AMERICAN ART DIRECTORY

50th EDITION

AMERICAN ART DIRECTORY

50th EDITION

Edited and Compiled by
JAQUES CATTELL PRESS

R. R. BOWKER COMPANY
New York & London

705
Am 35 a
1984
50th ed

Published by R. R. Bowker Co.
205 East 42nd Street, New York, NY 10017

Copyright © 1984 by Xerox Corporation

Contents

Preface

The *American Art Directory*, first published in 1898 as the American Art Annual, continues in its tradition of excellence with the 50th edition. The directory is a standard in the field of art, and an indispensible reference to art museums, libraries, organizations, schools and corporate art holdings.

The information for the directory is collected by means of direct communication whenever possible. Forms are sent to all entrants for corroboration and updating, and information submitted by entrants is included as completely as possible within the boundaries of editorial and space restrictions. Information is provided by new entrants in response to questionnaires. In those cases where no reply is received, data is obtained from secondary sources, and an asterisk (*) is shown to the right of the organizational name. Alphabetizing in the directory is strictly letter-by-letter. Those museums, libraries and organizations which bear an individual's name are alphabetized by the last name of that individual. Colleges and universities are alphabetized by the first word of their name, whether or not it is named for an individual.

Section I contains alphabetically arranged subsections of national and regional organizations in the United States and Canada. These 111 organizations administer and coordinate the arts within both countries. Two larger subsections, arranged geographically, contain listings for 1,586 main museums, 231 main libraries, 484 area associations, and 96 corporations with art holdings. There are an additional 2,000 listings for galleries, museums and libraries affiliated with main entries. A classification key is printed to the left of each entry to designate the type:

    C — Corporate Art
    L — Library
    M — Museum
    O — Organization or Association

The key "M" is assigned to organizations whose primary function is gathering and preserving the visual arts. The "O" designation is given to organizations supporting the arts through sponsorship of art activities.

Section II lists detailed information on 1,702 art schools, and college and university departments of art, art history, and architecture in the United States and Canada.

Section III provides reference to art museums and schools abroad, state arts councils, directors and supervisors of art education in selected school systems, art magazines, newspapers and their art critics, art scholarships and fellowships, open exhibitions, and traveling exhibitions booking agencies.

Section IV is composed of three alphabetical indexes, organizational, personnel, and subject. The subject index includes general art subjects and specific collections, along with the name and location of the holding organization.

The editors wish to thank the American Council for the Arts for the timely information that was provided. The editors thank the editorial assistants who worked so hard to make the *American Art Directory* a success. Every effort has been made to assure accurate reproduction of the material submitted. The publishers do not assume and hereby disclaim any liability to any party for any loss or damage caused by errors or omissions in the *American Art Directory* whether such errors or omissions resulted from negligence, accident or any other cause. In the event of a publication error, the sole responsibility of the publisher will be the entry of corrected information in succeeding editions.

As of June, 1984, the editorial offices of Jaques Cattell Press and R. R. Bowker Company will be combined. Please address any suggestions, comments or questions to The Editors, *American Art Directory*, R. R. Bowker Company, 205 East 42nd Street, New York, New York, 10017.

Martha Cargill, *Editor*
Renee W. Lautenbach, *Managing Editor*
Terence E. Basom, *General Manager*

JAQUES CATTELL PRESS

May, 1984

I ART ORGANIZATIONS

ARRANGEMENT AND ABBREVIATIONS
KEY TO ART ORGANIZATIONS

ARRANGEMENT OF DATA

Name and address of institution; telephone number, including area code.
Names and titles of key personnel.
Hours open; admission fees; date established and purpose; average annual attendance;
    membership.
Annual figures on income and purchases.
Collections, with enlarging collections indicated.
Exhibitions scheduled for 1980-82.
Activities sponsored, including classes for adults and children, dramatic programs and
    docent training; lectures, concerts, gallery talks and tours; competitions, awards,
    scholarships and fellowships; lending programs; museum or sales shops.
Libraries also list number of book volumes, periodical subscriptions, and audiovisual and
    micro holdings; subjects covered by name of special collections.

ABBREVIATIONS AND SYMBOLS

Admin — Administration, Administrative
Adminr — Administrator
Admis — Admission
A-tapes — Audio-tapes
Adv — Advisory
AM — Morning
Ann — Annual
Approx — Approximate, Approximately
Asn — Association
Assoc — Associate
Asst — Assistant
AV — Audiovisual
Ave — Avenue
Bldg — Building
Blvd — Boulevard
Bro — Brother
c — circa
Chap — Chapter
Chmn — Chairman
Circ — Circulation
Cl — Closed
Coll — Collection
Comt — Committee
Coordr — Coordinator
Corresp — Corresponding
Cur — Curator
Dept — Department
Dir — Director
Dist — District
Div — Division
Dr — Drive
E — East
Ed — Editor

Educ — Education
Enrl — Enrollment
Ent — Entrance
Estab — Established
Exec — Executive
Exhib — Exhibition
Exten — Extension
Fel(s) — Fellowship(s)
Fri — Friday
Fs — Filmstrips
Ft — Feet
Gen — General
Hon — Honorary
Hr — Hour
Hwy — Highway
Inc — Incorporated
Incl — Including
Jr — Junior
Lect — Lecture(s)
Lectr — Lecturer
Librn — Librarian
Mem — Membership
Mgr — Manager
Mon — Monday
Mss — Manuscripts
Mus — Museums
N — North
Nat — National
Per subs — Periodical subscriptions
PM — Afternoon
Pres — President
Prin — Principal
Prof — Professor

Prog — Program
Pub — Public
Publ — Publication
Rd — Road
Rec — Records
Res — Residence, Resident
S — South
Sat — Saturday
Schol — Scholarship
Secy — Secretary
Soc — Society
Sq — Square
Sr — Senior, Sister
St — Street
Sun — Sunday
Supt — Superintendent
Supv — Supervisor
Thurs — Thursday
Treas — Treasurer
Tues — Tuesday
Tui — Tuition
TV — Television
Univ — University
Vol — Volunteer
Vols — Volumes
VPres — Vice President
V-tapes — Videotapes
W — West
Wed — Wednesday
Wk — Week
Yr — Year(s)

*No response to questionnaire
† Denotes collections currently being enlarged
C Corporate Art Holding
L Library
M Museum
O Organization

National and Regional Organizations In The United States

O **ALLIED ARTISTS OF AMERICA, INC,** National Arts Club, 15 Gramercy Park S, New York, NY 10003. *Dir* William D Gorman; *VPres* Mervin Honig; *Pres* Reta Soloway; *Treas* Len Everett
Open daily 1 - 6 PM, Dec. Estab 1914, incorporated 1922, as a self-supporting exhibition cooperative, with juries elected each year by the membership, to promote work by American artists. Mem: 3601; dues $20 & up; annual meeting in Apr
Income: Financed by memorial funds, dues and donations
Exhibitions: Members' Regional AAA exhibitions; annual exhibition in the winter 1982; Annual held at National Arts Club; numerous awards and medals; prizes total approx $11,000 each year
Publications: Catalogs; newsletter
Activities: Lectures open to public, 2-4 visiting lecturers per year; gallery talks; competitions with awards; scholarships program for metropolitan art schools

O **AMERICAN ABSTRACT ARTISTS,** 17 West 16th St, New York, NY 10011. Tel 201-273-7394. *Pres* Merrill Wagner; *Secy* Douglas Sanderson; *Treas* Lucio Pozzi; *Exhibition Chair* James Juszczyk
Estab 1936, active 1937, to further cause; develop and educate through exhibitions and publications; maintains speakers bureau, museum & biographical archives. Mem: 60; dues $20; quarterly meetings
Income: Financed by membership
Exhibitions: (1983) Weatherspoon Art Gallery, University of North Carolina; Moody Gallery of Art, University of Alabama
Publications: Books and catalogs
Activities: Lectures open to public; gallery talks; tours; individual and original objects of art lent to responsible galleries, museums and universities; originate traveling exhibitions

O **AMERICAN ACADEMY AND INSTITUTE OF ARTS AND LETTERS,** 633 W 155th St, New York, NY 10032. Tel 212-368-5900. *Pres* Arthur Schlesinger Jr; *Exec Dir* Margaret M Mills
Open Tues - Sun 1 - 4 PM during exhibitions, by appointment other times. Estab 1898 as an honorary society of artists, writers and composers whose function it is to foster, assist and sustain an interest in literature, music and the fine arts. Formed by 1976 merger of the American Academy of Arts and Letters and the National Institute of Arts and Letters. Maintains two galleries separated by a terrace. Average Annual Attendance: 6000. Mem: 250; membership is by election; no dues; annual meeting May
Income: $1,200,000 (financed by endowment)
Purchases: $70,000
Collections: Works by members
Exhibitions: Exhibition of Candidates for Art Awards; Exhibition of Paintings Eligible for Hassam Fund Purchase; Memorial Exhibitions for Deceased Artist Members; Newly Elected Members & Recipients of Honors & Awards Exhibitions, art, scores & manuscripts
Publications: Proceedings, annual; exhibition catalogs
Activities: Awards given: Gold Medal, Richard and Hinda Rosenthal Foundation Award, Marjorie Peabody Waite Award, Arnold W Brunner Memorial Prize in Architecture, and Award of Merit of the Academy. No applications accepted
L **Library,** 633 W 155th St, 10032. *Librn* Casindania P Eaton; *Research Librn* Nancy Johnson
Open Mon - Fri 10 AM - 5 PM. Estab to collect books, papers and related articles concerning the members of the Academy-Institute. For reference only
Library Holdings: Vols 18,000; Other — Clipping files, exhibition catalogs, original art works, pamphlets
Collections: Books by and about members; manuscripts

O **AMERICAN ANTIQUARIAN SOCIETY,** 185 Salisbury St, Worcester, MA 01609. Tel 617-755-5221. *Dir* Marcus A McCorison; *Cur Graphic Arts* Georgia B Bumgardner
Open 9 AM - 5 PM; cl Sat, Sun & holidays. No admis fee. Incorporated 1812 to collect, preserve and encourage serious study of the materials of American history and life through 1876. Mem: 360 honorary; meetings third Wed in April & Oct
Income: $1,461,826 (financed by endowment, gifts and grants)
Purchases: $243,409
Collections: Early American portraits; Staffordshire pottery; †bookplates, †prints, †lithographs, †cartoons, †engravings; Colonial furniture; †photographs
Exhibitions: Temporary exhibitions
Publications: Proceedings, semi-annually; monographs
Activities: Undergraduate seminar in American Studies; lectures; fellowships; sales shop sells books
L **Library,** 185 Salisbury St, 01609. *Dir & Librn* Marcus A McConson
Library Holdings: Micro — Prints, reels; Other — Exhibition catalogs, manuscripts, memorabilia, original art works, pamphlets, photographs, prints, reproductions
Collections: †750,000 titles dating before 1877, including early American books on art and 20th century books and periodicals relating to the history and culture of the United States
Activities: Lectures; seminar; fellowships

O **AMERICAN ARTISTS PROFESSIONAL LEAGUE, INC,** * 215 Park Ave S, New York, NY 10003. Tel 212-475-6650. *Pres* Angelo John Grado; *Recording Secy* John Damron
Estab 1928 to advance the cause of fine arts in America, through the promotion of high standards of beauty, integrity and craftsmanship in painting, sculpture and the graphic arts; to emphasize the importance of order and coherent communication as prime requisites of works of art through exhibitions and publications. Mem: 1000; annual meetings
Income: Financed by membership
Exhibitions: Annually
Publications: AAPL News Bulletin, annually

O **AMERICAN ASSOCIATION OF MUSEUMS,** * 1055 Thomas Jefferson St NW, Washington, DC 20007. Tel 202-338-5300. *Pres* Kenneth Starr; *Dir* Lawrence L Reger; *Deputy Dir Admin* James Thomas; *Asst Dir Programs* Pamela Johnson; *Ed* Ellen C Hicks
Open Mon - Fri 9 AM - 5 PM. Estab 1906, to promote the welfare and advancement of museums as educational institutions, agencies of scientific and academic research and as cultural centers of the community; to encourage interest and inquiries in the field of museology; to increase and diffuse knowledge of all matters relating to museums. Average Annual Attendance: 6000
Publications: Aviso, monthly; books; Museum News, six per year; Official Museum Directory, annually; reprints

O **AMERICAN ASSOCIATION OF UNIVERSITY WOMEN,** * 2401 Virginia Ave NW, Washington, DC 20037. Tel 202-785-7700. *Exec Dir* Quincalee Brown
Estab 1881 to unite alumnae of different institutions for practical educational work; to further the advancement of women, lifelong learning, and responsibility to society expressed through action, advocacy, research and enlightened leadership. Mem: 190,000; holds biennial conventions
Publications: Action Alert, biweekly; Graduate Woman, bimonthly; Leader in Action, quarterly; brochures; research studies; study guides; booklets
Activities: Associations local branches develop and maintain programs in the arts. AAUW Foundation funds first professional degree in architecture, doctoral/post doctoral candidates in the arts

O **AMERICAN CERAMIC SOCIETY,** * 65 Ceramic Dr, Columbus, OH 43214. Tel 614-268-8645. *Pres* Robert J Beals; *Exec Dir* Arthur L Friedberg
Open Mon - Fri 8:30 AM - 4 PM. No admis fee. Estab 1899 to promote the arts, science and technology of ceramics. Mem: 10,050; dues $50; annual meeting May
Income: $2,000,000 (financed by membership)
Publications: American Ceramic Society Journal, monthly; Ceramic Engineering & Science Proceedings, bi-monthly; Journal and Abstracts, bi-monthly

O **AMERICAN COLOR PRINT SOCIETY,** * c/o Philadelphia College of Art, Broad & Spruce Sts, Philadelphia, PA 19102. Tel 215-893-3160. *Pres* Richard Hood; *VPres* Mildred Dillon; *VPres* Lois Johnson; *Treas* Bernard A Kohn; *Secy* Naomi Limonte
Estab 1939 to exhibit and sell color prints. Mem: 150; dues $10; annual meeting Oct
Activities: Sponsors annual national members exhibition of all media color prints; 6 annual prizes, 3 of which are purchase prizes

O **AMERICAN COUNCIL FOR THE ARTS,** 570 Seventh Ave, New York, NY 10018. Tel 212-354-6655. *Pres* Milton Rhodes; *Dir* William Keens; *Chmn* Marshall S Cogan; *Manager Conferences & Membership* Cecelia Fitzgibbon; *Manager Publishing* Robert Porter; *Manager Marketing* Joseph Ligammari
Open 9 AM - 5 PM. Estab 1960 as a national organization to provide management training, advocacy, news and publications services which address needs common to all the arts. Mem: 3500; dues organizations $35-$250, library $35, individual $30, student $20
Publications: American Arts, 6 times yr; Update, monthly; books on arts policy, management and issues
Activities: Sponsors competitions
L **Library,** 570 Seventh Ave, 10018. *Librn* Lisa Glover
Open Mon - Fri 9 AM - 5 PM. Estab 1965 to serve as a resource for a program of information services to the arts administration field. For reference only. Mem: 1200; dues $35-$250
Library Holdings: Vols 300; Per subs 60; documents; Other — Clipping files, manuscripts
Special Subjects: Cultural policy and management

O **AMERICAN CRAFT COUNCIL,** 22 W 55th St, New York, NY 10019. Tel 212-397-0600. *Board Chmn* Robert O Peterson; *Vice Chmn* Adele Greene; *Vice Chmn* Jack Lenor Larsen; *Executive Dir of Council* Lois Moran; *Secy* Sidney Rosoff; *Editor-in-Chief American Craft Magazine* Pat Dandignac
Estab 1943 to stimulate interest in and appreciation of contemporary American

crafts. The Council maintains the American Craft Museum (see entry under Museums). Mem: 35,000; dues $27.50 and higher; national conference every 3-4 years
Income: Financed by membership, private donations and government grants
Publications: American Craft Magazine (formerly Craft Horizons), bimonthly; exhibition catalogues
Activities: Regional workshops and conferences; sponsors Young Americans, a crafts competition every 6 years for persons 18-30 years old; lending collection contains over 100 slide kits, a national audio-visual service called Your Portable Museum; originate traveling exhibitions
L **American Craft Council Library,** 44 W 53rd St, 10019. Tel 212-397-0638. *Head* Joanne Polster
Library Holdings: Vols 3500; Per subs 40; AV — A-tapes, fs, slides, v-tapes; Other — Clipping files, exhibition catalogs, pamphlets, photographs

O **THE AMERICAN FEDERATION OF ARTS,** 41 E 65th St, New York, NY 10021. Tel 212-988-7700. *Pres Board of Trustees* Brooke Blake; *VPres* Donald M Cox; *VPres* Irvin L Levy; *VPres* Dr Evan H Turner; *VPres* John W Straus; *Treasurer* Carroll L Cartwright; *Dir* Wilder Green; *Assoc Dir & Exhibition Program Dir* Jane S Tai; *Exhibition Program Coordr* Jeffery J Pauelka; *Exhibition Coordr* James K Stave; *Coordr Exhibition Loans* Konrad G Kuchel; *Coordr Exhibition Scheduling* Amy V McEwen; *Registrar* Carol O'Biso; *Film Program Dir* Sam McElfresh; *Coordr Film Circ & Loans* Fred Riedel; *Business Mgr* James V Scarpat; *Development Officer* Charles Springman; *Membership Dir* Margot Linton; *Public Information Dir & Membership Coordr* Sandra Gilbert Estab 1909, a nonprofit educational institution which organizes circulating art exhibitions and film programs for museums, art centers, universities, colleges, schools and libraries. Mem: 1600; dues individual $35-$1250, institutions $35 - $150
Income: Financed by government agencies, corporations, foundations & membership
Publications: AFA Newsletter; exhibition catalogs
Activities: Originate traveling exhibitions

O **AMERICAN FINE ARTS SOCIETY,*** 215 W 57th St, New York, NY 10019. Tel 212-247-4510. *Pres* Stewart Klonis; *Secy* Arthur J Foster
Incorporated 1889; provides facilities for art activities at the American Fine Arts Society Building. Mem: Annual meeting Jan
Activities: Sponsors lect by prominent persons in the art world

O **THE AMERICAN FOUNDATION FOR THE ARTS,*** 3814 NE Miami Ct, Miami, FL 33137. Tel 305-573-0618. *Dir* Richard Levine
Open Mon - Fri 10 AM - 4 PM. No admis fee. Estab 1974. Mem: Dues founder $25,000, trustee $10,000, life $5000, benefactor $1000, business $250, friend $100, sustaining $50, family $25, individual $15, student annual $5
Collections: Architecture; comtemporary paintings; photography

O **AMERICAN INSTITUTE FOR CONSERVATION OF HISTORIC AND ARTISTIC WORKS (AIC),*** 1511 K St NW, Suite 725, Washington, DC 20005. Tel 202-638-1444. *Pres* Paul N Banks; *VPres* Perry C Huston; *Secy* Katherine Eirk; *Exec Secy* Martha Morales
Open 8 AM - 4 PM. Estab 1973 for professional organization of Conservators, people who take care of our cultural and historical patrimony. Mem: 1850; dues fellows $80, professional associates $65, associates $45, student $35; meetings in late May
Income: Financed by membership
Publications: Directory, annually; journal, semi-annually; newsletter, quarterly
Activities: Educ Committee to keep abreast of all conservation education facilities, programs; lect open to public; awards given
L **Library,*** 1522 K St NW, Suite 804, 20005. Tel 202-638-1444
Open 8 AM - 4 PM. For member's use and for students of conservation
Income: Financed by memberships, sales of publications, grants
Library Holdings: AV — Cassettes; Other — Clipping files, exhibition catalogs, pamphlets
Special Subjects: Conservation of artistic and historic works
Exhibitions: Know What You See

O **AMERICAN INSTITUTE OF ARCHITECTS,*** 1735 New York Ave NW, Washington, DC 20006. Tel 202-626-7300. *Pres* Robert M Lawrence; *First VPres* Robert C Broshar; *Secy* Harry W Harmon; *Exec VPres* David Olan Meeker Jr
Open Mon - Fri 8:30 AM - 5 PM. Estab 1857 to organize and unite the architects of the United States and to promote the esthetic, scientific and practical efficiency of the profession
Income: Financed by membership
Publications: AIA Journal, monthly; AIA Memo (newsletter), biweekly
Activities: Continuing education program; awards given, Gold Medal, Kemper Award, Architectural Firm Award, R S Reynolds Memorial Award and Reynolds Aluminum Prize Citation of Honor
L **Library,*** 1735 New York Ave NW, 20006. Tel 202-626-7493. *Librn* Susan Holton
Open to the public, lending provided for members
Library Holdings: Vols 23,000; Per subs 450; Micro — Reels 100; AV — Fs, motion pictures, slides, v-tapes
Special Subjects: Architecture, architectural history

O **AMERICAN INSTITUTE OF GRAPHIC ARTS,*** 1059 Third Ave, New York, NY 10021. Tel 212-752-0813. *Pres* David R Brown; *Exec Dir* Caroline Hightower
Open Mon - Fri 9:30 AM - 4:45 PM. No admis fee. Estab 1914 as a national nonprofit educational organization devoted to raising standards in all branches of the graphic arts. Maintains library and slide archives. Mem: 1900; dues resident $115, nonresident $65, student $20
Income: Financed by membership
Exhibitions: Book Show; Communication Graphics
Publications: 1981 AIGA Graphic Design USA:2 (hardbound annual)
Activities: Seminars on design and production problems; plant tours; awards AIGA Medal for distinguished contributions to the graphic arts; originate traveling exhibitions

O **AMERICAN NUMISMATIC ASSOCIATION MUSEUM,** 818 N Cascade, Colorado Springs, CO 80903. Tel 303-632-2646. *Pres* Q David Bowers; *Exec VPres* Edward C Rochette; *Museum Cur* Robert W Hoge
Open Tues - Sat 8:30 AM - 4 PM. No admis fee. Estab 1891 as an international organization to promote numismatics as a means of recording history. Maintains a museum and library; seven galleries display numismatic material from paper money through coins and art medals. Average Annual Attendance: 10,000. Mem: 40,000; to qualify for membership, a person must be at least eleven years of age and interested in coin collecting; dues $21 plus one-time initiation fee of $5; annual meetings held at National Conventions in Feb and August
Income: Financed by membership, endowment, donations and miscellaneous sources
Collections: Robert T Herdegen Memorial Collection of Coins of the World; Norman H Liebman Collection of Abraham Lincoln on Paper Money; Elliott Markoff Collection of Presidential Memorabilia; general and specialized collections from all other fields of numismatics
Exhibitions: Permanent galleries exhibiting coins of the American Colonial period, the United States 1792 to date and Modern Medallic Art from contemporary medals. Temporary exhibits on selected topics, including African Emblems of Wealth; (1983) The Olympic Games: A Numismatic Celebration
Publications: The Numismatist, monthly
Activities: Classes for adults and children; annual seminar on campus of Colorado College, Colorado Springs; lect open to public, visiting guest lectr; tours; sponsorship of National Coin Week third week in April (when members throughout the United States promote their avocations through exhibits in local areas); presentation of awards; scholarships; sales shop selling books, magazines, slides, medals and souvenir jewelry
L **Library,** 818 N Cascade Ave, 80903. *Librn* Nancy W Green
Open Mon - Fri 8:30 AM - 4:30 PM. Estab 1891 to provide research materials to the members of the Association and the general public. Open to the public for reference; lending restricted to members. Circ 4500
Library Holdings: Vols 15,000; Per subs 100; Auction catalogs, 20,000; Micro — Fiche, reels; AV — Motion pictures, slides; Other — Clipping files
Collections: Arthur Bradden Coole Library on Chinese Numismatics

O **AMERICAN NUMISMATIC SOCIETY,** Broadway at 155th St, New York, NY 10032. Tel 212-234-3130. *Dir & Secy* Leslie A Elam; *Chief Cur* William E Metcalf
Open Tues - Sat 9 AM - 4:30 PM, Sun 1 - 4 PM, cl Mon. Estab 1858 as an international organization for the advancement of numismatic knowledge. Maintains museum and library; two exhibition halls, one devoted to the World of Coins, the other to money in early America. Average Annual Attendance: 18,000. Mem: 2279; dues assoc $20; annual meeting second Sat in January
Income: Financed by endowment
Collections: Universal numismatics
Publications: Numismatic Literature, semi-annually; MuseumNotes, annually
Activities: Lect open to public, 2 visiting lectr per year; scholarships
L **Library,** Broadway at 155th St, 10032. Tel 212-234-3130, Ext 20. *Librn* Francis D Campbell Jr; *Assoc Librn* Margaret D'Ambrosio
Open to the public
Library Holdings: Vols 40,000; Per subs 70; auction catalogs; Micro — Reels 200; AV — Fs, slides; Other — Exhibition catalogs, manuscripts, pamphlets
Collections: Auction catalogs

O **AMERICAN PORTRAIT SOCIETY,** PO Box 666, Seal Beach, CA 90740. Tel 213-596-0139. *Pres* Robert Fleet Hubbell; *Administrator Editor* Joe Galliani; *Office Mgr* Debra Bushweit; *Administrative Asst* Monica J Matthews; *Systems Analyst* Kirk Nason
Open 9 AM - 5 PM. Estab 1982 to provide a unified effort in support of creative excellence & appreciation. Mem: 750; dues $35
Publications: American Portrait Society Directory, annual; Profile Magazine, quarterly
Activities: Leclтures open to public; competitions with awards; book traveling exhibitions; organizes traveling exhibitions

O **AMERICAN SOCIETY FOR AESTHETICS,*** C W Post Center of Long Island Univ, Greenvale, NY 11548. Tel 516-299-3054. *Pres* Francis Sparshott; *Journal Ed* John J Fisher; *Secy-Treas* Arnold Berleant
Estab 1942 for the advancement of philosophical and scientific study of the arts and related fields
Income: Financed by dues and subscriptions
Publications: Journal of Aesthetics and Art Criticism, quarterly; ASA Newsletter, quarterly

O **AMERICAN SOCIETY OF ARTISTS, INC,*** 1297 Merchandise Mart Plaza, Chicago, IL 60654. Tel 312-751-2500. *Pres* Nancy J Fregin; *VPres* Helen DelValle; *Secy* Arnold Jackson; *American Artisans Dir* Judy A EdBorg; *Festivals Committee Dir* Kathy Chan Barnes; *Dir Lecture & Demonstration Service* Charles J Gruner; *Special Arts Services Dir* Patricia E Nolan; *Dir Special Events* Marge Coughin
Estab 1972, membership organization of professional artists - American Artisans Division is professional craftspeople. Showroom for stores, shops, designers, and galleries contain original art work by American member artists and craftspeople. Mem: 600; qualifications for mem, must have work juried and pass jury to be accepted; dues $50, plus one initiation fee of $10
Income: Financed by membership
Collections: †Photographs and slides of members works
Exhibitions: Approximately 23 indoor and outdoor juried shows per year
Publications: Art Lovers' Art and Craft Fair Bulletin, quarterly; Members' Bulletin, quarterly
Activities: Lect and Demonstration Service
L **Library,*** 1297 Merchandise Mart Plaza, 60654. Tel 312-751-2500. *Librn* Don Metcoff
Estab 1978 to provide reference material for member artists only
Income: Financed by dues and fees
Library Holdings: Per subs 8; AV — Lantern slides; Other — Photographs
Special Subjects: Art and craft supplies, exhibition and gallery information

O **AMERICAN SOCIETY OF BOOKPLATE COLLECTORS AND DESIGNERS,** 605 N Stoneman Ave No F, Alhambra, CA 91801. Tel 213-283-1936. *Dir & Ed* Audrey Spencer Arellanes
Estab 1922 as an international organization to foster an interest in the art of the bookplate through the publication of a yearbook, and to encourage friendship and a greater knowledge of bookplates among members by an exchange membership list. Mem: 200 who are interested in bookplates as either a collector or artist, or just an interest in bookplates and graphic arts; dues $35 which includes yearbook and quarterly newsletter
Income: Financed by membership
Publications: Bookplates in the News, quarterly newsletter; Yearbook, annually
Activities: Lect given upon request; contributes bookplates to the Prints and Photographs Division of the Library of Congress and furnishes them with copies of Newsletter and Yearbook; originate traveling exhibitions

O **AMERICAN SOCIETY OF CONTEMPORARY ARTISTS,** 2820 Ave J, 1916 Ave K, Brooklyn, NY 11210. Tel 212-252-4736. *Pres* Edith L Abrams
Estab 1917. Mem: 151 elected on basis of high level of professional distinction; dues $20; annual meeting Apr
Exhibitions: 60th & 61st Annual at National Arts Club; 62nd, 63rd & 64th Annual at Salmagundi Club; Exhibitions at Lever House Gallery and US Customhouse Museum; 65th Annual at Federal Plaza
Activities: Educ dept; demonstrations in graphics, painting & sculpture; lectures open to the public; awards; originate traveling exhibitions

O **AMERICAN WATERCOLOR SOCIETY,** 14 E 90th St, New York, NY 10028. Tel 212-876-6622. *Pres* Mario Cooper; *First VPres* William D Gorman; *Second VPres* William Strosahl; *Third VPres* Serge Hollerbach; *Corresponding Secy* Janet Walsh; *Treas* Ann Ritchie; *Recording Secy* Mare Brutus; *Active Honorary Pres* Dale Meyers
Open during exhibitions 1 - 5 PM, cl Mon. Estab 1866 as a national organization to foster the advancement of the art of watercolor painting and to further the interests of painters in watercolor throughout the United States; rents space from the National Academy Galleries for four weeks each year for annual exhibition. Average Annual Attendance: 4000 - 5000. Mem: Approx 550; to qualify for membership, an artist must exhibit in three annuals within past ten years, then submit application to membership chairman; dues $20; annual meeting in April
Income: Financed by membership & donations
Publications: AWS Newsletter, semi-annually; exhibition catalog
Activities: Lectures open to the public; demonstrations during annual exhibitions; awards given at annual exhibitions; scholarships; originate traveling exhibitions

O **ARCHAEOLOGICAL INSTITUTE OF AMERICA,** PO Box 1901 Kenmore Station, Boston, MA 02215. Tel 617-353-9361. *Pres* Machteld Mcllink; *VPres* James R Wiseman; *Exec Dir* Raymond A Liddell; *Asst Dir* Martha Richardson
Estab 1879 as an international organization concerned with two major areas of responsibility: facilitating archaeological research and disseminating the results to the public. Mem: 9834 consisting of professionals and laypersons interested in archaeology; dues $30; annual meeting Dec 27-30
Income: Financed by endowment and membership
Publications: Archaeology Magazine, bimonthly; American Journal of Archaeology, quarterly
Activities: Lect open to the public, 270 visiting lectr per year; annual award given for distinguished archaeological achievement; one or more fellowships awarded for an academic year

O **ART DEALERS ASSOCIATION OF AMERICA, INC,** 575 Madison Ave, New York, NY 10022. Tel 212-940-8590; Cable: ARTDEALAS, NEW YORK. *Pres* Norman Hirschl; *VPres* Serge Sabarsky; *Secy & Treasurer* Gilbert S Edelson; *Admin VPres & Counsel* Ralph F Colin; *Public Relations* Susan M Wasserstein; *Admin Asst* Donna Carlson; *Admin Asst* Judith Irby
Estab 1962 as a national organization to improve the stature and status of the art-dealing profession. Mem: 110, membership by invitation
Income: Financed by membership
Publications: Activities and Membership Roster Update, newsletter 4-6 per yr
Activities: Lectures open to public; gives ADAA Award for Excellence & Doctoral Dissertation in Art History; scholarships; appraisal service for donors contributing works of art to nonprofit institutions; international art theft service including monthly publication of notices

O **ART DIRECTORS CLUB, INC,*** 488 Madison Ave, New York, NY 10022. Tel 212-838-8140. *Pres* Walter Kaprielian; *VPres* Lee Epstein; *Secy* Blanche Florenza; *Exec Dir* Diane Moore
Estab 1920 as an international organization to protect, promote and elevate the standards of practice of the profession of art directing. Owns gallery. Mem: 620, criteria for membership: qualified art director, at least 21 years of age, of good character and at least two years of practical experience in creating and directing in the visual communication of graphic arts industry. Dues regular $150, nonresident $75, junior $25
Income: Financed by membership
Exhibitions: Art Directors' Annual Exhibition of Advertising, Editorial and Television Art and Design. Bimonthly shows conceived to provide a showcase for works and ideas not readily viewed otherwise. They cover new art, design, lettering and graphics by illustrators, alumni art directors, ad agencies and individuals
Publications: The Art Directors Annual; Newsletter, bimonthly
Activities: Portfolio Review Programs; seminars; lect open to public; gallery talks; annual exhibition with Gold & Silver Medals, Gold, Silver and Distinctive Merit Certificates; scholarships; originate traveling exhibitions
L **Library,*** 488 Madison Ave, 10022
Open to the public for reference
Library Holdings: Vols 58

O **ARTISTS EQUITY ASSOCIATION, INC,*** Central Station, PO Box 28068, Washington, DC 20005. Tel 202-628-9633. *Pres* George Koch; *Secy* Ellouise Schoettler; *Exec Dir* Gail Simmons
Estab 1947 as a national nonprofit, aesthetically nonpartisan organization working for social, economic and legislative change for all artists. Mem: 4500 who are or ask to be recognized as professional contributors to the development of visual art and culture; dues $20 and $30; annual meeting
Income: $70,000 (financed by membership and grants)
Publications: AEA News, quarterly; Legislative Update, bimonthly
Activities: Approximately 20 conferences, seminars and other educational programs per year which are open to the general public; chapter occasionally organize and circulate traveling exhibitions

O **ARTISTS' FELLOWSHIP, INC,*** 47 Fifth Ave, New York, NY 10003. Tel 212-255-7740. *Pres* Arthur Harrow; *VPres* Peter Cox; *Treas* John R McCarthy; *Correspondence Secy* Robert J Riedinger; *Recording Secy* Janet Sumner; *Historian* Kent Day Coes
Estab 1859, reorganized 1889 as Artists' Aid Society, then incorporated 1925 as Artists' Fellowship; to aid artists and their families in need because of death, illness or financial reverses. Mem: 200; annual meeting Dec
Activities: Presbyterian Hospital awards the Gari Melchers Gold Medal for distinguished service to the arts, and Benjamin West Clinedinst Memorial Medal for outstanding achievement in the arts

O **ART LIBRARIES SOCIETY-NORTH AMERICA,*** 3775 Bear Creek Circle, Tucson, AZ 85715. Tel 602-749-9112. *Chmn Bd* Caroline Backlund; *Exec Secy* Pamela Jeffcott Parry
Open 9 AM - 5 PM, cl Sat & Sun. Estab 1972 to promote the profession of art librarians in the country. Mem: 1050; qualification for mem is an interest in art librarianship or related fields; dues institutional $60, personal $35; annual meeting Feb
Income: Financed by membership
Publications: Art Documentation, 5 per year; Annual Membership Directory

O **THE ART MUSEUM ASSOCIATION OF AMERICA,** 270 Sutter St, San Francisco, CA 94108. Tel 415-392-9222. *Pres* David H Katzive; *Chmn* Robert K Hoffman; *VPres* Ronald Gleason; *Executive Dir* Lynn Jorgenson; *Exhibition Prog Dir* Harold B Nelson; *Program Development Dir* Gigi Dobbs; *Professional Training Coordr* Davida Egherman
Open Mon - Fri 9 AM - 5 PM. No admis fee. Estab 1921 as a national nonprofit museum service organization which circulates traveling exhibitions, offers fine art insurance, and organizes educational seminars for museum professionals. Mem: Over 500, members selected by accreditation and approval of membership committee; dues active $200, individual $25; annual meeting Oct-Nov
Publications: Exhibition Catalogs; educational publications printed in conjunction with seminars
Activities: Seminars for museum professionals; lect; Publication Design Award competition is sponsored annually to award excellence in museum publications including posters, books, catalogs, annual reports, and others; scholarships and fellowships offered; book traveling exhibitions, 50 per yr; member and non-member institutions may rent exhibitions organized for circulation

O **ASSOCIATION OF AMERICAN EDITORIAL CARTOONISTS,*** 22 Mimosa Dr, Harrison, AR 72601. *Pres* Jim Berry; *VPres* Roy Peterson; *Secy & Treas* Bob Drebelbis
Estab 1957 as an international organization of professional editorial cartoonists for newspapers and newspaper syndicates. Mem: 250; to qualify for membership, an editorial cartoonists must produce at least three editorial cartoons per week for publication; dues $50
Income: Financed by membership
Exhibitions: University of Southern Mississippi Touring Exhibition of Association's editorial cartoons
Publications: Notebook, AAEC news magazine; Best Editorial Cartoons of the Year

O **ASSOCIATION OF ARCHITECTURAL LIBRARIANS,** 1735 New York Ave NW, Washington, DC 20006. Tel 202-626-7494. *Correspondent* Stephanie C Byrnes
Average Annual Attendance: 30. Mem: 400; annual meetings in conjunction with national convention of American Institute of Architects
Publications: Newsletter, quarterly

O **ASSOCIATION OF ART MUSEUM DIRECTORS,*** PO Box 10082, Savannah, GA 31402. Tel 912-234-1393. *Adminr* Millecent Hall Gaudiere
Estab 1916. Mem: 140; chief staff officers of major art museums
Income: Financed by membership dues
Publications: Conference Proceedings; Fine Arts Insurance: A Handbook for Art Museums; Professional Practices in Art Museums

O **ASSOCIATION OF COLLEGIATE SCHOOLS OF ARCHITECTURE,** 1735 New York Ave NW, Washington, DC 20006. Tel 202-785-2324. *Pres* C Hight; *VPres* W Gilland; *Secy* E Cherry; *Tres* R Beckley; *Executive Dir* R McCommons; *Asst Dir* Gary Haney; *Project Mgr* E Showen; *Admin Mgr* D Greene
Open daily 9 AM - 5 PM. No admis fee. Estab 1912 as an international organization furthering the advancement of architectural education. Mem: 3400 faculty members; membership open to schools (and their faculty) which offer professional degrees in architecture; school dues $1020-$1500; annual meeting in March or April
Income: $400,000 (financed by endowment, membership, state appropriation and grants)
Publications: ACSA News, 7 times per year; Journal of Architectural Education, quarterly; Annual Meeting Proceedings; Architecture Schools in North America, biennially; Architecture Off-Campus Study Programs: Abroad-US
Activities: Educational seminars; institutes; publications; services to member schools; sponsor competitions; awards; sales shop selling books and magazines

O **ASSOCIATION OF MEDICAL ILLUSTRATORS,** Route 5, Box 311F, Midlothian, VA 23113. Tel 804-794-2908. *Pres* Martin Finch; *Chmn of Board* Donald Biggerstaff; *Correspondence Secy* Diane Nelson; *Exec Dir* Margaret Henry
Estab 1945 as an international organization to encourage the advancement of medical illustration and allied fields of visual education; to promote understanding and cooperation with the medical and related professions. Mem: 552; dues active $100; annual meeting June
Income: Financed by membership
Publications: Journal of Biocommunications, 4 times per year; Medical Illustration, brochure; Newsletter, 6 times per year
Activities: Individual members throughout the world give lectures on the profession; awards given for artistic achievements submitted to salon each year; scholarships to members of AMI accredited schools only; originate traveling exhibition

O **AUDUBON ARTISTS, INC,*** 225 W 34th St, Suite 1510, New York, NY 10122. Tel 212-949-6142. *Pres* Hughie Lee-Smith; *VPres* Len G Everett; *Secy* William Behnken; *Exec Officer* Domenico Facci
Open during annual exhibition. Admis $.50. Estab 1940 as a national organization for the presentation of annual exhibitions in all media, oil, acrylics, watercolors, graphics, sculpture; open to nonmembers. Exhibitions held at the National Art Club. Mem: 650; membership by invitation; dues $20; annual meeting April
Income: $15,000 (financed by membership and exhibition admission)
Exhibitions: Annual exhibition lasting four weeks
Publications: Illustrated catalog, annual
Activities: Demonstrations in all media; medals and $4000 in cash prizes

O **COLLEGE ART ASSOCIATION OF AMERICA,** 149 Madison Ave, New York, NY 10016. Tel 212-755-3532. *Pres* Lucy Freeman Sandler; *VPres* John Rupert Martin; *Secy* Paul B Arnold; *Exec Secy* Rose R Weil
Estab 1912 as a national organization to further scholarship and excellence in the teaching and practice of art and art history. Mem: 9000; open to all individuals and institutions interested in the purposes of the Association; dues life $1000, institution $75, individual $35-$60 (scaled to salary), student $17.50 & $25; annual meeting in Feb
Income: Financed by membership
Publications: The Art Bulletin, quarterly; Art Journal, quarterly; CAA Newsletter, quarterly
Activities: Awards: Distinguished Teaching of Art History Award; Distinguished Teaching of Art Award; Charles Rufus Morey Book Award; Frank Jewett Mather Award for Distinction in Art and Architectural Criticism; Arthur Kingsley Porter Prize for Best Article by Younger Scholar in The Art Bulletin; Alfred H Barr, Jr Award for Museum Scholarship

O **CONFEDERATION OF AMERICAN INDIANS,** Council of American Indian Artists, Box 5474, New York, NY 10163. *Chmn* Adam Starchild; *Exec Dir* David McCord
Estab 1981 for promotion of American Indian art & design, particularly contemporary
Activities: Lectures open to public; awards; book traveling exhibitions; originates traveling exhibitions

O **CONGRESSIONAL ARTS CAUCUS,*** House of Representatives, House Annex 2, H2-338, Washington, DC 20515. Tel 202-225-0308. *Chmn Exec Board* Fred Richmond; *VChmn* James Jeffords; *Secy* Margaret Heckler; *Treas* Tony Coelho; *Exec Dir* Rhoda Glickman
Estab 1980 to keep members informed of the progress of arts legislation in Congress and provide them with analyses of issues affecting the arts community as a whole and within their own districts. Mem: The Caucus, which is bipartisan, is open to any member of the House of Representatives who is interested in supporting the arts

O **COUNCIL OF AMERICAN ARTIST SOCIETIES,*** 215 Park Ave S, New York, NY 10003. Tel 212-475-6650
Estab 1962, a national, tax-free, nonprofit incorporated educational council to educate, motivate and challenge art and artists; to further traditional art at the highest esthetic level; policies and management controlled by artists. Mem: 100 societies; no dues; annual meeting in May
Income: Financed by endowment
Publications: Annual Report; monographs
Activities: Presents awards to art organizations; awards and citations for excellence in art; medals and awards; provides some scholarships

O **THE DRAWING SOCIETY,*** 500 Park Ave, New York, NY 10022. Tel 212-688-7630. *Pres* Paul Cummings; *VPres* Wilder Green
Estab 1959 to encourage interest in, and understanding of drawing of all periods and cultures. Mem: Dues $100 and up for patrons, institutional $75, associate $25
Publications: Books and catalogues; Drawing, bi-monthly

O **FEDERATION OF MODERN PAINTERS AND SCULPTORS,*** 234 W 21st St, New York, NY 10011. Tel 212-568-2981. *Pres* Haim Mendelson; *VPres* Theo Hios; *VPres* Barbara Krashes; *Secy* Elisabeth Model
Estab 1940 as a national organization to promote the cultural interests of free progressive artists working in the United States. Mem: 3000; selected by membership committee; dues $10; meeting every two months
Income: Financed by membership and New York State Council on the Arts
Activities: Lect open to public, 1 - 2 visiting lectrs per year; originate traveling exhibitions

O **GENERAL SERVICES ADMINISTRATION,*** Art-in-Arch Program, Public Bldgs Service, F St between 18th & 19th NW, Washington, DC 20405. Tel 202-566-0950. *Dir Arts-in-Arch Program* Donald W Thalacker
The Arts-in-Arch Program office directs the work of artists commissioned to design and execute sculpture, murals, tapestries and other art work incorporated as part of the design of new Federal Buildings, except Post Offices and Veterans Administration Buildings. The scope of work is determined by the size and character of the building with allowances up to .5 percent of the estimated construction cost. Artists are commissioned by direct selection by agency upon recommendation by a panel of distinguished art professionals appointed by the National Endowment for the Arts and the Architect for the building
Income: $1,000,000

O **GUILD OF BOOK WORKERS,** 663 Fifth Ave, New York, NY 10022. Tel 212-757-6454. *Pres* Caroline F Schimmel; *VPres* Wilton Hale Wiggins; *Secy* Louise Kuflik
Estab 1906 as a national organization to establish and maintain a feeling of kinship and mutual interest among workers in the several hand book crafts. Mem: 560; membership open to all interested persons; dues New York City area $50, national $30; annual meeting May or June
Income: Financed by membership
Publications: Guild of Book Workers Journal, 2 times per year; Membership List, annually; Newsletter, quarterly; Supply List, biennially; Opportunities for Study in Hand Bookbinding and Calligraphy, directory and supplement
Activities: 2 - 4 lect annually, some open to public and some for members only; book traveling exhibitions; originate traveling exhibitions
L **Library,** Boston Athenaeum, 10 1/2 Beacon St, 02108. Tel 617-227-0270. *Librn* Stanley E Cushing
Open to Guild members for lending and reference
Library Holdings: Vols 500
Special Subjects: Related to the hand book crafts; bookbinding; manuals on book & paper making crafts

O **INDUSTRIAL DESIGNERS SOCIETY OF AMERICA,*** 6802 Poplar Pl, McLean, VA 22101. Tel 202-466-2927. *Pres* Robert Smith; *Exec VPres* Katherine McCoy; *Secy-Treas* Dana Mox; *Exec Dir* Brian J Wynne
Open daily 8 AM - 5 PM. No admis fee. Estab and incorporated 1965 as a nonprofit national organization representing the profession of industrial design. Mem: 2000; dues full, assoc, affiliate, sustaining and student from $50 to $175; annual meeting Oct
Publications: Innovations; IDSA Newsletter, monthly; Membership Directory; other surveys and studies
Activities: IDSA Student Chapters; IDSA Student Merit Awards; lect; competitions

O **INTERMUSEUM CONSERVATION ASSOCIATION,** Allen Art Bldg, Oberlin, OH 44074. Tel 216-775-7331. *Pres* William S Talbot; *VPres* Larry Hoffman; *Secy-Treas & Dir* Thom Gentle; *Admin Dir & Asst Cur* Caroli Asia
Estab 1952 as a non-profit conservation laboratory to aid in the maintenance of the collections of its member museums. Not open to public, maintains a technical conservation library. Mem: 24; must be a nonprofit cultural institution
Activities: 10 vis lectr per year

O **INTERNATIONAL ASSOCIATION OF CONTEMPORARY MOSAICISTS,** 10602 Bucknell Drive, Silver Spring, MD 20902. Tel 301-649-5019. *Pres* Jerry Carter; *Administration Officer* Tarja Cater
Estab 1980 to promote high aesthetic quality in mosaic, identify artists making quality work, promote the medium of mosaic as a fine art, act as a clearing house for architects and other buyers of mosaic art and provide a place to discuss mosaic art every two years

O **INTERNATIONAL CENTER FOR ADVANCED STUDIES IN ART,*** NY Univ Dept of Art & Art Education, 735 East Bldg, Washington Sq, New York, NY 10003. *Co-Chmn* Angiola Churchill
Estab 1979 to provide international studies through which the complex and multi-faceted field of visual arts can be viewed, examined, researched and developed on the highest scholarly and professional level. The most significant aspect of the Center is the firsthand contact with critics, theorists, aestheticians and other specialists and the opportunity to work with artists and other thinkers

O **INTERNATIONAL COUNCIL OF MUSEUMS COMMITTEE OF THE AMERICAN ASSOCIATION OF MUSEUMS,** 1055 Thomas Jefferson St NW, Washington, DC 20007. Tel 212-338-5300. *Prog Coordr* Maria Papageorge
Open 9 AM - 5 PM. No admis fee. Estab 1973, the AAM represents international museum interests within the United States through the AAM-ICOM office which disseminates information on international conferences, publications, travel and study grants and training programs. The AAM-ICOM office also maintains an international network of museum contacts around the world. Mem: 1000; members must be museum professionals or institutions holding membership in the American Association of Museums
Income: Financed by membership
Publications: AAM-ICOM Newsletter, quarterly; ICOM News, quarterly
Activities: Specialty committees; serves as liaison for the organization and circulation of traveling exhibitions

O **INTERNATIONAL FOUNDATION FOR ART RESEARCH, INC,*** 46 E 70th St, New York, NY 10021. Tel 212-879-1780. *Pres* Edwin L Weisl Jr; *Executive Dir* Bonnie Burnham; *Research Assoc, Art Theft Archive* Mary Ellen Guerra; *Research Assoc, Authentication Service* Virginia Pancoast
Open Mon - Fri 9:30 AM - 5 PM. Estab 1968 to provide a framework for impartial consideration by experts of questions concerning attribution and authenticity of major works of art; expanded in 1975 to include an Art Theft Archive for collection and cataloging of information on art theft
Income: Financed by donations, memberships and fees
Publications: Art Research News; Art Theft, Its Scope, Its Impact and Its Control; Stolen Art Alert
Activities: Lectures and symposia are conducted throughout the year on subjects relating to connoisseurship, authenticity and art theft and fraud
—**Art Theft Archive,***
A research program of the Foundation, the Art Theft Archive is devoted to collecting and cataloguing records of art thefts, and providing information on stolen objects to individuals, institutions, government agencies, and others in

order to prevent the circulation of stolen art and aid in its recovery. The Archive contains reports from a wide range of domestic and international sources. Stolen art reports are published free of charge in its monthly Stolen Art Alert. A comprehensive report that includes museum and dealer surveys, international statistics, and an evaluation of the legal context of the problem
—Collection Cataloguing and Research,*
At the request of the collector or institution, IFAR will provide cataloguing and inventory systems, and create written, automated, and visual records of the collection. Fees on a per-diem basis; estimates free of charge

O **INTERNATIONAL SOCIETY FOR THE STUDY OF EXPRESSIONISM,** Box 210-57 Campus Station, Cincinnati, OH 45221. Tel 513-961-8868. *Founder* Eva Lachman-Kalitzki
Founded 1979 and dedicated to the study of expressionism and related topics. Promotes literary, historical and political study and research concerning the life, work and times of various expressionists. Encourages study of twentieth century German history, art and literature and studies concerning antifascism and exile
Publications: Yearbook

O **INTER-SOCIETY COLOR COUNCIL,*** US Army Natick R&D Laboratories, Natick, MA 01760. Tel 617-651-5467. *Pres* William D Schaeffer
Estab 1931 as a national organization to stimulate and coordinate the study of color in science, art and industry; federation of 36 national societies & individuals interested in colors. Mem: 900; members must show an interest in color and in the aims and purposes of the Council; dues $15; annual meeting usually in April
Income: Financed by membership
Publications: Inter-Society Color Council Newsletter, bimonthly
Activities: Lect open to public; lect at meetings; gives Macbeth Award and Godlove Award

O **KAPPA PI INTERNATIONAL HONORARY ART FRATERNITY,** PO Box 7843, Midfield, Birmingham, AL 35228. Tel 205-428-4540. *Pres* Garnet R Leader; *VPres* Dr Ralph M Hudson; *Secy* Elmer J Porter; *Treas* Myrtle Kerr; *Ed* Arthur Kennon
Estab 1911 as an international honorary art fraternity for men and women in colleges, universities and art schools
Income: Financed by membership
Publications: Bulletin, annually in the fall; Sketch Book, annual spring magazine
Activities: Sponsors competition in photography; annual scholarships available to active members
Alpha, University of Kentucky, Lexington, KY 40506
Theta, Birmingham Southern College, Birmingham, AL 35254
Iota, Iowa Wesleyan College, Mount Pleasant, IA 52641
Kappa, Lindenwood College, Saint Charles, MO 63301
Mu, New Mexico Western University, Silver City, NM 88061
Xi, University of Montevallo, Montevallo, AL 35115
Omicron, Western Montana College, Dillon, MT 59725
Pi, University of Georgia, Athens, GA 30601
Rho, Mississippi University for Women, Columbus, MS 39701
Sigma, Huntingdon College, Montgomery, AL 36106
Phi, Central State University, Edmond, OK 73034
Chi, Eastern Illinois University, Charleston, IL 61920
Psi, Southern Illinois University, Carbondale, IL 62901
Omega, Indiana State University, Terre Haute, IN 47809
Alpha Alpha, Samford University, Birmingham, AL 35209
Alpha Beta, Central Washington State College, Ellensburg, WA 98926
Alpha Delta, University of Arkansas, Fayetteville, AR 72701
Alpha Epsilon, Mary Hardin Baylor College, Belton, TX 76513
Alpha Eta, Florida Southern College, Lakeland, FL 33802
Alpha Theta, Winthrop College, Rock Hill, SC 29730
Alpha Iota, DePauw University, Greencastle, IN 46135
Alpha Kappa, Baylor University, Waco, TX 76703
Alpha Lambda, Sam Houston State University, Huntsville, TX 77340
Alpha Mu, University of Minnesota, Duluth, MN 55812
Alpha Xi, Kansas Wesleyan University, Salina, KS 67401
Alpha Omicron, Georgetown College, Georgetown, KY 40324
Alpha Pi, Southwest Texas State University, San Marcos, TX 78666
Alpha Rho, Brenau College, Gainesville, GA 30501
Alpha Sigma, Our Lady of the Lake University, San Antonio, TX 78285
Alpha Tau, John B Stetson University, DeLand, FL 32720
Alpha Upsilon, Winona State University, Winona, MN 55987
Alpha Chi, Black Hills State College, Spearfish, SD 57783
Alpha Psi, University of South Carolina, Columbia, SC 29208
Alpha Omega, Wichita State University, Wichita, KS 67208
Alpha Alpha Alpha, Oregon College, Monmouth, OR 97361
Alpha Alpha Beta, Oklahoma Baptist University, Shawnee, OK 74801
Alpha Alpha Delta, Western State College, Gunnison, CO 81230
Alpha Alpha Epsilon, Southwestern College, Winfield, KS 67156
Alpha Alpha Eta, University of Southern California, Los Angeles, CA 90007
Alpha Alpha Theta, University of Tampa, Tampa, FL 33606
Alpha Alpha Iota, University of Miami, Coral Gables, FL 33124
Alpha Alpha Kappa, Arkansas State University, Jonesboro, AR 72467
Alpha Alpha Lambda, Southwestern Oklahoma State University, Weatherford, OK 73096
Alpha Alpha Mu, Eastern Washington State College, Cheney, WA 99004
Alpha Alpha Nu, University of Texas at El Paso, El Paso, TX 79968
Alpha Alpha Xi, Phillips University, Enid, OK 73701
Alpha Alpha Omicron, Eastern New Mexico University, Portales, NM 88130
Alpha Alpha Pi, Oregon State University, Corvallis, OR 97331
Alpha Alpha Rho, University of Southern Mississippi, Hattiesburg, MS 39401
Alpha Alpha Sigma, New Mexico Highlands University, Las Vegas, NM 87701
Alpha Alpha Tau, West Liberty State College, West Liberty, WV 26074
Alpha Alpha Upsilon, St Cloud State University, Saint Cloud, MN 56301
Alpha Alpha Phi, University of North Carolina, Chapel Hill, NC 27514
Alpha Alpha Chi, Murray State University, Murray, KY 42071
Alpha Alpha Psi, Eastern Kentucky University, Richmond, KY 40475
Beta Alpha, Baker University, Baldwin City, KS 66006
Beta Beta, Kearney State College, Kearney, NE 68847
Beta Gamma, Southeast Missouri State University, Cape Girardeau, MO 63701
Beta Delta, University of Alabama, University, AL 35486
Beta Epsilon, North Texas State University, Denton, TX 76203
Beta Zeta, Heidelberg College, Tiffin, OH 44883
Beta Eta, Marshall University, Huntington, WV 25701
Beta Theta, Wayne State College, Wayne, NE 68787
Beta Iota, Stephen F Austin State University, Nacogdoches, TX 75961
Beta Kappa, Queen's College of the City University of New York, Flushing, NY 11367
Beta Lambda, Hofstra University, Hempstead, NY 11550
Beta Mu, Frostburg State College, Frostburg, MD 21532
Beta Nu, Hunter College of the City University of New York, New York, NY 10021
Beta Xi, University of Evansville, Evansville, IN 47702
Beta Omicron, Lewis and Clark College, Portland, OR 97219
Beta Pi, West Texas State University, Canyon, TX 79016
Beta Rho, State College of Iowa, Cedar Falls, IA 50613
Beta Sigma, Drew University, Madison, NJ 07940
Beta Tau, Lamar University, Beaumont, TX 77710
Beta Upsilon, Harris Teachers College, Saint Louis, MO 63103
Beta Phi, Texas Wesleyan College, Fort Worth, TX 76105
Beta Chi, Hardin-Simmons University, Abilene, TX 79601
Beta Psi, Concord College, Athens, WV 24712
Beta Omega, Seattle Pacific College, Seattle, WA 98119
Gamma Alpha, Northwest Missouri State University, Maryville, MO 64468
Gamma Beta, Fairmont State College, Fairmont, WV 26554
Gamma Gamma, Union College, Barbourville, KY 40906
Gamma Delta, University of Wisconsin, Eau Claire, WI 54701
Gamma Epsilon, University of Houston, Houston, TX 77004
Gamma Zeta, Hastings College, Hastings, NE 68901
Gamma Eta, Nebraska State College, Chadron, NE 69337
Gamma Theta, Montclair State College, Upper Montclair, NJ 07043
Gamma Iota, Eastern Oregon College, LaGrande, OR 97850
Gamma Kappa, Madison University, Harrisonburg, VA 22802
Gamma Lambda, Abilene Christian University, Abilene, TX 79601
Gamma Mu, Northwestern State University, Natchitoches, LA 71457
Gamma Nu, University of Southwestern Louisiana, Lafayette, LA 70501
Gamma Xi, Louisiana College, Pineville, LA 71360
Gamma Omicron, Centenary College of Louisiana, Shreveport, LA 71104
Gamma Pi, Western Kentucky University, Bowling Green, KY 42101
Gamma Rho, Northwestern Oklahoma State University, Alva, OK 73717
Gamma Sigma, Adelphi University, Garden City, NY 11530
Gamma Tau, California State University, Los Angeles, CA 90032
Gamma Upsilon, University of Alaska, Fairbanks, AK 99701
Gamma Chi, Alaska Methodist University, Anchorage, AK 99504
Gamma Psi, San Diego State University, San Diego, CA 92115
Gamma Omega, West Virginia Wesleyan College, Buckhannon, WV 26201
Delta Alpha, Northeast Louisiana University, Monroe, LA 71201
Delta Beta, Mississippi College, Clinton, MS 39058
Delta Gamma, Mankato State University, Mankato, MN 56001
Delta Delta, Western Illinois University, Macomb, IL 61455
Delta Epsilon, University of Bridgeport, Bridgeport, CT 06602
Delta Zeta, State University of New York College at New Paltz, New Paltz, NY 12561
Delta Eta, Northern Montana College, Havre, MT 59501
Delta Iota, Morehead State University, Morehead, KY 40351
Delta Kappa, University of the Philippines, Quezon City, PI
Delta Lambda, Delta State University, Cleveland, MS 38732
Delta Mu, University of North Alabama, Florence, AL 35630
Delta Nu, Belhaven College, Jackson, MS 39202
Delta Xi, Arkansas Polytechnic College, Russellville, AR 72801
Delta Omicron, Long Island University, C W Post Center, Greenvale, NY 11548
Delta Pi, Asheville Biltmore College, Asheville, NC 28801
Delta Rho, Ottawa University, Ottawa, KS 66067
Delta Sigma, Keuka College, Keuka Park, NY 14478
Delta Tau, Alabama State University, Montgomery, AL 36104
Delta Upsilon, Troy State University, Troy, AL 36081
Delta Phi, College of Mount Saint Vincent, Bronx, NY 10471
Delta Psi, Waynesburg College, Waynesburg, PA 15370
Delta Omega, Louisiana Tech University, Rushton, LA 71270
Epsilon Alpha, Baldwin-Wallace College, Berea, OH 44017
Epsilon Gamma, Middle Tennessee State University, Murfreesboro, TN 37130
Epsilon Delta, Minot State College, Minot, ND 58701
Epsilon Zeta, Dickinson State College, Dickinson, ND 58601
Epsilon Eta, State College of Arkansas, Conway, AR 72032
Epsilon Theta, McMurray College, Abilene, TX 79605
Epsilon Iota, Harding College, Searcy, AR 72143
Epsilon Kappa, Montreat-Anderson College, Montreat, NC 28757
Epsilon Lambda, University of Wyoming, Laramie, WY 82071
Epsilon Mu, Boise State University, Boise, ID 83725
Epsilon Omicron, Herbert H Lehman College of the City University of New York, Bronx, NY 10468
Epsilon Pi, Carson Newman College, Jefferson City, TN 37760
Epsilon Rho, Friends University, Wichita, KS 67213
Epsilon Sigma, Ohio Northern University, Ada, OH 45810
Epsilon Tau, University of Alabama in Huntsville, Huntsville, AL 35807
Epsilon Upsilon, Saint Mary's College, Saint Mary's City, MD 20686
Epsilon Phi, Mississippi State University, Mississippi State, MS 39762
Epsilon Chi, Bethany College, Bethany, WV 26032
Epsilon Psi, University of Mississippi, Oxford, MS 38677
Epsilon Omega, Instituto Allende, San Miguel de Allende,
Zeta Alpha, Austin College, Box 1499, Sherman, TX 75090
Zeta Gamma, Union University, Jackson, TN 38301
Zeta Delta, Oklahoma Christian College, Oklahoma City, OK 73111
Zeta Zeta, University of Texas, Austin, TX 78712
Zeta Eta, Kilgore College, Kilgore, TX 75662
Zeta Theta, Belleuve College, Belleuve, NE 68005
Zeta Iota, Meridian Junior College, Meridian, MS 39301
Zeta Kappa, Nebraska Wesleyan University, Lincoln, NE 68504
Zeta Lambda, Salisbury State College, Salisbury, MD 21801
Zeta Mu, Jacksonville University, Jacksonville, FL 32211

O **MID-AMERICA ARTS ALLIANCE,** Suite 550, 20 W Ninth St, Kansas City, MO 64105. Tel 816-421-1388. *Chmn* Harry Seward; *VChmn* Robin Tryloff; *Secy* Marion Andersen; *Executive Dir* Henry Moran; *Dir Programs* Robert Pierle; *General Mgr* Will Conner; *Visual Arts Dir* Edean Martin
Estab 1973 to coordinate touring arts events and services (performing and visual arts), for people of Arkansas, Kansas, Missouri, Nebraska and Oklahoma.
Average Annual Attendance: 600,000
Income: $2,200,000 (financed by federal and state grants, private contributions and sponsorship fees)
Exhibitions: (1981-1983) Benton's Bentons; Light & Color - Images from New Mexico; Goin' to Kansas City - A Social History of Jazz in Mid America and the Southwest; Forever One Child - Toys Designed by Artists; The Joy and Arthur Addis Collection of 20th Century Mexican Art; Visions 83 - a juried biennial of regional artists; Lewis Hine - Human Documents; Frozen In Time - Photographs by Joseph Judd Pennell; Thomas Morans - Selling The West; Of Dustbowl Descent - Forty Years on the Great Plains; 500 Years of Botanical Illustrations; The Art Of The Mola; The Oklahoma State Art Collection; Crying For A Vision - A Rosebud Sioux Trilogy
Publications: Exhibition catalogues
Activities: Lectures open to public in conjunction with selected touring exhibitions; concerts; awards to artists selected for biennial exhibit; sponsor development assistance; book traveling exhibitions; originate traveling exhibitions

O **MIDWEST ART HISTORY SOCIETY,** Elvehjem Museum of Art, University of Wisconsin, Madison, WI 53706. *Pres* Jane C Hutchison; *Secy-Treasurer* Burton L Dunbar
Estab 1973 to further art history in the Midwest as a discipline and a profession.
Average Annual Attendance: 150 at meetings. Mem: 550; membership is open to institutions, students and academic and museum art historians in the Midwest; dues institution $10, professional $5; annual meeting March 29th-31st
Income: $1200 (financed by membership)
Publications: Midwest Art History Society Newsletter, Oct & April
Activities: Lect provided

O **NATIONAL ACADEMY OF DESIGN,** 1083 Fifth Ave, New York, NY 10028. Tel 212-369-4880. *Dir* John H Dobkin; *Asst* Barbara Krulik
Open Tues - Sun Noon - 5 PM, cl Mon, New Year's, Thanksgiving & Christmas.
Admis $1.50. Estab 1825, honorary arts organization for American artists and architects. Mem: 425
Collections: Permanent collection consists of 250 architectural drawings and portfolios, 1200 drawings and graphics, 2000 paintings, 500 sculptures, all are the gifts of the artist and architectural members of the Academy from 1825 to present; prints and watercolors dating from the 19th century; Hudson River School Portraits; American Impressionism; 30's & 40's Realism; American paintings, drawings & sculpture
Exhibitions: Annual juried exhibition of contemporary art; exhibitions of permanent collection & loan exhibitions
Publications: Annual exhibition catalogue; catalogues of exhibitions of permanent collection
Activities: Classes for adults; lectures open to public; awards; tours by appt; scholarships; individual paintings and original objects of art lent to other museums; museum shop sells books, posters, catalogues and postcards
L **Fine Arts Archives,** 1083 Fifth Ave & 89th St, 10028. *Archivist* Abigail Booth Gerdts
Open by appointment only
Library Holdings: Biographical files on all members, correspondence, exhibition records, news clips from 1826 to present

O **NATIONAL ANTIQUE AND ART DEALERS ASSOCIATION OF AMERICA,** 59 E 57th St, New York, NY 10022. Tel 212-355-0636. *Pres* Peter L Schaffer; *VPres* Emily M Manheim; *VPres* Philip Colleck; *Secy* James Berry Hill; *Treas* Christian Jussel
Estab 1954 to promote the best interests of the antique and art trade; to collect and circulate reports, statistics and other information pertaining to art; to sponsor and organize antique and art exhibitions; to promote just, honorable and ethical trade practices
Activities: Lect

O **NATIONAL ARCHITECTURAL ACCREDITING BOARD, INC,** 1735 New York Ave NW, Washington, DC 20006. Tel 202-783-2007. *Exec Dir* John Wilson-Jeronimo
Estab 1940 to produce and maintain a current list of accredited programs in architecture in the United States and its jurisdictions, with the general objective that a well-integrated program of architectural education be developed which will be national in scope
Publications: Criteria and Procedures, pamphlet; List of Accredited Programs in Architecture, annually

O **NATIONAL ART EDUCATION ASSOCIATION,** 1916 Association Dr, Reston, VA 22091. Tel 703-860-8000. *Exec Dir* Dr Daniel G Cannon; *Pres* Dr Nancy MacGregor; *Pres-Elect* Robert Curtis
Estab 1947 through the affiliation of four regional groups, Eastern, Western, Pacific and Southeastern Arts Associations. The NAEA is a national organization devoted to the advancement of the professional interests and competence of teachers of art at all educational levels. Promotes the study of the problems of teaching art; encourages research and experimentation; facilitates the professional and personal cooperation of its members; holds public discussions and programs; publishes desirable articles, reports, and surveys; integrates efforts of others with similar purposes. Mem: 6699 art teachers, administrators, supervisors and students; fee institutional comprehensive $150, active $50; National Conference held 1984 will be in Miami, FL
Income: Programs financed through membership, sales of publications, and occasional grants for specific purposes
Publications: Art Education, 8 issues per year; Studies in Art Education, 4 times per year; special publications

O **NATIONAL ASSEMBLY OF LOCAL ARTS AGENCIES,** 1625 Eye St NW, Suite 725A, Washington, DC 20006. Tel 202-293-6818. *Pres* Robert Camon; *VPres* Burton I Woolf; *Treasurer* Thomas J Heywood; *Executive Dir* Gretchen Wiest; *Program Coordr* Vivian McKibben; *Secy* Christine Gill
Open Mon - Fri 9 AM - 5 PM. No admis fee. Estab 1978 to provide services for and to represent the interests of local arts agencies. Mem: 500; annual meeting June
Income: $165,000 (financed by membership, grants and contracts)
Publications: Newsletter, semi-monthly

O **NATIONAL ASSEMBLY OF STATE ARTS AGENCIES,** 1010 Vermont Ave NW, Suite 316, Washington, DC 20005. Tel 202-347-6352. *Chmn* Peter de Chero; *VPres* Robert Yegge; *Secy* Ellen McCulloch-Lovell; *Executive Dir* Geoffrey Platt Jr
Estab 1975 to enhance the growth and development of the arts through an informed and skilled membership; to provide forums for the review and development of national arts policy. Mem: 56; members are the fifty-six state and jurisdictional arts agencies, affiliate memberships are open to public; annual meeting Oct
Income: Financed by membership and federal grants
Publications: Annual survey of state appropriations to arts councils; newsletter, monthly

O **NATIONAL ASSOCIATION OF SCHOOLS OF ART AND DESIGN,** 11250 Roger Bacon Dr, 5, Reston, VA 22090. Tel 703-437-0700. *Pres* George Bayliss; *Exec Dir* Samuel Hope
Formerly the National Conference of Schools of Design, holding its first conference in 1944. Changed name in 1948, at which time its constitution and by-laws were adopted. Changed its name again in 1960 from National Association of Schools of Design to National Association of Schools of Art. Name changed again in 1981 to National Association of Schools of Art and Design. NASAD is the national accrediting agency for higher educational institutions in the visual arts and design and is so recognized by the US Department of Education and the Council on Postsecondary Accreditation. The organization was established to develop a closer relationship among schools and departments of art and design for the purpose of educating designers and artists in the visual arts and giving evidence of permanence and stability, possessing an approved organization, administration, faculty and facilities and maintaining standards agreed upon by the Association
Publications: Directory of Member Institutions, annually; Handbook of Accreditation Standards, biennial

O **NATIONAL ASSOCIATION OF WOMEN ARTISTS, INC,** 41 Union Square, New York, NY 10003. Tel 212-675-1616. *Secy* C Costa
Estab 1889 as a national organization to provide opportunities for member women artists, to exhibit and sell their work. Mem: 650; member work is juried prior to selection; dues $25; meetings Nov and May
Income: Financed by membership
Exhibitions: Annual members' exhibition in spring with awards; annual traveling exhibitions of oils, watercolors and graphics; annual New York City shows of oils, watercolors, graphics and sculpture
Publications: Annual Exhibition Catalog
Activities: Lect open to the public, 1 visiting lectr per year; awards given during annual exhibition; originate traveling exhibitions

O **NATIONAL CARTOONISTS SOCIETY,** Nine Ebony Court, Brooklyn, NY 11229. Tel 212-743-6510. *Pres* John Cullen Murphy; *Secy* Frank Springer; *Scribe* Marge Duffy Devine
Estab 1946 to advance the ideals and standards of the profession of cartooning; to assist needy, or incapacitated cartoonists; to stimulate interest in the art of cartooning by cooperating with established schools; to encourage talented students; to assist governmental and charitable institutes. Mem: 480; annual Reuben Awards Dinner in April
Collections: Milt Gross Fund; National Cartoonists Society Collection
Publications: Newsletter, monthly; The Cartoonist; annually
Activities: Educ dept to supply material and information to students; individual cartoonists to lect, chalktalks can be arranged; cartoon auctions; proceeds from traveling exhibitions and auctions support Milt Gross Fund assisting needy cartoonists, widows and children; gives Reuben Award to Outstanding Cartoonist of the Year, Silver Plaque Awards to best cartoonists in individual categories of cartooning; original cartoons lent to schools, libraries and galleries; originate traveling exhibitions

O **NATIONAL COUNCIL OF ARCHITECTURAL REGISTRATION BOARDS,** 1735 New York Ave NW, Suite 700, Washington, DC 20006. Tel 202-783-6500. *Executive Dir* Samuel T Balen
Estab 1920 as a clearinghouse for architects registering from state to state. All now have laws regulating the practice of architecture. Mem: 54, including state architectural registration boards of the United States, Puerto Rico, Virgin Islands and Guam; annual meeting June 1983 in Philadelphia
Publications: Annual Report; Architect Registration Examination Handbook, annually; Newsletter, quarterly

O **NATIONAL ENDOWMENT FOR THE ARTS,** 2401 E St NW, Washington, DC 20506. Tel 202-682-2000. *Chmn* Livingston L Biddle Jr; *Deputy Chmn* David D Searles; *Deputy Chmn* Mary Ann Tighe
Open 9 AM - 5:30 PM. No admis fee. Estab 1965 as a national organization to make the arts available to more people across the country; to strengthen cultural institutions so they can better serve the people; to advance cultural legacy
Income: $139,660,000 appropriation for fiscal year 1979, for programming Federal funds that are given through grants to individuals and non-profit organizations. Grants to organizations must be matched at least dollar for dollar by private, state or local funds
Publications: Annual Report; Cultural Post, bi-monthly; Guide to Programs

L **Library,** 2401 E St NW, 20506. Tel 202-634-7640. *Librn* M Christine Morrison
Open Mon - Fri 9 AM - 5:30 PM. Estab 1971 to provide an effective
information service which will support program and division activities and
contribute to the accomplishment of agency goals
Income: Financed by federal appropriation
Library Holdings: Vols 5000; Per subs 150; Other — Clipping files, exhibition
catalogs
Special Subjects: Arts in contemporary America, arts administration, cultural
policy; government and the arts

O **NATIONAL INSTITUTE FOR ARCHITECTURAL EDUCATION,** 30 W
22nd St, New York, NY 10010. Tel 212-924-7000. *Chmn Board* Stanley
Salzman; *VChmn* John Stonehill; *Treas* Byron Bell; *Secy* Raymond F Pavia; *Dir
Education* Arthur Rosenblatt; *Executive Secy* Lilian Marus
Open Mon - Fri 9 AM - 5 PM. Incorporated 1894 as Society of Beaux-Arts
Architects, which was dissolved Dec 1941; Beaux-Arts Institute of Design estab
1916, name changed 1956 to present name. Mem: Approx 250; dues $25; annual
meeting first week in Dec
Exhibitions: Prize-winning drawings of competitions held during year
Publications: Yearbook, annually in October
Activities: Trustee for the Lloyd Warren Fellowship (Paris Prize in Architecture)
for study and travel abroad; William Van Alen Architect Memorial Award
(international competition) annual scholarship for further study or research
project of some architectural nature; and other trust funds for prize awards for
study and travel abroad and educational activities in the United States

O **NATIONAL LEAGUE OF AMERICAN PEN WOMEN,** 1300 17th St NW,
Washington, DC 20036. Tel 202-785-1997,Ext 785. *Chmn* Pauline D Lorfano;
Pres Virginia Avery; *First VPres* Wanda Rider; *Second VPres* Genevieve Randall;
Treasurer Edna Falbo; *Letters* M Louise Ray; *Music* Gladys Scalfe
Maintains member reference library. Mem: 6200; 212 state branches; dues $25
Collections: Purchase award
Exhibitions: Arts Club of Washington; 1986 in Boston
Publications: The Pen Woman, monthly magazine
Activities: Lectures open to members; competitions with awards; scholarships

O **NATIONAL MUSEUM & GALLERY REGISTRATION ASSOCIATION,**
1629 K St NW, Suite 520, Washington, DC 20006
Estab 1969 to record ownership & past ownership of artists' works & current
retail value of works of fine art. Maintains biographical archive covering artists
represented in members' collections, museums & galleries. Mem: 1293
Collections: Members' works
Activities: Speakers bureau; grants & awards

O **NATIONAL SCULPTURE SOCIETY,** 15 E 26th St, New York, NY 10010.
Tel 212-889-6960. *Pres* Charlotte Dunwiddie; *VPres* Domenico Facci; *Secy*
Donald Miller; *Executive Dir* Claire A Stein
Open Mon - Fri 9 AM - 5 PM. No admis fee. Estab 1893 as a national
organization to spread the knowledge of good sculpture. Average Annual
Attendance: 4000 at annual exhibition. Mem: 350; work juried for sculptor
membership; vote of Board of Directors for allied professional and patron
membership; dues $20-$50; annual meeting second Tues in Jan
Income: Financed by endowment, membership & donations
Exhibitions: Annual juried exhibition open to all United States residents
Publications: Exhibition catalog, annually; membership book, triennial; National
Sculpture Review, quarterly
Activities: Lect open to the public, 5 visiting lectr per year; gallery talks and
tours with annual exhibition; youth awards annually; exhibition prizes; Education
Committee chooses recipients for NSS scholarships; scholarships offered to
accredited art schools; exhibitions organized for other institutions
L **Library,** 15 E 26th St, 10010. Tel 212-889-6961
Open to the public for reference; a few volumes and periodicals, photographic
and original archival materials
Library Holdings: Per subs 6000; Micro — Fiche; AV — Slides; Other —
Clipping files, exhibition catalogs, photographs, sculpture
Special Subjects: Sculpture, American sculpture, biography, history

O **NATIONAL SOCIETY OF MURAL PAINTERS, INC,** 41 E 65th St, New
York, NY 10021. Tel 212-873-1095. *Pres* Dean Fausett; *Secy* Lloyd Lozes Goff
Estab and incorporated 1895 to encourage and advance the standards of mural
painting in America; to formulate a code for decorative competitions and by-laws
to regulate professional practice. Mem: 200; dues $20, non-resident $15
Publications: Biographies and articles pertinent to the mural painting profession;
Press Sheets of photographs and articles of the executed work of the members of
society
Activities: Exhibitions held in collaboration with allied professions; available for
booking - a traveling show of color sketches for murals on the subject of
momentous events in American History

O **NATIONAL SOCIETY OF PAINTERS IN CASEIN AND ACRYLIC, INC,**
225 W 34th St, Rm 1510, New York, NY 10001. Tel 212-686-2659. *Pres* Mark
Freeman; *VPres* Jack Bookbinder; *VPres* David Laska; *Secy* Lily Shuff
Open in March during annual exhibition. Estab 1952 as a national organization
for a showcase for artists in casein and acrylic. Galleries rented from National
Arts Club. Average Annual Attendance: 800 during exhibition. Mem: 120;
membership by invitation, work must pass three juries; dues $20; annual meeting
April
Income: $3000 (financed by membership)
Exhibitions: 27th and 28th Annual Exhibition
Publications: Exhibition Catalog, annually
Activities: Demonstrations; medals and $2500 in prizes given at annual
exhibition; originate traveling exhibitions

O **NATIONAL WATERCOLOR SOCIETY,** 2408 Daneland, Lakewood, CA
90712. *Pres* Dr Jae Carmichael; *First VPres* Pat Cox; *Treas* Betty Rodbard;
Correspondence Secy Ruth Eyrich
Estab 1921 to sponsor art exhibits for the cultural and educational benefit of the
public. Mem: 528; dues $25 beginning each year in March (must be juried into
membership); annual meeting Jan
Collections: Award-winning paintings from 1954 to present
Exhibitions: Spring Membership Exhibition; National Annual Exhibition
Activities: Docent training; slide-cassette program of members' works;
competitions; cash awards; originate traveling exhibitions

O **NEW ENGLAND WATERCOLOR SOCIETY,** 748 First Parish Rd, Scituate,
MA 02066. Tel 617-545-2025. *Pres* Charles A Mahoney; *VPres* Glenn MacNutt;
Secy Fletcher Adams
Estab 1886 to advance the practice of watercolor and its proficiency. Average
Annual Attendance: 8000. Mem: 125; dues $15; annual meeting Jan
Income: Financed by membership
Activities: Lectures open to the public

O **PRINT CLUB,** 1614 Latimer St, Philadelphia, PA 19103. Tel 215-735-6090.
Pres Donald W McPhail; *VPres* Cynthia Lister; *VPres* Peter Paone; *VPres*
Richard Jaffe; *Secy* Bobbye Burke; *Dir* Ofelia Garcia; *Asst to Dir* Marilyn Dix
Open Tues - Sat 10 AM - 5:30 PM. No admis fee. Estab 1915 as a non-profit,
educational organization dedicated to the promotion of fine prints and the
support and encouragement of printmakers and print collectors. Average Annual
Attendance: 2000. Mem: 4000; dues contributing $50, family $30, individual $25,
artists $15; annual meeting in Jan
Income: $80,000 (financed by endowment, membership and private and
government grants for some activities)
Collections: The Print Club Permanent Collection (prints and photograph
collection held at the Philadelphia Museum of Art); The Print Club Archives
(documents, books and catalogues held at the Historical Society of Pennsylvania)
Exhibitions: Changing monthly exhibitions of prints and photographs; Annual
International Competition (since 1924)
Publications: Counter Proof, bi-annual; News Print, monthly news sheet
Activities: Workshops for artists; lect series for print collectors; lect open to
public, 15 visiting lectr per year; gallery talks; competitions; various prizes and
purchase awards; originate traveling exhibitions
L **Library,** 1614 Latimer St, 19103
Open to members for reference
Special Subjects: Auction information, catalogs raisonnes, exhibitions, history of
prints, printmaking

O **PRINT COUNCIL OF AMERICA,** Museum of Fine Arts, Boston, MA 02115.
Tel 617-267-9300. *Pres* Sue W Reed; *Treas* Diana Johnson
Estab 1956 as a nonprofit organization fostering the study and appreciation of
fine prints, new and old. Mem: 100 museum and university professionals
interested in prints; annual meeting April or May
Publications: Occasional publications on old and modern prints

O **SALMAGUNDI CLUB,** 47 Fifth Ave, New York, NY 10003. Tel 212-255-
7740. *Chmn of Board* William C W Fames; *Pres* Carol L Thomson;
Correspondence Secy Linda E Scher
Gallery open during exhibitions 1 - 5 PM. No admis fee. Estab 1871,
incorporated 1880, building purchased 1917. Clubhouse with living quarters for
men, restaurant, gallery and library. Mem: 600; dues resident $288,
resident artist $212, nonresident layman $174, nonresident artist $162, junior
$120; scholarship graduated to scale
Exhibitions: Seven per year by artist members with cash awards
Publications: Centennial Roster published in 1972; Salmagundi Membership
Roster, biennially; Salmagundian, monthly except for summer
Activities: Lect; art classes; awards; scholarships and prizes; acts as organizing
and screening agency between the US Navy and all qualified American artists;
under its Naval Art Cooperation and Liaison (NACAL) Committee, artists are
chosen and sent on short painting trips around the world to interpret the daily
life and traditions of the US Navy; buys paintings to present to museums
L **Library,** 47 Fifth Ave, 10003
For reference only
Library Holdings: Vols 6000

O **SCULPTORS GUILD, INC,** 110 Greene St, New York, NY 10012. Tel 212-
431-5669. *Pres* Bill Barrett; *Executive VPres* Cleo Hartwig; *Secy* Legh Myers;
Treasurer Chaim Gross; *VPres Membership* Jean Woodham
Open Tues - Thurs 10 AM - 1:30 PM & by appointment. No admis fee. Estab
1937 to promote sculpture & show members' work in an annual show &
throughout the country. Mem: 100; dues $35; annual meeting in May
Publications: Exhibition catalogs
Activities: Lectures open to public; competitions; originates traveling exhibitions

O **SOCIETY FOR FOLK ARTS PRESERVATION, INC,** 308 E 70 St, New
York, NY 10021. Tel 212-734-4503. *Exec Dir* Evelyn Stern; *First VPres* Edward
Lauitt; *Second VPres* Dr Erika Moser; *Secy* Jude Burkhauser
Estab 1977 to document on film and video, living folk art and craft traditions,
worldwide. Mem: 350; dues $15
Income: Financed by donations
Exhibitions: Warli Womens Wall Paintings from Maharashtra, India; A Sense of
Beauty; Multi Image Slide Presentations - Crafts and People of Asia
Publications: Newsletter, three times per yr
Activities: Lectures open to the public, 3 vis lectr per yr; originate traveling
exhibitions
L **Library,** New York, NY 10021
Estab 1979. Reference only
Library Holdings: Vols 500; AV — A-tapes, slides 10,000, v-tapes; Other —
Clipping files, exhibition catalogs, memorabilia, original art works, pamphlets,
photographs
Special Subjects: Living folk arts and crafts
Collections: Indian textiles; folk art

O **SOCIETY OF AMERICAN GRAPHIC ARTISTS,** Room 1214, 32 Union Square, New York, NY 10003. Tel 212-260-5706. *Pres* Robert Broner; *VPres* George Nama; *VPres* Dan Welden; *Treas* Helen Gerardia; *Recording Secy* Christine Engler; *Corresponding Secy* Steven Yamin
Estab 1916 as a society of printmakers. Mem: 250 voted in by merit; dues $15; annual meeting May
Income: Financed by membership and associate memberships
Exhibitions: Semi-annual Open Competition National Print Exhibition; Semi-annual Closed Members Exhibit; National Traveling Exhibitions every two years
Publications: Exhibition Catalog, annually; Presentation Prints for Associate Membership
Activities: Lect open to public, 1 visiting lectr per year; sponsors competitive and members' exhibits with awards; original objects of art lent, lending collection contains original prints; originate traveling exhibitions

O **SOCIETY OF AMERICAN HISTORICAL ARTISTS,** Box 3635, Stamford, CT 06902. *Pres* Don Troiani; *VPres* James Muir; *Treasurer* Ron Tunison; *Secy* James Triggs
Estab 1980 for furthering American Historical Art, especially authenticity. Mem: 13; dues $150; meeting 3-4 per yr
Activities: Awards for excellence

O **SOCIETY OF ANIMAL ARTISTS, INC,** 151 Carroll St Box 24, City Island, Bronx, NY 10464. Tel 212-885-2181. *Pres* Albert Gilbert; *Treas* Joseph Vance Jr; *Secy* Patricia Allen Bott
Open during exhibitions. No admis fee. Estab 1960 to encourage internatinoal awareness of the artists who explore the beauty and habits of animals, and by so doing, help ecology and the environment. Mem: 250; artists must pass jury of admissions to become a member; dues $95, initiation fee $200; meetings twice a year, or more often if needed
Income: Financed by membership
Exhibitions: 1978 held at Sportsmans Edge, New York City, Owens Gallery, Oklahoma City, Philadelphia Museum of Natural History, Denver Museum of Natural History, Mulvane Art Center, Topeka Kansas and A M Adler Fine Arts, New York
Publications: Newsletter, every other month, sometimes more often
Activities: Lect for members only, 3 visiting lectr per year; gallery talks; conventions arranged with film lect and instruction; slide lect of trips with animal art by members; advisory board for those who want to study animal art and wildlife; paintings and individual objects of art lent to members, wildlife organizations, Audubon, World Wildlife Special Exhibitions; lending collection consists of catalogs, prints, color and framed reproductions, sculpture, photographs and slides; originate traveling exhibitions; prints, reproductions and original art sold at gallery shows

O **SOCIETY OF ARCHITECTURAL HISTORIANS,** 1700 Walnut St, Suite 716, Philadelphia, PA 19103. Tel 215-735-0224, 735-0246. *Pres* Damie Stillman; *First VPres* Carol Krinsky; *Second VPres* Osmund Overby; *Secy* Eileen Michels; *Executive Secy* Paulette Olson
Open daily 8:30 AM - 4:30 PM. Estab to provide an international forum for those interested in architecture and its related arts, to encourage scholarly research in the field and to promote the preservation of significant architectural monuments throughout the world. Mem: 4500 who show an interest in architecture, past, present and future; dues $48; annual meeting April
Income: Financed by membership
Publications: Journal, quarterly; Newsletter, bimonthly; Preservation Forum, biannual
Activities: Sponsors competitions; Alice Davis Hitchcock Book Award and Founders' Award given annually; scholarships given to student members for graduate work in architecture & architectural history to attend annual domestic tour; Rosann Berry Fellowship to help advanced grad student attend annual meeting; sales shop sells architectural guides and booklets and also back issues of the Journal

O **SOCIETY OF ILLUSTRATORS,** 128 E 63rd St, New York, NY 10021. Tel 212-838-2560. *Pres* D L Cramer, PhD; *Dir* Terry Brown
Open Mon - Fri 10 AM - 5 PM. No admis fee. Estab 1901 as a national organization of professional illustrators and art directors. Gallery has group, theme, one-man and juried shows, approx every three weeks. Mem: 900
Publications: Illustrators Annual
Activities: Lect open to public; holds annual national juried exhibition of best illustrations of the year; awards scholarships to college level art students; originate traveling exhibitions; sales shop sells books
L **Library,** New York, NY 10021
Reference Library
Library Holdings: Vols 5000; Per subs 10; American Illustration, 1880-present; AV — V-tapes; Other — Clipping files, memorabilia, original art works

O **SOCIETY OF MEDALISTS,** Old Ridgebury Rd, Danbury, CT 06810. Tel 203-792-3000. *Pres* Donald A Eifert; *Art Advisory Board* Elvira Clain-Stefanelli; *Art Advisory Board* Frank Eliscur; *Art Advisory Board* Marcel Jovine; *Art Advisory Board* Eric Sloane; *Art Advisory Board* Albert Weinman; *Exec Secy* Carol Cipot
Estab 1930 by the late art patron, George DuPont Pratt, to stimulate interest in medallic sculpture. The Society of Medalists has granted two commissions annually since 1930 to American sculptors to execute basrelief medallic sculpture. The finished high-relief fine art medals struck by the Society are then distributed to dues paying members of the non-profit organization. Mem: 1200
Collections: Complete collections of Society medals are on permanent exhibition at the R W Norton Gallery, Shreveport, Louisiana and the World Heritage Museum, University of Illinois, Urbana, Illinois
Publications: News Bulletin, annually

O **SOCIETY OF NORTH AMERICAN GOLDSMITHS,** 6707 N Santa Monica Blvd, Milwaukee, WI 53217. Tel 414-468-0204. *Pres* Arline M Fisch; *VPres* Michael Croft; *Treas* Douglas Steakley; *Business Mgr* Robert Mitchell
Mem: 1800; dues $45; annual meetings in June

Income: $150,000
Exhibitions: Distinguised Members of SNAG; Jewelry USA
Publications: Metalsmith, quarterly magazine; Newsletter, montly
Activities: Lectures open to members only; competitions

O **SOCIETY OF TYPOGRAPHIC ARTS,** 233 E Ontario, Suite 301, Chicago, IL 60611. Tel 312-787-2018. *Pres* Rick Valicenti; *VPres* K Groble; *Secy* W Goldsmith; *Exec Dir* Jane Dunne
Estab 1927 as a non-profit association of graphic designers. Mem: 1300; dues resident $60, nonres $40, student $30; annual meeting in June
Income: Financed by membership
Exhibitions: STA/100 Show
Publications: 100 Catalog, annually; annual membership directory; monthly newsletter; quarterly journal
Activities: Education dept; design office visitation program; annual design awards program; lectures open to public, 20 vis lectr per yr; tours; competitions; awards; scholarships; originate traveling exhibitions

O **SOUTHERN ASSOCIATION OF SCULPTORS, INC,** c/o Tim Murray, University of Alabama, Huntsville, AL 35805. Tel 205-895-6114
Estab 1965, incorporated 1967, to promote the exchange of ideas and information among its members; assist institutions, museums and the public in developing and understanding of sculpture through exhibitions, demonstrations and publications. Mem: 210; mem open to any United States sculptor; annual meeting in Fall
Exhibitions: Annual National Juried Sculpture Traveling Exhibition
Publications: Illustrated Sculptors Directory; Job Information Center Bulletin, 9 per year; periodic technical publications; Presidents Newsletter, quarterly
Activities: Competitions; originate traveling exhibitions

O **SPECIAL LIBRARIES ASSOCIATION,** Museum, Arts and Humanities Division,* 235 Park Ave S, New York, NY 10003. Tel 212-477-9250. *Chmn* Thomas V Hull; *Secy Treas* William B Neff; *Bulletin Ed* Sharon Sweeting
Estab 1928 to provide an information forum and exchange for librarians in the specialized fields of museums, arts and humanities. Mem: 731; dues $55; annual meeting early June
Publications: Museums, Arts and Humanities Division Bulletin, semi-annual

O **THE STAINED GLASS ASSOCIATION OF AMERICA,** c/o Norman Temme, 1125 Wilmington Ave, Saint Louis, MO 63111. Tel 314-353-5128. *Pres* John Kebrle; *First VPres* Bill Laws; *Second VPres* John Salisbury; *Treas* Richard L Hoover; *Ed* Norman Temme; *Secy* Richard E Mesmer; *Exec Secy* Naomi M Mundy
Estab 1903 as an international organization to promote the development and advancement of the stained glass craft. Mem: 850; there are five categories of membership - studio member, artist designer, craft supplier member, associate member and patron member (various criteria apply to each membership); dues vary for members with size of studio; associate members $60, patron members $30; semi-annual meetings Jan and June
Income: Financed by membership dues
Publications: Stained Glass magazine, quarterly
Activities: Educ dept with two and three week courses; apprenticeship program; competitions sponsored for apprentices only, every two years; cash prizes

O **SUMI-E SOCIETY OF AMERICA,** 4200 Kings Mill Ln, Annandale, VA 22003. *Corresponding Secy* Margaret McAdams
Estab 1963 by a diversified group of people whose common interest was the art of Japanese brush painting. Mem: 350
Publications: The Sumi-E Notes, newsletter

O **UKIYO-E SOCIETY OF AMERICA, INC,** 1692 Second Ave, New York, NY 10028. *Pres* Dr Rafaele A Roncalli; *VPres* Gabriele H Grunebaum; *Secy* Ruth Lansner; *Treasurer* James Kirkpatrick III
Estab 1972 as society of collectors of Japanese woodblock prints. Average Annual Attendance: 350. Mem: 200; dues $25
Income: $10,000 (financed by membership)
Publications: Impressions, bi-annual newsletter; President's Newsletter, 10 per yr
Activities: Lectures open to public, 8-10

O **UNITED STATES COMMITTEE OF THE INTERNATIONAL ASSOCIATION OF ART, INC,** 1438 Montague St, NW, Washington, DC 20011. Tel 212-787-7063. *Pres* George Koch
Estab 1952, incorporated 1955, to promote greater appreciation of contemporary fine arts, regardless of genre; to uphold the status of the artists and to defend their rights, primarily on the national level, then on the international level, evaluating by comparison and appraisal; also to stimulate international cultural relations and exchanges of art and artists free of any aesthetic or other bias. Mem: Twelve national art organizations of painters, sculptors and graphic arts in the United States
Publications: Information, three per year

O **UNITED STATES DEPARTMENT OF THE INTERIOR,** Indian Arts and Crafts Board, C St between 18th & 19th Sts (Mailing add: United States Dept Interior, Room 4004, Washington, DC 20240). Tel 202-343-2773. *Gen Mgr* Robert G Hart; *Program Dir* Myles Libhart
Open Mon - Fri 7:45 AM - 5 PM. No admis fee. Estab 1936 to promote contemporary arts by Native Americans of the United States. Board administers the Southern Plains Indian Museum, Anadarko; Museum of the Plains Indian, Browning; Sioux Indian Museum, Rapid City. Average Annual Attendance: 80,000
Income: Financed by federal appropriation
Collections: Contemporary Native American Arts
Exhibitions: 27-30 one-person exhibitions among the three museums
Publications: Source Directory of Native American Owned and Operated Arts and Crafts Businesses

Activities: Information and advice on matters pertaining to contemporary Native American arts and crafts; Gallery talks; tours; originate traveling exhibitions

O **VISUAL ARTISTS AND GALLERIES ASSOCIATION, INC,** VAGA, One World Trade Center, Suite 1535, New York, NY 10048. Tel 212-466-1390; Telex 42-4848. *Executive Dir* Dorothy M Weber; *Asst Exec Dir* Evelyn Torres
Open daily 9 AM - 5 PM, by appointment. Estab 1976 as a nonprofit venture to help artists control and police the reproduction of their works, from textile designs to photographs in textbooks; to act as a clearinghouse for licensing reproduction rights and set up a directory of artists and other owners of reproduction rights for international use. Mem: European 10,000, American 500; dues gallery and associate $70, estates $50, artist $20
Income: Financed by membership
Special Subjects: Copyright Law, Moral Rights, Fair Use, Droite Morale
Publications: Newsletter
Activities: Lectures by guest speakers

Museums, Libraries and Associations In The United States

ALABAMA

BIRMINGHAM

M ALABAMA MUSEUM OF PHOTOGRAPHY, 4322 Glenwood Ave, 35222. Tel 205-595-6980. *Pres & Cur* Ed Willis Barnett; *VPres* James S Larkin
Open by appointment and invitation. No admis fee. Estab 1974 to promote photography as a fine art; to procure outstanding photographs from over the world and mount exhibitions in America; to maintain a laboratory for experimentation. Collections are housed in a residence, on display for students and small groups
Income: Financed by donations, grants from National Endowment for the Arts, and Alabama State Council
Collections: Ed Willis Barnett (many photographs, color and black and white); Samuel Chamberlain (30 photographs used to illustrate his books); Man Ray (rayographs, portraits, scenes); collection of Enos, Fassbender, Fincken, Fisher, Gore, Litzel, Underwood, Widder and others
Activities: Organize and circulate traveling exhibitions

M BIRMINGHAM MUSEUM OF ART, 2000 Eighth Ave N, 35203. Tel 205-254-2565. *Asst Dir* Gail Andrews Trechsel; *Cur Painting & Sculpture* Edward F Weeks; *Cur Decorative Arts* Bryding Adams; *Cur Oriental Art* John Seto; *Cur Education* Claudia Esko; *Registrar* Betty Keen
Open Tues, Wed, Fri, & Sat 10 AM - 5 PM, Thurs 10 AM - 9 PM, Sun 2 - 6 PM. No admis fee. Estab 1951 as a general art museum with collections from earliest manifestation of man's creativity to contemporary work. Its goal is to illustrate the highest level of man's artistic work in an art historical context. The 36 galleries are climate controlled; lighting system is modern and controlled to latest safety standards. Average Annual Attendance: 100,000. Mem: 2000; dues $10 - $500
Income: $2,000,000 (financed by membership, city appropriation and annual donations)
Purchases: $200,000
Collections: †English ceramics and silver; American painting and sculpture; American decorative arts 19th - 20th centuries; †art of the American West; †Asian art; †contemporary American art; †old masters painting and sculpture; †Pre-Columbian; †prints and drawings; †Beeson Collection of Wedgwood; Lamprecht Collection of 19th century German cast iron; Frances Oliver Collection of Porcelain; Rives Collection of Palestinian Art
Exhibitions: Birmingham Collections; Man Ray Photographs; Sylvia Pizitz Collection; The Tiepolos: Painters to Princes and Prelates, Rubens and Humanism; William Spratling Silver; drawings; French Painting: 1870 - 1920; 20th Century Art; The Art of Healing: Medicine and Science in American Art
Publications: Annual bulletin; bi-monthly calendar
Activities: Classes for adults and children; docent training; lect open to the public, 12 - 15 vis lectr per year; concerts; gallery talks; tours; competitions; organize and circulate traveling exhibitions; museum shop sells reproductions, prints and gifts
L Library, 2000 Eighth Ave N, 35203
Open to the public by request
Library Holdings: Vols 6000; Per subs 18; Other — Clipping files, exhibition catalogs
Special Subjects: Oriental Art, American West
Collections: Kress Collection; Wedgwood Collection

L BIRMINGHAM PUBLIC LIBRARY, Art and Music Department, 2020 Park Place N, 35203. Tel 205-254-2551. *Head* Jane Fackler Greene; *Librn* Patricia Sears; *Librn* Norma Parsons
Open Mon - Thur 9 AM - 9 PM, Fri 9 AM - 6 PM. Estab 1909 to serve the Jefferson County area. For reference and lending
Library Holdings: Vols 29,000; Per subs 67; Micro — Fiche; AV — A-tapes, cassettes, Kodachromes, rec, slides; Other — Clipping files, exhibition catalogs, framed reproductions, memorabilia, pamphlets, photographs, sculpture
Special Subjects: Architecture, Art History, Crafts, Photography
Collections: Small permanent collection of prints, paintings and Mexican pottery

M BIRMINGHAM SOUTHERN COLLEGE, Doris Wainwright Kennedy Art Center,* Box A21, 35254. Tel 205-328-5250. *Dir* Bob Tucker
Mon - Fri 8:30 AM - 5 PM
Exhibitions: One person exhibitions

KAPPA PI INTERNATIONAL HONORARY ART FRATERNITY
For further information, see National and Regional Organizations

M UNIVERSITY OF ALABAMA, Visual Arts Gallery,* 900 13th St S, 35294. Tel 205-934-4941, 934-4011. *Pres* S Richardson Hill; *VPres* Thomas Hearn; *Dir* John M Schnorrenberg; *Registrar* M Antoinette Johnson; *Research Asst* Kevin Mitchell
Open Mon - Fri Noon - 6 PM except between exhibitions, holidays and vacation. No admis fee. Estab 1973 to exhibit works of students, faculty and others and to form and exhibit a permanent collection of art since 1750. Two galleries, each 1200 square feet and adjacent storage all on first floor of Humanities building with adjacent sculpture courtyard. All are temperature and humidity controlled and secured by alarms. Average Annual Attendance: 4100
Income: Financed by university and private donations
Purchases: $2200
Collections: Student and faculty works since 1950
Exhibitions: Prints and Drawings by Laquita Thomson; French 19th Century Bronzes; Works of Art by Students; Outdoor Sculpture and Installations; The Italian Poster as Mass Communication; Recent Work by Richard Urban; Recent Work by Dennis Harper; Folk Crafts of Mexico; Fifth Annual UAB Art Dept Students Juried Exhibition; Contemporary Works of Art from a Birmingham Collection; Works from the Visual Arts Gallery Permanent Collection
Publications: Visual Arts Gallery Paper, 10 per year; Selections I, first in the intended series; exhibition catalogs
Activities: Lectures open to public, 2 vis lectr per year; gallery talks; tours; competitions; individual and original objects of art lent; book traveling exhibitions

DECATUR

M JOHN C CALHOUN STATE COMMUNITY COLLEGE, Art Gallery, Highway 31 North, PO Box 2216, 35602. Tel 205-353-3102. *Pres* Dr James Chasteen; *Dir* Helen C Austin, PhD; *Cur* Richard Green; *Dir* Arthur Bond
Open Mon - Fri 8 AM - 3 PM, special weekend openings. No admis fee. Estab 1965 to provide temporary exhibits of fine art during the school year for the benefit of the surrounding three county area and for the students and faculty of the college. In a new fine arts building completed June 1979, the gallery has 105 linear feet of carpeted wall space with adjustable incandescent track lighting and fluorescent general lights in a controlled and well-secured environment. Average Annual Attendance: 20,000
Collections: Permanent collection consists of graphics collection as well as selected student and faculty works
Exhibitions: (1983-84) Space Illustration: Twenty-five Years in Space; Southern Printmakers; English Calligraphy Student Art Exhibit; Student Photographs
Publications: Announcements; exhibition catalogs
Activities: Classes for adults; lect open to the public, 3 visiting lectr per year; gallery talks; tours; competitions with awards; scholarships and fellowships; individual paintings and original objects of art lent to museums, galleries and college art departments; lending collection contains 40 original art works and 85 original prints; book traveling exhibitions, biannually

FAIRHOPE

O PERCY H WHITING ART CENTER, 401 Oak St, 36532. Tel 205-928-2228, 928-5188. *Pres* Robert Thompson; *Dir* Mary D Foreman; *Registrar* Fydella Evans
Open Tues - Sat 10 AM - 5 PM, Sun 2 - 5 PM, cl Mon, New Years Day, Thanksgiving, Christmas. No admis fee. Estab 1952 to sponsor cultural, educational and social activities for members. Center for Eastern Shore Art Association and Eastern Shore Art Academy; four galleries change exhibits monthly. Mem: 1200; dues: Benefactor: Life $500; Patron: Individual $50, Married Couple $100; Sustaining: Individual $25, Married Couple $50; Regular: Individual $8, Married Couple (including children under 18) $15; Junior $2; Sponsoring Memberships: Business and Professional (includes one single membership) $25
Income: $100,000
Collections: Herman Bischoff, drawings, oils & watercolors; Maria Martinez, pottery
Exhibitions: (1984) George White, photography; David Kessler, pastels, pen and ink, charcoal, photography; Tom Corcoran, photography; Ethel K Pollard Fund Exhibit: Drawings by American Artists; Elberta Arts and Crafts Club: Baldwin County Wallhangings; Eudora Welty; ESA Members' Exhibit; Mary Van Antwerp, photography; Carroll Case, watercolors; Floyd Norris, oils; Meg Heath, handmade paper; Caroline Kilgore, photography; Mobile Watercolor and Graphic Arts Society; Felipe Packard, oils, jewel-like miniatures; Janet Johnson, collage, mixed media; Harry Weeks, watercolors; Fibers and Clay Exhibit; Mickey Mullan, watercolors; Dorothy Summers, sculpture; David Simmons, graphics; Sylvia Rohmer, photography; Delta State Art Faculty Exhibit; Pat Regan,

watercolors; John W Robichaux, oils; Jerry Broadhurst, photography; Students of the Academy of Fine Arts; Children's Art Show, ESAA Students; Don Andrews, watercolors; Roy Thigpen, photography
Publications: Yearbook; monthly newsletter
Activities: Classes for adults and children; docent training; lectures open to the public, 5 vis lectr per yr; concerts; gallery talks; tours; competitions with awards; monthly membership dinners; movies; scholarships; outreach educational program arranges gallery tours, slide programs, and portable exhibits; book traveling exhibitions
L   **Library,** Fairhope, 36532
Reference only
Library Holdings: Vols 1500; Per subs 6; Micro — Cards; AV — Slides; Other — Clipping files, exhibition catalogs, prints

FAYETTE

M   **FAYETTE ART MUSEUM,*** 2nd Ave SE City Hall, Box 189, 35555. Tel 205-932-3300. *Board Chmn* Jack Black; *Dir* Ned Nichols
Open Mon - Fri 7:30 AM - 4 PM. No admis fee. Estab 1969 to offer on continuous basis exhibits of visual arts free to the public. Fayette City Hall auditorium and other wall space in the building serve as a gallery
Income: Financed by city appropriation and Annual Art Festival
Collections: Present collection consists of about 2000 paintings, mostly by Lois Wilson, a former resident
Activities: Gallery talks; tours; lending collection contains original objects of art and is available for other museums, libraries and schools; book traveling exhibitions, 1 per year; originate traveling exhibitions

HUNTSVILLE

O   **HUNTSVILLE ART LEAGUE AND MUSEUM ASSOCIATION INC,** Arts Council, 700 Monroe St, 35802. Tel 205-533-6565. *Pres* Linda Rinehart; *VPres* John Dodd; *Secy* Pat Jones; *Exhibitis Chmn* Olga Edwards; *Educational Chmn* Betty Foster; *Programming* Garnett Jennings; *Treas* Orin Richardson
Phones open 9 AM - 5 PM, studio by appointment. Estab 1957. The League is a nonprofit organization dedicated to promoting and stimulating the appreciation of the visual arts. Mem: 150; dues family $20, individual $15; meetings held 1st Thurs each month
Income: Financed by memberships, commissions, grants
Exhibitions: Annual Fall Mall Shows; annual juried show; continous exhibitions throughout Huntsville; Sunday Salons
Publications: Newsletter on activites and exhibition opportunities in the Southeast, monthly; membership books
Activities: Classes for adults and children; lectures open to the public, 6 vis lectr per yr; competitions; individual paintings & original objects of art lent to banks, restaurants, theaters; lending collection contains original art works, original prints, paintings, photographs, sculpture; sales shop sells original art, reproductions & prints

M   **HUNTSVILLE MUSEUM OF ART,** 700 Monroe St SW, 35801. Tel 205-534-4566. *Dir* Donald E Knaub; *Deputy Dir* James D Bowne; *Cur of Exhibitions* Bruce Hiles; *Cur of Education* Dennis A McAndrew; *Registrar* Barbara Bell
Open Tues - Sat 10 AM - 5 PM, Thurs 10 AM - 9 PM, Sun 1 - 5 PM; cl Mon. No admis fee, donations. Estab 1970 to provide art and educational exhibitions to the city of Huntsville, surrounding counties and educational districts; to encourage by appropriate means the cultivation of artistic talents and recognition of artistic achievements. Museum is located in the Von Braun Civic Center; 23,000 sq ft total including flex exhibition space. Atmospherically controlled galleries and storage; research library. Average Annual Attendance: 40,000. Mem: Due Champion $5000 - up, Sustaining $2500 - $4999, Participating $1000 - $2499, Benefactor $500 - $999, Sponsor $200 - $499, Patron $100 - $199, Contributing $25 - $99
Income: $500,000 (financed by membership, city appropriation, grants and support groups)
Purchases: $25,000
Collections: Works of art on paper with emphasis on 19th and 20th century prints and drawings; multiples
Exhibitions: (1982-84) Philippi Halsman; Georg Jensen Silver; Frank Stella Prints: 1976-1982; Benton's Bentons; The Lithographs of James McNeill Whistler; Viola Frey Ceramics; William Christenberry: Southern Views; The Alex Hillman Collection; The Gund Collection of Western Art
Publications: Catalogues, occasionally; Museum Newsletter, quarterly
Activities: Docent training; educational programs; lect; gallery talks; collection loan program; traveling exhibitions organized and circulated
L   **Reference Library,** 700 Monroe St SW, 35801. Tel 205-534-4566. *Librn* Patsy E Gray
Open Tues & Wed 9 AM - Noon & 2:30 - 5 PM, Thurs 9 AM - Noon & 1 - 4 PM, Fri 10 AM - Noon & 3:30 - 5 PM. For reference only
Library Holdings: Vols 1000; Per subs 36; AV — Slides; Other — Clipping files, exhibition catalogs 500
Special Subjects: Contemporary American art

SOUTHERN ASSOCIATION OF SCULPTORS, INC
For further information, see National and Regional Organizations

M   **UNIVERSITY OF ALABAMA IN HUNTSVILLE,** Gallery of Art,* 35899. Tel 205-895-6114. *Dir* Michael G Crouse; *Deputy Dir* Jeffrey J Bayer
Open Mon - Thurs 11:30 AM - 4 PM. No admis fee. Estab 1975. An intimate and small renovated chapel with a reserved section for exhibits. Average Annual Attendance: 1800
Income: Financed by administration
Exhibitions: Contemporary artwork (US and international); Annual Juried Exhibition
Activities: Lect open to the public, 7-10 visiting lectr per year; gallery talks; competitions with awards; individual paintings and original objects of art lent; book traveling exhibitions, 3 times per year; originate traveling exhibitions

MOBILE

O   **ART PATRONS LEAGUE OF MOBILE,** Box 8055, 36608. Tel 205-342-6074. *Pres* Mrs Calvin Clay; *VPres* Mrs Andrew Saunders; *Secy* Mrs William Reimers
Estab 1964 to promote the education and appreciation of the visual and graphic arts in the Mobile area. Mem: 435; dues associate $35, active $15
Income: $50,000 (financed by membership)
Purchases: $28,000
Exhibitions: Outdoor Arts and Crafts Fair; Christmas Tree Exhibit; Public Sculpture Program
Publications: Art Patrons League Calendar
Activities: Classes for adults and children; workshops; lectures open to the public; gallery talks

M   **FINE ARTS MUSEUM OF THE SOUTH,** Museum Dr, PO Box 8426, 36608. Tel 205-342-4642; Cable FAMOS. *Chmn of the Board* Lowell Friedman; *Dir* Mary O'Neill Victor; *Asst Dir* Harold M Wittmann; *Registrar* David McCann; *Secy* Hazel Mims
Open Wed - Sat 10 AM - 5 PM, Sun 10 AM - 5 PM, cl Mon & Tues. Estab 1964 to foster the appreciation of art and provide art education programs for the community. Average Annual Attendance: 100,000. Mem: 1800; dues business $1500, benefactor $500, associate $250, patron $100, supporting $50, family $25, individual $15
Income: Financed by membership and city appropriation
Collections: American Crafts; African Art; 19th and 20th century American and European paintings, sculpture, prints, and decorative arts; Oriental art; Miller Collection of Oriental Porcelain, Indian Miniatures, Chinese Ceramics, Medieval Art, European Paintings and Sculpture; 16th to 20th century and classical art; Wellington Collection of Wood Engravings
Exhibitions: American Impressionist; Anchutz Collection of Western Art; Duveneck and Chase; Ripening of American Art; (1982) Henry Wo Yu Kee, Chinese Watercolors and Brush Paintings; 5000 Year of Art from the Metropolitan Museum; Christine Smith; Alabama Women in Art: Our Heritage and Present; The Art of Holography; Provincetown Artist, Romanos Rizk; Chinese Cloisonne; Jim Gray; Noel Concept VII; Toys of the Past; Watercolor and Graphic Arts Society Annual Juried Exhibit
Publications: Calendar, quarterly
Activities: Classes for adults and children; docent training; lect open to the public; competitions; Junior Discovery Museum
L   **Library,** Langan Park, PO Box 8426, 36608. *Librn* Iras Smith
For reference only
Library Holdings: Vols 1800; AV — Slides; Other — Clipping files, exhibition catalogs, framed reproductions, pamphlets, photographs, reproductions
Collections: American & European paintings & decorative arts; contemporary crafts; Southern decorative arts; wood engraving

M   **MUSEUM OF THE CITY OF MOBILE,** 355 Government St, 36602. Tel 205-438-7569. *Dir* Caldwell Delaney
Open Tues - Sat 10 AM - 5 PM, Sun 1- 5 PM, cl Mondays and city holidays. Consists of three museums including: The Carlen House built in 1842 is a beautiful example of that style of architecture unique to this area, the Creole cottage; the Phoenix Fire Museum occupies the home station house of the Phoenix Steam Fire Company No 6, which was organized in 1838; the Bernstein-Bush House built in 1872. Average Annual Attendance: 68,000
Museum is located in the elegantly restored Bernstein-Bush townhouse, the museum houses exhibits bearing the history of Mobile and the Gulf Coast area since its founding as a French colony in 1702. This building is listed on the National Register of Historic Places. Displays illustrate life in Mobile under French, British and Spanish colonial rule, the rapid growth of the city in the pre-Civil War period, the rise and fall of the fortunes of Mobile as the best defended Confederate city, and the ever increasing importance of the city as an international seaport and center of culture, business and scholarly institutions.
Income: Financed by city appropriation
Collections: Fenollosa Room collection of books, manuscripts and family photographs, Japanese photographs, paintings, prints, china and textiles; Roderick D MacKenzie Room; McMillan Room; Queens of Mobile Mardi Gras; Admiral Raphael Semmes collection includes probably the finest Confederate presentation sword in existence, along with a presentation cased revolver and accessories, books, paintings, documents, personal papers and ship models; Alfred Lewis Staples Mardi Gras Gallery; 80,000 items reflecting the entire span of the history of Mobile
Activities: Classes for adults & children; docent training; lectures open to the public; tours; museum shop sells books, prints & slides
L   **Reference Library,** 355 Government St, 36602. Tel 205-438-7569. *Exec Asst* Alton Sheffield
For research only
Library Holdings: Vols 25,000
M   **Carlen House,*** 54 Carlen St, 36606. Tel 205-438-7486
The Carlen House is an important representation of Mobile's unique contribution to American regional architecture. It is a fine example of the Creole Cottage as it evolved from the French Colonial form and was adapted for early American use. The house was erected in 1842; furnishings are from the collections of the Museums of the City of Mobile and are typical of a house of that period
Activities: Group tours are conducted by guides in period costumes who emphasize aspects of everyday life in Mobile in the mid-nineteenth century. The making of material is demonstrated by the guide who cards wool, spins fibers and weaves cloth

L   **UNIVERSITY OF SOUTH ALABAMA,** Ethnic American Slide Library, College of Arts & Sciences, University Blvd, 36688. Tel 205-460-6337. *Head* James E Kennedy
Open daily 8 AM - 5 PM. Estab for the acquisition of slides of works produced by Afro-American, Mexican American and native American artists and the distribution of duplicate slides of these works to educational institutions and individuals engaged in research
Library Holdings: AV — Slides
Collections: 19th and 20th century ethnic American art works in ceramics, drawing, painting, photography, printmaking, sculpture
Publications: Slide Catalog

MONTEVALLO

M **UNIVERSITY OF MONTEVALLO,** The Gallery,* 35115. Tel 205-665-2521, Ext 285
Open Mon - Fri 9 AM - 5 PM. No admis fee. Estab Sept 1977 to supply students and public with high quality contemporary art. The gallery is 27 x 54 ft with track lighting; floors and walls carpeted; no windows. Average Annual Attendance: 2500 - 3000
Income: Financed by state appropriation and regular department budget
Publications: High quality catalogs and posters
Activities: Management classes; lect open to the public, 6 vis lectr per year; gallery talks; originate traveling exhibitions

MONTGOMERY

M **ALABAMA DEPARTMENT OF ARCHIVES AND HISTORY MUSEUM,** 624 Washington Ave, 36130. Tel 205-832-6510. *Dir* Fowin C Bridges; *Museum Cur* Robert A Cason
Open Mon - Fri 8 AM - 5 PM, Sat & Sun 9 AM - 5 PM. No admis fee. Estab 1901. Average Annual Attendance: 78,000
Income: Financed by state appropriation
Collections: William Rufus King Collection; Hank Williams; Fine Arts Room; French Room; Music Room
Exhibitions: History of Alabama
L **Library,** 624 Washington Ave, 36130. *Librn* Albert K Craig
Open Mon - Fri 8 AM - 5 PM. Estab 1901. Department has a Manuscripts Division where original manuscript collections are maintained
Library Holdings: Vols 32,000; Other — Clipping files, pamphlets, photographs

C **BLOUNT INC,** 4520 Executive Park Dr, PO Box 949, 36102. Tel 205-272-8020. *Coordr Cultural Affairs* Carol Ballard
Open 8 AM - 5 PM. No admis fee. Estab 1973, original collection began in response to commemorate America's bicentennial. Collection displayed at Corporate Headquarters Building
Collections: †American art—200 years; †international sculpture; †regional artists; †works by American artists from Revolutionary period to present
Exhibitions: Greenville Co Museum of Art; Selections from the Blount Collection; Highlights of the Blount Collection
Publications: Blount Collection Vol I, II & III, catalog; Blount Collection, quarterly newsletter
Activities: Lectures; concerts; gallery talks; toursposter employee art competition with award; individual paintings and original objects of art lent to museums; instrumental in the formation of Art, Inc, a traveling exhibition of corporate art
L **Library,** 36102
Library Holdings: Vols 75; Per subs 15; Micro — Fiche; AV — Motion pictures, rec; Other — Exhibition catalogs

M **MONTGOMERY MUSEUM OF FINE ARTS,** 440 S McDonough St, 36104. Tel 205-832-2976. *Pres* Ross C Anderson; *Asst Dir for Development* Grace M Hanchrow; *Actg Cur* Margaret Ausfeld; *Cur Education* Mary Sater Ward; *Registrar* Lynn W Cox; *Asst to Dir* Shirley Woods; *Pres* Vaughan Hill Robison; *Registrar* Ilene Whiteworth
Open Tues - Sat 10 AM - 5 PM, Thur evening until 9 PM, Sun 1 - 6 PM. No admis fee. Estab 1930 to generally promote the cultural artistic and higher education life of the city of Montgomery by all methods that may be properly pursued by a museum or art gallery. Gallery occupies the upper floor of a two-story museum-library structure built by the city in the late 1950's. Five galleries provide the necessary space for displaying the permanent collection and circulating shows; 180 seat auditorium. Average Annual Attendance: 50,000. Mem: 1800; dues leadership $250-$5000, associate $50-$150, individual $10-$30; annual meeting Oct
Income: Financed by membership, city and county appropriations and grants
Collections: †American & European Works on Paper; †Contemporary graphics and other works on paper by artists living in the South; decorative arts; master prints of the 15th and 19th Centuries; †paintings by American artists from early 19th Century through the present
Publications: Annual Report; Calendar of Events, quarterly; exhibitions catalogs for selected shows
Activities: Classes for children; docent training; lect open to public, 20 visiting lectr per year; films; concerts; gallery talks; tours; individual paintings and original objects of art lent to galleries which meet AAM standards for security and preservation; lending collection contains 330 original prints, 250 paintings, photographs, sculpture and 3500 slides; book traveling exhibitions, 12 per year; originate traveling exhibitions, national and international; museums shop sells books, original art, reproductions, prints and gift items
L **Library,** 440 S McDonough St, 36104. Tel 205-834-3490. *Librn* Elizabeth B Brown
Open Tues - Fri 10 AM - 5 PM. Estab 1975 to assist the staff and community with reliable art research material. For reference
Library Holdings: Vols 2200; Per subs 28; AV — Fs, motion pictures, slides; Other — Clipping files, exhibition catalogs, pamphlets, photographs, prints
Special Subjects: American Art

SELMA

M **STURDIVANT HALL,*** 713 Mabry St, PO Box 1205, 36701. Tel 205-872-5626. *Pres* J Mel Gilmer; *Cur* Mrs Jefferson Ratcliffe
Open Tues - Sat 9 AM - 4 PM, Sun & holidays 2 - 4 PM. Admis adults $2, student $1, children free. Estab 1957 as a museum with emphasis on the historical South. Period furniture of the 1850's in a magnificent architectural edifice built 1852-53. Average Annual Attendance: 10,000. Mem: 480; dues $10 - $1000; annual meeting April
Income: Financed by membership, city and state appropriations
Collections: Objects of art; †period furniture; textiles
Publications: Brochure
Activities: Lect open to public; tours

TALLADEGA

M **TALLADEGA COLLEGE,** Savery Art Gallery,* 627 W Battle St, 35160. Tel 205-362-2752. *Cur* Edward Jennings; *Cur Talladega Art Collection* James Huff
Open 9 AM - 5 PM. No admis fee. Estab to exhibit student art work, faculty art work and traveling exhibitions. Gallery, located in Library Building basement, is 25 x 35 ft and has adjustable lights. Average Annual Attendance: 1500
Income: Financed by college funds
Collections: Permanent collection maintained in the gallery
Exhibitions: Art Instructor Exhibit; Arts Festival Exhibit; Photo Exhibit; Student Exhibit
Activities: Lect open to the public, 12 visiting lectrs per year; concerts; gallery talks; individual paintings lent to faculty, students and administration personnel; lending collection contains prints of paintings; traveling exhibitions organized and circulated; museum shop and sales shop

THEODORE

M **BELLINGRATH GARDENS AND HOME,** Route 1, Box 60, 36582. Tel 205-973-2217. *General Mgr* John M Brown
Open daily 7 AM to dusk. Admis Gardens adults $3.60, children 6-11 $1.80, under 6 free; Admis Home $4.50. Estab 1932 to perpetuate an appreciation of nature, and display man-made objects d'art. The gallery houses the world's largest public display of Boehm porcelain, and the Bellingrath Home contains priceless antiques. Average Annual Attendance: 250,000
Income: Supported by Foundation and admissions
Collections: Antiques from Europe and America; Boehm Porcelain
Activities: Classes for children; tours; lending collection contains kodachromes, motion pictures, slides; sales shop sells books, magazines, prints, reproductions and slides

TUSCALOOSA

O **ARTS AND HUMANITIES COUNCIL OF TUSCALOOSA COUNTY, INC,*** Box 1117, 35401. Tel 205-758-5195. *Pres* John Owens; *Executive* Doug Perry
Open Mon - Fri 8 AM - 5 PM. No admis fee. Estab 1970 for the development, promotion and coordination of educational, cultural and artistic activities of the city and county of Tuscaloosa. Mem: 410 individual, 30 organization; dues organization $25, individual $10; annual meeting June, meetings quarterly
Income: Financed by endowment, membership, city, state and county appropriations
Publications: Arts Calendar, monthly; Newsletter - Arts Update, quarterly
Activities: Dramatic programs; concert series, Stars Fall on Ubama; sponsor of educational program called Sugar (Schools using greater arts resources)

TUSCUMBIA

O **TENNESSEE VALLEY ART ASSOCIATION AND CENTER,*** 511 N Water St, PO Box 474, 35674. Tel 205-383-0533. *Dir* Shirley Maize; *Asst Dir* Mary Settle-Cooney
Open Tues - Sat 1 - 5 PM, Sun 2 - 5 PM. No admis fee. Chartered 1963 to promote the arts in the Tennessee Valley. Building completed 1973. Main Gallery 60 x 40 ft; West Gallery for small exhibits, meetings and arts and crafts classes. Located one block from the birthplace of Helen Keller in Tuscumbia. During the Helen Keller Festival, TVAC sponsors the Arts and Crafts Fair. Average Annual Attendance: 10,000. Mem: Dues benefactor $100, sustaining $25, regular $10, student $5
Income: $50,000 (financed by donations, grants and memberships)
Collections: Helen Keller Crafts Collection; Reynolds Collection (aluminum)
Exhibitions: Exhibition South, (paintings, sculpture, prints), annual juried art show for mid-south states; Spring Photo Show, annual juried; feature work by national artists, members and students; handcraft exhibits; exhibit work by blind and handicapped individuals
Activities: Classes for adults and children; dramatic programs; class instruction in a variety of arts and crafts; String School provides music instruction for children and adults; workshops and performances in ballet and drama; lectures open to public; concerts; gallery talks; competitions with awards; illustrated slide lecture; book traveling exhibits

TUSKEGEE

M **TUSKEGEE INSTITUTE NATIONAL HISTORIC SITE,** George Washington Carver & The Oaks, 399 Montgomery Rd, 36088. Tel 205-727-3200. *Park Superintendent* Randolph Scott; *Museum Technician* Joan S Pryor
Open 9 AM - 5 PM, cl Thanksgiving, Christmas & New Years. Original museum estab 1941 and National Park in 1976 to interpret life and work of George Washington Carver and the history of Tuskegee Institute. Maintains small reference library
Income: Financed by federal funds
Collections: Artifacts interpreting life and work of George Washington Carver and history of Tuskegee Institute; life and contributions of Booker T Washington
Activities: Lectures open to public; gallery talks; guided tours; sponsor competitions with awards; individual and original objects of art lent to other parks and museums; lending limited to photos, films, slides and reproductions; book traveling exhibitions; originate traveling exhibitions; sales shop sells books, reproductions, prints and slides

UNIVERSITY

M **UNIVERSITY OF ALABAMA,** Moody Gallery of Art, Garland Hall, Box F, 35486. Tel 205-348-5967. *Dir* Angelo Granata
Open Mon - Sat 8 AM - 5 PM, Sun 2 - 5 PM. No admis fee. Estab 1946
Collections: Small collection of paintings, prints, photography, drawings, sculpture and ceramics; primarily modern
Exhibitions: Approx 15 exhibitions per year
Activities: Originate traveling exhibitions

ALASKA

ANCHORAGE

O **ALASKA ARTISTS' GUILD,** PO Box 101888, 99510. *Pres* John Peirce; *VPres* Helen Liston; *Secy* Pat Fridley; *Treasurer* Sam McClain; *Funding* Marie Shaughnessy; *Program* Belle Dawson; *Newsletter* Barbara Suddock
Estab 1954 to provide an association for the educational interaction of qualified artists and to provide an education focus for the visual arts in the community. Mem: 100; qualifications for membership include talent and training or experience in the visual arts; dues $20; meetings second Tues each month
Income: $1500 (financed by membership)
Exhibitions: All Alaska Juried Art Show; Alaska Festival of Music Art Exhibit; Exhibitions in Federal Office Building
Publications: Alaska Artists Guild Newsletter, monthly
Activities: Monthly meetings open to the public, 3 - 4 vis lectr per yr; gallery talks; competitions; $500 Betty Park Memorial Award given; annual workshop with vis instr of national repute; individual paintings and original objects of art lent to colleges and schools by members

M **ANCHORAGE HISTORICAL AND FINE ARTS MUSEUM,** Cook Inlet Historical Society,* 121 W Seventh Ave, 99501. Tel 907-264-4326. *Dir* R L Shalkop; *Cur of Education* Patricia Wolf; *Cur of Exhibits* Gary Marx; *Cur of Coll* Walter VanHorn
Open Mon - Sat 10 AM - 5 PM, Sun 1 PM - 5 PM. No admis fee. Estab 1955 to collect and display Alaskan art and artifacts of all periods; to present changing exhibitions of the art of the world. Average Annual Attendance: 138,000. Mem: 279; dues $10 and up, annual meeting third Thurs of April
Income: $12,000 (financed by members)
Purchases: $155,000
Collections: †Alaskan art; †Alaskan Eskimo and Indian art; Alaskan history; American art; Primitive Art (non-American); Photographs
Exhibitions: All Alaska Juried Annual; Earth, Fire and Fibre Juried Craft Annual; 20th Century Sculptors and Their Drawings; Eskimo Masks From The Sheldon Jackson Museum; A Pictorial History of Russian Alaska; World Print III; Young Americans: Metal; Thomas Hill; Vasarely; American Landscape Paintings From The High Museum Contemporary Native Art of Alaska; Polish Textiles; Prints from the Guggenheim Museum; Recent Latin American Drawings; Survival: Art and Life of the Alaskan Eskimo; With Captain Cook in the North Pacific
Publications: Exhibition catalogs; Newsletter, monthly; occasional papers
Activities: Classes for children; dramatic programs; lect open to the public, 10 vis lectr per year; concerts; tours; competitions, awards; individual paintings lent to municipal offices; organize and circulate traveling exhibitions; museum shop sells books, magazines, original art, prints, slides and Alaskan Native art

L **Archives,** 121 W Seventh Ave, Pouch 6-650, 99501. Tel 907-264-4326. *Museum Archivist* M Diane Brenner
Open Tues - Fri 9 AM - 5 PM. No admis fee. Estab 1968 to maintain archives of Alaska materials, chiefly the Cook Inlet area. Reference only
Income: $5000 (financed by city appropriation)
Purchases: $4000
Library Holdings: Vols 6000; Per subs 10; original documents; Micro — Fiche, reels; AV — A-tapes, cassettes, Kodachromes, motion pictures, rec, slides, v-tapes; Other — Clipping files, exhibition catalogs, memorabilia, pamphlets, photographs
Special Subjects: American art, Alaska history and culture, Alaska native peoples, museum techniques
Collections: Hinchey Alagco Photograph Collection of approximately 4000 pictures of the Copper River area; Alaska Railroad Collection, 6000 historical photos; Reeve Collection, historical maps; Ward Wells Anchorage Photo Collection 1950-80, 125,000 items
Exhibitions: Military History of Alaska, a photographic history; (1983) The Alaska Railroad: 60 Years and Going Proud

BETHEL

M **YUGTARVIK REGIONAL MUSEUM,** Third Ave, PO Box 388, 99559. Tel 907-543-2098. *Cur* Elizabeth A Mayock; *Arts & Crafts Dir* Martina Olson
Open Tues - Sat 11 AM - 6 PM. No admis fee. Estab 1967 to help preserve the native culture and lifestyle of the people of the Kuskokwim River. Average Annual Attendance: 10,500. Mem: 50; dues $25
Income: $35,000 (financed by city appropriation)
Purchases: $5000
Collections: †Native handmade objects of the Yupik Eskimo, both artifacts and contemporary art objects (included are full-size kayak, ivory carvings and wooden masks, wooden bowls, stone & ivory implements, Yupik toys, fishskin, sealgut, birdskin & fur clothing)
Publications: Newsletter, quarterly
Activities: Classes for adults and children; lect open to the public; book traveling exhibitions, 3-4 times per year; museum shop selling baskets, ivory jewelry, beaded work, skin & fur items, wooden & ivory masks & books relating to Yupik Eskimos

FAIRBANKS

O **ALASKA ASSOCIATION FOR THE ARTS,** PO Box 2786, 99707. Tel 907-456-6485, 456-2169. *Pres* Esther Weiss; *VPres* Terry P Dickey; *VPres* Jackie Goering; *Secy* Doreen Smith; *Treas* June Rogers; *Exec Dir* Jeanette C MacNeille
Office open Mon - Fri, 9 AM - 5 PM, gallery Tues - Sat 12:30 - 8:30 PM, Sun 12:30 - 6:30 PM. Estab 1965 to provide assistance and to help coordinate and promote the programs of other arts organizations, to encourage and develop educational programs designed to strengthen and improve the climate for the arts. To stimulate and facilitate the touring of professional and amateur performances and exhibits in the Fairbanks area, to inform the community of performing and creative arts awareness and development in the Fairbanks area. Average Annual Attendance: 50,000. Mem: 600; dues $25 & up; annual meeting Sept
Income: Financed by city and state appropriations, national grants, contributions
Publications: Arts in Fairbanks cultural calendar and newsletter each month; Envoy: Literary Arts Statewide Journal, monthly
Activities: Classes for adults and children; dramatic programs; docent training; lectures open to the public, 10 vis lectr per yr; concerts; gallery talks; tours; competitions with awards; book traveling exhibitions; museum shop sells prints & cards

UNIVERSITY OF ALASKA

M **Museum,** 907 Yukon Drive, 99701. Tel 907-479-7505. *Dir* Basil C Hedrick; *Coordr Exhibits & Exhibits Designer* Wanda W Chin; *Admin Asst* Hazel E Daro; *Coordr Pub Servs & Educ* Terry P Dickey; *Coordr Alaska Heritage Film Project* Leonard J Kamerling; *Coordr Ethnology* Dinah W Larsen; *Coordr Photog* Barry J McWayne
Open May 1 - Sept 30 9 AM - 5 PM, Oct 1 - April 30 Noon - 5 PM. No admis fee. Estab 1929 to collect, preserve and interpret the natural and cultural history of Alaska. Gallery contains 10,000 sq ft of exhibition space. Average Annual Attendance: 100,000. Mem: 186; dues $7; annual meeting in October
Income: Financed by state appropriation, public and private donations, grants and contracts
Collections: Contemporary Alaska photography; ethnographic collection; paintings & lithographs of Alaska subjects
Exhibitions: (1980-1983) Temporary exhibits rotate every 2 - 3 months
Activities: Classes for adults and children; docent training; monthly children's program; lectures open to the public, three visiting lecturers per year; docent tours for grades 1 - 12; individual and original objects of art lent to other museums or in-state institutions; traveling photographic exhibitions organized and circulated; museum shop sells notecards, slides, exhibition catalogues, pamphlets, charts, posters

L **Elmer E Rasmuson Library,** 99701. Tel 907-479-7224. *Dir* Robert H Geiman; *Head Information Access Services* Sharon West; *Head Alaska & Polar Regions Collections* Paul McCarthy; *Head Instructional Media Services* Edmund Cridge
Open Mon - Thurs 7:30 AM - 11 PM, Fri 7:30 AM - 10 PM, Sat 10 - 6 PM, Sun 10 - 10 PM, when school is not in session 8 AM - 5 PM. Estab 1922 to support research and curriculum of the university. Circ 147,000
Income: Financed by state appropriation
Library Holdings: AV — Slides; Other — Photographs
Collections: Lithographs of Fred Machetanz; paintings by Alaskan artists: Claire Fejes, C Rusty Heurlin; photographs of early Alaskan bush pilots; print reference photograph collection on Alaska and the Polar Regions

HAINES

M **SHELDON MUSEUM AND CULTURAL CENTER,** 25 Main St, 99827. Tel 907-766-2366. *Dir Sheldon Museum* Elisabeth S Hakkinen; *Pres Chilkat Valley Historical Society* John Poling; *VPres* Carl Heinmiller; *Secy* Vera B Smith; *Treas* Retha Young
Open summer Mon - Sun 1 - 4 PM, winter 3 days weekly. Admis adults $2, children free if with adult. Estab 1924, under operation of Chilkat Valley Historical Society since 1975, for the purpose of collecting, displaying and explaining local and Alaskan history, artifacts and mementoes. Average Annual Attendance: 10,000. Mem: 87; dues $10; annual meeting second Thurs of Jan
Income: Financed by membership and other sources
Collections: Indian artifacts, basically Tlingit; pioneer
Publications: Quarterly newsletter
Activities: Movie & slide/cassette programs; books published; lect open to the public; sales shop sells books; Children's Corner

L **Library,** 25 Main St, Box 236, 99827
Open to the public for reference only
Library Holdings: Vols 400; Micro — Reels; AV — A-tapes, cassettes, motion pictures, rec, slides; Other — Clipping files, memorabilia, original art works, photographs

JUNEAU

M **ALASKA STATE MUSEUM,** Whittier St, Pouch FM, 99811. Tel 907-586-1224. *Dir* Alan Munro; *Deputy Dir* Dan Monroe; *Cur Collections* Bette Hulbert; *Cur Visual Arts* Kenneth DeRoux; *Cur Education* Betty Bradlyn; *Conservator* Alice Houeman; *Field Services* Roxana Adams
Open Weekdays 9 AM - 4:30 PM, weekends 1 - 5:30 PM, summer weekdays 9 AM - 9 PM. No admis fee. Estab 1900 to collect, preserve, exhibit and interpret objects of special significance or value in order to promote publice appreciation of Alaska's cultural heritage, history, art and natural environment. Gallery occupies two floors; first floor houses permanent and temporary exhibits on 1400 sq ft with 14 foot ceiling; second floor houses permanent exhibits. Average Annual Attendance: 100,000 with more than 200,000 including outreach program. Mem: Dues sustaining $100, family $20, adults $5, student $1
Income: Financed by state appropriation and grants
Collections: Alaska ethnographic material including Eskimo, Aleut, Athabaskan, Tlingit, Haida and Tsimshian artifacts; Gold Rush and early Alaskan industrial and historical material; historical and contemporary Alaskan art
Publications: Museum Alaska, periodic

Activities: Education department; docent training; circulate learning kits to Alaska public schools; concerts; gallery talks; tours; competitions; individual paintings and original objects of art lent to other museums, libraries, historical societies; lending collection contains original prints, photographs; traveling exhibits of photographs and prints organized and circulated
L **Library,** Whittier St, 99811. *Cur of Education* Martha Stevens
Open to staff and other upon request
Library Holdings: Vols 1500; Per subs 25

KENAI

M **KENAI HISTORICAL SOCIETY INC,** Kenai Community Historical Center, PO Box 1348, 99611. Tel 907-283-3340. *Pres* Roger Meeks; *VPres* Louisa Miller; *Secy* Jetret S Petersen; *Treasurer* Francis Meeks
Average Annual Attendance: 5000. Mem: 30; dues $5; annual meeting first Sun in Feb
Income: Financed by membership
Publications: Annual report; newsletter
Activities: Sales shop sells post cards

KETCHIKAN

M **TONGASS HISTORICAL SOCIETY MUSEUM,** 629 Dock St, 99901. Tel 907-225-5600. *Pres* Bill Lattin; *VPres* Ann Thompson; *Dir* Virginia McGillvray; *Sr Cur* Marjorie Anne Voss
Open summer Wed - Mon 11 AM - 5 PM, cl Tues, winter Wed - Sun 1 - 5 PM, cl Mon & Tues. No admis fee. Estab 1961 to collect, preserve & exhibit area articles & collect area photographs. Maintains reference library. Average Annual Attendance: 34,000. Mem: 122; dues life $100, sustaining $25, annual $5; annual meeting third Thurs in Jan
Income: $10,000 (financed by membership, donations, sales & grants)
Purchases: $9950
Collections: †Ethnographic & development history, local artists contemporary artwork; †local area history artifacts; †works from local & Alaskan artists, photographs, manuscripts & newspaper archives
Publications: Newsletter
Activities: Classes for adults; docent training; lectures open to public; book traveling exhibitions, 5 vis lectr per yr; museum shop sells books, magazines, original art, reproductions & prints

NOME

M **CARRIE MCLAIN MUSEUM,*** 200 E Front St, PO Box 53, 99762. Tel 907-443-2566. *Dir* Roy D Iutzi-Johnson; *Museum Aide* Anette Martin
Open Mon - Fri 9 AM - 5 PM. No admis fee
Income: Financed by City of Nome and supplemental grant projects and donations
Collections: Permanent collection includes examples of art from 1890 thru 1980, including basketry, block prints, carved ivory, ink, oil, skin drawings, stone carving, watercolor paintings, woodworking
Exhibitions: Permanent exhibitions, with a large number of rotating exhibits plus temporary exhibits every other month; Annual Competitions include: Kivetoruk Moses Arts & Crafts Fair in March and Photographic Competition in April
Activities: Demonstrations; workshops; lect; film series

SITKA

O **ALASKA ARTS SOUTHEAST, INC,** PO Box 2133, 99835. Tel 907-747-8177, 747-8557, 747-5778. *Exec Dir* Clyde L Carraway; *Program Dir* Judith Harris; *Program Asst* James Westhusing; *Communications Coodr* Marie Giddings; *Office Mgr & Bookkeeper* Kathleen Van Horn
Open 8 AM - 5 PM. Estab in 1973 as a not-for-profit coordinating agency for arts organizations and community arts councils in Southeast Alaska. Mem: Individuals, art groups and supporters statewide
Income: Financed by membership dues, local school districts and municipalities, private contributions, and grants from the Alaska State Council on the Arts and National Endowment for the Arts
Publications: Annual statewide arts directory listing of Southeast Alaska arts organizations; annual anthology of stories and poems by young people; The Panhandle Post (bi-monthly newsletter on art happenings throughout the region and state); Artsline Update, (bi-weekly calendar of arts activities & opportunities)
Activities: Fine arts camp; radio series; arts consulting service

M **SHELDON JACKSON COLLEGE,** Sheldon Jackson Museum,* Lincoln St, PO Box 479, 99835. Tel 907-747-5228. *Dir* Peter L Corey
Open summer May 15 - Sept 15, 8 AM - 5 PM daily, winter hours Sept 16 - May 14, 1 - 4 PM Tues - Fri and Sun, cl Mon and Sat. Admis $1 over 18. Estab 1888, the first museum in Alaska, for the purpose of collecting and preserving the cultural remains of the Alaskan natives in the form of artifacts. The museum occupies one room with permanent displays concerned with Tlingit, Haida, Aleut, Athabascan, and Eskimo culture. Average Annual Attendance: 35,000
Income: $30,000 (financed by admission fee, sales, donation and college support)
Collections: Ethnographic material from Tlingit, Haida, Aleut, Athabascan, Eskimo and some Russian items
Publications: Brochures; catalogs of Ethnological Collection
Activities: Lect open to the public, 1 - 2 vis lectr per yr; gallery talks; tours; traveling exhibitions organized and circulated; museum shop sells books, magazines, original art, prints, slides
L **Stratton Library,** Lincoln & Jeff David Sts, Box 479, 99835. Tel 907-747-5259. *Dir Library Services* Evelyn K Bonner; *Librn* Deborah Saito; *Library Asst In Charge of Interlibrary Loan & Periodicals* Nancy Ricketts; *Library Asst In Charge of Circulation & Reserve* Pamela Kelly
Estab 1944 with Collection Library for curriculum support and meeting the needs of patrons interested in the arts. Circ 600

Purchases: $750
Library Holdings: Vols 22,500; Per subs 25; Micro — Reels; AV — A-tapes, cassettes, fs, Kodachromes, lantern slides, motion pictures, rec, slides, v-tapes; Other — Clipping files, exhibition catalogs, framed reproductions, memorabilia, original art works, pamphlets, photographs, reproductions, sculpture
Special Subjects: Alaskan and Native American Art Books, Alaska and the Northwest Pacific Coast, Harmon original pictures
Collections: Alaska Reference Collection (containing works on Native Arts and Crafts); E W Merrill Glass Plate Photo Collection (representative of Sitka at the turn of the century)
Activities: Annual programs held in April, includes dramatic presentations; lect; demonstrations

ARIZONA

DOUGLAS

L **COCHISE COLLEGE,** Charles Di Peso Library,* Art Dept, 85607. Tel 602-364-7943. *Libr Dir* Catherin Lincer
Open Mon - Fri 8 AM - 9 PM, Sat as posted. Estab 1965
Income: Financed by state & local funds
Library Holdings: Other — Exhibition catalogs, framed reproductions, memorabilia, original art works, photographs, prints, reproductions, sculpture
Special Subjects: Oriental Art
Collections: Oriental originals (ceramics and paintings); 19th century American & European Impressionists

O **DOUGLAS ART ASSOCIATION,** Little Gallery,* 11th St at Pan American Ave, PO Box 256, 85607. Tel 602-364-2633. *Pres* Joyce Smith
Open Tues - Sat 1:30 - 4 PM. No admis fee. Estab 1960 as a non-profit tax exempt organization dedicated to promoting the visual arts and general cultural awareness in the Douglas, Arizona and Agua Prieta, Sonora area. Little Gallery is operated in a city owned building with city cooperation. Average Annual Attendance: 2000. Mem: 100; dues $7.50 and $10
Income: Financed by membership and fund raising events
Collections: †Two Flags Festival International Collections for the cities of Douglas and Agua Prieta, Mexico
Publications: Newsletter, monthly
Activities: Classes for adults and children; workshops in painting and various art activities; lect open to the public; gallery talks; competitions with cash awards; sales shop sells books and donated items

DRAGOON

O **AMERIND FOUNDATION, INC,** Dragoon Rd, PO Box 248, 85609. Tel 602-586-3003. *Pres* William Duncan Fulton; *VPres* Peter L Formo; *Secy* Elizabeth F Husband; *Treas* Michael W Hard; *Foundation Dir* Open
Open Mon - Fri 8 AM - Noon and 1 - 5 PM, tours Sat & Sun 10:30 AM & 1 PM by appointment. No admis fee. Estab 1937 for archaeological research of the American Southwest and northern Mexico; includes the Amerind Foundation, Inc Museum and Fulton-Hayden Memorial Art Gallery. Average Annual Attendance: 6000. Mem: Annual meeting Nov
Income: $241,333 (financed by endowment)
Collections: Archaeological and ethnographic specimens of Native Americans of the Americas; art of the Southwest; miscellaneous collections of Dr and Mrs William Shirley Fulton
Publications: Amerind Publications on Arizona
Activities: Docent training; lect; tours; individual paintings and original objects of art lent, subject to Board of Directors approval, for temporary exhibitions; lending collection contains original art works and paintings; Brochure of Amerind and postcards available
L **Fulton-Hayden Memorial Library,** Dragoon Rd, PO Box 248, 85609. Tel 602-586-3003. *Librn* Mario N Klimiades
Estab 1961. Open to scholars by appointment
Purchases: $3500
Library Holdings: Vols 16,500; Per subs 100; Micro — Cards 50, fiche, reels 400; AV — Slides; Other — Clipping files, exhibition catalogs, manuscripts, memorabilia, original art works, pamphlets, photographs
Special Subjects: Archaeology, Ethnology
Collections: Parral Archives on microfilm; collections of research and technical reports
Publications: Recent Additions, irregular

FLAGSTAFF

M **MUSEUM OF NORTHERN ARIZONA,** Route 4, Box 720, 86001. Tel 602-774-5211. *Dir* Philip M Thompson; *Pres Board of Trustees* Dr David Chase; *Cur of Archaeology* Dr Donald E Weaver; *Actg Cur of Anthropology* Laura Graves Allen
Open Mon - Sun 9 AM - 5 PM. Admis adults $2, students and children $1. Estab 1928 to maintain a museum where the geological history and pre-history of northern Arizona can be explained and where archaeological and ethnological treasures of northern Arizona can be preserved; to protect historic and prehistoric sites, works of art, scenic places and wildlife from needless destruction; to provide facilities for research and to offer opportunities for aesthetic enjoyment. Average Annual Attendance: 100,000. Mem: 1750; dues $10 - $1000; annual meeting Jan
Income: $2,500,000 (financed by endowment, membership and earned income)
Collections: Archaeological collection; art collection, ethnographic collection; geneology collection
Exhibitions: (1982) The Navajo Way - One Artist's View: Beatien Yazz

Retrospective What In The World? (science show); Hopi Show; Navajo Show; Student Art Exhibition of Northern Arizona; Images of the Colorado Plateau - Selections from MNA Fine Arts Collection
Publications: Museum Notes, bimonthly; Plateau, quarterly
Activities: Classes for adults and children; docent training; expeditions; lectures open to the public; concerts; gallery talks; tours; competitions with awards; exten dept serves the Southwestern states; individual paintings and original objects of art lent to various institutions; lending collection contains nature artifacts, original art works, original prints, paintings, photographs, and sculpture; organize and circulate traveling exhibitions; museum shop sells books, magazines, original art and crafts

L **Harold S Colton Memorial Library,** Route 4, Box 720, 86001. Tel 602-774-5211, Ext 56
Open Mon - Fri 9 AM - 5 PM. Estab 1928, library is a repository of material relating to the Colorado Plateau, with its primary function to serve the needs of the Museum's research staff, although visiting scholars are welcome. Circulation restricted to Museum staff
Income: Financed by endowment
Special Subjects: Southwest Artists; Southwest Indian Art
Collections: Navajo sandpainting reproductions

M **NORTHERN ARIZONA UNIVERSITY,** Art Gallery, Creative Arts Building, Room 231, Box 6021, 86011. Tel 602-523-3471. *Dir Art Gallery* Joel S Eide; *Dean College Creative Arts* Charles H Aurand
Open Mon - Fri 8:30 AM - 5 PM, Tues 6:30 - 8:30 PM, Sun 3 - 5 PM, cl Sat. No admis fee. Estab 1968 for the continuing education and service to the students and the Flagstaff community in all aspects of fine arts
Collections: Master prints of the 20th century and American painting of the Southwest
Activities: Lectures open to public, 6 vis lectr per yr; concerts; gallery talks; tours; competitions with awards; scholarships; individual paintings & original objects of art lent to university departments; originate traveling exhibitions; museum shop sells books, reproductions, prints, slides, posters & lithos

GANADO

M **HUBBELL TRADING POST,** PO Box 150, 86505. Tel 602-755-3475. *Supt* L Edward Gastellum; *Cur* Liz Bauer
Open May - Sept 8 AM - 6 PM, Oct - Apr 8 AM - 5 PM. No admis fee. Estab 1965 to set aside Hubbell Trading Post as a historic site as the best example in Southwest of a Trader, an Indian Trading Post and people he served. Average Annual Attendance: 150,000
Income: Financed by federal appropriation
Collections: Contemporary Western artists; ethnohistoric arts & crafts; furnishings; photographs
Activities: Tours; gallery talks; individual paintings & art objects are lent to certified museums; sales shop sells books, Indian arts & crafts, magazines, original art, prints & slides

JEROME

O **VERDE VALLEY ART ASSOCIATION, INC,** Main Street, PO Box 985, 86331. Tel 602-634-5466. *Chmn* Terry Molloy; *VChmn* Seth Kellogg; *Secy* Susan Cloud; *Treas* Henry Vincent; *Dir* V Paige Peters
Open daily 10 AM - 5 PM. Admis by donation. Estab 1954 to promote and further the arts in Northern Arizona, particularly the Verde Valley, in all its forms; visual arts, performing arts and educational programs. Gallery is 1000 sq ft; changing monthly exhibitions. Average Annual Attendance: 40,000. Mem: 250; dues vary; annual meeting third Thur in June
Income: Financed by membership, federal and state grants, corporate gifts, foundation gifts, donations, fund raising projects
Collections: Small permanent collection of original works and prints
Exhibitions: (1982-83) Jerome Theme and Memorabilia Show; Verde Valley Christmas Exhibition & Sale; Young Artists Exhibition & Tour; one-artist shows & group shows of Arizona artists & craftspersons; monthly visual art exhibitions
Publications: Verde Artists Bulletin, quarterly
Activities: Performing arts & educational programs; Verde Valley Visual Artists Slide Registry

MESA

M **GALERIA MESA,** Cultural Activities Dept, 155 N Center, PO Box 1466, 85201. Tel 602-834-2053. *Coordr* Sue Hakala; *Specialist* Carol Miller
Open Mon - Fri 1 - 4 PM, Tues evening 7 - 9 PM. Estab 1981 to provide an exhibition for new and emerging artists. Average Annual Attendance: 1500
Income: Financed by city appropriation
Collections: †Permanent collection
Activities: Classes for adults and children; dramatic programs; lectures open to the public; competitions with awards; book traveling exhibitions, 2 per yr; originate traveling exhibitions

NOGALES

O **PIMERIA ALTA HISTORICAL SOCIETY,** 223 Grand Ave, PO Box 2281, 85621. Tel 602-287-5402. *Pres* Arthur M Doan; *Secy* Juanita Schock; *Dir* Susan Clarke-Spater
Open Mon - Fri 9 AM - 5 PM, Sat 10 AM - 4 PM, Sun 1 - 4 PM. Estab 1948 to preserve the unique heritage of northern Sonora Mexico and southern Arizona from 1000 AD to present; art is incorporated into interpretive exhibits. Also maintains a photo gallery. Average Annual Attendance: 10,000. Mem: 700; dues adults $7.50; meeting last February in Jan
Income: $40,000 (financed by memberships & grants)
Collections: Art and artifacts of Hohokam and Piman Indians, Spanish conquistadores and Mexican ranchers and Anglo pioneer settlement

Exhibitions: The Photography of Charles Brill; Regional Medicine
Publications: Centennial Book of Nogales; A Guide to Casas Grandes, Chihuahua, Mexico; newsletter, 10 per year
Activities: Educ dept; lectures open to public, 12 vis lectr per year; tours; originate traveling exhibitions; sales shop sells books, maps and pins

L **Library,** 85621. *Head* Alma D Ready
Collects books and archival material on Pimeria Alta, northern Sonora and southern Arizona
Income: $600
Purchases: $600
Library Holdings: Vols 600; Per subs 3; AV — Cassettes; Other — Clipping files, manuscripts, memorabilia, pamphlets, photographs
Collections: The Jack Kemmer Memorial Collection, books on the cattle industry of Texas, New Mexico, Arizona and California

PATAGONIA

M **STRADLING MUSEUM OF THE HORSE, INC,** Box 413, 85624. Tel 602-394-2264. *Dir* Anne C Stradling; *Cur* Marianna Bowers
Open daily & holidays 9 AM - 5 PM, cl Thanksgiving & Christmas. Admis adults $2, children under 12 $.50. Estab 1960
Collections: Bronzes, china, glass, paintings, prints, saddles, silver; Indian Painting and Kachinas; 40 carriages
Activities: Guided tours; sales shop sells saddlery, Indian rugs, art, china and jewelry

PHOENIX

O **ARIZONA ARTIST GUILD,** 8912 N Fourth St, 85020. Tel 602-944-9713. *Pres* Garnette Widdicield; *First VPres* Shirley Kleppe; *Second VPres Exhibitions* Paul Klein; *Recording Secy* Claudia McEchne; *Recording Secy* Joan Hale
Estab 1928 to foster guild spirit, to assist in raising standards of art in the community, and to assume civic responsibility in matters relating to art. Average Annual Attendance: 550. Mem: 220 juried, 35 assoc; dues $25; membership by jury; monthly meetings
Income: Financed by endowment and membership
Exhibitions: Horizons (annually in spring, members only); fall exhibition for members only
Publications: AAG news, monthly
Activities: Classes for adults; lectures sometimes open to the public, 12 or more vis lectrs per year; gallery talks; competions with awards; workshops by visiting professionals offered; paint-outs; sketch groups; demonstrations; schol offered

L **Library,** 8912 N Fourth St, 85020
Open to members for reference only

C **THE ARIZONA BANK,** 101 N First Ave, PO Box 2511, 85003. Tel 602-262-2826. *Chmn & Chief Executive Officer* Don B Tostenrud
Open Mon - Thurs 9 AM - 3 PM, Fri 9 AM - 6 PM. Estab as art sponsor to provide an opportunity for Southwest art to be seen by customers and others in downtown Phoenix. Displays continually changing exhibits which benefit charitable organizations through the sale of works being shown. Collection displayed in the Galleria, and in offices statewide. Galleria exhibits, including parts of permanent collection
Collections: Approximately 400 Hopi Indian Kachinas; 350 paintings and sculpture

O **ARIZONA COMMISSION ON THE ARTS,** 2024 N 7th St, Suite 201, 85006. Tel 602-255-5882. *Chmn* Richard H Whitney; *VChmn* Ronald H Warner; *Executive Dir* Adrienne Hirsch; *Deputy Dir* Shelley Cohn; *Expansion Arts Coordr* Lawrence Moore; *Arts Services Coordr* Tonda Gorton; *Community Development Coordr* Lynn Timmons; *Visual Arts Coordr* Rex Gulbranson; *Museum Special Projects Coordr* Deborah Whitehurst; *Education Coordr* Carol Jean Kennedy
Open 8 AM - 5 PM. No admis fee. Estab 1966 to promote and encourage the arts in the State of Arizona. Mem: Meetings, quarterly
Income: $1,152,800 (financed by state and federal appropriation)
Publications: Bi-Cultural Information, quarterly, annual report; Artists' Guide to Programs; monthly bulletin; guide to programs
Activities: Workshops; artists-in-education program; lect open to public; scholarships; bi-cultural arts program; Art in Public Places Program; Art in Arizona Towns Program; book traveling exhibitions; originate traveling exhibitions

L **Reference Library,** 2024 N 7th St, Suite 201, 85006
Library Holdings: Vols 1150; Per subs 35; AV — A-tapes, cassettes, slides; Other — Exhibition catalogs, pamphlets
Special Subjects: Topics related to the business of the arts

O **ARIZONA WATERCOLOR ASSOCIATION,** PO Box 7574, 85011. Tel 602-948-4887. *Pres* Ann McEachron; *Dir* Robert Oliver; *First VPres* Sidney Moxham; *Second VPres* Geraldine Beans; *Third VPres* Elaine Retherford; *Recording Secy* Kathleen Stuart; *Corresponding Secy* Julie Pollard; *Treas* Milton Lemberg
Estab 1960 to further activity and interest in the watercolor medium, promote growth of individuals and group and maintain high quality of professional exhibits. Average Annual Attendance: 125. Mem: 350; qualifications for juried membership, fall and spring jurying by Membership Committee; for Associate membership, application through First VPres; dues $15; meetings second Mon each month at AAG building
Income: Financed by dues and donations
Exhibitions: Two exhibitions yearly: fall juried members only and spring juried members & assoc members
Publications: AWA Newsletter, monthly
Activities: Workshops; lectures for members only; paint outs; competitions with awards; book traveling exhibitions; traveling exhibitions organized and circulated

M **HEARD MUSEUM,** 22 E Monte Vista Rd, 85004. Tel 602-252-8848. *Dir* Michael J Fox; *Chief Cur* Dr Robert Breunig; *Cur Coll* Ann Marshall; *Cur Exhib* Patrick Neary; *Public Program Coordr* Susan Slaffer; *Development Officer* Dr Joseph Schaffer; *Asst Cur* Diana Pardue; *Public Info Officer* David Campbell
Open Mon - Sat 10 AM - 4:45 PM, Sun 1 - 4:45 PM. Admis adult $2, senior citizen $1.50, student and children $.75. Estab 1929 to collect and exhibit anthropology and art; collections built around works of Indians of the Americas. Average Annual Attendance: 250,000
Collections: Archeology; Native American fine arts; sculpture, primitive arts from the cultures of Africa, Asia and Oceania; American Indian; Fred Harvey Fine Arts Collection
Exhibitions: (1982) Frontier Merchants & Native Craftsmen: The Fred Harvey Company Collects Indian Art; New Paintings by Joe Baker; Numkena & Mozart's Magic Flute; Generations in Clay: Pueblo Pottery of the American Southwest; Oscar Howe Retrospective; Heye Foundation: Native American Paintings; (1983) Pueblo & Navajo Textiles from the Silvermen Collection; The Tipi: Art & Architecture; Gifts from Mother Earth: Zuni Ceramics; Artist Hopid; Houser and Haozous: A Sculptural Retrospective
Publications: The Heard Museum Newsletter, bi-monthly; exhibition catalogs
Activities: Docent training; lect open to public, 15 vis lectr per year; lect at schools; original objects of art lent to accredited museums; lending collection contains framed reproductions, original prints, 1000 paintings, photographs, sculpture, and 600 slides; organize and circulate traveling exhibitions; museum shop sells books, original art, prints, reproductions and slides
L **Library,** 22 E Monte Vista Rd, 85004. Tel 602-252-8840. *Librn* Mary E Graham
Open Mon - Fri 10 AM - 4:45 PM. Estab 1929 as a research library for museum staff, members and the public (in-house only)
Income: $7600 (financed by membership & museum budget)
Library Holdings: Vols 44,000; Micro — Fiche, reels; AV — A-tapes, motion pictures, v-tapes; Other — Clipping files, exhibition catalogs, memorabilia, pamphlets, photographs, prints
Special Subjects: Anthropology, Primitive Art, American Indian

M **PHOENIX ART MUSEUM,** 1625 N Central Ave, 85004. Tel 602-257-1880. *Pres* Betsy Stodola; *VPres* Charles S Snead; *VPres* Howard McCrady; *Secy* Robert Ulrich; *Treas* L Roy Papp; *Dir* James K Ballinger
Open Tues - Sat 10 AM - 5 PM, Wed 10 AM - 9 PM, Sun 1 - 5 PM, cl Mon. Admis adults $2, students & senior citizens $1, members & school tours free. Estab 1925; museum constructed 1959. Average Annual Attendance: 250,000. Mem: 5300; dues $20 and up; annual meeting April
Income: $1,200,000
Collections: Contemporary paintings, sculptures and graphics; 19th century; Baroque; Mexican art; Oriental arts collection; Renaissance; Thorne Miniature Room; Western art; Medieval art
Exhibitions: (1984) 20th Century Masters: The Thyssen-Bornemisza Collection; Diego Rivera: The Cubist Years; Jim Dine: Five Themes
Publications: Annual report; Calendar, monthly; catalog of permanent collection; exhibition catalogs
Activities: Classes for adults and children; docent training; lectures open to public, 12 vis lectr per year; concerts; gallery talks; tours; competitions; originate traveling exhibitions; museum shop sells books, magazines, reproductions, prints, slides and gifts from around the world; junior museum at same address
L **Art Research Library,** 1627 N Central Ave, 85004. Tel 602-257-1222. *Librn* Clayton C Kirking
Open Tues - Fri 10 AM - 4:30 PM. Estab 1959 to serve reference needs of the museum staff, docents, membership, students and public. For reference only
Income: Financed by endowment and membership
Purchases: $13,700
Library Holdings: Vols 18,000; Per subs 85; Micro — Cards; AV — Motion pictures, slides, v-tapes; Other — Clipping files, exhibition catalogs, manuscripts, memorabilia, pamphlets, reproductions
Special Subjects: Painting - American, Prints
Collections: Ancient Architecture Collection; Ambrose Lansing Egyptian Collection; †Arizona Artist Index; †auction catalogs; †museum archives; Rembrandt etching catalogs; Whistler Prints

C **VALLEY NATIONAL BANK OF ARIZONA,** Fine Arts Department, PO Box 71, 85001. Tel 602-261-2966. *Cur Art* Judy Hudson
Open to public. Estab 1933 to support emerging artists throughout the state; encourage and promote talented high school students with Scholastic Art Awards; provide the public with beautiful, integrated art in branch banks. Several thousand pieces of art collection displayed in over 200 branches, business offices, and support facilities throughout the state of Arizona
Collections: Primarily Western, Southwestern art featuring many of the now classic Western artists; earliest lithograph dates back to the 1820's and collection continues through the present
Exhibitions: Employee's Art Show
Activities: Lect; gallery talks; tours by appointment; competitions; since 1942 state sponsor for Scholastic Art Awards throughout Arizona; purchase awards throughout the state, sponsor Employees' Art Show annually, with juried and popular choice awards, underwrite local art exhibitions on the Concourse of the Home Office Building; individual objects of art lent contingent upon bank policy

PRESCOTT

O **PRESCOTT FINE ARTS ASSOCIATION,*** 202 North Marina St, PO Box 1267, 86301. Tel 602-445-9853. *Pres* Robert Gray; *VPres* Ted Liese; *Secy* Jane Morgan
Gallery open Mon - Sun 1 - 5 PM during shows. No admis fee, donations accepted. Estab 1968 to promote arts within the county and local community. Art Gallery is one large room below theater section in what was previously a Catholic Church. Average Annual Attendance: 3000. Mem: 318; dues family $15, individual $10; annual meeting second Thurs of Dec
Income: $30,000 (financed by membership and grants from Arizona Arts and Humanities Council)
Activities: Docent training; concerts; competitions; book traveling exhibitions, 2-3 per year

SCOTTSDALE

O **COSANTI FOUNDATION,** 6433 Doubletree Ranch Rd, 85253. Tel 602-948-6145. *Pres* Paolo Soleri
Open Mon - Sun 9 AM - 5 PM. Admis $1. Estab 1956 as a non-profit educational organization by Paolo Soleri pursuing the research and development of an alternative urban environment. Arcosanti Gallery & the North Studio has a permanent exhibit of original sketches, sculptures, and graphics by Paolo Soleri. Average Annual Attendance: 40,000
Income: Financed by tuition, private donations and sales of art objects
Collections: Permanent collection of architectural designs and drawings by Paolo Soleri
Exhibitions: Toward Arcology, Works in Progress; Two Sun Arcology, The City Energized by the Sun, sponsored by Xerox Corporation
Publications: Arcosanti Newsletter, monthly
Activities: Classes for adults; docent training; Arcosanti Workshop Program, experiential workshops; lectures open to the public; gallery talks; tours; scholarships; traveling exhibits organized and circulated; sales shop sells books, original art, prints, reproductions, slides

O **SCOTTSDALE ARTISTS' LEAGUE,** PO Box 1071, 85252. Tel 602-948-3560. *Pres* Maxine Johnston; *Dir* Ronald F Caya
Estab 1961 to encourage the practice of art and to support and encourage the study and application of art as an avocation, to promote ethical principals and practice, to advance the interest and appreciation of art in all its forms and to increase the usefulness of art to the public at large. Maintains Upstairs Gallery in Camelview Plaza Mall and gallery in Scottsdale Hospital. Average Annual Attendance: 50 - 100 per month. Mem: 325; dues $12.50; monthly meetings first Tues
Exhibitions: Yearly juried exhibition for members only; yearly juried exhibition for all Arizona artists (open shows)
Publications: Art Beat, monthly
Activities: Classes for adults; lectures open to the public, 6 vis lectr per year; gallery talks; tours; awards given to art students

M **SCOTTSDALE CENTER FOR THE ARTS,** 7383 Scottsdale Mall, 85251. Tel 602-994-2301. *Dir* Ronald F Caya; *Arts Mgr* Lynn W White; *Arts Mgr* Errol Selsby; *Exhibits Coordr* Marvin Schenck; *Events Coordr* Mollie Trivers
Open Tues - Fri 10 AM - 5 PM, Sat & Sun Noon - 5 PM. No admis fee. Estab 1975 to provide a varied program of performance events & art exhibits. Center is a large contemporary space divided by movable walls, allowing viewing of large & small works in various media. Average Annual Attendance: 130,000. Mem: 2500; dues $20 and up
Income: $1,250,000 (financed by membership, city appropriation & corporate sponsorship)
Collections: Paintings, prints, sculptures
Exhibitions: (1983) Photography - Two Views; (1984) The Valley Collects - Western Art of the Past; New Artists from Arizona State University; Stephen DeStaebler
Publications: In Touch with the Arts, monthly membership newsletter; exhibition catalogs
Activities: Docent training; lectures open to public, 10 vis lectr per yr; competitions with awards; exten dept serves local schools; book traveling exhibitions; originates traveling exhibition; sales shop sells books, original art, reproductions, prints & craft items

SECOND MESA

M **HOPI CULTURAL CENTER,*** Box 38, 86043. Tel 602-734-2411. *Dir* Terrance Talaswalma
Open 8 AM - 6 PM
Collections: Hopi arts & crafts; pre-historic & historic pottery; weavings; wood carvings; silver

TEMPE

ARIZONA STATE UNIVERSITY
M **University Art Collections,** Matthews Center, 85287. Tel 602-965-2874. *Dir* Rudy H Turk; *Registrar* Mary Jane Williams; *Public Services Officer* Charlotte Lomeo; *Installationist* Paula Ganzel; *Museum Asst* Carol Miller
Open Mon - Fri 8 AM - 5 PM, Sun 1 - 5 PM. No admis fee. Estab 1950 to provide esthetic and educational service for student and the citizens of the state. Three permanent exhibition galleries featuring American, contemporary and Latin American art; two changing galleries and two changing areas; 48 shows annually. Average Annual Attendance: 40,000
Income: $150,000 (financed by state appropriations, donations and earnings)
Purchases: $15,000
Collections: †American crafts, especially ceramics; †American painting and sculpture 18th Century to present; †print collection 15th Century to present
Exhibitions: Continuous showing of Historical and Contemporary Print Exhibitions; Showing of historical American ceramic collection; Sculpture in the 70's; The Figure; The Collages of George Miyasaki; Illusion and Reality; Tony DeLap Multi-Media; Magiscopes by Feliciano Bejar
Activities: Educ dept; dramatic programs; docent training; special events; lect open to public, 12 visiting lectr per year; gallery talks; tours; competitions; individual paintings and original objects of art lent to other professional organizations; originate traveling exhibitions; museum shop sells books, original art and crafts
L **Hayden Library Art Dept,** Arizona State University, 85201. Tel 602-965-3605, 965-3417. *Chief Librn* Don Riggs; *Assoc Librn* Helen Gater; *Acting Asst Librn* Constance Corey; *Art Specialist* Win Berta Yao
Open Mon - Thurs 7 AM - Midnight, Fri 7 AM - 10 PM, Sat 9 AM - 5 PM, Sun 10 AM - Midnight
Library Holdings: Vols 30,000; Per subs 225; Micro — Cards, fiche, reels; AV — A-tapes, cassettes

M **Memorial Union Gallery,** 85287. Tel 602-965-6649. *Dir* Rosalyn Munk
Open Mon - Fri 9 AM - 5 PM. Estab to exhibit work that has strong individual qualities from the United States, also some Arizona work that has not been shown on campus. Gallery is contained in two rooms with 1400 sq ft space; fireplace; one wall is glass; 20 ft ceiling; 26 4 x 8 partitions; track lighting; one entrance and exit; located in area with maximum traffic. Average Annual Attendance: 30,000
Income: Financed by administrative appropriation
Purchases: $3000
Collections: Painting, print and sculpture, primarily Altman, Gorman, Mahaffey, Schoulder and Slater
Exhibitions: Arizona Designer Craftsmen; Bert Brouwer; Lois Coren; John Fox; Christian Heckscher; Diane Thomas Lincoln; Susan Meyer; Clarence Morgan; Jo Ann Morgan; Susan Pontious; M O'Hara Ure; Jan Wurm
Activities: Educ dept; internships; lect open to public, 4 visiting lectr per year; gallery talks; competitions; originate traveling exhibitions

L **Howe Architecture Library,** College of Architecture, Planning & Design Sciences, 85287. Tel 602-965-6400. *Librn* Katherine M Weir
Open Mon - Thurs 8 AM - 10 PM, Fri 8 AM - 5 PM, Sat Noon - 5 PM, Sun 5 - 10 PM. Estab 1959 to serve the architecture college and the university community with reference and research material in the subject of architecture. Circ 35,000
Income: Financed by state appropriation
Library Holdings: Vols 17,000; Per subs 133; Micro — Reels; AV — Cassettes; Other — Pamphlets
Collections: Paolo Soleri Archive; †Frank Lloyd Wright Rare Material

TUBAC

O **TUBAC CENTER OF THE ARTS,** Santa Cruz Valley Art Association, Box 1911, 84540. Tel 602-398-2371. *Pres* Robert Lasch; *Dir* Pat Marohn
Open Tues - Sat 10 AM - 4:30 PM, Sun & holidays 1 - 5 PM, cl Mon. No admis fee. Estab 1963 to exhibit local artists works. One gallery, Spanish Colonial Building, 139 running feet of exhibit space. Average Annual Attendance: 29,000. Mem: 750; dues $10 - $150
Collections: Works by present and former Tubac artists
Activities: Classes for adults and children; docent training; lectures open to public, 7 visiting lecturers per year; guided tours; films; art festivals; gallery talks; awards given; sales shop sells books, original art, pottery, jewelry, ethnic crafts (Indian, Mexican)

L **Library,** 84540
Library Holdings: Vols 800; Per subs 4

TUCSON

ART LIBRARIES SOCIETY-NORTH AMERICA
For further information, see National and Regional Organizations

C **FIRST INTERSTATE BANK OF ARIZONA,*** 150 N Stone Ave, 20551. Tel 602-271-6879. *Cur* Patsy Koldoff
Open Mon - Fri 10 AM - 3 PM. Collection displayed in Old West Gallery, three room gallery on second floor of Tucson Main
Collections: Western scenes
Activities: Tours; awards to various art associations around the state; objects of art lent to Tucson Museum & Phoenix Art Museum

M **TUCSON MUSEUM OF ART,** 140 N Main, 85705. Tel 602-624-2333. *Dir* R Andrew Maass; *Cur Collections* Annette Munzer; *Cur Exhibitions* Susanne Frantz; *Public Relations & Media* Jan Crebbs
Open Tues - Sat 10 AM - 5 PM, Sun 1 - 5 PM. No admis fee. Estab 1924 to operate a private nonprofit civic art gallery to promote art education, to hold art exhibitions and to further art appreciation for the public. Galleries display the permanent changing exhibitions; museum shop displays contemporary crafts by southern Arizona artists. Average Annual Attendance: 80,000. Mem: 2100; dues Angel $1000 or more, benefactor $500, patron $250, sponsor $100, donor $50, general $35; annual meeting May
Income: $551,000 (financed by endowment, membership, city and state appropriations and contributions)
Purchases: Endowment for purchase $70,000
Collections: †Pre-Columbian; †Spanish Colonial; †Western American
Exhibitions: (1982) Artists by Artists, George Bellows, Marsden Hartley; National Watercolor Society's 61st Annual; Dale Chihuly; Arizona Biennial; Contemporary German Tapestries; Warren Anderson; Jose Galvez; Patterns & Sources of Navajo Weaving; Paradigm, 8 Arizona Artists; Tokaido Road, Hikroshinge Prints; Inro & Netsuke; Patti Warashina; Mayumi Oda; Sculptural Glass; Collage & Assemblage; Making Paper; Selections from the Permanent Collections; Harry Benson; Nasca Lines; Arizona Collects the West, Campbell Collection
Publications: Calendar, bi-monthly; exhibition catalogs
Activities: Classes for adults and children; docent training; lect open to public; concerts; gallery talks; tours; competitions; exten department serving Tucson school districts; traveling exhibitions organized and circulated; museum shop features contemporary crafts by Arizona artists

L **Library,** 140 North Main Ave, 85705. Tel 602-623-4881. *Librn* Dorcas Worsley; *Cataloger* Dorothy Siebecker; *Slide Librn* Elinore Smith; *Bibliographer* Donald Powell; *Asst* Margaret Peck; *Asst* Jerry Albert
Open Mon - Fri 10 AM - 3 PM. Estab 1974 for bibliographic and research needs of Museum staff, faculty, students and docents. Open to public for research and study
Income: Financed by gifts and fund allocations
Library Holdings: Vols 6200; Per subs 23; AV — Cassettes, slides 20,000; Other — Clipping files, exhibition catalogs, pamphlets, photographs
Special Subjects: Pre-Columbian Art, Art of Africa, Oceania, Pre-Columbian Art Western art, Contemporary Art
Collections: Biographic material documenting Arizona artists for the Archives of Arizona Art

UNIVERSITY OF ARIZONA

M **Museum of Art,** Olive & Speedway Sts, 85721. Tel 602-621-7567. *Dir & Chief Cur* Dr Peter Bermingham; *Asst Dir* Kathryn C Jessup; *Cur of Education* Joshua Goldberg; *Assoc Cur of Education* Margaret Perkins; *Assoc Cur* Lee Karpiscak; *Admin Asst* Elvira Plewa; *Registrar* Kenneth D Little; *Asst Registrar* Richard Schaffer; *Public Relations* Jerre Johnston
Open Mon - Fri 9 AM - 5 PM, Sun 12 - 5 PM. Estab 1955 to share with the Tucson community, visitors and the university students the treasures of three remarkable permanent collections: the C Leonard Pfeiffer Collection, the Samuel H Kress Collection and the Edward J Gallagher Jr Collection. One of the museums' most important functions is to reach out to schools around Tucson through the education department. Special exhibitions are maintained on the first floor of the museum; the permanent collections are housed on the second floor. Average Annual Attendance: 45,000
Income: Financed by state appropriation
Collections: Edward J Gallagher Collection of over a hundred paintings of national and international artists; Samuel H Kress Collection of 26 Renaissance works and 26 paintings of the 15th century Spanish Retablo by Fernando Gallego; C Leonard Pfeiffer Collection of American Artists of the 30s, 40s and 50s; Jacques Lipchitz Collection of 70 plaster models
Exhibitions: Keith Crown Watercolors; Jose Luis Cuevas Illustrated Letters; Durer, Rembrandt, Hogarth Prints; The Moving Image; Whistler and his Contemporaries; New Work/New York; Beth Ames Swartz: Israel Revisited; Aaron Siskind: 50 Years; Splendors of the Sohites; Arakawa: The Mechanism of Meaning; Sewing Space; Santos: The Religious Folk Art of the Southwest; Clayton Bailey's Robots; John Sloan in Santa Fe; Texas on Paper; Manuel Neri; Hans Hofmann as Teacher; annual faculty and MFA exhibits
Publications: Fully illustrated catalogs on all special exhibitions
Activities: Docent training; tours of museum; lectr; gallery talks; out reach tours; traveling exhibitions organized and circulated; sales shop sells books, cards and poster reproductions

L **Museum of Art Library,** Speedway & Olive, 85721. Tel 602-621-7567. *Librn* Barbara Kittle
Estab to assist staff and students working at museum with reference information. Not open to public; telephone requests for information answered
Library Holdings: Vols 1000; Per subs 16; AV — Cassettes, slides; Other — Clipping files, exhibition catalogs, pamphlets

M **Center for Creative Photography,** 843 E University, 85719. Tel 602-626-4636. *Dir* James Enyeart; *Cur & Librn Photography Archive* Terence R Pitts; *Registrar* Lawrence Fong
Open Mon - Fri 9 AM - 5 PM, Sun Noon - 5 PM. Estab 1975 to house and organize the archives of numerous major photographers and to act as a research center in 20th century photography. Gallery exhibitions changing approximately every six weeks. Average Annual Attendance: 15,000
Income: Financed by state, federal, private and corporate sources
Collections: Archives of Ansel Adams, Wynn Bullock, Harry Callahan, Aaron Siskind, W Eugene Smith, Frederick Sommer, Paul Strand, Edward Weston and others
Publications: The Archive, approx 3 times per year; bibliography series; exhibitions catalogs; guide series
Activities: Lectures open to public, 8 vis lectr per year; gallery talks; tours; original objects of art lent to qualified museums; traveling exhibitions organized and circulated

L **Photography Library,** 843 E University, 85710. Tel 602-626-4636. *Librn* Terence R Pitts
Open Mon - Fri 9 AM - 5 PM, Sun Noon - 5 PM. Open to the public for lending and reference
Library Holdings: Vols 5000; Per subs 45; Micro — Fiche, reels; AV — A-tapes, cassettes, slides, v-tapes; Other — Clipping files, exhibition catalogs, manuscripts, memorabilia
Collections: Limited edition books; hand-made books; books illustrated with original photographs

WICKENBURG

M **DESERT CABALLEROS WESTERN MUSEUM,** 20 N Frontier St, Box 1446, 85358. Tel 602-684-2272. *Pres* Charles Klein; *Exec VPres and Dir* Harry T Needham; *Cur* Veeva Fletcher; *Chmn of the Board* Roy Coxwell; *Treas* Herald Arnt
Open Tues - Sat 10 AM - 4 PM, Sun 1 PM - 4 PM, cl Mon. Admis by donation. Estab 1975 to show the development of Wickenburg from prehistoric to present day. The museum houses western art gallery, mineral room, Indian room, period rooms and gold mining equipment. Average Annual Attendance: 16,500. Mem: 250; dues $15 and up; annual meeting 2nd Mon in April
Income: $50,000 - $60,000 (financed by membership)
Collections: Indian artifacts; period rooms; western art; George Phippen Memorial Western Bronze Collection, including Remington and Russell
Activities: Provides tours; lending collection contains original objects of art; book traveling exhibitions 2 per year; museum shop sells books, prints and postcards

L **Library,** 20 N Frontier St, Box 1446, 85358. Tel 602-684-2272
Open to members for reference only
Library Holdings: Vols 200

WINDOW ROCK

M **NAVAJO TRIBAL MUSEUM,** Highway 264, PO Box 308, 86515. Tel 602-871-6673. *Cur* Russell P Hartman
Open Mon - Fri 9 AM - 4:45 PM, cl national & tribal holidays. No admis fee. Estab 1961 to collect and preserve items depicting Navajo history and culture and natural history of region. Exhibit area approx 2500 ft. Average Annual Attendance: 13,000
Income: Financed by tribal budget
Collections: Works in all media by Navajo Indian artists, & non-Navajo artists who depict Navajo subject matter
Publications: Artist's directory & biographical file
Activities: Individual paintings and original works of art available for loan to other museums

L Navajo Nation Library, Highway 264, Box K, 86515. Tel 602-871-6457. *Librn* Deborah MacBeth
Open to public for reference only
Library Holdings: Vols 6000

YUMA

O YUMA FINE ARTS ASSOCIATION, Yuma Art Center, 281 Gila St, PO Box 1471, 85364. Tel 602-783-2314. *Dir & Cur* James Nelson; *Admin Asst* Gwen Robinson
Open Tues - Sun 10 AM - 5 PM. No admis fee. Estab 1962 to foster the arts in the Yuma area and to provide a showing space for contemporary Arizona artists. Gallery is housed in restored Southern Pacific Railway depot built in 1926. Average Annual Attendance: 15,000. Mem: 300, dues, $5 - $1000
Income: Financed by endowment, membership and city appropriation
Collections: Contemporary Arizona
Exhibitions: (1981-82) Curran, puppets; G Reckling; Mexican Folk Toys; 16th Southwestern Annual Exhibition; Mendoza; F Golding; Scholder-Peabody; (1982-83) Sam Scott; Artists in Yuma Residence; Hal Painter; David Kraisler; 17th Southwestern Annual Exhibition
Publications: Membership bulletin, bimonthly
Activities: Classes for children; dramatic programs; docent training; lect open to public; concerts; gallery talks; tours; individual painting and original objects of art lent to members and businesses; organize and circulate traveling exhibitions; museum shop sells original art, prints, and reproductions

ARKANSAS

CLARKSVILLE

L COLLEGE OF THE OZARKS LIBRARY, 214 College Ave, 72830. Tel 501-754-3964. *Library Dir* Stuart Stelzer
No admis fee. Estab 1834
Library Holdings: Vols 1500; Micro — Fiche, reels; AV — Cassettes, fs, rec, slides; Other — Clipping files, pamphlets
Collections: Original print collection; graduate students painting collection
Activities: Dramatic programs; lect open to the public, 9 vis lectr per yr; scholarships offered; individual paintings lent to schools; lending collection contains 100 color reproductions, 16mm films

EL DORADO

O SOUTH ARKANSAS ART CENTER,* 110 E Fifth St, 71730. Tel 501-862-5474. *Executive Dir* Pamela A Bosanko; *Pres* Penny Ralston; *Secy* Lilla Johnston
Open Mon - Fri 10 AM - 5 PM, Sat 2 - 5 PM. No admis fee. Estab 1965 for the promotion, enrichment and improvement of the visual arts by means of exhibits, lectures and instruction, and through scholarships to be offered whenever possible. Gallery maintained. Mem: 350; dues $5; annual meeting second Tues every month
Income: Financed by membership, city and state appropriation
Collections: All paintings and collections are under jurisdiction of South Arkansas Arts Center
Exhibitions: Various art shows in this and surrounding states; gallery shows, ten guest artists annually, two months dedicated to local artists, works by local artists displayed in corridor year-round
Publications: Newsletter, quarterly
Activities: Classes for adults and children; theater and dance workshops; lect open to public; gallery talks; competitions; scholarships
L Library,* 110 E Fifth St, 71730
Library Holdings: Vols 200

FAYETTEVILLE

UNIVERSITY OF ARKANSAS
M Fine Arts Center Gallery,* Dept of Art, FA 116, 72701. Tel 501-575-5202. *Gallery Dir* Robert Ross
Open Aug - May Mon - Fri 9 AM - 4 PM, Thurs - Sat evenings, Sun afternoon. No admis fee. Estab 1950 as a teaching and community art gallery in fields of painting, drawing, sculpture and architecture. One gallery with moveable display panels covers 80 x 40 ft, gallery is part of center for art and music
Income: Financed by state appropriation
Collections: Permanent collection of paintings, photographs, prints and sculpture
Exhibitions: Fifteen exhibitions per year, of which four are in-house, art deparment related; one regional competion; one public school exhibit; one architecture exhibit; visiting artists, traveling exhibitions; Five Contemporary Photographers: Crane, Jachna, Josephson, Larson, Metzger
Activities: Classes for adults; lect open to the public, 6-8 vis lectr per year; concerts; gallery talks; competitions with awards; traveling exhibitions
L Fine Arts Library, FNAR-104, Fayetteville, 72701. Tel 501-575-4708. *Librn* Joyce M Clinkscales
Open Mon - Thurs 8 AM - 10 PM, Fri 8 AM - 5 PM, Sat 10 AM - 4 PM, Sun 2 - 10 PM. Estab 1951 to support the curriculum in music, art and architecture. Circ 36,000
Library Holdings: Vols 33,000; Per subs 155; AV — Slides; Other — Exhibition catalogs

FORT SMITH

O FORT SMITH ART CENTER,* 423 N Sixth St, 72901. Tel 501-782-6371, 782-1156. *Dir* Polly Crews; *Pres* Marcia Edwards
Open daily 10 AM - 4 PM, Sun 2 - 4 PM, cl Mon, July 4, Labor Day, Thanksgiving and Christmas Eve - New Years. No admis fee. Estab 1957 to provide art museum, art association and art education. Library maintained. Average Annual Attendance: 10,000. Mem: 930; dues $15
Income: $69,000 (financed by endowment, mem, contributions & sales)
Collections: †American painting, graphics and drawings; †Boehm porcelain; local & regional art
Exhibitions: Five exhibitions monthly
Publications: Bulletin, monthly
Activities: Classes for children; Competitions with awards; artmobile; individual paintings and original objects of art lent to banks and schools; sales shop sells books and original art

HARRISON

ASSOCIATION OF AMERICAN EDITORIAL CARTOONISTS
For further information, see National and Regional Organizations

HELENA

M PHILLIPS COUNTY MUSEUM, 623 Pecan St, 72342. Tel 501-338-3537. *Pres* Mrs Dale Kirkman
Open Mon - Sat 9 AM - 5 PM, cl national holidays. No admis fee. Estab 1929 as an educational and cultural museum to impart an appreciation of local history and to display objects of art from all over the world. Average Annual Attendance: 5000. Mem: 250; dues $3-$5; annual meeting first Fri in May
Income: Financed by endowment, membership and city appropriation
Collections: China; glassware; paintings; Indian artifacts; Civil War memorabilia; Thomas Alva Edison Historical Display
Exhibitions: (1983) Antique Clothing from the Late 1800s to Early 1900s; Charles L Thompson Architectural Drawings

HOT SPRINGS

O SOUTHERN ARTISTS ASSOCIATION, Fine Arts Center,* 815 Whittington Ave, 71901. Tel 501-624-9836. *Pres* Margaret Pedersen; *VPres* Bruce Richards
Open Wed - Sat 10 AM - 4 PM, Sun 1:30 - 5 PM, cl Mon & Tues. Estab 1951 to provide the community with a yearly calendar of art exhibitions, to provide gallery space for members, to provide educational program in art for the community and serve as a statewide art association. Mem: 137; dues $15; meetings monthly
Income: Financed by membership, city appropriation and commission from sales of artwork
Activities: Classes for adults and children; art films; workshop; lect open to the public, 3-4 visiting lectrs per year; gallery talks; competitions with prizes, awards and honorable mentions given; book traveling exhibitions

JONESBORO

M ARKANSAS STATE UNIVERSITY ART GALLERY, JONESBORO, Caraway Rd (Mailing add: Box 2782, State University, 72467). Tel 501-972-3050. *Dir* Dr Charlott Jones; *Chmn Dept of Art* Dr William Allen; *Chmn Exhibits* Don Osborn
Open weekdays 9:30 AM - 4 PM. No admis fee. Estab 1967 for education objectives; recognition of contemporary artists and encouragement to students. Located in the Fine Art Center, the well-lighted gallery measures 45 x 45 ft plus corridor display areas. Average Annual Attendance: 10,500
Income: $3956 (financed by state appropriation)
Collections: Contemporary paintings; contemporary sculpture; †historical and contemporary prints; †photographs
Exhibitions: Roger Carlisle; Nancy Harris; Cheryl Trimarchi; Dale Maddox; Faculty of Northern State College; Craft Invitational; Young Artists Exhibition; Ellen Murray Meissinger; permanent collection
Publications: Exhibition catalogs
Activities: Lect open to public, 4 - 6 visiting lectr per year; gallery talks; competitions; originate traveling exhibitions
L Library, Caraway Rd (Mailing add: PO Box 2782, 72467)
Library Holdings: Vols 5500; Per subs 79; Micro — Fiche, reels; AV — Cassettes, fs, Kodachromes, motion pictures, slides; Other — Exhibition catalogs

LITTLE ROCK

M ARKANSAS ARTS CENTER, MacArthur Park, PO Box 2137, 72203. Tel 501-372-4000. *Exec Dir* Townsend D Wolfe III; *Asst to Dir* Bill Atkins; *Sr Dir* Evelyn McCoy
Open Mon - Sat 8 AM - 5 PM, Sun & holidays Noon - 5 PM. No admis fee to galleries, admission charged for theatre activities. Estab 1960 to further the development, the understanding and the appreciation of the visual and performing arts. Six galleries, three for permanent collections and three for temporary exhibits. Average Annual Attendance: 475,000. Mem: 4000; dues from benefactor $20,000 to basic $35; annual meeting in July
Income: Financed by endowment, membership, city and state appropriation and earned income
Purchases: Bierre Bonnard's Marthe Entrant Le Salon, Vincent Van Gogh's Man With A Spade Resting, Paul Cezanne's Le Pont D'Argenteuil & verso: Quais Avec Pont Et Barque, Edgar Degas' Trois Danseuses Nues, Georges Braque's Pommes
Collections: Paintings, prints and drawings prior to the 20th century; †drawings; †prints; decorative arts

Exhibitions: (1983-84) Annual Delta Art Exhibition; Robert Andrew Parker, watercolors; Jerome Witkin — A Decade of Work; British Watercolors & Drawings — 1775-1950; 11th Annual Toys Designed by Artists; Kassebaum Medieval & Renassiance Ceramic Collection; Art Nouveau, Art Deco & Modern; Canadian Crafts
Publications: Members bulletin, monthly; annual membership catalog; annual report; catalogue selections from the permanent collection
Activities: Classes for adults and children; docent training; lect open to the public, 6 - 10 visiting lectr per year; concerts; gallery talks; tours; competitions; childrens' theatre; dance; exten department serving the state of Arkansas; artmobile; individual paintings and original objects of art lent to schools, civic groups and churches; lending collection contains motion pictures, original prints, paintings, 4300 phonorecords and 16,000 slides; originates traveling exhibitions; museum shop sells books, slides, gifts, jewelry and crafts; junior museum
L **Elizabeth Prewitt Taylor Memorial Library,** MacArthur Park, 72203. *Dir* Evelyn McCoy; *Visual Arts Asst* Carolyn Phelps
Open Mon - Fri 10 AM - 5 PM. Estab 1963 to provide resources in the arts for students, educators, and interested public
Income: $25,120
Purchases: $6800
Library Holdings: Vols 6000; Per subs 104; AV — Cassettes, fs, Kodachromes, motion pictures, rec, slides; Other — Clipping files, exhibition catalogs, memorabilia, pamphlets
Collections: †George Fisher Cartoons; John Reid Jazz Collection

M **ARKANSAS TERRITORIAL RESTORATION,** 3rd & Scott, 72201. Tel 501-371-2348. *Dir* Bill Worthen; *Cur* Chris Serio; *Educ Coordr* Karen Norman
Open daily 9 AM - 5 PM, Sun 1 - 5 PM, cl New Year's, Easter, Thanksgiving, Christmas Eve and Christmas Day. Admis to museum houses adults $1, senior citizens (65 and over) and children 6 - 16 $.25, children 5 and under free; admis to Reception Center free. Restoration completed 1941. The Restoration is a group of homes including a recently restored log house, that represent the early and mid 19th century of Arkansas history. Average Annual Attendance: 40,000
Collections: Audubon prints; furnishing of the period; porcelain hands, prints and maps from the 19th century; silver collection; watercolors
Activities: Log House activities include educational program for students and adults in candle dipping, cooking and needlework; classes for children; docent training; Reception Center has slide show, exhibits and art gallery; tours; individual paintings & original objects of art lent to other museums & cultural institutions; lending collection contains 476 books, motion pictures, 40 original prints, 10 paintings, 50 photographs, 2000 slides, loan box (artifacts); craft store sells early Arkansas crafts
L **Library,** Territorial Square, 3rd & Scott Sts, 72201. *Dir* W B Worthen
Income: Financed by the state
Library Holdings: Vols 300; Per subs 10; Micro — Reels; AV — A-tapes, cassettes, slides; Other — Clipping files, framed reproductions, manuscripts, original art works, pamphlets, photographs, prints, reproductions
Special Subjects: Furniture, historical material, art, gardening, houses
Exhibitions: Contemporary art; historical exhibits

C **FIRST COMMERCIAL BANK IN LITTLE ROCK,** Capitol & Broadway, PO Box 1471, 72203. Tel 501-371-7284. *In Charge Art Coll & Program* Joy Greer
Open Mon - Fri 9 AM - 4 PM. Estab 1970 to support art community. Collection displayed in main bank building and 24 branch offices; annual amount of contributions and grants $5000 - $15,000
Purchases: $5000
Collections: Arkansas art, chiefly paintings; some sculpture and weavings, pottery
Exhibitions: One major exhibit per year
Activities: Tours; purchase awards in two annual festivals

M **QUAPAW QUARTER ASSOCIATION, INC,** Villa Marre,* 1321 Scott St, PO Box 1104, 72203. Tel 501-371-0075, 374-9979. *Pres* Donald W Evans
Open Sun 1 - 5 PM, and by appointment. Admis adults $2, sr citizens & students $1. Estab 1966. The Villa Marre is a historic house museum which, by virtue of its extraordinary collection of late 19th century decorative arts, is a center for the study of Victorian styles. Average Annual Attendance: 5000. Mem: 1000; dues $10 - $1000; annual meeting Nov
Income: $95,000 (financed by membership, corporate support, grants and fund raising events)
Collections: Artwork by Benjamin Brantley; curioes appropriate to an 1881 Second Empire Victorian home, late 19th & early 20th century furniture, textiles
Publications: Quapaw Quarter Chronicle, quarterly
Activities: Classes for adults and children; docent training; lect open to public, visiting lectr; tours; book traveling exhibitions; Originate traveling exhibitions; sales shop sells books and magazines
L **Preservation Resource Center,** 308 E Eighth St, 72202. Tel 501-371-0075. *Executive Dir* Ralph Megan
Open Mon - Thur 9 AM - 5 PM. Estab 1976 for the assembly of materials relevent to the design and furnishing of Victorian period homes
Purchases: $500
Library Holdings: Vols 130; Per subs 12; AV — Kodachromes, lantern slides; Other — Clipping files, manuscripts, pamphlets, photographs
Collections: Architectural drawings

L **UNIVERSITY OF ARKANSAS,** Art Slide Library,* Fine Arts Building, Rooms 262 & 263, Art Department, 33rd & University Ave, 72204. Tel 501-569-3182. *Slide Cur* Susan Terry Borne
Open Mon - Fri 8 AM - 5 PM. Estab 1975. For reference only
Income: Financed by state funds
Library Holdings: Vols 150; Per subs 15; AV — Fs, Kodachromes, slides 50,000; Other — Clipping files, exhibition catalogs, pamphlets
Special Subjects: Dutch, Renaissance, Baroque, Contemporary art
Activities: Classes for adults; gallery talks; tours; student competitions with awards; scholarships

MAGNOLIA

M **SOUTHERN ARKANSAS UNIVERSITY,** Art Dept Gallery & Magale Art Gallery, Jackson & S University, SAU Box 1414, 71753. Tel 501-234-5120. *Chmn Art Dept* Willard C Carpenter; *Pres* Harold Brinson; *VPres* Lowell Logan; *Assoc Prof* Fred Henry; *Asst Prof* Dianne O'Hern
Open Mon - Fri 9 AM - 4 PM. No admis fee. Estab 1970. Magale Library Art Gallery, foyer type with 120 running ft exhibition space, floor to ceiling fabric covered. Caraway Gallery preview type gallery, about 80 ft
Income: Financed by state funds
Collections: †American printmakers
Exhibitions: Mike Ellis—American Photographer; faculty exhibit; six student shows
Activities: Classes for adults & children; lectures open to public; gallery talks; tours; individual paintings & original objects of art lent to schools, non-profit organizations

PINE BLUFF

O **SOUTHEAST ARKANSAS ARTS AND SCIENCE CENTER,** Civic Center, 200 E Eighth Ave, 71601. Tel 501-536-3375. *Dir* Joe L Kagle; *Dir Education* David Robinson; *Dir Performing Arts* David Kent; *Business Mgr* Sara Wright; *Registrar* Ellen Stern
Open Mon - Fri 10 AM - 5 PM, Sat 10 AM - 4 PM. No admis fee. Opened in 1968 in Civic Center Complex; governing authority, city of Pine Bluff. Average Annual Attendance: 55,000. Mem: 750; dues family $25
Income: $250,000
Collections: †Works on paper by local, national & international artists; art deco/nouveau bronze sculptures
Exhibitions: Annual Crafts Festival; Annual National Competition; Art Gallery Exhibitions
Activities: Classes for adults & children; dramatic programs; docent training; lectures open to public, 5 vis lectr per yr; concerts; gallery talks; tours; competitions with awards; individual paintings & original objects of art lent; book traveling exhibitions; originate traveling exhibitions

SPRINGDALE

O **COUNCIL OF OZARK ARTISTS AND CRAFTSMEN, INC,** Arts Center of the Ozarks Gallery,* Arts Bldg, 216 W Grove Ave, PO Box 725, 72764. Tel 501-751-5441. *Pres* Mrs Fred McCuistion; *VPres Arts Division & Exhibit Chmn* Mrs Nicks Matthews; *Prog Dir* Kathi Blundell; *Dir of Theatre* Harry Blundell
Open Sun 1 - 5 PM, gallery open Mon - Fri 9 AM - 4 PM. No admis fee. Estab 1948, merged with the Springdale Arts Center to become Arts Center of the Ozarks in 1973 to preserve the traditional handcrafts, to promote all qualified contemporary arts and crafts, to help find markets for artists and craftsmen. Mem: 70; annual meeting third Mon in Aug
Income: Financed by membership and city and state appropriations
Exhibitions: Exhibitions change monthly
Publications: Arts Center Events, monthly; newsletter, bimonthly
Activities: Adult and children's workshops; instruction in the arts, music, dance and drama run concurrently with other activities; evening classes in painting; five theater productions per year

STUTTGART

O **GRAND PRAIRIE ARTS COUNCIL, INC,** Arts Center of the Grand Prairie, PO Box 65, 72160. Tel 501-673-1781. *Pres* Mrs Jack Jacobs
Open Tues - Fri 10 AM - Noon & 2 - 4 PM, Sat & Sun 2 - 4 PM, cl Mon. No admis fee. Estab 1956 & incorporated 1964 to encourage cultural development in the Grand Prairie area, to sponsor the Grand Prairie Festival of Arts held annually in Sept at Stuttgard. Established an arts center for junior & sr citizens. Average Annual Attendance: 2500. Mem: 250; dues $10 - $100; monthly meetings
Income: Financed by memberships & donations
Collections: Very small permanent collection started by donations
Exhibitions: Monthly exhibitions of Arkansas artists
Publications: Festival invitations; newsletter, monthly; programs
Activities: Classes for adults & children; dramatic programs; lectures open to public, 4-6 vis lectr per yr; gallery talks; competitions with awards; originate traveling exhibitions

CALIFORNIA

ALHAMBRA

AMERICAN SOCIETY OF BOOKPLATE COLLECTORS AND DESIGNERS
For further information, see National and Regional Organizations

BAKERSFIELD

M **MARIAN OSBORNE CUNNINGHAM ART GALLERY,** 1930 R St, 93301. Tel 805-323-7219. *Pres* Joyce Umbress; *VPres* Betty Gravis; *Second VPres* Eileen Meyer; *Secy* Jean Reimer; *Treas* Phil Urner; *Gallery Dir* Ann Brown; *Recording Secy* Zola Hylton
Open Tues - Sun Noon - 3:30 PM, cl Mon. No admis fee. Estab to provide art culture to community; encourage and educate amateur artists; assist artists in selling work. Gallery is a one story building located in Camellia Garden of

Central Park. Average Annual Attendance: 7500. Mem: 300; dues $7.50; annual meeting second Mon each month 8 PM, except July & Aug
Income: Financed by membership, fund raising events, dues and donations
Exhibitions: Guest artists, membership shows, past-presidents show
Publications: Perspective, monthly
Activities: Lect open to public (non-members pay fee), 9 visiting lectr per year; demonstrations; tours; fels

M **KERN COUNTY MUSEUM,** 3801 Chester Ave, 93301. Tel 805-861-2132. *Dir* Carola G Rupert; *Registrar* John Ohe
Open Mon - Fri 8 AM - 5 PM, Sat, Sun & holidays 10 AM - 5 PM. Admis Pioneer Village: adults $1, children 6-12 $.75, sr citizens and under 6 free. Estab 1945 to collect and interpret local history, mainly through a 14 acre Pioneer Village. Also has Randsburg Mining Museum. One main building houses changing exhibitions on assorted topics. Average Annual Attendance: 150,000
Income: $378,000 (financed by county appropriation and local volunteer support)
Purchases: Pier mirror, postcards & child's lounge
Collections: California primitive paintings; 56-structure Pioneer Village covering 14 acres; Photographic Image Collection; Material Culture; Paleontology
Exhibitions: Historic Kern Photography; Sharktooth Hill Fossils; Yokuts Baskets; Borax in Kern County; Guns of the West
Publications: Brochure on the Museum; The Forgotten Photographs of Carleton E Watkins
Activities: Docent training; lectures open to public; Victorian Christmas & Heritage Days celebrations; gift shop sells books, reproductions and slides; Lori Brock Junior Museum

L **Library,** 3801 Chester Ave, 93309
Estab 1950 to support the work of the museum. Open for reference only by appointment
Library Holdings: Vols 2000; Other — Clipping files, manuscripts, memorabilia, pamphlets, photographs

BELMONT

O **SAN MATEO COUNTY ARTS COUNCIL,*** 1219 Ralston Ave, 94002. Tel 415-593-1816. *Pres* Susan Swope; *VPres* Rene Conrad; *Secy* Catherine Worthingham; *Exec Dir* Nancy Jalonen; *Media Coordr* Elliot Klein; *Gallery Dir* Sharon Wallach; *Asst Gallery Dir* Lisa Kammersgard; *Admin Mgr* Kathleen Young
Open Mon - Fri 9 AM - 5 PM, Sun 1 - 4 PM. No admis fee. Estab 1972 to promote the cultural life of San Mateo County through programs in schools, business and to provide services for artists and arts organizations. Two galleries maintained on premises and one at the Hall of Justice in Redwood City, Calif. Each holds about 300 artworks. Average Annual Attendance: 100,000. Mem: 600; dues $7.50 - $100; annual meeting June
Income: $150,000 (financed by membership, state and county appropriation, corporate and foundation support and programs)
Exhibitions: Monthly exhibits in three galleries of local artists
Publications: Arts Talk; cultural calendar
Activities: Classes for adults and children; dramatic programs; docent training; lectures open to public; concerts; gallery talks; tours; competitions with awards; sales shop sells crafts

BERKELEY

O **BERKELEY ART CENTER,*** 1275 Walnut St, 94709. Tel 415-644-6893. *Dir & Cur* Robbin Henderson; *Preparator* Robin Kaneshiro
Open Fri - Sun 11 AM - 5 PM, Thurs evening 7 - 10 PM, cl holidays. No admis fee. Estab 1965 to display art works of Bay Area artists. Average Annual Attendance: 20,000. Mem: Dues sponsor $500, patron $250, supporting $100, sustaining $50, family $25, regular $15, sr citizen & student $10
Income: Financed by city appropriation and other grants
Collections: Paintings; sculptures; environments
Exhibitions: Loan exhibitions and shows by Bay Area artists
Activities: Classes for adults and children; docent training; lectures open to public, 15 vis lectr per year; concerts; gallery talks; competitions; cash awards

L **BERKELEY PUBLIC LIBRARY,** Art and Music Dept, 2090 Kittredge St, 94704. Tel 415-664-6787, 644-6785. *Head Art & Music Dept* Diane Davenport; *Librn* Heo Park; *Librn* Lynn Murdock
Open Mon - Thurs 10 AM - 8 PM, Sat 10 AM - 6 PM, Sun 1 - 5 PM, cl Fri
Income: $35,976
Library Holdings: Vols 20,560; Per subs 116; AV — Cassettes 1200, slides 12,560; Other — Framed reproductions 467

O **FIBERWORKS, CENTER FOR THE TEXTILE ARTS,** 1940 Bonita Ave, 94704. Tel 415-548-6030. *Dir* J Weldon Smith; *Dir Education* Sylvia Seventy; *Gallery Dir* Molly Lambert
Open Tues - Fri Noon - 5 PM, Sat 9 AM - 5 PM. No admis fee. Estab 1973 to promote the textile arts. Gallery is 18 x 36 ft. Average Annual Attendance: 10,000. Mem: 500; dues $25
Income: $125,000 (financed by membership, National Endowment for the Arts, donations & earnings)
Exhibitions: Joan Livingstone; Bella Feldman; Barbara Showcroft; Ed Rossbach; annual juried competition
Publications: Fiberworks Newsletter, quarterly; catalogues
Activities: Classes for adults; lectures open to public, 35 vis lectr per yr; competitions; scholarships; originates traveling exhibitions

M **JUDAH L MAGNES MUSEUM,** 2911 Russell St, 94705. Tel 415-849-2710. *Dir* Seymour Fromer; *Cur* Ruth Eis; *Registrar* Ted A Greenberg; *Public Relations* Malka Weitman; *Archivist* Ruth Rafael
Open Sun - Fri 10 AM - 4 PM, cl Jewish and legal holidays. No admis fee. Estab 1962 to preserve, collect and exhibit Jewish artifacts and art from around the world; the museum also does research in the establishment of the Jewish community in the Western part of the United States from 1849 to the present.

Museum's first floor has changing exhibition space and painting gallery, and the second floor contains the permanent exhibition area; Jacques & Esther Reutlinger Hall established 1981. Average Annual Attendance: 6000
Income: Financed by membership and donations
Purchases: Ethnic Costumes & Folk Art Pieces
Collections: †Hannukah lamps; Synagogue art and objects; †spice boxes; †graphics, †manuscripts, †prints, †rare books, †textiles
Exhibitions: (1982) Moshe Rynecki: View of Poland; The Twelve Tribes of Israel: Analee Reutlinger, tapestries; Journey's End in Galilee: Jakob Nussbaum; Images of Israel in War and Peace & Jews in Egypt: Micha Bar-Am, photographs; Kafka-Prague; My Beloved is Mine, ceremonial art from the Magnes' Collection; Israel Revisited: Beth Ames Swartz, sculptural paintings; The Name's of God: Chava Eshel, beadwork; The Russian Jews of Brighton Beach: Carl Glassman, photographs; Charlotte: Life or Theater?, paintings & text; In the Courtyard of the Ari: Shoshana Greenberg; Raphael Soyer: 65 Years of Printmaking; jewelry and ceremonial objects from Bezalel Academy in Jerusalem; The Jewish Experience in Prints and Drawings: Permanent Collection
Publications: Bibliographies; books of Western Jewish Historical themes; exhibition catalogs; pamphlets; biannual newsletter
Activities: Lectures open to the public; gallery talks; tours; concerts; individual paintings and original objects of art lent to museums, synagogues, exhibition halls and Jewish organizations; traveling exhibitions organized and circulated; museum shop selling books, magazines, original art, reproductions, prints, original jewelry, note cards, posters, postcards

L **Morris Goldstein Library,*** 2911 Russell St, 94705. Tel 415-849-2710. *Librn* Jane Levy
Open Sun - Fri 10 AM - 4 PM. Estab 1966 as a center for the study and preservation of Judaica. For reference only. Changing and permanent exhibitions of painting, sculpture, photography, ceremonial objects
Income: Financed by membership and private gifts
Library Holdings: Vols 12,000; Per subs 15; original documents; AV — Fs, motion pictures, slides; Other — Clipping files, exhibition catalogs, manuscripts, memorabilia, pamphlets, reproductions
Special Subjects: Ethics, Hebraica, Jewish art and music, Judaica, literature in English, Hebrew, Yiddish and Ladino, mysticism, music of the Yiddish theater, philosophy, rare book and manuscripts, religious thought
Collections: Community collections from Cochin, Czechoslovakia, Egypt, India and Morocco; Holocaust Material (Institute for Righteous Acts); Karaite Community (Egypt); Passover Haggadahs (Zismer); 16th to 19th century rare printed editions, books and manuscripts; Ukrainian programs (Belkin documents)
Activities: Docent training; lectures open to public, vis lectr 15 per year; concerts; gallery talks; tours; awards; book traveling exhibitions; originate traveling exhibitions nationwide

UNIVERSITY OF CALIFORNIA

M **University Art Museum,** 2626 Bancroft Way, 94720. Tel 415-642-1207. *Dir* James Elliott; *Assoc Dir* Ronald Egherman; *Cur of Coll* Open; *Registrar* Jack Coyle; *Head, Installation & Design* Nina Hubbs; *Business Mgr* Anne Aaboe; *Assoc Cur Exhibitions* Susan Teicholz; *Assoc Cur Matrix* Connie Lewallen
Open Wed - Sun 11 Am - 5 PM. Admis $1 - $2. Estab 1965, new museum bldg opened in 1970. Museum designed by Mario Ciampi, Richard Jorasch and Ronald E Wagner of San Francisco; eleven exhibition galleries, a sculpture garden, and a 200 seat theatre. Average Annual Attendance: Gallery 300,000, Pacific Film Archive 105,000. Mem: 2800; dues vary
Income: $1,743,000 (financed by university sources, Federal and other grants, earned income and private donations)
Purchases: Jonathan Borofsky: Hammering Man
Collections: Gift of 45 Hans Hofmann paintings housed in the Hans Hoffman Gallery; pre-20th century paintings and sculpture; Chinese and Japanese paintings; 20th century European and American painting and sculpture; over 4000 films and video tapes
Exhibitions: Twenty exhibitions annually; Matrix Project (a changing exhibition of contemporary art)
Publications: The Calendar, monthly; catalogs; handbills; exhibition brochures; Matrix artists sheets
Activities: Lectures open to the public; gallery talks; film programs for classes and research screenings; public service media program; book traveling exhibitions, 3 per year; traveling exhibitions organized and circulated; museum shop sells books, magazines, crafts, posters, jewelry, art materials, reproductions

M **R H Lowie Museum of Anthropology,** 103 Kroeber Hall, 94720. Tel 415-642-3681. *Dir* James J Deetz; *Asst Dir* Frank A Norick; *Senior Cur Anthropologist* Dave D Herod
Open Mon - Fri 10 AM - 4 PM, Sat and Sun Noon - 4 PM, cl major national holidays. Admis adults $1, children $.25. Estab 1901 as a research museum for the training and educating of students and graduate students, a resource for scholarly research and to collect, preserve, educate and conduct research. Average Annual Attendance: 65,000
Income: Financed principally by state appropriations
Collections: Over three million objects of anthropological interest, both archaeolgical and ethnological. Ethnological collections from Africa, Oceania, North America (Plains, Arctic and Sub-Arctic); archaeological collections from Egypt, Peru, California and Africa
Exhibitions: Basketry Traditions of Southwestern California; Pueblo Culture Images; Across the Waters: Boats of the World; The Panama-Pacific International Exposition
Publications: Annual Report; Exhibition Guides
Activities: Classes for adults; lectures open to the public; gallery talks; tours; book shop

L **Pacific Film Archive,** 2625 Durant Ave, 94720. Tel 415-642-1412. *Cur Film* Edith Kramer; *Film Librn* Nancy Goldman; *Gen Mgr* Tom Schmidt
Library Open Mon - Fri 1 - 5 PM. Estab 1971, the Archive is a cinematheque showing a constantly changing repertory of films; a research screening facility; a media information service and an archive for the storage and preservation of films
Income: Financed by earned box office income, grants, students fees and benefits
Library Holdings: Vols 3000; Per subs 30; Stills and posters; AV — Motion pictures 6000; Other — Clipping files

Collections: Japanese film collection; Soviet Silents; experimental and animated films
Publications: Monthly calendar
Activities: Nightly film exhibition; special daytime screening of films; lectures, fifty - seventy-five visiting filmmakers per year

L **Architectural Slide Library,** Wurster Hall, 94720. Tel 415-642-3439. *Librn* Maryly Snow; *Library Asst* Marika Wolfe
Open Mon - Fri 10 AM - Noon, 1 - 4 PM. Estab 1951 for instructional support for the Department of Architecture. In 1976 Library opened circulation on a 24 hour basis for educational presentations
Income: Financed by state appropriation
Library Holdings: AV — Motion pictures, slides; Other — Photographs
Special Subjects: History of Architecture, Slides and Photographs, Topography
Collections: Denise Scott Brown and William C Wheaton Collections: City Planning, 35 mm slides; Herwin Schaefer Collection: visual design, 35 mm slides

BEVERLY HILLS

L **BEVERLY HILLS PUBLIC LIBRARY,** Fine Arts Library, 444 N Rexford, 90201. Tel 213-550-4720. *Fine Arts Librn* Nicholas Cellini; *AV Librn* Camille Razadi-Kazadi
Open Mon - Thurs 10 AM - 9 PM, Fri & Sat 10 AM - 6 PM. Estab 1973 to make art materials available to the general public. The library concentrates on 19th and 20th century art
Income: Financed by city appropriation and Friends of Library
Library Holdings: Vols 20,000; Per subs 200; Micro — Fiche, reels; AV — Cassettes, Kodachromes, motion pictures, slides; Other — Clipping files, exhibition catalogs, pamphlets, photographs, prints
Special Subjects: Architecture, Film, Art, Costume, Dance
Collections: Dorthai Bock Pierre Dance Collection; Will Rogers Collection; Zita Zech Collection: Gifts of American Society of Interior Designers
Activities: Lectures open to the public, 3 vis lectr per year; gallery talks; tours

M **FRANCIS E FOWLER JR FOUNDATION MUSEUM,** 9215 Wilshire Blvd, 90210. Tel 213-278-8010. *Dir* Basil W R Jenkins
Open Mon - Sat 1 - 5 PM, cl Sun & holidays. No admis fee. Estab 1953
Collections: European & Asiatic decorative arts; 15th - 19th century English, early American & Continental silver; Russian silver
Activities: Lect; guided tours

BREA

M **BREA CIVIC CULTURAL CENTER GALLERY,*** Number One Civic Center Circle, 92621. Tel 714-990-7631. *Cultural Arts Mgr* Kathie Conrey; *Cur* Emily Keller
Open Wed - Sat Noon - 5 PM, cl holidays. No admis. Estab 1980
Activities: Docent training; lectures; tours; gallery talks; concerts; workshops

BURBANK

O **BURBANK PUBLIC LIBRARY,** Warner Research Collection, 110 North Glenoaks Blvd, 91501. Tel 818-953-9743. *Dir* Mary Ann Grasso; *Research Asst* Nancy Burns-McConnohie; *Research Asst* Joyce Kneisel
Open Mon - Fri 9 AM - 5 PM by appointment only. Estab 1936 to provide visual and historical documentation for use in the pre-production phase of motion picture and television production. Also used for prototype research by artist and architects
Library Holdings: Vols 30,000; Per subs 75; Other — Clipping files, exhibition catalogs, pamphlets, photographs, reproductions
Special Subjects: Advertising Design, Aesthetics, Afro-American Art, Afro-American Art, American Indian Art, American Western Art, Anthropology, Archaeology, Architecture, Costume Design & Construction, Decorative Arts, Fashion Arts, Flasks & Bottles, Folk Art, Furniture, Antiques, Glass, Graphic Arts, Graphic Design, Industrial Design, Period Rooms, Stage Design, Theater Arts
Activities: Lectures open to the public

CARMEL

M **CARMEL MISSION AND GIFT SHOP,*** 3080 Rio Rd, 93921. Tel 408-624-3600. *Cur* Richard J Menn; *Shop Mgr* Katherine Ambrosia
Open Mon - Sat 9:30 AM - 4:30 PM, Sun 10:30 AM - 4:30 PM, cl Thanksgiving and Christmas. No admis fee; donations accepted. Estab 1770
Collections: California's first library, founded by Fray Junipero Serra, 1770; library of California's first college, founded by William Hartnell, 1834; Munras Memorial Collection of objects, papers, furnishings of early California; large collection of eccleciastical art of Spanish colonial period; large collection of ecclesiastical silver and gold church vessels, 1670 - 1820; paintings, sculpture, art objects of California Mission period
Activities: Sales shop sells religious articles, souvenir books and postcards

L **Archive of Old Spanish Missions, Diocese of Monterey,*** 3080 Rio Rd, 93921. Tel 408-624-1271. *Cur* Harry Downie
Estab 1931 for research for Mission Restoration and Documents. Open to scholars by special appointment
Library Holdings: Vols 100; AV — Cassettes; Other — Clipping files, manuscripts, pamphlets, photographs
Special Subjects: Early California reference and photo library

O **THE FRIENDS OF PHOTOGRAPHY,** San Carlos at Ninth, PO Box 500, 93921. Tel 408-624-6330. *Chmn* Ansel Adams; *Pres* Peter C Bunnell; *VPres* Robert Baker; *VPres* Albert Dorskind; *VPres* Tim Hill; *VPres* Joan D Manley; *VPres* Otto Meyer; *Exec Dir* James Alinder; *Exec Assoc* David Featherstone; *Exec Asst* Mary Virginia Swanson; *Exec Asst* Claire Peeps; *Treas* Robert K Byers; *Secy* Julia Siebel

Open daily 1 - 5 PM. No admis fee. Estab 1967 to serve the field of serious art photography through exhibitions, workshops, publications and critical inquiry. Maintains an art gallery with continuous exhibitions. Average Annual Attendance: 25,000. Mem: 11,500; dues $28; annual meeting Feb
Income: $800,000 (financed by endowment, membership, city and state appropriations, federal grants and patrons)
Exhibitions: (1982) Thomas Barrow; The Unknown Ansel Adams; Four Color Photographers: William Christenberry, Avery Danziger, Emmet Gowin, Terry Husebye; Members Exhibition; Brett Weston: New York; Dyed Images: Recent Work in Dye Transfer; Renate Ponsold-Robert Motherwell: Apropos Robinson Jeffers; The Contact Print 1946-1982 (1983) Segmentations: Chuck Close, Robbert Flick, David Joyce, Ann Lovett, Robert Schiappaccasse, John Williams; Max Yavno: New York from Mexico; John Stewart; Mount Saint Helens, The Photographer's Response: Marilyn Bridges, Tod Gangler, Frank Gohlke, Emmet Gowin, Joel Sternfeld, Eve Sonneman, Mathias Van Hesemans; Beaumont Newhall: A Retrospective; Members Exhibition; Nicholas Nixon; Dave Read; Mary Ellen Mark: Photographs from Mother Theresa's Hospitals for the Dying, Calcutta
Publications: Journal of the Friends, quarterly; monthly newsletter; monographic publications
Activities: Classes for adults; lect open to the public, 6 vis lectr per year; competitions with awards; scholarships; book traveling exhibitions, 1-2 per year; originate traveling exhibitions; sales shop sells books

CHERRY VALLEY

M **RIVERSIDE COUNTY ART AND CULTURAL CENTER,** Edward-Dean Museum of Decorative Arts, 9401 Oak Glen Rd, 92223. Tel 714-845-2626. *Dir* Janice R Holmlund
Open Tues - Fri 1 - 4:30 PM, Sat & Sun 10 AM - 4:30 PM. Admis adults $1, children under 12 free. Built in 1957 and given to the county of Riverside in 1964, and is a division of the Parks Dept. The South Wing of the gallery displays antiques and decorative arts as permanent collections; the North Wing has monthly exhibits by contemporary artists. Average Annual Attendance: 20,000. Mem: 250; monthly meetings
Income: Financed by county funding
Collections: Antiques; Boulle Cabinet; Capo di Monte; Chinese export wares and other fine porcelains; decorative arts; Far Eastern bronzes; Lowestoft; Meissen; David Roberts (original watercolors); Sevres; 17th & 18th Century European & Asian decorative arts; Wedgwood
Exhibitions: Maria Martinez - 5 generations of potters; Women Painters of the West; Robert Hiram Meltzer, watercolors; George Jensen Silver; National Academy of Design; French Faience; Rods, Bundles and Stitches: A Century of Indian Basketry
Publications: Museum catalog
Activities: Classes for children; docent training; lectures open to public; tours; outdoor art shows; cultural festivals; concerts; gallery talks; original objects of art lent to local universities and colleges; museum and sales shop sells books, original art, reproductions, prints and slides

L **Library,** 9401 Oak Glen Rd, 92223
Open to the public for reference only
Library Holdings: Vols 1000; Per subs 5; Micro — Cards; Other — Manuscripts, original art works, prints
Special Subjects: Decorative Arts, Furniture, Glass, Porcelain, David Roberts (original lithograph set of Holy Land)

CHICO

M **CALIFORNIA STATE UNIVERSITY, CHICO,** Art Gallery,* Normal & Salem Sts, 95929. Tel 916-895-5331, 895-5218. *Dir* Ann T Pierce; *Secy* Janet Karolyi; *Gallery Dir* James W McManus
Open Mon - Fri 10 AM - 4 PM, Sun 1 - 5 PM, Tues - Thurs evenings 7 - 10 PM. No admis fee. Estab to afford broad cultural influences to the massive North California region. Average Annual Attendance: 15,000
Income: Financed by state appropriations and private funds
Collections: The Behrick Oriental Ceramics Collection; The Janet Turner Print Collection
Exhibitions: Donald Cleland Drawings & Paintings; Realism: A California Vision; Photography Exhibit, curated by Heinz Henisch; Prints & Drawings by Roy deForrest; works by Steve Wilson & Michael Monahan; Alice Hutchings Kinetic Sculpture; selected students drawings
Activities: Lectures open to public, 6-12 visiting lecturers per year; tours; competitions with awards; scholarships; individual and original objects of art lent to offices on campus; museum shop

L **Meriam Library,** First & Hazel, 95929. Tel 916-895-5833. *Actg Assoc Dir* Robert M Cookingham
Open to students and the public
Library Holdings: Book vols & periodicals 15,000; Micro — Cards, fiche, prints; AV — A-tapes, cassettes, fs, motion pictures, rec, slides, v-tapes; Other — Framed reproductions, photographs, prints, reproductions
Collections: Janet Turner Print Collection

CHULA VISTA

M **SOUTHWESTERN COLLEGE,** Art Gallery,* 900 Otay Lakes Rd, 92010. Tel 714-421-0349, 421-6700, Ext 340. *Dean Humanities* Ann Stephenson
Open Mon - Fri 10 AM - 2 PM; Wed - Thurs 6 - 9 PM. No admis fee. Estab 1961 to show contemporary artists' work who are of merit to the community and the school, and as a service and an educational service. Gallery is approx 3000 sq ft. Average Annual Attendance: 10,000
Income: Financed by city and state appropriations
Collections: Permanent collection of mostly contemporary work
Activities: Classes for adults; lect open to public, 3 vis lectr per year; gallery talks; competitions; individual paintings and original objects of art lent; lending collection contains color reproductions, photographs, and original art works; junior museum

CLAREMONT

M GALLERIES OF THE CLAREMONT COLLEGES, 91711. Tel 714-621-8000, Ext 2241. *Dir* Marjorie H Beebe; *Cur Exhibitions* Melinda Lorenz; *Cur Coll* Kay Koeninger; *Galleries Mgr* Richard Gerrish; *Admin Asst* Barbara Senn
Open daily 1 - 5 PM, cl National and school holidays. No admis fee. Estab 1974 to present balanced exhibitions useful not only to students of art history and studio arts, but also to the general public. Average Annual Attendance: 15,000
Income: $180,000 (financed by endowment)
Collections: Samuel H Kress Collection of Renaissance paintings; 19th century American painting; contemporary ceramics; Old Master and contemporary graphics; photographs; Oriental art; African Art
Exhibitions: (1982-83) The Claremont Colleges Faculty Exhibition: Printmaking in France, 1850-1900; Arts of Kenya; Contemporary Collage: Art from Southern California; Anne Ryan: Collages; Filaments of the Imagination; Photography 1983: An Invitational; 39th Scripps Ceramic Annual; Pomona and Scripps student and senior exhibitions; (1983-84) The Colleges Collect: Art from Three Continents; Mexican Folk Art; Suzanne Lacy: Performance Documentation; Paintings by Ted Kerzie; Helen Escobedo: Gentle Interferences; Site-Specific Sclpture; Early Twentieth Century German Prints from the Pomona College Collection; Slater Barron and Sheila Pinkel: Two Xerography Installations; Artists' Books; The Magic Show: An International Mail Art Exhibition; The Denver/Boulder Show; Earth and Fire: The Fred Marer Collection of Contemporary Ceramics; 40th Ceramic Annual; The Scripps Clay Connection; Pomona and Scripps student and senior exhibitions
Publications: Art Publications List, annual
Activities: Docent training; Museum Practices; lect open to the public, 7 - 10 vis lectr per yr; gallery talks; tours; competitions; originates traveling exhibitions; sales shop sells books, posters, and cards
M Montgomery Art Gallery of Pomona College,* 747 N Dartmouth, 91711. Tel 714-621-8000
Contains one large and two smaller galleries, with two exhibition corridors
M Lang Art Gallery of Scripps College,* 91711. Tel 714-621-8000
Contains one large and three smaller galleries, one of which can be closed off from the rest of the building

M SCRIPPS COLLEGE, Clark Humanities Museum, 91711. Tel 714-626-8000, Ext 3606. *Pres* Eric Haskell; *Admin Asst* Nancy Burson
Open Mon - Fri 9 AM - Noon and 1 - 5 PM, cl holidays and summer. No admis fee. Estab 1970 to present multi-disciplinary exhibits in conjunction with Scripps College's humanities curriculum, and to maintain a study collection. Museum has large room with storage and study area; reception desk
Collections: Nage Collection of Chinese, Tibetan Sculpture and Textiles; Wagner Collection of African Sculpture
Exhibitions: Hatian art; Japanese prints; masks and musical instruments
Publications: Exhibition catalogues
Activities: Lect open to public

CYPRESS

M CYPRESS COLLEGE, Fine Arts Gallery, 9200 Valley View St, 90630. Tel 714-826-2220, Ext 130. *Dir* Robert Hardy; *Secy* Maureen King
Open Mon - Fri 11 AM - 3 PM during exhibitions. No admis fee. Estab 1969 to bring visually enriching experiences to the school and community. Average Annual Attendance: 5000
Income: Financed by school budget, donations, and sales
Collections: †Student works; †purchase awards; †donor gifts
Exhibitions: (1983) Five Directions: Recent Color Photography; Javier Alvarez: Paintings & Drawings; annual holiday art sale; (1984) Biennial high school invitational; California Indian Basketry; annual student art show
Publications: Exhibition catalogs
Activities: Lectures open to public, 2 vis lectr per year; competitions; scholarships

DAVIS

M PENCE GALLERY, 212 D St, 95616. Tel 916-758-3370. *Pres* Gracie Goodpaster; *Cur* Edelgard Brunelle, PhD; *Secy* Joyce Wade
Open Tues - Sat Noon - 4 PM, except holidays and between shows. No admis fee. Estab 1975. A downtown non-commercial art space with changing exhibitions of contemporary, historical and ethnic art shows. Gallery has 86 running feet of wall space and 650 square feet of floor space. The walls are 8 feet high and provide 6 ft high exhibition areas. Average Annual Attendance: 6000.
Mem: 250; dues business $30, family $20, individual $15
Income: $14,000 (financed by membership, city appropriation and fund raisings)
Exhibitions: (1983) Dogs, Dogs, Dogs, Acrylic Paintings by Dian Leach; Chinese New Years Pictures, Folk Prints by Mary Fong; Contemporary Furniture Design; Young Artists from Davis Schools; Swimmers, Lisa Baack; MFA Candidates; Landscape Paintings—Nine Perspectives; Pueblo Pottery & Navajo Rugs; Lori Holland: New Adventures; (1984) Scientific Illustrators; Laura Raboff: Small Installations & Environments; Gloria Seborg: Paintings; Woodcuts from the 16th - 20th Century; University of California Davis 1984 MFA Exhibition; Peruvian Art (1982) Zea Morritz: Recent Work; Art from New Guinea; George Longfish: Paintings
Activities: Classes for adults; dramatic programs; docent training; concerts; gallery talks; tours; competitions

UNIVERSITY OF CALIFORNIA

M Memorial Union Art Gallery,* Second Floor Memorial Union, 95616. Tel 916-752-2285. *Dir* Arthur Hermann; *Program Coordr* Marilyn Berling Hunt
Open Mon - Fri 9 AM - 5 PM, also by appointment. No admis fee. Estab 1965 to provide exhibitions of contemporary and historical concerns for the students, staff and community. Gallery consists of North Gallery and South Gallery
Collections: Contemporary art
Exhibitions: Design dept exhibition; Sacramento Valley Landscapes
Publications: Exhibition catalogs
Activities: Classes for adults; lectures; concerts; poetry readings; films; competitions; internships

M Richard L Nelson Gallery, Department of Art, 95616. Tel 916-752-8500. *Dir* L Price Amerson Jr; *Cur & Registrar* Cynthia Charters
Open Mon - Fri Noon - 5 PM, Sun 2 - 5 PM. No admis fee. Estab 1976 to provide exhibitions of contemporary art as well as historical importance as a service to teaching program of the department of art, the university and the public. Contains main gallery and small gallery. Average Annual Attendance: 15,000
Income: Financed by university appropriation and grants
Collections: Fine Arts Collection of the Department of Art; general collection representing various periods of historical and contemporary art, with emphasis on Northern California art; also special collection includes: The Nagel Collection of Oriental Ceramics & Sculpture
Exhibitions: (1981) Elaine Wander, paintings; Luis Cruz Azeceta, paintings & drawings; Stephen Pring, drawings & constructions; Judy Moran, installation; Stephanie Weber, mixed media works on paper; Alan Kikuchi-Yngojo, metaphotos; Helen Oji, paintings; Joan Jonas, Performances: Double Lunar Dogs; Cowboys & Cowboys; photoetchings & mixed media; Robert Arneson: Alice Street; (1982) MFA exhibitions; Sculptors at University of California Davis: Past & Present; Contemporary California Prints; The Slant Step Revisited; Robert Hudson, sculpture & drawings; Directions In Bay Area Painting: A Survey of Three Decades, 1940s - 1960s; (1983) MFA exhibitions; Rita Yokoi: Paintings on Paper & Installation-Environment; Pierre Picot, paintings & drawings; Roy De Forest: The Early Constructions; Painters at University of California Davis: Part I 1950s - 1960s; painters at University of California Davis: Part II 1970s - 1980s; Glass: Twenty Artists; William Wegman, videos; (1984) MFA exhibitions
Publications: Exhibition catalogues, 2-3 per year
Activities: Lectures open to the public, three to five visiting lecturers per year; gallery talks
L Art Dept Library, University of California, Davis, 95616. Tel 916-752-3138. *Library Asst (Books)* Teri Markson; *Library Asst (Slides)* Karen Spence
Open Mon - Fri 8 AM - Noon, 1 - 5 PM. Estab 1966 to make readily accessible reference and research material to Art Department faculty, students and the general public
Income: Financed by state appropriation and college funds
Purchases: $3500
Library Holdings: Vols 4000; Per subs 25; DIAL (Decimal Index of Art of the Low Countries) photographs; Micro — Fiche; AV — Fs, slides; Other — Exhibition catalogs, reproductions

DOMINGUEZ HILLS

M UNIVERSITY ART GALLERY OF CALIFORNIA STATE UNIVERSITY AT DOMINGUEZ HILLS (Formerly Art Gallery of California State College), 1000 E Victoria, 90747. Tel 213-516-3334. *Gallery Dir* Kathy Zimmerer-McKelvie
Open Mon - Fri 11 AM - 5 PM. Estab 1973 to exhibit faculty, student and outside art. New 2000 sq ft gallery in 1978. Average Annual Attendance: 5000
Income: Financed by yearly grants from CSUDH Student Association; support from Friends of the Gallery
Exhibitions: (1982) Artists of Local or National Reputation; Figurative Notations; Art as Alchemy; Navajo Rugs; A Clay Preface; (1983) Michael Todd: Recent Sculpture; Janice U Weissman, The Wedding
Activities: Lectures open to public, 15 vis lectr per year; gallery talks; tours; book traveling exhibtions annually

DOWNEY

M DOWNEY MUSEUM OF ART, 10419 S Rives Ave, 90241. Tel 213-861-0419. *Dir* Lukman Glasgow
Open Wed - Sun Noon - 5 PM. No admis fee. Estab 1957 as an aesthetic and educational facility. Located in Furman Park, it is the only municipal art museum with a permanent collection in Southeast Los Angeles which includes in its area 27 neighboring communities of such significant ethnic range and a total population close to one million. The Museum is continuing a program for new artists which originally was funded by Los Angeles County but is now paid for by museum operating funds. The facility has five gallery areas plus classroom space. Gallery I covers 15 x 39 ft, Gallery II covers approx 12 x 12 x 24 ft, Gallery III covers 15 x 20 ft, and Gallery IV covers 23 x 39 ft. Average Annual Attendance: 7500. Mem: 475; dues $15 - $1000; annual meeting April
Income: $45,000 (financed by memberships, grants, donations, and city appropriation)
Collections: Many pieces produced by Southern California artists over the past 20 years, including Billy Al Bengston, Corita Kent, Don Emery, Sabato Fiorello, Stephen Longstreet, Anna Mahler, Shirley Pettibone, Betye Saar, Boris Duetsch, and Fredick Wight
Exhibitions: The New Batik; The Light Source, Larry Albright, Lili Lakich, Laddie Dill; Patterns, Peter Shire, Ed Forde, Larry Lubow; Fiber Structure National; Westwood Clay National; Vessels Aesthetic; Cactus and Palms, David Hockney, Richard Misrach, Frederick Wight, Bruce Houston, Ken Price
Activities: Lectures open to public, 4 vis lectr per year; gallery talks; tours; traveling exhibitions organized and circulated; museum shop selling reproductions and prints

EL CAJON

M GROSSMONT COMMUNITY COLLEGE GALLERY,* 8800 Grossmont College Dr, 92020. Tel 714-465-1700, Ext 450. *Dir* Gene Kennedy
Open by appointment. No admis fee. Estab 1970 as a co-curricular institution which cooperates with and supports the Art Dept of Grossmont College and which provides a major cultural resource for the general public in the eastern part of the greater San Diego area. Two galleries, one 30 x 40 ft; one 30 x 20 ft. Average Annual Attendance: 20,000
Income: Financed through College
Collections: Prints; photographs; clay objects; large Tom Holland painting
Publications: Exhibition catalogs; posters
Activities: Lect open to public, 6 vis lectr per year; concerts; original objects of art lent to institutions; lending collection photographs; originate traveling exhibitions

EUREKA

O **HUMBOLT ARTS COUNCIL,*** Humbolt Cultural Center, PO Box 221, 95501.
Pres Jeanne Fish; *Secy* Peggy Taylor
Estab 1966 to encourage, promote & correlate all forms of activity in the arts &
to make such activity a vital influence in the life of the community. Mem: 250;
annual meeting Oct
Income: $10,000 (financed by membership)
Collections: Art Bank, consisting of the yearly award winner from the juried
Redwood Art Association Sprint Show; other purchase & donated works of art;
photograph collection
Activities: Concerts; competitions; scholarships; individual paintings & original
objects of art lent; originate traveling exhibitions

FRESNO

M **FRESNO ARTS CENTER,** 2233 North First St, 93703. Tel 209-485-4810. *Dir*
Robert Barrett; *Asst to Dir* Marty Limbaugh
Open Mon - Sun 10 AM - 5 PM. Admis adults $2, students & senior citizens $1,
children 16 & under, school tours & museum mem free, Sat free to public. Estab
1949 as a visual arts gallery to provide Fresno and its environs with a community
oriented visual arts center. The Center exhibits works of internationally known
artists, and arranges shows of local artists. Three galleries plus entry for exhibits.
Average Annual Attendance: 95,000. Mem: 2000; dues $35; annual meeting
March
Income: Financed by membership and fund raising efforts
Collections: Works of prominent Central valley artists; contemporary American
artists; Mexican folk art; Mexican graphic arts; Oriental art
Activities: Classes for adults and children; docent training; lect open to public, 12
vis lectr per yr; gallery talks; concerts; tours; competitions; scholarships offered;
individual paintings and objects of art lent to city and county offices and other
institutions; lending collection contains framed reproductions, original art works,
original prints and slides; book and originate traveling exhibitions; traveling
exhibitions organized and circulated; museum shop sells books, magazines,
original art, reproductions, prints, cards and local crafts

FULLERTON

M **CALIFORNIA STATE UNIVERSITY FULLERTON,** Art Gallery, Visual Arts
Center,* 800 N State College Blvd, 92634. Tel 714-773-2011. *Dir* Dextra
Frankel; *Asst to Dir* Barbara Lamb; *Equipment Technician* Joseph Brubaker
Open during exhibits, Mon - Fri Noon - 4 PM, Sun 1 - 4 PM, cl Sat. No admis
fee. Estab 1963 to bring to the campus carefully developed art exhibits that
instruct, inspire and challenge the student to the visual arts, to present to the
student body, faculty and community exhibits of historical and aesthetic
significance; acting as an educational tool, creating interaction between various
departmental disciplines, and promotion of public relations between campus and
community. Four to five exhibits each year organizational activity stemming from
the Museum Studies and Exhibition Design Program. Undergraduate and
graduate students have the opportunity to focus within a professionally oriented
program directed toward the museum profession. Activity incorporates classes,
art gallery and local museums. The Dept of Art and the Art Gallery are the
holders of the permanent collection. Average Annual Attendance: 15,000-20,000
Income: Financed by state appropriation, grants and donations
Collections: Contemporary Lithographs (Gemini); works by artists in the New
York Collection for Stockholm executed by Styria Studio; lithographs by Lita
Albuquerque, Coy Howard, Ed Rusha and Alexis Smith; Pre-Columbian artifacts;
environmental and site-specific sculpture by Lloyd Hamrol, Ray Hein, Bernard
Rosenthal, Michael Todd, Jay Willis
Exhibitions: Itchiku Kubota: Kimono in the Tsujiguahana Tradition; Claire
Zeisler; Juan Quezada; Dimensional Fibers; The 100 Yard Canvas; Visions &
Figurations; Nine and the Wall; John Altoon Drawings; California Innovations;
Triptychs in Cast Paper; To Honor Our Mothers: The Gelede Tradition of
Yoruba; Artists in Academe; New Work by CSUE Faculty; Emerson Woelffer:
Profile of an Artist 1947-1981
Publications: Exhibition catalogs
Activities: Lectures open to public, 8-10 visiting lectures per year; workshops;
production of slide/sound interpretation programs in conjunction with specific
exhibitions; gallery talks; tours; scholarships; Four - six major exhibitions per
year; traveling exhibitions; originate traveling exhibitions
L **Library,** 800 N State College Blvd, 92634. *Actg Librn* Carolyn Kacena
Open to students for reference only
Library Holdings: AV — A-tapes, Kodachromes, motion pictures, slides, v-tapes;
Other — Clipping files, exhibition catalogs, photographs

O **MUCKENTHALER CULTURAL CENTER,** 1201 W Malvern, 92633. Tel 714-
738-6595. *Dir* Margaret Hammon; *Center Adminr* Grace Miranda; *Exhibition
Preparator* Norman Lloyd; *Secy* Billie Ann Watts
Open Tues - Sun Noon - 5 PM. No admis fee. Estab 1966 for the promotion and
development of a public cultural center for the preservation, display and
edification in the arts. Gallery is a National Historic Building, contains 2500 sq ft
and is on 8 1/2 acres of land; outdoor theatre facilities. Average Annual
Attendance: 60,000. Mem: 500; dues $10 and up; annual meeting in June
Income: $170,000 (financed by endowment, membership, and city appropriation)
Publications: Exhibition catalogs
Activities: Classes for adults and children; docent training; lect open to public, 40
vis lectr per year; concerts; 4 theatre productions annually; gallery talks; tour;
book traveling exhibitions; sales shop selling books, magazines and original art

GARDEN GROVE

M **MILLS HOUSE VISUAL ARTS COMPLEX,** 12732 Main St, 92640. Tel 714-
638-6707. *Dir* Lora P Brown; *Asst to Dir* Steven Callaway
Open Wed - Sun Noon - 4 PM, cl Mon & Tues. No admis fee. Estab 1974 to
promote the visual arts in the city of Garden Grove. Mills House West features
regional, local & student shows. Mills House East features contemproary
painting, drawing & sculpture & major collections. Average Annual Attendance:
12,000. Mem: 50
Income: Financed by city appropriation
Activities: Lect open to public; gallery talks; tours; gift shop

GILROY

M **GAVILAN COLLEGE,** Art Gallery,* 5055 Santa Teresa Blvd, 95020. Tel 408-
847-1400. *Gallery Advisor & Humanities Division Dir* Kent Child; *Community
Services Dir* Ken Cooper
Open Mon - Fri 8 AM - 9:30 PM. No admis fee. Estab 1967 to serve as a focal
point in art exhibitions for community college district and as a teaching resource
for the art department. Gallery is in large lobby of college library with 25 ft
ceiling, redwood panelled walls and carpeted floor
Income: Financed through college
Collections: Approx 25 paintings purchased as award purchase prizes in college
art competitions
Exhibitions: Monthly exhibits of student, local artist and traveling shows
Activities: Lending collection contains books, cassettes, color reproductions, film
strips, Kodachromes, paintings, sculpture

GLENDALE

L **BRAND LIBRARY AND ART CENTER,*** 1601 W Mountain St, 91201. Tel
213-956-2051. *Librn* Jane Hagan; *Gallery Dir* Burdette Peterson; *Asst Librn*
Ellen Dworkin
Open Tues & Thurs Noon - 9 PM, Wed, Fri, Sat Noon - 6 PM. No admis fee.
Estab 1956 as art and music departments of the Glendale Public Library. Two
galleries maintained with contemporary art program and crafts. Average Annual
Attendance: 72,000. Mem: Dues $15 - $500
Income: Financed by city and state appropriations
Library Holdings: Vols 28,000; color slides; AV — Cassettes, rec
Collections: Indexes and other guides to art and music literature; Dieterle picture
collection; early photography journals
Activities: Lect open to the public; tours; concerts; competitions; lending
collection contains color reproductions, Kodachromes

M **FOREST LAWN MUSEUM,** 1712 S Glendale Ave, 91209. Tel 213-254-3131.
Dir Frederick Llewellyn; *Mgr* Jane E Llewellyn
Open daily 10 AM - 6 PM. No admis fee. Estab 1951 as a community museum
offering education and culture through association with the architecture and the
art of world masters. There are four galleries in the museum and several smaller
galleries in buildings throughout the four parks. Recreation of room under the
Medici Chapel in Florence, Italy, where Michelangelo's drawings were recently
discovered. Average Annual Attendance: 200,000
Collections: American Western Bronzes; Ancient Biblical and Historical Coins;
Crucifixion by Jan Styka (195 x 45 ft painting); Resurrection (Robert Clark),
painting; reproductions of Michelangelo's greatest sculptures; stained glass
window of the Last Supper by Leonardo da Vinci; originals and reproductions of
famous sculptures, paintings, and documents
Exhibitions: History of Forest Lawn
Activities: Schol offered; lending collection contains reproductions of the crown
jewels of England; originate traveling exhibitions; memento shop selling books
and art works
L **Library,** 1712 Glendale Ave, 91209. Tel 213-254-3131
Open 10 AM - 6 PM. For use of employees
Library Holdings: Vols 3000

C **GLENDALE FEDERAL SAVINGS,*** 401 N Brand Blvd, 91209. Tel 213-956-
3800, 500-2000. *In Charge Art Coll* Barbara Cassel
Open 9 AM - 4 PM. Collection displayed in branches

GLEN ELLEN

M **JACK LONDON STATE HISTORIC PARK,** House of Happy Walls, 2400
London Ranch Rd, 95442. Tel 707-938-5216
Open daily 10 AM - 5 PM; cl Thanksgiving, Christmas, New Year's Day. Admin
$2 per car, $20 per bus. Estab 1959 for the interpretation of the life of Jack
London; the fieldstone home was constructed in 1919 by London's widow. The
collection is housed on two floors in the House of Happy Walls, and is operated
by Calif Dept of Parks & Recreation. Average Annual Attendance: 80,000
Income: Financed by state appropriation
Collections: Artifacts from South Sea Islands; original illustrations
Activities: Tours; sales shop sells some of Londons books

HAYWARD

M **CALIFORNIA STATE UNIVERSITY, HAYWARD,** University Art Gallery,
CSUH, Theresa Halula, 94542. Tel 415-881-3299. *Pres* Dr Ellis E McCune;
Executive Dean William G Vandinburgh; *Gallery Dir* Theresa Halula
Open Mon - Fri Noon - 4 PM, Sun 1 - 4 PM. No admis fee. Estab 1970 to
provide a changing exhibition program for the university & general public.
Gallery contains 2000 sq ft. Average Annual Attendance: 6800
Income: $13,500
Exhibitions: (1984) New Artists/New Art; Ellen Manchester & Frank Goelke:
Photography; CSUH Student Show; Australian Printmakers
Activities: Internships; certificate program in museum & gallery studies

M HAYWARD AREA FORUM OF THE ARTS, Son Gallery, 1015 E St, 94541.
Tel 415-581-4050. *Dir* Robertt Hanamura
Open Wed - Sat 10 AM - 4 PM, cl major holidays. No admis fee. Estab 1975.
Mem: Dues sustaining $35, nonprofit organization $25, family $20, single $15,
student and sr citizen $10
Income: Financed by city, county & membership funds
Collections: Contemporary art by Northern California artists
Activities: Educ dept; docent training; lectures; concerts; gallery talks; tours; arts
festivals with awards; scholarships; individual paintings & original objects of art
lent to city offices; sales shop sells original art, prints & crafts

IRVINE

M UNIVERSITY OF CALIFORNIA, IRVINE, Fine Art Gallery, 92650. Tel 714-
856-6610, 856-6648. *Dir* Melinda Wortz; *Asst Dir* Leah Vasquez
Open Sept - June, Tues - Sat Noon - 5 PM. No admis fee. Estab 1965 to house
changing exhibitions devoted to contemporary art
Income: Financed by city and state appropriations and by interested private
collectors
Exhibitions: (1983) James Ford, architectural sculpture, photographs, drawings;
Gunnar Asplund, Scandanavia Today Architecture; Bill Gregorius; Bill Broaders;
Christopher Stevens; (1984) Il Modo Italiano: Mario Merz; O Week, Carolyn
Armacost; Jeff Glab; Adam Sherman; Julie Medwedeff; Parvin Teharani;
Claremont Graduate Exchange Show; Terry Atkinson, Ross Rudel & Buzz
Harper; graduate show; Nancy Mooslin Art Performance; John Paul Jones; Linda
A Stark; Peggy Jones; Ann Chernenko; Ron Saito; Architects Building Toys;
undergraduate show; Vietnamese Artistic Association Show
Publications: Exhibition catalogs; mailers
Activities: Monthly lect on each exhibit; performances

KENTFIELD

M COLLEGE OF MARIN, Art Gallery,* 94904. Tel 415-485-9411. *Dir* Ann L
Jack
Open Mon - Fri 8 AM - 10 PM; open also during all performances for drama,
music and concert-lecture series. No admis fee. Estab 1970 for the purpose of
education in the college district and community. Gallery is housed in the
entrance to Fine Arts Complex, measures 3600 sq ft of unlimited hanging space;
has portable hanging units and locked cases. Average Annual Attendance: 100 -
300 daily
Income: Financed by state appropriation and community taxes
Collections: Art student work; miscellaneous collection
Exhibitions: Faculty and Art Student; Fine Arts and Decorative Arts
Publications: Catalogs, 1-2 per year
Activities: Gallery Design-Management course; gallery talks; tours

LAGUNA BEACH

M LAGUNA BEACH MUSEUM OF ART, Pacific Coast Highway at 307 Cliff Dr,
92651. Tel 714-494-6531. *Dir* William G Otton; *Admin Asst* Edythe E Mannes;
Dir of Education Suzanne Paulson; *Public Relations* Lauri Pelissero; *Bookstore
Mgr* Ruth Boyle
Open Tues - Sun 11:30 AM - 4:30 PM, cl Mon. No admis fee. Estab 1918 as an
art association. Two large galleries, two small galleries, museum store and offices.
Average Annual Attendance: 60,000. Mem: 1800; dues $20; annual meeting
September
Income: Financed by endowment and membership
Collections: Emphasis on early 20th century California painting
Exhibitions: Permanent collection
Activities: Classes for adults & children; docent training; lectures open to public;
concerts; gallery talks; tours; demonstrations; competitions with awards; museum
shop sells books, magazines, reproductions & prints

LA JOLLA

M LA JOLLA MUSEUM OF CONTEMPORARY ART, 700 Prospect St, 92037.
Tel 619-454-3541. *Dir* Hugh M Davies; *Pres Board of Trustees* Edgar J Marston
Jr; *Comptroller* Racthel Lindgren; *Cur* Lynda Forsha; *Cur* Burnett Miller
Open Tues - Fri 10 AM - 5 PM, Sat & Sun 12:30 - 5 PM, cl Mon, New Years,
Thanksgiving & Christmas. Admis adults $2, students and senior citizens $1,
children under 12 $.50. Founded 1941, to provide exhibitions and understanding
of the visual arts. Museum is a non-profit organization, tax exempt, and
maintains a 500-seat auditorium and 13,000 sq ft exhibition space; six-acre
sculpture garden is under development. Average Annual Attendance: 100,000.
Mem: 2000; dues $25 - $1000; annual meeting Oct
Income: $1,000,000 (financed by endowment, membership and Combined Arts
and Education Council of San Diego County)
Collections: Contemporary Art, primarily American, 1955 to the present
Publications: Exhibition catalogs; newsletter, bi-monthly
Activities: Docent programs; lectures open to the public, 6-8 vis lectr per year;
films; gallery talks; tours; concerts; individual paintings & original objects of art
lent to other museums; book traveling exhibitions, 3 - 4 per yr; originate traveling
exhibitions; museum bookstore sells books, magazines
L Helen Palmer Geisel Library, 700 Prospect St, 92037. *Librn* Gail Richardson
Open Tues - Fri 10 AM - 5 PM, Sat & Sun 12:30 - 5 PM. Estab 1941. For
reference use by staff and docents; by appointment only to other persons
Income: Financed by membership, gifts and grants
Library Holdings: Vols 2500; Per subs 27; AV — Micro — Cards;
AV — Slides, v-tapes; Other — Clipping files, exhibition catalogs, pamphlets
Special Subjects: Contemporary art, international in scope
Exhibitions: (1980) Richard Artschwager's Theme(s); Lynn Fayman
Photography; Sidney and Harriet Janis Collection; The McCrory Corporation
Collection; Roman Opalka; Selections from Permanent Collection

L LIBRARY ASSOCIATION OF LA JOLLA, Athenaeum Music and Arts
Library, 1008 Wall St, 92037. Tel 619-454-5872. *Adminr* Lynn Neumann
Open Tues - Sat 10 AM - 5:30 PM. Estab 1899 for the use of the people in the
community, endeavoring to provide material not otherwise available. No
established gallery. Circ 15,000
Library Holdings: Vols 4250; Per subs 48; AV — Cassettes, rec, v-tapes;
Other — Clipping files, memorabilia, pamphlets
Exhibitions: Monthly one-man shows
Activities: Lect open to public, 10 vis lectr per year; concerts; library tours

M MINGEI INTERNATIONAL INC, Mingei International Museum of World
Folk Art, University Towne Centre Bldg I-5, 4405 La Jolla Village Dr (Mailing
add: PO Box 553, 92038). Tel 619-453-5300. *Pres* Martha Longnecker; *VPres*
Sam Hinton; *Secy* Althea Lucic; *Program & Volunteer Coordr* Nan Danninger
Open Tues, Wed, Thurs & Sat 11 AM - 5 PM, Sun 2 - 5 PM. Admis fee
donation. Estab 1978 to further the understanding of arts of the people from all
parts of the world. 6000 sq ft museum, architecturally designed space, white
interior, hardwood floors, track lighting. Average Annual Attendance: 40,000.
Mem: 1500; annual dues $20-$1000; meetings in May
Income: Financed by membership, grants and contributions
Collections: †International Folk Art (in all media incl textiles, ceramics, metals,
woods, stone, paper, bamboo & straw); African, American, Ethiopian, East
Indian, Japanese, Pakistan, Himalayan & Mexican Folk Art
Exhibitions: International exhibitions utilizing permanent collection & loans from
other museums & private collectors
Publications: Exhibition related publications
Activities: Docent training; illustrated lectures; films; gallery talks; tours;
originate traveling exhibitions; collectors gallery sells original folk art
L Reference Library, 92038. *Librn* Maralys Hill
Library Holdings: AV — A-tapes, cassettes, fs, Kodachromes, lantern slides,
motion pictures, slides, v-tapes; Other — Clipping files, exhibition catalogs,
framed reproductions, manuscripts, memorabilia, photographs

M UNIVERSITY OF CALIFORNIA-SAN DIEGO, Mandeville Art Gallery,
B-027, 92093. Tel 619-452-2864. *Dir* Gerry McAllister Open Tues -
Sun Noon - 5 PM, cl Mon & holidays. No admis fee. Estab 1967 to
provide changing exhibitions of interest to the visual arts majors, university
personnel and the community at large, including an emphasis on contemporary
art. Located on the west end of Mandeville Center, flexible open space
approximately 40 x 70 ft. Average Annual Attendance: 12,000
Income: Financed by state appropriations and student registration fees
Collections: Small Impressionist Collection owned by UC Foundation, presently
on loan to San Diego Fine Arts Gallery, Balboa Park
Exhibitions: (1982-83) Drawings by Painters; Young American Artists; Amdur,
Budgett, Rice & Robbins; Video/TV: Humor/Comedy; At Home With
Architecture; Terry Allen Works; New Epiphanies Religious Contemporary Art;
(1983-84) Young American Artists II: Paintings & Painted Wall Reliefs; Chicago
Scene: Paintings, Drawings, Video; Diter Rot Graphics; Naive Painting,
Contemporary German; Lettrisme: Into The Present; Furnshings by Artists; UC
San Diego Faculty Exhibition: 1984
Publications: UC San Diego Catalog: At Home with Architecture; exhibition
catalogs
Activities: Ten visiting lecturers per year sponsored by the Department of Visual
Arts

LAKEWOOD

NATIONAL WATERCOLOR SOCIETY
For further information, see National and Regional Organizations

LONG BEACH

M CALIFORNIA STATE UNIVERSITY, LONG BEACH, University Art
Museum, 1250 Bellflower Blvd, 90840. Tel 213-498-5761. *Dir* Constance
W Glenn; *Administrative Dir* Jane K Bledsoe; *Admin Asst* Gloria B
Skovronsky; *Cur of Education* Sally Steiner
Open Mon - Thurs Noon - 8 PM, Fri Noon - 4 PM, Sun 1 - 5 PM. No admis
fee. Estab 1949 to be an academic and community visual arts resource. Three
galleries situated adjacent to the fine arts patio. Average Annual Attendance:
30,000
Income: Financed by university appropriation
Collections: 1965 Sculpture Symposium; contemporary prints, drawings &
†photographs; †monumental sculpture
Exhibitions: Jim Dine Figure Drawings: 1975-1979; Kathe Kollwitz at the Zeitlin
Bookshop 1937: CSULB 1979; Roy Lichtenstein: Ceramic Sculpture; Nathan
Oliveira Print Retrospective; Lucas Samaras: Photo Transformations; George
Segal: Pastels 1957-1965; Frederick Sommer at Seventy-five; The Photograph as
Artifice; Renate Ponsold-Robert Motherwell: Apropos Robinson Jeffers;
Francesco Clemente: Recent Works; Paul Wonner: Recent Works; Jacques
Hurtubise: Oeuvres Recentes-Recent Works; Bryan Hunt: A Decade of Drawings
Publications: Exhibition catalogs, three or four per year; color brochures
Activities: Docent training; scheduled tours; lectures, ten visiting lecturers per
year; traveling exhibitions organized and circulated

M JEWISH COMMUNITY CENTER, Center Lobby Gallery, 3801 East Willow
St, 90815. Tel 213-426-7601. *Pres* Don Saltman; *Executive Dir* Joe Permet;
Program Dir Lynne Rosenstein; *Gallery Dir* Dr Bernard Landes
Open Sun - Fri 9 AM - 5 PM, Mon - Thurs evening 7:30 - 10 PM. Estab to
provide a community service for local artists and the broader community as well
as offering exhibits of particular interest to the Jewish Community. The gallery is
the large lobby at the entrance to the building; panels and shelves are for exhibit
displays
Income: Finance by membership, United Jewish Welfare Fund, United Way and
Fund Raising Events
Exhibitions: Monthly exhibits throughout the year; Annual Holiday Gift Show;
Annual Youth Art Show; Paintings; Photography; Portraits; Sculpture; Soft

Sculpturing
Publications: Center Services, bimonthly; Jewish Federation News, bimonthly
Activities: Classes for adults and children; dramatic programs; lect open to the public; concerts; competitions with awards; sales shop selling books, Israeli and Jewish Holiday art objects and gift items

M **LONG BEACH MUSEUM OF ART,** 2300 E Ocean Blvd, 90803. Tel 212-439-2119. *Dir* Russell J Moore; *Cur* Kathy Huffman; *Asst Cur* Kent Smith; *Mgr Bookshop* Barbara Hendrick
Open Wed - Sun Noon - 5 PM; cl New Year's, Thanksgiving and Christmas. No admis fee. Opened in 1951 as a Municipal Art Center under the city library department; in 1957 the Long Beach City Council changed the center to the Long Beach Museum of Art, a department of municipal government. Six galleries & a bookshop with changing exhibitions. Average Annual Attendance: Approx 60,000. Mem: 1100; dues $20, annual meeting second Sun in June
Income: Financed by municipal & private funding
Collections: †Paintings, †sculpture, †prints, †drawings, crafts and photography; 850 items with emphasis on West Coast and California contemporary art; small collection of African artifacts; sculpture garden; Milton Wichner; Kandinsky; Jawlensky; Feininger; Maholy-Nagy
Exhibitions: (1983-84) At Home; Roles, Relationships & Sexuality; Diaries, Notebooks & Journals by Women Artists 1970-1983; Friends Christmas Bazaar; Toy Trains; The Second Link-Viewpoints on Video in the Eighties; 1984 video retrospective; Jennifer Bartlett: Up the Creek & Selected Works; Passion & Precision: The Photographer & Grand Prix Racing, 1895-1985; Second Western States Exhibition of American Paintings; Concepts in Construction: 1910-1980; West Coast Folk Art
Publications: Quarterly bulletin, catalogs, announcements
Activities: Workshops for adults & children; docent training; screening & lecture series open to public, 20 vis lectr per year; gallery talks; tours; individual paintings & original objects of art lent to other city offices; book traveling exhibitions; originate traveling exhibitions; museum shop sells books, magazines, original art, reproductions, prints & ethnic objectss
L **Library,** 2300 E Ocean Blvd, 90803. Tel 213-439-2119
Estab 1957. Open for staff reference with restricted lending of books, publications and slides
Library Holdings: Vols 2000; Per subs 4; AV — V-tapes; Other — Clipping files, exhibition catalogs
Special Subjects: Art History

L **LONG BEACH PUBLIC LIBRARY,** 101 Pacific Ave, 90802. Tel 213-437-2949. *Dir Libr Servs* Cordelia Howard; *Head Performing Arts Dept* Natalee Collier; *Assoc Dir Adult Servs* Doris Soriano
Open Mon 10 AM - 8 PM; Tues - Sat 10 AM - 5 PM; Sun 1:30 - 5 PM. Estab 1897
Library Holdings: Vols 734,009; Micro — Fiche, reels; AV — A-tapes, cassettes, rec, v-tapes; Other — Clipping files, exhibition catalogs, framed reproductions, memorabilia, original art works, pamphlets, photographs, prints
Collections: Miller Special Collections Room housing fine arts books and Marilyn Horne Archives

LOS ANGELES

O **ADVOCATES FOR THE ARTS,** University of California School of Law, 405 N Hilgard Ave, 90024. Tel 213-825-5670. *Dir* Amy Lawrence
Founded 1974 to provide free legal assistance to visual and performing artists, and art organizations who otherwise would be unable to afford counsel. Besides providing legal support to art groups and individuals, the program seeks to encourage research and understanding of arts-related issues by University of California, Los Angeles students. Over 100 volunteer lawyers
Activities: Research in arts-related topics and historic preservation, copyright, contracts, and libel; legal seminars; research into funding sources for community art; voluntary legal services and assistance to community groups fostering public arts

C **ARCO CENTER FOR VISUAL ART,** 505 S Flower St, 90071. Tel 213-488-0038. *Gallery Asst* Therese M McMahon; *Dir* Fritz A Frauchiger; *Cur Asst* Eddie L Fumasi
Open Mon - Fri 9:30 AM - 5:30 PM, Sat 11 AM - 5 PM. Estab 1976; the Atlantic Richfield Company is the corporate sponsor of the center, which is a not for profit gallery for changing exhibitions. The gallery has two show spaces, the larger used for painting, sculpture and installations; the smaller for photography and drawing. Shows are changed every six weeks, with a staggered opening schedule so that there is something new every three weeks. Average Annual Attendance: Approx 75,000
Exhibitions: Contemporary California Artists; Joe Goode, Paintings: Environmental Impact Series; The Art of the Movie Miniature; Peter Alexander, Velvets; Larry Bell, New Sculpture; Plank House Architecture of the Northwest Coast Indians

L **ART IN ARCHITECTURE,** Joseph Young Library, 7917 1/2 W Norton Ave, 90046. Tel 213-656-2286, 654-0990. *Dir* Dr Joseph L Young
Estab 1955 to provide background to history of art in architecture. Only availabe to students, associates and apprentices for reference only
Purchases: $2000
Library Holdings: Vols 2000; Per subs 10; AV — Kodachromes, motion pictures, slides, v-tapes; Other — Clipping files, exhibition catalogs, memorabilia, original art works, pamphlets, photographs, prints, reproductions, sculpture
Special Subjects: Art in Architecture
Activities: Lectures open to public, 2 vis lectr per yr; tours; scholarships; lending collection contains 2000 books, 200 color reproductions, 2000 Kodachromes, motion pictures, 100 original art works, 500 original prints, paintings, 500 photographs, sculpture & 2000 slides; book traveling exhibitions once a yr; originate traveling exhibitions

M **CALIFORNIA MUSEUM OF SCIENCE AND INDUSTRY,** * 700 State Dr, Exposition Park, 90037. Tel 213-744-7400. *Dir* Janis Berman; *Asst Dir* Sam C Cogan; *Dir Development* Karen King; *Dir Exhibits* Frank Glisson
Open daily 10 AM - 5 PM. Dynamically tells the story of science, industry and commerce to the public by tempting each visitor to take part in a sensory learning experience and education adventure. The museum has 9 halls housing 20 permanent exhibits and more than 60 temporary exhibits among which are Sister Cities Youth Art Exhib and Sister Cities in Focus which appear throughout the year; auditorium seating 500
Income: Financed by state appropriation and California Museum Foundation
Exhibitions: Permanent—Art Hall of Fame. Temporary—Annual Union Artist (paintings and sculpture by all unions in AFL-CIO); Bonsai, Care and Growing; children's Gametime playground exhibit; Key Art Awards (annual showing of posters, logos, word-styles promoting movies or TV shows); props from motion picture Alien
Publications: Notices of temporary exhibits, maps, pamphlets
Activities: Formal science-art education programs for school groups and the public; competitions; scholarships

M **CALIFORNIA STATE UNIVERSITY, LOS ANGELES,** Fine Arts Gallery, 5151 State University Dr, 90032. Tel 213-224-3521. *Dir* Daniel Douke; *Asst to Dir* Noel Quinn; *Gallery Asst* Paula Van Derlans
Open Mon - Thurs Noon - 5 PM; Sun 1 - 4 PM. No admis fee. Estab 1954 as a forum for advanced works of art and their makers, so that education through exposure to works of art can take place. Gallery has 1400 sq ft, clean white walls, 11 ft high ceilings with an entry and catalog desk. Average Annual Attendance: 30,000
Income: Financed by endowment and state appropriation
Exhibitions: (1982) Glen Lukens: Pioneer of the Vessel Aesthetic; Mark Lere: Installation; (1983) Works on Paper: American Art 1945-1975; New Artists: New Art
Publications: Exhibition catalogs, 3 per year
Activities: Educ dept; lect open to public, 10 - 20 per year; gallery talks; exten dept

M **CITY OF LOS ANGELES,** Cultural Affairs Dept, Room 1500 City Hall, 90012. Tel 213-485-2433. *General Mgr* Fred Croton; *Dir Municipal Art Gallery* Josine Ianco-Starrels; *Dir Performing Arts Division* George Milan; *Dir Cultural Heritage* Ileana Welch; *Dir Watts Towers Arts Center* John Outterbridge; *Dir William Grant Still Community Arts Center* Hakim Ali; *Pres Cultural Affairs Commission* Louise G Tate; *Pres Cultural Heritage Board* Patricia M Simpson
Estab 1925 to bring to the community the cultural and aesthetic aspects of Los Angeles; to encourage citizen appreciation and participation in cultural activities and developing art skills. The art areas are the Cultural Affairs Dept, the Junior Arts Center Gallery, and the Watts Towers Art Center Gallery. Average Annual Attendance: 250,000
Income: $1,907,073 (financed by city appropriation)
Collections: Works by local area artists; Portraits of Mayors of Los Angeles; gifts to the city from other countries
Exhibitions: Abstractions-Sources-Transformations; Approaches to Xerography; Artist as Social Critic 1979; The Blimp Show; Ideas Work-Art Works; Magical Mystery Tour; Newcomers; Portraits-1979; Secrets & Revelations II; Robert Sengstacke and Larry Sykes; The Stamp Act of 1979; Ruth Weisberg 1971-79
Activities: Classes for adults and children; dramatic programs; docent training; lect open to public; concerts; gallery talks; tours; competitions; sales show selling books, original art, reproductions, and prints; Junior Arts Center Gallery at Barnsdall Park

M **CRAFT AND FOLK ART MUSEUM,** * 5814 Wilshire Blvd, 90036. Tel 213-937-5544. *Prog Dir* Edith R Wyle; *Executive Dir* Patrick Ela; *Sr Curator* Sharon Emanuelli; *Registrar* Marcia Page; *Education Cur* Janet Marcus; *Graphic Designer* Max King; *Special Programs Coordr* Willow Young
Open Sat - Wed 11 AM - 5 PM; Fri 11 AM - 8 PM. No admis fee. Estab 1973 as The Egg and The Eye Gallery
Collections: Contemporary American Crafts; International Folk Art; Masks of the world
Exhibitions: Festival of Masks
Publications: Newsletter, quarterly; exhibition catalogs
Activities: Educ programs; workshops; films; lectures; tours; community outreach programs
L **Library-Media Resource Center,** 5814 Wilshire Blvd, 90036. Tel 213-934-7239, 937-5544. *Museum Librn* Joan M Benedetti
Open Tues & Wed 11 AM - 5 PM and by appointment. Estab 1975 to support and supplement the documentation and information activities of the Museum in regard to contemporary crafts and international folk art; visual material collected equally with print. For reference only
Income: Financed by grant from James Irvine Foundation
Library Holdings: Vols 1500; Per subs 70; AV — Cassettes, slides; Other — Clipping files, exhibition catalogs, memorabilia, pamphlets, photographs
Special Subjects: Decorative arts, folk art, contemporary crafts, vernacular architecture, masks & masking
Collections: Preserving Ethnic Traditions Project Archive (slides, cassette, a-tapes, and reports); †Slide Registry of Contemporary Craftspeople
Activities: Los Angeles Community Research Project

C **GOLDEN STATE MUTUAL LIFE,** * 1999 W Adams Blvd, 90018. Tel 213-731-1131. *Correspondence Secy & Dir Program Advisor* William Pajaud
Open to public by appointment through Personnel Department. No admis fee. Estab 1965 to provide a show place for Afro-American Art; to assist in the development of ethnic pride among the youth of our community. Collection displayed throughout building
Collections: Drawings, lithographs, paintings and sculpture
Activities: Tours by appointment

M HEBREW UNION COLLEGE, Skirball Museum,* 32nd & Hoover Sts (Mailing add: 3077 University Ave, 90007). Tel 213-749-3424. *Dir* Nancy Berman; *Admin Asst* Martha Bolinger; *Education Cur* Isa Aron; *Registrar* Georgia Harvey; *Cur Asst* Joanne Ratner; *Media Resources Coordr* Susanne Kester
Open Tues - Fri 11 AM - 4 PM; Sun 10 AM - 5 PM. No admis fee. Estab 1913 as part of library of Hebrew Union College in Cincinnati, Ohio, and moved in 1972 to the California branch of the college, and renamed the Hebrew Union College Skirball Museum; to collect and display artifacts of Jewish culture. 5575 sq ft in gallery, divided into four rooms, which are: main or permanent installation, mini-exhibit room (changing gallery), large changing exhibits gallery (north gallery), and ceremonial art gallery (northeast gallery). Average Annual Attendance: 30,000. Mem: 1300; dues life $5000, sponsor $1000, patron $500, sustaining $250, supporting $100, contributing $50, participating $30, sr citizen & student $10
Income: Financed by college appropriation; some private and public grants
Collections: 2000 archaeological objects from the Near East, primarily Israeli; 6000 ceremonial objects, primarily Western European, but some exotic Oriental and Indian pieces as well; Chinese Torah and India Torah cases; 4000 prints and drawings from Western Europe, spanning 4 - 5 centuries
Exhibitions: A Centennial Sampler-One Hundred Years of Collecting at Hebrew Union College; A Disappearing Community: Jewish Life on New York's Lower East Side (photographs, by Bill Aron); And There Was Light, Studies by Abraham Rattner for the Stained Glass Windows of the Chicago Loop Synagogue (selections from the Louis & Jennie Rattner Allen Collection); David Bennett: Illustrations to the Bible; The Custom Cut: Jewish Papercuts, Past & Present; For Meyer Shapiro: $38; Jerusalem—City of Mankind (photographs); Jewish Marriage Contracts: a Celebration in Art; Jews of Yemen, a Retrospective (textiles & ceremonial art); Krasnow: A Retrospective Exhibition of Paintings, Sculpture, and Graphics; Los Angeles Collects: Works on Paper and Graphic Art from Israel; Maranova: A Modern Graphic Interpretation of Kafka's The Trial; Mark Podwal: Drawings from A Book of Hebrew Letters; Segal: Praise Him with the Psaltery and the Harp (sculptural interpretation of Psalm 150); Spiritual Resistance: Art from Concentration Camps 1940-45; Twelve from the Soviet Underground; Ludwig Yehuda Wolpert. Permanent—A Walk Through the Past; The Five Sense Show (ceremonial art)
Publications: Museum News
Activities: Docent training; lect open to public; children's workshops; lending collection contains 1200 slides; originate traveling exhibitions; museum shop selling books, reproductions, prints, and ceremonial objects; lobby-gift shop area

O JUNIOR ARTS CENTER, 4814 Hollywood Blvd, 90027. Tel 213-485-4474. *Pres* Ann Boren; *Actg Dir* Tom Matthews; *Art Cur* James Volkert; *Dir Education* Joan De Bruin; *Handicapped Services Coordr* Dr Mary J Martz
Open Tues - Sat 10 AM - 5 PM, Sun Noon - 5 PM. No admis fee. Estab 1967 to stimulate and assist in the development of art skills and creativity. A Division of Cultural Affairs Department, City of Los Angeles, the gallery offers exhibitions of interest to children and young people and those who work with the young. Average Annual Attendance: 21,000. Mem: 350; dues $10 - $500; annual meeting of Friends of the Junior Arts Center, May
Income: Financed by city appropriation and Friends of the Junior Arts Center
Collections: Two-dimensional works on paper; 8mm film by former students
Publications: Schedules of art classes, quarterly; exhibition notices
Activities: Art classes for young people in painting, drawing, etching, general printmaking, photography, filmmaking, photo silkscreen, ceramics, film animation; workshops for teachers; lectures, 2 - 4 vis lectr per yr; films; musical instrument making, design, video festivals for students and the general public; gallery talks; tours; scholarships
L **Library,** 4814 Hollywood Blvd, 90027
Staff use only
Library Holdings: Vols 700; AV — Slides 15,000

C KAUFMAN & BROAD, INC, 10801 National Blvd, 90064. Tel 213-475-6711. *Cur* Michele DeAngelus
Estab 1981 in support and involvement of local art community
Collections: †Selection of works by Southern California artists; emphasis on artists who had not had a major retrospective prior to 1975
Activities: Individual paintings & original objects of art lent

O LOS ANGELES CENTER FOR PHOTOGRAPHIC STUDIES, 814 S Spring St, 3rd Floor, 90014. Tel 213-623-9410. *Pres* Darryl Curran; *Exec Dir* Howard Spector
Open Wed - Sun 11 AM - 5 PM. No admis fee. Estab 1974 to promote photography within the visual arts. Two gallery spaces, one of 1000 sq ft & one of 500 sq ft. Average Annual Attendance: 30,000. Mem: 400; dues $25
Income: $80,000 (financed by membership, city & state appropriation & federal funds)
Exhibitions: Theatre of Gesture; members exhibition; group exhibitions
Publications: Obscura, quarterly; Photo Calendar, monthly
Activities: Classes for adults; lectures open to public, 8-12 vis lectr per yr; competitions with awards; originates traveling exhibitions; sales shop sells books, magazines & original art

M LOS ANGELES CONTEMPORARY EXHIBITIONS, INC, 240 S Broadway, 3rd Floor, 90012. Tel 213-620-0104. *Dir* Joy Silverman; *Program Coordr* Jim Isermann; *Program Coordr* Lee Werbel; *Development Asst* Monique Safford
Open Wed - Sat 11 AM - 5 PM. No admis fee. Estab 1978 to exhibit all disciplines of new art, exhibitions, performance, video & film. Average Annual Attendance: 10,000. Mem: 1000; dues $15-$250
Exhibitions: Video LACE Presents, John Sandborn, Retrospective of Videotapes; Il Modo Italiano, Luigi Ontani
Publications: Headhunters - Catalog, video exchange; New York - Los Angeles Exchange, catalog
Activities: Lectures open to public; originates traveling exhibitions; museum shop sells books & magazines

M LOS ANGELES COUNTY MUSEUM OF ART,* 5905 Wilshire Blvd, 90036. Tel 213-937-2590. *Chmn* Richard E Sherwood; *Pres* Mrs F Daniel Frost; *VPres* Norman Barker Jr; *VPres* Hoyt B Leisure; *Treas* Daniel H Ridder; *Secy* Anna Bing Arnold; *Dir* Earl A Powell III; *Deputy Dir Admin* Morton Golden; *Asst Dir Museum Programs* Myrna Smoot; *Sr Cur of Prints and Drawings* Ebria Feinblatt; *Cur of European Sculpture* Peter Fusco; *Asst Cur of Decorative Arts* Leslie Bowman; *Sr Cur of Far Eastern Art* George Kuwayama; *Cur of American Art* Michael Quick; *Sr Cur of Modern Art* Maurice Tuchman; *Registrar* Renee Montgomery; *Public Information Officer* Pamela Jenkinson; *Dir of Film Programs* Ronald Haver; *Head Museum Education* William Lillys; *Head Conservation* William Leisher; *Head Membership & Development* Dia Dorsey
Open Tues - Fri 10 AM - 5 PM, Sat & Sun 10 AM - 6 PM, cl Mon, Thanksgiving, Christmas and New Years Day. Admis adults $1.50, students and senior citizens with ID, young people 5 - 17, $.75; free day, second Tuesday of each month; museum members and children under 5 admitted free. Estab 1910 as Division of History, Science and Art; estab separately in 1961, for the purpose of acquiring, researching, publishing, exhibiting and providing for the educational use of works of art from all parts of the world in all media, dating from prehistoric times to the present. Complex of three buildings and sculpture garden. Average Annual Attendance: 1,500,000. Mem: 45,000; dues $30 - $1000
Income: $9,000,000 (financed by endowment, membership and county appropriation)
Collections: †American art; †ancient art; †contemporary art; †decorative arts; †European painting and sculpture; †Far Eastern art; †Indian and Islamic art; †textiles and costumes; †modern art; †prints and drawings
Exhibitions: Southern California Photography 1900-1965: An Historical Survey; Gallery Six: Elaine Carhartt; Three Decades of Collecting: Gifts of Anna Bing Arnold; Silver in American Life: Selections from the Mabel Brady Garvan and other collections at Yale University; Gallery Six: Robert Graham; Ansel Adams and the West; The Great Bronze Age of China: An Exhibition from the Peoples Republic of China; That Red Head Gal: Fashions and Designs of Gordon Conway, 1916-1936; Monumental Silver: Selections from the Gilbert Collection; Gallery Six: Maren Hassinger; Los Angeles Prints 1883-1980; The Art of Mosaics: Selections from the Gilbert Collection; From the Far West: Carpets and Textiles of Morocco; Recent Acquisitions: Decorative Arts; Art in Los Angeles-17 Artists in the 60's, and The Museum as Site: 16 Projects; Netsuke: Japanese Sculpture in Miniature; A Mirror of Nature: Dutch Paintings from the Collection of Mr & Mrs Edward William Carter; Recent Acquisitions: Textiles and Costumes; The Human Image in German Expressionist Graphic Art from the Robert Gore Rifkind Foundation; American Portraiture in the Grand Manner: 1720-1920; Elephants and Ivories in South Asia; Arshile Gorky 1904-1948: A Retrospective; Ritzi and Peter Jacobi: Contemporary Fiber Art
Publications: Members Calendar, monthly; Bulletin, annually; Biennial Report; exhibition catalogs, 3 - 4 yearly; special installation brochures, 10 - 12 yearly
Activities: Classes for adults and children; dramatic programs; docent training; lect open to the public, 50 vis lectr per yr; concerts; gallery talks; tours; films; competitions with awards; individual paintings and original objects of art lent to other AAM-accredited museums for special exhibitions; lending collection contains original art works, original prints, paintings and 130,000 slides; traveling exhibitions organized and circulated; museum shop sells books, magazines, reproductions, prints, slides, gifts, posters, postcards and antiquities
L **Library,** 5905 Wilshire Blvd, 90036. Tel 213-857-6118. *Librn* Eleanor C Hartman
Open Tues - Fri 10 AM - 4 PM. For reference only
Library Holdings: Vols 64,000; Per subs 365; auction catalogues 26,000; Other — Clipping files, exhibition catalogs, pamphlets
L **Robert Gore Rifkind Center for German Expressionist Studies,** 5905 Wilshire Blvd, Los Angeles, 90036
Open by appointment
Library Holdings: Vols 4000; Other — Exhibition catalogs, manuscripts, memorabilia, original art works, pamphlets, photographs, prints, reproductions
Special Subjects: Decorative Arts, Drawings, Etchings & Engravings, Graphic Arts, Painting - German, Photography, Portraits, Posters, Printmaking, Prints, Sculpture, Watercolors, Woodcuts
Collections: German expressionist prints, drawings, books & periodicals
Activities: Individual paintings lent to qualified institutions

M LOS ANGELES INSTITUTE OF CONTEMPORARY ART, 2020 S Robertson Blvd, 90034. Tel 213-559-5033. *Dir* Robert L Smith; *Cur* Dan Wasil; *Dir Develop* Debra Burchett; *Membership Secy* Margaret Allen; *Financial Dir* Tobi Smith; *Journal Editor* Cindy Berry
Open Wed - Sat Noon - 6 PM. No admis fee. Estab 1974 to be a major resource for exhibition of contemporary art. The gallery maintains 4500 sq ft of exhibition space to be used for static and temporary work; film and video facilities. Average Annual Attendance: 50,000. Mem: 1500; dues patron-corporate $500, sponsor $100, contributing $50, active $25, artist $20
Income: $105,000 (financed by membership, state appropriation, NEA, California Arts Council and private donations)
Exhibitions: Artwords-Bookworks; William Brice; Clothing Constructions; One of a Kind; Pistoletto; Social Works; Sound; Survey Australia; Tableau; Architectural Sculpture; LeRoy Neiman-Andy Warhol; Wolf Vastell; Changing Trends; Cabin; Temple; Trailer-Architect; Charles Moore
Publications: LAICA Newsletter, monthly; Journal: A Contemporary Art Magazine, quarterly
Activities: Lectures open to public; gallery talks; individual paintings & original objects of art lent to corporations; book traveling exhibitions; originate traveling exhibitions; museum shop sells books, magazines & prints
L **Reference Library,** 2020 S Robertson Blvd, 90034
Open Tues - Sat Noon - 6 PM. Open to public for reference
Library Holdings: Vols 1000; Per subs 5; 100 artists in video library; AV — A-tapes, cassettes, fs, slides, v-tapes; Other — Clipping files, exhibition catalogs, manuscripts, original art works, pamphlets, photographs, prints, reproductions
Special Subjects: Art catalogs; periodicals on contemporary art, painting, sculpture, installation, performance, photography and video
Collections: Documentation of 34 arts groups covered by CETA Title VI grants

L   LOS ANGELES PUBLIC LIBRARY, Art and Music Dept, 630 West Fifth St, 90071. Tel 213-626-7461. *Dept Mgr* Mel Rosenberg
Open Mon, Wed, Fri & Sat 10 AM - 5:30 PM, Tues & Thurs Noon - 8 PM, cl Sun. No admis fee. Established 1872
Income: Financed by municipality
Library Holdings: Vols 200,000; Per subs 800; Prints including original etchings, woodcuts, lithographs & drawings; Other — Clipping files, exhibition catalogs, framed reproductions, original art works, photographs, prints
Collections: Twin Prints; Japanese prints, including a complete set of Hiroshige's Tokaido Series

L   LOS ANGELES TRADE-TECHNICAL COLLEGE LIBRARY, Art Dept,* 400 W Washington Blvd, 90015. Tel 213-746-0800, Ext 494. *Dir* Harold Eckes
Open daily 7 AM - 8:30 PM. Estab 1920 for academic, vocational, trade and technical education. Mini-gallery is located in new Learning Resources Center. Circ 21,500
Income: Financed by district tax base
Library Holdings: Micro — Fiche, reels; AV — A-tapes, cassettes, fs, Kodachromes, motion pictures, rec, slides, v-tapes; Other — Memorabilia, pamphlets, photographs, prints
Special Subjects: Art History, Graphic Arts, Illustration, Photography, Apparel Arts, Art Trades
Collections: Career Information; Vocational-Trade-Technology Education
Publications: LATTC Learning Resources Center Newsletter
Activities: Classes for adults; competitions; scholarships

M   LOYOLA MARYMOUNT UNIVERSITY, Art Gallery, Loyola Blvd at W 80th, 90045. Tel 213-642-2880. *Dir* Ellen Ekedal
Open Mon - Sat 11 AM - 4 PM. No admis fee. Estab 1971 to hold exhibitions. Gallery is 20 x 60 ft with 15 ft ceilings, track lighting and carpeted floors. Average Annual Attendance: 10,000
Income: $10,000 (financed by university)
Exhibitions: Contemporary Los Angeles Drawings; Edward Curtis-Image of the North American Indian; Alice Neel: Paintings 1933-1982
Publications: Catalogs
Activities: Classes for adults and children; docent training; lectures open to public, 2 vis lectr per year; concerts; gallery talks; films; competitions with awards; individual and original objects of art lent; book traveling exhibitions; sales shop sells books

M   MOUNT SAINT MARY'S COLLEGE, Fine Arts Gallery, Art Dept, 12001 Chalon Rd, 90049. Tel 213-476-2237. *Gallery Dir* Jake Gilson
Open Wed - Sun 12 - 4 PM. No admis fee. Estab to present works of art of various disciplines for the enrichment of students and community
Income: Financed by College
Collections: Collection of and by Jose Drudis-Blada
Publications: Exhibitions Catalogs, 2-3 per year
Activities: Lect open to public, 2-3 visiting lectrs per year; scholarships

M   THE MUSEUM OF CONTEMPORARY ART, 152 N Central Ave, 90012. Tel 213-382-6622. *Chmn* Eli Broad; *Pres* William F Kieschnick; *Dir* Richard Koshalek; *Admin* Sherri Geldin; *Dir Development* Robert Sain
Open Wed - Fri 11 AM - 8 PM, Sat - Mon 11 AM - 6 PM; cl Tues. Admis general $3, sr citizens & students $1.50, children under 12 free. Estab 1979, will focus on the arts since mid-century, encompassing traditional and non-traditional media. Will open in permanent building designed by Arata Isozaki in 1986. Currently operating the Temporary Contemporary, a 55,000 square foot warehouse renovated by Frank Gehry. Mem: 8000; dues $30
Special Subjects: Contemporary Art
Exhibitions: (1983-84) The First Show: Painting & Sculpture from Eight Collections; In Context (one-person exhibitions by Micael Heizer, Ian Flavin, Robert Therrien); The Automobile & Culture; In Context: Betye Saar, Doug Heubler, Mark Lere; Mobile Image
Activities: Lectures open to public; gallery talks; book traveling exhibitions; originate traveling exhibitions; sales shop sells books & reproductions

M   MUSEUM OF NEON ART, 704 Traction, 90013. Tel 213-617-1580. *Dir* Lili Lakich
Open Wed - Sat Noon - 5 PM. Admis $2.50. Estab 1981 to exhibit, document & preserve works of neon, electric & kinetic art. Consists of large main gallery for group or theme exhibitions & a small gallery for solo shows. Average Annual Attendance: 15,000. Mem: 300; dues $25 and up; annual meetings Dec 10
Income: Financed by memberships, donations & admission fees
Collections: †Antique electrical signs; contemporary neon art
Exhibitions: Ladies of the Night; Victoria Rivers: Neon/Fabric Construction; Electro-Kinetic Box Art
Publications: Transformer, quarterly
Activities: Classes for adults; lectures open to public; concerts; gallery talks; tours; original objects of art lent to motion picture sets & plays; book traveling exhibition; originates travelings exhibitions; museum shop sells books, magazines, original art, reproductions, prints, slides, electronic jewelry & posters

M   NATURAL HISTORY MUSEUM OF LOS ANGELES COUNTY, 900 Exposition Blvd, 90007. Tel 213-744-3411. *Dir* Dr Craig C Black; *Pres Bd of Governors* Ed Harrison; *Chief of Exhib* Frank Ackerman
Open Tues - Sun 10 AM - 5 PM, cl Mon. Admis adults $1.50, children, senior citizens and students $.75. Estab 1913 to collect, exhibit and research collection in history, art and science; now focuses on American history, science and earth science. Average Annual Attendance: 1,400,000. Mem: 11,000; dues $25 - $100; annual meeting in Sept
Income: Financed by county appropriation and private donations
Collections: †American historical works and decorative arts; †California and western paintings and prints; pre-Columbian artifacts
Exhibitions: Permanent Collection: Toy Trains; Along El Camino Real (mission paintings); California Faces From the Past (Hispanic Californian's Portraits)
Publications: Science Bulletin; Contributions in Science; Terra, bi-monthly Magazine

Activities: Classes for adults and children; docent training; lectures open to the public, 6 vis lectr per yr; school tours; film program; Saturday workshops; concerts; gallery talks; tours; artmobile; individual and original objects of art lent to recognized museums, educational galleries and similar institutions; lending collection contains 30,000 color reproductions, 8653 native artifacts, 35,670 slides, 5500 small mammals, historical & scientific models; originate traveling exhibitions; museum & sales shops sell books, magazines, original art, reproductions, prints, slides & ethnic art objects

L   Library, 900 Exposition Blvd, 90007. Tel 213-744-3414. *Librn* Katherine Donohue
Open to staff and to the public by appointment for reference only
Library Holdings: Vols 50,000; Per subs 900; Micro — Reels; AV — Slides; Other — Clipping files, exhibition catalogs, memorabilia, pamphlets, photographs, prints

M   OCCIDENTAL COLLEGE GALLERY,* Thorne Hall, 1600 Campus Rd, 90041. Tel 213-259-2737, 259-2749. *Dir* Linda Lyke
Open Mon - Fri 9 AM - 3 PM. No admis fee. Estab 1938 to support the academic program of the College and the community. Gallery is located in the foyer of the auditorium. Average Annual Attendance: 19,500
Income: $2600
Activities: Lect open to public; gallery talks

M   OTIS ART INSTITUTE OF PARSONS SCHOOL OF DESIGN GALLERY,* 2410 Wilshire Blvd, 90057. Tel 213-387-5288. *Dir* Al Nodal
Open Mon - Sat 9 AM - 5 PM. No admis fee. Estab 1954 as a forum for contemporary art. Gallery is flawless white drywall; two rooms measuring 35 x 40 ft each with 16 ft ceilings. Average Annual Attendance: 20,000. Mem: 670; dues $25 and up; meeting May and Dec
Income: Financed by endowment, membership
Collections: Contemporary art
Publications: On Kawara, 2 per yr; posters
Activities: Classes for adults; lect open to public and/or members, 2-3 visiting lectr per yr; gallery talks; individual paintings and original objects of art lent; museum shop sells books, magazines, posters, postcards

L   Library,* 2401 Wilshire Blvd, 90057. Tel 213-387-5288. *Library Dir* Neal Menzies; *Tech Svs & Ref Librn* Lyndy Zoeckler; *Libr Asst* Cheri Toomey
Open daily 9 AM - 5 PM for student & faculty use; open to public by appointment only; cl weekends. Estab 1918 as a visual arts library
Library Holdings: Vols 35,000; Per subs 250; AV — A-tapes, cassettes, motion pictures, rec 150, slides 25,000, v-tapes 100; Other — Clipping files, exhibition catalogs, original art works, pamphlets, prints, reproductions 2500

O   SAVING & PRESERVING ARTS & CULTURAL ENVIRONMENTS, 1804 N VanNess, 90028. Tel 213-463-1629. *Dir* Seymour Rosen
Estab 1978 for documentation & preservation of folk art environments
Collections: Archival materials about Americas folk art
Activities: Lectures open to public; lending collection; originates traveling exhibitions; sales shop sells books & slides

C   SECURITY PACIFIC NATIONAL BANK,* H46-2, PO Box 2097, Terminal Annex, 90051. Tel 213-613-5871. *Sr VPres* Ronald Azzolina
Estab 1970 to enhance the environment of Security Pacific banking offices throughout California as well as in other US & overseas offices. 6000 pieces are displayed in 200 banking offices. These collections in each banking office are permanent displays for the benefit of the public and staff
Collections: Contemporary American artists
Exhibitions: Sponsors a variety of art exhibitions & cultural programs throughout the year
Activities: Objects of art lent where appropriate & when available

M   SOUTHERN CALIFORNIA CONTEMPORARY ART GALLERIES OF THE LOS ANGELES ART ASSOCIATION, 825 N LaCienega Blvd, 90069. Tel 213-652-8272. *Pres* Stephen Longstreet; *Dir* Helen Wurdemann; *VPres* Shirley Burden; *Treas* Oscar Grossman
Open Tues - Fri Noon - 5 PM, Sat Noon - 4 PM, Sun 2 - 4 PM, cl Mon. Estab 1925 to discover and present young professional artists, and to exhibit the work of established California artists. North and South galleries and little gallery. Average Annual Attendance: 5000. Mem: 600; dues $40; annual meeting April & Oct
Income: Financed by membership
Exhibitions: All Creatures Great and Small; The Animal in Art; Avery Collection of Famous Photographers; Fantasy and Allegory; Los Angeles, Yesterday and Today
Publications: Announcements of exhibitions; pamphlets; folders
Activities: Lectures open to the public, 4 vis lectr per yr; gallery talks

M   SOUTHWEST MUSEUM, 234 Museum Drive, PO Box 42128, 90042. Tel 213-221-2164. *Pres* Dr Norman Sprague Jr; *Dir* Dr Patrick T Houlihan; *Cur* Dr Stephen LeBlanc; *Cur* Peter Welsh; *Registrar* Claudine Scoville; *Controller* Valerie F Dembrowski
Open Tues - Sat 11 AM - 5 PM, Sun 1 - 5 PM, cl Mon. Admis adults $1.50, children $.75. Estab 1907. Average Annual Attendance: 80,000. Mem: 1500; dues $25 and up
Income: $750,000 (financed by endowment and membership)
Collections: Anthropology and the science of man in the New World; Prehistorical, historical, Spanish Colonial and Mexican provincial arts; 20 galleries contain various collections
Exhibitions: Permanent exhibits of Plains, Northwest Coast, California and Southwest Indian art and culture
Activities: Classes for children and adults; docent training; lect; individual paintings and original objects of art lent to authorized museums; originate traveling exhibitions

L   Braun Research Library, 234 Museum Drive, 90065. *Librn* Ruth Christensen
Open Tues - Sat 1 - 4:45 PM, cl Sun & Mon. Estab 1907. For reference only
Library Holdings: Vols 200,000; Micro — Cards; Other — Clipping files, exhibition catalogs, framed reproductions, manuscripts, memorabilia, original art

works, pamphlets, photographs, prints, reproductions
Special Subjects: Man in the New World, Indians of the Western Hemisphere, Anthropology of the Americas, Western Americana

C **TIMES MIRROR COMPANY,** Times Mirror Square, 90053. Tel 213-972-3977, 972-3700. *Secy of Foundation* Charles R Redmond
Estab as part of corporate philanthropic activities. Annual amount of contributions and grants $100,000; supports museums by providing funds for acquisitions, constructions and operating (mostly in Southern California)

UNIVERSITY OF CALIFORNIA, LOS ANGELES
M **Grunwald Center for the Graphic Arts,** 405 Hilgard Ave, 90024. Tel 213-743-2311. *Dir & Cur* Dr E Maurice Bloch; *Asst to Dir* Lucinda H Gedeun; *Cur Asst* Gordon Fuglie
Open Mon - Fri 9 AM - Noon and 1 - 5 PM. No admis fee. Estab 1956 as a research and study center for the graphic arts
Collections: Contemporary Photography; German Expressionism; Japanese Woodblock; Matisse, Picasso, Ornament, Renoir, Rouault; prints and drawings 15th Century to present; Tamarind Lithography Workshop Impressions (complete)
Publications: Grunwald Center Studies, annual
M **Museum of Cultural History,** 55A Haines Hall, 405 Hilgard Ave, 90024. Tel 213-825-4361. *Dir* Dr Christopher B Donnan; *Asst Dir & Cur Africa, Oceania & Indonesia* Doran H Ross; *Admin Asst* Barbara Underwood; *Grants & Accessibility Coordr* Emily M Woodward; *Cur of Textiles & Folk Art* Patricia B Altman; *Consulting Cur of Costumes & Textiles* Patricia Anawalt; *Registrar* Sarah J Kennington; *Conservator* Benita Johnson; *Photographer* Richard Todd; *Collections Mgr* Robert V Childs; *Exhib Coordr* Betsy Quick; *Exhib Designer* George Johnson
Open Wed - Sun 12 - 5 PM. Estab in 1963 to collect, preserve and make available for research and exhibition objects and artifacts from cultures considered to be outside the Western tradition. Changing exhibitions on view Wed - Sun Noon - 5 PM. Museum's annual major exhibition opens at the UCLA Frederick S Wight Art Gallery, Tues - Fri 11 AM - 5 PM, Sat & Sun 1 - 5 PM
Income: Financed by endowment, state appropriation and private donations
Collections: Archaeological and ethnographic collections; 150,000 objects primarily from non-Western cultures - Africa, Asia, the Americas, Oceania, The Near East and parts of Europe
Exhibitions: (1983) Nigerian Textiles from the Museum of Cutural History; Asante Art & History; The Art of Benin; Honoring the Dead: Anasazi Ceramics from the Rainbow Bridge-Monument Valley Expedition; Dance Occasions & Festive Dress in Yugoslavia (1982) Armenian Archeological Monuments; The Dutch and America; Mexican Folk Art
Publications: Exhibition catalogues; filmstrips; monographs; pamphlets; papers; posters; slide sets
Activities: Satellite Museum Program; Hall Case Program; Early Man Program; Chumash Indian Program; Publications Program; lect open to public, 1 - 3 visiting lectr per year; seminars; symposia; book traveling exhibitions; originate traveling exhibitions
M **Frederick S Wight Art Gallery,** 405 Hilgard Ave, 90024. Tel 213-825-1461. *Dir* Dr Edith A Tonelli; *Admin Analyst* Marian Eber; *Design Dir* Thomas Hartman; *Registrar & Cur Asst* Katherine Hart
Open Tues 11 AM - 8 PM, Wed - Fri 11 AM - 5 PM, Sat & Sun 1 - 5 PM, cl Mon and during Aug. No admis fee. Estab 1952. Gallery serves the university and public; program is integrated with the curricula of the Art Department. Average Annual Attendance: 175,000
Collections: The Willitts J Hole Collection of approximately 50 paintings of the Italian, Spanish, Dutch, Flemish and English schools from the 15th - 19th century Franklin D Murphy Sculpture Garden; 66 sculptures from the 19th - 20th centuries, including Arp, Calder, Lachaise, Lipchitz, Moore, Noguchi, Rodin and Smith
Exhibitions: Twelve exhibitions annually. Architecture and design: operates in close conjunction with the Museum of Cultural History, and the Grunwald Center for the Graphic Arts; drawings, painting, prints and sculpture
Publications: Exhibition catalogues
Activities: Gallery talks; tours daily; book traveling exhibitions; originate traveling exhibitions; museum shop sells books, magazines, original art, reproductions and various gift items
M **Exploratorium, University Student Union,** 5154 State University Dr, 90039. Tel 213-224-2189. *Exploratorium Mgr* Lynda Lyons
Open Mon - Thurs 11 AM - 7 PM, Fri 11 AM - 1 PM. No admis fee. Estab 1975 as a fine art gallery-alternative space. Average Annual Attendance: 18,000
Income: Financed by city and state appropriations
Exhibitions: Works by new and established professional artists; art, cultural and scientific exhibitions
Publications: Catalogs, 3 - 4 per year
Activities: Hosts artists' performances; dance groups; dramatic productions; lectures open to the public, 10 vis lectr per yr; concerts; book traveling exhibitions; sales shop sells prints & crafts
L **Visual Resource Collection,** Art Department, 405 Hilgard Ave, 90024. Tel 213-825-3725
Library Holdings: AV — Slides 230,000
L **Art Library,** 2250 Dickson Art Center, 90024. Tel 213-825-3817. *Art Librn* Joyce P Ludmer; *Public Services Librn* Raymond Reece
Founded 1952
Library Holdings: Vols 70,000; Per subs 1500; Ephemera files; Micro — Fiche, reels; Other — Exhibition catalogs, manuscripts, memorabilia, original art works, pamphlets, photographs, prints, reproductions
Collections: †One of four copies of Princeton's Index of Christian Art; †Elmer Belt Library of Vinciana
L **Architecture and Urban Planning Library,** 1302 Architecture Bldg, 405 Hilgard Ave, 90024. Tel 213-825-2747. *Head Librn* Jon S Greene
Open Mon - Thurs 8:30 AM - 9 PM, summer and intersessions Mon - Fri 9 AM - 5 PM, cl Sat, Sun & evenings. Estab 1969 to provide the basic materials for the study of architecture and urban planning at the professional graduate level. Circ 21,000
Income: Financed by endowment and state appropriation

Purchases: $25,000
Library Holdings: Vols 16,161
L **Elmer Belt Library of Vinciana,** 405 Hilgard Ave, 90024. Tel 213-825-3817
Open Mon - Fri 9 AM - 5 PM. Estab 1961
Income: Financed by state appropriation
Library Holdings: Vols 9000; original documents; Other — Clipping files, exhibition catalogs, framed reproductions, manuscripts, original art works, pamphlets, photographs, reproductions
Special Subjects: Leonardo da Vinci
Collections: Special collection of rare books, incunabula, and related materials in Renaissance studies, with a focus on Leonardo da Vinci, his manuscripts, milieu, art and thought

UNIVERSITY OF SOUTHERN CALIFORNIA
M **Fisher Gallery,** 823 Exposition Blvd, 90089. Tel 213-743-2799, 743-7624. *Dir* Dr Selma Holo; *Cur* Marie de Alcuaz; *Admin Asst* Kay Allen; *Designer* Trevor Norris
Open Tues - Sat Noon - 5 PM, except for special exhibitions. No admis fee. Estab 1939 as an educational department of the University. Fisher Gallery consists of three rooms, two for changing exhibitions, the third for permanent collection display; Lindhurst Gallery displays student work. Average Annual Attendance: 20,000. Mem: 350; dues $200; meeting second Tues every month
Income: Financed by endowment
Collections: Galleries house the permanent collections of paintings of 17th century Dutch, Flemish and Italian, 18th century British, 19th century French and American landscape and portraiture schools; Elizabeth Holmes Fisher Collection; Armand Hammer Collection
Exhibitions: Subject: Women; LA Seen; Honore Daumier; Leonardo's Return to Vinci; Finland: Nature Design Architecture; Abhasa: Image Bearing Light; Hearst Castle; Ceci n'est pas le surrealisme (California: Idioms of Surrealism)
Publications: Exhibition catalogs, three annually
Activities: Docent training; lectures open to the public, 10 vis lectr per yr; concerts; gallery talks; tours; awards; scholarships; individual paintings & original objects of art lent; lending collection contains 200 original prints, 400 paintings, 15 sculpture; originate traveling exhibitions; sales shop
L **Architecture and Fine Arts Library,** Watt Hall, University Park, 90007. Tel 213-743-2798. *Librn* Alson Clark; *Library Asst* Thomas Gates; *Slide Cur* Andrea Hales; *Asst Librn* Nancy Smith
Open Mon - Thurs 8:30 AM - 10 PM, Fri 8:30 AM - 5 PM, Sat Noon - 5 PM, Sun 1 - 8 PM. Estab 1925 to provide undergraduate and graduate level students and the teaching and research faculty materials in the areas of architecture and fine arts needed to achieve their objectives. Branch library in the central library system is supported by the University. Circ 65,000
Income: Financed by University funds
Purchases: $56,000
Library Holdings: Vols 46,000; Per subs 260; architectural drawings 1000; Micro — Reels; AV — Slides 150,000; Other — Exhibition catalogs, pamphlets, photographs
Activities: Tours

MALIBU

M **J PAUL GETTY MUSEUM,** 17985 Pacific Coast Highway, 90265. Tel 213-459-2306; TWX 910-343-6873. *Dir* John Walsh Jr; *Cur Paintings* Burton Fredericksen; *Cur Antiquities* Dr Jiri Frel; *Cur Decorative Arts* Gillian Wilson; *Head Public Information* Jean Keefe
Open Tues - Sun 10 AM - 5 PM. No admis fee, parking reservations required, call 213-459-8402. Estab 1953 to display art objects for public viewing & to promote scholarly research in the fields represented. The museum building is a re-creation of an ancient Roman villa and consists of 38 galleries. Average Annual Attendance: 300,000
Income: Financed by endowment
Collections: †Greek & Roman antiquities; †French decorative arts; †Western European paintings
Publications: Calendar, monthly; Museum Journal, annually
Activities: Docent training; slide show for children; classroom materials; lectures open to public, 10-12 vis lectr per yr; concerts; original objects of art lent to other museums for special exhibitions; museum shop sells books, reproductions, slides & museum publications
M **J Paul Getty Center for the History of Art and Humanities,** 401 Wilshire Blvd, Suite 400, Santa Monica, 90401.
—**Photo Archives,** 401 Wilshire Blvd, Suite 400, Santa Monica, 90401. Tel 213-458-9811. *Head Photo Archives* Dr William Rieder
Open Mon - Fri 10 AM - 5 PM, by appointment. Estab 1972 to provide scholars with a research facility of photographs of works of art in international collections. Non-circulating
Income: Financed by endowment
Library Holdings: Micro — Fiche; Other — Photographs 300,000
Special Subjects: Ancient art (Greek, Etruscan & Roman); Western European painting (14th - 19th centuries); Western European decorative arts, particularly French 18th century; Medieval art & architecture; European sculpture
Collections: Bartsch series of early prints; Decimal Index of Art of Low Countries; microfiche of Witt Library Photo Collection; Itatti Collection; Dou Wes Archive of Old Master Paintings; Conway Library architecture collection on microfiche
—**Research Library,** 401 Wilshire Blvd, Suite 400, Santa Monica, 90401. Tel 213-458-9811. *Head Librn* Anne-Mieke Halbrook; *Assoc Librn* Bethany Mendenhall
Open Mon - Fri 10 AM - 5 PM, by appointment. Estab 1973 to support research by curatorial & other professional museum staff. For reference only, noncirculating
Library Holdings: Vols 20,000; Per subs 90; Micro — Fiche, reels; AV — V-tapes; Other — Clipping files, exhibition catalogs, pamphlets
Special Subjects: Classical archeology, 18th century French decorative art, Western European painting
Collections: Auction-sales catalogs 20,000

MENDOCINO

O **MENDOCINO ART CENTER,** Gallery, 45200 Little Lake St, Box 765, 95460. Tel 707-937-5818. *Executive Dir* Karen Kesler; *Gallery Mgr* Grace Rubasamen
Open Mon - Thurs 10 AM - 4 PM, Fri - Sun 10 AM - 5 PM, winter hours daily 10 AM - 5 PM. No admis fee. Estab 1959 as a rental-sales gallery for exhibition and sales of member work; also to sponsor traveling and museum exhibits. Two major gallery rooms, 1 gallery room available for rental of one-man shows. Average Annual Attendance: 25,000. Mem: 1000; dues $20
Collections: Graphics, paintings and sculpture
Publications: Arts & Entertainment, monthly
Activities: Classes for adults and children; docent training; lectures open to the public, 4 - 10 vis lectr per yr; concerts; competitions; scholarships; individual paintings and original objects of art lent to businesses and public places; sales shop sells books, original art, reproductions, prints and crafts
L **Library,** 45200 Little Lake St, Box 765, 95460. Tel 707-937-5818. *Librn* Joan Burleigh
Open Mon - Fri 9 AM - 1 PM for members only. Estab 1975 to provide members with access to art books and magazines. Lending library for members of Art Center only. Circ 1350 books & 18 magazines
Income: Financed by donations, grants from CAC and membership drive
Library Holdings: Vols 1827; Per subs 17; Picture File; AV — Cassettes, fs, slides; Other — Clipping files, exhibition catalogs, framed reproductions, prints, reproductions
Special Subjects: Women in Art

MISSION HILLS

O **SAN FERNANDO VALLEY HISTORICAL SOCIETY,*** 10940 Sepulveda Blvd, 91345. Tel 213-365-7810. *Cur* Elva Meline
Open Wed & Sun 1 - 4 PM, cl holidays. No admis fee. Estab 1943. The Society manages the Andres Pico Adobe (1834) for the Los Angeles City Department of Recreation, where they house their collection. Mem: Dues; active, sustaining and organization $10, Life $100
Income: Financed by membership and donations
Collections: Historical material; Indian artifacts; paintings; costumes; decorative arts; manuscripts
Activities: Lectures; films; guided tours; Permanent and temporary exhibitions
L **Library,*** 10940 Sepulveda Blvd, 91345
Library open by appointment. Estab 1970
Income: Financed by members and gifts
Library Holdings: Vols 3650; AV — Cassettes; Other — Clipping files, manuscripts, memorabilia, original art works, pamphlets, photographs, prints
Collections: Citrus; Communities; Historical landmarks; Olive; Pioneers; San Fernando Mission; San Fernando Valley
Exhibitions: Ethnic contributions to valley history (for local school dist); 200 years valley agriculture (for SFV Fair), Valley history (local malls)
Publications: The Valley, monthly newsletter

MONTEREY

M **CASA AMESTI,*** 516 Polk St, 93940. Tel 408-372-8173. *Chmn Monterey Council* Frederick S Farr
Open Sat & Sun 2 - 4 PM, cl 2 wks July. Admis $1, children & members no charge. Bequeathed to the National Trust in 1953 by Mrs Frances Adler Elkins. It is an 1833 adobe structure reflecting phases of the history and culture of the part of California owned by Mexico, after the period of Spanish missions and before development of American influences from the Eastern seaboard. It is a prototype of what is now known as Monterey style architecture. The Italian-style gardens within the high adobe walls were designed by Mrs. Elkins, an interior designer, and her brother, Chicago architect David Adler. The furnishings, largely European, collected by Mrs. Elkins are displayed in a typical 1930's interior. The property is a National Trust historic house. The Old Capital Club, a private organization, leases, occupies and maintains the property for social and educational purposes
Collections: Elkins Collection of largely European furnishings
Activities: Monterey History and Art Association volunteers provide interpretive services for visitors on weekends

O **MONTEREY HISTORY AND ART ASSOCIATION,** 550 Calle Principal, PO Box 805, 93940. Tel 408-372-2608. *Pres* Douglas C Despard Jr
No admis fee. Estab 1931. The Association owns the 1845 Casa Serrano Adobe, the 1865 Doud House, the 1845 Fremont Adobe and the Mayo Hayes O'Donnell Library. They operate and maintain the Allen Knight Maritime Museum, but do not own the premises. The Association celebrates the birthday of Monterey (June 3, 1770) with the Merienda each year on the Sat nearest that date. The Association commemorates the landing at Monterey by Commodore John Drake Sloat in 1846. Mem: Dues; individual life membership $500, sustaining couple $75, sustaining single $50, couple $25, single $15, junior $1
Income: Financed by memberships, donations & fund raising activities
Collections: Costumes, manuscripts and paintings, sculpture, †antique furniture
Exhibitions: Permanent and temporary exhibitions
Publications: Noticias Del Puerto De Monterey, quarterly bulletin
Activities: Guided tours
M **Allen Knight Maritime Museum,** 550 Calle Principal, 93940. Tel 408-375-2553. *Dir* Earl E Stone
Open Tues - Fri 1 - 4 PM, Sat & Sun 2 - 4 PM, Sept 1 - June 15 afternoons only, cl Mon and National holidays. No admis fee. Estab 1971
Collections: Marine Artifacts, ship models, paintings, photographs, Fresnel First Order Lens from Point Sur, California (on loan from US Coast Guard)
Exhibitions: Permanent and temporary exhibitions
Activities: Lectures; guided tours
L **Allen Knight Maritime Museum Library,** 550 Calle Principal, 93940. Tel 401-375-2553. *Librn* Mrs George St Jean

Open for research on the premises
Library Holdings: Maritime photo archive; Other — Manuscripts
Publications: Brochure of Museum with map

M **MONTEREY PENINSULA MUSEUM OF ART,** 559 Pacific St, 93940. Tel 408-372-7591. *Pres* Patricia Hall Lott; *VPres* Morgan Flagg; *VPres* Sarah Bonner; *VPres* Dr Kenneth Yost; *Recording Secy* James Nelson Algar; *Corresp Secy* Betty Bailey; *Treas* William H Cullen; *Dir* Tom Logan; *Special Cur & Registrar* Rick Deragon; *Museum on Wheels Dir* Kay Cline; *Projects Dir* Ilene Tuttle; *Extended Education Service* George DeGroat
Open Tues - Fri 10 AM - 4 PM; Sat & Sun 1 - 4 PM; cl Mon and holidays. No admis fee. Estab 1959 to perpetuate knowledge of and interest in the arts; to encourage a spirit of fellowship among artists and to bring together the artist and the community at large. It recognizes the need for the collection, preservation and exhibition of art works, especially the best of those done in the area. The main gallery (30 x 60 ft) houses monthly temporary exhibitions; Leonard Heller Memorial Gallery, shows promising young artists; Maurine Church Coburn Gallery, monthly temporary exhibitions of painting and photography; Asian Gallery, permanent collection; Armin Hansen Gallery, William Ritschel Memorial Gallery; Folk Art Gallery for collection of international folk arts and hallways which are used to show permanent collection. Average Annual Attendance: 45,000. Mem: 2200; dues individual $10; annual meeting Jan
Income: Financed by endowment, memberships and fund-raising functions
Collections: Armin Hansen Collection; international folk art, photography and graphics; regional art, past and present; William Ritschel Collection
Exhibitions: (1982) Artists from Monterey Peninsula 1875-1925; (1983) Artists of the Monterey Peninsula 1875-1925; Remington Russell, paintings, drawings & bronzes; 23 contemporary California artists including: Lundelburg, Feitelson, Thiebaud, Wiley, Bingston, Diebenkorn, Bischoff, Brown, Wonner & others; Percy Gray Retrospective; Rodin-Balzac; Japanese folk art; photography juried show; Brett Weston Retrospective
Publications: Courier, monthly; Yesterday's Artists on the Monterey Peninsula, book; exhibition catalogs
Activities: Classes for adults and children; docent training; lect open to public, 4 visiting lectr per year; concerts; gallery talks; tours; competitions; exten dept serves three rural county areas; Museum on Wheels teaches craft classes in schools; museum shop sells books, reproductions, prints, and museum replicas and folk art objects

L **MONTEREY PUBLIC LIBRARY,** Art & Architecture Dept, 625 Pacific St, 93940. Tel 408-646-3932. *Dir* Dorothy Steven
Open Mon - Thurs 9 AM - 9 PM; Fri 9 AM - 6 PM; Sat 9 AM - 5 PM; Sun 1 - 5 PM. Estab 1849
Income: Financed by membership and city appropriation
Purchases: $750,000
Library Holdings: Vols 10,000; Per subs 12; Micro — Reels; AV — Cassettes, motion pictures, rec, slides; Other — Clipping files, manuscripts, original art works, pamphlets, photographs, reproductions
Special Subjects: Local history
Collections: Adler; Elkins Collection on Architecture and Interior Design, especially 17th - 19th century English, Italian and French; Raiqueil; Robert Stanton

M **PRESIDIO OF MONTEREY ARMY MUSEUM,** 93944. Tel 408-242-8414. *Dir & Cur* Margaret B Adams; *Asst Cur* Victor D McNamara
Open Mon - Fri 9 AM - 4 PM. No admis fee. Estab 1965. Outlines Presidio Hill from Indian, Spanish and Mexican eras to present United States Army base. One gallery of historical artifacts. Average Annual Attendance: 45,000
Income: Financed by federal appropriations
Collections: Local artifacts: Rumsen Indian tools & decorations; Spanish and Mexican military items; Spanish paintings and utensils from Governor Arguello's residence; United States military items 1846 to present with emphasis on the pre-1940 horse cavalry; horse-drawn field artillery
Activities: Docent training; gallery talks; tours
L **Library,** 93940
Estab 1905 to offer military historical library to professional scholars. Open museum hours with advance arrangements for reference only
Library Holdings: Vols 300; Per subs 5; Micro — Fiche 350; AV — A-tapes, fs, motion pictures, slides; Other — Clipping files, exhibition catalogs, framed reproductions, memorabilia, original art works, photographs 600, prints, sculpture
Special Subjects: History of Monterey, United States Army

M **SAN CARLOS CATHEDRAL,*** 550 Church St, 93940. Tel 408-373-2628. *Rector* Brendan McGuiness
Open daily 8 AM - 6 PM. No admis fee. Built in 1770, now a branch of the Monterey Diocese. The art museum is housed in the 1794 Royal Presidio Chapel
Collections: Spanish religious paintings and sculpture of the 18th and 19th century
Activities: Guided tours

MORAGA

M **SAINT MARY'S COLLEGE OF CALIFORNIA,** Hearst Art Gallery, Box AE, 94575. Tel 415-376-4411, Ext 379. *Dir* Ann Harlow
Open Wed - Sun 11 AM - 4 PM. No admis fee. Estab 1977 to exhibit a variety of the visual arts for the benefit of college students, staff and members of surrounding communities. Maintains two 30 x 30 ft rooms with connecting rampway. Opened William Keith Room for permanent collection in 1983. Average Annual Attendance: 2000. Mem: 150; dues William Keith Assoc & patron $50 and up, family $15, students $10, senior citizens $5; annual meeting in May
Collections: Paintings by William Keith (1838-1911); East European icons; medieval sculpture
Exhibitions: (1982) Engravings by William Hogath; At Mono Lake: A Photographic Exhibition; Posters of the 1890s and 1980s; John Swanson and Alex Maldorado; (1983) Japanese Folk Arts and crafts; Know What You See:

The Examination & Treatment of Paintings; Poseidon's Realm: Ancient Greek Art from the Louie Museum; Bask Black: Contemporary International Prints in Black & White; Dia de los Muertos/Day of the Dead; A Growing Circle of Friends: Art Works from Members' Collections
Publications: Catalogue; newsletter, occasionally
Activities: Lectures open to the public, 3 - 4 vis lectr per yr; concerts; gallery talks; tours; book traveling exhibitions, 1 - 2 per yr

NEWHALL

M WILLIAM S HART MUSEUM, William S Hart Park, 24151 N Newhall Ave, 91321. Tel 805-259-0855. *Regional Park Supt* Mike Dortch
Open Wed - Fri 10 AM - 3 PM; Sat & Sun 10 AM - 5 PM. No admis fee. Estab 1958 to maintain the park and museum as center for leisure enjoyment to the population of Southern California. The retirement home of William S Hart is full of Western art. Average Annual Attendance: 120,000
Income: Financed by county appropriation
Collections: Christadoro; Joe de Yong; James M Flagg; Robert L Lamdin; Remington; Charles M Russell (bronzes, oils, watercolors, grisalle, pen & ink); Schrezvogel; Western art
Activities: Classes for children; docent training; lectures open to public, 4 vis lectr per yr; tours
L Reference Library, 24151 N Newhall Ave, Newhall, CA 91321
Library Holdings: Vols 1000; AV — Motion pictures, rec, slides, v-tapes; Other — Clipping files, manuscripts, memorabilia, original art works, photographs, sculpture

NEWPORT BEACH

M NEWPORT HARBOR ART MUSEUM, 850 San Clemente Dr, 92660. Tel 714-759-1122. *Dir* Kevin E Consey; *Cur Exhibitions* Paul Schimmel; *Assoc Cur* Tom Heller; *Cur Education* Ellen Breitman; *Administrator* Donna Cathey; *Public Relations* Kathleen Costello; *Operations Mgr* Richard Tellinghuisen; *Registrar* Kathleen Pferd; *Technical Supervisor* Luis De La Cruz
Open Tues - Sun 11 AM - 5 PM. Admis by contribution. Estab 1962 as a museum of the Art of our Time serving Orange County and Southern California. Building completed in 1977 contains four galleries of various sizes; 5000; 1600; 1200; 500 sq ft plus lobby and sculpture garden area. Average Annual Attendance: 80,000. Mem: 5500; dues business council $250, patron $150, general membership $30, student $10
Income: $800,000 (financed by special events, memberships, grants from NEA, private sector, sales from restaurant and bookstore)
Purchases: $100,000
Collections: Collections of contemporary American art; California artists
Exhibitions: William Baziotes Retrospective: Paintings, Drawings & Watercolors; Tony Berlant: The Eccentric Image; David Park Retrospective; The Prometheus Archives: A Retrospective Exhibition of Work by George Herms; Vija Celmins: A Survey Exhibition; Cy Twombly; David Amico: Sonata; Deborah Remington: Twenty Year Survey; Loren McIver: Five Decades; Shift: LA/NY; Alan Saret: Matter Into Aether; Action/Precision: Gestural Abstract Expressionism; New California Artists: Jerry Brane, painting; Leonard Koscianski, painting; Seth Seiderman, painting & installation; Dan McCleary, painting
Publications: Bimonthly calendar; exhibition catalogs; posters
Activities: Docent training; in-training session for teachers; lectures open to public, occasionally for members only; special guest lectures & meet-the-artist programs; gallery talks; docent tours; creative art workshops; concerts & performances; film & video programs; individual paintings and original objects of art lent to qualified art museums; lending collection contains original prints; paintings and sculptures; traveling exhibitions organized and circulated; museum shop selling books, magazines, original art
L Library, 850 San Clemente Dr, 92660. Tel 714-759-1122. *Librn* Ruth Roe
Open for reference by appointment
Library Holdings: Vols 2000; Per subs 20; AV — A-tapes, slides, v-tapes; Other — Exhibition catalogs
Special Subjects: Contemporary art

NORTHRIDGE

M CALIFORNIA STATE UNIVERSITY, NORTHRIDGE, Art Gallery, 18111 Nordhoff St, 91330. Tel 213-885-2192. *Dir* Louise Lewis; *Assoc Dir* Phil Morrison; *Admin Asst* Ann Burroughs
Open Mon Noon - 4 PM; Tues - Fri 10 AM - 4 PM. No admis fee. Estab 1971 to serve the needs of the four art departments and to provide a source of cultural enrichment for the community at large. Exhibitions in main gallery have average duration of four weeks. Gallery II for weekly MA candidate solo exhibitions. Average Annual Attendance: 35,000. Mem: Arts Council for CSUN 300; dues $25; annual meeting Sept
Income: $20,000 (financed by city and state appropriation, community support organizations)
Exhibitions: New/Now Narrative; Commercial Break; Jody Pinto; Carole Caroompas; Art Deco: Statues and Bronzes; Scandinavian Glass; West Coast Illustration; Alghierro Boetti: Il Modo Italiano; Negative Photography; Body Art; Marvin Harden: A Tribute; New Bay Area Painting and Sculpture; Vanadium Theater
Publications: Exhibition catalogs, 2 per yr
Activities: Docent training; 2 - 3 art performances per yr; gallery talks; tours; sales shop selling books, magazines, reproductions and gifts

OAKLAND

O BAY AREA ART CONSERVATION GUILD, Daedal Us, 6020 Adeline St, 94608. *Pres* Anita Noenning; *VPres* Genevieve Baird; *Secy* Robin Tichane

Estab 1974 to promote ethical preservation of art and artifacts and to carry on educational programs. Mem: 130; dues $15; 6 meetings per year
Income: $1500 (financed by membership)
Publications: Periodic Newsletter
Activities: Presentations; lect; exten dept serves San Francisco Bay Area

L CALIFORNIA COLLEGE OF ARTS AND CRAFTS, Meyer Library, 5212 Broadway & College Aves, 94618. Tel 415-653-8118, Ext 178. *Head Librn* Robert L Harper; *Asst Librn* Vanroy R Burdick
Open Mon - Thurs 8 AM - 7 PM, Fri 8 AM - 5 PM. Estab 1907 to support the studio and academic requirements for BFA and MFA
Income: $115,000(financed by tuition)
Purchases: $20,240
Library Holdings: Vols 29,132; Per subs 362; Micro — Reels; AV — Rec, slides 80,000; Other — Clipping files, exhibition catalogs, manuscripts, original art works, pamphlets, photographs, prints, reproductions
Collections: Jo Sinel Collection of pioneering work in industrial design
Exhibitions: Small exhibitions mounted on free standing panels

L LANEY COLLEGE LIBRARY, Art Section,* 900 Fallon St, 94607. Tel 415-763-4791. *Art Librn* Lucy Wilson
Open daily 8 AM - 8:45 PM. Estab 1954. Circ 78,000
Library Holdings: AV — A-tapes, cassettes, fs, Kodachromes, lantern slides, motion pictures, rec, slides, v-tapes; Other — Prints, reproductions
Exhibitions: Paintings, sculpture, ceramics, fabrics, photography by students, faculty and community persons

M MILLS COLLEGE, Art Gallery, Seminary & MacArthur Blvd, PO Box 9973, 94613. Tel 415-430-2164. *Dir* Philip E Linhares; *Asst to the Dir* Suzann Dunaway
Open Tues - Sun 10 AM - 4 PM. No admis fee. Estab 1925 to show contemporary and traditional painting, sculpture, and ceramics, exhibitions from permanent and loan collections. Gallery is Spanish-type architecture and has 4500 sq ft main exhibition space, with skylight full length of gallery. Average Annual Attendance: Approx 12,000
Income: Financed by college funds
Collections: †Regional collection of California paintings, drawings and prints; †extensive collection of European and American prints, drawings and ceramics; Asian and Guatemalan textiles; American Indian Artifacts; photographs; slides
Exhibitions: (1980-82) New California Views; China, A Personal View; Big Prints from Rome; Nell Sinton: A 30-Year Retrospective; Recollections: 10 Women of Photography; (1982-83) International Sculture Conference Exhibition; Quilts: A Tradition of Variations; (1983-84) The Shojiro Nomura Fukusa Collection; Joan Brown from the Studio; Narrative Painters; student exhibitions
Publications: Exhibition catalogs
Activities: Lect open to the public, 3 vis lectr per yr; gallery talks

M OAKLAND MUSEUM, Art Dept, 1000 Oak St, 94607. Tel 415-273-3005. *Dir & Chief Exec Officer* Julian T Euell; *Chief Cur Art* Christina Orr-Cahall; *Deputy Cur Art* Harvey L Jones; *Sr Cur Prints & Photographs* Therese Heyman; *Asst Cur* Terry St John; *Registrar* Arthur Monroe; *Preparator* Victor Oliver
Open Weds - Sat 10 AM - 5 PM, Sun 12 - 7 PM, cl Mon, Tues, New Year's, Thanksgiving and Christmas. No admis fee. The Oakland Museum is comprised of three departments: Natural Sciences (formerly the Snow Museum of Natural History, founded 1922); History (formerly the Oakland Public Museum, founded 1910); and the Art Department (formerly the Oakland Art Museum, founded 1916). Internationally recognized as a brilliant contribution to urban museum design. The Oakland Museum occupies a four-square-block, three storied site on the south shore of Lake Merritt. Designed by Kevin Roche, John Dinkeloo and Associates, the Museum is a three-tiered complex of exhibition galleries, with surrounding gardens, pools, courts and lawns, constructed so that the roof of each level becomes a garden and a terrace for the one above. The Art Department has a large hall with 20 small exhibition bays for the permanent collection and a gallery for one-person or group shows as well as the Oakes Art Observatory and Gallery
Income: Financed by city funds, private donations & Oakland Museum Association
Collections: Paintings, sculpture, prints, illustrations, photographs, artists dealing with California subjects, in a range that includes sketches and paintings by early artist-explorers; Gold Rush genre pictures; massive Victorian landscapes; examples of the California Decorative Style, Impressionist, Post-Impressionist, Abstract Expressionist, and other contemporary works
Exhibitions: (1982-83) Slices of Time: California Landscape 1860-1880 & 1960-1980; Three Etchers in California: Whistler, Pollack, Brown; 100 Years of California Sculpture; From the Sunny Side: 6 East Bay Painters; The Tapestries of Trude Guerniouprez; Deborah Butterfield; Attention: California Artists; In Color: Ten California Photographers; On & Off the Wall: Shaped & Colored; Masaui Teraoka; Site Strategies
Publications: The Museum of California, bi-monthly
Activities: Docent training; lectures for members only; tours; awards; individual paintings and original objects of art lent to other museums and galleries for specific exhibitions; originate traveling exhibitions; museum shop sells books, magazines, reproductions, prints, slides & jewelry
O Oakland Museum Association,* 1000 Oak St, 94607. Tel 415-273-3402
A separately incorporated auxiliary for all three departments with over 5000 members. From its membership, the OMA provides assistance and support for museum educational and cultural programs, through its Women's Board, Docent Council, and its Art, History, and Natural Sciences Guilds, which coordinate volunteer activities in the museum's three Departments.
L Library, 1000 Oak St, 94607. Tel 415-834-2413
Library maintained on archives of California art and artists
Library Holdings: Per subs 7; Bk vols & catalogues 6000; Micro — Fiche; AV — Cassettes, slides; Other — Clipping files, manuscripts, memorabilia, photographs

L OAKLAND PUBLIC LIBRARY, Art, Music & Recreation Section, Main Library, 125 14th St, 94612. Tel 415-273-3178. *Dir Library Services* Lelia White;

Sr Librn in Charge Richard Colvig
Open Mon Noon - 8:30 PM, Tues - Thurs 10 AM - 8:30 PM, Fri & Sat 10 AM -
5:30 PM, cl Sun & holidays. Library cooperates with the Oakland Museum and
local groups
Purchases: $30,000
Library Holdings: Posters; AV — A-tapes, cassettes, rec; Other — Framed
reproductions, reproductions
Collections: Picture Collections
Publications: Museum catalogs

OJAI

O **OJAI VALLEY ART CENTER,** 113 S Montgomery, PO Box 331, 93023. Tel
805-646-0117. *Pres* John Haag; *Dir* Cary Sterling
Open Mon - Sat 9 AM - 5 PM. No admis fee. Found 1936, dedicated to the
advancement and development of the arts. Gallery is 40 x 50 ft, high ceilings,
with a large hanging area. Average Annual Attendance: 52,000 - 60,000. Mem:
400; dues family $25, adult $10; annual meeting in Jan
Income: Financed by membership, class and special event fees
Exhibitions: Twelve monthly exhibitions
Publications: Newsletter, monthly
Activities: Classes for adults & children; dramatic programs; workshops; craft
fair; lectures open to public, 20 vis lectr per yr; concerts; tours; competitions with
awards; museum shop sells tee shirts

PACIFIC GROVE

O **PACIFIC GROVE ART CENTER,** 568 Lighthouse Ave, PO Box 633, 93950.
Tel 408-375-2208. *Pres* Frank Keillor; *Co-Dir* Irene Masteller; *Co-Dir* Barry
Masteller; *Secy* Barbara Davies; *Secy* Connie Callas
Open Tues - Sat 11 AM - 5 PM; cl Sun, Mon and holidays. No admis fee. Estab
1968 to promote the arts and encourage the artists of the Monterey Peninsula
and California. Two galleries consist of 4000 sq ft of exhibition space, showing
traditional and contemporary fine art and photography; galleries are available for
classes and lectures. Mem: 500; dues business and club $25, family $15, single
$10, annual meeting in Feb
Income: $50,000 (financed by rents, memberships & donations)
Collections: †Photography; †painting
Exhibitions: Contemporary Paper; Fibre Invitational; Western Surrealism
Publications: Monthly newsletter
Activities: Classes for adults and children; dramatic programs; docent training;
lectures open to public, 5-10 vis lectr per yr; concerts; gallery talks; competitions
with cash awards; sales shop sells original art, reproductions, prints, slides and
craft items
L **Library,** 568 Lighthouse Ave, PO Box 633, 93950. Tel 408-375-2208. *Asst Dir*
Mary Lou Stutzman
Open to members for reference only

PALM SPRINGS

M **PALM SPRINGS DESERT MUSEUM, INC,** 101 Museum Dr, PO Box 2288,
92263. Tel 619-325-7186. *Dir* Morton J Golden; *Asst Dir Administration &
Business* Gordon C O'Gara; *Cur Natural Science* James W Cornett; *Cur Art*
Katherine Plake Hough
Open Sept - June Tues - Fri 10 AM - 4 PM, Sat & Sun 10 AM - 5 PM, cl Mon.
Admis adults $2.50, students & children 8-17 $1.25, members & children under 8
free. Estab and inc 1938. Average Annual Attendance: 106,000. Mem: 4000;
dues life $5000, benefactor $1000, patron $500, business and sustaining $100,
supporting $75, contributing $50, family $35, individual $25
Income: Financed by private funds
Collections: Interpretation of natural sciences of the desert; 19th-20th century
American painting, prints & sculpture specializing in California artists;
Southwestern Native American art; William Holden Collection
Exhibitions: Approx 20 per year
Publications: Calendar of Events, monthly; special exhibition catalogs
Activities: Classes for adults & children; dramatic programs; docent training;
lectures open to public, 20 vis lectr per yr; concerts; gallery talks; tours;
individual paintings & original objects of art lent to museums; originate traveling
exhibitions; museum shop sells books, magazines, original art, reproductions,
slides, jewelry & cards
L **Library,*** 101 Museum Dr, PO Box 2288, 92262. *Librn* Frederick W Sleight
Open for reference only; art and natural science books available for use on
premises
Library Holdings: Vols 3000; Other — Photographs

PALO ALTO

O **PALO ALTO CULTURAL CENTER,** 1313 Newell Rd, 94303. Tel 415-329-
2366. *Dir* Laurie Eason; *Volunteer Coordr* Beverly Balanis; *Actg Cur* Mary
Drach; *Workshop Supv* Gary Clarien; *Office Mgr* Jean Haimson; *Children's
Program* Jamie Kugler
Open Tues - Sat 10 AM - 5 PM, Tues - Thurs evening 7 - 10 PM, Sun 1 - 5 PM,
cl Mon. No admis fee. Estab 1971 to stimulate aesthetic expertise & awareness in
the Palo Alto & surrounding communities. Average Annual Attendance: 55,000.
Mem: 200; dues $10
Income: Financed by city appropriation & private donations
Collections: Contemporary & historical art
Exhibitions: Eating Experience, Handcrafted Utensils; Relief Prints/Woodcuts;
Personal Adornment; Animal Spirit
Activities: Classes for adults & children; dramatic programs; docent training;
lectures open to public; concerts; gallery talks; tours; competitions; museum shop
sells books, original art, reproductions, prints & objects for sale related to
exhibitions;

M **PALO ALTO JUNIOR MUSEUM,*** 1451 Middlefield Rd, 94301. Tel 415-329-
2111. *Supv* Mearl Carson; *Instructor Arts & Crafts* Gale Bruce
Open Tues - Sat 10 AM - 5 PM, Sun 1 - 4 PM, cl New Years, Easter, July 4,
Thanksgiving & Christmas; Baylands Interpretive Center: Wed - Fri 2 - 5 PM,
Sat & Sun 10 AM - 5 PM, cl Thanksgiving & Christmas. No admis fee. Estab
1932, completely renovated in 1969. Average Annual Attendance: 100,000
Income: Financed by city appropriation
Collections: Art and artifacts
Publications: Notes, monthly; Prehistoric Palo Alto (brochure)
Activities: Classes; guided tours; exten dept; sciencemobile

PASADENA

L **ART CENTER COLLEGE OF DESIGN,** James Lemont Fogg Memorial
Library,* 1700 Lida St, 91103. Tel 213-577-1700, Ext 265. *Dir* Elizabeth
Stockly; *Asst Librn* Alison Holt; *Slide Librn* Marie Jordan; *Acquisitions Librn*
Margaret Rose; *Circulation Supvr* Maria Elena Bevan
Open Mon - Thur 7:30 AM - 10 PM, Fri 8:30 AM - 5 PM, cl Sat & Sun. Estab
to provide reference and visual resources for the designers who study and teach
at Art Center College of Design. For lending and reference. Circ 26,000
Purchases: $38,724
Library Holdings: Vols 22,493; Per subs 287; AV — Motion pictures 80, slides
37,088; Other — Clipping files, exhibition catalogs 950, reproductions
Special Subjects: Commercial art, graphic design, illustration, industrial
design, photography, fine arts, history of design, moving-pictures, product
design, transportation design

M **CALIFORNIA INSTITUTE OF TECHNOLOGY,** Baxter Art Gallery,* 1201 E
California Blvd, 91125. Tel 213-356-6811. *Dir* Michael H Smith; *Asst Dir &
Registrar* Barbara Alexander
Open daily Noon - 5 PM, cl July & Aug. No admis fee. Estab 1968 to exhibit
comtemporary art. Maintains 3,000 square feet on campus of Cal Tech in the
Humanities Department. Average Annual Attendance: 25,000. Mem: 300; dues
$25 - $500
Income: $115,000; (financed by membership, Cal Tech and Pasadena Art
Alliance)
Exhibitions: Michael Brewster; Robert Cumming and William Wegman; Laddie
John Dill; Hans Haacke; Nathan Oliveira: Survey of Monotypes; Bruce Richards;
Richard Tuttle; Visionary Drawings of Architecture; Watercolors: Ed Ruscha,
Sam Francis, Diebenkorn, etc
Publications: Exhibition catalogs
Activities: Lect open to the public, 10 visiting lectr per year; gallery talks; tours;
book traveling exhibitions; originate traveling exhibitions

M **PACIFIC - ASIA MUSEUM,*** 46 N Los Robles Ave, 91101. Tel 213-449-2742.
Dir David Kamansky; *Development Officer* Peggy Spear; *Admin Asst* Liz Corey;
Communications Coordr Susan Lerner; *Education Coordr* Karen Copeland;
Registrar Ruth Scherrer; *Bookstore Mgr* Irene Wright
Open Wed - Sun Noon - 5 PM, cl holidays. Adults & non-members $1, under 12
free. Estab 1971 to promote understanding of the cultures of the Pacific and Far
East through exhibitions, lectures, dance, music and concerts. Through these
activities, the museum helps to increase mutual respect and appreciation of both
the diversities and similarities of Eastern and Western cultures.. The building was
designed by Marston, Van Pelt and Mayberry, architects for Grace Nicholson.
The building is listed in the national register of historic places as the Grace
Nicholson Building. There is 11,000 sq ft of exhibition space. Average Annual
Attendance: 50,000. Mem: dues benefactor $1000, donor $500, sponsor $250,
patron $100, contributor $50, active $25
Collections: Oriental art objects
Exhibitions: Japan Day By Day; The Past and Present Art of the Australian
Aborigine; China's Inner Asian Frontiers; Bhutan: The Fabled Kingdom;
Japanese Woodblock Prints from the Henrietta Hill Swope Collection; Chinese
Folk Art: The Eternal in the Everyday; Amri Yahya, Contemporary Indonesian
Batiks; Southeast Asian Ceramics of Thailand and Annam; Ming, Moghul and
Momoyama, the Arts of Asia in Shakespear's Time; The Woodblock Prints of
Paul Jacoulet
Publications: The Past and Present Art of the Australian Aborigines;
Contemporary Australian Aborigine Paintings; The Woodblock Prints of Paul
Jacoulet; bi-monthly calendar of events; exhibition catalogs
Activities: Classes for adults & children; docent training; lectures open to public,
12-15 visiting lecturers per year; concerts; gallery talks; tours; original objects of
art lent to other museums and limited number of libraries; book traveling
exhibitions, 2-3 per year; originate traveling exhibitions; museum shop sells
books, original art and items for cooking and serving Oriental foods

M **PASADENA CITY COLLEGE,** Art Gallery,* 1570 E Colorado Blvd, 91106. Tel
213-578-7238. *Dir* Rolan Percy
Open Mon - Thurs 11 AM - 4 PM; Evenings Mon, Tues & Wed 7 - 9 PM. No
admis fee. Estab to show work that relates to class given at Pasadena City
College. Gallery is housed in separate building; 1000 sq ft. Average Annual
Attendance: 20,000. Mem: 2800 (financed by school budget)
Exhibitions: Clothing Design; painting; sculpture; Faculty Show; Advertising
Design; Student Show; Print Show
Publications: Mailers for each show

L **PASADENA PUBLIC LIBRARY,** Fine Arts Dept, 285 E Walnut St, 91101. Tel
213-577-4054. *Library Dir* Edward Szynaka; *Head Reference* Anne Cain
Open Mon - Thurs 9 AM - 9 PM, Fri & Sat 9 AM - 6 PM, Sun 1 - 5 PM. No
admis fee. Art department estab 1927
Income: Financed by endowments and gifts, for materials only
Library Holdings: Vols 27,500; Per subs 135; scrapbooks on local architecture
and artists; Micro — Cards, fiche, reels; AV — Cassettes, motion pictures, rec
14,200; Other — Clipping files, pamphlets, photographs, reproductions

M NORTON SIMON MUSEUM, Colorado & Orange Grove Blvds, 91105. Tel 213-449-6840. *Pres* Norton Simon; *Asst to Pres* Walter Timoshuk; *Cur* Tessa Helfet; *Cur* Sara Campbell; *Registrar* Andrea Clark; *Research Cur* Susan C Coffey
Open Thurs - Sun Noon - 6 PM. Admis Thurs: adults $2, students & sr citizens $.75; Sunday: all patrons $3; members and children under 12 accompanied by adults free. Estab 1924; this museum brings to the western part of the United States one of the worlds great collections of paintings, tapestries, prints, and sculptures for the cultural benefit of the community at large; the museum is oriented toward the serious and meticulous presentation of masterpiece art. Mem: dues $35 - $1000
Income: Financed by endowment, membership, city appropriation, tours, admissions, contributions, bookshop and grounds maintenance
Collections: Art spanning 14 centuries: including paintings, sculptures, tapestries and graphics from the early Renaissance through the 20th century; Blue Four Galka Scheyer Collection of German Expressionism; Indian and Southeast Asian sculpture; masterpieces by Cezanne, Degas, Matisse, Monet, Henry Moore, Picasso, Raphael, Rembrandt, Rodin, Rubens, Tiepolo, van Gogh, Zurbaran and others; paintings, graphic work by Rembrandt, Goya and Picasso; photography of Weston, Cunningham and others
Exhibitions: Degas bronze sculptures; Goya prints; Claude Lorrain drawings; Picasso; etchings of Rembrandt; Southeast Asian and Indian Sculpture
Publications: Selected Paintings at the Norton Simon Museum; The Blue Four Galka Scheyer Collection; Degas in Motion
Activities: Private guided tours; museum shop sells books, original art, reproductions, prints, slides and postcards

QUINCY

M PLUMAS COUNTY MUSEUM,* 500 Jackson, PO Box 776, 95971. Tel 916-283-1750. *Cur* Robert G Moon; *Asst Cur* Linda C Brennan
Open winter Mon - Fri 8 AM - 5 PM, summer Mon - Fri 8 AM - 5 PM, Sat 11 AM - 4 PM, cl holidays. No admis fee. Estab 1968 to preserve the past for the enjoyment and edification of the present and future generations. Average Annual Attendance: 13,000. Mem: 300; dues life $100, general per yr $5; meetings held bi-annually
Income: Financed by members and county budget
Purchases: $300
Collections: Antique period furnishing, Indian (Maidu) artifacts, dolls, clothing, mining & logging artifacts, domestic arts, quilts, handwork, paintings, photography, books, documents, jewelry, guns
Publications: Plumas County Museum Newsletter, three times a year
Activities: Lectures open to public; bookstore
L Museum Archives,* 500 Jackson, PO Box 776, 95971. Tel 916-283-1750
Open Jan - May & Sept - Dec 8 AM - 5 PM, June - Aug Mon - Fri 8 AM - 5 PM, Sat 11 AM - 4 PM, cl holidays. No admis fee. Founded 1964
Library Holdings: AV — A-tapes, cassettes, fs, Kodachromes, lantern slides, motion pictures, slides, v-tapes; Other — Clipping files, exhibition catalogs, framed reproductions, manuscripts, memorabilia, original art works, pamphlets, photographs, prints, reproductions
Special Subjects: Logging, Mining, Railroad
Collections: Crystal, china, bottles, musical instrument; Indian jewelry; Maidu Indian Basket Collection

RANCHO PALOS VERDES

O PALOS VERDES ART CENTER,* 5504 W Crestridge Rd, 90274. Tel 213-541-2479. *Exec Dir* Harriet S Miller; *Secy* Joyce Schrello; *Exhib Coordr* Arlene Havens
Open Tues - Fri 10 AM - 4 PM, Sat & Sun 1 - 4 PM, cl Christmas, New Years. No admis fee. Estab 1974, to provide a multifaceted program of classes, exhibits and lectures in the visual arts. Rental-Sales Gallery; also changing exhibits gallery. Mem: 1600; dues $25 - $100
Income: Financed by membership
Collections: Small purchase prize collection
Exhibitions: Eight museum exhibits per year
Publications: Chronicle, bimonthly
Activities: Classes for children; docent training; lect open to public; gallery talks

RED BLUFF

M KELLY-GRIGGS HOUSE MUSEUM,* 311 Washington St (Mailing add: 1248 Jefferson St, CA 96080). Tel 916-527-1129. *Pres* Helen McKenzie Owens; *Pres Emeritus* Fred B Godbolt
Open Thurs - Sun 2 - 5 PM, cl holidays. Donations welcome. Estab 1965, a history museum in a home built in 1880. Mem: Dues associate $10, sustaining $50, charter $100 plus $10 annually, memoriam $100, life $200, patron $500, benefactor $1000
Collections: Pendleton Art Collection spanning over a century of art; Indian artifacts; antique furniture; Victorian costumes
Exhibitions: Permanent and temporary exhibitions
Publications: Brochure; Kellygram (guides' newsletter and schedule)
Activities: Guided tours

REDDING

M REDDING MUSEUM AND ART CENTER, 1911 Rio Dr, PO Box 427, 96099. Tel 916-243-4994. *Pres* Ed Howland; *VPres* Cheri Gandy; *Secy* Dee Ray; *Treas* Cindy Howland; *Dir* Carolyn Bond; *Arts Cur* John Harper
Open summer Tues - Sat 10 AM - 5 PM, Sun Noon - 5 PM, winter Tues - Fri & Sun Noon - 5 PM, Sat 10 AM - 5 PM, cl Mon. Estab 1963 to encourage the understanding of and appreciation for, man's accomplishments throughout history and pre-history. Two galleries present changing monthly contemporary art exhibits. Average Annual Attendance: 50,823. Mem: 947; dues $10-$100; annual meeting second Wed June
Income: Financed by membership, city appropriation, fund raising activities
Collections: Mexican & Central American Pre-Columbian pottery; Native American baskets; Shasta County historical artifacts and documents
Exhibitions: (1982-83) Robert Strin, sculpture; David Kuraoka, ceramics; Howard Ikemoto, monotypes; Bob Nugent, handmake paper & prints; Timothy Hearsum, photography & serigraphs; Student Art Show; Orient & Flume, glass; Catherine Gibson, sculpture; Sylvia Seventy, paper vessels; Theresa May, paintings & quilts; Bob & Mark Hartman, paintings; Art Faire Annual Winners; Northern California Realist Painters; Christmas on 5th Avenue Gift Show
Publications: The Covered Wagon, published by Shasta Historical Society annually; occasional papers: Winter ethnography
Activities: Classes for adults and children; docent training; lect open to public; gallery talks; competitions; Children's Lawn Festival; Art Faire; Native American Heritage Day; Christmas Craft Show; affiliated natural science museum, quarterly art rental
L Museum Research Library, 1911 Rio Dr, PO Box 427, 96001. *Volunteer* Hazel McKim; *Volunteer* Agnes Orr
Open Wed - Thur 10 AM - 2 PM. Open for reference only by appointment

REDLANDS

L LINCOLN MEMORIAL SHRINE, 125 W Vine St, 92373. Tel 714-793-6622. *Cur* Larry E Burgess
Open Tues - Sat 1 - 5 PM, other hours by appointment; cl Sun, Mon & holidays. No admis fee. Estab 1932, operated as a section of the Smiley Public Library. Reference use only
Library Holdings: Vols 4500
Collections: Sculptures, paintings, murals
Activities: Docent training; temporary art exhibitions; lectures; guided tours

O REDLANDS ART ASSOCIATION, 12 E Vine St, 92373. *Pres* George E Riday
Open Tues - Sat 11 AM - 3 PM. No admis fee. Estab 1964 to promote interest in the visual arts and to provide a gallery for artists. Average Annual Attendance: 150. Mem: 275; dues $15; annual meeting in April
Exhibitions: Lyon Gallery exhibitions, 3 times per yr; many media juried shows
Publications: Bulletin, monthly
Activities: Classes for children and adults; lect open to public, 10 vis lectr per yr; tours; competitions with prizes; gallery talks; scholarships; lending collection contains nature artifacts & original prints; museum shop sells original art, reproductions, glass & ceramics

M SAN BERNARDINO COUNTY MUSEUM AND SATELLITES, Fine Arts Institute,* 2024 Orange Tree Lane, 92373. Tel 714-825-4825, 792-1334. *Pres* Bee Walsh; *VPres* Elizabeth Hopkins; *Dir* Dr Gerald Smith; *Asst Dir* Alan Izzo; *Cur Natural History* Gene Cardiff; *Cur Geology* Robert Reynolds; *Cur Archaeology* Ruth D Simpson; *Cur Herpetology* Robert Sanders; *Cur Entomology* Dr Charles Howell; *Cur Entomology & Registrar* Bobbie Miller; *Artist* Michael Cole; *Cur of Education* Ann Quinn
Open Tues - Sat 9 AM - 5 PM, Sun 1 - 5 PM. No admis fee. Estab 1952 for education. Maintains upper and lower dome auditoriums and foyer. Average Annual Attendance: 300,000. Mem: 2100; dues Fine Arts Institute $30, Museum Association $15 and up; annual Fine Arts Institute meeting June; annual Museum Association meeting May
Income: $280,000 (financed by membership)
Purchases: $1000 - $2000
Collections: Collection established through Annual Heritage Awards Exhibit Purchase Awards and Fine Arts Institue Exhibits
Publications: Newsletter, monthly; Quarterly
Activities: Classes for adults and children; docent training; lect open to the public, 150 visiting lectr per yr; competitions with awards; individual paintings and original objects of art lent to various schools and county organizations; lending collection contains books, nature artifacts, original art works, original prints, paintings, photographs, sculpture, slides; originate traveling exhibitions; museum shop selling books, original art, reproductions, prints and slides

M UNIVERSITY OF REDLANDS, Peppers Art Center and Gallery,* 1200 E Colton Ave, 92373. Tel 714-793-2121, Ext 366. *Gallery Dir* Louis Fox; *Dept Chmn* John Nava
Open Mon - Fri 1 - 5 PM, Sun 2 - 5 PM. No admis fee. Estab 1963 to widen students interest in art. Gallery is one large room with celestiary windows and movable panels for display. Average Annual Attendance: 1000-1500
Income: Financed by endowment
Collections: Ethnic Art; graphics; a few famous artists works
Exhibitions: Exhibitions during fall, winter, spring
Publications: Exhibition catalogs and posters
Activities: Lectures open to public, 4-5 vis lectr per year; gallery talks; tours; talent awards

RICHMOND

O RICHMOND ART CENTER, Civic Center, 25th and Barrett Ave, 94804. Tel 415-231-2163. *Coordr Art Ed* Linda Sanvels; *Exec Dir* Albert Stewart; *Admin Asst* Sarah Robinson; *Outreach Coordr* Stan Peterson; *Outreach Coordr* Valerie Otan
Open Mon - Thurs 10 AM - 4:30, Sat & Sun 12 - 4:30 PM, cl Fri & holidays. No admis fee. Estab preliminary steps 1936-44; formed in 1944 to establish artists studios and community center for arts; to offer to the community an opportunity to experience and to improve knowledge and skill in the arts and crafts at the most comprehensive and highest level possible. A large gallery, small gallery and entrance gallery total 4757 sq ft, and a rental gallery covers 1628 ft; an outdoor sculpture court totals 8840 sq ft. Average Annual Attendance: 7000. Mem: 1300; dues $20 up; annual meeting fourth Wed in May
Income: $175,000 (financed by membership, donation, grants, in-kind services from city and Art Center Association)
Collections: †Primarily contemporary art and crafts of Bay area

Exhibitions: Rotating: group theme, solo, invitational and juried annuals
Publications: Catalog for annual shows; newsletter, quarterly; show announcements for exhibitions
Activities: Classes for adults and children; docent training; lect open to the public, 6 visiting lectrs per year; gallery talks; competitions with awards; outreach program serving community; rental gallery, paintings and original objects of art lent to offices, businesses and homes, members of Art Center
L   **Library,** 25th and Barrett Ave, 94804
Open to Art Center members
Library Holdings: Books on paintings and crafts; AV — Slides

RIVERSIDE

M   **RIVERSIDE ART CENTER AND MUSEUM,** 3425 Seventh, 92501. Tel 714-684-7111. *Pres* Susan Davis; *Dir* H Ray Miller; *Cur Exhibits & Sales* Linda Lorenzi; *Exec Secy* Betty Pitts
Open Tues - Fri 10 AM - 5 PM, Sat 10 AM - 4 PM, cl Mon and holidays. No admis fee. Estab 1931 to enlighten and refine the thinking of interested people through the visual arts and crafts. Two galleries for changing exhibitions; permanent collection in lobby areas, members' sales and rental gallery. Average Annual Attendance: 20,000. Mem: 1000; dues life mem $1000 & up, patron $100, supporting $50, family $40, individual $20, senior citizen $10
Income: Financed by membership, grants and donations
Collections: Mixture of media dating from the late 1800s to the present; 50 pieces
Publications: Artifacts, monthly
Activities: Classes for adults and children; docent training; lectures open to public, 5 vis lectr per year; demonstrations; special events; competitions with prizes; gallery talks; tours; scholarships and fels offered; art program presented in public school system; sales shop sells magazines, original art & reproductions
L   **Library,** 3425 Seventh, 92501. Tel 714-684-7111
Open for reference upon request
Library Holdings: Vols 500; Per subs 5; Other — Exhibition catalogs, framed reproductions, pamphlets, photographs, reproductions

UNIVERSITY OF CALIFORNIA
M   **University Art Gallery,** 1208 Humanities, 92521. Tel 714-787-5924, 787-4592. *Dir* Katherine Diage; *Preparator* John Dingler
Open Mon - Fri 10 AM - 3 PM. No admis fee. Estab 1963, gallery presents major temporary exhibitions. Gallery contains 900 sq ft. Average Annual Attendance: 8000
Exhibitions: Master Prints from the Age of Durer; Contemporary Mexican Prints; Harry Callahan; Contemporary Black Art; Ikat: Art of the Ancient Peoples; Transformed Houses; program in art faculty exhibition; Photo-Mechanical Printmaking Competition
Publications: Exhibition catalogs
Activities: Tours; book traveling exhibitons, 3-4 per year
M   **California Museum of Photography,** 92521. Tel 714-787-5924, 787-4592. *Dir* Charles Desmarais; *Cur* Edward W Earle; *Membership Secy* Dorothy Evans; *Public Relations Coordr* Jerilyn Emori; *Registrar & Cur* Dan Meinwald; *Asst Dir Administration* Cathleen Walling
Open Mon - Sat 10 AM - 5 PM, Thurs 10 AM - 7 PM. No admis fee. Estab 1973 to preserve, protect and exhibit photography. Museum has two exhibition galleries which display changing exhibitons related to historical & contemporary photography. Average Annual Attendance: 10,000-15,000. Mem: 800; dues $25
Income: $250,000 (financed by university funds, grants, private donations & memberships)
Collections: Bingham camera and apparatus; Keystone-Mast stereo negatives; photographs of the 19th & 20th centuries
Exhibitions: (1982) Lee Friedlander; Samuel Bourne: Photographs of India; Exploring Society Photographically; Mary Ellen Mark: Falkland Road; (1983) Edward Weston in Mexico, 1923-1926; Philip Brigandi: Keystone Photographer; selections from the Graham Nash Collection; Tenth Anniversary Gifts
Publications: CMP Bulletin, 5 times per yr
Activities: Classes for adults & children; docent training; lectures open to public, 5-10 vis lectr per yr; gallery talks; tours; competitions; individual photographs & original objects or art lent to qualified museums, non-profit galleries & art organizations; lending collection contains 350,000 original art works; book traveling exhibition, 3 per year; originate traveling exhibitions; museum shop sells books, magazines, reproductions; exhibition catalogues & CMP bulletin
L   **Library,** PO Box 5900, 92517. Tel 714-787-3703. *Art Selector* Laine Farley
Open Mon - Thur 8 AM - 12 PM, Fri 8 AM - 6 PM, Sat 10 AM - 6 PM, Sun 1 - 12 PM. Open to faculty, students and staff
Library Holdings: Vols 32,000; Per subs 200; Micro — Cards, fiche, reels; AV — A-tapes, cassettes, fs, motion pictures, rec, slides, v-tapes; Other — Exhibition catalogs, manuscripts, original art works
O   **Friends of the Museum,** Calif Museum of Photography, 92521
Mem: 25

ROHNERT PARK

M   **SONOMA STATE UNIVERSITY ART GALLERY,** 1801 E Cotati Ave, 94928. Tel 707-664-2295. *Gallery Dir* Bob Nugent
Open Mon - Fri 10 AM - 4 PM, Sat & Sun Noon - 4 PM. No admis fee. Estab 1978 to provide exhibitions of quality to the college and northern California community. 2800 sq ft of exhibition space designed to house monumental sculpture and painting
Income: Financed through University and private funds
Collections: Asnis Collection of Prints; Garfield Collection of Oriental Art
Exhibitions: Major Artists from Northern California: Bill Allen, Larry Bell, Fletcher Benton, Joan Brown, de Forest, Diebenkorn, Sam Francis, Bill Geis, Wally Hendrick, Ed Moses, Harold Paris, Sam Richardson, Cornelia Schultz, Mark deSovero, Peter Voulkos, William Wiley; Sculpture '82; Thematic Exhibitions of Regional and National Art
Publications: Bulletins and announcements of exhibitions; exhibition catalog
Activities: Classes for adults; lect open to public, 30 vis lectr per yr; gallery talks; tours; competitions; exten dept

ROSS

O   **MARIN SOCIETY OF ARTISTS INC,** Sir Francis Drake Blvd, PO Box 203, 94957. Tel 415-454-9561. *Pres* Yvonne Beller; *VPres* Kendall King; *Office Mgr* Jo Smith; *Secy* Rae Stone Taub
Open Mon - Fri 11 AM - 4 PM; Sat & Sun 1 - 4 PM. No admis fee. Estab 1926 to foster cooperation among artists and to continually develop public interest in art. Gallery is located in a garden setting. It is approximately 3500 sq ft of well lighted exhibit space. Average Annual Attendance: 75,000. Mem: 600; Qualifications for membership: Previous exhibition in a juried show, and must reside in Bay Area if active; dues $20; meeting May & Sept
Income: Financed by membership, sale and rental of art
Exhibitions: (1984) Eleven exhibitions annually, some are open to non-member artists residing in San Francisco - Bay Area
Activities: Lect open to the public, 2-3 vis lectr per yr; competitions with cash awards; scholarships; sales shop selling original art, original prints, handcrafted jewelry, ceramics and fiberworks

SACRAMENTO

L   **CALIFORNIA STATE UNIVERSITY, SACRAMENTO, LIBRARY,** Humanities Reference and Media Services Center, 2000 Jed Smith Drive, 95819. Tel 916-454-6218. *University Librn* Joyce Ball; *Humanities Reference Librn* Herbert W Drummond Jr; *Assoc Humanities Reference Librn* Clifford P Wood; *Media Servs Librn* Sheila J Marsh; *Slide Cur* Delia Schalansky Krupp
Open Mon - Thurs 7:45 AM - 11 PM, Fri 7:45 AM - 5 PM, Sat 10 AM - 6 PM, Sun 1 - 9 PM (during school year), summer sessions vary during week, cl weekends. Estab 1947. The Art Department maintains a gallery in the Art Bldg and a gallery in the University Union
Income: Financed through the University
Library Holdings: Vols 21,138; Per subs 250; Micro — Cards, fiche, reels; AV — A-tapes, cassettes, fs, slides, v-tapes; Other — Clipping files, exhibition catalogs, pamphlets, reproductions
Special Subjects: Book Arts
Publications: Women Artists: A Selected Bibliography; bibliographic handouts

M   **CROCKER ART MUSEUM,** 216 O St, 95814. Tel 916-446-4677. *Dir* Barbara K Gibbs; *Chief Cur* Roger D Clisby; *Registrar & Asst Cur* Joanna Ownby; *Cur Education* K D Kurutz
Open Wed - Sun 10 AM - 5 PM, Tues 2 - 10 PM, cl Mon. Admis adult $1, children under 12 free. Estab 1873; municipal art museum since 1885; original gallery building designed by Seth Babson completed in 1873; R A Herold Wing opened in 1969. Average Annual Attendance: 100,000. Mem: 1700: annual meeting June
Income: $750,000 (financed by Crocker Art Museum Association and city appropriation)
Purchases: $30,000 - $50,000 per annum
Collections: †American Decorative Art and Costumes 1800-1950; †American painting of the 19th century, with emphasis on California painting 1850-1900; †contemporary California painting, sculpture and crafts; †prints and photographs; †European decorative arts; †European painting 1500 - 1900; †Old Master drawings; †Oriental art
Exhibitions: Welcome to the Candy Store; From Exposition to Exposition: Progressive and Conservative Painting in Northern California, 1915-1939; Large Spaces in Small Places: A Survey of Western Landscape Photograhy, 1850-1980; A Century of Women's Costume from the Collections of the Crocker Art Museum, 1814-1914; Steven Kaltonbach: Portrait of My Father; The Colored Print; Treasures of the Sacramento History Center; Viola Frey Retrospective; Nineteenth Century Photographs from the Rubot Collection; Impressionism in California; Art of the Mamhiks: Renaissance of Islam The Huichol creation of the World; Hungarian Art Noveau; Munich and American realism in the 19th Century; The Santa Show
Publications: Calendar, 11 times per annum: Report; biannually
Activities: Classes for children; docent training; lect open to the public; concerts; gallery talks; tours; annual juried competitions; museum shop selling books, magazines, original art, reproductions and slides
L   **Research Library,** 216 O St, 95814. Tel 916-446-4677. *Librn* Lois Courvoisier
Open to staff, docent, interns and others upon application
Library Holdings: Vols 1400; Per subs 24; Dissertations; Micro — Fiche; Other — Exhibition catalogs

SAINT HELENA

M   **SILVERADO MUSEUM,** 1490 Library Lane, PO Box 409, 94574. Tel 707-963-3757. *Dir* Norman H Strouse; *Cur* Ellen Shaffer
Open Tues - Sun Noon - 4 PM, cl Mon. No admis fee. Estab 1969; the museum is devoted to the life and works of Robert Louis Stevenson, who spent a brief but important time in the area; the object is to acquaint people with his life and works and familiarize them with his stay. The museum has five wall cases and three large standing cases, as well as numerous bookcases. Average Annual Attendance: 9000
Income: Financed by the Vailima Foundation, set up by Mr & Mrs Norman H Strouse
Collections: All material relating to Stevenson & his immediate circle
Exhibitions: A different exhibition devoted to some phase of Stevenson's work is mounted every two months
Activities: Lectures open to public; tours; sales desk sells books and post cards
L   **Reference Library,** 1490 Library Lane, PO Box 409, 94574
For reference only
Library Holdings: Vols 3000; AV — Kodachromes 300, motion pictures
Collections: First editions, variant editions, fine press editions of Robert Louis Stevenson, letters, manuscripts, photographs, sculptures, paintings and memorabilia

SALINAS

M **HARTNELL COLLEGE GALLERY,** * 156 Homestead Ave, 93901. Tel 408-758-8211, Ext 261 . *Dir* Gary T Smith
Open Mon - Thurs 10 AM - 1 PM and 6 - 9 PM, cl Fri, Sat & Sun. No admis fee. Estab 1959 to bring to students and the community the highest quality in contemporary and historical works of all media. Main gallery is 40 by 60 ft, south gallery is 15 by 30 ft, brick flooring. Average Annual Attendance: 7500
Collections: Approx 45 works on paper from the San Francisco Bay Area WPA
Exhibitions: Michael Arntz; Bolivian Textiles from the Collection of Jonathan S Hill; Children's Art; Classical Narratives in Master Drawings; Helen Escobedo; Faculty Show; Historical and Contemporary Objects; Alex Katz: Cutouts; Barry Le Va: Ten Years of Drawings; Ralph Eugene Meatyard; Orozco and Rivera: Prints and Drawings; Retablos; Selection; Student Show; Marjorie Post Woolcott
Publications: Three small catalogs per yr
Activities: Classes for adults; dramatic programs; gallery management training; individual paintings lent to qualifying educational institutions; lending collection contains original art works; individual and original objects of art lent to professional galleries or museums; book traveling exhibitions; traveling exhibitions organized and circulated

SAN BERNARDINO

M **CALIFORNIA STATE COLLEGE SAN BERNARDINO,** College Art Galleries,* 5500 State College Parkway, 92407. Tel 714-887-7459, 887-7450. *Chmn Art Dept* Julius Kaplan; *Dir* Don Woodford
Open Mon - Fri 9 AM - Noon, 1 - 3 PM, Sat 1 - 4 PM. No admis fee. Estab 1972 for the purpose of providing high quality exhibitions on varied subjects suitable for both campus and community. Gallery 2 opened 1978 as an exhibit area for senior shows and student work. Average Annual Attendance: 5500
Income: Financed by membership, city and state appropriations
Collections: Small collection of prints
Publications: Catalogs; Personas de los Tumbas - West Mexican tomb sculpture
Activities: Classes for adults; lect open to the public, 1-3 visiting lectrs per year; gallery talks; competitions

O **SAN BERNARDINO ART ASSOCIATION, INC,** 1640 E Highland Ave, 92404. *Pres* Mrs K G Stone; *First VPres* Majorie Mills; *Second VPres* Mrs P S Monroe; *Secy* Mrs Glen Stirnaman; *Corresp Secy* Mrs John Lawson
Open Tue - Sat 11 AM - 3 PM. No admis fee. Estab 1934 as a non-profit organization to generate interest in art for all ages. Open to the public; maintains gallery. Mem: 100; dues $20; monthly meetings
Publications: Newsletter
Activities: Lectures open to public; gallery talks; competitions with awards; scholarships; individual paintings lent; sales shop sells original art, books, pottery & glassware

SAN DIEGO

O **BALBOA ART CONSERVATION CENTER,** Balboa Park, 1649 El Prado, PO Box 3755, 92103. Tel 619-236-9702. *Pres* Barbara Walbridge; *VPres* Susan Kockritz; *Secy* Stephen Brezzo; *Exec Dir* Gary Wade Alden; *Chief Conservator* Betty Engel; *Conservator* Elizabeth Court; *Conservator* Alfredo Antognini; *Conservator* Marie Fox; *Conservator* Janet E Ruggles
Open Mon - Fri 9 AM - 4:30 PM. No admis fee. Estab 1975 for research and education in art conservation; services in exams, treatment and consultation in art conservation. One exhibition room with viewing window into treatment laboratory and changing exhibitions about art conservation history and techniques. Mem: 11; non-profit institutions are members, their members may contract for servs; annual meeting first Thurs in May
Income: $250,000 (financed by services performed)
Collections: †Illustrative photographs, †memorabilia, tools, equipment of profession; paintings for experimental & didactic purposes
Publications: BACC Newsletter, quarterly
Activities: Lectures open to public & some for members only; gallery talks; tours
L **Reference Library,** Balboa Park, PO Box 3755, 92103
Library Holdings: Vols 700; Per subs 35; Micro — Reels; AV — Cassettes, slides; Other — Clipping files, exhibition catalogs, memorabilia, pamphlets, photographs
Special Subjects: Art Conservation, Scientific Analysis of Materials

M **SAN DIEGO MARITIME MUSEUM,** 1306 N Harbor Dr, 92101. Tel 619-234-9153. *Pres* John E Hamrick; *Exec Dir* Edward H C Fredericks
Open daily 9 AM - 8 PM. Admis family $7, adults $3.50, service personnel, children 13-17 & sr citizens $2.50, children under 12 $1, in groups $.25, discount to adult groups. Estab 1948 for preservation & education of San Diego related maritime history. A maritime museum in a fleet of three ships: Star of India (1863); Berkeley (1898 ferryboat); and Medea (1904 steam yacht). Average Annual Attendance: 180,000. Mem: 1200; dues life $500, development $100, supporting $50, family $25, regular $20, student $5; annual meeting in Nov
Collections: Antiques; maritime art; maritime artifacts
Exhibitions: Temporary exhibitions
Publications: Mains'l Haul, quarterly newsletter; Star of India, They Came by Sea; Transpac 1900-1979
Activities: Educ dept; docent training; lectures for members & guests, 4 vis lectr per yr; tours; special programs; museum shop sells books, magazines, reproductions, prints, slides & related maritime items

M **SAN DIEGO MUSEUM OF ART,** Balboa Park, PO Box 2107, 92112. Tel 714-232-7931. *Dir* Steven L Brezzo; *Dep Dir* Jane G Rice; *Cur Exhib* Darcie Fohrman; *Cur Paintings* Martin E Peterson; *Cur Grant* Holcomb; *Cur Education* Carol Heepke; *Development Officer* Kerry Buckley; *Special Events Coordr* Sharon Hemus; *Public Information Officer* Tim Larrick
Open Tues - Sun 10 AM - 5 PM; cl Mon. Admis general public $3, children 6-12 $.50. Estab 1925. Gallery built in 1926 by a generous patron in a Spanish Plateresque design; the West wing was added in 1966 and the East wing in 1974. Average Annual Attendance: 417,000. Mem: 6362; dues Presidents Circle $1000, sponsoring friend $500, friend of museum $100, family $35, individual $30, senior citizens $20, student $15
Income: $1,800,000 (financed by endowment, membership, city and county appropriations)
Purchases: $207,917
Collections: Italian Renaissance and Baroque Paintings; 19th and 20th Century American and European Sculpture and Paintings; Oriental Arts - sculpture, paintings, ceramics, decorative arts, American furniture and glass, English and Georgian silver; Spanish Baroque, Flemish, Dutch and English Schools; extensive print collection containing American, European and Oriental schools
Exhibitions: The Golden Treasures of Peru; Lautrec, Baldwin M Baldwin Foundation Collection; The Cowboy; Musical Manuscripts; Turkish Treasures from Edwin Binney III; 5000 Years of Art From The Metropolitan Museum of Art; The Art of Motion Picture Posters; The Art of the Mamluks; Museum of Modern Art Collection, Modern Masters: 20th Century Paintings; Dale Chihuly: The Art of Glass; Leonardo's Return to Vinci; Corcoran Gallery Collection, Of Time and Place: American Art; Between Continents—Between Seas: Precolumbian Art of Costa Rica; The Art of Maurice Sendak; Andy Warhol: Portraits; The Savoy
Publications: Annual Report; catalogs of collections; exhibition catalogs; membership calendar, monthly; gallery guide
Activities: Classes for adults and children; docent training; lectr open to the public; gallery talks; tours; competitions; traveling exhibitions organized and circulated; sales shops selling books, reproductions, prints, cards, jewelry and ceramics
L **Art Reference Library,** Balboa Park, PO Box 2107, 92112. Tel 714-232-7931. *Librn* Nancy Andrews
Open Tues - Fri 10 AM - 3 PM. Estab 1926 for curatorial research and members reference. For reference only
Library Holdings: Vols 10,000; Per subs 35; AV — Slides; Other — Clipping files, exhibition catalogs, pamphlets
Special Subjects: Asian Art, Italian Renaissance, Spanish Baroque
Collections: Bibliography of artists in exhibition catalogues
Activities: Reading Club

L **SAN DIEGO PUBLIC LIBRARY,** Art & Music Section, 820 E St, 92101. Tel 619-236-5810. *Supv Librn* Barbara A Tuthill; *Picture Specialist* Linda Griffin; *Librn* Evelyn Kooperman; *Librn* Christina Clifford
Open Mon - Thurs 10AM - 9 PM, Fri & Sat 9:30 AM - 5:30 PM. Estab 1954 to provide information and reference service in the fine arts; an expanding collection of reference and circulating books available. Corridor Gallery exhibits work by local artists and art groups each month
Income: Financed by city and state appropriation
Purchases: $32,000
Library Holdings: Vols 75,000; postcards; AV — Rec 23,000; Other — Clipping files, exhibition catalogs
Collections: Former libraries of William Templeton Johnson, architect, and Donal Hord, sculptor; emphasis is on Spanish, Mediterranean, Italian and French Renaissance architecture and Oriental art, sculpture and ceramics; books on the theatre including biographies of famous actors and actresses as well as histories of the American, London and European stages, gift of Elwyn B Gould, local theatre devotee
Activities: Lect open to public; concerts; opera previews

M **SAN DIEGO STATE UNIVERSITY,** Art Gallery, 5402 College Ave, 92182. Tel 714-265-6511. *Dir* Fredrick Orth; *Dir* Dennis Komac
Open Wed - Sun noon - 4 PM. No admis fee. Estab 1977 to provide exhibitions of importance for the students, faculty and public of the San Diego environment; for study and appreciation of art and enrichment of the University. Average Annual Attendance: 35,000
Income: Supported by student fees, SDSU Art Council & grants
Collections: Crafts collection; contemporary print collection; graduate student sculpture and painting
Exhibitions: Contemporary national & international artists
Activities: Lect open to the public; original art objects lent to University
L **Love Library and Art Department Slide Library,** San Diego State University, 5402 College Ave, 92182. *Art Librn* Lee Sandelin; *Slide Cur* Lilla Sweatt
Love Library open Mon - Thurs 7:30 AM - 11 PM, Fri 7:30 AM - 5 PM, Sat 10 AM - 5 PM, Sun Noon - 10 PM; Slide Library open Mon - Fri 8 AM - 4:30 PM. Estab 1957 to aid and facilitate the faculty in teaching art and art history as well as aiding students in class reports
Library Holdings: Micro — Cards, fiche, prints, reels; AV — Cassettes, Kodachromes, slides 120,000; Other — Clipping files, exhibition catalogs, framed reproductions, manuscripts, memorabilia, pamphlets, reproductions
Exhibitions: Special Art collections, student and women's art shows

M **TIMKEN ART GALLERY,** * 1500 El Prado, 92101. Tel 714-239-5548. *Pres Bd* A J Sutherland; *VPres* Clara Weitzenhoffer; *Dir* Nancy Ames Petersen
Open Tues - Sat 10 AM - 4:30 PM, Sun 1:30 - 4:30 PM, cl Mon. No admis fee. Estab to display and preserve Old Master's paintings. Six galleries. Average Annual Attendance: 75,000
Income: Financed by endowment
Collections: †Dutch and Flemish, †French, †Spanish and American paintings; Russian icons; all paintings owned by Putnam Collection are on permanent display; Pissarro, Bords de l'oise 'a Pontoise - Il Guercino Return of the Prodigal Son
Publications: Pamphlets which are distributed free to visitors; catalog
Activities: Tours Tues - Thurs 11 AM - 1 PM

M **UNIVERSITY OF SAN DIEGO,** Founders' Gallery, Alcala Park, 92110. Tel 714-291-6480. *Dir* Therese T Whitcomb
Open Mon - Fri Noon - 5 PM. Estab 1971 to enrich the goals of the art department and university by providing excellent in-house exhibitions of all eras, forms and media, and to share them with the community. Gallery is an architecturally outstanding facility with foyer, display area and patio, parking in

central campus. Average Annual Attendance: 1500
Income: Financed by art department & private endowment
Collections: †19th & 20th century American folk sculpture; 17th, 18th & 19th century French tapestries and furniture; South Asian textiles and costumes of 19th and 20th centuries; Tibetan and Indian looms, Ghandi spinning wheels, bronze sculpture, watercolors
Exhibitions: Seven shows each year
Publications: The Impressionist as Printmaker; Child Hassam 1859-1935; Arbal de la Vida, The Ceramic Art of Metepec
Activities: Educ dept; seminars in art history; lectures open to the public, 4 vis lectr per yr; concerts; gallery talks; tours; awards; scholarships offered; individual paintings and original objects of art lent; lending collection contains paintings & sculpture; originate traveling exhibitions

SAN FRANCISCO

O **ACADEMY OF THE MUSEUM OF CONCEPTUAL ART,** 75 Third St, 94103. Tel 415-495-3193. *Dir* Tom Marioni; *Preparator* Tony Labot; *Video Cur* Burt Arnowitz
Open Wed PM or for events. Estab 1970 for actions and situational art, preservation of old site, and social activities for artists. Gallery maintained and covers 10,000 sq ft on two floors. Average Annual Attendance: 50. Mem: 2000; dues $25 & up
Income: Financed by endowment
Exhibitions: Vito Acconci; Robert Barry; Bar Room Video; Chris Burden; Lowell Darling; Howard Fried; Paul Kos; Masashi Matsumoto; Restoration of Back Wall
Publications: Vision, annually
Activities: Dramatic programs; gallery talks; original objects of art lent

L **Library,** 75 Third St, 94103
For reference only
Library Holdings: Original documents; Micro — Reels; AV — A-tapes, cassettes, fs, Kodachromes, motion pictures, rec, slides, v-tapes; Other — Exhibition catalogs, original art works, pamphlets, photographs, prints, sculpture

O **AFRICAN AMERICAN HISTORICAL AND CULTURAL SOCIETY,** Fort Mason Ctr, Bldg C-165, 94123. Tel 415-441-0640. *Pres* Toye Moses; *VPres* Ken Simmons; *Secy* Margaret Woody; *Exec Dir* Monica Scott; *Admin Asst* Hilda Robinson
Open Tues - Sat Noon - 5 PM. Estab 1955 as an archival & presentation institution of African American thought & culture
Income: $100,000 (financed by membership & donations)
Collections: African artifacts, sculpture; Haitian art; Sargent Johnson
Publications: Ascension, biennial; Praisesinger, newsletter
Activities: Classes for children; lectures open to public, 20 vis lectr per yr; gallery talks; tours; competitions with awards; individual paintings & original objects of art lent to museums; book traveling exhibitions; sales shop sells books, original art, reproductions, prints, t-shirts & African art

L **Library,** 94123
Library Holdings: Vols 3000; Oral history
Collections: 1000 periodicals; African-American newspapers

THE ART MUSEUM ASSOCIATION OF AMERICA (Formerly Western Association of Art Museums)
For further information, see National and Regional Organizations

M **ASIAN ART MUSEUM OF SAN FRANCISCO,** Avery Brundage Collection, Golden Gate Park, 94118. Tel 415-558-2993. *Dir & Chief Cur* Rene-Yvon Lefebvre d'Argence; *Sr Cur* Clarence F Shangraw; *Cur Chinese Art* Patricia Berger; *Cur Indian Art* Terese Tse Bartholomew; *Cur Japanese Art* Yoshiko Kakudo; *Cur Educ* Cecelia Levin
Open daily 10 AM - 5 PM, cl Christmas. Adult(18-64) $2, youth(5-17) and senior citizen $.50, children under 5 free; recognized educational group free; first Wednesday of each month free. Founded in 1969 by the City and County of San Francisco. Branch Display: Japan Center Extension, Japan Cultural and Trade Center, Webster Street Bridge
Income: Financed by city and county appropriation and the Asian Art Museum Foundation
Collections: Nearly 10,000 objects of Asian art, including the Avery Brundage Collection and the Roy C Leventritt Collection
Exhibitions: (1983) Treasures from the Shanghai Museum: 6000 Years of Chinese Art
Publications: Handbooks and catalogs on museum collections; exhibition catalogs
Activities: Docent training; intern prog for graduate students; lectures open to public, 12 visiting lectr per year; gallery talks; tours; films; concerts; scholarships; inter-museum loan; originate traveling exhibitions; museum bookshop sells books, magazines, prints and slides

L **Library,** Golden Gate Park, 94118. Tel 415-558-2993. *Librn* Fred A Cline Jr
Open Mon - Fri 1 - 4:45 PM. Estab 1967. For reference only
Income: Financed by membership, city appropriation and private gifts
Library Holdings: Vols 15,000; Per subs 150; Micro — Fiche, prints, reels; AV — A-tapes, cassettes, Kodachromes, lantern slides, motion pictures, rec, slides; Other — Clipping files, exhibition catalogs, pamphlets, photographs, prints, reproductions
Special Subjects: Oriental Art
Collections: Chinese painting collection; Khmer Art Collection

C **BANK OF AMERICA,** Concourse Gallery,* 241 California St, Dept 3021 Bank of America, 94103. Tel 415-622-1265, 622-6611. *Cur* Bonnie Earls-Solari
Open Plaza Gallery Mon - Fri 8 AM - 5:30 PM, Concourse Gallery Mon - Fri 8 AM - Midnight, SFMO Gallery Mon - Fri 8 AM - 7 PM. Estab 1970 to operate as a public service by Bank America Corporation for the downtown, financial district audience and art community. Average Annual Attendance: 520,000
Collections: Collection contains contemporary and historical art from international sources
Exhibitions: Bruce Johnson, outdoor sculpture
Activities: Individual paintings and original objects of art lent to bonafide exhibitions and exhibiting bodies which can protect and properly install the art

O **CALIFORNIA HISTORICAL SOCIETY,** Whittier Mansion, 2090 Jackson St, 94109. Tel 415-567-1848. *Pres* Louis H Heilbron; *VPres* Carol Terry; *Treas* George N Hale Jr; *Executive Dir* J S Holliday; *Assoc Dir* Pamela L Seager; *Dir Southern Calif* Louise Braunschweiger; *Cur* Beverly Denenberg; *Membership* Lorin Starr; *Programs Dir* Nancy Jones
Estab in 1871 (reorganized in 1922), to collect, preserve and disseminate information pertaining to history of California and the West. Organization designated California's state historical society in 1979
Income: Financed by endowment, membership and funding from private, corporate and public agencies
Collections: Fine arts include California lithography and other graphics; oils; watercolors; drawings; furniture and artifacts to 1915; research materials both original and published on California and Western artists
Exhibitions: National traveling photographic exhibitions; The American Farm; changing thematic exhibits relating to California history in the galleries of the Whittier Mansion from the society's collection. Permanent exhibition in San Francisco from the Society's collections
Publications: California History, quarterly magazine; California Historical Courier (newspaper), six times per yr; The Kemble Occasional, tri-annual
Activities: Classes for adults; docent training; programs; lectures, tours and films throughout the state; lectures open to the public; concerts; gallery talks; tours; awards given for participation in the field of California history; traveling exhibitions organized and circulated; bookshop

L **History Center Library,** 6300 Wilshire Blvd, 90048. Tel 213-651-5655
Open (archive) Tues - Thur 1 - 4 PM, (exhibit gallery) Mon & Fri 9 AM - 5 PM. Estab 1978 to collect, preserve and make available materials related to the history of California, focusing specifically on southern California
Income: Financed by endowment, members and grants
Library Holdings: Vols 2000; Micro — Fiche; Other — Clipping files, memorabilia, pamphlets, photographs
Collections: Historical photographs from the TICOR Collection which includes approximately 20,000 photographs by C C Pierce: Downtown Los Angeles; George Wharton James: Indians; M Rieder: Santa Barbara; Edward Vischer: Missions; the primary thrust of the collection is Los Angeles and surrounding communities, 1865-1930
Exhibitions: Man Made Los Angeles: An Inprobable Urban History
Publications: California History, quarterly magazine, The Courier, newspaper published 4 times a year, Calendar, monthly

M **El Molino Viejo,** 1120 Old Mill Rd, 91108. Tel 213-449-5450
Open Tues - Sun 1 - 4 PM, cl holidays. Historic adobe grist mill with changing exhibit room. Mem: Dues centennial $1000, benefactor $500, associate $250, patron $150, contributing $75, sustaining $40, active $25, student $15
Income: Financed by membership dues and contributions
Publications: California History, quarterly
Activities: Meetings & tours

L **Schubert Hall Library,** 2099 Pacific Ave, 94109. Tel 415-567-1848. *Dir* Bruce L Johnson; *Manuscripts* Waverly B Lowell; *Genealogy* Gerald D Wright; *Photography* Douglas M Haller; *Photography* Stephen J Fletcher; *Ref Librn* Jocelyn Moss; *Ref Librn* Glenn E Humphreys; *Ref Librn* Judy Sheldon; *Ref Librn* Joy Berry
Open Wed - Sat, 10 AM - 4 PM. Estab 1922 to collect books, manuscripts, photographs, ephemera, maps and posters pertaining to California and Western history. For in house reference and research only
Library Holdings: Vols 45,500; Per subs 150; original documents; 3-dimensional artifacts; Micro — Fiche, reels; AV — A-tapes, cassettes, Kodachromes, lantern slides, motion pictures, slides; Other — Clipping files, framed reproductions, manuscripts, memorabilia, original art works, pamphlets, photographs 300,000, prints, reproductions
Special Subjects: Early California imprints; county and municipal histories; early voyages of exploration, Genealogy; Gold Rush; Printing; Publishing.
Collections: C Templeton Crocker Collections; Florence Keen Collection of Western Literature; Genealogy Collection of the California Historical Society; Kemble Collection of Western Printing and Publishing
Exhibitions: The American Farm; Executive Order 9006
Publications: The Kemble Occasional, tri-annual newsletter

O **CHINESE CULTURE FOUNDATION,** Chinese Culture Center Gallery, 750 Kearny St, 3rd Floor, 94108. Tel 415-986-1822. *Pres* Rolland Lowe; *Exec VPres* Emory Lee; *Executive Dir* Lucy Lim; *Secy* William Gong; *Admin* Vivian Chiang
Open Tues - Sat 10 AM - 4 PM, cl holidays. No admis fee. Estab 1965 to promote the understanding and appreciation of Chinese and Chinese-American culture in the United States. Traditional and contemporary paintings and sculpture by Chinese and Chinese-American artists, photographs and artifacts illustrating Chinese-American history, and major international and cultural exchanges from China make the center a local and national focus of Chinese artistic activities. Mem: 1500
Income: Financed by membership, city appropriation and grants
Exhibitions: Shopping in China: The Artisan Community at Canton, 1825-1830; Chinese Kites: Flights of Fancy; Chinese Women of America: 1848-1982; Contemporary Chinese Painting: An Exhibition from the People's Republic of China; The Chinese of America: 1785-1980; Chinese American Artists
Activities: Classes for adults and children; dramatic programs; docent training; lect open to the public; concerts; gallery talks; tours; film programs; museum shop selling books, original art, reproductions, prints, jewelry, pottery, jade, material and papercuts

C **CROCKER NATIONAL BANK,*** 1 Montgomery St (Mailing add: 111 Sutter St, Suite 1300, CA 94104). Tel 415-477-5395. *Art Coordr* Felicia Cansino
Collection is centered around prominent California artists as well as work that depicts the history of California. Collection displayed in various corporate administrative offices and branches in California
Collections: Contemporary graphics; oils; Oriental screens

C **EMBARCADERO CENTER INC,** Four Embarcadero Center, Suite 2600, 94111. Tel 415-772-0585, 772-0500. *Executive Dir* Jim Bronkema
Open to public at all hours. No admis fee. Estab 1971, modern art has been a key element in the planning and development of the Embarcadero Center

complex; evidence of a desire to provide beauty on a smaller scale amid the harmony of its massive structures; to enhance the total environment, and provide a variety of dramatic views for pedestrians as they circulate through the complex. Collection displayed throughout the Center complex; Center supports San Francisco DeYoung Museum, Fine Arts Museum Downtown Center, American Conservatory Theatre, San Francisco Symphony, San Francisco Center for the Performing Arts, and others
Collections: Willi Gutmann, Two Columns with Wedge; Francoise Grossen; Michael Gibbers, Steel Sculptures; Nicholas Schoffer, Chronos XIV; Lia Cook, Space Continuum Two; Olga de Amaral, Citurs Wall; Anne Van Kleeck, Blocks, Stacks; Louise Nevelson, Sky Tree; Barbara Shawcroft, Yellow Leggs; Robert Russin, Chthonodynamis; Jean Dubuffet, La Chiffonniere; Sheila Hicks, Cristobal's Trapeze & Itaka's Cascade; John Portman Jr, The Tulip; Elbert Weinberg, Mistral; Charles O Perry, Eclipse; Adolph Gottlieb, Burst; Francoise Grossen; Olga de Amaral, Hojarasca en mil Rojos; Jagoda Buic, Souvenir en Blue; Josef Grau Garriga, Lapell D'un Poble; Candace Crockett, Revival; Armand Vaillancourt, 101 precast aggregate concrete boxes that allow visitors to walk over, under & through its waterfalls

O **EXPLORATORIUM,** 3601 Lyon St, 94123. Tel 415-563-7337. *Dir* Frank Oppenheimer; *Assoc Dir* Rob Semper; *Executive Assoc Dir* Virginia Rubin; *Assoc Dir Exhibit Design* Bob Miller; *Biology Lab* Charles Carlsen; *Artist Coordr* Peter Richards; *Professional Internship Prog* Sally Duensing
Open winter Wed - Fri 1 - 5 PM, Wed evening 7 - 9 PM, Sat & Sun 11 AM - 5 PM, summer Wed - Sun 11 AM - 5 PM, Wed evening 7 - 9 PM. Admis adult $3, sr citizen $1.50, under 18 free. Estab 1969 to provide exhibits and art works centering around the theme of perception, which are designed to be manipulated and appreciated at a variety of levels by both children and adults. Average Annual Attendance: 500,000. Mem: 1500; dues $30
Income: Financed by city and state appropriation, private foundations and corporation contributions
Publications: The Exploratorium Magazine, monthly; exhibition catalogs
Activities: Classes for adults, children and teachers; lect open to the public; concerts; tours; book traveling exhibitions, 3-4 per year; originate traveling exhibitions; museum shop selling books, magazines, reproductions, prints, slides and science related material

M **FINE ARTS MUSEUMS OF SAN FRANCISCO,** M H de Young Memorial Museum and California Palace of the Legion of Honor, Lincoln Park, 94121. Tel 415-221-4811. *Pres* Leonard E Kingsley; *Secy* Delores Malone; *Dir* Ian M White; *Chief Administrative Officer* F Whitney Hall; *Deputy Dir Admin* Stephen E Dykes; *Deputy Dir Education & Exhibition* Thomas K Seligman; *Deputy Dir Operations* Gus Teller; *Cur Painting* Charles S Moffett; *Cur European Decorative Arts & Sculpture* Laura Calmins; *American Decorative Arts* Donald L Stover; *Cur Prints & Drawings* Robert F Johnson; *Cur African Oceania & the Americas* Kathleen Berrin; *Mgr of Exhibitions* Debra Pughe; *Cur Interpretation* Renee Dreyfus; *Asst to Dir* Martha Williams; *Cur Textiles* Anna Bennet; *Chief Registrar* Virginia Mann; *Public Information Coordr* Gail C Docktor; *Public Information Officer* Charles Long; *Conservator Paper* Robert Futernick; *Conservator Painting* Teri Oikawa-Picante; *Conservator Furniture* Gene Munsch; *Ednah Root Cur of American Art* Margaretta Lovell; *Conservator Textiles* Birgitta Anderton; *Dir Art School* James Stevenson
Open Wed - Sun 10 AM - 5 PM. Admis adults $2, youth & sr citizen $.50, children under 5 free. Estab 1895 to provide museums of historic art from ancient Egypt to the 20th century. Two separate buildings are maintained, one in the Golden Gate Park (de Young Museum) with 65 galleries, and the other in Lincoln Park (California Palace of the Legion of Honor) with 22 galleries. Average Annual Attendance: 800,000. Mem: 55,000; dues patron $1000, sponsor $500, donor $250, supporting $100, sustaining $60, participating $35, individual $25, senior dual $20, senior single $15
Income: $6,000,000 (financed by endowment, membership, city appropriations)
Purchases: St John the Baptist Preaching, by Mattia Preti, Italian 1613-1699
Collections: American painting and decorative arts; ancient Egypt, Greece and Rome; Europe from the middle ages; graphic arts of all schools and eras; primitive arts of Africa, Oceania and the Americas
Exhibitions: The Art of Louis Comfort Tiffany; The Search For Alexander; The Vatican Collections: The Papacy & Art; Treasures of Early Irish Art; Treasure of Tutankhamun
Publications: Triptych, bi-monthly magazine; exhibition and collection catalogues
Activities: Classes for adults and children; dramatic programs; docent training; lect open to the public; concerts; gallery talks; tours; artmobile; individual paintings and original art objects are lent to other museums; book traveling exhibitions; originate traveling exhibitions to other museums; museum shop sells books, magazines, reproductions, prints, and slides

L **Library,*** Golden Gate Park, 94118. Tel 415-558-2887. *Librn* Jane Gray Nelson
Estab 1955 to serve museum staff in research on collections, conservation, acquisition, interpretations. Graphic arts are housed in the Achenbach Foundation Library in the California Palace of the Legion of Honor
Income: Financed by membership and city appropriation
Library Holdings: Vols 30,000; Per subs 105; AV — Slides
Special Subjects: American Indian Art, African, American, French and Oceanic art
Collections: Achenbach Foundation for Graphic Arts (prints and drawings)

O **The Museum Society,*** c/o de Young Museum, Golden Gate Park, 94118. Tel 415-752-2800. *Chmn* Gail Merriam; *2nd VChmn* Sylvia Hunter; *Secy* Jane Otto; *Treas* William A Stimson II; *General Mgr* Nativity D'Souza; *Executive Secy* Alice S Fischer; *Membership Coordr* Ann Knauber; *Mgr de Young Bookshop* Leroy Dutro; *Mgr Legion Bookshop* Lewis Thomas
Open Wed - Sun 10 AM - 5 PM. Admis adults $1.50, juniors 5-17 and senior citizens $.50, children under 5 free. Estab 1971 as a membership organization for Fine Arts Museums of San Francisco and the Asian Art Museum of San Francisco. Mem: 45,000; dues $10 to $1000; annual meeting in May
Income: $2,770,000 (financed by membership and bookshop revenues)
Publications: Triptuch, bimonthly magazine
Activities: Museum shop sells books, reproductions, prints and slides

M **GALERIA DE LA RAZA,** Studio 24, 2851 & 2857 24th St, 94110. Tel 415-826-8009. *Co-Dir* Ralph Maradiaga; *Co-Dir* Rene Yanez; *Asst Cur* Salvador Garcia; *Cur & Education Coordinator* Maria V Pinedo
Open Tues - Sat 1 - 6 PM, Galeria; Mon - Sat Noon - 6 PM, Studio 24. Estab 1969 as a community gallery and museum to exhibit works by Chicano-Latino artists, contemporary as well as cultural folk art. Average Annual Attendance: 35,000
Income: Financed by NEA, California Arts Council, private foundations and earned income from sales in studio
Exhibitions: Changing monthly with one traveling per year
Publications: Exhibition catalogs, small publications, yearly calendar, children's coloring book and postcards
Activities: Galeria tours, some lectures; gift shop sells books, prints, Mexican folk art & other culture materials

L **Chicano-Latino Arts Resource Library,** 2857 24th St, 94110. *Dir* Maria V Pinedo
Open Mon - Fri Noon - 6 PM. Estab 1978 as a reference and archive of Chicano and Latino arts
Income: $1000
Purchases: $500
Library Holdings: Vols 100; Per subs 5; AV — Slides; Other — Clipping files, exhibition catalogs, memorabilia, original art works, pamphlets, photographs, prints, reproductions
Special Subjects: El Dia de Los Muertas artifacts and resources
Collections: Chicano and Latino murals; Chicano Latino Youth; car clubs

O **LA MAMELLE INC,** 70 12th St, Box 3123 Rincon, 94119. Tel 415-431-7524. *Pres* Carl E Loeffler
Estab 1975 to support network for contemporary art. Gallery houses new contemporary art
Income: Financed by endowment, membership and state appropriation
Collections: Artists books; Marginal works; Video art
Exhibitions: Davi-Det-Hompson; Ecart; Photography and Language; Recorded Works; Rubber Stamp Art; Endre Tot; West Coast Conceptual Photographers; Women in the Printing Arts; All Xerox
Publications: Art Com, quarterly; Performance Anthology: Source book for a decade of California performance art; Videozine; Audiozine; Correspondence Art: Source Book for the Network of International Postal Art Activity
Activities: Lect open to public; concerts; gallery talks; original objects of art lent; lending collection contains video tapes; traveling exhibitions organized and circulated; sales shop sells books, magazines, original art

L **Contemporary Art Archives,** 70 12th St, Box 3123 Rincon, 94119
For reference only

M **MEXICAN MUSEUM,** Fort Mason Center, Bldg D, Laguna & Marina Blvd, 94123. Tel 415-441-0404. *Founder & Exec Dir* Peter Rodriquez; *Adminr* Terry Gerald; *Education Dir* Nora Wagner; *Education Coordr* Bea Carrillo Hocker; *Cur of Collections* Gloria Jaramillo
Open Wed - Sun Noon - 5 PM. No admis fee, donation adult $1, student $.50. Estab 1975 to foster the exhibition, conservation and dissemination of Mexican and Mexican American art and culture for all people. Average Annual Attendance: 50,000. Mem: 650; dues $20
Income: Financed by membership, city and state appropriation, federal grants and corporate support
Collections: Pre-Hispanic; Colonial; Folk; Mexican Fine Arts; Mexican American Fine Arts
Exhibitions: (1983) Rufino Tangyo
Publications: Catalog of permanent collection; newsletter, quarterly
Activities: Education dept; docent training; lectures open to public, 6 vis lectr per yr; gallery talks; tours; exten dept serves San Francisco Bay area; lending collection contains slides and educational kits; book traveling exhibitions; museum shop sells books, original art, reproductions, prints & folk art

M **MUSEO ITALO AMERICANO,*** 678 Green St, 94133. Tel 415-398-2660. *Chmn* Virgil D Dardi; *Pres* Richard P Figone; *1st VPres* James A Scatena; *Secy* Dorothy Casper; *Exec Dir* Giuliana Nardelli Haight; *Dir of Educ* Paola Bagnatori
Open Wed - Sun Noon - 5 PM. No admis fee. Estab 1978 to research, preserve and display works of Italian and Italian-American artists and to foster educational programs for the appreciation of Italian and Italian art, history and culture. The Museo is located on the third floor of Casa Fugazi, a building that has played an active role in San Francisco's Italian-American community. Floorspace is approximately 3600 square feet. Average Annual Attendance: 8000 - 10,000. Mem: 600; annual dues $25, $50 and up
Income: Financed by membership and city appropriation
Collections: †Collection consists of work done by Italian-American artists from mid-19th century and objects from ancient Rome
Exhibitions: Graphic Arts from Italy; Joe DiStefano (paintings & sculpture); Second Italian-American Women Artists Show; John Mancini (painting); Victor Bagno (painting); Mary and Anthony de Bone (mixed media); Italian-American Artists in California 1850-1925; An Exhibit of Italian-American Art for the Museo's Future Permanent Collection; New Paintings by John Sacarro; Paolo Portoghesi's Architectural Studies for the Citta Vallo di Diano Project; Young Emerging Italian-American painters, sculptors and photographers
Publications: Calendar of Events, quarterly
Activities: Classes for adults and children; Italian language classes; lectures open to public, 5 vis lectr per year; concerts; gallery talks; tours; book traveling exhibitions

L **Library,*** 94133. *Admin Asst* Wendy H King
Estab 1981 to serve as a resource center of Italian and Italian-American materials
Library Holdings: Vols 50; Per subs 2

M **NATIONAL MARITIME MUSEUM,*** Golden Gate National Recreation Area, Foot of Polk St, 94109. Tel 415-556-8177. *Chief Cur* Karl Kortum; *Cur* Harlan Soeten; *Photograph Librarian* John Maounis
Open winter Mon - Fri 10 AM - 5 PM, summer Mon - Fri 10 AM - 6 PM.

Admis adults $2, children $1. Estab 1951; museum built in 1939; a terazzo and stainless steel structure with a nautical theme
Income: Financed by federal funding, private support from National Maritime Museum Association and donations
Special Subjects: Maritime history with emphasis on San Francisco & Pacific Coast
Collections: Over 150,000 photographs and negatives of ships and other memorabilia; ship †models; paintings; †recordings; sailing ship and paddlewheeler
Publications: Newsletter; booklets, irregular
Activities: Tours; book traveling exhibitions; sales shop sells books, magazines, reproductions and misc materials
L **Library,*** Foot of Polk St, 94109. *Principal Librn* David Hull
Open to the public for research on premises
Library Holdings: Vols 11,000; Per subs 90; Micro — Fiche, reels; AV — A-tapes, cassettes, motion pictures; Other — Clipping files, manuscripts, memorabilia, pamphlets 1600, photographs 150,000

M **JOSEPHINE D RANDALL JUNIOR MUSEUM,*** 199 Museum Way, 94114. Tel 415-863-1399. *Dir* Dr A Kirk Conragan; *Cur Arts & Crafts* Dennis Treanor
Open summer 10 AM - 5 PM, winter Tues - Sat 10 AM - 5 PM, cl holidays. No admis fee. Estab 1945 as part of the San Francisco Recreation and Park Dept. Average Annual Attendance: 120,000
Collections: Children's art Indian Artifacts
Activities: Classes in ceramics; weaving; leaded glass; painting; art history; jewelry; stitchery; tours; lect; films; individual paintings and original objects of art lent to other museums; traveling exhibitions organized and circulated
L **Library,*** 199 Museum Way, 94114
Open for reference
Library Holdings: Vols 10,000; Map files

L **SAN FRANCISCO ACADEMY OF COMIC ART,** Library,* 2850 Ulloa St, 94116. Tel 415-681-1737. *Dir* Bill Blackbeard; *Dir* Barbara Tyger
Open daily by appointment 10 AM - 10 PM. Estab 1967 to locate, preserve and house all elements of American popular narrative culture in danger of destruction through oversight or misunderstanding. Gallery maintained
Income: Financed by grants, donations, fees from personnel writing and lect, research charges
Library Holdings: Vols 25,000; Per subs 31; AV — Cassettes, motion pictures, rec, slides, v-tapes; Other — Clipping files, exhibition catalogs, framed reproductions, manuscripts, memorabilia, original art works, pamphlets, photographs, prints, reproductions
Collections: †Adventure fiction; †the American comic strip; †the American newspaper; †the American popular fiction magazine; †children's books since 1850; †detective fiction; †motion pictures; †the popular illustrated periodical; radical and underground publications; †science fiction; †Victorian illustrated book; western fiction
Exhibitions: Permanent collection: Original art in the comic strip and popular fiction; comic strip exhibit; national science fiction
Activities: Lect, 10 visiting lectr per year; gallery talks; tours; originate traveling exhibitions

M **SAN FRANCISCO ART INSTITUTE,** 800 Chestnut St, 94133. Tel 415-771-7020. *Dir Exhibitions* David S Rubin; *Asst Dir Exhibitions* Michael Schwager
Open Tues - Sat 10 AM - 5 PM. No admis fee. Estab 1871, inc 1889 to foster the appreciation and creation of the fine arts and maintain a school and museum for that purpose. Atholl McBean Gallery and Emanuel Walter Gallery for exhibitions of contemporary artists of international repute; Diego Rivera Gallery for exhibitions of work by SFAI students; SFAI Photo Gallery for exhibition of photographs by participating photographers invited by SFAI Photo Dept. Average Annual Attendance: 60,000. Mem: 1300; dues $15 - $100 and up; annual meeting June
Exhibitions: (1982) Vito Acconci; (1983) Gold Coast: A Performance Festival; (1984) Arakawa Drawings
Activities: Traveling exhibitions organized and circulated
L **Anne Bremer Memorial Library,** 800 Chestnut St, 94133. *Media Dir* C Stephanian; *Librn* Jeff Gunderson; *Catalog Librn* Carolyn Franklin; *Library Asst* Amanda Rendall; *Catalog Asst* Diana Rossi
Open Mon & Fri 9 AM - 5 PM; Tues - Thurs 9 AM - 8 PM during school sessions. Estab 1871 to develop a collection and services which will anticipate, reflect and support the objectives and direction of the San Francisco Art Institute and the contemporary arts community. Circ 12,795
Library Holdings: Vols 22,500; Per subs 250; AV — Cassettes, fs, Kodachromes, motion pictures, slides 45,000; Other — Clipping files, exhibition catalogs, manuscripts, memorabilia, pamphlets, photographs
Collections: Archives documenting the history of the Art Institute; artists' books; audio-tapes of artists working in sound (experimental music, etc)

O **SAN FRANCISCO CAMERAWORK,*** 70 - 12th St, 94103. Tel 415-621-1001. *Pres* Arthur Ollman
Open Tues - Sat Noon - 5 PM. Estab 1973 to encourage and display fine arts photography. Average Annual Attendance: 25,000. Mem: 200; dues $15 per yr
Income: Financed by government agencies & private contributions
Collections: Contemporary fine arts photography
Publications: Camerawork Newsletter, quarterly
Activities: Educ dept; lectures open to public, vis lecturers 15 per year; bookstore sells books, magazines, posters and postcards

O **SAN FRANCISCO CITY AND COUNTY ART COMMISSION,** 45 Hyde St Suite 319, 94102. Tel 415-558-3463. *Pres Commission* Roselyne C Swig; *Dir Cultural Affairs* Claire N Isaacs; *Dir Neighborhood Art Program* Anne Marie Theilen; *Coordr Street Artist Program* Howard Lazar; *Art Coordr* Jill Manton; *Cur Capricorn Asunder Gallery* John McCarron; *Art Coordr* Regina Almaguer
Open daily 8 AM - 5 PM. No admis fee. Estab 1932. Average Annual Attendance: 100,000. Mem: Consists of 9 professional and 3 lay-members appointed by the Mayor with advice of art societies, and 5 ex-officio members; monthly meetings. Passes on all buildings and works of art placed on property of City or County; supervises and controls all appropriations made by the Board of

Supervisors of music and the advancement of art and music; may volunteer advice to private owners who submit plans for suggestions; maintains a State/Local Partnership Program and a Neighborhood Arts Program; administers ordinance providing two percent of cost of public construction for art; also, a municipal collection for art for embellishing public offices; maintains art gallery and Annual Symphony Pops Concerts and Annual Arts Festival; licenses street artists; responsible for cataloging and maintaining all public works of art
Activities: Classes for adults and children; dramatic programs; docent training; lectures open to the public; concerts; gallery talks; tours; competitions with awards; individual paintings & original objects of art lent

M **SAN FRANCISCO MUSEUM OF MODERN ART,*** Van Ness at McAllister, 94102. Tel 415-863-8800. *Dir* Henry T Hopkins; *Deputy Dir* Michael McCone; *Chief Cur* Suzanne Foley; *Controller* S C St John
Open Tues - Wed & Fri 10 AM - 6 PM, Thurs 10 AM - 10 PM, Sat & Sun 10 AM - 5 PM. Admis adults $2, sr citizens & students $1, Thurs no charge after 6 PM. Estab 1935 to collect and exhibit art of the 20th century. Museum occupies two floors; four major galleries 35 x 180 ft; six corridor galleries; six smaller galleries. Average Annual Attendance: 300,000. Mem: 8000; dues $15-$1000
Income: Financed by endowment, membership, city appropriation, earnings and grant
Collections: Clyfford Still; †California clay; †painting, †photography, †sculpture
Publications: Calendar, monthly
Activities: Classes for adults and children; docent training; lect open to public, 6-8 visiting lectrs per year; concerts; gallery talks; tours; traveling exhibitions organized and circulated; museum shop selling books, magazines, reproductions and slides
L **Louise Sloss Ackerman Fine Arts Library,*** Van Ness at McAllister, 94102. Tel 415-863-8800. *Librn* Eugenie Candau
Open to the public for reference
Library Holdings: Vols 8000; Per subs 100; artists files; museum archives; Other — Exhibition catalogs
Special Subjects: Modern and contemporary art including photography and architecture
Collections: Margery Mann Collection of books in the history of photography

L **SAN FRANCISCO PUBLIC LIBRARY,** Art and Music Dept,* Civic Center, 94102. Tel 415-558-3687. *Dir* John C Frantz; *Art & Music* Mary Ashe
Open Mon - Thurs 9 AM - 9 PM, Fri & Sat 9 AM - 6 PM. Estab 1878
Income: Financed by city and state appropriations
Library Holdings: AV — Rec; Other — Framed reproductions, prints

L **SAN FRANCISCO STATE UNIVERSITY,** J Paul Leonard Library, 1630 Holloway, 94132. Tel 415-469-1681. *Dir* Joanne Euster
Open Mon - Thur 8 AM - 9:50 PM, Fri 8 AM - 4:50 PM, Sat 10 AM - 4:50 PM, Sun 1 - 8:50 PM. Estab 1890. Circ 730,043
Library Holdings: Micro — Cards, fiche, prints, reels; AV — A-tapes, cassettes, fs, motion pictures, rec, v-tapes; Other — Exhibition catalogs, framed reproductions, manuscripts, memorabilia, original art works
Collections: John Magnani Collection of Arts and Crafts; Frank deBellis Collection on Italian Culture; Juliet Bredon Collection of Chinese Textiles; H Wilder Bentley Brush Painting Collection; Simeon Pelene Collection of Paintings & Drawings
Exhibitions: Arts of China; Inventive Wrappings & Packaging; Berlin Dada; The Vision Revisited; The Immigrant Oral History Project; Tibet: Land of Snow; What is Pennsylvania Dutch?; Radical Humor Art Show
Activities: Book traveling exhibitions; originate traveling exhibitions

M **TATTOO ART MUSEUM,** 30 Seventh St, 94103. Tel 415-864-9798. *Dir* Lyle Tuttle; *Consult* Jane E Falk
Open daily Noon - 6 PM. Admis donations. Estab 1974. Average Annual Attendance: 5000. Mem: 50; monthly meetings
Collections: Lyle Tuttle Collection, tattoo art, Memorabilia and Equipment, especially tattoo machines
Exhibitions: Ancient European Tattooing; Tattoo Pacific Exhibition
Publications: Bulletin of the Tattoo Art Museum, Tattoo Historian
Activities: Annual Tattoo Ball; lectures open to public, 12 vis lectr per yr; individual paintings and objects of art lent; bookstore sells books, original art work, reproductions, prints, slides and t-shirts

M **WINE MUSEUM OF SAN FRANCISCO,*** 633 Beach St, 94109. Tel 415-673-6990. *Dir* Ernest G Mittelberger; *Asst to Dir* Barbara W Thompson; *Dir of Visitor Services* Kip Lee-Bevier; *Preparator* Karl L Folsom
Open Tues - Sat 11 AM - 5 PM, Sun Noon - 5 PM, cl Mon. No admis fee. Estab 1974 for the purpose of learning about the rituals and history of wine and its enjoyment, and as a demonstration of the quality and diversity of artistic expressions created by man as a record of his appreciation of wine from the earliest times to the present. One large room is divided into following sections: Grape, Vineyard and Harvest; Winemaking and the Vintner; Ancient Drinking Vessels; Wine in Mythology; In Celebration of Wine and Life; and a changing exhibition area. Average Annual Attendance: 100,000
Income: Financed by private sponsor
Collections: †Christian Brothers Collection of original graphics and decorative arts; Franz W Sichel Collection of glass drinking vessels spanning 2000 years
Exhibitions: Wit and Wine; Traditions of Dining from the Roman era to the present
Publications: The Wine Museum of San Francisco, brochure; In Celebration of Wine and Life; Wine & the Artist; full color art reproductions
Activities: Docent training; gallery talks; tours; individual objects of art and individual prints lent to other museums who have proper security and insurance systems; originates traveling exhibitions; museum shop sells books, reproductions
L **Alfred Fromm Rare Wine Books Library,*** 633 Beach St, 94109
Open to writers, researchers, and scholars for reference only
Income: Financed by private sponsor
Library Holdings: Vols 1000
Special Subjects: History and Technology of Wine

SAN JOSE

M ROSICRUCIAN EGYPTIAN MUSEUM AND ART GALLERY, Park and Naglee, 95191. Tel 408-287-9171, Ext 229. *Dir* Ralph M Lewis; *Asst Dir & Cur* Curt Schild
Open Tues - Fri 9 AM - 4:40 PM, Mon & Sat Noon - 4:40 PM. No admis fee. Estab 1929, in present location 1966, to publicly show a collection of the works of the ancient Egyptians, reflecting their lives and culture. A Gallery contains the Babylonian and Assyrian collection of funeral works; B Gallery contains tomb replicas and mummies; C Gallery, Tel-El-Armana room with amulets, cosmetics and writing implements; D Gallery has jewelry, pottery, and King Zoser's tomb complex. Average Annual Attendance: 500,000
Income: Financed by Rosicrucian Order
Collections: Assyrian & Babylonian seals, coins & cylinders; Egyptian antiquities; French Room with Louis XIV - Louis XVI furniture
Exhibitions: Monthly exhibitions, mainly one-man
Publications: Egypt The Eternal - Museum Guide Book
Activities: Tours for children; lectures; Sales shop sells books, magazines, reproductions, prints, slides, jewelry, records and posters

M SAN JOSE INSTITUTE OF CONTEMPORARY ART,* 377 S First St, 95113. Tel 408-998-4310. *Dir* Susan Kirkpatrick
Open Tues - Sat 11 AM - 4 PM. No admis fee. Average Annual Attendance: 1200
Collections: Paintings including fibre painting, documents, sculpture

M SAN JOSE MUSEUM OF ART, 110 S Market St, 95113. Tel 408-294-2787. *Exec Dir* Russell J Moore; *Cur* Martha L Manson; *Office Mgr* Pamela Leach; *Admn Asst* Donna Carneghi
Open Tues - Thurs 11 AM - 5 PM, Fri 11 AM - 6 PM, Sat & Sun Noon - 4 PM. Admis Tues - Sat $1, Sun free. Estab 1968 to provide the citizens of San Jose and the South Bay region with a changing exhibition schedule featuring local, regional, national and international exhibitions. The museum is housed in an 1892 sandstone structure in the Romanesque style; it was a federal post office building in San Jose, and was renovated for museum use in 1975-76. Average Annual Attendance: 100,000. Mem: dues $20 - $1000; annual meeting June
Income: Financed by membership, city appropriation, fund-raising activities & corporate donations
Collections: Permanent Collection features work by nationally recognized artists of the Calif region, & †prints, †sculptures & paintings by American masters
Exhibitions: (1983) Alan Magee: Paintings; Paul Beattie: Paintings/Drawings; Good as Gold: Alternative Materials in American Jewelry; Harry Powers: Sculpture; Gertrude Bleiberg: Let Us Savor This Moment; Hassel Smith: Paintings; Artists & the Theatre; Jude Silva: New Work; Okudaira & Doering; Bill Heiderich & Barbara Hayes: Sculpture; Mary Anne Rose: Paintings; Gene Flores: Sculpture; Irish Silver; Clare Leighton: Prints; Gordon Parks Retrospective: Photos; Jorgen Haugen Sorensen; Helen & Newton Harrison; Robert Hartman: Photographs; Artists of the Sun Yat-Sen Art Society; Eisenstaedt: Germany; American & English Majolica; Cliff McReynolds: For God's Sake; Franklin Williams; Elena Sheehan: Journey Through Seven Circles; Lieberman, Slevoght, Corinth; Diana Krevsky; Reginald Marsh's New York; Milton Komisar; Lithographs of J M Whistler; Norman Lundin; (1984) Lithographs of J M Whistler; Campbell Soup Tureens; Norman Lundin; Milton Komisar; Paul Kubic; Toshiyasu Oi: Paintings; Traditional Crafts of Saudi Arabia; Lucy Hayward Parker; Sam Hernandez; Nancy Worthington; Children's Class Exhibition; Ann Rinehart; Fifty Years of Babar; The Collector's Eye
Publications: Newsletter monthly; exhibition catalogs
Activities: Classes for adults and children; docent training; lectures open to the public; tours; book traveling exhibitions, 8-10 per yr; traveling exhibitions organized and circulated; museum shop sells books, original art, reproductions
L Library, 110 S Market St, 95113. Tel 408-294-2787. *Asst* Mildred Chatton; *Asst* Jean Wheeler
Open to the museum staff and volunteers for reference only
Income: Financed by grants and donations
Library Holdings: Vols 970; AV — Slides 556; Other — Clipping files, exhibition catalogs 952, pamphlets, photographs

SAN JOSE STATE UNIVERSITY

M Art Gallery, Ninth and San Carlos, 95192. Tel 408-277-2579. *Dir* Erica Vegter-Kubic
Open Tues - Thur 11 AM - 4 PM during term. No admis fee. Estab 1960 as part of the university Art Dept. Gallery is 34 x 28 ft with 12 ft ceiling. Average Annual Attendance: 9000
Income: Financed by city and state appropriations
Collections: †Contemporary and historical graphics; †work by faculty, students and alumni; †Chagall Graphics Collection
Publications: Exhibition catalogs; brochures
Activities: Lectures open to the public, 6 vis lectr per yr; concerts; gallery talks; tours; paintings and original art objects lent to university offices; lending collection contains original prints, paintings (including Klee and Chagall), sculpture; originate traveling exhibitions; catalogs sometimes made
M Union Gallery, S Ninth St, Student Union, 95192. Tel 408-277-3221. *Dir* James Feeder; *Registrar* Lisa Mari Ramirez; *Cur Permanent Coll* Robert Yanes
Open Mon - Fri 9:30 - 4 PM, Wed & Thurs 6 - 8 PM. No admis fee. Estab 1968 to supplement the available art at San Jose State and to broaden the student's appreciation of art. The gallery consists of two main spaces: main gallery, with an additional back gallery for smaller exhibitions. Average Annual Attendance: 30,000
Income: Financed by state appropriation and through the University
Publications: Exhibition catalogs
Activities: Lect open to public, 9 visiting lectr per year; gallery talks; paintings and original art objects lent to other galleries or museums; lending collection contains cassettes
L Robert D Clark Library, Washington Sq, 95192. *Art Reference Librn* Edith Crowe; *Slide Cur* Rachel Hoffman
Purchases: $24,000
Library Holdings: Vols 31,500; Per subs 100; Micro — Cards, fiche, prints, reels; AV — A-tapes, cassettes, fs, Kodachromes, lantern slides, motion pictures, rec, slides, v-tapes; Other — Exhibition catalogs, framed reproductions, original art works, pamphlets, photographs, prints, reproductions

SAN LUIS OBISPO

L CUESTA COLLEGE LIBRARY, Art Dept,* PO Box J, 93406. Tel 805-544-2943. *Dir* Mary Lou Wilhelm
Open Mon - Thur 7:30 AM - 9 PM, Fri 7:30 AM - 4:30 PM, vacation hours vary. Estab 1965 to support the educational program of the college
Income: $305,970
Purchases: $26,610
Library Holdings: Micro — Fiche, reels; AV — A-tapes, cassettes, fs, slides, v-tapes; Other — Pamphlets
Activities: Flea market; originate traveling exhibits

SAN LUIS REY

M MISSION SAN LUIS REY MUSEUM, 4050 Mission Ave, 92068. Tel 619-757-3651. *Local Minister* Michael Weishaar; *Asst Mgr* Edith Eddy
Open 9 AM - 4 PM, Sun Noon - 4 PM. Admis adults $1, 12 - 18 $.50, 6 - 12 $.25. Estab 1798 to protect, conserve and show Mission history and artifacts
Income: Financed by property of Franciscan Friars Inc, of California
Collections: Artifacts, furniture, paints, statuary, religious vestments and vessels and other historical objects from early mission days in California

SAN MARCOS

M PALOMAR COMMUNITY COLLEGE, Boehm Gallery,* 1140 W Mission Rd, 92069. Tel 619-744-1150. *Gallery Dir* Russell W Baldwin
Open Mon - Thurs 8 AM - 8 PM, Fri 8 AM - 4 PM, Sat 10 AM - 2 PM. No admis fee. Estab 1964 to provide the community with fine art regardless of style, period or approach. The gallery is 35 x 35 ft, no windows, 18 in brick exterior, acoustic ceiling and asphalt tile floor. Average Annual Attendance: 50,000
Income: $8000 (exhibition budget). Financed by city and state appropriations
Collections: †Contemporary art by nationally acclaimed artists; 16th - 20th Century Art; California Artists
Exhibitions: Annual Student Art Show; Three Photographers: Edward, Cole and Kim Weston; Roland Reiss, The Morality Plays: An Installation Work; Eleanor Antin, A Look-Back 1969-1975; Robert Freeman; Native American; Etchings and Richard White; Table; Kazuo Kadonaga; Sculpture; D J Hall; Recent Paintings and Drawings Richard Allen Morris: Painting Retrospective; Christine Oatman: Fantasy Landscapes; Sam Richardson: Ten Year Retrospective of Sculpture and Drawing; Italo Sconga: Recent Sculpture; Masami Teraoka: Recent Paintings and Prints; Wayne Thiebaud: Recent Paintings and Drawings; William Wiley: Recent Sculpture and Drawings
Activities: Lect open to public, 12 vis lectr per year; competitions; individual paintings and original objects of art lent to reputable museums and galleries; lending collection contains original paintings, prints and sculpture

SAN MARINO

M HUNTINGTON LIBRARY, ART GALLERY AND BOTANICAL GARDENS, 1151 Oxford Rd, 91108. Tel 213-792-6141. *Dir* Robert Middlekauff; *Cur Art Coll* Robert R Wark; *Public Relations Officer* Katherine Ann Wilson
Open Tues - Sun 1 - 4:30 PM. No admis, call (213) 449-3901 for information regarding free Sun reservations. Estab 1919 by the late Henry E Huntington as a free research library, art gallery, museum and botanical garden; exhibitions open to the public in 1928 for educational and cultural purposes. Virginia Steele Scott Gallery will open in 1984. Average Annual Attendance: 500,000. Mem: 3000, supporters of the institution who give $35 - $999 annually are known as the Friends of the Huntington Library, Fellows give $1500 or more per year
Income: Financed by endowment and gifts
Collections: British and European art of the 18th and early 19th centuries with a strong supporting collection of French furniture, decorative objects and sculpture of the same periods
Exhibitions: Rotating exhibitions from the permanent collection
Publications: The Calendar, bimonthly
Activities: Lect open to public; gallery talks; tours; dramatic programs; fels offered; sales shop sells books, postcards, prints, reproductions and slides
L Art Reference Library, 1151 Oxford Road, 91108. Tel 213-792-6141. *Art Reference Librn* Diana Wilson
Open to qualified scholars for reference
Income: Financed by endowments and gifts
Library Holdings: Vols 16,000; Per subs 26; Photographic archive 100,000; Other — Clipping files, exhibition catalogs
Special Subjects: British art of the 18th and early 19th centuries
Collections: British drawings and watercolors; probably the largest collection of books, photographs and other materials for the study of British art that exists outside London

SAN MATEO

L COLLEGE OF SAN MATEO LIBRARY, Art Division,* 1700 W Hillsdale Blvd, 94402. Tel 415-574-6161. *Coordr* Gregg T Atkins
Open Mon - Fri 7:30 AM - 10 PM, Sun 1 - 5 PM, cl Sat. Estab 1922. An art gallery maintained with monthly exhibits
Income: Financed by state appropriation
Library Holdings: Original documents; Micro — Fiche, reels; AV — A-tapes, cassettes, fs, Kodachromes, lantern slides, motion pictures, rec, slides, v-tapes; Other — Pamphlets, photographs, reproductions
Special Subjects: Crafts, European and Oriental art
Exhibitions: Community college student show; faculty art show

SAN MIGUEL

M MISSION SAN MIGUEL MUSEUM, Mission St, 93451. Tel 805-467-3256. *Superior Reverend* Reginald McDonough; *Pastor Reverend* Maurus Kelly
Open daily 10 AM - 5 PM, cl New Year's, Easter, Thanksgiving and Christmas. Admis by donation. Estab 1797 as The Old Mission church, the original still in use as the parish church, and the entire Mission has been restored. The Mission contains paintings dating back to the 18th century, also original, untouched frescoes. Average Annual Attendance: 50,000
Income: Financed by Franciscan Friars
Activities: Concerts; tours; sales shop sells books, reproductions, prints, slides, gifts & religious articles

SAN RAFAEL

M FALKIRK COMMUNITY CULTURAL CENTER,* 1408 Mission Ave, PO Box 60, 94915. Tel 415-485-3328. *Dir* Consuelo Underwood; *Cur* Mary Dekker
Gallery open Mon - Fri 11 AM - 4 PM, Sat 10 AM - Noon, Office open Mon - Fri 9 AM - 5 PM. Estab 1974 to provide classes, lectures, concerts. Contemporary art gallery. Average Annual Attendance: 45,000. Mem: Dues patron $100, sponsor $50, contributing $25, regular $10, sr citizen & student $5
Income: Financed by state appropriation, rentals & classes
Activities: Classes for adults and children; docent training; lectures open to public, 6 vis lect per yr; concerts; tours; juried annual competition; cash awards; bookstore sells books and prints

SANTA ANA

M BOWER'S MUSEUM, 2002 N Main St, 92706. Tel 714-972-1900. *Dir* William B Lee; *Registrar* Margaret A Key; *Admin Asst* Pat Rice; *Museum Publicity Agent* Elaine Osborn; *Cur of Education* Joan Primm; *Exhibit Specialist* Paul John
Open Tues - Sat 9 AM - 5 PM, Sun 1 - 5 PM, cl Mon. No admis fee. Estab 1934 to provide an active general museum for the community. The Charles W Bower Museum is housed in an authenic California mission-style structure amid expansive fountain-studded grounds, originally devoted to the display of antique furniture, Indian relics and historical items of early California families. A new wing has been added with an exhibition program of contemporary art. Average Annual Attendance: 225,000. Mem: 1800; dues from student $15 - life $1000
Income: Financed by city appropriation supplemented by Foundation Board
Collections: Asian, African and contemporary American art; early California history; Indian artifacts; late 19th century Oriental costumes; 19th & Early 20th century North and South American costumes; Northwest American Indian; 19th & 20th century American Indian baskets; 19th century American textiles, decorative arts and patterned glass; Oceania; Orange County history; Pre-Columbian; †native North American Indian arts
Exhibitions: (1983) Art of Metal in Africa; A Sampler of Chinese Art; Paintings of Jerry Wayne Downs; (1983-84) Sky Watchers of Ancient California; (1984) Irish Silver; Native Harvest; Orange County Photograph; (1984-85) Flowering of Science; Tangata
Publications: Brochures; Calendar, monthly; exhibition catalogs
Activities: Classes for adults and children; docent guild; lect open to public; films; gallery talks; tours; study clubs; paintings and original art objects lent to other museums; organize and circulate traveling exhibitions; sales shop sells books, magazines, original art, reproductions, prints, jewelry, imported clothing, gift items

M ORANGE COUNTY CENTER FOR CONTEMPORARY ART, 3621 W Mac Arthur Blvd, Space 111, 92704. Tel 714-549-4989. *Dir* Suvan Geer; *Vice Dir* Claudia Kilby; *Secy* Nancy Mooslin; *Treas* Linda Stevens; *Gallery Dir* Ray Jacob; *Gallery Dir* Ruth Ann Anderson; *Finances* Richard Aaron; *Advisor to Board* Ivan Blum
Open Wed - Sun Noon - 5 PM. No admis fee. Estab 1980 as a non-profit exhibit space, alternative to commercial galleries and to provide support and exposure to contemporary work in visual arts; gallery houses artists slide registry. Average Annual Attendance: 1000. Mem: 100; general membership requires only annual dues, affiliate is a juried process; annual dues affiliate $420, general $25
Income: Financed by membership
Exhibitions: The gallery shows run 3-1/2 wks & 3 artists are shown concurrently
Publications: Art Week, monthly; Art Scene, monthly
Activities: Lectures open to public; concerts; gallery talks; sponsors juried exhibit annually; awards donated by local businesses

SANTA BARBARA

L BROOKS INSTITUTE PHOTOGRAPHY LIBRARY,* 2020 Alameda Padre Serra, 93103. Tel 805-969-2291. *Librn* James B Maher
Library Holdings: Vols 4990; Per subs 115
Special Subjects: Photography

O SANTA BARBARA CONTEMPORARY ARTS FORUM, 7 W De La Guerra St, 93101. Tel 805-966-5373. *Dir* Mona Worthington Kwan; *Pres Bd of Dirs* Joan Tanner; *VPres* Brian Beebe; *VPres* Teen Coxwell; *Treas* Paul Roberts; *Secy* Sally Lewis
Open Wed - Sun Noon - 5 PM. Estab 1976; committed to the presentation of contemporary art. Mem: Dues $20
Exhibitions: (1983-1984) Black On Black Show; Polacolor Prints; Dan Rice; Diamanda Galas; Kim Adams; Dana Reitz; Art As Science, Science As Art; Lyon Balliett; Joseph Clower
Activities: Lectures open to the public; competitions

M SANTA BARBARA MUSEUM OF ART,* 1130 State St, 93101. Tel 805-963-4364. *Dir* Richard V West; *Deputy Dir* Carl Vance; *Cur Exhibitions* Robert Henning Jr; *Cur Collections* Jane Baxter; *Cur Education* Penny Knowles; *Asst Cur Oriental Art* Susan Tai; *Registrar* Elaine Dietsch; *Public Relations* Kathleen M Monaghan

Open Tues - Sat 11 AM - 5 PM, Sun Noon - 5 PM, cl Mon. No admis fee. Estab 1941 as an art museum. Average Annual Attendance: 180,000. Mem: 2408; dues patron circle $1000, patron $500, supporting $250, gallery guild $100, business $100, individual $50, family $25, friends of Oriental art $24, individual $15, student $10
Income: $2,000,000 (financed by endowment, membership, state and federal grants)
Collections: Preston Morton Collection of American Art; Alice F Schott Doll Collection; American and European paintings, sculpture, drawings, prints; Greek and Roman Antiques; Oriental ceramics, paintings and sculpture
Exhibitions: Change throughout the year
Publications: Calendar and exhibition and collection catalogs monthly
Activities: Classes for adults and children; docent training; dramatic programs; lect open to the public, 70-80 visiting lectr per year; concerts; gallery talks; tours; films; competitions with awards; paintings and original art objects lent to museums and University galleries; originate traveling exhibitions
L Library, 1130 State St, 93101. *Librn* John Crozier
Open to public on an appointment basis. For reference only
Library Holdings: Vols 2500; Per subs 37; Other — Exhibition catalogs, pamphlets

L SANTA BARBARA PUBLIC LIBRARY, Faulkner Memorial Art Wing, 40 E Anapamu St, Box 1019, 93102. Tel 805-962-7653. *Dir* Robert A Hart; *Reference Librn* Myra J Nicholas
Open Mon - Thurs 10 AM - 9 PM, Fri & Sat 10 AM - 5:30 PM, Sun 1 - 5 PM. Estab 1930 and administered by the library trustees as a municipal art reading room and gallery
Library Holdings: Vols 200,000; Per subs 625; Micro — Fiche, prints, reels; AV — Cassettes, rec; Other — Clipping files, framed reproductions, pamphlets, reproductions
Exhibitions: Local contemporary paintings and sculpture
Activities: Lectures, programs and meetings; lending collections contains reproduction paintings

UNIVERSITY OF CALIFORNIA, SANTA BARBARA

M University Art Museum, Arts Bldg, 1626-B, 93106. Tel 805-961-2951, 961-3013. *Dir* Dr J David Farmer; *Cur* Phyllis Plous; *Designer of Exhib* Paul Prince; *Admin Asst* Judy Altschuler; *Registrar* Alice Wong
Open Tues - Sat 10 AM - 4 PM, Sun & holidays 1 - 5 PM, cl Mon, New Year's, Thanksgiving, Christmas and between exhibits. No admis fee. Estab 1961 & direct at both the needs of the university & the community; with a wide range of contemporary & historical exhibitions. Located on the UCSB campus and within the Museum complex; three galleries for changing exhibits; three which exhibit part of the permanent collection. Average Annual Attendance: 30,000
Income: Financed by university funds
Collections: Collection of Architectural Drawings by Southern California Architects, including Irving Gill, R M Schindler, George Washington Smith and Kem Weber; Morgenroth Collection of Renaissance Medals and Plaquettes; Sedgwick Collection of 16th - 18th Century Italian, Flemish and Dutch Artists; Ala Story Print Collection; Grace H Dreyfus Collection of Ancient Peruvian & Middle Eastern Art; Fernand Lungren Estate
Exhibitions: Annual undergraduate & MFA candidate exhibitions; studio faculty; Extensions of Photography; Arts of Kenya; Re-Exhumed Etruscan Bronzes; contemporary exhibition; undergraduate exhibition; graduate exhibition; The Santa Barbara Show; Contemporary Spanish Prints; First Thoughts & Final Studies; The French Oil Sketch; Contemporary Painting/Figuration; The Cubist Print; The Anglo-American Artists in Italy, 1750-1820; A Heritage Renewed: Contemporary Representational Drawing; Old Master Drawings from the Feitclson Collection The French Oil Sketch; Contemporary Painting/Figuration; The Cobbist Print; The Anglo American Artist in Italy, 1750-1820
Publications: Exhibition catalogs, 3 - 6 per year
Activities: Lect upon request; lending collection contains 3000 original art works; 800 original prints, 300 paintings, sculpture, 100,000 architectural drawings; originate traveling exhibitions; sales shop sells exhibition catalogs
L Arts Library, University of California, Santa Barbara, 93106. Tel 805-961-2850. *Head Arts Library* William R Treese
Open Mon - Thurs 9 AM - 11 PM, Fri & Sat 9 AM - 6 PM, Sun 2 - 11 PM. Estab 1966 to support academic programs. Circ 57,000
Income: Financed by state appropriation
Library Holdings: Vols 65,000; Per subs 250; Auction Catalogs 36,000; Micro — Fiche, reels; AV — V-tapes; Other — Exhibition catalogs 44,000, pamphlets, photographs
Special Subjects: Architecture, Oriental Art, Greek, Roman and Etruscan art, Medieval Art, Renaissance and Baroque Art, 18th, 19th and 20th Century Art, primitive and exotic arts
Publications: Catalogs of the Art Exhibition Catalogs of the Arts Library, University of California, Santa Barbara; Teaneck, New Jersey, Somerset House, 1978
Activities: Tours

SANTA CLARA

M TRITON MUSEUM OF ART, 1505 Warburton Ave, 95050. Tel 408-247-3754. *Dir* Jo Farb Hernandez; *Asst Dir* Marc D'Estout; *Development Dir* David de la Torre; *Pres* Orlando Maione; *VPres* Margaret Gleason
Open Tues - Fri noon - 4 PM, Sat - Sun noon - 5 PM. No admis fee. Estab 1965 to offer a rich and varied cultural experience to members of the community through the display of international folk art and of works of art by American artists, particularly artists of California, and through related special events and programs. The museum consists of four buildings constructed in an architectural style that blends Oriental and Spanish elements; each pavilion is designed somewhat differently so as to lend variety to the gallery space. Average Annual Attendance: 60,000. Mem: 500; dues $10-$1000
Income: $180,000 (financed by endowment, membership and city appropriation)
Collections: American Ceramics and Glass Collection, the heart of which is the Vivian Woodward Elmer Majolica Collection; American painting, prints and sculpture; oil paintings by Theodore Wores; international folk art

Exhibitions: American Indian Artifacts; Masami Teraoka; Ron Nelson; Raymond Saunders; Egyptian Antiquities; Roy De Forest; Contemporary Glass; Irene Dogmatic; Art of Portugal; Da Vinci; Views of California Past and Present; Art of Guatemala; Clayton Bailey: Scientific Curiosities & Inventions; The Day of the Dead: Tradition and Change in Contemporary Mexico; Irv Tepper and Kristi Hager: Stereo Views; The World of Haitian Painting; Ashanti Goldweights; Mexican India Dance Masks; Crime and Punishment; Carol Law; Art of the Cuna Indians; Stephanie Sanchez
Publications: Exhibition catalogs; newsletter, bimonthly
Activities: Classes for children; dramatic prog; docent training docent training; lect open to public, 10 per year; concerts; gallery talks; tours; museum shop sells books, postcards and reproductions

L **Library,** 1505 Warburton Ave, 95050. Tel 408-248-4585. *Admin Asst* Sheila B Braufman
Open by appointment only. Estab 1967 to enhance the resource of the art museum. Open to members for reference
Library Holdings: Vols 500; Per subs 10
Special Subjects: Folk Art, Twentieth Century American Art
Collections: †Special collection of artists books
Exhibitions: Working with Glass: A Survey of Bay Area Artists; Art of New Guinea; The Art of Instruments: 1450-1800; Scientific Inventions and Curiosities by Clayton Bailey; Miniatures
Publications: Newsletter, bi-monthly; exhibition catalogs
Activities: Classes for adults and children; docent training; outreach activities; lectures open to public, 5-10 vis lectr per year; concerts; gallery talks; tours; sponsor juried competitive exhibitions; awards; orginate traveling exhibitions to local & regional institutions

M **UNIVERSITY OF SANTA CLARA,** de Saisset Museum, 95053. Tel 408-984-4528. *Academic VPres* Paul Locatelli; *Dir* Dr Brigid S Barton; *Asst Dir* Georgianna Lagoria; *Preparator* Fred Shepard; *Museum Coordr* Rebecca Schapp
Open Tues - Fri 10 AM - 5 PM, Sat & Sun 1 - 5 PM, cl Mon and all holidays. No admis fee. Estab 1955 as a major cultural resource in Northern California. In recent years the museum has dramatically broadened its scope, exhibiting some of the world's leading avant-garde artists while not losing sight of the traditional. The gallery has 20,000 sq ft of floor space in a concrete structure adjacent to the Mission Santa Clara, two stories of galleries with a balcony for small exhibitions, plus offices and a gallery shop along with workrooms. Average Annual Attendance: 250,000. Mem: Dues patron $500, benefactor $250, sponsor $100, sustaining $25, annual $15, senior or student $7.50
Income: Financed by endowment, membership
Purchases: Prints by European & American artists
Collections: Kolb Collection of 17th and 18th century graphics; Arnold Mountfort Collection; D'Berger Collection of French furniture and ivories; African collection; New Deal art repository; paintings, antiques, sculture, †prints, china, silver and ivory collections; 17th and 18th century tapestries; photography
Exhibitions: Quarterly exhibitions of contemporary & modern art; annual exhibition of photography; Gallery IV program of recent work by Bay area artists
Publications: Calendar, quarterly; exhibition catalogs
Activities: Lect open to public, 15 visiting lectr per year; gallery talks; paintings lent to campus offices; originate traveling exhibitions; museum shop sells books, original art, prints, jewelry, antiques and artifacts

L **Library,** 95053
Open for reference only
Library Holdings: Vols 1500; Per subs 25; Micro — Cards; AV — A-tapes, cassettes, slides, v-tapes; Other — Clipping files, exhibition catalogs, framed reproductions, manuscripts, memorabilia, photographs, prints, sculpture
Collections: California mission period manuscripts and books

SANTA CRUZ

M **THE ART MUSEUM OF SANTA CRUZ COUNTY,** 224 Church St, 95060. Tel 408-429-3420. *Dir* Robert McDonald
Admis $1 general public, free to members, children, teachers with school groups. Estab 1981 to encourage and develop the study of fine arts and to foster and support educational and artistic interests in the county. The city of Santa Cruz has donated 1500 sq ft of space of the Santa Cruz Central Library, upstairs. There is 250 linear ft of exhibit space. Average Annual Attendance: 10,000. Mem: 700; dues $10 - $1000
Income: $100,000
Exhibitions: William Dole; Folk Art; Wayne Thiebaud, paintings; Walker Evans, photographs; Japanese Prints; Carrousel Animals; Manuel Neri, sculptures & drawings; Amish Quilts; Johan Hagemeyer, photographs; Picasso, Matisse & Giacametti: A Graphic View of the Human Form; Zandra Rhodes—Fashion as Art; New Prints from Cirrus Editions: Peter Alexander, Jedd Garet, Charles Christopher Hill, Craig Kauffman; Christo Wrapped Coast Documentation Exhibition; Greek & Russian Icons from the Charles Pankow Collection; Morris Graves; Imongen Cunningham; Henrietta Shore
Publications: Catalogues; newsletter, bi-monthly
Activities: Docent training; lectures open to public, 12 vis lectr per yr; gallery talks; tours; competitions; originate traveling exhibitions

O **CHILDREN'S ART FOUNDATION,** 915 Cedar St, PO Box 83, 95063. Tel 408-426-5557. *Pres* Gerry Mandel; *VPres* William Rubel; *Administrative Asst* Madalon Zorn
Open Mon - Fri 2 - 5:30 PM & by appointment. No admis fee. Estab 1973 to improve the quality of American art education. Gallery has 800 sq ft with rotating displays of art by children from around the world. Average Annual Attendance: 3500. Mem: 9000; dues $17.50; annual meeting Jan 15
Income: $130,000
Purchases: $5000
Collections: American children's drawings; drawings, paintings & prints from 40 countries
Exhibitions: (1983) Recent acquisitions from New Zealand & Bangladesh
Publications: Stone Soup, magazine 5 times per yr
Activities: Classes for children; individual paintings & original objects of art lent; originates traveling exhibitions; sales shop sells magazines, reproductions & slides

M **SANTA CRUZ ART CENTER,** 1003 Center St, 95060. Tel 408-429-1188. *Dir* M William Downey; *Office Mgr* Henry Hample; *Coordr* Nancy Meyberg
Open Noon - 8 PM. Estab 1976 to provide a space where artists can work in public and to enrich the cultural life of the area through exhibits, performance and cuisine. Three non-profit galleries providing exposure to regional artists. Average Annual Attendance: 5000. Mem: 15
Income: Financed by members, city & state appropriation
Exhibitions: Craft invitational, juried photography show, juried print show, handmade musical instrument
Activities: Concerts; competition; awards; bookstore sells books, handmade crafts and original artwork

O **SANTA CRUZ ART LEAGUE, INC,** 526 Broadway, 95060. Tel 408-426-5787. *Pres* Patricia Ferro; *Cur* June Baker
Open Tues - Sat 11 AM - 4 PM, cl Mon. No admis fee, $1 donation. Estab 1919, Incorporated 1949, to further interest in art. Monthly gallery displays of paintings by members. Average Annual Attendance: 11,000. Mem: 225; membership qualifications, Executive Board of Art League judge three original artworks; dues life $200, active artists $25, associate artists $15, membership $10, annual meeting 2nd Wed each month
Income: Financed by donations
Collections: Permanent display of life size wax figures of Last Supper from DaVinci painting
Exhibitions: (1984) 54th Annual Statewide Juried Show
Publications: Bulletin, monthly
Activities: Classes for adults; classes in painting; demonstration by professional artist at monthly meetings; 12 vis lectrs per year; gallery talks; competitions with awards; scholarships offered

L **SANTA CRUZ PUBLIC LIBRARY,** Art, Music, Film Dept,* 224 Church St, 95060. Tel 408-429-3530. *Dir* Anne M Turner; *Art & Music Librn* Alma Westberg; *Library Asst* Timothy G Bell; *Clerk* Mark Moore
Open Mon - Thurs 9 AM - 9 PM, Fri & Sat 9 AM - 5 PM. Estab 1881 for the cultural enrichment and enjoyment of the citizens. Gallery maintained in local and western art of variety of media. Circ 11,000
Income: $10,000 (financed by city and state appropriations)
Purchases: $10,000
Library Holdings: Vols 11,000; Micro — Reels; AV — A-tapes, cassettes, fs, motion pictures, rec, slides, v-tapes; Other — Clipping files, framed reproductions, pamphlets, prints
Activities: Classes for children; film programs; tours; exten dept serving Santa Cruz County

SANTA MONICA

M **THE MUSEUM OF AFRICAN AMERICAN ART,** 2617 Lincoln Blvd, Suite 207, 90405. Tel 213-450-5045. *Dir* Mary Jane Hewitt; *Cur* Samella Lewis
Open Mon - Fri 10:30 AM - 5 PM. No admis fee. Estab 1976. Maintains small reference library of African and African-American art, literature and history. Mem: Dues corporate $1000, patron $500, sponsor $250, active $100, family $50, individual $20
Collections: Makonde sculpture of East Africa; soapstone sculpture of Shona people of South East Africa; traditional sculpture of West African peoples; arts of African and African descendant peoples; paintings, prints and sculptures of leading contemporary American artists
Publications: Black Art, quarterly
Activities: Training programs for professional museum workers; docent training and counciling; lectures; films; gallery talks; permanent collection lent; originate traveling exhibitions; sales shop sells greeting cards and notes, The Black Art quarterly, posters and prints, periodicals on African-American art

M **SANTA MONICA COLLEGE ART GALLERY,** 1900 Pico Blvd, 90405. Tel 213-450-5150, Ext 340. *Dir* William M Hill; *Technical Asst* Camille Gonzales
Open Mon - Fri 10 AM - 3 PM, Thurs 7 - 9 PM, cl academic holidays. No admis fee. Estab 1973 to provide a study gallery for direct contact with contemporary and historic works of art. Average Annual Attendance: 25,000
Income: Financed by membership, city and state appropriations
Collections: Southern California prints and drawings
Exhibitions: 8 per year
Activities: Lect open to public; gallery talks; tours; original art objects lent

SANTA ROSA

O **ARTRIUM INC,** 1150-A Coddingtown Center, Suite 126, 95401. Tel 707-578-4142. *Pres* Barbara Harris; *VPres* Barbara Eggers
Open 10 AM - 2 PM. Estab 1965 to promote and encourge interest and appreciation of all phases of the arts. Mem: 250; dues $10 and up; annual meeting Oct
Income: Financed by membership and city appropriation
Exhibitions: (1982-83) Artium Festival; graphics, sculpture, painting, photography, paperworks
Publications: Newsletter & calander, monthly; crafts trail map
Activities: Concerts; tours; sponsor competitions; arts festival

M **SANTA ROSA JUNIOR COLLEGE ART GALLERY,** 1501 Mendocino Ave, 95401. Tel 707-527-4298. *Dir* John Watrous
Open Sun - Fri Noon - 4 PM, cl Sat. No admis fee. Estab 1973. Gallery is 40 x 42 ft, 12 ft walls, peaked roof with four skylights. Average Annual Attendance: 9000
Activities: Lectures open to the public; gallery talks

L **Library,** 1501 Mendocino Ave, 95401
For reference only
Library Holdings: Vols 100; Per subs 2

SARATOGA

O **MONTALVO CENTER FOR THE ARTS,** 15400 Montalvo Rd, PO Box 158, 95071. Tel 408-867-3421. *Executive Dir* Gardiner R McCauley
Open Tues - Sun 1 - 4 PM, cl Mon and holidays. Admis $1, 18 and under free. Estab 1930; administered by Montalvo Association, Villa Montalvo is part of a cultural center for the development of art, literature, music and architecture by artists and promising students. There are facilities for five artists-in-residence. The home of the late US Senator and Mayor of San Francisco, James Duval Phelan, was bequeathed as a cultural center, and is conducted as a non-profit enterprise by the Board of Trustees of the Montalvo Association. Average Annual Attendance: 7000. Mem: 1250; dues $25 and up; annual meeting in Nov
Income: $350,000 (financed by donation, grants & investments)
Exhibitions: 20 solo exhibitions per year of emerging artists in all media; occasional special or group exhibitions
Publications: Calendar, monthly
Activities: Lectures open to public, 8 vis lect per year; concerts; gallery talks; tours; competitions with awards; plays; winter workshops; scholarships; museum shop sells books, original art, reproductions, prints & gift items

SEAL BEACH

AMERICAN PORTRAIT SOCIETY
For further information, see National and Regional Organizations

STANFORD

M **STANFORD UNIVERSITY,** Museum of Art & Art Gallery, Museum Way & Lomita Dr, 94305. Tel 415-497-4177. *Dir* Dr Lorenz Eitner; *Assoc Dir & Cur Coll* Dr Carol Osborne; *Cur of Prints & Drawings* Betsy G Fryberger; *Dir of Oriental Art* Dr Patrick Maveety; *Cur of Photography* Anita V Mozley; *Registrar & Asst Cur* Nancy C Bavor; *Asst Cur* Kate Kimelman
Open Tues - Fri 10 AM - 5 PM, Sat & Sun 1 - 5 PM. No admis fee. Estab 1891 as a teaching museum and laboratory for University's Department of Art. Average Annual Attendance: 85,000. Mem: 1600; dues $10 - $100; annual meeting in May
Income: Financed by endowment, membership and university funds
Collections: †Native American art; †African art; †Ancient art; †B G Cantor Gallery of Rodin Sculpture; †Oriental art; Stanford Family Collection; †European art 16th-20th century; †American art of 19th & 20th centuries †Photography; †Pre-Columbian art †Contemporary Art; †Oriental Art; †20th Century Art; Stanford Family Collection; †Western Art of the 20th Century
Exhibitions: (1982) Fashion: 1850-1930; Nudes; Photographs by Harry Callahan; Laura Volkerding: Panoramic Photographs; Katherine Porter: Recent Works; Gwen John; Molas; Hollywood Posters; recent acquisitions; Paul Harris: Still Life; Ansel Adams: Ski-Experience; The Art of William Gropper; The Prints of William Nicholson; Early Lithography: 1803-1830; Portraits of Artists: From the Photography Collection; Contemporary Prints; Sue Ferguson Gussow: Paintings and Pastels; Navajo Blankets and Rugs; Beth Van Hoesen: Prints and Drawings; Gisele Freund: Photographs, 1933-1973
Publications: The Stanford Museum, biennial journal; exhibition catalogs
Activities: Classes for adults and children; docent training; lect open to the public, 15 vis lectr per year; gallery talks; tours; book traveling exhibitions; originate traveling exhibitions; museum shop sells books, magazines, reproductions, prints, slides and cards
L **Art Library,** 102 Cummings Art Building, 94305. Tel 415-497-3408. *Librn* Alex Ross; *Asst Librn* Marguerite Grady
Open Mon - Thurs 8 AM - 10 PM, Fri 8 AM - 5 PM, Sat 9 AM - 5 PM, Sun 1 - 10 PM. Limited service to non-Stanford students
Library Holdings: Vols 110,000; Per subs 500; Micro — Fiche; Other — Exhibition catalogs

STOCKTON

M **THE HAGGIN MUSEUM,** 1201 N Pershing Ave, 95203. Tel 209-462-4116. *Dir* Keith E Dennison; *Admin Asst* Setsuko Ryuto; *Cur of Exhibits & Design* Dave A Denney; *Registrar* Joanne Avant; *Librn & Archivist* Diane Freggiaro
Open Tues - Sun 1:30 - 5 PM. No admis fee. Estab 1928 to protect, preserve and interpret for present and future generations historical and fine arts collections that pertain to the museum's disciplines. The gallery covers 34,000 sq ft of exhibit space housing art and history collections. Average Annual Attendance: 50,000. Mem: 1130; dues $15 and up; annual meeting third Tues in Jan
Income: $350,000 (financed by endowment, membership, city and county appropriation & foundation grant)
Collections: 19th Century French, American and European paintings; decorative arts; graphics
Exhibitions: Six - eight temporary exhibits per year
Publications: Museum Calendar, quarterly
Activities: Classes for children; docent training; lect open to the public, 4 - 5 vis lectr per year; concerts; gallery talks; tours; competitions; individual paintings and original objects of art lent
L **Petzinger Memorial Library,** Victory Park, 1201 N Pershing Ave, 95203. Tel 209-462-4116. *Librn* Raymond Hillman
Open Tues, Thurs & Sat by appointment only. Estab 1941 to supply material to those interested in the research of California and San Joaquin County history as well as the history of Stockton
Income: $5400
Purchases: $700
Library Holdings: Vols 7000; original documents; AV — Lantern slides, motion pictures, slides; Other — Clipping files, exhibition catalogs, manuscripts, memorabilia, original art works, pamphlets, photographs, prints, reproductions
Special Subjects: California; San Joaquin & Stockton History
Collections: Earl Roland Art Collection
Activities: Lect open to the public, 3 vis lectr per year; concerts; gallery talks

M **UNIVERSITY OF THE PACIFIC,** University Center Gallery, 3601 Pacific Ave, 95211. Tel 209-946-2242. *Chmn Dept* J Ronald Pecchenino; *Dir* James F Paull
Open Mon - Fri 9 AM - 5 PM. No admis fee. Estab 1975 to expose the University community to various art forms. Gallery is 1200 sq ft with 80 ft wall space, well equiped ceiling spots and flat panels. Average Annual Attendance: 10,000
Income: Financed by student fees and sales
Exhibitions: Peter Voris (sculpture); Imperial Robes from Ching Dynasty; National League of Pen Women; Louise Lieber & Roger Berry (sculptures); Mixed Media Invitational; faculty and student works; Vasereler Prints: E M Escher; HS and alumnae exhibitions
Activities: Lectures open to the public, 3-4 vis lectr per year; gallery talks; juried contests; awards; tours

THOUSAND OAKS

M **CONEJO VALLEY ART MUSEUM,*** 197 N Moorpark Rd, 91360. Tel 805-495-3253. *Pres* Sylvia Sullivan; *VPres* Sandy Webrand; *Secy* Deanna Hackman; *Dir* Loretta Rubin
Open Wed - Sun Noon - 5 PM. No admis fee. Estab 1975 to exhibit works of nationally and internationally known artists. Average Annual Attendance: 8000.
Mem: 200; dues family $25, single $12.50
Income: Financed by membership, donations & grants
Collections: Large Serigraph by Ron Davis
Activities: Sponsor juried art exhibition; cash awards; scholarships offered; museum shop sells books, magazines and merchandise from around the world

TORRANCE

M **EL CAMINO COLLEGE ART GALLERY,** 16007 Crenshaw Blvd, 90506. Tel 213-532-3670. *Gallery Coordr* Judith Markwell
Open Mon - Fri 9 AM - 3 PM, Mon & Thurs 6 - 9 PM. No admis fee. Estab 1970 to exhibit professional, historical and student art. Average Annual Attendance: 1500-1800
Collections: Small print collection; small sculpture collection
Publications: Exhibit catalogs
Activities: Classes for adults; docent training; lectures open to public, 3000 vis lectr per yr; gallery talks; tours; awards; individual paintings & original objects of art lent to campus departments

TURLOCK

CALIFORNIA STATE COLLEGE, STANISLAUS
M **Art Gallery,** 800 Monte Vista, Turlock, 95380. Tel 209-667-3431
Open Mon - Fri 1 - 5 PM. No admis fee. Estab 1967, for the purpose of community and cultural instruction. Gallery is small, covering 250 ft running. Average Annual Attendance: 10,000
Income: Financed by state appropriation
Purchases: $500
Collections: Permanent collection of graphics and small contemporary works
Exhibitions: (1983-84) Albion Contemporary Arts Group; Prints from the Collection of Ernest de Soto; Prints from the Kala Institute; Richard Sauini; A Planar Perspective: Eight Photographers; California: Idioms of Surrealism; Slade; Vredaparis
Publications: Exhibition catalogs
Activities: Classes for adults; lect open to the public, 11 visiting lectrs per year; concerts; gallery talks; tours; exten dept serving summer school; individual paintings and original objects of art lent to the campus community; lending collection contains film strips, 35mm lantern slides, motion pictures, original art works, original prints; traveling exhibitions organized and circulated
L **Vasche Library,** 801 Monte Vista, 95380. Tel 209-667-3232. *Dir* R Dean Galloway
Open daily 8 AM - 10 PM. Estab 1960, as a college resource for liberal arts. Circ 129,000
Income: $8300 (financed by state appropriation)
Purchases: $8300
Library Holdings: Vols 8500; Per subs 150; Micro — Fiche, prints, reels; AV — A-tapes, cassettes, fs, Kodachromes, motion pictures, slides, v-tapes; Other — Framed reproductions, original art works, reproductions
Special Subjects: Emphasis on 19th and 20th century art
Collections: Art History Slide Library Collection; contemporary American prints

VALENCIA

L **CALIFORNIA INSTITUTE OF THE ARTS LIBRARY,*** 24700 McBean Parkway, 90038. Tel 805-255-1050. *Head* James Elrod; *Cataloger* Joan Anderson; *Head, Public Services* Frederick Gardner; *Film Librn* Margie Hanft; *Art & Slide Librn* Evelyn White
Open Mon - Thurs 9 AM - Midnight, Fri 9 AM - 5 PM, Sat 1 - 5 PM, Sun 1 - 9 PM. Estab 1961, first classes 1970, designed to be a community of practicing artists working in schools of art, design, film, music, theatre and dance
Income: Financed by endowment
Library Holdings: Vols 72,609; Per subs 545; Micro — Cards 3900, fiche 991, reels 6520; AV — A-tapes, cassettes, fs 731, motion pictures, rec 798, slides 59,302, v-tapes 376; Other — Exhibition catalogs, pamphlets
Special Subjects: Film, Theatre Arts, Video, art and design, critical studies, dance, music,
Exhibitions: Student work, approximately 20 per year
Publications: California Arts Admissions Bulletin

VAN NUYS

M LOS ANGELES VALLEY COLLEGE, Art Gallery, 5800 Fulton Ave, 91401.
Tel 213-781-1200, Ext 400. *Dir* Dennis Reed
Open Mon - Thurs Noon - 3 PM & 7 - 9 PM. No admis fee, donation requested.
Estab 1960 to show original changing exhibitions of ethnic, historical,
contemporary & nature art. Single gallery
Income: $50,000 (financed by state appropriation & fundraising)
Exhibitions: The Furniture of Gustav Stickley; Edie Ellis: Handmade Poems &
Books; Lena Rivkin: Visual Scores; Ormette's Way: An Art Performance/An
Opera
Activities: Lectures open to public, 2 vis lectr per yr

VENICE

O BEYOND BAROQUE FOUNDATION, 681 Venice Blvd, 90291. Tel 213-822-
3006. *Pres* Jocelyn Fisher; *VPres* Alexandra Garrett; *Co-Dir Reading Servs* Jack
Skelley; *Admin Asst* Marilyn Groch; *Dir Exhibition Series* Judith Czlonka;
Co-Dir Reading Series Benjamin Weissman
Open Tues - Fri 9 AM - 5 PM, Sat 9 AM - 1 PM. No admis fee, $2 donation.
Estab 1968 to promote & support literary arts projects & artists in Southern
Calif. Mem: 1200; dues $15
Income: $180,000 (financed by membership, city appropriation, state
appropriation, individual donations & National Endowment for the Arts)
Exhibitions: Joan Jonas Videotapes; The Time Machine, An Exhibition of 50's
Beat Art from California
Publications: Magazine, bi-monthly
Activities: Fiction writing workshops; lectures open to public; sales shop sells
books & magazines

WALNUT CREEK

M WALNUT CREEK CIVIC ARTS DEPARTMENT GALLERY, 1641 Locust St,
94596. Tel 415-943-5866. *Cur* Carl Worth
Open Tues - Sun Noon - 5 PM, Fri 7:30 - 9 PM, cl national holidays. No admis
fee. Estab 1963, to offer varied and educational changing exhibitions to the
community and surrounding area. Gallery contains 396 running ft, 2300 sq ft,
including mezzanine gallery. Average Annual Attendance: 24,000. Mem: 500;
dues $15
Income: Funded by city, public & private grants
Purchases: $2000
Collections: General city collection consisting of paintings, prints, photographs
and crafts
Exhibitions: (1982-84) Hard Edge; Geometric Abstraction; Early California
Landscapes; Social Commentary; Ceramics Competitive; Bay Area Contemporary
Sculptors & Painters; Musical Instruments; American Folk Art
Publications: City Scene (newsletter); three catalogs per year
Activities: Classes for adults and children; dramatic programs; docent training;
lect open to public, 6-10 visiting lectrs per year; concerts; gallery talks; tours;
competitions; sales shop selling books, original art, slides and catalogs
L Library, 1445 Civic Dr, 94596
Open to local schools, docents and civic arts members

WHITTIER

M RIO HONDO COLLEGE ART GALLERY, 3600 Workman Mill Road, 90608.
Tel 213-692-0921, Ext 361. *Gallery Dir* William Lane; *Chair Fine Arts* John R
Jacole
Open Mon - Fri 11 AM - 4 PM & 6:30 - 9 PM. No admis fee. Estab 1967 to
bring to the college students a wide variety of art experiences that will enhance
and develop their sensitivity and appreciation of art. Small gallery about 1000 sq
ft located within the art facility. Average Annual Attendance: 8000
Income: Financed through college
Collections: Contemporary paintings and graphics by Southern California artists
Exhibitions: Landscapes by Paul Donaldson, Carl Aldana, James Urstrom;
Sculptures by Joyce Kohl; Self Portraits by Selected California Artists; student
shows and area high school honor show
Activities: Classes for adults; lect open to public
L Fine Arts Dept Library, Fine Arts Dept, 3600 Workman Mill Rd, 90608. Tel
213-692-0921, Ext 361
Library Holdings: Vols 200; Per subs 8; AV — A-tapes, cassettes, fs,
Kodachromes, motion pictures, rec, slides, v-tapes; Other — Framed
reproductions, manuscripts, memorabilia, original art works, photographs, prints,
reproductions, sculpture

YOSEMITE NATIONAL PARK

M YOSEMITE COLLECTIONS, National Park Service, Box 577, 95389. Tel 209-
372-4461, Ext 281. *Chief Cur* David M Forgang; *Cur Ethnography* Craig D
Bates; *Registrar* Barbara L Beroza
Open daily 9 AM - 5 PM summer, Fri - Tues 9 AM - 5 PM winter. No admis
fee. Estab 1926 to interpret the natural sciences and human history of the
Yosemite area. Mem: 1700; dues $10 and up
Income: Financed by federal appropriation
Collections: Indian cultural artifacts; photographs (special collection on early
Yosemite); pioneer artifacts; Yosemite related ephemera
Activities: Classes for adults and children; lect open to public; paintings and
original art objects lent on special exhibits only; lending collection contains
prints, photographs; shop sells books, magazines, reproductions, prints, slides;
junior museum
L Research Library, Box 577, 95389. Tel 209-372-4461, Ext 280. *Librn* Mary
Vocelka
For reference only
Library Holdings: Vols 15,000; Per subs 85; Micro — Fiche, reels; AV —
Lantern slides; Other — Clipping files, exhibition catalogs, manuscripts,
memorabilia, pamphlets, photographs, reproductions
Special Subjects: Yosemite history

COLORADO

ALAMOSA

L ADAMS STATE COLLEGE, Library, 81102. Tel 303-589-7781, 589-7782. *Dir*
Nellie N Hasfjord; *Reference Librn* Shannon Patterson; *Reference & Special Coll
Librn* Christine E Moeny; *Cataloger* Dr Jerome Halpin
Open 8 AM - 10 PM. Estab 1924 to support the total educational mission of the
college
Income: $300,000
Purchases: $120,000
Library Holdings: Vols 3250; Per subs 15; AV — Cassettes, fs, motion pictures,
slides; Other — Original art works, photographs, prints, reproductions, sculpture

ASPEN

M ASPEN CENTER FOR VISUAL ARTS, 590 N Mill St, 81611. Tel 303-925-
8050. *Dir* Laurel Jones
Open Tues, Weds, Fri, Sat & Sun Noon - 6 PM, Thurs Noon - 8 PM, cl New
Years, July 4, Thanksgiving and Christmas. Admis $2. Estab 1979. Maintains
small reference library. Mem: Dues benefactor $5000 and up, patron $1501-
$5000, sponsor $501-$1500, contributor $150, charter $15
Activities: Classes for adults and childrens; docent training; lectures; tours; films;
gallery talks; concerts; originates traveling exhibitions

BLACKHAWK

M BLACKHAWK MOUNTAIN SCHOOL OF ART GALLERY,* 251 Main St,
80422. Tel 303-582-5235. *Dir* Michael S Parfenoff; *Dir* Michael J Reardon
Open 10 AM - 5 PM June, July and Aug. No admis fee. Estab 1972 to exhibit
works of art by students, faculty and friends of the School. The Gallery is part of
the educational experience for the students. They organize exhibits, staff the
gallery and carry out all necessary functions of the gallery. There is 300 sq ft of
exhibition space

BOULDER

O BOULDER CENTER FOR THE VISUAL ARTS, 1750 13th St, 80302. Tel
303-443-2122. *Dir* Karen Hodge
Open Tues - Sat 11 AM - 5 PM, Sun 1 - 5 PM. Admis exhibitions free, lectures
$1-$5. Estab 1976 to promote growth, development & appreciation of quality art
in the community and act as catalyst between broad community and the arts.
Two galleries totaling 5000 sq ft; workshop & lecture space; exhibitions focus on
contemporary Colorado & regional art. Average Annual Attendance: 20,000.
Mem: 700; dues from $12-$1000; annual meeting in Oct
Income: $90,000 (financed by endowment, membership, city appropriation and
grants)
Collections: Tom Hicks, Voyage, large outdoor sculpture
Exhibitions: Boulder Public School Art Show; Group Exhibitions of Colorado
Artists; Sculpture in the Park; (1983) Margaretta Gilboy-Chuck Forsman: Insides
and Out; John Fudge Retrospective; Once Upon a Time, children's book
illustrations; 25 Years on the Road, a Visual Tribute to Jack Kerouac; Further
Selections, from the Collection of Amoco Production Co; Models of Invention of
Leonardo da Vinci; New Tools/Machine & Image; Inventions: Twelve Around
One, prints by R Buckminster Fuller; 4 Potters: curated by Betty Woodman;
Atomic Symmetries,paintings & drawings by Clark Richert; Art 82, juried; Draw
82, juried; Colorado Artist-Craftsman Annual Exhibition, juried; Interlacements,
textiles
Publications: Art Review, bi-monthly
Activities: Classes for adults and children; docent training; lectures open to
public, 3-5 vis lect per yr; concerts; gallery talks; tours; competitions with awards;
book traveling exhibitions 1-2 per yr; sales shop sells magazines

L BOULDER PUBLIC LIBRARY AND GALLERY, Dept of Fine Arts Gallery,
1000 Canyon Blvd, PO Drawer H, 80306. Tel 303-441-3100. *Library Dir*
Marcelee Gralapp; *Asst Library Dir* Richard Luce; *Dir Media & Programing*
Richard Varnes
Open Mon - Thurs 9 AM - 9 PM, Sat 9 AM - 6 PM, Sun Noon - 6 PM, cl Fri.
Estab to enhance the personal development of Boulder citizens by meeting their
informational needs. Bridge Gallery, three shows change monthly. Average
Annual Attendance: 300,000
Income: Financed by city appropriations, grants and gifts
Library Holdings: Micro — Cards, fiche, prints; AV — A-tapes, cassettes, fs,
slides, v-tapes; Other — Clipping files, exhibition catalogs, framed reproductions,
manuscripts, original art works, pamphlets, photographs, prints, reproductions,
sculpture
Exhibitions: Barbara Bash (calligraphy); Ira Sherman (metal sculpture); Charles
Dowling (photography); Artifacts of the H'mong Tribe; Jalal Quinn
(watercolors); Colorado Music Festival, Between the Wars; Linda Stenzel
(stencils); Laura Marshall (watercolors); Historic Boulder, Architecture as Art -
Thomas MacLaren in Boulder; Karmen Effenberger-Thompson (watercolors);
Barbara Whipple (woodcuts); Ann Johnson (bronzes & batiks); Ceramic Art by
Local Children; Pat Braverman (photography); Embroiderers Guild of America
Display; Brian Gough (pen & ink); Gini Kircher (porcelain portraits); Barbara
Nielson & Phil Biltz (fiber art); Diane Hogan (quilts); Linda Lawsen (fabric to
metal); Boulder Valley Doll Collectors, A Doll's Christmas; Ron Chidester
(Chesdegango), Oil Paintings; Jim Hurrell (photography); Boulder Model
Railroad Club (trains); University of Colorado School of Fine Art (mixed media);
Steve Sutton (photography); Arawana Hayashi, Bugaku: Japanese Court Dance;
Colorado Artists Register Exhibit
Activities: Classes for adults and children; lect open to public; concerts; tours;
competitions; awards

M LEANIN TREE MUSEUM OF WESTERN ART, 6055 Longbow Dr, PO Box
9500, 80301. Tel 303-530-1442. *Art Adminr* Susan Blackstock
Open Jan - Sept Mon - Fri 8 AM - 4:30 PM, Oct - Dec Mon - Fri 8 AM - 4:30
PM, Sat 8 AM - 4 PM, cl all holidays. No admis fee. Estab 1974
Collections: Contemporary western cowboy and Indian art; western bronze
sculptures; paintings by major contemporary western artists
Activities: Self guided tours; museum shop sales prints, greeting cards and related
paper products with western art

M UNIVERSITY OF COLORADO ART GALLERIES, Sibell-Wolle Fine Arts
Building, Box 318, 80309. Tel 303-492-8300. *Dir* Jean-Edith V Weiffenbach;
Asst Cur Gabrielle Bershen
Open Mon - Fri 10 AM - 4 PM, Sat & Sun 1 - 5 PM. No admiss fee. Estab 1939
to maintain and exhibit art collections and to show temporary exhibits. The
galleries have 413 linear ft of wall space and a total of 5000 sq ft
Income: Financed through University
Collections: †19th and 20th century paintings and †prints; †prints, drawings,
watercolors, sculptures and ceramics of the 15th - 20th centuries
Exhibitions: (1982-83) Robert Kushner; Ed McGowin; Eric Fischl; April Gornik;
Jody Pinto; Mike Mandel/Larry Sultan; Meridel Rubenstein; Commentaries: Jo
Harvey Allen, Martha Rosler, Theodora Skiptares, Francesc Torres; monthly
selections from the permanent collection; recent acquisitions to the collection;
Rick Dingus & Steve Fitch; Frank Mechau: Artist of Colorado
Publications: Brochures; exhibition catalogs
Activities: Lect open to public, 12 visiting artists per year; paintings and original
art objects lent to museums; lending collection contains original art works and
prints, paintings, photographs, sculpture, original drawings
L Art and Architecture Library, Box 184, 80309. Tel 303-492-7955. *Head Art and
Architecture Library* Liesel Nolan; *Library Technician* Mary Larson; *Library
Asst* Martha Covey
Open Mon - Fri 8 AM - Midnight, Sat 10 AM - 5 PM, Sun Noon - Midnight.
Estab 1966 to support the university curriculum in the areas of fine arts, art
history and architecture. Maintains small gallery devoted to book exhibitions and
some photography exhibitions
Income: Financed by state appropriation
Library Holdings: Vols 54,000; Per subs 343; Micro — Fiche, reels; Other —
Clipping files, exhibition catalogs, memorabilia
Special Subjects: Photography, Artists books

BRECKENRIDGE

M COLORADO MOUNTAIN COLLEGE, Fine Arts Gallery,* 103 S Harris St,
80424
Exhibitions: Harry Callahan, color photographs; The Cranbrook Show, Polaroid
still lifes; Betty Hahn, images from the series It's a Mystery; Robert Fichter,
recent works; William Larson & Henry Wessel, Jr, recent works; Meridel
Rubenstein: Low Riders portfolio

CENTRAL CITY

O GILPIN COUNTY ARTS ASSOCIATION, Eureka St, 80427. Tel 303-582-
5952. *Pres* J Theodore Ellis; *VPres* Christine Emmert; *Secy* Billie DeMars;
Corresponding Secy Kay Russell; *Gallery Mgr* Open
Open daily 11 AM - 5 PM. No admis fee. Estab 1947 to offer a juried exhibition
of Colorado artists. A gallery is maintained. Average Annual Attendance: 20,000.
Mem: 200; dues $5 - $100; annual meeting third Sun in Aug
Income: Financed by membership, sales and entry fee
Publications: Catalog
Activities: Juried competitions with awards; scholarships; sponsor elementary
school art program; sales shop sells original art

COLORADO SPRINGS

AMERICAN NUMISMATIC ASSOCIATION MUSEUM
For further information, see National and Regional Organizations

M COLORADO SPRINGS FINE ARTS CENTER, 30 W Dale St, 80903. Tel
303-634-5581. *Dir* Paul M Piazza; *Adminr* G W Engle; *Cur Fine Arts Coll &
Exhib* Charles Guerin; *Actg Cur Taylor Mus* Jonathan Batkin; *Dir Development*
Jeffrey Haney; *Dir Educational Prog* Joyce Robinson; *Dir Public Relations*
DeAnn Hiatt; *Dir Sales Shop* Maggie Lombard; *Dir Museum Services* R E
Zendejas
Open Tues - Sat 10 AM - 5 PM, Sun 1:30 - 5 PM, cl Mon. No admis fee. Estab
1936 as a forum, advocate and programmer of visual and performing arts
activities for the community. Eleven galleries range in size from quite small to
large. Average Annual Attendance: 200,000. Mem: 2500; dues $25 - $1000;
annual meeting Feb
Income: $1,000,000 (financed by endowment, membership, city and state
appropriations, and revenue producing enterprises)
Library Holdings: Vols 19,000; Per subs 85; Other — Clipping files, exhibition
catalogs, pamphlets, reproductions
Collections: Taylor Collection of Southwestern Spanish Colonial and native
American art; American paintings, sculptures, graphics and drawings with
emphasis on art west of the Mississippi; ethnographic collections; fine arts
collections; 19th and 20th century art and survey collection of world art
Exhibitions: Bernard Arnest Retrospective; The Arts of the Indians of the
Northwest Coast; Frithjof Schuon: Scenes of Plains Indian Life; Whitney
Museum of American Art: American Painting of the 60's & 70's; Arthur
Amiotte: Paintings and Wall Hangings; New Images from Spain organized by the
Guggenheim; The Arts of the Great Lakes and Woodland Indians; Portraits from
the Permanent Collection; The Pueblos; Rauschenberg Prints; Mexican Influences
in the Hispanic Southwest; Bruce McGrew: One-man Show; Tom Cosgrove:
One-man Show; The Lost Keam Collection of Hopi Pottery; Annual Art
Auction; Colorado Springs Young People's Art; Gallery of Christmas Trees;
Colorado Springs Collects; John Sloan in Santa Fe; Henry Moore Shelter

Drawings; Woodworking in the Rockies; Photography of Gordon Parks; Heritage
Renewed-Representational Drawing Today
Publications: Annual report; Artsfocus; monthly calendar; educational programs
and tours; exhibition catalogs; gallery sheets; scholarly publication
Activities: Art classes for children and adults; dramatic programs; docent
training; lect open to public; concerts; films; gallery talks; competitions; art lent
to AAM accredited museums; shop sells books, art and gifts
L Library, 30 W Dale St, 80903. Tel 303-634-5581. *Librn* Roderick Dew
Open Tues - Sat 10 AM - 5 PM, cl Mon & Sun. Estab 1936 as a fine arts
reference library in support of the museum's collection and activities. Open for
public reference, lending is restricted to members of the center and local
university students and faculty
Income: Financed by endowment & membership
Library Holdings: Vols 20,000; Per subs 88; Other — Clipping files, exhibition
catalogs, memorabilia, pamphlets, prints, reproductions
Special Subjects: Art and anthropology of the Southwest
Collections: Taylor Museum Collection on the art & †anthropology of the
Southwest
Activities: Tours

M UNITED STATES FIGURE SKATING HALL OF FAME AND MUSEUM,
20 First St, 80906. Tel 303-635-5200. *Pres* George T Yonekura; *VPres* Hugh C
Graham Jr; *Secy* Betty Sonnhalter; *Actg Exec Dir* Ian A Anderson; *Cur* Pat
Cataldi; *Registrar* Deann Crider
Open winter Mon - Fri 10 AM - 4 PM, summer Tues - Sat 10 AM - 4 PM. No
admis fee. Estab 1979 to preserve the art and history of skating. Maintains 5000
square feet exhibit area. Average Annual Attendance: 8000
Collections: Skating In Art, the Gillis Grafstrom Collection; costumes of the
champions; Gladys McFerron Collection
Publications: Skating Magazine
Activities: Lect; gallery talks; tours; competitions with awards; video tape
showings; film showings; originate traveling exhibitions to skating organizations,
clubs and members; museum shop selling books, jewelry, figurines, medals,
decals, cards, decorations and music boxes
L Library, 20 First St, 80906
Open Tues - Sat 10 AM - 4 PM
Library Holdings: Micro — Reels; AV — A-tapes, cassettes, fs, lantern slides,
motion pictures, rec, slides, v-tapes; Other — Clipping files, exhibition catalogs,
framed reproductions, memorabilia, original art works, pamphlets, photographs,
prints
Special Subjects: Skating, the best reference collection in the world
Collections: First books published in English, French & German on skating

DENVER

AURARIA HIGHER EDUCATION CENTER
M Auraria Library Gallery, 1027 9th St, Denver, 80204. Tel 303-629-3291. *Cur*
Carol Keller
Open Mon - Fri 11 AM - 5 PM. Estab 1982. Library Gallery is located in the
Auraria Library and exhibits small one-person and group exhibitions. Average
Annual Attendance: 30,000
Income: Financed by colleges and Auraria Higher Education Center
Exhibitions: (1983) Visions on The Figure
Activities: Book traveling exhibitions
M Emmanuel Gallery, 1027 9th St, Denver, 80204
Open Mon - Fri 11 AM - 5 PM. Estab 1976. Gallery is in the oldest standing
church structure in Denver which has been renovated for exhibit space. This
historically designated building is used by the local campus institutions, Denver
Auraria Community College, Metropolitan State College and The University of
Colorado at Denver, and the Denver community. Average Annual Attendance:
30,000
Income: Financed by three above colleges and Auraria Higher Education Center
Exhibitions: (1983) University of Colorado at Denver Faculty Exhibit
Activities: Book traveling exhibitions

M COLORADO HISTORICAL SOCIETY, State Museum, Colorado Heritage
Center, 1300 Broadway, 80203. Tel 303-866-3682. *Executive Dir* Barbara Sudler;
Asst State Historic Preservation Officer for History Jim Hartman; *Asst State
Historic Preservation Officer for Archaeology* Bruce Rippeteau; *Cur of
Decorative & Fine Arts* Georgiana Contigulia; *Cur of Photographs* Eric Paddock;
Head of Publications David Wetzel; *Head of Education* Lola Farber; *Cur
Material Culture* Barbara Handy; *Asst Cur of Manuscripts* Margot Honan; *Head
Conservation & Registration* Eryl Platzer; *Head of Public Service & Access*
Katherine Kane; *Head of Design & Production* Gene Roberts
Open Mon - Sat 10 AM - 4:30 PM, Sun Noon - 4:30 PM, cl Mon & Christmas.
Admis adults $2.50, children 6 - 16 yrs & senior citizens $1, children under 6
free. Estab 1879 to collect, preserve and interpret the history of Colorado. Main
level exhibit space of 35,000 sq ft to be developed over the next 2 years; special
exhibit galleries. Average Annual Attendance: 200,000. Mem: 4683; dues $15;
annual meeting varies
Income: $1,600,000 (financed by endowment, membership, state and federal
appropriations)
Exhibitions: Puppets: Art & Entertainment; Buffalo Bill & The Wild West;
Landmarks of Liberty; continuing Colorado history exhibits; North American
Basketry; Native American Textiles - Southwest; Artists of America; R G Bellers,
photographs; Stobie Paintings; W H Jackson, chromolimographs; Mining in
Colorado; Dolores River Photographic Survey
Publications: Colorado Heritage, biannual; Colorado Heritage News, monthly
Activities: Classes for adults and children; dramatic programs; docent training;
lectures open to the public; concerts; gallery talks; tours; exten dept serving the
state; individual paintings & original objects of art lent; book traveling exhibitions
2-3 per yr; originate traveling exhibitions; museum shop sells books, magazines,
original art, reproductions, prints and slides
L Stephen H Hart Library, 80203. Tel 303-866-2305
Open to public for reference
Library Holdings: Vols 40,000; maps; Micro — Reels 26,000; AV — A-tapes,
rec; Other — Manuscripts 1,000,000, photographs 250,000
Collections: William Henry Jacson Glass Plate Negatives of Views West of the
Mississippi

M **COLORADO WOMEN'S COLLEGE**, Lyle True Gallery,* Montview at Quebec, 80220. Tel 303-394-6012. *Dir* Joyce Eakins
Gallery and Library maintained
Income: Financed by endowment and student tuition
Exhibitions: Six exhibitions per year by nationally-known artists; faculty and student exhibitions
Activities: Classes for adults; field trips to regional and national museums and galleries; dramatic programs; lect open to the public; concerts; ; scholarships offered; book shop

M **DENVER ART MUSEUM**, 100 W 14th Ave Parkway, 80204. Tel 303-575-2793. *Interim Dir* Lewis W Story; *Public Relations Dir* Helen Masterson
Open Sun & Mon Noon - 5 PM, Tues - Sat 9 AM - 5 PM, Wed evening till 8 PM. Admis $2, members free. Estab 1893, new building opened 1971, to provide a number of permanent and rotating art collections for public viewing, as well a variety of art education programs and services. The Museum is a seven story building composed of two cubes, placed like a square-cornered figure eight. The building contains 210,000 sq ft of space, 117,000 of which is exhibit space. Average Annual Attendance: 500,000. Mem: Dues family $25, individual $15; annual meeting April
Income: Financed by membership, city and state appropriations and private funding
Collections: †American art; †contemporary art; †European art; †Native American art; †native arts; †New World art; †Oriental art; †costumes and textiles
Exhibitions: A Century of French Masters: Corot to Braque; Andrew Dasburg Retrospective; Hawaii: The Royal Island; Journey of the Three Jewels; 19th and 20th Century Master Drawings; Song of the Brush; Travels With Pen, Pencil and Ink (David Hockney); Watercolors from the Baltimore Museum of Art; William T Wiley: 12 Years; Circles of the World; Traditional Plains Indian Art
Publications: Calendar, monthly; catalogues for exhibitions
Activities: Classes for adults and children; dramatic programs; docent training; lect open to the public, 20 vis lectr per year; concerts, gallery talks; tours; art mobile; individual paintings and original objects of art lent to museums; traveling exhibitions organized and circulated; museum shop sells books, jewelry, prints, reproductions, slides, and Native American Art

L **Frederic H Douglas Library**, 100 W 14th Ave Parkway, 80204. Tel 303-575-2256. *Librn* Margaret Goodrich; *Cur Native Arts Department* Richard Conn
Open by appointment only. Estab 1935 to facilitate research in anthropology and native arts. Reference only
Purchases: $1000
Library Holdings: Vols 7000; Per subs 300; Micro — Cards, fiche; AV — Slides; Other — Clipping files, exhibition catalogs, framed reproductions, manuscripts, memorabilia, original art works, pamphlets, photographs, prints, reproductions, sculpture
Special Subjects: Africa, American Indians, Native American linguistics, Oceania
Collections: †Native American, African & Oceanic linguistics

L **DENVER PUBLIC LIBRARY**, Arts & Recreation Dept, 1357 Broadway, 80203. Tel 303-571-2070. *Librn* Henry G Shearouse Jr; *Head Dept* Georgiana Tiff
Open Mon - Wed 10 AM - 9 PM, Fri & Sat 10 AM - 5:30 PM, cl Thur & Sun. Estab 1889
Income: Financed by city and county taxes
Library Holdings: Vols 65,391; original documents; Micro — Fiche, reels; AV — A-tapes, cassettes, fs, motion pictures 3000, rec, slides 15,000, v-tapes; Other — Clipping files, exhibition catalogs, framed reproductions 1000, manuscripts, memorabilia, original art works, pamphlets 177,726, photographs 14,752, prints 1384, reproductions, sculpture
Exhibitions: Frequent exhibitions from the book and picture collections
Activities: Tours; individual paintings lent to Denver Public Library card holders

M **THE TURNER MUSEUM**, 773 Downing St, 80218. Tel 303-832-0924. *Pres & Treas* Douglas Graham; *VPres & Secy* R Canady; *Librn & Registrar* Walden Porter
Open Sun 1 - 6 PM and by appointment. No admis fee. Estab 1972 to carry out the last will of J M W Turner to display his and his principal admirer's (Thomas Moran) works. The Atlantic Richfield Gallery; The Mediterranean Gallery; The Kurt Pantzer Gallery. Average Annual Attendance: 1000. Mem: 800; dues $25; annual meeting first Sun in Dec
Income: $10,000 (financed by endowment and membership)
Purchases: J M W Turner; Thomas Moran
Collections: Moran Collection; Turner Collection
Exhibitions: Turner & Moran; Turner & Switzerland; Turner's Versatility
Publications: Turner & Moran, yearly; Turner on Paper
Activities: Lect open to the public, 2 visiting lectr per year; concerts; gallery talks; tours; individual paintings and original objects of art lent to other museums and similar organizations; lending collection contains books, color reproductions, original art works, original prints, slides and posters; museum shop selling books, reproductions, prints and posters

FORT COLLINS

C **FIRST INTERSTATE BANK OF FORT COLLINS**,* 205 W Oak, PO Box 578, 80521. Tel 303-482-4861. *Community Relations Officer* Libby Dale
Open 9 AM - 5:30 PM. No admis fee. Estab 1977 to invest in art for enjoyment of bank customers. Collection displayed in lobby and mezzanine of main bank; supports Council on Arts and Humanities, Colorado State University, Symphony, Theater
Collections: Prints by Boulanger, Calder, Sam Francis, Japser Johns, Pali, Rauschenberg, Vasarely, Dave Yust and local artists
Activities: Originate traveling exhibitions; sponsors Colorado State University Traveling Print Collection

GOLDEN

O **FOOTHILLS ART CENTER, INC**,* 809 15th St, 80401. Tel 303-279-3922. *Exec Dir* Marian J Metsopoulos
Open Mon - Sat 9 AM - 4 PM, Sun 1 - 4 PM, cl holidays. No admis fee. Estab 1968 to provide a cultural center which embraces all the arts, to educate and stimulate the community in the appreciation and understanding of the arts, to provide equal opportunities for all people to participate in the further study and enjoyment of the arts, and to provide artists and artisans with the opportunity to present their work. Housed in the former First Presbyterian Church of Golden, the original structure was built in 1872, the manse (a part of the whole layout) was built in 1892; there are three galleries, offices, a kitchen and classrooms. Average Annual Attendance: 15,000. Mem: 950; dues $20; annual meeting in December
Income: $165,000 (financed by membership, city appropriation, donations, commissions and rental of rooms)
Exhibitions: North American Sculpture Exhibition; Rocky Mountain Watermedia Exhibition; numerous open juried competitions
Publications: Communique; one chapbook per year-winner of poetry competition (international); poetry newsletter, bi-monthly
Activities: Classes for adults and children; lect open to the public, 2 - 3 vis lectr per year; concerts; tours; competitions with awards; individual paintings and original objects of art lent to businesses

L **Mary S Robinson Art Library**, 809 15th St, 80401. Tel 303-279-3922
Open to members only
Library Holdings: Vols 800; Per subs 3

GRAND JUNCTION

L **MUSEUM OF WESTERN COLORADO ARCHIVES**, Fourth and Ute, 81501. Tel 303-242-0971. *Dir* John R Brumgardt; *Asst Dir* Larry Bowles; *Cur* William Tennent; *Archivist-Registrar* Judy Prosser
Open Tues - Sat 10 AM - 4:45 PM, Mon 1 - 4:45 PM, cl Sun, Christmas wk & major holidays. No admis fee. Estab 1965 to preserve and collect documents and art concerning Western Colorado. For reference only. Mem: Dues benefactor $1000, patron $800, sponsor $100, contributer and business $25, family $15, adult $7.50, retired adult $5
Income: Financed by membership and Mesa County
Library Holdings: Vols 1000; Per subs 25; Micro — Prints, reels; AV — Cassettes, lantern slides, motion pictures, slides; Other — Manuscripts, memorabilia, original art works, pamphlets, photographs
Special Subjects: Natural History; Social History of Western Colorado
Collections: Frank Dean Collection; †Al Look Collection; †Warren Kiefer Railroad Collection; Wilson Rockwell Collection; artwork, books, manuscripts and photographs on the history of Western Colorado; Mesa County Oral History Collection
Exhibitions: Denny Sanders Exhibit; Country School Legacy; Otavolo Indian Exhibit; Keith Phillips/Sheri Dunn Art Show; Lydia & Bob Maurer Art Show; World War I Exhibition & Lecture Series; Pearl Harbor Exhibition & Lecture Series; Classic Film Festival; Al Look Lecture Series
Publications: Museum Quarterly; Mesa County Cooking with History (3rd Ed); Footprints in the Trail (3rd printing); Familiar Insects of Mesa County Colorado; More Footprints in the Trail; Cross Ranch Cookbook
Activities: Classes for children; docent training; lectures open to the public, 10 vis lectr per year; concerts; tours; Cross Ranch Apple Jubilee; Cross Ranch Artisan's Festival; slides/tape & video tape presentations

O **WESTERN COLORADO CENTER FOR THE ARTS, INC**, 1803 N Seventh, 81501. Tel 303-243-7337. *Dir* Allen Dodworth; *Pres of Board of Trustees* Charles Cole; *Secy & Registrar* Louise Moore; *Development Officer* Susan Burkey; *Bookkeeper* Connie Kuyoth-Smith
Open Tues - Sat 10 AM - 5 PM, Sun Noon - 4 PM. No admis fee. Art Center incorporated in 1953 to provide an appropriate setting to involve individuals in the appreciation of, and active participation in the arts. Two exhibition galleries of 2000 sq ft each; small stage; four studio classrooms. Average Annual Attendance: 20,000 - 24,000. Mem: 800; dues family $15, individual $7.50; annual meeting in February
Income: Financed by endowment, membership, tuitions, gifts & grants
Collections: Ceramics, needlework, paintings; Navajo weavings
Exhibitions: Changing exhibits only in gallery
Publications: Newsletter for members, monthly
Activities: Classes for adults and children; dramatic programs; Childrens Theatre Company and Class Program; Community Theatre docent training; lectures open to the public, 4 - 5 vis lectr per yr; concerts; gallery talks; tours; competitions; book traveling exhibitions, 8 - 10 per yr; originate traveling exhibitions; sales shop sells books, magazines, original art, reproductions, Southwest Indian & contemporary craft items & notecards

L **Library**, 1803 N Seventh, 81501
Open to members and public for reference
Library Holdings: Vols 250; Per subs 8; Other — Exhibition catalogs

GREELEY

M **UNIVERSITY OF NORTHERN COLORADO**, John Mariani Art Gallery,* Department of Fine Arts, Eighth Ave & 18th St, 80639. Tel 303-351-2143, 351-1890. *Dir* Richard Luster; *Asst Dir* Ellen Martin; *Coordr* Magee Ferguson
Open Mon - Fri 9 AM - 4 PM. No admis fee. Estab 1973, to provide art exhibitions for the benefit of the University and the surrounding community
Income: Financed by endowment and city and state appropriations
Publications: Schedule of Exhibitions, quarterly
Activities: Classes for adults; lectures open to public; gallery talks; tours; competitions with awards; (1982) Faculty Exhibit; Teg Egri (sculpture); Joan Hiett (ceramics); Catherine Nicagetta (drawings); Printmakers Invitational Exhibit; Deborah Hohn (paintings); John Zimmer (ceramics); International Posters; Student Art Exhibit; Eleanor Huntley (weaving); Jerry Hubka (ceramics)

GUNNISON

M WESTERN STATE COLLEGE, Quigley Hall Art Gallery,* 81230. Tel 303-943-2045. *Dir* Harry Heil; *Dept Head* Pat T Julio; *Chmn* Dr Jess W Gern
Open Mon - Fri 1 - 5 PM. No admis fee. Estab 1967 for the purpose of exhibiting student, staff and traveling art. Nearly 300 running ft fireproof brick walls, security lock-up iron grill gate is contained in the gallery. Average Annual Attendance: 6000
Income: Financed by state appropriation
Collections: Original paintings and prints
Activities: Competitions; originates traveling exhibitions

LA JUNTA

M KOSHARE INDIAN MUSEUM, INC, 115 West 18th, 81050. Tel 303-384-4801. *Dir* J F Burshears
Open summer 9 AM - 5 PM, winter 1 - 4:30 PM. No admis fee. Estab 1949 for the exhibition of Indian artifacts and paintings. Average Annual Attendance: 100,000. Mem: 100
Income: Financed by donations and shows
Collections: Indian arts and crafts, of and by Indians; Taos Ten; prominent South Western artists
Activities: Classes for children; tours; Paintings and original art works lent; book traveling exhibitions; museum shop sells books, original art, reproductions & souvenirs & Indian jewelry & pottery
L Library, 115 West 18th, 81050. Tel 303-384-4801. *Librn* Sharon E Johnson
Open for reference only to members
Library Holdings: Vols 1657; Other — Clipping files

LEADVILLE

O LAKE COUNTY CIVIC CENTER ASSOCIATION, INC, Heritage Museum and Gallery, 100-102 W Ninth St, PO Box 962, 80461. Tel 303-486-1878. *Pres Board of Dir* Robert Cavalli; *Treas Board of Dir* Betti Bureau; *Secy Board of Dir* LeRoy Wingenbach
Open from Memorial Day through Labor Day Mon - Sun 9 AM - 5 PM. Admis adults $1.50, sr citizens $.75, children 6-18 $.50, under 6 free, members free. Estab 1971 to promote the preservation, restoration and study of the rich history of the Lake County area, and to provide display area for local and non-local art work, and also to provide an educational assistance both to public schools and interested individuals. The Museum and Gallery own no art work, but display a variety of art on a changing basis. Average Annual Attendance: 11,000 - 12,500. Mem: 350; dues donor $100, contributing $50, patron $25, associate $12.50; annual meeting Feb
Income: $10,000-$15,000 (financed by membership and admission fees)
Purchases: $500 - $1000
Exhibitions: Changing displays of paintings, photography and craft work
Publications: Mountain Diggings, annual; The Tallyboard, newsletter, quarterly
Activities: Lect open to public; competitions; shop sells books, slides, papers, postcards, rock samples

M TABOR OPERA HOUSE MUSEUM, 306-310 Harrison Ave (Mailing add: 815 Harrison Ave, 80461). Tel 303-486-1147. *Cur* Evelyn E Furman
Open June - Oct Sun - Fri 9 AM - 5:30 PM, Nov - May by appointment only. Admis adults $2, children under 12 $1. Estab 1955 as a historic theatre museum
Collections: Costumes; paintings
Activities: Lectures; tours; films; concerts; arts festivals; sales shop sells books, pictures and souvenirs

LITTLETON

M ARAPAHOE COMMUNITY COLLEGE, Colorado Gallery of the Arts, 5900 S Santa Fe Dr, 80120. Tel 303-797-5650. *Dir* Sally L Perisho; *Asst Cur* Jean S Wilson; *Development Dir* Sylvia S Cohen
Open Mon, Wed & Fri 1 - 5 PM, Thurs 5 - 9 PM, Sat 10 AM - 2 PM. Admis adults $1, sr citizens & students $.50, Arapahoe students, staff, gallery members & children under 12 free. Gallery contributes significantly to the cultural growth of the Denver-metro area. Average Annual Attendance: 13,000. Mem: 550; dues patron $100, friend $35-$99, family $15, individual $10, student $5
Income: $82,970 (Financed by membership & state appropriation)
Collections: Costume Collection
Exhibitions: (1983-84) Forgotten Dimension: Sculpture in California; New American Graphics 2; The Heritage of the Inuit: Masterpieces of the Eskimo; Images Without End: Imogen Cunningham Photographs
Publications: Artline, quarterly newsletter
Activities: Classes for children; docent training; workshops; lectures open to public, 10 vis lectr per yr; tours; concerts; book traveling exhibitions

LOVELAND

M LOVELAND MUSEUM AND GALLERY, 503 Lincoln, 80537. Tel 303-667-6070. *Dir* Susan Ison; *Cur Exhibits* Svein Edland; *Cur Education* Tom Ketsimpalis; *Secy* Sharon Thomas
Open Tues - Sat 9 AM - 5 PM. No admis fee. Estab 1956 to preserve and interpret history of Loveland area. Average Annual Attendance: 16,000. Mem: 40; dues individual $15
Income: Financed by city appropriation
Collections: Archaeology; art; dioramas; historical material; period rooms
Exhibitions: Victorian period rooms; pioneer cabin; Bureau of Reclamation relief map of Big Thompson Project
Activities: Classes for adults and children; lectures open to public; tours; inter-museum loan programs

PUEBLO

O SANGRE DE CRISTO ARTS & CONFERENCE CENTER, 210 N Santa Fe, 81003. Tel 303-543-0130. *Dir* Al Kochka; *Assoc Dir* Maggie Divelbiss; *Visual Art Cur* Jerry Schefcik; *Rentals Coordinator* Lynn Gregory; *Asst Development Mgr* Tallie Huber
Open Mon - Sat 9 AM - 5 PM. No admis fee. Estab 1972 to promote the educational and cultural activities related to the fine arts in Southern Colorado and the management of conventions, specifically those which may be concerned with and related to the fine arts. The Helen T White Gallery, opened in 1982, provided four new gallery spaces for permanent & temporary exhibitions. The Conference Gallery located in another building covers 6000 sq ft. Average Annual Attendance: 200,000. Mem: 840; dues $15-$1000; annual meeting second Wed in Dec
Income: $540,000 (financed by membership, city appropriation, county appropriation, grants, private underwriting and donations)
Collections: Francis King Collection of Western American Painting
Exhibitions: (1982-83) Annual Invitational Pottery Sale; Own-Your-Own Regional (eight state) Juried Exhibition: Artist of Rockies 10 Year Retrospective; Humanities Experience: Subject Is You; Theodore Wores: An American Impressionist; Japanese Visions of a Floating World-Edo Period; Second International Colorado Poster Exhibition, Western Skies/Western Eyes
Publications: Town and Center Mosaic, nine times a year; Catalogue of Frances' King Collection, annual report
Activities: Classes for adults and children; dramatic programs, docent training; workshops; classic film series; school of dance; artists-in-residence; lect open to the public; 3 vis lectr per year; concerts; gallery talks; tours; originate traveling exhibitions

M UNIVERSITY OF SOUTHERN COLORADO, School of Liberal Arts, 2200 N Bonforte, 81001. Tel 303-549-2817. *Art Dept Chmn* Edward R Sajbel; *Gallery Dir* Robert Hench
Open daily 10 AM - 4 PM. No admis fee. Estab 1972 to provide educational exhibitions for students attending the University. Gallery has a 40 x 50 ft area with 16 ft ceiling; vinyl covered wooden walls; carpeted and adjustable track lighting. Average Annual Attendance: 6000
Income: Financed through University and student government
Collections: Basketry of the Plains Indian, clothing of the Plains Indian; Orman Collection of Indian Art of the Southwest including Indian blankets of the Rio Grande and Navajo people; pottery of the Pueblo Indians (both recent and ancient)
Exhibitions: (1983-84) Patrick Rowan: Contemporary Sculpture; Communications Graphics; Drawings by Mesple; Polish Composers; graduate student exhibition; University of Southern Colorado alumni art exhibit; art open house for high school seniors; student art exhibit; Orman Collection
Publications: Catalogs
Activities: Lect open to the public; individual paintings and original objects of art lent; book traveling exhibitions 2-6 per year; traveling exhibitions organized and circulated

CONNECTICUT

AVON

O FARMINGTON VALLEY ARTS CENTER, Avon Park North, Box 220, 06001 Tel 203-678-1867. *Pres* Phil Zimmerman; *VPres* Jadee Kaeyman; *Secy* Sally Daly; *Executive Dir* Betty Friedman; *Program Asst* Marcia Bucl; *Admin Coordr* Pam Shauley
Open Tues - Sat 11 AM - 4 PM, Sun 1-4 PM. No admis fee. Estab 1971 to provide a facility with appropriate environment and programs, to serve as a focal point for public awareness of and participation in the visual arts by furthering quality arts education and exposure to dedicated artists and their works. Maintains 20 studios. Average Annual Attendance: 20,000. Mem: 1200; dues family $20, individual $15; Board of Directors annual meeting in April
Income: $140,000 (financed by membership, grants, tuitions, donations from corporations and individuals, special event earning)
Exhibitions: (1983) Local Artists, 9 exhibitions per year; regional art & crafts
Activities: Classes for adults and children; lect open to the public; tours; competitions; visits to artist's studios

BRIDGEPORT

O BRIDGEPORT ART LEAGUE,* 2200 North Ave, 06604. Tel 203-335-6250. *Pres* Alexander Mazur
Open Mon - Sat 10:30 AM - 5 PM, cl Sun. No admis fee. Organized 1895, inc 1916. Average Annual Attendance: 200. Mem: 150; annual meeting May
Exhibitions: Annual exhibition in April with jury and awards, open to non-members; Members Exhibition in May, of work completed in classes during the year; special monthly shows by local artists
Activities: Classes in arts and crafts; lect

M CARLSON GALLERY, 84 Iranistan Ave, 06602. Tel 203-576-4402. *Gallery Coordr* Christopher White
Open Mon - Fri 11 AM - 5 PM, Sat & Sun 1 - 5 PM. No admis fee
Collections: Contemporary art; prints
Exhibitions: (1983) Annual faculty show; The Paragon of Animals: Current Photography of the Human Figure; Dennis Letbetter: Photographs; Anni Albers Printmaking; (1984) Symbols of Man; 20 Year Retrospective: Albert Dorne Professors of Art; annual student exhibit
Activities: Lectures; gallery talks; concerts; originates traveling exhibitions

M HOUSATONIC COMMUNITY COLLEGE, Housatonic Museum of Art, 510 Barnum Ave, 06608. Tel 203-579-6727. *Dir* Burt Chernow; *Asst Dir* David Kintzler
Open Mon - Thurs 8 AM - 10 PM, Fri 8 AM - 4 PM. No admis fee. Estab 1968 for educational purposes. Collection is located on five floors throughout college facilities with changing exhibition galleries on the second and fourth floors. Average Annual Attendance: 12,000
Income: Financed by student government, other groups and donations
Collections: Extensive 19th and 20th Century drawings, paintings and sculpture - Avery, Baskin, Calder, Cassat, Chagall, Daumier, DeChirico, Derain, Dubuffet, Gottlieb, Lichtenstein, Lindner, Marisol, Matisse, Miro-Moore, Pavia, Picasso, Rauchenberg, Rivers, Shahn, Vasarely, Warhol, Wesselmann and others. Extensive ethnographic collections, including Africa, South Seas and others; smaller holdings from various historical periods
Exhibitions: Allied Sculptors and Painters of Bridgeport; Greater Bridgeport High School Student Show; Faculty Show; 19th and 20th Century Sculpture; Christo; Lindner; Housatonic Museum of Art: Selections From A Growing Collection
Publications: Exhibition catalogs
Activities: Classes for adults; college art courses; lect open to public, 2-4 vis lectr per year; concerts; gallery talks; tours; individual paintings and original objects of art lent to institutions; limited lending collection contains 2000 paintings, 25,000 slides; originate traveling exhibitions
L Library, 510 Barnum Ave, 06608. *Librn* Robert Martinson
Extensive art section open to students and community
Library Holdings: Vols 1000; Micro — Fiche

M MUSEUM OF ART, SCIENCE AND INDUSTRY,* 4450 Park Ave, 06604. Tel 203-372-3521. *Dir* Christine Stiassni; *Cur Art* Frank Bramblke; *Art Education Cur* Joan Hackett
Open Tues - Thurs, Sat & Sun 2 - 5 PM, Fri 10 AM - 5 PM, cl holidays. Admis adults $1, children, senior citizens & students $.50. Estab 1958 to provide exhibitions and educational programs in the arts and sciences for a regional audience. Average Annual Attendance: 164,000. Mem: Dues $10 - $2500; annual meeting June
Collections: Antique furniture; Indian artifacts; paintings
Exhibitions: Temporary and permanent exhibitions
Activities: Classes for adults and children; lect; gallery talks; tours

BROOKFIELD

M BROOKFIELD CRAFT CENTER, INC GALLERY, 286 Whisconier Rd, PO Box 122, 06804. Tel 203-775-4526. *Pres* Linda Millener; *VPres* Fred Marden; *Secy* Barrie Karasch; *Exec Dir* John I Russell
Open Mon - Sat 10 AM - 4 PM, Sun 2 - 5 PM. Estab 1954 to provide a wide spectrum of craft education and exhibition to the local and national audiences. Average Annual Attendance: 5500. Mem: 1200; dues $20-$1000
Income: $203,500 (financed by endowment, membership & tuition)
Exhibitions: Contemporary craft exhibitions changing every six weeks
Publications: Catalogs
Activities: Classes for adults and children; lectures open to public, vis lectr 180 per yr; concerts; gallery talks; tours; scholarships; book traveling exhibitions to other craft organizations; sales shop sells original art and handmade craft items
L Members' Library, PO Box 122, 06804
Open Mon - Sat 10 AM - 4 PM, Sun 2 - 5 PM. Estab 1962 to aid students and members of the Center with resource craft information. Reference only
Purchases: $250
Library Holdings: Vols 1200; Per subs 25; Other — Exhibition catalogs

BROOKLYN

M NEW ENGLAND CENTER FOR CONTEMPORARY ART,* Rte 169, PO Box 302, 06234. Tel 203-774-8899. *Dir* Henry Riseman
Open Apr - Dec Mon - Sat 10 AM - 5 PM, Sun Noon - 5 PM, cl Christmas. No admis fee. Estab 1975. Mem: Dues corporate $100, supporting $50, family $15, individual $10, senior citizen $6
Collections: Contemporary paintings and sculpture; print collection by Russian artists; woodblock print collection from the People's Republic of China
Activities: Classes for adults and children; lectures; tours; films; gallery talks; originates traveling exhibitions; sales shop sells paintings, prints and books

COS COB

M HISTORICAL SOCIETY OF THE TOWN OF GREENWICH, INC, Bush-Holley House, 39 Strickland Rd (Mailing add: PO Box 906, Greenwich, 06830). Tel 203-622-9686, 869-6899. *Cur* Lauren Kaminsky
Open Tues - Sun Noon - 4 PM, cl major holidays. Admis adults $2, senior citizens & students $1, children under 12 $.50. Average Annual Attendance: 5000. Mem: 700; dues $15 and up; annual meeting June
Collections: Outbuildings housing toys and collection of John Rodgers groups; 18th and 19th century decorative arts; paintings of American impressionists; antiques
Publications: Pamphlets
Activities: Classes for adults and children; docent training; lectures open to the public, 7 vis lectr per yr; concerts; tours
L Library, Greenwich, 06830
Reference library
Library Holdings: Vols 500; AV — Cassettes, slides; Other — Clipping files, exhibition catalogs, manuscripts, memorabilia, photographs

DANBURY

M DANBURY SCOTT-FANTON MUSEUM AND HISTORICAL SOCIETY, INC, 43 Main St, 06810. Tel 203-743-5200. *Pres* Donald C Wood; *Dir* Dorothy T Schling
Open Wed - Sun 2 - 5 PM, cl Mon, Tues & holidays. No admis fee. Estab June 24, 1941 as historic house. Merged with Museum and Arts Center by Legislative Act 1947. Operates the 1785 John and Mary Rider House as a museum of early Americana, and the 1790 Dodd Hat Shop with exhibits relating to hatting. Huntington Hall houses frequently changing exhibits. Ives Homestead, located at Rogers Park in Danbury is to be restored and opened to the public as a memorial to American composer Charles Edward Ives. At present there is a Charles Ives Parlor in the Rider House, recreating the period with Ives furnishings and memorabilia. Average Annual Attendance: 5000. Mem: 500; dues student $2 up to life $1000; annual meeting in Nov
Income: Financed by endowment and membership
Publications: Newsletter, monthly; reprints
Activities: Classes for adults and children; lectures; concerts; open house; special exhibits; tours
L Library, 43 Main St, 06810. Tel 203-743-5200. *Dir & Cur* Julie B Barrows; *Asst Dir & Registrar* Lucye Boland
Historic material for reference only
Library Holdings: Other — Clipping files, manuscripts, memorabilia, photographs
Collections: Charles Ives Photograph Collection

SOCIETY OF MEDALISTS
For further information, see National and Regional Organizations

O WOOSTER COMMUNITY ART CENTER,* Ridgebury Rd, 06810. Tel 203-743-6311, 744-4825. *Dir* Roger O Prince
Open Mon - Fri 9 AM - 10 PM. Estab 1965 as a Community Art Center for exhibitions and art classes. Average Annual Attendance: 3000
Exhibitions: Sperry Andrews; L Archacki; C Augusine; Will Barnet; Fred Baur; M Carstanjen; George Chaplin; Ed Giobbi; R Hare; Bryan Kay; Mike Nevelson; Andrew Parker; Roger Prince; R Riche; B Roll; Thomas Stearns; A Shundi; Nancy Tholen; P Warfield; A Werner
Activities: Classes for adults, high school and elementary students; 2-year Certificate Program for adults; Advanced Placement; Sales shop sells art materials
L Library,* Ridgebury Rd, 06801
Library Holdings: AV — Slides 2200; Other — Photographs 170

EAST WINDSOR

M EAST WINDSOR HISTORICAL SOCIETY INC, Scantic Academy Museum, Scantic Rd (Rte 191), PO Box 232, 06016. Tel 203-623-3144, 623-3623. *Pres* Bobbi Mazurek; *VPres* Terri Fawthrop; *Secy* Flicka Thrall; *Treasurer* Phyllis Bednarz; *Cur* Wanda Mazurek; *Cur* Bob Fawthrop
Open by appointment only. Estab 1965 to display household & farm implement used in East Windsor 1800-1930. Average Annual Attendance: 250. Mem: 100; dues $5; annual meeting fourth Wed in May
Income: $2000 (financed by membership and donations)
Collections: Paintings by local artists
Publications: East Windsor, Through the Years: a local history
Activities: Museum shop sells books

ESSEX

O ESSEX ART ASSOCIATION, INC,* N Main St, PO Box 193, 06426. Tel 203-767-8996. *Pres* Jessie Mayer; *Treas* Margaret Wilson; *Secy* Adele Clement
Open daily 1 - 5 PM (June - Labor Day). No admis fee. Estab 1946 as a non-profit organization for the encouragement of the arts and to provide and maintain suitable headquarters for the showing of art. Maintains a small, well-equipped one-floor gallery. Average Annual Attendance: 2500. Mem: 360; dues artists $7.50, associate $10; annual meeting in Sept
Income: Financed by membership
Exhibitions: Three annual exhibits each year plus one or two special exhibits

FAIRFIELD

O FAIRFIELD HISTORICAL SOCIETY, 636 Old Post Rd, 06430. Tel 203-259-1598. *Pres* Leon E Thomas Jr; *Dir* Catherine C Boisseau; *Cur* Christopher B Nevins
Open Mon - Fri 9:30 AM - 4:30 PM, Sun 1 - 5 PM. Suggested donation adults $1, children $.50. Estab 1902 to collect, preserve and interpret artifacts and information relating to the history of Fairfield. Average Annual Attendance: 3000. Mem: 750; dues $10 - $500; meeting date varies
Income: Approx 100,000 (financed by endowment, membership, admissions, donations and town contributions)
Collections: Ceramics, furniture, greeting cards, jewelry, paintings, photographs, prints, silver; local history; textiles & costumes
Exhibitions: (1982-83) Rotating exhibits; Hillside & Seaside: Four Centuries of Fairfield Life
Publications: Newsletter, quarterly
Activities: Classes for adults & children; dramatic programs; docent training; docent lectures open to public for a fee; gallery talks; tours
L Library, 636 Old Post Rd, 06430. Tel 203-259-1598. *Librn* Irene K Miller
Open to the public for reference only
Library Holdings: Vols 8000; Per subs 19; diaries, documents, maps; AV — Lantern slides, slides; Other — Clipping files, manuscripts, original art works, pamphlets, photographs, prints
Special Subjects: Genealogy & local history

FARMINGTON

O FARMINGTON ART GUILD,* Church St, 06032. Tel 203-677-6205. *Pres* Pam Everets; *Secy* Datsie Kagan; *Admin Dir* Kevin Loader; *Prog Dir* Sharmon Kennedy
Open Mon - Fri 10 AM - 5 PM, Sat & Sun 1 - 4 PM, when exhibits are ongoing. No admis fee. Estab 1976 to provide instruction in art and crafts and provide facilities for local artists. Mem: 370; dues $15 - $1000
Income: $40,000 (financed by membership, state, local and corporate grants, sales and fees)
Exhibitions: Faculty show; Xmas Crafts Show; The Finished Print; National Juried Photography Show
Publications: Bulletin
Activities: Classes for adults and children; tours; competitions; awards; scholarships; book traveling exhibitions, 2 vis lectr per yr; sales shop sells original art

C HEUBLEIN INC, Munson Rd, 06032. Tel 203-677-4061. *Corporate VPres* J M McGarry; *Dir Admin Services* J E Gluth
Open to public by appointment. Estab 1973 for the benefit of employees and to compliment the building interior design
Purchases: $15,000
Collections: Contemporary American art, large oils & sculptures, acrylics, watercolors, drawings, prints, photographs & tapestries
Activities: Selected pieces are loaned to qualifying organizations who must provide for all necessary packing requirements, insurance & transportation

M HILL-STEAD MUSEUM, 671 Farmington Ave, PO Box 353, 06032. Tel 203-677-9064. *Pres* Mrs Talcott Stanley; *Treas* Susan Galvin; *Trustee* Charles Ferguson; *Trustee* John C Pope; *Trustee* Frederick Emeny; *Cur* Philip C Wright
Open Wed - Sun 2 - 5 PM, cl holidays & between Jan 15 - Feb 15. Admis adults $2.50, children $1. Estab 1946. The art collection is housed in turn-of-the-century house by Stanford White and contains original furnishings and collection of Alfred Atmore Pope. The museum is kept as if lived in by original owners; paintings were collected between 1880 and 1907. Average Annual Attendance: 13,000. Mem: Dues $12 - $500; meetings Nov & June
Income: Financed by endowment, contributions, individual, corporate & foundations, admissions & sales
Collections: Nineteenth century art: Carriere, Cassatt, Degas, Manet, Monet & Whistler; sculpture: Barye; prints: Durer, Haden, Hiroshige, Hokusai, Utamaro, Whistler; Chinese ceramics; 18th century French and English furniture; Oriental rugs; Italian Majolica
Publications: Catalog of Hill-Stead Paintings, Hill-Stead Yesterdays; Theodate Pope Riddle, Her Life & Work
Activities: Docent training; lectures open to the public, 3 vis lectr per yr; concerts; gallery talks; tours; sales shop sells books, postcards and slides
L Library, 671 Farmington Ave, Farmington, 06032. Tel 203-677-4787
Open to authorized scholars
Income: Financed by trust fund, admissions & sales
Library Holdings: Vols 4000; Per subs 12
Collections: An aquatint by Mary Cassatt; Goya's Disasters of War; mezzotints after Joshua Reynolds; Japanese woodblock prints; Whistler etchings & lithographs

M STANLEY-WHITMAN HOUSE, FARMINGTON (Formerly Farmington Museum), * 37 High St, 06032. Tel 203-677-9222. *Chmn* Beatrice Stockwell; *Dir* Dorothy Lunde
Open May - Oct Tues - Sun 1 - 4 PM, Mar - April & Nov - Dec Sun 1- 4 PM. Admis adults $1.50, children $.75. Estab 1935. The museum is governed by a branch of the Farmington Village Green and Library Association and is housed in the circa 1660 Stanley-Whitman House. Mem: Dues life $500, supporting $150, contributing $75, sustaining $50, family $15, individual $10
Collections: American costumes and textiles; decorative arts; furniture; musical instruments; 17th century garden
Exhibitions: Permanent and changing exhibitions
Publications: A Guide to Historic Farmington, Connecticut; A Short History of Farmington, Connecticut
Activities: Guided tours; shop sells books and pamphlets

GLASTONBURY

O CONNECTICUT WOMEN ARTISTS, INC,* 202 Shallowbrook Lane, 06033. Tel 203-646-1990. *Pres* Jean Dalton; *VPres* Jean Mazo; *Secy* Gigi H Liverant
Estab 1929 to provide a forum for serious Connecticut women artists. Mem: 180; mem must have three juried acceptances in CWA exhibitions; dues $10; annual meeting in June
Income: Financed by members
Activities: Awards; scholarships

GREENWICH

O ART BARN, 143 Lower Cross Rd, 06830. *Pres* Carol Gatrall; *Exec Dir* Gail Nemeti
Open Tues - Sat 10 AM - 4 PM, Sun 1 - 4 PM. No admis fee. Estab Mar 1962 to provide a stimulating atmosphere which encourages growth without competitive pressures and by bringing sculptors, painters, printmakers, photographers and handcrafters from all parts of the country to exhibit at the Art Barn. The gallery is located in a converted dairy barn. Average Annual Attendance: 3500. Mem: 350; dues $25; annual meeting in Aug
Income: Financed by membership, from workshops, gallery and shop sales
Exhibitions: Nine per year
Publications: Bi-annual newsletter
Activities: Classes for adults and children; demonstrations; competitions with awards; scholarships offered; Handcraft Shop open March - Dec; nine gallery shows a year
L Library, 143 Lower Cross Rd, 06830
Library Holdings: Vols 500

M THE BRUCE MUSEUM, Museum Dr, 06830. Tel 203-869-0376. *Dir* John B Clark
Open Tues - Sat 10 AM - 5 PM, Sun 2 - 5 PM. Donations. Estab 1909 by Robert M Bruce as regional education center that collects & exhibits objects of artistic, historic & scientific importance to the development of our American culture. Small reference library for staff use only. Average Annual Attendance: 80,000. Mem: 1000; dues $10 - $500; annual meetings in May
Income: $215,000 (financed by the town of Greenwich); $75,000 (financed by the Bruce Museum Associates, Inc)
Collections: †19th & 20th century American paintings; North American Indian ethnology; Orientalia; American natural sciences
Exhibitions: (1982-83) The Whims of Whalemen; Outdoor Arts Festival; International Folk Arts Bazaar; Robots Alive; Needlework of the New Ornamentalism; Fabulous Fakes: An Overview of Art Fakes & Frauds; Earth, Wind & Fire: Contemporary Glass Works
Publications: Gallery Notes, 6 per year; calendar of events, 6 per year
Activities: Classes for adults and children; docent training; lectures open to public; concerts; gallery talks; tours; competitions; scholarships; exten dept serves 15 mile radius; museum shop sells books & international ethnic arts & crafts

O THE GREENWICH ART SOCIETY INC, 299 Greenwich Ave, 06830. Tel 203-629-1533. *Pres* Elizabeth Haas; *Dir Classes* Linda Laska; *Treasurer* Barbara Bradbury
Estab 1912 as a nonprofit organization to further art education and to awaken and stimulate broader interest in arts and crafts in the town of Greenwich. Art Center studio is used for classes, exhibitions and meetings. Mem: 400; dues family $35, regular $25, student 19-24 yrs $10
Income: Financed by membership, fees & contributions
Exhibitions: (1984) Outdoor-Indoor Show at the Arts Center, open to all artists; Members' Juried Annual Fall Show; additional exhibitions
Publications: The History of the Greenwich Art Society, booklet; bulletin of program for the year and class schedule
Activities: Day and evening classes for adults, special classes for children; critiques and demonstrations; lectures open to public; scholarships

M PROPERSI SCHOOL OF ART INC GALLERIES, 44 W Putnam Ave, 06830. Tel 203-869-4430. *Pres & Dir* August Propersi; *VPres* Joann Propersi; *Office Mgr* Michael Propersi; *Admin Asst* Linda Propersi
Open Tues - Sat 10 AM - 5 PM, cl Mon. No admis fee. Estab 1954. Gallery to exhibit professional works of art

HARTFORD

O CONNECTICUT HISTORICAL SOCIETY, 1 Elizabeth St, 06105. Tel 203-236-5621. *Dir* Christopher P Pickford; *Museum Cur* Philip H Dunbar; *Cur Exhibitions & Education* Robert F Trent; *Cur Prints & Photogs* Kate Steinway; *Registrar* Maura Feeney; *Managing Editor* Peter J Malia
Open Mon - Fri 9 AM - 5 PM, cl Sun, Sat and holidays (June 1 - Sept 1). Estab 1825 to collect and preserve materials of Connecticut interest and to encourage interest in Connecticut history. Exhibition space totals 6500 sq ft, two-thirds of which are devoted to permanent exhibitions; one-third changing exhibits
Income: Financed by endowment and membership
Publications: Connecticut Historical Society Bulletin, quarterly; Annual Report; Notes and News, five times a year
Activities: Gallery talks; originate traveling exhibitions
L Library, One Elizabeth St, 06105. *Dir* Christopher P Bickford; *Librn* Elizabeth Abbe
Open Mon - Sat 9 AM - 5 PM, summer Mon - Fri 9 AM - 5 PM
Library Holdings: Vols 90,000; Per subs 75; maps, posters, original documents; Micro — Reels; AV — Kodachromes; Other — Clipping files, exhibition catalogs, manuscripts, original art works, pamphlets, photographs, prints
Special Subjects: Local Connecticut history and genealogy, Connecticut printing, maps, prints, broadsides, printed ephemera, portraits, children's books and reference books on decorative arts of New England
Collections: Frederick K & Margaret R Barbour Furniture Collection; George Dudley Seymour Collection of Furniture; Morgan B Brainard Tavern Signs
Publications: Bulletin, quarterly; Notes & News, five times per year
Activities: Docent training; lectures open to public, 10 vis lectr per year; gallery talks; tours

L CONNECTICUT STATE LIBRARY, Raymond E Baldwin Museum, 231 Capitol Ave, 06106. Tel 203-566-3056. *Museum Dir* David O White; *Cur* David J Corrigan
Open Mon - Fri 9 AM - 4:45 PM, Sat 9 AM - 1 PM, cl holidays. Estab 1910 to collect, preserve and display artifacts and memorabilia reflecting the history and heritage of Connecticut. For reference only
Library Holdings: Vols 500,000; original documents; Micro — Fiche, reels; AV — Cassettes, motion pictures, v-tapes; Other — Clipping files, manuscripts, memorabilia, original art works, pamphlets, photographs, prints
Special Subjects: Coins & Medals, Connecticut, firearms
Collections: Portraits of Connecticut's Governors
Exhibitions: Changing exhibits

L HARTFORD PUBLIC LIBRARY, 500 Main St, 06103. Tel 203-525-9121, Ext 672. *Dept Head* Vernon Martin
Open hours vary. Estab 1774 as a free public library. A gallery is maintained on wall space and glass cases
Income: Financed by endowment, membership, and city appropriation
Library Holdings: 300,000 pictures; AV — Motion pictures, rec
Exhibitions: Changing exhibit each month
Activities: Dramatic prog; concerts

M **OLD STATE HOUSE,*** 800 Main St, 06103. Tel 203-552-6766. *Chmn* Wilson Wilde; *Pres* Stanly Schultz; *VPres* Elizabeth Capen; *Exec Dir* Joseph S MacLaughlin
Open Mon - Sat 10 AM - 5 PM, Sun 12 - 5 PM. No admis fee. Estab 1975 to preserve oldest state house in the nation and present variety of exhibitions on historic and contemporary subjects. Former executive wing is used for exhibitions of contemporary artists and craftsmen, paintings, decorative arts on a rotating basis. Average Annual Attendance: 60,000. Mem: 1500; dues individual $10, family $15, life $1000; annual meeting in the fall
Income: Financed by endowment, membership and appeals
Collections: †Connecticut portraits; documents; Restored Senate Chamber
Activities: Education department; lect open to the public, 25 vis lectr per yr; concerts; gallery talks; tours; individual paintings and original objects of art lent to museums for special exhibitions; museum shop sells books, magazines, original art, reproductions, prints, slides, Connecticut arts and crafts

O **STOWE-DAY FOUNDATION,** 77 Forest St, 06105. Tel 203-522-9258. *Pres* H Burton Powers; *VPres* Helen D Perkins; *VPres* Mrs Ellsworth Grant; *Secy* Thomas L Archibald; *Dir* Joseph S Van Why; *Cur* Ellice Schofield; *Vistors Center Adminr* Andrea Rudy
Open daily June - Aug 10 AM - 4:30 PM, Sept - May Tues - Sat 9:30 AM - 4 PM, Sun 1 - 4 PM. Estab 1941 to maintain and open to the public the restored Harriet Beecher Stowe House. The Foundation operates the Stowe-Day Library, oversees a publishing program of reprints of H B Stowe's works and new books and provides workshops and lectures. Average Annual Attendance: 22,000. Mem: 210; dues special $25, couple $15, single $12; fall and spring meetings
Income: $200,000 (financed by endowment)
Collections: †Architecture of 19th century: books, plans, drawings, trade catalogs; †decorative arts; study samples of wallpaper
Exhibitions: George Keller, Architect; 'Kaleidoscope' Selection of 150 Early Photographs; Nook Farm: Corner on the World; Portraits of a 19th Century Family (Lyman Beecher and Children); Trade Cards and Catalogs of the 19th Century; Victorian Christmas
Publications: The American Woman's Home; Eminent Victorian Americans; Joan of Arc (reprint of Mark Twain's work); George Keller, Architect; The Minister's Wooing; The Papers of Harriet Beecher Stowe; The Pearl of Orr's Island; Pognauc People; Portraits of a 19th Century Family; H B Stowe and American Literature
Activities: Classes for adults; teacher worshops; lect open to public, 1-2 visiting lectr per year; paintings and original art objects lent to institutions; shop sells books, prints, slides, Victorian game reproductions, stencil patterns and needlework

L **Library,** 77 Forest St, 06105. Tel 203-522-9258. *Head Librn* Diana Royce; *Asst Librn* Roberta Bradford; *Catalogue Librn* Thomas Harkins
Open Mon - Fri 8:30 AM - 4:30 PM, cl national holidays. Estab 1965 to concentrate on the architecture, decorative arts, history and literature of the United States in the 19th century emphasizing a Hartford neighborhood known as Nook Farm. Reference only
Income: $50,000 (financed by endowment)
Purchases: $15,000
Library Holdings: Vols 20,000; Per subs 18; original documents; Micro — Fiche, reels; AV — Lantern slides; Other — Clipping files, exhibition catalogs, manuscripts, memorabilia, original art works, pamphlets, photographs, prints, sculpture
Special Subjects: Hartford 19th Century Literature Community, Nook Farm & Residents; Mark Twain; Harriet Beecher Stowe; Chas Dudley Warner, William Gillette
Collections: Paintings by Harriet Beecher Stowe, oil & tempera; Theatrical broadside; Uncle Tom's Cabin, lithographs
Exhibitions: Paintings of Harriet Beecher Stowe
Activities: Adult classes & docent training; lectures open to public, 2 vis' lectr per yr

M **TRINITY COLLEGE,** Austin Arts Center, Summit St, 06106. Tel 202-527-3151. *Dir* John Woolley; *Chmn Dept Fine Arts* Michael Mahoney; *Dir Studio Arts Program* George Chaplin
Open daily 1 - 5 PM (when college is in session). No admis fee. Estab 1965. A building housing the teaching and performing aspects of music, theater and studio arts at a liberal arts college. Widener Gallery provides exhibition space mainly for student and faculty works, plus outside exhibitions
Income: Financed by college appropriation
Collections: Edwin M Blake Memorial and Archive; College Collection; Samuel H Kress Study Collection; George F McMurray Loan Collection
Activities: Lect open to public, 6 vis lectr per year; lending collection contains 500 original art works and 100,000 slides

M **MARK TWAIN MEMORIAL,** 351 Farmington Ave, 06105. Tel 203-247-0998. *Dir & Cur* Wynn Lee
Open June - Aug 9:30 AM - 4:30 PM; Sept - May Tues - Sat 9:30 AM - 4 PM; Sun 1 - 4 PM; cl Mon, Jan 1, Easter, Labor Day, Thanksgiving and Dec 25. Guided tours adults $3, children 16 and under $1.25; special group tour rates with advance arrangements. Estab 1929 to restore and maintain Mark Twain's Hartford home, to collect research materials needed for the project and to keep before the public the life and work of Mark Twain. Maintains Historic House Museum with period interiors, museum room of memorabilia. National Historic Landmark status, US Dept of Interior. Average Annual Attendance: 70,000. Mem: Approx 1000; dues $20 and higher; annual meeting May
Collections: Lockwood deForest Collection; Mark Twain memorabilia (photographs, manuscripts); period and original furnishings; Tiffany Collection; Candace Wheeler Collection
Exhibitions: occasional exhibits
Activities: Classes for adults and children; Lectures open to public; group tours; open house; Victorian Christmas; Book traveling exhibitions; museum shop

L **Nook Farm Research Library,** 351 Farmington Ave, 06105
Library Holdings: Vols 13,000; Other — Manuscripts, pamphlets

M **WADSWORTH ATHENEUM,** 600 Main St, 06103. Tel 203-278-2670. *Dir* Tracy Atkinson; *Cur European Paintings, Sculpture, Drawings & Prints* Jean Cadogan; *Cur Education* Danielle Rice; *Head Conservator* Stephen Kornhauser; *Cur Matrix* Andrea Miller-Keller; *Chief Cur* Gregory Hedberg; *Cur Textile & Costumes* Marianne Carlano; *Decorative Arts, Assoc Cur* William Hosley; *Registrar* David Parrish
Open Tues - Fri 11 AM - 7 PM, Sat & Sun 11 AM - 5 PM, cl Mon. Estab 1842 by Daniel Wadsworth as Atheneum Gallery of Fine Arts. There are more than 60 galleries in 5 interconnected buildings, plus lecture room, classrooms and 299-seat theater. 1968 renovation of facilities includes James Lippincott Goodwin Building, along with sculpture court, restaurant, additional classrooms, and offices. Average Annual Attendance: 152,000. Mem: 6000; dues $25 & up; annual meeting Nov
Income: Financed by private funds
Library Holdings: Vols 20,000; Micro — Fiche, reels; AV — A-tapes, rec, slides, v-tapes; Other — Clipping files, exhibition catalogs, manuscripts, memorabilia, pamphlets, photographs
Special Subjects: Decorative Arts, Museology; Visual Arts
Collections: Achival materials (Wadsworth Atheneum); Titles from the Watkinson Library of Reference, 19th Century; Hetty Gray Baker Bookplate Collection
Exhibitions: Archival materials from 1934 premiere of Four Saints in Three Acts
Publications: Newsletter, monthly to members; collections and exhibitions catalogs
Activities: Lect and gallery talks by staff; docent talks; seasonal concerts; gallery tours; outside lect; members' exhibition previews and various special events; Atheneum Shop selling books, reproductions, photographs, cards and gifts

L **Auerbach Art Library,** 600 Main St, 06103. Tel 203-278-2670, Ext 257. *Librn* John W Teahan; *Asst Librn* Catherine Colemon
Open Tues - Sat 11 AM - 5 PM, cl Sun & Mon. Estab 1934 as a reference service to the museum staff, members and public; to provide materials supporting work with museum collection. For reference only
Library Holdings: Vols 20,000; Per subs 150; Micro — Fiche, reels; AV — Lantern slides, rec; Other — Clipping files, exhibition catalogs, pamphlets
Special Subjects: Decorative Arts, Art sales and collections, museology
Collections: Sol Lewitt (contemporary art); Elizabeth Miles (English silver); Watkinson Collection (pre-1917 art reference)

KENT

M **CONNECTICUT HISTORICAL COMMISSION,** Sloane-Stanley Museum,* Rt 7 (Mailing add: Connecticut Historical Commission, 59 S Prospect St, Hartford, 06757). Tel 203-927-3849. *Dir* John W Shannahan; *Museum Dir* Marion K Leonard
Open May - Oct Wed - Sun 10 AM - 4:30 PM. Admis adults $1, sr citizens $.50, children $25. Estab 1969 to collect, preserve, exhibit historic American tools, implements and paintings of American scenes. Average Annual Attendance: 8000
Income: Financed by state appropriation
Collections: Paintings by Eric Sloane; American tools and implements

O **KENT ART ASSOCIATION, INC,** Box 202, Route 7, 06757. Tel 203-927-4289. *Pres* Laurence W Newquist; *First VPres* Barbara Goodspeed; *Second VPres* Norman Gardner; *Recording Secy* Maggie Smith; *Corresponding Secy* Lucille Lupke
Open during exhibitions only, 2 - 5 PM. Estab 1923, incorporated 1935. Maintains gallery for changing exhibitions. Average Annual Attendance: 2500. Mem: 335; dues assoc $8, sustaining $15, patron $25, life $100; annual meeting Oct
Income: Financed by memberships, donations
Exhibitions: Fall Show; Member's Show; President's Show; Spring Show
Publications: Kentara, newsletter 6 times a year; exhibition catalogues
Activities: Lect; demonstrations

LITCHFIELD

O **LITCHFIELD HISTORICAL SOCIETY,** On-the-Green, PO Box 385, 06759. Tel 203-567-5862. *Pres* Mrs C A MacDonald; *VPres* William M VanWinkle Jr; *Secy* Lewis M Wiggin; *Dir* Robert G Carrison
Open Tues - Sat 11 AM - 5 PM; Mid Apr - Mid Nov. Donation suggested. Estab 1856, incorporated 1897 for the preservation and interpretation of local historical collections. A gallery of portraits by Ralph Earl is maintained. Average Annual Attendance: 8000 - 10,000. Mem: 500; dues benefactor $100, donor $50, contributing $25, family $10, individual $6, senior citizen $4, student (under 21) $2; annual meeting second Fri in Sept
Income: $40,000 (financed by endowment and membership)
Collections: American and Connecticut decorative arts, pewter, costumes, textiles, paintings, silver, pottery, and graphics
Exhibitions: (1980) Three Centuries of Connecticut Folk Art, contemporary art from local collections; local architecture and preservation exhibits. (1981) Lost Litchfield, postcards, photographs, memorabilia of the past; (1982) Industrial Litchfield; Clock Exhibit; (1984) Anson Duckenson, Connecticut's miniature painter
Activities: Lect open to public, 5 vis lectr per year; competitions; individual and original objects of art lent to accredited museums with board approval; sales shop sells books and postcards

L **Ingraham Memorial Research Library,** On-the-Green, PO Box 385, 06759. Tel 203-567-5862. *Librn* Mrs Hugh Todd
Open Tues - Sat 10 - 12 AM, 1 - 4 PM. Estab 1856 as a center of local history and genealogy study
Income: $10,000 (financed by endowment and membership)
Library Holdings: Vols 10,000; Per subs 35; original documents; AV — Kodachromes, slides; Other — Clipping files, exhibition catalogs, manuscripts, memorabilia, original art works, pamphlets, photographs, prints, sculpture
Collections: 40,000 manuscripts in local history

MERIDEN

O **ARTS AND CRAFTS ASSOCIATION OF MERIDEN INC,** Gallery, 53 Colony St, PO Box 348, 06450. Tel 203-235-5347. *Pres* Stuart Grandy
Open Tues - Fri Noon - 4 PM, weekends on special exhibits. No admis fee. Estab 1907 to encourage appreciation of the arts in the community. One floor gallery to hold exhibits and art work studios above with meeting room. Average Annual Attendance: 500. Mem: 300; dues $8 and up; annual meeting June
Income: Financed by membership and fund raising
Collections: †Permanent collection of paintings & sculptors
Activities: Classes for adults and children; dramatic programs; lectures open to the public, 8 vis lectr per yr; workshops; gallery talks; tours; competitions with awards; scholarships; individual paintings and original objects of art lent to banks & public buildings; originate traveling exhibitions; sales shop sells original art & crafts
L **Library,** PO Box 348, 06450
Library Holdings: Vols 250
Collections: Indiana Thomas Book Collection

MIDDLETOWN

M **WESLEYAN UNIVERSITY,** Davison Art Center, 301 High St, 06457. Tel 203-347-9411. *Cur* Ellen G D'Oench; *Admin Asst & Registrar* Janette G Boothby
Open Tues - Fri 12 - 4 PM, Sat & Sun 2 - 5 PM cl Mon and academic vacations. No admis fee. Part of the collection was presented to Wesleyan University by George W and Harriet B Davison. Since 1952 the collection with its reference library has been housed in the historic Alsop House, now the Davison Art Center
Collections: †The print collection, extending from the 15th century to present day includes Master E S Nielli, Mantegna, Pollaiuolo, Durer, Cranach, Rembrandt, Canaletto, Piranesi, Goya, Millet, Meryon and others; †Japanese and contemporary American prints; 1840s to present, photographs
Exhibitions: Regularly changing prints, drawings and photograph exhibitions and other works on paper
Publications: Exhibition catalogues
Activities: Lectures open to the public, 8-15 per yr; concerts; gallery talks; tours; individual paintings and original objects of art lent; lending collection contains 16,000 art works, 100 original prints, 5000 photographs, drawings; traveling exhibitions organized & circulated
—**Art Library,** Middletown, 06457. Tel 203-347-9411, Ext 2697. *Art Librn* Richard H Wood
Open Mon - Fri 9 AM - 10 PM, Sat Noon - 4 PM, Sun 1 - 10 PM. Estab 1950 as research/reference library primarily supporting university courses in art history. Circ 10,000
Library Holdings: Vols 20,000; Per subs 125
Collections: †Print Reference Collection (books pertaining to the history of the graphic arts)
O **Friends of the Davison Art Center,** 301 High St, 06457
Estab 1961 for the support and augmentation of the activities and acquisition fund of the Davison Art Center by its members
M **Ezra and Cecile Zilkha Galleries,** Center for the Arts, Middletown, CT 06457. *Asst Cur* Jean F Feinberg
Open Tues - Fri Noon - 4 PM, Sat & Sun 2 - 5 PM, cl Mon & academic vacations
Exhibitions: Changing exhibitions of paintings, drawings and photographs
Publications: Exhibition catalogues

MYSTIC

O **MYSTIC ART ASSOCIATION, INC,** Water St, PO Box 259, 06355. Tel 203-536-7601. *Pres* Fritz Stein; *VPres* Paul L White; *Treas* John Lazerek
Open daily 11 AM - 5 PM. No admis fee. Estab 1920 to maintain an art museum to promote cultural education, local philanthropic and charitable interests. The association owns a colonial building on the bank of Mystic River with spacious grounds; there is one small gallery and one large gallery with L-shaped corridor. Average Annual Attendance: 2000 - 3000. Mem: 450, active mem must have high standards of proficiency and be elected by 2/3 vote; dues active $15, assoc $10; meetings held May and Sept
Income: Financed by membership
Collections: Works by deceased members donated, shown in Groton Savings Bank
Exhibitions: (All juried) Crafts Show; Members' Show (all media); Photo II; 24th Annual Regional (all media)
Activities: Occasional classes; lect open to public, 3 or 4 vis lectr per year; concerts; gallery talks; competitions with cash awards; individual paintings lent

NEW BRITAIN

M **CENTRAL CONNECTICUT STATE UNIVERSITY,** Art Dept Museum, 1615 Stanley St, 06050. Tel 203-827-7322. *Dir* A Walter Kendra
Estab to collect, display and interpret works of art and ethnic materials relating to the art education program. Center will be constructed within two years and collection will be on display in center, whole collection will not be on permanent display

M **NEW BRITAIN MUSEUM OF AMERICAN ART,*** 56 Lexington St, 06052. Tel 203-229-0257. *Dir* Charles B Ferguson; *Asst to Dir* Lois L Blomstrann
Open Tues - Sun 1 - 5 PM, cl holidays. No admis fee. Estab 1903 to exhibit, collect and preserve American art. Average Annual Attendance: 20,000. Mem: 1000; dues patron $100, contributing $50, family $25, individual $15
Income: Financed by endowment
Collections: American Art from Colonial Period (1740) to Contemporary (Copley, West, Bierstadt, Church, Homer, Eakins, Sargent, Whistler, Cassatt, Wyeth); Murals by Thomas Hart Benton
Publications: Newsletter, quarterly
Activities: Docent training; lect open to public, 4 vis lectr per year; gallery talks; tours; competitions; individual paintings and original objects of art lent to other museums and institutions; originate traveling exhibitions; museum shop selling books, reproductions, prints, slides and postcards

NEW CANAAN

O **SILVERMINE GUILD CENTER FOR THE ARTS,** Galleries, 1037 Silvermine Rd, 06840. Tel 203-966-5617. *Dir* Ira Flateman; *Pres Bd Trustees* Robert Bowman
Open Tues - Sun 12:30 - 5 PM; cl Mon. No admis fee. Estab 1922 as an independent art center to foster, promote and encourage activities in the arts and art education and to provide a place for member artists and invited artists to show and sell their work, and to offer the community a wide variety of artistic, cultural and educational activities. Four exhibition galleries and Farrell Gallery which contains paintings and sculpture for purchase. Average Annual Attendance: 20,000. Mem: 800; dues sustaining $125, individual $35
Income: Financed by membership, sale of art, contributions and tuitions
Collections: †Permanent print collection containing purchase prizes from National Print Exhibition
Exhibitions: Biennial National Print Exhibition; Art of Northwest USA - Exhibition of Painting and Sculpture (juried); 14 one-person exhibitions (juried); 2 group shows (juried); 2 invitational exhibtions (juried)
Publications: Exhibtion catalogs, member newsletter, quarterly
Activities: Classes for adults and children; docent training; workshops; lectures open to the public, 10 vis lectr per yr; concerts; gallery talks; tours; competitions with awards; scholarships; individual paintings and original objects of art lent to corporations and banks; lending collection contains books & original prints; originate traveling exhibitions; museum shop sells books, original art, reproductions & prints
L **Library,** 1037 Silvermine Rd, 06840
Library Holdings: Vols 2000; Per subs 6; AV — Motion pictures, slides

NEW HAVEN

M **MUNSON GALLERY,*** 33 Whitney Ave, 06511. Tel 203-865-2121. *Pres* Richard M Pelton; *Dir* Judy Birke
Open Mon - Sat 10 AM - 5:30 PM, Sat 11 AM - 5 PM. No admis fee. Estab 1860 to encourage interest in the arts by regular exhibitions of painting, sculpture, graphics, framing and restoration. Located in restored foundry building in New Haven Audubon Street Arts complex
Collections: Contemporary art in all mediums
Exhibitions: One person exhibits; regional work; international artists

M **THE NATIONAL ART MUSEUM OF SPORT,*** University of New Haven, 06516. Tel 203-934-6321, Ext 575. *Pres* Germain G Glidden; *VPres* Angelica Heller; *Secy* James Q Bensen
Open Mon - Fri 9 AM - 5 PM. No admis fee. Estab 1964 to expose the direct connection between art and sport. Average Annual Attendance: 1000. Mem: 3003; dues up to $1000; annual meeting in Jan
Income: $50,000 (financed by membership and corporate donations)
Collections: Paintings, sculpture and prints of leading past and present US sports champions
Publications: Newsletter, 2-3 per year
Activities: Lectures open to public, 2 visiting lecturers per year; individual and original objects of art lent to leading museums and corporate offices; originate traveling exhibitions

O **NEW HAVEN COLONY HISTORICAL SOCIETY,** 114 Whitney Ave, 06510. Tel 203-562-4183. *Pres* Brooks Shepard Jr; *Secy* Mrs Harry Perkins; *Dir* Floyd M Shumway; *Cur* Robert Egleston
Open Tues - Fri 10 AM - 5 PM; Sat, Sun & major holidays 2 - 5 PM; cl Mon. No admis fee. Estab 1862 for the preservation, exhibition and research of local scholarly materials, memorabilia and arts. Average Annual Attendance: 20,000. Mem: 1100; dues $20 - $50; annual meeting Nov
Collections: Morris House (c 1685-1780); †Connecticut Pewter; †New Haven silver, local furniture, paintings, drawings and graphics, and items of local historic interest
Publications: Newsletter; Quarterly Journal
Activities: Active school program; Exhibitions; morning and evening lect series; gift shop
L **Research Library,** 114 Whitney Ave, 06510. Tel 203-562-4183. *Librn & Manuscripts Cur* Ottilia Koel; *Ref Librn* Lysbeth Andrews-Zike; *Archivist* Anne Willard
Open Tues - Fri 10 AM - 5 PM. Estab 1862 to collect, preserve, make available, and publish historical and genealogical material relating to the early settlement and subsequent history of New Haven, its vicinity and incidentally, other parts of the USA. The Society has three departments: museum, library-archives, and educational, with the museum staff taking care of the gallery
Income: Financed by endowment, membership, and grants
Library Holdings: Vols 25,000; Per subs 55; original documents; 30,000 glass plate negatives; Micro — Fiche, reels; AV — Lantern slides; Other — Clipping files, exhibition catalogs, manuscripts, memorabilia, pamphlets, photographs, prints
Special Subjects: Decorative Arts, Historical Material, Photography
Collections: Afro-American Coll; Architectural Drawings; John W Barber Coll; Dana: New Haven Old and New; Durrie Papers; Ingersoll Papers; National & Local Historic Figures, A-Z; Ezra Stiles Papers; Noah Webster Collection
Publications: Journal, irregular; News and Notes, irregular; monographs; exhibition catalogs
Activities: Arrangement with local colleges for internship programs and work-study programs; students from Southern Connecticut State University Library School do on-site field work and give seminars for graduate students in library science; classes for children; docent training; lectures for members, 7 vis lectr per year; tours

O **NEW HAVEN PAINT AND CLAY CLUB, INC,** The John Slade Ely House, 51 Trumbull St, 06510. Tel 203-624-8055. *Pres* Edward J Kasper; *Secy* Elizabeth Greeley
Open Tues - Fri 1 - 4 PM; Sat & Sun 2 - 5 PM; cl Mon. Estab 1900, incorporated 1928. Permanent collection is on display in the Upstairs Galleries of

the John Slade Ely House at all times when the House is open. Mem: 254; open to artists working in any media whose work has been accepted two times in the Annual Juried Show; dues life $200, sustaining $20, assoc $5, active $10; annual meeting May
Income: $2500
Purchases: $1000
Exhibitions: Annual March Exhibition (New England artists); Annual Fall Exhibition (members only)
Publications: Catalog of spring show

M **SOUTHERN CONNECTICUT STATE COLLEGE,** Art Gallery,* 501 Crescent St, PO Box 3144, 06515. Tel 203-397-4262. *Dir* Olafs Zeidenbergs
Estab 1976 to build a collection of works of art for educational purposes, gallery developing now. Mem: 600; dues $5 and up
Income: $10,000 (financed by membership, state appropriation, and fund raising)
Activities: Lect open to public, 6 visiting lectr per year; gallery talks; national and international tours; exten dept; paintings and objects of art lent to administrative offices

YALE UNIVERSITY
M **Art Gallery,** 1111 Chapel St, Box 2006 Yale Station, 06520. Tel 203-436-0574. *Dir* Alan Shestack; *Cur Education* Janet S Dickson; *Cur Oriental Art* Mary G Neill; *Cur Prints, Drawings & Photographs* Richard S Field; *Assoc Cur Ancient Art* Susan Matheson; *Cur American Painting* Helen Cooper; *Cur American Decorative Arts* Patricia Kane; *Registrar* Rosalie Reed; *Membership, Sales & Publications* Caroline Rollins; *Supt* Robert Soule
Open Tues - Sat 10 AM - 5 PM, Sun 2 - 5 PM, cl Mon. No admis fee. Estab 1832 to exhibit works of art from ancient times to present. Building designed by Louis Kahn and completed in 1953. Average Annual Attendance: 120,000. Mem: 1500; dues $25 and up
Income: Financed by endowment, membership and annual fund-raising
Collections: †American and European painting and sculpture; Chinese painting and porcelains; Dura-Europos Archaeological Collection; †Garvan Collection of Decorative Arts; History paintings and miniatures by John Trumbull; Jarves Collection of Italian Renaissance Painting; Societe Anonyme Collection of twentieth century art; Stoddard Collection of Greek Vases; 20th Century Art; 25,000 Prints and Drawings
Publications: Exhibition catalogues; Yale University Art Gallery Bulletin, 3-4 times a yr
Activities: Sunday programs; gallery tours three times per week; Art a la Carte (lunchtime mini-lect); sales desk sells books, catalogues, reproductions, jewelry and postcards
M **Yale Center for British Art,** 1080 Chapel St, Box 2120 Yale Station, 06520. Tel 203-432-4594. *Dir* Duncan Robinson; *Asst Dir Education & Information* Constance Clement; *Cur Paintings* Malcolm Cormack; *Cur Prints & Drawings* Patrick Noon; *Cur Rare Books* Joan Friedman; *Registrar* Timothy Goodhue; *Conservator Paper* Theresa Fairbanks
Open Tues - Sat 10 AM - 5 PM, Sun 2 - 5 PM, cl Mon. Estab 1977 to foster appreciation and knowledge of British art; to encourage interdisciplinary use of the collections. Library for reference; maintains gallery
Income: Financed by endowment and annual gifts
Library Holdings: Vols 10,000; Per subs 60; Micro — Fiche 1000, reels; Other — Exhibition catalogs, pamphlets, photographs
Special Subjects: British Art circa 1500-1915
Collections: Paintings; drawings; prints; rare books & sculpture
Exhibitions: Painters and Engraving; Camden Town Group; The Conservation Piece: Arthur Devis and His Contemporaries; The Art of Alexander and John Robert Cozens; Selected Watercolors; Tom Eckersley: Posters & Other Graphic Work; Stanley Spencer: A Modern Visionary; Turner and the Sublime; Shakespeare and British Art; Recent Acquisitions; Classic Ground; Exhibition Watercolors, 1770-1870; Eight Figurative Painters; The English Miniatures; Biscuit Tins; The Great Exhibition: A Question of Taste; Victorian Womanhood; 18th & 19th British Architectural Drawings; Noble Exercise: The Sporting Ideal in 18th Century British Art; William Blake: His Art & Times; Presences of Nature: British Landscape 1780-1830; John Linnell: A Centenary Exhibition; Richard Wilson, R A (1713-1782); The Early Georgian Landscape; Vanxhall Gardens; Rembrandt in 18th Century Britain
Publications: Calendar of Events-Preview of Exhibitions, bi-annually; exhibition catalogues, five per year
Activities: Docent training; symposia; colloquia; lectures; concerts; gallery talks; tours; films open to the public; scholarships
—**Reference Library,*** 1080 Chapel St, Yale Sta, Box 2120, 06520. Tel 203-432-4097. *Librn* Dr Anne-Marie Logan
Library Holdings: Vols 13,000; Per subs 35; Micro — Reels 860
Special Subjects: British Art
L **Art and Architecture Library,** 180 York St, Box 1605 A Yale Station, 06520. Tel 203-436-1439. *Librn* Nancy Sifferd Lambert; *Asst Librn* Gary R Sipe; *Slide & Photograph* Helen Chillman
Estab 1868. Serves Schools of Art & Architecture, History of Art Dept & the Yale University Art Gallery
Library Holdings: Vols 78,000; Photographs and color prints 262,000; Micro — Fiche; AV — Slides 251,512; Other — Exhibition catalogs
Collections: †Faber Birren Collection of Books on Color
Publications: Faber Birren Collection of Books on Color: A Bibliography

NEW LONDON

M **LYMAN ALLYN MUSEUM,** 625 Williams St, 06320. Tel 203-443-2545. *Dir* Dr Edgar deN Mayhew; *Secy* Mrs Willard Shepard; *Cur* Mrs Arvin Karterud; *Educ Coordinator* Mrs Frederick Richartz; *Conservator* Lance Mayer; *Conservator* Gay Myers; *Docent* Mrs Edward Gipstein
Open Tues - Sat 1 PM - 5 PM, Sun 2 PM - 5 PM; cl Mon. No admis fee. Estab 1932 for the education and enrichment of the community and others. The current building consists of nine permanent galleries and four galleries for changing exhibitions. Average Annual Attendance: 50,000. Mem: 1000; dues range from individual $10 to life $1000
Income: $180,000 (financed by endowment, membership, and gifts)

Purchases: $20,000
Collections: Egyptian, Greek & Roman antiquities; Medieval & Renaissance art; Oriental material primitive art; American & European paintings; furniture; silver; decorative arts; Baratz Collection of dolls, doll houses & toys
Exhibitions: (1982) Pre-Columbian Exhibition; one man shows by Daniel Truth, Ricky Gipstein, Ted Hendrickson, Louise McCagg; Special 50th Anniversary Show; New London Revisited; Connecticut Watercolor Society; one man shows by Charles Moser, Rollie McKenna and Homer Pfeiffer; (1983) One man shows by Ann Latrobe, Gigi Liverant, Patty Kitchings, Richard Webb, Richard Lukosius, John Gregoropoulos; Eleven Phases of Art
Publications: Handbook of the Museum's Outstanding Holdings; New London County Furniture from 1640-1840; New London Silver
Activities: Classes for adults and children; docent training; school tours and programs; lect for members; museum shop sells small antiques
L **Library,** 625 Williams St, 06320
Open Tues - Sat 1 - 5 PM. Estab 1932 to provide an art reference library as an adjunct to the material in the Lyman Allyn Museum. Reference only
Library Holdings: Vols 16,000; Per subs 32; Other — Exhibition catalogs
Special Subjects: Decorative Arts, Artists & Related Areas; Art Objects
Collections: Decorative arts, furniture, drawings
Activities: Docent training; lectures open to public, 2 vis lectr per year; gallery talks; tours

M **US COAST GUARD MUSEUM,** 06320. Tel 203-444-8513. *Cur* Paul H Johnson
Open Mon - Fri 8 AM - 4:15 PM, also summer Sat & Sun 10 AM - 4 PM. Estab 1967 to preserve historical heritage of US Coast Guard, US Life Saving Service and US Lighthouse Service. Average Annual Attendance: 20,000
Income: Financed by federal appropriations and private donations
Purchases: $12,000
Collections: Maritime paintings; shipmodels
Exhibitions: Life Savings At Sea; permenent collection
Activities: Tours by appointment; competitions; sales shop sells souvenirs

NORWALK

M **LOCKWOOD-MATHEWS MANSION MUSEUM,** 295 West Ave, 06850. Tel 203-838-1434. *Pres* N Nicoll Snow; *Dir* David J Byrnes
Open Tues - Fri 11 AM - 3 PM, Sun 1 - 4 PM. Admis, suggested donation $3, students & senior citizens $2. Estab 1968 to completely restore this 19th century 50-room mansion as a historic house museum. Now a registered National Historic Landmark. Average Annual Attendance: 15,000. Mem: 700; annual meeting May
Income: $37,000 (financed by membership, city and state appropriation, federal grant)
Publications: Newsletter, quarterly
Activities: Docent training; lect open to public, 6 vis lectr per year; gallery talks; tours; museum shop selling books, reproductions, prints, Victorian toys and games

NORWICH

M **NORWICH FREE ACADEMY,** Slater Memorial Museum & Converse Art Gallery, 108 Crescent St, 06360. Tel 203-887-2505, Ext 218. *Dir* Joseph P Gualtieri; *Asst to Dir* Marie E Noyes; *Docent* Mary-Anne Hall; *Registrar* Carolynn A Foss
Open Sept - May Mon - Fri 9 AM - 4 PM; Sat & Sun 1 - 4 PM; June - Aug Tues - Sun 1 - 4 PM; cl holidays throughout the year. No admis fee. Estab 1888. The collection is housed in two buildings. Average Annual Attendance: 34,000. Mem: 400; sustaining over $25, patron $25, contributing $15, family $10, single $6; annual meeting usually April
Income: Financed by endowment
Collections: Vanderpoel Collection of Oriental Art; African Art; American Art and Furniture from the 17th - 20th Centuries; American Indian Artifacts; Egyptian Art Objects and Textiles
Exhibitions: Special exhibitions changed monthly
Publications: Exhibition catalogs
Activities: Lect open to public; competitions; individual paintings and original objects of art lent to museums and historical societies; shop sells postcards

OLD LYME

O **LYME ART ASSOCIATION, INC,*** Lyme St, PO Box 222, 06371. Tel 203-434-7802. *Pres* Sultana Hanniford; *VPres* Thomas Torrenti; *Recording Secy* Ann Moran; *Treas* H Gil-Roberts
Open seasonally Mon - Sat 12 - 5 PM, Sun 1 - 5 PM. Admis $.50, no fee to members. Estab 1901 to present fine arts in the traditional manner. Four large sky-lighted galleries are maintained. Average Annual Attendance: 4000. Mem: 38; dues invitational juried members $25, $10 associate membership, $2 season ticket
Income: Financed by membership and associate members
Exhibitions: Four annual exhibitions: 2 open, 2 member only
Activities: Sales shop sells original art

M **LYME HISTORICAL SOCIETY,** Florence Griswold Museum, 96 Lyme St, 06371. Tel 203-434-5542. *Pres* George J Willauer Jr; *Dir* Jeffrey W Andersen; *Cur & Librn* Debra A Fillos
Open (June - Aug) Tues - Sat 10 AM - 5 PM; Sun 1 - 5 PM; (Sept - May) Wed - Sun 1 - 5 PM. No admis fee. Estab 1936 for the purpose of collecting, preserving and exhibiting the art and history of the Lyme region. Average Annual Attendance: 7000. Mem: 1120; dues family $20, individual $15; annual meeting June
Income: $150,000 (financed by endowment, membership, grants, and town appropriation)
Purchases: $1500

Collections: Old Lyme Art Colony Paintings; Clara Champlain Griswold Toy Collection; Decorative Arts and Furnishings; Local Historical Collections
Exhibitions: The Ancient Town of Lyme; The Art Colony at Old Lyme; A Child's World; 19th Century Period Rooms; A Grave Business: New England Gravestone Art; Walker Evans Photographs; Clark Voorhees 1871-1933; Old Lyme: The American Barbizon; Dressed for Any Occasion: Patterns of Fashion in the 19th Century; Thomas W Nason, 1889-1971, A Personal Vision of New England
Publications: The Lyme Ledger, quarterly; Report of the Lyme Historical Society, annually; Miss Florence & The Artists of Old Lyme; A New Look at History; The Connecticut Impressionists at Old Lyme
Activities: Classes for adults and children; docent training; lect open to public; tours; museum shop selling books
L **Archives,** 96 Lyme St, 06371. Tel 203-434-5542
Open Mon -Fri 10 AM - 5 PM. Estab 1953 as a research facility for museum programs and the public. Open to the public for reference
Purchases: $1200
Library Holdings: Vols 1200; Per subs 15; AV — Cassettes, Kodachromes, motion pictures, slides; Other — Clipping files, exhibition catalogs, manuscripts, memorabilia, pamphlets, photographs, prints, reproductions
Special Subjects: The Art Colony at Old Lyme, American landscape paintings, local history

RIDGEFIELD

M **ALDRICH MUSEUM OF CONTEMPORARY ART,*** 258 Main St, 06877. Tel 203-438-4519. *Pres* Richard E Anderson; *Dir* Dorothy Mayhall; *Cur Education* Martha Scott
Open Wed - Fri 2 - 4 PM, Sat & Sun 1 - 5 PM; group visits by appointment. Admis adults $1, students, children and senior citizens $.50. Estab 1964 for the presentation of contemporary painting and sculpture and allied arts; to stimulate public awareness of contemporary art through exhibitions and education programs. Nine galleries on three floors of a totally renovated colonial building provide well-lit exhibition space; outdoor sculpture garden. Average Annual Attendance: 20,000. Mem: 450; dues $25 - $1000
Income: $130,000 (financed by membership, federal and state grants, corporate and private foundations)
Collections: Aldrich Collection; †extended loan collection; †museum collection of emerging artists; print collection
Exhibitions: Art in the Seventies; Contemporary Reflections: The Sixties Revisited; 15 New Talents; The Minimal Tradition; Sculptural Forms; Mysterious & Magical Realism; Acquisitions Plus; New Dimensions in Drawing; New Visions; A Look Back-A Look Forward
Publications: Exhibition catalogs; Newsletter, quarterly
Activities: Classes for adults; docent training; lect open to public, 6 vis lectr per year; concerts; gallery talks; tours; individual & original paintings lent to museums, university galleries, and corporate patrons; Artreach Program sends docents with slide lect into Fairfield County art classes

STAMFORD

C **CHAMPION INTERNATIONAL CORPORATION,*** 1 Champion Plaza, 06921. Tel 203-358-7695. *Interior Design Consultant* Mrs Vibeke Simonsen
Estab 1975 to create a pleasant environment and expose employees to art. Collection displayed on most floors and in executive offices
Collections: Antique European oils; antique Pennsylvania quilt; A Calder; large Helena Hernmark tapestry; oil paintings by Edward Hicks; oil painting by William Horton; tapestry by Michelle Lester; tapestry by Anna Petersen; two Henry Moore lithographs; etchings by R Nakian; oil painting by Millard Sheets; four 19 century weathervanes; 12 photographs

L **FERGUSON LIBRARY,** 96 Broad St, 06901. Tel 203-964-1000. *Dir* Ernest A DiMattia Jr; *Arts & Media Librn* Phyllis Massar; *Admin Asst* Edith Halverson
Open Mon - Fri 9 AM - 9 PM, Sat 9 AM - 5:30 PM, Oct - June Sun 1 - 5 PM. Estab 1880 as a public library dedicated to serving the information needs of the community
Income: Financed by city appropriation
Purchases: $11,000 (art and music books), $30,000 (films), $11,000 (records)
Library Holdings: Vols 12,600; AV — Cassettes, motion pictures, rec, slides; Other — Framed reproductions
Collections: Photography of Old Stamford
Exhibitions: Painting, sculpture, photography & posters under sponsorship of Friends of Ferguson Library
Publications: Art Currents

SOCIETY OF AMERICAN HISTORICAL ARTISTS
For further information, see National and Regional Organizations

M **STAMFORD MUSEUM AND NATURE CENTER,*** 39 Scofieldtown Rd, 06903. Tel 203-322-1646. *Pres* Haynes Johnson; *Dir* Gerald E Rasmussen; *Asst Dir* Philip Novak; *Art Dir* Dr Robert Metzger
Open Mon - Sat 9 AM - 5 PM, Sun & holidays 1 - 5 PM, cl Thanksgiving, Christmas & New Year's Day. Admis adults $2, children & sr citizens $1. Estab 1936, Art Department 1955. Average Annual Attendance: 250,000. Mem: 3000; dues $15 and up; annual meeting June
Collections: American crafts, American Indian, painting, sculpture, sculpture garden
Publications: Brochure; Newsletter, monthly
Activities: Classes in painting, drawing, sculpture, ceramics and modern dance; lect to school groups; museum shop sells books, prints and crafts

M **WHITNEY MUSEUM OF AMERICAN ART, FAIRFIELD COUNTY,*** One Champion Pl, 06921. Tel 203-358-7630. *Dir* Pamela Gruninger
Open Tues - Sat 11 AM - 5 PM. No admis fee. Estab 1981
Income: Financed by Champion International Corporation
Collections: 20th century American painting, sculpture, drawing, prints
Exhibitions: One-person exhibitions
Activities: Lectures; gallery talks; films; performances

C **XEROX CORPORATION,** Art Collection, Long Ridge Park, 06904. Tel 203-329-8700. *VPres* Robert M Schneider; *Program Consultant* Elizabeth T Kucklick
Collection on display at Xerox Headquarters
Collections: The art collection represents a broad spectrum of American fine art as well as art forms from other countries. The works range from abstraction to realism and consist of sculpture by David Lee Brown located in the lobby, fiberwork by Gerhardt Knodel located in the dining facility, collages, etchings, lithographs, graphics, mezzotints, mono-prints, montages, pastels, photography, pochoir, silkscreens, watercolors and xerography

STORRS

UNIVERSITY OF CONNECTICUT
M **William Benton Museum of Art,*** 06268. Tel 203-486-4520. *Dir* Paul F Rovetti; *Asst Dir & Cur 20th Century Art* Stephanie Terenzio; *Cur of Collections* Thomas P Bruhn; *Cur of Education* Hildegard Cummings; *Registrar* George Mazeika
Open during exhibitions Mon - Sat 10 AM - 4:30 PM, Sun 1 - 5 PM, cl summers. No admis fee. Estab 1966, a museum of art, operating as an autonomous department within the University, serving the students, faculty and general public; contributing to the field at large through research, exhibitions and publications and by maintaining a permanent collection of over 3000 objects. The main gallery measures 36 x 116 ft with a balcony (with exhibit walls) running on three walls and two small pendant galleries 20 x 31 ft. Average Annual Attendance: 25,000. Mem: 1200; dues double $16
Income: $9000 (financed by membership and state appropriation)
Collections: †American painting and graphics early 20th Century; †German and French graphics late 19th and 20th Century; †selected 17th and 18th Century European paintings, sculptures and graphics; Western European and American c 1600 to present; paintings, graphics
Exhibitions: American Decorative Tiles (1870 - 1915); Connecticut and American Impressionism; Selected Paintings of Anthony Terenzio; Drawings Into Color: Work by Graham Nickson
Publications: Annual report; bulletin, annually; exhibition catalogs, biannually
Activities: Lect open to the public, 5-8 vis lectr per year; concerts; gallery talks, tours; individual paintings and original objects of art lent to accredited institutions for exhibition purposes; lending collection contains original prints, paintings and sculpture; book traveling exhibitions; originate traveling exhibitions; sales shop sells books, original art, prints, reproductions and museum related art objects and jewelry
M **Jorgensen Gallery,** U-104, 06268. Tel 203-486-4226. *Dir Jorgensen Auditorium* Jack Clonan; *Assoc Dir* Edmund O Seagrave
Open Tues - Fri 11 AM - 4 PM, Sat & Sun 1 - 4 PM. No admis fee. Estab 1967 to present work by leading contemporary American artists. Since 1982, known as the Benton Connection, houses works from the permanent collection of the William Benton Museum of Art at the University of Connecticut. Serves the public as well as the university community. The gallery is 2872 square feet. Average Annual Attendance: 25,000
Activities: Gallery talks
L **Art and Design Library,** Box U-5AD, 06268. *Head* Thomas J Jacoby; *Asst Head* Tim Ann Parker
Open Mon - Thurs 9 AM - 10 PM, Fri 9 AM - 5 PM, Sat noon - 6 PM, Sun noon - 10 PM. Estab 1979 to support the Departments of Art, Interior Design, Landscape, Architecture & Garden History. Circ 14,000
Library Holdings: Vols 42,000; Per subs 120; Micro — Fiche; Other — Exhibition catalogs, original art works, pamphlets, photographs
Special Subjects: American Art, Western European Art
Exhibitions: Continuing exhibits of faculty work

WALLINGFORD

O **WALLINGFORD ART LEAGUE,** Box 163, 06492. *Pres* Manuel Gomes; *VPres* Jean Whitehouse; *Secy* B Jeanne Kovacs
Estab 1945. Average Annual Attendance: 200. Mem: 62; dues $5; meetings Oct - June, second Thurs each month
Income: Approx $500 (financed by membership)
Activities: Classes for adults; lect open to public, 5 visiting lectr per year; scholarships

WASHINGTON DEPOT

O **WASHINGTON ART ASSOCIATION,** 06794. Tel 203-868-2878. *Pres* R Dana Gibson; *VPres* Mrs Owen Eames; *VPres* Mrs Steven Lasar; *VPres* Mrs John Strawbridge; *Exec Secy* Mrs William Talbot; *Secy* Mrs Phillips Payson
Open Mon, Tues, Thurs - Sat 10 AM - 5 PM, Sun 2 - 5 PM, cl Wed. Estab 1952 to make available to the community a variety of art experiences through exhibitions and activities. Gallery is located in three rooms downstairs. Average Annual Attendance: 6400. Mem: 815; dues family $15, individual $10; annual meeting third week in Aug
Income: $32,000 (financed by endowment, membership and fund-raising events)
Exhibitions: (1982) Winifred van Duyl, paintings and drawings; Emily Nelligan, drawings; Francis Cook, etchings; Michael Gallatly, airbrush painting; John Norris, drawings of fire engines; Claude Saucy, woodcuts; Ten Artists from Woodbury and Bethlehem; Roger van Damme, paintings and drawings; Weymouth Somerset, handmade paper works; Ruth Miller, drawings; Vita Peterson, drawings; Members Show, oils and acrylics; Nancy Lasar, paintings and drawings; Georgia Middlebrook, paintings and prints; Tony Balloch, photographs; Clemens Kalisher, photographs; Christmas Show and Sale; (1983) Benigna Chilla, paper and canvas sculpture; John Christensen, sculpture and drawings; Joan Mathews, drawings; Paul Strand, photographs; Eleanor Hubbard, paintings; Susan Reeder, ceramics; Members Show, sculpture and works on paper; Al Martinez, installation; Wykeham Alumnae, mixed media; Werner Pfeiffer, sculpture, graphics and prints; Vincent Mastracco, large abstract paintings; Craft Exhibition: Joan Loveless, tapestries; Mark Cecula, ceramics; Kenneth Holsapple, furniture; Photographs: Paul Diamond, Debbie Fleming Caffery, Margaret Stewart;

Dorothea Goldys-Bass, paintings; Elizabeth Coleman, environmental sculpture; Wendell Minor, book covers - original artwork; Marjorie Walker, paintings; Christmas Show & Sale, crafts and small works of art
Publications: Events Bulletin
Activities: Classes for adults and children; trips to major museums and Tanglewood concerts; lectures open to the public, 4 vis lectrs per yr; sales shop sells original art
L **Library,** 06794. *Librn* Elizabeth Kihl
Open to members and teachers for reference
Library Holdings: Vols 350; Per subs 2; Other — Exhibition catalogs

WATERBURY

L **SILAS BRONSON LIBRARY,** Art, Music & Theatre Dept,* 267 Grand St, 06702. Tel 203-574-8236. *Dir* Stanford Warshasky; *Fine Arts* Eugenia Benson
Open Mon & Wed 9 AM - 9 PM, Tues, Thurs & Sat 9 AM - 5:30 PM, Fri Noon - 5:30 PM. Estab 1869 to provide a free public library for the community. A spotlighted gallery wall and locked glass exhibition case used for art exhibits
Income: Financed by endowment and city appropriation
Exhibitions: Local artists in various media
Publications: Books & Happenings, monthly newsletter
Activities: Lect open to the public; concerts; individual paintings lent

M **MATTATUCK HISTORICAL SOCIETY MUSEUM,** Mattatuck Museum,* 119 W Main St, 06702. Tel 203-753-0381. *Pres* Orton P Camp Jr; *VPres* W Fielding Secor; *Secy* Mrs William W Brown; *Dir* Ann Smith; *Educ Dir* Dorothy Cantor
Open Tues - Sat Noon - 5 PM, Sun 2 - 5 PM, cl Mon. No admis fee. Estab 1877 to collect and preserve the arts, history of the state of Connecticut, especially of Waterbury and adjacent towns. An art gallery is maintained. Average Annual Attendance: 25,000. Mem: 1000; dues $10 - 500; annual meeting in Nov
Income: Financed by endowment, membership and grants
Collections: Connecticut artists collection; decorative arts collection; local history and industrial artifacts; period rooms
Publications: Annual Report
Activities: Classes for adults and children; lect open to the public, 5 vis lectr per year; gallery talks; tours; lending collection contains photographs and slides
L **Library,*** 06702
Library Holdings: Vols 3000; Per subs 10

WATERFORD

M **HARKNESS MEMORIAL STATE PARK,*** 275 Great Neck Rd, 06385. Tel 203-443-5725. *Park Manager* Theodore J Tetreault Jr
Grounds open 8 AM - Sunset year round; buildings open Memorial Day to Labor Day 10 AM - 5 PM. Parking fee $1. Estab 1954. Average Annual Attendance: 125,000
Income: Financed by state appropriation
Collections: Complete collection of artist Rex Brasher: Birds of North American, (874 watercolor paintings)
Publications: Brochures
Activities: Sales shop sells black and white prints of the paintings

WEST HARTFORD

M **UNIVERSITY OF HARTFORD,** Joseloff Gallery,* Hartford Art School, 200 Bloomfield Ave, 06117. Tel 203-243-4393. *Dir* Edwin E Stein; *Gallery Coordr* Joan Saunders
Open Mon - Fri 9 AM - 4:30 PM. No admis fee. Estab 1964 primarily for the education of the students, but is also for the aesthetic enjoyment of the art interested public. The gallery is 40 x 60 x 13 ft high and can be divided into two rooms
Publications: The Hartfor Art School: The Early Years
Activities: Classes for adults; lectures open to the public, 20 - 30 vis lectr per yr; concerts; gallery talks; tours; competitions; individual paintings and original objects of art lent to area businesses and institutions; book traveling exhibitions; traveling exhibitions organized and circulated
L **Anne Bunce Cheney Library,*** University of Hartford, 200 Bloomfield Ave, 06117. Tel 203-243-4397. *Art Librn* Jean J Miller; *Library Asst* Anna Bigazzi
Open Mon - Thurs 8:30 AM - 10 PM, Fri 8:30 AM - 5 PM, Sat & Sun Noon - 5 PM. Estab 1964. Circ 9689
Income: Financed through university library
Library Holdings: Vols 11,000; Per subs 83; Other — Exhibition catalogs, pamphlets, reproductions

WILTON

M **CRAFT CENTER MUSEUM,** 78 Danbury Rd, PO Box 488, 06897. Tel 203-762-8363. *Pres* Kenneth Lynch; *VPres* Pat Nolan; *Secy* Grace Weitman; *Cur* Theodore Monnich
By invitation only. Estab 1927 for the exhibition of the tools of the armorer, the silversmith, goldsmith, coppersmith and blacksmith and products made by these tools. Maintains gallery for exhibitions
Library Holdings: Vols 3000; Other — Photographs
Collections: Armor, brass casting, copper, furnishing, lead, leather, lighting, silversmithing, wood, tools and finished products in areas of metal spinning
Publications: The Armorer & His Tools; Adventures in Metalwork
Activities: Lectures; scholarships
L **Library,** 78 Danbury Rd, Wilton, 06897
Reference library
Library Holdings: Vols 3000; Per subs 100; Micro — Cards, fiche; AV — A-tapes

DELAWARE

DOVER

M **DIVISION OF HISTORICAL AND CULTURAL AFFAIRS,** Bureau of Museums and Historic Sites, 102 S State St, PO Box 1401, 19901. Tel 302-736-5316. *Actg Division Dir* Dr Ann Houseman; *Chief Bureau of Museums and Historic Sites* Dean E Nelson; *Cur Coll* Ann Horsey; *Cur Exhib* Mrs Dominique C Western; *Cur Education* Madeline D Hite; *Cur Historic Buildings* James A Stewart; *Cur Registration* Claudia F Melson
Delaware State Museum, John Dickinson Mansion, Old State House, Zwaanendael Museum, Island Field Museum, New Castle Court House, Fort Christina; Tues - Sat 10 AM - 4:30 PM, Sun 1:30 - 4:30 PM; Prince George's Chapel, Memorial Day weekend - Labor Day weekend Sat 10 AM - 4:30 PM, Sun 1:30 - 4:30 PM; Allee House Sat & Sun 2 - 5 PM Octagonal School, by appointment only; Robinson House, Wed 11 AM - 4 PM, first Sun of month, 1 - 4 PM, cl state legal holidays; Visitor Center open Mon - Sat 10 AM - 4:30 PM, Sun 1:30 - 4:30 PM; Johnson Memorial Tues - Sat 10 AM - 4:30 PM, Sun 1:30 - 4:30 PM. No admis fee. Historic house museums were opened in the 1950s, Zwaanendael Museum 1931, to reflect the pre-historic and historic development of Delaware by exhibiting artifacts and interpreting the same through various facilities-those of early times. Average Annual Attendance: 110,000
Income: $650,000
Collections: Allee House—furniture and decorative arts; Delaware State Museum—changing exhibits; early Delaware industry & businesses; John Dickinson Mansion—decorative arts, furniture and Dickinson family artifacts; Island Field Museum—archaeological remains, artifacts; The Lindens—furniture and decorative arts; New Castle Court House—portraits of famous Delawareans, archaeological artifacts, furniture and maps; Old State House—legislative, judicial and governmental furniture and decorative arts; Prince George's Chapel—ecclesiastical furniture and decorative arts; Robinson House—furniture and decorative arts; Zwaanendael Museum—Indian artifacts and Colonial items pertaining to the early history of Lewes and lower Delaware, commemorative gifts to the State of Delaware from Holland, china, glass, and silver; Johnson Memorial—Talking machines, Victrolas, early recordings & Johnson memorabilia associated with the Victor Talking Machine Company (RCA)
Publications: Delaware State Museum Bulletins; Delaware History Notebook; miscellaneous booklets and brochures
Activities: Classes for children; docent training; special educational programs for school groups and adults which reflect the architecture, government, education and aspects of social history relevant to Delaware; individual paintings are lent to governmental facilities; inservice programs relating to Delaware history are offered to Delaware teachers; traveling trunk program circulated to elementary schools; museum shop sells books, magazines, prints & Delaware souvenirs

NEWARK

O **COUNCIL OF DELAWARE ARTISTS,** 112 Tanglewood Lane, 19711. Tel 302-737-2473. *Pres* Carol Gray
Estab 1955 to educate the membership and the public about significant aspects of the creative arts including discussions, lectures and exhibitions pertaining to the visual arts and to provide continuous exposure of member's work through exhibitions; to establish an atmosphere of fellowship and cooperation among professional artist members. Mem: 60; dues $15; annual meeting in May
Income: Financed by membership dues
Exhibitions: (1984) Division of Continuing Education, University of Delaware; Arthritis Foundation Exhibition
Publications: Newsletter
Activities: Lect open to public; 9 vis lectr per year; individual paintings lent to schools, public offices, retirement homes and banks; originate traveling exhibitions

UNIVERSITY OF DELAWARE
M **Student Center Art Gallery,*** 19711. Tel 302-738-2630. *Dir* Jack S Sturgell
Open daily Noon - 5 PM, shorter hours during vacation. Estab 1926 to enlarge the student's acquaintance with art in its various aspects. Average Annual Attendance: 10,000
Exhibitions: Change monthly; include traveling exhibitions from prominent museums and organizations as well as from the University collections; annual exhibition of University students' work; yearly juried show of regional artists
Activities: Book traveling exhibitions
M **University Art Collections,*** 19711. Tel 302-Archivist's Office 738-2750; Art History Collection 738-2418. *University Archivist & Dir Permanent Coll* John M Clayton; *Cur Slide & Photograph Library & Art History Teaching Coll* Charlotte Kelly
No admis fee. Estab to consolidate the gifts of art to the University and to provide exhibitions of art objects from these collections to increase visual awareness on the campus. Several exhibition areas around campus Morris Library, Clayton Hall, Smith Hall mini-exhibition cases. Average Annual Attendance: 4000
Income: Financed by state appropriation
Collections: Art History Teaching Collection of 600 art objects, including painting, sculpture (primarily American, African and pre-Columbian), and prints; permanent collection of 500 art objects including painting, sculpture and prints
Publications: Bulletins
M **University Gallery,** Museum Studies Program, University of Delaware, 19716. Tel 302-451-1251. *Dir* Barbara H Butler; *Cur* Gail Shrott
Open Mon - Fri 10 AM - 5 PM, Sun Noon - 5 PM, cl university holidays. No admis fee. Estab 1978. Average Annual Attendance: 6000
Exhibitions: (1982) James Turrell; Jida: A Space & Light Installations; Images of an Enlightened Age; Campion of the Enlightment: Goya as Printmaker
Publications: Exhibit catalog
Activities: Lectures open to public, 2-3 vis lectr per year; gallery talks; competitions with awards; individual and original objects of art lent to other museums and universities; book traveling exhibitions

L **Morris Library,** South College Ave, 19711. Tel 302-738-2231. *Dir Libraries* Susan Brynteson; *Chief Reference Librn* Jill Fatzer; *Reference Librn (Art & Art History)* Susan A Davi
Open Mon - Thurs 8 AM - 12:30 AM, Fri 8 AM - 10 PM, Sat 9 AM - 10 PM, Sun 11 - 12:30 AM (when in session). Estab 1834 as University Library
Income: Financed through the University
Purchases: $90,895
Library Holdings: Vols 50,000; Per subs 200; Micro — Fiche, reels; AV — Rec; Other — Exhibition catalogs, pamphlets
Collections: American Art and Architecture; Early 20th Century European Art; material on Ornamental Horticulture

REHOBOTH BEACH

O **REHOBOTH ART LEAGUE, INC,** Henlopen Acres, PO Box 84, 19971. Tel 302-227-8408. *Pres* Robert E Grigsby; *Exec Secy* Mary L Pearce
Open March 23 - Oct 31 daily 10 AM - 4 PM. No admis fee. Estab 1938 to provide art education and creative arts in Rehoboth Beach community and Sussex County, Delaware. Two galleries, the Corkran and the Tubbs built for exhibitions. New the Restored Homestead, and old home with small rooms planned for exhibitions of paintings and small sculpture and crafts. Average Annual Attendance: 18,000. Mem: 1100; dues $15 and up; annual meeting last Mon in Aug
Income: Financed by membership, donation and fund raising and sales of paintings
Collections: Small permanent collection from gifts
Exhibitions: Annual exhibitions
Publications: Brochure of yearly events
Activities: Classes for adults and children; lect open to public, 3 vis lectr per yr; concerts; gallery talks; competitions with awards; scholarships; sales shop selling original art and prints

WILMINGTON

M **DELAWARE ART MUSEUM,** 2301 Kentmere Parkway, 19806. Tel 302-571-9590. *Dir* Robert Frankel; *Assoc Dir & Chief Cur* Rowland P Elzea; *Assoc Cur & Cur John Sloan Archives* Elizabeth Hawkes; *Cur of Education* Diane B Stillman; *Asst Dir* Stephen Bruni; *Registrar* Mary Holahan
Open Mon - Sat 10 AM - 5 PM, Sun 1 - 5 PM. No admis fee. Incorporated 1912 as the Wilmington Society of Fine Arts; present building completed in 1938; a privately funded, non-profit cultural and educational institution dedicated to the increase of knowledge and pleasure through the display and interpretation of works of art and through classes designed to encourage an understanding of and a participation in the fine arts. Six galleries are used for exhibitions; five usually hold permanent or semi-permanent exhibitions which change at approximately six week intervals. Exhibitions are also held in the library and the education wing. Average Annual Attendance: 35,000. Mem: 2000; dues family $25, individual $15; annual meeting third Tues in Oct
Income: $1,075,500 (financed by endowment, membership and grants)
Purchases: $6500
Collections: Bancroft Collection of English Pre-Raphaelite Paintings; †Copeland Collection of Work by Local Artists Phelps Collection of Andrew Wyeth Works; †American Paintings and Sculpture, including many Howard Pyle works and complete etchings and lithographs of John Sloan
Exhibitions: (1980-81) Brooke Alexander: A Decade of Print Publishing; City Life Illustrated: 1890-1940; 23rd Contemporary Crafts Exhibition; Rememberances of Holidays Past: Dolls, Toys and Teddy Bears; Consumers Choice: The American Home 1890-1940; Gidney Goodman: Contemporary Crafts; Maria Rose C Blake, Jesoph Detweiler and Louise Briggs; Photography of the Fifties; From All Walks of Life; 66th Delaware Exhibition
Publications: DAM Bulletin, bi-monthly
Activities: Classes for adults and children; docent training; workshops; lect open to the public and occasionally to members only, 6 vis lectr per year; concerts; gallery talks; tours; competitions; exten dept serving schools and community groups offering two-week programs in visual education; originate traveling exhibitions; museum and sales shops sell books, candles, jewelry, note cards, paper, original art, prints, reproductions, slides and crafts

M **Downtown Gallery,*** Bank of Delaware, 901 Market St, 19801. Tel 302-658-4825. *Dir* Lial A Jones
Open Mon - Fri 10:30 AM - 3 PM. Serves businessmen and shoppers in downtown area
Exhibitions: Ten exhibitions a year of local and nationally known contemporary artists

L **Library,** 2301 Kentmere Parkway, 19806. Tel 302-571-9590. *Librn* Anne Marie Haslam
Open Mon - Fri 1:30 - 3 PM & by appointment. Estab 1923. Open to students, scholars for reference only
Library Holdings: Vols 25,000; Micro — Reels; Other — Clipping files, exhibition catalogs, manuscripts, memorabilia, original art works, pamphlets, photographs, prints
Special Subjects: American Art 19th - 20th Century, American Illustration, Pre-Raphaelite Art
Collections: John Sloan Archives
Exhibitions: Howard Pyle Collection; Bancroft Pre-Raphaelite Library

M **HAGLEY MUSEUM,** Eleutherian Mills-Hagley Foundation, Barley Mill Rd & Brandywine Creek (Mailing add: PO Box 3630, Greenville, 19807). Tel 302-658-2400. *General Dir* Dr Glenn Porter
Open Tues - Sat 9:30 AM - 4:30 PM; Sun 1 - 5 PM. Admis adults $4, sr citizens and students $3.50, children 6-14 $1, under 6 free. Estab 1952; museum first opened to public in 1957, to preserve and interpret the site of the original duPont black powder works and tell the story of the early history of industry on the Brandywine. The 1803 home of E I duPont, furnished to illustrate the lifestyle of five generations of duPonts, is open year round. Average Annual Attendance: 100,000. Mem: 1100; dues family $25, single $15
Income: Financed by endowment, grants, gifts & community support

Exhibitions: Changing exhibits
Publications: Annual Report; Guide Books; Newsletter, three per year
Activities: Classes for children; docent training; lectures for members; tours; concerts; gallery talks; Irish Day; Textile Craft Fair; Christmas tours; scholarships; individual and original objects of art lent; traveling exhibitions organized and circulated; museum shop selling books, original art, reproductions, prints, slides

L **Eleutherian Mills Historical Library,** PO Box 3630, 19807. Tel 302-658-2400. *General Dir* Glenn Porter; *Library Dir* Richmond T Williams
Open Mon - Fri to students, and to researchers by appointment
Library Holdings: Vols 150,000; Per subs 220; Other — Photographs 246,000

HISTORICAL SOCIETY OF DELAWARE
M **Old Town Hall Museum,*** Sixth & Market Sts, 19801. Tel 302-655-7161. *Exec Dir* Charles T Lyle; *Museum Cur* John H Braunlein; *Museum Asst* Ruth Anne Clarke
Open Tues - Fri Noon - 4 PM, Sat 10 AM - 4 PM. No admis fee
Collections: Children's toys; costumes; decorative arts; Delaware silver; local history
Exhibitions: Thomas Mendenhall, His Last Time: The Legacy of a Wilmington Qualeer Merchant

M **George Read II House,** 42 The Strand, 19720. Tel 302-322-8411. *Museum Cur* Rebecca J Hammell; *Site Adminr* Karin E Peterson
Open Tues - Sat 10 AM - 4 PM, Sun Noon - 4 PM, cl New Year's, Thanksgiving and Christmas. Admis adults $2, children $1. Estab 1864 to record and preserve Delaware History. Average Annual Attendance: 10,000. Mem: 1000; dues $10 and up
Collections: Costumes; †Delaware pictures; †furniture; manuscripts; †silver; Federal Period decorative arts
Activities: Lectures open to the public, 3 vis lectr per yr; concerts; walking tours; sales shop sells books & crafts

L **Library,** 505 Market St, 19801. Tel 302-655-7161. *Dir Libr* Dr Barbara E Benson
Open Mon 1 - 9 PM, Tues - Fri 9 AM - 5 PM
Library Holdings: Vols 75,000; Per subs 73; Micro — Fiche, reels; AV — Cassettes, fs, Kodachromes, lantern slides, motion pictures, rec, slides; Other — Clipping files, exhibition catalogs, manuscripts, memorabilia, pamphlets, photographs, prints
Special Subjects: American and Delaware history

C **WILMINGTON TRUST COMPANY,*** 100 W Tenth St, 19899. Tel 302-651-1649. *VPres* C R McPherson
Open to public by appointment only. No admis fee. Estab 1942 to support Delaware artists in watercolors. Collection displayed statewide in branch offices
Collections: Primarily Delaware scenes by Delaware artists

WINTERTHUR

M **WINTERTHUR MUSEUM AND GARDENS,** Route 52, 19735. Tel 302-656-8591 (offices), 654-1548 (reservations). *Pres Trustees* John A Herdeg; *Dir* James Morton Smith; *Deputy Dir Collections* Charles F Hummel; *Deputy Dir Interpretation* Scott T Swank; *Deputy Dir Finance & Administration* Wesley A Adams; *Head of Gardens* Walter O Petroll; *Advanced Studies Chmn* Kenneth L Ames; *Cur* Nancy E Richards; *Registrar* Nancy Goyne Evans; *Editor Publications Office* Ian M G Quimby; *Head Public Relations* Catherine Wheeler; *Deput Dir Public Affairs* Robert W Safrin
Main museum tours by reservation only, Jan - Apr & June - Nov museum hours Tues - Sat 10 AM - 4 PM, Sun & holiday Mondays Noon - 4 PM, cl New Years, Thanksgiving, Dec 24 & 25, all non-holiday Mondays. Admis varies with season, under 12 not admitted on reserved tours. Corporation estab in 1930, museum opened in 1951. Two hundred rooms and display areas featuring decorative arts made or used in America between 1640 and 1840; sixty acres of horticultural displays in the Gardens. Average Annual Attendance: 300,000. Mem: 11,535; dues $25 - $35
Income: Financed by endowment, membership, grants for special projects
Collections: Pennsylvania German Folk Art; ceramics, furniture, glassware, interior architecture, metals, needlework, paintings, prints and textiles
Publications: Publications and articles by staff, including Winterthur Portfolio, quarterly; Annual Report
Activities: Docent training; Winterthur Program in Early American Culture, a graduate program sponsored with the University of Delaware; Winterthur Program in the Conservation of Artistic and Historic Objects, a graduate program co-sponsored by the University of Delaware; lect open to the public and to members only; yuletide tours; individual paintings and original objects of art lent to museums and historical societies; museum shop sells books, gifts, postcards, plants and slides; Winterthur reproduction gallery sells over 200 reproductions of museum objects

L **Library,** Route 52, Winterthur, 19735. *Head, Library Div* Dr Frank H Sommer III; *Slides* Kathryn McKenney; *Manuscripts & Microfilm* Mrs James Taylor; *Archivist* Paul B Hensley; *Decorative Arts Photographic Coll* Bert Denker
Open Mon - Fri 8:30 AM - 4:30 PM. Estab for research in American Decorative Arts and their European antecedents through World War I. For reference only
Library Holdings: Vols 60,000; Per subs 300; Manuscripts, Slides & Photographs 200,000; Auction Catalogs; Architectural Drawings; Micro — Fiche, reels; AV — Motion pictures, rec, slides; Other — Exhibition catalogs, manuscripts, memorabilia, original art works, pamphlets, photographs, prints, reproductions
Special Subjects: Museology
Collections: Belknap Library; Edward Deming Andrews Memorial Shaker Collection; Decorative Arts Photographic Collection; Henry A duPont and Henry F duPont Papers; Thelma S Mendsen Card Collection; Maxine Waldron Collection of Children's Books and Paper Toys

M **Winterthur in Odessa,** Route 299 at Route 13 (Mailing add: Route 52, Winterthur, 19735). Tel 302-378-4069. *Cur* Horace L Hotchkiss Jr
Open Tues - Sat 10 AM - 4:30 PM, Sun 1 - 4:30 PM, cl Mon & holidays. Winterthur in Odessa is a cluster of 18th & 19th century domestic structures composing a historic village within the community of Odessa
Collections: Corbit-Sharp House containing Chippendale & Queen Anne furniture; Wilson-Warner House; 19th century Brick Hotel Gallery

DISTRICT OF COLUMBIA

WASHINGTON

AMERICAN ASSOCIATION OF MUSEUMS
For further information, see National and Regional Organizations

AMERICAN ASSOCIATION OF UNIVERSITY WOMEN
For further information, see National and Regional Organizations

AMERICAN INSTITUTE FOR CONSERVATION OF HISTORIC AND ARTISTIC WORKS (AIC)
For further information, see National and Regional Organizations

AMERICAN INSTITUTE OF ARCHITECTS
For further information, see National and Regional Organizations

M **AMERICAN INSTITUTE OF ARCHITECTS FOUNDATION,** The Octagon, 1799 New York Ave NW, 20006. Tel 202-638-3105. *Dir* Susan R Stein
Open Tues - Fri 10 AM - 4 PM; Sat & Sun 1 - 4 PM. Admis by donation; groups over 10 charges $1 per person except student and senior citizens groups $.50 per person. Opened as house museum in 1970; formerly a federal townhouse built by Col John Tayloe III to serve as a winter home; used by President & Mrs Madison as temporary White House during war of 1812. Furnished with late 18th and early 19th century decorative arts; changing exhibition program in second floor galleries. Average Annual Attendance: 18,000
Collections: Permanent collection of furniture, paintings, ceramics, kitchen utensils
Exhibitions: (1983-84) Honor & Intimacy: Architectural Drawings by AIA Gold Medalists, 1907-1983; Great Drawings from the Collection of the Royal Institute of British Architects; Chicago/New York Architects
Publications: Competition 1792-Designing a Nation's Capitol, book; Dolley and the Great Little Madison, book; exhibition catalogs; Octagon Being an Account of a Famous Washington Residence: Its Great Years, Decline and Restoration, book; Selections from the AIA Architectural Archives, book; William Thornton: A Renaissance Man in the Federal City, book
Activities: Educ dept; docent training; tours; lectr for members only, 2-3 vis lectr per yr; sales shop selling books, prints and slides
L **Library,** The Octagon, 1799 New York Ave, NW, 20006. *Librn* Joanna H Wos
Open to the public for reference but primarily used by staff
Library Holdings: Vols 200; Per subs 10
Special Subjects: Architecture, Decorative Arts, History of the Octagon and the Tayloe Family

M **AMERICAN UNIVERSITY,** Watkins Art Gallery, 4400 Massachusetts Ave NW, 20016. Tel 202-686-2114. *Chmn* Robert D'Arista
Open Mon - Fri 10 AM - Noon & 1 - 4 PM. No admis fee. Estab 1943 to exhibit art of interest to public and university art community; schedule includes occasional education or theme shows and student exhibits. Maintains large room with moveable panels and one small exhibit room with attendant's desk. Average Annual Attendance: 2000 plus art students
Collections: Watkins Collection of 19th and 20th century American and European paintings
Exhibitions: Jack Boul; Leonard Maurer; Selections from the Watkins Collection; Faculty Exhibition
Activities: Educ dept; docent training; lect open to the public, 3-5 vis lectr per yr; individual paintings and original objects of art lent to museums and university galleries; traveling exhibitions organized and circulated on occasion

M **ANACOSTIA NEIGHBORHOOD MUSEUM,*** 2405 Martin Luther King, Jr Ave SE, 20020. Tel 202-287-3369. *Dir* John R Kinard; *Exhib Program Dir* Victor M Govier; *Historian* Louise D Hutchinson; *Education Program Dir* Zora Martin-Felton
Open Mon - Fri 10 AM - 6 PM, Sat, Sun and holidays 1 - 6 PM, cl Christmas. No admis fee. Estab 1967, as a non-profit federally chartered corporation to record and research African, Black American and Anacostia history and urban problems
Income: Federally funded bureau of Smithsonian Institute
Collections: Afro-American and African art; Afro-American history
Publications: Educational booklets; exhibit programs; museum brochures accompany each major exhibit
Activities: Programs for children and adults; lect; tours; gallery talks; art festivals; competitions; extension department serves groups unable to visit the museum; traveling exhibitions organized and circulated; sales shop
L **Library,*** 2405 Martin Luther King, Jr Ave SE, 20020. Tel 202-357-1300
Open to the public for research on the premises
Library Holdings: Vols 1000

ARTISTS EQUITY ASSOCIATION, INC
For further information, see National and Regional Organizations

O **ART PAC,** 210 7th St SE Suite A18, 20003. Tel 202-547-5146. *Treas* Robert J Bedard
Estab 1981 to lobby for art's legislation & assist federal candidates supporting the arts. Mem: Dues $40
Income: Financed by membership
Publications: Newsletter/ART PAC News, quarterly
Activities: Legislator of Year Award

M **ARTS CLUB OF WASHINGTON,** James Monroe House,* 2017 Eye St NW, 20006. Tel 202-331-7282. *Pres* Dudley Brown; *Mgr* Edward Duea
Open Tues - Sun 10 AM - 4 PM. No admis fee. Founded 1916. The James Monroe House (1803-1805) was built by Timothy Caldwell of Philadelphia. It is registered with the National Register of Historic Places, the Historical Survey 1937 and 1968, and the National Trust for Historic Preservation. James Monroe, fifth President of the United States, resided in the house while he was Secretary of War and State. During the first six months of his Presidency (1817-1825) the house served as the Executive Mansion, since the White House had been burned in the War of 1812 and had not yet been restored. Mem: 250; annual meeting April
Activities: Monthly lect; exhibitions; scholarships

ASSOCIATION OF ARCHITECTURAL LIBRARIANS
For further information, see National and Regional Organizations

ASSOCIATION OF COLLEGIATE SCHOOLS OF ARCHITECTURE
For further information, see National and Regional Organizations

M **B'NAI B'RITH KLUTZNICK MUSEUM,*** 1640 Rhode Island Ave, Northwest, 20036. Tel 202-857-6583. *Dir* Anna R Cohn; *Assoc Dir* Linda Altshuler
Open Sun - Fri 10 AM - 5 PM, cl Sat and Jewish holidays. No admis fee. Estab 1957 for exhibits by Jewish artists. Five galleries
Income: Financed by B'nai B'rith International
Collections: Permanent collection of pre-twentieth century Jewish ceremonial and folk art; ancient coins; archives of B'nai B'rith
Exhibitions: Two to four changing exhibitions annually
Publications: Exhibitions brochures
Activities: Holiday family education program; children's program; lect; films
L **Library,*** 20036. Tel 202-857-6600
Estab 1957; staff use only
Library Holdings: Vols 12,000; Other — Manuscripts, photographs

L **CATHOLIC UNIVERSITY OF AMERICA,** Humanities Division, Mullen Library, 620 Michigan Ave NE, 20064. Tel 202-635-5075. *Head Humanities Division* B Gutekunst
Open fall & spring terms Mon - Thurs 9 AM - 10 PM, Fri & Sat 9 AM - 5 PM, Sun 1 - 10 PM. Estab 1958 to offer academic resources and services that are integral to the work of the institution
Library Holdings: Vols 6700; Other — Prints
Special Subjects: Religious Art

CONGRESSIONAL ARTS CAUCUS
For further information, see National and Regional Organizations

M **CORCORAN MUSEUM,** 17th St and New York Ave NW, 20006. Tel 202-638-3211. *Pres* David Lloyd Kreeger; *Dir* Michael Botwinick; *Assoc Dir* Jane Livingston; *Cur* Edward J Nygren; *Registrar* Judith Riley; *Archivist* Katherine M Kovacs
Open Tues - Sun 10 AM - 4:30 PM, Thurs 10 AM - 9 PM, cl Mon and holidays. No admis fee. Founded 1869 primarily for the encouragement of American art. The nucleus of the collection of American Paintings was formed by its founder, William Wilson Corcoran, early in the second half of the 19th century. In 1925 a large wing designed by Charles A Platt was added to house the European collection bequested by Senator William Andrews Clark of Montana. The Walker Collection, formed by Edward C and Mary Walker, added important French Impressionists to the collection upon its donation in 1937. Average Annual Attendance: 500,000. Mem: 3000; dues contributing $500 and up, sponsor $250, Friends of the Corcoran $125, family $50, single $35, student and senior citizen $15
Collections: The American collection of paintings, watercolors, drawings, sculpture and photgraphy from the 18th through 20th centuries; The European Collection includes paintings and drawings by Dutch, Flemish, English and French artists; 18th century French salon, furniture, laces, rugs, majolica; Gothic and Beauvais tapestries; Greek antiquities; 13th century stained glass window and bronzes by Antoine Louise Barye; tryptich by Andrea Vanni; Walker Collection of French Impressionists
Exhibitions: Changing exhibitions of Contemporary Art; Fine Art Photography; Works by regional artists; works drawn from the permanent collection
Publications: Calendar of Events (for members); Corcoran Shop Catalogue
Activities: Classes for adults and children; docent training; lectures open to public; concerts; gallery talks; tours; originates traveling exhibitions; shop sells books, magazines, reproductions, prints & slides
L **Library,** 17th St and New York Ave NW, 20006. Tel 202-628-9484, Ext 75. *Librn* Ann Maginnis
Available for inter-library loan and for public use by appointment only
Library Holdings: Vols 7000; Per subs 125; Micro — Fiche; AV — Slides; Other — Exhibition catalogs
Special Subjects: Art History

M **DAR MUSEUM,** National Society Daughters of the American Revolution, 1776 D St NW, 20006. Tel 202-628-1774. *Dir* Christine Minter-Dowd
Open Mon - Fri 9 AM - 4 PM, Sun 1 - 5 PM. No admis fee. Estab 1890 for collection & exhibition of decorative arts used in America from 1700 - 1840; for the study of objects, & the preservation of Revolutionary artifacts & documentation of American life. There are 29 period rooms which reflect the decorative arts of particular states, also a museum which houses large collections grouped by ceramics, textiles, silver, glass, furniture & paintings. Average Annual Attendance: 12,000. Mem: 205,000; dues $15 - $17; annual meeting in April
Income: Under $200,000 (financed by membership)
Purchases: Under $20,000
Collections: †Ceramics, †furniture, †glass, †paintings, †prints, †silver, textiles
Exhibitions: Special exhibitions arranged and changed periodically, usually every 2 - 3 months
Activities: Classes for children; docent training; lectures; gallery talks; tours; exten dept serves third to sixth grades; paintings and original art works lent to museums; sales shop sells books, slides, stationery, dolls and handcrafted gift items
L **Library,** 1776 D St NW, 20006
Open to public by advance notice; for reference only
Purchases: $1000
Library Holdings: Vols 2500; Per subs 4
Special Subjects: American Decorative Arts

M DECATUR HOUSE, 748 Jackson Pl NW, 20006. Tel 202-673-4210. *Dir* Earl James; *Asst Dir* Vicki Sopher; *Admin Asst* Barbara Ballantine
Open Tues - Fri 10 AM - 2 PM, Sat & Sun Noon - 4 PM, cl Mon. Admis adults $2, students & senior citizens $1, National Trust Members free. Estab 1958, bequeathed to National Trust for Historic Preservation by Mrs Truxton Beale to foster appreciation and interest in the history and culture of the city of Washington, DC. The House is a Federal period townhouse designed by Benjamin Henry Latrobe and completed in 1819. Average Annual Attendance: 11,000. Mem: National Trust members
Income: Financed by endowment and membership
Collections: Furniture and memorabilia of the Federal period; Victorian house furnishings
Exhibitions: Special exhibits
Activities: Lectures open to public, 2-3 vis lectr per yr; concerts; individual paintings & original objects of art lent; sales shop sells books, magazines, reproductions, prints & Christmas decorations

M DEPARTMENT OF STATE, Diplomatic Reception Rooms, 2201 C St NW, 20520. Tel 202-632-0298. *Cur* Clement E Conger; *Asst Cur* Gail F Serfaty; *Staff Asst* Patricia Heflin; *Cur Asst* Kathryn McCutchen
Open for 3 public tours by reservation only Mon - Fri. No admis fee. Estab unofficially 1961, officially 1971 to entertain foreign dignitaries. These rooms allow foreign visitors to view furniture of the American Colonial and Federal periods. Nine rooms are furnished in 18th and early 19th Century American furniture and silver, Chinese export porcelain and antique Oriental rugs, and American portraits and paintings. Average Annual Attendance: 70,000
Income: Financed by private donations, foundation and corporate grants and loans of furnishings and paintings
Collections: †American furniture (1740-1825); †American portraits and paintings; †Chinese export porcelain; †American silver
Publications: Guidebook; Reprints of articles on the Diplomatic Reception Rooms
Activities: Tours given Mon through Fri; decorative art objects lent to special museum exhibitions

L FOLGER SHAKESPEARE LIBRARY, 201 E Capitol St SE, 20003. Tel 202-544-4600. *Acting Dir* Philip A Knachel; *Dir Research Activities* John F Andrews
Open (exhibition gallery) Mon - Sat 10 AM - 4 PM, Sun also from April 15 - Labor Day. Estab 1932 as an international center for the study of all aspects of the European Renaissance and civilization in the 16th and 17th centuries. Maintains an art gallery and a permanent display of Shakespearean items and changing topical exhibits of books, manuscripts, paintings and sculpture. Contemporary art is exhibited in the lower gallery
Income: Financed by endowment
Library Holdings: Vols 220,000; Per subs 180; Original documents; Micro — Reels; AV — A-tapes, fs, motion pictures, rec, slides; Other — Exhibition catalogs, manuscripts, memorabilia, original art works, pamphlets, photographs, prints, reproductions, sculpture
Collections: Shakespeare, playbills and promptbooks; Continental and English Renaissance, 1450-1700
Exhibitions: Decade of Folger Acquisitions; Medicine and Health in the Renaissance; Renaissance Art of War; Shakespeare in American; Sir Thomas More, the Man and His Age; Books and Libraries of the Renaissance
Publications: Newsletter, five times yearly; Shakespeare Quarterly
Activities: Seminars for advanced graduate students; lect open to public; concerts; gallery talks; scholarships offered; originate traveling exhibitions

M FREER GALLERY OF ART, Jefferson Dr at 12th St SW, 20560. Tel 202-357-2104. *Dir* Thomas Lawton; *Asst Dir* Richard Louie; *Cur Chinese Art* Shen Fu; *Cur Japanese Art* Yoshiake Shimizu; *Asst Cur Japanese Art* Ann Yonemura; *Head Conservator & Technical Laboratory* W T Chase; *Conservation Scientist* John Winter; *Admin Officer* Sarah Newmeyer-Hill
Open daily 10 AM - 5:30 PM, cl Christmas. No admis fee. Estab 1906 under Smithsonian Institution to exhibit its outstanding masterpieces of American and Oriental art; to carry out research and publication in the history of civilizations represented by objects in the collections. Average Annual Attendance: 310,000
Income: Financed by endowment and Federal appropriation
Purchases: Oriental art
Collections: †Art of the Near and Far East: paintings, sculpture, objects in stone, wood, jade, glass, porcelain, bronze, gold, silver, lacquer, metalwork; manuscripts (early Christian); Collection of works by James McNeill Whistler and some of his contemporaries
Exhibitions: Asian art; Whistler paintings
Activities: Lectures, six vis lectr per year; tours; museum shop sells books, reproductions, slides, needlepoint, desk accessories, postcards, greeting cards and note cards
L Library, Twelfth and Jefferson Dr, Southwest, 20560. Tel 202-357-2091. *Librn* Ellen A Nollman; *Asst Librn* Ming Lung
Open to the public for reference
Library Holdings: Vols 30,000; Per subs 100
Special Subjects: Volumes related to cultural and historical background of the collection

GENERAL SERVICES ADMINISTRATION
For further information, see National and Regional Organizations

M GEORGETOWN UNIVERSITY, Art and History Museum,* Box 1595, Hoya Station, 20007. Tel 202-625-4085. *Cur* Clifford T Chieffo; *Assoc Cur* Patricia H Chieffo
Open during University hours according to yearly schedule, cl holidays. No admis fee. University estab 1789. The museum is on the Georgetown University campus in Healy Hall (1879)
Collections: American portraits; Works by Van Dycke and Gilbert Stuart; graphics, historical objects, paintings, religious art, paintings
Publications: Collection catalog, exhibit catalogs
Activities: Educational programs for undergraduate students; gallery talks, guided tours; art festivals, temporary exhibitions

M GEORGE WASHINGTON UNIVERSITY, The Dimock Gallery, Lower Lisner Auditorium, 730 21st St NW, 20052. Tel 202-676-7091. *Cur* Lenore D Miller; *Asst Cur* Gail M Mishkin
Open Mon - Fri 10 AM - 5 PM, cl Sat, Sun & national holidays. No admis fee. Estab 1964 to enhance graduate and undergraduate programs in fine art and research in art history; documentation of permanent collections, feature historical and contemporary exhibitions related to university art dept programs. Average Annual Attendance: 10,000
Collections: U S Grant Collection of Photographs; W Lloyd Wright Collection of Washingtoniana; Joseph Pennell Collection of Prints; graphic arts from the 18th, 19th and 20th centuries, with special emphasis on American art; historical material; paintings; prints; sculpture; works pertaining to George Washington
Exhibitions: 8 - 10 temporary exhibitions staged per year The Fine Art of Private Commissions; faculty, student, MFA thesis shows; Jerry Lake: Photographs; Frank Wright: Paintings and Prints; Marc Chagall Graphics
Publications: Exhibition catalogs
Activities: Lectures open to public, concerts and gallery talks; individual paintings and orginal objects of art lent; book traveling exhibitions

M HARVARD UNIVERSITY, Dumbarton Oaks Research Library and Collections, 1703 32nd St NW, 20007. Tel 202-342-3200; Cable: HARDOAKS. *Dir* Giles Constable; *Asst Dir* Judy Siggins
Open daily (Gardens) 2 - 6 PM, (Collections) Tues - Sun 2 - 5 PM, cl holidays. Conveyed in 1940 to Harvard University by Mr and Mrs Robert Woods Bliss as a research center in the Byzantine and Medieval humanities and subsequently enlarged. Average Annual Attendance: 100,000
Collections: †Byzantine devoted to Early Christian & Byzantine mosaics, textiles, bronzes, sculpture, ivories, metalwork, jewelry, glyptics & other decorative arts of the period; Pre-Columbian devoted to sculpture, textiles, pottery, gold ornaments & other objects from Mexico, Central & South America, dating from 800 BC to early 16th century; European & American paintings, sculpture & decorative arts
Publications: Handbooks and catalogs of the Byzantine and Pre-Columbian collection; scholarly publications in Byzantine, Pre-Columbian and landscape architecture studies
Activities: Lect; conferences
L Library, 1703 32nd St NW, 20007. *Librn* Irene Vaslef; *Serials Librn* Dina Giambi
Important resources for Byzantine research
Library Holdings: Vols 90,000; Per subs 818; Micro — Fiche, reels; Other — Exhibition catalogs
Collections: Dumbarton Oaks Census of Early Christian and Byzantine Objects in American Collection; Photographic copy of the Princeton Index of Christian Art; collection of photographs
L Pre-Columbian Library, 1703 32nd St NW, 20007. Tel 202-342-3265. *Assoc Cur* Elizabeth H Boone
Library Holdings: Vols 10,000
Publications: Handbooks of collections
L Garden Library, 1703 32nd St NW, 20007. *Librn* Laura Byers; *Dir Studies* Elisabeth B MacDougall
Library Holdings: Vols 10,000; Drawings; Micro — Prints
Special Subjects: History of Landscape Architecture, History of Horticulture, History of Botanical Illustration
Collections: †Rare books (2400)

M HIRSHHORN MUSEUM AND SCULPTURE GARDEN, Eighth & Independence Aves SW, 20560. Tel 202-357-3091. *Dir* Abram Lerner; *Deputy Dir* Stephen Weil; *Adminr* Nancy Kirkpatrick; *Chief Cur* Charles Millard; *Chief Education Dept* Edward P Lawson; *Registrar* Douglas Robinson; *Chief Exhib* Joseph Shannon; *Chief Conservator* Felrath Hines; *Chief Photography* Lee Stalsworth
Open Mon - Sun 10 AM - 5:30 PM. Estab 1966 under the aegis of the Smithsonian Institution; building designed by Gordon Bunshaft of the architectural firm of Skidmore, Owings & Merrill. Opened in 1974
Income: Financed by federal funds
Collections: Approx †7400 paintings and sculptures, the majority donated to the nation by Joseph H Hirshhorn, emphasizing the development of modern art from the latter half of the 19th century to the present; †American art beginning with a strong group of Thomas Eakins' and going on to Sargent, Chase, Hartley, Gorky, De Kooning, Rothko, Noland, Rivers and Frank Stella; †European paintings of the last 3 decades represented by Agam, Bacon, Balthus, Leger, Miro and Vasarely; †extensive sculpture collection includes works by Arp, Caro, Daumier, Brancusi, Degas, Giacometti, Manzu, Moore, Nadelman, Rodin and David Smith
Exhibitions: Permanent collection and special loan exhibitions
Publications: Exhibition catalogs, collection catalogs
Activities: Docent training; lectures open to public; concerts; gallery talks; tours; films; internships; education outreach; individual and original objects of art lent to museums; originate traveling exhibitions; sales shop sells books, magazines, reproductions, slides, jewelry and various gift items
L Library, Eighth & Independence Ave SW, 20560. Tel 202-357-3222. *Librn* Anna Brooke
Estab 1974. For reference only by appointment
Income: Financed by federal funds
Library Holdings: Vols 11,000; Per subs 45; Auction Cats; Micro — Fiche, reels; AV — A-tapes, cassettes, slides, v-tapes; Other — Clipping files, exhibition catalogs, memorabilia, photographs
Special Subjects: American painting 1850 to the present, international modern sculpture
Collections: Armory Show Memorabilia; Eakins Memorabilia; 5 Samuel Murray Scrapbooks

M HOWARD UNIVERSITY, Gallery of Art,* College of Fine Arts, 2455 Sixth St NW, 20001. Tel 202-636-7047. *Dir* Starmanda Bullock
Open Mon - Fri 9 AM - 5 PM, cl Sat & Sun. No admis fee. Estab 1928 to stimulate the study and appreciation of the fine arts in the University and community. Three air-conditioned art galleries are in Childers Hall, James V Herring Heritage Gallery, James A Porter Gallery, and the Student Gallery along with Gumbel Print Room. Average Annual Attendance: 24,000

Collections: †Agnes Delano Collection of contemporary American watercolors and prints; Irving R Gumbel Collection of prints; Kress Study Collection of Renaissance paintings and sculpture; Alain Locke Collection of African art; †University collection of painting, sculpture and graphic arts by Afro-Americans
Exhibitions: Changing monthly exhibits
Publications: Catalogue of the African and Afro-American collections; exhibition catalogues; informational brochures; Native American Arts (serial)
Activities: Bimonthly gallery lect and community programs

L **Architecture & Planning Library,*** Sixth St & Howard Pl NW, 20059. Tel 202-636-7773. *Librn* Mod Mekkawi
Library Holdings: Vols 18,755; Per subs 360; Doc 600; Micro — Reels 850; AV — Fs, lantern slides, slides 29,000; Other — Photographs
Special Subjects: Architectural History, Construction & Design, City Planning, Environmental Design
Collections: Dominick Collection of pre-1900 books & periodicals on architecture; K Keith Collection of books & photographs on indigenous African architecture

INTERNATIONAL COUNCIL OF MUSEUMS COMMITTEE OF THE AMERICAN ASSOCIATION OF MUSEUMS
For further information, see National and Regional Organizations

O **JOHN F KENNEDY CENTER FOR THE PERFORMING ARTS,** 20566. Tel 202-872-0466. *Chmn of the Board of Trustees* Roger L Stevens
Open Mon - Sun 10 AM - 12 Midnight. No admis to building, ticket prices vary. The Center opened in Sept 1971. Facilities include the 2200-seat Opera House, 2750-seat Concert Hall, 1130-seat Eisenhower Theater, 500-seat Terrace Theater and 224-seat film theater operated by the American Film Institute. Estab in 1958 by Act of Congress as the National Cultural Center. A bureau of the Smithsonian Institution, but administered by a separate independent Board of Trustees; the Center is the sole official memorial in Washington to President Kennedy. Although the Center does not have an official collection, gifts in the form of art objects from foreign countries are on display throughout the Center. Average Annual Attendance: 1,500,000 ticketed, 2,500,000-3,000,000 visitors. Mem: 16,000; dues from $25-$500; annual meetings in Jan
Income: $27,000,000 (financed by ticket revenue and private contributions)
Exhibitions: Changing exhibits on the performing arts are displayed in the Center's Performing Arts Library, a cooperative effort between Kennedy Center and the Library of Congress. Exhibits frequently include portraits, prints, engravings, sketches, etc, of relevance to the performing arts
Publications: John F Kennedy Center for the Performing Arts; Kennedy Center News, bi-monthly; Two on the Aisle, bi-monthly
Activities: Classes for adults and children; dramatic programs; performing arts series for young audiences; lectures open to public, 50 vis lectr per yr; concerts; tours; originate traveling exhibitions to Library of Congress; sales shop sells books, original art, reproductions, slides, souvenirs, needle point and posters

L **Performing Arts Library,** John F Kennedy Ctr for the Performing Arts, Roof Terrace Level, 20566. Tel 202-254-9803. *Deputy Dir of Operations & Center Liaison with the Library of Congress* Dr Geraldine M Otremba; *Head Librn* Peter Fay
Open Tues - Fri 11 AM - 8:30 PM, Sat 10 AM - 6 PM, cl Mon & Sun. Estab 1979 to provide a national information and reference facility for all areas of the performing arts, including film and broadcasting. For reference only. Access to all Library of Congress collections
Library Holdings: Vols 7000; Per subs 400; Micro — Fiche, reels; AV — A-tapes, cassettes, rec, slides, v-tapes; Other — Clipping files, exhibition catalogs, framed reproductions, manuscripts, memorabilia, pamphlets, reproductions
Special Subjects: Kennedy Center History, performing arts information
Exhibitions: (1982) Focus on the Performing Arts: The Portrait Photography of Bern Schwartz; (1983) The Kiralby Brothers Present

L **LIBRARY OF CONGRESS,** Prints and Photographs Division, First St Between E Capitol St & Independence Ave SE, 20540. Tel 202-287-6394 (reference), 287-5836 (offices). *Librn of Congress* Daniel J Boorstin; *Actg Chief* Renata Shaw; *Head Reference Section* Jerry L Kearns
Exhib Halls Open 8:30 AM - 9:30 PM; Sat & Sun 8:30 AM - 6 PM; Reading Room of the Division open Mon - Fri 8:30 - 5 PM; cl legal holidays. Estab 1897. For reference only
Income: Financed by congressional appropriation, gifts and endowments
Library Holdings: Architectural Items 100,000; Posters 70,000; Popular and Applied Graphic Art Items 40,000; Master Photographs 3500; Fine Prints 110, 000; Other — Photographs 9,000,000
Collections: Archive of Hispanic Culture; Japanese Prints; †Pennell Collection of Whistleriana; †Civil War drawings, prints, photographs and negatives; †early American lithographs; †pictorial archives of early American architecture including the Historic American Buildings Survey; †original drawings by American illustrators; original prints of all schools and periods, increased annually by the Gardiner Greene Hubbard and J & E R Pennell Endowments; Seagram County Court House Collection; Swann Collection of Cartoons and Caricatures; American Political Cartoons; †outstanding among the collection of photographs and photographic negatives are the Brady-Handy Collection, Farm Security Administration Collection, Alexander Graham Bell Collection, Red Cross Collection, Arnold Genthe, J C H Grabill, F B Johnston, Toni Frissell, Detroit Photographic Co W H Jackson Collection, George Grantham Bain Collection, H E French Washington Photographs, Matson Near Eastern Collection; †Presidential, †geographical, †biographical and †master photograph groupings and captured German photographs of the WW II period
Exhibitions: Permanent collection
Publications: A Century of Photographs, 1846-1946; America 1935-1945; American Prints in the Library of Congress; American Revolution in Drawings and Prints; Graphic Sampler; Historic American Buildings Survey; Middle East in Pictures; Viewpoints; Special Collections in the Library of Congress; The Prints and Photographs Division in the Library of Congress; Fine Prints in the Library of Congress; The Poster Collection in the Library of Congress; Popular and Applied Graphic Art in the Library of Congress
Activities: Internship program for advanced undergraduate and graduates who wish to work with and study the collections of the division

M **MARINE CORPS MUSEUM,** Art Unit,* Marine Corps Historical Center, Bldg 58 Washington Navy Yard, 20374. Tel 202-433-2820. *Dir* E H Simmons; *Deputy Dir* F B Nihart
Open Mon - Sat 10 AM - 4 PM, Sun Noon - 5 PM, summers Mon - Thurs & Sat 10 AM - 4 PM, Fri 10 AM - 4 PM & 6 - 11 PM, Sun Noon - 5 PM, cl Christmas & New Years. No admis fee. Large 20 ft x 100 ft gallery available for temporary exhibits; maintains 22,000 volume library directly relating to military and Naval history
Collections: Marine Corps art (original art work by, of and about Marines with the major emphasis of the collection on the Vietnam War); military music; personal papers
Activities: Tours; museum shop sells prints, books, models, miniatures and jewelry

M **MUSEUM OF MODERN ART OF LATIN AMERICA,*** 201 18th St, NW (Mailing add: 1889 F St, Washington, DC 20006). Tel 202-789-6016. *Dir* Jose Gomez-Sicre
Open Tues - Sat 10 AM - 5 PM, cl holidays. No admis fee. Estab 1976 by organization of American States to bring about an awareness and appreciation of contemporary Latin American art. The museum maintains an art gallery with the focus on contemporary Latin American art. Average Annual Attendance: 100, 000
Collections: Contemporary Latin American art
Activities: Lect open to public, 4 visiting lectr per year; gallery talks; tours; paintings and original art objects lent to museums; originate traveling exhibitions; museum shop sells films on Latin American art and artists

L **Archive of Contemporary Latin American Art,*** 201 18th St NW, 20006. Tel 702-789-3000
Open to scholars for research only
Special Subjects: Latin American Art

M **MUSEUM OF THE UNITED STATES,** C St between 18th & 19th Sts NW, Dept of the Interior, 20240. Tel 202-343-5016. *Dir* Stanley W Olsen; *Exhib Specialist* Open
Open Mon - Fri 8 AM - 4 PM. No admis fee. Estab 1938 to visualize and explain to the public through works of art and other media the history, aims and activities of the Department. Museum occupies one wing on the first floor of the Interior Department Building. Average Annual Attendance: 100,000
Collections: Antarctic Painting by Leland Curtis; Colburn Collection of Indian basketry; †general collection of Indian, Eskimo, South Sea Islands and Virgin Islands arts and crafts, documents, maps, charts, etc.; Gibson Collection of Indian materials; Indian arts and crafts; murals; miniature dioramas; oil paintings of early American Explorers by William Henry Jackson; oil paintings of Western Conservation Scenes by Wilfrid Swancourt Bronson; sculpture groups; watercolor and black and white illustrations; Wildlife Paintings by Walter Weber
Publications: Illustrated museum brochure

M **NATIONAL AIR AND SPACE MUSEUM,** 7th & Independence Ave SW, 20560. Tel 202-357-2700, 357-1745. *Dir* Walter J Boyne; *Deputy Dir* Donald Lopez
Open daily 10 AM - 5:30 PM, cl Christmas. No admis fee. Estab 1946 to memorialize the national development of aviation and space flight. One gallery comprised of 5000 sq ft devoted to the theme, Flight and the Arts. Average Annual Attendance: 10,000,000
Income: Financed through the Smithsonian Institution
Collections: Paintings, prints and drawings include: Alexander Calder, Lamar Dodd, Richard Estes, Audrey Flack, Francisco Goya, Lowell Nesbitt, Robert Rauschenberg, James Wyeth; major sculptures by Richard Lippold, Alejandro Otero, Charles Perry; Stuart Speiser Collection of Photo Realist Art
Exhibitions: Assignment: Aviation, Stuart M Speiser Collection (photo-realism space shuttle art); permanent, temporary and traveling exhibitions
Publications: Various publications relating to aviation and space science
Activities: Education dept; handicapped services; regional resource program; lectures open to public, 15 - 20 vis lectr per year; concerts; gallery talks; tours scholarships; individual paintings and original objects of art lent to non-profit educational institutions; book traveling exhibitions; originate traveling exhibitions; museum shop selling books, magazines, reproductions, prints, slides, posters, stamp covers, kites, models and jewelry

L **Library,** Smithsonian Institution, 7th & Independence Ave SW, 20560. Tel 202-357-3133
Open 10 AM - 5:15 PM. Estab 1972 to support research in aerospace field; Library is part of the Smithsonian Institution Libraries system. For reference. Average Annual Attendance: 4000
Income: Financed by federal funds
Library Holdings: Vols 30,000; Per subs 450; Micro — Fiche 200,000, reels 2000; AV — A-tapes 1400, motion pictures 2000, slides 1000; Other — Clipping files, manuscripts, pamphlets, photographs 900,000
Special Subjects: Ballooning (prints), Earth & Aerospace, Astronomy and Planetary Science
Collections: Aerospace Event Files; Aviation and Space Art; Illustrated Sheet Music; Archives of Personalities
Publications: NASM Library Guide; NASM Library Periodical Index
Activities: Educ dept; classes for children; docent training; lectures open to public; tours; awards; scholarships

NATIONAL ARCHITECTURAL ACCREDITING BOARD, INC
For further information, see National and Regional Organizations

NATIONAL ASSEMBLY OF LOCAL ARTS AGENCIES
For further information, see National and Regional Organizations

NATIONAL ASSEMBLY OF STATE ARTS AGENCIES
For further information, see National and Regional Organizations

NATIONAL COUNCIL OF ARCHITECTURAL REGISTRATION BOARDS
For further information, see National and Regional Organizations

NATIONAL ENDOWMENT FOR THE ARTS
For further information, see National and Regional Organizations

M **NATIONAL GALLERY OF ART,** Constitution Ave at Fourth St NW, 20565. Tel 202-737-4215. *Chmn Board of Trustees* Paul Mellon; *Pres* John R Stevenson; *VPres* Carlisle H Humelsine; *Dir* J Carter Brown; *Deputy Dir* John Wilmerdiuf; *Chief Cur* S J Freedberg; *Asst to Dir Music* Richard Bales; *Asst to Dir Public Information* Katherine Warwick; *Asst to Dir Special Events* Genevra Hissinson; *Admin Asst* Angela Lore; *Cur American Art* Nicholas Cikovsky; *Cur Dutch & Flemish Painting* Arthur K Wheelock Jr; *Cur Early Italian Painting* David Alan Brown; *Cur Northern & Later Italian Painting* Sheldon Grossman; *Cur Northern European Painting* John Hand; *Cur Prints & Drawings* Andrew Robison Jr; *Cur Sculpture* Douglas Lewis Jr; *Cur 20th Century Art* E A Carmean Jr; *Chief Design & Installation* Gaillard F Ravenel; *Chief Exhibition Programs* D D Thompson; *Cur Education* Margaret I Bouton; *Head Extension Prog Development* Ruth R Perlin; *Head Art Information Service* Elise V H Ferber; *Editor* Frances Smyth; *Conservator* Ross Merrill; *Registrar* Peter Davidock; *Chief Photographic Laboratory* William J Sumits; *Treas* Robert C Goetz; *Adminr* Joseph G English; *Construction Mgr* Hurley Offenbacher; *Secy & Gen Counsel* Carroll J Cavanagh; *Assoc Secy & Assoc Gen Counsel* Elizabeth A Croog
Open Mon - Sat 10 AM - 5 PM; Sun Noon - 9 PM; (Apr 1 through Labor Day) Mon - Sat 10 AM - 9 PM; Sun Noon - 9 PM; cl Christmas & New Year's Day. No admis fee. Administered by a board of trustees which consists of Chmn Paul Mellon, US Chief Justice, US Secy of State, US Secy of the Treasury, Secretary of the Smithsonian Institution, John R Stevenson, Carlisle H Humelsine, Franklin D Murphy and Ruth Carter Stevenson.
Estab 1937; The West Building opened 1941; East Building opened 1978. West Building was a gift from Andrew W Mellon; the East Building was a gift of Paul Mellon, Alisa Mellon Bruce, and Andrew Mellon Foundation. Average Annual Attendance: 6,500,000
Income: Financed by private endowment and federal appropriation
Collections: The Andrew W Mellon Collection of 126 paintings and 26 pieces of sculpture includes Raphael's Alba Madonna, Niccolini-Cowper's Madonna, and St George and the Dragon; van Eyck Annunciation; Botticelli's Adoration of the Magi; nine Rembrandts. Twenty-one of these paintings came from the Hermitage. Also in the original gift were the Vaughan Portrait of George Washington by Gilbert Stuart and The Washington Family by Edward Savage. The Samuel H Kress Collection, given to the nation over a period of years, includes the great tondo The Adoration of the Magi by Fra Angelico and Fra Filippo Lippi, the Laocoön by El Greco, and fine examples by Giorgione, Titian, Grlnewald, Dürer, Memling, Bosch, Francois Clouet, Poussin, Watteau, Chardin, Boucher, Fragonard, David and Ingres. Also included are a number of masterpieces of Italian and French sculpture. In the Widener Collection are paintings by Rembrandt, van Dyck, and Vermeer, as well as major works of Italian, Spanish, English and French painting and Italian and French sculpture and decorative arts. The Chester Dale Collection includes masterpieces by Braque, Cezanne, Degas, Gauguin, Manet, Matisse, Modigliani, Monet, Picasso, Pissarro, Renoir, Toulouse-Lautrec, van Gogh, and such American painters as George Bellows, Childe Hassam, and Gilbert Stuart. Several major works of art by Cezanne, Gauguin, Picasso and the American painter Walt Kuhn were given to the Gallery in 1972 by the W Averell Harriman Foundation in memory of Marie N Harriman. Paintings to round out the collection have been bought with funds provided by the late Ailsa Mellon Bruce. Most important among them are: portrait of Ginevra de' Benci (the only generally acknowledged painting by Leonardo da Vinci outside Europe), Georges de la Tour's Repentant Magdalen, Picasso's Nude Woman-1910, Rubens' Daniel in the Lions' Den, Claude Lorrain's Judgment of Paris, St George and the Dragon attributed to Rogier van der Weyden, and a number of American paintings, including Thomas Cole's second set of the Voyage of Life. The National Gallery's rapidly expanding graphic arts holdings, in great part given by Lessing J Rosenwald, numbers about 50,000 items and dates from the 12th century to the present. The Index of American Design contains over 17,000 watercolor renderings and 500 photographs of American crafts and folk arts. The National Gallery's Collection continues to be built by private donation, rather than through government funds, which serve solely to operate and maintain the Gallery
Exhibitions: Temporary exhibitions from collections both in the United States and abroad
Publications: A W Mellon Lectures in the Fine Arts; Studies in the History of Art; exhibition catalogs; annual report; monthly calendar of events
Activities: Sunday lect by distinguished guest speakers and members of the staff are given throughout the year; the A W Mellon Lect in the Fine Arts are delivered as a series each spring by an outstanding scholar; concerts are held in the East Garden Court each Sunday evening between September and June at 7 PM without charge; general tours and lect are given in the Gallery by members of the Education Department throughout the week; special tours are arranged for groups; films on art are presented on a varying schedule; color slide programs, films and video cassettes on gallery exhibitions and collections, free of charge, free catalog; programs to 4900 communities; provides art loans

L **Library,** Constitution Ave at Fourth St NW, 20565. Tel 202-737-4215. *Chief Librn* J M Edelstein; *Reader Services Librn* Caroline H Backlund
Open Mon Noon - 4:30 PM, Tues - Fri 10 AM - 4:30 PM. Estab 1941 to support the national curatorial, educational and research activities and serve as a research center for graduate students, visiting scholars and researchers in the visual arts. Supports the research programs of the Center for Advanced Study in the Visual Arts. For reference only
Income: Financed by federal appropriations and trust funds
Library Holdings: Vols 107,000; Vertical Files 103,000; Micro — Fiche, reels; Other — Clipping files, exhibition catalogs, pamphlets
Special Subjects: Western European & American art & architecture, illuminated manuscripts; surrealism
Collections: Art exhibition, art auction and private art collection catalogs; artist monographs; Leonardo da Vinci
Exhibitions: Changing exhibitions; art & history of books, printing & graphic arts
Publications: Guide to the Library, annual
Activities: Library tours on request

L **Photographic Archives,** Constitution Ave at 6th NW, 20565. Tel 202-842-6026. *Cur* Ruth Philbrick
Library Holdings: Micro — Fiche 3,000,000; Other — Photographs 1,000,000
Special Subjects: Black-white photographs of American and Western European art

L **Educational Division Slide Library,*** Sixth & Constitution Ave NW, 20565. Tel 202-842-6100. *Slide Librn* Anne vonRebhan
Library Holdings: AV — Slides 120,000
Special Subjects: Western European & American painting & sculpture

L **Index of American Design,*** Sixth & Constitution Ave NW, 20565. Tel 202-737-4215. *Cur* Lina Steele
Library Holdings: Water colors 17,000; Micro — Fiche; Other — Photographs
Special Subjects: Decorative Arts, Folk Art

NATIONAL LEAGUE OF AMERICAN PEN WOMEN
For further information, see National and Regional Organizations

NATIONAL MUSEUM & GALLERY REGISTRATION ASSOCIATION
For further information, see Regional and National Organizations

M **NATIONAL MUSEUM OF AFRICAN ART,** Smithsonian Institution, 318 A St NE, 20002. Tel 202-287-3490. *Dir* Sylvia H Williams; *Assoc Dir* Roy Sieber; *Asst Dir* Jean Salan; *Senior Scholar & Founding Dir Emeritus* Warren M Robbins; *Cur Coll* Lydia Puccinelli; *Cur* Roslyn Walker; *Cur Education* Edward Lifschitz; *Public Information Officer* Margaret Bertin; *Operations Mgr* Basil Arendse
Open Mon - Fri 10 AM - 5 PM; Sat & Sun Noon - 5 PM. Admis voluntary contribution. Estab 1963, open 1964 to reveal African art as one of the great cultural heritages of mankind; to help replace myth and misconception with valid scientific and historical information; to provide proper representation of African art in the spectrum of museums of Washington. Twelve galleries display 500 objects of traditional African sculpture, plus a period-furnished memorial room of Frederick Douglass, 19th century abolitionist, orator, publisher, statesman in whose first Washington, DC residence the Museum is located. Average Annual Attendance: 85,874. Mem: 1100; dues $15 - $5000
Income: $1,000,000 (federal funding, membership and contributions)
Collections: African sculpture, textiles, crafts, musical instruments (8000 items); 19th Century Afro-American Art; Eliot Elisofon Memorial Archives of 100,000 photos, slides and films
Exhibitions: The African Photography of Eliot Elisofon; The Influence of African Sculpture on Modern Art; Traditional African Art; Permanent Outdoor color wall mural of the N'Debele villages of South Africa
Publications: Exhibition Catalogs; multimedia slide kit; pamphlets; booklets
Activities: Credit courses in cooperation with area universities; classes for adults and children; docent training; lectures open to public, 12 vis lectr per year; concerts; gallery talks; tours; scholarships; individual paintings and original objects of art lent to museums, universities, public officials and conferences; lending collection contains motion pictures, paintings, photography, sculpture, slides and textiles; museum sales shop, (Boutique Africa), sells books, magazines, reproductions, prints, slides, quality crafts, original art, jewelry and other imports from Africa

L **Branch Library,*** 318 A St NE, 20002. Tel 202-287-3490. *Librn* Janet L Stanley
Open Mon - Fri 10 AM - 5 PM. Estab 1971 to provide major resource center for African art and culture; Library is part of the Smithsonian Institution Libraries system. For reference only
Income: Financed through Smithsonian budget
Library Holdings: Vols 6000; Per subs 50; Other — Clipping files, exhibition catalogs, pamphlets
Special Subjects: Afro-American Art, African Art: African artistic retentions in the New World

M **NATIONAL MUSEUM OF AMERICAN ART,** Eighth & G Sts NW, 20560. Tel 202-357-1959. *Dir* Charles C Eldredge; *Deputy Dir* Harry Lowe; *Asst Dir & Chief Cur* Elizabeth Broun; *Asst Dir, Museum Programs* Barbara Shissler Nosanow; *Asst Dir, Museum Resources* Charles J Robertson; *Sr Curatorial Advisor* Adelyn D Breeskin; *Cur 18th & 19th Century Painting & Sculpture* William H Truettner; *Cur 20th Century Painting & Sculpture* Harry Z Rand; *Cur Graphic Arts* Janet Altic Flint; *Cur Research & Fellowships* Lois M Fink; *Registrar* W Robert Johnston; *Chief Office of Design & Construction* David B Keeler; *Sr Conservator* Stafano Scafetta; *Chief Office of Research Support* Eleanor E Fink; *Ed-in-Chief* Carroll S Clark; *Chief Office Public Affairs* Margery Byers; *Chief Office Public Programs* Margaret P Cogswell; *Chief Office Intern Programs* Patricia H Chieffo; *Admin Officer* Sherwood A Dowling
Open daily 10 AM - 5:30 PM; cl Christmas. Estab 1829, and later absorbed by the Smithsonian Institution, it was designated the National Gallery of Art in 1906. The title was changed to the National Collection of Fine Arts in 1937: and, in 1980, to the National Museum of American Art. The museum is now primarily concerned with the acquisition, study and presentation of American art from its beginning to the present. Barney Studio House is administered by the National Museum. A unique 1902 showplace built by artist Alice Pike Barney as her home, studio and salon, it is open for guided visits by reservation and for series of cultural programs. Average Annual Attendance: 450,000
Collections: The collection of paintings, sculpture, photographs, prints, drawings, crafts and decorative arts number over 30,000, and include outstanding masterworks as well as important holdings by lesser-known artists. It represents a wide range of American work, particularly late 19th and early 20th century. Major collections include those of Harriet Lane Johnston (1906), William T Evans (1907), John Gellatly (1929), and the S C Johnson and Son Collection of paintings from the 1960s. There is a sizeable collection of portrait miniatures. All works not on display are available for examination by scholars
Exhibitions: A representative selection of works from the collection are on permanent display in the galleries, providing a comprehensive view of the varied aspects of American art. Most temporary exhibitions, some twenty a year, are originated by the staff, many as part of the program to investigate less well-known aspects of American art. They include both studies of individual artists and thematic studies. Major exhibitions for 1982-83 include: The Prints of Louis Lozowick; Joseph Cornell: An Exploration of Sources; Elizabeth Nourse (1859-1938): A Salon Career; American in Brittany and Normandy: 1860-1915; Sawtooths and Other Ranges of Imagination: Contemporary Art from Idaho
Publications: Major exhibitions are accompanied by authoritative publications; small exhibitions are accompanied by checklists
Activities: The Office of Public Programs carries on an active program with the

schools and the general public, offering imaginative participatory tours for children, and varied presentations of films, poetry readings, lectures, symposia and concerts. A research program in American art is maintained for visiting scholars and training is carried on through internship in general museum practice and conservation; the museum also circulates exhibitions throughout the United States on a regular basis

L Library of the National Museum of American Art and the National Portrait Gallery, Eighth & G Sts NW, 20560. Tel 202-357-1886. *Chief Librn* Cecilia Chin; *Asst Librn* Susan Gurney; *Cataloger* Charles H King Jr
Open Mon - Fri 10 AM - 5 PM. Estab 1964 to serve the reference and research needs of the staff and affiliated researchers of the National Collection of Fine Arts, the National Portrait Gallery, the Archives of American Art, and other Smithsonian bureaus. Open to graduate students and other qualified adult researchers. Circ 7940
Income: $160,000 (financed by federal appropriation)
Purchases: $30,000
Library Holdings: Vols 45,000; Per subs 800; Original documents; Micro — Fiche, reels; Other — Clipping files, exhibition catalogs, manuscripts, pamphlets, reproductions
Special Subjects: American art, especially printing, drawing, sculpture and graphic arts, contemporary art, American history and biography
Collections: Ferdinand Perret Art Reference Library: collection of scrapbooks of clippings and pamphlets; special section on California art and artists consisting of approx 325 ring binders on art and artists of Southern California; vertical file of 300 file drawers of material on art and artists, with increasing emphasis on American art and artists
Activities: Library tours by appointment only

M Renwick Gallery, 17th St & Pennsylvania Ave NW, 20560. Tel 202-357-2531. *Dir* Lloyd E Herman; *Cur* Michael Monroe
Open daily 10 AM - 5:30 PM; cl Christmas. Designed in 1859 by architect James Renwick, Jr, as the Corcoran Gallery of Art, the building was renamed for the architect in 1965 when it was transferred by the Federal government to the Smithsonian Institution for restoration. Restored to its French Second Empire elegance after 67 years as the United States Court of Claims, the building has two public rooms with period furnishings, the Grand Salon and the Octagon Room, as well as eight areas for temporary exhibitions of American crafts and design
Collections: Since its opening, the Renwick Gallery has presented 93 special exhibitions; American crafts and decorative arts
Exhibitions: (1982-83) Picnic Posters; The Inedible Renwick Birthday Cakes; Celebration: A World of Art and Ritual; The Grand Renwick Gallery Souvenir Show; Threads: Seven American Artists and Their Miniature Textile Pictures; Clay for Walls: Surface Reliefs by American Artists; Lafayette Square, 1963-1983: Architecture, Preservation and the Presidency; Scandinavian Modern: 1880-1980; Russel Wright: American Designer
Publications: Major exhibitions are accompanied by publications, smaller exhibitions by checklists
Activities: Docent training; film programs; lectures emphasizing the creative work of American designers and craftsmen as well as complementing the exhibitions from other countries; tours; concerts

M NATIONAL MUSEUM OF AMERICAN HISTORY, Smithsonian Institution, Constitution Ave between 12th & 14th Sts NW, 20560. Tel 202-357-1300. *Dir* Roger G Kennedy; *Deputy Dir* Douglas E Evelyn
Open daily 10 AM - 5:30 PM, Apr 1 - Labor Day 10 AM - 9 PM, cl Christmas Day. No admis fee. Estab 1964. The museum tells the story of American achievements from Colonial Times to the present, from man's basic needs of food, clothing and shelter, to the men and women who shaped our heritage and our progress in science and technology. Average Annual Attendance: 6 million
Collections: †Archaeology, †ceramics, †glass, †graphic arts, †numismatics, †photography, †textiles
Exhibitions: Atom Smashers; A Nation of Nations; We the People; and others
Publications: Exhibition catalogs; Studies in History and Technology Series
Activities: Docent training; Lectures open to public; concerts; tours; museum shop selling books, magazines, reproductions, prints and slides

O Society For Commercial Archeology, Room 5010, 20560. *Pres* Susan Shearer
Estab to promote public awareness, exchange information & encourage selective conservation of the commercial landscape. Mem: 150; dues $15
Publications: News Journal, bi-annual

L Branch Library, Constitution Ave between 12th & 14th Sts NW, 20560. Tel 202-357-2036. *Librn* Rhoda Ratner
Open Mon - Fri 8:45 AM - 5:15 PM. Library is part of the Smithsonian Institution Libraries system. Open to staff and visiting scholars
Income: Financed through SIL budgets

M NATIONAL PORTRAIT GALLERY, F St at Eighth NW, 20560. Tel 202-357-2137. *Dir* Alan Fern; *Admin Officer* Barbara A Hart; *Asst Dir for History & Public Programs* Marc Pachter; *Cur Paintings & Sculpture* Robert G Stewart; *Chief Design & Production* Nello Marconi; *Cur Exhib* Beverly Cox; *Cur Education* Kenneth A Yellis; *Cur Photographs* William F Stapp; *Cur Prints* Wendy W Reaves; *Registrar* Suzanne Jenkins; *Keeper Catalog of American Portraits* Mona Dearborn; *Catalog of American Portraits Survey Coordr* Richard K Doud; *Sr Conservator* Rosamond Westmoreland; *Editor & Historian American Archives* Charles Willson; *Audiovisual Media Coordr* Eugene Mantie; *Public Affairs Officer* Sandra Westin; *Ed* Frances Wein
Open daily 10 AM - 5:30 PM; cl Christmas. No admis fee. The National Portrait Gallery was estab by Act of Congress in 1962 as a museum of the Smithsonian Institution for the exhibition and study of portraiture depicting men and women who have made significant contributions to the history, development, and culture of the people of the United States. The Gallery is housed in one of the oldest government structures in Washington, the former US Patent Office Building constructed between 1836 and 1867, on the very site which Pierre L'Enfant, in his original plan for the city, had designated for a pantheon to honor the nation's immortals. The first floor of the Gallery is devoted to major loan exhibitions and photographs, prints, and drawings from the permanent collection. There are special galleries housing a collection of portrait engravings by C B J F de Saint-Memin, silhouettes by Auguste Edouart, portrait sculptures by Jo Davidson, and

selections from the Time Cover Collection. On the second floor are featured the permanent collection of portraits of eminent Americans and the Hall of Presidents containing portraits and associative items of our Chief Executives. The two-story Victorian Renaissance Great Hall on the third floor is used for special events and exhibitions. Average Annual Attendance: 414,000
Income: Approx $3,000,000 (financed by federal appropriation & private contributions)
Collections: The collections, which are constantly being expanded, include portraits of significant Americans, preferably executed from life, in all traditional media: oils, watercolors, charcoal, pen and ink, daguerreotypes, photographs; portraits of American Presidents from George Washington to Ronald Reagan. 900 original works of art from the Time Magazine Cover collection; more than 5000 glass plate negatives by Mathew Brady & studio in the Meserve Collection
Exhibitions: (1982-83) Charles Willson Peale & His World; The Meserve Collection; American Portraiture in the Grand Manner; Hollywood Portrait Photographers, 1921-1941; Mr Sully, Portrait Painter: The Works of Thomas Sully (1783-1872); Heroes, Martyrs & Villains: Printed Portraits of the Civil War; Portraits on a Page of History: The Career of James Barton Longacre; The New Deal; Gertrude Vanderbilt Whitney: Artists & Patron; The Eight; Masterpieces from Versailles: Three Centuries of French Portraiture; Blessed are the Peacemakers; Robert Gornelius: Portraits from the Dawn of Photogrpahy; Portraits from the New Deal
Publications: Large-scale, richly illustrated publications accompany major shows and provide comprehensive analysis of exhibition themes; descriptive brochures about the gallery; documentary, audio, and visual materials designed to be used as teaching guides; illustrated checklist; American portraiture; biographies
Activities: Outreach programs for elementary and secondary schools, senior citizens groups, hospitals, and nursing homes; docent training; teacher workshops; scheduled walk-in tours for special groups, adults, families, and schools; programs for handicapped and other special audiences; Portraits In Motion (special weekend musical & dramatic events); museum shop selling books, magazines, reproductions, prints, and slides
Library,
Shared with the National Museum of American Art; see library entry under National Museum of American Art

M NATIONAL TRUST FOR HISTORIC PRESERVATION, 1785 Massachusetts Ave NW, 20036. Tel 202-673-4000. *Pres* Michael Ainslie
Open to the public, hours and fees vary with the property, cl Christmas, New Years. Founded 1949, the National Trust for Historic Preservation is the only national, non-profit, private organization chartered by Congress to encourage public participation in the preservation of sites, buildings and objects significant in American history and culture. Its services, counsel and education on preservation, and historic property interpretation and administration, are carried out at national and regional headquarters in consultation with advisors in each state and U.S. Territory. Mem: 155,000; dues sustaining $100, active $15, student $5
Income: Financed by membership dues, contributions and matching grants from the U.S. Department of the Interior, National Park Service, under provision of the National Preservation Act of 1966
Collections: Fine and decorative arts furnishing nine historic house museums: Chesterwood, Stockbridge, MA; Cliveden, Philadelphia, PA; Decatur House and Woodrow Wilson House, Washington, DC; Drayton Hall, Charleston, SC; Lyndhurst, Tarrytown, NY; Oatlands, Leesburg, VA; The Shadows-on-the-Teche, New Iberia, LA; Woodlawn Plantation, Mt Vernon, VA. (For additional information, see separate listings)
Publications: Historic Preservation, quarterly; Preservation News, monthly newspaper

L Library, Information Services, 1785 Massachusetts Ave NW, 20036. Tel 202-623-4038. *Information Services Coordr* Susan Shearer; *Librn* Cary Schneider
Open Mon - Fri 9 AM - 5 PM for members only, cl legal holidays. For reference only
Library Holdings: Vols 10,000; Per subs 200; Vertical Files 13,000; AV — Slides 30,000; Other — Photographs 20,000

M NAVAL HISTORICAL CENTER, United States Navy Memorial Museum, Washington Navy Yard, Ninth & M Sts SE, 20374. Tel 202-433-2651. *Dir* T A Damon; *Assoc Dir* Dr Oscar Fitzgerald
Open Mon - Fri 9 AM - 4 PM, Sat, Sun & holidays 10 AM - 5 PM. Parking and admis free. Estab 1961 to present history & preserve heritage of US Navy. Average Annual Attendance: 150,000
Income: Financed by federal appropriations
Collections: History of US Navy from 1775 to Space Age; Naval Combat Art; Paintings; Prints; Watercolors
Exhibitions: Changing art exhibitions
Activities: Classes for children; docent training; museum shop sells books & prints

M THE PHILLIPS COLLECTION, 1600-1612 21st St NW, 20009. Tel 202-387-2151. *Dir* Laughlin Phillips; *Cur* Willem de Looper; *Registrar* Joseph Holbach; *Asst Registrar* Jan Johnson; *Adjunct Cur* Robert C Cafritz; *Assoc Cur* Sasha Newman; *Asst Cur Research* Martha Carey; *Asst Cur Research* Jan Lancaster; *Admin* Michael Green; *Dir Music* Charles Crowder; *Preparator* William Koberg; *Development Officer* Anne Hobler; *Coordr Spec Events & Mem* Karen Ritch; *Exec Asst* Louise Steffens; *Public Info Officer* Laura Lester; *Bookshop Mgr* Jane Godfrey
Open Tues - Sat 10 AM - 5 PM, Sun 2 - 7 PM, cl Mon, Christmas, Thanksgiving, July 4 and New Years. No admis fee. Opened to the public 1921 to show and interpret the best of contemporary painting in the context of outstanding works of the past; to underscore this intent through the presentation of concerts and lectures. The original building, a Georgian Revival residence designed in 1897 by Hornblower & Marshall, was added to in 1907. A modern annex connected by a double bridge to the old gallery was opened to the public in 1960. Average Annual Attendance: 100,000
Income: Financed by endowment, exhibition fees, sale of publications & private contributions
Purchases: David Blackburn, Philip Guston, Sherry Kasten, Herman Maril

Collections: 19th and 20th century American and European painting with special emphasis on units of particular artists such as Bonnard, Braque, Cezanne, Daumier, de Stael and Rouault, and Americans such as Avery, Dove, Gatch, Knaths, Marin, O'Keeffe, Prendergast, Rothko and Tack. The best known painting is Renoir's Luncheon of the Boating Party
Exhibitions: (1982) Georges Braque: The Late Paintings 1940-1963; (1983) Morris Graves: Vision of the Inner Eye; Paintings & Drawings from the Phillips Collection
Publications: Pierre Bonnard; Maurice Prendergast; Paul Klee; The Luncheon of the Boating Party; exhibition catalogs
Activities: Lectures open to public, 1-2 vis lectr per year; concerts; gallery talks; tours; individual paintings and original objects of art lent to national and international museums; book traveling exhibitions, 3 per year; originate traveling exhibitions to national and international museums; museum sales shop sells books, magazines & reproductions

L **Library,** 1600 21st St NW, 20009. Tel 202-387-2151. *Librn* Karen Schneider
Available to serious students, researchers and museum professionals, by appointment; reference only
Library Holdings: Vols 4000; Per subs 40; Vertical Files; Micro — Reels; Other — Clipping files 20, exhibition catalogs, pamphlets
Special Subjects: Monographs from the Phillips Collection, 19th & 20th century European & American art

M **MARJORIE MERRIWEATHER POST FOUNDATION OF DC,** Hillwood Museum,* 4155 Linnean Ave NW, 20008. Tel 202-686-0410. *Dir* Roy D R Betteley; *Cur* Katrina V H Taylor
Open Mon, Wed - Sat 9 - 10:30 AM & Noon & 1:30 PM for tours. Admis adults $7, students $4, children under 12 free. Estab 1976 to enable the general public to see extensive collection of Russian and French decorative art. Mansion in the Georgian style, home of the late Marjorie Merriweather Post, situated on 25 acres of landscaped grounds. Average Annual Attendance: 20,000
Income: Financed by endowment & admis
Collections: French decorative arts, furnishings & memorabilia; Russian decorative arts
Activities: Lectures open to public; gallery talks; tours; museum shop sells books, original art, reproductions and prints

PUBLIC LIBRARY OF THE DISTRICT OF COLUMBIA

L **Art Division,*** Martin Luther King Memorial Library, 901 G St NW, 20001. Tel 202-727-1291. *Dir Libr* Dr Hardy R Franklin; *Chief Art Div* Lois Kent Stiles
Open Mon - Thurs 9 AM - 9 PM, Fri & Sat 9 AM - 5:30 PM. No admis fee
Income: Financed by city government appropriation
Library Holdings: Vols 20,804; Per subs 100; Micro — Reels; Other — Clipping files, exhibition catalogs, framed reproductions, pamphlets, prints, reproductions
Collections: †Reference and circulating books and periodicals on architecture, painting, sculpture, photography, graphic and applied arts; †extensive pamphlet file including all art subjects, with special emphasis on individual American artists and on more than 400 artists active in the area; †circulating picture collection numbering over 65,000 mounted reproductions and 290 framed prints
Exhibitions: Special exhibitions held occasionally

L **Audiovisual Division,*** Martin Luther King Memorial Library, 901 G St NW, 20001. *AV Librn* Diane V Henry
Open Mon - Thurs 9 AM - 9 PM, Fri & Sat 9 AM - 5:30 PM
Library Holdings: AV — Fs, motion pictures

M **SMITH-MASON GALLERY AND MUSEUM,*** 1207 Rhode Island Ave NW, 20005. Tel 202-462-6323. *Dir* Helen S Mason; *Cur Graphics* James L Wells; *Cur Painting* Delilah W Pierce; *Cur Ceramics & Sculpture* Dr Leroy Gaskin
Open Tues - Fri Noon - 4 PM, Sat 10 AM - 5 PM, Sun 2 - 5 PM. No admis fee. Estab 1967 for the preservation and research of ethnology. Mem: Dues life $500, donor $250, contributing $100, supporting $25, sustaining $15, individual $10
Collections: Ethnology; decorative arts; graphics; paintings; sculpture; textiles
Publications: Exhibition brochures; newsletter, annually
Activities: Lect; gallery talks; tours; films

L **Library,*** 1207 Rhode Island Ave NW, 20005
Open to public for research and on premises reading only
Library Holdings: Vols 300

M **SMITHSONIAN INSTITUTION,*** 1000 Jefferson Dr SW, 20560. Tel 202-628-4422. *Secy* S Dillon Ripley; *Under Secy* Phillip Samuel Hughes; *Asst Secy for Art & History* Charles Blitzer; *Asst Secy Science* David Challinor; *Asst Secy for Museum Programs* Paul N Perrot; *Writer & Editor* Kathryn B Lindeman
Open daily 10 AM - 5:30 PM, extended spring and summer hours determined yearly, cl Christmas. Estab 1846, when James Smithson bequeathed his fortune to the United States, under the name of the Smithsonian Institution, an establishment in Washington for the increase and diffusion of knowledge among men. To carry out the terms of Smithson's will, the Institution performs fundamental research; preserves for study and reference about 78 million items of scientific, cultural and historical interest; maintains exhibits representative of the arts, American history, aeronautics and space exploration; technology; natural history; and engages in programs of education and national and international cooperative research and training. Responsibility for the administration of the trust is vested in the Board of Regents, which is comprised of the Chief Justice of the United States (Chancellor of the Board of Regents), the Vice President of the United States, three members of the Senate, three members of the House of Representatives and nine citizen members. Average Annual Attendance: 23,000,000
Income: Board of Regents meets three times yearly, Jan, May and Sept.
The individual bureaus concerned with art under the Smithsonian Institution are as follows. For complete information see separate listings.
—**Archives of American Art,** Eighth & G Streets, NW, 20560
—**Cooper-Hewitt Museum of Decorative Arts and Design,** 2 East 91st St, 20560
—**Freer Gallery of Art,** 12th & Independence Ave, SW, 20560. Tel 202-357-2104
—**Hirshhorn Museum and Sculpture Garden,** Eighth & Independence, SW, 20560
—**John F Kennedy Center for the Performing Arts,** 20566
Administered under a separate Board of Trustees
—**National Air and Space Museum,** Seventh & Independence Ave, SW, 20560
—**National Museum of American Art,** Ninth & G Streets, NW, 20560
Includes the Renwick Gallery
—**National Gallery of Art,** Constitution Ave at Sixth St, NW, 20565
Administered under a separate Board of Trustees
—**National Museum of History and Technology,** Constitution Ave between 12th & 14th Streets, NW, 20560
—**National Portrait Gallery,** Eighth & F Streets, NW, 20560

M **SOCIETY OF THE CINCINNATI,** Anderson House Museum, 2118 Massachusetts Ave NW, 20008. Tel 202-785-2040, 785-0540. *Dir* John D Kilbourne; *Conservator* Katheleen Betts
Open Tues - Sat 1 - 4 PM, special hours on request by groups for guided tours, cl National holidays. No admis fee. The Society of the Cincinnati was founded in May 1783; the museum was opened to the public in 1938. Anderson House Museum is a national museum for the custody and preservation of historical documents, relics and archives, especially those pertaining to the American Revolution. Because of its superb building (1905, Little and Browne, Boston architects), original furnishings and collections of Western and Oriental art, Anderson House Museum is also a Historic House Museum. On the first floor of the house are portraits of founding members of the Society by Gilbert Stuart, George Catlin, Ezra Ames, Ralph Earl and other early American painters. Average Annual Attendance: 12,000. Mem: 3000
Collections: Figurines of the French regiments that fought at Yorktown, Virginia in 1781 and others; †historical material; Japanese screens, bronzes, ceramics, jade; Oriental works of art; 16th and 17th Century Flemish tapestries, sculpture and period furniture; paintings
Exhibitions: Rotating exhibitions; the permanent collection
Publications: Annual Report of the Director; A Few Questions and Answers Regarding the Society of the Cincinnati, brochures; George Rogers Clark Lectures on American History (4 volumes published); The Sword and Firearm Collection of the Society of the Cincinnati; Oriental Art in Anderson House
Activities: Lectures open to the public; concerts; tours; scholarships and fels offered; individual paintings and original objects of art lent

L **Library,**
Library Holdings: Vols 10,000; Per subs 100; Micro — Reels 300; Other — Clipping files, manuscripts, memorabilia, original art works, photographs, prints
Special Subjects: American Revolution

M **THE SUPREME COURT OF THE UNITED STATES MUSEUM,** US Supreme Court Bldg, 20543. Tel 202-252-3298. *Cur* Gail Galloway
Open Mon - Fri 9 AM - 4:30 PM, cl federal holidays. No admis fee. Curator's office estab 1974
Collections: Portraits of all former Justices throughout history; marble busts of the Chief Justices and certain Associate Justices; historic images such as photos, etchings and drawings of the Justices and the architecture of the building; memorabilia, archival & manuscript materials on the Supreme Court history; 18th & 19th century American & English furniture & decorative arts
Exhibitions: Permanent and temporary exhibits
Publications: Exhibit brochures
Activities: Lectures in the courtroom every hour on the half hour; continuously running film describing the functions of the Supreme Court

M **TEXTILE MUSEUM,*** 2320 S St NW, 20008. Tel 202-667-0441. *Pres* Arthur D Jenkins; *Actg Dir* Patricia L Fiske; *Exec Asst* Mary Lee Berger-Hughes; *Asst Cur New World* Ann P Rowe
Open Tues - Sat 10 AM - 5 PM, Sun Noon - 4 PM. Admis adult $2, children $.50. Estab 1925 for the acquisition, study and exhibition of rugs and textiles. The gallery contains eight rooms for exhibition, storage areas, museum shop, conservation laboratory, library and offices. Average Annual Attendance: 20,000. Mem: 1500; dues $25
Income: Financed by endowment, membership and grants
Collections: Oriental rugs from antiquity to the present, as well as rugs and textiles from the Old and New Worlds with the general exception of Western Europe and the United States. The collection contains approximately 9000 textiles and 700 rugs; Coptic, Islamic textiles; Central & South American ethnographic textiles
Exhibitions: Caucasian Rugs; China Looms Resplendent; Ethnographic Textiles of the Western Hemisphere; History of Knitting; Masterpieces in the Textile Museum from 3 AD to 20th Century; Molas; Quilts; Spanish Silks and Carpets, 13th - 17th Centuries; Structures of Fabrics; Tribal Weavers of the Andes-a Fanfare of 19th and 20th Century Rugs; Uzbek Textiles; White-Ground Turkish Rugs
Publications: Irene Emery Round Table on Museum Textiles, irregular; Museum journal, annual; museum newsletter, quarterly; exhibition catalogs
Activities: Dramatic programs; docent training; internships in conservation and museum studies; lect open to public, 40 visiting lectr per year; concerts; gallery talks; tours; original objects of art lent to other museums for special exhibitions; originate traveling exhibitions; museum shop and sales shop selling books, original art, patterns, yarn and floss, ethnic folk jewelry, woven and knitted articles

L **Arthur D Jenkins Library,*** 2320 S St NW, 20008. Tel 202-667-0441. *Librn* Katherine T Freshley
Open Tues - Fri 10 AM - 5 PM, Sat 10 AM - 1 PM. Estab 1925 as a reference library dealing with ancient and ethnographic textiles and rugs of the world
Income: Financed by endowment, membership and gifts
Library Holdings: Vols 10,000; Per subs 144; Other — Clipping files, exhibition catalogs, pamphlets, photographs
Collections: Oriental rugs; Peruvian, Indonesian, American Indian and Indian Textiles

L **TRINITY COLLEGE LIBRARY,** Michigan Ave & Franklin St NE, 20017. Tel 202-269-2252. *Librn* Dorothy Beach; *Readers Services* Keneth Venet; *Acquisitions* Therest Marie Gaudreau; *Cataloger* Karen Leider; *Periodicals* Doris Gruber
Open during school semesters, Mon - Thurs 9 AM - 11 PM, Fri 9 AM - 8 PM, Sat 10 AM - 5 PM, Sun Noon - 11 PM. Estab 1897 as an undergraduate college library, serving the college community

Income: $253,548 (financed by college budget)
Library Holdings: Vols 5200; Per subs 16; Micro — Reels; AV — Cassettes, slides
Special Subjects: Art collection in both books and slides is general in content, including works on painting, sculpture and architecture principally

M **UNITED STATES CAPITOL MUSEUM,** 20515. Tel 202-225-1222. *Architect of the Capitol* George M White; *Chief Cur* Dr Anne-Imelda Radice; *Art Reference* Florian H Thayn
Open daily 9 AM - 4:30 PM, summer 9 AM - 10 PM. No admis fee.
Cornerstone layed 1793. Capitol is working building with museum value. Restored historic chambers. Average Annual Attendance: 10,000,000
Income: Financed by United States Congressional appropriation and appropriate donations
Collections: Works by Andrei; Brumidi; Crawford; Costaggini; Cox; Franzoni; French; Greenough; Leutze; Peale; Powers; Rogers; Trumbull; Vanderlyn; Weir;
Exhibitions: Architectural drawings relating to the Capitol
Publications: Catalog of collections; occasional pamphlets
Activities: Individual paintings and original art objects lent to qualified museums
L **Art Reference Library,** Office of the Architect, 20515. Tel 202-225-1222. *Art Reference* Florence H Florian
Open 8:30 AM - 5 PM. Estab for research on United States Capitol, its art and artists
Library Holdings: Vols 5000; Micro — Fiche; AV — Kodachromes, slides; Other — Clipping files, manuscripts, memorabilia, original art works, pamphlets, photographs, prints, sculpture
Collections: 55,000 architectural drawings; 50,000 photographs; archives pertaining to Capitol art and architecture 1793 to present

O **UNITED STATES COMMISSION OF FINE ARTS,** 708 Jackson Place NW, 20006. Tel 202-566-1066. *Chmn* J Carter Brown; *Secy* Charles H Atherton
Open daily 8:30 AM - 5 PM. Estab by Act of Congress in 1910 to advise the President, members of congress, and various governmental agencies on matters pertaining to the appearance of Washington, DC. The Commission of Fine Arts is composed of seven members who are appointed by the President for four-year terms. Report issued periodically, principally concerned with architectural review. Plans for all new projects in the District of Columbia under the direction of the Federal and District of Columbia Governments which affect the appearance of the city, and all questions involving matters of design with which the Federal Government may be concerned must be submitted to the Commission for comment and advice before contracts are made. Also gives advice on suitability of designs of private buildings in certain parts of the city adjacent to the various departments and agencies of the District and Federal Governments, the Mall, Rock Creek Park, and Georgetown
Publications: 15 publications on area architecture, 1964-1978

UNITED STATES COMMITTEE OF THE INTERNATIONAL ASSOCIATION OF ART, INC
For further information, see National and Regional Organizations

UNITED STATES DEPARTMENT OF THE INTERIOR, Indian Arts and Crafts Board
For further information, see National and Regional Organizations

M **UNITED STATES NAVY,** Combat Art Gallery, 9th and M Sts, Bldg 67 Washington Navy Yard, 20374. Tel 202-433-3816. *Cur* Charles D Lawrence; *Asst Cur* John D Barnett
Open Monday - Friday 8AM - 4PM. Estab 1941. Average Annual Attendance: 3000
Collections: Graphic arts, paintings, sketches
Exhibitions: Quarterly exhibits of art work from WWII through 1979 from the permanent collection
Publications: United States Navy Combat Art
Activities: Lending collection contains original objects of art

O **UNITED STATES SENATE COMMISSION ON ART AND ANTIQUITIES,** United States Capitol Bldg, Room S-411, 20510. Tel 202-224-2955. *Chmn* Howard H Baker, Jr; *VChmn* Robert C Byrd; *Executive Secy* William F Hildenbrand; *Cur* James R Ketchum; *Registrar* James S Haugerud; *Museum Specialist* Diane K Skvarla
Rooms in Capitol under jurisdiction of Commission are open daily 9 AM - 4:30 PM. No admis fee. Commission estab 1968 to acquire, supervise, hold, place and protect all works of art, historical objects, and exhibits within the Senate wing of the United States Capitol and Senate Office Buildings. Average Annual Attendance: 1,000,000
Income: Financed by United States Senate appropriation
Collections: Paintings, sculpture, historic furnishings and memorablilia located within the Senate wing of the Capitol and Senate Office Buildings; Preservation Projects: Old Senate and Old Supreme Court Chamber restored to their appearances 1850
Exhibitions: (1983-84) The Webster-Hayne Debate of 1850
Publications: Manners in the Senate Chamber: 19th Century Women's Views; Senatorial Fare: Recipes by and for the Members of the US Senate; The Senate Chamber 1810-1859; The Supreme Court Chamber 1810-1860
L **Reference Library,** United States Capitol Bldg Room S-411, 20510
A reference collection on fine and decorative arts; supplemented by the United States Senate Library
Library Holdings: Vols 250,000; Other — Clipping files, photographs
Special Subjects: Architecture, Decorative Arts

O **WASHINGTON WOMEN'S ARTS CENTER,** 420 7th St NW, PO Box 50182, 20004. Tel 202-393-8364, 393-0197. *Exec Dir of Bd* Dana Gordon; *Asst Exec Dir Bd* Harriet Lessey; *Coordr* Sylvia Snowden
Open Tues - Sat 11 AM - 5 PM. Estab 1975 to support women artists. Mem: 602; dues $30
Income: Financed by endowment, membership, city appropriation
Exhibitions: Dreams and Daydreams; Sculpture; Art for Gift's Sake

Publications: Exhibition catalogues, 6 per yr; Newsletter, monthly
Activities: Classes for adults; lectures open to the public, 8 vis lectr per yr; competitions with awards; individual paintings lent; book traveling exhibitions, two per yr; originate traveling exhibitions; gallery store sells books, magazines, original art

M **WHITE HOUSE,** 1600 Pennsylvania Ave NW, 20500. Tel 202-456-1414. *Cur* Clement E Conger; *Registrar & Assoc Cur* Betty C Monkman
Open winter Tues - Fri 10 AM - Noon, summer Tues - Sat 10 AM - 1 PM, cl Sun, Mon, most holidays. No admis fee
Collections: 18th & 19th century period furniture; 18th, 19th & 20th century †paintings & †prints; †glassware; †porcelain; †sculpture
Publications: The White House: A Historic Guide; The Presidents of the United States; The Living White House; The First Ladies; White House History, magazine

M **WOODROW WILSON HOUSE,** 2340 S St, NW, 20008. Tel 202-673-4034. *Dir* Earl James; *Asst Dir* Nancy McCoy; *Admin Asst* Cindy Guglielmo
Open Tues - Fri 10 AM - 2 PM, Sat & Sun Noon - 4 PM, cl Mon. Admis adults $2, students and senior citizens $1, National Trust Members free. Estab 1963, owned by the National Trust for Historic Preservation, it works to foster interest and appreciation of the 28th President, Woodrow Wilson. Wilson House is a 1915 Georgian-Revival townhouse designed by Waddy B Wood, with formal garden. From 1921 it served as the retirement home of President Wilson and Mrs Wilson. Average Annual Attendance: 15,000
Income: Financed by endowment and membership
Collections: Early 20th century clothing, furnishings, utensils
Exhibitions: The Architectural Drawings of Waddy Butler Wood; Civil Liberties in Washington, DC during the First World War; Kalorama: From Country Estate to Urban Elegance; Hornblower & Marshall, A $.25 Discovery; War Against Freedom; A Taste of the Twenties
Activities: Concerts; films; individual paintings and objects of art lent to qualified museums and non-profit corporations

FLORIDA

BOCA RATON

O **BOCA RATON CENTER FOR THE ARTS, INC,** 801 W Palmetto Park Rd, 33432. Tel 305-392-2500. *Pres* Frank Bennardo; *VPres* Charles Buck; *Dir* Maria Lawton; *Public Relations Dir* Marie Marche
Open Jan - June & Sept - Dec Tues - Fri 10 AM - 4 PM, Sat & Sun 1 - 4 PM, July & June Tues - Fri 10 AM - 4 PM, Sat 1 - 4 PM, cl holidays. No admis fee. Estab 1951 to foster and develop the cultural arts. Large Main Gallery, museum shop contained in one building. Second building houses art school and storage. Average Annual Attendance: 25,000. Mem: 1050; annual dues single $20, family $35; annual meeting April 15
Income: Financed by membership and school
Exhibitions: Student show
Publications: Exhibition catalogues; newsletter, 10 per year
Activities: Classes for adults and children; docent training; lect for members and guests, 2 vis lectr per yr; tours; two statewide compeitions per year and National outdoor art festival with awards given for Best in Show and Merit; scholarships offered; museum shop sells books, original art, reproductions, prints
L **Library of the Center,** 801 W Palmetto Park Rd, 33432. *Librn* Evelyn Capson
Open Mon - Fri 10 AM - 4 PM, Sat & Sun 1 - 4 PM. Estab 1970
Library Holdings: Vols 1000; Per subs 3

M **FLORIDA ATLANTIC UNIVERSITY,** Ritter Art Gallery, Art Department, 33431. Tel 305-393-2660. *Dir* Dr David Courtney; *Cur* Shirley F Fields
Open Tues - Sat 10 AM - 4 PM. No admis fee. Estab 1970 to provide exhibit space for faculty and students and to provide an opportunity to bring to the area exhibits which would expand the cultural experience of the viewers. Gallery is located in the University library. Average Annual Attendance: 15,000
Income: Financed by city and state appropriations and student activities fees
Collections: Slide collection; student work
Exhibitions: Annual juried student show; faculty and former students; work from area junior colleges; traveling exhibitions; '84 Folk Art
Publications: We Call This Art, newsletter
Activities: Classes for adults; dramatic programs; lectures open to public & some for members only; concerts; gallery talks; tours; competitions with awards; originate traveling exhibitions; traveling exhibitions organized and circulated

BRADENTON

O **ART LEAGUE OF MANATEE COUNTY,** Art Center, 209 Ninth St W, 33505. Tel 813-746-2862. *Office Mgr* Nancy Johnson
Open Sept - May, Mon - Fri 9 AM - 4:30 PM, Sat 9 AM - noon, Sun 2 - 4 PM, cl June July, Aug and holidays. No admis fee. Estab 1937. Average Annual Attendance: 25,000. Mem: 600; dues $5 and up; annual meeting in April
Exhibitions: Work by members, one person shows and circulating exhibitions changing at three week intervals from Oct to May
Activities: Art school instruction in painting, drawing, clay techniques and variety of handcrafts; creative development for children; special art programs; gallery talks
L **Library,** Art Center, 209 Ninth St W, 33505. Tel 813-746-2862. *Librn* Marguerite Matteson
Library Holdings: Vols 850

CLEARWATER

O FLORIDA GULF COAST ART CENTER, INC,* 222 Ponce De Leon Blvd, 33516. Tel 813-584-8634. *Managing Dir* Judith Boodon Powers; *President* Donald Ehrmann; *VPres* Mrs Gerald Keefe; *Treas* William Crown III; *Sr Secy* Emil Marquardt; *Cur Education* Karen Tucker Kuykendall; *Registrar* Jeanette Emrich
Open Sept - May Tues - Sat 10 AM - 4 PM, Sun 2 - 5 PM, June - July Tues - Sat 1 - 4 PM, Sun 2 - 4 PM, cl Mon & holidays. No admis fee, donations accepted. Estab 1948 as a regional center for the visual arts. Gallery has 1800 sq ft of space, carpeted walls, track lighting and a security system. Average Annual Attendance: 10,000. Mem: 1000; dues patron $100, contributing $50, family $30, individual $20; annual meeting in March
Income: Financed by membership and grants
Exhibitions: Average ten exhibitions a year including regional artists, traveling exhibits, permanent collections and those organized by Art Center Staff
Activities: Classes for adults and children; workshops; lectures; films, concerts
L Art Reference Library,* 222 Ponce de Leon Blvd, 33516
Open Tues - Sat 10 AM - 4 PM, Sun 2 - 5 PM, cl Aug. Estab 1949 to provide reference material and current periodicals to Art Center members and students. Average Annual Attendance: 8000. Mem: 1300; dues $20 and up; annual meeting in March or April
Library Holdings: Vols 1200; Per subs 10; AV — Fs, slides; Other — Exhibition catalogs
Activities: Classes for adults and children; docent training; lectures open to public, 8 vis lectr per year; concerts; gallery talks; tours; competitions with awards; book traveling exhibitions 2 per yr

CORAL GABLES

M METROPOLITAN MUSEUM AND ART CENTER, 1212 Anastasia Ave, 33134. Tel 305-442-1448. *Dir* Open; *Cur* Mark Ormond; *Dir School* Juanita May; *Educ Coordr* Phyllis Margulies; *Pres Board Trustees* Mrs R Kirk Landon; *Volunteer Coordr* Polly Ramos
Open Tues - Sat 10 AM - 5 PM, Wed evening 7 - 10 PM, Sun Noon - 5 PM. Admis adults $1, sr citizens and students 12-18 yrs $.50. Estab 1962 as a general museum of visual arts with emphasis on Latin America. Six gallery spaces are devoted to both temporary and permanent exhibitions. Average Annual Attendance: 150,000. Mem: 2000; dues life $5000, family $40, individual $30, student $10; annual meeting Sept
Income: $550,000 (financed by membership, contributions and grants)
Collections: Contemporary American painting and graphics; Fashion Group Collection of Historic Costumes; Latin art; contemporary art; Oriental and African art; Jacques Lipchitz Sculpture Center; Martinez-Canas Collection of Contemporary Latin American Paintings; Oriental; Pre-Columbian
Exhibitions: (1982) Twenties Fashions; selections from the Martinez-Canas collection; Photography: 50's Artists in the 80's; Fashion 1900-1910; National Street Furniture Design Competition; Spanish Art Tomorrow; 5th Miami International Print Biennial; Artists of Israel: 1920-1980; Art of India; Arango Multipurpose Furniture Design exhibition; New, New York: Contemporary Art; LeCorbusier: Models & Drawings; Rosenquist: F-111 & Flamingo Capsule; Alejandro Obregon, paintings; Colonial Silver from Central America; Bridal Costumes (1820-present); Seven in Miami; Watercolor Society Exhibition; (1983) Eight American Sculptors; student show; faculty exhibition; Hills & Streams; Chinese Export Porcelain; Paintings from the Martinez-Canas Collection; Dade Co Children's Art Exhibition; As New as Tomorrow: Fashions from the 30's & 40's; contemporary American prints from collection of Martin Margulies; Molly Luce: Eight Decades of the American Scene; tapes by pioneer video artists Nam June Paik, Peter Campus, Juan Downey & Les Levine; Irving Penn, portraits; Robert Thiele, sculptor; Gerald Winter, painter; Highlights of the 1983 Summer Art Camp; New Sculpture from the Collection of Martin Z Margulies; Lipchitz, Rodin, Glackens, Merritt-Chase, 19th & 20th Century Paintings & Sculpture; Benin bronzes from the Pre-Columbian & Japanese collections; paper works by students & faculty of the Museum School; Florida Artists Exhibition, selections from permanent collection including Jill Cannady, Duane Hanson, Martin Hoffman, Juan Gonzalez & Eugene Massin; photographs & objects relating to Coral Gables history & the Biltmore Hotel complex architecture & lifestyle
Publications: Catalogs for exhibitions; newsletter, bimonthly
Activities: Classes for adults & children; computer classes; lectures open to public, 5 vis lectr per yr; concerts; gallery talks; tours; scholarships; museum shop sells books, original art, reproductions, prints, jewelry, crafts, stationery & gift items
L Library, 1212 Anastasia Ave, 33134. *Dir* Arnold L Lehman
Open to members for reference only
Library Holdings: Vols 2500; Per subs 6
Collections: Fern B Muskat Collection

M UNIVERSITY OF MIAMI, Lowe Art Museum, 1301 Stanford Dr, 33146. Tel 305-284-3535. *Dir* Ira Licht; *Asst to Dir* Sharon Clark; *Cur* John Haletsky; *Registrar & Cur Oriental Art* Brian Dursum
Open Tues - Fri Noon - 5 PM, Sat 10 AM - 5 PM, Sun 2 - 5 PM. No admis fee. Estab 1952 to bring outstanding exhibitions and collections to the community and to the University; gallery maintained. Average Annual Attendance: 95,000
Collections: †African Art; Washington Allston Trust Collection; †Virgil Barker Collection of 19th & 20th Century American Art; Alfred I Barton Collection of Southwestern American Indian Textiles; †Decorative Arts; Esso Collection of Latin American Art; Samuel H Kress Collection of Renaissance and Baroque Art; Samuel K Lothrop Collection of Guatemalan Textiles; †Oriental Art; †Pre-Columbian Peruvian Arts
Exhibitions: (1983-84) Max Ernst: Books & Graphic Work; Larry Rivers Performing for the Family; Splendors of the Sohites; Goya's Disasters of War; Pat Steir Paintings; Edward Weston Photographs; Drawings & Watercolors by John Singer Sargent; Paul Sample: Ivy League Regionalist; Miami Collects: Asian Art; Alan Shields; Liebermann, Slerogt & Corinth; Master Drawings from the Museum of Art; Rhode Island School of Design; Gold of El Dorado; Futurism & Photography; Charlotte: Life or Theater?

Publications: Exhibition catalogs; newsletter, bimonthly
Activities: Classes for children; docent training; lectures open to public, 12 vis lectr per yr; concerts; gallery talks; individual paintings & original objects of art lent to other museums; museum shop sells books, original art, cards
L Reference Library, 1301 Hanford Dr, 33146. *Librn* Lucile Ball; *Librn* Zan Gay
For reference only
Library Holdings: Vols 5000; Per subs 1500; AV — Slides; Other — Exhibition catalogs
Special Subjects: Art History
Exhibitions: Dennis Oppenheim; Goya Graphics; Innovative Furniture; Shaker Furniture, textiles and inspired drawings; Graphic Works of Odilon Redon; Toulouse-Lautrec posters; Utagawa Kuniyoshi-Printmaker
Publications: Newsletter, bi-monthly
Activities: Classes for children; docent training; lectures open to public, 6 vis lectr per year; concerts; gallery talks; tours

DAYTONA BEACH

M MUSEUM OF ARTS AND SCIENCES, Cuban Museum, Planetarium, 1040 Museum Blvd, 32014. Tel 904-255-0285. *Dir* Gary Russell Libby
Open Tues - Fri 9 AM - 4 PM, Sat Noon - 5 PM, cl Mon, Sun & national holidays. Admis $2, museum members free. Estab 1955 to offer both educational and cultural services to the public. Large hexagonal main exhibition galleries, hall gallery and lobby gallery are maintained. Average Annual Attendance: 100,000. Mem: 6000; dues family $35; annual meeting Nov
Income: $400,000 (financed by endowment, membership, city and county appropriations and donations)
Collections: Aboriginal art including Florida Indian; American Illustration: Norman Rockwell; Cuban Collection; decorative arts including silver and furniture; Florida Contemporary Collection
Exhibitions: Great American Illustrations; Indian Cultures Exhibit; Masterpieces of Modern Art; Rockwell's America
Publications: Catalogs, monthly; magazine, quarterly
Activities: Classes for adults and children; docent training; lect open to public, 10 vis lectr per year; gallery talks; concerts; tours; competitions with awards; scholarships; exten dept serving area schools; individual paintings and original objects of art lent to other museums and educational institutions; lending collection contains books, nature artifacts, original art works, original prints, paintings and sculpture; traveling exhibitions organized and circulated; museum shop sells books, magazines, original art, reproductions & prints
L Library, 1040 Museum Blvd, 32014. *Librn* Marge Segerson
Open to members and school children; reference library
Library Holdings: Vols 10,000; Per subs 10; AV — Slides, v-tapes; Other — Clipping files, exhibition catalogs, manuscripts, photographs
Collections: Cuban: Jose Marti Library

DE LAND

M STETSON UNIVERSITY, Art Gallery, 32720. Tel 904-734-4121, Ext 208. *Dir* Fred Messersmith
Open Mon - Fri 9 AM - 4:30 PM. No admis fee. Estab 1964 as an educational gallery to augment studio teaching program. There is a large main gallery, 44 x 55 ft, with a lobby area 22 x 44 ft. Average Annual Attendance: 5000
Income: University art budget
Purchases: $1000
Collections: 20th Century American Prints, Oils, Watercolors
Exhibitions: (1983) American Watercolor Traveling Show; various regional artists exhibitions
Publications: Exhibition announcements, monthly
Activities: Lect open to public, 3 vis lectr per year, gallery talks; competitions

DELRAY BEACH

M PALM BEACH COUNTY PARKS AND RECREATION DEPARTMENT, Morikami Museum of Japanese Culture, 4000 Morikami Park Rd, 33446. Tel 305-499-0631. *Pres* Doris M Love; *VPres* Mrs Nicholas Gaglio; *Secy* Michael Botos; *Cur* Larry Rosensweig; *Asst Cur* Thomas Gregersen
Open Tues - Sun 10 AM - 5 PM. No admis fee; donations accepted. Estab 1977 to preserve and interpret Japanese culture and Japanese-American culture. Five small galleries in Japanese style building. Average Annual Attendance: 50,000. Mem: 400; dues $20; annual meeting March
Income: $100,000 (financed by membership and county appropriation)
Purchases: $9000
Collections: †Japanese folk arts (ceramics, dolls, tools, baskets, home furnishings); Japanese art (paintings, prints, textiles)
Exhibitions: The Soul of a Tree: Handmade Furniture by George Nakashima; Visit to a Japanese Discount Department Store; Manga Miscellany; Contemporary Japanese Ink Painting and Calligraphy; Folk Toys of Japan; Japanese Performing Arts Posters; Animal World of Japanese Art Color and Pattern: Stencil-dyed Fabrics by Eisha Nakano; Ghosts, Goblins and Gods; Luck 0' The Japanese; Animal World of Japanese Art
Publications: Newsletter, quarterly; Calendar bi-monthly; Exhibition catalogs 1-2 annually
Activities: Classes for adults and children; docent training; lect open to the public, 3-5 vis lectr per yr; concerts; tours; Lending collection contains books, film strips, phonorecords & photographs; book traveling exhibitions biannually; originate traveling exhibitions; museum shop sells books, reproductions, Japanese clothing, folk toys, original art, prints
L Donald B Gordon Memorial Library,* Morikami Museum, 33446. Tel 305-499-0631. *Librn* Tobie Heller
Open by appointment. Estab 1977 to provide printed and recorded materials on Japan
Purchases: $600
Library Holdings: Vols 450; Per subs 10; AV — Fs, rec, slides, v-tapes; Other — Clipping files, exhibition catalogs
Special Subjects: Japan, Japanese-Americans
Collections: Memorabilia of George S Morikami

FORT LAUDERDALE

L **ART INSTITUTE OF FORT LAUDERDALE,*** 3000 East Las Olas Blvd,
33316. Tel 305-463-3000. *Personnel* Brian McKinney
Open daily 7:45 AM - 5:15 PM. Estab 1973 as a technical library for the applied
and fine arts
Purchases: $8000
Library Holdings: Vols 500; Per subs 16; AV — A-tapes, cassettes, fs, motion
pictures, slides, v-tapes; Other — Clipping files, memorabilia, pamphlets, prints,
reproductions

M **FORT LAUDERDALE MUSEUM OF THE ARTS,** 426 E Las Olas Blvd,
33301. Tel 305-463-5184. *Dir* George S Bolge
Open Tues - Sat 10 AM - 4:30 PM, Sun Noon - 5 PM, cl Mon & national
holidays. Admis non-members $1, sr citizens $.75, student with identification
card $.50, no charge for members and children under 12. Estab 1958 to bring art
to the community and provide cultural facilities and programs. Library, reading
room, exhibit space and classrooms are maintained. Average Annual Attendance:
14,000. Mem: 2500; dues corporate $1000, patron $500, sustaining $100, family
$35, individual $20
Collections: American & European paintings, sculpture & graphics from late 19th
century - present; Pre-Columbian & historic American Indian ceramics, basketry
& stone artifacts; West African tribal sculpture; Golda & Meyer B Marks Cobra
Art Collection
Exhibitions: Changing monthly exhibitions
Publications: Annual Report; Bulletin, quarterly; Calendar of Events, monthly;
Exhibition Catalogs
Activities: Classes for adults and children; docent training; slide lecture program
in schools by request; lect; gallery talks; tours; films; competitions; individual
paintings and original objects of art lent to other museums; sales shop
L **Library,** 426 E Las Olas Blvd, 33301. *Librn* Ann Callan
Founded 1958. Staff and members only
Library Holdings: Vols 1670; Per subs 8; AV — Slides

FORT MYERS

M **EDISON COMMUNITY COLLEGE,** Gallery of Fine Art, College Parkway,
33907. Tel 813-489-9298. *Head Dept* Dr James Cain; *Dir* Jay Williams; *Registrar*
Dorothy Causey
Open Tues, Wed, Fri 10 AM - 4 PM, Thurs 10 AM - 4 PM, 5 - 9 PM. No admis
fee. Estab 1979. Main gallery 3000 sq ft designed with assistance of the
Smithsonian for high security; adjunct auditorium gallery. Average Annual
Attendance: 15,000. Mem: 400; annual dues $10
Income: Financed by endowment and state appropriation
Collections: Pre-Columbian
Exhibitions: (1982) Robert Rauschenberg; Art in the Schools; Images 82;
Photographs from the National Portrait Gallery; (IBM) Leonardo da Vinci; Jef
Whipple; Educator as Artist; Florida Craftsmen; 30 Florida Women Artists; 50
National Women in Art; Filaments of the Imagination; St Petersburg Museum
Photo Collection; Tony Eitharong; The Muse & the Marketplace; (1983)
Lichtenstein; African Sculpture; Hiram Williams Retrospective; Rubens & the
Flemish Baroque; Rauschenberg; American Drawings VI; Kathe Kollwitz; Art in
the Schools; Images 83; Bogdanowitsch and Page; History of the Movie Poster &
Animals in the Movies; Laura Wortzel; Photographs of Jewish Life Around the
World; (1984) Jamaican Art; End of the Road; Florida Artist Group Statewide
Competition; World Print IV; John Briggs; Marcel Duchamp; Edison Printshop;
Gordon and Lenny Bruno; Images 84; Images of Old Age in America;
Contemporary Dutch Prints
Activities: Classes for adults and children; docent training; lectures open to
public, 2-4 visiting lecturers per year; gallery talks; tours; competitions with
awards

GAINESVILLE

UNIVERSITY OF FLORIDA

M **University Gallery,** 32611. Tel 904-392-0201. *Dir* Roy C Craven Jr; *Secy*
Marjorie Z Burdick
Open Mon - Fri 9 AM - 5 PM, Sun 1 - 5 PM, cl Sat and holidays. No admis fee.
Estab 1965 as an arts exhibition gallery, open 11 months of the year, showing
monthly exhibitions with contemporary and historical content. Gallery located in
independent building with small lecture hall, limited access and completely
secure with temperature and humidity control, carpet covered walls and
adjustable track lighting; display area is in excess of 3000 sq ft. Average Annual
Attendance: 40,000. Mem: 200; dues professional $100 and up, family $20,
individual $10; annual meeting May
Income: $70,000 (financed by state appropriation and community memberships)
Purchases: $2000
Collections: †European and American prints, paintings and photographs;
†Oriental (India) miniatures and sculptures; †Pre-Columbian and Latin American
art (also folk art)
Exhibitions: Changing monthly exhibitions; Annual University of Florida Art
Faculty (January)
Publications: Exhibition catalogs; periodic bulletins
Activities: Docent training; lect open to public; exten dept serving area schools;
lending collection contains cassetts, original art works, photographs and slides;
traveling exhibitions organized and circulated
L **Architecture and Fine Arts Library,** 32611
Library Holdings: Vols 52,000; Per subs 194; Micro — Fiche, reels; Other —
Clipping files, exhibition catalogs
Special Subjects: Architecture, Art Education

HOLLYWOOD

M **HOLLYWOOD ART MUSEUM,*** 2015 Hollywood Blvd, 33020. Tel 305-927-
6455. *Dir* Herbert Tulk
Open Sept - June Mon - Fri 10 AM - 4 PM, Sat 1 - 4 PM. No admis fee. Estab
1962. Mem: Dues $5-$20
Collections: African, Bakuba and Zaire contemporary sculpture and paintings
Exhibitions: Permanent and temporary exhibits
Publications: H.A.M., annual magazine
Activities: Classes for children; lectures; tours; films; gallery talks; art festivals;
artmobile

JACKSONVILLE

M **CUMMER GALLERY OF ART,** DeEtte Holden Cummer Museum Foundation,
829 Riverside Ave, 32204. Tel 904-356-6857. *Dir* Robert W Schlageter; *Asst to
Dir* L Vance Shrum
Open Tues - Fri 10 AM - 4 PM, Sat noon - 5 PM, Sun 2 - 5 PM, cl Mon and
national holidays. No admis fee. Estab 1961 as a general art museum, collecting
and exhibiting fine arts of all periods and cultures. Average Annual Attendance:
45,000
Income: $600,000
Purchases: $125,000
Collections: †European and American Painting, Sculpture, Graphic Arts,
Tapestries and Decorative Arts; Netsuke, Inro and Porcelains; Oriental
Collection of Jade, Ivory; Early Meissen Porcelain (largest in United States)
Publications: Collection handbooks; exhibition catalogs; yearbooks
Activities: Lectures; concerts; gallery tours; gift shop
L **Library,** 829 Riverside Ave, 32204. Tel 904-356-6857
Open for reference
Purchases: $2000
Library Holdings: Vols 4000; Per subs 16; AV — Slides 10,000; Other —
Exhibition catalogs
Special Subjects: German porcelain, Meissen

M **JACKSONVILLE ART MUSEUM,** 4160 Boulevard Center Dr, 32204. Tel 904-
398-8336. *Dir* Bruce H Dempsey; *Assoc Dir* John S Bunker
Open Tues, Wed & Fri 10 AM - 4 PM, Thurs 10 AM - 10 PM, Sat & Sun 1 - 5
PM, cl Mon, holidays and month of Aug. No admis fee. Estab 1947 as an art
center for the greater Jacksonville area. Average Annual Attendance: 100,000.
Mem: 1500; dues $20; annual meeting spring
Income: Financed by membership and city appropriation
Collections: Pre-Columbian Art; Oriental Porcelains and Ceramics; 20th Century
Paintings and Prints
Exhibitions: Nevelson: Sculpture & Graphics; Picasso Portraits; Realism and
Metaphor; Leon Berkowitz; Duane Hanson; Modern European Masters from the
Norton Collection; Japanese Robes from the Metropolitan; Paintings by Robert
Gordy; Contemporary Photography Exhibition; Currents: A New Mannerism;
Peter Voulkos: Recent Works; Joseph Raffael: New Directions, Recent Works
Publications: Calendar, monthly; exhibition catalogues
Activities: Classes for adults and children; docent training; art enrichment
program; dramatic programs; lectures open to the public, 10 vis lectr per yr;
concerts; gallery talks; tours; competitions; scholarships; book traveling
exhibitions; originate traveling exhibitions; museum shop sells books, magazines,
original art, reproductions, prints, jewelry & children's toys
L **Library,** 4160 Boulevard Center Dr, 32207
Open to teachers in Duval County schools
Library Holdings: Vols 200

M **JACKSONVILLE MUSEUM OF ARTS AND SCIENCES,*** 1025 Gulf Life
Dr, 32207. Tel 904-396-7062. *Dir* Doris L Whitmore; *Admis Asst* Sally Taylor;
Program Developer Michael Coffman; *Cur Coll* Nada Wineman
Open Mon - Fri 9 AM - 5 PM; Sat 11 AM - 5 PM; Sun 1 - 5 PM; cl Mon, Sept
and major holidays. Admis adults $2, children 4-18 $1. Estab 1941. Lobby and
three floors contain exhibit areas, classrooms, and studios. Average Annual
Attendance: 225,000. Mem: 825; dues vary
Income: Financed by membership, city appropriation, and grants
Exhibitions: Dolls; health; wildlife
Publications: Teacher's Guide, annually; brochures, bimonthly; annual report
Activities: Classes for adults and children; dramatic programs; docent training;
lect open to public; tours; Art in the Park; traveling exhibitions organized and
circulated; museum shop and sales shop selling books, prints, museum-oriented
items and toys for children
L **Library,*** 1025 Gulf Life Dr, 32207
Open to staff, docents and volunteers for reference

L **JACKSONVILLE PUBLIC LIBRARY,** Art and Music Dept, 122 North Ocean
St, 32201. Tel 904-633-6870. *Dir* James Nelson; *Art and Music Dept Librn* Jeff
Driggers
Open Mon - Fri 9 AM - 9 PM, Sat 9 AM - 6 PM. No admis fee. Estab 1905 to
serve the public by giving them free access to books, films, phonograph
recordings, pamphlets, periodicals, maps, plus informational services and free
programming. Open area on the mezzanine of the building serves as a display
area for local artists
Income: Financed by city appropriation
Library Holdings: Vols 35,000; color reproductions; AV — Motion pictures
2125, rec 15,000, slides 5100; Other — Framed reproductions, photographs 3000
Publications: Annual Report
Activities: Classes for adults; weekly film programs

KEY WEST

O **KEY WEST ART AND HISTORICAL SOCIETY,** S Roosevelt Blvd, 33040.
Tel 305-296-3913. *Pres* Jack Church; *VPres* Ida Barron; *VPres* Colin Jameson;
Recording Secy Sally Lewis; *Corresp Secy* Ruth Munder; *Exec Dir* Barbara
Hodgens
Open Mon - Sun 9:30 AM - 5 PM. Admis $2.50 adults, children 7 - 15 $.50,
active military free. Estab 1966. The gallery is located in a restored 1861 brick
fort; there are four galleries, all contiguous. These galleries have arched ceilings,
are air conditioned and have moveable track lighting. Average Annual
Attendance: 40,000. Mem: 1100; dues couple $30, individual $15, student $2;
annual meeting first Wed in April
Income: $55,000 (financed by membership)
Collections: Small collection
Publications: Martello
Activities: Classes for adults & children; lectures open to public; sales shop sells
books, magazines, original art, reproductions, prints
L **Library,** South Roosevelt Blvd, 33040
Open by appointment only. Founded 1949. There are approximately 250
hisotrical items, such as ledgers, property abstracts, books on history, and others
Library Holdings: Vols 250; Per subs 10

LAKELAND

M **FLORIDA SOUTHERN COLLEGE,** Melvin Art Gallery, Ludd M Spivey Fine
Arts & Humanities Bldg, 33802. Tel 813-683-5521, Ext 310 or 316. *Dir*
Downing Barnitz
Open Mon - Fri 1:30 - 4:30 PM. No admis fee. Estab 1971 as a teaching gallery.
Small gallery dedicated to Frank Lloyd Wright (architect for college) covers 200
running ft. Average Annual Attendance: 3000 - 5000
Collections: Brass Rubbings Collection in Ronx Library; Laymon Glass
Collection in Annie Pfeiffer Chapel; Permanent Collection in various offices and
buildings
Exhibitions: (1983) Louise Cherwak & Ken Westerman; Balcomb Greene; Jane
Gross & John Tilton; Gerd Winner; (1984) Art Faculty Show: Joyce Davis, Gale
Doak, Beth Ford, Kate Huckabee, John Orecht & Downing Barnitz; An Art
Dealer Collects: Avery, Austin, Florsheim, Soyer; Lakeland Art Guild Juried
Show; Florida Southern College annual student exhibition
Activities: Lectures open to public, 3 vis lectr per yr; gallery talks

M **POLK PUBLIC MUSEUM,*** 800 E Palmetto, 33801. Tel 813-688-7744. *Dir*
Ken Rollins; *Cur Exhib* Kurt Gibson; *Pres* Corinne Sikora; *Secy* Laura Boatman;
Office Mgr Joann Davis
Open Tues - Fri 9 AM - 5 PM, Sat 10 AM - 4 PM, Sun 1 - 4 PM. No admis fee.
Estab 1966 to bring changing exhibits of art and educational programs to the
community; to provide cultural enrichment for the county. Average Annual
Attendance: 25,000. Mem: 850; dues benefactor $1000, sponsor $500, sustaining
$100, patron $50, family $25, individual $15, teacher $10, sr citizen and student
$5
Income: Financed by membership, city of Lakeland, Polk County School Board,
grants, fund drive
Purchases: $200
Collections: Barnum Collection; Ellis Verink Photographs; 14th - 19th Century
European ceramics; Pre-Columbian Collection; assorted decorative arts;
contemporary paintings featuring Florida artists
Exhibitions: Museum Graphics/American Pop Art; 500 Years of Wine in the
Arts; Daniel Putnam Brinley: American Impressionist; Christmas in a Doll's
House; Robert Gelinas/Masters of Photography; Creative Youth Exhibit; Edward
Hopper: The Early Years; Klevins-Wishnatzki; Audubon/Landscapes
Activities: Classes for adults and children; workshops; dramatic programs;
Suitcase Museum Program; docent training; lectures open to public; tours;
concerts
L **Library,*** 800 E Palmetto, 33801. Tel 813-688-7743. *Dir* Nancy H Thornberry;
Librn Marjorie Givins
Open Mon - Fri 10 AM - 5 PM, Sat 10 AM - 4 PM, Sun 1 - 4 PM. Estab 1970
as a reference library for Polk County residents
Library Holdings: Vols 500; Per subs 4; Other — Photographs, prints

MAITLAND

O **MAITLAND ART CENTER,** 231 W Packwood Ave, 32751. Tel 305-645-2181.
Dir James G Shepp
Open Tues - Fri 10 AM - 4 PM, Sat & Sun 1 - 4 PM, cl Mon. No admis fee.
Estab 1937 to promote exploration and education in the visual arts and
contemporary crafts; listed in National Register of Historic Places. Gallery is
maintained. Average Annual Attendance: 7500. Mem: 600; dues $15 - $1000;
annual meeting May
Income: Financed by membership, city and state appropriations, donations,
special events, endowment
Collections: Architectural work including 9-acre compound and memorial chapel
designed by Smith; graphics-paintings & sculptures of Andre Smith
Exhibitions: (1983) Robert E Singleton Retrospective; Linda Rose, fiber; Tim
Ludwig, ceramics; James Cook, ceramics; Raymond Decicco, paintings & prints;
members annual juried exhibition; Robert E Calvo, sculpture; David Fithian,
painting; photographs: Karen Albritton, Cheryl Bogdanowitsch, Anna Tomczak &
Jerry Uelsmann; Karen Smith Carter, sculpture
Publications: Imagination, bimonthly
Activities: Classes for adults and children; art training classes; docent training;
lectures open to public, 2 - 3 vis lectrs per year; gallery talks; tours; concerts;
competitions with awards; scholarships; individual paintings & original objects of
art lent; lending collection contains 50 original art works, 50 original prints, 50
paintings; book traveling exhibitions, 1 - 2 per yr; book shop
L **Library,** 231 W Packwood Ave, 32751
Open for reference
Library Holdings: Vols 430

MELBOURNE

M **BREVARD ART CENTER AND MUSEUM, INC,** 1510 Highland Ave, PO
Box EG 782, 32935. Tel 305-254-7782. *Pres* Laurie Brown; *VPres* Lee Saltzman;
Secy Philip Nohrr; *Exec Dir* Robert A Gabriel; *Dir Education* Burton B Van
Scoy; *Office Mgr* Barbara Marfuta
Open Tues - Fri 10 AM - 5 PM, Sat 10 AM - 4 PM, Sun Noon - 4 PM, cl Mon.
No admis fee. Estab 1978 to exhibit art for the education, information, and
enjoyment of the public. One story building with three galleries with
approximately 3000 sq ft of exhibition space for changing exhibits; a please touch
gallery for the blind. Average Annual Attendance: 30,000. Mem: 1500; dues
individual $20, family $35, patron $100 and up; annual meeting third Tues in
May
Income: $200,000 (financed by membership, city & county appropriation,
corporate gifts & grants)
Purchases: $1500
Collections: †Contemporary Regional Artists; Pre-Columbian Art
Exhibitions: (1982) 2000 Year of Oriental art
Publications: Bi-monthly newsletter; calendar for members
Activities: Classes for adults and children; docent training; lectures open to the
public, 4 vis lectr per yr; concerts; gallery talks; tours; competitions with awards;
book traveling exhibitions, 6-8 per yr; museum shop sells books, magazines,
original art, reproductions prints

MIAMI

THE AMERICAN FEDERATION OF ARTS
For further information, see National and Regional Organizations

M **MIAMI-DADE COMMUNITY COLLEGE,** South Campus, Art Gallery, 11011
SW 104th St, 33176. Tel 305-596-1281. *Dir Cur* Karen Valdes
Open Mon - Fri 8 AM - 4 PM. No admis fee. Estab 1970 as a teaching
laboratory and public service
Income: Financed by state appropriation
Purchases: $250,000
Collections: Contemporary American paintings, photographs, prints, sculpture
includes: Beal, Boice, Bolotowsky, Christo, Fine, Hepworth, Hockney, Judd,
Oldenburg, Pearlstein, Henry
Exhibitions: Tom Doyle; Max Cole; Ed McGowin; Fernando Garcia; David
Stoltz; Michael Flich; Lynn Gelfman; Vita Acconci; Jene Highstein; Jim Jacobs
Publications: Bi-annual catalog
Activities: Lectures open to public, 4 - 6 vis lectrs per year; gallery talks;
individual paintings and original objects of art lent; lending collection contains
original art works, original prints, paintings, photographs, sculpture; traveling
exhibitions organized and circulated

L **MIAMI-DADE PUBLIC LIBRARY,** One Biscayne Blvd, 33132. Tel 305-579-
5001. *Dir* Edward F Sintz; *Asst Dir* Mrs Micki Carden; *Supv Processing Center*
Lilliam Conesa; *Supv Traveling Libraries* Carol Gawron; *Public Relations Coordr*
Margarita Cano; *Supv Branches* Eleanor McLaughlin; *Coordr Work with
Children and Young Adults* Anne Boegen; *Art Librn* Barbara Young; *Artmobile
Librn* Loretta Waldman
Open Mon - Fri 9 AM - 6 PM, Sat 9 AM - 6 PM, Sun 1 - 5 PM. Estab 1947 to
provide the informational, educational and recreational needs of the community.
Gallery maintained
Income: Financed by special millage
Library Holdings: Micro — Fiche, reels; AV — Motion pictures, rec; Other —
Clipping files, exhibition catalogs, framed reproductions, original art works,
photographs, reproductions, sculpture
Special Subjects: Latin American Art, Black American Art
Collections: Black American Original Graphics; Latin American Original
Graphics; Oriental Collection of Original Graphics
Exhibitions: (1982) Sam Gilliam, Installation; Christo Surrounded Islands Project
for Biscayne Bay; Preliminary Drawings & Model
Publications: Exhibition catalogs
Activities: Lectures open to public; concerts; gallery talks; tours; exten dept;
artmobile; individual paintings & original objects of art lent; book traveling
exhibitions; originate traveling exhibitions

C **SOUTHEAST BANKING CORPORATION,*** 1699 Coral Way, 33145. Tel
305-285-3022. *Art Dir* Jean H Johnson; *Asst Art Dir* Lisa Sheres
Estab 1974 to benefit and provide an attractive working environment for
employees and bank customers; belief that support of the arts is one of the
corporation's links to the community. Collection displayed throughout more than
100 banks in Florida
Income: Financed by corporate funds
Collections: Mostly contemporary pieces consisting of graphics, oils, sculpture
and works on paper (1600 pieces)
Exhibitions: Traveling show of three different photo portfolios to various banks
in the Southeast system; portfolios owned by the corporation
Activities: In-house art department works closely with the local visual and
performing art organizations in the community; originates traveling exhibitions to
bank center throughout Florida

M **VIZCAYA MUSEUM AND GARDENS,** 3251 S Miami Ave, 33129. Tel 305-
579-4626. *Dir* Carl J Weinhardt Jr; *Cur Education* Zelie Tourais; *Cur Coll* Doris
B Littlefield; *Asst Cur* David Hertzberg; *Chief Conservator* Emilio Cianfoni;
Conservator Barbara Ward
Open daily 9:30 AM - 5 PM, cl Christmas. Admis house and gardens $5, group
$3.50, garden only $3.50, group $.50, annual ticket $10, Sound & Light (Sunday
evenings) $5, group, senior citizens & children $3.50. Estab 1952 to increase the
general public's appreciation of the European decorative arts, architecture and
landscape design through lectures and visits conducted by trained volunteer
guides. Vizcaya is a house museum with a major collection of European
decorative arts and elaborate formal gardens. The Villa, formerly the home of
James Deering, was completed in 1916 and contains approximately 70 rooms.

Upper Gallery, changing special exhibitions. Average Annual Attendance: 225,000. Mem: 1500; dues $25 and up; annual meeting third Wed in April
Income: $1,039,725 (financed by admission fees)
Collections: Italian and French Furniture of the 16th - 18th and Early 19th Centuries; Notable Specialized Collections of Carpets, Tapestries, Roman Antiques and Bronze Mortars
Exhibitions: Four - six changing annually
Publications: Vizcayan Newsletter, quarterly
Activities: Classes for children; docent training; lectures open to the public; concerts; tours; individual paintings and original objects of art lent to accredited museums; museum shop sells books, magazines, original art, reproductions, prints and slides
L **Library,** 3251 S Miami Ave, 33129. Tel 305-579-2808. *Vol Librn* Mrs A Miller
Open to museums volunteers and students of the decorative arts for reference only
Income: Financed by donations
Library Holdings: Vols 1570; Per subs 8; archival material; AV — Cassettes, Kodachromes, slides; Other — Exhibition catalogs, memorabilia, photographs
Special Subjects: Decorative Arts, Furniture, Interior Design
Collections: Original blueprints of Vizcaya 1914-1916; slide collection for reference and teaching

MIAMI BEACH

M **BASS MUSEUM OF ART,** 2100 Collins Ave (Mailing add: 2121 Park Ave, 33139). Tel 305-673-7530. *Dir* Diane W Camber; *Chmn of the Bd* Rob W Parkins
Open Tues - Sat 10 AM - 5 PM, Sun 1 - 5 PM. Admis $1, free on Tues. Estab 1963 to provide a pleasant atmosphere for the viewing of the various art and artifacts that have been donated to the city; all of the art in the museum was donated by Mr John Bass. The museum is a two-story building comprising of seven gallery rooms. Average Annual Attendance: 30,000
Income: $350,000 (financed by city and grants from state and county)
Purchases: Sculpture garden
Collections: Permanent collection of church vestments, Old Master paintings, Renaissance sculpture, Baroque sculpture, Oriental bronzes, ecclesiastical artifacts
Exhibitions: (1983-84) Concepts in Construction 1910-1980; American Women Artists: Impressionists and Post Impressionists; Art Deco USA and Project Skyline; The Precious Legacy; Mid Century Modern: The Decorative Arts (1940-60); Frank Lloyd Wright Drawings and Prints and the Posters of Alfonso Iannelli; permanent collection
Publications: Monthly newsletter; exhibition catalogues
Activities: Lectures open to public; concerts; films; individual and original objects of art lent to other museums; book traveling exhibitions; originate traveling exhibitions; sales shop selling photographs and postcards

L **MIAMI BEACH PUBLIC LIBRARY,** 2100 Collins Ave, 33139. Tel 305-673-7535. *Chief Librn* Phyllis A Gray
Open Mon & Wed 10 AM - 8 PM, Tues & Thurs - Sat 10 AM - 5:30 PM. Estab 1927 to serve the citizens of Miami Beach. Circ 350,000
Income: $850,000 (financed by city appropriation)
Purchases: $125,000
Library Holdings: Vols 190,000; Per subs 250; Micro — Reels; AV — Rec; Other — Clipping files, pamphlets

M **SAINT BERNARD FOUNDATION AND MONASTERY,** 16711 W Dixie Hwy, 33160. Tel 305-945-1462. *Exec Dir* Bruce E Bailey
Open Mon - Sat 10 AM - 5 PM, Sun Noon - 5 PM. Admis adults $3, sr citizens $2, children 7-12 $.75, under 6 free. A reconstruction of a monastery built in Segovia, Spain, in 1141, with original stones brought to the United States by William Randolph Hearst
Income: Financed by members and donations of visitors
Collections: Historic and Religious Material; paintings; sculpture
Activities: Tours; museum loan exhibitions; arts festivals; sales shop sells books, slides & religious objects

OCALA

M **CENTRAL FLORIDA COMMUNITY COLLEGE ART COLLECTION,*** 3001 SW College Rd, Box 1388, 32678. Tel 904-237-2111. *Pres* Henry Goodlett; *Gallery Dir* John Thursby
Open Mon - Fri 8 AM - 4:30 PM. No admis fee. Estab 1962 as a service to the community. Gallery is the lobby to the auditorium. Average Annual Attendance: 5000
Income: Financed by state appropriations
Collections: Contemporary Artists of Varied Media
Exhibitions: Changing monthly shows, with one show for the summer
Activities: Classes for adults; scholarships

ORLANDO

O **LOCH HAVEN ART CENTER, INC,** 2416 N Mills Ave, 32803. Tel 305-896-4231. *Dir* Marena Grant Morrisey; *Cur Education* Scottie Foss
Open Tues - Fri 10 AM - 5 PM, Sat Noon - 5 PM, Sun 2 - 5 PM. Generally no admis fee. Estab 1926 to encourage the awareness of and participation in the visual arts. Accredited by the American Association of Museums. Average Annual Attendance: 200,000. Mem: 2000; dues vary; annual meeting in May
Income: Financed by membership, city appropriation and grants
Collections: †20th century American, Pre-Columbian and African art
Exhibitions: Major exhibitions in various media and styles
Publications: Magazine, quarterly; various catalogs
Activities: Classes for adults and children; docent training; workshop; lect open to public, 3 - 5 vis lectr per year; concerts; gallery talks; tours; film series; visiting artists; exten dept serving central Florida; individual paintings and original objects of art lent to organizations within central Florida; lending collection contains original prints; originate traveling exhibitions; museum and sales shop sells books, cards, original art, prints and reproductions

L **Library,** 2416 N Mills Ave, 32803
Library Holdings: Vols 1800; Per subs 5; Other — Clipping files, exhibition catalogs

O **PINE CASTLE CENTER OF THE ARTS, INC,** 5903 Randolph St, 32809. Tel 305-855-7461. *Executive Dir* Suzanne Nicola; *Music Dir* Vickie Schultz; *Secy* Pauline O Pitter
Open 9 AM - 5 PM. No admis fee. Estab 1965 as a non-profit community cultural center which provides programs in visual arts, folk crafts, local history, music and drama, and sponsors special projects for handicapped and senior citizens. One room 15 x 15 ft in main building; 85 yr old cracker farm house. Average Annual Attendance: 19,000. Mem: Annual meeting in March
Income: Financed by membership, private foundation, state grants & United Arts Fund
Collections: Oral histories of area Old-timers, along with photographs, memorabilia and antiques
Exhibitions: Members' Exhibition
Publications: Pioneer Days Annual Historical Magazine; quarterly newsletter
Activities: Classes for adults and children; dramatic programs; lect open to the public, 2 vis lectr per yr; Folk Art Events; concerts

ORMOND BEACH

M **TOMOKA STATE PARK MUSEUM,** N Beach St, 32074. Tel 904-677-9463. *Dir* Ney C Landrum; *Museum Guide* Donna M Sibley
Open Wed - Sun 9 AM - 5 PM; cl Mon & Tues. No admis. Estab 1967
Income: Financed by state appropriation
Collections: Indian artifacts; Fred Dana Marsh, paintings & sculptures
Exhibitions: Florida geology; Florida history; Indian artifacts; wildlife
Publications: Richard Oswald: Tomoka State Park's Hero of the Revolution (brochure)
Activities: Tours

PALM BEACH

M **HENRY MORRISON FLAGLER MUSEUM,** Whitehall Way, Box 969, 33480. Tel 305-655-2833. *Pres & Trustee* George G Matthews; *Executive Dir* Charles B Simmons; *Cur* Phyllis Guy
Open Tues - Sat 10 AM - 5 PM, Sun Noon - 5 PM, cl Mon. Admis adults $3, children 6 - 12 $1. Estab 1960 for preservation and interpretation of the Whitehall mansion, the 1901 residence built for Standard Oil partner and pioneer developer of Florida's east coast, Henry Morrison Flagler. Fifty room historic house with restored rooms and special collections, plus addition used for Historical Society, special events and exhibitions. Average Annual Attendance: 110,000. Mem: 1105; dues $25; annual meeting Fri preceding first Sat in Feb
Income: Financed by endowment, membership and admissions
Collections: Original family furnishings, costumes; ceramics, lace, paintings and silver
Exhibitions: Various temporary exhibits
Publications: The Henry Morrison Flagler Museum
Activities: Docent training; lect open to public, 2 - 5 vis lectr per year; gallery talks; tours; individual paintings and original objects of art lent by request; museum shop sells books, slides and postcards
L **Library,** Whitehall Way, Box 969, 33480
For reference and by appointment only, in conjunction with Historical Society
Collections: Archives

O **SOCIETY OF THE FOUR ARTS,** Four Arts Plaza, 33480. Tel 305-655-7226. *Pres* Walter S Gubelmann; *VPres* Mrs James A dePeyster; *VPres* Philip Hulitar; *VPres* Mrs Robert A Magowan; *VPres* Earl E T Smith; *Secy-Treas* LeBaron S Willard Sr; *Dir* James M Brown; *Deputy Dir* Gabrielle Summerville
Open Dec to mid-April Mon - Sat 10 AM - 5 PM, Sun 2 - 5 PM. Admis to exhibition galleries free. Estab 1936 to encourage an appreciation of the arts by presentation of exhibitions, lectures, concerts, films and programs for young people and the maintenance of a fine library and gardens. Five galleries for exhibitions, separate general library, gardens and auditorium. Average Annual Attendance: 72,000 (galleries and library). Mem: 1500; dues life $5,000, sustaining $250, double $200, single $130; annual meeting third Fri in March
Income: Financed by endowment, membership, city appropriation toward maintenance of library and contributions
Collections: Small collection of approximately 20 works
Exhibitions: (1982-83) Paintings From the Royal Academy in London: Flowers of Three Centuries; (1983-84) 45th Annual Exhibition of Contemporary American Paintings; Selections from the Anschutz Collection, Masterpieces of the American West; Flowers of the Yalya: Yoruk Weavings of the Toros Mountains, handwoven crafts of one of the last nomadic tribes of southern Turkey; Odyssey: Mirror of the Mediterranean, photographs by Roloff Beny; Winterthur Miniature Rooms; Henry Moore: A New Dimension; Cecil Beaton: Fashion and Portraits
Publications: Calendar; Jan, Feb and March; Schedule of Events, annual
Activities: Programs for young people; lectures open to the public when space permits, otherwise limited to members, 13 vis lectr per year; concerts; films; competitions to artists resident in United States; juror selects about 90 paintings for inclusion in annual exhibition
L **Library,** Four Arts Plaza, 33480. Tel 305-655-2766. *Librn* Helen McKinney
Open Mon - Fri 10 AM - 5 PM, cl Sat May to Nov. Estab 1948. Circ 38,000
Income: Financed by endowment, membership and city appropriation
Library Holdings: Vols 28,777; Per subs 56
Collections: Addison Mizner Collection which consists of over 300 reference books and scrapbooks in Mizner's personal library
Activities: Library tours

PENSACOLA

O   HISTORIC PENSACOLA PRESERVATION BOARD, West Florida Museum of History, 205 E Zaragoza St, 32501. Tel 904-434-1042. *Dir* James W Moody Jr; *Chief Cur* Russell Belous; *Historian* Linda V Ellsworth
Open Mon - Fri 8 AM - 4:30 PM, Sat 10 AM - 4:30 PM, cl New Years, Thanksgiving, Christmas. No admis fee. Estab 1967 for collection, preservation, and interpretation of artifacts dealing with the history and culture of Pensacola and West Florida. Main gallery includes history of development of West Florida as well as area for temporary exhibits. Average Annual Attendance: 60,000
Income: Approx $400,000 (financed by city, county, and state appropriations, sales and rentals)
Collections: Costumes; decorative arts; local artists
Exhibitions: Galvez, The Unmentionables; Its A Dolls World; Artifacts of Christianity; Odds & Ends from the Museum Attic; Florida Basketry
Activities: Educ dept; docent training; sales shop selling books, reproductions and local crafts
L   Library, 200 E Zaragoza St, 32501
Open to the public for reference
Library Holdings: Vols 800; Per subs 15; AV — Slides; Other — Photographs
Special Subjects: Architecture, Decorative Arts, Historical Material, Regional history

M   PENSACOLA JUNIOR COLLEGE, Visual Arts Gallery, 1000 College Blvd, 32504. Tel 904-476-5410, Ext 2254. *Dir* Allan Peterson; *Secy* Nathalia White
Open Mon - Thurs 8 AM - 9 PM, Fri 8 AM - 3:30 PM, cl weekends. No admis fee. Average Annual Attendance: 20,000
Income: Financed by state appropriation
Collections: †Contemporary ceramics, †glass, †drawings, †paintings, †prints, †photographs, †sculpture
Exhibitions: The Glassmaker: Historic and Contemporary; Pensacola National Crafts Exhibition; Pensacola National Printmaking Exhibition; Pensacola National Watermedia Exhibition; New Orleans Sculpture Invitational; Realism: A Close Look; Kim Irwin & Lisa Williamson-Fabric Collage; Texas Sculpture Invitational
Publications: Catalog, brochure or poster for each exhibition
Activities: Lectures open to the public, 3 - 6 vis lectr per yr; workshops; gallery talks; competitions with awards given; scholarships offered for second year students; individual paintings and original objects of art lent to other museums and lending collection contains original art works; traveling exhibitions organized and circulated

M   PENSACOLA MUSEUM OF ART, 407 S Jefferson St, 32501. Tel 904-432-6247. *Dir* Mary H Takach
Open Tues - Sat 10 AM - 5 PM, cl Sun & Mon. No admis fee. Estab 1954 to further and disseminate art history and some studio instruction with regard to the general public and to increase knowledge and appreciation thereof. Museum is a historical building, old city jail built in 1908, and has 13,000 sq ft of exhibition area. Average Annual Attendance: 24,000. Mem: 850; dues $20 and up; annual meeting Oct
Income: Financed by membership
Collections: Contemporary collection
Exhibitions: Changing displays of permanent collection
Publications: Monthly newsletter
Activities: Studio classes for adults and children; docent training; art history lect open to public; film series; book traveling exhibitions; originate traveling exhibitions
L   Harry Thornton Library,* 407 S Jefferson St, 32501. Tel 904-432-6247
Open Tues - Sat 10 AM - 5 PM, Sun 1 - 4 PM. Estab 1968 to provide reference material for public and members
Income: Financed by membership, city appropriation and grants by state and federal government
Purchases: $250
Library Holdings: Vols 300; Per subs 10; AV — Cassettes, slides; Other — Exhibition catalogs
Collections: Complete set of E Benezit's Dictionaire des Peintres, Sculpteurs, Dessinateurs et Graveurs; Encyclopedia of World Art and other art references books
Publications: Exhibitions catalogs; Newsletter, 10 per year
Activities: Lect open to public, 5 visiting lectr per year; films; concerts; tours; competitions; purchase and category awards; fels

M   UNIVERSITY OF WEST FLORIDA, Art Gallery, 32504. Tel 904-474-2696. *Dir* Duncan E Stewart
Open Mon - Thurs 10 AM - 5 PM; Fri 10 AM - 1 PM; cl Sat & Sun. No admis fee. Estab 1970 to hold exhibitions which will relate to our role as a senior level university. Galleries includes a foyer gallery 10 x 40 ft, & a main gallery of 1500 sq ft. It is fully air-conditioned & has carpeted walls with full facilities for construction & display. Average Annual Attendance: 3000
Income: Financed by state appropriation
Collections: Photographs and prints by a number of traditional and contemporary artists
Activities: Lectures open to public, 3 vis lectr per year; gallery talks; tours; competitions with awards; films; scholarships; individual paintings & original objects of art lent to univ offices; book traveling exhibitions
L   Library, 32504
Library Holdings: Vols 8345; Per subs 176

M   T T WENTWORTH, JR MUSEUM, 8382 Palafox Highway, PO Box 806, 32594. Tel 909-438-3638. *Dir & Cur* T T Wentworth Jr; *Deputy Dir & Secy* T W Wentworth
Open Sat - Sun 2 - 6 PM. No admis fee. Estab 1957 to conserve historical items and make them available to the public; art sections to encourage art and exhibit local art work. Mem: Annual meeting Aug
Income: Financed by membership and founder's contributions
Collections: Works of local and some nationally famous artists; Indian artifacts; coins; porcelain
Exhibitions: Special yearly art exhibit of some distinguished local artist

M   EDNA HIBEL ART FOUNDATION, Hibel Museum of Art, 150 Royal Poinciana Plaza, PO Box 10607, 33480. Tel 305-833-6870. *Dir* Virginia Dieckman; *Asst Dir* Betty Sands; *Pres* Theodore Plotkin; *VPres* William Hibel
Open Tues - Sat 10 AM - 5 PM, Sun 1 - 5 PM. No admis fee. Estab 1977 to extend the appreciation on the art of Edna Hibel specifically & visual art in general. Average Annual Attendance: 12,000. Mem: 5000; dues $10; meeting Feb & July
Income: $80,000 (financed by city appropriation & museum store sales)
Purchases: $80,000
Collections: Craig Collection of Edna Hibel's Work; English & Italian 18th century furniture; ancient Chinese snuffbottles; 18th & 19th century paperweights; 19th & 20th century library art books
Exhibitions: Timeless Beauty; Peace Through Wisdom; The Aesthetic Roots of Edna Hibel
Publications: Edna Heibel Society Newsletter, 4 per yr; exhibition catalogs
Activities: Education dept; docent training; lectures open to public, 4 vis lectr per yr; concerts; exten dept serves Palm Beach County; individual paintings lent; originate traveling exhibitions; museum shop sells books, reproductions, prints & gift items

SAFETY HARBOR

M   SAFETY HARBOR MUSEUM OF HISTORY AND FINE ARTS, 329 S Bayshore Dr, 33572. Tel 813-461-6977. *Pres* J R Michael; *Dir* Dorothy Reynolds; *Secy* Sissy Bierman; *Treasurer* Mitzi Farrington; *Asst Neal Lube*
Open Wed, Thurs, Sat & Sun 1 - 4 PM. No admis fee. Estab 1977 to promote, encourage, maintain and operate a museum for the preservation of knowledge and appreciation of Florida's history; to display and interpret historical materials and allied fields. Average Annual Attendance: 10,100. Mem: 40; dues $10; annual meeting July
Income: $2000 (financed by membership and donations)
Collections: †Fossils; †dioramas, †Indian artifacts; †natural history exhibits
Exhibitions: (1983) Space Exhibit; Butterflies, Sharks; Sugar Mill
Activities: Classes for adults & children; docent; lectures open to public, 70 vis lectr per yr; gallery talks; tours; awards; individual paintings & original objects of art lent to city offices; originate traveling exhibitions

SAINT AUGUSTINE

O   HISTORIC SAINT AUGUSTINE PRESERVATION BOARD,* PO Box 1987, 32084. Tel 904-824-3355. *Dir* William R Adams
Open daily 9 AM - 5:15 PM, cl Christmas. Admis to six buildings adults $2.50, students $1.25, children under 6 free. Estab 1959
Collections: Spanish artifacts; fine and decorative arts; restored and reconstructed colonial buildings from the 18th and 19th centuries
Exhibitions: Permanent and temporary exhibitions
Publications: Brochures and booklets

M   LIGHTNER MUSEUM, 75 King St, Museum-City Hall Complex, PO Box 334, 32084. Tel 904-824-2874. *Dir* Robert W Harper III; *Cur* Ken John; *Registrar* Irene L Lawrie; *Chief Visitors Services* Lee Selby
Open 9 AM - 5 PM, cl Christmas. Admis adults $2, students $.75, children under 12 free when accompanied by adult. Estab 1948. Average Annual Attendance: 133,000
Collections: Art glass; clocks; cut glass; dolls; furniture; mechanical musical instruments; natural science wing; porcelains; stained glass
Activities: Classes for adults and children; dramatic programs; docent training; lectures open to public, 4 vis lectr per year; concerts; gallery talks; tours; individual paintings & original objects of art lent; book traveling exhibitions; sales shop sells books, reproductions, prints & dolls
L   Library, 32084. *Librn* Ruth Shugart
Library for reference only
Special Subjects: 19th Century Decorative Arts

O   SAINT AUGUSTINE ART ASSOCIATION GALLERY, 22 Marine St, 32084. Tel 904-824-2310. *Pres* Marshall Wolfe; *VPres* Enzo Torcoletti; *Secy* Betty Carr; *Gallery Dir* Cay Odell
Open Tues - Sat 11 AM - 3 PM, Sun 2 - 5 PM. Estab 1924, inc 1934 as a non-profit organization to further art appreciation in the community by exhibits and instruction. Average Annual Attendance: 8000. Mem: 425; dues $10 and up
Collections: Permanent collection of donated and purchased works
Exhibitions: Oct to June changing monthly
Activities: Classes; demonstrations; lectures; social events

SAINT AUGUSTINE HISTORICAL SOCIETY

M   Oldest House and Museums, 14 Saint Frances St, 32084. Tel 904-824-2872. *Exec Dir* Marcy-Jean Mattson; *Cur Exhibits* Valerie Jackson Bell; *Vol Coordr* Eddie Joyce Geyer; *Librn* Jacquelene Fretwell
Open Mon - Fri 9 AM - 5 PM; cl Christmas Day. Admis adults $1.50, students $.50. Estab 1883 to preserve the Spanish heritage of the United States through exhibits in historic museum with collection of furnishings appropriate to the periods in Saint Augustine history (1565 to date). The Oldest House was acquired in 1918; it is owned and operated by the Saint Augustine Historical Society; it has been designated a National Historic Landmark by the Department of the Interior and is listed in the national register of historic sites and places. Average Annual Attendance: 90,000. Mem: 500; dues $10; annual meeting Jan
Income: Financed by admissions
Collections: Archaeological material recovered from this area, both aboriginal and colonial; period furnishings: Spanish America (1565-1763 & 1783-1821); British (1763-1783); American (1821-present)
Exhibitions: (1984) Click: St Augustine Caught in the Camera's Eye; Military in St Augustine; Maritime History
Publications: El Escribano, annual; East Florida Gazette, quarterly; Imprints, quarterly
Activities: Classes for adults and children; docent training; lectures open to the public, 4 vis lectr per yr; original objects of art lent; museum shop sells books, reproductions, prints & slides

L **Library,** 271 Charlotte St, 32084. Tel 904-829-5512. *Mgr* J Carver Harris; *Library Dir* Jacqueline Bearden
Open Mon - Fri 9 AM - Noon and 1 - 5 PM; cl holidays. Research library
Income: Financed by endowment and admissions from Oldest House
Library Holdings: Vols 10,000; Per subs 40; original documents; Micro — Reels; AV — A-tapes, cassettes, Kodachromes, motion pictures, rec, slides; Other — Clipping files, manuscripts, memorabilia, original art works, pamphlets, photographs, prints, reproductions, sculpture
Special Subjects: Florida history (to 1821) with emphasis on early periods of Saint Augustine history to the present
Collections: Paintings of early artists and of early Saint Augustine; 200 linear feet of maps, photographs, documents and photostats of Spanish Archival Materials as touching directly on Saint Augustine's History during the early Spanish, British and American periods (1565 to present)
Publications: East Florida Gazette, quarterly; El Escribano, annually
Activities: Lect open to public, 4 vis lectr per year

SAINT PETERSBURG

M **SALVADOR DALI FOUNDATION MUSEUM,** 1000 Third St S, 33701. Tel 813-823-3767. *Foundation Pres* A Reynolds Morse; *Managing Dir* Stuart W Smith; *Cur* Joan Kropf; *Res Coordr* Jill Logan; *Volunteer Coordr* Sunny Schurr; *Pub Relations* Betsy Stalzer; *Bookstore Mgr* Maggie Smith
Open Tues, Wed, Fri & Sat 10 AM - 5 PM, Thurs 10 AM - 8 PM, Sun Noon - 5 PM, cl Mon. Admis $3. Estab 1971 to share the private Dali Collection of Mr and Mrs A Reynolds Morse with the public; formerly in Cleveland, Ohio, the museum re-opened March 7, 1982 in St Petersburg, Fla. Average Annual Attendance: 75,000
Income: Financed by private collector, State University System and donations
Collections: †93 oils and 5 large masterworks by Dali make up a retrospective of his work from 1914 to the present; numerous drawings and watercolors
Exhibitions: Important Dali Statements & Surrealist Documents; Women - Dali's View; Erotic Art by Dali; Homage to Gala; The Secret Life Drawings; Flor Dali; Dali & Halsman Photography; Dali's Surrealist Fruits and Flowers (graphic show); Hiram College Graphic Exhibit
Publications: Dali Adventure; Dali - A Panorama of His Art; Dali Draftmanship; Guide to Works by Dali in Public Museums; Introduction to Dali; Dali-Picasso; Poetic Homage to Gala-Dali; Dali Primer Dali's World of Symbols: Workbook for Children; Dali Newsletter; exhibition catalogues
Activities: Adult classes; docent training; lect open to public 2 per year; film series; gallery talks; tours; museum shop sells books, reproductions, prints, slides, postcards

L **Library,** 1000 Third St S, 33701. Tel 813-3767
Restricted use at present; contains 5000 references to Dali in books, periodicals and newspapers
Income: Financed privately by Salvador Dali Foundation
Purchases: $15,000-20,000
Library Holdings: Vols 5000; Per subs 20; Illustrated editions by Dali; AV — A-tapes, cassettes, Kodachromes 3000, motion pictures 10, slides, v-tapes; Other — Clipping files, exhibition catalogs, framed reproductions 1000, manuscripts, memorabilia, original art works 150, pamphlets, photographs, prints 750
Collections: Films and Tapes on or by Dali

M **MUSEUM OF FINE ARTS OF SAINT PETERSBURG, FLORIDA, INC,** 255 Beach Dr N, 33701. Tel 813-896-2667. *Dir* Michael Milkovich; *Asst Dir* Alan Du Bois; *Admin Asst* Bobbye Hoover; *Memberships* Diane Footlick; *Museum Shop* Mrs Edgar Andruss; *Registrar* Mrs Thomas C Laughlin
Open Tues - Sat 10 AM - 5 PM; Sun 1 - 5 PM; cl Mon. Admis by voluntary donation. Estab 1961 to increase and diffuse knowledge and appreciation of art; to collect and preserve objects of artistic interest; to provide facilities for research and to offer popular instruction and opportunities for esthetic enjoyment of art. Nine galleries of works including American and European painting, drawing, print, sculpture and photographs; Oriental sculpture; decorative arts; pre-Columbian art. Average Annual Attendance: 63,695. Mem: 3200; dues $20 and higher; annual meeting May
Income: $576,4000 (financed by endowment, membership, fund raising, city & state grants)
Collections: †Decorative arts; †drawings; †paintings; †photographs; †prints; †sculpture
Exhibitions: (1982) Transformations of the Roman Baroque; Exotic Kingdoms: China & Europe in the Eighteenth Century; Photographs by Arthur Rothstein; Robert Drapkin Collection of 19th Century Photographs; Berlin Porcelain; Florida Art Fellows, Part I & II; Steuben Glass: Elegance & Luxury; Leonardo Da Vinci; Surrealism; Contemporary Blown Glass by Southeastern Artists; The Print Transformed, from Durer to the Present; Fragonard & His Friends: Changing Ideals in Eighteenth Century Art; Pachner Landscapes; Murano Glass in the Twentieth Century; Wedgwood from Local Collections; Of Time & Place: American Figurative Art from the Corcoran Gallery; Judaica from Private Collections; selected recent acquisitions from the museums' photography collection; Upham Collection of Photographs; Selections from the Collection of the Alex Hillman Family Foundation; Later Japanese Painting; Picasso Aquatints
Publications: Mosaic, bi-monthly newsletter; Pharos, semi-annual scholarly magazine
Activities: Classes for adults and children; docent training; films; lectures; Brownbagger Special Lunch; concerts; videocassettes; 3 vis lectr per year; tours; individual paintings & original objects of art lent to other museums; lending collection contains color reproductions, films on art; originate traveling exhibitions; museum shop sells books, reproductions, prints, museum replicas, jewelry, pottery and crafts by local artisans

L **Art Reference Library,** 255 Beach Dr N, 33701. Tel 813-896-2667. *Coordr* Muriel S Kirk
Open Tues - Fri 10 AM - 5 PM; cl Mon; special arrangements for Sat or Sun hours. Estab 1962 as reference libr
Income: Financed by endowment, membership and city appropriation
Purchases: $4200
Library Holdings: Vols 9500; Per subs 30; AV — A-tapes, slides 20,000, v-tapes; Other — Exhibition catalogs, reproductions
Collections: †Photography
Publications: Mosaic, bi-monthly membership bulletin; Pharos, semi-annual
Activities: Classes for adults and children; lect open to the public, 6 vis lectr per year; concerts; gallery talks; exten dept serves public schools

SARASOTA

L **RINGLING SCHOOL OF ART LIBRARY,** 1111 27th St, 33580. Tel 813-351-4614. *Library Dir* Yvonne L Morse; *AV Librn* Allen Novak; *Library Technician* Patti Roberts
Open 8:30 AM - 4:30 PM, 7 - 9 PM. Estab 1932 to serve the curriculum needs of this school, Visual Art being the exclusive purpose of the school, therefore the library collection is built on that premise. Art gallery is maintained. Circ 22,100
Income: $35,000 (Financed by library association, parent institution & capital expense)
Purchases: $35,000
Library Holdings: Vols 10,000; Per subs 140; AV — Fs 24, slides 21,000; Other — Clipping files, exhibition catalogs, original art works, pamphlets, prints, reproductions, sculpture
Special Subjects: Art History, Graphic Design, Illustration, Interior Design, Fine Arts
Collections: Jackson Collection of Japanese Books and Prints; Simmens Collection of 17th, 18th and 19th Century Prints and Engraving (contains 500 portrait engravings of French Revolutionary characters) Cecil Duff-Stevens Collection of 17th and 18th Century Copper and Steel Engravings
Publications: The Compleat Library Handbook, bi-annual

O **SARASOTA ART ASSOCIATION,** 707 N Tamiami Trail, PO Box 2077, 33578. Tel 813-365-2032. *Pres* John G Patterson; *Gallery Dir* Virginia Klemmer
Open Oct - May, Mon - Fri 10 AM - 4 PM; Sat & Sun 1 - 4 PM. No admis fee. Estab 1926, inc 1940. Average Annual Attendance: 10,500. Mem: 936; dues $20; annual meeting March
Exhibitions: (1983-84) Members Gallery; Nostalgia - People, Places and Things; Realism and Impressionism; Members Gallery Christmas; Members All Media Gala Open; Arvida state of Florida all media juried; Salute to the Musical Arts Juried All Media; Circus - Circus Juried All Media; Annual Sarasota county schools art; members end of season
Publications: Bulletin, monthly; yearbook
Activities: Classes for adults & children; lectures open to the public, 5 - 6 vis lectr per yr; demonstrations; competitions with cash awards; gallery talks; museum shop sells books, original art, prints, crafts

L **Library,** Civic Center, 707 N Tamiami Trail, 33577
Open for art reference
Library Holdings: Vols 200

M **STATE ART MUSEUM OF FLORIDA,** John & Mable Ringling Museum of Art, 5401 Bayshore Rd, Box 1838, 33578. Tel 813-355-5101. *Dir* Richard S Carroll; *Assoc Dir & Admin* Mark Gotlob; *Assoc Dir Programs* John Daniels; *Cur Contemporary Art* Michael Auping; *Registrar* Elizabeth S Telford; *Cur Decorative Arts* Cynthia Duval; *Head Education & State Service* Nancy Glaser; *Chief Public Information* Robert L Ardren; *Comptroller* Gerald Boon
Open Mon - Fri 9 AM - 7 PM, Sat 9 AM - 5 PM, Sun 11 AM - 6 PM. Admis adults $4.50, children 6-12 $1.75, under 6 free. Estab 1946. Bequeathed to the State of Florida by John Ringling and operated by the state; built in Italian villa style around sculpture garden on 38 landscaped acres; original 18th century theater from Asolo, near Venice, in adjacent building; Ringling Residence and Ringling Museum of the Circus on grounds. Average Annual Attendance: 250, 000 paid combination, 700,000 free attendance and special events. Mem: 3000; dues benefactor $10,000, patron $5000, fellow $1000, friend $250, centennial $100, family $50, individual $30
Collections: Archaeology of Cyprus; Baroque pictures, especially those of Peter Paul Rubens; European painting, sculpture, drawings & prints from the 16th, 17th & 18th centuries; medals & 18th century decorative arts; developing collection of 19th & 20th century painting, sculpture, drawings & prints
Exhibitions: 500 Years of Decorative Arts from the Ringling Collections: 1350-1850; Common Ground: Five Artists in the Florida Landscape; The Art of India & Woven Gardens: The Persian Carpet; A Decade of Acquisitions: 1972-1982; John Chamberlain: Reliefs 1960-1983; Ancient Art From Cyprus in the Ringling Collection; Amish Quilts from the American Museum of Folk Art; The Photographs of Timothy O'Sullivan & Edward Weston; Marcel Duchamp; French Salon Paintings from Southern Collections
Publications: Calendar, monthly; Collection Catalogues; Exhibition Catalogues; Newsletter, quarterly; Program Schedule, annually
Activities: Education dept; docent training; state services;; lectures open to public and some for members only; concerts; gallery talks; tours; annual craft festival competition; cash awards;; extension dept serves the state; 1000 individual paintings and 1000 original objects of art lent to affiliates and other qualified museums nationaly and internationally on board approval; originate traveling exhibitions to affiliates; sales shop sells books, reproductions, prints and slides

L **Art Research Library,** 5401 Bayshore Rd, Box 1838, Sarasota, 33578. Tel 813-355-5101. *Librn* Lynell A Morr
Open Mon - Fri 9 AM - 4:30 PM. Reference only
Library Holdings: Vols 10,000; Per subs 70; Art Auction Catalogues, Rare Books; Other — Clipping files, exhibition catalogs, reproductions
Special Subjects: Art History, emblem books, iconography, Renaissance and Baroque art
Collections: European painting, sculpture, drawings & prints from the Renaissance to 20th century; Baroque paintings, especially those of Peter Paul Reubens; Archaeology of Cyprus, medals & decorative arts; developing collection of 19th & 20th century painting, sculpture, drawings & prints
Exhibitions: Pearlstein Paintings & Drawings; Audubon's Birds of Florida; Stephen Shore Photographs; Judy Pfaff: Installation, Collages & Drawings; Common Ground: Five Artists in the Florida Landscape; 500 Years of Decorative Arts 1350-1850; John Chamberlain Reliefs, 1960-1982; Ancient Art from Cyprus: The Ringling Collection; Marcel Duchamp

Publications: Monthly newsletter
Activities: Docent training; teacher workshops; resource material; lectures open to public; concerts; gallery talks; tours; exten dept serves state; originate traveling exhibitions to statewide sponsors, approx 250 yearly

STUART

M **HISTORICAL SOCIETY OF MARTIN COUNTY,** Elliot Museum, 825 NE Ocean Blvd, 33494. Tel 305-225-1961. *Pres* James R Waldie Jr; *VPres* David A Childs; *Secy* Jane E Dickerson; *Dir* Janet Hutchinson
Open daily 1 - 5 PM, including holidays. Admis adults $1.50, children $.50. Estab 1961. Average Annual Attendance: 20,000. Mem: 600; dues $10-$100; meetings in Jan, April, July & Oct
Income: Financed by endowment & members
Collections: Contemporary American artists (realistic) - Walter Brightwell, Cecilia Cardman, James Ernst, Diana Kan, Hui Chi Mau, Bruce Elliott Roberts, Courtland Roberts
Activities: Lectures open to public; concerts; artmobile; bookstore

TALLAHASSEE

M **FLORIDA STATE UNIVERSITY,** Art Gallery, Fine Arts Building, 32306. Tel 904-644-6836. *Dir* Allys Palladino-Craig; *Registrar* Susan Parks; *Preparator* Humberto Ramirez
Open Mon - Fri 10 AM - 4 PM; Sat - Sun 1 - 4 PM; cl school holidays. Estab 1950. Average Annual Attendance: 60,000
Income: Financed by state appropriations
Collections: Asian prints; Carter Collection of Peruvian Art; contemporary American graphics & paintings; European painting; Old Master Works on paper
Exhibitions: Permanent Collections; changing schedule of major art historical works & contemporary American art
Activities: Docent training; workshops; internships for graduate students; Lect; gallery talks; volunteer program
M **Four Arts Center,** Fine Arts Building, 32306. Tel 904-644-1554
Institute for contemporary Art-sponsored performances & events
Exhibitions: Contemporary regional artists; major national artists

M **LEMOYNE CENTER FOR THE VISUAL ARTS,** * 125 N Gadsden St, 32301. Tel 904-222-8800. *Artistic Dir* Judith M Stauffer; *Development Dir* Jo Parker Kaplan; *Business Mgr* Charlene Williams; *Pres* Nanette G Fischer
Open Tues - Sat 10 AM - 5 PM; Sun 2 - 5 PM; cl Mon. No admis fee. Estab 1964 as a non-profit organization to serve as gallery for contemporary, quality art; class center; sponsor the visual arts in Tallahassee; an educational institution in the broadest sense. Located in Meginnes-Munroe House, built c 1840; four main galleries and gallery shop. Average Annual Attendance: 7000. Mem: 800; dues $15 - $1000
Income: Financed by membership, sales, classes and fund raisers
Collections: Contemporary Florida Artists; William Watson Collection of Ceramics; Karl Zerbe Serigraphs
Publications: Newsletter, bi-monthly
Activities: Classes for adults and children; lect open to public, 4 vis lectr per year; gallery talks; tours; competitions; individual paintings and original objects of art lent to businesses and members; lending collection contains original art works, original prints; paintings and sculpture; sales shop sells original fine art, craft items and prints

M **TALLAHASSEE JUNIOR MUSEUM,** 3945 Museum Dr, 32304. Tel 904-576-1636. *Dir* Lane Green; *Asst Dir* Joel McEachin; *Education Coordr* John Modden; *Cur of Collections & Exhibitions* Gwendolyn Waldorf; *Animal Cur* Mike Jones; *Naturalist* Dana Bryan
Open Tues - Sat 9 AM - 5 PM; Sun 2 - 5 PM. Admis adults $2, children 4 - 18 $1; members free. Estab 1957 to educate children and adults about natural history, native wildlife, North Florida history, art and culture. Facilities include 1880's farm, historic buildings, exhibit and class buildings, 40 acres of nature trails, and animal habitats. Average Annual Attendance: 100,000. Mem: 2300; dues $10 - $100; annual meeting third Thurs in Jan
Income: $300,000 (financed by membership, fund raisers and county school board appropriations)
Collections: Decorative Arts; Figurines; Oriental Items; Pre-Columbian Florida Indian Pottery
Exhibitions: Changing exhibit on art, clothing, crafts, history, and science; permanent or semi-permanent (3 years) exhibits on local history and natural history
Publications: Guidebook Series; Newsletter, monthly; School Handbook
Activities: Classes for adults and children; lect open to public, 8-12 vis lectr per year; concerts; tours; original objects of art lent to local school groups, and to civic organizations occasionally; lending collection contains 150 boxed exhibits on art, culture, history and science; sales shop sells books, and mainly science and history objects
L **Library,** 3945 Museum Dr, 32304
Open to members
Library Holdings: Vols 500; Per subs 7
Collections: Ivan Gundrum Pre-Columbian Florida Indian Artifacts (reproductions) representing the Weeden Island culture 500 - 1500 AD

TAMPA

C **FIRST NATIONAL BANK OF FLORIDA,** * 111 Madison St, PO Box 1810, 33601. Tel 813-224-1427, 224-1111. *In Charge Art Coll* Art Wiggins
Open 8:30 AM - 5 PM. Estab 1973. Collection displayed on all floors of bank
Collections: Acrylic on canvas, aluminum sculpture, ceramic raku, collages (paper, Plexiglas and serigraph), lithographs, oils, silk screen, silk screen on mirrored Plexiglas and plastic, sculpture, serigraphs and wool tapestries
Activities: Tours; individual objects of art lent to Tampa Museum

M **TAMPA MUSEUM** (Formerly Tampa Bay Art Center), * 601 Doyle Carlton Dr, 33602. Tel 813-223-8130. *Dir* John H Nozynski; *Asst Dir* Genevieve Linnehan; *Preparator* Bob Hellier
Open Tues, Thurs & Fri 10 AM - 6 PM, Wed 10 AM - 9 PM, Sat 9 AM - 5 PM, Sun 1 - 5 PM, cl holidays. No admis fee. Estab 1979. Mem: 2000; dues benefactor $5000, sustainer $1000, business $300, sponsor $280, patron $125, family $25, individual $15, student & sr citizen $7.50
Income: Financed by membership, city and state appropriation and grants
Collections: C Paul Jennewein Collection of Sculpture; Pre-Columbian sculpture; 20th century paintings and prints
Publications: Annual Report, Exhibition catalogs; Newsletter, monthly
Activities: Classes for adults and children; workshops; docent training; lectures open to the public, 5 visiting lectr per year; concerts; gallery talks; tours; competitions with awards; book traveling exhibitions; originate traveling exhibitions; museum shop sells ceramics, original art, paintings, prints and reproductions
L **Library,** * 601 Doyle Carlton Drive, 33602
For reference only
Library Holdings: Vols 1000; Per subs 30; Micro — Fiche; AV — A-tapes, cassettes, fs, Kodachromes, slides; Other — Clipping files, exhibition catalogs 600, original art works, pamphlets, photographs, prints, sculpture

M **UNIVERSITY OF SOUTH FLORIDA,** Art Galleries, College of Fine Arts, 4202 E Fowler Ave, 33620. Tel 813-974-2375. *Dir* Margaret A Miller; *Asst Dir* Alexa A Favata; *Cur* Michelle S Juristo; *Exhibits Supv* Roy Trapp; *Galleries* Jane Ingolia; *Exhib Coordr* Jerry Bassett
Open Mon - Fri 10 AM - 5 PM; Sat 1 - 4 PM; cl Sun. No admis fee. Estab 1968 to provide visual art exhibitions covering a broad range of media, subject matter, time periods for the university community and general public. Fine Arts Gallery, Student Services Center, Teaching Gallery, Fine Arts Building, 110, Theatre Gallery, Theatre Building are all maintained. Average Annual Attendance: 55,000
Income: Financed by state appropriation and grants
Collections: African art, Pre-Columbian artifacts, folk and ethnic arts; †art bank collection of loan traveling exhibitions (approx 60 small package exhibitions) contemporary photography; †contemporary works on paper; painting, sculpture, ceramics
Exhibitions: (1983) Rafael Ferrer - Impassioned Rhythms; Wally Mason, ceramics; Cuts - Woodcut & Relief Prints; George Pappas: Recent Works; MFA thesis exhibitions; annual fine art auction; Precious Objects; (1984) Univ South Fla art faculty exhibition; Realism: Drawings & Watercolors; 23rd annual student art exhibition; Humanism: An Undercurrent; MFA thesis exhibitions; Jim Rosenquist: Recent Work
Publications: Exhibition catalogs; newsletter, twice a season
Activities: Lectures open to public, approx 12 vis lect per yr, some lectr for members only; gallery talks; tours; through Art Bank program original prints, paintings & records are lent to institutions, universities & arts organizations; book traveling exhibitions; traveling exhibitions organized and circulated
L **Library,** 4202 E Fowler Ave, 33620. *Librn* Mary Lou Harkness
Open to students and public
Special Subjects: Historical Material, contemporary
Collections: Rare art books

UNIVERSITY OF TAMPA
M **Henry B Plant Museum,** 401 W Kennedy Blvd, 33606. Tel 813-253-8861, Ext 400. *Dir* Emily Brownold; *Asst Dir* Susan Vasiloff
Open Tues - Sat 10 AM - 4 PM, cl holidays. No admis fee, donations $1. Estab 1933 in the old Tampa Bay Hotel built in 1891. This building is now on the register as a National Historic Landmark built by the railroad industrialist H B Plant
Income: Financed by city appropriation, University of Tampa & donations
Collections: Late Victorian furniture and objects d'art of same period; Venetian mirrors; wedgwood, Oriental porcelains
Exhibitions: Exhibits relating to 19th century
Publications: Member newsletter, quarterly
Activities: Classes for children; docent training; concerts; tours; book traveling exhibitions; museum shop sells books, reproductions, antique reproductions, jewelry, glassware & Victorian style toys
M **Lee Scarfone Gallery,** 410 W Kennedy Blvd, 33606. Tel 813-253-8861, Ext 217. *Pres* U T Richard Cheshire; *Dir* Dorothy Cowden
Open Mon - Fri 9 AM - 5 PM. No admis fee. Estab 1977 to exhibit works of art as an extension of the classroom and to utilize the space for public functions which would benefit from the artistic environment created by showing current trends of all art forms of artistic merit. Average Annual Attendance: 12,000. Mem: 75; donation dues $25-$100
Collections: Contemporary artists
Exhibitions: Three Man Show (Ellis, Arthur, McNerney); All Florida Art Competiton; Faculty & Student Exhibitons; King, Shauweker, Winsniewski; Pedro Perez; O V Shaffer; Southern Exposures; William Haney; Otto Neuman; William Pachner; William Walmsley; Kenneth Kersladke; Michael Minardi; Cheryl Goldsleger
Publications: Exhibiton brochures, 10 times a yr
Activities: Lectures open to public, 5 vis lectr per yr; gallery talks; sponsor All-Florida Exhibitions; awards

TEQUESTA

M **LIGHTHOUSE GALLERY,** * 373 Gallery Square N, Tequesta Dr, 33458. Tel 305-746-3101. *Pres* C D Norton; *Secy* Augusta Wells; *Exec Dir* E Faye Schrecengost
Open Tues - Sat 10 AM - 4 PM; cl Mon. No admis fee. Estab 1964 to create public interest in all forms of the fine arts. Mem: Dues $35 and up
Exhibitions: Temporary and Traveling Exhibitions
Publications: Calendar of Events, monthly
Activities: Classes for adults and children; lect; competitions
L **Library,** * 373 Gallery Square N, Tequesta Dr, 33458
Small library of art books and art magazines

VENICE

O FLORIDA ARTIST GROUP INC, 601 Apalachicola Rd, 33595. Tel 813-485-1150. *Pres* Anne Atz; *VPres* Dorothy Stewart; *Recording Secy* Margaret Kelly; *Second VPres* Mary Faulkner; *Treas* Beatric Rose
Estab 1949 for the stimulation of finer standards of the creative effort within the state of Florida. Mem: 200, qualification for mem by invitation based on artistic merit; dues $20; annual meeting April or May
Income: $4700 (financed by membership and donations)
Publications: Newsletter, 3 per year
Activities: Lectures and workshops open to members and public; competitions, one annual competition open to members only; Genievieve Hamel, Robert Carson, 2 Hilton Leech and Elden Rowland Memorial awards; originate traveling exhibitions

WEST PALM BEACH

M NORTON GALLERY AND SCHOOL OF ART, 1451 S Olive Ave, 33401. Tel 305-832-5194. *Dir* Richard A Madigan; *Pres* J Russell Duncan; *Asst Dir* Flanders Holland; *Treasurer* Paul Prosperi; *Cur* Bruce Weber; *Mem Secy* Theresa Hickman; *Pub Relations Dir* Sue Whitman; *Supt* C Phelps Merrell; *Registrar* Pamela Parry; *Cur Education* Richard Frank
Open Tues - Sat 10 AM - 5 PM; Sun 1 - 5 PM. Admis voluntary donation. The Norton Gallery of Art was founded in 1940, dedicated in 1941 for the education and enjoyment of the public; additions were made in 1946, 49, 52 and 66. Acquisitions and gifts are continually being made to the museum. Building and major collections were given by Ralph Hubbard Norton and Elizabeth Calhoun Norton. The Gallery, designed by the Palm Beach architects, Wyeth, King and Johnson, opened to the public in 1941, with an original collection of one hundred paintings. Mr Norton continued to acquire works of art for the museum until his death in 1953, when the remainder of his private collection was given to the museum. Sculptures are exhibited throughout the Gallery & in the patio garden. Average Annual Attendance: 100,000. Mem: 3500; dues family $50 & $35; annual meeting Apr
Income: Financed by endowment, membership, city appropriation, donations & special fund raising events
Collections: French Collection contains late 19th & early 20th century paintings including Impressionist & Post-Impressionist masterpieces; American holdings include works of art from 1900 to the present, Chinese collections contain archaic bronzes, archaic jades, Buddhist sculpture, jade carvings & ceramics
Exhibitions: (1983-84) Yasuo Kuniyoski: Painter-Photographer; The Sun & the Shade: Florida Photography 1886-1983; Masterpieces of 20th Century Canadian Painting; Photographs by Gordon Parks; Social Concern & Urban Realism
Publications: Monthly calendar
Activities: Classes for adults and children; docent training; lectures; films; concerts; gallery talks; tours; individual paintings and original objects of art lent to museums around the world; museum store
L Library, 1451 S Olive Ave, 33401. Tel 305-832-5194. *Consulting Librn* Hilda Scott
Open Tues - Sat 10 AM - 5 PM, Sun 1 - 5 PM. Admis voluntary donation. Estab 1941
Purchases: $3000
Library Holdings: Vols 3800; Per subs 30; Micro — Fiche; AV — Slides; Other — Clipping files, exhibition catalogs
Collections: †Individual Artist Reviews, †Catalogues, etc
Publications: Bi-monthly calendar of events

WHITE SPRINGS

O FLORIDA FOLKLIFE PROGRAMS, Box 265, 32096. Tel 904-397-2192. *Dir* Ormond H Loomis; *Folklife Adminr* Margaret Ann Bulger
The Bureau is under Secretary of State George Firestone, and carries on a year-round calendar of folk activities in an effort to encourage statewide public interest and participation in the folk arts and folklore
Activities: Folk festival; folk art conferences (presented at Center and throughout the state)
M Stephen Foster State Folk Culture Center,* Box 285, 32096. Tel 904-397-2733
Open 8:30 Am - 5 PM daily. Admis adults $2, children $1. Estab 1950 as a memorial to Stephen Collins Foster; operated by the Department of Natural Resources, a Division of Recreation and Parks; sponsors artists-in-residence program. Museum contains eight dioramas of Foster's best known songs. The north wing is a collection of minstrel materials; south wing contains 19th century furniture and musical instruments; the 200 foot tall Foster Tower contains a collection of bells and pianos. Average Annual Attendance: 90,000
Income: Financed by state appropriation and receipts
Publications: Florida Folk Arts Directory, annual; Florida Folklife Newsletter, six times annually
Activities: Concerts; tours; sales shop
L Library, Box 285, 32096
Open to public for reference
Library Holdings: Vols 500; Per subs 12; AV — V-tapes

WINTER PARK

M MORSE GALLERY OF ART,* 133 E Welbourne Ave (Mailing add: 151 E Welbourne Ave, 32789). Tel 305-644-3686. *Pres* Reid Ewing; *VPres* Bill Miller; *Secy & Dir of Gallery Activities* Nancy Abberger; *Dir* Hugh F McKean; *Cur* David Donaldson; *Gallery Mgr & Public Relations* Nancy Long; *Dir Exhibits* Jeannette G McKean
Open Tues - Sat 9:30 AM - 4 PM, Sun 1 - 4 PM, cl Mon, Christmas Day, New Years Day, Fourth of July and Thanksgiving. Admis adults $1.50, students and children $1, members free. Estab to display work of Louis Comfort Tiffany and his contemporaries from an extensive collection on a rotating basis. A small, intimate jewel box of a gallery consists of nine rooms and display areas. Mem: 345; dues from $5-$10,000

Income: $141,000 (financed by endowment and membership)
Collections: Art Nouveau Furniture by Galle, Guimard, Majorette, and others; Louis Comfort Tiffany collection of lamps, paintings, personal correspondence and effects, personal windows and photographs; Tiffany and other American art pottery numbering several hundred items; Tiffany studios photographers; items of blown glass; complete inventory of metalware desk sets; paintings by Tiffany's contemporaries; personal windows of others; photographs
Exhibitions: Art That Swings: European Art Nouveau; With Love From the Past: A Celebration of the Winter Park Centennial; Art That Sparkles: American Cut Glass; American the Beautiful: Landscape Paintings from the McKeon Collection; Mysteries from Laurelton Hall; The Art of Printing; personal windows and lamps, vases, metal wares and paintings of Louis Comfort Tiffany; decorative art objects, paintings, contemporaries
Publications: MORSELS, monthly newsletter to members
Activities: Classes for adults; docent training; lectures, 5 vis lectr per year; concerts; gallery talks; tours; competitions with awards; exten dept serves schools, nursing homes and public parks; original objects of art lent to nursing homes, bank lobbies and art center; museum shop sells books, prints, slides, silk-screened tote bags, skirts and pillows
L Library,* 32789
Library Holdings: Vols 30; Per subs 12; Tiffany posters; AV — Kodachromes, slides; Other — Clipping files, exhibition catalogs

M ROLLINS COLLEGE, George D and Harriet W Cornell Fine Arts Center Museum, Holt Ave, 32751. Tel 305-646-2526. *Adminr* Joan B Wavell; *Registrar* Eldora H Peeples; *Exhibits Designer* Richard D Colvin
Open Tues - Fri 10 AM - 5 PM; Sat & Sun 1 - 5 PM; cl Mon. No admis fee. Formerly the Morse Gallery of Art, estab 1942. New Fine Arts Center completed in 1976 and dedicated and opened on Jan 29, 1978. Rollins College is a liberal arts college and the Cornell Fine Arts Center is part of this process. Cornell Fine Arts Center was accredited by the American Asn of Museums in 1981. The museum houses the college's permanent collection and provides a focus for the arts in central Florida. Museum consists of the McKean, the Yust and Knapp Galleries. Average Annual Attendance: 10,000. Mem: 180; dues assoc $25, active $15; annual meeting monthly
Income: $100,000 (financed by endowment)
Collections: American paintings and portraits; European paintings from the 15th to 20th centuries; print; bronzes; decorative arts; Smith Watch Key Collection of 1200 keys
Exhibitions: (1983) Ancient Art from Cyprus: The Ringling Collection; Mid-Nineteenth Century American Landscapes and Portraits from the Rollins College Permanent Collection; The Gregorian Collection of Oriental Rugs; Portraits, Landscapes and Studies by Everett Raymond Kinstler; Rollins College, Class of '83 Senior Art Show; Contemporary Japanese Ink Painting and Calligraphy; Contemporary American Graphics from the Permanent Collection; Aboriginal Art from Australia; Hudson International Creche Exhibit; Rubens and the Flemish Baroque; Collected Light: Photography Collectors Show; Rollins College Class of '84 Senior Art Show; Selections from the Permanent Collection for Summer of 1984
Activities: Five vis lectr per yr; concerts; gallery talks; tours; individual paintings lent; originates traveling exhibitions

GEORGIA

ALBANY

M ALBANY MUSEUM OF ART,* 813 N Slappey, PO Box 571, 31707. Tel 912-435-0977. *Dir* Beverly Willson; *Financial Officer* Chris Cannon; *Sales Shop Mgr* D Zimmerman
Open daily 2 - 5 PM, also by special appointment. No admis fee. Estab 1964. Average Annual Attendance: 35,000. Mem: 1000; dues family $15; annual meeting, monthly board meeting
Income: Financed by membership and special funding
Collections: African Collection; small permanent collection of puchase awards from annual arts festivals
Publications: Bimonthly newsletter; exhibition catalogs
Activities: Classes for adults and children; docent training; workshops; films; special classes; lectures open to public, 5-10 vis lectr per yr; concerts; gallery talks; tours; statewide corporate collection competition; Spring Arts Festival Purchase awards; outreach dept serves special and general audience; individual paintings and original objects of art and photographs lent by request; museum-sales shop sells original art, reproduction, prints and misc items

AMERICUS

M GEORGIA SOUTHWESTERN COLLEGE, Art Gallery,* 31709. Tel 912-928-1279. *Chmn Fine Arts* Jack R Lewis
Open Mon - Fri 8 AM - 5 PM. No admis fee. Estab 1971
Collections: Contemporary prints; Indian art of the southwest

ATHENS

UNIVERSITY OF GEORGIA
M Georgia Museum of Art, Jackson St, 30602. Tel 404-542-3255. *Dir & Cur Graphic Art* Richard S Schneiderman; *Preparator* Ronald Lukasiewicz; *Assoc Dir & Cur Education* Marianne Doezema; *Registrar* Linda Steigleder; *Pub Relations Specialist* Dianne Penny Wilson
Open Mon - Sat 9 AM - 5 PM, Sun & Holidays, cl Christmas Day & New Year's Day. No admis fee. Estab 1945; open to the public 1948 as a fine arts museum. Five exhibition galleries. Average Annual Attendance: 21,000. Mem: 350; dues $10 - $1000; annual meeting May

Income: Financed through university
Collections: American Paintings, †Drawings; †European and American Graphics, 15th century to the present
Exhibitions: (1982) J M W Turner Watercolors from the British Museum; 19th & 20th Century American Landscape Paintings; American Folk Art; The Herbert Waide Hemphill, Jr Collection; Preston Dickinson 1891-1930; La Belle Epoque; (1983-84) Davis Cone Theatre Paintings; Graphic Works of Toulouse Lautrec; Lamar Doda: The Heart; The Landscape in American Art; Art Nouveau Glass; Reginald Marsh's New York
Publications: Bulletin, biannual; exhibition catalogs
Activities: Classes for adults and children; docent training; volunteer docents program; lect open to the public 3 - 5 vis lectr per year; tours; gallery talks; competitions with awards; individual paintings and original objects of art lent to other museums and galleries; traveling exhibitions organized and circulated

L **University of Georgia Libraries,** Fine Arts Collection, Jackson St, 30602. Tel 404-542-7462. *Head Fine Arts Office* Bela Foltin; *Art Librn* William Clayton
Open Mon - Thurs 8 AM - Noon, Fri 8 AM - 9 PM, Sat 9 AM - 6 PM, Sun 1 - Midnight; between quarters Mon - Fri 8 AM - 6 PM, Sat 9 AM - 6 PM, cl Sun
Income: Financed by state appropriation
Library Holdings: Vols 46,100; Per subs 250; Micro — Cards, fiche, prints, reels; AV — A-tapes, cassettes, motion pictures, rec, slides, v-tapes; Other — Exhibition catalogs, manuscripts, photographs
Special Subjects: History of Art & Architecture, History of Photography
Collections: Rare books & manuscripts collection; illustration archives on microfiche; stereographs from William C Darrah Collection; private press collection; handmade paper collections

L **Dept of Art Visual Center,** Visual Arts Building, 30602. Tel 404-542-1511. *Slide Librn* Frank D Jackson; *Photographer* Lewis C Bartlett
Open 8 AM - 5 PM and by special arrangement. Estab 1955 to house slides and AV equipment for use by faculty and students for classroom lecturing
Library Holdings: AV — Cassettes, slides 150,000, v-tapes

ATLANTA

L **ATLANTA COLLEGE OF ART LIBRARY,** 1280 Peachtree St NE, 30309. Tel 404-892-3600, Ext 419. *Dir* JoAnne Paschall; *Visual Coll Cur* Jan Avgikos; *Asst Librn* Kevin Fitzgerald
Open Mon & Fri 9:30 AM - 5 PM, Tues, Wed, Thurs 9:30 AM - 8 PM. Estab 1950 to provide art information and research facility to the Atlanta College of Art community and the southeast art community. Library has a small exhibition space for art. Circ 12,000
Purchases: $22,800
Library Holdings: Vols 16,000; Per subs 250; Artists' book collection; Micro — Fiche; AV — Cassettes, rec, slides, v-tapes; Other — Exhibition catalogs, memorabilia, original art works, photographs, prints
Special Subjects: , 20th century American art, with emphasis on art since 1950
Collections: †Artists' Books; †rare books
Exhibitions: Monthly exhibitions of art by students and faculty
Activities: Films; visiting artists program

M **ATLANTA MUSEUM,*** 537-39 Peachtree St NE, 30308. Tel 404-872-8233. *Dir* J H Elliott Jr; *Cur* Mary Gene Elliot
Open Mon - Fri 10 AM - 5 PM, cl Sat, Sun & holidays. Admis adults $2, children $1, special group rates. Estab 1938
Collections: Bronzes; Confederate Money; Decorative Arts; Early Chinese Art; Furniture; Indian Artifacts; Paintings; Porcelains; Sculpture; Glass
Activities: Lect; tours; sales shop sells antiques, china, furntiure, gifts, glass, paintings, porcelain, rugs and silver

L **ATLANTA PUBLIC LIBRARY,** Fine Arts Dept,* One Margaret Mitchell Square NW, 30303. Tel 404-688-4636. *Head Fine Arts Department* Julie M Compton; *Librn* Ella Yates Edwards
Open weekdays 9 AM - 9 PM; Sat 9 AM - 6 PM. Estab 1950 to provide materials in the fine arts. Some exhibit space maintained
Income: Financed by city and state appropriation
Library Holdings: AV — Cassettes, motion pictures 1100, rec; Other — Prints
Activities: Classes for adults; lect open to the public

L **GEORGIA INSTITUTE OF TECHNOLOGY,** College of Architecture Library, 225 North Ave NW, 30332. Tel 404-894-4877. *Librn* Kathryn S Brackney; *Library Asst* Eva McGuigan; *Library Asst* Mary Watson
Hours vary. Estab 1924 to give good library service to the college faculty and students. Circ 21,000
Income: Financed by state appropriation
Library Holdings: Vols 20,000; Per subs 100; Architectural drawings; Micro — Fiche; AV — Slides; Other — Pamphlets
Special Subjects: Art nouveau, Greek art and architecture, Japanese art and architecture

L **GEORGIA STATE UNIVERSITY,** Art Dept, Visual Resource Library & Reading Room, Art Department, University Plaza, 30303. *Dir* Frances Cullen; *Cur* Joan W Tysinger; *Photographer Asst* Susan Baugh
Open Mon - Fri 8 AM - 8 PM. No admis fee. Estab 1970 to make visual and literary resource materials available for study, teaching and research. Average Annual Attendance: 20,000
Library Holdings: Vols 2500; Per subs 18; AV — A-tapes, slides 130,000, v-tapes; Other — Exhibition catalogs, original art works, pamphlets, reproductions
Activities: Lectures open to public, 5-10 vis lectr per yr; gallery talks; competitions; individual paintings & original objects of art lent to university offices; lending collection contains 100 original prints, 50 paintings, 50 phonorecords, 50 photographs, 50 sculpture & 100 fine crafts; originate traveling exhibitions

O **GEORGIA VOLUNTEER LAWYERS FOR THE ARTS, INC,** 32 Peachtree St, Suite 521, 30358. Tel 404-577-7378. *Chairman* William F Welch; *Executive Dir* John Eaton
Open Mon - Fri 9 AM - 5 PM. Estab 1980 as legal reference for the arts
Income: Financed by city & state funds & private foundations
Collections: Copyrights; fundraising; art law related to literature
Publications: An Artists Handbook on Copyright
Activities: Lectures open to public, 5 vis lectr per yr

M **HIGH MUSEUM OF ART,** 1280 Peachtree St NE, 30309. Tel 404-892-3600. *Dir* Gudmund Vigtel; *Cur Decorative Arts* Donald Pierce; *Cur of 20th Century Art* Peter Morrin; *Cur European Art* Dr Eric Zafran; *Pres Bd of Directors* Albert Bows
Open Tues - Sat 10 AM - 5 PM; Sun Noon - 5 PM, cl Mon. Admis adults $2, sr citizens & students $1, children under 12, museum members & Thurs from 1 - 5 PM free. Estab 1929 to make the best in the visual arts available to the Atlanta public in exhibitions and supporting programs. The Museum building, 135,000 sq ft, was completed in 1983. Average Annual Attendance: 400,000. Mem: 15,500; dues $25 and up
Income: $1,260,000 (financed by endowment, membership, city and state appropriations, grants, and operating income)
Collections: African objects; American paintings, sculpture, graphics; European paintings, sculpture, graphics; Haverty Collection; Kress Collection of Paintings and Sculpture from the 14th - 18th Centuries; Oriental, Pre-Columbian, European and American decorative arts; Uhry Collection of Prints after 1850; photography
Exhibitions: (1983) The Rococo Age: French Masterpieces of the 18th Century; Mark Rothko: Subjects; permanent collection; Sensation, multi-sensory exhibition; (1984) Mark Rothko: Subjects; Sensation, multi-sensory exhibition; Richard Devore, contemporary ceramics; Part II: Subjective Vision: The Lucinda Bunnen Photography Collection; Folk Art Collection from Ukranian Families Living in Atlanta Area; Kandinsky: Russian & Bauhaus Years, 1915-1933; One Hundred Years of Metropolitan Opera Photography; A Century of Black Photographers; 19th Century French Drawings from the Collection of Emile Wolf; (1985) China 7000 Years of Discovery; Chinese Ceramics & Bronzes: Art & Technology; Extended Loan of Fifteen Sculptures from Guggenheim; Pressed Glass: 1825-1925; American Cutglass: The Brilliant Period; Photography in California: 1945-present; Harvey Littleton Retrospective; The Curtis Baer Drawing Collection; Figures from Rodin's Gates of Hell: Sculpture from the B G Cantor Collection; Honore Daumier: 1808-1879; The Ancient Regime: Atget Photographs; (1986) In Pursuit of Beauty: Americans & the Aesthetic Movement
Publications: Calendar of Events, monthly; exhibition catalogues
Activities: Programs & tours for children; docent training; lect open to public, 20 vis lectr per year; gallery talks; tours; exten dept serving city of Atlanta; individual paintings and original objects of art lent; traveling exhibitions organized and circulated; museum shop selling books, magazines, reproductions, slides and gift items; junior museum

AUGUSTA

M **AUGUSTA RICHMOND COUNTY MUSEUM,*** 540 Telfair St, 30901. Tel 404-722-8454. *Dir* Richard Wescott
Open Tues - Sat 10 AM - 5 PM, Sun 2 - 5 PM, cl holidays. No admis fee. Estab 1937; owns 1850 historic Brahe House at 426 Telfair St. Mem: Dues $5-$250
Collections: Archaeology; Decorative Arts; Graphics; Historical Material; Paintings; Sculpture
Activities: Training program for professional museum personnel; workshops; films; lect; guided tours; volunteer council; book traveling exhibitions

M **GERTRUDE HERBERT MEMORIAL INSTITUTE OF ART,** 506 Telfair St, 30901. Tel 404-722-5495. *Dir* Kay Allen
Open Tues - Fri 10 AM - 5 PM, groups by special appt, Sun 2 - 5 PM, cl Mon, Thanksgiving, Christmas & New Years. No admis fee. Estab 1937. 2 Adams Drawing Rooms. Average Annual Attendance: 2000. Mem: 250
Income: $20,000
Collections: European Renaissance; modern paintings, sculpture, graphics
Exhibitions: Circulating exhibitions; monthly exhibitions; one-person and group exhibitions
Activities: Classes for adults & children; docent training; lectures open to public; concerts; gallery talks; tours; competitions with awards; scholarships; book traveling exhibitions

COLUMBUS

M **COLUMBUS COLLEGE,** Experimental Gallery, Art Department, 31907. Tel 404-568-2047. *Dept Head* Donna Maddox; *VPres & Gallery Coordr* Zoe Allison
Open 10 AM - 4 PM during exhibits. Average Annual Attendance: 6000
Exhibitions: Annual art students show; faculty show; regional guest artist & nationally prominent artist
Activities: Classes for adults; lectures open to the public, 5 - 6 vis lectr per yr; gallery talks; competitions with awards; scholarships offered

M **COLUMBUS MUSEUM OF ARTS AND SCIENCES,*** 1251 Wynnton Rd, 31906. Tel 404-323-3617. *Dir & Secy Board* William F Scheele
Open Mon - Sat 10 AM - 5 PM, Sun 2 - 5 PM, cl Thanksgiving, Christmas, New Year's. No admis fee. Estab 1952 to build a permanent collection; encourage work by Georgia and Southern artists; establish loan shows and traveling exhibitions in all fields of art. Mem: dues $25 and up; annual meeting Jan
Collections: †American Art; American and Foreign Doll Collection; †Early Masters; †Georgia Artists; †Indian section with extensive Collection of Ethnological and Archaeological Material relating to local Indians; †Prints; reconstructed pre-Civil War Log House on Museum grounds; †Sculpture; permanent collection includes Landscapes, Paintings and Portraits by Dutch, Early and Contemporary American Painters, English, Flemish, and Italian
Publications: Newsletter
Activities: Workshops for adults and children; gallery talks; tours; lectr; active Museum Guild; originate traveling exhibitions

L Library, 1251 Wynnton Rd, 31906
Library Holdings: Vols 1572; Per subs 13
Special Subjects: All phases of Art, Indian History

DALTON

O CREATIVE ARTS GUILD, 520 W Waugh St, PO Box 375, 30722. Tel 404-278-0168. *Pres* John Hinkle; *Dir* Bernice Spigel
Open Mon - Fri 9 AM - 5 PM; Sat 11 AM - 2 PM. No admis fee. Estab 1963 to recognize, stimulate and popularize the arts. Average Annual Attendance: 55,000. Mem: 800; dues family $15; annual meeting Dec
Income: $200,000 (financed by membership, commissions, grants, tuitions & fund raising events)
Exhibitions: Changing monthly shows of Crafts; Graphics; Photography; Original Art; Sculpture
Publications: Bulletins to members, monthly
Activities: Classes for adults and children; dramatic programs; visual and performing arts programs for schools; concerts; gallery talks; competitions with awards; arts and crafts festivals; originate traveling exhibitions

DECATUR

M AGNES SCOTT COLLEGE, Dalton Gallery, College Ave & Candler St, 30030. Tel 404-373-2571. *Cur* Leland Staven
Open Mon - Fri 9 AM - 9 PM; Sat 9 AM - 5 PM; Sun 2 - 5 PM. No admis fee. Estab 1965 to enhance art program. Gallery consists of 4 rooms, 300 running ft of wall space, light beige walls and rug; Dana Fine Arts Bldg designed by John Portman
Income: Financed by endowment
Collections: Clifford M Clarke; Harry L Dalton; Steffen Thomas; Ferdinand Warren, NA
Exhibitions: (1983-84) Spotlight Germany: 11 German photographers; Terri S McGehee, paintings; student exhibit; faculty exhibit; work of senior art majors
Activities: Lect open to public

FORT BENNING

M NATIONAL INFANTRY MUSEUM, Bldg 396, Baltzell Ave, 31905. Tel 404-545-2958. *Dir* Dick Dewayne Grube; *Cur* Frank Hannen
Open Tues - Fri 10 AM - 4:30 PM; Sat - Sun 12:30 - 4:30 PM. No admis fee. Estab 1959 to honor the infantryman and his two centuries of proud history. Gallery contains 50,000 sq ft; Hall of Flags, Gallery of Military Art, Benning Room, West Gallery: 1750 - 1865, Center Galleries 1870 - 1970, Medal of Honor Hall and Airborne Diorama. Average Annual Attendance: 100,000. Mem: 9000; dues $10
Income: $200,000 (financed by federal funds)
Collections: †Military related art; Presidential Documents and Memorabilia; 1896 Vintage Sutler's Store
Exhibitions: Hail to the Chief; Minority Art and the Military; Henry Gassen: Watercolors of Military Training
Activities: Lect open to public
L Library, Bldg 396, Baltzell Ave, 31905. *Librn* Carol Sims
Open Tues - Fri 10 AM - 4:30 PM, Sat & Sun 12:30 - 4:30 PM. Estab 1959 to preserve the collection of field manuals and other military information. For reference only
Library Holdings: Vols 20,000; AV — Fs, motion pictures, slides; Other — Clipping files, manuscripts, memorabilia, original art works, pamphlets, photographs, sculpture
Special Subjects: The Infantryman

JEKYLL ISLAND

M JEKYLL ISLAND AUTHORITY MUSEUM, 375 Riverview Dr, 375 Riverview Dr, 31520. Tel 912-635-2727. *Dir Museum & Historic Preservation* Dr Thomas A Rhodes; *Exec Dir Jekyll Island* George Chambliss
Open Memorial Day - Labor Day - Sun 9 AM - 6 PM, Labor Day - Memorial Day Mon - Sun 10 AM - 5 PM. Admis adults $4, students $3 (6-18 years), children under 6 $1
Income: Financed by fees & admissions
Collections: 1890 Furniture; Tiffany Stained Glass Windows; portraits

MACON

M MUSEUM OF ARTS AND SCIENCES, INC, 4182 Forsyth Rd, 31210. Tel 912-477-3232. *Dir* Nancy B Anderson; *Prog Coordr* Sandra Skillen; *Cur* Steve Hartman; *Cur* Linda Bitley
Open Mon - Thurs 9 AM - 5 PM, Fri 9 AM - 9 PM, Sat 11 AM - 5 PM, Sun 2 - 5 PM. Admis adults $1.50, children $1, members no charge
Collections: European and American Drawings, Paintings, Prints and Sculpture; Historical Material
Activities: Classes for adults and children; arts festivals; guided tours; lectr; movies; special events; traveling art exhibits in Main Exhibit Hall

MOUNT BERRY

M BERRY COLLEGE, Moon Gallery, Art Dept Berry College, 30149. Tel 404-232-5374, Ext 219. *Pres* Dr Gloria Shatto; *VPres* Dr Doyle Mathis; *Secy* Joyce Morris
Open weekdays 9 AM - 4 PM. No admis fee. Estab 1971. Medium size gallery, carpeted floors and walls, tracking spots. Average Annual Attendance: 3500
Exhibitions: (1983) Alison Knowles, prints; Chuck Tomlins, drawings Dan Talley, conceptual pieces

Activities: Classes for adults and children; lectures open to the public, 8 - 10 vis lectr per yr; gallery talks; competitions with awards; scholarships offered; individual paintings and original objects of art lent; lending collection contains books, cassettes, color reproductions, 20 original prints, paintings, records, photographs and 5000 slides; book traveling exhibitions; originate traveling exhibitions
L Moon Library, 30149. Tel 404-232-5374. *Chmn* Dr T J Mew III
Open daily 9 AM - 4 PM. Estab 1972 for educational purposes
Library Holdings: Vols 50; Per subs 25; AV — A-tapes, cassettes, fs, motion pictures, rec, slides, v-tapes; Other — Clipping files, exhibition catalogs, manuscripts, memorabilia, original art works, pamphlets, photographs, prints
Special Subjects: Ceramics, Contemporary women artists

SAVANNAH

ASSOCIATION OF ART MUSEUM DIRECTORS
For further information, see National and Regional Organizations

M KIAH MUSEUM, 505 W 36th St, 31401. Tel 912-236-8544. *Dir & Founder* Virginia J Kiah; *Asst Cur* Nancy H Walker
Open Tues - Thurs 11 AM - 5 PM. No admis fee. Estab 1959 to expose this type of culture to the masses; to teach the relationship of art to everyday life
Collections: Civil War Period Collection; Harmon Foundation Collection of African Wood Carvings; Howard J Morrison Jr Osteological Collection; Marie Dressler Collection; Fine Arts Exhibit—all art work of students and adult artists from 18 countries; Folk Art; 18th, 19th & 20th Century Furniture; Hobby Collection; Indian Artifacts
Activities: Docent training; gallery talks; tours; paintings and original art objects lent to schools
L Library, 505 W 36th St, 31401
Open to adults and students for reference
Collections: John Speight Simpkins

M SHIPS OF THE SEA MUSEUM, 503 E River St, 31401. Tel 912-232-1511. *Exec Dir* David T Guernsey Jr; *Asst Dir* Ellen McDougall
Open Mon - Sun 10 AM - 5 PM. Admis adults $2, children 7 - 12 $.75, group rates available. Estab 1966 to bring a greater awareness to the general public of the great part in history that ships have played. Four floors of ship models & items which pertain to the sea with an outstanding exhibit of ships-in-bottles & scrimshaw. Average Annual Attendance: 36,000
Income: Financed privately
Collections: Figureheads; Porcelains; Scrimshaw; Ships Models, etc
Activities: Classes for children; sales shop sells books and gifts
L Library, 503 E River St, 31401. *Librn* Lee Vanger
Reference only
Library Holdings: Vols 350; Per subs 10; Other — Clipping files, framed reproductions, memorabilia, original art works, pamphlets, photographs, prints
Special Subjects: Maritime
Activities: Children summer classes in nautical lore

M TELFAIR ACADEMY OF ARTS AND SCIENCES INC, 121 Barnard St, PO Box 10081, 31401. Tel 912-232-1177. *Actg Dir & Cur* Feay Shellman; *Cur of Education* Janine Underwood; *Registrar & Cur* Elizabeth Scott
Open Tues - Sat 1 - 5 PM; Sun 2 - 5 PM; cl Mon. Admis adults $2, students $1, children under 12 $.50; free on Sun. Estab 1875; it is the oldest art museum in the southeast. The collections are housed in an 1818 Regency Mansion (with an 1883 Art Museum Wing) designed by English architect William Jay; Telfair has been designated a National Historic Landmark. Average Annual Attendance: 90,000. Mem: 1675; dues family $30, individual $20, junior citizen and senior citizen $5; annual meeting spring
Income: Financed by endowment, membership, city and state appropriation, banks and corporate foundations and federal government
Collections: American Impressionism; Ash Can Realism; Collections of 18th and 19th Century American Portraiture; Decorative Arts and Period Rooms; works of art on paper; costumes; 19th and 20th century French and German paintings
Exhibitions: Special and traveling exhibitions
Publications: The Octagon Room; We Ain't What We Used to Be
Activities: Docent training; special tours; lect open to the public, 5 vis lectr per yr; concerts; gallery talks; family Sunday programs; exten dept serving public schools and retired citizens centers; museum shop sells books, magazines, posters, postcards
L Library, 121 Barnard St, PO Box 10081, 31401. *Librn* Wilma Wierwill
For reference only, for scholars and the public
Library Holdings: Vols 1200; AV — Slides; Other — Clipping files, exhibition catalogs, manuscripts, pamphlets, photographs, reproductions
Special Subjects: American Art

VALDOSTA

M VALDOSTA STATE COLLEGE, Art Gallery, N Patterson St, 31601. Tel 912-333-5835. *Head Art Dept* R S McRae
Open Mon - Thurs 10 AM - 4 PM, Fri 10 AM - 2 PM. No admis fee. Estab 1970 to expose both art and general education students to a variety of visual expressions. Gallery is an open rectangular room with approximately 122 running ft of exhibition space. Average Annual Attendance: 12,000-15,000
Income: Financed by state appropriations
Exhibitions: 6-8 exhibitions per year
Activities: Classes for adults & children; lectures open to public, 3 vis lectr per yr; gallery talks; tours; competitions; scholarships; individual paintings & original objects of art lent to libraries & museums; book traveling exhibitions; originate traveling exhibitions

WAYCROSS

M OKEFENOKEE HERITAGE CENTER, INC,* North Augusta Ave (Mailing add: Route 5, Box 406A, 31501). Tel 912-285-4260. *Dir* Joseph B Schenk; *Art Coordr* Richard Waterhouse; *Exhibit Designer* Robert Ducham
Open Tues - Sat 10 AM - 5 PM, Sun 2 - 4 PM, cl holidays. Admis adults $2, youth 5-18 $1, under 4 & members free. Estab 1975 to house displays on arts, sciences, history and social sciences. Two gallery areas. Average Annual Attendance: 14,000. Mem: 300; annual meeting 3rd week in March
Income: $64,000 (financed by endowment, membership, grants, contributions, admis, special activities, gift shop)
Collections: Prints, crafts, paintings and photographs
Publications: Newsletter, monthly; exhibition catalogues
Activities: Classes for adults and children; dramatic programs; docent training; films; demonstrations; workshops; slide show; lectures open to public, 4 vis lectr per yr; concerts; tours; sponsor annual juried exhibition; cash awards; book traveling exhibitions, 6-12 per yr; museum shop sells books, original art, reproductions, prints, trinkets, gifts and souvenirs

HAWAII

HONOLULU

O ARTS COUNCIL OF HAWAII, 300 Ala Moana Blvd, PO Box 50225, 96850. Tel 808-524-7120. *Exec Dir* Karl K Ichida; *Admin Asst* William D Heyd
Open Mon - Fri 8:30 AM - 4:30 PM. Estab 1974 to provide technical assistance to the public on the arts. One floor of Federal Courthouse Building Lobby approximately 2000 sq ft of wall space that is covered and illuminated. Maintains resource library open to the public. Average Annual Attendance: 6000. Mem: 1100; dues $15; annual meeting May
Income: $85,000 (financed by membership, state appropriation, donations)
Exhibitions: Dept of Education/State Arts Teachers' Association
Publications: Cultural Climate, monthly
Activities: Lectures open to the public; competitions

O ASSOCIATION OF HONOLULU ARTISTS,* 2417A University Ave, PO Box 10202, 96822. Tel 808-235-6294. *Pres* Ernest Brickman
Estab 1934 to promote congeniality and stimulate growth by presenting programs; to contribute to the cultural life of the State of Hawaii. Average Annual Attendance: 1000. Mem: 350; dues $12; monthly meeting every third Tues
Income: Financed by membership
Publications: Paint Rag, monthly
Activities: Lect open to public, 12 visiting lectr per year; demonstrations; competitions; cash awards, plaques and rossettes; scholarships

M CONTEMPORARY ARTS CENTER, 605 Kapiolani Blvd, 96813. Tel 808-525-8047. *Dir* Laila Roster; *Chmn of Board* Russell Cades; *Asst Dir Publications* Mary Mitsuda; *Development Dir* Evelyn Twigg-Smith
Open Mon - Fri 8:30 AM - 5 PM; Sat 8 AM - Noon; cl Sun. No admis fee. Estab 1961 to provide a showcase for contemporary artists living and working in the Hawaiian Islands. Gallery occupies 1800 sq ft of space in the center of the newspaper building. Average Annual Attendance: 25,000. Mem: 500; dues $1 - $1000; annual meetings in October
Income: $120,000 (financed by private contributions, operating budget from public sources & memberships)
Purchases: $20,000
Collections: Permanent Collection hangs throughout the building & is continually augmented by purchase from in house & outside exhibitions
Exhibitions: Robert Bush, paintings; Satoru Abe, sculpture; Brian Isobe/Nina Peterson, ceramics; Marianna Pineda, bronze terracottas; Sally Fletcher Morrison/Sister Adele, ceramics, photographs; Steven V Correia, glass; Keichi Kimura, Jerome Wallace, Jean Charlot, Hank Murata Adams, Hasuyo Miller, Robert Lee Eskridge, Laura Ruby, Ron Nakayam, Tadashi Sato, Ann Miura, Mary Ann Lynch, Kaori Uamamoto, Frank Salmoiraghi, Mark Abildgaard, Nathan Oliveira, Mary Mitsuda, Mary Bonic, Madge Tennent, recent acquisitions show; Jeffrey Dunn, drawings; Darrell Orwig, paintings; Douglas Doi, sculpture; Harue McVay, ceramic, sculpture; John Morita, photo etchings; Moses/Don Yacoe, paper, paintings; Lewis Moore, paintings; Helen Gilbert, mixed media; Laura Ruby, sculpture, serigraphs; Kate Wade, paintings; John A Varnett, sculpture, Betty Jane Lau, mixed media; Doug Young, watercolors
Publications: Monthly exhibition catalogues

L HAWAII STATE LIBRARY, Fine Arts-Audiovisual Section, 478 S King St, 96813. Tel 808-548-2340. *Art Spec* Chitra Stuiver; *Head AV Unit* Mary Lu Kipilii; *Head Fine Arts-Audiovisual Section* Eloise Van Niel; *Art Specialist* Norma Hirota
Open Tues - Thurs 9 AM - 8 PM, Mon, Wed, Fri and Sat 9 AM - 5 PM. No admis fee. Estab 1930 as central reference and circulating collection for both city and county of Honolulu and for state of Hawaii
Library Holdings: Vols 25,000; Pictures 50,000; Art Magazines; Art Films
Special Subjects: Handicrafts, Photography, Costume Design, Chinese Art, Japanese Art
Activities: Approx 10,000 art items lent yearly

M HONOLULU ACADEMY OF ARTS, 900 S Beretania St, 96814. Tel 808-538-3693, 538-1006; Cable HONART. *Dir* George R Ellis; *Asst Dir* Selden Washington; *Senior Cur & Cur Graphic Arts* Joseph Feher; *Cur Western Art & Publications Ed* James F Jensen; *Cur Asian Art & Keeper of Ukiyo-e Center* Howard A Link; *Cur Textile Coll* Reiko Brandon; *Cur Gallery Program* Roger Dell; *Cur Program Development* James H Furstenberg; *Cur Art Center* Violet A Scott; *Keeper, Lending Center* Barbara F Hoogs; *Slide Coll* Doris Lutzky; *Registrar* Sanna Deutsch; *Fund Development* Gail Pratt; *Public Relations Officer*

Mark Lofstrom; *Consultant for Chinese Art* Tsen Yu-ho Ecke; *Consultant for Western Art* Gertrude Rosenthal
Open Tues - Sat 10 AM - 4:30 PM, Sun 1 - 5 PM, cl Mon & major holidays. No admis fee. Estab 1927 as the only art museum of a broad general nature in the Pacific; to provide Hawaii's people of many races with works of art representing their composite cultural heritage from both East and West. Main building is a Registered National Historic Place. Average Annual Attendance: 218,000. Mem: 4500; dues $10 and up
Income: $1,710,949
Collections: European and American Decorative Arts, Painting, Prints, Sculpture; Ancient Mediterranean and Medieval Christian Art; Kress Collection of Italian Renaissance Painting; Chinese Bronze, Ceramics, Furniture, Lacquerware, Painting, Sculpture Islamic Ceramics; Japanese Ceramics, Folk Arts, Painting, Prints, Screens, Sculpture; Korean Ceramics; Traditional Arts of Africa, Oceania and the Americas; Western and Oriental Textiles
Exhibitions: Approx 35 temporary exhibitions annually
Publications: Art Books and Pamphlets; Catalogs of Special Exhibitions; Honolulu Academy of Arts Journal, biennially
Activities: Classes for children; lectr; films; guided tours; gallery talks; arts festivals; workshops; research in Asian art; lending collection contains paintings, prints, textiles, reproductions, photographs, slides and miscellaneous objects (about 21,000); originate traveling exhibitions; sales shop sells books and gifts

L Robert Allerton Library, 900 S Beretania St, 96814. Tel 808-538-3693. *Librn* Anne T Seaman
Open Tues - Fri 10 AM - 4 PM, Sat 10 AM - 3 PM, cl Sun & Mon. Estab 1927. Reference library for staff and members
Library Holdings: Vols 35,000; Per subs 200; Micro — Reels; AV — Slides; Other — Clipping files, exhibition catalogs, pamphlets, photographs
Special Subjects: Art History, Oriental Art, National Palace Museum Photographic Archives

M TENNENT ART FOUNDATION GALLERY, 203 Prospect St, 96813. Tel 808-531-1987. *Dir* Elaine Tennent
Open Tues - Sat 10 AM - Noon; Sun 2 - 4 PM or by appointment. No admis fee. Estab 1954; dedicated to aesthetic portrayal of Hawaiian people and to house works of Madge Tennent. Gallery on slopes of Punchbowl below National Cemetery of Pacific. Average Annual Attendance: 1000-15000. Mem: Dues individual $10, family $15
Income: Financed by trust
Collections: Madge Tennent's Personal Art Books Collection
Publications: Prospectus, quarterly newsletter
Activities: Special exhibitions and social events sponsored by Friends of Tennent Art Gallery; lect; tours

L Library, 203 Prospect St, 96813
Open for reference
Library Holdings: Vols 350

M UNIVERSITY OF HAWAII AT MANOA, Art Gallery, 2535 The Mall, 96822. Tel 808-948-6888. *Dir* Tom Klobe; *Chmn Department Art* John Wisnosky
Open Mon - Fri 10 AM - 4 PM; Sun Noon - 4 PM; cl Sat. No admis fee. Estab 1976 to present a program of local, national and international exhibitions. Gallery is seen as a major teaching tool for all areas of specialization. It is located in the center of the new art building and is designed as a versatile space with a flexible installation system that allows all types of art to be displayed according to their own requirements. Average Annual Attendance: 50,000
Exhibitions: First Western States Biennial; Filaments of the Imagination; Koa Furniture of Hawaii; The First International Shoebox Sculpture Exhibition; Egyptian Antiquities from the Pankow Collection; Artifacts of the Pomare Family; 20th Century Photographs from the Museum of Modern Art; Selection II: European & American Art from Hawaii Collection; Deja Vu: Masterpieced Updated
Publications: Exhibition catalogs
Activities: Lect open to public; gallery talks; originate traveling exhibitions

KAHULAI

L MAUI COMMUNITY COLLEGE LIBRARY,* 310 Kaahumanu Ave, 96732. *Dir* Bill Lindstrom; *Reference* Gail Bartholomew
Open Mon - Fri 8 AM - 9 PM. Estab 1968 to serve the community and students
Library Holdings: Vols 2000; Per subs 10; Micro — Fiche; AV — A-tapes, cassettes, fs, Kodachromes, motion pictures, rec, slides, v-tapes; Other — Clipping files, pamphlets
Exhibitions: Five gallery exhibits of national importance borrowed from Honolulu Art Museum

LAHAINA

O LAHAINA ARTS SOCIETY, Art Organization,* 649 Wharf St, 96761. Tel 808-661-0111. *Pres* Esther Ross Wilks; *VPres* Helen Scantlin; *2nd VPres* Mary Diehl; *Secy* Janet Allan; *Treasurer* Thomas Wright
Open daily 10 AM - 4 PM. No admis fee. Estab 1968 as a nonprofit organization interested in perpetuating native culture, art and beauty by providing stimulating art instruction, lectures and art exhibits. Gallery located in old Lahaina Courthouse; Main Gallery is on ground floor; Old Jail Gallery is in the basement. Average Annual Attendance: 36,000. Mem: 250; dues $15; annual meeting Oct
Income: $12,000 (financed by membership and annual fundraising event, Beaux Arts Ball)
Exhibitions: Honolulu Academy of Arts Annual Traveling Exhibit; exhibits change each month; group, special or theme exhibits in Main Gallery; one or two-person shows are in Old Jail Gallery
Publications: Newsletter, monthly; exhibition catalogs
Activities: Classes for children; lectures for members only; gallery talks; competitions with scholarships; workshops; scholarships; gallery sales shop sells original art, prints, cards, ceramics, macrame, woodcarving and sculptures

LAIE

O **POLYNESIAN CULTURAL CENTER,** 96762. Tel 808-293-3333. *Chmn Board* Marvin J Ashton; *Gen Mgr* Ralph G Rodgers Jr
Open Mon - Sat 11 AM - 9 PM, cl Sun, Thanksgiving, New Years & Christmas. Admis adults $14, children $7. Estab 1963 by the Church of Jesus Christ of Latter Day Saints as an authentic Polynesian village. Center is a 42 acre living museum with two amphitheaters, it represents villages of Hawaii, Samoa, Tonga, Fiji, Tahiti, New Zealand & the Marquesas. Average Attendance: 1,000,000
Income: Financed by admissions
Collections: Decorative arts, ethnic material, graphics, paintings and sculpture
Publications: Polynesia in a Day, magazine
Activities: Classes for adults & children; workshop training in Polynesian arts & crafts; lectures open to public; scholarships; sales shop sells Polynesian handicrafts, books, reproductions, prints, slides, tapa cloth, Hawaiian quilting & pandanus-leaf items

LIHUE

M **KAUAI MUSEUM,** PO Box 248, 96766. Tel 808-245-6931. *Pres* Juliet Rice-Wichman; *Secy* Maureen Morrison; *Dir* David Penhallow; *Cur* Kenneth A Kapp; *Researcher* Robert Gahran; *Mgr Museum Shop* Hazel Ward Gahran
Open Mon - Fri 9:30 AM - 4:30 PM, cl Sat & Sun. Admis adults $3, children thru age 17 free when accompanied by an adult. Estab 1960 to provide the history through the permanent exhibit, the story of Kauai and through art exhibits; ethnic cultural exhibits in the Wilcox Building to give the community an opportunity to learn more of ethnic backgrounds. Average Annual Attendance: 23,000. Mem: 500; dues $100, $50, $25, $15 and $7.50; annual meeting Nov
Exhibitions: Annual Artists of Hawaii Exhibit; Annual Elementary and Senior Division School Art Exhibit; Attempted Russian Expansion of Kauai, 1815 - 1817; Captain James Cook Bicentennial Exhibit; Filipino Cultural Heritage Exhibit Featuring the Badillo Collection; Hawaiian Quilts; Oils by John Young; Pacific Northwest Indian Exhibit (watercolors by Wai Hang Lai); The First Americans; The First American Indian Exhibit in Hawaii; Watercolors and Prints of Emily Ehlinger; Watercolors by Hubert Buel; Filipino Exhibit 1906-1981
Publications: Hawaiian Quilting on Kauai; Early Kauai Hospitality; Amelia; Moki Goes Fishing
Activities: Classes for adults & children; lectures open to the public; concerts; tours; museum shop sells books, original art, reproductions, prints
L **Library,** PO Box 248, 96766. Tel 808-822-4080
For reference only
Library Holdings: Vols 1000; Micro — Cards; AV — Motion pictures, slides; Other — Prints
Collections: Photograph Collection

L **KAUAI REGIONAL LIBRARY,** 4344 Hardy St, 96766. Tel 808-245-3617. *District Adminr* Donna Marie Garcia
Open Mon - Wed 8 AM - 8 PM, Thurs - Fri 8 AM - 4:30 PM, Sat 8 AM - noon. Estab 1922 to serve the public of Kauai through a network of a regional library, three community libraries, community-school library, reading room in community center and a bookmobile service. These libraries provide exhibition space for a variety of art works and individual art shows as well as participate in joint art exhibits with the local schools, community college and museum. Gallery provides display and exhibit area for one-man and group art shows. Circ 431,678
Income: $753,912 (financed by state appropriation)
Library Holdings: Vols 183,055; Per subs 801; AV — A-tapes, cassettes, fs, rec, slides, v-tapes; Other — Clipping files, pamphlets
Collections: Curator for art in State Buildings Collection for the Island of Kauai funded through the statewide program by the State Foundation on Culture and the Arts. This collection is a revolving collection available for all state buildings and public schools
Exhibitions: Series of small one-man exhibits; average thirteen per year
Activities: Dramatic programs; film programs; lectr open to public, 4 - 8 vis lectr per year; library tours; craft exhibits; contests

WAILUKU

O **MAUI HISTORICAL SOCIETY,** Hale Hoikeike,* 2375A Main St, PO Box 1018, 96793. Tel 808-244-3326. *Pres* Steve Parker; *VPres* James Luckey; *Secy* Kaui Goring; *Treas* James Haynes; *Mus Dir* Virginia Wirtz
Open daily 9 AM - 3:30 PM. Admis adults $2; students $.50. Estab 1957 to preserve the history of Hawaii, particularly Maui County; housed in former residence of Edward Bailey (1814-1903). Average Annual Attendance: 5000. Mem: 400; dues $10 - $100; annual meeting March
Income: $50,000 (financed by membership, gift shop purchases and admission fees)
Collections: Landscape Paintings (1860-1900); Paintings of Hawaiian Scenes by Edward Bailey; Prehistoric Hawaiian Artifacts
Publications: LaHaina Historical Guide; La Perouse on Maui; Hale Hoikeike - A House and Its People
Activities: Lect open to the public, 5 vis lectr per year; sales shop selling books, slides, postcards, notepaper, jewelry and souvenirs

IDAHO

BOISE

M **BOISE GALLERY OF ART,** 670 S Julia Davis Dr, 83702. Tel 208-345-8330.

Dir Dennis O'Leary; *Asst Dir* Alberta Mayo; *Admin Asst* Barbara Streng; *Cur* David Willard; *Cur* Sandy Harthorn
Open Tues - Fri 10 AM - 5 PM, Sat & Sun Noon - 5 PM, cl Mon and holidays. Donation $1, sr citizens and children $.50. Estab 1931, incorporated 1961, gallery opened 1936. Average Annual Attendance: 147,000. Mem: 850; dues family $35, individual $25; annual meetings in May
Collections: American, European and Oriental Collections of Painting, The Minor Arts, Sculpture; Collection of works by Idaho Artists
Exhibitions: Biennial exhibition for Idaho artists; 10 exhibitions annually of all media, regional to international; (1983) Contemporary Trompe l'Oeil Painting and Sculpture; Arranged Image Photography
Publications: Annual report; bulletin; catalogs & posters of exhibitions, occasionally
Activities: Classes in art and art appreciation; lect open to public; docent tours; concerts; films; outdoor arts festival; Beaux Arts Societe (fund raising auxiliary); originate traveling exhibitions statewide and Northwest region; gallery shop

C **FIRST SECURITY BANK OF IDAHO,** 119 N Ninth St, PO Box 7069, 83730. Tel 208-384-6877. *In Charge Art Coll* Glenn Lungren
Open Mon - Fri 10 AM - 5 PM. Estab 1967. Collection displayed in most of our 140 banks on a monthly basis
Activities: Underwrite for all kinds of performing art activities all over the state; fels through our Foundation

CALDWELL

M **COLLEGE OF IDAHO,** Blatchley Gallery,* 83605. Tel 208-459-5321. *Dir* John Anderson; *Cur* Max Peter
Open Tues, Thurs & Sun 1 - 4 PM, cl academic holidays. No admis fee. Estab 1980, (formerly Jewett Exhibition Center 1962)
Collections: Paintings; Prints Collection
Exhibitions: Temporary and traveling exhibitions on an inter-museum loan basis
Publications: Exhibit Brochures
Activities: Lect; gallery talks; guided tours; films

MOSCOW

M **APPALOOSA MUSEUM, INC,** Moscow-Pullman Hwy, PO Box 8403, 83843. Tel 208-882-5578. *Pres* King Rockhill; *VPres* Ellis Burcaw; *Secy* George B Hatley; *Cur* Judy Emerson
Open Mon - Fri 8 AM - 5 PM, Sat & Sun by appointment. No admis fee. Estab 1962 to collect, preserve, study and exhibit those objects that illustrate the story of the Appaloosa Horse
Income: $6000 (financed by grants from Appaloosa Horse Club)
Purchases: $1600
Collections: Bronzes by Shirley Botoham, Less Williver, Don Christian & William Menshew; reproductions of Chinese, Euopean & Persian Art relating to Appaloosas; reproductions of Charles Russellart; original Western by George Phippen, Reynolds
Activities: Lectures open to the public; tours

POCATELLO

M **IDAHO STATE UNIVERSITY,** John B Davis Gallery of Fine Art, 83209. Tel 208-236-2361. *Dir* Tony Martin
Open Mon - Fri Noon - 5 PM. No admis fee. Estab 1956 to exhibit art. Gallery contains 130 running ft of space with 8 ft ceilings. Average Annual Attendance: 2600
Income: $2600 (financed by city appropriation)
Purchases: $350
Collections: †Permanent collection
Exhibitions: Ann Baddley-Fiberforms; Robert Barnum-Prints & Drawings; Group Graduate Exhibit; Anita Kapaun-Fiberforms; Marilyn Levine-Ceramics; MFA Thesis Exhibits, weekly one-man shows; Northwest Eccentric Art; Lorna Obermayr-Paper Pieces; Paper as Medium (from Smithsonian Institute); Mike Phippen-Ceramics; The Production Potter: A Question of Quality; Jacqui Steinberg- Metalsmithing; Undergraduate Exhibit; Janet Wright- Metalsmithing
Activities: Lectures open to public, 3 vis lectr per year; gallery talks; tours; competitions with awards; scholarships; individual paintings lent to school offices & community

TWIN FALLS

M **COLLEGE OF SOUTHERN IDAHO,** Art Gallery,* Box 1238, 83301. Tel 208-733-9554. *Dir* LaVar Steel; *Gallery Dir* Mike Green
Open Mon - Sat 8 AM - 5 PM, cl Sun. No admis fee. Estab 1967 as a college gallery for student and public enjoyment. Included is a fine arts building and auditorium. Average Annual Attendance: 15,000
Income: Financed by community college and local support
Collections: Permanent collection
Activities: Classes for adults and children; dramatic programs; lect open to public; scholarships
L **Library,** Box 1238, 83303. *Dir* William Beale; *Reference Librn* Stephen Poppino
Open Mon - Fri 8 AM - 9 PM. Estab 1965
Library Holdings: Vols 1850; Per subs 7; Micro — Cards, fiche, prints, reels; AV — A-tapes, cassettes, fs, motion pictures, slides, v-tapes; Other — Framed reproductions, manuscripts, original art works, photographs, prints

M COLLEGE OF SOUTHERN IDAHO, Herrette Museum,* 315 Falls Ave, PO Box 1238, 83301. Tel 208-733-9554. *Dir* Jim Woods; *Cur Collections* Phyllis Morgret
Open Tues 9:30 AM - 8 PM, Wed - Fri 9:30 AM - 4:30 PM, Sat 1 - 4:30 PM, cl holidays. No admis fee. Estab 1965. Average Annual Attendance: 10,000
Collections: Contemporary Art; Pre-Columbian Art
Activities: Classes for adults and children; dramatic programs; lectures open to public; concerts; gallery talks; tours; competitions with prizes; scholarships

ILLINOIS

BISHOP HILL

M BISHOP HILL STATE HISTORIC SITE, PO Box O, 61419. Tel 309-927-3345. *Site Supt* Martha J Downey
Open daily 9 AM - 5 PM, cl Thanksgiving, Christmas and New Years. No admis fee. Estab 1946 to interpret history of Bishop Hill Colony. Average Annual Attendance: 50,000
Income: Financed by state appropriation
Collections: Artifacts pertaining to Bishop Hill Colony 1846-1861; primitive paintings
Activities: Lect open to public

BLOOMINGTON

M ILLINOIS WESLEYAN UNIVERSITY, Merwin Gallery,* Alice Millar Center for Fine Arts, 210 E University St, 61701. Tel 309-556-3077, 556-3131. *Dir* Anna Calluori-Holcombe
Open Mon - Sun 1 - 4 PM, Tues evening 7 - 9 PM, cl Mon. Estab 1945
Income: Financed by endowment, and membership
Collections: 250 drawings, paintings and prints including works by Baskin, Max Beckmann, Helen Frankenthaler, Philip Guston, John Ible, Oliviera, Larry Rivers and Whistler
Exhibitions: Annual Illinois High School Art Exhibition; School of Art Faculty Exhibition; School of Art Student Exhibition
Publications: Exhibition Posters; Gallery Schedule, monthly
Activities: Dramatic programs; concerts; lect open to public, 5 vis lectr per year; tours; competitions; original objects of art lent, on campus only; book traveling exhibitions; traveling exhibitions organized and circulated
L Slide Library, 210 E University St, 61701. *Fine Arts Librn* Robert C Delvin
Library Holdings: AV — Slides 35,000

O MCLEAN COUNTY ART ASSOCIATION, Arts Center, 601 N East St, 61701. Tel 309-829-0011. *Pres* Flo Armstrong; *Secy* Trudy Brim; *Dir McLean County Arts Center* Judith D Spear; *Secy* Paula Monroe
Open Mon - Fri 10 AM - 5 PM, Sat Noon - 4 PM. No admis fee. Estab 1922 to enhance the arts in McLean County by providing display gallery and sales and rental gallery to aid local professional artists. Gallery is 2500 sq ft and hosts local shows and traveling exhibits. Mem: 600; dues family $15, single $10, students $5; annual meeting first Fri in May
Income: Financed by membership, art and book sales
Exhibitions: Annual Amateur Competition and Exhibition; Annual Holiday Sale
Activities: Classes for adults & children; lectures open to public; gallery talks; tours; competitions with awards; sales shop selling books, magazines, original art; operates both a used book store and art sales gallery

CARBONDALE

M SOUTHERN ILLINOIS UNIVERSITY, University Museum, Southern Illinois Univ at Carbondale, 62901. Tel 618-453-5388. *Dir* Dr John J Whitlock; *Cur Art* Evert A Johnson; *Cur Exhibits* Eugene P Moehring; *Cur History* Bonnie Krause; *Prog Educational-Community Services Coordr* Geraldine Kelley; *Registrar* Lorilee Huffman; *Exhibits Designer* Alan Harasimowicz; *Secy* Patricia Simmons; *Adj Cur Archaeology* Dr Robert L Rands; *Adj Cur Anthropology* Dr Carroll L Riley; *Adj Cur Geology* Dr George Fraunfelter; *Adjunct Cur Botany* Donald Ugent; *Adjunct Cur Zoology* Dr Brooks Burr
Open Mon - Fri 9 AM - 3 PM; Sun 1:30 - 4:30 PM. No admis fee. Estab 1874 to reflect the history and cultures of southern Illinois and promote the understanding of the area; to provide area schools and the University with support through educational outreach programs; to promote the fine arts in an unrestricted manner through exhibitions and provide support to the School of Art MFA program through exhibition of MFA graduate students. Two art galleries totaling 3500 sq ft, sculpture garden & 2 semi-permanent exhibit halls with 3500 sq ft featuring exhibits on southern Illinois. Average Annual Attendance: 50,000
Income: Financed by state appropriated budget, federal, state & private grants, donation, Museum & Art Galleries Association exhibition support
Purchases: Peter Markman; John Henry; Brent Kington; Reuben Nakian; Jack Zajak; Dennis Kowal; Harold Tovish
Collections: Decorative Arts; European & American paintings, drawings & prints from 13th - 20th century with emphasis on 19th & 20th century; photography, sculpture, blacksmithing & art & crafts; Oceanic Collection; Southern Illinois history; 20th century sculpture, metals, ceramics; Asiatic holdings; archaeology; costumes; textiles; geology; zoology
Exhibitions: Gaston Lachaise; Paper As Medium (S.I.T.E.S.); Joliet Photos; Evesong; Handmade Paper & Books; Adelaid Hanscom Leeson; Pictorialist Photographer; Ke & Jean Francis: Mixed Media; Herbert Fink: Retrospective; Illinois Ozark Crafts Guild; Southern Illinois Folk Artists; Rudy Pozzatti Retrospective; John Richardson Photographs; Amazonian Pottery from Ecuador; American Glassware 1850-1930; WPA: Models of the Past; 20 Years of Metals at SIU; Towards A New Iron Age; Kyoto Metal; Sculpture of Ernest Trova; Milton Avery; Louisiana Women in Contemporary Art; The Forest; Mapping

America; Geology of Southern Illinois; Southern Illinois Folk Artists; Ulysses S Grant: Man of War, Man of Peace/Contrasting Images
Publications: Annual report; annual museum newsletter; exhibition catalogs
Activities: Formally organized education programs for children; museum studies program; docent training; tours; lect; films; inter-museum loan; public outreach programs; active volunteer program; originates traveling exhibitions; museum gift shop
L Reference Library, 62901
Library Holdings: Vols 102; Per subs 11; AV — A-tapes, fs, slides, v-tapes; Other — Clipping files, exhibition catalogs, manuscripts, pamphlets

CHAMPAIGN

UNIVERSITY OF ILLINOIS
M Krannert Art Museum, 500 Peabody Dr, 61820. Tel 217-333-1860. *Dir* Stephen S Prokopoff; *Asst Dir* Mark Johnson; *Research Cur* Margaret Sullivan; *Registrar* Kathleen Jones
Open Tues - Sat 10 AM - 5 PM, Sun 2 - 5 PM. No admis fee. Estab 1961 to house and administer the art collections of University of Illinois, to support teaching and research program, and to serve as an area art museum. Average Annual Attendance: 190,000. Mem: 600; dues $20 and up
Income: Financed by endowment, membership, state appropriation
Collections: †American paintings, sculpture, prints and drawings; †Ancient Near Eastern Classical and Medieval Art; Krannert Collection of Old Masters; Moore Collection of European and American Decorative Arts; Olsen Collection of Pre-Columbian Art; †Oriental Arts: Class of 1908; Trees Collection
Exhibitions: (1983) Lorado Taft Retrospective; Psychomachia Drawings by Robert Morris; Raphael and the Ruins of Rome
Publications: Catalogs; Krannert Art Museum Bulletin, semi-annually
Activities: Classes for children; docent training; lect open to the public, 5-10 visiting lectrs per year; tours; original objects of art lent to museums and university galleries; originate traveling exhibitions; museum shop
M World Heritage Museum, College of Liberal Arts & Sciences, 484 Lincoln Hall, 61801. Tel 217-333-2360. *Dir* Dr Barbara E Bohen; *Cur of Numismatics* Dr James Dengate
Open Mon - Fri 9 AM - 4 PM, Sun 2 - 5 PM when classes in session. No admis fee. Estab 1911. Galleries devoted to different historic and ethnographic cultures. Average Annual Attendance: 13,000. Mem: 175
Income: $75,000
Purchases: John Needles Chester Vase - Apulian Krater ca 320 BC
Collections: Originals and reproductions of Greek, Roman, Egyptian, Mesopotamian, African, Oriental and European art objects, including sculpture, pottery, glass, implements, coins, seals, clay tablets, inscriptions and manuscrips
Exhibitions: (1982) Parthenon U-C; (1983) From Alexander to Augustus; Allerton Revisited; (1984) FDR and Mass Communications in the 30's; Olympics
Publications: Heritage, newsletter bi-annual; exhibition brochures
Activities: Lectures open to the public, 1 - 2 vis lectr per yr; concerts; gallery talks; tours; competitions with awards; original objects of art lent for special shows in established museums; book traveling exhibitions; museum shop sells books & reproductions
M Museum of Natural History, 438 Natural History Bldg, Urbana, 61801. Tel 217-333-2517. *Dir* Donald F Hoffmeister; *Cur Exhibits* Harry C Henriksen
Open Mon - Sat 8 AM - 5 PM
Activities: Docent training; tours
L Ricker Library of Architecture and Art, 208 Architecture Bldg, 608 E Lorado Taft Dr, 61820. Tel 217-333-0224. *Librn* Dee Wallace
Open Mon - Thurs 8 AM - 10 PM, Fri 8 AM - 6 PM, Sat 9 AM - 5 PM, Sun 1 - 10 PM. Estab 1878 to serve the study and research needs of the students and faculty of the university and the community. Ricker Library lends material through UIUC Interlibrary Loan. Circ 50,000
Income: $60,200 (financed by state appropriation, blanket order, gifts and UIUC Library Friends)
Purchases: $36,300
Library Holdings: Vols 45,000; Per subs 350; Micro — Fiche, reels; AV — Slides; Other — Clipping files, exhibition catalogs, pamphlets, photographs, reproductions, sculpture
Special Subjects: Aesthetics, Architecture, Art Education, Constructions, Drawings, Prints, Sculpture, History of Art & Architecture; Philosophy of Art, Practice and History of Painting, Vernacular Architecture
Collections: Architectural Folio; Prairie School Architects; Ricker Papers; Frank Lloyd Wright
Publications: Acquisitions list, 4 per year; annual periodicals list

CHARLESTON

M EASTERN ILLINOIS UNIVERSITY, Tarble Arts Center, Lincoln & Seventh Sts, 61920. Tel 217-581-5832, 581-2787. *Dir* Donald R Carmichael; *Cur* Mark Alexander; *Admin Asst* Ann Shafer
Open Tues - Fri 10 AM - 5 PM, Sun 1 - 5 PM, cl Mon & Sat. No admis fee. Estab as an exhibition gallery and fine arts center. Average Annual Attendance: 18,000. Mem: 1400; dues $10 - $25
Income: Financed by state appropriation, membership and through the University
Collections: Contemporary Art; Illinois Folk Art
Exhibitions: Temporary exhibition including ceramics, jewelry, paintings, photography, prints, sculpture and textiles; (1982-84) Lawrence Calcagno: A Retrospective; Survey of Illinois Clay; Al Allen: Recent Works; Dean Fausett: Selected Paintings; Ten Illinois Sculptors; Women Look at Women; Know What You See: Smithsonian; (1983) Rauschenberg/Rosenquist; Watercolor: Illinois '83; International Children Art; Joliet Prison Photographs; Mid-States Art Exhibition: 35th Annual Competition; American Masters of Photography; Johann Eyfells: Contemporary Sculpture; Iceland: Fire of the Arctic; Walter Sorge: A Retrospective; Netherlands—Art of Design Environments in Netherlands; Dan Howard: A retrospective
Publications: Exhibition catalogs
Activities: Classes for adults and children; docent training; lectures open to the

public, 7 vis lectr per yr; concerts; gallery talks; tours; competitions with awards; individual paintings & original objects of art lent to other institutions; lending collection contains 75 original prints, 50 paintings, 20 sculpture, 150 folk art objects; book traveling exhibitions; originate traveling exhibitions; museum & sales shops sell books, magazines, original art, reproductions & prints

CHICAGO

AMERICAN SOCIETY OF ARTISTS, INC
For further information, see National and Regional Organizations

M **ARTEMISA GALLERY,** 9 W Hubbard St, 60610. Tel 312-751-2016
Open Tues - Sat 11 AM - 5 PM. No admis fee. Estab 1973 as a non-profit women's cooperative to exhibit members' work and to promote public awareness of the achievements of women artists. Photography gallery is maintained. Mem: Dues benefactor $200 or more, patron $100, sponsor $50, members $15
Income: Financed by grants donations and gallery members
Exhibitions: Regular exhibitions by members; annual exhibit of established contemporary women artists; new artists and educational exhibits
Activities: Classes for adults; dramatic programs; lectures open to public; gallery talks; competitions; sales shops sells original art

L **Learning Resource Center,** 9 W Hubbard St, 60610
Open to school groups, organizations and the public, the Learning Resource Center houses a collection of video and audio tapes of locally and nationally known artists, with emphasis on women. A video monitor and replay equipment makes the tapes available for viewing during regularly scheduled hours (4 - 5 PM Tues - Sat) or at other times by appointment
Library Holdings: AV — A-tapes, slides, v-tapes

M **ART INSTITUTE OF CHICAGO,** Michigan Ave at Adams St, 60603. Tel 312-443-3600. *Chmn Board of Trustees* Arthur W Schultz; *Dir* James N Wood; *Pres* E Laurence Chalmers Jr; *VPres Admin Affairs* Robert E Mars; *VPres Develop & Public Relations* Larry Ter Molen; *Secy* Linda Starks; *Cur American Art* Milo M Naeve; *Cur European Painting & Sculpture* Richard R Brettell; *Conservator* Timothy Lennon; *Assoc Cur for Classical Art* Louise Berge; *Executive Dir Museum Education* Rex Moser; *Dir Museum Photography* Howard Kraywinkel; *Cur Photography* David Travis; *Cur Africa, Oceania & Americas* Richard Fraser Townshend; *Cur Prints & Drawings* Harold Joachim; *Cur Dept Architecture* John R Zukowsky; *Cur Textiles* Christa C Mayer Thurman; *Cur European Decorative Arts* Lynn Springer-Roberts; *Assoc Cur 20th Century Painting & Sculpture* Anne Rorimer; *Museum Registrar* Wallace Bradway; *Dir Public Relations* Helen M Lethert; *Editorial Coordr* Susan F Rossen; *Dir Annual Programs* Edith B Gaines; *Cur 20th Century Painting & Sculpture* A James Speyer
Open Mon - Wed & Fri 10:30 AM - 4:30 PM, Thurs 10:30 AM - 8 PM, Sat 10 AM - 5 PM, Sun & holidays Noon - 5 PM, cl Christmas. Admis adults $4 suggested, sr citizens and children $2 suggested, Thurs no admis fee. Estab and incorporated 1879 to found, build, maintain and operate museums of fine arts, schools and libraries of art, to form, preserve and exhibit collections of objects of art of all kinds, and to carry on appropriate activities conducive to the artistic development of the community. Average Annual Attendance: 1,200,000. Mem: 75,000; dues family $40, individual $30
Collections: Paintings, sculpture, oriental art, prints and drawings, photographs, decorative arts, primitive art and textiles; The painting collection reviews Western art, with an especially fine sequence of French Impressionists and Post Impressionists; the print collection illustrates the history of printmaking from the 15th - 20th centuries with important examples of all periods. It is particularly rich in French works of the 19th century including Meryon, Redon, Millet, Gauguin and Toulouse- Lautrec; The Thorne Miniature Rooms are on permanent view; textiles are displayed in the Agnes Allerton Textile Galleries, which includes a study room and new conservation facilities; the collection of primitive art consists of African, Oceanic and ancient American objects; The Architecture Collection includes all the 19th & 20th century drawings and architectural fragments in the Institute's permanent collection including the more than 40,000 architectural drawings that are in the Burnham Library of Architecture; The Columbus Drive Facilities include the reconstructed Trading Room from the Chicago Stock Exchange; Arthur Rubloff Paperweight collection is on view in Gunsaulus Hall; the America Windows, monumental stained glass windows designed by Marc Chagall, are on view in the gallery overlooking McKinlock Court
Exhibitions: (1982) Highlights of the Universal Limited Art Editions Collection; 74th American Exhibition; The Work of Atget: Old France; selected textile acquisitions since 1978; Frederic Remington: Painting & Sculpture from the George F Harding Collection; France in the Golden Age: Seventeenth-Century French Paintings in American Collections; Chicago Architects Design: A Century of Architectural Drawings; Paper and Light: The Calotype in France and Great Britain, 1838-1870; Living National Treasures of Japan; Mauritshuis: 17th-Century Dutch Painting from the Royal Picture Gallery; Perspectives on Contemporary Realism: The Jalane and Richard Davidson Collection; Ansel Adams: An American Place; Photography and Architecture: 1839-1939; New Chicago Architecture: Beyond the International Style; An Open Land: Photographs of the Midwest, 1852-1982
Publications: Masaic, every two months; Museum Studies; catalogs; Annual Report
Activities: Classes for adults; docent training; lectures open to public; concerts; gallery talks; guided lecture tours; competitions; individual paintings and original objects of art lent to museums around the world; originate traveling exhibitions to selected museums; museum shop sells books, magazines, original art, reproductions, prints, slides, decorative accessories, crafts, jewelry, greeting cards and postcards

L **Ryerson and Burnham Libraries,** Michigan at Adams St, 60603. Tel 312-443-3600. *Dir of Libraries* Daphne Roloff; *Assoc Librn & Head Reference Dept* Susan Glover Godlewski; *Head Technical Services* Louis Hammack; *Head Slide Librn* Nancy Kirkpatrick
Open Mon, Tues & Fri 10:30 AM - 4:30 PM, Thurs 12:30 AM - 7:45 PM, Sat 10 AM - 4:30 PM, cl Sats from June - Labor Day & legal holidays. Open to museum members, staff of museum, students and faculty of the School of Art Institute and visiting scholars and curators only
Income: $424,300
Purchases: $138,000
Library Holdings: Vols 131,000; Per subs 824; Micro — Fiche, reels; AV — Slides 300,000; Other — Exhibition catalogs, manuscripts, memorabilia, pamphlets, photographs
Collections: Burnham Archive: Chicago Architects, letters, reports; including special Louis Sullivan, Frank Lloyd Wright, and D H Burnham collections; Percier and Fontaine Collection; Chicago Art and Artists Scrapbook: newspaper clippings from Chicago papers from 1880 to present; Ryerson Collection of Japanese and Chinese Illustrated books; Mary Reynolds Collection: Surrealism
Exhibitions: Chicago Architects; Plan of Chicago; P B Wight; Walter Burley Griffin
Publications: Architectural Records In Chicago, research guide

O **Woman's Board,** 60603. *Pres* Mrs Robert O Delaney
Estab 1952 to supplement the Board of Trustees in advancing the growth of the Institute and extending its activities and usefulness as a cultural and educational institution. Mem: 98; annual meeting May
Income: Financed by contributions

O **Auxiliary Board,** 60603. *Pres* Mrs George M Covington
Estab 1973 to promote interest in programs and activities of the Art Institute amoung younger men and women. Mem: 58; dues $25; annual meeting June

O **Antiquarian Society,** 60603. Tel 312-443-3641. *Pres* Mrs James W Alsdorf
Open Tues & Wed 9 AM - 5 PM. Estab 1877. Makes gift of decorative arts to the Institute. Mem: 475; by invitation; annual meeting Nov
Activities: Lectures and seminars for members; tours; trips

O **Print and Drawing Club,** 60603. Tel 312-443-3660. *Pres* Edward A Bergman
Estab and incorporated 1922 to study prints and drawings and their purchase for the institute. Mem: 190; dues $25

O **Society for Contemporary Arts,** 60603. Tel 312-443-3630. *Pres* Sandra Guthman
Estab and incorporated 1940 to assist the Institute in acquisition of contemporary works. Mem: 180; annual dues $200 - $400; annual meeting May
Income: Membership contributions
Activities: Lectures, seminars and annual exhibition at the Institute

O **Oriental Dept,** 60603. Tel 312-443-3652. *Cur* Jack Sewell; *Assoc Cur* Osamu Ueda
Estab 1925 to promote interest in the Institute's collection of Oriental art. Mem: 50; dues $25 and $10

O **Textile Society,** 60603. Tel 312-443-3696. *Pres* George W Overtom
Open daily 10 AM - 4 PM by appointment only. Estab 1978 to promote appreciation of textiles through lectures, raising of funds, special publications and exhibitions for the Department of Textiles

O **Old Masters Society,** 60603. Tel 312-443-3615. *Pres* Julius Lewis
Estab 1977 to promote interest in the Department of European Painting & Sculpture, through lectures and fund raising for acquisitions. Mem: 175
Income: Financed by memberships & gifts
Activities: Lectures open to public; gallery talks; tours

M **Junior Museum,** Michigan Ave at Adams St, 60603. Tel 312-443-3680. *Dir* L Raasch
Open Mon - Wed and Fri 10:30 AM - 4 PM, Thurs 10:30 AM - 7 PM, Sat 10 AM - 4:30 PM, Sun & holidays Noon - 4:30 PM. Admission discretionary, no admis fee Thursday. Estab 1964. A facility including auditorium, lunchroom, galleries, offices and library. One main gallery with exhibits changing every two or three years and two corridor galleries changed every six months; Picnic Room for children. Average Annual Attendance: 150,000
Income: Financed by endowment
Exhibitions: (1983) Painting: From the Ground Up; Here's How: Drawing as Marking; Vatican Discovered; Works from Family Programs; Paintings That Tell A Story
Publications: Forms in Space I; Heritage Hike I, II, III, IV; yearly publications: Volunteer Directory; Information for Students and Teachers; bi-monthly brochures on family programs & teachers' services
Activities: Docent training; teacher & family workshops; lectures open to the public; gallery games; tours; junior museum shop sells books, postcards, toys

L **Little Library,** Michigan Ave at Adams St, 60603
Open for reference only
Income: Financed by endowment
Library Holdings: Vols 1500
Activities: Center for junior museum activities such as gallery games and architectural walks

O **ARTISTS GUILD OF CHICAGO,*** 664 N Michigan Ave, 60611. Tel 312-663-9300. *Pres* Corrie Glass; *VPres* Shlomo Krudo; *Secy* Gordon Hempel; *Executive Dir* M Gleeson
Open 10 AM - 4 PM Mon - Fri. No admis fee. Estab 1922 to secure and protect the independence of our members, to prevent their exploitation, to cooperate with groups with similar aims, to further the communicating arts and public knowledge and understanding of same. Galleries are located in headquarters building. Average Annual Attendance: 2000. Mem: 750; dues $65; annual meeting first Tues in Oct
Income: Financed by membership, employment service for artists, social and educational programs, exhibits
Collections: AGC Permanent Collection of over seventy fine art works
Exhibitions: Eight or nine juried shows each year; Members exhibitions; Annual Chicago Show

O **ARTS CLUB OF CHICAGO GALLERY,** 109 E Ontario St, 60611. Tel 312-787-3997. *Dir* Patricia M Scheidt; *Pres* Stanley M Freehling; *First VPres* James W Alsdorf; *Secretary* Mrs Sanger P Robinson
Open 10 AM - 5:30 PM. No admis fee. Estab 1916 to maintain club rooms for members and provide public galleries for changing exhibitions. Gallery has 200 running ft of wall space. Average Annual Attendance: 15,000. Mem: 1150; annual meeting in Nov
Income: Financed by membership
Purchases: Occasional purchases from bequests
Exhibitions: (1982-83) Mies van der Rohe: Interior Spaces; High Culture In the Americas Before 1500; Raoul Hague sculpture; Terence La Noue paintings;

David Smith paintings, sculpture, works on paper; 63rd Annual Artist Members Exhibition Arakawa, Paintings and Montypes; James Biederman, Mel Kenrick, Don Gummer, Sculpture; Harry Bowers, Photographs; Robert Curtis, Sculpture; John Evans, Collages; Nathan Oliveira, Paintings and Monotypes; 62nd Professional Members Exhibition of Drawings and Sculpture
Publications: Exhibition Catalogs
Activities: Dramatic programs; lect; concerts; traveling exhibitions organized and circulated

L **Reference Library,** 109 E Ontario St, 60611
Reference library
Library Holdings: Vols 2500; Per subs 6; Other — Exhibition catalogs
Special Subjects: 20th Century paintings, sculpture, drawings, prints & photography

M **BALZEKAS MUSEUM OF LITHUANIAN CULTURE,** 4012 Archer Ave, 60632. Tel 312-847-2441. *Pres* Stanley Balzekas Jr; *VPres* Joseph Katauskas
Open seven days a week 1 - 4 PM. Admis adults $1, children and senior citizens $.50. Estab 1966 as a repository for collecting and preserving Lithuanian cultural treasures. Mem: 1000; annual dues $15
Income: $5000 (financed by membership and donations)
Collections: Amber; Philately; †Coins; Textiles; Wooden folkart; Maps
Exhibitions: Will exhibit twenty-five paintings
Publications: Lithuanian Museum Review, bi-monthly
Activities: Classes for adults and children; lectures open to the public; gallery talks; tours; competitions with awards; scholarships offered; individual paintings are lent to the University and other institutions; book traveling exhibitions; Sales shop sells books, reproductions, textiles, amber, Lithuanian dolls, philately, numismatics

L **Research Library,** 4012 Archer Ave, 60632. *Head Librn* Jurgis Kasakaitis
Open Seven days 1 - 4 PM. Estab 1966. Open to public for reference; lending restricted to members
Library Holdings: Vols 15,000; Per subs 20; Micro — Cards; AV — A-tapes, cassettes, fs, rec, slides, v-tapes; Other — Clipping files, exhibition catalogs, framed reproductions, manuscripts, memorabilia, original art works, pamphlets, prints, reproductions, sculpture
Collections: Folk art; Reproductions of Lithuanian artists; Information on Lithuanian artists and their works
Exhibitions: Rare Book & Map Exhibits
Publications: Books

CHICAGO ARCHITECTURE FOUNDATION

M **Glessner House,*** 1800 S Prairie Ave, 60616. Tel 312-326-1393. *Cur* Elaine Harrington
Open Tues - Fri 11 AM - 4 PM, Sat - Sun 11 AM - 5 PM, cl Fri Nov - March. Admis adults $3, students and senior citizens $2, members free; group rates available. Estab 1966 for the restoration of the main floor of this architecturally significant residence, and for the promotion of good architecture in general. Designed by world-famous Henry Hobson Richardson, often known as the Father of Modern Architecture, Glessner House was completed in 1886. Its period furnishings give visitors an excellent idea of what Victorian life was like on this street once known as Millionaires' Row. Average Annual Attendance: 5000. Mem: 1800; dues life $500, contributing $100, family $30, individual $20, students and seniors $10
Income: Financed by membership, tours, and rentals of house
Collections: †House Furnishings
Publications: Chicago Architecture Foundation Members' Newsletter, bimonthly
Activities: Classes for adults and children; docent training; public service; visiting lectrs; tours; original objects of art lent to galleries which are mounting exhibitions on architecture; lending collection contains architectural ornaments; sales shop selling books, posters, stationery, small gift items

M **ArchiCenter,*** 330 S Dearborn, 60604. Tel 312-782-1776. *Mgr* Jane Lucas; *Asst Mgr* D Patti Marks
Open Mon - Fri 9 AM - 5 PM, Sat 9 AM - 4:30 PM, Sun Noon - 4:30 PM. No admis fee. Estab 1976 to make people more aware of the build environment through exhibits, lectures, films and tours. Approx 2500 sq ft of exhibit space offers various exhibit chronicling Chicago's contributions to the modern building arts. Average Annual Attendance: 40,000
Income: Financed by membership, book shop, foundation, government and private grants
Exhibitions: (1982) Issac Scott Reform Furniture; Academic Architecture; Walter Burley Griffins Parliment House
Activities: 30 visiting lectrs per year; sales shop selling books, magazines, slides, small gift items, stationery and posters

O **CHICAGO HISTORICAL SOCIETY,** Clark St at North Ave, 60614. Tel 312-642-4600. *Pres* Stewart Dixon; *VPres* Philip W Hummer; *Secy* Bryan S Reid Jr; *Dir* Ellsworth H Brown; *Cur Painting & Sculpture* Joseph B Zywicki; *Cur Decorative Arts* Sharon Darling; *Cur Costumes* Elizabeth Jachimowicz; *Editor* Timothy Jacobson; *Chief, Education and Public Programs* Judy Weisman; *Cur Architectural & Printed Collections* Wim de Wit; *Cur Manuscripts Collections* A J Motley
Open Mon - Sat 9:30 AM - 4:30 PM; Sun & holidays 12:00 - 5 PM; Library open Tues - Sat 9:30 AM - 4:30 PM, cl Christmas, Thanksgiving, and New Year's Day. Admis adults $1, children (6-17) $.50, senior citizens $.25; no admis fee Mon. Estab 1856 to maintain a museum and library of American history with special emphasis on the Chicago region. The Montgomery A Ward Costume Gallery provides a series of changing exhibitions. Average Annual Attendance: 200,000. Mem: 5200; dues $25; annual meeting in Oct
Income: $2,500,000 (financed by endowment, membership, city and state appropriations and public donations)
Collections: Architectural Archive; Chicago Decorative Arts; Costumes; Graphics; Manuscripts; Printed Collection
Exhibitions: Chicago Ceramics & Glass; Chromolithography in America 1840-1900; Red Head Gal: Fashions of Gorden Conway; Holabird & Roche, Holabird & Root: the First Two Generations; Puppets: Art & Entertainment; Fort Dearborn & Frontier Chicago (re-installed); Arthur Siegel: A Life In Photography; Maxwell Street: Nathan Lerner & James Newberry; Art, Craft, Industry: Chicago Furniture, 1833-1983; Illinois Toys: 1880-1980; continuing program of craft demonstrations and exhibits from the collections
Publications: Books; Calendar of Events, quarterly; Catalogs; Chicago History, quarterly
Activities: Classes for adults and children; lect open to public, 8-10 vis lectr per year; gallery talks; tours; sales shop selling books, magazines, prints, reproductions, slides

L **Library,** Clark St at North Ave, 60614
Open Tues - Sat 9:30 AM - 4:30 PM, except July & August when it is open Mon - Fri
Library Holdings: Vols 120,000; Micro — Reels; Other — Manuscripts 4,000,000, photographs, prints

L **CHICAGO PUBLIC LIBRARY,** Art Section, Fine Arts Division, Cultural Center, 78 E Washington St, 60602. Tel 312-269-2858. *Commissioner* Amanda S Rudd; *Chief Fine Arts Division* Rosalinda I Hack; *Asst Division Chief* Gerald Zimmerman; *Asst Division Chief* Yvonne S Brown; *Picture Coll Librn* Margarete K Gross; *Coll Development* Judith Rosenbaum-Cooper
Open Mon - Thurs 9 AM - 7 PM, Fri 9 AM - 6 PM, Sat 9 AM - 5 PM. Estab 1872 as a free public library and reading room. The present building was built in 1897. Audio-visual materials are restricted for use by Chicago area residents
Income: $100,000 (financed by city and state appropriations)
Library Holdings: Vols 57,000; Per subs 330; Micro — Fiche, reels; AV — V-tapes 75; Other — Clipping files, exhibition catalogs, pamphlets, photographs
Special Subjects: Architecture, Crafts, Decorative Arts, Photography, Theatre Arts, Chicago Architecture; Dance
Collections: Exhibition catalogues beginning in 1973, primarily English language catalogues; folk dance collection of 50 loose leaf volumes; picture collection of over one million items of secondary source material covering all subject areas; dance videocassettes documenting history styles & local choreography
Activities: Dramatic programs; lect open to public; concerts; interlibrary loan

M **Cultural Center,** 78 E Washington St, 60602. Tel 312-269-2820. *Board Pres* Sally Berger; *VPres* Peter J Fosco; *Cur Special Coll* Laura Linard; *Head Audio-visual Center* Barbara Flynn; *Coordr of Programs & Exhibits* Janet Carl Smith
Open Mon - Thurs 9 AM - 7 PM, Fri 9 AM - 6 PM, Sat 9 AM - 5 PM, Sun open for programs only. No admis fee. Estab 1977 to integrate in a single facility the functions of library gallery, museum and center for the arts and humanities. The Center maintains the Randolph Gallery, 2025 sq ft, the West Gallery, 92 running ft, the East Gallery, 150 running ft, G A R Memorial Hall, 5088 sq ft, and the Exhibit Hall, 6004 sq ft. Average Annual Attendance: 1,250,000
Income: Financed by city and state appropriations, grant monies and corporate support
Exhibitions: (1982-83) A Nation Divided: The War Between the States, 1861-1865; The Scandinavian Touch: Contemporary Scandinavian Textiles; Images of Shakespeare; Under the Spell: The Art of Haiti; ceremonial textiles from Chicago area churches and synagogues
Publications: Calendar of Events, monthly
Activities: Dramatic programs; lect open to public; concerts; tours; gallery talks; sales shop

O **CONTEMPORARY ART WORKSHOP,** 542 W Grant Place, 60614. Tel 312-525-9624. *Dir* John Kearney
Open daily 9 AM - 5:30 PM, Sat Noon - 5 PM. No admis fee. Estab 1950 as an art center and a Workshop-Alternative Space for artists; it is the oldest artist-run art workshop in the country. Studios for approximately 20 artists and two galleries for exhibition of developing and emerging artists from Chicago and other parts of the country are maintained. Average Annual Attendance: 4000
Income: Financed by contributions, foundations, Illinois Arts Council, National Endowment for the Arts, and earnings by the workshop fees
Exhibitions: Joe Agate; Roger Akers; Carol Bendell; Nancy Burket; Mimi Dolnick; Michael Dunbar; Walter Fydryck; Diana Foster; Julian Harr; W A S Hatch; Amy Kaiser; John Kearney; Mark Krastoff; Steven Lowery; Robert McCauley; John Mishler; Renate Ponsold Motherwell; Jacqueline Ruttinger; Bill Stipe; Marilyn Sward; Emerson Woelffer; Paul Zakoian Robert Stiegler; Mati Maldre; Rufus Zogbaum; Cameron Zebrun; Paul Caccia; Scott Sandusky; Peter Holbrook; Franze Schulze; Susan Michod; Dennis Goncher; Kevin Strandberg; Marilyn Schechter; Charles Derer; Christopher Kondrath; Peter Ratner; Seymour Rosofsky; Valerie Eickmeier; George Cohen; James Pizzillo; Michael Warrick; Sherry Healy; Ellen Lanyon; Sheri Klein; Kathleen Kehoe; Anna Horvath; Theresa Taylor; David Moose; Didier Nolet; Alex Nelson; Arnaldo Roche; Ellen Nadeau; Matthew de Genaro; Melinda Hunt; Laurel Fredrickson; Christopher Boyce; Michele Hemsoth; Jannifer Krantz; Kimbel Sadlon; Gonzalo Jesse Sadia; Elizabeth Knowles; Sydney Licht; Christine O'Connor; Cherri Rittenhouse
Activities: Classes for adults; lect open to the public, 5 vis lect per yr; tours; gallery sells artwork

M **DUSABLE MUSEUM OF AFRICAN AMERICAN HISTORY,** 740 E 56th Pl, 60637. Tel 312-947-0600. *Dir* Margaret T Burroughs; *Cur* Charles G Burroughs; *Art Cur* Ramon Price; *Dir Publications* Eugene P Feldman
Open Mon - Fri 9 AM - 5 PM, Sat & Sun Noon - 5 PM. Admis adults $1, children & students $.50, groups by appointment. Estab 1961 as history and art museum on African American history. Mem: Dues life $1000, general $15
Collections: Historical archives; paintings; photographs; prints; sculpture
Publications: Books of poems, children's stories, African and Afro-American history; Heritage Calendar, annually
Activities: Lect; guided tours; book traveling exhibitions; sales shop selling curios, sculpture, prints, books and artifacts

C **EXCHANGE NATIONAL BANK OF CHICAGO,*** 130 S LaSalle St, 60603. Tel 312-781-8079, 781-8000. *Cur* Herbert Kahn
Open to public. Estab 1968 as a community service by making a meaningful cultural contribution to the community. Collection displayed in public areas of the bank
Collections: Approximately 2000 photographs by important photographers since the founding of photography up to the present
Activities: Tours

M **FIELD MUSEUM OF NATURAL HISTORY,** Roosevelt Rd at Lake Shore Dr, 60605. Tel 312-922-9410. *Pres* Willard L Boyd; *Dir* Lorin I Nevling, Jr
Open daily 9 AM - 5 PM, cl Thanksgiving, Christmas, New Years. Admis family $4, adults $2, students $1, senior citizens $.50, no charge on Thurs. Estab 1893 to preserve and disseminate knowledge of natural history. 22 anthropological exhibition halls, including a Hall of Primitive Art are maintained. Average Annual Attendance: 1,200,000. Mem: 31,646; dues $20 & $25
Income: $8,000,000 (financed by endowment, membership, city and state appropriations and federal and earned funds)
Collections: Anthropological collections totaling over one third million specimens, including approx 100,000 art objects from North and South America, Oceania, Africa, Asia and prehistoric Europe
Exhibitions: Basketry of the Northwest Coast Indians; Between Friends; Gold of Eldorado; Great Bronze Age of China; Hopi; The People & Art of the Philippines; The Last & First Eskimo; Treasures from the Shanghai Museum: 6000 Years of Chinese Art; Masters Pyer's The World: Early Fabrics from India; A Celebration of Birds: Louis Agassiz & His Art; The Vanishing Race & Other Illusions: A New Look at the Work of Edward Curtis
Publications: Bulletin, monthly; Fieldiana (serial)
Activities: Classes for adults and children; lect open to the public, 25 visiting lectrs per year; concerts; gallery talks; tours; exten dept serving Chicago area; original objects of art lent to qualified museum or other scholarly institutions; traveling exhibitions organized and circulated; museum shop selling books, magazines, prints, slides

L **Library,** Roosevelt Rd at Lake Shore Dr, 60605. *Librn* W Peyton Fawcett
Library Holdings: Vols 202,000; Per subs 4000
Collections: Rare Bookroom housing 6000 vols

C **THE FIRST NATIONAL BANK OF CHICAGO,*** One First National Plaza, 60670. Tel 312-732-8939, 732-4000. *Cur* Robert Middaugh
Open to public by appointment only. No admis fee. Estab 1968 to assemble works of art to serve as a permanent extension of daily life. Collection displayed throughout bank building and overseas offices
Collections: Art from Africa, America, Asia, Australia, the Caribbean Basin, Europe, Latin America, Near East and the South Seas ranging from 6th Century BC to the present
Activities: Individual objects of art lent only to major exhibitions in museums

L **HARRINGTON INSTITUTE OF INTERIOR DESIGN,** Design Library, 410 S Michigan Ave, 60605. Tel 312-939-4975. *Head Librn* Adeline Schuster
Open daily 8 AM - 5 PM, Tues & Thurs 8 AM - 9 PM. Estab 1960
Purchases: $30,000
Library Holdings: Vols 6000; Per subs 95; Micro — Fiche 300; AV — Slides; Other — Clipping files, exhibition catalogs, pamphlets
Special Subjects: Architecture, Interior Design, Design Theory, Product Design, 20th Century Design
Collections: Furniture Manufacture Catalogs
Publications: Current Awareness, memos; subject bibliographies

C **ILLINOIS BELL,*** 225 W Randolph St, 60606. Tel 312-727-2158, 727-9411. *Mgr Art Program* Marion Butler
Lobby gallery open 8 AM - 5 PM. Estab 1967 to support the arts; to make the company a responsive member of the community; to provide uplifting atmosphere for employees. Collection displayed throughout building and in offices; Lobby exhibits art (not from company collection)
Collections: Approximately 2000 pieces, multi-media, mostly modern, non-representational works, many by Illinois artists
Activities: Gallery talks; tours for groups; originate traveling exhibitions from Lobby exhibits to various galleries and other public locations in Illinois

M **LOYOLA UNIVERSITY OF CHICAGO,** Martin D'Arcy Gallery of Art, 6525 N Sheridan Rd, 60626. Tel 312-274-3000, Ext 2677. *Dir* Donald F Rowe; *Asst Dir* Leo J Martin
Open Mon - Fri Noon - 4 PM, Tues & Thurs 6:30 - 9:30 PM, Sun 1 - 4 PM. No admis fee. Estab 1969 to display the permanent university collection of Medieval, Renaissance and Baroque decorative arts and paintings. One gallery set up as a large living room with comfortable seating, classical music, fresh flowers, view of Lake Michigan, and art objects in view. Average Annual Attendance: 10,000
Income: Financed by gifts
Purchases: $200,000
Collections: †Bronze, †enamel, †gold, †ivory, paintings, †sculpture, †silver, †textiles, †wax
Publications: Annual Report; The Art of Jewelry, 1450 to 1650; Enamels, the XII to the XVI century; The First Ten Years, Notable Acquisitions of Medieval, Renaissance and Baroque Art
Activities: Gallery talks; tours on request; paintings and original objects of art lent to qualified museums; lending collection contains original art works, paintings and sculpture

L **Library,** 6525 N Sheridan Rd, 60626
Open to university students and scholars
Library Holdings: Vols 15,000; Per subs 40

O **MUSEUM, FINE ARTS RESEARCH & HOLOGRAPHIC CENTER,** 1134 W Washington Blvd, 60607. Tel 312-226-1007. *Exec Dir* Loren Billings; *VPres* Patrick McCallig; *Secy* Robert Billings; *Dir Display & Design* Constance Kasprzak; *Dir Education* Terrence Kay; *Dir Research* John Hoffmann; *Dir System Development* Russell Hilton; *Dir Electronics* Ken Hilton
Open Wed - Sun 12:30 - 5 PM. Admis $1. Estab 1976 to display Holographic works; to carry on public education; to operate a school of Holography. 15,000 sq ft of exhibition space, oak panel walls, special display wings, sales gallery; school facilities comprise 4600 sq ft of fully equipped laboratories and darkrooms with additional lecture facilities. Average Annual Attendance: 7000
Income: $200,000 (financed by city & state appropriation, sales, research grants, teaching, consulting, museum store, school, tours & rentals)
Collections: Holograms from throughout the world
Exhibitions: Holography: A Perceptual Odessey
Publications: Holography; class text books
Activities: Classes for adults; lectures open to public, 6 vis lectr per yr; book traveling exhibitions; museum shop sells books, originals, slides & holograms

L **David Wender Library,** 1134 W Washington Blvd, 60607. *Librn* Ivan Dee
Open by appointment only
Library Holdings: Vols 200; Per subs 10; AV — Kodachromes, motion pictures, slides, v-tapes; Other — Exhibition catalogs, framed reproductions

M **MUSEUM OF CONTEMPORARY ART,** 237 E Ontario St, 60611. Tel 312-280-2660. *Chief Cur* Mary Jane Jacob; *Programming & Publicity Dir* Alene Valkanas; *Education Dir* Naomi Vine; *Adminr* Helen Dunbeck; *Asst Cur* Lynne Warren; *Dir Development* Russell Barnes; *Registrar* Debi Purden; *Store Mgr* Curistine Der Deridn; *Controller* Nancy Cook
Open Tues - Sat 10 AM - 5 PM, Sun 12 - 5 PM, cl Mon. Admis general $2. Estab 1967 as a forum for contemporary arts in Chicago. Average Annual Attendance: 110,000. Mem: 5700
Income: $1,000,000 (financed by endowment, membership, public and private sources)
Collections: Permanent collection of 20th century and contemporary, constantly growing through gifts and purchases
Exhibitions: Margaret Wharton; Charles Simonds; Selections from the Dennis Adrian Collection; Contemporary Art from the Netherlands; Melvin Charney, Chicago Construction; Laurie Anderson: United States I-IV; Magdalena Abakanowicz; Kenneth Josephson Retrospective; Naive and Outsider Painting in Germany and Paintings by Gabriele Munter; Dogs
Publications: Bimonthly calendar, exhibition catalogs
Activities: Docent training; lectures; performance, tours, films; originate traveling exhibitions; museum store selling books, designer jewelry and other gifts, magazines, original art & reproductions

L **Library,** 237 E Ontario St, 60611. Tel 312-280-2660
Library collection
Library Holdings: Vols 3500; Per subs 85; AV — Cassettes, rec, slides, v-tapes; Other — Clipping files, exhibition catalogs, memorabilia, pamphlets

M **MUSEUM OF SCIENCE AND INDUSTRY,** 57th St & Lake Shore Dr, 60637. Tel 312-684-1414. *Pres* Dr Victor J Danilov; *VPres & Dir Business Affairs* Audley G Lemmenes; *Dir Development* Thomas G Sanberg; *Dir Education* Theodore H Ansbacher; *Dir Building Servs* Robert B Diehl; *Special Asst to Pres* Sherry B Goodman; *Dir Operations* Bernice Martin; *Dir Public Relations* Irving Paley; *Dir Exhibits* Theodore J Swigon; *Dir Science* David A Ucko
Open summer Mon - Sun 9:30 AM - 5:30 PM, winter Mon - Fri 9:30 AM - 4 PM, Sat, Sun & holidays 9:30 AM - 5:30 PM. No admis fee. Estab 1926 to further public understanding of science, technology, industry, medicine & related fields. Visitor-participation exhibits depicting scientific principles, technological applications & social implications in fields of artscience. Average Annual Attendance: 4,000,000. Mem: 8090; dues life $1000, contributing $100, family $30, individual $20
Income: $16,200,000 (financed by endowment, membership, city & state appropriation, contributions & grants from companies, foundations & individuals)
Collections: Artscience Gallery, artworks based on scientific & technological principles; This is Photography, scientific, industrial & popular uses of photography; Chicago, industrial & scientific development; Newspaper in America, world events in photos; Colleen Moore's Fairy Castle
Exhibitions: (1983) Design: The Problem Comes First; Finland: Nature, Architecture; (1984) Muppets & Friends
Publications: Progress, bimonthly; calendar of events, bimonthly
Activities: Classes for adults & children; dramatic programs; field trips; summer camps; teacher workshops; lectures open to public, 4 vis lect per yr; competitions; outreach activities; lending collection contains communications, transportation & textile equipment; book traveling exhibitions; originate traveling exhibitions; museum shop sells books, magazines, prints, slides, postcards & souvenirs

M **N.A.M.E. GALLERY,** 9 W Hubbard St, 60610. Tel 312-467-6550. *Pres* Sharon Evans; *VPres* Buzz Spector; *Treas* John Ragir; *Secy* Victor Cassidy; *Gallery Dir* Christopher English
Open Tues - Sat 11 AM - 5 PM. Estab 1973, a non-profit, tax exempt, alternative exhibition space dedicated to the encouragement of ideas and communication. Gallery has 4000 sq ft of space with one main show area of 3200 sq ft, 210 ft running wall; first floor-loft building. Average Annual Attendance: 22,000
Income: Financed by city and state and federal grants, private donations and corporate-foundation grants
Exhibitions: Mike Glier Wall Drawings; Desiring Machines; Compassionate Images; Photographers Invite Photographers; Les Levine; Ellen Lanyon; New Talent; Ron Cohen; Semaphore at N.A.M.E; 19th Anniversary Show Drawing At N.A.M.E.; Steve Mannheimer; Leonard Titzer; Six Over Six; Connie Campbell-Eaton; Sandra Geiger; Michael Paxton; Phil Berkman; Othello Anderson; Lorenzo Pale; Patrick Thibert; Sam Krizan; Guy Whitney; L J Douglas; Vietnam Veterans Exhibit; Spiritual Perceptions
Publications: Exhibition catalogues
Activities: Lect open to public, vis lectr; concerts; gallery talks; tours; panel discussion of current issues; honorariums; originate traveling exhibitions

L **N.A.M.E. Documents,** 9 W Hubbard St, 60610
Open Tues - Sat 11 AM - 5 PM. Estab 1974 to preserve the history of N.A.M.E. Gallery
Library Holdings: AV — Lantern slides, slides; Other — Clipping files, exhibition catalogs, memorabilia, original art works, photographs, prints

M **NORTHEASTERN ILLINOIS UNIVERSITY,** North River Community Gallery,* 3307 W Bryn Mawr, 60659. Tel 312-583-4050, Ext 586. *Gallery Coordr* Frank J Fritzmann
Open Mon - Fri 1 - 5 PM. No admis fee. Estab Feb 1973 for the purpose of providing a link between the University and the local community on a cultural and aesthetic level, to bring the best local and Midwest artists to this community. Gallery is located in a relatively small storefront, on a commercial street, three blocks from the University. Average Annual Attendance: 500-900
Income: Financed by Department of Art funds and personnel
Publications: Flyers on each show
Activities: Competitions

M **NORTH PARK COLLEGE,** Carlson Tower Gallery, 5125 N Spaulding Ave, 60625. Tel 312-583-2700. *Gallery Dir* Gayle V Bradley-Johnson
Open Mon - Fri 9 AM - 3 PM. Educational exposure to campus and community
Activities: Educ dept

M **PALETTE AND CHISEL ACADEMY OF FINE ARTS GALLERY,*** 1012 N Dearborn St, 60610. Tel 312-337-9889. *Pres* Alfred Alfredson; *Secy* Elsie T Lowe
Open daily 2 - 5 PM, Tues & Thurs evenings 7 - 9 PM. No admis fee. Estab and incorporated 1895. Gallery owns building containing galleries, classrooms, studios and library. Mem: 100; dues $84; annual meeting Jan
Collections: Oil paintings by members
Activities: Educ events; lect; competitions; awards

M **PEACE MUSEUM,*** 364 W Erie St, 60611. Tel 312-440-1860. *Dir* Mark Rogovin
Open Tues to the public. Estab as a center for discussion and debate on how to build peace through art
Exhibitions: Works by 170 artists

C **PLAYBOY ENTERPRISES, INC,** 919 N Michigan Ave, 60611. Tel 312-751-8000. *VPres & Art Dir* Tom Staebler; *Admin Mgr* Barbara Hoffman
Open to public by appointment only in groups. No admis fee. Estab 1953 to gather and maintain works commissioned for reproduction by Playboy Magazine
Collections: Selected works from 4000 illustrations and fine art pieces, works include paintings and sculpture representing 20th Century artists such as Robert Ginzel, Roger Hane, Larry Rivers, James Rosenquist, Seymour Rosofsky, Roy Schnackenberg, George Segal, Andy Warhol, Robert Weaver, Tom Wesselman, Karl Wirsum, and others
Publications: Catalogs pertaining to Beyond Illustration - The Art of Playboy; The Art of Playboy - from the First 25 Years
Activities: Lectures; tours; annual illustration awards; individual paintings & original objects of art lent to museums & schools; originate traveling exhibitions to galleries, universities, museums and cultural centers
L **Library,** Chicago, 60611
Library Holdings: Other — Clipping files, exhibition catalogs, original art works, photographs

M **POLISH MUSEUM OF AMERICA,** 984 N Milwaukee Ave, 60622. Tel 312-384-3352. *Dir* Donald Bilinski; *Pres* Ted Swigon
Open daily Noon - 5 PM. No admis fee. Estab 1937, to gather and preserve items and records pertaining to Polish culture as well as Polish American culture. A specialized Museum and Gallery containing works of Polish artists, and Polish-American artists is maintained. Average Annual Attendance: 7500
Income: Financed by donations
Collections: Originals dating to beginning of 20th century, a few older pieces; Pulaski at Savannah (Batowski); works of Polish artists, Polish-American artists and works on a Polish subject; Nikifor, Jan Styka; Kossak Wojoiech
Publications: Polish Museum Quarterly
Activities: Lectures open to public; tours; traveling exhibitions organized and circulated; sales shop sells books, magazines and folk art of today
L **Research Library,** 984 N Milwaukee Ave, 60622
Library Holdings: Vols 25,000; Per subs 65
Special Subjects: Poland and works by Polish-American authors
Collections: Haiman

O **RENAISSANCE SOCIETY,** Bergman Gallery, 5811 S Ellis, 60637. Tel 312-962-8670. *Dir* Susanne Ghez
Open Tues - Sat 10 AM - 4 PM, Sun Noon - 4 PM, cl summer. Founded 1915 to advance the understanding & appreciation of the arts in all forms
Exhibitions: Six changing exhibitions per yr; annual art for young collectors sale
Activities: Lectures; gallery talks; film programs; performances

L **SAINT XAVIER COLLEGE,** Byrne Memorial Library,* Art Dept, 3700 W 103rd St, 60655. Tel 312-779-3300, Ext 365. *Dir* Chris Millson-Martula; *Sr Asst Librn* Susan Swords-Steffen
Open daily 8 AM - 10 PM. Estab 1847
Library Holdings: Vols 1733; Per subs 15; Micro — Cards; AV — Kodachromes, motion pictures, rec, slides 10,000, v-tapes; Other — Original art works
Collections: Permanent art collection

L **SCHOOL OF THE ART INSTITUTE OF CHICAGO LIBRARY,** Columbus Dr & Jackson, 60603. Tel 312-443-3748. *Dir* Nadene Byrne; *Head Readers Services* Roland Hansen; *Asst Dir & Head Technical Services* Fred Hillbruner; *Video Data Bank* Lyn Blumenthal; *Video Data Bank* Kate Horsfield
Open Mon - Thurs 8:30 AM - 9 PM, Fri 8:30 AM - 5 PM, Sat 9 AM - 5 PM, Sun 10 AM - 6 PM. Estab 1967 to provide a strong working collection for School's programs in the visual and related arts. Circ 30,000
Income: $260,100 (financed through the operational budgets of the School of Art Institute of Chicago)
Purchases: $44,500
Library Holdings: Vols 20,795; Per subs 210; AV — Cassettes, motion pictures, rec, v-tapes; Other — Exhibition catalogs, pamphlets, prints
Special Subjects: Art, Humanities
Collections: †Erens Film Scripts; Whitney Halstead Art History; †Film Study Collection; †Artists Interview Series; †Artist's Book Collection
Exhibitions: International Artists Book, 1981
Publications: Book Sak, quarterly newsletter; International Artists Book Show Catalog; Library Handbook for patrons, annually

C **SEARS ROEBUCK AND COMPANY,*** Sears Tower D 731-H, 60684. Tel 312-875-8570, 875-2500. *In Charge Art Coll* Michael C Lucia
No admis fee. Estab 1972 to present a comprehensive collection of original art of the highest quality, while providing additional decorative and color schemes throughout the Tower complex. Collection displayed throughout building; the gallery within the Tower is for the selection of art by employees for their own office. Tower is world's tallest building

Collections: Approximately 7000 pieces of art: etchings, lithographs, master graphics, oils, serigraphs and watercolors
Exhibitions: Annual Sear Employee Art Show
Activities: Tours of special events only; competitions with awards; Calders universe sculpture (Marquette 1/3 scale) on loan to Whitney Museum of Art, New York City

SOCIETY OF TYPOGRAPHIC ARTS
See National and Regional Organizations

M **SPERTUS MUSEUM OF JUDAICA,** 618 S Michigan Ave, 60605. Tel 312-922-9012, Ext 60. *Dir* Arthur M Feldman; *Cur Collections* Mary Larkin; *Asst to Dir* Bernadine Gierut; *Research Assoc* Olga Weiss; *Membership & Tours Coordr* Susan Warsager
Open Mon - Thurs 10 AM - 5 PM, Fri 10 AM - 3 PM, Sun 10 AM - 4 PM. Admis adults $2, children, students and senior citizens, $1, Fri free. Estab 1967 for interpreting and preserving the 3500-year-old heritage embodied in Jewish history. Museum houses a distinquished collection of Judaica from many parts of the world, containing exquisitely designed ceremonial objects of gold, silver, bronze and ivory. Average Annual Attendance: 25,000
Income: Contributions and subsidy from Spertus College
Collections: A pertinent collection of sculpture, paintings and graphic art; ethographic materials spanning centuries of Jewish experience; a permanent holocaust memorial; Judaica, paintings, ceremonial silver, textiles, archaeology
Publications: Catalog of Collection; special publications with exhibits; yearly Calendar of Events
Activities: Educ dept; docent training; lending collection contains 1500 slides & archaeological replicas; traveling exhibitions organized and circulated; museum store selling books, original art reproductions, slides and jewelry from Israel
L **Library,** 618 S Michigan Ave, 60605. *Librn & Dir* Richard Marcus
Reference library open to students and members
Library Holdings: Per subs 560
Special Subjects: Judaica

M **SWEDISH AMERICAN MUSEUM ASSOCIATION OF CHICAGO,** 5248 N Clark St, 60640. Tel 312-728-8111. *Pres* Sven Flodstrom; *First VPres & Mgr* Kurt Mathiasson; *Second VPres, Archivist & Board of Dir* Selma Jacobson; *Treas* Edith Johnson; *Secy* Vereen Ann Nordstrom
Open Tues - Fri 11 AM - 2 PM, Sat 11 AM - 3 PM. No admis fee, donations appreciated. Estab 1976 to display Swedish arts, crafts, artists, scientists, and artifacts connected with United States, especially Chicago. Material displayed in a store front in Andersonville, once a predominantly Swedish area in Chicago. Average Annual Attendance: 10,000. Mem: 210; dues $5 - $500; meetings April, June and Oct
Income: $10,000 (financed by membership & donations)
Collections: Artifacts used or made by Swedes, photographs, oils of or by Swedes in United States
Publications: Bulletins, bi-monthly
Activities: Educ dept for Swedish language and culture study; classes for adults; dramatic programs; docent training; lectures open to public, 2 vis lectr per yr; concerts

M **UKRAINIAN NATIONAL MUSEUM AND LIBRARY,** 2453 W Chicago Ave, 60622. Tel 312-276-6565. *Pres* Emil Basiuk; *Cur* Oksana Teodorowych
Open Sun Noon - 3 PM; office Mon - Fri 8 AM - 2 PM. Estab 1954, to collect and preserve Ukrainian cultural heritage
Income: Financed through membership and donations
Library Holdings: Vols 15,000; Per subs 100; Micro — Cards; AV — Kodachromes, slides; Other — Clipping files, framed reproductions, manuscripts, memorabilia, original art works, pamphlets, photographs, sculpture
Special Subjects: Large collection of Ukrainian Folk Arts: easter egg painting, embroidery, woodcarving
Activities: Classes for adults and children; tours; Book traveling exhibitions; traveling exhibitions organized and circulated

UNIVERSITY OF CHICAGO
M **Lorado Taft Midway Studios,*** 6016 Ingleside Ave, 60637. Tel 312-753-7234. *Dir* Thomas Mapp
Open Mon - Fri 9 AM - 5 PM, cl Sun. Studios of Lorado Taft and Associates, a Registered National Historic Landmark; now University of Chicago, Committee on Art & Design
Exhibitions: Maquettes and Portraits by Lorado Taft; student work in ceramics, graphics, painting and sculpture held in the Court Gallery
Activities: Special performances
M **David and Alfred Smart Gallery,** 5550 S Greenwood Ave, 60637. Tel 312-753-2121. *Actg Dir* Reinhold Heller; *Admin Asst* Vivian Heller; *Registrar* Mary Braun; *Secy* Jean Hall; *Cur* Richard Born; *Preparator* Rudy Bernal; *Asst Preparator* Muneer Bahauddeen; *Public Relations & Membership* Karen Bornstein
Open Tues - Sat 10 AM - 4 PM, Sun Noon - 4 PM, cl Mon. No admis fee. Estab 1974 to assist the teaching program of the Art Department of the University by maintaining a permanent collection and presenting exhibitions of scholarly and general interest. Gallery designed by E L Barnes; exhibit space covers 9500 sq ft and also contains conservation room, print and drawing study room, sculpture garden, storage and preparator's workroom. Average Annual Attendance: 25,000. Mem: 400; dues individual $25; annual meeting in Spring
Income: Financed by membership, university and special funds
Collections: †American, †Ancient, †Baroque, †Medieval, †Modern European, †Oriental and †Renaissance paintings, sculpture and †decorative arts
Exhibitions: (1982-84) Tulips, Arabesques & Turbans: Decorative Arts from the Ottoman Empire; Benton's Bentons; New Image/Pattern & Decoration from the Morton F Neumann Family Collection; Fernand Khnopff & the Belgian Avant-Garde; The Balloon: A Bicentennial Exhibition; An alle Kunstler War, Revolution-Weimar
Activities: Lectures open to public, 15 vis lectr per year; gallery talks; tours; book traveling exhibitions 2-3 per year; originate traveling exhibitions; sales shop sells books, post cards, posters, papers and photographs

M **Oriental Institute,** 1155 E 58th St, Chicago, 60637. Tel 312-753-2474. *Dir* Janet H Johnson; *Cur* John Carswell; *Assoc Cur* Barbara Hall; *Asst Cur* Anita Ghaemi
Open Tues - Sat 10 AM - 4 PM, Sun Noon - 4 PM, cl Mon. No admis fee. Estab 1894 as a museum of antiquities excavated from Egypt, Mesopotamia, Assyria, Syria, Palestine, Persia, Anatolia and Nubia, dating from 7000 years ago until the 18th Century AD. Average Annual Attendance: 58,000 - 62,000. Mem: 2650; dues $20 and up
Income: Financed by endowment, membership, federal and state grant
Collections: Ancient Near Eastern antiquities from pre-historic times to the beginning of the present era plus some Islamic artifacts; Egypt: colossal statue of King Tut, mummies, Assyrian bullman (40 tons); Mesopotamian temple interior, house interior, jewelry; Persian bull; column and capital from Persepolis; Megiddo ivories and horned altar
Exhibitions: (1982) The Quest for Prehistory: The Oriental Institute and the Origins of Civilization in the Near East; Publishing the Past: Oriental Institute Publications; (1983) The House on the Nile: Fifty Years of Chicago House at Luxor, Egypt; The Sacred Tree
Publications: Annual report; News and Notes, bimonthly
Activities: Classes for adults and children; docent programs; free film series; lectures open to the public, 8 - 10 vis lectr per yr; gallery talks; tours; original objects of art lent to museums and institutions; museum shop sells books, magazines, reproductions, prints, slides, original art, crafts, and near Eastern jewelry
—**Research Archives of the Oriental Institute,** 60637. *Librn* Charles Jones
Open to staff, students and members for reference
Library Holdings: Vols 19,000; Per subs 275; Micro — Reels; AV — A-tapes, cassettes, Kodachromes, lantern slides, motion pictures, slides; Other — Clipping files, exhibition catalogs, manuscripts, memorabilia, pamphlets 5715, photographs
Special Subjects: The ancient Near East
L **Art Library,** 1100 E 57th St, 60637. Tel 312-962-8438. *Asst Art Librn* April A Oswald
Art reserve available Mon - Thurs 8:30 AM - 9 PM, Fri 8:30 AM - 5 PM, Sat 9 AM - 5 PM, Sun 1 - 5 PM, interims Mon - Fri 9 AM - 1 PM; reference collection & stack books available Mon - Thurs 8:30 AM - 1 AM, Fri & Sat 8:30 AM - 10 PM, Sun Noon - 1 PM
Library Holdings: Vols 55,500; Auction sales catalogs, Union Catalog of Art Books in Chicago; Other — Pamphlets
L **Art Slide Collection,** * Goodspeed Hall, 80#1050 E 59th St, 60600. Tel 312-753-3896. *Cur* Olivera Mihailovic
Open Mon - Fri 8:30 AM - 4 PM; cl Sat & Sun. Estab 1938. For reference only
Library Holdings: AV — Slides 125,000
L **Max Epstein Archive,** 420 C Joseph Regenstein Library, Chicago, 60637. Tel 312-962-7080. *Cur* Holly B Hutchens
Open Mon - Fri 10 AM - 6 PM; cl Sat & Sun. Estab 1938. For reference only
Income: Financed by gifts and donations
Library Holdings: Mounted photographs of art 500,000; catalogued and mounted photographs added annually 8000
Collections: Photographs of architecture, sculpture, painting, drawing & decorative arts illustrating Far Eastern, South Asian & Western art history; illustrated Bartsch Catalogue; DIAL Index; Marburger Index; Papal Medals Collection; Courtauld Institute Illustrated Archive; Courtauld Photo Survey

CLINTON

O **FINE ARTS CENTER OF CLINTON,** * 119 W Macon St, 61727. Tel 217-935-5055. *Pres* Mrs William B Smith; *Dir* Vera MacGillivray; *Secy* Margaret Peltz; *Treas* John Warner III
Open Sept - July 1, Mon - Fri 10 AM - Noon, 1 - 5 PM, cl holidays. Estab 1960 in memory of John Smoot DeQuoin whose conviction it was that almost everyone is born with a latent talent and that developing that talent could be most rewarding. Average Annual Attendance: 1550
Income: Financed by tuition fees and supported by J Warner, III
Collections: Contemporary art, Aaron Bohrod, Emil Gruppe
Exhibitions: Batik; ceramics; needlework; oils; sculpture; watercolors; weaving
Publications: Bulletin of Center activities, annually
Activities: Classes for adults and children; dance, painting and writing workshops; school programs; concerts; scholarships offered

DANVILLE

M **VERMILION COUNTY MUSEUM SOCIETY,** 116 N Gilbert St, 61832. Tel 217-442-2922. *Dir* Ann Bauer
Open Tues - Sat 10 AM - 5 PM, Sun and Holidays 1 - 5 PM, cl Mon, Thanksgiving, Christmas. Admis 15 years over $1, 6 - 14 $.50, under 6 years no admis fee, school and scout groups no admis fee. Estab 1964, in 1855 doctor's residence and carriage house. Average Annual Attendance: 5500. Mem: 1230, dues life $150, patron $50, contributing $25, organization $10, family $12, individual $10, student & sr citizen $8
Collections: Costumes; decorative arts; graphics; historical material; paintings; sculpture
Exhibitions: Temporary exhibitions
Publications: Heritage, quarterly magazine
Activities: Gift shop
L **Library,** 116 N Gilbert St, 61832. Tel 217-442-2922
Open to the public and for inter-library loan
Library Holdings: Vols 300

DECATUR

M **MILLIKIN UNIVERSITY,** Kirkland Gallery, Kirkland Fine Arts Center, 1184 W Main St, 62522. Tel 217-424-6227. *Dir* Marvin L Klaven; *Asst Dir Kirkland Gallery & Art Prof* Ted Wolter
Open Mon - Fri Noon - 5 PM, Sat Noon - 4 PM. No admis fee. Estab 1970. Gallery has 3200 sq ft and 224 running ft of wall space

Income: Financed by university appropriation
Collections: Drawings; painting; prints; sculpture; watercolors
Exhibitions: (1983) Darryl Halbrooks, painting; Barbara Blades, paintings & wall pieces; David Bushman, paintings, drawings & prints; On My Own Time; Sonya Baysing, sculpture; Bill Heyduck, ceramics; Robert Maguire, draiwngs; Faculty Show; (1984) Jeanette Pasin Sloan, prints & drawings; Paul Sierra, paintings; Jeff Colby, wood constructions; Millikin University Student Exhibition
Publications: Annual bulletin; Center Activities
Activities: Classes for adults and children; guided tours; lect; gallery talks; junior museum

DE KALB

M **NORTHERN ILLINOIS UNIVERSITY,** Swen Parson Gallery and Gallery 200, Art Department, 60115. Tel 815-753-1936. *Dir* E Michael Flanagan; *Chmn Dept* Robert L Even
Open Mon - Fri 9 AM - 4 PM; Tues & Wed 7 - 9 PM; Sun 1 - 4 PM. No admis charge. Estab to bring wide range of art to the university and community. Swen Parson Gallery is 3200 sq ft for nationally prominent exhibitions, two other galleries 200 sq ft and 3000 sq ft for educational exhibits. Average Annual Attendance: 20,000
Income: Financed by state appropriation
Collections: Harold Gross Collection (Indian art); Mel Pfaelzer Collection †(prints, surrealist); Nause & Graff Collection (prints, contemporary)
Exhibitions: Changing exhibitions in both galleries
Publications: Show catalogs, four per year
Activities: Lectures open to public, 7-10 vis lectr per year; gallery talks; tours; print and drawing competition and student competitions with awards; individual paintings and original objects of art lent to on-campus recipients, also museums and galleries as requested; book traveling exhibitions, 1-2 per year
L **Library,** 60115. Tel 815-753-1094. *Arts Librn* Lester K Smith
Estab 1977 to provide reference service and develop the collection
Library Holdings: Vols 30,000; Per subs 234; Micro — Cards, fiche, reels

EDWARDSVILLE

SOUTHERN ILLINOIS UNIVERSITY, Lovejoy Library,* Art Dept, 62026. Tel 618-692-2711. *Friends of Lovejoy Library* Sheila Stimson; *Fine Arts Librn* Philip M Calcagno
Open Mon - Thurs 8 AM - 11 PM, Fri 8 AM - 5 PM, Sat 9 AM - 5 PM, Sun 2 - 9 PM. Estab 1957, as a source for general University undergraduate and graduate instruction, and faculty research
Library Holdings: Vols 16,700; Per subs 49

ELMHURST

M **LIZZADRO MUSEUM OF LAPIDARY ART,** * 220 Cottage Hill Ave, 60126. Tel 312-833-1616. *Dir* John S Lizzadro; *Exec Secy* Judith Greene
Open Tues - Fri & Sun 1 - 5 PM, Sat 10 AM - 5 PM, cl Mon. Admis adults $.50, ages 13-18 $.25, under 13 free, no charge on Fri. Estab 1962 to promote interest in the lapidary arts and the study and collecting of minerals and fossils. Main exhibit area contains hardstone carvings, gemstone materials, minerals; lower level contains education exhibits. Average Annual Attendance: 45,000. Mem: 600; dues $20 per year
Income: Financed by endowment
Collections: Hardstone Carving Collection
Exhibitions: Educational exhibits
Activities: Classes for adults and children; lectures open to the public, 3 - 15 vis lectr per yr; gallery talks; tours; hobby workshops; sales shop sells books, magazines, harstone & gemstone souvenirs

ELSAH

M **PRINCIPIA COLLEGE,** School of Nations Museum, 62028. Tel 618-374-2131. *Cur* Bonnie Gibbs
Open Tues & Fri by appointment only
Collections: American Indian collection including baskets, bead work, blankets, leather, pottery, quill work and silver; Asian art collection includes arts and crafts, ceramics, textiles from China, Japan and Southeast Asia; European collections include glass, metals, patch, snuff boxes, textiles and wood; costumes and dolls from around the world
Exhibitions: Changing exhibits on campus locations; permanent exhibits in School of Nations lower floor
Activities: Special programs offered throughout the year; objects available for individual study

EVANSTON

O **AMERICAN COMMITTEE FOR SOUTH ASIAN ART,** 1104 Asbury Ave, 60202. Tel 312-864-7382. *Pres* Sara L Schastok; *VPres* Holly Hutchens; *Treasurer* Janice Leoshko; *Newsletter Editor* Joan Raducha
Estab 1966 to support advancement of knowledge & understanding of the art & archaeology of S Asia & related countries. Mem: 150; dues institutions $20, regular $15, students $7.50; annual meetings in Feb-Mar
Publications: ACSAA Newsletter, biannual; ACSAA Bibliography of South Asian Art, biennial; slide sets

O **EVANSTON ART CENTER,** 2603 Sheridan Rd, 60201. Tel 312-475-5300. *Pres* Lucy Beighley; *Dir* Diane Gail Lazarus
Open Mon - Sat 10 AM - 4 PM, Thurs evening 7 - 10 PM, Sun 2 - 5 PM. No admis fee. Estab 1929 as a community visual arts center with exhibits, instruction, and programs. Includes Wieghardt Memorial Gallery, West Gallery for work of young artists, Octagon Gallery for Crafts & Photography Gallery.

Average Annual Attendance: 15,000. Mem: 1500; dues $20; annual meeting in April
Income: Supported by state & city arts councils & memberships
Publications: Concentrics, quarterly; exhibition catalogs
Activities: Classes for adults and children; lect, 6 vis lectr per year

NORTHWESTERN UNIVERSITY
M **Mary & Leigh Block Gallery,** 1967 Sheridan Rd, 60201. Tel 312-492-5209. *Dir* Kathy Kelsey Foley; *Cur* Suzanne Tanderup Wise; *Registrar & Prepartor* Karl Snoblin; *Dept Asst* Stephanie B May
Open Tues - Sat 10:30 AM - 4:30 PM, Sun 12 - 5 PM. No admis fee. Estab 1980, to serve the university, Chicago and North Shore communities. Average Annual Attendance: 30,000. Mem: 500; dues $25-$1000
Exhibitions: (1982) Chinese ceramics; (1983) Discoveries from Kurdish Looms
Publications: Exhibition catalogs
Activities: Lect open to public; concerts; gallery talks; tours; book traveling exhibitions; originate traveling exhibitions circulated through other university galleries and museums; sales shop will sell catalogs and posters
L **Art Library,** 60201. Tel 312-492-7484. *Head Art Collection* Sarah Sherman; *Bibliographer* Richard D Olson
Open Mon - Thurs 8:30 AM - 10 PM, Fri & Sat 8:30 AM - 5 PM, Sun 1 - 10 PM, after hours with prior permission. Estab 1970 as a separate collection. Serves curriculum & research needs of the Art & Art History Departments
Income: Financed through the university & endowment funds
Library Holdings: Vols 44,000; Other — Exhibition catalogs
Special Subjects: History of Art & Archaeology, 20th Century Art Movements

M **TERRA MUSEUM OF AMERICAN ART,** 2600 Central Park Ave, 60201. Tel 312-328-3400. *Pres* Daniel J Terra; *Dir* Ronald McKnight-Melvin; *Cur* David M Sokol; *Consultant* John I H Baur; *Asst to Dir* Mildred R Richards; *Registrar* Gloria Cooper
Open Tues - Sat 11 AM - 5 PM, Sun 1 - 5 PM, cl Mon. Admis adults $2, sr citizens, children & students $1. Estab 1980 to educate the public through the exhibition of the Terra Collection and visiting exhibitions of American paintings. Average Annual Attendance: 50,000. Mem: 1000; dues $25-$5000
Income: Financed by endowment and memberships
Collections: †Terra Collection of 18th, 19th and 20th century American oil, watercolor and pastel paintings
Exhibitions: American Naive Paintings from the National Gallery of Art; The Boston Tradition: Two Hundred Years of American Paintings, 1720-1920; American Masters of the Twentieth Century; Solitude—Inner Visions in American Art; An International Episode: Millet, Monet & Their North American Counterparts; The Lithographs of James McNeill Whistler; Early Rebels in American Art; George Bellows: Lithographs; Stuart Davis the Formative Years: 1910-1930; Two Hundred Years of American Painting from Private Chicago Collections; Reginald Marsh's New York; American Super Realism from the Morton G Neumann Family Collection; Down Garden Paths: The Floral Environment in American Art
Publications: Exhibition catalogues
Activities: Docent training; gallery talks; guided tours; individual and original objects of art lent to other museums; sales shop sells books, prints, slides and posters
L **Library,** 60201
Reference library
Library Holdings: Vols 500; Per subs 20; Auction Catalogs; Other — Exhibition catalogs, manuscripts, pamphlets

FREEPORT

M **FREEPORT AREA ARTS COUNCIL,** Freeport Art Museum, 121 N Harlem, 61032. Tel 815-235-9755. *Cur and Dir* Steven Broocks; *Business Mgr* Carolyn Brady
Open Fri, Sat & Sun Noon - 5 PM, and by appointment. No admis fee. Estab 1975 to house W T Rawleigh Art Collection and to promote the arts in the region. Five large galleries. Average Annual Attendance: 9000. Mem: 300; dues $20; annual meeting May
Income: $35,000 (financed by endowment, membership, city and state appropriations, and other grants)
Collections: American Indian pottery, basketry and beadwork; art from Madagascar; art nouveau pottery; European 19th century oil paintings; †oil paintings; †prints; sculpture; textiles; †antiquities from Egypt, Greece, Rome & MesoAmerica; †Oriental art
Exhibitions: W T Rawleigh European Art Collection; American Indian Art; Oriental Art; Kenneth Parvin Memorial Collection of Antiquities; Monthly Group & One-person Exhibitions
Activities: Classes for adults and children; docent training; lectures open to public; gallery talks; tours; competitions; exten dept serving Ogle, Carroll, Jo Daviess Counties; individual paintings and original objects of art lent to bona fide galleries with full insurance; lending collection contains paintings & sculpture; book traveling exhibitions; organize and circulate traveling exhibitions
L **Library,** 511 S Llberty, 61032
Open to members for research and reference
Library Holdings: Vols 200; Per subs 10; US Government materials

GALESBURG

O **GALESBURG CIVIC ART CENTER,** 114 E Main, 61401. Tel 309-342-7415. *Pres* Robert Mills; *VPres* Sarah Biorn; *Treas* Rose Sampson; *Secy* Isabelle Buncher; *Dir* Mary Lou Asaro
Open Tues - Fri 10:30 AM - 4:30 PM, Sat 10:30 AM - 3 PM, cl Sun & Mon. No admis fee. Estab 1923 as a non-profit organization for the furtherance of art. The main gallery has about 100 running feet of wall space for the hanging of exhibits. The sales-rental gallery runs on a commission basis and is open to professional artists as a place to sell their work under a consignment agreement. Average Annual Attendance: 20,000. Mem: 400; dues begin at $10; annual meeting 2nd Weds in May

Income: Financed by membership and grants
Collections: Some paintings and sculpture
Exhibitions: (1982-83) Annual Competitions: Galex, High School Invitational, Members & Friends; Isabelle Pera, Sculpture, Spaces-Places; Recent Etchings by Pam Carson and Robert McCauley; Ellen Sovony, Paintings; Gunther Wittenberg; Sculpture by Burlini; Farwinkle and Friends; George M Farbotko; The Shapiro Collection Prints; Matta; Miro; Dali; George Newton Watercolors; Black White Show, group; Realism 80's Style, group; (1983-84) Memi & Friends, Galex & High School Competitions; Annual Xmas Show; John Hartman of Kewanee; Local Photographers; Elmira Wilkey: Architecture Artist-In-Residence
Publications: The Artifacts, newsletter
Activities: Classes for adults and children; gallery talks; tours; competitions with awards; individual paintings and original objects of art lent to schools, library, activity centers; lending collection contains original art works, paintings, photographs & sculpture; museum shop sells books, magazines, original art, prints & note cards

GREENVILLE

M **GREENVILLE COLLEGE,** Richard W Bock Sculpture Collection, 62246. Tel 618-664-1840, Ext 321. *Dir & Cur* Guy M Chase
Open Mon - Wed 3:30 - 5:30 PM, Sat 10:30 AM - 12:30 PM & by appointment, cl summer & holidays. No admis fee. Estab 1975 to display an extensive collection of the life work of the American sculptor in a restored home of the mid-19th century period. Five large rooms and two hallways have approximately 320 running ft of exhibition space. Average Annual Attendance: 5000
Income: Financed by endowment, college appropriation, gifts and donations
Collections: Furniture and furnishings of the 1850-1875 era; Japanese prints; late 19th and early 20th century drawing, painting and sculpture; late 19th and early 20th century posters; Frank Lloyd Wright artifacts, designs and drawings
Exhibitions: (1983) Figurative Work of Richard Bock, sculpture & drawings
Publications: General museum brochures
Activities: Lect open to the public, 1-2 vis lectr per year; gallery talks; individual paintings and original objects of art lent to museums only; lending collection contains original art works, paintings, photographs, sculpture and drawings; traveling exhibitions organized and circulated; museum shop selling books, magazines
L **Research Library,** 62246. *Librn* Donald P Hallmark
For reference only
Library Holdings: Vols 1000; Micro — Prints; AV — Rec; Other — Exhibition catalogs
Special Subjects: Richard W Bock, The Prairie School of Architecture, Frank Lloyd Wright

JACKSONVILLE

M **ART ASSOCIATION OF JACKSONVILLE,** David Strawn Art Gallery,* 331 W College, 62650. Tel 217-243-6988. *Co-Dir* Alice Harrington; *Co-Dir* Jack Harrington; *Pres* Dr Tom Stevens
Open Sept - May Tues - Sun 2 - 5 PM; Fri 7 - 9 PM; cl Mon. No admis fee. Estab 1873, endowed 1915, to serve the community by offering monthly shows of visual arts and weekly classes in a variety of media. The two main rooms house the monthly exhibitions and a third large room houses a collection of Pre-Columbian pottery. The Gallery is in a large building, previously a private home. Average Annual Attendance: 1200. Mem: 400; dues $5 and up; annual meeting June
Income: Financed by endowment and membership
Collections: Pre-Columbian Pottery; pottery discovered in the Mississippi Valley
Exhibitions: (1981-1982) Robert R Malone (paintings & prints); Jack Decoteau (bronze sculpture); Robert Blue (ceramics); J Mitch Clark (paintings); Asian Arts & Crafts Exhibit; Prairie Fiber Guild; Alice & Jack Herrington (prints, paintings & sculpture); Sharon Hardin (watercolors); Illinois College Students Show; (1982-1983) Nick Kripal (sculpture); Robert Mejer (prints); Children's Show; Peter Slavish (ceramics); Charles Marsh (paintings & prints); John Rogers (paper cast); John Hawker (photography); Illinois College Students Show; Bruce McCoy (sculpture)
Activities: Classes for adults and children; lect open to public, 2 vis lectr per year; concerts

JOLIET

M **JOLIET JUNIOR COLLEGE,** Laura A Sprague Art Gallery, 1216 Houbolt Ave, 2nd Fl, J Building, 60436. Tel 815-729-9020, Ext 423. *Gallery Dir* Joe B Milosevich
Open Mon - Fri 9 AM - 2 PM, Wed & Thurs 6 PM - 8 PM. Estab 1978, exhibitions related to academic programs, the college and the community. Gallery, approx 20 x 25 ft, has burlap covered panels mounted on the walls, and also has track lighting
Income: Financed by state appropriations
Exhibitions: (1982-83) Carol Hammerman; Gary Allen Justis; John Link; Wayne Forbes; (1984) Illinois Community College Juried Art Exhibition
Activities: Lectures open to public, 2 - 3 visiting lecturers per year; gallery talks; tours; sponsor competitions with awards

LAKE FOREST

L **LAKE FOREST LIBRARY,** Fine Art Dept, 360 E Deerpath, 60045. Tel 312-234-0636. *Librn* Sydney S Mellinger; *Head of Reference* Nancy G Wallens; *Circulation Head* Judy Gummere
Open Mon - Fri 9 AM - 9 PM, Sat 9 AM - 5 PM; Sept - May, Sun 1 - 5 PM. Estab 1898 to make accessible to the residents of the city, books and other resources and services for education, information and recreation. Gallery carries sculptures and minimasters (framed art prints). Circ 212,000
Income: $535,000 (financed by city and state appropriations)

Purchases: $84,000
Library Holdings: Other — Framed reproductions, pamphlets, sculpture
Special Subjects: Local architects
Collections: Folk art; painting
Publications: The Open Book, three times per year

LONG GROVE

C **KEMPER GROUP,** Kemper Dr, 60049. Tel 312-540-2502. *Art Cur* Joan E Robertson
Open to public in groups of 5 - 25, by three weeks prior appointment. Estab 1973 to provide a better working environment for employees and to support Chicago and Midwest artists. Collection displayed in halls and offices of headquarters
Purchases: $20,000 - $57,000
Collections: Approximately 57 percent Chicago and Midwest artists, contemporary, with many young emerging artists
Exhibitions: One-person shows in private exhibition area
Publications: Art collection brochure
Activities: Lect; gallery talks; purchase awards at Chicago area shows and art fairs; individual objects of art lent to artists of works for retrospectives and shows, or works to institutions

MACOMB

M **WESTERN ILLINOIS UNIVERSITY,** * 61455. Tel 309-298-1355. *Pres* Leslie Malpass; *VPres* Bruce Carpenter; *Secy* Roseanne Ledbetter
Open weekdays 8:30 AM - 4:30 PM. No admis fee. Estab 1945 to present art as an aesthetic and teaching aid. Browne Hall Gallery in room with 200 running ft; exhibitions show at the University Union & the Library. Average Annual Attendance: 2000
Income: Financed through state appropriation
Exhibitions: Exhibits are changed monthly
Activities: Classes for adults; lect open to the public, 8 visiting lectrs per year; concerts; gallery talks; tours; competitions with awards; individual paintings lent; lending collection contains 30 paintings; traveling exhibitions organized and circulated

MOLINE

C **DEERE & COMPANY,** * John Deere Rd, 61265. Tel 309-752-8000
Guided tours Mon - Fri 10:30 AM - 1:30 PM. No admis fee. Estab 1964 to complement the offices designed by Eero Saarinen and Kevin Roche; to provide opportunities for employees and visitors to view and enjoy a wide variety of art pieces from many parts of the world. Collection displayed at Deere & Company Administrative Center
Collections: Artifacts, paintings, prints, sculpture and tapestries from over 25 countries
Activities: Concerts; tours

MOUNT VERNON

M **MITCHELL MUSEUM,** Richview Rd, Box 923, 62864. Tel 618-242-1236. *Pres* Jerome Glassman; *Secy* Ruby Miller; *Exec VPres* Kenneth R Miller
Open Tues - Sun 1 - 5 PM, cl Mon & national holidays. No admis fee. Estab 1973 to present exhibitions of paintings, sculpture, graphic arts, architecture and design representing contemporary art trends; to provide continued learning and expanded education. Museum has three galleries: Main Gallery, Hall Gallery and Lecture Gallery. Average Annual Attendance: 50,000. Mem: 850; dues $25; annual meeting in Nov
Income: Financed by endowment and membership
Collections: Paintings by late 19th and early 20th century American artists; some drawings and small sculptures; silver, small stone, wood and ivory carvings; vases; jade; cut glass; small bronzes; outdoor sculpture
Exhibitions: Changing exhibits
Publications: The Communicator, monthly; quarterly newsletter
Activities: Classes for adults and children; dramatic programs; docent training; lect open to public, 10 vis lectr per year; concerts; gallery talks; tours; competitions; exten dept serves local schools, colleges & local civic groups; individual paintings and original objects of art lent to museums and universities; sales shop selling books, magazines, reproductions, prints and slides
L **Library,** Richview Rd, Box 923, 62864. *Dir* K R Miller
Open to public for reference only
Library Holdings: Vols 1500; Per subs 12; AV — Slides; Other — Photographs

NILES

M **THE BRADFORD MUSEUM,** 9333 Milwaukee Ave, 60648. Tel 312-966-2770; Telex 72-4407. *Mgr Public Relations* Carrie Reckert; *Tour Coordr* Eloise Bartlebaugh
Open Mon - Fri 9 AM - 4 PM, Sat & Sun 10 AM - 5 PM. Admis adult $2, sr citizens $1, children under 12 accompanied by adult free, free on Sat. Estab 1977 to house and display limited-edition collector's plates for purposes of study, education and enjoyment. Average Annual Attendance: 10,000
Income: Financed by The Bradford Exchange
Collections: Traded Limited-Edition Collector's Plates, including Bing & Grondahl, Haviland, Lalique, Lenox, Rosenthal, Royal Copenhagen, Royal Doulton, and many more; †plates produced by more than 62 makers from 12 different countries, each plate series is updated yearly
Publications: The Bradford Book of Collector's Plates, annually
Activities: Docent training; lect open to public; tours; original objects of art lent for temporary exhibition purposes; lending collection contains motion pictures and limited-edition collector's plates; book traveling exhibitions; originate traveling exhibitions

NORMAL

ILLINOIS STATE UNIVERSITY

M **University Museums,** * 61761. Tel 309-829-6331. *Dir* Dr Gordon Davis; *Meseum Educator* Anita Bohn
Ewing Museum of Nations, open year round, Tues, Thurs, Sat, Sun 1 - 5 PM; Eyestone School Museum, fall and spring, Sun only 1 - 5 PM, summer, Tues, Thurs, Sun 1 - 5 PM; Funk Gem and Mineral Museum, year round, Tues, Thurs, Sun 1 - 5 PM; Hudelson Museum of Agriculture, fall and spring, Sun only 1 - 5 PM, summer, Tues, Thurs, Sun 1 - 5 PM; Stevenson Memorial Room, fall and spring, Mon - Fri 10 AM - 5 PM, summer, Tues, Thurs, Sun 1 - 5 PM; University Historical Museum, year round, Mon - Fri 10 AM - 5 PM, Sat, Sun 1 - 5 PM. No admis fee. Estab 1872, re-estab 1945 to collect, preserve and interpret museum objects directly related to academic programs of the university and the public schools; to support research related to exhibit collections; and to maintain general interest collections. The six museums house temporary and permanent exhibits on loan and from the permanent collection. Average Annual Attendance: 28,000
Income: Financed by state appropriation
Collections: †African Art; decorative arts; International Collection of Child Art; †international dolls; native American art; †Pre-Columbian art of Middle America; southeast Asian artifacts
Exhibitions: Temporary and permanent exhibits from permanent collections
Publications: Annual Report; exhibit brochures and catalogs
Activities: Lect open to the public; gallery talks; tours; original objects of art lent to local and county schools and local exhibits; lending collection contains cassettes, original art works, sculpture and slides; traveling exhibitions organized and circulated
L **Museum Library,** * 61761. *Librn* Arlene A Boggs
Museum library open to scholars, students and staff
Library Holdings: Vols 201; Per subs 22
Special Subjects: Decorative Arts, American Indian Art, Pre-Columbian Art, African Art and History
M **Center for the Visual Arts Gallery,** Beaufort St, 61761. Tel 309-436-5487. *Dir* Gordon A Davis; *Cur Art* Barry D Weer; *Registrar* Carolyn R McDonald; *Cur Exhibitions* David L Kuntz
No admis fee. Estab 1973 to provide changing exhibits of the visual arts for the students and community at large; also display student art work. The main Gallery I contains rotating exhibitions; Galleries II and III display student work, graduate exhibitions, studio area shows and works from the permanent collection. Average Annual Attendance: 25,000
Income: $100,000 (financed by university)
Collections: †20th century American art emphasis
Exhibitions: (1984) West Coast Realism; An Open Land: Photographs of the Midwest, 1852-1982; Tenth Biennial National Invitational Crafts Exhibition and Workshop; Normal Editions Workshop Print Exhibition; Raphael Soyer and John Stewart Curry; Illinois State University Graduate Student Biennial Exhibition
Publications: Exhibition catalogues; annual report
Activities: Lectures open to the public, 3 vis lectr per yr; gallery talks; tours; individual paintings and original objects of art lent for other exhibitions; lending collection contains original art works, original prints, paintings, photographs and sculpture; book traveling exhibitions, 4 - 6 per yr; originate traveling exhibitions

OAK PARK

M **FRANK LLOYD WRIGHT ASSOCIATION,** Chicago & Forest Aves, PO Box 2100, 60303. Tel 312-848-1976
Admis adults $3, students under 18 and senior citizens $1.50. Estab 1977 to collect & disseminate information of the life & work of Frank Lloyd Wright. Mem: dues supporting $50, family $25, individual $15
Collections: Decorative arts
Publications: Frank Lloyd Wright Newsletter, quarterly
Activities: Lectures; tours; individual paintings & original objects of art lent
L **Library,** PO Box 2100, 60303. *Librn* T A Heinz
Open by appointment only. Estab 1977
Library Holdings: Vols 10,000; Per subs 20; Micro — Reels 20; AV — A-tapes 10, cassettes 10, Kodachromes, motion pictures 3, rec 3, slides 40,000, v-tapes 6; Other — Clipping files, exhibition catalogs, framed reproductions, manuscripts, memorabilia, original art works, pamphlets, photographs, prints, reproductions, sculpture
Special Subjects: Architecture

PEORIA

M **BRADLEY UNIVERSITY,** Hartman Center Gallery,* Division of Art, 61625. Tel 309-676-7611. *Dir Div of Art* Walter Thompson
Open Tues - Fri 12 - 5 PM. Exhibition space 45 x 25 ft; new gallery: Hartmann Center. Average Annual Attendance: 2000
Income: Financed by University
Exhibitions: Bradley National Print & Drawing Exhibition
Activities: Classes for adults; lect open to the public, 10 vis lectr per year; gallery talks; tours; competitions with awards

M **LAKEVIEW MUSEUM OF ARTS AND SCIENCES,** 1125 W Lake Ave, 61614. Tel 309-686-7000. *Exec Dir* John E Buchanan; *Assoc Dir* Judy Geary-Furniss; *Cur Coll & Exhib* Henry Moy; *Asst Cur Exhibitions* Cory Dawson-Tibbitts; *Mgr Sales-Rental Gallery* Maryan Miller
Open Tues - Sat 10 AM - 5 PM, Sun 1 - 5 PM, Wed 7 - 9 PM, cl Mon. Estab 1960, new building opened 1965, to provide enjoyment and education by reflecting the historical, cultural and industrial life of the Central Illinois area. Average Annual Attendance: 250,000. Mem: 3600; dues family $25, individual $15, student $10; annual meeting in June
Income: $500,000
Collections: Archaeological; †decorative arts; extensive entomological and paleontological collections; paintings and graphics
Exhibitions: Monthly exhibitions dealing with the arts and sciences

Publications: Bi-monthly bulletin; Lake Views, bi-monthly; exhibition catalogues
Activities: Classes for adults and children; dramatic programs; docent trainings; lectures open to public, 8-10 vis lectrs per year; concerts; gallery talks; tours; competitions with awards; individual and original objects of art lent to sister institutions; sales shop sells books, magazines, original art, reproductions, prints and craft items

O **PEORIA ART GUILD,** 1831 N Knoxville, 61603. Tel 309-685-7522. *Pres* Howard Courtney; *VPres* Bonnea Tilton; *Dir* Janet M Jensen
Open Tues - Sat 10 AM - 4 PM, Sun 1 - 4 PM, cl Mon. No admis fee. Estab 1878 to encourage development of the arts. Average Annual Attendance: 5000. Mem: 600; dues $10 & up
Income: Financed by membership, Illinois Arts Council, sales & rental & private donations
Collections: Framed and unframed two-dimensional work, ceramics, sculpture, jewelry, weaving and wood designs; winning works from the Bradley Print and Drawing Exhibition
Exhibitions: One-person shows; group theme shows
Activities: Classes for adults and children; workshops; lect open to public, 4 vis lectr per year; gallery talks; competitions with purchase awards; individual paintings lent to businesses & members of the community; lending collection contains prints, paintings & photographs; sales shop sells original art

M **PEORIA HISTORICAL SOCIETY,** 942 N E Glen Oak, 61603. Tel 309-674-1921. *Pres* Joseph F Bartley III
Open Judge John C Flanagan House 2 - 4 PM, Pettengill-Morron House Sun 2 - 4 PM. Admis adults $1.50, children 12 & under $.50. Estab 1934 to acquire, preserve and display artifacts and records relating to the history of Peoria and the Central Illinois Valley; to encourage and support historical research and investigation and to promote and sustain public interest in history of Peoria and the Central Illinois Valley. Average Annual Attendance: 7000-8000. Mem: 584; annual meeting in May
Income: Financed by membership & endowments
Collections: Household items & artifacts from 1840; Library housed in special collections center of Bradley University
Publications: Monthly Newsletter to members
Activities: Docent training; lectures open to public, 6-8 vis lectr per yr; tours; awards; Boutique at Pettengill-Morron House

QUINCY

O **QUINCY ART CENTER,** 1515 Jersey St, 62301. Tel 217-223-5900. *Pres* Martha Didriksen; *Secy* Vera Magill
Open Tues - Fri 1 - 4 PM, Sat & Sun 2 - 5 PM, cl Mon, holidays, July & Aug. Estab 1923, incorporated 1951 to foster public awareness and understanding of the visual arts. Average Annual Attendance: 6000. Mem: 400; dues life membership $250, sustaining $100, annual patron $30, family $15, individual $10, student $5; annual meeting in July
Income: Financed by grants, donations, membership fees, antique shows and Beaux Art Ball
Collections: Crafts, graphics, †painting and sculpture by contemporary American and European artists
Exhibitions: Annual Quincy Art Show; annual students art show; Art Club's Artist Guild Show
Publications: Calendar, brochures and/or catalogs for temporary exhibitions; Quarterly Bulletin; quarterly bulletin
Activities: Classes for adults and children; lectures open to public, 6 visiting lecturers per year; films; gallery talks; tours; competitions with awards; scholarships; inter-museum loan; traveling exhibitions organized and circulated
L **Library,** 1515 Jersey St, 62301. *Dir* William C Landwehr
Library Holdings: Vols 350

M **QUINCY COLLEGE,** Art Gallery, 1831 College Ave, 62301. Tel 217-222-8020, Ext 371. *Gallery Dir* Robert Lee Mejer
Open Mon - Thur 8 AM - 10 PM, Fri 8 AM - 8 PM, Sat 11 AM - 5 PM, Sun 1 - 10 PM. No admis fee. Estab 1968 as a cultural enrichment and artistic exposure for the community. Exhibitions are held in the library foyer and the foundation room. Average Annual Attendance: 6000
Income: Financed through the College
Collections: †19th century Oriental and European prints; †permanent collection of student and faculty works; †20th century American prints and drawings
Exhibitions: (1982-83) QC Art Department Faculty Anniversary; J Michael Walsh - Souvenirs Series, mixed media; Donald Furst - Intaglio Prints; Wayne Forbes - Sculpture & Drawings; Joan Hall - Cast Paper Sculptures & Workshop; Richard Helmick - Silkscreen Prints; Susan Mart - Drawings; Larry Thall - Color Photographs; Michael Rubin - Black/White Photographs; Student Art Show; Baccalaurete - Senior Exhibition 83; Alumni Exhibition; (1983-84) QC art department faculty show; Beth Shadur - Watercolors; Mark Pascale - Lithographs; Dennis Goncher - Aquamedia; Lois Coren - Mixed Media Paper Constructions; Robert Wolfe Jr - Drawings; Lon Beck - Drawings; Nicholas Hill - Oil Paintings; Kathleen Sanjabi - Quilted Paintings; Win Bruhl - Silkscreen Prints & Drawings; student art show; baccalaureate - senior exhibition 84; alumni exhibition Clare Romano (recent collagraphs); Take A Good Look (contemporary works by Pennsylvania, Ohio and New York artists); annual alumni, faculty, senior, and student exhibits
Publications: Brochures, 3-5 times annually; gallery calendars, annually
Activities: Lectures open to public, 2 vis lectr per year; gallery talks; tours; student show with awards; individual paintings & original objects of art lent; book traveling exhibitions 2-4 per year
L **Library,** 1831 College Ave, 62301
Library Holdings: Vols 6800

O **QUINCY SOCIETY OF FINE ARTS,** 1310 Washington, 62301. Tel 217-222-3432. *Dir* Rob Dwyer
Open Mon - Fri 9 AM - 5 PM. Estab 1948 as a community arts council to coordinate and stimulate the visual and performing arts in Quincy and Adams

County. Mem: 19 art organizations
Income: Financed by endowment, membership and contribution
Publications: Cultural Calendars, semi-monthly; pamphlets & catalogs
Activities: Workshops for adults and students in visual and performing arts

ROCKFORD

O **ROCKFORD ART ASSOCIATION,** Burpee Art Museum, 737 N Main St, 61103. Tel 815-965-3131. *Dir* Martin DeWitt; *Admin Asst* Patricia Schueller; *Tech Asst* Chuck Ludeke; *Education Coordr* Jan Provenzano
Open Tues - Fri Noon - 5 PM, Sat & Sun 1 - 5 PM, cl Mon and holidays. No admis fee. Estab 1913 to promote and cultivate an active interest in all fields of fine and applied art, past and present, in the surrounding area. The main building is an Italian style villa which was redecorated and renovated to house six rooms for exhibition space; an auditorium was added later. Average Annual Attendance: 30,000. Mem: 700; dues gift-pledge $100, sponsor $50, family $25, individual $15, student $8
Income: Financed by membership and state appropriation
Collections: Permanent collection 19th & 20th century American oil paintings, graphics, sculpture, photography, ceramics, glassware, textiles, watercolors and mixed media
Exhibitions: (1982-83) Annual Rockford and Vicinity Show; Annual Young Artist's Exhibition; numerous one-person and group shows
Publications: Exhibition brochures and catalogs; newsletter, quarterly
Activities: Classes for adults and children; lectures open to public, 6 vis lectr per year; gallery talks; tours; competitions with cash awards; scholarships offered; book traveling exhibitions
L **Katherine Pearman Memorial Library,** 737 N Main St, 61103
Open to the public and members by appointment. For reference only
Library Holdings: Vols 500; Per subs 15
Special Subjects: The visual arts

ROCK ISLAND

M **AUGUSTANA COLLEGE,** Centennial Hall Gallery,* 61201. Tel 309-794-7341. *Head Art Dept* Mary Em Kirn; *Secy* Carol Petersen
Open Mon - Fri 1 PM - 4 PM. No admis fee. Estab to exhibit contemporary visual arts of local and regional artists. Main gallery serves as an extrance to large auditorium; lower gallery is much smaller than main gallery
Income: $3000
Purchases: $1000
Collections: Contemporary eastern and western prints
Activities: Classes for children; competitions; awards; art works lent to campus offices for display

SPRINGFIELD

L **ILLINOIS STATE LIBRARY,** Centennial Bldg, 62756. Tel 217-782-2994. *Dir* Bridget Lamont; *Deputy Dir* Vince Schmidt
Open weekdays 8 AM - 4:30 PM, cl Sat & Sun. Estab 1839. Reference services are available to patrons of Illinois public libraries on inter-library loan requested through library systems
Income: Financed by state appropriation
Library Holdings: Micro — Fiche, Other — Framed reproductions
Collections: Books; magazines; framed art prints
Activities: Tours

M **ILLINOIS STATE MUSEUM OF NATURAL HISTORY AND ART,** Spring & Edwards St, 62706. Tel 217-782-7125. *Dir* R Bruce McMillan; *Asst Dir* Edward A Munyer; *Head Art Section & Cur of Art* Robert J Evans; *Cur Decorative Arts* Lowell Anderson; *Asst Cur* Maureen McKenna; *Cur Asst* Terry Suhre
Open Mon - Sat 8:30 AM - 5 PM; Sun 1:30 - 5 PM. No admis fee. Estab 1877 as museum of natural history, art added in 1928. Collection and display of art produced by or of interest to Illinois and its citizens; art program is specialized to Illinois to a great degree. Five change exhibit galleries of approx 500 running feet of display. Permanent collection galleries of fine and decorative arts, a gallery for ethnographic arts & gallery of Illinois photography. Average Annual Attendance: 300,000. Mem: 900; dues $10 - $300
Income: $1,400,000 (financed by state appropriation)
Purchases: $35,000
Collections: Decorative art including †ceramics, †metal work, †textiles, †glass, †furniture; fine art including †paintings, †sculpture, †prints, †drawings, †photography, †contemporary crafts
Exhibitions: 22 exhibitions each yr featuring wide range of graphics, paintings, photogrpahy, sculpture & decorative arts with emphasis on Illinois
Publications: Living Museum (also in Braille), quarterly; exhibit and collection catalogs
Activities: Docent training; lect open to public and members; tours; competitions; exten dept; original objects of art lent to museums and art galleries; traveling exhibitions organized and circulated; museum shop selling books, reproductions and other miscellaneous items
L **Library,** Spring & Edwards St, 62706. Tel 217-782-6623. *Librn* Orvetta Robinson; *Library Asst* Ronald Sauberli
Open Mon - Fri 8:30 AM - 5 PM. Estab to provide informational materials and services to meet the requirements of the museum staff in fields pertinent to the purpose and work of the museum. Circ 100 per month
Income: Financed by state appropriation
Purchases: $2600
Library Holdings: Vols 1200; Per subs 32; AV — Motion pictures, slides
Special Subjects: Anthropology, art and natural sciences
Collections: Anthropology and Ornithology

O **SPRINGFIELD ART ASSOCIATION OF EDWARDS PLACE,** 700 N Fourth, 62702. Tel 217-523-2631, 523-3507. *Exec Dir* Nelson C Britt
Open Tues - Sun 2 - 4 PM, cl Mon. No admis fee. Estab 1913 to foster appreciation of art, to instruct people in art and to expose people to quality art.
Mem: 1000; dues $20 - $2000; monthly meeting
Income: $128,000 (financed by membership and grants, interests, tuition, and benefits)
Collections: †Contemporary American Indian; African sculpture; early American paintings; furniture; Mexican; Oriental and Japanese artifacts and textiles; †paintings; †pottery; †prints; †textiles
Exhibitions: Twelve to fifteen exhibitions are scheduled annually with 2 or 3 juried exhibitions; work is borrowed from museum and artist nationwide
Publications: Newsletters, membership brochures, membership roster, 12 - 15 per year
Activities: Classes for adults and children; docent training; art outreach program in school in community funded through CETA; lectr open to the public; gallery talks; tours; competitions with cash awards of $50 - $100; scholarships; individual paintings and original objects of art lent to businesses for displays; lending collection contains 300 framed reproductions, original art works, 1500 original prints and paintings, sculpture, pottery, furniture, textiles, craft items, 2500 books; book traveling exhibitions; sales shop sells original art, prints
L **Michael Victor II Art Library,** 700 N Fourth, 62702. Tel 217-523-0092. *Librn* Irene Boyer
Open 9 AM - 4 PM daily, Mon - Thurs 6:30 - 9:30 PM, Sat 9 AM - Noon, cl Sun. Estab 1965 to provide total community with access to art and art related books
Income: $900
Purchases: $700
Library Holdings: Vols 2500; Per subs 10; Micro — Cards; AV — Slides; Other — Clipping files, exhibition catalogs, pamphlets, reproductions
Activities: Film program; lecture series

WATSEKA

M **IROQUOIS COUNTY HISTORICAL MUSEUM,** 103 W Cherry, 60970. Tel 815-432-2215. *Pres* Lorraine V Schriefer; *VPres* Wayne Rosenberger; *Secy* Mary Hartke; *Exec Secy* Marie Hanford
Open Mon - Fri 10 AM - 4:30 PM, Sat & Sun 1 - 4 PM. Estab 1967 to further the interest in history, art & genealogy. Two rooms for county artists. Average Annual Attendance: 10,000. Mem: 700; dues $5-$3
Income: Financed by donations by visitors, artists & art committee sells crafts
Collections: Paintings, prints, posters & pictures
Publications: Genealogical Stalker, quarterly; newsletter, monthly; historic reprints
Activities: Lectures open to public; concerts; tours; competitions with awards; museum shop sells books, original art, maps & Indian items

WHEATON

O **DUPAGE ART LEAGUE,*** 219 West Front St, 60187. Tel 312-653-7090. *Pres* Louise Escott; *VPres* Doris Morris; *VPres* Lucille Jones; *VPres* Donna Crabtree; *VPres* Gloria Haffner; *VPres* Carol Hagerman; *Secy* Grace Haverty; *Treas* Joanne Stevens; *Pres Emeritus* Vicki Brucciani
Open daily 9 AM - 5 PM. No admis fee. Estab 1957, is primarily an educational organization founded to encourage artists and promote high artistic standards through instruction, informative programs and exhibits. Gallery is maintained where members exhibit and sell their work. Shows change monthly and based on a theme. Mem: 425; dues $15; annual meeting May
Income: Financed through membership, gifts and donations
Exhibitions: Monochromania; Palletations; Thoughts and Threads; From Adam to Aardvards; Papier...Papel...Paper; Anniversary Walls; Summer Daze; Annual Mini Show; Holiday Gift Gallery
Publications: Newsletter, monthly
Activities: Classes for adults and children; programs; demonstrations; lect open to the public, 6-7 visiting lectrs per year; gallery talks; competitions; awards; scholarships; traveling exhibitions organized and circulated; sales shop selling original art and prints

WINNETKA

O **NORTH SHORE ART LEAGUE,** Winnetka Community House, 620 Lincoln, 60093. Tel 312-446-2870. *Pres* Peg Spengler; *First VPres* Rita Price; *Second VPres* Sarah Danzig; *Recording Secy* LuAnn Herbold
Open Mon - Sat 9 AM - 6 PM. Estab 1924, inc 1954, to promote interest in creative art through education, exhibition opportunities, scholarship and art programs. Average Annual Attendance: 100,000. Mem: 900; dues $25; annual meeting May
Exhibitions: Midwest Craft Festival - New Horizons in Art; Old Orchard Art Festival - Members Show
Publications: Art League News, quarterly
Activities: Classes for adults and children; competitions with awards

INDIANA

ANDERSON

O **ANDERSON FINE ARTS CENTER,** 226 W Historical Eighth St, 46016. Tel 317-649-1248. *Executive Dir* Deborah McBratney-Stapleton; *Pres Board of Trustees* Francis Oleksy; *Cur* Neil C Cockerline; *Education Outreach* Robin Johnson; *Gallery Asst* Tim Swain

Open Sept - July Tues - Sat 10 AM - 5 PM, Sun 2 - 5 PM, cl Mon & national holidays. No admis fee. Estab 1967 to serve the community by promoting & encouraging interest in the fine arts through exhibitions, programs & education activities & the development of a permanent collection. Three galleries contain 1705 sq ft; also a small sales & rental gallery & a studio/theatre. Average Annual Attendance: 30,000. Mem: 700; dues benefactor $5000, corporate supporting $1000, donor $500, corporate sponsor $250, patron $100, family $25, individual $15, student $5; annual meeting in May
Income: Financed by memberships, endowments, grants, individual & corporate contributions
Collections: Primarily Indiana; †Mid-West & †American art; contemporary art; early Indiana artists; folk art
Exhibitions: (1983-84) Aiden Lassell Ripley, watercolors; The Art Record: Revolutions Per Minute; Alfred P Maurice: Chicago; AFAC Permanent Collection; 1983-84 Sales & Rental Gallery; Christmas Trees Around the World; Making It In Paper: An Indiana Paper Mill; Anderson Winter Show; Photography in Anderson; The Anderson Area Annual; The Anderson Area Student Exhibition; Twentieth Century Prints; New Masks; Hollywood 1924-28: Paintings of Batiste Madalena; Anderson Art League/Anderson Society of Artists
Publications: Calendar of Events, quarterly; catalogue of the permanent collection; exhibition catalogs
Activities: Classes for adults & children; dramatic programs; docent training; educational outreach; lectures open to public, 4-6 vis lectr per yr; concerts; gallery talks; tours; competitions with awards; individual paintings & original objects of art lent to businesses, educational facilities & other museums; lending collection contains 300 original art works, 150 original prints, 300 paintings, 10 sculpture & 1000 slides; book traveling exhibitions; museum shop sells books, original art, reproductions, prints, slides, pottery, handcrafted items, glass, fine cards & note papers
L **Library,*** 226 W Historicial Eighth St, Anderson, 46016. Tel 317-649-1248. *Librn* Judith Dillingham
Open Tues - Sat 10 AM - 5 PM, Sun 2 - 5 PM. Estab 1967 for reference needs & enjoyment by members of Arts Center & the community
Purchases: $500
Library Holdings: Vols 300; Per subs 14; AV — Cassettes, Kodachromes, motion pictures, slides; Other — Clipping files, exhibition catalogs, pamphlets
Collections: Contemporary American art

BLOOMINGTON

INDIANA UNIVERSITY
M **Art Museum,** Fine Arts 007, 47405. Tel 812-335-5445; Cable ARTMUSEUM INDVERS. *Dir* Thomas T Solley; *Cur Western Art to 1800* Adelheid Gealt; *Cur Ancient Art* Adriana Calinescu; *Registrar* Diane Drisch; *Editor* Linda Baden; *Public Relations* Virginia Jackson; *Cur Asian Art* Pamela Buell
Open Wed, Fri & Sat 9 AM - 5 PM, Thurs 10 AM - 8 PM, Sun 1 - 5 PM, cl Mon & Tues. No admis fee. Estab 1962 to serve as a teaching adjunct to the School of Fine Arts and as a cultural resource for the University community and the public at large. Average Annual Attendance: 50,000
Income: $386,000 (financed by state appropriation)
Collections: †African, †ancient to modern, Far Eastern, Oceanic, the Americas, prints, drawings and photography
Exhibitions: (1982-84) Animals in Ancient Art from the Leo Mildenberg Collection; Buffon Picasso Drawings; Masters of Fine Arts Thesis Shows; Recent Acquisitions of Old Master Drawings; Homage to James S and Elizabeth G Adams; Genji: The World of a Prince; The Hope Collection and Photographs by Henry Holmes Smith; Techniques of Old Master Prints I and II; Korean Drawing Now; School of Fine Arts Faculty Exhibition; Nineteenth Century Landscapes; Rembrandt and His Contemporaries; Finland Designs; The Plan of St Gall; Japanese Woodcuts: Artists of the Utagawa School; Italian Portrait Drawings 1400-1800 from North American Collections; German-American Celebration Exhibition
Publications: Bulletin, guide to the collection, exhibition catalogs
Activities: Lect open to public; gallery talks; tours
M **William Hammond Mathers Museum,** 416 N Indiana Ave, 47405. Tel 812-337-7224. *Dir* Geoffrey W Conrad; *Cur Exhibits* David Schalliol; *Registrar* Elaine Gaul; *Exhibit Preparator* David Bruker; *Conservator* Judith Sylvester
Open Tues - Fri 9 AM - 4:30 PM, Sat & Sun 1 - 4:30 PM. No admis fee. Estab 1964 as Indiana University Museum, institutes renamed in 1983. Museum of Anthropology, Folklore & History housing over 50,000 artifacts
Collections: Anthropology, folklore & history with collections of American primitives, Latin American primitives & folk art
Exhibitions: Somalia - In Word & Image; Road to the Rainbow: The Saga of Human Transport
Publications: Papers & monograph series
Activities: Docent program; museum training classes; lectures; tours; film series; scholarships; school loan collection; originate traveling exhibitions in state

ELKHART

M **MIDWEST MUSEUM OF AMERICAN ART,** 429 S Main St, PO Box 1812, 46515. Tel 219-293-6660. *Pres* Dr Richard D Burns; *VPres* Michael Nickol; *Dir* Jane Burns; *Cur Exhibitions & Education* Brian D Byrn; *Administrative Asst* Gertrude Baspuin
Open Tues - Sat 11 AM - 5 PM, Thurs Eve 7 - 9 PM, Sun 1 - 5 PM. Admis adults $1.50, children & senior citizens $.75, members free, Thurs eve free. Estab 1978, to promote the exhibitions and understanding of American art. Three galleries are maintained for changing exhibitions; and five galleries are maintained for the permanent collection. Average Annual Attendance: 20,000. Mem: 900; dues $10 - $250
Income: $100,000 (financed through membership, grants, foundations, contributions)
Collections: Paintings: Thomas Hart Benton; Albert Bierstadt; Arthur Bowen Davies; Adolph Gottlieb; Grace Hartigan; Childe Hassam; Conrad Marca-Relli; Joan Mitchell; Robert Natkin; Maurice Pendergast; †Grant Wood; Milton Avery;

Red Grooms; Hans Hoffman; Joan Mitchell; Rauschenberg; Carl Olaf Seltzer; Norman Rockwell; LeRoy Neiman; Roger Brown; Art Green; George Luks; Glen Cooper Henshaw; Pennerton West; Robert Reid; Sculpture: Louise Nevelson; Mark DiSuvero; Felix Eboigbe; Frederick MacMonnies; Photographs: Ansell Adams; Imogen Cunningham; Walker Evans; W Eugene Smith; Edward Steichen; Alfred Stieglitz; Clarence White; Minor White; Bernice Abbott; Edward Curtis; Arnold Genthe
Exhibitions: Changing Walls: Tactile Environment; Midwest Photo '80
Publications: Midwest Museum Bulletin, bimonthly
Activities: Classes for adults and children; dramatic programs; docent training; lect open to the public, 6 visiting lectrs per year; concerts; gallery talks; tours; competitions with awards; individual paintings and original objects of art lent; book traveling exhibitions, 8 per year; traveling exhibitions organized and circulated

EVANSVILLE

M EVANSVILLE MUSEUM OF ARTS AND SCIENCE, 411 SE Riverside Dr, 47713. Tel 812-425-2406. *Pres Bd Dir* Mrs D Patrick O'Daniel; *Dir* John W Streetman; *Dir Emeritus* Siegfried Weng; *Coordr Public Programs* Jean Lee; *Cur of Coll* Mary Schnepper; *Registrar* Patricia Sides
Open Tues - Sat 10 AM - 5 PM, Sun Noon - 5 PM, cl Mon. No admis fee. Estab 1926 to maintain and perpetuate a living museum to influence and inspire the taste and cultural growth of the community, to provide facilities for the collection, preservation and exhibition of objects and data and programs related to the arts, history, science and technology. Lower Level: 19th century village of homes, shops, offices and town hall, arms and armor gallery, science and technology gallery; Main Level furnished Gothic Room with linenfold paneling; Sculpture Gallery: Galleries for Dutch & Flemish Art, American Art and English Portraits; Gallery arts and crafts of Egypt, the Orient, Africa and the American Indian; Two Galleries for monthly exhibits; Upper Lever: Planetarium, classrooms. Average Annual Attendance: 100,000. Mem: 1500; dues donor $250, patron $100, contributing $35, participating $35, family $20, adult $10, and collegiate $5; annual meeting third Tues in May
Income: $174,000 (financed by membership, city and state appropriations)
Collections: American and European graphics; †American art; American paintings; arts and crafts of Black Africa, Egypt, Oceania and the American Indian; †18th & 19th century American crafts; European paintings; history archives; oriental art; sculpture from BC to contemporary; Victorian decorative arts
Exhibitions: (1984) All In Place; 24th Annual Mid-States Craft Exhibition; Harry Callahan: Master of Photography; 21st Annual High School Art Show; Realism Today; Auguste Rodin's Gates of Hell; Currier and Ives: American Middle Class Values, Recreation and Education; 37th Annual Mid-States Art Exhibition; Sarah Campbell Blaffer Golden Age of Dutch Painting; Textiles by Ed Oppenheimer; Artists Invitational; Here Comes the Bride; Annual Artist-In-Residence; Works in Wood
Publications: Bulletin, monthly; catalogs of exhibitions
Activities: Classes for adults and children; dramatic programs; docent training; lect open to public; concerts; gallery talks; tours; competitions; exten dept serving area schools; individual paintings and original objects of art lent to institutions; lending collection contains nature artifacts, original art works, original prints, paintings, photographs and sculpture; traveling exhibitions organized and circulated; museum shop selling books, original art, reproductions, prints, jewelry, and pottery
L Henry R Walker Jr Memorial Art Library, 411 SE Riverside Dr, 47713. Tel 812-425-2406
Open Tues - Sat 10 AM - 5 PM, Sun Noon - 5 PM. For reference only
Library Holdings: Vols 4000; Per subs 25; AV — Slides; Other — Clipping files, exhibition catalogs, manuscripts, memorabilia, original art works, pamphlets, photographs, prints, reproductions, sculpture

UNIVERSITY OF EVANSVILLE
M Krannert Gallery,* Lincoln Ave, PO Box 329, 47702. Tel 812-479-2043. *Chmn Art Dept* Les Miley; *Gallery Coordr* William Brown
Open Mon - Sat 9 AM - 5 PM. No admis fee. Estab 1969-70 to bring to the University and public communities exhibitions which reflect the contemporary arts, ranging from crafts through painting and sculpture. Public access exhibition space 80 x 40 ft and located in Fine Arts Building
Income: Financed by Department of Art funds
Collections: 20th century art primarily centered around paintings and prints acquired through purchase awards and private gifts
Exhibitions: Drawing Exhibition; Indiana Ceramics; New Aquisitions; Student Scholarship Exhibition; Undergraduate BFA Exhibition; Faculty Exhibition; Painting Invitational; Sculpture Invitational; Evansville Artists Guild Show; Photography Exhibition
Activities: Competitions; individual paintings and original objects of art lent to university community
L Clifford Memorial Library, 1800 Lincoln Ave, PO Box 329, 47702
Open 8 AM - 12 PM
Library Holdings: Vols 3550; Per subs 27; Micro — Cards, fiche, prints; Other — Exhibition catalogs, manuscripts, memorabilia, original art works, pamphlets, prints

L WILLARD LIBRARY, Dept of Fine Arts, 21 First Ave, 47710. Tel 812-425-4309. *Head Librn* Don Baker; *Asst Librn* David Locker; *Special Collections* Joan Elliott
Open Tues - Fri 9 AM - 5:30 PM, Sat 9 AM - 5 PM, Sun 1 - 5 PM. Estab 1885
Income: $5000 (financed by endowment and city appropriation)
Library Holdings: Vols 5000; Per subs 16; Micro — Fiche; AV — Rec; Other — Original art works, photographs

FORT WAYNE

L ALLEN COUNTY PUBLIC LIBRARY, Fine Arts Dept, 900 Webster St, 46802. Tel 219-424-7241. *Dir* Rick J Ashton; *Public Services Mgr* Steven Fortriede; *Head Fine Arts Dept* Kay Lynn Isca
Open Mon - Thurs 9 AM - 9 PM, Fri 9 AM - 6 PM, Sat 9 AM - 6 PM, Sun 1 - 6 PM. Estab 1968 to provide a reference collection of the highest quality and completeness for the community and its colleges, and a place where local artists and musicians could exhibit their works and perform; and to provide a circulating collection of art prints, slides and musical scores sufficient to meet the demand. The gallery is reserved for painting, sculpture, graphics, ceramics and other art crafts; photography exhibits are held in the lobby area
Income: $100,000 (financed by local property taxes)
Library Holdings: Vols 13,442; Per subs 170; Mounted pictures; AV — Cassettes, motion pictures, rec, slides, v-tapes; Other — Exhibition catalogs, framed reproductions, prints, reproductions
Activities: Concerts

O FORT WAYNE FINE ARTS FOUNDATION, INC, The Canal House, 114 E Superior St, 46802. Tel 219-424-0646. *Interim Dir* Jean Greenlee; *Pres* Charles Weinraub; *Secy* Stewart Spencer; *Mgr Community Arts Center* Janet McCaulay
Estab 1955 to raise funds for cultural organizations in Fort Wayne & to foster a positive atmosphere for arts growth
Income: Financed by public allocations & private donations
Collections: Bicentennial Collection
Publications: Discovery, quarterly newspaper; fine arts calendar
Activities: Own and manage Community Center for the Performing Arts

M FORT WAYNE MUSEUM OF ART, 311 E Main St, 46802. Tel 219-422-6467. *Dir* Valerie V Braybrooke
Open Tues - Sat 10 AM - 4 PM, Sun 1 - 4 PM; cl Mon. No admis fee. Estab 1921 to heighten visual perception of fine arts and perception of other disciplines. Average Annual Attendance: 30,000. Mem: 1200; dues $20 for an individual and up; annual meeting May
Income: Financed by endowment, memberships, fine arts foundation and grants
Collections: Paintings, prints, sculpture and minor arts; Dorsky and Tannenbaum Collection of Contemporary Graphics; Fairbanks Collection of Paintings and Prints; Hamilton Collection of Paintings and Sculpture; Thieme Collection of Paintings; Weatherhead Collection of Contemporary Paintings & Prints; William Moser Collection of African Art; contemporary pieces by living American artists (representing pop art, the 1950's & the Pluralism of the 1970's: Tworkov, Rosenquist, J Johns, Warhol & Arakawa)
Exhibitions: Annual Tri Kappa (Indiana, Ohio, Michigan artists juried show); Photographs by Photorealists; Painterly Abstraction: 4 Views for the 1980's; Alexander Gavalas; I U Printmaking; Annual National Watercolor Society
Publications: Heritage Crafts, books; calendar, bi-monthly; catalogs; fact sheets; posters
Activities: Classes for adults and children; docent training; lectures open to public; 32 visiting lecturers per year; gallery talks; tours; competitions with awards; individual and original objects of art lent to area universities, schools and libraries; originate traveling exhibitions; sales shop selling books, original art, ceramics and other gift items; junior museum in Young People's Wing

M LINCOLN NATIONAL LIFE FOUNDATION, INC, Louis A Warren Lincoln Library and Museum, 1300 S Clinton St, Box 1110, 46801. Tel 219-427-3864. *Dir* Mark E Neely Jr; *Asst* Ruth Cook
Open Mon - Thurs 8 AM - 4:30 PM, Fri 8 AM - 12:30 PM, May - Sept Mon - Fri 8 AM - 4:30 PM, Sat 10 AM - 4:30 PM. No admis fee. Estab 1928 for collection of Lincolniana; as research library and museum. Average Annual Attendance: 15,000
Collections: 6000†Lincoln portraits, †lithographs, †engravings, †paintings, †photographs,
Publications: Lincoln Lore, monthly; R Gerald McMurry Lecture, annually
Activities: Lect open to public with visiting lectr; original objects of art lent to museums and libraries

M SAINT FRANCIS COLLEGE, Lakeview Gallery, 1901 Spring St, 46808. Tel 219-432-3551, Ext 236
Open Mon - Fri 10 AM - 5 PM. No admis fee. Estab 1965, to provide art programs to students and community. Gallery, approx 25 x 15 ft each, is maintained in two rooms, located on the third floor, Bonaventure Hall. Average Annual Attendance: 1000
Collections: American Indian Collection; †Oriental Collection
Exhibitions: (1982-83) Saint Francis faculty exhibit; Robert Barnum; regional high school exhibit; student exhibit; Darren Walker; (1983-84) Marilyn Bock—To Bolski; faculty exhibit
Activities: Lectures open to public, 1-2 visiting lecturers per year; tours; competitions with awards; traveling exhibitions organized and circulated

HAMMOND

M PURDUE UNIVERSITY CALUMET, Bicentennial Library Gallery, 46323. Tel 219-844-0520, Ext 249. *Admin* Bernard H Holicky; *Chmn Art Committee* Barbara M Meeker
Mon - Thurs 8 AM - 9:30 PM, Fri 8 AM - 5 PM, Sat 10 AM - 4 PM, Sun 1 - 6 PM. No admis fee. Estab 1976 to present varied art media to the university community & general public. Average Annual Attendance: 25,000
Income: $2000
Collections: 19th century Chinese Scroll collection; 1930 art deco bronze sculptured doors from City Hall
Exhibitions: Area Professional Artists and Students Shows; group shows; traveling shows (Smithsonian Institution)
Activities: Book traveling exhibitions

INDIANAPOLIS

C ELI LILLY AND COMPANY, 307 E McCarty St, 46285. Tel 317-261-2489.
Department Head Community Relations Marilee Fraser
Supports museums, including Indianapolis Museum of Art and The Children's Museum
Activities: Supports construction, special projects and general operating

M HISTORIC LANDMARKS FOUNDATION OF INDIANA, Morris-Butler House, 1204 N Park Ave, 46202. Tel 317-636-5409. *Cur* Charles M Jacobs
Open Wed - Sun 1 - 5 PM; other times by appointment for groups; cl Mon & Tues. Admis adult $1.50, students $.50. Home built 1865 and restored by Historic Landmarks Foundation of Indiana. Estab in 1964 to document age of picturesque eclecticism in architecture & interior decoration. Twenty-one rooms completely furnished. Facilities for receptions and meetings. Average Annual Attendance: 8000
Collections: †Rococo, Renaissance & Gothic Revival furniture; paintings by early Indiana artists; †Victorian ceramics, silver & glass

O HOOSIER SALON PATRONS ASSOCIATION, Hoosier Salon Art Gallery, 47 S Meridian, 46204. Tel 317-632-1736. *Pres* Harry Riser; *Secy* Mrs G W Foster; *First VPres* Eugene Henderson; *Tres* David Shea; *Executive Dir* Mary Beck
Main gallery open Mon - Fri 9:30 AM - 4:30 PM. Estab 1925 to promote work of Indiana artists. Mem: Dues mem $15 and up, artist $10, annual meeting June
Income: Financed by memberships and art sales
Collections: Paintings, prints, sculpture
Exhibitions: Annual Hoosier Salon in Spring & then on tour
Publications: Annual Salon Catalog; History of the Hoosier Salon; Hoosier Salon Newsletter, three times a year
Activities: Competitions with awards; loan service to members; originate traveling exhibitions

M INDIANA CENTRAL UNIVERSITY, Leah Ransburg Art Gallery, 1400 E Hanna Ave, 46227. Tel 317-788-3253. *Dir* Gerald G Boyce
Open daily 9:30 AM - 4 PM. No admis fee. Estab 1964 to serve the campus and community. Average Annual Attendance: 40,000
Income: Financed by institution support
Purchases: $15,000
Collections: †Art Department Collection; †Krannert Memorial Collection
Publications: Announcements; annual catalog and bulletin
Activities: Classes for adults; lectures open to public; concerts; gallery talks; competitions with prizes; scholarships

L INDIANAPOLIS MARION COUNTY PUBLIC LIBRARY, Art Dept, 40 E St Clair St, 46204. Tel 317-635-5662. *Dir* Raymond Gnat
Open Mon - Fri 9 AM - 9 PM, Sat 9 AM - 5 PM, Sun 1 - 5 PM. Estab 1873
Income: Financed by state appropriation and county property tax
Library Holdings: Micro — Reels; AV — Motion pictures, rec; Other — Clipping files, exhibition catalogs, pamphlets, prints
Activities: Lect open to public; concerts; tours; competitions

M INDIANAPOLIS MUSEUM OF ART, 1200 W 38th St, 46208. Tel 317-923-1331. *Chmn Board of Trustees* Robert S Ashby; *Pres Board of Trustees* Clarence W Long; *Dir* Robert A Yassin; *Senior Cur* Dr Anthony F Janson; *Cur Oriental Art* Dr Yutaka Mino; *Cur Textiles and Ethnographic Art* Peggy S Gilfoy; *Assoc Cur Painting & Sculpture* Ellen W Lee; *Assoc Cur Decorative Arts* Catherine Beth Lippert; *Asst Cur Prints & Drawings* Martin F Krause; *Dir Education* Helen Ferrulli; *Chief Conservator* Martin J Radecki; *Registrar* Vanessa Burkhart; *Public Relations* Paula S Jackson; *Dir Development* Mark P McKinzie; *Dir Personnel* Gilbert Holmes; *Business Mgr* Matthew Wrnacchione
Open Tues - Sun 11 AM - 5 PM; cl Mon, Thanksgiving, Christmas & New Year's Day. No admis fee to permanent collection, charge for special exhibitions. Estab 1883 to maintain a museum, the grounds, pavilions, and other facilities for the display of art, a library for the collection of books, manuscripts, periodicals, photographs and other similar data or facilities relating to art of all kinds; to promote interest in art of all kinds by lectures, exhibitions, publications, programs and general sponsorship of art and artists in the City of Indianapolis and State of Indiana; to cooperate with national state and city government and civic, educational and artistic groups foundations. Maintains three galleries, the Krannert, Clowes and Lilly Pavilions. Average Annual Attendance: 500,000. Mem: 12,000; dues reciprocal $100, sustaining $50, family-double $25, individual $15, student $12.50
Collections: Classical to contemporary watercolors, including †J M W Turner Collection; American period rooms, †costumes and textiles; †decorative arts, including watch collection; †18th century English portraiture; 18 - 19th century European porcelain and furniture; †ethnographic art of North and South America, Africa and Oceania; Indiana paintings; †Oriental bronzes, ceramics, jade and paintings; †19th - 20th century American and European paintings; Holliday Collection of Neo-Impressionist paintings; 17th century European paintings; Renaissance to contemporary drawings and prints; Western American art
Exhibitions: (1982) The Print & Drawing Society Collects 100 Years of American Graphic Art; Forever Free: An Exhibition of Art by African-American Women 1862-1980; Radiance of Flowers: The Franklin Mead Collection of Chinese Ceramics; Chinese Fan Painting; The Museum Collects: 1883-1906; Masters of Taos; Recent Accessions, 1981; Japanese Stencils; Adolph Gottlieb: A Retrospective; Drawings by Gian Lorend Bernini From the Muzder Bildenden Kunste, Leipzig; Painting & Sculpture Today: 1982; Gifts of the Gamboliers 1930-1936; Fashion Technology: A Tribute to the Modiste; Batuz; Art of the Avat-Garde in Russia: Selections from the George Costakis Collection; Chinese Sleevebands; Original Teachers of the Herron School; (1983) Masterpieces of Prints & Drawings; Holliday Collection, The Aura of Neo-Impressionism; A Collector's Choices: Asian Art from the Collection of Dr Walter Compton; Museum in Bloom; 69th Indiana Artists Show; Party of the Century; Fabrics & Celebration from the Collection; Michael Cohen—Pottery, Carol Ward Textiles; Orchid Society; Beauty & Tranquility: The Eli Lilly Collection of Chinese Art;

Master Drawings & Watercolors from the Collection of the Indianapolis Museum of Art
Publications: Perceptions, annual journal; brochures; catalogs of permanent collection; quarterly magazine for members
Activities: Classes for adults and children; dramatic programs; docent training; lect open to the public and for members only; concerts; gallery talks; tours; competitions; originate traveling exhibitions; museum shop and sales shop selling books, magazines, original art, reproductions, prints, slides; Alliance Art Rental Gallery rents paintings to members and sells to members and public

M Clowes Fund Collection, Clowes Pavilion, 1200 W 38th St, 46208. Tel 317-923-1331. *Cur* Allen W Clowes; *Research Cur* A Ian Fraser
Open Tues - Sun 11 AM - 5 PM, cl Mon. No admis fee. Estab 1958 to display paintings of the Old Masters from the collection of the late Dr G H A Clowes. Average Annual Attendance: 62,000
Income: Financed by endowment
Collections: Italian Renaissance: Duccio, Fra Angelico, Bellini, Luini, Tintoretto, and others; Spanish-El Greco, Goya and others; Northern Renaissance-17th and 18th century Dutch, Hals, Rembrandt and others; French-Clouet, Corneille de Lyon; English-Reynolds, Constable and others; Flemish-Breughel, Bosch and others

M Downtown Gallery, American Fletcher National Bank, 101 Monument Circle, 46277. *Asst VPres* Linda D Paul
Open Mon - Fri 9 AM - 5 PM. No admis. Estab 1973

L Stout Reference Library,* 1200 W 38th St, 46208. Tel 317-923-1331. *Head Librn* Martha G Blocker; *Cataloger* Julie C Su
Open Tues - Fri 11 AM - 5 PM, Sat & Sun 1 - 4 PM. Estab 1908 to serve needs of Museum staff and Indianapolis community. For reference only
Income: Financed by endowment, membership, city appropriation and federal grants
Library Holdings: Vols 22,500; Per subs 150; Micro — Fiche, reels; Other — Clipping files, exhibition catalogs, pamphlets
Special Subjects: Architecture, Decorative Arts, Ethnology, Painting - American, Sculpture, Textiles
Collections: Indiana Artists
Exhibitions: British Watercolors & Watercolorist; Painting & Sculpture Today; Teo Chou Ware; Romantics to Rodin; Indiana Artists Show; Henri Cartier-Bresson Photos; Gustave Bauman; Forever Free
Publications: Exhibition catalogs as needed; Indianapolis Museum of Art Bulletin, irregularly; newsletter, bimonthly; 100 Masterpieces
Activities: Docent training; lectures open to public; concerts; gallery talks; tours; originate traveling exhibitions to Indiana area

L Visual Resources & Services, 1200 W 38th St, 46208. Tel 317-923-1331, Ext 35. *Coordr Visual Resources & Servs* Cynthia K Shipley; *Dir Visual Resources & Servs* Carolyn J Metz
Open Tues - Sat 1 - 5 PM. Estab 1972 to provide visuals on the history of art and to document and record the museum programs and activities. Circ 40,000
Income: Financed by endowment and museum budget
Purchases: $5000
Library Holdings: AV — Slides 80,000
Special Subjects: Art History
Collections: Exhibits and installation documentation of programs

M Indianapolis Museum of Art at Columbus Ind,* Fifth and Franklin Sts, 47201
Exhibitions: Exhibitions from the permanent collection quarterly

M INDIANA STATE MUSEUM,* 202 N Alabama St, 46204. Tel 317-232-1637. *Dir* Carl H Armstrong; *Cur Coll* Susan J Dickey; *Cur Exhib* Jack Moore; *Exhib Design Coordr* Wade Carmichael; *Cur Educ* Kathleen McLary; *Pub Relations Coordr* James McKean; *Grants & Memorial Liaison* Denver Howlett
Open daily 9 AM - 5 PM. No admis fee. Estab 1869 for collections; current museum building opened 1967 to collect, preserve and interpret the natural and cultural history of the state. Numerous galleries: Natural Interactions: The Flora and Fauna of Indiana; Earth Science; Pioneer Lifestyles and Fashions; Indiana Artists; Early Man in Indiana, Modes of Travel; and Abraham Lincoln. Average Annual Attendance: 130,000. Mem: 1300; dues $5 and up; annual meeting Apr
Income: Financed by state appropriation
Exhibitions: Three Indiana art shows annually
Publications: History-on-the-Move, bimonthly
Activities: Docent training; in-school programs; lect open to public, 4 vis lectr per year; sales shop selling books, reproductions and prints

L Library,* 202 N Alabama St, 46204
Open to staff for reference
Library Holdings: Vols 1000

INDIANA UNIVERSITY - PURDUE UNIVERSITY AT INDIANAPOLIS
M Herron School of Art Gallery, 1701 N Pennsylvania St, 46202. Tel 317-923-3651. *Dir Art Gallery* Martha Winans; *Gallery Asst* William C Grimes
Open Mon - Thurs 10 AM - 7 PM, Fri 10 AM - 5 PM, Sat 10 AM - 2 PM. No admis fee. School estab 1977. Gallery estab 1978 and is located in the Museum Building & exhibits contemporary art on an international scale, and is part of the original John Herron Art Institute. Average Annual Attendance: 40,000. Mem: 174; dues $25 - $250
Income: Financed by state appropriation
Collections: Student and faculty exhibits; temporary contemporary arts installations with documentation
Exhibitions: (1981) Imagery-Amstraction; Midwest Photo; Cynthia Carlson Installation; (1982) Edward Mayer Installation; (1983) Michael Smith, Mike's House
Activities: Classes for adults and children; lect; tours; film series; workshops; vis artists program; gallery talks; exten dept serving Indianapolis and surrounding communities; original objects of art lent
—Art Library, 1701 N Pennsylvania St, 46202. Tel 317-923-3651. *Head Librn* Maudine B Williams; *Asst Librn* Jennifer Hehman
Open Mon - Thurs 8 AM - 7 PM, Fri 8 AM - 5 PM, Sat 8:30 AM - 12:30 PM. Estab 1970 as a visual resource center for the support of the curriculum of the Herron School or Art. Circ 80,938
Income: $8200 (financed by state appropriation)
Purchases: $8200

Library Holdings: Vols 16,284; Per subs 162; AV — A-tapes, fs, lantern slides, rec, slides, v-tapes; Other — Clipping files, exhibition catalogs, pamphlets, photographs, prints, reproductions
Special Subjects: Art History, Art Education, Photography, Printmaking, Sculpture, visual communication, painting

C **LAUGHNER BROTHERS, INC,*** 4004 S East St, 46227. Tel 317-783-2907. *Pres* Charles Laughner
Open 11 AM - 2:30 PM and 4 - 8 PM. Estab 1963 to promote artists and their original paintings. Collection displayed in cafeterias. Mr Laughner uses original paintings from several artists as his main decor in all 9 locations in Indiana
Purchases: $2000

M **MARIAN COLLEGE,** Allison Mansion,* 3200 Cold Spring Rd, 46222. Tel 317-924-3291. *In Charge* Sr Mary de Paul-Schweitzer
Open Sun 2 - 4 PM and by appointment. No admis fee, donations accepted. Estab 1970, in the National Register of Historical Places, Allison Mansion houses the Art Department of Marian College, a four-year liberal arts college. The interior of the mansion is a work of art with its magnificent treatment of walls of hand carved marble and wood: oak, white mahogany and walnut. The grand stairway in the main hall leads to the balcony overlooking the hall, all hand-carved walnut. A private collection of 17th century paintings complement its beauty
Income: Financed by donations
Activities: Concerts; tours

LAFAYETTE

O **LAFAYETTE ART ASSOCIATION,** Greater Lafayette Museum of Art, 101 S Ninth St, 47901. Tel 317-742-1128. *Pres* Kendall Smith II; *Dir* Sharon A Theobald
Open Tues - Sun 1 - 5 PM, cl Mon & Jan. No admis fee. Estab 1909 to encourage and stimulate art and to present exhibitions of works of local, regional and national artists and groups as well as representative works of American and foreign artists. Three galleries. Average Annual Attendance: 10,000. Mem: 900; dues family $15, individual $10, student and senior citizen $5; annual meeting Oct
Income: Financed by art association foundation, endowment, membership, school of art & special events
Collections: Permanent collection of over 300 works of art obtained through purchase or donation since 1909; Laura Anne Fry American Art Pottery & Art Glass; Alice Baber Midwest Collection of Contemporary Art; American art collection specializing in Hoosier artist's work
Exhibitions: Monthly exhibitions; permanent collection
Publications: In Perspective, quarterly newsletter; exhibition catalogs
Activities: Classes for adults and children; docent training; lectures open to the public, gallery talks, tours, competitions with awards; Weil Gallery lecture series; scholarships; Art Smart (art-in-education) in area schools; sales shop selling books, original art, prints, reproductions
L **Library,** 101 S Ninth St, 47901. Tel 317-742-1128
Open to members
Library Holdings: Vols 350; Per subs 15; Other — Clipping files, exhibition catalogs, framed reproductions, prints

M **TIPPECANOE COUNTY HISTORICAL MUSEUM,** 909 South St, 47901. Tel 317-742-8411. *Dir* John M Harris; *Asst Dir & Librn* Carol N Waddell; *Cur of Photography* Rachel Road; *Cur of Educ* Paula Woods; *Archivist* Sarah Cooke
Open daily 1 - 5 PM, cl Mon. No admis fee. Estab 1925 to collect, preserve, research and interpret the history of Tippecanoe County and the immediate surrounding area. Housed in a Victorian house (1851-52), there are exhibits of various phases of county history in nine rooms. Average Annual Attendance: 20,000. Mem: 1000; dues $7 - $25; annual meeting Jan
Income: Financed by endowment, membership, county and state appropriation, sales and programs
Collections: Broad range, incorporating any object relative to county history
Exhibitions: Changing exhibits; fixed exhibits include Pioneer Development, Woodland Indians, miniature rooms, paintings and porcelains
Publications: Tippecanoe Tales, occasional series on various phases of Tippecanoe County history; Weatenotes, nine times a year
Activities: Classes for adults and children; docent training; lect open to the public; tours; individual paintings and original objects of art lent to other museums; sales shop selling books, reproductions, original crafts on consignment
L **Alameda McCollough Library,** 909 South St, 47901. *Librn Genealogical Section* Lyda Hilt; *Librn* Nancy Weirich
Open to serious researchers for reference only
Library Holdings: Vols 5000; Per subs 21; maps; Micro — Reels; AV — A-tapes; Other — Clipping files, manuscripts, pamphlets, photographs

MADISON

M **JEFFERSON COUNTY HISTORICAL SOCIETY MUSEUM,*** 412 Elm St, 47250. Tel 812-265-3546. *Pres* Emmett S Wood
Open Fri, Sat & Sun 1 - 4 PM. Estab 1900 to preserve and display art and artifacts worthy of note and pertinent to local area history and culture. Museum is on the grounds of the Madison Jefferson County Public Library and was the carriage house for the owners of the original mansion which later became the library. Average Annual Attendance: 1500. Mem: 45, dues $2 single, $5 family, $10 patron, monthly meetings on the fourth Thurs 8 PM
Collections: William McKendree Snyder Collection, paintings, portraits
Activities: Lectures open to public, 6 vis lectr per yr; paintings & art objects are lent to organization sponsored events

MUNCIE

BALL STATE UNIVERSITY
M **Art Gallery,** 47306. Tel 317-285-5242. *Dir* Alain Joyaux; *Cur Education* Anne Moore; *Secy* Betty Magill; *Preparator* Brian Moore
Open Mon - Fri 9 AM - 4:30 PM, Sat & Sun 1:30 - 4:30 PM, cl legal holidays. Estab 1936 as a university & community art museum. Eight galleries, sculpture court & mezzanine. Average Annual Attendance: 50,000
Collections: Kraft-Ball Collection of Roman and Syrian glass; Italian Renaissance art and furniture; 18th, 19th & 20th century European & American paintings, prints, and drawings
Exhibitions: Annual Art Faculty Exhibit; Annual Art Student Exhibit; Annual Drawing and Small Sculpture Show
Activities: Lect open to public, 2 - 3 vis lectr per year; concerts; gallery talks; competitions; individual paintings and original objects of art lent to other art galleries and museums, and to offices and special buildings on campus; originate traveling exhibitions
L **Architecture Library,** College of Architecture & Planning, McKinley at Neely, 47306. Tel 317-285-8497, 285-8498. *Librn* Marjorie Hake Joyner; *Clerical Asst* Barbara Ballinger
Open (academic year) Mon 8 AM - 8 PM, Tues - Thurs 8 AM - 10 PM, Fri 8 AM - 5 PM, Sat 9 AM - 5 PM, Sun 1 - 10 PM; (summer) Mon - Fri 8 AM - 5 PM. Estab 1965 to provide materials necessary to support the academic programs of the college of Architecture & Planning
Income: Financed through University
Library Holdings: Vols 24,500; Per subs 150; Manufacturers' catalogs; architectural drawings; maps and student theses; Micro — Fiche, reels; AV — Slides; Other — Clipping files, pamphlets
Special Subjects: Architectural history

NASHVILLE

O **BROWN COUNTY ART GALLERY ASSOCIATION INC,** 1 Artist Dr, PO Box 443, 47448. Tel 812-988-4609. *Pres* Frances Rogers; *First VPres* George Goehl; *Second VPres* Martin Saavi; *Exec Secy* Ann Bright
Open March - Dec 10 AM - 5 PM. Admis adult 50. Estab 1926 to unite artists and laymen in fellowship; to create a greater incentive for development of art and its presentation to the public; to estab an art gallery for exhibition of work of members of the Association. Average Annual Attendance: 35,000. Mem: 53 artists; 750 supporting members; dues individual $10 - life $500; annual meeting Oct
Income: Financed by memberships, foundation and trust
Collections: 75 oil paintings and pastels by the late Glen Cooper Henshaw
Exhibitions: 3 exhibits each year by the artist members
Publications: Annual catalog
Activities: Competitions with awards

M **T C STEELE STATE MEMORIAL,*** RR 1, 47448. Tel 812-988-2785. *Mgr* B D Weddle
Open Wed - Sat 9 AM - Noon & 1 - 5 PM, Sun & Tues 1 - 5 PM. Admis adults $.50, children under 12 no charge
Collections: Books; period furnishings; Steele paintings
Activities: Tours

NEW ALBANY

M **FLOYD COUNTY MUSEUM,** 201 E Spring St, 47150. Tel 812-944-7336. *Pres* Sara Newkirk; *VPres* Jane Anderson; *Secy* Dr Richard Smith; *Art Dir* Diana Todd; *Exec Secy* Nettie Skaggs
Open Tues - Sat 10 AM - 4 PM, Sun 2 - 5 PM. No admis fee. Estab 1971, to exhibit professional artists work on a monthly basis. Two galleries are maintained, approx dimensions: 18 x 25 ft and 15 x 25 ft. Average Annual Attendance: 7000. Mem: 300; dues $10 - $100
Income: Financed through membership
Collections: Permanent collection of †historical items
Exhibitions: Floyd County in World War I; 1920s to Depression Years; A History Sampler
Publications: Bulletins
Activities: Classes for adults and children; lect open to the public; gallery talks; tours; competitions; awards; book traveling exhibitions, 2-4 per year; museum shop sells original art, reproductions, prints

NEW HARMONY

M **THE NEW HARMONY GALLERY OF CONTEMPORARY ART,** Main St, PO Box 248, 47631. Tel 812-682-3156. *Pres* Ralph G Schwarz; *VPres* Neil Pagano; *Secy* Doris Manning; *Dir* John P Begley
Open Tues - Sat 9 AM - 5 PM, Sun 1 - 5 PM, cl Mon. No admis fee. Estab 1975 for exhibition of contemporary midwest art and artists. Average Annual Attendance: 20,000
Income: Financed by contributions and grants
Exhibitions: Monthly changing exhibitions
Activities: Classes for adults and children; workshops; lectures open to the public, 4 vis lectr per yr; gallery talks; awards; individual paintings & original objects of art lent; lending collection contains motion pictures; paintings & video; book traveling exhibitions; originate traveling exhibitions; sales shop sells books, magazines, original art & prints

NOTRE DAME

SAINT MARY'S COLLEGE

M **Moreau Gallery Three,** Art Department, 46556. Tel 219-284-4655. *Chmn, Ceramics & Sculpture* H James Paradis; *Gallery Dir* Bill Sandusky; *Gallery Dir* Giovanna Lenzi Sandusky
Open Mon - Fri 9:30 AM - Noon & 1 PM - 3 PM, Sun 1 PM - 3 PM, cl Sat.
Estab 1956 for education and community-related exhibits. Gallery presently occupies three spaces; all exhibits rotate. Average Annual Attendance: 6000
Collections: Cotter Collection; Dunbarton Collection of prints; Norman LaLiberte; various media
Exhibitions: (1982-83) Margo Hoff; Indiana Women's Caucus; Jim Paradis; Dolores Milmoe; Betsy Packard; International Holographers Invitational; senior comps; NASAD; Giuseppe Gattuso; Joseph Jachna; Jim Raymo; Barbara Blandeau; Douglas Tyler
Publications: Catalogs, occasionally
Activities: Classes for adults; dramatic programs; lect open to public; tours; concerts; gallery talks; competitions with awards; scholarships offered; individual paintings and original objects of art lent; originate traveling exhibitions
L **Cushwa-Leighton Library,** Saint Mary's College, 46556. Tel 219-284-5280. *Head Librn* Sr Bernice Hollenhorst; *Head Cataloguer* Sr Marjorie Johnes; *Reference Librn* Robert Hohl; *Periodicals Librn* Ann Johnson; *Order Librn* Marcia Burns; *Collection Development & ILL Librn* Lola M Philippsen; *AV Coordr* Sue Gutterman; *Archivist* Sr Bernadette Marie; *Reference* Julia Long
Open Mon - Fri 7:45 AM - Midnight, Sat 9 AM - Midnight, Sun 1 PM - Midnight. Estab 1855
Income: Financed through the college
Library Holdings: Vols 6000; Per subs 25; Micro — Reels; AV — A-tapes, cassettes, fs, Kodachromes, motion pictures, rec, slides

UNIVERSITY OF NOTRE DAME

M **Snite Museum of Art,** 46556. Tel 219-239-5466. *Dir* Dean A Porter; *Cur* Stephen B Spiro; *Cur* Douglas Bradley; *Admin Asst to Dir* Teri Larkin; *Admin Asst to Dir* Gwen Diehn; *Education Coordr* Barbara Rinehart; *Education Coordr* Diana Matthias; *Registrar* Robert Smogor; *Preparatorial* Greg Denby; *Secy* Anne Mills; *Auditorium Mgr & Librn* Lisa Stanczak
Open Tues - Fri 10 AM - 4 PM; Thurs 4 - 8 PM; Sat & Sun 1 - 4 PM. No admis fee. Estab 1842; Wightman Memorial Art Gallery estab 1917; O'Shaughnessy Hall Art Gallery estab 1951; Snite Museum estab 1980 to educate through the visual arts; during a four year period it is the objective to expose students to all areas of art including geographic, period and media, open 1980. Galleries consist of 35,000 sq ft. Average Annual Attendance: 95,000. Mem: 650; dues from $10 - $1000; annual meeting in May
Income: $600,000 (financed by endowment, university appropriation & gifts)
Purchases: $40,000
Collections: African art; American Indian and pre-Columbian art; Baroque paintings, northern and Italian; †18th and 19th century American, English and French paintings and drawings; Kress Study Collection; Oceanic Art; Oriental porcelains and sculpture; western culture; medieval, modern, and †contemporary paintings; 15th century to contemporary prints; †photographs; Renaissance paintings and sculpture; 16th-20th century prints; †ethnographic
Exhibitions: (1983) Religious Narrative in 16th Century Rome; Christo; Ivan Mestrovic: A Centennial; African Art from the Raymond E Britt Collection
Publications: Exhibition catalogs, 3-5 times per yr
Activities: Classes for adults & children; dramatic programs; docent training; lectures open to public, 4-6 vis lectr per year; concerts; gallery talks; tours; individual paintings and original objects of art lent to qualified institutions; book traveling exhibitions, 2-3 per year; originate traveling exhibitions; museum shop sells books, posters & post cards
L **Catalog Library,** 46556. Tel 219-239-5466. *Librn* Kimberlie Gumz
Open to students and faculty for reference only
Library Holdings: Vols 20,000; Per subs 6; Other — Clipping files, exhibition catalogs, manuscripts, memorabilia, pamphlets, prints, reproductions
L **Architecture Library,** 46556. Tel 219-283-6654. *Librn* Geri Decker
Open Mon - Thurs 8 AM - 10 PM; Fri 8 AM - 5 PM; Sat 9 AM - 5 PM; Sun 1 - 10 PM; Vacations Mon - Fri 8 AM - 5 PM. Estab 1890 as a branch of the university library. Circ 15,000
Income: $34,500 (financed by university)
Purchases: $9000
Library Holdings: Vols 15,000; Per subs 2100; AV — Fs, lantern slides, motion pictures, slides; Other — Clipping files, original art works, reproductions, sculpture
Special Subjects: Architecture, art, engineering, planning environment
Collections: Rare folio books on architecture
Exhibitions: Art of Robert Schultz; Models of Major Buildings; Models of Student Work; Student Thesis Projects; visiting exhibitis
Activities: Lectures open to public, 8 vis lectr per year; gallery talks; tours; awards; scholarships; exten dept serves Rome

RICHMOND

O **ART ASSOCIATION OF RICHMOND,** McGuire Memorial Hall, 350 Whitewater Blvd, 47374. Tel 317-966-0256. *Dir* Ruth B Mills; *Secy* Carolyn Jellison
Open Sept - Dec & Feb - June, Mon - Fri 9 AM - 4 PM, Sun 1 - 4 PM, cl Sat and school holidays. No admis fee. Estab 1898 to promote creative ability, art appreciation and art in public schools. Maintains an art gallery with four exhibit rooms: 2 rooms for permanent collection and 2 rooms for current exhibits. Average Annual Attendance: 10,000. Mem: 600; dues from student $2 - $1000; annual meeting second Wed in Oct
Income: Financed by membership
Collections: Regional and state art; American, European, Oriental art
Exhibitions: Annual Area Professional Artists Exhibition; Crafts Exhibition; Amateur Area Artists Exhibition; Annual Photographic Exhibition; High School Art Exhibition; Hands-On Exhibition for grade school children
Publications: Art in Richmond - 1898 - 1978; newsletter, quarterly

Activities: Docent training; lect open to public, 6 vis lectr per year; gallery talks; tours; competitions with merit and purchase awards; scholarships; individual paintings and original objects of art lent to businesses and schools; lending collection contains books, original art works, original prints and photographs; originate traveling exhib; sales shop selling original art
L **Library,** McGuire Memorial Hall, 350 Whitewater Blvd, 47374. Tel 317-966-0256
Open to members
Library Holdings: Vols 200; Per subs 3
Special Subjects: Art museums, art techniques

M **EARLHAM COLLEGE,** Leeds Gallery, National Road W, 47374. Tel 317-962-6561. *Pres College* DeWitt C Baldwin; *Dir* JoAnne D Sieger
Open daily 8 AM - Noon. No admis fee. Estab 1847 as a liberal arts college; Leeds Gallery estab 1970
Collections: Regional artist: George Baker, Bundy (John Ellwood), Marcus Mote; prints by internationally known artists of 19th & 20th centuries; regional artists
Activities: Dramatic programs; lect open to public, 5-6 vis lectr per yr; concerts; individual paintings and original objects of art lent; traveling exhibitions organized and circulated; sales shop selling books

SOUTH BEND

O **ART CENTER, INC,** * 120 S Saint Joseph St, 46601. Tel 219-284-9102. *Dir* John R Brice; *Cur* Judy Oberhausen
Warner Gallery open Tues - Sun Noon - 5 PM; WAL Gallery open Tues - Fri 12:30 AM - 4 PM, Sat & Sun Noon - 5 PM. No admis fee. Estab in 1947 for museum exhibitions, lectures, film series, workshops, and studio classes. The Art Center is located in a three-story building designed by Philip Johnson. There are two galleries: the Warner Gallery features travelling shows or larger exhibits organized by the Art Center, and The WAL Upper Level Gallery features one or two-person shows by local or regional artists. Average Annual Attendance: 40,000. Mem: 1,000; dues sustaining $100, family $35, active $20, student & senior citizens $10
Income: Financed by membership, corporate support, city and state appropriations
Collections: European and American paintings, drawings, prints and objects; †20th century American art
Publications: Bi-monthly newsletter, exhibition catalogues, and checklists
Activities: Studio classes for adults and children; docent training and tours; outreach educational program conducted by Women's Art League; workshops; lecture series; artist studio tours; film series; museum shop offering gifts and original works of art for sale
L **Library,** * 120 S Saint Joseph St, 46601. Tel 219-284-9102
Estab 1947 to provide art resource material to members of the Art Center. Open to public on request; for reference only
Library Holdings: Vols 963; Per subs 49; AV — Motion pictures, rec; Other — Exhibition catalogs

TERRE HAUTE

M **INDIANA STATE UNIVERSITY,** Turman Gallery,* 47809. Tel 812-232-6311. *Chmn Art Dept* Frederick Bunce, PhD; *Dir* Bert Brouwer
Open Mon - Fri Noon - 5 PM, Sat & Sun 1 - 5 PM, cl last two weeks Aug. No admis fee
Collections: Paintings and sculpture
Exhibitions: Regular traveling exhibitions for short periods during school terms; student and faculty exhibitions
Activities: Classes for children; lect

M **SHELDON SWOPE ART GALLERY,** 25 S Seventh St, 47807. Tel 812-238-1676. *Dir* Robert D Kinsman; *Gallery Asst* Martin Ryan; *Asst Registrar* Diane Bayless
Open Sept 1 - July 31 Tues - Sun 2 - 4:30 PM, cl national holidays. No admis fee. Estab 1942 to present free of charge works of fine art for the education and enjoyment of the public. Average Annual Attendance: 12,000. Mem: 750; dues individual $15; annual meeting third Wed in Sept
Income: $108,555 (financed by membership, city appropriation and trust fund)
Collections: American art of 19th and 20th centuries; European art from 14th century to present; ancient, Far Eastern and ethnographic art; decorative arts; glass
Exhibitions: (1982-84) Josef Albers: Formulation/Articulation; British Watercolors; Contemporary Hoosier Artists: Selections from the Collection of Indiana Bell Telephone Company; Herman Armour, prints, drawings, watercolors; For the Record: Historic American Buildings Survey in Indiana, 1933-1983; Kathe Kollwitz: An Exploration in Human Destinies; annual Wabash Valley exhibition; annual exhibition of art by students of the Vigo County School Corporation
Publications: Membership newsletter, bimonthly; color brochure of the Gallery; catalogs to special exhibitions
Activities: Docent training; lectures open to the public, 10 vis lectr per yr; concerts; gallery talks; tours; competitions with awards; individual paintings & original objects of art lent to other museums; originate traveling exhibitions; museum shop sells books, original art, reproductions, note cards, gift items & prints
L **Research Library,** 25 S Seventh St, 47807. *In Charge* R Colleen Coleman
Open to the public
Library Holdings: Vols 3000; Per subs 25; AV — Slides; Other — Clipping files, exhibition catalogs, memorabilia, pamphlets, photographs

UPLAND

M **TAYLOR UNIVERSITY,** Chronicle-Tribune Art Gallery,* Art Dept, 46989. Tel 317-998-2751, Ext 322. *Dir* Ray E Bullock, PhD
Open Mon - Sat 11 AM - 4 PM and Mon, Wed and Fri 7 - 9 PM, cl Sun. No admis fee. Estab 1972 as an educational gallery
Activities: Classes for children; competitions

VALPARAISO

M **VALPARAISO UNIVERSITY,** University Art Galleries and Collections, 46383. Tel 219-464-5365 or 464-5364. *Chmn* Dr Jack Hiller; *Dir* Richard Brauer
Open Mon - Fri 8 AM - 10 PM, Sat 9 AM - 5 PM, Sun 1 - 10 PM. No admis fee. Estab 1953 to present significant art to the student and citizen community for their education in the values of art. Gallery areas located in Moellering Library, Christ College Building and the Union
Income: $14,000 (financed by endowment)
Purchases: $10,000
Collections: †Sloan Collection: 19th and 20th Century American Landscape Paintings, Prints, and Drawings; Valparaiso University Collection: Art on Biblical Themes
Exhibitions: (1983) Wanda Rice, ceramics; recent acquisitions; Anthony Droege, painting & sculpture; Wendy Brusick, watercolors; Blanche Gallagher, mystical paintings; Diane Vatne, photographs; university art faculty; student art works
Activities: Lectures open to the public; gallery talks; individual paintings and original objects of art lent to museums and art centers

WEST LAFAYETTE

M **PURDUE UNIVERSITY GALLERIES,** Creative Arts Bldg 1, 47907. Tel 317-494-3061. *Gallery Dir* Mona Berg; *Asst Dir* Belena Chapp
Open Mon - Fri 9 AM - 5 PM & 7 - 9 PM, Sun 12:30 - 4:30 PM. No admis fee. Estab 1972 to provide aesthetic & educational programs for art students & the university & greater Lafayette community. Galleries are located in four different buildings to provide approximately 5000 sq ft of space for temporary exhibitions. Average Annual Attendance: 60,000
Income: Financed through the university
Purchases: $1500
Collections: Contemporary paintings, †prints, sculpture; †ceramics; †pre-Columbian textiles; American Indian baskets
Exhibitions: (1983-84) Approximately 40 per yr including work by faculty, students, regionally & nationally prominent artists; Renaissance & Baroque Prints; Amelia Earhart: Woman With Wings; Winslow Homer; The Elegance of the Scientific Image, Sir Francis Seymour Haden/James McNeill Whistler; The Geometric Vision; Arts of the Zulu
Publications: Exhibit catalogs
Activities: Lectures open to public; concerts; gallery talks; competitions with awards; individual paintings & original objects of art lent to university administrative offices; book traveling exhibitions, 1-2 per year; traveling exhib organized and circulated

IOWA

AMES

M **IOWA STATE UNIVERSITY,** Brunnier Gallery Museum,* Scheman Bldg, Iowa State Center, 50011. Tel 515-294-3342. *Iowa State Center Cur* Lynette Fohlman; *Registrar & Secy* Mary Atherly
Open Tues - Sun 11 AM - 4 PM, cl Mon. No admis fee. Estab 1975, to provide a high level of quality, varied and comprehensive exhibits of national and international scope; and to develop and expand a permanent decorative arts collection of the western world. Gallery is maintained and comprised of 10,000 sq ft of exhibit space, with flexible space arrangement. Average Annual Attendance: Approx 30,000-50,000
Income: $90,000 (financed through state appropriations)
Collections: Permanent collection of ceramics, dolls, furniture, glass, ivory, wood
Activities: Classes for children; docent training; lectures open to the public, 1 - 2 vis lectr per yr; competitions with awards; gallery talks; tours; arts festivals; original objects of art lent; lending collection contains decorative arts, original prints; book traveling exhibitions, 3-4 per year; traveling exhibitions organized and circulated; sales shop sells books, slides, catalogs

O **OCTAGON CENTER FOR THE ARTS,** 427 Douglas, 50010. Tel 515-323-5331. *Pres* Gloria Layton; *VPres* Robins Hawthorne; *Secy* Carol Grant; *Treas* Dean Steffens; *Dir* Martha Benson; *Dir Educ* Helene Kaplan
Open Tues - Fri 9 AM - 5 PM, Sat 10 - 5 PM, Sun 2 - 5 PM. Estab 1966 to provide year-round classes for all ages; exhibitions of the work of outstanding artists from throughout the world and also special programs in the visual and performing arts. Average Annual Attendance: 35,000. Mem: 600, open to anyone who is interested in supporting or participating in the arts; dues $8 - $500; annual meeting second Sun in April
Income: $150,000 (financed by membership, city and state appropriations, class fees and fund raising)
Collections: Crafts; local history
Exhibitions: (1982-84) Shamans & Spirits: Myths & Medical Symbolism in Eskimo Art; Monoprints by Annette Okner; Iowa Weavers & Spinners; Gail Kristensen, Ceramist; The Art of the Piano; Marquee on Main Street: Jack Liebenberg's Deco Theaters, 1928-41; Annual Clay & Paper Show; Hand, Mind & Spirit: Crafts Today; Glass & Wood: Jan Elfline & Galen Winchip; The Art of Puppetry; Impressions/Expressions: Black American Graphics; Drawings & Paintings by Richard Weis; The Lincoln Highway, Pathfinders Lost; Central Iowa Regional Scholastic Art Award Exhibition; Women in Clay: The Ongoing Tradition; Ames Public School Art Show
Publications: Exhibition catalogs; newsletter, monthly
Activities: Classes for adults and children; dramatic programs; docent training; special classes for elderly and handicapped; lectures open to public, 2-5 vis lectr per year; concerts; gallery talks; tours; competitions with awards; lending collection of 500 lantern slides; book traveling exhibitions; originate traveling exhibitions; sales shop sells books, magazines, original art, prints, original crafts and fiber art supplies

ANAMOSA

O **PAINT 'N PALETTE CLUB,** RR 3 - 204 N Huber St, 52205. Tel 319-462-2601, 462-2680. *Pres* Mildred B Brown; *VPres* Harlan Jacobsen; *Executive Dir* Dr Gerald F Brown; *Executive Dir* Wilbur Evarts; *Secy* Lorena Gray
Open June 1 - Oct 15; Sun 1 - 5 PM; other times by appointment. No admis fee (donations accepted). Estab 1955 to maintain Antioch School, the school attended by Grant Wood, a famous Iowa artist; to provide a studio and gallery for local artists and for public enjoyment. A log cabin art gallery on the grounds of the Grant Wood Memorial Park contains the work of some local and visiting artists. Average Annual Attendance: 2000 - 3000. Mem: 37, members must have art experience; dues $10
Income: $700 - $800 (financed by endowment and donations)
Collections: Prints of Grant Wood, Iowa's most famous artist
Exhibitions: Amateur Art and Craft Show; Grant Wood Art Festival; art sale and exhibit
Activities: Occasional classes for adults and children; films; lect open to public, 6-7 vis lectr per yr; tours; competitions; sales shop selling magazines, original art, prints, reproductions, memorial plates and coins, postcards

BURLINGTON

O **ART GUILD OF BURLINGTON,** Arts for Living Center, Seventh & Washington St, PO Box 5, 52601. Tel 319-754-8069. *Dir* Lois Rigdon; *Pres* Gordon Hunt; *Pres Elect* Dick Phillips; *VPres* John Siekert; *Treas* Jim O'Neill; *Secy* Kay Weiler; *Corresponding Secy* Jean Mahon
Open Tues - Sat Noon - 5 PM, special openings Sun 2 - 5 PM, cl Mon and all major holidays, with the exception of Thanksgiving. No admis fee. Estab 1966, the Art Guild purchased the Center (a church building built 1868) in 1974, which has now been placed on the National Register of Historic Places. Average Annual Attendance: 8000. Mem: 350: dues student $10 up to benefactor $1000, meeting first Thurs monthly
Income: Financed by membership and donations
Exhibitions: Exhibitions of regional professional artists
Publications: Newsletter, once-twice monthly
Activities: Classes for adults and children; films; special workshops; lectures open to the public, 6 vis lectr per yr; concerts; gallery talks; tours; book traveling exhibitions, 2 - 3 per yr; traveling exhibitions organized and circulated; sales shop sells books, original art, reproductions, prints

CEDAR FALLS

M **UNIVERSITY OF NORTHERN IOWA,** Gallery of Art, 27th St at Hudson Rd, 50614. Tel 319-273-6114. *Dir* Daniel Everett Stetson
Open Mon - Thurs 9 AM - 4 PM, Sat & Sun 1 - 4 PM, Mon evenings 7 - 9 PM, cl Fri. No admis fee. Estab 1978 to bring to the University and the community at large the finest quality of art from all over the world. One main gallery with 365 running feet; two upstairs galleries, each with 100 running feet and a photographic exhibition corridor. New Gallery will be completed in 1985. Average Annual Attendance: 10,000
Income: Financed by state appropriation
Purchases: 20th century art work
Collections: †20th century American & European Art
Exhibitions: Current Clay Works by Barbara Cassino and Ed Harris; Drawings and Sculpture of Gaston Lachaise; Mark Tobey, graphics; Annual Student Exhibition; Annual Faculty Group Exhibition; Colorado Photographers; The Contemporary American Potter; The Great West; The International Year of the Child; The Right to Art; The Stock Show; Marvin Cone Retrospective; Jacob Landau, A Retrospective; The Graphic Works; Contemporary Metals Focus on Idea; Leonard Baskin: Woodcuts and Etchings; Art Nouveau Glass & Pottery; 20th Anniversary Vogel Collection; Barbara Crane; Reuben Nakian: Leda and the Swan; Jose de Creeft (1898-1982); Philip Pearlstein: Painting to Watercolors
Publications: Exhibition catalogs
Activities: Docent training; lectures open to public, 20 vis lectr per year; concerts; gallery talks; tours; competition; individual paintings & original objects of art lent; book traveling exhibitions 2 - 8 per yr; originate traveling exhibitions; sales shop sells catalogs, postcards, posters, t-shirts

L **Art and Music Section Library,** 50613. Tel 319-273-6252. *Dir* Donald O Rod; *Asst Dir* Donald Gray; *Art & Music Librn* Verna Ford Ritchie
Open Mon - Thurs 7:30 AM - Midnight, Fri 7:30 AM - 6 PM, Sat 10 AM - 6 PM, Sun 1:30 PM - Midnight. Main Library estab 1964, addition 1975, to serve art and music patrons. For lending and reference. Circ 18,872
Income: Financed by state
Purchases: $33,383
Library Holdings: Vols 43,870; Per subs 162; Micro — Fiche, prints; AV — A-tapes, cassettes, rec, slides; Other — Clipping files, exhibition catalogs, original art works, pamphlets, prints, reproductions

CEDAR RAPIDS

M CEDAR RAPIDS MUSEUM OF ART, 324 Third St SE, 52401. Tel 319-366-7503. *Pres* Bea Huston; *Treas* F W Schlesselman; *VPres Program Planning* John Bickel; *Secy* Joanne Ribble; *Dir* Joseph Czestochowski; *Cur* Monica Kindraka
Open Tues - Sat 10 AM - 5 PM, Thurs 10 AM - 8:30 PM, Sun 2 - 5 PM. Estab art association 1905, art center 1966. First and second floors maintain changing exhibits and the third floor maintains the Permanent Collection. Mem: 1000; Dues family $25, individual $15, students and sr citizens $5; meetings 3rd Monday in January
Income: Financed by endowment, membership, city and state appropriations
Collections: Largest concentrated collection of Grant Wood & Marvin Cone art in existence; print collection
Exhibitions: Rotating exhibitions
Publications: Newsletter, bi-monthly
Activities: Classes for adults and children; docent training; lectures open to public, 2 - 3 vis lectr per yr; gallery talks; tours; individual paintings and original objects of art lent on request; book traveling exhibitions, 5 - 6 per yr; originate traveling exhibitions; museum shop sells books, original art, reproductions, prints & craft items including pottery, weaving, jewelry
L Herbert S Stamats Library, 324 Third Ave SE, 52401. Tel 319-366-7503
Open Tues - Sat 10 AM - 5 PM, Thurs 10 AM - 8:30 PM, Sun 2 - 5 PM. For reference
Library Holdings: Vols 1200; Per subs 5; AV — Cassettes, fs, Kodachromes, slides; Other — Exhibition catalogs, framed reproductions, manuscripts, photographs
Special Subjects: Archival materials on American Reginalism; Cuzzy-wood

M COE COLLEGE, Gordon Fennell Gallery & Marvin Cone Gallery, 1221 First Ave NE, 52402. Tel 319-399-8559. *Chmn Art Dept* John Beckelman; *Gallery Dir* Shirley Donaldson
Open daily 3 - 5 PM. No admis fee. Estab 1942 to exhibit traveling exhibitions and local exhibits. Two galleries, both 60 x 18 ft with 125 running ft of exhibit space. Average Annual Attendance: 5000
Income: $3500 (financed through college)
Collections: Coe Collection of art works; Marvin Cone Alumni Collection; Marvin Cone Collection of oils; Conger Metcalf Collection of paintings; Hinkhouse Collection of contemporary art
Exhibitions: Circulating exhibits; one-person and group shows of regional nature; rental print exhibitions
Publications: Exhibition brochures, 8 - 10 per year
Activities: Lect open to public, 5 - 6 vis lectr per year; gallery talks; tours; competitions; individual paintings and original objects of art lent to colleges and local galleries; lending coll contains framed reproductions, original art works, original prints, paintings, sculpture and slides; traveling exhib organized and circulated
L Art Library, 52402
Library Holdings: Per subs 10; Micro — Cards, fiche; AV — A-tapes, cassettes, fs, motion pictures, rec, slides, v-tapes; Other — Exhibition catalogs

M MOUNT MERCY COLLEGE, McAuley Gallery, 1330 Elmhurst Dr NE, 52402. Tel 319-363-8213. *Dir* Robert Naujoks
Open Sun - Thur 7 AM - 9 PM. No admis fee. Estab 1970 to show work by a variety of fine artists. The shows are used by the art department as teaching aids. They provide cultural exposure to the entire community. One room 22 x 30 ft; one wall is glass overlooking a small courtyard. Average Annual Attendance: 1000
Income: Financed through the college
Purchases: $300
Collections: †Small collection of prints & paintings
Exhibitions: (1981-83) Priscila Sage (fibers); Ashley Walker (polaroid paintings); Kathy Saccoupolos (photographs); Sharon Burns (paintings); Tom Jackson (paintings); Cornell College Faculty Exhibit; Fourth Annual High School Exhibit; Senior Thesis Exhibition: Norville Tucker; Dennis Jennings; Rhond Taggart; Peggy Snyder
Publications: Reviews in Fiber Arts; American Craft & Ceramics Monthly
Activities: Classes for adults; dramatic programs; lectures open to the public; gallery talks; competitions with awards; scholarships; museum shop
L Library, Art Dept, 1330 Elmhurst Dr NE, 52402
Library Holdings: Vols 1000; Per subs 30; Micro — Cards, fiche, prints, reels; AV — A-tapes, cassettes, fs, Kodachromes, lantern slides, motion pictures, rec, slides, v-tapes; Other — Exhibition catalogs, framed reproductions, original art works, pamphlets, photographs, prints, reproductions, sculpture

CLINTON

O CLINTON ART ASSOCIATION GALLERY, 708 25th Ave N, PO Box 132, 52732. Tel 319-242-9635. *Dir* Hortense Blake
Open Sat & Sun 1 - 5 PM, cl Christmas and New Years. No admis fee. Estab 1968 to bring visual art to the community. Small gallery is housed in an abandoned building of an army hospital complex and is loaned to the association by the Clinton Park and Recreation Board. A separate Pottery School has been maintained since 1975. Average Annual Attendance: 15,000. Mem: 400; dues single membership $7; annual meeting first Tues in May
Income: Financed by membership and through grants from the Iowa Arts Council
Collections: Painting (watercolor, oil, acrylic, pastel); beaded loin cloth; photographs; lithograph; engraving; sculptures; etching; prints; pottery; fabric; pencil; wood; slate; Ektaflex Color Printmaking System; glass; ink; lucite; rugs; woodcarving
Exhibitions: Michael Kranovich, paintings; Kurt Anderson, painting; association photography group; children's class exhibits; Christmas annual; Japanese needlework; David Kracht, paintings; Pat Hawkins, watercolors; association pottery; Kit Cherry, watercolors; Clarence Sherman, retrospective photography; Mae Domack, paintings; Denise Baker, photography; Sherrianna McKenrick, acrylic paintings; Karen Cossman, watercolors & drawings; Harriet Michels,

paintings
Publications: Newsletter every two months
Activities: Classes for adults and children in watercolor, oil, rosemaling, macrame, photography and pottery making; docent training; lectures open to public; gallery talks; tours; individual paintings lent by members to businesses; lending collection contains books, lantern slides and slides; sales shop selling original art and prints; sales shop

DAVENPORT

M DAVENPORT MUNICIPAL ART GALLERY, 1737 W 12th St, 52804. Tel 319-326-7804. *Dir* L G Hoffman; *Admin Secy* Marielou Lee; *Cur Educ* Joseph M Fury; *Registrar* Patrick Sweeney; *Cur* Ann C Madonia
Open Tues - Sat 10 AM - 4:30 PM, Sun 1 - 4:30 PM. No admis fee. Estab 1925 as a museum of art and custodian of public collection and an education center for the visual arts. Consists of three levels including a spacious main exhibition display area: six multipurpose art studies, childrens gallery; studio workshop; and an outdoor studio-plaza on the lower level. Average Annual Attendance: 150,000. Mem: 1009; dues $20 & $30, annual meeting April
Income: $512,000 (financed by private and city appropriation)
Collections: European including English, French, German and Italian; Grant Wood; Haitian; 19th and 20th century American; Oriental; Mexican-Colonial
Exhibitions: Beverly Pepper: The Moline Markers; Byron Burford; Mississippi Corridor; Grandma Moses; Selections: The Union League of Chicago Collection; Thomas Eakins (photographs); Joseph Sheppard; Mauricio Lasansky; Sol LeWitt
Publications: Bulletin, quarterly; catalogs
Activities: Classes for adults and children; docent training; lect open to the public; concerts; gallery talks; tours; competitions; artmobile; traveling exhibiton organized and circulated; sales shop selling original art; junior museum called Arterarium
L Art Reference Library, 1737 W 12th St, 52804. *Librn* Gladys Hitchings
Open for reference
Library Holdings: Vols 6000; Per subs 17
Special Subjects: General visual arts

M PUTNAM MUSEUM, 1717 W 12th St, 52804. Tel 319-324-1933. *Dir* Michael J Smith; *Cur of Coll* Janice Hall; *Cur of Education* Ann Mandolini; *Registrar* Carol Hunt
Open Tues - Sat 9 AM - 5 PM, Sun 1 - 5 PM, cl Mon and national holidays. Admis adults $1.50, ages 13-18 $1, no admis fee Sat 9 AM - Noon. Estab 1867 as Academy of Science. Average Annual Attendance: 60,000. Mem: 2500; dues life $500, sustaining $120, contributing $50, family $28, individual $18, senior citizen $12
Income: $300,000 (financed by endowments & earned income)
Collections: Natural history; American Indian, pre-Columbian; anthropology; arts of Asia, Near & Middle East, Africa, Oceanic; botany; ethnology; paleontology; decorative arts; local history
Exhibitions: Permanent and changing exhibition programs
Activities: Formally organized education programs for children and adults; films; lect; gallery talks; guided tours
L Library, 1717 W 12th St, 52804. Tel 319-324-1933
Available for use by special request
Library Holdings: Vols 10,000

DECORAH

M VESTERHEIM, Norwegian-American Museum, 502 W Water St, 52101. Tel 319-382-9682. *Dir* Marion John Nelson; *Cur* Darrell Henning; *Dir in Charge of Academic Relations* John Christianson; *Textiles Cur* Lila Nelson; *Conservator* Dana Jackson; *Asst Cur & Site Mgr* Steve Johnson
Open May - Oct 9 AM - 5 PM daily, Nov - Apr 10 AM - 4 PM, cl Thanksgiving, Christmas & New Years. Admis adults $3, children $1.25, (summer), adults $2.50, children $1 (winter). Estab 1877 for the collection, preservation and exhibition of all artifacts on the life of the people in the United States of Norwegian birth and descent, in their home environment in Norway and in their settlements in America. Numerous historic buildings, including two from Norway, make up the complex of Vesterheim. Average Annual Attendance: 30,000. Mem: 6000; dues $10; annual meeting Oct
Income: $190,000 (financed by endowment, membership, donations, admissions, sales)
Collections: Extensive collections combine those of Luther College and the Museum Corporation through house furnishings, costumes, tools and implements, church furniture, toys and the like, the Museum tells the story of the Norwegian immigrant
Exhibitions: Annual competitive exhibitions in Norwegian rosemaling, weaving & woodcarving; American rug hooking
Publications: Newsletter, quarterly; Norrona Sketchbook; Norwegian Tracks, quarterly; Pioneer Cookbook, Time Honored Norwegian Recipes; Rosemaling Letter, quarterly; Vesterheim: Samplings from the Collection
Activities: Classes for adults; genealogy center; workshops in & tours to Norway; competitions; museum shop sells books, original art, prints, and slides, related gift items, woodenware, artist supplies for rosemaling
L Library,* 502 W Water St, 52101
Reference library open to the public
Library Holdings: Vols 800
Special Subjects: Norwegian history, culture, crafts, genealogy

DES MOINES

M EDMUNDSON ART FOUNDATION, INC, Des Moines Art Center, Greenwood Park, 50312. Tel 515-277-4405. *Dir* James T Demetrion; *Asst Dir* Peggy Patrick; *Dir of Educ* Georgeann KudronKulh; *Pres Bd of Trustees* John R Taylor
Open Tues - Sat 11 AM - 5 PM, Sun Noon - 5 PM, cl Mon. No admis fee. Estab 1948 for the purpose of displaying, conserving and interpreting art. Large

sculpture galleries in I M Pei-designed addition; the main gallery covers 36 x 117 ft area. Average Annual Attendance: 108,000. Mem: 2600, dues $20 and up
Income: $935,000 (financed by endowment, membership, city and state appropriation)
Collections: African art; graphics; American & European sculpture & painting of the past 200 years
Exhibitions: (1982-83) Giorgio Morandi, retrospective; Super Realism From the Morton G Neumann Family Collection; Robert Graham: Statues; Awards in the Visual Arts I; Of Time & Place: American Figurative Art From the Corcoran Collection; Images of America: Precisionist Painting & Modern Photography; 34th & 35th Iowa Artists Exhibition
Publications: Bulletin, bimonthly; annual report; catalogs of exhibitions
Activities: Classes for adults and children; docent training; lect open to members only, 6 visiting lectr per year; concerts; gallery talks; tours; competitions; traveling exhibitions organized and circulated; museum shop sells books, original art, prints, and postcards
L **Des Moines Art Center Library,** Greenwood Park, 50312. Tel 515-277-4405. *Librn* Margaret Buckley
11 AM - 5 PM Tues - Sat. Estab 1948 for research for permanent collection, staff for class preparation and lectures. Open to the public for reference only
Income: $11,400
Purchases: $2000
Library Holdings: Vols 8350; Per subs 23; Other — Exhibition catalogs
Special Subjects: 20th Century Art
Collections: Pennington Collection of weaving samples, by appointment

M **IOWA STATE EDUCATION ASSOCIATION,** Salisbury House, 4025 Tonawanda Drive, 50312. Tel 515-279-9711. *Exec Dir* Fred Comer; *Museum Coordr* Caroline Moon; *Mgr Business Operations* C William Pritchard
Open daily 8 AM - 4:30 PM. Admis adults $2, mini-tour & 12 years and under $1. Estab 1954 as a cultural center. Gallery is maintained as a replica of King's House in Salisbury, England and contains Tudor age furniture, classic paintings, and sculpture from East and West, tapestries, Oriental rugs. Average Annual Attendance: 17,000
Income: Financed through membership and endowment
Collections: Collection of paintings by Hogarth, Raeburn, Romney, Sir T Lawrence, Van Dyck; permanent collection of tapestries by Brussels Brabant, Flemish, French Verdure; permanent collection of sculpture by Archapinko, Bordelle, Martini; permanent collection of Chinese, India and Oriental (Persian) rugs
Exhibitions: Permanent collection
Activities: Lect; tours; individual paintings and original objects of art lent; lending collection contains motion pictures, original art works, paintings; museum shop sells reproductions, brochures, postcards, stationery

DUBUQUE

M **DUBUQUE ART ASSOCIATION,** Old Jail Gallery, Box 1134, 52001. Tel 319-557-1851. *Pres* Richard Sturman; *Actg Dir* J Knox Coit
Open Wed - Sun 1 - 5 PM, cl Mon & Tues. No admis fee. Estab 1911, incorporated 1956. Occupies Old County Jail (now on Registry of Historic Places), built in 1857, converted in 1976. Average Annual Attendance: 1000. Mem: 240; dues $8-$100; annual meeting in May
Income: Financed by dues and donations
Collections: Permanent collection consists of drawings, paintings, prints and sculptures
Exhibitions: Crafts show; paintings, ceramics, drawings, sculptures
Activities: Classes for adults & children; lectures open to public, 3-4 vis lectr per yr; concerts; gallery talks; tours; competitions with awards; book traveling exhibitions

FAIRFIELD

L **FAIRFIELD PUBLIC LIBRARY AND MUSEUM,** Fairfield Art Association,* Court & Washington, 52556. Tel 515-472-6551. *Librn* James Rabis; *Chmn Museum Committee* Ben Taylor; *Chmn Art Gallery* Dr Paul Selzi
Open Mon - Fri 9 AM - 6 PM, Sat 9 AM - 1:30 PM, Winter Sun 1:30 - 4:30 PM, cl national holidays. No admis fee
Income: Library and museum financed by endowment and city appropriation; Art Association financed by endowment and membership
Library Holdings: Vols 53,000; Per subs 115
Collections: †Graphics; Indian art; †paintings
Activities: Classes for adults and children; lect open to the public; competitions

FORT DODGE

M **BLANDEN MEMORIAL ART MUSEUM,** 920 Third Ave S, 50501. Tel 515-573-2316. *Dir* M Jessica Rowe; *Asst Dir* Cheryl Ann Parker; *Membership* Catherine Deardorf; *Shop Mgr* Marcia Rich
Open Tues, Wed, Fri, Sat & Sun 1 - 5 PM, Thurs 1 - 8:30 PM, cl Mon. No admis fee. Estab 1932. houses works of art in permanent collection. Neo-Italian Renaissance architecture. Average Annual Attendance: 20,000. Mem: dues $5 - $1000; annual meeting July
Income: $100,000 (financed by city & state appropriation, membership, Blanden Art Gallery Charitable Foundation)
Collections: Twentieth century American and European masters; paintings and sculpture; 19th & 20th Century graphic art; 17th Century Oriental arts
Publications: Tri-monthly bulletin, BAG Charitable Foundation brochure; exhibition catalogues; annual report; membership information
Activities: Art classes and programs for children & adults; docent programs; museum internship program; guided tours; lectures; films; Art Appreciation program; slide programs for schools and community groups; book traveling exhibitions; originate traveling exhibitions; museum shop sells original art, prints, and prints

L **Library,** 920 Third Ave S, 50501. Tel 515-573-2316
Open Mon - Sun 1 - 5 PM, Thurs 1 - 8 PM. Estab 1972 as reference library for museum.
Income: $90,000 (financed by membership, city appropriation and charitable foundation)
Library Holdings: Vols 2500; Per subs 4; Micro — Cards; AV — Fs, slides, v-tapes; Other — Clipping files, exhibition catalogs, framed reproductions 148, pamphlets, reproductions, sculpture 9

INDIANOLA

M **SIMPSON COLLEGE ART GALLERY,** * 50125. Tel 515-961-6251. *Head Art Dept* Janet Heinicke
Collections: Creche figures from 18th century Italy; small permanent collection
Exhibitions: Student shows; visiting exhibits
Activities: Lect open to public, 2 visiting lectrs per year; concerts

IOWA CITY

ART LIBRARIES SOCIETY-NORTH AMERICA
For further information, see National and Regional Organizations

O **IOWA CITY, JOHNSON COUNTY ARTS COUNCIL,** The Arts Center, 129 East Washington, 52240. Tel 319-337-7447. *Pres* Judith Hurtig; *VPres* Jody Hovland; *Receptionist* Eve Dolch
Open Mon - Sat 10 AM - 4 PM. Estab 1975. Average Annual Attendance: 5000. Mem: 250 - 300; dues family $25, individual $15; annual meeting 1st Tues March & Nov
Income: $20,000 (financed by membership, sales & grants)
Exhibitions: Eleven exhibitions per year are mounted. In May a national exhibition of works using paper and/or fiber as a medium is organized and installed. Monthly exhibitions include works of local artists and from local collections. Summer show include work of fiber artists visitig University of Iowa
Publications: Exhibition catalogs
Activities: Workshops; competitions with awards

UNIVERSITY OF IOWA
M **Museum of Art,** Riverside Dr, 52242. Tel 319-353-3266. *Dir* Robert C Hobbs; *Cur of Education* Honee Hess; *Cur Coll* Joann Moser; *Registrar* Jo-Ann Conklin; *Installation Coordr* David Dennis
Open Tues - Sat 10 AM - 5 PM, Sun noon - 5 PM, cl Thanksgiving, Christmas & New Year's Day. No admis fee. Estab 1969 to collect, exhibit and preserve for the future, works of art from different cultures; to make these objects as accessible as possible to people of all ages in the state of Iowa; to assist the public, through educational programs and publications, in interpreting these works of art and expanding their appreciation of art in general. 48,000 sq ft in 16 galleries, including a central sculpture court. Average Annual Attendance: 50,000. Mem: 780; dues patron $100 - $499, supporting $25 - $99, student $5 - $24
Income: Financed by membership, state appropriation and private donations
Collections: African and Pre-Columbian art; Chinese and Tibetan bronzes; Oriental jade; 19th and 20th century European and American paintings and sculpture; prints, drawings, photography, silver
Exhibitions: The Elliott Collection of 20th Century European paintings, silver and jade; a major collection of African sculpture and a selection of prints by Mauricio Lasansky are on permanent exhibition. Approximately 14 changing exhibitions each year, both permanent collection and traveling exhibitions
Publications: Calendar (brochure), monthly; exhibition catalogs
Activities: Docent training; lect open to the public, 8 visiting lectr per year; concerts; gallery talks; tours; works of art lent to other museums; originate traveling exhibitions; sales area selling posters, postcards and catalogs
L **Art Library,** Riverside Dr, 52242. Tel 319-353-4440. *Librn* Harlan L Sifford
Open Mon - Fri 8 AM - 5 PM, Mon - Thurs 7 - 10 PM, Sat & Sun 1 - 4 PM. Estab 1937 to support the University programs, community and state needs. Circ 32,000
Income: Financed by state appropriation
Purchases: $65,000
Library Holdings: Vols 60,000; Per subs 230; Micro — Fiche, reels; Other — Clipping files, exhibition catalogs, memorabilia, pamphlets

KEOKUK

O **KEOKUK ART CENTER,** 9 1/2 7th St, Box 862, 52632. Tel 319-524-8354. *Pres* Randy Hill; *VPres* Pat Chaloupek; *Secy* Dorri Davis; *Treas* Jane Marion; *Dir* Tom Seabold
Open Mon - Fri 9 AM - 4:30 PM, Sat 9 AM - Noon. No admis fee. Estab 1954 to promote art in tri-state area. Gallery maintained in Keokuk Public Library, 210 N Fifth St. Average Annual Attendance: 2000. Mem: Dues sustaining $50, patron $25, family $12, individual $6, student $2; annual meeting first Mon in May
Collections: Paintings, sculpture
Publications: Newsletter, quarterly
Activities: Classes for adults and children; docent training; lect open to the public; gallery talks; tours; competitions with cash awards; scholarships; book traveling exhibitions; originate traveling exhibitions

LEMARS

M **WESTMAR COLLEGE** (Formerly Weidler Art Gallery), Mock Memorial Art Gallery, 51031. Tel 712-546-7081, Ext 231. *Gallery Dir* Charles Mertes
Open daily 8 AM - 5:30 PM, Sat 8 AM - 12:30 PM; inactive during summer. No admis fee. Estab 1973. The purpose of the gallery is to provide a forum for cultivating the sensitivity of our student body and the community to the world of visual arts through a regular schedule of art exhibits. Gallery covers 2000 sq ft floor space, 170 linear feet of display space, with track lighting. Average Annual

Attendance: 7500
Income: Financed by endowment, college appropriation and private gifts
Publications: Westmar College Fine Arts Schedule of Events
Activities: Educ dept; lectures open to the public; concerts; gallery talks
L **Mock Library Art Dept,** 51031. *Dir* Jarel Kledis
Open to students
Library Holdings: Vols 1600; Per subs 9; AV — Slides

MARSHALLTOWN

O **CENTRAL IOWA ART ASSOCIATION, INC,** Fisher Community Center, 709 S Center, 50158. Tel 515-753-9013. *Dir* Patrick Gillam
Open Mon - Fri 8 AM - 10 PM, Sat 8 AM - 5 PM, Sun 2 - 5 PM. Estab 1946, incorporated 1959. Average Annual Attendance: 10,000. Mem: 300; dues student $6, individual $12 and up; annual meeting May
Income: Financed by city funds, memberships, gifts
Collections: Fisher Collection—Utrillo, Cassatt, Sisley, Vuillard, Monet, Degas, Signac, Le Gourge, Vlaminck and Monticelli; sculpture—Christian Petersen, Rominelli, Bourdelle; ceramic study collection—Gilhooly, Arneson, Nagle, Kottler, Babu, Geraedts, Boxem, Leach, Voulkos; traditional Japanese wares
Exhibitions: Monthly exhibits beginning the first Sun of the month and open weekdays thereafter
Publications: Artsletter, monthly
Activities: Classes for adults and children in ceramics, sculpture, jewelry, painting; lectures open to the public, 2 vis lectr per yr; gallery talks; tours; individual paintings & original objects of art lent; book traveling exhibitions, 10 per yr; originate traveling exhibitions; sales shop sells original art, reproductions, prints, pottery, wood, fiber & metal
L **Art Reference Library,*** Fisher Community Center, 50158. *In Charge* Luann Putnam
For reference only
Library Holdings: Vols 1600

MASON CITY

M **CHARLES H MACNIDER MUSEUM,** 303 Second St SE, 50401. Tel 515-423-9563. *Dir* Richard E Leet; *Dir Education & Special Programs* Robert C Christensen
Open Tues & Thurs 10 AM - 9 PM, Wed, Fri & Sat 10 AM - 5 PM, Sun 1 - 5 PM, cl Mon & holidays. No admis fee. Estab 1964, opened 1966 to provide experience in the arts through development of a permanent collection, through scheduling of temporary exhibitions, through the offering of classes and art instruction, through special programs in film, music and other areas of the performing arts. The museum was estab in an English-Tudor style of brick and tile. It is located in a scenic setting, 2 1/2 blocks from the main thoroughfare of Mason City. Gallery lighting and neutral backgrounds provide a good environment for exhibitions. Average Annual Attendance: Over 30,000. Mem: 830; dues from contributions $5 - $250 or more
Income: $230,000 (financed by membership and city appropriation)
Collections: Permanent collection being developed with an emphasis on American art, with some representation of Iowa art; contains paintings, prints, pottery; artists represented include Baziotes, Benton, Burchfield, Burford, Cropsey, Davies, Dove, Francis, Gottlieb, Graves, Guston, Healy, Hurd, Lasansky, Levine, Maurer, Metcalf and Oliveira; Bil Baird: World of Puppets
Exhibitions: Light and Color: Images of New Mexico; Annual Area Competitive Show; Annual Iowa Crafts Competition; Art of the Puppet by Bil Baird; Bentons Bentons; Gund Collection of Western Art; Magic Carpets—Rugs of the Orient; Weathervanes, Carvings and Quilts, from the Chase-Manhattan Bank
Publications: Newsletter, monthly; occasional exhibit fliers or catalogs
Activities: Classes for adults and children; docent training; seminars and workshops; lect open to public, 2-4 vis lectr per yr; concerts; gallery talks; tours; competitions; individual paintings and original objects of art lent to other museums and art centers; museum shop selling original art
L **Library,** 303 Second St SE, 50401
Reference library within the structure of the museum. For reference only
Library Holdings: Vols 500; Per subs 24; AV — Slides
Special Subjects: American art

L **MASON CITY PUBLIC LIBRARY,*** 225 Second St SE, 50401. Tel 515-423-7552. *Dir* Steve Rogge; *Reference* Jean Casey; *Childrens Room* Lisa Hoyman; *Young Adult* Judy Sheriff; *Art Librn* Elizabeth Camarigg
Open Mon - Thurs 9 AM - 9 PM; Fri & Sat 9 AM - 5 PM; Sun 1 - 5 PM. Estab 1869 to service public in providing reading material and information. Gallery maintained in auditorium. Circ 197,635
Income: $327,909 (financed by city, county appropriation and Federal Revenue Sharings)
Purchases: $42,913
Library Holdings: Vols 127,146; original documents; Micro — Fiche, reels; AV — Cassettes, fs, motion pictures, rec; Other — Clipping files, framed reproductions, memorabilia, original art works, pamphlets, prints
Collections: Permanent collection of regional artists; signed letters of authors
Exhibitions: (1980) Joe Bittner (oil portraits); Jan Bowman (needlecraft); Larry Gregson (painting); Howard Hof and Ken McClemmons (painting); Pearl Krager (paintings); Josephine Olsen (painting); Fred Peterson (ceramics); Mike Sharp (painting); Mary Siberell (watercolor); Terry Vlademar (wild-life works); (1981) Art Educators of Mason City (mixed media); Corrine Severson (tole, decorative painting); Mason City Elementary Art Students; Elaine Hall, Marilyn Niemi (painting, mixed media); Vesta Brownell McCullough; Libraries New Framed Reproductions; Hane & Wagonner (mixed media); William Mitchell (painting); North Iowa Artists League; Elsie Laird (pastel, painting); Betty Winga; Photographers of Mason City; (1982) Tom Mitchell (North Iowa Heritage Sketches); Sharon Hays (b & w photos); Mason City High School Art Students Show; Allan Reynolds (wildlife artist); Iowa State University '82 Creative Visual Art Exhibit; Howard Hof (painting & mixed media); Paggy Spicknell; North Iowa Artists League (mixed media); Terry Vlademar (wildlife animal painting); Robert Noland (painting); Mame Furnish, Bev Motto (mixed media)

MOUNT VERNON

M **CORNELL COLLEGE,** Armstrong Gallery, 52314. Tel 319-895-8811. *Dir Gallery & Chmn Dept of Art* Hank Lifson
Open Mon - Fri 7:30 AM - 4:30 PM. Estab to display artists work
Income: Financed by Cornell College
Collections: Thomas Nast drawings & prints; Sonnenschein Collection of European Drawings of the 15th - 17th Century
Exhibitions: Four exhibits per yr plus 10-20 student thesis shows
Activities: Lect open to public, 1 vis lectr per yr

MUSCATINE

M **MUSCATINE ART CENTER** (Formerly Laura Musser Art Gallery and Museum), 1314 Mulberry Ave, 52761. Tel 319-263-8282. *Dir* William A McGonagle; *Asst Dir* Barbara C Longtin; *Pres* Richard Johnson
Open Tues - Fri 11 AM - 5 PM, Sat & Sun 1 - 5 PM, Thurs Eve 7 - 9 PM, cl Mon and legal holidays. No admis fee. Estab 1965. Mem: 600; dues sponsor $500, supporting $200, contributing $100, sustaining $50, family $25, individual $15, student & senior citizens $5
Income: Financed by city appropriation
Collections: African Collection; Civil War Collection; Muscatine History; Button Collection; Paperweight Collection; decorative arts, graphics, paintings; Great River Collection, prints and paintings depicting the Mississippi River and its environs
Publications: Newsletter, bimonthly; catalogs
Activities: Classes for children and adults; lectures open to the public, 6 vis lectr per yr; concerts; gallery talks; tours; competitions with awards; individual paintings & original objects of art lent; book traveling exhibitions; Sales shop
L **Library,** 1314 Mulberry Ave, 52761
For reference only
Library Holdings: Vols 2000; Per subs 10; Other — Memorabilia, pamphlets

ORANGE CITY

M **NORTHWESTERN COLLEGE,** Te Paske Gallery of Rowenhorst, Student Center, 51041. Tel 712-737-4904. *Exhib Coordr* Rein Van Derhill
Open Mon - Fri 8 AM - 5 PM. No admis fee. Estab 1968 to promote the visual arts in northwest Iowa and to function as a learning resource for the college and community. College art gallery for traveling exhibitions; local artists are sometimes invited. Average Annual Attendance: approx 2000
Collections: Approx 75 original works of art: etchings, woodcuts, serigraphs, lithographs, mezzotints, paintings, sculpture and ceramics by modern and old masters of Western World and Japan
Exhibitions: Contemporary American Artists Series; student and faculty shows
Activities: Classes for adults; lect open to the public, 2 - 3 vis lectr per yr; gallery talks; competitions; individual prints and original objects of art lent to schools and libraries

SIOUX CITY

O **SIOUX CITY ART CENTER,** 513 Nebraska St, 51101. Tel 712-279-6272. *Bd of Trustees* Harlan Soper; *Bd of Dirs Pres* Karen Chesterman; *Dir* Bruce Bienemann; *Asst Dir* Tom Butler; *Educ Cur* Marilyn Laufer
Open Tues - Sat 11 AM - 5 PM, Sun 1 - 5 PM, Mon 5 - 8 PM, cl holidays. No admis fee. Estab 1938 to provide art experiences to the general public. Gallery is 2 floors of exhibitions consisting of nationally known artists from the midwest regional area; includes a graphics gallery and changing exhibitions. Average Annual Attendance: 30,000. Mem: 500; dues $10 - $5000; monthly meetings
Income: Financed by membership, city and state appropriation
Collections: Permanent collection of over 700 works; consists of †paintings and †prints of nationally known regional artists, contemporary photography and sculpture and crafts
Exhibitions: Dan Howard: A Retrospective; Fall Biennial
Publications: Annual Report; Artifact, monthly magazine; exhibition catalogs
Activities: Classes for adults and children; docent training; workshops; outreach programs to schools; lectures open to public, 5 - 10 vis lectr per year; gallery talks, tours; film series; concerts; competitions; scholarships; original objects of art lent to qualified institutions with approved facilities and security; book traveling exhibitions, 2 - 3 per yr; traveling exhibitions organized and circulated; museum & sales shops sell books, original art and prints; junior museum
L **Library,** 513 Nebraska St, Sioux City, 51101
Reference library - non-circulating
Library Holdings: Vols 500; Per subs 10; AV — Cassettes, slides; Other — Exhibition catalogs

STORM LAKE

M **WITTER GALLERY,*** 609 Cayuga St, 50588. Tel 712-732-3400. *Pres* Christine Geisinger; *Dir* Cherie Thatcher
Open Mon - Fri 1:30 - 5 PM, Sat 1:30 - 4 PM. No admis fee. Estab 1972 to encourage the appreciation of fine arts and to support fine arts education, exhibits, lectures and workshops. Gallery occupies a wing of the Storm Lake Public Library building. It has about 1800 sq ft of floor space and 120 linear ft of hanging wall space. Average Annual Attendance: 10,000. Mem: 173; dues $5; annual meeting Jan
Income: $13,000 (financed by endowment, membership, city appropriation, fund raising projects)
Collections: Paintings & collected artifacts of Miss Ella Witter
Exhibitions: Paintings & drawings by Virginia Myers; Contemporary American Graphics; Thomas Colbert—Around a Fishbowl
Publications: Witter Gallery News & Events
Activities: Classes for adults and children; art appreciation program in area schools; lectures open to public, 8 vis lectr per yr; gallery talks; sponsors competition between area schools; awards; museum shop sells notecards and tote bags

WATERLOO

O **WATERLOO ART ASSOCIATION,** Eleventh Street Gallery, 420 W 11th St, 50702. Tel 319-232-1984. *Pres* James L Smith; *VPres & Dir Exhib* Doris Frandsen; *Secy* Jill Adams; *Gallery Dir* Joanne Wilson
Open Tues - Sat Noon - 4 PM. No admis fee. Estab 1944 to encourage area artists and provide for the exhibition of their work. Gallery is maintained in a rented building providing three gallery rooms, workshop, art supply sales room and storage. Average Annual Attendance: 2000. Mem: 150; dues $20; annual meeting last Tues Jan
Income: Financed by membership
Collections: Small collection of work by former members
Exhibitions: Amateur Iowa Artists Regional Show; Black Hawk County Art Show; Monthly exhibits by area professionals
Publications: Bulletin published six times a yr
Activities: Classes for adults; workshops; lectures open to public, 8-10 vis lectr per yr; gallery talks; tours; competitions with awards; sales shop sells original art, prints, pottery & sculpture

M **WATERLOO MUNICIPAL GALLERIES,** 225 Cedar St, 50704. Tel 319-291-4491. *Gallery Dir* Clarence Alling
Open Mon - Sat 9 AM - 5 PM; Sun 2 - 5 PM. No admis fee. Estab 1957 to provide an art forum for the Waterloo area. Average Annual Attendance: 35,000, plus junior museum attendance of 16,000. Mem: 500; dues single $5 and up; annual meeting second Thurs of Jan
Income: Financed by city funds and memberships
Collections: Small new collection of contemporary American paintings, prints and †sculpture; †Haitian paintings and sculpture
Exhibitions: Monthly exhibitions of regional painting, sculpture, prints and fine crafts
Activities: Classes for adults and children; docent training; lectures open to public; concerts; gallery talks; tours; sales shop sells original art; junior museum

WEST BRANCH

L **HERBERT HOOVER PRESIDENTIAL LIBRARY & MUSEUM,** 234 S Downey, 52358. Tel 319-643-5301. *Library Dir* Thomas T Thalken; *Museum Cur* Phyllis Foster
Open daily 9 AM - 5 PM, cl Thanksgiving, Christmas, New Year's Day. Admis $1, children 15 & under free. Estab 1962 as a research center to service the papers of Herbert Hoover and other related manuscript collections; a museum to exhibit memorabilia from Herbert Hoover's 90 years of public service and accomplishments
Income: Financed by federal appropriation
Library Holdings: Vols 25,000; Per subs 67; original documents, still photographs; Micro — Reels; AV — A-tapes, motion pictures, rec, slides; Other — Clipping files, manuscripts, memorabilia, pamphlets
Collections: 64 Chinese porcelains; oil paintings; 190 Original Editorial Cartoons; 340 posters; 26 World War I Food Administration; 464 World War I Painted and Embroidered Flour Sacks
Exhibitions: Permanent exhibits on Herbert and Lou Henry Hoover; subjects related to Hoover and the times
Activities: Sales shop sells books, prints, slides and medals

KANSAS

ABILENE

L **DWIGHT D EISENHOWER PRESIDENTIAL LIBRARY,** 67510. Tel 913-263-4751. *Dir* Dr John E Wickman; *Museum Cur* Dennis Medina
Open daily 9 AM - 5 PM, cl Thanksgiving, Christmas Day, New Year's Day. Admis $.75, under 16 free. Estab 1961 as library, in 1954 as museum. Average Annual Attendance: 400,000
Income: Financed by Federal Government appropriation
Library Holdings: Vols 23,000; Other — Prints 75,000
Collections: Research Library and Museum contains papers of Dwight D Eisenhower and his associates, together with items of historical interest connected with the Eisenhower Family. Mementos and gifts of General Dwight D Eisenhower both before, during, and after his term as President of the United States
Activities: Lectures open to the public, 4 - 12 vis lectr per yr; sales shop sells books, original art & reproductions

ATCHISON

M **MUCHNIC FOUNDATION AND ATCHISON ART ASSOCIATION,** Muchnic Gallery, 704 N Fourth St, Box 12, Route 2, 66002. Tel 913-367-1317. *Cur* Mrs Pennell Snowden
Open weekends 1 - 5 PM, Sun Sept - May. No admis fee. Estab 1970 to bring art to the people of Atchison. Gallery comprised of four rooms is maintained for visiting artists shows and occasional senior exhibits from Benedictine College students. Average Annual Attendance: 1000. Mem: 20; annual meeting second Tues of each month
Income: Financed by Muchnic Foundation, Atchison Art Asn art shows
Purchases: $7000
Collections: †Paintings by regional artists: Don Andorer; Thomas Hart Benton; John Stuart Curry; Raymond Eastwood; John Falter; Jim Hamil; Wilbur Niewald; Jack O'Hara; Roger Shimomura; Robert Sudlow; Grant Wood; Jamie Wyeth; Walter Yost
Exhibitions: Christmas Exhibition; exhibitions two - four weekends per month, Sept - May
Activities: Classes for adults; docent training; gallery talks; tours; book traveling exhibitions, annually; originate traveling exhibitions; sales shop sells original art

CHANUTE

M **MARTIN & OSA JOHNSON SAFARI MUSEUM,** 16 South Grant, 66720. Tel 316-431-2730. *Dir* Sondra Alden; *Cur* Barbara Henshall
Open Mon - Sat 10 AM - 5 PM, Sun 1 - 5 PM. Admis adults $1.50, students $1, children $.50, family group $5. Estab 1961 to exhibit & conserve the art & artifacts of Africa. Average Annual Attendance: 6000
Income: $30,000 (financed by membership, city appropriation, donations and gift shop)
Publications: Wait-A-Bit, newsletter; catalogs and other publications
Activities: Educ dept; tours; museum boxes for school use; individual paintings & original objects of art lent to qualified institutions; museum shop sells books, imported carvings, brass, fabric & ethnic toys
—Imperato Collection of West African Artifacts, 66720
Estab 1974
Collections: West African sculpture including masks, ancestor figures & ritual objects
Exhibitions: African culture exhibit of East & West African items; narrow strip loom; ceremonial masks
—Johnson Collection of Photographs, Movies & Memorabilia, 66720
Collections: Photographs & movies of the South Seas, Borneo & East Africa between 1971-1936
Exhibitions: Life of the Johnsons, photographs & film
—Selsor Gallery of Art, 66720
Estab 1981
Collections: Original paintings; scratch boards & sketches; bronze, ivory & amber sculpture; lithographs
—Scott Explorers Library, 66720
Estab 1980 for research and reference
Library Holdings: Vols 8000; Per subs 13; Nature artifacts 15; AV — A-tapes, motion pictures 6, slides 50; Other — Clipping files, manuscripts, memorabilia, original art works 300, pamphlets, photographs 10,000, prints 50, sculpture 50
Special Subjects: Natural History

ELLSWORTH

M **ROGERS HOUSE MUSEUM GALLERY,** Snake Row, 67439. Tel 914-472-3255. *Dir* Charles B Rogers; *Mgr* Ruth E Rogers
Open Mon - Sat 10 AM - 5 PM, Sun & holidays 1 - 5, cl Christmas. Adults $.50, children 6-12 $.25. Estab 1968 in a historic cowboy hotel
Collections: Original paintings, prints; miscellaneous art
Publications: Art Observations (book); Country Neighbor; The Great West; Quill of the Kansan (books)
Activities: Sales shop sells original paintings and prints

EMPORIA

M **EMPORIA STATE UNIVERSITY,** Norman R Eppink Art Gallery, 1200 Commercial, 66801. Tel 316-343-1200. *Dir* Donald Perry
Open Mon - Fri 9 AM - 5 PM, cl university holidays. No admis fee. Estab 1939 to bring a variety of exhibitions to the campus. Gallery is 25x50 feet & has a 50 ft wall for hanging items. Average Annual Attendance: 10,000
Income: Financed by state, grant & endowment funds
Collections: Artifacts; †contemporary drawings and paintings; †sculpture
Publications: Exhibition catalogs
Activities: Lectures open to public, 6-10 vis lectr per yr; gallery talks; tours; competitions with awards; scholarships; individual paintings & original objects of art lent to university offices; originate traveling exhibitions to schools

HAYS

M **FORT HAYS STATE UNIVERSITY,** Visual Arts Center, 600 Park St, 67601. Tel 913-628-4247. *Dir of Exhib* Zoran Stevanov
Open Mon - Fri 8:30 AM - 4 PM, weekends on special occasions. No admis fee. Estab 1953 to provide constant changing exhibitions for the benefit of students, faculty and other interested people in an education situation. Rarick Hall has 2200 sq ft with moveable panels that can be used to divide the gallery into four smaller galleries. Mem: 88
Income: Financed by state appropriation
Purchases: $2000
Collections: Vyvyan Blackford Collection; †contemporary prints; †national exhibition of small paintings, prints and drawings; regionalist collection (1930s); Oriental scroll collection
Exhibitions: (1982) Annual Faculty Exhibition; Annual Undergraduate Exhibition; Annual High School Exhibition & Art Conference; Annual Smoky Hill (State) Exhibition; Kansas Fifth National Small Paintings, Drawings & Prints Show; (1983-84) Annual Faculty Exhibition; Watercolor USA (MAA); New American Graphics (MAA); Joan Nuss, sculpture; Kansas Ninth National Small Paintings, Prints & Drawings; Graduate Theses Exhibitions; Annual Undergraduate Exhibition; Annual High School Exhibition & Art Conference; Annual Smoky Hill (State) Exhibition
Publications: Exhibitions brochures; Art Calendar, annually
Activities: Lectr open to public, 4 vis lectr per yr; gallery talks; tours; competitions with prizes; concerts; Exten dept serving western Kansas; individual paintings and original objects of art lent to individuals, organizations and institutions; lending collection of original art works and prints, paintings, sculpture and slides; traveling exhibitions organized and circulated
L **Art Library,** 67601
Reference Library
Library Holdings: Vols 6000; Per subs 107; AV — Fs, lantern slides, motion pictures, slides; Other — Exhibition catalogs

HUTCHINSON

O **HUTCHINSON ART ASSOCIATION,** 1520 North Main, 67501. Tel 316-663-1081. *Pres* Barbara Canfield; *VPres* Brad Dillon; *Dir of Gallery* Edith M Symns; *Treas* Louise Zink; *Secy* Shirley Schmidt; *Exhibitions* Marvel Senti
Open Tues - Sat 1 - 5 PM, Sun 2 - 4 PM. Estab 1949 to bring exhibitions to the city of Hutchinson and maintain a permanent collection in the public schools. Average Annual Attendance: 9000 - 10,000. Mem: 400-500; dues $8 and up or $15 for two; annaul meeting monthly
Income: Financed by memberships & donations
Collections: Permanent collection of watercolors, prints, and oils circulated
Exhibitions: Includes an all-member show
Activities: Annual Art Fair with prizes; lectures open to the public, 5 - 6 vis lectr per yr; gallery talks; tours; scholarships; exten dept serves entire state; lending collection contains original art works, original prints, paintings, phonorecords; book traveling exhibitions; shop sells original art, prints, ceramics, handblown galss, jewelry & sculpture

INDEPENDENCE

M **LADIES LIBRARY AND ART ASSOCIATION,** Independence Museum, 123 N Eighth, PO Box 294, 67301. Tel 316-331-3515. *Pres* Mrs Jim Housel; *Chmn* Mrs Clyde A Huff
Open Wed, Sat & Sun 1 - 4:30 PM. Donations. Inc 1882 to provide library facilities and the secure an art collection for the community. The museum has a large gallery which contains original paintings; Indian art & artifacts; Mexican Room, late 1800 & early 1900 costume room, country store, War & Peace Room, Oriental Room, period bedroom, early 1900 kitchen, childrens room, William Inge Memorabilia Room, historical oil room. Presently establishing a blacksmith shop. Mem: 150; dues $15 - $50; meeting monthly Oct - May
Income: Financed by membership, bequests, gifts, art exhibits and various projects
Collections: William Inge Memorabilia Collection; Oriental Collection
Exhibitions: Annual Art Exhibit; Photography Shows; various artists & craftsmen exhibits; Quilt Fair; Doll Fair; Gun Show; Afghan Fair; Needlework Show
Activities: Classes for adults; lectures; concerts; gallery talks; competitions

LAWRENCE

M **UNIVERSITY OF KANSAS,** Spencer Museum of Art, The University of Kansas, 66045. Tel 913-864-4710. *Dir* Open; *Actg Dir* Douglas Tilghman; *Cur Prints & Drawings* Jan Howard; *Cur Photography* Thomas Southall; *Research Cur* Marilyn Stokstad, PhD; *Registrar* Janet Dreiling; *Exhib Designer* Mark Roeyer; *Publishing Editor* Ruth Lawner; *Membership* Linda Bailey; *Programs* Sally Hoffmann; *Public Relations* Carol Shankel; *Docents* Sandy Praeger; *Bookshop* Ann Kathryn Ekstrom; *Cur Painting, Sculpture & Decorative Art* Marla Prather
Open Tues - Sat 9:30 - 4:30, Sun 1 - 4:30, cl Mon. No admis fee. Dedicated in Spooner Hall 1928, Spencer dedicated 1978. The Museum has traditionally served as a laboratory for the visual arts, supporting curricular study in the arts. Primary emphasis is placed on acquisitions and publications, with a regular schedule of changing exhibitions. Museum has a two level Central Court, seven galleries devoted to the permanent collections, and three galleries for temporary exhibitions; altogether affording 29,000 sq ft. Mem: dues $30
Income: Financed by membership, state appropriation and state and federal grants, contributions
Collections: †American Paintings; †ancient art; †graphics; †Medieval art; †17th and 18th Century art, especially German; †19th century European and American art; †Oriental art; †20th century European and American art
Exhibitions: (1982-83) Kassebaum Collection, medieval and renaissance ceramics; SITE Buildings and Spaces; Crawford Collection, Chinese calligraphy; Log Cabin Quilts; Charles Walter Stetson Paintings; Blaffer Foundation, American abstract expressionist paintings; McGovern Collection, images of foreigners; Pat Steir, prints and drawings; Contemporary Chinese Paintings; Esquire Collection, photographs; Gardens of the Middle Ages; Guggenheim Museum, early modern art; Dutch prints of daily life; Influences: Contemporary Quilts and Traditional Quilts; Nuremberg: A Renaissance City
Publications: The Register of the Spencer Museum of Art, annually; Calendar, bimonthly; exhibition catalogues 3 - 4 per year
Activities: Classes for children, docent training; lect open to the public, 24 vis lectr per yr; concerts; gallery talks; tours; traveling exhibitions organized and circulated; museum shop sells books, magazines and postcards

L **Murphy Library of Art History,** University of Kansas, 66045. Tel 913-864-3020. *Librn* Susan V Craig
Mon - Thurs 8 AM - 10 PM, Fri 8 AM - 5 PM, Sat 9 AM - 5 PM, Sun Noon - 10 PM. Estab 1970 to support academic programs and for research. Open to faculty, students and public
Library Holdings: Vols 56,000; Per subs 700; Auction catalogs; Micro — Fiche, reels; Other — Clipping files, pamphlets
Special Subjects: Oriental Art, Photography

LINDSBORG

BETHANY COLLEGE
M **Birger Sandzen Memorial Gallery,** 401 N First St, 67456. Tel 913-227-2220. *Dir* Larry L Griffis
Open Wed - Sun 1 - 5 PM, cl Mon, Tues & major holidays. Admis adults $1, grade and high school students $.25. Estab 1957 to permanently exhibit the paintings and prints by the late Birger Sandzen, teacher at Bethany College for 52 years. Ten exhibition areas. Average Annual Attendance: 7000 - 9000. Mem: 350; dues $5 - $100; annual meeting April for Board of Directors
Income: Financed by admission fees, sales and membership
Collections: H V Poor, Lester Raymer, Birger Sandzen
Exhibitions: Doran Barnum, watercolors; Tim Unruh, glass; Kent Ullberg and A J Obara, Jr, bronze sculpture; Lester Raymer and area artists, paintings; Angelo

Garzia and Robert Fromme, ceramics; Anders Zorn, etchings; Joseph Domjan, woodcuts
Publications: The Graphic Work of Birger Sandzen
Activities: Classes for children; lect open to the public 2 - 4 vis lectr per year; concerts; gallery talks; tours; sales desk sells books, reproductions, stationary
L **Library,** 401 N First St, 67456. *Librn* Dixie M Lanning
Wed - Sun 1 - 5 PM. Estab 1957 for use by art students. For reference only
Library Holdings: Other — Clipping files, exhibition catalogs, pamphlets, photographs
M **Mingenback Art Center,*** 401 N First St, 67456. *Department Head* Daniel Mason
Materials are not for public display, for educational reference only
Exhibitions: Oil paintings, watercolors, prints, etchings, lithographs, wood engravings, ceramics and sculpture

LOGAN

M **DANE G HANSEN MEMORIAL MUSEUM,*** 67646. Tel 913-689-4846. *Dir* Renee McElroy
Open Mon - Fri 9 AM - Noon & 1 - 4 PM, Sat 9 AM - Noon & 1 - 5 PM, Sun & holidays 1 - 5 PM, cl Christmas. No admis fee. Estab 1973. Mem: Dues business $10, individual $2
Collections: Coins; guns; oriental art
Activities: Tours

MANHATTAN

L **KANSAS STATE UNIVERSITY,** Paul Weigel Library, College of Architecture and Design, 66506. Tel 913-532-5968. *Librn* Patricia Weisenburger
Open Mon - Thurs 8 AM - 10 PM, Fri 8 AM - 5 PM, Sat 10 AM - 2 PM, Sun 2 - 10 PM. Estab 1917. Circ 21,855
Income: $22,200 (financed by state appropriations and gifts)
Library Holdings: Vols 27,400; Per subs 225; Micro — Fiche, reels
Special Subjects: Architecture, Landscape Architecture, Pre-Design Professions, Interior Architecture, Community and Regional Planning

MCPHERSON

M **MCPHERSON COLLEGE GALLERY,** Friendship Hall, 1600 E Euclid, 67460. Tel 316-241-0731. *Dir* Mary Ann Robinson
Open Mon - Fri 8 AM - 10 PM. No admis fee. Estab 1960 to present works of art to the college students and to the community. A long gallery which is the entrance to an auditorium, has four showcases and 11 panels 4 x 16 ft. Average Annual Attendance: 2500
Income: Financed through college
Collections: Oils, original prints, watercolors
Activities: Classes for adults; scholarships; book traveling exhibitions

NORTH NEWTON

L **BETHEL COLLEGE,** Mennonite Library and Archives, 67117. Tel 316-283-2500, Ext 213. *Dir* Robert Kreider; *Archivist* David A Haury; *Librn* Laurie Wolfe
Open Mon - Fri 8 AM - 5 PM. No admis fee. Estab 1936 to preserve resources related to Mennonite history for the use of researchers
Income: $50,000 (financed by college and church conference support)
Library Holdings: Micro — Fiche, reels; AV — A-tapes, cassettes, fs, Kodachromes, lantern slides, motion pictures, rec, slides, v-tapes; Other — Clipping files, exhibition catalogs, framed reproductions, manuscripts, memorabilia, original art works, pamphlets, photographs, prints, reproductions
Collections: 500 paintings and etchings by Mennonite artists
Exhibitions: Photographs of Hopi and Cheyenne Indians; The Dutch Setting: Mennonite Personalities & Their Environment
Publications: Gleanings from the Threshing Floor, bi-annual newsletter; Mennonite Life, quarterly journal
Activities: Sales shop sells books, magazines, reproductions, prints and slides

TOPEKA

O **ARTS COUNCIL OF TOPEKA,*** 215 SE Seventh St, 66603. Tel 413-295-3808. *Pres* Marlyn Burch; *Exec Dir* Don Lambert
Open Mon - Fri 9 AM - 5 PM. Estab 1959, an organization serving more than 70 organization members and 300 individual members in promoting the arts in Topeka. Mem: 370; dues $10; annual meeting Mar
Income: Financed by membership and city appropriation
Publications: Newsletter, monthly
Activities: Resource fair; competitions; art contest

M **KANSAS STATE HISTORICAL SOCIETY MUSEUM,** 6425 SW Sixth St, 66615. Tel 913-272-8681. *Exec Dir* Joseph W Snell; *Museum Dir* Mark A Hunt; *Asst Museum Dir* Martha D Kratsas; *Cur Fine Art* James R Kratsas; *Cur of Decorative Art* Mary Ellen Hennessey Nottage
Open Mon - Sat 9 AM - 4:30 PM, Sun 12:30 - 4:30 PM. No admis fee. Estab 1875 to collect, preserve and interpret the historical documents and objects of Kansas history. Average Annual Attendance: 70,000. Mem: 4100; dues life $500, regular $15; annual meeting in spring and fall
Income: $1,114,000 (financed by endowment and state appropriation)
Collections: Regional collection for period from middle 19th century to present, especially portraiture, native art, political cartoons and folk art
Exhibitions: (1980) From the Prairie (photog); (1981) Standing Rainbows: Railroad Promotion of Art, the West and It's Native Peoples, paintings from the Santa Fe RR Collection; (1982) Marijana: Images of Strawberry Hill, paintings depicting Croatian immigrant life in Kansas City, Kansas

Publications: Kansas History: Journal of the Great Plains, quarterly
Activities: Classes for adults and children; docent training; annual film program; craft demonstration program; lect open to public; lect provided by staff to public organizations on request; tours; slide tape programs; sales shop sells books, prints, cards, souvenirs and jewelry

L **TOPEKA PUBLIC LIBRARY,** Fine Arts Dept & Gallery of Fine Arts, 1515 W Tenth St, 66604. Tel 913-233-2040, Ext 330. *Dir* James C Marvin; *Asst Dir* Tom J Muth; *Fine Arts Dept Head* Robert H Daw; *Gallery Dir* Larry D Peters; *Adult Serv Dept* Jim Rhodes; *Childrens Dept Head* Sheila Radell; *Exten Head* Dick Brown; *Tech Serv Head* Helen Spencer; *Cir Dept Head* Alene Giesy
Open Mon - Fri 9 AM - 9 PM; Sun in winter 2 - 6 PM. Estab 1870 to serve the city and the Northeast Kansas Library System residents with public information, both educational and recreational; to be one of the areas cultural centers through services from the unique Fine Arts Dept and Gallery of Fine Arts within the library. Circ 1,000,000
Income: $1,500,000 (financed by endowment & city appropriation)
Purchases: $72,713
Library Holdings: Vols 267,782; Per subs 497; Documents, Postcards; Micro — Fiche, reels; AV — Cassettes, fs, motion pictures, rec, slides; Other — Clipping files, exhibition catalogs, framed reproductions, manuscripts, memorabilia, original art works, pamphlets, photographs, reproductions, sculpture
Special Subjects: Topeka Room of Topeka artists and authors
Collections: Hirschberg Collection of West African Arts; Johnson Collection of Art; Rare Book Room; Wilder Collection of Art Glass & Pottery
Exhibitions: Carpets of the Caucasus; Topeka Crafts Exhibition 5; Gustave Bauman Woodcuts; Australai Clay; Robert Motherwell; A la Pintura A la Pintura Walter Hatke
Publications: Creative Expression in Rural West Africa; Rookwood Pottery: One Hundred Year Anniversary
Activities: Classes for adults and children, dramatic programs, docent training; lectures open to public; concerts; gallery talks; library tours; competitions; awards; exten dept serves outlying areas within city limits

M **WASHBURN UNIVERSITY,** Mulvane Art Center, 17th & Jewell, 66621. *Dir* R J Hunt; *Asst Dir* Edward Navone
Open 9 AM - 4 PM, Sun 2 - 5 PM, cl Sat & holidays. Estab 1924. Building gift of Margaret Mulvane; provides three galleries with 319 running ft of hanging space with carpeted walls and temperature and humidity controlled. Average Annual Attendance: 15,000-20,000. Mem: 750; dues $7.50 and up
Income: Approx $60,000
Purchases: Approx $2000
Collections: International paintings, sculpture, prints and ceramics
Exhibitions: Continuous program of exhibitions; students exhibition
Publications: Exhibition brochures
Activities: Classes for adults and children; popular art lectures in Topeka by staff and visiting artists; frequent gallery programs; films open to the community without charge; gallery talks and tours; scholarships
L **Library,** 17th & Jewell, 66621
Library Holdings: Vols 3000

WICHITA

FRIENDS UNIVERSITY
M **Whittier Fine Arts Gallery,*** 2100 University, 67213. Tel 316-261-5800
Open daily 7:45 AM - 10 PM. No admis fee. Estab 1963 to bring art-craft exhibits to campus as an educational learning experience and to supply the local community with first class exhibits. 1224 sq ft of exhibit space. Average Annual Attendance: 15,000-20,000
Publications: Exhibition catalogs
Activities: Lectures open to public, 4 vis lectr per year; gallery talks; tours; exten dept
L **Edmund Stanley Library Gallery,*** 67213
Estab 1979. 500 sq ft of exhibition space, ideal for crafts and locked cases

M **THE INDIAN MUSEUM,** Mid American All Indian Center, 650 N Seneca, 67203. Tel 316-262-5221. *Exec Dir* Randy Greenfeather; *Dir Museum Services* Lorraine Zongker; *Gift Shop Mgr* Macil Harris
Open April 15 - Oct 30 Mon - Sat 10 AM - 5 PM, Sun 1 - 5 PM, Oct 30 - April 15 cl Mon & legal holidays. Admis adults $1.50, students with ID $1, senior citizens $.75, children 7 - 12 $.50, children under 7 free. Estab 1975. Maintains small reference library. Average Annual Attendance: 36,000. Mem: 300 - 400; dues patron over $1000, benefactor $500 - $1000, donor $250 - $499, subscriber $100 - $249, sustainer $50 - $99, sponsor $25 - $49, individual $15, student $7
Income: Financed by admissions, donations, memberships & gift shop sales
Collections: Native American arts and artifacts; Mildred Many Memorial Collection; Lincoln Ellsworth Collection
Publications: Gallery Notes, quarterly newsletter
Activities: Lectures open to the public; gallery talks; tours; museum shop sells books, original art, reproductions, prints & Indian items
L **Library,** Wichita, 67203
Reference only
Library Holdings: Vols 500; Indian art & history; AV — Fs, motion pictures, slides; Other — Pamphlets

O **KANSAS WATERCOLOR SOCIETY,** Wichita Art Museum, PO Box 7235, 67207. Tel 316-684-7056. *Pres* Jim Rigg; *Secy* Donna Brigman
Open during shows Tues - Sat 10 AM - 4:50 PM, Sun 1 - 4:50 PM. No admis. Estab 1968 to promote watercolor in Kansas. Three levels, space is triangulated, sales-rental gallery & childrens area. Average Annual Attendance: 450. Mem: 200; dues $10; annual meeting in Mar
Income: Financed by membership and entry fees
Exhibitions: Annual Tri-State (Kansas, Oklahoma, Missouri) Exhibition; traveling and invitational exhibitions in Kansas
Publications: Newsletter, bi-monthly
Activities: Demonstrations & workshops; lectures open to public, 2 vis lectr per yr; competitions with awards; traveling exhibitions organized and circulated; sales shop

O **WICHITA ART ASSOCIATION INC,** 9112 E Central, 67206. Tel 316-686-6687. *Chmn of Board* Mrs Karl T Wiedemann; *Dir & Cur* Glenice L Matthews; *Treas* John T Sheffield
Open Tues - Sun 1 - 5 PM, cl Mon, August, National holidays. No admis fee. Estab 1920, inc April 1932. Average Annual Attendance: 25,000. Mem: 1000; dues $25 and up, annual meeting May
Income: Financed by private contributions
Collections: Prints and drawings, paintings, sculpture, †decorative arts and crafts
Exhibitions: Traveling exhibitions change each month; one man shows, special programs
Publications: Newsletter, monthly
Activities: Lectures; concerts; gallery talks; workshops; films; demonstrations; Sales gallery
L **Maude Schollenberger Memorial Library,** 9112 East Central, 67206
Open 1 - 5 PM daily, cl Mon. Estab 1965. For reference
Income: Financed by private contributions
Library Holdings: Vols 3000

M **WICHITA ART MUSEUM,** 619 Stackman Dr, 67203. Tel 316-268-4621. *Dir* Howard E Wooden; *Cur of Coll-Exhib* Howard D Spencer; *Executive Asst* Mary Lee Archer; *Financial Officer* Alma Gilley; *Registrar* Barbara Odevseff; *Cur Education* Novelene Ross
Open Tues - Sat 10 AM - 4:50 PM, Sun 1 - 4:50 PM, cl Mon and holidays. No admis fee. Estab 1935 to house and exhibit art works belonging to permanent collection; to present exhibits of loaned art works, to ensure care and maintain the safety of works through security, environmental controls and appropriate curatorial functions and to interpret collections and exhibitions through formal and educational presentations. Facility designed by Edward Larrabee Barnes opened Oct 1977. Average Annual Attendance: 60,000 - 75,000. Mem: Dues $7.50 - $1000
Income: $800,000 (financed by endowment, membership, city appropriation, restricted gifts for art acquisition)
Collections: Roland P Murdock, American Art; M C Naftger Collection of Charles M Russell (paintings, drawings and sculpture); Kurdian Collection of Pre-Columbian Mexican Art; Virginia and George Ablah Collection of British Watercolors; L S & Ida L Naftzger Collection of Prints & Drawings; Gwen Houston Naftzger Collection of Boehm and Doughty Porcelain Birds; Florence Naftzger Evans Collection of Porcelain and Faience; Hands-on Collection for the Blind Gwen Houston Naftzger Collection of Boehm and Doughty Porcelain Birds; M C Naftzger Collection of Charles M Russell Paintings, Drawings and Sculpture; L S and Ida L Naftzger Collection of Prints and Drawings
Exhibitions: (1982) Benton's Bentons; Sculptures to Touch: Jane B Armstrong; Molly Luce: Painter of the American Scene; Edward Laning: American Realist; The Legendary Wichita Bill: A Retrospective Exhibition of Paintings by John Noble; Ned Jacob: The Kenyan Portfolio; Lily Harmon: Fifty Years of Painting; The Urban Scene: Realitites & Myths of the Big City; (1983) Will Barnet: Paintings & Prints; Max Weber Paintings; The Romance of the American Southwest; The Art of Alvar; American Painting, 1920-1960, Two Sides of the Coin; Les Enfans Terribles by Favarni; Margit Varga: Paintings, 1929-1980; Trends in American Art since 1960; Scenes of Rural America
Publications: Monthly Newsletter; Catalog of Roland P Murdock Collection; Charles M Russell Collection; exhibition brochures
Activities: Classes for adults & children; dramatic prog; docent training; lectures open to public; concerts; gallery talks; tours; competitions with awards; individual paintings and original objects of art lent; originate traveling exhibitions to Kansas communities; sales shop sells books, magazines, original art, reproductions, prints, slides, also a sales-rental gallery
L **Library,** 619 Stackman Drive, 67203
Open Tues - Fri 10 AM - 4:30 PM. Estab 1963 as research library for museum staff. Reference only. Library is a dept of Wichita Art Museum which shows portions of its permanent collection plus 1-2 special exhibitions a month
Income: $3500
Library Holdings: Vols 2500; Per subs 13; auction catalogs, museum handbooks; Other — Exhibition catalogs, pamphlets
Special Subjects: History of American Art
Collections: Roland P Murdock Collection of American Art, paintings, sculpture, graphics; LS & Ida L Naftzger Collection of Prints, old master prints; Charles M Russell Collection of Western Art, paintings, graphics, sculpture
Exhibitions: Chuck Forsman, Meditations on Realist Content & Theory; Neglected Generation of American Realist Painters 1930-1948; Ernest Shaw, scultures, paintings and drawings

L **WICHITA PUBLIC LIBRARY,** 223 S Main, 67202. Tel 316-262-0611. *Head Librn* Richard J Rademacher; *Asst Librn* Gary D Hime; *Circulation Dept Head* Virginia Dillon; *Reference Dept Head* Viola Tidemann; *Acquisitions Dept Head* Bonnie Rupe; *Art & Music Dept Head* Len Messineo Jr; *Children's Room Dept Head* Barbara Fischer; *Business & Technical Dept Head* William Hoffman; *State-Wide Film Service* Sondra Koontz; *Talking Books for the Blind* Betty Spriggs
Open Mon - Thurs 8:30 AM - 9 PM, Fri & Sat 8:30 AM - 5:30 PM. Estab 1876 and grown to be informational center and large free public library to improve the community with educational, cultural and recreational benefits through books, recordings, films, art works and other materials. Circ 1,100,000
Income: $1,400,000 (from local taxes)
Library Holdings: Micro — Reels; AV — Motion pictures, rec; Other — Framed reproductions
Collections: Kansas Book Collection; John F Kennedy Collection; Harry Mueller Philately Book Collection; Driscoll Piracy Collection
Exhibitions: Annuals, Kansas Scholastic Art Show; Best News Photographs Exhibit; Senior High School Students Spring Exhibit; Wichita Area Girl Scout Exhibit; Wichita Women Artists; plus numerous other exhibits throughout the year
Activities: Lect; tours

M **WICHITA STATE UNIVERSITY,** Edwin A Ulrich Museum of Art, McKnight Art Center - Box 46, 67208. Tel 316-689-3664. *Dir* Dr Martin H Bush; *Cur* Gary Hood; *Asst Cur* Tom Gormally; *Asst Cur* Gary Buettgenbach; *Secy* Karin Glenn
Open Wed 9:30 AM - 8 PM, Thur & Fri 9:30 AM - 5 PM, Sat, Sun & holidays 1 - 5 PM. No admis fee. Estab 1974 to provide exhibitions of major artists for the benefit of the university and community by accepting and putting together traveling shows and to build and exhibit a permanent collection of outstanding quality. A 6000 sq ft main gallery has movable walls that can be changed to accomodate different exhibitions
Income: Financed by endowment
Collections: The Outdoor Sculpture Collection of 37 pieces featuring a 28 by 52 ft mosaic mural designed by Joan Miro; The Permanent Collection, with emphasis on 20th century American and European artwork; Ulrich Collection of Frederick J Waugh paintings; collection of prints by Honore Daumier, Albrecht Altdorfer, Harry Sternberg, Anthony van Dyck; collections of sculpture by Ernest Trova and Charles Grafly
Exhibitions: Milton Avery (paintings, drawings, prints), Frederic Church (paintings), John DeAndrea (sculpture) Honore Daumier (prints), Alberto Giacometti (sculptures, drawings, prints), George Grosz (paintings, drawings, prints); Duane Hanson (sculpture), David Hockney (drawings, paintings), Andre Kertesz and France (photographs), Kathe Kollwitz (drawings and prints), Oskar Kokoschka (prints), Dorothea Lange (photographs), Henry Manguin Retrospective (paintings); Joan Miro (paintings), Robert Motherwell (paintings, prints), Moses Soyer (paintings), Josef Presser (paintings), Realists in Hamburg (paintings), Pierre Alechinsky (prints), Joseph Cornell (box constructions), Holography: Through the Looking Glass (holograms); Georges Rouault (prints), Gustav Klimt and Egon Schiele (drawings) Abraham Walkowitz Retrospective (paintings), Antwerp's Golden Age, as well as various visiting artists
Publications: College catalog
Activities: Lect open to public; concerts; gallery talks; tours by arrangement; traveling exhibits organized and circulated; sales shop sells books

WINFIELD

L **SOUTHWESTERN COLLEGE,** Memorial Library - Art Dept, 100 College, 67156. Tel 316-221-4150, Ext 225. *Dir* Daniel L Nutter
Open school year Mon - Thurs 8 AM - 10 PM, Fri 8 AM - 4 PM, Sat 1 - 5 PM, Sun 3 - 10 PM, summer Mon - Fri 8 AM - 4 PM. Estab 1885 as a four-year liberal arts college. Circ 30,000
Income: Financed by college budget
Collections: Arthur Covey Collection of paintings, mural sketches, etchings, lithographs, drawings and watercolors; Cunningham Asian Arts Collection of books, catalogues & exhibition catalogs
Exhibitions: Arthur Covey Centennial Exhibit
Activities: Tours

KENTUCKY

BEREA

M **BEREA COLLEGE,** Art Department Gallery, 40404. Tel 606-986-9341, Ext 292. *Dir* Lester F Pross
Open Mon - Fri 8 AM - 5 PM, Sun 1 - 5 PM. No admis fee. Estab 1936 for educational purposes. Three gallery areas; exhibitions change monthly; loan and rental shows, regional artists, work from Berea College collections
Income: Financed by college budget
Collections: Kress Study Collection of Renaissance art; Doris Ulmann photographs; prints, textiles, paintings, sculpture, ceramics; Asian Art
Exhibitions: (1982-83) Egyptian Children's Tapestries from Harrania; Ted Saupe (sculptural claywork); Alden Addington (sculpture); Dale Leys (drawings); Steve Bishop (cast metal sculpture); Elizabeth Kershner (batik cloth sculpture); Clare Verstegen (kites); Stanley Mace Anderson and Diana Gillispie (ceramics); Greek Art and Goya's Tauromachia, prints, and Renaissance paintings from the departmental collection; student and staff exhibits; (1983-84) More Than Land or Sky: Art From Appalachia; David Capps (photography); Tom Dimig (ceramics); Daniel Dutton and Carolyn Hisel (paintings); Dennis Whitcopg (sculpture); Wally Hyleck (ceramics); William Morningstar (sculpture); West African Art; Indigo Fabrics from the Choi and Counts Collection; Ron Meyers (ceramics); student shows; special exhibits from the departmental collection
Activities: Education Dept; lectures open to the public, 2 - 6 vis lectr per yr; gallery talks; tours; scholarships; individual paintings and original objects of art lent to other colleges, museums, and galleries; lending collection contains 500 framed reproductions

L **Art Dept Library,** 40404
Open Mon - Fri 8 AM - 5 PM. Estab 1936. Reference library only
Income: Financed by college budget
Purchases: $1200 annually
Library Holdings: Vols 3000; Per subs 30; AV — Cassettes, fs, Kodachromes, lantern slides, rec, slides, v-tapes; Other — Clipping files, exhibition catalogs, framed reproductions, manuscripts, memorabilia, original art works, pamphlets, photographs, prints, reproductions, sculpture

O **KENTUCKY GUILD OF ARTISTS AND CRAFTSMEN INC,*** PO Box 291, 40403. Tel 606-986-3192. *Exec Dir* James E Seidelman; *Admin Asst* Maggie Rifai
Open Mon - Sat 10 AM - 5 PM. No admis fee. Estab 1961 for the pursuit of excellence in the arts and crafts and to encourage the public appreciation thereof. Maintains an art gallery. Average Annual Attendance: 20,000. Mem: 500; must be a Kentucky resident and be juried for exhibiting status; dues individual $15; annual meeting Nov
Income: $62,000 (financed by grants, contributions, admissions and membership fees)

Exhibitions: Two annual fairs include a members exhibit
Publications: The Guild Record, 6 times per yr
Activities: Classes for adults and children; docent training; workshops; lectures open to public, 4-5 visiting lecturers per year; demonstrations; competitions with awards; individual and original objects of art lent to corporate offices and museums; traveling exhibitions organized and circulated

BOWLING GREEN

WESTERN KENTUCKY UNIVERSITY

M **Kentucky Museum,** 42101. Tel 502-745-2592. *Cur* Diane L Alpert; *Assoc Exhib* Bob Brigl; *Public Information Officer* Doug Nesbit; *Registrar* Debbie Smith; *Asst Cur Educ* Vicki Middlesworth-Kohn
Open Tues - Sat 9:30 AM - 4 PM, Sun 1 PM - 4:30 PM. No admis fee. As well as offering exhibits and programs of wide interest, the museum also serves as a research and educational resource for scholars, specialists, and academic units of the University. The museum's subject area is the history and art of Kentucky, with supportive areas in American art and decorative arts, and European art. Average Annual Attendance: 21,000
Income: Financed by state appropriation and University
Exhibitions: (1983) Growing Up Victorian
Activities: Classes for adults and children; docent training; lect open to the public; gallery talks; tours; competitions; individual paintings lent; originate traveling exhibitions; museum shop sells books, original art & reproductions

L **Kentucky Library,** 42101
Open to the public for reference
Library Holdings: Vols 30,000; Per subs 35; Maps, broadsides, postcards; Other — Clipping files, manuscripts, photographs
Collections: Ellis Collection of steamboat pictures; Gerard Collection of Bowling Green Photographs; McGregor Collection of rare books; Neal Collection of Utopian materials

M **University Gallery,** Ivan Wilson Center for Fine Arts, Rm 200, 42101. Tel 502-745-2345. *Dir* John Warren Oakes
Open Mon - Fri 8:30 AM - 4 PM. No admis fee. Estab 1973 for art exhibitions relating to university instruction and regional cultural needs. Average Annual Attendance: 12,000
Income: Financed by state appropriation
Exhibitions: (1983-84) Generation to Generation, Sharing the Intangible; Library of Congress, photographs; Rauschenberg/Rosenquist, two print suites of the mid-70's; Students Weaving; Selected Students; Invitational Ceramic; American Drawings IV; Folk Art Festival; faculty recent work; Neil Peterie: Sabbatical Exhibtion; 16th annual high school art competition; 24th annual student art competition; selected seniors

DANVILLE

M **MCDOWEL HOUSE AND APOTHECARY SHOP,** 125 S 2nd St, 40422. Tel 606-236-2804. *Dir* Susan Nimocks
Open Mon - Sat 10 AM - Noon & 1 PM - 4 PM, Sun 2 PM - 4 PM. Admin adults $2, children under 12 $.50. Estab 1939 to show the town house of a prominent professional man in Danville, 1795-1830. Average Annual Attendance: 3000. Mem: 600; dues $15-$1000
Income: $36,000 (financed by endowment, members, private contribution from groups & individuals)
Collections: Portraits & folkart, 1795-1830
Publications: Annual newsletter
Activities: Docent training; lectures open to public, vis lecturers 5 per year, tours; museum shop sells books, magazines, original art, reproductions, prints, slides, American gift items

FORT MITCHELL

M **THOMAS MORE COLLEGE,** TM Gallery, Crestview Hills, 41017. Tel 606-341-5800. *Dir* Sr M deDeo Rauf; *Asst Dir* Marissa Murphy
Open Mon - Thurs 8 AM - 9:45 PM, Fri 8 AM - 4:30 PM, Sat & Sun 1 - 5 PM. No admis fee. Estab for cultural & educational enrichment for the institution & area. Average Annual Attendance: 2000
Exhibitions: Works on Paper; Diane Fishbein, ceramic sculpture & drawing; Gayle H Marsh, photographs; Christine & Barry Stevens; Valerie Shesko: Deconstruction; Thomas Frank: Cliche Verre; Honore Daumier 1801-1879: A Centenary Tribute; senior exhibition; student exhibition
Activities: Lectures open to public, 1-2 vis lectr per yr; book traveling exhibitions

FRANKFORT

M **KENTUCKY HISTORICAL SOCIETY,** Old State Capitol & Annex, Broadway at Saint Clair, PO Box H, 40602. Tel 502-564-3016. *Dir* Robert B Kinnaird; *Cur* Elizabeth Perkins
Open Mon - Sat 9 AM - 4 PM, Sun 1 - 5 PM. No admis fee. Estab 1836 as a general history and art museum emphasizing the history, culture and decorative arts of the Commonwealth of Kentucky and its people. The Old Capitol Galleries located in the Old State House consist of two rooms totaling 2740 sq ft which are used by the Museum to display its fine arts exhibitions, painting, silver, furniture and sculpture, one temporary exhibits gallery in Old Capitol Annex. Average Annual Attendance: 50,000. Mem: 9000; dues from life $300 to individual $18
Income: $450,200 (financed by state appropriation)
Collections: Kentucky and American china, coverlets, paintings, quilts, silver, textiles
Exhibitions: (1982) Patrick Henry Davenport: Itinerant Portraitist; (1983) Vitro Girone: The Beaux Arts Education of an Architect
Publications: The Register, The Bulletin, quarterly
Activities: Lect open to public, 4 vis lectrs per year; tours; individual paintings and original objects of art lent to qualified museums; lending collection consists of original art works, original prints; paintings; sculpture and historical artifacts; book traveling exhibitions; traveling exhivitions organized and circulated; museum shop sells books and reproductions

L **Library,** Broadway at Saint Clair, PO Box H, 40602
Library Holdings: Vols 50,000

M **KENTUCKY STATE UNIVERSITY,** Jackson Hall Gallery,* Art Department, E Main St, 40601. Tel 502-564-5996. *Gallery Coordr* Jo Leadingham
Open Mon - Fri 8 AM - 4:30 PM. No admis fee. Gallery. Average Annual Attendance: 2000
Income: Financed through small grants and University appropriations
Collections: A small permanent collection of graphic arts
Activities: Lect open to the public, 4 visiting lectrs per year; competitions; scholarships; book traveling exhibitions, 2-3 per year

M **LIBERTY HALL MUSEUM,** 218 Wilkinson St, 40601. Tel 502-277-2560. *Chmn* Mrs Edward C O'Rear; *Cur* Mrs Harvey R Bixler
Open Tues - Sat 10 AM - 5 PM, Sun 2 - 5 PM, cl Mon and holidays. Admis adults $2, children and students $.50. Estab 1937 as an historic museum. A Georgian house built in 1796, named Historic Landmark in 1972
Collections: 18th century furniture; china; silver; portraits
Activities: Guided tours
L **Library,** 218 Wilkinson St, 40601
Open to the public during scheduled hours, with supervision
Library Holdings: Vols 4000
M **Orlando Brown House,** 202 Wilkinson St, 40601. Tel 502-875-4952. *Chmn* Sarah Stanfill; *Cur* Ora Gordon Taylor
Open Tues - Sat 10 AM - 4 PM, Sun 2 - 4 PM, cl Mon and holidays. Admis adults $1.50, children $.50. Estab 1956. Built in 1835 by architect Gilbert Shryock
Collections: Paul Sawyier paintings; original furnishings
Activities: Guided tours
L **Orlando Brown House Library,** 202 Wilkinson St, 40601
Open to public
Library Holdings: Vols 500

GEORGETOWN

M **GEORGETOWN COLLEGE GALLERY,** Mulberry St, Box 83, 40324. Tel 502-863-8106. *Chmn* James McCormick
Open Mon, Wed & Fri 12:30 - 4:30 PM. No admis fee. Estab 1953 as educational gallery with various mediums & styles. Gallery has 100 running ft wall space, portable screens. Average Annual Attendance: 2000
Collections: †Contemporary graphics; †contemporary painting & sculpture; crafts; artifacts
Exhibitions: Alma Lesch, fiber art; Anna Faye Crockett & Dennis Shaffner; alumni artists; Arturo Sandoval, fabric art
Activities: Lectures open to public; competitions with awards

HENDERSON

M **AUDUBON STATE PARK,** John James Audubon Museum,* U S 41 N, PO Box 576, 42420. Tel 502-826-2247. *Dir* Samuel W Jones
Open summer 9 AM - 5 PM, winter Sat & Sun 9 AM - 5 PM. Admis adults $1.50, adult groups $1, children 12 and under $.75, children groups $.50. Average Annual Attendance: 12,000
Collections: John James Audubon's original paintings

HIGHLAND HEIGHTS

M **NORTHERN KENTUCKY UNIVERSITY GALLERY,** 41075. Tel 606-572-5420
Open Mon - Fri 8 AM - 10 PM, Sat & Sun 10 AM - 5 PM. No admis fee. Estab 1968, new location 1976, to provide an arts center for the University and community area. Two galleries are maintained, the smaller 15 X 30. Average Annual Attendance: 2500
Income: Financed by university and state funds
Collections: Permanent collection of Red Grooms Monumental Sculpture in Metal; Donald Judd Monumental Sculpture; earth works, other outdoor sculpture, prints, painting, photographs, folk art
Exhibitions: Student exhibitions; state, regional & national visiting artists
Publications: Bulletins, 4-5 per year
Activities: Lectures open to public, 5-6 vis lectr per yr; gallery talks; individual paintings & original objects of art lent to university community

LEXINGTON

M **HEADLEY-WHITNEY MUSEUM,** 4435 Old Frankfort Pike, 40510. Tel 606-255-6653. *Pres* Claude W Trapp; *VPres* Edna-French Johnstone; *Dir* Anne Gobar
Open Wed - Sun 10 AM - 5 PM, cl major holidays. Admis adults $2.50, students $1.50, children 5 and under free. Estab 1968 for the collection & dissemination of art in central Kentucky. Five principal galleries are maintained. Average Annual Attendance: 20,000. Mem: 500; dues $35 & $100
Income: Financed by admissions, membership, benefits, sales, grants & contributions
Collections: European and American paintings; antique boxes, gemstones, jeweled bibelots, minerals; Oriental porcelains; seashells
Publications: Headley Treasure of Bibelots & Boxes (catalog of Bibelot Collection); newsletters, quarterly
Activities: Educ dept; docent training; symposia; lect open to the public; concerts; tours; individual paintings and original objects of art lent; lending collection contains slides, selected works from permanent collections by special arrangement; book traveling exhibitions; museum shop sells books, original art, reproductions, slides, jewelry, shell items & porcelains

L **Library,** 4435 Old Frankfort Pike, 40511
Open Wed - Sun 10 AM - 5 PM. Estab 1968. For reference, research and visitors' use
Library Holdings: Vols 1400; Per subs 14; Other — Exhibition catalogs, memorabilia, original art works, pamphlets, photographs, reproductions, sculpture
Special Subjects: Goldsmithing, Oriental Art, Gemstones, minerals, seashells

O **LEXINGTON ART LEAGUE, INC,** Loudoun House, Castlewood Park Castlewood Drive, 40505. Tel 606-269-8602. *Pres* James E Seidelman; *VPres* Paddy Lisk; *Secy* Nancy Smith
Open daily 1 - 4 PM. No admis fee. Estab 1957, to engender and encourage an active interest in the creative arts among its members and the community as a whole. Average Annual Attendance: 1200. Mem: 400; dues $17.50; annual meeting April
Income: Financed by membership, art fairs, donations
Exhibitions: Changing monthly exhibitions; member, group, one person exhibitions
Publications: Annual Membership Book; newsletter, monthly
Activities: Demonstrations; programs; workshops; lect open to the public; competitions; awards

L **LEXINGTON PUBLIC LIBRARY,** Skydome Gallery, 251 W Second St, 40507. Tel 606-252-8871. *Dir* Ronald Steensland; *Head Information Center* Rebecca Croft; *Gallery Dir* Marcia Greyman
Open Mon - Thurs 9 AM - 9 PM, Fri & Sat 9 AM - 5 PM, Sun 1 - 5 PM. Estab 1798 to provide books, periodicals and audiovisual materials for the community. Gallery is maintained. Circ 700,000
Income: Financed by city, state and federal appropriations
Library Holdings: Vols 200,000; Per subs 800; Micro — Fiche, prints, reels; AV — Cassettes, fs, motion pictures, rec, slides; Other — Framed reproductions, manuscripts, original art works, photographs, sculpture
Special Subjects: Photograph Collection of early Lexington Audubon Prints
Collections: 19th century American Portraits
Exhibitions: Monthly exhibits of regional artists; Quilts Up-To-Date; Fibers; The Art of Drawing; Michael Brechner; Aline Winkler; Rachel Naupin; Anne Roberts; Quentin Colgan
Activities: Artist in residence programs; demonstrations; lect open to the public, 50 visiting lectrs per year; gallery talks; competitions; exten dept serves inmates, elderly and hospitalized; book traveling exhibitions

M **LIVING ARTS SCIENCE CENTER,** 362 Walnut St, 40508. Tel 606-252-5222. *Dir* Susan B Thompson
Open Mon - Fri 9 AM - 5 PM, Sat 10 AM - 4 PM, cl New Years, July 4, Thanksgiving, Christmas. No admis fee. Estab 1968. Mem: Dues $15 - $500
Publications: Exhibition catalogs
Activities: Classes for adults and children; lectures

M **TRANSYLVANIA UNIVERSITY,** Morlan Gallery,* Mitchell Fine Arts Center, 40508. Tel 606-255-6861. *Coordr* Nancy Wolsk
Open Mon - Fri 11:30 AM - 3 PM, Sun 1 - 5 PM, cl Sat
Income: Financed by endowment
Exhibitions: Debbie Fredricks; Hume Collection Textile Art; Alma Lesch Collage in Cloth - Tapestry; Terrie Mangat - Quilts and Prints; Oriental Shadow Puppets; Arturo Sandovol; Soft Sculpture and Woven Collage

UNIVERSITY OF KENTUCKY

M **Art Museum,** Center for the Arts, 40506. Tel 606-257-5716. *Dir* William Hennessey; *Registrar* Robin Mitchell; *Cur* Harriet Fowler; *Admin Asst* Maureen Saxon; *Preparator* Michael Brechner; *Asst Preparator and Designer* Tom Baker
Estab 1975 to collect, preserve, exhibit and interpret world art for the benefit of the University community and the region. new building completed and opened November 1979; 20,000 sq ft of galleries and work space
Income: $225,000 (financed by state appropriation and gifts)
Collections: African; American Indian; European and American paintings, sculpture and graphics, 15th - 20th century; Oriental; Pre-Columbian
Exhibitions: Beginnings: A University Art Museum Collects
Publications: Art Museum Notes; exhibition catalogs; posters
L **Art Library,** M I King Library, North, 40506. Tel 606-257-3938. *Librn* Meg Shaw
Open to students and the general public
Library Holdings: Vols 26,196; Per subs 138; Micro — Fiche, reels; Other — Clipping files, pamphlets

LOUISVILLE

O **ART CENTER ASSOCIATION,** The Water Tower, 3005 River Rd, 40206. Tel 502-896-2146. *Pres* Thomas Dieruf; *Exec Dir* John Begley; *Executive Secy* Lois Madden; *Asst Dir* Suellen Joy
Open Mon - Fri 9 AM - 5 PM, Sun Noon - 4 PM, cl Sat. No admis fee. Estab 1907 to serve area artists and citizens; slide registry. Gallery area: Price Gallery 125-150 running ft, Brown Hall 125-150 running ft, 3500 sq ft total. Average Annual Attendance: 30,000. Mem: 1225; dues $15 - $100; monthly meeting of Board of Dir
Income: $200,000 (financed by endowment, membership, state appropriation, Greater Louisville Fund for the Arts, grants and rental of space)
Exhibitions: Kentucky Watercolor Society Annual Competition; group invitational; regional artist emphasis
Publications: Art Center News, 10 times per yr
Activities: Classes for adults and children; docent training; lectures open to the public, 12 vis lectrs per yr; gallery talks; tours; competitions with awards; scholarships; book traveling exhibitions; originate traveling exhibitions; sales shop sells magazines, original art, crafts and prints

O THE FILSON CLUB, 118 W Breckinridge St, 40203. Tel 502-582-3727. *Dir* Martin F Schmidt
Open Mon - Fri 9 AM - 5 PM, cl national holidays. No admis fee. Estab 1884 to collect, preserve and publish historical material, especially pertaining to Kentucky. Mem: 3000; dues life $360, annual $18
Income: Financed by membership dues & private funds
Collections: †Books and manuscripts; large collection of portraits of Kentuckians; artifacts
Publications: Filson Club History Quarterly; Series 1 and Series 2 Publications (38 volumes)
L Reference and Research Library, 118 W Breckinridge St, 40203. Tel 502-582-3727. *Librn* Martin F Schmidt
Open Mon - Fri 9 AM - 5 PM, Sat 9 AM - Noon. Estab 1884 to collect, preserve and publish Kentucky historical material and associated material
Income: Financed by endowments, memberships and gifts
Library Holdings: Vols 38,000; Other — Photographs
Exhibitions: Portraits of Kentuckians
Publications: Filson Club History Quarterly

M LOUISVILLE ART GALLERY, 301 York St, 40203. Tel 502-583-7062. *Exec Dir* Roberta L Williams
Open Mon - Sat 9 AM - 5 PM, cl Sun and holidays. No admis fee. Estab 1950 to develop understanding and appreciation of man's effort to communicate visually. The gallery attempts to achieve this goal through exhibitions, workshops for adults and children, and special events. The gallery is housed in the Louisville Free Public Library. There is a 1500 sq ft exhibition area. Five or six exhibitions a year of work by professional artists. Each exhibition is planned around a theme and in context for special interest to school-age children as well as adults.
Average Annual Attendance: 30,000. Mem: 500
Income: Financed by membership, united arts fund, grants
Exhibitions: (1984) The Artists & The Computer; Painting in the Eighties: Two Trends; For the Masses, product design; Contemporary Iron, Close Encounters with Art and Technology;
Publications: Exhibition catalogs
Activities: Classes for adults & children; dramatic programs; docent training; hands-on gallery activities; demonstrations; gallery games; lectures open to public; gallery talks; tours; exten dept; book traveling exhibitions; originate traveling exhibitions

M SOUTHERN BAPTIST SEMINARY MUSEUM, 2825 Lexington Rd, 40206. Tel 502-897-4807. *Cur* Dr Ronald F Deering
Open Mon - Sat 9:30 AM - 10 PM, cl Sun & national holidays. No admis fee. Estab 1961
Collections: Archeology; glass; numismatics; religious materials from Caesarea, Machaerus; sculpture; textiles
Activities: Guided tours; films

M J B SPEED ART MUSEUM, 2035 S Third St, P O Box 8345, 40208. Tel 502-637-1925. *Chmn Board of Governors* Dillman A Rash; *Pres Board Governor* W L Lyons Brown Jr; *Dir & Cur* Addison Franklin Page; *Cur Asst & Registrar* Mary E Carver; *Communications Officer* Kelly Scott Reed; *Technician* William E Kruetzman
Open Tues - Sat 10 AM - 4 PM, Sun 2 - 6 PM. Donation. Estab 1925 for the collection and exhibition of works of art of all periods and cultures, supported by a full special exhibition program and educational activities. Galleries are arranged to present painting, sculpture and decorative arts of all periods and cultures; special facilities for prints and drawings. Average Annual Attendance: 120,000. Mem: 2800; dues $25; annual meeting Jan
Income: $520,000 (financed by endowment)
Purchases: $150,000
Collections: Comprehensive permanent collection
Exhibitions: Matthew Boulton Silver; Retrospective of Paintings by Sam Gilliam; An Auditory Environment by Joe Moss; An Exhibition for Corporate Collecting; British Watercolors: A Golden Age 1750-1850; French 19th Century Landscape Watercolors; Ruskin and Venice; In Pursuit of Perfection: The Art of J A D Ingres
Publications: Calendar, monthly; Bulletin, semiannually
Activities: Classes for children; docent training; lect open to public, 10 - 12 vis lectr per yr; concerts; gallery talks; tours; competitions; individual paintings and original objects of art lent to museums and galleries; lending collection contains 200 paintings; museum shop sells books, original art, reproductions
L Art Reference Library, 2035 S Third St, PO Box 8345, 40208. Tel 502-636-2893. *Librn* Mary Jane Benedict
Open Tues - Fri 10 AM - 4 PM
Library Holdings: Vols 12,000; Per subs 50; Vertical Files 48; AV — Slides; Other — Clipping files, exhibition catalogs, pamphlets
Collections: J B Speed's Lincoln Books; Frederick Weygold's Indian Collection
Publications: Acquisitions list, bibliographies, in-house periodical index, index to J B Speed Art Museum bulletins, index to dealers catalogs

UNIVERSITY OF LOUISVILLE
M Allen R Hite Art Institute Gallery, Belknap Campus, 40292. Tel 502-588-6794. *Dir* Stephanie J Maloney; *Secy* Linda Rowley
Estab 1935 for education and enrichment. Open by appointment
Income: Financed by endowment, and state appropriation
Collections: drawings; paintings; †prints
Publications: Exhibition catalogs, occasionally
Activities: Lect open to public, 4 vis lectr per yr; Winthrop Allen Memorial Prize for creative art; scholarships
L Margaret M Bridwell Art Library, Belknap Campus, 40292. Tel 502-588-6741. *Head Art Library* Gail R Gilbert; *Asst to Art Librn* Kathleen Moore
Open Mon - Thurs 8 AM - 9 PM, Fri 8 AM - 5 PM, Sat 10 AM - 2 PM, Sun 2 - 6 PM. Estab 1956 to support the programs of the art department. For reference only
Income: Financed by endowment and state appropriation
Purchases: $36,300
Library Holdings: Vols 40,000; Per subs 200; Micro — Fiche, reels; AV — Rec;

Other — Clipping files, exhibition catalogs, manuscripts, memorabilia, pamphlets, prints
Special Subjects: Photography, American Art and Architecture, German Gothic Sculpture
Collections: Original Christmas cards; †original prints; †posters
L University of Louisville Photographic Archives, 40292. Tel 502-588-6752. *Cur* James C Anderson; *Asst Cur* David Horvath
Open Mon - Wed & Fri 8 AM - 4:30 PM, Thurs 8 AM - 8 PM. Estab 1967 to collect, preserve, organize photographs and related materials; primary emphasis on documentary photography
Income: Financed through the University
Library Holdings: Vols 500; Micro — Reels; Other — Clipping files, exhibition catalogs, photographs 750,000
Exhibitions: (1983-84) Kentucky: Two Surveys, 1903 & 1976; The Faculty Show: Lexington Area Artists & Instructors; Finding a Needle in a Haystack: The Computer Assisted Street Index Show; American Spectrum: Color Works from the Standard Oil of New Jersey Collection 1943-1951; The Road Show: Contemporary Photographers & the American Road; Royal Photos: Photographs from the Royal Photographic Studio; Summer Show '84
Activities: Lectures open to public, 3-5 vis lectr per yr; gallery talks; tours; competitions; original objects of art lent to museums and galleries; book traveling exhibitions; originates traveling exhibitions
L Slide Collection, 40208. Tel 502-588-5917. *Cur Slides* Ann S Coates; *Asst to Cur* Lana Stokes
Open Mon - Fri 8:30 AM - 4:30 PM. Estab 1930's to provide comprehensive collection of slides for use in the University instructional program; 250,000 catalogued slides illustrating history of Western art. Circ 40,000
Library Holdings: AV — Kodachromes, slides; Other — Clipping files
Special Subjects: Architecture, Furniture, Painting - American, Photography, Porcelain, Pottery
Collections: American Studies; Calligraphy; Manuscript of Medieval Life

MAYSVILLE

M MASON COUNTY MUSEUM, * 215 Sutton St, 41056. Tel 606-564-5865. *Dir* Louis Browing; *VPres* S A Glass; *Secy* M M Kendall; *Dir* Mrs C C Calvert
Open Tues - Sat 10 AM - 4 PM. Admis adults $1, children $.50, students in groups $.25. Estab 1879 to maintain historical records and artifacts for area. Average Annual Attendance: 500. Mem: 200; dues $10-$25
Income: $30,000 (financed by endowment and members)
Collections: Paintings & maps related to area
Activities: Gallery talks; tours; individual paintings and original objects of art lent; book traveling exhibitions; bookstore sells books, prints and postcards

MOREHEAD

M MOREHEAD STATE UNIVERSITY, Claypool-Young Art Gallery,* Art Dept, PO Box 714, 40351. Tel 606-783-2193. *Dir* Dr Bill R Booth; *Assoc Dir* Gene Plye
Open Mon - Fri 8 AM - 4:30 PM, Sat & Sun 1 - 4 PM, by appointment. Estab 1922 to provide undergraduate and graduate programs in studio and art education. An exhibition gallery is maintained for traveling exhibitions, faculty and student work. The Claypool-Young Art Gallery is tri-level with 2344 sq ft of exhibition space
Income: Financed by appropriation
Collections: Establishing a permanent collection which to date consists principally of prints by major contemporary figures; several works added each year through purchase or bequest. Additions to lending collection include: The Maria Rilke Suite of lithographs by Ben Shahn consisting of 23 pieces; the Laus Pictorum Suite by Leonard Baskin, consisting of 14 pieces; and three lithographs by Thomas Hart Benton: Jesse James, Frankie and Johnny, and Huck Finn
Exhibitions: A large number of one-man exhibitions along with invitational shows and group exhibits
Activities: Lect open to the public, 5 visiting lectr per year; concerts; gallery talks; tours; competitions; individual paintings lent to schools; lending collection contains 200 items, prints, photographs; traveling exhibitions organized and circulated
L Library, * Art Dept, PO Box 714, 40351. *Dir* Jack D Ellis
Library Holdings: Vols 5000

MURRAY

M MURRAY STATE UNIVERSITY, Clara M Eagle Gallery, Price Doyle Fine Arts Center, 42071. Tel 502-762-3784. *Chmn* Robert W Head; *Gallery Dir* R Michael Watts
Open Mon - Fri 7:30 AM - 9 PM, Sat 10 AM - 4 PM, Sun 1 - 4 PM. No admis fee. Estab 1971. Gallery houses the permanent collection of the University; the Main Gallery is located on the fourth floor and its dimensions are 100 x 40 ft; the upper level is divided into three small galleries that may be used as one or three. Average Annual Attendance: 100,000
Income: Financed by state appropriation and grants
Collections: Asian Collection (given by Asian Cultural Exchange Foundation); Collection of Clara M Eagle Gallery; Harry L Jackson Print Collection; WPA prints, drawings
Exhibitions: Biennial Alumni Invitational; Annual Magic Silver Show; Annual Student Exhibition Biennial Faculty Exhibition; Dennis Gould: Paintings; Shereen LaPlantz: The Woven Form; Dale Leys: Drawings 1973-83; African Arts: Beauty in Utility; Metals Invitational; NCECA Traveling Exhibition
Publications: Brochures and posters for individual shows
Activities: Classes for adults and children; films; visiting artists; workshops; demonstrations; lect open to public, 8 visiting lectr per year; gallery talks; tours; competitions with merit & purchase awards; exten dept serving Jackson Purchase Area of Kentucky; individual paintings and original objects of art lent; lending collection consists of original prints, paintings, records, photographs & sculpture; books traveling exhibitions; traveling exhibitions organized and circulated

OWENSBORO

M **BRESCIA COLLEGE,** Art Gallery, 120 W 7th St, 42301. Tel 502-685-3131.
Coordr Dept Gerald A Matlick, MFA; *Gallery Dir* Dan McGuire, MFA
Open Mon - Fri 8 AM - 4:30 PM, Sat 8 AM - Noon. No admis fee. Estab 1950.
Gallery space is 20 x 30 ft, walls are covered with neutral carpeting. Average
Annual Attendance: 4000
Exhibitions: (1983-84) National Paper Works Exhibition; Alisa Payne; Lynn
Donaldson; Kenneth Taylor; Randy Johnson; Terry Bailey; Regional High School
Art Competition; Brescia College Annual Student Juried Show
Activities: Lectures open to public, 2-3 vis lectr per yr; competitions with awards;
scholarships; book traveling exhibitions; originate traveling exhibitions

M **OWENSBORO MUSEUM OF FINE ART,** 901 Frederica St, 42301. Tel 502-685-3181. *Dir* Mary Bryan Hood; *Dir Operations* David Atkinson; *Educ Dir & Registrar* Jane Wilson; *Business Mgr* Mary Ellen Clark
Open Mon - Fri 10 AM - 4 PM, Sat & Sun 1 - 4 PM. No admis fee. Estab 1976.
Average Annual Attendance: 60,000. Mem: 1000; annual dues $5-$10,000
Income: Financed by endowment, membership, city and county appropriations,
grants
Collections: 14th - 18th century drawings, graphics, decorative arts; 19th -
20th century American and English paintings
Exhibitions: (1982-83) The Sara Roby Foundation Collection; Annual Christmas
Exhibition: Holiday Forest; The Academic Approach (one-person exhibitions by
art faculty members); The Naive Approach, Kentucky's Primitive Painters; The
Regionalists: Three Dimensional Forms; 116th American Watercolor Society
Exhibition; Watercolor East and West; Aqueous '83, the Kentucky Watercolor
Society's annual watercolor competition; (1983-84) The Kentucky Tradition in
American Landscape Painting: From the Early 19th Century to the Present;
Kentucky Quilts; Helen Turner: A Retrospective (1858-1958); Area Architecture:
1840 to the Present; Kentucky Expatriates; Mid America Biennial, a national
juried exhibition
Publications: Exhibition catalogues; newsletters
Activities: Classes for adults and children; docent training; dramatic programs;
seminars & critiques led by major American artists; lectures open to the public,
8-10 vis lectrs per year; concerts; gallery talks; tours; competitions with awards;
pre-visit visits to the classroom; film series; individual & original objects of art
lent to museums; book traveling exhibitions; traveling exhibitions organized and
circulated; museum shop sells books, original art, reproductions, prints
L **Library,** 901 Frederica Street, 42301. Tel 502-685-3181
Open Mon - Fri 10 AM - 4 PM, Sat & Sun 1 - 4 PM, cl holidays. Estab 1977
Library Holdings: Vols 2,000; Per subs 15; AV — Slides, v-tapes; Other —
Clipping files, exhibition catalogs, manuscripts, pamphlets, photographs,
reproductions
Collections: 19th & 20th century American & English paintings, drawings &
graphics; 14th - 18th century decorative arts
Publications: Exhibition brochures and catalogs
Activities: Classes for adults and children; docent training; lectures open to
public, 12-20 vis lectr per yr; concerts; gallery talks; tours; sponsor Mid America
Biennial Exhibition; purchase awards; 6 book traveling exhibitions per yr

PADUCAH

O **PADUCAH ART GUILD,** 200 Broadway, PO Box 634, 42001. Tel 502-442-2453. *Pres* Juanita Gilliam; *Dir* Earl W Lock; *VPres* Barbara Livingston; *Secy* Jane Bright; *Treas* Dick Holland
Open Tues - Sat 10 AM - 4 PM, Sun 1 - 5 PM, cl Mon & major holidays. No
admis fee. Estab 1957 as a non profit cultural and educational institution to
provide the community and the membership with visual art exhibitions, classes
and related activities of the highest quality. Average Annual Attendance: 10,000.
Mem: Monthly programs and membership meetings
Income: $35,000 (membership fees, donations, commissions, grants)
Collections: Primarily regional/contemporary with some 19th century works on
paper & Japanese prints; †teaching collection
Exhibitions: Changing exhibitions of historical and contemporary art of regional,
national, and international nature; Two regional juried art shows held annually
Publications: Monthly Newsletter
Activities: Classes for children and adults; workshops; lectures open to public, 4
vis lectr per yr; demonstrations; gallery talks; receptions; special fund raising
events; competitions with awards; individual and original objects of art lent to
qualified institutions; originate traveling exhibitions; sales shop sells books,
original art and regional crafts

RUSSELL

C **ASHLAND OIL, INC,** 1000 Ashland Dr (Mailing add: PO Box 391, Ashland,
41114). Tel 606-329-3283, 329-3333. *Dir* Teo Nutini
Collection may be viewed through special arrangements. Estab 1972, primary
function is decorative art, but also to establish a creative atmosphere; to enhance
community cultural life. Collection displayed in public areas of corporate office
buildings
Collections: Mainly contemporary printmaking, emphasis on Americans;
paintings, sculpture, wall hangings
Activities: Tours; competitions; sponsorship consists of purchase awards for local
art group and museum competitions; provides purchase and merit awards for
certain museum and university competitions; individual objects of art lent;
originate traveling exhibitions to museums, colleges, universities and art centers
in general marketing areas

WILMORE

M **ASBURY COLLEGE,** Student Center Gallery,* Lexington Ave, 40390. Tel 606-858-3511. *Head Art Dept* Dr Rudy Medlock
Open 1 - 9 PM. No admis fee. Estab 1976 for the purpose of exhibiting the
works of national, local, and student artists. Carpeted walls, and tract lighting in
a 20 by 20 ft space. Average Annual Attendance: 2000
Publications: Newsletter
Activities: Classes for children; dramatic programs; lect open to public, 6 vis lectr
per yr; gallery talks; competitions

LOUISIANA

ALEXANDRIA

M **CENTRAL LOUISIANA ART ASSOCIATION,** Alexandria Museum Visual
Art Center,* 933 Main St, PO Box 1028, 71301. Tel 318-443-3458. *Pres* Mrs
Malcolm Holloway; *VPres* Thilo Steinschulte; *Secy* Mrs William Long; *Dir*
Timothy S Allen; *Chief Cur & Registrar* Sheila Stewart; *Cur Educ* Wendy Starn
Open Tues - Fri 9 AM - 5 PM, Sat 10 AM - 2 PM. No admis fee. Estab 1977, to
encourage appreciation, education and active participation in art and culture; and
to sponsor exhibitions. Gallery is located in an 1890's bank with 2014 sq ft of
installation space, with a 20 ft ceiling and track lighting; gallery is the only
facility in Central and North Louisiana for hanging exhibits of major size.
Average Annual Attendance: 10,000. Mem: 900; dues Presidents Club $1000, to
individual $10; annual meeting April
Income: $175,000 (financed by membership, grants, state and city
appropriations)
Purchases: $5000
Collections: Permanent collection of art work by 20th century artists
Exhibitions: Travers Green: Watercolors; Louisiana Collegiate Competition;
Clyde Connel: Sculpture; Paul Harris: Soft Sculpture; Louisiana Painters of the
Past Decade; Salvadore Pecararo; The Wichner Collection; Southern Illinois
Foundry Exhibition: Multiples
Publications: Museum News, monthly; Doing It Right and Passing It On: North
Louisiana Folk Art Catalog; Common Ground, fibers competition catalog;
newsletter, quarterly
Activities: Classes for adults and chilren; docent training; workshops;
demonstrations; lect open to the public, 6 visiting lectrs per year; gallery talks;
tours; competitions; awards; individual paintings and original objects of art lent;
lending collection contains original art works, original prints, paintings; book
traveling exhibitions; traveling exhibitions organized and circulated; museum
shop sells books, original art, reproductions, prints, crafts

BATON ROUGE

M **JAY R BROUSSARD MEMORIAL GALLERIES,** Division of the Arts, Old
State Capitol, Corner North Blvd & River Rd, PO Box 44247, 70804. Tel 504-925-3930. *Div of the Arts Exec Dir* Albert B Head; *Visual Arts Coordr* Kevin
Brown
No admis fee. Estab 1938 as showcase of visual arts and crafts in Louisiana,
particularly contemporary work. Contemporary collection housed in National
Historic Landmark (Gothic revival building 1848). Standing collection includes
400 works, including works circulated under art in public places program. Closed
during building renovation. Average Annual Attendance: 85,000
Income: $80,000 (financed by state appropriation)
Purchases: $60,000
Collections: †Louisiana artists
Publications: Exhibition Catalogs
Activities: Lectures, 6 vis lectr per year; concerts; gallery talks; tours; variety of
competitions; awards; scholarships; individual 400 paintings and original objects
of art lent to non-profit tax exempt agencies; lending collection contains original
prints, paintings, photographs and sculpture; originate traveling exhibitions to tax
exempt non-profit agencies in Louisiana
L **Library,** 70804
Library Holdings: Vols 200; Per subs 6; AV — A-tapes, cassettes, fs,
Kodachromes, lantern slides, motion pictures, slides, v-tapes; Other — Clipping
files, exhibition catalogs, original art works, pamphlets, photographs, sculpture

M **LOUISIANA ARTS AND SCIENCE CENTER,** 100 S River Rd, PO Box 3373,
70821. Tel 504-344-9463. *Exec Dir* Carol S Gikas
Open Tues - Sat 10 AM - 4:30 PM, Sun 1 - 4:30 PM, cl Mon. Admis
Planetarium only adults $1.50, children $.50. Estab 1960. General museum - art,
history and science. Center administers the Riverside Museum in the renovated
Old Illinois Central Railroad Station with an auditorium, restaurant & sculpture
garden. Museum contains changing & permanent exhibits of art, Louisiana
history & science. Center administers the Zeiss Planetarium & Old Governor's
Mansion, a restored historic house.. Average Annual Attendance: 300,000. Mem:
Dues $15 - $1000
Income: Financed by membership, city appropriation and donations
Collections: 18th & 20th century European & American paintings; contemporary
photographs; Clementine Hunter paintings; Ivan Mestrovic; sculpture; Egyptian
artifacts; Eskimo graphics & soapstone carvings; North American Indian crafts;
Tibetan religious art; memorabilia of former Louisiana governors; graphics;
North American Indian crafts; Tibetan religious art
Exhibitions: Changing & permanent collection; Country Store & Acadian House;
Egyptian Mummies & Artifacts; Miniature Train; Discovery Depot, a
participatory gallery that introduces children to art
Publications: Happenings, Heavenly Facts, quarterly
Activities: Classes for adults & children; docent training; lectures open to public;
concerts; gallery talks; tours; book traveling exhibitions; museum shop
L **Library,** 100 S River Rd, 70821
Small reference library open to staff only

LOUISIANA STATE UNIVERSITY

M **Anglo-American Art Museum,** 114 Memorial Tower, 70803. Tel 504-388-40003. *Pres* Mrs Bert S Turner; *Secy* John C Fisher; *Dir & Cur* H Parrott Bacot
Open Mon - Fri 8 AM - Noon & 12:30 - 4:30 PM; Sat 9 AM - Noon & 1 - 4 PM; Sun 1 - 4 PM. No admis fee. Estab 1959 to serve as a constant reminder of the major cultural heritage the United States received from the British People. Two temporary galleries house loan exhibitions and local art work. Average Annual Attendance: 25,000. Mem: 400; dues $10 - $25
Income: Financed by endowment, membership & state funds
Special Subjects: Hogarth and Caroline Durieux Graphics Collection, New Orleans Silver
Collections: Hogarth & Caroline Durieux (largest collection of graphic works); early Baton Rouge subjects; early New Orleans-made silver (largest public collection); English and American drawings, decorative arts, paintings, watercolors
Exhibitions: (1984) Rhoda B Stokes: A Retrospective
Publications: Catalogues; newsletter
Activities: Lect, 2 vis lectr per year; gallery talks; tours; competitions; originate traveling exhibitions

L **Anglo-American Art Museum Library,** 114 Memorial Tower, 70803
Reference library
Library Holdings: Vols 600; Per subs 7
Special Subjects: Anglo-American decorative arts, drawings, paintings

M **Union Art Gallery,*** PO Box BU, 70803. Tel 504-388-5117. *Art Dir* Judith R Stahl
Open Mon - Fri 9 AM - 5 PM, Sat & Sun Noon - 5 PM. Estab 1964, designed for exhibitions for university and community interests. Gallery is centrally located on the main floor of the LSU Union with 1725 sq ft. Average Annual Attendance: 55,000
Publications: Brochures for local exhibitions, quarterly
Activities: Lect open to public, 2 vis lectr per year; free art films

L **Union Art Gallery Library,*** PO Box BU, 70803. Tel 504-388-5117
Collections: Photography Collection

M **Dept of Fine Arts Gallery,*** 114 Memorial Tower, 70803. Tel 504-388-5402. *Head Department* Dr Walter E Rutkowski
Open daily 8 AM - 5 PM. No admis fee. Estab 1934 for special exhibitions planned by faculty committee. Circulates exhibitions of student's arts consisting of 30 - 40 works by students. Average Annual Attendance: 10,000
Collections: Department collection of contemporary graphic works, prints and drawings
Activities: Lect; gallery talks

L **Design Resource Center,*** 136 Atkinson Hall, 70803. Tel 504-388-2665. *Librn* Doris A Wheeler
Estab 1959
Library Holdings: Vols 7600; Per subs 90; VF 12; AV — Slides 10,100
Special Subjects: Architecture, Interior Design, Landscape Architecture, Restoration & Conservation

L **SOUTHERN UNIVERSITY,** Art and Architecture Library, Southern University Post Office Branch, 70813. Tel 504-771-3290. *Librn* Dorothy Lewis
Open Mon - Fri 8 AM - 10:45 PM. Estab 1971, to encourage support of fine arts and architecture. Circ 12,000
Income: Financed by state appropriation
Library Holdings: Vols 5200; Per subs 92; Micro — Fiche, reels; AV — Cassettes, motion pictures, slides; Other — Pamphlets

JENNINGS

M **ZIGLER MUSEUM,** 411 Clara St, 70546. Tel 318-824-0114. *Chmn Board Trustees* Mrs C A Storer; *Pres Board Trustees* Walter C Peters; *Dir* Ivan Mira; *Dir* Evalyn Mira
Open Tues - Fri 10 AM - Noon & 2 - 4:30 PM, Sat & Sun 2 - 4:30 PM, cl Mon. No admis fee. Estab 1963 to create an art gallery for Southwest Louisiana. West Wing has permanent collection of American and European paintings and sculptures. East Wing contains nine dioramas of Southwest Louisiana wild life. Central Galleries are reserved for a new art exhibit each month. Average Annual Attendance: 15,000
Collections: Bierstadt; Chierici; Constable; Crane; Gay; Heldner; George Inness Jr; Pearce; Pissarro; Reynolds; Sloan; Frank Smith; Vergne; Whistler; Gustave Wolff; Robert Wood; Sculpture: Euphemia Glover; Charles Parks
Exhibitions: Twenty-four Louisiana Artists
Publications: Brochure
Activities: Docent training, art appreciation

LAFAYETTE

M **LAFAYETTE NATURAL HISTORY MUSEUM, PLANETARIUM AND NATURE STATION,** 637 Girard Park Dr, 70503. Tel 318-261-8350. *Pres* John T Green III; *VPres* Sylvia P Ross; *Secy* Mary Jane Broadhurst; *Dir* Beverly D Latimer; *Cur of Exhibits* Allision H Pena; *Cur of Natural Science* Diane Laborde; *Cur of Planetarium* David Hostetter; *Asst Naturalist* Stephen Shively; *Registrar* Kathy Ball; *Secy* Rose Must
Open Mon, Wed, Fri 9 AM - 5 PM, Tues, Thurs 9 AM - 9 PM, Sat, Sun 1 - 5 PM. No admis fee except to out of parish school groups-$1 per student. Estab 1969 to provide a focus on the physical world in order to benefit the citizens of the community. 30 by 130 space with architectural glass window walls, interior walls constructed as needed. Average Annual Attendance: 60,000. Mem: 900; annual meeting in Oct
Income: $250,000 (financed by membership, city appropriation)
Purchases: $4000
Collections: Acadian artifacts; Audubon prints; Historical Louisiana maps; Louisiana Indian artifacts; Louisiana landscape art; Louisiana related Harper's Weekly prints; Louisiana shells; Louisiana moths & butterfiles
Exhibitions: L'Amour de Maman: the Acadian Textile Heritage; Life in the Louisiana Marsh; Elemore Morgan, Jr: Paintings, Drawings & Photographs; Outlook Universe; Waterways of Louisiana; Wildflowers of Louisiana; Rain or Shine: Louisiana Weather
Activities: Classes for adults and children; docent training; lectures open to public, 2 lectr per yr; sponsor juried contemporary craft show; cash awards; lending collection contains 20 nature artifacts, original art works, 400 photos, 1000 slides, 200 Louisiana Indian & Acadian artifacts; book traveling exhibitions; originate traveling exhibitions in Louisiana; shop sells books, regional crafts, posters and souvenirs

UNIVERSITY OF SOUTHWESTERN LOUISIANA

M **University Art Museum,** PO Drawer 42571, 70504. Tel 318-231-5326. *Dir* Herman M Hire; *Dir Foundation* Nancy Ricahrd; *Asst to Dir* Lou Rabe
Open Mon - Fri 10 AM - 4 PM, cl Sat. No admis fee. Estab 1968 as an art museum, for education of the population of the region. Average Annual Attendance: 36,000. Mem: Dues $1000 - $10
Income: Financed by membership, university, university foundation, state & federal grants
Collections: Paintings by 19th & 20th century American artists; 19th century Japanese prints
Exhibitions: Victorian Decorative Arts in Louisiana (1837-1901); American Pop Art; Robert Ramschenberg; Arakawa; Van Deren Coke; East Indian Textiles; West African Sculpture & Textiles; Images of the Eighties: Washington Photography from the Corcoran; Architectural Drawings of the Italian Renaissance; Tribal Weavings: Persia & Afghanistan; Henry Botkin: Paintings, Drawings, Collages, 1928-1981; Tina Gironard; SECCA Seven VI; Peruvian Colonial Paintings; 20th Century Sculpture from The Virlane Foundation
Publications: Newsletter, quarterly
Activities: Classes for adults and children; docent training; lectures open to the public; concerts; gallery talks; tours;; traveling exhibitions organized and circulated

LAKE CHARLES

M **IMPERIAL CALCASIEU MUSEUM,** 204 W Sallier St, 70601. Tel 318-439-3797. *Dir* Samuel B Carleton
Open Mon - Sat 10 AM - Noon, Sun 2 - 5 PM. No admis fee. Estab March 1963 by the Junior League of Lake Charles and housed in City Hall. After several moves in location, the museum is now housed in a building of Louisiana Colonial architecture which incorporates in its structure old bricks, beams, balustrades, and columns taken from demolished old homes. In December 1966 administration was assumed by The Fine Arts Center and Museum of Old Imperial Calcasieu Museum, Inc, with a name change in 1971. Site of the building was chosen for its historic value, having been owned by the Charles Sallier family, the first white settler on the lake, and the town named for him. The museum depicts the early history of the area. Average Annual Attendance: 12,500. Mem: 150; dues $12 - $350
Income: Financed by membership
Collections: Artifacts of the Victorian Period, especially Late Victorian
Exhibitions: American Indian Artifacts in Calcasieu Collections; Antique Quilts and Coverlets; Calcasieu People and Places in 19th Century Photographs; Christmas Around The World; special exhibitions every six weeks, with smaller exhibits by other organizations at times
Activities: Tours; museum shop sells books and museum stationery

M **Gibson Barham Gallery,** 204 W Sallier St, Lake Charles, 70601
Activities: Lectures open to the public; gallery talks

L **Gibson Library,** 204 W Sallier St, 70601. *Dir* Open; *Secy* Kathleen Collins
Open Mon - Fri 10 AM - Noon & 2 - 5 PM, Sat 10 AM - Noon, Sun 2 - 5 PM. Estab 1971, to display early school books, bibles, etc. Reference Library
Income: Financed by memberships, memorials & gifts
Library Holdings: Vols 100; Per subs 100; AV — A-tapes, cassettes, slides, v-tapes; Other — Memorabilia, original art works, pamphlets, photographs, sculpture
Collections: Audubon animal paintings; Audubon bird paintings; Calcasieu photographs; Boyd Cruise
Exhibitions: History of Imperial Calcasieu Parish, with settings & objects

MONROE

M **TWIN CITY ART FOUNDATION,** Masur Museum of Art, 1400 S Grand St, 71201. Tel 318-329-2237. *Dir* William C Pratt
Open Tues - Thurs 10 AM - 6 PM, Fri - Sun 2 - 5 PM. No admis fee. Estab 1963 to encourage art in all media and to enrich the cultural climate of this area. Gallery has 500 running ft hanging space. Average Annual Attendance: 5000. Mem: 250; dues $200, $100, $50, $25
Income: $46,000 (financed by membership and appropriations)
Purchases: $3000
Collections: †Contemporary art all media, approximately 100 works
Publications: Brochures of shows, monthly
Activities: Classes for adults and children; lectures open to public, 4 vis lectr per yr; tours; competitions

NEW IBERIA

M **SHADOWS-ON-THE-TECHE,** 117 East Main St, PO Box 254, 70560. Tel 318-369-6446. *Dir* Shereen H Minivielle
Open daily 9 AM - 4:30 PM, cl Christmas, New Years Day and Thanksgiving Day. Admis adults $4, students $2, group rates available. The Shadows is a property of the National Trust for Historic Preservation. Preserved as a historic house museum; operated as a community preservation center, it is a National Historic Landmark. A townhouse on the Bayou Teche, it faces the main street of modern New Iberia, but is surrounded by three acres of landscaped gardens shaded by live oaks. Built in 1831, the Shadows represents a Louisiana adaptation of classical revival architecture. Fashionable balls and masquerades as well as everyday activities are reflected in the possessions of four generations of the Weeks family on display in the house. It fell into ruin after the Civil War, but was restored during the 1920's by Weeks Hall, great grandson of the builder Mr

Hall bequeathed the Shadows to the National Trust in 1958. Property serves as a focal point for advancement of historic preservation, it develops new relationships among cultural community preservation groups and National Trust members in its area. Responds to community preservation needs by acting as a link between community and appropriate regional or headquarters offices of National Trust. Average Annual Attendance: 30,000. Mem: 300
Income: Financed by memberships in Friends of the Shadows, admission fees & special events
Collections: Paintings by Louisiana's itinerant artist Adrian Persac (1857-72); paintings by Weeks Hall; furnishings typical of those owned by a planter's family between 1830 and 1865
Activities: Docent training; interpretive programs which are related to the Shadows historic preservation program; Members Day during National Historic Preservation Week; concerts; tours; museum shop sells books, original art and prints

NEW ORLEANS

M **HISTORIC NEW ORLEANS COLLECTION,** Kemper and Leila Williams Foundation, 533 Royal St, 70130. Tel 504-523-4662. *Chmn of Board* Benjamin W Yancey; *Dir* Stanton M Frazar; *Chief Cur* Dode Platou; *Cur* John Mahe; *Cur & Syst Dir* Rosanne McCaffrey; *Cur* John Lawrence; *Registrar* Priscilla O'Reilly; *Education Cur* Elsa Schneider; *Dir Publications & Academic Affairs* Patricia Schmit
Open Tues - Sat 10 AM - 4:45 PM. No admis fee to Gallery, admis to Williams Residence and ten gallery tour by guide $2. Building constructed in 1792 by Jean Francois Merieult; recently renovated by Koch & Wilson to accommodate the ten galleries which house a collection of paintings, prints, documents, books & artifacts relating to the history of Louisiana from the time of its settlement, gathered over a number of years by the late L Kemper Williams & his wife. The foundation was established with private funds to keep original collection intact & to allow for expansion. Average Annual Attendance: 35,000
Income: Financed by endowment
Collections: Charles L Franck, photographs (1900-1955); Dan Leyrer, photographs (1930-1970); Clarence Laughlin, photographs (1935-1965); James Gallier Jr & Sr, architectural drawings (1830-1870); Morries Henry Hobbs, prints (1940); B Lafon, drawings of fortifications (1841); B Simon, lithographs of 19th-century businesses; Alfred R & William Waud, drawings of Civil War & post-war; †maps, †paintings, †photographs, †prints, †three-dimensional objects
Exhibitions: Alfred R Waud, Special Artist on Assignment (Profiles of American Cities 1850-1880); Crescent City Silver (19th-Century New Orleans Silver & Silversmiths); The Changing Face of Canal Street; The Roast of the Town (coffee); It's the Law; Charles H Reinike (watercolors); Joseph Rusling Meeker: Images of the Mississippi Delta, painting; Off the Track: Southern Plantation Photographs; Piney Woods People; In Dixieland I'll Take My Stand: Confederate Music of Civil War; Orleans Gallery: The Founders, painting & sculpture; Bound to Please, books; Music in the Street: Photographs by Ralston Crawford; I Remember New Orleans: The Movies; Sugar Bowl 50th Anniversary; Rex, Mardi Gras Memorabilia; Louisiana Alphabet
Publications: Guide to Research at the Historic New Orleans Collection; exhibition brochures & catalogs; historic publications; monograph series
Activities: Docent training; lectures open to public; tours; competitions with awards; gallery talks; individual paintings & original objects of art lent to museums, institutions, foundations, libraries & research centers; lending collection contains 2500 original prints, 200 paintings, 125,000 photographs, 100 sculptures, 6000 rare pamphlets; sales shop sells books, original art, reproductions and prints

L **Library,** 533 Royal St, 70130. Tel 504-523-4662. *Head Librn* Florence Jumonville
Open Tues - Sat 10 AM - 4:30 PM. Open to researchers
Income: Financed by private endowment
Library Holdings: Vols 12,000; Per subs 50; Maps 500; AV — Motion pictures 100; Other — Pamphlets 15,000
Special Subjects: Material pertaining to Louisiana, New Orleans architecture
Collections: Archives Division: unique textural sources on New Orleans and Louisiana History and Culture (broadsides, libretti, newspapers, sheet music)
Publications: The Vieux Carre Survey, a guide to a collection of material on New Orleans architecture

M **LOUISIANA DEPARTMENT OF CULTURE, RECREATION AND TOURISM,** Louisiana State Museum,* 751 Chartres St, PO Box 2458, 70176. Tel 504-568-6968. *Pres* William Cristovich; *VPres* Roulhac Toledano; *Secy* Mary Davis; *Dir* Robert R Macdonald; *Chief Cur Museum Services* Vaugh Glasgow; *Chief Cur Education* Tamra Carboni; *Registrar* Amy Husten
Open Tues - Sun 9 AM - 5 PM. Admis adult $1, student $.50, educational groups free by appointment. Estab 1906, to collect, preserve and present original materials illustrating Louisiana's heritage. Gallery is maintained, and has eight historic buildings containing paintings, prints, maps and photographs. Average Annual Attendance: 320,000. Mem: 2500; dues $10; annual meeting May
Income: $2,580,000 (financed by state appropriation)
Purchases: $40,000
Collections: Carnival costumes (200 items); Colonial documents (500,000 folios); †decorative art (8000 items); †flat textiles (1000 items); historic costumes (6000 items); jazz and Louisiana music (40,000 objects); Louisiana silver (300); maps and cartography (2500); Newcomb pottery and allied arts (750); †paintings (1500 canvases); †photography (70,000 images); †post Colonial manuscripts (500,000); †prints (3000 works); †rare Louisiana books (40,000); sculpture (125 works)
Exhibitions: L'Amour de Maman: The Acadian Textile Heritage; Louisiana's Legal Heritage; John Henry Belter and the Rococo Revival; Recent Accessions; Played with Immense Success; Matters of Life and Death
Publications: Louisiana's Black Heritage; Louisiana Portrait Gallery, Vol I
Activities: Classes for children; docent training; lect open to the public, 4-6 visiting lectrs per year; tours; artmobile; individual paintings and original objects of art lent to museums; book traveling exhibitions, 2-4 per year; originate traveling exhibitions, circulated through SITES; museum shop sells books, original art, reproductions, prints, maps and crafts

L **Louisiana Historical Center Library,*** 400 Esplande Ave (Mailing add: 751 Chartres St, 70116). Tel 504-568-8214. *Chief Cur* Dr Edward F Haas; *Archives* Dr Steve Webre; *Librn* Rose Lambert
Archives open by appointment only Tues - Fri 8:30 AM - 5 PM. Estab 1930, to collect materials related to Louisiana heritage
Library Holdings: Vols 40,000; Per subs 5; Non-circulating Louisiana historical material; Other — Clipping files
Special Subjects: Colonial judicial documents

O **LOUISIANA HISTORICAL ASSOCIATION,** Confederate Museum, 929 Camp St, 70130. Tel 405-523-4522. *Chmn Memorial Hall Committee* Bernard Eble; *Cur* Pat Eynard
Open Mon - Sat 10 AM - 4 PM. Admis adults $2, students & sr citizens $1, children $.50. Estab 1891 to collect and display articles, memorabilia and records from Louisiana history and particularly the era surrounding the Civil War. Gallery is maintained in a one story brick building; one main hall paneled in cypress, one side hall containing paintings of Civil War figures and display cases containing artifacts. Average Annual Attendance: 13,000. Mem: 2000; dues $8; annual meeting March
Income: Financed by membership and admissions
Publications: Louisiana Historical Association Newsletter; Louisiana History, quarterly
Activities: Lect open to the public; competitions; sales shop sells books, reproductions and novelties

M **NEW ORLEANS ACADEMY OF FINE ARTS GALLERY,*** 5256 Magazine St, 70115. Tel 504-899-8111. *Dir* Allison Collins

M **NEW ORLEANS MUSEUM OF ART,** Lelong Ave, PO Box 19123, 70179. Tel 504-488-2631. *Dir* E John Bullard; *Pres of Board* Ernest A Carrere Jr; *Asst Dir for Art* William A Fagaly; *Asst Dir for Admin* Jaqueline Sullivan; *Asst Dir for Develop* Barbara Neiswender; *Chief Cur Collections* Valerie L Olsen; *Cur Decorative Arts* John W Keefe; *Cur European Paintings* Edward P Caraco; *Cur Photography* Nancy Barrett; *Research Fellow Japanese Art* Patricia Fister; *Adjunct Cur Japanese Art* Stephen Addiss; *Adjunct Cur Photography* Tina Freeman; *Registrar* Dan Piersol; *Asst Registrar & Cur Travelling Exhibitions* Paul Tarver; *Principal Cur Education* Alice Rae Yelen; *AV Coordr* Debra Bryant; *Chief Preparator* Thomas E Herrington
Open Tues - Sun 10 AM - 5 PM, cl Mon. Admis adults (18-64) $2, children (3-17) $1. Estab 1911; building given to city by Isaac Delgado, maintained by municipal funds to provide a stimulus to a broader cultural life for the entire community. Stern Auditorium, Ella West Freeman wing for changing exhibitions; Wisner Education wing for learning experiences; Delgado Building for permanent display; Hyams Room for Barbizon and late 19th century salon painting. Average Annual Attendance: 150,000. Mem: 10,000; dues $20 - $100; annual meeting Nov
Income: Financed by membership, city appropriation, federal, state & foundation grants, corporate contributions & individual donations
Collections: †Victor Kiam Collection of Fauve and Surrealist Paintings; Samuel H Kress Collection of Renaissance Masterpieces; Latter-Schlesinger Collection of Portrait Miniatures; Stern-Davis Collection of Peruvian Colonial Painting; †African Art; †Graphics; †Latin American Colonial Painting and Sculpture; Japanese Painting of the Edo Period; †19th and 20th Century American Art; 19th and 20th Century Louisiana Painting and Furniture; †Old Masters Paintings of various schools; †Pre-Columbian Masterworks
Exhibitions: Photography in Louisiana; Contemporary Art of Senegal; Treasures from Chatsworth; Gold of El Dorado; The Art of the Muppets; Creativity, the Human Resoure; Elena Karina; Art, Myth & Culture: Greek Vases from Southern Collections; The Search for Alexander; Edward Weston & Clarence John Laughlin; Lisette Model; Photographs of Mother Saint Croix; The Geometric Impulse: The Lillian Florsheim Foundation Collection; Constructivism & the Geometric Tradition: The McCrory Corporation Collection; Louisiana World Exposition International Water Sculpture Competition; The Faberge Collection from the Matilda Geddings Gray Foundation; Paintings from the Royal Academy; Great Architectural Drawings from the Royal Institute of British Architects; Elizabeth Catlett; A Myriad of Autumn Leaves: Japanese Art from the Kurt & Millie Gitter Collection; 1983 New Orleans Triennial
Publications: Arts Quarterly; catalogs of exhibitions
Activities: Classes for children; docent training; lect open to public, 20 vis lectr per year; concerts; gallery talks; tours; competitions; individual paintings and original objects of art lent to museums; book traveling exhibitions 5 per year; originate traveling exhibitions; museum shop sells books, original art, reproductions, prints, cards, toys and jewelry

L **Felix J Dreyfous Library,** Lelong Ave, PO Box 19123, 70179. *Librn* Jeanette Downing; *Library Asst* Nancy Jacobs; *Library Asst* Barry Cantin
Open Mon - Fri 9 AM - 5 PM. Estab 1971 to provide information for reference to the curators, museum members and art researchers. Open to staff and members; general public by appointment
Income: Financed by membership, donations and gifts
Library Holdings: Vols 10,000; Per subs 115; Micro — Fiche, reels; AV — Slides; Other — Clipping files, exhibition catalogs, photographs
Special Subjects: Photography, African art, Pre-Columbian art
Collections: WPA Project - New Orleans Artists

TULANE UNIVERSITY

M **University Art Collection,*** Tulane University Library, 7001 Freret St, 70118. Tel 504-865-5685. *Cur* William R Cullison
Open Mon - Fri 8:30 AM - 5 PM, Sat 10 AM - Noon, cl school holidays and Marti Gras. No admis fee. Estab 1889
Collections: Architectural Drawings; Photograph Collection; 19th and 20th century European and American Paintings and Prints; 19th and 20th century Japanese Block Prints
Activities: Lectures

M **Dept Art Newcomb Col Art Galleries,** 1229 Broadway, New Orleans, 70118. Tel 504-865-4631. *Chmn & Dir Galleries* John Clemmer
Open Tues - Fri 9 AM - 4:30 PM, Sat & Sun (during exhibitions) 1 - 5 PM. Average Annual Attendance: 5000 - 7000

Exhibitions: Exhibitions as an integral part of the Art Department Program
Activities: Lectures open to the public, 10 - 12 vis lectr per yr; gallery talks; tours; awards; scholarships; book traveling exhibitions, 2 - 3 per yr; originate traveling exhibitions

L **Architecture Library,** Howard-Tilton Memorial Library, Rm 202 Richardson Memorial Hall, 70118. Tel 504-865-5391. *Head* Frances E Hecker
Open fall & spring Mon - Thurs 8 AM - 9:50 PM, Fri 8 AM - 4:50 PM, Sat 10 AM - 4:50 PM, Sun 2 - 9:50 PM; summer Mon - Fri 8:30 AM - 4:50 PM, cl Sat & Sun
Library Holdings: Vols 7802; Per subs 163; Other — Clipping files, prints
Special Subjects: Architecture

M **UNIVERSITY OF NEW ORLEANS,** Fine Arts Gallery, Lake Front Dr, 70148. Tel 504-286-6493. *Gallery Dir* Ron Todd; *Secy* Molly Guarisco
Open Mon - Fri 8 AM - 4:30 PM. No admis fee. Estab 1974 to expose the students and community to historic and contemporary visual arts. Gallery consists of 1800 sq ft, 165 lineal ft of wall space, 20 ft ceilings, natural and artificial lighting. Average Annual Attendance: 15,000
Income: Financed by state appropriation
Activities: Classes for adults; lectures open to public, 10 vis lectr per yr; gallery talks; tours; book traveling exhibitions

PORT ALLEN

M **WEST BATON ROUGE MUSEUM,** 845 N Jefferson Ave, 70767. Tel 504-383-2392. *Pres & Dir Art* Mary Jane Kahao; *Cur* Mary Vlcek Pramuk; *Custodian* Laura Mae Dunstane; *Asst Custodian* Dorothy Landry; *Exhib Chmn* Evelyn B Terrill
Open Tues - Sat 10 AM - 4:30 PM. No admis fee. Estab 1968, Museum opened 1970, to foster interest in history, particularly that of West Baton Rouge Parish; to encourage research, collection and preservation of material illustrating past and present activities of the parish; to operate one or more museums; to receive gifts and donations; to accept exhibits and historical materials on loan. One room housing a collection of American Empire (circa 1840) bedroom furniture; a large room housing a scale model of a sugar mill (one to one, dated 1904) with a plantation railroad and parish memorabilia, two old printing presses; a room 31 x 40 ft for art exhibits; restored plantation quarters cabin (circa 1850). Average Annual Attendance: 6000. Mem: 235; dues $10; annual meeting Jan
Income: $44,500 (financed by membership, gifts and millage levied on parish)
Collections: †Art collection of parish artists; †contemporary Louisiana paintings, drawings & prints, sculpture; †needlework; †Newcomb pottery; old duck decoys
Exhibitions: The Peaceable Kingdom; Photography in Louisiana: The Documentary Photograph; Alice Peak Reiss; Useful Objects-Handmade; Wooden Imposters V; Miserere-Rouault Prints; A View of the Water; The West Bank Collects: Fine & Decorative Art; A Sugar Parish Revisted: West Baton Rouge 1890 to 1910; Ann Harding, paintings
Publications: Ecoutez, twice a year
Activities: Gallery talks; tours; competitions

SAINT MARTINVILLE

M **ACADIAN HOUSE MUSEUM,*** Hwy 31, PO Box 497, 70582. Tel 318-394-4284. *Historic Site Mgr* Michael Henderson; *Cur Asst* Charles R Brassieur
Open Mon - Sat 9 AM - 5 PM, Sun 1 - 5 PM. Admin $1 per carload. Estab 1931 to display and describe 18th century French lifeways & folk items. Artworks are displayed in an 18th century plantation home, in the visitors center of the park and in the craft shop
Income: Financed by state appropriations
Collections: Early 19th century portraits; 18th, 19th & 20th century textile arts; religious art of the 19th century; wood carvings; local craft & folk art
Activities: Lectures open to public, tours; museum shop sells books, craft and folk items and original art work

SHREVEPORT

M **CENTENARY COLLEGE OF LOUISIANA,** Meadows Museum of Art, 2911 Centenary Blvd, PO Box 4188, 71104. Tel 318-869-5169. *Cur* Willard Cooper; *Programs Dir* Judy Godfrey
Open Tues - Fri 1 - 5 PM, Sat & Sun 2 - 5 PM. No admis fee. Estab 1975 to house the Indo-China Collection of Drawings & Paintings by Jean Despujols. Eight galleries; main gallery on first floor 25 x 80 ft; other galleries 25 x 30 ft; linen walls, track lights and no windows. Average Annual Attendance: 6000
Income: $60,000 (financed by endowment)
Collections: 360 works in Indo-China Collection, dealing with Angkor Region, The Cordillera, Gulf of Siam, Laos, The Nam-Te, The Thai, Upper Tonkin, Vietnam
Exhibitions: Charles Burchfield; Edward Hopper, German Expressionists; Leonardo da Vinci Exhibit; Centennial Celebration of American Cut Glass; Olga Hirshhorn Collection; John Sloan; American Indian Art; William T Richards
Publications: Partial Catalog of Permanent Collection with 21 color plates
Activities: Docent training; lectures open to public, 4 vis lectr per yr; gallery talks; tours; competitions with awards; individual paintings & original objects of art lent to qualified museums

M **LOUISIANA STATE EXHIBIT MUSEUM,*** 3015 Greenwood Rd, 71109. Tel 318-635-2323. *Dir* R E Baremore Jr
Open Mon - Sat 9 AM - 5 PM, Sun 1 - 5 PM, cl Christmas. No admis fee. Estab 1939 to display permanent and temporary exhibitions demonstrating the state's history, resources and natural beauty. Art Gallery is maintained. Average Annual Attendance: 600,000
Income: Financed by state appropriation
Collections: Archaeology; china; coins; dioramas; glass; historical relics; Indian artifacts; murals
Publications: History of Art; brochures
Activities: Art workshops; films; concerts

M **R W NORTON ART GALLERY,** 4747 Creswell Ave, 71106. Tel 318-865-4201. *Pres of the Board* Mrs Richard W Norton Jr; *Building & Grounds Supt* Frank Todaro; *VPres of the Board* A W Coon
Open Tues - Sun 1 - 5 PM. cl Mon & holidays. No admis fee. Estab 1946, opened 1966. Founded to present aspects of the development of American and European art and culture through exhibition and interpretation of fine works of art and literature, both from the Gallery's own collections and from those of other institutions and individuals. Average Annual Attendance: 25,000
Income: Financed by endowment
Collections: American Miniatures and Colonial Silver; Contemporary American & European Painting and Sculpture; Painting and Sculpture relating to Early American History; Paintings by 19th Century American Artists of the Hudson River School; Portraits of Famous Confederate Leaders; 16th Century Flemish Tapestries; large collection of Wedgwood Pottery; large collection of paintings and sculpture by western American artists Frederic Remington & Charles M Russell
Exhibitions: (1981) Sevres Porcelain; Louisiana Landscape & Genre Paintings; Scenes from Operas of Richard Wagner; 14th Annual Christmas Exhibition; (1982) American Landscape Paintings; American Gemstones; Richard Earl Thompson, American Impressionist; 15th Annual Christmas Exhibition; (1983) American Pressed Glass & Victorian Novelties; Peter Ellenshaw: Selected Works, 1929-1983; 16th Annual Christmas Exhibition
Publications: Announcements of special exhibitions; catalogs (39 through 1983); catalogs of the Frederic Remington & Charles M Russell Collections and of the Wedgwood Collection
Activities: Educ dept; lect open to public; gallery talks; tours; museum shop sells magazines, exhibition catalogs, catalogs of permanent collection

L **Library,** 4747 Creswell Ave, 71106. *Librn* Jerry M Bloomer; *Asst Librn* Eva W Moses
Open Wed & Sat 1 - 5 PM. Estab 1946 to acquire and make available for public use on the premises, important books, exhibition catalogs, etc relating to the visual arts, literature, American history and genealogy, as well as other standard reference and bibliographic works for reference only
Income: Financed by endowment
Library Holdings: Vols 6500; Per subs 125; Original documents; Auction catalogs; Micro — Reels; AV — Slides; Other — Clipping files, exhibition catalogs, manuscripts, memorabilia, pamphlets, photographs
Special Subjects: Bibliography, fine arts, history, literature, ornithological works by J J Audubon (elephant folio edition of Birds of America) and John Gould (complete set), rare books and atlases
Collections: James M Owens Memorial Collection of Early Americana (725 volumes on Colonial history, particularly on Virginia)

L **SOUTHERN UNIVERSITY LIBRARY,*** 3050 Martin Luther King Jr Dr, 71107. Tel 318-674-3400. *Librn* Mrs Orella R Brazile
Estab 1967 to supplement the curriculum and provide bibliographic as well as reference service to both the academic community and the public
Library Holdings: Micro — Fiche, reels; AV — Cassettes, fs, motion pictures, rec, slides, v-tapes; Other — Clipping files, framed reproductions, original art works, pamphlets, prints, reproductions, sculpture
Collections: Black Collection, pictures, clippings & motion pictures; Louisiana Collection
Exhibitions: High School Art Exhibit; Ceramic Exhibit; Nan's Japanese Art Embroidery
Activities: Book traveling exhibition annually; originate traveling exhibitions to YWCA

MAINE

AUGUSTA

M **UNIVERSITY OF MAINE AT AUGUSTA GALLERY,*** University Heights, 04330. Tel 207-622-7131. *Dir* Patricia McGraw Anderson
Open Mon - Thurs 9 AM - 9 PM; Fri 9 AM - 5 PM. No admis fee. Estab 1970 to provide changing exhibitions of the visual arts for the university students and faculty and for the larger Augusta-Kennebec Valley community; the principal exhibition area is a two level combination lounge and gallery. Average Annual Attendance: 9000
Income: Financed by university budget
Collections: Drawings, paintings, prints, sculpture by students and faculty
Exhibitions: Six major art exhibits
Activities: Lect open to public, 2 - 3 vis lectr per year; gallery talks; tours

BATH

M **MAINE MARITIME MUSEUM,** 963 Washington St, 04530. Tel 207-443-6311. *Exec Dir* John S Carter; *Asst Cur* Nathan Lipfert
Open daily 10 AM - 5 PM (mid-May - mid-Oct), Mon - Sat 10 AM - 3 PM, Sun & holidays 1 PM - 4 PM remainder of the year. Summer admis adults $5.50, under 16 $2.25, under 6 free, winter rates reduced. Estab 1964 for the preservation of Maine's maritime heritage. Average Annual Attendance: 30,000. Mem: 1400; dues $15 and up; annual meeting Oct
Income: Financed by membership, gifts and grants
Collections: Marine art; ship models; shipbuilding tools; shipping papers; navigational instruments
Exhibitions: Century of Maine Steamers; memorabelia; small craft; building of a wooden ship; permanent and changing exhibits
Publications: Long Reach Log, quarterly
Activities: Apprenticeshop Boatbuilding School; Lect open to public; group tours; individual paintings and original objects of art lent; museum shop selling books, reproductions, prints and related novelties

L **Archives Library,** 963 Washington St, 04530. Tel 207-443-6311
Open Mon - Sun 10 AM - 5 PM May 20 - Oct 20, Mon - Fri Nov - April.
Admis adults $5.50, children $2.25. Estab 1964 to preserve Maine's maritime
heritage and disseminate to public ship portraits and ship models. Maintains
small reference library. Average Annual Attendance: 30,000. Mem: 1400; dues
$15 and up; annual meetings last Wed of Oct
Income: Financed by membership, admis, gifts and grants
Library Holdings: Vols 6500; Per subs 50; original documents; AV —
Kodachromes, slides; Other — Clipping files, memorabilia, original art works,
pamphlets, photographs
Special Subjects: Maine maritime history & art, especially shipbuilding
Collections: Sewall Ship Papers, shipbuilding firms business papers
Publications: Long Reach Log, quarterly
Activities: Individual paintings and original objects of art lent to other museums;
sales shop sells books and prints

BLUE HILL

M **PARSON FISHER HOUSE,** Jonathan Fisher Memorial, Inc,* 04614. Tel 207-
374-2780. *Pres* William P Hinckley
Open Tues - Fri 2 - 5 PM, Sat 10 AM - Noon (summer only). Admis $.50. Estab
1954 to preserve the home and memorabilia of Jonathan Fisher. The house was
designed and built by him in 1814. Average Annual Attendance: 300. Mem: 320;
dues endowment $1000, contributing $100, sustaining $25, annual $2; annual
meeting August
Income: Financed by endowment and membership
Collections: Furniture, Manuscripts, Paintings and Articles made by Fisher
Activities: Sales shop sells books, reproductions and copies of Fishers works and
books relating to him

BOOTHBAY HARBOR

O **BOOTHBAY REGION ART FOUNDATION, INC,** Brick House Gallery,
Brick House, Oak St, 04538. Tel 207-633-2703. *Pres* Jean Andrews; *VPres*
Richard Wiggins Johnson; *Secy* Eleanor Miller; *Treas* William Burley
Open Mon - Sat 11 AM - 5 PM; Sun 2 - 5 PM (June 27 through Sept 9). Admis
adults 25, children free. Estab 1966, originated to help develop an art curriculum
in the local schools, presently functions to bring art of the region's artists to
enrich the culture of the community. Located in historic Brick House, built in
1807, two exhibition rooms on the first floor and two on the second, one of
which features prints, drawings and small watercolors. Average Annual
Attendance: 3000. Mem: 475; dues $1 - $25; annual meeting Oct
Income: Financed by memberships, contributions and commissions
Exhibitions: Three juried shows of graphics, paintings and sculpture by artists of
the Boothbay Region and Monhegan Island; (1983-84) One week exhibition of
the best work of local school art department
Activities: Scholarships

BRUNSWICK

M **BOWDOIN COLLEGE,** Museum of Art & Peary-MacMillan Arctic Museum,
04011. Tel 207-725-8731, Ext 275. *Dir* Katharine J Watson; *Admin Asst to Dir*
Roxlyn Yanok; *Cur* John W Coffey III; *Secy to Dir* Suzanne Bergeron; *Registrar*
Henrietta MacBee; *Museum Receptionist & Shop Mgr* Marilyn Dwyer; *Cur
Education* Patricia M Anderson; *Registrar & Cur MacMillan Arctic Museum*
Richard Condon
Open Tues - Fri 10 AM - 4 PM; Sat 10 AM - 5 PM; Sun 2 - 5 PM; cl Mon &
holidays. No admis fee. Estab Museum of Art 1894, Peary-MacMillan Artic
Museum 1967. The Walker Art Building, designed by McKim, Mead and White,
houses a collection begun in 1811 at the bequest of James Bowdoin III. There are
eight galleries housing the permanent collection and one for temporary
exhibitions. Average Annual Attendance: 50,000. Mem: 800
Collections: Colonial and Federal Portraits by Copley, Feke, Smibert, Stuart;
19th and 20th Century Works by Leonard Baskin, Thomas Eakins, Martin
Johnson Heade, Robert Henri, George Inness, John Sloan; The Molinari
Collection of Coins, Medals, Plaquettes; The Warren Collection of Classical
Antiquities; The Winslow Homer Collection and Memorabilia; Old Master Prints
and Drawings
Exhibitions: (1981) Permanent Collections; The Haystack Tradition: Art in Craft
Media; John Sloan: Prints & Drawings; Maine Festival Shows; Treasures From
Near Eastern Looms; (1982) Cubism in American Photography, 1910-1930;
(1983) Winslow Homer Watercolors; Maine Artists Invitational; The Prints of
Edvard Munch: Mirror of His Life
Publications: Exhibition catalogs; Handbook of the Collection, 1982; Winslow
Homer Watercolors, 1983
Activities: Docent training; lecture open to public; concerts; gallery talks; tours;
individual paintings and original objects of art lent to qualified institutions;
museum shop sells books, magazines, reproductions, prints, slides and jewelry

DEER ISLE

M **HAYSTACK MOUNTAIN SCHOOL OF CRAFTS GALLERY,** 04627. Tel
207-348-6946. *Chmn Board* Ronald Hayes Pearson; *Pres* Mary Nyburg; *Admin
Asst* Ethel Clifford; *Dir* Howard M Evans; *Treas* Lloyd Capen
Open Thurs - Sun, June - Sept. Estab 1951 for research and instruction in crafts
and related extension services of exhibitions, consultation and conferences.
Gallery maintained for continuous summer exhibition of important American and
other national craftsmen. Average Annual Attendance: 3000
Income: $150,000 (financed by tuition income plus annual donations)
Collections: †American Ceramics; †Jewelry
Publications: Annual brochure
Activities: 13 week summer session in ceramics, graphics, glass, jewelry, weaving,
blacksmithing, papermaking & fabrics; lect; gallery talks; scholarships
L **Library,** 04627. Tel 207-348-6946
For reference only
Library Holdings: Vols 500; AV — Kodachromes

ELLSWORTH

M **COLONEL BLACK MANSION,** 04605. Tel 207-667-8671. *Pres* Sylvia C
Whitcomb; *Secy* Mrs Paul Marshall
Open June 1 - Oct 15, Mon - Sat 10 AM - 5 PM; cl Sun. Donations adults $2,
children $1. Historical mansion operated by the Hancock County Trustees of
Public Reservations. Average Annual Attendance: 5500. Mem: 225; annual
meeting second Thurs in August
Collections: Authentic period China, Decorative Objects, Glass, Furniture in
original setting
Activities: Guided tours

HALLOWELL

O **KENNEBEC VALLEY ART ASSOCIATION,** Harlow Gallery, 160 Water St,
PO Box 213, 04347. *Pres* Phyllis Wicks; *Dir* Adele Nichols; *VPres* Nancy Fraser;
Treas Madge Ames
Open Tues - Sat 1 - 4 PM, cl Mon & Sun. No admis fee. Estab 1963 to foster an
interest in and appreciation of fine art. Single gallery on ground level having
central entrance and two old storefront windows which provide window display
space, peg board covering walls, with two large display screens providing extra
display area. Average Annual Attendance: 700. Mem: Approx 100; dues $10;
annual meeting first Mon in Jan
Income: Financed by membership and donations
Publications: Newsletter, monthly
Activities: Classes for adults; lectures open to the public, 10 - 12 vis lectrs per
year; gallery talks; scholarships; museum shop sells original art

KENNEBUNK

M **BRICK STORE MUSEUM,** 117 Main St, PO Box 177, 04043. Tel 207-985-
4802. *Dir* Sandra S Armentrout
Open Tues - Sat 10 AM - 4:30 PM. Admis $1. The Museum is composed of a
block of 19th century commercial buildings, including William Lord's Brick Store
(1825), exhibiting fine and decorative arts, historical and marine collections.
Average Annual Attendance: 5000. Mem: 600; dues $15 - $50; annual meeting
Sept
Income: Financed by endowment, membership, small grants
Collections: Taylor-Barry Period House (circa 1803, sea captain's house); 19th
century Americana; costumes; household furnishings; marine artifacts; paintings;
tools; manuscripts
Exhibitions: Crafts, fine arts, local history, decorative arts
Publications: Exhibition catalogues
Activities: Lect series; architectural walking tours, field trips; teas and receptions
at Taylor-Barry House; sales shop sells books, crafts
L **Library,** 117 Main St, 04043. Tel 207-985-4802. *Manuscripts Cur* Joyce Butler
Non-circulating reference library only
Library Holdings: Other — Manuscripts
Special Subjects: Architecture, Fine Arts, Local and State History, New England
19th Century Decorative Arts

KENNEBUNKPORT

M **ROGER DEERING STUDIO - GALLERY,*** Ocean Ave, 04046. Tel 207-967-
2273. *Dir* Winifred Deering
Open to the public during the summer season and by appointment only the
remaining months
Collections: Deering Painting Collection

LEWISTON

M **BATES COLLEGE,** Treat Gallery, 04240. Tel 207-786-6158. *Cur* Kathryn
Hargrove
Open Tues - Sun 1 - 4 PM, mornings by appointment, cl major holidays. No
admis fee. Estab 1955 in honor of Mr & Mrs George W Treat to acquaint the
student body and the community with the works of recognized artists. Average
Annual Attendance: 6800
Collections: Marsden Hartley Drawings (99) Paintings (2); Freeman Hinckley
(former Bates College Trustee) Collection of Chinese Objects; Sylvan Lehman
Joseph Collection of Prints including one Rembrandt and 19 Cassattas; Four
Thompson Family Portraits (ancestors of George W Treat); One Zorach
Sculpture; The Little Family Antique Collection; 19th & 20th Century American
and European Paintings and Prints; 17th & 18th Century Dutch, English, French
and Italian Landscapes and Portraits
Exhibitions: Changed monthly
Activities: Lectures open to public; concerts; gallery talks; individual paintings &
original objects of art lent

MACHIAS

M **UNIVERSITY OF MAINE AT MACHIAS,** Torrey Gallery, 04654. Tel 207-
255-3313. *Dir of Gallery* David B Boggs; *Chmn Cultural Affairs* Dr Alvin
Bowker
Open 8 AM - 5 PM. No admis fee. Estab 1972. Average Annual Attendance:
2000
Income: Financed by city and state appropriation
Collections: Norma & John C Marin Collection
Exhibitions: (1982-83) Univ of Maine at Machias Faculty Exhibition;
Midwestern Artists; Works on Paper, international invitational; Chicago Artist
One Person Show; American Folk Art; Student Exhibitions
Publications: Exhibition schedule, annually
Activities: Classes for adults; lectures, 2 vis lects per year; exten dept serves
Eastern Maine; material available to residents & summer visitors; individual
paintings & original objects of art lent; lending collection contains 100 color
reproductions, 2000 lantern slides, 6400 Kodachromes, 1200 film strips; traveling
exhibitions organized and circulated to Calais Technical Institute

L **Library,** 04654
Lending and reference library
Library Holdings: Vols 56,000; Other — Prints

OGUNQUIT

M **MUSEUM OF ART OF OGUNQUIT,** Shore Rd, Box 815, 03907. Tel 207-646-4909. *Dir* Henry Strater; *Cur* Michael Culver; *Asst Dir* John Dirks
Open (July through Labor Day, 10 wks only) Mon - Sat 10 AM - 5 PM, Sun 1 - 5 PM. No admis fee. Estab 1951. Gallery has 3 large rooms in a cinder-block building overlooking a grove of cedar trees and a rocky cove on the coast of southern Maine. Average Annual Attendance: 16,000. Mem: 200; dues couple $25, individual $15; annual meeting Aug
Income: Financed by endowment, membership
Purchases: Recent additions to Collection: works by Willian Von Schlegell, Frank London, and Elyot Henderson
Collections: Paintings and sculpture by contemporary Americans, including Marsh, Burchfield, Luks, Hartley, Demuth, Kuniyoshi, Lachaise, Tobey and Zorach
Exhibitions: (1981) Works of Sixty Two Years by Henry Strater; (1982) Harmon Neill Memorial; (1983) Five Ogunquit Artist; (1984) Museum of Art of Ogunquit Permanent Collection Show
Publications: Exhibition catalog, annually
Activities: Individual paintings and original objects of art lent (restricted list only, available for short periods to museums and galleries)

L **Reference Library,** 03907
Library Holdings: Vols 200; Other — Clipping files, exhibition catalogs, manuscripts, memorabilia, original art works, pamphlets, photographs, reproductions

O **OGUNQUIT ART ASSOCIATION,** The Barn Gallery, Bourne's Lane, PO Box 206, 03907. Tel 207-646-5370. *Pres* Gregory Kelleher; *VPres* Valfred Thelin; *Secy* Fran Scully; *Treas* Evelyne Harper; *Cur* Jamie Reynolds
Open Mon - Sat 10 AM - 5 PM; Sun 2 - 5 PM (mid-June through mid-Sept), evenings Tues & Thurs 7 - 9 PM, Fri 7 - 10 PM. No admis fee. Estab 1928 as a charitable, educational institution. Maintains two main galleries, the Collector's Gallery of unframed works and J Scott Smart outdoor sculpture court. Average Annual Attendance: 15,000. Mem: 59; dues $30; meetings June & Aug
Income: Financed by sale of works
Exhibitions: Exhibitions during the summer
Activities: Classes for adults and children; workshops; films and demonstrations; art auction; lect open to public; concerts; gallery talks

O **OGUNQUIT ART CENTER,*** Hoyt's Lane, 03907. Tel 207-646-2453. *Dir* Florence W Nims
Open daily 10 AM - 5 PM, Sun 2 - 5 PM. No admis fee. Estab 1920, to provide a high quality of paintings on exhibition. Main gallery is large enough to accomodate over 300 paintings, also three small galleries can hang 30 paintings. Average Annual Attendance: 1200-1500. Mem: 300; dues $12; annual meeting Sept
Income: Financed through patrons
Exhibitions: 60th Annual National Exhibition of Paintings
Activities: Competitions; awards; individual paintings lent; art gallery sells original art

ORONO

M **UNIVERSITY OF MAINE AT ORONO,** Art Collection, Carnegie Hall, 04469. Tel 207-581-3255. *University Pres* Paul Silverman; *Cur* Diana Emery Hulick; *Exhibits Preparator* Kenneth Matthews; *Secy* Julie Cota
Open Mon - Fri 8 AM - 4:30 PM. Estab 1946 to add to the cultural life of the university student; to be a service to Maine artists; to promote good & important art, both historic and modern. There are seven galleries, four in Carnegie Hall, and three in campus buildings. Average Annual Attendance: 15,000. Mem: 180; dues $100, $50, $25
Income: Financed by membership and state appropriation
Collections: The University Collection has grown to a stature which makes it a nucleus in the state for historic & contemporary art, in all media. It includes more than 4300 original works of art
Publications: Annual catalogs & exhibition notes
Activities: Lectures open to public & some for members only; competitions; individual paintings & original objects of art lent other museums & galleries; book traveling exhibitions

PEMAQUID POINT

O **PEMAQUID GROUP OF ARTISTS,** Lighthouse Park (Mailing add: c/o Mrs Edward Wise, New Harbor, 04554). *Co-Pres* Donald Bowman; *Co-Pres* Ernest T Thompson; *Secy* Mrs Edward Wise; *Gallery Hostess* Jean Smyder
Open Mon - Sat 10 AM - 4:30 PM; Sun 1 - 4:30 PM. No admis fee. Estab 1929 to exhibit and sell paintings, sculpture, carvings by members. Maintains an art gallery, open July through Sept 14. Average Annual Attendance: 8000. Mem: 310, must be residents of the Pemaquid Peninsula; dues $5; annual meeting Sept 15
Exhibitions: Summer members exhibition
Activities: Scholarships; gallery sells original art

POLAND SPRING

M **SHAKER MUSEUM,** Sabbathday Lake, 04274. Tel 207-926-4597. *Dir & Librn* Theodore E Johnson; *Cur Manuscripts* R Mildred Barker; *Archivist* Frances A Carr
Open Mon - Sat 10 AM - 4:30 PM. Admis adults $2.50, children (6-12) $1.25, under 6 free with adult. Estab 1931, incorporated 1971, to preserve for educational and cultural purposes Shaker artifacts, publications, manuscripts and works of art; to provide facilities for educational and cultural activities in connection with the preservation of the Shaker tradition; to provide a place of study and research for students of history and religion
Collections: †Drawings & paintings by Shaker artists; †Shaker textiles; †community industries; †furniture; †manuscripts; †metal & wooden ware
Publications: The Shaker Quarterly
Activities: Classes for adults; workshops in summer for herb dyeing, cultivating, weaving, spinning, baskets; lect open to public; gallery talks; tours; museum shop sells books, reproductions, prints, slides, herbs produced in the community, yarn from flock, woven items

L **Library,** Sabbathday Lake, 04274
Open to qualified scholars by appointment
Library Holdings: Vols 15,363; Per subs 104; ephemera; Micro — Prints 317, reels 353; Other — Manuscripts, photographs
Special Subjects: History of Art & Archaeology, American Communal Societies, Early American Technology, Herbology
Collections: The Koreshan Unity; The Religious Society of Friends

PORTLAND

O **MAINE HISTORICAL SOCIETY,** 485 Congress St, 04101. Tel 207-774-1822. *Dir* William H Toner Jr
Open June - Sept Mon - Fri 10 AM - 5 PM, cl State & Federal holidays. No admis fee. Estab 1822, a society that owns and operates an historical research library & a 1785 house, The Wadsworth-Longfellow House. Mem: 1750; dues $20 - $250 per yr
Publications: Maine Historical Society, quarterly; tri-annual monograph

M **Wadsworth-Longfellow House,** 485 Congress St, Portland, 04101
Open June - Sept Tues - Sat 10 AM - 4 PM. Admis adults $2, children $1. Average Annual Attendance: 7500
Collections: Maine furniture; glass; historic artifacts; paintings; photographs; pottery; prints; textiles; Maine artists; Maine portraits, seascapes

L **Library,** 485 Congress St, 04101. *Librn* Mary-Kate Murphy; *Manuscripts Asst* Arthur J Gerrier
Open Tues - Fri 9 AM - 5 PM, 2nd Sat each month, cl Mon, Sun & most Sat. Admis $2. Average Annual Attendance: 4000
Library Holdings: Vols 60,000; Other — Manuscripts

M **PORTLAND MUSEUM OF ART,** 7 Congress Sq, 04101. Tel 207-775-6148. *Dir* John Holverson; *Assoc Dir* Jane Begert; *Cur Collections* Michael Preble; *Registrar* Barbara Redjinski; *Education Dir* Margaret Burchenal; *Public Information Officer* Megan Thorn; *Development Mgr* Joanne Bayreuther; *Financial Officer* Rebecca Hingston; *Sales Mgr* Judith McCabe; *Chief Security* Edward Elliott
Open summer Tues - Sat 10 AM - 5 PM, Thurs until 9 PM, Sun Noon - 5 PM, winter Wed - Sat 10 AM - 4 PM, Thurs until 9 PM, Sun Noon - 4 PM. Admis adults $2, sr citizens & students $1, children 6-16 yrs $.75, children under 6 free, Thurs 5 - 9 PM free. Estab 1882 as a non-profit educational institution based on the visual arts and critical excellence. The Museum includes the McLellan-Sweat House, built in 1800, a Registered National Historic Landmark; the LDM Sweat Memorial Galleries, built in 1911; & the Charles Shipman Payson Building, built in 1983, designed by Henry N Cobb. This building is named for Mr Charles Shipman Payson, whose gift of 17 Winslow Homer paintings spurred expansion. Average Annual Attendance: 150,000. Mem: 3000; dues $15 - $5000
Income: $988,425 (financed by endowment, membership, private & corporate donations, grants from national, state & municipal organizations)
Purchases: $10,000
Collections: †19th & 20th century American & European paintings; neo-classic American sculpture; †contemporary prints; †State of Maine Collection of artists associated with Maine including Winslow Homer, Andrew Wyeth & Marsden Hartley; †American decorative arts of the Federal period; †American glass
Exhibitions: (1983) The State of Main Collection; The Nineteenth Century Glass Industry in America; The Charles Shipman Payson Collection of Winslow Homer Paintings; Main Light: Temperas by Andrew Wyeth; James Brooks: Paintings & Works on Paper, 1946-1982; America Observed: Wood Engravings by Winslow Homer; Maine Biennial Drawing Exhibition; Marsden Hartley
Publications: Bulletin, monthly; exhibition catalogs; general information brochure
Activities: Classes for adults & children; docent training; lectures open to public; tours; gallery talks; concerts; films; competitions; members' openings of exhibitions; individual paintings and original objects of art lent to museums; museum shop sells books, reproductions, prints, posters, cards, jewelry, gifts & items by Maine craftsmen

L **PORTLAND PUBLIC LIBRARY,** Art Dept, 5 Monument Square, 04101. Tel 207-773-4761. *Dir* Edward V Chenevert; *Asst Dir* Barbara Smith; *Art Librn* Judith Wentzell
Open July - Aug Mon, Wed & Fri 9 AM - 6 PM, Tues & Thurs 9 AM - 9 PM, cl Sat; Sept - June Mon, Wed & Fri 10 AM - 6 PM, Tues & Thurs Noon - 9 AM, Sat 9 AM - 5 PM. Estab 1867 as the public library for city of Portland. Circ 33,503
Income: Financed by endowment, city & state appropriation
Purchases: $11,400
Library Holdings: Vols 16,108; Per subs 99; Micro — Fiche, reels; AV — Cassettes, motion pictures, rec, v-tapes; Other — Clipping files, exhibition catalogs, original art works, pamphlets, sculpture
Collections: †Costume Book Collection; †Maine Sheet Music; Press Books - †Anthoensen Press, Mosher Press
Exhibitions: Monthly exhibits concentration on Portland & Maine artists; Lin Lisberger, sculpture; Ed Holcomb, photography; Liz Wagner, paintings; Jacqueline Field, tapestry weaving Spiegel; Etching - Susan Amons; Photography - Michael Rowell
Activities: Lectures open to the public; gallery talks

L   PORTLAND SCHOOL OF ART LIBRARY, 619 Congress St, 04101. Tel 207-761-1772. *Libm* Joanne Waxman; *Asst Libm* Jeffory Clough
Open Mon - Thurs 8 AM - 9:30 PM, Fri 8 AM - 5 PM, Sun 11 AM - 4 PM. Estab 1973, to support the curriculum and serve the needs of students and faculty. Circ 12,000
Income: $20,000
Purchases: $15,000
Library Holdings: Vols 15,000; Per subs 72; AV — Cassettes, lantern slides, slides 30,000, v-tapes; Other — Clipping files, exhibition catalogs, pamphlets, photographs, reproductions
Special Subjects: Advertising Design, Aesthetics, Anthropology, Archaeology, Architecture, Art Education, Art History, Bookplates & Bindings, Bronzes, Calligraphy, Cartoons, Ceramics, Coins & Medals, Collages, Conceptual Art, Antiquities, Costumes, Crafts, Decorative Arts, Dolls, Drafting, Drawings, Enamels, Etchings & Engravings, Ethnology
Activities: Book traveling exhibitions

M   VICTORIA SOCIETY OF MAINE, Victoria Mansion and Morse Libby Mansion, 109 Danforth St, 04101. Tel 207-772-4841. *Pres* Mrs A Holmes Stockly; *Secy* Mrs Ann M McCullum; *Cur* Dr Roger D Calderwood
Open mid-June to Labor Day, Tues - Sat 10 AM - 4 PM; cl Sun, Mon & holidays. Admis adults $2, children under 12 $.50. Estab 1943 to display Italian Villa, Victorian Period, built by Henry Austin of New Haven, Connecticut in 1859-1863. Average Annual Attendance: 5000. Mem: 365; dues $15; annual meeting Apr
Income: Financed by membership, tours and special activities
Collections: Original Interior-Exterior and Original Furnishings, Gifts and Loans of the Victorian Period
Activities: Lectures open to public; concerts; tours

M   WESTBROOK COLLEGE, Joan Whitney Payson Gallery of Art, 716 Stevens Ave, 04103. Tel 207-797-9546. *Dir* Judith E Sobol; *Asst Dir* Gael May McKibben
Open Tues - Fri 10 AM - 4 PM, Sat & Sun 1 - 5 PM, cl Mon & holidays. No admis fee. Estab May 1977 for cultural exhibits. Payson Gallery is a tri-level cube 32 x 32 ft
Income: Financed by college operating budget
Collections: American masters of the 19th and 20th century; French Impressionist paintings; French Post-impressionist paintings
Exhibitions: The Gregorian Collection of Oriental Rugs; Women Pioneers in Maine Art; New Architecture Maine Traditions; regularly changing special exhibitions
Publications: The Joan Whitney Payson Gallery of Art, Women Pioneers in Maine Art; New Architecture - Maine Traditions, one catalogue yearly
Activities: Lectures open to public, 4 vis lectr per year; gallery talks; tours; individual paintings and original objects of art lent to selected institutions; book traveling exhibitions, one per year; museum shop sells catalogs and postcards

ROCKLAND

M   WILLIAM A FARNSWORTH LIBRARY AND ART MUSEUM, 19 Elm St, Box 466, 04841. Tel 207-596-6457. *Dir* Marius B Peladeau; *Dir Education* Valerie N Duffy; *Membership Secy* Sharon Merrow; *Admin Asst* Barbara J Entwistle
Open Tues - Sat 10 AM - 5 PM; Sun 1 - 5 PM; Mon (June - Sept) 10 AM - 5 PM. Admis by donations. Estab 1948 to house, conserve and exhibit American art. Four galleries house permanent and changing exhibitions. Average Annual Attendance: 60,000. Mem: 1200; dues $20 and up
Collections: American Art; American Decorative Arts; European Fine Arts and Decorative Arts
Exhibitions: Annual Open Show; Childrens Art Show
Publications: Annual report, quarterly newsletter, exhibit catalogs
Activities: Classes for adults and children; lect open to public; concerts; gallery talks; competitions; individual paintings and original objects of art lent to other museums and galleries; originate traveling exhibitions; museum shop sells books, original art, reproductions, prints
L   Library, 19 Elm St, 04841. Tel 207-596-6457. *Cur* Christine Podmaniczky; *Dir Education* Val Duffy
Estab 1948. Art reference only. Archives on American artists, including papers of Louise Nevelson, Andrew Wyeth, N C Wyeth, George Bellows, Robert Indiana
Library Holdings: Vols 4000; Per subs 20; Other — Clipping files, exhibition catalogs

ROCKPORT

O   MAINE COAST ARTISTS, Russell Ave, Box 147, 04856. Tel 207-236-2875. *Gallery Dir* Sylvie Skira
Open Tues - Sat 10 AM - 6 PM; Sun 1 - 6 PM; cl Mon (June - Sept). No admis fee. Estab 1958 to show the works of artists who paint in Maine, full or part time. Gallery building was an old large livery stable overlooking Rockport Harbor. Average Annual Attendance: 10,000. Mem: 300; dues $30; annual meeting August
Income: Financed by members, sales, contributions and special events
Activities: Classes for adults and children; lectures open to the public, 7 vis lectr per yr; gallery talks; tours; sales shop sells books, reproductions & prints

O   MAINE PHOTOGRAPHIC WORKSHOPS, 2 Central St, 04856. Tel 207-236-8581. *Founder & Dir* David H Lyman; *Assoc Dir* Kate Carter; *Assoc Dir* Craig Stevens; *Dir Information* Carol Stevens
Open Mon - Sun 9 AM - 5 PM & 7 - 9 PM June - Aug. Admis lectures $2.50. Estab 1973 as photographic center. Contains four separate spaces for the display of vintage & contemporary photographers. Average Annual Attendance: 10,000. Mem: 1400; dues $20; annual meetings Nov
Income: $2,000,000 (financed by membership, tuitions, sales & accommodations
Collections: Eastern Illustrating Archive containing 100,000 vintage glass plates; The Kosti Ruohomaa Collection, prints of Life photographers; Master Work

Collection; Paul Caponigro Archive, prints
Exhibitions: Forty photographic exhibitions
Publications: The Work Print, bi-monthly newsletter; Catalogues - Programs, semi-annual
Activities: Classes for adults & children; dramatic programs; lectures open to public, 50 vis lectr per yr; competitions with awards; scholarships; lending collection contains photographs; book traveling exhibitions; originate traveling exhibitions; sales shop sells books, magazines, original art, reproductions, prints, photographic equipment & supplies
L   Workshop Library, Union Hall, 2 Center St, 04856
Open Mon - Wed 9 AM - 5 PM & 7 - 9 PM, Thur - Sun 9 AM - 5 PM. Estab 1975 to support student studies
Purchases: $2500
Library Holdings: Vols 500; Per subs 45; Micro — Cards, prints; AV — A-tapes, cassettes, fs, Kodachromes, lantern slides, motion pictures, rec, slides, v-tapes; Other — Clipping files, exhibition catalogs, framed reproductions, memorabilia, original art works, pamphlets, photographs, reproductions
Special Subjects: Photographic technical & esthetic subjects, photographic history

SACO

M   YORK INSTITUTE MUSEUM, 375 Main St, 04072. Tel 207-282-3031, 283-3861. *Exec Dir* Stephen J Podgajny
Open May 1 - Nov 1 1 - 4 PM, by appointment. No admis fee. Estab 1867. 48 ft x 32 ft windowless gallery, 5 period rooms, national history room, printing shop, exhibition hall. Average Annual Attendance: 3000. Mem: 300; dues, perpetual $1000, life $500, contributing $50, family $25, single $10
Income: Financed by endowment & municipal support
Collections: Colonial decorative arts; glass; historical material; paintings; sculpture
Exhibitions: (1982) John Brewster, paintings; (1983) Outdoors & Maine
Activities: Classes for children; dramatic programs; docent training; lectures open to public, 6 vis lectr per yr; concerts; tours; inter-museum loan; individual paintings and original objects of art lent to other museums; museum shop sells books, notepaper; junior museum

SEARSPORT

M   PENOBSCOT MARINE MUSEUM, Church St, 04974. Tel 207-548-6634. *Dir* C Gardner Lane Jr; *Secy* Marilyn Kenney; *Teacher* Janice Kasper
Open Memorial Day weekend - Oct 15, Mon - Sat 9:30 AM - 5 PM, Sun 1 - 5 PM. Admis adults $2.50, sr citizens $2, youth 7 - 15 $.75, 6 & under free. Estab 1936 as a memorial to the maritime record of present and former residents of the State of Maine in shipbuilding, shipping and all maritime affairs. The Museum consists of six buildings, including the Old Town Hall (1845), Nickels-Colcord-Duncan House (circa 1880); new Phillips Library & a classroom building. Average Annual Attendance: 10,000. Mem: 650; dues $15 and up; annual meeting July
Income: Financed by endowment, membership and admissions
Collections: Marine Hardware; Oriental Exports; †Paintings; †Ships Models; Small Craft
Exhibitions: Permanent exhibit: The Challenge of the Downeasters; Marine Painting of Thomas and James Buttersworth
Publications: Annual report; newsletter, when appropriate
Activities: Classes for children; individual paintings and original objects of art lent to other institutions; Sales shop sells Marine books, original art and prints
L   Library, Church St, 04974. Tel 207-548-6634. *Libm* Charles H Howard
Open for reference to researchers
Library Holdings: Vols 3000; Per subs 10; nautical charts; Other — Photographs

SKOWHEGAN

L   SKOWHEGAN SCHOOL OF PAINTING AND SCULPTURE, Margaret Day Blake Library, Box 449, 04976. Tel 212-861-9270
Estab 1946, to serve the students at the School. For reference only
Income: Financed by special gifts
Purchases: $500
Library Holdings: Vols 7500; Per subs 5; AV — A-tapes, Kodachromes, lantern slides, motion pictures; Other — Exhibition catalogs
Special Subjects: Art History, Studio Arts Methods and Materials

SPRINGVALE

L   NASSON COLLEGE, Anderson Learning Center, Art Dept,* Bradeen St, 04083. Tel 207-324-5340. *Dir* Robert J Berkley; *Cur* George Burk
Open Mon - Fri 8:30 AM - 5 PM, Sat 9 AM - 5 PM, Sun 1 - 5 PM. Estab 1969 to provide facilities for the study of humanities and a location for the display of the college's permanent art study collection. Maintains an art gallery with exhibition and lecture area and an adjoining outdoor sculpture court
Income: Financed by endowment and through college
Library Holdings: Micro — Fiche, reels; AV — A-tapes, fs, lantern slides, motion pictures, rec, slides, v-tapes; Other — Clipping files, exhibition catalogs, framed reproductions, memorabilia
Collections: Selective 18th, 19th & 20th Century Graphic Works; Paintings; Photographs; Sculpture
Exhibitions: Seven exhibitions of prominent artists per year; Historical Exhibitions; Student Shows
Publications: Posters for each exhibit

WATERVILLE

M COLBY MUSEUM OF ART, 04901. Tel 207-873-1131, Ext 2228. *Dir* Hugh J Gourley III
Open Mon - Sat 10 AM - Noon, 1 - 4:30 PM, cl major holidays. No admis fee. Estab 1959 to serve as an adjunct to the Colby College Art Program and to be a museum center for Central Maine. Mem: Friends of Art at Colby, 625; dues $15 & higher
Income: Financed by college funds, membership & donations
Collections: Bernat Oriental ceramics and bronzes; American Heritage collection; The Helen Warren and Willard Howe Collection of American Art; American Art of the 18th, 19th and 20th centuries; Jette Collection of American painting in the Impressionist Period; John Marin Collection of twenty-five works by Marin; Adelaide Pearson Collection; William J Pollock Collection of American Indian Art; Pulcifer Collection of the works of Winslow Homer; Pre-Columbian Mexico; Etruscan art;
Exhibitions: (1983) Maine Biennial
Publications: Exhibition catalogs; periodic newsletter
Activities: Docent training; lectures open to public; gallery talks; tours; individual paintings lent to other museums; originate traveling exhibitions; museum shop sells gift items, jewelry & sundries
L Library, 04901. Tel 207-873-1131, Ext 2232. *Librn* Paula D Matthews
For reference only
Library Holdings: Vols 9000; Per subs 50; AV — Cassettes, lantern slides, rec, slides; Other — Clipping files, prints

M THOMAS COLLEGE GALLERY, W River Rd, 04901. Tel 207-873-0771. *Pres* Paul G Jensen; *Dir* Ford A Grant
Open Mon - Fri 8 AM - 5 PM. No admis fee. Estab 1968 for presentation of instructional shows for student audience. Average Annual Attendance: 1500
L Library, W River Rd, 04901
For reference only
Library Holdings: AV — Slides

M WATERVILLE HISTORICAL ASSOCIATION, Redington Museum,* 64 Silver St, 04901. Tel 207-873-3817. *Pres Historical Society* William B Miller; *Resident Cur* Charles Magoon; *Resident Cur* Mrs Charles Mogoon; *Librn* Ernest C Marriner
Open May - Oct Tues - Sat 2 - 6 PM. Admis adults $1, under 18 free. Average Annual Attendance: 1500. Mem: Dues sponsor $25-$50, family $15, single $10
Income: Financed by membership and city appropriation
Collections: 19th century drug store, 19th century furniture, portraits of early local residents, early silver and china, Victorian clothing
Activities: Tours

WISCASSET

O LINCOLN COUNTY CULTURAL AND HISTORICAL ASSOCIATION, *
04578. Tel 207-882-6817. *Pres* Prescott Currier
Inc 1954, to preserve buildings of historic interest. Presents 200 years of Maine's crafts and skills including the work of craftsmen who spend part of the year in Maine. Gallery presents the work of contemporary professional artists, working in Maine, by means of two juried summer exhibitions. Three museums and one art gallery maintained. Average Annual Attendance: 3000. Mem: 650; dues $10 and up; annual meeting July
Collections: Furniture; hand tools; household articles; prison equipment; textiles
Exhibitions: Changing exhibits on 200 years of Maine crafts and skills; Lincoln County Museum, permanent exhibit on the history of punishment
Publications: Newsletter and occasional monographs
Activities: School programs; tours; slide shows; lect
L Library, * 04578. Tel 207-882-6817
Open by appointment for reference and research
M Lincoln County Museum, * Federal St, 04578. Tel 207-882-6817. *Dir* Carol Adams
Open daily 10 AM - 5 PM, Sun 12:30 - 5 PM Jul 1 - Aug 30
M Lincoln County Fire Museum, * Federal St, 04578. Tel 207-882-6817
Open by appointment only 10 AM - 4 PM, Jul 1 - Aug 30
M Maine Art Gallery, Old Academy, Warren St, PO Box 815, 04578. Tel 207-882-7511. *Chmn & Dir* Roger Johnson; *Treas* F Wenderoth Saunders; *Secy* Warren Spaulding
Open summer daily 10 AM - 4 PM, Sun 1 - 4 PM, winter Sat 10 AM - 4 PM, Sun 1 - 4 PM. No admis fee, donations appreciated. Estab 1958 as a cooperative, non-profit gallery created by the Artist Members of Lincoln County Cultural & Historical Association to exhibit the work of artists living or working in Maine. Gallery occupies a red brick federal two-story building built in 1807 as a free Academy. The building is now on National Historical Register. Average Annual Attendance: 6000. Mem: 100; annual dues $10; annual meeting Sept
Income: Financed by patrons
Exhibitions: Summer Exhibition: A juried show in two parts of 5 weeks each featuring approx 100 painters and sculptors living or working in Maine. Winter series of one-person invited exhibitions
Activities: Lectures open to public, 16 vis lectr per year; gallery talks

YORK

M OLD GAOL MUSEUM, York St and Lindsay Rd, PO Box 188, 03909. Tel 207-363-3872. *Dir* Eldridge H Pendleton; *Chmn Committee* Robert Lord; *Cur* Kerry O'Brien; *Educator* Juliet Mofford
Open June - Oct Mon - Fri 10:30 AM - 4:30 PM, Sun 1:30 - 4:30 PM. Admis $3. Estab 1900 as a local history museum to maintain, care for and develop historical collections of a regional nature and to promote historic research and historically educational programs. Museum consists of the oldest jail in the United States and an 18th century tavern arranged as period rooms. Two exhibition rooms house traveling shows and temporary exhibitions of an historical nature. Average Annual Attendance: 10,000. Mem: 600; dues family $15, single $10; annual meeting Aug

Income: $70,000 (financed by endowment)
Collections: Regional collection of American furniture & decorative arts; rare books; manuscripts
Publications: Old Gaol Museum (history), E H Pendleton; York Maine Then and Now; Enchanted Ground, George Garrett; Old Gaol Newsletter, quarterly
Activities: Classes for adults & children; dramatic programs; docent training; lectures open to public, 6 vis lectr per yr; sales shop sells books
L Library, Box 188, 30909
Open daily 10 AM - 4 PM. Reference only
Library Holdings: Vols 5000; original documents; Micro — Prints, reels; AV — Kodachromes, slides, v-tapes; Other — Clipping files, exhibition catalogs, manuscripts, memorabilia, pamphlets, photographs
Special Subjects: Decorative Arts, genealogy, local history

O SOCIETY FOR THE PRESERVATION OF HISTORIC LANDMARKS, *
140 Lindsay Rd, Box 312, 03909. Tel 207-363-4974. *Dir* Mary P Harding
Open summer Mon - Sat 10:30 AM - 5 PM, Sun 1:30 - 5 PM. Admis adults $1.50 per building, children $.50. Estab 1941 to operate buildings of historic interest. Mem: 350; dues $2; annual meeting August
Collections: American & European furniture; decorative arts; ceramic & glass collection; tools & maritime artifacts
M Elizabeth Perkins House, * 03909. Tel 207-363-4723
Late June - Labor Day 10:30 AM - 5 PM daily. Admis adults $1. A Colonial house as lived in by a Victorian family, built in 1730; contains 18th and 19th century furniture, china, and prints. Average Annual Attendance: 2300
M Old School House, * 03909. Tel 207-363-4974
Open Memorial Day - Mid October. Original school built in 1745; figures of the schoolmaster and children are in period costumes. Average Annual Attendance: 6000
M Jefferds Tavern, * 03909. Tel 207-363-4974
Open Memorial Day - Mid-October Mon - Sat 10:30 AM - 5 PM. Admis adults $1, children under 12 free. An ancient hostelry built before the Revolution by Captain Samuel Jefferds
M John Hancock Warehouse, * 03909. Tel 207-363-4974
Open Mon - Sat 10:30 AM - 5 PM, Sun 1:30 - 5 PM. Admis adults $.50, children under 12 free. Owned by a signer of the Declaration of Independence at the time of his death; listed in the National Register of Historic Places. Average Annual Attendance: 1000
Income: Financed by endowment
Exhibitions: Old tools; antique ship models
Activities: Lectures open to public, 12 visiting lecturers per year; originate traveling exhibitions

MARYLAND

ANNAPOLIS

M HAMMOND-HARWOOD HOUSE ASSOCIATION, INC, 19 Maryland Ave, 21401. Tel 301-269-1714. *Admin* Barbara A Brand
Open Nov - March Tues - Sat 10 AM - 4 PM, Sun 1 - 4 PM, Apr - Oct Tues - Sat 10 AM - 5 PM, Sun 2 - 5 PM. Admis adults $2, students $1, children $.50. Estab 1938 to preserve the Hammond-Harwood House (1774), a National Historic Landmark; to educate the public in the arts and architecture of Maryland in the 18th century. Average Annual Attendance: 15,000. Mem: 400; dues varied; meeting May and Nov
Income: Financed by endowment, membership, attendance and sales
Collections: Paintings by C W Peale; Chinese export porcelain; English and American furnishings, especially from Maryland; prints; English & American silver; colonial architecture
Publications: Maryland's Way (Hammond-Harwood House cookbook); Hammond-Harwood House Guidebook
Activities: Interpretive programs; docent training; lect open to public; individual paintings and original objects of art lent to bonafide museums within reasonable transporting distance; sales shop sells books, slides, postcards and notepaper

M SAINT JOHN'S COLLEGE, Art Gallery,* 201 Mellon Hall, 21404. Tel 301-263-2371. *Dir* Burton Blistern
Open Sept-May, 1-6 PM; Fri 7-8 PM
Exhibitions: (1981-82) Prints by Peter Milton; Ryohei and Tajima; Mythprints; Geometric Images and Figurative Art; Master Printmakers and Painter Printmakers; Paintings by Bernard Lennon; Lithographs of Honore Daumier; community art exhibition
Activities: Educ dept offers studio courses in painting, lifedrawing and sculpture

M UNITED STATES NAVAL ACADEMY MUSEUM, 21402. Tel 301-267-2108. *Dir* William W Jeffries; *Senior Cur* James W Cheevers; *Cur of Ship Models* Robert F Sumrall; *Cur of Robinson Coll* Sigrid Trumpy; *Sr Exhibit Specialist* Robert D Mimms
Open Mon - Sat 9 AM - 5 PM, Sun 11 AM - 5 PM. No admis fee. Estab 1845 as Naval School Lyceum for the purpose of collecting, preserving and exhibiting objects related to American naval history. Museum contains two large galleries totaling 9000 sq ft, with other exhibits in other areas of the campus. Average Annual Attendance: Approx 600,000
Income: Financed by Federal Government appropriations and private donations
Purchases: $36,170
Collections: †Ceramicwares; Drawings, †Paintings, †Prints, †Sculpture of Naval Portraits and Events; †Medals; †Naval Uniforms; †Ship Models; †Silver; †Weapons
Exhibitions: (1982) Life on New Frontiers: Retrospective of Fred Freeman; Sailing Ships in Dutch prints; (1983) Currier and Ives Navy
Publications: Collection catalogs and special exhibition brochures, periodically
Activities: Lect; tours upon request; individual paintings and original objects of art lent to other museums and related institutions for special, temporary exhibitions; originate traveling exhibitions

L **Library,** 21402
Open to students, scholars and public with notice, reference only
Library Holdings: Vols 2500; Per subs 15

BALTIMORE

M **BALTIMORE MUSEUM OF ART,** Art Museum Dr, 21218. Tel 301-396-7101. *Dir* Arnold L Lehman; *Dir Education* Susan S Badder; *Dir Membership & Development* Martha Parkhurst; *Dir Public Information* Faith M Holland; *Dir Programs* Brenda Edelson; *Asst Dir & Cur Paintings & Sculpture* Brenda Richardson; *Asst Dir Admin* Ann Boyce Harper; *Cur Decorative Arts* William Voss Elder III; *Asst Cur Decorative Arts* M B Munford; *Cur Prints & Drawings* Victor I Carlson; *Assoc Cur Prints, Drawings & Photographs* Jay M Fisher; *Assoc Cur Painting & Sculpture* Sona Johnston; *Cur Textiles* Dena Katzenberg; *Assoc Cur Art of Africa, Americas, Oceania* Frederick Lamp; *Registrar* L Carol Murray; *Museum Shop Mgr* Steven Rostkowski
Open Tues - Fri 10 AM - 4 PM, Thurs evening 6 - 10 PM, Sat & Sun 11 AM - 6 PM, cl Mon & holidays. Admis $2 for non-members. Estab 1914 to house & preserve art works, to present art exhibitions, art-related activities & offer educational programs & events. The original building was designed by John Russell Pope in 1929; new wing opened 1982 with cafe, auditorium & traveling exhibition galleries. Average Annual Attendance: 250,000. Mem: 7000; dues $15 - $150
Income: $2,000,000 (financed by endowment, membership, city & state appropriation & federal & county funds)
Collections: Blanche Adler Collection of Graphic Art; Antioch Mosaics; Ellen H Bayard Collection of 18th & 19th Century American Paintings, European Ceramics, Chinese Export Porcelain, Irish Glass, 19th Century European Jewelry & American & English Silver; General Lawrason Riggs Collection of Old Master Prints & Chinese Ceramics; Thomas E Benesch Memorial Collection of Drawings by 20th Century American & European artists; Harry A Bernstein Memorial Collection of Contemporary American Paintings; Cone Collection of 19th & 20th Century French Paintings, Sculpture; Drawings & Prints, Near Eastern & European Textiles, Laces, Jewelry, Furniture & other Decorative Arts; Elise Agnus Daingerfield Collection of 18th Century English, French & American Paintings with emphasis on Portraiture; Hanson Rawlings Duval Jr Memorial Collection of 19th Century Baltimore Architectural Elements, American Furniture, Paintings, European & Chinese Ceramics; Abram Eisenberg Collection of Paintings, primarily 19th Century French; Jacob Epstein Collection of Old Master Paintings; Edward Joseph Gallagher III Memorial Collection of American Paintings between 1921 & 1955; T Harrison Garrett Collection of Graphic Art 15th - 19th Century; Nelson & Juanita Greif Gutman Memorial Collection of 20th Century Paintings, Sculpture & Drawings; Charles & Elsa Hutzler Memorial Collection of Contemporary Sculpture; Mary Frick Jacobs Collection of 15th - 18th Century European Paintings, Tapestries, Furniture & Objects d'Art; Julius Levy Memorial Fund Collection of Oriental Art; George A Lucas Collection of 19th Century Drawings, Prints, Paintings & Bronzes; Saidie A May Collection of 20th Century Paintings, Sculpture & Graphics, Ancient, Medieval & Renaissance Sculpture & Textiles; McLanahan Memorial Collection of 1720 Bedchamber & its Furnishings; Samuel & Tobie Miller Memorial Collection of Contemporary Painting & Sculpture; J G D'Arcy Paul Collection of 18th Century American Furniture; Peabody Institute Collection of 19th & 20th Century American Paintings; White Collection of Ceramics, Furniture, Needlework, Glass & Decorative Art Books; White Collection of Early Maryland Silver; William Woodward Collection of 18th & 19th Century Paintings of English Sporting Life; Wurtzburger Collection of Art of Africa, the Americas & Oceania; Janet & Alan Wurtzburger Collection of 20th Century Sculpture
Exhibitions: Painting, sculpture, textiles, furniture & other decorative arts, prints, drawings and photography
Publications: Calendar, bi-monthly; exhibition catalogs
Activities: Classes for children; docent training; lect open to the public; concerts; gallery talks; tours; competitions; dance performances; exten dept serves shopping malls in White Marsh & Columbia; originate traveling exhibitions; museum shop selling books, original art, reproductions, prints, slides

L **E Kirkbride Miller Art Research Library,** Art Museum Dr, 21218. Tel 301-396-6317. *Librn* Anita Gilden; *Asst Librn* Margaret Prescott
Open Tues - Fri 10 AM - 4 PM. Open by appointment for reference only
Library Holdings: Vols 40,000; Per subs 75; Auction Catalogs; Micro — Fiche, reels; Other — Clipping files, exhibition catalogs, pamphlets
Special Subjects: Photography, American decorative arts, 19th and 20th century French art, arts of Africa, the Americas & Oceania

M **COMMUNITY COLLEGE OF BALTIMORE,** Art Gallery, 2901 Liberty Heights Ave, 21215. Tel 301-396-7980. *Gallery Dir* Allyn O Harris
Open Mon - Fri 10 AM - 4 PM. No admis fee. Estab 1965 to bring to the Baltimore and college communities exhibitions of note by regional artists, and to serve as a showplace for the artistic productions of the college art students and faculty. Consists of one large gallery area, approx 120 running ft, well-lighted through the use of both natural light (sky domes) and cove lighting which provides an even wash to the walls
Income: Financed through the college
Collections: Graphics from the 16th century to the present; paintings by notable American artists and regional ones
Exhibitions: Baltimore High School Art Students Show; Two Man Show of ceramist Carlton Leverette & painter David Bahr; Community College of Baltimore Fall Students Show; Annual Art Faculty Exhibition; One Woman Exhibition by sculptor-printmaker Frieda Sohn; Community College of Baltimore Spring Students Show
Publications: Gallery anouncements
Activities: Lect open to public; gallery talks

JOHNS HOPKINS UNIVERSITY

M **Archaeological Museum,*** Charles & 34th St, 21218. Tel 301-338-7561. *Archaeological Museum Cur* Dr John Pollini
Open Mon - Wed 11 AM - 3 PM. Estab 1876. Small exhibit space in Gilman Hall
Collections: Egyptian through Roman material 3500 BC to 500 AD

M **Evergreen House,*** 4545 N Charles St, 21210. Tel 301-338-7641. *Dir Univ Collections* Susan G Tripp
Open Mon - Fri 2 - 5 PM, second Tues every month tours 10 AM - 5 PM. No admis fee second Tues, special appointments $1 per person. Estab 1952 for promotion of cultural and educational functions and research. Formerly the residence of Ambassador John W Garrett which he bequeathed to the University. Average Annual Attendance: 10,000
Collections: Bakst Theater Decorations; European Ceramics; Japanese Inro, Netsuke & Lacquer: Chinese Ceramics; Oriental Rugs; Rare Book Collection; Tiffany Glass; Twentieth Century European Paintings
Exhibitions: Changing exhibitions
Activities: Continuing Education course given each semester by Dir on the Art; lectures for various groups, 10 vis lect per yr; concerts; tours; individual paintings and original objects of art lent to other museums, national and international

L **George Peabody Library,** 17 E Mount Vernon Place, 21202. Tel 301-659-8197. *Libr* Lyn Hart
Open Mon - Sat 9 AM - 5 PM
Special Subjects: Architecture, Decorative Arts

M **MARYLAND HISTORICAL SOCIETY MUSEUM,** 201 W Monument St, 21201. Tel 301-685-3750, Ext 70. *Dir* Mrs Romaine S Somerville; *Cur* Stiles T Colwill
Open Tues - Fri 11 AM - 4:30 PM, Sat 9 AM - 4:30 PM, cl Sun. Admis $2. Estab 1844 to collect, display and interpret the history of the State of Maryland. Average Annual Attendance: 60,000. Mem: 7000; annual meeting Oct
Income: Financed by endowment, membership, city and state appropriations
Collections: †Architectural drawings; †crystal and glassware; †ethnic artifacts, all of Maryland origin or provenance; †metalwork; †paintings, both portrait and landscape; †porcelain and †pottery; †silver; †textiles and †costumes; †furniture
Exhibitions: Continually changing exhibitions reflecting the history and culture of the state
Publications: Maryland Historical Society Magazine, quarterly; News and Notes, bimonthly; Maryland Magazine of Genealogy, biannually
Activities: Lectures open to the public, 6 vis lectr per yr; gallery talks; tours; individual paintings and original objects of art lent to other organizations; sales shop selling books, magazines, prints and reproductions; museum shop sells books, magazines, original art, reproductions, prints, slides

L **Library,** 201 W Monument St, 21201. Tel 301-685-3750. *Head Librn* William B Keller
Open Tues - Fri 11 AM - 4:30 PM. Estab 1844
Library Holdings: Vols 70,000; Per subs 350; Micro — Fiche, reels; AV — A-tapes, cassettes, fs, Kodachromes, lantern slides, motion pictures, rec, slides, v-tapes; Other — Clipping files, exhibition catalogs, manuscripts, memorabilia, pamphlets, photographs, prints, reproductions
Collections: Robert G Merrick Collection of Prints
Exhibitions: Vanished Maryland; (1982) Mapping of Maryland; (1983) Silver in Maryland
Activities: Lectures open to the public

M **MARYLAND INSTITUTE,** College of Art Galleries,* 1300 W Mount Royal Ave, 21217. Tel 301-669-9200. *Pres* Fred Lazarus IV; *Dir* Robin Coplan
Open Mon, Tues, Fri & Sat 10 AM - 5 PM, Wed & Thurs 10 AM - 9 PM, Sun Noon - 5 PM. No admis fee. Estab 1826, including the Decker & Meyerhoff Galleries & the Graduate Thesis Gallery. Average Annual Attendance: 10,000
Income: Financed by endowment and student tuition
Collections: Maryland Institute-George A Lucas Collection donated in 1909 comprising over 400 paintings and drawings by Corot, Daumier, Delacrox, Greuze, Manet, Millet, Pissarro, Whistler; bronzes by Antoine Barye, and a collection of 17,000 graphics
Publications: Handouts of the works in the Lucas Collection; several small catalogs; two major publications per year
Activities: Dramatic programs; lect open to the public; concerts; gallery talks; tours; original objects of art lent; traveling exhibitions organized and circulated; sales shop selling books

L **Library,*** 1400 Cathedral St, 21201. *Librn* John Stoneham
Library Holdings: Vols 40,000; Per subs 200

M **MEREDITH CONTEMPORARY ART GALLERY** (Formerly Arts, Limited), 805 N Charles St, 21201. Tel 301-837-3575. *Dir* Judith Lippman; *Asst Dir* Mandy Lippman
Open Tues - Fri 10 AM - 5 PM, Sat 11 AM - 5 PM, cl Mon; summer hours Mon - Fri 10 AM - 5 PM. No admis fee. Estab 1977 to show a variety of contemporary art forms by living American artists, variety includes paintings, sculpture, prints, clay, fiber, and mixed media. The building is divided into two floors to display art, the first floor is for monthly exhibits and the second floor is for gallery artists and a poster gallery. The poster gallery displays signed and unsigned contemporary art posters. Average Annual Attendance: 3500-4000
Exhibitions: Ed Baynard; Gene Davis; Dorothy Gillespie; Paul Jenkins; Margie Hughto; Alex Katz; Brian Kavanagh; David Lund; Robert Milnes; Robert Motherwell; Gayil Nalls; Elizabeth Osborne; Kaete Brittin Shaw
Activities: Classes for adults and children; educational lect on current exhibitions; lect open to public; gallery talks; tours

M **MORGAN STATE UNIVERSITY GALLERY OF ART,*** Cold Spring Lane & Hillen Rd, 21239. Tel 301-444-3030. *Dir* James E Lewis; *Cur* Gabriel S Tenabe; *Secy* Lorena D Meadows
Open Mon - Fri 9 AM - 5 PM, Sat, Sun, holidays by appointment only, cl Easter, Thanksgiving, Christmas. No admis fee. Estab 1950. Average Annual Attendance: 5000
Income: $5500
Collections: 19th and 20th century American and European sculpture; graphics; paintings; decorative arts; archaeology; African and New Guinea sculptures
Exhibitions: Recent Acquisitions; Eugene R Coles Exhibition; Robert T Francis II and John Lewis Collection of Traditional African Art Exhibition; Paul F Keene Jr, One-man Exhibition; Mr & Mrs Leonard Whitehouse African Art Collection Exhibition; Egyptian Folkloric Exhibition; 1981 Annual Undergraduate Student Art Exhibition; Build Environment Studies Exhibition

Architect; Architect City; Regional Planning; Romare Bearden: Prints & Watercolors
Publications: Catalogs, monthly
Activities: Lect open to the public, visiting lectrs; lending collection contains 500 Kodachromes; traveling exhibitions organized and circulated

L **Library,*** Cold Spring Lane & Hillen Rd, 21239. *Dir* Karen Robertson
Library Holdings: Other — Photographs

O **MUNICIPAL ART SOCIETY OF BALTIMORE CITY,** c/o Beverley C
Compton Jr, 135 E Baltimore St, 21202. Tel 301-727-1700. *Pres* Beverley C Compton Jr; *Treas* Alan P Hoblitzell
Estab 1899; the society contributes primarily public sculpture and worthy public art projects in Baltimore City
Income: Financed by endowment
Activities: Support public art in Baltimore City

M **NATIONAL SOCIETY OF COLONIAL DAMES OF THE STATE OF
MARYLAND,** Mount Clare Mansion, Carroll Park, 21230. Tel 301-837-3262.
Chmn House Committee Anne S Cantler; *Cur* Pamela Ford Charshee
Open Tues - Sat 11 AM - 4 PM, Sun 1 - 4 PM. Admis adults $2, students & sr citizens $1, children under 12 $.50. Estab 1917 to preserve the home of Charles Carroll, barrister & teach about the colonial period of Maryland history. Maintained by the National Society of Colonial Dames. Rooms of the house are furnished with 18th & early 19th century decorative arts, much of which belonged to the Carroll family who built the house in 1756. Average Annual Attendance: 4500
Income: Financed by admission, gift shop sales and contributions from public and private sectors
Collections: American paintings; 18th and early 19th century English and American furniture; English silver; Irish crystal; Oriental export porcelain; archaelogical artifacts found on property; other English and American decorative arts
Exhibitions: (1983-84) Changing Exhibits: Mount Clare Archaeology
Publications: Brochure on Mount Clare; Mount Clare: Being an Account of the Seat Built by Charles Carroll, Barrister Upon His Lands at Patapsco; booklet on the house
Activities: Historical slide shows for schools and organizations; tours; competitions; individual paintings and original objects of art lent to local museums on occasion; sales shop sells slides, gifts & colonial candlelight Christmas; Childrens Touch Museum

L **Library,** Carroll Park, 21230
Open to members and the public
Library Holdings: Vols 1000
Special Subjects: Decorative Arts, 18th Century Culture
Collections: 18th century furniture; decorative arts; part of the library of Charles Carroll, Barrister-at-law, builder of the house, 1756

M **PEALE MUSEUM,** 225 Holliday St, 21202. Tel 301-396-3523. *Pres* M Chace Davis; *VPres* George K Reynolds; *Treas* Francis Contino; *Dir* Nancy Brennan; *Asst Dir* Barry Dressel
Open Tues - Sat 10 AM - 5 PM, Sun 1 - 5 PM. No admis fee. Estab 1931 as the museum of the life and history of Baltimore. Built in 1814 as Rembrandt Peale's Baltimore Museum and Gallery of Fine Arts, a national historical landmark. Also operates the Carroll Mansion, historic house built in 1812. Average Annual Attendance: 21,000. Mem: 450; dues $15 - $500
Income: $235,000 (financed by endowment, membership, city appropriation)
Collections: †Baltimore Painters; The A Aubrey Bodine Collection; paintings by members of the Peale family; photographs of Baltimore of the 19th and 20th centuries; prints of Baltimore
Exhibitions: Rowhouse: A Baltimore Style of Living; The Peale Family
Publications: City Past-Time, quarterly newsletter
Activities: Lect open to public, 1 - 2 visiting lectr per year; museum shop sells books

L **Library,** 225 Holliday St, 21202
Open to staff for reference only
Library Holdings: Vols 1300; Per subs 43; AV — Lantern slides, slides; Other — Clipping files, exhibition catalogs, framed reproductions, manuscripts, memorabilia, original art works, pamphlets, photographs, prints, reproductions

L **ENOCH PRATT FREE LIBRARY OF BALTIMORE CITY,** Fine Arts Dept, 400 Cathedral St, 21201. Tel 301-396-5491. *Dir* Anna Lurry; *Chief Public Relations Division* Averil Kadis
Open Mon - Thurs 9 AM - 9 PM, Fri - Sat 9 AM - 5 PM; Oct - May Sun 1 - 5 PM. Estab 1882 to provide materials, primarily circulating on the visual arts and music. Exhibition space in display windows, interior display cases, corridors and special departments
Income: Financed by city and state appropriation
Purchases: $38,000
Library Holdings: Framed prints, unframed pictures; AV — Fs, motion pictures, rec, slides; Other — Framed reproductions, reproductions
Publications: Booklets, periodically
Activities: Lect and film showings; concerts

O **STAR-SPANGLED BANNER FLAG HOUSE ASSOCIATION,** 844 E Pratt St, 21202. *Pres* Hugh Benet Jr; *VPres* Herbert R Preston; *VPres* Mrs Miles B Hopkins; *VPres* Louis V Koerber; *Treasurer* John H Ensor; *Secy* Mrs Turner Moore; *Dir* Linda Vahrenkamp
Open Mon - Sat 10 AM - 4 PM, Sun 1 - 4 PM, cl Mon. Admis adults $1.50, students 12 - 18 $1, children 6 - 12 $.50, under 6 free. Estab 1927 for the care and maintenance of 1793 home of Mary Pickersgill, maker of 15 star, 15 stripe flag used at Fort McHenry during Battle of Baltimore, War of 1812, which inspired Francis Scott Key to pen his famous poem, now our national anthem; also to conduct an educational program for public and private schools. Museum houses artifacts, portraits and library. 1793 house furnished and decorated in Federal period to look as it did when Mary Pickersgill was in residence. Average

Annual Attendance: 20,000. Mem: 500; dues corporate $100, family $20, individual $10; annual meeting May
Collections: Flag collection; original antiques of Federal period
Exhibitions: Old and Historic Flag Exhibit
Publications: The Star (newsletter), quarterly
Activities: Educ dept; lectures open to public; concerts; gallery talks; tours; original objects of art loaned to other historical sites; museum sales shop sells books, reproductions, prints, slides, Baltimore souvenirs, flags from all nations, country crafts & small antiques

L **Library,** 844 E Pratt St, 21202. *Education Coordr & Registrar* Margaret Fowler; *Cur* Jane D Woltereck
Open to public for reference
Library Holdings: Vols 1500; Per subs 4; Government Documents; AV — A-tapes, slides; Other — Clipping files, exhibition catalogs, framed reproductions, manuscripts, memorabilia, original art works, pamphlets, photographs, prints, reproductions

M **UNITED METHODIST HISTORICAL SOCIETY,** Lovely Lane Museum, 2200 Saint Paul St, 21218. Tel 301-889-4458. *Pres* William Louis Piel; *Executive Secy* Edwin Schell
Open Mon & Fri 10 AM - 4 PM, Sun after church; groups by appointment. No admis fee. Estab 1855; a religious collection specializing in Methodism. The main museum room contains permanent exhibits; three other galleries are devoted largely to rotating exhibits. Average Annual Attendance: 5000. Mem: 509; dues $3 - $100; annual meeting May
Income: $29,187 (financed by membership, and religious denomination)
Collections: Church edifices, furniture, medallions and emblems, photographs, quilts, and statuary
Exhibitions: Our Ethnic Church Heritage; (1981) 100 Years of The World Methodist Council; (1982) Preparation For The Ministry; (1984) General Conferences
Publications: Third Century Methodism, quarterly; annual report
Activities: Docent training; lectures open to public, 1 vis lectr per year; gallery talks; tours; competitions with awards; sales shop sells books, prints, and cards

L **Library,** Lovely Lane Museum, 2200 Saint Paul St, 21218. *Librn* Edwin Schell; *Asst Librn* Betty Ammons
Open to general public for reference
Library Holdings: Vols 4500; Per subs 25; Archives; Micro — Reels; AV — A-tapes, cassettes, fs, Kodachromes, lantern slides, motion pictures, rec, slides; Other — Clipping files, manuscripts, memorabilia, original art works, pamphlets, photographs, prints, sculpture

M **WALTERS ART GALLERY,** 600 N Charles St, 21201. Tel 301-547-9000. *Pres* Board of Trustees Jay M Wilson; *Dir* Robert P Bergman; *Asst Dir Curatorial Affairs* William R Johnston; *Asst Dir Admin* Roy G Corbett; *Cur of Egyptian and Ancient Near Eastern Art* Jeanny Vorys Canby; *Cur of Greek and Roman Art* Diana M Buitron; *Cur of Manuscripts and Rare Books* Lilian M C Randall; *Cur of Medieval Art* Richard H Randall Jr; *Dir of Education* Diane Lynn Arkin; *Editor of Publications* Carol Stronecker; *Dir of Conservation Dept* Terry Drayman Weisser; *Registrar* Leopoldine Arz; *Sales Mgr* Mary Bahus
Open Tues - Sun 11 AM - 5 PM, cl Mon, New Year's Day, Fourth of July, Thanksgiving, Christmas Eve, Christmas. Admis adults $2, students & senior citizens $1, free admin on Wed. Estab 1931 by the will of Henry Walters and opened in 1934 as an art museum. A Renaissance revival museum of 1905 with a contemporary wing of five floors opened in 1974, covering 126,000 sq ft of exhibition space with auditorium, library and conservation laboratory. Average Annual Attendance: 222,000. Mem: 5000; dues $15 - $5000
Income: $2,400,000 (financed by endowment, membership, city and state appropriation and grants)
Collections: The Collection covers the entire history of art from Egyptian times to the beginning of the 20th century. It includes important groups of Roman Sculpture, Etruscan, Byzantine and medieval art; Sevres porcelains; Near Eastern Art and European paintings
Exhibitions: (1984) Japanese Art from the Gitter Collection; The Taste of Maryland; Prix de Rome French Paintings; Masterpiece of Medieval Painting: Illuminated Manuscripts from The Walters Collection
Publications: Bulletin, bi-monthly; journal, annually; exhibition catalogues
Activities: Classes for adults and children; docent training; seminars; lectures open to the public; concerts; gallery talks; tours; films; individual paintings and original objects of art lent; lending collection contains 25,000 original art works, 2000 paintings, 2500 sculpture; book traveling exhibitions, 3 - 4 per yr; originate traveling exhibitions; museum shop sells books, reproductions, slides, Christmas cards, notepaper

L **Library,** 600 N Charles St, 21201. Tel 301-547-9000, Ext 20. *Librn* Muriel L Toppan
Open Tues - Fri 11 AM - 5 PM. Estab 1934 chiefly to serve the curatorial staff; also provides art reference services for students and the general public. For reference only
Income: $68,000
Purchases: $36,300
Library Holdings: Vols 80,000; Per subs 500; Other — Exhibition catalogs
Special Subjects: History of art from prehistoric times to the end of the 19th century, with emphasis on manuscript illumination and decorative arts

CHESTERTOWN

O **HISTORICAL SOCIETY OF KENT COUNTY,*** 101 Church Alley, PO Box 665, 21620. *Pres* J Hurst Purnell Jr
Open May - Sept Sun 1 - 4 PM. Admis adults $1, children & students $.50. Estab 1936 to foster an appreciation of our colonial heritage, to encourage restoration, to enlighten and to entertain. Headquarters are in an early 18th century town house, beautifully restored and furnished. Mem: 525; dues family $10, single $7; annual meeting Apr
Income: Financed by membership and a Candlelight Tour
Collections: Furniture, pictures, some silver; Indian artifacts
Exhibitions: Annual Decorative Arts Forum
Activities: Lect for members and guests, 4 visiting lectr per year; tours; open house with traditional costuming

CHEVY CHASE

C GOVERNMENT EMPLOYEES INSURANCE COMPANY,* 5260 Western
Ave (Mailing add: GEICO Plaza, Washington, DC 20076). Tel 301-986-2502. *In
Charge Art Coll* Walter R Tinsley
Open to public by special arrangement. No admis fee. Estab 1959 for edification
and pleasure of officers, employees and visitors; to adorn the offices and common
areas. Collection displayed throughout office building
Collections: American contemporary art, 19th century and early 20th century
figurative art

COLLEGE PARK

M UNIVERSITY OF MARYLAND, COLLEGE PARK, Art Gallery,
Art-Sociology Bldg, 20742. Tel 301-454-2763. *Dir* Dr Arthur R Blumenthal; *Asst
to Dir* Vicki C Wright; *Exhibition Designer* John Birmingham
Open Mon - Fri 10 AM - 4 PM, Wed evening until 9 PM, Sat & Sun 1 - 5 PM,
cl summer & holidays. No admis fee. Estab 1966. Gallery has 4000 sq ft of
space, normally divided into one large & one smaller gallery. Average Annual
Attendance: 12,000
Income: Financed by university & dept funds
Collections: †Small collection of 20th century paintings, sculpture and prints,
including works executed on the WPA Federal Art Project and the Department
of the Treasury, †Section of Painting and Sculpture; small collection of West
African sculpture; collection of Andy Warhol paintings
Exhibitions: (1982-83) Louis Faurer: Photographs from Philadelphia & New
York, 1937-1973; David Driskell: A Survey; Ralston Crawford Photographs: Art
& Process; Traditional Forms & Modern Africa: West African Art at the
University of Maryland; 350 Years of Art & Architecture in Maryland
Publications: Catalogs for exhibitions, 6-8 per year
Activities: Lectures, symposiums & films open to public; gallery talks; tours;
originate traveling exhibitions; exhibition catalogs sold in gallery
L Art Library, Art-Sociology Bldg, 20742. Tel 301-454-2065. *Head Art Library*
Courtney Shaw; *Ref Librn* Patricia Lynagh; *Libr Asst* Patricia Lange; *Libr Asst*
Leslie May
Open Mon - Thurs 8:30 AM - 10 PM, Fri 8:30 AM - 5 PM, Sat 10 AM - 5 PM,
Sun 1 - 10 PM. Estab 1979 in new building to serve the needs of the art
department and campus in various art subjects
Purchases: Deloynes Collections; Alinari; Victoria & Albert; Southeast Asia
Collection; French Photography Collection; Index Iconologicus
Library Holdings: Vols 50,000; Per subs 234; Micro — Fiche, reels; Other —
Exhibition catalogs, reproductions
Collections: Decimal index to art of Low Countries; Marburg Index; Index of
American Design
Publications: Bibliography; Checklist of Useful Tools for the Study of Art
Activities: Tours
L Architecture Library, 20742. Tel 301-454-4316. *Head* Berna E Neal
Open Mon - Thurs 8:30 AM - 10 PM, Fri 8:30 AM - 5 PM, Sat 1 - 5 PM, Sun 5
- 10 PM. Estab 1967. Circ 13,810
Library Holdings: Vols 20,000; Per subs 154; Bd per 5000; Micro — Fiche 200,
reels 500
Special Subjects: Architecture, Landscape Architecture
Collections: World exhibitions, books & pamphlets on buildings, art work &
machinery
Publications: Acquisitions List, bi-monthly

COLUMBIA

M MARYLAND MUSEUM OF AFRICAN ART, PO Box 1105, 21044. Tel 301-
730-0011. *Dir* Claude M Ligon; *Cur* D Regina Hillain-Ligon
No admis fee. Estab 1980. Mem: Dues contributing $100, family $25, individual
$15, student $10
Collections: African art consisting of sculpture, textiles, masks and musical
instruments
Publications: Museum Memos, quarterly
Activities: Classes for children; lectures; tours

EASTON

M ACADEMY OF THE ARTS, Harrison & South Sts, PO Box 605, 21601. Tel
301-822-0455, 822-0457. *Pres* Judith S Straub; *Cur* Sydney K Hamburger; *Dir*
Anna C Larkin
Open Mon - Fri 10 AM - 4 PM, Sat 1 - 4 PM, cl Sun & bank holidays. No
admis fee. Estab 1958 to enrich the lives of the people in the community with
the arts through exposure and instruction. Two galleries are maintained. Average
Annual Attendance: 6000. Mem: 1200; dues individual $18, junior $10; annual
meeting May
Income: Financed by endowment, membership, city and state appropriation
Collections: †Permanent art collection
Publications: Newsletter, quarterly
Activities: Classes for adults and children; dramatic programs; docent training;
lectures open to the public; concerts; gallery talks; tours; competitions; film
series; exten dept serving tri-county area; individual paintings lent to different
organizations locally and to other galleries; lending collection contains books,
original art works, original prints, paintings, photographs
L Library,* Harrison & South Sts, PO Box 605, 21601
Open to members only
Library Holdings: Vols 500
Collections: Print Collection

FORT MEADE

M FORT GEORGE G MEADE MUSEUM, 4674 Griffin Ave, 20755. Tel 301-
677-6966; FTS 938-6966. *Cur* David C Cole; *Exhibit Specialist* Alan
Archambault; *Museum Technician* James A Speraw Jr
Open Wed - Sat 11 AM - 4 PM, Sun 1 - 4 PM, cl Mon, Tues and holidays. No
admis. Estab 1963 to collect, preserve, study and display military artifacts
relating to the United States Army, Fort Meade and the surrounding region.
Average Annual Attendance: 22,000
Income: Financed by federal and military funds
Collections: Military art; World War I, World War II and Civil War Periods
Exhibitions: (1984) The Civil War As Seen By Currier & Ives
Activities: Lect open to the public, 20 visiting lecturers per year; gallery talks;
tours; concerts

FROSTBURG

M FROSTBURG STATE COLLEGE, The Stephanie Ann Roper Gallery, 21532.
Tel 301-689-4109. *Head* Dustin P Davis
Open Wed - Fri & Sun 1:30 - 4 PM. No admis fee. Estab 1972 for educational
purposes. Average Annual Attendance: 3000
Income: Financed by state appropriation
Collections: Folk art; prints
Exhibitions: Duane Hanson; Mid-Atlantic Region Print Exhibition; Tenth Street
Days
Activities: Educ dept; lectures open to the public, 5 vis lectr per yr; gallery talks;
competitions with awards; individual and original objects of art lent for
exhibition; book traveling exhibitions, 4 per yr; junior museum
L Library, Frostburg, 21532
Library Holdings: Micro — Fiche; AV — A-tapes, cassettes, fs, Kodachromes,
motion pictures, slides, v-tapes

HAGERSTOWN

M WASHINGTON COUNTY MUSEUM OF FINE ARTS, City Park, PO Box
423, 21740. Tel 301-739-5727. *Pres Board of Trustees* Richard G Wantz; *Dir*
Jean Woods; *Cur* Robert E Preszler; *Secy* Mabert E Fox; *Educ Dir* Elizabeth
Altman
Open Tues - Sat 10 AM - 5 PM, Sun 1 - 6 PM, cl Mon. No admis fee. Estab
1939 and opened to the public in 1931 for the purpose of preserving, protecting,
promoting, displaying and educating through the arts. The museum consists of
the William H Singer Memorial Gallery, Sculpture Court, Concert Gallery, South
Gallery and North Gallery. Average Annual Attendance: 32,000. Mem: 600;
dues family $50, individual $15; annual meetings Nov
Income: $194,000 (financed by membership, city and county government)
Collections: American pressed glass; antique laces; †contemporary painting,
drawing, prints and sculpture; †European and †American sculpture, †prints and
drawings; illuminated manuscripts; Oriental jades and art; †ethnographic art;
decorative art; textiles; folk art
Exhibitions: Annual Exhibition of Cumberland Valley Artists; Annual
Photographic Salon; Fiber and Metal; Old Master Drawings; Paintings by Alice
Neel; Paintings by American Indians; Paintings by the Peale Family; American
Drawings II; English Landscapes by Philip Jackson; Victorian Art Glass; Crafts
Invitational; Data-Paintings by Charles Field and Richard Lutzke; David
Hatfield; Discovery in Stone; American Indian Baskets; Sculpture Fibers;
Germanic Heritage; Cullen Yates: American Impressionist; Dorothy Gillespie;
William H Singer, Jr (1868-1943)
Publications: The Fiftieth Year; American Pressed Glass; Old Master Drawings;
annual reports; bulletin, monthly; catalogs of major exhibitions; catalog of the
permanent collection; bi-monthly bulletin
Activities: Classes for adults and children; dramatic programs; docent training;
lectures open to public, 10 vis lectr per yr; concerts; gallery talks; tours;
competitions with awards; scholarships and fels offered; exten dept serving
Pennsylvania, Virginia, West Virginia, western Maryland; individual paintings
and original objects of art lent to other museums and galleries, as per museum
policy regarding security; book traveling exhibitions; sales shop selling books,
magazines, original art, reproductions, prints, slides and original art objects and
hand crafted items
L Library,* City Park, PO Box 423, 21740
Open to the public for reference only
Library Holdings: Vols 6000; Per subs 5; Micro — Cards; AV — Cassettes, fs,
motion pictures, rec, slides; Other — Clipping files, exhibition catalogs

MONKTON

M BREEZEWOOD FOUNDATION MUSEUM AND GARDEN, 3722 Hess Rd,
21111. Tel 301-472-9438. *Pres* A B Griswold
Open May - Oct, first Sun each month 2 - 5:30 PM. Admis $2. Estab 1956 to
exhibit Breezewood's collection of sculpture and other art from Southeast Asia.
Museum has one large room and two small rooms. Average Annual Attendance:
280
Income: Financed by endowment and private means
Collections: Buddhist art from India; sculpture and art from Southeast Asia

ROCKVILLE

M JUDAIC MUSEUM OF THE JEWISH COMMUNITY CENTER, Goldman
Fine Arts Gallery, 6125 Montrose Rd, 20352. Tel 301-881-0100. *Pres* Philip N
Margolius; *Exec Dir* Lester Kaplan; *Dir* Susan W Morgenstein
Open Mon - Thur Noon - 4 PM & 7:30 - 9:30 PM, Sun 2 - 5 PM. No admis fee.
Estab 1925 to preserve, exhibit and promulgate Jewish culture. Average Annual
Attendance: 25,000
Income: Financed by endowment, corporate, private and public gifts and grants
and sales

Exhibitions: Beth Ames Swartz: Israel Revisited; The Jews in the Age of Rembrandt; First Generation: Jewish Immigrant Artists in America; ?Charlotte: Life or Theater
Publications: Exhibition catalogues; brochures
Activities: Classes for adults & children; docent training; lectures open to public; concerts; gallery talks; tours; book traveling exhibitions; originate traveling exhibitions; museum shop sells books, original art, reproductions & prints

SAINT MICHAELS

M **CHESAPEAKE BAY MARITIME MUSEUM,** Navy Point, PO Box 636, 21663. Tel 301-745-2916. *Dir* R J Holt
Open Oct - May, Tues - Sun 10 AM - 4 PM; cl Mon; Jan-March weekends only; May - Oct daily 10 AM - 5 PM. Admis adults $2.50, children $1. Estab 1968 as a waterside museum dedicated to preserving the maritime history of the Chesapeake Bay. Consists of fifteen buildings on approximately 16 acres of waterfront property including Hooper's Strait Lighthouse, 1879. Average Annual Attendance: 70,000. Mem: 3000; dues $10 - $35
Income: Financed by membership and admissions
Collections: Paintings; ship models; vessels including skipjack, bugeye, log canoes, and many small crafts; waterfowling exhibits; working boat shop
Publications: Weather Gauge (newsletter), quarterly
Activities: Classes for adults and children; lectures open to public, 10 vis lectr per year; concerts; gallery talks; tours; museum shop books, original art, reproductions, prints, slides
L **Library,** Navy Point, PO Box 636, 21663. *Cur Collection* Sandra Bult
Small library for research only by appointment with curator
Income: Financed by endowment
Library Holdings: Vols 3000; Per subs 5; Micro — Cards; Other — Clipping files, pamphlets
Special Subjects: Local art, maritime history

SALISBURY

SALISBURY STATE COLLEGE
M **College Gallery,** College & Camden Aves, Art Department, 21801. Tel 301-543-6000. *Acting Pres* Dr A N Page; *Gallery Dir* John R Cleary
Open 10 AM - 10 PM. No admis fee. Estab 1967, to provide a variety of fine arts to the college and community, with emphasis on educational value of exhibitions. Gallery open to public, and is located on the second floor of Blackwell Library, hours vary. Average Annual Attendance: 3200
Income: Financed by state appropriations
Collections: Contemporary prints
Exhibitions: (1982-83) Baskets of the Southwest; Chagall's Exodus; faculty show; permanent collection; Eastern Shore Potters; Images of Christianity, Mandarin Squares; Korean Drawing Now; Kent English, recent paintings; Roy Scott; Barye's Animals, Pages of Kitaj; student show; senior show; Alice Aycock; John Cleary: New Work; Marie Tator, sculpture; Myth Prints
Publications: Announcements
Activities: Classes for adults; dramatic programs; lectures open to public; gallery talks; tours; scholarships; originate traveling exhibitions
L **Blackwell Library, Art Department,** College & Camden Aves, 21801. Tel 301-546-6130. *Library Dir* James R Thrash
Open Mon - Thurs 8 AM - Midnight, Fri 8 AM - 10 PM, Sat 10 AM - 5 PM, Sun Noon - Midnight. Estab 1925, to support the curriculum of Salisbury State College. Library has total space of 66,000 sq ft. Circ 2500
Library Holdings: Vols 128,618; Per subs 36; Micro — Cards, fiche, reels; AV — A-tapes, cassettes, fs, motion pictures, rec, slides, v-tapes; Other — Clipping files, pamphlets
M **Wildfowl Art Museum,*** Camden Ave, PO Box 703, 21801. Tel 301-742-4988. *Dir* Ken Basile; *Chmn* Tom George; *Vice Chmn* Max Hughes; *Secy* Bill Humphreys; *Treas* Ted Crockett; *Cur* Cindy Doerzbach; *Asst Cur* Katie Fox; *Secy* Barbara Gehrm; *Gift Shop Coordr* Peggy Parsons; *Gift Shop Coordr* Elmer Lowe
Open daily 1 - 5 PM. Admis $1, members & children under 12 free. Estab 1976, a non-profit organization dedicated to the preservation and conservation of wildfowl carving. Main gallery and balcony contain 2000 carvings, prints and paintings of wildfowl related items, including the World Championship carvings. Average Annual Attendance: 5000. Mem: 4000; dues family $25, individual $15, student $5; annual meeting March
Income: $77,297 (financed by membership, city and state appropriations, grants, donations, gift shop sales)
Collections: Permanent collection of 2300 bird carvings
Exhibitions: (1980) Annual Fall Exhibition (October); Annual Spring Competition (April)
Publications: Newletter, four times per year
Activities: Lectures for members only; carving workshop held once a year in the spring; individual paintings and original objects of art lent; lending collection contains color reproductions, framed reproductions, original art works, original prints, paintings, photographs, sculpture; museum shop sells books, magazines, original art, reproductions, prints, slides, decoys and video show

SILVER SPRING

INTERNATIONAL ASSOCIATION OF CONTEMPORARY MOSAICISTS
For further information, see National and Regional Organizations

L **MARYLAND COLLEGE OF ART AND DESIGN LIBRARY,** 10500 Georgia Ave, 20902. Tel 301-649-4454. *Head Librn* Laura C Pratt; *Librn* M Elizabeth Stites
Open Mon - Thurs 8:30 AM - 9:30 PM, Fri 8:30 AM - 5 PM, some evenings. Estab 1977 to facilitate and encourage learning by the students and to provide aid for the faculty. College maintains Gudelsky Gallery. Circ 7200
Purchases: $6153
Library Holdings: Vols 10,000; Per subs 25; AV — Cassettes, motion pictures, rec 117, slides 14,000; Other — Clipping files
Special Subjects: Drawings, Illustration, Sculpture, Design, Painting, Visual Communications

SOLOMONS

M **CALVERT MARINE MUSEUM,** PO Box 97, 20688. Tel 301-326-3719. *Dir* Ralph E Eshelman; *Registrar* David J Bohaska; *Exhib Designer* Bette Bumgarner; *Master Woodcarver* Pepper Langley; *Educational Coordr* Scott Rawlins
Open May - Sept, Mon - Sat 10 AM - 5 PM, Sun 1 - 5 PM, Oct - April, Mon - Fri 10 AM - 4:30 PM, Sat & Sun 1 - 4:30 PM. No admis fee. Estab 1970, to provide the public with a marine oriented museum on maritime history, estuarine natural history and marine paleontology. Gallery is maintained on the history of sail. Average Annual Attendance: 50,000. Mem: 1000; dues family $15, individual $12
Income: $130,000 (financed by county appropriation)
Purchases: $1000
Collections: J S Bohannon Folk Art Steamboat Collection; †local Chesapeake Bay Ship Portraits; Tufnell Watercolor Collection; †watercolor decoys
Exhibitions: Fossils of Calvert Cliffs: A 10 x 7 ft mural depicting Marine Miocene life; John Olsen Chapter of American Shipcarving Guild Exhibit; War on the Patuxent: 1814; History of an Underwater Archaeological Search for the Ill Fated Chesapeake Flotilla
Publications: Newsletter 'Bugeye Times', quarterly; Flotilla: Battle for the Patuxent; War on the Patuxent, 1814: A Catalog of Artifacts; miscellaneous special publications on history; A History of Drum Point Lighthouse; Fossils of Calvert Cliffs; Watercraft Collection, brochure; The Drum Point Lighthouse, brochure
Activities: Classes for adults and children; docent training; lect open to the public, 16 visiting lectrs per year; gallery talks; tours; competitions; awards; individual paintings and original objects of art lent; lending collection contains motion pictures, nature artifacts, photographs, slides; sales shop sells books, prints, slides, hand crafts
L **Library,** PO Box 97, 20688. Tel 301-326-3719
Open May - Sept, Mon - Sat 10 AM - 5 PM, Sun 1 - 5 PM, Oct - April, Mon - Fri 10 AM - 4:30 PM, Sat & Sun 1 - 5 PM. Estab 1974. Library open for research and reference
Activities: Originate traveling exhibitions

TOWSON

M **GOUCHER COLLEGE,** Kraushaar Auditorium Lobby Gallery,* Department of Art, 1021 Dulaney Valley Rd, 21204. Tel 301-337-6256. *Chmn Dept* Lincoln F Johnson
Open Mon - Fri 9 AM - 5 PM during the academic calendar and on evenings and weekends of public events. No admis fee. Estab 1964 to display temporary and continuously changing exhibitions of contemporary and historically important visual arts. Gallery space located in the lobby of the Kraushaar Auditorium; 150 running feet of wall space. Average Annual Attendance: 15,000
Income: Financed privately
Collections: Elizabeth Morris Collection; ceramics; coins; drawings; paintings; prints; sculpture; textiles containing over 200 objects representing textiles from Egypt, Peru, Java, China, Japan, Europe and America
Exhibitions: Jeff Powley, Stained Glass Window Installation; Carol Linnsley, Paintings 1975-1980 Contemporary Redism in Graphic Art; Afro-American Painting, sculpture, works on paper 1864-1981; Baltimore Currents: Intimate Interiors; Baltimore Currents: Dimensions in Abstraction; Annual Student Exhibition; Machine Messages: Uses of the Xerox Image; Maryland Arts Council Award Exhibiton III; Configurations: A Selection of Contemporary Photography; Selections from the Goucher Collection; Contemporary Watercolors; Paintings by Wil Brunner, Sigrid Trumpy & Ceramics by Kovner-Lewin; Ed Worteck, Recent Photographs
Activities: Lect open to public, 3 visiting lectrs per year; gallery talks; individual paintings and original objects of art lent to museums and university galleries

TOWSON STATE UNIVERSITY
M **The Holtzman Art Gallery,** Osler Dr, 21204. Tel 301-321-2808. *Dir* Christopher Bartlett
Open Mon - Fri 11 AM - 4 PM, Tues & Thurs 6 - 9 PM, Sat & Sun 1 - 5 PM. Estab 1973 to provide a wide variety of art exhibitions, primarily contemporary work, for students, faculty and community. The main gallery is situated in the new fine arts building directly off the foyer. It is 30 x 60 ft with 15 ft ceiling and 15 x 30 ft storage area. Average Annual Attendance: 10,000
Income: $10,000 (financed by state appropriation, cultural services fees and private gifts)
Purchases: $1000
Collections: African art; †Asian arts, through Roberts Art Collection; †contemporary painting and sculpture
Exhibitions: Art department faculty; art student show; Chao-Hwa Tung, Chinese brush painting; Drawings USA 77; Haitian Paintings; John Mitchell, plastics & prints; Leonard Baskin, new graphics & watercolors; Milton Avery, prints; Morningstar Quilts; Naive Art in Yugoslavia; National Ceramic Invitational: Function - Non-Function; New American Monotypes; New Directions in Fabric Design, national invitational; Colleen Browning, paintings; Theatre Design, A Student Perspective; Tyler School of Art Faculty Exhibit, painting, drawing & sculpture; Low Fire Clay Sculpture; Mary Frank (works on paper); Push Pin Posters; Contemporary Australian Printmakers; Century of American Landscape Photography; Philip Pearlstein, lithographs & etchings; Sculptors Who Teach Maryland Artists Exhibition; Mary Ann Krutsick, paintings; Christopher Bartlett, sculpture & watercolors; Korean Drawings Now; 20th Century American Watercolor
Publications: Calendar, each semester; exhibition posters and catalogs
Activities: Lectures open to public, 5 - 10 visiting lectr per year; gallery talks; tours; artmobile; book 2 - 3 traveling exhibitions per year; sales shop selling exhibition catalogs and posters
L **Roberts Gallery,** Fine Arts Building, Osler Dr and Cross Campus Dr, 21204. Tel 301-321-2807. *Cur* Harriet McNamee
Open during academic year Mon - Fri 10 AM - Noon and 2 - 4 PM; summers Mon - Fri 10 AM - Noon and 1 - 3 PM. No admis fee. Estab 1972 to provide an area to display the Asian art collections of the University and for the benefit of

both the university community and the public. The gallery is located on the second floor of the Fine Arts Building. Average Annual Attendance: 3000
Income: Financed by state appropriation and university budget
Collections: Asian Ceramics; ivory; metalwork; furniture; paintings; prints; textiles
Exhibitions: Permanent collection
Activities: Lectures open to public; 2 vis lectr per year; gallery talks; tours; workshops; concerts; performances; individual and original objects of art lent to educational and cultural institutions

WESTMINSTER

M **WESTERN MARYLAND COLLEGE,** Gallery One, Department of Art, 21157. Tel 301-848-7000, Ext 596. *Gallery Dir* Wasyl Palijczuk
Open Mon - Fri 10 AM - 4 PM. No admis fee. Estab to expose students to original works by professional artists
Exhibitions: Six visiting artists shows; student shows; faculty & alumni show

MASSACHUSETTS

AMHERST

M **AMHERST COLLEGE,** Mead Art Museum, 01002. Tel 413-542-2335. *Dir* Frank Trapp; *Cur* Judith Barter
Open Mon - Fri 10 AM - 4:30 PM, Sat & Sun 1 - 5 PM (fewer hours during summer), cl Aug. No admis fee. Estab 1949. Average Annual Attendance: 13, 500. Mem: 500; dues $10; annual meetings in the spring
Collections: †Ancient art; †American art; †English art; Western European and Oriental collections
Exhibitions: (1982) Joseph Ablow; Isabel Bishop; Henry Buksztynowicz; Jim Frazer; E Powis Jones; Gabriel Aderman; Michael Mazur; Jan Menses; Herbert W Plimpton Collection of American Art; Bill Ravanesi; Iwa Yoruba Art; changing exhibitions for college curriculum needs
Publications: American Art at Amherst: A Summary Catalogue of the Collection at the Mead Art Gallery; Mead Museum Monographs, annually; catalogs for major exhibitions
Activities: Education dept; lectures open to public; 3 vis lect per yr; gallery talks; tours; individual paintings and original objects of art lent for exhibition only to other museums
L **Art Library,** Mead Art Bldg, 01002
Library Holdings: Vols 20,000

L **JONES LIBRARY, INC,** 43 Amity St, 01002. Tel 413-256-0246. *Dir* Bonnie Isman; *Asst Dir* Sondra M Radosh; *Reference Librn* Pauline M Peterson; *Adult Service Librn* Beth Girshman; *Cur* Dan Lombardo
Open Mon, Wed, Fri and Sat 9 AM - 5:30 PM, Tues & Thurs 9 AM - 9:30 PM, Sun 1 PM - 5 PM; Special Collections has limited hours. Estab 1919 as a public library. Gallery. Circ 210,000. Average Annual Attendance: 100,000
Income: Financed by endowment and city appropriation
Library Holdings: Micro — Reels; AV — A-tapes, cassettes, rec, slides; Other — Clipping files, framed reproductions, manuscripts, memorabilia, original art works, pamphlets, photographs, sculpture
Collections: †Emily Dickinson; Harlan Fiske Stone; Ray Stannard Baker; †Robert Frost; †Sidney Waugh Writings; †local history & geneology; J J Lankes
Exhibitions: Gallery has monthly exhibits by local artists and craftspeople
Activities: Lect open to public; concerts; tours

UNIVERSITY OF MASSACHUSETTS, AMHERST

M **University Gallery,** Fine Arts Center, 01003. Tel 413-545-3670. *Gallery Mgr* Craig Allaben; *Actg Dir & Registrar* Betsy Siersma; *Actg Dir & Cur* Helaine Posner; *Cur Asst* Karen Koehler
Open Tues - Fri 11 AM - 4:30 PM, Sat & Sun 2 - 5 PM during school year. No admis fee. Estab 1962. Main gallery 60 x 60 ft; East, West and Lower Galleries 20 x 60 ft each. Average Annual Attendance: 65,000. Mem: 150; dues $8 and up
Collections: †20th century American works on paper including drawings, prints and photographs
Exhibitions: Judy Pfaff; Richard Nonas; Michael Brewster; Barbara Zucker; Donald Evans; Contemporary Prints: The Figure Beside Itself; Vito Acconci; Do Did Done (performance series): Alex Gray, Fab Five Freddie, Ann Magnuson, Jeff Way; Eleven Alumni; Jim Roche; Fred Sandback; The Prints of Barnett Newman; Martin Puryear
Publications: Exhibition catalogs
Activities: Lect open to the public; gallery talks; tours; film program; individual art works from the permanent collection loaned to other institutions; originate traveling exhibitions
L **Dorothy W Perkins Slide Library,** Bartlett Hall, 01003. Tel 413-545-3595. *Dir* Louise Bloomberg
Open Mon - Fri 8 AM - 3:30 PM. Circ 60,000 (slides)
Library Holdings: Study Plates 7000; Micro — Fiche 1000; AV — Rec, slides 260,000

ANDOVER

M **PHILLIPS ACADEMY,** Addison Gallery of American Art,* 01810. Tel 617-475-7515. *Dir* Christopher C Cook; *Cur Photography* James L Sheldon; *Registrar* Antoinette Thiras
Open Tues - Sat 10 AM - 5 PM, Sun 2:30 - 5 PM. No admis fee. Estab 1931 in memory of Mrs Keturah Addison Cobb, to enrich permanently the lives of the students by helping to cultivate and foster in them a love for the beautiful. The gift also included a number of important paintings, prints and sculpture as a nucleus for the beginning of a permanent collection of American art. Maintains

small reference library for museum use only. Average Annual Attendance: 35,000
Income: Financed by endowment
Collections: 18th, 19th and 20th century drawings, paintings, prints, sculpture; photographs; film; videotapes
Exhibitions: The American Still Life, 1835-1979; Photographs by Lotte Jacobi; Masterworks from the Permanent Collection; Wall Drawing by Sol Lewitt; Sandy Skoglund-Radioactive Cats; Photographs by Berenice Abbott (1930's); Photo Sculptures by Douglas Prince
Activities: Lect open to public, 8-10 visiting lectrs per year; concerts

ATTLEBORO

M **ATTLEBORO MUSEUM, CENTER FOR THE ARTS,** Capron Park, 199 County St, 02703. Tel 617-222-2644. *Pres* Mrs Charles O'Connell; *VPres* Mrs Richard Sweet; *Treas* Mervell T Cronin; *Dir* Mrs F K Cross
Open Tues - Fri 12:30 - 4 PM, Sat & Sun 2 - 5 PM, cl Mon & holidays. No admis fee. Estab 1927 to exhibit the works of current artists, as well as the art works of the museum's own collection. There are preview openings for members and guests, plus several competitive exhibits with awards and an outdoor art festival. Three galleries, with changing monthly exhibits of paintings, drawings and prints as well as glass cases for jewelry and crafts, are maintained. All three galleries are carpeted with grass cloth walls and excellent track lighting. Average Annual Attendance: 7200. Mem: 300; dues life mem $250, sustaining mem $25, associate mem $20, family $15, individual $10; annual meeting May
Income: Financed by membership, gifts
Collections: Paintings and prints
Exhibitions: (1983-84) The Lacemakers; 1980 Sumac; Holiday Show; Annual Area Artist Exhibit; Japanese Brushwork; Two Members; One Man Show; Competitive Painting Show; Journey Into Africa; Art in the Park; Summer Members Show
Publications: Newsletter, monthly; school brochures; yearly program booklet
Activities: Classes for adults and children; lect open to public; concerts; gallery talks; competitions, painting and photography; original objects of art lent; museum shop sells original art

BEVERLY

M **BEVERLY HISTORICAL SOCIETY,** Cabot, Hale and Balch House Museums, 117 Cabot St, 01915. Tel 617-922-1186. *Pres* Harold Pinkham; *Treas* Ray Standley
Three museums open May 20 - Oct 20 Wed - Sat 10 AM - 4 PM, Sun, Memorial Day & Columbus Day 1 - 4 PM, Cabot Museum open Oct 16 - May 19 Thur - Sat 10 AM - 4 PM. Admis adults $2 (all three museums for $5), children under 16 $.50 (all three museums for $1). The Balch House built in 1636 by John Balch contains period furniture. The Hale House was built in 1694 by the first minister, John Hale. Cabot House built in 1781-82 by prominent merchant and private owner, John Cabot. Average Annual Attendance: 2000. Mem: 450; dues families $15, single $10; annual meeting Oct
Collections: 120 paintings containing portraits, folk and Revolutionary War scenes; 200 pieces furniture, toys, doll houses, military and maritime items and pewter
Exhibitions: Beverly Mariners and the China Trade; Two Hundred Years at the House of Cabot; Christmas in New England
Publications: Quarterly newsletter, annual report
Activities: Docent training; lectures open to public and some for members only; gallery talks by arrangement; tours; indivudual paintings and original objects of art lent to other museums and libraries; sales shop sells books and postcards
L **Library,** 117 Cabot St, 01915
Library Holdings: Vols 4000; Per subs 2; AV — A-tapes, motion pictures, slides; Other — Clipping files, manuscripts, memorabilia, pamphlets, photographs, prints, sculpture
Special Subjects: New England Maritime and Transportation History; Beverly History

BOSTON

ARCHAEOLOGICAL INSTITUTE OF AMERICA
For further information, see National and Regional Organizations

M **THE ART INSTITUTE OF BOSTON,** Gallery West, Gallery East, 700 Beacon St, 02215. Tel 617-262-1223. *Dir* William H Willis; *Chmn Gallery* Angelo Fertitta
Open Mon - Fri 9 AM - 5 PM, Mon - Thurs 6 - 7 PM. No admis fee. Estab 1969 to show work by young New England artists, all disciplines and work by well known artists from any locale, especially in less exhibited disciplines such as graphic design, and to show work by students and faculty of the Institute. 3000 sq ft of gallery. Average Annual Attendance: 2500
Exhibitions: Alternatives '81 national juried traveling photography exhibiton; Outer Boston Project, NEA funded photography survey; Ulises Carrion artist's books; Masond Yasami (paintings); Thirty-one selected shows
Activities: Classes for adults; lectures open to the public, five visiting lecturers per year; lecture series coordinated with exhibitions; gallery talks; competitions, local and regional, usually student oriented; extension department serving metropolitan Boston; individual paintings and original objects of art lent to other galleries; book traveling exhibitions 2-3 per yr
L **Library,** 700 Beacon St, 02215. Tel 617-262-1223. *Librn* Andrea DesJardins
Open Mon - Thurs 9 AM - 9 PM, Fri 9 AM - 5 PM. Estab 1969 to support school curriculum
Purchases: $12,200
Library Holdings: Vols 6500; Per subs 65; AV — Kodachromes, slides; Other — Clipping files, exhibition catalogs

O **BOSTON ARCHITECTURAL CENTER,** 320 Newbury St, 02115. Tel 617-536-3170
Open Mon - Thurs 9 AM - 11 PM, Fri - Sun 9 AM - 5 PM. No admis fee. Estab 1883 for education of architects and designers. Small exhibition space on first floor. Average Annual Attendance: 2000. Mem: 300; dues $25; annual meeting June
Activities: Classes for adults; lect open to public, 16 visiting lectrs per year; competitions; exten dept serving professional architects; traveling exhibitions organized and circulated
L **Memorial Library,*** 320 Newbury St, 02115. *Chief Librn* Susan Lewis; *Asst Librn* Margaret Bartley
Open by appointment only
Library Holdings: Vols 2000
Collections: 18th, 19th and early 20th century architectural books from the collections of practicing architects

O **BOSTON ART COMMISSION OF THE CITY OF BOSTON,** 1 City Hall Square, 02201. Tel 617-725-3850. *Chmn* William B Osgood; *Exec Secy* Mary O Shannon; *Commissioner* Carol A Bratley; *Commissioner* Stephen D Paine; *Commissioner* Donald L Stull; *Commissioner* Robert Cormier
Estab 1898 to accept and maintain the art collection owned by the City of Boston. Mem: 5; one representative from each organization: Boston Society of Architects, Massachusetts Institute of Technology, Boston Public Library, Copley Society, and Boston Museum of Fine Arts; meetings approx once per month
Income: Financed by city appropriation
Collections: City of Boston art collection, including fountains, paintings, sculpture, †statuary
Publications: Catalog and guide to the art work owned by the City of Boston, in preparation; Passport to Public Art
Activities: Competitions

L **BOSTON ATHENAEUM,*** 10 1/2 Beacon St, 02108. Tel 617-227-0270. *Dir & Librn* Rodney Armstrong; *Art Librn* Jack Jackson; *Art Gallery Dir* Donald C Kelley; *Print Dept Cur* Sally Pierce; *Honorary Cur of Prints* Charles E Mason Jr
Open Mon - Fri 9 AM - 5:30 PM, Sat 9 AM - 4 PM; cl Sun also Sat June 1 - Sept 1. Estab 1807 to serve New England living artists in the fine arts and crafts
Income: $750,000 (financed by endowment and membership)
Purchases: $75,000
Library Holdings: Original documents; Micro — Reels; Other — Clipping files, exhibition catalogs, manuscripts, memorabilia, original art works, pamphlets, photographs, prints, reproductions, sculpture
Collections: †19th century Boston prints & photographs
Exhibitions: Change monthly
Publications: Exhibition catalogs
Activities: Lect open to the public, 6 vis lectr per year; concerts; gallery talks; tours

M **THE BOSTONIAN SOCIETY,** Old State House, 206 Washington St, 02109. Tel 617-242-5655. *Pres* Joshua A S Young; *Treasurer* Lee R Forker Jr; *Asst Treasurer & Clerk* Roger Allan Moore; *Dir* Thomas W Parker; *Museum Mgr* Donald J Conn
Open Apr - Oct Mon - Sun 9:30 AM - 5 PM, Nov - Mar Mon - Fri 10 AM - 4 PM, Sat 9:30 AM - 5 PM, Sun 11 AM - 5 PM. Admis adult $.75, sr citizens $.50, children $.25, free for Massachusetts school children. Estab 1881 to collect and preserve the history of Boston. Mem: 1200; dues life $150, family $25, individual $15; annual meeting
Income: Financed by endowment, membership, city and state appropriation
Collections: Paintings and artifacts relating to Boston history; Maritime art
Exhibitions: Marine Art at State Street Bank Gallery; 350 Years of State Street at State Street Bank Gallery; permanent collection
Publications: Proceedings of The Bostonian Society
Activities: Lectures for members only, 3 vis lectr per yr; tours; individual paintings and original objects of art lent to museums for special exhibits; sales shop sells books, reproductions, prints, slides, brass, pewter and china
L **Library,** 15 State St, 3rd Floor, 02109. *Librn* Mary Leen; *Cataloger* Andrea DesJardins
Open Mon - Fri 9:30 AM - 4:30 PM. Estab 1881 to collect and preserve material related to the history of Boston
Purchases: $1000
Library Holdings: Vols 8000; Per subs 10; Postcards, Ephemera, Scrapbooks, Documents; AV — Slides; Other — Clipping files, manuscripts, memorabilia, original art works, pamphlets, photographs, prints, reproductions
Special Subjects: History of Boston

BOSTON PUBLIC LIBRARY
L **Central Library,** Copley Square, 02117. Tel 617-536-5400. *Actg Dir* Liam Kelly
Building contains mural decorations by Edwin A Abbey, John Elliott, Pierre Puvis de Chavannes, and John Singer Sargent; bronze doors by Daniel Chester French; sculptures by Frederick MacMonnies, Bela Pratt, Louis Saint Gaudens, Francis Derwent Wood; illustratons by Howard Pyle; paintings by Copley and Duplessis; and bust of John Deferrari by Joseph A Coletti
Income: Financed by city and state appropriation
Publications: Exhibition catalogues
Activities: Lectures open to the public; concerts; gallery talks; tours; book traveling exhibitions
L **Fine Arts Dept,** Copley Square, 02117. Tel 617-536-5400; Telex 710-321-0513. *Coordr Art & Architecture* Theresa D Cederholm
Open Mon - Thurs 9 AM - 9 PM, Fri & Sat 9 AM - 5 PM, Sun 2 - 6 PM, clo Sun June - Sept. Non-circulating
Library Holdings: Vols 138,000; Per subs 350; Micro — Fiche, reels; AV — Lantern slides; Other — Clipping files, exhibition catalogs, manuscripts, memorabilia, pamphlets, photographs, prints, reproductions
Collections: Vertical files on local artists, architects & organizations
Activities: Lectures open to public; concerts; gallery talks; tours

M **Albert H Wiggin Gallery (Prints),** Copley Square, 02117. *Keeper of Prints* Sinclair H Hitchings
Open Mon - Fri 9 AM - 9 PM, Sat 9 AM - 6 PM, Sun 2 - 6 PM in winter. Print Study Room Mon - Fri 9 AM - 5 PM, cl Sat & Sun
Collections: Alfred H Wiggin Collection of 18th & 19th Centuries French & English Prints; large photographic holdings; architectural archives; paintings
Exhibitions: Eight or nine per year
Activities: Individual paintings & original objects of art lent; lending collections contains 70,000 original prints, paintings, 500,000 photographs
L **Rare Book & Manuscripts Dept,** Copley Sq, 02117. Tel 617-536-5400, Ext 425. *In Charge* Dr Laura Monti; *Keeper* Ellen Oldham; *Asst Keeper* Berta Zonghi
Open 9 AM - 5 PM. Average Annual Attendance: 1000
Income: Financed by trust funds
Special Subjects: Navigation & Travel, Sciences, Spanish & Portugese, West Indies
Collections: †Abolitionism; †Americana: anti-slavery, history, colonization & discovery; Spanish & Portuguese: literature, history & economics; theater: playbills, plays, programs; juvenilia; women: authors, marriage, manners & customs; science: astronomy, physics & mathematics; English: literature, history & laws; classical literature; history of printing; botany; landscape & gardening; religion

O **CHILDREN'S ART CENTRE,*** 36 Rutland St, 02118. Tel 617-536-9666. *Exec Dir* Frieda Garcia; *Coordr* Pat Wirtenberg; *Admin Asst* Kim Moriarty
Open July - Aug Mon - Fri 9 AM - 3 PM, Sept - June Mon 2 - 5 PM, Tues - Fri 9 AM - 5 PM, Sat 10 AM - Noon. Estab 1916 to provide an aesthic environment conducive to learning about, viewing & creating art. Art gallery exhibits a variety of artwork in all media created by local artists. Average Annual Attendance: 5500. Mem: 500; meetings in June
Income: Financed by the United Way, Institute of Museum Services, Massachusetts Council on the Arts & Humanities
Collections: American Indian objects, baskets, blankets; small Egyptian artifacts
Activities: Classes for adults and children, teacher training course; scholarships

C **EASTERN GAS AND FUEL ASSOCIATES,*** One Beacon St, 02108. Tel 617-742-9200. *Pub Rel* Eleanor A Tishler
Open to public by appointment only. 1977 to educate employees in the various forms of art
Purchases: $10,000
Collections: Acrylic, collagraphs, fiber weaving, oil, paper, posters, quilts, serigraphs, watercolors
Activities: Individual objects of art lent to local exhibits

C **FEDERAL RESERVE BANK OF BOSTON,*** 600 Atlantic Ave, 02106. Tel 617-973-3000. *In Charge Art Collection* Anne M Belson
Open Mon - Fri 9 AM - 5 PM by appointment only. No admis fee. Estab 1978 for educational and cultural activities. Collection displayed on 3rd, 4th, 31st and 32nd floors and elsewhere throughout building. A permanent gallery, 27 x 178 ft with an adjoining 420-seat auditorium, located on the ground floor; open Mon - Fri 10 AM - 4 PM; is reserved for traveling exhibitions
Collections: Focus of the collection is on United States art since the mid-1950's
Activities: Lect; gallery talks; tours; book traveling exhibitions

M **ISABELLA STEWART GARDNER MUSEUM,*** 280 Fenway (Mailing add: 2 Palace Rd, 02115). Tel 617-566-1401. *Dir* Rollin van N Hadley; *Asst Dir* Linda V Hewitt; *Cur* Deborah Gribbon
Open Sept - June Tues Noon - 9 PM, Wed - Sun Noon - 5 PM, July - Aug Tues - Sun Noon - 5 PM, cl Mon & national holidays. No admis fee, suggested donation $1. Estab 1903, the museum houses Isabella Stewart Gardner's various collections. Museum building is styled after a 16th century Venetian villa; all galleries open onto a central, glass-roofed courtyard, filled with flowers that are changed with the seasons of the year. Mem: 170,000
Income: Financed by endowment and membership donations
Collections: Gothic and Italian Renaissance, Roman and classical sculpture; Dutch and Flemish 17th century; Japanese screens; Oriental and Islamic ceramics, glass, sculpture; 19th century American and French paintings
Publications: Guide to the Collection; Oriental and Islamic Art in the Isabella Stewart Gardner Museum; European and American Paintings in The Isabella Stewart Gardner Museum, Drawings-Isabella Stewart Gardner Museum; Titian's Rape of Europe; Isabella Stewart Gardner and Fenway Court; A Checklist of the Correspondence of Isabella Stewart Gardner at the Gardner Museum; Sculpture in the Isabella Stewart Gardner Museum; The Isabella Stewart Gardner Museum
Activities: Sales shop selling books, reproductions, prints, slides
L **Library,*** 2 Palace Rd, 02115. Tel 617-566-1401. *Librn* Hope Coolidge; *Archivist* Susan Sinclair
Open to scholars who need to work with museum archives
Library Holdings: Vols 800; Per subs 6
Special Subjects: Art History

M **GIBSON SOCIETY, INC,** Gibson House Museum, 137 Beacon St, 02116. Tel 617-267-6338. *Pres* George R Ursul; *Mgr* Rebecca A Guild
Open May - Oct Tue - Sun, Nov - April Sat & Sun 2 - 5 PM, cl holidays. Admis $2. Estab 1957 as a Victorian House museum. Average Annual Attendance: 1500
Collections: Decorative arts; paintings; sculpture; Victorian period furniture
Activities: Guided tours; sales shop selling books and postcards

O **GUILD OF BOSTON ARTISTS,** 162 Newbury St, 02116. Tel 617-536-7660. *Pres* Robert J Cormier; *VPres* Kenneth L Gore; *Secy* Maris Platais; *Cur* Gretchen K Stone
Open Tues - Sat 10:30 AM - 5:30 PM; cl Sun & July & Aug. No admis fee. Estab and incorporated 1914, cooperative organization. Guild owns building; one gallery with continuous exhibitions in which each member is entitled to show one work; second gallery devoted to one-man shows, each member by turn at regular intervals. Mem: Active 65-80, associates under 100; annual meeting April
Exhibitions: Three yearly general exhibitions

M **INSTITUTE OF CONTEMPORARY ART,** 955 Boylston St, 02115. Tel 617-266-5152. *Dir* David A Ross; *Business Mgr* Jack DeBeradinis; *Development Dir* Thaleia Schlesinger; *Cur* Elisabeth Sussman; *Cur* Gillian Levine; *Membership Dir* Jane G Kennedy
Open Tues & Thurs - Sun 11 AM - 7 PM, Wed 11 AM - 8 PM. Admis adults $2.50, students and senior citizens $1, members free. Estab 1936 to organize, document, & exhibit works of contemporary masters of new & innovative talents. A full range of contemporary working methods including painting, sculpture, photography, film & video & performance are shown. Gallery is comprised of three floors gallery space 4000 sq ft & a video & performance theatre, offices are located on the third floor; building is 19th century renovated police station. Average Annual Attendance: 55,000. Mem: 2000; dues $20 and up; annual meeting Oct
Income: Financed by membership, city and state appropriations, gifts and grants
Publications: Exhibition catalogs; newsletter, bimonthly
Activities: Classes for adults & children; dramatic programs; docent training; lectures open to public, 20 vis lectr per yr; dance performances; film series; video; concerts; gallery talks; tours; competitions; originate traveling exhibitions; museum shop sells books, magazines, jewelry, t-shirts, catalogues, cards, records & posters

M **THE LOADING DOCK GALLERY,** 46 Waltham St #102 (Mailing add: 20 St Lukes Rd #3, Allston, MA 02118). Tel 617-782-9235. *Dir* John J Higgins; *Pres* William Harby; *Coordr* Debra Claffey; *Member* Linda Pollen; *Member* Gema Phillips; *Member* Pat Gordon; *Member* Oscar Lakeman; *Member* Andy Zimmermann; *Member* Carolyn Baker; *Member* Alice Hutter; *Member* Christus Murphy; *Member* Helen Bronikowski
Open Wed - Sat Noon - 3 PM. Estab 1982 to provide alternative exhibition space for artists. The Gallery is an artist-owned and artist-operated alternative gallery comprised of working, professional artists in various media. Average Annual Attendance: 2000. Mem: 15 - 25; dues $350; monthly meetings
Income: Financed by endowment, membership, city and state appropriation
Collections: Members artwork
Exhibitions: Portraits of the Artists: Group Exhibition; Debra Claffey, recent works; Antoinette Prince & Helen Bronikowski: Species-Calla Lilly
Publications: Newsletter, monthly
Activities: Competitions; individual paintings lent

O **MASSACHUSETTS HISTORICAL SOCIETY,*** 1154 Boylston St, 02215. Tel 617-536-1608. *Dir* Louis L Tucker
Open Mon - Fri 9 AM - 4:45 PM, cl Sat, Sun & holidays. No admis fee. Estab 1791
Income: Financed by endowment
Collections: Archives; historical material; paintings; sculpture
Exhibitions: Temporary exhibitions
Publications: Annual brochure; irregular leaflets; various books
Activities: Lectures; special exhibits for members and their guests
L **Library,** 1154 Boylston St, 02215. *Librn* John D Cushing
Open Mon - Sat 9 AM - 4:45 PM. Average Annual Attendance: 3000
Library Holdings: Vols 400,000; Other — Manuscripts
Activities: Lectures

M **MUSEUM OF AFRO-AMERICAN HISTORY,*** PO Box 5, Dudley Station, 02119. Tel 617-445-7400. *Pres* Byron Rushing
Estab 1965 to collect & secure for permanent exhibiton, historical material to be found in Boston & in all parts of the United States pertaining to the life, thought & heritage of three centuries of Afro-Americans in New England

M **MUSEUM OF FINE ARTS,** 465 Huntington Ave, 02115. Tel 617-267-9300. *Dir* Jan Fontein; *Assoc Dir* Ross Farrar; *Dir of Finance* John J Higgins; *Dir Resource Develop* Charles Taggert; *Registrar* Linda Thomas; *Conservator Asiatic Art* Yashiro Iguchi; *Cur American Decorative Arts* Jonathan Fairbanks; *Cur European Decorative Arts & Sculpture* Anne Poulet; *Cur Contemporary Art* Kenworth Moffett; *Cur Textiles* Jean Michel Tushscherer; *Cur Prints & Drawings* Eleanor A Sayre; *Cur Egyptian Art* William Kelly Simpson; *Cur Classical Art* Cornelius C Vermeule; *Cur Asiatic Art* James Watt; *Cur American Photography* Theodore Stebbins; *Conservator Paintings* Alain Goldrach; *Dir Research Laboratory* Lambertus vanZelst; *Dir Education* William Burback; *Librn* Nancy S Allen
Open Tues 10 AM - 5 PM, Wed 10 AM - 10 PM, Thurs - Sun 10 AM - 5 PM, cl Mon. Admis adults $4, sr citizens $3, members & children under 16 free, Sat 10 AM - Noon free. Estab and inc 1870; present building opened 1909. Average Annual Attendance: 800,000. Mem: 20,000; dues donor $60, family $40, individual $30
Collections: Outstanding Chinese, Japanese and Indian art; exceptional †Egyptian, †Greek and †Roman art; †master paintings of Europe and America; †superb print collection from 15th century to present; †sculpture, †decorative and minor arts including period rooms, porcelains, †silver, †tapestries, †textiles, †costumes, †musical instruments
Exhibitions: Specially organized exhibitions are continually on view; exhibitions of the permanent collections
Publications: Bulletin, yearly; Calendar of events, monthly
Activities: Classes for adults & children; docent training; lectures open to public; concerts; gallery talks; tours; museum shop sells books, magazines, original art, reproductions, prints & slides; junior museum arranged through education dept
L **William Morris Hunt Memorial Library,** 465 Huntington Ave, 02115. Tel 617-267-9300. *Librn* Nancy S Allen
Estab 1879 to support curatorial research. For reference only
Income: $80,000 (financed by endowment and membership)
Library Holdings: Vols 150,000; Per subs 650; AV — Slides 70,000; Other — Clipping files, exhibition catalogs, pamphlets
Activities: Classes for adults and children; docent training; dramatic programs; lect open to public; concerts; gallery talks; tours; book traveling exhibitions
L **Dept of Photographic Services,*** Slide & Photographic Library, 465 Huntington Ave, 02115. Tel 617-267-9300. *Mgr* Janice Sorokow
Library Holdings: AV — Slides 90,000
Special Subjects: Architecture, Decorative Arts, Photography, Prints, Sculpture

M **MUSEUM OF THE NATIONAL CENTER OF AFRO-AMERICAN ARTISTS,*** 300 Walnut Avenue, 02119. Tel 617-442-8014. *Dir* Edmund B Gaither; *Asst Dir* Harriet F Kennedy; *Artistic Dir* Elma Lewis
Open June - Aug daily 1 - 6 PM, Sept - May daily 1 - 5 PM. Admis adult $1.25, children $.50. Estab 1969 to promote the use of the visual art heritage of Black people in the Americas and Africa. Suite of three special exhibition galleries; suite of three African Art Galleries; suite of three permanent collection galleries; one local artist gallery. Average Annual Attendance: 10,000. Mem: 250; annual dues $25
Income: $250,000 (financed by private gifts, contracts, etc)
Collections: Art from Western Africa; Early 20th century Afro-American Prints and Drawings
Exhibitions: African Artists in America; Stone Churches of Ethiopia
Publications: Newsletter, quarterly
Activities: Dramatic programs; lectures open to the public; concerts; gallery talks; tours; competitions with awards (Edward Mitchell Barrister Award); book traveling exhibitions; traveling exhibitions organized and circulated; sales shop sells books, magazines, prints and small sculpture

PRINT COUNCIL OF AMERICA
For further information, see National and Regional Organizations

O **RELIGIOUS ARTS GUILD,** Unitarian Universalist Association, 25 Beacon, 02108. Tel 617-742-2100. *Executive Secy* Barbara M Hutchins
Tues - Thurs 9 AM - 5 PM. No admis fee. Estab 1923 to promote the use of the arts in worship services & programs of churches. Mem: 120; dues $20; annual meeting in June
Income: $3500
Activities: Workshops

O **SOCIETY FOR THE PRESERVATION OF NEW ENGLAND ANTIQUITIES,** Harrison Gray Otis House, 141 Cambridge St, 02114. Tel 617-227-3956. *Admin Dir* Nancy R Coolidge
Open Mon - Fri, tours at 10 AM, 11 AM, 1 PM, 2 PM & 3 PM. Admis adults $2, children under 12 $1. Estab and inc 1910, the Otis House serves as both headquarters and museum for the Society. Society owns over 40 historic houses throughout New England, 23 of which are open to the public. Average Annual Attendance: 3000. Mem: 3200; dues $15 and up; annual meeting May
Special Subjects: Historic preservation, interpretation of historic properties
Collections: American and European decorative arts and antiques with New England history; photographs; houses
Publications: Old Time New England, occasional bulletin; SPNEA News, quarterly; house guide, annual
Activities: Classes for adults; lectures open to public, 5-10 vis lectr per yr; originate traveling exhibitions; museum shop sells books
L **Library,** Otis House, 141 Cambridge St, 02114. *Librn* Elinor Reichlin
Library Holdings: Other — Clipping files, manuscripts, memorabilia, original art works, prints
Collections: Study collections of New England Architecture in the form of fragments, measured drawings, 200,000 photographs, pattern books; other collections include textiles and wallpaper

O **THE SOCIETY OF ARTS AND CRAFTS,** 175 Newbury St, 02116. Tel 617-266-1810. *Co-Pres* Rudolf Talbot; *Co-Pres* Herta Loeser; *VPres* Nina Nielsen; *Secy* Suzanne Martin; *Asst Dir* Merye Zassman; *Gallery Mgr* Barbara Heller
Open Mon - Sat 10 AM - 5:30 PM. No admis fee. Estab 1897 to serve craftspeople in the US and to educate the public about fine crafts. Two galleries on the second level house special exhibitons. Average Annual Attendance: 8000. Mem: 600; dues party or joint $50, single $25, craft $15; annual meeting in May of June
Income: $110,000 (financed by membership, shop sales, grants)
Collections: Contemporary one-of-a-kind furniture
Exhibitions: Special exhibitions on a single craft medium presented year round
Activities: Visiting lectr, 4-5 per yr; gallery talks; awards; sales shop sells fine handmade crafts in wood, glass, metal, fiber & leather

BROCKTON

O **BROCKTON ART MUSEUM,** Fuller Memorial, Oak St, 02401. Tel 617-588-6000. *Dir* Marilyn Hoffman; *Cur* Elizebeth Haff; *Dir of Development and Public Relations* Michael Calmes; *Business Mgr* James Keneklis; *Dir of Education* Susan Braham; *Graphic Designer* Andrea Haroldsson; *Museum Technician* Patrick Bell; *Dir Museum School* Beverly Edwards
Open Tues - Sun Noon - 5 PM. Admis donations. Estab 1969 to provide a variety of art exhibitions and education programs of regional and national interest. The center houses six galleries; one gallery is reserved for important works of art on loan from the Museum of Fine Arts, Boston. Average Annual Attendance: 35,000. Mem: 1500; dues $20
Income: $784,000 (financed by endowment, membership, gifts and government grants)
Collections: Contemporary American art; Early American and Sandwich glass; 19th century American and European paintings
Exhibitions: Biennial of Boston painting and sculpture; regional and national contemporary exhibits; temporary exhibits of 19th century American contemporary crafts
Publications: Newsletter and calendar of events, 4 per year
Activities: Classes for adults and children; dramatic programs; docent training; special programs for children; lect open to the public, 4 vis lectr per year; gallery talks; tours; competitions; concerts; scholarships; individual paintings and original objects of art lent to accredited museums of the American Association of Museums; lending collection contains paintings and slides; originate traveling exhibitions; museum shop sells original art, reproductions, prints and contemporary crafts
L **Library,** Fuller Memorial, Oak St, 02401. *Librn* Deedee Andrea DesJardins
Open to members, staff and students
Library Holdings: Vols 1200; Per subs 8

L **BROCKTON PUBLIC LIBRARY SYSTEM,** Municipal Art Gallery, 304 Main St, 02401. Tel 617-587-2515. *Dir* Ernest J Webby
Open Mon - Thurs 9 AM - 9 PM, Fri & Sat 9 AM - 5 PM, cl Sun. No admis fee. Special room for monthly art exhibitions. Average Annual Attendance: 20,000
Library Holdings: Vols 5000
Collections: W C Bryant Collection of 19th and 20th century American paintings, chiefly by New England artists; gifts of 20th century paintings which includes four paintings by Hendricks Hallett and an oil painting by Mme Elisabeth Weber-Fulop; loan collection of 20th century painters from the Woman's Club of Brockton; mounted photographs of Renaissance art and watercolors by F Mortimer Lamb
Exhibitions: Monthly exhibitions by local and nationally known artists

BROOKLINE

O **BROOKLINE ART SOCIETY,** 361 Washington St, 02146
Estab 1950. Mem: Dues $20
Exhibitions: Annual juried show; rotating exhibits by individual members, local artists and photographers; members' show
Publications: Newsletter, monthly
Activities: Workshops and programs open to public

CAMBRIDGE

O **CAMBRIDGE ART ASSOCIATION,*** 25 Lowell St, 02138. Tel 617-876-0246. *Dir* Joyce Eriksson-Rylander
Open Tues - Sat 11 AM - 5 PM, cl in July and Aug. No admis fee. Estab 1944 to exhibit, rent and sell members' work and to encourage an interest in fine arts and crafts in the community. Mem: 400; dues artists $25, friends $20, students $7.50; annual meeting Jan
Exhibitions: Invited shows in Rental Gallery and Craft Gallery; foreign exhibition each year; members' juried exhibitions in Main Gallery every month
Publications: Bulletin, monthly
Activities: Classes for adults; dramatic programs; open workshops; lect and demonstrations; competitions with prizes; sales shop sells books, original art, prints, cards, jewelry and crafts

HARVARD UNIVERSITY

M **Busch-Reisinger Museum,** 29 Kirland St, 02138. Tel 617-495-2317. *Cur* Charles W Haxthausen; *Curatorial Asst* Emilie Dana; *Development* Dagmar Kohring
Open Tues - Fri Noon - 5 PM, Sat 10 AM - 5 PM, Sun 1 - 5 PM. No admis fee. Estab 1901 and opened in 1920, it has one of the most important and extensive collections of Central and European art outside of Europe, ranging from the Romanesque to the present day. This collection serves the teaching program of the Department of Fine Arts, outside scholars and the general public. Average Annual Attendance: 39,000. Mem: 200; dues $20
Income: $180,000 (financed by endowment and membership)
Collections: Late Medieval, Renaissance and Baroque sculpture; 16th century paintings & 18th century porcelain; 20th century German works, sculpture, paintings, drawings and prints; largest collection of Bauhaus material outside Germany
Exhibitions: Horst Janssen; Klee and Kandinsky; Prints and Drawings of Ernst Barlach; Gabriele Munter: From Munich to Murnau; 19th Century German Drawings and Watercolors; Graphic Works of Max Klinger; 20th Century Works from the Permanent Collection
Publications: Newsletter, quarterly
Activities: Tours by appointment; lect open to public; concerts; gallery talks; originate traveling exhibitions
M **Harvard Semitic Museum,** 6 Divinity Ave, 02138. Tel 617-495-4631. *Dir* Frank Moore Cross Jr; *Cur* Dr Carney E S Gavin
Open Mon - Fri 11 AM - 5 PM, Sun Noon - 5 PM. No admis fee, $2 donation. Estab 1889 to promote sound knowledge of Semitic languages and history; an archaeological research museum. Average Annual Attendance: 3000-15,000. Mem: 250; dues $20 and up
Income: Financed by endowment, membership, federal research grants and contracts
Collections: †Historic photographs, E E Hale Egyptian Collection; Excavated material from Nuzi and various other Palestinian and Near Eastern sites; Islamic metal, weapons, garments (Ottoman Empire); Phoenician glass
Exhibitions: (1984) Crossroads of the Ancient World; A Tale of Two Cities: Jewish Life in Frankfurt & Istanbul 1750-1870
Publications: Harvard Semitic Series; exhibit catalogues
Activities: Docent training; lecture-film series; lectures open to public, 5-8 vis lectr per yr; gallery talks; tours; exten dept serves Harvard University; original objects of art lent to universities and museums; book traveling exhibitions; originate traveling exhibitions; sales shop sells books, reproductions & prints
M **William Hayes Fogg Art Museum,** 32 Quincy St, 02138. Tel 617-495-7768. *Actg Dir* John M Rosenfield; *Assoc Dir* Robert Rotner; *Asst Dir Cultural Affairs* Caroline Jones; *Asst Dir Finance* Lisa Flanagan; *Archivist* Phoebe Peebles; *Dir Conservation* Arthur Beale; *Assoc Conservator* Kate Olivier; *Assoc Conservator* Marjorie Cohn; *Sr Conservator of Science* Eugene Farrell
Open Mon - Fri 9 AM - 5 PM, Sat 10 AM - 5 PM, Sun 1 - 5 PM. Admis adults $2, students $1, Sat free. University estab 1891; museum estab 1927; serves both as a public museum and as a laboratory for Harvard's Dept of Fine Arts, which trains art historians and museum professionals. The Center for Conservation and Technical Studies operates a training program for conservators and technical specialists. Average Annual Attendance: 200,000. Mem: 2600; dues $35 and up
Income: Financed by endowment, membership and federal grants
Collections: Ancient coins; Egyptian antiquities; English and American silver; European and American painting and sculpture; Greek and Roman sculpture and vases; Oriental bronzes, ceramics, jades, paintings, prints and sculpture; Romanesque and Gothic sculpture; Sculpture from Persepolis; Wedgwood; Maurice Wertheim Collection of Impressionist and Post-Impressionist Art
Publications: Annual report; newsletter, 4 - 5 per year
Activities: Docent training; lectures open to the public, up to 50 vis lectrs per yr; concerts; gallery talks; tours; individual paintings and original objects of art lent to exhibitions; book traveling exhibitions, 1 - 2 per yr; originate traveling exhibitions; museum shop sells books, reproductions and prints

M **Arthur M Sackler Museum,*** 32 Quincy St, Cambridge, 02138
Will open in 1985
L **Fine Arts Library,*** 02138. Tel 617-495-3373. *Librn* Wolfgang Freitag; *Acquisitions Librn* James Hodgson; *Cur Visual Coll* Helene Roberts; *Chief Cataloguer* Jane Kaufman
Open to Harvard community Mon - Fri 9 AM - 5 PM, Sat 10 AM - 5 PM. Estab 1895 to support the teaching department of fine arts and the research needs of the curatorial department of the Fogg Art Museum and an international community of scholars in art history. Circ 116,000
Income: $460,000 (financed by endowment)
Purchases: $105,000
Library Holdings: Vols 195,000; Per subs 1090; Micro — Fiche, reels; AV — Lantern slides, slides; Other — Clipping files, exhibition catalogs, pamphlets, photographs
Special Subjects: All areas of art history with emphasis on Italian primitives, architectural history, art and architecture of Eastern Europe, conservation and restoration of works of art, Dutch 17th century, history of photography, Italian Renaissance, master drawings, Romanesque sculpture, Islamic art and architecture
Collections: DIAL Index; Foto Marburg Collection; The Index of Jewish Art; The Knoedler Library Microfiche; Manuscript Archives of American artists and art scholars; Oriental and Islamic Art; Rübel Asiatic Research Collection: Library collection on the arts of the Far East; 25,000 catalogued auction sales catalogs
Publications: Catalog of Auction Sales Catalogs, and First Supplement; Fine Arts Library Catalog
L **Frances Loeb Library,** Graduate School of Design, Gund Hall, 02138. Tel 617-495-2574. *Asst Librn* Christopher Hail; *Visual Servs Librn* Katherine Poole
Estab 1900 to serve faculty and students of graduate school of design. Circ 55,000
Income: $450,000 (financed by endowment and tuition)
Purchases: $95,000
Library Holdings: Vols 221,000; Per subs 850; Drawings; Micro — Fiche, reels; AV — A-tapes, cassettes, fs, Kodachromes, lantern slides, motion pictures, rec, slides, v-tapes; Other — Clipping files, exhibition catalogs, manuscripts, pamphlets, photographs
Special Subjects: Architecture, City and Regional Planning; Landscape Architecture
Collections: Cluny; Le Corbusier; Charles Eliot; John C Olmsted; H H Richardson; Mulford Robinson
Exhibitions: Student work 1954-1958; Olmsted; Marcel Breuer; Eleanor Raymond
Publications: Frances Loeb Library Users' Guide, annual
Activities: Tours

M **LONGFELLOW NATIONAL HISTORIC SITE,** 105 Brattle St, 02138. Tel 617-876-4491. *Cur* Kathleen Catalano; *Supervisory Park Technician* Frank Buda
Open daily 10 AM - 4:30 PM. Admis 50 (16 years of age and older). Estab 1973 to acquaint the public with the life, work, and time of the American poet Henry W Longfellow
Income: Financed by US Department of the Interior
Collections: Paintings, sculpture, prints, furniture and furnishings once belonging to Henry W Longfellow and his daughter Alice; 19th century photographic collection including views of China and Japan
Publications: Newsletter, biannually
Activities: Concerts; tours; individual paintings and original objects of art lent to qualified institutions; sales shop selling books, slides and postcards

MASSACHUSETTS INSTITUTE OF TECHNOLOGY

M **MIT Committee on Visual Arts (Hayden Gallery and MIT Permanent Collection),** Rm 7-145, 160 Memorial Drive, Rm 7-145, 02139. Tel 617-253-4400. *Dir Exhib* Kathy Halbreich
Open Mon - Fri 10 AM - 4 PM, Sat & Sun 1 - 5 PM, cl holidays. No admis fee. Estab 1950 to house the Hayden Gallery's and MIT's permanent collection and temporary exhibitions. The MIT Committee on the Visual Arts organizes an active program in contemporary visual arts that includes exhibitions in Hayden Gallery and Hayden Corridor Gallery; more than 1200 works of art contained in the permanent collection are sited throughout the Institute's public spaces and offices; the outdoor sculpture collection is on view 24 hours a day to the public. Average Annual Attendance: 20,000
Income: Financed by MIT, public and private endowments, art councils, corporations and individuals
Collections: MIT Permanent Collection of †20th century painting, sculpture and works on paper
Exhibitions: Twelve exhibitions per year of contemporary art in all mediums
Publications: Exhibition catalogs
Activities: Educ Dept; symposia; artist-in-residence programs; lectures open to public; gallery talks; individual paintings & original objects of art lent to museums & institute offices; lending collection contains 600 original art works, 600 original prints, 100 paintings, 100 photographs; originate traveling exhibitions
M **Hart Nautical Museum,** Building 5, first floor, 77 Massachusetts Ave, 02139. Tel 617-253-4444. *Cur Coll* John Waterhouse
Open daily 9 AM - 10 PM
Collections: Forbes Collection of whaling prints; rigged models and half models of merchant and warships, engine models, marine paintings, prints, photos, ship plans and working drawings; nautical prints, paintings and drawings
M **Margaret Hutchinson Compton Gallery,** Cambridge, 02139
Open Mon - Fri 9 AM - 5 PM, Sat 10 AM - 4 PM
M **Creative Photography Gallery,*** 120 Massachusetts Ave, W31-310, 3rd Floor, 02139. Tel 617-253-4424. *Dir* Starr Ockenga
Open Mon - Fri 9 AM - 10 PM, Sat 10 AM - 6 PM, Sun Noon - 8 PM. No admis fee. Estab 1965
Income: Financed by institute and special funding projects
Exhibitions: Six exhibitions of contemporary photography per year
Publications: Positive, annual magazine
Activities: Lectures open to public, 6 vis lectr per year; book traveling exhibitions; originate traveling exhibitions to professional galleries

M **Museum,** Building N52-260, 265 Massachusetts Ave, 02139. Tel 617-253-7052. *Dir* Warren A Seamans; *Facilities Mgr* Barbara Linden; *Asst Dir Exhibits* Joan Loria; *Asst Dir Coll* Michael Yeates; *Reference Librn* Michael Leininger; *Asst Cur Exhibits* Donald Stidsen
Open Mon - Thurs 8:30 AM - 10 PM, Fri 8:30 AM - 7 PM, Sat 11 AM - 6 PM, Sun 2 - 10 PM, special hours when school is not in session. No admis fee. Estab 1971 as a museum facility documenting the development of the Institute and of 19th and 20th century science and technology
Special Subjects: Historical Material
Collections: Architectural drawings; biographical information; furniture; objets d'art; scientific instruments and apparatus
Exhibitions: Twenty exhibitions per year
Publications: Selected publications of the faculty, School of Architecture and Planning, annually
Activities: Classes for adults and children; lectures open to the public; 5 -10 vis lectr per yr; gallery talks; tours; book traveling exhibitions, 1 - 2 per yr; originate traveling exhibitions; museum shop sells books & prints

L **Rotch Library of Architecture and Planning,*** Room 7-238, 77 Massachusetts Ave, 02139. *Librn* Margaret DePopolo; *Assoc Librn* Micheline Jedrey; *Coll Librn* Rona Gregory; *Librn Aga Khan Program for Islamic Architecture* Omar Khalidi; *Visual Coll Librn* Merrill W Smith
Open Mon - Thurs 8:30 AM - 10 PM, Fri 8:30 AM - 8 PM, Sat 10 AM - 6 PM, Sun 2 - 10 PM, special hours when school is not in session. Estab 1868 to serve the students and faculty of the School of Architecture and Planning and other members of the MIT community
Library Holdings: Vols 149,000; Per subs 650; Micro — Fiche, reels; AV — A-tapes, cassettes, Kodachromes, lantern slides, motion pictures, slides, v-tapes; Other — Exhibition catalogs, pamphlets, photographs
Special Subjects: Architecture, Historical Material, Art History, Contemporary Islamic architecture, environmental designs
Exhibitions: Student and faculty work
Publications: Selected Rotch Library Acquisitions; Selected Publications of the Faculty, School of Architecture and Planning, annually

CONCORD

M **CONCORD ANTIQUARIAN SOCIETY MUSEUM,** 200 Lexington Rd, Box 146, 01742. Tel 617-369-9609. *Pres* Sarah K Hindle; *Dir* Dennis Fiori; *Treas* Wyane Thornbrough; *Administrator* Mrs Thomas G Doig
Open Mon - Sat 10 AM - 4:30 Pm, Sun 2 - 4:30 PM. Admis adults $3, sr citizens $2, children $1. Estab 1886 to collect and preserve objects of antiquarian interest to Concord and towns originally a part of Concord; to interpret life in Colonial America, range of American arts, role of Concord in the American Revolution, and contributions of Concord authors-Thoreau, Emerson, Alcotts and Hawthorne-to American literature. Fifteen Period rooms showing life in Concord from 1685 to 1840; Ralph Waldo Emerson study. Average Annual Attendance: 20,000. Mem: 950; dues $20 and up; annual meeting Feb or March
Income: $320,000 (financed by membership, admission, grants, endowment & giving)
Publications: Newsletter, quarterly; The Flavour of Concord, cookbook; Concord: Climate for Freedom by Ruth Wheeler
Activities: Classes for adults and children; docent training; lectures open to the public; 8 vis lectrs per yr; concerts; gallery talks; tours; museum shop sells books, reproductions, prints, slides, gift items and crafts made by local craftspeople which compliment the museum collection

L **Library,** 200 Lexington Rd, 01742. *Chmn* M Clark; *Librn* Rosalie Frost; *Librn* Annie Reece
Open to members only for lending reference
Purchases: American Decorative Arts
Library Holdings: Vols 800; Per subs 14
Special Subjects: Decorative Arts, Concord Collection, Costumes, Early American Decorative Arts

O **CONCORD ART ASSOCIATION,** 37 Lexington Rd, 01742. Tel 617-369-2578. *Pres* John W Hill Jr; *VPres* Loring W Coleman; *Cur* Patsy B McVity; *Treasurer* Robert Booth; *Secy* Beatrice Synnott
Open Tues - Sat 11 AM - 4:30 PM, Sun 2 - 4:30 PM. Admis adult $1, members, children under 14, student groups & sr citizens free. Estab 1916 for the encouragement of quality art by New England artists. Average Annual Attendance: 10,000. Mem: 600; dues life member $500, business & patron $30, associate $20, artist $15, student $2
Income: Financed by membership
Collections: Bronze sculptures; colonial glass; miniatures
Exhibitions: Changing exhibits
Publications: Exhibition notices
Activities: Lect open to public, 4 - 6 vis lectr per year; tours; sales gallery selling original art, prints and reproductions

DEERFIELD

M **DEERFIELD ACADEMY,** Hilson Gallery, Dept Fine Arts, 01342. Tel 413-772-0241, Ext 221. *Dir* Daniel Hodermarsky; *Cur* Robert Moorhead
Open Mon - Fri 9 AM - 4 PM. No admis fee. Estab 1955 to exhibit the work of regional artists and members of the Deerfield community; to serve as a focus for visiting lecturers, concerts and similar events; to be a logical extension of the academic program of the Fine Arts Department; to enrich the Academy. A single large exhibition space with its own entrance and central fireplace. Average Annual Attendance: 2000. Mem: 130
Income: Financed through Academy
Collections: Charles P Russell Collection
Publications: Term schedule, three times a year
Activities: Lectures open to public, 3 lectr per year

M **HISTORIC DEERFIELD INC,*** The Street, PO Box 321, 01342. Tel 413-774-5581. *Pres* Henry N Flynt Jr; *VPres* Hugh B Vanderbilt; *Executive Dir & Secy* Donald R Friary; *Cur* Joseph P Spang; *Dir of Education* J Ritchie Garrison; *Business Mgr* Carol Wenzel
Open Mon - Sat 9:30 - 4:30 PM, Sun 11 AM - 4:30 PM. Admis per house adults $1 - $2.50, children $2.50. Estab 1952 to collect, study and interpret artifacts related to the history of Deerfield, the culture of the Connecticut Valley and the arts in early American life. Maintains 12 historic house museums. Average Annual Attendance: 50,000. Mem: 762; dues $25; annual meeting 2nd Sun in Nov
Income: $1,025,000 (financed by endowment, membership, rental, royalty and museum store income)
Purchases: $36,434
Collections: †American and English silver; American and European textiles and costume; †American needlework; †American pewter; †Chinese export porcelain; †early American household objects; †early American paintings and prints; †early New England furniture; †English ceramics
Exhibitions: (1980) A Christmas Exhibit of Antique Toys; (1981) Punch Bowls in the Historic Deerfield Collections; (1982) Candlesticks from the Historic Deerfield Collections
Publications: Historic Deerfield Quarterly
Activities: Educ dept; Lect open to public, 8 visiting lectr per year; gallery talks; tours; scholarships and fellowships; museum shop selling books, reproductions, slides and local crafts

L **Henry N Flynt Library,*** Memorial Street, PO Box 53, 01342. Tel 413-774-5581, Ext 125. *Librn* David R Proper; *Library Asst* Louise H M Perrin
Open Mon - Fri 9 AM - 4:30 PM. Estab 1970 to support research on local history and the museum collections; also for staff training. Circ 1250
Income: $2157
Purchases: $2679
Library Holdings: Vols 8500; Per subs 28; Micro — Reels 120; AV — Motion pictures, slides; Other — Clipping files, exhibition catalogs, manuscripts, memorabilia, pamphlets, photographs, prints
Special Subjects: Decorative Arts
Collections: Works dealing with the Connecticut River Valley
Publications: Research at Dearfield, An Introduction to the Memorial Libraries
Activities: Scholarships; sales shop sells books, reproductions, slides, craft items, souvenirs, ceramics, glass and candles

O **POCUMTUCK VALLEY MEMORIAL ASSOCIATION,** Memorial Hall,* Memorial St, Box 174, 01342. Tel 413-773-8929, 773-5206. *Pres* Rus A Miller; *VPres* William Hubbard; *Secy* Mary Hawkes; *Cur & Dir* Timothy C Neumann
Open Mon - Fri 10 AM - 4:30 PM, Sat - Sun 12:30 - 4:30 PM. Admis adults $2, students $1.50, children (6-12) $.75, tour $1. Estab 1870 to collect the art and other cultural artifacts of the Connecticut River Valley and Western Massachusetts. Maintains 15 galleries. Average Annual Attendance: 10,000. Mem: 800; dues $5; annual meeting last Tues in Feb
Income: $45,000 (financed by endowment, membership and sales)
Collections: Folk art; furniture; Indian artifacts; paintings; pewter; textiles; tools; toys; dolls
Publications: PVMA Newsletter, quarterly
Activities: Classes for children; lect open to the public; concerts; tours; artmobile; individual paintings and original objects of art lent to other museums; lending collection contains original art works, original prints, paintings and artifacts; museum shop selling books, original art, reproductions and slides

DORCHESTER

M **NATIONAL ARCHIVES AND RECORDS SERVICE,** John F Kennedy Library and Museum, Columbia Point, 02125. Tel 617-929-4500. *Dir* Dan H Fenn Jr; *Cur* David F Powers
Open daily 9 AM - 5 PM. Admis adult $1.50, children free. Estab 1964 to preserve collections of Kennedy papers and other material pertaining to his career; to educate public about J F Kennedy's career and political system; to make materials available to researchers. Library is a nine-story building overlooking Boston Harbour, has two theaters and an exhibition floor. Average Annual Attendance: 500,000
Income: Financed by federal government and national archives trust fund
Library Holdings: Micro — Cards, fiche, prints; AV — A-tapes, cassettes, fs, lantern slides, motion pictures, slides, v-tapes; Other — Memorabilia, original art works, pamphlets, photographs, prints, reproductions
Collections: 32,000,000 documents and personal papers of John F Kennedy, Robert Kennedy and many others associated with life and career of John F Kennedy; 6,000,000 ft of film relating to political career, 150,000 photographs, 3000 oral histories, 11,000 paintings and museum objects (personal)
Activities: Tours; museum shop sells books, reproductions, prints and slides

DUXBURY

M **ART COMPLEX MUSEUM AT DUXBURY,** 189 Alden St, PO Box 1411, 02331. Tel 617-934-6634. *Museum Dir* Charles A Weyerhaeuser; *Assoc Dir* Lillian E Bengtz; *Dir Public Affairs* Lanci Valentine
Open Fri - Sun 2 - 5 PM. No admis fee. Estab 1971 to exhibit art. Gallery is 40 x 60 ft; entrance also used for exhibition purposes. Average Annual Attendance: 8500
Collections: American, European and Oriental art; Shaker furniture
Exhibitions: Arts of Japan from museum collection, and others; Boston Printmakers; Shaker Furniture; various Boston & South Shore Artists
Publications: The Lithographs of Ture Bengtz (book); Theater Prints, 1850-1950; The Shakers: Pure of Spirit, Pure of Mind
Activities: Educ dept; outreach to Duxbury schools; lectures open to public, 2-3 vis lectr per year; concerts; gallery talks; tours of visiting groups

L **Library,** 189 Alden St, PO Box 1411, 02331. *Librn* Nancy W Grinnell
Open to the public for reference
Library Holdings: Vols 3400; Per subs 5; Other — Clipping files, exhibition catalogs, pamphlets
Special Subjects: Oriental Art

FITCHBURG

M **FITCHBURG ART MUSEUM,** Merriam Parkway, 01420. Tel 617-345-4207.
Pres Andre A Gelinas; *VPres* Roger W Foster; *Dir* Peter Timms; *Asst to the Dir*
Aliki Katsaros; *Secy* Nelde Drumm; *Treas* Mrytle Parcher; *Exhib Interpreter*
Ursula Pitman; *Dir Education & Public Relations* E Linda Poras
Open Tues - Sat 10 AM - 4:30 PM, Sun 1 - 5 PM. No admis fee. Estab 1925.
Two large galleries and entrance hall on the first floor; two large galleries with
connecting hall gallery on the second floor. Average Annual Attendance: 15,000.
Mem: 900; dues $15 - $500; annual meeting Dec
Income: Financed by endowment and membership
Collections: †Drawings, †paintings and †prints
Publications: Exhibitions catalogs; event notices
Activities: Classes for adults & children; docent training; lectures open to public,
12 vis lectr per yr; concerts; gallery talks; tours; competitions with awards;
scholarships; individual paintings & original objects of art lent to colleges &
museums; sales shop sells original art & reproductions

FRAMINGHAM

M **DANFORTH MUSEUM OF ART,** 123 Union Ave, 01701. Tel 617-620-0050.
Pres Board of Trustees Paul B Rosenberg; *Treas* Bruce Garvin; *Dir* Joy L
Gordon; *Education Coordr* Vicki Reikes Fox; *Exhibitions Coordr* Eileen Carew
Open Wed - Fri Noon - 4:30 PM, Sat & Sun 1 - 4:30 PM. No admis fee. Estab
1974 to provide fine arts and art-related activities to people of all ages in the
South Middlesex area. There are six galleries, including a children's gallery with
hands-on activities. Average Annual Attendance: 30,000. Mem: 1000; dues vary
from $6-$25
Income: Financed by membership, Framingham State College and Town of
Framingham
Collections: †Old master and contemporary prints; †19th century American
paintings
Exhibitions: (1982-83) Usable Art; Ex Voto: Italian Votive Tablets; Works from
the Sara Roby Foundation Collection; Three Regionalists: Benton, Curry &
Wood; Bay State Photography; German Expressionist Prints from the Permanent
Collection; Photographs by August Sander; American Artists in Dusseldorf:
1840-1865; The Art of William Gropper; Spanish Drawings & Graphics from the
Guggenheim Museum; Abstract Art in New England; Indiana's Indians;
Photographs by Rollie McKenna; Grandma Moses: The Artist Behind the Myth;
PROJECTS: A Series of Five Site-Specific Installations; The Emmets: A Family
of Women Painters
Publications: Calendar of events, monthly; exhibition brochures & catalogues,
occasionally; museum school brochure, quarterly
Activities: Classes for adults and children; docent training; programs for area
schools; lectures open to public; concerts; gallery talks; tours; trips; originate
traveling exhibitons to other museums; museum shop sells original art, prints,
original glass art, crafts, jewelry and ceramics
L **Library,** 123 Union Ave, 01701. Tel 617-620-0050. *Head of the Library
Committee* Maureen Krier
Open Weds - Fri Noon - 4:30, Sat & Sun 1 - 4:30. Estab 1975 as an educational
resource of art books and catalogues. For reference only; research as requested
Library Holdings: Vols 2500; Other — Clipping files, exhibition catalogs,
pamphlets
Special Subjects: Rare and valuable books
Collections: Bibliographies for the museum exhibitions; museum school book
collection

GARDNER

M **MOUNT WACHUSETT COMMUNITY COLLEGE,** Art Galleries,* Green St,
01440. Tel 617-632-6600, Ext 180. *Coordinator Dept Art* Jean C Tandy; *Dir
Fine Arts Gallery* Gene Cauthen
Open Mon 8 AM - 9:30 PM. No admis fee. Estab 1971 to supply resources for a
two-year art curriculum; develop an art collection
Income: Financed by city and state appropriations
Collections: †Approx 100 works; framed color art posters and reproductions
Exhibitions: Annual student competition of painting, sculpture, drawing,
ceramics, printmaking; local, New Hampshire and former students works
Publications: Annual brochure
Activities: Dramatic program; evening and summer studio courses; workshops;
lect open to public, several visiting lectr per year; concerts; gallery talks; tours;
competitions; art club, visual arts film series
L **Library,** Green St, 01440. *Dir* Mason Parker; *Asst Librn* Linda Oldach
Open Mon - Thurs 8 AM - 9:30 PM, Fri 8 AM - 5 PM, Sun 2 - 6 PM (when
school is in session). Estab 1964. Circ 12,998
Income: Financed by state appropriation
Library Holdings: Vols 51,137; Per subs 256; Micro — Fiche, reels; AV —
Cassettes, fs, rec, slides; Other — Memorabilia, pamphlets
Exhibitions: Periodic exhibitions

GLOUCESTER

O **CAPE ANN HISTORICAL ASSOCIATION,*** 27 Pleasant St, 01930. Tel 617-
283-0455. *Cur* Deborah L Goodwin
Open Tues - Sat 1 - 5 PM, cl Sun, Mon & holidays. Admis adults $2, students,
$1, children no charge if accompanied by adult. Incorporated in 1876 for the
preservation of ancient houses. One built in 1650, one in 1750 and one in 1803.
Average Annual Attendance: 5000. Mem: 950; dues $10 and up; annual meeting
May
Income: Endowment, contribution, memberships
Collections: Paintings and drawings by Fitz Hugh Lane, antique furniture, glass,
jewelry, mementos of the Revolutionary period, porcelain, ship models, silver
Activities: Occasional classes; children's programs; lectures open to the public;
tours; concerts
L **Reference Library,*** 27 Pleasant St, 01930
Library Holdings: Vols 500; Per subs 3; Other — Clipping files, exhibition
catalogs, pamphlets, photographs

M **HAMMOND CASTLE MUSEUM,** 80 Hesperus Ave, 01930. Tel 617-283-2080.
Executive Dir Ben J Deluca Jr; *Cur* Joanna Soltan; *Dir Education* John Petibone
Open winter Mon, Tues & Thur - Sat 10 AM - 4 PM, Sun 1 - 4 PM, cl Wed,
spring and summer daily 10 AM - 4 PM. Admis adults $3, children under 12 $1.
Estab 1931 by a famous inventor, John Hays Hammond Jr. Incorporated in 1938
for the public exhibition of authentic works of art, architecture and specimens of
antiquarian value and to encourage and promote better education in the fine arts,
with particular reference to purity of design and style. Built in style of a medieval
castle with Great Hall, courtyard and period rooms, Mr Hammond combined
elements of Roman, Medieval and Renaissance periods in his attempt to recreate
an atmosphere of European beauty. Average Annual Attendance: 60,000. Mem:
300; dues vary
Income: Financed by tours, concerts, membership and grants, special events
Collections: Rare collection of European artifacts; Roman, Medieval and
Renaissance Periods
Exhibitions: (1983) John Hays Hammond Jr: Renaissance Man in the 20th
Century; The Polish Theatre Posters; (1983-84) The Glorious Company: Saints at
Hammond Castle Museum
Publications: Museum guidebook; exhibition catalogs
Activities: Classes for adults and children; dramatic programs; docent training;
special activities; lectures; films; concerts; gallery talks; tours; extension
dept serves neighboring schools; individual paintings and original objects of art lent to
sister institutions for special exhibitions; originate traveling institutions to sister
institutions; sales shop sells books, original art, reproductions, prints, slides and
gift items

O **NORTH SHORE ARTS ASSOCIATION, INC,** Art Gallery, 197 E Main St
(Rear), 01930. Tel 617-283-1857. *Pres* Beverly DeMont; *VPres* Ken Gore; *Treas*
Roger Curtis; *Secy* Winifred Curtis
Open 10 AM - 5:30 PM, Sun 2:30 - 5:30 PM, July, Aug & Sept. No admis fee.
Estab in 1922 to promote American art by exhibitions. Gallery owned by
Association. Average Annual Attendance: 4000. Mem: 300; dues artist $15,
patron $10, associate $5; annual meeting Aug
Income: Financed by dues, contributions & rentals
Publications: Calendar of Events
Activities: Art classes in painting & drawing from life; lectures open to public, 4
vis lect per yr; gallery talks; competitions with awards

GRAFTON

M **WILLARD HOUSE AND CLOCK MUSEUM, INC,** 3 Willard St, 01519. Tel
617-839-3335. *Pres* Dr Roger W Robinson; *VPres* George McEvoy; *Dir* Mrs
Roger W Robinson; *Secy* Marguerite Longstreet
Open Tues - Sat 10 AM - 4 PM, Sun 1 - 5 PM. Admis adults $1.50, children $.
75. Estab 1968 for education in fields of decorative arts and antiques. Maintains
seven rooms open in house museum. Average Annual Attendance: 3000. Mem:
200; dues $5; annual meeting Oct
Income: Financed by endowment, membership, admissions, gifts and sales
Purchases: Three Willard Clocks
Collections: Early Country Antique Furniture, 17th & 18th Century; 44 Willard
Clocks by Benjamin, Simon, Ephraim and Aaron Willard; 16 paintings of various
members of the Willard Clockmaking Family
Exhibitions: Doll Show; Fashion Show of 18th & 19th Century Gowns
Activities: Lect, 4 visiting lectr per year; museum shop sells books and antiques

GREAT BARRINGTON

M **SIMON'S ROCK OF BARD COLLEGE,** Alford Rd, 01230. Tel 413-528-0771.
Chmn Art Dept William Jackson
Estab 1964 as a liberal arts college
Exhibitions: A continuing exhibition program of professional and student works
in drawing, painting, graphics, sculpture and crafts; Graphic Design Workshop of
Simon's Rock (poster); Barbara Baranowska (photographs); Jim Cave (prints);
Peter Homestead (sculpture); Tom Shepard (sculpture and drawings); Evan
Stoller (sculpture); Niki Berg, photograph; Dennis Connors, sculpture; Cynthia
Picchi, painting; Lyalya, painting & sculpture; Nick Farina, photography; Richard
Webb, painting; William Jackson, sculpture; Jane Palmer, ceramics; Arthur
Hillman, prints; The African-Afro-American Connection, photos; Brigitte Keller,
painting; Harriet Eisner, painting; Linda Kaye-Moses, jewelry; Taff Fitterer,
painting
Activities: Gallery talks; tours
L **Library,** Alford Rd, 01230. Tel 413-528-0771, Ext 273. *Librn* Karen Carney
Library Holdings: Vols 3000; Per subs 20; Micro — Fiche, reels; AV —
Cassettes, rec

HARVARD

M **FRUITLANDS MUSEUMS,** Rural Rte 2, Box 87, Prospect Hill, 01451. Tel
617-456-3924. *Dir* Richard S Reed; *Admin Secy* Jean L Crispen
Open May 30 - Sept 30, Tues - Sun 1 - 5 PM, cl Mon. Admis adults $2, children
$.50. Estab 1914, incorporated 1930 by Clara Endicott Sears. Fruitlands was the
scene of Bronson Alcott's Utopian experiment in community living. The
Fruitlands Farmhouse contains furniture, household articles, pictures, handicrafts,
books and valuable manuscript collection of Alcott, Lane and Transcendental
group. The Shaker House, built in the 1790's by the members of the former
Harvard Shaker Village, was originally used as an office. Moved to its present
location, it now forms the setting for the products of Shaker Handicrafts and
Community Industries. American Indian museum contains ethnological exhibits.
Picture gallery contains portraits by itinerant artists of the first half of the 19th
Century and landscapes by Hudson River School. Average Annual Attendance:
12,000
Exhibitions: (1983) Specimens of Indian lore, art, culture & dioramas illustrating
historical events of the Indians of the region; Edward S Curtis, Photographs of
the American Indian; Black Ash Shaker Baskets; select works of the 19th century
American artists
Activities: Individual & original objects of art lent to other museums in the area;
museum shop sells books, magazines, reproductions & prints

L Library, Rural Rte 2, Box 87, Prospect Hill Rd, 01451. Tel 617-456-3924
  Library Holdings: Vols 10,000; Per subs 10; AV — Fs, motion pictures, slides;
  Other — Manuscripts, memorabilia, original art works, photographs
  Special Subjects: Art History, Transcendental Movement, Shakers, American
  Indian North of Mexico

HAVERHILL

L HAVERHILL PUBLIC LIBRARY, Art Dept, 99 Main St, 01830. Tel 617-373-
1586. *Dir* Howard W Curtis
  Open Mon - Wed 9 AM - 9 PM, Thurs - Sat 9 AM - 5:30 PM. Estab 1873
  Library Holdings: Vols 8500; Per subs 16; AV — A-tapes, cassettes, fs,
  Kodachromes, lantern slides, motion pictures, v-tapes; Other — Clipping files,
  manuscripts, original art works, photographs, prints, sculpture
  Collections: Illuminated manuscripts; mid-19th century photographs, work by
  Beato and Robertson, Bourne, Frith, Gardner, Naya, O'Sullivan, and others; 19th
  & 20th century prints, including Cassatt, Chagall, Daumier, Degas, Dufy,
  Kollwitz, Legros, Picasso, Renoir, Sloan, Toulouse-Lautrec, Whistler, and others;
  small group of paintings including Joseph A Ames, Henry Bacon, Sidney M
  Chase, William S Haseltine, Thomas Hill, Harrison Plummer, Winfield Scott
  Thomas, Robert Wade
  Exhibitions: The Many Worlds of Bob Eastman, paintings
  Publications: Architectural Heritage of Haverhill
  Activities: Slide presentations; lectures open to public; concerts; periodic films

HOLYOKE

M CITY OF HOLYOKE MUSEUM-WISTARIAHURST, 238 Cabot St, 01040.
Tel 413-536-6771. *Museum Dir* Marie S Quirk; *Chmn Holoyoke Historical
Commission* Philip Cote
  Open Tues - Sat 1 - 5 PM, Sun 2 - 4 PM on special event days, cl national and
  state holidays. No admis fee. Sponsored by the City of Holyoke under the
  jurisdiction of the Holyoke Historical Commission. Average Annual Attendance:
  18,000. Mem: 350; dues regular $10, active $10 and up, junior $3; annual
  meeting May
  Income: $77,000 (financed by city appropriation)
  Collections: †Antique furniture; china; glass; historical dioramas; †Oriental art;
  †paintings; period rooms; silver
  Activities: Classes for children; dramatic programs; special art shows; concerts;
  gallery talks; sponsors films and lectures; special exhibits and festivals of ethnic
  culture featured periodically; special programs and illustrated lectures planned for
  visiting school classes; tours; sales shop selling booklets and items relating to
  exhibitions
M Youth Museum,* 238 Cabot St, 01040. Tel 413-534-3350
  Open Mon - Sat 1 - 5 PM, Sun when a concert, special program or opening of
  art exhibit is scheduled. Opened May 3, 1964 in Carriage House on Wisteriahurst
  estate; sponsored by the City of Holyoke, under jurisdiction of Holyoke
  Historical Commission. North American Indian Hall opened May 1973 on the
  second floor. Average Annual Attendance: 18,000
  Exhibitions: Scrimshaw, an Early Folk Art Exhibit; twelve exhibits encompassing
  Northeast, Southeast, Plains, Southwest, Northwest Coast and California Indian
  tribes
  Activities: Art classes for children; lect on arts and crafts; guided tours including
  film and slides on Indians; individual paintings and original objects of art lent;
  traveling exhibitions organized and circulated

LEXINGTON

M MUSEUM OF OUR NATIONAL HERITAGE, 33 Marrett Rd, Box 519,
02173. Tel 617-861-6559. *Dir & Librn* Clement M Silvestro; *Asst Dir &
Designer* Addis M Osborne; *Registrar* Jacquelyn Oak; *Gen Servs* Raymond
Wilkinson; *Admin Asst* Susan Balthaser; *Asst Librn* Gloria Jackson; *Cur of
Collection & Exhibition Coordr* Barbara Franco; *Cur Exhibits* John Hamilton;
Publicity Dir Marlene Gray
  Open Mon - Sat 10 AM - 5 PM, Sun Noon - 5:30 PM, Nov - Mar Mon - Sat 10
  AM - 4:30 PM, Sun Noon - 5:30 PM. No admis fee. Estab 1972 as an American
  history museum, including art and decorative art. Five modern galleries for
  changing exhibits, flexible lighting and climation control. Two galleries of 3000
  sq ft, two 1500 sq ft, atrium area used for print and photo exhibits. Average
  Annual Attendance: 110,000. Mem: 200; dues friend for life $250, family $20,
  individual $15
  Income: $1,063,310 (financed by endowment & appeal to Masons)
  Purchases: $25,000
  Collections: General American & American Paints; American decorative art;
  objects decorated with Masonic, patriotic & fraternal symbolism
  Exhibitions: American Dolls; Decorated Masonic Apron in America; Democratic
  Art, 1840-1900; John Henry Belter & Rococco Revival; Molly Luce-American
  Genre; Reflections of 19th Century America
  Publications: Exhibition catalogs
  Activities: Curriculum packets for exhibits; lectures open to public, 7 vis lectr per
  yr; concerts; gallery talks; tours for school groups; sponsor Symposium of Belter
  Furniture; paintings and art objects lent; originate traveling exhibitions to Belter,
  Art Institute of Chicago, Cooper-Hewett & Lousiana; museum shop sells books
  and a variety of gift items related to exhibit program

LINCOLN

M DECORDOVA AND DANA MUSEUM AND PARK, Sandy Pond Rd, 01773.
Tel 617-259-8355. *Actg Dir & Asst Dir for Educ* Eleanor Lazarus; *Asst to Dir*
Joan Kennedy; *Cur* Rachel Lafo; *Membership Dir* Joan Sinatra; *Corp Program
Dir* Joan Bragen; *Public Relations Dir* Susan Jaeger; *School Mgr* Linda Foster
  Open Tues - Fri 10 AM - 5 PM, Wed 10 AM - 9:30 PM, Sat Noon - 5 PM, Sun
  1:30 - 5 PM. Admis adults $1.50, under 21 $.50, Wednesday nights free. Estab
  1948 to offer a variety of exhibitions, build an important collection of

contemporary art and to support living New England artist, in its collecting and
exhibitions. 4500 sq ft is broken into five galleries. Average Annual Attendance:
60,000. Mem: 3200; dues $40 - $500
  Income: $1,000,000 (financed by endowment and membership)
  Purchases: $20,000
  Collections: †Works of living New England artists
  Exhibitions: African Art: The Spirit Manifest; An American Dream: The Art of
  Free Enterprise; Born in Boston; Boston Printmakers National; By the People,
  For the People: New England; The China Trade: Romance and Reality; Barbara
  Busteter Falk: Paintings; Finnish Constructivism; Homer to Hopper: Sixty Years
  of American Watercolors; Peter Milton: Prints; New England in Winter; Patron's
  Choice: New England Artists Under 36; Donald Stoltenberg: Collagraphs;
  Francisco Zuniga: Sculpture and Drawing; New England Drawing Competition;
  Photography-Recent Directions; The DeCordova-Three Decades; Modern
  American Masterworks from the William H Lane Foundation; Three
  Installations-Catherine Jansen, Mario Kon & Michael Timpson; Glass Routes;
  New Englands Relief-Patrons Choice; Being and Nothingness; John Sloan/
  Buckminster Fuller; Boston Printmakers 34th National; Super Realism from the
  Morton G Neumann Family Collection; Beyond Measurement; Mags Harries;
  Harold Cohen, Computer Drawings/From Pong to Pac-Man; Settings: Three
  Boston Painters; student faculty exhibition; Wegman's World; Jack Wolfe; Art of
  the State; Magdalena Abakanowicz
  Publications: Exhibition catalogs; newsletter
  Activities: Classes for adults and children; docent training; lect open to public, 6
  visiting lectr per year; concerts; gallery talks; tours; competitions; paintings and
  original objects of art lent to corporate membership; traveling exhibitions
  organized and circulated
L DeCordova Museum Library,* Sandy Pond Rd, 01773. *Librn* Bee Warren
  Open Mon - Fri 9 AM - 5 PM, for members only
  Library Holdings: Vols 1700; Per subs 10; AV — Slides, v-tapes; Other —
  Exhibition catalogs, pamphlets
  Special Subjects: Fine Arts and Crafts, 20th Century Northeast Contemporary
  Art

LOWELL

O LOWELL ART ASSOCIATION, Whistler House and Parker Gallery, 243
Worthen St, 01852. Tel 617-452-7641. *Pres* Catherine L Goodwin; *VPres* David
K Reppucci; *Corresp Secy* Anastasia Porter; *Recording Secy* Robert W McLeod
Jr; *Whistler House Dir* Florence Marion
  Open Whistler House Tues - Fri 1 - 4 PM, Parker Gallery Tues - Fri 1 - 4 PM,
  open Sun for special exhibits only, cl Mon. Admis adults $1, senior citizens $.50,
  members no charge. Estab 1878 to preserve the birthplace of James McNeil
  Whistler; to promote the arts in all its phases; and to maintain a center for the
  cultural benefit of all the citizens of the community. Parker Gallery built in 1960
  to house permanent collection. Average Annual Attendance: 2000. Mem: 300;
  dues sustaining $50, individual $10, student $5
  Income: Financed by endowment and membership
  Collections: Early 20th century America: Hibbard, Benson, Noyes, Spear,
  Paxton, Phelps; Whistler etchings & lithographs
  Exhibitions: Monthly exhibits by contemporary artists
  Publications: Brochures
  Activities: Classes for adults and children; docent training; lectures open to
  public, 10 vis lectr per yr; concerts; gallery talks; tours; competitions with
  awards; programs of historical interest; originate traveling exhibitions; sales shop
  sells books, original art, reproductions, prints, postcards, mugs, tote bags &
  souvenir medals

MALDEN

L MALDEN PUBLIC LIBRARY, Art Dept & Gallery, 36 Salem St, 02148. Tel
617-324-0218. *Librn* Dina G Malgeri
  Open Mon - Thurs 9 AM - 9 PM, Fri & Sat 9 AM - 6 PM, cl Sun & holidays, cl
  Sat during summer months. Estab 1879, incorporated 1885 as a public library
  and art gallery. Maintains an art department with three galleries. Circ 239,493
  Income: $421,530 (financed by endowment, city and state appropriations)
  Purchases: $91,000
  Library Holdings: Other — Exhibition catalogs, framed reproductions,
  manuscripts, memorabilia, original art works, pamphlets, photographs, prints,
  reproductions, sculpture
  Publications: Thirty Paintings in the Malden Collection (art catalog); annual
  report; art reproduction note cards
  Activities: Lect open to public, 6-12 vis lectr per year; concerts; gallery talks;
  tours

MARBLEHEAD

O MARBLEHEAD ARTS ASSOCIATION, INC, 8 Hooper St, 01945. Tel 617-
631-2608. *Pres* Nancy Ferguson; *VPres* William E McKeon; *Secy* R Tate
Simpson; *Executive Secy* Mrs James Livengood
  Open Tues - Sun 1 - 4 PM, cl Mon. Admis $1 for tours, no admis to art galleries.
  Estab 1922. Owns and occupies the historic King Hooper Mansion (1728).
  Contains fine paneling, ballroom, gallery, and garden by Shurclif. Maintains an
  art gallery. Mem: 350; membership application must be signed by two members
  in good standing; dues $12 and up; annual meeting June
  Income: Financed by memberships & rentals
  Activities: Classes for adults; lectures open to the public; concerts; gallery talks;
  tours; competitions with cash & ribbon awards

O MARBLEHEAD HISTORICAL SOCIETY, 161 Washington St, PO Box 1048,
01945. Tel 617-631-1069. *Executive Secy* Mrs John P Hunt Jr
  Open May 15 - Oct 15, Mon - Sat 9:30 AM - 4 PM, cl Sun. Admis $2.25. Estab
  1898, incorporated 1902 for the preservation of Lee Mansion and historical
  material and records of Marblehead. Average Annual Attendance: 3000
  Income: Financed by endowment, membership, and admissions

Collections: China and glass; collection of portraits; documents; furniture; pictures of ships
Activities: Lect open to the public; tours; sales shop selling books, prints, reproductions
L **Library,** 161 Washington, PO Box 1048, 01945. Tel 617-631-1069
Open to qualified visitors for reference only

MARION

O **MARION ART CENTER,** 80 Pleasant, Box 602, 02738. Tel 617-748-1266. *Pres* Mancy L Putnam
Open Tues - Sat 1 - 4:30 PM. Estab 1957 to provide theater and visual arts exhibitions for the community and to provide studio classes for adults and children. Gallery is 70 ft of wall space, 280 sq ft floor space; indirect lighting; entrance off Main St. Average Annual Attendance: 1200. Mem: 450; dues family $15, single $10; annual meeting second Tues in July
Publications: Annual membership folder; monthly invitations to opening; Newsletter, monthly
Activities: Classes for adults and children; dramatic programs; lect open to the public, 5 visiting lectrs per year; concerts; competitions; scholarships; original objects of art lent; rental of paintings and prints available to anyone for a fee of $10-$20 per two month period

MEDFORD

M **TUFTS UNIVERSITY,** Gallery Eleven, Cohen Arts Center - Fine Arts Dept, Talbot Ave, 02155. Tel 617-628-5000, Ext 2800. *Dir* Nancy Doll
Open fall & spring semesters, Mon - Sat 10 AM - 4 PM, Wed evenings 6 - 8 PM. No admis fee. Estab 1955 to display works of art by University students and faculty and special exhibitions of traditional and experimental works in all visual art media. Average Annual Attendance: 5000
Income: Financed through the Fine Arts Department
Purchases: Roger Kizik, Animal
Exhibitions: 14 shows annually, including theses exhibits of candidates for the MFA degree offered by Tufts in affiliation with the School of the Boston Museum of Fine Arts; Audrey Flack: Photographs & Prints; A Boston School: Four Artists; Nine Photographers; Mira Cantor: Tufts Beach; Private Lives: Personal Narrative Painting; Chuck Close: Handmade Paper Editions
Publications: Exhibition brochures
Activities: Lectures open to the public, 1-2 vis lectrs per year; gallery talks; tours; competitions; individual and original objects of art lent to locations on campus and occasionally outside sources; book traveling exhibitions

MILTON

M **CHINA TRADE MUSEUM,*** 215 Adams St, 02186. Tel 617-696-1815. *Pres* Mark Claff; *Secy* Joseph Hinkle; *Dir* Betty Wurth Hirsch; *Cur* H A Crosby Forbes; *Assoc Cur* William Sargent; *Dir of Development & Public Relations* Linda M Abegglen; *Registrar* Dana D Ricciardi; *Asst Cur* Carol A Kim
Open Tues - Sun 1 - 4 PM; group tours 9 AM - 1 PM. Admis adults $3, sr citizens and students (with ID) $1.50, members and children under 12 free. Estab 1964 to promote understanding of the cultural, historical, economic and political implications of the early Western trade with East Asia. Robert Bennet Forbes House 1833, National Historic Landmark, Greek Revival mansion, nine exhibition rooms; Amos Holbrook House 1800, Federalist mansion, exhibition rooms and lecture hall. Average Annual Attendance: 15,000. Mem: 1000; dues benefactor $2500, patron $1000, sponsor $500, donor $250, friend $100, contributing $50, participating $25
Income: $319,000 (financed by endowment, membership, contributions and grants from government, private foundations and admission fees)
Purchases: $12,000
Collections: Archives of documents, Chinese art, fancy goods, furniture, Oriental export porcelain, paintings, 19th century photographs, silver, textiles
Exhibitions: Silk As Ceremony; Tradition of Splendor: Chinese Silver for the West
Publications: China Trade Register, membership newsletter, quarterly; exhibition catalogs
Activities: Classes for adults and children; school outreach; docent training; lect open to public, some for members only, 12 visiting lectr per year; concerts; gallery talks; tours; Samuel Shaw Award; exten dept serves nationwide; original objects of art lent to other institutions; lending collection contains original art works, original prints, paintings and decorative arts; originate traveling exhibitions; museum shop sells books, reproductions, prints and imported arts and craft items
L **Library and Archives,*** 215 Adams St, 02186. *Archivist* Dana D Ricciardi
Open by appointment only. Estab 1965 as reference for staff, members and visitors
Library Holdings: Vols 1500; Per subs 20; Micro — Reels; AV — Slides, v-tapes; Other — Clipping files, exhibition catalogs, manuscripts, memorabilia, pamphlets, photographs
Special Subjects: United States - China Trade
Collections: Documents (letters, logbooks, etc) of the United States - China trade; history of China and China trade; history of art; early photographs of China and Japan

NANTUCKET

O **ARTISTS ASSOCIATION OF NANTUCKET,** Kenneth Taylor Gallery, 02554. Tel 617-228-0722. *Administrator* Penny Dey; *Pres* Barbara Capizzo
Open daily 9 AM - 10 PM (May 1 - Dec 6). No admis fee. Estab 1944 to provide gallery space to approximately 290 exhibiting artist members, to promote the arts; to provide arts and crafts workshops year round. Maintains two galleries: The Kenneth Taylor Gallery, two floors in historic building, and The Little Gallery, one small floor for one-person shows. Average Annual

Attendance: 50,000 - 75,000. Mem: 500; dues patron $25 - $500, artist $20; annual meeting Aug
Income: $12,000 - $15,000 (financed by membership, fund raising and commissions)
Collections: Permanent collection on loan to hospital and town buildings
Exhibitions: Annual Craft Show; Nantucket Craftspeople; 53rd Annual Sidewalk Art Show; changing one-person and group member shows during summer; occasional off-season shows
Publications: Newsletter, three times per year; annual brochure
Activities: Classes for adults and children; workshops; lectures open to public, 3-4 vis lectr per year; gallery talks; competitions with awards; scholarships; individual paintings and original objects of art lent to local hospital and public offices

M **NANTUCKET HISTORICAL ASSOCIATION,** Fair Street Museum,* 2 Union, PO Box 1016, 02554. Tel 617-228-1894. *Pres* Leroy H True; *VPres* Albert T Egan; *Secy* Richard Austin; *Treas* John N Welch
Open June - Oct 10 AM - 5 PM. Admin $1. Estab 1979. Gallery has 2 floors & displays 100 paintings, rotating monthly. Mem: 2500, dues $7.50 per year, annual meeting in July
Income: $350,000 (financed by endowment, membership and admissions)
Collections: Pre-20th Century Oil Paintings
Activities: Classes for adults and children; lectures open to public; museum shop sells books, reproductions, prints and slides

NATICK

INTER-SOCIETY COLOR COUNCIL
For further information, see National and Regional Organizations

NEEDHAM

O **BOSTON PRINTMAKERS,** c/o Sylvia Rantz, 299 High Rock St, 02192. Tel 617-444-2692. *Pres* Sidney Hurwitz
Estab 1947 to aid printmakers in exhibiting their work; to bring quality work to the public. Average Annual Attendance: 15,000. Mem: 180; dues $15; annual meeting June
Income: Financed by membership, entry fees, and commission on sales
Purchases: $4700
Exhibitions: Exhibitions are held at Brockton Art Center, Rose Art Museum, Brandeis University and Decordova Museum, Boston University
Publications: Exhibition catalogs
Activities: Lectures open to the public; gallery talks; competitions with awards and prizes; individual paintings and original objects of art lent to local musuems, galleries, libraries and schools; book 5 traveling exhibitions per year; traveling exhibitions organized and circulated

NEW BEDFORD

L **NEW BEDFORD FREE PUBLIC LIBRARY,** Art Dept,* 613 Pleasant St, 02740. Tel 617-999-6291. *Dir* Laurence H Solomon; *Dept Head Reference* Thelma Paine; *Dept Head Genealogy & Whaling Coll* Paul Cyr; *Dept Head AV* Phillip Dimor; *Dept Head Technical Service* Pauline Bolduc
Open Mon - Sat 9 AM - 5 PM, cl Sun & holidays. Estab 1852. Circ 478,828
Income: $640,900 (financed by endowment, city and state appropriation)
Purchases: $111,178
Library Holdings: Micro — Reels; AV — Cassettes, fs, motion pictures, rec, slides, v-tapes; Other — Framed reproductions, photographs
Special Subjects: Whaling, New Bedford Artists
Collections: Paintings by Clifford Ashley, Albert Bierstadt, F D Millet, William Wall
Activities: Scholarships; individual and original objects of art lent to city offices

M **OLD DARTMOUTH HISTORICAL SOCIETY,** New Bedford Whaling Museum, 18 Johnny Cake Hill, 02740. Tel 617-997-0046. *Dir* Richard C Kugler; *Asst Dir* Barbara H Collins; *Sr Cur* Philip F Purrington; *Cur Coll* Elton W Hall; *Cur Ethnology* John R Bockstoce; *Cur Photography* Nicholas Whitman
Open Mon - Sat 9 AM - 5 PM, Sun 1 - 5 PM. Admis adults $2, children 6 - 14 $1, children under 6 free. Estab 1903 to interest and educate the public in the history of the whaling industry and the greater New Bedford area. Average Annual Attendance: 100,000. Mem: 2300; dues $10 - $500; annual meeting May
Income: $603,469 (financed by endowment, membership, special events and admissions)
Purchases: $78,088
Collections: Russell-Purrington Panorama of a Whaling Voyage; domestic crafts; †furniture and domestic arts; †New Bedford artists; paintings and prints; †scrimshaw; ship models; Whaleship Lagoda (1-2 scale model); †whaling arts and crafts
Exhibitions: (1982) Portugal & the East Through Embroidery; Marine Prints by Philip Kappel; The Manhattan in Japanese Waters; The Ernestina - A Human Story; Sailing Ships in Dutch Prints: Four Centuries of Naval Art From the Rijksmuseum; Albert Van Beest: Paintings & Drawings; Photographs of New Bedford, 1895-1920; Watercolors by Joseph S Russell; (1983) Ken Davies: 35 Years--A New Bedford Homecoming
Publications: Bulletin from Johnny Cake Hill, quarterly; exhibition catalogs; calendar, quarterly
Activities: Classes for adults and children; docent training; lect open to public, 6 vis lectr per yr; gallery talks; tours; individual paintings and original objects of art lent to other museums; traveling exhibitions organized and circulated; museum shop sells books, magazines, reproductions, prints and gift items
L **Whaling Museum Library,** 18 Johnny Cake Hill, 02740. Tel 617-997-0046
For reference only
Library Holdings: Vols 15,000; Per subs 12; Micro — Reels; Other — Clipping files, exhibition catalogs, manuscripts, memorabilia, pamphlets
Special Subjects: Charles F Batchelder Whaling Collection, Charles A Goodwin Collection, History of Whaling Industry, Andrew Snow Logbook Collection

M SWAIN SCHOOL OF DESIGN, William W Crapo Gallery, 19 Hawthorn St, 02740. Tel 617-997-7831. *Dir* Bruce Yenawine; *Gallery Dir* Sarah Benham
Open Mon - Fri 10 AM - 4 PM, cl Sat, Sun & holidays. Estab 1881
Income: Financed by private funds, school budget & grants
Exhibitions: Lester Johnson; Lennart Anderson; Wolf Kahn; Harvey Breverman; Tyler Smith; Michael Couch; David Loffler Smith
Publications: Catalogs
L Library, 19 Hawthorn St, 02740. *Library Dir* Angela M Sciotti
Open Mon - Fri 8:30 AM - 4:30 PM and 6 - 9 PM during school term. Estab 1967 for reference and research supporting fine arts curriculum. Circ 800
Purchases: $9500
Library Holdings: Vols 16,000; Per subs 45; AV — Kodachromes, slides; Other — Clipping files, exhibition catalogs
Special Subjects: Art History, Fine Arts, Design
Collections: New Bedford Area Artist File

NEWBURYPORT

M HISTORICAL SOCIETY OF OLD NEWBURY, Cushing House Museum, 98 High St, 01950. Tel 617-462-2681. *Cur* Wilhelmina V Lunt
Open May - Oct Tues - Sat 10 AM - 4 PM, Sun 2 - 5 PM, cl Nov - Apr, except by appointment. Admis adults $2, children under 16 $.50, special group rates. Estab 1877. Mem: Dues individual life $200, annual benefactor $100, annual sustaining $25, family $15, individual $10
Income: $30,000 (financed by dues, tours, endowments, fund-raisers)
Collections: China; dolls; furniture; glass; miniatures; needlework; paintings; paperweights; sampler collection; silver; other historical material
Activities: Lect; guided tours

M NEWBURYPORT MARITIME SOCIETY, Custom House Maritime Museum,* 25 Water St, PO Box 306, 01950. Tel 617-462-8681. *Pres* Josiah Welch; *Dir & Cur* Regina Tracy; *Secy* Jean Reardon
Open Mon - Sat 10 AM - 4:30 PM, Sun 2 - 5 PM. Admis adults $1, children to 15 $.50, under 5 free, adult tours $.75, children's tours $.35. Estab 1975 to exhibit the maritime heritage of the Merrimack Valley; Valley. Housed in an 1835 custom house designed by Robert Mills. The structure is on the National Register of Historic Places. Average Annual Attendance: 8000. Mem: 525; dues $350, $100, $50, $15 or $10; annual meeting March
Income: $30,000 (financed by membership, admission and fundraisers)
Collections: Collection of portraits and decorative art objects 1680-1820; original collection of ethnographic items owned by Newburyport Marine Society Members; half hull models of Merrimack River Valley Ships; portraits of sea captains; navigational instrument and models
Exhibitions: Lithographs of George C Wales; Run of the Mill - Photos of New England Milling
Publications: Newsletter, bimonthly
Activities: Classes for adults and children; lect open to the public, 6 visiting lectr per year; gallery talks; tours; individual paintings and original objects of art lent to other museums and historical agencies; museum shop selling nautical items

NORTHAMPTON

L FORBES LIBRARY, 20 West St, 01060. Tel 413-584-8550. *Dir* Blaise Bisaillon; *Art & Music Librn* Angela M Sciotti
Open Mon, Tues & Thurs 9 AM - 6 PM, Wed 9 AM - 9 PM, Fri & Sat 9 AM - 5 PM, cl holidays. Estab 1894 to serve the residential and academic community as a general public library and a research facility. Gallery and exhibit cases for regional artists, photographers and craftspeople. Circ 292,950
Income: $350,000 (financed by endowment, city and state appropriation, federal funds)
Purchases: $53,500
Library Holdings: Vols 17,000; Per subs 47; original documents; AV — Cassettes, motion pictures; Other — Exhibition catalogs, framed reproductions, manuscripts, memorabilia, original art works, photographs, prints
Special Subjects: Art, music
Collections: Bien Edition of Audubon Bird Prints; Library of Charles E Forbes; Lyman Collection of Japanese Wood Block Prints and Japanese Books; Walter E Corbin Collection of Photographic Prints and Slides; The Coolidge Collection; Connecticut Valley History; Genealogical Records; Official White House Portraits of President Calvin Coolidge and Grace Anna Coolidge; The Holland House Collection of English Miniatures; World War I and II Poster Collection
Exhibitions: Monthly exhibits of works by regional artists, photographers and craftspeople
Activities: Lect program; concerts; tours; weekly film; exten dept to elderly and house bound

M SMITH COLLEGE, Museum of Art, Elm Street at Bedford Terrace, 01063. Tel 413-584-2700, Ext 2236, 740. *Dir & Chief Cur* Charles Chetham; *Assoc Dir & Cur of Paintings* Betsy B Jones; *Asst Cur Prints* Inga Christine Swenson; *Asst Dir Admin* Kathryn Woo; *Asst Cur Paintings* Linda Muehlig
Open Tues - Sat Noon - 5 PM, Sun 2 - 5 PM, cl Mon & academic holidays; June by appointment; July - August Tues - Sat 1 - 4 PM. No admis fee. Collection founded 1879; Hillyer Art Gallery built 1882; Smith College Museum of Art established 1920; Tryon Art Gallery built 1926; present Smith College Museum of Art in Tryon Hall opened 1973. Average Annual Attendance: 36,000. Mem: 700; dues student $10 and higher
Collections: Examples from most periods and cultures with special emphasis on European and American paintings, sculpture, drawings, prints, photographs and decorative arts of the 17th-20th centuries
Exhibitions: 12-24 temporary exhibitions and installations annually
Publications: Catalogues
Activities: Gallery tours; lectures; gallery talks; concerts; individual works of art lent to other institutions; sales desk selling publications, post and note cards, posters

L Hillyer Art Library, Elm Street at Bedford Terrace, 01063. *Librn* Karen J Harvey
Open Mon - Thurs 8 AM - 11 PM; Fri 8 AM - 10 PM; Sat 10 AM - 10 PM, Sun 12 Noon - 10 PM. Estab 1900 to support courses offered by art department of Smith College
Income: Financed by endowment
Library Holdings: Vols 43,000; Per subs 200; Micro — Fiche, reels; AV — Cassettes; Other — Exhibition catalogs, photographs

NORTH ANDOVER

M MERRIMACK VALLEY TEXTILE MUSEUM,* 800 Massachusetts Ave, 01845. Tel 617-686-0191. *Pres* Samuel S Rogers; *Dir* Thomas W Leavitt; *Secy* Clifford E Elias; *Cur* Laurence F Gross; *Assoc Cur* Paul Hudon; *Museum Conservator* Robert A Hauser; *Textile Conservator* Jane Hutchins
Open Tues - Fri 9 AM - 4 PM, Sat & Sun 1 - 5 PM. Admis adults $1, minors and senior citizens $.50, free to all on Sat. Estab 1960 to preserve artifacts, documents and pictorial descriptions of the American textile industry and related development abroad. Two permanent exhibit galleries: Homespun to Factory Made; Woolen Textiles in America, 1776-1876. Average Annual Attendance: 6000
Income: Financed by endowment
Collections: Hand looms, industrial machinery, spinning wheels, †textile collection
Exhibitions: All Sorts of Good Sufficient Linen Cloth: Linen Making in New England 1640-1860
Publications: Exhibition catalogs
Activities: Classes for adults; docent training; tours; competitions; lending collection contains slides; originate traveling exhibits; sales desk selling books, prints and postcards
L Library,* 800 Massachusetts Ave, 01845. Tel 617-686-0191. *Librn* Helena Wright
Open Tues - Fri 10 AM - 5 PM
Income: Financed by endowment
Library Holdings: Vols 33,500; Per subs 30; ephemera, original documents, trade literature; Micro — Reels; AV — Motion pictures; Other — Exhibition catalogs, manuscripts, original art works, pamphlets, photographs, prints
Special Subjects: History of textile industry, textile design and manufacturing, textile mill architecture
Publications: Checklist of prints and manuscripts

NORTON

WHEATON COLLEGE
M Watson Gallery, East Main St, 02766. Tel 617-285-7722, Ext 428. *Dir* Sandra Davidson; *Asst Cur* Morag Murray
Open Mon 10 AM - 12 Noon, 2 - 4 PM, Tues - Sun 1 - 5 PM. No admis fee. Estab 1960, gallery program since 1930 to provide a wide range of contemporary one person and group shows as well as exhibitions from the permanent collections of paintings and graphics. Gallery is of fireproof steel-frame, glass and brick construction; there are no windows. Average Annual Attendance: 5000
Income: Financed by college budget
Purchases: Marble portrait bust of Roman boy & Etruscan antefix head
Collections: Ancient Coins from the Newell Bequest; Ashley Collection of Textiles; Helen Mead Wires Collection of Textiles; Laila G Raab Collection of American Glass; †paintings; †drawings; †prints; †sculpture; †glass & other decorative arts; Cass Wedgewood Collection; Collins Candlestick Collection
Exhibitions: (1982-83) Adrienne Farb: Recent Works - Paris & Provence, paintings & drawings; Francesco Spicuzza: An American Impressionist, paintings & drawings; Carol Aronson: Circus Performer Series, paintings; Randy Mersel Goldberger: Inner Thoughts, sculpture; Recent Acquisitions, paintings, drawings & watercolors, prints; Women Look at Women, photography; Cliff Prokop & Beth Burkhauser, metal sculpture & jewelry; student exhibition, paintings, drawings, prints, sculpture & photography; (1983-84) Judith Nulty: Recent Landscapes, paintings, drawings & lithographs; Rose Imhoff: Stations of the Cross Series, collage; Jozeph Zaremba: Hat People - A Series of Watercolors & Pastels; Jacalyn Brookner: Bronze Sculpture; Evelyn Stehle: Space & Reality - Abstract Landscapes; Clarence Washington: Recent Paintings; Sue Standing & Katherine Kadish: Waterworks, Poetry & Monotypes; local artists, invitational, paintings, prints, drawings, photographs; Vaino Kola: Recent Work, etchings & colored pencil drawings; Majors' Works II, senior art majors
Publications: Gallery notes, semi-annually; exhibition catalogs; Prints of the Nineteenth Century: A Selection from the Wheaton College Collection; Collage; Eleanore Norcross; Amy Cross; Edith Loring Getchell; Hugh Townley; Patterns: Period Costumes; Francesco Spicuzza; Waterworks
Activities: Lectures open to the public, five - eight visiting lecturers per year; concerts; gallery talks; tours; individual paintings and original objects of art lent to college and other museums and galleries; traveling exhibitions organized and circulated; original prints and reproductions for annual rental
L Art Collection, Wheaton College, 02766. *Fine Arts Librn Liaison* Open
Open Mon - Fri 8:30 AM - 10 PM, Sat 9 AM - 10 PM, Sun 10:30 Am - 10 PM. Estab 1962 in Watson Hall; consolidated in 1980 as special collection in Main library to support curricular and other needs of the Wheaton community
Library Holdings: Vols 14,500; Per subs 65; AV — Slides; Other — Clipping files, exhibition catalogs, pamphlets

PAXTON

M ANNA MARIA COLLEGE, Saint Luke's Gallery, Moll Art Center, Sunset Lane, 01612. Tel 617-757-4586. *Chmn Art Dept* R A Parente Jr
Open 9 AM - 4 PM. No admis fee. Estab 1968 as an outlet for the art student and professional artist, and to raise the artistic awareness of the general community. Main Gallery is 35 x 15 ft with about 300 sq ft of wall space. Average Annual Attendance: 600
Collections: Small assortment of furniture, paintings, sculpture

Exhibitions: Annual senior art exhibit; local artists, faculty and students shows
Publications: Exhibit programs
Activities: Lect open to public; individual paintings & original objects of art lent to campus offices; museum sales shop

PITTSFIELD

L BERKSHIRE ATHENAEUM, Music and Arts Department, 1 Wendell Ave, 01201. Tel 413-442-1559, Ext 26. *Librn* Larry Price; *Head Dept Music and Arts Services* Mary Ann Knight; *First Asst Music and Arts Services* Irene Knott; *First Asst Music and Arts Services* Margaret Bartolomucci
Open Mon, Wed, Fri & Sat 10 AM - 5 PM, Tues & Thurs 10 AM - 9 PM. Estab 1872, music and arts dept 1937
Income: Financed by city and state appropriations and gifts
Library Holdings: Vols 7500; AV — Cassettes 1000, rec 13,000; Other — Prints 2000
Collections: †Mary Rice Morgan Ballet Collection: a reference room of programs, prints, original art, rare and current books on the dance; 1350 piece sheet music reference collection
Exhibitions: (1980-81) Presidential Campaign Memorabilia by Woodward S Bousquet; Stenciled Toleware by Dr Elizabeth C Carton; Eric Carles Childrens World In Books & Illustration; Antique Boxes by Donald & Edna Tench; Contemporary Quilts by Deborah Hollingsworth; Kites by Ellen Plageman; Pottery by Emily Rose; Photography by Joel Librizzi; Jacobs Pillow Dance Festival - 50th Anniversary; Fantasy In Soft Sculpture by Vlada Roussef; William Cumpianos Stringfellow Guitars; Paintings & Jewelry by Chandra & Kenn Holsten; (1981-82) Berkshire Seasons In Photography, Catherine & Stephen Gatti; Memorabilia of World War I, A David Rutstein; Artistry In Metals, Nina Fersen; Cottages & Castles In English Ceramics; Steel Sculpture & Jewelry, Gladys Novick; Early Scrimshaw, the Willis I Milham Collection; Contemporary Scrimshaw, Andrew Bell; Weavers Guild of Southern Berkshire; Lincoln Memorial 60th Anniversary, Chesterwood Collection & Daniel Chester French; Costumes of the Hancock Shakers; Blown Glass by Josh Simpson; Native Wood Arts by Don Kelly; Arabic Calligraphy by Norman Najimy
Activities: Library Series; lect & performances open to public; films

M BERKSHIRE MUSEUM, 39 South St, 01201. Tel 413-443-6721. *Dir* Gary C Burger; *Cur Science* Bartlett Hendricks; *Cur Art* Debra Balken; *Financial Secy* Samuel A Spratlin; *Dir of Environmental Education Dept* Thomas G Smith; *Mem Secy* Avery Spencer; *Dir of Art Education* Maureen Hickey; *Asst to the Dir & Registrar* Marjorie N Hall
No admis fee. Estab 1903 as a museum of art, science and history. Mem: 1620; dues sustaining $25 and up; family $20; single $10; annual meeting February
Income: Financed by endowment, membership and gifts
Collections: Paintings of the Hudson River School (Inness, Moran, Blakelock, Martin, Wyant, Moran, Church, Bierstadt and others); American Abstract: Art of the '30s; early American portraits; Egyptian, Babylonia and Near East arts; grave reliefs from Palmyra; Paul M Hahn Collection of 18th century English and American silver; Old Masters (Patinir, Pons, de Hooch, Van Dyck, Reynolds, Raeburn, Lawrence and others); †contemporary sculptures; two Norman Rockwell paintings
Exhibitions: The Emmetts, A Family of Women Painters; The Suspended Object; Nancy Davidson; New Decorative Art
Publications: Schedule of events, quarterly
Activities: Classes for adults and children; lectures open to the public; museum shop sells gifts; junior museum

M HANCOCK SHAKER VILLAGE, INC, US Rte 20, PO Box 898, 01201. Tel 413-443-0188, 447-7284. *Pres* Mrs Lawrence K Miller; *Dir* Jerry V Grant; *Cur Coll* Tomas Harrington; *Cur Educ Service* Susan Markham
Open June 1 - Oct 31 9:30 AM - 5 PM daily. Admis family of 2 adults & 2 or more children $10, adults $4.50, children $1.50. Estab 1960 for the preservation and restoration of Hancock Shaker Village and the interpretation of Shaker art, architecture and culture. Period rooms throughout the village. Exhibition Gallery contains Shaker inspirational drawings and graphic materials. Average Annual Attendance: 50,000. Mem: 1000; dues individual $15
Income: Financed by membership, donations
Library Holdings: Micro — Fiche, reels; AV — Cassettes, Kodachromes, motion pictures, rec, slides; Other — Exhibition catalogs, manuscripts, memorabilia, pamphlets, photographs
Special Subjects: Shaker Books & Manuscripts; Agricultural and Mechanical Research Material
Collections: Shaker architecture, furniture and industrial material; Shaker inspirational drawings
Publications: Newsletter, biannually; specialized publications
Activities: Classes for adults and chilren; workshops, seminars; lect open to public, 6 visiting lectr per year; concerts; tours; original objects of art lent to accredited museums; lending collection contains 1 film strip, 4 motion pictures, 250 photographs, 40 slides; museum shop selling books, magazines, reproductions, prints, slides
L Hancock Shaker Village Library,* US Rte 20, PO Box 898, 01201. Tel 413-447-7284. *Librn* Robert F W Meader
Reference library open to students and scholars by appointment
Library Holdings: Vols 1000; graphic, maps; Other — Manuscripts, photographs

PLYMOUTH

O PLYMOUTH ANTIQUARIAN SOCIETY,* 27 North St, 02360. Tel 617-746-9697. *Pres* Mrs Gordon Holland; *Cur* Dorothea Anderson; *Registrar* Dorothy B Reed
Open May - Oct Tues - Sat 9 AM - 5 PM, cl Mon & Sun, Nov & April mornings only, cl winter. Admis adults $1.25, children $.25, combination ticket adults $3.25. Estab 1919 to maintain and preserve the three museums: Harlow Old Fort House (1677), Spooner House (1747), and Antiquarian House (1809). Average Annual Attendance: 2000. Mem: 7800; dues $15-$100; annual meeting July
Income: Financed by membership
Collections: Antique dolls
Activities: Classes for children; lect open to the public; sales shop at Harlow House selling hand woven items

PROVINCETOWN

O PROVINCETOWN ART ASSOCIATION AND MUSEUM,* 460 Commercial Street, 02657. Tel 617-487-1750. *Pres* Ciriaco Cozzi; *VPres* Mischa Richter; *Dir* Ellen O'Donnell
Open daily 12 - 4 PM & 7 - 9 PM Memorial Day to Oct. Admis adults $1, children & senior citizens $.50, members free. Estab in 1914 to promote and cultivate the practice and appreciation of all branches of the fine arts, to hold temporary exhibitions, forums, and concerts for its members and the public. Four galleries are maintained. Average Annual Attendance: 40,000. Mem: 626; mem open to artists only; dues range from $25-$50
Income: Financed by membership
Collections: Permanent collection consists of artists work who have lived or worked on the Lowe Cape
Exhibitions: Permanent Collection, Members' Exhibitions
Publications: Exhibitions catalogues and newsletters
Activities: Classes for adults and children, dramatic programs, symposia, and childrens theater arts programs; lect open to the public, 30 vis lectr per year; concerts; film series; gallery talks; tours; scholarships; individual paintings and original objects of art lent to other museums; book traveling exhibitons; originate traveling exhibition; museum shop selling books, original art, prints, reproductions, slides, postcards and notecards, craft items by members
L Library,* 460 Commercial Street, 02657
Open to members only
Library Holdings: Vols 500; Other — Exhibition catalogs
Special Subjects: Provincetown artists
Collections: Memorabilia of WHW Bicknell

QUINCY

M ADAMS NATIONAL HISTORIC SITE, 135 Adams St, PO Box 531, 02269. Tel 617-773-1177. *Supt* Wilhelmina S Harris
Open daily April 19 - Nov 10 9 AM - 5 PM. Admis adults $.50, children under 16 admitted free if accompanied by an adult. Estab 1946. The site consists of a house, part of which dates to 1731; a library containing approx 12,000 books, (most of which belonged to John Quincy Adams); a carriage house; a woodshed and grounds which were once owned and enjoyed by four generations of the Adams family. Average Annual Attendance: 20,000
Income: Financed by Federal Government
Collections: Original furnishings belonging to the four generations of Adamses who lived in the house between 1788 and 1937
Activities: Lectures (one week each spring); tours

ROCKPORT

O ROCKPORT ART ASSOCIATION, Old Tavern, 12 Main St, 01966. Tel 617-546-6604. *Pres* John Manship; *Cur* George Faddis; *VPres* Michael Stoffa; *Secy* Helen Faddis; *Treas* Penn Westman; *Dir* Ann Fisk; *Publicity* Miriam Lippincott
Open Summer: daily 9:30 AM - 5 PM, Sun 1 - 5 PM, Winter: daily 9:30 AM - 4:30 PM, Sun 1 - 5 PM. No admis fee. Estab 1921 as a non-profit educational organization established for the advancement of art. Three galleries are maintained in the Old Tavern Building; two large summer galleries are adjacent to the main structure. Average Annual Attendance: 75,000. Mem: 1000; dues artists $40; annual meeting second Thurs in August
Income: Financed by endowment and membership
Collections: Permanent collection of works by former and current association artist members
Exhibitions: Amateur Art Festival; Annual Spring Ten-Man Show; bi-monthly one artist shows and monthly one artist revolving screen show; four major summer shows, second & third juried; monthly group shows year-round, representing over 200 artist members; Rockport Public Schools Show; Special Annual Exhibitions: Amateur Members' Show; various community shows
Publications: Exhibition catalogs, yearly; Rockport Artist Book (1970), every 10 years
Activities: Classes for adults and children; sketch groups; workshops demonstrations; lect open to the public; competitions with awards given; concerts; slide lect; individual paintings and original objects of art lent to colleges, art schools, churches and hospitals for short term exhibition; lending collection contains original art works of paintings, graphics and sculpture; Tavern Door shop sells books, cards and notes by artist members

SALEM

M ESSEX INSTITUTE, 132 Essex St, 01970. Tel 617-744-3390. *Dir* Bryant F Tolles Jr; *Asst to Dir* Katherine W Richardson; *Cur* Anne Farnam; *Public Relations* Phyllis Shutze
Open June 30 - Sept 5 Mon - Sat 9 AM - 6 PM, Sun 1 - 5 PM, Sept - May Mon - Sun 9 AM - 4:30 PM, cl Thanksgiving, Christmas & New Years. Admis adults $2, children $1. Estab 1848 to display the Institute's collections of artifacts and historic houses representing the richness of Salem's and Essex County's material culture from the early 17th into the 20th centuries. The Museum is housed in Plummer Hall built in 1857 and is an excellent example of Victorian Italian Revival architecture. On the first floor is the John A McCarthy Gallery devoted to changing displays and loan exhibitions. The second floor has a portrait gallery, and the main gallery containing three early period rooms; a special collections and print room used for small exhibitions. Average Annual Attendance: 100,000. Mem: 1200; dues from $15 to corporate-institutional $100-$300; annual meeting April
Income: $687,542 (financed by endowment, membership, gifts and admissions)
Collections: Architectural fragments, buttons, ceramics, clocks, dolls, furniture, glassware, pewter, sculpture, silver and toys all associated with the civil history of Essex County and adjacent areas since the early 17th century
Exhibitions: Charles Osgood (1809-1890); Child Life in Early America; Costume Exhibition, CEL Greene; Crazy Quilts (1875-1885); Early American Woodworking Tools; Essex County Landscape artist; Fashions and Draperies for

Windows and Beds; Library Exhibit - Conservation: Some Problems and
Solutions; Life and Times in Shoe City: The Shoe Workers of Lynn; Nathaniel
Hawthorne Exhibition; Olive Prescott: Weaver of Forge Village; Prints at the
Essex Institute; Rare Book Exhibit; Recent Acquisitions and Basement Treasures
in the Essex Institute Collections; Salem on the Grand Tour; Salem Willows in
Retrospect; Salem Witches: Myth and Reality; Sights and Sound from the Past:
The Television Age is Born; The First Church of Salem: 350 Years; The Prolific
Portrait Painter of Salem, MA; The Salem Redevelopment Authority: The
Changing Picture of Urban Renewal in an Historic City; To My Valentine (1880-
1929); Selections from Quilts & Woven Coverlets; Children of Essex County;
Scratching Birds and Profile Mountain: Prints from the Collection; Salem
Witches: Documentary of an Early American Drama; 98 Years of Play; the
Games of Parker Brothers; William Morris Hunt and the Summer Art Colony of
Magnolia 1876-1979; Architectural Fragments; Salem the Home Front: 1941-
1945; Conservation: Keeping Americas Neighborhoods Together; The Joy of
Dining as Shown in Art; Salem Witches: Documents of an Early Drama;
Architecture of Salem: A Century of Changing Styles, 1800-1900
Publications: Historical Collections, quarterly; newsletter, quarterly; occasional
books
Activities: Classes for adults and children; docent training; lect open to public, 6
visiting lectr per year; gallery talks; tours; concerts; films; scholarships; paintings
and original objects of art lent to museums and institutions; sales shop sells folk
art, books, magazines, original art, reproductions, prints and slides
L   **James Duncan Phillips Library,** 132 Essex St, 01970
Open Mon - Fri 9 AM - 4:30 PM. For reference only
Library Holdings: Vols 400,000; Other — Manuscripts, memorabilia, pamphlets
Collections: Frederick T Ward China Collection, the history of China and
Chinese-American relations to the early 20th century
M   **Gardner-Pingree House,** 128 Essex St, 01970
Open Tues - Sat 10 AM - 4 PM; Sun 1 - 4:30 PM (June 1 - Oct 15). Admis
adults $1.50, sr citizens $1, children $.75. Built in 1804-1805 and illustrates the
Federal Style of Salem master-builder and carver, Samuel McIntire; furnished in
that period
M   **Crowninshield-Bentley House,** 126 Essex St, 01970
Open Tues - Sat 10 AM - 4 PM; Sun 1 - 4:30 PM (June 1 - Oct 31). Admis
adults $1.50, sr citizens $1, children $75. Built in 1727, added to and remodeled
after 1800. It illustrates the styles of interior architecture and furnishings of much
of the 18th century in Salem
M   **John Ward House,** 132 Essex St, 01970
Open Tues - Sat 10 AM - 4 PM; Sun 1 - 4:30 PM (June 1 - Oct 31). Admis
adults $1.50, sr citizens $1, children $.75. Built 1684, restored 1910-1912 under
direction of George Francis Dow, architectural historian. Furnished in the
manner of the time. The rear lean-to contains a later apothecary's shop, a
weaving room with operable loom and a small cent shop
M   **Andrew-Safford House,** 13 Washington Square, 01970
Open Thurs 2 - 4:30 PM. Admis $1.50. Built in 1818-1819, and purchased by the
Institute in 1947 for the purpose of presenting a vivid image of early 19th
century urban life. It is the residence of the Institute's director
M   **Peirce-Nichols House,** 80 Federal St, 01970
Open Tues - Sat 2 - 4:30 PM. Admis $1.50. Built in 1782 by Samuel McIntire.
Maintains some original furnishings and a counting house
M   **Assembly House,** 138 Federal St, 01970
Open for functions & by special appointment. Admis $1. Built in 1782 as a hall
for social assemblies; remodeled in 1796 by Samuel McIntire as a home
residence. The interior features a Victorian sitting room and an unusual Chinese
parlor
M   **Lye-Tapley Shoe Shop (1830) and Vaughan Doll House,** 132 Essex St, 01970
Open June 1 - Oct 31 Tues - Sat 9 AM - 4:30 PM, Sun 1 - 5 PM.
Accommodates special collections
M   **Beebe Summer House,** 132 Essex St, 01970
The Summer House (c. 1800) is the focal point of the Institute Gardens

M   **PEABODY MUSEUM OF SALEM,** East India Square, 01970. Tel 617-745-
1876, 745-9500. *Dir* Peter Fetchko
Open Mon - Sat 10 AM - 5 PM, Sun 1 - 5 PM, cl New Years, Thanksgiving,
Christmas. Admis adults $2, children $1. Estab 1799 for the conservation of
American maritime history, art objects; ethnology of non-European peoples;
natural history of Essex County. Gallery is a conglomeration of old and new
buildings, 45,000 sq ft of exhibit space, 95,000 sq ft total. Average Annual
Attendance: 100,000. Mem: 2700; dues $20 - $1000; annual meeting Sept
Income: $1,100,000 (financed by endowment, grants, gifts & membership)
Library Holdings: marine photographs archive; photo reproductions
Collections: †American Maritime History (paintings, objects); †Ethnology of
Pacific Islands and Far East; †Natural History of Essex County, Massachusetts;
1,000,000 Negative Collection
Exhibitions: The Art & Science of Navigation: Instruments from the Collection
of the Peabody Museum; American Traders in European Ports, watercolors,
charts & broadslides; Steam & the Sea: Chinese Rice
Grain Porcelain from the H Nelson Hartstone Collection; Beyond Tradition,
contemporary ceramics; The Tribal Style, African arts & crafts
Publications: The American Neptune, quarterly journal of maritime history;
annual report of the Director
Activities: Classes for adults and children; docent training; lect open to public, 4
visiting lectrs per year; gallery talks; tours; museum shop selling books,
reproductions, prints
L   **Phillips Library,** East India Square, 01970. *Librn* Barbara Edkins
Open Mon - Fri 10 AM - 4:30 PM. Staff library, but open to qualified
researchers
Income: Financed by endowment
Library Holdings: Vols 100,000; Per subs 225
Special Subjects: Ethnology of non-European peoples, maritime history of New
England, natural history of Essex County, voyages of discovery

SANDWICH

M   **HERITAGE PLANTATION OF SANDWICH,*** Grove and Pine Sts, 02563.
Tel 617-888-3300. *Dir* Gene A Schott; *Cur Arts & Crafts* Lewis Stedman; *Cur
Military History* James Cervantes; *Cur Botanical Science* Jean Gillis; *Registrar*
Allota Whitney; *Cur Education* Richard Ressmeyer; *Cur Antique Auto Museum*
Robert Melber
Open daily 10 AM - 5 PM, May - Oct. Admis adults $4, children $1.50, special
rates for school groups. Estab 1969 as a museum of Americana. Heritage
Plantation is a Massachusettes charitable corporation. Maintains three galleries
which house collections. Average Annual Attendance: 100,000. Mem: 2000; dues
family $25, individual $20; annual meeting May
Income: Financed by endowment, membership, admissions
Collections: †American Indian artifacts; folk art; primitive paintings; †Scrimshaw
Exhibitions: An American Flower Show; Travels With Mermaids; Bark, Beads,
Maize and Whales; (1981) Across The Wide Missouri: The American West In
Art; Firemen and Folk Art; Angels of the Mounds: Leaders in Indiana
Archaeology
Publications: The Cupola, quarterly
Activities: Classes for adults and children; lect for members only, 4 - 5 vis lectr
per year; concerts; gallery talks; tours; exten dept serving Cape Cod area;
artmobile; individual paintings and original objects of art lent
L   **Library,*** Grove & Pine Sts, 02563. *Cur* Richard Ressmeyer
Open to staff and members for reference only
Library Holdings: Vols 1000; Per subs 10
Special Subjects: Antique automobile, art, military history

SCITUATE

NEW ENGLAND WATERCOLOR SOCIETY
For further information, see National and Regional Organizations

SHARON

M   **KENDALL WHALING MUSEUM,** 27 Everett St, PO Box 297, 02067. Tel
617-784-5642. *Dir* Stuart M Frank; *Cur* Robert H Ellis Jr
Open Tues - Fri 1 - 4 PM, Sat 10 AM - 4 PM; cl holidays. Admis adults $1,
children under 14 $.50. Estab 1956 to collect, preserve & interpret materials
relating to the history & fine arts of whaling & the natural history of the whale.
Nine galleries hold the maritime collections. Average Annual Attendance: 10,
000. Mem: 250
Income: Financed by foundations, grants, admissions, gifts and publications
Collections: American, European, British, Dutch & Japanese paintings;
scrimshaw; ship models; tools; small craft; decorative arts & carvings; Eskimo
(Inuit) art; maritime art; marine paintings
Exhibitions: (1983-84) American Whaling in the Western Arctic; American
Whaling & the Civil War; Arctic Whaling, 1596-1925; British Whaling Paintings
& Prints; Old Master Whaling Prints; Dutch Whaling; British & American
Paintings & Prints; Modern Whaling; Arctic Whaling & Seal Hunting; American
Whaling, 19th century
Publications: Kendall Whaling Museum Newsletter, quarterly; original
publications; exhibition catalogs; monograph series
Activities: Classes for adults & children; musical programs; lectures open to
public, 15 vis lectr per year; concerts; gallery talks; tours; exten dept serves New
England & anywhere else by arrangement; individual paintings & original objects
of art lent to qualified museums only; originate traveling exhbitions; museum
shop sells books, original art, reproductions, prints, apparel, stationery, gifts,
curriculum kits & educational materials
L   **Library,** 27 Everett St, PO Box 297, 02067. *Librn* Robert L Webb
For reference only
Library Holdings: Vols 5000; Per subs 25; Micro — Cards, reels; AV —
Kodachromes, motion pictures, rec, slides; Other — Clipping files, framed
reproductions, manuscripts, memorabilia, original art works, pamphlets,
photographs, prints, reproductions, sculpture
Special Subjects: Whaling history & literature, fine arts, natural history, marine
mammal preservation

SOUTH HADLEY

M   **MOUNT HOLYOKE COLLEGE ART MUSEUM,** 01075. Tel 413-538-2245.
Dir Teri J Edelstein; *Chief Cur* Wendy Watson; *Sr Admin Asst* Margery Roy
Open Mon - Fri 11 AM - 5 PM; Sat - Sun 1 - 5 PM; summer Wed - Sun 1 - 4
PM. No admis fee. Estab 1875 to display permanent collection and temporary
exhibitions. Building erected in 1971 to house the equipment and collections of
the Department of Art and Art Museum of Mount Holyoke College. Contains
lecture rooms, painting and sculpture studios, art library; art museum with five
galleries houses the permanent collection. Mem: Dues $50 - $500
Income: Financed by endowment, membership and college funds
Collections: †Asian art, European and American paintings, sculpture, prints and
drawings; Egyptian, Greek, Roman, Pre-Columbian
Exhibitions: (1980-81) Milton Avery-Works on Paper; Suffragettes and Women's
Rights: English Posters of the Early 20th Century; Roma Resurgens: Papal
Medals from the Age of the Baroque; (1981-82) Master Drawings Rediscovered;
Savoy; (1982-83) Louisa Matthiasdottir, paintings; Samuel F B Morse: Educator
and Champion of the Arts of America; Transformations of Hellenistic Art; (1983-
84) The Harvest of a Quiet Eye: Selections from an Alumna Collection;
Apocalyptic Visions: The Impact of the Bomb in Recent American Art
Publications: Newsletter, twice yearly
Activities: Lect open to the public, 5 - 6 vis lectr per year; individual paintings
lent to exhibitions sponsored by museums
L   **Art Library,** 01075. Tel 413-538-2000
Open to college community only
Library Holdings: Vols 15,000; Per subs 60; AV — Slides

SOUTH SUDBURY

M LONGFELLOW'S WAYSIDE INN, Wayside Inn Road off Route 20, 01776. Tel 617-443-8846. *Innkeeper* Francis Koppeis; *Chmn Trustees* Daniel J Coolidge
Open daily 9 AM - 6 PM; cl Christmas Day. Admis $.50; no charge for dining room and overnight guests. Estab 1702 as the oldest operating Inn in America. The ancient hostelry continues to provide hospitality to wayfarers from all over the world. 18th century period rooms including Old Barroom, Longfellow Parlor, Longfellow Bed Chamber, Old Kitchen, Drivers and Drovers Chamber. Historic buildings on the estate include Redstone School of Mary's Little Lamb fame, grist mill, and Martha Mary Chapel. Average Annual Attendance: 250,000
Collections: Early American furniture and decorative arts; Howe family memorabilia; paintings; photographs of the Inn
Activities: Classes for adults; docent training; colonial crafts demonstrations and workshops; lect open to public, 10 vis lectr per year; gallery talks; tours; sales shop selling books, original art, reproductions, prints and slides

SPRINGFIELD

M CONNECTICUT VALLEY HISTORICAL MUSEUM, 194 State St, 01103. Tel 413-732-3080. *Cur Education & Dir* Elizabeth Newell; *Cur Coll* Margaret Bleecker
Open Tues - Sun Noon - 5 PM, cl Mon, New Year's Day, July 4, Thanksgiving & Christmas. No admis fee. Estab 1876. Average Annual Attendance: 30,000.
Mem: Dues $25
Collections: Decorative arts of the Connecticut Valley; furniture; paintings
Activities: Classes for adults and children; docent training; lectures open to the public, 30 vis lectr per yr; concerts; gallery talks; tours; scholarships; exten dept; artmobile; book traveling exhibitions 3 - 4 per yr; originate traveling exhibitions; sales shop sells books, records & prints

M MUSEUM OF FINE ARTS,* 49 Chestnut St, 01103. Tel 413-732-6092. *Dir* Richard Muhlberger; *Secy* Gerri Lockwood; *Cur Education* Janet Gelman; *Assoc Cur* Mary Suzor; *Asst Cur Education* Lisa Italiano; *Publicist* Patricia Cahill; *Coordr Volunteers* Ruth Sulser
Open Tues 12 - 9 PM, Wed - Sun 12 - 5 PM, cl Mon and holidays. No admis fee. Estab 1933 as a unit of the Springfield Library and Museums Association through the bequests of Mr & Mrs James Philip Gray. Building contains 18 galleries, theater, offices
Collections: American paintings, sculpture, and graphics, primitive to contemporary; Chinese, Prehistoric to 19th Century; European paintings and sculpture, early Renaissance to contemporary; Japanese woodblock prints
Exhibitions: Special exhibitions, historic to contemporary, are continually on view in addition to permanent collection
Publications: Handbook to the American and European Collection, Museum of Fine Arts, Springfield; Quadrangle News, monthly newsletter; exhibition catalogs
L Reference Library,* 49 Chestnut St, 01103
Library Holdings: Vols 5000; AV — Slides

M GEORGE WALTER VINCENT SMITH ART MUSEUM,* 222 State St, 01103. Tel 413-733-4214. *Chmn Trustee Committee* Irving Meyer; *Dir* Richard Muhlberger; *Assoc Cur* Mary E Suzor; *Registrar* Laura Olmstead; *Cur Education* Janet Gelman; *Asst Cur Education* Lisa Italiano; *Conservator* Emil G Schnorr
Open Tues Noon - 9 PM, Wed - Sun Noon - 5 PM. No admis fee. Estab 1889 to preserve, protect, present, interpret, study and publish the collections of fine and decorative arts; administered by the Springfield Library & Museums Association. Maintains eleven galleries housing permanent collection and one gallery reserved for changing exhibitions. Average Annual Attendance: 35,000. Mem: 2000; dues $15 and up; annual meeting June
Income: Financed by endowment, membership, city and state appropriations
Collections: American and European Paintings; Japanese Bronzes; Near Eastern Carpets; Oriental Arts (calligraphy, ceramics, lacquer, painting, sculpture, textiles); Oriental Cloisonne; Plaster Casts
Exhibitions: Ceramics of Weston Priory-Brother Thomas; Tom Patti (glass); Young Americans (metals); Arcadian Vales: Views of the Connecticut River Valley; Fifteen Massachusetts Artists: An Invitational
Publications: Annual report; quadrangle calendar; special exhibition catalogs
Activities: Classes for adults and children; docent training; lectures open to public, 30 vis lect per yr; concerts; gallery talks; tours; scholarships; original objects of art lent to members; book traveling exhibitions one per yr; originate traveling exhibitions

O SPRINGFIELD ART LEAGUE,* George Walter Vincent Smith Art Museum, 222 State St, 01103. Tel 413-733-4214. *Pres* Maureen Keough
Estab 1918 to stimulate art expression and appreciation in Springfield. Mem: Dues $2.50; annual meeting May
Income: Financed solely by membership
Exhibitions: Non-juried show in Nov open to all members; annual juried exhibition in April open to all artists
Activities: Lect; demonstration; tours

L SPRINGFIELD CITY LIBRARY, Art & Music Dept, 220 State St, 01103. Tel 413-739-3871. *Pres* John J Canavan Jr; *Dir* James H Fish; *Head Fine Arts Department* Karen A Dorval
Open Mon - Thurs 9 AM - 9 PM, Fri 9 AM - 5 PM, Sat 9 AM - 5 PM, cl Sun and holidays. No admis fee. Estab 1857, Department opened 1905. In addition to the City Library system, the Springfield Library and Museums Association owns and administers, as separate units, the George Walter Vincent Smith Museum, the Museum of Fine Arts, the Science Museum and the Connecticut Valley Historical Museum
Income: $160,000 (financed by city appropriations and private endowments)
Library Holdings: Vols 20,000; Per subs 34; pictures 125,000; American wood engravings and blockprints; Micro — Fiche, reels; AV — Cassettes, rec; Other — Clipping files, exhibition catalogs, pamphlets, photographs, reproductions
Exhibitions: Monthly exhibitions from the Library's collections and of work by local artists; loan exhibitions

L SPRINGFIELD COLLEGE, Hasting Gallery, 263 Alden St, 01109. Tel 413-788-3307. *Cultural Affairs Committee* David P Micka
Open daily 8 AM - 4:30 PM. Estab 1975 to bring a wide range of quality exhibits in all areas of the visual arts to the Springfield College campus and surrounding community
Income: Financed by Cultural Affairs Committee
Library Holdings: Vols 112,000; Per subs 10; Micro — Prints; AV — Cassettes, fs, motion pictures, v-tapes; Other — Original art works, prints
Activities: Lect open to public, 6 vis lectr per year; concerts; tours; gallery talks; competitions

STOCKBRIDGE

M CHESTERWOOD, Box 248, 01262. Tel 413-298-3579. *Dir* Paul W Ivory; *Asst Dir* Susan Frisch Lehrer; *Admin Asst* Kathleen Oppermann
Open daily 10 - 5, May 1 through Oct 31. Admis adults $3.50, students 18 and under $1, group rates available, free to National Trust Members & Friends of Chesterwood. Chesterwood, a museum property of the National Trust for Historic Preservation, was the Berkshire Hill summer estate of Daniel Chester French (1850-1931), sculptor of the Lincoln Memorial and Minute Man. The 150 acre property includes: French's studio (1898) and colonial revival residence (1900-1901), both designed by Henry Bacon, architect of the Lincoln Memorial; Barn Sculpture Gallery, a c 1825 barn adapted for use as exhibition, museum storage and sales space; a period garden and nature walks laid out by French in the woods to the North of the studio. Average Annual Attendance: 30,000
Collections: Plaster models, marbles and bronze casts of French's work and paintings; decorative arts and furnishings representing his family's taste and lifestyle
Exhibitions: Annual Antique Car Show; Christmas at Chesterwood; outdoor contemporary sculpture exhibitions; special exhibits dealing with aspects of historic preservation in the Berkshire region and French's life, career, social and artistic milieu, and summer estate; outdoor sculpture shows
Activities: College summer intern programs; guide training program; sculptor in residence program; guided and school group tours; National Trust Members Day; Berkshire Day Open House; National Trust Preservation Bookstore
L Library,* Box 248, 01262. *Program Asst* Susan Frisch
Open by appointment only. Estab 1969. Library consists of art, reference, gardening, architecture and personal books collected by Daniel Chester French and Margaret French Cresson (Daughter) as well as archival material; serves art, social and architectural historians and historic preservationists
Library Holdings: Vols 5000; Per subs 2; AV — Cassettes, lantern slides, motion pictures, rec, slides; Other — Clipping files, manuscripts, memorabilia, original art works, photographs, prints, sculpture
Special Subjects: Chesterwood, late 19th, early 20th century classical sculpture
Collections: Oral histories: Daniel Chester French and Chesterwood; Berkshire region historic preservation clipping file; blueprints and plans of work; photographs of Daniel Chester French and his family, summer estate and works

M THE TRUSTEES OF RESERVATIONS, The Mission House, Box 115, 01262. Tel 413-298-3383. *Adminr* Ellen Molloy
Open Memorial Day through Columbus Day Tues - Sat 10 AM - 5 PM, Sun 11 AM - 4 PM. Admis. Built 1739, the home of John Sergeant, first missionary to the Stockbridge Indians, it is now an Early American Museum containing an outstanding collection of Colonial furnishings. Museum opened in 1930. Average Annual Attendance: 3000

TYRINGHAM

M TYRINGHAM ART GALLERIES, Tyringham Rd, 01264. Tel 413-243-0654, 243-3260. *Co-Dir* Ann Marie Davis; *Co-Dir* Donald Davis; *Co-Dir* Gary Davis
Admis $.50, children under 12 free. Estab 1953 to exhibit and sell paintings, prints and sculptures by recognized artists, including world masters. The building was designed as a sculpture studio by the late Sir Henry Kitson. Average Annual Attendance: 30,000
Income: Financed privately
Collections: Santarella Sculpture Gardens
Exhibitions: Frequent one-person shows by established artists from New York City
Publications: Occasional auction catalogs
Activities: Gallery talks; tours

L TYRINGHAM INSTITUTE, Jean Brown Archive, Shaker Seed House, 02164. Tel 413-243-3216. *Dir* Mrs Leonard Brown
Open to public by appointment. No admis fee. Estab 1971 for research in dada, surrealism, fluxus for scholars on graduate and advanced research levels. For reference only. Average Annual Attendance: 50
Income: Privately financed
Collections: Concrete Poetry; Dada; Fluxus; Happenings; Intermedia
Activities: Lending collection contains original art works, original prints and photographs
L Library, Shaker Seed House, 01264. *Dir* Jean Brown
Open Mon - Fri 2 - 5 PM. Estab 1971 for reference only
Library Holdings: Per subs 25; AV — Cassettes, rec; Other — Clipping files, exhibition catalogs, framed reproductions, manuscripts, memorabilia, original art works, pamphlets, prints
Special Subjects: Dada, fluxus, mail art, performance art, surrealism, visual art
Collections: Artists' books

WALTHAM

O AMERICAN JEWISH HISTORICAL SOCIETY, 2 Thornton Rd, 02154. Tel 617-891-8110. *Pres* Ruth B Fein; *Chmn Executive Council* Saul Viener; *Dir* Bernard Wax
Open (summer) Mon - Fri 8:30 AM - 5 PM, (winter) Mon - Thurs 8:30 AM - 5 PM, Fri 8:30 AM - 2 PM. No admis fee. Estab 1892 to collect, preserve, catalog

and disseminate information relating to the American Jewish experience. Two galleries with exhibitions mounted, 15 x 50 ft. Average Annual Attendance: 3000. Mem: 3600; dues $20; annual meeting May
Income: $400,000 (financed by endowment, membership, Jewish Federation allocations, grants and donations)
Collections: Manuscripts; Portraits; Yiddish Motion Pictures; Yiddish Theater Posters
Exhibitions: (1983) Haym Salomon: A Gentleman of Precision and Integrity; Jews in Colonial America; On Common Ground: The Boston Jewish Experience, 1649-1980
Publications: American Jewish History, quarterly; books; newsletters
Activities: Lectures open to public, 3 vis lectr per year; gallery talks; tours; competitions with awards; individual paintings & original objects of art lent to museums & historical societies; lending collection contains motion pictures, paintings, books, original art works, original prints & photographs; originate traveling exhibitions

L **Lee M Friedman Memorial Library,** 2 Thornton Rd, 02154. Tel 617-891-8110. *Librn* Dr Nathan M Kaganoff
Open Mon - Fri 8:30 AM - 5 PM, winter hours on Fri 8:30 AM - 2 PM. Estab 1892 to collect, preserve & catalogue material relating to American Jewish history. Open to qualified researchers for reference
Income: $370,000 (financed by endowment, membership, contributions, grants, allocations from Jewish welfare funds)
Purchases: $10,000
Library Holdings: Vols 67,000; Per subs 100; archives; AV — Cassettes, motion pictures, rec, slides; Other — Exhibition catalogs, manuscripts, memorabilia, original art works, pamphlets, photographs, prints, reproductions, sculpture
Special Subjects: Colonial American Jewry, philanthropic institutions, synagogues
Collections: Stephen J Wise Manuscripts Collection; Rutenberg & Everett Yiddish Film Library; Archives of Major Jewish Organizations
Exhibitions: Colonial American Lowry; 19th Century Jewish Families; On Common Ground: The Boston Jewish Experience, 1964-1980
Activities: Lectures open to public, 2-3 vis lectr per year; gallery talks; tours; sponsor competitions; awards; originate traveling exhibitions to libraries, museum societies, synagogues

M **BRANDEIS UNIVERSITY,** Rose Art Museum, 415 South St, 02254. Tel 617-647-2402. *Dir* Carl I Belz; *Cur* Nancy Miller; *Registrar* Susan Stoops; *Preparator* Roger Kizik; *Coordr Patrons & Friends* Tina Grill-Sferlazzo
Open Tues - Sun 1 - 5 PM, cl Mon and holidays. No admis fee. Estab 1961 for the organization of regionally and nationally recognized exhibits of contemporary painting and sculpture. A additional gallery is located in the Spingold Theatre Building. All galleries are used for changing exhibitions; there are no permanent exhibitions. Average Annual Attendance: 20,000
Collections: The permanent collections consist of: African art; American Indian art; contemporary art (post World War II); Japanese prints; modern art (1800 to World War II), including the Riverside Museum Collections and the Teresa Jackson Weill Collection; Pre-Columbian art; pre-modern art (before 1800); Mr and Mrs Edward Rose Collection of early ceramics; Helen S Slosberg Collection of Oceanic art; Tibetian art
Exhibitions: Frank Stella; Mavericks (Guston, Jensen, Samaras, Golub); Frankenthaler; Ancient American Art; Maat: Charles Garabedian
Publications: Exhibition catalogs
Activities: Classes for children; docent training; lectures open to public; gallery talks; tours; individual paintings and original objects of art lent to students and individuals within the university; lending collection contains original art works, original prints, paintings; book traveling exhibitions, one per year

WELLESLEY

WELLESLEY COLLEGE
M **Museum,** 02181. Tel 617-235-0320, Exten 2051. *Dir* Ann Gabhart; *Asst Dir* Eleanor M Hight; *Membership & Publicity* Marjorie Dings
Open Mon - Sat 10 AM - 5 PM; Sun 2 - 5 PM; cl New Years Day, Thanksgiving, Dec 24, 25 and 31, mid-June, July and Aug. No admis fee. Estab 1889, dedicated to acquiring a collection of high quality art objects for the primary purpose of teaching art history from original works. Main gallery houses major exhibitions; Corridor Gallery, works on paper; Sculpture Court, permanent installation, sculpture, reliefs, works on wood panel. Average Annual Attendance: 18,000. Mem: 650; dues donor $100, contributor $50, regular $25
Income: Financed by membership, through college and gifts
Collections: Paintings; sculpture; graphic & decorative arts; Asian, African, ancient, medieval, Renaissance, Baroque, 19th & 20th century European & American art; photography
Exhibitions: One Century Wellesley Families Collects of paintings, sculpture and graphics by Degas, Picasso, Matisse, Monet and Renoir; Salvator Rosa in America and those artists he influenced, West, Colr, Allston, Bingham, Trumbull and Mount; Sitework by Stephen Antonakos, Nancy Holt, Robert Irwin and Ned Smyth; The Railroad in the American Landscape 1850-1950 by Asher B Durand, George Inness, Alfred Stieglitz, John Sloan, Charles Sheeler and Walker Evans
Publications: Exhibition catalogs; Wellesley College Friends of Art Newsletter, annually
Activities: Docent training; lectures open to public and members only; gallery talks; tours; original objects of art lent to students; lending collection contains original prints; book traveling exhibiton; originate traveling exhibitions; sales desk sells catalogs, postcards and notecards

L **Art Library,** 02181. Tel 617-235-0320, Ext 2049. *Librn* Katherine D Finkelpearl
Circ 22,000
Income: Financed by College appropriation
Purchases: $25,000
Library Holdings: Vols 30,000; Per subs 75; AV — Kodachromes, lantern slides; Other — Exhibition catalogs, pamphlets, photographs
Special Subjects: American art and architecture, Western European art and architecture, Far Eastern art, Ancient art and architecture

WENHAM

O **WENHAM HISTORICAL ASSOCIATION AND MUSEUM, INC,** 132 Main St, 01984. Tel 617-468-2377. *Dir* Eleanor E Thompson; *Doll Cur* Lorna Lieberman; *Office Admin* Felicia Connolly; *Pres* Mrs Henry Streeter
Open Mon - Fri 1 - 4 PM, Sun 2 - 5 PM, mornings by appointment. Admis adults $1.50, children (6-14) $.50. Estab 1921 as Historical Society, incorporated 1953, to acquire, preserve, interpret, and exhibit collections of literary and historical interest; to provide an educational and cultural service and facilities. Maintains three permanent galleries and one gallery for changing exhibits. Average Annual Attendance: 10,000. Mem: 650; dues family $10, individual $5; annual meeting April
Income: Financed by endowment, membership, earned income
Collections: Dolls; doll houses; figurines; costumes and accessories 1800 - 1960; embroideries; fans; needlework; quilts; toys
Exhibitions: Portraits, Still Lifes; Quilts Old and New; Samplers; Tin and Woodenware; Weavers; Wedding Dresses
Publications: Annual report; newsletter
Activities: Classes for children; lectures open to the public; gallery talks; tours; museum shop sells books, miniatures, original needlework, dolls and small toys

L **Timothy Pickering Library,** 132 Main St, 01984. *Librn* Mary L Corning
Open to members and the public for reference
Library Holdings: Vols 2000; Other — Manuscripts, memorabilia, pamphlets, photographs

WESTFIELD

M **WESTFIELD ATHENAEUM,** Jasper Rand Art Museum, 6 Elm St, 01085. Tel 413-568-7833. *Pres* James P Stow III; *Treas* Leslie A Chapin; *Dir* Franklin P Taplin; *Secy* John J Palezynzki
Open Mon, Tues, Thurs & Fri 8:30 AM - 8 PM, Wed 9 AM - 6 PM, Sat 8:30 AM - 5 PM, cl Sat in summer. No admis fee. Estab 1927 to provide exhibitions of art works by area artists and other prominent artists. Gallery measures 25 x 30 x 17 feet, with a domed ceiling and free-standing glass cases and wall cases. Average Annual Attendance: 13,500. Mem: 250; no dues; annual meeting fourth Mon in Oct
Income: Financed by endowment, city appropriation
Exhibitions: Original Currier & Ives (lithographs); Southwick, Art League (paintings); Catherine Brodeur (portraiture); George Gore (paintings); Frank Gugliemo (oils, pastels & charcoals); The Five Women Painters of Greater Springfield; Sarah Stifler Lucas (portraits); Athenaeum Gifts from the Past
Activities: Classes for children

WESTON

M **REGIS COLLEGE,** L J Walters Jr Gallery, 235 Wellesley St, 02193. Tel 617-893-1820, Ext 237. *Dir* Sr Louisella Walters
Open Mon - Fri 9 AM - 4:30 PM. No admis fee. Estab 1964 for education, visiting exhibits and student use. Gallery is one room, 20 x 30 ft. Average Annual Attendance: 1500
Income: Financed by donations
Exhibitions: Local Painters and Sculptors; Student Exhibits

WILLIAMSTOWN

M **STERLING AND FRANCINE CLARK ART INSTITUTE,** 225 South St, PO Box 8, 01267. Tel 413-458-8109, 458-9545. *Dir* David S Brooke; *Assoc Dir* John H Brooks; *Cur Prints & Drawings* Rafael A Fernandez; *Assoc Cur* David B Cass; *Assoc Cur* Beth Carver Wees; *Registrar* Martha Asher; *Comptroller* Virginia Riorden; *Photograph & Slide Librn* J Dustin Wees; *Supt* G Louis McManus
Open Tues - Sun 10 AM - 5 PM, cl Mon, New Year's Day, Thanksgiving & Christmas. No admis fee. Estab 1955 as a museum of fine arts with galleries, art research library and public events in auditorium. Average Annual Attendance: 100,000
Collections: Antique silver; Dutch, Flemish, French, Italian Old Master paintings from the 14th-18th centuries; French 19th century paintings, especially the Impressionists; 19th century sculpture; Old Master prints and drawings; porcelains; selected 19th century American artists (Homer and Sargent)
Exhibitions: The Permanent Collection and Traveling Exhibitions
Publications: Calendar of Events, quarterly
Activities: Docent training; organized educ programs for children; graduate program for MA in art history in collaboration with Williams College; lect; concerts; movies; gallery talks; book traveling exhibitions; museum shop sells books, reproductions, prints, slides and postcards

L **Clark Art Institute Library,** 225 South St, 01267. *Librn* Michael Rinehart; *Asst Librn* Marshall A Lapidus
Open Tues - Fri 10 AM - 5 PM. Estab 1962. For reference only
Purchases: $50,000
Library Holdings: Vols 76,000; Per subs 483; Auction sales catalogues; Micro — Fiche, reels; Other — Clipping files, exhibition catalogs, pamphlets, photographs, reproductions
Special Subjects: European and American Art
Collections: Mary Ann Beinecke Decorative Art Collection; Duveen Library and Archive; Juynboll Collection

M **WILLIAMS COLLEGE,** Museum of Art, Main St, 01267. Tel 413-597-2429. *Dir* Thomas Krens; *Co-Dir* Charles Parkhurst; *Asst Dir* Russell Panczenko; *Secy* Hanne Booth; *Asst Cur & Registrar* Lise Holst; *Asst Cur* Vivian Patterson; *Preparator* Joseph Thompson
Open Mon - Sat 10 AM - 5 PM, Sun 1 - 5 PM, cl Mon. No admis fee. Estab 1926 for the presentation of the permanent collection and temporary loan exhibitions for the benefit of the Williams College community and the general public. Central rotunda, built in 1846 by Thomas Tefft; other period galleries & loan exhibitions galleries are maintained, new galleries, entrance, atrium & non-public work areas added in 1983. Building also houses Art Department of

Williams College. Average Annual Attendance: 38,000
Collections: African and Asian art; ancient and medieval sculpture and glass; British and American portraits; contemporary art; 19th & 20th century American painting and sculpture; Renaissance and Baroque paintings; prints, drawings and photographs
Publications: Exhibition catalogs, 3 - 4 per year
Activities: Occasional lect open to public; gallery talks; tours; originate traveling exhibitions
L **Sawyer Library,** Main St, 01267. Tel 413-597-2501. *Librn* Lawrence E Wikander
Income: $11,500
Library Holdings: Vols 17,250; Per subs 63; AV — Slides; Other — Reproductions

WORCESTER

AMERICAN ANTIQUARIAN SOCIETY
For further information, see National and Regional Organizations

M **CLARK UNIVERSITY,** Little Center Gallery,* 950 Main St, 01610. Tel 617-793-7260. *Dir* Donald W Krueger; *Intern* James Geanakos
Open Mon - Fri Noon - 6 PM, Sat & Sun 2 - 6 PM, cl University holidays. No admis fee. Estab 1977 primarily for one and two-person shows of young, unknown as well as well-known artists; to help artists get recognition and to educate the community. Gallery 40 x 50 ft with moveable panels. Average Annual Attendance: 10,000
Income: Financed through the University
Exhibitions: Ten exhibitions a year of lesser known young artists and well-known artists
Publications: Announcements of exhibitions
Activities: Dramatic programs; lectures open to public, 2-5 vis lectr per yr; gallery talks; competitions of student art and graduate students with awards

M **HIGGINS ARMORY MUSEUM,** 100 Barber Ave, 01606. Tel 617-853-6015. *Pres* Harold Cabot Jr; *Dir* Warren M Little; *Assoc Cur & Librn* Walter J Karcheski Jr
Open Tues - Fri 9 AM - 5 PM, Sat & Sun Noon - 5 PM, cl Mon and National holidays. Admis adults $2, children 5 - 16 & sr citizens $1. Established 1928. Museum is in a Gothic Hall with high vaulted ceilings. Average Annual Attendance: 40,000. Mem: 490; dues $5 - $500; annual meeting Apr
Income: Financed by admissions, membership, grants, gift shop and endowment
Collections: Arms and armor from Stone Age through the 19th century; artistic objects of the iron smith's craft; art from related periods: paintings; tapestries; stained glass; woodcarvings
Exhibitions: (1982) Battle of Poitiers, Military Miniatures; (1983) Spirit of the Samurai; Dragons
Publications: Catalogue of Armor; Booklet on Armor; Ventail Voice, quarterly
Activities: Classes for adults & children; dramatic programs; docent training; lectures open to public, 6 vis lectr per yr; concerts; gallery talks; tours; competitions; original objects of art lent to other museums; museum shop sells books, magazines, reproductions, slides & souvenirs
L **Library,** 100 Barber Ave, 01606. *Librn* Walter J Karcheski Jr
Open for reference Tues & Thurs by appointment
Library Holdings: Vols 3000; Per subs 3; Other — Clipping files, exhibition catalogs, manuscripts, memorabilia, photographs
Special Subjects: Arms & armor, medieval & Renaissance history & warfare
Publications: Higgins Catalogue of Armor; Higgins Catalogue of Books; Ventail Voice, quarterly

M **WORCESTER ART MUSEUM,** 55 Salisbury St, 01608. Tel 617-799-4406. *Dir* Tom L Freudenheim; *Asst Dir Development & Membership* Susan Courtemanche; *Dir Public Information* Jennifer B Weininger; *Dir Publications* Gaye L Brown; *Cur American Art* Susan Strickler; *Chief Cur* James A Welu; *Cur of Education* Ellen R Berezin; *Coordr Programs & Special Events* Elizabeth Page; *Cur Photography* Stephen B Jareckie; *Registrar* Sally Freitag; *Cur Oriental Art* Elizabeth de Swinton; *Admin* W Arthur Gagne; *Conservator* Paul F Haner
Open Tues - Sat 10 AM - 5 PM, Sun 2 5 PM, cl Mon, New Year's, July 4th, Thanksgiving & Christmas. Admis adults $1.50, children under 14 and senior citizens $.50, children under 5 accompanied by adult free, members free. Estab Museum 1896, School 1898. The Museum and School were founded for the promotion of art and art education in Worcester; for the preservation and exhibition of works and objects of art and for instruction in the industrial, liberal and fine arts. There are 42 galleries housed in a neoclassical building. The Higgins Education Wing, built in 1970, houses the Museum School and contains exhibition space for shows sponsored by the Education Department and the School. Average Annual Attendance: 95,000. Mem: 3200; dues $15 - $1000 and over; annual meeting Oct
Income: $2,000,000 (financed by endowment, membership, admission fees, private corporate contributions and government grants)
Collections: John Chandler Bancroft Collection of Japanese Prints; †American Paintings of 18th - 20th Centuries; †British Paintings of 18th and 19th Centuries; †Dutch 17th Century Paintings; †Egyptian, Classical, Oriental and Medieval Sculpture; †French Paintings of 16th - 19th Centuries; †Flemish 16th Century Paintings; †Italian Paintings of the 13th - 18th Centuries; †Mosaics from Antioch; †Pre-Columbian Collection; 12th Century French Chapter House
Exhibitions: (1980) Sculpture by Hugh Townley; Treasures of the Royal Photographic Society; (1982) From the Courts of India: Indian Miniatures in the Collection of the Worcester Art Museum; John Ritto Penniman (1782-1841); An Ingenious New England Artist; Around Abstract Expressionism; Close-Ups; Late 20th Century Art from the Sidney and Frances Lewis Foundation; The Edward A Bigelow Collection Exhibition; Worcester Art Museums Asiatic Collection; (1982-83) Bruce Davidson; Angels in American Prints; The Vision of Landscape in 19th Century France; (1983) Twins; Jean-Francois Millet, Claude Monet and Their North American Counterparts; Herbert Barnett Exhibition; Flemish Exhibition; The Painter and Printer: Robert Motherwells' Graphics
Publications: Calendar of Events, quarterly
Activities: Classes for adults and children; docent training; lect open to public, 5 - 6 vis lectr per year; concerts; gallery talks; tours; museum shop sells books, reproductions, prints, jewelry, and others

L **Library,** 55 Salisbury St, 01608. Tel 617-799-4406, Ext 30. *Librn* Kathy L Berg; *Asst* Anne P Walsh; *Slide Librn* Cynthia L Bolshaw
Open Tues - Fri 10 AM - 5 PM, Sun 2 - 5 PM during the academic year. Estab 1909 to provide resource material for the Museum Departments. Participate in Worcester Area Cooperating Libraries. Maintains non-circulating collection only
Purchases: $22,000
Library Holdings: Vols 35,000; Per subs 90; Auction & sale catalogues; Micro — Fiche; AV — Kodachromes, lantern slides, slides; Other — Exhibition catalogs, pamphlets
Special Subjects: Auction Sale Catalogs, Fine Arts, Museum Exhibition Catalogs, Prints and Drawings, Western European Paintings
Collections: Japanese prints
Activities: Tours

M **WORCESTER CRAFT CENTER GALLERY,** 25 Sagamore Rd, 01605. Tel 617-753-8183. *Executive Dir* Cyrus D Lipsitt
Open Mon - Sat 9 AM - 5 PM, Sun 2 - 5 PM. No admis fee. Estab 1952 for educational exhibits of historic and contemporary crafts. Professionally lighted and installed 40 x 60 gallery with six major shows per year. Average Annual Attendance: 5000. Mem: 1100; dues $28 and up
Income: Financed by membership and grants
Collections: Collection contains 200 books, 2000 Kodachromes, 300 photographs
Exhibitions: 5 exhibits annually, juried, invitational or traveling; Its About Time: American Woodcarvers; Michael James: Quiltmaker; Fabric Constructions: The Art Quilt
Publications: Exhibition catalogs; On-Center, newsletter
Activities: Classes for adults and children; weekend professional workshops; lectures open to the public, 12 visiting lecturers per year; gallery talks; tours; traveling exhibitions organized and circulated; supply shop and gift shop sell books, original craft objects
L **Library,** 25 Sagamore Rd, 01605
Open Mon - Fri 9 AM - 5 PM. Established 1958. For reference only
Library Holdings: Vols 100; Per subs 50; AV — Slides; Other — Photographs

MICHIGAN

ADRIAN

M **SIENA HEIGHTS COLLEGE,** Little Gallery, Studio Angelico, 1257 Siena Heights Dr, 49221. Tel 313-263-0731. *Dir* Jeannine Klemm
Open Mon - Fri 9 AM - 4 PM, cl Easter, Christmas and semester breaks. No admis fee. Estab 1919 as an arts center and institute. Average Annual Attendance: 5000
Collections: Paintings; sculpture; graphics; decorative arts; art history; textiles
Exhibitions: Invitational Artists Shows; temporary exhibitions
Activities: Classes for adults and children; dramatic programs; lectures open to public; concerts; gallery talks; tours; competitions with awards; scholarships offered
L **Art Library,** 1257 Siena Heights Dr, 49221
Library Holdings: Vols 10,000; Per subs 35; Micro — Fiche, reels; AV — A-tapes, cassettes, fs, rec, slides, v-tapes; Other — Clipping files, exhibition catalogs, manuscripts, memorabilia, pamphlets, photographs, reproductions, sculpture

ALBION

M **ALBION COLLEGE,** Bobbitt Visual Arts Center, 49224. Tel 517-629-5511, Ext 246. *Gallery Dir* Frank Machek
Open Mon - Thurs 9 AM - 4:45 PM & 6:30 - 10 PM, Fri 9 AM - 4:45 PM, Sat 10 AM - 1 PM, Sun 2 - 5 PM. No admis fee. Estab 1835 to offer art education at college level and general art exhibition program for campus community and public. Maintains one large gallery and three smaller galleries
Income: Privately funded
Purchases: $2000 - $4000
Collections: African Art; ceramics; glass; †prints
Exhibitions: From The Print Collection; Pieces from the Permanent Collection; various one-man and group shows
Activities: Lect open to public, 2 - 4 vis lectr per year; gallery talks; original objects of art lent to faculty and students

ALPENA

M **JESSE BESSER MUSEUM,** 491 Johnson St, 49707. Tel 517-356-2202. *Dir* Dennis R Bodem; *Asst Dir* Eugene A Jenneman; *Pres* Alan Walker; *VPres* William Zeller; *Secy* Avis Hinks; *Treas* J Austin Sobczak
Open Mon - Fri 9 AM - 5 PM, Sat & Sun 1 - 5 PM, Thurs evenings 7 - 9 PM. Admis by donation. Estab association 1962, building open to public 1965, a museum of history, science, and art serving northern Michigan. Museum has a planetarium and the Foucault Pendulum. Three galleries are utilized for shows, traveling exhibits, and changing exhibitions of the Museum's collection of modern art and art prints. There is 104 running ft of wall space on lower level, 1250 sq ft and 1645 sq ft on upper level galleries. Average Annual Attendance: 30,000. Mem: 500; dues family $15, individual $8; annual meeting in Sept
Income: Financed by Besser Foundation, federal and state grants, private gifts and donations, Museums Founders Society
Collections: Photography of Daniel Farber; †art prints; †modern art
Exhibitions: (1982) National Association of Women Artists Painting Exhibition; selected works; Birds as Art; European & American Sculpture, 1830-1930; Glass Sculpture: Four Artists-Four Views; Michigan Printmakers Exhibit; Lina Dean, Weavings & Cast Paper; Shirley Ritzler; Victorian Kaleidoscopes; Paper Cutouts; Richard Vian, Paintings; watercolors from area collectors; From IBM -

Inventions of Leonardo da Vinci; Misha Gordin, photographs; Alpena: The Beginnings to 1880; National Association of Women Artists Graphics Exhibition; Northeast Michigan Artists Juried Exhibition; (1983) From Art Train Inc: Break Through - Post War Modern; new acquisitions; Transitions: Paintings by Michael Estkowski; John Hubbard, drawings; James Deloria, raku; Cranbrook Institute of Science: Michigan Wildlife Art Awards; From CMU, Mt Pleasant: Chairs; Masterworks: Glass, Wood, Clay, Fibers; selected works; Alma College: Michigan Printmakers; Krasl Art Center: Michigan Corporations Collect Art; Lorraine Chambers McCarty, paintings; Sam Pope, paintings & drawings; Jan Richardson, works in clay; From the DIA: Forest, Praire, Plains - Native American Art from the Chandler-Pohrt Collection; Alpena - The 1890's; Maps of the Great Lakes; Images of Old Age in America: 1790 to the Present; Northeast Michigan Artists Juried Exhibition; Brian Gougeon: Recent Works; Furniture & Decorative Arts
Activities: Classes for adults and children; docent training; lectures open to public, 2 - 4 vis lectr per year; gallery talks; tours; competitions with awards; exten dept serves area schools; individual paintings & original objects of art lent to museums & art centers; book traveling exhibitions; originate traveling exhibitions; museum shop sells books, magazines, original art, reproductions & prints
L **Library,** 491 Johnson St, 49707
Open to public for reference only
Library Holdings: Vols 700; Per subs 14; Other — Clipping files, exhibition catalogs, manuscripts, pamphlets
Special Subjects: Art History, Antiques, Museum Management

ANN ARBOR

O **ANN ARBOR ART ASSOCIATION,** 117 W Liberty, 48103. Tel 313-994-8004. *Pres* Doni Lystra; *VPres* Mary Campbell; *Secy* Paul Stein; *Executive Dir* Marsha Chamberlin; *Asst to the Dir* Susan Monaghan; *Exhibit Gallery Dir* Susan Froelich; *Gallery Shop Dir* Pat Bantle; *Gallery Shop Asst* Bettina Pollock
Open Mon Noon - 5 PM, Tues - Sat 10 AM - 5 PM. Estab 1909 to further the welfare of visual art in Ann Arbor by encouraging local art interests. Maintains 750 square feet of exhibit gallery space with monthly shows; sales - rental gallery next to exhibit area. Average Annual Attendance: 10,400. Mem: 475; dues $15; annual meeting May
Income: Financed by membership, Michigan Council for the Arts grant, rental of studios and retail sales
Exhibitions: Monthly Shows
Publications: Class catalog, quarterly; gallery announcements, monthly; lecture listings, quarterly; newsletter, monthly
Activities: Classes for adults and children; lect open to the public, 4-6 visiting lectr per year; gallery talks; tours; awards; scholarships; individual paintings and original objects of art lent to organizations and community facilities; sales shop selling original art

UNIVERSITY OF MICHIGAN

M **Museum of Art,** 525 S State St, 48109. Tel 313-764-0395. *Dir* Evan M Maurer; *Cur of Asian Art* Marshall Wu; *Asst to Dir* Lauren Arnold; *Registrar* Carole A Cunningham; *Cur of Western Art* Anne I Lockhart; *Cur of Educ* Mary Kujawski
Open (Sept - May) Tues - Fri 10 AM - 4 PM, Sat & Sun 1 - 5 PM; (June - Aug) daily 11 AM - 4 PM. No admis fee. Estab 1946, as a university art museum and museum for the Ann Arbor community. Average Annual Attendance: 55,000. Mem: 1500; dues individual $30
Income: Financed by state appropriation
Collections: Arts of the Western world from the 6th century AD to the present; Asian, Near Eastern, African and Oceanic, including ceramics, †contemporary art, †decorative art, †graphic arts, manuscripts, †painting, †sculpture
Exhibitions: Works from the Collection of Jean Paul Slusser; Masterworks from the Collection; 20th Century Russian Prints; (1982) School of Arts: A Rackham Grant Exhibition; Inuit Prints from the Collection of Mr and Mrs Eugene B Power; Dutch Art Margaret Watson Parker: A Collector's Legacy; Leonardo's Return to Vinci; Quilts and Ceramics; Gifts from University of Michigan Alumni; Kyoto Metal; Nudes from Michigan Collections; Frank Stella: Prints 1967-1982; Major Works from the Collection of Phillip Kassebaum; Jean Paul Slusser: 1886-1981; An American Treasury in Southeastern Michigan Jan Beekman; Howard Bond Photographs; Forest, Prairie and Plains: Native American Art from the Chandler-Pohrt Collection; Jean-Louis Forain: Artist, Realist, Humanist, Tiffany Glass from the Permanent Collection; Austrian and German Expressionist Drawings from a Private Collection; Gerome Kamrowski: A Retrospective Exhibition; Prints from the Reformation and Counter-Reformation Period
Publications: Bulletin of the Museums of Art and Archaeology, annually
Activities: Educ dept; docent training; 10 visiting lectr per year; gallery talks; tours; museum shop selling publications and postcards
M **Kelsey Museum of Ancient and Medieval Archaeology,** 434 State St, 48109. Tel 313-764-9304. *Dir* John G Pedley; *Assoc Cur* Elaine K Gazda; *Assoc Cur* Sharon Herbert; *Asst Cur* Margaret C Root; *Assoc Cur* Amy Rosenberg; *Registrar* Pamela Reister; *Technician* David W Slee
Open Mon - Fri 9 AM - 4 PM, Sat & Sun 1 - 4 PM. No admis fee. Estab 1928. Four small galleries are maintained. Average Annual Attendance: 25,500
Collections: Objects of the Graeco-Roman period from excavations conducted by the University of Michigan in Egypt and Iraq; Greece, Etruria, Rome and provinces: sculpture, inscriptions, pottery, bronzes, terracottas; Egyptian antiquities dynastic through Roman; Roman and Islamic glass, bone and ivory objects, textiles, coins
Exhibitions: Faces of Immortality; Art of the Ancient Weaver; A Victorian View of Ancient Rome; Greek Sculpture In Transition; Decorative Arts of Gothic & Islamic Egypt; Vaults of Memory, Jewish & Christian Imagery in the Catacombs of Rome; Wondrous Glass: Reflections on the World of Rome; Karanis: An Egyptian Town in Roman Times; In Pursuit of Antiquity: Thomas Spencer Jerome and the Bay of Naples (1899-1914)
Publications: Bulletin of the Museums of Art and Archaeology
Activities: Lect open to the public, 10-12 visiting lectr per year; gallery talks; tours; sales shop selling books and exhibition catalogs

M **Slusser Gallery,** School of Art, 2000 Bonisteel Blvd, 48109. Tel 313-764-0397. *Exhib Dir* Louis Marinaro
Open Mon - Fri 9 AM - 5 PM, Sat 9 AM - 12 Noon. No admis fee. Estab 1974, primarily used as an educational facility with high volume of student and faculty participation. Gallery is located on the main floor of the Art & Architecture Building and is comprised of 3,431 sq ft of exhibition space and is a well lighted area. Average Annual Attendance: 4000
Collections: Artifacts of the schools history
Publications: Abstraction-Creation; Fugitive Color; catalogs
Activities: Lect open to the public, 10-15 visiting lectr per year; gallery talks
L **Asian Art Archives,** Ann Arbor, 48109. *Cur* Wendy Holden
Open Mon - Fri 9 AM - 5 PM. Estab 1962 to study and research. Library also houses the Asian Art Photographic Distribution, a non-profit business selling visual resource materials dealing with Chinese and Japanese art
Income: $4000 - $5000 (financed by endowment, federal funds)
Purchases: $4000 - $5000
Library Holdings: Vols 50; Black/white negatives 26,000; Other — Exhibition catalogs, photographs 55,000
Collections: †National Palace Museum, Taiwan, photographic archive; †Chinese art, painting, decorative arts; Southeast Asian Art Archive, sculpture, architecture; Islamic Art Archive; †Asian Art Archive, Chinese & Japanese arts, painting
L **Fine Arts Library,** 103 Tappan Hall, 48109. Tel 313-764-5405. *Head Fine Arts Library* Margaret P Jensen
Open Mon - Thurs 8 AM - 11 PM, Fri 8 AM - 5 PM, Sat 10 AM - 6 PM, Sun 1 - 10 PM, summer hours vary. Estab 1949, to support the academic programs of the History of the Art Dept, including research of faculty and graduate students. Circ 17,200
Income: Financed by state appropriation
Library Holdings: Vols 51,970; Per subs 215; Marburger index of photographic documentation of art in Germany; Micro — Fiche, reels; Other — Exhibition catalogs, pamphlets
Special Subjects: Art History, Oriental Art
L **Slide and Photograph Collection,** History of Art Department, 107 Tappan Hall, 48109. Tel 313-764-5404. *Cur* Joy Alexander; *Assoc Cur* Eleanor Mannikka; *Assoc Cur* Marjorie Panadero; *Photographer* Patrick Young
Open Mon - Fri 8:30 AM - 1 PM, 2 - 5 PM. Estab 1911, as a library for teaching and research collection of slides and photos of art objects; limited commercial distribution; non-profit slide distribution projects; (Asian Art Photographic Distribution; Univ of Mich Slide Distribution). Circ 3,600 weekly
Income: Financed by state appropriation
Library Holdings: AV — Lantern slides, slides; Other — Photographs, reproductions
Special Subjects: History of Art & Archaeology
Collections: Berenson's I Tatti Archive; Courtauld Institute Illustration Archive; Palace Museum Archive (Chinese painting); Romanesque Archive (sculpture and some architecture concentrating on Burgundy, Southwestern France, †Spain and southern Italy; †SE Asian and Indian Archives; †Islamic Archives
Activities: Materials lent only to University of Michigan faculty and students
L **Art & Architecture Library,** 2106 Bonisteel Blvd, 98109. Tel 313-764-1303. *Librn* P A Kusnerz; *Asst Librn* Dot Shields
Estab to support the teaching and research activities of the School of Art and the College of Architecture
Library Holdings: Vols 45,000; Per subs 450; Micro — Cards, fiche, prints, reels; AV — A-tapes, cassettes, fs, Kodachromes, lantern slides, slides, v-tapes; Other — Clipping files, exhibition catalogs, manuscripts, original art works, pamphlets, photographs, sculpture

BATTLE CREEK

M **ART CENTER OF BATTLE CREEK,** 265 E Emmett St, 49017. Tel 616-962-9511. *Dir* Ann Worth Cancannon; *Admin Asst* Linda Skidmore; *Assoc Dir* Ruth M Sundberg; *Cur* Linda Poirier
Open Mon - Thurs 10 AM - 5 PM, Fri 10 AM - 1 PM, Sat & Sun 1 - 4 PM, cl August & legal holidays. No admis fee. Estab 1947 to offer classes for children and adults, and to present monthly exhibitions of professional work. Mem: 1000; dues $10.00 and up; annual meeting Sept
Income: Financed by endowment fund, grants MCA, MCH, UAC and special projects
Collections: Michigan Art Collection featuring 19th & 20th century Michigan artists
Exhibitions: C M Russell; Crafts; Drawings; Group and One-Man Shows; Paintings; Photography; Prints; Student Exhibits
Publications: Newsletter, monthly
Activities: Classes for adults and children; dramatic programs; docent training; lectures open to public; gallery talks; tours; competitions with prizes; scholarships; individual paintings and original objects of art lent to professional art agencies; book traveling exhibitions; originate traveling exhibits; museum and sales shop sells original art
L **Michigan Art & Artist Archives,** Tel 616-962-9511. *Dir* Ann Concannon
Library Holdings: Vols 400; Per subs 3; AV — Slides; Other — Clipping files, exhibition catalogs, original art works, photographs, sculpture
Special Subjects: Afro-American Art, American Indian Art, Antiquities-Egyptian, Art History, Mexican Art, Oriental Art

BIRMINGHAM

O **BIRMINGHAM-BLOOMFIELD ART ASSOCIATION,** 1516 S Cranbrook Rd, 48009. Tel 313-644-0866. *Pres* Victor L Klein; *VPres* Leo G Shea; *Secy* Susanne Velick; *Dir* Kenneth R Gross; *Asst Dir* Leslie Masters; *Office Mgr* Mrs Douglas Garrison; *Business Mgr* Frances St Lawrence
Open Mon - Thurs 9 AM - 10 PM, Fri 9 AM - 7 PM, Sat 9 AM - 5 PM, cl Sun. No admis fee. Estab 1956 to provide a community-wide, integrated studio-gallery art center. Average Annual Attendance: 10,000. Mem: 1300; dues $25 and up; annual meeting May
Income: $200,000 (financed by membership, tuitions and special events funding)

Collections: Very small collection of craft objects and prints by local artists
Publications: Newsletter, eleven a year
Activities: Classes for adults and children; docent training; Picture Lady Program; Career Program; Teen Volunteer Service; lect open to public, 4 - 8 vis lectr per year; tours; competitions, cash awards, ribbons and certificates; local scholarships; exten dept serving public schools; individual paintings and original objects of art lent to public on a rental basis; lending collection contains original art works and prints, paintings, photographs; sales and rental gallery; sales shop sells original art, prints, photographs, paintings and crafts

BLOOMFIELD HILLS

M **CRANBROOK ACADEMY OF ART MUSEUM,** 500 Lone Pine Rd, PO Box 801, 48103. Tel 313-645-3312. *Dir Museum* Roy Slade; *Museum Adminr* Michele Rowe-Shields; *Cur of Coll* John Gerard; *Asst Cur* Susan Waller
Open Tues - Sun 1 - 5 PM, cl major holidays. Admis adults $1.50, students & senior citizens $1, group rates available. Estab 1924 as part of Cranbrook Academy of Art. Average Annual Attendance: 60,000
Collections: Ceramics by Maija Grotell; decorative arts by Eliel Saarinen; porcelains by Adelaide Robineau; sculpture by Carl Milles; contemporary paintings; 19th century prints; study collection of textiles
Exhibitions: Annual Student Exhibition; contemporary architecture, crafts, design, paintings and sculpture
Activities: Lect; tours; film program

L **Library,** 500 Lone Pine Rd, PO Box 801, 48103. Tel 313-645-3328. *Head Librn* Diane L Vogt
Visitors with a scholarly interest in the Fine Arts are allowed to use the facilities Mon - Fri 1 - 5 PM. No browsing is permitted. Library is for Academy students, faculty and staff use only
Income: Financed by academy
Library Holdings: Vols 23,000; Per subs 70; AV — A-tapes, cassettes 600, Kodachromes, lantern slides, motion pictures, rec, slides 22,000, v-tapes; Other — Clipping files, exhibition catalogs, manuscripts, memorabilia, original art works, pamphlets
Special Subjects: Ceramics, Graphic Arts, Sculpture, Architecture, Design, Fiber Arts, History of Art, Metal Working, Painting, Photography
Publications: How to Research a Work of Art, an Artist & How to Reseach From Primary Sources; Detroit Area Fine Arts Libraries & Art Historical Bibliographies

DETROIT

O **ARTRAIN, INC** (Formerly Michigan Artrain, Inc), 316 Fisher Building, 48202. Tel 313-871-2910. *Chmn* Charlotte Lyeth Dively; *VPres* James Buschmann; *Pres & Dir* John J Hohmann; *Exhibition Coordr* Joan Krueger; *Community Coordr* James Tottis
No admis fee. Estab 1971 to tour major art exhibits throughout the nation and provide catalyst for on-going development. Consists of converted railroad cars with large walls and cases. Average Annual Attendance: 225,000
Income: Financed by endowment, state appropriation, individual foundation and corporation campaigns
Exhibitions: (1983-84) Michigan: State of the Art; Creative Impulse; Contemporary Texas Art
Publications: Exhibition catalogs; newsletter
Activities: Classes for children; docent training; lectures open to public; competitions; book traveling exhibitions; sales shop selling books, prints and slides

L **CENTER FOR CREATIVE STUDIES - COLLEGE OF ART & DESIGN LIBRARY,*** 245 E Kirby, 48202. Tel 313-872-3118. *Librn* Jean Peyrat; *Slide Librn* Susan Campbell
Open Mon - Thurs 8:30 AM - 7 PM, Fri 8:30 AM - 4:30 PM. Estab 1966 to serve students and faculty of an undergraduate art school. Primarily a how-to collection
Income: Financed by private school
Library Holdings: Vols 13,000; Per subs 72; AV — Slides 28,000; Other — Exhibition catalogs

M **DETROIT INSTITUTE OF ARTS,** 5200 Woodward Ave, 48202. Tel 313-833-7900. *Dir* Frederick J Cummings; *Art Museum Adminr* Robert T Weston; *Cur American Art* Nancy Rivard-Shaw; *Cur Ancient* William H Peck; *Deputy Dir & Cur Ethnographic Art* Michael Kan; *Cur European Paintings* J Patrice Marandel; *Cur Education* Linda Downs; *Graphic Arts* Ellen Sharp; *Actg Cur Modern Art* Davira Taragin; *Cur Oriental Art* Suzanne Mitchell; *Registrar* Judith Schulman; *Photographer* Dirk Bakker; *Head Conservator* Abraham Joel; *Cur Emeritus Medieval Art* Francis W Robinson; *Cur European Sculpture & Decorative Art* Alan Darr; *Registrar* Karen Serota; *Cur Performing Arts* Audley M Grossman
Open Tues - Sun 9:30 AM - 5:30 PM, cl Mon & holidays. Estab and incorporated 1885 as Detroit Museum of Art; chartered as municipal department 1919 and name changed; original organization continued as Founders Society Detroit Institute of Arts; present building opened 1927; Ford Wing addition completed 1966; Cavanagh Wing addition opened 1971. Midwest area office of Archives of American Art
Collections: Elizabeth Parke Firestone Collection of 18th Century French Silver; William Randolph Hearst Collection of Arms and Armor and Flemish Tapestries; Grace Whitney Hoff Collection of Fine Bindings; Paul McPharlin Collection of Puppetry, Theatre and Graphic Arts; Robert H Tannahill Bequest of Impressionist and Post-Impressionist Paintings, traditional African Objects, French Silver; Comprehensive Collection of Textiles and of American Decorative Arts; Representative examples of the Arts from prehistory to the present time, including Egypt, Mesopotamia, Greece and Rome, the Orient, Europe, Africa, the South Seas, and the Americas. Central court decorated with Diego Rivera frescoes (1932-33). Whitby Hall, furnished with important collection of furniture
Exhibitions: John Singer Sargent and the Edwardian Age (drawings, paintings, watercolors); Michigan Artists and Michigan Artist-Craftsmen (alternate years)
Publications: Exhibition catalogues; bulletin; annual report; collection catalogues

Activities: Classes for adults and children; dramatic programs; docent training; lectures open to the public; concerts; gallery talks; tours; individual paintings & original objects of art lent; book traveling exhibitions; originate traveling exhibitions; museum shop sells books, magazines, prints & slides, also rental gallery

L **Research Library,** 5200 Woodward Ave, 48202. *Librn* F Warren Peters; *Asst Librn & Cataloguer* Constance Wall; *Asst Librn & Reference* Lynne Garza
Open Mon - Fri 9 AM - 5 PM. Estab 1905 to provide material for research, interpretation and documentation of museum collection. For reference only
Income: Financed by city
Library Holdings: Vols 65,000; Per subs 140; Micro — Cards, reels; AV — Lantern slides, slides; Other — Clipping files, exhibition catalogs, pamphlets, photographs
Special Subjects: Archaeology, Architecture, Art History, applied arts
Collections: Albert Kahn Architecture Library; Paul McPharlin Collection of Puppetry; Grace Whitney-Hoff Collection of Fine Bindings

O **Founders Society,** 5200 Woodward Ave, 48202. Tel 313-833-7900; Cable DETINARTS. *Chmn of Board* Stanford C Stoddard; *VChmn* Norman B Weston; *Pres* Walter B Ford; *VPres* Mrs Gaylord W Gillis Jr; *Treas* Alfred M Pelham; *Secy* Mrs Alan E Schwarz
Estab and incorporated 1885; public membership philanthropic society contributing to the growth of the Detroit Institute of Arts; underwrites Educ Dept activities, publications, special exhibitions and purchases of works of art. Mem: 26,000; dues corporate patron $10,000, corporate sponsor $5000, corporate contributor $1000, corporate $250, patron $150, family $40, individual $25
Activities: Museum shop rents original work by Michigan artists and reproductions

L **DETROIT PUBLIC LIBRARY,** Fine Arts Dept, 5201 Woodward Ave, 48202. Tel 313-833-1467. *Library Dir* Jane Hale Morgan; *Chief Fine Arts Department* Shirley Solvick; *First Asst Fine Arts Department* Jean Comport; *Reference Librn* Ruth Barton; *Reference Librn* Dora Deitch; *Clerk* Barbara Goff
Open Tues, Thurs, Fri & Sat 9:30 AM - 5:30 PM, Wed 1 - 9 PM. Estab 1921. Serves residents of Michigan with circulating and reference materials in all fields of art
Income: Financed by city and state appropriation
Purchases: $15,000
Library Holdings: Vols 60,000; Per subs 290; Micro — Fiche, reels; Other — Clipping files, exhibition catalogs, framed reproductions, pamphlets, photographs, reproductions
Activities: Tours

M **WAYNE STATE UNIVERSITY,** Community Arts Gallery, 450 Reuther Mall, 48202. Tel 313-577-2400. *Dir* Richard J Bilaitis
Open Mon - Fri 9 AM - 5 PM. No admis fee. Estab 1956 as a facility for university and community oriented exhibitions and programs. Has a slide library
Collections: Small collection of American and European graphics, painting, sculpture
Exhibitions: (1982) John Egner & Robert Wilbert, paintings; Sights of Canadian History; Michigan Watercolor Society 36th Annual Exhibition; Olga Constantine, pastel drawings; (1983) Photographs from the Institute of Design, Illinois Institute of Technology
Activities: Lect for adults, students and the community; concerts

M **YOUR HERITAGE HOUSE, INC,*** 110 East Ferry Ave, 48202. Tel 313-871-1667. *Dir* Josephine H Love; *Development Officer* Dawson Lewis
Open daily 10 AM - 4 PM. Estab 1980. Average Annual Attendance: 15,000 - 20,000. Mem: 100; dues $50; annual meeting Sept
Income: Financed by endowment, membership, city and state appropriation, individuals, groups and business donations
Collections: †Art for Youth; Black Heritage; graphics; Puppetry; Paintings; objects and works of interest to children
Publications: Catalogues; imprints; I Remember a Southern Christmas, book
Activities: Classes for adults and children; lect open to the public, 3-6 visiting lectr per year; concerts; gallery talks; tours; scholarships; artmobile; sales shop selling books, cards and catalogues of exhibits

L **Library,*** 110 East Ferry Ave, 48202
Open daily 10 AM - 4 PM. Estab 1969 to provide fine arts material for children. For reference only
Library Holdings: Micro — Cards; Other — Clipping files, exhibition catalogs, manuscripts, memorabilia, pamphlets, photographs, prints
Special Subjects: Fine Arts for Youth
Collections: Black Heritage; Music for children by notable French composers; Puppetry of the World

EAST LANSING

M **MICHIGAN STATE UNIVERSITY,** Kresge Art Center Gallery, 48824. Tel 517-355-7610, Gallery 355-7631. *Chmn Dept Art* Paul W Deussen; *Dir of Gallery* Joseph Ishikawa
Open Mon & Wed - Fri 9:30 AM - 4:30 PM, Tues 12 - 8 PM, Sat & Sun 1 - 4 PM, Summer hours: Mon - Fri 10 AM - 4 PM, Sat & Sun 1 - 4 PM, cl Aug - mid-Sept. No admis fee. Estab 1959. Average Annual Attendance: 50,000. Mem: 500; dues $5 - $1000
Collections: Permanent collection of paintings, †prints, †sculptures
Exhibitions: Shows making up a yearly calendar of about 14 exhibitions supplementing the permanent collection; special exhibits; rental shows; staff and student shows
Publications: Exhibition calendar, annually; announcements of art lectures and films; catalogs
Activities: Classes for adults and children; docent training; workshops; lectures open to public, 10 - 12 vis lectr per yr; gallery talks; tours; awards; individual paintings and original objects of art lent to qualified institutions or galleries; museum shop sells catalogs, postcards and stationary

L   Art Library, 48824. Tel 517-353-4593. *Art Librn* Shirlee A Studt
Open Mon - Fri 8 AM - 11 PM, Sat 9 AM - 11 PM, Sun Noon - 11 PM. Estab
1973 to support the research and teaching needs in the visual arts of Michigan
State University
Income: Financed by state appropriation
Library Holdings: Vols 42,000; Per subs 150; Other — Clipping files, exhibition
catalogs, photographs, reproductions
Special Subjects: Architecture, Illuminated manuscripts facsimiles, Italian
Renaissance art

ESCANABA

M   WILLIAM BONIFAS FINE ART CENTER GALLERY,* 7th St & 1st Ave S,
49829. Tel 906-786-3833. *Dir* Norbert Laporte; *Exec Secy* Estelle Smyth
Open Tues & Wed Noon - 4 PM, 7 - 9 PM, Thurs - Sat Noon - 4 PM, cl
Memorial Day, July 4, Labor Day, Thanksgiving, Christmas. No admis fee. Estab
1974. Mem: Dues club $50, patron $30 and up, family $25, individual $15,
student and senior citizen $10
Collections: Local artists work
Publications: Passage North, monthly newsletter
Activities: Gallery talks; concerts

FLINT

M M FLINT INSTITUTE OF ARTS, 1120 E Kearsley St, 48503. Tel 313-234-
1695. *Dir* Dr Richard J Wattenmaker; *Asst Dir* Joan Ranadive; *Cur Collections
& Registrar* Christopher R Young; *Program Coordr & Educator* Jessie Sirna;
Museum Shop Mgr Virginia Inman
Open Tues - Sat 10 AM - 5 PM, Sun 1 - 5 PM, Tues (May - Oct) 7 - 9 PM. No
admis fee. Estab 1928 as a community art museum serving the citizens of the
area. Average Annual Attendance: 100,000. Mem: 2200; dues $15 and up; annual
meeting third Tues in June
Collections: African Sculpture; French Paperweights; Modern Art; 19th & 20th
Century European & American Art; 19th Century Germanic Glass; Oriental
Gallery; Renaissance Gallery of Decorative Arts
Exhibitions: Auguste Rodin; Art of the Twenties; European Tools from the 17th
to the 19th Century; American Native Paintings: The Edgar William and Bernice
Chrysler Garbisch Collection; Alexander Calder
Publications: Exhibition catalogs; monthly Calendar for members
Activities: Classes for adults and children; docent training; lectures open
to public, 12 vis lectr per year; concerts; gallery talks; tours; Flint Art Fair; individual
paintings and original objects of art lent to other museums; museum shop sells
books, gift items, stationery, cards and jewelry

L   FLINT PUBLIC LIBRARY, Fine Arts Dept, 1026 East Kearsley, 48502. Tel
313-231-7111. *Dir* John A Oliver; *Head Art, Music & Drama Dept* James
Kangas
Open Mon - Thurs 9 AM - 9 PM, Fri & Sat 9 AM - 6 PM. Art, Music and
Drama Department established in 1958 a division of Flint Board of Education
Library Holdings: Vols 40,700; Per subs 165; Other — Clipping files, exhibition
catalogs, photographs, reproductions

GRAND RAPIDS

M   CALVIN COLLEGE CENTER ART GALLERY, 49506. Tel 616-949-4000, Ext
326. *Dir of Exhib* Macyn Bolt; *Asst Dir* Marlene Vanderhill
Open Sept - May Mon - Thurs 9 AM - 9 PM, Fri 9 AM - 5 PM, Sat Noon - 4
PM, cl Sun. No admis fee. Estab 1974 to provide the art students, and the
college community and the public at large with challenging visual monthly
exhibitions. Gallery is well lighted, air-conditioned 40 x 70 ft with 10 ft ceiling
along the sides and 8 ft ceiling in the center. Average Annual Attendance: 12,
000
Income: Financed through private budget
Collections: Dutch 17th & 19th century paintings and prints; Japanese prints;
†contemporary paintings, prints, drawings, sculpture, weaving and ceramics
Exhibitions: Invitational exhibits by various artists, exhibits of public and private
collections and faculty and student exhibits
Publications: Various exhibition brochures
Activities: Classes for adults; lectures open to public; concerts; gallery talks;
competitions
L   Library, 49506. *Librn* Marvin Monsma
Open to students and the public
Library Holdings: Vols 280,000; Per subs 1800; Curriculum Center of
demonstration teaching materials; Micro — Cards, fiche, reels
Collections: H H Meeter Calvinism Research Collection; Cayvan Collection of
Recordings; Colonial Origins Collection of the Christian Reformed Church;
Government Documents

M   GRAND RAPIDS ART MUSEUM, 155 Division N, 49503. Tel 616-459-4676.
Actg Dir Elizabeth Crouch
Open Tues - Sat 10 Am - 5 PM, Sun 2 - 5 PM, cl Mon & legal holidays. Admis
adults $1.25, students $.75, children free. Museum located in a 1910 Beaux
Arts former post office and courthouse, renovated and opened in Sept 1981.
Average Annual Attendance: 100,000. Mem: 2750; dues $15 - $1000; annual
meeting May
Income: $919,000 (financed by endowment, membership, state appropriation and
federal grants)
Purchases: $30,000
Collections: Staffordshire Pottery; American 19th & 20th century paintings;
decorative arts; drawings; French 19th century paintings; German expressionist
paintings; master prints of all eras; Renaissance paintings; sculpture
Publications: Catalogs of major exhibitions; newsletter, monthly
Activities: Classes for children; dramatic programs; docent training; lectures open

to public, 15 vis lectr per year; gallery talks; tours; competitions; concerts;
scholarships; artmobile; individual paintings and original objects of art lent to
museums; lending collection contains books, color reproductions, framed
reproductions, original art works, original prints, paintings, photographs,
sculpture and slides; book traveling exhibitions; originate traveling exhibitions;
museum & sales shops sell books, reproductions, jewelry, arts and crafts objects;
Passage-ways Children's Gallery

L   McBride Art Reference Library, 155 Division N, 49503. Tel 616-459-4676
Open Tues - Fri 12:30 - 4 PM, and upon request. Estab 1969. Reference library
Income: Financed by membership, endowment, community fund drive support
Purchases: $2600
Library Holdings: Vols 4500; Per subs 31; AV — A-tapes, cassettes, slides;
Other — Clipping files, exhibition catalogs, pamphlets, reproductions

L   GRAND RAPIDS PUBLIC LIBRARY, Music & Art Dept, Library Plaza NE,
49503. Tel 616-456-4410. *Dir Library* Robert Raz; *Head Music & Art Dept*
Lucija Skuja; *Music Librn* Helen Vanden Engel
Open Tues & Weds Noon - 9 PM; Thurs - Sat 9 AM - 5:30 PM. Estab 1871 to
provide information and library materials for people in Grand Rapids and
Lakeland Library Federation area. Circ 871,859
Income: $2,032,478 (financed by city and state appropriations)
Purchases: $156,000
Library Holdings: Vols 17,000; Per subs 44; Micro — Reels; AV — Cassettes,
motion pictures, rec; Other — Clipping files, pamphlets
Collections: The Furniture Design Collection
Activities: Art talks; tours

HARTLAND

O   HARTLAND ART COUNCIL, PO Box 126, 48029. Tel 313-632-5200. *Pres*
John Galloway
Estab 1967 to promote arts in Hartland community. Gallery space in local library
and Hartland High School Media Center. Mem: 25; dues $1 - $100
Income: $3000 - $4000 (financed by membership and local foundation)
Purchases: $1500 - $2000
Collections: †Paintings, †photographs, †sculptures, †fibers, works of Michigan
artists exhibited in local public buildings
Exhibitions: 4 - 5 one man - woman shows annually
Activities: Dramatic programs; lect open to public; concerts; competitions;
scholarships; exten dept serving Michigan art councils and schools, lending
collection contains kodachromes and photographs; originate traveling exhibitions

HOLLAND

M   HOPE COLLEGE, De Pree Art Center & Gallery, 49423. Tel 616-392-5111,
Ext 3170. *Dir* John Montgomery Wilson
Open Mon - Sat 10 AM - 9 PM, Sun 1 PM - 9 PM. No admis fee. Estab as a
place for the college & community to enjoy art. Average Annual Attendance:
5000
Exhibitions: (1983-84); Bruce Mc Combs; Robert Vickers Sabatical Shows; Walls
of the 70's; Bertha Urdang Photography; Korean Drawing; Ceramics; Mexican
Art; senior art major show
Publications: Exhibition catalogs
Activities: Classes for adults and children; lect open to the public; tours;
competitions with awards; gallery talks; scholarships and fellowships; individual
paintings and original objects of art lent to faculty; lending collection contains
original art works; original prints, paintings and sculpture

INTERLOCHEN

L   INTERLOCHEN ARTS ACADEMY LIBRARY,* 49643. Tel 616-276-9221,
Ext 320. *Head Librn* Patricia Scheffler
Open daily 8:30 AM - 5 PM & 7 - 9:30 PM. Estab 1963. Circ 9000
Library Holdings: Vols 14,000; Per subs 140; Micro — Reels; AV — Cassettes,
fs, rec
Publications: Interlochen Review, annual
Activities: Dramatic programs; lect open to the public, 10 visiting lectr per year;
concerts; tours; competitions; awards; scholarships or fellowships; originate
traveling exhibitions

JACKSON

M   ELLA SHARP MUSEUM, 3225 Fourth St, 49203. Tel 517-787-2320. *Dir*
Millie Hadwin; *Asst Dir* Lynnea Loftis; *Cur Art Education* Elise Cole; *Assoc Cur
Art* Robin Blocksma; *Registrar* Carole Loll; *Exhibit Preparator* James
Richardson; *Membership Secy* Norma Cook; *Historian* Natalie Field; *Gift Shop
Mgr* Sally Reynolds
Open Tues - Fri 10 AM - 5 PM, Sat & Sun 1:30 - 5 PM, cl Mon, Jan and major
holidays. Admis adults $1, children $.50, local school tours free. Estab 1965 to
serve the people of Jackson and to provide a place for cultural education in the
community and a temporary gallery where a variety of exhibits are held.
Included are a large and small gallery; small library is maintained. Average
Annual Attendance: 70,000. Mem: 10,000; dues $1000 and up, $500, $125, $65,
$35, $20, $15, $5; annual meeting May
Income: Financed by endowment and membership along with grants
Collections: China; coverlets and quilts; furniture from Victorian period; †oil
paintings; porcelain; †prints
Publications: Annual Report; bulletins and catalogs; newsletter, monthly;
research material as requested
Activities: Classes for adults and children; dramatic programs; lect open to
public, 7 visiting lectr per year; concerts; gallery talks; tours; competitions; art
objects lent to schools; lending collection contains photographs; gift shop

---

KALAMAZOO

M KALAMAZOO INSTITUTE OF ARTS, Genevieve and Donald Gilmore Art Center, 314 S Park St, 49007. Tel 616-349-7775. *Exec Dir* Thomas A Kayser
Open Tues - Sat 10 AM - 5 PM, Sun 1 - 5 PM, cl Aug, Sun during July & Aug and holidays. No admis fee. Incorporated 1924 to further interest in the arts, especially in the visual arts; new building opened in 1961. There is one large gallery, four small exhibition galleries, with exhibitions changed monthly. One or more galleries always devoted to pieces from the permanent collection. Average Annual Attendance: 80,000. Mem: 1600; dues $15 and up; annual meeting Sept
Income: $543,000 (financed by endowment, membership)
Collections: †Art on Paper - Drawings, Graphics, Photographs and Watercolors; †sculpture; †20th century American art
Exhibitions: Bronson Park Art Fair; Kalamazoo Area Show
Publications: Exhibition catalogs, issued irregularly; newsletters, monthly
Activities: Classes for adults and children; doncent training; lectures open to the public; concerts; tours; scholarships; individual paintings and original objects of art lent to other institutions; lending collection contains books and slides; originate traveling exhibitions; museum shop sells craft items, jewelry, cards
L Library, 314 S Park St, 49007. Tel 616-349-7775. *Head Librn* Helen Sheridan; *Librn* Marianne L Cavanaugh
Open Tues - Sat 10 AM - 5 PM, Sun 1 - 5 PM, Thurs evenings 7 - 9 PM. Estab 1961, reference for Kalamazoo Institute of Arts curatorial staff and school faculty. For public reference only, open to members for circulation
Library Holdings: Vols 6000; Per subs 50; AV — Slides; Other — Clipping files, exhibition catalogs, original art works, pamphlets
Special Subjects: Photography, American art, especially art of the 20th century printmaking, history and technique
Activities: Lect; tours

M WESTERN MICHIGAN UNIVERSITY, Gallery II, Department of Art, 49008. Tel 616-383-0407. *Chairperson* John Link; *Exhibitions Dir* Margaret McAdams
Open Mon - Fri 10 AM - 5 PM. No admis fee. Estab 1965 to provide visual enrichment to the university and Kalamazoo community. Gallery II is a space located in the ground floor of Sangren Hall. Average Annual Attendance: 10,000
Income: $8000 (financed by state appropriation)
Purchases: $1000
Collections: Contemporary print collection
Exhibitions: (1982-84) John Gill, ceramics; Against the Grain, prints; Bea Nettles, non-silver photographs; Deborah Butterfield, sculpture; Paul Earls, multi-media & laser
Activities: Educ dept; lectures open to public, 8 vis lectrs per year; gallery talks; tours; competitions with awards; scholarships; individual and original objects of art lent to other offices on campus; lending collection contains 800 original art works, 350 original prints; originate traveling exhibitions

LANSING

M LANSING ART GALLERY, 425 S Grand Ave, 48933. Tel 517-374-6400. *Pres* Jackie Stebbins; *VPres* Raymond Joseph; *Exec Dir* Phyllis Adams; *Bookkeeper* Bernita Sage; *Field Representative* Pati Brush; *Field Representative* Sheldon Kemp
Open Tues - Fri 10 AM - 4 PM, Sun 1 - 4 PM. No admis fee. Estab 1965 to promote the visual arts in their many forms to citizens of the greater Lansing area. Maintains large exhibit area, gallery shop and rental gallery. Average Annual Attendance: 18,000. Mem: 500; dues $12 - $500; annual meeting May
Income: $90,000 (financed by membership, sales, grants, contributions and fees)
Publications: Gallery News, bimonthly
Activities: Docent training; lect open to the public, 10 visiting lectr per year; gallery talks; tours; competitions with awards; individual paintings and original objects of art lent to other art organizations, schools, library, Chamber of Commerce, etc; lending collection contains 350 books, 250 Kodachromes, original art works, original prints, paintings, photographs and sculpture; book traveling exhibitions, 1-2 per year; sales shop sells books, jewelry, pottery, original art and prints
L Art Reference Library, 425 S Grand Ave, 48933
Open Tues - Fri 10 AM - 4 PM, Sun 1 - 4 PM. Estab 1965 to enhance the meaning of visual art to our patrons
Library Holdings: Vols 350; Per subs 50; AV — Slides
Special Subjects: History of Macrame, Glass Blowing

MARQUETTE

M NORTHERN MICHIGAN UNIVERSITY, Lee Hall Gallery,* 49855. Tel 906-227-2194. *Exhib Coordr* William C Leete
Open Mon - Fri 8 AM - 5 PM. No admis fee. Estab 1975 to bring exhibits of the visual arts to the University, community and the upper peninsula of Michigan. Gallery covers approx 1500 sq ft of space, with security system and smoke detectors. Average Annual Attendance: 4000-6000
Income: $6500 (financed by University funds)
Collections: †Permanent collection; student collection
Exhibitions: Average of one to two major exhibits each month, with a reduction of exhibits during the summer months
Publications: Exhibit Announcement, monthly
Activities: Lect open to the public, 3-4 visiting lectrs per year; gallery talks; competitions; individual paintings and original objects of art lent contains original art works; traveling exhibitions organized and circulated

MIDLAND

L GRACE A DOW MEMORIAL LIBRARY, Fine Arts Dept, 1710 W Saint Andrews, 48640. Tel 517-835-7151. *Dir* Rosemarie Byers; *Fine Arts Reference Librn* Margaret Allen
Open Mon - Fri 10 AM - 9 PM, Sat 10 AM - 5 PM; during school year, Sun 1 - 5 PM. Estab 1955 as a public library. Maintains art gallery
Income: Financed by city appropriation and gifts
Purchases: $25,000
Library Holdings: Vols 12,000; Per subs 80; AV — Cassettes, motion pictures, rec; Other — Clipping files, framed reproductions, original art works, reproductions
Collections: Alden B Dow Fine Arts Collection
Exhibitions: (1983) Joe Viest; photographs from 1984 UNICEF calendar; fine arts film festival; Central Michigan University Sculpture; exhibits from local artists, art groups & schools Eunice Y Smith Canterbury Tales Etchings; Washington Square Prizewinners; exhibits from local art groups and schools
Publications: Arts Newsletter, 3 times per year
Activities: Films; originate traveling exhibitions

O MIDLAND ART COUNCIL,* 1801 W St Andrews, 48640. Tel 517-631-3250. *Dir* Michael S Bell; *Admin Asst* Shirley King; *Business Mgr* Mary L Dalton; *Studio School Coordr* Diane O'Brien; *Secy* Pamela Loertscher
Open Mon - Wed, Fri - Sun 1 - 5 PM, Thurs 1 - 9 PM. No admis fee. Estab 1956. Exhibition space consists of three galleries, one 40 x 80 ft and two smaller 20 x 40 ft space; spot tracking lighting. Mem: 350; dues $25; meetings held in spring and fall
Income: $100,000 (financed by endowment and membership)
Publications: Calendar of events; monthly newsletter for members; yearly report
Activities: Classes for adults and children; docent training; volunteer Show Me a Picture Program in public schools; lect open to public; gallery talks; tours; competitions; originate traveling exhibitions; sales shop sells books, magazines, original art and reproductions

MONROE

O MONROE CITY-COUNTY FINE ARTS COUNCIL, 1555 S Raisinville Rd, 48161. Tel 313-242-7300. *Pres* Robert Merkel; *Secy* Catherine Gibson; *Treas* Elaine Rugila
Estab 1967 to promote the arts. Average Annual Attendance: 120. Mem: 50; dues $2
Income: $1000 (financed by endowment, membership and county appropriation)
Activities: Classes for children; gallery talks; competitions with awards; scholarships

MOUNT CLEMENS

M THE ART CENTER, 125 Macomb Pl, 48043. Tel 313-469-8666. *Pres Bd of Trustees* Norma Stone; *Exec Dir* Douglas A Nordrum
Open Tues - Sat 11 AM - 5 PM, Sun 1 - 4 PM, cl Mon. No admis fee. Estab 1969 to foster art appreciation and participation for people of Macomb County. The only public art facility of its kind in the northeast Detroit metro area; The Center has two rooms, 17 x 27 ft, connected by lobby area in the former Carnegie Library Bldg, a Historical State Registered building. Average Annual Attendance: 10,000. Mem: 500; dues individual $15; annual meeting June
Income: Financed by membership, city and state appropriation, commissions from sales, class fees, special fund raising events & the Michigan Council for the Arts
Exhibitions: Several all state open competitive exhibitions, including painting and sculpture; crafts; two county wide student shows, one is regional scholastic art awards shows
Publications: Newsletter, quarterly
Activities: Classes for adults and children; docent training; tours; competitions; gallery & gift shops sell original art

MOUNT PLEASANT

M CENTRAL MICHIGAN UNIVERSITY, Art Gallery,* S Art Studio, 48859. Tel 517-774-3800. *Dir* Virginia Jenkins
Open Mon - Fri 10 AM - 4 PM, Tues 7 - 9 PM, Sat & Sun Noon - 3 PM. No admis fee. Estab to serve Mount Pleasant and university community; offer contemporary and traditional forms of art. Gallery has 114 ft running space; track lighting in all areas; motion monitoring alarm system. Average Annual Attendance: 4500
Income: Financed by art department
Activities: Classes for adults; lect open to public, 3 - 5 visiting lectr per year; gallery talks; tours upon request; competitions; cash awards; book traveling exhibitions

MUSKEGON

M MUSKEGON MUSEUM OF ART, 296 W Webster Ave, 49440. Tel 616-722-2600. *Dir* Mary Riordan; *Asst Cur* Richard Nelson; *Asst Cur* Douglas A Fairfield
Open Tues - Sat 10 AM - 4 PM. Estab 1912, Hackley Gallery designed by S S Beman, Chicago architect. Average Annual Attendance: 12,000. Mem: 400; dues benefactor $500, patron $250, sponsor $100, contributing $50, family $25, individual $15, students & sr citizens $5
Income: $100,000 (financed by school board and membership)
Collections: American paintings; glass by Louis Comfort Tiffany; The Home Signal by Winslow Homer; Impressionist paintings; modern & Old Masters prints; Study in Rose and Brown by James Whistler; Tornado Over Kansas by John Steuart Curry; New York Restaurant by Edward Hopper
Exhibitions: 56th Annual West Michigan Juried Competition; Michigan Fibers; Seaway Festival Juried Exhibition; Watercolors by Six Michigan Artists; changing exhibitions from the permanent collection; Great Lakes Marine Paintings of the 19th Century
Publications: Catalogs of American & European paintings from the Permanent Collection
Activities: Classes for adults and children; docent training; workshops; lectures open to public; gallery talks; tours; competitions with awards; individual and original objects of art lent to qualified museums; book traveling exhibitions; originate traveling exhibitions; museum shop sells books and reproductions

L **Library,** 296 W Webster, 49440
Membership estab 1977. Reference only

OLIVET

M **OLIVET COLLEGE,** Armstrong Museum of Art and Archaeology,* 49076. Tel 616-749-7000. *Pres* Donald Morris; *Dir* Donald Rowe
Open Mon - Fri 9 AM - 5 PM; while college is in session. Estab 1960 to collect artifacts and display for educational purposes. Average Annual Attendance: 1200
Collections: American Indian, Mesopotamian, Philippine and Thailand Artifacts; Modern American Prints; Primitive Art; Sculpture
Exhibitions: Invitational shows; one-man shows; student shows; traveling shows
Activities: Book traveling exhibitions
L **Library,** * 49076
Library Holdings: Vols 70,000; Micro — Prints

ORCHARD LAKE

M **ORCHARD LAKE SCHOOL GALERIA,** 48033. Tel 313-682-1885. *Dir* Marian Owczarski
Open Mon - Fri 1 - 5 PM, First Sun of the Month 1 - 4 PM and anytime upon request. No admis fee. Estab to house major Polish and Polish-American art. Average Annual Attendance: 8000
Collections: Contemporary Polish Painting by Andrzej Luczynski; John Paul II: The First Year (Pictorial exhibit); Sculpture by Marian Owczarski; History of Polish Printing: Rare Books and Documents; Polish Folk Art; Polish Tapestry; Paintings of A Wierusz Kowalski; Watercolors by J Falat; Watercolors by Wojciech Gierson; Louvre by Night, a sketch by Aleksander Gierymski; Oil paintings by Jacek Malczewski; lithographs by Irena Snarski and Barbara Rosiak
Exhibitions: (1983) The Lithographs of Barbara Rosiak, centennial exhibition of the Battle of Vienna; Majewska, graphics and sketches; Krystyna Owczarska, solidarnosc; Lois Wood, watercolors
Activities: Lectures open to the public; concerts; tours

PONTIAC

O **PONTIAC ART CENTER,** 47 Williams St, 48053. Tel 313-333-7849. *Educ Coordr* Carol S Goodale; *Exec Dir* Mary C Lilley; *Exhibition Coordr* James R Gilbert; *Office Coordr* Ann Waddell
Open Mon - Sat 9 AM - 5 PM, cl holidays. No admis fee. Estab 1968 to educate and uplift minority and culturally deprived people through the exposure of art. Gallery is maintained. Mem: 400; dues corporation $500, sponsor $100, supporting $50, family $35, individual $20; annual meeting March
Income: Financed by endowment, membership, city and state appropriation
Exhibitions: (1982) Michigan Council for the Arts, Grant Recipients Exhibit; (1983) Studio Artists of Pontiac Exhibit
Activities: Classes for adults and children; dramatic programs; lectures open to the public, 6 vis lectrs per year; gallery talks; competitions with awards; tours; scholarships; exten dept services Oakland University; originate traveling exhibitions; sales shop sells books & original art work

PORT HURON

M **MUSEUM OF ARTS AND HISTORY,** 1115 Sixth St, 48060. Tel 313-982-0891. *Dir* Stephen R Williams
Open Wed - Sun 1 - 4:30 PM. No admis fee. Estab 1968 to preserve area historical and marine artifacts; exhibit living regional artists; exhibit significant shows of national and international interest. Two galleries are maintained for loaned exhibitions and the permanent collection; also a doecorative arts gallery and a sales gallery. Average Annual Attendance: 40,000. Mem: 1100; dues family $15
Income: $120,000 (financed by endowment, membership, city appropriation, state & federal grants & earned income through program fees)
Collections: Thomas Edison; Civil War; Marine Artifacts; 19th Century American Decorative Arts, Painting and Prints
Publications: Newsletter, monthly; exhibit catalogs
Activities: Classes for adults and children; docent training; lect open to public, 6 vis lectr per year; gallery talks; tours; competitions with awards; film series; festivals; music & theatre programs; book traveling exhibitions, 8 per year; museum shop sells books, magazines, original art

M **SAINT CLAIR COUNTY COMMUNITY COLLEGE,** Jack R Hennesey Art Galleries,* 323 Erie, 48060. Tel 313-894-3881, Ext 340. *Coordr of Galleries* Ray Pierotti
Open Mon - Fri 8 AM - 5 PM. No admis fee. Estab 1975 to serve the community as an exhibition site and to serve the faculty and students of the college as a teaching tool. Maintains three galleries connected by common hall with approximately 2,000 sq ft. Average Annual Attendance: 3000
Collections: Paintings, print, and sculpture (wood and metal)
Activities: Educ dept; lect open to the public, 6 visiting lectr per year; concerts; competitions with awards; scholarships; artmobile

ROCHESTER

M **OAKLAND UNIVERSITY,** Meadow Brook Art Gallery, 48063. Tel 313-377-3005. *Dir Office Cultural Affairs Oakland Univ* Robert Dearth; *Dir* Kiichi Usui; *Secy* Eileen Arseneau; *Pres Meadow Brook Gallery Assocs* Mrs David Handleman
Open Tues - Fri 1 - 5 PM, Sat & Sun 2 - 6:30 PM, evening 7:30 - 8:30 PM in conjunction with Meadow Brook Theater Performances. No admis fee. Estab 1962 to provide a series of changing exhibitions and to develop an art collection to serve the university community and the greater community of southern Michigan. Average Annual Attendance: 50,000. Mem: 300; dues $20 - $500

Income: Financed by university budget, membership, fees and contributions
Collections: Art of Africa, Oceania and Pre-Columbian America; contemporary art and Sculpture Park; Oriental art
Exhibitions: (1984) Meadow Brook Invitational: Outdoor Sculpture Exhibition; Installation of Six Outdoor Sculpture in The Meadow Brook Sculpture Park
Publications: Exhibition catalogs
Activities: Educ dept; lect open to public, 2 visiting lectr per year; slide presentations in conjunction with exhibitions; paintings and original art objects lent within university; originate traveling exhibitions

SAGINAW

M **SAGINAW ART MUSEUM,** 1126 N Michigan Ave, 48602. Tel 517-754-2491. *Dir* William E Story
Open Mon - Fri 11 AM - 5 PM, Sat & Sun 1 - 5 PM. Estab 1948 to offer the cultural and educational services of an art museum to the regional community and to foster a love and understanding of the visual arts. Historic Georgian Revival Mansion (Charles Adams Platt, architect); approx 2600 sq ft of gallery space; formal outdoor garden. Average Annual Attendance: 15,314. Mem: 530; dues $10 - $500; annual meeting Sept
Income: $124,000 (financed by endowment, membership and grants)
Collections: American Sculpture and Painting (especially John Rogers sculpture); European painting, sculpture 3000 BC - present; Oriental prints, and textiles; †contemporary painting, †prints, and sculpture
Publications: Annual report; bulletin, monthly
Activities: Classes for adults and children; docent training; lectures open to the public, 14 vis lectr per yr; gallery talks; tours; competitions with awards; individual paintings and original objects of art lent to other museums and other small extension exhibitions in community; traveling exhibitions organized and circulated; sales shop sells books, original art, reproductions & prints
L **Library,** 1126 N Michigan Ave, 48602. *Librn* Deborah Schell
Open to public for reference only
Library Holdings: Vols 1000; Per subs 8

SAINT JOSEPH

O **SAINT JOSEPH ART ASSOCIATION INC,** Krasl Art Center,* 707 Lake Blvd, 49085. Tel 616-983-0271. *Dir* Darwin R Davis; *Asst Dir* Vicky Nemethy; *Educ Coordr* Marna Fisher
Open Mon - Thurs & Sat 10 AM - 4 PM, Fri 10 AM - 1 PM, Sun 1 - 4 PM. No admis fee. Estab 1962 to increase the level of aesthetic understanding in the area through exhibitions and studio art history classes. Maintains two galleries, 20 x 20 ft and 30 x 40 ft with humidity and temperature controls. Average Annual Attendance: 10,000. Mem: 1000; dues family $25, individual $15
Income: Financed by endowment and membership
Exhibitions: Dehn Ohara Show; Henri Douzil Show; C M Russell Show; juried competition
Publications: Newsletter, monthly
Activities: Classes for adults and children; lect open to the public, 3 visiting lectr per year; gallery talks; tours; competitions with awards; art fair; museum shop selling original art, reproductions, prints, crafts and gift items

TRAVERSE CITY

L **NORTHWESTERN MICHIGAN COLLEGE,** Mark Osterlin Library, 1701 E Front St, 49684. Tel 616-969-5650, Ext 541. *Library Dir* Bernard C Rink
Open Mon - Thurs 8 AM - 10 PM, Fri & Sat 9 AM - 4 PM, Sun 1 - 5 PM. Estab 1961, the library is charged with providing the resources needed to fulfill the educational and cultural task of the college. Permanent sculpture and print display in lobby and throughout building whenever wall space permits
Income: $414,000 (financed by state and county appropriation)
Purchases: $2000 - $5000
Library Holdings: Vols 46,000; Per subs 400; Micro — Reels; AV — A-tapes, cassettes, fs, Kodachromes, motion pictures, rec, slides, v-tapes; Other — Original art works 250, prints, sculpture 240
Special Subjects: Italian Renaissance art history
Collections: Canadian Eskimo sculpture and prints collected and for sale
Exhibitions: Annual Eskimo Sculpture and Print Exhibit

YPSILANTI

M **EASTERN MICHIGAN UNIVERSITY,** Ford Gallery, 48197. Tel 313-487-1268. *Dept Head* John Van Haren; *Gallery Dir* Jay Yager
Open Mon - Fri 8 AM - 5 PM. No admis fee. Estab 1925, in present building since 1982, for educational purposes. Art Dept gallery is maintained displaying staff and student exhibitions from a wide variety of sources; also one large, well-lighted gallery with lobby and a satellite student-operated gallery are maintained
Income: Financed by state appropriation
Purchases: $500
Exhibitions: Children's art; conceptual art; faculty art; international ceramics; international jewelry and metal; international textiles; National Student Photography Exhibition; student art; G Mennen Williams African art
Publications: Campus Life, bi-annual bulletin
Activities: Classes for adults; lect open to public, 6 visiting lectr per year; gallery talks; concerts; competitions; Community Art House
L **Art Dept Book Collection,** Sill Hall, Room 112, 48197. Tel 313-487-1849. *Librn* Virginia Stein
Open 9 AM - 5 PM. Estab 1978 as reference source for faculty and graduate students
Library Holdings: Vols 350

MINNESOTA

BROOKLYN PARK

M NORTH HENNEPIN COMMUNITY COLLEGE, Art Gallery,* 7411 85th
Ave N, 55445. Tel 612-425-4541
Open Mon - Fri 8 AM - 4 PM. Estab to show works of art. Consist of two
gallery spaces: small gallery for students, large gallery for local, state and national
personalities
Income: Financed by state appropriation
Collections: Student works and local artists in Minnesota
Activities: Lect open to the public; concerts; gallery talks; tours; competitions
with awards

DULUTH

M SAINT LOUIS COUNTY HISTORICAL SOCIETY,* 506 W Michigan St,
55802. Tel 218-727-8025, 722-8011. *Dir* Shirley Swain
Open Mon - Sat 10 AM - 5 PM, Sun Noon - 5 PM. Admis adults $2.50, sr
citizen $2, children 6-17 $1.50, under 6 free. Incorporated in 1971. Includes St
Louis County Historical Society, Chisholm Museum, Duluth Ballet, Duluth-
Superior Symphony, Duluth Playhouse, Duluth Art Institute, Matinee Musicale,
Lake Superior Museum of Transportation and Industry. Arts Center consists of
three galleries interspersed in viewing areas. Average Annual Attendance:
125,000. Mem: 2000; annual dues $25; meetings semi-annually
Income: $445,960; (financed by earned profit & public support)
Collections: E Johnson Collection; drawings; paintings
Exhibitions: Each of the three museums has its own acquisitions policy
Publications: Newsletter, quarterly; books and pamphlets on topics related to the
history of northeastern Minn
Activities: Classes for adults and children; dramatic programs; lect open to the
public, 2-3 visiting lectr per year; gallery talks; tours; awards; individual paintings
and original objects of art lent to other museums; sales shop sells books,
magazines, original art, reproductions, prints and gifts

M UNIVERSITY OF MINNESOTA, Tweed Museum of Art, 2400 Oakland Ave,
55812. Tel 218-726-8222. *Dir* William G Boyce; *Technician* Larry Gruenwald;
Secy Sharon Alexander; *Mgr Tweed Museum Gift
Shop* Joyce Nelson; *Museum Intern* Jane Johnson
Open Tues - Fri 8 AM - 4:30 PM, Sat & Sun 2 - 5 PM, cl Mon. No admis fee.
Estab 1950 to serve both the University and community as a center for
exhibition of works of art and related activities. Six galleries within the Museum.
Average Annual Attendance: 80,000. Mem: 680; dues $10 - $100
Income: Financed by membership, state appropriation and foundation
Purchases: $80,000
Collections: Jonathan Sax Collections of 20th Century American Prints; George
P Tweed Memorial Art Collections of 500 paintings with emphasis on Barbizon
School and 19th Century American; †20th century American paintings and
sculptures; Potlatch Collection of 349 Paintings of Royal Mounted Police
Exhibitions: (1982-83) Cheng-Khee Chee, watercolors; Travels with the
President: Diane Magrath; Sharon Roberts Macy, interiors; Barbara Fumagalli,
drawings and prints; John Taylor Arms, prints; Phyllis Ames Wiener,
retrospective; Lake Superior Watercolor Society; Fairs and Rodeos: Ron Geibert;
Ben Effinger, sculpture; Plates and Photographs from Camera Work; Art and the
Circus; Techniques, Textures and Trends; Hunter of the Sacred Game; Works
from the Zhejiang Academy; People's Republic of China; Photography
Invitational
Publications: Catalogues, irregular
Activities: Docent training; lect open to public, 1 - 2 vis lectr per yr; concerts;
gallery talks; tours; individual paintings and original objects of art lent to
qualifying museums and institutions; lending collection contains original art
works, original prints and paintings; traveling exhibitions organized and
circulated; museum shop sells books, original art, reproductions, craft objects and
cards

ELYSIAN

M LESUEUR COUNTY HISTORICAL SOCIETY MUSEUM, Box 240, 56028.
Tel 507-267-4620, 362-8350. *Dir & Secy* James E Hruska; *VPres* Michael
LaFrance; *Co-Dir & Museologist* Dorothy Irene Hruska
Open May - Sept Sat & Sun 1:30 PM - 5:30 PM; June - Aug Wed - Sun 1:30 PM
- 5:30 PM. No admis fee. Estab 1966 to show the works of Adolf Dehn, Roger
Preuss and David Maass; to preserve early heritage and artifacts of the pioneers
of LeSueur County. Museum is depository for Dehn, Preuss and Maass, and
Lloyd Herfindahl, examples of originals, prints and publications of the Artists are
on display. Average Annual Attendance: 5000. Mem: 700; dues life $25, annual
$1; annual meeting quarterly
Income: $12,000 (financed by membership, county appropriation, county
government and by grants)
Purchases: $51,000
Collections: †Adolf Dehn; David Maass; Roger Preuss; Lloyd Herfindahl; Albert
Christ-Janer
Exhibitions: (1982) Lloyd Herfindahl; (1983) Albert Christ-Janer
Publications: Newsletters, quarterly
Activities: Slide carousel to show the sites and early history of the County and
works of the Artists; lect open to public; gallery talks; tours; lending collection
contains 300 books, cassettes, color reproductions, 400 lantern slides, original
prints, paintings, motion pictures and 300 photographs; museum shop sells books,
original art and prints
L Collections Library,* Box 557, 56028. Tel 507-362-8350, 267-4620
Open by appointment only. Estab 1970 to collect local and state purposes for
geneaology; history of the artists
Income: $300
Purchases: $450

Library Holdings: Vols 350; Per subs 3; Micro — Reels 120; AV — A-tapes,
cassettes, lantern slides, slides; Other — Clipping files, framed reproductions,
original art works, prints, reproductions
Special Subjects: Prints of four Artists
Collections: Adolf Dehn Watercolors and Lithographs; Duck Stamp Prints of
Roger Preuss and David Maass; Lloyd Herfindahl, all mediums
Exhibitions: Lloyd Herfindahl
Publications: Newsletters, 4 per yr

INTERNATIONAL FALLS

M KOOCHICHING COUNTY HISTORICAL SOCIETY MUSEUM, 214 6th
Ave, PO Box 1147, 56649. Tel 218-283-4316. *Pres* Lillian Kaufman; *VPres* Bruce
Polkinghorne; *Secy* Hermoine Schwanki; *Exec Secy & Cur* Mary Hilke
Open Mon - Sat 10 AM - 4 PM. Admis adults $.50, children $.25. Estab 1967 to
collect, preserve and interpret the history of Koochiching County and of the state
of Minnesota
Income: Financed by county, membership & admission funds
Collections: 50 paintings relating to the history of the county, including many by
local artists, and six of which were commissioned for the museum
Exhibitions: Permanent collection
Publications: Gesundheit, monthly newsletter; descriptive brochure about
paintings
Activities: Classes for adults and children; dramatic programs; lectures open to
public, 1-2 vis lectr per year; tours; originate traveling exhibitions; sales shop sells
books, Indian craft items, note and post cards

MANKATO

M MANKATO STATE UNIVERSITY, Nichols Gallery,* 56001. Tel 507-389-2463
Open Mon - Fri 8 AM - 4:30 PM. No admis fee. Estab 1960 to provide cultural
enrichment in the visual arts to the campus and community through a program of
exhibitions from local, regional, and national sources, and student exhibitions.
Gallery has 180 running feet of carpeted display area, track lighting and climate
controlled
Income: Financed by city appropriation
Collections: American bookplates; contemporary prints, drawings, paintings,
photographs, sculpture and crafts; student works in all media

MINNEAPOLIS

M AMERICAN SWEDISH INSTITUTE, 2600 Park Ave, 55407. Tel 612-871-
4907. *Dir* Dr John Z Lofgren; *Pres* Irving Dahlstrom
Open Tues - Sat Noon - 4 PM, Sun 1 - 5 PM, cl Mon and National holidays.
Admis adults $2, students under 21 and senior citizens $1, children under 6 free.
Estab and inc 1929. Building donated by Swan J Turnblad and contains, in a
home setting, a fine collection of Swedish artifacts, plus many items of general
cultural interest pertaining to Scandinavia. The Grand Hall, paneled in African
mahogany, is considered to be a fine installation. Throughout the gallery there
are eleven porcelain tile fireplaces; nine Swedish and two German design.
Average Annual Attendance: 50,000. Mem: Dues—students attending school,
below the age of 21, $10, non-resident single, or husband and wife outside a fifty
mile radius of Twin Cities $15, regular (single)$20, regular (husband and wife)
$25, sustaining (husband, wife and all children under age 21, living at home) $40,
supporting $55, patron $100, life $1000
Collections: Paintings, sculpture, tapestries, ceramics, china, glass, pioneer items
and textiles
Publications: ASI Posten (newsletter), monthly
Activities: Films; lect; concerts; gift shop and bookstore

C DAYTON HUDSON CORPORATION,* 777 Nicollet Mall, 55402. Tel 612-
370-6948. *Arts Grants Adminr* Margaret Wurtele
No admis fee. Estab for works by artists living and working in Minneapolis.
Collection displayed on 15th Floor, IDS Building, Minneapolis
Activities: Corporate Giving Program has designated 40% of its funds to
community art organizations

C FEDERAL RESERVE BANK OF MINNEAPOLIS,* 250 Marquette Ave,
55480. Tel 612-340-2345. *Art Dir* Kathy Balkman
Open to public by appointment with Art Dir or Asst. No admis fee. Estab 1973
to enhance the working environment of bank; to support the creative efforts of
9th district artists. Collection displayed throughout the bank in offices, lounges,
public areas and work areas
Collections: Regional collection consists of works by artists living and working in
the 9th District
Activities: Tours with 10 minute slide presentation; individual objects of art lent
for special exhibitions upon request

C GENERAL MILLS, INC,* 9200 Wayzata Blvd, PO Box 1113, 55440. Tel 612-
540-2311. *Art Cur* Donald B McNeil
Open to public by appointment only. No admis fee. Estab 1959 to enhance
employee work areas and alternative community art resource. Collection
displayed in office building
Collections: 20th Century multi-media works, original prints, paintings and
sculptures (1000 pieces)
Activities: Lect; gallery talks; tours; individual objects of art lent at request of
museums, galleries, and artists for specific exhibitions; originate traveling
exhibitions to colleges, art centers and museums

C HONEYWELL INC,* Honeywell Plaza, 2701 Fourth Ave S, 55408. Tel 612-
870-2403, 870-5200. *In Charge Collection* Lloyd H Kirk
Open Mon - Fri 9 AM - 4 PM. Collection displayed in main lobby, second and
fifth floors
Collections: Variety of paintings, abstracts and statues

C **LUTHERAN BROTHERHOOD GALLERY,*** 625 Fourth Ave S, 55415. Tel 612-340-7353. *In Charge Art Program* David Swanson
Collections: Bing and Grondahl Plate Collection; Martin Luther Coin Collection
Exhibitions: 8-10 Exhibitions per year
Activities: Competitions with awards; purchase awards

O **METROPOLITAN CULTURAL ARTS CENTER,*** 1834 Emerson Ave N, 55411. Tel 612-522-7796. *Chmn Board* Robert Samples
Open 9:30 AM - 9 PM. Small fee gallery. Estab 1967 to offer training in the arts to people who could not afford it otherwise and to bring people of different cultural backgrounds together to experience art. Average Annual Attendance: 400. Mem: 100; dues $10; annual meeting Sept
Income: Financed by endowment, membership, state appropriation and grants
Publications: Newsletter, monthly
Activities: Classes for adults and children; dramatic programs

L **MINNEAPOLIS COLLEGE OF ART AND DESIGN,** Library and Media Center, 200 E 25th St, 55404. Tel 612-870-3291, 870-3292, 870-3139. *Dir* Richard Kronstedt; *Asst Librn* Mary Miller; *Slide Librn* Peggy Rudberg; *Media Center Dir* Tim Perkins
Open Mon - Thurs 8 AM - 8 PM, Fri 8 AM - 5 PM, Sat & Sun 12:30 - 4:30 PM, summer 8 AM - 5 PM; slide library and media center have different hours. Estab to provide library and media services and materials in support of the curriculum of the College; includes a library, slide library and media center. 40,000. Circ Limited to students & staff
Income: Financed by student tuition, grants and gifts
Library Holdings: Vols 50,000; Per subs 180; AV — Cassettes, rec, slides, v-tapes; Other — Clipping files, exhibition catalogs, pamphlets
Special Subjects: Drawings, Film, Graphic Design, Illustration, Architecture, Photography, Printmaking, Sculpture, Video, Contemporary painting, Product design

M **MINNEAPOLIS INSTITUTE OF ARTS,** 2400 Third Ave S, 55404. Tel 612-870-3046. *Dir* Samuel Sachs II; *Assoc Dir* Timothy Fiske; *Chmn Communications* Marcy Dahlquist; *Acting Chmn Education* Kathryn C Johnson; *Dir Upper Midwest Conservation Assoc* David Dudley; *Cur Prints & Drawings* John Ittmann; *Cur Photography* Carroll T Hartwell; *Cur Oriental Arts* Robert Jacobsen; *Registrar* Marilyn Bjorkland
Open Tues, Wed, Fri & Sat 10 AM - 5 PM, Thurs 10 AM - 9 PM, Sun Noon - 5 PM cl Mon. Admis adults $2, student $1, free to members, senior citizens, those under twelve, school groups. Estab 1883 to foster the knowledge, understanding and practice of the arts. The first gallery was opened in 1889, and the original building was constructed in 1911-15. The south wing was added in 1926, and the entire structure features the classical elements of the day. The museum was expanded to twice the original size in 1972-74, and has incorporated modern themes designed by Kenzo, Tange and URTEC of Tokyo. Average Annual Attendance: 350,000. Mem: 11,862; dues household $25, individual $15; annual meeting in Oct
Income: Financed by endowment, membership, county and state appropriations, and admissions
Collections: Collection representing all schools and periods of art: American and European paintings, decorative arts, period rooms, photography, prints and drawings, sculpture; Ancient, African, Oceanic, Oriental and native North and South American arts
Exhibitions: Arts of China and Japan; Carl Chiarenza: Photographs; Drawings by Arakawa: Mechanism of Meaning; Leger's Grand Dejeuner: a Masterpiece from the Museum of Modern Art; Millet's Gleaners: a Masterpiece from the Louvre; New Treasure at the Institute; Sculpture from the David Daniels Collection; James Jacques Joseph Tissot: The Complete Printer; Victorian High Renaissance Art of Norway 1750 - 1914
Publications: Bulletin, biannually; exhibitions catalogs; member's magazine, monthly
Activities: Classes for adults and children; docent training; workshops; lect open to public, 15 visiting lectr per year; concerts; gallery talks; tours; artmobile; paintings and original art objects lent to other professional arts organizations; originate traveling exhibitions; museum shop sells books, original art, reproductions, prints, slides and jewelry

L **Art Reference Library,*** 2400 Third Ave S, 55404. *Librn* Harold Peterson; *Asst Librn* Barbara Lassonde
Open Tues - Sat 10 AM - 5 PM, Sun Noon - 5 PM, cl Mon. Estab 1915 to provide a reference collection based around the museum's collection of works of art for use primarily by curatorial staff but to be available to students and museum visitors. Maintains an art gallery, Leslie Memorial Room and has exhibitions of books and prints
Library Holdings: Vols 35,000; Per subs 100
Special Subjects: History of books, printings, decorative arts, prints and photography
Collections: Leslie Collection: History of Books and Printing; Minnick Collection: Botanical, Floral and Fashion Books
Exhibitions: Artist as Book Illustrator; Artists Books of the Seventies; Eye of the Composer; 19th Century English Book Illustrators; Private Presses; Bruce Rogers: Book Designer

O **Friends of the Institute,*** 2400 Third Ave S, 55404. Tel 612-870-3046. *Pres* Barbara M DeLaittre
Estab 1922 to broaden the influence of the Institute in the community and to provide volunteer support within the museum. Mem: 1900; annual meeting May
Activities: Coordinates docent program, museum shop, sales and rental gallery, speaker's bureau, information desk, special lect, exhibitions and fund-raising projects

C **THE PILLSBURY COMPANY,*** 608 Second Ave S, 55402. Tel 612-330-4966. *Executive VPres* Walter D Scott
Estab to create exciting and attractive environment and support the arts. Collection displayed on internal walls of corporate headquarters building
Collections: Contemporary and Western American art, primarily oil paintings, prints and watercolors

UNIVERSITY OF MINNESOTA

M **University Art Museum,** 110 Northrop Memorial Auditorium, 84 Church St SE, 55455. Tel 612-373-3424, 373-3425. *Dir* Lyndel King; *Asst Dir* Susan Brown; *Cur* Charles Helsell; *Editor & Cur* Valerie Turdik; *Asst Dir for Outreach* Rebecca Keim; *Registrar* Abigail Terrones; *Asst Cur* Laura Andrews-Mickman; *Preparator* William Lampe
Open Mon - Wed & Fri 11 AM - 4 PM, Thurs 11 AM - 8 PM, Sun 2 - 5 PM, cl Sat & holidays. Estab 1934; the program of the University Art Museum is one geared to meet broad objectives of an all-University museum, as well as the specific teaching and research needs of various University of Minnesota departments. Average Annual Attendance: 50,000
Income: Financed by state appropriation, grants and gifts
Purchases: Earth Projects, 1969, by Robert Morris; Warm on Cool, 1958, Cameron Booth
Collections: Paintings, drawings and prints by American artists working in the first half of the 20th century, and contains notable works by Avery, Dove, Feininger, Hartley, MacDonald-Wright, Marin, Maurer and O'Keefe; Nordfeldt collection on extended loan from Mrs. B J O Nordfeldt; print collection includes works by artists of all schools and periods; sculpture collection of major works by contemporary artists including: Baizerman, Bertoia, Richier, David Smith and others; Third Ave El at 14th St, 1931: Edward Laning; Study of New York 1939 Worlds Fair Mural, 1938: Ilya Bolotowsky; decorative arts
Exhibitions: The University Art Museum stresses a program of major loan exhibitions, held concurrently with smaller exhibitions organized for specific teaching purposes or from the permanent collection
Activities: Programs; lending program to University, staff & students of Minnesota faculty of framed two-dimensional material; originate traveling exhibitions

M **Coffman Union Gallery,*** 110 Northrop Memorial Auditorium, 84 Church St SE, 55455. Tel 612-373-1051. *Coordr* Roselyn Rezac
Open Daily 10 AM - 5 PM. No admis fee. Estab 1976 for campus and local artists
Income: Financed by student fees
Activities: Lect; films; demonstrations

L **Art Library,** 208 Walter Library, 117 Pleasant Street SE, 55455. Tel 612-373-2875. *Librn* Herbert G Scherer
Open Mon - Thurs 8 AM - 9 PM, Fri 8 AM - 5 PM, Sat & Sun 1 - 5; Summer Mon, Wed, Fri 8 - 4:30, Tues 8 AM - 9 PM. Estab 1950 to serve undergraduate and graduate teaching programs in Art History to PhD level and in Studio Art to MA level. To provide art related books to other departments and to the entire academic community as best we can
Library Holdings: Vols 61,000; Per subs 339; trade and post card albums; Micro — Fiche; Other — Exhibition catalogs 7150, pamphlets
Special Subjects: Scandinavian art history
Activities: Tours; single lectures

O **Architecture Library,** 89 Church St SE, 55455. Tel 612-373-2203. *Head* Kris Johnson
Open Mon - Fri 8 AM - 5 PM. Circ 34,000
Library Holdings: Vols 20,000; Per subs 200; Micro — Reels; AV — V-tapes; Other — Manuscripts, pamphlets
Special Subjects: Architecture, Decorative Arts, Furniture, Graphic Arts, Graphic Design, Interior Design, Landscape Architecture

M **WALKER ART CENTER,** Vineland Place, 55403. Tel 612-375-7600. *Pres* Harriet S Spencer; *VPres* Erwin A Kelen; *Chmn Board* Thomas M Crosby Jr; *Dir* Martin Friedman; *Admin Dir* D C Borrman; *Chief Cur* Robert M Murdock; *Cur* Marge Goldwater; *Asst Cur* Elizabeth Armstrong; *Cur Design* Mildred S Friedman; *Registrar* Carolyn Clark DeCato; *Asst Registrar* Jane E Falk; *Dir Development* Dolores Johnson; *Dir Education* Adam Weinberg; *Dir Performing Arts* Robert Stearus; *Dir Media* Melinda Ward; *Dir Film & Video* Richard Peterson; *Public Information* Mary Abbe Martin; *Graphic Designer* Robert Jensen; *Dir Membership* Lockie Rawstad
Open Tues - Sat 10 AM - 8 PM; Sun 11 AM - 5 PM, cl Mon. No admis fee. Estab 1879 by T B Walker, reorganized 1939 as Walker Art Center, Inc; building erected 1927; new museum building opened 1971. The Center consists of nine galleries, three sculpture terraces, the Center Bookshop and the Gallery 8 restaurant. Average Annual Attendance: 450,000. Mem: 5000; dues household $35, individual $25, special $20; annual meeting September
Income: $1,983,625 (financed by endowment, membership, state appropriation, grants and book shop)
Collections: †Graphics; 19th century American landscape paintings by Church, Cole, Durand, Kensett, Inness, Ryder; †photography; †sculpture; †20th century paintings
Exhibitions: George Segal Sculptures; William Wiley: Twelve Years; Picasso: From the Future Musee Picasso, Pans; City Segments; Close Portraits, Kay Kurt Paintings; Artist & Printer: Six American Print Studios; Wayne Thiebaud Painting; Robert Moskowitz; Recent Paintings; Robert Graham; Statues; De Stijl: 1917-1931, Visions of Utopia; The Frozen Truage; Scandinavian Photography; Weginau's World; Mark Rothko: Seven Paintings from the 1960's; Hockway Paints the Stage
Publications: Brochures; calendar of events, 11 issues a year; Design, quarterly; exhibition catalogs
Activities: Classes for adults and children; tour guide training; family workshops; lect open to public; concerts; gallery talks; school & adult tours; films; exten dept serving Minnesota and surrounding states; individual paintings and original objects of art lent to museums; traveling exhibitions organized and circulated; museum shop selling books, magazines, posters, jewelry and gift items

L **Staff Reference Library,** Vineland Place, 55403. Tel 612-375-7680. *Librn* Rosemary Furtak
Open to museum personnel, librarians, graduate students by appointment. For reference only
Library Holdings: Vols 5000; Per subs 100; AV — A-tapes, v-tapes; Other — Clipping files, exhibition catalogs 20,000
Special Subjects: Architecture, Film, Photography, Sculpture, Design, Graphics, catalogs dating back to 1940

O WOMEN'S ART REGISTRY OF MINNESOTA GALLERY, 414 First Ave N, 55401. Tel 312-332-5672. *Executive Dir* Catherine Jordan
Open Tues, Wed & Fri 11 AM - 4 PM, Thurs 11 AM - 7:30 PM, Sun 12 - 5 PM. No admis fee. Estab 1975. Maintains gallery. Average Annual Attendance: 9000. Mem: 400; dues $20 - $100; annual meeting Feb
Income: Financed by membership, grants for projects & operating expenses
Collections: Members work on display in one area
Exhibitions: (1983) Annual Juried Show for Minnesota Women Artists; special shows, theme shows and invitiational space for emerging women artists from the midwest region
Publications: WARM Journal, quarterly
Activities: Educ dept; lect open to the public; concerts; gallery talks; tours; competitions with awards; scholarships and fels offered; individual paintings lent and original objects of art lent to non-profit groups for fee; originate traveling exhibitions; sales shop sells magazines, original art & prints

MOORHEAD

PLAINS ART MUSEUM

M **Main Gallery,** 521 Main Ave, PO Box 37, 56560. Tel 218-236-7171. *Dir & Secy Board Dir* James O'Rourke; *Pres Board Dir* Stan Ryland; *VPres Board Dir* Catherine Mulhigan; *Business Mgr* Constance Brust; *Cur* Scott Ferris; *Cur* Barry Rosenman; *Education & Registrar* Susan Talbot-Stanaway; *Membership* Kate Roberts; *Development* Marilyn Doolan
Open Wed - Sat 10 AM - 5 PM, Sun 1 - 5 PM, Tues by appointment, cl holidays. Admis $1. Estab 1960 to foster and promote a knowledge and love of art in the community and to provide a repository for the artistic heritage of this area; to operate and maintain an art gallery and museum; to promote the extension and improvement of education in the arts; to provide facilities for the exhibition and conservation of the art in this area, past and present. Former Moorhead Federal Building (1913), Oscar Wenderoth, architect, houses the museum. This stately classical revival style building has a vari-colored marble lobby, ionic columns and tall arched windows; currently undergoing a major restoration-reconstruction project. Average Annual Attendance: 26,000. Mem: 1200; dues $10 - $1000; annual meeting April
Income: Financed by membership, NEH, NEA & foundation grants & charitable gaming
Collections: African, Pre-Columbian and North American Indian; Eskimo sculpture; 19th & 20th century prints and drawings; 19th century decorative arts; 20th century paintings from local, regional and national artists; photography
Exhibitions: (1982-83) Twenty in-house exhibitions yearly; major exhibitions include Inuit art from private collections; Catherine Mulligan: Sculpture; Leonard Baskin: Woodcuts, Etchings & Sculpture; Jack Youngquist Retrospective; George Pfeifer: Paintings; Red River & Midwestern Juried Invitationals
Publications: Museum & Gallery News, every other month; exhibition checklist & catalogs, monthly
Activities: Classes for adults; docent training; lect open to public; concerts; gallery talks; tours; individual paintings & original objects of art lent to art galleries, historical museums, college & schools; lending collection contains more than 1000 original art works, 550 original prints, 450 paintings, 400 photographs; museum shop sells books, magazines, original art, posters & prints
M **Rourke Art Gallery,** 523 S Fourth St, 56560. Tel 218-236-7171
Open Wed - Sun Noon - 5 PM. Admis fee $1. Estab 1960 to foster and promote a knowledge and love of art in our community and to provide a repository for the artistic heritage of this area; to operate and maintain an art gallery and museum. Former Martinson family home built in 1884, remodeled 1903, renovations have preserved the period details and historical features; three floors for exhibitions. Average Annual Attendance: 16,000. Mem: 1200; dues $10 - $1000; annual meeting April
Income: Financed by membership, NEH, NEA foundation grants & charitable gaming
Purchases: $5000
Collections: Contemporary visual arts; 19th century decorative art; North American Indian Art; Pre-Columbian Art; West African Art
Exhibitions: (1982-83) George Pfiefer Paintings; 24th Midwestern Invitational; Gordon Mortensen Woodcuts
Publications: Catalogs; checklists; membership newsletter

OWATONNA

O OWATONNA ARTS CENTER, 435 Dunnel Dr, PO Box 134, 55060. Tel 507-451-4540. *Pres* Robert Allyn; *VPres* Dee Teller; *Treas* James Birdsall; *Bldg Mgr* John M Spencer; *Secy* Bea Spencer; *Cur* Silvan A Durken; *Performing Art Chmn* Nancy Hockenberry
Open Tues - Sat 1 - 5 PM, Sun 2 - 5 PM. No admis fee except for specials. Estab 1975 to preserve local professional artists' work and promote the arts in the community. The West Gallery (32 x 26 x 12 ft) and the North Gallery (29 x 20 x 12 ft) provide an interesting walk through space and a versatile space in which to display two and three dimensional work; the two galleries can be combined by use of moveable panels; and the Sculpture Garden which was completed in 1979 of multi-level construction. Average Annual Attendance: 5000. Mem: 400; dues, individual $10, family $15; annual meeting first Tues in Oct
Income: $20,394 (financed by membership and fund raising activities plus sustaining fund from industries and business)
Purchases: $500
Collections: Marianne Young World Costume Collection of garments and jewelry from 27 countries; painting, prints, sculpture by local professional artists; 3 Bronzes by John Rood, Paul Grandland & Charles Gagnon
Exhibitions: Annual Outdoor Arts Festival; Annual Steel Country Show; An Old Fashioned Christmas
Publications: Monthly newsletter to members only
Activities: Classes for adults and children; festivals; concerts monthly; tours; sales shop sells original art
L **Library,** 435 Dunnel Dr, 55060
Open to members only; for reference
Library Holdings: Vols 180

PARK RAPIDS

M NORTH COUNTRY MUSEUM OF ARTS,* Third and Court Streets, PO Box 328, 56470. Tel 218-732-5237. *Chmn* Grace Privratsky; *Cur* Pamela Teslow; *Secy* Sandy Perez; *Treas* Blanche Szuszitzky
Open Tues - Sun 11 AM - 5 PM May - Oct. Admis adults $1, students $.50. Estab 1977 to provide a cultural and educational center in which to house our permanent study collection of old school European paintings and additional traveling exhibitions from which all ages may benefit by being exposed to and working with art in its many forms. Maintins Great Gallery, Members Gallery, four Revolving Galleries and studio. Average Annual Attendance: 6000. Mem: 120; dues family $20, individual $15; annual meeting Oct
Income: $40,000 (financed by membership, individual and corporate grants and gifts)
Collections: †Nigerian arts, crafts and artifacts; †30 Old School European paintings; †Contemporary Prints
Exhibitions: Drawings by Gendron Jensen; Juried High School Fine Art Exhibition; Learning to See - Conservation of Paintings by Louis Pomerantz Once Upon a Time: Illustrations of Children's Tales from Around the World; Scandinavian Wood, Traditional Scandinavian Woodworking; Juried High School Fine Arts Exhibition; The Human Comedy: Daumier & His Contemporaries from University Gallery, University of Minnesota; Contemporary Guilting: A Renaissance from University of Wisconsin, Green Bay; Minnesota Governors Residence Dinnerware & Table Linens Competition Finalists
Activities: Classes for adults and children; docent training; lect open to the public, 2-3 lectr per year; concerts; gallery talks; tours; competitions; book traveling exhibitions, 5-6 per year; Originate traveling exhibits; museum shop selling original art

ROCHESTER

O ROCHESTER ART CENTER, 320 E Center St, 55904. Tel 507-282-8629. *Dir* Betty Jean Shigaki
Open Tues - Sat 10 AM - 5 PM, cl Sun & Mon. No admis fee. Estab 1946 as a center for contemporary arts and crafts of the Upper Midwest region, to sponsor an on-going program of exhibitions, educational classes, lectures, workshops and community services in the arts. Included are the Upstairs Gallery of Contemporary Crafts, and the main exhibitions space, the Holland Gallery. Average Annual Attendance: 30,000
Income: Financed by endowment, contributions, city and state appropriations, fund raising and tuition
Collections: Local and regional artists' work
Exhibitions: Varied exhibits in Contemporary Fine Arts and Crafts
Publications: Newsletter, quarterly
Activities: Classes for adults and children; lectures open to public, 2 vis lectr per year; concerts; gallery talks; tours; competitions; film series
L **Library,** 320 E Center St, 55901
Open to staff and members only
Library Holdings: Vols 500; Per subs 12

SAINT CLOUD

SAINT CLOUD STATE UNIVERSITY

M **Atwood Center Gallery Lounge,** Atwood Center, 56301. Tel 612-255-2205. *Program Dir* Brant Greene
Open Mon - Fri 7:30 AM - 11 PM, Sat 8 AM - 11 PM, Sun Noon - 11 PM. No admis fee. Estab 1967 as a university student union facility. Gallery area is part of program, designed for maximum exposure, where students may relax or study while enjoying exhibits; space is flexible; also area for music listening and small theatre; additional exhibits displayed in prominent area
Income: Financed by student enrollment fee assessment
Exhibitions: 1 - 3 exhibits monthly, many by students
Activities: Artists' residencies, lectures & workshops that coincide with exhibits
M **Kiehle Gallery,*** 56301. Tel 612-255-4283. *Dir* Kingsly Dorholt
Open Mon - Fri 8 AM - 4:30 PM. No admis fee. Estab 1974 to expose college community to ideas and attitudes in the field of visual arts and crafts. The gallery has 1600 sq ft of enclosed multi use gallery floor space and 2500 sq ft outside sculpture court. Average Annual Attendance: 15,000
Income: Financed by student fund appropriation
Collections: Works donated by Master of Arts degree program (visual arts)
Activities: Lect open to the public, 5 vis lectr per yr; gallery talks; competitions; individual paintings and original objects of art lent to other departments on campus; lending collection contains original prints, paintings, photographs and sculpture; traveling exhibitions organized and circulated

SAINT JOSEPH

M COLLEGE OF SAINT BENEDICT, Art Gallery,* Benedict Arts Center, 56374. Tel 612-363-5785. *Pres* Sr Emmanuel Renner, PhD; *Chmn of Art Dept & Gallery Dir* Stanley Shafer
Open daily 9 AM - 4:30 PM. No admis fee. Estab 1963
Income: Financed by college
Collections: Contemporary collection of crafts, drawings, paintings, prints and sculpture; East Asian Collection of ceramics, crafts, drawings, fibers and prints; Miscellaneous African, New Guinea, Indian and European
Activities: Lect open to the public, 8 visiting lectr per year; gallery talks; tours; scholarships; individual paintings and original objects of art lent to faculty and staff members of the college

SAINT PAUL

C BURLINGTON NORTHERN, INC,* 176 E Fifth St, 55101. Tel 612-298-2121
Estab 1910
Collections: American art of the first half of the 20th century; landscape of
North Western US; Blackfeet Indian portraits
Activities: Lectures; Collection travels to museums throughout the US 4 times a
year

M CATHOLIC HISTORICAL SOCIETY OF SAINT PAUL, 2260 Summit Ave,
55105. Tel 612-690-4355. *Dir* Leo J Tibesar
No admis fee. Estab 1905 to collect and preserve materials of historic interest
relating to the Catholic history of the ecclesiastical province of Saint Paul. Open
by appointment only
Income: Financed by endowment
Collections: Architectural drawings; ecclesiastical memorabilia; liturgical
vestments

M HAMLINE UNIVERSITY LEARNING CENTER GALLERY, 55104. Tel 612-
641-2296. *Cur Permanent Collection* Roslye B Ultan; *Exhib Dir* James Conaway
Open Mon - Fri 8 AM - 8 PM. Estab 1943 to display outstanding works of art in
all media for instruction of and appreciation by the public and students. Average
Annual Attendance: 7000 - 10,000
Income: Financed by the University
Collections: Contemporary paintings, prints, drawings and sculpture
Exhibitions: (1983-84) Gabriele Ellertson Drawings; Barbara Gluck Photography;
Friends of Hamline Auction; National Invitational Watercolor Show; New
Acquisitions to Hamline University Permanent Art Collection; Barbara Fumagalli
Prints; Hamline University faculty show; student exhibition
Publications: Exhibition catalog
Activities: Classes for adults; lectures open to the public, 6 vis lectr per year;
gallery talks; individual paintings and original objects of art lent to faculty and
staff; originate traveling exhibitions to galleries, historical societies and colleges
L Library, 55104
Rental Library of original modern works and reproductions; extensive color slide
library of paintings, architecture, sculpture, minor arts and graphics

M MACALESTER COLLEGE GALLERIES, 1600 Grand Ave, 55105. Tel 612-
696-6416. *Cur* Cherie Doyle
Open Mon - Fri 10 AM - 9 PM, cl June - Aug, national holidays & school
vacations. No admis fee. Estab 1964 as a college facility to bring contemporary
art exhibitions to the students, faculty and community. Average Annual
Attendance: 10,000 - 18,000
Collections: Jerome Collection; Collection of Henry Wolf Prints; Davis
Collection of African Art; †Oriental Art; contemporary & historical crafts, fine
art, design
Exhibitions: Temporary, traveling and student exhibitions
Activities: Lectures open to the public; concerts; gallery talks; tours; competitions
with awards; individual paintings and original objects of art lent; lending
collection contains original prints, paintings & sculpture; book traveling
exhibitions; traveling exhibitions organized and circulated; sales shop selling art
books and supplies
L Weyerhaeuser Library, 1600 Grand Ave, 55105. Tel 612-696-6345. *Dir* Jean K
Archibald
Circ 66,531
Library Holdings: Vols 291,720; Per subs 850; Micro — Cards, fiche, reels;
AV — Cassettes; Other — Framed reproductions, pamphlets
Special Subjects: Art History
Exhibitions: individual paintings and original objects of art lent to students,
faculty and staff of the college

O MINNESOTA HISTORICAL SOCIETY,* 690 Cedar St, 55101. Tel 612-296-
2747. *Pres* Paul L Parker; *Dir* Russell W Fridley; *Assoc Dir* Robert C Wheeler;
Deputy Dir John J Wood; *Asst Dir* June Holmquist; *Asst to Dir for Libraries
and Museum Coll* Lila J Goff
Estab 1849 to collect, preserve and make available to the public the history of
Minnesota. Mem: 6000
Income: Financed by endowment, membership and state appropriation
Collections: Archives; †art works; †books; †maps; †manuscripts; †museum
artifacts relating to the history of Minnesota; newspapers; †photographs
Exhibitions: The Clothes Off Our Backs
Publications: Minnesota History, quarterly; Minnesota History News, 6 issues
per year
Activities: Classes for adults; lect open to the public; tours; sales shop selling
books, magazines, prints, reproductions
L Library,* 690 Cedar St, 55101. *Chief Reference Librn* Patricia Harpole
Open to the public for general reference; library contains only a few works
relating to art
Library Holdings: Vols 500,000
Collections: Seth Eastman (watercolors); maps; Minnesota photographs; Edwin
Whitefield (watercolors)

M MINNESOTA MUSEUM OF ART, St Peter at Kellogg Blvd, 55102. Tel 612-
224-7431. *Chmn Board Trustees* Richard C Magnuson; *Dir* M J Czarniecki III;
Asst Dir Auxillary Activities Gloria Kittleson; *Asst Dir Support Services* Open;
Deputy Dir Planning & Development Joanna Baymiller; *Cur Education* Ben
Braverman; *Asst Cur Education* Nell McClure; *Asst Cur Education* Marcie
Soderman-Olson; *Supvr Information* Patricia S Heikenen; *Cur Collections*
Thomas S Holman; *Asst Cur Register* Katherin Van Tassell; *Cur Exhibitions*
James D Ristine; *Membership Specialist* Susan Fitzgerald; *Supvr Plant & Security*
Terry Hildebrand; *Supvr Personnel* Jean Hunter
Open Tues - Sat 10 AM - 5 PM, Sun 1 - 5 PM. Admis by donation. Estab 1927.
The museum is housed in a beautiful four-story Art Deco building built in 1931
by architect Magnus Jemne, his wife did inlays of brass in foyer floors; designer
Frank Post did curving brass stair rail and lighting fixtures; the first floor
auditorium has gold leaf on the walls, and the upstairs dining room sits amid art
works. Special Exhibition Galleries, Museum School, Kidspace, Museum Store

and administrative and education offices in late 19th century former Federal
Courts Bldg renamed Landmark Center. Average Annual Attendance: 160,000.
Mem: 1500; dues household $30, individual $20; annual meeting Sept
Income: $940,000 (financed by endowment, individual contributions,
membership, allocation from United Arts Fund and foundation and governmental
grants)
Collections: American Art 1900-1940; Asian sculpture & ceramics; Paul
Manship; contemporary art of the Upper Midwest; 19th & 20th century
American; Asian, Oceanic, African art
Exhibitions: Artists and Writers; Melanesian Images; The Painter and
Printer: Robert Motherwell's Graphics; Design for Urban Living: Germany in the
1920's; The Art Fabric: Mainstream; American Style: Early Modernist Works in
Minnesota Collections; Eduard Munch; Prarie School Architecture;
Scandanavian Modern; Benton's Bentons; Stieglitz & O'Keefe; Stuart Davis; The
Preston Morton Collection of American Art
Publications: Exhibition catalogues; Newsletter, bi-monthly
Activities: Classes for adults and children; docent training; lectures open to
public, 10 visiting lectr per year; gallery talks; tours; competitions; art works are
lent to businesses and professional offices in the community for a specified fee;
originates traveling exhibitions
L Library, St Peter at Kellogg Blvd, 55102. Tel 612-292-4350. *Librn* Leanne Klein
Open to members, students and staff for reference only
Library Holdings: Vols 1500; Per subs 10; Documented Museums Collection
Special Subjects: Asian Art, American Art of the 20th century
Collections: Art of Korea
M Landmark Center,* 75 W Fifth St, 55102. Tel 612-292-4355
Open Tues - Sat 10 AM - 5 PM, Sun 1 - 5 PM. No admis fee
Income: Financed by Minnesota Museum of Art
Exhibitions: Changing exhibition of wide community interest

L SAINT PAUL PUBLIC LIBRARY, Art & Music Dept, 90 W Fourth St, 55102.
Tel 612-292-6186. *Dir Library* Gerald W Steenberg; *Supv Art & Music Dept*
Delores A Sundbye
Open Mon & Thurs 9 AM - 9 PM, Tues, Wed, Fri & Sat 9 AM - 5:30 PM. Estab
1857. Circ 92,642
Income: Financed by city appropriation
Purchases: $30,000
Library Holdings: Vols 16,000; Per subs 50; AV — Cassettes, rec; Other —
Clipping files, exhibition catalogs, framed reproductions, sculpture

M SCHOOL OF THE ASSOCIATED ARTS GALLERIES,* 344 Summit Ave,
55102. Tel 612-224-3416. *Dir* Virginia Rahja
Open Mon - Fri 9 AM - 4 PM. No admis fee. Estab 1948; galleries were
established in adjunct to art education. Average Annual Attendance: 400-500
Income: Financed by endowment
Exhibitions: Ten shows per year of the work of local artists, faculty, students,
traveling shows, and work from our own collection. The emphasis is on Modern
Art
L Library,* 344 Summit Ave, 55102
Estab 1948 to have reference material for our own students. Not open to public.
Maintains an art gallery
Library Holdings: Vols 7500; Per subs 5; AV — Slides; Other — Original art
works, pamphlets, photographs, reproductions

M UNIVERSITY OF MINNESOTA, Paul Whitney Larson Gallery, 2017 Buford,
55108. Tel 612-373-1046 or 373-1051. *Dir* Charles Rausch; *Asst Dir* Timothy L
McCarty; *Gallery Cur* Esther Neely
Open Mon, Tues, Thurs & Fri 9 AM - 6 PM, Wed 9 AM - 8 PM, Sun 1 - 5 PM,
cl Sat. No admis fee. Estab 1979 to bring art of great variety into the daily lives
of students & university community
Income: Financed by student fee
Publications: Annual Report and Activity Summary
Activities: Mini-courses in crafts; opening receptions; lectures open to public, arts
& crafts sales
M Goldstein Gallery,* 241 McNeal Hall, 55108. Tel 612-373-2851. *Dir* Dr Mary
Stieglitz; *Costume Cur* Suman Shenoi; *Cur Decorative Arts* Dr Timothy T Blade
Estab 1976
Collections: Historic costumes; 20th century designer garments; historic &
contemporary decorative arts; furniture; glass; metal ceramics; historic flat
textiles
Activities: Tours; gallery talks

WORTHINGTON

O NOBLES COUNTY ART CENTER GALLERY,* 318 Ninth St, PO Box 281,
56187. Tel 507-372-7711. *Pres* Mrs Howard Dixon; *Cur and Secy* Genevieve
Peterson
Open Mon - Sat 2 - 4:30 PM, Mon - Fri in summer. No admis fee. Estab 1961 to
nourish the arts and to bring the arts and cultures of other communities, nations
and civilizations to Nobles County and the surrounding area, so that its residents
may become more universal in their thinking. Room on lower level of building
housing county library and information center; 25 x 51 ft. Average Annual
Attendance: 1000. Mem: 150; dues family $5; annual meeting January
Income: Financed by county appropriation
Exhibitions: Art in the Park; the work of area artists
Publications: Monthly newsletter
Activities: Classes for adults; gallery talks; competitions; original art work for sale
during exhibitions

MISSISSIPPI

BILOXI

O BILOXI ART ASSOCIATION, Gallery, 137 Rue Magnolia, PO Box 667, 39530. Tel 601-435-3521. *Gallery Dir* Ellen Morrison O'Brian; *Asn Pres* Vera Lee; *Asn VPres* Melanie Platt; *Asn Recording Secy* Ruth Schleiniger; *Asn Corresp Secy* Bobbie Slade; *Asn Treas* Mary Kate Platts
Open Tues - Sat 11 AM - 4:30 PM. No admis fee. Estab to upgrade the level of art, art education and participation in the creative process. Maintains small reference library. Average Annual Attendance: 150. Mem: 150; dues $5
Income: $750 (financed by membership)
Collections: Works by local artists
Exhibitions: Annual art exhibit
Publications: Biloxi Art Asn newsletter & Gallery Newsletter, every other month
Activities: Educ dept; workshops; lectures open to public; 3 vis lectr per yr; competitions with awards; original objects of art lent; lending collection contains original prints & paintings; sales shop sells fine art, original art, reproductions & prints

CLEVELAND

M DELTA STATE UNIVERSITY, Fielding L Wright Art Center, Box D-2, 38733. Tel 601-843-2151. *Chmn Dept* Malcolm M Norwood; *Exhib Chmn* Terry K Simmons; *Chmn Art Education* Carolyn Stone, PhD
Open Mon - Fri 8 AM - 5 PM, Sun 3 - 5 PM on opening shows, cl school holidays. No admis fee. Estab 1968 as an education gallery for the benefit of the students, but serves the entire area for changing art shows; it is the only facility of this nature in the Mississippi Delta Region. Three gallery areas. Average Annual Attendance: 2500-3000
Income: Financed by state appropriation
Collections: Delta State University permanent collection; Ruth Atkinson Holmes Collection; Marie Hull Collection; Smith-Patterson Memorial Collection; Whittington Memorial Collection
Exhibitions: (1982-83) Southern Works on Paper; Pat Brown, fibers; Win Bruhl, serigraphs; Masterworks from The National Palace Museum, Taiwan; Hugh Williams - Shirts, A Drawing Show; DSU Art Student Show; 1983 Collage; DSU Former Student Show; DSU Art Faculty Show
Publications: Announcements of exhibitions, monthly during fall, winter and spring
Activities: Classes for adults & children; lect open to public, 10 vis lectr per yr; gallery talks; tours; competitions; exten department serving the Mississippi Delta Region; individual paintings and original objects of art lent to offices of campus; lending collection contains color reproductions, film strips, motion pictures, original art works, 6000 slides; traveling exhibitions organized and circulated
L Library, Box D-2, 38733
Reference only
Library Holdings: Vols 17,858; Per subs 52; Micro — Cards, fiche, prints, reels; AV — A-tapes, cassettes, fs, Kodachromes, motion pictures, rec, slides, v-tapes; Other — Clipping files, exhibition catalogs, framed reproductions, original art works, photographs, prints

COLUMBUS

M COLUMBUS AND LOWNDES COUNTY HISTORICAL SOCIETY MUSEUM, 316 Seventh St N, 39701. Tel 601-328-5437. *Pres* Jeff Artz; *VPres* Harvley Brown; *Secy* Josie Shumoke; *Cur* Grace Balch; *Dir* Mrs George S Hazard
Open Tues & Thurs 1 - 4 PM. No admis fee. Estab 1960 for a memorabilia 1832-1907 pertaining to Lowndes County preserved & exhibited. Average Annual Attendance: 2000. Mem: 210; dues $3; annual meeting third Thurs in Nov
Income: $600 (financed by membership, bequests, donations, memorials, sale of souvenirs)
Collections: 100 years of artifacts, books, †china, †crystal, clothes, flags, †furniture, †jewelry, pictures, portraits, swords, wedding gowns
Activities: Docent training; tours for school children; awards; museum shop sells books and souvenirs

M MISSISSIPPI UNIVERSITY FOR WOMEN, Art Gallery and Museum, Fine Arts Bldg, 39701. Tel 601-329-4750. *Dir of Gallery, Cur of Museum & Permanent Coll* Eugenia Summer
Open Mon - Fri 8 AM - 5 PM. No admis fee. Estab 1948. Average Annual Attendance: 600
Income: Financed by state appropriation
Collections: †American Art; †paintings, sculpture, photographs, drawings, ceramics, prints; †Permanent collection of Mississippi artists
Exhibitions: Frequent special and circulating exhibitions; Selections from permanent collection, periodically
Activities: Visiting artists program; visiting foreign artists; workshops; lectures open to public, 4 vis lect per year; gallery talks; tours; scholarships; individual paintings & original objects of art lent to offices & public student areas on the campus; lending collection contains 400 original prints, 300 paintings, 100 records; book traveling exhibitions; originate traveling exhibitions

HATTIESBURG

M TURNER HOUSE MUSEUM,* 500 Bay, 39401. *Cur* J H Turner Jr
Open by appointment. No admis fee. Estab 1970
Collections: 18th century furniture; silver; crystal chandelier; Persian rugs; old masters; tapestries
Activities: Tours

JACKSON

L MISSISSIPPI DEPARTMENT OF ARCHIVES AND HISTORY, State Historical Museum, 100 State St, PO Box 571, 39205. Tel 601-354-6218, 354-6222. *Pres Board Trustees* William F Winter; *Dir State Historical Museum* Patti Carr Black; *Dir Archives & Library* Madel Morgan; *Dir Historic Preservation* Robert J Bailey; *Dir Public Information* Christine Wilson; *Dir Special Projects* Dr Patricia Galloway
Open Mon - Fri 8 AM - 5 PM, Sat 9:30 AM - 4:30 PM, Sun 12:30 PM - 4:30. Estab 1902 for the care and custody of official archives; to collect material relating to the history of the State from the earliest times and to impart a knowledge of the history and resources of the State. Maintains the State Historical Museum. Maintains a portrait gallery of distinguished Mississippians and holds monthly exhibitions, folk song and folk crafts programs. Average Annual Attendance: 90,000
Income: Financed by state appropriation
Library Holdings: Vols 33,000; Per subs 250; original documents; Micro — Fiche, reels; AV — A-tapes, cassettes, fs, motion pictures, rec, slides, v-tapes; Other — Clipping files, exhibition catalogs, manuscripts, pamphlets, photographs, prints
Special Subjects: Archaeology, Civil War, genealogy, Mississippiana
Collections: Maps; photographs; newspapers; all pertaining to Mississippi
Publications: Journal of Mississippi History, quarterly; Mississippi Newsletter, monthly
Activities: Folk crafts programs; lectures; concerts; gallery talks; tours; book traveling exhibitions, 4-5 per year; originate and circulate traveling exhibitions; sales shop sells books, original art, reproductions, prints, slides and folk crafts

M MISSISSIPPI MUSEUM OF ART, Pascagoula at Lamar Sts, PO Box 1330, 39205. Tel 601-960-1515. *Dir Coll & Exhibitions* John B Henry III; *Coll & Registrar* Elise Brevard
Open Tues - Thurs, Sat 10 AM - 4 PM, Fri 10 AM - 8 PM, Sun Noon - 4 PM. Admis adult $1, students, senior citizens, handicapped $.25. Chartered in 1911. Museum opened April 22, 1978; East Exhibition Galleries, 6400 sq ft; West Exhibition Galleries, 2600 sq ft; Graphics Study Center, 800 sq ft, houses exhibition area, study and seminar rooms; Open Gallery, 2000 sq ft, includes special power, lighting and water requirements for technological media; Upper and Lower Atrium Galleries and outdoor Sculpture Garden; Non-Profit Corporation. Mem: 3400; dues student $5, individual $15, artist $20, family $25, patron $100, donor $250, benefactor $500, grand benefactor $1000
Income: $550,000 (financed by endowment, membership, contributions, public sector grants & appropriations, earned income)
Collections: 19th & 20th Century American; Smaller non-western art collection, oceanic, Eskimo, Native American, Asian, African; Southern Photographers; Western art history sample collection
Exhibitions: To Live Upon Canvas, the Portrait Art of Thomas Cantwell Healy (1820-1889); Dance Image: A Tribute to Serge Diaghiley; Southern Realism; Dimensionions & Directions: Black Artists of the South; Collage & Assemblage; Russian Stage Designs
Publications: Newsletter, bi-monthly; selected exhibition catalogs
Activities: Classes for adults and children; docent training; lect open to public, some for members only, 6 vis lectr per yr, 10 vis artists per yr; tours; competitions; scholarships offered; Art Cart; travel lecture program; original objects of art lent to accredited museums; book traveling exhibitions 4-6 per yr; originate traveling exhibitions; museum shop sells books, magazines, reporductions, prints, slides, paper goods, designer items, Mississippi crafts
L Media Center Library,* Pascagoula at Lamar Sts, 39205. *Media Center Supv* Margaret Tucker
For reference only, open to the general public
Library Holdings: Vols 3000; Per subs 28; AV — Kodachromes, motion pictures, slides, v-tapes; Other — Clipping files, exhibition catalogs
Collections: Walter Anderson Collection on Slides; Marie Hull Collection of Art Reference Books; Metropolitan Miniature Album; Museums permanent collection

M MISSISSIPPI STATE HISTORICAL MUSEUM, 100 South State St, PO Box 571, 39201. Tel 601-354-6222. *Pres* William Winter; *Dir* Patti Carr-Black; *Cur Exhibits* Cavett Taff; *Cur Collections* Mary Jordan; *Programs Coordr* Ann Morrison
Open Mon - Fri 8 AM - 5 PM, Sat 9:30 AM - 4:30 PM, Sun 12:30 - 4:30 PM. No admis fee. Estab 1902 to exhibit portraits of renown Mississippians and to have temporary exhibitions. Oil portraits hung throughout the 3-story Greek Revival former capitol; two rooms set aside for temporary exhibits. Average Annual Attendance: 80,000
Income: $500,000
Collections: 98 oil portraits
Activities: Talks for children and adult groups; docent training; lectures; concerts; book traveling exhibitions, 4-6 per year; originate traveling exhibitions; sales shop sells books, original art, prints, and Mississippi Craftsmen's Guild items

LAUREL

M LAUREN ROGERS LIBRARY AND MUSEUM OF ART,* Fifth Avenue & Seventh St, PO Box 1108, 39440. Tel 601-428-4875. *Dir Admin* Betty Mulloy; *Cur & Registrar* Amorita Gordon
Open Tues - Sat 10 AM - Noon, 1 - 5 PM, Sun 2 - 5 PM, cl Mon. No Admis fee. Estab 1923 as a reference and research library and museum of art for public use and employment. Five smaller galleries open off large American Gallery; these include European room, Contemporary room, Gardiner Basket collection, Western and Indian room, and temporary exhibit gallery. Average Annual Attendance: 7000. Mem: Dues $10 - $100
Income: Financed by endowment (Eastman Memorial Foundation)
Collections: European Artists of the 19th Century; Georgian Silver; Indian Basketry; 19th and 20th Century American artists
Exhibitions: Annual schedule of monthly exhibitions by regional and nationally recognized artists
Publications: Gibbons Silver Catalog; Exhibition announcements
Activities: Classes for adults and children; docent training; lect open to the public, 2 - 3 vis lectr per yr; concerts; competitions; individual paintings lent to AAM Accredited museums or galleries

L **Library,*** 39440. Tel 601-428-4875
   For reference only
   Library Holdings: Vols 14,000; Per subs 74; Micro — Fiche, reels; AV —
   Cassettes, Kodachromes, slides; Other — Clipping files, exhibition catalogs,
   framed reproductions, memorabilia, original art works, pamphlets, photographs,
   reproductions, sculpture
   Special Subjects: Art, genealogy, Mississipiana, Laurel history
   Collections: Edward S Curtis books and photogravure portfolios on American
   Indian

MERIDIAN

M **MERIDIAN MUSEUM OF ART,*** Seventh St at Twenty fifth Ave, PO Box
   5773, 39301. Tel 601-693-1501. *Pres* Bob Merson; *Dir* Dan W Griffin; *Secy*
   Janet Tinnin
   Open Tues 10 AM - Noon & 1 - 5 PM, Wed - Sun 1 - 5 PM, cl July. No admis
   fee. Estab in 1969 to give cultural enrichment and educational benefits to the
   people of eastern Mississippi, western Alabama and the South. Five galleries.
   Average Annual Attendance: 6500. Mem: 350; dues $2 - $1000; annual
   membership meeting second week of Dec
   Income: Financed by membership and appropriation
   Collections: Ink drawings; lithographs; paintings (oil, acrylic and water color);
   photographs; pottery; sculpture
   Activities: Classes for adults, teens, children; workshops; lectures and special
   exhibitions; museum receptions; gallery talks; tours; competitions; Museum Guild
   for Education gift shop
L **Library,*** Seventh St at Twenty fifth Ave, 39301
   For reference only
   Library Holdings: Vols 220

O **MISSISSIPPI ART COLONY,** c/o Alex M Loeb, 2741 38th St, 39301. Tel
   601-482-2827. *Dir* Bess Dawson; *Pres* Alex M Loeb; *VPres* R B Jacoby; *Secy &
   Treas* Jean R Loeb
   Estab 1945 to hold workshops at least twice yearly, for painting instruction and
   occasionally other areas; to organize juried show, with prizes awarded, which
   travels state of Mississippi between workshops. Mem: 40; dues $12; annual
   meeting in Oct
   Income: Financed by membership
   Exhibitions: Two travel exhibitions each year
   Publications: Bulletin, newsletter
   Activities: Traveling exhibitions organized and circulated

OXFORD

M **UNIVERSITY OF MISSISSIPPI,** University Museums, University Ave and
   Fifth St, 38677. Tel 601-232-7073. *Actg Dir & Cur of Classics* Lucy Turnbull;
   Collections Mgr Jill Thomas-Clark; *Cur Millington-Barnard Coll* A B Lewis
   Open Tues - Sat 10 AM - 4 PM, Sun 1 - 4 PM, cl Mon. No admis fee. Estab
   1977 to collect, conserve and exhibit objects related to history of the University
   of Mississippi and to the cultural and scientific heritage of the people of the state
   and region. Main gallery contains 3000 sq ft with 12 ft ceilings for permanent
   collections and 800 sq ft with 18 ft ceilings for temporary exhibits; meeting room
   has 1100 sq ft for temporary wall hung exhibits; each of the four galleries of the
   Mary Buie Museum contains 400 sq ft for permanent collection. Mem: 125; dues
   student $10, individual $15, family $25, contributing $50, organizational $50,
   patron $100 up
   Income: $100,000 (financed by membership and state appropriation)
   Collections: Theora Hamblett Collection (paintings, glass, drawings); Lewisohn
   Collection of Caribbean Art; Fulton-Meyer Collection of African Art; Millington-
   Barnard Collection of 18th and 19th Century Scientific Instruments; David
   Robinson Collection of Greek and Roman antiquities; antique dolls; Victorian
   memorabilia and American decorative arts
   Exhibitions: (1982) Southern Works on Paper; Graphic Studio; Metalsmiths;
   Photojournalism of the 1960's by D Gorton; Image of the Black in Western Art;
   Appalachian Crafts; Children's Discovery Exhibit; Comparisons and Contrasts:
   American vs Russia; Michael Rogers One-Man Exhibit; Women's Centennial at
   Ole Miss; (1983) More Than Land or Sky: Art from Appalachia; Paintings by
   Clementine Hunter; Children's Discovery Exhibit; Sculpture by Tom Douglas;
   Yoknapatawpha Through Other Eyes; Pottery of George E Ohr; Dreams and
   Visions of Theora Hamblett; Mississippi: The Thirties; Selections from the Hal L
   and Mae Ballew Collection; Selections from the Lewisohn Collection; An Oxford
   Christmas Album
   Publications: Newsletter, quarterly
   Activities: Classes for children; docent training; gallery talks and tours; school
   outreach program
L **Library,** University Ave and Fifth St, 38677
   Open to members, students, researchers for reference
   Library Holdings: Vols 600; Per subs 7
   Special Subjects: Graphic Arts, Art History, Victorian Decorative Arts,
   American Art, Philosophy of Art

PASCAGOULA

O **SINGING RIVER ART ASSOCIATION INC,** L & N Railroad Depot Gallery,
   PO Box 262, 39567. *Pres* Guy Harris; *VPres* Sara Kirkland; *Secy* Gin Bemrends
   Open Tues - Fri 10 AM - 4 PM, Sat 10 AM - 1 PM. No admis fee. Estab 1964
   to promote and encourage interest in art and exhibition art works. Gallery
   exhibits members works in an old railroad station restored as Bicentennial project
   1976. Average Annual Attendance: 2000 - 3000. Mem: 250; dues $5 and up, $12
   and contributions; monthly meetings second Thurs
   Income: $1100 (financed by membership and commissions on sales)
   Collections: Paintings by local prominent artists, some purchase prize winners,
   some by memorial loan; some donations by artists
   Exhibitions: Exhibitions on a six week rotating basis; (1981-83) Mall Art Show
   Publications: Members newsletter, monthly

Activities: Classes for adults; educational workshops; competitions with awards;
scholarships; lending collection contains cassettes, film strips, 200 lantern slides,
original art work, original prints, paintings, phonorecords, slides; book traveling
exhibitions; sales shop sells original art
L **Library,** PO Box 262, 39567
   Open to members only for reference
   Library Holdings: Vols 100; Other — Clipping files, original art works

RAYMOND

M **HINDS JUNIOR COLLEGE DISTRICT,** Marie Hull Gallery, 39154. Tel 601-
   857-3275. *Dir* Gayle McCarty
   Open Mon - Thurs 8 AM - 3 PM, Fri 8 AM - Noon. No admis fee. Estab 1971
   as a community service and cultural agent for the visual arts. Main gallery
   measures 60 x 60 ft; an adjacent gallery 8 x 45 ft; reception area 15 x 25 ft.
   Average Annual Attendance: 2500
   Income: $2900 (financed by Art Department budget)
   Collections: †Permanent collection of state artist, with 150 pieces in prints,
   sculptures and paintings
   Exhibitions: Sponsors 7 exhibits during college session
   Activities: Lect open to the public; gallery talks; tours; competitions; individual
   paintings and original objects of art lent to faculty and staff offices on three
   campuses; lending collection contains original art works

TOUGALOO

TOUGALOO COLLEGE
M **Art Collection,*** 39174. Tel 601-956-4941, Ext 327. *Pres* Dr George A Owens;
   Academic Dean Dr Van S Allen; *Photographer* Bruce O'Hara; *Cur* Hermona
   Dayal
   Open Wed 2 - 5 PM, Sun 1 - 4 PM, and by appointment. No admis fee. Estab
   1963 to service the community and the metropolitan Jackson area. Located in
   Student Union Building and Library. Average Annual Attendance: 1000
   Income: Financed by endowment and department budget
   Collections: †Afro-American; African; International Print Collection with
   emphasis on European art; New York School (abstract, expressionism, minimal
   art, surrealism)
   Exhibitions: African Collection; Afro-American Collection; AMISTAD II
   (originated at Fisk University, Nashville); Works in Metal; German
   Expressionists; faculty and student shows, local artists
   Publications: Mississippi Museum of Art, African Tribal Art; Calder-Hayter-
   Miro; G M Designs of the 1960's; Hans Hofmann, Light Prints; catalog;
   newspaper of special events
   Activities: Dramatic programs; lect open to public, 2-3 visiting lecturers per year;
   concerts; gallery talks; tours by appointment; scholarships; exten dept; individual
   paintings and original objects of art lent to libraries, universities and museums;
   lending collection contains 8000 lantern slides, 700 original art works, 350
   original prints, 140 paintings, 150 sculpture, industrial designs and typography;
   originate traveling exhibitions
L **Coleman Library,** 39174. Tel 601-951-4941, Ext 271. *Librn* Jeannetta C Roach
   Open by appointment. No admis fee. Estab 1963. Open to students and faculty
   Library Holdings: Vols 5000; Per subs 14
   Special Subjects: Afro-American Art
   Collections: Tracy Sugerman (wash drawings, civil rights studies 1964); African
   masks & sculpture
   Publications: Tougaloo College Art Collections
   Activities: Lectures open to public, 2 vis lectr per yr; gallery talks; tours

TUPELO

C **BANK OF MISSISSIPPI,*** 1 Mississippi Plaza, Spring & Troy, PO Drawer
   789, 38801. Tel 601-842-6661. *Pres* J W Collins
   Open 9 AM - 4:30 PM. Estab to encourage local artists and provide cultural
   enrichment for customers and friends
   Purchases: $500
   Collections: Oils, prints, watercolors
   Activities: Grants available

L **LEE COUNTY LIBRARY,** 219 Madison, 38801. Tel 601-844-2377. *Chmn
   Board of Trustees* Peggy Webb; *Dir* Betty R Kemp; *Technical Services Librn*
   Barbara Anglin; *Children's Librn* Ann Ballard
   Open Mon - Thurs 9 AM - 8PM, Fri & Sat 9 AM - 5 PM, cl Sun. Estab 1941 to
   provide books and other sources of information to serve the intellectual,
   recreational and cultural needs of its users. Maintains art gallery; The Mezzanine
   Gallery and Helen Foster Auditorium are used as exhibit space for works by
   University Art students, local professional artists and traveling exhibitions
   Income: $398,000 (financed by city, state and county appropriations)
   Library Holdings: AV — Cassettes, motion pictures, rec; Other — Framed
   reproductions
   Collections: The Tupelo Gum Tree Festival purchase prizes, these include
   paintings and pottery
   Publications: Bi-monthly newsletter
   Activities: Book traveling exhibitions

UNIVERSITY

M **UNIVERSITY OF MISSISSIPPI,** University Gallery, Fine Arts Center,
   38677. Tel 601-232-7193. *Dir* Margaret Gorove
   Open daily 8:30 AM - 4:30 PM. No admis fee. Estab 1954 as a teaching gallery.
   Average Annual Attendance: 1000
   Income: Financed by state appropriation and tuition
   Collections: Faculty and student work; some work bought from traveling
   exhibitions
   Exhibitions: Herbert Fink; Peter Thompson; faculty, students and junior colleges

Publications: Gallery Schedule, yearly
Activities: Lect open to public, 1-2 visiting lectrs per year; gallery talks; individual paintings and original objects of art lent to departments within the University Complex; lending collection contains original art works, original prints, paintings and sculpture

MISSOURI

ARROW ROCK

M **ARROW ROCK STATE HISTORIC SITE,** PO Box 1, 65320. Tel 816-837-3392. *Administrator* Richard R Forry, PhD
Open Memorial Day - Labor Day 10 AM - 4:30 PM, and by appointment. Admis $2. Estab 1923 to preserve, exhibit and interpret the cultural resources of Missouri, especially those associated with George Caleb Bingham and his era in central Missouri. The 1837 home of G C Bingham serves as a museum house and the 1834 Tavern has exhibitions space for the Bingham Collection. Average Annual Attendance: 80,000
Income: Financed by state appropriation
Collections: Bingham Collection; Central Missouri Collection (textiles, furnishing and glass of the 19th century)
Exhibitions: Annual Art Fair; Annual Summer Workshop Exhibit; Annual Craft Festival
Activities: Docent training; tours

CAPE GIRARDEAU

L **SOUTHEAST MISSOURI STATE UNIVERSITY,** Kent Library, 63701. Tel 314-651-2235. *Dir* James Zink
Open Mon - Thur 8 AM - 10:30 PM, Fri 8 AM - 6 PM, Sat 9 AM - 5 PM, Sun 1:30 - 10:30 PM. Exhibition areas on second and third levels; Atrium Gallery on fourth level. The Jake K Wells Mural, 800 sq ft covers the west wall of the library foyer, depicting the nature and the development of the southeast region of the state
Collections: Charles Harrison Collection (rare books including some of the finest examples of the book arts); books and manuscripts from the 13th to the 20th century
Exhibitions: Missouri Arts Council touring exhibits; exhibits by local artists
Activities: Tours

COLUMBIA

L **DANIEL BOONE REGIONAL LIBRARY,** Art Dept, 100 W Broadway, PO Box 1267, 65205. Tel 314-443-3161. *Dir* Gene Martin
Open Mon - Thurs 9 AM - 9 PM, Fri 9 AM - 6 PM, Sat 9 AM - 5 PM, Sun 1 - 5 PM. Estab 1959
Library Holdings: Micro — Reels; AV — Cassettes, fs, motion pictures, rec, slides; Other — Framed reproductions, original art works, pamphlets, photographs, sculpture
Exhibitions: Exhibits by local artists through the year

O **STATE HISTORICAL SOCIETY OF MISSOURI,** 1020 Lowry, 65201. Tel 314-882-7083. *Dir* Dr Richard S Brownlee; *Cur* Sidney Larson
Open Mon - Fri 8 AM - 4:30 PM. No admis fee. Estab 1898 to collect, preserve, make accessible and publish materials pertaining to the history of Missouri and Western America. Average Annual Attendance: 800. Mem: 11,500; dues $5; annual meeting held in the fall
Income: Financed by state appropriation
Collections: Works by Thomas H Benton, George C Bingham, Karl Bodmer, Fred Geary, Carl Gentry, William Knox, Roscoe Misselhorn, Frank B Nuderscher, Charles Schwartz, Fred Shane, Frederick Sylvester; contemporary artists collection containing work of over fifty outstanding Missouri related artists; original cartoon collection of works by Tom Engelhardt, Daniel Fitzpatrick, Don Hessee, Bill Mauldin, S J Ray and others
Publications: Missouri Historical Review, quarterly
L **Library,** Hitt and Lowry Sts, 65201. *Librn* Richard S Brownlee
Open to public
Library Holdings: Vols 420,000; Per subs 900
Special Subjects: Missouri and the midwest
Collections: J Christian Bay Collection; Eugene Field Collection; Mahan Memorial Mark Twain Collection; Bishop William Fletcher McMurray Collection; Francis A Sampson Collection of rare books

M **STEPHENS COLLEGE,** Lewis James & Nellie Stratton Davis Art Gallery,* 65201. Tel 314-442-2211, Ext 302. *Actg Dir* Ralph Komizes
Open Mon - Fri 8 AM - 4 PM, Sat - Sun 1 - 5 PM, cl school holidays, summer. No admis fee. Estab 1964 to provide exhibitions of art for the general interest of the local community and for the education of the student body in general. Average Annual Attendance: 5000
Income: Operating budget $2500 (financed by endowment)
Collections: †Modern paintings; †modern graphics; primitive sculpture
Exhibitions: Women Look At Women; Keith Crown Watercolors; Missouri Quilts; Lind Trauth Sculpture; Amy Panek Paintings; New Acquisitions; Stephens Historical Costume Collection
Activities: Lect open to the public, 6 vis lectr per yr; gallery talks; exhibitions

UNIVERSITY OF MISSOURI

M **Museum of Art and Archaeology,** 1 Pickard Hall, 65211. Tel 314-882-3591.
Interim Dir Ruth E Witt; *Cur Renaissance & Modern Art* Richard Baumann; *Cur Ancient Art* Jane C Biers; *Coordr Education & Registrar* David Butler; *Assoc Cur Exhib* Jeffrey Wilcox; *Assoc Cur & Graphics Designer* John Huffstot

Open Tues - Sun 12 - 5 PM, cl Mon and Holidays. No admis fee. Estab 1957 to exhibit a study collection for students in Art History and Archaeology; a comprehensive collection for the enjoyment of the general area of Missouri. Nine separate galleries, each devoted to specific collections. Average Annual Attendance: 25,000. Mem: 800; dues family $25
Income: $250,000 (financed by membership, and state appropriation)
Purchases: $35,000
Collections: †Ancient Art—Egypt, Near and Middle East, Greek and Roman; †Old Masters, painting and sculpture; †Early Christian—Byzantine and Coptic; †Modern painting and sculpture; †Prints and drawings; Primitive—Oceanic, African, Pre-Columbian; Oriental—Chinese and Japanese; South Asian—Indian, Thai, Tibetan, Nepalese
Exhibitions: Changing exhibitions from permanent collections, mainly in the archaeological material of the Near East and in Prints and Drawings
Publications: Muse, annually; exhibition catalogues; Museletter, 5 per year
Activities: Classes for children; docent training; workshops on conservation; lect open to public, 6 - 8 vis lectr per yr; tours; gallery talks; scholarships offered; original objects of art lent to institutions; book traveling exhibitions 2 - 3 per year; museum shop sells books, prints, reproductions, prints and slides
L **Museum of Art and Archaeology Library,** 1 Pickard Hall, 65211. Tel 314-882-3591
Open to the public
Library Holdings: Vols 6000; Per subs 2; Sales catalogs of three major auction houses; bulletins; exhibitions catalogs and annual reports of other institutions; coin catalogs and journals in Near Eastern Archaeology
L **Art, Archaeology and Music Library,** 4D32 Ellis Library, Ninth & Lowry St, 65201. Tel 314-882-7634. *Librn* Open
Open 8 AM - 5 PM, Mon - Fri . Estab 1841 to house material for the faculty and students of the University
Income: Financed by state appropriation
Library Holdings: Vols 65,000; Per subs 300; AV — Rec; Other — Exhibition catalogs
Special Subjects: European prehistory, Near Eastern & Mediterranean art & archeology, Renaissance art history

FULTON

M **WILLIAM WOODS COLLEGE,** Art Gallery,* 65251. Tel 314-642-2251, Ext 367. *Dir* Paul Clervi
Open Mon - Fri 9 AM - 4:30 PM. No admis fee. Estab 1967 to be used as a teaching aid for the Art Center. Maintains 3200 sq ft sky-lighted gallery with a mezzanine
Income: Financed by endowment
Activities: Lect open to the public, 2 per year; gallery talks; scholarships

INDEPENDENCE

M **JACKSON COUNTY HISTORICAL SOCIETY,** 1859 Marshal's House, Jail & Museum, 217 N Main St, 64050. Tel 816-252-1892. *Exec Dir* Sarah F Schwenk
Open Tues - Sat 10 AM - 4 PM, Sun 1 - 5 PM Sept-May, Mon - Sat 9 AM - 5 PM, Sun 1 - 5 PM June - Aug. Admis adult $1.50, student $1, under 13 free, group rates available. Estab 1958 for interpretation of Jackson County history. 1859 Federal town house of county marshal, attached limestone jail which served as federal headquarters during the Civil War. Restored historical interior c 1860's. Restored cell of Frank James c 1882. Average Annual Attendance: 20,000. Mem: 2000; dues $15 - $500; annual meeting in Jan
Income: Financed by membership
Collections: Archival & artifact collection 1800-present
Exhibitions: Jackson County Goes to the Inaugurating
Publications: Jackson County Historical Society Journal
Activities: Classes for adults & children; docent training; lectures open to public & some for members only, 1-10 vis lect per yr; tours; original objects lent to educational & historical institutions; originate traveling exhibitions; museum shop sells books, reproductions & prints
L **Research Library and Archives,** Independence Square Courthouse, Room 103, 64050. Tel 816-252-7454. *Dir* Nancy Ehrlich
Open Mon - Thurs 10 AM - 3 PM. Estab 1960
Library Holdings: Vols 1000; Per subs 15; Micro — Reels; AV — A-tapes, Kodachromes, lantern slides, motion pictures, slides, v-tapes; Other — Clipping files, photographs
Special Subjects: Collection limited to the history of Jackson County
Collections: Photograph collection for reference
M **John Wornall House Museum,** 146 W 61 St Terrace, 64113. Tel 816-444-1858. *Dir* Janet Bruce; *Staff Asst* Genrose Welsh
Open Tues - Sat 10 AM - 4 PM, Sun 1 - 4 PM. Admis adults $1.50, children under 12 & senior citizens $1. Restored to interpret the daily lives of frontier farm families in the 1850s - 1960s in early Kansas City. House was used as field hospital during the Civil War. Built in 1858; opend to public in 1972. Average Annual Attendance: 10,000. Mem: 400; dues $15 - $25
Income: Financed by memberships, tours & fund raisings
Collections: Home furnishings of prosperous farm families
Exhibitions: Special exhibitions on subjects dealing with interpretation of home & Civil War period
Activities: Classes for adults & children; docent training; lectures open to public; tours; museum shop sells books, herbs, holiday & gift items

M **HARRY S TRUMAN LIBRARY AND MUSEUM,** 64050. Tel 816-833-1400. *Dir* Benedict K Zobrist; *Asst Dir* George H Curtis
Open 9 AM - 5 PM, cl Thanksgiving, Christmas & New Years. Admis $1. Estab 1957 to preserve and make available for study and exhibition the papers, objects and other materials relating to President Harry S Truman and to the history of the Truman administration. Gravesite of President Truman in the courtyard. Administered by the National Archives and Records Service of the Federal Government. Average Annual Attendance: 200,000
Income: Financed by federal appropriation and federal trust fund
Library Holdings: Vols 300; Per subs 10; Documents; Micro — Reels; AV — A-

tapes, motion pictures, rec, slides; Other — Clipping files, framed reproductions, manuscripts, memorabilia, original art works, pamphlets, photographs, prints, sculpture
Collections: Papers of Harry S Truman, his associates, and of officials in the Truman administration; Portraits of President Truman; paintings, prints, sculptures and artifacts presented to President Truman during the Presidential and Post—Presidential periods; original political cartoons; mural by Thomas Hart Benton
Exhibitions: Permanent and temporary exhibits relating to the life and times of Harry S Truman; the history of the Truman administration; the history and nature of office of the Presidency
Publications: Historical materials in the Truman Library
Activities: Educ dept; tours for school groups; sales shop sells books, reproductions, slides and postcards

JEFFERSON CITY

M **MISSOURI STATE MUSEUM,** State Capitol, 65101. Tel 314-751-2854. *Cur* Bill Fannin; *Site Adminr* Martin Shay; *Cur Special Programs* Beth Hunter; *Cur Coll* L T Shelton
Open daily 8 AM - 5 PM, cl holidays. No admis fee. Estab 1920. Average Annual Attendance: 250,000
Income: Financed by state appropriation, affiliated with Missouri Department of Natural Resources
Collections: Art murals by T H Benton, Berninghaus, Frank Brangwyn, N C Wyeth; historical material and natural specimens representing Missouri's natural and man-made resources; Indian artifacts
Exhibitions: Permanent and temporary exhibits
Publications: Pamphlets
Activities: Guided tours of Capitol; audio-visual presentations; book traveling exhibitions, 4-5 per year
M **Elizabeth Rozier Gallery,** Union Hotel, Jefferson City, 65101. Tel 314-751-4210
Open 10 AM - 4 PM. No admis fee. Estab 1981 to provide art, crafts & educational exhibits. Located in mid-nineteenth century building with a large & small gallery. Average Annual Attendance: 6000
Activities: Lectures open to public, 15 vis lectr per yr; concerts; gallery talks; tours; competitions with awards; book traveling exhibitions

JOPLIN

L **POST MEMORIAL ART REFERENCE LIBRARY,** 300 Main St, 64801. Tel 417-782-5419. *Dir* Leslie T Simpson
Open Mon & Thurs 10 AM - 9 PM, Tues, Wed & Fri 10 AM - 5 PM, Sat 10 AM - 4 PM. Estab 1981 to provide information on the fine and decorative arts to members of the community. Located in a wing of the Joplin Public Library. Average Annual Attendance: 6000
Library Holdings: Vols 2500; Per subs 25; Other — Clipping files, exhibition catalogs, pamphlets, reproductions
Special Subjects: Architecture, Art History, Decorative Arts, Furniture, Historical Material, Photography
Collections: 16th-17th Century Antiques & Artworks
Activities: Lectures open to public, 4-5 vis lectr per yr

O **SPIVA ART CENTER, INC,** Newman & Duquesne Rds, Missouri Southern State College Campus, 64801. Tel 417-623-0183. *Dir* V A Christensen; *Exec Secy* Sharon McGuire
Open Tues - Sat 10 AM - 4 PM, Sun 2 - 5 PM, cl Mon & national holidays. Estab June 1959, inc 1969, as a non-profit, cultural center with the purpose of increasing knowledge and appreciation of the visual arts in Joplin and surrounding area; to offer educational classes, workshops, and to exhibit works of educational and artistic value. Average Annual Attendance: 15,000. Mem: 650; dues $5 - $1000; annual meeting in Dec
Publications: Calendar; newsletter
Activities: Classes in various phases of the visual arts for adults and children; lect; gallery tours; competitions
L **Library,** Newman & Duquesne Rds, 64801
Art books for reference only

KANSAS CITY

O **ART RESEARCH CENTER,** * 922 E 48th St, 64110. Tel 816-531-5483, 931-2541. *Coordr* Michael Stephens; *Education Consultant* Virginia Hillix; *Photographer* John Baird; *Photographer* Kathryn Howard; *Technical Asst* Steve Collins; *Graphic Designer* Gerard Eisterhold
Open Sat & Sun 2 - 6 PM, other hours by appointment. No admis fee. Estab 1966 as an independent collective of artists, stressing multi-disciplinary activity and open experiment in the Constructive Arts. No gallery spaces. Average Annual Attendance: 3000 - 5000. Mem: 30; monthly meetings
Income: $30,000 (financed by grants, contributions, sales and subscriptions)
Exhibitions: Telic 81 International Exhibitions Series (more than 100 artists from 20 countries)
Publications: ARC Magazine, regularly; BioMechanic International Journals, annually
Activities: Seminars for adults; lect open to public, 2 visiting artists per year; concerts; gallery talks; films
L **New Circle Publications,** * 922 E 48th St, 64110. Tel 816-531-5483
Library open to memebers, artists, students and interested or subscribing public
Income: Financed by sales and subscriptions
Library Holdings: Vols 2000; Per subs 6
Special Subjects: Architecture, Art History, Photography, Art in politics, design, structuralist activity
Collections: Constructivist catalogs; films and video tapes (abstract) by contemporary film-makers; survey of historic and contemporary structural art, architecture, design in slides; also documentary films and video tapes
Exhibitions: Ken Gray, Participatory Saind Constructions; Cris Hawkins (drawings); Will Elton (paintings); International TELIC 81 Exhibition Series, 100 artists from 20 countries; 15th Anniversary Series, 30 artists 1963-1981
Publications: ARC Magazine; BioMechanic, international journal

M **ATKINS MUSEUM OF FINE ART,** 4525 Oak St, 64111. Tel 816-561-4000. *Dir & Cur Oriental Art* Marc F Wilson; *Asst Dir & Samuel Sosland Cur American Art* Jay Gates; *Dir Development* James Forbes; *Registrar* Martha S Stout; *Cur Decorative Arts & Assoc Cur European Decorative Arts* Jospeh Kuntz; *Assoc Cur Oriental Art* Jeanne Harris; *Asst Cur Southeast Asian & Indian Art* Dorothy H Fickle; *Cur Prints & Photography* George L McKenna; *Asst Cur European Painting & Sculpture* Dr Roger B Ward; *Sanders Sosland Cur 20th Century Art* Deborah R Emont-Scott; *Asst Cur Africa, Oceania & New World Cultures* Mary Jo Arnoldi; *Cur Exhibitions & Designs* Michael Hagler; *Consult Cur Medieval Art* Dr Marilyn Stokstad; *Res Cur Far Eastern Art* Chu-tsing Li; *Conservator* Forrest Bailey; *Assoc Conservator of Paper* Nancy Heugh; *Assoc Conservation* Anton Rajer
Open Tues - Sat 10 AM - 5 PM, Sun 1 - 5 PM, cl Mon. Admis adults $2, students & children under 18 free. Estab 1933 to enrich, enliven and present the arts of the ancient and modern world to the Midwest and the remainder of the US; develop activities relating to art education, the interpretation of the collections and their general enjoyment. Average Annual Attendance: 310,051. Mem: 7000; dues $35 - $250
Income: Financed by endowment, membership and gifts
Collections: †Burnap Collection of English pottery, Oriental ceramics, paintings, sculpture, bronze, Egyptian tomb sculpture, American painting, period rooms and furniture; Coloisters; †contemporary works of art; †Impressionist painting; the finest Oriental furniture collection outside of the Orient; sculpture garden
Exhibitions: Christo's Wrapped Walkways Documentation; Richard Estes Urban Landscape; Monet's Water Lilies Triptych; various loan shows and displays of permanent exhibitions
Publications: Eight Dynasties of Chinese Paintings; bulletin; handbook
Activities: Classes for adults and children; docent training; lect open to the public; concerts; gallery talks; tours; competitions; films; scholarships offered; individual paintings and original objects of art lent to other museums, city institutions requesting display; traveling exhibitions organized and circulated; museum sales shop sells books, magazines, reproductions, prints, slides; sales and rental gallery sells or rents original art; junior musuem
L **Kenneth and Helen Spencer Art Reference Library,** 4525 Oak St, 64111. Tel 816-561-4000, Ext 216. *Librn* Stanley W Hess; *Head Cataloger* Karen L Meizner; *Cataloger* Jane Cheng; *Slide Librn* Jan B McKenna
Open Tues - Fri. For reference only
Library Holdings: Vols 35,000; Per subs 425; Auction catalogues, international auction records; Micro — Fiche; AV — Rec, slides; Other — Clipping files, exhibition catalogs, pamphlets, photographs
Special Subjects: Oriental Art, Graphic Arts
Collections: Bender Library is comprised of books on prints and drawings; Oriental study collection of materials on Oriental art
O **Friends of Art,** * 4525 Oak St, 64111. *Pres* Open; *VPres* Open; *Secy* Open; *Executive Secy* Judith M Drake
Open Tues - Sat 10 AM - 5 PM, Sun 2 - 6 PM. Admis adults $1.50, children $.75, under 6 free. Estab 1934 as a non-profit organization supporting the Nelson Gallery and serving as a membership department. Mem: 6500; dues $15-$35; annual meeting Nov
Income: Financed by membership and contributions
Publications: Membership communication
Activities: Classes for adults and children; docent training; lectures open to public; gallery talks; tours; sales shop sells books, magazines, reproductions and slides; junior museum
M **Junior Gallery and Creative Arts Center,** 4525 Oak St, 64111. *Dir* Ann Brubaker
Open Tues - Sat 10 AM - 5 PM, Sun 2 - 6 PM. Estab 1960 to create a greater awareness of the world around us through art. Average Annual Attendance: 144,249
Activities: Creative art classes; adult sculpture, drawing, painting, Oriental brushwork and design classes; workshops; docent training; tours

M **AVILA COLLEGE,** Thornhill Art Gallery, 11901 Wornall Rd, 64110. Tel 816-942-8400. *Dir* Carol Zastoupil; *Pres* Sr Olive Louise Dallavis; *Academic Dean* G Richard Scott; *Chmn Fine Arts* William Louis
Open Mon - Fri 10 AM - 4 PM. No admis fee. Estab 1978 to present the visual arts in a contemporary sense to the student community as well as the Greater Kansas City community. Gallery space 60 x 35 ft is maintained with carpeted floor and walls, an Artist-in-Residence studio, and track lighting. Average Annual Attendance: 2000
Income: Financed through school budget
Exhibitions: (1983-84) Animals from the collection of the Kansas Grassroots Art Association; Jesse Dominguez, Silent Seasons; Warren Mackenzie, pottery; Minga Sota, pottery; senior exhibition; annual student art exhibition; Black on Black Crime Paintings, John Newman; Margo Kren, Dreams & Memories, prints & drawings; Roger Kraft, architect
Activities: Classes for adults; dramatic programs; lectures open to public; gallery talks

O **COWBOY ARTISTS OF AMERICA,** * 922 Walnut St, Rm 602, 64106. Tel 816-471-5323. *Mgr* T M Watson
Estab 1965 to educate collectors & the public in the authentic reproduction of the American West, as it was & is. Maintains biographical archives. Mem: 25
Publications: Catalog, annual

HALLMARK CARDS, INC

C **Hallmark Collections,** 25th & McGee, 64108. Tel 816-274-5298. *Cur* Keith F Davis; *Mgr, Collections & Archives* Sally Hope
Collections: Hallmark Photographic Collection; Hallmark Art Collection; Hallmark Historical Collection; antique greeting cards and playing cards; antique toys and Christmas ornaments; paintings; photographs; prints
Exhibitions: (1981-83) Harry Callahan: Photographs; (1982) Edward Weston: One Hundred Photographics; (1983-85) Andre Kertesz: Forum & Feeling; Saul Steinberg: Drawings & Watercolors
Activities: Lect; purchase awards for art shows; individual objects of art lent to reputable institutions for temporary exhibitions

L **Creative Library,** 25th & McGee, 64108. Tel 816-274-5525. *Mgr Library Services* Jon M Henderson
Open to Hallmark personnel only. Estab to provide pictorial research
Income: Financed by corp funds
Library Holdings: Vols 12,000; Per subs 120; AV — Slides; Other — Clipping files

M **KANSAS CITY ART INSTITUTE,** Charlotte Crosby Kemper Gallery, 4415 Warwick Blvd, 64111. Tel 816-561-4852. *Chmn Board of Governors* Robert H Lange; *Dir Exhibitions* Sherry Cromwell-Lacy
Open Tues - Fri 11 AM - 4 PM, Sat & Sun Noon - 5 PM. Estab 1963 to provide exhibitions of interest to the college and regional community
Exhibitions: Changing exhibitions
L **Library,** 4421 Warwick Blvd, Box 10360, 64111. Tel 816-561-4852. *Library Dir* Ellen Lignell
Open Mon - Thurs 8:30 AM - 5 PM and 6 - 10 PM, Fri 8:30 - 5 PM, Sun 1 - 6 PM. Estab 1924 to serve students and Faculty of Art Institute
Income: $75,622 (financed by Art Institute budget)
Library Holdings: Vols 31,000; Per subs 112; Other — Clipping files, exhibition catalogs, pamphlets
Special Subjects: Photography, Fine arts

L **KANSAS CITY PUBLIC LIBRARY,** Art & Music Department, 311 East 12th St, 64106. Tel 816-221-2685. *Librn* Marjorie Kinney; *Art & Music Reference Librn* Carol Wallace
Open Mon - Sat 9 AM - 5 PM, cl Sun. Established 1873
Library Holdings: Vols 30,000; Per subs 1315; Micro — Fiche, reels; AV — Motion pictures, rec, slides; Other — Clipping files, exhibition catalogs, framed reproductions, memorabilia, pamphlets, prints, reproductions

MID-AMERICA ARTS ALLIANCE
For further information, see National and Regional Organizations

C **UNITED MISSOURI BANCSHARES, INC,** PO Box 1771, 64141. Tel 816-283-1100. *Chmn* R Crosby Kemper
Estab 1973 to provide good art for viewing by customers. Collection is displayed in lobbies and customer access areas in various United Missouri Banks
Collections: Americana Collection, including American portraits (George Caleb Bingham, Benjamin Blythe, Gilbert Stuart, Charles Wilson Peale), regional collection (William Commerford, Peter Hurd, J H Sharp, Gordon Snidow), modern art (Fran Bull, Olive Rush, Wayne Thiebaud, Ellsworth Kelly)
Activities: Objects of art lent to galleries for special exhibits

MARYVILLE

M **NORTHWEST MISSOURI STATE UNIVERSITY,** DeLuce Gallery, 64468. Tel 816-582-7141. *Chmn Dept Art* Lee Hageman; *Olive DeLuce Art Gallery Coll Cur* Philip Laber; *Percival DeLuce Art Gallery Coll Cur* Robert Sunkel
Open Mon - Fri 1 - 4 PM. No admis fee. Estab 1965 to provide exhibitions of contemporary works in all media as part of the learning experiences in the visual arts. Gallery is maintained with 150 running feet exhibition space with high security, humidity controlled air conditioning and flexible lighting. Average Annual Attendance: 6000
Income: Financed by city appropriation
Collections: Percival DeLuce Memorial Collection consisting of American paintings, drawings, prints and decorative arts; some European furniture and prints
Exhibitions: (1983-84) New Photographics Traveling Exhibit; Solo Exhibit: Jennie Frederick, sculpture; Alumni Exhibit: Dwaine Crigger, mixed media, sculpture; Faculty Exhibit; Art Club Fall Show & Sale
Activities: Classes for adults; Lect open to public, 6 visiting lectrs per year; gallery talks; tours; scholarships; individual and original objects of art lent within the institution; lending collection contains original art works, original prints, paintings and drawings; book 3 traveling exhibitions per year

MEXICO

L **MEXICO-AUDRAIN COUNTY LIBRARY,** 305 W Jackson, 65265. Tel 314-581-4939. *Pres* Charles Crow; *Dir* Kurt H Lamb; *Children's Librn* Margaret Jones; *Acquisitions Librn* Violet Lierheimer; *Reference Librn* Christal Brunner; *Bookmobile Librn* Linda Griffin
Open winter hours, Mon - Thurs 9 AM - 9 PM, Fri & Sat 9 AM - 5:30 PM. No admis fee. Estab 1912 to provide library services to the residents of Audrain County, Missouri. Exhibit room with different exhibits each month; childrens department has a continuously changing exhibit
Income: Financed by donations
Library Holdings: Vols 112,529; Per subs 127; art print reproductions; newspapers; AV — Fs, slides, motion pictures, rec
Collections: Audrain County history; paintings by Audrain County artists
Exhibitions: Local Federated Womens Club sponsored a different exhibit each month during the fall, winter and spring, these included local artists, both adult and young people, and recognized artists of the area; The Missouri Council of the Arts also provide traveling exhibits that we display
Activities: Classes for children; story hour 1 hr 4 days a week; individual paintings and original objects of art lent

SAINT CHARLES

M **LINDENWOOD COLLEGE,** Harry D Hendren Gallery, Department of Art, 63301. Tel 314-946-6912, Ext 240. *Chmn* W Dean Eckert
Open Mon - Fri 9 AM - 5 PM, Sat & Sun Noon - 5 PM. No admis fee. Estab 1969 as a college exhibition gallery. Gallery is approximately 3600 sq ft with skylight and one wall of side light. Average Annual Attendance: 4000
Income: Financed by endowment
Collections: Contemporary American and European prints in various media

including works by Paul Jenkins, William Hayter, Will Barnet, Mauricio Lazansky
Activities: Lectures open to the public, 5-6 vis lectr per year; gallery talks; tours; original objects of art lent; lending collection contains photographs; traveling exhibitions organized and circulated through the Missouri State Council on the Arts

SAINT JOSEPH

M **ALBRECHT ART MUSEUM,** 2818 Frederick Blvd, 64506. Tel 816-233-7003. *Dir* Jim Ray; *Secy Registrar* Margo Prentiss
Open Tues - Fri 10 AM - 4 PM, Sat & Sun 1 - 4 PM, cl Mon. Admis adults $1, children $.10, free to members. Estab 1914 to increase public knowledge and appreciation of the arts. Mem: 600; dues $15 up; annual meeting second Wed in April
Income: $90,000 (financed by membership)
Collections: †Henry D Bradley Memorial Collection of Prints; Forrest C Campbell Collection of Prints; †Drawing America Collection; †Hax Memorial Collection; Eugene S Juda Jr Memorial Collection of American Engravings; Kemper Collection of American Paintings; Saint Joseph Photographic Collection of Architecture and Stained Glass Windows; William Toben Memorial Collection
Exhibitions: Thomas Hart Benton's Illustrations from Mark Twain; Drawing Missouri 1976; Magic Carpets; Rugs of the Orient; Stained Glass Windows of St Joseph
Publications: Calendar of events, monthly
Activities: Classes for children; lectures open to public
L **Library,** 2818 Frederick Blvd, 64506
Library open to museum members only
Library Holdings: Vols 600; Per subs 4

M **MISSOURI WESTERN STATE COLLEGE,** Fine Arts Gallery,* 4525 Downs Dr, 64507. Tel 816-271-4282. *Pres* Dr M O Looney; *VPres* Dr Robert Nelson; *Chmn Department of Art* William Eickhorst, EdD; *Gallery Coordr* John T Hughes
Open 8 AM - 4:30 PM. No admis fee. Estab 1971 to bring an awareness of contemporary directions in art to students and to the community. Gallery is in front of building, next to theater; 120 ft long, 30 ft wide, with 25 ft high ceiling; rug paneling on walls; modern decor. Average Annual Attendance: 10,000
Income: Financed by state appropriation
Exhibitions: Invitational or juried art exhibitions
Activities: Classes for adults; lect open to public; gallery talks; tours; competitions; scholarships; exten dept; individual paintings and original objects of art lent to staff offices within college; lending collection contains original art works, original prints, paintings and sculpture; book traveling exhibitions

M **SAINT JOSEPH MUSEUM,** 11th and Charles, 64501. Tel 816-232-8471. *Dir* Richard A Nolf; *Asst Dir & Cur Pony Express Stables* Don L Reynolds; *Executive Secy* June M Swift; *Registrar & Cur Collections* Bonnie K Harlow; *Cur Ethnology* Marilyn S Taylor; *Cur Hist & Librn* Jacqueline Lewin
Open April to Oct Mon - Sat 9 AM - 5 PM, Sun & holidays 2 - 5 PM, Oct to April Tues - Sat 1 - 5 PM, cl Mon, Christmas, Thanksgiving and New Years Day. Admis adults $.50, children 12 and under $.25. Estab 1926 to increase and diffuse knowledge and appreciation of history, art and the sciences and to aid the educational work that is being done by the schools of Saint Joseph and other educational organizations. Mini-gallery, usually for small, low security traveling exhibits. Average Annual Attendance: 100,000. Mem: 209; dues $15 and up; annual meeting Jan
Income: $100,000 (financed by membership, and city appropriation)
Publications: The Happenings (newsletter), bimonthly
Activities: Classes for children; craft program; lect open to public; museum shop selling books, reproductions, prints, slides, gift items
L **Library,** 11th & Charles, 64501
Open Mon - Sat 9 AM - 5 PM, Sun 2 -5 PM. Estab 1926 to hold museum collections. Mini gallery for traveling exhibits
Purchases: $1200
Library Holdings: Vols 4500; Per subs 35; Other — Clipping files, framed reproductions, manuscripts, memorabilia, original art works, photographs, prints, sculpture
Special Subjects: Area History; Native American; Natural History
Publications: The Happenings, bi-monthly newsletter
Activities: Classes for children; docent training; tours; originate traveling exhibitions to schools

SAINT LOUIS

O **ARTS AND EDUCATION COUNCIL OF GREATER SAINT LOUIS,** 40 N Kingshighway, 63108. Tel 314-367-6330. *Chmn* Robert R Hermann; *Pres* H O Johnston; *Exec Dir* Mel J Loewenstein; *Dir Public Information* Gloria Hogbin Luitjens
Estab 1963 to coordinate, promote and assist in the development of cultural and educational activities in the Greater St. Louis area; to offer generally, planning, coordinating, promotional and fund-raising service to eligible organizations and groups, thereby creating a valuable community-wide association. Mem: 130
Income: Financed by private funds
Publications: Artist registry, annually; calendar of cultural events, monthly; media guide, annually
Activities: Arts festival for children; CAMELOT auction

M **CONCORDIA HISTORICAL INSTITUTE,** 801 DeMun Ave, 63105. Tel 314-721-5934. *Dir* Dr August R Suelflow
Open Mon - Fri 8 AM - 5 PM, cl international holidays. No admis fee. Estab 1847, affiliated with The Lutheran Church, Missouri Synod. Mem: Dues Life $300, over 65 $200, corporation $200, organization $75, patron $50, sustaining $25, active & subscription $15
Collections: Church archives and vast historical materials; crafts; handcrafts; Reformation and Lutheran coins and medals; Works by Lutheran artists and

paintings and artifacts for Lutheran worship; Native artwork from Foreign Mission Fields, especially China, India, Africa & New Guinea
Exhibitions: Temporary exhibitions
Publications: Concordia Historical Institute Quarterly; Historical Footnotes, a quarterly newsletter; Regional Archivist, a newsletter and 'how to' serial for archives; bulletins
Activities: Lectures open to public; competitions with awards; sales shop sells books, magazines, slides & craft items

O **FIRST STREET FORUM,** 717 N First St, 63102. Tel 314-421-3791. *Pres* Douglas B MacCarthy; *Executive Dir* Laurel Meinig; *Asst to Dir* Deana Barron
Open Tues - Sat 9 AM - 6 PM. Admis $1 donation. Estab 1980 to provide a comprehensive program of exhibitions, performances, lectures & symposia. Mem: 300; dues $25 and up
Income: $120,000 (financed by membership, corporations & foundation funds)
Exhibitions: Pop & After: Sculpture by Johns, Lichtenstein, Oldenburg & Segal; Selections From the Fabric Workshop
Activities: Docent training; workshops; lectures open to public; competitions; book traveling exhibitions; originates traveling exhibitions

M **LAUMEIER SCULPTURE PARK,** 12580 Rott Rd, 63127. Tel 314-821-1209. *Dir* Beej Niergarten-Smith; *Registrar* Debbie Reinhardt
Park open daily 8 AM - half hour past sunset; Gallery open Wed - Sat 10 AM - 5 PM, Sun 12 - 5 PM. Estab 1976 to exhibit contemporary sculpture by internationally acclaimed artists. Average Annual Attendance: 200,000. Mem: 500; dues corporate $500, patron $200, contributing $100, regular $35 and students $10; bi-annual meetings Jan & June
Income: Art program financed by Federal & State Grants, membership & donations
Collections: Outdoor contemporary sculpture collection by Jackie Ferrara, Charles Ginnever, Richard Hunt, William King, Alexander Liberman, Mary Miss, Robert Morris, Clark Murray, Louise Nevelson, Beverly Pepper, Tony Rosenthal, David Von Schlegell, Richard Serra, Michael Steiner, Mark Di Suvero and Ernest Trova
Exhibitions: (1982) Artists' Gardens & Parks; Beverly Pepper; Cast in Carbondale; Mary Miss; DeWain Valentine; (1983) Japanese Kites; Great Sculptors at Laumeier; Manuel Neri; Walter Dusenbery; Alan Siegel
Activities: Classes for adults and children; dramatic programs; docent training; lect open to the public, 4 visiting lectures per year; concerts; gallery talks; tours; competitions with awards; original objects of art lent to established institutions; lending collection contains 40 sculptures; book traveling exhibitions; originate traveling exhibitions; shop sells books and posters

O **MARYVILLE COLLEGE SAINT LOUIS,** Beaumont Gallery, 13550 Conway Rd, 63141. Tel 314-576-9300. *Gallery Dir* Nancy N Rice
Open Mon - Fri 9 AM - 5 PM. No admis fee. Estab to show work of artists, many of whom have no gallery affiliation. Average Annual Attendance: 3000
Income: $1140
Exhibitions: (1983-84) Richard Helmick; Kent Addison; Joan Elkin; Rodney M Winfied; Jim Reed; William Weidner

M **MISSOURI HISTORICAL SOCIETY,** Jefferson Memorial Bldg, Forest Park, 63112. Tel 314-361-1424. *Pres* Hal Stuhl; *Dir* Raymond Pisney; *Cur* Gary Smith; *Cur Education* Kathy Corbett; *Cur Art* Karen Goering; *Registrar* Marie Schmitz; *Cur Special Projects* Duane Sneddeker
Open Tues - Sun 9:30 AM - 4:45 PM. No admis fee. Estab 1866 to collect and preserve objects and information relating to the history of St Louis, Missouri and the Louisiana Purchase Territory. Average Annual Attendance: 450,000. Mem: 3000; dues from $25; annual meeting Sept
Income: Financed by private endowment, membership and special events
Collections: †19th & 20th century art of St Louis and the American West; †paintings; †photographs; †prints
Exhibitions: Lindbergh Memorabilia; Decorative Arts; Lewis and Clark Exhibition; St Louis Women Artists; Five St Louis Artists: Their City and Their World
Publications: Gateway Heritage, quarterly journal; Spirit, quarterly newsletter
Activities: Classes for adults and children; lectures open to public, 3-5 vis lectr per year; gallery talks; tours; sales shop sells books, prints, slides, souvenirs, china, antique items
L **Library,** Jefferson Memorial Bldg, Forest Park, 63112. Tel 314-361-1424. *Librn & Archivist* Stephanie A Klein; *Researcher-in-Residence* Janice L Fox; *Asst Librn* Carol Verble
Admis fee for non-members. Library open to members for reference
Library Holdings: Vols 120,000; Per subs 250; Micro — Reels; Other — Clipping files, manuscripts, pamphlets, photographs, prints
Special Subjects: Midwestern and Western Artists: Bodmer, Catlin and Russell

O **SAINT LOUIS ARTISTS' GUILD,** 227 E Lockwood, 63119. Tel 314-962-2056. *Pres* Ann Metzger; *Secy* Barbara Ayot; *Treas* Michael Cramer
Open daily Noon - 4 PM, Sun 1 - 5 PM, cl Tues. No admis fee. Estab for the purpose of exhibiting art. Average Annual Attendance: 5000. Mem: 600; dues $35
Income: Financed by membership
Exhibitions: (1983) Guild membership, unjuried; Retrospective: Tanasko Milovich, 1900-1964; 60th Annual Watercolors & Pastels; portraits; (1984) art section, juried; oil, sculpture, acrylic; guild membership, juried; prints, crafts, drawings; young artists (15-21 years of age); art fair & flea market; photography; guild weaving class exhibit
Publications: Monthly newsletter
Activities: Lect open to the public; competitions with awards

M **SAINT LOUIS ART MUSEUM,** Forest Park, 63110. Tel 314-721-0067. *Dir* James D Burke
Open Tues 1:30 - 8:30 PM, Wed - Sun 10 AM - 5 PM, cl Mon. No admis fee. Estab 1907, erected as Palace of Art for 1904 World's Fair; designed by Cass Gilbert in Beaux Art architecture; the main sculpture hall is fashioned after Roman Baths of Caracalla. Average Annual Attendance: 650,000. Mem: 11,000; dues Beaux Arts Council $1000, associate $500, sustaining $100, contributing $50, participating $25, student $15
Income: $5,930,903 (financed by endowment, membership, county, grants, sales and contributions)
Purchases: Judith & Helofernes by Vasari; View Along the Amstel by Hobbema; Landscape with Goatherd by Pynacker; Sada in Search of the Waters of Oblivion by John Martin; 13th century terra cotta, African Maternity Group, Djenne
Collections: Holdings range from Egyptian to contemporary art. A new department of prints, drawings and photographs displays works from the Museum's 6000 holdings; outstanding art collection of works from Oceania, Africa, Pre-Columbian and American Indian objects; paintings emphasize Northern European works from the Renaissance to Rembrandt as well as colonial to contemporary American, French Impressionist and Post Impressionist and German Expressionist works; 20th century European sculpture, American and European decorative art; Chinese bronzes and porcelains
Exhibitions: (1982) Michelle Stuart; Deborah Butterfield; James Surls; Kim Strommen; Black on Black; Viola Frey; Impressionism Reflected: American Art 1890-1920; Art of the Old West; Treasures of the East; (1983) Expressions: New Art from Germany; Dale Chihuly; Cindy Sherman; Mary Sprague; Ellsworth Kelly: Sculpture
Publications: The St Louis Art Museum Bulletin, semi-annual; annual report; bi-monthly calendar
Activities: Classes for adults and children; lect; concerts; gallery talks; tours; individual paintings and original objects of art lent to other museums; traveling exhibitions organized and circulated
L **Richardson Memorial Library,** Forest Park, 63110. Tel 314-721-0067. *Librn* Ann B Abid; *Asst Librn* Dana Beth; *Archivist* Doris Sturzenberger; *Archives Technician* Norma Sindelar; *Asst to Librn* Deborah Hopper; *Libr Asst* Cheryl Vogler
Open Wed - Fri 10 AM - 4:45 PM. Estab 1915 to provide reference and bibliographical service to the museum staff and the adult public; to bibliographically support the collections owned by the museum
Income: Financed by endowment and city appropriation
Library Holdings: Vols 30,000; Per subs 300; Art auction catalogs; Micro — Fiche, reels; AV — Lantern slides, slides; Other — Clipping files, exhibition catalogs, pamphlets, photographs, reproductions

L **SAINT LOUIS PUBLIC LIBRARY,** Art Dept, 1301 Olive St, 63105. Tel 314-241-2288. *Librn* Joan Collett; *Chief Art Dept* Martha Hilligoss
Open Mon 9 AM - 9 PM, Tues - Sat 9 AM - 5 PM. Estab Art Department in 1912
Library Holdings: Vols 44,000; Micro — Fiche, reels; AV — Cassettes, motion pictures, rec, slides, v-tapes; Other — Clipping files, exhibition catalogs, framed reproductions, pamphlets, prints, reproductions, sculpture
Collections: Steedman Architectural Library

THE STAINED GLASS ASSOCIATION OF AMERICA
For further information, see National and Regional Organizations

M **UNIVERSITY OF MISSOURI, SAINT LOUIS,** Gallery 210,* Art Department, 8007 Nahral Bridge Rd, 63121. Tel 314-553-5975. *Dir* Sylvia Solochek Walters, MFA
Open Mon - Thurs 9 AM - 9 PM, Fri 9 AM - 5 PM. Estab 1972 to provide visual enrichment to campus and community. Average Annual Attendance: 5000
Income: Financed by state appropriation
Publications: Exhibition catalogs: Color Photography; Light Abstractions
Activities: Educ dept on art history; studio courses; lect open to public; book traveling exhibitions; originate traveling exhibitions

WASHINGTON UNIVERSITY
M **Gallery of Art,** Steinberg Hall, Box 1214, 63130. Tel 314-889-5490. *Dir* Gerald D Bolas; *Cur & Registrar* Joseph D Ketner II; *Admin Secy* Natalie Mondschein; *Facilities Tech* Jonathan Edwards
Open Mon - Fri 10 AM - 5 PM, Sat & Sun 1 - 5 PM. No admis fee. Estab 1881, present building opened 1960, for the students of Washington University and the community at large. A modern building containing two floors of gallery space for exhibit of the permanent collection and special exhibitions. Also houses a library of art, archaeology, architecture, and design
Income: Financed by university & private support
Collections: Emphasis on †modern artists, including Miro, Ernst, Picasso, Leger, Moore; many †Old Masters, 19th & 20th century European & American paintings, sculpture, draiwngs & prints
Exhibitions: (1982) The Architectural Heritage of St Louis; (1983) Baroque Theatre & Stage Design; (1984) The Beautiful, The Sublime, & the Picturesque: British Influences on American Landscape Painting
Publications: Exhibition catalogs
Activities: Lect open to public, 24 visiting lectr per year by artists, art historians & architects; symposia; music concerts; films; scholarships; traveling exhibitions organized and circulated; sales shop sells exhibition catalogs & postcards
L **Art and Architecture Library,** Steinberg Hall, Box 1189, 63130. Tel 314-889-5268. *Librn* Imre Meszaros; *Circulation Supv* Julie Arnott; *Library Records* Betty Daniel; *Reserve Supv* Madeleine Illies; *Serials and Rare Books* Paula Ferrario
Open Mon - Thurs 8:30 AM - 11 PM, Fri 8:30 AM - 5 PM, Sat 11 AM - 6 PM, Sun 11 AM - 10 PM, cl nights and weekends during vacations and intersessions. Estab 1879 to support the academic programs of the three departments of the University: the School of Fine Arts, the School of Architecture, and the Department of Art & Archaeology
Income: Financed through the university
Library Holdings: Vols 50,000; Per subs 300; Micro — Cards, fiche, prints, reels; Other — Exhibition catalogs, pamphlets, reproductions
Special Subjects: Archaeology, Architecture, Costume Design & Construction
Collections: Baker Collection: 50 examples of fine binding; Bryce Collection: 576 volumes of early books on Architectural History; Eames and Young Collection: 273 volumes of 19th and pre-19th century imprints on architectural history; East Asian Art Collection; Exhibitions: Fashion Design of the 19th century; Eames & Young Architectural Library: Printed Books and Photo-Albums; Rare Book Room; Sorger Collection: 243 volumes of 19th century historic costume books with lithographs and hand-coloured fashion or costume plates, and 4 drawers of plates
Activities: Library tours

M **WEBSTER COLLEGE,** Loretto-Hilton Center Gallery,* 130 Edgar Rd, 63119.
Tel 314-968-6915. *Admin* Charles F Madden
Open Mon - Fri 9 AM - 6 PM, Sat & Sun 1 - 5 PM, cl Christmas. No admis fee.
Estab 1966
Publications: Monthly news releases; exhibition catalogs; books
Activities: Classes for adults and children; lectures; gallery talks; guided tours;
concerts; films; competitions; temporary and traveling exhibitions
L **Library,*** 130 Edgar Rd, 63119
Open to the public for researching on the premises
Library Holdings: Vols 300
Special Subjects: 20th century paintings, prints, sculpture and photography

SPRINGFIELD

O **SOUTHWEST MISSOURI MUSEUM ASSOCIATES INC,** 1111 Brookside
Dr, 65807. Tel 417-866-2716, Ext 2
Estab 1928 to inform and interest citizens in appreciation of art, and to maintain
an art museum as an essential public institution. Mem: 1300; dues sustaining life
$1000, life $250, supporting $25, family $20, at large $15, art group: resident
$10, extension groups $6
Income: $14,000 (financed by membership)
Publications: Bi-monthly newsletter, in cooperation with the Museum
Activities: Gift shop sells books, prints, reproductions, stationery and gift items

M **SOUTHWEST MISSOURI STATE UNIVERSITY,** University Gallery, 901 S
National, 65804. Tel 417-836-5000. *Dir* Teresa Rohrabaugh
Open Tues - Sat 11 AM - 3 PM, cl Mon & Sun. No admis fee. Estab 1963 to
present exhibitions of interest and educational worth to the university community
and general public. Average Annual Attendance: 2000
Income: Financed by state appropriation
Collections: †Contemporary and historical prints
Publications: Catalogs, 2 or 3 per year
Activities: Traveling exhibitions organized and circulated

M **SPRINGFIELD ART MUSEUM,** 1111 E Brookside Dr, 65807. Tel 417-866-
2716. *Dir* William C Landwehr; *Cur of Coll & Registrar* Greg G Thielen; *Cur
Education* Ray Smenner; *Secy* Diane Carr
Open Tues - Sat 9 AM - 5 PM, Weds 6:30 - 9 PM, (except July & Aug), Sun 1 -
5 PM, cl Mon. No admis fee. Estab 1928 to encourage appreciation and foster
education of the visual arts. Museum has three temporary exhibition galleries
totaling approximately 7500 sq ft; new wing opened in 1975 contains 400-seat
auditorium and sales gallery. Average Annual Attendance: 100,000. Mem: 1300;
dues $10 - $1000; annual meeting second Wed in May
Purchases: $10,000 - $15,000
Collections: †American drawing and photography; †American painting and
sculpture of all periods; †American prints of all periods with emphasis on the
20th century
Exhibitions: The Etchings of Anders Zorn from the Collection of the Springfield
Art Museum; The Lithographs and Etchings of Philip Pearlstein
Publications: Annual Accessions catalog and temporary exhibition catalogs;
Watercolor USA, annually
Activities: Classes for adults and children; lect open to public; concerts; gallery
talks; tours; competitions; originate traveling exhibition; sales shop selling books,
original art, prints
L **Library,** 1111 E Brookside Dr, 65807. Tel 417-866-2716. *Librn* Alice Brooker
Open Tues - Sat 9 AM - 5 PM. Estab 1946 to assist those persons interested in
securing information regarding art and artists, craftsmen from ancient times to
the present. Circ 750-800
Income: Financed by city
Purchases: $2500
Library Holdings: Vols 3699; Per subs 42; AV — Slides; Other — Clipping files,
exhibition catalogs, pamphlets

STOUTSVILLE

M **MARK TWAIN BIRTHPLACE MUSEUM,** Box 54, 65283. Tel 314-565-3449.
Site Admin Stanley P Fast; *Guide* Madeline Loutenschlager
Open Mon - Sat 10 AM - 4 PM, Sun Noon - 5 PM. Admis adults $1, ages 6-12
$.50. Estab 1960 to preserve the birth cabin of Samuel L Clemens, interpret his
life and inform visitors of local history. Foyer and two large exhibt areas.
Average Annual Attendance: 12,000
Income: Financed by state appropriation
Collections: Samuel Clemens memorabilia; manuscripts; period furnishings and
paintings
Exhibitions: Permanent exhibits depicting the life of Samuel Clemens
Activities: Lectures; tours; craft demonstrations

WARRENSBURG

M **CENTRAL MISSOURI STATE UNIVERSITY,** Art Dept Gallery, 64093. Tel
816-429-4498. *Dir* Richard A Luehrman
Open Mon - Fri 8 AM - 5 PM, cl holidays. No admis fee. Estab 1958 for the
purpose of education through exhibition. Small university oriented gallery located
in the Art Department. Average Annual Attendance: 2000
Income: Financed by state appropriation and university funding
Activities: Lect open to the public, 2 visiting lectr per year; gallery talks;
competitions; traveling exhibitions organized and circulated

MONTANA

ANACONDA

O **COPPER VILLAGE MUSEUM & ARTS CENTER,** 110 E Eighth St, 59711.
Tel 406-563-8421, Ext 242. *Dir* Mary Blaskovich; *Gallery Hostess* Catherine
Stone; *Gallery Hostess* Helen Peterson; *Pres Board of Dir* Marian Geil; *VPres*
Millie Avery
Open Tues - Fri 10 AM - 5 PM, Sat & Sun 1 - 4 PM. No admis fee. Estab 1971
as Community Arts Center, gallery and local historical museum. Average Annual
Attendance: 15,000. Mem: 370; dues family $3-$10; annual meeting Oct
Income: Financed by endowment, membership and city appropriation
Collections: Permanent collection
Exhibitions: Monthly exhibits
Activities: Classes for adults and children; traveling exhibitions organized and
circulated; sales shop selling original art, reproductions, prints and pottery
L **Library,** 110 E Eighth St, 59711. Tel 406-563-8421, Ext 242
Library open to the public for reference
Library Holdings: Vols 30; Per subs 5; AV — Motion pictures, slides; Other —
Clipping files, memorabilia, original art works, pamphlets, reproductions,
sculpture
Special Subjects: Western History and Art
Publications: Newletters, quarterly; brochures
Activities: Book traveling exhibitions

BILLINGS

O **YELLOWSTONE ART CENTER,** 401 N 27th St, 59101. Tel 406-259-1869.
Pres of Board Pat Etchart; *Dir* Donna M Forbes; *Asst Dir* Gordon McDonnell;
Cur Chris Warner
Open Tues - Fri 11 AM - 5 PM, Sat & Sun Noon - 5 PM, Thurs 7 - 9 PM. No
admis fee. Estab 1964 to offer a broad program of art exhibitions, both historical
and contemporary, of the highest quality, to provide related educational
programs. Two large galleries and four smaller ones in a large brick structure.
Average Annual Attendance: 25,000. Mem: 850; dues $15 and up; annual
meeting third Wed June
Income: $270,000 (financed by membership, contributions and county
appropriations)
Collections: †Contemporary Print Collection; Mackay Collection of Olaf
Wieghorst Painting; Mary Mulloy Carmichael Collection of 20th Century French
Prints; Poindexter Collection of Abstract Expressionists
Exhibitions: (1982) Clarice Dreyer: Recent Sculpture; Chinese Robes: 1750-
1900; Frank Ferguson; Neil Parsons; (1983) Fifteenth Annual Art Auction
Exhibition; Edith Freeman Woodcuts; Marilyn Swartwood Duke: Desert Gardens
& Other Drawings; Robert Irwin Installation; Naomi Lazard: Ordinances; James
Reineking; Ken Little; Our Land/Our People; James Poor
Publications: Monthly exhibition announcements; newsletter, monthly; exhibition
catalogues
Activities: Docent training; lect open to public, 6 visiting lectr per year; gallery
talks; tours; competitions; individual paintings and original art objects lent to
museums and art centers; originate traveling exhibitions; museum shop selling
books, original art, reproductions, prints, jewelry, pottery and posters

BOZEMAN

MONTANA STATE UNIVERSITY
M **Museum of the Rockies,*** 59717. Tel 406-994-0211, 994-2251. *Dir* Michael W
Hager; *Construction Specialist* Jim Goosey; *Administrative Asst* Judy Weaver;
Registrar Wanda J Walker; *Sales Shop Manager* Jeri Walton; *Photo Technician*
Steve Jackson; *Cur History* Ken Karsmizki
Open Mon - Fri 9 AM - 4:30 PM, Sat & Sun 1 - 4:30 PM, cl Mon in winter
months. No admis fee. Estab in 1958 to interpret the physical and social
heritages of the Northern Rockies region. Rotating gallery features monthly
showings of local work and traveling exhibits. Average Annual Attendance:
60,000. Mem: 800; dues sponsor $20,000, special patron $5000, benefactor $1000,
patron $500, life $250, contributing $100, sustaining $50, family $20, individual
$10
Collections: Art Works by R E DeCamp; Edgar Paxton; C M Russell; O C
Seltzer; William Standing; Geology; paleontology; archaeology; history and
western art
Publications: Quarterly newsletter; papers
Activities: Classes for adults; docent training; lectures open to public and
members only, 3 vis lectr per yr; tours; book traveling exhibitions; originate
traveling exhibitions; museum shop sells books, magazines, original art,
reproductions and prints
M **Fine Arts Gallery,*** 59717. Tel 406-994-4501. *Dir* Elizabeth Guheen
Open Mon - Fri 8:30 AM - 4:30 PM. No admis fee. Estab 1894 to present
exhibitions of national interest. A new building with a small gallery space
adjacent to offices and studio classrooms. Average Annual Attendance: 10,000
Income: Financed by university appropriation
Activities: Lectures open to the public, ten visiting lecturers per year; gallery
talks; competitions
L **Creative Arts Library,** 207 Cheever Hall, Creative Arts Complex, 59717. Tel
406-994-4091. *Librn* Linda Swieszkowski; *Slide Cur* Emily Gadd
Open Mon - Thurs 7:30 AM - 11 PM, Fri 7:30 AM - 5 PM, Sat 10 AM - 6 PM,
Sun Noon - 11 PM. Estab 1974 to support the Schools of Architecture and Art.
Maintains art gallery
Income: Financed by state appropriation
Library Holdings: Vols 16,000; Per subs 100; Architectural Plans; Micro —
Reels; AV — Slides; Other — Framed reproductions
Exhibitions: Stephen Lehmer, photography; Robert Demachy, photography;
Gary D'Este, pre-thesis show; Jessie Wilber, print retrospective

BROWNING

M MUSEUM OF THE PLAINS INDIAN, US Hwy 89, PO Box 400, 59417. Tel 406-338-2230. *Acting Cur* Rosemary Ellison
Open June - Sept, daily 9 AM - 5 PM, Oct - May Mon - Fri 10 AM - 4:30 PM, cl New Year's Day, Thanksgiving Day and Christmas. No admis fee. Estab 1941 to promote the development of contemporary Native American arts, administered and operated by the Indian Arts and Crafts Board, US Dept of the Interior. Average Annual Attendance: 80,000
Income: Financed by Federal appropriation and gifts
Collections: Contemporary Native American arts and crafts; historic works by Plains Indian craftsmen
Exhibitions: Historic Plains Indian Arts; permanent exhibit of historic Plains Indian arts; continuing series of one-person exhibitions
Publications: Continuing series of brochures for one-person shows
Activities: Gallery talks; traveling exhibitions organized and circulated; sales shop selling books, original art

BUTTE

M BUTTE SILVER BOW ARTS CHATEAU,* 321 W Broadway, 59701. Tel 406-723-7600. *Dir* P J Wright
Open Sept - May - Sun 1 - 5 PM, June - Aug Tues - Sat 10 AM - 5 PM, Sun 1 - 5 PM, cl major holidays. No admis fee. Estab 1977. Mem: Dues Business: benefactor $1000, patron $750, sustaining $500, contributing $100, active $10; Individual: benefactor $1000, patron $500, sustaining $100, contributing $50, family $25, active $10
Collections: Contemporary regional art
Publications: Newsletter
Activities: Lectures; gallery talks; tours; sales shop

CHESTER

M LIBERTY VILLAGE ARTS CENTER AND GALLERY, Box 269, 59522. Tel 406-759-5652
Open Tues - Fri & Sun 1 - 5 PM, cl New Years, Easter, Thanksgiving & Christmas. No admis fee. Estab 1976 to provide community with traveling exhibitions & education center. Average Annual Attendance: 1500-2000. Mem: 50; dues patron $100 and up, Friend of the Arts $50-$99, family $10, individual $5, student $1; annual meeting Oct
Collections: Works by local artists, paintings & quilts
Activities: Classes for adults & children; workshops; film series; lectures open to public, 5 vis lectr per yr; gallery talks; competitions with awards; book traveling exhibitions; originate traveling exhibitions; museum shop sells books, original art & prints

DILLON

M WESTERN MONTANA COLLEGE, Art Gallery, 59725. Tel 406-683-7232. *Dir* Jim Corr
Open Mon - Fri 8 AM - 10 PM, Sat 2 - 4 PM, Sun 7 - 10 PM. No admis fee. Estab 1970 to display art works of various kinds, used as an educational facility. Art Gallery located in the College library. Average Annual Attendance: 7000
Income: Financed through college funds
Collections: †Emerick Art Book Collection
Activities: Education dept; scholarships; artmobile
L Library,* 59725. *Librn* Ken Cory
Library open to the public
Library Holdings: Vols 4000; Per subs 10

GREAT FALLS

M CASCADE COUNTY HISTORICAL SOCIETY MUSEUM,* 1400 First Ave N, 59401. Tel 406-452-3462. *Pres* Joyce Wohlgemuth; *VPres* Phil Faccenda; *Secy* Mildred Dalich; *Dir & Cur* Janet W Postler; *Cur History* Gail Thies
Open Mon - Fri 10 AM, Sat & Sun 1 - 4 PM, cl holidays. No admis fee. Estab 1976 to preserve and interpret the history of the Cascade County area. The historical museum is housed in a school building built in 1896, which is functioning as an art center and historical museum. Paris Gibson Square has art galleries showing contemporary and historic art. Mem: 300; dues sponsor $20, family $15, single $10; annual meeting third Thur in Feb
Income: $12,000 (financed by membership)
Collections: Art, documents, manuscripts, photographs, objects reflecting the history of the local area; clothing, furniture & memorabilia from Great Falls & Cascade County
Exhibitions: Haynes collection of photos (Montana Historical Society); rotating exhibits from the permanent collections
Activities: Lectures open to public; tours; book traveling exhibition, 1-4 times per year; sales shop sells books, prints

M PARIS GIBSON SQUARE, 1400 First Ave N, 59401. Tel 406-727-8255. *Dir* Vicki S Everson; *Cur* Mark Leach
Open Tues - Fri 10 AM - 5 PM, Sat & Sun 1 - 4 PM, cl Mon. No admis fee. Estab 1976 for contemporary arts. Maintains 3 galleries. Average Annual Attendance: 30,000. Mem: 650; dues $15-$500; annual meetings in June
Income: $160,000 (financed by classes, sales shop, restaurant & county mill)
Collections: †Contemporary regional artists
Exhibitions: H Schlauzhauer; C Ching & S Newall; James Castle
Publications: Newsletter, bi-monthly
Activities: Classes for adults & children; docent training; lectures open to public, 6 vis lectr per yr; book traveling exhibitions; sales shop sells original art, reproductions & prints

M C M RUSSELL MUSEUM, 1201 Fourth Ave N, 59401. Tel 406-727-8787. *Dir* Ray W Steele
Open Mon - Sat 10 AM - 5 PM, Sun 1 - 5 PM, cl Mon during winter, summer Mon - Fri until 8 PM. Estab 1953. Museum includes Russell's original studio. Average Annual Attendance: 50,000. Mem: Dues sponsor $500, sustaining $100, supporting $50, associate $35, non-resident and family $20, student $2
Income: Financed by operating budget
Collections: Works by Charles M Russell and other Western works, historical and contemporary
Exhibitions: Traveling exhibitions in contemporary arts; more than a dozen exhibitions are offered yearly, along with related programs within the arts
Publications: Newsletter, quarterly
Activities: Creative dramatics; creative workshops; children's theatre; film program; Arts-Science Fair; Annual C M Russell Auction; traveling exhibitions organized and circulated; gift shop selling books, reproductions, jewelry, pottery

HAMILTON

M RAVALLI COUNTY MUSEUM, 205 Bedford, Old Court House, 59840. Tel 406-363-5177. *Pres* Lavern Vance; *VPres* Dick Babcock; *Secy* Winona Linn; *Dir* Erma L Owings
Open summer Mon - Fri 10 AM - 4 PM, Sun 2:30 - 5 PM, winter Mon - Fri 1 - 4 PM, Sun 2:30 - 5 PM. No admis fee. Estab 1979 to preserve the history of the Bitterroot Valley. Museum contains Indian exhibit kitchen, living room, parlor, schoolroom, dental office & tack room. Average Annual Attendance: 9000. Mem: 150; dues regular $5, sr citizen $2; meetings third Mon of each month
Income: Financed by county appropriation & gifts from Bitterroot Valley Historical Society
Purchases: $5000
Collections: Home furnishings reflecting early life of the Bitterroot Valley; Indian Railroad
Exhibitions: Montana Collage; R McKay Sepea photos of Flathead Indians
Publications: An Old Bitter Rooters Thoughts in Poetry, Joe Hughes; McIntosh Apple Cookbook: Bitterroot Trials
Activities: Book traveling exhibitions; sales shop sells locally made china & cards

HELENA

O MONTANA HISTORICAL SOCIETY, 225 N Roberts, 59620. Tel 406-449-2694. *Dir* Dr Robert Archibald; *Pres* George O'Connor; *VPres* Mike Malone; *Secy* Bruce Enniz; *Business Mgr* Linda Gamble-Depew
Open daily 8 AM - 5 PM (Sept - May), 8 AM - 6 PM (June - August). No admis fee. Estab 1865 to collect, preserve and present articles relevant to history and heritage of Montana and the Northwest. C M Russell Art Gallery, western artists; Poindexter Gallery; Haynes Gallery. Average Annual Attendance: 200, 000. Mem: 11,000; dues $15
Income: Financed by membership, state appropriation and donations
Purchases: $400,000
Collections: †Haynes Collection of Art and Artifacts; MacKay Collection of C M Russell Art; Poindexter Collection of Contemporary Art
Exhibitions: Three Photographers: Ansel Adams, Edward Weston, Wynn Bullock; Rudy Auto: A Retrospective, ceramic & sculpture; Montana Views & Visions, paintings, drawings, sculpture; Children in Montana, photography
Publications: Montana, Magazine of Western History, quarterly; Montana Post (newsletter), quarterly
Activities: Classes for adults and children; docent training; lect open to public, 2 visiting lectr per year; gallery talks; special guided tours; individual painting and original objects of art lent only with approval of Board of Trustees; traveling exhibitions organized and circulated; sales shop selling books, magazines, prints, reproductions, slides, bronzework
L Library, 225 N Roberts, 59601. *Art Cur* Mike McCourt; *Photographs* Lori Morrow
For reference and research only
Library Holdings: Vols 5000; Per subs 100
Collections: Newspaper Collection; Photographic Collection

KALISPELL

O HOCKADAY CENTER FOR THE ARTS, Flathead Valley Art Association & Art Gallery, Second Ave East and Third St, Box 83, 59901. Tel 406-755-5268. *Dir* Magee Ferguson; *Asst Dir* Sue Rolfing; *Secy* Becky Lucas
Open Tues - Sat 10 AM - 5 PM. No admis fee. Estab 1968 to foster and encourage a growing interest in and understanding of all the arts; to provide the opportunity to take a place in the main current of the arts today, as well as to observe and learn from the arts of the past. Center is housed in the former Carnegie Library near downtown Kalispell; has two spacious exhibition galleries and a sales gallery. Mem: 1000; dues benefactor $50; patron $25; family $20; individual $10; student and sr citizen $5
Income: $110,000 (financed by memberships, contributions, grants, exhibition sponsors, corporate donations and city-county funds)
Collections: Main collection includes eight portrait studies by Hugh Hockaday, artist of regional significance & the center's late namesake, as well as several other of his works
Exhibitions: A variety of art exhibitions of all mediums, mostly curated by staff
Publications: Exhibition catalogs; newsletter, monthly
Activities: Classes for adults and children; drama programs; pottery lab with full-time potter; docent training; gallery talks open to public; annual film tour; summer and winter art festival; sponsors competitions with awards; book traveling exhibitions, 3-7 per year; originate traveling exhibitions; sales shop sells local artists' paintings

LEWISTOWN

O **LEWISTOWN ART CENTER,** 108 8th Ave North, PO Box 644, 59457. Tel
406-538-8278. *Dir* Tammy L Hedges; *Pres* Keay Cowen; *VPres* Kathleen Clasby-
LeTellier; *Secy* Cynthia Denton; *Treas* Kathy Fleharty
Open Tues - Thurs & Sat 1:30 - 5 PM, Fri 11 AM - 6 PM, Tues evening 7 - 9
PM, cl Mon. Estab 1971 for the advancement in and education of all of the arts.
The exhibits gallery changes monthly providing a variety of local, state and
national exhibits. There is also a sales gallery which features Montana artists and
a gallery for local artists. Average Annual Attendance: 3300. Mem: 650; dues
$10 - $25; annual meeting second wk in Sept
Income: $28,000 (financed by membership, various grants, programs sponsored
by the Center)
Exhibitions: Don Greytak, drawings; Local Artist's Show; Annual Auction, open
to Montana artists
Activities: Classes for adults and children; dramatic programs; docent programs;
lectures open to the public, 2 - 3 vis lectr per yr; book traveling exhibitions, 6 per
yr; sales shop sells books, original art, reproductions

MILES CITY

O **CUSTER COUNTY ART CENTER,** Water Plant Rd, PO Box 1284, 59301. Tel
406-232-0635. *Exec Dir* Julia A Cook; *Asst* Sandy Meidinger; *Asst* Bob Shy
Open Tues - Sun 1 PM - 5 PM, cl holidays. No admis fee. Estab 1977 to provide
an arts program of exhibits and workshops to Southeastern Montana. Maintains
The Water Works Gallery, located in the old Miles City pumping plant holding
tanks; pottery workshop; printing workshop. Average Annual Attendance:
10,000. Mem: 450; dues benefactor $500, patron $300, sponsor $100, sustaining
$50, contributing $35, family $25, individual $15, student & sr citizens $7.50
Income: $60,000 (financed by membership, county appropriation, fund raising
events and grants)
Exhibitions: Custer County Art Center Juried Art Exhibit; Annual Art Auction
Exhibit
Publications: Newsletter, monthly; exhibit announcement, monthly; catalog, biannually
Activities: Classes for adults and children; docent training; lect open to the
public, 4 visiting lectr per year; gallery talks; tours; competitions; films; exten
dept serves schools; book traveling exhibitions; originate traveling exhibitions;
sales shop selling books, magazines and original art

MISSOULA

M **FORT MISSOULA HISTORICAL MUSEUM,*** Building 322, Fort Missoula,
59801. Tel 406-728-3476. *Pres* Donna Heilman; *VPres* Jack Weidenfeller; *Secy*
Lois Blevins; *Dir* Frank R Grant; *Cur* Kathi Olson; *Registrar* Sharon Hoefler
Open Tues - Sun Noon - 5 PM. No admis fee. Estab July 4, 1976 to collect and
exhibit artifacts related to the history of western Montana. Changing gallery, 900
sq ft used for temporary exhibits; Meeting room gallery, 200 sq ft; Permanent
gallery, 1200 sq ft. Average Annual Attendance: 14,000. Mem: 225; annual dues
$10; meetings third Thursday in May
Income: $70,000 (financed by membership, county appropriation and fund raising
events)
Collections: Photograph collection
Exhibitions: A J Gibson: Architect for a Proud Missoula; Woven from Nature:
Native American Art and Artifacts; Curtis Photographs of Native Americans, F J
Haynes, photographer; View from the Street: Architecture; Toy Shoppe:
Christmas Exhibit
Activities: Classes for adults and children; lectures open to public; gallery talks;
tours; book traveling exhibitions; sales shop sells books, magazines, original art

M **MISSOULA MUSEUM OF THE ARTS,** 335 N Pattee, 59802. Tel 406-728-
0447. *Dir* Mary Cummings; *Cur* Lawrence E Eick; *Executive Secy* Billie Blom
Open Mon - Sat Noon - 5 PM. No admis fee. Estab 1975. Housed in renovated
Carnegie Library (1903) featuring soft-panel covered walls; moveable track
lighting; approx 3500 sq ft of exhibits space on two floors; fire and security alarm
systems; meeting rooms. Average Annual Attendance: 18,000. Mem: 600
Income: $135,000 (financed by membership, grants, fund raising events & and
annual permissive mill levy by Missoula County)
Purchases: Contemporary art of Western Montana
Collections: †Contemporary Art of Western Montana
Exhibitions: Asian Di-Visions: A Contrast of the Art of China & Japan;
Theodore Wores: American Working in Wishes; Still as the Grass; Dana
Boussard
Publications: Exhibition catalogs; FOCUS, monthly membership newsletter;
mailers and posters advertising shows
Activities: Classes for adults and children; lect open to public, 6 - 8 visiting lectr
per year; gallery talks; tours; competitions; prize and purchase awards; films;
book traveling exhibitions 8-10 per year

M **UNIVERSITY OF MONTANA,** Gallery of Visual Arts,* 59801. Tel 406-243-
0211. *Prof in Charge* Mary Warner; *Gallery Clerk* Gayl Teichert
Open Mon - Fri summer and academic year, 12 - 5 PM. No admis fee. Estab
1970 to provide exhibit space for students and faculty of the Art Department at
the University of Montana and for periodical showings of the University's
permanent art collection; to sponsor outside exhibitions in an effort to acquaint
the community and the university with significant contemporary artists
nationwide; to provide guest lecturers to the community. Gallery covers 60 x 40
ft exhibit space with spot and flood lighting, moveable panels and 14 ft ceilings.
Average Annual Attendance: 10,000
Income: Financed by city and state appropriation
Collections: Dana Collection; Poindexter Collection
Exhibitions: Faculty, student and traveling exhibitions are shown in both
galleries; shows from the permanent collection
Activities: Lect open to the public, 5 vis lectr per yr; competitions; Scholarships
offered; original objects of art lent; lending collection contains Kodachromes

PRYOR

M **CHIEF PLENTY COUPS STATE MONUMENT MUSEUM,** Box 35, 59066.
Tel 406-252-1289. *Dir* James Flynn; *Deputy Dir* Ron Holliday; *Cur* Harley R
Sorrells
Open Mon - Sat 9 AM - 5 PM, Sun Noon - 5 PM. No admis fee. Estab 1932
Income: Financed by state appropriation; affiliated with Montana Fish, Wildlife
and Parks
Collections: Ethnographic materials of the Crow Indians; paintings; drawings;
prehistoric artifacts
Exhibitions: Crow clothing and adornment
Activities: Sales shop sells books, prints, sculpture, and handicrafts of the Crow
Indians

SIDNEY

M **J K RALSTON MUSEUM AND ART CENTER,** 221 Fifth Ave SW, PO Box
50, 59270. Tel 406-482-3500. *Chmn County Museum Board* Gene Krueger; *Dir*
Anne Schneider
Open Wed - Fri & Sun 1 - 5 PM, cl Mon, Tues & Sat. No admis fee. Estab 1972
to preserve history of area and further interest in fine arts. Average Annual
Attendance: 4500. Mem: 300; dues $7.50 and up; annual meeting March
Income: Financed by county and state appropriations & membership dues
Exhibitions: (1982) Hmon Textiles; All-Montana Art Show; Second Annual
Quilt Show; Jade: The Stone of Heaven; John Bashor Paintings; Helen McAuslan
Retrospective; Maureen Curtis, An Artist from Circle; Beth Moffit - Absaroka
Wilderness Series; Between Art & Craft; Remington - Black & White Wood
Engravings; Blank Walls; Eighth Annual Art Show; F Jay Haynes: Fifty Views,
photography; Mary Hardy, photography; Photography Guild of Sidney; (1983)
Second Annual All-Montana Art Show; Third Annual Quilt Show; Flathead
Wellsprings: The Art of Juane Quick-To-See Smith; Don Ruth Watercolors; New
Work in Montana: 5 Montana Artists; Maribeth Dietrich: Handmade Paper;
Native American Prints; Gene Tierney: 20 Photographs Hand-painted with Oils;
Dinnerware Artists Cooperative: Exhibition; Miniature Art Show - Migration
'83; Nineth Annual Art Show; Emphasis: Local Artists; Front Range: Women in
the Arts
Publications: Mondak Historical & Arts Society Newsletter, 3-4 times yearly
Activities: Classes for adults and children; dramatic programs; competitions; book
traveling exhibitions; sales shop sells books, magazines, original art, reproductions
& prints
L **Willo Ralston Library for Historical Research,** 59270. Tel 406-482-3279.
Executive Dir Charles Evanson
Open to the public for historical reference
Library Holdings: Vols 400; Other — Exhibition catalogs
Activities: Tours

SOMERS

M **KALAMUNDA MUSEUM OF WESTERN ART,** 1485 Montana Hwy 82,
59932. Tel 406-857-3802. *Pres* Cecil Smith; *VPres* Marie W Smith; *Secy*
Rockwell L Smith; *Museum Attendant* La Priel Smith; *Museum Attendant*
Raychelle R Smith; *Framer* Stephen L Smith; *Asst Framer* Carey Smith
Open daily 9:30 AM - 3 PM. No admis fee. Estab 1980 to promote and
encourage national interest in Masterpiece Western and Genre Art. Maintains
two four wall galleries: one gallery accomodates permanent collection and the
other accomodates temporary exhibits
Income: Financed by endowment
Collections: †Buckaroo Artists of America; †Original Art by the Rare Brede
Artists; †Work by Renown Painters and Sculptors
Publications: Art Service Associate, catalogue; Full Color Listing of Paintings
and Prints
Activities: Individual paintings and original objects of art lent to state and
national museums; lending collection contains paintings, photographs and
sculpture; museum and sales shop selling original art, reproductions, prints and
slides

NEBRASKA

AURORA

M **PLAINSMAN MUSEUM,*** 210 16th , 68818. Tel 402-694-6531. *Pres* Wesley
Huenefeld; *VPres* Louis Oswald; *Secy* Gwen Allen
Open April 1 - Oct 31 Mon - Sat 9 AM - 5 PM, Sun 1 - 5 PM, Nov 1 - Mar 31
Mon - Sun 1 - 5 PM. Admis adults $1, sr citizens & children $.50. Estab 1976 to
tell the story of Plainsman using mosaics, murals, house, shop and other settings
to add to use of artifacts. Average Annual Attendance: 8000. Mem: 150; dues
couples $10, singles $6; annual meeting second Tues in Jan
Income: $50,000 (financed by membership, county allowance and individual
donations)
Collections: Murals by Sidney E King; Pioneer Scene Mosaic Floor
Exhibitions: School art; Australian pottery
Activities: Sales shop sells books and prints

CHADRON

M **CHADRON STATE COLLEGE,** Arts Gallery, Tenth and Main Sts, 69337. Tel
308-432-4451, Ext 6317. *Coordr* Charles J Harington
Open Mon - Fri 8 AM - 5 PM. No admis fee. Estab 1967 to offer opportunities
for students, faculty and local artists to present their works; to bring in shows to
upgrade the cultural opportunities of students and the general public. Main

gallery has space for traveling and larger shows; little gallery suffices for small shows. Average Annual Attendance: 5000
Income: Financed by college budget and state appropriation
Exhibitions: Arts and Crafts Fair; Bosworth, Rickenbach Exhibits; DaVinci Model show by IBM; Edges: Hard and Soft; Faculty Art Show; Former Students Works; Hands in Clay; Greg Lafler: Handmade Jewelry; Tony Martin: Ceramics and Crafts; Photographs of the Farm Security Administration; Roten Galleries: Graphics Show; National Cone Box Traveling Show; Iowa Arts & Crafts; Mathew Brady, photographs; State of the Print; Student Art Show
Activities: Lectures open to public; gallery talks; competitions with awards

CHAPPELL

L CHAPPELL MEMORIAL LIBRARY AND ART GALLERY, 289 Babcock, 69129. Tel 308-874-2626. *Head Librn* Doris McFee; *Asst Librn* Gladys Smith
Open Tues - Thurs 2 - 5 PM, Tues & Thurs evening 7 - 9 PM. No admis fee. Estab 1935 by gift of Mrs Charles H Chappell
Income: Financed by city of Chappell
Library Holdings: Vols 10,446; Per subs 29
Collections: Permanent personal collection of art works from many countries, a gift from Mrs Charles H Chappell
Activities: Gallery talks; library tours

HASTINGS

M HASTINGS MUSEUM,* 1330 N Burlington Ave, 68901. Tel 402-463-7126. *Dir* Ed Bisaillon; *Pres Board Trustees* Harry A Borley; *Cur Exhib* Burton R Nelson; *Museum Coordr* Geraldine S Shuman; *Cur Astronomy* Robert S Craighead; *Exhib Specialist* Jerome Dierfeldt
Open Mon - Sat 9 AM - 5 PM, Sun 1 - 5 PM. Admis adults $1.25, children (6-11) $.50, tots free. Estab 1926 for a program of service and exhibits to augment and stimulate the total educative program of schools and the general public. Animal displays in natural habitat settings. Average Annual Attendance: 45,000. Mem: 1750; dues life $100, family $5, individual $2.50
Income: Financed by city appropriation
Collections: American Indian artifacts; glassware; Irma Kruse Collection; Richards Coin Collection
Publications: Yester News, monthly except July-August-Sept
Activities: Sales shop selling books and selected gift items

HOLDREGE

M PHELPS COUNTY HISTORICAL SOCIETY MUSEUM, N Burlington St, PO Box 215, 68949. Tel 308-995-5015. *Pres* Don Lindgren; *VPres* Eileen Schrock; *Secy* Faye Stevens; *Treas* Bernice Lindgren
Open daily 2 - 5 PM. No admis fee. Estab 1966 for preservation of County History and artifacts. Average Annual Attendance: 4000. Mem: 450; dues life $100, annual $5; annual meeting May
Income: Financed by membership and county mill levy
Collections: Agriculture equipment, China, furniture, historical items, photos
Publications: History of Phelps County, 1873-1980; Centennial History of Holdrege, 1883; Holdrege Centennial Coloring Book
Activities: Lectures open to the public, 4 - 6 vis lectr per yr; tours; book traveling exhibitions; sales shop sells books, labels & souvenir plates
L Library, Holdrege, 68949
Reference only
Library Holdings: Vols 500; AV — A-tapes, cassettes, Kodachromes, lantern slides, v-tapes; Other — Clipping files, manuscripts, pamphlets, photographs, prints

LINCOLN

O LINCOLN COMMUNITY ARTS COUNCIL,* Room 508, Lincoln Center Bldg, 68508. Tel 402-477-5930. *Executive Dir* Jackie Hall; *Pres* Dr Dick Hay; *Sr Arts Coordr* Dixie Moss
Open 8:45 AM - 4:45 PM. Estab 1966 to promote and encourage the community at large and all its arts organizations to grow, develop, use all the resources available, avoid over-lapping of energy, money, talent and to enrich the entire community; clearing house for arts activities scheduling. Mem: 175; 60 groups; dues prorated; meetings monthly Sept - May
Income: Financed by endowment, membership, city and state appropriation, community arts fund
Publications: Arts calendar; newsletter
Activities: Arts festival; awards; outreach to handicapped

M NEBRASKA WESLEYAN UNIVERSITY, Elder Gallery, 50th & Huntington, 68504. Tel 402-466-2371. *Dir* Betty Wallace
Open Tues - Fri 10 AM - 4 PM, Sat & Sun 1 - 4 PM. No admis fee. Estab 1966 as a cultural addition to college and community. Average Annual Attendance: 10,000
Collections: Campus collection; †permanent collection of prints, paintings and sculpture
Exhibitions: Annual Fred Wells 10-state juried exhibition; Nebraska Art Educators; faculty show; students shows; other changing monthly shows
Activities: Classes for adults

UNIVERSITY OF NEBRASKA, LINCOLN
M Sheldon Memorial Art Gallery, 68588. Tel 402-472-2461. *Dir* George W Neubert; *Asst Dir* Donald Bartlett Doe; *Dir Educational Services* Mrs A Douglas Anderson; *Dir Sheldon Film Theatre* Dan Ladely
Open Tues 10 AM - 10 PM, Wed - Sat 10 AM - 5 PM, Sun 2 - 5 PM. No admis fee. Estab 1888 to exhibit the permanent collections owned by the University and to present temporary exhibitions on an annual basis. These activities are accompanied by appropriate interpretive programs. The Sheldon Gallery, a gift of

Frances & Bromley Sheldon, was opened in 1963 & is the work of Philip Johnson. Facilities in addition to 25,000 sq ft of exhibition galleries, include an auditorium, a print study, members room and an outdoor sculpture garden. Average Annual Attendance: 110,000
Income: Financed by endowment, state appropriation and Nebraska Art Association
Purchases: $30,000
Collections: †Frank M Hall Collection of contemporary paintings, sculpture, prints, drawings, photographs and ceramics; †Nebraska Art Association Collection of American paintings and drawings; Bertha Schaefer Bequest; †University Collections
Exhibitions: Annual Faculty Exhibition; Annual Undergraduate Exhibition; Prints and Drawings by Sigmund Abeles; Paintings by James Bama; Photographs by Cirrus Bonneau; Photographs by Jim Butkus; Paintings by John Dawson; Paintings and Drawings by Preston Dickinson; Photographs by Elliot Erwitt; Of Dust Bowl Descent, photographs by Bill Ganzel; Kadinsky's Small Worlds; Paintings, Drawings & Collages by Weldon Kees; Graphics by Michael Mazur; Fiberworks by Trudy Morgenstern; Photographs by Dave Read; Paintings & Drawings by David Routon; Graphics by Mark Tobey; Photographs by Kelly Wise
Publications: Exhibition catalogs, 2 per yr
Activities: Docent training; lect open to the public; tours; individual paintings and original objects of art lent to campus offices; traveling exhibitions organized and circulated; museum shop sells books, original art, prints, jewelry and ceramics
L Architecture Library, 11th and R Sts, 68588. Tel 402-472-1208. *Assoc Prof* Kathleen A Johnson
Open Mon - Thurs 8 AM - 5 PM, 7 - 10 PM, Fri 8 AM - 5 PM, Sat 10 Am - 5 PM, Sun 6 - 10 PM, summer hours Mon - Fri 7:30 AM - 4 PM. Circ 8700
Purchases: $20,000
Library Holdings: Vols 28,000; Per subs 135; Micro — Fiche, reels; AV — A-tapes, cassettes, fs, rec, slides; Other — Clipping files, exhibition catalogs, photographs
Special Subjects: Architecture; Community and Regional Planning
Collections: Architecture: Urban Documents Microfiche; Historic American Building Survey Measure and Drawings
O Nebraska Art Association, 68588. *Pres* Mrs Wallace Richardson; *VPres* Mrs Tom Larsen; *VPres* Dr Larry Lusk; *VPres* Mrs William Miller; *Secy* Art Thompson
Open Tues 10 AM - 10 PM, Wed - Sat 10 AM - 5 PM, Sun 2 - 5 PM, cl Mon. Estab 1888 as the Haydon Art Club, inc 1900 to study and prepare papers on art, to form a collection, to acquire a suitable art museum, to encourage young artists, to interest public school children and to attract industry and keep abreast of a growing city; a supportive organization to the Sheldon Memorial Art Gallery. Mem: 950; dues family $20; annual meeting May
Income: $18,865 (financed by endowment, membership)
Purchases: $15,000
Collections: †Paintings, †drawings, †prints, †photographs, †crafts, †sculpture
Exhibitions: (1982) Annual art faculty exhibition; annual art & home economics student exhibition; Great Plains Outdoor Sculpture Exhibition; Ranchos De Taos: An Exploration of Photographic Style; Four Native Americans, John Hoover, Randy Lee White; Jaune Quick-to-See-Smith, Dan Namingha; Larry Bell Retrospective, Works in Glass; Chicago, Some Other Traditions; Ron Slowinski: A Retrospective; Santa Fe/Taos Exhibition; Larry Fink, photographs; Don Williams, pastels; Treasures from the Millicent Rogers Museum Collection; Andre Kertesz, photographs; (1984) Chicago: Some Other Traditions: Ron Slowinski: A Retrospective; MFA/Art Undergrad Exhibtions, textiles, clothing, design; Dan Howard Retrospective; Victor Schrager, photographs; Gordon Holler; Linda Conner; Michael Geiger
Publications: Annual report; exhibition catalog
Activities: Docent training; gallery talks; tours; Scholarships offered; individual paintings and original objects of art lent to corporations; lending collection contains film strips & motion pictures; sales shop sells magazines, reproductions, original art & cards

MCCOOK

M HIGH PLAINS MUSEUM,* 423 Norris Ave, 69001. Tel 308-345-3661. *Chmn Bd* Mrs Alan Redfern; *Pres* Lester Harsh
Open Mon - Sun 1:30 - 4:30 PM, cl legal holidays. No admis fee. Estab 1966 to preserve the items pertaining to the local history and to interpret them for the public. Museum is located in former Carnegie Library mission style building. New additions include complete pioneer kitchen; Railroad section (inside and out);complete Old Time Pharmacy. Morning tours by appointment. Average Annual Attendance: 8000. Mem: 230; dues $5 - $150
Income: Financed by membership
Collections: Paintings made on the barracks walls of prisoner of war camp near McCook; paintings donated by local artists
Activities: Lect open to the public; gallery talks; tours; Book shop

MINDEN

M HAROLD WARP PIONEER VILLAGE FOUNDATION, 68959. Tel 308-832-1181. *Pres* Harold Warp; *Cur* Larry Nielsen
Open daily. Admis adults $4, children $2, children under 6 free; special rates to groups. Estab 1953 to preserve man's progress from 1830 to present day. Average Annual Attendance: 135,000
Collections: Folk art; graphics; historical materials; paintings; sculpture
Activities: Classes for adults; elderhostel; lectures for members only; tours; museum shop sells books, reproductions, prints & slides

NEBRASKA CITY

M GAME AND PARKS COMMISSION, Arbor Lodge State Historical Park,*
Rural Route Two, 68410. Tel 402-873-3221. *Supt* Randall Fox; *Asst Supt*
Kathleen Moore; *Dir* Eugene Mahoney
Open April - May Mon - Sun 1 - 5 PM, May - Sept Mon - Sun 10 AM - 8 PM,
Sept - Nov Mon - Sun 1 - 5 PM. Admis adults $.50, children 6-15 $.25, children
under 6 no charge. Estab 1923. Art collection of members of the J S Morton
family and outdoor scenes spread through a 52 room mansion. Average Annual
Attendance: 40,000
Income: Financed by state appropriation
Activities: Lect open to public; tours; awards, Arbor Day Tree plantings on April
22; sales shop sells books, Arbor Day Tree and stick pins and postcards

OMAHA

M ARTISTS' COOPERATIVE GALLERY, 424 S 11th St, 68102. Tel 402-342-
9617. *Dir* Elizabeth J Brougham; *Board Dir* Lee Lubbers; *Board Dir* Marcia
Joffe-Bouska; *Board Dir* Stephen Roberts; *Board Dir* L Zenaide Luhr; *Board Dir*
Mary Keogh
Open Tue - Thurs 11 AM - 5 PM, Fri & Sat 11 AM - 10 PM, Sun Noon - 5 PM.
No admis fee. Estab 1975 to be gathering place for those interested in visual art;
to display quality local, contemporary art; to offer programs, panels & discussions
on related issues to the public. Gallery contains 1300 sq ft consisting of large
open area with 2 small, self-contained galleries. Average Annual Attendance:
21,000. Mem: 33; dues $300; monthly meetings
Income: $10,000
Exhibitions: Alumni Show; Michael Flelcky; Lee Lubbers; Harry Jordan; Steve
Roberts; Mary Jane Krance; All Member Show; Marcia Joffe-Bouska; Kristin
Hoffman; Nancy Parks Carlson; Thomas Wise; Cindy Jane Menolascino; Escape;
Garage Sale; Duane Adams; John C Miller; L Zenaide Luhr; Allen Vap; Margie
Schimenti; Sue Devlin; C Robert Chenoweth; Joan Frost; Lin McKeown; Jim
Williams; Robert Willits; Nick Chiburis; Barbara Hesse; Annual All-Member
Holiday Show
Activities: Lectures open to public, 3-4 vis lectr per yr; book traveling
exhibitions; originates traveling exhibitions

M CREIGHTON UNIVERSITY ART GALLERY,* 2602 California St, 68178. Tel
402-449-2509. *Dir* Roger C Alkin; *Chmn Fine & Performing Arts Dept* Donald
A Doll
Mon - Fri 9 AM - 4 PM, Sat & Sun 12 - 4 PM. Mus estab 1973. Gallery handles
10 exhibits per academic year; space provided for student thesis exhibits; 150
running ft. Average Annual Attendance: 2000
Collections: Ceramics; drawings; graphics; paintings; photography; pottery and
sculpture
Exhibitions: Linda Pepper; Sandy Kinnll; Robert Therien; Don Doll; S J;
Riccardo Marchio; Jim Butkint
Activities: Lect open to the public

M JOSLYN ART MUSEUM, 2200 Dodge St, 68102. Tel 402-342-3300. *Dir*
Henry Flood Robert Jr; *Assoc Dir Admin* Audrey Kauders; *Assoc Dir Art* Ted
James; *Development Dir* Burdette M Frederickson; *Cur European Art* Hollister
Sturges; *Curatorial Asst* Ruby Hagerbaumer; *Asst to Dir* Cynthia Christensen;
Cur Western Art David Hunt; *Cur Western History* Joseph Porter; *Cur Material
Culture* Marsha Gallagher; *Cur Manuscripts* William Orr; *Cur American Art*
Holliday T Day; *Admin Asst Cur Western Studies* Marilyn Shanewise; *Registrar*
Berneal Anderson; *Head Registration & Prep* Edward R Quick; *Museum Shop*
Denise Lorey; *Cur Educ* Anne El-Omami; *Cur Educ* Jan Braden; *Cur Educ*
Allison Perkins
Open Tues - Sat 10 AM - 5 PM, Sun 1 - 5 PM, cl Mon & holidays. Admis adults
$2, children under 12 & sr citizens $1, members free. Joslyn Art Museum was
incorporated 1928, opened 1931, to care for and expand the collections; offer
exhibitions; promote education in and cultivation of the fine arts. Museum was a
gift of Mrs Sarah H Joslyn in memory of her husband, George A Joslyn.
Museum is a marble building covering a two-block area; contains ten large
galleries with small exhibit areas surrounding a large central court and 1200-seat
Witherspoon Concert Hall on the main floor. The concert hall is used for
programs by major community music and cultural organizations. The ground
floor includes exhibit areas, library, studios, lecture hall, museum shop, rental and
sales gallery and offices. Mem: 5000; dues $12.50 - $2500; annual meeting 2nd
Tues in Dec
Collections: America Art from Colonial to present; European Art from Middle
Ages to present; Maximilian-Bodmer Collection (including works by Karl
Bodmer, Alfred Jacob Miller, George Catlin, Frederick Remington and Charles
Russell); Native American from pre-Columbian to present; works from the Orient
and Ancient Mediterranean civilizations
Exhibitions: The Joslyn Biennial Exhibition, a juried show open to artists in a 22
state area around Nebraska, is held in even-numbered years; it includes paintings,
sculpture and graphics; additions to the Museum's permanent collection are
purchased from the exhibition. Temporary exhibitions include traveling shows of
national significance, Joslyn-organized shows, one-person and group shows in all
media; (1981-82) The Shape of Space: The Sculpture of George Sugarman; (1982)
Jules Breton; Legacy of the West; (1984) Views of a Vanishing Frontier
Publications: Members calendar, bi-monthly; exhibition catalogs
Activities: Creative and art appreciation classes for adults and children (pre-
school through high school); special workshops; film programs; special tour
program of permanent collections and special exhibitions maintained for public
school children; lect and exhibition gallery talks; tours of the collections and
special exhibitions; book traveling exhibitions

L Art Reference Library, 2200 Dodge St, 68102. *Librn* Ann E Birney
Open Tues - Sat 10 AM - 12 & 1 - 5 PM, Sun 1 - 5 PM. Estab 1931, reference
only
Library Holdings: Vols 17,000; Per subs 100; circulating material of
reproductions: 140 vertical files; Stereographs; Micro — Fiche, reels; AV — A-
tapes, fs, motion pictures, slides 20,000, v-tapes; Other — Clipping files,
exhibition catalogs, framed reproductions, memorabilia, original art works,
pamphlets, reproductions, sculpture
Special Subjects: Tran-Mississippi West, Native American Art

L NEBRASKA ARTS COUNCIL LIBRARY, 1313 Farnam On-the-Mall, 68102.
Tel 402-554-2122. *Chmn* LaVon Crosby; *VChmn* Dick C E Davis; *Executive Dir*
Robin Tryloff
Open Mon - Fri 8 AM - 5 PM. Estab circa 1970 to provide information on arts
administration topics to constituents
Income: $100 (financed by state appropriation and federal grants)
Purchases: $100
Library Holdings: Vols 550; AV — Motion pictures, slides, v-tapes; Other —
Pamphlets
Publications: Guidelines, annually; Nebraska touring program brochures,
annually; newsletters, quarterly
Activities: Grants to non-profit community organizations and schools for projects
related to the arts; workshops; lect open to public, 2 - 3 visiting lectr per year;
grant awards to non-profit organizations in Nebraska for arts projects

M OMAHA CHILDREN'S MUSEUM, INC, 515 S 18th, 68102. Tel 402-342-
6164. *Pres* Bob Schorr; *VPres* Nancy Roberts; *Exec Dir* Robert L Russell; *Asst
Dir* Linda Roush; *Educ Dir* Jo Ann Cutler; *Floor Mgr* Connie Conway; *Secy*
Julie Resenberger; *Vol Dir* Martha Jacobs
Open Tues - Sat 10 AM - 5 PM, Sun 1 - 5 PM, cl Mon. Admis $1.75. Estab
1978 to provide hands-on Museum experience for children in art and science.
Average Annual Attendance: 45,000. Mem: 800 families; dues $18
Income: Financed by membership, admissions, grants, donations from individuals
and corporations
Exhibitions: 10 Hands-On exhibit-learning centers; workshops by local
professional educators and artists; traditional gallery shows with related open
studio
Publications: Museum newsletter, quarterly
Activities: Classes for adults and children; docent training; gallery talks; exten
dept serves Greater Metro Omaha; book traveling exhibitions two per year;
originate traveling exhibitions; museum shop sells books, educational games and
toys

M UNIVERSITY OF NEBRASKA AT OMAHA, Art Gallery, 133 S Elmwood
Rd, 68132. Tel 402-554-2420. *Dir* Earl Lock
Open Mon - Fri 8 AM - 5 PM. No admis fee. Estab 1967 to heighten cultural
and aesthetic awareness of the metropolitan and midlands area. Average Annual
Attendance: 14,000
Income: Financed by state appropriation
Purchases: $5000
Collections: University Visiting Printmaker's Collection
Exhibitions: Wayne Kimball, lithographs; Dennis Guastella, paintings; Juergen
Strunck, relief prints; Drawings: Terry Allen, Power Boothe, Harold Boyd, Ann
Karlsen, Fran Noel & Jim Roche
Publications: Exhibition catalogs
Activities: Lect open to public, 2 vis lectr per year; gallery talks; tours;
competitions; scholarships

SEWARD

M CONCORDIA COLLEGE, Koenig Art Gallery, 800 N Columbia Ave, 68434.
Tel 402-643-3651. *Dir* Richard Wiegmann
Open weekdays 8 AM - 5 PM, Sun 2 - 5 PM. No admis fee. Estab 1959 to
provide the college and community with a wide variety of original art; both
monthly exhibitions and permanent collection serve primarily an educational
need; spacious gallery has additional showcases
Collections: Ceramics; †Contemporary Original Prints
Exhibitions: Nebraska Crafts Touring Exhibition; shows drawn from
permanent collection; Annual Student Exhibitions; The Indignant Artist; Images
of Independence; Wood: A Common Material; Nebraska Places & Spaces; 1 & 2
artists exhibitions Milton Heinrich; 1981 Nebraska Crafts Touring Exhibition;
American Prints of the 30's and 40's; works from the artist's cooperative;
occasional shows drawn from Permanent Collection and Annual Student
Exhibitions
Activities: Gallery talks; original objects of art lent; lending collection of framed
reproductions, original prints and paintings; book traveling exhibitions, 12 per
year

WAYNE

M WAYNE STATE COLLEGE, Nordstrand Visual Arts Gallery, Fine Arts Center,
68787. Tel 402-375-2200, Ext 360. *Division Chmn of Fine Arts* Dr Jay O'Leary
Open Mon - Fri 9 AM - 5 PM. No admis fee. Estab January 1977 to provide art
students with a space to display work; to enhance student's education by viewing
incoming regional professional work; to enrich cultural atmosphere of college and
community. Small gallery, carpeted floors and walls, ceiling spotlights on tracts.
Average Annual Attendance: 800
Income: Financed by city and state appropriation, as well as Wayne State
Foundation
Collections: †Wayne State Foundation Print Collection
Exhibitions: (1983-84) Lawrence Anderson, prints & drawings; Candra Guenther
& Lance Hankins; student show; Priscilla Fenton, fibers & soft sculpture; Craig
Schmidt & Traci Blom; annual undergraduate competitive; Cindia Willers &
Cercelia Werner; Bob Lewis & Sheri Tacner; faculty show (1982) Colleen Victor
& Susan Madden Senior Exhibit; Ray George, Illinois State University Drawings
& Prints; Marla Mantey & Ken Hladky Senior Exhibit; Faculty Show; Spring
Juried Student Show; Fine Arts Open House
Activities: Lect open to public, 1 - 2 vis lectr per year; competitions

WILBER

M **WILBER CZECH MUSEUM,** Box 652, 68465. Tel 402-821-2485. *Pres* Irma Ourecky
Open by appointment. No admis fee. Estab 1953 to preserve Czech culture. Average Annual Attendance: 4000. Mem: Meetings second Monday of each month
Income: Financed by donations
Collections: Bronzes; photography; portraits; religious artifacts
Exhibitions: 22nd Annual Czech Festival
Activities: Tours for school groups; Sales shop sells books, magazines and Czech crafts

NEVADA

ELKO

M **NORTHEASTERN NEVADA HISTORICAL SOCIETY MUSEUM,** 1515 Idaho St, PO Box 2550, 89801. Tel 702-738-3418. *Dir* Howard Hickson; *Registrar* Bevette Moore; *Office Mgr* Laura Hawkins
Open weekdays & Sat 9 AM - 5 PM, Sun 1 - 5 PM. No admis fee; admis charge for theatre program. Estab 1968; general museum concentrating on Northeastern Nevada; also area cultural center. Gallery is 3000 sq ft also has round theatre with three-dimensional narrated exhibits and 8-projector slide-sound history show. Average Annual Attendance: 55,000. Mem: 2100; dues $10 - $1000; annual meeting date varies
Income: $150,000 (financed by private funding)
Exhibitions: (1984) Nevada 84: 10th Statewide Touring Photography Exhibition
Publications: Historical, quarterly; Northeastern Nevada Historical Society Quarterly
Activities: Lect open to public, 2 vis lectr per year; gallery talks; photography competitions; exten dept serving Nevada; lending collection of film strips, slides (complete programs); originate traveling exhibitions; museum shop sells books and local craft items
L **Library,** 1515 Idaho St, 89801
Open to public for reference
Library Holdings: Vols 2200; Per subs 5; Other — Photographs
Special Subjects: Concentration on Northeastern Nevada History
Collections: Newspaper and negative files

LAS VEGAS

L **CLARK COUNTY LIBRARY DISTRICT,** 1401 E Flamingo Rd, 89109. Tel 702-733-7810. *Dir* Charles W Hunsberger; *Admin* Joel McKee; *Admin* Jack Gardner; *Young People's Coordr* Beryl Andrus; *Ref* David Wells; *Exten Admin* Ann Langevin; *Regional Service Librn* Richard Stegman; *Asst Dir* Nancy Hudson; *Programming Coordr* Peggy Trasatti
Open Mon - Thurs 9 AM - 9 PM, Fri & Sat 9 AM - 5 PM, Sun 1 - 5 PM. Estab 1965 to provide information in all its varieties of form to people of all ages. Gallery provides regularly rotating art exhibitions of regional and national repute as well as three solo local shows a year, and a regional mixed media competition every spring. Circ 1,645,758
Income: $3,185,158 (financed by state and county appropriation)
Purchases: $570,000
Library Holdings: Vols 455,289; Per subs 535; Micro — Fiche, reels; AV — A-tapes, cassettes, fs, motion pictures, rec; Other — Clipping files, framed reproductions, original art works, pamphlets, photographs, prints, reproductions, sculpture
Collections: Nevada materials
Exhibitions: Art-a-Fair: Nevada Watercolor Society; Kenneth S Osthimer: Three Portfolios; Greg Kennedy: Fireworks; Rodolfo Fernandez: Colors in Concert; Bill Leaf: Desert Series; Landscapes & Interiors: Alan Platzer; Converging Views: Jim Kearns & Terry Weetling; Welcome to Las Vegas: Greg Allred & James Stanford; It's a Small, Small World: Kimberly House; Silver Performance: David Brown
Publications: Exhibition brochures, monthly; library program, bimonthly
Activities: Lectures open to the public; concerts; tours; competitions with awards; exten dept and regional service dept serving the area; bookmobiles; artists traveling through Southern Nevada giving demonstrations and lect; book traveling exhibitions; used book store sells books, magazines & original art
M **Flamingo Gallery,** * 1401 E Flamingo Rd, 89109. Tel 702-733-7810
Open Mon - Thurs 9 AM - 9 PM, Fri 9 AM 5 PM, Sat 9 AM - 5 PM, Sun 1 - 5 PM. Estab 1970. Gallery is located in Clark County Library, main gallery has 80 running feet of exhibit space, upstairs gallery is used for photographic displays. Average Annual Attendance: 10,000 - 15,000
Income: Financed by tax support, Federal and State grants
Exhibitions: Art-A-Fair (judged and juried); Spirit Impressions; The Potter & the Weaver; Nevada Watercolor Society Annual exhibit
Publications: Bi-monthly library calendar of events
Activities: Clases for adults and children; dramatic programs; string quartet; feature films; lectures open to public, 10 vis lectr per year; concerts; Art-A-Fair competition; monetary awards

M **LAS VEGAS ART MUSEUM,** 3333 W Washington, 89107. Tel 702-647-4300. *Pres* Lorrie Maultsby; *Secy* Kaye Thompson; *Museum Dir* Kay Focht
Open Mon - Sat 11 AM - 4 PM, Sun 1 - 4 PM. No admis fee. Estab 1950 to offer fine arts to the citizens of Las Vegas; to offer artist a place to show, work and study; to offer good education in fine arts to adults and children of the community. Average Annual Attendance: 15,000. Mem: 400; dues benefactor $1000, patron $500, sponsor $100, family $25, individual $18, senior citizens (65 and over) $10
Income: Financed by membership

Collections: Contemporary artists
Publications: Bulletin, monthly
Activities: Classes for adults presented by leading artists and craftsmen; Junior Art League sponsors classes for youths; self-help workshops; competitions

M **UNIVERSITY OF NEVADA, LAS VEGAS,** Art Gallery,* 4505 Maryland Parkway, 89109. Tel 702-736-6111, 739-3011, Ext 237. *Dir* Lee T Sido; *Art Preparator* John Kane
Open Sept - June Tues - Sat Noon - 4 PM. Gallery measures 26 x 22 ft. Average Annual Attendance: 5000. Mem: 50; dues $10
Income: Financed by membership and appropriation
Collections: †Ceramics; Oriental Art; †Paintings; Prints; †Sculpture
Exhibitions: Regularly exhibits work by students and faculty; sponsors exhibits throughout the year by several nationally-renowned artists
Activities: Classes for adults and children; dramatic programs; lect open to the public, 2 vis lectr per year; concerts; gallery talks; tours; competitions; scholarships; lending collection contains 15,000 Kodachromes and 70,000 slides; originate traveling exhibitions

RENO

O **SIERRA ARTS FOUNDATION,** * 135 N Sierra St, PO Box 2814, 89505. Tel 702-329-1324. *Pres* Thomas R C Wilson; *VPres* J Craig Sweeney; *Secy* Rosemary D McMillan; *Exec Dir* Carol Mousel
Estab as a service organization to construct downtown center for visual and performing arts on land owned by Foundation. Mem: 504
Income: Financed by endowment, membership, city, state and federal appropriations, and gifts
Publications: Art Works; How Do I Feel? What Do I Need?; Marketing Survey Report; A Celebration, Encore, monthly newsletter; Master Calendar; Services Booklet; Art Resources Guide
Activities: Educ dept; Arts-In-Education; concerts; festivals; exten dept

M **SIERRA NEVADA MUSEUM OF ART,** 549 Court St, 89501. Tel 702-329-3333. *Pres* Clifton B Shoolroy; *VPres* Timothy Collins; *Secy* Maureen Barrett; *Treasurer* Robert Seale; *Dir* Dr Marcia Cohn Growdon; *Asst Cur* Alice Cerniglia; *Astist-in-Residence* Kerry Dion; *Registrar* Bernie Antone; *Bus Mgr* Tina Nesler; *Cur Education* Nancy Peppin
Open Tues - Fri 10 AM - 4 PM, Sat & Sun Noon - 4 PM, cl Mon. No admis fee. Estab 1931 to collect, conserve, exhibit and interpret art for the enrichment and heritage of the citizens of Nevada. Museum is a nonprofit educational institution operated in the community's interest. Located in the Hawkins House, a Historic Landmark building designed in the Georgian style by Elmer Grey in 1911. Maintains drawing rooms, dining room, library and suite of rooms that house the galleries. Average Annual Attendance: 12,000. Mem: 650; dues corporation $100, individual $25; annual meeting April 1
Income: Financed by endowment, membership, federal and private foundation grants, individual grants and earned income
Collections: Charles Cutts Collection (†art glass, †graphic art, †manuscripts, oriental carpets, paintings and †rare books); †Samuel Houghton Great Basin Collection
Exhibitions: (1983) Fritz Scholder, Monotypes; Stanton MacDonald-Wright, watercolors & drawings; Kirk Robertson, West Nevada Waltz; Traditions in Western American Art; (1984) Historic Photography of the Great Basin; The Art of Theodore Wores
Publications: Annual Bulletin; brochures; catalogues; calendar newsletter, bi-monthly
Activities: Classes for adults & children; workshops; docent training; lectures open to the public, 3-6 vis lectr per year; concerts; gallery talks; tours; competitions with awards; outreach services to schools, senior citizens and other community groups in Greater Reno-Carson-Tahoe area; individual paintings and original objects of art lent to museums and galleries; book traveling exhibitions, 3-4 times per year; originate traveling exhibitions; museum shop sells books, prints & gift items
L **Art Library,** * 549 Court St, 89501. Tel 702-329-3333
Open by arrangement only. Estab 1951. For reference only
Library Holdings: Vols 1000; Other — Exhibition catalogs, manuscripts, memorabilia, pamphlets, photographs, reproductions

M **UNIVERSITY OF NEVADA, RENO,** 89557. Tel 702-784-6682. *Gallery Cur* Walter McNamara; *Art Dept Chmn* Howard Rosenberg
Open Mon - Fri 8 AM - 5 PM, cl Sat, Sun & holidays. Estab 1960. Gallery has 800 sq ft finished exhibition space. Average Annual Attendance: 12,000-15,000
Activities: Lectures open to public, 2-4 vis lectr per yr; competitions with awards; scholarships; individual paintings & original objects of art lent; book traveling exhibitions; museum shop

NEW HAMPSHIRE

CONCORD

O **LEAGUE OF NEW HAMPSHIRE CRAFTSMEN,** Concord Gallery, 205 N Main St, 03301. Tel 603-224-3375. *Dir* Richard Fitzgerald; *Education Coordr* Evelyn Zimmerman
Open Mon - Fri 10 AM - 4 PM. Estab 1932 to encourage the economic development & education of the crafts; gallery displaying traveling shows & exhibits of members' works. Average Annual Attendance: 5000. Mem: 3000; dues $6; annual meeting in Oct
Exhibitions: Annual Craftsmen's Fair; Living with Crafts; Annual Juried Exhibit
Publications: Newsletter, six times per year
Activities: Classes for adults; seminars; lect open to public; tours; competitions with awards; scholarships; lending collection of books and slides

L **Library,** 205 N Main St, 03301. Tel 603-224-3375
Open to members
Income: Financed by league operating funds
Library Holdings: Vols 1000; Per subs 24; AV — Cassettes, slides; Other —
Clipping files, exhibition catalogs, manuscripts, original art works, pamphlets,
photographs
Special Subjects: Crafts, Marketing Crafts

O **NEW HAMPSHIRE HISTORICAL SOCIETY,** 30 Park, 03301. Tel 603-225-
3381. *Pres* John K Gemmill; *VPres* David H Souter; *VPres* Timothy W
Woodman; *Dir & Secy* John F Page; *Cur* James L Garvin
Open Mon - Sat 9 AM - 4:30 PM, summer Wed 9 AM - 8 PM. No admis fee.
Estab 1823 to collect, preserve and make available books, manuscripts and
artifacts pertaining to the history of New Hampshire; art gallery maintained.
Maintains a reference library. Average Annual Attendance: 10,000. Mem: 2000;
dues family $20, active $15; annual meeting first Sat in April
Income: $300,000 (financed by endowment, membership and grants)
Purchases: $10,000
Collections: Artifacts made or used in New Hampshire including collections of
glass, furniture, metals, paintings, silver and textiles; Fine and Decorative Arts;
Historical Memorabilia
Exhibitions: Concord's Count & Countess Rumford; Documented New
Hampshire Furniture; Linen Making in New England
Publications: Historical New Hampshire, quarterly; annual report; exhibition
catalogues; quarterly newsletter
Activities: Classes for children; lectures open to public, 6-8 vis lect per year;
concerts; gallery talks; tours; sales shop sells books, postcards and folders

M **SAINT PAUL'S SCHOOL,** Art Center in Hargate, 03301. Tel 603-225-3341,
Ext 258. *Dir Art Center* Thomas R Barrett
Open Tues - Sat 10 AM - 4:30 PM, during school year. Estab 1967 to house the
Art Department of St Paul's School, to provide a cultural center for the school
community as well as the central area of New Hampshire. Secure gallery
consisting of subdivided room approximately 60 x 40 ft. Average Annual
Attendance: 10,000
Income: Financed by endowment
Collections: Painting, sculpture, drawings, graphics, chiefly gifts to the school;
collection represents varied periods and nationalities
Exhibitions: (1982) Pages, An Exhibition of Contemporary American
Bookworks, circulated through the New England Foundation for the Arts; The
Hargate Faculty Biennial; Color/Material/Form: Painting & Sculpture by Loving,
Bowling & Mohr; A Persistence of Vision: Edwin Hale Lincoln; Contemporary
American Print Workshop; (1983) Classical Greek, Etruscan & Roman Art from
the Boston Museum of Fine Arts; Three American Regionalists - lithographs by
Thomas Hart Benton, John Steuart Curry & Grant Wood; Ben Shahn
Photographs of the 1930's; Eugene Atget: 45 Vintage Photographs of France;
Sandy Walker - Very Large Drawings
Activities: Classes for students; Lectures for members only, four visiting lecturers
per year; gallery talks; tours; original objects of art lent to qualifying institutions
L **Sheldon Library,** St Paul's School, 03301. *Librn* R Cassels-Brown
Estab 1967 for art reference only. Circ 600
Income: Approx $1000
Purchases: Approx $1000
Library Holdings: Vols 450; Per subs 12; AV — Slides; Other — Exhibition
catalogs, reproductions

CORNISH

M **SAINT-GAUDENS NATIONAL HISTORIC SITE,** off New Hampshire Route
12A (Mailing add: RR 2, 03745). Tel 603-675-2175; FTS 834-1620. *Supt &
Chief Cur* John H Dryfhout
Open daily 8:30 AM - 4:30 PM (end of May - Oct 31). Admis (16 and over)
$.50. Estab 1926, transferred to Federal Government (National Park Service) in
1965 to commemorate the home, studios and works of Augustus Saint-Gaudens
(1848-1907), one of America's foremost sculptors. The site has historically
(1907) furnished rooms, studios and gardens displaying approximately half of the
work of Augustus Saint-Gaudens. Sculptor-in-residence program. Average
Annual Attendance: 40,000
Income: Financed by federal appropriation (National Park Service)
Purchases: Works by Augustus Saint Gaudens; original furnishings of the Cornish
Property
Collections: Historic furnishings and plaster, bronze and marble works by
Augustus Saint-Gaudens
Exhibitions: Contemporary and Historic Paintings; Drawings; Photographs;
Prints; Sculpture
Publications: Brochures
Activities: Individual paintings and original objects of art lent to museums and
societies; sales shop sells books, slides and souvenir items
L **Library,** 03102
Open for reference
Library Holdings: Vols 600
Special Subjects: 19th and early 20th Century American art

DURHAM

M **UNIVERSITY OF NEW HAMPSHIRE,** University Art Galleries, Paul
Creative Arts Center, 03824. Tel 603-862-3712. *Dir* Susan Faxon Olney; *Asst
Dir* Susan Frankenbach
Open Mon - Fri 8 AM - 4:30 PM. No admis fee
Exhibitions: temporary exhibitions
Publications: Exhibition catalogs; miscellaneous booklets
Activities: Educational program for area schools; workshops; lectures open to
public, 8-10 vis lectrs per year; gallery talks; tours
L **Dept of the Arts Slide Library,** Paul Creative Arts Center, 03824. Tel 603-862-
2190. *Slide Librn* Diane C White
Estab as a teaching collection for the university. Slides do not circulate off-
campus
Library Holdings: AV — Slides 85,000
Special Subjects: Western art

EXETER

M **PHILLIPS EXETER ACADEMY,** Frederic R Mayer Art Center & Lamont
Gallery, 03833. Tel 603-772-4311, Ext 324. *Principal* Stephen G Kurtz; *Dir*
Nichols Clark
Open Mon, Tues & Thurs - Sat 9 AM - 5 PM, Wed 9 AM - 1 PM & Sun 2 - 5
PM. No admis fee. Estab 1953 to provide an Art Center and studios for art
instruction Dedicated to the memory of Thomas William Lamont II, lost in
action in 1945. Four bays with moveable walls to alter number of rays, sky lit
with sol-r-veil screen
Exhibitions: Peter Milton, contemporary photos; Glen Krause; Robert Murray;
Vincent Mastracco; Picasso Vollard Suite; Time-Life Photos; Asmat
Activities: Classes for Academy students; dramatic programs; lectures open to
public, 4 vis lectr per year

HANOVER

M **HOOD MUSEUM OF ART,** Dartmouth College, Hopkins Center, 03755. Tel
603-646-2808. *Dir* Richard Stuart Teitz; *Assoc Dir* Richard L Stucker; *Chief Cur*
Jacquelynn Baas; *Exhibitions Designer & Asst Cur* Malcolm Cochran; *Asst Cur*
Barbara MacAdam; *Registrar* Hazel Burrows; *Asst to Exhibitions Designer*
Evelyn Marcus; *Asst to Exhibitions Designer* Robert Raiselis; *Admin Asst*
Joanne M Sugarman; *Cur Ethnographic & Archeological Collections* Tamara
Nothern; *Assoc Registrar & Asst Cur* Gregory Schwarz; *Business Asst* Meredith
Kendall; *Dir Public Relations* Marion Bratesman; *Dir External Relations*
Kenneth P Spritz; *Cur Arts Educ Servs* Mary Sue Glosser; *Sr Secy* Patricia
Cherrier
Open Mon - Sat 10 AM - 10 PM, Sun 10 AM - 4 PM. No admis fee. Estab
1771; anticipate completion of new facilites by 1985
Income: Financed through Dartmouth College
Collections: The Hood Museum has about 15,000 art objects and about 35,000
anthropology objects; especially strong in areas such as 19th and 20th century
American art, 17th century paintings and European and American prints; also
has a survey of Native American, African, Oriental and Pre-Columbian artifacts
Exhibitions: (1982) Annual regional selections; annual student art show; Super
Realism from the Mortin G Neumann Family Collection; Don Nice, Winter
Artist-in-Residence; Leonardo Lasansky, Spring Artists-in-Residence; (1983)
Annual Regional Selections; annual student art show; Peter Milton, Winter
Artist-in-Residence; Outdoor Sculpture; Arakawa: Drawings; John Singer Sargent
Drawings; Architecture on Paper; (1984) Annual Regional Selections; annual
student art show; Architecture on Paper; Dogs; The AAS & Crafts Movement;
Old Master Drawings from Rhode Island School of Design
Activities: Undergraduate museum studies courses offered; gallery talks;
originates traveling exhibitions
L **Sherman Art Library,** Carpenter Hall, 03755. Tel 603-646-2305. *Librn* Jeffrey L
Horrell
Open Mon - Fri 8 AM - 12 PM; Sat 9 AM - 5 PM, Sun 1 - 12 PM. Estab 1928
Library Holdings: Vols 54,540; Per subs 380; Micro — Cards 400, fiche 7500,
reels; Other — Exhibition catalogs, pamphlets

KEENE

M **KEENE STATE COLLEGE,** Thorne-Sagendorph Art Gallery, Appian Way,
03431. Tel 603-352-1909, Ext 382. *Dir* Maureen Ahearn
Open Mon - Fri 12 - 5 PM, Sat & Sun 1 - 4 PM, Wed evenings until 8 PM. No
admis fee. Estab 1965 to provide a year-round calendar of continuing exhibitions;
to sponsor related programs of artistic and educational interest; and to maintain
small permanent collection displayed on campus. Two adjacent galleries occupy
space in a wing of Mason Library on campus. Average Annual Attendance: 9000.
Mem: 400; dues $10
Income: Financed by endowment, state appropriation and annual College budget
Collections: Paintings and Prints of Historical Interest included: Pierre
Alechinsky; Milton Avery; Paul Pollaro; Gregorio Prestopino; George Rickey;
Sidney Twardowicz; Artists of National Prominence; Paintings by Regional
Artists
Exhibitions: (1983-84) Graphics/New Hampshire; Marson LTD; Esme
Thompson; Christmas Greens Festival; Eye of the Child; Round the Mountain -
The Best of Monadnock Regional Art; Masks from Montgomery, VT
Publications: Small catalogs or brochures to accompany exhibitions
Activities: Lectures open to public; concerts; gallery talks; competitions;
individual paintings lent to departments on campus, other museums and galleries;
lending collection consists of original prints, paintings and sculpture; book
traveling exhibitions; originate traveling exhibitions; sales shop sells catalogues

MANCHESTER

M **CURRIER GALLERY OF ART,** 192 Orange St, 03104. Tel 603-669-6144. *Pres*
Kimon S Zachos; *VPres* Mrs Lawrence W Shirley; *Treas* Davis P Thurber; *Clerk*
Mrs Norman F Milne; *Dir* Robert M Doty; *Coordr Public Relations* Sharon G
Callahan; *Coordr Membership* Virginia Eshoo; *Supv Currier Art Center* Robert
Eshoo; *Dir Educ* Marian Woodruff
Open Tues, Wed, Fri, Sat 10 AM - 4 PM, Thurs 10 AM - 10 PM, Sun 2 - 5 PM,
cl Mon and national holidays. No admis fee. Estab and incorporated 1915 by will
of Mrs Hannah M and Governor Moody Currier, which included endowment,
building opened in 1929. Building contains six galleries, library and auditorium,
two pavilions. Currier Art Center is housed in adjacent building acquired in 1938,
and offers after school and Sat classes for children. Average Annual Attendance:
40,000. Mem: 1200; dues $15 and up; annual meeting in March
Income: Financed by endowment
Collections: American Furniture, glass and textiles 18th-20th century; †American
Paintings and Sculpture 18th century to present; European Paintings, prints and
sculpture, 13th-20th century; †European Masters 13th-20th century; †Fine
American Decorative Art 17th-19th century including furniture, glass textiles and
silver
Exhibitions: (1982) Decorative arts, photography, painting & sculpture

Publications: Bulletin, semi-annually; calendar, quarterly; exhibition catalogs, occasionally
Activities: Classes for children; docent training; lectures open to public; concerts; gallery talks; tours; awards; extension dept serves NH schools; individual paintings and original objects of art lent; lending collection contains cassettes, 500 color reproductions, film strips and 2000 slides

L **Library,** 192 Orange St, 03104. Tel 603-669-6144. *Librn* Maria K Graubart
Open to gallery staff, docents and research students by appointment for reference only
Library Holdings: Vols 5000; Per subs 40; Other — Exhibition catalogs

L **MANCHESTER CITY LIBRARY,** Carpenter Memorial Building, 405 Pine St, 03104. Tel 603-624-6550. *City Library Dir* John J Hallahan; *Fine Arts Librn* Theresa Snow Toy
Open Mon, Tues & Thurs 9 AM - 9 PM, Wed & Fri 9 AM - 6 PM, Sat 9 AM - 5 PM, cl Sun
Income: Financed by city appropriations
Purchases: $4000
Library Holdings: Vols 17,000; mounted pictures; Micro — Reels; AV — Fs
Exhibitions: Patron's art works, crafts, collectibles
Activities: Monthly film program to public; Canadian travel films available to groups, cooperative film collection available for loan and interlibrary loan

O **MANCHESTER HISTORIC ASSOCIATION,** 129 Amherst St, 03104. Tel 603-622-7531. *Pres* Kathleen Mirabile; *Dir* George Comtois
Open Tues - Fri 9 AM - 4 PM, Sat 10 AM - 4 PM, cl Sun & Mon, national & state holidays, & Tues following Mon holidays. Inc 1896 to collect, preserve and make known Manchester's historical heritage. Average Annual Attendance: 10,000. Mem: 250; dues active $1000, patron $100 or more, contributing $15 - $99; annual meetings in April
Income: $45,000
Collections: †Furniture, †glass, †pewter, †maps, †prints, †paintings, †ceramics, †costumes, †textiles, †artifacts of all types; †Indian artifact collection of over 10,000 pieces found at Manchester sites; historical material
Exhibitions: Permanent and changing exhibitions reflecting all aspects of Manchester history
Publications: Annual report; bulletin, quarterly; catalogs, occasionally
Activities: Spring and fall program series; docent training; lectures open to public, 4 vis lectr per year; concerts; gallery talks; tours; competitions; individual and original objects of art lent to educational, business organizations and other museums; book traveling exhibitions; sales shop sells books, original art, reproductions and prints

L **Library,** 129 Amherst St, 03104. *Librn* Elizabeth Lessard; *Education Dept Coordr* Denise Arel; *Registrar* Mary Lou Ashooh
Income: $47,000 (financed by endowment)
Library Holdings: Per subs 1500; maps; early textiles mill records; swatch sample books; 19th century music; Amoskeag Mfg Co Archives, publications of local history; AV — Cassettes; Other — Clipping files, manuscripts, memorabilia, pamphlets, photographs, prints, reproductions
Exhibitions: Manchester Made; Sharing Manchester's Past Through Photographs; Franco-American; Ulric Bourgeois; The Hermit Images
Publications: Manchester Historic Association Bulletin, annual

M **MANCHESTER INSTITUTE OF ARTS AND SCIENCES GALLERY,** 148 Concord St, 03104. Tel 603-623-0313. *Gallery Dir* Angelo Randazzo; *Program & Education Coordr* Adrienne LaVallee; *Educ Coordr* Pamela Riel
Open Mon - Thurs 9 AM - 9 PM, Fri & Sat 9 AM - 5 PM, cl Sun. No admis fee. Estab 1898, as a private non-profit educational institution in order to promote, encourage and stimulate education in the arts and sciences. Gallery has limited space which is devoted to a variety of exhibitions including historical as well as contemporary themes. Mem: 450; dues family $30, individual $20; annual meeting in June
Income: Financed by endowment, membership, tuition and grants
Publications: Exhibition catalogs; schedule of courses, exhibitions and programs, 2 or 3 times per year
Activities: Classes for adults; films; lect; concerts; sales shop selling handcrafted items & fine arts prints

O **NEW HAMPSHIRE ART ASSOCIATION, INC,*** 24 W Bridge St, Box 1075, 03105. Tel 603-622-0527. *Executive Dir* Grace Casey
Sales and rental gallery open year-round, Mon - Fri 9 AM - 5 PM. Estab 1940, incorporated 1962, as a non-profit organization, to promote the public's understanding and appreciation of the arts; to provide the artist with a forum for his work and ideas. It offers a year-round exhibition and sales gallery at its headquarters in Manchester; a summer gallery in the Joshua Wentworth House, Strawbery Banke, Portsmouth; an August exhibition and sales program at Sunapee State Park. Mem: 300; dues $20; annual meeting June
Exhibitions: Annuals at Currier Gallery of Art; Summer Annual combined with New Hampshire League of Arts and Crafts at Mount Sunapee State Park; Summer Annual Juried Exhibition at Prescott Park; Spring Annual Juried Exhibit at the Nashua Arts and Science Center; various one-man and group shows
Activities: Educ program for schools; patron program; Lect demonstrations by member artists; awards; originate traveling exhibitions

M **SAINT ANSELM COLLEGE,** Chapel Art Center, 03102. Tel 603-669-1030, Ext 328. *Arts Admin* Beverly Zisla Welber; *Coordr Exhibitions* Schuyler Bemis; *Gallery Asst* Patricia Morris
Open Mon - Fri 10 AM - 4 PM, Wed evenings 7 - 9 PM. No admis fee. Large gallery, formerly college chapel with painted, barrel-vaulted ceiling, stained glass windows; one small gallery. Average Annual Attendance: 5000
Income: Financed through College
Collections: †Photographs; †prints; †New Hampshire artists and craftsmen
Exhibitions: (1982-83) Sistine Ceiling Reproduction; Paintings by Peder Johnson; Prints by Al Hirschfeld; Paintings by John White; Sculpture by Eleanor Prager; Watercolors by Willard Sunstein; Sculpture by Susan Donovan; Graphics New Hampshire; Paintings by Rose Labrie
Publications: The View, periodically
Activities: Lectures open to the public; gallery talks

PLYMOUTH

L **PLYMOUTH STATE COLLEGE,** Herbert H Lamson Library, 03264. Tel 603-536-1550, Ext 257. *Dir Library Services* Philip Wei; *Coordr Public Services* Robert V McDermand; *Slide & ILL Librn* William Kietzman
Open Mon - Thurs 8 AM - 12 PM, Fri 8 AM - 5 PM, Sat 10 AM - 5 PM, Sun Noon - 12 PM. Estab 1871 to serve the academic and personal needs of the college's students and faculty. Maintains exhibition space, an 18 ft exhibition wall. Circ 98,500
Income: $630,000 (one-fourth financed by state appropriation)
Purchases: $185,100
Library Holdings: audio discs 6300; Micro — Fiche 275,000, reels 7600; AV — Cassettes 1770, fs 3200, rec 6000, slides 32,700; Other — Pamphlets
Exhibitions: Lucien Aigner; Patricia Benson; James Fortune; Margaret Houseworth; Winthrop Pratt; Leslie Snow; Viola Sutton; John McDonnell; Warren Mason
Publications: Brochures; handbook
Activities: Lectures open to public; library tours; bibliographic instruction

PORTSMOUTH

M **JOHN PAUL JONES HOUSE,*** Middle and State St, 54 Court St, 03801. Tel 603-436-8420. *Pres* Albert W Arkroyo; *VPres* Wyman P Boynton; *Secy* Rita Conant; *Dir* E S Laraway
Open mid-May - mid-Oct Mon - Sat 10 AM - 4 PM. Admis adults $2, children $.50, children under 6 free. Estab 1920 to identify and retain local history. The House was built in 1758 by Gregory Purcell, a merchant sea-captain. Purchased and restored in 1920 by the Portsmouth Historical Society. Average Annual Attendance: 7000. Mem: 245; dues $5; annual meeting May
Income: Financed by membership, investment and admission fees
Collections: Books, china, costumes, documents, furniture, glass, portraits and silver pertaining to the early history of Portsmouth
Activities: Lectures, 1-2 vis lectr per year; museum shop sells books, prints and slides

M **PORTSMOUTH ATHENAEUM NR, INC 1817,** 9 Market Square, Box 848, 03801. Tel 603-431-2538. *Pres* Joseph G Sawtelle Jr; *VPres* Open; *Treas* James S Millar; *Secy* Cynthia Wills Harriman; *Librn* Jeannette Mitchell
Open yearly Thurs 1 - 4 PM or by appointment. No admis fee. Estab 1817 to house museum of historical objects of local, statewide and national interest and is listed on National Register of Historical Sites. Average Annual Attendance: 2800. Mem: 200; dues $40; annual meeting 2nd Wed in Jan
Income: Financed by endowment and membership
Collections: American paintings; Colonial portraits; ship models & half-models; New England history; maritime history
Exhibitions: American Portraiture in the Grand Manner, 1720-1920
Activities: Lectures; 6 vis lect per year; gallery talks; tours; Lending collection contains individual and original objects of art and is lent to the Los Angeles County Museum of Art & National Portrait Gallery

L **Library,** 9 Market Square, Box 848, 03801. *Librn* Mrs William Boesch
Open Thurs 1 - 4 PM or by appointment. Estab 1817. For reference only
Library Holdings: Vols 31,000; Per subs 45; AV — Cassettes, lantern slides; Other — Clipping files, manuscripts, memorabilia, original art works, pamphlets, photographs, prints
Special Subjects: 18th Century American Shipping; United States Marine History

NEW JERSEY

ATLANTIC CITY

L **PRINCETON ANTIQUES BOOKSERVICE,** Art Marketing Reference Library, 2915-17 Atlantic Ave, 08401. Tel 609-344-1943. *Pres* Robert E Ruffolo Jr; *Cur* Martha Ireland; *Adminr* Robert Eugene
Open by appointment 10 AM - 4 PM. Estab 1974 for pricing documentation of books and antiques. Open by appointment only; maintains art gallery. Average Annual Attendance: 1000
Income: $25,000 - $30,000
Purchases: $20,000
Library Holdings: Vols 12,500; Per subs 20; exhibition catalogs, original art works and prints; AV — Slides
Special Subjects: The function in US of art and the book market, Price information history from 1900
Collections: 19th century art; Post-card Photo Library Information Bank, 1900 - 1950, consisting 250,000 post-cards
Activities: Sales shop sells books & original art

BAYONNE

L **BAYONNE FREE PUBLIC LIBRARY,** Art Dept, 697 Avenue C, 07002. Tel 201-858-6981. *Dir* M E O'Connor
Open Mon, Tues, Thurs 9 AM - 12PM, 1 - 5 PM, 6 - 9 PM, Wed, Fri, Sat 9 AM - 12 PM, 1 - 5 PM. Estab 1894. Art Gallery has 194 running feet exhibition space
Income: Financed by city appropriation and state aid
Library Holdings: Vols 8560; AV — Fs, rec 6676, slides 736; Other — Clipping files
Activities: Concerts; adult and children film programs weekly

BLOOMFIELD

M HISTORICAL SOCIETY OF BLOOMFIELD, 90 Broad St, 07003. Tel 201-429-9292. *Pres* Elizabeth Kingsley; *Cur* Lucy SantAmbrogioe; *Cur* William Smith
Open Wed 2 - 4:30 PM, Sat 11 AM - 3 PM & by appointment. No admis fee.
Estab circa 1968 to collect, preserve and exhibit items which may help to establish or illustrate the history of the area. Museum located in the gallery of the Bloomfield Public Library. Average Annual Attendance: 1436. Mem: 232; dues life $50, commercial organization $25, non-profit organization $10, couple $8, individual $5, student under 18 $1; meeting second Wed of alternate months Sept - May
Income: Financed by membership, Ways and Means Committee
Collections: Miscellaneous items of books, †clothing and †accessories, †deeds and other documents, †dioramas, early †maps and †newspapers, furniture, †household articles, letters, †memorabilia, †paintings, postcards, posters, tools, toys
Activities: Lect open to public, 3 - 5 visiting lectr per year; tours; $100 award to student graduating from Bloomfield Senior High School who has attained an outstanding achievement in American History; sales shop sells books, prints, postcards, medallions, wallets, phonorecords and fruit cake (seasonal)

BURLINGTON

O BURLINGTON COUNTY HISTORICAL SOCIETY, 457 High St, 08016. Tel 609-386-4773. *Pres* Susan Bradman; *VPres* James Greene; *Secy* H Elizabeth Heyl; *Dir* M M Pernot
Open Wed 1 - 4 PM, Sun 2 - 4 PM. Admis by contribution. Estab 1923 to maintain collections relating to Burlington County History and residents. Average Annual Attendance: 2300. Mem: 450; dues $5; annual meeting May
Income: Financed by endowment
Library Holdings: Vols 2000; Per subs 15; Other — Clipping files, manuscripts, memorabilia, pamphlets, photographs, prints
Collections: China; Glass; Quilts; Sampler
Publications: Newsletter, quarterly
Activities: Docent training; lectures open to public; concerts; tours; individual paintings and original objects of art lent; originate traveling exhibitions; museum shop sells books, magazines, reproductions and slides

CALDWELL

M CALDWELL COLLEGE, Art Gallery,* 07006. Tel 201-228-4424. *Dir* Sr M Gerardine
Open Mon - Fri 8:30 AM - 5 PM, weekends by appointment. No admis fee. Estab 1970 to provide students and area community with exposure to professional contemporary talent, to afford opporunities for qualified artists to have one-person shows
Activities: Education department in connection with the college art department; lect open to public, 3 vis lectr per yr; scholarships offered; lending collection contains 12,000 kodachromes, motion pictures

CAMDEN

C CAMPBELL MUSEUM, Campbell Place, 08101. Tel 609-342-6440. *Pres* Ralph Collier
Open Mon - Fri 9 AM - 4:30 PM. No admis fee. Estab 1966 to collect soup tureens of silver, porcelain and pewter of the 18th Century. Collection displayed at Campbell Museum. Museum has red velvet walls and Plexiglas cases
Collections: 18th Century soup tureens by leading porcelain makers and silversmiths
Activities: Lectures; competitions; original objects of art lent; book traveling exhibitions; originate traveling exhibitions to museums only; museum shop sells catalogues & postcards

M RUTGERS UNIVERSITY, Stedman Art Gallery, Fine Arts Center, 08102. Tel 609-757-6176, 757-6245. *Dir* Virginia Oberlin Steel
Open Mon - Sat 11 AM - 4 PM. No admis fee. Estab 1975 to serve educational needs of the campus and to serve community of southern New Jersey. Average Annual Attendance: 7000
Income: Financed by endowment, state appropriation and gifts from private sources
Collections: Modern & contemporary art; †works on paper
Exhibitions: Changing exhibitions of visual arts & interdisciplinary exhibitions
Publications: Catalog for a major exhibition, yearly
Activities: Visiting lecturers, symposia, concerts & gallery talks open to public; competition with purchase prizes

CLINTON

M CLINTON HISTORICAL MUSEUM VILLAGE, 56 Main St, PO Box 5005, 08809. Tel 201-735-4101. *Dir* Catherine West; *Cur* Claire Young
Open Apr 1 - Oct 31, Mon - Fri 1 PM - 5 PM, Sat & Sun Noon - 6 PM. Admis adults $2, seniors $1.50, children under 12 $1, pre-schoolers free. Estab 1960 for the preservation and display of artifacts from the 18th and 19th century for educational and cultural purposes. Four-floor grist mill, blacksmith shop, general store, schoolhouse, log cabin and herb garden. Average Annual Attendance: 26,000. Mem: 350; dues $10 - $1000; annual meeting April
Income: $85,000 (financed by membership and donations)
Collections: Artifacts pertaining to 18th and 19th centuries
Exhibitions: Craft Show; Antique Show; Harvest Jubilee
Publications: The Old Mill Wheel, newsletter, four times a year
Activities: Docent training; lectures; concerts; sales shop selling books and gift items
L Library, 56 Main St, PO Box 5005, 08809
For historical reference
Library Holdings: Vols 500

O HUNTERDON ART CENTER, 7 Center St, 08809. Tel 201-735-8415. *Pres* Jane Reading; *VPres* Larry Carlbon; *Secy* Richard Dieterly; *Exec Dir* Linda Constant Buki; *Asst to Dir* Barbara Wolock; *Cur Education* David Kinney; *Public Relations* Martha Cahn
Open Tues - Fri 1 - 4 PM, Sat & Sun 1 - 5 PM, cl Mon. No admis fee. Estab 1952 as a non-profit organization to provide opportunity for adults and children to participate in the enjoyment of the arts and crafts in all forms. The first and second floors provide gallery space. The old stone mill has been remodeled retaining the original atmosphere with open broad wooden beams, white walls and plank flooring. Average Annual Attendance: 40,000. Mem: 1000; dues patron $150, endowment $100, sustaining $75, family $25, single $20, student & sr citizens $10
Income: Financed by membership, city, state and county appropriations, federal funding, donations
Purchases: $100
Collections: †Print collection
Exhibitions: (1983-84) Invitational group shows; members show; National Print Exhibition Craft Exhibitions; Invitational Group Shows; Members Show; National Print Exhibition
Publications: Newsletter, bimonthly
Activities: Classes for adults & children; dramatic programs; lectures open to public; concerts; gallery talks; tours; films; scholarships offered; individual paintings and original objects of art lent to Newark Museum and corp membership; originate traveling exhibitions to Newark Museum and corp membership; sales shop sells books, original art, reproductions, prints & handmade items

CONVENT STATION

L COLLEGE OF SAINT ELIZABETH, Mahoney Library, 07961. Tel 201-539-1600, Ext 365. *Librn* Sr Marie Rousek
Open weekdays 9 AM - 5 PM. Estab 1899 for academic purposes
Income: Financed by private funds
Library Holdings: Vols 7100; Per subs 50; Micro — Fiche, reels; AV — Cassettes, fs, rec; Other — Exhibition catalogs, original art works, photographs, prints, reproductions, sculpture
Special Subjects: The Madonna
Exhibitions: Russian artifacts; Lithuanian hooked rugs; Bruce Welch, color photos; Annie Lenney, paintings; (1982) Fashions of Four Centuries; (1983) Anne Ryan, selected works; Sacred Art
Activities: Original objects of art lent

ELIZABETH

L FREE PUBLIC LIBRARY OF ELIZABETH, Fine Arts Dept, 11 S Broad St, 07202. Tel 201-354-6060. *Library Dir* Hazel Hulbert Elks; *Supervising Art Librn* Roman Sawycky; *Sr Art Librn* Daisy Tamayo
Open Mon - Wed 9 AM - 9 PM, Thurs - Sat 9 AM - 5 PM, cl Sun. No admis fee. Estab 1913, the art department functions within the area library system; it offers free service to patrons of Elizabeth and also to patrons of neighboring towns, Roselle Park, Kenilworth, Union and Cranford. Special exhibit area displays paintings and miscellaneous objects d'art
Income: Financed by city and state appropriations
Library Holdings: Vols 15,000; Photographs & Illustrations 200,000; Other — Reproductions 800
Collections: Japanese prints by various artists
Exhibitions: Works by artists and photographers; other special exhibitions from time to time
Activities: Dramatic programs; lect open to the public, 15 visiting lectrs per year; concerts; material available to patrons of Union, Kenilworth, Roselle Park & Cranford; lending collection contains film strips, projection equipment & motion pictures; printed catalogues of film strips & films available to the public

ENGLEWOOD

L ENGLEWOOD LIBRARY, Fine Arts Dept, 31 Engle St, 07631. Tel 201-568-2215. *Dir Library* Patricia Anderson; *Head Programming Dept* Mary Beall
Open Mon - Thurs 9 AM - 9 PM, Fri & Sat 9 AM - 5 PM, Sun 1 - 5 PM (Oct-May). Estab 1901 to establish a free public library for citizens. Area of library is used for exhibitions; special panels and cases
Income: $510,000 (financed by endowment, city and state appropriation)
Library Holdings: Micro — Reels; AV — Cassettes, fs, motion pictures, rec, slides; Other — Clipping files, framed reproductions, original art works, pamphlets
Exhibitions: Faculty of Old Church Cultural Center; Members of Salurre to Women In The Arts; Quilts; Rare Books & Manuscripts; World of Renaissance
Activities: Lectures open to public; concerts; tours

HOPEWELL

M HOPEWELL MUSEUM, 28 E Broad St, 08525. Tel 609-466-0103. *Pres* James Kettle; *Cur* Beverly Weidl
Open Mon, Wed & Sat 2 - 5 PM, cl national holidays. No admis fee, donations suggested. Estab 1922 as a museum of local history from early 1700 - 1900, to show what the community was like for almost 300 years. Average Annual Attendance: 2000
Income: Financed by endowment, membership and donations
Collections: Antique china, glass, silver & pewter; colonial furniture; colonial parlor; early needlework; Indian handicrafts; photograph collection; Victorian parlor
Publications: Hopewell Valley Heritage; Pioneers of Old Hopewell; maps

JERSEY CITY

M JERSEY CITY MUSEUM ASSOCIATION, 472 Jersey Ave, 07302. Tel 201-547-4513. *Pres* J Owen Grundy; *VPres* Theodore Conrad; *Secy* Adelaide Dear; *Treas* Arthur Hansen; *Trustee & Cur* Cynthia Sanford; *Asst Cur* Robert Ferguson
Open Tues - Sat 11:30 AM - 4:30 PM, Wed evening untill 8 PM, cl Mon; open to children Tues 3 - 5 PM. No admis fee. Estab 1932 for the purpose of advancing interest in the Arts, Sciences and History. Maintains an art gallery housing the Will Collection. Average Annual Attendance: 10,000. Mem: 189; dues from Junior $1 to Benefactor $1000; meetings Jan, Mar and Nov
Income: $1000 (financed by endowment)
Collections: Will Collection of Paintings & Drawings (1850's - 1910) of Jersey City Scenes; Antiques; Local Historical Pictures and Artifacts; Modern and Old Paintings; Posters; Sculpture
Publications: Year Book
Activities: Educ dept; lect open to public, 4 - 5 vis lectr per year; competitions

M JERSEY CITY STATE COLLEGE, Courtney Art Gallery,* Dept of Art, 2039 Kennedy Blvd, 07307. Tel 201-547-3214. *Dir* Harold Lemmerman
Open Mon - Fri 10 AM - 5 PM. No admis fee. Estab 1969 to bring examples of professional work to the campus in each of the areas in which students are involved: Painting, sculpture, film, photography, textiles, weaving, ceramics, graphic design. Gallery is operated by students, and with the Jersey City Museum form a student internship training program. Average Annual Attendance: 5000
Income: Financed by city, state appropriation, and Art Department
Collections: Small collection of prints and paintings
Activities: Lect open to public, 5 visiting lectrs per year; gallery talks; exten dept serving community organizations; individual paintings and original objects of art lent; lending collection contains color reproductions, film strips, Kodachromes, motion pictures, photographs; traveling exhibitions organized and circulated
M Zigfelt Gallery,* 2039 Kennedy Blvd, 07307. Tel 201-547-6000
Gallery maintained for student exhibitions

M SAINT PETER'S COLLEGE, Art Gallery,* 2641 Kennedy Blvd, 07306. Tel 201-333-4400. *Dir* Oscar Magnan
Open Mon, Tues, Fri & Sat 11 AM - 4 PM, Wed & Thurs 11 AM - 9 PM. No admis fee. Estab 1971 to present the different art trends. Gallery is maintained with good space, lighting and alarm systems
Income: Financed by the college
Activities: Classes for adults; docent training; lect open to public, 20 visiting lectrs per year; concerts; gallery talks; tours; exten dept serving students

LAKEWOOD

M GEORGIAN COURT COLLEGE GALLERY,* Lakewood Ave, 08701. Tel 201-364-2200, Ext 48. *Dir* Sr Mary Christina Geis
Open Mon - Fri 9 AM - 4 PM. No admis fee. Estab 1964 to offer art students the opportunity to view the works of professional artists and also to exhibit student work. Gallery is one large room with 100 running feet of wall area for flat work; the center area for sculpture. Average Annual Attendance: 1000
Income: Financed through the college

LAWRENCEVILLE

M RIDER COLLEGE ART GALLERY, 2983 Lawrenceville Rd, PO Box 6400, 08648. Tel 609-896-5327. *Asst Dir Student Activities* Sarah-Ann Harnick
Open Mon - Thurs 1 - 10 PM, Fri - Sun 1 - 5 PM. No admis fee. Estab 1970 to afford members of the Rider College community the opportunity to expand their knowledge and exposure to art. Gallery has 1513 sq ft of space divided into two rooms of different height. Average Annual Attendance: 5000
Income: $700 (financed by college appropriation)
Exhibitions: (1983-84) Photography; landscape prints; fiber arts; painting; ceramics
Activities: Lectures open to public, 2 vis lectr per yr; gallery talks; book traveling exhibitions

LAYTON

L PETERS VALLEY INC CRAFT CENTER LIBRARY,* 07851. Tel 201-948-5202. *Executive Dir* Philip C Homes
Not open to public. Estab 1978 to serve as resource library for residents, interns and students at Peters Valley Craft Center. Located at Valley Brook Farm Administrative Offices
Library Holdings: Vols 1000; Per subs 5; AV — Slides; Other — Exhibition catalogs, memorabilia, original art works
Special Subjects: Ceramics, Crafts
Collections: Encyclopedias of Japanese wood-fired pottery; slides of contemporary craft work

LINCROFT

M MONMOUTH MUSEUM AND CULTURAL CENTER, Brookdale Community College, Newman Springs Rd, 07738. Tel 201-747-2266. *Dir* Dorothy V Morehouse; *Pres* Howard R Berger; *First VPres* Philip C Carling; *Second VPres* Lois Rathman; *Program Adminr* Catherine Jahos
Open Tues - Sat 10 AM - 4:30 PM, Sun 1 - 5 PM. Admis adults $1.50 children and Senior citizens $.75, free to Museum members and students. Estab 1963 to advance interest in art, science and nature in this area. Museum houses two large galleries, a children's gallery, the Wonder Warehouse and the main gallery which changes exhibitions four times yearly; also an educational area and a conference area. Average Annual Attendance: 50,000. Mem: 1600; dues family $25, individual $15; annual meetings Jan
Income: $220,000 (financed by membership, donations and county funds)

Exhibitions: Puppets for the Present, Monmouth County Arts Council Annual Juried Exhibition; Porcelain to Ping Pong (China Trade); Sitting Pretty, From this Day Forward (Wedding Gowns 1810-1930); Holiday Playland—An Arcade of Amusements; Tom Toms to Tranquilizers (History of Medicine); New Jersey Watercolor; Great Gatherings, Monmouth Collects
Publications: Calendar of events; catalogues of exhibitions; newsletter
Activities: Classes for adults and children; docent training; lect open to public; originate traveling trunks for use in schools; museum shop sells books and gift items

LONG BRANCH

M LONG BRANCH HISTORICAL MUSEUM, 1260 Ocean Ave, 07740. Tel 201-229-0600, 222-9879. *Pres* Edgar N Dinkelspiel
By appointment only. No admis fee. Estab 1953 as post Civil War historical museum. Average Annual Attendance: 10,000. Mem: Dues $1
Income: Financed by art shows
Collections: Period furniture
Exhibitions: Annual Art Exhibition
Publications: Annual Art Show Book

MADISON

M DREW UNIVERSITY, College Art Gallery,* 07940. Tel 201-377-3000, Ext 321. *Dean* Robert Ackerman; *Chmn Art Dept* Martyvonne Dehoney
Open weekdays 1 - 4 PM, Sat 9 AM - Noon, and by appointment. Estab 1968 to provide exhibitions each school year to augment program of courses and to serve the community
Income: Financed by University instructional budget, general budget and donations
Collections: Study collection of serigraphs, lithographs and intaglio prints; pottery; large sculpture by Robert Mallary
L Art Dept Library,* Rt 24, 07940. Tel 201-377-3000. *Dir* Dr Arthur E Jones Jr; *Assoc Dir* Dr Caroline M Coughlin
Library maintained for art history courses
Library Holdings: AV — Slides

M UNITED METHODIST CHURCH COMMISSION ON ARCHIVES AND HISTORY,* PO Box 127, 07940. Tel 704-456-9433. *Secy* Dr Charles Yrigoyen Jr; *Asst Secy* Louise Queen
Open Mon - Fri 9 AM - 5 PM, summer Sat 9 AM - 5 PM, cl Sun and holidays, Sept - May cl Sat & Sun. No admis fee. Estab 1885 as a religious history museum
Collections: John Wesley Busts; Paintings of Church Leaders and Historic Buildings; Religious Church Materials
Publications: Historian's Digest, bimonthly; Methodist History, quarterly
Activities: Guided tours in summer; sales shop sells books, plates, cards, slides and prints
L Library,* PO Box 127, Madison, 07940
Library Holdings: Vols 40,000

MERCERVILLE

L JOHNSON ATELIER TECHNICAL INSTITUTE OF SCULPTURE, Library, 60 Ward Ave Extension, 08619. Tel 609-890-7777. *Librn* Eden R Bentley
Not open to public. Estab 1977 to provide an information center for apprentices, instructors and staff on sculpture, art appreciation and art history. Library provides space for lectures, movies, slides, classes on art history & critique sessions
Income: $3000
Purchases: $3000
Library Holdings: Vols 2000; Per subs 24; AV — Cassettes, slides; Other — Clipping files, exhibition catalogs
Special Subjects: Art History, Sculpture, Art Appreciation, Health & Legal Issues Concerning Art
Collections: Exhibition catalogues on sculptors and group shows; slides of about 30 sculptor's work

MONTCLAIR

M MONTCLAIR ART MUSEUM, 3 South Mountain Ave, PO Box 1582, 07042. Tel 201-746-5555. *Pres* Brenda Bingham; *Dir* Robert j Koenig; *Coordr Public Relations* Lillian Bristol; *Curatorial Registrar* Hope Morrill; *Asst Dir* Roy Davis; *Bursar* Adelaide R Birnie; *Development Coordr* Eileen M Tokar
Open Tues - Sat 10 AM - 5 PM, Sun 2 - 5 PM. No admis fee. Estab 1914. Five galleries of changing exhibitions; one gallery of permanent exhibitions; student gallery. Average Annual Attendance: 50,000. Mem: 2500; dues $30
Income: Financed by endowment and membership
Collections: American costumes; The Lang Collection and Tomlin Collection of Chinese Snuff Bottles; the Rand Collection of American Indian Art; Whitney Silver Collection; †American paintings, 18th - 20th century; †prints and drawings
Exhibitions: (1981-82) American Indian jewelry; Portraits from the Museum Collection; Sacred Voyage: Chris Matens; Sadie Kurtz, folk artist; Josef Albers, His Art and His Influence; Montclair Art Colony; Currier and Ives Prints, George Raimes Beach Collection; Two Hundred Years of American Masterpiece, 1755-1955; Prints from the Collection: The American Scene, 1900-1950; A Woman's Day, 19th-20th Century Costume; Jack Roth; The Vernon Mona Lisa; Who Speaks to Me in My Own Voice?, Southwestern Indian watercolors from the John Sloan Collection
Publications: Bulletin, bi-monthly, five issues; Newsletter, three issues; exhibition catalogues
Activities: Classes for adults and children; docent training; workshops coordinated programs with school groups; dramatic programs; lectures open to the public, 6 - 10 vis lectrs per year; concerts; gallery talks every Sunday; tours; museum shop sells books, reproductions, slides, handcrafted textiles, pottery, jewelry and objects for children

L **LeBrun Library,** 3 South Mountain Ave, PO Box 1582, 07042. Tel 201-746-5555. *Librn* Edith A Rights
Open Tues - Fri 10 AM - 5 PM, Sat 10 AM - 1 PM, cl July and August. Estab 1924 to support research and exhibitions of the museum. For reference only
Library Holdings: Vols 10,000; Per subs 50; Micro — Fiche; AV — A-tapes, cassettes, lantern slides, slides; Other — Clipping files, exhibition catalogs, pamphlets, reproductions
Special Subjects: American Art, American Indian, Japanese Culture
Collections: †Bookplates; †posters

MORRISTOWN

M **MORRIS MUSEUM OF ARTS AND SCIENCES,** Normandy Heights & Columbia Rds, PO Box 125, Convent, 07961. Tel 201-538-0452. *Dir* John D Peterson; *Asst Dir* Donald A Madson; *Fine Arts Cur* Harry F Orchard; *Public Relation Dir* Judith Boyd; *Exhibition Technician* Michael Rizzo
Open Mon - Sat 10 AM - 5 PM; Sun 2 - 5 PM. Summer, July and August, Tues - Sat 10 AM - 4 PM; cl major holidays. Admis adults $1, students & senior citizens $.50, children & groups of 15 or more $.25. Inc 1943. Average Annual Attendance: 173,000. Mem: 1550; dues benefactor $100, patron $50, organizations $25 and up, family $25, couple $15, individual $10, students and senior citizens $5; annual meeting third Wed in Jan
Collections: American historic and foreign; decorative arts; dolls; North American Indians
Activities: Classes for adults and children; dramatic programs; docent training; lectures open to the public, 6 - 8 vis lectr per yr; concerts; gallery talks; individual paintings & original objects of art lent to other museums & art organizations; museum shop sells books, original art, reproductions, prints, slides, jewelry, games & crafts; Five Sense Center
L **Library,** Normandy Heights and Columbia Rds, PO Box 125, Convent, 07961
Library Holdings: Vols 1000; AV — Slides

M **SCHUYLER-HAMILTON HOUSE,*** Five Olyphant Place, 07960. Tel 201-267-4039. *Regent* Sally Fairchild-Foy; *Cur* Mrs F K Newcomber
Open Tues - Sun 2 - 5 PM, other times by appointment. Admis adults $.50, children under 12 free. Estab 1923 for preservation of historical landmark. House is furnished with 18th Century antiques; five large portraits of General & Mrs Philip Schuyler, their daughter, Betsey Schuyler Hamilton, Alexander Hamilton and Dr Jabez Campfield; old lithographs, silhouette of George Washington, needle and petit point. Average Annual Attendance: 350. Mem: 106; dues $20; annual meeting May, Chapter meets Sept - May
Income: Financed by membership
Collections: China - Canton, blue willow, Staffordshire; doll china; pewter; brass candlesticks; rugs; tunebooks
Activities: Docent training; lect open to public; tours; competitions with awards; scholarships; exten dept; sales shop sells colonial dolls, miniature furniture and rugs, stationery, cards and reproductions

NEWARK

M **NEWARK MUSEUM,** 49 Washington St, PO Box 540, 07101. Tel 201-733-6600. *Pres* David J Sherwood; *Dir* Samual C Miller; *Asst Dir & General Adminr* David Collins; *Business Adminr* Dominic A Lisanti; *Cur Adminr & Registrar* Audrey Koenig; *Dir Programs & Publications & Spec Asst to Dir* Mary Sue Sweeney; *Cur Classical* Susan Auth; *Cur Coins* Dorothy Budd Bartle; *Cur Decorative Arts* Ulysses G Dietz; *Cur Oriental Coll* Valrae Reynolds; *Cur Painting & Sculpture* Gary Reynolds; *Cur Ethnology* Anne Spencer; *Dir Education* Susan Newberry; *Lending Dept* Joan Brown; *Planetarium* Jerome Vinski; *Cur Zoology* Kenneth Gosner; *Cur Geology* Alice Blount; *Arts Workshop* Jean West; *Dir Mem & Musuem Services* Barbara Lowell; *Public Relations* Mary Chris Rospond; *Development* Elizabeth Kopley
Open Mon - Sun Noon - 5 PM, cl Christmas, New Year's Day, July 4 & Thanksgiving. No admis fee. Estab 1909 to exhibit articles of art, science, history and technology, and for the study of the arts and sciences. The building was a gift of Louis Bamberger, opened 1926; held in trust by the Museum Association for the City of Newark, which gave the site. The adjoining building purchased by Museum in 1937. Average Annual Attendance: 412,000. Mem: 5000; dues $12.50 and up; annual meeting Jan
Income: $2,000,000 (financed by city and state appropriations, county funds)
Collections: †American painting and sculpture of all periods with primitives well represented; †African, †American Indian, †Chinese, †Indian, †Islamic, †Japanese, †South Pacific, †Tibetan; †Mediterranean Antiquities, including Eugene Schaefer Collection of ancient glass; †decorative arts; †Pre-Columbian material; †crosses and crucifixes; †coins
Exhibitions: American Folk Art; American paintings and sculptures; Tibet: A Lost World; Japanese Art; Chinese Ceramics; Art in African Living; Contemporary African Political Cloths; 1820 House; Victorian Furniture; The Ballantine House; Lee Gatch; Myth and Gospel, Art of Coptic Egypt; Survival: Life and Art of the Alaskan Eskimo; Southwest Indian pottery; The Two Worlds of Japenese Art; 2000 Years of Chinese Ceramics; Murals Without Walls; Arshile Gorky's Aviation Murals Rediscovered
Publications: New Notes, monthly; The Newark Museum, quarterly; catalogs and bulletins on major exhibitions
Activities: Classes for adults and children; dramatic programs; docent training; lect open to the public, 15 - 20 vis lectr per yr; concerts; gallery talks; tours; competitions; extention department serving community neighborhoods; individual paintings and original objects of art lent to other museums; lending collection contains nature artifacts; museum shop sells books, magazines, original art, reproductions, prints, original craft items from around the world
L **Library,** 49 Washington St, PO Box 540, 07101. Tel 201-733-6640, 733-6584. *Librn* Margaret DiSalvi; *Libr Asst* Helen Olsson
Open Mon - Fri 9 Am - 5 PM. Estab 1926 to serve the Museum staff and to provide information on the collections
Library Holdings: Vols 22,000; Per subs 143; AV — Kodachromes, lantern slides, slides; Other — Clipping files, exhibition catalogs, pamphlets, photographs
Special Subjects: American Indian Art, Decorative Arts, Oriental Art, Primitive Art, American Art, Tibet, general art subjects
Publications: Acquisitions list, monthly to staff

M **Junior Museum,** 49 Washington St, 07101. Tel 201-733-6608. *Supv* Jane Caffrey; *Asst Supv* Stephen Kneisel; *Art Asst* Marsha Smith
Open daily Noon - 5 PM. No admis fee. Estab 1926 to supply art and science programs designed to stimulate the individual child in self discovery and exploration of the world, and to teach effective use of the Museum as a whole, which may lead to valuable lifetime interests. Art and Science education resource information and workshops, after school, Saturday and summer workshops in art and science for children ages 3 - 18; preschool workshops Tues - Fri mornings; special holiday festivals for children; awards; field trips. Average Annual Attendance: 16,700. Mem: 10,123; dues 10; annual meeting May
Income: Financed through The Newark Museum
Exhibitions: Changing exhibitions; annual exhibition of childrens work
Activities: Parents art workshops; special education workshops for exceptional children and adults

L **NEWARK PUBLIC LIBRARY,** Art & Music Dept, 5 Washington St, Box 630, 07101. Tel 201-733-7840. *Supv Art & Music Department* William J Dane
Open Mon, Wed & Thurs 9 AM - 9 PM; Tues & Fri 9 AM - 5:30 PM; Sat 9 AM - 5 PM. Estab 1888. Provides materials on all aspects of the visual arts to the New Jersey Library Network of New Jersey. Maintains an art gallery: three separate galleries with a total of 375 running feet. Circ 70,000
Income: Financed by city and state appropriations
Purchases: $45,000
Library Holdings: Vols 65,000; Per subs 215; original documents; Micro — Fiche, reels; AV — Cassettes, slides 15,000, v-tapes; Other — Clipping files, exhibition catalogs, manuscripts, original art works, pamphlets, photographs, prints, reproductions
Special Subjects: Artist's Books, Fine Prints, History of Fine Printing, Illustrated Books, Japanese Books and Prints
Collections: †R C Jenkinson Collection of fine printing; †Autographs; †Bookplates; †Fine Print Collection (13,000); †Picture Collection (1,000,000 illustrations); †Posters (4000)
Exhibitions: It's On the Bag (Shopping Bag Design); Prints, Posters, Illustrated Books from Puerto Rico; A Salute to Clare Leighton; Sculpture & Architecture in Contemporary Posters; illustration from L'Illustration; The Art of Cartography
Publications: Calendar of events, bimonthly
Activities: Concerts; gallery talks; films; tours; traveling exhibitions organized and circulated

M **NEW JERSEY HISTORICAL SOCIETY MUSEUM,** 230 Broadway, 07104. Tel 201-483-3939. *Pres & Exec Dir* Joan C Hull; *Chmn of the Board* Robert B O'Brien Jr; *Cur* Alan D Frazer
Open Wed 10:30 AM, 12:30 PM, 2:30 PM for guided tours; Tues, Thurs - Sat by appointment only. Admis adults $2.50, students & senior citizens $2, groups $1.50 per person. Estab 1845 to collect, preserve, exhibit and make available for study the materials pertaining to the history of New Jersey and its people. The museum has five period rooms and lobby display cases on the main floor; three galleries on second floor totaling 3900 sq ft devoted to permanent or changing exhibitions. Average Annual Attendance: 45,000. Mem: 3163; dues adults $25 and up; annual meeting third Wed in April
Income: Financed by endowment, membership, gifts, grants and benefits
Collections: Ceramics; glassware; furniture; important technical drawings from 1790-1815; Indian relics; New Jersey portraits, landscapes, prints and photographs; sculpture; silhouettes and miniatures; silver; toys; World War I posters
Exhibitions: Painted in Crayon: Pastel Portraits from the Collection; Steam: Power to Move the World; Things Once Common, a collection of household implements and every day tools from the late 18th - 19th centuries interpreting the social history of New Jersey's past; Period Rooms, four Victorian & one Colonial; Rembrandt Peale and Gilbert Stuart from permanent collection
Publications: Exhibition catalogs; New Jersey History, quarterly; New Jersey Messenger, monthly newsletter; Instructional Bulletin; Crossroads, Jersey Journeys
Activities: Classes for children; docent training; school history clubs; lectr open to the public; tours; competitions; individual paintings and original objects of art lent to established institutions; traveling exhibitions organized and circulated; sales shop selling books, reproductions, prints and items for children
M **New Jersey Historical Society at Morven,** 55 Stocketon St, Princeton, 08540. *Adminr* Gregory Coin
Open Wed 10:30 AM - 12:30 PM, 2:30 Pm for guided tours. Admis adults $2.50, students and senior citizens $2, groups $1.50 per person. In 1701 a tract was purchased by Richard Stockton, the elder, from William Penn in West Jersey; on 600 acres of this land was built the 18th century mansion later called Morven by Annis Stockton, wife of the grandson Richard Stockton, a signer of the Declaration of Independence. Morven is an early Georgian house and reflecting classical Renaissance architecture and, with its gardens and ancient trees, covers five acres. Average Annual Attendance: 36,500
Income: Financed by endowment, membership, gifts, grants & benefits
Exhibitions: Period Rooms in Federal and Jacksonian Era; Statesmen Gallery
Activities: Tours; orientation films; museum shop

C **PRUDENTIAL INSURANCE COLLECTION,*** Prudential Plaza, 07101. Tel 201-877-6000. *Dir of Design* Lois Dickson
Estab 1969 to enhance the surroundings and living up to social responsibility in supporting art as a genuinely important part of life
Collections: Approximately 1059 holdings of paintings, sculptures and unique works on paper; 2558 signed graphics; 1182 posters; 241 billboards; 52 photographs

NEW BRUNSWICK

RUTGERS UNIVERSITY
M **Jane Voorhees Zimmerli Art Museum,** Voorhees Hall, Hamilton Street, 08903. Tel 201-932-7237. *Dir* Phillip Dennis Cate; *Cur Painting & Sculpture & Asst Dir* Jeffrey Wechsler; *Cur of Education* Stephanie Grunberg; *Cur of Children's Literature* Elaine-Carol Stanis; *Cur Prints & Drawings* Patricia Boyer; *Registrar* Marilyn Tatrai

Open Mon, Tues, Thurs & Fri 10 AM - 4:30 PM; Sat & Sun noon - 5 PM, cl
Wed. No admis fee. Estab 1966 to house Fine Arts Collection and present
exhibitions through the school year. Average Annual Attendance: 40,000. Mem:
Dues $30 family, $10 student
Income: Financed by state appropriation
Purchases: $50,000
Collections: Original artwork and manuscripts for children's books; 15th and
17th century Italian; 17th century Dutch; 18th, 19th and 20th century American;
18th and 19th century English paintings; †19th and 20th century French and
American prints; †Rutgers University Collection of Children's Literature;
†Rutgers Archives for Printmaking Studios
Exhibitions: (1982) Durer to Cezanne: Northern European Drawings from the
Ashmolean Museum; Realism & Realities: The Other Side of American Painting,
1940-1960; Theophile Alexandre Steinlen (1859-1923) Retrospective; (1983)
Haarlem: The Seventeenth Century; Rutgers Archives for Printmaking Studios;
Henri Riviere (1864-1951) Retrospective; Harry Gottlieb: The Silkscreen &
Social Concern in the WPA Era
Publications: Friends Newsletter; exhibition catalogs
Activities: Classes for adults & children; docent training; lect open to public;
concerts; gallery talks; tours; individual paintings & original objects of art lent to
museums; traveling exhibitions organized and circulated
L **Art Library,** Voorhees Hall, Hamilton St, 08903. Tel 201-932-7739. *Art Librn*
Ferris Olin; *Asst to Art Librn* Elaine Risch; *Assoc Librn* Halina Rusak
Open Mon - Thurs 9 AM - 12 PM, Fri 9 AM - 5 PM, Sat 12 - 5 PM, Sun 1 - 12
PM. Estab 1966 for academic research. For reference only
Library Holdings: Vols 40,000; Per subs 280; Micro — Fiche, reels; Other —
Clipping files, exhibition catalogs, pamphlets
Special Subjects: Architectural History; Western Art
Collections: Mary Bartlett Cowdrey Collection of American Art; Louis E Stern
Collection of Contemporary Art; Western Art-Architectural History
Activities: Bibliographic instruction; tours; lect

OCEAN CITY

O **CULTURAL ART CENTER OF OCEAN CITY,*** 409 Wesley Avenue, 08226.
Tel 609-399-7628. *Executive Dir* Frances Taylor; *Asst to Dir* Eunice Bell;
Publicity Coordr Shirley A Waldron
Open Mon - Sat 9 AM - 4 PM, Evenings Mon - Fri 7 - 10 PM. Estab 1966 to
promote the arts. Two galleries are maintained; upper gallery houses the
permanent collection; lower gallery is for monthly changing exhibitions
throughout the year. Average Annual Attendance: 10,000. Mem: 1000; dues
individual $8, family $15; annual meeting in mid-March
Income: $70,000 (financed by membership, city appropriation, New Jersey State
Council on the Arts Grant 1981)
Exhibitions: Annual: Membership Show, Juried Show, Boardwalk Art Show
Winners Exhibition, Christmas Crafts Fair, Juried Photography Show;
Needlework Show in 1980
Publications: Newsletters, quarterly
Activities: Classes for adults and children; lectures open to the public, 12 visiting
lecturers per year; concerts; competitions with awards; scholarships offered;
museum shop sells books, original art and crafts
L **Art Library,*** 409 Wesley Ave, 08226. Tel 609-399-7628
Open 9 AM - 4 PM daily, & Mon - Sat, 7 - 10 PM evenings. Estab 1972 to
make art and research materials available to instructors, students and members
Income: $70,000
Library Holdings: Vols 700; Per subs 2; AV — Slides; Other — Clipping files,
exhibition catalogs
Special Subjects: Art History, Photography

PARAMUS

M **BERGEN MUSEUM OF ART & SCIENCE,** E Ridgewood and Farview Ave,
07652. Tel 201-265-1248, 265-1255. *Dir* Joan Kuyper; *Educational Liaison*
Aaron Fish; *Secy* Helen L Meyer
Open Tues - Sat 10 AM - 5 PM; Sun 1 - 5 PM, cl Mon & some holidays. Admis
adults $1, children $.50. Estab May 1956 to maintain a museum which will
provide a creative and recreative center to stimulate youth and adult interest in
arts, science, history and industry
Income: Financed by membership, contributions, county appropriations, grants &
corporation
Collections: Mainly works of New Jersey artists
Publications: Calendar, bi-monthly
Activities: Concerts; gallery talks; tours; competitions with awards; museum shop
sells books, jewelry, dolls, toys, rocks, minerals

PATERSON

M **PASSAIC COUNTY HISTORICAL SOCIETY,** Lambert Castle Museum,
Valley Rd, 07503. Tel 201-881-2761. *Dir* Catherine Keene
Open Wed - Sun 1 - 4 PM. Admis adults $1, children under 15 free. Estab 1926.
Located in Lambert Castle built in 1892. Average Annual Attendance: 15,000.
Mem: Society dues sustaining $25; family $15; regular $10; student $3
Collections: Koemple Spoon Collection; textiles; local historical material;
paintings; photographs; decorative arts; folk art
Exhibitions: Passaic Falls; Gaetano Federici; Victorian Costumes; quilts &
coverlets; World War I posters; Passaic County Folk Art
Publications: Castle Lite, bi-monthly newsletter; pamphlets; exhibition catalogues
Activities: Lectures; guided tours; museum shop sells publications, postcards,
souvenirs, gifts
L **Library,** Lambert Castle, Valley Rd, 07503. Tel 201-881-2761
Open Mon - Fri 9 AM - 4 PM by appointment
Library Holdings: Vols 10,000
Special Subjects: Local History, Silk Industry, Local Geneology

PITTSTOWN

O **ASSOCIATED ARTISTS OF NEW JERSEY,** RD 1, 08867. Tel 201-735-5831.
Pres Harry Devlin; *VPres* Joseph Konopka; *Secy* Anne Steele Marsh; *Treas* Hella
Bailin
Estab 1941 to hold one or two exhibitions a year, with informational meetings in
summer. Mem: Members selected by invitation of the board; dues $15; annual
meeting April-May
Income: Financed by membership

PLAINFIELD

L **PLAINFIELD PUBLIC LIBRARY,** Eighth St at Park Ave, 07060. Tel 201-
757-1111. *Dir* Thomas H Ballard
Open Mon, Tue & Thur 9 AM - 9 PM; Wed 1 PM - 9 PM; Fri - Sat 9 AM - 5
PM. Estab 1881. Maintains an art gallery with original artworks on permanent
display, group shows as scheduled. Circ 135,000
Income: Financed by state appropriation, and Federal funds
Library Holdings: Vols 190,000; Per subs 400; Micro — Fiche, reels; AV —
Cassettes, fs, Kodachromes, motion pictures, rec, slides, v-tapes; Other —
Exhibition catalogs, original art works, photographs
Special Subjects: Arts of the United States (slides), Lincoln Fine Arts Collection
(books & periodicals)
Exhibitions: Annual National Print Exhibition; Associated Artists of New Jersey;
Invitational Exhibits; student work

M **TWEED ARTS GROUP,** 112 E Front St, PO Box 2957, 07062. Tel 201-754-
9350. *Pres* Alfred Munoz; *VPres* A Kimberlin Blackburn; *Secy* Ernest Jaeger;
Exhibit Chair Maria Mijares
Open Wed - Sat Noon - 5 PM. No admis fee. Estab 1980. Mem: 250; dues $15
Exhibitions: (1983) Fear & Trembling; Peace on Earth: Pastorals & Politics;
Maximalism
Publications: Tweedgram, quarterly newsletter
Activities: Competitions; originates traveling exhibitions

PRINCETON

O **PRINCETON ART ASSOCIATION,** Rosedale Rd, PO Box 3019, 08540. Tel
609-921-9173. *Chmn Bd of Trustees* Gordon Strauss; *VChmn* Jean Lindabury;
Secy Patricia J Labaw; *Treas* David Walter; *Exec Dir* Mary Yess
Open Mon - Fri 9 AM - 3 PM, Tues - Fri evenings 4 - 7:30 PM. Estab 1964 to
establish and maintain educational and cultural programs devoted to art.
Exhibitions are held at McCarter Theatre and at various locations throughout the
community. Average Annual Attendance: 1500. Mem: 1000; annual meeting
May
Income: Financed by membership, class fees, workshops and demonstration fees,
trip fees, entry fees and donations
Activities: Classes for adults and children; lectures open to the public, 3 vis lectr
per yr; tours; competitions with awards; scholarships offered
L **Library,** Princeton, 08540
Reference library
Library Holdings: Vols 200; AV — Slides

PRINCETON UNIVERSITY
M **Art Museum,** 08544. Tel 609-452-3788. *Dir* Allen Rosenbaum; *Cur Coll* Frances
F Jones; *Dir Community Services* JoAnn Carchman; *Registrar* Robert LaFond;
Custodian Prints & Drawings Barbara T Ross; *Publication Ed* Jill Guthrie
Open Tues - Sat 10 AM - 4 PM; Sun 1 - 5 PM; Summer 2 - 4 PM; cl Mon &
major holidays. No admis fee. Estab 1882 to make original works of art available
to students in the Department of Art & Archeology and also for the enjoyment
of the University, community and general public. About 24,000 sq ft of gallery
space for permanent, semi-permanent and changing installations. Average Annual
Attendance: 90,000. Mem: 1250; dues $20 and up
Income: Financed by endowment and University
Collections: †Ancient Mediterranean; †British and American; †Chinese ritual
bronze vessels; †Far Eastern, especially Chinese and Japanese paintings;
†mediaeval and later European; †Pre-Columbian
Publications: Catalogs, occasionally; Record of the Art Museum, semi-annually
Activities: Docent training; lect; gallery talks; tours
L **Index of Christian Art,** McCormick Hall, 08544. Tel 609-452-3773. *Dir* Nigel
Morgan
Open Mon - Fri 9 AM - 5 PM, cl holidays. Estab 1917 as a division of the
Department of Art and Archaeology. It is a research and reference collection of
cards and photographs designed to facilitate the study of Christian iconography
in works of art before 1400. Duplicate copies exist in Washington, DC in the
Dumbarton Oaks Research Center and in Los Angeles in the Library of the
University of California. European copies are in Rome in the Vatican Library and
in Utrecht in the University

C **E R SQUIBB & SONS, INC,*** Lawrenceville-Princeton Rd, PO Box 4000,
08540. Tel 609-921-4261, 921-4000. *Dir Community Affairs* Lora W Jones
Estab as a community service, in appreciation of beauty. Maintains a Fine Arts
Gallery which mounts 8 exhibitions per year
Activities: Competitions; financial assistance to museums and art association's
juried shows throughout New Jersey; for medical charities, have initiated large
photograph exhibitions; awards; originate traveling exhibitions

RINGWOOD

M **RINGWOOD MANOR HOUSE MUSEUM,** Sloatsburg Rd, PO Box 1304,
07456. Tel 201-962-7031. *Cur* Elbertus Prol
Open May - Oct Tues - Fri 10 AM - 4 PM; Sat, Sun & holidays 10 AM - 5 PM.
No admis fee. Estab 1935
Income: Financed by state appropriation
Collections: Decorative arts; furniture; graphics; historical material; paintings;
New Jersey iron making history
Activities: Guided tours; special events; sales shop sells books, magazines,
reproductions & prints

RIVER VALE

L **RIVER VALE PUBLIC LIBRARY,** Art Dept,* 644 River Vale Rd, 07675. Tel 201-391-2323. *Dir* Dorothy Cornell
Open Mon - Thurs 10 AM - 9 PM, Fri 10 AM - 5 PM, Sat 10 AM - 4 PM, cl Sat July and Aug
Income: $90,000 (financed by city appropriation)
Library Holdings: AV — Cassettes, rec, slides, v-tapes; Other — Framed reproductions, prints, sculpture
Collections: Fine arts: music and art, history, artists, techniques; Theatre history: Broadway; movies; Beginning photography collection
Exhibitions: Local artists exhibits
Activities: Individual paintings lent to valid library card holders

SOUTH ORANGE

O **NEW JERSEY WATERCOLOR SOCIETY,** 48 Duffield Dr, 47B Cheshire Square, 07079. Tel 201-747-6141. *Pres* Nessa Grainger; *First VPres* William Senior; *Second VPres* Anthony Ventura; *Treas* Thomas A Bavolar
Estab 1942 to bring to the public the best in New Jersey watercolorists - teachers. Mem: 121; dues $15; annual meeting last Sun in April
Exhibitions: Annual Members Show in spring; Annual Open Statewide Juried Exhibition in fall - alternating between Morris Museum of Arts and Sciences, Morristown NJ and the Monmouth Museum, Lincorft NJ
Publications: Illustrated Catalogue; Newsletter; Open Show
Activities: Annual dinner; receptions for Open Show and Members Show; competitions with awards

M **SETON HALL UNIVERSITY,** Student Center Art Gallery,* S Orange Ave, 07079. Tel 201-761-9459, 761-9000. *Dir* Petra Ten-Doesschate Chu; *Cur Exhib* Barbara W Kaufman
Open Mon - Fri 10 AM - 5 PM, Sat & Sun 2 - 4 PM. No admis fee. Estab 1963. Troast Memorial Gallery, estab 1974, houses permanent collection of contemporary American art; Wang Fang-Yu Collection of Oriental art was estab in 1977. Average Annual Attendance: 35,000
Exhibitions: Henry Grasser: American-Indian Artists From The Southwest
Activities: Lect open to the public; gallery talks
L **Library,*** 405 S Orange Ave, 07079. Tel 201-761-9431. *Librn* James C Sharp; *Assoc Librn* Paul Chao
Library Holdings: AV — Slides 11,000

SPRINGFIELD

L **SPRINGFIELD FREE PUBLIC LIBRARY,** Donald B Palmer Museum, 66 Mountain Ave, 07081. Tel 201-376-4930. *Library and Museum Dir* Cynthia A Josephs; *Head Technical Servs & Ref Dept* Joan L Meyer; *Head Circulation Department* Rose Searles; *Head Childrens Department* Patricia Fennimore; *Bookeeper* Erna Kitzing
Open Mon, Wed, Thurs Noon - 9 PM, Tues, Fri, and Sat Noon - 5 PM. No admis fee. Estab 1975 as a museum addition to a public library established to preserve local history and to present cultural exhibits throughout the year. The library, including a meeting room with and the museum's bimonthly exhibits of art, crafts and history, serves as a cultural center
Collections: †Permanent collection of circulating framed art reproductions
Activities: Films; lectures; puppet shows; individual reproductions lent to library patrons; lending collection contains books, framed reproductions, records, photographs, slides & periodicals

SUMMIT

O **SUMMIT ART CENTER, INC,** 68 Elm St, 07901. Tel 201-273-9121. *Pres* Mrs Paul Stein; *Dir* Paul Master-Karnik, PhD
Exhibits open daily Noon - 4 PM, Sat & Sun 2 - 4 PM. Estab 1933 to develop art education and appreciation. Two gallery spaces specializing in contemporary American Art. Average Annual Attendance: 27,000. Mem: 2500; dues Friends Membership $35, general membership $25; annual meeting April
Exhibitions: (1982) American Realism 1930s - 1980s; Philip Pearlstein; Hoboken, USA; William Zorach; sculpture, drawings; Connections: Science into Art; American Landscape Photography Intertwining Native American Art Bouquet; one and two-man shows
Publications: Class & exhibition catalogs; monthly newsletter
Activities: Art classes for adults, children and community groups; docent training; lectures open to public and for members, 10 vis lectr per year; concerts; gallery talks; tours; competitions with awards; scholarships; extension dept serves four counties; individual paintings and original objects of art lent to public organizations; sales shop sells original art, prints and art crafts
L **Library,** Summit, 07901
Reference library
Library Holdings: Vols 2000; Per subs 6; AV — Slides

TRENTON

L **FREE PUBLIC LIBRARY,** Art and Music Dept, 120 Academy St, PO Box 2448, 08607. Tel 609-392-7188, Ext 24. *Dir* Harold W Thompson Jr; *Head Art and Music Dept* Alice F Fullam
Open Mon , Wed, Thurs 9 AM - 9 PM, Tues, Fri and Sat 9 AM - 5 PM, cl Sun and holidays. Estab 1900
Income: Financed by city appropriation
Library Holdings: Vols 7000; Per subs 35; 2000 Mounted pictures; Micro — Reels; AV — Motion pictures, rec; Other — Clipping files, exhibition catalogs, memorabilia, pamphlets, photographs, prints, reproductions
Exhibitions: Paintings; photographs; crafts; antiques collections

M **MERCER COUNTY COMMUNITY COLLEGE GALLERY,** 1200 Old Trenton Rd, 08690. Tel 609-586-4800. *Dir* Frank G Butorac
Open 9 AM - 5 PM. No admis fee. Triangle Gallery primarily for exhibiting student work
Collections: Ceramics collection; Cybis Collection; Kelsey Collection; Mexican art and handicrafts; painting by Wolf Kahn
Exhibitions: Faculty, student and children's art exhibits as well as exhibits from the permanent collection
Activities: Classes for adults and children; lect open to the public; gallery talks; extension dept; lending collection contains motion pictures; book traveling exhibitions
L **Library,** 1200 Old Trenton Rd, 08690
Estab 1891 to provide library services for the college; portion of the main floor is devoted to permanent display cabinets. In addition display panels are used for faculty exhibits, community exhibits and traveling exhibits
Library Holdings: Vols 70,000; Other — Prints
Publications: Audio-visual materials catalog, biannually; college catalog, every two years; film catalog, annually; library handbook, biannually; library newsletter, quarterly; The Book Bynder

M **NEW JERSEY STATE MUSEUM,** 205 W State St, 08625. Tel 609-292-6300. *Dir* Leah P Sloshberg; *Asst Dir* Karen Cummins; *Cur Fine Arts* Zoltan Buki; *Cur Cultural History* Sue Crilley; *Cur Exhibits* Wallace Conway; *Cur Education* Raymond Howe; *Cur Archaeology-Ethnology* Lorraine Williams; *Cur Science* Ray Stein
Open Mon - Sat 9 AM - 4:45 PM, Sun 1 - 5 PM, cl Mon and most state holidays. No admis fee. Estab 1891 by legislation to collect, exhibit and interpret fine arts, cultural history, archaeology-ethnology and science with a New Jersey focus; changing exhibit gallery, Hall of Natural Science, projected hall for permanent collection. Average Annual Attendance: 450,000. Mem: 1000; dues $25 and up; annual meeting June
Income: $1,300,000 (financed by state appropriation)
Purchases: $60,000, plus $30,000 - $60,000 from Friends
Collections: American fine and decorative arts of the 18th, 19th and 20th century; American painting from 1910-1950 with special emphasis on the †Steiglitz circle, Regionalist, Abstract Artists; †New Jersey fine and decorative arts
Exhibitions: Changing exhibitions focus on New Jersey artists and cultural history; Long-term teaching exhibitions on language of the visual arts and Indian culture
Publications: Bulletins; catalogs, and irregular serials; Investigators; reports
Activities: Classes for adults & children; dramatic programs; docent training; lectures open to the public, 10 vis lectr per yr; concerts; gallery talks; tours; competitions; individual paintings and original objects of art lent to other institutions; lending collection contains 3000 motion picture titles, 2613 reels, nature artifacts, original art works, original prints, paintings, photographs, sculpture, slides; book traveling exhibitions; traveling exhibitions organized and circulated; museum shop sells books, international folk crafts or items related to collection
L **Library,** 205 W State St, 08625
Open to staff for reference only
Library Holdings: Vols 5000; Per subs 12; AV — Slides, v-tapes; Other — Exhibition catalogs, photographs
Publications: NEWS, bi-monthly; annual report

M **OLD BARRACKS MUSEUM,** Barrack St, 08608. Tel 609-396-1776. *Dir* Cynthia Koch; *Cur Education* Douglas Winterich; *Cur Coll* Caroline Webb; *Admin Asst* Sharon Wysocki
Open Mon - Sat 10 AM - 5 PM, Sun 1 - 5 PM. Admis adults $.50, children 12 and under $.25, senior citizens and educational groups free. Built 1758, estab 1902 as museum of history and decorative arts. Located in English barracks that housed Hessian Soldiers Dec 1776. Average Annual Attendance: 28,000. Mem: 385; dues $10 - $200; annual meeting Nov, March, May
Income: Financed by membership and state appropriation
Collections: †American decorative arts 1750-1820; patriotic paintings and prints; military artifacts; early American tools and household equipment
Exhibitions: The Trenton Barracks 1758-1918; Washington & The Battle of Trenton; 18th Period Rooms and Soldiers Quarters
Publications: The Barracks Bugle, quarterly newsletter; The Old Barracks at Trenton, book; The Old Barracks, Trenton, NJ: A Historic Structure Report, book
Activities: Classes for children; dramatic programs; docent training; lectures open to the public, 3 vis lectr per yr; concerts; tours; individual paintings and original objects of art lent to museums; lending collection contains slides & reproduction military objects/costumes; book traveling exhibitions; museum shop sells books, reproductions, prints, slides, historical toys, ceramics

M **TRENTON STATE COLLEGE,** Holman Gallery,* Hillwood Lakes, 08625. Tel 609-771-2198, 771-1855. *Pres* Dr Harold Eickoff; *Dir* Dr Howard Goldstein; *Gallery Coordr* Fame Dileo
Open Mon - Fri 12 - 3 PM, Thurs 7 - 9 PM, Sun 1 - 3 PM. No admis fee. Estab to present students and community with the opportunity to study a wide range of artistic expressions and to exhibit their work. Average Annual Attendance: 2000
Income: Financed by art dept budget and grants including NJ State Council on the Arts, Mercer County Cultural and Heritage Commission
Collections: Purchases from National Print and Drawing Show
Exhibitions: Craft Show; Faculty Show; Mercer County Competitive Art; Mercer County Competitive Photography; National Drawing Exhibition; National Print Exhibition; Selections from the State Museum; Sculpture Shows; Student Exhibition
Publications: Catalog for National Print Exhibition; catalog for National Drawing Exhibition
Activities: Classes for adults and children; Lectures open to the public, five visiting lecturers per year; gallery talks; tours; competitions with awards; individual paintings and original objects of art lent to other offices and departments on campus; lending collection contains original art works; original prints; paintings; traveling exhibitions organized and circulated to other state colleges and art schools

UNION

M KEAN COLLEGE OF NEW JERSEY, College Gallery, Morris Avenue, 08063. Tel 201-527-2307, 527-2347. *Pres* Dr Nathan Weiss; *Chmn Art Dept* James Howe; *Gallery Dir* Zara Cohan
Open Mon - Thurs 10 AM - 2 PM, 5 - 8 PM, by appointment at other times. No admis fee. Estab 1971 as a forum to present all art forms to students and the community through original exhibitions, catalogues, fine art, art history and museum training. One gallery 22 x 34 ft plus an alcove 8 x 18 ft on first floor of arts and humanities building. Average Annual Attendance: 3000
Income: Financed by state appropriation
Collections: American painting by Audubon, L Baskin, Lamar Dodd, W Homer, P Jenkins, J Stella, Tony Smith, Walter Darby Bannard, Werner Drewes, B J O Norfeldt, James Rosen Quist, Robert Rauschenberg, Odilon Redon; prints and photographs
Exhibitions: (1983-84) John Cotton Dana: Visionary; Robin Krueger Gallery 1935-1974: Reconstructed; Local Limners; Another Side of Thomas Nast; Giulio Bonasone; John Button; Fine Arts Faculty 83 Local Limners; Mount, Homer & their contemporaries; Piranesi: Real & Imaginary; Problems in Connoisseurship; Tony Smith, 81 More & the Sculptural Process; Art Directors Club of New Jersey Awards Exhibition; Hans Weingaertner 1896-1970, paintings; works by candidates for graduate degree; exhibition of works by undergraduate fine arts majors
Publications: Catalogues for exhibitions
Activities: Dramatic programs; lect open to public; individual paintings lent to colleges, institutions, and departments on the campus; lending collection contains original art works, original prints, photographs, sculpture and slides
L Nancy Thompson Library, Morris Avenue, 08063. *Acquisitions Librn* Tamara Avdzej
Open Mon - Thurs 8 AM - 11:30 PM, Fri 8 AM - 10 PM, Sat 9 AM - 4 PM, Sun 1 - 8 PM. Estab 1855 to support instruction
Purchases: $6000
Library Holdings: Vols 7628; Per subs 45; AV — A-tapes, fs, slides; Other — Exhibition catalogs

UPPER MONTCLAIR

M MONTCLAIR STATE COLLEGE, Gallery One, 07043. Tel 201-893-5112. *Dir* Harry Rosenzweig; *Asst Dir* Julie Marchini; *Pres* Dr David W D Dickson; *VPres* Rolland Garret; *Dean* Donald Mattran; *Chmn Fine Arts Department* Helen Ross
Open Mon - Fri 9:30 AM - 4:30 PM. No admis fee. Estab 1973. Three galleries with 1200 sq ft, 600 sq ft & 600 sq ft. Average Annual Attendance: 5000
Collections: Cosla Collection of Renaissance Art
Exhibitions: (1982-83) Josef Albers Formulation: Articulation; National Council of Education for the Ceramic Arts; Montclair State, Ellis Island Photography Project; Printmaking Council of New Jersey; selected high school art; selected Latin American artists; BFA exhibition
Activities: Classes for adults; lectures open to public; concerts; gallery talks; scholarships
L Slide Library, Fine Arts Department, 07043. *Slide Librn* Rosanne Martin
Open Mon - Thurs 8:30 AM - 8 PM, Fri 8:30 AM - 1:30 PM. Estab 1968 to provide audio visual material and information about the art world for faculty, visiting artists and community. Circ 40,000
Library Holdings: Per subs 15; announcements of art shows throughout the country; AV — Cassettes, fs, Kodachromes, lantern slides, slides; Other — Clipping files, exhibition catalogs, framed reproductions, pamphlets, photographs, reproductions
Special Subjects: Prehistoric to contemporary art

WESTFIELD

O FEDERATED ART ASSOCIATIONS OF NEW JERSEY, INC, 720 Lawrence Ave, 07090. Tel 201-232-7623. *Dir* Jane Whipple Green; *VPres for South Jersey* Barbara L McIlvain; *VPres for North Jersey* Dolores A Z Powell; *Secy* Wilhelmine Holler
Estab 1969 to provide communications and exchange of ideas among visual art groups. Mem: 9000 (50 member groups); dues per club $25, individuals $10; composed of four districts which meet separately, annually
Publications: Directory of Visual Art Organizations in New Jersey, periodically; newsletter, quarterly; Views; Judge & Jury Selector
Activities: Annual Art Seminar; lectures open to the public, 8 vis lectr per yr

NEW MEXICO

ABIQUIU

M GHOST RANCH LIVING MUSEUM, Carson Nation Forest, Canjilon District, General Delivery, 87510. Tel 505-685-4312. *Dir* Albert Martinez
Open April - Sept 8 AM - 6 PM, Oct - March Tues - Sun 8 AM - 4:30 PM. No admis fee. Estab 1959 as an outdoor interpretive project for the conservation of natural resources. Average Annual Attendance: 100,000
Income: Financed by federal and private contributions
Collections: Paintings and prints related to natural resources conservation; art objects
Publications: Ghost Ranch Museum & More, bulletin; Museum at Ghost Ranch, bulletin; We Called it Ghost Ranch, book
Activities: Lectures open to the public; tours; museum shop sells books & prints
L Library, Abiquiu, 87510
Reference library
Library Holdings: Vols 1000; AV — Fs, motion pictures

ALBUQUERQUE

M ALBUQUERQUE MUSEUM OF ART, HISTORY AND SCIENCE, 2000 Mountain Road NW, PO Box 1293, 87103. Tel 505-766-7878. *Dir* James C Moore; *Admin Asst* Irene Kersting; *Cur of Art* Ellen J Landis; *Cur of History* Byron Johnson; *Cur of Exhibits* Robert Woltman; *Cur of Collections* Tom Lark; *Asst Cur Collections* Jackie Cunningham; *Cur of Education* E A Mares
Open Tues - Fri 10 AM - 5 PM; Sat & Sun 1 - 5 PM. Estab 1967 as a city museum which with Mexico diffusing knowledge and appreciation of history, art and science, establishing and maintaining a museum and related reference library, of collecting and preserving objects of historic, artistic and scientific interest, of protecting historic sites, works of art and works of nature from needless destruction, of providing facilities for research and publication and of offering popular instruction and opportunities for aesthetic enjoyment. Average Annual Attendance: 110,000. Mem: 1075; dues donor $5000, business $100, sustaining $50, family $20, individual $15, sr citizen $7.50
Income: Financed by city appropriation and Albuquerque Museum Foundation
Collections: Decorative arts; costumes; fine arts and crafts; objects and artifacts relevant to our cultural history from 20,000 BC to present; photography
Exhibitions: Explore; New Images From Spain; Enabled; Treasures, People, Ships and Dreams; The Moving Image: The Art of Film Animation; The Transcendental Painting Group: New Mexico 1938-1941 The American Gemstone Jewelry Collection; Contemporary Western Art in New Mexico; A Feast of Color: Dance Costumes From Ecuador; The History of Albuquerque; Autochromes: Color Photography Comes of Age
Publications: Las Noticias, bimonthly
Activities: Classes for children; docent training; lect; monthly vis lectr per year; gallery talks; tours; competitions; extension department serving Albuquerque Public Schools; artmobile; sales shop selling original magazines, reproductions, prints, Indian jewelry and local crafts
L Library, 2000 Mountain Road NW, 87103
Open to staff, docents and volunteers for reference
Library Holdings: Vols 1000; Per subs 10
Special Subjects: New Mexico history, art and material culture

M CLASSICAL SCHOOL GALLERY, 614 Indian School Rd NW, 87102. Tel 505-843-7749. *Pres* Dr C M Flumiani
Open daily 10 - 12 AM and 3 - 5 PM. No admis fee. Estab 1969 to foster the classical approach to the arts and art education. New 2500 sq ft building. Mem: 15; dues $200
Income: Financed by endowment
Collections: Italian masters
Publications: Art & Life, quarterly
Activities: Classes for adults; lect; book shop
L Library, 614 Indian School Rd NW, 87102
Library Holdings: Vols 2000

O INDIAN ARTS & CRAFTS ASSOCIATION,* 4301 Lead SE, 81108. Tel 505-265-9149. *Exec Dir* Dave Lewis
Estab 1974 to promote, preserve, protect & enhance the understanding of authentic American Indian arts & crafts
Publications: Directory, annual; Newsletter, monthly

C LOVELACE MEDICAL FOUNDATION, Art Collection,* 5400 Gibson Blvd, SE, 87108. Tel 505-842-7000. *Chief Executive Officer* Dr David J Ottensmeyer; *Cur Art Coll* Will Taylor
Open daily. No admis fee. Estab 1940. Foundation utilizes patient waiting lobbies throughout medical clinic and hospital complex to display collection
Collections: Indian (American Southwest) Textiles; Santa Fe School paintings; Taos School paintings
Activities: Tours; individual paintings lent to requesting museums

O NEW MEXICO ART LEAGUE, Gallery, 3401 Juan Tabo NE, 87111. Tel 505-293-5034. *Pres* Janice Mudd; *VPres* Glynda Fleming; *Dir* Florence Christison; *Secy* Helen Nielsen
Open Mon - Sat 10 AM - 5 PM; Sun 1 - 4 PM. No admis fee. Estab 1929 to promote artists of New Mexico; art gallery. Mem: 400; dues $20; monthly meetings
Income: Financed by membership and sales
Collections: Best of show of National Small Painting Show
Publications: Catalog of National Small Painting Show; newsletter, monthly
Activities: Workshops for adults; lectures open to the public; gallery talks; competitions with awards; museum & sales shop sells reproductions and prints

UNIVERSITY OF NEW MEXICO
M University Art Museum, Fine Arts Center, 87131. Tel 505-277-4001. *Interim Dir* Emily Kass; *Cur Coll* Peter Briggs; *Preparator* David Wagoner
Open Tues - Fri 10 AM - 5 PM & 7 - 10 PM; Sat & Sun 1 - 5 PM. No admis fee. Estab 1963. Maintains four galleries; a print and photograph room which is open to the public at certain hours. Mem: 300; dues $5 - $1000; annual meeting May
Income: Financed by university appropriations, grants and donations
Collections: 19th and 20th century American paintings, drawings, prints, photographs and sculpture; The Lahard Collection, photography; prints by American and European masters; 19th and 20th century lithographs
Exhibitions: Certain Realities; FSA Color Photographs; The Self as Subject: Visual Diaries by 14 photographers; American Lithographers 1900-1960
Publications: Bulletin, yearly; exhibition catalogs
Activities: Lectures open to the public; inter-museum loans; traveling exhibitions organized and circulated; museum shop sells books, catalogs, magazines, cards
M Jonson Gallery, 1909 Las Lomas Rd NE, 87106. Tel 505-277-4967. *Dir* Emily Kass; *Staff Asst* Lynn Adkins Varner
Open Tues - Fri Noon - 5 PM; Sat & Sun 1 - 5 PM, cl Mon. No admis fee. Estab 1948 for the assemblage and preservation of a comprehensive collection of the works of Raymond Jonson; a depository for works of art by other artists and their preservation; the exhibition of works of art. The structure includes a main gallery, four storage rooms, work room & office, a reception room and living

quarters for the curator. Average Annual Attendance: 4000
Income: Financed through University
Collections: Jonson reserved retrospective collection; other artists works by Jonson students
Publications: Exhibition announcements
Activities: Individual paintings and original objects of art lent to museums
L **Jonson Gallery Library,** 1909 Las Lomas Rd NE, 87106
Open to students and others doing research
Library Holdings: Vols 1000; Per subs 1
Collections: The Jonson Archives containing books and magazines relating to Raymond Jonson, his letters, his diaries, catalogs, clippings, photographs and slides of works
L **Fine Arts Library,** Fine Arts Center, 87131. Tel 505-277-2357. *Head Fine Arts Library* James Wright; *Asst Head Fine Arts Library* Nancy Pistorius
Open Mon - Thurs 8 AM - 11 PM; Fri 8 AM - 6 PM; Sat 9 AM - 5 PM; Sun Noon - 11 PM. Estab 1963 to provide library assistance and literary, microform and sound recording materials to support the programs of the university in the areas of art, architecture, music and photography
Library Holdings: Vols 44,000; Per subs 180; Micro — Cards, fiche, reels; AV — Cassettes, rec; Other — Exhibition catalogs, pamphlets, photographs
Special Subjects: History of Photography, Modern American & European, Native American, Spanish Colonial

CHURCH ROCK

M **RED ROCK STATE PARK MUSEUM** (Formerly Gallup Museum of Indian Arts), PO Box 328, 87311. Tel 505-722-6196. *Cur* Belinda Casto-Landolt
Open Mon - Fri 9 AM - 5 PM. Admis adults $1. Estab 1959 to acquaint visitors with the arts and crafts of the Navajo, Zuni and Hopi Indians. A small museum manned by Red Rock State Park; displaying Indian arts and crafts and exhibitions on natural history. Average Annual Attendance: 20,000. Mem: Dues $8
Income: Financed by city of Gallup, private contributions and admission fees
Exhibitions: Rock Art of the Early Navajo
Publications: Exhibitions catalog
Activities: Lectures open to public, 6 vis lectr per year; gallery talks; tours; sales shop sells books, reproductions and Indian arts and crafts
L **Library,** 87311
Library Holdings: Vols 1000; Other — Clipping files, photographs

DEMING

M **LUNA COUNTY HISTORICAL SOCIETY, INC,** Deming Luna Mimbres Museum, 301 S Silver St, PO Box 1617, 88031. Tel 505-546-2382. *Coordr* Ted Southerland; *Asst Coordr* Alden Fay; *Treas* John Plantz; *Dolls & Toys* Louise Southerland; *Frontier Life* Gene Todd
Open Mon - Sat 9 - 11:30 AM & 1:30 - 4 PM, Sun 1:30 - 4 PM, cl New Year's Day, Thanksgiving & Christmas Day, open by appointment during evenings for special interest groups. Admis free with donations. Estab 1969, moved into Old Armory 1978. Sponsored by Luna County Historical Society, Inc. Mem: 100; dues $3; annual meeting in Jan
Income: Financed by donations & endowment earnings
Collections: Chuck wagon, clothing, dolls, frontier life objects and other items on the local history; Indian artifacts; mine equipment; minerals; paintings and saddles; camera display; phone equipment; quilt room; old lace display
Exhibitions: Centennial Exhibition
Publications: History of Luna County
Activities: Museum shop sells books, magazines, original art, reproductions, prints, Indian jewelry & pottery

LAS CRUCES

M **NEW MEXICO STATE UNIVERSITY,** Art Gallery, Box 3572, 88003. Tel 505-646-2545. *Gallery Dir* Richard A Gehrke
Open Mon - Fri 11 AM - 4 PM, Sun 1 - 4 PM. No admis fee. Average Annual Attendance: 17,000
Collections: Photographs; limited edition prints & drawings & works on paper; collection of Retablos; paintings on canvas; sculpture
Exhibitions: Malcolm Grear Desiners Inc, graphic design exhibition; Dorthea Lange, Dorthea Lange Looks at American Country Women; NMSU Faculty Exhibition
Activities: Lectures open to public, 10-12 vis lectr per yr; competitions with awards; lending collection to campus departments; book traveling exhibitions; originate traveling exhibitions; museum shop sells books & magazines

LAS VEGAS

M **NEW MEXICO HIGHLANDS UNIVERSITY,** Arrott Art Gallery, Donnelly Library, National Ave, 87701. Tel 505-425-7511. *Chmn of Fine Arts* Lawrence Wise; *Art Dir* Paula Geisler
Open Mon - Sun 8 AM - 5 PM. No admis fee. Estab 1956 to acquaint University and townspeople with art of the past and present. Gallery dimensions approximately 20 x 20 ft. Average Annual Attendance: 1000
Income: Financed by state appropriation
Collections: †Permanent collection
Publications: University general catalog, annually
Activities: Classes for adults & children; lectures open to public, 1 vis lectr per yr; concerts; gallery talks; tours; competitions; book traveling exhibitions

LOS ALAMOS

M **FULLER LODGE ART CENTER,** 2132 Central Ave, PO Box 790, 87544. Tel 505-662-9331. *Dir* Karen Noll Purucker
Open Mon - Fri 10 AM - 4 PM, Sun 1 - 4 PM. No admis fee. Estab 1977 to provide an art center to the regional area; to foster the interests of the artists and art interested public of the Community. Center is approx 210 running ft; located in the Fuller Lodge; national Historical Site; gallery area has been renovated. Average Annual Attendance: 7500. Mem: 263; dues memorial $1500, life $1000, corporate $300, patron $100, sponsor $50, contributing $25, member $15, sr citizens and student $5
Income: $18,000 (financed by membership, county appropriation and grants)
Exhibitions: (1984) Siggraph '83: Computor Art; Intermountain Weaver's Guild Biennial Convention; Public Schools Annual Youth Art Exhibit; African Crafts; Personal Visions: Women Artists; New Mexico Formations: Mountains & Architecture; Third Biennial Juried Craft Exhibition;; The Body Beautiful; Art Through the Loom Weaver's Guild; The Consortium: Impressions of New Mexico; Men at Work; Annual Affordable Art Benefit; Toys for all Ages; (1985) Sister Adele, a Sculptor; juried humorous art; annual youth art; Grant Exhibit of Carole Steinke Costume Designs; Pajarito Art League Exhibit; Aliza Mandel, Catherine Fels & Lois Stouffer; Pajarito Painting, Drawing & Sculpture Exhibit; Invitational Quilt Exhibit; Pajarito Chapter of EGA
Publications: Bulletin, quarterly
Activities: Classes for children; docent training; seminars for artists; competitions with awards; individual paintings & original objects of art lent; museum shop sells books, original art, cards, art related toys & calendars

PORTALES

M **EASTERN NEW MEXICO UNIVERSITY,** Art & Library Gallery, Liberal Arts Bldg 101, 88130. Tel 505-562-2652. *Dir* Chris Gikas
Open 7 AM - 9 PM. No admis fee. Estab 1935 for exhibiting student artwork; gallery is room coverted for student works
Income: Financed by University funds
Collections: Student works in Art Department Collection
Activities: Individual paintings and original objects of art lent to the University
L **Golden Library,** Liberal Arts Bldg 101, Portales, 88130
Library Holdings: Vols 5400; Per subs 54; Micro — Cards, fiche; AV — A-tapes, cassettes, fs, Kodachromes, motion pictures, slides, v-tapes; Other — Exhibition catalogs, framed reproductions, original art works, pamphlets, photographs, prints, sculpture

ROSWELL

M **ROSWELL MUSEUM AND ART CENTER,** 100 W 11th St, 88201. Tel 505-622-4700. *Pres Board Trustees* Donald B Anderson; *VPres* Robert V Ely; *Secy* Martha Gillespie; *Treas* Ralph McIntyre; *Dir* Wendell Ott; *Asst Dir* William D Ebie; *Registrar & Cur* Wesley A Rusnell
Open Mon - Sat 9 AM - 5 PM, Sun & holidays 1 - 5 PM. No admis fee. Estab 1937 to promote and cultivate the fine arts. The basis of the fine arts collection being paintings and sculptures with emphasis on the artistic heritage of the Southwest. Ten galleries are maintained for art works; plus Robert H Goddard display . Average Annual Attendance: 50,000. Mem: 750; dues $10.50 and up
Income: $200,000 (financed by membership, city and county appropriation)
Collections: Witter Bynner Collection of Chinese Paintings & Jade; ethnological and archaeological collection of Southwestern Indian art; †international graphics collection; New Mexico regional; †20th century Southwestern paintings & sculpture; Plains Indians & Western Art
Exhibitions: Permanent collection plus 10-14 temporary exhibitions annually
Publications: Bulletin, quarterly; Exhibition Catalogs
Activities: Classes for adults and children; lect open to public, 4 visiting lectrs per year; concerts; gallery talks; tours; scholarships; individual paintings and original art objects lent to museums; lending collection contains books, kodachromes and motion pictures; book traveling exhibitions; museum shop selling books, magazines, reproductions, prints, and Indian jewelry
L **Library,** 11th and Main Sts, 88201
Reference only
Library Holdings: Vols 2000; Per subs 6
Special Subjects: Southwestern Art

SANTA FE

M **GUADALUPE HISTORIC FOUNDATION,** Santuario de Guadalupe, 100 Guadalupe, 87501. Tel 505-988-2027. *Pres* Gregory Salinas; *VPres* Rudy Lujon; *Secy* Elvira Ogard; *Dir* Virginia Castellano
Open Tues - Sat 9 AM - 4 PM. No admin fee. Estab 1790, became an international museum 1975 to preserve and extend the community's awareness through education and in culture areas. Gallery space is used for exhibits of local artists which are mainly Hispanic. Average Annual Attendance: 37,000. Mem: 400; dues $10 and up; annual meeting Apr
Income: $41,000 (financed by membership, grants, corporate & private donations)
Collections: Archidioces Santa Fe Collection, 16th century books, 18th-19th century religious artifacts; Mexican Baroque paintings; Our Lady of Guadalupe mural; Renaissance Venetian paintings
Exhibitions: Francisco Rodriguez Onate-Casa de la Cultura de Michoacan; Memorial to Patrocino Barela, master woodcarver; Commemoration to Our Lady of Guadalupe 450th Anniversary; Santos; Carvings; Needlepoint; Cordova Woodcarvers Exhibition; Senior Citizens Exhibition; Embroidery; Rio Grande Wetwings
Publications: Noticias, quarterly
Activities: Dramatic programs; docent training; performing arts; visual arts, poetry readings; lectures open to public, 1-2 vis lectr per year; concerts; tours

M **INSTITUTE OF AMERICAN INDIAN ARTS MUSEUM,** 1369 Cerillos Rd, 87501. Tel 505-988-6281; WATS 800-476-1281. *Dir* Charles Dailey
Open summer Mon - Sat 9 AM - 5 PM, Thurs Evenings 7:30 - 9:30 PM, Sun 1 - 5 PM, winter daily 9 AM - 5 PM, weekends by appointment only. No admis fee. Estab 1962 to train Native American students to own, operate and manage their own museums; to collect, preserve and exhibit materials relating to the Native American; act as a resource area for Indian Museums nationwide. Small museum of 5 principal galleries; approx 10,000 ft of exhibit area. Average Annual Attendance: 15,000
Income: $25,000 (financed by Bureau of Indian Affairs, Washington DC)
Purchases: $5000
Collections: Only major collection of contemporary Indian arts and crafts in America; Vital and comprehensive collection in fields of paintings, graphics, textiles, ceramics, sculpture, jewelry, photographs, printed textiles, costumes, ethnological materials such as drums and paraphernalia for general living
Exhibitions: Photograph traveling show; yearly student sales exhibit; annual faculty & alumni; annual national high school Indian art show
Publications: Exhibition catalogs; museum workbooks
Activities: Assisting any Indian reservation in setting up their own visitor centers or museums in America; material available to Indian reservations, museum, cultural centers and universities, with fees, transportation and insurance provided; classes for adults; lect open to public, 2-3 visiting lectr per year; concerts; gallery talks; competitions; awards; scholarships; individual paintings and original objects of art lent; book traveling exhibitions 6-8 per year; originate traveling exhibitions; sales shop sells student arts and crafts, books, magazines, original art, and prints
L **Library,** CSF Campus, Saint Michaels Dr, Santa Fe, 87501. Tel 505-988-6356.
Librn Karen Highfill; *Libr Technician* Bernadette Townsend; *Libr Technician* Lorraine Hayes
Open daily 8 AM - 5 PM, cl weekends. Estab 1962 to support college curriculum. Circ 30,000
Income: $10,000
Purchases: $8000
Library Holdings: Vols 700; Per subs 20; Indian Reference Books 200; Micro — Prints, reels; AV — A-tapes, Kodachromes 40,000, motion pictures, v-tapes 1000; Other — Clipping files, exhibition catalogs, original art works, photographs, prints, sculpture
Special Subjects: Native American subjects

M **MUSEUM OF NEW MEXICO,*** 113 Lincoln Ave, PO Box 2087, 87503. Tel 505-827-7356. *Dir* Jean M Weber; *Asst Dir* William Holmes; *Cur Fine Arts* Ellen Bradbury
Open March - Oct Mon 1 - 8:45 PM, Tues - Sun 9 AM - 4:45 PM, Oct - March Tues - Sun 9 AM - 4:45 PM. Admis adults $1, senior citizens & students 12 - 18 $.50, children under 12 free. Estab 1909. Museum is a state institution and operates in four major fields of interest: Fine Arts, International Folk Art, History and Anthropology. Four separate buildings, each with galleries: Southwestern art, Indian arts and crafts. Average Annual Attendance: 850,000.
Mem: 800; dues $25 - $1000; annual meeting in Nov
Income: Financed by state appropriation
Collections: Over 185,000 items in collections
Publications: Annual report; books; El Palacio, quarterly; exhibition catalogs; guides; magazines; monographs; pamphlets
Activities: Educ kits with hands-on materials are sent to schools throughout the state; docent program serving 15,000 school children; films; lectures open to public, 12 vis lectr per year; gallery talks; tours; extension dept serves United States & Mexico; original objects of art lent to other cultural institutions; lending collection 7000 original art works; book traveling exhibitions 2-3 per yr; originate traveling exhibitions; museum-sales shop sells books, magazines, reproductions, prints, slides, posters and Indian arts & crafts
L **Library,*** PO Box 2087, 87503. Tel 505-827-2343. *Librn* Orlando Romero; *Anthropology Librn* Laura Holt; *Fine Arts Librn* Albert Donlan
Museum houses four separate research libraries on folk art, fine arts, history and anthropology
Library Holdings: Vols 24,000
Special Subjects: Spanish colonial history, Southwestern art and archaeology, worldwide folk art
M **Museum of Fine Arts,** 105 W Palace, PO Box 2087, 87503. Tel 505-827-4455.
Dir David Turner; *Chief Cur* Don Humphrey; *Cur* Sandra D'Emilio; *Cur* Steve Yates; *Asst Cur* Cynthia Sanchez
Open daily 9 AM - 4:45 PM, cl Mon in winter. No admis fee. Estab 1917 to serve as an exhibitions hall, chiefly for New Mexican and Southwestern art. Building is of classic Southwestern design (adobe); attached auditorium used for performing arts presentations. Average Annual Attendance: 290,000
Income: Financed by state appropriation
Collections: Drawings, paintings, photographs, prints and sculpture with emphasis on New Mexican and regional art, including Native American artists
Exhibitions: (1982-83) Eliot Porter Photographs; Juan Hamilton; Video as Attitude; Images of Ranchos Church; Larry Bell; A California Connection: The Gifford and Joann Phillips Collection
Activities: Classes for adults and children; docent training; lect open to public, 10 visiting lectr per year; concerts; gallery talks; tours; competitions; individual paintings and original objects of art lent to art museums; lending collection contains original prints, paintings, photographs and sculpture; originate traveling exhibitions; museum shop sells books, magazines, reproductions and slides
L **Museum of Fine Arts Library,** 105 W Palace, PO Box 2087, 87503. *Librn* Sue Critchfield
Open Mon - Fri 9 AM - 4 PM, cl Mon in winter. Estab 1917 to provide fine arts research materials to museum staff, artists, writers and community
Purchases: $4000
Library Holdings: Vols 5050; Per subs 50; Micro — Fiche; AV — Slides; Other — Clipping files, exhibition catalogs, manuscripts, memorabilia, pamphlets, photographs
Special Subjects: American art and artists with emphasis on Southwestern art and artists
Collections: Biography files of artists

M **Museum of International Folk Art,*** 706 Camino Lejo, 87501. Tel 505-827-7356. *Dir* Dr Yvonne Lange; *Asst Dir* James H Pahl; *Cur American & Latin American Coll* Charlene Cerny; *Cur Coll* Carol Steiro; *Cur European Coll* Judith Chiba-Cohen; *Cur Spanish Colonial Coll* Christine Mather; *Cur Textiles* Nora Fisher; *Conservator* Claire Munzenrider
Open daily 9 AM - 4:45 PM, cl Mon in winter. No admis fee. Estab 1953 to collect, exhibit and preserve worldwide folk art. Average Annual Attendance: 80,000
Income: Financed by endowment, grants and state appropriation
Collections: Costumes; folk art, with emphasis on Spanish Colonial and Hispanic-related cultures; textiles; worldwide carvings, ceramics and toys
Exhibitions: (1978-79) Baroque to Folk; Girard Foundation Collection; Palestinian Costumes; Spanish Textiles; 25th Anniversary Show
Publications: Celebrate, 25th anniversary catalog; El Palacio, quarterly
Activities: Docent training; lect open to public; tours; original objects of art lent to responsible museums nationwide; originate traveling exhibitions; museum shop sells books, magazines, original art and reproductions
L **Museum of International Folk Art Library,*** 706 Camino Lejo, 87501. Tel 505-827-7356. *Librn* Judith Sellars
Open Mon - Fri 9 AM - Noon and 1 - 4:45 PM, cl Mon in winter. Estab 1953 to support museum's research needs
Income: Financed private and state support
Purchases: $5000
Library Holdings: Vols 6500; Per subs 80; AV — A-tapes, cassettes, rec, slides; Other — Clipping files, exhibition catalogs, manuscripts, pamphlets, photographs
Special Subjects: Costume Design & Construction, Textiles, Folk art of various countries, religious folk art of New Mexico
Collections: Folk literature and music of the Spanish Colonist in New Mexico circa 1800-1971
M **Palace of Governors,*** 87503. Tel 505-827-6483
Built in 1610
Exhibitions: The Palace Press, a working exhibit of Frontier printing; Southwestern History, Spanish-Colonial and Territorial Periods
M **Hall of the Southwestern Indian,*** 87503. Tel 505-827-7356
Collections: Contemporary Indian Civilizations of the Southwest
M **Laboratory of Anthropology,*** Old Santa Fe Trail, 87501. Tel 505-827-3241
Open Mon - Sat 8 AM - Noon and 1 - 5 PM. Estab 1936 as a research laboratory in archaeology and ethnology
Collections: Materials from various Indian cultures of the Southwest: jewelry, pottery and textiles
Exhibitions: Ceremonial paraphernalia; Indian silverwork

M **SCHOOL OF AMERICAN RESEARCH,** 660 Garcia St, PO Box 2188, 87501. Tel 505-982-3583. *Pres* Douglas W Schwartz; *Mgr Coll* Michael J Hering
Estab 1907. Dedicated to advance studies in anthropology, support advanced seminars for post-doctoral scholars, archaeological research, anthropological publication, and a public education program. Open to members and special scholars by appointment. Southwest Indian Arts Building houses collections for research. Mem: 875; dues family $35, individual $25
Income: Financed by endowment, membership, special grants and individuals
Purchases: J J Mora prints
Collections: Basketry, paintings, Southwest Indian pottery, silver jewelry, textiles, Kachinas
Publications: Discovery, once a year; Explorations, once a year; Publications of Advanced Seminar Series
Activities: Lectures for members only, 5 vis lectr per yr; scholarships
L **Library,** 660 Garcia St, PO Box 2188, 87501. Tel 505-982-3583. *Coll Mgr* Barbara Stanislawski
Open to scholars of the School of American Research; staff and members by appointment
Library Holdings: Vols 6000; Per subs 27; Government publications
Special Subjects: Anthropology

M **WHEELWRIGHT MUSEUM,** 704 Camino Lejo, PO Box 5153, 87502. Tel 505-982-4636. *Dir* Richard Lang; *Cur* LaRayne Parrish
Open Mon - Sat 10 AM - 5 PM, Sun 1 - 5 PM, cl Mon from Nov - May. No admis fee. Estab 1937 to preserve Navajo ceremonialism and promote the culture of the American Indian. Main gallery has changing exhibitions dealing with contemporary Indian themes; lower gallery is a recreation of a turn-of-the-century trading post and functions as a museum shop. Average Annual Attendance: 50,000. Mem: 1400; dues $25 and up; annual meeting
Income: Financed by endowment and membership
Collections: Jewelry; masks; photographs; ritual material; sandpainting reproductions of various Navajo ceremonies; tapes
Exhibitions: (1984) World of the Navajo Child
Publications: Bulletins and books on Navajo culture
Activities: Lect open to public, 15 visiting lectrs per year; tours; individual paintings and original objects of art lent to museums; lending collection contains books, color reproductions, film strips, framed reproductions, Kodachromes, nature artifacts, original art works, original prints, paintings and phonorecords; museum shop selling books, magazines, original art, reproductions, prints, slides and authentic American Indian arts and crafts
L **Mary Cabot Wheelwright Research Library,** 704 Camino Lejo, PO Box 5153, 87502
Open to members for reference
Library Holdings: Vols 4000; Per subs 3000

TAOS

O **KIT CARSON MEMORIAL FOUNDATION,*** Old Kit Carson Rd, PO Box B, 87571. Tel 505-758-1000. *Executive Dir* Jack K Boyer
Estab 1949 to maintain and operate the home of Kit Carson and to perpetuate his name and deeds. The Kit Carson Home is now classified as a Registered National Historic Landmark. In 1962 the home of Ernest L Blumenschein was given to the Foundation by Miss Helen C Blumenschein; it is now classified as a Registered National Landmark. In 1967 Mrs Rebecca S James gave the Foundation the Ferdinand Maxwell House and Property. In 1972, acquired the

Hacienda de Don Antonio Severino Martinez, prominent Taos merchant and official during the Spanish Colonial Period; designated a Registered National Historic Landmark. Acquired in 1972, site of the Simeon Turley Trading Post, Grist Mill and Distillery, built in 1830 and destroyed in Taos Rebellion of 1847; entered in National Register of Historic Places. Acquired in 1977 La Morada de Don Ferdnando de Taos, Chapel and meeting place of Los Penitentes, an early religious organization; entered in National Register of Historic Places. Average Annual Attendance: 53,000. Mem: 230; dues patron $1000, sponsor $750, benefactor $500, supporting $250, subscribing $100, sustaining $50, share $25, participating $15, contributing $10; annual meeting March
Income: $75,000 (financed by admissions, museum shops, rentals, donations and grants)
Purchases: $70,000
Collections: †Historical and Archaeological Collection; Western Americana
Publications: Director's Annual Report, monthly; Las Noticias Alegres de Casa Kit Carson, quarterly newsletter; Publications on the Life of Kit Carson; technical reports
Activities: Tours; lect
L **Foundation Library,*** PO Box B, 87571. Tel 505-758-9898
For reference only
Purchases: $500-$1000
Library Holdings: Vols 5109; maps; AV — Cassettes, Kodachromes, lantern slides, motion pictures, rec, slides; Other — Clipping files, exhibition catalogs, framed reproductions, manuscripts, memorabilia, original art works, pamphlets, photographs, prints, reproductions, sculpture
Special Subjects: Archaeology, Kit Carson
M **Ernest Blumenschein Home,*** PO Box B, 87571. Tel 505-758-4741
Open daily - summer, spring and autumn 9 AM - 5 PM, winter 10 AM - 4 PM. Admis family rate $2.50, adults $1, youths $.50, children $.25, children under 6 years free with parents, group tour rates available. Home of world renowned artist and co-founder of famous Taos Society of Artists. Average Annual Attendance: 5000
Collections: Original antique furniture; pieces of art by the Blumenschein family and members of Taos Society of Artists and other Taos artists - 1890-1930
Exhibitions: Temporary exhibits of arts and crafts of the Taos area and of New Mexico
Activities: Education dept; docent training; tours; annual children art show; original objects of art lent to qualified art museums; book traveling exhibitons; museum shop sells books, reproductions, prints and slides
M **Kit Carson Home and Museum,*** 207 Old Kit Carson Rd, PO Box B, 87571. Tel 505-758-4741. *Cur* Jack R Dyson
Open daily - summer 8 AM - 6 PM, spring and autumn 8 AM - 6 PM, winter 8 AM - 5 PM. Admis family rate $2.50, adults $1, youths $.50, children $.25, under 6 years free with parents, group tours available. Home of the famous Western Scout and Fur Trapper. Built in 1825, bought by Kit in 1843 as a wedding gift for his beautiful bride, Josefa Jaramillo, member of prominent Taos family. They lived in the home for 25 years, their lifetime together as both died in 1868
Collections: Period furniture and furnishings
Exhibitions: Life of Kit Carson and Personal Items; clothing; guns; saddles; tools; Spanish articles; archaeological artifacts
M **La Hacienda de Don Antonio Martinez,*** 87571. Tel 505-758-1000
Open summer Mon - Sun 9 AM - 5 PM, winter 10 AM - 4 PM. Admis family rate $2.50, adults $1, youth $.50, children $.25, under 6 free with parents, group tour rates and combination tickets available. Built and occupied by Don Antonio, 1800-1827. Last remaining hacienda in New Mexico. Martinez, an important trader with Mexico, also served as Alcalde of Northern New Mexico. Spanish Colonial fortress hacienda having 21 rooms and two large patios
Collections: Furniture, furnishings, tools, and other articles of Spanish Colonial period and personal family articles

M **HARWOOD FOUNDATION OF THE UNIVERSITY OF NEW MEXICO,** Box 766, 87571. Tel 505-758-3063. *Dean* Dr Rupert A Trujillo; *Pres Board* Dr Wallace Bacon; *Dir* David L Caffey; *Cur* David Witt
Open Mon & Thurs 10 AM - 8 PM, Tues, Wed, Fri 10 AM - 5 PM, Sat 10 AM - 4 PM. No admis fee. Estab 1923, Buildings and contents given to the University by Elizabeth Case Harwood, 1936, to be maintained as an art, educational and cultural center; maintained by the University with all activities open to the public. Foundation was added to the National Register of Historic Places in 1976; two main galleries plus smaller display areas throughout the Harwood
Collections: Spanish Colonial New Mexico Santos; †permanent collection of works by Taos artists; Persian miniatures; wood sculptures by Patrocinio Barela
Exhibitions: Changing exhibits
Publications: Exhibit catalogs; newsletter, 4 per yr
Activities: Classes for adults and children; lectures open to public, 10 vis lectr per yr; concerts; gallery talks; tours; individual paintings and original objects of art lent to museums; lending collection contains original prints, paintings, photographs and sculpture; book traveling exhibitions
L **Library,** 25 Ledoux St, 87571. *Librn* Bernice P Martinez
Open Mon, Thurs 10 AM - 8 PM; Tues, Wed, Fri 10 AM - 5 PM; Sat 10 AM - 4 PM. Estab 1936 as a public library. Circ 59,000
Library Holdings: Vols 27,000; Per subs 10; AV — Slides; Other — Clipping files, exhibition catalogs, framed reproductions, manuscripts, original art works, pamphlets, photographs, prints, reproductions, sculpture
Special Subjects: Southwestern Art
Activities: Lect; concerts; films; plays

M **MILLICENT ROGERS MUSEUM,** Museum Rd, PO Box A, 87571. Tel 505-758-2462. *Dir* Arthur H Wolf; *Registrar* Margot Julian; *Cur* Michael Stephens; *Secy* Carmen Woodall; *Museum Asst* Rick Romancito; *Museum Asst* Guadalupe Tafoya; *Store Mgr* Georgette Ely
Open winter Wed - Sun 9 AM - 5 PM, cl Mon & Tues, summer Mon - Sun 10 AM - 4 PM. Admis adults $3 ($2 groups of 10 or more), under 16 $1, family groups $6. Estab 1956 for the acquisition, preservation, research, display and interpretation of art and material cultures of Native American and Hispanic cultures of the southwest focusing on northern New Mexico. The museum's

permanent home is a traditional adobe building, once the private residence of Claude J K Anderson. Average Annual Attendance: 20,000. Mem: 600; semi-annual Board of Directors meeting in spring and fall
Income: Financed by endowment, membership, donations, admissions, grants and revenue from museum store
Collections: American Indian Art of Western United States, emphasis on Southwestern groups; paintings by contemporary Native American artists; religious arts and non-religious artifacts of Hispanic cultures; Nucleus of collection formed by Millicent Rogers
Exhibitions: (1982) The Weaver & the Wool; Native American Painting; San Ildefonso Painting; In Deer's Heart I Travel; Frederico Vigil: Sentidos y Aficiones; Contemporary Acquistions 1982; Taos Pueblo Painting; 3rd Annual Art of Taos Pueblo; Hebras de Vision/Threads of Vision; (1983) Selection from the Collection of Native American Graphics; With Eagle Glance: American Indian Photographic Images, 1868-1931; Transfigurations: The Photographic Imagery of Alejandro Lopez; R C Gorman: A Portrait; 4th Annual Art of Taos Pueblo; Seven Views of Hopi
Publications: Las Palabras, quarterly newsletter for members of the museum
Activities: Classes for adults and children; lectures open to the public, 2 - 3 visiting lecturers per year; gallery talks; tours; competitions; field trips; seminars; film series; individual paintings and original works of art lent to similar institutions and special interest groups; book 1 - 3 traveling exhibitions per year; museum shop sells books, magazines, original art, reproductions, prints, art and craft work by contemporary Southwest Indian and Hispanic artisans
L **Library,** Museum Rd, 87571. *Librn* May Harrover
Estab 1977 as reference library for members and staff
Library Holdings: Vols 64; Per subs 15; Other — Exhibition catalogs, pamphlets
Special Subjects: Archaeology, Ethnology, Art & Architecture, Material Culture & Art, Museology, Southwestern Hispanic History
Collections: Limited edition, special edition and out of print books on Southwestern Americana

O **TAOS ART ASSOCIATION INC,** Stables Art Center, PO Box 198, 87571. Tel 505-758-2052. *Pres* Richard Crawley; *Executive Dir* Donald Thompson; *Secy* Johanna Jones; *Dir Stables Gallery* Connie Evans
Open Mon - Sat 10 AM - 5 PM, Sun 1 - 5 PM. No admis fee. Estab Oct 1981 as a nonprofit community art center to promote the arts in Taos for the benefit of the entire community. Average Annual Attendance: 20,000. Mem: 525; annual meeting April
Income: Financed by memberships, contributions, grants and sales of art works
Exhibitions: Annual Awards Show for Taos County; 12 exhibitions per year, including Animal Kingdom, Institute of American Indian Art, Faces of Taos & Visual Technology
Publications: Monthly calendar of events to membership and with map to hotels
Activities: Classes for adults and children; children's program in painting and theater; dramatic programs; lect open to the public; concerts; competitions; traveling exhibitions organized and circulated

TOME

M **TOME PARISH MUSEUM,*** Hwy 47, PO Box 397, 87060. Tel 505-865-7497. *Dir* Robert M Beach
Open daily dawn to dusk. No admis fee. Estab 1966 as a religious museum
Collections: Paintings; religious material

NEW YORK

ALBANY

M **ALBANY INSTITUTE OF HISTORY AND ART,** 125 Washington Ave, 12210. Tel 518-463-4478. *Chmn* Herbert A Jones; *Dir* Norman S Rice; *Pres* John C Byron
Open Tues - Sat 10 AM - 4:45 PM, Sun 2 - 5 PM, cl Mon & most NY state holidays. No admis fee. Estab 1791, inc 1793 as the Society for the Promotion of Agriculture, Arts, and Manufactures; 1829 as Albany Institute; 1900 as Albany Institute and Historical and Art Society. Present name adopted 1926. Provides curatorial services to Empire State Plaza contemporary art collection. Maintains luncheon gallery, museum shop & sales-rental gallery. Average Annual Attendance: 80,000. Mem: 2000; dues $15 and up; annual meeting Oct
Income: Financed by endowment, membership, sales, city, county and state appropriations, special gifts
Collections: †Art and historical material, chiefly related to regional artists and craftsmen or people who lived in the area; †contemporary paintings and sculpture; †18th & 19th century painting and sculpture by artists of the Hudson River area; paintings; ceramics, especially Staffordshire with local historic scenes and export ware; †New York (especially Albany) furniture, glass, pewter, silver, and other regional decorative arts; textiles; costumes
Exhibitions: (1983) Inventors and Inventions in the Upper Hudson Area; In Search of the Picturesque (19th century images of industry along the Hudson River Valley); Pride of Place (Early American Views from the Collection of Leonard Milberg); People of the Great Peace (Iroquois-European Relations in Early New York); Golden Day & Silver Night; selections from the permanent collection; co-sponsors annual show of regional artists
Publications: Catalogues; several books about the history of New York State
Activities: Classes for adults and children; dramatic programs; lectures open to the public, 5 - 12 vis lectr per yr; concerts; gallery talks; tours; competitions with awards; exten dept serving area schools; originate traveling exhibitions; sales-rental gallery sells books, original art & prints
L **McKinney Library,** 125 Washington Ave, 12210. *Actg Librn* Daryl J Severson; *Photo Librn* Suzanne Roberson; *Libr Asst* Catharine Tobin
Open Mon - Fri 8:30 AM - 4 PM. Estab 1793 to collect historical material concerning Albany and the Upper Hudson region, as well as books on fine and

decorative art related to the Institute's holdings. For reference only
Library Holdings: Vols 10,000; Per subs 50; Other — Clipping files, exhibition
catalogs, manuscripts, memorabilia, pamphlets, photographs
Special Subjects: Albany social and political history, American painting and
sculpture, Dutch in the Upper Hudson Valley, 17th to 19th century manuscripts

M **COLLEGE OF SAINT ROSE,** Art Gallery,* 324 State Street, 12210. Tel 518-
454-5111. *Dir* Jeanne Flanagan
Open Sun - Fri 12:30 - 4:30 PM, cl Sat. No admis fee. Estab 1969 to provide a
facility that presents fine art both to the college community and to the public and
provide a place for college art students to display their works
Income: Financed by college funds
Collections: Paintings, prints, sculpture
Activities: Traveling exhibitions

M **HISTORIC CHERRY HILL,** 523-1/2 S Pearl St, 12202. Tel 518-434-4791.
Pres Edward Frisbee; *VPres* Charles Shoudy; *Secy* Clark Daggett; *Cur* Jacqueline
Calder; *Educ Dir* Rebecca Watrous
Open Tues - Sat 10 AM - 4 PM, Sun 1 - 4 PM. Admis adults $2, seniors $1.50,
students $1, children $.75. Estab 1964 to preserve and research about the house
and contents of Cherry Hill, built for Philip Van Rensselaer in 1787, and lived in
by him and four generations of his descendents unitl 1963. Georgian mansion
having 14 rooms of furniture, ceramics, paintings and other decorative arts &
garden. Average Annual Attendance: 8000. Mem: 200; dues $10 & up
Collections: Catherine Van Rensseaer Bonney Collection of Oriental decorative
arts; New York State furniture, silver, ceramics, textiles & paintings dating from
the early 18th thru 20th centuries
Exhibitions: Not Just Another Pretty Dress: Clothing and Textiles of an Albany
Family from 1740-1963
Publications: New Gleanings, bi-monthly newsletter
Activities: Educ dept; classroomm materials; lectures open to public; gallery
talks; tours; paintings and art objects are lent to other museums and exhibitions;
museum shop sells books, postcards and slides

M **MUSEUM OF THE HISTORICAL SOCIETY OF EARLY AMERICAN
DECORATION,*** 19 Dove St, 12210. Tel 518-462-1676. *Pres* Mrs L Corey;
VPres Mrs A Duvall; *Secy* Mrs A E Jones; *Cur* Doris H Fry
Open Wed - Fri 9:30 AM - 4 PM, Sat Noon - 3 PM. No admis fee. Estab 1946
to perpetuate Early American Decoration as an art and to promote research,
record and preserve examples, maintain exhibits and publish works on the
subject. Four exhibit areas, two 9 by 9 ft, two 16 by 16 ft, 20 wall cases, six table
cases, study storage area of about 10 ft by 10 ft. Library maintained. Mem: 815;
dues $20; meetings in May & Sept
Income: Financed by endowment, membership, city appropriation &
contributions
Collections: Decorated japanned ware, tin wood, papier mache; country painted
items; †stenciled furniture; piano; boxes; looking glasses; trays; cornices; metal
leaf, Victorian painted; †pontypool trays & objects; †reversed painting on clocks,
looking glasses
Exhibitions: The Ornamental Painter 1820-1860, Neglected But Not Forgotten
Publications: The Decorator, twice yr; The Ornamented Tray; The Ornamented
Tray; The Ornamented Chair; Illustrated Glossary of Decorated Antiques;
Antiques
Activities: Classes for adults; workshops; teacher training; judges training;
lectures open to public, 4 vis lectr per yr; gallery talks; tours; sponsors
competitions; awards; lending collection contains photographs & slides

L **NEW YORK STATE LIBRARY,** Manuscripts and Special Collections, Eleventh
Floor, Cultural Education Center, Empire State Plaza, 12230. Tel 518-474-4461.
State Librn-Assoc Commissioner for Libraries Joseph Shubert; *Dir* Peter J
Paulson; *Manuscripts and Special Coll* Peter Christoph
Open Mon - Fri 9 AM - 5 PM
Collections: Over 50,000 items: black and white original photographs, glass
negatives, daguerreotypes, engravings, lithographs, original sketches and
drawings, cartoons, stereograms, and extra illustrated books depicting views of
New York State and portraits of its citizens past and present
Exhibitions: Exhibit program involves printed and manuscript materials

M **NEW YORK STATE MUSEUM,** Empire State Plaza, 12230. Tel 518-474-5877.
Asst Commissioner Martin E Sullivan; *Museum Servs Div* Robert D Sullivan;
Science Service Division Dir Richard Monheimer; *Historical Service Division
Dir* Paul Scudiere; *Planning & Program Develop Dir* G Carroll Lindsay
Open 10 AM - 5 PM. No admis fee. Estab 1836 to research, collect, exhibit and
educate about the natural & human history of New York State for the people of
New York; to function as a cultural center in the Capital District of the Empire
State. Museum has 1 1/2 acres of exhibit space; 3 permanent exhibit halls
devoted to man & nature (history & science) themes of Adirondack Wilderness,
Metropolitan New York, upstate New York; 3 temporary exhibit galleries of art,
historical and technological artifacts. Average Annual Attendance: 500,000
Income: $5,700,000 (financed by state appropriation, government and foundation
grants and private donations)
Collections: Ethnological artifacts of Iroquois-Algonkian (New York area)
Indians; circus posters, costumes, decorative arts, paintings, photographs,
postcards, prints, toys, weapons
Exhibitions: (1983-84) Ancient Inspirations, Contemporary Interpretations;
Design in Buffalo; Images of Experience: Untutored Older Artists; Oom Pah Pah:
The Great American Band; Eight Pound Livelihood: Chinese Laundry Workers
in the United States; Brooklyn Before the Bridge; Paintings as a Pastime: The
Paintings of Winston S Churchill; Community Industries of the Shakers...A New
Look; Seneca Ray Stoddard: Adirondack Illustration; The Humanities
Experience, The Subject is You; Grandma Moses: The Artist Behind the Myth;
Collectors' Choice: Treasures from the Schomburg Center; Two Hundred Years
of Education in New York State; Three Generations: Immigrants & Their
Families in Broome County; Roman Vislmiac: A Vanished World; Lou Stourmen:
Forty Years on Times Square; The New York Landscape
Publications: NAHO, quarterly
Activities: Classes for adults and children; lect open to public; concerts;

individual paintings and original objects of art lent to museums; lending
collection contains nature artifacts, original art works, original prints, paintings,
photographs and slides; book traveling exhibitions 6 per year; originate traveling
exhibitions; museum shop sells books, magazines, original art, reproductions,
prints, slides, toys, baskets, pottery by local artists, jewelry, stationery and
posters

M **SCHUYLER MANSION STATE HISTORIC SITE,** 32 Catherine St, 12202.
Tel 518-474-3953. *Site Mgr* Susan L May; *Historic Site Asst* Mary Ellen
Grimald; *Historic Site Asst* Robert Falk
Open Wed - Sat 10 AM - 5 PM, Sun 1 - 5 PM, cl Mon & Tues, call for winter
hours. No admis fee. Estab 1917 for the preservation and interpretation of the
18th century home of Philip Schuyler, one of the finest examples of Georgian
architecture in the country. Period rooms: informal parlour, formal parlour,
dinning room, study, ballroom, young ladies bedroom, winter bedroom, summer
bedroom. Average Annual Attendance: 15,000
Income: Financed by state appropriation
Collections: American furnishings of the Colonial and Federal Periods,
predominantly of New York and New England origins
Publications: Schuyler Masion: A Historic Structure Report
Activities: Educ dept; lect; tours

M **STATE UNIVERSITY OF NEW YORK AT ALBANY,** University Art Gallery,
1400 Washington Ave, 12222. Tel 518-457-3375. *Dir* Nancy Liddle; *Asst Dir*
Marijo Fasulo; *Preparator* Jason Stewart; *Admin Asst* Joanne Lue
Open Tues, Wed & Fri 9 AM - 5 PM; Thurs 9 AM - 8 PM; Sat & Sun 1 - 4 PM;
cl Mon. No admis fee. Estab 1968 to augment the teaching program of the Fine
Arts Department, to present exhibitions of community interest, and to be of
service to the University System, particularly Albany. Gallery has 6400 sq ft on
first floor, 3200 sq ft on second floor. Medium security gallery, students as
security personnel. The University Art Gallery is custodian for the Fine Arts
Study Collection, a collection of contemporary prints which is available on
premises for study purposes. Average Annual Attendance: 25,000
Income: Financed by state appropriation
Collections: Paintings, prints, drawings & sculpture of 20th century
contemporary art; photographs
Exhibitions: (1982) Edward Koren; Lotte Jacobi; Thom O'Connor; (1983) New
Decorative Art; Rollie McKenna
Publications: Exhibition catalogs
Activities: Lectures open to public, some for members only; gallery talks; tours;
competitions with awards; individual paintings lent to offices on the university
campus only; lending collection contains 300 art works, 150 original prints and
75 sculptures; book traveling exhibitions; originate traveling exhibition

L **Art Dept Slide Library,*** Fine Arts Building, Room 121, 12222. Tel 518-457-
3408. *Art Historian* Mojimir Frinta
Open daily 9 AM - 4 PM. Estab 1967 to provide instruction and reference for
the university and community
Library Holdings: Per subs 8; AV — Fs, Kodachromes, lantern slides, slides
80,000; Other — Exhibition catalogs, pamphlets, photographs
Collections: Slides, mainly of Western art and architecture

ALFRED

L **NEW YORK STATE COLLEGE OF CERAMICS AT ALFRED
UNIVERSITY,** Scholes Library of Ceramics, Harder Hall, State St, 14802. Tel
607-871-2494. *Dir* Bruce E Connolly; *Head Cataloging & Serials* Martha A
Mueller; *Head Technical Ref & ILL* Paul T Culley; *Head Art Reference & Slide
Room & Archivist* Susan R Strong
Open daily year Mon - Thurs 8:30 AM - 10:30 PM, Fri 8:30 AM - 4:30 PM,
Sat 10 AM - 10:30 PM, Sun 1 - 10:30 PM, other periods Mon - Fri 8:30 AM -
4:30 PM. Estab 1947 to service art education to the Master's level in fine art and
the PhD level in engineering and science related to ceramics. The College has a
2500 sq ft Art Gallery which is managed by the Art and Design Division
Income: $390,000 (financed by endowment, state appropriation, and federal
grant)
Purchases: $29,000
Library Holdings: Vols 18,000; Per subs 150; Micro — Fiche, reels; AV —
Cassettes, fs, slides 85,000; Other — Original art works, pamphlets
Special Subjects: Graphic Arts, Ceramics, Painting - American, Photography,
Pottery, Printmaking, Sculpture, Video, Fine Art, Wood Design
Collections: Silverman Collection (glass)
Activities: Tours

AMENIA

O **AGES OF MAN FELLOWSHIP,** Sheffield Rd, 12501. Tel 914-373-9380. *Pres*
Dr Nathan Cabot Hale; *VPres* Niels Berg; *Secy* Alison B Hale
Open 10 AM - 5 PM. Estab 1968 for the building and design of a sculpture
chapel based on the thematic concepts of the Cycle of Life. Mem: 20; dues $100;
meetings May and Nov
Income: Financed by membership and contributions
Collections: Sculpture and architectural models of the chapel
Publications: Project report, yearly
Activities: Art history; apprenticeship and journeyman instruction in Cycle of
Life design; lect open to the public, 20 visiting lectr per year; gallery talks;
original objects of art lent to museums, art associations, educational institutions;
originate traveling exhibitions

AMHERST

M **DAEMEN COLLEGE,** Daemen Gallery, 4380 Main St, 14226. Tel 716-839-
3600, Ext 241. *Dir* Bruce Marzahn
Open Mon - Fri 9 AM - 4 PM. No admis fee. Estab to add dimension to the art
program and afford liberal arts students opportunity to view art made by
established artists as well as art students. Gallery area is part of main building
protected by folding gate. Average Annual Attendance: 1500
Income: Financed by College Art Department
Activities: Lect open to public, 4 - 5 visiting lectr per year; competitions

ANNANDALE-ON-HUDSON

M BARD COLLEGE, William Cooper Procter Art Center,* 12504. Tel 914-758-8494, Ext 138. *Dir* Tom Wolf
Open daily 10 AM - 5 PM. Estab 1964 as an educational center. Art center has a gallery, slide library and uses the college library for its teaching
Collections: Assorted contemporary paintings and sculptures; photograph collection of prints
Exhibitions: Two student exhibitions per year; faculty and traveling exhibitions
Publications: Catalogs
Activities: Children's art classes; lect open to the public; gallery talks; scholarships

ARDSLEY

C CIBA-GEIGY CORPORATION, Art Collection, 444 Saw Mill River Rd, 10502. Tel 914-478-3131. *Dir, Corporate Art Services* Markus J Low
Open to public by appointment. No admis fee. Estab 1959 to add color and warmth to interior of its new headquarters, and to support of promising artists. Collection displayed at various company facilities
Collections: †New York School of Painting, abstract expressionist, geometric and figurative art; Swiss Art
Exhibitions: CIBA GEIGY Collects: Aspects of Abstraction
Publications: Catalogues of collection and exhibition
Activities: Individual objects of art lent upon request to museums and educational institutions for limited periods; originate traveling exhibitions upon request to museums and educational institutions

AUBURN

M CAYUGA MUSEUM OF HISTORY AND ART,* 203 Genesee St, 13021. Tel 315-253-8051. *Dir* Walter K Long
Open Tues - Fri 1 - 5 PM, Sat 9 AM - 5 PM, Sun 2 - 5 PM, cl Mon, New Year's, Labor Day, Thanksgiving, Christmas. No admis fee. Estab 1936 for research and Indian history. Average Annual Attendance: 40,000. Mem: 500; dues $10 - $30; annual meeting in Jan
Income: Financed by endowment, membership, county and city appropriation
Collections: Beardsley Filipino; Herter textiles; †sound on film; †permanent paintings by Americans
Exhibitions: Bicentennial, 12 Ethnic Group Shows
Activities: Classes for adults and children; docent training; lect open to public, 6 visiting lectr per year; gallery talks, tours; competitions; lending collection contains motion pictures, paintings, slides; museum shop sells original art, reproductions and small gifts
L Library,* 203 Genesee St, 13021
Open to researchers for reference
Library Holdings: Vols 15,000
Special Subjects: Indians, local history
Collections: Clarke Collection

BAYSIDE

L QUEENSBOROUGH COMMUNITY COLLEGE LIBRARY, 56th Ave & Springfield Blvd, 11364. Tel 212-631-6226. *Actg Chief Librn* Carol A Sanger; *Music & Art Librn* Donald Bryk
Open Mon - Thurs 8:30 AM - 9 PM, Fri 8:30 AM - 5 PM, Sat 10 AM - 2 PM. Estab 1961 to serve the students and faculty of the college
Income: $750,000
Purchases: $55,000
Library Holdings: Book and periodical collection which includes material on painting, sculpture and architecture; reproductions of famous paintings on walls throughout the library and reproductions of artifacts and sculpture
Collections: Extremely valuable vertical file collection; print collection
Exhibitions: (1983) Winners of the First Annual Juried Exhibition; Works on Paper - Annual Juried Exhibition; SITES: Perfect in Her Place; (1984) student art exhibit; 4 Arts: Politics in Art; Holocaust

BINGHAMTON

M ROBERSON CENTER FOR THE ARTS AND SCIENCES, 30 Front St, 13905. Tel 607-772-0660. *Pres of the Bd* Richard W Botnick; *Dir* Richard Stine; *Asst Dir* Laura B Martin; *Chief Cur & Cur of History* Ross McGuire; *Cur Exhibitions & Design* Philip Carey; *Cur Coll* Gary Dayton; *Cur Art* Roslyn Tunis; *Cur Educ* Richard DeLuca; *Cur Roberson Kopernik Observatory* Jay Sarton
Open Tues - Thurs 10 AM - 5 PM, Fri 10 AM - 10 PM, Sat & Sun Noon - 5 PM, cl Mon. Admis special exhibitions $1.50. Estab 1954. The Roberson Mansion, built in 1905-06 contains eight galleries; the Martin Building, built in 1968, designed by Richard Neutra, contains five galleries; the A Ward Ford Wing, completed in 1983 contains the Irma M Ahearn Gallery. Average Annual Attendance: 300,000. Mem: 3000; dues $30 - $35
Income: $900,000 (financed by endowment, membership, city, county and state appropriations, federal funds and foundations)
Collections: Fine and decorative arts, crafts, furniture; archeological and ethnological collections; natural history specimens; historical archives and photographic collections
Exhibitions: Our Shining Heritage; Charles Eldred: Sculpture and Drawings; Fine Arts Society Members' Show; The Forest: Susque Hanna: Images of the Settles Landscape; Working Lives: Broome County, 1890-1930; Made in Broome, Parts I - IV; Photo Exhibition; Scholastic Art; annual student show and Christmas Forest; (1984) Scholastic Art and Photography Exhibition; Contemporary Artist; A Family Quilt Collection; Arctic Vision/Art of the Canadian Inuit; New Sculpture: Icon and Environment
Publications: Bulletin, monthly; exhibition catalogs; Newsletter, quarterly

Activities: Classes for adults and children; docent training; workshops; lectures open to the public; concerts; gallery talks; tours; competitions with awards; scholarships; programs sent to schools in eleven counties; individual paintings and original objects of art lent; lending collection contains cassettes, color reproductions, film strips, framed reproductions, Kodachromes, motion pictures, nature artifacts, original art works, original prints; book traveling exhibitions, 50 - 100 per yr; originate traveling exhibitions to schools in 5 - 6 different counties; museum & sales shops sell books, original art, reproductions, prints, slides & a wide range of contemporary crafts
L Broome County Historical Library, 30 Front St, 13905
For reference and research only

M STATE UNIVERSITY OF NEW YORK AT BINGHAMTON, University Art Gallery, 13901. Tel 607-798-2634. *Dir* Josephine Gear; *Cur* Barbara Perkins; *Technician* Michael O'Kane; *Secy* Norma Moses
Open Mon - Fri 9 AM - 4:30 PM, Sat & Sun 1 - 4:30 PM, cl university holidays. Estab 1967
Income: $15,000 (financed by state appropriations)
Collections: †Teaching collection from Egyptian to contemporary art
Exhibitions: Student-Faculty Show; 19th Century Painters of the Delaware Valley; Selections from Permanent Collection; David Hare, Susquehanna Region Works in Clay
Publications: Cobra; The Sara Roby Foundation Collection of American Art; Traditional Art of West Africa (Harowitz Collection)
Activities: Lectures open to the public; gallery talks; seminars; internships
L Gallery Library, 13901
The Library is supplemented with the University Library and is very adequate for research

BLUE MOUNTAIN LAKE

M ADIRONDACK HISTORICAL ASSOCIATION, Adirondack Museum, 12812. Tel 518-352-7311. *Pres* A Hochschild; *Dir* Craig A Gilborn; *Cur* William Crowley; *Education Dir* Hallie Bond
Open June 15 - Oct 15 daily 10 AM - 6 PM. Admis adults $4.50, children 7 - 15 $2.75, under 7 free, special group rates. Estab 1955 to show the relationship of man to the Adirondacks. Museum contains two large galleries for paintings. Average Annual Attendance: 80,000. Mem: 150; annual meeting August
Collections: †Paintings, †prints and †photographs
Exhibitions: One special exhibition each year (has included the work of Winslow Homer, A F Tait and Eliot Porter)
Publications: A F Tait & Rustic Furniture (newsletters) annual
Activities: Classes for adults and children; lectures open to public, 8-10 vis lectrs per year; concerts; tours; individual paintings and original objects of art lent to museums and galleries; sales shop sells books, magazines, reproductions, prints, slides and postcards
L Library, 12812. Tel 518-352-7312. *Librn* Vijay Nair
Open Mon - Fri 9:30 AM - 4:30 PM by appointment. Estab to provide research materials for museum staff (exhibit documentation) and researchers interested in the Adirondack, and to preserve written materials relating to the Adirondack. For research only
Library Holdings: Vols 5000; maps; Micro — Fiche, reels; AV — A-tapes, cassettes, Kodachromes, motion pictures, rec, slides; Other — Clipping files, exhibition catalogs, manuscripts, memorabilia, original art works, pamphlets, photographs
Special Subjects: All Adirondackiana

O ADIRONDACK LAKES CENTER FOR THE ARTS, 12812. Tel 518-352-7715. *Pres* Michael F Nerney; *VPres* L Robert Webb; *Treas* Karen P Joyce; *Dir* Elizabeth Folwell; *Secy* Holly Burke; *Program Coordr* Pamela L Gang
Open Mon - Fri 9 AM - 4 PM, summers Mon - Sun 9 AM - 4 PM & evenings. Admis concerts films $2, concerts $4. Estab 1967; the Community Art Center offers both community and artist - craftsmen the opportunity for creative exchange. 7000 sq ft facility with 4 studios and black-box theatre. Average Annual Attendance: 12,500. Mem: 500; dues $5 and up; annual meeting in July
Income: $100,000 (financed by private contributions, county, state and federal assistance, foundations, local businesses, memberships & fundraising events
Exhibitions: (1983-84) Annoel Krider, weavings; Judy Natale, photographs; (1984) resident artists & students
Publications: Newsletter - Program, quarterly
Activities: Classes for adults and children; lectures open to public, 8 vis lectr per yr; concerts; competitions; gallery talks; tours; scholarships; exten dept serves Adirondack Park; sales shop sells original art, prints, crafts made locally and records by musicians appearing at the art center

BRIARCLIFF MANOR

M PACE UNIVERSITY GALLERY,* Elm Road, 10510. Tel 914-769-3200, Ext 716. *Gallery Dir* Beth A Treadway
Open Sun - Fri 1 - 5 PM, cl Sat. No admis fee. Estab 1978 to exhibit the works of nationally known professional artists and groups, and to serve as a focal point for artistic activities within the university and surrounding communities. The gallery is located on the ground floor of the Arts Building and has a commanding view of the center of campus; it is both spacious and modern
Income: Financed by the university
Exhibitions: (1981-1982) Pace - The First 75 Years; Hudson River Contemporary Artists; Sculptors Studies circulated by GANYS; Love Tapes - a video exhibition circulated by MOMA; The Street Painters; Pace University Selected Art Students
Activities: Lectures open to public, 8-10 visiting lecturers per year; gallery talks; tours
L Arts Building Library,* Elm Rd, 10510. *Dir* William Murdock
Estab 1963
Library Holdings: Vols 7565; Per subs 40

BRONX

M **BRONX MUSEUM OF THE ARTS,** 1040 Grand Concourse, 10456. Tel 212-681-6000. *Pres of Board* Jane Lee Garcia; *Dir* Luis R Cancel; *Asst Dir* Carmen Vega-Rivera; *Cur* Philip Verre; *Cur Satellite Galleries* Betty Wilde; *Dir Public Relations* Sondra Jaffe
Open Mon - Thurs & Sat 10 AM - 4:30 PM, Sun 11:30 AM - 4:30 PM. Admis adults $1.50, senior citizens & students $1, children under 6 free. Estab 1971 as a conduit for other museums of the city to bring their works to the community and for local artists to have their works viewed, making art available, free and easily accessible to the Bronx community. Museum also maintains five Satellite Galleries in public spaces in the Bronx. Mem: 761; dues sponsor $1000, donor $500, contirbutor $250, sustaining $100, family $35, individual $25, student & senior citizens $15
Income: Financed by membership, city, state & federal appropriations
Collections: Artist's file on Bronx artists
Exhibitions: (1983-84) Sculptural Statements; Narration in Art; (1984) Native American Paintings; New Talent Display; Bronx Express
Publications: Catalogs of exhibitions; educational workbooks; walking tours of the Bronx
Activities: Classes for adults & children; docent training; lectures open to the public, 20 vis lectr per yr; concerts; gallery talks; tours; originate traveling exhibitions; museum shop sells books, original art, prints, jewelry, weavings, African art & children's items

L **HUNTINGTON FREE LIBRARY AND READING ROOM,** Depository Library for the Museum of the American Indian, 9 Westchester Square, 10461. Tel 212-829-7770. *Pres Board Trustees* Edward A Morgan; *Librn* Mary B Davis
Open Mon - Sat 9:30 AM - 4:30 PM by appointment. Estab 1891, the Reading Room was established as a library for the people of Westchester Square. Materials are for reference only
Income: Financed by endowment
Library Holdings: Vols 40,000; Per subs 120; Original documents; Micro — Fiche; AV — Rec; Other — Clipping files, exhibition catalogs, manuscripts, pamphlets
Special Subjects: Indians of North, South and Central America

C **PROSPECT HOSPITAL,*** 730 Kelly St, 10455. Tel 212-542-1500, Ext 296. *Executive Dir* Dr Jacob B Freedman
Open to public. No admis fee. Estab 1969 to bring joy to the dissadvantaged of the South Bronx; to provide a pleasant and cheerful environment for patients, visitors, staff and employees. Collection displayed throughout hospital
Collections: Lithographs, paintings, posters, reproductions by Calder, Chagal, Matise, Modigliani, Picasso, and others
Exhibitions: Art exhibitions by unknown artists, who hang their works in the lobby of the hospital
Activities: Lect; sponsored art and cultural concerts; individual objects of art lent to Bronx Borough President, Banks in the Bronx, Bronx Museum of Art

SOCIETY OF ANIMAL ARTISTS, INC
For further information, see National and Regional Organizations

M **VAN CORTLANDT MANSION & MUSEUM,*** Van Cortlandt Park, N 242nd St, 10471. Tel 212-546-3323
Open AM - 4:30 PM, Sun 2 - 4:30 PM, cl Mon. Admis adult $.50, children under 12 free, Fri & Sat free to all. Estab 1898. Average Annual Attendance: 30,000
Collections: Furniture and objects relating to the Colonial period of American history; also Delftware, pottery and glass
Activities: Classes for children; slide programs for visitors

BRONXVILLE

L **BRONXVILLE PUBLIC LIBRARY,** 201 Pondfield Rd, 10708. Tel 914-337-7680. *Dir* Jane Cumming Selvar
Open (winter) Mon, Wed & Fri 9:30 AM - 5:30 PM, Tues 9:30 AM - 9 PM, Thurs 1 - 9 PM, Sat 9:30 AM - 5 PM, Sun 1 - 5 PM, (summer) Mon, Wed & Fri 9:30 AM - 5:30 PM, Tues 9:30 AM - 9 PM, Thurs 9:30 AM - 5:30 PM, Sat 9:30 AM - 1 PM. No admis fee
Income: Financed by city and state appropriations
Collections: American painters: Bruce Crane, Childe Hassam, Winslow Homer, William Henry Howe, Frederick Waugh; Japanese Art Prints; 25 Original Currier and Ives Prints
Exhibitions: Current artists, changed monthly; original paintings and prints

L **SARAH LAWRENCE COLLEGE LIBRARY,** Esther Raushenbush Library, Glen Washington Rd, 10708. Tel 914-337-0700. *Librn* Rose Anne Burstein; *Exhibits Librn* Carol Shaner; *Slide Librn* Renee Kent
Open 9 AM - 5 PM. Estab to provide library facilities for students and members of the community with an emphasis on art history. Slide collection closed to the public; non-circulating reference materials available to the public
Library Holdings: Vols 20,000; Per subs 951; AV — Slides 60,000
Exhibitions: Changing exhibits
Activities: Lectures in connection with exhibits; tours on request

BROOKLYN

AMERICAN SOCIETY OF CONTEMPORARY ARTISTS
For further information, see National and Regional Organizations

M **BROOKLYN MUSEUM,** 188 Eastern Parkway, 11238. Tel 212-638-5000; Telex 12-5378; Cable BRKLYN-MUSUNYK. *Chmn Board of Governors* Robert A Levinson; *Dir* Robert T Buck; *VDir Cur* Patrick D Cardon; *VDir Finance & Personnel* Roy Eddey; *Acting VDir Operations* Dan Wiedmann; *Special Asst Dir* B J van Damme; *Public Relations Mgr* Arthur Lindo; *Publications & Marketing*

Division Head Brian N Rushton; *Cur Egyptian & Classical Art* Richard Fazzini; *Assoc Cur Egyptian & Classical Art* Robert Bianchi; *Assoc Cur Egyptian & Classical Art* James Romano; *Cur European & Contemporary Paintings & Sculpture* Sarah Faunce; *Cur American Paintings & Sculpture* Linda Ferber; *Assoc Cur Sculpture Garden* Barbara Millstein; *Cur Oriental Art* Robert Moes; *Assoc Cur Oriental Art* Amy Poster; *Cur Costumes & Textiles* Elizabeth A Coleman; *Cur Decorative Arts* Dianne H Pilgrim; *Assoc Cur Decorative Arts* Kevin Stayton; *Asst Cur* Christopher Wilk; *Consultant Cur Prints & Drawings* Charlotte Kotik; *Assoc Cur Prints & Drawings* Barry Walker; *Conservator* Ken Moser; *Cur African, Oceanic & New World Cultures* Diana Fane; *Security* Edward Pisano; *Registrar* Barbara LaSalle; *Librn* Dierdre Lawrence; *Community Gallery Coordr* Richard Waller; *Graphic Designer* Daniel Weidmann
Open Wed - Sat 10 AM - 5 PM, Sun Noon - 5 PM, cl Mon & Tues. Voluntary admis fee. Estab 1823 as an art museum with educational facilities. Five floors of galleries maintained, seventh largest museum of art in the United States. Average Annual Attendance: 575,000. Mem: 4500; dues donor $500, patron $250, contributor $100, sustaining $75, family $40, individual $25, senior citizens & students $15
Income: $8,073,062 (financed by endowment, membership, city and state appropriation)
Collections: Art from the Americas and South Pacific; American period rooms; European and American paintings, sculpture; prints and drawings; costumes and textiles, decorative arts; Major collections of Egyptian and Classical; Oriental, Middle Eastern and African art; Sculpture Garden of ornaments from demolished New York buildings
Exhibitions: The American Artist as Printmaker; Homer, Sargent and the American Watercolor Tradition; Japanese Folk Art
Publications: Annual Report; calendar, monthly; catalogs of major exhibitions; handbooks
Activities: Classes for adults and children; dramatic programs; docent training; lect open to the public, 150 visiting lectr per year; gallery talks; tours; individual paintings and original objects of art lent to other museums; originate traveling exhibitions; museum and sales shop sells books, original art, reproductions, prints, slides

L **Art Reference Library,*** 11238. Tel 212-638-5000, Ext 307. *Asst Librn* Mildred G Iriberry
Open Wed 1:30 - 5 PM, Thurs & Fri 1 - 5 PM. Estab 1823 to serve the staff of the museum and local researchers
Income: $31,300 (financed by city, state and private appropriation)
Library Holdings: Vols 100,000; Per subs 400; Micro — Fiche; AV — A-tapes, slides 21,000, v-tapes; Other — Clipping files, exhibition catalogs, original art works, pamphlets
Special Subjects: Am painting & sculpture, decorative arts, Oriental art, Middle Eastern art & archit, primitive art & New World cultures, 19th & 20th century prints, costumes & textiles
Collections: Fashion plates; original design sketches 1900-150
Exhibitions: African Furniture & Household Objects; Begian Art, 1880-1914; Brancusi as photographer; Buffalo Bill & the Wild West; The Dinner Party - Jude, Chicago Indian Botanical Paintings; In China-Photography by Ere Arnold; The Realist Tradition; Romare Bearden, 1970-1980; Art of the Archaic Indonesians; 22nd National Print exhibition
Publications: Exhibition catalogues, 2 or 3 annually
Activities: Classes for children; docent training; programs relating to current exhibitions; lectures open to public, 30 vis lectr per year; gallery talks; tours; book traveling exhibitions, 2-3 per year; originate traveling exhibitions to other museums

L **Wilbour Library of Egyptology,** 11238. Tel 212-638-5000, Ext 215. *Librn* Diane Guzman
Open Wed - Fri 10 AM - 5 PM, cl Mon & Tues. Estab 1916 for the purpose of the study of Ancient Egypt. For reference by appointment only
Income: Financed by endowment and city appropriation
Purchases: $6000
Library Holdings: Vols 20,000; Per subs 150; original documents; Micro — Fiche; Other — Exhibition catalogs, pamphlets
Collections: Seyffarth papers
Publications: Wilbour Monographs; general introductory bibliographies on Egytian art available to visitors

L **BROOKLYN PUBLIC LIBRARY,** Art and Music Division, Grand Army Plaza, 11238. Tel 212-780-7784. *Dir* Kenneth F Duchac *Chief Art & Music Division* Sue Sharma; *Chief AV Division* Kenneth Axthelm
Open Mon - Thurs 9 AM - 8 PM; Fri & Sat 10 AM - 6 PM; Sun 1 - 5 PM. No admis fee. Estab 1892
Income: Financed by city and state appropriation
Library Holdings: Vols 168,500; Per subs 420; mounted picture; Micro — Cards, fiche, prints, reels; AV — Cassettes, fs, motion pictures, rec, slides; Other — Exhibition catalogs, pamphlets
Collections: Checkers Collection; Chess Collection; Costume Collection
Publications: Brooklyn Public Library Bulletin, bimonthly
Activities: Classes for children; programs; films

O **LONG ISLAND HISTORICAL SOCIETY,** 128 Pierrepont St, 11201. Tel 212-624-0890. *Pres* Irving Choban; *Exec Dir* David M Kohn
Open Tues - Sat Noon - 5 PM. No admis fee for members, non members $1 per day for library use. Estab in 1863 to collect, preserve and interpret documentary and other materials relating to the history of Brooklyn and the adjoining geographical areas. Gallery used for exhibits on Brooklyn history. Average Annual Attendance: 15,000. Mem: 1300; dues $25 - $250, annual meeting May
Income: Financed by endowment, membership
Collections: Paintings, drawings, watercolors, prints, sculpture, decorative arts, archeological artifacts relating to Brooklyn's history and key citizens
Exhibitions: (1982) Brooklyn Before the Bridge; (1983) Two Centuries of Commuting in Brooklyn; (1984) Origins of the Black Churches of Brooklyn; Antiques, Relics and Curiosities; Old Dutch Homesteads of Brooklyn; (1985) Brooklynites at Home
Publications: Journal of Long Island History, biannual
Activities: Educ dept; docent training; Lect open to the public, 15 vis lectr per year; concerts; gallery talks; individual paintings and original objects of art lent to other institutions; lending collection contains 6000 original prints, 275 paintings, 20 sculptures; shop sells books and prints

L **Library,** 128 Pierrepont St, 11201. *Librn* Patricia Flavin; *Asst Librn* Judy Metzger
Open Tues - Sat 9 AM - 5 PM. General admis $1. Open for reference only
Library Holdings: Vols 125,000; Per subs 150; Micro — Fiche 500, reels 1000; Other — Photographs 10,000
Exhibitions: Brooklyn Before The Bridge, paintings from the Long Island Historical Society

NATIONAL CARTOONISTS SOCIETY
For further information, see National and Regional Organizations

M **NEW MUSE COMMUNITY MUSEUM OF BROOKLYN, INC,*** 1530 Bedford Ave, 11216. Tel 212-774-2900, 774-2901. *Chmn Bd of Dir* Joseph Jiggetts; *Exec Dir* Jackie Woods; *Secy Bd of Dir* Lucille Bell; *Exec Secy* Ima Zawadi; *Coordr Exhib* Teresia Bush; *Coordr of Cultural Arts* Gaylord Hassan; *Coordr Music* Reginald Workman; *Coordr Public Relations* Mark Irving
Open Tues - Sat 10 AM - 6 PM, Sun 2 - 6 PM, cl Mon. No admis fee. Estab 1973 to effect an African-American educational and cultural institution of high calibre in the Crown Heights and Bedford-Stuyvesant sections of Brooklyn. Gallery contains cultural and historic exhibitions; fine art exhibitions. Average Annual Attendance: 650,000. Mem: 150; dues $100 - $5; annual meeting Jan 31
Income: Financed by membership, city and state appropriation
Collections: Small nucleus of Haitian, African and African-American Artifacts
Publications: Bulletins, announcing activities and workshops, monthly
Activities: Classes for children and adults; dramatic programs; music lectures open to the public

L **NEW YORK CITY TECHNICAL COLLEGE,** Namm Hall Library and Learning Resource Center,* 300 Jay Street, 11201. Tel 212-643-5240. *Chief Librn* Prof Catherine T Brody; *Admin Services Librn* Prof Paul T Sherman
Open Mon - Thurs 9 AM - 9 PM, Fri 9 AM - 5 PM, Sat 10 AM - 2 PM, cl Sun. Estab 1947
Library Holdings: Other — Reproductions
Special Subjects: Advertising Design, Graphic Arts
Exhibitions: Antique Christmas Cards; Impressions of Peru; Polish Folk Art
Publications: Library Notes, occasional publication
Activities: Tours

L **PRATT INSTITUTE LIBRARY,** Art & Architecture Dept, 215 Ryerson St, 11205. Tel 212-636-3685. *Dir* Dr George Lowy; *Art and Architecture Librn* Dr Sydney Starr Keaveney
Open Mon - Thurs 9 AM - 9 PM, Fri and Sat 9 AM - 5 PM, Sun 12 AM - 6 PM. Estab 1887 for students, faculty, staff and alumni of Pratt Institute. The school has several galleries, the library has exhibitions in display cases
Income: $50,000 Art & Architecture Dept
Library Holdings: Vols 50,000; Micro — Fiche, reels; AV — Cassettes, slides; Other — Clipping files, reproductions

M **ROTUNDA GALLERY,** Brooklyn War Memorial, 209 Joralemon St, 11201. Tel 212-643-5102. *Dir* Jackie Battenfield; *Education Program Dir* Merle Temkin
Open Tues - Sat Noon - 5 PM. No admis fee. Estab 1981 to exhibit the works of professional Brooklyn affliated artists. Average Annual Attendance: 14,000
Exhibitions: Fragment From Everyday Life: Interiors; Sculptor's Drawing; Photographic Narration; On, Of & About Paper; The Carribbean Influence
Activities: Classes for adults & children; competitions with awards

BUFFALO

L **BUFFALO AND ERIE COUNTY PUBLIC LIBRARY,*** Lafayette Square, 14203. Tel 716-856-7525. *Dir* Paul M Rooney; *Deputy Dir Public Services* Diane S Chrisman; *Deputy Dir Support Services* Donald Cloudsley
Open Mon - Thurs 10 AM - 9 PM, Fri and Sat 9:30 AM - 5:30 PM. Estab 1954 through a merger of the Buffalo Public, Grosvenor, and Erie County Public Libraries
Income: $10,835,000 (financed by county appropriation)
Library Holdings: Vols 33,200; Per subs 75; AV — Motion pictures; Other — Exhibition catalogs, manuscripts, original art works, photographs, prints
Collections: Drawings by Fritz Eichenberg; etchings by William J Schwanekamp; Niagara Falls prints; original woodcuts of J J Lankes; posters (mostly WW I); Rare Book Room with emphasis on fine printing
Publications: Library Bulletin, monthly
Activities: Dramatic programs; consumer programs; gallery talks; tours; concerts; book talks; architectural programs

M **THE BUFFALO FINE ARTS ACADEMY,** Albright-Knox Art Gallery, 1285 Elmwood Ave, 14222. Tel 716-882-8700. *Chmn* Seymour H Knox; *Pres* Samuel D Magavern; *VPres* Mrs John T Elfvin; *VPres* Northrup R Knox; *VPres* Robert E Rich; *Secy* Roy W Doolittle Jr; *Treas* William J Magavern II; *Actg Dir & Chief Cur* Douglas G Schultz; *Cur Education* Christopher Crosman; *Cur* Susan Krane; *Asst Cur* Cheryl A Brutuan; *Registrar* Sarah Ulen
Open Tues - Sat 11 AM - 5 PM, Sun Noon - 5 PM, cl Thanksgiving, Christmas and New Year's Day. No admis fee, voluntary contribution. Estab 1862 as The Buffalo Fine Arts Academy, gallery opened in 1905, with a new wing added in 1962. Average Annual Attendance: 250,000. Mem: 6700; dues $25; annual meeting in Oct
Income: $2,300,000 (financed by contributions, endowment and county appropriations)
Collections: †Paintings and drawings; †prints ranging from 3000 BC to the present with special emphasis on American and European contemporary art; †sculpture and constructions
Exhibitions: (1982) Fernand Leger; 39th Western New York Exhibition; Buffalo Architecture; Twelve Contemporary French Artists; John Cage: Scores and Prints; SURFACING IMAGES: The Painting of Joe Zucker 1969-1982; Adolph Gottlieb; Judy Pfaff: Rock-Paper-Scissors; Chryssa: Urban Icons; (1983) Golden Day-Silver Night: Perceptions of Nature in American Art 1850-1910; Alan Saret - Installation; In Western New York 1983; Milton Avery; Clyfford Still: Thirty-

Three Works From the Permanent Collection; Robert Motherwell; American Still Life: 1945-1982; (1984) The Painterly Object: Works by Jan Kotik; Mario Merz; 40th Western New York Exhibition; William Wegman - Recent Polaroids; The Photo-Secession: The Golden Age of Pictorial Photography in America; The Expendable Ikon—John McHale and Early British Pop Art; Francois Morellet: Systems; Hollis Frampton: Recollections-Recreations; Jim Dine: Five Themes
Publications: Annual report; calendar (monthly); exhibition catalogs
Activities: Classes for adults and children; docent training; lect open to public; concerts; gallery talks; tours; community outreach program; lending collections contain paintings, photographs and sculptures; originate traveling exhibitions; gallery shop sells books, magazines, original art, reproductions, prints, slides, cards, stationery, toys and jewelry

L **Art Reference Library,** 1285 Elmwood Ave, 14222. Tel 716-882-8700, Ext 225. *Librn* Annette Masling; *Asst Librn* Mary Bell
Open Tues - Fri 2 - 5 PM, Sat 1 - 3 PM. Estab 1933 to support the staff research and to document the Gallery collection, also to serve the fine art and art history people doing research in the western New York area. Exhibits are prepared in a small vestibule just outside the library, rare items in the library collection and print collection are displayed
Library Holdings: Vols 20,000; Per subs 150; original documents; Micro — Fiche; AV — A-tapes, cassettes, v-tapes; Other — Clipping files, exhibition catalogs, manuscripts, memorabilia, original art works, pamphlets, photographs, prints, reproductions
Special Subjects: American Art; Contemporary Art
Collections: †Artists books; †illustrated books
Exhibitions: Books and Prints of Maillol; Photography in Books; Rare Art Periodicals; Woodcuts from the Library Collection
Activities: Classes for adults and children; docent training; lectures open to public; concerts; gallery talks; tours; sponsors competitions

L **BUFFALO MUSEUM OF SCIENCE,** Research Library, Humboldt Parkway, 14211. Tel 716-896-5200, Ext 239. *Librn* Marcia Morrison
Open Mon - Fri 10 AM - 5 PM. Estab 1861 to further the study of natural history among the people of Buffalo. Reference only to members. Museum has exhibition space for permanent and temporary exhibitions. Circ 650
Income: Financed by endowment, membership, county & state appropriation, grants, gifts
Purchases: $12,000
Library Holdings: Vols 10,000; Per subs 650; Micro — Fiche, reels; AV — A-tapes; Other — Clipping files, exhibition catalogs, manuscripts, original art works, pamphlets, photographs, prints
Collections: African, Asian, American, European, Oceanic & Oriental Peasant Art; E W Hamlin Oriental Library of Art & Archaeology; Milestones of Science: First Editions Announcing Scientific Discoveries or Advances
Publications: Bulletin of the Buffalo Society of Natural Sciences, irregular; Collections, quarterly
Activities: Classes for adults and children; docent training; travel talks; lectures open to public, 5 vis lectr per year; gallery talks; tours; sponsor Camera Club Photo Contests; book traveling exhibitions, 2-3 per yr

M **BURCHFIELD ART CENTER,** 1300 Elmwood Ave, 14222. Tel 716-878-6011. *Chmn* R William Doolittle Jr; *Dir* Dr Edna M Lindemann; *Archivist & Registrar* Nancy Weekly; *Admin Asst* Suzanne Murray; *Technical Asst to Dir* Micheline Lepine
Open Tues - Sat 10 AM - 5 PM, Sun 1 - 5 PM. No admis fee. Estab 1966 to develop a total center concept including a regional center for the exhibition, study and encouragement of art expression in the Western New York area. This includes building a permanent collection of works by Charles Burchfield and other artists of the area, both living and historical. Museum has a main gallery with four supplemental galleries and the Burchfield studio gallery. Average Annual Attendance: 40,000. Mem: 1600; dues sustaining $50, family $30, regular $20, student, artist & sr citizen $10
Income: Financed by endowment, membership, SUNY and other sources
Collections: †Charles Burchfield collection; †works by contemporary and historical artists of the western New York area
Exhibitions: Charles Burchfield, permanent collection; Bruce Kurkland: Insight Into Still Life, Charles Cary Rumsey 1879-1922; Design in Buffalo, Charles Clough; Milton Rogovin; The Kitchen & the Gallery: The Artist & the Chef; 150 Years of Portraiture in Western New York
Publications: Exhibition catalogues
Activities: Docent training; lect open to the public; concerts; tours; competitions; exten dept serves area schools and community organizations; original objects of art lent to students and teachers; lending collection contains books, cassettes, color reproductions, film strips, framed reproductions, original art works slides, magazine articles, periodicals; originates traveling exhibitions; shop sells books, magazines, reproductions and wallpapers designed by Charles Burchfield

L **Burchfield Center Archives,** RH 317, 1300 Elmwood Ave, 14222. Tel 716-878-6020, 878-6011
Open Mon - Fri 9 AM - 5 PM. Estab 1967. For public reference only
Library Holdings: Vols 1000; AV — A-tapes, cassettes, motion pictures, slides, v-tapes; Other — Clipping files, exhibition catalogs, framed reproductions, manuscripts, memorabilia, original art works, pamphlets, photographs, prints, reproductions
Special Subjects: Works of Charles Burchfield, Western New York art and artist, American art
Collections: Charles Burchfield Archive, George William Eggers Archive
Exhibitions: Archive materials relating to the life and career of Charles Burchfield

L **STATE UNIVERSITY OF NEW YORK AT BUFFALO,** Lockwood Memorial Library,* Art Dept, Room 106, Talbert Hall, 14260. Tel 716-636-2748. *Librn* Shirley Hesslein; *Collection Development* M Stern
Open Mon - Thurs 9 AM - 10 PM, Fri 9 AM - 5 PM, Sat 9 AM - 5 PM. Estab 1913 to support curriculum in the history of art and architecture, and in the fine arts. Library has microfiche holdings on a reciprocal exchange basis, of the Albright-Knox Art Gallery Catalog
Library Holdings: Vols 38,000; Micro — Fiche
Exhibitions: Monthly exhibitions of bibliothecal interest

CANAJOHARIE

M **CANAJOHARIE LIBRARY AND ART GALLERY,** Erie Blvd, 13317. Tel 518-673-2314. *Pres* Mrs John Fenno; *Cur* Edward Lipowicz; *Secy* Mrs James Dern
Open Mon - Wed and Fri 9:30 AM - 4:45 PM, Thurs 9:30 AM - 8:30 PM, Sat 9:30 AM - 1:30 PM, cl Sun. No admis fee. Estab 1927 as a memorial to Senator James Arkell. Average Annual Attendance: 3000 - 5000. Mem: Annual meeting in Jan
Income: Financed by endowment and village grants
Collections: †Paintings by American artists
Exhibitions: Permanent collection
Activities: Gallery talks; tours; individual paintings lent to community residents and business institutions
L **Library,** Erie Blvd, 13317. Tel 518-673-2314. *Librn* Marie Moore
Library Holdings: Vols 21,000; Per subs 50

CANTON

M **ST LAWRENCE UNIVERSITY,** Richard F Brush Art Gallery,* Romoda Dr, 13617. Tel 315-379-6003. *Dir* Betsy Cogger Rezelman
Open Mon - Fri 8 AM - 5 PM, cl holidays. No admis fee. Estab 1968 as an adjunct of the Department of Fine Arts. The Gallery's programs are intended to compliment the University's art courses as well as benefit the general public of northern New York state and southern Canada
Income: Financed by university funds
Collections: Contemporary prints, paintings, sculture and photography; 19th century American art; Old Master graphics; Oriental and African art; Frederic Remington collection
Exhibitions: Two Contemporary Canadian Artists; Video Festival by CAPS Fellows; Charles Ehricke (watercolors); Selection from the permanent collection; American Representational Artists of the 1930's and 1940's; Schemes: A Decade of Installation Drawings; Joint Faculty Exhibition: State University College of Potsdan and St Lawrence
Publications: Annual report; exhibition brochures
Activities: Lect open to public, 4 visiting lectr per year; competitions; individual paintings and original art objects lent to student loan program and museums

CAZENOVIA

M **CAZENOVIA COLLEGE,** Chapman Art Center Gallery, 13035. Tel 315-655-9446. *Dir Art Prog* John Aistars
Open Mon - Fri 1 - 4 PM & 7 - 9 PM, Sat 10 AM - 7 PM, Sun 1 - 5 PM. No admis fee. Estab 1977 as a college gallery for students and community. Gallery is 1084 sq feet with track lighting and movable display panels. Average Annual Attendance: 1000
Income: Financed through College
Collections: A small permanent collect of work donated to college
Exhibitions: (1983-84) Annual shows of faculty, alumni, students & invitational work; Cazenovia Arts; Richard Pascucci & Andrew Schuster; Jacqueline Goldman, Ceramics Invitational Exhibition; David MacDonald, Joan Riccardi & Lin Underhill

CHAUTAUQUA

M **CHAUTAUQUA ART ASSOCIATION GALLERIES,** Wythe Ave, PO Box 1365, 14722. Tel 716-357-2771. *Pres* Perry Dvidson; *Dir* William Waite; *Chmn of Board* George Weaver; *Secy* Mariam Lewis; *VPres* Gayle C Johnson; *VPres* Suzanne Gray
Open Mon - Sun 1 - 8 PM July - Aug. No admis fee. Estab 1948 to promote quality art, culture and appreciation of the arts at Chantanque Institution. Winter address: PO Box 518, Dept D, Celoron, NY 14720. Average Annual Attendance: 20,000. Mem: 1200; dues $5; six annual meetings
Income: Financed by membership
Exhibitions: 12 exhibitions including crafts, prints, paintings, glass, metals and sculpture; 27th Chautauqua National Exhibition of American Art
Publications: Chautauqua National, catalog; Calendar of Events, yearly; Chautauqua National Prosetus
Activities: Classes for adults and children; dramatic programs; art appreciation; lect open to public, 24 visiting lectr per year; concerts; gallery talks; docent tours; competitions; museum shop sells books, original art and hand-crafted items from around the world

CLINTON

M **HAMILTON COLLEGE,** Fred L Emerson Gallery, 13323. Tel 315-859-4396. *Dir* William Salzillo
Open Sept - May Mon - Fri 9 AM - 5 PM, Sat & Sun 1 - 5 PM. Estab 1982 to make available to Hamilton College students and to the entire community fine examples of art. Housed in 1920 building. Average Annual Attendance: 20,000
Income: Financed by Hamilton College appropriations
Exhibitions: Six exhibitions throughout the academic year
Publications: Exhibition catalogues
Activities: Lectures open to the public; gallery talks; tours; individual paintings & original objects of art lent; book traveling exhibitions; originate traveling exhibitions
L **Library,** 13323. Tel 315-859-7135
Books on art and related subjects
M **Bristol Campus Center,*** 13323. Tel 315-859-7194. *Dir* Andrew W Wertz
Exhibitions: Six throughout the academic year arranged under the direction of a Student Faculty Committee
L **Art Lending Library,*** 13323
Over 200 paintings and prints which may be rented by the semester by students for a nominal fee

O **KIRKLAND ART CENTER,** On-the-Park, 13323. Tel 315-853-8871. *Dir* Dare Thompson; *Asst Dir* Andree Leidig
Open Tues - Fri 9:30 AM - 5 PM, Sun 2 - 4 PM, cl Mon; Tues - Fri 9:30 - 3 PM, Sun 2 - 4 PM July & Aug. No admis. Estab 1960 to promote the arts in the town of Kirkland. The center has a large main gallery, studio space. Average Annual Attendance: 15,000 - 17,000. Mem: 1100; dues adults $7; annual meeting June
Income: Financed by endowment, memebership, state, county & town appropriation, fund raising events, thrift & gift shops
Exhibitions: Works by contemporary artists
Publications: Newsletter, monthly
Activities: Classes for adults and children; lectures open to public; competitions; gift shop sells original art, crafts & purchased items

COOPERSTOWN

O **COOPERSTOWN ART ASSOCIATION,*** 22 Main St, 13326. Tel 607-547-9777. *Exec Dir* Olga Welch
Open Mon - Sat 10 AM - 4 PM, Sun 1 - 4 PM. Estab 1928 to provide a cultural program for the central part of New York State. An art gallery is maintained. Average Annual Attendance: 14,000. Mem: 1284; dues $10 and up
Income: Financed by membership
Collections: †Crafts; †paintings; †sculpture
Exhibitions: (1982) Annual National Juried Exhibitions; 49th Annual National Art Exhibition (juried show)
Publications: Newsletter, annual
Activities: Classes for adults; competitions; prizes; individual paintings and original objects of art lent; lending collection contains paintings, sculpture, crafts
L **Reference Library,*** 22 Main St, 13326
For reference only

O **LEATHERSTOCKING BRUSH & PALETTE CLUB INC,** PO Box 446, 13326. Tel 607-547-8044. *Publicity* Dorothy V Smith
Estab 1965 to encourage original arts and crafts work and foster general art appreciation and education. Fire House Arts & Crafts Gallery in local historical building. Mem: 100; dues $3, meetings May & Oct
Income: Financed by membership and outdoor show revenues
Exhibitions: Annual Labor Day Weekend Outdoor Art Show; annual fall fine arts exhibition
Publications: Information Bulletin, quarterly
Activities: Classes for adults; lectures open to public, 2-3 vis lectr per yr; originate traveling exhibitions; sales shop
M **Firehouse Gallery,** 59 Pioneer st, PO Box 446, 13326
Open June - Aug 30, Mon - Sat 9 AM - 5 PM, Sun 1 - 5 PM. No admis fee. Privately owned firehouse built in 1842, leased to Club from June to August

M **NATIONAL BASEBALL HALL OF FAME AND MUSEUM, INC,** Art Collection,* PO Box 590, 13326. Tel 607-547-9988. *Dir* Howard C Talbot Jr; *Registrar* Peter P Clark; *Public Relations* William J Guilfoile; *Historian* Clifford Kachline; *Cur Exhibits* Ted Spencer
Open May - Oct daily 9 AM - 9 PM, Nov - April daily 9 AM - 5 PM. Admis adults $4, children ages 7-15 $1.50. Estab 1936 to collect, preserve and display memorabilia pertaining to the national game of baseball. Average Annual Attendance: 200,000
Income: $1,500,000 (financed by admis & gift shop sales, Hall of Fame Game & contributions)
Collections: Baseball & sport-related art & memorabilia
Publications: National Baseball Hall of Fame & Museum Yearbook, annually; Newsletter, quarterly
Activities: Orginate traveling exhibitions to museums, banks, baseball clubs, shopping malls; bookstore sells books, t-shirts, caps, glassware, postcards, mugs and jackets

NEW YORK STATE HISTORICAL ASSOCIATION
M **Fenimore House,** Rte 80, Lake Rd, 13326. Tel 607-547-2533. *Dir* Daniel R Porter; *Assoc Dir and Chief Educ* Milo V Stewart; *Assoc Cur* A Bruce MacLeish
Open May - Oct daily 9 AM - 5 PM, cl Mon in April, Nov & Dec, cl all Jan - March. Admis adults $3.50, children $1.25, members free. Estab 1899 as a historical society whose purpose is to promote the study of New York State through a statewide educational program, the operation of two museums, and graduate programs offering master's degree in conjunction with the State University College at Oneonta. Fenimore House is an art museum with an extensive collection of art. Average Annual Attendance: 45,000. Mem: 5800; dues $15; annual meeting July
Collections: †American folk art; Browere life masks of famous Americans; James Fenimore Cooper (memorabilia); genre paintings of New York State; landscapes; †portraits
Exhibitions: (1983) A Shifting Wind: Views of American Folk Art; Cooper's America
Publications: Director's Report, annual; Newsletter, biannual; New York History, quarterly journal; The Yorker, junior magazine
Activities: Classes for adults and children; docent training; seminars on American culture; junior program; conferences; lect open to the public; gallery talks; tours; individual paintings and original objects of art lent to selected museums
M **Farmers' Museum, Inc,** Lake Rd, PO Box 800, 13326. Tel 607-547-2593. *Dir* Daniel R Porter III; *Assoc Dir* David L Parke Jr; *Asst Cur* Kathryn A Boardman
Open May - Oct Mon - Sun 9 AM - 5 PM, Nov - Apr cl Sun mornings & Mon. Admis adults $4, children $1.50, under 7 and members free. Estab 1943 as an outdoor folk museum of rural life in upstate New York, 1785-1860. Main buildings with collections and craft demonstrations are maintained; recreated Village Crossroads with 13 buildings are brought in from nearby area. Average Annual Attendance: 90,000
Collections: †Folk art; 19 century tools & implements; period house; drawn vehicles; farm horse drawn equipment
Activities: Classes for adults & children; docent training; lectures open to public, 2-3 vis lectr per yr; concerts; tours; special events; museum shop sells reproductions & gifts

L **Library,** Lake Rd, 13326. Tel 607-547-2509. *Librn* Amy Barnum
Open to public for reference only
Library Holdings: Vols 62,000; Per subs 160; Micro — Reels; AV — Cassettes, rec; Other — Manuscripts
Special Subjects: Decorative Arts, Folk Art, New York State History

CORNING

M **CORNING MUSEUM OF GLASS,** Corning Glass Center, 14831. Tel 607-937-5371; Cable CORMUS. *Dir* Dwight P Lanmon; *Deputy Dir Admin* John H Martin; *Research Scientist* Robert H Brill; *Chief Cur* Sidney M Goldstein; *Cur American Glass* Jane Shadel Spillman; *Asst Cur 20th Century Glass* William Warmus; *Registrar* Priscilla B Price; *Managing Editor* Charleen K Edwards
Open all year daily 9 AM - 5 PM. Admis family $6, adult $2.50, senior citizen $2, children 6 - 17 $1.25, children under 6 free. Estab 1951 to present to the public the art and history of glass. New building opened May 1980. Average Annual Attendance: 750,000
Income: Financed by state appropriations
Purchases: $2,300,000
Collections: Over 20,000 objects representing all periods of glass history from 1500 BC to the present
Exhibitions: Glassmaking: America's First Industry (traveling); New Glass: A Worldwide Survey (traveling); The Crystal Palace (traveling)
Publications: Journal of Glass Studies annually; New Glass Review, annually; annual catalog for special exhibitions
Activities: Classes for children; annual seminar on glass; lectures open to the public, 20 vis lectr per year; film series; competitions; original art objects lent to other museums; originates traveling exhibitions; sales shop sells books and slides
L **Library,*** 14831. Tel 607-937-5371; Cable CORMUS. *Librn* Norma P H Jenkins; *Assoc Librn* Virginia L Wright
Open Mon - Fri 9 AM - 5 PM. Estab 1951 for the purpose of providing extensive and comprehensive coverage of the art, history, archaeology and early manufacture of glass. The library is primarily for research reference only
Library Holdings: Vols 25,000; Per subs 500; Original documents; 650 rare books; Micro — Fiche 6500, reels 360; AV — A-tapes, cassettes, motion pictures, slides 79,000, v-tapes 120; Other — Clipping files, exhibition catalogs, original art works, pamphlets, photographs, prints 400
Special Subjects: Glass history, manufacturing, painting and staining, glassware, ornamental glass
Collections: Archival and historical materials relating to glass and its manufactures; 800 manufacturers' trade catalogs on microfiche

M **THE ROCKWELL MUSEUM,** Cedar St at Denison Parkway, 14830. Tel 607-937-5386. *Supv Museum Coll* Kristin A Swain; *Supv Museum Prog* P Jensen Monroe; *Business Mgr* Pamela Michlosky; *Dir* Michael Duty
Open Mon - Sat 10 AM - 5 PM, Sun Noon - 5 PM. Admis adults $1.50, senior citizens $1, students $.75, maximum family rate $4.50. Estab 1976 to house and exhibit the collections of the Robert F Rockwell Foundation and Family and to serve the Corning community with major funding provided by the Corning Glass Works. Average Annual Attendance: 40,000. Mem: 2000; dues $10 - $1000
Income: $400,000 (financed by a grant from the Corning Glass Works
Purchases: $50,000
Collections: Carder Steuben glass (1903-1933); bronzes; etchings; 19th century western paintings & illustrations; Plains Indian beadwork and artifacts; prints; Pueblo Indian pottery; Navajo rugs; 19th century popular western fiction
Exhibitions: Best of Rockwell's Western Art Collection; seasonal exhibits featuring smaller parts of Rockwell collections
Publications: Exhibition catalog; Newsletter, quarterly
Activities: Volunteer & docent training; programs for students; film series; lect open to public and for members only, 2 visiting lectr per year; gallery talks; tours; paintings and original objects of art lent to established museums; lending collection contains reproductions, original art works, original prints, Victorian toys, Carder Steuben Glass; originate traveling exhibitions; shop sells books, magazines, reproductions, prints, Indian jewelry, postcards, needlepoint, T-shirts, Pueblo pottery, Hopi Kachinas
L **Library,** Baron Steuben Place, 14830. Tel 607-937-5386. *Librn* Carolyn Lovejoy
Open to the public by prior arrangement for reference only
Library Holdings: Vols 350; Per subs 15; Micro — Cards; Other — Exhibition catalogs

CORTLAND

M **CORTLAND COUNTY HISTORICAL SOCIETY,** Suggett House Museum, 25 Homer Ave, 13045. Tel 607-756-6071. *Pres* Joan Siedenburg; *VPres* Mary Ann Kane; *Secy* Linda Ruthig; *Treas* Ruth Webster; *Dir* Dr Leslie C O'Malley
Open Tues - Sat 1 - 4 PM, mornings by appointment. Estab 1925 to collect, store and interpret the history of Cortland County through programs, exhibits and records in our 1869 Suggett House. Average Annual Attendance: 30,000. Mem: 602; dues $10; meetings second Sat of Jan, Apr, June & Oct
Income: $50,000 (financed by endowment, memberships, county appropriations, grants, sales and fund raisers)
Purchases: Antique furniture & paintings from Cortland County
Collections: †Antique furniture, †children's toys, †china, †folk art, †glass, †military memorabilia, †paintings, †textiles & clothing
Exhibitions: (1984) Historic textiles including samplers, coverlets & quilts; The Architecture of Stearns & Bickford, photos; The Suggett Family & Their House; locally produced Empire-style furniture on permanent exhibit; permanent gallery of local artists and/or local subjects including F B Carpenter, Susan Waters & Jere Wickwire
Publications: Roots & Branches, 4 times per yr; books on local history; bulletin, 4 times per yr; newsletter, 6 times per yr
Activities: Classes for adults & children; docent training; lectures open to public, 12 vis lectr per yr; gallery talks; tours; exten dept serves Cortland & surrounding counties; individual paintings & original objects of art lent to other museums & college galleries; book traveling exhibitions; originates traveling exhibitions; museum shop sells books, reproductions & prints

L **Kellogg Memorial Reading Room,** 13045. *Librn* Shirley Heppell
Open Tues - Sat 1 - 5 PM, mornings by appointment. Estab 1976 to collect, preserve and interpret information about the history of Cortland County
Purchases: $500
Library Holdings: Vols 2000; Per subs 10; Micro — Reels; AV — Slides; Other — Clipping files, exhibition catalogs, manuscripts, memorabilia, original art works, pamphlets, photographs, prints

L **CORTLAND FREE LIBRARY,** Art Gallery, 32 Church St, 13045. Tel 607-753-1042. *Dir* Warren S Eddy
Open Mon - Thurs 10 AM - 9 PM, Fri and Sat 10 AM - 5:30 PM, cl Sun. No admis fee. Estab 1938
Library Holdings: Vols 1400
Exhibitions: Monthly exhibitions held

L **STATE UNIVERSITY OF NEW YORK COLLEGE AT CORTLAND,** Art Slide Library,* 13045. Tel 607-753-4316. *Cur* Jo Schaffer
Open Mon - Fri 8:30 AM - 5 PM, and by appointment. Estab 1967 to provide visual resources to faculty, students and community
Income: Financed by state appropriation
Library Holdings: Vols 300; Per subs 10; Micro — Fiche; AV — Fs, Kodachromes, lantern slides, slides 75,000; Other — Exhibition catalogs, photographs
Special Subjects: Pop Art

DOUGLASTON

O **NATIONAL ART LEAGUE INC,** 44-21 Douglaston Parkway, 11360. Tel 212-229-9495. *Pres* Daniel Stone; *VPres* Al Camurati
Estab 1932, inc 1950, as Art League of Long Island, Inc. Mem: 224
Income: Financed by membership dues & contributions
Exhibitions: Six annual major shows, one national; gallery exhibitions
Publications: Brochures; bulletins; catalogs; newsletter, monthly
Activities: Art classes for adults and children; demonstrations; lectures open to public, 10 vis lectr per yr; gallery talks; competitions with awards

EAST HAMPTON

M **GUILD HALL OF EAST HAMPTON, INC,** Museum Section, 158 Main St, 11937. Tel 516-324-0806. *Chmn* Robert B Menschel; *First VChmn* Eloise Spaeth; *Secy* Robert F Denny; *Treasurer* James Marcus; *Dir* Open; *Consultant Cur* Helen A Harrison; *Assoc Cur* Rae Ferren
Open Oct - Apr Wed - Sat 10 AM - 5 PM, Sun 2 - 5 PM. No admis fee. Estab 1931 as a cultural center for the visual and performing arts with a State Board of Regents Educational Charter. Emphasis on art collection and exhibitons is chiefly on the many artists who live or have lived in the area. Museum has three galleries and a sculpture garden. Average Annual Attendance: 80,000. Mem: 4000; dues $25-$1000; annual meeting Nov
Income: $1,500,000 (financed by memberships, federal, state, county & town appropriations, corporate, foundation, individual contributions, benefits, fund drives & museum shop)
Purchases: $20,000
Collections: Mainly American artist associated with the regions of eastern Long Island, including James Brooks, Jimmy Ernst, Adolf Gottlieb, Childe Hassam, Willem de Kooning, Roy Lichtenstein, Thomas Moran, Jackson Pollock and Larry Rivers: paintings, works on paper, prints, sculpture, photographs
Exhibitions: (1982) Winterscape, landscapes by artists of the region; Artist & Printer; Edward Hopper Works on Paper: A Personal Collection; Five Distinguished Alumni: The WPA Federal Art Project; E L Henry's Country Life; The Townspeople of Bridgehampton, photos by Frank Stiefel; William Tarr, sculpture; Selections from the Collection: Recent Acquisitions; Val Telberg Photomontages; Artists from the Edward F Albee Foundation; Twins on Twins, photos by Kathryn Abbe & Frances McLaughlin-Gill; Poets & Artists; John Little Retrospective; Enez Whipple Print & Drawing Collection; Stanley Kearl Sculpture; 44th Annual Members' Exhibition; The World of George Bellows; (1983) On Hard Water: Iceboating Past & Present; The World of George Bellows; Pressed on Paper, nature prints & fish rubbings; Universal Limited Art Editions: The First Ten Years; Arrivals, Artists New to the Region; Ted Davies; Cyril David/Penny Kaplan; Multiple Portraits: Recent Work by Elaine de Kooning; John Day, Memorial Exhibition; John Hall Wheelock: A Photographic Portrait by Robert Blaisdell; Larry Rivers: Performing for the Family; 45th Annual Members' Exhibition; The South Fork Tercentennial Series: Everett Rattray's South Fork, Our Children's South Fork, Robert Giard's South Fork
Publications: Newsletter, exhibition catalogues
Activities: Classes for adults; docent training; cooperative projects with area schools; lect open to public, 12 visiting lectr per year; concerts, gallery talks; tours, competitions; original art objects lent to museums, libraries, schools, public building; lending collection contains cassettes, original art works and prints, paintings, photographs, sculpture, slides; book traveling exhibitions; originate traveling exhibitions; museum shop sells mainly posters created for Guild Hall by artists of region; also gift items and local crafts

ELMIRA

M **ARNOT ART MUSEUM,*** 235 Lake St, 14901. Tel 607-734-3697. *Dir* Kenneth H Lindquist; *Cur Coll* Allen C Smith
Open Tues - Fri 10 AM - 5 PM, Sat 9 AM - 5 PM, Sun 2 - 5 PM, cl Mon & national holidays. No admis fee. Estab 1911 to serve the people of the community with a regular schedule of changing exhibits from the permanent collection and traveling shows, as well as providing other free cultural activities not ordinarily available in the area. Average Annual Attendance: 40,000. Mem: 650; dues $5 and up; annual meeting in May
Collections: †American and European sculpture; †contemporary prints; Flemish, Dutch, French, English, German, Italian, Spanish and †American paintings
Exhibitions: Changed monthly; Annual Regional Exhibition with prizes; Annual Craft Exhibition with prizes
Activities: Classes for adults and children; lect open to public

M **ELMIRA COLLEGE,** Hamilton Art Gallery, Park Place, 14901. Tel 607-734-3911, Ext 354. *Dir* Leslie Kramer
Open Tues - Sat 1 - 4 PM, cl Mon & Sun. No admis fee. The Gallery is located in a Gothic Cathedral-like building with 100 x 35 feet of space. Average Annual Attendance: 1000
Income: Financed by school budget
Exhibitions: Ten exhibitions per year

O **SOUTHERN TIER ARTS ASSOCIATION, INC,*** PO Box 641, 14902. Tel 607-734-0885. *Pres* Mary Louise Donovan
Estab 1974 to improve the Fine Arts in the Southern Tier of New York State. Mem: 130; dues $12; annual meeting Dec
Income: $5700 (financed by membership, decentralization grants)
Purchases: $5000
Exhibitions: Arts in the Parks
Activities: Lectures open to the public, 2 visiting lecturers per year; gallery talks; competitions with awards; individual paintings and original objects of art lent to area museums, banks, cultural institutions, businesses

FLUSHING

M **BOWNE HOUSE,** 37-01 Bowne St, 11354. Tel 212-359-0528. *Pres* Franklin F Regan, Jr; *VPres* Mrs John H Tennent; *Treas* Kenneth Kupferberg; *Corresp Secy* Mrs E V Bowen; *Recording Secy* Marjorie Wilmot; *Dir* Michael May
Open Tues, Sat & Sun 2:30 - 4:30 PM. Admis adults $1, children $.25, children under 14 free. Estab 1945 for historic preservation, education, collection of 17th & 18th century furnishings and examples of colonial life. Average Annual Attendance: 5000. Mem: 620; dues $10, $15, $25, $100, $250; annual meeting third Tues in May
Income: Financed by membership and private & public contributions
Collections: Furnishings from the 17th, 18th and early 19th Centuries Furniture, pewter, fabrics, china, portraits, prints and documents
Exhibitions: (1983) Three Centuries at Bowne House; (1984) Needlework exhibit
Publications: Booklets regarding John Bowne and the House; quarterly newsletter
Activities: Classes for children; docent training; tours; museum shop sells books, reproductions, prints, slides, products of herb garden, plates and tiles

M **GODWIN-TERNBACH MUSEUM,** Queens College, City University of New York, Kissena Blvd & Long Island Expressway, 11367. Tel 212-520-7049. *Dir & Cur* Suzanne M Heim
Open Mon - Thurs 12:30 - 4 PM, Tues evening 6 - 8 PM. No admis fee. Estab 1957 for a study collection for Queens College students & in 1981 independently chartered. Collection located in one large exhibition gallery on Queens College Campus. Average Annual Attendance: 500. Mem: 15; dues $25
Income: Financed by state appropriation, NEA & Friends of the Museum
Collections: Ancient & antique glass; Egyptian, Greek, Luristan antiquities, Old Master & WPA prints; Renaissance & later bronzes; 16th - 20th century paintings
Exhibitions: Anni Albers (prints); Rudolph Baronik (collages); Naomi Boretz (watercolors); Lois Dodd (paintings); Blance Dombek (sculpture); Evelyn Eller (collages); M C Escher (prints); Sally Friedman (paintings); Un Voyage Heliographique A Faire; The Mission of 1851; The First Photographic Survey of Historical Monuments in France; Latin American Artists in the US Before 1950; Zofia Griffen (drawings); Richard McDermott Miller (sculpture); Emily Nelligan (prints and drawings); Peri Schwartz (paintings); Zelda Tannenbaum (drawings); Latin American Artists in the US 1950-1970; 20th Century Prints
Publications: Brochures; exhibition catalogs
Activities: Lectures open to public, 3-4 vis lectr per yr; gallery talks; individual paintings & original objects of art lent to qualified museums; book traveling exhibitions; originate traveling exhibitions

L **Paul Klapper Library,** Kissena Blvd and Long Island Expressway, 11367. *Art Librn* Irene Avens
Open to City University students for reference
Library Holdings: Vols 35,000; Per subs 115; Micro — Fiche, reels; AV — Slides; Other — Exhibition catalogs, original art works, pamphlets, photographs, reproductions

M **QUEENS MUSEUM,** New York City Bldg, Flushing Meadow Park, 11368. Tel 212-592-2405. *Dir* Janet Schneider; *Program Admin* Ileen Sheppard; *Asst Dir Operations* James Mesler; *Cur Education & Community Servs* Kathryn Adamchick; *Administrator* Barbara Sperber; *Chmn* Raplh Brotter; *Pres* Carola Michael; *Secy* Joseph Morsellino
Open Tues - Sat 10 AM - 5 PM, Sun 1 - 5 PM, cl Mon. No admis fee, contributions requested. Estab 1972 to provide a vital cultural center for the more than 2 million residents of Queens County; it provides high quality fine art exhibition & a wide-range of educational and community services. Museum has approx 25,000 sq ft gallery space, Panorama of the City of New York (18,000 sq ft detail-perfect scale model of New York City), theatre, workshops, offices. Average Annual Attendance: 100,000. Mem: 500; dues $5 - $1000
Income: $1,000,000 (financed by membership, city and state appropriation, corporation, foundation, National Endowment for Humanitites and individual grants)
Collections: Panorama of the City of New York (scale model); Small collection of paintings, photographs and prints
Exhibitions: (1983-84) Made in Queens; 20th Century Art From the Metropolitan Museum of Art: Selected Recent Acquisitions; A Printer's Perspective; Indian Miniatures; Michelangelo: A Sculptor's World; Aspects of Indian Art & Life; Streamline Design: How the Future Was; Annual Juried Exhibition 1984
Publications: Catalogs; newsletter, quarterly
Activities: Classes for adults and children; docent training; projects involving elementary school children; films; drop-in arts & crafts workshops on Sun; lect open to public and some for members only, with visiting lectr; concerts; gallery talks; tours; competitions; book traveling exhibitions, 4 per yr; museum shop sells books, reproductions, prints, exhibition catalogs and children's items

FREDONIA

M **STATE UNIVERSITY OF NEW YORK COLLEGE AT FREDONIA,** M C Rockefeller Arts Center Gallery, 14063. Tel 716-673-3217. *Ctr Dir* Jefferson Westwood
Open Wed & Thurs 11 AM - 3 PM, Fri & Sun 3 PM - 8 PM. No admis fee. Estab 1963 and relocated in 1969 to new quarters designed by I M Pei and Partners. The gallery serves as a focal point of the campus, uniting the college with the community. Average Annual Attendance: 10,000. Mem: 100
Income: Financed by state appropriation and student groups
Collections: Primarily 20 century American art and architectural archival material, with an emphasis on †prints and †sculpture
Exhibitions: (1983-84) New York Landscape; Collected Visions; Art Faculty Exhibit; CAPS Painting Exhibit; Annual Student Exhibit; Graduating Seniors Exhibit I; Graduating Seniors Exhibit II
Publications: Exhibition catalogs
Activities: Small slide library; Lect open to public, 2 - 4 vis lectr per year; gallery talks; tours; competitions; individual paintings and original objects of art lent to offices and public lobbies on campus; lending collection contains framed reproductions original prints, paintings, photographs, sculpture; traveling exhibitions organized and circulated

GARDEN CITY

L **ADELPHI UNIVERSITY,** Fine Arts Library, 11530. Tel 516-663-1042. *Head Fine Arts Library* Erica Doctorow; *Performing Arts Librn* Gary Cantrell
Open Mon - Thurs 8:30 AM - 10 PM, Fri & Sat 9 AM - 5 PM, Sun 1 - 5 PM. The Fine & Performing Arts Library builds print and nonprint collections and provides reference service in fine and applied arts, music, dance, theater and photography
Income: Financed by state appropriations and through the University
Library Holdings: Vols 21,800; Per subs 150; original documents; Micro — Fiche, reels; AV — Cassettes, fs, motion pictures, rec, slides, v-tapes; Other — Exhibition catalogs, manuscripts, memorabilia, original art works, pamphlets, photographs, prints, reproductions
Collections: Americana; William Blake; Cuala Press; Expatriate Writers: Cobbett, Morley, Hauptman and Whitman; University Archives
Activities: Lectures

M **Swirbul Library Gallery,** 11530
Open Mon - Thurs 8 AM - 11 PM, Sat 9 AM - 5 PM, Sun 1 - 11 PM. No admis fee. Estab 1963 to enrich cultural life, provide a showcase for faculty research and art works and interdisciplinary exhibitions. Average Annual Attendance: 30,000. Mem: 150
Exhibitions: (1982) Gnome d'Afrique: African Musical Instruments from the American Museum of Natural History; Handicrafts of India; Richard Vaux: Iconographic Images; Peter Porcupine Exposed: The Pungent Pen of William Cobbett in England and America; (1983) Homage to Alice: A Wonderland Vision by Martin Barooshian; Resounding Performance: The Acoustic Phonograph, 1895-1926; Airy Aggression: Fighter Kites of India; Humor as a Weapon: The Art of Robert Cenedella
Activities: Lectures open to the public, 4 vis lectrs per yr; gallery talks; individual and original objects of art lent to university offices only

M **NASSUA COMMUNITY COLLEGE,** Firehouse Gallery, Stewart Ave, 11530. Tel 516-222-7165. *Dir* Helen B Muller; *Cur* Janet Marzo
Open Mon - Fri 11 AM - 4:30 PM Sept - May. Estab 1964 to exhibit fine art and varied media. Two exhibition spaces, carpeted fabric walls, and track lighting
Income: Financed by state, college & county appropriation
Collections: Painting; sculpture; prints
Exhibitions: (1983) Open Competition; David Porter
Activities: Lectures open to the public; competitions with awards

GENESEO

M **STATE UNIVERSITY OF NEW YORK COLLEGE AT GENESEO,** Bertha V B Lederer Gallery,* 14454. Tel 716-245-5657. *Dir* Paul Hepler; *Chairman Exhibitions Committee* Richard Beale
Open 2 - 5 PM for exhibitions. No admis fee. Estab 1967; the gallery serves the college and community. Average Annual Attendance: 6000
Income: Financed by state appropriation
Collections: Ceramics, furniture, graphics, paintings, sculpture
Publications: Exhibition catalogs
Activities: Lectures open to public; lending collection contains 400 - 600 books

GLENS FALLS

M **HYDE COLLECTION,** 161 Warren St, 12801. Tel 518-792-1761. *Dir* Frederick J Fisher; *Adjunct Cur* James Kettlewell; *Asst to Dir* Cecilia Esposito
Open Tues - Sun Noon - 5 PM. Admis adults $1, children, students, senior citizens $.50. Estab 1952 to promote & cultivate the study & improvement of the fine arts. Average Annual Attendance: 14,000. Mem: 700; dues $15-$5000
Income: Financed by endowment, membership, contributions, municipal support and grants
Collections: Drawings by da Vinci, Degas, Tiepolo, Matisse, Lorraine and others; Paintings by El Greco, Rembrandt, Rubens, Botticelli, Tintoretto, Renoir, Picasso, Homer and others; furniture, sculpture, tapestries
Exhibitions: Six temporary exhibitions throughout the year
Publications: American Quilts: European and American Samplers; Annual Report; The Art of Henry Ossawa Tanner; Rembrandt's Christ; The Sculpture of John Rogers; David Smith of Bolton Landing; Rockwell Kent (1882-1971); Elihu Vedder; Hyde Collection Catalogue; History of Glens Falls
Activities: Classes for adults and children; docent training; lectures open to the public, 5-10 vis lectr per year; concerts; gallery talks; tours; competitions with purchase awards; scholarships; original objects of art lent to accredited museums; book traveling exhibitions; originate traveling exhibitions; museum sales shop sells books, reproductions, prints & slides

L Library, 161 Warren St, 12801
Library Holdings: Vols 600; Per subs 3; Hyde Family Archives containing 3000 original documents; Other — Clipping files, exhibition catalogs, memorabilia, photographs

GOSHEN

M HALL OF FAME OF THE TROTTER, 240 Main St, 10924. Tel 914-294-6330.
Dir Philip A Pines; *Graphics Designer* Janet S Hack; *Registrar & Educational Officer* Kathyann Dirr; *Asst Treas* Heidi Ellgren; *Admin Asst* Walter Latzko
Open Mon - Sat 10 AM - 5 PM, Sun & holidays 1:30 - 5 PM. Discretionary admis fee. Estab 1951 to preserve the artifacts of harness racing. There are two galleries; one usually has the museum's permanent collection; the smaller one is used for visiting art shows. Average Annual Attendance: 27,000 - 35,000. Mem: 800; dues $100, $50, $25; annual meeting in July
Income: Financed by endowment and membership
Collections: Large collection of lithographs by Currier and Ives pertaining to harness racing, plus other leading printers of the 19th century; bronzes, dioramas, statuary, wood carvings
Exhibitions: Visiting art shows
Publications: Newsletter, quarterly
Activities: Classes for children; lect open to public; concerts; gallery talks; tours; museum shop sells books, reproductions, prints, jewelry and harness racing memorabilia

M ORANGE COUNTY COMMUNITY OF MUSEUMS AND GALLERIES,*
101 Main St, PO Box 527, 10924. Tel 914-294-5657. *Pres* Philip A Pines; *VPres* R E Kuehne; *Secy* M A Booth
Open Mon - Wed 9 AM - 4 PM, Thurs & Fri 9 Am - Noon, cl holidays. No admis fee. Estab 1961 to coordinate the programs and activities of the member museums and galleries. Promotional agency for local museums. Mem: 100; dues $10 individual, $25 institutional
Income: Financed by membership and CTEA
Activities: Lectures open to the public; extension department serves Orange County and adjacent areas; museum shop sells books
L Library,* 101 Main St, 10924. *Secy* Malcolm Booth
Open Mon - Fri, 9 AM - 5 PM. Estab 1966
Income: Financed by membership and CTEA
Purchases: $76
Library Holdings: Vols 200; Per subs 8; AV — Motion pictures, slides; Other — Manuscripts, photographs
Special Subjects: Architecture
Activities: Lectures open to the public; extension department serving Orange County and adjoining counties

GREENVALE

AMERICAN SOCIETY FOR AESTHETICS
For further information, see National and Regional Organizations

M C W POST COLLEGE OF LONG ISLAND UNIVERSITY, Hillwood Art Gallery, 11548. Tel 516-299-2788 & 299-2789. *Dir* Dr Judith K Van Wagner; *Asst Dir* Leslie Roth
Open Mon - Fri 10 AM - 5 PM, Sun 1 - 5 PM. No admis fee. Estab 1973. Gallery has great appeal to the surrounding North Shore community as well as the student body. The gallery is located in a multimillion dollar student complex; it occupies a space of approx 46 x 92 ft. Average Annual Attendance: 25,000
Income: Financed by university budget, grants and donations
Collections: Contemporary graphics, including works by Rauschenberg, Max Ernst, Pearlstein, Mark di Suvero and Salvador Dali
Exhibitions: Monumental Drawings, including R Serrs, R Nonas, M Westerlund-Roosen, J Highstein; Painting from the Mind's Eye, including B Jensen, T Nozkowski, N Brett, P Brown, D Nelson, L Fishman; The Raw Edge: Ceramics of the 80's, including M Lucero, T Rosenberg, P Gourfain, A Gardner, V Frey; Floored, including L Benglis, C Andre, T Girouard, K Park, H Hammond, L Katzen; The Expressionist Vision, including A Rattner, J Solmon, M Hartley, K Schrag, Ben-Zion, U Romano, K Zerbe; Futurism and Photography; The Artist in the Theatre, including R Grooms, R Lichtenstein, J Shea, E Murray, V James, R Kushner, A Katz; Reflections: New Conceptions of Nature, including P Norvell, J Bartlett, L Nesbitt, A Sonfist, M Stuart, T Winters, J Robbins
Publications: Exhibition catalogs
Activities: Lectures open to public, 20 - 25 vis lectrs per year; concerts; gallery talks; tours; individual paintings & original objects of art lent; lending collection contains books, cassettes, 5000 original art works, 4970 original prints, paintings & sculpture; originate traveling exhibitions; sales shop sells books, original art, reproductions, prints and museum cards

HAMILTON

M COLGATE UNIVERSITY, Picker Art Gallery, Charles A Dana Arts Center, 13346. Tel 315-824-1000, Ext 632. *Dir* Dewey F Mosby, PhD; *Registrar* Leslie Ann Eliet
Open Mon - Fri 10 AM - 5 PM, Sat, Sun, holidays 1 - 5 PM, by appointment academic recesses. No admis fee. Estab 1966, as an educative adjunct to study in the fine arts and liberal arts curriculum. Building designed by architect Paul Rudolph. Average Annual Attendance: 10,000. Mem: 100; dues $5 - $5000
Income: Financed by the University and Friends of the Visual Arts at Colgate
Collections: Herman Collection of Modern Chinese Woodcuts; Herbert Meyer Collection; †Gary M Hoffer '74 Memorial Photography Collection; Luis de Hoyos Collection of Pre-Columbian Art; paintings; photographs; posters; prints; †sculpture
Exhibitions: (1982) Matisse: Jazz; (1983) Dutch Painting in the Age of Rembrandt; Invisible Light: Infra-red Photography by Contemporary Artists; (1984) Old Master Painting and Sculpture
Publications: Exhibiton catalogs
Activities: Lectures open to the public & some for members only; individual paintings & original objects of art lent; book traveling exhibitions; originate traveling exhibitions

HEMPSTEAD

M HOFSTRA UNIVERSITY, Emily Lowe Gallery, Hempstead Turnpike, 11550. Tel 516-560-3275 & 560-3276. *Dir* Gail Gelburd; *Admin Asst* Mary Wakerford; *Asst Cur* Lenore Golub; *Cur Collections* Eleanor Rait; *Assoc Registrar* Susan Albrams; *Assoc Registrar* Barry Trona
Open Wed - Fri 10 AM - 5 PM, Tues 10 AM - 9 PM, Sat & Sun 1 - 5 PM. No admis fee. Estab 1963; a university museum that serves the needs of its student body and the surrounding Nassau County community. Average Annual Attendance: 35,000 - 40,000. Mem: 500; dues $20 - $100
Income: Financed by endowment, membership, foundation and University
Collections: †American paintings & prints; African, Pre-Columbian, New Guinea, Japanese & Indian art; 17th & 18th century European painting; contemporary prints, painting & photographs
Publications: Exhibition catalogs
Activities: Classes for children; lect open to public, 10 - 15 vis lectr per year; gallery talks; tours; individual paintings lent; originate traveling exhibitions

HEWLETT

L HEWLETT-WOODMERE PUBLIC LIBRARY, 1125 Broadway, 11557. Tel 516-374-1967. *Actg Dir* Rebecca Rockmuller; *Art Librn* Clarice Henry
Open Mon - Thurs 9 AM - 9 PM, Fri 9 AM - 6 PM, Sat 9 AM - 5 PM, Sun 1 - 5 PM. Estab 1947 as a Co-Center for art and music. Gallery maintained. Circ 286,819
Income: Financed by state appropriation and school district
Library Holdings: Vols 124,980; Per subs 473; Micro — Reels; AV — Fs, Kodachromes, motion pictures, rec, slides; Other — Clipping files, exhibition catalogs, framed reproductions, pamphlets, photographs, prints, reproductions
Special Subjects: Architecture, Crafts, Film, Photography, antiques
Exhibitions: Hold local exhibits
Publications: Index to Art Reproductions in Books (Scarecrow Press)
Activities: Classes for adults and children; lect open to the public; concerts; gallery talks; tours

HUDSON

M OLANA STATE HISTORIC SITE, RD 2, Off Route 9-G, 12534. Tel 518-828-0135. *Historic Site Mgr* James Ryan; *Interpretive Programs Asst* Yvonne Smith
Open Memorial Day weekend to Labor Day, Wed - Sat 10 AM - 4 PM, Sun 1 - 4 PM, by tour only. Opened as a museum June 1967 to promote interest in and disseminate information of the life, works and times of Frederic Edwin Church, landscape painter of the Hudson River School. The building is a Persian-style residence overlooking the Hudson River. Average Annual Attendance: House 20,000; Grounds 170,000. Mem: 300; dues $15; annual meeting May or June
Income: Financed by state appropriation
Collections: Extensive 19th Century Furniture Collection; Oil Sketches & Drawings by Church; Paintings by Church and other artists; Textile Collection; Decorative Arts
Publications: The Crayon, quarterly (journal produced by Friends of Olana)
Activities: Slide programs, lectures; concerts; original objects of art lent to other institutions who qualify
L Archives, Rd 2, Off Route 9-G, 12534. Tel 518-828-0135
Open to the public with approval of Site Manager; for reference only
Library Holdings: Other — Exhibition catalogs, memorabilia, original art works, photographs, prints
Collections: Family papers, photographs, books, correspondence diaries, receipts

HUNTINGTON

M HECKSCHER MUSEUM, Prime Ave, 11743. Tel 516-351-3250. *Chairman Board Trustees* Miner D Crary Jr; *Dir* Katherine Lochridge; *Assoc Cur* Anne Cohen DePietro; *Registrar* William Titus
Open Tues - Fri 10 AM - 5 PM, Sat, Sun & holidays 1 - 5 PM, cl Mon. No admis fee. Estab 1920, inc 1957, for the maintenance, preservation and operation of the museum building together with the preservation, exhibition and display of all objects and works of art therin. Four galleries, each 20 x 40 ft with 15 ft ceilings, track incandescent and diffused ultraviolet-free fluorescent lighting. Two galleries are used for changing exhibition and two for permanent collections. Average Annual Attendance: 50,000. Mem: 800; dues $20 and up; annual meeting in June
Income: $400,000 (financed by endowment, membership, town appropriations and grants)
Collections: Major works by the Moran family, George Grosz, Thomas Eakins, Lucas Cranach the Elder are included; paintings, sculpture, drawings and prints by 16th - 20th century artists, primarily American with some European
Exhibitions: Land of Whitman; Watercolors and Drawings by Stanton MacDonald Wright; The Photo Secession: The Golden Years of Pictorial Photography in America; From the Pens of the Masters: Eighteenth Century Venetian Drawings From the Robert Lehman Collection of the Metropolitan Museum of Art; A Feast for the Eyes: Contemporary Representations of Food; Tonalism, An American Experience; The Eight Americans and the Canadian Group of Seven; Long Island Painters & Portraits; Huntington Township Art League sponsors annual Long Island Artists Exhibition; regional artists are featured in contemporary exhibitions
Publications: Heckscher News, bi-monthly newsletter
Activities: Classes for adults and children; docent training; lectures open to the public; gallery talks; tours; competitions with awards; scholarships; individual paintings and original objects of art lent to art institutions and galleries; lending collection contains original art works, paintings, sculpture; book traveling exhibitions; originate traveling exhibitions; sales shop sells books, reproductions & slides
L Library, Prime Ave, 11743
Open Tues - Fri 10 AM - 4 PM. Estab to provide range of research materials and unique resources. Open to researchers by appointment, for reference only
Library Holdings: Vols 1000; Per subs 10; AV — Fs, Kodachromes, slides; Other — Clipping files, exhibition catalogs, memorabilia, pamphlets, photographs, reproductions

HYDE PARK

M **FRANKLIN D ROOSEVELT LIBRARY AND MUSEUM,** Albany Post Rd, 12538. Tel 914-229-8114. *Dir* William R Emerson; *Cur Museum* Marguerite B Hubbard
Open daily 9 AM - 5 PM, cl Christmas Day and New Year's Day. Admis adults $1.50 for combination ticket to the Roosevelt Home, Museum and Vanderbilt Mansion, children, senior citizens and school groups free. Estab 1941; contains display on President and Mrs Roosevelt's lives, careers and special interests, including personal items, gifts and items collected by President Roosevelt. Average Annual Attendance: 225,000
Income: $750,000 (financed by congressional appropriation, trust fund)
Purchases: $63,400
Collections: Papers of President & Mrs Roosevelt & of various members of his administration; prints, paintings & documents on the Hudson Valley; paintings, prints, ship models, documents & relics of the history of the United States Navy as well as other marine items; early juvenile books
Publications: The Museum of The Franklin D Roosevelt Library; Historical Materials in the Franklin D Roosevelt Library; The Era of Franklin D Roosevelt
Activities: Tours to school groups upon request; individual paintings and original objects of art lent to museums and other qualified educational institutions; sales shop sells books, prints, slides, postcards, philatelic items, medals, campaign buttons and posters

L **Library,** 259 Albany Post Rd, 12538. Tel 914-229-8114. *Librn* Joseph W Marshall; *Catalog Librn* Sheryl Griffith
Open 9 AM - 4:30 PM, cl national holidays. Estab 1939. Open to scholars for reference only
Income: $325,000 (financed by US government & Trust Fund)
Purchases: $5000
Library Holdings: Newspapers, maps, broadsides; Micro — Fiche, reels; AV — A-tapes, cassettes, fs, motion pictures, rec, v-tapes; Other — Clipping files, manuscripts, memorabilia, original art works, pamphlets, photographs, prints, sculpture
Special Subjects: Franklin-Eleanor Roosevelt; American history & politics, 1913-45; NY colonial history; Hudson Valley history; US Naval history
Collections: Naval history; Hudson River Valley history; early juvenile books; illustrated ornithology; Eleanor and Franklin Roosevelt; US History: 20th Century
Publications: The Era of Franklin D Roosevelt: A Selected Biliography of Periodicals, Essays & Dissertation Literature, 1945-1971; Franklin D Roosevelt and Foreign Affairs

M **ROOSEVELT-VANDERBILT NATIONAL HISTORIC SITES,** 12538. Tel 914-229-9115. *Superintendent* Duane Pearson
Open 9 AM - 5 PM. Admis $1.50, under 16, over 62 and school groups free admis. Estab to preserve the home of Franklin D Roosevelt and the Frederick W Vanderbilt Mansion. Average Annual Attendance: 280,000
Income: Financed by Federal Government
Collections: Furnishings which are original to the historic periods and owners
Publications: Two park brochures, annually
Activities: Tours; sales shop sells books, postcards and slides

M **EDWIN A ULRICH MUSEUM,** Wave Crest on-the-Hudson, Albany Post Rd, 12538. Tel 914-229-7107. *Dir* Edwin A Ulrich
Open May to Oct, Fri - Sun 11 AM - 4 PM. Admis $1. Estab 1956 to exhibit three generation of the Waugh family of painters, 1813 - 1973. Average Annual Attendance: 500
Income: Financed by owner and director
Collections: Collections by Samuel Bell Waugh, 1813-1884; Fred J Waugh 1860-1940; Coulton Waugh, 1896-1973
Exhibitions: Fine art and works by the Waugh family
Activities: Lect open to the public; gallery talks; tours; individual paintings lent to other recognized museums; lending collection contains 300 Kodachromes; sales shop sells books, reproductions, slides and prints

L **Library,** Wave Crest on-the-Hudson, Albany Post Rd, 12538
Open Thurs - Mon 11 AM - 4 PM. Estab 1956. For reference only
Library Holdings: Vols 100; Per subs 1; Micro — Prints; AV — Kodachromes, slides; Other — Clipping files, exhibition catalogs, framed reproductions, memorabilia, original art works, pamphlets, photographs, prints, reproductions
Collections: Early Original Drawings by Fred J Waugh

ITHACA

M **CORNELL UNIVERSITY,** Herbert F Johnson Museum of Art, 14853. Tel 607-256-6464. *Dir* Thomas W Leavitt; *Cur Asian Art* Martie Young; *Assoc Cur* Barbara Blackwell; *Assoc Cur* Gwendolyn Owens; *Coordr Educ* Vas Prabhu; *Coordr Crafts* Louise Haupin; *Registrar* Cathleen Anderson; *Administrator* Nancy Scoones
Open Tues - Sun 10 AM - 5 PM, cl Mon. No admis fee. Estab 1973, replacing the Andrew Dickson White Museum of Art, originally founded in 1953 as Cornell University's Art Museum to serve students, the Tompkins County community & the Finger Lakes region. The collection and galleries are housed in an I M Pei designed building on Cornell University campus overlooking downtown Ithaca and Lake Cayuga. Average Annual Attendance: 80,000. Mem: 1200; dues $10 - $1000
Income: $800,000 (financed by endowment, membership, grants and university funds)
Purchases: $100,000
Collections: †Asian art; †arts of primitive societies; †European & American paintings, †drawings, †sculpture, †graphic arts & †photographs

Exhibitions: Abstract Expressionism: The Formative Years; Architecture and Media: Visual Communications in Environmental Design; Cornell Then, Sculpture Now; Landscape: New Views; Robert Smithson; Painting Up Front; Golden Day, Silver Night: Perceptions of Nature in American Art, 1850-1910; Joshua Neustein; Emerging From the Shadows: The Art of Martin Lewis; Ten Years of Collecting: The Herbert F Johnson Museum of Art 10th Anniversary Exhibition; Olaf Brauner; Jewelry Design: New York State Artists; Twenty Five Years of Discovery at Sardis; Watercolers of David Milne
Publications: Bi-monthly newsletter; exhibition catalogs, 10 per yr
Activities: Workshops for adults and children; lect open to public, 5 - 10 vis lectr per year; gallery talks; tours; individual paintings and original objects of art lent to Cornell University community upon official permission; lending collection contains paintings, sculpture, drawings; originate traveling exhibitions; museum shop sells exhibition catalogs, postcards & notecards

L **Herbert F Johnson Museum Library,** 14853. Tel 607-256-6464. *Asst Cur* Suzette Lane; *Librn Intern* Hope Kuniholm
Open to public by appointment only. Estab 1973. For reference only, primarily for museum and university staff
Income: Financed by museum funds
Library Holdings: Vols 4000; Per subs 20; Monographs; Other — Exhibition catalogs, pamphlets, photographs

L **Fine Arts Library,** Sibley Dome, 14853. Tel 607-256-3710. *Librn* Judith Holliday; *Asst Librn* Patricia Sullivan
Open Sat 10 AM - 5 PM, Sun 1 - 11 PM, Mon - Thurs 9 AM - 11 PM, Fri 9 AM - 6 PM, hours change for University vacation and summer session. Estab 1871 to serve Cornell students. Circ 56,000
Income: Financed through University funds
Purchases: $84,000
Library Holdings: Vols 114,000; Per subs 1800; Micro — Fiche, reels; Other — Exhibition catalogs

JAMAICA

M **JAMAICA CENTER FOR THE PERFORMING & VISUAL ARTS, INC,** Jamaica Arts Center, 161-OA Jamaica Ave, 11432. Tel 212-658-7400. *Pres* Thomas Nemet; *VPres* Celedonia Jones; *Exec Dir* Steven Tennen; *Deputy Dir* William P Miller; *Educ Coordr* Efeyinwa Acosta
Open Mon - Sat 10 AM - 5 PM. Estab 1974 to provide educational opportunity in the visual and performing arts, exhibitions and performances. Three exhibition galleries each. Average Annual Attendance: 55,000
Income: $320,000 (financed by city dept of cultural affairs, foundations, corporations, workshop tuitions, state council of the arts & city youth board)
Exhibitions: (1982) Master Drawings; Spanish Colonial Paintings from the Brooklyn Museum; Ceremonies & Spirits—Art from Africa, Oceania & the Americas; Queens: A Borough of Neighborhoods; Dictadores y Caudillos; Sculpture from the Collection of the Grey Art Gallery & Study Center; American Paintings from the Heckscher Museum; Wallworks; William Henry Johnson: Paintings from the Collection of the National Museum of American Art
Publications: Exhibition catalogs
Activities: Classes for adults and children; dramatic programs; concerts; tours; scholarships; exten dept serves New York City; photographs and blow ups of original photogragh lent; book traveling exhibitions annually; museum shop sells books, reproductions, prints, postcards and ethnic crafts

L **QUEENS BOROUGH PUBLIC LIBRARY,** Art and Music Division, 89-11 Merrick Blvd, 11432. Tel 212-990-0755. *Dir* Constance B Cooke; *Head, Art & Music Division* Claire Kach; *Asst Head Art & Music Division* Esther Lee
Open Mon - Fri 10 AM - 9 PM, Sat 10 AM - 5:30 PM, Sun, Sept - May, Noon - 5 PM. Estab 1933 to serve the general public in Queens, New York
Income: $44,000
Purchases: $44,000
Library Holdings: Vols 84,000; Per subs 265; Micro — Fiche, reels; AV — Cassettes 2500, rec 10,000; Other — Exhibition catalogs, framed reproductions 180, original art works, pamphlets, photographs, prints, reproductions 1,500,000
Collections: The WPA Print Collection

M **SAINT JOHN'S UNIVERSITY,** Chung-Cheng Art Gallery, Sun Yat Sen Hall, Grand Central and Utopia Parkways, 11439. Tel 212-969-8000, Ext 582. *Cur* Abraham P Ho
Open Mon - Sun 10 AM - 8 PM. No admis fee. Estab Oct 1977 to make available Oriental art objects to the public, and to expose the metropolitan area to the Oriental culture through various exhibits and activities. Gallery displays contemporary as well as ancient objects, mainly Oriental with a few western subjects. Average Annual Attendance: 50,000
Income: Financed by the University, endowments and private contributions
Collections: Harry C Goebel Collection containing 595 pieces of rare and beautiful art objects dating from the 7th - 19th century - jades; ivory carvings; netsuke; procelains; lacquerware and paintings from Japan and China; permanent collection contains 650 pieces of Chinese porcelain, paintings, textiles and calligraphy dating from 7th - 20th century
Exhibitions: (1980) Monkey King: A Celestial Heritage; (1981) Graphic Artists; (1982) The Art of Korean Handicraft Exhibit; (1983) Chinese Coins Through The Dynasties; (1984) The Paintings of Master Chang Da-chien
Publications: Exhibition catalogues
Activities: Lectures open to the public, 3 vis lectr per yr; concerts; gallery talks; tours; competitions with awards; individual paintings & original objects of art lent; lending collection contains 200 original art works; original prints; 200 paintings; traveling exhibitions organized and circulated

L **Asian Collection,** Saint Augustine Hall, 11439. *Librn* Hou-Ran Ferng
Open to the public for reference only
Library Holdings: Vols 50,000; Per subs 100
Collections: Collected Works of Chinese and Japanese Calligraphy; Japan Foundation Collection includes 200 volumes on various Japanese art subjects; Series of Chinese Arts

M **STORE FRONT MUSEUM,*** 162-02 Liberty Ave, 11433. Tel 212-523-5199.
Dir & Cur Tom Lloyd; *Asst Dir* Janet DeSisso
Open Tues - Fri 9:30 AM - 4 PM. No admis fee. Estab 1970 to preserve Black
art and history, and for use as a cultural center
Collections: Drawings; paintings; sculpture; tribal African art
Exhibitions: temporary exhibitions
Activities: Classes for adults and children; training programs for professional
museum workers; lect; gallery talks; guided tours; concerts; competitions; hobby
workshops; TV programs; artmobile; traveling exhibitions organized and
circulated
L **Library,*** 162-02 Liberty Ave, 11433
Open to the public; material also for inter-museum loan
Library Holdings: Vols 500
Special Subjects: Black history and culture

JAMESTOWN

L **JAMES PRENDERGAST LIBRARY ASSOCIATION,** 509 Cherry St, 14701.
Tel 716-484-7135. *Dir* Murray L Bob
Open Mon - Fri 9 AM - 9 PM, Sat 9 AM - 5:30 PM, Sun 1 - 4 PM, shorter
hours in summer. Estab 1891 as part of library. Maintains art gallery
Income: Financed by state & local funds
Library Holdings: Vols 5000; Micro — Prints; AV — Motion pictures, rec,
slides; Other — Reproductions, sculpture
Collections: Prendergast paintings, 19th & 20th century paintings; Roger Tory
Peterson, limited edition print collection; Alexander Calder mats
Exhibitions: Traveling Exhibitions; local one-person and group shows
Publications: Mirror Up To Nature, collection catalog
Activities: Lectures open to the public; concerts; competitions; lending collection
contains books, cassettes, film strips, framed reproductions, Kodachromes,
phonorecords & slides; books traveling exhibitions

KATONAH

M **JOHN JAY HOMESTEAD STATE HISTORIC SITE,** New York State Rte
22, PO Box AH, 10536. Tel 914-232-5651. *Historic Site Manager II* Linda M
Connelly; *Interpretive Programs Asst* Jane D Begos; *Cur* Lino S Lipinsky
Open Wed - Sat 10 AM - 4 PM, Sun 1 - 4 PM, May - Sept, Wed - Sat Noon - 4
PM, Sun 1 - 4 PM Sept & Oct, Sat & Sun 1 - 4 PM Nov & Dec. No admis fee.
Estab 1968 to inform public on John Jay and his contributions to national, state
& local history. Ten restored period rooms reflecting occupancy of John Jay and
5 generations of Jay family, 1801-1953; art distributed throughout. Average
Annual Attendance: 25,000. Mem: 200; annual dues $10 and up; annual meetings
in April
Income: Financed by state appropriation
Collections: American art and American decorative arts 1801-1953; John Jay
memorabilia and archives; Westchester mansion with estate and out-buildings
Activities: Classes for adults and children; docent training; lectures open to
public; concerts
L **Library,** New York State Rte 22, PO Box AH, 10536. Tel 914-232-5651
Open by appointment. Owned and administrated by New York State Office of
Parks Recreation & Historic Preservation
Library Holdings: Vols 4000; Other — Clipping files, manuscripts, memorabilia,
original art works, photographs, prints, reproductions, sculpture
Special Subjects: John Jay; National, State & Local History; American Art &
American Decorative Arts
Publications: John Jay, pamphlet

M **KATONAH GALLERY,** 28 Bedford Rd, 10536. Tel 914-232-9555. *Pres* Deborah
McCain; *VPres* Linda Nordberg; *Treas* Richard Weinland; *Adminr* Anne H
Baren; *Secy* Ellen Cabell
Open Tues - Fri 2 - 5 PM, Sat 10 AM - 5 PM, Sun 1 - 5 PM, cl Mon. No admis
fee. Estab 1953 to present exhibitions created with loaned works of art, programs
for schools, films, lectures, demonstrations and workshops. Located on the
ground floor of the Katonah Village Library; the Katonah Gallery consists of
1800 sq ft of exhibition space with a meeting room of 1200 sq ft. Average
Annual Attendance: 25,000. Mem: 1040; dues $15 - $500
Income: Approx $160,000 (financed by membership, contributions, and grants)
Exhibitions: (1982-83) Three Dimensions: Glass, Clay, Fiber; Rodin Bronzes;
Area Artists Group Show; Many Trails: Indians of the Lower Hudson Valley;
Robert Osborn Drawings; Four Masters of Haitian Art; (1983-84) Arthur Dove:
Paintings & Watercolors; Shaker Masterpieces; Forms That Function; The
Product of Design: American Industrial Design; Helen Frankenthaler: Monotypes
Publications: Forgotten Instruments, 1980; exhibition catalogs; Shelter: Models
of Native Ingenuity, 82; Many Trails: Indians of the Lower Hudson Valley, 1983
Activities: Docent training; teacher workshops; programs for schools; lect & films
open to the public, 2 - 10 vis lectr per year; gallery talks; tours; original paintings,
prints & photos lent; lending collection contains motion pictures, photographs,
slides; originate traveling exhibitions

KINDERHOOK

M **COLUMBIA COUNTY HISTORICAL SOCIETY,** 12106. Tel 518-758-9265.
Pres Barbara Rielly; *Secy* Jane Mills; *Exec Dir* Sally A Bottiggi
Open Memorial Day - Labor Day weekends, Tues - Sat 10:30 AM - 4:30 PM,
Sun 1:30 - 4:30 PM, open by appointment Sept - May Mon - Fri 9 AM - 5 PM.
Admis one museum adults $2, children over 12 $1.25, both museums adults $3,
children over 12 $2. Estab 1924 as House of History & Van Alen House to
interpret local and regional, colonial and federal period history, including art of
18th and 19th century and decorative arts. In large hall, wall space used for
exhibition of paintings. Average Annual Attendance: 8000. Mem: 630; dues $5 -
$75; annual meeting third Sat in Oct

Income: $25,000 (financed by membership, endowment, activities, projects,
events and grants)
Purchases: $1800
Collections: Historical objects pertaining to history of county; New York regional
decorative arts; paintings of 18th and 19th centuries
Publications: Newsletter, quarterly; exhibition
Activities: Classes for children; docent training; lectures open to the public, 4 - 6
vis lectr per year; concerts; tours; individual paintings and original objects of art
lent to other museums; lending collection contains books, cassettes, original art
works, original prints, paintings, photographs & sculpture; originate traveling
exhibitions; museum shop sells books, magazines, gifts, prints
M **Library,** Broad St, 12106. *Exec Dir* R Piwonka
Open June - August Tues - Sat 10:30 AM - 4:30 PM, Sun 1:30 - 4:30 PM;
September - May Mon - Fri 9:30 AM - 5:00 PM, appointment advisable. Estab
1926 to maintain research files on the county and regional art history. For
reference only
Library Holdings: Vols 3000; Per subs 2; AV — Cassettes, lantern slides;
Other — Clipping files, exhibition catalogs, manuscripts, memorabilia, original art
works, pamphlets, photographs, prints, sculpture
Collections: County and Regional history; Hudson Valley architecture, Dutch
culture; Local and Regional paintings and decorative arts
Activities: Classes for adults; docent training; lectures open to public, 4-6 vis
lectr per year

KINGSTON

M **PALISADES INTERSTATE PARK COMMISSION,** Senate House State
Historic Site, 296 Fair St, 12401. Tel 914-338-2786. *Historic Site Mgr* Leigh
Rehner Jones
Open Wed - Sat 10 AM - 5 PM, Sun 1 - 5 PM; cl Mon & Tues. No admis fee.
Estab 1887. The site is one of 38 New York State historic sites. Senate House is
where the first New York State Senate met in 1777; furnished as 18th century
middle-class dwelling
Collections: 18th and 19th century decorative arts; 18th and 19th century
paintings and other works of art, particularly those by James Bard, Jervis
McEntee, Ammi Phillips, Joseph Tubby and John Vanderlyn
Publications: Exhibition catalogs
Activities: Classes for children; lect open to the public, 4-6 vis lectr per yr; concerts
L **Reference Library,** 12401. Tel 914-338-2786
Open Weds - Sat 10 AM - 5 PM, Sun 1 - 5 PM, cl Jan - Mar. Estab 1887. Open
by appointment to scholars, students & researchers for reference only
Library Holdings: Vols 2500; Other — Manuscripts
Collections: Collection of letters relating to the artist John Vanderlyn
Publications: Exhibit catalogs

LAKE PLACID

M **LAKE PLACID CENTER FOR MUSIC, DRAMA & ART,** Fine Arts Gallery,
Saranac Ave, 12946. Tel 518-523-2512. *Board Pres* Charles L Ritchie; *Dir* Mary
Ann Ricketson
Open 9 AM - 5 PM. Estab 1972 to serve as an art resource center for national
organizations & individual artists of national prominence in visual & performing
arts. Average Annual Attendance: 6000
Income: Financed by foundation funds, grants & tuition
Exhibitions: Gallery offers 10 exhibitions a year; Center programs reflects
fellowship program
Activities: Classes for adults; workshops; concerts; scholarships; book traveling
exhibition; originate traveling exhibitions
L **Nettie Marie Jones Fine Arts Library,** Saranac Ave, 12946. Tel 518-523-2512.
Library Dir Suellen Linn
Open Mon - Fri 9 AM - 5 PM. Estab 1972 to serve as a unique resource center
for visual and performing arts to the Center for Music, Drama and Art, and the
surrounding North Country. Circ 1500
Income: $38,000 (financed by private foundation and memberships)
Purchases: $9400
Library Holdings: Vols 9500; Per subs 120; Micro — Fiche; AV — Rec, slides;
Other — Exhibition catalogs, memorabilia, original art works, photographs,
prints, sculpture
Collections: Stedman and Moses Glass Plate Negative Collection; Victor Herbert
Memorabilia
Exhibitions: monthly exhibitions featuring work by North Country artists

LONG BEACH

O **LONG BEACH ART ASSOCIATION,*** 111 W Park Ave, 11561. Tel 516-432-
7201. *Co-Pres* Clar Olin Schaenfeld; *Co-Pres* David B Hecht
Founded in 1952 by a group of interested residents determined to form an
organization to promote art activity and appreciation with emphasis on quality
Exhibitions: Artists-of-the-Month Shows; July Outdoor Show and Sale, co-
sponsored by the City of Long Beach; May Open Juried Show; Material Awards
Shows; three Membership Shows annually
Publications: Exhibitions brochures
Activities: Workshops; demonstrations; lect; discussions

L **LONG BEACH PUBLIC LIBRARY,** Art Dept, 111 W Park Ave, 11561. Tel
516-432-7201. *Dir* George Trepp
Open Oct - May Mon, Wed, Thurs 9 AM - 9 PM, Tues & Fri 9 AM - 6 PM, Sat
9 AM - 5 PM, Sun 1 - 5 PM. Estab 1928 to serve the community with
information and services, including recreational, cultural and informational
materials. The Long Beach Art Association in cooperation with the library
presents monthly exhibits of all types of media in a room 32 ft x 22 ft with
seating capacity of 50
Library Holdings: Micro — Fiche, reels; AV — Cassettes, fs, motion pictures,

rec; Other — Memorabilia, pamphlets, photographs
Collections: Local history; 300 photographs of Long Beach
Exhibitions: Local talent; membership shows; juried exhibitions; politician myth and reality; Telma Hillman's spectra sculpture
Publications: Monthly newsletter
Activities: Dramatic programs; lectures open to public, 18-20 vis lectrs per year; concerts; gallery talks; films; tours

LONG ISLAND CITY

O **THE INSTITUTE FOR ART AND URBAN RESOURCES, INC,** 46-01 21st St, 11101. Tel 212-784-2084
Open Thurs - Sun Noon - 6 PM. Admis $1 donation. Estab 1972 as a non-profit arts organization providing low-cost studios for national and international artists as well as exhibitions in galleries on the premises and special project rooms in which artists can work out experimental ideas. Project Studios One was rehabilitated from an abandoned 19th century school house in Long Island City with spaces for over 50 artists; The Clocktower, located at 108 Leonard St in Manhattan is on the 13th floor of a city office building where there are 2 exhibition spaces and more studios for national artists. Both Project Studios One and The Clocktower are opened throughout the year with three main project periods. Average Annual Attendance: 35,000
Collections: Contemporary art; sculpture
Publications: Exhibition catalogs
Activities: Lectures open to public; concerts; gallery talks; tours; book traveling exhibitions; originate traveling exhibitions; museum shop sells catalogues
M Project Studios One, 46-01 21st St, 11101. Tel 212-784-2084.
Exec Dir Alanna Heiss; *Program Dir* Ronald Lynch;
Fiscal Administrator Gwen Darien; *Publicity Dir* Thomas Finkelpearl;
Executive Asst Rita Sirignano; *Fiscal Asst* Laura Spitzer
Open Thurs - Sun Noon - 6 PM. Admis donation $1. Estab 1972 as artists studios & exhibitions of contemporary & experimental art. Gallery contains 25,000 sq ft of space. Annual Attendance: 35,000. Mem: Dues leadership council $5000, patrons council $1000
Collections: Painting; sculpture; photography; fashion; video; film; architecture
Exhibitions: Changing exhibitions of permanent collection
Publications: Studio Artists Yearbook, annually; exhibition catalogs
Activities: Childrens classes; lectures open to public; book traveling exhibitions; originate traveling exhibitions; sales shop sells exhibition catalogues, posters & postcards

MOUNTAINVILLE

M **STORM KING ART CENTER,** Old Pleasant Hill Rd, 10953. Tel 914-534-3115.
Dir David R Collens
Open Mid-May - Oct Mon, Wed - Sun 2 - 5:30 PM, cl Tues, grounds cl Nov - Mar. Admis $2. Estab 1960. Average Annual Attendance: 30,000. Mem: Dues life $10,000, patron $1000, contributing $100
Collections: 200 acre sculpture garden with over 95 large scale outdoor contemporary sculptures, including works by: Bourgeois, Calder, Caro, di Suvero, Grosvenor, Hepworth, LeWitt, Liberman, Moore, Noguchi, Rickey, David Smith, Snelson, Stankiewicz, Von Schlegell, Westerlund, Witkin
Exhibitions: Changing exhibitions of contemporary sculpture in the Museum; permanent collection of outdoor sculpture plus loan sculptures in special exhibtions
Publications: Sculpture at Storm King; brochures; exhibition catalogs; poster
Activities: Gallery and garden tours; lect

MOUNT VERNON

L **MOUNT VERNON PUBLIC LIBRARY,** Fine Art Dept, 28 S First Ave, 10550. Tel 914-668-1840. *Library Dir* Marcia Schwartz
Open Mon - Thurs 9 AM - 9 PM, Fri 9 AM - 6 PM, Sat 9 AM - 5 PM, Sun 1 5 PM, cl Sat & Sun during July and Aug. No admis fee. Estab 1854. Library contains Doric Hall with murals by Edward Gay, NA; Exhibition Room with frescoes by Louise Brann Soverns; and Norman Wells Print Alcove, estab 1941
Income: $1,836,730 (financed by city & other funds)
Library Holdings: Vols 17,000; Art books 17,000; AV — A-tapes 1293, cassettes 1293, rec 11,500; Other — Framed reproductions 200, photographs 11,500
Special Subjects: Architecture, Ceramics, Costume Design & Construction, Decorative Arts, Painting — American, Photography, Prints
Exhibitions: Costume dolls; fans; metalwork; one-man shows of painting, sculpture & photographs porcelains; silver; woodcarving; jewelry; other exhibits changing monthly cover a wide range of subjects from miniatures to origami
Activities: Lectures open to public, 6 vis lectr per yr; concerts; gallery talks; tours; individual paintings & original objects of art lent to library members

MUMFORD

M **GENESEE COUNTRY MUSEUM,** * Flint Hill Rd (Mailing add: Box 1819, Rochester, 14603). Tel 716-538-6822. *Dir* Stuart B Bolger
Open Mon - Fri 10 AM - 4 PM, Sat - Sun 10 AM - 5 PM, July - Labor Day Daily & Holidays 10 AM - 5 PM. Admis adults $6, children and students $2.50, special rates for groups and tours. Mem: Dues Advisor $1000, Crier $500, Overseer & Corporate $100, Selectman $50, Neighbor $30, Friends $20
Collections: 18th, 19th & 20th century paintings, sculptures & graphics
Publications: Booklets; Genesee Country Village; Sporting Art Gallery; monthly newsletter

NEW PALTZ

M **STATE UNIVERSITY OF NEW YORK AT NEW PALTZ,** College Art Gallery, Smiley Art Bldg, 12562. Tel 914-257-2439. *Dir* Neil C Trager; *Admin Asst* Christine Morse
Open Mon - Fri 10 AM - 4 PM. No admis fee. With an exhibition schedule of 12 major shows per year, the College Art Gallery provides support for the various art curricula and serves as a major cultural resource for the College and surrounding community. There are two adjoining galleries, South Gallery 59 x 56 ft, North Gallery 42 x 23 ft. Average Annual Attendance: 15,000 - 20,000
Collections: Oriental Prints, Sculpture, Artifacts, Photographs, Folk Art, Posters; Pre-Columbian Art; Painting, principally 20th Century America; Prints, Primitive African and New Guinea
Exhibitions: (1982) Hermann Junger, jewelry; John Ferro, sculpture; Aldo Argiro Memorial Ceramics Exhibition; BFA & MFA Presentation; Oriental prints from permanent collection
Activities: Lect open to public; concerts; gallery talks; competitions; individual paintings and original objects of art lent to museums and galleries; lending collection contains artifacts; original prints; paintings, photographs, sculpture, folk art, textiles, drawings, posters

NEW ROCHELLE

M **COLLEGE OF NEW ROCHELLE,** Castle Gallery,* Castle Place, 10801. Tel 914-632-5300, Ext 423. *Dir* Ellen Kenny; *Asst to Dir* Kathy Ferrerri
Hours open vary with shows. No admis fee. Estab 1979 as a professional art gallery to serve the college, city of New Rochelle and lower Westchester. Located in Leland Castle, a gothic revival building, listed in National Register of Historic Places; gallery is modern facility, with flexible space
Exhibitions: (1980) Quiltforms 1980; International Mail Art Show; The Domesticated Sublime-Picturesque Palaces of Westchester County; Shouts in Silence-works by Deaf Children; Feline Ephemera-Victorian Trade Cards; (1981) Henry Moore Maquettes; David Finn: A Photographic Exploration of the Sculpture of Henry Moore; The Person and the Planet; 12 Latin American Artists; Art & Technology; The Great American Circus: Imagery in the Folk Art Tradition; Jennifer Cecere; Ona Lindquist: Synthetic Interiors; New Rochelle in the Ragtime Era (1982) Contemporary American Realists: The Figure (consortium exhibition); London College of Fashion-Works by students
Publications: Newsletter
Activities: Docent training; lectures; gallery talks; tours

L **NEW ROCHELLE PUBLIC LIBRARY,** Art Section, Library Plaza, 10801. Tel 914-632-7878. *Dir* Eugene L Mittelgluck; *Head of Reference* Ethelynn Williams
Open Mon 10 AM - 6 PM, Tues 10 AM - 9 PM, Wed Noon - 6 PM, Thurs Noon - 9 PM, Fri & Sat 10 AM - 5 PM, Sun 1 - 5 PM, Oct - May. Estab 1894
Library Holdings: Vols 7800; Per subs 22; Micro — Fiche, reels; AV — Slides; Other — Clipping files, framed reproductions, original art works, pamphlets, photographs
Exhibitions: All shows, displays and exhibits are reviewed and scheduled by professional advisory panel
Activities: Lect and demonstrations; lending collection contains framed prints and art slides
O **New Rochelle Art Association,** * Library Plaza, 10801. Tel 914-632-7878. *Pres* Inga Meyer
Estab 1912. Mem: 200; dues $20; monthly meeting
Income: Financed by membership
Exhibitions: 4 per year, including one open juried show
Activities: Classes for adults; Lectures open to public, 4 vis lectrs per year; competitions with awards

NEW YORK

O **ACTUAL ART FOUNDATION,** Seven Worth St, 10013. Tel 212-226-3109. *Pres* Valerie Shakespeare; *VPres* Susan Davis; *Secy* Fred Seeman; *Treasurer* Margaret Thatcher; *Board Member* Clyde Lynds; *Board Member* Naomi Newman
Estab 1983 to promote Actual Art
Income: $75,000 (financed by endowment & public fund raising)

M **AFRICAN-AMERICAN INSTITUTE,** * 833 United Nations Plaza, 10017. *Dir Admin* Wilbur Jones; *Dir Art Exhibitions Programs* Marie Therese Brincard
Open Mon - Fri 9 AM - 5 PM, Sat 11 AM - 5 PM, cl national holidays. No admis fee
Collections: Traditional and modern African arts and crafts
Publications: Africa Report, bi-monthly magazine; South Africa Namibia Report, monthly newsletter; brochures; pamphlets
Activities: Tours

M **AFRO ARTS CULTURAL CENTRE, INC,** African Arts Museum & Gallery, 2191 Adam C Powell, Jr Blvd, 10027. Tel 212-831-4410. *Pres* Emma Robertson; *VPres* Andrew Campbell; *Secy* Lillie Ward; *Exec Dir* Simon Bly Jr; *Mus Dir* Ruby M Owooh; *Business Mgr* Isaiah Bly
Open daily 9 AM - 6 PM including holidays. No admis fee, groups adults $1.75, children $1.50. Estab 1947 to project the grandeur of the African history and the greatness of its culture, heritage and art; thereby improving and strengthening the American cultural and educational pattern. Afro Arts gallery has the largest collection of African fine arts in America. The larger collection consists of Congolese paintings created between the 40's and 60's during the Patrice Lamumba period, First Premier of Congo. Average Annual Attendance: 15,000. Mem: 35; dues $24; meetings second & fourth Sat each month; members must have abiding respect & interest in African history, culture, heritage & education
Income: $12,000 (financed by members and fund raising concerts and cultural educational programs)
Collections: Congolese Art, Religious Art from Ethiopia, Sand Art from Ghana, Silk Thread Art from Nigeria, US paintings

Exhibitions: Mr & Miss United Nations Children's Program for Public & Parochial School
Publications: Afro Arts Book, irregular
Activities: Classes for adults & children; dramatic programs; docent training; inservice training for board of education teachers; lectures open to public, monthly vis lectr; concerts; gallery talks; tours; competitions with awards; individual paintings & original objects of art lent; museum shop sells original art; reproductions; prints & African artifacts

M **A I R GALLERY,*** 63 Crosby St, 10012. Tel 212-966-0799. *Dir* Renata Lac
Open Tues - Sat 10 AM - 6 PM. No admis fee. Estab 1972 as cooperative women's gallery representing 20 American women artists; also provides programs and services to women artists community. Average Annual Attendance: 20,000. Mem: 20; dues $350
Income: Financed by membership, city and state appropriation
Exhibitions: One-woman exhibitions; invitational which can be international, regional and performance or theme shows
Publications: Invitational exhibition catalogues, bi-annually
Activities: Lect open to public

ALLIED ARTISTS OF AMERICA, INC
For further information, see National and Regional Organizations

AMERICAN ABSTRACT ARTISTS
For further information, see National and Regional Organizations

AMERICAN ACADEMY AND INSTITUTE OF ARTS AND LETTERS
For further information, see National and Regional Organizations

AMERICAN ARTISTS PROFESSIONAL LEAGUE, INC
For further information, see National and Regional Organizations

AMERICAN COUNCIL FOR THE ARTS
For further information, see National and Regional Organizations

M **AMERICAN CRAFT COUNCIL MUSEUM,** 44 W 53rd St, 10019. Tel 212-397-0630. *Dir* Paul J Smith; *Registrar* Doris Stowens
Open Tues - Sat 10 AM - 5 PM, Sun & Holidays 11 AM - 5 PM, cl Mon. Admis adults $1.50, children under 16, students and senior citizens $.75. Estab 1956 by the American Craft Council (see National Organizations). Average Annual Attendance: 47,000. Mem: Dues benefactors $1000, patrons $500, friends $250, sponsors $100, contributors $50, subscribing $29.50
Collections: Works of American craftsmen since 1900 in ceramics, paper, fiber, wood, metal, glass, plastics, enamels
Exhibitions: Young Americans (metal); Felting;   For the Tabletop; Beyond Tradition;   Art for Use; Young Americans: Metal; Exhibitions from the Permanent Collection
Publications: American Craft, bi-monthly magazine; exhibition catalogs; bibliographies, directories and manuals on crafts
Activities: Book traveling exhibitions
L **Library,*** 44 W 53rd St, 10019. Tel 212-397-0638. *Librn* Joanne Polster
Open Tues, Wed & Fri Noon - 4:30 PM, Sat Noon - 4:30 PM. Estab 1956 to promote the work of contemporary American crafts and crafts people. The Library is open to members Tues, Wed & Fri, general public on Sat, and is owned and maintained by the American Craft Council (see entry under National Organizations)
Library Holdings: Vols 3500; Per subs 40; data on craft courses, suppliers, organizations and the state arts councils; AV — A-tapes, slides, v-tapes; Other — Clipping files, exhibition catalogs, pamphlets, photographs
Collections: Archives of the American Craft Museum; Photo-Archives of the American Craft Museum; Portfolio Files of 2500 contemporary American craftspeople working in all media
Publications: Books; bibliographies; directories

THE AMERICAN FEDERATION OF ARTS
For further information, see National and Regional Organizations

AMERICAN FINE ARTS SOCIETY
For further information, see National and Regional Organizations

AMERICAN INSTITUTE OF GRAPHIC ARTS
For further information, see National and Regional Organizations

M **AMERICAN MUSEUM OF NATURAL HISTORY,** Central Park West at 79th St, 10024. Tel 212-873-1300. *Pres* Robert G Goelet; *Dir* Dr Thomas D Nicholson
Open Mon, Tues, Thurs & Sun 10 AM - 5:45 PM, Wed, Fri & Sat 10 AM - 9 PM, cl Thanksgiving and Christmas. Admis by contribution (suggested, adults $3, children $1.50). Estab 1869 as a museum for the study and exhibition of all aspects of natural history. Exhibition spaces include Roosevelt Memorial Hall, Gallery 3, Naturemax Gallery, Akeley Gallery, Center Gallery & Gallery 1 opening Apr 1984. Average Annual Attendance: 2,500,000. Mem: 470,000
Income: Financed by special presentations, contributions
Exhibitions: Permanent exhibitions include: Hall of Asian People; Hall of Ocean Life & Biology of Fishes; Arthur Ross Hall of Meteorites; John Lindsley Hall of Earth History; Hall of Man in Africa; Hall of Mexico and Central America; Morgan Memorial Hall of Minerals and Gems; Margaret Mead Hall of Pacific Peoples
Publications: Natural History, magazine; Curator; Bulletin of the American Museum of Natural History; Anthropological Papers of the American Museum of Natural History; American Museum of Natural History Novitates; annual report
Activities: Classes for adults and children; dramatic programs; lectures open to the public; concerts; gallery talks; tours; scholarships
L **Library,** Central Park West at 79th St, 10024. *Chairwoman Library Services* Nina J Root
Library Holdings: Vols 400,000; AV — A-tapes, fs, Kodachromes, lantern slides, motion pictures, rec, slides, v-tapes; Other — Clipping files, exhibition catalogs, manuscripts, memorabilia, original art works, pamphlets, photographs, prints, reproductions, sculpture

AMERICAN NUMISMATIC SOCIETY
For further information, see National and Regional Organizations

O **AMERICAN SCANDINAVIAN FOUNDATION GALLERY,** 127 E 73rd St, 10021. Tel 212-879-9779. *Pres* Patricia McFate; *Dir* Lynn Carter; *Dir Programs* Christian Malcolm; *Programs Asst* Florence Seery
Open Tues - Sat Noon - 5 PM. No admis fee. Foundation estab 1911, gallery estab 1980 as an exhibition space for art from Denmark, Finland, Iceland, Norway & Sweden. Gallery occupies the second floor of the American Scandinavian Foundation. Average Annual Attendance: 5000. Mem: 4500; annual dues $25
Exhibitions: Antero Kare, Evening Whispers Darkly; Bjorn Ruriksson Photographs; Olli Lyytikainen Paintings; artwork is selected for exhibition by a committee of professional arts advisors, the gallery presents five exhibitions a year varying the art according to media & country
Publications: The Scandinavian Review, quarterly; SCAN, newsletter 8 times a yr
Activities: Lectures open to public, 10 vis lectr per yr; awards; scholarships

AMERICAN WATERCOLOR SOCIETY
For further information, see National and Regional Organizations

O **THE ARCHITECTURAL LEAGUE,** 457 Madison Ave, 10022. Tel 212-628-4500. *Pres* Emilio Ambasz; *Executive Dir* Marita O'Hare
Open Mon - Fri 10 AM - 5 PM. Admis seminars $5, mem free. Estab 1881 to promote art and architecture; serves as a forum for new and experimental ideas in the arts. Sponsors Archive of Women in Architecture. Mem: 1200; dues over 35 years $85, under 35 years $50, students $25; annual meeting April
Exhibitions: Annual Juried Exhibition of Architectural Renderings
Publications: Art tour map of New York City; exhibition catalogues; posters
Activities: Lect; slide lect; walking tours; competitions; awards

M **ARCHIVES OF AMERICAN ART,** Smithsonian Institution, National Headquarters, 41 East 65th St, 10021. Tel 212-826-5722. *Chmn* Mrs Otto L Spaeth; *Pres* A Alfred Taubman; *Dir* Richard N Murray
Open Mon - Fri 9 AM - 5 PM. No admis fee. The Archives of American Art, founded in 1954, has assembled the world's largest collection of material documenting the history of the visual arts in this country. Eight million items of original source material are available on microfilm to scholars, students, writers and researchers. Affiliated with the Smithsonian Institution since 1970, the Archives preserves its original documents in Washington with microfilm copies in its regional branches. Mem: 2000; dues $50 and Up
Income: Financed by federal appropriation, private contributions, gifts & foundation grants
Collections: †Manuscript collection pertinent to the study of art in America
Publications: Archives of American Art: A Directory of Resources; Arts in America: A Bibliography; card catalog of the manuscript collections; quarterly journal
—**Washington Center,*** AA-PG Building, Eighth & F Streets, NW, Washington, DC 20560. Tel 202-357-2781. *Sr Cur* Garnett McCoy
—**New York Area Center,*** 41 East 65th St, New York, NY 10021. Tel 212-826-5722. *Dir* William McNaught
—**Midwest Area Center,*** 5200 Woodward Ave, Detroit MI 48202. Tel 313-226-7544. *Dir* Dennis Barrie
—**New England Area Center,*** 87 Mount Vernon St, Boston, MA 02108. Tel 617-223-0951. *Dir* Robert Brown
—**M H de Young Memorial Museum,*** Golden Gate Park, San Francisco, CA 94118. Tel 414-556-2530. *Dir* Paul Karlstrom
Special Subjects: Art History
Publications: The Archives of American Journal, quarterly
—**Texas Area Center: Museum of Fine Arts,*** Houston, TX 77052. Tel 713-526-1361. *Area Collector* Sandra J Curtis
Special Subjects: Art History
Publications: The Archives of American Art Journal, quarterly

O **ART COMMISSION OF THE CITY OF NEW YORK,*** City Hall, 10007. Tel 212-566-5525. *Pres* Muriel R Silberstein-Storfer; *VPres* Norval White; *Secy* Margot Gayle; *Adminr* Annette Kuhn
Open by appointment only. No admis fee. Estab 1898 to review designs for city buildings and the works of art proposed for their embellishment. Portraits are installed in Governors Room and other areas in City Hall. Mem: 11
Income: Financed by city appropriation
Collections: 100 portraits of historic figures, state, city and national
Publications: City Hall, A Guide To It's Art and Architecture
Activities: Lending collection contains 100 paintings, sculpture
O **Associates of the Art Commission, Inc,** City Hall, 10007. Tel 212-566-5525. *Pres* David Levine; *VPres* Francis D Rogers; *Secy* Allyn Cox
Estab 1913 to advise and counsel Art Commission as requested. Mem: 35; dues $35; annual meeting in Jan
Income: Financed by membership

ART DEALERS ASSOCIATION OF AMERICA, INC
For further information, see National and Regional Organizations

ART DIRECTORS CLUB, INC
For further information, see National and Regional Organizations

O **ART INFORMATION CENTER, INC,** 280 Broadway #412, 10007. Tel 212-227-0282. *Pres* Anne Chamberlain; *Dir* Dan Concholar; *Treas* George Tanier; *Board Dir Member* Stanley William Hayter; *Board Dir Member* Jacob Lawrence; *Board Dir Member* Sylvan Cole; *Board Dir Member* Inger Tanier
Open 10 AM - 5 PM. Organized 1959, inc 1963, as a free tax-deductible clearing house of contemporary fine arts. Maintains international files of living artists with their gallery affiliations and where they have shown since 1960 (c 65,000 artists); files of galleries, their rosters of artists and catalogs of current and recent shows (c 550 in New York, 300 in other US cities, 50 in foreign cities); files of slides of work by unaffiliated artists (c 750 artists and 8-12 slides each) for use by dealers

looking for new talent. The Center helps to channel the many artists in New York, and those coming to New York, seeking New York outlets for their work. It aids new galleries to start, helps artists to find out where they can learn special disciplines and skills. Furnishes information on many aspects of contemporary art to museums, art schools, collectors and the public. All documentation kept constantly up-to-date

O **ARTIST-CRAFTSMEN OF NEW YORK,*** 130 E 28th St, 10016. Tel 212-679-8154. *Pres* Monona Rossol
Estab 1958 as successor to New York Society of Craftsmen and New York Society of Ceramic Arts. Exhibitions and demonstrations are arranged for the purpose of broadening public interest in and knowledge of crafts; developing standards of taste in design and workmanship. Affiliated with American Craftsmen's Council. Mem: 300; qualification for mem: by submission of work by artist-craftsman member to membership jury with emphasis laid upon professional standards of craftsmanship and the quality of work; non-craftsman may become associate or contributing member on election by the Board of Governors; annual meeting in March, with six membership meetings per year
Exhibitions: Annual exhibition in New York City; periodic exhibitions at National Design Center and other New York City locations
Publications: Newsletter, 4 - 6 per year

ARTISTS' FELLOWSHIP, INC
For further information, see National and Regional Organizations

ARTISTS GUILD INC OF NEW YORK
For further information, see National and Regional Organizations

O **ARTISTS TECHNICAL INSTITUTE,*** 207 W 106th St, 10025. Tel 212-749-7819. *Pres* Herb Aach; *VPres & Secy* Bena F Mayer; *Treas* Felicia Van Veen; *Dir* Ralph Mayer
Estab 1959 for the publication of results of scientific laboratory investigations of the materials of creative painting and sculpture
Income: Financed by appropriations and grants from NEA and private donations
Publications: Journal, quarterly; publication of audio-visual materials

O **ARTS & BUSINESS COUNCIL,*** 130 E 40th St, 10016. Tel 212-683-5555. *Exec Dir* Sybil C Simon
Estab 1973 and serves as a liaison agency between the arts and business communities and establishes and administers projects benefiting to both
Publications: Winterfare Directory, annual

O **ART STUDENTS LEAGUE OF NEW YORK,*** 215 W 57th St, 10019. Tel 212-247-4510. *Pres* R D Franza; *Men's VPres* R Reid; *Women's VPres* Anne Gordon; *Exec Dir & Dir Libr* Rosina A Florio
Open Sun - Fri 8:45 AM - 10 PM, Sat 8:45 AM - 4:45 PM. No admis to members. Estab 1875 to maintain art school and membership activities. Maintains an art gallery open to public for league exhibits. Average Annual Attendance: 2400. Mem: 6000; dues $5; annual meeting Dec
Income: Financed by tuitions and investments
Exhibitions: Exhibitions by members, students and instructors
Publications: Art Students League News, monthly
Activities: Lectures open to public; scholarships
L **Library,** 215 W 57th St, 10019
Reference library for students and members

M **ASIA SOCIETY, INC,** Gallery, 725 Park Ave, 10021. Tel 212-288-6400. *Chmn Society Board of Trustees* Roy Huffington; *Pres* Robert Oxnam; *Dir Gallery* Allen Wardwell; *Asst Dir Gallery* Sarah Bradley
Open Tues - Sat 10 AM - 5 PM, Thurs until 8:30 PM, Sun Noon - 5 PM. Admis fee $2. Inc 1957 as a non-profit organization to further greater understanding and mutual appreciation between the US and peoples of Asia. The Asia House Gallery was inaugurated in 1960 to acquaint Americans with the historic art of Asia. In 1981 the Asia Society came into possession of a permanent collection, the John D Rockefeller 3d Collection of Asian Art, which is shown in conjunction with four temporary exhibitions each year. Average Annual Attendance: 60,000. Mem: 6000; dues $25 and up; annual meeting in May
Income: Financed by membership, contributions and grants
Collections: †Mr & Mrs John D Rockefeller 3d Collection of Asian Art; loans obtained from the US and foreign collections for special exhibitions
Exhibitions: (1982) Arts of the Solamic Book; (1983) Euralsi, Narrative Scrolls from Japan
Activities: Three or more lectures for members given by guest specialists in connection with each exhibition and recorded lectures by the gallery education staff available to visitors; loan exhibitions originated; sales shop selling exhibition catalogs, cards & publications concerned with Asian art, culture, political & economic affairs & crafts

O **ASSOCIATION OF ARTIST-RUN GALLERIES,** 164 Mercer St, 10012. Tel 212-226-3107. *Exec Dir* Joellen Bard; *Exhibitions Coordr* Linda Schonfeld; *Asst Program Dir* Dennis Corbett
Open Tues & Thurs 11 AM - 4 PM. No admis fee. Estab 1974 as a non-profit membership association composed of artist-run galleries & spaces. Sponsors an information resource center for member galleries, artists & general public. Thirty five artist-run galleries. Mem: Dues patron $100, sponsor $50, contributor $25, individual $10
Income: Financed by endowment, membership, city and state appropriation
Exhibitions: US Customhouse-World Trade Center; Museum of the City of New York
Publications: AAR Guide; Fly Tracks, reviews; Time & Space Concepts in Art; The 10th St Days; How to Begin & Maintain an Artist Run Space; Newsletter
Activities: Educ program in conjunction with various schools off-campus programs; lectures open to public; concerts; gallery talks; tours

O **ASSOCIATION OF HISPANIC ART,*** 200 E 87th St, 10028. Tel 212-369-7054. *Exec Dir* Elsa Ortiz Robles
Estab 1975 to promote the general concept of Hispanic arts as an intergral part of the arts community in the US. Maintains central information office & a mailing list of active arts organizations
Publications: Hispanic Artist & Arts Organization Directory; Newsletter, bimonthly; Spanish Calendar, monthly

M **ATLANTIC GALLERY,*** 458 W Broadway, 10012. Tel 212-228-0944. *Dir & Pres* Rich Samuelson; *Asst Dir* Stephanie Lebowitz; *Secy* Carol Levin
Open Tues - Sun Noon - 6 PM. No admis fee. Estab 1974 as an artist-run gallery presenting the work of members and guests artists in solo exhibitions and group shows. Gallery is 25 x 75 ft second-floor space. Average Annual Attendance: 12,000. Mem: 32; dues $360; monthly meetings
Income: Financed by membership and artists of the gallery
Exhibitions: Continuing series of solo shows
Publications: Periodic flyers
Activities: Life-drawing sessions; concerts; poetry readings, all open to public; sales shop sells original art

AUDUBON ARTISTS, INC
For further information, see National and Regional Organizations

O **LEO BAECK INSTITUTE,** 129 E 73rd St, 10021. Tel 212-744-6400. *Exec Dir* Dr Fred Grubel; *Pres* Max Grunewald; *Art Cur* Dr Aline Pritchard
Open daily 9 AM - 5 PM; Fri 9 AM - 3 PM Nov - March. Estab 1955 for history of German-Speaking Jewry. Center includes library & archives. Mem: 1000; dues $12.50 - $35
Collections: Drawings, paintings, prints, sculpture, ritual objects, textiles from 15th - 20th centuries; 19th - 20th Century German-Jewish Artists, including Max Siebermann, Lesser Ury, Ludwig Meidner, Hugo Steiner-Praj
Exhibitions: Berlin 1900-1930; selected oil paintings
Publications: Year Book; LBI News, semi-annually
Activities: Educ dept; lectures open to the public, 10 vis lectr per yr

M **BARTOW-PELL MANSION MUSEUM AND GARDEN,*** Pelham Bay Park, 10464. Tel 212-885-1461
Open Tues, Fri, Sun 1 - 5 PM, cl 3 wks in summer. Admis adults $.50, children under 12 free, special group rates. Estab 1914
Collections: Greek revival restoration; period furnishings; paintings; sunken gardens

M **CANADIAN CONSULATE GENERAL DEPT OF EXTERNAL AFFAIRS,** 49th Parallel Centre for Contemporary Canadian Art, 420 W Broadway, 10012. Tel 212-925-8349. *Dir* France Morin; *Cultural Asst* Elodie Lauten; *Installation Mgr* Robert Keay
Open Tues - Sat 11 AM - 6 PM. Estab 1981 as a showcase for leading edge of contemporary Canadian art. There are three galleries and a video room
Income: Financed by Dept of External Affairs
Exhibitions: Robin Collyer, installations and mixed media; Videotapes by: Marshalore, Tom Dean, Elizabeth Vander Zaag, Paul Wong

O **CARAVAN OF EAST AND WEST, INC,** Caravan House Galleries,* 132 65th St, 10021. Tel 212-744-4793. *Gallery Dir* John Lally; *Asst Dir* Franca P Lally
Open Tues - Sat 11:30 AM - 5:30 PM, cl Sun & Mon. No admis fee. Estab 1928 as a non-profit foundation, chartered to help artists show their work to the general public & chartered to help communication between peoples of the world. The Caravan House has two galleries located in a town house with a gallery downstairs & one upstairs. Average Annual Attendance: 14,000. Mem: 690; dues $10; annual meeting in April
Income: Financed by endowment, membership
Collections: Two exhibitions every month January to May, September to December
Publications: Pen Friend Guide, biannually
Activities: Classes for adults; lect open to public, 12 vis lectr per year; concerts; gallery talks

O **CARTOONISTS GUILD,*** 156 W 72nd St, 10023. Tel 212-873-4023. *Executive Dir* Ron Wolin
Estab 1967 to create new market areas for cartoons & cartoonists; to provide legal & credit services to members; to increase public appreciation of cartooning as an art form. Mem: 275
Publications: Newsletter, monthly; cartooning books

M **THE CATHEDRAL MUSEUM,*** Cathedral of Saint John the Divine, 1047 Amsterdam Ave, 10025. Tel 217-678-6923, 678-6913. *Dir* Barbara Bonner-Socarides; *Asst Dir* Susan Schreiber
Open Mon - Fri 11 AM - 4 PM, Sat & Sun 1 PM - 4 PM. No admis fee. Estab 1974. The museum building was erected in the 1820's and forms part of the complex of the Cathedral of Saint John the Divine. Average Annual Attendance: 500,000
Income: Financed by federal government appropriations and Cathedral assistance
Collections: Old Master Paintings; decorative arts; sculptures; silver; tapestries; vestments
Exhibitions: Monthly Photography Exhibitions; annual exhibitions planned to spotlight specific areas of the Cathedral's permanent art collection
Activities: Lectures open to public, 10 vis lectr per year; concerts; gallery talks; tours

O **CENTER FOR ARTS INFORMATION,** 625 Broadway, 10012. Tel 212-677-7548. *Exec Dir* Ellen Thurston; *Assoc Dir* Jana Jevnikar
Open weekdays 11 AM - 5 PM, Wed 11 AM - 7 PM. Estab 1976 to furnish management and funding information to artists and arts organizations. Maintains small reference library dedicated to art information
Publications: Artist Colonies; Careers in the Arts: A Resource Guide; Film Service Profiles; International Cultural Exchange; Catalog III
L **Library,** New York, 10012
Reference only
Library Holdings: Vols 5000; Per subs 310; Other — Clipping files

M CENTER FOR INTER-AMERICAN RELATIONS ART GALLERY, 680 Park Ave, 10021. Tel 212-249-8950; Telex 22-6000. *Dir Visual Arts Program* John Stringer; *Deputy Dir* Kathleen McGuire; *Gallery Asst* Denise Vito
Open Tues - Sun Noon - 6 PM, cl Mon (during exhibitions). Admis suggested $1 contribution. Estab 1967 to enlarge knowledge and appreciation in the United States of the art and cultural heritage of other areas in the Western Hemisphere. Three galleries with 8-9 loan exhibitions a year of Latin American and Canadian art. Average Annual Attendance: 10,000. Mem: 900
Income: $120,500
Exhibitions: (1982-83) A Century of Change in Guatemalan Textiles; Nazca Lines: Ancient Peruvian Desert Art; Performance Cycle: Maler/Marin/ MacLennan/Pena/Ripley/Vater; Women of the Americas; Recent Editions; New Spaces: Castles/Rabinovich/Ragazzoni; Homage to Simon Bolivar; Printed Matta: Highlights from 4 Decades; Printmaking by Roberto Matta Objects of Bought Pride: Northwest Coast Indian Art; Pioneer Photographers of Brazil; Warp-patterned Weaves of the Andes
Publications: Exhibition catalogs
Activities: Classes for adults and children; lect open to the public, 20 vis lectr per year; gallery talks; tours; originate traveling exhibitions; sales shop sells books

C THE CHASE MANHATTAN BANK, NA,* 410 Park Ave, 10022. Tel 212-223-6131. *Advisor on the Arts* Jack Boulton; *Second VPres & Mgr* Merrie Good
Estab 1959 to enhance Bank offices world-wide. Collection displayed in branches, offices in New York City, state and world-wide
Collections: Largely contemporary American, approximately 6500 works in all media
Exhibitions: Selection from the Chase Manhattan Bank Art Collection
Publications: Acquisitions report, annual
Activities: Lectures for employees; individual objects of art lent to museum and gallery exhibitions; originate traveling exhibitions

M CHINA INSTITUTE IN AMERICA, China House Gallery, 125 East 65th Street, 10021. Tel 212-744-8181. *Dir* Wan-go H C Weng; *Asst Dir* Anita Christy
Open Mon - Fri 10 AM - 5 PM, Sat 11 AM - 5 PM, Sun 2 - 5 PM.
Contribution. Estab 1966 to promote a knowledge of Chinese culture. One-room gallery. Average Annual Attendance: 12,000. Mem: 800; dues resident $50, non-resident $35, academic $25
Income: $30,000 (financed by membership government grants and sponsors)
Exhibitions: Art of the Han; Embroidery of Imperial China; Origins of Chinese Ceramics; Treasures from The Metropolitan Museum of Art; Treasures from The Newark Museum; Chinese Porcelain in European Mounts; Tz'u-chou Ware; Masterpieces of Sung & Yuan Dynasty Calligraphy; Communion of Scholars: Chinese Art at Yale; Chinese Bamboo Carving; Chinese Ceramics of the Transitional Period: 1620-1683; Chinese Traditional Architecture; Chinese Printed Books
Publications: Exhibition catalogs, 2-3 a year
Activities: Classes for adults & children; lectures open to public; concerts; gallery talks; originate traveling exhibitions; sales shop sells books

C CITIBANK, NA,* 399 Park Ave, 10043. Tel 212-559-1000. *In Charge Art Coll* Laura Lynn Miner
Estab to enhance the environment. Collection displayed in offices of the corporate headquarters
Collections: Art reflects the working environment of the various departments, including international, American and New York themes
Activities: Individual objects of art lent for museum exhibitions

L CITY COLLEGE OF NEW YORK, Cohen Art Library, Convent Ave & 138th St, 10031. *Chief Librn* Ann K Randall; *Chief Reference Div* Mary Cope; *Special Collections & Archives* Barbara Dunlap
Open Mon - Thur 9 AM - 8 PM, Fri 9 AM - 5 PM, Sat Noon - 6 PM. Estab 1847 to support the education at the City College
Library Holdings: Vols 22,000; Per subs 40; Micro — Fiche; Other — Clipping files, exhibition catalogs, memorabilia, pamphlets
Collections: History ofCostume
L Architecture Library,* 3300 Broadway, Rm 206, 10031. Tel 212-690-5329. *Librn* Sylvia H Wright
Library Holdings: Vols 14,000; Per subs 149; Other — Pamphlets 11,000
Special Subjects: Architecture, Landscape Architecture

COLLEGE ART ASSOCIATION OF AMERICA
For further information, see National and Regional Organization

L COLUMBIA UNIVERSITY, Avery Architectural and Fine Arts Library, 117th St W of Amsterdam Ave, 10027. Tel 212-280-3501. *Librn* Angela Giral
Open Mon - Thurs 9 AM - 11 PM; Fri 9 AM - 5 PM; Sat 12 AM - 6 PM; Sun 2 - 10 PM. Estab 1890 for reference only
Library Holdings: Vols 200,000; Per subs 1000; original documents; Micro — Fiche, reels; Other — Clipping files, exhibition catalogs
Special Subjects: Architecture, Art History
Collections: Over 100,000 original architectural drawings, mainly American
Exhibitions: Selected acquisitions 1960-1980; exhibition in honor of Adolf K Placzek; Low Memorial Library
Publications: Catalog of Avery Memorial Architectural Library; Avery Index to Architectural Periodicals
L Dept of Art History & Archeology,* Photographic Collection, 420 Schermerhorn Hall, 10027. Tel 212-280-5203. *Prof* Jane Rosenthal
Library Holdings: Gallery announcements 15,000; Other — Photographs 155,000
Collections: Berenson I-Tatti Archive; Dial Iconographic Index; Haseloff Archive; Bartsch Collection; Gaiglaere Collection; Arthur Kingsley Porter Collection; Ware Collection; Courtauld Collection; Marburger Index; Windsor Castle; Chatsworth Collection; Bibles; Millard Meiss Collection; James Q Reber Collection

O COMMITTEE FOR THE VISUAL ARTS, INC, 105 Hudson St, 10013. Tel 212-254-8310. *Pres* Donald Droll; *VPres* Mary Miss; *Secy* Claire Copley; *Exec Dir* Linda Shearer; *Asst Dir* Susan Wyatt; *Development Dir* Judith Lyczko; *Cur* Valerie Smith; *Installation Coordr* Frank Farmer; *Program Coordr* Kenji Fujita
Open Tues - Sat 11 AM - 6 PM. Estab 1973 as a non-profit contemporary art exhibition space & artists service organization that provides artists with professional & financial support while presenting the most exciting new art developments to the public
Activities: Administers two grant programs
M Artists Space Gallery, 105 Hudson St, New York. Tel 212-226-3970
Open Tues - Sat 11 AM - 6 PM. No admis fee for exhibitions, films & events $4. Estab 1973 to assist emerging & unaffiliated artists. Five exhibition rooms & hall gallery. Average Annual Attendance: 20,000
Income: Financed by National Endowment for the Arts, New York State Council, corporate & foundation funds & private contributions
Exhibitions: (1983) Selections; 3 Artists Select 3 Artists; Ernst Benkert; International Projects: Canada; Benefit Exhibition: Works on Paper; Group Exhibition; International Projects: Belgium; Sally Hazelet Drummond; International Projects: Holland; Mowry Baden; International Projects: Italy; A Decade of New Art: Artists Space
Activities: Gallery talks by appointment; financial aid to artists for public presentation; book traveling exhibitions; originate traveling exhibitions; junior museum
L Unaffiliated Artists File, Committee for the Visual Arts, 105 Hudson St, New York, 10013
Open Tues - Sat 11 AM - 6 PM. Slide file of over 2000 New York state artists. Available to dealers, critics, curators & artists for reference only

CONFEDERATION OF AMERICAN INDIANS
For further information, see National and Regional Organizations

M COOPER-HEWITT MUSEUM, Smithsonian Institution, 2 E 91st St, 10028. Tel 212-860-6868. *Dir* Lisa Taylor; *Asst Dir for Coll* Christian Rohlfing; *Cur Decorative Arts* David McFadden; *Cur Drawings & Prints* Elaine Evans Dee; *Cur Textiles* Milton Sonday; *Exhib Coordr* Dorothy Twining Globus; *Librn* Robert Kaufman
Open Tues 10 AM - 9 PM, Wed - Sat 10 AM - 5 PM, Sun Noon - 5 PM, cl Mon and major holidays. Admis $1.50, no admis Tues after 5 PM. Founded 1895 as the Cooper Union Museum, to serve the needs of scholars, craftsmen, students, designers and everyone who deals with man's living world. Museum is based on large and varied collections of decorative arts, architecture and a library strong in those fields. Exhibitions are based on the Museum's vast collections or loan shows illustrative of some phase of design & make available the best examples of man's creative genius from the past and present. Its emphasis on education is expanded by special courses and seminars related to design in all forms and of all periods. The Main galleries occupy the first and second floors; exhibitions relate to the collections and some aspects of design; the Contemporary Design Gallery has changing exhibitions relating to architecture and design. Average Annual Attendance: 200,000. Mem: 7000; dues $25-$1000
Income: Financed by private contributions, membership and partly Smithsonian Institution
Collections: Drawings and paintings including works by Frederic Church, Winslow Homer, Thomas Moran and other 19th century American artists; ceramics, furniture and woodwork, glass, original drawings and designs for architecture and the decorative arts; 15th - 20th century prints; textiles, lace, wallpaper; 300,000 works representing a span of 300 years
Exhibitions: Gardens of Delight, writing; Oceanliner; Hair; Now I Lay Me Down to Eat; Alvar Aalto; Cooper-Hewitt Collection on Furniture, Glass, Silver and Porcelain Puppets and Japanese Holdings; Fantastic Design and Illustration in Britain 1850-1930; Indelible Images: Contemporary Advertising Design; Ludwig II of Bavaria, The Dream King; Ma, Space-Time in Japan; Roma Interrotta; The Shopping Bag: Portable Graphic Art; Smithsonian (whole show); Urban Open Spaces: Streets-Street Graphics and Street Furniture; Take Your Choice: Contemporary Product Design; The Suburbs, Resorts
Publications: The Smithosian Illustrated Library of Antiques; books on decorative arts; collection handbooks; exhibition catalogues; quarterly newsletter
Activities: Classes for adults and children; dramatic programs; docent training; Master's Degree program in European Decorative Arts through Parsons & New School; lect open to public; tours; seminars; concerts; gallery talks; paintings and original objects of art lent to museums and cultural institutions; lending collection contains over 300,000 original prints; book traveling exhibitions; originate traveling exhibitions; museum and sales shop sells books, reproductions, slides, posters
L Cooper-Hewitt Museum Branch Library,* Two E 91st St, 10028. Tel 212-860-6887
Open Mon - Fri 9 AM - 5:30 PM
Income: Financed through SIL budgets
Library Holdings: Vols 30,000; Per subs 47; picutres and photographs 1,500,900, original documents; Other — Exhibition catalogs, manuscripts, memorabilia, photographs, prints, reproductions
Special Subjects: Advertising Design, Decorative Arts, Graphic Design, Industrial Design, Interior Design, Color, Materials of Design
Collections: Donald Deskey Archive; Henry Dreyfuss Archive; Nancy McCelland Archive; Ladislav Sutnar Archive

L COOPER UNION FOR THE ADVANCEMENT OF SCIENCE & ART, Library, Cooper Square, 10003. Tel 212-254-6300, Ext 360. *Head Librn* Elizabeth Vajda; *Art & Architecture* Ginni Weimer; *Slide & Picture* Carol Abatelli; *Engineering & Science* Irene Perry
Estab 1859 to support the curriculum of the three professional schools: Art, Architecture, Engineering
Library Holdings: Vols 76,000; Per subs 350; Micro — Fiche 250, reels 3400; AV — Lantern slides 12,000, slides 34,000; Other — Clipping files 75,000
Special Subjects: Antiquities-Greek, Antiquities-Roman, Architecture, Art History, Calligraphy, Commercial Art, Drawings, Etchings & Engravings, Graphic Arts, Landscape Architecture, Painting - Dutch, Painting - European, Painting - French, Painting - German, Painting - Italian, Painting - Spanish, Photography
Activities: Non-degree classes for adults; lectures open to the public, 20 - 30 vis lectr per yr; scholarships

O **LOVIS CORINTH MEMORIAL FOUNDATION, INC,** 145 E 16th St, 10005.
Tel 212-674-6514. *Dir* H Borchardt; *Treasurer* M Weinstein; *Secy* Thomas
Corinth; *Art Ed* M Klopfer
Open by appointment. No admis fee. Estab 1969-70 as tax-exempt, non-profit,
educational. Organized to dispense information about German art as represented
by the painter Lovis Corinth to the inquiring public at large. Mem: Members
must be over 21 years of age; dues $120; annual meeting Oct
Income: Financed by membership
Exhibitions: Charlotte Berend Show

COUNCIL OF AMERICAN ARTIST SOCIETIES
For further information, see National and Regional Organizations

O **CREATIVE TIME,** 66 West Broadway, 10007. Tel 212-619-1955. *Exec Dir*
Anita Contini; *Public Relations Dir* Andrea Pedersen; *Program Dir* Gerard
McCarthy
Open 10 AM - 5 PM. Estab 1973 to present visual and performing art programs
in public spaces throughout New York City. Spaces include a variety of
temporarily unused and artistically public locations. Average Annual Attendance:
50,000
Income: $200,000 (financed by National Endowment for the Arts, NY State
Council on the Arts, private corporations and foundations)
Publications: Creative Time, documentation book
Activities: Lectures open to the public, 10 vis lectr per yr

M **CULTURAL COUNCIL FOUNDATION,** Fourteen Sculptors Gallery, 164
Mercer St, 10012. Tel 212-966-5790. *Board of Dir* Harold Olejarz; *Board of Dir*
Shaw Stuart
Open Tues - Sun 11 AM - 6 PM. No admis fee. Estab 1973 to offer the artist
exhibition space, possible reviews by art periodicals, and a forum for the
exchange of ideas and techniques; to offer the public the chance to see fresh new
work. Average Annual Attendance: 20,000. Mem: 20; dues $480
Income: Financed by membership
Activities: Originate traveling exhibitions

O **DIA ART FOUNDATION, INC,*** 107 Franklin St, 10013. Tel 212-431-9232.
Pres Philippa Pellizzi; *VPres* Heiner Friedrich; *VPres* Helen Winkler; *Cur* Jeffrey
Krass
Estab 1974 for planning, realization and presentation of important works of
contemporary art. Committment to artist's participation in display of works in
long term, carefully maintained installations. Galleries in US & abroad
Collections: Works by 13 contemporary American & European artists,
retrospective in nature
Publications: The Foundation has published collections of poetry, translations of
poetry and religious writings
Activities: Paintings & art objects lent to established museums or galleries

O **THE DRAWING CENTER,** 137 Greene St, 10012. Tel 212-982-5266. *Dir*
Martha Beck; *Assoc Cur* Marie Keller; *Dir Development* Jane Fluegel
Open Tues - Sat 11 AM - 6 PM, Wed 11 AM - 8 PM. Estab 1977 to express the
quality and diversity of drawing through exhibition and education. Average
Annual Attendance: 125,000. Mem: 300; dues $35 and up
Income: $285,000 (financed by foundations and corporations)
Exhibitions: Group show of emerging artists: Selections 23, Selections 24,
Selections 25; Reading Drawings: Selections from the Victoria and Albert
Museum
Publications: Exhibition catalogs
Activities: Classes for adults and children; lectures open to the public; originate
traveling exhibitions

THE DRAWING SOCIETY
For further information, see National and Regional Organizations

O **ELECTRONIC ARTS INTERMIX, INC,** 84, Room 301, 10011. Tel 212-989-
2316, 989-2317. *Pres* Howard Wise; *Distribution* Lori Zippay; *Editing Post
Production Facility* Mathew Danowski
Open daily 9:30 - 5:30. Estab as a non-profit corporation to assist artists seeking
to explore the potentials of the electronic media, particularly television as a
means of personal expression
Income: Financed by videotape and editing fees and in part by federal and state
funds and contributions
Collections: Several hundred video cassettes
Publications: Electronic Arts Intermix Videocassette Catalog, annual

M **EL MUSEO DEL BARRIO,** 1230 Fifth Ave, 10029. Tel 212-831-7272. *Dir*
Jack Agueros; *Cur* Gladys Pena; *Co-Dean of Fine Arts School* Jorge Soto;
Co-Dean of Fine Arts School Oscar Ciccone; *Co-Dean of Fine Arts School* Pepe
Castillo
Open Tues - Fri 10:30 AM - 4:30 PM, Sat & Sun 10 AM - 4 PM. No admis fee.
Estab 1969 to conserve and display works by Puerto Rican artists and other
Hispanic artists. Located on Museum Mile. Gallery space divided into 4 wings:
Northwest Wing houses Santos de Palo, East Gallery will house Pre-Columbian
installation, F-Stop Gallery devoted to photography and Childrens Wing opened
fall of 1982. Average Annual Attendance: 15,000. Mem: 400; dues $15
Collections: 16mm Films on History, Culture and Art; †300 Paintings and †5000
Works on Paper, by Puerto Rican and other Latin American Artists; Pre-
Columbian Caribbean Artifacts; Santos (Folk Religious Carvings)
Exhibitions: Permanent and temporary traveling exhibitions
Activities: Classes for adults and children; dramatic programs; lectures open to
public, 25 visiting lecturers per year; concerts; gallery talks; tours; awards;
scholarships; individual and original ojbects of art lent to other museums and
galleries; originate traveling exhibitions; sales shop sells books, magazines, jewelry
and posters; Junior Museum to open in fall of 1982

C **EQUITABLE LIFE ASSURANCE SOCIETY,*** 1285 Ave of the Americas,
10019. Tel 212-554-1234. *Dir Corporate Support* William P Epke
Annual amount of contributions and grants $75,000; supports employee gifts to
all arts organizations; direct grants to 8 national arts service organizations
Activities: Support technical assistance programs

M **FASHION INSTITUTE OF TECHNOLOGY,** Galleries,* 277 W 27th St,
10001. Tel 212-760-7675, 760-7700. *Dir* Marty Bronson
Open Tues & Wed 10 AM - 8 PM, Thurs - Sat 10 AM - 5 PM, cl Sun, Mon and
holidays. No admis fee. Estab May 1975 to bring to the student body and the
community at large a variety of exhibitions in the applied and fine arts. Gallery
contains 11,500 sq ft of space divided into four galleries. The gallery on the main
floor is used for small exhibits while the three galleries located in the lower level
are used for major exhibitions. Average Annual Attendance: 50,000
Income: Financed by endowment and grants
Collections: Largest working costume and textile collection in the world
Publications: Facades by Bill Cunningham (book); Poiret (book)
Activities: Classes for adults; docent training; lect open to the public, 2 visiting
lectrs per year; gallery talks; tours; exten dept serving the museum personnel;
individual paintings and original objects of art lent to major museums and art
institutions; traveling exhibitions organized and circulated

L **Library,*** 277 W 27th St, 10001. Tel 212-760-7695. *Dir* Barbara Jones; *Art Librn*
Marjorie Miller; *Art Librn* Lorraine Weberg
Open Mon - Fri 9 AM - 10 PM, Sat Noon - 5 PM, Sun Noon - 8 PM. Estab
1948 to meet the academic needs of the students and faculty and to serve as a
resource for the fashion industry. Open for reference only
Library Holdings: Vols 125,000; Per subs 600; sketchbook collections; Micro —
Reels; AV — A-tapes, cassettes, fs, motion pictures, rec, slides, v-tapes; Other —
Clipping files, exhibition catalogs, memorabilia, pamphlets, photographs
Special Subjects: Costume Design & Construction, Fashion Arts
Collections: Oral History Project on the Fashion Industry; several sketchbook
collections
Publications: Re:Sources, quarterly
Activities: Originate traveling exhibitions

FEDERATION OF MODERN PAINTERS AND SCULPTORS
For further information, see National and Regional Organizations

M **55 MERCER,** 55 Mercer St, 10013. Tel 212-226-8513. *Pres* Tom Nozkowski;
Secy Elfi Schuselka
Open Tues - Sat 10 AM - 6 PM. No admis fee. Estab 1970 to give unaffiliated
artists a space to show their work. Average Annual Attendance: 8000. Mem: 16;
dues $750; meeting every 2 months
Income: Financed by membership dues and grants
Exhibitions: One person & group shows including: TzviBen-Aretz, Geneen
Estrada, Susan Gardner, Brigid Kennedy, China Marks, Jane Rosenberg, Gail
Swithenbank, Ellen Weider, Russell Maltz, Jane Handzel, Arden Scott, Robert
Porter, Maggie Saliske, Peter Brown, Joan Gardner, Tom Clancy, Nicolas
Collins, Elfi Schuselka, Gerry Griffin, Grace Wapner, Gloria Greenberg, Joan
Gillman Negron, Dominick Capobianco, Diane Karol, Chip Duyck, Andrew
Nash, Donna Page, Sandy Strauss, Elisa D'Arrigo, Carla Tardi, Arlyne Bayer,
Rolando Briseno, Carol Hepper, Dana Crooks, Tom Thorson, Duane Schat, Don
Boyd, Ellen Levy, Carol J Steen, Jerilea Zempel, Margo Herr, Robert Buxbaum,
Bruce Cunningham, Elizabeth Dworkin, Hank de Ricco, Beckerman Balkan,
Denise Corley, Douglas Hilson, Eliot Lable, Dennis Leder, Susan Morningstar,
Gerald Nichols, Drew Shiflett, Charles Searles, Richard Snyder, Mary Ann
Unger, Gerald Wolfe
Activities: Apprenticeship program; competitions; individual paintings and
original objects of art lent to college shows

C **FORBES MAGAZINE,*** 60 5th Ave, 10011. Tel 212-620-2200
Collections: Faberge Imperial Eggs Collection; Peter Paul Rubens canvas; van
Gogh drawing; Renoir oil; Victorian paintings

O **FOUNDATION FOR THE COMMUNITY OF ARTISTS,** 280 Broadway
Suite 412, 10007. Tel 212-227-3770. *Exec Dir* Jimmie Durham; *Pres* Walter
Weissman; *VPres* Lori Antonacci; *Adminr* Paul Smith
Non-profit membership organization. Mem: 3000; dues $17.50
Income: $100,000 (financed by membership, state appropriation, federal funds,
grants, individual contributions)
Publications: Art & Artists, monthly; The Art Law Primer; Health Hazards
Manual for Artists
Activities: Seminars; workshops; lectures open to the public

L **FRANKLIN FURNACE ARCHIVE, INC,** 122 Franklin St, 10013. Tel 212-925-
4671. *Executive Dir* Martha Wilson; *Cur* Matthew Hogun; *Publicist* Ann
Rosenthal; *Performance Coordr* Bill Gordh
A non-profit corporation dedicated to the cataloging, exhibition and preservation
of book-like work by artists
Library Holdings: Vols 9000; Per subs 25; AV — A-tapes, cassettes, slides, v-
tapes; Other — Exhibition catalogs, pamphlets
Special Subjects: Artists' use of language, Latin American, Japanese & Icelandic
artists' books; Cubist books
Publications: Flue, quarterly
Activities: Intern training program; performance program; lectures open to public;
concerts; gallery talks; book traveling exhibitions 2-3 per year; originate traveling
exhibitions

M **FRAUNCES TAVERN MUSEUM,** 54 Pearl St, 10004. Tel 212-425-1778.
Chmn Bd James F Stebbins; *VChmn* Stephen Ball; *Dir* Christine Miles;
Development Officer Jeffrey Ryan; *Cur Collection* Robert Goler; *Public
Information Officer* Mary Stiles
Open Mon - Fri 10 AM - 4 PM. No admis fee. Estab 1907 for focus on early
American history, culture, historic preservation & New York City history.
Museum is in historic Fraunces Tavern & four adjacent 19th century buildings on
the National Register. Contains 18th & 19th century period rooms, galleries for
permanent collection, changing exhibits & an auditorium. Average Annual
Attendance: 100,000-150,000. Mem: 250; dues $15-$25
Income: $250,000 (financed by endowment & memberships)
Collections: 17th, 18th, 19th & 20th century prints, paintings, artifacts &
decorative arts relating to early American history, culture & historic preservation;
New York City history; George Washington & other historic figures in American
history

Exhibitions: Taverns: For the Entertainment of Friends & Strangers; Irish Silver from the 17th-19th Centuries; A Toast to Freedom: New York Celebrates Evacuation Day; Legacy of LaFayette; City Streets: Paintings of New York City, Heidi Pagremanski
Publications: The Jewish Community in Early New York, booklet; Early American Taverns; For the Entertainment of Friends & Strangers
Activities: Classes for adults & children; dramatic programs; docent training; lectures open to public, 30 vis lectr per yr; originates traveling exhibitions; museum shop sells books, reproductions & postcards

L **FRENCH INSTITUTE-ALLIANCE FRANCAISE LIBRARY,** 22 E 60th St, 10022. Tel 212-355-6100. *Librn* Fred J Gitner
Open Mon - Thurs 10 AM - 8 PM, Fri 10 AM - 6 PM, Sat 10 AM - 1:30 PM. Estab 1911 to encourage the study of the French language and culture. Maintains art gallery. Circ 27,500
Income: Financed by endowment and membership
Library Holdings: Vols 37,500; Per subs 80; AV — Cassettes, rec; Other — Exhibition catalogs
Special Subjects: French Art
Collections: Architecture, costume, decorative arts, paintings
Exhibitions: Rogi Andre: Portraits; Sam Levin: French Stars, portraits
Publications: Acquisitions list, quarterly
Activities: Classes given; lect open to public, 50 vis lectr per year; concerts; originate traveling exhibitions

L **FRICK ART REFERENCE LIBRARY,** 10 E 71st St, 10021. Tel 212-288-8700. *Librn* Helen Sanger; *Asst Librn & Indexer of Photographs* Marie C Keith; *Cataloguer* Blanche V Houston; *Reference Librn* Frances E Young; *Assoc Reference Librn* William Russell Ferguson
Open Mon - Fri 10 AM - 4 PM, Sat 10 AM - Noon; cl Sun, holidays & month of August. Estab 1920 as a reference library to serve adults and graduate students interested in the history of European and American painting, drawing, sculpture, illuminated manuscripts. For reference only
Library Holdings: Vols 85,872; 54,711 sales catalogs; Other — Exhibition catalogs, pamphlets 68,074, photographs 420,000
Publications: The Story of the Frick Art Reference Library: The Early Years, by Katharine McCook Knox

M **FRICK COLLECTION,** 1 E 70th St, 10021. Tel 212-288-0700. *Pres* Henry Clay Frick II; *Dir* Everett Fahy; *Cur* Edgar Munhall; *Research Cur* Bernice Davidson; *Adminr* David M Collins; *Mgr Sales & Info* Martha Hackley; *Supt* Fred Jakob
Open Tues - Sat 10 AM - 6 PM, Sun 1 - 6 PM; cl Jan 1, July 4, Thanksgiving, Dec 24 & 25. Admis adults $1, students & senior citizens $.50; children under 10 not admitted. Estab 1920; opened to public 1935 as a gallery of art. The Frick Collection is housed in the former residence of Henry Clay Frick (1849-1919), built in 1913-14 and alterations and additions were made 1931-1935 and a further extension and garden were completed in 1977. The rooms are in the style of English and French interiors of the 18th century. Average Annual Attendance: 266,290. Mem: 300 Fellows; dues $250 minimum contribution
Income: $3,100,000 (financed by endowment, membership, admissions)
Collections: 15th-18th century sculpture, of which Renaissance bronzes are most numerous; 14th-19th century paintings, with fine examples of Western European masters and suites of Boucher and Fragonard decorations; Renaissance and French 18th century furniture; 17th-18th century Chinese and French porcelains; 16th century Limoges enamels; 16th-19th century drawings and prints
Publications: French Clocks in North American Collections; The Frick Collection, An Illustrated Catalog; Guide to the Galleries; Handbook of Paintings
Activities: Lect open to public; concerts; museum shop selling books, prints, slides, postcards, greeting cards

M **GALERIA VENEZUELA,** 7 E 51st St, 10022. Tel 212-826-1660. *Dir* Graciela Pantin
Open Mon - Fri 9 AM - 4 PM. Estab in 1974 as a center for the promotion of Venezuelan art in the context of cross-cultural manifestations. Average Annual Attendance: 3000
Income: Financed by private & government institutions
Collections: Paintings & prints by Venezulan artists
Exhibitions: Group show: Textos Infernos, Bonevardi, Maler, Mazzei, Zerpa, Cvevas; Nos Americas, Photographers: Villar, Antman, La Rosa, Rojas, Vengochea, Perezluna, Ranney, Plachy; Bolivar X15X New York: Irazabal, Gutierrez, Bermudez, Nunez, Capriles & Fernandez
Activities: Individual paintings lent to other galleries

M **GALLERY OF PREHISTORIC PAINTINGS,** 220 Fifth Ave, 10001. Tel 212-689-7518. *Dir* Douglas Mazonowicz
Open Mon - Fri 9 AM - 5 PM, Sat 9 AM - Noon, other times by appointment. No admis fee. Estab 1975 to make available to the public the art works of prehistoric peoples, particularly the cave paintings of France, Spain and the Sahara Desert. Large display area. Average Annual Attendance: 10,000
Income: Financed by private funds
Collections: Early American Indian Rock Art; Rock Art of Eastern Spain; Rock Art of the Sahara; serigraph reproduction editions of Cave Art of France and Spain
Publications: Newsletter, quarterly
Activities: Classes for adults and children; Cave Art-in-Schools Program; lect open to the public; gallery talks; tours; lending collection contains books, cassettes, framed reproductions, 1000 Kodachromes, motion pictures, original prints, 1000 photographs, 2000 slides; traveling exhibitions organized and circulated; sales shop selling books, magazines
L **Library,*** 20 E 12th St, 10003
Open Mon - Fri 9 AM - 5 PM, Sat 9 AM - Noon. Estab 1975 to make information available to the general public concerning the art works of prehistoric peoples. For reference only
Library Holdings: Vols 200; Per subs 10; AV — Cassettes, Kodachromes, motion pictures, slides; Other — Clipping files, exhibition catalogs, framed reproductions, manuscripts, pamphlets, photographs, prints, reproductions, sculpture

C **THE GILMAN PAPER COMPANY,*** 111 W 50th St, 10020. Tel 212-246-3300. *Cur* Pierre Apraxime
Collections: Al Reinhardt; Robert Mangold; Ellsworth Kelly; Dan Flavin; Robert Morris; conceptual art; Robert Smithsons Script for the Spiral Jetty; Claes Oldenburg drawing Potatoe; architectural drawings; photography; Cameron; Duchamp; Steiglitz; Sheeler; Moholy-Nagy
Activities: Tours

L **GROLIER CLUB LIBRARY,** 47 E 60th St, 10022. Tel 212-838-6690. *Pres* F S Sheeter; *Secy* G T Tonselle; *Librn* Robert Nikirk
Open Mon - Fri 10 AM - 5 PM, Sat 10 AM - 3 PM, cl Sun. Estab 1884, devoted to the arts of the book. Mem: 625
Purchases: $15,000
Library Holdings: Vols 65,000; Per subs 35; Other — Prints
Special Subjects: Bibliography
Collections: †Bookseller and auction catalogs from 17th century
Exhibitions: (1983-84) Four centennial exhibitions bearing on Grolier history and activities
Publications: The Grolier Club 1884-1984: Bibliography, Its History and Development

C M **GRUMBACHER INC,** 460 W 34th St, 10001. Tel 212-279-6400. *In Charge Art Coll & Dir Public Relations* Dan Daniels
Activities: Lectures; factory tours; cash awards; medallions; certificates to various art societies

O **JOHN SIMON GUGGENHEIM MEMORIAL FOUNDATION,** 90 Park Ave, 10016. Tel 212-687-4470. *Pres* Gordon N Ray; *VPres* G Thomas Tanselle; *Secy* Stephen L Schlesinger; *Treas* Robert P Bergin
Estab and incorporated 1925; offers fellowships to further the development of scholars and artists by assisting them to engage in research in any field of knowledge and artistic creation in any of the arts under the freest possible conditions and irrespective of race, color or creed. For additional information see section devoted to Scholarships and Fellowships

M **SOLOMON R GUGGENHEIM MUSEUM,** 1071 Fifth Ave, 10128. Tel 212-360-3500. *Dir* Thomas M Messer; *Deputy Dir* Diane Waldman; *Adminr* William M Jackson; *Cur* Vivian Endicott Barnett; *Cur Emer* Louise Averill Svendsen; *Auditor* Agnes R Connolly; *Asst Cur* Susan B Hirschfeld; *Asst Cur* Lisa Tabak; *Ed* Carol Fuerstein; *Archivist* Ward Jackson; *Conservator* Leni Potoff; *Preparator* Saul Fuerstein; *Photographer* Carmelo Guadagno; *Development and Public Affairs Officer* Mimi Poser; *Public Affairs Coordr* Deborah J Greenberg; *Public Affairs Assoc* Richard Pierce; *Membership Assoc* Elizabeth K Lawson; *Development Assoc* Ann Kraft; *Development Assoc* Carolyn Porcelli; *Admin Asst* Rebecca H Wright; *Admin Asst* Jill Snyder
Open Wed - Sun 11 AM - 8 PM, Tues 11 AM - 8 PM, cl Mon & holidays. Admis general $2.50, students with valid ID cards and visitors over 62 $1.50, group rates for students when accompanied by a teacher, children under seven free, Tues eve free. Estab 1937 as a nonprofit organization which is maintained by the Solomon R Guggenheim Foundation; founded for the promotion and encouragement of art and education in art; to foster an appreciation of art by acquainting museum visitors with significant paintings and sculpture of our time. The gallery was designed by architect Frank Lloyd Wright. Average Annual Attendance: 530,000. Mem: 2000; dues $35 - $1000
Income: Financed by endowment, membership and state and federal appropriations
Purchases: Anthony Caro, Richard Long, Robert Rauschenberg, Cy Twombly
Collections: Reflects the creative accomplishments in modern art from the time of the Impressionists to the constantly changing experimental art of today. The collection of nearly four thousand works, augmented by the Justin K Thannhauser Collection of 75 Impressionists and Post-Impressionist masterpieces, including the largest group of paintings by Vasily Kandinsky; one of the largest and most comprehensive collection of paintings by Paul Klee; largest number of sculptures by Constantin Brancusi in any New York museum; paintings by Chagall, Delaunay, Lager, Marc, Picasso, Bacon, Bonnard, Braque, Cezanne, Malevitch, Modigliani, Moore, Reusseau and Seurat, with concentration of works by Dubuffet, Miro and Mondrian among the Europeans; Americans such as Davis, deKooning, Diebenkorn, Gottlieb, Guston, Johns, Lichenstein, Agnes Martin, Motherwell, Nevelson, Noguchi, Pollack, younger artists include Andre, Flavin, Judd, Christensen, Hamilton, Hesse, Mangold, Nauman, Stella and Serra; paintings, drawings and sculpture collections are being enlarged
Exhibitions: (1984) Kandinsky: Russian and Bauhaus Years, 1915-1933; Julius Bissier; Walter Stein; Michael Singer; Postwar American and European Art from the Collection and Major Loans; Eduardo Arroyo; Juan Gris; Will Insley; Exxon International Exhibition; Robert Motherwell
Publications: Exhibition catalogs
Activities: Education dept; dramatic programs; docent, intern and fellow training; lect open to the public, 6 - 12 visiting lectrs per year; concerts; gallery talks; acoustiguide tours; individual paintings and original objects of art lent to other museum and galleries; lending collection contains original art works, original prints, paintings, 4000 photographs, sculpture, 10,000 slides; book traveling exhibitions; originates traveling exhibitions; museum shope sells books, prints and slides
L **Library,** 1071 Fifth Ave, 10028. Tel 212-360-3538, 360-3541. *Librn* Sonja Bay; *Asst Librn* Marian Wolf
Open by telephone appointment only, Mon - Fri 11 AM - 5 PM. Estab 1952 to document the Museum's collection of 20th century art. For reference only
Library Holdings: Vols 25,000; Per subs 50; Micro — Reels; AV — A-tapes, cassettes, slides, v-tapes; Other — Clipping files, exhibition catalogs
Collections: Rebay Library; Aye Simon Reading Room

GUILD OF BOOK WORKERS
For further information, see National and Regional Organizations

M **HALLWALLS GALLERY,*** 700 Main St, 14202. Tel 212-256-3277. *VPres*
Charles Clough; *Dir* William Currie; *Asst to Dir* Diane Bertolo
Open Tues - Sat 11 AM - 5 PM, Sun 1 - 4 PM. No admis fee except for special
events. Estab 1974 to provide exhibition space for anyone wishing to exhibit.
Three large rooms, one small room (the Matrix Room), and office space; the
building was originally a 1900's ice factory. Average Annual Attendance: 50,000.
Mem: 130; dues $15, $25, $100; meeting dates January and September
Income: Financed by endowment
Collections: Vito Acconci; Jared Bark; Jon Borofsky; Chris Burdon; Rafael
Ferrer; Judy Haffif; Suzy Lake; Sol Lewitt; Gregoire Muller; Charles Simonds
Publications: Top Stories; catalog
Activities: Lectures open to the public; internships; concerts; gallery talks; tours;
traveling exhibitions organized and circulated throughout the United States and
Canada; museum sales shop sells books
L **Library,*** 700 Main St, 14203
Estab 1977 to provide access to art periodicals. Open to public for viewing video
tapes and documentation of work exhibited in the gallery
Income: Financed by endowment, New York State Council for the Arts,
donations, memberships
Library Holdings: Vols 400; Per subs 20; postcards (artists); AV — A-tapes,
lantern slides, rec, slides, v-tapes; Other — Clipping files, exhibition catalogs,
memorabilia, original art works, pamphlets, photographs, prints

M **HISPANIC SOCIETY OF AMERICA,** Museum, Broadway, Between 155th
and 156th Sts, 10032. Tel 212-926-2234. *Pres* George S Moore; *Dir* Theodore S
Beardsley Jr; *Cur Mus Paintings & Metalwork* Priscilla E Muller; *Cur Applied
Arts* Isadora Rose DeViejo; *Cur Applied Arts* Irene Soriano; *Cur Archaeology*
Vivian A Hibbs; *Cur Iconography* Lydia A Dufour; *Cur Emeritus Sculpture*
Beatrice G Proske; *Cur Emeritus Textiles* Florence L May
Open Tues - Sat 10 AM - 4:30 PM, Sun 1 - 4 PM. No admis fee. Estab 1904 by
Archer Milton Huntingon as a free public museum and library devoted to the
culture of Hispanic peoples. Average Annual Attendance: 35,000. Mem: 100 plus
300 corresponding members; membership by election
Income: Financed by endowment
Purchases: Hispanic objects in various media
Collections: †Archaeology; †costumes; customs; †decorative arts of the Iberian
peoples; †paintings; †photographic reference files; †sculpture; †prints
Exhibitions: Gifts to the Collection; gallery exhibits are representative of the
cultures of Iberian Peninsula from prehistory to the present
Publications: Works by members of the staff and society on Spanish art, history,
literature, bibliography, with special emphasis on the collections of the society
Activities: Some individual paintings and original objects of art lent; sales shop
selling books, reproductions and slides
L **Library,** 613 West 155th St, 10032. Tel 212-926-2234. *Cur* Jean R Longland;
Asst Cur Irene S Frye; *Cur of Mss & Rare Bks* Martha M de Narvaez
Open Tues - Fri 1 - 4:30 PM, Sat 10:30 AM - 4:30 PM, cl Aug, Christmas
holidays & other holidays. Estab 1904 as a free reference library to present the
culture of Hispanic peoples. Reference only. The museum is a department of the
Society on the same basis as the library
Income: Financed by endowment
Library Holdings: Vols 200,000; Micro — Fiche, prints, reels; AV — Cassettes,
fs, lantern slides, motion pictures, rec, slides, v-tapes; Other — Clipping files,
exhibition catalogs, manuscripts, memorabilia, original art works, pamphlets,
photographs, prints, reproductions, sculpture
Special Subjects: Art, history, literature, general culture of Spain & Portugal
Publications: Catalogues

O **INDEPENDENT CURATORS INCORPORATED,** 799 Broadway Suite 642,
10003. Tel 212-254-8200. *Exec Dir* Susan Sollins; *Assoc Dir* Judith Olch
Richards; *Exhibitions Coordr* Mike Harwig; *Asst Registrar* Elisabeth L Hahn
Estab 1975 as a non-profit traveling exhibition service specializing in
contemporary art
Income: $230,000
Exhibitions: Sculpture from Germany; Selections from the Sol Lewitt Collection;
Drawings: After Photography; Verbally Charged Images; Large Scale Drawings;
Texas on Paper; Points of View; Four Painters; Concepts in Construction; New
Sculpture; Icon and Environment
Publications: Exhibition catalogues; The List
Activities: Originate traveling exhibitions

L **INSTITUTE OF FINE ARTS,** Slide Collection,* 1 E 78th St, 10021. Tel 212-
988-5550, Ext 31, 772-5800. *Cur* Suzanne Babineau-Simenauer; *Asst Cur*
Dorothy Simon
Estab 1941 to serve as a teaching and research collection for the faculty of the
institute. reference only
Income: Financed by New York University budget
Library Holdings: AV — Kodachromes, lantern slides, slides 300,000; Other —
Clipping files, exhibition catalogs, pamphlets, photographs, prints
Collections: Art history

M **INTAR LATIN AMERICAN GALLERY,** 420 W 42nd St, 2nd Floor, 10036.
Tel 212-695-6135. *Dir* Inverna Lockpez
Open Mon - Fri 10 AM - 6 PM. No admis fee. Estab 1978 as one of New
York's principal alternative spaces providing exposure for emerging Hispanic
artists & facilitating an all-important link to museum curators & collectors. Only
Hispanic gallery in area. Average Annual Attendance: 7000
Income: Financed by endowment
Exhibitions: (1983) Papo Colo; Juan Boza; Luis A Solari; Women & Politics;
Omar Rayo; Lydia Cabrera
Activities: Originates traveling exhibitions

INTERNATIONAL CENTER FOR ADVANCED STUDIES IN ART
For further information, see National and Regional Organizations

O **INTERNATIONAL CENTER OF MEDIEVAL ART, INC,** The Cloisters, Fort
Tryon Park, 10040. Tel 212-923-3700. *Pres* Robert G Calkins; *VPres* Ilene
Forsyth; *VPres* Madeline Caviness; *Treas* Paula Gerson; *Secy* Leslie A Bussis
Estab 1956 as The International Center of Romanesque Art, Inc. The
International Center of Medieval Art was founded to promote greater knowledge
of the arts of the Middle Ages, & to contribute to & make available the results of
new research. Mem: 985; dues benefactor $1000, sustaining $500, contributing
$100, institutions $50, active foreign countries $35, active US $30, student $15;
annual meeting Feb, in conjunction with College Art Association of America
Publications: Gesta (illustrated journal), two issues per year; ICMA Newsletter,
3 issues per year; Romanesque Sculpture in American Collections, New England
Museums; Etudes d'Art Medieval offertes a Louis Grodecki
Activities: Sponsor sessions at the annual conferences of The Medieval Institute
of Western Michigan University, Kalamazoo; keeps its members informed as to
events of interest to medievalists; public lect, exhibitions and symposia

M **INTERNATIONAL CENTER OF PHOTOGRAPHY,** 1130 Fifth Ave, 10128.
Tel 212-860-1777; Telex 42-0752. *Executive Dir* Cornell Capa; *Dir Exhib*
William Ewing; *Dir Education* Anne White; *Development Dir* Ann Doherty;
Adminr Steve Rooney; *Public Information Dir* Phyllis Levine; *Cur of Coll* Miles
Barth
Open Tues - Thurs Noon - 8 PM, Fri - Sun Noon - 6 PM. Admis adults $2,
students & senior citizens $1. Estab 1974 to encourage and assist photographers
of all ages and nationalities who are vitally concerned with their world and time,
to find and help new talents, to uncover and preserve forgotten archives and to
present such work to the public. Maintains five exhibition galleries showing a
changing exhibition program of photographic expression and experimentation by
over 350 photographers. Average Annual Attendance: 75,000. Mem: 3000; dues
$25 and higher
Income: Financed by public and private grants
Collections: The core of the collection is 20th century documentary photography,
with a companion collection of examples of master photographs of the 20th
century including Siskind, Abbott, Callahan, Feininger, Hine and Cartier-Bresson.
Major holdings include works from the documentary tradition as well as fashion
and other aesthetic genres
Exhibitions: (1983) Bonjour Monsieur Lartigue; A Day in the Life of Australia;
The Frozen Image: Scandinavian Photography; Sarah Moon: Improbable
Memories; Len Jenshel: Era of Extravagance; Photographs by Bill Brandt;
London/New York: 1909-1950; Joe Steinmetz/Killing Time; Lou Stouman/Forty
Years on Times Square; Ghost Trains: Railroad Photographs of the 1950s by O
Winston Link; The American Image: Photographs from the National Archives/
1860-1960; The Metropolitan Opera Centennial: A Photographic Album; Yousef
Karsh: A Fifty Year Retrospective; High Light: The Mountain in Photography
from 1840 to the Present; Roman Vishniac: A Vanished World; (1984) David
Bailey's Sixties; El Salvador; People; Lewis W Hine; Arnold Genthe: A
Pictorialist and Society; Gyorgy Kepes; Kenneth Josephson; Gertrude Blom:
Bearing Witness; Shooting for the Gold: The Olympics; Lucas Samaras: Polaroid
Photographs 1969-1983; Horst (Masters of Fashion Photography III); Years of
Challange, Years of Hope/Life: The Second Decade, 1946-1955
Publications: Annual report; monographs; exhibition catalogs
Activities: Classes for adults and children; docent training; workshops; lect open
to public, 75 vis lectr per yr; gallery talks; tours; scholarships; original objects of
art lent to other museums and educational institutions; book traveling exhibitions,
3 per yr; originate traveling exhibitions; museum shop selling books, magazines,
original art, reproductions, prints and postcards
L **Library,** New York, 10028
Reference only
Library Holdings: Vols 4000; Per subs 25; AV — A-tapes, cassettes, fs,
Kodachromes, slides, v-tapes; Other — Clipping files, exhibition catalogs,
pamphlets

INTERNATIONAL FOUNDATION FOR ART RESEARCH, INC
For further information, see National and Regional Organizations

JAPAN SOCIETY, INC
M **Japan House Gallery,** 333 E 47th St, 10017. Tel 212-832-1155. *Pres Japan
Society* David MacEachron; *Dir* Rand Castile
Open daily 11 AM - 5 PM, Fri 11 AM - 7:30 PM. No admis fee to members;
contribution for nonmembers. Estab 1907, bi-cultural membership organizations
to deepen understanding and friendship between Japan and the United States.
Average Annual Attendance: 50,000 - 100,000. Mem: 3000 individual; dues
$200, $60, $45, $20; annual meeting Oct
Income: Financed by membership, grants and donations
Exhibitions: Shiko Munakata (1903-1975); Works on Paper; Shinohara; The
Great Age of Japanese Buddhist Sculpture 600-1300 AD; Kanban: Japanese Shop
Signs; Autumn Grasses & Water: Motif in Japanese Art; From the Suntory
Museum
Publications: Japan Society Newsletter, monthly; exhibition catalogs
Activities: Classes for adults; concerts; movies; tours
L **Library,** 333 E 47th St, 10017. Tel 212-832-1155. *Librn* Tomie Mochizuki
Open Mon - Fri Noon - 5 PM. Estab 1971
Income: Financed by membership
Library Holdings: Vols 4500; Per subs 113; Other — Clipping files, pamphlets
Publications: What Shall I Read on Japan

M **JEWISH MUSEUM,*** 1109 Fifth Ave, 10128. Tel 212-860-1888. *Dir* Joan H
Rosenbaum; *Adminr* Ruth M Dolkart; *Chief Cur* Susan Goodman; *Cur of
Judaica* Vivian Mann; *Dir Public Information* Barbara Kaplan Lane; *Dir of
Education* Andrew Ackerman; *Registrar* Rita Feigenbaum; *Mgr of Museum Shop*
Michael Freiser; *Dir of Development* Rosemarie Garipoli
Open Mon, Wed & Thurs 12 - 5 PM; Tues Noon - 8 PM; Sun 11 AM - 6 PM.
Admis adults $2.50, children (6-16), students with ID card and senior citizens
$1.50, members free. Estab 1904 to preserve and present the Jewish cultural
tradition. Three exhibition floors devoted to the display of ceremonial objects in
the permanent collection, special exhibitions from the permanent collections and
photographs and contemporary art on loan. Average Annual Attendance: 85,000.
Mem: 6700; dues $10 - $250 and up

Income: Financed by membership, grants, individual contributions and organizations
Collections: Contemporary art; graphics; Jewish ceremonial objects; paintings; textiles; comprehensive collection of Jewish ceremonial art
Exhibitions: (1982-83) A Tale of Two Cities: Jewish Life in Frankfurt and Istanbul 1750-1870; (1983) Frank Stella: Plish Wooden Synagogues, Constructions from the 1970s; George Segal: The Holocaust; The Immigrant Generations: Jewish Artists in Britain 1900-1945; (1983-84) Kings and Citizens: The History of the Jews in Denmark 1622-1983; Form and Fantasy in the Hanukkah Lamp; Soviet Jews: Photographs by Bill Aron & Nodar Djindjihashvili; (1984) The Precious Legacy: Judaic Treasures from the Czechoslovak State Collections
Publications: Calendar, bimonthly; exhibition catalogs; program brochures; posters and graphics
Activities: Classes for children; docent training; lect open to public; traveling exhibitions organized and circulated; museum shop selling books, magazines, original art, reproductions, prints, slides, needlecrafts, posters, catalogs and postcards

L **Library,** 1109 Fifth Ave, 10028
Reference library open to staff only
Special Subjects: Judaica
Collections: Comprehensive collection of Judaic textiles; Harry G Friedman Collection of Ceremonial Objects; Samuel Friedenberg Collection of Plaques & Medals; Rose and Benjamin Mintz Collection of Eastern European art; Harry J Stein-Samuel Friedenberg Collection of Coins from the Holy Land

M **JUST ABOVE MIDTOWN GALLERY, INC,** 178 Franklin St, 10013. Tel 212-966-7020. *Executive Dir* Linda Goode Bryant; *Special Projects* Wade Miller; *Preformance Cur* Tony Whitfield; *Asst Cur* Dorothy Desir; *Publicity & Marketing* Cathey Billian; *Project Administration* Ann Schoenfield
Open Tues - Sat 10 AM - 6 PM. No admis fee. Estab 1974 as a non-profit contemporary visual arts exhibition & performance media space with emphasis on exhibiting work by emerging artists & experimental art forms. Average Annual Attendance: 15,000-25,000
Exhibitions: Ten-tweleve exhibition annually
Publications: Blachcurrant, quarterly

L **KENNEDY GALLERIES,** Art Library,* 40 W 57th St, 10019. Tel 212-541-9600. *Librn* Cynthia Seibels
Open to public with restrictions
Library Holdings: Vols 6500; Per subs 25; VF 10
Special Subjects: American Painting & Sculpture
Publications: American Art Journal

L **LANDMARK SOCIETY OF WESTERN NEW YORK, INC,** Wenrich Memorial Library,* 130 Spring St, 14608. Tel 212-546-7029. *Exec Dir* Mrs Patrick Harrington; *Asst Dir* Ann B Parks; *Res Coordr* Cynthia Howk
Open Mon - Fri 8:30 AM - 5 PM and by appointment. Estab 1970 to preserve landmarks in Western New York; information center containing drawings, photographs, slides, books and periodicals, as well as archives of local architecture and information on preservation and restoration techniques
Income: Financed by membership and special grants
Purchases: $900
Library Holdings: Vols 2500; Per subs 25; AV — Kodachromes, slides; Other — Clipping files, exhibition catalogs, manuscripts, pamphlets, photographs
Special Subjects: Architecture, Architectural History, Historic Preservation, Local Architecture
Collections: Claude Bragdon Collection of Architectural Drawings; Historic American Buildings Survey drawings of local architecture; John Wenrich & Walter Cassebeer Collection of prints & watercolors
Exhibitions: Adaptive Use: New Uses for Old Buildings; The Architecture of Ward Wellington Ward; Rochester Prints, from the drawings of Walter Cassebeer
Publications: Newsletter, bi-monthly
Activities: Classes for adults and children; docent training; lectures open to public, tours; originate traveling exhibitions to area schools, colleges, banks, community centers

M **LINCOLN CENTER FOR THE PERFORMING ARTS,** Cork Gallery, Avery Fisher Hall, 140 W 65th, 10023
Open Mon - Sun 10 AM - Midnight. Admis varies. The first building in Lincoln Center opened in 1962, the entire center was compleated in 1969 to present the performing arts to the community. Cork Gallery was estab in 1971 to provide a show case for young & unknown artists. Average Annual Attendance: 550,000. Mem: Center has guilds, associations & constituents which support it; dues $1000-$25
Income: $71,000,000 (financed by endowment, membership, city, state & federal appropriation)
Purchases: $76,000,000 (center)
Exhibitions: 26 exhibitions annually
Activities: Classes for adults; sales shop

C **MCCRORY CORPORATION,** 888 Seventh Ave, 10106. Tel 212-621-4606. *Cur* Celia Ascher
Estab 1968. Collection in traveling exhibitions
Collections: Modern art with special emphasis on Constructivism
Exhibitions: Constructivism and the Geometric Tradition & Constructive Concepts: Willy Rotzler
Activities: Gallery talks; tours; individual objects of art lent to museum exhibitions; originate traveling exhibitions; previously a two-year exhibition through Europe, at present, two-year exhibition at major United States museums

M **MANHATTAN LABORATORY MUSEUM,** 314 W 54th St, 10019. Tel 212-765-5904. *Founder & Exec Dir* Bette Korman; *Dir Public Affairs & Speical Programs* Helen Silverstein; *Museum Education Dir* Lisa Garrison; *Dir Museum Programs* Daniel Dixon; *Dir Harlem Youth Bd Program* Amapola Morales
Open Wed - Fri & Sun 1 - 5 PM, Sat 11 AM - 5 PM. Admis suggested adults $2, children $3. Estab 1973 as a children's museum and art center featuring participatory nature, science and art exhibits, programs and activities focusing on the child and the world. It is the only children's museum in Manhattan featuring high quality painting, film, sculpture, printmaking and art program and exhibitions. Administered by Growth Through Art and Museum Experience. Average Annual Attendance: 50,000. Mem: 300; dues $15-$100
Income: $300,000 (financed by endowment, membership, city and state appropriation, admission fees, store sales, foundations and corporate funding)
Exhibitions: (1983-84) The Mystery of Time, 10th anniversary exhibition; Children's Hands in Harlem, Harlem Youth Bd Project Exhibition; Origami & Japanese Fold-out Books
Publications: Participations, biannual newsletter; monthly bulletins, calendars and announcements
Activities: Classes for children; dramatic programs; docent training; parent/child workshops; lectures open to public, 20 visiting lecturers per year; concerts, theatrical performances, resident artist & performing artists; gallery talks; tours; scholarships; sales shop sells books, original art, reproductions, games and ceramic prints

O **MANHATTAN PSYCHIATRIC CENTER'S SCULPTURE GARDEN,** Ward's Island, 10035. Tel 212-369-0500
Open Mon - Sun 10 AM - sundown. No admis fee. Estab 1977 to enhance hospital environment & offer exhibition area to new as well as 122 acres of hospital grounds are used to site outdoor sculptures, mostly on temporary basis. Project is organized in affiliation with two art organizations, Artists Representing Environmental Art (AREA) & the Organization of Independent Artists (OIA)
Collections: The Emerging Sun, Vivienne Thaul Wechter; Silent Columns, Penny Kaplan; Rock Garden Sanctuary, Gigi & Paul Franklin; The Map of Time/The Time of Map, Toshio Sasaki
Exhibitions: Sculpture on Shoreline Sites; Ward's Island Inland Show Continued; Roman Garden Sites Continued
Publications: Manhattan Psychiatric Center's Sculpture Garden, yearly
Activities: Educ dept; lectures open to public; competitions

M **MARYMOUNT MANHATTAN COLLEGE GALLERY,** 221 E 71 St, 10021. Tel 212-472-3800. *Dir* June Rosner
Open 12:30 - 8 PM. No admis fee. Estab 1982 as a showcase for unaffiliated artists. Gallery is 30 x 40 ft. Average Annual Attendance: 2500
Exhibitions: Dorothy Gillespie; Liz Whitney Quisgar
Activities: Lectures by artist

M **METROPOLITAN MUSEUM OF ART,** Main Bldg, Fifth Ave at 82nd St, 10028. Tel 212-535-7710 (General Information), 879-5500 (Museum Offices). *Chmn Bd Trustees* J Richardson Dilworth; *Pres* William B Macomber; *Dir* Philippe de Montebello; *Dep Dir* James Pilgrim; *VDir for Education* Merribell Parsons; *VPres Architecture & Planning* Arthur Rosenblatt; *VPres, Secy & Counsel* Ashton Hawkins; *VPres Operations* Richard Morsches; *VPres Finance* Daniel Herrick; *VPres Public Affairs* Richard Dougherty; *VPres & Publisher* Bradford D Kelleher; *Consultant Film & Television* Karl Katz; *Admin Personnel* Michael Sparacino; *Chmn American Art Dept* John K Howat; *Cur American Decorative Art* Morrison H Hecksher; *Chmn Ancient Near Eastern Art* Prudence O Harper; *Cur Arms & Armor* Helmut Nickel; *Chief Librn* William B Walker; *Cur Drawings* Jacob Bean; *Cur Egyptian Art* Christine Lilyquist; *Lila Acheson Wallace Research Cur Egyptology* Henry G Fischer; *Consultative Chmn European Paintings* John Pope-Hennessy; *Cur European Paintings* Elizabeth E Gardner; *Cur & Admin European Paintings* Katharine Baetjer; *Chmn European Sculture & Decorative Arts* Olga Raggio; *Cur European Sculpture & Decorative Arts* James Parker; *Cur Textile Study Room* Jean Mailey; *Cur & Admin Far Eastern Art* Jean K Schmitt; *Cur Far Eastern Art* Martin Lerner; *Chmn Greek & Roman Art* Dietrich von Bothmer; *Cur Greek & Roman Art* Joan R Mertens; *Cur Robert Lehman Collection* George Szabo; *Cur Musical Instruments* Laurence Libin; *Cur Medieval Art* Margaret E Frazer; *Chmn Primitive Art* Douglas Newton; *Cur Primitive Art* Julie Jones; *Chmn Twentieth Century Art* William S Lieberman; *Conservator Objects* James H Frantz; *Conservator Paintings* John M Brealey; *Conservator Prints & Drawings* Helen K Otis; *Conservator Textiles* Nobuko Kajitani; *Museum Education Community Education* Joan Sandler; *Program Mgr Concerts & Lectures* Hilde Limondjian
Open Tues 10 AM - 8:45 PM, Wed - Sat 10 AM - 4:45 PM, Sun 11 AM - 4:45 PM, cl Mon. Admis contribution suggested adults $4 students & sr citizens $2. Estab 1870 to encourage and develop the study of the fine arts, and the application of arts to life; of advancing the general knowledge of kindred subjects, and to that end of furnishing popular instruction and recreation. Average Annual Attendance: 3,800,000. Mem: 82,173; dues patron $2500, sponsor $1000, donor $500, contributing $300, sustaining $150, participating $65, individual $45, student $20
Income: $54,316,665 (financed by endowment, membership, city and state appropriations and other)
Collections: Acquisitions-Departments: American decorative arts, paintings and sculpture; Ancient Near Eastern art; arms and armor; Costume Institute; The Astor Court and the Douglas Dillon Galleries for Chinese painting; drawings; Egyptian art; European paintings, sculpture and decorative arts; far Eastern art; Greek and Roman, Islamic art; Lehman Collection, medieval art and The Cloisters; musical instruments; primitive art; prints and photographs; Twentieth Century Art Exhibitions
Exhibitions: (1982-83) Spirit and Ritual: The Morse Collection of Ancient Chinese Art; Buildings on Paper: Rhode Island Architectural Drawings, 1825-1945; Hendrik Goltzius and His Circle; The Cimabue Crucifix; The Celestial Pen: Islamic Calligraphy; Notable Acquisitions in Indian and Southeast Asian Art; The Search for Alexander; Tokens of Friendship: Miniature Watercolors from the Manney Collection; Eighteenth through Twentieth Century: American, Dutch, English, German, Italian and Spanish Drawings from the Lehman Collection; The Frank Lloyd Wright Room; Annual Christmas Tree and Baroque Creche Display; Annual Christmas Display at The Cloisters; Albrecht Durer and the Holy Family; La Belle Epoque; Devotional Images from the Old and New Worlds from the Howard Collection; Ruth and Harold D Uris Center for Education; 15th and 16th Century Italian Drawings; Recent Gifts, 1982; The Vatican Collections: The Papacy and Art; Working America: Industrial Imagery in American Prints, 1900-1940; Color and Shape in American Indian Art; Karl

Bitter's Pulpit; Constable's England; Islamic Jewelry; Nineteenth-Century Porcelains; Architecture of the Vatican; Raphael in Prints; Henry Moore: 60 Years of His Art; Intalian Bronzes and Other Small Sculptures of the Renaissance and Baroque Periods; Charles Willson Peale and His World; Alfred Stieglitz; The Lawrence A and Barbara Fleischman Gallery of Late Medieval Secular Art
Publications: Bulletin, quarterly; Calendar/News, bi-monthly; The Journal, annually
Activities: Classes for adults and children; docent training; films; programs for the disabled touch collection; lectures open to public; concerts; gallery talks; tours; outreach; scholarships; exten dept serves community programs for greater New York City area; color reproductions, individual paintings & original objects of art lent to other institutions; book traveling exhibitions; originate traveling exhibitions to US museusm through the American Federation of the Arts; museum shop sells books, magazines, original art, reproductions, prints, slides, children's activities, records, post cards & posters

L **Thomas J Watson Library,** Fifth Ave at 82nd St, 10028. Tel 212-879-5500, Ext 221. *Museum Librn* Donya-Dobrila Schimansky
Open Tues - Fri 10 AM - 4:45 PM, cl holidays and Aug. Estab 1880 for the use of the curatorial, educational and other staff; privileges are extended to qualified researchers and graduate students with appropriate identification. Circ 208,500
Income: Financed by endowment
Library Holdings: Vols 230,000; Per subs 1500; original documents; Micro — Fiche, reels; Other — Clipping files, exhibition catalogs, manuscripts, memorabilia, pamphlets
Special Subjects: Archaeology, Architecture, Decorative Arts, Sculpture, Painting, Prints and drawings of all countries and periods
Collections: Art Auction Catalogs
Exhibitions: Outstanding Art Books of the Year; The Vatican Frescoes of Michelangelo

L **Dept of Prints & Photographs,** Fifth Ave at 82nd St, 10028. Tel 212-570-3920. *Cur in Charge* Colta Ives; *Cur* Janet S Byrne; *Cur* Mary L Myers; *Cur Photography* Weston J Naef
Open Tues - Fri 10 AM - 12:30 PM & 2 - 5 PM. Estab 1917 to collect & preserve prints, photos, illustrated books & drawings for ornament & architecture. Has 3 exhibition galleries
Library Holdings: Other — Original art works, prints
Special Subjects: Architecture, Art History, Bookplates & Bindings, Costume Design & Construction, Decorative Arts, Drawings, Etchings & Engravings, Landscape Architecture, Photography, Portraits, Printmaking, Prints, Woodcuts

L **Photograph and Slide Library,*** Fifth Ave at 82nd St, 10028. Tel 212-879-5500, Ext 3261. *Chief Librn* Margaret P Nolan
Open Tues - Fri 10 AM - 4:45 PM. Estab 1907 to provide a circulation (rental) library of slides covering the history of art; to provide color transparencies and photographs of the collections of the Metropolitan Museum of Art for publication purposes; to maintain a reference collection of photographs and mounted color prints covering the history of art. Circ 170,000 slides; 3600 color transparencies
Library Holdings: Color transparencies; Micro — Cards 500; AV — Lantern slides, slides 170,000; Other — Photographs, prints
Special Subjects: Collections of the Metropolitan Museum of Art, particularly complete coverage of Western and European decorative arts
Collections: William Keighley Slide Collection covering Asia Minor, Austria, France, Germany, Italy and Spain; architecture and other arts of various periods

L **Robert Goldwater Library of Primitive Art,*** Fifth Ave at 82nd St, 10028. Tel 212-879-5500, Ext 3707. *Museum Librn* Allan D Chapman
Estab 1957 as the library of the Museum of Primitive Art; holding of the Metropolitan Museum as of 1976; open Feb 1982
Library Holdings: Vols 25,000; Per subs 175; Black and white photographs of primitive art 150,000; Micro — Fiche, reels
Special Subjects: Anthropology, Archaeology, Ethnology, African, American Indian, Eskimo, Oceanic, Pre-Columbian and Primitive art
Publications: Primitive Art Bibliographies

L **Robert Lehman Collection Library,*** Fifth Ave at 82nd St, 10028. Tel 212-879-5500, Ext 2946. *Asst Cur Research* Victoria S Galban
Estab 1941 to provide general public with a resource from which to obtain information about the museum & its collections. Open by appointment only
Income: Financed by endowment
Library Holdings: Vols 9000; Per subs 49; Original documents; Other — Clipping files, exhibition catalogs, manuscripts, pamphlets, photographs, reproductions
Special Subjects: Western European arts from the 13th - 20th Centuries with special emphasis on the art of Siena, Old Master drawings and Renaissance decorative arts
Collections: Archives containing books, correspondence, manuscripts and reproductions; photograph collection

L **Irene Lewisohn Costume Reference Library,*** Fifth Ave at 82nd St, 10028. Tel 212-879-5500, Ext 3908. *Assoc Museum Librn* K Gordon Stone
Open Tues - Fri 10 AM - 1 PM, and 2 - 4:30 PM. Estab 1946 to study costume history, fashion and theatre design and any subject related to the subject of dress. For reference only
Income: Financed by bequest
Library Holdings: Vols 42,000; Per subs 52; fashion plates, original fashion sketches; Other — Clipping files, memorabilia, photographs, prints
Special Subjects: Costume Design & Construction
Collections: Mainbocher Fashion Sketches by Douglas Pollard from 1940-1970
Uris Library, Fifth Ave at 82nd St, 10028. Tel 212-879-5500, Ext 3379. *Librn* Beverly Robertson
Open Tues - Fri 2:30 - 4:30 PM, Tues until 7 PM. The Uris Library & Resource Center is part of the Uris Center for Education
Library Holdings: Vols 5300; AV — Cassettes, fs, rec, slides; Other — Exhibition catalogs
Special Subjects: Afro-American Art, Archaeology, Architecture, Art Education, Art History, Crafts, Decorative Arts, Drawings, Etchings & Engravings, Folk Art, Graphic Arts, Historical Material, Islamic Art, Period Rooms, Photography, Antiquities, Portraits, Primitive art, Sculpture, Tapestries
Activities: Classes for children; lectures

M **The Cloisters,*** Fort Tryon Park, 10040. Tel 212-923-3700; Cable CLOMUSE. *Chmn* William D Wixom; *Cur* Jane Hayward; *Consultative Cur* Kurt Weitzman
Open Tues - Sat 10 AM - 4:45 PM, Sun & holidays Oct - April 1 - 4:45 PM, May - Sept Noon - 4:45 PM. Estab 1938 to display in an appropriate setting works of art and architecture of the Middle Ages. Medieval French cloisters incorporated into the building, as well as the chapter house, a chapel, and Romanesque apse; also Medieval herb garden. Average Annual Attendance: 240,000
Collections: Frescoes, ivories, precious metalwork, paintings, polychromed statues, stained glass, tapestries, and other French and Spanish architectural elements
Exhibitions: The Wild Man: Medieval Myth and Symbolism; The Royal Abbey of Saint-Denis in the Time of Abbot Suger (1122-1151)
Publications: A Walk Through The Cloisers; exhibition catalogs
Activities: Classes for adults and children; dramatic programs; lect open to public; concerts; original objects of art lent to other museums; museum shop sells books, reproductions and slides

L **The Cloisters Library,*** Fort Tryon Park, 10040. Tel 212-923-3700, Ext 54. *Librn* Suse C Childs; *Library Asst* David Adams
Open Tues - Fri 10 AM - 1 PM and 2 - 4:45 PM. Estab 1938 to be used as a small highly specialized reference library for the curatorial staff at The Cloisters; scholars and accredited graduate students are welcome. For reference only
Income: Financed by endowment
Library Holdings: Vols 6500; Per subs 48; original documents; AV — Slides; Other — Exhibition catalogs, photographs
Collections: George Grey Barnard Archive

L **MIDMARCH ASSOCIATES,** Women Artists News Archive, 300 Riverside Dr, Box 3304 Grand Central Sta, 10163. Tel 212-666-6990. *Editor* Rena Hausen; *Exec Dir* Cynthia Navaretton
Open by appointment. Estab 1975 to maintain archival material on women artists world wide
Library Holdings: Other — Clipping files, exhibition catalogs, manuscripts, memorabilia, original art works, pamphlets, photographs, sculpture
Special Subjects: Architecture, Art History, Ceramics, Conceptual Art, Constructions, Crafts, Decorative Arts, Drawings, Film, Latin American Art, Mixed Media, Pre-Columbian Art, Sculpture, Theatre Arts, Watercolors
Publications: Guide to Women's Art Organizations Directory For The Arts; Voices of Women; Women Artists of the World; Women Artists News, bimonthly
Activities: Education department; lectures provided

L **M KNOEDLER & CO, INC,** Library, 19 East 70th St, 10021. Tel 212-794-0567. *Asst Librn* Vernon Shetley
Open Mon - Fri 9:30 AM - 5:30 PM by appointment only. Research for gallery staff, and by appointment for scholars, museum curators, students
Income: Financed by memberships
Library Holdings: Vols 50,000; Per subs 20; Micro — Fiche; Other — Clipping files, exhibition catalogs, memorabilia, original art works, pamphlets, photographs, sculpture
Special Subjects: American Western Art, Art History, Painting - American, Painting - European

L **PIERPONT MORGAN LIBRARY,** 29 E 36th St, 10016. Tel 212-685-0008. *Pres* Haliburton Fales; *Dir* Dr Charles Ryskamp; *Asst Dir* Francis S Mason Jr; *Research Fellow for Texts Emeritus* Dr Curt F Buhler; *Cur Printed Books and Bindings* Paul Needham; *Cur Medieval and Renaissance Manuscripts* Dr John H Plummer; *Cur Medieval and Renaissance Manuscripts* William M Voelkle; *Cur Drawings and Prints* Felice Stampfle; *Cur Drawings and Prints* Cara D Denison; *Cur Autograph Manuscripts* Herbert Cahoon; *Cur Music Manuscripts* J Rigbie Turner; *Cur of Gilbert & Sullivan Coll* Reginald Allen; *Cur Early Chldren's Books* Gerald Gottlieb; *Assoc Cur Printed Books* Anna Lou Ashby; *Asst Cur Gilbert & Sullivan Coll* Fredric W Wilson; *Reference Librn* Barbara Paulson; *Registrar* David W Wright; *Public Affairs* Frederick Schroeder; *Honorary Cur Seals and Tablets* Dr Edith Porada
Open Tues - Sat 10:30 AM - 5 PM, Sun 1 - 5 PM, cl Mon, cl Sun during July, cl month of Aug; reading room open to scholars Mon - Fri 9:30 AM - 4:45 PM. No admis fee; suggested donation $2. Estab 1924 by endowment; collection placed in custody of a Board of Trustees for research and exhibition purposes. The Gallery has changing exhibition with Old Master drawings, Medieval and Renaissance illuminated manuscripts, rare printed books, and literary, historical, and music manuscripts. Average Annual Attendance: 200,000. Mem: 1100; dues $35, $50
Income: $1,601,709 (financed by endowment and membership)
Purchases: $975,050
Library Holdings: Vols 45,000; Per subs 170; original documents; AV — Slides; Other — Manuscripts, original art works
Collections: †Ancient written records including seals, cuneiform tablets and papyri; art objects; †autograph manuscripts; †book bindings; †early children's books; †Medieval & Renaissance illuminated manuscripts; †later printed books; †letters and documents; mezzotints; modern calligraphy; †music manuscripts; †original drawing from 14th-19th centuries; †printed books before 1500; Rembrandt prints
Exhibitions: (1983-84) Holbin and the Court of Henry VIII; Four Centuries of Opera; Letters from Notable Children; 50 Italian Drawings, 1375-1775; Flowers of Three Centuries; Gothic Painting in Manuscripts; Belle da Costa Greene: A Centenary Celebration; Renaissance Painting in Manuscripts: Treasures from the British Library; Chamber Music from Mozart to Webern; The Centennial of the Grolier Club: Fine Bindings from its Library Bzyantium and 19th Century France: A Tribute to John S Thacher; Building the Collections of the Morgan Library; French Drawings, 1565-1825; Master Drawings from the National Gallery of Ireland
Publications: Report to the Fellows, biennial; books; catalogs; facsimiles
Activities: Lect open to the public, 8 vis lectr per year; tours; sales shop sells books, reproductions, prints, slides, cards, calendars, address books and posters

O **MUNICIPAL ART SOCIETY OF NEW YORK,*** 457 Madison Ave, 10022. Tel 212-935-3960. *Pres* Ralph C Menapace Jr; *Secy* Gordon Hyatt; *Executive Dir* Margot Wellington
Estab 1892, incorporated 1898. The Society is the one organization in New York where the layman, professional and business firm can work together to encourage high standards for public art, architecture, planning, landscaping and preservation in the five boroughs. Mem: 4500; dues $25 and up; annual meeting June
Publications: The Livable City, quarterly

L **Information Exchange,*** 457 Madison Ave, 10022. Tel 212-935-3960. *Dir* Darlene McCloud; *Asst Dir* Sue Radmer
Open Mon - Fri 10 AM - 4 PM. Estab 1979. For reference only
Library Holdings: Vols 1000; Per subs 100; Other — Clipping files, exhibition catalogs, pamphlets
Special Subjects: Architecture, historic preservation, landscape architecture, public art, urban planning
Publications: Information sheets, irregular

M **MUSEUM OF AMERICAN FOLK ART,** 49 W 53rd St, 10019. Tel 212-581-2475. *Dir* Dr Robert Bishop; *Asst Dir* Gerard C Wertkin
Open Wed - Sun 10:30 AM - 5:30 PM, Tues 10:30 AM - 8 PM, cl Mon. Admis adults $1, students & sr citizens $.50. Estab 1961 for the collection & exhibition of American folk art in all media, including painting, sculpture, textiles & painted & decorated furniture. Average Annual Attendance: 50,000. Mem: 4000; dues $25 and up
Income: Financed by membership, state appropriation, personal donations
Collections: American folk paintings & watercolors; folk sculpture including shop & carousel figures, shiphead figures, decoys, weathervanes, whirligigs, wood carvings & chalkware; painted & decorated furniture; tradesmen's signs; textiles including quilts, coverlets, stenciled fabrics, hooked rugs & samplers
Publications: The Clarion, quarterly magazine
Activities: Classes for adults and children; docent training; lectures open to public; gallery talks; tours; outreach programs; originate traveling exhibitions; museum shop sells books, magazines, reproductions & prints

L **Library,** 49 W 53rd St, 10019
Not open to public; reference library
Library Holdings: Vols 5000; Per subs 25; AV — Fs, motion pictures, slides; Other — Clipping files, exhibition catalogs, manuscripts, memorabilia, pamphlets, photographs, prints, reproductions

M **MUSEUM OF HOLOGRAPHY,** 11 Mercer St, 10013. Tel 212-925-0581, 925-0526. *Dir* Rosemary H Jackson; *Asst Dir* Shoshanah G Cooper; *Admin Asst* Ada P Cruz; *Dir Finance & Development* Mona H Rubin; *Cur Collections & Exhibitions* Rene P Barilleaux; *Dir Exhibitions* Gerhard Schlanzky; *Dir Educational Servs* Fred Unterseher; *Admin Asst Educational Servs* R Scott Lloyd; *Bookstore Mgr* Leanne Krause; *Dir Traveling Exhibitions* Paul D Barefoot; *Cur Collection* Rene Daul Barilleaux
Open Wed - Sun Noon - 6 PM. Admis $2.75, children & sr citizens $1.50, group rates if booked in advance. Estab 1976 to provide a focal point for the growing art form of holography and serve as an information center for the field. Consists of temporary exhibition gallery, permanent historical gallery, downstairs gallery for the permanent collection & downstairs theatre-education room. Average Annual Attendance: 60,000. Mem: 400; dues $30 and up
Income: Financed by membership, federal funds, state appropriation, corporate and foundation grants and admissions
Collections: †Contemporary art holography collection; †contemporary and historic commercial holography collection including data; †historic collection early prototypes and firsts, with date, early machines and books, tapes and photographs, major bequest from inventor of the medium, Dr Dennis Gabor and other pioneers of the medium
Exhibitions: One woman retrospective of work by Margaret Benyon, pioneer of holography as art; Futuresight: 12 NY Holographers; Stages: Dan Schweitzer; Its All Waves Anyway, retrospective work of Abe Rezny, holography, neon, photography; Light Years Contemporary Holography from Permanent Collection; Fringescapes 81; Contemporary Art Holography; Shadowgrams, one man retrospective work of Rick Silberman; Contemporary Portrait Gallery; Light Years: 4 Contemporary Art Holographers from the Permanent Collection; Recent work by Peter Van Riper; Similar Visions, the history and development of dimensional imaging systems, guest curated by Dr Stephen A Benton of Polaroid Corporation; Flux: Sam Moree; Light Lines: Andy Pepper; Sterealities: Aaron Kurzen; Clockwork Concerto: Scott Nemtzow; Contemporary Art Holography
Publications: Holosphere, quarterly newsletter; exhibition catalogs; general information packets; reprints on holography
Activities: Docent training; study notes for exhibitions; artist in residence program; lectures open to the public; gallery talks; tours; concerts; scholarships offered; individual holograms and original objects of art lent to museums and other non-profit cultural organizations; lending collection contain photographs, holograms; book traveling exhibitions; traveling exhibitions organized and circulated to art museums, science centers; museum shop sells books, magazines, holograms, exhibition catalogs, original art objects, postcards, posters, reproductions and optical art objects

L **Reference Library,*** 11 Mercer St, 10013. Tel 212-925-0526. *Librn* Laura Mack; *Admin Asst* Mary Duffy
Open Wed - Sun noon to 6 PM, by appointment only. Estab 1976 to provide data from a wide variety of disciplines that relate to holography, lasers, artists working in the field, equipment and opportunities in holography
Income: $370,000 (financed by endowment, membership, city and state appropriation)
Library Holdings: Vols 580; Per subs 52; AV — A-tapes, cassettes, fs, motion pictures, slides, v-tapes; Other — Clipping files, exhibition catalogs, manuscripts, memorabilia, pamphlets, photographs
Special Subjects: 3-D design, holography
Collections: Nobel Prize for Holography awarded to Dr Dennis Gabor; Papers, technical manuscripts, books and photographs from Dr Dennis Gabor, inventor of holography; early books about holography, including holograms
Publications: Holosphere, monthly; Holography Directory, every 2 years;

exhibition catalog
Activities: Docent training; lectures open to public, 30 vis lectr per year; concerts; gallery talks; tours; video and slide presentations; offer artists in residence program; orginate traveling exhibitions to non-profit museums, art galleries, science centers

M **MUSEUM OF MODERN ART,** 11 W 53rd St, 10019. Tel 212-956-6100. *Chmn of Board* William S Paley; *VChmn* Gardner Cowles; *VChmn* Mrs Henry Ives Cobb; *VChmn* David Rockefeller; *Pres* Mrs John D Rockefeller 3rd; *VPres* Mrs Frank Y Larkin; *VPres* Donald B Marron; *VPres & Treas* John Parkinson III; *Dir Museum* Richard E Oldenburg; *Deputy Dir Admin* Robert L Howe; *Dir Painting & Sculpture Coll* William Rubin; *Dir Drawings* John Elderfield; *Dir Prints & Illustrated Books* Riva Castleman; *Dir Dept Architecture & Design* Arthur Drexler; *Dir Dept Photography* John Szarkowski; *Dir Dept Film* Mary Lea Bandy; *Coordr Exhib* Richard Palmer; *Dir International Prog* Waldo Rasmussen; *Asst Dir Dept Education* Philip Yenawine; *Assoc Dir Dept Publications* Louise Chinn; *Dir Membership & Development* John Limpert; *Dir Public Information* Luisa Kreisberg
Open Mon, Tues, Fri, Sat & Sun 11 AM - 6 PM; Thurs 11 AM - 9 PM; cl Wed and Christmas. Admis adults $3, students $2, children and senior citizens $.75, Tues pay-what-you-wish. Estab 1929 to help people enjoy, understand and use the visual arts of our time. New gallery addition designed by Cesar Pelli, opening May 1984 is a nonprofit education organization. Average Annual Attendance: 1, 300,000. Mem: 49,000; dues student $15, others $35 and up
Income: Financed by admissions, membership, sales of publications and other services and contributions
Collections: Painting and sculptures over 3000; drawings 6000; prints 35,000-40,000; illustrated books 1000; posters and graphics 3500; photographs 20,000; architectural drawings over 1250; architectural models 60; design objects over 4000; films 10,000; film stills over 3,000,000
Exhibitions: (1982) Giorgio De Chirico; The Architecture of Richard Neutra; Five Artists; The Work of Atget: Old Paris; Louise Bourgeois; (1983) Three New Skyscrapers; Prints from Blocks: Gauguin to Now; Big Pictures by Contemporary Photographers; The Modern Drawing: 100 Works on Paper
Publications: Books on exhibitions and artists; monographs; catalogs; exhibitions catalogs
Activities: Symposia; film showings, international in scope, illustrating the historic and esthetic development of the motion picture; lectr; concerts; art lending service; originates traveling exhibitions; circulating film programs and video programs; bookstore selling publications, reproductions, postcards, note and seasonal cards, posters, slides, calendars and gift items

L **Library,** 11 W 53rd St, 10019. Tel 212-956-7236. *Dir* Clive Phillpot; *Asst Dir* Janis Ekdahl; *Assoc Librn Cataloguing* Daniel Starr; *Assoc Librn Reference* Paula Baxter
Open Mon - Fri 1 - 5 PM. Estab 1929 as a research library. For museum staff, art researchers & the public
Library Holdings: Vols 40,000; Per subs 250; Artists files 15,000; Micro — Reels; AV — Cassettes, v-tapes; Other — Clipping files, exhibition catalogs 50,000, manuscripts, pamphlets, photographs
Special Subjects: Architecture, Drawings, Film, Graphic Arts, Mixed Media, Photography, Sculpture, Design, Painting
Collections: †Artists' books; †Dada & Surrealism; †archive of museum publications; †Latin American art; †personal papers of past members, staff and trustees; †personal papers of artists, writers, dealers
Publications: Catalog of the Library of the Museum of Modern Art

M **MUSEUM OF THE AMERICAN INDIAN,** Broadway at 155th St, 10032. Tel 212-283-2420. *Dir* Dr Roland W Force; *Asst Dir* George Eager; *Cur North America* Dr James G E Smith; *Cur South America* Dr Anna C Roosevelt; *Registrar* David Fawcett; *Public Information* Nancy Henry; *Development Officer* Elizabeth Beim; *Designer* Don Werner
Open Tues - Sat 10 AM - 5 PM, Sun 1 - 5 PM, cl Mon & holidays. Admis adults $2, sr citizens & students $1, group rates. Estab in 1916 by George G Heye & devoted to the collection, preservation, study & exhibition of culture & history of the native peoples of Americas. Exhibition halls are arranged to show geographic distribution of peoples with objects ranging in age from 10,000 BC to the present. Museum building is accessible to the physically handicapped, visitors guide in braille & interpreter-on-request program is available. Average Annual Attendance: 75,000. Mem: 1500; dues benefactor $5000, Calumet Circle Corporate Memberships $1000, patron $1000, supporting $500, associate $250, contributing $100, sustaining $50, family $35, regular $20, senior citizen and student $10
Income: Financed by endowment, grants, contributions & memberships
Collections: Decorative arts; numismatic; outstanding collections of pre-Columbian art and historical materials; world's largest collection of art and culture of the Indians of North, Central and South America, West Indies and the Eskimo
Exhibitions: (1983) Star Gods of the Ancient Americas; Glimpses of Algonquin Culture: Indians of Southern New York State; Native American Painting: Selections From the Museum of the American Indian; Iroquois Silverwork; With Eagle Glance: Indians Photographic Images 1868-1931
Publications: Indian Notes; annual book; annual monograph; catalogs; newsletter
Activities: Classes for adults & children; internship & volunteer programs; gallery talks; tours; outreach program to classrooms & audience beyond museum's immediate location; originate traveling exhibition; museum shop sells Indian crafts, jewelry, masks, pottery, beadwork, basketry, weavings, carvings, paintings & prints, books slides, postcards & notepaper

M **MUSEUM OF THE CITY OF NEW YORK,** 1220 Fifth Ave, 10029. Tel 212-534-1672. *Dir* Joseph Veach Noble; *Controller* Thomas McNamara; *Public Affairs* Felice Axelrod
Open Tues - Sat 10 AM - 5 PM, Sun & holidays 1 - 5 PM, cl Mon. No admis fee. Estab 1923 to preserve the cultural accomplishments of New York City's ancestors and to meet the needs and interests of the community of today. Average Annual Attendance: 850,000. Mem: 2500; dues $20 and up

Income: $2,000,000
Collections: Costume collection; decorative arts collection; paintings and print and photograph collection; theatre and music collection; toy collection
Publications: Annual Report; Bulletin, Fall and Spring
Activities: Classes for adults and children; dramatic programs; demonstrations; docent training; lectures open to public; gallery talks; concerts; city walking tours; individual paintings and original objects of art lent to affiliated institutions; museum shop selling books, reproductions, cards
L Library,* 10029. Tel 212-534-1672. *Librn* Nancy Kessler-Post
Library Holdings: Vols 8000; Per subs 10; Other — Clipping files, manuscripts, memorabilia, original art works, pamphlets, photographs, prints, reproductions
Special Subjects: History of New York City

NATIONAL ACADEMY OF DESIGN
For further information, see National and Regional Organizations

NATIONAL ANTIQUE AND ART DEALERS ASSOCIATION OF AMERICA
For further information, see National and Regional Organizations

M **NATIONAL ART MUSEUM OF SPORTS, INC,*** 375 Park Ave, Suite 3408, 10022. Tel 212-755-9679. *Dir* Germain G Glidden
Open daily 9 AM - 5 PM. Admis adults $.50, children $.25. Estab 1959 as an art museum covering sports subjects. Mem: Dues sponsor $5000, general $100, sustaining $25, individual $10
Income: Financed by the State University of New York and governed by the Board of Regents
Collections: Paintings, prints and sculpture of sporting subjects
Exhibitions: Permanent, temporary and traveling exhibitions
Publications: News from the Museum, quarterly newsletter
Activities: Guided tours; rental gallery; book traveling exhibitions

NATIONAL ASSOCIATION OF WOMEN ARTISTS, INC
For further information, see National and Regional Organizations

O **NATIONAL COUNCIL ON ART IN JEWISH LIFE,** 15 E 84th St, 10025. Tel 212-879-4500. *Pres* Julius Schatz; *Secy* Cain Newell; *Treasurer* Sam Levine; *VPres* Dr Mark Podwal; *VPres* Michael Ehrenthal
Open to public. Estab 1965 to advance Jewish art & aid Jewish artists. Average Annual Attendance: 500. Mem: 200; dues $15-$100
Collections: Bibliographic & resource files
Publications: First Jewish Art Annual; Art in Judaism
Activities: Classes for adults; lectures open to public; sales shop sells books, original art, prints & slides
L Library, 15 E 84th St, 10088
Open Mon - Fri 9 AM - 4 PM. Estab 1965
Library Holdings: Micro — Cards; Other — Clipping files, exhibition catalogs, manuscripts, memorabilia, pamphlets, reproductions

NATIONAL INSTITUTE FOR ARCHITECTURAL EDUCATION
For further information, see National and Regional Organizations

NATIONAL SCULPTURE SOCIETY
For further information, see National and Regional Organizations

NATIONAL SOCIETY OF MURAL PAINTERS, INC
For further information, see National and Regional Organizations

NATIONAL SOCIETY OF PAINTERS IN CASEIN AND ACRYLIC, INC
For further information, see National and Regional Organizations

M **NEW MUSEUM,*** 65 Fifth Ave, 10003. Tel 212-741-8962. *Dir* Marcia Tucker; *Dir Planning & Development* Dieter Morris Kearse; *Adminr* Maureen Stewart
Open Mon, Thurs - Fri Noon - 6 PM, Wed Noon - 8 PM, Sat Noon - 5:30 PM; cl Tues, Sun & holidays. Estab 1977 to present to the public new, provocative art that does not yet have wide public exposure or critical acceptance. The gallery space is 2500 sq ft which has been given by the New School for Social Research on an extended basis. Average Annual Attendance: 60,000. Mem: 400; dues $15 and up
Income: Financed by endowment, membership, state appropriation, corporations, foundations and Federal grants
Publications: Newsletter; exhibition catalogs
Activities: Lect open to public; gallery talks

M **NEW SCHOOL FOR SOCIAL RESEARCH ART CENTER GALLERY,*** 65 Fifth Ave, 10003. Tel 212-746-5600
Estab 1919, as a university for adults to advance education of both the scholar and the layman, with work centering in the social sciences and the humanities. Gallery includes large non-credit program; Graduate Faculty of Political and Social Science, Center for New York City Affairs and undergraduate New School College. In 1970 the Parsons School of Design affiliated with The New School. Gallery occupies six buildings, dedicated 1931, 1956, 1959, 1969 and 1972. Mural decorations by Thomas Hart Benton, Michael Cadoret, Camilo Egas, Gonzalo Fonseca and Jose Clemente Orozco. Average Annual Attendance: 17,000
Collections: Paintings by Carlo Dolci, Cleve Gray, Rattner, Youngoman; †sculpture including works by Baskin, Gross, King, Konzal, Lipchitz, Lipton, Hadzi, Noguchi, Penalba, Trajan, Zogbaum and others
Publications: Monthly Bulletin; Social Research, quarterly
M **Collectors Institute of the New School,*** 65 Fifth Ave, 10003. Tel 212-741-5600. *Dir* Paul Mocsanyi
Estab to teach connoisseurship in many fields of art, ancient and modern, as well as the ways and means of collecting. Open to members only. Mem: Dues $650 annually or $325 semi-annually

O **NEW YORK ARTISTS EQUITY ASSOCIATION, INC,** 225 W 34th St, Suite 1510, 10001. Tel 212-736-6480. *Pres* Bert Diener; *VPres* Roy Gussow; *VPres* Carol Hamann; *VPres* Elizabeth Horman; *VPres* Isobel Folb Sokolow; *Exec Dir* Eve Wilen; *Treas* Bea Begman; *Recording Secy* Wendy Jackel
Open 10 AM - 5 PM. Estab 1947 as a politically non-partisan group to advance the cultural, legislative, economic and professional interest of painters, sculptors, printmakers, and others in the field of visual arts. Various committees concerned with aims. Administrators of the Artists Welfare Fund, Inc. Mem: Over 1700; dues $24; meetings Oct - May
Income: Financed by dues
Publications: NY Artists Equity, Association newsletter, quarterly
Activities: Symposiums; seminars; trips to cultural institutions; advocacy; information services; artists benefits
O **Artists Welfare Fund, Inc,** 225 W 34 St, Rm 1510, 10001. Tel 212-736-6480. *Exec Officer* Elias Newman
Artists Welfare Fund, Inc is a non-profit tax-deductible service organization, administered by officers of New York Artists Equity Association, Inc. Formed to help artists in need of financial assistance in health emergencies, with loans without interest
Income: Financed by contributions
Activities: Art Symposia, free to the public

M **NEW YORK CITY DEPARTMENT OF CULTURAL AFFAIRS,** City Gallery,* Second Floor, 2 Columbus Circle, 10019. Tel 212-974-1150
Open Mon - Fri 10 AM - 5:30 PM. No admin fee
Exhibitions: Exhibitions are curated by outside organizations on application basis
Activities: Concerts; loan exhibitions

O **NEW YORK HISTORICAL SOCIETY,** 170 Central Park W, 10024. Tel 212-873-3400. *Pres* Robert G Goelet; *VPres* Robert S Beekman, MD; *Dir* James B Bell; *Coordr Exhibition* Elizabeth M Currie; *Secy* Jarvis Cromwell; *Librn* Dr Larry Sullivan
Open Tues - Fri 11 AM - 5 PM; Sat 10 AM - 5 PM; Sun 1 - 5 PM. No admis fee, donations. Estab 1804 to collect and preserve material relating to the history of New York City and State. Maintains art gallery. Average Annual Attendance: 300,000. Mem: 2000; dues corporate member $1000, family member $75, annual member $50
Income: $750,000 (financed by endowment and membership)
Collections: American landscape and genre paintings; American portraits; European paintings prior to 1850
Activities: Lect for members only, 5 vis lectr per yr; concerts; gallery talks; tours; individual paintings and original objects of art lent to museums; lending collection contains 8000 paintings, 500,000 photographs, 2500 sculptures; sales shop selling books, magazines and prints
L Library, 170 Central Park West, 10024. *Librn* Larry E Sullivan; *Assoc Librn* Katherine Richards
Open Tues - Sat 10 AM - 5 PM. Estab 1804. For reference only
Income: $750,000 (financed by endowment & membership)
Library Holdings: Vols 630,000; Per subs 300; Micro — Cards, fiche, reels; Other — Exhibition catalogs, manuscripts, memorabilia, original art works, pamphlets, photographs, prints, sculpture
Special Subjects: American Art to 1900
Collections: Civil War material; New York City & State History; 19th century advertising

L **NEW YORK PUBLIC LIBRARY,** Astor, Lenox & Tilden Foundations, Fifth Ave & 42nd St, 10018. Tel 212-930-0736. *Pres* Vartan Gregorian
Estab 1895. Entire library contains over 7,000,000 volumes
L Prints Room, Fifth Ave & 42nd St, Rm 308, 10018. Tel 212-930-0817. *Keeper of Prints* Robert Rainwater
Open by application to Special Collection Office, Mon, Wed, Fri & Sat 1 - 6 PM, cl Sun, Thurs & holidays. Estab 1899
Library Holdings: Vols 20,000; Other — Prints 175,000
Special Subjects: Graphic artists and catalogs of their works, original fine prints of the past six centuries with special emphasis on 19th century French and American, contemporary American and European, prints, techniques and illustrated books
Collections: Samuel Putnam Avery Collection of bookplates; Radin Collection of Western European bookplates; British and American caricatures; Beverly Chew bequest of Milton and Pope portraits; Eno Collection of New York City Views; McAlpin Collection of George Washington Portraits; Smith Collection of Japanese prints; Phelps Stokes Collection of American views
L Spencer Collection, Fifth Ave & 42nd St, Room 324, 10018. Tel 212-930-0818. *Cur* Joseph T Rankin
Open by application to Special Collections Office, Mon, Wed, Fri & Sat 1 - 6 PM, cl Sun, Thurs & holidays
Library Holdings: Vols 8000
Special Subjects: Rare illustrated and illuminated manuscripts and books in all languages of all countries and of all periods, constituting the development of book illustration and fine bindings
L Art, Prints and Photographs Division, Fifth Ave & 42nd St, Room 313, 10018. Tel 212-930-0834. *Chief* Joseph T Rankin
Open Mon, Wed, Fri & Sat 10 AM - 6 PM, Tues 10 AM - 9 PM, cl Sun & Thurs. Estab 1911 for reference
Library Holdings: Vols 100,000; Other — Clipping files, exhibition catalogs, pamphlets
Special Subjects: Ceramics, costume design & construction, furniture, glass, interior design, jewelry, silversmithing, textiles, architectural design, history, painting and sculpture and the decorative arts of all countries from prehistoric times to the present, special emphasis on scholarly works in history, post-Columbian American art and Oriental art
Collections: †Private and public collection catalogs; individual artists and architects
L Schomburg Center for Research in Black Culture, 515 Lennox Ave, 10030. Tel 212-862-4000. *Chief* Kathy Lennonx Hooker
A reference library devoted to Black people throughout the world
Library Holdings: Vols 70,000; broadsides, maps, playbills, programs; Micro —

Reels; AV — Fs, rec; Other — Clipping files, photographs, prints
Special Subjects: Black people throughout the world with major emphasis on Afro-American, Africa and Carribbean, nucleus of collected rarities of Arthur A Schomburg, a Puerto Rican of African descent
Collections: Largest collection in the country of books on Black Culture and Art; permanent collection of African Art

L **Mid-Manhattan Library, Art Collection,*** 455 Fifth Ave, 10016. *Supervising Librn* Open
Open Mon - Thurs 9 AM - 9 PM, Fri & Sat 10 AM - 6 PM
Library Holdings: Vols 22,984; Per subs 100; Vertical files of catalogs & clippings on comtemporary artists & art movements; Micro — Reels; Other — Clipping files
  —**Mid-Manhattan Library, Picture Collection,** 455 Fifth Ave, 10016. *Cur* Open
Open Mon, Wed & Fri Noon - 6 PM, Tues Noon - 8 PM, Thurs 10 AM - 6 PM, cl Sat, Sun & holidays. Estab 1915
Library Holdings: Vols 20,000; Per subs 100
Collections: Approximately 2,378,000 classified picture encyclopedic in subjects. May be borrowed by those who live, work or study in New York State, except for exhibition of classroom use

M **Shelby Cullom Davis Museum, Library & Museum of the Performing Arts,** Lincoln Center, 111 Amsterdam Ave, 10023. Tel 212-870-1630. *Chief* Dr Robert Morton Henderson; *Admin Assoc* Joan Canale; *Dance Cur* Genevieve Oswald; *Theatre Cur* Dorothy Swerdlove; *Recordings Cur* Frank Campbell; *Recordings Cur* David Hall; *Librn* George Mayer; *Public Relations Dir* Sue Fontaine; *Publications Dir* Dr David V Erdman
Open Mon & Thurs 10 AM - 8 PM, Tues 10 AM - 6 PM, Wed, Fri & Sat Noon - 6 PM. No admis fee. Estab 1964 to present exhibitions of high quality pertaining directly with the performing arts. Main Gallery is 140 x 40 x 20 ft and has large glass space designed by Saarinen; Astor Gallery measures 80 x 30 x 30 ft; Amsterdam Gallery is 30 x 50 x 10 ft; Plaza Gallery 20 x 20 x 20 ft
Income: Financed by endowment and city appropriation
Collections: Prints; letters; documents; photographs; posters, films; video tapes; memorabilia; dance music; recordings
Activities: Sales shop sells books, magazines, reproductions, prints, slides and various material related to the performing arts

L **NEW YORK SCHOOL OF INTERIOR DESIGN LIBRARY,** 155 E 56th St, 10022. Tel 212-753-5365. *Librn* Malcolm E Scheer
Open Mon & Thurs 9 AM - 4:30 PM, Tues & Weds 11:30 AM - 6:30 PM, Fri 9 AM - 2 PM. Estab 1924 to supplement the courses given by the school and to aid students and faculty in their research and projects
Income: $14,000
Purchases: $5000
Library Holdings: Vols 2700; Per subs 53; AV — Slides; Other — Exhibition catalogs
Special Subjects: Interior Design, Architecture

O **NEW YORK SOCIETY OF ARCHITECTS,*** 16 E 42nd St, 10017. Tel 212-682-3594. *Pres* Donald E Freed; *VPres* Richard Bender; *VPres* Joseph Feingold; *Secy* Samuel Horn; *Treas* Robert A Brisson; *Executive Dir* Margot A Henkel
Open 10:30 AM - 5 PM. Incorporated 1906. Mem: 450; dues $72; meetings third Wed of every month
Income: $32,000 (financed by dues and sales)
Publications: Bulletin, monthly; New York City Building Code Manual; New York City Electrical Code; New York City Fire Prevention Code
Activities: Matthew W DelGaudio Award for Excellence in Design to architectural students, Honorary Membership Certificate to other than architect, Distinguished Service Award to members, Sidney L Strauss Memorial Award to architect or layman

NEW YORK UNIVERSITY
M **Grey Art Gallery and Study Center,** 33 Washington Place, 10003. Tel 212-598-7603. *Dir* Robert R Littman; *Asst Dir* James Clearwater; *Registrar* Michele Wong
Open Tues & Thurs 10 AM - 6:30 PM; Weds 10 AM - 8:30 PM; Fri 10 AM - 5 PM; Sat 1 - 5 PM. No admis fee. Estab 1975 as university art museum to serve public as well as university community. The New York University Art Collection of approx 3500 works is now under the Grey Art Gallery. Gallery space of approx 4000 sq ft used for changing exhibitions
Collections: American and European 20th Century Paintings, Watercolors, and Prints; Ben and Abby Grey Foundation Collection of Comtemporary Asian and Middle Eastern Art; New York University Art Collection
Exhibitions: (1982) A Sense of Place: Edward Burra & Paul Nash; Sculpture by David Hare & Frederick Kiesler; Audubon & Sons; Samuel F B Morse; Faces Photographed; Eva Hesse; Frida Kahlo & Tina Modatti; Tulips, Arabesques & Turbans, Art from the Ottoman Empire; Louise Dahl Wolf & Paul Outerbridge
Publications: Exhibition catalogs
Activities: Individual paintings and original objects of art lent to other cultural institutions; originate traveling exhibitions; sales shop selling exhibition catalogs
M **80 Washington Square East Galleries,** 80 Washington Sq E, 10003. Tel 212-598-2163. *Faculty Dir* Dr Marilynn Karp; *Co-Dir* Ruth D Newman; *Co-Dir* C Allen Coleman
Open Tues 11 AM - 7 PM, Wed & Thurs 11 AM - 6 PM, Fri & Sat 11 AM - 5 PM. No admis fee. Estab 1975 for exhibitions of works by graduate student artists. Six gallery rooms containins one man shows. Average Annual Attendance: 10,000
Exhibitions: (1983-84) Five one man shows; 8th Annual Small Works Competition
Publications: Press releases
Activities: Lectures open to public; competitions with awards
L **Stephen Chan Library of Fine Arts,*** One E 78th St, 10021. *Dir* Evelyn K Samuel; *Cataloger* Francis G Bondurant
Estab to provide scholarly materials for graduate studies in art history and archaeology. Open to the public upon application to the librarian
Library Holdings: Vols 78,807; Per subs 676; Micro — Fiche, reels; AV — Slides

L **Photographic Archive,*** One E 78th St, . Tel 212-772-5800. *Cur* Suzanne Babineau-Simenauer
Library open to qualified researchers
Collections: Offner, Florentine painting; Coor, Sienese painting; Berenson, Italian painting; DIAL Collection; I Tatti Archive; Gernsheim Corpus, 60,000 drawings

O **THE ONE CLUB FOR ART & COPY,** 251 E 50th St, 10022. Tel 212-935-0121. *Dir* Beverley Daniels; *Asst to Dir* Patricia Reilly
Estab 1975 to support the craft of advertising, informal interchange among creative people, develop advertising excellence through advertising students who are tomorrow's professionals. Mem: 500; dues individual $60, student $45; annual meeting in Jan
Income: $200,000 (financed by membership & awards show)
Publications: The One Show Annual, Advertising's Best, annually
Activities: Lectures open to public & some for members only; competitions with awards; scholarships

O **ORGANIZATION OF INDEPENDENT ARTISTS,** 201 Varick St, PO Box 146, 10014. Tel 212-929-6688. *Pres* Rubin L Gorewitz; *VPres* Corinne Robins; *Exec Dir* Debi Feiman; *Artistic Dir* Warren Tanner; *Public Relations* Pennelope Goodfriend
Mon - Fri 11 AM - 5 PM. Estab 1976 to facilitate artist-curated group exhibitions in public spaces throughout NY. Exhibit in public spaces. Average Annual Attendance: 10,000. Mem: 1000; registration $5
Income: $25,000 (financed by membership, state appropriation, federal funds, corporate & foundation funds)
Exhibitions: South Beach Psychiatric Center Sculpture Garden; 16 Printmakers From the Printmaking Workshop; Personal Expressionism
Activities: Scholarships

C **PAINE WEBBER INC,*** 140 Broadway, 10005. Tel 212-437-2105, 437-2121. *Pres* Donald B Marron
Collection displayed throughout offices
Collections: Contemporary American paintings, drawings and prints
Activities: Tours; individual objects of art lent

L **PARSONS SCHOOL OF DESIGN,** Adam & Sophie Gimbel Library, 2 W 13th St (Mailing add: 66 Fifth Ave, New York, NY 10011). Tel 212-741-8914, 741-8915. *Head Librn* Sharon Chickanzeff; *Reference Librn & Cataloguer* Claire Petrie
Open Mon - Thurs 9 AM - 9 PM, Fri 9 AM - 6 PM, Sat 10 AM - 6 PM. Estab as a school in 1896, with the Adam L Gimbel Library moving at present location in 1974, as a support to the curriculum of the school
Library Holdings: Vols 32,000; Per subs 160; Picture files; Other — Clipping files, exhibition catalogs, memorabilia, original art works, prints
Special Subjects: Architecture, Crafts, Fine Arts, Furniture, Industrial Design, Photography, Sculpture, Costume Design, City Planning, Environmental Design, Graphics, Painting, Typography
L **Library,** 66 Fifth Ave, New York, 10011
Library Holdings: Vols 32,000; Per subs 160; Other — Clipping files, exhibition catalogs, memorabilia, original art works, pamphlets, reproductions

O **PEN AND BRUSH, INC,*** 16 E Tenth St, 10003. Tel 212-475-3669. *Pres* Mercy Dobell Wolfe; *First VPres* Helen Slottman; *Recording Secy* Harriet M Hagerty; *Corresp Secy* Arthur Ray Nichols; *Exec Secy* Camilla Belding; *Treas* Jennie M Palen
Open Noon - 4 PM except holidays during exhibitions. Estab 1893, incorporated 1912. The Clubhouse was purchased in 1923, and contains rooms, dining room and exhibition galleries. Mem: Approx 250 professional women writers, artists, sculptors, and craftsmen; annual meeting Feb
Collections: Paintings; graphics; pastels; sculpture
Exhibitions: Ten annual exhibitions of members' work; occasional one-man shows
Activities: Workshops; lect
L **Library,*** 16 E Tenth St, 10003
For members only
Library Holdings: Vols 1500

C **PHILIP MORRIS INCORPORATED,*** 100 Park Ave, 10017. Tel 212-880-3470. *Mgr Cultural Affairs* Odile Basch
Estab 1960's to enhance the creative and aesthetic environments of offices. Collection displayed in offices and corridors; annual amount of contributions and grants $1,000,000; supports museums, exhibitions, theater, groups, symphony orchestras, art associations, libraries, historical societies, opera companies, commissions
Collections: Prints by artists around the world, tobacco memorabilia, works by emerging artists
Activities: Supports arts organizations located in Philip Morris plant communities; individual objects of art lent to museums exhibitions only

M **PRATT INSTITUTE,** Pratt Manhattan Center Gallery, 160 Lexington Ave, 10016. Tel 212-685-3169. *Dir* Andrew Stasik; *Staff* Ellen Schwartz
Open Mon - Fri 10 AM - 6 PM, Sat 10 AM - 5 PM. No admis fee. Estab to present to the public exhibitions of interest vital to the concerns of the New York artists and collectors. Average Annual Attendance: 10,000. Mem: 2500; dues $18 and up
Exhibitions: International Miniature Print Competition; Molas: Art of the Cuna Indians; mini-competition and annual exhibition of Artists of the Pratt Graphics Center
Publications: Print Review magazine, semi-annually
Activities: Classes for adults in printmaking, book arts, papermaking & graphic design; lect for members only, 5 - 10 lectr visiting per year; gallery talks; competitions; awards; book traveling exhibitions; originate traveling exhibitions
L **Phoenix School of Design Library,*** 160 Lexington Ave, 10016. Tel 212-685-2973
Library Holdings: Vols 2000; Per subs 32; VF 8; AV — Motion pictures 7500
Special Subjects: Decorative Arts, Interior Design, Costume Design & Construction, Fashion Arts, Textiles, Photography

M **PRINCE STREET GALLERY,** 121 Wooster St, 10012. Tel 212-226-9402
Open Tues - Sun Noon - 6 PM. Estab 1970 to provide a showing place for
members, mainly figurative art; cooperative artist run gallery. Gallery has about
25 members who have shown in New York as well as throughout the Country
and internationally. Average Annual Attendance: 6000. Mem: 25; dues $420;
monthly meetings
Income: Financed by membership
Exhibitions: (1982-83) Season: Monica Bernier, Marion Lerner Levine, Marcy
Rosenblat, Selina Trieff, Donald Kimes, Gerald Marcus, Christopher Semergieff,
Arthur Levine and group shows
Publications: Catalog of Gallery Artists 1973

O **PRINTMAKING WORKSHOP,*** 114 W 17th St, 10011. Tel 212-989-6125,
242-9884. *Dir* Robert Blackburn
Open Mon - Fri 8 AM - 11 PM, Sat & Sun 9 AM - 5 PM. Estab 1949 as a
workshop space for artists to print etchings and lithographs including night
classes and edition printing. Gallery is maintained with 2000 contemporary prints
for sale and exhibition rental. Mem: 800; dues vary
Income: Financed by endowment, membership, city and state appropriation
Collections: Impressions-Expressions, Black American Graphics; Artists Who
Make Prints, Independent Artists; Prints & Monotypes From Bob Blackbur
Exhibitions: Contemporary Images From the Printmaking Workshop; Selections
from the Printmaking Workshop Collection; Diverse Directions of Selected
Prints; Printmakers-New Offerings
Activities: Classes for adults; classes in graphic arts; lect open to the public;
scholarship; original objects of art lent; material available to local areas with
mobile print programs; traveling exhibitions organized and circulated

O **PUBLIC ART FUND, INC,** 25 Central Park West, Suite 25R, 10023. Tel 212-
541-8423. *Exec Dir* Jenny Dixon; *Project Dir* Jessica Cusick; *Percent for Art
Program Coordr* Jennifer McGregor
Open Mon - Fri 10 AM - 6 PM. Estab 1977 as an umbrella organization to fund
the activities of the Public Arts Council and City Walls; to bring art outside and
into a daily urban environment; for temporary exhibitions; administrates New
York City Percent for Art program
Income: $220,000 (financed by National Endowment for the Arts, New York
State Council of the Art, endowments, private & corporate contributions)
Exhibitions: Jean Dubuffet, Richard Serra, Noguchi, Jeffrey Brosk, George
Sugarman, Linda Howard, Louise Nevelson, George Rickey, David Wells, Alice
Adams, Jack Youngerman, Kit-Yin Snyder, California Billboards; Boyant Park,
AIR; Messages to the Public
Publications: A walking tour guide to Lower Manhattan
Activities: Competitions to commission new works of art; originated traveling
exhibitions; sales shop sells slides, postcards, catalogs and manuals on public art
L **Library,** 25 Central Park West, 10023
Estab as a reference library on public art
Library Holdings: AV — Slides 4000
Collections: Murals; outdoor sculpture

M **NICHOLAS ROERICH MUSEUM,** 319 W 107th St, 10025. Tel 212-864-
7752. *Pres* Katherine Campbell Stibbe; *Secy* Elina Yussupoff; *Exec Dir* Daniel
Entin; *Cur* Edgar Lansbury
Open daily 2 - 5 PM; cl Mon & holidays. No admis fee. Estab 1958 to show a
permanent collection of paintings by Nicholas Roerich, internationally known
artist, to promote his ideals as a great thinker, writer, humanitarian, scientist, and
explorer, and to promote his Pact and Banner of Peace. There is a gallery in
which works of contemporary artists are shown. Average Annual Attendance:
5000. Mem: Dues sustaining $50, contributing $25, assoc $10
Income: Financed by membership and donations
Collections: Permanent collection of paintings by Nicholas Roerich
Activities: Lect open to public, 3 vis lectr per year; concerts; tours; museum shop
selling books, reproductions and postcards
L **Library,** 319 W 107th St, 10025
Pamphlets and publications being catalogued for reference

C **RUDER & FINN FINE ARTS,*** 110 E 59th St, 10022. Tel 212-593-6475. *Pres*
Nina Wright
Estab to link corporations which support the arts with museum exhibitions and
performing arts events, to develop major corporate sponsored exhibitions and
special projects created for public spaces. Assistance given for marketing and
publicity assignments for cultural institutions and the selection, installation and
documentation of corporate art collections. We are in the business of linking
corporations with museums and other arts organizations in support of exhibitions;
also council both small business and large corporations on how they can
contribute to their communities through the visual arts. Ruder & Finn Fine Arts
is a division of the public relations firm of Ruder & Finn Inc
Activities: Originate traveling exhibitions to museums nationwide

SALMAGUNDI CLUB
For further information, see National and Regional Organizations

M **SCALAMANDRE MUSEUM OF TEXTILES,*** 950 Third Ave, 10022. Tel
212-361-8500. *Founder & Pres* Franco Scalamandre; *Dir* Serena Hortian
Open Mon - Fri 9 AM - 5 PM. Estab 1947 to encourage interest in textile design
for decoration
Collections: Contemporary textiles showing modern motifs in textured weaves of
today; reproductions of old textiles; 2000 old documentary pieces of textile
Exhibitions: 15 small student exhibits for art schools, colleges (must be requested
by faculty member); permanent display of textiles used in Historic Restorations
Activities: Lect given on history of textile design, including the classification of
textiles, both period and modern; traveling exhibits in the various periods of
decorative art for circulation throughout the United States to museums only

L **SCHOOL OF VISUAL ARTS LIBRARY,** 380 Second Ave (Mailing add: 209 E
23rd St, 10010). Tel 212-679-7350, Ext 412. *Chief Librn* Zuki Landau; *Cataloger*
Rosemary Pandolfi; *Cataloger* Joan Arnold; *Slide Cur* Dr Eriko Amino
Open Mon - Thurs 9 AM - 7:30 PM, Fri 9 AM - 5 PM, Sat 11 AM - 4 PM

exclusively for student and faculty use. Estab 1962 to serve needs of School of
Visual Arts students and faculty. Small gallery space for student work.
Circ 32,500
Income: Financed by tuition
Purchases: $37,785
Library Holdings: Vols 40,000; Per subs 178; AV — Cassettes, rec, slides;
Other — Clipping files, exhibition catalogs, framed reproductions, original art
works, pamphlets, photographs 28,000, prints 38,000, reproductions, sculpture
Special Subjects: Art History, Film, Photography, Sculpture, Painting
Exhibitions: Master Eagle Family of Companies' exhibition; student exhibitions
Publications: Library Handbook; monthly accessions lists
Activities: Poetry readings are held

SCULPTORS GUILD, INC
For further information, see National and Regional Organizations

M **SCULPTURE CENTER,** 167 E 69th St, 10021. Tel 212-879-0430, 737-9870.
Pres Arthur F Abelman; *Treas* Victor Tamerlis; *VPres* Barbara Lekberg; *Secy*
John Gilman; *Gallery Dir* Marion Giffiths; *School Dir* Gary Sussman
Open Tues - Sat 11 AM - 5 PM. No admis fee. Estab 1928 as Clay Club of New
York to further the interest of student and professional sculptors. Incorporated in
1944 as the Sculpture Center, a nonprofit organization for the promotion of the
art of sculpture and to provide work facilities. Moved into the new building in
1950, when the present name was adopted. Slide file maintained for unaffiliated
sculptors for use by consultants, curators, collectors & architects. A gallery is
maintained, and has represented in it professional sculptors. School and studio
space can be provided for beginning, intermediate and advanced students.
Average Annual Attendance: 35,000
Exhibitions: Solo and group exhibitions throughout the year
Publications: Announcements (for the gallery and school); brochures; exhibition
catalogs
Activities: Classes for adults and children; lectures open to public; concerts;
gallery talks; tours; scholarships; original objects of art lent to private galleries
and corporate lobbies; sales shop sells tools and supplies for sculptors
L **Library,** 167 E 69th St, 10021
Library Holdings: Vols 300; Per subs 3; Other — Exhibition catalogs,
memorabilia, original art works, pamphlets, photographs, sculpture

C **JOSEPH E SEAGRAM & SONS, INC,** 375 Park Ave, 10152. Tel 212-572-
7379. *In Charge Art Coll* Carla Caccamise Ash
Open to public. Estab 1958 for the enjoyment of Seagram employees. Collection
displayed in offices and reception areas; permanent gallery on 4th floor, used for
temporary art exhibitions, both loan and in-house
Collections: 19th and 20th century American photographs of urban life; antique
glass, European and American; 20th century drawings, graphics, paintings,
posters and tapestries
Exhibitions: Temporary installations of notable sculpture on Plaza; several loan
exhibitions
Activities: Lect; tours Tues 3 PM; individual objects of art lent for selected
musuem exhibitions; originate traveling exhibitions

SOCIETY FOR FOLK ARTS PRESERVATION, INC
For further information, see National and Regional Organizations

SOCIETY OF AMERICAN GRAPHIC ARTISTS
For further information, see National and Regional Organizations

SOCIETY OF ILLUSTRATORS
For further information, see National and Regional Organizations

O **SOCIETY OF SCRIBES, LTD,** PO Box 933, 10150. *Pres* Edward Francolini;
VPres Barry Morentz; *Treasurer* Judith B Kastin
Estab 1975. Mem: 1300; dues $15; annual meeting in Feb
Exhibitions: Calligraphy in the Graphic Arts
Publications: Newsletter, 3 per yr; Journal, annual
Activities: Workshops; lectures open to public; book traveling exhibitions

O **SOHO CENTER FOR VISUAL ARTISTS,*** 110-114 Prince St, 10012. Tel
212-226-1993. *Founder & Pres* Larry Aldrich
Open Tues - Sat Noon - 6 PM. No admis fee. Estab 1974, a non-profit activity
sponsored by the Aldrich Museum of Contemporary Art and the Mobil
Foundation. An exhibition center was established for the purpose of showing the
work of new artists who are not represented by a commercial gallery. Average
Annual Attendance: 50,000
Exhibitions: Changing monthly
L **Library,*** 110-114 Prince St, 10012. Tel 212-226-1993. *In Charge* Kristen
Cooney-Crawford
Open Tue - Sat Noon - 6 PM. Estab 1974 for art reference of working artists.
Nonprofit gallery gives shows to selected NYC artists not represented by a
commercial gallery. Average Annual Attendance: 600
Income: Financed by Aldrich Museum of Contemporary Art and the Mobil
Foundation
Library Holdings: Vols 2000; Per subs 35; museum catalogs; Other — Exhibition
catalogs, pamphlets, prints, reproductions
M **Soho 20,*** 469 Broome St, 10013. Tel 212-226-4167. *Coordr* Reine Hauser
Open Tues - Sat Noon - 6 PM. Estab as a women's co-operative gallery
Activities: Lectures open to public, 12 vis lectr per year; gallery talks; tours;
originate traveling exhibitions to other museums

M **SOUTH STREET SEAPORT MUSEUM,*** 203 Front St, 10038. Tel 212-766-
9020. *Pres* John B Hightower; *Dir Educ* Jane Clark
Open daily 11 AM - 5 PM. Admis adults $3.50, children $1.50, members no
charge. Estab 1967 to preserve the maritime history and traditions of the Port of
New York. Several gallery spaces: The Seaport Gallery for art exhibits; the
model ship gallery; the printing press gallery at Bowne & Co Stationers; the
museum orientation center. Mem: 9000; dues family $25, individual $15; annual
meeting May

Income: Financed by membership and corporate grants
Collections: Collection is mainly the buildings and ships and the neighborhood they define; small permanent collection of marine art and artifacts; Palmer Collection of ship models
Publications: South Street Packet, bi-monthly; South Street Reporter, quarterly
Activities: Classes for adults and children; walking tours of area; lect open to public, 10 - 15 visiting lectr per year; concerts; individual paintings and original objects of art lent to institutions; lending collection contains 200 original prints, paintings, ship models; museum shop sells books, magazines, original art, reproductions, prints and slides

L **Library,*** 16 Fulton, 10038. Tel 212-766-9047. *Librn* Gerard Boardman
For reference
Library Holdings: Vols 3000; Per subs 20; negatives; Other — Photographs

SPECIAL LIBRARIES ASSOCIATION, Museum, Arts and Humanities Division
For further information, see National and Regional Organizations

M **STUDIO MUSEUM IN HARLEM,** 144 W 125th St, 10027. Tel 212-864-4500.
Executive Dir Mary S Campbell; *Deputy Dir* Kinshasha Conwill; *Controller* Al Bolton; *Develop Dir* Patricia Cruz; *Cur* Terrie Rouse; *Cur Education* Schroeder Cherry; *Art Dir* Alfred Cucci; *Gift Shop Mgr* Joan Deroko
Open Wed - Fri 10 AM - 5 PM, Sat & Sun 1 - 6 PM. Admis adults $1, children, students & sr citizens $.50, members free. Estab 1967 to exhibit the works of contemporary Black American artists, mount historical and informative exhibitions, and provide culturally educational programs and activities for the general public. 10,000 sq ft of exhibition and education space. Average Annual Attendance: 40,000. Mem: 707; dues $15 - $1000
Income: Financed by membership, city and state appropriation, corporate and foundation funding, federal funding, rental income, gift shop sales & individual contributions
Collections: James Van Der Zee Collection of Photography; 1000 works of art by Afro-American artists including sculpture, painting and works on paper; †Caribbean art
Exhibitions: Ritual Myth: A Survey of African American Art; Images of Dignity: A Retrospective of the Works of Charles White; Harlem Heyday: The Photography of James VanDerZee; An Ocean Apart: American Artists Abroad; Anthony Barboza: Introspect; Red & Black to D; Photographs by Sam Gilliam; The Sound I Saw: The Jazz Photographs of Roy DeCarava; Alma Thomas: A Life in Art; Richards Yarde: Savoy; Jack Whitten: Ten Years; Gifts & Promised Gifts: Selections From the Permanent Collection
Publications: Catalogues of major black artists
Activities: Classes for adults & children; docent training; workshops; panel discussions; demonstrations; cooperative school program; internship program; lectures open to public, 10 vis lectr per yr; concerts; gallery talks; tours; scholarships; book traveling exhibitions; originate traveling exhibitions; museum shop sells books, magazines, original art, reproductions, prints, jewelry, baskets, crafts, pottery & catalogues

O **LOUIS COMFORT TIFFANY FOUNDATION,*** 1083 Fifth Ave, 10028. Tel 212-431-9880. *Pres* Lewis Iselin; *VPres* Paul Smith; *Secy* Gerard Jones; *Exec Dir* Elizabeth Stevens
Estab 1918 to give grants to painters and sculptors and in the crafts. Applications available Jan, applications due Sept. Mem: Annual meeting May
Income: Financed by endowment
Activities: Open competition for painters and sculptors every two years; twenty grants of $5000 each are given

M **TRAPHAGEN SCHOOL OF FASHION,** Museum Collection, 257 Park Ave S, 10010. Tel 212-673-0300. *Cur Museum Coll* Phyllis Spenser
Open to public by appointment only. No admis fee. Estab 1923 to record fashion changes through the centuries; to use the collection as another means of teaching history of costume; to use the items as inspiration for new design ideas. Exhibition area in Reception Hall. Trunk showings for students, guests or designers (by appointment) in Museum Workroom are also given
Collections: Bride and bridegroom folk costumes around the world; ethnic dolls in native costume; extensive African and American Indian costumes and jewelry; famous women in history; famous women in the theatre; four doll collections, including children of the 19th and 20th centuries; over 1000 period and ethnic costumes, plus fashion accessories
Exhibitions: Antique Laces; Beaded Chemises of the Twenties; Children of the 19th and 20th Centuries; Gloves and Fans; Period Bridal Gowns; Undercover Fashions 1840-1910; Chinese Costumes, Textiles, Fans and Shoes
Activities: Educ dept; docent training; tours

L **Library,** 257 Park Ave S, 10010. Tel 212-673-0300. *Librn* Mrs Allyn Rice Bloeme
Open to public by appointment. Estab 1923 to stimulate inquiry into new areas of fashion and allied fields; to give students of fashion design, illustration, or interior design the opportunity to explore related subjects in depth
Library Holdings: Vols 17,000; Per subs 5; AV — Slides; Other — Clipping files, memorabilia, pamphlets
Special Subjects: Fashion Arts, Interior Design
Collections: Bound volumes of early fashion magazines including: Godey's Magazine; Journal des Dames et Modes (1798-1840); Journal des Demoiselles (1870-1907); La Art et La Mode (1880-1915); Ladies' Companion; Les Modes (1903-1936); Les Modes et Usages du temps de Marie Antoinnette (1787-1792), 2 vols; Studio and Illustration Magazine of Fine and Applied Arts, 41 Vols
Exhibitions: (1983) American Indian Exhibit; French Provences Costumes; Diamond Jubilee Celebration: Traphagen Salute to Brooklyn Bridge in its Centennial; Swiss Exhibit: Collection Geszler; Polish Exhibit of Native Costume
Activities: Library tours

M **22 WOOSTER GALLERY,** 22 Wooster St, 10013. Tel 212-431-6445. *Executive Member* Julie Graham; *Executive Member* Samia A Halaby; *Executive Member* Charlotte Hastings; *Executive Member* Kevin Hylton; *Executive Member* Lorenzo Pace; *Executive Member* Georgeann Packard; *Executive Member* Carey

Rosemarin; *Executive Member* Sumayyah Samaha; *Executive Member* Ted Thirlby
Open Tues - Sat Noon - 6 PM. No admis fee. Estab 1978 as a non-profit alternative exhibition space run by artists. Average Annual Attendance: 11,200
Exhibitions: (1983) Halaby & McClelland; Anna B Bresnick; (1984) On Rhythms & Form; Making Marks: Works on Paper
Publications: On Trial: Yale School of Art, catalog
Activities: Lectures open to public; artist talk on art series

UKIYO-E SOCIETY OF AMERICA, INC
For further information, see National and Regional Organizations

O **UKRAINIAN INSTITUTE OF AMERICA, INC,*** Two East 79th St, 10021. Tel 212-288-8660. *Pres* Theodore Dzus; *VPres* W Nazarevicz; *Secy* M Honczarenko; *Admin Dir* John M Samilenko; *Board of Dir* Dr Stepan Woroch; *Chmn of Membership Committee* Dr Rostyslaw Sochynsky; *Chmn of Pub Rel* V Hnatkowsky
Open Tues - Sat 10 AM - 6 PM, Sun by appointment. Admis by contribution. Estab 1948 to develop, sponsor and promote educational activities which will acquaint the general public with history, culture and art of Ukrainian people. Average Annual Attendance: 8500. Mem: 280; dues life $100, associate $25; annual meeting Nov 6
Income: $60,000 (financed by endowment, membership and contributions)
Purchases: $2500
Collections: Church & religious relics; folk art, ceramic & woodwork; patents of Ukrainian-American engineers; Gritchenko Foundation Collection; sculptures by Archipenko, Kruk, Mol & others; Ukrainian paintings
Exhibitions: Fifteen Young Ukrainian Artists; Slavic & Baltic Ethnic Groups; Y Kalmanovsky & Turowsky—new emigrants from Kiyev; M Morozov, Z Onishkevycz, Arka Petryshyn, International Art Exhibit
Publications: UIA Newsletter, monthly; Fifteenth Anniversary of UIA; Thirtieth Anniversary of UIA
Activities: Classes for adults; dramatic programs; seminars; symposiums; workshop seminars; literary evenings; lectures open to public, 3000 vis lectr per yr; concerts; gallery talks; tours

M **UKRAINIAN MUSEUM,** 203 Second Ave, 10003. Tel 212-228-0110. *Dir* Maria Shust; *Admin Dir* Daria Bajko; *Educational Dir* Lubow Wolynetz; *Public Relations* Lydia Hajduczok; *Archivist* Chrystyna Prvry
Open Wed - Sun 1 - 5 PM. Admis adults $1, sr citizens, students & children $. 50. Estab 1976 to preserve, maintain, expand and exhibit its permanent collection of Ukrainian folk art and its photographic and document collection on Ukrainian immigration. Average Annual Attendance: 13,000. Mem: 1200; dues family $50, adults $25, sr citizens & students $10
Income: $139,000 (financed by membership, donations and grants)
Purchases: $2000
Collections: Major crafts in Ukrainian folk art; Ukrainian Easter eggs; ceramics, documents, fine arts, metalwork, photographs, woodwork, woven and embroidered textiles (including costumes), kilims; photographic archival collection on Ukrainian immigration in the USA
Exhibitions: Ukrainian Folk Costumes; Folk Art from the Cospathian Mountains; Pysanky, Ukrainian Easter Eggs; Rushnyky, Ukrainian Ritual Cloths; The Lost Architecture of Kiev; To Preserve a Heritage: The Story of the Ukrainian Immigration in the United States
Publications: Annual report; bulletins; bilingual exhibition catalogs or brochures
Activities: Classes for adults & children; workshops on Ukrainian Easter eggs & Christmas decorations; embroidery and woodcarving courses; lect open to public, tours; original objects of art lent to museums; lending collection contains 300 slides, 200 Ukrainian woven and embroidered textiles; originate traveling exhibitions; sales shop sells books, reproductions, prints, slides, embroideries, ceramics, wooden inlayed items and jewelry

L **Library,** 203 Second Ave, 10003
Library for internal use only
Library Holdings: Vols 200; AV — Slides 600; Other — Exhibition catalogs, photographs
Special Subjects: Ukrainian Fine and Folk Art

L **UNION OF AMERICAN HEBREW CONGREGATIONS,** Synagogue Art and Architectural Library, 838 Fifth Ave, 10021. Tel 212-249-0100. *Dir* Myron E Schoen
Open Mon - Fri 9:30 AM - 5 PM; cl Sat & Sun. Estab 1957. Books for use on premises only
Library Holdings: Vols 200; AV — Slides 3000
Special Subjects: Synagogue architecture, ceremonial objects and Judaic art
Publications: An American Synagogue for Today and Tomorrow (book); Contemporary Synagogue Art (book)
Activities: Slide rental service

L **UNIVERSITY CLUB LIBRARY,*** One W 54th St, 10019. Tel 212-572-3428. *Dir* Guy Saint-Clair; *Asst Dir* R Smith
Open to members and qualified scholars (inquire by letter first) Mon - Sat 10 AM - 5 PM. Estab 1865 for the promotion of the arts and culture in post-university graduates. Art is displayed in all areas of the building. Average Annual Attendance: 7000. Mem: 4250
Income: Financed by endowments and membership
Library Holdings: Vols 135,000
Collections: Art; architecture, fine bindings

VISUAL ARTISTS AND GALLERIES ASSOCIATION, INC
For further information, see National and Regional Organizations

M **WARD-NASSE GALLERY,** 178 Prince St, 10012. Tel 212-925-6950. *Dir* Rina Goodman; *Asst Dir* Tamara Sandy
Open Tues - Sat 11 AM - 5:30 PM, Sun 1 - 4 PM. No admis fee. Estab 1969 to provide an artist-run gallery; also serves as resource center for artists and public; to provide internships for students. Cooperative gallery with four-person and larger salon shows. Average Annual Attendance: 7000. Mem: 150; dues $700 for

2 years: 4 person show, slide and salon, $200 for sustaining membership
Income: Financed by membership
Exhibitions: Four person shows changing every three weeks
Publications: Brochure; gallery catalog, every two years
Activities: Work study programs; lectures open to public; concerts; poetry readings; multi-arts events; extension dept

L **Library,** 178 Prince St, 10012
Open Tues - Sat 11 AM - 5:30 PM. Estab 1969 to provide biographical information and slides of artists' work; to provide information on the art events in the area
Library Holdings: Vols 100; Per subs 4; Other — Clipping files, exhibition catalogs, memorabilia, original art works, pamphlets, photographs, prints, sculpture

M **WASHINGTON HEADQUARTERS ASSOCIATION,** Morris-Jumel Mansion, W 160th St & Edgecombe Ave, 10032. Tel 212-923-8008. *Pres* Mrs Paul E Parker Jr; *Dir* Audrey Daniels Braver
Open Tues - Sun 10 AM - 4 PM. Admis adults $1, students & sr citzens $.50, guided tours $1.50. Estab 1904 as a Historic House Museum. There are 9 rooms furnished in three periods of American history. Average Annual Attendance: 35,000. Mem: 200; dues $10 - $500; annual meeting May
Income: Financed by membership and fund raising
Collections: Decorative art; furniture of 18th and 19th centuries
Publications: Morris-Jumel News, quarterly; exhibitions catalogs
Activities: Educ dept; docent training; lectures open to the public; concerts; tours; traveling exhibitions organized and circulated; sales shop selling books, postcards

M **WHITNEY MUSEUM OF AMERICAN ART,** 945 Madison Ave, 10021. Tel 212-570-3600. *Dir* Thomas N Armstrong III; *Asst Dir Operations* Madeline McWhinney; *Asst Dir Program* Jennifer Russell; *Cur* Barbara Haskell; *Assoc Cur Permanent Collection* Patterson Sims; *Assoc Cur, Hopper Collection* Gail Levin; *Assoc Cur, Exhibitions* Richard Marshall; *Adjunct Cur, 18th & 19th Century Art* Patricia Hills; *Adjunct Cur, Drawings* Paul Cummings; *Head, Public Educ* Russell Connor; *Development Officer* Jane E Heffner; *Cur, Film & Video* John G Hanhardt; *Public Relations Officer* Linda Gordon; *Finance Officer* Michael Wolfe; *Registrar* Nancy McGary; *Head Publications* Doris Palca
Open Tues 11 AM - 8 PM, Wed - Sat 11 AM - 6 PM, Sun & holidays Noon - 6 PM, cl Christmas. Admis $2.50, senior citizens $1.25, Tues 6 - 8 PM free, children under 12 with adult, full time college students and New York City secondary school groups free. Estab 1930, incorporated 1931 by Gertrude Vanderbilt Whitney for the advancement of contemporary American art; Museum opened 1931 and moved to 54th Street in 1954; new building opened in 1966. Average Annual Attendance: 500,000. Mem: 5100; dues $35 and up
Income: Financed by endowment, admissions, grants, membership
Purchases: Numerous annual acquisitions
Collections: †Drawings, †paintings, †prints, †sculpture of mainly 20th century American artists
Exhibitions: Calder's Circus; Charles Simonds Dwellings; 20th Century American Art: Highlights of the Permanent Collection; (1982) Selected Paintings and Sculpture Acquired since 1978; The Katherine Schmidt Shubert Bequest and A Selective View of Her Art; Robert Smithson: Sculpture; John Cage: Scores and Prints; Focus on the Figure: Twenty Years; Nam June Paik; Abstract Drawings, 1911-1981; New American Art Museums; The Works of Edward Ruscha; Sculpture of the Late Sixties: Selections from the Permanent Collection; Block Prints; Milton Avery; Joel Shapiro; Jasper Johns: Savarin Monotypes; (1983) Ellsworth Kelly: Sculpture; Frank Stella: Prints 1967-1982; The Eight; Biennial Exhibition; Minimalism to Expressionism: Painting and Sculpture Since 1965 from the Permanent Collection; Prehistoric Pottery of the Southwest; Grant Wood: The Regionalist Vision; Morris Graves: Vision of the Inner Eye; The Sculptor as Draftsman; Dennis Oppenheim: Lecture #1; The Drawings of Willem de Kooning; (1984) The Theodore Roszak Bequest; Reflections of Nature: Flowers in American Art; Five Painters in New York; Konrad Cramer; R M Fischer; Fairfield Porter; Abstract Painting and Sculpture in America 1927-1944; Viola Frey; Print Acquisitions 1974-1984; The American Avant Garde 1958-1964; Morgan Russell; Abstract Expressionism: The Third Dimension; Claire Zeisler; Jonathan Borofsky
Publications: Exhibition catalogues; annual report; annual members' newsletter; bi-monthly calendar
Activities: Classes for adults; docent training; symposia & panel discussions; performances; teachers' workshops; lectures open to the public; concerts; gallery talks; tours; fels; Artreach provides introductory art education to elementary and high school students; individual paintings and original objects of art lent; originate traveling exhibitions for museums here and abroad; sales shop sells books, magazines, reproductions, slides, cards & posters

L **Library,*** 945 Madison Ave, 10021. Tel 212-570-3649. *Librn* May Castleberry
Open Tues - Fri 10 AM - Noon & 2 - 5 PM by appointment for advanced research. No admis fee. Estab 1931 for encouragement and advancement of American art and art scholarship
Purchases: $15,000
Library Holdings: Vols 16,000; Per subs 50; Micro — Cards, fiche, reels; AV — A-tapes, cassettes, rec, slides; Other — Clipping files, exhibition catalogs, manuscripts, memorabilia, pamphlets, photographs, reproductions
Special Subjects: Focuses on 20th century American drawing, graphics, painting and sculpture

M **Downtown Branch,** Federal Hall National Memorial, 26 Wall St At Broad St, 10041. Tel 212-431-1620. *Asst Mgr* Karl E Willers; *Senior Instructor* Richard Armstrong; *Sr Instructor* Nan Rosenthal
Open Mon - Fri 11 AM - 3 PM. No admis fee. Operated by students participating in the Education Department Independent Study Program
Income: Branch Museum financed by lower Manhattan business community
Exhibitions: (1982) Frames of Reference - Video-Music; New Correlations; Universal Limited Art Editions; A Tribute to Tatyana Grosman; Portraits on a Human on a Human Scale; Phototypes; The Development of Photography in New York City; The Comic Art Show; Cartoons in Painting and Popular Culture; Spectators of Life; Guy Penedu Bois and John Sloan Cinematograph, Newsreal and Movie - Early Nonfictional Films (1895-1937); The Prison Show; Con Flicks; Roy Lichtenstein: Graphic Work 1970-1980; Lower Manhattan from Street to Sky
Activities: Performances; gallery talks; films; walking tours

M **Whitney at Philip Morris,** 120 Park Ave, 10017. Tel 212-570-3643. *Head* Lisa Phillips; *Branch Mgr* Susan Lubowsky; *Asst Mgr* Sarah Warren
Open Mon - Sat 11 AM - 6 PM, Thurs 11 AM - 7:30 PM. No admis fee. Estab 1983 to extend American art to a wider audience. Sculpture court with major works & adjacent gallery for changing exhibitions. Average Annual Attendance: 71,602
Exhibitions: Reginal Marsh's New York; Three American Families: A Tradition of Artistic Pursuit; Still Life: Hollywood Photographs; Raymond Hood: City of Towers; Flowers in American Folk Art; Alexander Calder
Publications: Exhibition brochures
Activities: Lectures open to public; sales shop sells books

O **Friends of the Whitney Museum of American Art,*** 945 Madison Ave, 10021
Since their founding in 1956, the Friends have contributed a large number of important works of art to the permanent collection as well as supporting other parts of the museum's program. Mem: 4500; dues Corporate $2000 and up, Whitney Circle $1000, Friend $250, Associate $100, Family/Dual $45, individual $30

O **CATHARINE LORILLARD WOLFE ART CLUB, INC,** 802 Broadway, 10003. Tel 212-254-2000. *Pres* Andrea Rimberg
Estab 1896, inc 1963, to further fine, representational American art. A club of professional women painters and sculptors. Mem: 250; dues $15, associate membership $10; monthly meetings
Exhibitions: 88th Open Annual Exhibition; members exhibition
Activities: Metropolitan Museum Benefit, annually; lect; demonstration programs; scholarships offered

O **WOMEN IN THE ARTS FOUNDATION, INC,** 325 Spring St, Room 200, 10013. Tel 212-691-0988. *Exec Coordr* Erin Butler; *Exec Coordr* Roberta Crown; *Recording Coordr* Freda Pond; *Newsletter Editor* Jackie Skiles; *Financial Coordr* Terry Furlong
Open Mon & Weds 2 - 5 PM. Estab 1971 for the purpose of overcoming discrimination against women artists both in government and the private sector. Sponsors discussions, workshops, panels and exhibits the work of women artists, both established and unknown. Average Annual Attendance: 1000. Mem: 300; dues $25
Income: $12,000 (financed by endowment, membership)
Exhibitions: (1983) Pace University Group Show; Cork Gallery: Works on Paper Show
Publications: Women in the Arts, bulletin-newsletter, bi-monthly
Activities: Classes for adults; public education as to the problems and discrimination faced by women artists; lect open to the public, 10 vis lectr per year; competitions; individual paintings and original objects of art lent to museum and university art galleries for special exhibitions; lending collection contains 1500 slides; original art works for exhibitions are obtained from member artists; traveling exhibitions organized and circulated; sales shop selling catalogs of own exhibitions

L **Library,** 325 Spring St, 10013
Library Holdings: Vols 50; Per subs 5; AV — Slides; Other — Clipping files, exhibition catalogs, memorabilia, pamphlets

M **WOMEN'S INTERART CENTER, INC,** Interart de St Amand Gallery, 549 W 52 St, 10019. Tel 212-246-1050. *Pres* Marquerite A L Lewitin; *VPres* Bill Pertman; *Mgr Dir* Sam Sweet; *Cur* Inverna Lockpez
Open Mon - Fri 1 - 6 PM. No admis fee. Estab 1970 to present to the public the work of significant, emerging women artists. Average Annual Attendance: 9000. Mem: Dues $35
Income: Financed by state appropriation, National Endowment for the Arts, private foundations, corporations & individuals
Exhibitions: (1983-84) Women Artists of the Southwest; Interiors; Warm Show; The Circus Arene: Martha Edelheit; All's Fair: Love and War in New Feminist Art; Intakt: Women's Artist Collection in Vienna; Not Far From Mocando: Irene Barki, photographs
Publications: Women's Interart Center Newsletter, quarterly
Activities: Classes for adults; lect open to public, 2 visiting lectr per year; originate traveling exhibitions

M **YESHIVA UNIVERSITY,** Museum, 2520 Amsterdam Ave at 185th St, 10033. Tel 212-960-5390, 960-5429. *Dir* Sylvia A Herskowitz; *Educ Dir* Carol Kaufman Newman; *Office Mgr* Joan D Schwartzappel; *Asst Cur* Ariel Hurwich; *Secy* Eve Liss
Open Tues - Thurs 11 AM - 5 PM, Sun Noon - 6 PM. Admis adults $1, students and senior citizens $.50. Estab 1973 to collect, preserve & interpret Jewish art & objects of material culture in the light of Jewish history. 6000 sq ft of upper & lower galleries including a little theatre with seats for 80, two rear view projection screens. Average Annual Attendance: 10,000 - 20,000. Mem: 200; dues $10 - $100
Collections: Biblical Garden; Synagogues through the Centuries
Exhibitions: Raban Remembered: Jerusalem's Forgotten Master; A Fantastic Voyage: Original art from children's books on Jewish themes plus an imaginative environment where children can read the books on exhibit; The Art of Celebration: Environment on Jewish Holiday's
Publications: Catalogs
Activities: Docent programs; museum shop sells books, original art, reproductions, prints & slides

NIAGARA FALLS

M **NATIVE AMERICAN CENTER FOR THE LIVING ARTS,** 25 Rainbow Mall, 14303. Tel 716-284-2427. *Dir* Duffy Wilson; *Museum Dir* Elwood Green; *Dir Enterprise & Marketing* Valerie Staats
Open Mon - Fri 10 AM - 5 PM, Sat & Sun Noon - 5 PM; summer daily 10 AM - 8 PM, cl New Years, Easter, Thanksgiving, Christmas. Admis adults $3, children and seniors $1.75, group rates avail. Estab 1970 to preserve & promote American Indian art & culture. Average Annual Attendance: 100,000. Mem: 500; dues $25

Income: $1,500,000 (Financed by earned income & state arts councils programs funding)
Collections: Native American Archaeological, Ethnographic & Contemporary Art from Mexico, US & Canada; Native American Archive & Iconography
Publications: Turtle, quarterly tabloid; art catalogues
Activities: Classes for adults & children; dramatic programs; docent training; lectures open to public, 10 vis lectr per yr; concerts; gallery talks; tours; AV presentations; competitions with awards; individual paintings & original objects of art lent to museums & galleries; originate traveling exhibition; sales shop sells books, magazines, original art, reproductions, prints, slides, crafts & records

M **NIAGARA UNIVERSITY,** Buscaglia-Castellani Art Gallery, 3100 Lewiston Rd, 14305. Tel 716-284-2816. *Dir* Sandra H Olsen; *Preparator* Kim Yarwood; *Cur Education* Linda Breth
Open Wed - Sat 10 AM - 5 PM, Sun 1 PM - 5 PM. Estab 1978. The gallery is a ten thousand square feet house that displays the permanent collection of over four hundred pieces encompassing 17th century to present with a concentration in contemporary art
Income: $120,000
Collections: Modern paintings, sculpture & works on paper (19th -20th centuries); pre-Columbian pottery
Exhibitions: Glass Art; Sawyer Legacy; John Moore; Michael Vessler; Taking of Niagara: History of the Falls through Photography
Publications: Exhibition catalogs, 4 per yr
Activities: Concerts; tours; individual paintins lent; originate traveling exhibitions

NORTHPORT

L **NORTHPORT-EAST NORTHPORT PUBLIC LIBRARY,** Art Dept, 151 Laurel Ave, 11768. Tel 516-261-6930. *Dir* Victoria Wallace; *Asst Dir* Eileen Minogve
Open Mon - Fri 9 AM - 9 PM, Sat 9 AM - 5 PM, Sun 1 - 5 PM, Sept - June. Estab 1914. Circ 476,240
Income: $1,412,721 (financed by state appropriation, local tax levy)
Purchases: $140,000 (book budget)
Library Holdings: Other — Reproductions

NORTH SALEM

M **HAMMOND MUSEUM,** Museum of the Humanities, Deveau Rd, 10560. Tel 914-669-5033. *Dir* Natalie Hays Hammond; *Assoc Dir* Elizabeth H Taylor
Open May - Dec, Wed - Sun 11 AM - 5 PM. Admis to Museum, adults $2, senior citizens $1.50, children $1; to the Gardens, adults $2.50, senior citizens $1.50, children $1. Incorporated in 1957 as a non-profit, educational institution; absolute charter from New York State Board of Regents 1962. A Museum of the Humanities, it presents changing exhibitions of international scope and varied historic periods and topics, supplemented by programs of related special events. The Oriental Stroll Gardens comprising 15 individual gardens on 3 1/2 acres, include a lake, a reflecting pool, a dry landscape, a waterfall, and a Zen Garden. Average Annual Attendance: 35,000. Mem: 1800; Qualifications for mem: Open to all who are in sympathy with its aims and purposes
Activities: Dramatic programs; lect open to the public; concerts; documentary films; museum shop; Terrace Restaurant, luncheon by reservation

OGDENSBURG

M **FREDERIC REMINGTON ART MUSEUM,** 303 Washington St, 13669. Tel 315-393-2425. *Exec Dir* Bruce B Eldredge; *Dir* Mildred Dillenbeck; *Cur Education* Dr Carol R Wenzel-Rideout
Open Mon - Sat 10 AM - 5 PM, Sun 1 - 5 PM. Admis adults $2, senior citizens & students 12 and over $1. Estab 1923 to house and exhibit works of art of Frederic Remington (1861-1909), a native of northern New York. The museum is in the converted Parish Mansion, built 1809-10, and the recently constructed Addie Priest Newell Wing. Remington's last studio has been reconstructed with most of the original furnishings. Average Annual Attendance: 15,000
Income: Financed by endowment and city appropriation
Collections: Remington paintings, bronzes, watercolors, drawings, photographs, letters & personal art collection; studies in plaster by Edwin Willard Deming; sculpture by Sally James Farnham; Haskell Collection of 19th century American and European paintings; Parish Collection of Belter furniture; Sharp Collection of period glass, china, silver and cameos
Activities: Educ dept; lectures open to the public; tours; sales shop sells books, prints, slides, post cards, plates, spoons and rings

OLD CHATHAM

M **SHAKER MUSEUM,** Shaker Museum Rd, 12136. Tel 518-794-9100. *Dir* Viki Sand; *Admin Asst* Claire Wheeler; *Cur & Registrar* Maria Larsen
Open May - Oct daily 10 AM - 5:30 PM. Admis adults $3, senior citizens $2.50, youths $2, children $1. Estab 1950 to promote interest in and understanding of the Shaker cultural heritage. The exhibits are housed in a complex of eight buildings. Average Annual Attendance: 20,000. Mem: 300; dues $10 - $100
Income: $150,000 (financed by endowment and membership)
Purchases: $3000
Collections: †19,000 artifacts representing 200 years of Shaker history and culture
Exhibitions: Intro to Shaker History, Crafts and Industries; workshops and period rooms; changing exhibits
Publications: Newsletter; The Shaker Adventure; Shaker Seed Industry; Pamphlets; booklets; gallery guide; catalogs; postcards; slides, reprints, and broadsides
Activities: Seminars; lect open to public; festivals; craft fairs; gallery talks; tours; community showcase program of regional contemporary art, other special events; traveling exhibitions organized and circulated; museum shop sells books, magazines, original art, reproductions, prints and slides

L **Emma B King Library,** Shaker Museum Rd, 12136. *Archivist-Librn* Ann Kelly
Open to qualified persons by appointment, for reference only
Income: $8000
Purchases: $1000
Library Holdings: Vols 2000; Per subs 15; Micro — Reels; AV — A-tapes, cassettes, fs, Kodachromes, motion pictures, rec, slides, v-tapes; Other — Manuscripts, memorabilia, original art works, pamphlets, photographs
Collections: Manuscripts and records; Photographic and map archive

OLD WESTBURY

M **NEW YORK INSTITUTE OF TECHNOLOGY GALLERY,** Wheatly Rd, 11568. Tel 516-686-7542. *Associate Dir Fine Arts Dept* John Murray
Open Mon - Fri 9 AM - 5 PM. Estab 1964. Gallery maintained for the many exhibits held during the year. Average Annual Attendance: 5000
Exhibitions: Annual faculty and student shows; some traveling exhibitions
Publications: Graphic Guild Newsletter, quarterly
Activities: Classes in custom silk-screen printmaking; gallery talks; awards; scholarships; Exten Dept serves all areas
L **Art & Architectural Library,*** Old Westbury, 11771. Tel 516-686-7579. *Librn* Stephen H Van Dyk
Open Mon - Thurs 8:30 AM - 9 PM; Fri 8:30 AM - 5 PM. No admis fee. Estab 1976
Income: $16,000
Library Holdings: Vols 8800; Per subs 100; Micro — Reels; AV — Cassettes, motion pictures, slides, v-tapes; Other — Clipping files, exhibition catalogs, pamphlets
Special Subjects: Architecture
Exhibitions: Architecture dept student projects
Activities: Tours

ONEIDA

M **MADISON COUNTY HISTORICAL SOCIETY,** Cottage Lawn,* 435 Main St, PO Box 415, 13421. Tel 315-363-4136. *Pres* Harry Hood; *VPres* William Cassell; *VPres* V Rann; *Dir* Barbara J Giambastiani; *Cur* Mildred Stress
Open Mon - Fri 9 AM - 5 PM & by appointment. No admis fee. Estab 1898 to collect, preserve and interpret artifacts indigenous to the history of Madison County. 1849 AJ Davis Gothic dwelling with period rooms, library and Craft Archive. Average Annual Attendance: 4000. Mem: 1000; dues $5; annual meeting second Monday of November
Income: $51,000 (financed by endowment, membership, county, city and state appropriation, Annual Craft Fair)
Collections: Locally produced and or used furnishings, paintings, silver, textiles and ceramics
Exhibitions: Madison County Hop Industry; Too Much is Not Enough: Victorian America; Morse-Mott House, Eaton: Family History Through Furnishings; Windsor Chair Making
Publications: Monthly Newsletter; Madison County Heritage, published annually; Studies in Traditional American Crafts, annually
Activities: Educational outreach programs for nursing homes and schools; lectures open to the public, 11 visiting lecturers per year; slides, tapes and movies documenting traditional craftsmen at work; individual paintings and original objects of art lent to qualified museums and galleries for special exhibits; sales shop sells books, magazines, prints and slides
L **Library,*** 435 Main St, 13421. Tel 315-363-4136
Open Mon - Fri 9 AM - 5 PM. Estab 1975 as a reference library of primary and secondary sources on Madison County History
Library Holdings: Vols 2500; AV — Cassettes, lantern slides, motion pictures, rec, slides, v-tapes; Other — Clipping files, exhibition catalogs, manuscripts, memorabilia, pamphlets, photographs, prints
Special Subjects: Madison County and New York State History, Civil War, Oneida Indians
Collections: Gerrit Smith family papers

ONEONTA

M **HARTWICK COLLEGE FINE ART GALLERY,** Anderson Center for the Arts, 13820. Tel 607-432-4200, Ext 481. *Cur* Dr K Christine Flom
Open Mon - Fri 1 - 4 PM, or by appointment; cl last half of Dec. No admis fee. Estab 1928, college collections and exhibitions for benefit of faculty, students and community
Collections: Painting, prints, drawings, sculpture, ceramics, and tapestry from 16th through 20th centuries: Renaissance and Baroque paintings and drawings; 19th century American Landscapes; 260 American political cartoons by John H Cassell
Exhibitions: Changing Exhibitions to meet curriculum needs
Publications: Exhibition catalogues
Activities: Classes in museum studies; lectures open to the public; book traveling exhibitions, 2 - 4 per yr; originate traveling exhibitions
M **Yager Museum,** Hartwick College, 13820. Tel 607-432-4200, Ext 464. *Dir* Jane des Grange
Open Mon - Fri 10 AM - 4 PM, cl holidays. No admis fee. Estab 1928
Collections: Collection of North American, Mexican & South American Indian art & artifacts
Exhibitions: Changing exhibitions
Activities: Classes in museum studies; lectures; tours; films

M **STATE UNIVERSITY OF NEW YORK COLLEGE AT ONEONTA,** Art Gallery & Sculpture Court,* Fine Arts Center, 13820. Tel 607-431-3500. *Chmn Art Dept* Robert Doyle
Estab 1972 to offer students, staff and visitors an opportunity to view current as well as past artistic styles and works. Art Gallery and Sculpture Court are major features of the Art Wing
Income: Financed by city and state appropriation
Activities: Lect open to the public, 8 visiting lectrs per year; extensive exhibition program

OSSINING

M MUSEUM OF OSSINING HISTORICAL SOCIETY, 196 Croton Ave, 10562. Tel 914-941-0001. *Dir* Roberta Y Arminio; *Pres* Margaret Brennan
Open Mon, Weds and Sun 2 - 4 PM & by appointment. No admis fee. Estab 1931 to educate the public in the history and traditions of the vicinity. East Gallery contains changing exhibitions and a portion of the permanent collection; West Gallery contains permanent collection. Average Annual Attendance: 2500. Mem: 279; dues patron $100, civic, commercial & contributing $25, family $15, individual $10, sr citizens & student $5
Income: Financed by membership and city appropriation
Collections: Costumes; textiles and quilts; slides and films of old Ossining; old photographs and daguerreotypes; Victorian dollhouse complete in minute detail, contains antique dolls, toys, miniatures, old school books & photographs
Publications: Monthly brochure
Activities: Education dept; class visits; special assignment guidance; lecutres open to public, 4 vis lectr per yr; gallery talks; tours; competitions & awards; individual paintings & original objects of art lent to schools, banks & industry; sales shop sells books, magazines
L Library, 10562
Library Holdings: Vols 1000; Micro — Reels; AV — A-tapes, cassettes, lantern slides, slides; Other — Clipping files, exhibition catalogs, framed reproductions, memorabilia, original art works, photographs, prints, reproductions

OSWEGO

M STATE UNIVERSITY OF NEW YORK AT OSWEGO, Tyler Art Gallery, Tyler Art Gallery, 13126. Tel 315-341-2113. *Dir* Coy L Ludwig; *Asst Dir* Mindy Ostrow; *Secy* Kathleen Jackson
Open Mon - Fri 9:30 AM - 4:30 PM, Sept - May; summer hours as posted. No admis fee. Estab 1969 to provide cultural stimulation and enrichment of art to the college community and to the residents of Oswego County. Two gallery spaces in Tyler Hall, the North Gallery is approximately 2400 sq ft and the South Gallery is approximately 1300 sq ft. Average Annual Attendance: 20,000
Income: Financed by University funds
Collections: Arnold Collection of Fine Prints; Contemporary American Prints and Paintings
Exhibitions: Two galleries show a combined total of 20 exhibitions per school year
Publications: Brochures; occasional catalogs for exhibitions; posters
Activities: Lect open to public, 8-10 vis lect per year; concerts, gallery talks; lending collection contains individual and original objects of art; originates traveling exhibitions
L Library, 13126
Library Holdings: Vols 8141; Per subs 59; AV — A-tapes, cassettes, motion pictures, slides, v-tapes

PLATTSBURGH

M STATE UNIVERSITY OF NEW YORK, Myers Fine Arts and Rockwell Kent Galleries, 12901. Tel 518-564-2813 Kent, 564-2288 Myers. *Dir* Edward R Brohel
Open Tues - Wed & Fri 10 AM - 5 PM, Thurs 10 AM - 9 PM, Sun 2 - 5 PM, cl university holidays. No admis fee. Estab 1978
Collections: Rockwell Kent Collection, paintings, prints, drawings, sketches, proofs & designs, books; china; ephemera
Exhibitions: Sixteen exhibitions each year; antique and contemporary, all media
Publications: Exhibition catalogs; monthly exhibition announcements; semi-annual calendar of events
Activities: Programs for undergrad students, elementary and secondary schools and community groups in area; docent programs; lectures open to the public, 10 vis lectr per yr; tours; competitions with awards; individual paintings lent

PORT CHESTER

M MUSEUM OF CARTOON ART, Comly Ave, 10573. Tel 914-939-0234. *Pres* Mort Walker; *Dir* Charles Green; *Dir* Brian Walker; *Secy* Veronica Nasca
Open Tues - Fri 10 AM - 4 PM, Sun 1 - 5 PM, cl Sat and Mon. Admis adults $1.50, sr citizens and children under 12 $.75. Estab 1974 as world's first museum dedicated solely to the unique art form of cartooning. Consists of two floors with a total of 10 large display rooms. Average Annual Attendance: 20,000. Mem: 600; dues $30
Collections: Animated Film Collection, videotape; Cartoon Hall of Fame; Comics collection from 1896 to the present; early and contemporary original cartoon art; Walt Disney display showing the various steps used to produce animated cartoons
Exhibitions: Original artwork from all of the various genres of cartoon art including comic strips, comic books, animation, caricature & illustration
Publications: Tad Dorgan, Story of America in Cartoons; Dick Tracy: The Art of Chester Gould
Activities: Lectures open to public, 12 vis lect per year; competitions with cash, prize, print & certificate awards; individual paintings & original objects of art lent to other museums, galleries, schools & universities & arts organizations; book traveling exhibitions; originate traveling exhibitions; museum sales shop sells books, magazines, original art, reproductions, prints & various cartoon oriented souvenirs
L Library, Comly Ave, 10573
Library Holdings: Vols 1500; Per subs 5; Other — Memorabilia, photographs, prints, reproductions
Collections: Archives collection

L PORT CHESTER PUBLIC LIBRARY, Fine Arts Dept, One Haeeco Ave, 10573. Tel 914-939-6710. *Dir* Robin Lettieri; *Art Dir* Lillian Adams
Open Mon 9 AM - 9 PM, Tues & Wed 9 AM - 8 PM, Thurs - Sat 9 AM - 5 PM. Estab 1876 to circulate books, records, magazines, to the general public to provide reference services. Maintains an art gallery. A small gallery with about

ten shows per year, mostly local artists. Circ 117,515
Income: $365,000 (financed by endowment, city and state appropriation)
Purchases: $40,000
Library Holdings: Vols 73,642; Per subs 181; Micro — Reels; AV — Fs, rec, slides; Other — Framed reproductions, pamphlets, prints
Exhibitions: Water colors, oils, acrylics, photographs
Activities: Lectures, concerts, films; open to the public; career seminars and workshops

PORT WASHINGTON

M LONG ISLAND GRAPHIC EYE GALLERY, 301 Main St, 11050. Tel 516-883-9668. *Pres* Viggo Holm Madsen; *VPres* Shellie Schneider; *VPres* Ann Pellaton; *Treasurer* David B Hecht; *Secy* Mary Ann De Carlo
Open Wed - Sun Noon - 5 PM. No admis fee. Chartered 1974 as a non-profit educational gallery to educate the public in the understanding & appreciation of prints, and to promote art techniques. Mem: 27; dues $350; monthly meetings
Income: Financed by memberships & individual project grants
Collections: †Slide collection
Exhibitions: (1983) Black & White Plus One Color; Eat, Drink & Have a Merry; (1984) Olga Polokhine; Andrew Stasik
Activities: Education dept; lectures & demonstrations in print media open to public, 2 vis lectr per yr; competitions with awards; sales shop sells original art & prints

POTSDAM

M POTSDAM PUBLIC MUSEUM, Civic Center, 13676. Tel 315-265-6910. *Pres of Board* Robert John McGill; *Dir-Cur* Katherine F Wyant; *Asst Dir* Betsy Travis; *Registrar* Aimee L Ay; *Secy* Mrs F A Ramsdell
Open Tues - Sat 2 - 5 PM, cl Sun & Mon. No admis fee. Estab 1940 as an educational institution acting as a cultural and historical center for the Village of Potsdam and surrounding area. Educational services taken to area schools. Museum occupies a sandstone building, formerly a Universalist Church built in 1876. Maintains small reference library. Average Annual Attendance: 9000
Income: Financed by city and state appropriation
Collections: Burnap Collection of English Pottery; costumes of the 19th and 20th centuries; Mandarin Chinese hangings, china and costumes; photograph collection and artifacts and material on local history; pressed glass and art glass of the 19th and early 20th century
Exhibitions: Cranberry Glass; Charles Edison Fund Exhibit; Faberge-Style Decorated Eggs; From Old China; Ironside China; History of Lighting; Local History; New York State Forces Exhibit; Wedding Party; Wrapping Up (coats and capes)
Publications: Bi-monthly newsletter
Activities: Classes for adults and children; programs for schools craft days; lectures open to public, 8 vis lectr per year; concerts; tours

M STATE UNIVERSITY OF NEW YORK COLLEGE AT POTSDAM, Brainerd Art Gallery, Pierrepont Ave, 13676. Tel 315-267-2254, 267-2251. *Art Department Chmn* Arthur Sennett; *Gallery Dir* Georgia Coopersmith; *Secy* Mary Haught
Open Mon, Wed, Fri, Sat & Sun 1- 5 PM, Tues & Thurs 7 - 9 PM. No admis fee. Estab 1967 to serve college and community as a teaching gallery. Gallery associated with Art Department. Gallery has 2500 square feet of exhibition space on three levels with security & environmental controls. Average Annual Attendance: 18,000
Collections: †Contemporary Japanese, Italian & American art (painting, sculpture & prints); †contemporary drawing collection
Exhibitions: Contemporary Patrons of the Arts; American Folk Art
Publications: Exhibition catalogs
Activities: Lectures open to public, 10-12 vis lectr per yr; concerts; gallery talks; tours; competitions; original objects of art lent to public institutions, art museums and art organizations; book traveling exhibitions, 1-3 times per yr; traveling exhibitions organized and circulated

POUGHKEEPSIE

M MID-HUDSON ARTS AND SCIENCE CENTER,* 228 Main St, 12601. Tel 914-471-1155. *Pres* Leonard Zimmerman
Open Tues - Sat 10 AM - 6 PM, Sun Noon - 5 PM, Thurs 10 AM - 9 PM. Admis adults $.25, children $.10. Estab 1977 as a museum for all people. Main gallery approx 35 x 60 ft, community gallery approx 15 x 20 ft, theatre gallery approx 35 x 35. Average Annual Attendance: 5000. Mem: 350; dues $15 family, $10 individual, $5 student
Income: Financed by membership, state appropriation, and foundation grants
Activities: Classes for adults and children; dramatic programs; lectures open to the public; concerts; gallery talks; tours; competitions with awards; individual paintings and original objects of art lent to local businesses, schools, government buildings; traveling exhibition organized and circulated to schools, government buildings; museum shop sells books, magazines, original art, reproductions, prints and import gift items

M VASSAR COLLEGE ART GALLERY, Raymond Ave, 12601. Tel 914-452-7000, Ext 2645. *Dir* Joan Mickelson Lukach; *Cur* Sally Mills; *Secy* Anna Conforti; *Friends of the Art Gallery Exec Dir* Joan Grennan; *Preparator* John P Miller
Open Mon - Sat 9 AM - 5 PM, Sun 1 - 5 PM, summers by appointment. No admis fee. Estab 1864; collects Eastern and Western art of all periods. The museum has 6000 sq ft of exhibition space in 1915 Gothic style building. Average Annual Attendance: 12,000. Mem: 650; dues $25 and up; bi-annual meeting fall and spring
Income: Financed by Vassar College, endowment and membership
Purchases: $60,000
Collections: Charles M Pratt gift of Italian Renaissance paintings; †Matthew

Vassar collection of 19th century American paintings of Hudson River School and 19th century English watercolors; †Felix M Warburg Collection of medieval sculpture and graphics including Durer & Rembrandt; Charles Pratt Collection of Chinese Jades; †20th century art of all media including photography; †European paintings, sculpture and drawings ranging from the Renaissance to the 20th century, including Bacchiacca, Cezanne, Salvator Rosa, Claesz, Tiepolo, Robert, Corot, Cezanne, Delacroix, Gifford, Van Gogh, Tanner, Munch, Klee, Bourdelle, Laurent, Davidson, Gabo, Calder, Moore; †20th century American and European paintings including Henri, Hartley, O'Keeffe, Bacon, Nicholson, Rothko, de Kooning, Hartigan, Weber; graphics ranging from Barocci to Rembrandt to Goya to Picasso, Matisse, Braque, Kelly, Grooms and Graves; photography from Anna Atkins, Cameson, Gilpin Steichen, Abbott, Lange, Lynes and Linda Connor; †The Classical Collection includes Greek vases, Egyptian, Etruscan, and Mycenaean objects, Roman glass, portrait busts, jewelry; other archaeological finds
Exhibitions: Recent Latin American Drawings; Works on Paper from Winston-Malbin Coll
Publications: Gallery, biannually
Activities: Lect open to public, 10 - 12 vis lectr per yr; gallery talks; tours; concerts; internships offered; individual paintings and original objects of art lent to other museums; book and originate traveling exhibitions
L **Art Library,** Raymond Ave, 12601. Tel 914-452-7000, Ext 2136. *Librn* Janet Clarke-Hazlett
Open Mon - Thurs 8:30 AM - midnight, Fri 8:30 - 10 PM, Sat 9 AM - 10 PM, Sun 10 AM - 12 PM, cl summers. Estab 1937. Circulation to students and faculty only
Library Holdings: Vols 35,000; Per subs 180

PURCHASE

M **MANHATTANVILLE COLLEGE,** Brownson Art Gallery, 10577. Tel 914-694-2200, Ext 331. *Pres* Barbara Knowles Debs; *Dean of Faculty* Dr Cate Myers
Open 9 AM - 4:30 PM. No admis fee. Average Annual Attendance: 300 per wk
Income: Financed by endowment and tuition
Publications: Magazine, bimonthly; catalogs
Activities: Lectures open to public, 5 vis lectr per yr; concerts; gallery talks; scholarships; original objects of art lent; originate traveling exhibitions; sales shop sells books, magazines, reproductions & prints
L **Manhattanville Library,** 10577. *Librn* Edward O'Hara
Library Holdings: Vols 13,100; Per subs 50

C **PEPSICO INC,** Anderson Hill Rd, 10577. Tel 914-253-2900. *Chmn* Donald M Kendall
Open Mon - Sun 9 AM - 5 PM. No admis fee. Estab 1970 to present sculpture of museum quality. Average Annual Attendance: 10,000
Collections: Thirty-three large outdoor sculptures, works of Henry Moore, Louise Nevelson, David Smith, Arnaldo Pomodoro, Jacques Lipchitz, Henri Lauren and Auguste Rodin, Miro, Giacometti

M **STATE UNIVERSITY OF NEW YORK AT PURCHASE,** Neuberger Museum, 10577. Tel 914-253-5087. *Dir* Suzanne Delehanty; *Asst Dir* Laurence Shopmaker; *Museum Mgr* Douglas Caulk; *Registrar* Marina Walker; *Asst to the Dir* Teresa Vettoretti; *Cur Asst* Olga D'Angelo; *Coordr of Public Programs* Marjorie Tuttle; *Coordr Education Services* Jacqueline Sheinberg; *Coordr of Musuem Education* Eleanor Brackbill; *Public Information Coordr* Ann Marie Duross
Open Tues - Fri 10 AM - 4 PM, Sat & Sun 1 - 5 PM, cl Mon and major holidays. No admis fee. Estab 1968, opened May 1974 to serve university and residents of New York State and Connecticut. 78,000 sq ft facility with nine total galleries, five outside sculpture courts. Average Annual Attendance: 50,000. Mem: Dues sustaining $1000, patron $500, donor $250, contributing $100, family-dual $50, individual $35
Income: Financed by State University of New York, endowment fund, government grants, private foundations, donors and membership
Collections: The Neuberger Museum's permanent collection includes 5000 20th century European and American paintings, sculpture, drawings, prints, and †photographs; †African and ancient art; †large scale sculpture
Exhibitions: Changing contemporary art exhibitions
Publications: Exhibition catalogues, brochures, quarterly calendars, and annual reviews
Activities: Education dept; docent training; internships for Purchase College students; tours for children, adults and citizens with special needs; lectures open to public, 10-12 vis lectr per year; concerts; gallery talks; tours; scholarships and internships; original objects of art lent to other museums; book traveling exhibitions, 2-3 per year; originate traveling exhibitions to other museums; sales shop sells books, magazines, prints, small gift items and cards
L **Library,** 10577. *Dir* Robert W Evans; *Reference-Visual Arts Specialist* RosAnn Auchstetter
Library Holdings: Vols 15,400; Per subs 120; Micro — Cards, fiche, reels; AV — A-tapes, cassettes, motion pictures, rec, slides, v-tapes; Other — Clipping files, exhibition catalogs, pamphlets
Special Subjects: 20th Century American Art

RIVERHEAD

O **EAST END ARTS & HUMANITIES COUNCIL,** 133 E Main St, 11901. Tel 516-727-0900
Open Mon - Sat 10 AM - 5 PM. No admis fee. Estab 1972. Average Annual Attendance: 11,000. Mem: 3000; dues $4-$25
Publications: East End Arts News & Arts Calendar, monthly; Suffolk County Art Source
Activities: Lectures open to public, competitions with awards; book traveling exhibitions; originates traveling exhibitions; sales shop sells books, original art & crafts

ROCHESTER

O **AMERICAN BAPTIST HISTORICAL SOCIETY,** 1106 S Goodman St, 14620. Tel 716-473-1740. *Exec Dir* William H Brackney
Open daily 8:30 AM - 3:30 PM. No admis fee. Estab 1853 as a religious museum affiliated with American Baptist Convention. Average Annual Attendance: 100. Mem: 250
Collections: Paintings; pewter; religious historical material; silver
Publications: American Baptist Quarterly
L **Library,*** 1106 S Goodman St, 14620
Open to the public, under staff supervision
Library Holdings: Vols 55,000; Other — Manuscripts
Collections: Archives; Baptistiana; records

M **INTERNATIONAL MUSEUM OF PHOTOGRAPHY AT GEORGE EASTMAN HOUSE,** 900 East Ave, 14607. Tel 716-271-3361. *Chmn* Andrew D Wolfe; *Dir* Robert A Mayer; *Dir Film Coll* John Kuiper; *Dir Photography Coll* Robert Sobieszek; *Dir Technology Coll* Philip Condax; *Dir Interdept Services* Andrew Eskind; *Dir Development* Dan Meyers; *Assoc Cur Photography Coll* Janet Buerger; *Asst Cur Photography Coll* Marianne Fulton
Open Tues - Sun 10 AM - 4:30 PM. Admis adults $2, students & senior citizens $1, children under 12 $.75. Estab 1949 for photography exhibitions, research and education. Average Annual Attendance: 110,000. Mem: 3000; dues family $35, individual $25, students & senior citizens $15
Income: Financed by corp & individual gifts, foundation & government grants, earned income
Collections: Equipment (photographic); film; 19th and 20th century photography
Exhibitions: (1982-84) Faces and Fabrics/Feathers and Furs; Jerry Uelsmann; Contemporary Photographers VIII & IX; Eikoh Hosoe: The Human Figure, 1960-1981; Color as Form: A History of Color Photography; The Era of the French Calotype; Robert Fichter: Photography and Other Questions; Aaron Siskind: Fifty Years; Naya's Italy; Particulars: Selections from the Miller-Plummer Collection of Photography; The Wise Silence: Photographs by Paul Caponigro; The Last Decade
Publications: Image, quarterly; books & catalogs
Activities: Classes for children; docent training; teacher workshops; school exhibition program; lectures open to the public; gallery talks; tours; scholarships; exten dept; lending collection contains photographs & original objects of art; traveling exhibitions organized and circulated; museum shop sells books, magazines & reproductions; junior museum
L **Library,** 900 East Ave, 14607. Tel 716-271-3361, Ext 235. *Chief Archivist* Joan Pedzich; *Asst Archivist* David A Wooters; *Asst Librn* Norma Feld; *Librn* Rachel Stuhlman
Research facility temporarily closed
Library Holdings: Vols 30,000; Per subs 300; Micro — Fiche, reels 75; AV — A-tapes, rec, slides; Other — Clipping files, exhibition catalogs, manuscripts, pamphlets, reproductions
Special Subjects: History and Aesthetics of Photography
Collections: Largest collection in the US of photographs and related material dealing with the history and aesthetics of photography: 600,000 photographs including major collections of Edward Steichen, Alvin Langdon Coburn, Southworth & Howes, Louis Walton Sipley, Lewis Hine, Edward Muybridge and Nickolas Muray
Exhibitions: Glamour Stills; Colar as Form; French Calotypes; R W Fichter
Publications: Image, quarterly

M **LANDMARK SOCIETY OF WESTERN NEW YORK, INC,*** 130 Spring St, 14608. Tel 716-546-7029. *Dir* Mrs Patrick Harrington
Campbell-Whittlesey House open Tues - Fri 10 AM - 5 PM, Sun 1 - 4 PM; Stone-Tolan House open Wed - Fri 10 AM - 4 PM, Sat & Sun 1 - 4 PM. Admis adults $1, students $.25, children under 14 $.10. Estab 1937. Campbell-Wittlesey House, 123 S Fitzhugh St; Stone-Tolan House, 2370 East Ave. Mem: Dues life $1000, cornerstone $250, pillar $100, patron $50, family $25, active $20, student & associate $10
Collections: Art, furnishings and decorative arts of the 1830s; furnishings and decorative arts of early 19th century; country-style architecture
Publications: Landmarks of Rochester and Monroe County; quarterly newsletter, booklets; brochures; guides
Activities: Classes for adults and children; docent program; workshops; lectures; tours

O **ROCHESTER HISTORICAL SOCIETY,** 485 East Ave, 14607. Tel 716-271-2705. *Pres* Elizabeth G Holahan; *First VPres* Charles Shepard; *Cur* Mary R Shannon; *Cur* Melinda Pittman; *Treas* Clinton Steadman; *Secy* Mrs David Falk
Open Mon - Fri 10 AM - 4 PM. Admis adults $1, senior citizens $.75, students $.50. Headquarters at Woodside, Greek Revival Masion built 1839. Maintains major collection of portraits and scenes relating to Rochester, Reference Library and other collections. Average Annual Attendance: 2500. Mem: 600; dues $15 - $1000
Income: Financed by membership
Activities: Lectures open to public, 5 vis lectr per year; tours

L **ROCHESTER INSTITUTE OF TECHNOLOGY,** Information Services Library, Technical & Education Center of the Graphic Arts, 14623
The library houses an extensive international collection of graphic arts periodicals, technical reports and conference proceedings. These are used to compile a monthly publication which offers subject-categorized, fully indexed informative abstracts of the literature. It represents an expanded effort into current awareness and retrospective retrieval capability. The library is open to Rochester Institute of Technology graduate printing students and Technical and Education Center staff for research
Publications: Graphic Arts Literature Abstracts, monthly

UNIVERSITY OF ROCHESTER

M **Memorial Art Gallery,** 490 University Ave, 14607. Tel 716-275-3081. *Pres Bd of Mgrs* Marilyn Kayser; *Dir* A Bret Waller; *Asst Dir* Langdon F Clay; *Admin Officer* Edmund W Pease; *Develop Officer* Christine D Hyer; *Chief Cur* Donald A Rosenthal; *Public Relations Mgr* David Richards; *Membership Mgr* Melissa Hopkins; *Exhibitions & Facilities Mgr* Mark Donovon; *Assoc Cur American Art* Patricia Anderson
Open Tues 2 - 9 PM, Wed - Sat 10 AM - 5 PM, Sun 1-5 PM, cl Mon. Admis adults $2, senior citizens & students $1, children $.50; No admis fee Tues 5 - 9 PM and to members, University Rochester students and children accompanied by adults. Estab 1913 as a university art museum and public art museum for the Rochester area involved in a broad variety of community programs. The building is built in an Italian renaissance style, a new wing built in 1968 reflects a comtemporary style. Average Annual Attendance: 160,000. Mem: 7000; dues $25 and up
Income: $1,500,000
Collections: Covers all major periods and cultural area from Assyria and predynastic Egypt to the present, paintings, sculpture, prints, drawings, decorative arts; special strengths are medieval, renaissance and 17th century art, 19th and early 20th century French painters, American tribal arts, folk art and contemporary prints
Exhibitions: (1984-85) Charles Rand Penney Collection; Artists of La Revue Blanche: Bonnard, Toulouse-Lautrec, Vallotton, Vuillard; The Course of Empire: The Erie Canal and the New York Landscapes, 1825-1875; Frank Stella Prints, 1967-1982; Neumann Collection; Frans Wilderheim; Albert Paley Retrospective; American Art Between the Wars; Rochester-Finger Lakes Exhibition
Publications: Gallery Notes, 11 times yr; Porticus, journal of the Memorial Art Gallery; exhibition catalogs
Activities: Classes for adults and children; docent training; lect open to the public, 30 vis lectr per yr; concerts; gallery talks; tours; exten department serving Rochester area and surrounding nine counties; individual paintings lent and original objects of art lent to cultural institutions; lending collection contains books, cassettes, color reproductions, framed reproductions, kodachromes, motion pictures, original art works, original prints, paintings, photographs, sculpture and slides; traveling exhibitions organized and circulated; gallery store sells original art, fine crafts, prints, books & paper products

M **Charlotte W Allen Memorial Art Gallery Library,** 490 University Ave, 14607. Tel 716-275-4765. *Librn* Stephanie Frontz
Open Tues 2 PM - 5 PM & 6 PM - 9 PM, Wed - Fri & Sun 1 PM - 5 PM, cl Sat. Estab as a research library
Income: Financed by endowment, membership and city appropriation
Library Holdings: Vols 16,000; Per subs 55; Other — Clipping files, exhibition catalogs, pamphlets

L **Fine Arts Library,** River Campus, 14627. Tel 716-275-4476. *Librarian* Stephanie J Frontz; *Slide Cur* William A Taylor
Open Mon - Thurs 9 AM - 10 PM, Fri 9 AM - 8 PM, Sat 12 - 5, Sun 2 - 10 PM. Estab to support academic programs of Fine Arts Department and other academic departments within the University. Small gallery is maintained by Fine Arts Department
Library Holdings: Vols 35,000; Per subs 220; Micro — Fiche; AV — Kodachromes, lantern slides, motion pictures, slides; Other — Exhibition catalogs

M **VISUAL STUDIES WORKSHOP,*** 31 Prince St, 14607. Tel 716-442-8676. *Dir* Nathan Lyons; *Chmn Board of Trustees* William Parker; *Coordr Exhib* Nancy Gonchar; *Coordr Print Shop* Joan Lyons; *Coordr Book Distribution* Don Russell; *Coordr Summer Institute* Brian Kirkey; *Media Center* Nancy Norwood; *Copy Center* Greg Erf
Open Mon - Thurs 9:30 AM - 12 PM, 2 - 5 PM, Mon & Tues 5 - 9 PM. No admis fee. Estab 1969 to establish a center for the transmission and study of the visual image. At this time there are three exhibition spaces at the workshop; one for contemporary imagemakers, one for historical material and one for area artists and artists-in-residence. Average Annual Attendance: 300,000. Mem: 2300; dues $18
Income: $460,000 (financed by membership, state appropriation, federal and corporate sources and earned income)
Purchases: $5000
Special Subjects: Photography, Prints, Artist's Books
Exhibitions: John Pfahl, Picture Windows; Joe Babcock, Scientific Portfolio; Charles Traub, People: Works in Progress; Paul Berger, Camera Text or Picture; Eric Baden; Woman Bookworks; Film Posters for Nazi Popular Cinema; Bernard Faulon, Phyllis Galembo, Martha Madigan; John Brumfield, Esther Parada; Michael Bishop, On Photography and Vision; selected Gallery artists; William Paris, Photographs; Works by John Wood; The Artist and the Magazine; Books From The Coach House Press; The Photographic Book; E O Goldbeck, Panoramic Views; The Sequential Image in Photographic Books; Bern Porter Joseph Jachna; Mario Giacomelli; Joan Lyons; Eric Renner; Murray Riss
Publications: Afterimage, monthly
Activities: Classes for adults and children; workshop program in museum studies; summer Institute program with intensive short term workshops for artists and museum professionals; lectures open to the public, 15 visiting lecturers per year; gallery talks; tours (by appointment); original objects of art lent to institutions with proper exhibition facilities; lending collection contains 27,000 photographs of original artwork; traveling exhibitions organized and circulated to museums, colleges and universities; museum shop sells books, magazines, original art and prints

L **Research Center,*** 31 Prince St, 14607. Tel 716-442-8676. *Coordr Research Center* Helen M Brunner; *Librn* Robert Bretz; *Conservation Asst* Linn Underhill; *Research Asst* Joanne Ross
Open Mon - Thurs 9 AM - Noon, Mon & Tues 9 AM - Noon, 2 - 9 PM. Estab 1971 to maintain a permanent collection for the study of the function and effect of the visual image. For reference only
Income: $80,000 (financed by grants)
Purchases: $5000
Library Holdings: Vols 15,000; Per subs 746; posters; AV — A-tapes, cassettes, fs, Kodachromes, lantern slides, motion pictures, slides, v-tapes; Other — Clipping files, exhibition catalogs, manuscripts, original art works, photographs, prints, reproductions

Special Subjects: Photography
Collections: Illustrated book collection; photographic print collection
Exhibitions: Exhibitions are shown
Publications: Various publications
Activities: Internship programs; workshops; graduate museum studies program; lectures open to public; gallery talks; tours

ROME

O **ROME ART AND COMMUNITY CENTER,** 308 W Bloomfield St, 13440. Tel 315-336-1040. *Dir* Scott Severance; *Gift Shop* Bernardine Lohden
Open Tues - Sat 9 AM - 5 PM, Sun 2 - 4 PM. No admis fee. Estab 1968 for art exhibits and classes. Three galleries. Average Annual Attendance: 30,000. Mem: 1000; dues family with 2 children $10, individual $5
Income: Financed by city appropriation
Exhibitions: Various art and craft exhibitions every six weeks
Publications: Quarterly calendar; invitations to programs, etc
Activities: Classes for adults and children; lectures open to the public; tours; readings; scholarships to gifted children

M **ROME HISTORICAL SOCIETY,** Rome Information and Cultural Center,* 200 Church, 13440. Tel 315-336-5870. *Pres* Richard F Kahler; *VPres* P F Scripture; *Secy* Mrs F E Henze; *Dir* Joseph G Vincent; *Admin Asst* Mrs C E Flack; *Registrar & Conservator* M L Campbell; *Assoc Dir* W T Macmaster
Open Mon - Sat 10 AM - 4 PM & by appointment, cl holidays. No admis fee. Estab 1936 as a historical museum and society. Average Annual Attendance: 79,000. Mem: 800; dues $7.50; annual meeting in Dec
Income: Financed by membership and city appropriation
Collections: E Buyck; P F Hugunine; Forest Moses; Ann Marriot; Joseph G Vincent; Will Moses; Revolutionary War period paintings
Exhibitions: Statewide tours; local artists on tour
Publications: Annuals and Recollections
Activities: Lectures open to the public, 12 visiting lecturers per year; tours; awards; lending collection contains books, original art works, original prints, paintings, sculpture; traveling exhibitions organized and circulated; museum shop sells reproductions, prints, history related art works

L **William and Elaine Scripture Memorial Library,*** 113 W Court St, 13440. *Librn* B Dehimer
Open 9 AM - 4 PM, Mon - Fri. Estab 1936 for historical research of Rome and the Mohawk Valley
Library Holdings: Vols 3500; Per subs 5; Other — Clipping files, manuscripts, pamphlets, photographs, prints, reproductions
Collections: Area paintings from the Revolutionary War period to the present

ROOSEVELT

M **ROOSEVELT PUBLIC LIBRARY** , Black Artists Association Arts Center,* Rose & Mansfield Aves, 11575. Tel 516-378-1408, 378-9872. *Pres* Eliot Israel; *Dir* Margaret Kisselof
Open Mon - Fri 2 PM - 5 PM, Sat 11 AM - 2 PM. No admis fee. Estab 1972 to develop and maintain a viable art program for education and information of surrounding community and its outside patrons. Small community centered gallery, 88 sq ft of wall space. Average Annual Attendance: 2050
Income: Financed by endowment, state appropriation and Roosevelt Public Library
Collections: Various works of art
Exhibitions: Monthly exhibit
Publications: Press release; invitations to special events
Activities: Classes for adults and children; lect open to the public, 4 visiting lectr per year; gallery talks; original objects of art lent

ROSLYN

M **NASSAU COUNTY MUSEUM OF FINE ART,** Northern Blvd, PO Box D, 11576. Tel 516-484-9337. *Dir Office of Cultural Development* Marcia E O'Brien; *Dir Museum of Fine Art* Thomas A Saitzman
Open Tues - Fri 10 AM - 4:30 PM, Sat & Sun 1 - 5 PM, cl Mon. No admis fee. Estab 1975 for exhibits of historical and contemporary nature for Nassau County Residents. The building houses ten galleries, three on the first floor, and seven on the second floor, which are utilized for rotating exhibitions. Average Annual Attendance: 250,000. Mem: 2500; dues $20 - $1000
Income: Financed by membership and county appropriation
Collections: Contemporary prints; contemporary sculpture (outdoor)
Exhibitions: (1984) Sculpture: The Tradition In Steel; Works by Ray Johnson; Peter Bela Mayer: American Impressionist; Roots of Modernism in America
Publications: Catalogs for exhibitions
Activities: Classes for adults and children; dramatic programs; docent training; lectures open to the public; concerts; gallery talks; tours; original paintings and original objects of art lent to other qualified institutions; book traveling exhibitions; traveling exhibitions organized and circulated to the Gallery Association of New York State

SAINT BONAVENTURE

M **SAINT BONAVENTURE UNIVERSITY ART COLLECTION,** 14778. Tel 716-375-2323, Ext 6. *Art Cur* Bro John Capozzi
Open Mon - Thurs 8 AM - Midnight, Fri 8 AM - 5 PM, Sat 8 AM - 8 PM, Sun 10 AM - Midnight. No admis fee. Estab 1856 to provide artistic surroundings for students. Average Annual Attendance: 4000
Income: Financed by university budget
Collections: Paintings; porcelains and American Indian pottery; ivories, jade miniatures; cloisonne
Exhibitions: Rotating exhibitions
Publications: Art Catalog of Collection
Activities: Museum shop sells reproductions

SANBORN

M NIAGARA COUNTY COMMUNITY COLLEGE ART GALLERY, 3111
Saunders Settlement Rd, 14132. Tel 716-731-3271, Ext 159. *Gallery Dir*
Dorothy H Westhafer
Open hours vary from semester to semester; generally, Mon - Fri 11 AM - 3 PM,
occasional Sun hours. Estab 1973 for varied exhibits that will be of interest to
students and the community. There are two galleries with 270 sq ft of area and
approx 250 running ft. Average Annual Attendance: 7500
Income: $3000
Collections: Prints (contemporary)
Exhibitions: Professor Richard Robideau; People, photos by Joseph Benenate;
Robert Mark & Charles Roth (etchings); Elizabeth Bennett (pen sketches);
Barbara Johansen Newman (soft sculpture); Photo-Realism & The Geometric
Image; Buffalo Art Communicators & Directors; Abstraction & Landscape:
photos by Roman Zabinski; Kenneth Klier (drawings); Robert L Flock (paintings)
About Face: Ellen Carrey, photographer and Bruce Morosko, sculptor
Publications: Catalogs
Activities: Classes for adults; dramatic programs; lectures open to the public;
tours

SARATOGA SPRINGS

M NATIONAL MUSEUM OF RACING, INC, Union Ave, 12866. Tel 518-584-
0400. *Dir* Elaine E Mann; *Secy to Dir* Ann Genaro; *Asst to Dir* Elizabeth Clute
Open Jan - Mar Mon - Fri 10 AM - 4 PM; April - May & Oct - Nov Mon - Fri
9:30 AM - 5 PM, Sat Noon - 5 PM; June - Sept Mon - Fri 9:30 AM - 5 PM, Sat
& Sun Noon - 5 PM; August racing season daily 9:30 AM - 7 PM; cl New
Year's, Thanksgiving, Christmas. No admis fee, children under 12 must be
accompanied by parents. Estab 1950 as a museum for the collection, preservation
and exhibition of all kinds of articles associated with the origin, history and
development of horse racing. There are 10 galleries of sporting art. The
handsome Georgian-Colonial design brick structure houses one of the world's
greatest collections of equine art along with trophies, sculptures and memorabilia
of the sport from its earliest days. Average Annual Attendance: Approx 45,000.
Mem: Annual meeting Aug
Income: Financed through annual appeal and individual contributions
Collections: Oil paintings of thoroughbred horses, trophies, racing silks, bronzes,
prints, racing memorabilia
Publications: Catalog; Hall of Fame booklets
Activities: Lect open to public, 2-4 visiting lectrs per year; gallery talks; exten
dept serving Northeast; original objects of art lent on special occasions; museum
shop selling books, reproductions, prints, jewelry, figurines and other items
L Reference Library, Union Ave, 12866
Open to researchers, students and authors by appointment
Library Holdings: Per subs 6; AV — Fs; Other — Clipping files, exhibition
catalogs, memorabilia, original art works, pamphlets, photographs
Special Subjects: Thoroughbred horse, horses

M SKIDMORE COLLEGE, Art Gallery,* North Broadway, 12866. Tel 518-584-
5000, Ext 370. *Dir* David Miller
Open Sept - May Mon - Fri 9 AM - 5 PM, Sat & Sun Noon - 5 PM; summer:
hours variable according to summer class schedules. No admis fee. Estab 1927
for educational enrichment of the college and community. Exhibitions are
intended to bring awareness of both contemporary and historical trends in art.
Average Annual Attendance: 6000
Income: Financed through College
Collections: American and European Prints; Saratoga Springs Historical
Collection
Publications: Exhibition catalogs, occasionally
Activities: Lect open to public, 5-6 visiting lectr per year; gallery talks; traveling
exhibitions organized and circulated
L Lucy Scribner Library, Art Reading Area, North Broadway, 12866. Tel 518-
584-5000, Ext 640. *Fine Arts Librn* Jane Graves
Open Mon - Sat 8 AM - 11 PM, Sun Noon - 11 PM. Estab 1925
Library Holdings: Vols 12,000; Per subs 130; Micro — Cards; AV — Fs,
Kodachromes, lantern slides, motion pictures, rec, slides 53,000; Other —
Exhibition catalogs, memorabilia, original art works, photographs, prints 600,
reproductions, sculpture
Collections: Anita Pohndorff Yates Collection of Saratoga History

SCHENECTADY

O SCHENECTADY COUNTY HISTORICAL SOCIETY, 32 Washington Ave,
12305. Tel 518-374-0263. *Pres* Wayne H Harvey; *Cur* Marilyn Freitas
Open Mon - Sun 1 - 5 PM, cl national holidays. No admis fee. Estab 1905, for
the preservation of local historical materials. Located within area of original
Schenectady stockade by the Dutch in 1661; contains 50 paintings of the 19th
century dealing with prominent Schenectady residents. Average Annual
Attendance: 6500. Mem: Dues organization $25, patron $10, regular $5
Collections: Decorative arts; historical material; Indian artifacts; paintings;
photographs
Exhibitions: Temporary exhibitions from other museums
Publications: Newsletter, monthly
Activities: Lect for members only, 10 lectr a yr, tours; individual paintings and
original objects of art lent; sales shop sells books, maps and postcards
L Library, 32 Washington Ave, 12305. *Librn* Elsa K Church
Open Mon - Fri
Library Holdings: Vols 2500; Per subs 7; Micro — Reels; AV — Cassettes,
motion pictures, slides; Other — Clipping files, manuscripts 16,000, photographs

M SCHENECTADY MUSEUM, Nott Terrace Heights, 12308. Tel 518-382-7890.
Actg Dir George Weinheimer; *Cur Exhibits* Georgia Cascio; *Cur Exhibits*
Dorothy Dietrich; *Cur Education* Alfred Hulstrunk; *Public Information* Carol J
Hadson

Open Tues - Fri 10 AM - 4:30 PM, Sat & Sun Noon - 5 PM. Museum only
admis adults $1, children $.50; museum & planetarium adults $2, children $1.
Founded 1934, chartered by the New York State Regents in 1937 to increase
and diffuse knowledge in appreciation of art, history, industry, and science by
providing collections, exhibits, lectures and other programs. Sales and rental
gallery is maintained. Average Annual Attendance: 80,000. Mem: 2200; dues
annual $60, regular $25, individual $15, student & senior citizens $7.50; annual
meeting Oct
Collections: African Art; decorative arts; 19th and 20th century art; 19th and
20th century costumes and textiles; North American Indian Art
Exhibitions: (1983) Amazing World of Electronics; A Woman's Perspective;
Designer Crafts Council Craft Exhibit; Collected Visions; Mohawk-Hudson
Regional Art Exhibition; Rockwell Kent; Clayton Pond; Family Images; Portrait
of an Atom; Lines & Waves; Jubilee Collection: 50 Years of Costume Collecting
at the Schenectady Museum
Publications: Annual Report; Calendar, monthly; Museum Notes, monthly;
exhibition catalogues
Activities: Art and craft classes; Festival of Nations; Crafts Fair; Rock Festival;
Haunted House; Museum Ball; docent training; lectures open to the public;
concerts; gallery talks; tours; loan materials and exhibits for area schools, colleges
and libraries; book traveling exhibitions, 3 - 4 per yr; museum shop sells books,
original art, reproductions, prints & crafts
L Library, 12308. *Librn* Sue C Welch
For reference and technical information only
Library Holdings: Vols 5000

SENECA FALLS

M SENECA FALLS HISTORICAL SOCIETY MUSEUM, 55 Cayuga St, 13148.
Tel 315-568-8412. *Pres* Philip Olmstead; *VPres* William Ottemiller; *Secy* Gen
Collins; *Dir* Lisa Fern Johnson; *Education Cur* Geralyn Heisser; *Registrar* Dawn
Emerson; *Photo Archivist* George Covert
Open 9 AM - 5 PM. Admis adult $1, children $.50. Estab 1904 as an educational
institution dedicated to the preservation and interpretation of local history.
Victorian 23 room house with decorative arts collection. Average Annual
Attendance: 4000. Mem: 350; dues family $25, single $12; annual meetings
Income: $85,000 (financed by endowment, membership, city, state & federal
appropriation, United Way)
Collections: Local painters; central New York State folk art & crafts; Currier &
Ives prints; nineteenth century decorative arts
Exhibitions: (1982) Lost & Found: Nineteenth Century Architecture in Seneca
Falls; (1984) Ambivalent Pioneers on a New Frontier
Publications: Reprints of archival material
Activities: Classes for adults and children; docent training; school group
programs; lectures open to public, 11 vis lectr per yr; concerts; gallery talks;
tours; poster competitions; outreach programs to shutins; individual paintings and
original objects of art lent to other institutions; lending collection contains books,
motion pictures, slides; sales shop sells books and reproductions

SETAUKET

M GALLERY NORTH, 90 N Country Rd, 11733. Tel 516-751-2676. *Dir* Elizabeth
Goldberg; *Pres* Elizabeth Phraner Davis; *VPres* Marjorie Bishop; *Secy* Sharon
Cowles; *Treasurer* Helen McCorkle
Open Tues - Sat 10 AM - 5 PM, Sun 1 - 5 PM. No admis fee. Estab 1965 to
exhibit the work of contemporary Long Island artists & crafts people. Gallery is
housed in Victorian building with 3 main exhibition rooms. Average Annual
Attendance: 10,000. Mem: 150; dues $10-$100; quarterly meetings
Income: $57,000 (Financed by membership & sales)
Exhibitions: Eight changing exhibitions per yr
Activities: Lectures open to public; competitions with awards; sales shop sells
crafts from local artists & imported crafts

SKANEATELES

M JOHN D BARROW ART GALLERY, 49 E Genesee St, 13152. Tel 315-685-
5135. *Chmn of Trustees* Frovies Milford; *Secy* Frederick Martin
Open summer Thurs & Sat 2 - 4 PM, Tues & Thurs 7 - 8:30 PM, winter Thurs &
Sat 2 - 4 PM. no admis fee. Estab in 1900 to exhibit paintings of John D Barow.
Three rooms with unusual feature of tiered paintings built in a wainscoting. Mem:
160
Activities: Lectures open to public

O SKANEATELES LIBRARY ASSOCIATION, 49 E Genesee St, 13152. Tel
315-685-5135. *Pres* G W Gregory; *Secy* Judy Gelston
Open 10 AM - 5 PM, cl Sun. Estab 1877
Income: Financed by annual fund raising drive and endowments
Collections: Paintings by American artists; etchings by American and foreign
artists; 300 paintings by John D Barrow, in separate wing
Exhibitions: Occasional special exhibitions

SOUTHAMPTON

M PARRISH ART MUSEUM, 25 Jobs Lane, 11968. Tel 516-283-2118. *Dir* Trudy
Kramer; *Assoc Dir & Cur Affairs* Maureen C O'Brien; *Cur* Robert Lehman; *Cur*
Klaus Kertess; *Educ Dir* William Henry; *Asst to Dir* Anke Jackson
Open Mon, Thurs, Sat 10 AM - 5 PM, Fri 10 AM - 9 PM, Sun 1 - 5 PM, cl
Tues & Wed Oct - May, cl Tues May - Oct. No admis fee. Estab 1898 to exhibit,
care for and research permanent collections and loaned works of art with
emphasis on American 19th and 20th century paintings. Three main galleries are
maintained; total dimensions 4288 sq ft, 355 running feet. Average Annual
Attendance: 70,000. Mem: 2000; dues $15 - $1000 and up; annual meeting Dec
Income: Approx $170,000 (financed by endowment, membership)
Collections: †American paintings, 19th and 20th century; Carney Collection of

Chinese ceramics; D Doughty porcelains; Dunnigan Collection of 19th century etchings; Japanese woodblock prints and stencils; Oriental decorative arts; Samuel Parrish Collection of Italian Renaissance panel paintings; Phillips Collection of 17th and 18th century portraits
Exhibitions: Annual Juried Exhibition; Renaissance Paintings from the Collection; Alive at The Parrish; The World of Kabuki Theatre, Woodblock Prints by Kunisada; Annual School Art Festival; Still Life Paintings & Drawings by East End Artists; Americans Abroad at the Turn of the Century; An American Place; The Long Island Landscape, 1865-1914: The Halcyon Years; Alexander Brook
Publications: Exhibition Catalogs (10 per year); Newsletter, quarterly
Activities: Classes for adults and children; dramatic programs; lectures open to the public 3 vis lectr per yr; concerts; gallery talks; films; exten dept serving area schools; lending collection contains color reproductions, film strips, original art works, original prints; book traveling exhibitions, 1 - 3 per yr; traveling exhibitions organized and circulated; museum shop sells books, magazines, reproductions, prints, craft items
L **Aline B Saarinen Library,** 25 Jobs Lane, 11968. *Librn* Penelope Henry
Reference library is open to the public
Library Holdings: Vols 4200; Per subs 6; Other — Clipping files, exhibition catalogs, memorabilia
Special Subjects: Architecture, Oriental Art, Painting - American
Collections: William Merritt Chase Archives; original documents, photographs, memorabilia, research materials pertaining to the life and work of Chase (1849-1916)

STAATSBURG

M **NEW YORK STATE OFFICE OF PARKS, RECREATION & HISTORICAL PRESERVATION,** Mills Mansion State Historical Site, Old Post Road, 12580. Tel 914-889-4100. *Historic Site Mgr* John Feeney
Open May 26 - Oct 31, Wed - Sun 10 AM - 4:30 PM. No admis fee. Estab 1938 to interpret lifestyle of the very affluent segment of American society during the period 1890-1929. Average Annual Attendance: 10,000
Collections: Original furnishings, paintings, prints, decorative art objects and tapestries from Mr and Mrs Mills
Activities: Docent training; workshops; lectures open to the public; concerts; gallery tours; loans of paintings or original art objects have to be approved by New York State Office of Parks and Recreation, Division of Historic Preservation

STATEN ISLAND

M **JACQUE MARCHAIS CENTER OF TIBETAN ARTS, INC,** 338 Lighthouse Ave, New York, 10306. Tel 212-987-3478. *Asst Dir* Rod W Preiss
Open April 1 - November 30, Sat & Sun 1 - 5 PM; June, July & Aug, open Fri 1 - 5 PM. Admis adults $2, children under 12 $1. Estab 1946 for maintenance of library and museum in Buddhist philosophy, art and religion, with particular emphasis on Tibetan Buddhism. Buildings planned for and collection amassed by Mrs Harry Klauber, (known professionally as Jacques Marchais) who ran an Oriental art gallery from 1938 until her death in 1948.
Average Annual Attendance: 5000. Mem: 300; dues $15-$100; annual meeting Oct
Income: Financed by contributions, admissions, county, state & federal appropriations & gift shop sales
Collections: Jacques Marchais permanent collection of Tibetan and Buddhist Art
Activities: Classes for adults & children; dramatic programs; lectures open to public; concerts; gallery talks; tours; exten servs New York City; individual paintings & original objects of art lent to museums for special exhibits; museum shop sells books, original art, reproductions, prints, Tibetan carpets, wooden masks, jewelry & antiques
L **Library,** 338 Lighthouse Ave, 10306. *Librn* Sigred Sidrow
For reference only
Library Holdings: Other — Photographs

M **STATEN ISLAND INSTITUTE OF ARTS AND SCIENCES,** 75 Stuyvesant, Saint George, 10301. Tel 212-727-1135. *Pres* William Siebenheller; *Dir* A Mae Seeley; *Cur of Art* Barry Leo Delaney; *Editor & Librn* Gail K Schneider; *Museum Lectr* Freda Mulcahy Esterly
Open Tues - Sat 10 AM - 5 PM, Sun & holidays 2 - 5 PM, cl Mon, Thanksgiving, Christmas, New Years, Fourth of July, Labor Day. No admis fee. Estab 1881, inc 1906. Average Annual Attendance: 105,000. Mem: 900; dues $10 and up
Collections: †American paintings of the 19th and 20th centuries; Oriental, Greek, Roman and primitive art objects; †prints and small sculptures
Exhibitions: Exhibitions in decorative arts; design exhibitions in various media; major loan shows of paintings and prints; special exhibitions of graphic arts and of photography; four Weissglass awards totaling $400 presented each year
Publications: Proceedings, 3 times a yr; catalogs; Annual Reports
Activities: Fall and spring terms of adult classes; lectures on art and science; complete program of lectures, art and natural history, for school children with annual registration of 30,000
L **Library,** 75 Stuyvesant PL, St George, 10301. *Librn* Eloise Beil
Library Holdings: Vols 30,000; Per subs 6
Collections: George W Curtis Collection of books, manuscripts, and memorabilia; reference collection of 30,000 publications in science and art history; a choice collection of Staten Island newspapers from 1834-1934 on microfilm; letters, documents, journals, files of clippings and old photographs relating to the history of Staten Island and the metropolitan region

STONE RIDGE

M **ULSTER COUNTY COMMUNITY COLLEGE,** Visual Arts Gallery, 12484. Tel 914-687-7621, Ext 76. *Coordr* Allan L Cohan
Open Mon - Fri 10 AM - 3 PM, fall and spring semesters, Noon - 3 PM summer. No admis fee. Estab 1963 as a center for creative activity. Gallery is maintained as an adjunct to the college's cultural and academic program; John Vanderlyn Hall has 40 x 28 ft enclosed space and is located on the campus. Average Annual Attendance: 3000
Income: Financed by college funds
Purchases: $750
Collections: Contemporary drawings, paintings, photographs, prints, sculpture, historical works
Publications: Flyers announcing each exhibit, every four to six weeks
Activities: Lect open to the public, 2-3 visiting lectrs per year; concerts

STONY BROOK

M **THE MUSEUMS AT STONY BROOK,** 1208 Route 25A, 11790. Tel 516-751-0066. *Dir* Susan Stitt; *Public Information Officer* Connie Hoebich
Open Wed - Sun 10 AM - 5 PM, cl Mon & Tues. Admis adults $2.75, students and sr citizens $2.25, children 6 - 12 $.50, under 6 and members free. Estab 1942 as a nonprofit educational institution whose purpose is to collect and preserve objects of historic and artistic interest. The Museums' 19 buildings, 13.5 acre complex include a History Museum, Art Museum, Carriage Museum (open Apr - Nov), various period buildings, a museum store, the Stony Brook Grist Mill (open Sundays, June - Oct) and the Hawkins-Mount House (open for one week of guided tours in Dec). Average Annual Attendance: 55,000. Mem: 600; dues $10 - $500
Collections: Paintings, drawings and memorabilia of artist William Sidney Mount; other 19th century American artists costumes; dolls; decoys; textiles; carriages
Exhibitions: Changing exhibitions in Art Museum and History Museum
Publications: Annual Report; Quarterly Newsletter; exhibition catalogs; brochures
Activities: Classes for adults and children; docent training; lect open to public, vis lectrs; gallery talks; tours; loans to other museums; museum shop sells books, reproductions, prints, childrens toys, early American housewares, miniatures
L **Kate Strong Historical Library,** 1208 Route 25A, 11790. Tel 516-751-0066. *Librn & Registrar* Jan Armstrong
Reference library open to researchers by appointment
Library Holdings: Vols 1500; Per subs 15; trade catalogs; Other — Manuscripts, photographs
Collections: William Cooper, shipbuilder, 19th century, Sag Harbor; Israel Green Hawkins, Edward P Buffet, Hal B Fullerton; Archives: Papers of William Sidney Mount and family; Daniel Williamson and John Williamson, Stony Brook

M **STATE UNIVERSITY OF NEW YORK AT STONY BROOK,** Art Gallery,* 11794. Tel 516-246-5000. *Coordr* Lynn Silbonm; *Tech Asst* Stephen Larise
Open Mon - Fri Noon - 5 PM. No admis fee. Estab 1967 to serve both the campus and the community by exhibitions of professional artists. One gallery 42 x 74 with 22 ft ceiling; second space 22 x 60 ft with 12 ft ceilings. Average Annual Attendance: 1500 students and members of the community per show
Income: Financed by state appropriation
Exhibitions: Benny Andres: Bicentennial Series; Alex Katz: Recent Paintings; Otto Piene: Sculpture; Senior Art Show, Mixed Media
Activities: Lectures weekly

SYRACUSE

M **EVERSON MUSEUM OF ART,** 401 Harrison St, 13202. Tel 315-474-6064. *Pres* William C Egan; *VPres* Dr John J Prucha; *VPres* Mrs William Hall; *VPres* Mrs Frederic J Durkin; *VPres* John S Ferguson; *Dir* Ronald A Kuchta; *Asst Dir* Sandra Trop; *Cur Contemporary Art* John Perreault; *Cur Education* Jeffrey York; *Secy* Henri E Bonvin; *Treas* William A Hider; *Registrar* Rita Alexandrides
Open Tues - Fri 12 - 5 PM, Sat 10 AM - 5 PM, Sun 12 - 5 PM, cl Mon. No admis fee. Estab 1968 to present free exhibitions by lending artists, chiefly American to serve as an educational element for the cultural and general community. Main Sculpture Court - indoor and 50 x 50 x 40 ft, four large upper galleries 40 x 50 x 28 ft, lower gallery 40 x 50 x 15 ft, four small galleries, Sales Gallery & Luncheon Gallery, Inner Court in Administration Wing 28 x 40 x 32 ft, square block of outdoor Community Plaza with monumental sculpture. Mem: 2609; dues general $25, senior citizens $12.50, student $7.50
Income: Financed by membership, city and state appropriation, New York State Council on the Arts, National Endowment for the Arts, Institute for Museum Services, private corporate grants, individual grants
Collections: African Collection; †contemporary American ceramics; †contemporary American painting & sculpture; 17th, 18th & 19th century English porcelain; traditional American painting & portraiture; video-tape collection; Cloud Wampler Collection of Oriental Art
Exhibitions: (1982) Boobies, Boojums and Snarks: The Ceramic Curiosities of the Martin Brothers (1880-1914); African Art; Asian Art; Memorabilia Celebrating the Everson Museum's 85th Anniversary Year; Selections from the Permanent Collection of Photography; Photographs by Misha Gordin: Silence in Light; Recent Acquisitions and Selections from the Permanent Collection; On My Own Time; Ceramics of the World from the Permanent Collection; Stoneware from the New York State: Richard J Giarrusso Collection; William Rose: Metaphysical Australian Structures, paintings; Selection from the Permanent Collection of American and English Painting; Permanent Collection of Prints and Drawings; Selected Videotapes; American Painting and Decorative Arts: Arts and Crafts Period c 1900; Abbott Handerson Thayer; Rivers, Gorges, and Canyons: Watercolors by Samuel Vann; Merlin Pollock: Four Decades of Painting; Work by Instructors in the Syracuse City School Districts; Paintings by George Wingate; Children's Book Week; Golden Day, Silver Night: Perceptions of Nature in American Art; Kyo Ikebe: Grand Cosmos and Elementary Domain; Nafsika Bersentes: Astron II; The Syracuse Ceramic Guild: Recent Works; (1983) Adrian Saxe: Between Sevres and Momoyama; Focus on the Permanent

Collection; MONY Scholastic Art Exhibition; Images of Buddha; Late Twentieth Century Art: Sydney and Frances Lewis Foundation; David Chamberlain: Frozen Music; Stella Waitzkin: Selected Work 1973-1983; Ceramic: The Vessel Through Time and Culture; Black Artists from Five Countries: USA, Haiti, Ethiopia, Jamaica, Zaire; Anthony Panzera, drawings
Publications: Art books; bulletin, monthly; Educational materials; exhibition catalogs
Activities: Educ dept; classes for children; docent training; lect open to the public, 10 visiting lectr per year; concerts; gallery talks; tours; competitions; exten dept serves public schools of Syracuse; individual paintings and original objects of art lent; originate traveling exhibitions; museum and sales shop selling books, magazines, original art, reproductions, prints, slides, ceramics, local and national arts and crafts

L **Art Reference Library,** 401 Harrison St, 13202
Library Holdings: Vols 8000; Per subs 35; Micro — Cards, prints; AV — Kodachromes, slides, v-tapes; Other — Clipping files, exhibition catalogs, memorabilia, pamphlets, photographs

M **LEMOYNE COLLEGE,** Art Gallery,* LeMoyhe Heights, 13214. Tel 315-446-2882. *Chairperson & Librn* Dr Tanya Popovic; *Asst Prof of Philosophy* William McKenna; *Asst Prof of Philosophy* Dr Donald Arentz; *Periodical Librn* Lynnette Stevens
Open Mon - Thurs 9 AM - 11 PM, Fri 9 AM - 9 PM, Sat & Sun 9 AM - 5 PM. No admis fee. Estab 1966. Average Annual Attendance: 1500
Income: Financed through the Faculty Art Gallery Committee
Collections: Paintings, etchings, prints and watercolors
Activities: Individual paintings and original objects of art lent

SYRACUSE UNIVERSITY

M **Joe and Emily Lowe Art Gallery,** Sims Hall, 13210. Tel 315-423-4098. *Dir* Joseph A Scala; *Cur* Ruth Appelhof; *Secy* Betty LaPlante; *Registrar & Preparator* Leonard Eichler
Open Tues - Sun Noon - 5 PM, cl Mon. No admis fee. Estab 1952 to present art exhibitions to inform university and communities of central upstate New York areas of international heritage of art, new advances in contemporary art with emphasis on the discovery of regional values, outstanding local art including faculty and student work. Museum Training Program complements our exhibition program. 6300 sq ft of space normally divided into separate galleries by movable walls. Average Annual Attendance: 20,000
Income: Financed through University with additional outside grants
Exhibitions: (1982) Design in Lace; Outside New York City; From Drawing to Sculpture; Perspectives of an Era; Sir Francis Seymour Hayden, MD; George Vandersluis - Homage to the Barn; The Personal Apocalypse; (1983) Margaret Bourke-White: The Humanitarian Vision; MFA Show; Symbols of Change: British Prints of the Last Two Decades; Native American Contemporary Art
Publications: Exhibition catalogs each show
Activities: Private tours on request; traveling exhibitions organized and circulated

M **Art Collection,** Sims Hall, 13210. Tel 315-423-4097. *Dir* Alfred T Collette; *Cur Coll* Domenic J Iacono; *Asst to Cur* Thomas Piche; *Asst to Registrar* Philip A Ladoucuer
The Art Collection is housed in a temperature & humidity-controlled area of Sims Hall, adjacent to the Art Gallery. Used primarily for storage & care of the 25,000 object collection, this facility also includes a teaching display area to accommodate classes & individuals involved in research
Income: Financed by university funds
Purchases: Jim Dine, Martin Lewis, Everett Shinn, Peggy Bacon, John Steuart Curry
Collections: West African tribal art; Korean, Japanese & American ceramics; Indian folk art; Pre-Columbian & contemporary Peruvian ceramics; Scandinavian designs in metal, wood, clay & textiles; 20th century American works with an emphasis on the Depression and War years (paintings); 19th century European Salon paintings; history of printmaking (emphasis on American artists); decorative arts; Mary Petty-Alan Dunn Center for Social Cartooning
Publications: Art Nouveau Glass & Pottery; collection catalogs

L **Ernest Stevenson Bird Library,** Fine Arts Dept, 13210. *Librn* Randall Bond; *Fine Arts Dept Head* Donald C Seibert; *Architecture Librn* Barbara A Opar; *Slide Cur* Johanna W Prins
Open Mon - Thurs 8 AM - 10 PM, Fri 8 AM - 6 PM, Sat 10 AM - 6 PM, Sun 10 AM - 10 PM. Estab 1870 for reference and research in the history of art
Purchases: $110,616
Library Holdings: Vols 53,000; Per subs 130; Picture file 26,000; Micro — Cards, fiche, prints, reels; AV — A-tapes, cassettes, fs, lantern slides, motion pictures, rec, slides 200,000, v-tapes; Other — Exhibition catalogs 10,000, manuscripts, photographs
Collections: Manuscript Collections of many American artists

TARRYTOWN

M **LYNDHURST,** 635 S Broadway, 10591. Tel 914-631-0046. *Dir* John L Frisbee III
Open April - Oct Tues - Sun 10 AM - 5 PM, Nov - Mar by advance reservation. Admis adults $4, senior citizens $3, students $2, group rates by arrangement; free to National Trust members. A property of the National Trust for Historic Preservation as a National Historic Landmark and operated as a community preservation center. Lyndhurst is a Gothic revival castle designed in 1838 for General William Paulding by Alexander Jackson Davis, one of America's most influential 19th century architects. Commissioned by second owner, George Merritt, to enlarge the house, Davis, in 1865, continued the Gothic revival style in the additions. It was purchased in 1880 by Jay Gould and willed to his daughter, Helen. Later acquired by another daughter, Anna, Duchess of Talleyrand-Perigord, Lyndhurst was left to the National Trust in 1964. The property is located on spacious grounds along the Hudson River. Visitors are free to explore the magnificent park which is being restored. Other highlights include a carriagehouse, stocked with period vehicles, stables, and the remains of private greenhouses. Windows attributed to L C Tiffany. The preservation of Lyndhurst is a composite of the contributions of the three families who lived in it. Property serves as a focal point for advancement of historic preservation. Through it are developed new relationships amoung cultural, community preservation groups and National Trust members in its area. Responds to community preservation needs by acting as a link between community and appropriate regional or headquarter offices of National Trust. Provides interpretive programs which are related to Lyndhurst's particular case study in historic preservation. The National Trust Restoration Workshop, located in a portion of the stable complex carries out restoration craft services for National Trust properties. Average Annual Attendance: 51,000
Income: Financed by admission fees, memberships, private contributions, special events and federal appropriations
Collections: Collection of Gothic furniture designed by architect A J Davis in the 1830s and 1870s; 19th century furnishings and paintings; Tiffany glass
Activities: Summer outdoor concerts; antique and auto shows; Christmas programs; guided tours; individual paintings and original objects of art lent as requested for special exhibitions by museums and historical societies; museum shop sells books, reproductions, slides and gift items

M **SLEEPY HOLLOW RESTORATIONS INC,** 150 White Plains Road, 10591. Tel 914-631-8200. *Pres* Dana S Creel; *Exec Dir* John W Harbour Jr; *Assoc Dir* Willialm B Pfeifer; *Cur* Joseph T Butler
Open 10 -AM - 5 PM, cl Thanksgiving Day, Christmas and New Years. Admis to Sunnyside, Philipsburg Manor and Van Cortland Manor adults $4 each property, sr citizens and juniors 6-14 $2.50 each property; three visit tickets valid one year, adults $10, sr citizens and juniors $6.50; groups of 20 or more must make reservations in advance. Chartered 1951 as a nonprofit educational foundation. Owns and operates historic properties which are Sunnyside in Tarrytown, the home of author Washington Irving; Philipsburg Manor in North Tarrytown, a Dutch-American gristmill-farm site of the early 1700s; Van Cortlandt Manor in Croton-on-Hudson, a manorial estate of the Revolutionary War period. Average Annual Attendance: 150,000
Collections: Memorabilia of Washington Irving, Van Cortlandt and Phillips families; 17th, 18th and 19th century decorative arts; Philipsburg Manor, Upper Mills, Four Centuries of History, A Decade of Restoration
Exhibitions: Exhibitions of collections; (1982) Alhambra; Officers and Gentlemen: Historic West Point in Photographs; (1983) Sleepy Hollow Restorations, A Cross Section of the Collection
Publications: American Industrialization, Economic Expansion, and the Law; America's Wooden Age; Aspects of Early New York Society and Politics; Bracebride Hall; Business Enterprise in Early New York; Diedrich Knickerbocker's A History of New York; An Emerging Independent American Economy: 1815-1875; The Family Collections at Van Cortlandt Manor; The Howe Map; The Hudson River 1850-1918, A Photographic Portrait; Life Along the Hudson; Life of George Washington; The Loyalist Americans; Material Culture of the Wooden Age; The Mill at Philipsburg Manor, Upper Mills, and a Brief History of Milling; Old Christmas; Party and Political Opposition in Revolutionary America; Philipsburg Manor: A Guidebook; A Portfolio of Sleepy Hollow Prints; Rip Van Winkle & the Legend of Sleepy Hollow; Six Publications related to Washington Irving
Activities: Classes for adults and children; docent training; demonstrations of 17th and 18th century arts and crafts; lectures open to the public; guided tours; gallery talks; sales shop sells books, reproductions & slides

L **Library,** 150 White Plains Rd, 10591. Tel 914-631-8200. *Librn* Hollee Haswell; *Asst Librn* Sherri Paul
Specialized reference library with particular emphasis on 17th, 18th and 19th century living in the Hudson River Valley
Library Holdings: Vols 12,000; Per subs 123; Micro — Reels; Other — Exhibition catalogs, manuscripts
Special Subjects: Washington Irving

TICONDEROGA

M **FORT TICONDEROGA MUSEUM,** Box 390, 12883. Tel 518-585-2821. *Pres* John G Pell; *Cur & Librn* Jane M Lape
Open daily, mid-May - mid-Oct 9 AM - 5PM. Admis adults $5, children 10 - 13 $3. Estab 1909 to preserve and present the Colonial and Revolutionary history of Fort Ticonderoga. the museum is the restored barracks of the Colonial fort. Average Annual Attendance: 200,000
Income: Financed by admission fees
Collections: Artifacts; manuscripts; paintings
Exhibitions: Exhibitions are held in mid-May - mid-Oct
Publications: Bulletin of the Fort Ticonderoga Museum
Activities: Classes for adults; individual paintings and original objects of art lent to qualified museums; sales shop sells books, reproductions, slides

L **Library,** 12883
Open by appointment for reference only
Library Holdings: Vols 5000

TROY

O **RENSSELAER COUNTY HISTORICAL SOCIETY,** Hart-Cluett Mansion, 1827, 59 Second St, 12180. Tel 518-272-7232. *Pres* David B Klingaman; *Dir* Breffny A Walsh; *Cur* Stacy F Pomeroy; *Secy* Sandra Reizen
Open Tues - Sat 10 AM - 4 PM. Admis donation for adults $1. Estab 1927 to promote historical research and to collect and exhibit materials of all kinds related to the history of the Rensselaer County area including books, papers, fine and decorative arts. The Hart-Cluett Mansion is a historic house museum with 11 period rooms. Average Annual Attendance: 10,000. Mem: 550; dues $5 - $1000; annual meeting Sept
Income: Approx $80,000 (financed by endowment and membership)
Collections: Ceramics; costumes; Elijah Galusha 19th century furniture; paintings by local artists including C G Beauregard, Joseph Hidley and Abel Buel Moore; portraits; quilts and coverlets; silver
Exhibitions: Canes; Currier and Ives; Troy-Bilt Rototiller
Publications: Newsletter, monthly
Activities: Lect open to public, 8 visiting lectr per year; internships; lending collection contains cassettes, motion pictures, slides; traveling exhibitions organized and circulated; sales shop selling books, prints and gifts

L **Library,*** 59 Second St, 12180. Tel 518-270-6673. *Dir* James C Andrews
Library Holdings: Vols 1000; Per subs 3; AV — Slides; Other — Photographs

M **RENSSELAER NEWMAN FOUNDATION CHAPEL AND CULTURAL CENTER,** 2125 Burdett Ave (Mailing add: 2008 19th St, 12180). Tel 518-274-7793. *Pres* Paul Catan; *Dir* William McQuiston; *Treasurer* Thomas Phelan; *Secy* Mack Stewart
Open 9 AM - 11 PM. Estab 1968 to provide religion and culture for members of the Rensselaer Polytechnic Institute and Troy area, a broadly ecumenical service. Gallery maintained. Average Annual Attendance: 100,000
Income: $150,000 (supported by contributions)
Collections: Contemporary paintings, sculpture and needlework; liturgical vestments and artifacts; medieval sculpture
Exhibitions: Laliberte banners; Picasso traveling exhibition New York State Council on the Arts; Smithsonian Institution Traveling Exhibition; local one man shows
Publications: Sun and Balance, three times a year
Activities: Dramatic programs; classes for adults and children; lect open to public, 10 vis lectr per yr; concerts

M **RUSSELL SAGE COLLEGE,** New Gallery,* Schacht Fine Arts Center, 12180. Tel 518-270-2248. *Gallery Dir* Ruth Healey
Open Mon - Fri 9 AM - 5 PM, Sun 2 - 5 PM. No admis fee. Estab 1970 for exhibition of contemporary art for college and public. Gallery is one room, with 150 running ft. Average Annual Attendance: 3000
Income: Financed by the college
Collections: Drawings (contemporary); paintings (contemporary); sculpture of New Guinea and Africa
Exhibitions: Faculty and student shows; paintings, drawings, sculpture from New York City galleries and area artists; photography; traveling exhibitions
Activities: Gallery talks; original objects of art lent on campus; lending collection contains original prints, paintings, sculpture; traveling exhibitions organized and circulated

UTICA

M **MUNSON-WILLIAMS-PROCTOR INSTITUTE,** Museum of Art, 310 Genesee St, 13502. Tel 315-797-0000. *Pres* Paul J Farinella; *Dir* Paul D Schweizer; *Cur Painting & Sculpture* Sarah Clark-Langager; *Cur of Education* David Stark; *Cur of Decorative Arts* Chris Bensch
Open Tues - Sat 10 AM - 5 PM, Sun 1 - 5 PM, cl Mon. No admis fee. Estab 1919 through an endowment granted a provisional charter by the Board of Regents of the University of the State of New York, changed to an absolute charter in 1941, and amended in 1948 to empower the Institute to provide instruction at the college level in the field of fine arts. The Institute became active in 1935 with the purpose of establishing & maintaining a gallery & collection of art to give instruction & to have an auxiliary library. It consists of a School of Art estab 1941; a Museum of Art opened in 1960; Fountain Elms, a house-museum was restored in 1960; a Meetinghouse opened in 1963 & a Performing Arts Division. Average Annual Attendance: 200,000. Mem: 2500; dues $15
Income: Financed by endowment, tuition and private contributions
Purchases: 19th & 20th century American, European paintings, sculpture, graphic & decorative arts
Collections: †Arts of Central New York; † contemporary European paintings and sculpture; Greek, Persian and pre-Columbian art; †18th, 19th and 20th century American paintings, sculpture, and decorative arts; †drawings and prints
Exhibitions: (1981-83) Pop Art & Photo Realism Prints; Wolf Kahn; Arthur B Davies Retrospective; Sculpture of George Sugarman; Artists of the Stieglitz Circle; Annual of Artists of Central New York; The Painter's West; New Sculpture by John Von Bergan; E L Henry's Country Life; Rural Vistas; North Country Folk Art; Realist Painting Today; Utica Stained Glass; Light in American Landscape Painting; Abstract Expressionism in Permanent Collection; Sidewalk Arts Exhibition; Recent Paintings by Raymond Han; Next to Nature; Evolution of the American Chair; Rodney Ripps; Coles, Couger of Empire; Lachaise Sculpture; D Oppenheim
Publications: Bulletin, monthly; exhibition catalogues
Activities: Educ dept; docent training; lect open to public; visiting lectureres; concerts; tours; film series; competitions; art and gift shop sells books, original art, reproductions, prints, slides

L **Art Reference Library,** 310 Genessee St, 13502. Tel 315-797-0000, Ext 23. *Head Librn* Linda L Lott; *Slide Librn* Lisa Pennella; *Music Librn* Kim R Wheatley
Open Tues - Sat 10 AM - 5 PM. Estab 1940 to support School of Art, Museum of Art staff, Institute Membership and general public; circulation only to members of the Institute. Circ 5000
Purchases: $5000
Library Holdings: Vols 15,000; Per subs 60; Micro — Fiche; AV — Rec 5500, slides 25,000; Other — Clipping files, pamphlets
Special Subjects: Decorative Arts, Painting - American
Collections: Fountain Elms Collection; autographs, rare books and manuscripts, book plates; 19th century pictorial sheet music covers
Publications: Bibliographies related to museum exhibitions; bibliographic instructional materials

WATERTOWN

M **ROSWELL P FLOWER MEMORIAL LIBRARY,** Art Gallery, 229 Washington St, 13601. Tel 315-788-2352. *Dir* Anthony F Cozzie
Open Sept - June Mon - Thurs 8:30 AM - 9 PM, Fri 8:30 AM - 8:30 PM, Sat 9 AM - 5:30 PM; July & Aug Mon 8:30 AM - 8:30 PM, Tues - Fri 8:30 AM 5:30 PM, cl Sat. Estab 1904. The art gallery contains murals, paintings and sculptures scattered throughout the building. Circ 184,325
Income: $380,000
Special Subjects: Murals and paintings of local history and local interest
Collections: Military history (US); New York State material and genealogy
Exhibitions: Local Artists Guild; North Country Artist Guild
Publications: Focus, quarterly; Community Calendar, bi-monthly
Activities: Lectures open to public; concerts; library tours; film programs

WATKINS GLEN

L **AMERICAN LIFE FOUNDATION & STUDY INSTITUTE,** American Research Library,* Old Irelandville, Box 349, 14891. Tel 607-535-4737. *Dir* John Crosby Freeman; *Cur* Ruth Freeman; *Cur Decorative Arts Libr* Larry Freeman
Library Holdings: Vols 5000; Per subs 25; AV — Slides 5000; Other — Pamphlets 3000
Special Subjects: Architecture, Decorative Arts

WESTFIELD

L **PATTERSON LIBRARY & ART GALLERY,** 40 S Portage St, 14787. Tel 716-326-2154. *Dir* Michael Nyerges; *Art Dir* Joseph Koshute
Open Mon - Sat 9:30 AM - 5 PM, Mon, Wed & Thurs 7 - 9 PM. Estab 1896 to provide opportunity for education and recreation through the use of literature, music, films, paintings and other art forms. Octagon Gallery is 1115 sq ft with 11 ft ceilings & 100 ft running space. Circ 100,000
Income: Financed by endowment, city and state appropriation
Library Holdings: Vols 31,773; Per subs 164; AV — A-tapes, cassettes, fs, motion pictures, rec, slides; Other — Framed reproductions, memorabilia, original art works, pamphlets, photographs, sculpture
Special Subjects: Glass plate negatives of local history, WW I posters, seashells, mounted birds
Activities: Classes for adults and children; lect open to the public; concerts; gallery talks; tours; traveling exhibitions organized and circulated

WEST POINT

M **UNITED STATES MILITARY ACADEMY,** West Point Museum, 10996. Tel 914-938-2203, 938-3100; Autovon 8-688-2203/3201. *Dir Museum* Richard E Kuehne; *Cur Arms* Robert W Fisch; *Cur History* Michael J McAfee; *Cur Art* Michael E Moss; *Museum Specialist* Walter J Nock; *Registrar* Renee Klish; *Cur Design* Richard Clark
Open 10:30 AM - 4:15 PM. No admis fee. Estab 1854, supplementing the academic, cultural and military instruction of cadets. Collections open to the public. Average Annual Attendance: 370,000
Purchases: $5000
Collections: Rindisbacher watercolors; Sully Portrait Collection; †cadet drawings from 1820 - 1940; †military paintings and prints; †military artifacts including weapons, flags, uniforms, medals, etc; paintings and prints of West Point; Jonas Lie Collection of Panama Canal Oils; Liedesdorf Collection of European Armor; European and American posters; extensive holdings from World War I and World War II, military and homefront subjects
Exhibitions: The Toy Soldier—a Historical Review; Whistler and Others—Cadet Drawings from the 19th Century to World War I; Jonas Lie and the Building of the Panama Canal; The Land of Counterpane: Toy Soldiers; The US Cavalry in the West; Exhibition of Don Spaulding's art and private collection; American and French Zouaves
Publications: Posters for Victory; West Point Museum Bulletin, irregularly
Activities: Individual paintings and original objects of art lent

WHITE PLAINS

O **HUDSON VALLEY ART ASSOCIATION,*** 15 Minivale Rd, Stamford, CT 06907. Tel 203-322-1110. *Pres* Peter Matulavage; *Treas* Perry Alley; *Secy* Richard Pionk
Estab 1928, inc 1933 to perpetuate the artistic traditions of American artists such as made famous the Hudson River School of painting through exhibitions of painting and sculpture with public support. Mem: 300; membership by invitation; dues $15, special exhibits extra; annual meeting May
Exhibitions: Annual juried exhibition each May, open to all artists of the US who work in realistic tradition, to compete for money awards and gold medals of honor; other exhibits from time to time
Activities: Free demonstrations, exhibitions, lectures

WILLIAMSVILLE

O **BUFFALO SOCIETY OF ARTISTS,** 163 Millbrook Dr, 14221. Tel 716-633-8962. *Pres* Jane Clary Miner; *VPres* Russell Ram; *Treas* Maggie Headrick; *Recording Secy* Norine Spurling; *Corresponding Secy* Adele Becker
Estab 1891 for practicing and exhibiting artists. Mem: 160; dues $20; annual meeting May
Publications: Annual Exhibition Catalogue
Activities: Lectures open to the public; competitions with awards

YONKERS

M **HUDSON RIVER MUSEUM,** 511 Warburton Ave, Trevor Park-on-Hudson, 10701. Tel 914-963-4550. *Dir* Peter Langlykke; *Assoc Dir* Rick Beard; *Admin* Richard B Carlson; *Dir Marketing & Development* Inge Brovard; *Registrar* Lynne Addison; *Research Cur* Margaret Conrads; *Tech* John Matherly; *Dir Education* Bonnie Levinson Rosenblum
Open Wed - Sun Noon - 7 PM, Thurs until 9 PM. Admis by voluntary contribution. Estab 1924 as a general museum of art, history and science
Income: $700,000 (financed by membership, city and county appropriation, state arts council, federal grants, donations)
Collections: 19th & 20th century American art, decorative arts, furniture, toys, dolls, costumes, accoutrement, silver, china, paintings, sculpture, photography
Publications: Bimonthly calendar of events; special exhibitions catalogs; annual report
Activities: Docent training; lectures and special events open to public; concerts; gallery talks; tours; art lent to other museums for exhibition purposes; lending collection contains original art works, paintings, photographs, sculpture; book traveling exhibitions; traveling exhibitions organized and circulated to museums, college galleries - regional & national; museum shop selling books, inexpensive items for children

L **Library,** 511 Warburton Ave, Trevor Park-on-Hudson, 10701
For staff use only
Library Holdings: Vols 3000

M **PHILIPSE MANOR HALL STATE HISTORIC SITE,** 29 Warburton Ave,
PO Box 496, 10702. Tel 914-965-4027. *Historic Site Mgr* Mary Dougal;
Education Dir Suzanne Cleary
Open Memorial Day Weekend - Oct 30 Wed - Sat Noon - 5 PM, Sun 1 - 5 PM,
other seasons by appointment only. No admis fee. Estab 1908 to preserve
Georgian manor house owned by the Frederick Philipse family; to interpret
Philipse Manor Halls architecture, its significance as the home of an American
Loyalist and its importance as an example of 17th and 18th century Anglo-
Dutch patterns in landholding and development. The State Historic Site is part of
the New York State Office of Parks and Recreation; the Hall houses
contemporary style exhibits of history, art and architecture hung against a
backdrop of fine 18th and 19th century architectural carvings
Income: Financed by state appropriation
Collections: Cochran Portrait Collection of Famous Americans
Activities: Classes for children; lectures open to public; concerts; tours;
demonstrations; films

L **YONKERS PUBLIC LIBRARY,** Fine Arts Dept, 1500 Central Park Ave,
10710. Tel 914-337-1500, Ext 21. *Librn III & Head Department* Joan Stevenson;
Librn II Lois Herzberg; *Librn I* Valerie Schneer
Open Mon - Wed, Fri 10 AM - 9 PM, Thurs 10 AM - 5 PM, Sat 9 AM - 5 PM,
Sun 1 - 5 PM. Estab 1962 to serve the general public with a special interest in
the arts, especially the fine arts, performing arts, and the decorative and applied
arts. Circ printed material approx 22,000; recorded material approx 66,000
Income: $28,000 (financed by city appropriation)
Purchases: $46,000
Library Holdings: Vols 14,000; AV — Cassettes 787, rec 14,000, slides 2000;
Other — Clipping files, pamphlets 7000
L **Will Library,** 1500 Central Park Ave, 10710
Exhibitions: Exhibits work by local artists and craftsmen

NORTH CAROLINA

ASHEVILLE

M **ASHEVILLE ART MUSEUM,** Civic Center Complex, Haywood St, 28801. Tel
704-253-3227. *Dir* Edwin Ritts Jr; *Program Coordr* Wendy W Burns; *Business
Mgr* Patricia Smith
Open Tues - Fri 10 AM - 5 PM, Sat & Sun 1 - 5 PM, cl Mon. No admis fee.
Estab 1948 to provide educational services to the western North Carolina area
through exhibitions. Three galleries maintained, with movable walls. Average
Annual Attendance: 20,000. Mem: 750; dues family $25, single $15, student $10;
annual meeting March
Income: Financed by membership, United Arts Fund Drive & auxiliary
Exhibitions: Sections from the Magul Collection; James A Haverny Collection;
Jasper Johns: Serigraphs; Highwater Invitational
Publications: Quarterly membership; newsletter
Activities: Classes for adults & children; docent training; lectures open to public;
gallery talks; tours; competitions; original objects of art lent to other museums

O **SOUTHERN HIGHLAND HANDICRAFT GUILD,** Folk Art Center, Riceville
Rd & Blue Ridge Parkway, P O Box 9545, 28815. Tel 704-298-7928. *Dir* James
Gentry; *Asst Dir* Blair White
Open Mon - Sun 9 AM - 5 PM, cl Thanksgiving, Christmas and New Year's. No
admis fee. Estab 1930 to encourage wider appreciation of mountain crafts; raise
and maintain standards of design and craftsmanship, and encourage individual
expression. Mem: 700; open to eligible craftsmen from Southern Appalachian
Mountain Region upon approval of applicant's work by Standards Committee
and Board of Trustees; dues group $30, single $10; annual meeting in April
Income: Financed by membership and merchandising
Exhibitions: (1983-84) New Works '83; About Paper; Christmas with the Guild;
Furniture Making: Berea College; Woven Wearables
Publications: Highland Highlights; bimonthly newsletter
Activities: Education dept; workshops for adults and children; lectures open to
public and some for members only; gallery talks; tours; competitions; retail shops
open

BREVARD

M **BREVARD COLLEGE,** Coltrane Art Center, 28712. Tel 704-883-8292, Ext 245.
Dir Tim Murray
Open Mon - Thurs 8 AM - 10 PM, Fri 8 AM - 5 PM. No admis fee. Estab 1969
as Art Department with on-going gallery. Center has three areas, 160 ft running
space, and 1500 sq ft floor space
Income: Financed by departmental appropriation
Collections: Contemporary art; 1940-1970 paintings and watercolors; print and
pottery collection
Exhibitions: Student and visiting artist exhibitions
Activities: Classes for adults; dramatic programs; college classes and continuing
education; 4 vis lectr per yr; 4 gallery talks; competitions with cash awards;
scholarships; lending collection contains books, cassettes, color reproductions,
film strips, photographs, slides
L **Jones Library,*** Brevard College, 78712. *Dir* Mary Margaret Houk
Open Mon - Thurs 8 AM - 6:30 PM, Fri 8 AM - 5 PM, Sat 10 AM - Noon and
1 - 4 PM, Sun 2 - 5 PM. Estab 1934
Library Holdings: Vols 3000; Per subs 10; AV — Cassettes, fs, slides; Other —
Clipping files, pamphlets, prints
Activities: Film series, weekly; shows

CHAPEL HILL

SOUTHEASTERN COLLEGE ART CONFERENCE
For further information, see National and Regional Organizations

UNIVERSITY OF NORTH CAROLINA
M **The Ackland Art Museum,** Columbia & Franklin Streets, 27514. Tel 919-966-
5736. *Dir* Innis H Shoemaker
Open Tues - Sat 10 AM - 5 PM, Sun 2 - 6 PM, cl Mon and University holidays.
No admis fee. Estab 1958 as an art museum which serves the members of the
university community as well as the public. The Museum houses a permanent
collection in two galleries and foyer, a period room, a prints and drawings gallery
and an exhibition gallery. Average Annual Attendance: 40,000. Mem: 427, dues
$25
Income: Financed by endowment, membership and state appropriation
Collections: †Collection of paintings, sculpture, photographs, prints and drawings
covering the history of primarily Western art from ancient Egypt to the present
day; decorative arts
Publications: Newsletter, fall and spring; The Ackland Art Museum (handbook)
Activities: Docent tours; gallery talks open to public; lectures; films; receptions
for members; exhibition catalogs available for sale
L **Art Library,** Art Classroom Studio Bldg, 27514. Tel 919-962-2397. *Art Librn*
Philip Rees; *Libr Asst* Rachel Frew
Open Mon - Thurs 8 AM - 10 PM, Fri 8 AM - 5 PM, Sat 10 AM - 5 PM, Sun 2
- 10 PM
Income: Financed by state appropriation
Library Holdings: Vols 46,000; Per subs 325; Micro — Fiche, reels; Other —
Exhibition catalogs, pamphlets

CHARLOTTE

C **KNIGHT PUBLISHING COMPANY,** 600 S Tryon St, PO Box 32188, 28232.
Tel 704-379-6896. *In Charge of Collection* D Fleck
Open 8 AM - 8 PM. No admis fee. Collection estab 1971 to enhance the interior
decoration of the building; monthly changing exhibits in lobby gallery. Lobby
gallery is 30 X 100 for showing regional arts, crafts & photography. Average
Annual Attendance: 500-1000
Purchases: $2500
Collections: Collection contains wide variety of regional contemporary art,
paintings, drawings, weavings and pottery
Activities: Purchase awards in regional art competitions

M **MINT MUSEUM OF ART,*** 501 Hempstead Place, PO Box 6011, 28208. Tel
704-334-9723. *Dir* Milton J Bloch; *Asst Dir* Stephen W Musgrove; *Cur of Exhib*
Jerald Melberg
Open Tues 10 AM - 10 PM, Wed - Sat 10 AM - 5 PM, Sun 2 - 5 PM, cl Mon &
holidays. No admis fee. Estab 1936 as an art museum in what was the first
branch of the US mint erected in 1837. Museum houses three changing galleries:
a permanent gallery, Delhom Decorative Arts Gallery; two Charlotte Gold
Rooms; and a sales and rental gallery. Average Annual Attendance: 150,000.
Mem: 1850; dues student and senior citizens $7.50, up to $150 for others; annual
meeting Jan
Income: Financed by endowment, membership and city appropriation
Collections: Decorative arts, paintings, sculpture with emphasis on Baroque,
Renaissance, 18th century English, 19th and 20th century European and
American paintings, and pre-Columbian art
Publications: Mint Museum Newsletter and calendar of events, six times a year
Activities: Classes for adults; docent training; lect open to the public, 25 visiting
lectrs per year; concerts; gallery talks; tours; competitions; original objects of art
lent to other museums; museum shop selling books, original art, prints, gifts,
museum replicas, jewelry, cards
L **Library,*** 501 Hempstead Place, PO Box 6011, 28208. *Librn* Sara Wolf
Open to members for reference only
Library Holdings: Vols 6000

L **PUBLIC LIBRARY OF CHARLOTTE AND MECKLENBURG COUNTY,**
310 N Tryon St, 28202. Tel 704-374-2725. *Dir* Ronald S Kozlowski; *Assoc Dir*
Judith Sutton; *Art Librn* Carolyn Hunter
Open Mon - Fri 9 AM - 9 PM, Sat 9 AM - 6 PM, Sun 2 - 6 PM, cl Sun June -
Aug. Estab 1903 to provide free public library service to citizens of Mecklenburg
County. Gallery contains 90 linear feet of wall space
Income: $5,500,000 (financed by state and county appropriations)
Purchases: $713,068
Library Holdings: Vols 792,393; maps 6865; AV — Cassettes, fs, motion pictures
2772, rec 27,869, slides 9261; Other — Prints 424, sculpture
Exhibitions: Local artists exhibit for one month
Activities: Individual paintings loaned to residents

M **SCIENCE MUSEUMS OF CHARLOTTE, INC,** Discovery Place,* 301 Tryon
St, 28202. Tel 704-372-6261. *Chief Exec Officer* Freda Nicholson; *Education
Coordr* Jo Duckett; *Exhibits Coordr* Thom Roberts; *Operations Coordr* Darrell
Harrison
Open Mon - Sat 9 AM - 6 PM, Sun 1 - 6 PM, cl Christmas. Admis adult $2.50,
students & sr citizens $1.50, children under 5 free, no charge for members. Inc
1947 to develop an appreciation of man and nature. small staff reference library
is maintained. Average Annual Attendance: 500,000. Mem: 3000; dues - family
$35, sr citizen $20, student $15; meetings 2nd Mon of May
Income: $1,350,000 (financed by city & county appropriations, fees & sales shop
Collections: Arthropods; gems & minerals; Lepidoptera; †Pre-Columbian: Mayan,
North American, Puruvian; †primitive art: African, Alaskan Eskimo, Oceania,
South American; reptillia
Publications: Discovery-Nature Bulletin, bi-monthly; activities bulletin, quarterly
Activities: Classes for adults and children; docent training; volunteer training
program for demonstrators & guides; lectures open to public, major programming
for school lectures; tours; acceptable for internship from UNCC and Queens
College; book traveling exhibitions; sales shop sells books, prints and gift related
items; junior museum is primarily geared to pre-school and early elementary age
children

DALLAS

M GASTON COUNTY MUSEUM OF ART & HISTORY, 131 N Gaston St, PO Box 429, 28304. Tel 704-866-3437. *Pres* Jeanne Rauch; *VPres* Lucy Penegar; *Secy* Constance Houser; *Treas* Ray Jimison; *Dir* Alan D Waufle; *Cur of Education* Melissa Jones
Open Tues - Fri 10 AM - 5 PM, Sat 10 AM - 2 PM, Sun 2 - 5 PM. No admis fee. Estab Nov 1975, opened July 1976 to promote the fine arts and local history in Gaston County, through classes, workshops and exhibitions; to preserve Historic Dallas Square; promote the history of the textile industry. The museum is located in an 1848 Greek Revival Courthouse; the Hands-On Gallery includes sculpture and weaving which may be touched; the two small galleries are on local history, with the major gallery for changing and traveling exhibitions. Average Annual Attendance: 20,000. Mem: 400; dues $10 - $1000; annual meeting Nov, with monthly meetings the first Thurs in Feb, May, August and Nov
Income: Financed by membership and county appropriation
Collections: †Contemporary sculpture; †documents; †19th - 20th century American art; objects of local history; †paintings by North Carolina artists living and dead; photographs; †textile history
Publications: The Register, quarterly newsletter
Activities: Classes for adults and children; docent training; dramatic programs; puppet performances; lectures open to the public, 6 vis lectr per year; concerts; competitions with awards; gallery talks; tours; individual paintings & original objects of art lent to other museums & galleries; lending collection contains original art works & original prints; book traveling exhibitions, 3 per year; originate traveling exhibitions; sales shop sells books, magazines, original art, reproductions, prints stationery
L Library, 131 N Gaston St, 28304
Open to public for reference only
Library Holdings: Vols 150; Per subs 10

DAVIDSON

M DAVIDSON COLLEGE ART GALLERY, Box 2495, 28036. Tel 704-892-2000. *Dir* Herb Jackson
Open Mon - Fri 10 AM - 5 PM. No admis fee. Estab 1952 to provide exhibitions of educational importance. Gallery covers 4000 sq ft. Average Annual Attendance: 6000
Income: Financed by college budget
Collections: Primary emphasis in graphics
Activities: Lect open to public, 6 vis lectr per year; gallery talks
L Library, Box 2495, 28036. *Librn* Dr Leland Park
Open to students and visitors

DURHAM

M DUKE UNIVERSITY UNION GALLERIES,* 6877 College Station, 27708. Tel 919-684-5135. *Dir* W K Stars; *Staff Asst* Jessie W Petcoff; *Cur Classical Coll* Dr Keith Stanley
Open Mon - Fri 9 AM - 5 PM, Sat 10 AM - 1 PM, Sun 2 - 5 PM. No admis fee. Estab 1969 as a study museum with the collections being used and studied by various university departments, as well as the public school system and surrounding communities. The museum is located on the East Campus in a renovated two-story Georgian building; gallery space includes part of the first floor and entire second floor with the space divided into eight major gallery areas. Average Annual Attendance: 8000 - 10,000
Income: Financed by University
Collections: African; classical; graphics; Medieval decorative art and sculpture; Oriental jade and porcelain; paintings; †Pre-Columbian; textiles (Peruvian, Navajo)
Publications: Exhibition catalogs, 1 - 2 per year
Activities: Lect open to public, 2 - 4 lectr per year; gallery talks; tours; individual paintings and original objects of art lent to other museums which are equipped with proper security and insurance
O Union Galleries Committee, Box KM, Duke Station, 27706. Tel 919-684-2911. *Union Dir* Jon J Phelps
Louise Jones Gallery open Sun - Sat 7 AM - 1 AM; West Gallery & Hanks Gallery open Mon - Fri 8 AM - 5 PM; East Gallery open Sun - Sat 8 AM - Midnight. No admis fee. Estab to bring to the university community exhibits of every type of graphic arts; to bring artists to campus for workshops. Louise Jones Gallery, room with waist high bookshelves in east campus library; West Gallery, small gallery next to main auditorium lobby; Hanks Gallery & East Gallery, two galleries in Bryan Center (performing arts complex). Mem: 15; monthly meetings
Income: Financed by endowment and commission on exhibit works sold
Exhibitions: Professional and Local Artist, approx four monthly (one in each gallery)
Activities: Classes for adults; lectures open to public, 1 vis lectr per year; competitions; gallery talks
L East Campus Library,* 6877 College Station, 27708. Tel 919-684-6227. *Librn* Betty Young
Open 8 AM to Midnight. Estab 1930 to support the study of art at Duke University
Purchases: $20,000
Library Holdings: Vols 52,000; Per subs 179; Micro — Cards, fiche, reels; Other — Clipping files, exhibition catalogs, pamphlets
Collections: Emphasis on European and American Art

M NORTH CAROLINA CENTRAL UNIVERSITY, Museum of Art, PO Box 19555, 27707. Tel 919-683-6211. *Dir* Norman E Pendergraft; *Secy Registrar* Janice Pointer
Open Tues - Fri 9 AM - 5 PM, Sun 2 - 5 PM. No admis fee. Estab 1971 in a former black teaching institution with a collection of contemporary art, many Afro-American artists, reflecting diversity in style, technique, medium and subject. Three galleries are maintained; one houses the permanent collection and two are for changing shows. Average Annual Attendance: 4000
Income: Financed by state appropriation

Purchases: $174,359
Collections: African and Oceanic; †Contemporary American with a focus on minority artists; †Contemporary, non-American
Exhibitions: (1983-84) Recent acquisitions; California Black Printmakers; Robert S Duncanson (1817-1872) Paintings; The Museum's Choice; North Carolina Central University Artists: New Horizons
Publications: Artis, Bearden & Burke: A Bibliography & Illustrations List; exhibition catalogs
Activities: Lect open to public; gallery talks; tours

FAYETTEVILLE

M FAYETTEVILLE MUSEUM OF ART, INC, 539 Stamper Rd, PO Box 35134, 28303. Tel 919-485-5121. *Pres* Charlotte Yarborough; *Dir* Phyllis A McLeod; *Adminr* Barbara A C Hennig
Open Tues - Fri 10 AM - 5 PM, Sat & Sun 1 - 5 PM. No admis fee. Estab 1971 to promote in the area an active interest in the fine and applied arts; to establish and maintain a permanent collection. Lobby and main gallery is 996 sq ft, 143 ft wall space (231 ft wall space with temporary walls). Average Annual Attendance: 17,000. Mem: 532; dues $100, $50, $25, $15, $10; annual meeting in the spring
Income: $87,000 (financed by membership and city appropriation)
Collections: Contemporary Southeastern Artists
Exhibitions: Frederick Carl Frieseke - An American Impressionist; The London Collection-100 Years of American Art; Kinetic Sculpture and Color Painting by Rudy Ayoroa; Annual Competitions for North Carolina Artists; Master Artists: Black Waters of the Carolinas and other Photographs by Jerome Kohl
Publications: Annual competition catalogue; quarterly calendar
Activities: Classes for adults and children; docent training; lect open to public, 12-15 visiting lectr per year; concerts; gallery talks; competitions with cash awards; book traveling exhibitions 3 - 4 per year; originate traveling exhibitions

GREENSBORO

M GREEN HILL CENTER FOR NORTH CAROLINA ART, 200 N Davie St, 27401. Tel 919-373-4515. *Pres* Alice Isaacson; *VPres* Ann Lineweaver; *Secy* Virginia Booker; *Treas* Jan Blackford; *Dir* Cynthia K Ference
Open Tues - Fri 10 AM - 5 PM, Sat & Sun 2 - 5 PM, cl Mon & holidays. No admis fee. Estab and incorporated 1974 as a non-profit institution offering exhibitions and educational programming featuring the visual arts of North Carolina. Average Annual Attendance: 35,000. Mem: 450; dues $500 - $5
Income: Financed by memberships, United Arts Council of Greensboro and various grants
Publications: Newsletter; catalogues
Activities: Classes for adults & children; docent training; artists-in-the-schools program; lectures open to public, 5-6 vis lectr per yr; concerts; gallery talks; tours; competitions with awards; originate traveling exhibitions; sales shop sells books, magazines & original art

O GREENSBORO ARTISTS' LEAGUE,* 200 N Davis St, 27401. Tel 919-373-4514. *Pres* John R Beaman Jr; *Exec Dir* Stuart Norman; *Bus Officer* Mrs William Sharpe; *Cur* Joe Whisnant; *Cur Competitions* Shirley Gibson; *Treasurer* Hope S Beaman
Open Mon - Fri 9 AM - 5 PM, cl New Year's Day, Easter Monday, July 4, Labor Day, Thanksgiving, Christmas. No admis fee. Estab 1956. Gallery housed is Old Greensboro Daily News Record Newspaper building. Mem: Dues life $100, sustaining $50, patron $25, single $15, senior citizen $10
Publications: Art News, monthly newsletter
Activities: Programs for adults and children; lectures; gallery talks; juried competition arts festivals

M GREENSBORO COLLEGE, Irene Cullis Gallery, 815 W Market St, 27401. Tel 919-272-7102. *Asst Prof* Robert Kowski
Open Mon - Fri 10 AM - 4 PM, Sun 2 - 5 PM. Estab to exhibit visual art by visiting professional artists, Greensboro College art students and others. Average Annual Attendance: 1500
Exhibitions: (1983) Regional high school sr art competition; Abner Hershberger, paintings and prints; Greensboro College Art Alumni Exhibit; Gretchen Williams, paintings; African Sculpture
Activities: Lectures open to public; gallery talks; competitions; cash awards; scholarships; book traveling exhibition

M UNIVERSITY OF NORTH CAROLINA AT GREENSBORO, Weatherspoon Art Gallery, Walker Ave at McIver St, 27412. Tel 919-379-5770. *Dir* Gilbert F Carpenter; *Secy* Scott Keener; *Cur* James E Tucker; *Asst Dir* Donald Droll
Open Tues - Fri 10 AM - 5 PM, Sat & Sun 2 - 6 PM, cl Mon, University holiday periods and between academic sessions. No admis fee. Estab 1942 as a teaching arm of the University Department of Art. The gallery houses modern art for the Greensboro and Piedmont area; the main gallery is large and can exhibit large shows, or several small shows at once; the outer lobby gallery is used mainly for student shows; a sculpture court contains permanently installed modern sculptures. A downtown branch is located in the Greensboro Arts Center, 200 N Davie St, and exhibits rotating shows from the Weatherspoon permanent collection. Mem: 500; dues $5 and up; annual meeting April or May
Income: $60,000 (financed by university budget)
Purchases: $60,000
Collections: 20th Century American & European Drawings, Paintings, Prints & Sculpture; †Oriental Art
Exhibitions: Teacher Artist-Artist Teacher; MFA Thesis Exhibition; Recent Acquisitions; New York Artists of the Fifties in the Eighties; Photographs by Timothy Greenfield-Sanders; Annual Student Art Exhibition; Selections from the Permanent Collection
Publications: Weatherspoon Gallery Association Bulletin, annually
Activities: Lect open to the public, 6 - 8 vis lectr per year; gallery talks; tours; individual paintings and original objects of art lent to other museums, and local corporate and individual benefactors contributing $1000 or more per year; lending collection consists of original art works, original prints, paintings, photographs, sculpture and videotapes; originate traveling exhibitions; postcard reproductions sold at reception desk

GREENVILLE

M **EAST CAROLINA UNIVERSITY,** Gray Art Gallery, Jenkins Fine Arts Center, 27834. Tel 919-757-6665, 757-6336. *Gallery Dir* Randolph Osman
Open Mon - Fri 10 AM - 5 PM, Sun 1 - 4 PM. No admis Fee. Estab 1977 as a teaching gallery offering visual experiences to students and general public. The gallery is a large, modern 5000 sq ft facility with track lighting and modular moveable walls
Income: Financed by state appropriation, Friends of Art and state and federal grants
Special Subjects: 20th Century Art; Historical Art from Different Cultures and Civilizations
Exhibitions: National and Regional Exhibitions; faculty and student (undergraduate and graduate) exhibitions
Publications: Exhibition catalogs
Activities: Lectures open to public, 4 vis lect per yr; gallery talks; tours; scholarships; book traveling exhibitions semi-annually
L **Art Library,** Leo Jenkins Fine Arts Center, 27834
Open daily 8 AM - 5 PM. Estab 1977 for Art School study of current and selected periodicals and selected reference books and slides. For lending and reference
Library Holdings: Per subs 60; Micro — Cards; AV — Fs, motion pictures, slides, v-tapes; Other — Exhibition catalogs, manuscripts

O **GREENVILLE MUSEUM OF ART,** 802 Evans St, 27834. Tel 919-758-1946. *Exec Dir* Mary Anne Pennington
Open Tues 10 AM - 9 PM, Weds, Thurs, Fri 10 AM - 6 PM, Sat 11 AM - 3 PM, cl Sun & Mon. Estab 1939, incorporated as East Carolina Art Society in 1956, to foster public interest in art and to form a permanent collection. Average Annual Attendance: 12,000. Mem: 500; dues $25 and higher; annual meeting each Spring
Income: $60,000 (plus Foundation income for acquisition of art; financed by contributions, memberships, appropriations & grants)
Collections: 20th Century Contemporary paintings; drawings; graphics; †regional and national sculpture
Exhibitions: Exhibitions change monthly, featuring work of regional artists; national traveling exhibits; works from the North Carolina Museum of Art, of which our museum is an Affiliate Gallery
Publications: Bi-monthly newsletter
Activities: Classes for adults and children; demonstrations; dramatic programs; docent training; workshops; lect open to public; gallery talks; tours; sponsors competitions; traveling exhibitions organized and circulated
L **Library,** 802 Evans St, 27834
Library Holdings: Vols 300; Per subs 150

HICKORY

M **HICKORY MUSEUM OF ART, INC,** Third St & First Ave NW, PO Box 2572, 28601. Tel 704-327-8576. *Pres* Donald R Fuller Jr; *VPres* Robert T Hambrick; *Secy* Marilyn Kopp; *Treas* Sherrill F Young; *Exec Dir* Mildred M Coe; *Asst to Dir* V Stephen Jones; *Cur Education* Susanne Hall; *Registrar* Ellen Schwarzbek
Open Mon - Fri 10 AM - 5 PM, Sun 3 - 5 PM. No admis fee. Estab 1944 to collect and foster American art and serve the western Piedmont area as an exhibiting and training art center. One large gallery is used mainly for traveling exhibitions; eight small galleries are used for permanent collections. Average Annual Attendance: 19,000. Mem: 670; dues $20 - $1000; meetings second Tues of each month
Income: Financed by membership and donations
Collections: Small European collection; very fine collection of 19th and 20th century American paintings; Oriental works, Pre-Columbian
Activities: Classes for adults and children; docent training; periodic art classes; films; lectures open to the public, 6 vis lectr per yr; gallery talks; tours; competitions with awards; individual paintings & original objects of art lent to other museums & galleries; traveling exhibitions organized and circulated
L **Library,** Hickory, 28601
Library Holdings: Vols 2000; Per subs 8; AV — Cassettes 50, slides 500; Other — Clipping files, exhibition catalogs, manuscripts, memorabilia, pamphlets, photographs, reproductions

KINSTON

O **COMMUNITY COUNCIL FOR THE ARTS,** 111 E Caswell St, PO Box 3554, 28501. Tel 919-527-2517. *Exec Dir* S Reid Cone; *Pres* Jimmy Moore; *VPres* Sarita Minges; *Secy* Val Carmine; *Asst Dir* Leigh Riggs; *Art Coordr* Susan Jones; *Bookkeeper* Adelle Taylor
Open Mon - Thurs 8:30 AM - 5:30 PM, Fri 8:30 AM - 12:30 PM. No admis fee. Estab 1965 to promote the arts in the Kinston area. Maintains a library of art magazines available for research by approval, two exhibition galleries & one sales gallery. Mem: Dues benefactor $1000, sustaining patron $500-$999, sustaining $250-$499, patron $100-$249, sponsor $50-$90, donor $30-$49, family $15-$29, single $10-$14
Income: Financed by county appropriations
Publications: Kaleidscope, monthly newsletter
Activities: Arts festivals; classes for adults and children; tours; concerts; gallery talks; competitions with awards; lending collection contains original art works, 52 original prints, 102 paintings, sculpture; book traveling exhibitions; sales shop sells original art; Art Center Children's Museum

LOUISBURG

M **LOUISBURG COLLEGE,** Art Gallery,* 405 W Noble St, 27549. Tel 919-496-5448. *Dir* Julia Kornegay
Open Jan - Apr, Aug - Dec Mon - Fri 10 AM - 5 PM, cl holidays. No admis fee. Estab 1957
Collections: American Impressionist Art; Primitive Art
Activities: Arts festivals; lectures; gallery talks; tours

MONROE

M **UNION COUNTY PUBLIC LIBRARY GALLERY,** 316 E Windsor St, 28110. Tel 704-283-8184. *Dir* Barbara M Johnson
Open Mon, Wed & Fri 9 AM - 6 PM, Tues & Thurs 9 AM - 8 PM, Sat 9 AM - 5 PM, Sun 2 - 5:30 PM. Gallery accomodates 25 large paintings & monthly exhibits of local work or traveling exhibitions
Collections: North Carolina collection
Exhibitions: Bruce Curlee, Louise Napier, photography & paintings; Vermont Group; Old Bergen Traveling Exhibit; Dick Worley; Bohdan Osyckzka
Activities: Book traveling exhibitions

NEW BERN

M **TRYON PALACE RESTORATION COMPLEX,** 610 Pollock St, 28560. Tel 919-638-5109. *Dir* Kay P Williams; *Chmn* Robert L Stallings Jr; *Communications Specialist* Dabney M Coddington; *Museum Hist Specialist* Nancy C Blades; *Registrar* Grace C Ipock; *Maintenance* James A Thomas; *Horticulturist* W H Rea
Open Tues - Sat 9:30 AM - 4 PM, Sun 1:30 - 4 PM, cl Mon. Admis adults $6, children $2. Estab 1959. Maintained are the historic house museums (Tryon Palace, Stevenson House, John Wright Stanly House) with fine portraits, paintings, Federal and Empire antiques, furnishings, silver, porcelain and object d'art. Average Annual Attendance: 62,000. Mem: meetings April & Oct
Income: Financed by state & private bequests
Collections: Paintings by Nathaniel Dance; Thomas Gainsborough; School of Sir Godfrey Kneller; Claude Lorrain; David Martin; Richard Paton; William Peters; Charles Phillips; Alan Ramsay; Jan Siberechts; E Van Stuven; Richard Wilson; Graphics
Publications: Nine books, many leaflets
Activities: Classes for adults & children; audio-visual orientation program; annual symposium on 18th century decorative arts; interpretive drama program; docent training; lectures open to public, 6-8 vis lectr per yr; museum sales shop sells books, reproductions, prints & slides
L **Library,** 610 Pollock St, 28560
Open for use with permission
Library Holdings: Vols 3000; Other — Photographs
Special Subjects: Royal Governor William Tryon's Inventory, bks, 18th Century Collection of Books, Decorative Arts

NORTH WILKESBORO

M **WILKES ART GALLERY,** 800 Elizabeth St, 28659. Tel 919-667-2841. *Dir* Martha B Baker; *Cur* Carolina F Finley
Open Mon - Fri 10 AM - 5 PM, Sun 3 - 5 PM, evenings for special events, cl New Years, Easter, Easter Monday, July 4, Christmas. No admis fee. Estab 1962. Mem: Dues patron and corp $100 and up, donor $60, sponsor $30, family $15, student-senior $10
Income: Financed by membership, local governments, state arts council & corporations
Collections: Contemporary paintings, graphics, sculpture, primarily of NC artists
Exhibitions: Temporary exhibitions
Publications: Title of Exhibition, monthly brochures & catalogues; Wilkes Art Gallery Newsletter, monthly
Activities: Programs for adults and children; docent program; arts festivals; films; art & craft classes; lectures; gallery talks; tours; mobile vans; school and community loan service; book traveling exhibitions

RALEIGH

O **NORTH CAROLINA ART SOCIETY,** 2110 Blue Ridge Blvd, 27607. Tel 919-833-1935. *Pres* Mrs Frank A Daniels Jr; *VPres* Mrs Edward G Lilly; *Secy* Melissa Peden; *Treasurer* Peter VanGraafeiland; *Executive Dir* Elizabeth C Fentress
Estab 1927 to formulate programs to promote public appreciation of visual art, to encourage talent, to disseminate information on art through publications, to encourage private acquisition of works of art and to support the State Art Museum's programs by membership. The Art Society's collection has been given to the North Carolina Museum of Art and all purchases are given either to that or other art centers in the state. Mem: 4000; dues $15 and up; annual meeting Apr
Income: $75,000
Purchases: $60,000

M **NORTH CAROLINA MUSEUM OF ART,** 2110 Blue Ridge Blvd, 27607. Tel 919-833-1935. *Dir* Edgar Peters Bowron; *Asst Dir* Gay M Hertzman; *Chief Cur* William J Chiego; *Dir Education* Joseph F Covington; *Chief Designer* Patrick H Sears; *Conservator* David Goist; *Registrar* Peggy Jo Kirby
Open Tues - Sat 10 AM - 5 PM, Sun 1 - 5 PM, cl Mon & holidays. No admis fee. Estab 1947, open to public 1956, to acquire, preserve, and exhibit works of art for the education and enjoyment of the people of the state, and to conduct programs of education, research, and publications designed to encourage interest in and an appreciation of art. Average Annual Attendance: 250,000. Mem: 5000; dues $25 & up
Income: Financed by state appropriation

Collections: Ancient art; Mary Duke Biddle Education Gallery; European and American painting, sculpture & decorative arts; Samuel H Kress Collection; Pre-Columbian, African, Oceanic & New World art
Exhibitions: North Carolina Artists Exhibitions; wide range of temporary exhibitions
Publications: Bulletin, irregular; Preview, bimonthly; exhibition & permanent collection catalogs
Activities: Classes for adults & children; docent training; lectures open to public; concerts; gallery talks; tours; exten dept serving North Carolina; individual paintings and original objects of art lent to other museums; originate traveling exhibitions to North Carolina museums & galleries; museum shop sells books, magazines, reproductions, prints and slides
L   **Reference Library,** 2110 Blue Ridge Blvd, Raleigh, 27607. Tel 919-833-1935. *Librn* Dr Anna Dvorak
Open 10 AM - 5 PM. Open to public for reference
Income: $6275
Purchases: $4125
Library Holdings: Vols 17,000; Per subs 51; transparencies 1370; AV — Slides 13,700; Other — Clipping files, exhibition catalogs, pamphlets, photographs 18,900
Special Subjects: Costume Design & Construction, Decorative Arts, Fine Arts

L   **NORTH CAROLINA STATE UNIVERSITY,** Harrye Lyons Design Library, 209 Brooks Hall, 27650. *Librn* Maryellen LoPresti; *Library Asst* Lynn Crisp; *Library Asst* Christine Bach; *Library Asst* Dot Hunt
Open Mon - Thurs 8:30 AM - 9:30 PM, Fri 8:30 - 5 PM, Sat 9 AM - 1 PM, Sun 2 - 9:30 PM. Estab 1942 to serve the reading, study, reference and research needs of the faculty, students and staff of the School of Design and the University campus, as well as off-campus borrowers. Circ 50,514
Income: Financed by membership, state appropriation and private funds
Purchases: $40,000
Library Holdings: Vols 27,280; trade literature, vertical files; Micro — Fiche, reels; AV — Cassettes, fs, motion pictures, slides, v-tapes; Other — Clipping files, exhibition catalogs, pamphlets, photographs, prints, reproductions
Special Subjects: Art History, Architecture, Landscape Architecture, Urban and Product Design, Visual and Basic Design
Collections: John L Skinner Collection (etchings of the Raphel Loggia); File on measured Drawings of North Carolina Historic Sites; 458 maps and plans; 300 bibliographies compiled by the Design Library staff; and a 370 item print collection
Publications: Index to the School of Design, student publication book Vols 1 - 25

REIDSVILLE

M   **UNIVERSITY OF NORTH CAROLINA AT GREENSBORO,** Chinqua-Penn Plantation House, Route 8, Box 682, 27320. Tel 919-349-4576. *Dir* Douglas Merritt; *House Mgr* Vivian Forrester; *Supt of Grounds* Steve Gunn
Open March - third Sun in Dec, Wed - Sat 10 AM - 4 PM, Sun 1:30 - 4:30 PM. Admis adults $3, senior citizens $2, children $1. Estab 1966 as part of University's total educational program to make the house with its collection and the gardens available to the public. Average Annual Attendance: 37,000
Income: Financed by state appropriation
Collections: Antique European Furniture; Oriental Art Objects
Activities: Sales shop sells Chinqua-Penn Book and postcards

RESEARCH TRIANGLE PARK

C   **BURROUGHS WELLCOME COMPANY,*** 3030 Cornwallis Rd, 27709. Tel 919-541-9090, 248-3000, Ext 4449. *In Charge Art Coll* Thack Brown
Open 9 AM - 4 PM, groups only by prior arrangement. No admis fee. Estab 1979 to develop a meaningful collection of American Contemporary Art for enjoyment and enrichment for employees and communities. Collection displayed in Corporate Headquarters Building
Collections: Paintings and sculpture from permanent collection and on-loan from The Whitney Museum in New York City
Activities: Tours

ROCKY MOUNT

O   **ROCKY MOUNT ARTS AND CRAFTS CENTER,** Old Nashville Rd, PO Box 4031, 27801. Tel 919-972-1163, 972-1164. *Dir* Julia Jordan; *Dir Theatre* William A Rawls
Open Mon - Fri 8:30 AM - 5 PM, Sun 3 - 5 PM, cl Sat except for classes. Estab 1957 to promote the development of the creative arts in the community through education, participation and appreciation of music, dance, painting, drama, etc; to provide facilities and guidance for developing talents and enriching lives through artistic expression and appreciation. Maintains the Hines Art Gallery. Average Annual Attendance: 25,000. Mem: 600; dues $7.50 and up
Income: Financed by City Recreation Department with supplemental support by membership
Exhibitions: Outdoor Art Exhibition in the Spring, part of the Arts Festival; Permanent collection and traveling shows change each month
Activities: Conducts art classes; year-round theatre program; classes for adults and children; lect; concerts; book traveling exhibitions

SALISBURY

M   **SUPPLEMENTARY EDUCATIONAL CENTER,** Art Gallery,* 1637 Parkview Circle, 28144. Tel 704-636-3462. *Dir* Herbert C Rhodes; *Cur Visual Art* Rosemary Johnson
Open Mon - Fri 8 AM - 4 PM. No admis fee. Estab 1968 to exhibit art work of public schools, supplemented by exhibits of local artists from time to time during the school year; primary purpose is to supplement art education activities in the public schools. The Center is comprised of two areas, one approximately 24 x 65

ft, the other 15 x 70 ft with an adjoining classroom for instruction and demonstrations. Average Annual Attendance: 4500
Income: Financed by membership, state and county appropriation, and from local foundations
Activities: Classes for adults and children; lectures open to public, 5 visiting lecturers per year; gallery talks; tours; individual and original objects of art lent

M   **WATERWORKS GALLERY,*** One Water St, 28144. Tel 704-636-1882. *Pres* Loyd Hill; *VPres* Joe Finn; *Secy* Barbara Whitner; *Exec Dir* Robert E Haywood; *Admin Asst* Barbara Setzer
Open Mon - Fri 10 AM - 5 PM, Sun 2 - 5 PM. No admis fee. Estab 1978 for exhibition & instruction of visual arts. Two galleries with monthly changing exhibitions. Average Annual Attendance: 10,000. Mem: 639; dues $15
Income: $105,000 (financed by memberships, city & state appropriation & businesses)
Collections: North Carolina art
Exhibitions: Sculpture: Inside/Outside; Fifth North Carolina Artists Invitational; Jogtown Pottery & NC Quilts
Publications: Salisbury Rennaisance, Understanding Abstract Art
Activities: Classes for adults and children; classes for handicapped; docent training; lectures open to public, vis lectrs 10 per year; concerts; gallery talks; tours; annual photography & members competitions; cash awards; paintings and art objects lent to nursing homes and hospitals; books, original art work, reproductions, prints are sold in Museum shop

STATESVILLE

M   **ARTS AND SCIENCE MUSEUM,*** Museum Rd, PO Box 585, 28677. Tel 704-873-4734. *Pres* A F Walser; *VPres* E H McJunkin; *Secy* Sue Dishman; *Cur* Frank Sherrill; *Asst Cur* Trudy Van Bergen
Open Tues - Sun 2 - 5 PM, mornings by appointment. No admis fee. Estab 1956 to promote interest in and enthusiasm for arts and sciences. Bowles, Grier and Henkel Galleries features monthly changing exhibits (except August); Artifacts Room features permanent displays, including Egyptian mummy. Average Annual Attendance: 10,000. Mem: 1000; dues $5-$100; meetings quarterly
Income: Financed by membership and business profit percentile
Collections: Egyptian mummy; early American glassware; antique dolls & toys
Exhibitions: Jack Conkwright (paintings); J Brandon (lucite sculpture); Annual Statesville Artist Guild Exhibit
Activities: Lectures open to public; concerts; gallery talks; tours; sponsors competitions with awards; individual and original objects of art lent to museums and responsible organizations; book traveling exhibitions, 2-3 per year

WILMINGTON

O   **NORTH CAROLINA MUSEUMS COUNCIL,** PO Box 27647, 28401. Tel 919-763-0852. *Pres* Stuart C Schwartz; *Secy-Treas* Janet Seaker
Estab 1964 to stimulate interest, support and understanding of museums. Mem: 250; dues individual $5; meetings spring and fall
Income: Financed by membership
Publications: Newsletter, summer and winter

M   **SAINT JOHN'S MUSEUM OF ART,** 114 Orange St, 28401. Tel 919-763-0281. *Dir* Alan Aiches
Open Tues - Sat 10 AM - 5 PM. No admis fee. Estab 1962 to promote interest in the fine and applied arts; to establish and maintain an art collection; and to provide exhibitions for the enjoyment of creative ability and artistic achievement; the museum is a non-profit educational and cultural center serving southeastern North Carolina. Average Annual Attendance: 25,000. Mem: 700; dues $20 - $1000; annual meeting in May
Income: Financed by membership, city, county and state appropriation, and grants
Collections: Jugtown Pottery; †paintings; scent bottles; sculpture; works on paper
Exhibitions: Bi-monthly exhibitions including artwork from regional artists, loans from North Carolina Museum of Art and other museums in Southeastern United States
Publications: Quarterly bulletin; exhibition announcements
Activities: Classes for adults and children; docent training; lect open to public, 2 vis lectr per year; concerts; gallery talks; tours; originate traveling exhibitions; sales shop sells original art
L   **Library,** 114 Orange St, 28401. Tel 919-763-0281
Estab 1962. Open to members by appointment
Library Holdings: Vols 250; Per subs 3; Other — Exhibition catalogs, reproductions

M   **USS NORTH CAROLINA BATTLESHIP MEMORIAL,** Cape Fear River, PO Box 417, 28402. Tel 919-762-1829. *Dir* F S Conlon; *Maintenance Dir* Jerry Blanchard; *Prom Dir* A F Judd
Open daily 8 AM to approx sunset. Admis fee adult $3, 6 - 11 $1.50, under 6 free. Estab 1961 as historic ship museum to memorialize the World War Two dead of the state of North Carolina. Average Annual Attendance: 225,000
Income: Admissions only
Collections: World War II Battleship Memorabilia
Activities: Lectures open to public; sales shop sells booms, reproduction, prints, slides & souveniers

WILSON

M   **ATLANTIC CHRISTIAN COLLEGE,** Case Art Gallery, 27893. Tel 919-237-3161. *Museum Dir* Edward Brown
Open Mon - Fri 10 AM - 4:30 PM, Sat 1 - 3 PM. No admis fee. Estab 1967 to provide art exposure for our students and community. Gallery is 50 x 50 ft. Average Annual Attendance: 1800
Income: Financed by college budget
Collections: Ceramics; recent drawings; painting; prints; sculpture
Activities: Classes for adults; lect open to public, 1 vis lectr per year; gallery talks; competitions; scholarships

L Library, 27893
Library Holdings: Vols 2000; Per subs 8; AV — Rec; Other — Exhibition
catalogs, pamphlets
Special Subjects: Art History

WINSTON-SALEM

O ARTS COUNCIL, INC,* 305 W Fourth St, 27101. Tel 919-722-2585. *Pres &
Executive Dir* Milton Rhodes; *Facilities Mgr & Exhibitions Cur* Patrick Clancy
Open Mon - Fri 9 AM - 5 PM. Estab 1949 as a housing, coordinating, promoting
and fund-raising organization for 39 member groups, including Associated
Artists, Arts and Crafts Association, the Winston-Salem Symphony Association,
The Little Theatre, South Eastern Center for Contemporary Art and Childrens'
Theatre, member groups are autonomous of Arts Council. Housing facilities
include a theatre, rehearsal rooms, art and craft studios and an exhibition gallery.
Mem: 8400; annual meeting May
Income: Financed by fund drives, public and private grants and endowments
Exhibitions: Student Art Exhibiton; Build Art-Built Arts; Associated Artists
Juried Show; Arts and Crafts Retrospect; More Than Land or Sky (Art from
Appalachia); Appalachia Regional Comm Traveling Exhibition
Activities: Classes for adults and children; docent training; lectures, 4 vis lect per
year; concerts; gallery talks; tours; competitions; book traveling exhibitons, six
per year; sales shop sells book, magazines, original art and art supplies

O ASSOCIATED ARTISTS OF WINSTON-SALEM, 226 N Marhsall St, 27101.
Tel 919-722-0340. *Exec Dir* Vonda Blackburn; *Asst Dir* Tom Perryman
Open daily 10 AM - 6 PM. No admis fee. Estab 1956 to promote educational &
creative activities in fine arts. the Association rents the walls of the Gallery from
the Arts Council. Average Annual Attendance: 50,000. Mem: 600; dues $15;
monthly meetings
Income: $63,000 (financed by membership and funds)
Publications: Newsletter, monthly
Activities: Classes for adults; educational trips; lectures open to public, 12 vis
lectr per yr; gallery talks; tours; competitions with awards; scholarships; exten
dept serves city; individual paintings & original objects of art lent to various
businesses; book traveling exhibitions; originate traveling exhibitions; gallery shop
sells original art

M OLD SALEM INC, Museum of Early Southern Decorative Arts, 924 S Main St,
PO Box 10310, Salem Station, 27108. Tel 919-722-6148. *Dir* Frank L Horton;
Educ Coordr Sally Gant; *Assoc Educ* Elizabeth Putney; *Publications Dir* John
Bivins Jr; *Research Assoc* Luke Beckerdite; *Photographer Technician* Wes
Stewart; *Secy* Carolyn Head
Open Mon - Sat 10:30 AM - 5 PM, Sun 1:30 - 4:30 PM. Admis adult $3, student
$1.50. Estab 1965 to bring to light the arts and antiquities produced in Maryland,
Virginia, Kentucky, Tennessee, North and South Carolina, and Georgia through
the first two decades of the 19th century. Three galleries are furnished with
Southern decorative arts or imported objects used in the South, and fifteen period
settings from Southern houses dating from 1690 to 1821. Average Annual
Attendance: 21,000. Mem: 650; dues $15-$500; annual meeting Spring
Income: $225,000 (financed by endowment, membership, state appropriation, and
other funds)
Purchases: Approx $50,000
Collections: †Southern decorative arts in general, and specifically furniture,
paintings, silver, ceramics, metalwares, and woodwork of southern origin
Exhibitions: Ongoing Research in Southern Decorative Arts
Publications: Journal of Early Southern Decorative Arts, semiannually; catalog of
the collection 1979, Museum of Early Southern Decorative Arts; The Luminary,
newsletter, semiannually
Activities: Classes for adults and children; graduate Summer Institute; lect open
to public, 15 visiting lectr per year; gallery talks; scholarships; exten dept serves
eight Southern States; individual paintings and original objects of art lent to
museums and cultural institutions, and with special permission from staff are
available for special exhibits; lending collection contains 2000 original art works,
100 paintings, 9000 photographs and 30,000 slides; originate traveling
exhibitions; sales shop selling books, slides
L Library, 924 S Main St, Box 10310, Salem Station, 27108. Tel 919-722-6148.
Research Fellow Bradford L Rauschenberg; *Archivist* Rosemary Estes
Open Mon - Sat 10:30 AM - 5 PM, Sun 1:30 PM - 4:30 PM. Estab 1965 to
display and study southern decorative arts through 1820
Library Holdings: Vols 2400; Per subs 20; Micro — Fiche, prints, reels; AV —
Slides
Special Subjects: Research of regional artists
Publications: Journal of Early Southern Decorative Arts, bi-annually; Luminary,
bi-annually

M REYNOLDA HOUSE, INC,* Reynolda Village, Reynolda Rd, PO Box 11765,
27106. Tel 919-725-5325. *Exec Dir* Nicholas B Bragg; *Cur of Education* Marjorie
Northup; *Admin Asst* Diane Wise; *Development Asst* Elen Knott; *Secy* Marge
Wagstaff
Open Tues - Sat 9:30 - 4:30 PM, Sun 1:30 - 4:30 PM, cl Mon. Admis adults $2,
senior citizens $1, students $.75. Estab 1964 to offer a learning experience
through a correlation of art, music and literature using the house and the
Collection of American Art as resources. Gallery located in the 40 rooms of the
former R J Reynolds mansion. Average Annual Attendance: 38,500. Mem: 600;
annual meeting of Board of Directors in May and Nov
Income: Financed by endowment, Friends' contributions, local and state
government grants for specific programs, as well as foundation grants
Collections: Doughty Bird Collection; Costume Collection; †Permanent
Collection of Paintings and Prints on permanent loan
Publications: Annual Report; Calendar of Events, biannually
Activities: Classes for adults and children; dramatic programs; docent training;
lect open to public, 20 vis lectr per year; concerts; gallery talks; tours; individual
paintings and original objects of art lent to specific museums with reciprocity
agreement; lending collection contains original prints, paintings; slides of
paintings are sold
L Library,* Reynolda Village, Reynolda Rd, 27106. *Librn* Ruth Mullen
Open to public
Library Holdings: Vols 1000; Per subs 30

M SOUTHEASTERN CENTER FOR CONTEMPORARY ART, 750 Marguerite
Dr, 27106. Tel 919-725-1904. *Pres* Roberta W Irvin; *Dir* Ted Potter; *Assoc Dir*
McChesney S Dunn; *Business Mgr* Lucy P Wilson; *Education Coordr* Laura
Carpenter; *Cur* Vicki S Kopf
Open Tues - Sat 10 AM - 5 PM, Sun 2 - 5 PM, cl Mon. No admis fee. Estab
1956 to identify and exhibit the southeast's major artists of exceptional talent; to
present educational programs for children and adults; to bring the viewing public
in direct contact with artists and their art. Maintained are nine indoor and
outdoor exhibition areas. Average Annual Attendance: 80,000. Mem: 1500; dues
varying categories; annual meeting June
Income: Financed by endowment, membership, local arts council, grants and
sales commissions
Publications: Catalogs, 3-4 per yr; newsletter, quarterly
Activities: Classes for adults and children; docent training; workshops; lectures
open to public; concerts; gallery talks; tours; competitions with awards;
scholarships; original objects of art lent to non-profit tax exempt organizations;
originate traveling exhibitions; center shop sells books, magazines, original art,
gifts, paper products, crafts

C WACHOVIA BANK & TRUST COMPANY, NA,* 300 S Main, PO Box 3099,
27101. Tel 919-748-5000. *Asst VPres* Janet S Walters
Estab to support the arts and enhance the environment for customers and
employees. Collection displayed throughout the 204 offices
Collections: Traditional and contemporary work, primarily by North Carolina
and Southeastern United States artists

NORTH DAKOTA

DICKINSON

M DICKINSON STATE COLLEGE, Mind's Eye Gallery, Department of Art,
58601. Tel 701-227-2312. *Co-Dir* Dennis Edward Navrat; *Co-Dir* Benni
Privatsky
Open daily during academic year, regular library hours. No admis fee. Estab
1972 as a visual arts gallery presenting monthly exhibits representing the work of
local, national and international artists. Gallery is a secure, large room approx 50
x 20 ft, with a 20 ft ceiling and approx 120 running ft of sheetrock display space.
Average Annual Attendance: 10,000
Income: $9000 (financed by endowment, state appropriation, Badlands Art
Association, student fees, memberships)
Purchases: Approx $1000
Collections: Zoe Beiler paintings; contemporary graphics
Exhibitions: (1981-82) The Plastic Arts; Indian Summer; Lithography: An
Introduction by Bella Petheo; 1981 Governor's Student Art Show; Asian Pauses;
Pysanky; Feathered Impressions; Jim Dow/North Dakota; (1982-83) Pots from
Mount Saint Helens/Reynolds & McDowell; Janne Quick-To-See Smith,
drawings; Oil: Photographs from the Williston Basin; The New West; Ash Coulee
Pottery; 1982 Governor's Student Art Show; The Collection Connections; (1983-
84) Badlands North Dakota/David Christy; Allen Nelson, wildlife photographs;
Jack Ross, All Is A Circle Within; Den Navrat, Colorado Papers; Station Breaks;
Inuit Art; The Art of Jack Youngquist; Iron Spirits; 1983 Governor's Student Art
Show; Pysanky
Publications: Exhibit announcements
Activities: Lectures open to public, 2 - 4 vis lectr per year; gallery talks; originate
traveling exhibitions
L Stoxen Library, Art Department, 58601. *Library Dir* Bernnett Reinke; *Librn*
James Martz
Mon - Fri 8 AM - 10 PM, Sat & Sun 3 - 10 PM. Open to college students
Income: Financed by state appropriation
Library Holdings: Vols 3150; Per subs 16

FARGO

M NORTH DAKOTA STATE UNIVERSITY, Memorial Union Art Gallery,*
58105. Tel 701-237-8236. *Dir* Carol Morrow Bjorklund
Open Sept - May Mon - Fri 10 AM - 8 PM, Sun 1 - 5 PM
Exhibitions: Contemporary works by American artists

FORT RANSOM

M SVACA - SHEYENNE VALLEY ARTS AND CRAFTS ASSOCIATION,
Bjarne Ness Gallery,* PO Box 52, 58033. Tel 701-973-2351. *Pres* Wayne
Hankel; *VPres* Helen Bjone
Open Sat, Sun and holidays 1 - 6 PM, June 1 - Sept 30. No admis fee, donations
accepted. Estab 1971 to preserve and care for the Bjarne Ness Gallery and to
sponsor and promote interest in arts and crafts by conducting seminars,
workshops, and an annual festival. The Gallery is the former studio of the late
Bjarne Ness. Average Annual Attendance: 2400. Mem: 205; dues couple $5,
single $3; annual meeting Nov
Income: Financed by membership and grants
Collections: Paintings of Bjarne Ness; paintings and wood carvings by area artists
in SVACA's Bear Creek Hall
Exhibitions: Annual Arts and Crafts Festival; one or two members' shows
Activities: Classes for adults; gallery talks; individual paintings lent to banks,
libraries, cafes
L Library,* PO Box 52, 58033
Open to members for reference
Library Holdings: Vols 150
Special Subjects: Arts and crafts

GRAND FORKS

M NORTH DAKOTA MUSEUM OF ART, University Ave, Box 7305, Univ Station, 58202. *Dir & Head Cur* Laurel J Reuter; *Asst Dir* Marilyn Fundingsland
Open Mon - Thurs 10 AM - 5 PM & 7 - 9 PM, Fri 10 AM - 5 PM, Sat & Sun 1 - 5 PM. No admis fee. Estab 1971 as an exhibition gallery, historical as well as contemporary arts and crafts; galleries are also involved in educational and humanities projects. Galleries occupy three large sections on third floor of University Center, offices adjacent; mobile gallery housed in trailer. Average Annual Attendance: 18,000
Income: Financed by endowment, state appropriation and grants
Publications: Exhibition catalog
Activities: Lectures open to the public, 3 - 5 vis lectr per yr; gallery talks; book traveling exhibitions; originate traveling exhibitions
L Bierce Library, University Ave, 58202. *Librn* H Paul Schrank Jr
Open Mon - Fri 7:30 AM - Noon, Sat 9 AM - 5 PM, Sun 2 PM - 12 AM. Estab 1870
Library Holdings: Vols 9000
Activities: Classes for adults and children; lect open to public, 12-15 visiting lectr per year; gallery talks; art mobile; paintings lent to University offices; originate traveling exhibitions

MAYVILLE

M MAYVILLE STATE COLLEGE GALLERY,* 58257. Tel 701-786-2301, Ext 197. *Dir* Lila Hauge
Open Mon - Fri 9 AM - 5 PM
Exhibitions: Contemporary American & North Dakota artists; student exhibitions

MINOT

M MINOT ART GALLERY, Minot Art Association, State Fair Grounds, PO Box 325, 58701. Tel 701-838-4445. *Dir* Shelly Ellstrom
Open Tues - Sun 1 - 5 PM, Feb - Dec. Estab 1970 to promote means and opportunities for the education of the public with respect to the study and culture of the fine arts. Average Annual Attendance: 2500. Mem: 300; dues $5 - $100; annual meeting 2nd Wed of month
Income: Financed by endowment, membership and contributions
Purchases: $500
Collections: Macrame; paintings; pottery; prints; sculpture; all done by local and national artists
Exhibitions: Art competitions; artfests; one-person exhibits; traveling art exhibits; exhibitions change monthly
Publications: Calendar of Exhibits, five times per year; newsletter
Activities: Classes for adults and children; lectures open to public, 1 - 2 vis lectrs per year; concerts; gallery talks; tours; competitions; scholarships; individual paintings and original objects of art lent to local businesses, schools and libraries; lending collection contains original art works, original prints, paintings & pottery; book traveling exhibitions, 2 - 3 per yr; traveling exhibitions organized and circulated; junior museum

VALLEY CITY

M FINE ARTS CLUB, Second Crossing Gallery, Room 210, McFarland Hall, Valley City State College, PO Box 1319, 58072. Tel 701-845-2690. *Dir* Mrs Riley Rogers; *Asst Dir* Bev Werner
Open Mon - Fri 1 - 3 PM, cl Aug. No admis fee. Estab 1973 to provide local, state, national and international shows for people in this area. Small but professional gallery consists of a room 28 x 40 ft with track lighting and movable standards. Average Annual Attendance: 3500. Mem: 130; dues $15 and up
Income: $12,000 (financed by endowment and membership)
Collections: †The Fine Arts Club has 75 pieces; †Second Crossing Gallery has 25 pieces
Exhibitions: 11 or 12 exhibitions a year of material from American Federation of Arts, Smithsonian, Western Association of Art Museums, local, national & state shows
Publications: Calendar, annually
Activities: Gallery talks; competitions with awards; scholarships; original objects of art lent to campus offices; book traveling exhibitions

OHIO

AKRON

M AKRON ART MUSEUM, 70 E Market St, 44308. Tel 216-376-9185. *Dir* I Michael Danoff; *Cur of Art* Carolyn Kinder Carr; *Cur of Education* Marcianne Herr; *Registrar* Brenda Mitchell; *Admnr* Anne Palmer; *Dir Public Relations & Special Events* Sandra Hensel; *Dir of Development* James Szubski
Open Tues - Fri Noon - 5 PM, Sat 10 AM - 5 PM, Sun 1 - 5 PM. No admis fee. Estab 1921 as a museum to exhibit and collect art. In Sept 1981, opened new Akron Art Museum in restored and reconstructed 1899 Neo-Renaissance style old post office; total of four galleries; two house the permanent collection and two have changing exhibitions. Average Annual Attendance: 50,000. Mem: 1500; dues general $30; annual meeting Sept
Income: $550,000 (financed by membership, endowment, corporate, foundation

and government grants)
Purchases: Frank Stella, Jim Dine, Raphael Gleitsmann
Collections: Photography; 20th century American and European painting and sculpture; Mark Di Suvero; Philip Pearlstein; Sol Lewitt; Richard Estes; Lois Lane; Philip Guston; Cindy Sherman
Exhibitions: (1982-84) Tod Papageorge, Malcolm Morley, Susan Rothenberg: Paintings; John & Andrea Gill: Ceramics; Jack Earl: Ceramics; Terry Dike: Wearable Art; H C Westerman: Sculpture & Watercolor; James Surls: Sculpture & Drawings; Jacob Lawrence: The Legend of John Brown; American Landscapes: Photographs; American Abstract Expressionist Paintings; Lee Friedlander: Factory Valleys; Claire Zeisler: Fiber Sculptures; William Merritt Chase: American Portraits; Jackie Windsor: Sculpture; The Mondrian Room; American Folk Art: The Herbert Waide Hemphill Jr Collection; Abe Frajndlich: Recent Color Photographs; American Watercolors and Drawings; Collaboration: Artists & Architects; Akron Collaboration: Artists & Architects; Recent American Woodcuts; Jack Teemer: Color Photographs; The Art Fabric: Mainstream; Three European Photographers; O Winston Link: Railroad Photographs of the 1950s; Julian Schnabel & Georg Baselitz: Paintings; Helen M Turner: A Retrospective Exhibition; Jonathan Borofsky Installation
Publications: Calendar, bi-monthly; exhibition catalogs; annual report
Activities: Education dept; docent training; lectures open to public, 6 - 8 lectr per year; gallery talks; concerts; tours; film series; artist demonstration-workshop series; individual paintings & original objects of art lent; originates traveling exhibitions; sales desk sells books, original art and catalogues
L Martha Stecher Reed Art Library, 69 E Market St, 44308
Open for reference, not open to public
Library Holdings: Vols 6500; Per subs 42; Contemporary Art; AV — A-tapes, cassettes, Kodachromes, slides, v-tapes; Other — Clipping files, exhibition catalogs, pamphlets
Special Subjects: Contemporary art
Collections: Edwin Shaw Volumes, to accompany collection of American Impressionistic Art

M STAN HYWET HALL FOUNDATION, INC,* 714 N Portage Path, 44303. Tel 216-836-5533. *Exec Dir* John Franklin Miller; *Bus Mgr* Donald Starner; *Public Relations* Hillary Prueitt; *Dir Volunteers* Bea Kannel; *Admin Asst* Maida Bevington
Open Tues - Sat 10 AM - 4 PM, Sun 1 - 4 PM, cl Mon & major national holidays. Admis adults $4.50, children 6 - 12 $1.50. Incorporated 1956, Stan Hywet Hall is a house museum, serving as a civic and cultural center. All restoration and preservation work is carefully researched to retain the original concept of the property, which represents a way of life that is gone forever. The mansion, the focal point of the estate, is a 65-room Tudor Revival manor house, furnished with priceless antiques and works of art dating from the 14th century. The property is the former home of Frank A Seiberling, (Akron rubber industrialist) and was completed in 1915. There are 70 acres of formal gardens, meadows, woods and lagoons. Average Annual Attendance: 135,000. Mem: 2900; dues $20 and up; annual meeting third Sun in March
Income: $600,000 (financed by endowment, membership, admissions, gifts, grants, rentals and special events)
Collections: Antique furniture; china; crystal; paintings; porcelain; rugs; sculpture; silver; tapestries
Publications: Stan Hywet Hall Newsletter, monthly
Activities: Classes for children; dramatic programs; docent training; lect open to public, 20 vis lectr per year; concerts; gallery talks; tours; competitions; lending collection contains photographs, slides and slide show with soundtrack, available with operator; sales shop sells books, original art, slides and wide variety of gift items
L Library,* 714 N Portage Path, 44303
Currently being developed, with reference materials relative to Stan Hywet Hall and Gardens
Library Holdings: Vols 2000

UNIVERSITY OF AKRON
M University Galleries,* 44325. Tel 216-375-7111. *Head Dept* Earl L Ertman
Open Mon - Fri 10 AM - 4 PM, Wed 6 - 9 PM. Estab 1974 to exhibit the work of important contemporary artists working in all regions of the United States, as well as to provide a showcase for the work of artists working within the university community. Two galleries: Emily H Davis Art Gallery, 1500 sq ft of wall space; Guzzetta Hall Atrium Gallery, 120 running ft of wall space. Average Annual Attendance: 8000
Income: Financed by university funds
Publications: Catalogs and artists books in conjunction with exhibitions
Activities: Lectures open to the public, six to eight visiting lecturers per year; gallery talks; traveling exhibitions organized and circulated

ASHLAND

M ASHLAND COLLEGE ARTS AND HUMANITIES GALLERY,* College Ave, 44805. Tel 419-289-4142. *Chmn* Albert W Goad; *Dir Gallery* Carl M Allen
Open Tues - Sun 1 - 4 PM, Tues evenings 7 - 10 PM. No admis fee. Estab 1969. Gallery maintained for continuous exhibitions
Exhibitions: Mostly contemporary works, some historical, occidental and Oriental
Activities: Classes for children; dramatic programs; lect open to public; 2 - 3 gallery talks; tours and regular tours to leading art museums; concerts; scholarships; original objects of art lent to Akron Art Institute and Cleveland Museum of Art

ASHTABULA

O **ASHTABULA ARTS CENTER,** 2928 W 13th St, 44004. Tel 216-964-3396.
Exec Dir Caron Van Gilder; *Admin Asst* Rosemary Humphery; *Bus Mgr* Roberta
Raisanen; *Visual Arts & Exhibits Coordr* Nancy Vasse; *Theatre Coordr* Thom
Miller; *Public Relations Coordr* Melinda Shenk; *Tech Coordr* Stephen Hansell;
Pres Terry Persily; *VPres* Victor Rossetti; *Secy* Michael Stone
Open Mon - Sat 8:30 AM - 5 PM, Sun 1 - 4 PM. No admis fee. Estab 1953 as a
non-profit, tax exempt art organization, to provide high quality instruction. One
major gallery area with smaller anex-fixed panals on all walls. Average Annual
Attendance: 5000. Mem: 1000; dues family $25, individual $15; annual meeting
Oct 20th
Income: Financed by membership, earned, NEA, OAC, WSL, CETA
Collections: Local and regional contemporary work, small international
contemporary print collection, regional wood sculpture (major portion of
collection represents local and regional talent)
Publications: Ashtabula Arts Center News, monthly; exhibit information monthly
Activities: Classes for adults and children; dramatic program; lect open to public,
5 - 10 visiting lectr per year; concerts; gallery talks; tours; competitions; cash
awards; scholarships; exten dept serves Ashtabula County hospitals and public
buildings; individual paintings and original objects of art lent to schools and
public buildings; lending collection contains books, cassettes, color reproductions,
framed reproductions, original art works, original prints, paintings, phonorecords,
photographs, sculpture and slides; book traveling exhibitions; originate traveling
exhibitions; museum shop sells books, gift items, jewelry, original art, prints,
reproductions and stationery

ATHENS

M **OHIO UNIVERSITY,** Gallery of Fine Arts, 48 E Union St, 45701. Tel 614-
594-5664. *Dir* Henry H Lin; *Asst to Dir* Kim S Schinder
Open Mon - Fri Noon - 4 PM. No admis fee. Estab 1974 to provide cultural
exposure to the university community and to the residents of the surrounding
region. Gallery has four rooms with carpeted walls and floors. Average Annual
Attendance: 9,000-12,000. Mem: 350; dues $5; monthly meeting
Income: Financed by state appropriation
Purchases: $6,000 (plus grant funds)
Collections: †Contemporary prints, some paintings, photographs and sculpture
Exhibitions: (1981-1982) Berenice Abbott (photographs); Larry Bell (furniture &
vapor drawings); Contemporary Prints from Ashland Oil Co; Hillside News
(invitational from Cincinnati); Richard Koslow (paintings); Alumni Invitational;
Harriett Anderson (paintings & textiles); Moroccan Textiles & Prints; (1983-84)
Trisolini Print Project, prints created at Ohio University by artists not normally
considered printmakers; Young New York Artists, paintings & sculpture; The
Solomon Collection, primitive art; Chicago Artists, paintings
Publications: Scholarly exhibition catalogs, two or three times a year
Activities: Lect open to public, 50-75 visiting lecturers per year; gallery talks;
tours; sponsors competitions with awards; traveling exhibitions organized and
circulated; museum shop sells books, original art, prints, crafts, pottery,
handmade jewelry, quilts
M **Seigfred Gallery,*** School of Art, Seigfred Hall 528, 45701. Tel 614-594-5667.
Dir Abner Jonas; *Gallery Dir* Mary Manusos
Open Mon - Fri 10 AM - 4 PM. No admis fee. Gallery is used for faculty
exhibitions, student exhibitions and visiting artist shows
L **Fine Arts Library,** Alden Library, 45701. Tel 614-594-5065. *Art Librn* Anne
Braxton
Open Mon - Thur 8 AM - Midnight, Fri 8 AM - 10 PM, Sat 10 AM - 10 PM,
Sun Noon - Midnight
Income: Financed by state appropriation
Library Holdings: Vols 40,000; Other — Exhibition catalogs, photographs, prints
Collections: Research collection in history of photography; small collection of
original photographs for study purposes

BAY VILLAGE

O **BAYCRAFTERS, INC,** Huntington Metropark, 28795 Lake Rd, 44140. Tel 216-
871-6543. *Dir* Sally Irwin Price
Open Mon - Fri 9 AM - 5 PM, weekends during shows. Estab 1948 for
advancement & enjoyment of arts & crafts in the area. Average Annual
Attendance: 30,000. Mem: 1800, dues $12 & $15
Exhibitions: Christmas Show; Emerald Necklace Juried Art Show; Juried Art
Show; Octoberfair; Renaissance Fayre; Student competition; Individual gallery
shows
Publications: Bulletins & competition notives
Activities: Classes for adults and children; lectures open to public, 9-12 vis lectr
per yr; gallery talks; tours; sponsors two juried art shows for adults and one for
children; monetary prizes awarded; scholarships; individual paintings lent to
public; book traveling exhibitions annually; orignate traveling exhibitions to local
libraries; shop sells books, magazines, original art, reproductions, prints and craft
items

BEREA

M **BALDWIN-WALLACE COLLEGE,** Art Gallery,* 95 E Bagley Rd, 44017. Tel
216-826-2239. *Dir* Dean Drahos
Open Thur, Fri 2 - 5 PM and 7 - 10 PM, Sat & Sun 2 - 5 PM, cl Mon, Tues,
Wed and holidays. No admis fee. The Art Gallery is considered to be a part of
the art program of the department of art; its purpose is that of a teaching
museum for the students of the college and the general public. Average Annual
Attendance: 2500
Income: Financed through budgetary support of the college
Collections: Approx †200 paintings and sculptures by Midwest artists of the 20th
century; approx †1900 drawings and prints from 16th - 20th century, with a
concentration in 19th & 20th century examples
Exhibitions: Traveling and student exhibitions

Publications: Exhibition catalogs are published for important exhibitions, 1 - 2
per year
Activities: Lect open to public; gallery talks; tours; competitions; individual
paintings lent to schools; book traveling exhibitions

BOWLING GREEN

M **BOWLING GREEN STATE UNIVERSITY,** Fine Arts Gallery,* School of Art,
43403. Tel 419-372-2787. *Dir School Art* Maurice J Sevigny, PhD
Open Mon - Fri 8:30 AM - 5 PM, Sun 2 - 5 PM. Estab 1964 to provide
enrichment to School of Art program by furnishing research materials,
exhibitions and related events; to provide for the growth of public sensitivity to
the visual arts. Gallery is a multi-level facility located in the Fine Arts building
with approximately 1500 running feet of exhibition space. Average Annual
Attendance: 7500
Income: Financed by state appropriation and foundation

CANTON

M **CANTON ART INSTITUTE,** 1001 Market Ave N, 44702. Tel 216-453-7666.
Pres Leander P Zwick Sr; *VPres* Mrs Ronald Cullen; *Treas* Donald J Lundstrom;
Secy Mrs John Reeves; *Gallery Dir* Joseph R Hertzi; *Assoc Dir* Manuel J
Albacete; *Admin Asst* Mrs Kenneth D Adams
Open Sept - July 15, Tues - Sat 10 AM - 5 PM, Tues, Wed & Thurs 7 - 9 PM,
Sun 2 - 5 PM. Summer, July 15 - Aug 16, Tues - Sat 10 AM - 4 PM. Estab
1935, incorporated 1941. Average Annual Attendance: 75,000. Mem: 1200; dues
$15 and higher; annual meeting Fall
Collections: American, Italian, and Spanish paintings; art objects; costumes;
decorative arts; 18th & 19th century English and American portraiture; graphics;
sculpture; 20th century regional art
Exhibitions: Approx 40 to 50 traveling or collected exhibitions of Commercial
and Industrial Arts; Painting; Sculpture annually (1981) French Music Hall
Posters from 1890 to 1940s; ALL OHIO 1981; Photographs by Ansel Adams;
Ohio Quilts: A Living Tradition; Tomb of Tutankhamun Photo Exhibition;
(1982) Other Worlds than Ours: Science Fiction and Fantasy Art; William
Gropper Graphics; (1983) Impressionism: An American View; ALL OHIO 1983;
African Elegance: The Traditional Art of Southern Africa; Fritz Eichenberg: 70
Wood Engravings
Activities: Formally organized education programs for adults and children;
docent training; guided tours; lectures open to public, 3 visiting lecturers per
year; films; gallery talks; arts festivals; competitions with awards; scholarships;
individual and original objects of art lent; book traveling exhibitions; originate
traveling exhibitions
L **Art Library,** 1001 Market Ave N, 44702
Library Holdings: Vols 2000; Per subs 15; AV — A-tapes, slides, v-tapes;
Other — Clipping files, exhibition catalogs, pamphlets, prints

CINCINNATI

O **CINCINNATI ART CLUB,** 1021 Parkside Place, 45202. Tel 513-241-4591. *Pres*
Sherman L Peeno; *Secy* Clarence J Sekerak; *Treas* Horace C Daughters
Open Sun afternoon Sept - May. Estab 1890, incorporated 1923. Gallery
contains a small collection of paintings by American artists. Average Annual
Attendance: 3500. Mem: 250; dues active $65, associate $55
Exhibitions: Exhibition of members' work changed monthly. Annual Club Shows
Sept, Jan, Spring (March-April) and Christmas Art Bazaar
Publications: Dragonfly, monthly member newsletter
Activities: Lectures for members only, 4 - 6 vis lectr per yr; competitions with
awards; scholarships; original objects of art lent

M **CINCINNATI ART MUSEUM,** Eden Park, 45202. Tel 513-721-5204. *Dir*
Millard F Rogers; *Business Mgr* George E Snyder; *Cur Decorative Arts* Anita
Ellis; *Cur Costumes, Textiles, Tribal Arts* Carolyn R Shine; *Cur Prints, Drawings
& Photographs* Kristin L Spangenberg; *Cur Ancient, Near and Far Eastern Arts*
Daniel S Walker; *Cur Painting* Denny T Young; *Asst Dir Development* Robert
Helmholz; *Conservator* Elizabeth Batchelor; *Registrar* Kathryn Taulbee
Open Tues - Sat 10 AM - 5 PM, Sun 1 - 5 PM, cl Mon & holidays. Admis adults
$2, children ages 12 - 18 & sr citizens $1, children ages 3 - 11 $.25, free to
members, special rates for school tour groups, free to all on Sat. Estab 1881 to
collect, exhibit, conserve and interpret works of art from all periods and
civilizations (range of 5000 years of major civilizations of the world). Exhibition
galleries cover an area of approx 4 acres, occupying two floors, with a few
exhibition galleries, assembly areas and social center on ground level; altogether
some 100 galleries given over to permanent collections, with additional galleries
set aside for temporary exhibitions. Average Annual Attendance: 210,000. Mem:
5500; dues $27.50 and up; annual meeting March
Income: $1,500,000 (financed by endowment, membership, city appropriation,
Cincinnati Fine Arts Fund, museum shop earnings, federal, state and private
grants)
Collections: Ancient musical instruments; artists; art in Cincinnati; Cincinnati
Art Museum; Egyptian, Greek, Roman, Near and Far Eastern arts; paintings
(European and American); world costumes, textiles and tribal arts; world prints,
drawings and photographs; world sculpture; world decorative arts and period
rooms
Exhibitions: (1983) Italian Art: New Acquisitions & Reinstallation of the
Permanent Collection; Concepts in Construction 1910-1980; (1984) Aaron
Siskind: Fifty Years; Irish Silver from the National Museum of Ireland;
Cincinnati Selections; New Acquisitions; Mystic North: Symbolist Landscape
Painting in Northern Europe & North America, 1890-1940; Art Academy of
Cincinnati Annual Student Exhibition; Jiri Anderle: Master Printmaker; Silk
Roads/China Ships
Publications: Annual Report; bi-monthly calendar; catalogues for exhibitions
Activities: Seminars; lectures open to public; gallery talks; tours; exten dept
serving Greater Cincinnati; individual paintings and original objects of art lent to
established art institutions meeting aesthetic and security standards approved by
Director and Board of Trustees; museum shop sells books, original art,
reproductions, prints, slides, postcards and others

L **Library,** Eden Park, 45202. Tel 513-721-5204, Ext 51. *Dir* Millard F Rogers Jr; *Librn* Patricia R Rutledge; *Archivist* Carole Schwartz
Open Tues - Fri 10 AM - 4:45 PM, Sat 1 - 4:30 PM. Estab to satisfy research needs of museum staff, academy faculty and students
Income: Financed by endowment
Library Holdings: Vols 45,851; Per subs 102; Micro — Fiche; Other — Clipping files, exhibition catalogs, pamphlets, reproductions
Collections: Files on Cincinnati Artists, Art in Cincinnati, the Cincinnati Art Museum, and the Art Academy of Cincinnati

O **CINCINNATI INSTITUTE OF FINE ARTS,*** 2649 Erie Ave, 45208. Tel 513-871-2787. *Pres* Paul George Sittenfeld; *Secy* Fletcher E Nyce
Estab and inc 1927 to provide for the continuance and growth of education and culture in the various fields of fine arts in the metropolitan community of Cincinnati. Mem: Annual meeting Oct
Income: Financed through endowments by Cincinnati Symphony Orchestra, Cincinnati Art Museum, Cincinnati Opera, Taft Museum, May Festival, Cincinnati Ballet, Contemporary Arts Center, Playhouse in the Park, Special Projects Pool
Publications: Quarterly Calendar

M **CONTEMPORARY ARTS CENTER,** 115 E Fifth St, 45202. Tel 513-721-0390. *Chmn* Stuart Schloss; *Pres* Theresa Henderson; *VPres* Al Vontz; *Treas* Robert Bonini; *Secy* Suzi Stone; *Dir* Dr Dennis Barrie; *Business Mgr* Nancy Glier; *Publications Coordr* Carolyn Krause; *Membership & Gallery Coordr* Jennifer Schooler; *Preparator* Mark Rohling; *Cur* Sarah Rogers-Lafferty; *Dir Communications* Amy Banister
Open Mon - Sat 10 AM - 5 PM. Admis adults $1, students & sr citizens $.50, mem free. Estab 1939. The Center is a museum for the presentation of current developments in the visual and related arts. It does not maintain a permanent collection but offers changing exhibitions of international, national and regional focus. Average Annual Attendance: 30,000 - 40,000. Mem: 1000; dues from $10 - $100
Income: $475,000 (financed by endowment, city and state appropriations)
Exhibitions: (1983) Body Language: Siah Armajani, Jennifer Bartletl, Johnathan Borofsky, R M Fischer, Robert Longo, Cindy Sherman, Julian Schnabel; Representing Reality: Francesco Clemente, Joel Fisher, Robert Kushner, Pat Steir, William R Wiley, Scott Burton; Off the Streets and Onto the Wall: Lee Quinones; Recent Work by Connie Sullivan; Wegman's World; Object '83; The End of the Road: Vanishing Highway Architecture in America; Christo; Abstraction: Two Views Paintings by Scott Davis & Ted Stamm; Joann Callis, photographs; Expresssions: New German Art of the 1970s & 1980s; Arbitrary Order: Paintings by Pat Steir
Publications: Catalogs of exhibitions
Activities: Classes for adults and children; docent training; lectures open to public, 8 vis lectr per year; concerts; gallery talks; programs for adults and children; tours; lending collection contains slides and videotapes; book traveling exhibitions 6 per year; traveling exhibitions organized and circulated; museum shop sells books, magazines, cards, reproductions & prints

L **Library,** 115 E Fifth St, 45202. *Cur* Sarah Rogers-Lafferty; *Dir Communications* Amy Banister
Open to members and others by appointment for reference
Library Holdings: Per subs 10; Other — Exhibition catalogs
Exhibitions: Dennis Oppenheim-Constructions II; Rick Paul; R S M Fisher; John Baldessari; Counterparts: Emotion and Form in Photography; Tableaux; Scott Burton Chairs; Christo; William Wegman

M **HEBREW UNION COLLEGE,** Gallery of Art and Artifacts,* 3101 Clifton Ave, 45220. Tel 513-221-1875. *Coordr* Susan W Newmark
Open Mon - Fri 11 AM - 4 PM, Sun 2 - 4 PM. No admis fee. Estab 1923 to interpret Judaism to the general public; also the archaeologic work of the college in Isreal. 1350 sq ft of exhibition space. Average Annual Attendance: 4000
Income: $15,203 (financed by endowment)
Collections: Jewish ceremonial art; archaeologic artifacts; paintings, drawings and sculpture by Jewish artists; photography
Publications: A Walk Through The Past
Activities: Docent training; lectures open to public; tours; individual and original objects of art lent

INTERNATIONAL SOCIETY FOR THE STUDY OF EXPRESSIONISM
For further information, see National and Regional Organizations

L **PUBLIC LIBRARY OF CINCINNATI AND HAMILTON COUNTY,** Art and Music Dept, 800 Vine St, Library Square, 45202. Tel 513-369-6954. *Head Art & Music Department* Jayne Craven; *Head Librn* James R Hunt
Open Mon - Fri 9 AM - 9 PM, Sat 9 AM - 6 PM, cl Sun. Estab 1872 to provide the community with both scholarly and recreational materials in area of fine arts. Have display cases in the department to exhibit collections
Income: $56,100 (financed by intangible taxes, state and county appropriations)
Library Holdings: Vols 121,790; Per subs 631; Vertical file; Micro — Cards, fiche, prints, reels; AV — A-tapes, cassettes, fs, Kodachromes, lantern slides, motion pictures, rec, slides, v-tapes; Other — Clipping files, exhibition catalogs, manuscripts, memorabilia, original art works, pamphlets, photographs, prints, reproductions
Special Subjects: Architecture, Costume Design & Construction, Film, Photography
Collections: Langstroth Collection - Chromolithographs of the 19th Century: also scrapbooks on the history of Chromolithography; Eda Kuhn Loeb Collection - The Artist and the Book 1875 to present; 156 Titles with Original signed Lithographs by Artists from Manet to Dali
Exhibitions: (1982-84) Children's Book Illustrators; Decorative Textiles; Arms and Armor St Francis of Assisi; Advertising Art of the 19th Century; Animals in Art; Opera; The Art of Metalwork; The Artist and the Book (from Manet to Shahn)
Activities: Lect open to public, 2 or 3 visiting lectr per year; sales shop sells books, reproductions, prints, tote bags, toys & stationery items

M **TAFT MUSEUM,** 316 Pike St, 45202. Tel 513-241-0343. *Dir Taft Musuem* Dr Ruth K Meyer; *Assoc Dir Taft Museum* Jan Weigel; *Asst Cur Taft Museum* Heather M Hallenberg; *Chmn Cincinnati Inst of Fine Arts* Henry W Hobson Jr; *Chmn Museum Committee* William J Williams
Open Mon - Sat 10 AM - 5 PM, Sun & Holidays 2 - 5 PM, cl Thanksgiving and Christmas. No admis fee. Estab 1927, a gift of Mr and Mrs Charles P Taft's art collection to the Cincinnati Institute of Fine Arts including the house and an endowment fund for maintenance. Active control was taken in 1931; museum opened in 1932. The historic house, built in 1820, is one of the finest examples of Federal architecture in this country, and was designated a National Landmark. Its interior is decorated in the style of the period. An architectural formal (green) garden was opened in 1949. Average Annual Attendance: 60,000. Mem: Annual meeting Sept
Income: $475,000 (financed by endowment and annual fine arts fund drive)
Collections: Furnishings include antique toiles and satins and a notable collection of Duncan Phyfe furniture; paintings including works by Rembrandt, Hals, Turner, Goya, Corot, Gainsborough, Raeburn and other Masters; 200 notable Chinese Porcelains K'ang Hsi and Ch'Ien Lung; 120 French Renaissance enamels; Renaissance jewelry and 18th century watches from many countries
Exhibitions: Contemporary American Landscape Painting; Circus Posters; The 1930's Remembered, Part I: The High Style; The 1930's Remembered, Part II: Cincinnati, Do You Remember?; The 1930's Remembered, Part III: The Fine Arts; Old Toys at Taft; MacDowell: The Vital Beginning; Material Illusions-Unlikely Materials; Recent Portrait Photography; A Beautiful Order: Figures and Landscapes from the Butler Institute of American Art
Activities: Docent training; lect open to public, 10 vis lectr per year; gallery talks; tours; individual paintings lent to special museum exhibitions; museum shop sells reproductions, prints, slides, needlework and titles

UNIVERSITY OF CINCINNATI
M **Tangeman Fine Arts Gallery,** 403 Tangeman, Mail Location 15, 45221. Tel 513-475-3462. *Dir* Christopher T Eagen; *Asst to the Dir* Leslie Ann Sharps
Open Mon - Fri 9 AM - 5 PM, Sat 1 - 3 PM. No admis fee. Estab 1967 to preserve and maintain the University's art collection; Gallery reorganized and separated from University Collection in 1978. Gallery is maintained and presents quality contemporary and historical exhibitions of works by artists of local, regional and national reputation. Average Annual Attendance: 39,000
Income: Financed through university
Exhibitions: (1980-83) Art Nouveau from Cincinnati Collections; Great Ideas; Artist Television on the Cable; Art of Emotionally Disturbed Adolescents; The Art of the Composers; Fragments
Publications: Fragments, catalogue
Activities: Lectures open to the public; concerts; gallery talks; tours; individual paintings and original objects of art lent, 10 items lent in an average year; book traveling exhibitions, 1 - 3 per yr; small traveling exhibitions organized and circulated

L **Design, Architecture, Art & Planning Library,** 800 Alms Bldg, 45221. Tel 513-475-3238. *DAA Librn* Elizabeth Douthitt Byrne
Open Mon - Thurs 8 AM - 10 PM, Fri 8 AM - 5 PM, Sat 9 AM - 5 PM, Sun 1 - 8 PM (Academic Year); summer hours vary. Estab 1925 to support the programs of the College of Design, Architecture, Art and Planning. Circ 42,000
Purchases: $37,000
Library Holdings: Vols 40,000; Per subs 230; Micro — Fiche, reels; Other — Exhibition catalogs
Special Subjects: Art Education, Art History, Architecture, Graphic Design, Industrial Design, Interior Design, Fashion Design, Fine Arts, Planning

L **Art History Slide Collection Library,*** Art History Dept, 45220. Tel 513-475-8000
Library contains 125,000 slides

M **XAVIER UNIVERSITY,** Emery Galleries, 2220 Victory Parkway, 45206. Tel 513-961-3770. *Dir* Ann Beiersdorfer
Open Mon - Sat 1 - 5 PM, cl Sun. No admis fee. Estab to present to students and public outstanding artists of local, national and international fame
Income: Privately financed
Exhibitions: Professional artists; qualified students of Edgecliff College
Activities: Lectures open to public; gallery talks; tours; book traveling exhibitions

CLEVELAND

C **AMERITRUST COMPANY,*** 900 Euclid Ave, 44101. Tel 216-687-5000. *Sr VPres* L Louis Amoroso; *Operations Officer* Donald D Rolla
Collection estab 1971 to enhance the executive offices of the bank; supports and promotes the performing and visual arts. Collection displayed in executive offices
Collections: Primarily 19th Century American oils with few contemporary pieces
Activities: Tours; individual objects of art lent to traveling exhibit touring United States and Europe

M **CLEVELAND INSTITUTE OF ART,** University Circle, 11141 East Blvd, 44106. Tel 216-421-4322. *Pres* Joseph McCullough; *Dean* Robert D Weitzel, Jr
Open Mon - Fri 9 AM - 4:30 PM, Tues & Wed 7 - 9 PM, Sat 9 AM - noon, Sun 2 - 5 PM. No admis fee. Estab 1882 as a five-year, fully accredited professional college of art. Gallery is maintained with extensive exhibitions
Publications: Link (alumni magazine), quarterly; posters to accompany each exhibit; bi-annual school catalog
Activities: Classes for adults and children; lect open to public

L **Jessica Gund Memorial Library,*** University Circle, 11141 East Blvd, 44106. Tel 216-421-4322. *Librn* Karen Tschudy; *Special Collection Librn* Cristine Rom; *Technical Services Librn* Hyosoo Lee; *Media Center Librn* Patricia Lynagh
Open Mon - Thurs 9 AM - 9:30 PM, Fri 9 AM - 5 PM, Sat 9 AM - 4:30 PM, cl Sun. Estab 1882 to select, house and distribute library material in all media that will support the Institute's studio and academic areas of instruction
Income: Financed by tuition, gift, endowments
Library Holdings: Vols 40,000; Per subs 225; original documents; Micro — Fiche, prints; AV — A-tapes, cassettes, lantern slides, slides, v-tapes; Other — Clipping files, exhibition catalogs, manuscripts, memorabilia, original art works, pamphlets, photographs, prints, reproductions

Special Subjects: Anthropology, art, humanities, natural science , social and behavioral sciences, 20th century literature
Collections: Archival collection of clippings and exhibition notices; late 19th and early 20th century textiles; mounted pictures; nature study; posters & graphics
Activities: Library tours

O **Cleveland Art Association,*** University Circle, 11141 East Blvd, 44106. Tel 216-421-4322. *Pres* Ann Roulet
Estab and inc 1916, re-incorporated 1950 as a non-profit organization. Mem: 200; dues $45; annual meeting Nov
Income: $6000 (financed through endowment and donations)
Purchases: $5200
Activities: Competitions; awards; scholarships; individual paintings of local artists purchased for loan to members

M **CLEVELAND MUSEUM OF ART,** 11150 East Blvd, 44106. Tel 216-421-7340. *Pres* James H Dempsey, Jr; *Dir* Dr Evan H Turner; *Asst Dir Administration & Assoc Cur Paintings* William S Talbot; *Asst Dir Operations & Finance* Albert G Grossman; *Chief Cur Modern Art* Edward B Henning; *Cur Contemporary Art* Tom E Hinson; *Chief Cur Later Western Art* Henry Hawley; *Cur Paintings* Ann T Lurie; *Chief Cur Prints & Drawings* Louise S Richards; *Cur Early Western Art* Patrick M deWinter; *Cur Textiles* Anne E Wardwell; *Research Consultant Textiles & Islamic Art* Dorothy G Shepherd; *Sr Research Cur Chinese Art* Wai-Kam Ho; *Cur Indian Art* Stanislaw Czuma; *Asst in East Indian Art & Museum Designer* William E Ward; *Cur Ancient Art* Arielle P Kozloff; *Cur Education* James A Birch; *Chief Cur Musical Arts* Karel Paukert; *Chief Editor Museum Publications* Merald E Wrolstad; *Mgr Public Information & Membership* Adele Z Silver; *Registrar* Delbert R Gutridge
Open Tues, Thurs, Fri 10 AM - 6 PM, Wed 10 AM - 10 PM, Sat 9 AM - 5 PM, Sun 1 - 6 PM, cl Mon & four holidays. No admis fee. Estab and incorporated 1913; building opened 1916; New Wing 1958; New Education Wing 1971. Average Annual Attendance: 500,000. Mem: 10,000; dues $15 and up; annual meeting Nov
Income: $7,210,879
Purchases: $4,984,193
Collections: †Leonard C Hanna Jr; †Holden; †Mr and Mrs William H Marlatt; Elisabeth Severance Prentiss; Grace Rainey Rogers; †John L Severance; †J H Wade; Classical and Egyptian Art; Drawings and Prints; European and American Decorative Arts of all periods, notably medieval and 18th Century; European and American Paintings of all periods and styles, especially strong in works of 17th and 19th Centuries; Near Eastern Art; Oriental Art, including important Collections of Chinese and Japanese Painting and Ceramics, and Indian Sculpture; Textiles
Exhibitions: (1982) Artists & Craftsmen of the Western Reserve, annually; Year in Review, recent acquisitions annually; The World of Ceramics: Masterpeices from the Cleveland Museum of Art; A Century of Modern Drawing
Publications: Bulletin, 10 times a yr; Faberge & His Contemporaries; Rodin; Fifty Years of Modern Art; European Paintings Before 1500; European Paintings of 16th, 17th & 18th Centuries; Eight Dynasties of Chinese Painting; Reflections of Reality in Japanese Art; The World of Ceramics: Masterpieces from the Cleveland Museum of Art; News & Calendar, 6 times a yr; exhibition book-catalogs
Activities: Classes for adults & children, studio workshops; teacher resource center; lectures open to public, 14 vis lectr per yr; concerts; gallery talks; tours; competitions; exten dept serves local schools & public buildings; individual paintings & original objects of art lent to schools, libraries & cultural art centers; book traveling exhibitions; originate traveling exhibitions; museum shop sells books, reproductions & slides

L **Library,** 11150 East Blvd, 44106. *Librn* Jack Perry Brown
Estab 1916. Open to Museum members, visiting graduate students, faculty, curators only
Library Holdings: Vols 120,000; Per subs 1500; Micro — Fiche, reels; AV — Slides; Other — Clipping files, exhibition catalogs, photographs

O **Print Club of Cleveland,** 11150 East Blvd, 44106. Tel 216-421-7340. *Pres* Phyllis Seltzer; *VPres* Joseph Meals; *VPres* Betty Cavano; *Secy* Martina Grenwis; *Treasurer* Robert Lewis
Estab 1919 to stimulate interest in prints and drawings through education, collecting and commissioning of new works and enhancement of the museum's collection by gifts and purchases. Mem: 250; dues $100 and up; annual meeting Jan
Income: Financed by membership
Publications: The Print Club of Cleveland 1919-1969. Available at Museum Sales Desk, $10 plus postage
Activities: Lect open to the public

L **CLEVELAND PUBLIC LIBRARY,** Fine Arts & Special Collections Dept, 325 Superior Ave, 44114. Tel 216-623-2800, 623-2848. *Dir* Ervin J Gaines; *Head Fine Arts & Special Coll Dept* Alice N Loranth; *Planning & Research* Helen V Azusenis
Open Mon - Sat 9 AM - 6 PM, cl Sun. Estab 1869. Circ 3,605,627
Income: $18,461,473 (financed by county intangibles tax and by the city school district property tax levy and state subsidy)
Library Holdings: Vols 147,300; Per subs 166; original documents; special collection vol 134,700 & per sub 414; Micro — Fiche, reels; Other — Exhibition catalogs, manuscripts, original art works, pamphlets, photographs
Special Subjects: Architecture, Art History, Decorative Arts, Oriental Art, Primitive Art, Music, Rare Books
Collections: Cleveland Artist Original Graphics; John G White Collection of Folklore, Orientalia and Chess
Activities: Collections open to the public; tours available for groups

L **CLEVELAND STATE UNIVERSITY,** Library - Art Services, Rte 322, 44115. Tel 216-687-2492. *Supv Art Services* Candace Shireman
Estab 1965 to house collection of visual arts
Purchases: $16,000
Library Holdings: Vols 10,000; Per subs 96; Color Reproductions; Micro — Cards, fiche, prints, reels; AV — A-tapes, cassettes, fs, motion pictures, rec, slides 50,000, v-tapes; Other — Clipping files, exhibition catalogs, original art works, pamphlets, photographs, prints, reproductions
Collections: 19th & 20th century European & American art; medieval art

M **DEZIGN HOUSE III,** 1701 E Twelfth St, 44114. Tel 216-621-7777. *Dir* Ramon J Elias; *Assoc* Margery M Elias
Open only to clients. Estab 1962 for the encouragement of original art. Private gallery
Income: Financed privately
Collections: Original American and European

L **Library,** 1701 E Twelfth St, Cleveland, 44114. Tel 216-621-7777
Estab 1953. Open for private research only
Library Holdings: Vols 7000; Per subs 40; AV — Kodachromes 2000, rec; Other — Clipping files, exhibition catalogs, manuscripts, memorabilia, original art works, pamphlets, photographs, prints, sculpture
Special Subjects: North Eastern Ohio Art of the 60's

M **THE NEW GALLERY OF CONTEMPORARY ART,** 11427 Bellflower Rd, 44106. Tel 216-421-8671. *Dir* Marjorie Talalay; *Preparator* Andy Yoder; *Dir of Sales* Toby Lewis; *Admin Asst* Vicky Paras; *Dir Development* Barbara McLean; *Dir Education* Ginna Brand
Open Tues - Sat 10 AM - 5:30 PM. No admis fee. Estab 1968 to present the best and most innovative works by national figures in the contemporary visual arts as well as works by talented area artists. Two galleries for special exhibitions which change every 4-6 weeks, 1 small photography gallery, 1 gallery/office space to display recent acquisitions and consigned works of art. Mem: 700; annual dues $7.50 and up
Income: $175,000 (financed by membership, state appropriation, federal and state agencies and local foundations)
Exhibitions: Berencia Abbott: Documentary Photography of 1930's; Robert Rauschenberg Recent Works; Furniture As Sculpture; Color Photographs by John Ofahl; Insights: Small Works From the Past 15 Years; Art Materialized Works from the Fabric Workshop; (1982) Red Grooms' Welcome to Cleveland; David Hockney: Prints & Drawings; Frank Gehry: Drawings, Models & Furniture; New Italian Art; Five Modern American Metalsmiths; Julian Stanczak: Recent Prints & Drawings
Publications: Exhibition catalogues
Activities: Classes for children; lectures open to the public, 5 vis lectr per yr; gallery talks; tours; individual and original objects of art lent to other galleries and museums for special exhibitions; originate traveling exhibitions; sales shop sells original art works, books, magazines & posters

L **Library,** Cleveland, 44106
Reference only
Library Holdings: AV — Slides; Other — Clipping files, exhibition catalogs, photographs

M **SAINT MARY'S ROMANIAN ORTHODOX CHURCH,** Romanian Ethnic Museum, 3256 Warren Rd, 44111. Tel 216-941-5550. *Pres* Daniel Miclau; *VPres* Jean Dobrea; *Secy* Leona Barbu; *Dir* Jane Martin
Open Mon - Fri 8:30 AM - 4:30 PM, Sun & holidays 10 AM - 1 PM; by appointment only. No admis fee. Estab 1960. Average Annual Attendance: 10,000
Income: Financed by parish appropriation
Collections: Anisoara Stan Collection; O K Cosla Collection; Gunther Collection; Romanian art, artifacts, costumes, ceramics, painters, rugs, silver and woodwork
Activities: Lect open to public; tours; individual paintings and original objects of art lent locally for exhibits; lending collection contains 100 original art works, 250 original prints, 50 paintings, sculpture, 2000 costumes, rugs and artifacts

C **THE STANDARD OIL COMPANY (OHIO),*** Midland Bldg, 44115. Tel 216-575-4141. *In Charge Art Program* C D Shields
Estab to enhance quality of life in communities where the company has employees or operations. Supports performing theatres, museums, orchestras and art education
Activities: Operating support, facilities and production sponsorship

M **TEMPLE MUSEUM OF JEWISH RELIGIOUS ART,** University Circle & Silver Park, 44106. Tel 216-791-7755. *Dir* Daniel Jeremy Silver
Open by appointment only. No admis fee. Estab 1950. Branch museum on Shaker Blvd, Beachwood
Collections: Archaelogy; ceremonial art; decorative arts; paintings; prints; sculpture
Activities: Classes for adults and children; tours; museum shop

L **Library,** Cleveland, 44106
Reference only
Library Holdings: Vols 500; Per subs 20; AV — A-tapes, fs, slides, v-tapes; Other — Manuscripts, photographs

M **WESTERN RESERVE HISTORICAL SOCIETY,** 10825 East Blvd, 44106. Tel 216-721-5722. *Exec Dir* Theodore A Sande; *Dir History Museum* Jairus B Barnes; *Dir Auto Museum* John Rees; *Librn* Kermit J Pike; *Comptroller* Donald M Morse
Open Tues - Sat 10 AM - 5 PM, Sun Noon - 5 PM, cl Mon. Admis adult $2, senior citizens, students, children $1. Estab 1867 to collect and preserve items of historical interest to Western Reserve (Northeastern Ohio) such as manuscripts and maps, furniture and decorative arts. Average Annual Attendance: 80,000. Mem: 3200; dues $25 and up; annual meeting Oct
Income: $2,500,000 (financed by endowment, membership, admissions, gifts, county appropriations and special grants)
Collections: Period rooms including a Renaissance Revival Parlor, 1865-1875
Exhibitions: People at the Crossroads-Settling the Western Reserve, 1796-1870
Publications: Books on Regional History; Western Reserve Historical Society News, bi-monthly
Activities: Docent training; classes for adults and children; lect open to public; gallery talks; tours; individual paintings and objects of art lent to institutions; originate traveling exhibitions; sales shop sells books and magazines

L **Library,*** 44106
Library Holdings: Vols 220,000; Micro — Cards 100, fiche 2000, reels 25,000; AV — A-tapes, rec, slides; Other — Manuscripts 5,000,000

O **WOMEN'S CITY CLUB OF CLEVELAND,** Gallery,* 850 Euclid Ave, 44114. Tel 216-696-3760. *Exec Dir* Norma Huey; *Pres* Sandra M Johnson; *1st VPres* Mrs Stanley Stone Jr; *VPres* Mrs H G Weidner Jr; *Secy* Joanne Durante
Open Mon - Fri 9 AM - 5 PM, closes at 4:30 PM during July & Aug. No admis fee. Estab 1916 to promote a broad acquaintance, provide a central meeting place, maintain an open forum and promote the welfare of the City of Cleveland. Maintains an art gallery featuring monthly exhibitions by local professional artists. Average Annual Attendance: 25,000. Mem: 1000; dues resident member $100, junior member $50
Income: Financed by membership
Exhibitions: Continous exhibitions changing every four to six weeks
Publications: Bulletin, monthly
Activities: Classes for adults; art appreciation classes; lect open to public; gallery talks

COLUMBUS

AMERICAN CERAMIC SOCIETY
For further information, see National and Regional Organizations

M **CAPITAL UNIVERSITY,** Schumacher Gallery, 2199 E Main St, 43209. Tel 614-236-7108. *Dir* Prof Richard G Bauer; *Secy* Janet E Popp
Open Mon - Fri 1 - 5 PM, Sat and Sun 2 - 4 PM. No admis fee. Estab 1966 to provide the best available visual arts to the students; to serve the entire community with monthly traveling shows, community programming and permanent collections. Gallery is 16,000 sq ft, that includes six display galleries, fabrication room, community reception room, lecture hall seating 60 and lecture space seating 250. Average Annual Attendance: 9000 - 12,000
Income: Financed by endowment, foundation grants, individual gifts, corporate funding
Collections: American Indian & Eskimo; †American paintings, sculpture and graphics of 20th century; Flemish paintings from 16th - 17th century; 19th century paintings; Oceanic collection of tribal arts and artifacts; †Major Ohio painters; †prints; Oriental Collection
Exhibitions: Nine individual and group visiting shows per year; group exhibits include Central Ohio Watercolor Society, Bexley Area Art Guild, Ohio Liturgical Art Guild, Senior Student and Alumni Show, Art Faculty Show; individual exhibits include out of state contemporary artists and loans from major national museums; selected works from permanent collection
Activities: Lect open to public, 4 visiting lectr per year; concerts; gallery talks; tours; competitions; individual paintings and original art objects lent by special request only;; originate traveling exhibitions; gallery shop open to the public
L **Art Library,** 2199 E Main St, 43209. Tel 614-236-6615. *Dir* Dr Albert Maag
Open to students, faculty, staff, and for reference only to the public
Library Holdings: Vols 4000; Per subs 12

L **COLUMBUS COLLEGE OF ART AND DESIGN,** Packard Library, 47 N Washington Ave, 43215. Tel 614-224-9101. *Librn* Chilin Yu
Open Mon & Fri 8 AM - 5 PM, Tue - Thurs 8 AM - 8 PM. Estab 1879. Open to public for reference only
Income: $137,000 (financed by tuition fees and grants)
Purchases: $35,400
Library Holdings: Vols 18,819; Per subs 138; AV — Cassettes, Kodachromes, lantern slides, rec, slides; Other — Clipping files, exhibition catalogs, original art works, pamphlets, photographs, reproductions, sculpture
Exhibitions: Students' work
Publications: Botticelli, annually
Activities: Classes for adults and children; lectures open to the public, 25 vis lectr per yr; tours; competitions with awards; scholarships; artmobile; lending collection contains original prints, paintings, sculpture & slides; originate traveling exhibitions

M **COLUMBUS CULTURAL ARTS CENTER,** 139 W Main St, 43215. Tel 614-222-7047. *Dir* Susan Ann Wells
Open Mon - Thur 8 AM - 4 PM & 7 - 10 PM, Fri 8 AM - 5 PM, Sat & Sun 1 - 5 PM. No admis fee. Estab 1976. Maintains small reference library. Average Annual Attendance: 20,000
Income: Financed and city appropriation
Activities: Classes for adults; dramatic programs; docent training; lectures open to public; concerts; gallery talks; tours; artmobile

M **COLUMBUS MUSEUM OF ART,** 480 East Broad St, 43215. Tel 614-221-6801. *Pres* Arthur D Herrmann; *Dir* Budd Harris Bishop; *Chief Cur* Steven W Rosen; *Development Dir* James V Buchanan; *Registrar* Susan R Visser; *Dir Programs* Susan Page Tillett; *Business Mgr* Wayne C King; *Public Information Coordr* Linda Latimer
Open Tues, Thurs, Fri & Sun 11 AM - 5 PM, Wed 11 AM - 8:30 PM, Sat 10 AM - 5 PM, cl Mon & holidays. Admis adults $1.50, children (6 - 17) senior citizens & students with valid school ID $.50, Fri free. Estab 1878. Present main building constructed in 1931 in an Italianate palatial style; addition built in 1974; Sculpture Park and Garden added in 1979. Average Annual Attendance: 110,000. Mem: 5300; dues $35
Income: Financed by annual contributions, endowment, membership and public support
Collections: †16th - 20th century European paintings, drawings and prints; †19th and 20th century American paintings, works on paper, and sculpture; †Chinese and Japanese ceramics; †sculpture collection
Exhibitions: Woman: Artist and Image; Beaux Arts Designer-Craftsman; Images of Ancient Mexico: Pre-Columbian Art from Columbus Collections; Looms of Splendor; Oriental Rugs from Columbus Collections; Art of Glass: Selections from Columbus Collection; Lithographs by George Wesley Bellows; The Cutting Edge: Prints of Protest & Satire; Niki De Saint Phalle Monumental Projects; Shadow of the Dragon: Chinese Trade Ceramics; Robert Natkin; Morton Livingston Schamberg: An American Modernist; The Prints of Edward Munch; Arnoldo Pomodoro: A Quarter Century; Made in Ohio: Furniture 1788-1888; Henry Moore: The Reclining Figure
Publications: Exhibition & permanent collection catalogs; free interpretive

handouts; monthly members bulletin; three-month calendar
Activities: Workshops for adults and youth; docent training; Lectures open to public, 24 visiting lecturers per year; concerts; gallery talks; tours; film series; members trips; competitions; lending collection contains original prints, paintings and sculpture; museum shop sells contemporary crafts
L **Resource Center,** 480 East Broad St, 43215
Estab 1974 as a reference center for staff, members & volunteers
Library Holdings: Vols 3500; Per subs 24; AV — Slides; Other — Clipping files, exhibition catalogs, pamphlets

O **THE OHIO FOUNDATION ON THE ARTS, INC,** 440 Dublin Ave, PO Box 2572, 43216. Tel 614-221-4300. *Exec Dir* Dennison W Griffith; *Dir Fine Arts Transportation Service* Rod Bouc; *Dir Touring Exhibitions Program* Maureen McCormick
Estab 1975 to promote the sharing of visual arts resources. Mem: 99; dues $25 - $200
Income: $465,000 (financed by endowment, membership, state appropriation)
Publications: Dialogue, bimonthly journal
Activities: Originate traveling exhibitions

O **OHIO HISTORICAL SOCIETY,** I 71 & 17th Ave, 43211. Tel 614-746-8691. *Dir* Gary C Ness; *Assoc Dir* William G Keener; *Chief Educ Division* Dr Amos Loveday; *Head Archaeology* Martha Otto; *Actg Head History* Don Hutslar; *Head National History* Dr William Schultz; *Head Historic Preservation* Ray Luce
Open Mon - Sat 9 AM - 5 PM, Sun 10 AM - 5 PM. No admis fee. Estab 1885, Ohio Historical Society was chartered on this date, to promote a knowledge of history, natural history and archaeology, especially of Ohio; to collect and maintain artifacts, books and archives relating to Ohio's history. Main gallery covers over one acre of floor space and includes exhibits on history, natural history, archaeology and furniture; also houses a natural history demonstration laboratory and several audio-visual theatres. Average Annual Attendance: 500,000. Mem: 11,350; dues individual $25; annual meeting September
Income: Financed by endowment, membership, state appropriation and contributions
Collections: Archaeology; †artifacts; ceramics; †clothing; †furniture; †glassware; †paintings
Publications: Museum Echoes, newsletter, monthly; Ohio History, scholarly journal, quarterly
Activities: Docent training; lect; individual paintings and original art objects lent; lending collection contains film strips; books traveling exhibitions; originate traveling exhibitions; sales shop sells books, magazines, reproductions, prints, slides and other souvenir items, post cards, jewelry
L **Archives-Library Division,** 1982 Velma Ave, 43211. Tel 614-466-1500. *Division Chief* Dennis East; *Head Librn* James B Casey; *Head Manuscripts* William Myers; *Actg State Archivist* David Levine; *Head Microfilming Dept* Bob Jones; *Head Conservation* Vernon Will
For reference only
Income: $1,100,000 (Financed by state appropriation and private revenue)
Purchases: $30,000
Library Holdings: Vols 100,000; Per subs 300; maps, lithographs; Micro — Reels; AV — A-tapes, cassettes, fs, Kodachromes, lantern slides, motion pictures, rec, slides, v-tapes; Other — Exhibition catalogs, manuscripts, memorabilia, pamphlets, photographs, reproductions
Collections: †Broadsides; †Ohio government documents; †Ohio newspapers; †Temperance Collection maps; Ohio government documents and papers from early Ohio leaders; Ohio newspapers, posters; rare books

OHIO STATE UNIVERSITY 43210
M **Gallery of Fine Art,** 128 North Oval Mall, Hopkins Hall, 43210. Tel 614-422-0330, 422-2395. *Dean, College of the Arts* Andrew J Broekema; *Dir* Jonathan Green; *Administrative Mgr* Stephanie K Blackwood; *Chief Exhib Preparator* Jim Scott; *Exhib Preparator* Ben Knepper; *Secy* Martha Logan
Hopkins Gallery open Mon - Fri 9 AM - 5 PM; Sullivan Gallery open Mon - Fri 9 AM - 5 PM, Tues & Thurs 6 - 8 PM, Sat 10 AM - 4 PM, Sun 2 - 5 PM. No admis fee. Estab 1968 to provide quality contemporary exhibitions for students and faculty, to promote interaction with the regional art community and to maintain and extend our collection of contemporary art. The Gallery administers the permanent collection as well as exhibits in 2 corridor galleries and 2 professionally equipped galleries. It is the center for long-range planning in visual arts. Average Annual Attendance: 70,000
Income: $180,000 (financed by state and federal grant, funds raised through the University development fund, and state appropriation)
Purchases: $100,000
Collections: Art of the 70's collection; †contemporary collection; †historical collection; †manuscript collection
Exhibitions: (Solo Exhibitions) Gary Bower; Kathryne Field; Jim Friedman; Richard Harned; Roy Lichtenstein; O Winston Link; Hoyt L Shermank; Bill Whorrall; Allen Zak; (Group Exhibitions) Structure/Constructions: Works in Paper/Fiber by Diane Katsiaficas, Susan Lyman & Paul Wong; Festival of Cartoon Art; All's Fair: Love & War in New Feminist Art, works by 20 feminist artists; Writing On The Wall: Work in Progress by New York City Graffiti Artists; Painters' Painters: Avery, Balthus, Guston, Morandi
Publications: Dialogue, bi-monthly visual arts magazine
Activities: Lectures open to public, 12 vis lectr per year; concerts; gallery talks; tours; invitational juried exhibitions; individual paintings & original objects of art lent to institutions for exhibition; original art & prints rented to students, staff & faculty through the circulating collection; rent traveling exhibitions, 1-5 per year; originate traveling exhibitions
L **Fine Arts Library,** Room 166 Sullivant Hall, 1813 North High St, 43201. Tel 614-422-6184. *Head Librn* Susan E Wyngaard; *Asst* Diana Robinson
Open Mon - Thurs 8 AM - 10 PM, Fri 8 AM - 5 PM, Sat 10 AM - 4 PM, Sun 2 - 10 PM, while classes are in session; vacation, 8 AM - 5 PM daily. Estab during 1930's to support teaching and research in art, art education, design and history of art. Average Annual Attendance: 54,012
Income: $77,000
Purchases: $70,150

Library Holdings: Vols 70,000; Per subs 258; Micro — Cards, fiche, reels; AV — Slides; Other — Exhibition catalogs, original art works
Special Subjects: Medieval and Renaissance
Collections: †Archival materials on microfiche

L **Visual Resource Collection, Dept of History of Art,** 204 Hayes Hall, 108 N Oval Mall, 43210. Tel 614-422-7481. *Cur* Mark McGuire
Open Mon - Fri 8 AM - 5 PM. Estab 1925 to provide visual resources for instruction and research in history of art. Teaching - Reference Collection, restricted circulation
Income: Financed by state funds through State University System
Purchases: University of Denver slides
Library Holdings: Vols 150; Per subs 2; AV — A-tapes, slides 200,000; Other — Exhibition catalogs, framed reproductions, original art works, photographs 250,000, prints, reproductions
Collections: Asian art photographs; contemporary African art; history of Islamic art; Medieval manuscript illuminations; survey sets; ACSAA sets; Saskia slides; Rosenthal slides; British Library manuscripts; contemporary photographs; history of western art and architecture

L **PUBLIC LIBRARY OF COLUMBUS AND FRANKLIN COUNTY,** Humanities, Fine Arts and Recreation Division, 96 S Grant Ave (Mailing add: 28 S Hamilton Rd, Columbus, OH 43213). Tel 614-222-7189. *Dir* Richard Sweeney; *Division Head* Suzanne Fisher; *Exhib Coordr* Patti Kinsinger
Open Mon - Thurs 9 AM - 9 PM, Fri & Sat 9 AM - 6PM, cl Sun. Estab 1873 to serve informational, educational and cultural needs of Columbus and Franklin County. Gallery is 130 running ft
Income: $141,000 (financed by state and county appropriation)
Library Holdings: Vols 33,000; Per subs 112; Classified picture file; Micro — Reels; AV — Cassettes, motion pictures, rec, v-tapes; Other — Exhibition catalogs, pamphlets
Special Subjects: Architecture, Decorative Arts, Film, Photography, Theatre Arts, Antiques, music, television
Exhibitions: Milton Caniff: Art for Everybody; The Wonderful T: The Art of James Thurber; innovative and informative exhibits with emphasis on local professional artists and traveling exhibits; (1981) Creative Best of Columbus Society of Communicating Arts; Ohio Folk Traditions: A New Generation
Publications: Novel Events, newsletter, bimonthly
Activities: Classes for adults and children; film series; lect open to public; concerts; tours; exten dept serves Franklin County; book traveling exhibitions 3 - 4 per year; originate traveling exhibitions

COSHOCTON

M **JOHNSON-HUMRICKHOUSE MUSEUM,*** 300 Whitewoman St, Roscoe Village, 43812. Tel 614-622-8710. *Dir* Mary M Shaw
Open daily 12:00 - 5 PM May through Oct, 1 - 4:30 PM Nov through April, cl Mon, Thanksgiving, Christmas and New Year's Day. No admis fee. Estab 1931, as a gift of two pioneer residents. Museum occupies a school building erected in 1853 and managed by Library Board. Historical Roscoe Village is a restored 19th century canal town
Collections: American Indian baskets and bead work; Aztec, Toltec and Mayan pottery heads; Chinese and Japanese amber, brass, bronze, cloisonne, copper, embroideries, ivory, jade, lacquers, pewter ware, porcelains, prints, wood carvings; European glass, laces, pewter, porcelains, prints; Eskimo artifacts; material from Coshocton County Mound Builders; Miller-Preston bequest of furnishings and implements used by Coshocton County pioneer families
Exhibitions: Permanent collection exhibitions changed periodically; traveling exhibitions
Activities: Educ Dept; gallery talks, lect
L **Library,*** 300 Whitewoman St, Roscoe Village, 43812
Technical books for research supplied by City Library on permanent loan

CUYAHOGA FALLS

L **CREATIVE SCHOOL OF DESIGN LIBRARY,** 2250 Front St, 44221.
Open Tues - Fri 11:30 AM - 5 PM, Sat 11 AM - 1:30 PM. Estab 1960
Library Holdings: Vols 1000; Per subs 20; AV — Slides; Other — Clipping files, exhibition catalogs, framed reproductions, original art works, photographs, prints, reproductions
Activities: Programs on art

M **RICHARD GALLERY AND ALMOND TEA GALLERY,** Divisions of Studios of Jack Richard, 2250 Front St, 44221. *Dir* Jack Richard; *Agent* Jane Williams
Open Tues - Fri 11:30 AM - 5:00 PM, Sat 11 AM - 1:30 PM, Tues Eve 7 PM - 10 PM, cl Sun & Mon, other hours by appointment. No admis fee. Estab Richard Gallery 1960, for exhibition of local, regional and national works of art. Average Annual Attendance: 12,000
Income: Financed privately
Collections: Ball; Brackman; Cornwell; Grell; Gleitsmann; Loomis; Terry Richard; †Oriental
Exhibitions: 50 Women Plus; student exhibits; Japanese Prints; members exhibits; 30 one-person exhibits; Pastel Exhibit Great American Nude; Flowers, Flowers, Flowers; Age Old Masters; Progress and Change in Paintings; Brackman Masterpieces
Activities: Classes for adults and children; Lectures open to public; 5 visiting lectrs per year; 20 gallery talks; 20-25 tours; competitions with awards; scholarships; individual paintings and original objects of art lent; lending collection contains 300 paintings and prints, and 300 cassettes; book traveling exhibitions; originate traveling exhibitions; sales shop sells books, magazines, original art, reproductions, prints and slides; frame shop
L **Library,** 2250 Front St, 44221. Tel 216-929-1575
For reference and limited lending only
Library Holdings: Vols 1000; AV — Kodachromes, motion pictures, rec, slides, v-tapes; Other — Clipping files, framed reproductions, original art works, photographs, prints, reproductions

DAYTON

M **DAYTON ART INSTITUTE,** Forest & Riverview Ave, PO Box 941, 45401. Tel 513-223-5277. *Dir* Bruce H Evans; *Chief Cur* Kent Sobotik; *Asst Cur European Painting & Registrar* Dominique Vasseur; *Asst Cur Decorative Arts* Sue Walsh; *Asst Cur Asian Art* Clarence Kelley; *Assoc Cur Textiles* Helen Pinkney; *Dir Development* Roy Parsons; *Adminr* Marie D Ferguson; *Chmn Education Dept* Doramae O'Kelley; *Public Relations* Peggy Magill
Open Tues - Sun Noon - 5 PM. No admis fee. Estab 1919 for the public benefit. Some of the galleries include: Ancient Gallery, Contemporary Gallery, European 16th-18th Century Gallery, Experiencenter Gallery, Tapestry Gallery, Print Gallery, Special Exhibitions Gallery and an Asian Wing and an American wing. Average Annual Attendance: 150,000. Mem: 2000; dues $20 - $1000; annual meeting April
Collections: †American Collection; European Art From Medieval Period to Present; Oriental Collection;
Exhibitions: The Lines of Art Nouveau; Edward Colonna: 1862-1948; The Bicycle-Evolution of Design; Ink Under Pressure; Saints & Sinners: Old Master Drawings; Eighteenth Century French Prints; The Photography of Imogen Cunningham: A Centennial Selection; Ceramics from Ohio Collections; Chinese Gold & Silver from the Tang Dynasty (AD 618-907) Late 20th Century Art; George Cruikshank, Printmaker; Gene Davis Paintings; Robert Murray Sculpture; Books forms: Patterns Plus; Japanese House; Containers: Japanese Way of Design. Brooke Alexander, A Decade of Print Publishing; Americans in Glass; Classical Tradition in Rajput Painting; Louise Nevelson at 80; Surrealism in Photography
Publications: Annual report, bulletin
Activities: Docent training; classes for adults and children; lect open to public, 3-6 per year; gallery talks; tours; concerts; competitions; Annual Oktoberfest; Guild Volunteer Organization; scholarships; book 6 traveling exhibitions per year; museum store selling books, original art, toys and jewelry
L **Library,** Forest & Riverview Aves, PO Box 941, 45401. Tel 513-223-5277. *Librn* Helen Pinkney
Open Mon - Fri 9 AM - 5 PM. Estab 1922. Open to the public for art reference only
Library Holdings: Vols 23,220; Per subs 124; Auction catalogs; Micro — Fiche; AV — Slides; Other — Clipping files, exhibition catalogs, pamphlets, reproductions
Special Subjects: Architecture
Collections: Louis J P Lott and Walter G Schaeffer, architecture

M **PATTERSON HOMESTEAD,*** 1815 Brown St, 45409. Tel 513-229-9724. *Staff Site Interpreter* Kendal Kleinfeldt; *Staff Site Interpreter* Heather Slade; *Staff Site Interpreter* Marjorie McGraw
Open Apr - Dec Tues - Fri 10 AM - 4 PM, Sun 1 - 4 PM, cl legal holidays. No admis fee. Estab 1953. Patterson Homestead is an 1816 Federal style farmhouse
Collections: Antique & period furniture, ranging from the hand-hewn to highly decorative Victorian Eastlake pieces, including Chippendale, Hepplewhite, Sheraton & American Empire styles; Oil Portraits of members of the Patterson family; Manuscript Collection
Exhibitions: Temporary exhibitions
Activities: Programs for children & grad students affiliated with Wright State Univ; docent program; lectures; tours

C **THE THIRD NATIONAL BANK AND TRUST COMPANY,*** 34 N Main St, 45402. Tel 513-226-6000. *In Charge Art Coll* Judith L Mitchell
Open Mon - Fri 9 AM - 2 PM. No admis fee. Collection estab 1979 dedicated to the people of Dayton and displays in lobbies, offices and public spaces throughout bank
Collections: Collection centers on three major works by Dr R Buckminster Fuller and is augmented by paintings and photographs of Spaceship Earth; paintings, photographs and sculpture
Activities: Tours

WRIGHT STATE UNIVERSITY

M **Fine Arts Gallery,** 45435. Tel 513-873-2896. *Dir* Open
Open Mon - Fri 9:30 AM - 5 PM, Wed & Thur evenings 5 - 8 PM. No admis fee. Estab 1974, devoted to exhibitions of and research in comtemporary art. The gallery is a multi-level contemporary building with 1500 sq feet on each of two levels and 150 running feet of wall space on each level. Available also are areas outside on the campus and selected sites in Dayton. Average Annual Attendance: 20,000
Income: Financed through the university and grants
Collections: Small collection of contemporary art on paper
Exhibitions: Installation or project works by Cecile Abish, Vito Acconci, Patrick Ireland, Robert Irwin, Barry Le Va, Loren Madsen, Dennis Oppenheim, Athena Tacha, John Willenbecher and George Woodman; Exhibitions of existing works by Rudolf Baranik, Richard Fisher, Simone Forti, Jan Groover, Robert Morris, Micchelle Stuart, Paul Sharits and Mary Beth Edelson; regional artists and traveling exhibitions
Publications: Artist's books and exhibition catalogs, 6 per year
Activities: Lect open to public, 4 visiting lectr per year; gallery talks; competitions; individual paintings and art objects lent to faculty and administrative areas; lending collection contains original art works, original prints, paintings, photographs and sculpture; book traveling exhibitions; originate traveling exhibitions; sales desk sells books
L **Dept of Art and Art History Resource Center & Slide Library,** 45435. Tel 513-873-2981. *Slide Cur* Kimberly Sugrue
Open Mon - Fri 8:30 AM - 5 PM. Estab 1970 to serve Wright State University and art professionals in the greater Dayton area. For lending and reference. Circ Approx 300 slides per week
Library Holdings: Vols 200; Per subs 10; Art school catalogs; AV — A-tapes, cassettes, slides, v-tapes; Other — Exhibition catalogs

DELAWARE

M OHIO WESLEYAN UNIVERSITY, Dept of Fine Arts Gallery, Humphreys Art Hall, 43015. Tel 614-369-4431, Ext 650. *Chair* Marty J Kalb; *Dir Exhibitions* Betty Heald
Open daily 9 AM - 4 PM, Sat 9 AM - Noon. No admis fee. Estab 1915
Collections: †Drawings; †photography; †prints
Exhibitions: (1984-85) Invitational Sculpture, Fiber, Metal, Photography, Painting & Prints; faculty & student shows; one person & group shows
Activities: Classes for children; visiting artists workshops; lect open to the public, 10 visiting lectrs per year; art programs; gallery talks; lending collection contains 40,000 slides
L Beeghly Library, 43015. Tel 614-369-4431, Ext 650
Open to the public
Library Holdings: Vols 2400; Per subs 16

FINDLAY

M FINDLAY COLLEGE, Egner Fine Arts Center, 1000 N Main St, 45840. Tel 419-422-8313. *Dir* Douglas Salveson
Open Mon - Fri 9 AM - 4:30 PM. Estab in 1962 as a college art department. Gallery is maintained
Income: Financed by endowment
Collections: †Contemporary prints
Exhibitions: Contemporary Art & Crafts
Activities: Classes for adults and children; dramatic programs; concerts; competitions; scholarships; book shop

GALLIPOLIS

O FRENCH ART COLONY, INC,* 530 First Ave, PO Box 472, 45631. Tel 614-446-3834. *Dir* Jerry Skaggs; *Cur* Janice M Thaler; *Secy* Beth Cherrington; *Treasurer* Peggy Evans; *Public Relations* Pat Houck
Open Tues & Thurs 10 AM - 3 PM, Sat & Sun 1 - 5 PM. No admis fee. Estab 1964 to promote the arts throughout the region. Mem: 275; dues $12 and up; annual meeting last Thurs in Feb
Income: Financed by membership and donations
Exhibitions: Photography, bi-annual; visual arts - annual
Publications: Newsletter, monthly
Activities: Classes for adults and children; dramatic programs; community programs; creative writing; visual art programs and classes; lect open to public; concerts; tours; competitions; 10 - 12 purchase awards; book traveling exhibitions
L Library,* 530 First Ave, PO Box 472, 45631. Tel 614-446-3834
Open Tues & Thurs 10 AM - 3 PM, Sat & Sun 1 - 5 PM. Estab 1972 as small reference library dealing primarily with visual arts
Library Holdings: Vols 2000; Per subs 5; AV — Lantern slides; Other — Exhibition catalogs, pamphlets, prints, reproductions

GAMBIER

M KENYON COLLEGE, Colburn Gallery,* 43022. Tel 614-427-2244. *Coordr* Florence S Lord
Open Mon - Fri 8:30 AM - 8:30 PM, Sat & Sun 1:30 - 8:30 PM, through school year only. No admis fee. Estab 1973 as teaching arm of the Art Department of Kenyon College. Gallery was built 1904 with neo-gothic architecture, and has 153 ft running space. Average Annual Attendance: 1500
Income: Financed by college
Collections: Art collection and items of some historical importance
Exhibitions: Turbulence and Other Commotion, Barry L Gunderson, sculpture; Four Contemporary Photographers: Divola, Henkel, Park, Pfahl; Home Again, Home Again, Martin J Garhart, painter; Two Printmakers: Carl Grupp, Lithographs & James Munce, Intaglio Prints; Contemporary Quilts; Indoor/Outdoor Sculpture, Jeff Fauser; The Faculty Exhibition: Garhart, Parr, Schupbach, Spaid; Procession: The Parthenon Frieze; The Applique Art of Nell Sonneman; GLCA Artists Sponsors Exhibition; Small Sculpture: Don Johnson, metalsmith; Collages and Other Recent Work, David Burkett; Photography Invitational; Annual Mini-Art Show & Sale; Annual Multi-Media Competitive Show
Activities: Lect open to public, visiting lectr; tours; competitions; Honors Day cash awards; individual paintings and original objects of art lent; Book traveling exhibitions

GRANVILLE

M DENISON UNIVERSITY ART GALLERY, Burke Hall of Music & Art, 43023. Tel 614-587-6255. *Dir* George Bogdanovitch; *Registrar & Cur* Letha Schetzsle; *Honorary Cur Burmese Coll* J Terry Bailey
Open Mon - Fri 10 AM - 4 PM; Sun 1 - 4 PM, cl Sat. No admis fee. Estab 1946 for educational and exhibition purposes
Income: Financed through University
Collections: American and European paintings, prints, drawings and sculpture; Burmese textiles, lacquerware and Buddhist sculpture; Chinese bronzes, robes and porcelains; Cuna Indian Molas, Uchus and ceremonial objects; American Indian pottery, baskets and rugs; African sculpture and basketry
Exhibitions: Visiting artists exhibitions; student and senior shows; faculty show; in house show
Publications: Catalogs
Activities: Lect open to public; individual paintings and art objects lent
O American Committe for South Asian Art, Art Dept, Denison, 43023
Estab 1966 to further the study of South & Southeast Asian art history. Publishes slide sets & microfiche on South Asian art. Mem: 200; dues sustaining $100, institutions $20, regular $15, student $7.50; annual meeting in Feb
Publications: Newsletter
Activities: Biennial symposium on all aspects of South & Southeast Asian art history; outreach committee prepares slide sets & film strips for educational purposes

L Art Dept Slide Library,* 43023
Open to students and faculty for reference only
Library Holdings: 50,000 slides

KENT

KENT STATE UNIVERSITY
M School of Art Gallery,* 44242. Tel 216-672-7853. *Dir* Dr Stuart Schar
Open Mon - Fri 9 AM - 4 PM, Sun by appointment, cl school holidays. No admis fee. Estab 1950 as part of the instructional program at Kent State. One main gallery 2200 sq ft; two student galleries; James A Michener Gallery. Average Annual Attendance: 500 weekly
Collections: †Michener Collection, contemporary prints & paintings; permanent collection †sculpture, painting & †prints
Exhibitions: Annual Invitational Painting and Sculpture Show; exhibitions originating at this gallery; faculty and student one-man and group exhibitions; traveling exhibitions from museums
Publications: Brochures; catalogs
Activities: Classes for students in museum preparation; classes for children; lectures open to public, 10-15 vis lect per yr; gallery talks; tours; competitions; individual paintings and original objects of art lent to offices on campus; book traveling exhibitions, 3 per yr

LAKEWOOD

O KENNETH C BECK CENTER FOR THE CULTURAL ARTS, 17801 Detroit Ave, 44107. Tel 216-521-2540. *Pres* Joseph H Albrecht; *VPres* Erna L Berkey; *Secy* Barbara N King; *Managing Dir* Karl A Mackey
Open Mon, Wed, Thurs, Fri & Sat 2 - 5 PM, Sun 2 - 5 PM and 6:30 - 8:30 PM, Performance evenings 7:30 - 9:30 PM, cl Tues. No admis fee. Estab 1976 to present a wide variety of the fine and graphic arts including exhibits from the Cleveland Museum of Art. A North and South Gallery separated by an indoor garden under a skylight roof; total sq footage: approx 3400 sq ft; part of a cultural center which includes a legitimate theatre. Average Annual Attendance: 50,000
Income: Financed by operating cost of the center
Collections: Contemporary pieces including acrylics, collages, etchings, oils, sculpture and watercolors
Exhibitions: Richard Treaster Exhibit, A Show of His Paintings; Proscenium '83; Consuming Passions: The Art of Food & Drink; A Clevelander Collects Clevelanders, 1895-1983; North American Indian Paintings; Art Faculty at Beck Center; An Exhibit by the Laessig Family: Robert, Tom, Nancy, Mark Constance, Joanne; Cleveland Museum of Art Exhibit, Art and the Stage; Cleveland Art Festival Exhibit, Women View Men Telotaxis or Temerity; Fifth Annual Juries Art Show, Proscenium '81; Invitational Preview Reception; Cleveland Museum of Art Exhibits, Cleveland Pottery 1920-1970; Photographs by the Photorealists; Paul Travis, Africa 1927-1928; Cleveland Institute of Art Faculty Show; Industrial Designers of Northern Ohio
Publications: Bulletins; Programs, every five weeks
Activities: Classes for adults and children; dramatic programs; concerts; gallery talks; tours; competitions; cash awards; book traveling exhibitions 5 per year; sales shop sells original art and prints

MANSFIELD

O MANSFIELD FINE ARTS GUILD, Mansfield Art Center, 700 Marion Ave, 44903. Tel 419-756-1700. *Dir* H Daniel Butts III; *Exec Secy* Mrs Henry Van Horn
Open Tues - Sat 11 AM - 5 PM, Sun 12 - 5 PM, cl Mon & national holidays. No admis fee. Estab 1945, incorporated 1956, to maintain an art center in which exhibitions, lectures, gallery talks, special programs, symposia and series of classes for adults and children are provided for the North Central Ohio area; maintained by membership, commission on sales and classes. Gallery dimensions 5000 sq ft with flexible lighting, movable walls, props, etc to facilitate monthly exhibition changes. Average Annual Attendance: 15,000. Mem: 1050; dues $10 - $500; annual meeting in Apr
Exhibitions: Changing exhibitions of member artists' work; traveling shows & locally organized one-man, group and theme exhibitions changing monthly throughout the year
Publications: Annual report; class schedules; monthly newsletter
Activities: Classes for adults and children; lectures open to public, an average of 6 visiting lectr per year; gallery talks mainly for school groups; competitions; scholarships
L Library, 700 Marion Ave, 44903
The library is basically a collection of monographs and studies of styles and periods for teacher and student reference
Library Holdings: Vols 500

MARIETTA

M MARIETTA COLLEGE, Grover M Hermann Fine Arts Center,* 45750. Tel 614-373-4643. *Dir* M Jeanne Tasse
Open Mon - Fri 8 AM - 10:30 PM, Sat 8 AM - 5 PM, Sun 1 - 10:30 PM. No admis fee. Estab 1965. Gallery maintained. Average Annual Attendance: 20,000
Collections: Permanent collection of contemporary American paintings, sculpture and crafts; significant collection of African and pre-Columbian art
Activities: Lect open to public; competitions; book shop

M THE OHIO HISTORICAL SOCIETY, INC, Campus Martius Museum and Ohio River Museum, 601 Second St, 45750. Tel 614-373-3750. *Mgr* John B Briley; *Asst Mgr* Juanita Etter
Open Wed - Sat 9:30 AM - 5 PM, Sun Noon - 5 PM, cl Dec, Jan, Feb, holidays, Mon & Tues Day. Admis adult $2, children 6-12 $1, children 5 and under free. Estab 1920 as part of the Ohio Historical Society to collect, exhibit and interpret

historical items, including art and manuscripts, pertaining to the history of Marietta, the Northwest Territory (Ohio portion) and the Ohio River. Campus Martius Museum has 2500 sq ft of exhibition space on three floors plus a two-story home, a portion of the original fort of 1790-95 enclosed within the building. The Ohio River Museum has approximately 1500 sq ft of exhibition space in three separate buildings connected by walkway. Average Annual Attendance: 70,000

Income: Financed by membership, state appropriation, grants, fund raising, admissions and sales

Collections: Tell City Pilothouse, a replica of the 18th century flatboat; Steamer W P Synder, Jr; decorative arts from 19th century Ohio; early Ohio Paintings, prints, and photographs; items from early Putnam, Blennerhassett and other families; Ohio Company and Marietta materials; Ohio River landscapes

Exhibitions: Ohio Longrifle Exhibit; temporary exhibits

Activities: Classes for adults and children; museum tours; original art objects lent to other museums for exhibitions; sales shop sells books, reproductions, prints, slides, crafts, and souvenir items

MASSILLON

M **MASSILLON MUSEUM,** 212 Lincoln Way E, 44646. *Dir* John Klassen; *Education* Kathy Starr; *Registrar* Margaret Vogt; *Clerk & Treas* Raymond Ruwadi

Open Tues - Sat 9:30 AM - 5 PM, Sun 2 - 5 PM. No admis fee. Estab 1933 as a museum of art and history. The museum places emphasis on the Ohio area by representing the fine arts and crafts and the Massillon area with an historical collection. Average Annual Attendance: 24,000. Mem: 1254; dues $5 and higher

Income: Financed by county appropriations

Collections: †Ceramics, china, costumes, drawings, furniture, †glass, †jewelry, †paintings, prints

Exhibitions: Monthly exhibitions

Publications: Pamphlet of activities and exhibitions, twice yearly

Activities: Classes for adults and children; docent training; lectures open to public; 3 vis lectr per yr; gallery talks; tours; exten dept serves public schools; individual paintings & original objects of art lent to area museums; museum shop sells local arts & crafts

MIDDLETOWN

O **MIDDLETOWN FINE ARTS CENTER,*** AIM Bldg, 130 N Verity Parkway, 45042. Tel 513-424-2416. *Pres* Jo Ashworth; *VPres* Louise Malarky; *Secy* Jane Nerison; *Dir* Larry B Doud

Open Mon - Thurs 9 AM - 9 PM, Fri 9 AM - 4 PM, Sat 9 AM - Noon. Estab 1957 to provide facilities program and instruction, for the development of interests and skills in the visual arts, for students of all ages from Middletown and its surrounding communities. Average Annual Attendance: 5000

Income: Endowment through funds donated to Arts in Middletown (funding agency)

Exhibitions: 10 to 12 exhibitions per year including American Art Annual; Annual Area Art Show; Annual Clay Day; Annual Student Show; plus one and two-man invitational shows of artists throughout the US

Publications: Brochures publicizing exhibitions, schedule of classes, bi-monthly

Activities: Classes for adults and children Sat mornings; competitions; awards; scholarships; original art work and reproductions sold in bookstore

L **Library,** 130 North Verity Parkway, PO Box 441, 45042. Tel 513-424-2416. *Librn* Pat Butt

Open Mon - Thurs 9 AM - 9 PM, Fri 9 AM - 4 PM, Sat 9 AM - Noon, cl Sun. Estab 1963, to provide information and enjoyment for students and instructors. Library open for lending or reference. Circ 30

Purchases: $131

Library Holdings: Vols 711; Per subs 4; AV — Slides

Collections: All books pertain only to art subjects: Art history; ceramics; crafts; illustrations; references; techniques; theory

MOUNT SAINT JOSEPH

M **COLLEGE OF MOUNT SAINT JOSEPH ON THE OHIO,** Studio San Giuseppe, Art Department, 45051. *Dir* Sr Elizabeth Brown

Open Mon - Fri 8:30 AM - 5 PM, Sun 1:30 - 4:30 PM. No admis fee. Estab 1920 to exhibit a variety of art forms by professional artists, collectors & students. Average Annual Attendance: 3500

Collections: Original prints, paintings & sculpture

Activities: Lectures open to public; concerts; gallery talks; tours; competitions with awards; scholarships; individual paintings & original objects or art lent to staff, faculty & administration

L **Archbishop Alter Library,** Art Department, Mount Saint Joseph, 45051. *Dir* Cheryl C Alb:echt

Estab 1920 to serve students of art department. Circ 1200

Library Holdings: Vols 3400; Per subs 24; AV — A-tapes, fs, slides; Other — Exhibition catalogs, prints

NEWARK

M **LICKING COUNTY ART ASSOCIATION GALLERY,*** 391 Hudson Ave, 43055. Tel 614-349-8031. *Pres* Robert Mentzer; *Exec Secy* Alice Woolard; *Main Gallery Chairperson* Helen Crumet

Open Oct - June Tues - Sun 1 - 4 PM; school tours by appointment. No admis fee. Estab 1959 to offer nine monthly art exhibits of Ohio and mid-west artists. Three large rooms for monthly shows, also a youth gallery, members gallery and a permanent collection. Second building located at 19 North St adjoining, for art classes and houses a large kiln for ceramics. Average Annual Attendance: 4000. Mem: 400; dues life $150, $50, $10; annual meeting third Tues in May

Income: Financed by membership, annual art auction and Guild's Craft and Art Fair

Collections: Paintings

Publications: Art Print, monthly newsletter

Activities: Classes for adults and children; docent training; monthly programs; lect open to public, 4 visiting lectr per year; gallery talks; tours; demonstrations; competitions; cash awards; fellowships; book traveling exhibitions; sales shop sells, books, original art, prints, craft items, ceramics, jewelry, wood mirrors and stitchery

NORTH CANTON

L **NORTH CANTON PUBLIC LIBRARY,** Little Art Gallery, 185 N Main St, 44720. Tel 216-499-4712. *Library Dir* James Elfrank; *Chmn Art Committee* Mrs William Willis; *Cur Gallery* Mrs John L Zumkehr

Open Mon - Fri 10 AM - 9 PM, Sat 10 AM - 5 PM. No admis fee. Estab 1936 to encourage and promote appreciation and education of fine art, graphic arts, commercial art and other related subjects; also recognizes and encourages local artists by promoting exhibitions of their work. Circ 446. Average Annual Attendance: 5000

Income: Financed by city and state appropriation

Purchases: $500

Library Holdings: Vols 54,014; Per subs 180

Collections: †Original works by contemporary artists

Activities: Classes for adults and children; lectures open to the public; gallery talks; tours; competitions with awards; scholarships; lending collection contains color reproductions

OBERLIN

INTERMUSEUM CONSERVATION ASSOCIATION

For further information, see National and Regional Organizations

M **OBERLIN COLLEGE,** Allen Memorial Art Museum, Main & Lorain Sts, 44074. Tel 216-775-8665. *Actg Dir* William Olander; *Sr Cur* Chloe H Young; *Actg Cur* Elizabeth Shepherd; *Honorary Cur Modern Art* Ellen H Johnson; *Museum Technician & Preparator* Henry Paustain

Open during school year Tues - Fri 11 AM - 5 PM, Sat & Sun 2 - 5 PM, cl Mon; during vacations, summer and spring term Wed - Sun 2 - 5 PM, cl Mon & Tues. No admis fee. Estab 1917 to serve teaching needs of Oberlin College Art Department and other departments of the college and the college community. Original building was designed by Cass Gilbert, a new addition opened in 1977 and was designed by Venturi and Rauch. Average Annual Attendance: 27,000. Mem: 650; dues from $10 for students to $30

Income: Financed by endowment and membership

Collections: †Decorative Arts, †Graphics, †Painting, †Sculpture, from Early Egyptian Period to Present Day

Exhibitions: Frequent traveling exhibitions and specially assembled exhibitions

Publications: Allen Memorial Art Museum Bulletin; catalogues of permanent collections

Activities: Tours; lect open to public; competitions; individual paintings and original objects of art are lent to other institutions for special exhibitions; lending collection contains 250 original art works for lending to students on a semester basis; traveling exhibitions organized and circulated; sales desk selling reproductions, slides and museum publications

L **Clarence Ward Art Library,** Allen Art Bldg, Main & Lorain Sts, 44074. Tel 216-775-8635. *Art Librn* Dr Jeffrey Weidman

Open Mon - Thurs 8 AM - 5:30 PM and 7 - 11 PM, Fri 8 AM - 5:30 PM and 7 - 10 PM, Sat 9 AM - 5 PM, Sun 1 - 5 PM and 7 - 11 PM. Estab 1917 to serve the library needs of the Art Department, the Allen Memorial Art Museum and the Oberlin College community in the visual arts

Income: Financed by appropriations from Oberlin College Libraries

Library Holdings: Vols 43,500; Per subs 250; Auction - sales catalogs 8500; Micro — Fiche, reels; Other — Clipping files, exhibition catalogs 6500, pamphlets, reproductions

Special Subjects: Rare books and periodicals

Collections: Jefferson and Artz Collections of Early Architectural Books; †artists' books

Publications: Bibliographies and library guides, irregular

Activities: Tours

OXFORD

M **MIAMI UNIVERSITY ART MUSEUM,** Patterson Ave, 45056. Tel 513-529-2232. *Dir* David Berreth; *Cur* Sterling Cook; *Educ Coordr* Edna Southard; *Program & Public Relations Coordr* Bonnie C Mason; *Preparator & Registrar* Larry Sheldon

Open Tues - Sun Noon - 5 PM, cl Mon and university holidays. Estab 1972, Art Museum facility opened Fall 1978, to care for and exhibit University art collections, to arrange for a variety of exhibitions from other sources, and for the educational and cultural enrichment for the University and community. Gallery is maintained with exhibition space of 6,363 sq ft, 571 lin ft wall space. Average Annual Attendance: 25,000. Mem: 410

Income: Financed by gift and state appropriation

Purchases: $10,000 - $30,000

Collections: Decorative Arts; †Folk Art, largely Middle European, Middle Eastern, Mexican, Central and South America; †paintings, †prints and †sculptures; Charles M Messer Leica Camera Collection; African art; Gandhara art

Exhibitions: 15 exhibitions per year

Publications: Brochures; catalogs, approx 6-8 per year

Activities: Docent training; lectures open to the public, 4 vis lectr per yr; tours; originate traveling exhibitions

L **Library,*** Patterson Ave, 45056. *Librn* Joann Olson

For reference only

Library Holdings: Vols 1500; Other — Exhibition catalogs

PORTSMOUTH

M **SOUTHERN OHIO MUSEUM CORPORATION,** Southern Ohio Museum & Cultural Center, 825 Gallia St, PO Box 990, 45662. Tel 614-354-5629. *Pres* C Clayton Johnson; *Dir* Craig McDaniel; *Cur* Bryan Sieling; *Public Relations* Kay Bouyack
Open Wed & Thurs 11 AM - 4 PM, Fri 11 AM - 6 PM, Sat & Sun Noon - 4 PM. Admis adults $1, children $.75. Estab 1977 to provide exhibitions & performances. Museum facility is a renovated & refurbished neo-classical building, 21,000 sq ft, constructed in 1916 as a bank. Facility has two temporary exhibit galleries & a theatre. Average Annual Attendance: 30,000. Mem: 800; dues family $20
Income: $100,000 (financed by endowment, membership & city appropriation)
Exhibitions: Focus on: North American puppetry, masks (international), contemporary paintings & sculpture, antique quilts & glass, holography & art of the 1930's
Publications: Annual report; exhibition catalogs, biannual
Activities: Classes for adults & children; dramatic programs; docent training; lectures open to public, 3 vis lectr per yr; exten dept serves county; book traveling exhibitions; originates traveling exhibitions; museum shop sells books, magazines & prints

SALEM

O **G G DRAYTON CLUB,** 864 Heritage Lane, 44460. Tel 216-332-0959. *Pres* Patricia Bauman; *VPres* Thomas Bauman; *Secy* Geraldine Wine; *Treasurer* Jerry Wine
Estab 1979 to research Grace Drayton's art work. Mem: 80; dues $6 per yr
Income: $500 (financed by membership)
Collections: †Grace G Drayton Collection
Publications: International G G Drayton Association Newsletter, quarterly
Activities: Lectures open to public

SPRINGFIELD

M **CLARK COUNTY HISTORICAL SOCIETY,*** Memorial Hall, 45504. Tel 513-324-0657. *Pres* Linda Davis; *Executive Dir & Cur Museum* George H Berkhofer
Open Tues - Fri 9 AM - 4 PM; Sat 9 AM - 1 PM. Estab 1897 for collection and preservation of Clark County history and historical artifacts. Mem: 600; dues family $7.50, individual $5; annual meeting Nov
Income: $25,000 (financed by appropriation)
Collections: European Landscapes; Oil Paintings, mostly mid-late 19th century, of prominent Springfielders
Publications: Newsletter, monthly; annual monograph
Activities: Monthly meetings and lect open to public; restoration project: The David Crabill House (1826), located at Lake Lagonda in Buck Creek State Park; Sales shop sells books
L **Library,*** Memorial Hall, 45504. Tel 513-324-0657
Open to public
Library Holdings: Vols 3000
Collections: Photograph Collection

M **SPRINGFIELD ART CENTER,** 107 Cliff Park Rd, 45501. Tel 513-325-4673. *Chmn Board* Ralph H Wetherbee Jr; *Pres* John C McGregor Jr; *VPres* Dr Jacob C Baas; *Secy* Glenn W Collier; *Treas* Robert E Zinser; *Dir* Patricia D'Arcy Catron
Open Tues - Fri 9 AM - 5 PM; Sat 9 AM - 3 PM; Sun 2 - 4 PM; cl Mon. No admis fee. Estab 1951 for educational and cultural purposes, particularly the encouragement of the appreciation, study of, participation in and enjoyment of the fine arts. Average Annual Attendance: 30,000. Mem: 1000; dues benefactor $100, sustaining $50, family $30, individual $20; meetings third Tues in June
Income: $120,000 (financed by endowment, membership, and tuition fees)
Collections: 19th & 20th Century Artists (mostly American, some French)
Exhibitions: Monthly exhibits
Publications: Newsletter, monthly
Activities: Classes for adults and children; docent training; lect open to public, 6 vis lectr per year; tours gallery talks; competitions with prizes; individual paintings and original objects of art lent; book traveling exhibitions; originate traveling exhibitions; sales shop selling original art and prints
L **Library,** 107 Cliff Park Rd, 45501. Tel 513-325-4673. *Librn* Mary M Miller
Open Tues - Fri 9 AM - 5 PM; Sat 9 AM - 3 PM; Sun 2 - 4 PM. Estab 1973 for art study. For reference only
Income: Financed by endowment and membership
Library Holdings: Vols 2500; Per subs 20; AV — Slides 400; Other — Clipping files, exhibition catalogs, framed reproductions, pamphlets
Special Subjects: Photography
Collections: Axel Bahnsen Photograph Collection
Activities: Lectures open to public

TOLEDO

M **BLAIR MUSEUM OF LITHOPHANES AND CARVED WAXES,** 2032 Robinwood Ave (Mailing add: 2243 Ashland Ave, 43620). Tel 419-243-4115. *Cur* Laurel G Blair
Open by appointment for groups of 10-20. Admis $3. Estab 1965 for the purpose of displaying lithophanes and carved waxes; the only museum of its kind in the world. There are five galleries. Average Annual Attendance: 2500. Mem: 175; dues $12.50
Income: Financed by membership and sales to members
Collections: Lithophane Collection, with 2300 examples is the world's largest (only 1000 can be shown at once); †Wax Collection
Publications: Bulletin, bi-monthly
Activities: Lectures open to the public; original objects of art lent to other museums
L **Library,** 2243 Ashland Ave, 43620
For reference only
Library Holdings: Vols 200; Per subs 25

C **OWENS-CORNING FIBERGLAS CORPORATION,*** Fiberglas Tower, Jefferson & Saint Clair Sts, 43659. Tel 419-248-8000. *Cur* Penny McMorris
Open to public. Estab 1968 to create a pleasant and stimulating work environment for employees; to provide a focal point for contemporary art; supporting the arts both through purchase of works and display of the collection. Collection displayed in company offices in Toledo and other cities
Collections: Approximately 1000 works of art by contemporary American artists

O **SPECTRUM, FRIENDS OF FINE ART, INC,** 5304 Elmer Dr, 43615. Tel 419-531-7769. *Pres* Martin W Nagy; *First VPres* Lou Ann Glover; *Second VPres* Jack Beardsley; *Treas* Richard Mariasy; *Secy* Reen Beatty
Open Tues - Sun 1 - 4 PM; cl Mon. No admis fee. Estab 1976 to encourage and support public appreciation of Fine Art and to organize and promote related activities; promote mutual understanding and cooperation among artists, artist groups and the public; promote beautification of Toledo through use of art work. Clubhouse (3 galleries, sales room office and working studio) part of Crosby Village in Crosby Gardens; large adjacent Art Education Center. Average Annual Attendance: 15,000-20,000. Mem: 350; dues adult $20 - $75, student $12; annual meeting April
Income: Approximately $15,000 - $20,000 (financed by membership & fund-raising events, sales of art, donations)
Exhibitions: (1983) Edison Juried Membership Show; Spectrum Touring Show; Crosby Festival of the Arts; Toledo Festival; spot exhibitions; Summer Fiesta
Publications: Spectrum (newsletter), bi-monthly
Activities: Classes for adults and children; lect open to the public, 4-5 vis lectr per year; competitions; traveling exhibitions organized and circulated; sales shop selling original art

O **TOLEDO ARTISTS' CLUB,*** 5430 Elmer Dr, PO Box 7430, 43615. Tel 419-531-4079. *Pres* Edith D Shears; *First VPres* Ernest Spring; *Second VPres* Dale Keiser; *Secy* Helen Packard; *Treas* Lowell Skilliter
Open Mon - Fri 12 - 4 PM, Sat 9 AM - 1 PM, July - Oct open Sun. Estab 1943. New Clubhouse-Gallery opened at Crosby Gardens, Toledo in August 1979. Mem: 400-500; dues $15 (variable)
Income: Financed by membership and exhibitions
Exhibitions: Approximately 80 pieces of artwork exhibited each month in new Gallery; includes paintings, pottery, sculpture, stained glass
Publications: Newsletter, monthly
Activities: Classes for adults and children; workshops; demonstrations; lect open to the public; competitions; jointly present Crosby Gardens Arts Festival in June with Crosby Gardens, Toledo Forestry Division and the Arts Commission of Greater Toledo; sales shop selling original art

O **TOLEDO FEDERATION OF ART SOCIETIES,** PO Box 5588, 43613. *Pres* Eleanor Bacon; *First VPres* Stephen Johnston; *Second VPres* Louise Egnew; *Recording Secy* Betty Jenkins; *Treas* Robert Martin; *Corresponding Secy* Mary McGowan
Estab 1917 to arrange for annual area exhibition. Mem: 15 area clubs; dues $10; meetings first Sat after first Fri (Sept - May)
Income: Financed by membership, community contributions and fund drive
Collections: †Permanent collection
Exhibitions: Annual Exhibition
Activities: Competitions with cash awards; individual paintings and original objects of art lent to civic organizations; lending collection contains original art works, original prints, paintings, sculpture and fibers

M **TOLEDO MUSEUM OF ART,** Monroe St at Scottwood Ave, Box 1013, 43697. Tel 419-255-8000; Cable TOLMUSART. *Pres* Robert G Wingerter; *Dir* Roger Mandle; *Dir Education* Charles F Gunther; *Registrar* Patricia Whitesides; *Cur of Contemporary Art* Robert F Phillips; *Cur Ancient Art* Kurt T Luckner; *Chief Cur & Cur Decorative Arts* Roger M Berkowitz; *Sr Cur* William Hutton; *Cur of Graphic Arts* Roberta Waddell; *Supv Music* Joyce Smar; *Supt* George Hartman; *Asst Dir* Greg Smith; *Public Relations Coordr* Sandra Krawetz
Open Tues - Sat 9 AM - 5 PM; Sun 1 - 5 PM; cl Mon and legal holidays; Collector's Corner open Tues - Sat 10 AM - 4:30 PM, Sun 1 - 4:30 PM. No admis fee. Estab and incorporated 1901; building erected 1912, additions 1926 and 1933. Museum contains Canaday Gallery, Print Galleries, Glass Gallery, School Gallery, Collector's Corner for sales & rental & a bookstore. Average Annual Attendance: 320,000. Mem: 8000; dues $20 and higher
Collections: Ancient to modern glass; European paintings & decorative arts; American paintings & decorative arts books & manuscripts; Egyptian, Greek, Roman, Near & Far East art
Exhibitions: (1982-83) El Greco of Toledo: An International Exhibition; Twentieth Century Masters: The Thyssen-Bornemisza Collection; Art & Dance; 35th Annual Toledo Area Artists' Exhibition; Earthworks: Land Reclamation as Sculpture; World Print III; Rembrandt: A Matter of Comparison; Mapped Art: Charts, Routes & Regions; Alternatives: A History of Non-traditional Photography; Recent Acquisitions: Old Master & Early 20th Century Prints; Recent Acquisitions: Late 19th Century French Prints; Recent Acquisitions: Photographs; Recent Acquisitions: Contemporary American Prints; Students of the School of Design: An Overview; New Instructors: The School of Design; School of Design Sculpture Students; Showcase II-Art Instructors of the Toledo Area; Linda Ames-Bell, painting; Tom Lingeman, sculpture; Jr & Sr High Students in Saturday Classes; Painting Students of the School of Design; Alumni Exhibition, University of Toledo/Toledo Museum of Art Joint Degree Program; School of Design Ceramics Students; Graduating BFA Students
Publications: American Paintings; Art in Glass; Corpus Vasorum Antiquorum; European Paintings; Guide to the Collections; Museum News
Activities: Classes; lect; talk; concerts; book traveling exhibitions; originate traveling exhibitions
L **Library,** Box 1013, 43697. Tel 419-255-8000, Ext 37. *Librn* Anne O Reese; *Asst Librn* Joan L Sepessy
Open Tues - Fri 9 AM - 5 PM (Tues & Thurs 5 - 8:30 PM during university sessions). Estab 1901 to provide resources for the museum's staff
Library Holdings: Vols 44,600; Per subs 300; Micro — Fiche, reels; AV — Lantern slides, slides; Other — Clipping files, exhibition catalogs, photographs

VERMILION

M GREAT LAKES HISTORICAL SOCIETY, 480 Main St, 44089. Tel 216-967-3467. *Pres* Alexander C Meakin; *VPres* Alexander B Cook; *Secy* T A Sykora; *Business Mgr* Arthur N O'Hara
Open daily 11 AM - 5 PM. Admis adults $2, children $.75. Estab 1944 to promote interest in discovering and preserving material about the Great Lakes and surrounding areas. Maintains an art gallery as part of the Maritime History Museum. Average Annual Attendance: 35,000. Mem: 3000; dues from $12 - $1000; meetings May and Oct
Income: $130,000 (financed by endowment, membership and sales from museum store)
Collections: †Collection of Ship Models, †Marine Relics, †Paintings and †Photographs dealing with history of the Great Lakes
Exhibitions: Annual Model Boat Show Exhibition
Publications: Chadburn (newsletter), quarterly; Inland Seas, quarterly journal
Activities: Educ dept; lect open to public, 2 vis lectr per year; tours; competitions; awards; book traveling exhibitions, 2 per year; sales shop selling books, magazines, original art, reproductions, prints, slides and gifts

WELLINGTON

M SPIRIT OF '76 MUSEUM, Southern Lorain County Historical Society, 201 N Main, PO Box 76, 44090. Tel 216-647-4531. *Pres* Howard Arndt; *VPres* Albert Grimm; *Secy* Margaret Henes; *Museum Dir* Ernst L Henes
Open April - Nov 2:30 - 5 PM, groups of ten or more by reservation. No admis fee. Estab 1970 to memorialize Archibald M Willard who created the Spirit of '76, nation's most inspirational painting. Average Annual Attendance: 2000. Mem: 237; dues couples $5, individual $3; annual meeting April
Income: $10,000 (financed by membership, city appropriation, gifts and gift shop)
Purchases: $10,000
Collections: Archibald M Willard Paintings; artifacts of local interest
Publications: Newsletters
Activities: Sales shop sells books, reproductions, prints and miscellaneous items

WEST LIBERTY

M PIATT CASTLES,* 10051 Rd 47, 43357. Tel 513-465-2821. *Pres* William N Piatt Sr; *Secy & Treas* Frances Piatt
Mac-A-Check Castle open Mar - Nov daily 11 AM - 5 PM; Mac-O-Chee Castle May - Sept daily 11 AM - 5 PM. Castle Piatt Mac-A-Cheek, modeled on French fortified castle, 1864; Castle Mac-O-Chee, modeled on Flemish castle, 1879
Collections: Early American & French period family furnishings; Rare Art
Publications: Brochures, historic castles
Activities: Tours

WILLOUGHBY

O FINE ARTS ASSOCIATION, School of Fine Arts, 38660 Mentor Ave, 44094. Tel 216-951-7500. *Pres* Alan D Wright; *Executive Dir* James J Savage; *Secy* Mrs Arthur P Armington; *Visual Arts Coordr* Doris Foster
Open Mon - Fri 9 AM - 8 PM, Sat 9 AM - 5 PM, and performance times. No admis fee. Estab 1957 to bring arts education to all people regardless of their ability to pay, race or social standing. Gallery maintained. Average Annual Attendance: 30,000. Mem: 500; dues $20 and up; annual meeting Sept
Income: Financed by class fees and donations
Exhibitions: (1983-84) Monthly exhibitions, theme, one man and group; Annual juried exhibit for area artists; Annual outdoor Arts Festival
Activities: Classes for adults and children; dramatic programs; lectures open to the public, 10 - 15 vis lectr per year; gallery talks; tours; concerts; theatre productions; competitions awards; scholarships; three county area served by extension department; material available to schools and organizations

WOOSTER

M COLLEGE OF WOOSTER ART CENTER MUSEUM, University St, 44691. Tel 216-264-1234, Ext 388. *Dir* Dr Arnold Lewis; *Asst Mus Dir* Phyllis Blair Clark; *Installations* Walter Lurka; *Installations* Kathleen McManus
Open Mon - Sat 9 AM - Noon & 1 - 5 PM; Sun 2 - 5 PM. No admis fee. Estab 1944 to provide an opportunity for students, faculty and the local community to view original works of art. The gallery is housed in a former library; Main floor has large open areas and upper balcony more intimate exhibition space. Average Annual Attendance: 5000
Income: $7000 (financed through college)
Collections: Chinese bronzes & porcelains; paintings; prints; sculpture; tapestries
Exhibitions: Invitational Functional Ceramics Exhibition; traveling and monthly exhibitions
Publications: Functional Ceramics Catalogue, annually
Activities: Lect open to public, 10 - 15 vis lectr per year; gallery talks; books traveling exhibitions

YELLOW SPRINGS

M ANTIOCH COLLEGE, Noyes, Read and Grey Galleries, 45387. Tel 513-767-7331, Ext 464. *Project Dir* Karen Shirley
Open Mon - Fri 1 - 4 PM. No admis fee. Estab 1972. Noyes Gallery to offer works to students and the community that both challenge and broaden their definitions of Art; Grey Gallery is a small photo gallery; Read Gallery is primarily a student gallery. Average Annual Attendance: 3000
Exhibitions: (1982-83) Three Ohio Artists: Calkowal, photographs; The Armchair Sailor; Mark Soppeland, sculpture; Betty Collings, sculpture; visiting artist Peter Berg, drawings

YOUNGSTOWN

M BUTLER INSTITUTE OF AMERICAN ART, 524 Wick Ave, 44502. Tel 216-743-1107. *Dir* Dr Louis A Zona; *Assoc Dir* Clyde Singer; *Education* Peggy Kaulback
Open Tues, Thur - Sat 11 AM - 4 PM; Wed 11 AM - 8 PM; Sun Noon - 4 PM. No admis. Estab 1919, and is the first museum building to be devoted entirely to American Art. Twelve galleries containing 11,000 works of American artists. Average Annual Attendance: 90,000. Mem: 1114 (Friends of American Art, art auxiliary organization); dues $5 - $250; annual meetings in May
Income: Financed by endowment, grants and gifts
Collections: American Paintings Dating from 1719 to Present: Oils, Watercolors, Drawings, Sculpture and Ceramics; Glass Bells; Paintings and Drawings of the American Indian; Seven Ship Scale Models; †32 Paintings of Clipper Ships from Sail to Steam; prints
Exhibitions: Annual Midyear Show (national painting); Area Artists Annual; Ohio Ceramic Annual; Polish Arts Club Show; Youngstown State University Annual; Photo Show; one-person exhibitions
Publications: Exhibition catalogues
Activities: Classes for children; docent training; lect open to the public, 15 lectr per year; concerts; gallery talks; tours; competitions with awards; individual paintings and original objects of art lent to qualified museums, institutions, world wide; book traveling exhibitions, 1-2 per year; traveling exhibitions organized and circulated; museum shop sells books, original art, reproductions, prints, slides, crafts and art related materials
L Library, 524 Wick Ave, 44502. Tel 216-743-1107, 743-1711
For reference only
Income: Financed by endowment, grants and gifts
Library Holdings: Vols 1500; Per subs 10; AV — Kodachromes, slides; Other — Clipping files, exhibition catalogs, memorabilia, pamphlets, photographs
Special Subjects: American Art

M YOUNGSTOWN STATE UNIVERSITY, Kilcawley Center Art Gallery, 410 Wick Ave, 44555. Tel 216-742-3560. *Art Gallery & Craft Center Coordr* Sherri Hill
Open Mon & Fri 10 AM - 4 PM, Tues - Thurs 10 AM - 8 PM, Sat 11 AM - 3 PM. Estab 1974 to provide the university and the community with a diversified art program. Gallery is 120 running ft. Average Annual Attendance: 10,000
Income: Financed by university appropriation
Purchases: $1000
Collections: †Kilcawley Collection includes works by Alan Davie, Gene Davis, Jim Dine, Don Eddy, Sam Gilliam, Robert Indiana, Jasper Johns, Alfred Leslie, Roy Lichtenstein, Robert Motherwell, Claes Oldenburg, Robert Rauschenberg, James Rosenquist, Alen Shields, Jack Tworkov, Andy Warhol
Activities: Lect open to the public, 2-3 vis lectr per year; gallery talks; concerts; competitions with awards; original objects of art lent

ZANESVILLE

O ZANESVILLE ART CENTER, 620 Military Rd, 43701. Tel 614-452-0741. *Dir* Dr Charles Dietz; *Secy & Registrar* Mrs Joseph Howell; *Pres Board Trustees* Dr Paul Jones; *Pres Board Dir* Bert Hendley; *Cur Oriental Art* Mrs Willis Bailey; *Cur Glass* William Brown
Open Tues - Sun 1 - 5 PM; cl Fri & holidays. No admis fee. Estab 1936 to provide a public center for the arts and crafts, permanent collections and temporary exhibitions, classes in art and crafts, library of art volumes and a meeting place for art and civic groups. There are twelve galleries for Old and Modern Masters' paintings, sculpture, prints, ceramics, glass, photography, children's art and gift art; handicapped facilities. Average Annual Attendance: 25,000. Mem: 300; dues $10 and up
Income: Financed by endowment, membership
Collections: †American, European and †Oriental Paintings, Sculptures, Ceramics, Prints, Drawings, and Crafts; †Children's Art; †Midwestern and †Zanesville Ceramics and Glass
Exhibitions: (1983) Selections of permanent collection; recent accessions; Edwin Shuttleworth & Don Getz, paintings; April Grigsby, ceramics; American Association University Women's Sponsored Children's Scholastic Art; Hal Scroggy, water colors; Michele Colopy, photographs; 41st Annual May Art & Crafts Exhibition; Spring Flower Show; Richard Phipps, water colors; Ray Mylius, color photos; Ohio Governor's Regional Scholastic Show; Dr Robert Morrison, paintings & drawings; Sally Emslie, water colors; Mrs Henry Luburgh, button collections; Southeastern Ohio Watercolor Society Exhibition; Marson Graphics Inc, original graphics; Madaline Pepper, water media paintings; Janet Bailey, minimacrame jewelry; Jo Hune, floral & plant arrangements; Celeste Wince, color photographs; Paula Cassady, quilts & pillows; Elaine Balderston, landscape photos & fibre hangings
Publications: Bulletin, monthly
Activities: Classes for adults and children; docent training; lectures open to public, 5 vis lectr per year; concerts; gallery talks; tours; competitions with awards; individual paintings lent to public institutions; lending collection contains 6000 pieces of original art works, 500 original prints, 2000 paintings, 200 photographs & 50 sculpture; sales shop sells books & original art
L Library, 620 Military Rd, 43701. Tel 614-452-0741. *Librn* Mrs Joseph Howell
Open Mon - Thur 1 - 5 PM, cl Fri and major holidays. Estab 1936 to provide fine arts and crafts information
Income: Financed by endowment, membership, trust funds and investments
Library Holdings: Vols 6000; Per subs 10; AV — Fs 20, Kodachromes 10,000, lantern slides, slides 10,000; Other — Clipping files, exhibition catalogs, framed reproductions 10, original art works, pamphlets, photographs, prints, reproductions, sculpture
Special Subjects: Midwestern Glass and Ceramics
Publications: Bulletins

OKLAHOMA

ANADARKO

M NATIONAL HALL OF FAME FOR FAMOUS AMERICAN INDIANS, Box 808, 73005. Tel 405-247-5795. *Pres* Allie Reynolds; *Executive VPres & Dir* Paul T Stonum; *Treas & Secy* Sally Stonum
Open during daylight hours, seven days a week. No admis fee. Estab 1952 to honor famous American Indians who have contributed to the culture of America, including statesmen, innovators, sportsmen, warriors; to teach the youth of our country that there is a reward for greatness. An outdoor Museum in a landscaped area containing bronze sculptured portraits of honorees. Average Annual Attendance: 10,000. Mem: 1000; dues life $100, family $10, individual $5; annual meeting August
Income: Financed by membership, city and state appropriation and donation
Purchases: $2500 - $5000
Collections: Bronze sculptured portraits and bronze statues of two animals important to Indian culture
Publications: Brochure
Activities: Seminars of American Indian culture held during dedication ceremonies for honorees in August

M SOUTHERN PLAINS INDIAN MUSEUM, US Hwy 62, PO Box 749, 73005. Tel 405-247-6221. *Cur* Rosemary Ellison
Open (June - Sept) Mon - Sat 9 AM - 5 PM; Sun 1 - 5 PM; (Oct - May) Tues - Sat 9 AM - 5 PM; Sun 1 - 5 PM; cl New Year's Day, Thanksgiving and Christmas. No admis fee. Estab 1947-48 to promote the development of contemporary native American arts and crafts of the United States. Administered and operated by the Indian Arts and Crafts Board, US Department of the Interior. Average Annual Attendance: 80,000
Income: Financed by federal appropriation
Purchases: Primarily dependent upon gifts
Collections: Contemporary native American arts and crafts of the United States; Historic Works by Southern Plains Indian Craftsmen
Exhibitions: Contemporary Southern Plains Indian Metalwork; continuing series of one-person exhibitions; changing exhibitions by contemporary native American artists and craftsmen; Historic Southern Plains Indian Arts
Publications: One-person exhibition brochure series, monthly
Activities: Gallery talks; traveling exhibitions organized and circulated

ARDMORE

O CHARLES B GODDARD CENTER FOR THE VISUAL AND PERFORMING ARTS, First & D St SW, 73401. Tel 405-226-0909. *Pres* Mrs Leon Daube; *Secy* Richard Colvert; *Managing Dir* Laurence London; *Treas* John Snodgrass; *Dir* Robert Batis; *Dir* James E Thompson; *Office Secy* Lonna Martin
Open Mon - Fri 9:30 AM - 4 PM; Sat 11 AM - 4 PM. No admis fee. Estab March 1970 to bring fine art programs in the related fields of music, art and films to local community at minimum cost; gallery to bring traveling exhibitions to Ardmore. Average Annual Attendance: 35,000. Mem: 400; dues $5 - $1000; monthly advisory board meeting, and semi-annual primary board meeting
Collections: Portraits, paintings and drawings
Publications: Outlook, monthly
Activities: Classes for adults and children in dancing, art, pottery, piano, adult ballroom dancing, ladies exercise and movement classes; dramatic programs; lectures open to the public, 5 vis lectr per yr; concerts; gallery talks; competitions with awards; books for sale

BARTLESVILLE

M FRANK PHILLIPS MUSEUM, Woolaroc Museum, State Hwy 123, Route 3, 74003. Tel 918-336-0307. *Dir* Robert R Lansdown; *Cur Art* Linda Stone; *Museum Artist* Francis Letchworth
Open Mon - Sun 10 AM - 4:30 PM, cl Thanksgiving Day, Christmas Day. No admis fee. Estab 1929 to house art and artifacts of the Southwest. Museum dedicated to Frank Phillips. Gallery has two levels, 6 rooms upstairs and 3 rooms downstairs. Average Annual Attendance: 200,000
Income: Financed by endowment
Collections: American Indian artifacts; prehistoric artifacts; paintings, drawings, graphics, minerals, oriental material, sculpture, weapons
Publications: Woolaroc Story; Woolaroc, museum guidebook
Activities: Gallery talks; tours; lending collection contains transparencies to be used to illustrate educational publications; book traveling exhibitions; museum & sales shops sell books, magazines, original art, reproductions, prints, slides, Indian-made jewelry and pottery, postcards

CLAREMORE

M WILL ROGERS MEMORIAL AND MUSEUM, W Will Rogers Blvd, PO Box 157, 74017. Tel 918-341-0719. *Dir* Dr Reba Neighbors Collins; *Cur* Gregory Malak; *Secy* Marjorie Williams
Open Daily 8 AM - 5 PM. No admis fee. Estab 1938 to perpetuate the name, works, and spirit of Will Rogers. There are three main galleries, diorama room, foyer and gardens. The large Jo Davidson statue of Will Rogers dominates the foyer; the north gallery includes photographs and paintings of Will Rogers and his ancestors (including a family tree, explaining his Indian heritage), and many other personal items; east gallery has saddle collection and other Western items; Jo Mora dioramas; additional gallery, research library and theatre. Average Annual Attendance: 500,000
Income: $300,000 (financed by state appropriation)
Collections: Borein Etchings; Busts by James Hamilton; Bust by Electra Wagoner Biggs; Collection of Paintings by Various Artists commissioned by a calendar company with originals donated to Memorial; Count Tamburini Oil of Will

Rogers; Jo Mora Dioramas (13); Large Equestrian Statue by Electra Wagoner Biggs; Mural by Ray Piercey; Original of Will Rogers by Leyendecker; Paintings of Will and his Parents by Local Artists; original of Will Rogers by Charles Banks Wilson
Publications: Brochures and materials for students
Activities: Lect; films; assist with publishing project of Will Rogers works at Oklahoma State University; lending collection contains motion pictures, 50 photographs, 144 slides, 20 minute documentary of Will Rogers available to nonprofit organizations; originate traveling exhibitions; museum shop selling books, magazines, reproductions of original photographs in sepiatone, slides

L Media Center Library, W Will Rogers Blvd, PO Box 157, 74017
Reference library for research by appointment only; A new media center scheduled to open Nov 1982 will be used to show films and documentaries
Library Holdings: Vols 600; Per subs 15; original writings; AV — A-tapes, cassettes, fs, Kodachromes, motion pictures, rec, slides, v-tapes; Other — Clipping files, framed reproductions, manuscripts, memorabilia, original art works, pamphlets, photographs, prints, reproductions, sculpture
Collections: Will Rogers Collection

ENID

M PHILLIPS UNIVERSITY, Grace Phillips Johnson Art Gallery, University Station, 73701. Tel 405-237-4433. *Cur* Pricilla Bain-Smith, PhD
Open Tues - Fri 10 AM - 5 PM; Sat, Sun & holidays 2 - 5 PM; cl national holidays. No admis fee. Estab 1966
Collections: Decorative arts; historical material of the University; paintings, prints, sculpture
Exhibitions: Exhibitions from the collection; traveling exhibitions
Publications: Exhibition catalogs, bi-annual
Activities: Lect; gallery talks; tours; competitions; book traveling exhibitions

GOODWELL

M NO MAN'S LAND HISTORICAL SOCIETY MUSEUM, Sewell St, PO Box 278, 73939. Tel 405-349-2670. *Pres* Henry C Hitch, Jr; *Museum Dir* Dr Harold S Kachel; *Cur & Secy* Joan Overton Kachel
Open Tues - Fri 9 AM - 5 PM, Sun 1 - 5 PM; cl Mon, Sat & holidays. No admis fee. Estab 1934 to procure appropriate museum material with special regard to portraying the history of No Man's Land (Oklahoma Panhandle) and the immediate adjacent regions. The gallery is 14 ft x 40 ft (560 sq ft). Average Annual Attendance: 4000. Mem: 59; dues life $100, organization $10, individual $10
Income: Financed by state appropriation and donations
Collections: Duckett Alabaster Carvings; Oils by Pearl Robison Burrows Burns
Exhibitions: Nine exhibits each year by local artists; six exhibits by local craftsmen each year
Activities: Lect open to public, 2 vis lectr per year; gallery talks; tours

LANGSTON

M LANGSTON UNIVERSITY ART GALLERY,* 73050. Tel 405-466-2231
Open Mon - Fri 8 AM - 5 PM. No admis fee. Estab 1959 to exhibit pertinent works of art, both contemporary and traditional; to serve as a teaching tool for students. Average Annual Attendance: 6000
Income: Financed by state appropriation
Collections: Award purchases
Activities: Classes for adults; lect, 2 vis lectr per year; gallery talks; tours

LAWTON

M INSTITUTE OF THE GREAT PLAINS, Museum of the Great Plains, 601 Ferris, PO Box 68, 73502. Tel 405-353-5675. *Dir* Steve Wilson; *Cur Anthropology* Dan Provo; *Cur Exhibits* William Austin; *Cur Education* Linda Miles; *Archaeologist* John Northcutt; *Exhibits Technician* Andy Gallup; *Photo Technician* Gil Nunn
Open Mon - Fri 8 AM - 5 PM, Sat 10 AM - 5:30 PM, Sun 1:30 - 5:30 PM. No admis fee. Estab 1961 to collect, preserve, interpret, and exhibit items of the cultural history of man in the Great Plains of North America. Galleries of the Museum of the Great Plains express a regional concept of interpreting the relationship of man to a semiarid plains environment. Average Annual Attendance: 90,000. Mem: 700; dues $7.50
Income: Financed by endowment, city and state appropriations
Collections: Archaeological, ethnological, historical, and natural science collections relating to man's inhabitance of the Great Plains; photographs relating to Plains Indians, agriculture, settlement, ranching
Exhibitions: Lawton Jr Service League Annual Juried Art Show; history, archaeology, and ethnological exhibits
Publications: Great Plains Journal, annual; Contributions to the Museum of the Great Plains 1-9, irregular; Museum Newsletter, irregular
Activities: Classes for children; dramatic programs; docent training; lect open to public, 6 vis lectr per year; gallery talks; museum shop selling books, magazines, original art, reproductions, prints

L Research Library, Sixth & Ferris, 73502. Tel 405-353-5676. *Cur Special Coll* Paula Williams
Open Mon - Fri 8 AM - 5 PM. Estab 1961 to provide research materials for the 10-state Great Plains region. Lending to staff only
Income: Financed by endowment, city and state appropriations
Library Holdings: Vols 20,000; Per subs 100; Documents 200,000; Micro — Reels; Other — Photographs 20,000
Special Subjects: Archaeology, Anthropology
Collections: Archives; photographic collections

MUSKOGEE

M BACONE COLLEGE MUSEUM,* Ataloa Lodge, 74401. Tel 918-683-4581,
Ext 212. *Dir* Frances Donelson
Open Mon - Fri 10 AM - 4:30 PM. No admis fee. Estab to enhance Indian
culture by having a collection of artifacts from various Indian tribes. One large
room. Average Annual Attendance: 1000
Income: Financed through Bacone College
Collections: Indian crafts and artifacts: silverwork, weapons, blankets, dolls,
beadwork, pottery, weaving and basketry; Indian Art
Activities: Tours

M FIVE CIVILIZED TRIBES MUSEUM, Agency Hill, Honor Heights Dr,
74401. Tel 918-683-1701. *Pres* John T Griffin Jr; *Secy* Charlene Adair; *Dir* Mrs
Spencer Denton
Open Mon - Sat 10 AM - 5 PM, Sun 1 - 5 PM. Admis adults $1, students $.25.
Estab 1966 to exhibit artifacts, relics, history, and traditional Indian art of the
Cherokee, Chickasaw, Choctaw, Creek, and Seminole Indian Tribes. Average
Annual Attendance: 42,500. Mem: 1400; dues $10-$300; annual meetings Apr
and Oct
Income: $48,000 (financed by membership, and admissions)
Collections: †Traditional Indian art by known artists of Five Tribes heritage
Exhibitions: Annual Judged Exhibition and Sale of Beadwork, Pottery, Basketry
and Silver; Competitive Art Show; Students Competitive Show
Publications: Newsletter, bimonthly
Activities: Competitions with awards; museum shop selling books, magazines,
original art, reproductions, prints, beadwork, pottery, basketry and other
handmade items
L Library, Agency Hill, Honor Heights Dr, 74401. *Chmn* Frances R Brown
Open Mon - Sat 10 AM - 5 PM, Sun 1 - 5 PM. Estab 1966 to preserve history,
culture, traditions, legends, etc of Five Civilized Tribes (Cherokee, Creek,
Choctaw, Chickasaw, and Seminole tribes). Maintains an art gallery
Income: Financed by museum
Library Holdings: Vols 3500; Per subs 5; original documents; AV — Cassettes,
lantern slides; Other — Clipping files, exhibition catalogs, framed reproductions,
manuscripts, memorabilia, original art works, pamphlets, photographs, prints,
reproductions, sculpture
Publications: Newsletter, every three months

NORMAN

UNIVERSITY OF OKLAHOMA
M Museum of Art, 410 W Boyd St, 73019. Tel 405-325-3272. *Dir* Sam Oklinetzky;
Asst Dir Edwin J Deighton; *Museum Secy* Mary Cook; *Public Programs
Specialist* Lyn Rowden; *Exhibition Asst* Randy Scott
Open Tues - Fri 11 AM - 4 PM, Sat 11 AM - 2 PM, Sun 1 - 4 PM, cl Mon &
holidays. Estab 1936 to provide cultural enrichment for the people of Oklahoma;
to collect, preserve, exhibit and provide research in art of all significant periods.
Approx 15,000 sq ft for permanent and temporary exhibitions on two indoor
levels; 30 ft high, carpeted walls in 3 galleries; 2 galleries 120 sq ft each. Average
Annual Attendance: 50,000. Mem: 360; dues $15 - $100; meetings Sept & Jan
Income: Financed by university allocation
Collections: African sculpture; †American all media; †crafts; European all media;
oceanic art; †photography
Exhibitions: (1982) Autochromes: Color Photography Comes of Age; Artists
Quilts; Stanton MacDonald-Wright Watercolors; (1983) Eisenstadt's Germany;
China From Within; First International Shoebox Sculpture Exhibition; The
California Flea Market Series--Joel D Levinson Photographs; Visions '83; (1984)
Second US Biennial; Marjorie Strider: 10 years 1970-80
Publications: Calendar of activities; posters; announcements
Activities: Docent training; lect open to public; concerts; gallery talks; tours;
competitions; individual paintings and original objects of art lent to other
museums and galleries; lending collection contains original art works and prints,
paintings; museum shop selling books, magazines, original art, slides
L School of Architecture Library,* 73019. Tel 405-325-5521. *Libr Technician* Ilse
Davis
Library Holdings: Vols 10,044; Per subs 85
Special Subjects: Architecture, Landscape Architecture, Urban & Environmental
Design
L Art Library, 550 Parrington Oval, Room 203 Jacobson Hall, 73019. Tel 405-325-
2841. *Art Library Supervisor* Don Koozer
Open Mon - Thurs 8 AM - 5 PM, 7 - 9 PM, Fri 8 AM - 5 PM, Sun 1 - 4 PM, cl
Sat. Estab to provide instructional support to the academic community of the
university and general service to the people of the state. Circ 6900
Income: Financed by state appropriation
Library Holdings: Vols 11,000; Per subs 50; Micro — Fiche, reels

OKLAHOMA CITY

**M NATIONAL COWBOY HALL OF FAME AND WESTERN HERITAGE
CENTER,** 1700 NE 63rd St, 73111. Tel 405-478-2250. *Exec Dir* Dean Krakel;
Managing Dir Rich Muno; *Pub Relations Dir* Marsi Staggs; *Cur Coll* Don
Reeves; *Art Dir* Ed Muno; *Registrar* David Williams
Open daily 9:30 AM - 5:30 PM; summer 8:30 AM - 6 PM; cl New Year's Day,
Thanksgiving & Christmas Day. Admis adults $3, children $1, group rates
available for 10 or more persons. Estab 1965 as a memorial shrine to great
Westerners. Museum includes western history and art. Mem: 5000; dues $25 and
up; annual meeting Apr
Income: Financed by membership
Collections: Albert K Mitchell Russell-Remington Collection; †contemporary
western art; Fechin Collection; Schreyvogel Collection; Taos Collection; John
Wayne Collection, kachinas, guns, knives & art; western art; James Earle &
Laura G Fraser Studio Collection; Great Western Performers Portrait Collection;
Rodeo Portrait Collection
Publications: Persimmon Hill Magazine, quarterly
Activities: Western Heritage Awards in April; Rodeo Hall of Fame Inductions in
December

L Library, 1700 NE 63rd St, 73111
For reference only
Library Holdings: Vols 7000; Per subs 75

O OKLAHOMA ART CENTER, Plaza Circle-Fair Park, 3113 Pershing Blvd,
73107. Tel 405-946-4477. *Pres* Richard D Harrison; *VPres* Jack Tway; *VPres*
Mrs Dan Hogan; *Dir* Lowell Adams; *Assoc Dir* Mary Kathryn Adams; *Public
Relations Dir* Kate Hammett
Open Tues - Sat 10 AM - 5 PM, Sun 1 - 5 PM, cl holidays. Admis $2. Estab
1936 and incorporated 1946 to encourage regional art activity and to present an
educational program for adults and children. Three facilities of 35,000 sq ft.
Average Annual Attendance: 80,000. Mem: 2000; dues $25 and up; annual
meeting in June
Income: Financed by Private funding, memberships, donation grants
Purchases: Lowell Nesbitt, Parrott Tulip; Jack Levine, Old Mortality; Frank
Collection of Geonian, expressionist prints
Collections: †American contemporary paintings and sculpture (including
Washington Gallery of Modern Art complete collection and Eight State purchase
awards); †American masters paintings; †contemporary prints, drawings,
watercolors; †historical survey of prints and drawings
Exhibitions: Annual Eight State Exhibition of Painting and Sculpture; National
Exhibition of Prints and Drawings; Oklahoma Designer-Craftsmen Exhibition;
Young Talent of Oklahoma (juried high school show with awards of seven
college scholarships); (1982) Francoise Gelot Retrospective; Major American
Show; The Phillips Collection: Impressionism and The Modern Vision
Publications: Exhibition catalogs
Activities: Classes for adults & children; dramatic programs; docent training;
lectures open to public, 6-10 vis lectr per yr; concerts; gallery talks; tours;
competitions with awards; exten dept serves downtown public; individual
paintings & original objects of art lent to state agencies & other museums; book
traveling exhibitions; originate traveling exhibitions; museum shop sells books,
magazines, original art, reproductions, prints & gifts
L Library, 3113 Pershing Blvd, 73107. Tel 405-946-4477
Open Tues - Fri 10 AM - 4 PM. Estab 1965 to provide art reference materials
Income: Financed by endowment, membership and Allied Arts contributions
Library Holdings: Vols 1500; AV — Slides
Collections: Doughty Bird Ceramics; 20th century American art and graphics
Publications: Catalogues of exhibitions
Activities: Classes for adults and children; dramatic programs; docent training;
lect open to public; 5-10 vis lectr per year; concerts; gallery talks; tours;
competitions with awards; scholarships; exten dept serves center of metro area,
downtown gallery and Artsplace II; originate traveling exhibitions to other
regional museums
O Arts Place II,* 115 Park Ave, 73116. Tel 405-232-1787. *Mgr* June C Parsons;
Dir Pat Gallagher
Open Mon - Fri 10 AM - 4 PM. No admis fee. Estab 1977 to promote the visual
and performing arts by providing these experiences to downtown and offering
fine arts and crafts for sale and rental by offices and houses. Exhibition gallery,
performing arts area, sales and rental gallery
Income: Financed by membership and donations
Publications: OAC Bulletin; bi-monthly mailer listing exhibitions and
performances
Activities: Classes for adults and children; dramatic programs; docent training;
lect open to public, 12-15 vis lectr per year; concerts; gallery talks; tours;
competitions; artmobile; individual paintings and original objects of art lent;
lending collection contains original art works and prints, paintings, photographs,
sculpture; traveling exhibitions organized and circulated; sales shop selling books,
magazines, original art, reproductions, prints

M OKLAHOMA CENTER FOR SCIENCE AND ART, Kirkpatrick Center, 2100
NE 52nd, 73111. Tel 405-424-5545 (Omniplex); 427-5461 (Kirkpatrick Center);
424-1443 (Air Space Museum). *Pres, Board Governors* John E Kirkpatrick; *Dir
Kirkpatrick Ctr* Dr William L Hommel; *Cur Kirkpatrick Ctr* Peggie McCracken;
Coordr Indian Gallery Douglas Cummings; *Coordr Sanamu African Gallery*
Hannah Atkins; *Coordr Japanese Gallery* Earl Nichols; *Coordr Photography Hall
Fame* Edye Draper; *Dir Omniplex* Sheman Kent; *Dir Air Space Museum*
Clarence Page
Open Mon - Sat 10 AM - 5 PM, Sun 12 - 5 PM. Admis galleries free; admis
Omniplex: adults $2.50; children 12 and under and sr citizens $1.25, children
under 5 free; admis Air Space Museum: adults $2.50, children $1.50. Estab 1958
to focus on the inter-relationships between science, arts and the humanities and
to supplement educational facilities offered in the public schools in the areas of
arts and sciences. The Kirkpatrick Center houses Omniplex, a hands-on science
museum; museum shop; George Sutton bird paintings; Oklahoma Aviation and
Space Hall of Fame and Museum; Center of American Indian Gallery; Sanamu
African Gallery; Oriental Art Gallery; International Photography Hall of Fame;
Oklahoma Zoological Society Offices; Kirkpatrick Planetarium; miniature
Victorian house; antique clocks; US Navy Gallery; retired sr volunteer program;
Oklahoma City Zoo offices. Average Annual Attendance: 200,000
Income: Financed by membership, private donations, Allied Arts Foundation,
admission fees, and class tuition
Collections: European and Oriental Ivory Sculpture; Japanese Woodblock Prints;
Oceanic art; Pre-Columbian and American Indian art; Sutton paintings;
Traditional and Contemporary African art; 1,000 photographs in Photography
Hall of Fame
Exhibitions: Changing exhibitions every six to 10 weeks
Publications: Insights, quarterly; Omniplex Newsletter, monthly
Activities: Classes for adults and children; docent training; lect open to public;
tours; book traveling exhibitions; museum shop sells books and prints

M OKLAHOMA HISTORICAL SOCIETY, Central Museum, Historical Bldg,
73105. Tel 405-521-2491. *Pres Board Trustees* Jack T Conn; *Executive Dir* C E
Metcalf; *Interpretations & Publications* Bob Blackburn; *Museums & Historical
Sites* Mac Harris; *Library Resources* Andrea Clark; *Preservation Dir* Melvena
Thurman
Open Mon - Fri 9 AM - 5 PM. No admis fee. Estab 1893 to provide an overview
of the history of the State of Oklahoma presented in graphic and three-

dimensional forms through the use of artifacts with which the history was made, to tell the story in chronological order, pointing out the highlights of history. Average Annual Attendance: 50,000. Mem: 2000; dues $10; annual meeting Apr
Income: Financed by state appropriations and membership; society depends on donations for additions to its collections
Collections: Anthropology; archaeology; art history; costumes; ethnology; folk art; Indian art; numismatic art; specialized collections at historic sites and museums over the state
Exhibitions: Permanent chronological displays depicting pre-history, Plains Indian history, the Five Civilized Tribes' occupancy of Indian territory, the land openings of the late 19th and early 20th centuries, statehood, and progress since statehood
Publications: Mistletoe Leaves, monthly newsletter; The Chronicles of Oklahoma, scholastic quarterly; various brochures and reprints
Activities: Special presentations and study programs for children and adults; other interpretive programs; lectures open to the public, approx 40 vis lectr per year; gallery talks; tours; book shop
L **Library,** Central Museum, Historical Bldg, 73105. *Dir Reference Library* John Heisch
For reference only
Library Holdings: Vols 40,000; Other — Photographs

M **OKLAHOMA MUSEUM OF ART,** 7316 Nichols Rd, 73120. Tel 405-840-2759. *Dir* David Mickenberg; *Asst to Dir* Mary Scorlock; *Program Coordr* Barbara Fagin; *Financial Mgr* Barbara Kennedy; *Development Officer* Missy Kelly; *Admin* Beverly Glover; *Preparator & Registrar* David Rust; *Asst Cur* Debra Ogle; *Asst Program Coordr* Ann Swisher
Open Tues - Sat 10 AM - 5 PM, Tues evening 6:30 - 9 PM, Sun 1 - 5 PM, cl Mon & major holidays. Admis adults $2, young people under 12, Tues evening & members free. Estab 1960 and reorganized 1975; the Museum is committed to those ideals which hold that the great traditional values of art not only provide the soundest basis for continuing artistic expression, but offer a stability against which the merits of contemporary art can be weighed. The Museum sponsors exhibitions and offers studio and lecture art classes which familiarize the visitor and student with all art idioms. Twelve galleries are used for permanent collection and monthly changing temporary loan shows. Average Annual Attendance: 70,000. Mem: 1800; dues $25 - $1000; annual meeting Jan
Income: Financed by membership, private contributions, grants, admissions & endowment
Collections: †Old Master paintings including works by Lawrence, Crespi, Jordaens, Solimena; 19th - 20th century America paintings including works by Blakelock, Cropsey, Benton, Moran & Marsh; 19th - 20th century French paintings & sculpture including works by Courbet, Michel, Boudin, L'hermitte, Harpignies; Old Master prints & drawings including works by Rembrandt, Carracci, Goltzius & Durer
Publications: Calendar, bi-monthly, exhibition catalogs, posters
Activities: Studio training for adults & children; fine arts and crafts fairs; lectures open to public, 25 vis lectr per yr; concerts; gallery talks; tours; scholarships; book traveling exhibitions; originate traveling exhibitions; sales shop sells books, magazines, reproductions, prints & slides
L **Library,** 7316 Nichols Rd, 73120. Tel 405-840-2759
Library for reference only
Library Holdings: Vols 2000; Per subs 10; Other — Clipping files, exhibition catalogs

OKMULGEE

M **CREEK COUNCIL HOUSE AND MUSEUM,** Council Square, 74447. Tel 918-756-2324. *Dir* Bruce M Shackelford
Open Tues - Sat 9 AM - 5 PM. No admis fee. Estab 1867, first Council House Built, present Council House erected in 1878, to collect and preserve artifacts from the Creek History. Five rooms downstairs containing artifacts; four rooms upstairs showing art work, early time of Okmulgee; rooms of House of Warriors and House of Kings. Average Annual Attendance: 8000-10,000
Income: Financed by membership and city appropriation
Collections: †Creek Artifacts
Activities: Seminars on Creek Culture and history; lectures open to public, 5-10 per yr; gallery talks; artmobile; book traveling exhibitions; museum shop sells books, original art, reproductions, prints and Native American art and craft items
L **Library,** Town Square, 74447
Open Tues - Fri 9 AM - 5 PM. Estab to collect Creek and related books and documents for research and historical purposes. For reference only
Library Holdings: Vols 100; Per subs 15; Micro — Reels; AV — A-tapes, motion pictures; Other — Clipping files, exhibition catalogs, framed reproductions, manuscripts, memorabilia, original art works, pamphlets, photographs, prints, sculpture

PONCA CITY

O **PONCA CITY ART ASSOCIATION,** Box 1394, 819 East Central, 74601. Tel 405-765-9746. *Office Mgr* Lucille King
Open Wed - Sun 1 - 5 PM. No admis fee. Estab 1947 to encourage creative arts, to furnish place and sponsor art classes, art exhibits and workshops. Mem: 600; dues $10 family; annual meeting third Tues in April
Income: $10,000 (financed by membership and flea market)
Collections: Permanent fine arts collection; additions by purchases and donations
Exhibitions: Eight per year
Publications: Association Bulletin, 6 per yr
Activities: Classes for adults and children; lectures open to public; tours; competitions for members only with awards; scholarships; individual paintings lent to city-owned buildings; sales shop sells original art, reproductions and prints

M **PONCA CITY CULTURAL CENTER & MUSEUM,** 1000 E Grand Ave, 74601. Tel 405-762-6123. *Supervisor* La Wanda French
Open Mon, Wed - Sat 10 AM - 5 PM, Sun and holidays 1 - 5 PM; cl Tues, Thanksgiving, Christmas Eve and Christmas Day, New Year's Eve and New

Year's Day. Admis adults $1. The Cultural Center & Museum, a National Historic House since 1976, houses the Indian Museum, the Bryant Baker Studio, the 101 Ranch Room, and the DAR Memorial museum. The Indian Museum, established in 1936, places an emphasis on materials from the five neighboring tribes (Ponca, Kaw, Otoe, Osage, and Tonkawa) whose artistic use of beading, fingerweaving and ribbon-work are displayed throughout the Museum. The Bryant Baker Studio is a replica of the New York Studio of Bryant Baker, sculptor of the Pioneer Woman Statue, a local landmark, and the studio contains original bronze and plaster sculpture. The 101 Ranch Room exhibits memorabilia from the world renowned Miller Brothers' 101 Ranch, located south of Ponca City in the early 1900s. The Museum is the former home of Ernest Whitworth Marland, oilman and philanthropist, and the tenth governor of Oklahoma. Average Annual Attendance: 25,000
Income: Financed by the City of Ponca City and donations
Collections: Bryant Baker original sculpture; 101 Ranch memorabilia; Indian ethnography and archeology of Indian tribes throughout the United States
Exhibitions: Smithsonian Indian Images; Indian costumes, jewelry, pottery, baskets, musical instruments and tools
Publications: Brochure
Activities: Tours; Sales shop selling books, arrowheads, Indian arts and crafts
L **Library,** 1000 E Grand Ave, 74601
Primarily research library
Library Holdings: Vols 200; Per subs 15
Special Subjects: Anthropology, Archaeology, Indian art

L **PONCA CITY LIBRARY,** Art Dept, 515 E Grand, 74601. Tel 405-762-6311. *Dir* Steve Skidmore; *Head Public Services* Laurie Anderson; *Head Technical Services* Judy Johnson
Open Mon - Thurs 9 AM - 9 PM, Fri & Sat 9 AM - 5 PM, cl Sun. Estab 1904 to serve the citizens of Ponca City. Gallery maintained. Circ 150,000
Library Holdings: AV — Cassettes; Other — Framed reproductions, original art works, pamphlets, photographs, sculpture
Collections: Oriental Art Collection; Sandzen Collection; paintings

SHAWNEE

M **SAINT GREGORY'S ABBEY AND COLLEGE,** Mabee-Gerrer Museum of Art, 1900 W MacArthur Dr, 74801. Tel 405-273-9999. *Dir* John L Walch; *Cur* Justin Jones; *Conservator* Martin Wiesendanger; *Conservator* Margaret Wiesendanger
Open daily 1 - 4 PM, cl Mon. No admis fee. Estab 1904 to contribute to the cultural growth and appreciation of the general public of Oklahoma as well as of the student body of Saint Gregory's College. A new 16,000 sq foot gallery was completed in 1979. All collections are being enlarged by purchases and by gifts. Average Annual Attendance: 50,000
Income: Financed by endowment, membership and foundation funds
Purchases: Appeal to the Great Spirit by Dalin
Collections: †Artifacts from ancient civilizations: Egyptian, Roman, Grecian, Babylonian, Pre-Columbian North, South and Central American Indian, and South Pacific; †etchings, †engravings, †serigraphs and †lithographs; †oil paintings by American and European artists
Exhibitions: Robert C Lamell, paintings; Leonard Good, paintings; Joe Taylor, sculpture; Oklahoma Sculpture Society; Native American; Icons: Greek, Russian & Balkan; Art of the Mola; Drawings: An Eclectic Collection of Old Masters & Modern; Retablos from Mexico & New Mexico
Activities: Classes for adults and children; docent training; lectures open to public, 4 vis lectr per yr; gallery talks; tours; individual paintings and original objects of art lent to other museums and galleries; lending collection contains nature artifacts, original art works and prints, paintings, sculpture; book traveling exhibitions, 3 - 4 per yr; museum shop sells books, magazines, original art, reproductions & prints
L **Library,** Mabee-Gerrer Museum of Art, 1900 W MacArthur Dr, 74801. Tel 405-273-9999
Reference library open to art students and researchers
Income: Financed by grants, trust funds and private sources
Library Holdings: Vols 1262; Per subs 17; Other — Clipping files, exhibition catalogs, framed reproductions, original art works, prints, reproductions
Collections: †Benezit Index of Painters, Sculptors & Engravers; Thierne Becker Index & Volmer Supplement

STILLWATER

M **OKLAHOMA STATE UNIVERSITY,** Gardiner Art Gallery, Dept of Art, Bartlett Center of the Studio Arts, Morrill & Knoblock Sts, 74074. Tel 405-624-6016. *Dir* B J Smith
Open Mon - Fri 8 AM - 5 PM, Sun 2 - 5 PM. No admis fee. Estab 1970 as a visual and educational extension of the department's classes and as a cultural service to the community and area. One gallery located on the ground floor in new annex behind the renovated building. 250 running feet of wall space, 12 ft ceiling. Average Annual Attendance: 5000
Income: Financed by college
Collections: Fifty plus prints, mostly post World War II
Exhibitions: Exhibitions changed every 3 - 4 weeks year round; faculty, student, invitational and traveling shows
Publications: Exhibition schedule, annually; exhibition brochures
Activities: Book traveling exhibitions
L **Architecture Library,** 74078. Tel 405-624-6047. *Librn* William Harroff
Open Mon - Thurs 8 AM - 5 PM & 7 - 10 PM, Fri 8 AM - 5 PM, Sun 1:30 - 5:30 PM. Estab 1976 to meeet the combined needs of the faculty & students of the School of Architecture
Purchases: $12,000
Library Holdings: Vols 10,000; Per subs 65; Micro — Reels; AV — Slides; Other — Clipping files, exhibition catalogs, original art works, pamphlets
Special Subjects: Underground Housing
Activities: Lectures open to public

TAHLEQUAH

O CHEROKEE NATIONAL HISTORICAL SOCIETY, INC, PO Box 515, 74465. Tel 918-456-6195. *Pres* Ross O Swimmer; *Exec Dir* Dr Duane King; *Secy* James C Leake; *Office Mgr* Tom Mooney
Open Mon - Sat 10 AM - 5 PM, Sun 1 - 5 PM. Admis adult $2, children $1. Estab 1963 to commemorate and portray the history, traditions and lore of a great Indian tribe, and to assist in improving local economic conditions. Maintains an art gallery, primarily Indian art. Average Annual Attendance: 130,000. Mem: 1500; dues $25 and up
Income: Financed by membership, admissions and grants
Collections: Indian artists interpretations of Trails of Tears
Exhibitions: Trail of Tears Art Show, annually
Publications: The Columns, quarterly
Activities: Lectures open to public; competitions with cash awards; museum shop sells books, reproductions, prints & slides
L Library, PO Box 515, 74464
Open Mon - Sat 8 AM - 5 PM, Sun 1 - 5 PM. Estab 1976 to preserve remnants of Cherokee history and to educate the general public about that cultural heritage; a repository of Indian art and documents. Maintains an art gallery with work by artists of several different tribes; heavy emphasis given to the Cherokee experience
Income: Financed by membership, admissions and grants
Library Holdings: Vols 3000; Per subs 10; manuscripts; archival materials in excess of 500 cu ft; Micro — Reels 127; AV — A-tapes, cassettes, fs, Kodachromes, slides; Other — Clipping files, framed reproductions, manuscripts, memorabilia, original art works, pamphlets, photographs, prints, sculpture
Special Subjects: Cherokee history
Exhibitions: Annual Trail of Tears Art Show (Indian artists' interpretation of the Trail of Tears theme); Cherokee Artists Exhibition; rotating exhibitions; special exhibitions, periodically (primarily Indian artists)

TULSA

C BANK OF OKLAHOMA,* Williams Plaza, 74136. Tel 918-588-6000. *Chmn Executive Committee* Eugene Swearingen
Open 8 AM - 5 PM. No admis fee. Estab 1968 to enhance work environment. Collection displayed on 7 floors of the Bank of Oklahoma Tower
Purchases: $15,000
Collections: Approximately 300 pieces of Modern Art
Activities: Lect; tours; scholarships offered to University of Tulsa

M THOMAS GILCREASE INSTITUTE OF AMERICAN HISTORY AND ART, 1400 N 25 West Ave, 74127. Tel 918-582-3122. *Dir* Fred A Myers
Open Mon - Sat 9 AM - 5 PM, Sun & holidays 1 - 5 PM, cl Christmas. No admis fee. Estab by the late Thomas Gilcrease as a private institution; acquired by the City of Tulsa 1954 (governed by a Board of Directors and City Park Board); building addition completed 1963. Average Annual Attendance: 100,000. Mem: 1600; dues $15 and up
Income: Financed by city funds
Collections: American art from Colonial period to present, with emphasis on art of historical significance, sculpture, painting, graphics. Much of the work shown is of documentary nature, with considerable emphasis on the American Indian and the opening of the West. Art collections include 8000 paintings by 400 American artists; artifact collections include 10,000 objects from Mid-Americas, and North America, and include both prehistoric and historic materials from most of the Indian cultures of these areas
Exhibitions: Public school art exhibit; special exhibitions periodically; a special or rotating exhibit during fall, winter, spring seasons
Publications: The Gilcrease Magazine, quarterly
Activities: Film program; lect on art and history; gallery tours; lect to school groups outside the museum; book shop
L Library, 1400 N 25 West Ave, 74127
Open daily, cl weekends and holidays. Library open for research contains 65,000 books and documents, many rare books and manuscripts of the American discovery period, as well as materials concerning the Five Civilized Tribes
Library Holdings: Vols 40,000; Per subs 10; Other — Exhibition catalogs, manuscripts, memorabilia, pamphlets, photographs

M PHILBROOK ART CENTER, 2727 S Rockford Rd, PO Box 52510, 74152. Tel 918-749-7941. *Actg Dir* Marcia Manhart; *Cur Non-Western Art* Edwin L Wade PhD; *Dir Development* Helen G Sanderson; *Membership Coordr* Elizabeth Thomas; *Volunteer Coordr* Joan Hoar; *Dir Communications* Rocky Vesanen; *Graphic Designer & Publications Editor* Carol Haralson; *Museum Shop Mgr* Babs Richardson; *Registrar* Chris Knop; *Preparator* Charles Taylor; *Cur Education* Olivia Marino; *Asst Cur Native American Art* Isabel McIntosh; *Exhibitions & Publications Research* Gloria A Young, PhD
Open Tues - Sat 10 AM - 5 PM, Sun 1 - 5 PM. Admis adults $3, college students and sr citizens $1.50, high school students and younger free. Estab 1939 as a general art museum in an Italian Rennaissance Revival Villa, the former home of philanthropist & oil baron Waite Phillips. Twenty-three acres of formal and natural gardens. Also contains a special exhibition gallery. Average Annual Attendance: 120,000. Mem: 4500; dues $25 and up; annual meeting April
Income: Financed by endowment, membership, earned income, corporate & private gifts & public grants
Collections: Laura A Clubb Collection of American & European Paintings; Clark Field Collection of American Indian Baskets and Pottery; Gillert Collection of Southeast Asian Ceramics; Gussman Collection of African Sculpture; Samuel H Kress Collection of Italian Renaissance Paintings and Sculpture; Roberta C Lawson Collection of Indian Costumes and Artifacts; Elizabeth Cole Butler Collection of American Indian Art; Tabor Collection of Oriental Art; American Indian paintings and sculpture; European, early American and contemporary American oils, watercolors and prints; period furniture
Exhibitions: (1983) As in a Vision: The Elizabeth Cole Butler Collection; Reflections in Glass: 50 Years of Collecting; (1984) The Armand Hammer Collection: Five Centuries of Masterpieces; Nature's Forms/Nature's Forces;

The Art of Alexandre Hogue; Auspicious Spirits: Korean Painting & Folk Art Masters of Line and Shadow; Philbrook: Past-Present-Future; The Art Fabric; Of Time and Place: Figurative Paintings; The Art of South Italy; Butler Collection; Three Centuries of Italian Still-Life Painting; Photography; Jewelry, Ancient to Modern; Thyssen Collection
Publications: Bi-monthly bulletin; exhibition catalogs
Activities: Classes for adults and children; dramatic programs; docent training; lectures open to public, 27 visiting lecturers per year; concerts; gallery talks; tours; scholarships; individual and original objects of art lent to museums, corporations and city government; book traveling exhibitions, 3-5 per year; originate traveling exhibitions; museum shop sells books, magazines, original art, reproductions, prints, slides and gift items
L Library, 2727 S Rockford Rd, O Box 52510, 74152. Tel 918-749-7941. *Librn* Thomas E Young
Open Tues - Fri by appointment. Reference-resource center for the curatorial staff, teaching faculty, volunteer element and their education, as well as the membership
Library Holdings: Vols 5500; Per subs 90; AV — Slides; Other — Clipping files, exhibition catalogs, pamphlets, reproductions
Collections: Roberta Campbell Lawson Library of source materials on Indians

WOODWARD

M PLAINS INDIANS & PIONEER HISTORICAL FOUNDATION, Pioneer Museum & Art Center, 2009 Williams Ave, Box 1167, 73802. Tel 405-256-6136. *Cur* Sarah Taylor; *Asst Cur* Maedine Jones
Open Tues - Sat 10 AM - 5 PM, Sun 1 PM - 4 PM, cl Mon. No admis fee. Estab 1957 to preserve local history and to support visual arts. Average Annual Attendance: 15,000. Mem: 450; dues $10 - $15; annual meeting Nov
Income: Financed by membership and trust fund
Collections: Early day artifacts as well as Indian material
Publications: Woodward County Pioneer Families, 1907-57 (newsletter) quarterly; brochures; Below Devil's Gap (historical book)
Activities: Classes for adults and children; docent training; lectures open to public, 3 vis lectr per year; tours; competitions with prizes; book traveling exhibitions, 3 per year; museum shop sells books, magazines, original art and prints

OREGON

ASHLAND

SOUTHERN OREGON COLLEGE
M Stevenson Union Art Gallery, 97520. *Dir* Katharine Danner; *Asst Dir* Jerry Findley
Open Mon - Thurs 8 AM - 9 PM, Fri 8 AM - 5 PM. No admis fee. Estab 1966 to provide members of the Southern Oregon College community and the greater Ashland area an opportunity to experience a well rounded selection of art and crafts. Average Annual Attendance: 20,000
Income: Financed by student fees
Collections: †Small permanent collection of prints, paintings by local artists and a sculpture by Bruce West
Exhibitions: Ceramics, graphic design, paintings, photography, sculpture, weaving, works of professional artists
Activities: Short programs for educ television; exhibiting artists lect to art classes when possible; workshops; special lect; lect open to public, 3 visiting lectr per year; eight gallery talks per year; competitions with prizes
M Central Art Gallery, 97520. Tel 503-482-6386. *Dir* Robert Alston
Open Mon - Fri 8:30 AM - 5 PM
Income: Financed by Department of Art
Exhibitions: Primarily students works, also professional and local artists

ASTORIA

M COLUMBIA RIVER MARITIME MUSEUM, 1792 Marine Dr, 97103. Tel 503-325-2323. *Dir* Michael Naab; *Cur* Larry Gilmore
Open May - Sept daily 9:30 AM - 5 PM; Oct - Apr Tues - Sun 9:30 AM - 5 PM. Admis adults $2.50, children & sr citizens $1.50. Estab 1962 as a maritime museum. Maintains seven galleries of nautical history including works of art. Average Annual Attendance: 100,000. Mem: 2000; dues 15; annual meeting in Oct
Income: $300,000 financed by admissions, sales, memberships & individual & corporate donations
Collections: Maritime Paintings, Prints and Photography; Ship Models and Sailing Memorabilia
Exhibitions: Shipwrecks & Lifesavers; The Salmon Fishers; Fishing Boats of the Oregon Coast, watercolors
Publications: The Quarterdeck Review, quarterly
Activities: Classes for adults & children; dramatic programs; docent training; lectures open to the public, 3 - 4 vis lectr per year; tours; competitions; exten dept serves states of Oregon & Washington; outreach program to schools; originate traveling exhibitions; sales shop sells books, original art, reproductions, prints, slides, model kits & decorative items
L Library, 16th & Exchange Sts, 97103
Library for use on the premises
Library Holdings: Vols 5000; Per subs 55; AV — A-tapes, cassettes, motion pictures, rec, slides; Other — Clipping files, exhibition catalogs, manuscripts, pamphlets, photographs, prints, reproductions

COOS BAY

M COOS ART MUSEUM, 515 Market Ave, 97420. Tel 503-267-3901. *Chmn Bd* Armin Wehrle; *1st VChmn Bd* James Graeser; *Treas* Virginia Maine; *Co-Treas* Sharen Reese; *Secy* Hiltraud Volk; *Dir* Kay Lorence
Open Tues - Sun 1 - 4 PM. No admis fee. Estab 1966 to bring contemporary art to southwestern Oregon, and to have classes in related art subjects. There are two large spacious galleries with a wide entrance hall. Average Annual Attendance: 15,000. Mem: 800; dues family $25, single $15; annual meeting first Sat of the year
Income: $32,000 (financed by membership, fund raisers, memorials & contributions)
Collections: †Contemporary American Printmakers; †paintings, †photographs, †sculpture
Exhibitions: Crafts, functional; Sculpture, Painting and Nonfunctional Pottery, Weaving; monthly exhibits; three juried shows a year; one photography show
Publications: Bulletins, monthly
Activities: Classes for adults and children; dramatic programs; film festivals; lect open to the public, 2 - 3 vis lectr per year; concerts; tours; competitions;; individual paintings and original objects of art lent to members; museum and sales shops selling books, original art, prints, photographs, pottery, stained glass, blown glass

COQUILLE

O COQUILLE VALLEY ART ASSOCIATION, Fairview Route, Box 625, 97423. Tel 503-396-3294. *Pres* Katherine Callahan; *VPres* Leona Siglin; *Secy* Leola Hultin; *Treas* Lola Kysar
Open Tues - Sun 1 - 4 PM, cl Mon & holidays. No admis fee. Estab 1950 to teach art and art appreciation. Gallery maintained on main floor of Art Association owned old refurbished schoolhouse. Mem: 220; dues $15, sr citizens $12; annual meetings first Wed in April
Income: Financed by membership, annual bazaar & Coos County Fair
Exhibitions: Exhibits by local members, as well as by others throughout the state
Publications: Monthly newsletter
Activities: Classes for adults and children; lectures open to public, 4-5 vis lectr per yr; gallery talks; tours; awards; scholarships; individual paintings lent to banks, lobbies, automobile showrooms & music stores; traveling exhibitions organized and circulated; sales shop sells original art, miniatures & handicraft
L Library,* Fairview Route, Box 625, 97423. *Librn* Sharon Orchard

CORVALLIS

OREGON STATE UNIVERSITY

M Horner Museum, Gill Coliseum, 26th near Western, 97331. Tel 503-754-2951. *Dir* Lucy Skjelstad; *Asst Dir* Loretta Harrison
Open Tues - Fri 10 AM - 5 PM, Sat 10 AM - 2 PM, Sun 2 - 5 PM, cl Mon, winters; Mon - Fri 10 AM - 5 PM, Sun 2 - 5 PM, cl Sat, summers. No admis fee. Estab 1877 to collect, preserve and exhibit the history and natural history of Oregon. Average Annual Attendance: 15,000. Mem: 175; dues individual $10
Income: Financed by state appropriations and donations
Collections: Ethnographic, Worldwide; Geological and Biological Specimens; Historic Objects, Pioneer Period to Present; Oral History
Publications: Horner Museum Tour Guide Series, a set of thematic history guidebooks; exhibition catalogs
Activities: Lectures open to public; tours; individual paintings & original objects of art lent to museums & non-profit agencies; museum shop sells books, reproductions, posters & T-shirts
M Fairbanks Gallery, 97331. Tel 503-754-4745. *Chmn* Mark Sponenborgh
Open 8 AM - 5 PM. No admis fee. Estab 1933 to display work of contemporary American artists. One gallery space 20 x 50 ft
Income: Financed by state appropriation and grants
Collections: Wendel Black Print Collection; Richard Blow Inlaid Stone Reliefs Collection; OSU Japanese Woodcut Collection
Exhibitions: (1983-84) Annual faculty & student exhibition; New York Artists of the 1960's; Drawings of Wendel Black; Distinguished Alumni
Publications: Posters and flyers announcing shows
M Memorial Union Art Gallery, 97331. Tel 503-754-2416. *Secy & Dir* George F Stevens
Open daily 8 AM - 10 PM. Estab 1928. Average Annual Attendance: 50,000. Mem: 15,000; annual meeting May
Income: $70,000
Collections: William Henry Price Memorial Collection of Oil Paintings
Publications: Calendar and exhibition pamphlets
Activities: Educ program; lect; exten dept serving the State; individual paintings lent to schools; material available to responsible galleries for fees; traveling exhibitions organized and circulated

THE DALLES

O THE DALLES ART ASSOCIATION,* The Dalles Art Center, Fourth & Washington, 97058. Tel 503-296-4759. *Pres* Pat Rayburn
Open Tues - Sat 10 AM - 4 PM. No admis fee. Estab 1959 for presentation of community arts activities. Gallery maintained. Average Annual Attendance: 4500. Mem: 150; dues $10; meetings held each month on 3rd Mon
Income: Financed by dues, fund-raising events
Exhibitions: Member and guest exhibits; state services exhibits
Publications: Monthly bulletin
Activities: Classes for adults and children; summer children's program; lect open to public; competitions; individual paintings lent to schools

EUGENE

M BUTLER MUSEUM OF AMERICAN INDIAN ART,* 1155 W First, 97402. Tel 503-345-7055. *Dir* Elizabeth Butler
Open Tues - Sat 10 AM - 5 PM, cl major holidays. Admis adults $1.50, students 12-18 $.75, children under 12 $.25. Estab 1974. Maintains small library of books on Amerian Indian art forms and history
Collections: Baskets, pottery, weavings, jewelry, clothing, masks & carvings, dating from the early 1800's, representing the nine culture areas of the North American Continent-Southwest, California, Northwest Coast, Eskimo & Athabascan, Plateau, Great Basin, Plains, Woodlands & Southeast
Activities: Lectures; tours

M MAUDE I KERNS ART CENTER, Henry Korn Gallery,* 1910 E 15th Ave, 97403. Tel 503-345-1571. *Dir* Leslie Copland; *Pres* Kelly Beckley; *Secy* Candice Rohr
Open daily 10 AM - 5 PM. No admis fee. Estab 1951, the Center is a nonprofit educational organization dedicated to promoting quality in the arts and crafts through classes, exhibitions, workshops, community projects, and special events. The Center houses the Henry Korn Gallery, the Main Gallery featuring monthly shows of contemporary artists; the Mezzanine Gallery, suited to photographs, prints, drawings and smaller works of art. Average Annual Attendance: 9000. Mem: 500; dues family $25, individual $15; annual meeting second Mon in April
Income: $60,000 (financed by membership, class tuition, art sales, contributions, grants)
Collections: Sculpture and painting of Oregon artists
Exhibitions: (1982) Hayder Amir, Margaret Viw; Communication Arts, Barbara Kensler, Kacey Joyce, Jennifer Guske, Lyle Matoush, Libby Unthank, Don Sprague, Stan Beppu, Nils Lou, Ruri, Faye Nakamura, Dan Schwoerer, Howard Meehan, James Kingwell, Bill and Sally Worcester, annual Christmas Sale, faculty and student show
Publications: State of the Crafts, Maude Kerns; membership newsletter, monthly
Activities: Classes for adults and children; dramatic programs; volunteer program; lect open to the public and for members only on request; concerts; gallery talks; tours; competitions; book traveling exhibitions; the Rental-Sales Gallery, featuring an artist of the month, as well as a stock of a variety of art works

UNIVERSITY OF OREGON

M Museum of Art, 97403. Tel 203-686-3027. *Dir* Richard C Paulin; *Designer-Preparator* Tommy L Griffin; *Supv, Visual Art Resources* Michael Whitenack; *Admin Asst* Norine M Arens; *Registrar* Barbara Zentner
Open Wed - Sun Noon - 5 PM, cl Mon and university holidays. No admis fee. Estab 1930 to promote among university students and faculty and the general public an active and continuing interest in the visual arts of both Western and Oriental cultures. Average Annual Attendance: 100,000. Mem: 962; dues $15-$500; annual meeting May
Income: $201,000 (financed by state appropriation and private donations)
Collections: African; Contemporary Northwest Collection; Greater Pacific Basin Collection; Oriental Art representing the cultures of China, Japan, Cambodia, Korea, Mongolia, Tibet, Russia, and American and British works executed in the traditional Oriental manner
Exhibitions: (1982) Danzig 1939: Treasurers of a Destroyed Community; Morris Graves, paintings; Ceramic Traditions; Philippe Halsman, portrait photography; First International Shoebox Sculpture; Decoding Dragons: Status Garments of Ch'ing Dynasty China
Publications: Exhibition catalog
Activities: Docent training; exten dept serving Oregon and Washington; lending collection contains individual and original works of art; originate traveling exhibitions; sales shop sells books, reproductions and slides
M Aperture: Photo Gallery,* 13th & University Sts, 97403. Tel 503-686-4373. *Dir* Adell McMillan; *Asst Dir* Frank Geltner; *Craft Center Coordr* Thomas Urban
Open Mon - Sat 7:30 AM - 11:30 PM, Sun Noon - 11:30 PM. No admis fee. Estab 1981 to provide space for work of university community
Income: Financed by student fees
Collections: †Pacific Northwest Art
Exhibitions: Periodic art exhibitions on portable display boards in various rooms; display in the art gallery of selections from the permanent collection
Activities: Classes for adults; craft workshops; lectures
L School of Architecture and Allied Arts Library, 277A Lawrence Hall, 97403. Tel 503-686-3637. *Librn* Reyburn R McCready; *Librn* James H Carmin; *Slide Cur* Carmi Weingrod
Open Mon - Thurs 8 AM - 11 PM; Fri 8 AM - 6 PM; Sat 9 AM - 5 PM; Sun 10 AM - 10 PM. Estab 1919 to provide resources for the courses, degree programs, and research of the departments in the School of Architecture and Allied Arts and related Institute for Community Art Studies and Center for Environmental Research. Circ 58,882
Income: Financed by state appropriation
Purchases: $35,600
Library Holdings: Vols 40,000; Per subs 250; Micro — Fiche; AV — Slides 162,000; Other — Exhibition catalogs, pamphlets, photographs 50,000

FOREST GROVE

M PACIFIC UNIVERSITY, Old College Hall, Pacific University Museum, 97116. Tel 503-357-6151. *Cur* Karen Shield
Open Wed, Thurs & Fri 12:30 - 4:30 PM, Sat 9:30 AM - 1:30 PM & by appointment, cl school vacations. No admis fee. Estab 1949
Collections: Indian Artifacts; Oriental Art Objects; Pacific Univ & Forest Grove Artifacts
Publications: Annual of the Curator
Activities: Tours

JACKSONVILLE

M SOUTHERN OREGON HISTORICAL SOCIETY, Jacksonville Museum, 206 N Fifth St, PO Box 480, 97530. Tel 503-899-1847. *Dir* C William Burk; *Registrar of Collections* Gregory Gualtieri; *Exhib Cur* Jime Matoush; *Programs Dir* Dawna Curler; *Historian-Newsletter Editor* Marjorie Edens; *Photographer* Douglas Smith
Open Tues - Sat 9 AM - 5 PM; Sun Noon - 5 PM; summers, Mon 9 AM - 5 PM. No admis fee. Estab 1950 to collect and exhibit materials showing the history of Southern Oregon. Included are the Peter Britt Gallery (19th Century photography artifacts); the Costume Gallery; Children's Museum (a touching museum for children); Pinto's Theater. The historic houses include the Cornelius C Beekman House (1876), Catholic Rectory (circa 1861) and Cool-Beekman-Armstrong House (1858). Average Annual Attendance: 90,000. Mem: 1700; dues $7.50 and up; annual meeting June
Income: Financed by membership and county tax
Exhibitions: (1981) Dorland Robinson Artwork; (1983) Eugene Bennett Retrospective Artwork
Publications: Table Rock Sentinel, monthly; Eugene Bennett: A Retrospective (catalog)
Activities: Handcraft workshops for children; docent training; film program; lect open to the public; sales shop selling books
L Library, 206 N Fifth St, PO Box 480, 97530. Tel 503-899-1847. *Librn* Richard H Engeman
Open to public for reference only
Income: Financed by membership, sales and county tax
Library Holdings: Vols 4000; Per subs 75; Ephemera, art on paper; Other — Manuscripts, photographs
Special Subjects: Historic preservation, museum techniques, Southern Oregon History

KLAMATH FALLS

M FAVELL MUSEUM OF WESTERN ART & INDIAN ARTIFACTS, 125 W Main, PO Box 165, 97601. Tel 503-882-9996. *Pres* Gene H Favell; *VPres & Treas* Winifred L Favell; *Admin* Walter Havens; *Asst Admin* Bev Jackson
Open Mon - Sat 9:30 AM - 5:30 PM, cl Sun. Admis adults $2, youth 6 - 16 years $1. Estab 1972 to preserve Western heritage as represented by Indian artifacts and contemporary Western art. Gallery features contemporary western artists combined with art and artifacts displays. Average Annual Attendance: 15,000 - 20,000. Mem: Annual meeting May
Income: $200,000 - 250,000 (financed by owners)
Purchases: Paintings by: Grace Hudson, McCarthy, Arlene Hooker Fay & James Bama
Collections: †Contemporary western art; †western Indian artifacts: pottery, stonework, baskets, bead and quillwork; †miniature firearms
Activities: Gallery talks; Museum shop selling books, original art, reproductions, prints, slides

M KLAMATH COUNTY MUSEUM, 1451 Main St, 97601. Tel 503-882-2501, Ext 208. *Dir* Sandy Pratt
Open Tues - Sat 9 AM - 5 PM; cl Sun and Mon. Admis adults $2, students & sr citizens $1, families $5, under 5 free. Estab 1953 to tell the story of the Klamath Country and to preserve and exhibit related material. Average Annual Attendance: 30,000
Income: Financed by county appropriation
Collections: Four Original Rembrandt Etchings; Indian Artifacts; Pioneer Artifacts
Publications: Museum Research Papers, every 2 years
Activities: Lect open to public; tours; junior museum located at Baldwin Hotel; book traveling exhibitions; traveling exhibitions orgainzed and circulated; museum shop sells books, reproductions & prints; junior museum located at 31 Main St
L Research Library, 1451 Main St, 97601
Open to the public for reference by appointment
Library Holdings: Vols 10,000; Micro — Reels; AV — Motion pictures, slides; Other — Clipping files, pamphlets, photographs
Collections: Modoc Indian War Books, Documents and Manuscripts
M Baldwin Hotel Museum Annex, 31 Main St, 97601. Tel 503-882-2501, Ext 207
Open Tues - Sat 9:30 AM - 4 PM, winter Fri & Sat only. Admis adults $2, students & sr citizens $1.50, family $5. A state and national historic landmark purchased by Klamath County in January 1978. Restoration of building began in February 1978 and it was dedicated as a museum by Oregon's Governor Robert Straub June 3, 1978. Opened to the public August 19, 1978. May be viewed by tour only

O KLAMATH FALLS ART ASSOCIATION, Klamath Art Gallery,* 120 Riverside Dr, PO Box 955, 97601. Tel 503-883-1833. *Pres* Warren Kerr; *Chmn Exhib* Nina Pence; *Dir* Dorothy Hale
Open Mon - Sat 1 - 4 PM, Sun 2 - 5 PM, and special occasions. No admis fee. Estab 1948 to provide art training for local residents. Gallery estab 1960 to provide display and teaching space for the Association's activities. Average Annual Attendance: 5000. Mem: 200; dues $7 and higher; annual meeting Sept
Income: Financed by membership, gallery sales, tuition
Collections: Ceramics; paintings; weaving (owned by members)
Exhibitions: Twelve annually; one membership show, one juried show, and the remainder varies
Activities: Classes in painting, drawing, ceramics, weaving; children's summer art classes; workshops; lect, visiting lectrs; annual arts festival, mid-Sept

MEDFORD

O ROGUE VALLEY ART ASSOCIATION, 40 S Bartlett, PO Box 763, 97501. Tel 502-772-8118. *Pres* Jean Boyer-Root; *Exec Dir* Janeth Trowbridge
Open Mon - Fri 10 AM - 5 PM, Sat 10 AM - 4 PM (winter), 9 AM - 4 PM (summer), cl Sun & national holidays. Estab 1960 to provide the surrounding area with changing exhibits in what is going on in the world of art; Auxiliary Board initiated in 1971. Mem: 800; dues $10 - $30; annual meeting Apr
Publications: Newsletter, approx 4 annually
Activities: Art education for children; adult education classes throughout year have included calligraphy, drawing and workshops in stained glass and printmaking; tours and artist lect
M Rogue Gallery, 40 S Bartlett, Medford, 97501
Estab for exhibition, education & sales as tools for stimulating regional awareness of quality in the arts. Gallery is 1400 sq ft, 2 solid walls with 5 movable panels for exhibition. Average Annual Attendance: 8000
Exhibitions: New exhibit each month
Activities: Gallery talks; competitions; sales shop sells original art, paintings & hand crafts

MONMOUTH

M WESTERN OREGON STATE COLLEGE GALLERY, 345 Monmouth Ave, 97361. Tel 503-838-1220. *Head Art Dept* James T Mattingly
Open Mon - Fri 8 AM - 5 PM during scheduled exhibits. No admis fee. Estab to bring contemporary art work to the community and the college for study and visual understanding. Library maintained. Average Annual Attendance: 3000-4000
Income: $1200 (financed by state appropriation and student fees)
Collections: †Permanent collection
Exhibitions: Contemporary Northwest Visual Art
Activities: Lect open to the public, 3 - 5 vis lectr per year; gallery talks; tours; lending collection contains 8000 slides
M Campbell Hall Gallery, 97361. Tel 503-838-1220
Open Mon - Fri 8 AM - 5 PM. No admis fee. Estab to provide exposure to art. Average Annual Attendance: 4000
Exhibitions: Original Art; generated by the Visual Art Gallery Chairman; varies per academic year
Activities: Lectures open to public, 3 vis lectr per yr; competitions with awards; originate traveling exhibitions
M Gallery 107,* 97361. Tel 503-838-1220
Exhibitions: Original art generated by the Creative Arts Department Performance & Exhibitions Committee

PORTLAND

M BASSIST COLLEGE, Collections Library, 2000 SW 5th Ave, 97201. Tel 503-228-6528. *Pres* Donald B Bassist; *Secy* Ernest Buhlinger
Open 9 AM - 5 PM. No admis fee. Estab 1964 to provide practical instruction in retail merchandising, interior design, display, fashion design, advertising and promotion, fashion history and textiles. Average Annual Attendance: 200
Library Holdings: Vols 9000; Per subs 102; AV — Slides; Other — Clipping files
Collections: Collection of Fashion and Costume History Books; Collection in Furniture and Interior Decoration Fields
Activities: Lect open to the public; scholarships; lending collection of 150 motion pictures; book shop

M CONTEMPORARY CRAFTS ASSOCIATION AND GALLERY, 3934 SW Corbett Ave, 97201. Tel 503-223-2654. *Dir* Marlene Gabel
Open Mon - Fri 11 AM - 5 PM, Sat Noon - 5 PM, Sun 1 - 4 PM. No admis fee. Estab 1938 to promote, exhibit and sell contemporary crafts. Gallery is maintained also as a consignment outlet, and holds exhibits monthly. Average Annual Attendance: 30,000. Mem: 1400; dues $9 - $1000 depending on classification
Income: $114,000 (financed by membership)
Collections: †Craft objects including ceramics, glass, textiles, wood collected over a 40-year period
Publications: Contemporary Crafts News, quarterly
Activities: Artists-in-the-Schools program; lectures open to the public, 5 visiting lectrs per year; gallery talks; tours; lending collection contains books, cassettes, slides; sales shop selling books, magazines, original art
L Library,* 3934 SW Corbett Ave, 97201. Tel 503-223-2654. *Actg Librn* LaVerne Kuchler
Open to members
Library Holdings: Vols 430; Per subs 260

O METROPOLITAN ARTS COMMISSION, 1120 SW 5th, Rm 518, 97204. Tel 503-796-5111. *Chmn* Clifford Carlsen Jr; *Dir* Selina M Roberts
Open Mon - Fri 8 AM - 5 PM. No admis fee. Estab 1973, to promote and encourage programs to further the development and public awareness of and interest in the visual and performing arts
Income: Financed by city and county appropriation
Collections: Works by local artists
Publications: Newsletter, bi-monthly
Activities: Competitions with awards

L MULTNOMAH COUNTY LIBRARY, Henry Failing Art and Music Dept,* 801 SW Tenth Ave, 97205. Tel 503-223-7201. *Librn* James H Burghardt; *Head Art & Music Dept* Barbara K Padden
Open Tues - Thurs 10 AM - 9 PM; Fri & Sat 10 AM - 5:30 PM. Estab 1864 as a public library service to Multnomah County
Library Holdings: Vols 23,000; AV — Rec, slides; Other — Clipping files, framed reproductions

O   OREGON HISTORICAL SOCIETY, 1230 SW Park Ave, 97205. Tel 503-222-1741. *Dir* Thomas Vaughan; *Assoc Dir* Millard McClung; *Asst Dir* Robert Stark
Open Mon - Sat 10 AM - 4:45 PM. No admis fee. Estab 1873, incorporated 1898, to collect, preserve, exhibit and publish materials pertaining to the Oregon country. Approx 20,000 sq ft of exhibit space; Society maintains historic 1856 Bybee-Howell House, Sauvie Island. Average Annual Attendance: 130,000.
Mem: 8000; dues individual $15, family $25; annual meeting Nov
Income: Financed by endowment, membership, state appropriation
Collections: Approx 60,000 museum objects
Exhibitions: (1982) Soft Gold: Trade & Cultural Exchanges On The Pacific Northwest Coast (in cooperation with Harvard University Peabody Museum & National Endowment For The Humanities); The Genius of Ivan Collins: Wagons in Miniature; Indians of the Oregon Country; (1983) Iron Horse West: The Burlington Northern Collection, western painting; The American Image: Photographs from the National Archives; The Artists Patecky: A Place in History, regional artists; Passage Through Time: The Columbia Gorge, photographs, art, artifacts
Publications: Oregon Historical Quarterly; books; maps; pamphlets; newsletter
Activities: Seminars for adults; classes for children; docent training; educational programs; lectures open to the public; tours; individual paintings & original objects of art lent; originate traveling exhibitions; sales shop sells books, original art, reproductions & prints
L   Library, 1230 SW Park Ave, 97205. *Chief Librn* Louis Flannery; *Managing Editor* Priscilla Knuth
Open Mon - Sat 10 AM - 5 PM
Library Holdings: Vols 60,500; original documents; Micro — Cards, fiche, prints, reels; AV — A-tapes, cassettes, fs, lantern slides, motion pictures, rec, slides, v-tapes; Other — Clipping files, exhibition catalogs, framed reproductions, manuscripts, memorabilia, original art works, pamphlets, photographs, prints, reproductions, sculpture
Collections: 3000 separate manuscript collections containing 15,000,000 pieces; 1,000,000 historic photographs; 10,000 maps

M   OREGON SCHOOL OF ARTS AND CRAFTS, Hoffman Gallery, 8245 SW Barnes Rd, 97225. Tel 503-297-5544. *Executive Dir* Mary Greeley; *Curriculum Dir* Judith Chambliss
Open Mon - Thurs 9 AM - 9 PM, Fri 9 AM - 5 PM, Sat & Sun 10 AM - 4 PM. No admis fee, except for special events and classes. Estab 1906 to teach standards of quality in crafts. Average Annual Attendance: 3000. Mem: 2900; dues $25 - $1000
Income: Financed by tuitions, endowment, membership, state appropriation and National Endowments of the Arts, Washington, DC
Publications: Course catalogues, quarterly; gallery announcements, 12 per year; newsletter to members, 6 per year
Activities: Classes for adults and children; docent training; lect open to public, 10 visiting lectr per year; gallery talks; tours; competitions; book traveling exhibitions 2 per year; sales shop sells books, magazines, original art, prints & crafts
L   Library, 8245 SW Barnes Rd, 97225. Tel 503-297-5544. *Librn* Beverly B Stafford
Open Mon - Thurs 9:30 AM - 7 PM, Fri 9:30 AM - 4 PM, Sat 11 AM - 4 PM, cl Sun. Estab 1979 to serve as a craft reference library for students and faculty and others interested in crafts
Library Holdings: Vols 1500; Per subs 78; AV — Slides; Other — Pamphlets
Special Subjects: Calligraphy, Ceramics, Drawings, Metalwork, Photography, Printmaking, Stained Glass, Textiles, Craft history, weaving, woodworking
Activities: Interlibrary loan services available

O   PORTLAND ART ASSOCIATION, 1219 SW Park Ave, 97205. *Exec Dir* Stephen E Ostrow; *Development Officer* Steve Ritchie; *Business Mgr* Gary Ettinger
M   Portland Art Museum, 1219 SW Park Ave, 97205. Tel 503-226-2811. *Dir* Donald Jenkins; *Asst Cur* Mary Priester; *Cur Prints & Drawings* Gordon Gilkey; *Cur Education* Pauline Eyerly; *Registrar* Kathryn Gates
Open Tues, Wed, Thurs, Sat & Sun Noon - 5 PM, Fri Noon - 10 PM, cl Mon. Admis adults $1.50, students $1, children under 12, senior citizens and members free. Estab 1892 to make a collection of works of art and to erect and maintain a suitable building in which the same may be studies and exhibited, and to develop and encourage the study of art. Average Annual Attendance: 200,000. Mem: 6300; dues $20 and up; annual meeting Sept
Collections: †American painting, 19th & 20th centuries; †European painting, 17th-20th centuries; Gebauer Collection of Cameroon Art; †Vivian & Gordon Gilkey Graphics Art Collection; Hirsh Collection of Oriental Rugs; Samuel H Kress Collection of Renaissance Painting & Sculpture; Mary Andrews Ladd Collection of Japanese Prints; Lawther Collection of Ethiopian Crosses; Lewis Collection of Classical Antiquities; †Alice B Nunn Collection of English Silver; †Oriental sculptures, paintings, bronzes, ceramics and other decorative arts; Persian & Hindu miniatures; Pre-Columbian art; Rasmussen Collection of Northwest Coast Indian and Eskimo Arts; Evan H Roberts Memorial 19th & 20th Century Sculpture Collection; Margery H Smith Collection of Asian Art; †20th century photographs
Exhibitions: (1982) Rene Rickabaugh Works from 1975-1981; Social and Political Commentary in Prints; Honore Daumier, 1808-1879, from the Armand Hammer Daumier Collection; Lee Friedlander Photographs; Texture in Prints; The Art Fabric: Mainstream; Pacific Northwest College of Art Thesis Exhibition; Avant-Garde Photography in Germany: 1919-1939; Kandinsky Watercolors: A Selection from the Solomon R Guggenheim Museum and the Hilla von Rebay Foundation; Kandinsky and the Avant-Garde in Germany; Speaking a New Classicism: American Architecture Now; Big Prints from Rome; Henk Pander Drawings; Lucas Samaras Pastels; Northwest Print Council; Arthur B Davies; Of Time and Place: American Figurative Art from the Corcoran Gallery; American Figurative Art from the Portland Art Museum; Cartes de Visite
Publications: Annual report; Art Of Cameroon; Calendar, monthly; exhibition catalogs; Art in the Life of the Northwest Coast Indian; collection catalogs
Activities: Classes in art history for adults & children; docent training; lectures open to the public, 25 vis lectr per yr; gallery talks; tours; individual paintings & original objects of art lent; book traveling exhibitions, 6 - 10 per yr; originate traveling exhibitions; museum shop sells books, gifts & cards

L   Museum Library, 1219 SW Park Ave, 97205. Tel 503-226-2811, Ext 32. *Librn* Emily Evans-Elsner; *Slide Librn* Dan Lucas
Open Tues - Fri 9 AM - 5 PM, cl Mon; special schedules for holidays. Estab 1892 to provide a reference collection for Pacific Northwest Col Art as well as supportive materials for the museum collection
Income: $19,000 (financed by endowment and grants)
Purchases: $19,000
Library Holdings: Vols 15,900; Per subs 70; AV — Motion pictures, slides; Other — Clipping files, exhibition catalogs
Special Subjects: Silver, Northwest Coast Indian art & culture; Japanese art; contemporary art
O   Northwest Film Study Center,* 1219 SW Park Ave, 97225. Tel 503-221-1156. *Dir* Bill Foster
Estab 1972. Maintains film archives and circ film library
Exhibitions: Annual Northwest Film and Video Festival; Young Peoples Film Festival
Publications: Animator, quarterly
Activities: Film screening program; courses in film and video; Filmmaker-in-the-Schools program

M   PORTLAND CENTER FOR THE VISUAL ARTS, 117 NW Fifth Ave, 97209. Tel 503-222-7107. *Pres* Paul Magnusson; *Dir* Donna J Milrany; *Program Coordr* Randy Davis; *Secy* Jeannette Bugge
Open Tues - Sun Noon - 5 PM. Estab 1972 to bring a cross section of nationally known contemporary performing and visual arts to the Northwest. Main gallery covers 5000 sq ft and north gallery covers 2800 sq ft. Average Annual Attendance: 25,000. Mem: 1000; dues $20-$1000
Income: Financed by membership, city and state appropriation, contributions, fund raising events, foundation grants and NEA grants
Exhibitions: (1982) Selected performances: Magdalena Abakanowicz; Laurie Anderson; Trisha Brown; John Cage; Leo Castelli & His Artists; Ping Chong & the Fiji Company; Chico Freeman; Leroy Jenkins; Komar & Melamid; Donald Lipski; Roscoe Mitchell; Terry Riley; Robert Stackhouse
Publications: Bi-monthly calendar; annual report
Activities: Lectures open to public, 6-10 vis lectr per yr; concerts; dance & theater performances; site specific installations; traveling exhibitions organized and circulated

M   PORTLAND CHILDREN'S MUSEUM, 3037 SW Second Ave, 97201. Tel 503-248-4587. *Dir* Robert G Bridgeford
Open Mon - Fri 9 AM - 5 PM; Sat 9 AM - 4 PM. Estab 1949; sponsored by Portland Bureau of Parks and Recreation. Average Annual Attendance: 100,000.
Mem: 200; dues $16 family, $9 individual
Income: Income includes city appropriation
Collections: Children's art; natural history, toys, dollhouses, miniatures
Exhibitions: (1983-84) City Streets - 10 Best & 10 Worst Toys
Publications: Boing, quarterly for children
Activities: Classes for children; lectures; tours; book traveling exhibitions

M   PORTLAND COMMUNITY COLLEGE, North View Gallery,* 12000 SW 49th St, 97219. Tel 503-244-6111. *Dir* Sharon Bronzan
Open Mon - Fri 9 AM - 5 PM
Exhibitions: Contemporary art of the Northwest

PORTLAND STATE UNIVERSITY
M   Littman Gallery, PO Box 751, Portland, 97207
Open Mon - Fri Noon - 4 PM. No admis fee. Estab 1980 to exhibit art in variety of media, style & geographic distribution. Gallery space has 146 running ft
Exhibitions: (1983-84) China From Within, photos from China; Marly Stone, paintings & photography; FredKline, painting retrospective; Dwight Coburn, painting & prints; Ken Butler, installation; Michael Bliven, ceramic sculpture; Lou Ocepek, Jim Hubbard, Michihiro Kosuga, painting, prints, sculpture; Nancy McKimmens, photographic installation; Paul Trautman, neon
Activities: Lectures open to public; gallery talks
M   White Gallery, PO Box 751, Portland, 97207. Tel 503-229-3020. *Dir* Claudi Borvck
Open Mon - Fri 8 AM - 10 PM, Sat 9 AM - 7 PM. No admis fee. Estab 1970 as a student operated gallery exhibiting works by professional artists representing primarily photography
Collections: Permanent collection contains work by local professional artists with a few nationally recognized artists
Exhibitions: China From Within; Anthony Sanna, Canyons of the Colorado River System; David Inkpen, Two Big Paintings; Douglas T Hall; Stewart A Harvey; Jim Lommasson
Activities: Lectures open to public; gallery talks; individual paintings & original objects of art lent to other schools or museums; lending collection contains original prints, paintings & sculpture

M   REED COLLEGE ART GALLERY, 3202 SE Woodstock Blvd, 97202. Tel 503-771-1112. *Dir* Greg Ware
Open Sat & Sun Noon - 5 PM, or by appointment. No admis fee. Estab 1962 to bring to the college and the community shows of significant contemporary art not previously available in the Northwest. Many shows relate to advanced art courses at the college and to important exhibitions at the Portland Art Museum, the PCVA or other Northwest institutions. Mem: 75 Art Associates; dues $100
Income: $20,000 (financed by endowment, membership, state appropriation, individual donations and NEA grants)
Purchases: Marcus oil & pastel drawing
Collections: †pre-20th century prints; 20th century prints, drawings, paintings and sculptures
Exhibitions: (1982) John Avery Newman, sculpture; Frank Lobdell, summer mural; Eve Arnold, photographs; Richard Berger, sculpture; American Photography of the Thirties, Paul Berger, photography; Michael Kentson, paintings; Judy Rifka, paintings; Janis Provisor, paintings; (1983-84) Terry Winters, paintings & drawings; Whistler Lithographs; Oliver Jackson, paintings; Joe Zucker, paintings; Tad Sarinar, installation
Publications: Poster with introductory write-up on back published for each show
Activities: Lectures open to public, 4-6 vis lectr per yr; gallery talks; individual paintings and original objects of art lent to other museums only for major exhibitions

L **UNIVERSITY OF PORTLAND,** Wilson W Clark Memorial Library, 5000 N Willamette Blvd, 97203. Tel 503-283-7111. *Dir* Joseph P Browne; *Reference Librn* Jane Ozura; *Technical Services Librn* Susan Hinken; *Special Services Librn* Bro Frank Drury
Open Sun 1 - 11 PM; Mon - Thurs 8 AM - 11 PM; Fri 8 AM - 5 PM; Sat 9 AM - 4 PM. Estab 1901 to support the University curriculum. Maintains an art gallery with a rotating exhibit. Circ 50,000
Income: Financed through the University
Exhibitions: (1983) Reta Soloway, acrylics; Leslie Fliegel, water colors; Sally Kugelmeyer, etchings; Patricia Reynolds, water colors; Tom Griffith, water colors; San Diego Water Color Society; models of inventions of Leonardo da Vinci & facsimiles of his anatomical drawings
Publications: Art Objects, holdings list

O **WEST HILLS UNITARIAN FELLOWSHIP,** 8470 SW Oleson Rd, 97223. Tel 503-246-3351. *Pres* Rosie Hamilton; *VPres* Beverly Conaway; *Office Admin* Connie Morgan; *Secy* Sylvia McFarland; *Fine Arts Chmn* Doll Gardner
Open Mon - Fri 9 AM - Noon. No admis fee. Estab 1970 to give professional artists one or two-man shows in a lovely gallery space and to expose the congregation and public to fine visual art. The entire sanctuary wall space is like a large gallery and the building is light, airy with a woodsy backdrop. Average Annual Attendance: 10,000
Income: $30,000 (financed by membership)
Collections: Paintings, wall sculptures by local artists
Exhibitions: (1982) Gail Johnson, batiks; Eric Johnson, paintings; Gerald Wilson, paintings; Arch Diack, etchings; Lynne Oulman-Johnston, oil pastels and small bronze sketches; Manya Shapiro and Vickie Ayers, soft sculpture and mixed media collages; Mar Gorman, paintings, Nancy Cushwar Blake, paintings; (1983) Harold Johnson, paintings; Mary Greeley, Lois McClellan and Angela Dworkin, calligraphy; Elizabeth Rocchia, watercolors; Jay Shisler, silkscreens
Publications: Bulletin, weekly; newsletter, monthly
Activities: Classes for adults and children; dramatic programs; lect open to the public, 8 vis lectr per yr; concerts; sales shop selling books

SAINT BENEDICT

L **MOUNT ANGEL ABBEY & SEMINARY LIBRARY,** 97373. Tel 503-845-3318. *Head Librn* Bede Partridge; *Acquisitions Librn* Rev Jeremy Driscoll; *Cataloger* Susan Barnes
Open 8:30 AM - 5 PM. Estab 1882. The library serves Mount Angel Abbey, Mount Angel Seminary & visitors. It sponsors art exhibits in the foyer designed for this purpose & makes the auditorium available for concerts
Exhibitions: Local artists; Alvar Aalto

SALEM

O **SALEM ART ASSOCIATION,** 600 Mission St SE, 97302. Tel 503-363-4714, 581-2228. *Exec Dir* Doris Helen Nelson; *Cur* Jenny Hagloch
Incorporated 1938. Average Annual Attendance: 35,000. Mem: 2000; dues $10 and higher; annual meeting in Sept
Income: $250,000 (financed by sales gallery, art fair, special events, admission & membership)
Exhibitions: Changed monthly
M **Bush Barn Art Center,** 600 Mission St SE, Salem, 97302
Open Tues - Fri 9:30 AM - 5 PM, Sat & Sun 1 - 5 PM. No admis fee. Estab 1965 to preserve the best of the past & encourage the arts of the present. Average Annual Attendance: 20,000. Mem: 2000; dues $15; annual meeting third Mon Sept
Activities: Classes for adults & children; lectures for members only, 12 artists per yr; gallery talks; scholarships; book traveling exhibitions; originate traveling exhibitions; sales shop sells original art
M **Bush House,** 600 Mission St SE, Salem, 97302
Open summer Tues - Sun Noon - 5 PM, winter Tues - Sun 2 - 5 PM. Admis adults $1.50, students & sr citizens $1, children $.50. Estab 1953 to preserve & interpret the Victorian Era of 1870-1900. Contains 16 room mansion with original furnishings. Average Annual Attendance: 10,000
Collections: Furniture, books, documents & antiques
Activities: Lectures open to public; tours; original objects of art lent to organizations for display; museum shop sells books, post cards & brochures
L **Archives,** 600 Mission St SE, 97301
Library Holdings: Vols 150; AV — A-tapes, cassettes, motion pictures, v-tapes; Other — Clipping files, manuscripts, memorabilia, photographs
Collections: Bush family papers 1840-1950

M **WILLAMETTE UNIVERSITY,** George Putnam University Center,* 900 State St, 97301. Tel 503-370-6267. *Dir* Sally Howell
Open Mon - Sun 8 AM - 11 PM. No admis fee. Estab 1970 to enrich the atmosphere of the University Center and to acquaint students, faculty and staff with various forms of art. Two separate areas are used: one area is a paneled wall; the other area is comprised of free standing art panels with surface area of approx 54 x 54 inches. Average Annual Attendance: 45,000
Income: Financed through the University
Exhibitions: China exhibit; Robert Hess; Betty LaDuke; sculptures; several exhibits from Visual Arts Resources (University of Oregon); several local artists and photographers
Activities: Lect; gallery talks

SPRINGFIELD

O **EMERALD EMPIRE ARTS ASSOCIATION,*** 421 North A, 97477. Tel 503-726-8595. *Pres* Mrs Frank Light
Estab 1957 to advance art in community, and to build up funds for a workshop and gallery. Downtown area is 3000 sq ft. Mem: 150; dues $20; monthly meetings third Tues
Exhibitions: Exhibitions twice a year at local shopping centers

Publications: Monthly Art League Bulletin
Activities: Classes for adults, material available to anyone; lectures for members; picture of the month award; individual paintings and original objects of art lent; traveling exhibitions organized and circulated; sales shop sells crafts, magazines and original art

PENNSYLVANIA

ALLENTOWN

M **ALLENTOWN ART MUSEUM,** Fifth & Courts Sts, PO Box 117, 18105. Tel 215-432-4333. *Pres Board Trustees* Bernard Berman; *Dir* Richard N Gregg; *Cur* Peter F Blume; *Cur Educ* Mimi Miley; *Comptroller* Barbara Strohl; *Registrar* Patricia Delluva; *Development* Jeanne Beldon; *Sales Desk Mgr* Diana Maguire
Open Tues - Sat 10 AM - 5 PM, Sun 1 - 5 PM, cl Mon. No admis fee. Estab 1939 to acquire, protect, display and interpret the visual arts from the past and present, world wide. Building and land cover three quarters of a city block; 28,000 sq ft wing was added in 1975 to more than double the space. Average Annual Attendance: 100,000. Mem: 3600; dues benefactor $500, student $7.50
Income: $750,000 (financed by endowment, membership, city and state appropriations, and contributions)
Collections: †American 18th, 19th & 20th century paintings, sculptures and prints; Chinese porcelains; English and American silver; Samuel H Kress Memorial Collection of European paintings & sculpture, c 1350-1750 (Bugiardini, Hals, de Heem, Rembrandt, Ruisdael, Steen and others); †Textile study room; Frank Lloyd Wright period room, 1912
Exhibitions: Art for the Private Citizen in the Early Renaissance; Aspects of Ancient Greece; Beyond Nobility; Valley Collects: American Decorative Arts, 1780-1880
Publications: Calendar of events, monthly; catalogs of major exhibitions
Activities: Docent training; lect open to public; gallery talks; tours; competitions; individual paintings lent to museums; lending collection contains original art works, original prints, paintings and textiles; traveling exhibitions organized and circulated; museum shop selling books, original art, reproductions, prints, slides, cards and catalogs

M **MUHLENBERG COLLEGE CENTER FOR THE ARTS,*** 24th & Chew Sts, 18104. Tel 215-433-2163
Open daily during school term. No admis fee. Estab 1976. The building was designed by architect Philip Johnson; the focal point of its design and function is a 220 ft glass-covered galleria which bisects the structure
Collections: Contemporary art collection has recently been initiated
Exhibitions: Three exhibitions each semester

AUDUBON

M **AUDUBON WILDLIFE SANCTUARY,** Mill Grove, Box 25, 19407. Tel 215-666-5593. *Cur & Dir* Edward W Graham
Open daily 10 AM - 5 PM, cl Mon. No admis fee. Estab 1951 to display the major artwork of John James Audubon, artist-naturalist, who made Mill Grove his first home in America, 1804-06. This is a National Historic Site and features two original artworks by Audubon, plus examples of all his major publications. Average Annual Attendance: 25,000 - 30,000
Income: Financed by county appropriation
Collections: Birds of America (double elephant folio, 4 vols, Audubon & Havell); Birds of America (first ed Octavo, 7 vols, Audubon, Lithos by Bowen); Quadrupeds of North America (Imperial size, 2 vols, Audubon & Bachmann); Quadrupeds of North America (Octavo, 3 vols, Audubon, Lithos by Bowen)

BETHLEHEM

M **ANNIE S KEMERER MUSEUM,** 427 North New St, 18018. Tel 215-868-6868. *Pres* Mrs Peter P Prichett; *VPres* Mrs Donald Trautlein; *Secy* Ray R Brennen; *Dir* Deborah L Evans; *Secy* Mary Elizabeth Biggs; *Secy* Susan I Adleman; *Treas* William Mannering; *Asst Treas* Vernon H Nelson
Open Mon - Fri 1 - 4 PM, second and fourth Sun 2 - 4 PM, Sat April - December 10 AM - 4 PM, cl January. No admis fee, donation appreciated. Estab 1954 for public education. Devoted to the display of antiques and historical and other objects illustrative of the growth of the museum's geographical area. Gallery on second floor of the south wing provides monthly exhibits; showcase for local, national and international artists. Average Annual Attendance: 10,000. Mem: 200; dues donated
Income: $50,000 (financed by endowment and membership)
Collections: Bohemian Glass, Early Bethlehem Oil Paintings and Prints, 18th and 19th Century Furniture, Oriental Rugs, Pennsylvania German Frackturs, Victoriana, quilts and coverlets, locally made tall case clocks, and tinware
Exhibitions: Changing gallery exhibitions; changing temporary museum; private collection exhibits
Publications: Newsletter, quarterly
Activities: Docent training; lect for members only; gallery talks; tours; competitions; individual paintings and original objects of art lent to individuals and organizations; museum shop sells books, original art, reproductions, prints and handicrafts

M **LEHIGH UNIVERSITY ART GALLERIES,** Fine Arts Bldg, Chandler-Ullmann Hall, No 17, 18015. Tel 215-861-3615. *Dir Exhib & Coll* Ricardo Viera; *Asst to Dir* Judith Goldworm
Open Mon - Fri 9 AM - 10 PM, Sat 9 AM - Noon, cl Sun (DuBois Gallery). 9 AM - 5 PM, Sat 9 AM - Noon, Sun 2 - 5 PM (Ralph Wilson Gallery). Estab to bring diverse media and understanding to the Lehigh students and general public of the Lehigh Valley area. Collection is maintained in two galleries: DuBois

Gallery has four floors of approx 250 running ft of wall hanging space per floor; Ralph Wilson Gallery has two rooms of exhibition space; hall gallery consists of two corridors. Average Annual Attendance: 25,000 (per all galleries)
Income: Financed by endowment and gifts
Collections: Adler Collection of Paintings; Baker Collection of Porcelain; Berman Collection of Paintings; Driebe Collection of Paintings; Grace Collection of Paintings; Kempsmith Collection of Sculpture and Graphics; photography collection; Ralph Wilson Collection of Paintings and Graphics
Exhibitions: (1983-84) Art & Technology: Graphic Prints; European Paintings & Drawings from the Fearnside; Grace & Dreyfus Collection; Harold Edgerton, photographs; New American Photographs; Dorothy Gillespie, sculptured paintings; WCA '84 National Juried Exhibition; Richard Redd: Art From the Copy Machine; Siggraph '83 Philadelphia, Past & Present; the Deutscher Werkbund; Transformed Houses (sites); Lehigh Valley Artists Biennial (DuBois Gallery)
Publications: Calendar, twice per year; exhibition catalogs
Activities: Classes for adults; lect open to the public, 6 visiting lectrs per year; gallery talks; individual paintings and original objects of art lent to other schools and galleries; originate traveling exhibitions

BLOOMSBURG

M **BLOOMSBURG UNIVERSITY OF PENNSYLVANIA,** Haas Gallery of Art, 17815. Tel 717-389-4184. *Dir* John F Cook Jr; *Chmn Dept of Art* Barbara Strohman
Open Mon - Fri 9 AM - 5 PM. No admis fee. Estab 1966 as an educational and cultural extension of the College's Department of Art. Gallery covers 2350 sq ft with track lighting and three dome skylights. Average Annual Attendance: 16,000
Income: Financed by community activities and grants
Collections: Permanent Collection
Exhibitions: Ten monthly exhibitions in a variety of media
Publications: Exhibition catalogs and brochures, monthly
Activities: Lect open to the public, 6-8 vis lectr per yr; gallery talks; tours

BOALSBURG

M **COLUMBUS CHAPEL, BOAL MANSION AND MUSEUM,** Rte 322, 16827. Tel 814-466-6210. *Pres* Mathilde Boal Lee; *Dir* Christopher G Lee
Open June - Labor Day 10 AM - 5 PM; May, Sept & Oct 2 - 5 PM. Admis adults $3.50, students $2.50, children $1.50. Estab 1952 as a nonprofit educational organization devoted to preservation of this historic homestead built in 1789. Average Annual Attendance: 3,000
Income: Financed by admissions
Collections: Chapel contains 16th & 17th century Spanish, Italian and Flemish art; furniture, china and glassware; mansion contains 18th and 19th century French, Spanish, Italian, Flemish and American art; weapons: American, French and German (1780-1920)
Activities: Sales shop selling books, slides and postcards

BRYN MAWR

L **BRYN MAWR COLLEGE,** Art and Archaeology Library, Thomas Library, 19010. Tel 215-645-5088, 645-5087. *Head Librn* Eileen Markson; *Library Asst* Babette Bauerle
Open during academic year Mon - Thurs 9 AM - 12 PM; Fri 9 AM - 10 PM; Sat 9 AM - 5 PM; Sun 2 - 12 PM, summer Mon - Fri 9 AM - 5 PM. Estab 1931 to serve the needs of the general college program, the undergraduate majors and graduate students through the PhD degree in both history of art and Classical and Near Eastern archeology. Non-circulating
Income: Financed by college funds
Library Holdings: Vols 50,000; Per subs 400
Special Subjects: Early Christian and Byzantine, Italian Renaissance, Italian Baroque, Impressionism, Greek architecture and sculpture, Near Eastern archaeology, Aegean archaeology

CHADDS FORD

M **BRANDYWINE RIVER MUSEUM,** PO Box 141, 19317. Tel 215-388-7601, 459-1900. *Dir* James H Duff; *Business Mgr* Charles Burns; *Dir Public Relations* John Sheppard; *Cur Coll* Ann Barton Brown; *Cur* Gene E Harris; *Registrar* Jean A Gilmore; *Coordr Education & Visitor Servs* Cynthia Repplier; *Bookstore Mgr* Sue Coleburn
Open daily 9:30 AM - 4:30 PM, cl Christmas. Admis adults $2, senior citizens, students and children $1.00. Estab 1971, devoted to the preservation, documentation and interpretation of art history in the Brandywine Valley, the history of American illustration, American still-life painting, and the relationship of regional art to the natural environment. Three main galleries are housed in a renovated 1864 grist mill with contemporary additions for public services, storage, offices, restaurant and bookstore. Average Annual Attendance: 175,000. Mem: 2800; dues $20-$1000
Purchases: $64,000
Collections: †American illustration; †art of the Brandywine Valley from early and mid-19th century; †regional artists of the 20th century; †American still-life painting, drawing and sculpture, including a major Andrew Wyeth Collection
Exhibitions: (1982) Walter Elmer Schofield; Not for Publication-Landscapes, Still Lifes & Portraits by N C Wyeth; John W McCoy; Thornton Oakley Retrospective; Drawings by Palmer Cox; Natural History Illustrations from the National Geographic Collection; American Illustration: Recent Accessions from the Jane Collette Wilcox Collection
Publications: The Catalyst, quarterly; exhibition catalogs
Activities: Classes for children; tours; individual paintings and original objects of art lent to other museums for exhibition purposes; traveling exhibitions organized and circulated; museum shop selling books, reproductions, slides, postcards and catalogs

L **Library,** PO Box 141, 19317. Tel 215-459-1900, 388-7601. *Librn* Mary Bassett
Open daily 9:30 AM - 4:30 PM. For reference to staff and volunteers; by appointment to the public
Purchases: $2000
Library Holdings: Vols 4700; Per subs 20; Posters; Other — Clipping files, exhibition catalogs, manuscripts, memorabilia, pamphlets, photographs, reproductions
Special Subjects: The History of American illustration in books and periodicals; The History of Regional Art
Collections: Howard Pyle's published work; N C Wyeth memorabilia; Andrew Wyeth Memorabilia
Exhibitions: Illustrated Books From The Museum Library

CHESTER

M **WIDENER UNIVERSITY,** Alfred O Deshong Museum,* 11th St and Avenue of the States, 19013. Tel 215-499-4474, 499-4000. *Dir* Rebecca M Warda; *Asst to Dir* Anne Fabbri Butera
Open Mon - Fri 10 AM - 4 PM. Estab 1916
Income: Financed by endowment and University functions
Collections: 18th and 19th century Oriental art objects; 19th century European landscape and genre pictures; 20th century American paintings and sculpture
Exhibitions: (1980) Peter Lipman-Wulf (sculpture); Tom Ewing (sculpture and painting); Joseph Amarotico (painting); Architectural Fantasy; Isaiah Zagar, No Mirror Now; 7 Afro-American Artists of the Delaware Valley; Tradition and Innovations (9 Delaware County Artists); Social Realism and the Figure; Eleanor Bruegel (wood carvings); Greek Vases
Publications: Exhibition catalog
Activities: Lectures; guided tours

CLARION

M **CLARION UNIVERSITY,** Hazel Sandford Gallery, 16214. Tel 814-226-2000; WATS 800-669-2000. *Dir* Judy B Bond
Open Mon - Fri 10 AM - 1 PM, Sun 2 - 4 PM. No admis fee. Estab 1970 for aesthic enjoyment and artistic education of students. Gallery is 66 ft long, 17ft 3 inches wide; lit by some 50 adjustable spot lights; one side of gallery is glassed in; other side is fabric-covered panels; and a dozen free standing panels, available for hanging. Average Annual Attendance: 4000. Mem: 85
Income: Financed by university & memberships
Purchases: Lidded basket by Chris Richard; High Country paintings and refrigerator by Norman Scott Quinn
Collections: Original paintings, drawings and prints, purchased from selected artists who have shown at gallery; sculpture and †ceramics; †photographs
Publications: Monthly announcements of shows
Activities: Lectures open to the public, 2 - 3 vis lectr per yr; concerts; gallery talks; tours; competitions; individual paintings and original objects of art lent to departments on campus and other state colleges; lending collection contains original art works, original prints, paintings, photographs and sculpture; book traveling exhibitions

DOYLESTOWN

M **BUCKS COUNTY HISTORICAL SOCIETY,** Mercer Museum, Pine & Ashland Sts, 18901. Tel 215-345-0210. *Pres* William F Heefner; *Chief Cur* James Blackaby
Open Tues - Sat 10 AM - 5 PM; Sun 1 - 5 PM; Mar - Dec. Admis adults $2 and students $1. Estab 1880. Inside this poured, re-inforced concrete building, four galleries wrap around a towering central court where different hand crafts are exhibited inside small cubicles. Additional artifacts hang from ceilings, walls and railings. A six story tower on each end completes the building. Average Annual Attendance: 40,000. Mem: 2400; dues $20 and up; annual meeting Nov
Collections: Over 40,000 artifacts representing more than 40 early American crafts, their tools and finished products; large American folk art collection; the history and growth of our country as seen through the work of the human hand
Exhibitions: Continuous small changing exhibits
Publications: Journal, semi-annually; newsletter, monthly
Activities: Classes for adults and children; lect open to public, 6-7 vis lectr per year; Annual Folk Festival; museum shop selling books, magazines, reproductions and prints

L **Spruance Library,** Pine & Ashland Sts, 18901. Tel 215-345-0210. *Librn* Terry A McNealy
Open to the public for reference only
Library Holdings: Vols 18,000; Per subs 50; Archives; Other — Manuscripts
Special Subjects: Folk Art, Crafts and Early Industries of America

DUNCANSVILLE

M **LEE ATKYNS STUDIO-GALLERY,** Box 120, Route 2, 16635. Tel 814-695-0186. *Dir* Lee Atkyns
Open by appointment. No admis fee. Estab 1950, original gallery was in Washington, DC; present studio gallery opened in 1975 in what was once an abandoned chapel, the old cemetery adjacent has been converted into a flower garden
Income: Financed personally
Collections: Paintings by Lee Atkyns of Liberated Lines Series, showing the derivative trends through the years from 1947 to the present time: Landscapes, Abstractions and Music Expressionist paintings; Paintings in oils, watercolor, acrylic. From around the world: Paintings, tapestry, weavings, ceramics, prints and small sculptures including primitive old New Guinea and early Egyptian works
Activities: Individual paintings lent to galleries

EASTON

M LAFAYETTE COLLEGE, Morris R Williams Center for the Arts, Hamilton &
High St, 18042. Tel 215-250-5361. *Gallery Administrator* Michiko O Taylor;
Center Dir H Ellis Finger; *Center Administrator* Barbara Kerridge
Open Mon - Fri 10 AM - 5 PM & by appointment. No admis fee. Estab 1983 to
present a variety of exhibitions for enrichment of campus & community's
exposure to visual arts. Versatile space with movable panels & 160 running ft of
wall space, climate control & track lighting
Income: Financed by endowment
Collections: 19th & 20th century American painting, prints & photographs
Exhibitions: Ibram Lassaw, sculpture; George Arden Collection, 19th century
American paintings; Aaron & Rosa Esman Collection, 20th century paintings,
sculpture & drawings; Doug Sanderson, painting; Grace Hartigan, painting;
photography
Publications: Brochures; exhibition catalogues; handouts
Activities: Lectures open to public

ERIE

M ERIE ART MUSEUM, 411 State St, 16501. Tel 814-459-5477. *Pres* Marvin
Gold; *VPres* Charles Roberts; *Secy* Michele Ridge; *Treas* John Freeman; *Exec
Dir* John Vanco
Open Tues - Sat 11 AM - 5 PM, Sun 1 - 5 PM. Admis $1 for non-members.
Estab 1898 for the advancement of visual arts. Galleries are located in historic
building. Average Annual Attendance: 20,000. Mem: Dues family $25, individual
$15
Income: $190,000 (financed by membership)
Collections: Contemporary graphics, paintings, photographs, sculpture; historical
paintings and graphics; American ceramics both contemporary & historic
Exhibitions: Ansel Adams & Edward Weston, photo; Richard Anuszkiewicz
1965-79, graphic work; Art Nouveau; PHOTONATIONAL; Steven & Susan
Kemenyffy - Raku Plus; annual spring show; Wood Invitational; David Gilhooly,
ceramics; Daumier Lithography; National Glass Art Invitational; Take A Good
Look; Clay National
Publications: Catalogs for exhibitions; flyers for shows, monthly
Activities: Classes for adults and children; docent training; gallery talks; tours;
competitions; individual paintings and original objects of art lent to public
buildings, community centers, colleges; lending collection contains original art
works; traveling exhibitions organized and circulated; sales shop selling frames

L ERIE COUNTY LIBRARY SYSTEM, Art Dept,* 3 S Perry Square, 16501. Tel
814-452-2333. *Dir* Michele M Ridge
Open, winter Mon - Fri 9 AM - 9 PM, Sat 9 AM - 5:30 PM, cl Sun, summer
Mon & Fri 9 AM - 9 PM, Tues, Wed & Thurs 9 AM - 9 PM, Sat 9 AM - 5:30
PM, cl Sun. No admis fee. Estab 1899 to provide public library services to the
community. Gallery contains original paintings, drawings, prints and
reproductions of paintings and sculpture. Mem: 117,000
Income: Financed by county and state appropriations
Library Holdings: Micro — Cards, fiche, reels; AV — Cassettes, motion pictures;
Other — Clipping files, original art works, pamphlets, photographs, sculpture
Exhibitions: Exhibitions by local artists
Activities: Original paintings, prints, drawings and sculpture reproductions lent;
lending collection contains color reproductions and photographs

M ERIE HISTORICAL MUSEUM, 356 W 6th St, 16507. Tel 814-453-5811. *Pres*
William Garvey; *Exec Dir* Charles Alan Watkins; *Admin Asst & Shop Mgr* June
C Pintea
Open Tues - Sun 1 - 5 PM, extended summer hours. Admis adults $.75, children
under 18 free. Estab 1899 to display and collect regional and maritime history
and art. Museum is located in a Victorian mansion built in 1891-1892 and
designed by Green & Wicks of Buffalo, NY. Average Annual Attendance: 30,000
Income: $120,000 (financed by city appropriation)
Collections: Moses Billings (paintings); George Ericson-Eugene Iverd (paintings);
genre paintings; Native American pottery; Southwest & Northwest Coast baskets;
Victorian decorative arts; †Marx Toys
Exhibitions: Rotating exhibits of historical and art interest
Publications: Exhibition catalogs
Activities: Docent tours; film programs; lesson tours for students; lectures open
to public, 3 vis lectr per yr; gallery talks; tours; competitions; book traveling
exhibitions; originate traveling exhibitions; museum shop sells books, magazines
and prints

FRANKLIN CENTER

M FRANKLIN MINT MUSEUM, 19091. Tel 215-459-6168. *Supvr Guest
Relations* Judie Ashworth
Open Tues - Sat 9 AM - 4:30 PM, Sun 1 - 4:30 PM, cl Mon. No admis fee.
Estab 1973 to make available to the general public a location where the
collectibles created by The Franklin Mint can be viewed. Average Annual
Attendance: 55,000
Income: Financed by Franklin Mint funding
Collections: Etchings and woodblock prints; foreign coinage - coins minted for
19 foreign governments; heirloom furniture; medallic collections; heirloom dolls;
leather bound books ornamented in 22 karet gold; porcelain, crystal, bronze and
pewter art
Activities: Franklin Mint Gallery Store selling jewelry, medals, greeting cards
and collectibles

GLENSIDE

M BEAVER COLLEGE, Richard Eugene Fuller Gallery of Art, Church & Easton
Rds, 19038. Tel 215-572-2900. *Gallery Dir* Zina Goldsmith; *Dept Chmn* Jack
Davis
Open Mon - Fri 10 AM - 4:30 PM, Sat & Sun 1 - 4:30 PM. No admis fee. Estab
1969 to show contemporary art generally. Gallery dimensions 20 x 50 ft.
Average Annual Attendance: 5000
Collections: Benton Spruance Print Collection
Exhibitions: (1982-83) Barry Le Va, installations & drawings; Arakawa, paintings
& prints; Katherene Porter, paintings
Publications: Brochures for major exhibitions, 3 per year
Activities: Lectures open to public, 4 vis lectr per yr; gallery talks; competitions;
awards

GREENSBURG

M WESTMORELAND COUNTY MUSEUM OF ART, 221 N Main St, 15601.
Tel 412-837-1500. *Dir* Dr Paul A Chew; *Admin Asst* Regina L Narad;
Membership Secy Barbara Yeager; *Registrar* Jeffrey P Rouse; *Conservator*
Michael Mosorjak; *Gift Shop* Helen Hartzell
Open Tues - Sat 10 AM - 5 PM; Sun 1 - 5 PM, cl Mon & holidays. No admis
fee. Estab 1949 to create, establish and maintain a memorial foundation of a
public, charitable, cultural, literary and educational nature and in conjunction
therewith, to maintain a public art museum. The museum houses two large
galleries and one small gallery for changing exhibitions, two English 18th century
pine-panelled rooms. Woods-Marchand Memorial Gallery installed for permanent
collection of paintings, sculpture, furniture and decorative arts. Average Annual
Attendance: 18,000. Mem: 550; dues $5 - $1000
Income: Financed by endowment
Collections: †American art (paintings, drawings, sculpture and decorative arts);
†American prints; †antique toys; British drawings; Continental and British
paintings
Exhibitions: (1982-84) Molly Luce; Dorothy Davids; Aqueous '82; Anne Elliott,
paper sculptures, wall reliefs and drawings; Joseph Sheppard, paintings, drawings,
watercolors and sculpture; The Armchair Collector, an exhibition & sale of small
paintings, watercolors, drawings, prints & sculpture; Charles Rosen: The
Pennsylvania Years (1903-1920); Gertrude Quastler, 1909-1963; Impressionism:
An American View; Frederic Tuabes; Pittsburgh Print Group; Waterways of
Pennsylvania; Diane Burko, drawings and prints; Lawrence Calcagno,
retrospective
Publications: Calendar of events, twice a year; exhibition catalogs
Activities: Classes for adults; docent training; lectures open to the public, 6 vis
lectr per yr; concerts; gallery talks; tours; films; awards; individual paintings &
original objects of art lent to accredited museums & galleries; lending collection
contains books, cassettes, color reproductions, film strips, framed reproductions,
Kodachromes, lantern slides, motion pictures, nature artifacts, original prints,
paintings, phonorecords, photographs, sculpture & slides; book traveling
exhibitions, 3 per yr; museum shop sells books, original art, reproductions, slides,
toys and cards
L Art Reference Library, 221 N Main St, 15601
Open Tues - Sat 10 AM - 5 PM; Sun 1 - 5 PM. Estab 1959 for art reference. For
reference only
Purchases: $3600
Library Holdings: Vols 5900; Per subs 40; Other — Clipping files, exhibition
catalogs, pamphlets, photographs
Special Subjects: American art

GREENVILLE

M THIEL COLLEGE, Sampson Art Gallery, College Ave, 16125. Tel 412-588-
7700, Ext 265. *Dir* Alvin Dunkle; *Dir of Permanent Collection* Richard Hayes;
Student Dir Lori Stevenson
Open Mon - Fri 1 - 9 PM, Sat 11 AM - 5 PM, Sun 11 AM - 9 PM. No admis
fee. Estab 1971 to provide students, faculty, college staff and the community
with a gallery featuring a variety of exhibitions, and give students an opportunity
to show their work. Gallery has white walls, track floodlighting system, linoleum
tile floor, and one window wall. Average Annual Attendance: 1000
Activities: Lectures open to the public, gallery talks

HARRISBURG

M ART ASSOCIATION OF HARRISBURG, School and Galleries,* 21 N Front
St, 17101. Tel 717-236-1432. *Executive Dir* Charles A Schulz
Open Mon, Tues, Thurs & Fri 9 AM - 4 PM, Wed 9 AM - Noon, Sat Noon - 4
PM. No admis fee. Estab 1926 to act as showcase for member artists and other
area professionals; community services offered. Building is historic Brownstone
Building, former Governor's mansion (1817) and holds 5 galleries, 4 classrooms
and a garden. Average Annual Attendance: 5000. Mem: 350; dues $15 - $250;
annual meeting May
Income: Financed by endowment and membership
Collections: Old area masters; member's work; Laverty and Lebret
Exhibitions: Annual juried exhibition
Publications: Exhibition announcements, 12 times per year; newsletter, 12 times
per year; school brochure 3 times per year; bus trips 4 times per year
Activities: Classes for adults and children; lectures open to public, 6 vis lectr per
year; gallery talks; tours; competitions open to all states; monetary awards; sales
shop sells original art, prints and craft items

**O DOSHI CENTER FOR CONTEMPORARY ART,* 1435 N Second St, 17102.
Tel 717-232-3039. *Pres* Reed Hamilton; *VPres* L vonBarann; *Secy* Steven
Neiman; *Executive Dir* Judith Ann Westlake; *Dir* Randy Gohn
Open Mon - Fri 11 AM - 4 PM, Sun 3 - 5 PM. No admis fee. Estab 1972 as a
non-profit gallery offering exposure to artists and enlightenment to the
community. Main gallery is on street level, also two smaller rooms termed the

Upper Gallery. Average Annual Attendance: 5000. Mem: 125; dues family $25, artist $20, individual $15; board meeting second Thur every month
Income: $12,500 (financed by endowment)
Exhibitions: (1982) Restiary (Thematic Group Show); Steven Hulbert (photojournalism); Kathleen Piunti (painting); Sue Donmoyer (drawing); Daniel Fitch (painting); Alberto Weller (painting); Noreen Boggs (painting); Henry Casilli (clay sculpture); Cecil J Brooks (photography); Edith Socolow (painting); Henry Troup (photography); Harrisburg Area Community College Student Exhibit; Michael Heberlein (painting); Catherine Prescott (painting); Gerald Hoffman (xerographic photography); Charles Hickok (sculpture); Daniel Herman (stained glass); Lawrence von Barann (paintings & drawings); Kutztown State Student Exhibit; Fire & Ashes (traveling ceramic exhibit); Judith Westlake (constructions)
Activities: Lect open to public, 6 visiting lectr per year; gallery talk; Maya Schock Educational Fund awarded; sales shop sells original art, crafts (ceramics and jewelry)

O **PENNSYLVANIA DEPARTMENT OF EDUCATION**, Arts in Education Program, 8th Floor, 333 Market St, 17108. Tel 717-783-3958. *Senior Adviser* Dr Joseph B DeAngelis; *Dir Arts in Special Education Project* Lola Kearns; *Dir Governor's School for the Arts* Arthur Gatty
The Arts in Education Program provides leadership and consultative and evaluative services to all Pennsylvania schools in arts program development. Infusion of arts processes into differentiated curriculums for all students is a particular thrust. The program offers model programs at several sites, ongoing staff development programs, assistance in designing aesthetic learning environments and consultation in identifying and employing regional and community resources for arts education

O **PENNSYLVANIA HISTORICAL AND MUSEUM COMMISSION**, William Penn Memorial Museum and Archives Bldg, 17120. Tel 717-787-3362. *Executive Dir* Dr Larry E Tise; *Asst Exec Dir* Nancy D Kolb
Open Tues - Sat 9 AM - 5 PM, Sun 9 AM - 4 PM, cl Mon. Estab 1945 when the State Museum, Archives, Historical Commission and Historical Properties combined into one agency. Average Annual Attendance: 231,000. Mem: 200; dues $15
Income: $9,000,000 for entire commission
Publications: Pennsylvania Heritage, quarterly
Activities: Classes for children; docent training; lectures open to the public, 2 - 3 vis lectr per yr; tours; individual paintings & original objects of art lent to other museums; lending collection contains color reproductions, kodachromes, motion pictures & slides; originate traveling exhibitions; museum shop sells books, reproductions, prints & slides
M **William Penn Memorial Museum**, 17120. Tel 717-787-4980. *Cur of Fine Arts* Donald A Winer
Open Mon - Sat 9 AM - 5 PM; Sun 1 - 5 PM. Offices Mon - Fri 8:30 AM - 5 PM. Average Annual Attendance: 200,000
Collections: Anthropology; archaeology; china; decorative arts; folk art; glass; period rooms; silver; textiles Indian artifacts
Publications: Books, brochures
Activities: Classes for adults and children; docent training; lectures open to public; concerts; tours; museumobile; original objects of art lent to qualified museums and art organizations; museum shop sells books and magazines
L **Library**, Box 1026, Harrisburg, 17108. Tel 717-783-9898. *Librn* Carol W Tallman
Open to the public for use on premises only
Library Holdings: Vols 17,000
Special Subjects: Archaeology, Folk Art, Historical Material

HAVERFORD

O **MAIN LINE CENTER OF THE ARTS**, Old Buck Rd & Lancaster Ave, 19041. Tel 215-515-0272. *Pres* Helen Grayson; *VPres* Shirley Lund; *Exec Dir* Eleanor Daitzman; *Secy* Jane Trippe; *Corresp Secy* Dr Myra Haskin
Open Mon - Fri 10 AM - 12 PM & 1 - 4 PM. No admis fee. Estab 1937 to develop and encourage the fine arts. Three large, well lit galleries, completely modernized to accommodate over one hundred sculptures and paintings. Average Annual Attendance: Several thousand. Mem: 800; dues family $30, adult $22 and children $15; meetings once a month except Aug
Income: Financed by membership and fund raising
Exhibitions: Craft Show; Membership Shows; One-man and group Graphic Shows; Porcelain Show
Publications: Brochures, three times a year
Activities: Classes for adults, teens and children; dramatic programs; lect open to public and for members only, 12 vis lectr per yr; gallery talks; concerts; tours; competitions; individual paintings and original objects of art lent to libraries, schools, hospitals, etc; lending collection contains original art works, original prints and sculpture; sales shop sells original art, prints

HERSHEY

M **HERSHEY MUSEUM OF AMERICAN LIFE,** PO Box 170, 17042. Tel 717-534-3439. *Dir* Eliza C Harrison
Open daily 10 AM - 5 PM, summer daily 10 AM - 6 PM. Admis adults $2.50, 5-18 yrs $1.25, under 4 free. Estab 1937 to educate people and help them to enjoy various aspects of American life. Average Annual Attendance: 100,000. Mem: 225; dues $18
Collections: 19th century American Indian; Pennsylvania German life & arts; American decorative arts; western eskimo
Exhibitions: Amish Quilts; MS Hershey; Navajo Images; PA German Printing; Treasure of the Concepcion
Publications: Newsletter, 3 times per year
Activities: Classes for adults and children; docent training; open house; family programs; programs in schools; lectures open to public; tours; book traveling exhibitions; museum shop sells books and craft items relating to museum collections; childrens room

INDIANA

M **INDIANA UNIVERSITY OF PENNSYLVANIA**, Kipp Gallery, Sprowls Hall, 15705. Tel 412-357-2530. *Chmn Exhib* Ned O Wert
Open Mon - Fri Noon - 4 PM; Sat & Sun 2 PM - 4 PM. No admis fee. Estab 1970 to make available a professional gallery program to Western Pennsylvania and to the university community. Versatile space with portable wall system, track lighting, secure, humidity controlled. Average Annual Attendance: 12,000
Income: Financed by Student Coop Assn
Exhibitions: Solo and group shows annually; (1983-84) Connections - Handmade fiber by Elena Hiatt Houlihan; IUP Alumni Photographers Invitational; Art for the Computer Age; IUP Art Faculty Exhibition; Student Show: Winter 1984; IUP Hosts: A Ceramic Invitational; National Printmakers: Together at IUP; Robert Chotiner - Large and Small Works; Student Show: Summer - 1984
Activities: Lect open to public, 3-5 vis lectr per yr; gallery talks; tours; traveling exhibitions organized and circulated; sales shop selling original art and prints

KUTZTOWN

KUTZTOWN UNIVERSITY
M **Sharadin Art Gallery**, 19530. Tel 215-683-4224. *Gallery Dir* Tom Schantz
Open Mon - Fri 10 AM - 4 PM; Sat 12 - 5 PM; Sun 2 - 5 PM. No admis fee. Estab 1956 to make the best of the contemporary arts available to the town and college communities
Income: Financed by city, state & private appropriations
Collections: Approximately 400 works in prints, drawings and paintings
Publications: Brochure listing a gallery season's of shows
Activities: Artist-in-residence series; lectures; European travel tours
L **Rohrbach Library**, 19530. Tel 215-683-4480. *Univ Librn* John K Amrhein
Open Mon - Thurs 7:45 AM - 11 PM; Fri 7:45 AM - 5 PM; Sat 11 AM - 5 PM; Sun 2 - 11 PM. Estab 1866. Circ 90,000
Library Holdings: Vols 330,000; Per subs 2000; Micro — Cards, fiche, prints, reels; AV — A-tapes, cassettes, fs, motion pictures, rec, slides; Other — Exhibition catalogs, pamphlets
Special Subjects: Art Education, Art History, Russian Art

LANCASTER

M **COMMUNITY GALLERY OF LANCASTER COUNTY**, 135 N Lime St, 17602. Tel 717-394-3497. *Pres* Judith F Fulton; *Dir* Shirley M Reed
Open Mon - Sat 10 AM - 4 PM; Sun 12 - 4 PM. No admis fee. Estab 1965 to present the best quality in art exhibits. Average Annual Attendance: 17,000. Mem: 1000; dues, various categories
Income: $50,000 (financed by membership, local business and county commissioners)
Exhibitions: David Brumbach; Pfannebecker Collection; Joseph Raffael; Christo; Moses Soyer; Stanley William Hayter; Charles Demuth; National Watercolor Society; Pennsylvania Academy of Fine Arts; Alice Neal; Josef Albers; Toshiko Takaezu
Activities: Docent training; lect; gallery talks; bus trips

O **LANCASTER COUNTY ART ASSOCIATION**, Art Center, 22 E Vine St, 17602. Tel 717-392-9258. *Pres* Charles I Kent
Open Mon - Sun 7 - 9:30 PM, during shows 9 AM - 4 PM, 6 - 10 PM. No admis fee. Estab 1936, incorporated 1950. Average Annual Attendance: 250. Mem: 403; dues $15; annual meeting second Tues in May
Income: Financed by house tours, classes, contributions & volunteer service
Collections: Currently being enlarged by purchases
Exhibitions: Monthly exhibitions; Spring and Fall member and student shows; 3 three-man shows, and others
Publications: Prexys Corner, monthly newsletter
Activities: Classes for adults & children, free classes for sr retirees; lectures for members only, 12 vis lectr per yr; gallery talks; tours; competitions with awards; scholarships; individual paintings & original objects of art lent to Lancaster library & other museums

M **PENNSYLVANIA FARM MUSEUM OF LANDIS VALLEY,** 2451 Kissel Hill Rd, 17601. Tel 717-569-0401. *Dir* Robert N Sieber; *Cur Crafts & Education* John B Brooks; *Cur Collections* Vernon S Gunnion
Open Tues - Sat 9 AM - 5 PM, Sun Noon - 5 PM, cl holidays. Admis adults $2, sr citizens $1.40, children under 12 free. Estab 1925 to collect, preserve and interpret Pennsylvania rural life and culture, circa 1750 to 1900; farm implements, crafts, tools, domestic furnishings and folk art. The outdoor museum has 25 exhibit buildings, including restored 18th and 19th century structures. Average Annual Attendance: 80,000. Mem: 1000; dues $5 and up; annual meeting third Tues in Oct
Income: Financed by state appropriation
Collections: Folk art including ceramics, textiles, furniture and decorative ironware
Publications: Newsletter, monthly; special exhibit catalogs
Activities: Classes for adults and children; lect open to public, 4 vis lectr per year; traditional crafts programs; occasional loans made from permanent collections; museum shop selling books, crafts items and period reproductions
L **Library,** 2451 Kissel Hill Rd, 17601
Open to staff, scholars by appointment for reference only
Library Holdings: Vols 12,000; Per subs 25
Special Subjects: Crafts, Decorative Arts, Folk Art, Historical Material

LEWISBURG

M **BUCKNELL UNIVERSITY**, Center Gallery, 17837. Tel 717-524-3792. *Dir* Joseph Jacobs
Open Mon - Fri 11 AM - 4 PM, Sat & Sun 1 - 4 PM, evenings Tues - Thurs 7 - 10 PM. Estab 1979. Gallery contains a study collection of 20 paintings and one sculpture of the Renaissance given by the Samuel H Kress Foundation. Average

Annual Attendance: 25,000
Income: Financed by endowment, tuition and gifts
Exhibitions: Faces Since the 50s: A Generation of American Portraiture; Objects, Structures, Artifice: American Sculpture 1970-1982; Rodney Ripps; Two Presses, Two Processes: Simca and Parasol; Black on White, The Experience of the Black Artist Since the 20s
Activities: Lectures open to the public, 6 vis lectr per yr; concerts; gallery talks; tours; competitions; individual paintings & original objects of art lent; originate traveling exhibitions; sales shop

M FETHERSTON FOUNDATION, Packwood House Museum, 15 N Water St, 17837. Tel 717-524-0323. *Pres* Miriam Fisher; *VPres* Dr James Turnure; *Secy* Fred Kessler; *Dir* David W Dunn; *Secy* Tracy Knaus
Open Wed - Sat 1 - 4 PM, Sun 2 - 4 PM. Admis adults $1.75, groups over 15 $1.50, senior citizens $1.25. Estab 1976 to serve the community as an educational institution. Average Annual Attendance: 5000. Mem: 340; dues sponsor $1000, benefactor $500, patron $250, friend $100, family $25, individual $15
Income: Financed by endowment, admissions, memberships and museum shop
Collections: American Fine Arts; Paintings by Edith H K Fetherston; Fine Period Clothing ranging from 1890's to 1960's; 1800 - 1940 accessories, ceramics, furniture, glass, metalwork, textiles
Exhibitions: (1981) David Ginter—Lewisburg Chair Maker; John Wesley Little—Watercolor Artist 1867-1923; Oriental Rugs in the Collection of the Packwood House Museum; (1982) Sampler Exhibit; Hats Made in Old Lewisburg Milinery Shop; Packwood's Collection with Tasha Tudor, exhibit of children's book illustrator; (1983) English transfer printed earthenware; restoration of kitchen to a turn-of-the-century kitchen; (1983-84) David Armstrong Family Collection
Publications: Chanhcleer, quarterly newsletter for members
Activities: Classes for adults and children; docent training; lectures open to the public, 3 - 4 vis lectr per yr; tours; competitions with awards; lending collection contains books, cassettes & slides; book traveling exhibitions; originate traveling exhibitions; museum shop sells books, original art, reproductions and local handcrafted items

LORETTO

M SOUTHERN ALLEGHENIES MUSEUM OF ART,* Saint Francis College Mall, PO Box 8, 15940. Tel 814-472-6400. *Dir* Michael M Strueber; *Cur* Michael Allison; *Registrar* Edward Burda; *Admin Asst* Deborah Davis Grazier; *Community Outreach Coordr* Corliss Cavalieri; *Community Outreach Coordr* Kathleen Bearer
Open Tues - Fri 9:30 AM - 4:30 PM, Sat & Sun 1:30 - 5:30 PM. No admis fee. Estab and dedicated June 1976 to facilitate interest, understanding and the appreciation of the visual arts of the past, present and future through the exhibition of our permanent as well as temporary collections. Large open main gallery with flexible space, second floor graphics gallery. Average Annual Attendance: 10,000. Mem: 650; dues variable
Income: Financed by membership, business, corporate and foundation grants
Collections: †American paintings; 19th & 20th century drawings †graphics and sculpture; 19th century ceramics and crafts
Exhibitions: Invitational Contemporary Fibre Exhibition; Selections of Photo-Realist Paintings from New York City Galleries; Twenty-Five Pennsylvania Women Artists
Activities: Education dept; intern program in cooperation with area colleges; lect open to public, 5 vis lectr per year; concerts; gallery talks; tours; extension dept serves Altoona and Blair County; individual paintings and original objects of art lent to other institutions on request for special exhibitions; lending collection contains 2000 lantern slides; book traveling exhibitions, 1-3 per year; originate traveling exhibitions to instate institutions
L Library,* 15940
Library Holdings: Vols 450; Per subs 25; AV — Lantern slides, slides; Other — Clipping files, exhibition catalogs, pamphlets, photographs
M Museum Extension,* Central Counties Bank Building, 16603. Tel 814-942-1486. *Community Outreach Coordr* David Wilt
Open Mon - Fri 9:30 AM - 4 PM. Only one of its kind in the state
Income: financed by grants and private donations
Activities: Video programs air on local public access cable; lectures open to public, 12 vis lectr per year

MEADVILLE

M ALLEGHENY COLLEGE, Bowman, Megahan and Penelec Galleries, 16335. Tel 814-724-3371. *Gallery Dir* Fran Resch
Open Tues - Fri 12:30 - 5 PM, Fri evening 7 - 9 PM, Sat 1:30 - 5 PM, Sun 2 - 4 PM, cl Mon. No admis fee. Estab 1971 as one of the major exhibition spaces in northwest Pennsylvania; the galleries present exhibits ranging from works of contemporary artists to displays relevant to other fields of study. Galleries are housed in three spacious rooms, white walls, stone floor, 13 ft ceilings. Average Annual Attendance: 8000
Income: Financed by college funds
Collections: Alleghany College Permanent Collection; General David M Shoup Collection of Korean Pottery; Samuel Pees Collection of Contemporary Painting
Exhibitions: (1982-83) Gwen Cooper, handmade paper; Terry Wild, photographs; Stained Glass Invitational; Philadelphia, Past & Present; Man Ray Letters Surrealist Posters; Dynamix; faculty exhibition; student show; Clay Space Invitational; Mitchell Smith, paintings; (1983-84) Alumni Invitational in Photography; Face It; permanent collection; faculty exhibition; Florence Putterman, prints; Mark Perleman, paintings; Ed Malliard, photographs; Andrzel Strumillo, paintings & prints; Installation by Al Charley; Bruce Kastiff, photographs; student show
Activities: Lect open to the public; gallery talks; tours; individual paintings and original objects of art lent to local organizations

O MEADVILLE COUNCIL ON THE ARTS, Meadville Market House, PO Box 337, 16335. Tel 814-336-5051. *Exec Dir* Deb Reichart
Open Tues - Fri 9 AM - 4:30 PM, Sat 9 AM - Noon. No admis fee. Estab 1975 for local arts information and programming; to create community arts center. Gallery has 50 ft of wall space. Average Annual Attendance: 1500. Mem: 500; dues businesses $25 - $250, individual $10 - $50; annual meeting Jan
Income: $20,000 (financed by membership and state appropriation)
Exhibitions: Annual October Evenings Exhibition; annual county wide exhibits; local artists and crafters exhibits
Publications: Monthly calendar; monthly newsletter
Activities: Classes for adults and children; dramatic programs; lectures open to the public, 8 - 10 vis lectr per yr; concerts; competitions with awards; scholarships

MERION

M BUTEN MUSEUM OF WEDGWOOD, 246 N Bowman Ave, 19066. Tel 215-664-6601. *Pres* Mrs Harry M Buten; *Dir* Caroline M Stuckert; *Admin Asst* Marian Schofield; *Public Programs & Vol* Liz Jarvis; *Museum Shop Adminr* Sharon Bean
Open Tues - Fri 2 - 5 PM; Sat 10 AM - 1 PM; cl Sun & Mon . Admis adults $1.50, sr citizens & students $1, children $.50. Estab 1957 for study and exhibition of Wedgwood ceramics. Mem: 1600; dues $25; meetings first Sun of month (Sept to May)
Income: Financed by membership
Collections: Over 10,000 examples of Wedgwood ware made from 1759 to the present
Publications: Bulletin, 5 - 6 times per yr; Monographs in Wedgwood Studies, annually
Activities: Classes for adults and children; docent training; lectures open to public, 7 vis lectr per yr; original objects of art lent to other museums and colleges; lending collection contains kodachromes and original art works; museum shop sells books, magazines & original art
L Library, 246 N Bowman Ave, 19066. Tel 215-664-6601. *Librn* Mrs S Arthur Levy
Open to scholars by appointment for reference only
Library Holdings: Vols 1600
Special Subjects: English ceramics, especially Wedgwood ware

NAZARETH

M MORAVIAN HISTORICAL SOCIETY, Whitefield House Museum,* 214 E Center St, 18064. Tel 215-759-0292. *Pres* H Williams; *Cur* E B Clewell; *Secy* Mary Henry Stites
Open Tues, Fri & Sat 2 - 5 PM, 2nd & 4th Sun of each month 2 - 5 PM, other times by appointment. No admis fee; donations requested. Built in 1740 by George Whitefield, famous preacher, and bought by the Moravians in 1741 and continued in use by various segments of the church until its present occupation as a missionary home and the seat of the Moravian Historical Society which was organized on April 13, 1857 to elucidate the history of the Moravian Church in America; not however, to the exclusion of the general history of the Moravian Church; the museum houses many unique and distinctive items pertaining to early Moraviana and colonial life. Average Annual Attendance: 1500. Mem: 400; dues $5 - $100; annual meeting second Thurs in Oct
Income: Financed by endowment, membership and donation
Collections: Clothing and textiles; John Valentine Haidt Collection of Paintings; handwrought and cast bells; Indian and foreign mission artifacts; musical instruments; pottery and Stiegel glass; rare books; manuscripts
Publications: Transactions, bi-annual
Activities: Lending collection contains individual and original objects of art

NEW BRIGHTON

M MERRICK ART GALLERY, 5th Ave & 11th St, PO Box 312, 15066. Tel 412-846-1130. *Dir & Education Dir* Sandra Bierer; *Trustee* Robert S Merrick
Open Tues - Sat 10 AM - 4:30 PM; Sun 1 - 4:30 PM, cl Mon & holidays; reduced hours during summer. No admis fee. Estab 1880 to preserve and interpret the collection of paintings and other objects owned by Edward Dempster Merrick, the founder. Also to foster local art through classes and one-man shows. All galleries are on the second floors of two parallel buildings with a connecting bridge; there are three small rooms and one large one. Three rooms have clerestory monitors overhead. Average Annual Attendance: 6000. Mem: 350; dues $25, $15 and $10; annual meeting Jan or Feb
Income: Financed by endowment and membership
Collections: Most paintings date from the 18th & 19th century. American artists Emil Bott; Birge Harrison; Thomas Hill; A F King; Edward and Thomas Moran; E Poole; F K M Rehn; W T Richards; W L Sonntag; Thomas Sully; Charles Curran; John F Kensett; Andrew Melrose; Ralph A Blacklock; Asher B Durand; Worthington Whittredge. European artists Gustave Courbet; Hans Makart; Pierre Paul Prud'hon; Richard Westall; Franz Xavier; Winterhalter; Peter Baumgartner; Leon Herbo; Jaques Bertrand
Exhibitions: (1983) Susan Weimer, paintings; David Ludwick, paintings; 8-10 one-man shows yearly; Noel Reifel, prints; John Greco; John Regney; AVAC juried show; annual Christmas show & Christmas trees through the arts train display Howard Worner, Watercolors of Pittsburgh; Christmas Trees Through the Arts
Publications: Newsletter, monthly
Activities: Classes for adults & children; lectures open to public, 2 vis lectr per yr; concerts; gallery talks; tours; scholarships; museum shop

NEW CASTLE

M HOYT INSTITUTE OF FINE ARTS, 124 E Leasure Ave, 16105. Tel 412-652-2882. *Pres Board of Trustees* John L Wilson; *Exec Dir* David P Ludwick
Open Tues - Sat 9 AM - 4 PM. No admis fee. Estab 1968 to encourage the development of the arts within the community. Average Annual Attendance: 27,000. Mem: 850; dues $100, $50, $20, $13
Income: Commission on sales of arts and crafts
Collections: National artists
Exhibitions: Hoyt National Painting Show
Publications: Newsletter, quarterly
Activities: Classes for adults and children; dramatic programs; lect open to public; concerts; competitions; movies on arts and crafts; scholarships

NEWTOWN

M BUCKS COUNTY COMMUNITY COLLEGE, Hicks Art Center, Fine Arts Department, Swamp Rd, 18940. Tel 215-968-8425. *Chairperson* Bruce Katsiff
Open Mon - Fri 8 AM - 10 PM, Sat 9 AM - 5 PM. No admis fee. Estab 1970 to bring outside artists to the community. Gallery covers 960 sq ft. Average Annual Attendance: 5000
Income: Financed by county and state appropriation
Exhibitions: Six exhibits each academic year, ending with student annual exhibit
Activities: Lect open to the public, 8 visiting lectr per year; competitions; artmobile

NEW WILMINGTON

M WESTMINSTER COLLEGE ART GALLERY, 16142. Tel 412-946-8761. *Dir* Nelson E Oestreich
Open Mon - Sat 10 AM - 7 PM, Sun 2 - 7 PM. No admis fee. Estab 1854 to organize and present 6 exhibitions per season, to organize traveling exhibitions, publish art catalogs of national interest, and to conduct visiting artists program. Average Annual Attendance: 15,000
Income: Financed by endowment
Collections: 19th and 20th century paintings; †20th century drawings and prints
Publications: Catalogs; Westminster College Art Gallery, annually
Activities: Lect open to public, 4 visiting lectrs per year; gallery talks; traveling exhibitions organized and circulated

PAOLI

M WHARTON ESHERICK MUSEUM, Horseshoe Trail, Box 595, 19301. Tel 215-644-5822. *Pres* Ruth E Bascom; *Secy* Miriam Phillips; *Dir* Mansfield Bascom
Open Sat 10 AM - 5 PM, Sun 1 - 5 PM, by reservation only. Admis adults $3, children under 12 $2. Estab 1971 for the preservation and exhibition of the Studio and collection of sculptor Wharton Esherick (1887-1970), one of America's foremost artist/craftsmen. Esherick worked mostly in wood and is best known for his sculptural furniture. Studio is set high on hillside overlooking the Great Valley, and is one of Wharton Esherick's monumental achievements. He worked forty years building, enlarging and altering it. Average Annual Attendance: 3000. Mem: 350; dues family $25, individual $15
Income: $30,000 (financed by membership, endowment, admissions and sales)
Collections: 200 pieces of the artist's work, including furniture, paintings, prints, sculpture in wood, stone and ceramic, utensils and woodcuts
Publications: Brochures; catalog of Studio and Collection; Drawings by Wharton Esherick
Activities: Tours; individual paintings and original objects of art lent to museums or exhibitions; museum shop sells books, reproductions, prints and slides

PHILADELPHIA

M AFRO-AMERICAN HISTORICAL AND CULTURAL MUSEUM, 7th and Arch Sts, 19106. Tel 215-574-3671. *Exec Dir* Teri Y Doke; *Cur Fine Arts* Deryl Mackie; *Prog Dir* Spencer Weston; *Education* Shirley Parham; *Education* Muriel Feelings; *Education* Naomi Nelson
Open Tues - Sat 10 AM - 5 PM, Sun Noon - 6 PM, cl New Years, Martin Luther King's Birthday, Memorial Day, July 4, Labor Day, Columbus Day, Thanksgiving, Christmas. Admis adults $1.50, sr citizens, children & students $.75; group rates adults $1, children & students $.50. Estab 1976. Mem: Dues patron $500, friend $150, donor $100, sponsor $50, family $25, individual $10, student $5
Purchases: Bas relief in plaster by Henry O Tanner
Collections: African sculpture and artifacts; Afro-Americana; artifacts relating to Slave Trade, American Revolution, Black Church, Civil War, Reconstruction Period, Westward Movement, Harlem Renaissance, Civil Rights Movement, Black Scientists & Inventors; paintings, prints and sculpture by black artists; †archival documents
Exhibitions: Focus on West Sudan; Focus on South Africa; Swahli Culture; Collections from Ile Ife Humanitarian Center
Publications: Annual report; brochure; exhibition catalog; newsletter
Activities: Classes for adults and children; docent training; workshops; lectures open to the public; concerts; gallery talks; tours; awards; individual paintings & original objects of art lent; museum shop sells books, magazines, original art, reproductions, prints & African crafts

AMERICAN COLOR PRINT SOCIETY
For further information, see National and Regional Organizations

M AMERICAN SWEDISH HISTORICAL FOUNDATION AND MUSEUM, 1900 Pattison Ave, 19145. Tel 215-389-1776. *Dir* Lynn C Malmgren; *Cur* Katarina Cerny; *Admin Asst* Karin Persson
Open Tues - Fri 10 AM - 4 PM, Sat Noon - 4 PM, cl Sun, Mon & holidays.

Admis adults $1.50, students $1, children under 12 free. Estab 1926 to preserve Swedish heritage in America and to promote continued cultural interchange between Sweden & USA. 14 galleries containing materials interpreting 300 years of Swedish influence on American life. Average Annual Attendance: 6000. Mem: 1000; dues family $35, individual $20; annual meeting in June
Collections: †History and culture of Americans of Swedish descent
Exhibitions: Temporary exhibitions of paintings, arts and crafts by Swedish and Swedish-American artists; Scandinavian history and culture
Publications: Newsletter, bi-monthly
Activities: Classes for adults & children; workshops; lectures open to public, 5 vis lectr per year; gallery talks; tours; individual paintings and original objects of art lent to other museums; book traveling exhibitions; museum shop sell books, magazines, folk art & Swedish decorative arts
L Library, 1900 Pattison Ave, 19145. Tel 215-389-1776
For general reference
Library Holdings: Vols 12,000; Per subs 5; Micro — Reels; AV — Rec, slides; Other — Clipping files, exhibition catalogs
Special Subjects: Fredrika Bremer, John Ericsson, Jenny Lind, Rambo Research of genealogical and colonial material

L ART INSTITUTE OF PHILADELPHIA LIBRARY, 1622 Chestnut St, 19103. *Librn* Lesia Krych
Open daily 9 AM - 9 pM. Estab 1966
Library Holdings: AV — A-tapes, cassettes, fs, Kodachromes, v-tapes; Other — Clipping files, exhibition catalogs, memorabilia, photographs

M ATHENAEUM OF PHILADELPHIA, 219 S Sixth St, 19106. Tel 215-925-2688. *Dir* Roger W Moss Jr; *Program Coordr* Eileen Magee; *Architectural Librn* Sandra Tatman; *Circulation Librn* Ellen Batty; *Bibliographer* Keith Kamm
Open Mon - Fri 9 AM - 5 PM. No admis fee. Estab 1814 to collect, preserve and make available original sources on American cultural history, 1814-1914. The fine and decorative arts are arranged in room settings. Average Annual Attendance: 10,000. Mem: 1000; annual meeting first Mon in Apr
Collections: †Permanent study collection of American decorative arts, 1810-1850; 19th and 20th century architectural books; architectural drawings; trade catalogues
Publications: Annotations, quarterly newsletter; Athenaeum Architectural Archive; Annual Report; Bookshelf, six per year; Monographs, three to five per year
Activities: Lect open to public, 6-10 visiting lectr per year; concerts; gallery talks; tours; sales shop selling books, prints and slides
L Library, 219 S Sixth St, 19106
Open Mon - Fri 9 AM - 5 PM by appointment for reference only
Library Holdings: Vols 100,000; Per subs 200; Architectural drawings and related materials; Micro — Fiche, reels; AV — Cassettes; Other — Exhibition catalogs, manuscripts, original art works, photographs, prints, reproductions
Special Subjects: Architecture, Decorative Arts
Collections: Nineteenth century fiction and literary periodicals; trade materials relating to the building arts

M ATWATER KENT MUSEUM,* 15 S 7th St, 19106. Tel 215-686-3630. *Chmn of Board of Trustees* A Atwater Kent Jr; *Exec Dir* John V Alviti; *Cur* Sandra Gross; *Historian* Jeffrey P Roberts; *Treasurer* A Atwater Kent III
Open Tues - Sun 9:30 AM - 5 PM, cl holidays. No admis fee. Estab 1938. The museum is dedicated to the history of Philadelphia. The main interpretive gallery covers the growth of Philadelphia from 1680-1880. Smaller galleries on William Penn, his life & times; The History of the city through maps; Municipal services: fire, police, gas & water. Average Annual Attendance: 63,000
Income: $200,000 (financed by endowment & city appropriation)
Collections: Artifacts of the colonial city; costumes; folk art; print and painting collection; manufactured and trade goods; maritime artifacts; toys & dolls; ceramics & glassware; urban archaeology
Exhibitions: Fairmount Park & the Fairmount Waterworks; Fine Art from the Atwater Kent Collections; Poetry of Motion-Eadweard Muybridge & Children's Action Toys; Sights for City Eyes; Travelling Neighborhood Exhibits
Publications: Philadelphia: A City for All Centuries (in conjunction with KYW Newsradio)
Activities: Lectures open to public, concerts, gallery talks, tours; 500 original art works, 2500 original prints, 100 paintings available on loan to museums with adequate security systems; originate traveling exhibitions to community organizations & schools

M CLIVEDEN, 6401 Germantown Ave, 19144. Tel 215-848-1777. *Staff* Hope Coppage Hendrickson; *Office Mgr* Jean S Mitchell
Open April - Dec Tues - Sat 10 AM - 4 PM, Sun 1:30 - 4:30 PM, cl Easter, Thanksgiving & Christmas. Admis adults $2, senior citizens $1.50, students $1. Average Annual Attendance: 4000. Mem: 254
Activities: Lectures open to the public, 4 vis lectr per yr; tours; museum shop sells books, magazines, original art & reproductions

M DREXEL UNIVERSITY MUSEUM, Chestnut & 32nd Sts, 19104. Tel 215-895-2424, 895-2423. *Dir & Cur* Dr Jean Henry
Open Mon - Fri 10 AM - 4 PM, cl Sat, Sun & holidays. No admis fee. Estab 1891; Picture Gallery 1902. Main Gallery contains the John D Lankenau and the Anthony J Drexel Collections of German and French paintings, sculpture & decorative arts of the 19th century and a changing exhibition gallery. Average Annual Attendance: 10,000
Income: Financed by Drexel University
Collections: 19th century sculpture, academic European painting, decorative arts & costumes; ceramics; hand printed India cottons, European textiles; decorative arts of China, Europe, India and Japan
Activities: Lectures open to the public, 8 - 10 vis lectr per yr; concerts; gallery talks; book traveling exhibitions

O **FAIRMOUNT PARK ART ASSOCIATION,** 256 South 16th St, 19102. Tel 215-546-7550. *Pres* Theodore T Newbold; *VPres* Charles E Mather III; *VPres* Henry W Sawyer III; *Executive Secy* Karel Polch
Estab 1872 for the purpose of buying sculpture which is then given to the City of Philadelphia. Mem: 350; dues $15 - $100; annual meeting April
Income: Financed by membership and endowment
Publications: Annual Report

O **FOUNDATION FOR THE ADVANCEMENT OF ARTISTS,*** PO Box 11617, 19116
Estab 1977 to seek recognition for living American professional painters, sculptors, graphic artists & photographers

M **FOUNDATION FOR TODAY'S ART,** Nexus Gallery, 2017 Chancellor St, 19103. Tel 215-567-3481. *Trustee* Alexandra Lerner; *Trustee* Vivian Goldstein; *Trustee* Suzanne Horuitz
Open Tues - Sat 11:30 AM - 5 PM. No admis fee. Estab 1975 to educate the public in trend of contemporary art and performance; for artists to have opportunity to exhibit. Average Annual Attendance: 5000. Mem: 25; dues $35 per month; meeting first Mon each month
Income: Financed by endowment, membership and state appropriation
Activities: Classes; lect open to public, 5 or more visiting lectr per year; concerts; gallery talks; tours upon request; internship

FREE LIBRARY OF PHILADELPHIA
L **Art Dept,** Logan Square, 19103. Tel 215-686-5403. *Dir Library* Keith Doms; *Head Art Dept* Marianne Promos
Open Mon - Wed 9 AM - 9 PM, Thurs - Fri 9 AM - 6 PM, Sat 9 AM - 5 PM, Sun 1 - 5 PM. Estab 1891, art department estab 1896, to serve the citizens of the City of Philadelphia. Circ 39,000
Income: Financed by endowment, city and state appropriations
Purchases: $30,540
Library Holdings: Vols 150,000; Per subs 193; Micro — Fiche, reels; Other — Clipping files, exhibition catalogs, pamphlets
Collections: 18th and 19th century architectural pattern books; Index of exhibition catalogs of The Pennsylvania Academy of the Fine Arts 1870 to date; John Frederick Lewis Collection of books on fine prints and printmaking; 368 original measured drawings of colonial Philadelphia buildings, Philadelphia Chapter, American Institute of Architects
Exhibitions: Rotating exhibitions
L **Print and Picture Dept,** Logan Square, 19103. Tel 215-686-5405. *Head* Robert F Looney
Open 9 AM - 5 PM, cl Sat. Estab 1954 by combining the Print Department and the Picture Collection
Collections: (non-circulating) †Americana (1200); Hampton L Carson Collection of Napoleonic prints (3400); †graphic arts (2000); †greeting and tradesmen's cards (27,000); †John Frederick Lewis Collection of portrait prints (211,000); †Philadelphiana (8000); Rosenthal Collection of American Drawings (900); (circulating) †picture collection of pictures in all media and universal in subject coverage (800,000)
L **Rare Book Dept,** Third Floor, 19103. Tel 215-686-5416. *Rare Book Librn* Marie E Korey
Open Mon - Fri 9 AM - 5 PM. Estab 1949
Collections: American Sunday-School Union; Alfred Bendiner Collection of 300 caricatures, prints and drawings; early American children's books including Rosenbach Collection (1682-1836); Elisabeth Ball Collection of Horn books; †Borneman and Yoder Collection of Pennsylvania German Fraktur; Hampton L Carson Collection of legal prints; Frederick R Gardner Collection of Robert Lawson original drawings; Kate Greenaway; early American prints and engravings; Grace Clark Haskell Collection of Arthur Rackham; John Frederick Lewis Collection of cuneiform tablets and seals, †Medieval and Renaissance manuscripts and miniatures, Oriental manuscripts and miniatures (mostly Mughul, Rajput and Persian); Thornton Oakley Collection of †Howard Pyle and His School, books and original drawings; †Beatrix Potter, including H Bacon Collamore Collection of original art; Evan Randolph Collection consisting of angling prints from the 17th to the 20th century, and †prints of Philadelphia from 1800-1950; †original drawings, paintings, prints and other illustrative material relating to the works of Dickens, Goldsmith, Poe and Thackeray

O **HISTORICAL SOCIETY OF PENNSYLVANIA,*** 1300 Locust St, 19107. Tel 215-732-6200. *Dir* James E Mooney; *Chief of Manuscripts* Peter J Parker; *Dir Development* Lawrence Naftulin; *Cur* William T Oedel; *Public Relations* Harmon Harris; *Membership Coordr* Darthe C Hauck; *Head Librn* John H Platt
Open Mon 1 - 9 PM, Tues - Fri 9 AM - 5 PM. Admis $1 to library and manuscript department; no admis fee to museum. Estab 1824 to collect and preserve records relating primarily to Pennsylvania history; also collects various artifacts and paintings of persons relevant to Pennsylvania history. Art gallery is comprised of four exhibit rooms: two contain changing exhibits from the collections; and two serve as meeting rooms and contain numerous early American paintings and furniture. Mem: 3350; dues $15; meetings four per year
Income: Financed by endowment and membership
Collections: Unmatched collection of papers, prints, paintings, furniture, household and personal effects from pre-Revolution through 1800; more than 800 paintings and miniatures by early American artists Birch, Copley, Inman, Neagle, Peale, Stuart, Sully, Wright and others; more than 14 million manuscripts
Publications: The Pennsylvania Magazine of History and Biography, quarterly
Activities: Lect for members, 4 visiting lectr per year; individual paintings and original art objects lent primarily to other museums

C **INA CORPORATION,*** 1600 Arch St, PO Box 7728, 19101. Tel 215-241-4894, 241-4000. *Dir & Cur* Debra J Force; *Asst Cur* Melissa Hough; *Asst Cur* Leanna Lee-Whitman
Lobbies open Mon - Fri 8 AM - 5 PM; Gallery by appointment. No admis fee. Organized in 1926 to preserve the company's interest in its history through the collection of marine, fire, and Americana objects. Collection displayed in Lobbies, Gallery and throughout buildings. Lobbies of 2 buildings have artifacts in cases and on mounts; Gallery has artifacts on walls and hanging on movable cabinets which are also storage units
Collections: Fire: fire marks, full-size apparatus, equipment, models, prints; INA-related: furniture, manuscripts, portraits; Marine: figureheads, paintings, ship models; †19th & early 20th century paintings and works on paper; contemporary paintings, graphics & sculpture
Activities: Lectures open to public, vis lectrs; gallery talks; tours; individual and original objects of art lent (about one-third of collection) throughout the United States

M **INDEPENDENCE NATIONAL HISTORICAL PARK,** 313 Walnut St, 19106. Tel 215-597-7132. *Supt* Hobart G Cawood; *Asst Supt* Bernard Goodman; *Chief Museum Operations* John C Milley
Open daily 9 AM - 5 PM. No admis fee. Estab 1948 to preserve and protect for the American people, historical structures, properties and other resources of outstanding national significance, and associated with the Revolution and growth of the Nation. Seventeen public buildings with 54 period rooms & 38 on-site exhibits. Average Annual Attendance: 4,500,000. Mem: Dues $85
Collections: †18th century American period furnishings; decorative arts; American portraits from 1740-1840
Activities: Dramatic programs; docent training; lectures open to public, 6 vis lectr per yr; tours; individual paintings & original objects or art lent to qualified professional institutions; museum shop selling books, reproductions, prints, slides
L **Library,** 120 S Third St, 19106
Open to public Mon - Fri 8 AM - 4:30 PM
Library Holdings: Vols 5500; Per subs 23; Research notecard file; Micro — Reels; AV — Motion pictures, slides, v-tapes; Other — Pamphlets, photographs
Collections: Decorative arts of Philadelphia and Pennsylvania for the 18th century

M **KLING GALLERY,** 2301 Chestnut St, 19103. Tel 215-569-2900. *Dir* George Young
Open Mon - Fri 9 AM - 5 PM & by appointment. No admis fee. Estab 1965 as a not-for-profit gallery to present contemporary art works of emerging & established artists. Average Annual Attendance: 5000
Exhibitions: Solo & group shows

M **LA SALLE COLLEGE ART MUSEUM,** 20th & Olney Ave, 19141. Tel 215-951-1221. *Dir* Daniel Burke; *Asst Cur* Caroline Wistar
Open Tues - Fri 11 AM - 3 PM, Sun 2 - 4 PM; cl Mon. No admis fee. Estab 1975 for educational purposes and to house the collection begun in 1965, also as support for the art history program and as a service to the community. Average Annual Attendance: 11,000. Mem: 60; dues $5 - $1000
Income: Financed by endowment
Collections: 15th through 20th century paintings, drawings, watercolors, Old Master & those of 19th & 20th centuries prints; Western, European & American art, with a few pieces of sculpture & decorative art; rare illustrated 15th - 20th century Bibles; books illustrated with portrait prints
Exhibitions: Two special exhibitions are held each semester
Publications: Exhibition illustration; guide to the collection
Activities: Classes for adults; lectures open to public, 2-3 vis lectr per year; concerts; gallery talks; tours; individual paintings & original objects of art lent to museums

L **LIBRARY COMPANY OF PHILADELPHIA,** Dept of Art, 1314 Locust St, 19107. Tel 215-546-3181. *Librn* Edwin Wolf II; *Asst Librn* Gordon Marshall; *Cur of Printed Books* James Green; *Cur of Prints* Kenneth Finkel; *Chief of Reference* Phillip Lapsansky; *Chief Conservation* Jennifer L Woods
Open Mon - Fri 9 AM - 4:45 PM. No admis fee. Estab 1731 for the purpose of scholarly research. Average Annual Attendance: 2500. Mem: 800; dues $8; annual meeting first Mon May
Income: Financed by endowment, membership, city appropriation, and federal grants
Library Holdings: Other — Exhibition catalogs, original art works, pamphlets, photographs, prints, sculpture
Collections: †American Printing; †Philadelphia prints, watercolors, drawings and photography; collection of Americana
Exhibitions: (1981) On Stage in Philadelphia 1700-1900; Quarter of a Millennium: The Library Company 1731-1981 (1982) Bibliophiler Philadelphia Style; Ruin Upon Ruin; (1983) Philadelphia Revisions; Germantown and the Germans
Publications: Annual Report; Occasional Miscellany, 2-4 times per year; exhibition catalogues
Activities: Lectures open to public; gallery talks; tours; individual and original objects of art lent to museums, libraries and cultural institutions; sales shop sells books and publications

M **MOORE COLLEGE OF ART GALLERY,** 20th & Race Sts, 19103. Tel 215-568-4515. *Gallery Dir* Elsa Weiner
Open Mon - Fri 10 AM - 5 PM, Sat Noon - 4 PM. No admis fee. Estab 1831 to offer the Philadelphia community and its students the opportunity to view contemporary artwork that is usually not available locally. Gallery is housed in moderate exhibition space with flexible panels to accommodate current exhibit. Average Annual Attendance: 5000
Income: Financed by endowment
Publications: Bulletins, irregularly; Catalogs for major exhibitions
Activities: Lectures open to public, 10 vis lectr per yr; gallery talks; tours
L **Library,** 20th & The Parkway, 19103. Tel 215-568-4515. *Library Dir* Deborah Alterman; *Catalog Librn* Lorraine Heuser; *Slide Cur* Helen F McGinnis
Open Mon - Thurs 8 AM - 9:30 PM, Fri 8 AM - 6 PM, Sat 8:30 AM - 5 PM, Sun 1 PM - 5 PM, for student use; public use Mon - Fri 8:30 AM - 4:30 PM and by appointment. Estab to serve Moore Staffand students. For reference only
Purchases: $26,000
Library Holdings: Vols 33,000; Per subs 250; Picture files; AV — Lantern slides, rec, slides 74,000; Other — Clipping files, exhibition catalogs, manuscripts, memorabilia, reproductions
Special Subjects: Women in the Visual Arts
Collections: Sartain Family Collection; Bookworks Artists Books Collection

M **MUSE ART GALLERY,** 1915 Walnut St, 19103. Tel 215-963-0959. *Coordr* Carol Clamer; *Coordr* E Sherman Hayman
Open Tues - Sat 11 AM - 5 PM. No admis fee. Estab 1977, gallery provides a professional opportunity and place for qualified women artists to exhibit their work and let it speak for itself. Average Annual Attendance: 5500. Mem: 15, qualifications: highly qualified professional women artists who are juried by members; dues $360; monthly meetings first or second Sun
Income: Financed by membership, NEA grants and Pennsylvania State Council of the Arts
Publications: Catalogues; MUSE Gallery and Her Own Space
Activities: Docent training; workshops; student interns, volunteers group; art consultant program; lectures open to the public; slide presentations; poetry readings; gallery talks; tours; competitions; originate traveling exhibitions; original art for sale

M **MUSEUM OF THE PHILADELPHIA CIVIC CENTER,** Civic Center Blvd at 34th St, 19104. Tel 215-925-3804. *Dir* Ronald L Barber; *Chief Cur* Robert Nobel; *Cur Exhibitions* Robert Carter; *Cur Education* Edward Grusheski; *Dir Design* Zenon L Feszczak; *Promotion & Publicity Specialist* Henry Spector; *Registrar* Robert Eskind
No admis fee. Estab 1894 to present exhibitions of contemporary local, national and international art, craft, photography and design. Average Annual Attendance: 200,000
Income: Financed by city appropriation
Collections: Latin American crafts; New Caledonian ethnographic material; Oriental and African crafts; Philippine ethnographic collection; Southeastern Siberian ethnographic collection
Exhibitions: Changing exhibitions of contemporary local, national and international art, craft, design and photography
Activities: Classes for children; lect for scheduled school class only; suitcase exhibits on foreign countries loaned to schools

M **Port of History Museum,** Delaware Ave at Walnut St, 19106. Tel 215-925-3804
Open Wed - Sun 10 AM - 4:30 PM, cl Mon, Tues & legal holidays. Admis $1. Estab 1981 for international exhibitions of design, fine arts & crafts. Museum is 10,000 sq ft. Average Annual Attendance: 100,000
Exhibitions: The Buchheim Collection: German Expressionism; Philadelphia: Visions & Realities
Publications: Florence to Philadelphia; exhibition catalogs
Activities: Classes for children; book traveling exhibitions

M **PENNSYLVANIA ACADEMY OF THE FINE ARTS,** Galleries, Broad & Cherry Sts, 19102. Tel 215-972-7600. *Chmn Bd* Charles E Mather III; *Pres* Frank H Goodyear Jr; *Dir Museum* Open; *Dir School* Ephraim Weinberg; *Dir Development* Elaine Breslow; *Dir Admin & Finance* Harvey Gold; *Membership & Special Events Coordr* Jodie Borie; *Public Information Officer* Kirby F Smith; *Head Cur* Kathleen Foster; *Assoc Cur* Linda Bantel; *Asst Cur* Judith Stein; *Museum Registrar* Janice Stanland; *Museum Educ* Elizabeth Kolowrat; *Rights & Reproductions* Robert Harman; *Museum Shop Mgr* Fred Kelley
Open Tues - Sat 10 AM - 5 PM, Sun 1 - 5 PM. Admis adults $2, sr citizens $1. 50, students $1. Estab 1805 by C W Peale, Thos Sully, Benj West, et al, to cultivate collecting, training, and development of the fine arts in America. The Academy building, opened in 1876, was restored for the American Bicentennial. Considered the masterpiece of its architect, Philadelphian Frank Furness, its style is called, alternately, polychrome picturesque and High or Gothic Victorian. It was designated a Registered National Historic Landmark in 1975. The Peale House and Morris Galleries are maintained for exhibitions of contemporary artists. Average Annual Attendance: 108,000. Mem: 5000; dues $30 and up, $10 for student membership
Income: Financed by endowment, membership, city and state appropriation, contributions and federal grants
Purchases: Cascades Perpendiculars by Louise Nevelson; Dark Mother by Richard Stankiewicz; Jimmy and Liz & Under the Elms by Fairfield Porter; Night by Alex Katz; Woman Lying Down by Mark Frank; Behind the Store at Prospect by Rackstraw Downes
Collections: American contemporary works; 18th, 19th and early 20th century American paintings, sculpture, drawings and prints, including Allston, West, the Peale family, Stuart, Sully, Rush, Neagle, Mount, Eakins, Homer, Hopper, Hassam, Carles, Bellows, Henri, Beaux, Pippin
Exhibitions: (1983-85) Arthur B Carles: Painting with Color; Philip Pearlstein: A Retrospective; Philadelphia Pictorial Photography: The Academy's Salons; Frank Stella: Prints 1967-1982; The Pennsylvania Academy of the Fine Arts: A Growing American Treasure; Red Grooms: A Retrospective; Marcy Hermansader; Tom Judd; Contemporary American Photographers; Peter Gorny; Woofy Bubbles; Brian Meunier; Lisbeth Stewart
Publications: Annual report; exhibition and school catalogues; In This Academy (newspaper), three times yearly
Activities: Classes for adults and children; docent training; lectures open to public, some for members only, 6 vis lectr per year; concerts; gallery talks; tours; competitions; 50 awards; original objects of art lent to other art institutions, the White House, the Governor of Pennsylvania and Embassies abroad; book traveling exhibitions, 4-6 per year; traveling exhibitions organized and circulated; museum shop sells books, magazines, original art, reproductions, prints, slides, student work, ceramics, games and stationary

L **Library,** Broad & Cherry Sts, Philadelphia, 19102. Tel 215-972-7611. *Librn* Marietta P Bushnell
Open Mon - Fri 9 AM - 7 PM, open by appointment to public, clo during school vacations. Estab 1805, the library serves students of painting, sculpture & printmaking. Open to public for reference by appointment
Income: Financed by school funds
Library Holdings: Vols 9000; Per subs 35; Clipping files include biography of American artists; AV — Slides; Other — Clipping files, exhibition catalogs

L **Archives,** Broad & Cherry Sts, 19102. Tel 215-972-7641
Open weekdays by appointment only
Library Holdings: Artifacts; AV — A-tapes, fs, Kodachromes, lantern slides, slides; Other — Clipping files, exhibition catalogs, manuscripts, memorabilia, pamphlets, photographs
Special Subjects: History of Penn Academy
Publications: Brochure about the archives

O **Fellowship of the Pennsylvania Academy of the Fine Arts,** The Peale House, 1820 Chestnut St, 19103. Tel 215-972-7632. *Pres* Jack Gerber; *Exec Secy* Tish Byrne; *Treas* L A D Montgomery
Estab 1897 to provide opportunities for creative incentive and sharing in responsibilities for the development of facilities and activities in the field of art for its members and to maintain relations with the students of the Pennsylvania Academy of the Fine Arts. Mem: 1200; dues resident $15, students $8, nonresidents and associate $10; meetings held Sept, Nov, Feb & May
Income: Approx $3000
Collections: Paintings and sculpture
Exhibitions: Annual Fellowship Show
Publications: History of the Fellowship; quarterly newsletter
Activities: Classes; Lectures; films; open house; workshops

O **PHILADELPHIA ART ALLIANCE,** 251 S 18th St, 19103. Tel 215-515-4302. *Pres* Hal L Bemis; *VPres Admin* James Scheck; *Executive Dir* Marilyn J S Goodman
Open Mon - Sat 10:30 AM - 5 PM. No admis fee. Estab 1915, a unique, educational and cultural organization catering to all the arts: music, drama, painting, sculpture, prints, design, literary arts, illustration, architecture, photography. Average Annual Attendance: 100,000. Mem: Approx 2400 individuals and various organizations; dues from $50-$200; annual meeting Mar
Publications: The Art Alliance Bulletin, published 11 times a year, Sept to July; Philadelphia Art Alliance Press publishes 3 or 4 art-related volumes, annually
Activities: Classes for adults; lectures open to public, 70 vis lectr per year; concerts; gallery talks; tours

O **PHILADELPHIA ART COMMISSION,*** 1329 City Hall Annex, 19107. Tel 215-686-4470, 686-1776. *Pres* F Eugene Dixon Jr; *Exec Dir* Kathleen H McKenna
Open 8:30 AM - 5 PM. No admis fee. Estab 1911 under Philadelphia Home Rule Charter as the Art Jury, later retitled Art Commission. An Art Ordinance passed in 1959 provides for art work in city buildings and on city owned property. The Art Commission reviews architectural designs and art work covering all media for municipal locations or other locations in which municipal funds are expended. The Art Commission's files are open to inspection by anyone since the information contained therein qualifies as public information. As indicated, the material deals solely with art proposals and architectural designs. Designs cover all buildings, major highways, and bridges. Mem: 9; between 20 and 24 meetings annually
Income: Financed by city appropriation

M **PHILADELPHIA COLLEGE OF ART,** Broad & Spruce Sts, 19102. Tel 215-893-3100, 893-3188. *Pres* Peter Solmssen; *Dean of Faculty* Joanne Ryan; *Dir Exhibitions* Elaine J Cocordas
Open Mon, Tues, Thurs & Fri 10 AM - 5 PM, Wed 10 AM - 9 PM, Sat Noon - 5 PM. No admis fee. College contains two galleries: Howard A Wolf Gallery & Edith Rosenwald Gallery. Varied exhibition programs serve to stimulate its own community as well as the general public. The work of younger but innovative, recognized artists is featured
Income: Financed by city, state and federal appropriations, private & corporate support
Exhibitions: Contemporary & 20th century work in visual arts and design
Publications: Catalogs and posters accompany gallery exhibitions
Activities: Lectures; opening receptions; tours; slide presentations; gallery talks; workshops

L **Library,** Broad & Spruce Sts, 19102. Tel 215-893-3126. *Library Dir* Hazel Gustow; *Readers' Services Librn* Martha Hall; *Tech Servs* Deborah Stagg
Open Mon - Thurs 8:15 AM - 8 PM, Fri 8:15 AM - 5 PM, Sat 9 AM - 3 PM; (shorter hours during the summer). Estab 1876 to support the academic programs of the School. Circ 41,000
Library Holdings: Vols 47,000; Per subs 185; Micro — Fiche, reels; AV — A-tapes, cassettes, motion pictures, rec, slides; Other — Clipping files, exhibition catalogs, pamphlets, photographs, reproductions
Special Subjects: Visual Arts, particularly contemporary

M **PHILADELPHIA COLLEGE OF TEXTILES AND SCIENCE,** Paley Design Center, 4200 Henry Ave, 19144. Tel 215-951-2860. *Dir* Patricia Chapin O'Donnell; *Registrar* Jean Mapes
Open Tues - Sat 10 AM - 4 PM, cl Mons & holidays. Estab 1978 to provide a study collection of textiles and related materials as a design resource. Average Annual Attendance: 8000
Special Subjects: 19th and 20th century textile design
Collections: Historic and contemporary textiles 2nd - 20th Centuries, International; Fabric Library, 19th and 20th Centuries, American and Western European; manuscripts, records, textile fibers, tools, and related materials
Exhibitions: Works from permanent collection; local artists and designers of international repute

M **PHILADELPHIA MARITIME MUSEUM,** 321 Chestnut St, 19106. Tel 215-925-5439. *Pres* J Welles Henderson; *Actg Dir* Theodore T Newbold; *Asst Dir* Howard J Taylor; *Registrar* John Groff; *Instructor* William Ward
Open Mon - Sat 10 AM - 5 PM, Sun 1 - 5 PM. Admis adults $1, children under 12 $.50; group rates available. Estab 1960 to preserve and interpret the maritime heritage of the Bay and River Delaware, and the Port of Philadelphia. Gallery 1, Man and the Sea, general maritime history; Gallery 2, The Titanic & Her Era, collection of the Titanic Historical Society; Gallery 3, Waterway of History, history of Bay and River Delaware and Port of Philadelphia; Gallery 4, changing exhibits. Average Annual Attendance: 40,000. Mem: 950; dues $10 minimum; annual meeting May
Income: Financed by endowment, membership and private and corporate gifts
Collections: †Paintings by major American marine artists; Philadelphia Views; †17th-20th century maritime prints; †small craft
Exhibitions: (1982) Combat Art of World War II; From Rivers to Rinks - Ice Skating Philadelphians; (1983) Hand Crafts of the Sea--Alive & Well & Living in Philadelphia; Past Port--Future Port; A Flowing Tide: British Marine Artist W L Wylie; (1984) Two by Two: Animals & Arks in Toyland

Publications: Annual Report; books and catalogs, intermittently; Spindrift (newsletter), quarterly
Activities: Classes for adults and children; lect for members only, 10 visiting lectr per year; concerts; gallery talks; competitions; individual paintings and original objects of art lent to recognized non-profit museums with adequate facilities and pertinent need, six months only; museum shop selling books, magazines, reproductions, prints, postcards, models and souvenirs

L **Library,*** 321 Chestnut St, 19106. *Librn* Dorothy Mueller
Open Mon - Fri 9 AM - 4:45 PM by appointment. Open to members and scholars, for reference only
Library Holdings: Vols 7000; Per subs 75; rare books and maps; Micro — Fiche, reels; AV — Cassettes, Kodachromes, lantern slides, motion pictures, slides; Other — Exhibition catalogs, manuscripts, original art works, pamphlets, photographs, prints
Special Subjects: Traditional Small Craft Plans, Maritime Art and History Reference Works; Shipbuilders of the Delaware River, Maritime History of Philadelphia
Collections: Photographic file of Birch prints; photographic file of ships built by New York Shipbuilding Corp; art reference books on marine artists

M **PHILADELPHIA MUSEUM OF ART,** 26th and Parkway, Box 7646, 19101. Tel 215-763-8100. *Chmn of the Bd* Henry P McIlhenny; *Pres* Robert Montgomery Scott; *The George D Widener Dir* Anne d'Harnoncourt; *VPres Operations* Lawrence H Snyder; *VPres Finance* A Wesley Bryan; *Asst Dir Program* Cheryl McClenney; *Cur 20th Century Art* Mark Rosenthal; *Cur Paintings before 1900* Joseph Rishel; *Cur American Art* Darrel Sewell; *Cur American Decorative Arts* Beatrice Garvan; *Cur European Decorative Arts after 1700* Kathryn B Hiesinger; *Cur Medieval and Renaissance Decorative Arts* David DuBon; *Assoc Cur Prints* Ellen Jacobowitz; *Assoc Cur Drawings* Ann Percy; *Adviser to the Alfred Stieglitz Center* Michael Hoffman; *Cur Far Eastern Art* Jean Gordon Lee; *Asst Cur Costume and Textiles* Susan Anderson; *Conservator* Marigene Butler; *Chief Div Educ* Theodore Katz; *Registrar* Irene Taurins; *Public Relations Mgr* Sandra Horrocks; *Mgr Museum Shop* Terrell Baxter; *Development Dir* Maria Giliotti; *Special Exhibitions Coordr* Suzanne Wells
Open Tues - Sun 10 AM - 5 PM. Admis adults $2.50, senior citizens, students & children over 5 $1.50, Tues half-price. Estab 1876 as an art museum and for art education; known as Pennsylvania Museum of Art until the present name was adopted in 1938. Buildings owned by the City, opened 1928; wings 1931 and 1940; fashion galleries 1949, 1951 and 1953; Gallatin and Arensberg Collections 1954; Far Eastern Wing 1957; decorative arts galleries 1958; Charles Patterson Van Pelt Auditorium 1959; Napalese-Tibetan Gallery 1960; new galleries of Italian and French Renaissance Art 1960; American Wing, galleries of contemporary painting, sculpture, and decorative arts and special exhibitions galleries 1976; Alfred Stieglitz Center of Photography 1978; print and drawing gallery 1979; 19th century decorative arts galleries 1980 and 1981. Museum contains 200 galleries. Average Annual Attendance: 600,000. Mem: 18,000; dues $15 - $1000; annual meeting Oct
Income: $11,400,000 (financed by endowment, membership, city and state appropriations, grants, bequests and auxiliary activities)
Purchases: $465,000
Collections: †Indian sculpture and miniature painting, and the installation of 16th century South Indian temple; †Chinese and Southwest Asian sculpture, ceramics, and decorative arts from the Crozier, Crofts, Williams, McIlhenny, Thompson, and other collections, with installations of a Ming period Chinese palace hall and temple and a Ch'ing scholar's study; †Japanese scroll paintings, prints, and decorative arts, with installations of a tea house and a 14th century temple; Himalayan sculpture and painting; Middle Eastern tile, miniatures, and decorative arts from the White and other collections; Oriental carpets from the McIlhenny, Williams, and other collections; Pre-Columbian sculpture and artifacts from the Arensberg Collections; †Medieval and Renaissance sculpture, painting, and decorative arts from the Foulc, Barnard, and other collections; installations of a Gothic chapel, Romanesque cloister, French Renaissance choir screen, and period rooms; Barbarini-Kress Foundation tapestry series; Kienbusch Collection of Arms and Armor; †French, Dutch, English, and Italian painting and decorative arts of the 14th - 19th centuries, from the †Wilstach, Elkins, McFadden, Tyson, John G Johnson, and other collections; †Italian, Dutch and French drawings from the Clark and other collections; †French and English 17th and 18th century decorative arts from the Rice, Bloomfield-Moore, and other collections, with period rooms; †French and English art-nouveau decorative arts; costume and textiles from all periods of western and eastern art, including the Whitman sampler collection; †American collections include painting, sculpture, and decorative arts from the colonial era to the present, with period rooms, Philadelphia furniture and silver, Tucker porcelain, Lorimer Glass Collection, and the Geesey Collection of Pennsylvania German folk art; †20th century painting, sculpture and works on paper from the Gallatin, Arensberg, Tyson, White, Stern, Stieglitz, Zigrosser, Greenfield, Woodward, and other collections; †Ars Medica Collection of prints on the subject of sickness and healing from all periods of western art; †Alfred Stieglitz Center Collection of Photography; †20th century decorative arts
Exhibitions: (1983) Cezanne in Phildelphia Collections; Pennsylvania Modern: Charles Demuth of Lancaster; Particulars: Selections from the Miller-Plummer Collection of Photography; (1984) Design Since 1945; Tabu-Dada: Jean Crotti and Suzanne Duchamp, 1915-1922; Masters of Seventeenth-Century Dutch Genre Painting; Dutch Tiles from the Collection of the Philadelphia Museum of Art; Philadelphia and the China Trade; Jonathan Borofsky; The Golden Age of British Photography, 1839-1900
Publications: Bulletin, quarterly; exhibitions catalogs; newsletter, monthly
Activities: Classes for adults and children; dramatic programs; guide training; lect open to public, 20 visiting lectr per year; concerts; gallery talks; tours; exten dept serving all Philadelphia communities; artmobile; traveling exhibitions organized and circulated; museum shop selling books, magazines, original art, reproductions, prints, slides, jewelry, needlework, and postcards

M **Rodin Museum,*** 22nd & Benjamin Franklin Parkway, 19101. Tel 215-763-8100; Cable PHILMUSE. *Cur* Joseph Rishel
Open Wed - Sun 10 AM - 5 PM, cl holidays. Admis by donation. Estab 1926. Rodin Museum houses one of the largest collections outside of Paris of works by the major late 19th Century French sculptor, Auguste Rodin. Average Annual Attendance: 30,000
Income: Financed through Museum
Library Holdings: Vols 80,000
Collections: Collection includes many of the most famous subjects created by Rodin, as well as drawings, prints, letters, books and a variety of documentary material
Activities: Classes for adults and children; dramatic programs; docent training; lect open to public, 35-40 visiting lectr per year; concerts; gallery talks; tours; individual paintings and original objects of art lent to museums for exhibitions; originate traveling exhibitions; museum shop sells books, reproductions, prints, slides, jewelry, cards, glass, ceramics and memorabilia

M **Mount Pleasant,*** Fairmount Park, 19101. Tel 215-787-5431
Open daily except Mon, cl major holidays. Admis adults $.50, children $.25. Built 1761, an elaborate example of 18th century building and carving; a perfect model of Georgian symmetry. Some of the finest achievements of the master craftsmen in the Philadelphia area are well preserved in the boldly ornate woodwork and Chippendale style furnishings
Collections: Contents of the house from the Museum represent the elegant way of life in Philadelphia in the 1760's

M **Cedar Grove,*** Lansdowne Dr, Fairmount Park, 19101. Tel 215-787-5431
Open Wed - Mon 10 AM - 5 PM, cl Tues. Admis adults $.50, children $.25. Built in 1740's, a country farmhouse for Elizabeth Coates Paschall. The house was enlarged in the 1790's and a piazza added in the 1840's. In 1926, Lydia Thompson Morris, fifth generation owner of Cedar Grove, had the house dismantled stone by stone and moved to Fairmount Park as her gift to the city
Collections: The furniture was given with the house and reflects changes in styles through the 17th, 18th and 19th centuries

M **John Johnson Collection,** Parkway & 25th, PO Box 7646, 19101. Tel 215-787-5401. *Cur* Joseph Rishel; *Asst Cur* Carl B Strehlke
Open Tues - Sun 10 AM - 5 PM. Admis to Philadelphia Museum of Art $2.50. Upon his death in 1917, prominent Philadelphia lawyer, John Graver Johnson left his extensive collection intact to the city of Philadelphia; since 1933 the collection has been housed in the Philadelphia Museum of Art; administration and trusteeship of the collection is maintained separately from the other collections in the museum
Income: Financed by trust established by John G Johnson, contributions city of Philadelphia and Philadelphia Museum of Art
Collections: Early and later Italian Renaissance paintings; French 19th century paintings; northern European schools of Flanders, Holland and Germany in the 15th, 16th and 17th century
Exhibitions: In house exhibitions featuring works from permanent collection
Publications: Several catalogs for various parts of the collection including Catalog of Italian Paintings and Catalog of Flemish and Dutch Paintings
Activities: Special lect and related activities; occasional lending of collection to significant exhibitions
—**Library,** Parkway & 25th St, 19101. *Librn* Barbara Sevy
For reference only
Library Holdings: Vols 4500; rare sales catalogues

M **Samuel S Fleisher Art Memorial,** 719 Catharine St, 19147. Tel 215-922-3456. *Pres* James Nelson-Kise; *Dir* Thora E Jacobson
Open during exhibitions Mon - Fri Noon - 5 PM, Mon - Thurs 7 - 9:30 PM, Sat 1 - 3 PM. No admis fee. Estab 1898 as a free art school and sanctuary (Museum of Religious Art). It is housed in an Italian Romanesque Revival building; Gallery is primarily used for school-related exhibitions, also for special shows of contemporary artists. Mem: 2400; dues $5
Income: $350,000 (financed by endowment)
Collections: Medieval and Renaissance religious paintings and sculpture; 18th - 19th century Portuguese liturgical objects; 17th - 20th century Russian icons; some sculpture
Exhibitions: Challenge Series, annual schedule of 4 exhibitions featuring work by emerging Philadelphia area artists; annual student, faculty, adult and childrens' exhibitions
Activities: Classes for adults and children; lect open to the public; 4 vis lectrs per year; concerts; gallery talks; competitions with awards; sales shop sells art materials

L **Library,** Philadelphia Museum of Art, PO Box 7646, 19101. Tel 215-763-8100, Ext 259. *Librn* Barbara Sevy; *Cataloguer* Carol Homan; *Archivist* Louise Rossmassler
Open Wed - Fri 10 AM - 4 PM. Estab 1876, as a research source for Museum staff, and to serve the public three days per week. For reference only
Library Holdings: Vols 120,000; Per subs 525; Micro — Fiche, reels; AV — Slides; Other — Clipping files, exhibition catalogs, pamphlets
Special Subjects: Decorative Arts, Drawings, Photography, Prints, 20th century art
Collections: Art auction sale catalogs; Kienbusch collection of arms and armor; Museum archives
—**Slide Library,** 26th St & Benjamin Franklin Pkwy, PO Box 7646, 19101. Tel 215-764-8100, Ext 320. *Slide Librn* Thomas S Donio
Provides slides to museum staff, not open to public
Library Holdings: AV — Slides 110,000

O **Women's Committee,** Box 7646, 19101. Tel 215-803-8100, Ext 448. *Pres* Mrs W Brian McLarnon
Open Tues - Sun 10 AM - 5 PM. Admis $2.50. Estab 1883, incorporated 1915; takes an active interest in the museum. Organization sponsors art sales and rental, park houses, museum guides, Craft Show, classes for blind artists and tours for the deaf. Average Annual Attendance: 600,000
Income: Financed by fund raising events
Collections: European, American, Oriental paintings & decorative arts
Activities: Classes for adults & children; docent training; lectures open to public, 52 vis lectr per yr; concerts; gallery talks; tours; exten dept; individual paintings & original objects of art lent to other museums; museum sales shop sells books, magazines, original art, reproductions, prints & slides

O **PHILADELPHIA SKETCH CLUB INC,** 235 S Camac St, 19107. Tel 215-545-9298. *Pres* Herbert E Armstrong
Open Wed - Sun 1 - 5 PM. No admis fee. Estab 1860 for artistic practice, exhibitions, and education as well as social functions. Club owns building and maintains sky-lit gallery on the second floor; dimensions approximately 30 x 42 ft. Average Annual Attendance: 3000. Mem: 100; dues $80; monthly meeting on first Fri
Income: Financed by endowment, and membership
Collections: Forty Thomas Anshutz Portraits; J Pennell Citiscapes; deceased members collection
Publications: The Portfolio, (bulletin), monthly
Activities: Classes for adults and children from Sept - June; lect open to the public, 8 visiting lectr per year; gallery talks; competitions with cash prizes, purchase awards and certificates; individual paintings and original objects of art lent on a very limited basis; lending collection contains books, original art works, original prints, paintings

O **PLASTIC CLUB,** Art Club for Women,* 247 S Comac St, 19107. Tel 215-545-9324. *Acting Pres* Mary Bolden; *VPres* Mrs George Taylor; *Secy* Isabel Stone; *Treas* Sara Sharpe; *Finance* Mrs Wallace Jones; *House Chmn* Mrs William Gibson
Open Mon 10 AM - 3 PM, Tues 10 AM - 2 PM, Wed 10 AM - 3 PM. Estab 1897 to promote wider knowledge of art and to advance its interest among artists. Art gallery maintained in small club house. Mem: 70; must qualify for membership by submitting three framed paintings or two sculptures to be juried; annual meeting first Wed May
Income: Financed by membership and money-making projects
Exhibitions: Monthly exhibitions of paintings by members
Activities: Lect open to public and members; gallery talks; competitions with cash awards and medals; individual paintings lent to hospitals and public buildings; sales shop selling books, original art and small craft items

M **PLEASE TOUCH MUSEUM,** 210 N 21st St, 19103. Tel 215-963-0667, 567-5551. *Chmn* Dr Ruth Murray Klein; *Executive Dir* Portia Sperr; *Admin* Margaret Dungan; *Development Dir* Peter Geyelin; *Dir Education* Susan Brown; *Dir Exhibits* Greta Levitan; *Dir Public Affairs* Sharla Feidscher
Open Tues - Sat 10 AM - 4:30 PM, Sun 12:30 - 4:30 PM. Admis $2.50. Estab 1976 to provide a developmentally appropriate museum for young children, their parents and teachers. Gallery spaces are small-scaled, objects are accessible; dual interpretation is being developed for use by adults and children (arts, crafts, ethnic materials and exhibits). Average Annual Attendance: 100,000. Mem: 1100; dues family $35
Income: $250,000 (financed by memberships, governmental appropriations, admissions, foundation, corporate support & individuals)
Collections: †Art works by contemporary artists, sculpture, environmental, craft; †cultural artifacts from around the world: costumes, playthings, musical instruments, objects from daily life; †Materials from the natural sciences; †contemporary toys
Exhibitions: (1982) Responses: Art for Young Children; The Lenapes; (1983) Head to Toe
Publications: Newsletters, quarterly; annual report; thematic exhibition catalogs, bi-annually; follow-through materials for groups and parents
Activities: Classes for adults and children; dramatic programs; docent training; work with area colleges and art schools; coop programs; lectures open to public, 3 vis lectr per yr; concerts; competitions with awards; originate traveling exhibitions; museums shop sells books, posters & toys
L **Library,** Philadelphia, 19103
Library Holdings: Vols 200; Per subs 4; AV — Cassettes, v-tapes; Other — Clipping files, pamphlets

O **PRESBYTERIAN HISTORICAL SOCIETY,** 425 Lombard St, 19147. Tel 215-627-1852. *Dir* William B Miller; *Mgr Cataloging Servs* Barbara Roy
Open Mon - Fri 9 AM - 5 PM. No admis fee. Estab May 1852 to collect and preserve official records and memorabilia of the Presbyterian Church USA, its predecessors and affiliates. Portraits displayed in the Reading Room, Museum Room, Mackie Room, Board Room & hallways. Six Alexander Stirling Calder statues representing American Presbyterian personalities who played a significant role in the history of the Church are displayed outside in front of the building. Average Annual Attendance: 1845. Mem: 1250; dues $10; annual meeting first Fri Mar
Income: Financed by membership & General Assembly
Collections: †Paintings & sculptures; †church plates; †relics; †silver and pewter communionware
Publications: Journal of Presbyterian History, quarterly
Activities: Tours
L **Art Library,** 425 Lombard St, 19147. *Librn* William B Miller
Open to the public for reference
Library Holdings: Other — Manuscripts 3,000,000
Collections: Jackson Collection; National Council of Churches Collection; Scotch-Irish Society Archives; Shane Collection

PRINT CLUB
For further information, see National and Regional Organizations

M **THE ROSENBACH MUSEUM AND LIBRARY,** 2010 DeLancey Place, 19103. Tel 215-732-1600. *Dir* Ellen S Dunlap; *Cur Literature* Patricia C Willis; *Cur History & Bibliography* Open; *Cur Arts* Open
Open daily 11 AM - 4 PM except Mon, open to scholars 10 AM - 5 PM, cl August and national holidays. Admis adults $2.50, students $1.50, groups of 8 or more $2 per person; exhibits only $1.50. Estab 1953 as a nonprofit corporation
Collections: 18th century English antiques and silver, paintings, prints and drawings, porcelain, rugs and objets d'art; rare books and manuscripts, consisting of British and American literature, Americana, and book illustrations; 130,000 manuscripts; 30,000 books, Marianne Moore Archive; Maurice Sendak Archive
Exhibitions: (1981) Cortes in the New World; The Medieval Scriber and His Books; Maurice Sendak Toys; (1982) Cook: Choice; Art of the Picture Book; Passing Through; (1983) Rosenwald E Rosenbach
Publications: A Selection from Our Shelves; Fantasy Sketches; Lewis Carroll's Photographs of Nude Children; Marianne Moore Newsletter

M **ROBERT W RYERSS LIBRARY AND MUSEUM,** Burholme Park, Central & Cottman Aves, 19111. Tel 215-745-3061. *Park Historian & Admin Supv* John McIlhenny
Library open Fri - Sun 10 AM - 5 PM, Museum Sun 1 - 4 PM or by appointment. No admiss fee. Estab 1910. House (Historic Register) left to City complete with contents in 1905; three period rooms, three other museum rooms with art objects - predominately Victorian. Average Annual Attendance: 20,000. Mem: 75; dues $5; meeting first Mon every month
Income: Financed by endowment, city appropriation, volunteer fund raising and trust fund
Collections: Static collection; export china, ivory, paintings, period rooms, prints, sculpture, weapons
Activities: Tours; lending collection contains 12,000 books
L **Library,** Burholme Park, Central & Cottman Aves, 19111. *Librn* Mary L Campbell; *Asst Librn* Kathy LePore
Open Wed - Sun 10 AM - 5 PM. Estab 1910. Victoriana Collection available to scholars by appointment only
Library Holdings: Vols 20,000; Per subs 40; AV — Cassettes, fs, slides; Other — Framed reproductions, memorabilia, original art works, photographs, prints, sculpture
Collections: Victoriana

SOCIETY OF ARCHITECTURAL HISTORIANS
For further information, see National and Regional Organizations

TEMPLE UNIVERSITY
M **Tyler School of Art-Galleries,** Beech and Penrose Aves, Elkins Park, 19126. Tel 215-224-7575. *Actg Dean* Philip Betancourt; *Dir Exhibitions* Ann Jarmusch
Open Tues & Wed 10 AM - 8 PM, Thurs - Sun 10 AM - 4 PM. No admis fee. Three galleries (Elkins, Tyler, Penrose); track lighting. Average Annual Attendance: 7000
Income: Financed by state appropriation and grants
Exhibitions: (1982) Handmade Cameras: Contemporary Images; (1983) In a Basket Way; Brett Taylor: The Aegean Years, A Memorial Exhibition; Fears; (1984) Floored; Cover to Cover: Magazine Covers from 1890 - Present; Philadelphia Glass
Publications: The Tyler Offset Workshop; posters, announcements or exhibition catalogs for major shows
Activities: Lectures open to the public, 10-15 vis lectr per yr; concerts; gallery talks; special events
L **Tyler School of Art Library,** Beech and Penrose Ave, 19126. Tel 215-224-7575, Ext 245. *Librn* Ivy Bayard
Open Mon - Thurs 8:30 AM - 9 PM, Fri 8:30 AM - 6 PM, Sat 9 AM - 5 PM, Sun 1 - 9 PM. Estab 1935 to provide library services to students and faculty. Circ 26,022
Income: $86,845 (financed by appropriation from Central University Library)
Purchases: $27,200
Library Holdings: Vols 24,267; Per subs 77; Auction Sale Catalogs; Micro — Fiche, reels; AV — Cassettes, v-tapes; Other — Exhibition catalogs, pamphlets, prints
—**Slide Library,** Beech & Penrose Aves, 19126. Tel 215-224-7575. *Slide Cur* Edith Zuckerman
Library Holdings: AV — Slides 238,000
Special Subjects: Art History, Ceramics, Decorative Arts, Graphic Design, Photography

M **UNIVERSITY OF PENNSYLVANIA,** University Museum of Archaeology & Anthropology, 33rd and Spruce St, 19104. Tel 215-898-4000. *Dir & Near East Section Cur* Dr Robert H Dyson Jr; *Assoc Dir & Asian Cur* Dr Gregory L Possehl; *African Section Keeper of Coll* Dr Paula Ben-Amos; *Am Hist Arch Assoc Cur* Dr Robert L Schuyler; *Am Section Cur* Dr William R Coe; *Babylonian Section Tablet Coll Cur* Dr Ake W Sjoberg; *Akkadian Cur* Dr Erle Leichty; *Egyptian Section Assoc Cur* Dr David O'Connor; *European Archives Assoc Cur* Dr Bernard Wailes; *Mediterranean Section Cur* Dr Spyros Iakovidis; *Oceanian Section Cur* Dr William H Davenport; *Physical Anthropology Cur* Dr Francis E Johnston
Open Tues - Sat 10 AM - 4:30 PM, Sun 1 - 5 PM, cl Mon. Admis free; suggested donation $2. Estab 1887 to investigate the origins and varied developments of man's cultural achievements in all times and places; to preserve and maintain collections to document these achievements, and to present to the public the results of these investigations by means of permanent exhibits and temporary exhibitions. Average Annual Attendance: 160,000. Mem: 8188; dues from individual $18 - Loren Eiseley Assoc $1000
Income: $4,400,000 (financed by endowment, membership, state appropriation and University)
Collections: Archaeological and ethnographic displays relating to the Old and New World; the classical civilization of the Mediterranean, Egypt, Mesopotamia, Iran, Southeast Asia and the Far East, North, Middle and South America, Oceania; physical anthropology
Exhibitions: Changing exhibitions in the Nevil Gallery for the Blind and Sighted; permanent galleries have exhibits from each of the broad geographical areas represented in collections; temporary exhibitions composed of ethnological and archaeological specimens from the Museum's own collections and from other institutions
Publications: Expedition Magazine, quarterly; Museum Applied Science Center for Archaeology Journal; Museum Mimographs
Activities: Classes for adults and children; docent training; lectures open to public, 20 vis lectrs per year; concerts; gallery talks; tours; exten dept serving Pennsylvania Commonwealth; original objects of art lent to libraries and instructional centers in the state; lending collection contains motion pictures, original art works and slides; traveling exhibitions organized and circulated; museum shop selling books, magazines, reproductions, slides, jewelry and craft items
M **Henry Clews Memorial,** La Napoule Art Foundation, 133 Bennett Hall, 19104. Tel 215-898-5000. *Pres* Paul O Gaddis
Open June - Sept Tues - Sun 3 - 6 PM, Oct - May Mon - Fri 3 - 6 PM, cl Dec 1 - 20. Admis adult $1.50, children under 10 free, group rates. Estab 1950
Collections: Sculpture and paintings of Henry Clews Jr
Activities: Tours; concerts; art festivals

L **John and Ada Lewis Memorial Library,** * 33rd and Spruce St, 19104. Tel 215-243-7840. *Librn* Jean Shaw-Adelman; *Asst Librn* Anita Fahringer; *Asst Librn* Carol Tang
Open to staff and students of the University and the public
Library Holdings: Vols 75,000; Per subs 900; Micro — Fiche, reels; Other — Exhibition catalogs, manuscripts, pamphlets
Special Subjects: Anthropology, Archaeology
Collections: Brinton Collection

O **Institute of Contemporary Art,** * 34th and Walnut St, 19104. Tel 215-243-7108. *Dir* Janet Kardon; *Asst Dir* Paula Marincola
Open Tues 10 AM - 7:30 PM, Wed - Fri 10 AM - 5 PM, Sat & Sun Noon - 5 PM, cl holidays. No admis fee. Estab 1963 to provide a continuing forum for the active presentation of advanced development in the visual arts. Two large gallery spaces devoted to exhibiting contemporary art in all media. Average Annual Attendance: 80,000. Mem: 600; dues $30, $75, $150, $300 and up
Income: Approx $400,000 (financed by endowment, membership and grants)
Exhibitions: ICA Street Sights 1 & 2; Masks, Tents, Vessels & Talismans; Paul Thek: Processions; Urban Encounters; Art Architecture Audience; Drawings: The Pluralist Decade; Made in Philadelphia 4 & 5; Machineworks; Vito Acconci, Alice Aycock, Dennis Oppenheim; Robert S Zakanitch; Photography: A Sense of Order
Publications: Annual newsletter; calendar of events; exhibition catalogs
Activities: Lect open to the public, 5-10 visiting lectrs per year; concerts; gallery talks; tours; traveling exhibitions organized and circulated; sales shop sells original art and catalogs

M **WOODMERE ART MUSEUM,** 9201 Germantown Ave, 19118. Tel 215-247-0476. *Chmn of the Board* Dr John H Wolf; *Pres* Mrs Harry G Kuch; *VPres* Dr Patricia Allison; *Treas* Joseph Baxter; *Dir* Michael W Schantz
Open Tues - Sat 10 AM - 5 PM, Sun 2 - 5 PM, cl holidays. No admis fee. Estab 1940; founded by Charles Knox Smith, in trust for benefit of the public. A large addition in 1965 provides additional gallery and studio space. Average Annual Attendance: 14,000. Mem: 1500; dues $20 and higher; annual meeting April
Income: Financed by endowments and gifts
Collections: Contemporary American †paintings, †sculpture, and †graphics; European porcelains and furniture; European and American sculpture; Oriental rugs, furniture, porcelains; Smith Collection of European and American paintings
Exhibitions: 8 current exhibitions annually; prizes awarded in Members' Annual Juried and Special Exhibitions
Activities: Classes for adults and children; Philadelphia Guild of Handweavers' classes; concerts, lect, gallery tours

L **Library,** Philadelphia, 19118
Reference only
Library Holdings: Micro — Cards; Other — Clipping files, exhibition catalogs

PITTSBURGH

M **ART INSTITUTE OF PITTSBURGH GALLERY,** 536 Penn Ave, 15222. Tel 412-263-6600. *Pres* John R Knepper
Open Mon, Tues & Thurs 9 AM - 8 PM, Weds, Fri 9 AM - 5 PM, Sat 9 AM - 1 PM. No admis fee. Estab 1921 as an art school and proprietary trade school
Exhibitions: Local art group shows; local artists; loan exhibitions; student and faculty members; technical art exhibits
Publications: Brochures; Catalog; School Newspaper
Activities: Classes for adults and teens; lectures open to public, 2-4 visiting lectures per year; Scholarships available

L **Resource Center,** 526 Penn Ave, 15222. *Admin* Diana K Hunt
Open Mon - Fri 7:30 AM - 3 PM, Mon, Tues & Thurs 6 - 10 PM. Estab 1971 to supply our students with readily available reference materials. Circ Approx 2600
Purchases: $1295
Library Holdings: Vols 2030; Per subs 78; Micro — Fiche; AV — Cassettes, fs, rec, slides; Other — Clipping files, exhibition catalogs, framed reproductions, memorabilia, pamphlets
Special Subjects: Architecture, Art History, Commercial Art, Crafts, Fashion Arts, Graphic Arts, Interior Design, Mixed Media, Photography

O **ARTS AND CRAFTS CENTER OF PITTSBURGH,** * Mellon Park, Fifth & Shady Aves, 15232. Tel 412-361-0873. *Dir* Audrey Bethel
Open Tues - Sat 10 AM - 5 PM, Sun 2 - 5 PM. Estab 1944, incorporated 1947. Galleries maintained for monthly contemporary exhibitions, group and one-man shows. Headquarters for non-profit organizations in the creative arts consists of fifteen resident and two affiliated member groups. Average Annual Attendance: 85,000. Mem: 1600; dues resident members pay per capita according to own membership; affiliated members, group dues
Publications: Class brochure 4 times a year; Center brochure
Activities: Arts and crafts classes for adults and children; workshops; rental facilities provided for outside groups for art programs

O **ASSOCIATED ARTISTS OF PITTSBURGH ARTS AND CRAFTS CENTER,** Fifth & Shady Aves, 15232. Tel 412-361-4235. *Pres* Adrienne Heinrich; *VPres* Frances Gialamas; *Secy* Charlotte Toal; *Exec Dir* Anna Marie Sninsky
Open Tues - Sat 10 AM - 5 PM, Sun 2 - 5 PM, cl Mon. Estab 1910 to give exposure to member artists and for education of the area in the field of art. A small art gallery is maintained. Average Annual Attendance: 25,000. Mem: 550 (must be juried into the group); dues $30
Income: Financed by membership
Activities: Lectures open to public; competitions with awards

M **CARNEGIE INSTITUTE,** Museum of Art, 4400 Forbes Ave, 15213. Tel 412-622-3200. *Dir* John R Lane; *Asst Dir* Barbara L Phillips; *Cur Fine Arts* Henry Adams; *Cur Education* Vicky A Clark; *Adjunct Cur Contemporary Art* John Caldwell; *Conservator* Karen B Crenshaw; *Cur Film and Video* William Judson; *Registrar* Eleanor Vuilleumier; *Cur Section of Antiquities, Oriental & Decorative Arts* Phillip Johnston; *Dir Public Relations* Mary C Poppenberg; *Dir Development* Michael McGrael; *Pres* James M Walton; *Chmn Museum of Art Committee* Richard M Scaife

Open Tues - Sat 10 AM - 5 PM, Sun 1- 5 PM, cl Mon and major holidays. Admis by suggested contribution adults $2, children & students $1, members free, Sat free to students & children. Estab 1896, incorporated 1926. Original building 1896-1907. Average Annual Attendance: 800,000. Mem: 11,500; dues $22.50 and up
Income: Financed by endowment, membership, city and state appropriation and other funds
Collections: American and European paintings & sculpture, especially Impressionist and Post-Impressionist; Ailsa Mellon Bruce Furniture Collection; Japanese woodblock prints; Oriental & decorative arts; antiquities, drawings, photographs, films, video tapes, photographs, prints and watercolors
Exhibitions: (1982) Associated Artists of Pittsburgh, annually; Neopolitan Presepe, annually; Three Rivers Art Festival, annually; Carnegie International; Buffalo Bill & Wild West; American Photographers & the National Parks; (1983) Abstract Painting & Sculpture in America 1927-1944; one-artist exhibitions of contemporary artists; Images of a Changing World: Japanese Prints of the Twentieth Century; Recent Acquisitions in Contemporary Art; Collages by Irwin Kremen 1976-1983; Statements in Collecting: Selected Recent Acquisitions of American & European Decorative Art; Pennsylvania Modern: Charles Demuth of Lancaster; Great Drawings from the Collection of the British Institute of Architects; Susan Rothenberg; Fairfield Porter (1907-1975): Realist Painter in an Age of Abstraction; Japanese Prints by Utagawa Kunisada I (Toyokuni III) 1786-1864; Joan Witek: Paintings & Drawings; Six in Bronze; Philip Pearlstein; Mark Rothko: Works on Paper 1925-1970; Jewelry: Ancient to Modern, from the Collection of the Walters Art Gallery
Publications: Annual report; Carnegie Magazine, six times per year; catalogue of permanent collection; exhibition catalogs
Activities: Classes for adults and children; docent training; lectures open to public, concerts; gallery talks; tours; inter-museum loans; originate traveling exhibitions; museum shop sells books, periodicals, original art, reproductions, prints, slides, textiles, jewelry, pottery, sculpture, china and postcards

L **Library,** 4400 Forbes Ave, 15213
Open to staff and museum docents for reference only

L **CARNEGIE LIBRARY OF PITTSBURGH,** Music and Art Department, 4400 Forbes Ave, 15213. Tel 412-622-3105. *Head* Ida Reed; *Asst Head* Peggy Dusch; *Staff Librn* Kirby Delworth; *Staff Librn* Katherine Kepes; *Staff Librn* Ann Safley; *Staff Librn* Catherine Tack
Open Mon, Tues, Fri & Sat 9 AM - 9 PM, Wed & Thurs 9 AM - 5:30 PM, cl Memorial Day and Labor Day. Estab 1930 to provide reference and circulating materials on all aspects of art
Income: Financed by city, state and county appropriation
Library Holdings: Vols 40,000; Per subs 60; AV — Fs, slides; Other — Clipping files, exhibition catalogs, pamphlets
Collections: Architecture; Costume

CARNEGIE-MELLON UNIVERSITY *

M **Forbes Street Gallery,** * 5000 Forbes Ave, 51213. Tel 412-578-2000. *Dir* Margaret Bauman; *Co-Dir* Karen Kacurak
Open Tues & Thurs 7 - 9 PM, Wed & Sun Noon - 4 PM. Estab 1969 to offer exhibition space to students, and an opportunity to learn about gallery management through practice. Gallery is approximately 20 x 40 ft plus small back room space. Average Annual Attendance: 750
Income: $1700 (financed by university funding)
Exhibitions: Weekly student exhibitions

L **Hunt Library,** Schenley Park, 15213. Tel 412-578-2451. *Fine Arts Librn* Henry Pisciotta; *Dir of University Libraries* Thomas J Michalak
Open Mon - Thurs 8 AM - Midnight, Fri 8 AM - 9 PM, Sat 9 AM - 6 PM, Sun Noon - Midnight. Estab 1912. The Fine Arts Library is on the 4th floor of the Hunt Library. Its collection supports the College of Fine Arts programs
Income: Financed by the University Libraries general operating funds
Library Holdings: Vols 30,500; Per subs 179; Micro — Fiche, reels; AV — A-tapes, rec, slides 80,000; Other — Clipping files, exhibition catalogs, reproductions
Special Subjects: Architecture, Design, Modern Art
Exhibitions: (1983) Artists Books

M **CHATHAM COLLEGE,** Art Gallery, Woodland Rd, 15232. Tel 412-441-8200. *Co-Dir* Jerry L Caplan; *Co-Dir* Joseph Shelper
Open Tues - Sun 2 - 5 PM, cl Mon. No admis fee. Estab 1960 as an art gallery in a small liberal arts college, serving both the college and community by mounting exhibitions of high quality. Gallery is 100 running ft, is located in Jennie King Mellon Library, and is fitted with track lighting. Average Annual Attendance: 1500
Income: Financed by college
Exhibitions: Linda Benglis; Don Reitz; Idelle Weber; Jerry L Caplan
Activities: Lect open to the public, 2 visiting lectr per year; gallery talks; scholarships; individual paintings & original objects of art lent

C **FISHER SCIENTIFIC COMPANY,** Fisher Collection of Alchemical and Historical Pictures, 711 Forbes Ave, 15219. Tel 412-562-8480. *Adminr* John Pavlik
Open Mon - Fri 9 AM - 4 PM. Estab 1917 to preserve for scientists a record of their professional ancestors. To maintain paintings and other graphics regarding science history, especially chemistry, for the public. Collection is housed in two small rooms and a hallway with 4000 sq ft of wall space, housed within Fisher Scientific Company's headquarters. Average Annual Attendance: 1000
Collections: Permanent collection consists of 40 oil paintings, engravings and etchings dealing with science history, especially alchemy; works executed by 17th century Dutch and Flemish artists: D Teniers, Hellemont, Wyck and Heerschopp; Louis Pasteur Special Collection, books, artworks, letters

M **FRICK ART MUSEUM,** 7227 Reynolds St, 15208. Tel 412-371-7766. *Dir* Virginia E Lewis; *Exec Secy* Catherine Rudy Kiefer; *Registrar* Kathryn D Cox; *Supv of Maintenance* Thomas L Dennis
Open Wed - Sat 10 AM - 5:30 PM, Sun Noon - 6 PM. No admis fee. Estab 1970 as an art museum for public enjoyment and education. Average Annual

Attendance: 17,000
Income: Financed by endowment
Collections: Chinese 18th century porcelains; English and Irish 18th century silver; French 18th century period room; French 18th century furniture: †Italian, Flemish, French paintings from the early Renaissance through the 18th century; Italian and Flemish bronzes of the 15th, 16th and 17th centuries; Italian 16th to 18th century furniture; Russian 18th century silver; Sculpture, Houdon, Clodion, tapestries, French mille fleurs and Flemish 16th century
Publications: Five Lectures; The Arts in Changing Societies; Madame Jean Antoine Houdon (reprinted from the Art Bulletin); Reflections Inspired by Works of Art in the Frick Art Museum, Pittsburgh, Check List; The Treasures of Frick Art Museum
Activities: Lect open to the public, 3-5 visiting lectrs per year; 24 gallery talks; 50 tours; concerts; small working library

C **PAPERCRAFT CORPORATION,*** Papercraft Park, 15238. Tel 412-362-8000. *Pres* Marshall P Katz
Estab to support Western Pennsylvania artists and place collection in view for our visitors. Displayed in executive offices
Collections: Oils, watercolors and sculpture by local artists
Activities: Awards to local art societies; individual objects of art lent

M **PITTSBURGH HISTORY AND LANDMARKS FOUNDATION,** Old Post Office Museum,* One Landmarks Square, 15212. Tel 412-322-1204. *Pres* Arthur P Ziegler; *VPres* Barbara Hoffstot; *Secy* Anne S Genter; *Chmn of Board* Charles C Arensberg; *Asst Museums & Special Projects* Patricia A Wiley
Open Tues - Fri 10 AM - 4:30 PM, Sat & Sun 1 - 4:30 PM. Admis adults $1, children $.40. Estab 1971 to preserve our historical and architectural heritage. Museum is housed in the Old Allegheny Post Office; main gallery is in rotunda room; additional galleries in basement and on third floor; also artifacts garden court. Average Annual Attendance: 15,000. Mem: 3000; dues patron $500, sustaining $100, family $30, couples $25, active $15
Income: $30,000 (financed by membership, private donations and private foundation grants)
Collections: Architectural artifacts from demolished buildings and sites, decorative arts, documents, fashions, furniture, industrial artifacts, paintings, prints, stained glass and toys
Exhibitions: Art Deco International; John Bower Riverboat Collection; Recent Acquisitions; Stained Glass in Pittsburgh
Activities: Classes for adults and children; restoration seminars; preservation conferences; historic district survey training; lect, 5 visiting lectr per year; concerts; gallery talks; tours; exten dept serves Allegheny County; original objects of art lent to museums in Pittsburgh area; book traveling exhibitions; museum shop sells books, magazines, reproductions, prints, slides, gift items and artifacts; Toy Museum
L **James D Van Trump Library,*** One Landmarks Sq, 15212. Tel 412-322-1204
Library Holdings: Vols 5000; Per subs 20; VF 30
Special Subjects: Architecture, Landscape Architecture, Urban Planning

C **PITTSBURGH NATIONAL BANK,*** Fifth Ave & Wood St, 15222. Tel 412-355-2609. *Real Estate Adminr* Robert F Lew
No admis fee. Estab 1970 to enhance offices. Collection displayed at Pittsburgh National Building
Collections: Eclectic media and periods
Activities: Awards to local groups only; individual objects of art lent

O **PITTSBURGH PLAN FOR ART GALLERY,** Gallery 407, 407 S Craig St, 15213. Tel 412-683-7600. *Pres* Robert J Dodds III; *Dir* Ms Kennedy B Nelson
Open Tues - Sat 10 AM - 5 PM, Sun 1 - 5 PM; cl Mon. No admis fee. Estab 1955 as a nonprofit organization under aegis of Education to Learn by Looking. Maintains an art gallery for rental and-or sale of artworks; two floors over 6000 sq ft. Average Annual Attendance: 20,000. Mem: 567; dues public $25
Income: Financed by membership, rental and sales fees
Exhibitions: One-person and group shows every month
Activities: Lect open to public; tours; lending collection contains original art works of all media; originate traveling exhibitions

C **ROCKWELL INTERNATIONAL CORPORATION TRUST,** 600 Grant St, 15219. Tel 412-565-2000. *Secy* J J Christin
Annual amount of contributions and grants $667,800; supports fine and performing arts

UNIVERSITY OF PITTSBURGH
M **University Art Gallery,** 15260. Tel 412-624-4121. *Dir* David G Wilkins
Open Tues - Sat 10 AM - 4 PM, Sun 2 - 5 PM; cl Mon. No admis fee. Estab 1970 to provide exhibitions for the university community and the community at large and to provide students with gallery experience. Gallery comprised of 350 running ft in five areas. Average Annual Attendance: 4000
Income: Financed through the University
Collections: Drawings, paintings, prints and sculpture
Exhibitions: (1982-83) Kenneth Snelson, sculpture; Duane Michals, photographs; Ruttenberg Collection; Pittsburgh's Public Sculpture; Hazlett Awards; Lowenthal Gift
Publications: Exhibition catalogs, three per year
Activities: Original objects of art lent; lending collection contains 922 original art works, 700 original prints, paintings, 100 photographs, 100 sculptures and drawings; originate traveling exhibitions
L **Henry Clay Frick Fine Arts Library,** Henry Clay Frick Fine Arts Bldg, 15260. Tel 412-624-4124. *Librn* Anne W Gordon
Open Mon - Thurs 9 AM - 9 PM, Fri & Sat 9 AM - 5 PM, Sun 12 - 5 PM. Estab 1928 to support the teaching activities of the Departments of Fine Arts and Studio Arts. For reference only
Library Holdings: Vols 54,000; Per subs 400; Micro — Fiche, reels; AV — Slides; Other — Clipping files, exhibition catalogs, pamphlets
Special Subjects: Architecture, Art History, Graphic Arts, Sculpture, Medieval, Renaissance and Modern Art
Collections: Facsimile mss

C **WESTINGHOUSE ELECTRIC CORPORATION,*** Stanwix St, Westinghouse Building, 15222. Tel 412-255-3513, 255-3800. *In Charge Art Coll* Jon Philip Andrews
Open 8:15 AM - 5:15 PM. No admis fee. Estab 1970 to create pleasant working environment for employees. Collection displayed in headquarter building; is a working collection used by the employees
Collections: 1300 pieces: American Contemporary Abstract Paintings and Prints, 1965 to present; American Indian Tapestries; †Poster Classics
Activities: Individual objects of art lent

READING

M **ALBRIGHT COLLEGE,** Freedman Gallery, 13th & Exeter Sts, 19604. Tel 215-921-2381, Ext 312. *Pres* David G Ruffer; *Dean* Eugene S Lubot; *Treas* A Van Bodegraven; *Dir of Gallery* Judith Tannenbaum
Open Mon - Fri Noon - 4 PM, Tues evenings 6 - 8 PM, Sun 2 - 5 PM, also by appointment. No admis fee. Estab 1976 to present primarily contemporary art in a context of teaching. Gallery is 30 x 45 ft with flexible wall arrangements. Average Annual Attendance: 12,000. Mem: 220; dues $20, students $5; annual meeting Feb
Income: $100,000 (financed by endowment, college, membership and grants)
Purchases: $3000
Collections: †Contemporary Painting, Prints, Sculpture; Photography
Exhibitions: (1982-83) Messages: Words & Images; Harry Koursaros 1955-1980, paintings; Landscape in Sculpture; Usable Art; Wall-Size Works; Robert Colescott; Black American Folk Art; Thomas Watcke; Day In/Day Out; Ordinary Life as a Source For Art; Contemporary Landscape Painting; Bernd & Hilla Becher: Winding Towers; Tracking, Tracing, Marking, Pacing; The World of Japanese Theater
Publications: Neil Anderson (four-color limited edition poster); exhibition catalogues
Activities: Lectures open to public, 4-6 vis lectr per year; gallery talks; tours; Freedman Gallery Student Award; produce video-tapes on exhibitions, these include interviews with artists and commentary, tapes are available for rent; film series; individual paintings and original objects of art lent to galleries and museums; originate traveling exhibitions; sales desk sells catalogues, prints, t-shirts

O **BERKS ART ALLIANCE,*** Wyomissing Institute of Art Bldg, Trent & Belmont St, 19610. Tel 215-376-1576. *Pres* Suazanne Whitehouse; *First VPres* Polly Kinginger; *Second VPres* Joanne Post; *Record Secy* Rose Ann Dowty; *Correspondence Secy* Rose Ann Dowty; *Treasurer* Sylvia Umberger
Estab 1941 to maintain active art center in Reading and Berks county. Mem: 150; dues $12; annual meetings 2nd Tues of odd months
Income: Financed by dues; art auction; commisions from members shows
Exhibitions: Three annual membership shows, plus solo or two-persons shows of a two week period each; juried show
Publications: Palette, every other month
Activities: Life or costume drawing workshop Thurs morning; open painting workshop Thurs afternoon; life drawing workshop Thurs evening; three day seminars by professional artists; sponsors annual trip to American Watercolor Society Show in New York

M **READING PUBLIC MUSEUM AND ART GALLERY,** 500 Museum Rd, 19611. Tel 215-371-5850. *Dir* Bruce L Dietrich; *Cur Fine Arts* Jefferson A Gore
Open Mon - Fri 9 AM - 5 PM, Sat 9 AM - Noon, Sun 2 - 5 PM. No admis fee; suggested donation $1 adults, $.50 children. Estab 1904 to promote knowledge, pleasure, and cultivation of the arts and sciences. Ground floor: natural and social sciences exhibits. Second floor: permanent and temporary art exhibitions. Average Annual Attendance: 100,000. Mem: 500; dues $1000 - $5
Income: $600,000 (financed by government)
Collections: 19th Century Paintings; Old Masters Gallery; Pennsylvania-German Room
Exhibitions: (1983-84) Jon Carssman Watercolor Exhibition; Room for Thought; Peace Corps
Activities: Classes for children; docent training; lectures open to public, 6 vis lect per year; concerts; gallery tlaks; tours; competitions with purchase awards; individual paintings & original objects of art lent to AAM accredited museums; lending collection contains 600 original prints, 700 paintings, 100 photographs & 85 sculpture; museum shop sells books, reproductions & gift items
L **Library,** 500 Museum Rd, 19611
Open Mon - Fri 9 AM - 4 PM
Library Holdings: Vols 12,000; Per subs 30; Original documents; Other — Exhibition catalogs, manuscripts, memorabilia, pamphlets, prints, reproductions
Collections: American Bureau of Ethnology Collection

SCRANTON

M **EVERHART MUSEUM OF NATURAL HISTORY, SCIENCE AND ART,** Nay Aug Park, 18510. Tel 717-346-7186. *Chmn Trustees* Edwin M Kosik; *Dir* Kent Ahrens, PhD; *Cur Science & Natural History & Planetarium Dir* William E Speare; *Cur Art & Educ* Robert E Schweitzer; *Office Mgr* Helen E Kane
Open Tues - Sat 10 AM - 5 PM, Sun 2 - 5 PM, cl major holidays. No admis fee. Estab and incorporated 1908, a gift to the city from Dr Isiah F Everhart; building rebuilt 1928-29. Average Annual Attendance: 200,000. Mem: 1200; dues $5 and higher; annual meeting June
Income: Financed by endowment and city appropriation
Collections: African Art; †American Folk Art; †American Indian material; European and American painting, prints and sculpture; Dorflinger Glass (1852-1921); Oceanic Art; Oriental Art
Exhibitions: Monthly exhibitions
Activities: Weekly classes in art and science for children and adults; lect series in art and science for members; outside lect; guided tours; artists-in-residence programs
L **Library,** Nay Aug Park, 18510
For reference only
Library Holdings: Vols 8500

SHIPPENSBURG

M SHIPPENSBURG UNIVERSITY, Kauffman Gallery, Prince St, 17257. Tel 717-532-1530. *Secy* Veronica Mowrey; *Dir* William Hynes
Open Mon - Fri 9 AM - 4 PM, Wed evenings 6:30 - 9 PM. No admis fee. Estab 1972 to bring art to the college community. Average Annual Attendance: 1500
Income: Financed by Student Association funds and university
Activities: Classes for adults; lectures open to the public, 4 vis lectr per yr; concerts; gallery talks

SWARTHMORE

L SWARTHMORE COLLEGE, Friends Historical Library, 19081. Tel 215-447-7496. *Dir* Dr J William Frost; *Assoc Dir* Albert W Fowler; *Cur Peace Collection* Dr Jean R Soderlund
Open Mon - Fri 8:30 AM - 4:30 PM, Sat 9 AM - Noon; cl August and Sat when college not in session. Estab 1871 to preserve and make available to the public material by and about Quakers and their concerns, records of non-sectarian peace organizations and papers of peace movement leaders. Circ 4885
Income: $150,487 (financed by endowment and college)
Purchases: $7677
Library Holdings: Vols 43,190; Per subs 456; charts; maps; original documents; posters; Micro — Reels; AV — A-tapes, cassettes, Kodachromes, lantern slides, motion pictures, rec, slides, v-tapes; Other — Clipping files, manuscripts, memorabilia, original art works, pamphlets, photographs, prints, sculpture
Collections: Quaker paintings; Quakers as subject in art; †Meeting House Picture Collection; †portraits, group pictures, †residence pictures, †silhouettes and sketches of individual Friends; †Swarthmore College pictures; Swarthmore College Peace Collection consists primarily of archival material, records of non-sectarian peace organizations in the United States and 59 foreign countries, papers of peace leaders including Jean Addams, Emily Greene Balch, Elihu Burritt, A J Muste, †Wilhelm Sollmann and others; †1400 peace posters and war posters
Publications: Collection guides

UNIONTOWN

C FAYETTE BANK AND TRUST COMPANY,* 50 W Main St, 15401. Tel 412-438-4531. *Pres* Jay C Leff
Collection estab 1957. Collection viewed regular banking hours throughout the bank
Collections: North American Indian art and gold objects
Activities: Tours; individual objects of art lent for specialized museum exhibits

UNIVERSITY PARK

PENNSYLVANIA STATE UNIVERSITY
M Museum of Art, 16802. Tel 814-865-7672. *Interim Dir* William D Davis; *Cur* Olga Preisner; *Registrar* Richard Porter; *Preparator* Ronald Hand
Open Tues - Sun 11 AM - 4:30 PM, cl Mon & legal holidays. No admis fee. Estab 1972 to promote a program of changing exhibitions; a window to the world for the university community. Museum is a three-story brick building with one large gallery on each floor which can be sub-divided with movable panels. Average Annual Attendance: 60,000
Income: Financed by state appropriation
Collections: American and European painting, drawings, graphics and sculpture with some emphasis on Pennsylvania artists; Oriental ceramics, posters, painting, sculpture and prints; limited material in Ancient, African and Near Eastern areas; Kehl and Nina Markley Collection of Ancient Peruvian Ceramics
Exhibitions: (1982-84) Danish Ceramic Design; Architectural Fantasy and Reality: Drawings from the Accademia di San Luca in Rome, Concorsi Clementini 1700-1750; The England of William Penn 1644-1718; Jerome Witkin - Paintings and Drawings: A Decade of Work; Chinese Jade Carvings; Henry Varnum Poor, 1887-1970; A Retrospective Exhibition; The Language of Michael Graves Heritage Sampler: An Introduction to the Domestic Arts and Crafts of Central Pennsylvania 1750 - 1900; The Intimate Worlds of Faust and Titolo; John F Kensett Drawings; Robert Kulicke, Painter, Designer, Craftsman; Pennsylvania Prints from the Collection of Ralph M Yeager and John C O'Connor; The Song of Roland (Art of the Heroic Era); Recent Paintings and Drawings by George Zoretich
Publications: Brochures; bi-monthly calendar of events; exhibition catalogs; posters
Activities: Docent training; lect open to public, 8 visiting lectr per year; concerts; gallery talks; tours; museum store sells books, original art and reproduction prints
L Pattee Library, Arts Library, E 405, 16802. Tel 814-865-6481. *Arts & Architecture Librn* Jean Smith; *Music Librn* Daniel Zager
Open Mon - Thurs 8 AM - 9 PM, Sat 8 AM - 9 PM, Sun Noon - Midnight. Estab 1957 to support the academic programs of the College of Arts and Architecture and the Division of Art and Music Education; to provide information on the arts to members of the university and community
Income: Financed through University Libraries
Library Holdings: Vols 70,000; Per subs 400; Micro — Fiche; AV — Cassettes, rec; Other — Prints
Special Subjects: Medieval, Baroque and Renaissance art and architecture history, history of printmaking, illuminated manuscripts
Collections: †Fine Print Collection (original prints)

WASHINGTON

M WASHINGTON & JEFFERSON COLLEGE, Olin Art Gallery, E Wheeling St, Olin Art Center, 15301. Tel 412-222-4400. *Chmn* Paul B Edwards
Open Mon - Sun Noon - 7 PM during school yr. No admis fee. Estab 1982 to provide college & community with art shows. Flexible lighting, air conditioned gallery. Average Annual Attendance: 5000-6000

Exhibitions: Monthly exhibits
Publications: Exhibition catalogs
Activities: Lectures open to public; concerts; gallery talks; competitions with awards; individual paintings & original objects of art lent to students, faculty & staff

WAYNE

O WAYNE ART CENTER,* 413 Maplewood Ave, 19087. Tel 215-688-3553. *Pres* Mary Anne Dutt-Justice; *VPres* Rosemary Beardsley; *Secy* Terry Boyle; *Treas* John J Nesbitt III
Open Mon - Fri 10 AM - 4 PM. No admis fee. Estab 1930 as a community art center. Two galleries offer rotating exhibits of work by local artists. Average Annual Attendance: 2000. Mem: 400; dues $15; annual meeting May
Income: $25,000 (financed by membership, grants, corporations and Pennsylvania Council on the Arts)
Exhibitions: 10-12 changing exhibitions per year
Activities: Classes for adults and children; lect for members, 6 visiting lectr per year; gallery talks; competitions

WEST CHESTER

O CHESTER COUNTY HISTORICAL SOCIETY, 225 N High St, 19380. Tel 215-692-4800. *Treas* H B Beale; *Exec Dir* Roland H Woodward; *Cur* Ruth K Hagy
Estab 1893 for the acquisition and preservation of property and information of historic value or interest to the people of Chester County. Maintains small reference library. Average Annual Attendance: 7000. Mem: 1200; dues family $35, individual $25; annual meeting third Tues in May
Income: Financed by endowment and membership
Collections: Museum houses regional collections of furniture, from William & Mary through Victorian; ceramics, needlework, glassware, pewter, textiles, clocks, iron, dolls and costumes
Exhibitions: Chester County Furniture; dolls; decorative arts
Publications: Chester County History, occasionally; Newsletter, bi-monthly
Activities: Docent training; lectures open to the public; tours; individual paintings and original objects of art lent to other museums; museum shop selling books, reproductions and prints

WILKES-BARRE

M WILKES COLLEGE, Sordoni Art Gallery, 150 S River St, 18766. Tel 717-824-4651, Ext 388. *Dir* Judith H O'Toole
Open Mon - Fri 1 - 5 PM, Thur 6 - 9 PM, Sat 10 AM - 5 PM, Sun 1 - 5 PM. No admis fee. Estab 1973 to encourage the fine arts in the Wilkes-Barre and the northeastern Pennsylvania areas. The Gallery has one exhibition space, 30 x 40 ft, with adjustable flats used for hanging. Average Annual Attendance: 20,000. Mem: 450; dues $10-$500
Income: Financed by memberships, foundation endowment, and Wilkes College appropriations
Collections: Nineteenth century European sculpture & paintings; 19th & 20th century American paintings & prints; mining photography collection
Exhibitions: They consist of loan exhibitions from other college galleries, independent galleries, major museums and loan services; group and one-person exhibits feature established modern masters and contemporary artists
Publications: Calendar of Events, bimonthly; scholarly catalogs; illustrated brochures
Activities: Gallery talks; tours; competitions with awards; scholarships; loans to other universitites & museums; book traveling exhibitons; originate traveling exhibitions to schools and museums

WILLIAMSPORT

M LYCOMING COLLEGE GALLERY, 17701. Tel 717-326-1951. *Co-Dir* Diane Lesko; *Co-Dir* Roger Shipley
Open Mon - Thurs 8 AM - 11 PM, Fri 8 AM - 4:30 PM, Sat 10 AM - 5 PM, Sun 1 - 11 PM. No admis fee. Estab 1980 to bring quality art work to the students and faculty as well as to the interested community. The new gallery, 30 x 60 ft, is located in the College Library. Average Annual Attendance: 5000
Income: Financed by school budget
Collections: †Paintings and prints of 19th and 20th century artists
Exhibitions: One-man shows of regional and area artists and alumni of the Department; traveling exhibitions
Activities: Gallery talks; tours; individual paintings lent; book traveling exhibitions; originate traveling exhibitions

YORK

O HISTORICAL SOCIETY OF YORK COUNTY, 250 E Market St, 17403. Tel 717-848-1587. *Exec Dir* Philip D Zimmerman; *Cur Education* Gail Dennis
Open Mon - Sat 9 AM - 5 PM, Sun 1 - 5 PM, Historic Houses Mon - Sat 10 AM - 4 PM, Sun 1 - 4 PM, cl New Years, Easter, Thanksgiving, Christmas. Admis adults $2.75, children $1.25, senior citizen group rates for Historic Houses. Estab 1895 to record, preserve, collect and interpret the history of York County and Pennsylvania, including music and art of the past and present. Restoration Properties: General Gates House (1751); Golden Plough Tavern (1741) and Log House (1812), 157 W Market; Bonham House (1870), 152 E Market. Average Annual Attendance: 30,000. Mem: 3500; dues $15 and higher; annual meeting in April
Income: $300,000 (financed by endowment & membership)
Collections: Fraktur and other Pennsylvania folk art; works by Lewis Miller and other local artists; James Shettel Collection of theater and circus material; furniture & decorative arts; local paintings

Exhibitions: Four gallery shows per year featuring various subjects of regional interest
Publications: The Kentucky Rifle; Lewis Miller Sketches and Chronicles; Monthly Newsletter; Regional Aspects of American Folk Pottery
Activities: Educ program; classes for adults and children; summer internship program; guided tours; lect; concerts; museum shop sells books, magazines, reproductions, prints and slides
L   **Library,*** 250 E Market St, 17403. *Librn* Landon C Reisinger
Open to the public, cl Sun. For reference only
Library Holdings: Vols 21,000; Per subs 50; Maps, 156 VF; AV — Slides; Other — Manuscripts, photographs

L   **MARTIN MEMORIAL LIBRARY,** 159 E Market St, 17401. Tel 717-843-3978. *Dir* William H Schell; *Fine Arts* Paula Gilbert
Open Mon - Fri 9 AM - 5:30 PM, Sat 9 AM - 5 PM. No admis fee. Estab 1935
Library Holdings: Vols 115,000; Per subs 350; mounted pictures; AV — Motion pictures, rec; Other — Pamphlets
Publications: Annual Reports; Bulletin, monthly; Martin Memorial Library Historical Series; occasional bibliographies of special collections
Activities: Programs for adults and children; lect; concerts

RHODE ISLAND

BRISTOL

M   **BRISTOL ART MUSEUM,*** Wardwell St, Box 42, 02809. Tel 401-253-8800. *Pres & Chmn* Sally D Wilson; *VPres* David Habershaw; *Secy* Dory Boland; *Treas* Earl Rounds
Open May - Oct daily 1 - 5 PM, Fri evenings 7 - 9 PM. No admis fee, donations accepted. Estab 1963 for the cultural and aesthetic advantage of the community, exhibiting artists and tourists to this 300 year old salt water seaport. Building was designed in 1905 as a ballroom on the grounds of Linden Place, the old De Wolf Mansion built in 1810. Made available by owners, heirs of Samuel Pomeroy Colt. Average Annual Attendance: 6000. Mem: 350; dues $100, $25, $10, $5; executive officers and board meeting three times a year
Income: Financed by membership, donations and jury show entry fees
Activities: Lect open to public, 2-4 visiting lectr per year; jury show; awards; original art sold by exhibiting artists

KINGSTON

O   **SOUTH COUNTY ART ASSOCIATION,** Helme House, 1319 Kingstown Rd, 02881. Tel 401-783-2195. *Pres* Lynn Woodson; *VPres* William Gilroy; *Recording Secy* Gail Ambrose; *Cur & Caretaker* Lynda W O'Malley
Open Wed - Sun 3- 6 PM during exhibitions. No admis fee. Estab 1929 to promote an interest in art and to encourage artists and to support, in every way, the aesthetic interests of the community. Average Annual Attendance: 400; applicants for membership must submit three paintings and be accepted by a committee; dues lay member & artist $15, student $7.50; annual meeting Oct
Collections: No large permanent collection; paintings by early members, usually not on display
Publications: Newsletter, 3-4 annually
Activities: Classes for adults and children; lectures open to the public, 4 vis lectr per yr; gallery talks; competitions with awards; scholarships; original objects of art lent to other art associations; lending collection contains books, lantern slides, sculpture, original art works and slides

M   **UNIVERSITY OF RHODE ISLAND GALLERY,** 02881. Tel 401-792-2131. *Dir Exhibition* Marjorie Keller
Open Mon - Fri Noon - 3 PM, Tues - Fri 7:30 - 9:30 PM. No admis fee. Estab 1970 to expose campus and community to contemporary and historical art. Average Annual Attendance: 5000
Income: Financed through University
Collections: Contemporary artists in various media
Publications: Catalogs, occasionally; brochures for each exhibit
Activities: Concerts; gallery talks; tours; competitions

NEWPORT

O   **NEWPORT ART MUSEUM AND ART ASSOCIATION,** 76 Bellevue Ave, 02840. Tel 401-847-0179. *Dir* Frederick P Walkey; *Asst Dir* Stephanie Shoemaker; *Cur* Allison Cywin; *Archivist* Jane Walsh
Open Tues - Sat 10 AM - 5 PM, Sun & most holidays 1 - 5 PM; cl Mon, Christmas, New Year's Day, Thanksgiving. The Griswold House, designed by Richard Morris Hunt for John N A Griswold in 1862-1863, has been the home of the Art Association since 1916. Retaining some of the original interior decor of the era, the building is listed in the National Register of Historic Places. The Swanhurst Villa on Bellevue Avenue, a historically registered house built by Alexander MacGregor in 1851. Swanhurst Theatre on the estate is a carriage house theatre with two resident companies in production most of the year. Cushing Memorial Gallery was built in 1920, commissioned from the firm of Delano and Aldrich, by friends and associates of artist Howard Gardiner Cushing. Buildings contain 6 galleries exhibiting contemporary visual arts, historic and regional exhibits. Average Annual Attendance: 20,000. Mem: 900; dues $30; annual meeting July
Income: Financed by donations, endowment, membership, school and admissions
Exhibitions: Annual Exhibition of Contemporary American Art (juried); Annual All Media Members' Show; Harrison Morris Annual Exhibit
Publications: The Newport Review; The Art Association Newsletter, bi-monthly; The Newsletter Of The Artists Guild, monthly
Activities: Art school with day and evening classes for adults and children; dramatic programs; docent training; lectures open to the public & some for members only, 18 vis lectr per yr; concerts; gallery talks; competitions with awards; individual and original objects of art lent to galleries and museums

L   **Library,*** 02840
Library Holdings: Vols 500; Per subs 6; Other — Exhibition catalogs, memorabilia, pamphlets, photographs

O   **NEWPORT HISTORICAL SOCIETY,** 82 Touro St, 02840. Tel 401-846-0813. *Pres* William A Sherman; *VPres* Dr George Woodbridge; *Secy* Patrick O'Hayes; *Exec Dir* Dr Daniel Snydacker
Open Tues - Fri 9:30 - 4:30 PM, Sat 9:30 AM - Noon; summer, Sat 9:30 AM - 4:30 PM, Sun 1 - 5 PM. No admis fee. Estab 1853 to collect and preserve items of historical interest pertaining to the city. Maintains a regional art gallery and small marine museum. Also owns and exhibits the first Seventh Day Baptist Church in America (1729); the Wanton-Lyman-Hazard House (1675), the first home to be restored in Newport; the Friends Meeting House (1699), site of the annual New England Quakers Meeting for over 200 years. Average Annual Attendance: 5000. Mem: 850; dues $20 and up; annual meeting May
Income: Financed by endowment, membership, state appropriation and other contributions
Collections: Artifacts, china, Colonial silver, dolls, glass, furniture, Newport scenes and portraits, pewter and toys
Publications: Newport History, quarterly
Activities: School programs; lect open to public, 4-6 visiting lectr per year; tours; original objects of art lent to museums
L   **Library,** 82 Touro St, Newport, 02840. *Librn* Thomas G Brennan
Open Tues - Fri 9:30 - 4:30 PM, Sat 9 AM - Noon; summers, Sat 9:30 AM - 4:30 PM. Estab 1853 to provide resource materials. For reference only
Library Holdings: Vols 14,000; Per subs 30; Micro — Fiche, reels; AV — Kodachromes, slides; Other — Clipping files, exhibition catalogs, manuscripts, memorabilia, original art works, pamphlets, photographs, prints, sculpture
Special Subjects: Decorative Arts

L   **REDWOOD LIBRARY AND ATHENAEUM,** 50 Bellevue Ave, 02840. Tel 401-847-0292. *Pres* Dr Donald B Fletcher; *Librn* Donald T Gibbs
Open Mon - Sat 9:30 AM - 5:30 PM, 9:30 AM - 5 PM in July & August. Estab 1747 as a general library. Art gallery consists of three rooms with 100 paintings. Circ 53,000
Income: Financed by endowment and membership
Library Holdings: Vols 142,000; Per subs 175; AV — Rec
Collections: Portraits by Feke, Healy, Charles Willson Peale, Rembrandt Peale, Stuart, Sully, and other early American painters; many paintings by Charles B King; pictures, statues
Activities: Library tours

PAWTUCKET

O   **RHODE ISLAND WATERCOLOR SOCIETY** (Formerly Providence Water Color Club), Slater Memorial Park, Armistice Blvd, 02861. Tel 401-726-1876. *Pres* Norman R McKittrick; *VPres* Rosamond D Elliott; *Recording Secy* A E S Peterson; *Corresp Secy* Clara M Stewart; *Treas* John A Stewart; *Asst Treas* Robert F Pomfret
Open Tues - Sat 10 - 4 PM, Sun 1 - 5 PM; cl Mon. Estab 1896 to encourage & promote the advancement of watercolor painting. Housed in a former boathouse which is on the National Historic Register. Two large galleries, one small permanent gallery & a classroom. Mem: 230; dues $30; annual meeting May; must submit work for jurying for membership
Income: Financed by dues, commissions, contributions & assessments
Collections: Paintings & drawings by early members; prints & paintings by contemporary members
Exhibitions: (1983-84) Annual Exhibition of Member's Work; Annual Members Summer Sketch Exhibit; Annual Christmas Exhibitions; Annual Open Graphics Show; Annual Open Juried Watermedia Show; Annual New Members Show; 12 or more member exhibitions per yr
Activities: Classes for adults & children; lectures open to public, 6 vis lectr per yr; competitions; originate traveling exhibitions

PROVIDENCE

BROWN UNIVERSITY
M   **Bell Gallery,*** 64 College St, 02912. Tel 401-863-2421. *Dir* Nancy R Versaci; *Assoc Cur* Nancy Dickinson
Open Mon - Fri 11 AM - 4 PM, Sat & Sun 1 - 4 PM; cl holidays. No admis fee. Estab 1971 to present exhibitions of interest to the university and community. The gallery is modern, covers 2625 sq ft, 14 ft ceilings, and has track lighting. Average Annual Attendance: 12,000
Income: Financed by endowment and university funds
Collections: Substantial collection of Modern Masters; prints dating from the 15th - 20th century
Exhibitions: O louis Guglielmi; Manet and the Execution of Maximilian; Frank Stella - The Prints; Pat Steir; Marcy Miss: Interior Works; Brown Faculty Exhibition
Publications: Exhibition catalogs
Activities: Lect open to public, 14 visiting lectr per year; individual paintings and original objects of art lent to museums and galleries; lending collection contains 1200 original prints, 50 paintings and 20 sculptures
M   **Annmary Brown Memorial,*** 21 Brown St, PO Box 1905, 02912. Tel 401-863-2429. *Cur* Catherine Denning
Open Mon - Fri 9 AM - 5 PM. Estab 1907 to offer representatives of schools of European and American painting. There are three galleries which house early printed books (to 1501 AD), the art collection of the founder and his wife, and portraits of the Brown family. Average Annual Attendance: 3000
Activities: Lectures open to public, 10-20 visiting lecturers per year; concerts; tours
L   **Slide & Photo Collection,** Providence, 02912. Tel 401-863-3218. *Cur* Norine D Cashman; *Assoc Cur* Kathleen James
Open Mon - Fri 8:30 AM - 5 PM. Circ 44,000
Income: $125,000 (financed by university funds)
Library Holdings: Vols 200; Per subs 6; Micro — Fiche; AV — Slides; Other —

Exhibition catalogs, photographs, reproductions
Special Subjects: Architecture, Art History, Decorative Arts, Drawings, Etchings & Engravings, Folk Art, Industrial Design, Ivory, Landscapes, Manuscripts, Metalwork, Mosaics, Photography, Portraits, Religious Art, Antiquities, Paintings, Sculpture, Stained Glass, Watercolors

O **PROVIDENCE ART CLUB,** 11 Thomas St, 02903. Tel 401-331-1114. *Pres* A W Calder Jr; *VPres* Raynor Ahmuty; *Secy* Alice Teixeira; *Gallery Secy* Majory Dalenius
Open Mon - Fri 10 AM - 4 PM, Sun 3 - 5 PM. No admis fee. Estab 1880 for art culture, and to provide exhibition space for artists. Gallery maintained in two rooms of an historic building built in 1790. Average Annual Attendance: 4000. Mem: 710, to qualify, artists' work must pass a board of artists; no qualifications for non-artists; dues non-artist $200, artist $130; annual meeting first Wed in June
Income: Financed by endowment and membership
Collections: Small permanent collection of paintings and sculpture
Exhibitions: Eighteen shows a season of which two-three are juried open shows
Publications: Newsletter for members
Activities: Lectures for members only; gallery talks; competitons with awards; scholarships; work in shows usually for sale

M **PROVIDENCE ATHENAEUM,** 251 Benefit St, 02903. Tel 401-421-6970. *Pres* Jane Langmuir; *Treas* Merton P Stolz; *Secy* Rosemary Colt; *Exec Dir* Sally Duplaix
Open Mon - Fri 8:30 AM - 5:30 PM, Sat 9:30 AM - 5:30 PM, cl Sun. No admis fee. Estab 1753 to provide cultural services, information, rare and current materials in an historic setting. Maintains a rare book library. Mem: 1367; dues $60; annual meeting in the Fall
Income: $234,351 (financed by endowment & memberships)
Purchases: $32,761
Collections: Strength in the 19th century
Exhibitions: Exhibitions vary each month
Publications: The Athenaeum Bulletin, summer; Annual Report, Fall
Activities: Dramatic programs; film programs; lectures open to the public and some to members only; tours; festivals; concerts; day trips; Burnsnight; original objects of art lent to bonafide institutions, libraries or societies; lending collection contains phonorecords & videotapes; The center sells Audubon prints in limited editions, and stationery
L **Library,** 251 Benefit St, 02903. *Pres* Robert S Davis; *Secy* Robert T Clapp; *Executive Dir* Sylvia Moubayed
Open Mon - Fri 8:30 AM - 5:30 PM, Sat 9:30 AM - 5:30 PM, cl Sun. Estab 1753 to provide cultural services, information rare and current materials in a historic setting. Circ 106,000
Library Holdings: Vols 153,946; Per subs 133; posters; AV — Cassettes, motion pictures, rec; Other — Clipping files, exhibition catalogs, framed reproductions, manuscripts, memorabilia, original art works, pamphlets, photographs, prints, reproductions, sculpture
Special Subjects: Biography, old fiction, fiction, history
Collections: 19th century Robert Burns collection; Audobon, Old Fiction, Holder Border Bowen collection
Activities: Docent training; childrens programs; film programs; festivals; readings and lectures; tours; trips

L **PROVIDENCE PUBLIC LIBRARY,** Art and Music Dept, 150 Empire St, 02903. Tel 401-521-7722, Ext 235. *Head* Susan R Waddington; *Asst* Margaret Chevian; *Asst* Barbara Cook; *Asst* Jane E Duggan
Open Mon - Thurs 9:30 AM - 9 PM, Fri & Sat 9:30 AM - 5:30 PM; summer hours vary. Estab 1878 to serve needs of the public. A gallery is maintained in large exhibit hall
Income: $2,700,000 (financed by endowment, city and state appropriations and federal funds)
Purchases: $1500 (ciruclating art)
Library Holdings: Vols 40,000; Per subs 85; posters; AV — Fs, rec; Other — Clipping files, framed reproductions, original art works, photographs, prints
Special Subjects: Architecture, Crafts, Jewelry, design
Collections: †Nickerson Architectural Collection; art & music books
Exhibitions: (1982-83) Selections from the Library's circulating art collectin; Abracadabra; Children's Books for Holiday Giving; Photographs by Carol Batista and John Shaw; A History of Printing; China from Within, contemporary photographs; Sources II: The Creative Eye at Work

M **RHODE ISLAND COLLEGE,** Edward M Bannister Gallery, 600 Mount Pleasant Ave, 02908. Tel 401-456-8000, 456-9765. *Coordr* Dennis M O'Malley; *Asst* Michele Saillant
Open Mon - Fri 11 AM - 4 PM, Thurs evenings 6 - 9 PM, cl weekends. No admis fee. Estab 1977 to provide the Rhode Island community with a varied and progressive exposure to the visual arts, to offer to the college community, with its liberal arts perspective, access to top quality exhibits, artists and workshops. Gallery consists of one room, 25 x 60 ft separated by supports; a 12 ft ceiling on one side and an 8 ft ceiling on the other; a total of 55 spots and floods on tracks. Average Annual Attendance: 16,000
Income: Financed by state appropriation
Collections: Groundwork is presently being laid for the establishment of a permanent collection with annual purchases and possible gifts
Exhibitions: (1982) Steven Smalley Paintings and Drawings; juried alumni show; Prints and Drawings from the Collection of the Rhode Island School of Design; (1983) Lawrence Sykes, photography; faculty show; Robert Nelson, prints and drawings; Drawings by Marcos Bento, Brazilian Artist and Prints from the Collection of the Portuguese Consulate; senior and graduate show; Karen Dienstbier, watercolors; Drawings for Riverside Studios Project, London, England by Gareth Jones; Photo Show from University of Arkansas; Watercolors by Spencer Crooks; juried alumni show; Dimensions in Paint, Works by J E Newman; Collage Show Works by: Ron Bikel, Therese Bisceglia, Craig Mock and Lonny Schiff
Publications: Brochures, 6-8 per year; calendars, 1-2 per year
Activities: Competitions; workshops; open forums

O **RHODE ISLAND HISTORICAL SOCIETY,** 52 Power St, 02906. Tel 401-331-8575. *Dir* Albert T Klyberg; *Ed, Nathanael Green Papers* Richard K Showman; *Ed, Roger Williams Corresp* Glenn LaFantasie; *Museum Cur* Ann LeVeque; *Cur Education* Laura Roberts; *Public Relations* Linda Lotridge-Levin
Admis adults $2.50, students $1. Estab 1822 to preserve, collect and interpret Rhode Island historical materials, including books, manuscripts, graphics, films, furniture and decorative arts. Mem: 2500; dues $15 and up; annual meeting in Jan
Income: Financed by endowment, membership and city and state appropriation
Exhibitions: Changing exhibitions on Rhode Island history and decorative arts
Publications: American Paintings in the Rhode Island Historical Society, (catalogue); The John Brown House Loan Exhibition of Rhode Island Furniture; Nathanael Green Papers; Rhode Island History, quarterly; Roger Williams Correspondence; occasional monographs; newsletter, bimonthly
Activities: Classes for adults and children; children's tours; film programs; lect open to public, 4-6 visiting lectr per year; concerts; gallery talks; tours; lending collection contains 10,000 prints for reference and copying; traveling exhibitions organized and circulated locally; bookshop
M **John Brown House,** 52 Power St, 02906. Tel 401-331-8575
Open Tues - Sat 11 AM - 4 PM, Sun 1 - 4 PM; cl weekdays Jan & Feb except by appointment. Estab 1942, the 1786 house carefully restored and furnished with fine examples of Rhode Island heritage. Average Annual Attendance: 7000
Collections: Carrington Collection of Chinese export objects; McCrellis Collection of Antique Dolls; †Pieces by Rhode Island Cabinetmakers, some original to the house; †portraits, †china, †glass, †pewter, and †other decorative objects; Rhode Island furniture, silver, porcelain, paintings, textiles
Activities: Classes for children; docent training; lectures open to public, 10 vis lectr per year; tours; museum shop sells books, reproductions, prints and slides
M **Aldrich House,** 110 Benevolent St, 02906. Tel 401-421-6567. *Cur* Nina Zannieri
Open Tues - Sat 11 AM - 4 PM, Sun 1 - 4 PM. Estab 1974. Galleries for changing exhibitions of Rhode Island artists
Income: Financed by endowment, state & local funds, grants (state & federal) and admission rates
L **Library,*** 121 Hope St, 02906. Tel 401-331-0448. *Dir* Paul R Campbell
Open Tues - Sat 10 AM - 5 PM; June, July & Aug Mon 1 - 9 PM, Tues - Fri 10 AM - 5 PM. No admis fee. Estab 1822 to collect, preserve and make available materials relating to state's history and development. Small exhibit area at library, also galleries at John Brown and Aldrich houses. Average Annual Attendance: 9000. Mem: 3000; dues individual $20; annual meetings in January
Library Holdings: Per subs 80
Collections: †1000 manuscripts dating from 17th century; †Rhode Island Imprints, 1727-1800; †Rhode Island Broadsides; †Providence Postmaster Provisional Stamps; †Rhode Island Post Office Covers; †genealogical sources, all state newspapers, maps, films, TV news films and movies, graphics, architectural drawings; †200,000 reference volumes; †20,000 photographs; business archives
Exhibitions: Rhode Island photography
Publications: Rhode Island History, quarterly
Activities: Classes for adults and children; docent training; lectures open to public, 12 vis lectr per year; concerts; gallery talks; tours; awards; individual paintings lent; originate traveling exhibitions to educational and governmental institutions; museum shop sells books and prints

M **RHODE ISLAND SCHOOL OF DESIGN,** Museum of Art, 224 Benefit St, 02903. Tel 401-331-3511, Ext 341. *Dir* Franklin Robinson; *Chmn Museum Council* Nancy Angier; *Cur Decorative Arts* Christopher Monkhouse; *Cur Education* Ronnie Zakon; *Museum Shop Mgr* Susan Handy; *Museum Shop Mgr* Alice Westervelt
Open Tues, Wed, Fri, Sat 10:30 AM - 5 PM, Thurs 1 - 9 PM. Admis adults $1, children 5 - 18 $.25, children under 5 free. Estab 1877 to collect and exhibit art for general education of the public. Present buildings opened in 1897, 1906 and 1926. Average Annual Attendance: 95,000. Mem: 3500
Income: Financed by endowment, membership, state and federal appropriation, private and corporate contributions
Collections: Lucy Truman Aldrich Collection of European porcelains and Oriental textiles; Ancient Oriental and ethnographic art; American painting; contemporary graphic arts; Nancy Sayles Day Collection of modern Latin American art; English watercolors; 15th through 18th century European art; 19th and 20th century French art from Romanticism through post-Cubism; Albert Pilavin Collection of 20th century American Art; Pendleton House collection of 18th century American furniture and decorative arts; Abbey Aldrich Rockefeller collection of Japanese birds and flower prints
Exhibitions: Art For Your Collection XVIII; Clay; Buildings On Paper: Rhode Island Architectural Drawings 1825-1945; Jacquard Loom; California Photography
Publications: Museum Notes, annually; Calendar of Events, five per year
Activities: Classes for adults and children; dramatic programs; docent training; field trips; lectures open to the public, 15 - 20 visiting lecturers per year; gallery talks; concerts; tours; extension department serves schools in the area; lending collection contains color reproductions, original artwork and slides; traveling exhibitions organized and circulated; museum shop sells books, original art, reproductions, prints, jewelry, posters and postcards
L **Library,** 2 College St, 02903. Tel 401-331-3511. *Dir* James A Findlay
Open to the public for reference
Library Holdings: Vols 66,000; Per subs 315; Micro — Fiche; AV — Lantern slides, motion pictures, rec, slides; Other — Clipping files, exhibition catalogs, framed reproductions, memorabilia, pamphlets, photographs, prints, reproductions
Special Subjects: Fine Arts and Crafts

SAUNDERSTOWN

M **GILBERT STUART BIRTHPLACE,** Gilbert Stuart Rd, 02874. Tel 401-294-3001. *Cur* Mrs Kenneth W Pettigrew; *Pres* Richard Viall
Open daily 11 AM - 5 PM; cl Fri & winters. Admis adults $1.50, children under 12 $.50. Estab 1966 as a national historic landmark, the furnished birthplace of America's foremost portrait painter; the home was built 1751. Average Annual Attendance: 10,000. Mem: 180; dues $10 - $25; annual meeting June
Income: Financed by endowment, membership and grants
Activities: Guided tours of the home

WARWICK

M COMMUNITY COLLEGE OF RHODE ISLAND, Art Department Gallery, Knight Campus, 400 East Ave, 02886. Tel 401-825-2268. *Chmn* Donald F Gray
Open Mon - Fri 8 AM - 9:30 PM. Library maintained
Exhibitions: Exhibitions are changed bi-monthly
Activities: Lect open to public; original objects of art lent; lending collection contains 300 color reproductions, 20 filmstrips, 10,000 Kodachromes, motion pictures & clippings & small prints; book shop
M Blackstone Valley Campus Art Gallery,* Louisquisset Pike, Lincoln, 02865. Tel 401-825-2220
Open Mon - Fri 8 AM - 4 PM

WESTERLY

L WESTERLY PUBLIC LIBRARY, Broad St, 02891. Tel 401-596-2877. *Dir* David J Panciera; *Asst Dir* Susan Collins; *Art Dir* Helen Marsh
Open Mon - Wed 8 AM - 9 PM, Thurs - Sat 8 AM - 5 PM. Estab 1892 as a memorial to soldiers of the Civil War, and to provide a library and activities center for the community. Art gallery maintained, 30 x 54 ft, 16 ft ceiling, with incandescent track lighting. Circ 130,000
Income: Financed by endowment, city and state appropriation
Purchases: $40,000
Library Holdings: Vols 115,000; Per subs 250; Micro — Reels; AV — Rec; Other — Framed reproductions, original art works
Exhibitions: Ten - twelve exhibitions scheduled per year
Publications: First Westerly Coloring Book; Life's Little Pleasures; Westerly Photographys 1890-1910
Activities: Lect open to public; library tours

SOUTH CAROLINA

ANDERSON

O ANDERSON COUNTY ARTS COUNCIL,* 405 N Main St, 29621. Tel 803-224-8811. *Pres* Helen Camak; *VPres* Janet Bowen; *Secy* Fred Raetsch; *Executive Dir* Carol Tokarski; *Programs Coordr* Rebecca Michaels
Open Mon - Fri 9 AM - 5 PM, Sun 2 - 5 PM, cl holidays. No admis fee. Estab 1972 as a non-profit institution, serving as a clearinghouse for individuals and organizations interested in the promotion of visual, literary and performing arts. Gallery rotates exhibits monthly, featuring locally, regionally and nationally known artists. Average Annual Attendance: 10,000. Mem: 550; dues $1000, $500, $100, $50, $25, $18, $10, $5; annual meeting last Tues of Sept
Income: Financed by membership, foundations, donations, county appropriation and grants
Publications: Calendar of events; newsletter, bi-monthly
Activities: Classes for adults and children; gallery talks; tours

CHARLESTON

M CAROLINA ART ASSOCIATION, Gibbes Art Gallery, 135 Meeting, 29401. Tel 803-722-2706. *Pres Board* J Philip Kassebaum; *Dir* Charles L Wyrick Jr; *Adminr* Mary M Muller; *Cur Collections* Martha R Severens; *Cur Education* Paul C Figueroa; *Asst Cur* Angela Mack; *Public Information* Roberta Kefalos; *Gallery Shop Mgr* Dorothy Holton
Open Tues - Sat 10 AM - 5 PM, Sun & Mon 1 - 5 PM; cl national holidays. Admis adults $2, children $1. Estab 1858 as an art gallery and museum. Gallery is 31,000 sq ft. Average Annual Attendance: 50,000. Mem: 3200; dues family $35, individual $25; annual meeting third Mon in Oct
Income: $600,000 (financed by endowment, membership, city & county appropriation, grants & contributions)
Purchases: Contemporary paintings, sculpture, prints, drawings & photographs
Collections: Colonial and Federal Portraits; †Contemporary American Paintings and Prints; Japanese Woodblock Prints; †Miniature Portraits; Oriental Art Objects; Bombardment of Ft Moultrie, Charleston Harbor, SC by Conrad Wise Chapman
Exhibitions: (1982) The Magic of Japanese Woodblock Prints; American Landscapes; The American Comic Strip; Nena Allen: Landscape & the Storm; The New Color: A Dacade of Color Photographs; (1983) The Art of Sam Doyle; Femmes Fatals of the Fifties; Contemporary Works; From Settlement to Rebellion: The British in Charleston 1670-1782; Children in Art; Elena Darina: Recent Porcelain Sculptures; Charles Fraser of Charleston; Andre Harvey: Bronze Sculpture; Louise Nevelson: Spoleto Festival USA; The Art of Robert Courtwright: Spoleto Festival USE; Sandra Baker - Photographs: Spoleto Festival USA; Charles Fraser of Charleston; Oystering: A Way of Life
Publications: Bulletins, bi-monthly; books
Activities: Classes for adults and children; docent training; lect open to public, 4 visiting lectr per year; concerts; gallery talks; tours; extension dept serves tri-county area; individual paintings and original objects of art lent to museums; book traveling exhibitions, 4-8 per year; originate traveling exhibitions; museum shop sells books, magazines, original crafts & jewelry
L Library, 135 Meeting, 29401. Tel 803-722-2706
Open to scholars for reference only, by appointment
Income: Financed by public and private support
Library Holdings: Vols 3500; Per subs 20; Other — Clipping files, exhibition catalogs, manuscripts, memorabilia, pamphlets, photographs, reproductions
Special Subjects: Oriental art, American art

M CHARLESTON MUSEUM, 360 Meeting St, 29403. Tel 803-722-2996. *Pres* John F Hassell Jr; *Dir* W E Freeman; *Cur Anthropology* Allen Liss; *Cur Decorative Arts* J Kenneth Jones; *Cur Historic Houses* Mrs Edward Webb; *Cur Natural History* Albert E Sanders; *Registrar* Jan Hiester; *Cur Ornithology* William Post
Open daily 9 AM - 5 PM. Admis adults $2, children $.75. Estab 1773 as a museum and library to diffuse knowledge of history, decorative arts, art, natural history, anthropology and technology; also to preserve houses and monuments. It is the oldest museum in the United States. Average Annual Attendance: 100,000. Mem: 3000; dues $15 and up; annual meeting March
Income: $530,000 (financed by membership, city and county appropriations, admissions and sales)
Collections: Ceramics, decorative arts, furniture, glass, maps, photos, prints and textiles
Publications: Newsletter, bi-monthly
Activities: Classes for adults and children; dramatic programs; docent training; lectures open to public; concerts; book traveling exhibitions, 8 per year; sales shop sells books, magazines and prints related to collections
L Library, 350 Meeting St, 29403. Tel 803-722-2996, Ext 57. *Librn* K Sharon Bennett; *Library Technician* Myrtle Brown
Open daily 9 AM - 5 PM. Estab 1773 as an educational institution, collects, preserves and uses artifacts of natural history, history, anthropology and decorative arts
Income: Financed by city & county appropriations & memberships
Library Holdings: Vols 5000; Per subs 120; Maps; AV — Rec; Other — Clipping files, exhibition catalogs, manuscripts, memorabilia, pamphlets, photographs, prints
Special Subjects: Decorative Arts, Natural History
M Heward-Washington House,* 87 Church St, 29403. Tel 803-722-2996
Open daily 10 AM - 5 PM. Admis adults $2.25, students $.50. Built 1772; home of Thomas Heyward, Jr; purchased by the Museum in 1929. Museum is furnished with Charleston-made furniture of the period; a National Historic Landmark
M Joseph Manigault House,* 350 Meeting St, 29403
Open daily 10 AM - 5 PM. Admis adults $2.25, students $.50. Built 1803 as Adam style mansion designed by Gabriel Manigault. Museum contains Charleston-made furniture of the period; a National Historic Landmark

CLEMSON

CLEMSON UNIVERSITY

M Rudolph E Lee Gallery,* College of Architecture, 29631. Tel 803-656-3081, Ext 2-30. *Coordr Educational Media & Exhib* Tom Dimond
Open Mon - Fri 9 AM - 4:30 PM, Sun 2 - 5 PM, cl Sat. No admis fee. Estab 1956 to provide cultural and educational resources; to collect, preserve, interpret and display items of historical, educational and cultural significance. Average Annual Attendance: 20,000
Income: Financed by state appropriation
Collections: †Clemson Architectural Foundation Collection; Contemporary American Paintings and Graphics
Publications: Exhibition Bulletin, annually; Posters on Exhibits, monthly
Activities: Lect open to public, 12-15 visiting lectr per year; gallery talks; tours; exten dept serving southeast United States; individual paintings and original objects of art lent to museums, universities; lending collection contains original prints, paintings, sculpture; originate traveling exhibitions
L Emery A Gunnin Architectural Library, College of Architecture, 29631. Tel 803-656-3081
For reference only
Library Holdings: Vols 10,000; Per subs 200; AV — Slides
Collections: Rare Book Collection
M Fort Hill, 29631. Tel 803-656-2061. *Cur* Mrs Revelie Brannon
Open Tues - Sat 10 AM - Noon & 1 - 5:30 PM, Sun 2-6 PM, cl holidays and Christmas week. No admis fee. An historic museum located in the home of John C Calhoun. Restoration of the Shrine and furnishings are an on-going project of the John C Calhoun Chapter of the United Daughters of the Confederacy
Income: Clemson University
Collections: Flemish paintings; family portraits; period rooms and furnishings of original family heirlooms and memorabilia
Publications: Fort Hill, brochure
Activities: Lect; guided tours; sales shop

CLINTON

L PRESBYTERIAN COLLEGE, James H Thomason Library, 29325. Tel 803-833-2820. *Librn* Dr Lennart Pearson
Sun - Fri 2 - 10 PM, Sat 2 - 5 PM. Estab 1974 to serve educational institution. Small gallery with monthly exhibits
Income: Financed by college
Library Holdings: Vols 125,000; Per subs 665; Micro — Cards, fiche; AV — A-tapes, cassettes, fs, rec; Other — Framed reproductions, original art works
Exhibitions: Regional artists exhibits
Activities: Lect open to public; gallery talks

COLUMBIA

M COLUMBIA MUSEUMS OF ART AND SCIENCE, 1112 Bull St, 29201. Tel 803-799-2810. *Chmn Museum Commission* W Croft Jennings; *Pres* Dr John G Sproat; *VPres* Michael H Quinn; *Dir* Walter M Hathaway; *Registrar* Harriet Green; *Admin Asst* Renee Chevalier; *Dept of Education* Judy Kennedy; *Controller* Fred Panasiuk; *Chief Cur* Nina Parris
Open Mon - Fri 10 AM - 5 PM, Sat & Sun 1 - 5 PM. No admis fee. Estab 1950 to extend and increase art understanding, to assist in the conservation of a valuable cultural heritage, and to recognize and assist contemporary art expression. Library for reference of staff only. Average Annual Attendance: 100,000. Mem: 1799; dues family $25 and up, single $15; annual meeting Jan
Income: $500,000 (financed by membership, city, county and state appropriation)

Purchases: Works of art on paper, Southeastern artists & textiles
Collections: Barringer Collection; Erin Kohn Collection of Dolls; Samuel H Kress Collection of Renaissance Paintings; Neuhoff Collection of English Furniture; Scotese Collection of Graphics; Seibels Collection; European and American paintings and decorative art; South Carolina dispensary bottles; Spanish Colonial Collection; textiles; South Carolina collection of paintings & graphics; †decorative arts & textiles
Exhibitions: (1982-83) Jerome Witkill; Romane Beardeu; Export China; Teu Eyes on the Cameroons; Print Making Process; Bogd Saunders; Linda McCune; Wood & Fiber; Phillip Mullen; Karl Bodmer; Paints & Indian artifacts; Dealer's Choice; Holiday Trees; Charles Jacques; Hee Bing, photographs; Southeastern Photography Jack and Charlotte Girard; Dealer's Choice; Seibels, Bruce Carolina Watercolor Competition; Viginia Warren Smith; American Water Color Society; James F Cooper; Southeastern Crafts Invitational; Josef Albers: Interaction of Color; American Abstract Artists; (1981) Weekend Gallery; Jean McWhortor; Springs Mills; Carolinian's in New York; Contemporary Prints in Columbia; Photographs of Greece; Juried Columbia Guilds; Thomas Bayrle; SC Crafts Guild; Carolyn Brady; Guy Lipscomb; Worth Keeping Found Artists of the Carolinas; Samurai Arms & Armor; The 80's Sigmund Abeles; Collections; Sidney & Francis Lewis Collection; Jeanet Dreskin-Haig
Publications: Annual Report; exhibition folders and catalogs, occasionally
Activities: Classes for adults and children, docent training; lectures open to public, 15 vis lect per year; concerts; gallery talks; tours; awards for docent hours; exten dept serving Metropolitan area; individual paintings and original objects of art lent to qualified galleries, historic houses, and approved city and state facilities; originate traveling exhibitions; museum shop sells postcards, exhibition catalogs and crafts
L **Library,** 1112 Bull St, 29201. Tel 803-799-2810. *Librn* Cassandra Gissendanner
Open Mon - Fri 10 AM - 5 PM. Open to members and scholars for reference only
Library Holdings: Vols 5200; Per subs 16; Vertical files; Other — Exhibition catalogs, pamphlets
Special Subjects: Reference relating to the permanent collection, plus general art sources
O **Columbia Art Association,** 1112 Bull St, 29201. *VPres* Michael H Quinn; *Secy* Mrs Hugh M Chapman
Estab 1915, the association is the operating agent for the Museum

M **MCKISSICK MUSEUMS,** University of South Carolina, 29208. Tel 803-777-7251. *Dir & Archivist* George D Terry; *Assoc Dir & Cur of Collections* John R Heiting; *Chief Cur* Lynn R Myers; *Office Administrator & Asst to Dir* Terry Riemer; *Asst Archivist & Cur Exhibitions* Catherine W Horne; *Cur Geology* Karin L Willoughby; *Cur Community Servs* Barbara B Tartaglia; *Cur Education Museum* William W Savage
Open Mon - Fri 9 AM - 4 PM, Sat 10 AM - 5 PM, Sun 1 - 5 PM, cl Sat & Sun in summer. No admis. Estab 1976 to centralize the university's museum collections. Contains 4 major galleries for temporary & changing exhibitions in art, science & history. Average Annual Attendance: 60,000
Income: Financed by state appropriation & donations
Purchases: Southern Folk Art
Collections: Bernard Baruch Collection of 18th Century Silver; Movietonews Photographs; James F Byrnes Collection; Howard Gemstone Collection; Richard Mandell: Art Nouveau Collection; Colburn Gemstone Collection; university memorabilia; †southeastern folk art; minerals, fossils, rocks & meteorites; contemporary art works
Exhibitions: Changing exhibits of permanent collections; Mirror of Time: Elizabeth O'Neill Verner's Charleston; Prints Today: Holland/USA; Spring Mills annual traveling exhibit; Atget: Old Paris; 10,000 Years of Indian Culture in South Carolina; Carolina Athletics; Robert Mills: His Drawings & Buildings; South Carolina Women; The War in Print: 1861-1865; Medical Illustrations; Wildlife Photographs; Shark; Henry Evans Prints; World Under the Sea; Creatures of Darwin's Galapagos
Publications: Exhibition catalogs
Activities: Dramatic programs; docent training; lect open to public, 4-5 visiting lectr per year; concerts; gallery talks; tours; competitions; slide-tape programs & classes for students & sr citizens; community outreach to sr citizens groups & children's hospital wards; book traveling exhibitions; originate traveling exhibitions
L **Art Library,** Sloan College, Room 202, 29208. Tel 803-777-7260. *Instructional Media Specialist* Linda D Morgan
Open Mon - Fri 8 AM - 4 PM. Estab as a major teaching resource for the Art Department
Library Holdings: Vols 2000; Per subs 10; Slide-tape Programs; AV — Cassettes, motion pictures, slides 96,000, v-tapes; Other — Clipping files, exhibition catalogs, manuscripts, pamphlets, photographs
Special Subjects: Decorative Arts, Museology

O **SOUTH CAROLINA ARTS COMMISSION,** 1800 Gervais St, 29201. Tel 803-758-3442. *Chmn* Samuel J Tenenbaum; *Exec Dir* Scott Sanders; *Dir Support Services* Joyce Huey; *Dir Arts Development* Susie Surkamer; *Public Information* Jayne Darke
Open 8:30 AM - 5 PM. No admis fee. Estab 1967 to promote and develop the arts in South Carolina
Income: Federal, state and private sources
Collections: †State Art Collection
Exhibitions: Annual Exhibition
Publications: Artifacts, bi-monthly newsletter; F.Y.I., newsletter
Activities: Educational programming; lectures open to the public; concerts; gallery talks; competitions with awards; grants-in-aid & fellowships; exten dept serves state; art mobile; individual paintings & original objects of art lent to other galleries & museums; lending collection contains lantern slides, 235 original art works, paintings, photographs, sculpture & slides; originate traveling exhibitions
L **Media Center,** 29201
Library Holdings: AV — A-tapes, cassettes, motion pictures, slides, v-tapes

C **SOUTH CAROLINA NATIONAL BANK,** 101 Greystone Blvd, PO Box 168, 29226. Tel 803-765-3756. *VPres* Virginia M Grose
Open to public. Estab 1971 to recognize & promote artists who have or have had a connection with South Carolina. Collection displayed in offices throughout South Carolina
Collections: Contemporary South Carolina art
Activities: Sponsor purchase and merit awards for selected competitions in the state; individual objects of art lent to museums for display; originate traveling exhibitions, have carried-out two statewide tours from collection, work was displayed in a number of cities at museums, libraries, court houses and banks

FLORENCE

M **FLORENCE MUSEUM,*** 558 Spruce St, 29501. Tel 803-662-3351. *Dir* Dr William A Burns; *Board Pres* L A McCall; *Treas* O S Aiken; *Secy* Eileen Blackwell
Open Tues - Sat 10 AM - 5 PM, Sun 2 - 5 PM, cl Mon. No admis fee. Estab 1936 as a general museum of art, natural science, and history of South Carolina, with emphasis on the region known as the Pee Dee, and to acquaint the public with fine art. Twelve galleries exhibit artwork. Average Annual Attendance: 50,000. Mem: 500; dues $15-$1000; annual meeting third Thurs in April
Income: $40,000 (financed by membership, county & city appropriation, and donations)
Collections: African, Chinese, Japanese and Korean Collections; artifacts; works of local Black artists, particularly William H Johnson; works of local and regional artists
Exhibitions: Batiks, Prints and their Makers; Bicentennial Year in SC History Hall; Charles Councell; Children's Art; Janet Dreskin-Haig paintings; Dixie Dugan; 50th Annual Art Exhibition of Florence Art Association; Flora Exotics; Steve Gately; Nell LaFaye; Papal Coins; South Carolina Guild of Artists; SC State Artists; Southern Phenomena; 54th Pee Dee Regional Art Exhibition
Publications: Florence Museum, quarterly
Activities: Classes for adults and children; docent training; puppet shows; lect open to the public, 8 visiting lectrs per year; gallery talks; tours; competitions with prizes; lending collection contains 2000 books, 1000 framed reproductions, 300 original art works, 50 original prints, 300 paintings and 500 photographs; traveling exhibitions organized and circulated
L **Evans Research Library,*** 29501
Open to students, for reference only
Library Holdings: Vols 2000

GREENVILLE

M **BOB JONES UNIVERSITY,** Museum and Art Gallery, 29614. Tel 803-242-5100. *Chmn of the Board* Bob Jones; *Dir* Joan C Davis; *Staff Supv* Janice Churdar; *Conservator* Barbara Votaw
Open Tues - Sun 2 - 5 PM; cl Mon, Dec 20 - 25, New Year's Day and July 4. No admis fee. Estab 1951 to show how universal the Word of God is in its appeal to human hearts in every generation. Average Annual Attendance: 23,000
Income: Financed by University and gifts
Collections: Religious art by the Old Masters from the 13th - 19th centuries including Benson, Botticelli, Cranach the Elder, G David, Murillo, Rembrandt, Ribera, Rubens, Solimena del Piombo, Tintoretto, Titian, Van Leyden, Veronese; Zurbaran Bowen Collection of Biblical antiquities and illustrative material from Palestine, Syria, Lebanon, Egypt and Jordan; Revealed Religion by Benjamin West, 7 paintings; furniture; sculpture Because of the illness of the King, plans for the construction of the Chapel were abandoned and the completed paintings were returned to the painter. The posthumous sale of West's works in 1829 included a number of the pictures on Revealed Religion. Joseph Neeld, MP, was the successful bidder and the pictures hung in his home until 1962. At that time they were offered for sale by Christie's of London. Six were acquired for the Bob Jones University with funds provided for that purpose by an anonymous friend of the University, a seventh painting of this series was also acquired by gift
Publications: Catalogs; illustrated booklets
Activities: Tours for school and adult groups by appointment; individual paintings lent to other galleries in the US and abroad; sales shop sells reproductions and prints

M **GREENVILLE COUNTY MUSEUM OF ART,** 420 College St, 29601. Tel 803-271-7570. *Executive Dir* Thomas W Styron; *Head Development & Interpretive Programs* Sylvia L Marchant; *Head Exhibitions & Education* Sharon Campbell; *Head Collections Management & Security* Claudia Beckwith; *Head Operations* Rudy Gary
Open Tues - Sat 10 AM - 5 PM; Sun 1 - 5 PM. No admis fee. Estab 1958 for the collection and preservation of North American Art. Average Annual Attendance: 100,000. Mem: 1500; dues graduated schedule
Income: Financed by membership, donations & county appropriation
Collections: Limited to North American art with emphasis on contemporary. 26 works by Andrew Wyeth plus 230 preliminary studies by Wyeth on long term loan from the Holly & Arthur Magill Collection
Exhibitions: Jamie Wyeth; Ansel Adams & the West; Fairfield Porter, Morris Graves, From the Streets; Art Fabric: Mainstream
Publications: Museum Notes, three times per yr
Activities: Classes for children & adults; workshops; lect; films; gallery talks; extension dept serves Greenville County schools; museum shop and cafe

C **LIBERTY LIFE INSURANCE COMPANY,** 2000 Wade Hampton Blvd, PO Box 789, 29602. Tel 803-268-8111. *Pres* Glenn Hilliard
Open Mon - Thurs 8:30 AM - 5 PM, Fri 8:30 AM - 12:30 PM. Estab 1978 to collect textile art selections from various cultures & historical periods. Collection displayed throughout corporate headquarters
Collections: Limited edition prints, graphics and silkscreens; textile art works from around the world
Exhibitions: (1982) Columbia Museum of Art
Activities: Tours; original objects of art lent to regional museums

GREENWOOD

M THE MUSEUM, 106 Main St, PO Box 3131, 29648. Tel 803-229-7093. *Pres* Edwin F Lau; *Dir* Frederick C Schlein; *Secy* Joyce Wimmer
Open Tues - Fri 9 AM - 5 PM, Sat & Sun 2 - 5 PM, cl Mon. No admis fee. Estab June 1967 for educational purposes. Average Annual Attendance: 9000.
Mem: 220; dues $25; meeting Jan, March, May and Nov
Income: Financed by memberships, contributions & grants
Collections: Frank E Delano Gallery of African animal mounts and rare African works of art by the now extinct Katanga Tribe; bone, wood and ivory carvings; chinaware; crystals; glassware; limited art works; photographs
Exhibitions: Individual artists; Siebozs; Bruce; South Carolina arts & crafts; South Carolina Watercolor Society
Activities: Lectures open to public; book traveling exhibitions; sales shop sells original art

HARTSVILLE

M CECELIA COKER BELL GALLERY, Coker College, Gladys C Fort Art Building, 29550. Tel 803-332-1381, Ext 512
Open during school hours. No admis fee. Estab 1983
Income: $2000
Collections: American prints
Exhibitions: Small Works Competition; area artists; annual student juried show; senior students show
Publications: Collection catalog

MURRELLS INLET

M BROOKGREEN GARDENS, 29576. Tel 803-237-4218. *Pres* Joseph Veach Noble; *First VPres* Marshall M Fredericks; *Second VPres* John H Lumpkin Sr; *Dir & Librn* Gurdon L Tarbox Jr; *Secy* Eric S Malm; *Treas* Robert R Coker
Open 9:30 AM - 4:45 PM, cl Christmas. Admis adults $3, 6-12 years $1, under six free. Estab 1931 to exhibit the flora and fauna of South Carolina and to exhibit objects of art. The outdoor museum exhibits American sculpture, while smaller pieces are shown in the Small Sculpture Museum and indoor gallery. Average Annual Attendance: 180,000. Mem: 1350; dues $5 - $2500; annual meeting in Oct
Income: Financed by endowment, membership, gifts, grants and admission
Collections: †Representative collection of American sculpture, by 196 sculptors
Exhibitions: Permanent Collection
Publications: Brookgreen Bulletin, quarterly; Brookgreen Gardens Newsletter, bimonthly; A Century of American Sculpture, catalog
Activities: Classes for adults and children; lectures for members only, 1 vis lectr per yr; concerts; gallerytalks; tours; competitions; museum shop sells books, reproductions, prints and slides

L Library, 29576
For reference only to staff
Library Holdings: Vols 406; Per subs 72; maps, architectural and engineering drawings and plans; Micro — Prints; Other — Clipping files
Special Subjects: American sculpture

ORANGEBURG

M PINCKNEY BROTHERS MUSEUM,* 212 Wilkinson Ave NE (Mailing add: 1351 Monroe ST, 29115). Tel 803-534-9746. *Pres* Robert E Pinckney; *VPres* S M Pinckney Sr; *Cur* Dr Lawrence R Pinckney; *Asst Dir* Tommy Snell
Open Mon - Fri Noon - 5 PM, Sat & Sun 10 AM - 5 PM. Admis adults $1, students $.50, children $.25. Estab to serve the Land-Grant College community with portable exhibits, as well as local needs. Maintains a small reference library. Average Annual Attendance: 10,000. Mem: 500; annual meeting Nov 15
Income: $20,000 (financed by members & family)
Exhibitions: Paintings & photographs which compliment historical exhibits
Publications: Newsletter; tour guides; descriptive folders of museum activities
Activities: Classes for adults and children; lectures open to public, vis lecturers 10 per year; gallery talks; tours; poster contest to schools; awards; originate traveling exhibitions to Land-Grant College community; museum shop sells books, magazines, original art, reproductions, prints and slides

ROCK HILL

M WINTHROP COLLEGE GALLERY OF ART, 701 Oakland Ave, 29733. Tel 803-323-2191. *Dir* Edmund D Lewandowski
Open Mon - Fri 8:30 AM - 4 PM, Sun 2 - 5 PM, cl Sat. No admis fee. Estab 1970 to present area viewers with a wide variety of exhibitions, local, regional and national in scope; and to provide an opportunity for regional artists to exhibit. Two galleries 40 x 80 x 20 ft and 15 x 15 x 12 ft. Average Annual Attendance: 15,000
Income: Financed by city appropriation
Collections: Limited collections
Exhibitions: Annual Textile Invitational; Foundry Art; South Carolina Architectures 1670-1970; South Carolina State Art Collection; Spring Mills Annual Traveling Exhibition; several one-person shows
Activities: Classes for adults; lectures open to the public; concerts; gallery talks; scholarships; originate traveling exhibitions; museum shop sells original art and prints

SPARTANBURG

O ARTS COUNCIL OF SPARTANBURG COUNTY, INC, Spartanburg Arts Center, 385 S Spring St, 29301. Tel 803-583-2776. *Executive Dir* Cassandra Baker; *Asst Executive Dir* Mrs Danny R Hughes; *Business Mgr* William C Taylor Jr
Open Mon - Fri 9 AM - 5 PM, Sun 3 - 5 PM. No admis fee. Estab 1968 to coordinate all cultural activities in the area; to promote its member organizations; maintain an Arts Center with changing and permanent exhibitions. Average Annual Attendance: 100,000
Income: $170,000 (financed by private donations & project grants)
Collections: †Over 60 pieces mixed media
Exhibitions: Changing exhibits
Publications: Spartanburg Arts, bi-monthly
Activities: Classes for adults and children; dramatic programs; docent training; arts camp for children; drama festival; lect open to public; concerts; gallery talks; tours; competitions with awards; scholarships; exten dept serves schools in county; book traveling exhibitions, 2-3 per yr; sales shop sells books, original art and prints

M CONVERSE COLLEGE, Milliken Art Gallery,* PO Box 29, 29301. Tel 803-585-6421, Ext 251. *Dir* Henry Fagen Jr, EdD
Open Mon - Fri 11 AM - 4 PM, cl holidays. No admis fee. Estab 1971 for educational purposes. A brick and glass structure of 40 x 60 ft; movable panels 4 x 6 ft for exhibition of work, 16 panels, 12 sculpture stands. Average Annual Attendance: 1500
Income: Financed by endowment
Exhibitions: Invitational exhibits of regional artists
Activities: Lectures provided 2-3 per yr

O SPARTANBURG COUNTY ART ASSOCIATION, 385 S Spring St, 29301. Tel 803-582-7616. *Cur* Pamela Nienhuis
Open mon - Fri 10 AM - Noon & 2 - 4 PM, Sun 3 - 5 PM. No admis fee. Estab 1969 to promote the works of contemporary artists in the southeastern United States. Gallery is located in the Spartanburg County Arts Center and contains both a permanent sales section and a changing exhibit area. Average Annual Attendance: 1500. Mem: 450; dues $15 - $500
Income: Financed by endowment, membership
Collections: †Contemporary Southeastern Artists
Publications: Newsletter, quarterly
Activities: Classes for adults and children; docent training; lectures open to public, 2 vis lectr per yr; gallery talks; tours; competitions; sales shop sells books, original art

M UNIVERSITY OF SOUTH CAROLINA SPARTANBURG, Library Art Gallery,* 29303. Tel 803-578-1800. *Dir* Kathryn Hicks
Exhibitions: Works by South Carolina & Southeastern artists

M WOFFORD COLLEGE, Sandor Teszler Library Gallery,* 29301. Tel 803-585-4821. *Dir* Frank J Anderson
Open daily 9 AM - 5 PM
Exhibitions: US & regional & international works in all media

SUMTER

M SUMTER GALLERY OF ART,* 421 N Main St, PO Box 1316, 29150. Tel 803-775-0543. *Chmn Board Dir* J T Robertson; *Gallery Dir* Laura E Ayers
Open Tues - Fri 11 AM - 5 PM, Sat & Sun 2 - 5 PM, cl Easter, Thanksgiving & Christmas. No admis fee. Estab 1970 to bring to area exhibits of works of recognized artists, to provide an outlet for local artists for showing and sale of their work, and to serve as a facility where visual art may become a part of life and education of the people, particularly children of this community. The Gallery is the 1850 home of the late Miss Elizabeth White, well-known artist of Sumter, which was deeded to the gallery in 1977 under the terms of her will. Presently using hall, four downstairs rooms, back studio and rooms upstairs. Average Annual Attendance: 8500. Mem: 460; dues commercial patron $40, patron $30, family $15, individual $10; annual meeting May
Income: $18,000 (financed by membership, earned income, personnel development grant from SC Arts Com, CETA employee)
Collections: Approximately sixty paintings, etchings and drawings of Elizabeth White given to the gallery by trustees of her estate
Exhibitions: Annual Young People's Exhibit; Individual and group exhibits of paintings, sculpture, collages, photography and crafts by recognized artists primarily from Southeast
Publications: Newsletter, monthly
Activities: Classes for adults and children; lect open to public, 8 vis lect per yr; gallery talks; competitions, awards given; sales shop selling original art and prints

SOUTH DAKOTA

ABERDEEN

M DACOTAH PRAIRIE MUSEUM, Lamont Gallery, 21 S Main St, PO Box 395, 57401. Tel 605-229-1608. *Dir* Evearad Stelfox; *Cur of Education* Helen Bergh; *Asst Dir & Cur* Kevin Gramer
Open Mon - Fri 9 AM - 5 PM, Sun 1 - 4 PM. No admis fee. Estab 1969 to preserve the heritage of the peoples of the Dakotas; to maintain and develop exhibits that educate people about the heritage of the Dakotas. Average Annual Attendance: 25,000
Income: Financed by county funds
Collections: Sioux and Arikara Indian artifacts; local and regional artists; photography

Exhibitions: (1983) Illustrated Maps of England, Other Times, Other Places; Midwest Photography; Textiles: A Century of Handwork from the Collection of the Dacotah Prairie Museum; Our Land/Our People; The Costumer's Art; F Jay Haynes: Fifty Views; Prairie Visions & Circus Wonders: The Complete Lithographic Suite of John Steuart Curry; Plains Indian Art from the Ben Reifel Collections; Renaissance on the Missouri: The South Dakota Capitol; Marquee on Main
Publications: Annual Report; Dacotah Prairie Times, 6 per year
Activities: Lectures open to public, 5 vis lectr per yr; gallery talks; tours; individual paintings and original objects of art lent to museums, art centers and some materials to schools; originate traveling exhibitions; museum shop sells books, magazines, original art and reproductions
L **Ruth Bunker Memorial Library,** 21 S Main St, PO Box 395, 57401. Tel 605-229-1608. *Education Cur* Helen Berch
Open Mon - Fri 9 AM - 5 PM, Sat & Sun 1 -4 PM, cl holidays. Estab 1980 to store books, archives, maps, blueprints, etc. Reference only
Income: Financed by county funds
Exhibitions: 12 monthly exhibts of regional or national art
Publications: Annual report; newsletter, monthly
Activities: Special classes; lectures open to public, 4 vis lectr per year; gallery talks; tours; 12 book traveling exhibitions per year; orginate traveling exhibitions in midwest

BROOKINGS

M **SOUTH DAKOTA STATE UNIVERSITY,** South Dakota Memorial Art Center,* Medary Ave at Harvey Dunn St, 57006. Tel 605-688-5423. *Dir* Joseph Stuart; *Asst Dir* Sheila Agee; *Cur of Marghab Collection* Cora Sivers; *Secy* Elaine Hietbrink
Open Mon - Fri 8 AM - 5 PM, Sat 10 AM - 5 PM, Sun 1 - 5 PM. No admis fee. Estab 1969 as the state center for visual arts with various programs. The facility was designed by Howard Parezo, AIA, Sioux Falls, and occupies 112 x 90 foot site. There are seven galleries and a 147 seat auditorium. Average Annual Attendance: 140,000. Mem: 3000; annual meeting in April
Income: Financed by state appropriation, endowment, gifts and grants
Collections: Art of South Dakota; Harvey Dunn Paintings; Marghab Linens; Native American Art; Northwestern Art; United States Art
Publications: Annual report; bulletin, quarterly; exhibition catalogues; newsletter, monthly
Activities: Docent training; lect; films; tours; competitions; traveling exhibitions; sales shop
L **Jeannette Lusk Library Collection,** Medary Ave at Harvey Dunn St, 57006. Tel 605-688-5423
Open to the public for lending through the main library
Library Holdings: Vols 1500; Per subs 15; AV — Slides
Special Subjects: Archives of South Dakota Art

MITCHELL

O **OSCAR HOWE ART CENTER,** 119 W Third Ave, 57301. Tel 605-996-4111. *Dir* Margaret Quintal
Open 10 AM - 5 PM; cl holidays. No admis fee; donations accepted. Center is housed in a former Carnegie Library building constructed in 1902 and designated as a National Historic Site. Mem: Dues benefactor $250, sustaining $100, patron $50, sponsor $35, family $18 and individual $12.50
Income: Financed by private & public funds
Collections: †19 paintings by Sioux artist & South Dakota artist laureate, Oscar Howe
Exhibitions: (1983-84) Grete B Heikes: Weaving for Body & Soul; Bill Greiner: New Images for 1983; Young Artists Competition; Indiana University Graduate Printmaking Exhibition; Peg Nickerson: Watercolors; Vermillion 7 Print Exhibition; The Inspiration of Oscar Howe; Wallace Dow: Builder on the Prairie; George Catlin Lithographs; Gutzon Borglum Exhibit
Activities: Classes; workshops; tours; concerts; competitions; originate traveling exhibitions; Garret Museum Shop sells original art work of regional artists including pottery, watercolors, weavings, oils and acrylics, books, Indian beadwork & reproductions of Oscar Howe paintings

PINE RIDGE

M **HERITAGE CENTER, INC,** Red Cloud Indian School Box 100, 57770. Tel 605-867-5491. *Pres* E J Kurth; *VPres* E E Zimmerman; *Secy* D Edward Mathie; *Dir* C M Simon
Open Mon - Fri 9 AM - 5 PM. Estab 1974 to exhibit Indian art and culture. Museum has four changing galleries of American and Canadian Native American art. Mainly paintings and sculpture. Average Annual Attendance: 9000
Income: Financed by donations and grants
Collections: †Native American paintings and prints; †native American sculpture; †star quilts and tribal arts
Exhibitions: Selections from permanent collection; Eskimo prints; Northwest coast prints
Activities: Tours; awards; individual paintings lent; book traveling exhibitions, 4 - 6 per yr; originate traveling exhibitions; sales shop sells books, original art, beads & quilt work

RAPID CITY

M **DAHL FINE ARTS CENTER,** 713 7th St, 57701. Tel 605-394-4101. *Pres* Ardis I Barber; *Pres Elect* Patrick Wyss; *Exec Dir* Ruth Brennan; *Bookkeeper* Diane Bullard
Open Mon - Sat 9 AM - 5 PM, Sun 1 - 5 PM. No admis fee. Estab 1974 to promote, educate & serve the arts. The art center contains 3 galleries: Cyclorama Gallery, a 200 ft oil mural of American history; Central Gallery, touring exhibitions & some invitationals; Dakota Gallery for juried original works for

sale. Average Annual Attendance: 37,000. Mem: 285; dues $125; annual meeting third Mon in July
Income: $81,710 (financed by memberships & city appropriation, rentals & grants)
Purchases: $151,000
Collections: Grace French, oils & watercolors; †original prints; inks & washes; Hazel Schwentker, watercolors
Exhibitions: Toys Designed by Artists; Richard DuBois, watercolors; Robert Kusserow, acrylics
Publications: The French Sisters
Activities: Classes for adults & children; dramatic programs; docent training; workshops for non-profit organizations; lectures open to public, 1-2 vis lectr per yr; competitions with awards; lending collection contains books of play scripts, reproductions series & art slides; book traveling exhibition; sales shop sells books, magazines, original art & reproductions

M **SIOUX INDIAN MUSEUM,** Box 1504, 57709. Tel 605-348-0557. *Museum Asst* Paulette Montileaux
Open June - Sept, Mon - Sat 9 AM - 5 PM, Sun 1 - 5 PM; Oct - May, Tues - Sat 10 AM - 5 PM, Sun 1 - 5 PM; cl New Year's Day, Thanksgiving, Christmas. No admis fee. Estab 1939 to promote the development of contemporary native American arts and crafts of the United States. Average Annual Attendance: 80,000
Income: Financed by federal appropriation
Collections: Contemporary native American arts and crafts of the United States; Historic works by Sioux craftsmen
Exhibitions: Contemporary Sioux Quillwork; Photographs and Poems by Sioux Children; continuing series of one-person exhibitions
Publications: One-person exhibition brochure series, monthly
Activities: Gallery talks; tours; traveling exhibitions organized and circulated; sales shop selling books and original art

SIOUX FALLS

O **AUGUSTANA COLLEGE,** Center for Western Studies, 57197. Tel 605-336-4007. *Executive Dir* Sven G Froiland; *Promotion Dir* Wayne L Petersen; *Secy* Barbara Ries
Open 8 AM - 5 PM. Estab 1976 for collection and preservation of historic material for the promotion of South Dakota and its Western artists. New gallery open May 1980. Average Annual Attendance: 5000. Mem: 200; dues $15; annual meeting November
Income: Financed by endowment and membership
Collections: South Dakota Art
Exhibitions: 3-4 Art Shows per year featuring SD Artists
Publications: Manfred's Bibliography-Timmerman and Mulder; Natural History of the Black Hills, by S G Froiland; Norwegians in America--Translation by Blegen; Sundancing at Pine Ridge and Rosebud by Thomas Mails; The Wind Blow Free by Fred Manfred
Activities: Lectures open to the public; gallery talks; awards; tours; scholarships offered; artmobile serving South Dakota; individual paintings and original objects of art lent; lending collection contains books, cassettes, motion pictures, nature artifacts, original art works, paintings, photographs, sculpture, slides; six to eight traveling exhibitions booked per year; traveling exhibitions organized and circulated; museum shop sells books, original art, prints and slides, beadwork & silver jewelry
L **Resource Center,** 57197. Tel 605-336-4007
Library Holdings: Vols 30,000
Special Subjects: Western Americana

M **CIVIC FINE ARTS ASSOCIATION MUSEUM,** 235 W Tenth St, 57102. Tel 605-336-1167. *Pres* Joe Henkin; *VPres* Koula Fotis; *Executive Dir* Raymond Shermoe; *Office Mgr* Kathy Koons; *Treas* Manfred Szameit
Open Tues - Sat 11:30 AM - 5 PM; Sun 2 - 5 PM; cl Mon. No admis fee. Estab 1961 as a contemporary museum . Art gallery maintained. Circ museum. Mem: 1200; dues $15
Collections: Poster collection; regional art
Publications: Newsletter, monthly
Activities: Classes for adults and children; lect open to the public, 2 vis lectr per yr; concerts; gallery talks; tours; competitions with awards; scholarships; museum shop sells books; museum shop selling books, magazines, original art, prints, reproductions, pottery and imports, cards
L **Library,** 235 W Tenth St, 57102
Open to members only

SPEARFISH

M **BLACK HILLS ART CENTER,** Little Gallery,* Main St, 57783. Tel 605-642-3752. *Dir* Joan Marie Rudell
Open Mon - Fri 8 AM - 10 PM, Sat & Sun Noon - 6 PM. Estab 1936 to encourage art expression and greater appreciation in the Black Hills area. Work of the Art Center is promoted jointly by Black Hills State College Art Department and the Student Union. Average Annual Attendance: 1500. Mem: 500; dues $5 and up
Activities: Classes for adults; programs held each semester; summer workshop; competitions; traveling exhibitions
L **Library,** Little Gallery, 57783
Library Holdings: Vols 200; AV — Motion pictures; Other — Reproductions
Collections: Carnegie gift library containing 1000 prints and 150 books

VERMILLION

M **UNIVERSITY OF SOUTH DAKOTA ART GALLERIES,** W M Lee Center for the Fine Arts, 57069. Tel 605-677-5481. *Dir* John A Day
Open Mon - Fri 10 AM - 4:30 PM; Sat & Sun 1 - 5 PM. No admis fee. Estab 1965. Primary mission is educational, serving specifically the needs of the college and augmenting the university curriculum as a whole. There are two galleries. One is a changing gallery 50' x 50' located in the Fine Arts Center. The second houses the university collection of Works by Oscar Howe, a native American painter. This facility is approximately 30' x 20'. Average Annual Attendance: 15,000
Income: $12,000 (financed by state appropriation and student fee allotment)
Purchases: $4000
Collections: 35 Works by Oscar Howe; variety of media by contemporary artists
Exhibitions: (1982-83) USD Faculty Show; Senior Exhibition; Student Awards Exhibition; Oscar Howe Retrospective Exhibit
Publications: Catalogues for major exhibitions
Activities: Lect open to public; gallery talks; tours; competitions, awards given; exten dept serves 150 miles in general region; individual paintings and original objects of art lent to professional museums and galleries; book traveling exhibitions, 2 per year; originate traveling exhibitions

YANKTON

M **YANKTON COLLEGE,** Durand Art Collection,* James Lloyd Library, Rm 151, Forbes Hall, 57078. Tel 605-665-3661. *Cur* Hans Jansen
Estab 1909. Chiefly serves the Art Department. Open to students, faculty and townspeople
Collections: Some original paintings, sculpture and prints
Exhibitions: Frequently changed exhibitions
Activities: Lect for schools and clubs; loan exhibits circulated

TENNESSEE

CHATTANOOGA

M **HOUSTON ANTIQUE MUSEUM,** 201 High St, 37403. Tel 615-267-7176. *Dir & Cur* Libby Workman
Open Tues - Sat 10 AM - 4:30 PM; Sun 2 - 4:30 PM; cl Mon & holidays. Estab 1961, incorporated 1949, collection willed to Chattanooga by the late Anna Safley Houston. Average Annual Attendance: 8000. Mem: 600; dues $100, $25, $10 & $7; annual meeting April
Collections: Early American Furniture; Rare Collection of Glass (15,000 pitchers, 600 patterns of pressed glass, all types of art glass, steins and Tiffany glass); dolls
Publications: The Fabulous Houston
Activities: Classes for adults; docent training; lectures open to public, 2 vis lectr per year; tours; sales shop sells books, magazines, slides and antique items

M **HUNTER MUSEUM OF ART,** 10 Bluff View, 37403. Tel 615-267-0968. *Dir* Cleve K Scarborough; *Cur Education* Diana W Suarez; *Cur of Exhib* J Bradley Burns; *Admin Asst* Kay S Parish; *Registrar* Kay T Morris; *Cur Collections* William T Henning, Jr
Open Tues - Sat 10 AM - 4:30 PM; Sun 1 - 4:30 PM; cl Mon. No admis fee. Estab 1924, chartered in 1951, to present a visual arts program of high quality, maintain a fine collection of American art, and to carry out a vigorous educational program in the community and the schools. The permanent collection of American art is housed in the George Thomas Hunter Mansion constructed in 1904; a contemporary addition was opened in 1975 with 50,000 sq ft of space in four major gallery areas, a classroom wing and an auditorium. In 1982, the Twentieth Century Gallery, which features American art since 1945 to the present from the permanent collection, was introduced. Average Annual Attendance: 60,000. Mem: 3000; dues benefactor $1000, patron $500, sponsor $250, donor $100, advocate $50, general $30, student & sr citizen $15
Collections: American paintings including works by Bierstadt, Benton, Burchfield, Cassatt, Davies, Hassam, Henri, Inness, Marsh, Twachtman, Whistler & others; Recent contemporary acquisitions include Beal, Bechtle, Fish, Golub, Goodman, Johns, LeWitt, Oliveira, Park, Rauschenberg, Schapiro, Stackhouse, Tworkov, Wonner & Youngerman; contemporary American prints; sculpture by Calder, Snelson, Sugarman & others
Exhibitions: (1984) Davis Cone: Theatre Paintings; Five American Impressionist Women; Two by Two (local artists' group show); Chinese Painting from Wuxi; Bernard D'Andrea, paintings; Art Scene 1984—juried high school exhibit; Kentucky Quilts; Sidney Nisbet, paintings; Joe Falsetti, sculpture; The Graphics Collection of Daniel Brown; The Magic of Japanese Woodblock Prints; Southern Sculpture: Outdoors, 4-year shared exhibition; John Singer Sargent: Drawings & Watercolors from the Corcoran; Byron Browne Retrospective, paintings & drawings; Charles Hawthrone Watercolors; Art of Designed Environments from the Netherlands; The Lithographs of James McNeill Whistler; Tennessee Watercolor Society Show, 1984; Peter Poskas, paintings Hunt Slonem (paintings); Bill Whorall: 41 from 41; Spectrum 1981; Photographs from the National Portrait Gallery; Peter Moreno-Lacalle; Young Americans; Metal; 1981 Tenn Watercolor Society Annual Exhibition; Denise Frank (photographs); American Photography in the 30's; Ellyn Bivin (paintings); Brooke Alexander: A Decade of Print Publishing
Publications: Brochures and announcements; bulletin, monthly; Bluff and Magic Mansion: A Children's guide book to the Permanent Collection
Activities: Classes for adults and children; docent training; lect open to public, approximately 12 vis lectr per yr; gallery talks; concerts; tours; competitions; individual paintings are lent to other museums ; museum shops sells miscellaneous items

L **Reference Library,** 10 Bluff View, 37403. Tel 615-267-0968
Open Tues - Sat 10 AM - 4:30 PM, Sun 1 - 4:30 PM, cl Mon, open to public by appointment. Estab 1958
Library Holdings: Vols 1300; Per subs 38; Micro — Cards; AV — Cassettes, motion pictures, slides; Other — Clipping files, exhibition catalogs, memorabilia, original art works, pamphlets, photographs, prints, sculpture
Special Subjects: Architecture, American Art

M **UNIVERSITY OF TENNESSEE AT CHATTANOOGA ART GALLERY,*** Baldwin St, 37402. Tel 615-755-4177. *Dir* George Cress
Open Mon - Fri 9 AM - 5 PM, cl university holidays. No admis fee. Estab 1952
Collections: Graphics; paintings; students work
Activities: Gallery talks; loan program; temporary and traveling exhibitions

CLARKSVILLE

M **AUSTIN PEAY STATE UNIVERSITY,** Margaret Fort Trahern Gallery, Art Department, 37040. Tel 615-648-7333. *Dir* Larry Hortenbury
Open Mon - Fri 9 AM - 4 PM. No admis fee. Estab 1962 as a university community service to exhibit a variety of visual media from regional professionals and university art majors
Income: Financed by university appropriations
Collections: Graphics and sculpture; primarily watercolors; regional artists
Exhibitions: Average 6-10 per year
Publications: Announcements of shows and artist biographies, monthly
Activities: Classes for adults & children; lectures open to the public, 2-3 vis lectr per yr; gallery talks; tours; competitions with awards; scholarships; individual and original objects of art lent
L **Art Dept Library,** 37040. Tel 615-648-7333. *Gallery Cur* Lewis B Burton; *Slide Librn* Philancy Holder
Noncirculating department library
Library Holdings: AV — Fs, motion pictures, slides; Other — Clipping files, original art works, photographs, prints, reproductions, sculpture

COOKEVILLE

O **CUMBERLAND ART SOCIETY,** Cookeville Art Center, 186 S Walnut, 38501. Tel 615-526-2424. *Pres* Froun Felker; *VPres* Florence Kolhoff
Open Tues - Fri & Sun 1 - 4 PM. No admis fee. Estab 1961 to promote arts in the community and area. A new building with adequate gallery and studio space. The gallery is carpeted and walls are finished with wallscape and track lighting. Average Annual Attendance: 3000. Mem: 100; dues $10; meetings every other month
Income: $5500 (financed by membership, city & state appropriations)
Exhibitions: Changing exhibits, monthly
Activities: Classes for children & children; lectures open to public, 6 vis lectr per yr; gallery talks; tours; competitions with awards

FAYETTEVILLE

O **SURFACE DESIGN ASSOCIATION, INC,** 311 E Washington St, 37334. Tel 615-433-6804. *Pres* Donald Bujnowski; *VPres* Zoe Lancaster; *Secy* Patricia Mansfield; *Treasurer* Lenore Davis; *Editor Surface Design Journal* Stephen Blumrich
Estab 1976. Mem: 1100
Publications: Surface Design Journal, quarterly
Activities: Lectures open to public; competitions

JOHNSON CITY

EAST TENNESSEE STATE UNIVERSITY
M **Carroll Reece Museum,** 37614. Tel 615-929-4392, 929-4283. *Museum Coordr* Helen Roseberry; *Museum Secy* Margaret S Carr; *Installation Supervisor* Charles E Moore
Open Mon - Fri 9 AM - 4 PM, Sun 1 - 5 PM. No admis fee. Estab 1964 to enhance the cultural and educational advantages of the university and the people of upper east Tennessee. The purpose of Friends of the Reece Museum is to acquire fine arts works for the permanent collection. Average Annual Attendance: 23,500. Mem: 400; dues President's trust $10,000 plus, President's partners $500, Century Club $100-$499, supporting $25, family $15, individual $10, student $1
Collections: Frontier Exhibit, an exhibit of historical Tennessee household & farming items, includes a log cabin & conestoga wagon; Marks Collection of Pre-Columbian Art; Music From the Past, a collection of early musical instruments; Old Master & contemporary paintings; Printshop of the Past; Reece Room, an exhibition of memorabilia of former United States Congressman from Tennessee, B Carroll Reece; John Steele Collection of Contemporary Prints; contemporary paintings; historical material
Exhibitions: (1983-84) Three galleries of traveling exhibitions, some rented and some organized by museum staff
Publications: CRM Newsletter
Activities: Lectures, 6 vis lectr per yr; concerts; gallery talks; tours; competitions with awards; scholarships; individual paintings & original objects of art lent to inner administrative offices on campus; lending collection contains 354 original prints, 25 paintings, 400 original art works, 6 sculpture & 1000 slides; book traveling exhibitions; originate traveling exhibitions; rotating exhibitions at Kingsport University Center
M **Elizabeth Slocum Gallery,** Art Department, 37601. Tel 615-929-4292, 929-4247. *Chmn Art Dept* John E Schrader; *Dir Exhibitions* Gerald G Edmundson
Open daily 8 AM - 4 PM. No admis fee. Estab 1950 to augment all the programs and areas of instruction within the Art Department and to foster interest in various modes of artistic expression in the campus at large. Average Annual Attendance: 5000
Collections: A small teaching collection of prints, paintings, ceramics & weaving

Publications: Catalogs; posters
Activities: Classes for adults and children; art education program; seminars and workshops; lect, gallery talks, tours and competitions; scholarships and fellowships; originate traveling exhibitions
L **C C Sherrod Library,** Art Collection Box 22,450A, 37614. Tel 615-929-5308
Open Mon - Thur 8 AM - 12 PM, Fri 8 AM - 4:30 PM, Sat 9 AM - 5 PM, Sun 1 PM - 12 PM
Income: Financed by the state
Library Holdings: Vols 24,235
Special Subjects: Architecture, Decorative Arts, Photography
Collections: Appalachian Culture and Arts; photographs archives; slides of local; videotape archives

KINGSPORT

O **KINGSPORT FINE ARTS CENTER,** Church Circle, 37660. Tel 615-246-9351.
Pres David Pond; *Secy* Juanita Eaton
Open Mon - Fri 9 AM - 5 PM. No admis fee, charge for special events. Estab 1968 to promote and present all the arts to all the people in area; this includes performing arts, visual arts and classes. Mem: Dues $10 - $250; annual meeting May
Income: $40,000 (financed by membership)
Publications: Newsletter, bimonthly
Activities: Classes for adults and children; lectures open to public; competitions with awards; scholarships; individual paintings lent to clubs & businesses

KNOXVILLE

M **DULIN GALLERY OF ART,** 3100 Kingston Pike, 37919. Tel 615-525-6101.
Chmn Dean Anderson; *VChmn* Melvin White Jr; *2nd VChmn* L Caesar Stair III; *Secy* Mrs George White; *Treas* Mrs David Stair; *Dir* Rebecca Massie-Lane
Open Tues Noon - 8 PM, Wed - Fri Noon - 4 PM, Sat & Sun 1 - 5 PM, cl holidays. No admis fee. Estab 1962 as a nonprofit private corporation. The Gallery is located in the historic house designed in 1915 by John Russell Pope for H L Dulin and is listed in the National Register. Average Annual Attendance: 20,000. Mem: 1000; dues from $25 - $1000
Income: Financed by membership, contributions, foundations and state and federal grants
Collections: American paintings; Southeast regional art; works from last fifteen National Print and Drawing Competitions
Exhibitions: American Folk Art; Annual National Print and Drawing Competition; Art in East Tennessee from Private Collections; Community Project; Contemporary Art from Southeast Region; Photography; Tennessee Watercolor Society; Young People's Gallery
Publications: Russell Briscoe - An American Folk Artist; calendar, bi-monthly; H L Dulin Residence; Thorne Miniature Rooms
Activities: Classes for adults and children; docent training; arts to the schools; lectures open to public, 1-2 visiting lectures per year; tours; competitions with awards; inner city outreach Art Van; sales shop sells books, original art, jewelry and cards

UNIVERSITY OF TENNESSEE
M **Frank H McClung Museum,** 1327 Circle Park Dr, 37916. Tel 615-974-2144.
Dir Dr Paul Parmalee; *Exhib Coordr* Joseph W Hopkins; *Cur Coll* Elaine A Evans
Open Mon - Fri 9 AM - 5 PM. No admis fee. Estab 1961 to collect, maintian and interpret paintings, works of art, items of natural history and historical objects with emphasis placed on the Tennessee area. A major purpose is to provide research materials for students and faculty of the university. The museum, galleries and all cultural related departments will move to a new Art and Architecture Building in Jan 1981. Average Annual Attendance: 35,000
Income: Financed by city and state appropriations
Collections: Frederick T Bonham Collection (18th - 20th Century furniture, art objects); Lewis-Kneberg Collection (Tennessee archaeology); Grace Moore Collection (memorabilia of her career 1920's - 1940's)
Activities: Lect open to public; gallery talks; tours; competitions; exten dept serves the Southwest; original objects of art lent; lending collection contains prints and photographs
M **Eleanor Dean Audigier Art Collection,** Frank H McClung Museum, Circle Park Drive, 37916. Tel 615-974-2144
Open Mon - Fri 9 AM - 5 PM. No admis fee. Estab 1934. Average Annual Attendance: 19,600
Income: Financed by state appropriations
Collections: The Audigier Collection contains over 800 art objects: Ancient Egyptian scarabs, shawbtis; 19th Century Cameos; Chinese, French and German porcelain; Greco-Roman objects; 19th Century copies of Italian Renaissance paintings, furniture and sculpture; ivory miniatures; personal jewelry; Turkish and Arabic trays; early 20th Century decorative arts objects
Activities: Lectures open to public; tours; individual and original objects of art lent
M **Art & Architecture Gallery,** University of Tennessee, 921 Volunteer Blvd, 37916. Tel 615-974-6081
Open Mon - Fri 9:30 AM - 4 PM, Mon - Thurs 7 - 9 PM, Sat & Sun 1 - 4 PM. Estab 1981 to provide quality exhibitions focusing on contemporary art and architecture. Gallery consists of 3500 sq ft exhibition space. Average Annual Attendance: 15,000
Collections: †Contemporary American prints; †Japanese prints
Exhibitions: Corporation collections, fund raising, professional and student exhibitions
Activities: Lectures open to public, 12 vis lectr per year; gallery talks; tours; sponsor competitions; scholarships offered; lending collection contains individual and original objects of art; book traveling exhibitions, 2-3 per year; originate traveling exhibitions

O **University of Tennessee Exhibits Committee,** 305 University Center, 37996. Tel 615-974-5455. *Program Advisor* Lucy Hamilton
Open Mon - Fri 7:30 AM - 10:30 PM, Sat 7 AM - 10 PM, Sun 1 - 8 PM. No admis fee. Estab to provide cultural arts for the students of the university. Two major galleries: Gallery Concourse has 300 running ft & Barton Music Lounge & Gallery has 60 running ft for intimate shows. Average Annual Attendance: 20,000
Income: Financed by state appropriation and student activities fees
Purchases: Dunford Collection purchased annually
Collections: †Dunford Collection; †Marion Heard Collection of Crafts
Exhibitions: 20 exhibits per year - student shows and traveling shows
Activities: Lect open to public, 3 visiting lectr per year; originate traveling exhibitions

MARYVILLE

C **BANK OF MARYVILLE,** PO Box 528, 37801. Tel 615-977-5100. *In Charge of Art Coll* Ruth C Fouche
Estab to provide community interest in the arts; to aid participating artists; to enhance lobby. Supports local artists and art forms or displays that lend an interest to the community
Activities: Sponsors Wildlife Artist Guy Coheleach

M **MARYVILLE COLLEGE,** Fine Arts Center Gallery,* 37801. Tel 615-982-6412.
Chmn James Albert Bloy
Open daily except Sun
Collections: †Print collection
Activities: Gallery programs in connection with circulating exhibitions; art movies, four times a year; Ten to twelve traveling exhibitions during college year

MEMPHIS

M **DIXON GALLERY AND GARDENS,** 4339 Park Ave, 38117. Tel 901-761-5250. *Dir* Moussa M Domit; *Asst to Dir* Katherine Lawrence; *Cur* Reba Russell; *Asst to Dir & Public Relations* Madge Clark; *Registrar* Lawrence Wang
Open Tues Sat 11 AM - 5 PM; Sun 1 - 5 PM; cl Mon. Admis adults $1, children 2-11 years, students & senior citizens $.50, Tues free. Estab 1976 as a bequest to the public from the late Margaret & Hugo Dixon. Their Impressionist Art Collection & their Georgian-style home & gardens, situated on 17 acres of landscaped woodland, serve as the museum's foundation. Ten additional galleries, added in 1977, house the developing permanent collection & accomodate loan exhibitions. Formal & informal gardens, a camellia house & greenhouses are located on the site. A new wing of 13,000 sq ft is being built. Average Annual Attendance: 50,000. Mem: 1800; dues corporate patron $1000 and up, corporate donor & patron $500, donor $100, supporting $50, family $30, individual $20, student $10
Income: Financed by endowment
Collections: French Impressionist painting; Barbizon, Post-Impressionist & related schools; British paintings, 18th & 19th centuries; Georgian period furniture & decorative arts; English porcelain, 18th & 19th centuries Works by Pierre Bonnard, Eugene Boudin, A F Cals, Jean-Baptiste Carpeaux, Mary Cassatt, Marc Chagall, William Merritt Chase, John Constable, J B C Corot, Kenyon Cox, Henri-Edmond Cross, Charles Francois Daubigny, Edgar Degas, Julien Dupre, Sir Jacob Epstein, Henri Fantin-Latour, Thomas Gainsborough, Paul Gauguin, Francesco Guardi, Paul Guigou, Armand Guillaumin, Henri Joseph Harpignies, William James, Johan Jongkind, S V E Lepine, Maximilien Luce, Albert Marquet, Paul Mathey, Henri Matisse, Claude Monet, Berthe Morisot, Henriette A Oberteuffer, Ludovic Piette, Camille Pissarro, Sir Henry Raeburn, Auguste Renoir, Sir Joshua Reynolds, Sebastino Ricci, George Romney, Henri Rouart, Paul Signac, Alfred Sisley, Allen Tucker, J M W Turner, Horatio Walker and Richard Wilson
Exhibitions: (1982-83) Maurice Prendergast, watercolors; Five Hundred Years of Botanical Illustration; Vincent Van Gogh; 19th & 20th Century American & European Animal Sculpture; French Impressionist Prints, SAF; An International Episode - Millit, Monet & their North American counterparts; Jules Breton & the French Rural Tradition; An Assemblage of Decorative Arts; A View of Tennessee Silversmiths; Marc Chagall, selected works, 1911-1981; Matisse Prints, 1903-1929, SAF; H Lartigue Photographs, International Exhibitions Foundation; Communication Architecture; Drawings of the French Revolution & First Empire from the Musee Carnavalet; Bingham's World, MAAA
Publications: Exhibition catalogues; newsletter, bi-monthly; Paintings and Sculpture, Volume One
Activities: Classes for adults; docent training; film series; lect open to the public; concerts; gallery talks; tours; individual paintings and original objects of art lent to museums and galleries; lending collection contains original paintings, prints and sculpture, porcelain, silver and antique furniture
L **Library,** 4339 Park Ave, 38117. Tel 901-761-5250
Open to the public during museum hours for reference only

MEMPHIS ACADEMY OF ARTS
M **Frank T Tobey Gallery,** Overton Park, 38112. Tel 901-726-4085. *Pres* John S Slorp
Open Mon - Fri 9 AM - 5 PM, Sat 9 AM - Noon, cl summers, Sat & Sun & school holidays. No admis fee. Estab 1936 as an adjunct educational program. The Standing Committee on Exhibitions arranges visiting shows
Collections: Jacob Marks Memorial Collection; works by college graduates
Exhibitions: Juried student shows; one and two-man faculty shows; senior exhibition; summer student shows; traveling exhibitions
Publications: Exhibition catalogs
Activities: Classes for adults, children and undergraduate college students; lect; guided tours; films; competitions; book traveling exhibitions
L **G Pillow Lewis Memorial Library,** Overton Park, 38112. Tel 901-726-4085.
Librn Robert Scarlett; *Asst Librn* Bette Ray Callow
Open Mon - Fri 8 AM - 5 PM, Sat 9 AM - Noon, Mon & Wed evenings until 10 PM
Income: $10,000 (financed by city and county appropriations)
Library Holdings: Vols 16,000; Per subs 120; Original prints; AV — Slides 30,000; Other — Reproductions

M **MEMPHIS BROOKS MUSEUM OF ART,** Overton Park, 38112. Tel 901-726-5266. *Dir* Douglas Hyland; *Dir Office Operations* Gail Chumley; *Secy to Dir* Rhonda Russell; *Cur Education* Patty Bladon; *Asst Education Dir* Darla Linerode; *Cur Coll* Open; *Registrar* Marilyn Masler; *Asst Registrar* Palmer Thomason; *Coordr of Public Information & Special Educator* Lisa Shelby; *Public Information Asst* Pamela Hopper; *Exhibition Preparator* Elbert L Sharp III; *Exhibition Preparator Asst* Paul Tracy
Open Tues - Sat 10 AM - 5 PM; Sun 1 - 5 PM; cl Mon. No admis fee. Estab 1914 by gift from Mrs Samuel H Brooks to promote interest and development in cultural arts; to present a diversity of exhibitions; to assist people in their quest for knowledge and aesthetic experiences as well as contributing to their mental health through art education. The original building was opened in 1916 with additions in 1955 and 1973. Maintained by the city of Memphis, Public Service Department. Average Annual Attendance: 229,000. Mem: Dues $35 and up; annual meeting Sept
Income: Financed by city appropriation
Collections: American Paintings and Sculpture, 18th-20th centuries; Dutch and Flemish Paintings, 16th-18th centuries; Eastern and Near-Eastern Decorative Arts Collection (Han, T'ang and Ching Dynasty Chinese); English Paintings, 17th-19th centuries; French Paintings, 16th-19th centuries; †International Collection of Paintings and Sculpture, 19th & 20th centuries; Kress Collection of Italian Paintings and Sculpture, 13th-18th centuries; Dr Louis Levy Collection of American Prints; Mid-South Collection of 20th century paintings and sculptures; glass, textile and porcelain collection
Publications: Newsletter, bimonthly
Activities: Education Department; lect open to public; concerts; gallery talks; tours; competitions; originate traveling exhibitions; sales shop sells books, reproductions, prints and museum replicas
L **Library,** Overton Park, 38112. *Librn* Letitia Proctor
Open to the public for reference only
Library Holdings: Vols 10,000; Per subs 20; Other — Clipping files, exhibition catalogs, manuscripts, pamphlets

L **MEMPHIS-SHELBY COUNTY PUBLIC LIBRARY AND INFORMATION CENTER,** Dept of Art, Music and Recreation, 1850 Peabody, 38104. Tel 901-725-8828. *Dir* Robert Croneberger; *Chief Main Library* Sallie Johnson; *Head Art, Music, Recreation Dept* Lynn Whitson
Open Mon - Thurs 9 AM - 9 PM, Fri & Sat 9 AM - 6 PM. Estab 1895 to serve the reference, informational, educational and recreational needs of residents of Memphis-Shelby County. Turner-Clark Gallery exhibits promising and established local and regional artists of various media
Income: Financed by city and state appropriation
Library Holdings: Vols 62,015; Per subs 245; Other — Clipping files, framed reproductions

MEMPHIS STATE UNIVERSITY
M **University Gallery,** Southern Ave, 38152. Tel 901-454-2216. *Dir Exhib* C H Allgood
Open Tues 10 AM - 4 PM, Wed & Thurs 10 AM - 9 PM, Fri & Sat 10 AM - 4 PM, Sun 2 - 5 PM. No admis fee. Estab 1968 to provide information for the general public and instruction for students. Average Annual Attendance: 12,000
Income: Financed by state appropriation
Collections: Neil Nokes Collection of African Masks and other artifacts; Ancient Egyptian Art from the Boston Museum of Fine Arts; collection of over 100 prints, an overview
Publications: Flyers
Activities: Lectures open to the public, 6 visiting lecturers per year; gallery talks; tours; competitions; book traveling exhibitions
L **Art History Slide Library,** Jones Hall, Room 220, 38152. Tel 901-454-2216. *Slide Cur* Belinda C Patterson
Open Mon - Fri 8:00 AM - 4:30 PM. Estab 1967 to provide slides for Art Faculty, University Faculty, and some outside organizations. Circ 90,000
Library Holdings: Vols 100; AV — A-tapes, cassettes, fs, motion pictures, rec, slides; Other — Clipping files, exhibition catalogs, original art works, reproductions, sculpture

M **SOUTHWESTERN AT MEMPHIS,** Jessie L Clough Art Memorial for Teaching, Clough Hall, 2000 N Parkway, 38112. Tel 901-274-1800, Ext 248. *Cur* Dr Alice Merrill Hyland
Collection donated by the late Miss Floy K Hanson of her fine and valuable collection of oriental objects of art to be known as the Jessie L Clough Art Memorial for Teaching in memory of her first art teacher and friend Miss Clough
Collections: Brass; copper; Japanese prints; jewelry; pottery; precious metals; textiles; woodcarvings; lacquer
Exhibitions: Selections from the Jessie L Clough Art Memorial for Teaching

MURFREESBORO

M **MIDDLE TENNESSEE STATE UNIVERSITY,** Photographic Gallery, Box 305, 37132. Tel 615-898-2491. *Cur* Harold L Baldwin
Open Mon - Fri 8 AM - 4:30 PM; Sat 9 AM - Midnight; Sun 1 - 6 PM. No admis fee. Estab 1969 for the exhibition of outstanding photographers and beginners. Gallery has 42 panels lighted individually. Average Annual Attendance: 8,000-10,000
Income: Financed by the University
Collections: Ansel Adams; Richard Avedon; Harold Baldwin; Harry Callahan; Geri Della Rocea de Candal; Jim Ferguson; Minor White & Others; Jim Norton; Aaron Siskind; Marianne Skogh; H H Smith; Jerry Velsman; Ed Weston by Cole; Kelly Wise
Publications: Lightyear, annually
Activities: Original objects of art lent to responsible organizations; lending collection contains photographs; traveling exhibitions organized and circulated

NASHVILLE

M **FISK UNIVERSITY MUSEUM OF ART,** 17th and Jackson Sts, 37203. Tel 615-329-8685. *Dir* Earl J Hooks; *Cur* Robert Hall; *Asst to Cur* Pearl Creswell
Open Mon - Fri 9 AM - 12 PM & 1 - 5 PM; cl Sat & Sun; June, July & Aug. No admis fee. Estab 1949 as an education resource center for the Fisk and Nashville communities and for the promotion of the visual arts. Van Vechten Gallery houses the library, temporary exhibits and art offices; Library Gallery houses the permanent collection and African Art. Average Annual Attendance: 4000
Income: Financed through the University
Collections: †Afro-American Collection; Alfred Stieglitz Collection of Modern Art; †Traditional African Art Collection
Exhibitions: (1982) Nathan Jones: Drawings, Watercolors & Lithographs; Directions in Afro-American Abstract Art; Recent Works: Robert Hall, Earl Hooks, Gregory Ridley & Jerry Waters
Publications: Fisk Art Report, yearly
Activities: Lectures open to public, 3 vis lectr per yr; gallery talks; tours; individual paintings and original objects of art lent to institutions, organizations, community groups; lending collection contains original prints and paintings; traveling exhibitions organized and circulated; sales shop selling reproductions and exhibition catalogs
L **Florine Stettheimer Library,** 18th and Jackson Sts, 37203
Open Mon - Fri 9 AM - 12 PM & 1 - 5 PM. Estab 1949. Publications are used by students and instructors for research
Library Holdings: Vols 1100; AV — Kodachromes, motion pictures; Other — Exhibition catalogs

M **THE PARTHENON,** Centennial Park, West End Ave (Mailing add: Metro Postal Service, Centennial Park Office, Nashville, TN 37201). Tel 615-259-6358. *Dir* Wesley M Paine; *Museum Guide* Gary Pace; *Pres Board* Dr George Richardt
Open Tues - Sat 9 AM - 4:30 PM, Sun 1 - 4:30 PM, cl Mon & legal holidays. No admis fee, suggested donations: adult $1, children $.50. Estab 1897 to offer Nashville residents and tourists quality art for viewing and sale in a historical setting of significance and beauty. two large and two small galleries in the basement of the only, exact size, replica of the Parthenon in the world. Average Annual Attendance: 900,000
Income: Financed by city and county taxes and donations
Collections: Cowan Collection, sixty three paintings by 19th and 20th century American artists, donated by James M Cowan; †Contemporary collection, thirty paintings purchased out of the annual Central South Exhibition by John Canaday in celebration of Tennessee's bicentennial, The Century III Collection
Exhibitions: Exhibitions change monthly
Publications: The Cowan Catalog
Activities: Co-sponsor, with Tennessee Art League of Annual Central South Exhibition, juried show with awards given; sales shop sells books, magazines, souvenirs, prints and slides

M **TENNESSEE BOTANICAL GARDENS AND FINE ARTS CENTER, INC,** Cheekwood, Forrest Park Dr, 37205. Tel 615-352-5310, 352-8632. *Exec Dir* Guy Hairston; *Dir Fine Arts Center* Kevin Grogan
Open Tues - Sat 9 AM - 5 PM, Sun 1 - 5 PM, cl Mon. Admis adults $2.50, children 7-17 $1, children under 7 free. Estab 1957, the Fine Arts Center is housed in a Georgian style mansion built in 1929, originally adapted for museum use in 1960; contemporary gallery spaces added in 1981 renovation. Main galleries maintained for major exhibitions; Mary Cheek Hill Gallery maintained for smaller exhibitions; Nashville Artist Guild holds members shows; Permanent Collection Gallery maintained. Mem: 8400; dues $20
Income: Financed by membership and private donation
Collections: Works by American artists; English Worcester porcelain; Oriental snuff bottles; graphics all periods and schools
Publications: Newsletter, monthly; Trees of Christmas (book); exhibition catalogues and posters
Activities: Classes for adults and children; dramatic programs; docent training; educational trips; lectures open to the public, 5 - 10 vis lectr per yr; concerts; gallery talks; tours; awards; individual paintings and original objects of art lent to museums and corporations; lending collection contains original art works, paintings and sculpture; book traveling exhibitions, 10 per yr; traveling exhibitions organized and circulated to museums and cultural institutions; museum shop sells books, slides, posters, toys, jewelry, gifts & stationary items; junior museum
L **Botanic Hall Library,** Cheekwood, Cheek Rd, 37205
Open to staff and members for reference
Library Holdings: Vols 5000; Per subs 45
Collections: Extensive snuff bottle collection

O **TENNESSEE HISTORICAL SOCIETY,** Ground Floor, War Memorial Bldg, 37219. Tel 615-741-2660. *Exec Dir* James A Hoobler
Open Mon - Sat 8 AM - 4:30 PM, cl national holidays. No admis fee. Estab 1849. Mem: Dues life $250, sustaining $30, regular $15; monthly meetings
Collections: Paintings, some contemporary; The Tennessee State Museum holds the entire collection belonging to the Society in trust
Exhibitions: Temporary exhibitions
Publications: History Imprints, eight times per year; Tennessee Historical Quarterly
Activities: Guided tours

M **TENNESSEE STATE MUSEUM,** Polk Cultural Center, 505 Deaderick, 37219. Tel 615-741-2692. *Dir* Lois Riggins; *Admin Asst* Dancy Jones; *Chief Cur of Collections* Dr James Kelly; *Chief Researcher* Dan Pomeroy; *Chief of Exhibits* Philip Kreger; *Cur of Education* Patricia Rasbury; *Coordr of Museum Information* Sally Jones; *Coordr of Tennessee State Museum Association Inc* Sherry Caldwell; *Cur of Military History* William Baker
Open Sun 1 - 5 PM; Mon - Sat 10 AM - 5 PM, cl Christmas, Easter, Thanksgiving, New Year's Day. No admis fee. Estab 1937 to preserve and interpret the historical artifacts of Tennessee through museum exhibits and statewide outreach and educational programs. A military history museum in the

War Memorial Building depicts Tennessee's involvement in modern wars (Spanish-American to World War II). The new State Museum in the multimillion dollar Polk Cultural Complex opened June 18, 1981 with exhibits highlighting Life in Tennessee from early man to present. An art gallery houses changing exhibits. Maintains small art reference library. Average Annual Attendance: 250,000. Mem: 600; dues $10
Income: Financed by state appropriation
Purchases: Tennessee related early 19th century paintings and prints; 19th century Tennessee made silver; 19th century Tennessee made firearms
Collections: The museum collection of objects relating to Tennessee history from pre-historic times to the present. It holds in trust the collection of the Tennessee Historical Society as well as portraits and paintings of and by prominent Tennesseans; contemporary Tennessee related artists works
Exhibitions: William Edmondson: A Retrospective; Revival; Eleanor Dickinson; Charles Shannon (watercolors); Tennessee Arts Competition Show; Needle Expressions; Early Eighties; Peter Max Exhibit; Benton's Bentons (retrospective of Thomas Hart Benton's art); Carroll Cloar: A Retrospective; Made in Tennessee Show; The Homeplace: A Southern Portfolio (photograph exhibit by Robin Hood); Carl Sublett Retrospective; Is It True What They Say About Dixie? Myths & Realities of the Antebellum South
Publications: The Cabinet; newsletter, quarterly; The Open Eye, two times per yr; exhibition catalogues
Activities: Classes for adults and children; docent training; lectures open to the public; gallery talks; tours; competitions; extensive speaker's bureau serving entire state; exten dept serving statewide; individual paintings & original objects of art; book traveling exhibitions, 4 per yr; originate traveling exhibitions; museum shop sells books, Tennessee crafts, items relating to the collection; junior museum
L **Library,** 505 Deaderick, 37219
Library Holdings: Vols 1500; Per subs 15; AV — Slides, v-tapes; Other — Exhibition catalogs, pamphlets, photographs

M **VANDERBILT UNIVERSITY,** Art Gallery, West End Ave at 23rd, Box 1801 B, 37235. Tel 615-322-2831. *Dir* F Hamilton Hazlehurst, PhD; *Gallery Dir* Allison Price
Open Mon - Fri 1 - 4 PM; Sat & Sun 1 - 5 PM, cl holidays and some University vacations. No admis fee. Estab collection 1956, gallery 1961, to provide exhibitions for the University and Nashville communities, and original art works for study by Vanderbilt students. The gallery is included in the Old Gym, built in 1880 and listed in the National Register of Historic Places. Mem: 300; dues $10 - $500
Income: Financed by university resources and Art Association dues
Collections: †Vanderbilt Collection of Western, Eastern, Ancient and Modern Cultures; Harold P Stern Collection of Oriental Art; Anna C Hoyt Collection of Old Master Prints; former Peabody College Art Collection including Kress Study Collection of Italian Renaissance Paintings
Exhibitions: (1983-84) Selections from the Vanderbilt Art Collection, and exhibitions including The Show: An Extension in Time and Space, drawings by Edith Frohock; Olen Bryant: A Retrospective; Contemporary Selections: The Hospital Corporation of America Collection; City Fragments: Jack Robertson Photographs
Activities: Art Association lect open to members only
L **Arts Reference Library,** 419 21st Ave S, 37203. Tel 615-322-3485. *Librn* Jack Robertson
Library Holdings: Vols 37,000; Per subs 250; Micro — Fiche; AV — Fs, motion pictures, slides 110,000; Other — Clipping files, exhibition catalogs, pamphlets, reproductions 5500
Special Subjects: British 18th & 19th century landscape painting & the Norwich School

O **WATKINS INSTITUTE,*** Sixth Ave at Church St, 37219. Tel 615-242-1851. *Dir* C H Sargent; *Art Dir* Nancy Rogers; *Exec Secy* Dorris Stone
Open Mon - Thurs 9 AM - 9 PM; Fri 9 AM - 1:30 PM, cl Sat & Sun, Christmas, New Years, July 4, Labor Day, Thanksgiving Day. No admis fee. Estab 1885 as an adult education center for art, home economics, business education, adult evening high school, and courses of a general nature
Income: Financed by rent from business property
Collections: All-State Artist Collection (oldest collection of Tennessee art in the state); this is a purchase-award collection of oil, pastels, watercolors, graphics and sculpture; several other collections of lesser value
Exhibitions: Six or eight exhibitions per year
Publications: Art brochure; quarterly catalogue listing courses
Activities: Classes for adults and children; lect open to public, 6-8 visiting lectrs per year; competitions; individual paintings lent to schools; original objects of art lent; traveling exhibitions organized and circulated
L **Library,*** Sixth Ave at Church St, 37219. Tel 615-242-1851. *Librn* Mildred Egan
Open 9 AM - 8:30 PM. Estab 1885
Library Holdings: Vols 23,000; Per subs 15; AV — Fs, lantern slides, slides, v-tapes

OAK RIDGE

O **OAK RIDGE COMMUNITY ART CENTER & MUSEUM OF FINE ARTS,** PO Box 105, 37830. Tel 615-482-1182. *Pres* Victor McLaughlin; *Dir* Rose Kenney
Open Tues 1 - 9 PM, Wed - Fri 9 AM - 5 PM, Sat & Sun 1 - 4 PM; cl Mon. Admis $1 adults $.50 18 and under. Estab 1952 to help fulfill the cultural needs of the community and encourage enjoyment and understanding of the arts. Temporary gallery for 8 touring exhibitions, permanent collection exhibitions, quarterly classes and 3 studio areas. Average Annual Attendance: 25,000. Mem: 650; dues $15 - $500; annual meetings first Mon in May
Income: $30,000 (financed by membership)
Collections: †The Mary and Alden Gomez Collection
Publications: Vison, monthly bulletin
Activities: Classes for adults and children; docent training; forums; workshops; lectures open to public, 6 vis lectr per year; recorded concerts; gallery talks; tours; juried and unjuried competions; ribbons and certificate awards; scholarships; individual paintings and original objects of art rented to individuals and businesses on semi-annual basis; sales shop sells fine arts and fine crafts, magazines and original art

L **Library,** PO Box 105, 37830. *Librn* Gen Stoughton
Open to members for reference only
Library Holdings: Vols 600; Per subs 3; Micro — Cards; AV — Rec; Other — Clipping files, exhibition catalogs, memorabilia, pamphlets, photographs
Special Subjects: Music

SEWANEE

M **UNIVERSITY OF THE SOUTH GALLERY OF FINE ARTS,** Guerry Hall, 37375. Tel 615-598-5931. *Dir* Dr Susan Kaufman
Open daily 2-4 PM except holidays and non-university sessions. Estab 1938; museum chambers estab 1972. Average Annual Attendance: 5000 - 6000
Collections: Period Rooms; drawings, furniture and artifacts, paintings, photography, prints, sculpture
Exhibitions: Monthly exhibitions during school year, 1 per month; changing shows
Activities: Four lectures per year; tours

TEXAS

ABILENE

M **ABILENE FINE ARTS MUSEUM,** 801 S Mockingbird, 79605. Tel 915-673-4587. *Dir* Open
Open Tues - Fri 9 AM - 5 PM; Sat & Sun 1 - 5 PM; cl Mon. No admis fee. Estab 1937 as an art and history education institution. Two galleries and gift shop, built in 1964, cover approximately 5000 sq ft. Average Annual Attendance: 17,000. Mem: 700; dues $15 and up; meeting 2nd Tues
Income: Financed by membership, grants, fund-raising, events
Collections: American Paintings and Prints
Exhibitions: (1983-84) The Gutenberg Bible; The History of Printing; Artists' Books; Texas Painterly Monoprints; Oriental Rugs; Luis' Bend; American Painting from the Old Jail Foundation; The American Scene: Prints; Art from Public Schools; A Childlike Vision: Contemporary Prints from the Permanent Collection; 40th Annual Painting Competition; Panorama Photographs by E O Goldbeck
Publications: Newsletter, quarterly; Annual Report; Annual Exhibit Guide
Activities: Classes for adults and children; docent training; lectures open to the public, 6 vis lect per yr; gallery talks; competitions; scholarships; individual paintings and original objects of art lent to local civic and business organizations; lending collection contains paintings; book traveling exhibitions, 6 - 12 per yr; sales shop sells original art, reproductions, prints, books

M **MCMURRY COLLEGE,** Ryan Fine Arts Center, Sayles Blvd, Box 8, 79697. Tel 915-692-4130, Ext 307. *Dept Chmn & Gallery Dir* Sherwood E Suter
Open Mon - Fri 8 AM - 5 PM, cl Sat & Sun (open some Sun 2 - 5 PM for Opening Receptions). No admis fee. Estab 1970 when building was completed. Large room overlooking larger sculpture garden. Average Annual Attendance: 2500
Income: Financed by college art budget
Collections: Artists represented include Picasso, Jack Levine, Adolph Dehn, Frelander
Publications: Art Through the Ages (color reproductions and slides to accompany text)
Activities: Classes for adults; lect open to the public; gallery talks; competitions; individual paintings and original objects of art lent to college offices

AMARILLO

M **AMARILLO ART CENTER,** 2200 S Van Buren, PO Box 447, 79178. Tel 806-372-8356. *Actg Dir* Jackie Wilson; *Cur Education* Mark Morey; *Designer* Beverly Cook Perry; *Bus Mgr* Emma Avara; *Admin Asst* Claire Main; *Registrar* Devery Burch; *Membership* Viola Johnson
Open Tues - Fri 10 AM - 5 PM; Sat & Sun 1 - 5 PM; Wed 7 - 9 PM. No admis fee. Estab 1972 for cultural enrichment and education in the visual arts. Gallery 100, 90 x 30 ft, atrium area 45 ft; Gallery 200 & 203, 90 x 32 ft, 11 ft ceiling; Gallery 305 & 307, each 32 x 28 ft, 10 ft ceiling. Average Annual Attendance: 100,000
Income: Financed by membership, college, endowment & sponsorship program
Collections: American Images, a collection of Farm Security Administration (FSA) photographs; Contemporary American Drawings
Publications: Annual Report; Calendar of Events, bimonthly; catalogs on exhibits; brochures, as needed
Activities: Classes for adults; lect open to the public; 10 vis lectr per year; gallery talks; tours; competitions; originate traveling exhibitions; museum shop selling books, magazines, original art, reproductions, prints
L **Library,*** 2200 S Van Buren, PO Box 447, Amarillo, 79178. *Librn* Micheal P Kiefer; *Asst Librn* Ruby Caldwell
For reference only
Library Holdings: Vols 5000; Per subs 14
O **Amarillo Art Center Association,*** 2200 S Van Buren, PO Box 447, 79178. *Chmn of the Board of Trustees* Dr Merrill Winsett; *Secy* Gerry McKay; *Treas* Robert Hucker
Open Tues - Fri 10 AM - 5 PM; Sat & Sun 1 - 5 PM; Wed 7 - 9:30 PM. Estab 1972 to provide quality visual and performing arts to the Texas Panhandle. Mem: 1200; dues $50-$5000, family $25, single $15, student $5
Income: Financed by endowment, membership and Amarillo College funds
Activities: Classes for adults and children; docent training; classes in art appreciation and film appreciation; lect open to the public, 10 vis lectr per year; concerts; gallery talks; tours; individual paintings and original objects of art lent to other institutions; originate traveling exhibitions

M **MPK OMEGA CO,** Mike Kiefer Bio-Art Museum, 3615 Carson, 79109. Tel 806-355-9369. *Pres* Dr Mike Kiefer; *VPres* June Kiefer; *Librn* Jacques Cantrell
Open Mon - Sat 9 AM - 5 PM. Estab 1971. Average Annual Attendance: 200,000. Mem: 300; dues $15; annual meeting Jan 5
Income: $500,000 (financed by endowment and membership)
Collections: †American Paintings, †sculpture, †photos, †motion pictures
Exhibitions: The Art of Renfenstahl, underwater photography
Publications: Kiefer Bio-Art Museum Annual
Activities: Lectures open to the public; competitions with awards

ARLINGTON

M **UNIVERSITY OF TEXAS AT ARLINGTON,** University Art Gallery, Fine Arts Bldg, 601 Monroe St, 76019. Tel 817-273-2790. *Dir* Max W Sullivan; *Asst Dir-Registrar* Sherry R Dunaway
Open Mon - Fri 9 AM - 4 PM; Sun 1 - 4 PM; cl Sat and major holidays. No admis fee. Estab 1975 on completion of Fine Arts Complex. The Gallery serves the entire university; exhibitions draw on all cultures and all periods. Main and Mezzanine Galleries are air cooled, carpeted, fabric wall covered with incandescent light. Average Annual Attendance: 15,000
Income: $56,000 (financed by state appropriation and private gifts)
Collections: Very small collection mainly American and Contemporary
Exhibitions: (1982) Robert Einbeck: The First Six Ways of the Life's Tree; Fabric Collages, Ludy Strauss Collection; David Keens and Jamie Bennett Exhibition, Metal Sculpture and Enameled Metals; Calvin D Grigg: Recent Work; Rex Dyer: Pen and Ink Drawings; University of Texas at Arlington Art Faculty: Recent Works; Beyond the Box: Architecture of Philip Johnson and John Burgee, Photographed by Richard Payne; Navajo Blankets, Anthony Berlant Collection; (1983) German Art 1900-1924, Prints and Watercolors; The Plan of St Gall, A Carolingian Master Plan for Monastic Settlements; Sixth Annual Student Competition; Gustav Klimt, 1862-1918, Austrian Painter; University of Texas at Arlington Art Faculty: Recent Work; Photo-Flow 2, Symposium and Juried Photo Exhibition, Modern Masters
Activities: Undergraduate course on museum techniques; lect open to the public, 3 vis lect per year; catalogs on sale

AUSTIN

O **COMMITTEE FOR HISPANIC ARTS & RESEARCH,** PO Box 12865, 78711. Tel 512-469-9748. *Pres* Dr Armando Gutierrez; *VPres* Dr Alberto Mata; *Dir* Romeo Rodriguez
Estab to promote Chicano and Latin artists. Average Annual Attendance: 4000. Mem: 500; dues $12
Income: $50,000 (financed by state appropriation, membership & fund raisers)
Collections: †Mexican American Art; †Latin American Art
Publications: Arriba Magazine, monthly
Activities: Competitions with awards

M **LAGUNA GLORIA ART MUSEUM,** 3809 West 35th St, PO Box 5568, 78763. Tel 512-458-8192. *Dir* Laurence Miller; *Dir Prog* Judith Sims; *Cur* Annette DiMeo Carlozzi; *Dir Development* Penny Burnett; *Dir Public Information* Sherry Smith; *Dir Planning* Sharon Greenhill
Open Tues - Sat, 10 AM - 5 PM, Thur 10 AM - 9 PM, Sun 1 - 5 PM. No admis fee. Three galleries downstairs, one upstairs. Average Annual Attendance: 80,000. Mem: 2200; dues $1000 - $25; annual meeting September
Income: Financed by City of Austin, Fiesta, memberships, annual fund, grants, Art School, corporate donations
Special Subjects: 20th Century American Art
Exhibitions: Changing exhibitions of 20th Century American Art, its roots and antecedents
Publications: Calendar, bi-monthly; Estate-Planning, quarterly
Activities: Art School classes for children and adults; cultural and educational programs in conjunction with exhibitions; museum guides program; art after school; museum shop

M **ELIZABET NEY MUSEUM,** 304 E 44th, 78751. Tel 512-458-2255. *Dir* James Fisher; *Cur* Louis Hicks; *Cur* Lynn Lichtenfels; *Specialist* Willie Nunn
Open Tues - Fri 11 AM - 4:30 PM, Sat & Sun 2 - 4:30 PM. No admis fee. Estab 1908 to preserve & exhibit the studio & works of Elisabet Ney. Administered by the city of Austin. Eclectic limestone castle, one of four 19th century American sculpture studios to survive intact with its contents. Average Annual Attendance: 40,000. Mem: 300; dues $25
Income: $69,000 (financed by city appropriation)
Collections: Works of Elizabet Ney in the form of original plaster casts, supplemented by bronze and marble works and tools, furnishings and memorabilia; nineteenth century sculpture
Publications: Sursum (annotated letters of Elizabet Ney)
Activities: Classes for adults; dramatic programs; docent training; lect open to public, 5 vis lectr per year; concerts; gallery talks; tours; original objects of art lent to museums; lending collection contains 300 books, motion pictures, 400 original art works, paintings, photographs, 400 sculpture, 1500 slides; book traveling exhibitions; museum shop sells books
L **Library,** 304 E 44th, 78751. Tel 512-458-2255
Open Tues - Fri 11 AM - 4:30 PM, Sat - Sun 2 - 4:30 PM. Estab 1908 to collect background material on subjects relevant to the Museum's history and period. For reference only
Library Holdings: Vols 300; Per subs 3; Letters; AV — Slides; Other — Clipping files, exhibition catalogs, manuscripts, memorabilia, original art works, pamphlets, photographs
Special Subjects: 19th Century Sculpture; Elisabet Ney
Exhibitions: A Life in Art; Elisabet Ney in Austin
Publications: SURSUM, collected letters of Elisabet Ney
Activities: Classes for adults and children; dramatic programs; docent training; AV programs; lectures open to public, 3-5 vis lectr per year; concerts; gallery talks; tours; exten dept serves Austin area school systems

M **SAINT EDWARD'S UNIVERSITY,** Fine Arts Exhibit Program,* 78704. Tel 512-444-2621, Ext 327
Open Mon - Fri 8 AM - 6 PM, Sun 1 - 5 PM. No admis fee. Estab 1961 to present for the university population and general public a monthly schedule of exhibits in the visual arts, as a means of orientation toward established and current trends in art styles in terms of their historical-cultural significance and aesthetic value, through teaching exhibitions, art films, public and private collections from distributing and compiling agencies, museums, galleries and artists. Average Annual Attendance: 10,000
Exhibitions: Annual and art student exhibitions
Activities: Classes; lect, one visiting lectr per year; tours; literature

UNIVERSITY OF TEXAS AT AUSTIN

L **Fine Arts Library,** 23rd at Red River, 78712. Tel 512-471-4777. *Fine Arts Librn* Carole Cable; *Art Librn* Joyce Hess
Open Mon - Thurs 8 AM - 11 PM; Fri 8 AM - 5 PM; Sat 10 AM - 5 PM; Sun 2 - 11 PM. Estab 1948 to support teaching and research to the PhD level in art history, and to the master's level in art education and studio art. Circ 140,000
Income: Financed by state appropriation
Library Holdings: Vols 60,000; Per subs 498; Micro — Fiche, reels; AV — V-tapes; Other — Clipping files, exhibition catalogs
M **Archer M Huntington Art Gallery,** College of Fine Arts, 78712. Tel 512-471-7324. *Dir* Dr Eric McCready; *Asst Dir* Dr Forrest McGill; *Chief Cur* Dr Andrea Norris; *Cur of Prints and Drawings* Judith Keller; *Educational Coordr* Susan M Mayer; *Educational Cur* Becky Duval Reese
Open Mon - Sat 9 AM - 5 PM, Sun 1 - 5 PM. No admis fee. Estab 1963 to serve the students and faculty of the university and the general public. Galleries in the art building house temporary exhibitions; galleries in the Harry Ransom Center house the permanent collections. Average Annual Attendance: 125,000. Mem: 650; dues $40 & up
Collections: †Greek and Roman art; †19th & 20th century American paintings, including James and Mari Michener Collection of 20th Century American Art and the C R Smith Collection of Western American Painting; contemporary Australian paintings; †20th century Latin American art; †prints and drawings from all periods
Exhibitions: (1982) Adolph Gottlieb: A Retrospective; 17th Century Dutch Landscape Drawings; Next to Nature: 19th - 20th Century American Landscape Paintings, National Academy of Design; 43rd Annual Art Faculty Exhibition; Collaboration: Artists and Architects; MFA Thesis and Art Student Exhibition; Medieval Art, Metropolitan Museum of Art; Mapped Art, Charts, Routes, Regions; MFA Thesis Show; Medieval Indian Sculpture, Museum of Fine Art, Boston; The Painter and the Printer: Robert Motherwell's Graphics; Art in Our Time: Contemporary Art, HHK Foundation; Prints of the Seventies from the Permanent Collection; (1983) 44th Annual Art Faculty Exhibition; Konrad Cramer, 1917-1963: A Retrospective; Images of Texas; Paul Cret at Texas: Architectural Drawing and the Image of the University in the 1930s; MFA Thesis and Art Student Exhibition; Medieval Art, Metropolitan Museum of Art; Ornamentalism: The New Decorativeness in Architecture and Design; Nuremberg: A Renaissance City, 1500-1618; 45th Annual Art Faculty Exhibition; Latin American Art, University of Texas Collections; Henry Farny, 1847-1916; MFA Thesis Exhibition; (1984) Recent Acquisitions; Netherlandish Art, permanent collection; Dutch Prints of Daily Life; Electronic Arts Intermix: A Video Sampler; MFA Thesis and Art Student Exhibition; Russian Stage Design: Scenic Innovation 1900-1930
Publications: Exhibition catalogues; children's publications
Activities: Classes for adults; project for gifted and talented children; docent training; lect open to public; concerts; gallery talks; tours; exten dept serves Texas and the region; individual paintings and original objects of art are lent to other museums; originate traveling exhibitions to other university art museums and city museums; museum shop sells books, reproductions

BANDERA

M **FRONTIER TIMES MUSEUM,** PO Box 563, 78003. Tel 512-796-3864. *Pres* Mrs D W Hicks; *Cur & Mgr* John V Saul
Open daily 10 - 12 AM, 1 - 4:30 PM; cl Mon. Admis adults $1, children under 10 years $.25 (free when accompanied by teachers). Estab 1933 to preserve records, photographs, and artifacts of the American West with emphasis on the local Texas hill country area. Average Annual Attendance: 10,000. Mem: 17; no dues; meetings 3 times a year
Income: $10,000 (financed by endowment, $5000 from F B Doane Foundation)
Collections: F B Doane Collection of Western Paintings; Louisa Gordon Collection of Antiques, including bells from around the world; J Marvin Hunter Collection of Photographs, Artifacts, Memorabilia of American West and the Texas Hill Country; Photograph Collection; many rare items
Exhibitions: Occasional one-man shows by Texas artists whose work coincides with the theme of the museum
Activities: Book shop

BEAUMONT

M **BEAUMONT ART MUSEUM,** 1111 Ninth St, 77702. Tel 713-832-3432. *Exec Dir* Kay Paris; *Asst to Dir* Georgia Baier; *Registrar & Public Information* Dorothy Jensen; *Cur Education* Chris Steiner; *Asst Cur Education* Meg Birmingham; *Preparator & Bldg Mgr* Kerry Hopper; *Member Secy* Kathy Mitchell; *Museum Secy* Karin Martin; *Admin Asst* Christina Gordon; *Asst Preparator* Ed Byerly
Open Tues 10 AM - 9 PM, Wed - Fri 10 AM - 5 PM, Sat & Sun 2 - 5 PM, cl Mon & holidays. No admis fee. Estab 1950 as a non-profit institution to serve the community- through the visual experience and its interpretation as an instrument for education, cultural enrichment and aesthetic enjoyment. The museum has 2785 sq ft of exhibition space, four galleries. Downstairs areas are devoted to temporary exhibitions which change monthly, and upstairs is devoted to the permanent collection. Average Annual Attendance: 65,000. Mem: 1223; dues $20 - $10,000; annual meeting May
Income: Financed by endowment, membership, city appropriation, Kaleidoscope,

grants, museum shop and contributions
Collections: 20th century American painting, sculpture, graphics and photography
Exhibitions: (1983-84) Jean Despujols: Scenes from Southeast Asia; The Gutenberg Bible; Paul Manes; Watercolors & Drawings by Stanton MacDonald-Wright; Henry Moore: A New Dimension; Flowers of Three Centuries; Graphic Works by Toulouse-Lautrec; Fathers and Daughters of Texas; Beaumont Art Museum Annual Members Exhibition; (1984-85) Annual Members Exhibition Winner: Susan Smith; Wine, Bach and All: 500 Years of Wine in the Arts; Nineteenth Century American Pressed Wine Glasses; Marsden Hartley; Saints & Sinners: Master Drawings from the Crocker; Sam Francis: Paintings on Paper and Monotypes; West Coast Realism; Frank Stella: A Print Retrospective, 1967-1982
Publications: Newsletter, bi-monthly
Activities: Classes for adults and children; docent training; lectures open to public, 9 vis lectr per year; slide lectures, monthly lecture/workshops for 8th grade classes; gallery talks; tours; sponsors competitions with awards; scholarships; individual and original objects of art lent to other institutions; book traveling exhibitions, 10 per year; traveling exhibitions organized and circulated; museum shop sells books, original art and reproductions
L **Library,*** 77702. Tel 713-832-3432. *Library Cur* Julie Redding
Open Tues - Fri 10 AM - 5:30 PM, Sat & Sun 2 - 5 PM. Open to staff and docents for reference only
Library Holdings: Vols 3400; Per subs 27; AV — Slides; Other — Exhibition catalogs
Publications: Bi-monthly newsletter; exhibition catalogs

O **BEAUMONT ARTS COUNCIL,** 3360 Beard St, 77703. Tel 409-892-0336. *Chmn* Jeannette Doiron
Estab 1969 to foster total esthetic involvement in the community and improve communications among cultural organizations
Activities: Sponsored forum for city election candidates to discuss their attitudes toward cultural environment

BROWNSVILLE

M **BROWNSVILLE ART LEAGUE MUSEUM,*** 230 Neale Dr, PO Box 3404, 78520. Tel 512-542-0941. *Dir* Clara Ely; *Librn* Claire Hines
Open Mon - Fri 9 AM - 4 PM, cl Thanksgiving & Christmas. No admis fee. Estab 1936, museum opened 1977 to offer cultural advantages to lower Rio Grande Valley. Permanent collection on rotating basis housed in 90 ft x 14 ft galley; loan exhibitions and members' work in 90 ft x 26 ft gallery. Average Annual Attendance: 1000. Mem: 125; dues $35; meeting first Thurs each month
Collections: Paintings by H A DeYoung, M Enagnit, Augustus John, Dale Nichols, Fredric Taubes, Hauward Veal, James Whistler, N C Wyeth, Milford Zornes
Exhibitions: Arts and Crafts; International Art Show; loaned exhibitions
Publications: Brush Strokes, six per year
Activities: Classes for adults; lectures open to public; tours; International Art Show competition; monetary Best of Show Award; individual paintings lent to local businesses

CANYON

M **PANHANDLE-PLAINS HISTORICAL SOCIETY MUSEUM,** 2401 Fourth Ave, 79015. Tel 806-655-7194. *Dir* B Byron Price; *Asst Dir* James R Pfluger
Open Mon - Sat 9 AM - 5 PM, Sun 2 - 6 PM, cl New Years Day, Thanksgiving, Christmas. No admis fee. Estab 1921 to preserve history of the region, including all phases of history, fine arts and natural sciences. Average Annual Attendance: 125,000. Mem: 1000; dues contributing $500, life $250, annual $10, student $5; annual meeting May
Collections: Over 1300 paintings by early and contemporary American painters
Exhibitions: Exhibitions normally changed monthly
Publications: Panhandle-Plains Historical Review, annually
L **Library,** 2401 Fourth Ave, 79015. *Archivist & Librn* Claire Kuehn
Reference library
Library Holdings: Vols 10,000; Other — Photographs

COLLEGE STATION

M **TEXAS A & M UNIVERSITY,** University Art Exhibits, PO Box 5718, 77844. Tel 713-845-8501. *Dir Art Exhib and Special Asst to the Pres for Development of Cultural Programs* J W Stark; *Coordr University Art Exhib* J R Arredondo Jr; *Registrar Art* J C Hanks
Open 8 AM - 11 PM. No admis fee. Estab 1974 to bring art exhibits of state and national importance to Texas A & M University. Exhibit space is 35 ft x 100 ft by 35 ft in height; exhibits are hung on portable panels. Average Annual Attendance: 29,500
Income: Financed by university funds from bookstore profits and student fees
Collections: Paintings by Texas artists
Exhibitions: (1982) Fransisco Goya: The Disasters of War; A Golden Age of Painting: Dutch Flemish German Paintings of the 16th and 17th Century; The American Vision: Paintings from the C Thomas May Family Collection; (1983) Nine Realities; Matisse: Jazz; Robert Henri and His Influence of American Art; (1984) Alfred Stieglitz: Photographs, Photogravures and Publications; American Abstract Expressionists
Activities: Docent training; lectures open to the public, 2 vis lectr per yr; gallery talks; tours; individual paintings and original objects of art lent to qualified exhibitors and to publishers for use in books or catalogues; lending collection contains 100 books, 35 cassettes, 11 framed reproductions, 15 original prints, 120 paintings & 5 sculptures; book traveling exhibitions, 4 - 6 per yr
O **Memorial Student Center Arts Committee,*** Memorial Student Center, PO Box 5718, 77840. Tel 409-845-5201. *Chmn* Kerri Kernan; *Gallery Chmn* Sheri Williams; *Asst Program Coordr* Bart Block; *Asst Program Coordr* Karen Penny
Open daily 8 AM - 8 PM. No admis fee. Gallery is 35 x 35 ft with movable

hanging partitions and lighting; two exterior walls are glass for partial viewing after hours. Mem: 45; meetings are held each week
Income: Financed by student service fees allotment
Publications: Exhibition borchures; gallery calendar, two per year
Activities: Lect open to public, 10 visiting lectr per year; concerts; gallery talks; competitions; cash awards and honorable mention certificates; book traveling exhibitions 3-4 per year; sells prints

COMMERCE

M **EAST TEXAS STATE UNIVERSITY,** Art Dept Gallery,* 75428. Tel 214-468-2216. *Co-Dir* Barbara Frey; *Co-Dir* Jerry Dodd
Open Mon - Fri 9 AM - 5 PM. No admis fee. Estab 1977 to house all student exhibitions; 9-month exhibition calendar of exchange and traveling shows. Gallery 55 x 69 ft
Income: Financed by state appropriation
Collections: Collection of Student Work
Activities: Lect open to the public, 30 vis lectr per year; gallery talks; tours; competitions; individual paintings and original objects of art lent to regional citizens; traveling exhibitions organized and circulated; sales shop selling original art

CORPUS CHRISTI

M **ART MUSEUM OF SOUTH TEXAS,*** 1902 N Shoreline, 78401. Tel 512-884-3844. *Dir* Ric Collier; *Cur Educ* Donna Hamm; *Admin Asst* Marilyn Smith; *Cur Exhibits* James Edwards
Open Tues - Sat 10 AM - 5 PM; Sun 1 - 5 PM, cl Mon, New Year's, Christmas, Thanksgiving. No admis fee. Estab 1960 as a non-profit organization offering a wide range of programs to the South Texas community in an effort to fulfill its stated purpose to stimulate and encourage the fullest possible understanding and appreciation of the fine arts in all forms. A large central area, the Great Hall, and a small gallery. The sky-lighted Upper Gallery on the second floor level has over 1900 sq ft of space. Average Annual Attendance: 100,000. Mem: 1000; dues $10 - $2500
Income: $466,000 (financed by membership, city and state appropriations, school district)
Collections: Works on Paper (permanent drawing collection); paintings; sculpture; graphics; photographs
Publications: Exhibition catalogs
Activities: Classes for adults and children; dramatic programs; docent training; symposiums; lectures open to public, 9 vis lectr per year; concerts; gallery talks; tours; annual competitions; awards; art festivals; individual paintings and original objects of art lent to museums and exhibiting institutions; book traveling exhibitions, 6 per year; originate traveling exhibitions; sales shop sells books, magazines, reproductions, one-of-a-kind crafts
L **Library,*** 1902 N Shoreline, PO Box 1010, 78403
Open Tues - Fri 10 AM - 5 PM. Estab 1965, to provide reference information for visitors to museum and docent students. For reference only
Income: $2723
Purchases: $2100
Library Holdings: Vols 2100; Per subs 33; AV — A-tapes, slides; Other — Clipping files, exhibition catalogs, reproductions

M **CORPUS CHRISTI STATE UNIVERSITY,** Weil Art Gallery, Center for the Arts, 6300 Ocean Dr, 78412. Tel 512-991-6810, Ext 316. *Coordr* Amy Conger; *Asst Dir* Patricia J Fugitt
Open Mon - Fri 9 AM - 5 PM, cl school holidays. No admis fee. Estab 1979 to provide high quality art exhibitions to the university and the public. Average Annual Attendance: 10,000
Income: Financed by private and state funding
Purchases: Corpus Christi Star, Vernon Fisher
Exhibitions: Mrs John Allen King Collection; Clayworks by Texans; Goya, The Disasters of War; Indiana Print; Suzanne Klotz-Reilly; Southwest Artists Invitational; Permanent Collection of the Art Museum of South Texas; It's On the Bag; Return to Beyond the Valley of Photography; Bruno Andrade; Caras Y Mascaras: Zarco Guerrero; Texas Fine Arts Association; Oso Bay Biennial; Contemporary American Potter: New Vessels; Paul Outerbridge; Creatures in Print; US Mexico Interface: Luis Carlos Bernal; Golden Age of Painting
Publications: Exhibition catalogs
Activities: Classes for adults and children; dramatic programs; docent training; lectures open to the public; gallery talks; tours; scholarships; extension dept serves regional and local communities
M **South Texas Artmobile,*** 6300 Ocean Dr, 78412. *Asst Dir* Nora Rios; *Cur Education* Terri Cummings
Open school hours. No admis fee. Estab 1969 to take original works of art to the people throughout south Texas who would not have the opportunity to see art of this calibre; also where there are no museums available at this time. Average Annual Attendance: 35,000
Income: Financed by James R Dougherty Jr foundation
Publications: Exhibition catalogs; handbook
Activities: Docent training; lectures open to public; tours; originate traveling exhibitions

M **DEL MAR COLLEGE,** Joseph A Cain Memorial Art Gallery, Baldwin at Ayers, 78404. Tel 512-881-6216
Open Mon -Thurs 7:30 AM - 9 PM, Fri 7:30 AM - 4 PM. No admis fee. Estab 1932 to teach art and provide exhibition showcase for college and community. Gallery consists of over 300 running feet space, plus other smaller areas. Average Annual Attendance: 1000
Income: Financed by city and state appropriation
Collections: Purchases from Annual National Drawings and Small Sculpture Show
Activities: Originate traveling exhibitions

M **MUSEUM OF ORIENTAL CULTURES,** 426 S Staples St, 78401. Tel 512-883-1303. *Chmn* James M Goldston; *Educational Dir* Hisako Ochiai; *Gift Shop Mgr* Luclare Robinson
Open Tues - Sat 10 AM - 4 PM, Sun 2 - 5 PM, also by appointment, cl New Years, Easter, Memorial Day, July 4, Labor Day, Thanksgiving and Christmas. Admis adults $1, sr citizens $.75, student $.50, children $.35. Estab 1973. Maintans 500 vol library for research. Mem: Dues patron $500, sustaining $100, supporting $50, family $25, individual $15
Collections: Buddhist decorative arts; oriental & decorative arts including Hakata dolls, porcelains, metal ware, cloisonne and lacquerware; historical and cultural dioramas, architectural models of famous shrines and temples; oriental fan collection
Publications: Monthly newsletter
Activities: Educ dept; lectures; tours; films; culture festivals

DALLAS

M **BIBLICAL ARTS CENTER,** 7500 Park Lane, 75225. Tel 214-691-4661. *Managing Dir* Paul F Scheibe, Jr; *Asst Dir* Thomas J Gleason, Jr; *Registrar & Cur* Kathleen Brooks
Open Tues - Sat 10 AM - 5 PM, Sun 1 - 5 PM, cl New Years Day, Thanksgiving, Christmas Eve and Christmas Day. Admis adults $3.50, sr citizens $3, children 6-12 $1.75. Estab 1966. Mem: Dues patron $100, family $50, individual $25
Collections: Duyckinck's The Naming of John The Baptist; founder's collection of oriental art; Roberto Lupetti's The Rabbi; Miracle at Pentecost painting; Miracle at Pentecost pilot painting; Torger Thompson
Exhibitions: (1982) The Icon: Enduring Images of Sacred Art; (1983) Thomas Upshur: A Modern Vision; (1984) Iron Spirits; Symbols of Faith
Publications: Books, Creation of a Masterpiece; People of The New Testament, Coloring Book
Activities: Educ programs; docent training; tours; competitions with awards; individual paintings & original objects of art lent; museum shop sells books, reproductions, prints, slides

O **DALLAS HISTORICAL SOCIETY,** Hall of State, Fair Park, PO Box 26038, 75226. Tel 214-421-5136. *Dir* John W Crain; *Accountant* Polly Tynes; *Dir Museum Services* Ronnie Roese; *Dir Research & Public Programs* Peggy Riddle; *Dir Libr & Archives* Casey Greene
Open Mon - Sat 9 AM - 5 PM, Sun 1 - 5. No admis fee. Estab 1922 to collect & preserve materials relative to the history of Texas and Dallas. The Hall of State is an example of Art-Deco architecture. Average Annual Attendance: 200,000. Mem: 2000; annual meeting in Apr
Income: Financed by membership and city appropriation
Collections: Texas/Dallas Gallery; Dallas Fashion Gallery
Publications: Dallas Historical Society Report, newsletter bimonthly; Dallas Rediscovered: A Photographic Chronicle of Urban Expansion; When Dallas Became a City: Letters of John Milton McCoy, 1870-1881; A Guide to Fair Park, Dallas
Activities: In-class programs; docent training; summer children's workshops; lectures open to public; tours; awards; individual & original objects of art lent; gift and bookstore

L **Research Center Library,** Hall of State, Fair Park, PO Box 26038, 75226
For reference only
Library Holdings: Vols 14,000; Per subs 25; Archives, pages 2,000,000; Micro — Cards, reels; AV — Cassettes, fs, motion pictures, rec, slides; Other — Clipping files, exhibition catalogs, framed reproductions, memorabilia, original art works, pamphlets, photographs, prints, reproductions, sculpture
Collections: R M Hayes Photographic Collection of Texas Historic Sites; J J Johnson & C E Arnold Photographs of Turn-of-the-Century Dallas; Frank Reaugh Paintings; Allie Tennant Papers; Texas Centennial Papers
Publications: Dallas Historical Society, quarterly

M **DALLAS MUSEUM OF FINE ARTS,** * Fair Park, PO Box 26250, 75226. Tel 214-421-4187. *Dir* Harry S Parker III; *Asst Dir Admin* Thomas A Livesay; *Asst Dir Public Affairs* Carolyn Foxworth; *Asst Dir & Chief Cur* Steven A Nash; *Dir Operations* Larry Francell; *Senior Cur* John Lunsford; *Cur Exhibitions* Barney Delabano; *Assoc Cur Contemporary Art* Sue Graze; *Cur Educ* Dr Anne R Bromberg; *Cur Exhibitions* Anna McFarland; *Public Relations* Robert V Rozelle; *Registrar* Deb Richards
Open Tues - Sat 10 AM - 5 PM; Sun 1 - 5 PM; cl Mon. No admis fee. Estab 1903 to purchase and borrow works of art from all periods for the aesthetic enjoyment and education of the public. Fifteen galleries for permanent collection; five for temporary exhibition. Average Annual Attendance: 350,000. Mem: 4000; dues $20 - $5000; annual meeting May
Income: $2,000,000 (financed by endowment, membership and city appropriation)
Purchases: $1,000,000
Collections: †European and American painting and sculpture; †ancient Mediterranean, Pre-Columbian, African, Oceanic and Japanese art; †decorative arts; †drawings; †prints
Exhibitions: (1982-83) Impressionism And The Modern Vision; Master Paintings from the Phillips Collection; El Greco of Toledo
Publications: Newsletter, bimonthly; annual report; president's newsletter; exhibition catalogs; quarterly bulletin
Activities: Classes for children; docent training; lectures open to public, 10 vis lectr per year; concerts; gallery talks; tours; competitions; films; exten dept serving Dallas County; artmobile; museum shop selling books, magazines, original art, reproductions, prints and slides

L **Library,** * PO Box 26250, 75226. Tel 214-421-4187. *Librn* Donna E Rhein
For reference only
Income: Financed by city and private funds
Library Holdings: Vols 18,000; Per subs 40; Other — Exhibition catalogs
Special Subjects: Pre-Columbian Art, African & Contemporary Art

L **DALLAS PUBLIC LIBRARY,** Fine Arts Division,* 1515 Young St, 75201. Tel 214-749-4100. *Division Head* Jane Holahan; *First Asst* Jon Held; *Art Librn* William R Haddaway; *Music Librn* Jim Calhoun; *Recordings Librn* Donna Mendro; *Theatre Librn* Robert Eason
Open Mon - Fri 9 AM - 9 PM; Sat 9 AM - 6 PM; cl Sun. Estab 1901 to furnish the citizens of Dallas with materials and information concerning the arts
Income: $63,000
Purchases: $63,000
Library Holdings: Vols 52,662; Per subs 500; Micro — Fiche, reels; AV — A-tapes, fs, rec, slides; Other — Clipping files, exhibition catalogs, framed reproductions, manuscripts, memorabilia, original art works, pamphlets, photographs, prints, reproductions
Collections: W E Hill Collection (history of American theater); Lawrence Kelly Collection of Dallas Civic Opera Set and Costume Designs; Manuscript Archives (music); Margo Jones Theater Collection; original fine print collection; John Rosenfield Collection (art and music critic); Interstate Theatre Collection; USA Film Festival Files; Local Archival Material In Film, Dance, Theatre & Music

O **Dallas Print and Drawing Society,** * 1515 Young St, 75201. Tel 214-749-4100. *Pres* Cheryl Westgard; *VPres* Jeannot Barr; *Treas* Barbara Brown
Estab 1935 to study history, techniques and to collect prints and drawings. Mem: 75; annual dues $10; meeting six times per year
Income: Approx $1000 (financed by membership and income from legacy)
Purchases: $250 - $500
Activities: Lect open to the public, 5 - 6 vis lectr per year

M **D-ART, A VISUAL ARTS CENTER FOR DALLAS,** 2917 Swiss Ave, 75204. Tel 214-821-2522. *Pres* Patricia B Meadows; *VPres* Judy Smith Hearst; *Admin Dir* Cheryl Mick; *Program Dir* Patricia B Meadows; *Publicity Dir* Patricia Regan; *Facility Chmn* Norman Kary
Open Mon - Sat 9 AM - 5 PM, Sun 1 - 5 PM, evenings Tues, Wed & Thurs 5 - 9:45 PM. Estab to provide necessary space for artists & art organizations to hold exhibitions, classes, meetings, artist demonstrations & performances. D-Art center is 24,000 sq ft & maintains 3 galleries. Average Annual Attendance: 2000. Mem: 15,000-20,000; dues corporate $1000, sustaining $250, Michelangelo patron $100, patron $50, friend & artists $35
Exhibitions: (1983) Southwestern Watercolor Society Annual Award Show; Marilyn Louis; Betty Leonardo & Sherry Mick; Olivia Pinion Powell & Mary Gandy; Wendi Frahm; Skyline Architecture Cluster, Photography Contest; David Hart Holder; David Herriott; Polaroid National Touring Show, Instants '83; Tyler Mercier; Norman Kary; Rich McNeill; Artists & Craftsmen Assoc; Cheryl Christiansen; Robert Neal Williams; Annual Membership Show; Texas Fine Arts Association Membership Show; Presenting Nine
Publications: D-Art Newsletter, monthly; exhibition programs & catalogues
Activities: Classes for adults; dramatic programs; docent training; lectures open to public, 40 vis lectr per yr; competitions with awards; book traveling exhibitions

SOUTHERN METHODIST UNIVERSITY
M **Meadows Gallery,** 75275. Tel 214-692-2516. *Acting Dir* Irene Martin; *Registrar* Peggy Buchanan
Open Mon - Sat 10 AM - 5 PM; Sun 1 - 5 PM. No admis fee. The exhibitions scheduled in the gallery are primarily for the purpose of study and the committee selects them according to the needs of the classes. A one-room gallery with movable walls used for changing exhibitions. Average Annual Attendance: 10,000
Income: Financed through the University
Exhibitions: (1983-84) Ed Bearden: Landscapes 1944-1978; Laurence Scholder: Prints; Neil Welliver: Paintings; Victor Mira: Spanish Expressionist Painting; Edvard Munch: Prints; BFA & MFA qualifying exhibitions
Publications: Exhibition catalogs
Activities: Lectures open to public; book traveling exhibitions; originate traveling exhibitions

L **Fine Arts Library,** Central University Libraries, 75275. Tel 214-692-2796. *Asst Music & Fine Arts Librn* Kay Krochman-Marks
Open Mon - Thurs 8 AM - 10 PM, Fri 8 AM - 5 PM, Sat 9 AM - 5 PM, Sun 1 - 10 PM. No admis fee. Estab to support educational curriculum of art & art history dept of univ. Open to public for reference and research
Library Holdings: Vols 11,000; Per subs 53; Micro — Fiche, reels; AV — Slides; Other — Exhibition catalogs, pamphlets
Publications: Ars Nova, newsletter, 3 per year

M **Meadows Museum,** 75275. Tel 214-692-2727 . *Cur of Education* Nancy Berry
Open Mon - Sat 10 AM - 5 PM; Sun 1 - 5 PM. No admis fee. Estab 1965 to preserve and study the art of Spain. Average Annual Attendance: 44,000
Income: Financed by endowment
Collections: Spanish Paintings from Late Gothic to Modern including works by Juan de Borgona, Velazquez, Murillo, Zurbaran, Ribera, Goya, Miro, Juan Gris, and Picasso
Exhibitions: (1982) Goya and the Art of His Time
Activities: Classes for children; docent training; outreach program; lect open to public; concerts; tours; scholarships; individual paintings and original objects of art lent to other museums and galleries in US and Europe for scholarly exhibitions; traveling exhibitions organized and circulated; Sales shop sells slides and catalogs
—**Meadows Collection Fine Arts Library,** 75275
Open for reference to scholars
Library Holdings: Vols 1300; Per subs 10; Micro — Fiche, reels; AV — Slides; Other — Exhibition catalogs, pamphlets
Special Subjects: Spanish art

DENTON

M **NORTH TEXAS STATE UNIVERSITY,** Art Gallery, Mulberry and Ave A, North Texas Box 5098, 76203. Tel 817-565-4005. *Gallery Dir* C Kenneth Havis
Open Mon - Fri Noon - 5 PM, Sat 10 AM - 3 PM. No admis fee. Estab 1960 as a teaching gallery directed to students of North Texas State University and the Denton community. The gallery covers 193 running ft of exhibition wall space, approximately 10 ft high, which may be divided into smaller spaces by the use of semi-permanent portable walls; the floor is carpeted-terrazzo. Average Annual Attendance: 10,000

Income: Financed by state appropriation
Collections: †Fashion collection; †Voertman Collection (student purchases); †permanent collection; †permanent student collection
Publications: Exhibition announcements
Activities: Lect open to the public, 4-8 vis lectr per year; tours; competitions; individual paintings and original objects of art lent to the university offices; originate traveling exhibitions to other univs & museums
L **Art Slide Library,** Art Department, 76203. Tel 817-788-2855. *Slide Librn* Karen Olvera
Open during school term Mon - Fri 7:45 AM - 9 PM. Estab to provide art slides for instruction. For reference only
Income: Financed by state taxes
Purchases: $6000
Library Holdings: AV — Cassettes, fs, lantern slides, motion pictures 60, slides 90,000, v-tapes 10
Collections: Female artists; architectural subject index for buildings
L **Willis Library, Humanities Division,** 76203. Tel 817-788-2411, Ext 211.
Humanities Librn Johnnye Louise Cope; *Asst Humanities Librn* Harry A Butler
Open Mon - Thurs 8 AM - 12 PM; Fri 8 AM - 6 PM; Sat 10 AM - 6 PM; Sun 2 - 10 PM. Estab 1903 to support the academic programs and faculty and student research
Library Holdings: Vols 46,800; Per subs 151; AV — Fs, motion pictures, slides; Other — Exhibition catalogs
Special Subjects: Art Education, Interior Design, Renaissance - 20th century art, advertising, museum catalogs
Collections: †Artists and Exhibitions File (for local artists); †Interior Design Product File

M **TEXAS WOMAN'S UNIVERSITY ART GALLERY,** TWU Station, Box 22995, 76204. Tel 817-382-8923. *Dir* Mark S Smith
Open Mon - Fri 8 AM - 5 PM, Sat & Sun upon request. No admis fee. Administration Conference Tower Building maintains 2000 sq ft of exhibition area; Fine Arts Building consists of two galleries, each consisting of 3000 sq ft. Average Annual Attendance: 4000
Income: Financed by Art Department and student activities fees
Exhibitions: A C T Building Gallery has approx nine exhibits per school year; departmental galleries have approx twelve exhibits per school year
Activities: Concerts; gallery talks; tours; competitions with awards; scholarships

EL PASO

M **EL PASO MUSEUM OF ART,** 1211 Montana, 79902. Tel 915-543-3800, 541-4043. *Dir* Leonard P Sipiora; *Cur Educ* Patricia Davenport; *Cur History* Barbara Ardus; *Cur Coll* William Rakocy; *Asst Cur Coll* Loretta Martin; *Cur Science* Alex Apostolides; *Asst Cur Educ* Don Hoover
Open Tues - Sat 10 AM - 5 PM, Sun 1 - 5 PM, cl Mon & national holidays. No admis fee. Estab 1960 as a cultural and educational institution. One gallery houses a permanent display of the Kress Collection; second gallery is used for monthly changing exhibits; Heritage Gallery has decorative arts from 18th, 19th and 20th centuries. Average Annual Attendance: 80,000. Mem: 1036; dues $10 - $10,000; meetings Jan, Mar, Apr, Sept, Nov
Income: Financed by membership and city appropriation
Collections: 19th - 20th century American art; Kress Collection; Mexican Colonial paintings and sculpure; decorative arts of the 18th, 19th & 20th centuries; graphics
Publications: Artline (newsletter), quarterly
Activities: Classes for adults and children; dramatic programs; docent training; lectures open to the public, 12 vis lectrs per year; concerts; gallery talks; tours; competitions; individual paintings and original objects of art lent to other museums on request; book traveling exhibitions, 16 per yr; museum shop sells books, magazines, original art, reproductions & prints
L **Library,** 1211 Montana, 79902
Open to the public and members for reference only
Library Holdings: Vols 500; Per subs 18
M **Wilderness Park Museum,*** 2000 Transmountain Rd, 79924. Tel 915-755-4332
Estab 1977. Museum contains replica of Olla Cave and Mogollon cliff dwelling. Average Annual Attendance: 33,000
Collections: Five dioramas depict life styles and climate changes of Paleo Indians including the hunting and gathering era and the Hueco Tanks site
Exhibitions: (1981) The Masks of May; Messages From Yesterday; Rock Art Exhibit
Activities: Lectures open to public; sales shop sells books, original art, reproductions and prints

M **UNIVERSITY OF TEXAS AT EL PASO,** Department of Art Galleries, 79968. Tel 915-747-5181. *Dept Chmn* Charles Fensch
Department Studios and Galleries open Mon - Fri 8 AM - 5 PM. No admis fee. University established 1916, Department of Art established 1940. Main gallery features professional shows & glass gallery features student work. Average Annual Attendance: 3000-5000
Income: Financed by city and state appropriation
Collections: Small collection of prints from old and modern Masters; †Collection of student works
Publications: Exhibition catalogs
Activities: Classes for adults and children; lectures open to the public, 2-4 gallery talks per year; tours; competitions; extension work offered through university extension service to anyone over high school age; fees vary

FORT WORTH

M **AMON CARTER MUSEUM,** 3501 Camp Bowie Blvd, PO Box 2365, 76113. Tel 817-738-1933. *Pres* Ruth Carter Stevenson; *Dir* Jan Keene Muhlert; *Asst Dir Publ & History* Ron Tyler; *Cur Paintings* Carol Clark; *Cur Photographic Coll* Martha Sandweiss; *Registrar* Anne Adams; *Dir Special Programs* William Howze; *Business Manager* Glynatta Richie; *Public Affairs Coordr* Irvin Lippman
Open Tues - Sat 10 AM - 5 PM; Sun & holidays 1 - 5:30 PM; cl Mon. No admis

fee. Estab 1961 for the study and documentation of westering North America through permanent collections, exhibitions and publications. Main gallery plus ten smaller galleries. Average Annual Attendance: 150,000
Income: Financed by endowment
Collections: †American paintings and sculpture; †print collection; †photographs
Exhibitions: Amon Carter Museum; Carleton Watkins (photographs); Charles Wilson Peak 1741-1827; Important Information Inside: The Still-Life Paintings of John F Peto; Whistler to Wood: Prints from the Amon Carter Museum Collection; The Lane Collection: 20th Century Paintings in the American Tradition; Karl Bodmer: Views of a Vanishing Frontier
Publications: Calendar of Events, quarterly
Activities: Classes for adults; docent training; produces films and TV cassettes; lect open to public, 15 vis lectrr per year; gallery talks; tours; works of art lent to museums; traveling exhibitions organized and circulated; museum shop selling books, magazines, reproductions, prints and slides

M **FORT WORTH ART MUSEUM,** 1309 Montgomery, 76107. Tel 817-738-9215. *Dir* David Ryan; *Business Mgr* James Corser; *Ed & Coordr Public Information* Rosalind de Rolon; *Cur Education* Suzanne Levy; *Membership Coordr* Suzi Atkins; *Registrar* James Fisher
Open Tues 10 AM - 9 PM; Wed - Sat 10 AM - 5 PM; Sun 1 - 5 PM. No admis fee. Estab 1901 as a museum of 20th century art. Five large galleries on the main floor. Average Annual Attendance: 80,000. Mem: 800; dues $1000, $100, $25
Income: Financed by membership, city appropriations, grants and private donations
Collections: 20th Century Paintings, Sculpture, Drawings and Prints
Publications: Bi-monthly calendar
Activities: Classes for adults and children; docent training; lectures open to the public; traveling exhibitions organized and circulated
L **Library,*** 1309 Montgomery, 76107
Estab 1971 as a reference library for museum staff
Income: $4348 (trust)
Purchases: $4348
Library Holdings: Vols 5000; Per subs 35; Other — Clipping files, exhibition catalogs, pamphlets, photographs
Special Subjects: 20th Century Art

C **THE FORT WORTH NATIONAL BANK,** * 500 Throckmorton St, PO Box 2050, 76101. Tel 817-338-8011. *VPres* Archie L Nance
Estab 1974 to enhance the public areas of bank lobby and building; to provide art for offices of individual bank officers. Collection displayed throughout bank building, offices and public space
Collections: Alexander Calder sculpture; more than 400 pieces of drawings, graphics, paintings, prints, sculpture and tapestries, focusing on art of the Southwest, including artists throughout the nation and abroad
Activities: Tours for special groups only; sponsor two art shows annually; provide cash prizes; scholarships

L **FORT WORTH PUBLIC LIBRARY,** Fine Arts Section, 300 Taylor St, 76102. Tel 817-870-7739. *Arts Unit Mgr* Heather Goebel; *Asst* Thomas K Threatt; *Librn* Shakuntala Gokhale
Open Mon - Thurs 9 AM - 9 PM, Fri & Sat 10 AM - 6 PM, cl Sun. No admis fee. Estab 1902. Not a commercial gallery, but exhibit areas for framed and matted reproductions of paintings
Income: Financed by appropriation
Library Holdings: Books, sheet music, music scores, tune cards, framed and matted reproductions of paintings, special files of clipped pictures, articles, pamphlets and programs; AV — A-tapes, cassettes, fs, motion pictures, rec, slides, v-tapes; Other — Clipping files, memorabilia, pamphlets, photographs, reproductions
Collections: Hal Coffman Collection of original cartoon art; Nancy Taylor Collection of bookplate; historic picture and photograph collection autographed by various celebrities; rare books
Exhibitions: Antiques, crafts, framed and matted reproductions of paintings, prints, original photographs and original works, annual original kite exhibition in March
Publications: Bibliographies; catalogs; monthly Focus

M **KIMBELL ART MUSEUM,** 3333 Camp Bowie Blvd, PO Box 9440, 76107. Tel 817-332-8451. *Pres* Kay Fortson; *Dir* Dr Edmund P Pillsbury; *Deputy Dir* Dr William Jordan; *Asst Dir Academic Programs & Servs & Cur Asian Art* Emily Sano; *Cur Education* Marilyn Ingram; *Assoc Cur European Art* Michael Mezzatesta; *Business Mgr* Barbara White; *Public Relations Dir* Ruth Ann Rugg; *Research Cur* Ruth Sullivan; *Registrar* Foster Clayton; *Conservator* Perry Huston; *Librn* Erika Esau
Open Tues - Sat 10 AM - 5 PM, Sun 1 - 5 PM, cl Mon, July 4, Thanksgiving, Christmas and New Year's. No admis fee. Open to public 1972 for the collection, preservation, research, publication and public exhibition of art of all periods. Average Annual Attendance: 200,000
Income: Financed by endowment
Collections: Highly selective collection of European paintings, sculpture and graphic arts from ancient to early 20th century; African sculpture; Asian sculpture, painting and ceramics; Pre-columbian sculpture and ceramics
Exhibitions: (1982) The Great Age of Japanese Buddhist Sculpture, AD 600-1300; Mauritshuis: Dutch Painting of the Golden Age; The Paintings of Jusepe de Ribera; Elisabeth Louise Vigee Lebrun; Jean-Baptiste Oudry; The Art of Gian Lorenzo Bernini: Selected Sculpture; Faberge: The Forbes Collection; Wealth of the Ancient World: The Hunt Collection
Publications: Catalogue of the Collection; Light is the Theme: Louis I Kahn and the Kimbell Art Museum; Louis I Kahn: Sketches for the Kimbell Art Museum; Handbook of the Collection; exhibition catalogs
Activities: Classes for children; docent training; lect open to public, 20-25 visiting lectr per year; concerts; gallery talks; tours; film series; book traveling exhibitions; originates traveling exhibitions; museum shop sells books, magazines and slides

L   Library, Will Rogers Rd W, PO Box 9440, 76107. *Librn* Ilse S Rothrock
Open Tues - Fri 10 AM - 5 PM by appointment. Estab 1967 to support museum staff, docents and research in area. For reference use of curatorial staff
Purchases: $65,000
Library Holdings: Vols 25,000; Per subs 135; Micro — Cards, fiche, reels; AV — Motion pictures, slides, v-tapes; Other — Exhibition catalogs, original art works

M   SID W RICHARDSON FOUNDATION, Collection of Western Art, 309 Main St, 76102. Tel 817-332-6554. *Dir* Jan Fraser
Open Tues - Fri 10 AM - 5 PM, Sat 11 AM - 6 PM, Sun 1 - 5 PM. No admis fee. Estab 1982 to enable downtown visitors & workers to view the paintings in a metropolitan setting. Average Annual Attendance: 36,000
Collections: 52 original paintings by Frederic Remington & Charles M Russell
Activities: Sales shop sells books, prints, postcards, note cards & posters

M   TEXAS CHRISTIAN UNIVERSITY, Student Center Gallery,* Brown-Lupton Student Center, PO Box 292-80A, 76129. Tel 817-921-7928. *Dir* Pat Crowley
Open Mon - Fri 10 AM - 4 PM, Sat & Sun Noon - 4 PM. No admis. Estab to present the best art possible to the student body; to show faculty and student work. Gallery consists of one large room, 30 x 40 ft, with additional moveable panels. Average Annual Attendance: 10,000
Income: Financed by college funds
Exhibitions: Art of the Spirit: The Search for Spiritual Signifcance Made Visual; John Majerowicz: Chairs; Juried Student Exhibition; MFA Thesis Exhibition: Jan Pierce; Don Ivan Punchatz: Commercial Artist Par Excellence; Senior Exhibition; TCU Faculty Exhibition; University of Dallas Sixth National Invitational Print Exhibition
Publications: Exhibition notes, mailers and posters
Activities: Classes for adults; lect open to the public, 15 vis lectr per year; gallery talks; competitions

GAINESVILLE

L   COOKE COUNTY COLLEGE LIBRARY, Art Dept,* Highway 51, PO Box 240, 76240. Tel 817-668-7731. *Dir Library Services* Patsy Wilson
Open Mon - Thur 8 AM - 9:30 PM, Fri 8 AM - 4:30 PM, Sun 2 - 5 PM. Estab 1924 to serve the needs of the administration, faculty and students. Circ 500
Purchases: $1500
Library Holdings: Vols 1800; Per subs 10; Micro — Cards, fiche; AV — A-tapes, cassettes, fs, Kodachromes, lantern slides, motion pictures, rec, slides, v-tapes; Other — Clipping files, pamphlets, prints, reproductions

GALVESTON

L   ROSENBERG LIBRARY, 2310 Sealy, 77550. Tel 409-763-8854. *Librn* John D Hyatt; *Cur Special Coll* Jane Kenamore; *Rare Books Librn* Van Ferguson; *Museum Cur* Lise Darst
Open Mon - Sat 9 AM - 5 PM; cl Sun and national holidays. No admis fee. Estab 1900 to provide library services to the people of Galveston, together with lectures, concerts, exhibitions. Library includes the Harris Art Gallery, The James M Lykes Maritime Gallery, The Hutchings Gallery, together with miscellaneous art and historical exhibit galleries and halls. Mem: 820; dues $5 - $100
Income: $1,107,289 (financed by endowment, city and state appropriation)
Purchases: $125,778
Collections: †Contemporary American graphics; †historical artifacts relating to Texas, 15th century to present; Lalique crystal; 19th century American and European paintings and sculptures; 19th century Japanese art; photographic reference collection; †maritime history, maps & charts; incunabula; †Russian icons, 15th - 20th centuries
Exhibitions: Approx 18 per year; numerous one-man shows
Activities: Classes for adults and children; lect; gallery talks; concerts; dramatic programs; exten dept serves Galveston County; material available to individuals and organizations; original objects of art lent; lending collection contains 7071 photographs, 18,527 color reproductions, 708 motion pictures, 311 film strips, 615 framed pictures, 10 sculptures; 3600 items lent in average year; originate traveling exhibitions

HOUSTON

O   ART LEAGUE OF HOUSTON,* 1953 Montrose Blvd, 77006. Tel 713-523-9530. *Pres* Mrs Allen Gibson; *VPres* William Davis; *Secy* Barbara Minter; *Coordr* Ginger Taylor
Open Tues - Fri 10 AM - 4 PM; Sat Noon - 4 PM. No admis fee. Estab 1948 to promote public interest in art and the achievements of Houston area artists. Gallery maintained for monthly exhibits. Average Annual Attendance: 10,000 - 15,000. Mem: 750; annual dues $10 - $1000; annual meeting May
Income: $50,000 (financed by membership and fund-raising functions)
Exhibitions: Dimension Houston; Membership Exhibits; Student Exhibits
Publications: Newsletter, monthly; year book and membership roster, annually; exhibition catalogs
Activities: Classes for adults; lectures open to the public, 6 vis lectr per year; competitions with prizes; workshops

M   CONTEMPORARY ARTS MUSEUM,* 5216 Montrose, 77006. Tel 713-526-3129. *Dir* Linda L Cathcart; *Cur* Marty Mayo; *Development & Membership Officer* Pamela A Riddle; *Registrar* Jean Story; *Coordr Special Projects* Sally Gall
Open Tues - Sat 10 AM - 5 PM; Sun Noon - 6 PM; cl Mon, New Year's Day, July 4, Thanksgiving, Christmas. Estab 1948 to promote a better understanding of contemporary art. The 15,000 sq ft building was designed by Detroit architect Gunnar Birkerts; the parallelogram shaped structure consists of two floors. The upper level houses a 3000 sq ft gallery with a ceiling height of 20 ft. The lower level houses shipping and receiving, research library, multipurpose room, staff offices and storage. Average Annual Attendance: 90,000. Mem: 2000; dues $15 -

$1000; annual meeting May
Income: $650,000
Collections: Damaged in the 1976 flood. †New collection of contemporary paintings, sculpture and constructions
Exhibitions: Contemporary Art in Painting, Sculpture, Drawing, Video, Dance, Theater, Poetry and Music, with an emphasis on Texas artists
Publications: Exhibition catalogs; tri-monthly calendar; annual report
Activities: Wide ranging educational program including the prototypical Art After School, a program of art classes in selected elementary schools; docent programs; special events; lectures open to public; tours; gallery talks; films; originate traveling exhibitions; sales shop sells books, magazines, original art, reproductions, prints

M   HOUSTON BAPTIST UNIVERSITY, Museum of American Architecture and Decorative Arts,* 7502 Fondren Rd, 77074. Tel 713-774-7661. *Supvr* Dr E V Tapscott
Open Tues - Thurs 10 AM - 4 PM and by appointment, cl Easter, first three weeks in August, Christmas vacation. No admis fee. Estab 1964. Small reference library maintained
Collections: African art; dolls; furniture and decorative arts; pre-Columbian art; toys
Activities: Lectures; tours; films

L   HOUSTON PUBLIC LIBRARY, Fine Arts and Recreation Department, 500 McKinney, 77002. Tel 713-224-5441, Ext 336, 337, 338. *Head, Fine Arts & Recreation* John Harvath Jr; *First Asst* Gloria Selene Hinojosa
Open Mon - Fri 9 AM - 9 PM, Sat 9 AM - 6 PM, Sun 2 - 6 PM. Estab 1848 as a private library for the Houston Lyceum and opened to the public in 1895. Monthly exhibits, including art shows are spread throughout the Central Library Building. Circ 70,000
Income: Financed by endowment, city appropriation, federal and state aid (LSA & LSCA), Friends of the Library
Purchases: $175,000
Library Holdings: Vols 98,074; Per subs 380; exhibition posters, portrait file, sheet music collection, auction catalogs; Micro — Fiche, reels; AV — A-tapes, cassettes, fs, Kodachromes, rec, slides; Other — Clipping files, exhibition catalogs, framed reproductions, pamphlets, reproductions, sculpture
Special Subjects: Decorative Arts, Oriental Art
Activities: Lect open to public; tours

M   MUSEUM OF FINE ARTS, HOUSTON, 1001 Bissonnet, PO Box 6826, 77005. Tel 713-526-1361; Telex 77-5232; Cable MUFA HOU. *Dir* Peter C Marzio; *Chmn Board* Isaac Arnold Jr; *Assoc Dir* Board Warren; *Asst Dir Administration & Assoc Cur* Katherine Howe; *Cur Oriental Art* Celeste Adams; *Cur of Photography* Anne Tucker; *Assoc Cur* Michael Brown; *Registrar* Edward B Mayo
Open Tues - Sat 10 AM - 5 PM, Thurs evening until 9 PM, Sun 1 - 6 PM. No admis fee. Estab 1924 as an art museum containing works from prehistoric times to the present. Exhibition space totals 75,000 sq ft. Average Annual Attendance: 375,000. Mem: 10,000; dues $35; annual meeting May
Collections: †African, Oceanic, Pre-Columbian and American Indian art objects; †American and European graphics, paintings & sculpture; †European and American decorative arts including Bayou Bend Collection of American Decorative Arts; major collection of Impressionist and Post-Impressionist paintings; †Medieval and Early Christian work; †Oriental art; †Western Americana; †antiquities; †photography
Exhibitions: (1983) A Century of Modern Sculpture: 1882-1982; Poussin & the Classical Ideal; Ansel Adams; The Pennsylvania Germans: A Celebration of Their Arts 1683-1850; Heart Mountains & Human Ways: Japanese Landscape & Figure Painting; Paris, Rome, Athens: Explorations of Antiquity by French Architects After 19th & 20th Centuries; Lee Krasnel: A Retrospective; Eugene Atget: The Ancient Regime; Paul Strand, photographs Early Chinese Art: Selections from the Asia House Rockefeller Collection; Honore Daumier Prints from the Collection; Frederick Sommer at 75: A Retrospective; The Diaghilev Heritage; Ethiopia: The Christian Art of an African
Publications: Bulletin, quarterly; calendar of events, bimonthly; catalogs of exhibitions
Activities: Classes for adults & children; docent training; lectures open to public, 25 vis lectr per yr; concerts; gallery talks; tours; individual paintings & original objects of art lent to other art institutions; originate traveling exhibitions; museum shop sells books, magazines, prints & slides

L   Hirsch Library, 1001 Bissonnet, PO Box 6826, 77005. Tel 713-526-1361. *Librn* Linda N Shearouse
Open Tues - Sat 10 AM - 5 PM, Sun 1 - 6 PM. For reference only
Library Holdings: Vols 15,000; Per subs 75; Other — Clipping files, exhibition catalogs
Special Subjects: Art History, Photography

M   RICE UNIVERSITY, Institute for the Arts, Rice Museum,* University at Stockton Sts, PO Box 1892, 77251. Tel 713-522-0886. *Dir* Mrs John de Menil; *Exec Adminr* Harris Rosenstein; *Production Mgr* Jesse Lopez; *Registrar* Linda Goldstein; *Publicist* Paula Webb
Open Tues - Sat 10 AM - 5 PM, Sun Noon - 6 PM. No admis fee. Estab to organize and present art exhibitions. Average Annual Attendance: 38,000
Exhibitions: (1982) Yves Klein (1928-1962): A Retrospective; William Christenberry: Southern Views; (1983) Recent Acquisitions; Black Folk Art in America; Tibet; The Sacred Realm
Publications: Exhibition catalogues
Activities: Lectures open to public; originate traveling exhibitions; museum shop sells books and exhibition posters

L   Art Library, Fondren Library, PO Box 1892, 77001. Tel 713-527-4832, 527-4800. *Art Librn* Jet M Prendeville
Open Mon - Thurs 1 - 5 PM and 7 - 10 PM, Fri 1 - 5 PM, Sat 2 - 5 PM, Sun 2 - 5 PM and 7 - 10 PM. Estab 1964
Income: $13,000 (financed by Rice Univ)
Library Holdings: Vols 36,981; Per subs 427; Other — Exhibition catalogs 6000
Special Subjects: Art History, Film, Photography

M **Sewall Art Gallery,** 6100 S Main (Mailing add: PO Box 1892, 77005). Tel 713-527-8101. *Dir* Esther DeVecsey
Open Mon - Sat Noon - 5 PM. No admin fee. Estab 1981 as an extension of the teaching activities in the dept of art & art history. Gallery is an activity of the dept of Fine Arts, directed by a member of the faculty. Average Annual Attendance: 15,000
Income: $4400 (financed by Rice University)
Collections: Pre Columbian, prints, photos
Exhibitions: Bracquemond & the Ething Process; Houston Corporations; Emerging Texas Photographers; Leonardo da Vinci: Return to Vinci; Selections from the Menil Collection
Publications: Catalogs
Activities: Classes for adults; lectures open to public, 2 vis lectr per yr; gallery talks; tours; lending to offices of Rice University, original art works, original prints, paintings, photographs; book traveling exhibitions annually; originate traveling exhibitions to university & museums

O **SOUTHWEST ARTS FOUNDATION,** 9 Greenway Plaza, Suite 2002, PO Box 13037, 77019. Tel 713-961-7794. *Pres* W E Freckleton; *VPres* Gary Libby; *Secy* Dolores A Jansa; *2nd VPres* John K Sloan; *Treas* John F Moore; *Asst to Pres* Coma N Richardson; *Assoc Dir* Tony Falcone
Open 9 AM - 5 PM for exhibition. Estab 1980 to preserve the arts of the American West, to promote them for study and to present them to a national audience. Mem: 641, dues $10
Income: $1,000,000 (financed by endowment and members)
Collections: Art indigenous to the American West, basketry, paintings, pottery, sculpture
Exhibitions: Art of the American West
Activities: Docent training, administrative internship program in conjunction with Houston High School for the Preforming and Visual Arts; lectures open to public, gallery talks; scholarships; paintings and art objects available on loan to public institutions that conform with goals & philosophies of Southwest Arts Foundation; originate traveling exhibitions in all cities in the 17 states comprising the American West

C **TRANSCO ENERGY COMPANY INC,** 2800 S Post Oak Rd, PO Box 1396, 77001. Tel 713-439-2000. *Admin VPres* W H Cook; *Cur* Martha Terrill
Open to public by appointment only. Estab 1974 to enhance atmosphere for employees. Transco gallery to open mid 1984. Collection displayed within office spaces and hallways; annual amount of art contributions and grants $50,000; supports Museum of Fine Arts, Houston Ballet, Houston Symphony, Grand Opera, Business Committee for the Arts, Public Library, Public Television, Combined Arts Corporation Campaign, Houston Business Committee For The Arts and various Houston Cultural Arts Council projects
Collections: †1100 original works, mostly on paper by living contemporary artists; †American master watercolors including artists: Homer, Sargent, LaFarge, Demuth, Borchfield, Wyeth & Bricher
Exhibitions: Employee's Annual Juried Competition
Publications: Catalog of American Master Watercolors
Activities: Competitions with awards; Loans of original prints, drawings and watercolors to non-profit institutions for exhibition purposes may be arranged

M **UNIVERSITY OF HOUSTON,** Sarah Campbell Blaffer Gallery,* Entrance 5 off Cullen Blvd, 4800 Calhoun, 77004. Tel 713-749-1329. *Dir* William A Robinson; *Asst Dir* Toni Beauchamp; *Exhib Coordr* William Frazier; *Registrar* Nancy S Hixon
Open Tues - Sat 10 AM - 6 PM; Sun 1 - 6 PM; cl Mon, major holidays, Aug, and between exhibitions. Estab 1973 to present a broad spectrum of visual arts, utilizing the interdisciplinary framework of the University, to the academic community and to the rapidly increasing diverse population of greater Houston. Main gallery is 5000 sq ft, ceiling height varies from 10-25 ft; Mezzanine gallery is 1500 sq ft. Average Annual Attendance: 22,000
Income: Financed by state appropriation, university, local funds, grants, gifts
Collections: Charles & Katherine Blaffer Pre-Columbian Collections; Freda and Clara Radoff Mexican Print Collection; †Print Study Collection; Roy Hofheinz Tapestry Collection
Exhibitions: Pierre Alechinsky: A Print Retrospective; Ancient Roots - New Visions; Beyond the Box: Architecture of Philip Johnson and John Burgee Photographed by Richard Payne; Houston Area Juried Exhibition; Frida Kahlo; Texas Crafts; Vienna Moderne: 1898-1918; Way West: Artist-Explorers of the Frontier; American Fiber Art; A New Definition
Publications: Exhibition catalogues
Activities: Lect open to public; concerts; gallery talks; tours; competitions; originate traveling exhibitions; sales shop selling books
L **Franzheim Architecture Library,** Houston, TX 77004. Tel 713-749-1193. *Librn* Margaret Culbertson; *Asst* Lynn Sterba
Open Mon - Thurs 8 AM - 8 PM, Fri 8 AM - 5 PM, Sat 1 - 5 PM. Reference
Income: Financed by state appropriation
Library Holdings: Vols 14,000; Per subs 106; Micro — Fiche, reels; Other — Pamphlets
Special Subjects: Architecture

INGRAM

O **HILL COUNTRY ARTS FOUNDATION,** Hwy 39, PO Box 176, 78025. Tel 512-367-5121. *Pres* Arney M Davis; *VPres* Sally Ritch; *Secy* Kathy Benbow; *Treasurer* Justa Walsh; *Art Dir* Jeanne Bowman; *Theatre Dir* Larry Seymour; *Business Mgr* Lane Tait
Open 10 AM - 5 PM. No admis fee except for special events. Estab 1959 to provide a place for creative activities in the area of visual arts and performing arts; and to provide classes in arts, crafts and drama. Art Gallery maintains small reference library. Average Annual Attendance: 30,000. Mem: 850; annual meeting second Sat Sept
Income: Financed by endowment, membership, benefit activities and donations
Exhibitions: Annual craft exhibit; juried art exhibit; photography-graphics exhibit; young artists exhibit; art festival
Publications: Spotlight, quarterly newsletter
Activities: Classes for adults & children; competitions with awards; scholarships; sales shop sell original art & original crafts

KERRVILLE

M **COWBOY ARTISTS OF AMERICA MUSEUM,** 1550 Bandera Highway, PO Box 78028, 78028. Tel 512-896-2553. *Dir* Griffiths C Carnes
Open Tues - Sat 9 AM - 5 PM, Sun 1 - 5 PM, open Mon during summer. Admis adults $2, children 6 - 12 $.50. Estab 1983 to display contemporary art of American West. Average Annual Attendance: 30,000. Mem: 700; dues $25 - $10,000
Income: Financed by donations, membership
Collections: Western American Realism Art
Exhibitions: Visions of Cowboy Artists of America - 110 pieces of art by the 29 members of the Association
Publications: Visions West: History of the Cowboy Artists Museum, newsletter, quarterly
Activities: Classes for adults and children; docent programs; lectures
L **Library,** Kerrville, TX 78028. *Librn* Mary Meyers
Reference
Library Holdings: Other — Clipping files, exhibition catalogs, framed reproductions, manuscripts, memorabilia, original art works, pamphlets, photographs, prints
Special Subjects: Western Art, History of Range Cattle Industry

KINGSVILLE

M **TEXAS A AND I UNIVERSITY,** Art Gallery, Art Department, Santa Gertrudis, 78363. Tel 512-595-2619. *Dir* Dr Richard Scherpereel
Open 8 AM - Noon & 1 - 5 PM. No admis fee. Estab to exhibit art work of students, as well as visitors. Average Annual Attendance: 3000
Income: Financed by state appropriations

LONGVIEW

M **LONGVIEW MUSEUM AND ARTS CENTER,** 102 W College, Box 562, 75606. Tel 214-753-8103. *Dir* Joan Nachbaur Rathbun; *Secy* Dianna Zerban
Open Mon - Fri 9 AM - 5 PM; Sun 1 - 3 PM. No admis fee. Estab 1970 for the encouragement of art through a program of exhibition of professional quality work, education & participation of all interested persons. East Gallery 40 x 60 ft, overhead lights; West Gallery smaller but similar; galleries between are rooms that were once a private home, plus two class rooms. Average Annual Attendance: 12,000 - 15,000. Mem: 500; dues patron $500, sponsor $200, contributing $100, family $40; Board of Trustees monthly meetings
Income: Financed by membership and guild projects
Purchases: Contemporary Southwestern artists work
Collections: †Regional Artists Collection formed by purchases from Annual Invitational Exhibitions over the past 20 years
Publications: Exhibition catalogs
Activities: Classes for adults and children; docent training; day at museum with artist in residence for all 4th grade students; graduate course, Art for Elementary Teachers, offered by Univ of Texas-Tyler extension department; lectures open to the public, 6 vis lectr per year; talks; tours; competitions with cash awards; individual paintings and original objects of art lent; lending collection contains books, cassettes, film strips; book traveling exhibitions; originate traveling exhibitions
L **Library,** 102 W College, Box 562, 75606. Tel 214-753-8103
Open Mon - Fri 9 AM - 5 PM; Sun 1 - 3 PM, cl holidays. Estab 1970 for the enjoyment of members and public
Income: Financed by membership, guild fundraising, local & state grants
Library Holdings: Vols 300
Collections: Photography Collection
Activities: Films and slide shows when available with exhibition

LUBBOCK

O **LUBBOCK ART ASSOCIATION, INC,** Municipal Garden & Art Center, 4215 University Ave, 79413. Tel 806-762-6411, Ext 2724. *Pres* Carol Meek; *VPres* Myrtle Rochelle; *Secy* Caroline Day; *Treas* Ray Lawerence
Open Mon - Fri 9 AM - 5 PM, Sat & Sun 1 - 5 PM. No admis fee. Estab 1951 to promote art in Lubbock-South Plains. Located in beautiful Municipal Garden & Art Center near arboretum and is 54 x 64 ft. Average Annual Attendance: 100,000. Mem: 435; dues $8; meeting first Tues every month
Income: Financed by membership
Collections: Regional and nationally known artists; works representing professional quality in graphics, painting, sculpture and crafts
Exhibitions: Membership show, permanent collection, special one and three-person exhibitions, state level invitationals
Publications: Quarterly newsletter
Activities: Workshops for adults; lectures open to public, 4 vis lectr per yr; gallery talks; competitions with awards; scholarships; lending collection contains 1000 books; book traveling exhibitions; originate traveling exhibitions; studio art and gallery sales

M **TEXAS TECH UNIVERSITY MUSEUM,** Fourth St & Indiana, PO Box 4499, 79409. Tel 806-742-2442. *Dir of Museums & Cur Ethnology* Dr James Goss; *Asst Dir* Linda Vengroff; *Business Mgr* Janice Cooper; *Registrar* Rose Montgomery; *Cur Archaeology & Lubbock Lake Site Dir* Dr Eileen Johnson; *Cur Botany* Dr David Northington; *Cur Educ* Terry Zeller; *Cur Exhibits* Pat Allgood; *Cur Entomology* Dr Oscar Francke; *Cur Herpetology & Ichthyology* Dr John Mecham; *Cur Historic Textiles & Costumes* Betty Mills; *Cur Mammalogy & Living Tissues* Dr Robert Baker; *Cur Medical Zoology* Dr Danny Pence; *Cur Paleontology* Dr Sankar Chatterjee
Open Museum Mon - Wed, Fri & Sat 9 AM - 4:30 PM; Thurs 9 AM - 8:30 PM, Sun 1 - 4:30 PM; Ranching Heritage Center Mon - Sat 9 AM - 4:30 PM, Sun 1 - 4:30 PM; Moody Planetarium Mon - Wed & Fri 2:30 PM, Thurs 2:30 - 7:30 PM, Sat Sun 2 - 3 PM. No admis fee museum; $1 Ranching Heritage Center; $1 Moody Planetarium. Estab 1929 for public service, research, and teaching. One

permanent gallery for art; four temporary galleries. Average Annual Attendance: 132,000. Mem: 2500; dues $15, annual meetings WTMA in Feb and RMA in Sept
Income: Financed by state appropriations, West Texas Museum Association, Ranching Heritage Association, Women's Council
Collections: Archeology; ceramics; contemporary paintings; ethnology; graphics; history; Museum Complex Theme: The relationship of man, land, water & energy to an arid and semi-arid environment; photography; science; sculpture; western art; Indian artifacts; historical furniture; costumes
Exhibitions: Fourteen Acre Outdoor Museum of 30 Restructures display history of Southwest ranching; changing exhibitions of art, sciences and history; permanent exhibitions of anthropology, archeology and history; Paleo Indian archeological site, Lubbock Lake project
Publications: Museum Digest, quarterly; Ranch Record, quarterly; Museum Journal; occasional papers
Activities: Classes for children; docent training; lectures open to public, 15 vis lectr per year; gallery talks; tours; scholarships; book traveling exhibiton, 8 per year; two museum shops sell books, magazines, original art, reproductions, prints and slides
L **Art Dept Library,*** 79409
   Library Holdings: Vols 1800; Per subs 35; Other — Clipping files, exhibition catalogs, manuscripts, pamphlets

LUFKIN

O **LUFKIN HISTORICAL AND CREATIVE ARTS CENTER,** 2nd and Paul St, PO Box 771, 75901. Tel 409-639-4434. *Exec Dir* Rudolph V Pharis; *Admin Asst* Ruth Helen Cotharn; *Programs Coordr* Roschelle Springfield; *Develop Coordr* Marianna Duncan
   Open Tues - Fri 10 AM - 4 PM, Sun 1 - 5 PM, cl Thanksgiving & Christmas. No admis fee. Estab 1975. Average Annual Attendance: 12,000. Mem: 500; dues benefactor $5000, guarantor $1000, patron $500, sustainer $250, sponsor $150, family $60, individual $30 & $20
   Exhibitions: East Texas Art
   Publications: Bi-monthly newsletter
   Activities: Classes for adults & children; docent training; trips; film series; lectures open to public; gallery talks; tours; competitions with awards; book traveling exhibitions

MARSHALL

M **HARRISON COUNTY HISTORICAL MUSEUM,** Old Courthouse, Peter Whetstone Square, 75670. Tel 214-938-2680. *Pres* Dr Gwin Morris; *Dir* Inez H Hughes
   Open Sun & Mon 1:30 - 5 PM, Tues - Sat 9 AM - 5 PM, cl holidays. Admis adults $2, students $1, children under 6 free, groups of 10 or more half price. Estab 1965, housed in a 1901 courthouse. Average Annual Attendance: 3000. Mem: 350; dues couples $15, individual $8
   Income: Financed by membership, donations & admissions
   Collections: Cut and Pressed Glass; 400 BC - 1977 Ceramics; Hand-painted China; Historical Material; Religious Artifacts; etchings; jewelry; paintings; porcelains; portraits
   Publications: Historical Newsletter
   Activities: Guided tours; genealogical records researched; competitions with awards

MCALLEN

M **MCALLEN INTERNATIONAL MUSEUM,** 1900 Nolana, 78501. Tel 512-682-1564. *Exec Dir* David A Ross; *Cur Coll* Lori Jacobson; *Exhibits Coordr* Jerry Moore; *Education Coordr* Mary Speer; *Public Relations* Jane H Parker
   Open Tues - Sat 9 AM - 5 PM, Sun 1 - 5 PM, cl holidays. No admis fee. Estab 1969 to exhibit arts & sciences. Average Annual Attendance: 50,000. Mem: 500; dues $15 and up
   Income: Financed by membership, city appropriation and other funds
   Collections: †Local, state and regional artists; †Mexican folk art; †original prints; regional natural sciences
   Exhibitions: Continous traveling exhibits for one to two month duration
   Publications: Bulletins and brochures periodically; Newsletter, monthly
   Activities: Classes for adults and children; docent training; art and craft demonstrations; lect open to the public; concerts; gallery talks; tours; traveling exhibitions organized and circulated; museum shop selling books, reproductions, prints, slides, jewelry, museum related science kits
L **Library,** 1900 Nolana, PO Box 2495, 78501
   Open to staff, volunteers, and researchers for reference only
   Library Holdings: Vols 2000; Per subs 10; AV — Slides; Other — Photographs

MIDLAND

M **MUSEUM OF THE SOUTHWEST,** 1705 W Missouri, 79701. Tel 915-683-2882. *Dir* Jerry C Porter; *Asst to Dir* Stuart Chase; *Cur* Sue Devine; *Development & Public Relations* Anne Sherburn; *Building & Grounds* Bill Johnson; *Secy* Helen Boydstun
   Open Tues - Sat 10 AM - 5 PM, Sun 2 - 5 PM, cl Mon. No admis fee. Incorporated 1965 as an art and history museum with a separate planetarium providing various science exhibits. Average Annual Attendance: 12,000. Mem: 100; dues couple $30; board meeting third Wed monthly
   Income: Financed by endowment and membership
   Collections: †Art and historical materials of the Southwest; European fan collection; †Indian art collection; Oriental furniture collection; and permanent art collection
   Exhibitions: (1983) The Hillin Collection of New Western Images; China from Within, photographs; From Modest Beginnings; student art festival; Southwest Area Art Show; Progressions; Lithographs of Merritt Mauzey; Prints from

Tamarind; quilt exhibit; Mexican Folk Retablos; Molas from the Midland Community; Edward S Curtis, photographer/ethnographer; Aspects of Color, the First National Collection; Pueblo Pottery & Basketry from the Naomi Tackett Collection; Jim Bones, photographs
   Publications: Annual Report; Museum Bulletin, bimonthly
   Activities: Classes for adults and children; docent training; arts and crafts classes; movie series; lectures open to public, 5 visiting lecturers per year; gallery talks; tours; competitions with awards; individual and original objects of art lent to those who inquire; book traveling exhibitions, 2-3 per year; originate traveling exhibitions; museum shop sells books, magazines, original art, reproductions, prints and Native American Indian crafts
L **Library,** 1705 W Missouri, 79701. Tel 915-683-2882. *Planetarium Dir* John Hicks; *Asst to Dir* Stuart A Chase
   Open Tues - Sat 10 AM - 5 PM, Sun 2 PM - 5 PM. No admis fee. Estab 1966. Average Annual Attendance: 20,000. Mem: 795; dues $15-$1000
   Income: Financed by foundations, county and private donations
   Purchases: Fine arts and cultural anthropology material from the US Southwest
   Library Holdings: Vols 400; Per subs 15; Other — Clipping files, exhibition catalogs
   Collections: †Southwestern
   Publications: Quarterly bulletin; catalog

NACOGDOCHES

M **STEPHEN F AUSTIN STATE UNIVERSITY,** Art Gallery,* North St, 75962. Tel 409-569-2011. *Dir* Mary McCleary
   Open Mon - Fri 9 AM - 4 PM, Sun (for special exhibits). No admis fee. Estab as a teaching gallery and to bring in art from outside this area for our students and the entire community. One large room approx 42 x 27 ft, plus storage. Average Annual Attendance: 5300
   Income: Financed by state education funds
   Collections: Student works; Donation of Prints & Mulitiples from Martin Ackerman Foundation
   Exhibitions: Goya Disasters of War Etchings, First Edition from the Blaffer Foundation; Old Master Paintings from the Sarah Campbell Blaffer Foundation; James Surls, Charmaine Lock; Undergraduate and Graduate Shows; Documenta, Exhibit from Goethe Institute; Two-Person Show: Bill Komodore & Rick Maxwell; National Invitational Works on Paper Exhibit; James Hill: A Texan Living in New York; Abstract Expressionist Paintings from the Blaffer Foundation; Two Painters; Frederick Ortner & Lisa Zwerling; German Carnival Masks from the Goethe Institute; Works by Women from the Gihon Foundation; German Expressionists Works from the Fisher Collection
   Activities: Lectures open to the public, six visiting lecturers per year; gallery talks; competitions with awards; book two traveling exhibitions per year

ODESSA

M **PRESIDENTIAL MUSEUM,** 622 N Lee, 79761. Tel 915-332-7123. *Exec Dir* G F Crabtree; *Cur & Registrar* Valerie Christensen
   Open Mon - Fri 10 AM - 5 PM. No admis fee. Estab 1965 & dedicated to the study & understanding of constitutional government & the election process culminating in the Presidency. Average Annual Attendance: 10,000. Mem: 244; dues $500 - $25
   Income: Financed by Ector county & Presidential Museum board of trustees
   Collections: Campaign memorabilia; original signatures; portraits
   Exhibitions: Long-term exhibitions on the presidency; special temporary exhibitions
   Activities: Educational programs; tours; museum shop sells books & assorted objects relating to the presidency
L **Library,** 622 N Lee, 79761. Tel 915-332-7123
   For reference only
   Library Holdings: Vols 3500; books relating to the presidency; AV — A-tapes; Other — Photographs

ORANGE

M **STARK MUSEUM OF ART,** 712 Green Ave, PO Box 1897, 77630. Tel 409-883-6661. *Chmn* Nelda C Stark; *VChmn* Eunice R Benckenstein; *Secy* Clyde V McKee; *Registrar* Anna Jean Caffey
   Open Wed - Sat 10 AM - 5 PM, Sun 1 - 5 PM. No admis fee. Estab 1978 to preserve and display the Stark collection of art and promote interests in subjects relative to the same through exhibitions, publications and educational programs. Five galleries and lobby exhibition area. Average Annual Attendance: 30,000
   Income: Financed by endowment
   Collections: American Indian art; Western American art; porcelain and crystal
   Exhibitions: Paul Kane, Wanderings of an Artist; The Sculpture of Nicolai Fechin; The Expressed Personality of C M Russell; Nature in Porcelain & Glass; A Mirror Unto Nature: The Printed Art of Natural History
   Publications: Exhibition catalogs
   Activities: Gallery talks; museum shop sells books, posters and postcards

PANHANDLE

M **CARSON COUNTY SQUARE HOUSE MUSEUM,*** Fifth and Elsie Sts, Box 276, 79068. Tel 806-537-3118. *Dir & Cur Educ* Tim Shickles; *Bookkeeper* Pat Pollan; *Chmn Bd* Jo Randel; *VChmn* Margaret Surratt; *VChmn* Clarence Williams
   Open Mon - Sat 9 AM - 5:30 PM, Sun 1 - 5:30 PM, cl Thanksgiving, Christmas and New Years. No admis fee. Estab 1965 as a general museum with art galleries, area and State and National historical displays. Wildlife building and displays; Historic house, listed in National Register of National Trust. Two enclosed security controlled art galleries. New gallery is being designed and will be open to the public by September 1980. Average Annual Attendance: 25,000
   Income: Financed by endowments, county funds and public contributions

Collections: Paintings of area pioneers by Marlin Adams; Sculpture and bronze by Jim Thomas, Grant Speed and Keith Christi; Kenneth Wyatt paintings; Ben Carlton Mead and Harold Bugbee paintings; Indian art beadwork, water colors, Acoma pottery; costumes; antiques

Exhibitions: Karl Bodmer's Maxmilian Exhibit of aquatints and sketches from Northern Natural Gas, Joslyn Museum in Omaha; The Big Bend, Photographs by Bank Longmore, Amon Carter Museum; Goya's Disasters of War, 84 aquatints and sketches owned by the Sarah Blaffer Foundation of Houston; changing monthly exhibits of state artists

Publications: A Time To Purpose, book; Land of Coronado, coloring book; The Square House Cook Book; Voices of the Square House, poems

Activities: Classes for adults and children; dramatic programs; docent training; lectures open to the public, 50 vis lectr per year; gallery talks; tours; hobby workshops; films; scholarships; book four traveling exhibitions per year; museum shop sells books, magazines, reproductions and prints

SAN ANGELO

M ANGELO STATE UNIVERSITY, Houston Harte University Center, Box 11027, 76901. Tel 915-942-2062. *Dir* Wes Davis; *Chmn Art Committee* Kippy Edge; *Program Consult* Sue Parman
Open Mon - Fri 8 AM - 7:30 PM, Sat & Sun 2 - 5 PM. No admis fee. Estab 1970 to provide entertainment and informal education for the students, faculty and staff. Gallery is maintained
Income: $3000 (financed by city and state appropriations)
Collections: Wax drawings done by Guy Rowe for illustration of the book In Our Image by Houston Harte
Exhibitions: Historical artifacts; modern drawings; photography; pottery; weaving; childrens, students and faculty exhibitions
Activities: Lect open to public, 2 visiting lectr per year; gallery talks, tour; concerts, dramatic programs; compeitions

M SAN ANGELO ART CLUB, Helen King Kendall Memorial Art Gallery, 119 W First St, 76903. Tel 915-653-4405. *Pres* Roxa Bynum; *Secy* Dolores Wood
Open Wed 9:30 AM - 3:30 PM, Sat & Sun 2 - 5 PM. No admis fee. Club estab 1928 & gallery estab 1948 to promote the visual fine arts in San Angelo. Average Annual Attendance: 1500. Mem: 100; dues $20; meeting first Mon each month
Income: $8000 (financed by Memorial Endowment Fund)
Collections: Paintings by George Biddle, Gladys Rockmore Davis, Xavier Gonzales, Iver Rose and Frederick Waugh, Hazel Janick
Exhibitions: Monthly exhibits from area artists
Publications: Splashes, monthly newsletter
Activities: Classes for adults & children; tours; competitions with awards; individual paintings & original objects of art lent to libraries, churches & businesses

SAN ANTONIO

O COPPINI ACADEMY OF FINE ARTS, 115 Melrose Place, 78212. Tel 512-824-8502. *Pres* Dr Warren Hester; *Correspondence Secy* Ruth Rogers Wilcox; *Exhib Chmn* Erwin O Wesp
Open Sat & Sun 2 - 5 PM or by appointment. No admis fee. Estab 1945 to foster a better acquaintance and understanding between artists and patrons; to encourage worthy accomplishment in the field of art and to serve as a means of public exhibition for active members works and other works of art. Upstairs gallery donated by founder Dr Pompeo Coppini to the academy for exhibition of works. Mem: 191; dues $2 - $100; annual meeting third Sun in Jan
Income: Financed by membership
Collections: Oil paintings by Rolla Taylor; sculpture by Waldine Tauch and Pompeo Coppini; photography collection; paintings
Publications: Coppini News Bulletin, monthly
Activities: Lectures open to the public, 6 vis lectr per yr; gallery talks; tours; competitions; scholarships; individual paintings & original objects of art lent; originate traveling exhibitions
L Library, San Antonio, 78212
Library Holdings: AV — Slides; Other — Clipping files, original art works, photographs, sculpture

M MARION KOOGLER MCNAY ART MUSEUM, 6000 N New Braunfels Ave, 78209. Tel 512-824-5368. *Pres* Jesse Oppenheimer; *Dir* John Palmer Leeper; *Cur* Norris J Fergeson; *Development* Terrell Smith; *Registrar* Edward Bann Williams; *Secy* Helen M Armstrong
Open Tues - Sat 9AM - 5 PM, Sun 2 - 5 PM cl Mon. No admis fee.
Incorporated 1950 for the encouragement and development of modern art. Average Annual Attendance: 100,000. Mem: 1390; dues business patrons $1000, individual $500, gallery of friends $250, friends $125, members $25
Income: Financed by endowment, memberships & private gifts
Collections: 19th & 20th century paintings, sculptor & graphic arts of Europe & the Americas; Oppenheimer Collection of Gothic & Medieval art
Exhibitions: Edvard Munch: Paradox of Woman; Darrel Austin Retrospective; The World of Donald Evans; Paul Wonner: Abstract Realist; Robes from the Imperial Court of Faberge; Bonsai Society; permanent collection; Graphic Works of Toulouse-Lautrec; Collectors' Gallery XVI
Publications: Annual report, illustrated; exhibition catalogs & announcements
Activities: Docent training; lectures open to public; concerts; gallery talks; tours; individual paintings & original objects of art lent to members of American Association of Museums & accredited foreign museums; originates traveling exhibitions; sales shop sells material published by McNay, post cards & catalogues
L Reference Library, 6000 N New Braunfels St, 78209. *Librn* Mrs John P Leeper
Open Tues - Fri 9 AM - 5 PM to the public. Estab 1970 as an adjunct to the museum. For reference only
Income: Financed by endowment and gifts
Library Holdings: Vols 15,000; Per subs 20; Other — Clipping files, exhibition catalogs, pamphlets
Special Subjects: Visual arts
Collections: Far Eastern art, especially Japanese woodblock prints; 19th - 20th century Western visual arts

O SAN ANTONIO ART LEAGUE, 310 W Ashby, 78212. Tel 512-732-6048. *Pres* Mrs Jow Carroll Rust; *Secy* Mrs Hubert Verschoyle; *Executive Secy* Mrs Jack Casey; *Museum Consultant* Charles Long
Open Tues - Fri 10 AM - 4 PM, weekends 1 - 4 PM, cl Mon. No admis fee. Estab 1912 as a public art gallery for San Antonio, and for the promotion of a knowledge and interest in art by means of exhibitons. Mem: 1000; dues $15 - $300; meetings monthly Oct - May
Income: Financed by membership and fund raising projects
Collections: Crafts, paintings, prints and sculpture
Publications: Exhibiton catalogs; monthly calendar of events
Activities: Lect open to public; gallery talks; tours; competitions; paintings and original art objects lent; originate traveling exhibitions
L Library, 310 W Ashby, 78212
For reference only
Library Holdings: Vols 350

O SAN ANTONIO MUSEUM ASSOCIATION, INC, PO Box 2601, 78299. Tel 512-226-5544. *Exec Dir* Helmuth J Naumer; *Assoc Dir* Pamela Johnson
Open 10 AM - 5 PM weekdays, weekends and holidays. Admis adult $2, children under 12 $1. Estab 1922 to further education and awareness of local and regional history, art, science and technology. Consists of Museum of Art, Witte Memorial and Museum of Transportation. Average Annual Attendance: 400,000. Mem: 3500; contributions $25, $50 & $100
Income: $3,000,000 (financed by endowment, membership, city appropriation and other fund raising projects)
Purchases: $300,000
Publications: Monthly calendar; books
Activities: Educ dept sponsors classes for adults and for children; docent training; dramatic programs; Lect open to public, 10 - 12 visiting lectr per year; concerts; gallery talks; tours; paintings and original art objects lent; museum loans must be approved by the Associations' Board; book traveling exhibitions 25 - 30 per year; originate traveling exhibitions; shop sells books, magazines, original art, prints, reproductions, slides and local crafts
L Ellen S Quillin Memorial Library, 3801 Broadway, 78029. *Librn* Linda M Hardberger; *Slide Librn* George Anne Cormier
Open 8:30 AM - 5 PM weekdays. Estab 1942 as a reference library for curators and the general public on the subjects of art, decorative arts, history and natural science
Library Holdings: Vols 12,000; Per subs 24; AV — Slides 22,000; Other — Clipping files, exhibition catalogs, manuscripts, memorabilia, pamphlets, photographs, reproductions
Special Subjects: Decorative Arts, Primitive Art, American Indian Art, American and Texan Art
M San Antonio Museum of Art,* 200 W Jones Ave, 78215. Tel 512-226-5544. *Dir* Kevin E Consey; *Chief Cur of Art* Nancy Pressly; *Sr Cur* Cecilia Steinfeldt; *Cur Contemporary Art* Sally Boothe-Meredith
Open summer 10 AM - 6 PM; Sept 1-May 31, 10 AM - 5 PM Wed - Sun; cl Mon & Tues. Adults $2; children $1; group discount rates available. Estab 1981; a renovation project, the Brewery was originally chartered in 1883. Anheuser-Busch Brewing Asn of St Louis, during the early 1900, replaced the original wooden structures with a castle-like brick complex. Twin towers, housing glass elevators can be seen for miles. 6600 sq ft of exhibition space. Average Annual Attendance: 127,825
Collections: †American Indian Art; †Contemporary & Modern Art; †18th & 19th & 20th Century Paintings & Sculpture; †American Photography since 1920; †Mexican Folk Art; †Pre-Columbian Art; †Paintings & Decorative Arts; †Spanish Colonial Art;
Exhibitions: (1982) American Art of the 1930s (permanent collection of the Whitney Museum); Russell Lee, Photographer of the 1930; Pre-Columbian Art of Costa Rica; American Landscape (photography); Ed Ruscha. (1983) The Age of Carlos III
M Witte Memorial Museum,* 3801 Broadway, 78209. Tel 512-226-5544. *Dir* Mark Lane
Open winter Mon - Sun 10 AM - 5 PM, summer Mon - Sun 10 AM - 6 PM. Admis adults $2, children $1; group discount rates; Sat free until noon . The Witte Museum, a historical building, is located in Brackenridge Park near the old San Pedro Springs and ancient Indian encampment area. Average Annual Attendance: 208,229
Activities: Exten dept sponsors gallery talks, tours and an artmobile; museum shop sells reproductions, art works, folk art, posters, antique picture frames, pottery and ceramics
—Research Library,* Box 2601, 87299. Tel 512-226-5544
Library Holdings: Vols 10,000; Per subs 35; Documents 20 drawers; AV — Slides 22,000; Other — Photographs
Special Subjects: Decorative Arts, Indian Art, Natural History, Texana

L SAN ANTONIO PUBLIC LIBRARY, Dept of Fine Arts, Art, Music & Films Dept, 203 S Saint Marys St, 78205. Tel 512-299-7797. *Dir* Irwin Sexton; *Asst Dir* Geraldine LeFevre; *Dept Head* Mary A Wright
Open Mon - Fri 9 AM - 9 PM, Sat 9 AM - 6 PM. Estab to provide art reference and lending materials to the residents of Bexar County. Art gallery is maintained. Also serves as a major resource center to regional libraries in South Texas
Income: Financed by city, state and federal appropriation
Purchases: $250,000
Library Holdings: Micro — Fiche, reels; AV — A-tapes, cassettes, fs, motion pictures, rec, slides, v-tapes; Other — Clipping files, exhibition catalogs, memorabilia, pamphlets, photographs, reproductions
Exhibitions: Monthly exhibit of local artists work
Activities: Classes for children; dramatic programs; lectures open to the public, 2 vis lectr per yr; concerts; gallery talks; tours; competitions with awards; exten dept; lending collection contains 320,000 books, 400 video cassettes, 10,000 audio cassettes, 15,000 motion pictures; book traveling exhibitions

O SOUTHWEST CRAFT CENTER, Ursuline & Villita Galleries,* 300 Augusta St, 78205. Tel 512-222-0926, 224-1848. *Exec Dir* Darrell Bohlsen
Open daily 10 AM - 5 PM. Estab 1963, shop estab 1968, to keep crafts alive by giving craftsmen an outlet for their work, to educate the public in crafts by

putting good crafts before them and also maintaining a school where these medias can be taught. Average Annual Attendance: 100,000. Mem: 1500 students, 35 craftsmen; dues $10 and up; annual meeting May
Income: Financed by endowment and membership
Exhibitions: Student-Faculty Show; approx twelve one-man and group craft shows
Publications: Opening Invitations; Yearbook
Activities: Classes for adults and children; crafts workshop programs with visiting artists; sales shop selling juried crafts of over 110 craftsmen
L **Library,** 300 Augusta St, 78205. Tel 512-224-1848. *Librn* Mrs William Larsen Reference library contains craft books, slides and films

SHERMAN

M **AUSTIN COLLEGE,** Ida Green Gallery, Box 1651, 75090. Tel 214-892-9101, Ext 251. *Dir* Carl R Neidhardt
Open 9 AM - 5 PM weekdays. No admis fee. Estab 1972 to serve campus and community needs. Average Annual Attendance: 5000
Income: Financed by endowment
Collections: Prints
Exhibitions: Monthly, except summer
Activities: Lect open to public, 2 - 4 visiting lectrs per year; tours

SNYDER

M **DIAMOND M FOUNDATION MUSEUM,** 909 25th St, 79549. Tel 915-573-6311. *Assoc Dir* Janet R Parker; *Asst* Nona Bunch; *Secy* Beth Titus
Open Tues - Fri 10 AM - 4 PM, Sat & Sun 1 - 4 PM. No admis. Estab 1964. Average Annual Attendance: 6000
Purchases: American realist art of the 19th & 20th century
Collections: Bronzes & other sculpture; Currier and Ives lithographs; jade; ivory; paintings by Koerner, N C Wyeth; American illustrators; artists of the American West
Exhibitions: (1982) Eskimo Prints & Sculpture; (1983) Where the West Begins
Publications: The Museums, quarterly newsletter; Where the West Begins, occasional catalogs; You're a Cowboy, educational booklets
Activities: Educ dept; docent training; lectures open to public, 3-4 vis lectr per yr; gallery talks; tours; individual paintings & original objects of art lent to college & businesses; book traveling exhibition; originate traveling exhibitions; museum shop sells books, magazines & postcards

TYLER

M **TYLER MUSEUM OF ART,** 1300 S Mahon Ave, 75701. Tel 214-595-1001. *Dir* James D Weaver; *Cur of Education* Rebecca Bendel; *Cur of Exhib* Terry Keane; *Admin Asst* Carol Pianta
Open Tues - Sat 10 AM - 5 PM, Sun 1 - 5 PM. No admis fee. Estab 1971 as a museum of 19th and 20th century art. Two galleries are 40 x 60 ft with 20 ft ceilings; one gallery covers 25 x 45 ft. Average Annual Attendance: 42,000. Mem: 775; dues $25 - $10,000
Income: $230,000 (financed by endowment, membership and auction)
Activities: Classes for children; docent training; lect open to public, 5 - 6 visiting lectr per year; concerts; gallery talks; tours; individual paintings and original art objects lent; originate traveling exhibitions; shop sells books
L **Reference Library,** 1300 S Mahon Ave, 75701. Tel 214-595-1001
Open for reference only
Library Holdings: Vols 1500; Per subs 24; AV — Motion pictures, slides; Other — Exhibition catalogs

VERNON

M **RED RIVER VALLEY MUSEUM,** 2030 Cumberland, PO Box 2004, 76384. Tel 817-553-4682. *Pres* James King; *VPres* Helen Willingham; *Secy* Ann Slaugenhop; *Executive Dir* Kathleen P Grima; *Clerical Hostess* Bettye Coffey; *Clerical Hostess* Jessie Marlow
Open daily 1 - 5 PM. No admis fee. Estab 1976 to provide for and preserve local heritage while maintaining national exhibits in the arts, history, and science programs. One gallery with one hundred linear feet of hanging space. Average Annual Attendance: 4000. Mem: 500; dues family $25, individual $15; annual meeting third Tuesday in October
Income: Financed by membership, contributions
Collections: Electra Waggoner Biggs Sculpture Collection; J H Ray Indian Artifacts; Taylor Dabney mineral collection
Publications: Museum Newsletter, quarterly
Activities: Classes for children; lectures open to the public, three visiting lecturers per year; gallery talks; tours; book traveling exhibitions; museum shop selling books, art supplies; brochures; collectors items

WACO

M **THE ART CENTER,** 1300 College Dr, 76708. Tel 817-752-4371. *Dir* Paul Rogers Harris; *Cur* Patrick McCracken; *Education Coordr* Ann Skye
Open 10 AM - 5 PM Tues - Sat, 1 - 5 PM Sun. No admis fee. Estab 1972 to provide a variety of exhibitions for appreciation, and classes for participation. Former residence of William Cameron, now renovated and contains one large main gallery and a small adjacent gallery, also additional exhibition space on the second floor. Average Annual Attendance: 20,000. Mem: 900; dues $30
Income: $100,000 (financed by endowment, membership and grants)
Collections: Contemporary regional art
Exhibitions: (1983) Posters: Beauty & the Beast; Visual Short Stories: Five from Austin; Larry McIntire: Photographs; Joe Guy, Waiting, Listening; Peter Brown: Seasons of Light; Martin Delabano: Constructions; Five on Paper; (1984) The Art Center 1983 Competition; Jim Woodson: Paintings; Mitch Byers:

Photographs; Haynes Ownby: Paintings; Honey Harrison: Drawings
Publications: Catalogs; newsletter
Activities: Classes for adults and children; docent training; lect open to the public, 2 - 3 visiting lectr per year; gallery talks; tours; competitions; exten dept serves ethnic minorities and low socio-economic groups; originates traveling exhibitions; museum shop sells books, reproductions and gift items
L **Library,** PO Box 5396, 76708. Tel 817-752-4371
Open 10 AM - 5 PM Tues - Sat, 1 - 5 PM Sun. Estab 1976 as a reference source for staff, faculty and patrons of the Art Center
Income: $500
Purchases: $650
Library Holdings: Vols 250; Per subs 20; Other — Exhibition catalogs

BAYLOR UNIVERSITY
M **Martin Museum of Art,** 76798. Tel 817-755-1867. *Dir* Dr William M Jensen; *Cur* Vernie M Logan, MFA
Open Tues - Fri 1 - 5 PM, cl Mon, Sat & Sun. No admis fee. Estab 1967 as a teaching arm of the university to serve the area. Gallery contains one large room with storage and preparation room. Average Annual Attendance: 2000
Income: Financed through the art department
Collections: Graphics; local artists; prints; sculpture from Sepik River area, New Guinea
Activities: Lectures open to public, 4 vis lectr per yr; gallery talks
L **Armstrong Browning Library,** Eighth & Speight Sts, PO Box 6336, 76706. Tel 817-755-3566. *Dir* Dr Jack W Herring; *Librn* Betty A Coley; *Admin Asst* Rita S Humphrey; *Hostess* Nancy Dobbins
Open Mon - Fri 9 AM - Noon and 2 - 4 PM, Sat 9 AM - Noon. Estab 1918 to provide a setting for the personal possessions of the Brownings and to have as complete as is possible a collection for the use of Browning scholars. Gallery is maintained. Mem: Dues individual $25
Income: Financed by endowment and private university
Library Holdings: Vols 10,000; Per subs 25; original documents; Micro — Reels; AV — A-tapes, cassettes, fs, motion pictures, rec, slides; Other — Clipping files, manuscripts, memorabilia, original art works, pamphlets, photographs, prints, reproductions, sculpture
Special Subjects: Robert and Elizabeth Barrett Browning, Victorian Era of Literature
Collections: Hagedorn; Kress Foundation Gallery Collection of Portraits; Meynell; Pen Browning; photograph collection of prints; portraits of Robert Browning and Elizabeth Barrett Browning; portraits of donors; shields; Julia Margaret Cameron, photographs
Publications: Armstrong Browning Library Newsletter, semiannual; Baylor Browning Interests, irregular; Browning Music 1973, music catalog; Studies in Browning and His Circle, semiannual
Activities: Lect open to the public, 2 visiting lectrs per year; concerts; tours; scholarships

M **TEXAS RANGER HALL OF FAME AND MUSEUM** (Formerly Fort Fisher and Homer Garrison Memorial Museum), Interstate 35 West, Box 1370, 76703. Tel 817-754-1433. *Cur* Gaines de Graffenried; *Supt* B G Smith
Open 9 AM - 5 PM daily (winter), 9 AM - 6 PM daily (summer). Admis adults $2.50, children (6 and up) $1.50, special group rates
Collections: Texas Ranger items; Western history; paintings and sculpture
Exhibitions: Temporary and traveling exhibitions
Activities: Lectures, guided tours, research on Texas Rangers; sales shop
L **Library,** Waco, 76703
Reference library
Library Holdings: Vols 1034; Per subs 3; Micro — Reels; AV — Cassettes, slides, v-tapes; Other — Clipping files, photographs

WICHITA FALLS

M **WICHITA FALLS MUSEUM AND ART CENTER,** Two Eureka Circle, 76308. Tel 817-692-0923. *Dir* Larry Francell
Open Mon - Sat 9:30 AM - 4:30 PM, Sun 1 - 5 PM. No admis fee. Estab 1967 for the purpose of serving the community. Three galleries house art exhibits, science and history exhibits. Average Annual Attendance: 60,000. Mem: 1500; dues $15 - $1000; annual meeting April
Income: Financed by endowment, membership, city appropriation and schools
Collections: †American prints
Publications: Events calendar, Sept, Jan, May
Activities: Classes for adults and children; docent training; lect open to public, 2 - 5 visiting lectr per year; gallery talks; tours; lending collection has original prints; originate traveling exhibitions; shop sells books, prints, crafts and jewelry

WIMBERLEY

M **PIONEER TOWN,** 7A Ranch Resort, Box 259, Route 1, 78676. Tel 512-847-2517. *Dir* Raymond L Czichos
Open Memorial Day - Labor Day 9 AM - 10 PM daily, rest of the year, Sat & Sun afternoons, cl Dec, Jan & Feb. No admis fee. Estab 1956 as a village and art museum
Collections: Contemporary Western artists; sculpture and metalwork; Jack Woods, sculpture

UTAH

BRIGHAM CITY

M **BRIGHAM CITY MUSEUM-GALLERY,*** 24 N Third W, PO Box 583, 84302. Tel 801-723-6769. *Dir* Larry Douglas; *Chmn* Colleen H Bradford
Open Mon - Sat 11 AM - 7 PM, cl Sun. No admis fee. Estab 1970 to promote and preserve artistic and cultural opportunities and appreciation of the history and accomplishment of local citizens, and to further promote understanding of the natural resources and wildlife of the area. Average Annual Attendance: 13,000
Income: Financed by Brigham City Corporation
Collections: Crystal and glass; 19th century clothing, artifacts and furniture
Activities: Lectures, 5 visiting lectr per year; concerts, gallery talks, competitions; Monthly rotating exhibits of art and varied collections; shop sells souvenirs

CEDAR CITY

M **SOUTHERN UTAH STATE COLLEGE,** Braithwaite Fine Arts Gallery,* Old Administration Bldg, 84720. Tel 801-586-5432. *Dir* Thomas A Leek; *Asst Cur* June Miller Adams
Open Mon - Fri 10 AM - 5 PM, Sat 1 - 6 PM, cl mid-Aug & major holidays. No admis fee. Estab 1976 to provide a quality visual arts forum for artists' work and the viewing public. The gallery has 2000 sq ft of space with 300 lineal ft of display surface; it is equipped with facilities for two and three-dimensional media with electronic security system. Average Annual Attendance: 10,000. Mem: Association dues $50
Income: Financed by city and state appropriations and private donations
Collections: 18th, 19th & 20th century American art; currently purchasing three-dimensional media
Exhibitions: Annual Faculty Exhibition; Annual Printmaking West; Annual Student Exhibition; Annual Watercolor West; Recent Art Gifts to College
Publications: Exhibition announcements, monthly
Activities: Classes for adults; lect open to public, 4 visiting lectrs per year; gallery talks; tours; competitions; lending collection contains kodachromes, original art works, oroginal prints, paintings, slides; book traveling exhibitions

FILLMORE

M **UTAH NATURAL RESOURCES & ENERGY, PARKS & RECREATION,** Territorial Statehouse, 50 W Capital Ave, PO Box 657, 84631. Tel 801-743-5316. *Park Mgr* C Max Martin
Open 8 AM - 7 PM June 1 - Sept 1, all other months 8 AM - 5 PM. Admis 12 & over $.50. Estab 1930, as a museum for pioneer relics. Restored by the state and local Daughters of Utah Pioneers; run by Utah State Division of Parks and Recreation. Average Annual Attendance: 25,000
Income: Financed by state appropriations
Collections: Charcoal and pencil sketches; paintings by Utah artists; photograph prints collection; pioneer portraits in antique frames; silk screen prints; furniture arranged in household settings
Activities: Educ dept; lectures; gallery talks; tours

OGDEN

O **ECCLES COMMUNITY ART CENTER,** 2580 Jefferson Ave, 84401. Tel 801-392-6935. *Pres* Vera Eccles; *VPres* Dean Brunson; *VPres* Chris Christensen; *Treas* Marilyn Garner; *Secy* F L Winder; *Dir* Sandy Havas; *Asst Dir* Karen Poggemeyer
Open 9 AM - 5 PM Mon - Fri, 10 AM - 4 PM Sat, cl Sun & holidays. No admis fee. Estab 1959 to serve as a pivot and focal point for community cultural activities and to promote cultural growth. Maintains an art gallery with monthly exhibits. Average Annual Attendance: 25,000. Mem: 300; dues $15 - $100; annual meeting Nov
Income: $75,000 (financed by membership, state appropriation and fund raising)
Exhibitions: (1984) Utah Water Color Society; Palette Club; Women's Works; Gary Collins; John Eccles Ten Utah Photographers; Marilyn Garner; Invitational 25th Anniversary Exhibit; Robert Call
Publications: Newsletter, quarterly
Activities: Classes for adults and children; lect open to public; concerts; competitions with awards; book traveling exhibitions

PARK CITY

O **KIMBALL ART CENTER,** 638 Park Ave, PO Box 1478, 84060. Tel 801-649-8882. *Dir* Choral C Pepper; *Asst Dir* Peggy Black
Open Mon - Sun 10 AM - 6 PM. Estab 1976 for monthly gallery shows & workshops in arts & crafts. Main gallery has portable walls & is 80 x 180 ft, little gallery measures 17 x 20 ft. Average Annual Attendance: 500,000. Mem: 600; dues $35; meetings in June & Jan
Income: $400,000 (financed by endowment, membership & contributions)
Exhibitions: Desert Revisited - Seven Artists Whose Creativity is Influenced by the Desert; Joan Arnold Milligan, oil paintings
Publications: Kimball Canvas, newsletter; exhibition brochures
Activities: Classes for adults & children; dramatic programs; docent training; lectures open to public; book traveling exhibitions; originates traveling exhibitions; sales shop sells original art & prints

PRICE

M **COLLEGE OF EASTERN UTAH,** Gallery East,* 451 East Fourth North, 84501. Tel 801-637-2120, Ext 239. *Dir* James L Young
Open daily 8:30 AM - 5 PM, open special nights. No admis fee. Estab 1975 to provide an educational and aesthetic tool within the community. Average Annual Attendance: 5000
Income: $1600 (financed by school appropriation)
Collections: Broad collection of contemporary prints & painting
Exhibitions: Changing exhibits
Activities: Lectures open to the public, 9-10 visiting lecturers per year; gallery talks; tours; competitions with awards; scholarships; traveling exhibits organized and circulated to colleges

PROVO

BRIGHAM YOUNG UNIVERSITY

M **B F Larsen Gallery,** Harris Fine Arts Center F-303, 84602. Tel 801-378-2881. *Dir & Preparator* J Clyff Allen; *Dir of Art Acquisitions* Dr Wesley M Burnside; *Chmn Art Acquisitions Committee* Franz M Johansen; *Art Gallery Secy* Sharon Lyn Heelis
Open 8 AM - 10 PM Larsen Gallery; 8 AM - 5 PM Secured Gallery. No admis fee. Estab 1965 to bring to the University students and faculty a wide range of new experiences in the visual arts. B F Larsen Gallery is a three story atrium shaped gallery with exhibition areas in center floor and upper levels; Secured Gallery is large room with foyer and single entrance-exit; total exhibition space 15,260 sq ft. Average Annual Attendance: 55,000 Secured; 100,000 Larsen
Income: Financed by university
Collections: †Contemporay American Lithographs; †Maynard Dixon Collection; European Art; Oriental Art; International Collection of Antique Prints; †State Painter; Julian Alden Weir Collection (paintings, prints and drawings); †Western Americana; †Mahonri M Young Collection (paintings, prints and drawings and sculptures); †19th & 20th Century American Paintings, drawings and sculpture
Exhibitions: Monthly invitational exhibits by students and faculty, from the permanent collections and circulating exhibits
Activities: Lectures open to public; tours; competitions; monetary and certificate awards; individual paintings and original objects of art lent to university executive, faculty and university library; lending collection contains original prints, paintings and sculpture; book traveling exhibitons monthly
L **Harold B Lee Library,*** 84602. Tel 801-378-4005. *Dir Libraries* Sterling Albrecht; *Mus and Art Librn* Beth R Webb
Open 7 AM - 11 PM Mon - Sat. Estab 1875 to support the university curriculum
Income: Financed by endowment, membership and church funds
Library Holdings: Vols 34,835; Per subs 158; Micro — Fiche, reels; AV — A-tapes, cassettes, fs, motion pictures, slides; Other — Memorabilia, pamphlets, photographs, prints
Collections: George Anderson Collection of early Utah photographs; 15th and 16th century graphic art collection; C R Savage Collection; Vough indexed and mounted art print collection
Activities: Tours

SAINT GEORGE

M **DIXIE COLLEGE,** Southwestern Utah Art Gallery,* 84770. Tel 801-673-4811, Ext 297. *Dir* Gerald Olson
Open 8 AM - 6 PM. No admis fee. Estab 1960 to serve southwestern Utah as a visual arts exhibit center. Gallery is located in Fine Arts Center. Average Annual Attendance: 8000
Income: Financed by state appropriation
Collections: Early and contemporary Utah painters
Activities: Classes for adults; dramatic programs; lect open to public, visiting lectrs; gallery talks

SALT LAKE CITY

M **CHURCH OF JESUS CHRIST OF LATTER-DAY SAINTS,** Museum of Church History and Art, 45 North West Temple, 84150. Tel 801-531-2299. *Arts & Sites Dir* Florence S Jacobsen; *Conservator* Brook Bowman; *Cur Coll* Richard G Oman; *Cur Exhib & Sites* Paul L Anderson; *Sr Registrar* T Michael Smith; *Coordr Education* Shirley Ann Cox; *Research Supv* Steven L Olsen; *Media Specialist & Librn* Ronald W Read; *Store Supv* Gary M Conners
Open Mon - Fri 9 AM - 9 PM, Sat, Sun, Holidays & Jan - Mar 10 AM - 7 PM. No admis fee. Estab 1869 to disseminate information and display historical memorabilia, artifacts and art to the visiting public. Assists in restorations and furnishing of Church historic sites; galleries reopen in 1984
Income: Financed by Church
Collections: †Mostly 19th and 20th century Mormon art and historical artifacts: †portraits, paintings, drawings, sculpture, prints, American furniture, china, pottery, glass; †Mormon quilts and handwork; †decorative arts; †clothing and textiles; architectural elements and hardware; †Oceanic and American Indian pottery, basketry, and textiles; Pre-Columbian pottery and sculpture
Exhibitions: Permanent Installations: Presidents of the Church; Portraits of Church Leaders; Western Themes; Masterworks of Mormon art; (1984) Paintings & Prints by Contemporary Latter-Day Saints Artists; Church Museums: Past and Present; C C A Christensen: Mormon Immigrant Artist; Mola Art; LeConte Stewart; Immigration Prints; Biblical Paintings by Margetson
Publications: Exhibition catalogs
Activities: Docent training; seminars; gallery demonstrations; lectures open to the public; gallery talks; tours; individual paintings & original objects of art lent; museum shop sells books, reproductions, prints, slides & posters
L **Library,** 50 E North Temple, 84150
Reference library
Library Holdings: Vols 800; Per subs 25; Micro — Fiche, reels; AV — Slides, v-tapes; Other — Clipping files, exhibition catalogs, pamphlets
Special Subjects: Latter-Day Saints art, artists, history & historic sites

O **SALT LAKE ART CENTER,** 20 S W Temple, 84101. Tel 801-328-4201. *Pres* Marcia Price; *Treas* John Jorman; *Dir* Richard M Johnston
Open Tues - Sat 10 AM - 5 PM, Fri 10 AM - 9 PM, Sun 1 - 5 PM, cl Mon. No admis fee. Estab 1931 to educate the community in the visual arts through exhibitions and classes. Center has one large gallery of 5800 sq ft; one small gallery of 1000 sq ft; sales shop and rental sales gallery 1400 sq ft. Average Annual Attendance: 60,000. Mem: 1250; dues for one year family $30, individual $20; annual meeting Sept
Income: $295,000 (financed by membership, city & state appropriation, earned income, gifts, & private & corporate contributions)
Purchases: $70,000 Bolotowsky Sculpture
Collections: American and European prints 19th and 20th century; Utah artists
Exhibitions: (1983-84) Moishe Smith Retrospective; Christmas Exhibition: Toys of Our Lives; Celebration of Birds; Don Olsen Retrospective; Art Auction '84; John Schaefer/Fred Wright Election Campaign Council Design Exhibit; Contemporary Trompe L'oeil Paintings & Sculpture; Treasures from the BYU Collections, paintings & sculpture; Gund Collection of Western Art; Off the Walls of Utah; Parade, Rothstein Exhibit; Holiday Sale: The Art of Giving; George Janecheck Photographs; The Great Salt Lake Photographs, John Telford; Yule Bowl; Saul Steinberg Drawings; Photographic Abstraction
Publications: Bulletin, quarterly
Activities: Classes for adults & children; studio & lecture courses; lectures open to public, 30 vis lectr per yr; concerts; gallery talks; tours; competitions with awards; originate traveling exhibitions; sales shop sells books, original art, reproductions & prints

L **SALT LAKE CITY PUBLIC LIBRARY,** Fine Arts Department and Atrium Gallery,* 209 E Fifth S, 84111. Tel 801-363-5733, Ext 41. *Dir* J Dennis Day; *Head Fine Arts Department* Margaret Edmundson; *Coordr Atrium Gallery* Lori Arnall
Open Mon - Fri 9 AM - 9 PM, Sat 9 AM - 6 PM, Sun 1 - 5 PM winter only. Estab 1898. Maintains an art gallery with monthly exhibitions
Income: $1,599,345 (financed by endowment and city appropriation)
Library Holdings: Micro — Fiche; AV — Cassettes, fs, rec, slides; Other — Clipping files, exhibition catalogs, framed reproductions, original art works, pamphlets, reproductions
Special Subjects: Film, Contemporary art, dance
Collections: Art of Western United States; Utah Artists
Exhibitions: Mary Atwater Weaver's Guild; one-person and group shows such as Utah Watercolor Association; traveling exhibits from state-wide Museum on the Road Program; From the Smithsonian; special exhibits from private collections and museum collections
Publications: Brochures accompanying individual shows
Activities: Folk-Life Festival; concerts; gallery talks; tours; slide presentations; book traveling exhibitions

M **UNIVERSITY OF UTAH,** Utah Museum of Fine Arts, 101 Art and Architectural Center, 84112. Tel 801-322-7332. *Dir* E F Sanguinetti; *Cur of the Coll* Thomas Southam; *Gallery Supt & Preparator* David Hardy; *Asst Gallery Supt & Preparator* James A Williams; *Cur Educational Services* Elinor Sue McCoy; *Registrar* William R Balken; *Membership & Vol Coordr* Jean Mueller; *Executive Secy* Josephine Theodore; *Sr Citizens Coordr* Ann Stewart; *Coordr Museum Programs & Public Relations* Judith Kurtz
Open 10 AM - 5 PM Mon - Fri, Sat & Sun 2 - 5 PM. No admis fee. Estab 1951 as a museum of fine arts under the administration of the College of Fine Arts. Average Annual Attendance: 75,000. Mem: 800; dues family $25, single $15
Income: Financed by state appropriations
Collections: Winifred Kimball Hudnut Collection; Natacha Rambova Egyptian Collection; Marion Sharp Robinson Collection; Trower & Michael Collections of English, American & Peruvian Silver; Bartlett Wicks Collection; English 17th and 18th century furniture and pictures; Egyptian antiquities; French 18th century furnishings and tapestries; graphics, contemporary silver; Italian Renaissance paintings and furniture; objects from the Buddhist culture
Exhibitions: American Painting of 1850; Cities on Stone; Graphic Styles of the American Eight; Jo Hanson: Crab Orchard Cemetery; Images of Women; Indian Basket Designs of the Greater Southwest; Sol Lewitt; masterpieces of English watercolor from the Victoria & Albert Museum; Recent Work by Manuel Neri; 19th Century French Prints
Activities: Classes for adults; docent training; lect open to public, some members only; concerts; gallery talks; tours; paintings and art objects lent; originate traveling exhibitions

L **Owen Library,** Art and Architecture Center, 84112. *Dir* Robert S Olpin; *Librn* Elizabeth Knudson
Open 10 AM - 5 PM Mon - Fri. Estab 1978 as a reference library for art students
Library Holdings: Vols 2000; Per subs 50; AV — Cassettes, Kodachromes, slides; Other — Clipping files, exhibition catalogs, manuscripts, memorabilia, original art works, pamphlets

M **UTAH ARTS COUNCIL,** Glendinning Gallery, 617 E South Temple St, 84102. Tel 801-533-5895, Ext 5757. *Chmn* Ray Kingston; *Executive Dir* Ruth R Draper; *Visual Arts Coordr* Dan Burke
Open Mon - Fri 8 AM - 5 PM. Estab 1899 as the Utah Art Institute by Utah State Legislature to promote the fine arts in Utah. Now a division within the Department of Development Services, Utah. Average Annual Attendance: 12,000
Income: Financed by state and federal appropriations
Collections: Crafts, paintings, photography, prints, watercolors and sculptures with an emphasis on WPA period
Exhibitions: Annual visual arts competition; special exhibits
Activities: Lectures open to the public, 5 vis lectr per yr; gallery talks; tours; competitions with awards; individual paintings & original objects of art lent to non-profit organizations in Utah; lending collection contains 1000 original art works, 50 original prints, 800 paintings, 50 photographs, 20 sculpture, 1500 slides, 80 ceramic, mixed media; originates traveling exhibitions

O **UTAH TRAVEL COUNCIL,** Council Hall, Capitol Hill, 84114. Tel 801-533-5681. *Dir* James Braden; *Asst Dir* Ann King; *Deputy Dir* Macel Thurmond; *Travel Publications Specialist* Denise Bale; *Media Dir* Pat Eyre; *Travel Development Specialist* Alison Barnett
Open Memorial Day - Labor Day 8 AM - 6 PM, Sat & Sun 9:30 AM - 6 PM, rest of year Mon - Fri 8 AM - 5 PM. No admis fee. Constructed in 1866 and served as seat of government for 30 years; reconstructed on Capitol Hill and presented to Utah state in 1963; contains small museum of pioneer and historic items, paintings and furniture
Income: Financed by legislative appropriation
Publications: Brochures; two newsletters
Activities: Lending collection contains motion pictures, photographs, transparencies for public use; originate traveling exhibitions

SPRINGVILLE

M **SPRINGVILLE MUSEUM OF ART,** 126 E 400 South, 84663. Tel 801-489-9434. *Dir* Vern G Swanson; *Office Mgr* Rayma Allred
Open Tues - Sat 10 AM - 5 PM, Wed 10 AM - 9 PM, Sun 2 - 5 PM, cl Mon. No admis fee. Estab 1903 for the collection and exhibition of fine arts, and as an educational resource. Built in 1935-1937, is one of the largest museums in the mountain west, it has eleven galleries with 20,000 sq ft of exhibit space; maintains a small reference library for staff use. Average Annual Attendance: 55,000. Mem: 400; dues family $25, individual $15
Income: $165,000 (financed by membership, city and state appropriations)
Purchases: $5000 - $10,000 of fine art
Collections: †Cyrus Dallin Bronzes; †Traditional American Art of the 20th Century; †Utah Artists from 1850-1984 of all styles; †Western Americana
Exhibitions: (1984) Annual April Salon (national invitational painting); June Quilt Show; High Schools of Utah Show; Waldo Midgley: Utah Expatriate, Women Artists of Utah & Utah '84 Exhibit
Publications: Exhibition catalogs, quarterly bulletin
Activities: Classes for adults and children; docent and intern training; lectures open to public, 10 visiting lecturers per year; concerts; sponsors competitions with awards; exten dept serves NEBO, Alpine & Provo school districts; individual paintings and original objects of art lent to Springville High School and Public Library; lending collection contains original prints, paintings and sculpture; museum shop sells books, magazines, original art, reproductions, prints, catalogs and postcards

VERMONT

BENNINGTON

M **BENNINGTON MUSEUM,** W Main St, 05201. Tel 802-447-1571. *Dir* David W Dangremond; *Cur Art & Decorative Arts* Kirk Nelson; *Cur History* Eugene R Kosche; *Cur Peter Matteson Tavern* John Mills; *Registrar* Ruth Levin; *Dir Education* Kate Philbin; *Museum Shop Mgr* Nancy Walsh; *Business Mgr* Peggy L Morache; *Membership & Volunteer Coordr* Tricia N Hayes
Open March 1 - Nov 30 9 AM - 5 PM daily. Admis $2.50 adult, discounts for students, sr citizens, children and groups. Estab 1875 as resource for history and fine and decorative arts of New England. Local historical museum with gallery, Grandma Moses Schoolhouse Museum. Average Annual Attendance: 100,000. Mem: 650; dues $15-$1000; annual meeting May
Income: $400,000
Collections: Bennington pottery; Bennington battle flag; American Blown & pressed glass; American painting & sculpture; American furniture & decorative arts; dolls & toys; Grandma Moses paintings; rare documents
Exhibitions: The Shaping of Vermont: From the Wilderness to the Centennial, 1749-1877; Always in Season: Folk Art & Traditional Culture in Vermont; From Head to Toe: Women's Costumes from the Bennington Museum Collection, 1820-1920; Indomitable Vermont Women: Women in Vermont, 1800-1920
Publications: Exhibition catalogs
Activities: Classes for adults and children; docent training; lectures open to public, 5-10 vis lectr per year; concerts; gallery talks; tours; individual paintings and original objects of art lent through a rental program; book traveling exhibitions; originate traveling exhibitions to other northern New England museums; museum shop sells books, magazines, original art, reproductions, prints and slides

L **Library,** W Main St, 05201. Tel 802-447-1571. *Librn* Gladys Coghlan
Library Holdings: Vols 5000; Per subs 10; Micro — Reels; AV — Lantern slides, slides, v-tapes; Other — Clipping files, exhibition catalogs, manuscripts, memorabilia, pamphlets, photographs
Special Subjects: American Decorative Arts, New England Genealogy

BRATTLEBORO

M **BRATTLEBORO MUSEUM AND ART CENTER,** * Old Railroad Station, Box 662, 05301. Tel 802-257-0124. *Pres* Mary Blair; *VPres* John Davidson; *Secy* Jean Allen; *Treas* Lorene O'Bryan; *Admin Dir* W Rod Faulds
Open May - mid-Dec Tues - Sun Noon - 4 PM, cl Mon. No admis fee but donations encouraged. Estab 1972 to promote and make accessible to the community the field of art and cultural history of Brattleboro. The museum is located in a railroad station built in 1915, now a registered historic site. Average Annual Attendance: 7000. Mem: 325; dues $10 - $500; annual meeting Jan
Income: $40,000 (financed by membership, donations, town, state and federal appropriations)
Collections: Estey Organ Exhibit; permanent collection is being developed relating to Brattleboro and southern Vermont region
Activities: Classes for adults and children; lect open to public; concerts; gallery talks; competitions; sales shop

M **ONE STEP BEYOND,** 113 Main St, 05301. *Dir* Matt Richards; *Dir* Klaus Postler
Open Mon - Wed 10 AM - 3 PM, Fri & Sat 10 AM - 4 PM. No admis fee. Estab 1983 to show contemporary work by artists generally outside conventional gallery framework; artists gallery for artists by artists. Average Annual Attendance: 3000. Mem: Meetings Jan 10 & Aug 20; members work must be approved
Exhibitions: Paul Hoedecker, paintings & objects; Peter Lefcourt, photos; The Great Brattleboro Mail Art Show; Group Show

BROOKFIELD

M **COLLEGE OF THE AMERICAS,** Museum of the Americas, Rte 14, 05036. Tel 802-276-3386. *Pres* Earle W Newton
Estab 1971 to gather materials in support of Anglo American and Hispanic-American studies
Income: Financed by endowment & gifts
Collections: Anglo-American 16th - 19th century paintings; English mezzotints; Hispanic-American decorative arts; Hogarth prints and paintings; Latin American folk art; maps of the colonies; Pre-Columbian artifacts
L **Library,** Rte 14, 05036. Tel 802-276-3386. *Dir* Earle W Newton
For reference only
Income: Financed by endowment & gifts
Library Holdings: Vols 5000; Per subs 10; AV — V-tapes; Other — Clipping files, original art works
Collections: Anglo-American and Latin American art and history

BURLINGTON

M **UNIVERSITY OF VERMONT,** Robert Hull Fleming Museum, 05405. Telex 656-2090. *Dir* Ildiko Heffernan; *Admin Asst* Carol Wood; *Secy* Candi Barrows; *Exhibition Designer & Preparator* Merlin Acomb
Open Tue - Fri 10 AM - 5 PM, Sat & Sun 1 - 5 PM. No admis fee. Estab 1873 as a fine arts museum for the area and a teaching facility for the University. Four permanent galleries, three of changing exhibits. Average Annual Attendance: 15,000. Mem: 500; dues Fleming Society $1000, patron $250-$999, contributing $100-$249, family $30, individual $20, faculty, admin, employees and alumni $15, student $5
Income: Financed by endowment, membership, state and university appropriations and grants
Collections: American, European, Pre-Columbian and Oriental art including paintings, sculpture, decorative arts and artifacts; costumes; ethnographic collection, especially native American; prints and drawings of various periods
Exhibitions: American historic and contemporary; Asian; Ethnographic; Medieval and Ancient; European; Egyptian
Publications: Exhibition catalogs; quarterly museum calendar
Activities: Classes for adults & children; docent training; lectures open to public, 20 vis lectr per yr; concerts; gallery talks; tours; community outreach serves all Vermont; individual paintings & original objects of art lent to museum community; lending collection contains 2000 original prints, 500 paintings & 50 sculptures; book traveling exhibitions; originate traveling exhibitions; museum shop sells books, magazines, reproductions, prints & Vermont crafts
M **Francis Colburn Gallery,** Williams Hall, 05405. Tel 802-656-2014
Open Sept - May 9 AM - 5 PM. No admis fee. Estab 1975
Exhibitions: Student, faculty and visiting artist works

FAIRLEE

M **WALKER MUSEUM,** 37 Main St, PO Box 6, 05045. Tel 802-333-9572. *Dir* Herbert Brooks Walker II; *Asst Dir* Noel Gahagan Walker
Open by appointment only. No admis fee, donations accepted. Estab 1960. Average Annual Attendance: 1000
Collections: †American decorative arts; †American Indian art; 18th and 19th century American paintings; †Canadian displays; †Chinese porcelains; furniture; Iranian Bazaar; †Japanese room; †Polynesia; prints, sculpture
Exhibitions: Temporary exhibitions
Activities: Materials and items lent to libraries and schools; wagon loans by appointment; traveling exhibitions organized and circulated
L **Library,*** Rt 5, PO Box 6, 05045. Tel 802-333-9572. *Dir* Brooks Walker
For reference only
Library Holdings: Vols 1000; AV — Kodachromes; Other — Photographs

MANCHESTER

O **SOUTHERN VERMONT ART CENTER,** 05254. Tel 802-362-1405. *Pres* Frank L Hutchins; *Dir* Thomas Reilly Dibble; *Dir Public Relations* Margaret S Pierce; *Sales Dir* Anthony Holberton-Wood
Open June - mid-Oct daily, 10 AM - 5 PM, cl Mon. Estab 1929 to promote education in the arts and to hold exhibitions of art in its various forms. Average Annual Attendance: 20,000. Mem: 1100; dues layman $25 and higher, artist $15; annual meeting in Sept
Income: Financed by membership and sales
Collections: Contemporary American sculptors and painters; loan collection
Exhibitions: (1984) Annual exhibitions for members; Fall Show; one-man and special exhibitions
Publications: Annual catalog and brochures
Activities: Classes for adults in painting, drawing, graphic arts, photography, sculpture and pottery
L **Library,** 05254
Library Holdings: Vols 500

MIDDLEBURY

M **FROG HOLLOW CRAFT CENTER,** Frog Hollow Road, 05753. Tel 802-388-3177. *Exec Dir* Ann Roth; *Secy* Elaine Turpin; *Gallery Dir* Nancy Dunn; *Sales Mgr* Pat Pope; *Public Relations & Education* Melissa Pope
Open Mon - Sat 9:30 AM - 5 PM. No admis fee. Estab 1971 to provide craft educational, informational and marketing services to school children, adults and professionals. The building was once a working mill. Average Annual Attendance: 40,000. Mem: 450; dues $15 - $50; annual meeting Sept
Income: $275,000 (financed by membership, federal and state grants, fund raising activities, consignment receipts and tuition)
Purchases: $100-$1000
Collections: †Vermont Crafts
Exhibitions: (1984) Resident Potter Judith Bryant, Pieces of the Puzzle; Second Annual Youth Art & Craft Exhibit; Studio Potter; Handwoven Clothing, Barnyard Boogie, Christine Taylor & Madeline Fraioli; Ann Young & Preston McAdoo, Handmade Christmas Tapestries by Elinor Steele; Winter Wearables, textiles; Partners, jewelry & pewter
Publications: Information services bulletin; exhibition catalogs; calendar
Activities: Classes for adults and children; craft demonstrations; lect open to public, 3 vis lectr per yr; original objects of art lent to non-profit organizations; traveling exhibitions organized and circulated; sales shop

M **MIDDLEBURY COLLEGE,** Johnson Gallery, 05753. Tel 802-388-3711, Ext 5234. *Dir* David M Bumbeck; *Asst Dir* Glenn Andres
Open Mon - Fri Noon - 5 PM, Sat 9 AM - 5 PM, Sun Noon - 5 PM. No admis fee. Estab 1968 as a teaching collection and also to sponsor exhibitions of selected artists
Income: Financed through the college
Collections: †Drawings; †paintings; †prints; †sculpture
Exhibitions: Annual Student Show; Graphic Works by Isabel Bishop; Fibre Works by Sheila Hicks, Clare Zeisler and Daniel Griffin; Permanent Collection; Sculpture by Eric Nelson
Publications: Annual report

M **SHELDON ART MUSEUM,** Archaeological & Historical Society, One Park St, Box 126, 05753. Tel 802-388-2117. *Pres* Deborah P Clifford
Open June - Oct Mon - Sat 10 AM - 5 PM, winter hours by appointment. Admis adults $2, children $.50. Estab 1882 for the preservation of portraits, furniture and artifacts of Middlebury. Twelve rooms arranged as a 19th century Vermont home. Average Annual Attendance: 3500. Mem: 450; dues $5 and up
Collections: China; Glass; Pewter; Historical material; Portraits
Activities: Classes for children; guided tours; out-reach program to county schools; museum shop sells books, prints & crafts
L **Library,** One Park St, PO Box 126, 05753. *Librn* Polly C Darnell
Open Mon - Fri 10 AM - 5 PM
Library Holdings: Vols 8000; Library has 40,000 documents; bound copies of newspapers, manuscripts; Other — Manuscripts

MONTPELIER

M **WOOD ART GALLERY,** 135 Main St, 05602. Tel 802-229-0036. *Cur* Ronald Slayton; *Asst Cur* Olivia Bravakis
Open Tues - Sat Noon - 4 PM. No admis fee. Estab 1895; set up by the late Montpelier artist Thomas Waterman Wood as a place to house and exhibit a portion of his oils and watercolors of his genre paintings & portraits & copies of masters. Also an exhibit place for local and regional artists. The gallery has two exhibit areas; a large room 50 ft square and a small room 20 ft square; rooms are lighted with fluorescent lights. Average Annual Attendance: 4000. Mem: 300; dues $5 - $100; annual meeting Dec
Income: Financed by endowment and partial funding from city
Collections: Paintings by contemporaries J G Brown, DeHass, Durand, Wyant; Paintings by Thomas Waterman Wood; a collection of American artists of the 1920s & 1930s including Reginald Marsh, Louis Boucher, Joseph Stella & Paul Sample
Exhibitions: Group shows by artists and craftsmen; monthly exhibits by local and regional artists
Publications: Monograph on the Wood Collection
Activities: Lectures open to public, 5 vis lectr per yr; concerts; gallery talks; tours; competitions; individual paintings & original objects of art lent to local organizations, businesses & other museums; book traveling exhibitions

RUTLAND

O **RUTLAND AREA ART ASSOCIATION, INC,** Chaffee Art Gallery, 16 S Main St, PO Box 403, 05701. Tel 802-775-0356. *Pres & Co-founder* Henry Carris; *Senior Trustee & Co-founder* Katherine King Johnson
Open daily 10 AM - 5 PM, June - Oct. No admis fee. Estab and incorporated 1961 and sponsored by the Rutland Area Art Association to promote and maintain an educational and cultural center in Rutland for the area artists, photographers, craftsmen and others in the art field. Average Annual Attendance: 8000. Mem: 500; dues $10; annual meeting in Oct
Income: Financed by memberships, special funding and contributions
Exhibitions: Annual Members Exhibit, juried; Art-in-the-Park outdoor festival; Autumn Members Exhibit, juried; Foliage Festival: displays of photography, flower arrangements, hobby collections, special shows; one-man and invitational exhibits
Publications: Calendar of events, annually
Activities: Gallery talks; tours; individual paintings lent to banks; sales shop sells original art, reproductions, prints & crafts

SAINT JOHNSBURY

M **FAIRBANKS MUSEUM AND PLANETARIUM,** Main and Prospect Sts, 05819. Tel 802-748-2372. *Pres* Dr Arnold Waters; *VPres* Arnold Munkittrick; *Secy* Peter Crosby; *Actg Co-Dir* Howard B Reed; *Actg Co-Dir* Charles C Browns; *Registrar* Ruth Crane
Open Mon - Sat 10 AM - 4 PM, Sun 1 - 5 PM, extended summer hours. Admis families $5, adults $2, students and seniors $1.50, children $1.00, group rates available. Estab 1889 as a center for exhibits, special exhibitions, and programs; special exhibitions and programs on science, technology, the arts and the humanities. Art gallery for special exhibitions and work of regional artists. Average Annual Attendance: 35,000. Mem: 500; dues $25; monthly meeting
Income: $220,000 (financed by admissions income, grants, endowment, membership and city appropriation)
Collections: Hudson River School, primarily oil paintings; 19th century American and European art; Extensive natural science, history and anthropology collections
Exhibitions: Technology and Perception, the Photographic Vision of Nature; Victorian Legacies, the Fairbanks Family and their Peers; Swedish Nature Photography; Strong & Spirited: Women of the Northeast Kingdom
Publications: Newsletter
Activities: Classes for adults and children; docent training; lectures open to the public; concerts; gallery talks; tours; exten dept serving Northeast Vermont; artmobile; individual paintings and original objects of art lent to other accredited museums; lending collection contains 500 nature artifacts, 50 original art works, 10 paintings & 500 photographs; book traveling exhibitions; museum shop sells books, magazines, original art, reproductions, prints, slides, science kits, kites and crafts; junior museum

M **SAINT JOHNSBURY ATHENAEUM,** 30 Main St, 05819. Tel 802-748-8291. *Librn* Jean F Marcy
Open Mon - Sat 9:30 AM - 5 PM, Mon & Wed open to 8 PM. No admis fee. Estab 1873 and maintained as a 19th century gallery; given to the townspeople by Horace Fairbanks. It is the oldest art gallery still in its original form in the United States; a one-room addition to the public library building
Income: Financed by endowment and city appropriation
Collections: 19th century American landscape paintings of the Hudson River School (Bierstadt, Colman, Whittredge, Cropsey, Gifford, Hart brothers); copies of masterpieces; sculpture
Exhibitions: Permanent Collection
Publications: Art Gallery Catalogue

SHELBURNE

M **SHELBURNE MUSEUM,** Route 7, 05482. Tel 802-985-3346. *Dir* Benjamin Mason; *Comptroller* Joseph Mullen; *Registrar* Celia Y Oliver
Open 9 AM - 5 PM, mid-May - mid-Oct. Admis adults $8.50, children $3.50; special group and student rates. Estab 1947 as Museum of the American Spirit to collect, preserve and exhibit American fine, decorative and utilitarian arts, particular emphasis on Vermont. 35 buildings on 45 acres. Average Annual Attendance: 160,000
Income: Financed primarily by admissions and fund raising from members
Collections: American paintings, folk art, decoys, architecture, furniture, quilts and textiles, dolls, sporting art and sculpture, ceramics, tools, sleighs and carriages, toys, farm and home implements; European material: Impressionist and Old Master paintings; English furniture and architectural elements; seven period houses; Native American ethnographic artifacts; Sidewheeler Ticonderoga, railroad memorabilia including steam train, circus material and carousel animals
Activities: Classes for adults & children; docent training; lectures open to public, 5-10 vis lectr per yr; concerts; tours; individual paintings & original objects of art lent to other institutions around the US; originate traveling exhibitions; museum shop sells books, reproductions & slides
L **Library,** Route 7, 05482
Open to public by appointment
Library Holdings: Vols 10,000

SPRINGFIELD

O **SPRINGFIELD ART & HISTORICAL SOCIETY,** 9 Elm St, 05156. Tel 802-885-2415. *Pres* Mrs Kent Kirkland; *Treas* Mrs Bruce H Zeiser; *Clerk* David Shuffleburg; *Dir* Mrs Fred R Herrick
Open Tues - Fri 1 - 5 PM, Sat 1 - 4 PM. No admis fee. Estab 1955 for the purpose of presenting history, art and classes in the arts to the community. Gallery maintained for monthly exhibits. Average Annual Attendance: 3000. Mem: 150; dues $25, $15, and $7.50; annual meeting in Sept
Income: $15,000 (financed by endowment and membership)
Collections: Primitive portraits by H Bundy, Aaron D Fletcher, and Ashel Powers; Richard Lee, pewter; Bennington pottery; paintings by local artists; toys, costumes, sculpture, crafts
Exhibitions: Historical exhibits: costumes, toys; photography;
Publications: Annual schedule of events and monthly notices
Activities: Classes for adults and children; lect open to the public; gallery talks; individual paintings lent; lending collection contains original art work, paintings, photographs, sculpture, slides; sales shop sells books, original art, slides
L **Library,** 9 Elm St, 05156
Open to the public
Library Holdings: Vols 300; Per subs 3

WAITSFIELD

M **MILLHOUSE-BUNDY PERFORMING & FINE ARTS CENTER,*** Route 100, 05673. Tel 802-496-3713. *Dir & Pres* David Millstone; *VPres* Linde Millstone; *Asst Dir* Mary Schipa; *Cur* Gene Sousa
Open summer & fall 10 AM - 5 PM, cl Wed, winter Sat 10 AM - 5 PM, special events. No admis fee. Estab 1962, inc 1963 to make contemporary art and an art

library accessible to the public and to enhance the cultural life of surrounding communities. Multilevel modern gallery. Average Annual Attendance: 2000.
Mem: 125; dues $25
Collections: †Contemporary painting and sculpture
Exhibitions: traveling exhibitions
Activities: Educ dept; classes for adults andchildren; dramatic programs; docent training; workshops; seminars; lectures open to public; concerts; gallery talks; tours; competions with awards; individual paintings and original objects of art lent for lease or contribution; museum-sales shop sells original art
L **Library,*** Route 100, PO Box 19, 05673. Tel 802-496-3712
Library Holdings: Vols 450; Per subs 6; Other — Original art works, photographs, prints, sculpture

VIRGINIA

ALEXANDRIA

O **ART LEAGUE,** 105 N Union St, 22314. Tel 703-683-1780. *Pres* Cora J Rupp; *VPres* Lella Lee Edwards; *Secy* Kay Kaiser; *Gallery Co-Dir* Betsy Anderson; *Gallery Co-Dir* Geri Gordon
Open 10 AM - 5 PM daily. No admis fee. Estab 1953 to promote and maintain standards of art through membership juried exhibitions and a large school which teaches all facets of the fine arts and some high skill crafts. Three rooms in the Torpedo Factory Art Center in Old Town Alexandria, Virginia. Average Annual Attendance: 100,000. Mem: 700; annual dues $25; meetings in June
Exhibitions: Monthly juried shows for members
Activities: Classes for adults and children; docent training; lectures open to public, 6-10 vis lectr per year; gallery talks; tours; sponsors competitions with awards

O **NORTHERN VIRGINIA FINE ARTS ASSOCIATION,** The Athenaeum, 201 Prince St, 22314. Tel 703-548-0035. *Exec Dir* Betsy Mansmann; *Asst Dir* Nancy Morgan
Open Tues - Sat 10 AM - 4 PM, Sun 1 - 4 PM, cl Mon & holidays. No admis fee. Estab 1964 to promote education, appreciation, participation and pursuit of excellence in all forms of art and crafts; to enrich the cultural life of the metropolitan area and Northern Virginia. Main gallery space on main floor, with additional area available. Average Annual Attendance: 15,000. Mem: 350; dues $25 - $30
Income: Financed by membership & fund raisers
Exhibitions: Costumes of the 18th Century; An Audience with Fanny Kemble; The Frog Prince; History of Printmaking; Artists as Printmakers: A Personal Viewpoint; Mountain Tunes and Tales; The Little Red Hen; 12th Annual Athenaeum Multi-media Juried Show; Qualities of Printmaking; The Works of Victor Hammer; Sculpture by Murney Keleher; (1983) Wood Engravings: Barry Moser; Sculpture: Genna Watson; Matisse Prints; Peter Thomas
Publications: Newsletter, monthly
Activities: Classes for children; dramatic programs; docent training; lectures open to public, 4 - 6 vis lectrs per year; gallery talks; tours; competitions with awards; concerts; scholarships; book traveling exhibitions

ANNANDALE

SUMI-E SOCIETY OF AMERICA
See National and Regional Organizations

ARLINGTON

L **ARLINGTON COUNTY DEPARTMENT OF PUBLIC LIBRARIES,** Fine Arts Section, 1015 N Quincy St, 22201. Tel 703-527-4777. *Head* Jody Haberland
Open Mon - Thur 9 AM - 10 PM, Fri & Sat 9 AM - 5 PM, Sun 1 - 9 PM. Estab 1935 to serve needs of a urban-suburban population in all general subjects
Exhibitions: Local artists, crafts people and photographers have exhibitions at the central library each month in second floor lounge gallery, and first floor display cases. Six branch libraries also have special exhibits of similar nature
Publications: Monthly almanac of programs, library activities & exhibits
Activities: Lectures open to public, 10 vis lectr per year; extended learning institute video-tapes from Northern Virginia Community College available

BLACKSBURG

O **BLACKSBURG REGIONAL ART ASSOCIATION,** PO Box 525, 24060. Tel 703-552-0769. *Pres* Dr Donald R Fessler; *VPres* Dr Whitfield Cobb; *Secy* JoAnn Underwood; *Treas* Ellen Glover
Estab 1950, a chapter of the Virginia Museum of Fine Arts dedicated to the encouragement and the enjoyment of the arts. Mem: Dues including membership to the Virginia Museum, family $12, individual $8
Income: Financed by membership & patron contributions
Collections: †Collection of paintings by contemporary artists who have exhibited in Blacksburg
Activities: Dramatic programs; lectures open to public, 3 - 5 vis lectr per year; concerts; competitions; artmobile; originate traveling exhibitions

VIRGINIA POLYTECHNIC INSTITUTE AND STATE UNIVERSITY
M **University Art Gallery,** Visual Arts Bldg, 24061. Tel 703-961-5547. *Head Art Dept* Victor Huggins
Open Mon - Sun 9 AM - 5 PM. No admis fee. Estab 1969; new location Sept 1975 to serve needs of Art Department as a teaching gallery as well as to meet community needs in an area where there are few large art centers and museums.

Gallery is located in same building as Art Department; exhibition area is approx 30 x 30 ft. Average Annual Attendance: 1000 plus student use
Income: Financed through Departments Operational Budget
Collections: Student print collection
Exhibitions: Walter Darby Bannard; William Noland
Publications: Exhibition calendar; gallery announcements
Activities: Docent training to college students; lect open to the public, 3 vis lectr per yr; gallery talks; individual paintings and original objects of art lent to faculty and staff offices on campus, as well as library and continuing education center; traveling exhibitions organized and circulated

M **Squires Art Gallery,** Squires Student Center, Virginia Tech, Blacksburg, 24061. Tel 703-961-5661. *Dir Arts* Thomas F Butterfield
Open Mon - Sat 8 AM - Midnight, Sun 9 AM - Midnight. Estab 1969 to provide exhibits on the local and national level for the students, faculty and the college community. Weekly meetings of students and advisors to plan shows and events. Average Annual Attendance: 50,000
Income: Financed by student activity fee and building operation
Activities: Lect open to the public, 3 vis lectr per yr; competitions

L **Architecture Library,** Cowgill Hall, 24061. Tel 703-961-6182. *Dean* Charles W Steger; *Librn* Robert E Stephenson
Open Mon - Thurs 8 AM - 11 PM, Fri & Sat 8 AM - 5 PM, Sun 2 - 11 PM. Estab 1928 to provide service to the College of Architecture and Urban Studies and the other divisions of the University. Circ 30,890
Income: $57,700 (financed by state appropriation & gifts)
Purchases: $57,700
Library Holdings: Vols 42,124; Per subs 466; Micro — Fiche, reels; AV — Cassettes, slides, v-tapes; Other — Clipping files, exhibition catalogs, pamphlets
Special Subjects: Architecture, Art Education, Building Construction, Urban Affairs & Planning
Collections: Planning file, including urban affairs and planning, (1823 books and pamphlets)

CHARLES CITY

M **SHIRLEY PLANTATION,*** Route 2, Box 57, 23030. Tel 804-795-2385. *Owner* Charles Hill Carter Jr
Open daily 9 AM - 5 PM, cl Christmas Day. Admis adults $3.50, students $2.50, sr citizens $2, children $1.50, group rates. Estab 1723 to show the history of one distinguished family from colonial times to the present. Average Annual Attendance: 36,000
Income: $75,000 (maintained by admission fees)
Collections: Original portraits; silver and furniture: English and American
Activities: Individual paintings and original objects of art lent occasionally for exhibitions staged by such organizations as Virginia Museum and Colonial Williamsburg; museum shop sells books, reproductions, prints and slides

M **WESTOVER,** Rte 2 Box 94, 23030. Tel 804-829-2882. *Owner* Mrs B C Fisher; *Mgr* F S Fisher
Grounds and garden open daily 9 AM - 6 PM. Admis $2, children $.50; house interior not open. Built about 1730 by William Byrd II, Founder of Richmond, the house is considered an outstanding example of Georgian architecture in America, with steeply sloping roof, tall chimneys in pairs at both ends, elaborate Westover doorway, a three story central structure with two end wings. The path from the Caretakers House to the house is lined with tulip poplars over 100 years old; former kitchen is a separate small brick building. East of the house (open to vistiors) is the Necessary House, an old icehouse and a dry well with passageways leading under the house to the river. The Westover gates of delicate ironwork incorporate initials WEB; lead eagles on the gateposts, fence columns topped with stone finials cut to resemble pineapples, beehives, and other symbolic designs. Long established boxwood garden with tomb of William Byrd II. Members of his family, and Captain William Perry, who died August 1637, are buried in old church cemetary one-fourth mile west of the house

CHARLOTTESVILLE

M **MONTICELLO,** Thomas Jefferson Memorial Foundation,* PO Box 316, 22902. Tel 804-295-2657. *Cur-Dir* James A Bear Jr
Open Mar - Oct Mon - Sun 8 AM - 5 PM, Nov - Feb Mon - Sun 9 AM - 4:30 PM, cl Christmas. Admis adults $3, children 6 - 11 $1, school groups $.50. Monticello is owned and maintained by the Thomas Jefferson Memorial Foundation, a non-profit organization founded in 1923. The home of Thomas Jefferson, designed by him and built 1769-1809, contains many original furnishings and art objects
Collections: Jeffersonian furniture; memorabilia; art objects & manuscripts

M **SECOND STREET GALLERY,** 116 N E Second St, 22901. Tel 804-977-7284. *Pres* Gail McIntosh; *VPres* Cynthia Davis; *Secy* Anneliese Henry; *Executive Dir* Marilyn Mars
Open Tues - Sat 10 AM - 4 PM, Sun 1 - 4 PM. No admis fee. Estab 1973 to exhibit and aquaint the Piedmont area with new and innovative visual art by local, state and national artists. Gallery has second story exhibition space, consisting of three rooms (largest is 25 sq ft), uncluttered and well-lit. Average Annual Attendance: 3000. Mem: 200; dues $30 family, $20 individual, $10 artists
Income: Financed by membershiop, state appropriation, art auction and fund-raising
Exhibitions: (1983-84) Von Zur Muehlen x 2; The Piedmont: Landscape Images by Artists of the Virginia Piedmont; Art in Business & Industry; Better Than a Necktie II: An Exhibition of Small, Affordable Works; Flash: An Aesthetic; Willie Hall, sculpture; Walter Garde, drawing; Try Brinkly, drawing; David Noyes, painting; Aggie Zed, sculpture; Mark Krastoff, photography; Greg Leach, drawing; Foon Sham, sculpture; National Exhibition of Works on Paper
Publications: Juried Exhibition catalogue
Activities: Classes for adults & children; films; video; performances; lectures open to public, 3 vis lectr per yr; gallery talks; compeittons with awards; book traveling exhibitions

UNIVERSITY OF VIRGINIA

M **Art Museum,** Thomas H Bayly Memorial Bldg, Rugby Rd, 22903. Tel 804-924-3592. *Cur* David B Lawall; *Cur Pre-Columbian Art* Dicey Taylor Burhans; *Dir of Education* Jane Anne Young; *Registrar* Sue F Deter; *Cur Asst* Stephen Margulies; *Secy* Ruth C Cross
Open Tues - Sun 1 - 5 PM, cl Mon. No admis fee. Estab 1935 to make original works of art available to students of the University and to the general public. Average Annual Attendance: 22,000. Mem: 800
Income: Financed by membership and state appropriation
Collections: †American art; †European Art in the age of Jefferson; †East Asian art; †contemporary art; †20th century prints; ethnic art; †Pre-Columbian Art; †African Art; †Oceanic Art; †prints and drawings
Exhibitions: (1982-83) Somalia in Word & Image; Lowell Nesbitt, paintings, drawings, prints; German Art 1909-1924; Dr Ernst & Anne Fischer, prints & watercolors; contemporary German Art; Peruvian ceramics from the Arthur M Sackler Collection Conrad Felixmuller; Post Modern Man; Renewal of Classicism
Publications: May Ceramic Vases from the Late Classic Period; Leon Kroll: A Spoken Memoir
Activities: Docent training; extensive program of tours for school children; lect open to public, 3 vis lectr per yr; individual paintings lent to other museums; museum shop sells books, original art, reproductions, jewelry, cards

L **Fiske Kimball Fine Arts Library,** Bayly Dr, 22903. Tel 804-924-7024. *Librn* Mary C Dunnigan; *Slide Librn* Lynda White; *Bibliographer* Christie Stephenson
Open school year Mon - Fri 8 AM - 11 PM, Sat 9 AM - 6 PM, Sun 1 - 11 PM. Estab 1970; combination of existing Art and Architecture libraries to provide a research facility providing printed, microfilm and audio visual materials for the art, architecture and drama curriculum. Fifty percent of collection is noncirculating. Circ 127,244
Income: $117,000
Purchases: $127,244
Library Holdings: Vols 75,753; Per subs 258; Rare Books; Micro — Fiche, reels; AV — A-tapes, cassettes, fs, Kodachromes, lantern slides, motion pictures, rec, slides; Other — Exhibition catalogs, manuscripts, memorabilia, pamphlets, photographs
Special Subjects: Archaeology, Architecture, Art History, Film, Photography, Drama, Landscape Architecture, Planning and Urban Design
Collections: Francis Benjamin Johnson Photographs of Virgina Architecture; playbills, primarily New York Theatre; Rare books
Activities: Lect; tours

COURTLAND

M **WALTER CECIL RAWLS MUSEUM,*** Hwy 58 (Mailing add: PO Box 318, 23837). Tel 804-653-2821. *Chmn* Euan G Davis; *VChmn* L William Ballard; *Secy* Rebecca Beale; *Dir* William R Swinson; *Admin Asst* Carol Davis
Open Mon & Wed 9 AM - 8:30 PM, Tues, Thurs, Fri 9 AM - 5 PM, Sat 9 AM - 3 PM. Estab 1958 to promote the arts in the city of Franklin and the counties of Isle of Wight, Southampton, Surry and Sussex. Main gallery is 45 by 50 ft, 12 ft high with track design. Average Annual Attendance: 3000. Mem: 248; dues $12, $15, $30, $50; annual meeting in April, Board of Trustees meet monthly
Income: $17,500 (financed by endowment and membership)
Library Holdings: Paintings 20
Collections: Antique glass & silver; Southeastern Virginia Artists
Exhibitions: Form & Function - 500 years of the Chair as Art; The Romantic Bronzes
Publications: The Regional Arts Calendar, monthly
Activities: Classes for adults and children; lectures open to public, 3 vis lectr per yr; chamber concert series; sponsor annual 4 county art show; awards; paintings and art objects lent to museums and libraries; book traveling exhibitions, 2 per yr

DANVILLE

M **VIRGINIA MUSEUM,** Danville Museum of Fine Arts and History, 975 Main St, 24541. Tel 804-793-5644. *Pres* Haywood Thomas; *VPres* James Daniel; *Exec VPres & Dir* Dr James W Jennings; *Chmn Finance Committee* Loyd Harvey; *Museum Shop Mgr* Martha Corr; *Guild Dir* Doris Jones; *Office Secy* Betty Jones; *Dir Development* Louise Bendall; *Publicity & General Asst* Dianne McDonald
Open Tues - Fri 10 AM - 5 PM, Sun 2 - 5 PM. No admis fee. Estab 1974. Museum has two galleries: 27 x 35 ft with track lighting; two smaller galleries: 24 x 17 ft with track lighting. Average Annual Attendance: 8000. Mem: 779; annual meeting March & Sept
Income: Financed by membership, city and state appropriation and grants
Collections: Lithography Collection: Thomas Hart Benton, Regionalist School, Grant Wood; Taiwan Collection: Modern Scrolls, porcelain and bronzes; textiles (15th - 19th century); furnishings and wood carvings - European - 15th & 17th centuries; regional photographs, late 19th and early 20th century, letters and documents; Civil War Period: Contemporary Paintings
Exhibitions: Historic artifacts and memorabilia, brass, porcelain, Civil War objects
Publications: Last Capital of the Confederacy, book; Activities Report, quarterly newspaper; Record of Davis' government in Danville, Last week of Civil War
Activities: Classes for adults and children; dramatic programs; docent training; lectures open to the public, 6 vis lectr per yr; concerts; gallery talks; tours; original objects of art lent to other museums or galleries; museum shop sells books, original art and reproductions

L **Library,** Danville, 24541
Reference only
Library Holdings: Vols 5; Other — Manuscripts, memorabilia, photographs

FARMVILLE

M LONGWOOD COLLEGE, Bedford Gallery, Pine St, 23901. Tel 804-392-9359.
Dir Barbara L Bishop
Open Mon - Fri 9 AM - Noon, 1 - 5 PM, Sat 2 - 5 PM, Sun 5 - 9 PM, cl college holidays. No admis fee. Estab 1970 to present educational exhibits of professional artists for students and community
Income: Financed by state appropriation
Purchases: Work of a contemporary Virginia artist - annually
Collections: †Art Department collection; †collection of works by contemporary Virginia artists; †Thomas Sully Gallery Collection of 19th and 20th Century Art
Exhibitions: Survey of American Illustration (Society of Illustrators); Craft Collectables (Virginia Craftsmen); Works by a Contemporary Virginia Artist; Current Directions: Explorations in Clay (National Council on Education for Ceramic Arts); Stones, Bones, and Clay - An Archeological View of the Indians of the Virginia Piedmont
Publications: Exhibition catalogues
Activities: Lect open to public, 2 - 4 vis lectr per year; gallery talks; Individual paintings and original objects of art lent

FREDERICKSBURG

M MARY WASHINGTON COLLEGE, Belmont, The Gari Melchers Memorial Gallery, 224 Washington St, 22405. Tel 703-373-3634. *Dir* Richard S Reid
Open 1 - 5 PM. Admis adults $1.50, students $.50, group rates available. Estab 1975 to exhibit, preserve and interpret the works of art and memorabilia of the late American Artist Gari Melchers, in his former estate and studio. Studio consists of three gallery rooms, a work room, and storage rooms. Average Annual Attendance: 4000
Income: $100,000 (financed by endowment and state appropriation)
Collections: Over six hundred works of art, paintings, drawings and etchings by Gari Melchers; Over 1000 sketches and studies by Gari Melchers; Paintings and drawings by Berthe Morisot, Franz Snyders, Puvis de Chavannes, Rodin and others; Furnishings from Europe and America
Exhibitions: (1984) Melchers in Holland
Activities: Lectures open to the public; gallery talks; tours; book traveling exhibitions; sales shop sells postcards, pamphlets, magazines and reproductions

M JAMES MONROE LAW OFFICE - MUSEUM AND MEMORIAL LIBRARY, 908 Charles St, 22401. Tel 703-373-8426. *Dir* Rosalie Mercein Sullivan
Open daily 9 AM - 5 PM, cl Thanksgiving, Dec 24, 25, 31 & Jan 1. Admis adults $1.50, children $.50, group rates available. Estab to keep in memory the life and service of James Monroe and of his contribution to the principles of government, to preserve his treasured possessions for present and future generations. Open to the public in 1928; owned by Commonwealth of Virginia and under the control of Mary Washington College; a National Historic Landmark
Collections: Louis XVI furniture purchased by the Monroes in France in 1794 and later used by them in the White House; portraits; sculpture; silver; china; jewelry
Publications: Library of James Monroe, catalog
Activities: Tours; museum shop sells books, reproductions, prints, slides, history related objects & exclusive items from local crafts people
L Library, 908 Charles St, 22401. *Chmn Libr Committee* Ruby Weinbrecht
Open by appointment only
Library Holdings: Vols 20,000; letters; documents; Other — Manuscripts

HAMPTON

O HAMPTON CENTER FOR ARTS AND HUMANITIES, 22 Wine St, 23669. Tel 804-723-1776, 723-1779. *Cultural Center Manager* Charles Smith; *Visual Arts Coordr* Nancy Parker; *Performing Arts Coordr* Gail Faxon; *Staff Secy* Barbara Wood
Open year round Mon - Fri 10 AM - 5 PM. No admis fee. Estab 1966 as a non-profit organization; now a division of the city of Hampton Recreation Department
Income: Financed by municipal funds & arts grants
Collections: Archaeology; paintings; photography; sculpture;
Exhibitions: Regional artists, monthly; special event art show
Activities: Classes for adults & children; dramatic programs; workshops; demonstrations; lectures open to public, 3 vis lectr per yr; concerts; gallery talks; tours; competitions with awards; book traveling exhibitions

M HAMPTON INSTITUTE, College Museum, 23668. Tel 804-727-5308. *Dir* Jeanne Zeidler
Open Mon - Fri 8 AM - 5 PM, Sat & Sun Noon - 4 PM. No admis fee. Average Annual Attendance: 10,000
Income: Financed by college funds
Collections: American Indian and Oceanic Art; Contemporary Afro-American Art; Traditional African
Activities: Lect open to public; film series; gallery talks; tours; individual paintings and original objects of art lent to other museums and art galleries with appropriate security

HARRISONBURG

M JAMES MADISON UNIVERSITY, Sawhill Gallery, Duke Fine Arts Center, 22801. Tel 703-433-6216. *Gallery Dir* Stuart C Downs
Open Mon - Fri 8 AM - Noon, 1 - 5 PM, 7 - 9 PM, Sat & Sun 1 - 5 PM. No admis fee. Estab 1967 to schedule changing exhibitions for the benefit of students and citizens of this area. One-room gallery of 1040 sq ft with movable panels. Average Annual Attendance: 7000 - 10,000
Income: Financed by state appropriation, and is part of operation in Art Department budget

Collections: Sawhill Collection, mainly artifacts from classical civilizations; Staples Collection of Indonesian Art; †small group of modern works
Exhibitions: Annual James Madison University Faculty Exhibition; Annual James Madison University Undergraduate Student Exhibition; 32nd Annual Exhibition, Art Directors Club of Metropolitan Washington; Seven Former James Madison University Students; Visual Articuletion of Idea from Visual Studies Workshop; Broken Surfaces (paintings); Debbera Stelling Ceramic Wall Pieces; Robert A Fisher (Persian rugs); James Madison University Graduate Students Group Show; Recent Italian Political Posters; New Works on Paper from Kathryn Markel Fine Arts, New York City; Exposure Time VI (photo competition); Southeastern Graphics Invitational
Activities: Competitions

LEESBURG

M OATLANDS OF THE NATIONAL TRUST, INC, Route 2, Box 352, 22075. Tel 703-777-3174. *Exec Dir* Nicole Sours
Open April - late Nov Mon - Sat 10 AM - 5 PM, Sun 1 - 5 PM. Admis adults $4, sr citizens and youth (7-18) $3, under 7 free; special events at special rates, group rates by arrangement, free to National Trust members except during special events. Oatlands is a Classical Revival Mansion constructed by George Carter, son of Robert (Councillor) Carter (circa 1800-06). It was partially remodeled in 1827 when the front portico with hand carved Corinthian capitals was added. Confederate troops were billeted here during the Civil War. The home remained in possession of the Carters until 1897. In 1903 Mr and Mrs William Corcoran Eustis, of Washington DC, bought Oatlands. Their daughters gave the property to the National Trust for Historic Preservation; the property is protected by preservation easements which help insure the estates continuing role as a center for equestrian sports and cultural events which are produced by Oatlands and various groups. Average Annual Attendance: 38,000
Income: $260,000 (financed by grants, endowments, admis, fund raising events and shop sales)
Collections: Carter and Eustis Collection of Furniture; Greek-Revival ornaments adorn interior
Exhibitions: All-Virginia Pewter Show; American Patriotic Poster Show; Annual Needlework Show; Two changing exhibits per year
Activities: Special events

LEXINGTON

WASHINGTON AND LEE UNIVERSITY

M Gallery of DuPont Hall, 24450. Tel 703-463-9111, Ext 351. *Dir* Debora Rindge; *Dir* Dr Albert C Gordon
Open Mon - Fri 9 AM - 5 PM, Sat 11 AM - 3 PM, Sun 2 - 4 PM, June, July & Aug. No admis fee. Estab 1929 in separate gallery, in existence since 1742, as teaching resource of the Art Department of the College of Liberal Arts. One room, 30 x 60 ft, is maintained for temporary exhibits; also maintained are offices, studios and one storeroom. Average Annual Attendance: 40,000
Income: Financed by the university
Collections: Collections of university contemporary works (students, faculty, alumni & gifts); European paintings from 17th-mid 19th centuries; Reeves Collection of Chinese Export Porcelain; Louise Herreshoff paintings
Exhibitions: Annual faculty show; annual student show; monthly exhibitions; traveling exhibitions
Publications: Exhibition catalogs
Activities: Lectures open to public, 5 vis lectrs per year; gallery talks; tours; book traveling exhibitions
L Art Dept Library, 24450. Tel 703-463-9111, Ext 403. *Librn* Maurice D Leach Jr
Open for reference to students, scholars, public; this library is part of the main University library
Library Holdings: Vols 8000; Per subs 50; AV — Slides 80,000
Special Subjects: American Art of 18th & 19th centuries
Collections: Rare Books, 17th - 19th centuries
M Lee Chapel and Museum, 24450. Tel 703-463-9111, Ext 289. *Dir* Robert C Peniston
Open mid-Apr to mid-Oct Mon - Sat 9 AM - 5 PM, Sun 2 - 5 PM, mid-Oct to mid-Apr Mon - Sat 9 AM - 4 PM, Sun 2 - 5 PM. No admis fee. Estab 1868 as a part of the University. It is used for concerts, speeches and other events. Museum is used also to display the paintings, collections and personal items of the Washington and Lee families. The Lee Chapel is a National Historic Landmark. Average Annual Attendance: 38,000
Income: Financed through the University
Collections: Custis-Washington-Lee Art Collection; Lee archives; Lee family crypt; Lee's office; recumbent statute of General Lee by Valentine
Publications: Brochure
Activities: Sales shop sells books, prints, souvenirs

LORTON

M GUNSTON HALL PLANTATION, Gunston Rd, 22079. Tel 703-550-9220. *First Regent* Mrs Franklin W Hobbs; *Dir* Donald R Taylor; *Asst Dir* Mary L Allen
Open daily 9:30 AM - 5 PM, except Christmas. Admis adults $3, students (6 - 15) $1. Estab 1949 to acquaint the public with George Mason, Colonial patriot and his 18th Century house and gardens, covering 555 acres. Owned and operated by the Commonwealth of Virginia. Average Annual Attendance: 50,000
Income: Financed by state appropriation and admis fee
Collections: 18th century English and American decorative arts, furniture and paintings; 18th and 19th century family pieces
Activities: Docent training; tours; individual paintings and original objects of art lent to other museums; lending collection contains cassettes, film strips, motion pictures, slides; sales shop sells books, reproductions; Childrens Touch Museum located in basement

L **Library,** Gunston Rd, 22079. Tel 703-550-9220. *Librn & Archivist* Bennie Brown Jr
Open Mon - Fri 9:30 AM - 5 PM by appointment. Estab 1974 to recreate an 18th Century Virginia gentlemen's library as a research source plus acquiring a working reference collection on George Mason and the decorative arts
Income: Financed by endowment
Library Holdings: Vols 7500; Per subs 50; original documents; Micro — Fiche, reels; AV — Cassettes, fs, motion pictures, rec, slides; Other — Exhibition catalogs, manuscripts, memorabilia, pamphlets, photographs, reproductions
Special Subjects: Decorative Arts, Mason family, Early Virginiana
Collections: Pamela C Copeland Collection; Robert Carter Collection; Mason-Mercer Collection; Elizabeth L Frelinghuysen Collection

LYNCHBURG

O **LYNCHBURG FINE ARTS CENTER INC,** 1815 Thomson Dr, 24501. Tel 804-846-8451. *Art Coordr* Ron Boehmer; *Secy* Donna M Hudson
Open Mon - Fri 9 AM - 5 PM, Sun 1 - 5 PM; other hours depending upon programs. No admis. Estab 1958 to promote interest in and appreciation and talent for art, music, dramatic literature and other fine arts. Mem: Dues student $20, single $45, double $70; annual meeting in June
Income: Financed by membership, corporate & private donation, earned income from programs & performances
Exhibitions: Eighteen per year
Publications: FACets, (newspaper), monthly except July
Activities: Classes for adults and children; dramatic programs; docent training; dance, theatre, music & visual arts workshops; lect open to public, 2 - 3 vis lectr per yr; concerts; gallery talks; tours; competitions with cash awards; scholarships; exten dept serving youth; concerts for youth and theatre classics in public schools; book traveling exhibitions; originate traveling exhibitions; sales shop sells original art

M **RANDOLPH-MACON WOMANS COLLEGE,** Maier Museum of Art, Quinlan St, 2500 Rivermont Ave, 24503. Tel 804-846-7392, Ext 362. *Cur* Nancy Mowll Mathews
Open Tues - Sun 1 - 5 PM, cl Mon. No admis fee. Estab in 1952 as a collection of American painting for general and specific educational use. Museum was built in 1952 in cooperation with the National Gallery of Art, it houses part of the permanent collection and is used for special exhibitions
Income: Financed by endowment
Collections: Extensive collection of American paintings; European and American graphics
Exhibitions: Abstract Art in the 80's; Quilts and Collages; American Art in Pieces;
Publications: Maier Museum of Art Newsletter, quarterly
Activities: Dramatic programs; lectures open to public, 5 vis lectr per year; concerts; gallery talks; tours; objects of art lent; originate traveling exhibitions

MCLEAN

INDUSTRIAL DESIGNERS SOCIETY OF AMERICA
For further information, see National and Regional Organizations

MIDDLETOWN

M **BELLE GROVE PLANTATION,*** PO Box 137, 22645. Tel 703-869-2028. *Pres* Belle Grove; *Exec Dir* Michael Gore
Open April - Oct Mon - Sat 10 AM - 4 PM, Sun 1 - 5 PM, Nov - March by appointment. Admis adults $2.50 sr citizens $2, students $1.25, special rates. Open to the public in 1967, it is preserved as an historic house and is the property of the National Trust for Historic Preservation and managed by Belle Grove, Inc, an independent local nonprofit organization. It serves as a local preservation center and resource for the interpretation of regional culture in the Shenandoah Valley. Built in 1794 for Major Isaac Hite, Jr, a Revolutionary War officer and brother-in-law of James Madison, Belle Grove was designed with the help of Thomas Jefferson. During the Battle of Cedar Creek in 1864, the house served as headquarters to General Phillip Sheridan. The property is a working farm, and Belle Grove maintains an active program of events for the visiting public
Activities: Seminars on various subjects in museum field offered through the year; gift shop open all year

MIDLOTHIAN

ASSOCIATION OF MEDICAL ILLUSTRATORS
For further information, see National and Regional Organization

MOUNT VERNON

M **MOUNT VERNON LADIES' ASSOCIATION OF THE UNION,** 22121. Tel 703-780-2000. *Regent* Mrs Thomas Duneway Anderson; *Resident Dir* John A Castellani
Open to the public every day in the year from 9 AM: entrance gate closes Mar 1 - Oct 1 at 5 PM, Oct 1 - Mar 1 at 4 PM. Admis $4. The home of George Washington, purchased in 1858 from his great-grand-nephew by the Mount Vernon Ladies Association of the Union, which maintains it. The estate includes spinning house, coach house, various quarters, restored flower and kitchen gardens; also the tomb of George and Martha Washington. Average Annual Attendance: 1,000,000. Mem: Semi-annual meeting Oct & May
Income: Financed by admission fees
Library Holdings: Vols 12,000; Other — Manuscripts 15,000
Collections: Mansion is fully furnished with original and period furniture, silver, portraits and prints; large collection of original Washington memoribilia
Publications: Annual Report

M **POPE-LEIGHEY HOUSE,** 22121. Tel 703-557-7881. *Asst Admin* Gordon Alt
Open Mar - Oct, Sat & Sun 9:30 AM - 4:30 PM. Pope-Leighey is a house museum of the National Trust for Historic Preservation, located on the grounds of Woodlawn. This residence was designed in 1940 by Frank Lloyd Wright for his client, the Loren Pope Family. Built of cypress, brick and glass, the Usonian structure contains such features as a flat roof, radiant heat, indirect lighting and built in furniture, all designed by Frank Lloyd Wright, and all considered unusual for their time. Threatened by proposed construction of an interstate highway in 1964, Mrs Marjorie Folson Leighey, second owner, presented the property to the National Trust for Historic Preservation. It was then moved to the Woodlawn grounds
Publications: Brochure and paperback history of house

M **WOODLAWN PLANTATION,** 22121. Tel 703-557-7881. *Adminr* George M Smith; *Asst Adminr* Gordon Alt
Open 9:30 AM - 4:30 PM, except Thanksgiving Day, Christmas Day, and New Years Day. Admis adults $3, senior citizens $2.50, students $1.50, group rates by arrangement. Originally part of Mount Vernon. Built in 1800-05 for George Washington's foster daughter upon her marriage to Lawrence Lewis. It was designed with central pavilion and flanking wings by Dr William Thornton, winner of the architectural competition for the design of the United States Capitol. A group of Quakers, a pioneer anthropologist, a playwright and Senator Oscar W Underwood of Alabama were among Woodlawns residents after the Lewises. In 1951 the foundations trustees decided that the visiting public would be better served if Woodlawn was administered by the National Trust. The mansion furnishings are largely from the Federal and early Empire periods and include Lewis family memorabilia and gifts from the Robert Woods Bliss and Colonel Garbish Collection. Average Annual Attendance: 60,000. Mem: 305; dues family $35, individual $25
Exhibitions: Candlelight, Music and Champagne in July; Carols by Candelight in December; Fall Festival of Needlework, seminar in October; Needlework Exhibit each March
Publications: Friends of Woodlawn Newsletter, quarterly
Activities: Classes for children; docent training; lectures; concerts; tours; competitions with awards; museum shop sells books, slides, handmade & craft items

NEWPORT NEWS

M **MARINERS MUSEUM,*** One Museum Dr, 23606. Tel 804-595-0368. *Pres* George W Passage; *Dir* William D Wilkinson; *Assoc Dir* Dr Nancy Melton; *Assoc Dir* Alene N Cofer; *Asst Dir for Coll* John O Sands
Open Mon - Sat 9 AM - 5 PM, Sun Noon - 5 PM, cl Christmas Day. Admis adults $1.50, children 6 - 16 years $.75, children under 6 free. Estab 1930, the museum is devoted to the culture of the sea and its tributaries, its conquest by man and its influence on civilization. Museum has thirteen galleries. Average Annual Attendance: 150,000. Mem: 1000, dues family $15, individual $10, student $7.50
Collections: †Crabtree Collection of miniature ships; †thousands of marine artifacts; †over 10,000 paintings; †over 1000 ship models
Publications: The Journal, quarterly
Activities: Classes for adults and children; dramatic programs; lect open to public, 10 visiting lectr per year; gallery talks; tours; competitions; individual paintings and original objects of art lent; lending collection contains 120 motion pictures, 2000 original art works, 8000 original prints, 1000 paintings; museum shop sells books, reproductions, prints, slides, decorative items (maritime related)

L **Library,*** One Museum Dr, 23606. Tel 804-595-0368. *Librn* Ardie L Kelly; *Asst to Librn* Kathryn B Braig; *Archivist* Roger T Crew Jr
Open Mon - Sat 9 AM - 5 PM. Estab 1930. For reference only
Income: Financed by endowment
Library Holdings: Vols 60,000; Per subs 200; original documents; AV — Fs, motion pictures, rec; Other — Clipping files, manuscripts, memorabilia, pamphlets, photographs 150,000
Special Subjects: Maritime and Naval history

O **PENINSULA FINE ARTS CENTER,*** Mariners Museum Park, PO Box 6438, 23606. Tel 804-596-8175. *Pres* David Peebles; *VPres* Mrs Ward Scull III; *Dir* Mary M Lake
Open Tues - Sat 10 AM - 4 PM, Sun 1 - 4 PM. No admis fee. Estab 1962 to bring the best art possible; to educate the people of the Virginia Peninsula; to encourage local artists. Three galleries maintained with changing exhibitions. Mem: 850; dues family (including membership) $25, individual $18; annual meeting fourth Mon in March
Income: Financed by membership
Publications: Art class schedules; newsletter to members, quarterly; notification of special events
Activities: Classes for adults and children; lect open to public, 8 visiting lectr per year; gallery talks; competitions; cash awards and certificates of distinction; gallery shop sells books, original art and crafts

NORFOLK

M **CHRYSLER MUSEUM,** Olney Rd and Mowbray Arch, 23510. Tel 804-622-1211. *Dir* Dr David W Steadman; *Admin Asst* Shirley Woodward; *Dir Public Relations & Development* James F Sefcik; *Chief Cur* Thomas W Sokolowski; *Cur Glass* Nancy O Merrill; *Cur Decorative Arts* Mark A Clark; *Cur of Photography* Brooks Johnson; *Dir Education* Ann D Vernon; *Pres of Board of Trustees* Thomas H Willcox, Jr; *Chairman Board of Trustees* Walter P Chrysler, Jr
Open Tues - Sat 10 AM - 4 PM, Sun 1 - 5 PM, cl Mon. No admis fee. Museum originates from a memorial association established in 1901 to house a collection of tapestries and paintings donated in memory of and by Irene Leache. The Norfolk Society of Arts was founded in 1917, which raised funds throughout the 1920's to erect a building to permanently hold the collection. A Florentine Renaissance style building, named the Norfolk Museum of Arts and Sciences, opened to the public in 1933. The Houston Wing, housing the Museum Theatre and Lounge, was added in 1956, followed by the Centennial Wing in 1976. The

building has been designated the Chrysler Museum since 1971, when the collection of Walter P Chrysler, Jr was given to Norfolk. Average Annual Attendance: 120,000. Mem: 3500; dues benefactor $10,000, fellow $5000, sponsor $2500, director's circle $1000, patron $500, friend $250, sustaining $100, associate $60, family $35, individual $25, student & sr citizen $20, corporate memberships also available

Income: Financed by municipal appropriation and state appropriations as well as federal grants

Collections: African artists; American art from 18th century primitives - 20th century Pop Art; Bernini's Bust of the Savior; Francoise Boucher, The Vegetable Vendor; Mary Cassatt, La Famille; Thomas Cole, The Angel Appearing to the Shepherds; Decorative arts including furniture, silver, gold, enameled objects and Worcester porcelain; 18th century English paintings; 14th-18th century Italian paintings; 15th-18th century Netherlandish and German works; Gauguin's Loss of Virginity; Bernice Chrysler Garbisch and Edgar William Garbish (Native American paintings); Institute of Glass; Matisse, Bowl of Apples on a Table; Near and Far East artists; Oriental artists; photography collection including Alexander Gardner, Lewis W Hine, Walker Evans, Ansel Adams, W Eugene Smith & contemporaries Joel Meyerowitz & Sheila Metzner; Pre-Columbian artists; Reni, The Meeting of David & Abigail; 16th - 20th century French paintings; works from Spanish school

Exhibitions: (1982) A Tricentennial Celebration: Norfolk 1682-1982; Norfolk, 300 Years Later: Three Days; American Silver; 26th Irene Leache Memorial Juried Exhibition; Andre Kertesz Retrospective; Visions & Dreams, surrealist art; Art Deco; Eastern Shore, Virginia, Raised-Panel Furniture, 1730-1830; Light Images '82, photography; Still Modern After All These Years; Tiffany's Flower Garden; Recent Photography Acquisitions; (1983) The Sailor, 1930-1945: The Image of an American Demigod; George Krause, photographs; Tidewater Documentary 1982, photographs; French Salon Paintings from Southern Collections; Nineteenth Century French Photography; Reallegory, contemproary; Seventeenth Century Dutch Paintings & Drawings from the collection of Emile Wolf; Richard Haas: Now You See It; Aspects of Color: Works on Paper from the Hirshhorn Museum & Sculpture Garden; Old Gods & Young Heros: The Pearlman Collection of Maya Ceramics; Contemporary Latin American Artists; Ghost Trains: Railroad Photographs of the 1950's by O Winston Link (1984) Mystique & Identity: Women's Fashions of the Fifties; Eye For Elegance: the Photography of George Hoyningen-Huene; The Year One (1984-2001); Artists in Arcadia: The International Inspiration of Italy 1760-1915; Alfred Stieglitz, photographs; 27th Irene Leache Memorial Juried Exhibition Treasures from Greece

Publications: Monthly members' newsletter; exhibition catalogues

Activities: Educ program; family programs; docent training; teacher workshops; outreach information packages; lectures open to public, 20 vis lectr per year; concerts; gallery talks; tours; competitions (juried); exten dept operates three historic homes; individual paintings and original objects of art lent to accredited museums; book traveling exhibitions; traveling exhibitions organized and circulated; museum shop sells books, original art, reproductions, prints, slides, glass, gold & silver jewelry, ceramics, stationary, postcards and toys

L **Jean Outland Chrysler Library,*** Olney Rd & Mowbray Arch, 23510. Tel 804-622-1211. *Librn* Amy Navratil Ciccone
Open by appointment only. Estab 1959 to collect materials in support of the collections of the Chrysler Museum. Reference only
Income: Financed by city appropriation
Library Holdings: Vols 75,000; Per subs 50; Micro — Fiche; Other — Clipping files, exhibition catalogs
Special Subjects: Glass, Art Nouveau, American Art; Western European Art
Collections: M Knoedler & Co, London Library: Western European painting, monographs, auction & exhibition catalogues; M Knoedler & Co, New York, microfiche, auction & exhibition catalogues, international, 18th century-1970
Activities: Lectures open to public; concerts; gallery talks; tours

M **HERMITAGE FOUNDATION MUSEUM,** 7637 North Shore Road, 23505. Tel 804-423-2052. *Dir* Philip R Morrison; *Cur & Registrar* Lela M Hine; *Asst to Dir* Michael Farrell; *Pres of Board* W P Chilton
Open daily 10 AM - 5 PM, Sun 1 - 5 PM, cl New Years Day, Thanksgiving Day, Christmas Day. Admis adults $2, children 6 - 18 $.50. Estab 1937 to disseminate information concerning arts, and maintain a collection of fine art materials. Mansion on 16-acre site houses major collections as well as two small changing exhibition galleries. Average Annual Attendance: 20,000. Mem: 400; dues $30; meeting four times per yr
Income: $110,000 (financed by endowment and membership)
Collections: English oak and teakwood woodcarvings; Major collection of decorative arts from various periods and countries; Oriental collection of Chinese bronzes and ceramic tomb figures, lacquer ware, jades and Persian rugs; Spanish and English furniture; 20th century paintings
Exhibitions: American Illustrator; Art on Paper; Isabel Bishop; Bernard Chaet (paintings); Contemporary American Graphics; Currier and Ives; Export Porcelain from a Private Collection; Freshwork (Virginia photographers); Alexandra Georges (photographs); The Photographs of Wright Morris; Henry Pitz (one man show); student exhibitions from summer workshops
Activities: Classes for adults and children; dramatic programs; lect open to public and auxiliary lect for members only, 10 - 12 vis lectr per yr; concerts; tours; scholarships; individual paintings & original objects of art lent to institutions; lending collection contains 750 original art works, 300 paintings, 150 records & 50 sculpture; book traveling exhibitions; originate traveling exhibitions

L **Library,** 7637 North Shore Rd, 23505. Tel 804-423-2052
Open to students for reference only
Library Holdings: Vols 800; Per subs 6

M **MACARTHUR MEMORIAL MUSEUM,** MacArthur Square, 23510. Tel 804-441-2965. *Dir* Lyman H Hammond Jr; *Secy* Janice Stafford Dudley; *Cur* Joseph M Judge
Open Mon - Sat 10 AM - 5 PM, Sun 11 AM - 5 PM, cl Thanksgiving, Christmas, New Years Day. No admis fee. Estab 1964 to memorialize General Douglas MacArthur. Located in the 1850 Court House which was rebuilt in 1962; eleven galleries contain memorabilia. Average Annual Attendance: 85,000
Income: $272,941 (financed by city appropriation and Federal revenue

sharing funds)
Collections: Objects d'art, murals, portraits, photographs
Publications: Proceedings of symposia on the occupation of Japan, every 2 years
Activities: Concerts; gallery talks; tours; fellowships offered; individual paintings and original objects of art lent to schools, museums, and municipal agencies; sales shop created by MacArthur Memorial Foundation sells books, reproductions, prints, slides

M **Library & Archives,** One MacArthur Square, 23510. Tel 804-441-2965. *Archivist* Edward J Boone; *Asst Archivist* Ellen E Folkama
Library Holdings: Vols 4000; original documents; Micro — Fiche, reels; AV — A-tapes, cassettes, motion pictures, rec, slides, v-tapes; Other — Clipping files, framed reproductions, manuscripts
Activities: Lect open to the public, 2-3 vis lectr per yr; tours; Scholarships offered

M **NAVAL AMPHIBIOUS MUSEUM,*** Naval Amphibious Base, Little Creek, 23510. Tel 804-464-7923, 464-8130. *Dir* Harold Farley Jr; *Cur* John M Stroud
Open Sat & Sun 1 - 5 PM, during week by appointment only, cl New Year's, Easter, Christmas. No admis fee. Estab 1970 to preserve the history of the Amphibious Force of the United States Navy. Average Annual Attendance: 30,000
Income: Financed by federal appropriation
Collections: Naval historical memorabilia, ship models, paintings, sculpture and silver
Activities: Lectures open to the public; tours; individual paintings and original objects of art lent to on base facilities

L **NORFOLK PUBLIC LIBRARY,** Feldman Fine Arts & Audio Visual Dept, 301 E City Hall Ave, 23510. Tel 804-441-2426. *Head* Audrey G Hays; *Librn* Bill Baker
Open Mon - Thurs 9 AM - 9 PM, Fri 9 AM - 5:30 PM, Sat 9 AM - 5 PM. Estab 1972 to offer free use of all types of materials in the performing, audio and visual arts. Circ 52,816
Income: Financed by city and state appropriation
Purchases: $56,000
Library Holdings: Vols 20,800; Per subs 108; Micro — Fiche, reels; AV — Cassettes, fs, motion pictures, rec, slides, v-tapes; Other — Clipping files, exhibition catalogs, framed reproductions, manuscripts, memorabilia, original art works, pamphlets, photographs, prints, reproductions, sculpture
Collections: Original Art by Local Artists; Postcard Collection

M **OLD DOMINION UNIVERSITY GALLERY,*** 5215 Hampton Blvd, 23508. Tel 804-440-4059, 440-3000. *Coordr Arts* Glen A Ray; *Art Chmn* E May Dreyer
Open Mon - Sun 1 - 5 PM. No admis fee. Estab 1972 for the exhibition of contemporary work; also established as a public forum for contemporary artists, with student exposure. Average Annual Attendance: 3000
Income: Financed by endowment and city appropriation
Activities: Lect open to public, 10 visiting lectrs per year; gallery talks; tours; competitions; exten dept

L **Art Library,** 5215 Hampton Blvd, 23508. *Art Libr Asst* Lynda Erickson
Open Mon - Thurs 8 AM - 11 PM, Fri 8 AM - 9 PM, Sat 10 AM - 5 PM, Sun 1 - 11 PM. Open to students and faculty; open to the public for reference
Income: Financed by state, gifts and grants
Library Holdings: Vols 9000; Micro — Cards, fiche, prints, reels; AV — A-tapes, fs, rec, slides, v-tapes; Other — Clipping files, exhibition catalogs, framed reproductions, manuscripts, memorabilia, original art works, pamphlets, photographs, prints, reproductions
Activities: Lectures; concerts; gallery talks; tours

PETERSBURG

M **CENTRE HILL MANSION,*** Centre Hill Court, 15 West Bank Street, 23803. Tel 804-732-8081. *Cur* Elizabeth T Lyon; *Hostess* Jane B Holt
Open Mon - Sat 9 AM - 5 PM, Sun 1 - 5 PM, cl holidays. No admis fee. Estab 1978 as a historic house museum, built in 1823. Twenty five rooms with period interiors. Average Annual Attendance: 11,000
Collections: Period furnishings of mid 19th century America
Activities: Concerts, gallery talks, tours

PORTSMOUTH

M **PORTSMOUTH MUSEUMS, COMMUNITY ARTS CENTER DIVISION,** 400 High St, PO Box 850, VA 23705. Tel 804-393-8543, 393-8718. *Dir* Frederick S Bayersdorfer Jr; *Admin Asst* Albert F Harris; *Cur* Suzanne Seidman
Open Tues - Sun 11 AM - 4 PM, cl Mon. To offer a wide variety of the visual and performing arts to the citizens of Tidewater area. Average Annual Attendance: 30,000. Mem: 350; dues $15; meetings third Tues of each month
Income: $280,000 (financed by city appropriation)
Purchases: $3000
Collections: Contemporary drawings by American artists
Publications: Bi-monthly calendar; bi-annual catalog of American Drawings shows; newsletter, monthly
Activities: Classes for adults and children; dramatic programs; workshops; lectures open to public, 5 vis lectr per yr; concerts; gallery talks; tours; competitions with awards; outreach program; individual paintings & original objects of art lent to art organizations; originate traveling exhibitions

RESTON

NATIONAL ART EDUCATION ASSOCIATION
For further information, see National and Regional Organizations

NATIONAL ASSOCIATION OF SCHOOLS OF ART AND DESIGN
For further information, see National and Regional Organizations

RICHMOND

O **AGECROFT ASSOCIATION,** Agecroft Hall, 4305 Sulgrave Rd, 23221. Tel 804-353-4241. *Dir* Dennis H Halloran; *Coordr of Educ* Elizabeth H Schmidt
Open Tues - Fri 10 AM - 4 PM, Sat & Sun 2 - 5 PM. Admis adults $2, students $1, group rates by prior arrangements. Estab 1968 to exhibit 15th century Tudor Manor House brought over from Lancashire, England in 1925-26 and rebuilt in Richmond. Furnished with period objects of art. Average Annual Attendance: 18,000
Income: Financed by endowment and admission
Purchases: 1560 portrait of William Dauntesey
Collections: 16th & early 17th century furniture & objects of art depicting Elizabethan lifestyle, when Agecroft Hall was at its pinnacle
Activities: Classes for adults; docent training; lectures open to public; concerts; gallery talks; specialized tours
L **Library,** Agecroft Hall, 4305 Sulgrave Rd, 23221. *Cur* William C McKemie
Open Tues - Fri 10 AM - 4 PM, Sat & Sun 2 - 5 PM. Estab to interpret 16th Century English lifestyle. Lending to universities only
Library Holdings: AV — Fs, lantern slides, slides; Other — Original art works

O **ASSOCIATION FOR THE PRESERVATION OF VIRGINA ANTIQUITIES,** 2705 Park Ave, 23220. Tel 804-359-0239. *Pres* Florence W Cabaniss; *Exec Dir* Robert A Murdock; *Cur* Stephenson B Andrews
Estab 1889 to acquire and preserve historic buildings, grounds and monuments in Virginia. Branches administer forty properties in Virginia. Among the properties: Jamestown Island; Walter Reed Birthplace, Gloucester County; Bacon's Castle and Smith's Fort Plantation, Surry County; John Marshall House, Richmond; Scotchtown, Hanover County; Mary Washington House, Hugh Mercer Apothecary Shoe and Rising Sun Tavern, St James Cottage, Fredericksburg; Smithfield Plantation, Blacksburg; Farmers Bank, Petersburg; Cape Henry Lighthouse and Lynnhaven House, Virginia Beach; Powder Magazine, Williamsburg; Holly Brook, Eastville. Hours and admissions vary according to location. Mem: 5997; dues $10; annual meeting first Sunday in May
Income: Financed by membership, endowment fund and donations
Collections: Decorative arts; 17th - 19th century furniture, glass, ceramics, metalwork and textiles
Publications: Discovery (magazine) annually; Newsletter, quarterly
Activities: Lectures open to public; Sales shop sells books, reproductions, prints and slides
L **Library,** 2705 Park Ave, 23220. Tel 804-359-0239
Library Holdings: Vols 5000
Special Subjects: Architecture, Decorative Arts, Historical Material

C **FEDERAL RESERVE BANK OF RICHMOND,*** 701 E Byrd St, 23219. Tel 804-643-1250. *Art Coordr* Jackson L Blanton
Open to public by appointment only. No admis fee. Estab 1978 to provide enjoyment, education and a stimulating work environment for employees and visitors; to give encouragement and support to artists of the Fifth Federal Reserve District. Collection displayed throughout building
Collections: Primarily a regional collection, representing artists who live or who formerly lived in the Fifth Federal Reserve District
Exhibitions: Rotating cameo exhibits in lobby
Activities: Tours

O **FEDERATED ARTS COUNCIL OF RICHMOND, INC,*** Heritage Square, 23219. Tel 804-643-4993. *Chmn* Adrienne G Hines; *Pres* Charles B Davis; *Exec Dir* Kathy L Dwyer
Open daily 9 AM - 5 PM. Established to promote and support the arts and to act as a unified voice for member agencies. Mem: 350; dues Active $30, Associate $15
Income: Financed by grants, contributions, membership and city appropriation
Publications: Monthly newsletter; Cultural Calendar of Events; PR Handbook; Membership Directory
Activities: Management seminars; downtown arts festival, lunchtime concerts; biannual art show; Outreach program to hospitals, senior centers and prisons

C **FIRST AND MERCHANTS NATIONAL BANK,*** F & M Center, PO Box 27025, 23261. Tel 804-788-2148. *In Charge Art Coll* Constance Cann
Certain areas open to public 9 AM - 5 PM, or by appointment with tour guides. No admis fee. Estab 1974 to support the arts (mostly Virgina artists), to enhance bank surroundings and as an investment. Collection displayed on 2nd floor (monthly exhibits); permanent collection in reception areas and offices throughout 24 floors
Collections: Contemporary works of art in different media, mostly local and Va artists, and some known artists
Activities: Tours by appointment; sponsored employee art exhibit; individual objects of art lent; Monthly exhibits by local, employee and Virginia artists; paintings on loan by local gallery

C **REYNOLDS METALS COMPANY,*** 6601 W Broad St, 23261. Tel 804-281-2965
Open Mon - Fri 8:30 AM - 5 PM, cl holidays. Estab 1957. Art collection displayed in lobby of headquarters offices
Collections: Aluminum sculpture by American sculptors; new pieces commissioned annually as symbol of annual R S Reynolds Memorial Award for distinguished architecture
Activities: Competitions, awards

C **UNITED VIRGINIA BANK,*** 900 E Main St, 23219. Tel 804-782-5000. *In Charge Art Coll* Lucy B Turlington
Estab 1970. Collection displayed in banks and offices; separate gallery used for new exhibit each month
Collections: Contemporary Art
Activities: Competitions with awards

M **VALENTINE MUSEUM,** 1015 E Clay St, 23219. Tel 804-649-0711. *Dir Coll* Jean DuVal Kane; *Asst Dir* Dr Bruce King; *Admin Asst* Roberta Carew; *Cur of General Coll* Elizabeth Childs
Open Tues - Sat 10 AM - 5 PM, Sun 1 - 5 PM. Admis adults $2, children and students $1. Estab 1894 as a museum of the life and history of Richmond. Average Annual Attendance: 27,000. Mem: 700; dues individual $20
Income: Financed by endowment, membership, city and state appropriation and gifts
Collections: Conrad Wise Chapman (oils, almost entire life works); William Ludlow Sheppard (drawings and watercolors); Edward Virginus Valentine (sculpture); outstanding collection of Southern photographs; †candlesticks, ceramics, costumes, glass, jewelry, lace, †paintings, †photographs, prints, sculpture, local history, regional art and decorative arts
Publications: Silhouette, bimonthly; Visitor, monthly
Activities: Classes for adults and children; docent training; dramatic programs; lectures open to the public, 5 vis lectr per year; competitions; concerts; tours; exten dept serving city and area counties; individual paintings lent to member corporations and other museums; lending collection contains color reproduction, paintings, photographs, decorative art objects; originate traveling exhibitions; museum & sales shops sell books, original art, reproductions, prints, slides and silver; Junior Museum
L **Library,** 1015 E Clay St, 23219. Tel 804-649-0711. *Cur of Library* Sarah Shields; *Librn* Edith Jeter
Open to the public by appointment only; non-lending, reference library
Library Holdings: Vols 6000; Per subs 20; Other — Clipping files, exhibition catalogs, manuscripts, memorabilia, original art works, pamphlets, photographs 50,000, prints 600, reproductions
Special Subjects: Photography, Local history, tobacco, Virginia's art

VIRGINIA COMMONWEALTH UNIVERSITY
M **Anderson Gallery,** 907 1/2 W Franklin St, 23824. Tel 804-257-1522. *Dir* Marilyn Zeitlin
Open Tues - Fri 10 AM - 6 PM, Sat 1 PM - 5 PM, Sun 1 - 5 PM, cl Mon except by appointment. Estab 1930, re-opened 1970 as the showcase for the contemporary arts in Richmond; to expose the university and community to a wide variety of current artistic ideas and expressions. Gallery is situated on campus in a four-story converted stable. There are seven galleries with a variety of exhibition spaces. Average Annual Attendance: 20,000
Collections: †Contemporary prints & paintings; cross section of prints from the 15th to 20th century covering most periods; vintage & contemporary photography
Exhibitions: Frances Barth, Jake Berthot, Lester Van Winkle; Andy Warhol: Selected Works from the Still Life Group of 1976; Joan Snyder; Messages: Words & Images; Transforming Nature; Jud Fine; Kent Floeter; Paul Rotterdam; The Stations of the Cross; Michael Goldberg; Pat Adams; Francese Torres; Komar & Melamid; Craig Kauffman; Lune Garcia; Terry Berkowitz; Masters of Contemporary Drawing
Publications: Catalogs, posters & brochures, periodically
Activities: Lectures open to public, 10 vis lectr per yr; concerts; gallery talks; competitions; lending collection contains 100 original art works, 100 original paintings & photographs; originate traveling exhibitions
L **School of The Arts Library,** 325 N Harrison St, 23284. Tel 804-257-1683. *Dir* Joan L Muller
Open Mon - Thurs 9 AM - 7 PM, Fri 9 AM - 4:30 PM, Sat 1 - 5 PM. Estab 1926 to support the teaching program of the eleven departments of the School of the Arts
Income: Financed by state appropriation
Library Holdings: Micro — Fiche; AV — Slides 350,000; Other — Exhibition catalogs 17,000
Collections: †Transparencies (2 x 2 inch) of works of art; †exhibition catalogs, worldwide in scope

O **VIRGINIA HISTORICAL SOCIETY,*** 428 North Blvd, PO Box 7311, 23221. Tel 804-358-4901. *Dir* Paul C Nagel; *Assoc Dir* Virginius C Hall Jr; *Asst Dir* Robert Strohm; *Cur Special Coll* Rebecca Perrine
Estab 1831 for collecting, preserving and making available to scholars research material relating to the history of Virginia, its collections include extensive holdings of historical portraiture. Gallery maintained housing historical portraiture and paintings. Mem: Dues $15 - $500
Income: Financed by endowment and membership
Collections: Manuscripts, books, maps, charts, prints, engravings, portraits, sculpture, firearms, flags
Publications: Virginia Magazine of History and Biography, quarterly; bulletin
L **Library,*** 428 North Blvd, PO Box 7311, 23221. Tel 804-358-4901. *Librn* Howson W Cole
Open Mon - Fri 9 AM - 5 PM, Sat & Sun 2 - 5 PM. Estab 1831 for the study of Virginia history
Income: Financed by endowment, membership, state appropriation and private donations
Library Holdings: Vols 200,000; Micro — Fiche, reels; Other — Clipping files, exhibition catalogs, manuscripts, memorabilia, original art works, pamphlets, photographs, prints, reproductions, sculpture
Publications: Bulletin, semi-annually; Virginia Magazine of History and Biography, quarterly
Activities: Lect open to public

M **VIRGINIA MUSEUM OF FINE ARTS,** Boulevard & Grove, Box 7260, 23221. Tel 804-770-6344. *Pres* Bruce C Gottwald; *Actg Dir* Charles L Reed Jr; *Deputy Dir* Steve Brown; *Dir Art Servs* Richard Woodward; *Chief Cur* Pinkney Near; *Programs Dir* William Gaines; *Registrar* Lisa Hummel; *Development*

Dir Paul Hood
Open Tues - Sat 11 AM - 5 PM, Sun 1 - 5 PM, cl Mon. Estab 1934; theatre opened 1955; South Wing added 1970. Participating in the museum's programs are the Fellows of Virginia Museum, who meet yearly to counsel the museum on its future plans; the Women's Council, which sponsors and originates special programs; the Collector's Circle, a group of Virginia art lovers which meets four times a year to discuss various aspects of collecting; the Corporate Patrons, state and local business firms who lend financial support to museum programs; Virginia Museum Youth Guild; and the Institute for Contemporary Art, which presents exhibitions of works by state, nationally and internationally known contemporary artists. Average Annual Attendance: 1,250,000. Mem: 16,500; dues $35 and higher; annual meeting in May
Collections: Lady Nancy Astor Collection of English China; Branch Collection of Italian Renaissance Paintings, Sculpture and Furniture; Ailsa Mellon Bruce Collection of 18th Century Furniture and Decorative Arts; Mrs Arthur Kelly Evans Collection of Pottery and Porcelain; †Arthur and Margaret Glasgow Collection of Flemish and Italian Renaissance Paintings, Sculpture and Decorative Arts; Nasli and Alice Heeramaneck Collection of Art of India, Nepal, Kashmir and Tibet; T Catesby Jones Collection of 20th Century European Paintings and Drawings; Dr and Mrs Arthur Mourot Collection of Meissen Porcelain; The John Barton Payne Collection of Paintings, Prints and Portuguese Furniture; Lillian Thomas Pratt Collection of Czarist Jewels by Peter Carl Faberge; †Adolph D and Wilkins C Williams Collection of Paintings, Tapestries, China and Silver; archaic Chinese bronzes; archaic Chinese jades; comprehensive collections of early Greek vases (8th century to 4th century BC); representative examples of the arts from early Egypt to the present time, including paintings, sculpture, furniture and objects d'art
Exhibitions: (1983-84) Painting in the South; Wealth of the Ancient World; Paintings from the Royal Academy
Publications: Arts in Virginia, 3 times per year; Virginia Museum Bulletin, monthly; brochures; bulletins, nine per year; catalogues for special exhibitions and collections; programs
Activities: Classes for adults and children in painting, drawing, graphics, ceramics and weaving; workshops; demonstrations; lectures; concerts; drama productions; fels offered (10 - 15 per year) to Virginia artists; art mobile; originate traveling exhibitions throughout the state of Virginia
L **Library,** Boulevard & Grove, 23221. Tel 804-257-0827. *Librn* Betty Stacy
Open Tues - Fri 9 AM - 5 PM. Estab 1954 for art history research. For reference only
Income: Financed by private funds
Library Holdings: Vols 48,000; Per subs 210; Micro — Fiche, prints, reels; AV — Slides; Other — Clipping files, exhibition catalogs, pamphlets
Special Subjects: Art History, Decorative Arts, Sculpture, Crafts
Collections: Wecdon Collection; Hayes Collections; Strause Collection

ROANOKE

O **ROANOKE MUSEUM OF FINE ARTS,** Center in the Square, One Market Square, 24011. Tel 703-342-8945. *Executive Dir* Peter Rippe; *Cur* Ann D Masters; *Business Mgr* Virginia B Porten; *Membership & Education Coordr* Dori B Fitzgerald; *Downtown Gallery Curator* Carol D Bivens
Open Tues, Wed & Sat 10 AM - 5 PM, Thurs & Fri 10 AM - 8 PM, Sun 1 PM - 5 PM. No admis fee. Estab 1951 to encourage and develop interest in the study of the arts; to provide ways and means for the purchase of works in the arts, and to exhibit fine arts and other works of art. The center is housed in an old home with extremely fine architectural detail. The main rooms have been turned into galleries. Average Annual Attendance: 30,000. Mem: 1500; dues $25 and up; annual meeting in Sept
Income: Financed by endowment and membership
Collections: Contemporary Art (predominately by regional artists); Classical Collection; Decorative Arts; Oriental Artifacts; Print Collection
Activities: Classes for adults and children; docent training; lect open to the public; gallery talks; tours; competitions with awards; individual paintings lent to qualified museums; museum shop selling books, original art, prints, reproductions, handmade crafts including jewelry and children's items

STAUNTON

M **WOODROW WILSON BIRTHPLACE FOUNDATION,** 20 N Coalter St, PO Box 24, 24401. Tel 703-885-0897. *Dir* Katharine L Brown
Open daily 9 AM - 5 PM, cl Sun of Dec, Jan & Feb, Thanksgiving, Christmas and New Year's Day. Admis adults $2.50, senior citizens $2, children 6-16 $1. Estab 1938 in the 1846 Presbyterian Manse which was the birthplace of Woodrow Wilson. Mem: Dues $15 - $1000
Collections: Historical Material pertinent to the Wilson family; decorative arts, furniture, manuscripts, musical instruments, paintings, photographs, prints and drawings, rare books, textiles
Exhibitions: (1983) Woodrow Wilson: Professor, President, Peacemaker
Publications: Brochures; guides; Newsletter, semi-annually; pamphlets
Activities: Classes for adults & children; lectures open to public, 4 vis lectr per yr; concerts; tours; competitions with awards; scholarships; original objects of art lent to museums & government agencies; sales shop sells books, reproductions & slides
L **Library,** 20 N Coalter St, PO Box 24, 24401. *Librn* Trudy Davis

STRASBURG

M **STRASBURG MUSEUM,** E King St, 22657. Tel 703-465-3175. *Pres* J J Crawford; *VPres* Mrs John F Cadden; *Secy* Carole Hunt; *Treas* Mrs Paul Hatmaker; *Resident Potter* Mrs A L Dryer
Open May to Oct, daily 10 AM - 4 PM. Admis adults $1, children $.50. Estab 1970 to present the past of a Shenandoah Valley community and to preserve the pottery-making tradition of Strasburg. The museum is housed in the former Southern Railway Depot, which was orginally built as a steam pottery. Average Annual Attendance: 2300. Mem: 169; dues $2.50; annual meeting in March

Income: Financed by membership, admission fees and gifts
Collections: Indian Artifacts; pottery
Activities: Classes for adults and children in pottery making; museum shop selling books, original art, pottery and other local crafts

SWEET BRIAR

L **SWEET BRIAR COLLEGE,** Martin C Shallenberger Art Library, 24595. Tel 804-381-6138, 381-3315. *Dir* John G Jaffe; *Asst Dir* Patricia Wright; *Public Service* Christopher Bean; *Cataloger & Branch Coordr* Kathleen Lance
Estab 1961, when it was separated from the main library, the library serves an undergraduate community. There is a small gallery in the lobby which is overseen by the asst in art history
Income: Financed by college funds
Library Holdings: Vols 10,000; Per subs 30; AV — Cassettes, Kodachromes, lantern slides; Other — Original art works, prints

VIRGINIA BEACH

O **VIRGINIA BEACH ARTS CENTER,** 1711 Arctic Ave, 23451. Tel 804-428-9294. *Dir* Frederick Schmid; *Administrator* Robert Kelley; *Asst Cur* Elizabeth Wallace; *Public Relations & Events Coordr* Dan Goldblatt; *Admin Asst* Susan Blum; *Secy* Telathia Harrell; *Preparator* Larry Johnson
Open Mon - Sat 10 AM - 5 PM. No admis fee. Estab 1952, as a non-profit organization serving residents of the greater Hampton Roads area with exhibits & programming in the visual arts. Exhibition space 20 x 30 ft and 140 ft in hall gallery. Average Annual Attendance: 43,000. Mem: 1000; dues family $20 and up
Income: Financed by memberships, public grants, private donations, various fund raising events & art sale commissions
Collections: Best-in-Show winners from Boardwalk Art Show
Exhibitions: 12-14 temporary art shows per yr covering painting, photography, printmaking, sculpture, clay & fine crafts
Publications: ArtLetter, monthly
Activities: Classes & workshops for adults & children; preview openings for gallery exhibitions; art shows & festivals; Speakers' Bureau; lecture series

WILLIAMSBURG

M **COLLEGE OF WILLIAM AND MARY,** Joseph & Margaret Muscarelle Museum of Art,* 23185. Tel 804-253-4000. *Chmn Fine Arts Dept* James D Kornwolf
Open Mon - Fri 9 AM - 5 PM
Income: Financed by endowment, state appropriations and donations
Collections: Museum houses the paintings, drawings, prints, sculpture, ceramics & porcelain that composes the college art collection
Exhibitions: Sponsors changing exhibitions of art in the museum & in the Andrews Hall Gallery, which houses contemporary 2-D & 3-D art work

M **COLONIAL WILLIAMSBURG FOUNDATION,** PO Drawer C, 23187. Tel 804-229-1000. *Pres* Charles R Longsworth; *Dir Media Relations* Albert O Louer; *VPres Media & Government Relations* Norman G Beatty; *Dir & Cur Coll* Graham S Hood
Open 9 AM - 5 PM, Folk Art Center 11 AM - 7 PM. The colonial area of this 18th century capital of Virginia, encompassing 173 acres with nearly 500 homes, shops, taverns, public buildings, dependencies, has been carefully restored to its original appearance. Included are 90 acres of gardens and greens. The work was initiated by the late John D Rockefeller, Jr. There are more than 30 exhibition homes, public buildings and craft shops where guides and craftsmen in colonial costume show visitors the arts and decoration as well as the way of life of pre-Revolutionary Virginia. Included are the historic Bruton Parish Church, the Abby Aldrich Rockefeller Folk Art Center, The Courthouse of 1770, Bassett Hall (local residence of the Rockefellers), and Carter's Grove plantation. The exhibition properties include 225 furnished rooms. Average Annual Attendance: 1,000,000
Income: $74,615,352 (financed by endowment, ticket sales, products, restaurants & hotels)
Collections: 18th Century English and American Painting; English Pottery and Porcelains; English and Early American Silver; Collections of American and English furnishings, with frequent additions, include representative pieces, rare English pieces in the palace; exceptionally fine textiles and rugs; extensive collection of primary & secondary materials relating to British North America, the Colonial Period & the early National Period
Exhibitions: Brush-Everard House (small well-appointed home, typical of a comfortable but not wealthy colonial); The Capitol (one of colonial America's most important buildings, scene of Patrick Henry's oration against the Stamp Act); Craft Shops (the trades and crafts of 200 years ago are carried on in 20 authentically furnished craft shops where artisans use the tools and methods of the 18th century); The Gaol (where debtors, criminals and Blackbeard's pirates were imprisoned); James Geedy House (original dwelling and workshop of a well-known colonial silversmith and businessman); Governor's Palace and Gardens (residence of royal governors. Outstanding English and American 18th century furnishing and extensive formal colonial gardens); Public Magazine (arsenal of the Virginia colony, now exhibiting colonial arms); Raleigh Tavern (one of the most famous taverns of colonial times, where Virginia patriots plotted Revolutionary action, and social center of the capital); Peyton Randolph House (original residence of the first president of the Continental Congress); Wetherburn's Tavern (among the most famous of the 18th century Virginia hostelries, over 200 years old); Wren Building of the College of William and Mary (the oldest academic building in British America in Continuous Use with six room open to the public and the remainder still in use for college classes and faculty offices); Wythe House (home of George Wythe, signer of Declaration of Independence and teacher of Jefferson and John Marshall)
Publications: The foundation publishes many books on a wide range of subjects
Activities: Classes for adults & children; docent training; lectures open to public, 30 vis lectr per yr; concerts; gallery talks; tours; individual paintings & original objects of art lent; museum shop sells books, magazines, reproductions, prints & slides

O **Information Center**, PO Drawer C, 23185
Outside the historic area this modern center houses graphic exhibits of the restoration and colonial life. Continuous showings of a full-color, vista vision film, Williamsburg: The Story of a Patriot
Publications: Books and brochures on Williamsburg and colonial life; gallery book of the Folk Art Collection
Activities: Limited grant-in-aid program for researchers; Annual events including Antiques Forum; Garden Symposium; regular performance of 18th century dramas, organ recitals and concerts; slide lectures
L **Library**, PO Drawer C, 23185
Library Holdings: Vols 55,000

M **ABBY ALDRICH ROCKEFELLER FOLK ART CENTER,** The Colonial Williamsburg Foundation, 307 S England St, PO Drawer C, 23185. Tel 804-229-1000, Ext 2424. *Dir* Beatrix T Rumford
Open Mon - Sun 11 AM - 7 PM. Admission by donation. Estab 1939 for research, education and the exhibition of one of the country's leading collections of American folk art of the 18th, 19th and 20th centuries. Nine galleries of American folk art, including a craft gallery. Average Annual Attendance: 150,000
Collections: Decorative usefulwares, decoys, needlework, painted furniture, paintings, sculpture and shop signs
Exhibitions: (1982) Conrad Gilbert - Fraktur Artist; Three Centuries of Popular Tastes (Folk Art in Review); Lewis Miller's Virginia Sketches from the Abby Aldrich Rockefeller Folk Art Center; Santos: The Religious Folk Art of the Southwest; Home Sweet Home - Town Views, Farmscapes & House Portraits from the Permanent Collection; English Folk Pottery: Three Centuries of Slip-Decorated Earthenware; The Toys & Joys of Christmas; (1983) English Folk Pottery: Three Centuries of Slip-Decorated Earthenware; Recent Acquisitions & Loans; Williamsburg Collects: A Sampling of Notable Accessions at the Abby Adrich Rockefeller Folk Art Center; The Toys & Joys of Christmas
Publications: Exhibition catalogs
Activities: Lectures open to public; paintings & sculpture lent to other museums; book traveling exhibitions
L **Library**, 307 S England St, PO Drawer C, 23185
Open to serious scholars of folk art for reference
Library Holdings: Vols 2500; Per subs 11; AV — Slides; Other — Clipping files, exhibition catalogs, manuscripts, photographs
Special Subjects: Folk Art

WASHINGTON

BELLEVUE

M **PACIFIC NORTHWEST ARTS AND CRAFTS ASSOCIATION,** Bellevue Art Museum, 301 Bellevue Square, 98004. Tel 206-454-3322. *Dir* John Olbrantz; *Development Officer* Suzanne Hittman; *Business Mgr* Pat Lyon; *Secy* Lou Gerard
Open Tues - Fri Noon - 8 PM, Sat - Sun 10 AM - 6 PM, cl Mon and major holidays. Admis adults $1, senior citizens and students $.50, children under 6 free, family groups $2, Tues free. Estab 1975 to bring visual arts to Bellevue East King County area. Maintains 5000 sq ft for changing and temporary exhibitions. Average Annual Attendance: 48,000 - 60,000. Mem: 1000; dues $25; annual meetings in Oct
Income: $500,000 (financed by memberships, private contributions, art sales, store sales, grants, fund raising events and arts and crafts fair)
Collections: 20th Century American Art with an emphasis on regional art
Exhibitions: Exhibitons of local, regional and national significance, with an emphasis on archaeology, ethnography, American and regional art; annual Pacific Northwest Arts and Crafts Fair
Publications: Annual report; quarterly calendar of events; exhibiton catalogs; posters
Activities: Classes for adults and children; docent training; lectures open to public, 8-12 vis lect per year; films; concerts; dance performances; symposia; hands-on activities for children; awards through an art and craft juries; original works of art lent to other museums and galleries; lending collection contains original prints, paintings, photographs, sculpture and crafts; book traveling exhibitions, 2 per year; originate traveling exhibitons regionally and nationally; museum store sells books, magazines, reproductions, prints, cards, wrapping paper, puzzles and kits

BELLINGHAM

M **WHATCOM MUSEUM OF HISTORY AND ART,** 121 Prospect St, 98225. Tel 206-676-6981. *Dir* George Thomas; *Cur* Michael Warner; *Education Coordr* Richard Vanderway; *Registrar* Janis Olson; *Public Relations* Kathleen Green; *Secy & Bookkeeper* Denise Hoffman
Open Tues - Sun noon - 5 PM, cl Mon and holidays. No admis fee. Estab 1940 to collect, preserve and use, through exhibits, interpretation and research, objects of historic or artistic value, and to act as a multi-purpose cultural center for the Northwest Washington area providing presentations in all aspects of the arts. Twelve galleries cover 3750 sq ft floor space and 625 linear ft wall space, plus a permanent history exhibit space. Average Annual Attendance: 55,000. Mem: 700; dues family $35, individual $20; annual meeting in February
Income: Financed by private and public funds
Collections: Contemporary Northwest Arts; Darius Kinsey and Wilbur Sandison Historic Photograph Collection; Northwest Native American Artifacts; Regional Historic Photographs and Artifacts; H C Hanson Naval Architecture Collection
Publications: Art and Events Calendar, monthly; Exhibit catalogs; History texts
Activities: Classes for adults and programs for children; decent training; lectures open to the public; concerts; gallery talks; tours; individual paintings and original objects of art lent to other museums and galleries; originate traveling exhibitions; museum shop selling books, craftwork from around the world, original art and prints

L **Library**, 122 Prospect St, 98225
Open to public by appointment only. For reference only
Library Holdings: Vols 500

CLARKSTON

O **VALLEY ART CENTER INC,** 842 Sixth St, PO Box 65, 99403. Tel 509-758-8331. *Executive Dir* Pat Rosenberger; *Co-Chmn & Secy* Veda Taylor; *Treas* Richard Schutte
Open Mon - Fri 9 AM - 4 PM, Sat & Sun 10 AM - 3 PM. No admis fee, donations accepted. Estab 1968 to encourage and instruct in all forms of the visual arts and to promote the cause of art in the community. A portion of the Center serves as the gallery. Average Annual Attendance: 9500-11,000. Mem: 275; dues $10 and up; annual meetings in Jan
Income: Financed by membership and class fees
Exhibitions: Annual Heritage Show; Annual Western Bronze Show; Lewis-Clark Art Association Show
Publications: newsletter, semi-annually
Activities: Classes for adults and children; lectures open to the public, 3 vis lectr per yr; concerts; gallery talks; tours; competitions with awards; individual paintings lent to banks, business offices and professional people; lending collection contains original prints & paintings; museum shop sells books, magazines and prints

ELLENSBURG

M **CENTRAL WASHINGTON UNIVERSITY,** Sarah Spurgeon Gallery, 98926. Tel 509-963-2665. *Dir* George Stillman; *Dir Art Gallery* James Sahlstrand
Open Mon - Fri 8 AM - 5 PM. No admis fee. Estab 1970 to serve as university gallery and hold regional and national exhibits. The gallery is a large, single unit. Average Annual Attendance: 20,000
Income: Financed by state appropriations
Publications: Catalogs for all National shows
Activities: Lect open to the public; competitions

GOLDENDALE

M **MARYHILL MUSEUM OF ART,** Star Route 677, Box 23, 98620. Tel 509-773-4792. *Adminr* Dorothy Brokaw; *Dir Coll* Harvey Freer; *Pres Board of Dir* Herbert Frank
Open daily 9 AM - 5 PM Mar 15 - Nov 15. Admis adults $2.50, students (6-16) $1, under six free. Estab 1923 as a museum of art. Average Annual Attendance: 65,000. Mem: 100; dues $15
Collections: American Indian baskets; antique and modern chessmen; Columbia River Basin prehistoric arts; European and American paintings; 19th century American and French sculpture; Rodin sculpture and drawings; royal furniture designed by Marie, Queen of Romania and memorabilia; World War II costumed French fashion mannequins
Publications: Brochure and souvenir booklet

OLYMPIA

M **EVERGREEN STATE COLLEGE,** Evergreen Galleries,* 98505. Tel 206-866-6000, Ext 62. *Dir* Sid White
Exhibitions: Contemporary West Coast art; functional & sculptured ceramics

M **STATE CAPITOL MUSEUM,*** 211 W 21st Ave, 98501. Tel 206-753-2580. *Dir* Kenneth R Hopkins; *Cur* Delbert J McBride; *Registrar* Derek R Valley
Open Tues - Fri 10 AM - 4 PM, Sat & Sun Noon - 4 PM, cl Mon. No admis fee. Estab 1941 to interpret history of the State of Washington and of the capital city. The one-room gallery presents changing monthly shows. Average Annual Attendance: 40,000. Mem: 400; dues family $12, individual $6; annual meeting in June
Income: Financed by city and state appropriation and local funds
Collections: Etchings by Thomas Handforth; Winslow Homer Woodcuts; Northwest Indian serigraphs; small collection of paintings by Washington artists
Publications: Museum newsletter, monthly
Activities: Classes for adults and children; dramatic programs; docent training; lect open to the public; concerts; gallery talks; tours; individual paintings and original objects of art lent to State offices; lending collection contains original prints, paintings; originate traveling exhibitions; sales shop selling books and slides

PULLMAN

M **WASHINGTON STATE UNIVERSITY,** Museum of Art, 99164. Tel 509-335-1910, 335-1603. *Dir* Sanford S Shaman; *Cur* Patricia Watkinson; *Exec Secy* Margaret Johnson
Open Tues - Fri 10 AM - 5 PM, Tues evening 7 - 10 PM, Sat & Sun 1 - 5 PM. No admis fee. Estab 1974 to contribute the humanistic and artistic educational purpose and goal of the university for the direct benefit of the students, faculty and surrounding communities. Gallery covers 5000 sq ft and is centrally located on campus. Average Annual Attendance: 35,000. Mem: 200; dues $5 - $250; annual meeting in the spring
Income: Finance by the state of Washington and private and public grants and contributions
Collections: Late 19th century to present-day American art, with particular strength in the areas of the Ash Can School and North West regional art; photography collection; contemporary American and British prints
Exhibitions: The American Eight from permanent collection; Americans in Glass; Diverse Directions: The Fiber Arts; Drawing 1900-45, A Survey of American Works; Earthworks; Canaletto Etchins; Form and Figure; Historic Visions: Early Photography as Document; Imperial Robes from the

Ch'ing Dynasty; Young Photographers in the Northwest; Regionalism: Northwest Artists; Richard Smith: Recent Work 1972-77; Spectrum - New Directions in Color Photography; Contemporary American Potter; Swords of the Samurai; British Landscape Photography; Contemporary Metals; Arts of Kenya; British Prints; Noritake Art Deco Porcelains; Living With the Volcano; Artists of Mt St Helens; Philip Pearlstein: Paintings to Watercolor; annual faculty and student exhibitions

Publications: Special exhibition catalogs, two per year

Activities: Docent training; lectures open to the public, 4 vis lectr per yr; concerts; gallery talks; tours; competitions; exten dept serves state of Washington; individual paintings and original objects of art lent to art community of the state of Washington; originate traveling exhibitions; museum shop sells books and gift items

RICHLAND

O **ARTS COUNCIL OF THE MID-COLUMBIA REGION,** * PO Box 735, 99352. Tel 509-943-0524. *Pres* Louise Gustafson
Open Mon - Fri 8 AM - 4:30 PM. Estab April 1968 to encourage, promote and coordinate the arts. Mem: 300; dues $25, $15, $7.50; Board meeting 3rd Thurs monthly
Income: Financed by membership
Publications: Calendar and Newsletter, monthly
Activities: Creative arts development; Consultant Service on grant writing; dramatic programs; lect; Talent Bank, art awards; scholarships

SEATTLE

O **ALLIED ARTS OF SEATTLE, INC,** 107 S Main St, 98104. Tel 206-624-0432. *Pres* Henry M Aronson; *Executive Dir* Dick Lilly
Open Mon - Fri 9 AM - 5 PM. No admis fee. Estab 1954 to promote and support the arts and artists of the Northwest and to help create the kind of city that will attract the kind of people who support the arts. Mem: 1000; dues $10 - $250 depending on category; annual meeting Jan
Income: $70,000 (financed by membership and fund raising events)
Exhibitions: (1982) NW Regional Crafts
Publications: Allied Arts Newsletter, 10 times per year; Access: The Lively Arts, directory of arts organizations in Puget Sound, biannual; Art Deco Seattle
Activities: Self-guided tours; NW Regional crafts competition; awards; scholarships

O **AND-OR,** Resources in Contemporary Arts, 911 E Pine St, 98122. Tel 206-324-5880. *Librn* Claudia Clement
Open Tues - Sat Noon - 5 PM, Thurs evening 5 - 9 PM. No admis fee. Estab 1975 to provide a focused and accessible resource of information about recent activities in the contemporary arts. Exhibition space. Average Annual Attendance: 12,000. Mem: 150; annual dues $20
Income: Financed by National Endowment for the Arts and locally matched funds
Collections: †Artists' video tapes; †new music tapes; †periodicals pertaining to contemporary arts; †library of books pertaining to contemporary arts; †artists' books collection
Activities: Lectures open to public, 6 vis lectr per yr; book traveling exhibitions; originate traveling exhibitions
L **Library,** * 911 E Pine, 98122. Tel 206-324-5880
Open Tues & Wed 9 AM - 6 PM, Thurs & Fri Noon - 9 PM. Estab 1975. Library maintains Soundwork Listening Center with A-tapes of experimental music. For reference only
Library Holdings: Vols 1000; Per subs 130; original documents; AV — A-tapes, cassettes, rec, v-tapes; Other — Clipping files, exhibition catalogs, original art works, pamphlets
Special Subjects: Contemporary Art; business for artists; media arts, video, film, photography; new writing; performance art
Activities: Lectures open to public, 1-2 vis lectr per yr

M **CORNISH INSTITUTE,** Cornish Gallery, 710 E Roy St, 98102. Tel 206-323-1400. *Dir* Christopher Watts
Open Mon - Fri 10 AM - 5 PM, Sat 1 - 4 PM. No admis fee. Estab 1975 to support and enhance the visual arts curricula and reflect current trends in art. Gallery is 36 x 22 ft and has a lite-trak system, double door entry, 120 ft of free wall space, 10 ft ceilings, and tile floor
Income: Financed through Institute
Publications: Gallery mailers
Activities: Classes for adults; dramatic programs; lect open to public; gallery talks; competitions; exten dept serving adults interested in part-time study; traveling exhibitions organized and circulated
L **Library,** * 710 E Roy St, 98102. Tel 206-329-0901. *Librn* Ron McComb
Open to students and faculty
Library Holdings: Vols 7500; Per subs 100; AV — Cassettes, rec 3000, slides 6000; Other — Exhibition catalogs, memorabilia
Special Subjects: Design, fine arts, music, dance, theatre, liberal arts

O **CORPORATE COUNCIL FOR THE ARTS,** 730 Skinner Bldg, 98101. Tel 206-682-9270. *Chmn* D E Skinner; *Pres* William G Reed, Jr; *Secy* Christopher T Bayley; *Treas* John D Mangels; *Executive Dir* Robert E Gustavson; *Assoc Dir* John Renforth
Open 8:30 AM - 5 PM. Estab 1968 as a clearinghouse for corporate contributions to the arts, to monitor budgeting of art agencies and assess ability of business to provide funding assistance. Gallery not maintained. Mem: 300; minimum contribution of $500 to qualify for membership; annual meeting in Sept
Income: $1,012,000 (financed by membership)
Publications: Annual Report; brochures; periodic membership reports
Activities: Annual fund-raising event and campaign

M **CHARLES AND EMMA FRYE ART MUSEUM,** 704 Terry Ave, PO Box 3005, 98114. Tel 206-622-9250. *Pres & Dir* Mrs W S Greathouse
Open weekdays 10 AM - 5 PM, Sun noon - 5 PM. No admis fee. Estab 1952 to display and preserve the Frye Art Collection. Three galleries cover 30 x 60 ft and four galleries cover 30 x 30 ft, plus foyer; Alaskan Wing for showing art work, small auditorium with stage, space for sculpture & two studios on balcony for art work shops. Average Annual Attendance: 60,000
Income: Financed by endowment
Collections: Charles and Emma Frye Collection represents 13 nationalities and includes Baer, Boudin, Carlsen, Corrodi, Dahl, Diaz, Degregger, Grubner, Hoch, Jongkind, Kaulbach, Koester, Lenbach, Leibl, Liebermann, Lier, Llermitte, Manet, Gabriel Max, Monticelli, Slevogt, Soren, Stuck, Thoma, Willroider, Winterhalter, Uhde, Ziem, Zugel, Zumbusch
Publications: Frye Vues, monthly
Activities: Lect open to the public; gallery talks; tours; one competition yearly with awards
L **Library,** 704 Terry Ave, PO Box 3005, 98114. Tel 206-622-9250
For reference only
Income: Financed by private funds
Purchases: American 19th Century and Alaskan Paintings

O **KING COUNTY ARTS COMMISSION,** 828 Alaska Bldg, Second and Cherry, 98104. Tel 206-344-7580. *Dir* Dr Morton Kroll; *Actg Exec Dir* Mickey Gustin; *Performing Arts Coordr* Amy Larkin; *Community Arts Coordr* Lyn Waring; *Editor & Public Information* Joan Mann
Open Mon - Fri 8:30 AM - 4:30 PM. Estab 1967 to provide cultural arts opportunities to the citizens of King County. The Arts Commission purchases and commissions many works of art for public buildings. Mem: 18; membership by appointment of King County Executive; monthly meetings third Tues
Income: Approx $800,000 (financed by county government, including one percent for commissioned art in county construction projects)
Publications: The Arts, monthly newsletter; The Catalog, yearly; exhibition catalog, yearly; programs
Activities: Workshops; performances; originate traveling exhibitions

C **PACIFIC NORTHWEST BELL,** * 1600 Bell Plaza, 98191. Tel 206-345-6349. *Staff Specialist* Joycelyn Dixon
Open Mon - Fri 8:30 AM - 5 PM. No admis fee. Estab 1977 to display the varying cultural traditions which have contributed to Pacific Northwest Art. Collection displayed throughout 32 floors of Bell Plaza
Collections: Reflects the Pacific Northwesterner's eye and shows the influence of the region (restricted to include only artists who live in Washington, Oregon and Idaho)

C **RAINIER NATIONAL BANK,** * 1301 Fifth Ave, PO Box 3966, 98124. Tel 206-621-5736. *In Charge Art Coll* Jeanne Loughmuller
Open to public by appointment. No admis fee. Estab 1976 to support art and artists indigenous to the Northwest and Alaska. Collection displayed in main section in the corporate headquarters building
Purchases: $50,000
Collections: Oriental Porcelain Collection
Activities: Gallery talks; tours; individual objects of art lent to museums, galleries and public displays

C **SEAFIRST CORPORATION,** Corporate Affairs Dept, 1001 Fourth Ave, 98104. Tel 206-583-5563. *Corp Art Cur* Lawney Reyes
Open 9 AM - 4 PM by appointment only. Estab 1968 for complementing the interiors, the appreciation of the general public, and for the support of the fine arts. Collection displayed in state of Washington and overseas; supports visual and performing arts
Purchases: $1,750,000
Collections: Contemporary World Class, paintings, prints, sculpture, tapestries
Activities: Lect; gallery talks; tours; awards at local art exhibitions; individual objects of art lent to museums and exhibitions; book traveling exhibitions; originate traveling exhibitions to other public exhibitions spaces

M **SEATTLE ART MUSEUM,** * Volunteer Park, 98112. Tel 206-447-4710. *Pres of Board* Kenneth Fisher; *Dir* Arnold H Jolles; *Asian Art Cur* Henry Trubner; *Asian Art Cur* William Jay Rathbun; *Development Officer* John Hembroff; *Controller* David Ingham; *Public Relations Mgr* Annie Searle
Open Tues, Wed, Fri & Sat 10 AM - 5 PM, Thurs 10 AM - 9 PM, Sun & holidays Noon - 5 PM. Admis adults $2, students & senior citizens $1, children under 6 with adult, members & Thurs free. Estab 1906, incorporated 1917, building opened 1933; gift to the city from Mrs Eugene Fuller and Richard Eugene Fuller, for recreation, education and inspiration of its citizens. Average Annual Attendance: 300,000. Mem: 10,000; dues $12 and up
Collections: LeRoy M Backus Collection of Drawings and Paintings; Manson F Backus Collection of Prints; Norman Davis Collection (with emphasis on classical art); Eugene Fuller Memorial Collection of Chinese Jades from Archaic through 18th Century; Eugene Fuller Memorial Collection (with special emphasis on Japan, China, India, and including Egypt, Ancient Greece and Rome, European, Near Eastern, primitive and contemporary Northwest art); Alice Heeramaneck Collection of Primitive Art; Henry and Marth Issacson Collection of 18th Century European Porcelain; H Kress Collection of 14th - 18th Century European Paintings; Thomas D Stimson Memorial Collection (with special emphasis on Far Eastern art); Extensive Chinese and Indian Collection; 18th Century Drawing Room (furnished by the National Society of Colonial Dames of American in the State of Washington); major holdings in Northwest art, including Tobey, Callahan, Graves as well as all contemporary art, especially American artists Gorky, Pollock, Warhol and Lichtenstein; selected highlights on Asian collection on permanent display (with special emphasis on on Japanese screens, paintings, sculpture and lacquers); Katherine C White Collection of African Art
Publications: Annual Report; Japanese Paintings from the Sanso Collection; Johsel Namking: An Artist's View of Nature; Newsletter, 10 per year; Northwest Traditions; Song of the Brush
Activities: Docent service; film programs; double lecture course under the Museum Guild; adult art history classes; lect open to the public, 12 visiting lectr per year; tours; program for senior citizens; museum store sells books, gifts and jewelry

WASHINGTON 255

L **Library,*** Volunteer Park, Seattle, 98112. *Librn* Elizabeth de Fato; *Photography & Slide Librn* Jo H Nilsson
For reference only
Library Holdings: Vols 9000; Per subs 50; AV — Slides 44,000; Other — Exhibition catalogs 3000

M **Modern Art Pavilion,*** Seattle Center, 2nd N & Thomas St, 98109. Tel 206-447-4670. *Cur* Charles Cowles; *Assoc Cur* Bruce Guenther; *Mgr* Tore Hoven
Open Tues - Sun 11 AM - 6 PM, Thurs 11 AM - 8 PM, cl Mon, New Year's Day, Thanksgiving, Christmas. A branch of the Seattle Art Museum in the former British Pavilion at Seattle World's Fair, remodeled through a gift from Poncho Association and a bequest from the late Richard Dwight Merrill into a year round exhibition facility, officially opened June 4, 1965. Average Annual Attendance: 108,000
Collections: 20th century art
Exhibitions: Permanent Collection
Activities: Docent service; Rental and Sales Gallery; museum store sells books, gifts and jewelry

O **SEATTLE WEAVER'S GUILD,*** Museum of History and Industry, 2161 East Hamlin St, 98112. Tel 206-324-1125. *Pres* Becky Barnes; *Recording Secy* Helen Sandvig; *Corresp Secy* Donna Kaplan
Estab 1937 to further interest in hand weaving. Mem: 302; dues $15; monthly meetings except Dec, June, July & Aug
Income: Financed by membership dues
Exhibitions: Northwest Association of Handweavers biannual conference; Guild Show
Publications: Bulletin, 8 per year
Activities: Workshops throughout the year

UNIVERSITY OF WASHINGTON

M **Henry Art Gallery,** 98195. Tel 206-543-2280. *Dir* Harvey West; *Asst Dir* Vickie L Maloney; *Dir Henry Gallery Association* Mrs John E Z Caner; *Facilities Mgr* Chris Bruce; *Registrar* Judy Sourakli; *Editor of Publications* Jospeh N Newland
Open Tues - Fri 10 AM - 5 PM, Sat & Sun 1 - 5 PM, Thurs evenings 5 - 7 PM, cl Mon. Estab 1927 by gift of Horace C Henry. 8 galleries, 6000 sq ft of exhibition space. Average Annual Attendance: 100,000. Mem: 650; dues $15 and up
Collections: 19th century American landscape painting; contemporary West Coast ceramics; †works on paper, prints, drawings & photographs; 20th century Japanese folk pottery; Elizabeth Bayley Willis Collection of Textiles from India; †western & ethnic textiles; †19th & 20th century western dress (formerly Costume & Textile Study Center)
Exhibitions: American Impressionism; The Washington Year: A Contemporary View, 1980-1981; William Merritt Chase (1849-1916) Retrospective Exhibition; Radical Rational Space Time: Idea Networks in Photography
Publications: Books, exhibition catalogues; monographs
Activities: Symposia; lect; originate traveling exhibitions; sales shop sells books and posters

L **Architecture, Urban Planning Library,*** 334 Gould Hall, JO-30, 98195. Tel 206-543-4067. *Librn* Betty L Wagner
Estab 1923
Library Holdings: Vols 24,875; Per subs 307; Other — Pamphlets 7397
Special Subjects: Architecture, Landscape Architecture, Building Construction, Urban Planning

L **Suzzallo Library,*** Arch History Collection, 98195. Tel 206-543-0742
Library Holdings: Architectural plans, drawings & renderings 100,000

L **Art Library,** 101 Art Bldg, DM 10, 98195. Tel 206-543-0648. *Librn* Connie Okada
Open Mon - Thurs 8 AM - 9 PM, Fri 8 AM - 5 PM, Sat 1 - 5 PM, Sun 1 - 5 PM. Estab 1940 primarily to provide resources for the courses, degree and research programs of the School of Art; and serves as the Art Library for university community as a whole. Circ 69,800
Income: Financed by state appropriation
Library Holdings: Vols 34,153; Per subs 365; Other — Clipping files, exhibition catalogs, photographs, reproductions
Special Subjects: Art History, Ceramics, Graphic Design, Industrial Design, Metalwork, Painting - American, Photography, Printmaking, Sculpture, Fiber Arts
Activities: Library tours
—Art Slide Collection,* 120 Art Bldg, DM-10, 98195. Tel 206-543-0649.
Preparator Mildred Ellquist Thorson
Library Holdings: AV — Slides 190,000
Costume and Textile Study Center
For collection see Henry Art Gallery

M **Thomas Burke Memorial Washington State Museum,** 98195. Tel 206-543-5590. *Dir* George I Quimby; *Asst Dir* Robert M Free; *Cur Ethnology & Anthropology* Dr James Nason; *Cur Northwest Coast Indian Art* Bill Holm; *Registrar* Roxana Augusztiny
Open Tues - Fri 11 AM - 5:30 PM, Sat & Sun 10 AM - 4:30 PM. No admis fee. Estab 1885 for research and exhibitions. Mem: Dues $15 - $5000 and up
Collections: Anthropology and natural history of the Northwest and the Pacific, specializing in Primitive Art of these regions
Activities: Museum classes; circulates study collection

SPOKANE

M **EASTERN WASHINGTON STATE HISTORICAL SOCIETY,** Cheney Cowles Memorial Museum, 2316 W First Ave, 99204. Tel 509-456-3931. *Dir* Glenn Mason; *Cur Art* Beth Sellars
Open Tues - Sat 10 AM - 5 PM, Sun 2 - 5 PM, cl Mon. No admis fee. Estab 1916, Museum of history and art. Fine arts gallery with regular monthly art exhibitions. Average Annual Attendance: 60,000. Mem: 900; dues $15 per person; annual meeting usually in May
Income: Financed by membership, county and state appropriations, private sector support
Collections: Regional history including collection of Indian arts and handicrafts; historic house of 1898 by architect Kirtland K Cutter, interior designed and

decorated with period furnishings; 19th & 20th century American & European art; representative works of Pacific Northwest artists
Publications: Museum Notes, six per year; exhibitions catalogs
Activities: Docent training; have a lending collection; traveling exhibitions organized and circulated; museum shop

L **Library,** 2316 W First Ave, 99204. *Librn* Elinor Kelly
For reference only
Library Holdings: Vols 100; Per subs 10; Manuscripts for library use only, copies available upon request; Other — Clipping files, exhibition catalogs, pamphlets, reproductions

M **GONZAGA UNIVERSITY,** Ad Art Gallery, 502 East Boone Ave, 99258. Tel 509-328-4220, Ext 3211. *Dir* J Scott Patnode
Open Mon - Fri 10 AM - 4 PM. No admis fee. Estab 1971 to service the art program and art department at Gonzaga University. One room 24 ft x 40 ft, with moveable trac lighting. Average Annual Attendance: 5000
Income: Financed by Art Department funds
Purchases: Jiri Anderle, Honore Daumier print
Collections: Student art collection; †Contemporary and old master print collection
Exhibitions: (1983) Czechoslovakian Prints; Robert Doisneau: Photo Portfolio; National Watercolor Society Exhibit; Garry Winorand, photos
Activities: Classes for adults; lectures open to public, 2 vis lectr per yr; gallery talks

L **SPOKANE PUBLIC LIBRARY,** Art Dept, W 906 Main St, 99201. Tel 509-838-3361. *Chairperson Board of Trustees* Leonard Pearson; *Dir* Betty W Bender; *Asst Dir* Nancy P White
Open Mon, Tues & Thurs 9 AM - 9 PM, Weds 1 - 6 PM, Fri & Sat 9 AM - 6 PM. Estab 1894 basically to meet citizens education, information, recreation and cultural lifelong learning needs through a variety of programs and facilities. Gallery maintained to exhibit mainly local work and changed monthly
Library Holdings: original documents; Micro — Fiche, prints, reels; AV — A-tapes, cassettes, fs, Kodachromes, motion pictures, rec, slides, v-tapes; Other — Clipping files, exhibition catalogs, framed reproductions, manuscripts, memorabilia, original art works, pamphlets, photographs, reproductions, sculpture
Collections: Rare books
Exhibitions: One each month in picture gallery
Activities: Classes for adults and children; dramatic programs; lect open to the public, 9 vis lectr per yr; concerts, gallery talks; tours

TACOMA

M **TACOMA ART MUSEUM,** 12th and Pacific Ave, 98402. Tel 206-272-4258. *Dir* Jon W Kowalek; *Educ Head* Gail Janes
Open Mon - Sat 10 AM - 4 PM, Sun Noon - 5 PM. No admis fee. Estab 1895 to perpetuate the finest in the visual Fine Arts. Museum features galleries for permanent collection, traveling exhibitions and a specialized Childrens Gallery. Average Annual Attendance: 250,000. Mem: 1400; dues $25 - $1000 plus; annual meetings in June
Income: $400,000 (financed by gifts & membership)
Collections: †American & French paintings; American sculpture European & Asian works of art
Exhibitions: Japanese Drawings; Contemporary Calligraphy and Painting from Republic of China; Randy Jeter Photography; Philip McCracken Sculpture; Out of Africa; California Now; Debbie Foster Photography; New Talent for Christmas Giving; Lenore Tawney; Robert Haft Photography; Paul Clinton; Thomas Hill; Dona Anderson, Caroline Cooley Browne, William Richards; University-College art faculty; University-College student work; Children's Art; Contemporary American Photography; Dale Chihuly Glass; Japanese Calligraphy; Earth, Wind, Water & Fire; Charles Demuth Watercolors
Publications: Bulletin, monthly; exhibit catalogs
Activities: Docent training; lect open to the public, 12 vis lectr per yr; gallery talks; tours; competitions with awards; individual paintings and original objects of art lent to other professional museums; lending collection contains paintings, sculpture; museum shop sells books, magazines, original art, reproductions, prints

L **Reference Library,** 12th and Pacific Ave, 98402. Tel 206-272-4258. *Librn* Sadie Uglow; *Librn* Sarah Norris
Open to the public for reference only
Income: Financed by membership, donations and grants
Library Holdings: Vols 1000; Per subs 28
Collections: Unique collection of research material on Japanese woodcut
Publications: Monthly bulletins

L **TACOMA PUBLIC LIBRARY,** Handforth Gallery,* 1102 Tacoma Ave S, 98402. Tel 206-572-2000. *Dir* Kevin Hegarty; *Dir Handforth Gallery* Janice Olsen
Open Mon - Thurs 9 AM - 9 PM, Fri & Sat 9 AM - 6 PM. Estab 1952 to extend library services to include exhibits in all media in the Thomas S Handforth Gallery. Circ 1,237,000
Income: Financed by city appropriation
Library Holdings: Vols 594,700; Per subs 1759; Micro — Reels; AV — A-tapes, cassettes, fs, motion pictures, rec, slides; Other — Clipping files, exhibition catalogs, framed reproductions, memorabilia, original art works, pamphlets, photographs, prints
Special Subjects: Genealogy, manuscripts, Northwest Collection, photographs of local and regional subjects
Collections: Kaiser Collection; Lincoln Collection; city, county, federal and state documents
Exhibitions: Monthly changing exhibits
Activities: Classes for children; dramatic programs; lect open to public, 3 - 4 visiting lectr per year; originate traveling exhibitions

M **UNIVERSITY OF PUGET SOUND,** Kittredge Art Gallery, 15th and
Lawrence, 98416. Tel 206-756-3356. *Dir* Bill D Colby
Open Mon - Fri 10 AM - 4 PM. No admis fee. Estab for showing of student and
professional works. University operated. Average Annual Attendance: 1000
Collections: Abby Williams Hill, painter of Northwest scenes from 1880s to
1930s
Exhibitions: (1983) Arts and the Law; Goya: Los Disparates; (1984) New York
Prints
Publications: Monthly show bulletins
Activities: Lectures open to the public, 2 vis lectr per yr; gallery talks;
scholarships; book traveling exhibitions, 3 per yr

M **WASHINGTON STATE HISTORICAL SOCIETY,** 315 N Stadium Way,
98403. Tel 206-593-2830. *Dir* Anthony G King
Open Tues - Sat 9:30 AM - 5 PM, Sun 2 - 5 PM, cl Mon & holidays. Estab 1891
to promote and preserve Washington state's history. Society owns three
buildings; art gallery under the direction of the Society. Average Annual
Attendance: 300,000. Mem: 851; dues $10 and up; annual meeting May
Income: Financed by membership and other funding
Collections: Pre-historic relics; †Indian and Eskimo artifacts, baskets, clothing,
utensils; Oriental items; †Washington-Northwest pioneer relics
Publications: History Highlights and sponsors Pacific Northwest Quarterly with
the State University; books and pamphlets on Pacific-Northwest history
Activities: Classes for adults and children; lectures open to public, 6 vis lectr per
year; gallery talks; tours; scholarships offered; individual paintings and original
objects of art lent to other non-profit musuems; traveling exhibitions organized
and circulated; museum shop sells books, magazines
L **Hewitt Memorial Library,** 315 N Stadium Way, 98403. Tel 206-593-2830. *Librn*
Frank L Green; *Asst Librn* Jeanne Engerman
Open Tues - Sat 9:30 AM - 5 PM. Estab 1941 for research in Pacific Norhtwest
history. For reference only
Income: Financed by membership, state appropriations and gifts
Library Holdings: Vols 20,000; Micro — Reels; Other — Clipping files,
manuscripts, memorabilia, pamphlets, photographs, prints
Special Subjects: Railroads, lumber, fishing, Indians, missions, labor
Collections: Asahel Curtis Photograph Collection
Publications: History Highlights (newsletter) quarterly; Pacific Northwest
Quarterly (scholarly journal)
Activities: Lectures open to public

WALLA WALLA

O **CARNEGIE CENTER OF THE ARTS,** 109 S Palouse, 99362. Tel 509-525-
4270. *Dir* Carolyn Cron Ogden
Open Tues - Sat 11 AM - 4:30 PM, June - Aug Noon - 4 PM. No admis fee.
Estab 1970 in 1905 Carnegie Library, built of Kansas brick and paneled with oak,
inc 1971 as a non-profit educational organization. Average Annual Attendance:
12,000. Mem: 500; dues from student $5 to life $1500 or more
Income: Financed by endowments, dues, contributions, art sales and rentals, and
gift shop
Activities: Classes for adults and children; docent training; lectures open to the
public, 10 vis lectr per yr; gallery talks; tours; competitions with awards;
individual paintings lent; book traveling exhibitions; sales shop sells books,
original art & handcrafted gifts

WENATCHEE

M **WENATCHEE VALLEY COLLEGE,** Gallery 76, 1300 Fifth St, PO Box 573,
98801. Tel 509-662-1213. *VPres* Marcia Van Doren; *Pres* Ruth Allan; *Coordr*
Paul Janzen
Open Mon - Fri 1 - 4 PM, Mon and Thurs Eve 7 - 9 PM. Donation accepted.
Estab 1976 to serve a rural, scattered population in North Central Washington
State, which without Gallery 76, would not have access to a non-sales gallery.
Non-profit community art gallery housed in Sexton Hall on Wenatchee Valley
College Campus. Average Annual Attendance: 3150. Mem: 235; dues $10;
annual meeting February
Income: $12,000 (financed by membership, grants, donations, fund raising events,
art auction, Casino Night)
Collections: Oil Painting, Stephen Tse
Exhibitions: (1984) Bay Area Painters; The Collagraph Print: Glen Alps;
Painting and Pottery: Stephen Tse; Seattle First National Bank Corporate Art
Collection; Kenneth Callahan; Charles Russell; Pilchock Schoolof Glass;
Francisco Goya: Los Disparates; Edward Steichen; Immogen Cunningham; Space
Art from the USSR
Publications: Annual Brochure
Activities: Lectures open to the public; one or two visiting lecturers per year;
gallery talks; tours; Invitational Exhibit for North Central Washington Artists;
sales shop, located in another building, sells and rents original art

YAKIMA

O **ALLIED ARTS COUNCIL OF THE YAKIMA VALLEY,** 5000 W Lincoln
Ave, 98908. Tel 509-966-0930. *Pres* Jan Mendenhall; *Exec Dir* John Genette
Open 9 AM - 4 PM. No admis fee. Estab 1962 to encourage, promote and
coordinate the practice and appreciation of the arts among the people of Yakima
Valley. General gallery shows changing monthly exhibits; attic gallery rents art in
addition to selling it. Mem: 600; dues $15 - $250
Income: Financed by membership
Exhibitions: Monthly exhibits by local and area artists
Publications: Artscope (arts calendar) monthly
Activities: Lect open to the public
L **Warehouse Library,** * 5000 W Lincoln Ave, 98908. Tel 509-966-0930. *Librn* Fran
Marble

WEST VIRGINIA

CHARLESTON

O **SUNRISE FOUNDATION, INC,** Sunrise Museums, 746 Myrtle Rd, 25314. Tel
304-344-8035. *Exec Dir* J Hornor Davis IV; *Cur Fine Arts* Isabelle Umpleby;
Business Mgr Mary Ann Steed; *Asst Cur Fine Arts* Bonnie Stauffacher; *Cur
Childrens Museum* Carolyn Okoomian; *Planetarium Dir* Robert Gardner; *Public
Information Dir* Morgan Peyton; *Asst Cur Children's Museum* Robert Booher;
Shops Mgr Alma McMillan
Open Tues - Sat 10 AM - 5 PM, Sun 2 - 5 PM, cl national holidays. No admis
fee. Estab 1960. Sunrise is located on a 16 acre estate containing two restored
stone mansions and a carriage/nature trail. The Colonial Revival Sunrise
Mansion, built in 1905, houses a children's museum, planetarium and nature
center. The Georgian Torquilstone Mansion, built in 1928, houses the art
museum. Average Annual Attendance: 70,000. Mem: 1800; dues family $30,
organizational & double $25, single $15; annual meeting mid-April
Income: $425,000 (financed by endowment, membership, government grants and
general contributions)
Collections: Botany; †native American, African and Oceanic artifacts; †natural
history specimens in geology, mineralogy; †19th and 20th century American
paintings, prints, decorative arts and sculpture
Exhibitions: Numerous exhibitions held throughout the year
Publications: Monthly newsletter
Activities: Classes for adults and children; docent training; lectures open to
public, 8 vis lectrs per year; gallery talks; concerts; guided tours; planetarium
programs; recitals; art festivals; garden clinics; individual and original objects of
art lent to other museums and public institutions; book traveling exhibitions, 5
per yr; museum shop sells books, magazines, original art, reproductions, prints,
slides, variety of scientific, educational and decorative gift items including
jewelry; junior musuem

HUNTINGTON

M **HUNTINGTON GALLERIES,** Park Hills, 25701. Tel 304-529-2701. *Dir*
Roberta Shinn Emerson; *Adminr* James C Lawhorn; *Cur Collections* G Eason
Eige; *Cur Exhib* Louise Polan; *Cur Education* Marilyn Davidson; *Development
Officer* James F Weidman; *Registrar* Daniel Silosky; *Public Relations* Gay
Jackson; *Comptroller* Coral Nutter
Open Tues - Sat 10 AM - 6 PM, Wed evening 6 - 8 PM, Sun Noon - 6 PM; cl
Mon. No admis fee. Estab 1952 to own, operate and maintain an art museum for
the collection of paintings, prints, bronzes, porcelains and all kinds of art and
utility objects; to permit the study of arts and crafts and to foster an interest in
the arts. Three building complex on 52-acre site includes ten galleries, two
sculpture courts, seven studio workshops, a 10,000 volume capacity library, 300
seat auditorium, two and one-half miles of nature trails, (one marked with braille
signs for the visually handicapped), an observatory with Celestron-14 telescope
and an amphitheatre. Average Annual Attendance: 75,000. Mem: Membership
dues vary; annual meeting June
Income: Financed by endowment, membership, city, state and county
appropriations
Collections: American and European Paintings and Prints; American Decorative
Arts; Georgian silver; firearms; historical and contemporary glass; Turkish prayer
rugs
Publications: Bulletin, bi-monthly; catalogues for exhibitions
Activities: Classes and workshops for adults and children; docent training; public
lectures; concerts; theatre productions; gallery talks; tours; individual paintings
and original objects of art lent to museums; traveling exhibitions organized and
circulated; museum shop sells books, original art, reproductions, prints and crafts;
Junior Art Museum

MORGANTOWN

WEST VIRGINIA UNIVERSITY
M **West Virginia University Galleries,** Division of Art, College of Fine Arts, 26506.
Tel 304-293-2140. *Dean* Wayne M Sheley; *Chmn Art Dept* Gary Edson; *Cur
CAC Galleries* Urban Couch
Open 1 - 5 PM. Estab 1968 primarily as teaching galleries for art majors and for
the pleasure of students, public and campus community. Two galleries, 22 x 42 ft,
flexible arrangements, approximately 600 running ft. Average Annual
Attendance: 30,000
Income: Financed by state appropriation and funds from the private sector
Collections: Ceramics, drawings, paintings, prints, sculpture
Exhibitions: Graduate Thesis Exhibits of ceramics, paintings, and prints
produced by candidates for the degree of Fine Arts in the Division of Art;
Contemporary Photography; Watercolorist; undergraduate exhibits of ceramics,
drawings and prints; exhibits by art faculty; permanent collection Norfolk,
Virginia Invitational National Potters Teachers Exhibit
L **Library,** Evansdale Campus, 26506. Tel 304-293-5039
Library Holdings: Vols 9850; Per subs 49
M **Creative Arts Center and Gallery,** * Evansdale Campus, 26506. Tel 304-293-
0111. *Cur Art and Dir Acquisition* John D Clarkson
Open Mon - Fri 1 - 4 PM, cl national holidays. No admis fee. Estab 1867
Collections: Costumes; music; paintings; theatre
Activities: Lectures; gallery talks; tours; concerts; drama; competitions;
temporary traveling exhibitions
L **Creative Arts Center Library,** * Evansdale Campus, 26506. Tel 304-293-0111.
Librn Mrs Thomas Canning
Library Holdings: Vols 10,000; Music scores; records

PARKERSBURG

O **PARKERSBURG ART CENTER,** 220 Eighth Street, PO Box 131, 26101. Tel 304-485-3859. *Dir* Jane Ellen Osborn; *Exhibition Coordr* Mark Fleming
Open Tues - Fri 10 AM - 4 PM, Sat & Sun 1 - 4 PM, Mon evenings 7 - 9 PM. No admis fee. Estab 1938 for the operation and maintenance of an art center and museum facility for the appreciation and enjoyment of art, both visual and decorative, as well as art history, crafts, and other related educational or cultural activities. Main gallery 43 x 27 ft and upper gallery 38 x 27 ft, completely carpeted, airconditioned and climate controlled. Average Annual Attendance: 18,000. Mem: 500; dues individual $15, family $25, sustaining $75, corporate or patron $125; annual meeting June
Income: $100,000 (financed by endowment, membership and state appropriation)
Collections: Advice of Dreams (oil by Beveridge Moore); Patrick Henry Land Grant Document; The Hinge (watercolor by Rudolph Ohrning; Parmenides (sculpture by Beverly Pepper)
Exhibitions: (1983-84) Wendell Upchurch, abstract impressionist; Eye of the Beholder, photos; Alternative '83, photos; Masquerade; Circus in the Wild, photos; Katherine Talbot Burnside Retrospective, abstract painter; Visions - Robert Hutton, drawings & paintings; Pac '84 Photo Competition; Presenting W V Artist Lynn Budde; Ceramics & Drawings: E N Seligman; Bill Hopen: Sculpture; Adult Amateur Exhibition; 1984 Pac Print, Painting & Drawing Competition West Virginia Artists George Snyder; Victor Vasarely
Publications: Calendar of events, bimonthly; annual report; exhibition catalogs
Activities: Classes for adults and children; docent training; workshops; concerts; gallery talks; tours; competitions with awards
L **Library,** 220 Eighth St, 26101
Open to the public
Library Holdings: Vols 500; Per subs 5

ROMNEY

L **HAMPSHIRE COUNTY PUBLIC LIBRARY,** Main St, 26757. Tel 304-822-3185. *Librn* Helen Scott; *Asst Librn* Bernard Bowman
Open Mon - Sat 10 AM - 5 PM. No admis fee. Estab 1942. 7 Display cases changed every month. Average Annual Attendance: 25,000-30,000. Mem: 8469
Income: $57,000
Purchases: $8000
Library Holdings: Vols 28,460; Per subs 9; Micro — Reels; AV — Cassettes, fs, motion pictures, rec, v-tapes; Other — Clipping files, exhibition catalogs, framed reproductions, memorabilia, original art works, pamphlets, photographs, prints
Exhibitions: Children's art; private collections of rocks, antiques, displays of items of other countries; various local artists collection; weaving
Activities: Lectures open to public; concerts; tours; competitions with awards; individual paintings lent

WHEELING

M **OGLEBAY INSTITUTE MANSION MUSEUM,*** Oglebay Park, 26003. Tel 304-242-7272. *Executive Dir* Stanley H Coulling; *Dir* John A Artzberger; *Cur* T Patrick Brennan
Open Mon - Sat 9:30 AM - 5 Pm, Sun & holidays 1 - 5 PM, cl New Years, Thanksgiving, Christmas. Admis adults $2.50, sr citizens $2, students $1.50, children under 12 free. Estab and incorporated 1930 to promote educational, cultural and recreational activities in Wheeling Tri-State area. Building and grounds are the property of the city; an exhibition wing adjoins the main house. Average Annual Attendance: 30,000. Mem: 1000; dues $35-$5500
Collections: †Early china; †early glass made in Wheeling and the Midwest; period rooms; †pewter
Exhibitions: Current exhibits of art and other allied subjects change monthly
Activities: Antique seminars, twice per yr; antique classes; gallery talks
L **Library,*** Oglebay Park, 26003
Founded 1934. Highly specialized on the early history of the area
Library Holdings: Vols 750; Documents bound 100, Maps, VF 4; Micro — Prints 20; AV — Slides
Special Subjects: Decorative Arts, local hist
Collections: Brown Collection of Wheeling History, photographs; Wheeling City Directories; Wheeling & Belmont Bridge Company Papers

WISCONSIN

APPLETON

M **LAWRENCE UNIVERSITY,** Worcester Art Center,* 112 S Union, 54912. Tel 414-735-6644. *Dir* Arthur Thrall
Open Mon - Fri 10 AM - 4 PM, Sat & Sun 2 - 4 PM
Exhibitions: Graphics; Japanese woodcuts; German expressionists; early to contemporary American & European artists

BELOIT

M **BELOIT COLLEGE,** Wright Museum of Art, 53511. Tel 608-365-3391. *Dir* Debora Donato; *Registrar* Carol Simon
Open Mon - Fri 9 AM - 5 PM, Sat 11 AM - 5 PM, Sun 1 - 5 PM. No admis fee. Estab 1893; Wright Art Center built 1930 to house the collection for the enrichment of the college and community through exhibition of permanent collection and traveling and temporary regional art exhibitions of cultural and aesthetic value. A Georgian building architecturally styled after The Fogg Museum in Cambridge, Mass. Three galleries on main floor, on a large center court; Art Department shares other floors in which two student galleries are

included. Average Annual Attendance: 10,000 - 20,000
Collections: European and American (paintings, sculpture and decorative arts); Fisher Memorial Collection of Greek Casts; graphics, emphasis on German Expressionist and contemporary works; Gurley Collection of Korean Pottery, Japanese Sword Guards, Chinese Snuff Bottles and Jades; Morse Collection of Paintings and Other Art Objects; Neese Fund Collection of Contemporary Art; Oriental; Pitkin Collection of Oriental Art; Prints by Durer, Rembrandt, Whistler and others; sculpture of various periods; 19th century photography
Exhibitions: (1982-83) Beloit Collects III; Alinari: Italian Architectural Photography UW-Milwaukee Invitational; Black History in Posters & Prints; Paintings from the Samuel J & Ileen Campbell Collection; Sally Kovach; Glass & Works on Paper; Annual Beloit & Vicinity Exhibition; Annual Beloit College Student Art Exhibition; Wisconsin Painters & Printmakers (1983-84) Robert Arneson: Lithography & Sculpture; Sculpture for the Visually Impaired; Wisconsin Painters & Sculptors' Exhibition of Wisconsin Art; Artifacts at the End of A Decade; Rauschenberg/Rosenquist; Annual Beloit & Vincinity Exhibition; Beloit College Student Art Exhibition; student exhibitions; permanent collection
Publications: Exhibition catalogs
Activities: Classes; supportive programs; docent training; lectures open to public; gallery talks; tours; traveling exhibitions organized and circulated
O **Friends of the Wright Museum of Art,** Beloit, 53511
Mem: 200; dues $5 and up; holds annual meeting

CEDARBURG

O **WISCONSIN FINE ARTS ASSOCIATION, INC,** Ozaukee Art Center,* W63 N645 Washington Ave, 53012. Tel 414-377-8230. *Pres* Jack Zweck
Open Mon - Fri Noon - 4 PM, Sat & Sun 1 - 4 PM, cl holidays. no admis fee. Estab 1971. Mem: Dues business patron $500, patron $200, sustaining $100, associate sustaining $50, family $20, individual $12, student $10
Collections: Paintings, sculpture, prints, ceramics
Publications: Monthly newsletter
Activities: Classes for adults and children; lectures; tours; arts festivals

GREEN BAY

M **NEVILLE PUBLIC MUSEUM,** 210 Museum Place, 54303. Tel 414-497-3767. *Cur Art* James W Kreiter
Open Mon, Tues, Fri & Sat 9 AM - 5 PM, Wed & Thurs 9 AM - 9 PM, Sun Noon - 5 PM. No admis fee. Estab 1915 as Green Bay Public Museum; names changed 1926. Average Annual Attendance: 150,000. Mem: 1630; dues family $15, individual $10; annual meeting in the spring
Income: Financed by county appropriation
Collections: David Belasco Collection of Victoriana antique furniture, †china, †glass, †silver, fans, lace, costumes and †accessories; †contemporary and historical paintings; †drawings; Neville family portraits; †prints and sculpture
Exhibitions: Local art clubs exhibit annually; Northeastern Wisconsin Art Show annually with cash awards; rotating monthly exhibits
Publications: Museletter, 8 times per yr; Musepaper, quarterly
Activities: Classes for adults and children; dramatic programs; docent training; lectures open to the public, some for members only; concerts; gallery talks; tours; competitions; individual paintings and original objects of art lent other museums or galleries; traveling exhibitions organized and circulated; gallery shop sells books, magazines, original art, reproductions & prints
L **Library,** 129 S Jefferson St, 54301
Open to the public for reference

M **UNIVERSITY OF WISCONSIN, GREEN BAY,** Lawton Gallery, Nicolet Rd, 54301. Tel 414-465-2271. *Cur Art* Karon Winzenz
Open Tues - Sun Noon - 4 PM, cl Mon. No admis fee. Estab 1974 to show changing exhibitions of contemporary & 20th century art & recent ethnic art. Gallery is 2000 sq ft. Average Annual Attendance: 5000
Income: $5000
Exhibitions: (1984) Woven Works: Tradition & Innovation
Publications: Exhibition catalogs
Activities: Lectures open to public, 2-3 vis lectr per yr; competitions; book traveling exhibitions; originates traveling exhibitions

KENOSHA

M **KENOSHA PUBLIC MUSEUM,*** 5608 Tenth Ave, 53140. Tel 414-656-6026. *Dir* Stephen H Schwartz; *Cur Education* Paula Touhey
Open Mon - Fri 9 AM - 5 PM; Sat 9 AM - Noon; Sun 1 - 4 PM. No admis fee. Estab 1936 to promote interest in general natural history and regional art. The gallery has 8000 sq ft of permanent exhibition space and 1000 sq ft for temporary exhibits. Average Annual Attendance: 40,000. Mem: 250; dues $10; annual meeting April
Income: $175,000 (financed by city appropriation)
Purchases: $2200
Collections: Historic Wisconsin pottery; Oriental decorative arts; regional artists; regional natural history; worldwide ethnology
Exhibitions: Yousouf Karsh: People Who Make Our World; Roses
Publications: Newsletter, bi-monthly
Activities: Classes for adults and children; lect open to public, 12 vis lectr per yr; gallery talks; tours; competitions; lending collection contains cassettes, color reproductions, film strips, framed reproductions, motion pictures, nature artifacts and slides; museum shop selling original art
L **Library,** 5608 Tenth Ave, 53140. Tel 414-656-8026
Open to public for reference only
Income: $175,000 (financed by municipal tax)
Purchases: $500
Library Holdings: Vols 2000; Per subs 20; AV — A-tapes, cassettes, fs, Kodachromes, lantern slides, motion pictures, rec, slides, v-tapes
Special Subjects: Natural history
Activities: Six book traveling exhibitions per year

KOHLER

C KOHLER COMPANY,* 44 Kohler Memorial Dr, 53044. Tel 414-457-4441. *Dir Public Affairs* Jim Stiner
Estab 1973. Collection displayed in Kohler Company general office
Collections: Original ceramic art pieces, some of which were created in Kohler Company Pottery
Activities: Individual objects of art lent

LA CROSSE

M VITERBO COLLEGE ART GALLERY, 815 S Ninth St, 54601. Tel 608-784-0040. *Dir* Tim Crane
Open Mon - Fri 8 AM - 5 PM. Estab 1964 to exhibit arts and crafts which will be a valuable supplement to courses offered. Gallery is located in the center of the Art Department; 100 running feet; soft walls; good light
Income: Financed by school appropriation
Collections: Mrs Lynn Miller Collection of contemporary United States primitives; Peter Whitebird Collection of WPA project painting
Activities: Classes for adults; dramatic programs; lect open to public; gallery talks
L Zoeller Fine Arts Library, S Ninth St, 54601. *Librn* Sr Rosella Namer
Open 8 AM - 9:30 PM for students of Viterbo College. Estab 1971 to service the Music-Art-Theatre Arts Departments
Library Holdings: Vols 1326; Per subs 30; AV — Cassettes

MADISON

M CENTER GALLERY, 426 W Gilman St, 53703. Tel 608-251-8498. *Pres* George Pasdirtz
Open Tues - Sat Noon - 5 PM. No admis fee. Estab 1978 as an artist-run membership gallery showing emerging & experimental local artists. Store front, street level gallery with 1500 sq ft of space. Average Annual Attendance: 2000. Mem: 120; dues active $30, supporting $20; annual meeting in Feb
Income: $13,000 (financed by membership, fundraisers, art auction & grants)
Exhibitions: Landscape Six; A B Cox, painting; Colleen O'Reilly, abstract watercolors
Publications: Center Gallery Newsletter, bi-monthly
Activities: Lectures open to public; competitions with awards

M EDGEWOOD COLLEGE, DeRicci Gallery,* 855 Woodrow, 53711. Tel 608-257-4861. *Pres* Sr Alice O'Rourke; *Art Department Chmn* Sr M Stephanie Stauder
Open 9 AM - 5 PM Mon - Fri. Estab 1965 to serve local artists, and provide educational opportunity for students. Large room; carpeted walls. Average Annual Attendance: 5000
Collections: Edgewood College Collection
Exhibitions: Old Bergen Art Guild; Local Artists

M MADISON ART CENTER, 211 State St, 53703. Tel 608-257-0158. *Dir* Thomas H Garver; *Cur Coll* Janet Ela; *Exhibitions & Collections Mgr* Robert Schroeder; *Office Mgr* Michael Paggie; *Dir Development & Community Relations* Kathy Silbiger; *Membership & Program Liaison* Barbara Scherz; *Secy* Lori Haak; *Technical Services Supvr* Michael Holubar; *Cur Exhibitions* Trent Myers; *Chief Security* Candace Tschirki; *Gallery Shop Mgr* Susan Clewley; *Shop Asst* Amy Grimm; *Cur Education & Public Programming* Lanny Silverman
Open Tues - Fri 11 AM - 5 PM, Sat 10 AM - 5 PM, Fri night till 9 PM, Sun 1 - 5 PM. No admis fee. Estab 1901 to promote the visual arts. Five galleries, artists workshop and multi-media hall. Average Annual Attendance: 100,000. Mem: 1500; dues $10 and up; annual meeting May
Income: $100,000
Purchases: $10,000
Collections: Emphasis on Contemporary Americans; large print and drawing collection (Japanese, European, Mexican and American); paintings; sculpture; drawings; prints of America, European, Mexican and Japanese schools
Exhibitions: Sylvia Mangold; Chicago: Some Other Traditions; Kaethe Kollwitz; Georgia O'Keeffe; The Eiler Collection ... Now; Wisconsin Biennial
Publications: Catalogs; posters and announcements usually accompany each exhibition
Activities: Classes for adults and children; docent training; lectures open to the public, 10 vis lectr per yr; concerts; tours; competitions; films; loan program to public schools; originate traveling exhibitions; sales shop sells books, magazines, original art, reproductions and prints
L Library, 53703
Open for research only
Library Holdings: AV — Slides; Other — Exhibition catalogs

L MADISON PUBLIC LIBRARY, Art & Music Division, 201 West Mifflin St, 53703. Tel 608-266-6311. *Supervisor* Beverly Brager
Open Mon - Wed 8:30 AM - 9 PM, Thurs - Sat 8:30 AM - 5:30 PM. Estab 1875 to serve the people of Madison. Gallery maintained; an unsupervised area used primarily by local artists
Library Holdings: Vols 500,000; Per subs 1480; Micro — Fiche, reels; AV — A-tapes, cassettes 1000, fs, motion pictures 1000, rec 15,000, v-tapes; Other — Clipping files, exhibition catalogs, framed reproductions 450, pamphlets
Activities: Lectures open to public; concerts; tours; traveling exhibitions organized and circulated to other libraries in the service area; sales shop sells books

MIDWEST ART HISTORY SOCIETY

For further information, see National and Regional Organizations

M STATE HISTORICAL SOCIETY OF WISCONSIN, 816 State St, 53706. Tel 608-262-3266. *Dir* Richard A Erney; *Assoc Dir* Robert Thomasgard; *Dir Museum* Thurman O Fox; *Dir Research* William F Thompson; *Cur Decorative Arts* Anne Woodhouse; *Cur of Textiles* Joan Severa

Open Mon - Thurs 9 AM - 9 PM, Fri & Sat 9 AM - 5 PM, Sun Noon - 5 PM, cl holidays. No admis fee. Estab 1846, museum added 1854; organized to promote a wider appreciation of the American heritage, with particular emphasis on the collection, advancement and dissemination of knowledge of the history of Wisconsin and of the Middle West. Average Annual Attendance: 100,000. Mem: 7000; dues $15 and up
Income: Financed by state appropriation, earnings, gifts and federal grants
Collections: Historical material; iconographic collection; ceramics, coins, costume dolls, furniture, paintings, prints, photographs and slides
Exhibitions: Frequent special exhibitions; four annual gallery changes
Publications: Wisconsin Magazine of History, quarterly
Activities: Docent training; lectures open to public; competitions; individual paintings & original objects of art lent to other museums & individuals for educational purposes; book traveling exhibitions; originate traveling exhibitions; sales shop sells books, magazines, reproductions, slides & post cards
L Archives, 816 State St, 53706. *Archivist* F Gerald Ham
Includes the Iconography Section and the Wisconsin Center for Film and Theater Research
Library Holdings: Original documents, maps; AV — Motion pictures; Other — Photographs, prints

UNIVERSITY OF WISCONSIN

M Memorial Union Gallery, 800 Langdon St, 53706. Tel 608-262-2214. *Dir & Secy* Ted Crabb; *Art Coordr* Jan Marshall Fox
Open 10 AM - 8 PM. No admis fee. Estab 1907 to provide a cultural program for the members of the university community. Owns two fireproof buildings with four galleries. Also maintains Union South at 227 N Randall Ave. Average Annual Attendance: 193,000. Mem: 50,000 faculty, alumni and townspeople, plus 41,000 students; dues $35; annual meeting Nov
Purchases: $1500
Collections: Oil and watercolor paintings, prints and sculptures, mostly by contemporary American artists
Activities: Informal classes in arts and crafts; films; gallery talks; loan collection availble on rental to students and members
M Elvehjem Museum of Art, 800 University Ave, 53706. Tel 608-263-2246. *Actg Dir* Dr Stephen C McGough; *Cur Coll* Carlton E Overland; *Registrar* Lisa C Calden; *Cur Education* Anne Lambert; *Coordr Membership & Outreach* Susan Latton; *Dir of Development* Joel Skornicka
Open Mon - Sat 9 AM - 4:45 PM; Sun 11 AM - 4:45 PM; cl holidays. No admis fee. Estab 1962, building opened 1970 to display, preserve and build a general art collection of high quality for the study and enjoyment of students, community and state. Three levels, 12 galleries covering 25,000 sq ft of exhibition space. Average Annual Attendance: 100,000. Mem: 2500; dues $15-$1000
Income: Financed by endowment, membership, state appropriation and private sources
Purchases: Vary according to income
Collections: Ancient Egyptian and Greek pottery, sculpture, glass and coins; Joseph E Davies Collection of Russian Icons, Russian and Soviet Paintings; Vernon Hall Collection of European Medals; Indian sculpture; Medieval painting and sculpture; Renaissance painting and sculpture; Edward Burr Van Vleck Collection of Japanese Prints; Ernest C and Jane Werner Watson Collection of Indian Miniatures; 16th - 20th century prints - †general collection; 17th - 20th century European painting, sculpture, furniture and decorative arts; 18th, 19th and 20th century American painting, sculpture and furniture
Exhibitions: Twelve to fourteen temporary exhibitions per year in all media from varied periods of art history
Publications: Annual bulletin; calendar, bimonthly; special exhibition catalogs
Activities: Classes for children; docent training; lect open to the public, 10-15 vis lectr per yr; concerts; gallery talks; tours; individual paintings lent to qualified art museums and galleries for special exhibitions; traveling exhibitions organized and circulated; museum shop selling reproductions, gift items, catalogs, posters, exhibition related articles
M Art Dept Gallery,* 6241 Humanities, 455 N Park Street, 53706. Tel 608-262-1660. *Chmn* Prof Richard Lazzaro
Open hours varied. No admis fee. Estab 1968 for MA and MFA exhibitions. Average Annual Attendance: 10,000
Income: Financed by state appropriation
Exhibitions: Graduate student exhibitions
L Kohler Art Library, 800 University Ave, 53706. Tel 608-263-2256. *Dir* William Bunce; *Reference Librn* Louise Henning
Open Mon - Fri 8 AM - 4:45 PM & 7 - 9:45 PM; Sat & Sun 1 - 4:45 PM. Estab 1970 to support the teaching and research needs of the Art and Art History Departments and the Elvehjem Museum of Art. Circ 43,000
Income: Financed by state appropriation and private funding
Library Holdings: Vols 85,000; Per subs 288; Micro — Fiche, reels; Other — Clipping files, exhibition catalogs, manuscripts, pamphlets
Activities: Tours

MANITOWOC

M RAHR-WEST MUSEUM, Park St at N Eighth, 54220. Tel 414-683-4501. *Dir* Richard Quick; *Cur* George Tomko
Open Tues - Fri 9 AM - 4 PM; Sat & Sun 1 - 4 PM; cl Mon. No admis fee. Estab 1950 as an art center to serve the city of Manitowoc. Transitional gallery in new wing built 1975; period rooms in Victorian Rahr Mansion built c 1891; a Registered Historic home. Average Annual Attendance: 5000. Mem: 500; dues $5-$500
Income: $110,000 (financed by membership and city appropriation)
Collections: 19th and 20th Century American Paintings and Prints; Schwartz Collection of Chinese Ivories; contemporary art glass; porcelain
Exhibitions: Monthly changing exhibitions
Activities: Classes for adults and children; docent training; lect open to the public, 4-5 vis lectr per yr; gallery talks; tours; traveling exhibitions organized and circulated
L Library, Park St at N Eighth, 54220
Open to the public for reference only
Library Holdings: Vols 1500; Per subs 6
Special Subjects: Art reference

MENOMONIE

M UNIVERSITY OF WISCONSIN-STOUT, Gallery 209,* 54751. Tel 715-232-1141. *Cur* Eddie Wong
Open Mon - Fri 9 AM - 5 PM. No admis fee. Estab 1966 to serve university and local community with exhibits of art. A single room gallery; cloth walls and track lighting. Average Annual Attendance: 9500. Mem: Financed by state appropriation
Collections: African Art; paintings including works by Warrington Colescott, Roy Deforest, Walter Quirt, George Rovalt and Raphael Sover; drawings; prints; sculpture
Exhibitions: Changing exhibits
Activities: Classes for children; lect, 2-3 vis lectr per yr; gallery talks

MEQUON

M CONCORDIA COLLEGE WISCONSIN, Fine Arts Galleries, 12800 N Lake Shore Dr, 83092. Tel 414-243-5700. *Pres* John Buuck; *Academic Dean* Ronald Berg; *Cur* William L Chandler
Open Sun Tues, Wed, Thurs 1 - 4 PM, Tues 7 - 9 PM. No admis fee. Estab 1972 to exhibit work of area and national artists as an educational arm of the college. Average Annual Attendance: 1000
Income: Financed through college budget
Collections: Russian bronzes and paintings; graphics include Roualt, Altman and local artists; John Wiley Collection; American landscape; religious art

MILWAUKEE

M CHARLES ALLIS ART MUSEUM, 1801 N Prospect Ave (Mailing add: 1630 E Royall Place, Milwaukee, WI 53202). Tel 414-278-8295. *Cur* Margaret Fish Rahill; *Programs Cur* Richard Morgan
Open Wed - Sun 1 - 5 PM, Wed evenings 7 - 9 PM. Estab 1947 as a house-museum with 850 art objects from around the world & spanning 2500 years, collected by Charles Allis, first president of the Allis-Chalmers Company & bequeathed to the people of Milwaukee. The Museum is part of the Milwaukee County War Memorial Complex. Average Annual Attendance: 40,000. Mem: 700; dues $5 - $100; annual meetings in Oct
Income: $120,000 (financed by endowment)
Collections: Chinese, Japanese and Persian ceramics; Greek and Roman antiques; 19th century French and American paintings; Renaissance bronzes
Exhibitions: 12 exhibitions of work by Wisconsin artists and craftsmen
Publications: Exhibition catalogs
Activities: Docent training; lectures open to public, vis lectr; concerts; gallery talks; tours

M ALVERNO COLLEGE GALLERY, 3401 S 39th St, 53215. Tel 414-671-5400. *Dir* Priscilla Weissen-Flutt
Open Mon - Fri 11 AM - 3 PM, Sun 1 - 3 PM, by appointment. No admis fee. Estab 1954 for the aesthetic enrichment of community and the aesthetic education of students
Income: $2000
Exhibitions: (1983) Paul Donhauser; (1984) Earl Lindeman
Activities: Docent training; lectures open to the public, 4 vis lectr per year; concerts; gallery talks; tours; competitions with awards; book traveling exhibitions, 1-2 per year

M CARDINAL STRITCH COLLEGE, Studio San Damiano, 6801 N Yates Rd, 53217. Tel 414-352-5400. *Head Department* Sr Mary Tomasita
Open daily 10 AM - 5 PM. No admis fee. Estab 1947 to encourage creative art in each individual
Income: Financed by endowment, city and state appropriations and tuition
Collections: Folk Crafts; paintings
Exhibitions: Acquisitions from distant lands, children's art, professor's works, senior graduating exhibitions, well-known area artists
Publications: CSC News, monthly
Activities: Classes for adults and children; dramatic programs; lect open to public, 20 visiting lectr per year; competitions; concerts; scholarships; individual paintings and original objects of art lent; originate traveling exhibitions; book shop
L Library, Studio San Damiano, 6801 N Yates Rd, 53217
Reference only
Library Holdings: Vols 2800; Per subs 21; AV — Kodachromes; Other — Clipping files, photographs, prints, reproductions

L INSTITUTE OF ART & DESIGN, Library,* 207 North Milwaukee St, Fifth Floor, 53202. Tel 414-276-7889. *Librn* Terry Marcus
Open Mon & Fri 8 AM - 4 PM, Tues - Thurs 8 AM - 8 PM. Estab 1976 as an Art and Design Library for the art school
Income: $4500
Purchases: $4500
Library Holdings: Vols 10,000; Per subs 45; AV — Slides; Other — Clipping files, exhibition catalogs, pamphlets, reproductions
Special Subjects: Industrial Design, Photography, Art and Design

C THE MARINE CORPORATION, 111 E Wisconsin, PO Box 481, 53201. Tel 414-765-3000. *In Charge Art Coll* Mary Louise Roozen; *Gallery Coordr* Marylee McRae
Estab to encourage Wisconsin art and artists; to enhance the environment of Marine personnel. Collection displayed in offices, conference rooms and corridors of headquarters of bank holding company
Collections: Acrylics, batik, bronze sculpture, lithographs, oils, wall sculpture, watercolors by Wisconsin artists
Activities: Invitational competitions in 1965, Wisconsin Renaissance in 1976; cash and purchase awards sponsored for college university and community art exchange; individual ojbects of art lent

M MARQUETTE UNIVERSITY, Museum of Art, 402 Varsity Bldg, 1324 W Wisconsin Ave, 53233. Tel 414-224-7290, 224-1669. *Dir* Curtis L Carter; *Cur Asst* Mary Ladish
Open daily 8 AM - 5 PM. No admis fee. Estab 1955 to house the University's permanent collection of art, sponsor fine arts museum programs
Income: Financed through the university
Collections: 16th - 20th century paintings and prints, sculpture and decorative art
Exhibitions: Changes: Art in America 1881-1981; Marquette University's Centennial Art Exhibition
Publications: Catalogs of Exhibitions
Activities: Lectures open to the public, 4 - 6 vis lectr per yr; concerts; tours; individual paintings & original objects of art lent to other museums; museum shop sells books, reproductions, prints & slides

M MILWAUKEE AREA TECHNICAL COLLEGE, Kronquist Craft Gallery,* 1015 N Sixth St, 53203. Tel 414-278-6600. *Gallery Dir* John Strachota
Open daily. No admis fee. Estab 1961 to stimulate appreciation for fine metalwork. Gallery is 30 x 40 ft located on sixth floor of central building; glass display cases house permanent collection, spotlit walls for artwork, carpeted lounge area. Average Annual Attendance: 2500
Collections: Sculpture, bronze castings and other metalcraft by Emil F Kronquist; sterling holloware, flatware and jewelry by Danish Silversmiths, Jensen, Rhode and Anderson

M MILWAUKEE ART MUSEUM, 750 N Lincoln Memorial Dr, 53202. Tel 414-271-9508. *Pres Bd Trustees* David Kahler; *Dir* Gerald Nordland; *Exec Dir* Christopher Goldsmith; *Cur Education & Acting Cur Decorative Arts* Barbara Brown-Lee; *Chief Cur* Russell Bowman; *Assoc Cur* Verna Curtis; *Communications & Marketing* Alberta Darling; *Registrar* Open; *Communications & Marketing* Andrea Van Dyke
Open Tue, Wed, Fri & Sat 10 AM - 5 PM, Thurs Noon - 9 PM, Sun 1 - 6 PM, cl Mon. Admis adults $2, students, handicapped & sr citizens $1, children under 12 with adult free. Estab 1888 to create an environment for the arts that will serve the people of the greater Milwaukee community. Large, airy, flexible galleries, including a sculpture court and outdoor display areas. Fine arts and decorative arts are mixed to create an overview of a period, especially in the fine American Wings; small galleries provided for specific or unique collections. Average Annual Attendance: 150,000. Mem: 5000; dues $35, senior citizens & students $15; annual meeting May
Income: Financed by endowment, membership, county and state appropriations and fund drive
Collections: 19th and 20th Century American and European Art, including the Bradley and Layton Collections: The American Ash Can School and German Expressionism are emphasized; All media from Ancient Egypt to Modern America; The Flagg Tanning Corporation Collection of Haitian Art; a study collection of Midwest Architecture—The Prairie Archives; The von Schleinitz Collection of 19th Century German Painting, Mettlach Steins, and Meissen Porcelain
Exhibitions: Masters in Depth: Selections From the Permanent Collection; Recent Acquisitions; Controversial Public Art Symposium & Exhibition; Recent Directions: Selection for the Permanent Collection & Extended Loans; Currents 4: Art & Use; Selections From the Hope & Abraham Melamed Collection; American Indian Portraits From the Collection of Kurt Koegler; Linton Godown
Publications: Exhibitions and program brochure, tri-yearly; numbers calendar, bi-monthly
Activities: Classes for adults and children; docent training; lectures open to public, 5 vis lectr per yr; concerts; gallery talks; tours; competitions; films; originate traveling exhibitions; museum shop sells books, magazines, original art, reproductions, slides and cards
L Library, 750 N Lincoln Memorial Dr, 53202. *Librn* Betty Karow
For reference Tues & Thurs 10 AM - 4 PM
Library Holdings: Vols 15,000; Per subs 31; Vertical files, 27 drawers
Special Subjects: 19th Century German painting
Collections: Prairie Archives material (architecture and decorative arts of the Frank Lloyd Wright period) gift of Jacobson; von Schleinitz bequest of material on Meissen porcelain and 19th Century German painting

L MILWAUKEE PUBLIC LIBRARY, Art, Music & Recreation Dept, 814 West Wisconsin Ave, 53233. Tel 414-278-3000. *City Librn* Donald J Sager; *Supv Central Services* Kirk L Pressing; *Coordr Fine Arts* June M Edlhauser
Open Mon - Thurs, 8:30 AM - 9 PM, Fri & Sat 8:30 AM - 5:30 PM. No admis fee. Estab 1897. Circ 60,000
Income: $47,000 (financed by budgeted funds and endowments)
Library Holdings: Vols 138,712; auction catalogs, original documents, theatre programs; Micro — Fiche, reels; AV — Cassettes, motion pictures, rec, v-tapes; Other — Clipping files, exhibition catalogs, framed reproductions, manuscripts, memorabilia, original art works, pamphlets, photographs, prints, reproductions, sculpture
Special Subjects: Architecture, Art History, Coins & Medals, Costume Design & Construction, Crafts, Decorative Arts, Landscape Architecture, Photography, City Planning, Philately, Recreation
Collections: Record Collection; Historic Popular Song Collection

M MOUNT MARY COLLEGE, Tower Gallery,* 2900 Menomonee River Parkway, 53222. Tel 414-258-4810. *Chmn* Sr M Regina Collins
Open Mon - Fri 8 AM - 4:30 PM, Sat & Sun 1 - 4 PM. No admis fee. Estab 1940 to provide both students and local community with exposure to art experiences and to provide artists, both estab professionals and aspirants with a showplace for their work
Income: Financed by private funds
Collections: Antique furniture, 16th Century and Victorian period; contemporary print collection; watercolors by Wisconsin artists
Exhibitions: Six exhibitions a year

SOCIETY OF NORTH AMERICAN GOLDSMITHS
For further information, see National and Regional Organizations

UNIVERSITY OF WISCONSIN

M **University Art Museum,** 3253 N Downer Ave, 53201. Tel 414-963-6509. *Dir* Suzanne Foley; *Cur* Mark Chepp; *Registrar* Angela Jacobi
Open Mon - Thurs 11 AM - 3 PM, Wed 6 - 8 PM, Sun 1 - 3 PM, cl Fri, Sat & holidays. No admis fee. Estab 1982 to function as university museum; also oversees operations of art history gallery & fine arts galleries
Income: Financed by state appropriation
Collections: †Large graphic collection, primarily 20th century; †19th & 20th century painting, sculpture, drawings and photography; Oriental art; Greek & Russian icons & religious objects; Renaissance through 18th century sculpture, paintings & drawings
Exhibitions: Permanent, temporary & traveling exhibitions; faculty, student & MFA shows; MFA & MS thesis shows
Publications: Catalogs; checklists; handouts
Activities: Lect; gallery talks; concerts; inter-museum loans
—**Dept of Art History Gallery,** Mitchell Hall, 53201. Tel 414-963-4060
Open Mon, Tues, Thurs & Fri 1 - 4 PM; Wed 6 - 9 PM. No admis fee. Estab 1964 to support gallery-museum for an academic department. Average Annual Attendance: 7500
Publications: Exhibition schedules
Activities: Lectures open to public; gallery talks; tours; individual paintings lent to other galleries; book traveling exhibitions
➻—**Union Art Gallery,** 2200 E Kenwood Blvd, 53211. Tel 414-963-6310
Open Mon & Fri 10 AM - 4 PM, Wed 6 - 8 PM, Sun 1 - 3 PM. No admis fee. Estab 1971 to provide space for student art, primarily undergraduate, to be shown in group exhibits established by peer selection and apart from faculty selection

NEENAH

M **BERGSTROM MAHLER MUSEUM,** 165 N Park Ave, 54956. Tel 414-722-3348. *Dir* Alex Vance; *Cur* Geraldine Casper; *Secy* Kathy Smits
Open Wed - Fri 12 - 4:30 PM; Sat & Sun 1 - 4:30PM; June - Aug Tues 1 - 5 PM. No admis fee. Estab 1959 to provide cultural and educational benefits to the public. Average Annual Attendance: 29,000
Income: $200,000 (financed by endowment, state and county appropriations and gifts)
Collections: Evangeline Bergstrom Collection of Antique and Modern Glass Paperweights; †Ernst Mahler Collection of Germanic Glass; †Wisconsin and Midwestern Paintings; sculpture
Exhibitions: Monthly exhibitions in varied media
Publications: Museum Quarterly
Activities: Classes for adults and children; docent training; lect open to public; concerts; gallery talks; tours; individual paintings and original objects of art lent to museums; museum shop selling books, original art, prints, ceramics, paperweights and needlework
L **Library,** 165 N Park Ave, 54956
Open to the public for reference only
Library Holdings: Vols 2000; Per subs 10
Special Subjects: Art History, Glass

NEW GLARUS

M **CHALET OF THE GOLDEN FLEECE,** 618 2nd, 53574. Tel 608-527-2614. *Cur* Virginia Henning
Open May - Oct 9 AM - 4:30 PM. Admis adults $1.50, students 12-17 $1, children 6-11 $.50. Estab 1955. Authentic Swiss style chalet which was once a private residence. Average Annual Attendance: 13,000
Income: Financed by admission fees
Collections: Swiss wood carvings and furniture; antique silver and pewter samples; prints; exceptional glass and china
Activities: Lectures open to public; tours

OSHKOSH

M **OSHKOSH PUBLIC MUSEUM,** 1331 Algoma Blvd, 54901. Tel 414-424-0452. *Pres of Board* Donna Greischar; *Dir* John H Kuony; *Asst Dir & Cur Anthropology* Robert J Hruska; *Registrar* Brenda Acker; *Cataloger* Debra Daubert
Open Tues - Sat 9 AM - 5 PM; Sun 1 - 5 PM; cl Mon. No admis fee. Estab 1924 to collect and exhibit historical, Indian and natural history material relating to the area and fine and decorative arts. Steiger Memorial Wing opened in 1983 for additional exhibition space. Museum housed in city owned mansion near University campus. Average Annual Attendance: 90,000
Income: Financed by city appropriation
Collections: †American Artists; †Indian Artifacts; †Local & Wisconsin History; †Pressed Glass
Exhibitions: Monthly changing exhibits
Publications: Introductions to the Art & Artists Exhibited
Activities: Classes for adults and children; art school; offers museology & graduate history internship; dramatic programs; lectures open to public, 4 - 6 vis lectr per year; art fair; individual paintings and original objects of art lent to City of Oshkosh Depts, schools & nursing homes; originate traveling exhibitions; sales shop sells books, reproductions, prints, toys, memorabilia
L **Library,** 1331 Algoma Blvd, 54901. Tel 414-424-0452. *Archivist* Kitty A Hobson
Open Tues - Sat 9 AM - 5 PM; Sun 1 - 5 PM. Estab 1923. Research for museum exhibits and general public. For reference only
Income: Funded by city appropriation
Purchases: $2000
Library Holdings: Vols 10,000; Per subs 25; Maps; AV — Slides; Other — Clipping files, exhibition catalogs, manuscripts, memorabilia, original art works, pamphlets, photographs, prints, reproductions, sculpture
Special Subjects: Archaeology, Art Reference, Wisconsin, Upper Midwest
Publications: Exhibition catalogs
Activities: Classes; lect

O **PAINE ART CENTER AND ARBORETUM,** 1410 Algoma St, 54901. Tel 414-235-4530. *Exec Dir* Donn L Young; *Business Mgr* Dale D Wood; *Dir Public Relations* Jean Peters; *Arboretum Mgr* Allen Singstock; *Cur Education* Marti Norton; *Gift Shop Mgr* Lee Kester; *Registrar* Bea Halfen
Open Tues - Sat 10 AM - 4:30 PM, Sun 1 - 4 PM; cl national holidays. Admis $1. Estab 1948 as a non-profit corporation to serve the needs of the upper midwest by showing fine and decorative arts and horticulture. Average Annual Attendance: 30,000. Mem: 950; dues individual $15, youth & senior citizens $12, family $30
Income: Financed by endowment, membership and donations
Collections: American glass; Chinese collection; †decorative arts; †icons; †19th century English and French paintings; period rooms; oriental rugs; †arboretum contains displays of native and exotic trees, shrubs and herbacious plants
Exhibitions: American Antique Furniture; Antique Toys 1875-1950; Contemporary Polish Posters; English Brass Rubbings European Masters in Portraiture; Icons from Orthodox Church Museum of Finland; Retrospective: John McCrady (1983) The Mounties: North American Heroes; John Taylor Arms: The Gothic Aesthetic; Opening of Gothic Gallery; The True and Incredible Adventures of Doktor Thrill: Earl Lindermann Retrospective, 1972-1982; Earth, Air, Fire and Water: The Ceramic Art of Korea; The Paine Permanent Collection; Shakespeare's Flowers; French Master Caricaturists: Daumier and Gavarni; The New Epiphanies; The Divided Heart: Scandinavian Immigrant Artists, 1850-1950
Publications: Catalogues; Helen Farnsworth Mears; newsletter, bi-monthly
Activities: Classes for adults and children; dramatic programs; docent training; lect open to public, 3-6 vis lectr per yr; concerts; gallery talks; tours; competitions; scholarships; individual paintings and original objects of art lent to other museums and institutions; lending collection contains cassettes, original art works, original prints, paintings, photographs, sculptures and slides; book traveling exhibitions; traveling exhibitions organized and circulated; sales shop selling books, magazines, original art, reproductions and jewelry
L **George P Nevitt Library,** 1410 Algoma St, 54901. *Librn* Corinne H Spoo
Open Mon - Fri 8 AM - 5 PM upon request. Estab primarily for staff use as an art reference but also open to public. For reference only
Library Holdings: Vols 500; Per subs 12; Other — Exhibition catalogs
Special Subjects: Architecture, Decorative Arts, English furniture

M **UNIVERSITY OF WISCONSIN,** Allen Priebe Gallery, Arts and Communications Center, Elmwood & Woodland, 54901. Tel 414-424-0147, 424-2235. *Dir* David W Hodge; *Asst to Dir* Nancy Marks
Open Mon - Fri 10 AM - 3 PM, Mon - Thurs 7 - 9PM, Sat & Sun 1 - 4 PM. No admis fee. Estab 1971 for the purpose of offering exhibits which appeal to a wide range of people. Gallery is 60 x 40 with additional wall space added with partitions, a skylight along back ceiling. Average Annual Attendance: 15,000
Income: Financed by student allocated monies & Dept of Art
Purchases: $1500
Collections: Works Progress Administration Collection; †prints and drawings
Exhibitions: Art Teachers of Wisconsin; Joanne Kindt (paintings and drawings); Prismatic Constructions by Pecoraro; Eight in Eighty Show; Fiber Show; Lewis Foundation Exhibition; Paul Donhauser (ceramics) & Jean Stamsta (fiber); 1981 Faculty of UW-O Art Dept Show; William Whiley (lithos & etchings); Michael Brandt (jewelery) & Norman Keats (paintings); Invitation Wisconsin Glass Show; High School Art Show; Invitation Drawing Show; Invitational Doll Show (contemporary); Lewis Foundation Collection; Contemporary Images Watercolor; Dennis Gallagher, sculpture
Activities: Classes for adults and children; lectures open to the public, 2 - 4 visiting lecturers per year; gallery talks; tours; competitions with awards; individual paintings and original objects of art lent to University staff, and area museums

PLATTEVILLE

M **UNIVERSITY OF WISCONSIN,** Harry Nohr Art Gallery, 725 W Main St, 53818. Tel 608-342-1398. *Dir* John Mominee
Open Mon - Fri 11 AM - 4 PM, Mon - Wed evenings 6 - 8 PM, Sat & Sun Noon - 4 PM. No admis fee. Estab 1978. Average Annual Attendance: 9000
Income: Financed by state appropriation
Purchases: $3000
Activities: Lectures open to the public, 4 vis lectr per yr; gallery talks; tours; competitions with awards; individual paintings & original objects of art lent; lending collection contains color reproductions, framed reproductions, original art works, original prints, paintings, photographs, sculpture & ceramics; book traveling exhibitions; sales shop sells framing supplies

RACINE

O **THE RACINE ART ASSOCIATION, INC,** 2519 Northwestern Ave, 53404. Tel 414-636-9177. *Pres of Board* R J Carbonneau; *VPres of Board & Pres* Roger Lacock; *VPres* James T Gibson Jr; *Treasurer* Earl W Hammill; *Secy of Board* Edna M Olson; *Dir* Bruce W Pepich; *Asst Dir* Jane Aldrich
Open Sun - Sat 1 - 5 PM and 1 - 9 PM Mon & Thurs. Estab 1941 to foster and aid the establishment and development of public art galleries and museums, programs of education and training in the fine arts, and to develop public appreciation and enjoyment of the fine arts. Maintains an art gallery with six galleries. Average Annual Attendance: 40,000. Mem: 400; dues $15 and up; annual meeting May
Income: $130,000 (financed by membership, grants, and fund raising)
Publications: Newsletter, quarterly
Activities: Classes for adults and children; docent training; lectures open to public, 4-6 vis lectr per year; gallery talks; tours; competitions with awards; individual and original objects of art lent to qualified museums and galleries; sales shop sells books and original art
M **Charles A Wustum Museum of Fine Arts,** 53404. Tel 414-636-9177. *Dir* Bruce W Pepich
Open Sun - Sat 1 - 5 PM & Mon & Thurs 5 - 9 PM. No admis fee. Estab 1940 to serve as cultural center for greater Racine community. There are five galleries

in old (1856) residence converted for exhibition purposes. Average Annual Attendance: 40,000. Mem: 400; dues $10 - $1000; annual meeting in May
Income: $300,000 (financed by endowment, city and county appropriations, private gifts and programs)
Purchases: $500 - $1000
Collections: Contemporary Wisconsin Watercolors; WPA Project paintings and prints; contemporary graphics
Exhibitions: (1982) Watercolor Wisconsin; Edward Weston: Photographs; Fishing Lure/Fishing Lore; (1983) Wisconsin Photography 83; Wisconsin Wood 1983; Chicago Works on Paper-Abstracted
Publications: Newsbriefs, monthly
Activities: Classes for adults and children; docent training; lect open to public, 4 vis lectr per yr; gallery talks; tours; competitions with awards; individual paintings and original objects of art lent to other institutions; lending collection contains original prints, paintings, photographs & watercolors; book traveling exhibitions; originate traveling exhibitions; museum shop sells original art
L **Wustum Art Library,** 2519 Northwestern Ave, 53404. Tel 414-636-9177. *Dir* Bruce W Pepich
Open Sun - Sat 1 - 5 PM & Mon & Thurs 5 - 9 PM. Estab 1941 to provide museum visitors and students with exposure to art history and instructional books. For reference only
Income: $2500
Library Holdings: Vols 1000; Per subs 12; Micro — Cards; Other — Clipping files, exhibition catalogs
Special Subjects: 20th Century Art & Architecture

RIPON

M **RIPON COLLEGE ART GALLERY,*** Harwood Union Bldg, 54971. Tel 414-748-8110. *Dir* E M Breithaupt
Open Mon - Fri 9 AM - 4 PM. No admis fee. Estab 1965 to provide student body with changing exhibits. Average Annual Attendance: 4000
Collections: Paintings, print, sculpture, multi-media
Activities: Individual paintings lent to schools

RIVER FALLS

M **UNIVERSITY OF WISCONSIN,** Gallery 101, Cascade St, 54022. Tel 715-425-3236. *Gallery Dir* Michael Padgett
Open Mon - Fri 9 AM - 5 PM & 7 - 9 PM; Sat & Sun 1 - 5 PM. No admis fee. Estab 1973 to exhibit artists of regional and national prominence and for educational purposes. Maintains one gallery. Average Annual Attendance: 21,000
Income: $5000 (financed by state appropriation and student activities funds)
Collections: †National and International Artists; †Regional Artists; WPA Artists
Exhibitions: (1983-84) Area High School Exhibit; Invitational Photography; Art Faculty Exhibit; Fine Arts Festival; Senior Exhibit; Student Juried Exhibit; Student Photography Exhibit; James Tamer, ceramics; Jacqueline Kielkopf, paintings
Activities: Lect open to public; gallery talks; originate traveling exhibitions

SHEBOYGAN

O **JOHN MICHAEL KOHLER ARTS CENTER,** 608 New York Ave, 53081. Tel 414-458-6144. *Dir* Ruth Kohler; *Assoc Cur Exhibitions* Joanne Cubbs; *Assoc Cur Exhibitions* Anita Dowthat; *Registrar* Emil Donoval
Open Sun - Sat 12 - 5 PM, Mon 7 - 9 PM; cl national holidays. No admis fee. Estab 1967 to provide aesthetic and educational opportunities in the creative, visual and performing arts. Contains five exhibition galleries, theatre, four studio-classrooms, library, sales gallery. Average Annual Attendance: 128,000. Mem: 950; dues contributing membership categories $35 - $500 plus, family $22, individual $18, student $9
Publications: Annual report; exhibition catalogues; newsletter, bimonthly
Activities: Classes for adults and children; summer theatre; dramatic programs; docent training; lectures open to the public, 12 vis lectr per yr; concerts; gallery talks; tours; scholarships; originate traveling exhibitions; sales gallery sells books, magazines & original art
L **Library,*** 608 New York Ave, PO Box 489, 53081. Tel 414-458-6144. *Admin Asst* Nancy N Dummer
Open by appointment only. Estab 1967 to provide reference materials for staff and others. Reference only
Income: Financed by membership, grants, corporate-foundation donations
Library Holdings: Per subs 45; AV — Slides; Other — Clipping files, exhibition catalogs, memorabilia
Special Subjects: Contemporary American Crafts & Folk Art Environments
Collections: Contemporary Ceramics; Historical Decorative Arts; Prehistoric Wisconsin Indian Artifacts
Exhibitions: Paint on Clay; Murray Lemley Arts-Industry; A Woman's Place; Perspectives: Moty 2 Fibers; Filaments of the Imagination; Steeped in Tradition; Spouting Ideas; 3 from Baltimore, Perspectives: Graham Marks, Wisconsin; Art on the Road; Las Artistas del Valle de San Luis; Basketworks; Seasonal Stockings; Kristine Gunther; Earl Kittelson; Beverly Harrington; T P Speer; Thomas Hovorka
Publications: Annual Report; Exhibition checklists, qtr; Exhibition catalogues, 2 annually; Newsletter, bi-monthly
Activities: Classes for adults and children; dramatic programs; docent training; bus trips; demonstrations; lectures open to public, 5-10 vis lectr per yr; concerts; gallery talks; tours; sponsor competitions; cash awards; scholarships offered; book traveling exhibitions annually; originate traveling exhibitions to universities and museums

WAUSAU

M **LEIGH YAWKEY WOODSON ART MUSEUM, INC,** 700 North 12th St, Franklin and Twelfth Sts, 54401. Tel 715-845-7010, 848,6140. *Pres* T A Duckworth; *VPres* Alice Forester; *Secy* Helen Scholfield; *Dir* David J Wagner; *Cur of Exhibitions* Andrew J McGivern; *Cur of Education* Judith A Polus; *Assoc Cur* Jane Weinke; *Office Mgr* Marcia M Theel
Tues - Fri 9 Am - 4 PM, Sat & Sun 1 - 5 PM. No admis fee. Estab 1973 for acquisition of a creditable permanent collection of wildlife art; program of changing exhibits; art education. 7575 net square feet of exhibition space; galleries on three floors; parquet and carpeted floors; 628 running feet in galleries. Average Annual Attendance: 40,000. Mem: 100; dues $200
Income: $400,000 (financed by membership and private foundation)
Purchases: $30,000
Collections: Historical period pieces of Royal Worcester porcelain; 19th and 20th century art glass; wildlife theme paintings and sculptures with birds as the main subject
Publications: Americans in Glass; Birds in Art; Rembrandt's Etchings; The Group of Seven: Selections from the McMichael Canadian Collection
Activities: Docent programs; lectures open to the public; gallery talks; tours; competitions for participation in exhibitions; student competitions; Scholarships; individual paintings and original objects of art lent to recognized museums and art centers; book 12 - 15 traveling exhibitions per year
L **Art Library,** 54401
Open by appointment. Estab 1976. For reference only
Income: $1500
Purchases: $1500
Library Holdings: Vols 500; Per subs 20; AV — Cassettes, motion pictures, slides; Other — Clipping files, exhibition catalogs, pamphlets

WEST BEND

M **WEST BEND GALLERY OF FINE ARTS,** 300 S Sixth Ave, PO Box 426, 53095. Tel 414-334-9638. *Pres* Joan Pick; *Executive Dir & Librn* Thomas D Lidtke; *Cur* E G Kocher
Open Wed - Sun 1 - 4:30 PM; cl Mon & Tues. No admis fee. Estab 1961 to encourage the varied art interests of the community. The large colonial style building contains eight gallery exhibit rooms and three basement art classrooms. Average Annual Attendance: 8500. Mem: 450; annual meeting Feb
Income: Financed by endowment, membership and donations
Purchases: $2000
Collections: Carl von Marr Collection; †current Wisconsin art
Exhibitions: Monthly exhibitions; annual juried show
Publications: Bulletin, monthly
Activities: Classes for adults and children; lect open to public, 8 vis lectr per yr; gallery talks; tours; competitions; Art Aware, educational outreach of art appreciation serves local schools; individual paintings lent to business organizations; lending collection contains books and paintings; book traveling exhibits
L **Library,** 300 S Sixth Ave, 53095. Tel 414-334-9638
Open to members, museum & education professionals only
Library Holdings: Vols 300; Per subs 4
Publications: Carl Von Marr (catalogue)

WYOMING

BIG HORN

M **BRADFORD BRINTON MEMORIAL RANCH MUSEUM,** State Rd 335, PO Box 23, 82833. Tel 307-672-3173. *Dir* James Taylor Forrest; *Asst Dir* Dan Nelson; *Asst Dir* Osea Nelson
Open May 15 - Labor Day daily 9:30 AM - 5 PM. No admis fee. Estab 1961 to show a typical well-to-do ranch of the area of northern Wyoming as established in the late 19th century. Two galleries and house museum are maintained. Average Annual Attendance: 13,000
Income: $100,000 (financed by endowment)
Collections: Plains Indians Artifacts; Western American Art by Frederic Remington and Charles M Russell; American art and a few pieces of European art, largely of the 19th and 20th century; china; furniture; silver
Exhibitions: American Quilts; Art of Bill Gallings; Photo History of Ranch Life; Art of Winold Reise
Publications: Monographs on artists in the collection from time to time
Activities: Sales shop selling books, original art, reproductions, prints and slides
L **Library,** State Rd 335, 82833
Open to staff and to the public by appointment
Library Holdings: Vols 1200

CASPER

M **NICOLAYSEN ART MUSEUM,** 104 Rancho Rd, 82601. Tel 307-235-3347. *Chmn Board* Jon C Nicolaysen; *VChmn* Kenneth Gorder; *Secy* Peri Lathrop; *Dir* J M Neil; *Asst to Dir* Darlene Y Litalo
Open Mon - Sun 10 AM - 4 PM. No admis fee. Estab 1967 to exhibit permanent collection, nationwide traveling exhibits and provide school art classes and workshops. Two galleries, 2600 sq ft and 500 sq ft. Average Annual Attendance: 12,000. Mem: 200; annual meeting second Tues in June
Income: $200,000 (financed by membership, Wyoming Council for the Arts, NEA contributions)
Collections: Matisse prints (lithographs); Joseph Mugnaini Intaglio print; Montana Naegle, watercolor; Stephen Naegle, watercolor; Russian sculpture
Publications: Museum newsletter; brochures; exhibition catalogues

Activities: Classes for adults and children; docent training; lectures open to the public; tours; gallery talks; concerts; awards; lending collection contains original art works, original prints, paintings, sculpture; book traveling exhibitions; originate traveling exhibitions
L **Library,** 82601
Library Holdings: Vols 66; Per subs 8; AV — Slides; Other — Exhibition catalogs, pamphlets

CHEYENNE

M **WYOMING STATE ART GALLERY,** Barrett Building, 82002. Tel 307-777-7510. *Dir Wyo State Archives, Museums & Hist Dept* Robert D Bush; *Dir Wyo State Art Gallery* Steven R Cotherman
Open Mon - Fri 8 AM - 5 PM; Sat 9 AM - 5 PM. No admis fee. Estab 1969 to collect, preserve and to exhibit the work of Wyoming and Western artists. Average Annual Attendance: 50,000
Income: Financed by state appropriation
Collections: Works by Wyoming and Western artists
Exhibitions: Regional & Wyoming contemporary art, western art

CODY

O **BUFFALO BILL MEMORIAL ASSOCIATION,** PO Box 1000, 82414. Tel 307-587-4771. *Chmn* Mrs Henry H R Coe; *Secy* Melvin C McGee; *Dir* Peter H Hassrick; *Executive Secy* Judie Schmidlapp; *Cur Plains Indian Museum* George P Horse Capture; *Cur Winchester Arms Museum* Herbert Houze; *Cur Buffalo Bill Museum* Paul Fees
Open Mon - Sun 8 AM - 5 PM May & Sept, Mon - Sun 7 AM - 10 PM June - Aug, 1 - 5 PM Mar, Apr, Oct & Nov. Admis adults $4.50, sr citizens $3.75, students $3, children $2. Estab 1917 to preserve and exhibit art, artifacts and memorabilia of the Old West; to operate Buffalo Bill Museum, Plains Indian Museum, Whitney Gallery of Western Art and Winchester Arms Museum
Income: Financed by admissions & private funds
Activities: Educ dept; docent training; lectures open to public; scholarships; museum shop sells books, original art, reproductions,, prints, slides, jewelry, collectible items, Indian crafts & Kachina dolls
M **Whitney Gallery of Western Art,*** PO Box 1000, 82414. Tel 307-587-4771
Collections: Catlin, Bierstadt, Miller, Remington, Russell and all documentary artists of the Old West
Exhibitions: Annual exhibition of prominent contemporary Western artists; loan exhibitions
Publications: Exhibition catalogs
Activities: Gallery talks; sales shop selling books, prints, Indian artifacts and postcards
L **Harold McCracken Research Library,** PO Box 1000, 82414. Tel 307-587-4771. *Librn & Archivist* Michael Kelly
Open 9 AM - 4 PM. Estab 1980 for research in Western history. Open to the public for reference only
Library Holdings: Vols 12,000; Per subs 100; Micro — Reels; AV — Cassettes, motion pictures, slides; Other — Clipping files, exhibition catalogs, manuscripts, memorabilia, pamphlets, photographs, prints
Special Subjects: Firearms, Plains Indians, Western Art & History
Collections: WHD Koerner Archives; Buffalo Bill Cody Archives; Photo Collections; Rare Books
Publications: American West Magazine
Activities: Classes for children; docent training; lectures open to public, 10 vis lectr per year; gallery talks; tours

O **CODY COUNTRY ART LEAGUE,*** 836 Sheridan Ave, 82414. Tel 307-587-3597. *Pres* Mrs George W Tresler; *Dir* Mrs Gordon Way
Open Noon - 8 PM. No admis fee. Estab 1964 for promotion of artistic endeavor among local and area artists; also established for exhibits, displays and sales. Average Annual Attendance: 15,000. Mem: 115; dues $10; annual meeting Dec
Income: Financed by endowment, membership, grants from Wyoming Council on the Arts, yearly auction, and sponsors
Activities: Classes for adults and children; dramatic programs; films; workshops; lect open to public, 2-3 visiting lectrs per year; competitions

LARAMIE

M **UNIVERSITY OF WYOMING,** Art Museum, Fine Arts Building, 19th St and Willett St, 82071. Tel 307-766-2374. *Dir* James T Forrest; *Asst Dir & Cur Collections* Jerry A Berger; *Asst Cur* Kenneth L Schuster; *Asst Cur* James F Jackson
Open Sun - Fri 1:30 - 5 PM during spring and fall semester; Sun - Fri 1 - 4:30 PM during summer sessions; cl holidays. Estab 1968 to serve as an art resource center for faculty, students and the general public; the museum serves as a training ground for students interested in museums as a profession. Exhibition space consists of two galleries totaling 5625 sq ft; work room, receiving room, storage vault, offices and outdoor sculpture court. Average Annual Attendance: 12,000. Mem: 300; dues $10 and up
Income: $75,000 (financed by state appropriation and friends organization)
Purchases: $2500
Collections: 19th and 20th century European paintings, graphics and sculpture; 19th century American paintings, graphics and sculpture; 20th century American †paintings, †graphics and †sculpture
Exhibitions: Special exhibits from the permanent collections as well as traveling exhibitions on a regular basis during the fall and spring semesters; faculty shows; student shows
Publications: Annual report; exhibition catalogs
Activities: Lect open to the public, 6 vis lectr per yr; gallery talks; tours; individual paintings and original objects of art lent to other museums; lending collection contains 5000 original art works, 3000 original prints and 2000 paintings; originates traveling exhibitions

ROCK SPRINGS

O **SWEETWATER COMMUNITY FINE ARTS CENTER,** 400 C St, 82901. Tel 307-362-6520. *Dir* Allen L Keeney; *Secy* Diane V Gil; *Finance Officer* Mary Kornitnik
Open Mon & Thurs Noon - 8:30 PM, Tues & Wed 10 AM - 5 PM, Fri 1 - 6 PM, Sat Noon - 5 PM. No admis fee. Estab 1966 to house permanent art collection and hold various exhibits during the year; Halseth Gallery houses permanent art collection. Average Annual Attendance: Approx 5000
Income: Financed by endowment, city appropriation, county funds and school district # 1
Collections: †Rock Springs High School permanent collection
Exhibitions: Monthly
Publications: Calendar of events, two or three a year
Activities: Classes for adults; dramatic programs; concerts; competitions

SUNDANCE

M **CROOK COUNTY MUSEUM AND ART GALLERY,*** Box 63, 82729. Tel 307-283-3666. *Chmn Board* Nora Reimer
Open Mon - Fri 9 AM - 5 PM, cl holidays. No admis fee
Collections: Furniture, pictures, Western historical items
Publications: Brochure

PACIFIC ISLANDS

PAGO PAGO, AMERICAN SAMOA

M **JEAN P HAYDON MUSEUM,** PO Box 1540, 96799. Tel 809-633-4347. *Chmn Board of Trustees* Palauni Tuiasosopo; *Executive Dir* Enosa Pili; *Cur* Fa'ailoilo Lauvao
Open Mon - Fri 10 AM - 4 PM, Sat 10 AM - Noon. No admis fee. Estab 1971 to establish, maintain, acquire and supervise the collection, study preservation, interpretation and exhibition of fine arts, and objects and such relics, documents, painting, artifacts and other historical and related materials as will evidence and illustrate the history of the Samoan Islands, and the culture of their inhabitants, particularly of American Samoa. New extension of the museum is an Art Gallery displaying local artists work and student arts. Average Annual Attendance: 42,000
Income: Financed by city or state appropriations and grants from NEA
Collections: Natural Sciences; Polynesian Artifacts; Samoan Village Life; US Navy History; †painting, drawing, slides, †photographs, †artifacts
Activities: Classes for adults and children; dramatic programs; museum & sales shop sell books, original art
L **Library,** PO Box 1540, 96799
Reference library
Library Holdings: 16 mm films; AV — Motion pictures, slides, v-tapes; Other — Photographs
Collections: Photograph Collection

PUERTO RICO

PONCE

M **MUSEO DE ARTE DE PONCE,** Ponce Art Museum,* The Luis Ferre Foundation (Mailing add: Avenida de las Americas, PO Box 1492, 00731). Tel 809-842-6215, 840-1510. *Dir* Dr Rene Taylor; *Asst to Dir* Haydee Venegas; *Conservator* Anton Konrad
Open Mon & Wed - Fri 10 AM - Noon and 1 - 4 PM, Sat 10 AM - 4 PM, Sun 10 AM - 5 PM, cl Tues. Admis adults $1.50, children under 12 $.75. Estab 1965 to exhibit a representative collection of European paintings and sculpture; Puerto Rican art. Seven hexagonal galleries on upper floor; three rectangular galleries on lower floor. Mem: 600; dues $25
Income: Financed by endowment and membership
Collections: African, Latin American, Pre-Columbian and Puerto Rican Santos Art; 19th century art, contemporary art, 14th - 18th century paintings and sculpture
Exhibitions: El Paisaje Puertorriqueno; Arquitectura Barroca y Moderna; Ceramica del Grupo Manos Auspiciador; Grabados de Jose Luis Cuevas y Actualidad Grafica Panamericana; Colectiva Juan Ramon Velazquez Carmelo Sobrino y Joaquin Reyes; El Puerto Rico que nunca fue; Artistas Puertorriquenos residentes in NY; Juan Ramon Jimenez y los ninos;
Activities: Lect open to public, 6 visiting lectr per year; concerts; talks; tours; individual paintings and original objects of art lent to government offices; book traveling exhibitions; originate traveling exhibitions; museum shop sells books, original art, reproductions, prints, slides and plaster copies of Pre-Columbian artifacts
L **Library,*** Avenida de las Americas, PO Box 1492, 00731. *Librn* Ana Zayas
Open for reference
Library Holdings: Vols 4000; Per subs 4

RIO PIEDRAS

M UNIVERSITY OF PUERTO RICO, Museum of Archaeology, History and Art,* 00931. Tel 809-764-0000. *Dir* Dr Arturo V Davila; *Cur Archaeology* Luis A Chanlatte; *Cur Art* Pedro J Gispert
Open Mon - Fri 9 AM - 9 PM, Sat & Sun 8 AM - 3:30 PM, cl national holidays. No admis fee. Estab 1940
Collections: Archaeology; Puerto Rican paintings of the past and present; sculpture
Exhibitions: Temporary exhibitions from the collection and from museum loans
Activities: Lect; guided tours; concerts

SAN JUAN

M ATENEO PUERTORRIQUENO,* Ponce de Leon, Stop One, 00902. Tel 809-725-1265. *Pres* Eduardo Morales Coll
Open Mon - Fri 9 AM - 9 PM, Sat 9 AM - 5 PM, cl Sun & holidays. No admis fee. Estab 1876 and is the oldest cultural institution in Puerto Rico. Mem: Dues $25
Collections: Decorative arts; drawings; historical material; prints; Puerto Rican paintings; sculpture
Exhibitions: Temporary exhibitions
Publications: Annual catalogs; reports
Activities: Lect; gallery talks; guided tours; films; concerts; dance recitals; competitions; dramas; book shop
L Library,* Ponce de Leon, Stop One, 00902. *Librn* Clara S Lergier
Library Holdings: Vols 12,000

INSTITUTE OF PUERTO RICAN CULTURE
M Escuela de Artes Plasticas Galleria, 00905
Open daily 8 AM - 4 PM. Exposition of drawing, painting and art work of the students of visual school
Collections: †Permanent collection of student art work
—Library, 00905
Reference only
Library Holdings: Micro — Fiche; AV — Slides; Other — Exhibition catalogs, manuscripts, original art works, pamphlets, reproductions, sculpture
O Instituto de Cultura Puertoriquena, 98 Avenida Norzagaray, 00901. Tel 809-724-0700. *Exec Dir* Luis M Rodriquez Morales
Open Mon - Sun 8 AM - Noon & 1 - 5 PM. No admis fee. Estab 1955 to stimulate, promote, divulge and enrich Puerto Rico's cultural and historical heritage. The institute has created 16 museums around the island and has five more in preparation, including museums of historical collections, art museums and archaeological museums
Income: Financed by endowment, and state appropriation
Collections: Puerto Rican art, archaeology and historical collections
Publications: Revista del Institute de Cultura Puertoriquena, quarterly
Activities: Educ dept; lect open to public; gallery talks; concerts; tours; competitions; exten dept serving cultural centers around the Island; artmobile; individual paintings and original objects of art lent to Government agencies, universities and cultural centers; lending collection contains motion pictures, original art works; original prints, paintings, photographs; originates traveling exhibition; sales shop sells books, records and craft items; junior museum
M Museo de Bellas Artes, PO Box 4184, San Juan, 00905. Tel 809-723-2320. *Dir* Victor M Gerena
Open 9 AM - 4:30 PM. No admis fee. Estab 1977 for the exhibition of paintings and sculpture of Puerto Rican artists in a chronological way from 18th - 20th centuries. Show the techniques and trends in fine arts development in Puerto Rico
Income: Financed by state appropriation
Collections: Campeche-Oller Hall-religious and profane paintings of these two painters; 1900 Hall-exhibitions of paintings of the period by Oscar Colon Delgado, Ramon Frade and Miguel Pou; Primitive Paintings Hall-works of Manuel Harnandez Acevedo; documental and folklorical painting of the history of Puerto Rico; contemporary artists
Exhibitions: Works from permanent collection
Activities: Lect open to public; gallery talks; tours; exten dept; individual paintings and original objects of art lent to educational and cultural orgainzations and government offices; lending collection contains original art works, original prints, paintings; originate traveling exhibitions
M Dr Jose C Barbosa Museum and Library, San Juan, 00905
Open 9 AM - 5 PM. No admis fee. The house where patriot Jose Celso Barbosa was born and raised, restored to its original status as representative of a typical Puertorrican family home of the 19th century. Contains a small library geared to children's books
Income: Financed by state appropriations
Collections: Furniture, personal objects and documents belonging to Dr Barbosa, including medical instruments, manuscripts and books
M Centro Ceremonial de Caguana, San Juan, 00905
Open daily 8:30 - 5 PM. No admis fee. Caguana Indina Ceremonial Park and Museum includes the ceremonial center of the Taino Indians in Caguana, Utuado, a small town in the center of the Island, constituting the most important archeological find of the Caribbean and the most outstanding exposition of Indian primitive engineering. The plazas and walks where the Indians held their ceremonies, celebrations and games were restored and excavated to form an archeological park. Numerous petroglyphs are exhibited in the monoliths bordering the plazas, and a museum exhibits Indian objects found during the excavations at the site
Income: Financed by state appropriations
M Casa Blanca Museum, San Juan, 00905. Tel 809-724-4102, 724-5477
Open 9 AM - 4:30 PM. No admis fee. This magnificent restored building constructed in 1521 by the sons of Juan Ponce de Leon and inhabited by their descendents until mid 18th century. The Museum present domestic life in San Juan during the first three centuries of Spanish colonization. The furniture and decorations correspond to the 16th and 17th centuries, with the architectural details recreating the interior of a typical 16th century home. Average Annual

Attendance: 110,000
Collections: 16th and 17th century furniture; Ponce de Leon II, office, throne hall; kitchen, library paintings
Activities: Lectures open to the public; concerts; guided tours; museum shop
M Colonial Architecture Museum, San Juan, 00905. Tel 809-725-5250
Open 8:30 AM - 4:30 PM. No admis fee. A typical San Juan house of the 18th century has been restored to present not only its original structural splendor but also, plans, drawings, photos, maquettes and other details of San Juan colonial architecture. The exposition also includes ceramic tiles, iron works and stone masonry decorative items
Income: Financed by state appropriations
Collections: Colonial architecture
M Dominican Convent Museum, San Juan, 00905
Open 8 AM - 4:30 PM. No admis fee. Restored building constructed in 1523 to serve as a convent for Order of Dominican Monks. Use primarily as the main offices of the Institute of Puerto Rican Culture, the chapel and library have been restored to their original splendor. Average Annual Attendance: 52,000
Income: Financed by state appropriations
Collections: Manuscripts, books, religious objects and paintings; Magnificent 18th century ornate altar
Activities: Lectures open to the public; concerts; gallery talks; tours
M Museo de Arte Religioso Porta Coeli, San Juan, 00905
Open 8:30 AM - 5 PM. No admis fee. In the first years of the 17th century the Dominican monks constructed a convent in the townof San German, with a chapel they called Porta Coeli, the convent has now disappeared, but the chapel has been restored as a valuable example of missionary architecture in America
Income: Financed by state appropriations
Collections: Paintings and sculptures from between the 11th and 19th century obtained from different churches in the island
M Museo de Historia Naval y Militar de Puerto Rico, San Juan, 00905
Open 8:30 AM - 4:30 PM. No admis fee. The Museum of Naval and Military History is the historic fort of San Jeronimo del Boqueron at the entrance to the Condado lagoon, whose origins date to the second half of the 16th century, now restored to present a collection of weapons, flags and uniforms used by the Spaniards in the island. The major attacks and invasions to Puerto Rico are also illustrated
Income: Financed by state appropriations
Collections: Naval and Military canons, pistols, flags
M Museo de Imagineria Popular, San Juan, 00905
Open 8:30 AM - 4:30 PM. No admis fee. The Museum of Popular Imagery presents a collection of works called santos consisting of carved figures of saints and other religious symbols. A traditional form of Puertorrican art from the 18th century, the collection includes a rich variety of pieces representing the most outstanding santeros from the island
Income: Financed by state appropriations
M Museo de la Familia Puertorriquena del Siglo XIX, San Juan, 00905. Tel 809-725-5250
Open 8:30 AM - 4:30 PM. No admis fee. This museum presents furniture and decoration that illustrate the ambiance and lifestyle characteristic of Puerto Rico in the 19th century. All the rooms in this museum are furnished with artistic as well as historic furniture of the epoch
Income: Financed by state appropriations
Collections: Paintings, piano, complete furnishings
M Museo de la Farmacia Puertorriquena, San Juan, 00905
Open 8:30 AM - 4:30 PM. No admis fee. The Museum of the Puertorrican Pharmacy contains a rare and valuable collection of porcelain and crystal pharmacy jars, as well as objects and furnishings characteristic of 19th century Puertorrican pharmacies
Income: Financed by state appropriations
M Museo del Grabado Latinoamericano, San Juan, 00905. Tel 809-724-0700
Open 8:30 AM - 4:30 PM. No admis fee. A magnificent collection is presented in the Museum of Latin American Graphics which houses representative samples of graphic art of past and contemporary Puertorrican artists along with outstandingworks of Latin American graphic engravers. This collection of prized works from the San Juan Biennal of Latin American Graphics also forms part of this museum
Income: Financed by state appropriations
Collections: Works from Orozco, Matta, Tamayo, Martorell, Alicea, Cardillo, Nevarez, Hernandez Acevedo
M Museo del Indio, San Juan, 00905
Open 8:30 AM - 4:30 PM. No admis fee. Dedicated to the Indian culture of Puerto Rico, the Indian Museum also portrays the emerge of man in America and his development. Amongst its objects in exposition are archeological finds, photos, maps, graphics designs and paintings pertaining to the Indians in North, Central and South America, with emphasis in the Caribbean area
Income: Financed by state appropriations
M Museo y Parque Historico de Caparra, San Juan, 00905. Tel 809-781-4795
Open 8:30 AM - 4:30 PM. No admis fee. The Caparra Museum and Historic Park contain ruins of Caparra, first nucleus of colonization in Puerto Rico, founded by Ponce de Leon in 1508 and 1509, now excavated and transformed into a park memorial plaques indicating the historic significance. While the restoration and excavation were being conducted, numerous objects related to the period were discovered, which are now exhibited at this museum
Income: Financed by state appropriations
Collections: Cannos, flags, pistols, ceramics
L Library, Avenida Ponce de Leon 500, 00905. *Librn* Miguel A Nieves
Open for reference to public, investigators & students
Library Holdings: Vols 12,000; AV — A-tapes, cassettes, fs, Kodachromes, lantern slides, motion pictures, slides, v-tapes; Other — Clipping files, exhibition catalogs, framed reproductions, manuscripts, memorabilia, original art works, pamphlets, photographs, prints, reproductions, sculpture
Collections: Pre-Columbian Archaeological Collection

L LA CASA DEL LIBRO, Library, Calle del Cristo 255, 00901. Tel 809-723-0354. *Dir* David Jackson McWilliams
Open Mon - Fri 11 AM - 5 PM, Sat 2 - 5 PM. No admis fee. Estab 1955 as a museum-library devoted to the history and arts of the book and related graphic

arts. Average Annual Attendance: 14,000. Mem: 350; dues $10 and up
Income: Financed by state appropriation
Collections: Bibliography of graphic arts; binding; book illustration; calligraphy; early printing, especially 15th and 16th Century Spanish; modern fine printing; papermaking
Exhibitions: Gallery has displays on the first floor relating to printing and other arts of the book, such as: Bookplates, The Boundaries of the World, Concrete Poetry, Editions of the Quixote, Fifteen Years of Posters at La Casa del Libro, The Illustrated Book in Puerto Rico, Objetivos de Julio Plaza, Original Art Work for the Emperor's New Clothes, Por los Caminos del Dia, Printing of Music in Books, Spanish Incunables
Activities: Visits from school groups; students of library science and workers in graphic arts; material available, no fees; gallery talks; original objects of printing arts, material must be used on premises; originate traveling exhibitions

SANTURCE

M MUSEO HISTORICO DE PUERTO RICO INC,* 1396 Giorgetti St, 00909. Tel 809-725-4426. *Pres* Rosa G Coll Vidal; *VPres* Josefina Villafine; *Secy* Alba Raquel
Open 8:30 - 11:30 AM & 1 - 3 PM. Admis $.50 and $.25. Estab 1969 to study Puerto Rican art, culture and history. Twenty three rooms. Average Annual Attendance: 2000. Mem: Annual dues $100
Income: Financed by state appropriation
Collections: Puerto Rican painters
Exhibitions: Permanent exhibitions
Activities: Classes for children; docent training; lectures open to the public; gallery talks; tours; original objects of art lent to the government and to other museums

National and Regional Organizations In Canada

O **ASSOCIATION OF CANADIAN INDUSTRIAL DESIGNERS, ONTARIO,***
55 University Ave, Suite 600, Toronto, ON M5J 2H7. Tel 416-862-1799. *Admin Secy* Audrey Shaw
Estab 1948 to promote and foster a high standard of design in industrial products as a service to the public, the manufacturing industries, and the national culture and economy. Mem: 87; dues $125; annual meeting Jan

O **CANADIAN CONFERENCE OF THE ARTS,** 141 Laurier Ave W, Suite 707, Ottawa, ON K1P 5J3. Tel 613-238-3561. *National Dir* Jeffrey Holmes; *Assoc Dir* Open; *Dir Information* Brian Anthony
Estab 1945 to encourage and to advance the role of the arts and culture in Canada's national life, and to serve the interests of Canadian artists and the Canadian public. Mem: 1150; dues individuals $20, organizations based on budget: annual meeting May
Income: Financed by membership and grants
Publications: Arts Bulletin, bimonthly; Handbook Series: Who's Who, Who Does What, updated annually; Policy Papers and Reports: A Strategy for Culture, More Strategy for Culture, Culture as a Growth Sector in Canadian Development, A Little Applebert, How Government Works, Pay TV and the Regulatory Requirements of the CRTC, annually
Activities: Awards-Diplome d'Honneur to persons who have contributed outstanding service to the arts in Canada; Financial Post Awards: in collaboration with The Council for Business and the Arts in Canada, encourages the corporate sector's involvement with the visual and performing arts in Canada and recognizes those corporations whose involvement is already at a high and productive level

O **CANADIAN CRAFTS COUNCIL,** Conseil Canadien de l'Artisanat, 16-46 Elgin St, Ottawa, ON K1P 5K6. Tel 613-235-8200. *Exec Dir* Peter H Weinrich; *Pres* Patricia McLelland; *VPres* Adrienne VanRiemsdijk; *VPres* George Fry; *Secy* Joan Chalmers
Open Mon - Fri 9 AM - 5 PM. Estab 1974 to encourage the highest quality Canadian crafts and improve standards of craftsmen through education and information. Mem: 30,000; dues individuals $27.50; annual meeting Sept
Income: $100,000 - $250,000 (financed by membership and federal appropriation)
Collections: Artisan '78 Contemporary Canadian Crafts Collection
Publications: Artisan, bimonthly
Activities: Originate traveling exhibitions
L **Library,** 16-46 Elgin St, K1P 5K6
Open to the public for reference only
Library Holdings: Vols 700; Per subs 40; AV — A-tapes, v-tapes; Other — Exhibition catalogs, pamphlets
Special Subjects: Crafts

O **CANADIAN MUSEUMS ASSOCIATION,** Association des Musees Canadiens, 280 Metcalfe St Suite 202, Ottawa, ON K2P 1R7. Tel 613-233-5653. *Pres* Guy Vadeboncoeur; *Executive Dir* John G McAvity
Estab 1947 to advance public museum services in Canada, to promote the welfare and better administration of museums, and to foster a continuing improvement in the qualifications and practices of museum professions. Mem: 1800; dues $30 - $2000; annual meeting May/June
Income: Financed by membership, and government grants
Publications: Muse, quarterly; Museogramme, monthly
Activities: Correspondence course in basic museology; bursary program; travel grants; book sales
L **Museum Documentation Centre,** 280 Metcalfe Suite 202, K2P 1R7. Tel 613-233-5653. *Library Technician* Denis Roussel
Open for reference only
Library Holdings: Vols 1200; Per subs 80
Special Subjects: Museology
Publications: Directory of Canadian Museums and Related Institutions

O **CANADIAN SOCIETY FOR EDUCATION THROUGH ART,*** 1713 Bathurst St, Toronto, ON M5P 3K4. Tel 306-584-4546. *Pres* John M Emerson; *Secy General* Dr Les Groome
Estab 1954 to promote art education in Canada. Average Annual Attendance: 300. Mem: 1000; dues professional $20, affiliate $2; annual meeting Oct
Income: Financed by membership
Publications: Journal; Newsletter, quarterly; Research Bulletin
Activities: Workshops; research; annual conference; scholarships

O **CANADIAN SOCIETY OF PAINTERS IN WATERCOLOUR,*** 119 Glen Rd, Toronto, ON M4W 2W1. *Pres* Julius Griffith; *Secy* Aimee Millin
Exhibitions: Annual Exhibition

O **MARITIME ART ASSOCIATION,*** 767 Churchill Row, Fredericton, MB E3B 1P7. *Pres* Allan Rankin; *Treas* Edward Rice
Estab 1934 to coordinate work of art societies in New Brunswick, Newfoundland, Nova Scotia and Prince Edward Island. Mem: 13 societies paying corporate dues of $25; annual meeting May. Member Organizations: Conseil Acadien de Cooperation Culturele, Moncton, NB; Fredericton Art Club, NB; Fredericton Society of Artists, NB; Moncton Art Society Inc, NB; St Andrews Music, Art and Drama Club, NB; Woodstock Art Club, NB; Art Society of Newfoundland and Labrador, St John's, NF; Acadia University Art Gallery, Wolfville, NS; Contemporary Art Society, Halifax, NS; Dartmouth Heritage Museum, NS; Town of Amherst, NS; Western Counties Regional Library, Yarmouth, NS; Yarmouth Art Society, NS; plus individual members
Activities: Lect tours; lending collection contains lantern slides; regional and traveling exhibitions organized

O **PRINTING AND DRAWING COUNCIL OF CANADA,** Dept Art & Design,* Univ Alberta, Edmonton, AB T6G 2C9. *Pres* Walter Jule; *VPres* Roger Silvester; *Secy* Bonnie Sheckter
Estab 1977, following merger of the Society of Canadian Painter-Etchers and Engravers and the Canadian Society of Graphic Arts. Maintains three print cabinets in Royal Ontario Museum, Toronto; Public Library and Museum, London, Ontario; University of Toronto
Exhibitions: Annual exhibition in March
Activities: Administers G A Reid Silver Memorial Award, Nicholas Hornyansky Memorial Award; maintains Archives and Prints of 3-4 purchase awards per year; originate traveling exhibitions

O **PROFESSIONAL ART DEALERS ASSOCIATION OF CANADA,** 111 Elizabeth St, Suite 1100, Toronto, ON M5G 1P7. Tel 416-979-1276. *Pres* Jean-Pierre Valentin; *Executive Admin* Edith Yeomans; *VPres* Olga Korper
Estab 1966 for the promotion of art and artists of merit in Canada. Mem: 56, members must have five years in operation plus approved reputation, general exhibitions, financial integrity; dues $350; annual meeting May
Income: Financed by membership and appraisal fees
Publications: General information brochure; print brochure
Activities: Scholarships

O **ROYAL ARCHITECTURAL INSTITUTE OF CANADA,** 328 Somerset St West, Ottawa, ON K2P 0J9. Tel 613-232-7165. *Pres* Patrick Blouin; *Dir Programs* W Shields
Open 9 AM - 5 PM. Estab 1908 to promote a knowledge and appreciation of architecture and of the architectural profession in Canada and to represent the interests of Canadian architects
Publications: RAIC Directory, annually
L **Library,** 328 Somerset St W, K2P 0J9. Tel 613-232-7165
Special Subjects: Architecture, building and construction

O **ROYAL CANADIAN ACADEMY OF ARTS,*** 601-11 Yorkville Ave, Toronto, ON M4V 1L3. Tel 416-922-5535. *Pres* Christopher Chapman; *VPres* Gene Kinoshita; *Executive Dir* Rebecca Sisler
Estab 1880 to better the visual arts field in Canada through exhibitions. Mem: 550; membership open to visual artists concerned with excellence in their own medium; dues $50; annual meeting late Nov
Income: Non-profit association financed by membership
Exhibitions: Special exhibitions of the History of the Royal Canadian Academy 1880-1980; national, multi-disciplined, juried exhibition
Publications: Passionate Spirits: A History of the Royal Canadian Academy of Arts 1880-1980; limited edition of original prints
Activities: Originate traveling exhibitions

O **SASKATCHEWAN ARTS BOARD,*** 2550 Broad St, Regina, SK S4P 3V7. Tel 306-565-4056. *Executive Dir* Joy Cohnstaedt
Open 8 AM - 4:30 PM. Estab 1948 as an autonomous agency for promotion and development of the arts in Saskatchewan; Board is composed of 7-15 appointed members whose major concern at the present time is the support and development of professionals and professional standards within the province
Income: Financed by annual provincial government grant
Collections: †Permanent collection containing over 1000 works by Saskatchewan artists and artisans only, dating from 1950 to present; part of collection hangs in the Saskatchewan Centre of the Arts, Regina
Publications: Annual Report; brochures for Saskatchewan School of the Arts classes; services and programs brochure
Activities: Programs include individual and group assistance grants; workshop assistance; aid for exhibitions; community assistance for the performing arts; script reading service; play-script duplication subsidy; community artists program; consultative services; operates Saskatchewan School of the Arts at Echo Valley Centre, summer classes for young people and fall and spring classes for adults are offered in a wide variety of crafts, visual and performing arts

O **SCULPTOR'S SOCIETY OF CANADA,*** Visual Arts Ontario, 357 Glencairn Ave, Toronto, ON M5N 1V2. Tel 416-782-5782. *Pres* Andrew Boszin; *Cur of Collections* Aileen Hooper-Cowan

Estab 1928 to promote the art of sculpture; to present exhibitions (some to travel internationally); to educate the public about sculpture. Mem: 108, qualifications: professional sculptor; dues $45; meetings once a month

Income: $10,000 (financed by membership, provincial appropriation and sales commission)

Exhibitions: Sculptures for the Eighties; McMichael Canadian Collection; Member Show; Canadian National Exhibition

Publications: Exhibition catalogues

Activities: Workshops; lect open to public

O **SOCIETY OF CANADIAN ARTISTS,** Visual Arts Ontario, 417 Queen's Way W, Toronto, ON M5V 1A2

Estab in 1957 as the Society of Cooperative Artists and operated the first cooperative gallery in Toronto. In 1967 the name was changed to the Society of Canadian Artists and the gallery moved to larger premises. In 1968 the members elected to give up the gallery and concentrate on organizing group art shows for members in galleries across Canada. Mem: 120, membership by jury, open to artists throughout Canada

Income: Financed by membership, community fundraisings and commissions

Exhibitions: (1983-84) Southern Ontario Touring Exhibition

Publications: Two Decades, members' biographical catalog; bi-monthly newsletter

Activities: Sponsorship of art conferences and workshops; promotion of Canadian artists; originate traveling exhibitions

Museums, Libraries and Associations In Canada

ALBERTA

BANFF

M **BANFF CENTRE,** Walter Phillips Gallery, PO Box 1020, T0L 0C0. Tel 403-762-6283. *Cur* Lorne Falk
Open daily 1 - 5 PM. No admis fee. Estab 1977 to serve the community and students of the visual arts department at the Banff Centre, School of Fine Arts. Gallery is 15.24 x 21.34 m with 60.96 m of running space. Average Annual Attendance: 15,000
Income: Financed by provincial and public funding
Collections: Contemporary works; Group of Seven; Walter J Phillips Collection
Activities: Lect open to public; individual paintings and original objects of art lent
L **School of Fine Arts Library,*** PO Box 1020, T0L 0C0. Tel 403-762-6100. *Librn* Bob Foley; *Music Librn* Norah McCloy
Library Holdings: Per subs 200

M **PETER AND CATHARINE WHYTE FOUNDATION,** Peter Whyte Gallery,* 111 Bear St, Box 160, T0L 0C0. Tel 403-762-2291. *Pres* Cliff White; *Adminr & Head Archivist* E J Hart
No admis fee. Estab 1968 to preserve and collect materials of importance in the Canadian Rocky Mountain regions; to exhibit, publish and make material available for research, study and appreciation. Gallery consists of three main areas: the large main gallery and the Swiss Guides' Room downstairs and the George Brown and Belmore Brown Room upstairs. Average Annual Attendance: 75,000
Income: Financed by endowment, state appropriation, federal and provincial special activities grants
Collections: Canadian Artists, particularly Western Canadian, such as Belmore Browne, Illingworth Kerr, Walter Phillips, Sandy Spencer, Takao Tanabe, Catharine Whyte, Peter Whyte
Exhibitions: Approximately 47 per year: local, regional and national interest; ceramics, paintings, photographs, sculpture, textiles both historic and contemporary. One gallery contains works from the permanent collection at all times and changing
Publications: The Cairn, quarterly
Activities: Lect open to public, 10 visiting lectr per year; concerts; gallery talks; tours; individual paintings and original objects of art lent to accredited art galleries and museums; lending collection contains 2000 original art works, 500 original prints, 2000 paintings, 100 sculptures; book traveling exhibitions; originate traveling exhibitions; sales shop sells books, reproductions, note cards (all items sold pertain to the Foundation only)
L **Peter Whyte Gallery Library,*** 111 Bear St, PO Box 160, Banff, T0L 0C0. Tel 403-762-2291. *Librn* Mary Andrews
Open Tues & Sat 10 AM - 5 PM, Wed - Fri 1 - 9 PM, Sun 1 - 5 PM. For reference only
Library Holdings: Vols 563; Other — Clipping files, exhibition catalogs

CALGARY

M **ALBERTA COLLEGE OF ART GALLERY,** 1301 - 16th Ave NW, T2M 0L4. Tel 403-284-8661. *Cur* Valerie Greenfield; *Asst Cur* Kathleen Combton; *Gallery Display Artist* Bradley Struble; *Public Relations* Nancy Dodds
Open Mon - Fri Noon - 8 PM, Sat 2 - 5 PM, cl Sun & holidays. No admis fee. Estab 1958 as an academic-didactic function plus general visual art exhibition service to public. Two galleries: 450 sq meters of floor space; 131 meters running wall space; full atmospheric and security controls
Collections: Permanent collection of ceramics, graphics, paintings, photography, student honors work
Exhibitions: Contemporary art in all media by local, provincial, national and international artists; Western Association of Art Museums, North American public and commercial gallery offerings; monthly catalogues; Annual Wild West Show
Publications: Exhibition catalogs; posters
Activities: Lectures open to public, 20 vis lectr per year; book traveling exhibitions
L **Library,*** 1301 - 16th Ave NW, T2M 0L4. Tel 403-284-8661. *Library Supv* Mike Parkinson
Open Mon - Thurs 8 AM - 10 PM, Fri 8 AM - 4:45 PM, Sat 10 AM - 5 PM. Estab 1972 to support both college academic and studio programs. Circ 45,000
Purchases: $25,000
Library Holdings: Vols 550; Per subs 70; AV — Cassettes, fs, lantern slides, motion pictures, slides, v-tapes; Other — Clipping files, exhibition catalogs, pamphlets, reproductions
Collections: Art History and Studio (40,000 slides)
Activities: Lectures open to public, 25 visiting lecturers per year; concerts; gallery talks; competitions; individual and original objects of art lent to galleries

O **ALBERTA SOCIETY OF ARTISTS,*** Alberta College of Art, 1301 16th Ave, Rm S545, T2M 0L4. Tel 403-284-8656. *Pres* Barbara Roe Hicklin
Estab 1926 as an association of professional artists designed to foster and promote the development of visual and plastic fine arts primarily within the province. Mem: Approx 100; dues $15; annual meeting May
Publications: Highlights (newsletter), bimonthly

M **GLENBOW MUSEUM,*** 130 9th Ave SE, T2G 0P3. Tel 403-264-8300; Telex 03-825523. *Chmn Board* D E Lewis; *Dir* Duncan F Cameron; *Chief Cur* H A Dempsey; *Cur of Art* Jeremy Adamson; *Cur of Cultural History* Ron Getty; *Cur of Ethnology* Julia Harrison; *Head Extension & Education* Joyce Gibson; *Mgr Museum Shop* Carol Smith; *Head Security* L Lockhart; *Public Information* Joyce Mallman-Law
Open daily 11 AM - 9 PM. Admis adult $1, student & sr citizen $.50, children under 12 with adult free. Estab 1966 for art, books, documents, Indian and pioneer artifacts that lead to the preservation and better understanding of the history of Western Canada. Museum has three exhibition floors; 100,000 sq ft of exhibition space. Average Annual Attendance: 160,000. Mem: 23,000; dues family $25, individual $15, sr citizen & student $5
Income: $4,500,000 (financed by endowment, provincial and federal appropriation)
Purchases: $100,000
Collections: †Art: Representative collections of Canadian historical and contemporary art, Indian and Inuit. Large collection of natural history illustration and works of art on paper; †Ethnology: Large collection of material relating to Plains Indians; representative holdings from Africa, Australia, Oceania, Central and South America, Inuit and Northwest Coast; †Library and Archives: Western Canadian historical books, manuscripts and photographs
Exhibitions: Aspects of Canadian Painting; 150 Years of Watercolour Art in Alberta; Treasures of Ancient Nigeria; Pipes that Won't Smoke, Coal that Won't Burn; 19th century art from the Glenbow Collection
Publications: Chautauqua in Canada; Max Ernst; Four Modern Master; exhibiton catalogs
Activities: Classes for children; docent training; lectures open to public; gallery talks; tours; exten dept; individual paintings and original objects of art lent to public museums and galleries; lending collection contains 10,000 original prints, 10,000 paintings, 3000 sculpture and 5000 drawings; book traveling exhibitions 25 per year; originate traveling exhibitions; museum shop sells books, magazines, reproductions and prints; Luxton Museum, Banff, Alberta
L **Library,*** Ninth Ave & First St SE, T2G 0P3. *Librn* William McKee; *Librn* Len Gottselig
Open for reference
Income: Financed by endowment and government of Alberta
Library Holdings: Vols 50,000; Per subs 300; Micro — Cards, fiche, reels; Other — Clipping files, exhibition catalogs, pamphlets
Special Subjects: Western Canadian Art
Collections: †Western Canadian Art

M **MUTTART GALLERY ASSOCIATES,*** 1221 Second St SW, T2R 0W5. Tel 403-266-2764, 233-7337. *Pres* Frank Stewart; *VPres* Dennis Anderson; *Secy* Elizabeth Allen; *Treas* Robert J Lemmon; *Cur* Roberta Snyder; *Secy* Eva Tym
Open Tues - Fri Noon - 9 PM, Sat 10 AM - 5 PM. No admis fee. Estab 1978 to exhibit the works of amateur and emerging professional artists and to provide artists information for the Calgary community. Top floor of the restored Memorial Park Library (old Carnegie Library). Average Annual Attendance: 15,000. Mem: 1000; dues $6; annual meeting February
Income: $140,950 (financed by membership, city and state appropriation, private donations and corporate funds)
Exhibitions: Life Drawing Workshop; Dorothy Dausett; Morning Starr Perdue; Frances Chapman; Calgary Community Painters; Cam Steele; Harry Palmer; Glen Colin; Raymond Flatekral; Group Show Illustrators; G Leiser; M Morris; J Burgess; Violet Beaumont; Tribute Show; Jim & Marion Nicoll; Les Platt; Gwen Keenan; Jean Charles Ferri; Calgary Sketch Group; The Group; Bow Valley Group; E Luke Shwart; Helene Saint Claire; Gordon Milne & Don Wells; Salute to Art of Young Calgarians; Art Through the Schools; Eggsperience; Calgary Artists Society; Mount Pleasant Studio; Alice Williams; Jackie Anderson; Pam Rodgers; R F M McInnis; Calgary Corporation Collect; High Realism; Norma Gibson; Karen Brownlee; Charles Mitchell; Liv Pedersen; Ceramics Seminar; Tribute Show; A C and Barbara Leighton; Life Drawing Workshop; Calgary Community Painters; Alberta Society of Artists; Phil Mix; Courtney Andersen; Janusz Malinowski; Carolyn Christenson-Qualle/Eileen Oxendale; Karen Christensen; Coleen Anderson-Millard; Calgary Sketch Club; The Group; Bow Valley Group; Steve Burger/Masami Takahashi; Felicity Caron; Janet Morgan; Calgary Artists Society; Alex Jadah; Ruth Syme; Alberta Potters Association; Robert Benn; Barbara Amos; Marilyn Sagert, Janice Wong, Amy Gogarty; Calgary Public School Board; Calgary Separate School Board; Jean Biccum, Jane Pawson, Ilse Salkauskas; Marcia Perkins; Peter Raabe; Alberta Society of Artists; Hilda Fast; Jacques Rioux; Esso Resources Collection; Civic Collection of the

Calgary Allied Arts Foundation; Art & the Handicapped Exhibition; Jeff Stellick; Jill Percival; Jim Davis; Calgary Community Painters; Alberta Porcelain Artists of Calgary; Paul Shykora; Frances Chapman
Publications: Annual Report (One and One Third); Visual Arts Information Project
Activities: Classes for children; lect open to public, 2-3 visiting lectr per year; gallery talks; tours; competitions; book traveling exhibitions three per year

L SOUTHERN ALBERTA INSTITUTE OF TECHNOLOGY, Alberta College of Art Library, 1301 16th Ave NW, T2M 0L4. Tel 403-284-8665. *Head Librn* Christine Sammon; *Slide Librn* Monika Croydon
Open Mon - Thurs 8 AM - 10 PM, Fri 8 AM - 4:45 PM, Sat 10 AM - 5 PM. Estab 1972 to serve the educational needs of the Alberta College of Art. Gallery is separate
Income: Financed by SAIT via Alberta govt
Purchases: $60,000
Library Holdings: Vols 6000; Per subs 96; Micro — Fiche; AV — Cassettes, fs, slides, v-tapes 60,000; Other — Exhibition catalogs
Activities: Classes for adults and children; lectures open to public, 35-40 vis lectr per year; gallery talks; tours; awards; scholarships; book traveling exhibitions

M UNIVERSITY OF CALGARY, The Nickle Arts Museum, 2500 University Drive NW, T2N 1N4. Tel 403-284-7234. *Dir* Richard K Graburn; *Cur Art* Karyn Elizabeth Allen; *Cur Numismatics* Colin Orton
Open Tues - Fri 10 AM - 5 PM, Thur evenings until 7 PM, Sat & Sun 1 - 5 PM, cl Mon & holidays. In 1970 an Alberta pioneer, Mr Samuel C Nickle, gave the University a gift of one million dollars and the museum was opened in 1979. His son, Carl O Nickle, presented the University with an immensely valuable collection of some 10,000 ancient coins, covering over 1500 years of human history which is housed in the Numismatics department of the museum. Museum houses the permanent collection of the University; exhibitions are presented on a continuous basis in the gallery on the main floor (15,000 sq ft) A smaller numismatic gallery displays rotating collections. The smaller Gallery II on the second floor (1500 sq ft) is used for small exhibitions lectures, films & seminars. Average Annual Attendance: 25,000
Income: Financed by state appropriation through the Univ
Purchases: $15,000
Collections: Contemporary ceramics; paintings; photography; sculpture; prints and watercolors
Exhibitions: Local, national and international exhibitions are presented on a continuous basis
Publications: Exhibition catalogues
Activities: Docent training; seminars; lect open to public; gallery talks; films; originate traveling exhibitions

EDMONTON

O ALBERTA ART FOUNDATION, 4th Floor, Beaver House, 10158 103rd St, T5J 0X6. Tel 403-427-9968. *Chmn* Dale M Simmons; *Secy* Glen Buick; *Exec Dir* W Tin Ng
Open Mon - Fri 8:15 AM - 4:30 PM. No admis fee. Estab 1972 to collect and to exhibit art works pertinent to the Province of Alberta
Income: Financed by the Province of Alberta & Western Canada Lottery & Alberta Division
Collections: Alberta Art Foundation Collection
Exhibitions: Art Foundation; Little by Little; Westcape; Canada Day Exhibit; Fired Earth; Paper & Clay; Studio Ceramics in Alberta: 1947 - 1952; What Was New in '82; Recent Acquisitions 80/81; Choices; Bridging the Gap; Tribute - To Jim & Marion Nicoll; Studio Ceramics in Alberta II, 1953 - 1963; Ten - 83; Presence; Latitude 53: A Decade; In Celebration; Texas Energy Trade Show; Offshore Europe '83; Canadian National Exhibition; Crafts of the World Little by Little
Publications: Annual Report; exhibition catalogs
Activities: Acquisition of art works by Alberta artists; exhibition program in and outside Canada; individual paintings & original objects of art lent to public government buildings; originate traveling exhibitions

DEPARTMENT OF CULTURE, GOVERNMENT OF THE PROVINCE OF ALBERTA
O Beaver House Gallery, 10158 103rd St 3rd Floor, T5J 0X6. Tel 403-427-2031. *Dir Visual Arts* Leslie F Graff; *Consultant Exposure Programs* E Ross Bradley
Open Mon - Fri 8:15 AM - 4:30 PM, Sat 10 AM - 4:30 PM. No admis fee. Estab to provide assistance to the Province of Alberta in the development of the visual arts and crafts. Beaver House Gallery, approx 2000 sq ft, created for the purpose of increasing exposure to the visual arts in all their forms. Average Annual Attendance: 5000-10,000
Income: Financed by provincial appropriations
Exhibitions: Paintings, sculpture, graphics, crafts and children's work
Publications: Professional development manuals; quarterly newsletter; technical journals
Activities: Classes for adults & children; lectures open to the public; competitions; exten dept serves the Province of Alberta; artmobile; individual paintings & original objects of art lent to other institutions; lending collection contains 4000 original art works, 2000 original prints, 1000 paintings, 500 photographs, 100 sculptures, 400 craft objects; book traveling exhibitions; originate traveling exhibitions
L Visual Arts Library, 10158 103rd St, T5J 0X6. Tel 403-427-2031. *Librn* Zenobia Hurley
Reference library
Library Holdings: Vols 1200; Per subs 34; Other — Clipping files, pamphlets
M Provincial Museum of Alberta, 12845 102nd Ave, T5N 0M6. Tel 403-427-1730. *Dir* John Forlier; *Asst Dir Natural History* Dr P S Stepney; *Asst Dir Human History* E Waterton
Open Mon - Sun 10 AM - 8 PM, cl Christmas. No admis fee. Estab 1967 to preserve and interpret the human and natural history of the province of Alberta. Four major areas divided equally into human and natural history under broad themes of settlement history, anthropology, natural history habitat groups and

natural history interpretive displays. Average Annual Attendance: 500,000. Mem: 300; dues $3 - $8; annual meeting in April
Income: $3,817,511
Purchases: $46,000
Collections: Archaeological; ethnographical; fine and decorative arts; folk life; geology; historical; palaeontology
Exhibitions: Approx 20 feature exhibits
Publications: Museum Notes; occasional papers; occasional series; Publication Series
Activities: Classes for children; lectures open to public, 3 vis lectr per year; competitions; gallery talks; exten dept serving province of Alberta; Museumobiles; individual artifacts lent; originate traveling exhibitions; sales shop sells books
L Provincial Archives of Alberta, 12845 102nd Ave, T5N 0M6. *Provincial Archivist* A D Ridge; *Asst Provincial Archivist* W B Speirs; *Sr Archivist* J E Dryden; *Historical Resources Librn* J Toon
Open Mon - Fri 9 AM - 4:30 PM, Wed evening until 9 PM. Estab 1967 to identify, evaluate, acquire, preserve, arrange and describe and subsequently make available for public research, reference and display those diversified primary and secondary sources that document and relate to the overall history and development of Alberta
Income: Financed by provincial appropriation
Purchases: $39,000
Library Holdings: Vols 20,000; Per subs 180; Original documents; Micro — Fiche, reels; AV — A-tapes, cassettes, motion pictures, rec, slides; Other — Clipping files, manuscripts, original art works, pamphlets, photographs, prints
Special Subjects: Ethno-cultural groups and activities, genealogy, immigration and land settlement, local histories, religious archives
Exhibitions: Several small displays each year highlighting recent accessions

M EDMONTON ART GALLERY, 2 Sir Winston Churchill Square, T5J 2C1. Tel 403-422-6223. *Dir* T Fenton; *Assoc Cur* Russell Bingham; *Assoc Cur* Wayne Staples; *Registrar* Kate Davis; *Communications Mgr* Monty Cooper; *Public Relations* Deborah Witwick; *Head Art Education* John King; *Admin Services Mgr* Alma Garneau
Open Mon, Tues & Sat 10:30 AM - 5 PM, Wed - Fri 10:30 AM - 9 PM, Sun 1 - 5 PM, cl New Years, Christmas. Admis adults $2, senior citizens & students $1, members & children 12 & under free. Estab 1923 to collect and exhibit paintings, sculptures, photographs and other works of visual art and to teach art appreciation. Gallery covers 63,000 sq ft; exhibition area 20,000 sq ft. Average Annual Attendance: 200,000. Mem: 1700; dues $35
Income: $1,300,000 (financed by donations, fees, membership, city appropriation, state appropriation and federal grants)
Purchases: $119,000
Collections: †Contemporary Canadian art; † contemporary & historical photography; † contemporary international art; † historical Canadian art; historical European and American art
Exhibitions: 29 in-house exhibitions and 23 extension shows
Publications: Update Magazine, six copies per yr; exhibition catalogues
Activities: Classes for adults and children; docent training; workshops; lect open to the public, 6 visiting lectrs per year; concerts; gallery talks; tours; exten dept serving Alberta and across Canada; individual paintings and original objects of art lent to smaller galleries in area, and other large galleries; book traveling exhibitions; traveling exhibitions organized and circulated; sales shop selling books, magazines, original art, reproductions, craft items; junior museum maintained
L Library, 2 Sir Winston Churchill Square, T5J 2C1. Tel 403-429-6781. *Librn* Brenda Banks
Open to the public for reference use
Library Holdings: Vols 8000; Per subs 38; Micro — Fiche, reels; AV — Cassettes, slides, v-tapes; Other — Clipping files, exhibition catalogs
Activities: Classes for adults and children; docent training; lectures open to public and members only; gallery talks; tours; competitions; extension dept; originate travel;ing exhibitions; sales shop sells books, magazines, original art, reproductions

L EDMONTON PUBLIC LIBRARY, Foyer Gallery and Photography Gallery,* 7 Sir Winston Churchhill Sq, T5J 2V4. Tel 403-423-2331. *Coordr* Barbara Hartmann
Foyer Gallery has 120 running feet with extra panels available and 420 square feet of floor space; Photography Gallery has 84 running feet
Exhibitions: Twenty-four exhibitions per year

O LATITUDE 53 SOCIETY OF ARTISTS, 9749 111th St, T5K 1J7. Tel 403-488-6007. *Pres* Trudie Heiman; *Special Projects Researcher* M Moore
Open Wed - Sun Noon - 5 PM. Estab 1973 to present quality work of an alternative nature to the city of Edmonton. Average Annual Attendance: 2000. Mem: 225; dues voting $25, non-voting $15; annual meeting Oct 25
Income: $125,000 (financed by grants, donations, public & private funding, membership & fund raising events)
Exhibitions: (1983) Studio Survey: Sculpture; Barbara Todd; In House Show; Linda Krause; Stacy Spiegel; Greg Carleton & John Nagel; Laura Vickerson; Gregory Pyra; Cynthia Short & Moy Mah; Karen Curry; Photography: Jayce Salloum; Daryl Cote; Diana Selsor; Pat Morrow; Marla Strong; David Belcher; Ken Straiton; Banff Group; Doug Curran; Daniel Bagan; (1984) Michael Miller & Margaret Stewart; Doug Donely; Tommie Gallie; Molly McDonald; Visual Arts & Poetry; Photography: members show & sale; Justin Wonnacott; Shelagh Alexander; Fringe Research; TBA
Publications: Exhibition catalogues
Activities: Lectures open to the public, 1 vis lectr per yr; concerts; book traveling exhibitions; originate traveling exhibitions

**M UKRAINIAN MUSEUM OF CANADA,* 10611 - 110 Ave, T5H 1H7. Tel 403-424-7580. *Pres* N Seniw; *Dir* J Verchomin
Open by appointment, July & Aug Sun 2 - 5 PM. No admis fee. Estab 1941
Collections: Drawings, historical material, national costumes, paintings, prints, sculpture and textiles
Activities: TV and radio programs; study clubs; lect; guided tours; films; loan service

L Library, * 10611 - 110 Ave, T5H 1H7. Tel 403-424-1530. *Librn* Mrs O Lukomsky
Library Holdings: Vols 2500; Other — Manuscripts
Special Subjects: Ukrainian arts and crafts, general culture

M UNIVERSITY OF ALBERTA, Ring House Gallery,* T6G 2E2. Tel 403-432-5834, 432-5818. *Cur* Helen Collinson; *Registrar* Susan Heth; *Departmental Secy* Marlis Cooke; *Exhib Coordr* Darrell Colyer
Open Mon, Wed & Fri 11 AM - 4 PM, Thurs 11 AM - 9 PM, Sun 2 - 5 PM. No admis fee. Estab 1968 to display items from the University's permanent collection and from traveling exhibitions from outside sources. Gallery is located in former residence of the University President, which has been converted to an art gallery; three exhibition areas on first floor; two on second; space totals 350 running ft. Average Annual Attendance: 4000
Income: Financed by state appropriation and university funds
Collections: Antiquities, ethnographic material, furniture, graphics, paintings, sculpture and textile
Activities: Book traveling exhibitions; originate traveling exhibitions

FORT SASKATCHEWAN

L FORT SASKATCHEWAN MUNICIPAL LIBRARY, Exhibit Room, 10011 102nd St, Box 3060, T8L 2T1. Tel 403-998-4271. *Dir* Marcia Redford
Open winter Mon, Tues & Thurs 1 - 9 PM, Wed & Fri 10 AM - 5 PM, Sat & Sun 1 - 5 PM, cl Sat & Sun in summer. Estab 1980 as a gallery available for local artists & for interested citizens. Exhibit Room has 78 running feet of exhibition space and a floor space of approximately 731 square feet
Income: Financed by town grant, provincial grant, fees & fines
Exhibitions: Monthly exhibitions

GRANDE PRAIRIE

M GRANDE PRAIRIE COLLEGE GALLERY, * 10726 106th Ave, T8V 4C4. Tel 403-539-2911. *Cur* Carmon Hackstead
Activities: Painting classes; tours; originates 16 traveling exhibitions; gallery shop

LETHBRIDGE

O ALLIED ARTS COUNCIL OF LETHBRIDGE, Bowman Arts Center, 811 Fifth Ave S, T1J 0V2. Tel 403-327-2813. *Pres* Shirley Hamilton
Open Mon - Fri 10 AM - 10 PM, Sat & Sun 1 - 5 PM. No admis fee. Estab 1958 to encourage and foster cultural activities in Lethbridge, to provide facilities for such cultural activities, and to promote the work of Alberta and Western Canadian artists. Average Annual Attendance: 20,000. Mem: 300; dues $15; annual meeting Feb
Income: $67,000 (financed by membership and city appropriation, Alberta Culture granting & fund raising)
Exhibitions: Local exhibitions: Children's art, fabric makers, painters, potters; one-man shows: Paintings, photography, prints, sculpture, silversmithing; provincial government traveling exhibits
Publications: Calendar of Arts, weekly
Activities: Classes for adults and children; dramatic programs; concerts; competitions; scholarships; traveling exhibitions organized and circulated; sales shop selling original art

M LETHBRIDGE COMMUNITY COLLEGE GALLERY, * Buchanan Research Centre, T1K 1L6. Tel 403-320-3352. *Supvr* K Lea
Estab 1978. Gallery consists of 207 running feet of wall space in the library of the Buchanan Resource Centre
Collections: Canadian Perspectives Collection

M LETHBRIDGE PUBLIC LIBRARY, Art Gallery,* 810 Fifth Ave, S, T1J 4C4. Tel 403-329-3233. *Cur* Ann Reids
Estab 1974 to expand human experience, to encourage people to look at art as well as read and attend library programs
Activities: Originates traveling exhibitions

M SOUTHERN ALBERTA ART GALLERY, * 601 3rd Ave S, T1J 0H4. Tel 403-327-8770. *Pres* Peter Green; *VPres* Doug Lint; *Secy* Nancy Popovich; *Dir* Alf Bogusky; *Gallery Asst* Joan Stebbins
Open Tues - Sat 10 AM - 5 PM, Thurs & Fri 6:30 - 9 PM, Sun 1 - 5 PM. No admis fee. Estab 1975 to present historical and contemporary art programmes designed to further the process of art appreciation. Three gallery spaces contained in historical Lethbridge building remodelled as art gallery. Average Annual Attendance: 25,000. Mem: 500; dues $15 family, $10 single; meeting Feb 15
Income: Financed by membership, city, state and federal appropriation
Collections: Buchanan Collection of City of Lethbridge containing mid-20th Century Canadian work and various international pieces
Exhibitions: Historical and contemporary art changing monthly
Publications: Exhibition catalogues; monthly mailer
Activities: Lectures open to public, 5 vis lectr per yr; concerts; gallery talks; tours; artmobile; book traveling exhibitions, 12 per yr; originate traveling exhibitions
L Library, * 601 Third Ave S, T1J 0H4. Tel 403-327-8770
Reference library by appointment only
Library Holdings: Vols 2000; Per subs 10; AV — Slides; Other — Clipping files, exhibition catalogs, pamphlets

M UNIVERSITY OF LETHBRIDGE, Art Gallery,* 4401 University Dr, T1K 3M4. Tel 403-379-2691. *Chmn Art Dept* L E Weaver; *Gallery Dir* B J McCarroll
Open Mon - Fri 8:30 AM - 4:30 PM, Sun 1 - 4 PM. No admis fee. Estab 1968 for public service and the teaching mechanism. 21 ft x 40 ft gallery, adjoining hall and roof terrace available for exhibition space

Income: Financed by city and state appropriations
Collections: Some professional prints and drawings; student work
Exhibitions: Local and regional shows in addition to those traveling exhibitions by the National Gallery, The Winnipeg Gallery and the Western Association of Art Museums, approx ten shows per year
Activities: Lect open to the public; gallery talks; tours; individual paintings and original objects of art lent; lending collection contains Kodachromes and motion pictures

O WESTERN CANADA ART ASSOCIATION INC, Southern Alberta Art Gallery, 601 Third Ave S, T1J 0H4. Tel 403-327-8770. *Pres* Elizabeth Brown; *Secy & Treas* Joan Stebbins
Estab 1970 as art lobby & support association. Mem: 100
Income: Financed by membership
Publications: Wagon, 3 times a yr
Activities: Seminars; competitions with awards
L Library, 601 Third Ave S, T1J 0H4
For members only

MEDICINE HAT

M MEDICINE HAT MUSEUM ART GALLERY, National Exhibition Centre,* 299 College Dr SE, T1A 3Y6. Tel 403-527-6266 museum, 526-0486 gallery. *Dir* Tom Willock
June - Aug Mon - Fri 9 AM - 9 PM, Sat, Sun & holidays 1 - 5 PM, cl New Year's, Good Friday & Christmas. Admis adult $1. Estab 1951. Gallery has 1400 square feet of main exhibition space, smaller second gallery and downstairs display area of 3000 square feet. Average Annual Attendance: 10,000
Collections: Pioneer artifacts of city & the district; Indian artifacts
Activities: School programs; films; gallery talks

L MEDICINE HAT PUBLIC LIBRARY, * 414 First St SE, T1A 0A8. Tel 403-527-5551. *Chief Librn* R M Block; *Asst Dir* Erin T Doyle
Open Mon - Fri 9 AM - 9 PM. No admis fee. Library has a display area for traveling and local art shows. 600 sq ft room with track lighting and alarm system
Library Holdings: Vols 2000; Micro — Reels 175; AV — Cassettes 100, motion pictures 280, rec, v-tapes; Other — Clipping files, original art works, pamphlets, photographs, prints, sculpture
Activities: Dramatic programs; lect open to public, 10 vis lectr per year; concerts

MUNDARE

O BASILIAN FATHERS, Box 379, T0B 3H0. Tel 403-764-3860. *Dir* Myron Chimy
Open May - Oct, Mon - Sat 10 AM - 6 PM. Donations accepted. Estab 1951
Collections: Ukrainian Folk Art, Arts and Crafts; Historical Church Books
L Library, * Box 379, T0B 3H0
Library Holdings: Vols 650

RED DEER

M RED DEER AND DISTRICT MUSEUM AND ARCHIVES, Exhibition Centre, 45th St and 47th Ave, T4N 1M4. Tel 403-343-6844. *Dir* Morris Flewwelling
Estab 1978. The Exhibition Centre has 150 usable running feet of exhibition space and the Stewart Room has about 50-60 running feet of exhibition space. Average Annual Attendance: 31,000
Activities: Docent training; book traveling exhibitions
M Red Deer Recreation Centre Gallery, * T4N 1M4. Tel 403-343-6844. *Creative & Cultural Program Supvr* Barb McFarland
Estab 1974. The gallery is located upstairs from the Recreation Centre. It contains 1016 square feet of exhibition space
Activities: Book traveling exhibitions

STONY PLAIN

M STONY PLAIN MULTICULTURAL CENTRE, 5411 51st St, T0E 2G0. Tel 963-2777. *Cur* Anette Deib
Open Mon - Sun 10 AM - 4 PM. No admis fee. Estab 1974 to provide exposure to high quality art with priority given to local Alberta artists, to develop an appreciation for good art, to provide exposure for upcoming artists. Gallery has 900 square feet of exhibition space. Average Annual Attendance: 80,000. Mem: 200; dues $10; annual meeting Oct
Exhibitions: 14 exhibitions per yr
Publications: Newsletter, every 4 months
Activities: Classes for adults & children; gallery talks; tours; competitions; sales shop sells handicrafts

BRITISH COLUMBIA

BURNABY

M BURNABY ART GALLERY, * 6344 Gilpin St, V5G 2J3. Tel 604-291-9441. *Pres Board of Trustees* E Eakins; *Dir* Roger Boulet; *Gallery Asst* Elisa Anstis; *Educator* Judith O'Keeffe; *Chief Preparator* Brent Beattie; *Dir* Mary Fox; *Secy* Jennifer Harrard
Open Mon, Tues, Thurs, Fri 10 AM - 5 PM, Wed 10 AM - 9 PM, weekends & holidays Noon - 5 PM. No admis fee. Estab 1967 to present continually

changing exhibitions of the prints, paintings, sculpture, ceramic, fabric and other arts of local and other Canadian artists both contemporary and historic. Gallery is situated in a house built in 1909 surrounded by the 25 acres of Century Park. Average Annual Attendance: 45,000. Mem: 500; dues sponsor $100, group $25, family $15, single $10, student $5; annual meeting May
Income: Financed by endowment, membership, city and state appropriation and federal grants
Collections: Collection of Canadian prints from the earliest to those by contemporary artists
Exhibitions: Biennial Prints Exhibition; juried exhibitions
Publications: Catalogues and brochures to accompany exhibitions; Paper BAG, quarterly members bulletin
Activities: Classes for adults and children; docent training; lect open to public, 20 vis lectr per year; gallery talks; tours; competitions, sponsors juried exhibitions, offers biennial prints exhibition purchase awards; exten dept; book traveling exhibitions once or twice per year; originate traveling exhibitions; museum shop sells books, magazines, original art, reproductions, prints, crafts and pottery by local and other artists

M SIMON FRASER UNIVERSITY, Simon Fraser Gallery, V5A 1S6. Tel 604-291-4266. *Dir* James Warren Felter; *Gallery Asst* Suzie Young
Open Mon 1:30 - 4 PM and 5 - 8 PM, Tues - Fri 10 AM - 1 PM and 2 - 4 PM, cl Sat & Sun & Holidays. No admis fee. Estab 1971 to collect, conserve and display original works of art, principally contemporary Canadian. Gallery is 150 to 310 running ft, 1200 sq ft. Permanent works are installed throughout the university campus. Average Annual Attendance: 12,000
Income: Financed by public university appropriations, government grants and corporate donations
Purchases: $9000
Collections: Simon Fraser Collection, including contemporary and Inuit graphics; international graphics
Exhibitions: (1982) Musical Manuscripts; Canaletto Etchings: The William A Gumberts Collection; Recent Acquisitions to the Simon Fraser Collection; Rites of Passage: The Symbolic Textiles of Indonesia; Emma Lake '79; Shipibo: Conibo Painting of the Upper Amazon; Insights: 20 Vancouver Painters; Two Views of China; Woven Images: Bolivian Weaving from the 19th Century; Swedish Graphics: 8 Temperaments; (1982) The 2nd Canadian Biennale of Prints & Drawing; Selections: The Simon Fraser Collection; Recent Projects: A Survey of Work from the Centre for the Arts' Visual Arts Programme; Graphic Newfoundland; Rene Magritte: The Cinematograph and the Photograph; Nanga: Idealistic Painting of Japan; The World of Donald Evans; Gordon Smith: Prints 1954-1980; Laserienoire: The Blackseries; Andy Sinats: Photo Screenprints 1972-1982; Solidarity with Solidarnosc; Native Canadian Graphics from the Simon Fraser Collection; Past Laespiantao de Demain; North American Time Zone: VSI Simultaneity; Photographic Studies; Graham Cantieni: Recent Collages; Images of India; British Columbia Broadsides
Publications: Annual Report, every yr; occasional exhibition catalogues; posters
Activities: Lectures open to public, 1-2 vis lectrs per year; gallery talks; international exten dept; individual paintings and original objects of art lent; lending collection contains 900 original art works, 900 original prints, paintings and sculpture; book traveling exhibitions; originate traveling exhibitions
L Library,* Centre for the Arts, Academic Quadrangle 3004, Burnaby, V5A 1S6. Tel 604-291-3265. *Librn* Theodore C Dobb
Reference library
Library Holdings: AV — A-tapes, fs, slides, v-tapes; Other — Clipping files

CHILLIWACK

O COMMUNITY ARTS COUNCIL OF CHILLIWACK (Formerly Formerly Chilliwack Arts Council),* Box 53, V2P 6H7. Tel 604-792-2069. *Pres* J J VanderHoek; *VPres* D Renwick; *Secy & Coordr* Sherry Baker
Open 9 AM - 4 PM. Estab 1959 as Arts Council, Arts Centre estab 1973 to encourage all forms of art in the community. Mem: 5000; dues organizational $7.50, individual $5; annual meeting September
Income: Financed by endowment, membership and grants
Collections: 26 Salish Weavings
Exhibitions: Local artists' exhibitions, including oils, pottery, prints, weavings, wood carving and other fabric arts
Publications: Arts Council Newsletter, 11 per year
Activities: Classes for adults and children; dramatic programs; concerts; scholarships

COQUITLAM

O PLACE DES ARTS, 1120 Brunette Ave, V3K 1G2. Tel 604-526-2891. *Dir* Lenore Peyton
Open Mon - Thurs 9 AM - 10 PM, Fri 3 - 10 PM, Sat 9 AM - 4 PM. No admis fee. Estab Sept 1, 1972 as a cultural, community crafts and resource center, an art school and gallery. Average Annual Attendance: 3000
Income: Financed by municipal grant
Exhibitions: Bi-weekly shows of artists and craftsmen throughout the year
Publications: Program (12 weeks), every three months
Activities: Special Educ Dept serving retarded young adults, school children, senior citizens and women's groups; satellite courses within the school of the district on request; classes for adults and children; dramatic programs; lect open to public; concerts; gallery talks; scholarships

DAWSON CREEK

M SOUTH PEACE ART SOCIETY, Dawson Creek Art Gallery, 101-816 Alaska Ave, V1G 4T6. Tel 604-782-2601. *Pres* Edna McPhail; *Cur* Elizabeth Hillman; *Secy* Marg Baker; *Treas* Lois Roberts
Open winter Tues - Sat 10 AM - 5 PM, summer daily 9 AM - 9 PM. Admis individual $1. Estab 1961 to promote art appreciation in community. Art Gallery in elevator annex in NAR Park which includes museum and Tourist Information

Office. Average Annual Attendance: 40,000 - 50,000. Mem: 60; dues $5; annual meeting third Thurs of March
Income: Financed by membership, city appropriation and commissions on sales
Exhibitions: Approximately 15 - 18 per year, local and traveling
Activities: Classes for adults and children; gallery talks; tours; competitions with awards; paintings lent to members; lending collection contains color reproductions and slides; book traveling exhibitions, 4-6 per year; gallery shop sells original art, Hasty Notes of local scenes by local artists

KELOWNA

M KELOWNA CENTENNIAL MUSEUM AND NATIONAL EXHIBIT CENTRE, 470 Queensway Ave, V1Y 6S7. Tel 604-763-2417. *Pres* J D Wilson; *Secy* Sadie Conrad; *Dir & Cur* Ursula Surtees; *Asst Cur* Dan Bruce; *Museum Educator* Leslie Hopton; *Display Coordr* Debbie Griffith; *Registrar* Helga Sauthoff
Open summer Mon - Sat 10 AM - 5 PM, Sun 2 - 5 PM, winter Tues - Sat 10 AM - 5 PM. No admis fee. Estab 1935 as a community museum, a national exhibit center where traveling exhibits are received and circulated. Mem: Annual meeting March
Income: Financed by membership, city and state appropriation
Collections: Local history; natural history; costumes; textiles; ethnography
Exhibitions: (1983) First Alarm; All About Kitchens; Birds of Alberta; Oliver Jackson Nightwings; Woodworkers Art; Dreams of Empire
Publications: A Short History of Early Fruit Ranching Kelowna; Lak-La-Hai-Ee Volume III Fishing; Nan, A Childs Eye View of the Okanagan; Sunshine and Butterflies; The Games Grandpa Played, Early Sports in BC
Activities: Classes for adults and children; lect open to public; individual items lent to schools; lending collection contains 2000 lantern slides; book traveling exhibitions; originate traveling exhibitions
L Library,* 470 Queensway Ave, V1Y 6S7. Tel 604-763-2417
Library Holdings: Other — Photographs
Collections: Photograph Collection

NELSON

M THE MACGREGOR GALLERY (Formerly Kootenay School of Art Gallery),* 1111 Selby St, V1L 1C8. Tel 604-352-2241. *Gallery Curator & Dir* E H Underhill
Open Mon - Fri 10 AM - 4 PM, Sat & Sun by appointment. No admis fee. Estab 1962. Gallery is 50 x 50 ft with 96 running ft, 296 running ft with optional partitions; fluorescent lighting and adjustable floodlamps; office and two storage rooms. Average Annual Attendance: 10,000
Income: Financed by provincial appropriation
Collections: Permanent collection consists of graduate student examples in painting, drawing, sculpture, ceramics and applied design
Exhibitions: ...And the Rains Came; Animatoon; Art History; How Now; Inuit Games and Contest (printmaking); KSA Graduation Exhibition of Graphic Arts and Fine Arts; Painting and Sculpture; Photography; Small Delights and Greater Mysteries; Student Prints - Osaka/Alberta; Watercolors; What Happened at Emma Lake; Young Artists of the Prairies; applied design, ceramics, faculty exhibition, painting, printmaking
Publications: Calendar, yearly; exhibition catalogs
Activities: Classes for adults; dramatic programs; graphic arts training; lect open to public, 10-15 vis lectr per year; concerts; gallery talks; tours; scholarships and fels; exten dept; individual paintings and original objects of art lent to educational institutions; lending collection contains cassettes, film strips, motion pictures, original art works, original prints, paintings, phonorecords and 25,000 slides; book traveling exhibition; originate traveling exhibitions

PRINCE GEORGE

M PRINCE GEORGE ART GALLERY, 2820 15th Ave, V2M 1T1. Tel 604-563-6447, 563-9484. *Pres* June Parker; *Treas* Rowland Green; *Dir* Mimi Gely; *Asst Coordr* Lauren Cox
Open Tues - Fri Noon - 5 PM, Wed 7 - 9 PM, Sat 10 AM - 5 PM. No admis fee. Estab 1970 to foster development of arts and crafts in the community; to foster and promote artists. Gallery is wood frame building, 5849 sq ft including two 1200 sq ft galleries, with track-lighting and carpet. Average Annual Attendance: 18,000. Mem: 323; dues business $40, family $15, single $10; annual meeting May
Income: $33,550 (financed by membership, city and provincial appropriations and grants)
Collections: Individual paintings and original art
Publications: Newsletter, monthly
Activities: Classes for children; docent training; lect open to public, 8 vis lectr per year; gallery talks; tours for school children; competitions; exten dept serving northern British Columbia; individual paintings and original objects of art rented to members; lending collection contains books, original art works, paintings; originate traveling exhibitions; sales shop sells original paintings, drawings, pottery, handicrafts, prints, cards, art books and catalogues and Opus frames
L Library, 2820 15th Ave, V2M 1T1
Open to members for reference only
Library Holdings: Vols 20; Per subs 13; AV — Cassettes, slides; Other — Original art works

PRINCE RUPERT

M MUSEUM OF NORTHERN BRITISH COLUMBIA, Prince Rupert Museum Art Gallery, McBride St & First Ave, PO Box 669, V8J 3S1. Tel 604-624-3207. *Pres Board Dir* Herman Seidemann III; *VPres Board of Dir* F Stewart; *Dir & Cur* R Denman
Open Sept - April Mon - Sat 10 AM - 5 PM, May - Aug Mon - Sun 9 AM - 9 PM. Estab 1924, new building opened 1958, to collect, maintain and display the

history of the north coast, particularly of the Prince Rupert area. One main hall has two small side galleries, and a third gallery is the museum art gallery. Average Annual Attendance: 90,000. Mem: 200; dues $2; annual meeting May
Income: $130,000 (financed primarily by municipality and province)
Collections: †Contemporary North Coast Indian art; †historical collections; †native Indian collections; natural history; †photographs
Exhibitions: A continually changing display program; fine arts exhibitions from large galleries; local artists shows
Activities: Classes for adults and children; lect open to public; concerts; gallery talks; tours
L **Library,** McBride St and First Ave, PO Box 669, Prince Rupert, V8J 3E7. Tel 604-624-3207. *Dir* Ron Denman; *Asst Dir* Gail Blayney
Open June - Aug Mon - Sun 9 AM - 9 PM, Sept - May Mon - Sat 10 AM - 5 PM, cl Mon. No admis fee. Reference library for staff
Income: $130,000 (financed by city, province, donations & gift shop)
Library Holdings: Vols 100; Per subs 3; Some archival materials
Special Subjects: Concentration on British Columbia pre-modern history
Publications: Newsletter, twice a yr

REVELSTOKE

O **REVELSTOKE ART GROUP,** 315 W First St, PO Box 2655, V0E 2S0. Tel 604-837-3067. *Pres & Dir* Pat Anderson; *VPres* Heinz Pirnke; *Secy* Betty Olynyk; *Treasurer* Greta Speerbrecker; *Dir* Wyn Haggerstone; *Dir* Lorraine Romeo
Open May - Aug Tues - Sat 10 AM - 8 PM. Estab 1949 to promote and stimulate interest in art by studying art, artists methods and work, developing local interest and interchanging ideas. Average Annual Attendance: 2500. Mem: 30; dues $5; annual meeting in April
Income: $2200 (financed by art show commissions, donations and raffles)
Purchases: $460
Collections: Centennial collection contains 50 watercolours, acrylics and oils by Sophie Atkinson, Art Phillips, Mel Abbott, Mary Wells
Exhibitions: Landscapes by Jack Davis; Weaving & Pottery by Local Artisans; Sr Citizens' Paintings; Snowflake Porcelain Painters; Works by members of the Revelstoke Art Group; Annual fall art show; winter gallery 1981
Activities: Education dept; classes for adults; lectures open to public, 3 vis lectr per yr; competitions; original objects of art lent to Selkirk Health Clinic, Moberly Manor and Royal Bank; sales shop sells original art

RICHMOND

O **RICHMOND ARTS CENTRE,** 7671 Minoru Gate, V6Y 1R8. Tel 604-278-3301. *Mgr Cultural & Heritage Servs* Mary Gazetas; *Arts Centre Coordr* Page Hope-Smith
Open Mon - Fri 9 AM - 9 PM, Sat 10 AM - 4 PM, Sun 1 - 4 PM. No admis fee. Estab 1967 to provide stimulation and nourishment to the arts in the community. Gallery is 1200 sq ft; exhibitions change every two weeks. Average Annual Attendance: 40,000
Income: Financed by city appropriation
Collections: Oil paintings, ink and wash, pencil and ink sketches of local or related importance; photograph collection of 200 prints; theatre posters (world-wide)
Publications: Newsletter, monthly
Activities: Classes for adults & children; dramatic programs; workshops; special festivals; lectures open to public, 6 vis lectr per year; gallery talks; tours; scholarships; lending collection contains framed reproductions, sculpture & slides; book traveling exhibitions; originate traveling exhibitions to galleries in British Columbia; sales shop sells original art and prints; junior museum
L **Library,*** 7671 Minoru Gate, V6Y 1R8. Tel 604-278-3301
Reference Library
Library Holdings: Vols 60; AV - Taped interviews on local history, summarized and indexed 600 hours

SURREY

M **SURREY ART GALLERY,** 13750 88th Ave, V3W 3L1. Tel 604-596-7461. *Dir & Cur* Rosa Ho; *Cur* Jane Young; *Asst Cur* Gordon Rice; *Education & Events Coordr* Ingrid Kolt
Open Mon - Fri 9 AM - 4:30 PM, Tues - Thurs evenings 7 - 9:30 PM, Sat & Sun 1 - 5 PM, cl statutory holidays. No admis fee. Estab 1975. Average Annual Attendance: 32,000
Income: $264,000 (financed by city and provincial appropriation, special private foundations grants, and federal grants per project application)
Purchases: $3000
Collections: Contemporary Canadian Art, mostly works on paper
Exhibitions: (1982) Morphe: An Installation by Laara Cassells; Joan Ross Bloedel Recent Paintings; Bill Brandt, photographs; Recent Paintings by Richard Bond; Mark Adair & Bill Burns, sculpture; Four Painters: Dan Goorevitch, Susan Louden, Laure Makaseff & Doug Rowed; Gloria Masse, paintings; Word & Images; Tom Knott/John Wertschek; Drawings by Contemporary Sculptors; Patrick Gowley; Mark and Surfaces; (1983) Didna Dean & Sheila Tennenhouse, paintings & drawings; Evan Mathison, photographs; Olga Froelich, Deborah Koenker & Andre Patterson, sculptures; Andre Kertesz: A Lifetime of Perception; Anna Gustafson & Suzy Birstein, sculpture; Raphael Soyer; Jim Adams, paintings; Structures for Play: Projects by Michael Banwell; Winnipeg West; E J Hughes: 1931-1982; Judy Williams: Reflection/Extension
Publications: Exhibition catalogues; Surrey Arts Center, bi-monthly calendars
Activities: Workshops for school and community groups; docent training; lect open to public, 6 visiting lectr per year; concerts; gallery talks; tours; lending collection contains cassettes, slides and packaged workshop kits; book traveling exhibitions 2 or 3 per year; originates traveling exhibitions
L **Library,*** Surrey Centennial Arts Centre, 13750 88th Ave, V3W 3L1. Tel 604-596-7461
Estab 1975, reference for staff and docents only
Purchases: $300
Library Holdings: Vols 300; Per subs 20; Micro — Cards; AV — Slides; Other — Clipping files, exhibition catalogs

VANCOUVER

M **ARTISTS GALLERY,** 555 Hamilton St, V6B 2R1. Tel 604-687-1345. *Dir* Paul Bolding; *Mgr* Christine Elving
Open Tues - Fri 10 AM - 5 PM, Sat Noon - 5 PM. No admis fee. Estab 1971 as an exhibition space for contemporary Canadian art; as a non-profit gallery for the City of Vancouver Art Collection and Loan program. The Gallery has a medium sized exhibition area with collection storage and framing area. Average Annual Attendance: 20,000
Income: Financed by Federal Government, consulting fees, British Columbia Cultural Fund, city of Vancouver, and Federal Tax Exemption status under the name of the Greater Vancouver Artists Gallery Society
Purchases: Contemporary Canadian art
Collections: †City of Vancouver Art Collection; †Artists Gallery Society Collection
Exhibitions: Contemporary Canadian Artists; special exhibitions of recent acquisitions; juried competitions
Publications: Context, monthly forum-style newsletter
Activities: Competitions; individual paintings and original objects of art lent; sales shop sells miniature prints, original graphic art
L **Art Library Service,** 555 Hamilton St, V6B 2R1. Tel 604-687-1345. *Dir* Paul Bolding
Open Tues - Fri 10 AM - 5 PM. Estab 1971 for public enhancement, the Gallery provides this service to public agencies for free, commercial agencies pay a fee. Circ 3000
Income: Financed by British Columbia Cultural Fund, Vancouver Civic Cultural Grant, federal grant, consulting, sales
Library Holdings: Micro — Cards; AV — Slides; Other — Clipping files, original art works, pamphlets, photographs, prints, sculpture

O **COMMUNITY ARTS COUNCIL OF VANCOUVER,** 315 W Cordova St, V6B 1E5. Tel 604-683-4358. *Pres* Dr Allen Clingman; *First VPres* Bruce Hunter; *Secy* Shannon Norris; *Treas* Carlos Yep; *Honourary Secy* Barry Webster; *Exec Dir* Anne Macdonald; *Admin Asst* Mary Plant
Open 9 AM - 5 PM. No admis fee. Estab 1946 as a society dedicated to the support of arts, with a wide range of interest in the arts; to promote standards in all art fields including civic arts; also serves as a liaison centre. Small gallery-office shows works of emerging artists who have not exhibited before. Mem: 500; dues $20; annual meeting Oct
Income: Financed by membership, donations and British Columbia Cultural Fund
Exhibitions: Approx 12 shows per year
Publications: Newsletter, 6 issues per year
Activities: Lectures open to the public & members only; museum shop

M **EMILY CARR COLLEGE OF ART & DESIGN,** The Charles H Scott Gallery, 1399 Johnston St, V6H 3R9. Tel 604-687-2345, 687-8251. *Dir* E Theodore Lindberg; *Gallery Asst* Lois Redman
Open Sun - Tues & Thurs - Sat Noon - 5 PM, Wed 9 AM - 1 PM & 4 - 9 PM. Estab 1980 to exhibit historically and critically significant visual art from regional, national and international sources. Average Annual Attendance: 27,500
Income: $95,000 (financed by provincial appropriation)
Exhibitions: (1983) Stephen De Staebler, bronze sculpture; Prints and Plates: 23 Quebec Printmakers; Arnaud Maggs: An Exhibition of Selected Works, photo-installations; (1984) Robert Young: Ten Years, painting
Publications: Exhibition catalogues
Activities: Classes for adults; docent training; lectures open to the public; competitions; scholarships; outreach dept serves BC & Yukon; printmobile; book traveling exhibitions
L **Library,** Vancouver, V6H 3R9. Tel 604-681-2345. *Head Librn* Ken Chamberlain; *Library Asst* Liselotte Boender
Open May - Aug Mon - Fri 9 AM - 5 PM, Sept - Apr Mon - Thurs 9 AM - 9 PM, Fri 9 AM - 5 PM
Income: Financed by government funding
Library Holdings: Vols 8200; Per subs 150; Micro — Fiche; AV — A-tapes, slides, v-tapes; Other — Clipping files, exhibition catalogs
Publications: Acquisitions List, monthly

UNIVERSITY OF BRITISH COLUMBIA

M **Fine Arts Gallery,** Main Library Bldg, V6T 1Y3. Tel 604-228-2759, 228-4381. *Cur* Glenn Allison; *Asst Cur* Mary Williams
Open summer Mon - Fri 10 AM - 5 PM, cl holidays. No admis fee. Estab 1948, the exhibitions are organized from numerous sources and thus the gallery is able to bring to the university the widest variety of material representative of the principal trends in art, past and present. Gallery covers 27,000 sq ft. Average Annual Attendance: 15,000
Income: Financed by departmental funds
Publications: Catalog, annually; announcements; posters
Activities: Lect open to public, 2 vis lectr per year; gallery talks; originate traveling exhibitions; original art pieces by exhibiting artists available for sale
L **Fine Arts Division Library,** 1956 Main Mall, V6T 1Y3. Tel 604-228-2720; Telex 04-53296. *Head Librn* Melva J Dwyer; *Reference Librn* Diana Cooper; *Reference Librn* Peggy McBride
Open Mon - Thurs 8 AM - 11 PM, Fri 8 AM - 5 PM, Sat 9 AM - 5 PM, Sun 1 - 9 PM. Estab 1948 to serve students & faculty in all courses related to fine arts, architecture, planning & dance
Library Holdings: Dial Iconographic Index; Micro — Fiche, prints, reels; Other — Clipping files, exhibition catalogs, pamphlets, photographs, reproductions
Special Subjects: Architecture, fashion design & planning (emphasized in clipping files), Canadian art
Publications: Fine Arts Masters Theses, updated annually; List of Canadian Artists' Files, 1977 - present; Starts Here (short introductory bibliographies), produced as needed; Theses Related To Planning, updated annually
Activities: Classes for adults and children; workshops; lect open to public, awards; scholarships; exten dept; book traveling exhibitions

M **Museum of Anthropology,** 6393 NW Marine Dr, V6T 1W5. Tel 604-228-5087. *Dir* M M Ames; *Admin Officer* Jennifer Doran Kendon; *Cur Ethnology* Marjorie M Halpin; *Cur Ethnology & Education* Madeline Bronsdon Rowan; *Cur Ethnology & Education* Margaret Stott; *Extension Cur* Hindy Ratner; *Public Information Officer* Ruth Anderson; *Cur Documentation* Audrey Shane; *Cur Collections* Elizabeth Johnson; *Graphic Designer, Photographer* Bill McLennan; *Designer* Herb Watson; *Museum Technician* Len McFarlane
Open Sept - Apr Tues Noon - 9 PM, Wed - Sun Noon - 5 PM, May - Aug Tues Noon - 9 PM, Wed - Sun Noon - 7 PM. Admis adults $2, sr citizens & students $1, children $.75, group rates for 20 or more, Tues free. Estab 1976 to develop a high quality institution that maximizes public access & involvement while also conducting active programs of teaching, research & experimentation. Average Annual Attendance: 126,000. Mem: 1000; dues family $25, individuals $15, student & sr citizens $10
Collections: Ethnographic tribal areas around the world; oriental art and history; museum journals
Exhibitions: Permanent and temporary exhibitions
Activities: Classes for adults & children; dramatic programs; docent training; field trips; lectures open to public, some for members only, 10 vis lectr per yr; gallery talks; tours; exten dept; original objects of art lent to institutions for special exhibits; book traveling exhibitions; originate traveling exhibitions; museum shop sells books, original art, reproductions, prints, slides & jewelery

M **VANCOUVER ART GALLERY,** 750 Hornby St, V6Z 2H7. Tel 604-682-5621. *Pres* Robert G Brodie; *Dir* Luke Rombout; *Cur* Jo-Anne Birnie Danzker; *Cur* Scott Watson; *Cur* Lorna Farrell-Ward; *Educ Officer* Ann Morrison; *Information Officer* Dorothy Metcalfe; *Vanguard Ed* Russell Keziere; *Registrar* Helle Viirlaid
Open Tues, Thurs - Sat 10 AM - 6 PM, Wed 10 AM - 9 PM, Sun 1 - 6 PM, cl Mon, Christmas & News Years Day. Admis adults $2, students with cards & senior citizens $1, children under 12 free, Tues free. Estab 1931 to foster the cultural development of the community and a public interest in the arts. Four floors 41,000 sq ft of changing exhibitions. Main floor houses permanent Emily Carr Gallery and historical works from the permanent collection; second and third floor galleries show changing exhibitions of works on loan from various institutions, locally, nationally, and internationally as well as the permanent collection; fourth floor is reserved for prints and drawings; children's gallery is housed in the annex. Average Annual Attendance: 750,000. Mem: 20,000; dues $15 - $25; annual meeting last Thurs of March
Income: Financed by local, provincial and federal government grants
Purchases: Contemporary art
Collections: Emily Carr Collection; Canadian and American Painting, Sculpture and Graphics; 17th - 20th Century European Paintings; Contemporary American Painting and Graphics
Exhibitions: (1982) Geoffrey Smedley; 19th Century British Paintings; Sybil Andrews; Jock Macdonald the Inner Landscape; narrative works from the permanent collection; Emily Carr; Mannerism: A Theory of Culture; Mise En Scene - Kim Adams, Mowry Baden, Roland Brener, Al McWilliams, Liz Magor and Jerry Pethick; Canada Family Album: Tom Graff; Emily Car Paintings, Drawings and Watercolors; sculpture from the permanent collection - Robert Murray and Anthony Caro; Stoned Gloves by Roy Kiyooka; contemporary works from the permanent collection; landscapes from the permanent collection; Dennis Oppenheim Launching Structure #2; The Works of Edward Ruscha; historical works from the permanent collection; Children's Gallery; Canadian Pictures 1951; Cy Twombly Prints; (1983) Masterworks from the Collection of the National Gallery of Canada; Vancouver: Art & Artists 1931-1983; Emily Carr Paintings and Drawings from the Permanent Collection; Children's Gallery Inaugural Programme
Publications: Vanguard, ten times a year; exhibition catalogs
Activities: Docent training; lectures open to the public; gallery talks; tours; exten dept serving Province of British Columbia; individual paintings and original objects of art lent to museums who comply with security and climate control standards; lending collection contains 20,000 slides; originate traveling exhibitions; gallery shop sells books, reproductions, prints, slides, calendars & original Inuit art

L **Library,** 750 Hornby St, V6Z 2H7. *Librn* Catherine M Cowan; *Library Asst* Nora Blair
Open Tues - Fri 10 AM - 4 PM, Sat 10 AM - 1 PM, cl Sun & Mon. Estab to serve staff, docents, students and the public. For reference only
Library Holdings: Vols 8304; Per subs 122; Micro — Fiche; Other — Clipping files, exhibition catalogs 13,000, memorabilia, pamphlets, photographs
Special Subjects: Fine arts specializing in Canadian and contemporary art

L **VANCOUVER CITY ARCHIVES AND LIBRARY,** 1150 Chestnut St, V6J 3J9. Tel 604-736-8561. *Dir* Sue M Baptie; *Deputy Dir* John R Chang; *Chief Cur* Mrs Sheelagh Draper; *Cur Coll* Paul Yee
Open Mon - Fri 9:30 AM - 5:30 PM, other times by appointment, cl weekends and legal holidays. No admis fee. Estab 1933
Income: Financed by city appropriation
Library Holdings: Charts, Civic Records, Drawings, Maps, Paintings; Other — Manuscripts, prints
Exhibitions: Temporary exhibitions
Activities: Classes for adults and children; docent training; lect; tours

VERNON

M **VERNON ART ASSOCIATION,** Topham Brown Gallery,* 3009 - 32 Ave, PO Box 433, V1T 6M3. Tel 604-545-3173. *Pres* Rick Thorburn; *VPres* Dorothy Gower; *Secy* Marie Hill; *Treas* Larry Hill; *Public Relations* Lee Kowalski; *Cur* Jude Clarke
Open Mon - Sat 10 AM - 1 PM and 2 - 5 PM. No admis fee. Estab 1967 to display exhibits by local artists, Valley Jury Shows, and other significant shows by well known artists. Gallery professionally designed measuring approx 34 x 34 sq ft. Average Annual Attendance: 20,000. Mem: 150; dues family $8, individual $5; annual meeting first Mon of March
Income: Financed by membership, city appropriation and grants
Collections: Permanent collection consists of ceramics, paintings, prints, sculpture and serigraphs
Exhibitions: 25 exhibits annually; Okanagan Valley Jury Show
Publications: Art Quarterly
Activities: Classes for adults and children; docent training; supports the Vernon Resident Artists League; lect for members only; tours; competitions; fels; individual paintings and original objects of art lent to Chamber of Commerce, City Hall Vernon; originate traveling exhibitions

VICTORIA

M **ART GALLERY OF GREATER VICTORIA,** 1040 Moss St, V8V 4P1. Tel 604-384-4101. *Pres* George Kidd; *Dir* Patricia A Bovey; *Chief Cur of Contemporary Art* Greg Bellerby; *Cur Historical Art* Nicholas Tuele; *Cur Asian Art* Barry Till; *Educ Officer* Julia Wallace
Open Mon, Tues, Wed, Fri, Sat 10 AM - 5 PM, Thurs 10 AM - 9 PM, Sun 1 - 5 PM, cl Mon in winter. Admis $2 for nonmembers, $1 students, children under 12 free. Estab 1949. Six modern galleries adjoin 19th Century Spencer Mansion-Japanese Garden. Average Annual Attendance: 56,500. Mem: 3000; dues family $25, individual $20, student $10
Income: $500,000 (financed by membership, city, federal and state appropriation)
Collections: Chinese, Indian, Persian and Tibetan Art; Contemporary Canadian, American and European; European Painting and Decorative Arts from 16th - 19th Centuries; Japanese Art from Kamakura to Contemporary; Primitive Arts
Exhibitions: (1984) Susan Scott; Emily Carr; Drawings by A Y Jackson; Contemporary Japanese Prints; Mortimer-Lamb; Photographs; Samuel Maclure; Contemporary Chinese Woodblock Prints; Arts of the Samarai; Ralph Stanbridge; Eric Bergman; Michael Snow; Kamer Collection; Jack Kidder; Seatle Art Now; Pacific Northwest Conncetion; Albers Prints; Ukiyo-e Prints; Jeff Spalding; Ceramic Spectrum; American Prints; Menzies Chinese Embroideries; Oriental Costumes & Textiles
Publications: Membership newsletter, 8 times a year
Activities: Classes for children; docent training; gallery in the schools program; noon hour films; workshops; lectures open to public, 12 vis lectr per year; concerts; tours; exten dept serves Vancouver Island; artmobile; individual paintings and original objects of art lent to museums and local public buildings; lending collection contains works from permanent collection; book traveling exhibitions, 7-9 per year; originate traveling exhibitions; sales shop sells books, magazines, reproductions, stationary, jewellery, pottery, ornaments and glass

L **Library,** 1040 Moss St, V8V 4P1. *Asst Dir* Mrs J M Paige
Open Tues - Thur 10 AM - 5 PM. Estab 1951. only for staff and public
Income: $1000
Purchases: $1000
Library Holdings: Vols 3560; Per subs 49; Micro — Fiche; AV — Slides; Other — Clipping files, exhibition catalogs, pamphlets
Special Subjects: Oriental Art, Canadian Art, Oriental Art
Activities: Used book sale

M **OPEN SPACE GALLERY,** Photography at Open Space, 510 Fort St, PO Box 5207, Station B, V8R 6N4. Tel 604-383-8833. *Cur* Tom Gore
Open Tues - Sat 12 - 5 PM, Thurs 12 - 9 PM. No admis fee. Estab 1975 for the encouragement and promotion of photography as a fine art and of those photographers, particularly in Western Canada, who are engaged in making photographs as art. The program emphasis is on new forms of photography. Gallery has 3000 sq ft, 220 running ft with full light grid controlled to level for works of art on paper. Average Annual Attendance: 10,000. Mem: 230; dues $10
Income: $110,000 (financed by federal & provincial appropriations, city grants, donations & membership fees)
Exhibitions: The Stereo Show Motion, Sorel Cohen & Suzy Lake; Soundspace Collaboratory, John Celona; Television, Video, and the Future, Part II, National Cablecast; Colour Columns, Carole Sabiston; Open Space Invitational, works by Don Gill, Alan Storey, Terryl Atkinson, Christine Cousineau, Bill Pechet, Alison Pugh, Mary-Lynn Ogilvie, Sydney Condrashoff and Vilio Celli; Jericho Detachment, Joey Morgan; Grillwork Suite, Mary Arnold; The Stereo Show, Tom Gore (3-D photography); Fractured Visions: Peter Titenberger, Jon Baturin, Brian Laurey, Shara Corsaut; Grant Arnold, Randy Bradley, Susan McEachern; Photo Journalism: Lynne Cohen, David Miller & Richard Holdin
Publications: B C Photos 1978, Photos 1979; Secession Excerpts from the Literature of Photography, periodic; Stereo Bookwork
Activities: Lectures; concerts; gallery talks; tours; book traveling exhibitions, 2-3 per yr; originate traveling exhibitions

L **Library,*** 510 Fort St, PO Box 5207 Stn B, V8R 6N4
Open daily 11 AM - 5 PM. Estab 1975. Reference library
Library Holdings: Vols 350; Per subs 7; AV — Slides, v-tapes; Other — Exhibition catalogs
Special Subjects: Contemporary Canadian photography

L **PROVINCIAL ARCHIVES OF BRITISH COLUMBIA,*** 655 Belleville St, V8V 1X4. Tel 604-387-5885, 387-6505. *Dir* John A Bovey; *Head, Paintings, Drawings, Prints & Historic Photographs* J Mossop
Open Mon - Fri 9 AM - 5 PM. Estab 1893 to collect and preserve all records relating to the historical development of British Columbia. Maintains a small gallery for exhibiting collections
Income: Financed by provincial appropriation
Library Holdings: Vols 51,000; Per subs 300; original documents; maps; Micro — Reels; AV — A-tapes; Other — Clipping files, exhibition catalogs, manuscripts, original art works, pamphlets, photographs
Special Subjects: British Columbia history
Publications: Sound Heritage, quarterly

M **UNIVERSITY OF VICTORIA,** Maltwood Art Museum and Gallery, Ring Rd, PO Box 1700, V8W 2Y2. Tel 604-721-8298; Telex 049-7222. *Dir & Cur* Martin Segger; *Pres* Dr H Petch; *VPres* T Matthews; *Chmn of Board* Dr M Fraser; *Secy-Registrar* B Jackson
Open Mon - Fri 10 AM - 4 PM, Sun Noon - 4 PM. No admis fee. Estab 1968 to collect, preserve and exhibit the decorative arts. Gallery has 3000 sq ft of environmentally controlled exhibition space. Average Annual Attendance: 150, 000
Income: $100,000 (financed by endowment and state appropriation)

Purchases: $25,000
Collections: †Maltwood Collection of Decorative Art; †contemporary art (Canadian)
Exhibitions: Permanent collections, continuing and rotating
Publications: Painting During the Colonial Period in British Columbia 1845-1871; Herbert Siebner; Katharine Emma Maltwood Artist 1878-1961; The Cabinetmaker/Designer - Furniture Makers in the Victoria Region
Activities: Lect open to public, 3 visiting lectr per year; gallery talks; tours; individual paintings lent to offices and public spaces on campus; lending collection contains 500 original prints, 300 paintings and sculpture; book traveling exhibitions 5 per year; originate traveling exhibitions

MANITOBA

BRANDON

O **BRANDON ALLIED ARTS COUNCIL,*** 1036 Louise Ave, R7A 0Y1. Tel 204-727-1036. *Dir* Mary Louise Perkins
Open Mon - Sat 9 AM - 5 PM, Sun 2 - 5 PM. No admis fee. Estab 1960 to promote and foster cultural activities in Western Manitoba. Average Annual Attendance: 2400. Mem: 700; dues $6 - $20; annual meeting May
Income: Financed by membership, city and provincial appropriations and federal grants
Publications: Bulletin, every 2 months
Activities: Classes for adults and children; lect open to public, 2 visiting lectrs per year; gallery talks; tours; competitions; individual paintings and original objects of art lent to members; lending collection contains original art works, original prints, paintings, weavings
L **Brandon Allied Arts Center Library,*** 1036 Louise Ave, R7A 0Y1. *Librn* Joyce Holland
Open to members
Library Holdings: Vols 2000

CHURCHILL

M **ESKIMO MUSEUM,** 242 La Verendrye, Box 10, R0B 0E0. Tel 204-675-2252.
Dir Omer Robidoux; *Cur* Bro Jacques Volant; *Asst Cur* Lorraine Brandson
Open Mon - Sat 9 AM - Noon and 1 - 5 PM, Sun 1 - 4 PM. No admis fee. Estab 1944 to depict the Eskimo way of life through the display of artifacts. Museum has large single display room. Average Annual Attendance: 10,000
Income: Administered and funded by the Roman Catholic Episcopal Corporation of Churchill Hudson Bay
Collections: †Contemporary Inuit carvings; ethnographic collections; prehistoric artifacts; wildlife specimens
Publications: The Churchill Eskimo Museum by Jeannine Veisse
Activities: Films and slide shows for school groups upon request; tours upon request; original objects of art lent to special exhibits and galleries; sales shop sells books, magazines, and original art
L **Library,*** 230 La Verendrye, Box 10, R0B 0E0
Estab mainly for Arctic Canada material
Purchases: $200
Library Holdings: Vols 500; Other — Clipping files, exhibition catalogs, photographs
Special Subjects: European exploration of Arctic Canada

FREDERICTON

MARITIME ART ASSOCIATION
For further information, see National Organizations in Canada

PORTAGE LA PRAIRIE

O **PORTAGE AND DISTRICT ARTS COUNCIL,*** PO Box 215, R1N 3B5. Tel 204-239-6029. *Pres* Virginia Miller; *Secy* Helen Ebel
Estab 1976 as a coordinating body of local arts groups
Income: Financed by commission on sale of art, memberships, fees, govt grants, tickets sales

WINNIPEG

O **MANITOBA ASSOCIATION OF ARCHITECTS,** 2nd Fl, 100 Osborne St S, R3L 1Y5. Tel 204-477-5290. *Pres* J C Petersmeyer; *Executive Secy* H C Peters
Open Mon - Fri 9 AM - 4:30 PM. Established 1906: Provincial Architectural Registration Board and professional governing body. Mem: 300; dues $300; annual meeting Feb
Income: Financed by annual membership dues
Publications: Newsletter, 9 times a yr
Activities: The Manitoba Association of Architects has established a joint lectureship fund with the School of Architecture at the University of Manitoba, and has established a practice of bringing three or more outstanding lecturers to Winnipeg each year for university and public lectures. The Association has a yearly donation of $600 in prizes awarded to students pursuing the course at the School of Architecture; scholarships

M **MANITOBA HISTORICAL SOCIETY,** Dalnavert - MacDonald House Museum, 61 Carlton St, R3C 1N7. Tel 204-943-2835. *Secy* A Mulder; *Chmn Management Committee* Alan Crossin; *Pres Manitoba Historical Society* Shirley Smith; *Cur* Tim Worth; *Registrar* Nancy Foster
Open summer 10 AM - 6 PM, winter Noon - 5 PM. Admis adults $2, senior

citizens and students $1.50, children $1. Estab 1975 to preserve and display the way of life of the 1895 upper class family. Average Annual Attendance: 8000
Income: $40,000 (financed by membership, city and state appropriation and private donation)
Collections: Home furnishings of the 1895 period: clothing, decorative arts material, furniture, household items, paintings and original family memorabilia
Activities: Classes for children; docent training; lectures open to the public, 6 vis lectr per yr; sales shop sells books, postcards and tourist material

O **MANITOBA SOCIETY OF ARTISTS,** 549 Montrose St, R3M 3M3. Tel 204-284-0141. *Pres* Eleanor Golfman; *Secy* Barbara Cook-Endres; *Treas* Pat Kettner
Estab 1901 to further the work of the artist at the local and community levels. Mem: 60; dues $20; annual meeting Oct
Income: Financed by memberership and commission on sales
Exhibitions: Annual competition & exhibition open to all residents of Manitoba
Activities: Educ aspects include teaching by members in rural areas and artist-in-residence work in public schools; lect open to public; gallery talks; tours; competitions with awards; scholarships; originate traveling exhibitions

L **PROVINCIAL ARCHIVES OF MANITOBA,** 200 Vaughan St, R3C 1T5. Tel 204-944-3971. *Provincial Archivist* Peter Bower
Open Mon - Fri 8:30 AM - 5 PM, cl holidays. No admis fee. Estab 1952
Income: Financed by provincial appropriation through the Minister of Culture, Heritage & Recreation
Collections: Documentary & archival paintings, drawings, prints & photographs relating to Manitoba
Activities: Individual paintings & original objects of art lent to public institutions with proper security; book traveling exhibitions

M **UKRAINIAN CULTURAL AND EDUCATIONAL CENTRE MUSEUM,** 184 Alexander Ave E, R3B 0L6. Tel 204-942-0218. *Exec Dir* Sophia Kachor; *Cur* Sophia Lada; *Archivist* Zenon Hluszok; *Educ/Extension Coordr* Christine Korbutiak; *Registrar* Tania Drepko; *Secy* Cathy Dueck; *Secy* Nadia Melnyk
Open Tues - Sat 10 AM - 4 PM, Sun 2 - 5 PM, cl Mon. No admis fee. Estab as the largest Ukrainian cultural resource centre and repository of Ukrainian historical and cultural artifacts in North America. Mem: 2000; dues $15; annual meeting Oct
Income: $216,328 (financed by province of Manitoba, federal government, donations, memberships, trust fund, fund raising events)
Collections: Ukrainian Folk Art; †folk costumes; †embroidery; †weaving; †pysanky (Easter eggs); †woodcarving; †ceramics; coins, postage stamps and documents of the Ukrainian National Republic of 1918-1921; works of art by Ukrainian, Ukrainian Canadian and Ukrainian American artists: †prints, †paintings, †sculpture; archives: †Ukrainian immigration to Canada, †music collections
Exhibitions: (1983) The Great Western Canadian Screen Shop: A Print Legent; (1983-84) IKON, Byzantine ikons; John Paskiewich; About Free Lands; (1984) Pysanka, Symbolism of the Ukrainian Easter Egg; Russell Yuristy, paintings and drawings; Ukrainian Manitoba artists group show; Robert Kost, paintings, prints, 3 Women Artists, Manitoba: Machinsky, Sokulsky, Pisichko; Alex Suprowich, Manitoba landscapes; Folk Art from Bukovyna
Publications: Visti Oseredku/News from Oseredok, members' bulletin, 2 - 3 times per yr
Activities: Classes for adults and children; workshops; lectures open to the public; gallery talks; tours; competitions; scholarships; individual paintings and original objects of art lent to educational institutions, galleries and museums; lending collection contains color reproductions, framed reproductions, motion pictures, phonorecords, 40,000 photographs, 2000 slides; book traveling exhibitions, annually; originate traveling exhibitions; sales shop sells books, original art, reproductions, prints, folk art, phonorecords, casettes
M **Gallery Oseredok,*** 184 Alexander Ave E, R3B 0L6. Tel 204-942-0218
Mem: Dues family & organization $25, individual $15, student & senior citizen $5
Collections: 18th Century Icons; Contemporary Graphics (Archipenko, Gritchenko, Trutoffsky, Krycevsky, Hluschenko, Pavlos, Kholodny, Hnizdovsky, Mol, Levytsky, Shostak, Kuch)
Exhibitions: Works by visiting Ukrainian, Canadian, American and European artists; permanent collection
L **Library and Archives,** 184 Alexander Ave E, R3B 0L6
Library Holdings: Vols 30,000; Newspapers and periodicals in the Ukrainian language; AV — Motion pictures, rec, slides, v-tapes; Other — Clipping files, exhibition catalogs, pamphlets
Special Subjects: Ukrainian Studies

M **UNIVERSITY OF MANITOBA,** Gallery III, School of Art, R3T 2N2. Tel 204-474-9367. *Dir Exhib* Dale Amundson; *Cur Coll* Grace Thomson
Open Mon - Fri 8:30 - 4:30 PM. No admis fee. Estab 1965. Gallery III estab 1965 to provide exhibitions for students and faculty on the university campus; exhibitions also open to the public. Average Annual Attendance: 20,000
Collections: †Contemporary Canadian and American painting, prints and sculpture; Fitzgerald Study Collection
Exhibitions: Exhibitions of Canadian, European and American Art, both contemporary and historical; special exhibitions from other categories; annual exhibitions by the graduating students of the School of Art
Publications: Exhibition catalogues
Activities: Discussion groups; workshops; lectures open to the public, 3 - 6 vis lectr per yr; gallery talks; individual paintings & original objects of art lent; book traveling exhibitions, 2 - 4 per yr; originate traveling exhibitions
M **Faculty of Architecture Exhibition Centre,*** Architecture Bldg, R3T 2N2. Tel 204-474-9286. *Dir of Exhib* Donald Ellis
Open Mon - Fri 9 AM - 10:30 PM, Sat 9 AM - 5 PM. Estab 1959 with the opening of the new Faculty of Architecture Building to provide architectural and related exhibitions for students and faculty on the University campus and particularly for architecture students. Exhibitions also open to the public. Average Annual Attendance: 15,000
Exhibitions: Exhibitions from National Gallery of Canada, Smithsonian Institution, American Federation of Arts, Museum of Modern Art and from other private and public sources; annual exhibitions by the students in the Faculty of Architecture
Activities: Lect; gallery talks; symposia

—Library, Winnipeg, MB R3T 2N2. Tel 204-474-9216. *Head Librn* Peter Anthony; *Reference Librn* Michele Laing
Open Mon - Thurs 8:30 AM - 9 PM, Fri 8:30 AM - 5 PM, Sat 10 AM - 4:30 PM, Sun Noon - 4:30 PM. Estab 1916 to serve the needs of students and faculty in the areas of architecture, fine arts, landscape architecture, environmental studies, city and regional planning, design, interior design and photography. Circ 99,923
Library Holdings: Per subs 370; Micro — Fiche 560, reels 210; AV — A-tapes 75; Other — Clipping files, exhibition catalogs 1000, pamphlets, photographs, reproductions 776
Special Subjects: Aesthetics, Afro-American Art, American Indian Art, Art History, Asian Art, Calligraphy, Ceramics, Decorative Arts, Eskimo Art, Etchings & Engravings, Furniture, Glass, Islamic Art, Lettering, Oriental Art, Antiquities, Paintings, Period Rooms, Pre-Columbian Art, Reproductions, Sculpture, Stained Glass, Video, Woodcarvings
Collections: Fowler Collection of Early Architectural Books

M **WINNIPEG ART GALLERY,** 300 Memorial Blvd, R3C 1V1. Tel 204-786-6641. *Pres* Donald E Vernon; *Dir* Dr Terrence Heath; *Chief Cur* Nancy Dillow; *Business Admnr* James Bristow; *Head Marketing Dept* Brent Mooney; *Head Educ & Public Programs* Claudette Lagimodiere; *Head Design Dept* Lee Newton Kinrade
Open Tues - Sat 11 AM - 5 PM; Sun Noon - 5 PM; cl Mon. No admis fee. Estab 1912, incorporated 1963. Rebuilt and relocated 1968, opened 1972, to present a diversified, quality level program of art in all media, representing various cultures, past and present . Building includes 9 galleries as well as displays on mezzanine level, sculpture court and main foyer. Average Annual Attendance: 225,000. Mem: 4400; dues family $45, couple $40, individual $30, student $15, sr citizens couple $20, sr citizen single $15; annual meeting in June
Income: $2,300,000 (financed by endowment, membership, city, state and federal appropriation)
Collections: Canadian art; contemporary Canada; contemporary Manitoba; decorative arts; Inuit art; European art; Gort Collection; Master prints & drawings; modern European art; †photography
Exhibitions: (1983-85) Henri Cartier-Bresson, photographs; Transformation of Vision: The Works of H Eric Bergman; Grasp Tight the Old Ways: Selections from the Klamer Family Collection of Inuit Art; Andre Kertesz: A Lifetime of Perception; A A Chesterfield; Hills and Streams: Landscape Decoration on Chinese Export Blue and White Porcelain; Rosemary Kowalsky: Recent Works; Joan Kaufman: Recent Works; The Winnipeg Perspective 1984; Reflections on Three Plains: Contemporary Crafts; 19th Century Canadian Ceramics; The Canada Packers Collection: Selected Oil Paintings & Works on Paper; Purvis - MacAulay Collections: Founders Exhibition; Sculpture from Germany; Bruno Bobak; Do You Own a Canadian Painting? A Tribute to the Volunteer Committee; Manitoba Series #7; Inua Revealed: Art and Culture of the Bering Sea Eskimo; Tony Tascona: 1974-1984—Aluminum Constructions; Worchester Ceramics; Autochromes: Colour Photography Comes of Age; 20th Century Pottery; Manitoba Series #8; Oscar Cahen; From the Heart: Folk Art in Canada; Manitoba Series #9; Manitoba Two Person: William Pura, Milly Giesbrecht; Watercolours from BC: Fim Willer, Joe Plaskett, Takao Tanabe, John Koerner, Jack Shadbolt; Documentary; Playing the Game; Winnipeg Perspective: Video: Expanded Forms; Animalier
Publications: The WAG Magazine (calendar of events), monthly; exhibition catalogs
Activities: Classes for adults and children; docent training; lect open to public, 20-30 visiting lectr per year; concerts; gallery talks; tours; exten dept serves Manitoba, Canada and United States; individual paintings and original objects of art lent to centres and museums; lending collection contains 10,500 books and 10,000 slides; book traveling exhibitions; originate traveling exhibitions; sales shop sells books, gift items, prints, reproductions and slides
L **Clara Lander Library,** 300 Memorial Blvd, R3C 1V1. Tel 204-786-6641, Ext 58. *Chief Librn* David William Rozniatowski; *Library Asst* Beverley Phillips
Open Tues - Fri 11 AM - 5 PM, Sat Noon - 4 PM. Estab 1954 to serve as a source of informational and general interest materials for members and staff of the Winnipeg Art Gallery and to art history students. Circ 1500
Income: Financed by membership, city and provincial appropriations
Purchases: $10,000
Library Holdings: Vols 14,500; Per subs 47; original documents; Micro — Fiche, reels; AV — Slides; Other — Clipping files, exhibition catalogs, manuscripts, memorabilia, pamphlets, photographs, prints, reproductions
Special Subjects: Eskimo Art, Canadian Art, George Swinton Collection
Collections: Archival material pertaining to Winnipeg Art Gallery; Rare Books on Canadian and European Art; George Swinton Collection on Eskimo and North American Indian art and culture

O **WINNIPEG SKETCH CLUB,*** 434 Assiniboine Ave, R3C 0Y1. Tel 204-943-4772. *Pres* Arvie Anderson
Estab 1914 to provide a ground where members may meet for the purpose of advancing their studies by means of sketch meetings and for the encouragement of work done independently. Open to members only. Mem: 90; dues $15; annual meeting first week in Feb
Income: Financed by membership
Collections: Archives collection of work by past and present members
Exhibitions: Annual juried exhibition in Manitoba Archive Building; exhibits at the Assiniboine Park Conservatory; many local shows
Publications: All About Us, biannual newsletter
L **Library,*** 434 Assiniboine Ave, R3C 0Y1. *Librn* Helga Miller
Open to members only

NEW BRUNSWICK

CAMPBELLTON

M **GALERIE RESTIGOUCHE GALLERY,** 39 Andrew St, PO Box 674, E3N 3H1. Tel 506-753-5750. *Dir & Cur* Paul Soucy; *Secy* Gloria Richard; *Preparator* Leopold Thibeault; *Animator* Geraldine Grant
Open Mon - Fri 9 AM - 5 PM, Tues - Thurs evenings 7 - 9 PM, Sat 2 - 5 PM. No admis fee. Estab 1975 for exhibitions and activities. Building has 4800 sq ft; the Exhibition Hall is 1500 sq ft, small gallery 400 sq ft; 230 running feet. Average Annual Attendance: 20,000-25,000. Mem: 185; dues $10
Income: $80,000 (financed by federal, provincial, & city appropriations, by Art Society & by private donations)
Exhibitions: (1979-84) Couleurs d'Acadie, a color photography traveling exhibition illustrating the phenomenon of brightly painted houses along the Acadian areas of the Atlantic provinces
Publications: Exhibitions catalogues; Restigouche Gallery brochure
Activities: Classes for adults and children; art and craft workshops; lectures open to public, 10 vis lectr per year; concerts; gallery talks; tours; traveling exhibitions exten service; originate traveling exhibitions

FREDERICTON

M **BEAVERBROOK ART GALLERY,** 703 Queen St, PO Box 605, E3B 5A6. Tel 506-455-6551, 455-5316. *Dir* Ian G Lumsden; *Asst Cur* Paul A Hachey
Tues - Sat 10 AM - 5 PM, Sun & Mon Noon - 5 PM. Admis adults $1, students and members free; also booked tours. Estab 1959 to foster and promote the study and the public enjoyment and appreciation of the arts. Major galleries upstairs: British, Canadian & High Galleries & Pillow Porcelain Room. East wing galleries: Hosmer, Pillow-Vaughan Gallery, Sir Max Aitken Gallery & Vaulted Corridor Gallery. Downstairs galleries: exhibition gallery & Foyer Gallery. Average Annual Attendance: 40,000. Mem: 850; dues couple $15, single, firms & organizations $10, students, sr citizens & people outside 50 mile radius of Fredericton $5
Income: $400,000 (financed by endowment, and private foundation)
Purchases: $51,000
Collections: British drawings, paintings, prints & sculpture, 16th century to contemporary; 18th & 19th century British porcelain; Canadian drawings, paintings & prints, early 19th century to contemporary; continental European fine & decorative arts from 15th - 19th century
Exhibitions: Hosmer-Pillow-Vaughan Collection: Continental European Fine & Decorative Arts: 15th - 19th Century; British Portraits, Conversation Pieces & Landscapes: 17th - 19th Century; Recent Acquisitions: Highlights 1978-1983; Chairs: 400 Years of Social & Stylistic Changes; The Mature Years; James Kerr-Lawson; John O'Brien: Marine Painter; The Ceramic Art of Japan
Publications: The New Brunswick Landscape Print: 1760-1880; The Murray and Marguerite Vaughan Inuit Print Collection; The Beaverbrook Art Gallery; exhibition catalogs; bulletin announcing gallery's program
Activities: Lect open to the public, 3 - 4 visiting lectr per year; concerts; gallery talks; tours; exten dept serving New Brunswick as well as the rest of Canada; individual paintings lent to recognized art galleries and museums which operate as educational institutions; collection contains 1575 original art works, sculpture; book traveling exhibitions; originate traveling exhibitions; sales shop sells books, magazines, reproductions, exhibition catalogs, Christmas cards, postcards and hasty-notes
L **Library,*** 703 Queen St, E3B 5A6
Open to gallery personnel only, for reference

M **FREDERICTON NATIONAL EXHIBITION CENTRE,** Queen St, PO Box 6000, E3B 5H1. Tel 506-453-3747. *Exhib Dir* Linda Kelly-Quinlan
Open summer Mon - Thurs & Sat 10 AM - 5 PM, Fri 10 AM - 9 PM, Sun 1 - 5 PM. No admis fee. Estab 1976. Gallery deals with traveling exhibitions only. Average Annual Attendance: 18,000
Income: Financed by federal and provincial appropriation
Activities: Classes for adults and children; lect open to public, 10 visiting lectr per year; concerts; gallery talks; tours; book traveling exhibitions 10 - 12 per year

M **NEW BRUNSWICK CRAFT SCHOOL AND CENTRE GALLERY,** PO Box 6000, E3B 5H1. Tel 506-453-2305. *Dir of Crafts* George Fry
Open Mon - Fri 8:30 AM - 4:30 PM. Estab 1947 as a training school for professional craftspeople. Small gallery, craft related shows monthly. Average Annual Attendance: 1800
Income: Financed by provincial government
Collections: New Brunswick Permanent Craft Collection
Exhibitions: Student and staff juried shows
Publications: Provincial Craft Directory
Activities: Classes for adults; lectures open to public, 12 vis lectr per year; concerts; competition with award; scholarships; original objects of art lent; craft objects lent; originate traveling exhibitions
L **Library,** PO Box 6000, E3B 5H1. Tel 506-453-2305. *Librn* Sylvia Deranyi
A very small but growing library which is primarily for students & craftsmen
Income: Financed by government & book donations
Library Holdings: Vols 3500; Per subs 35; AV — Fs, Kodachromes, motion pictures; Other — Exhibition catalogs, memorabilia, pamphlets, photographs
Special Subjects: Crafts
Publications: Computerized catalogue

M **UNIVERSITY OF NEW BRUNSWICK,** Art Centre, University Ave, PO Box 4400, E3B 5A3. Tel 506-453-4623; Telex 014-46202. *Dir* Bruno Bobak; *Cur* Marjory Donaldson
Open Mon - Fri 10 AM - 5 PM, Sun 2 - 4 PM, cl Sat. No admis fee. Estab 1941 to broaden the experience of the university students and serve the city and province. Two galleries, each with approx 100 running ft of wall space; display case. Average Annual Attendance: 23,000
Income: Financed by university and from province

Collections: Chiefly New Brunswick Artists; some Canadian (chiefly printmakers)
Publications: Catalogues
Activities: Classes for adults and children; lect open to public, 2 visiting lectr per year; gallery talks; tours; individual paintings and original objects of art lent to public but secure areas on this campus and the university campus in Saint John, and reproductions to students; lending collection contains 200 framed reproductions, 100 original prints, 300 paintings, photographs and sculpture; book traveling exhibitions 4 per year; originate traveling exhibitions

HAMPTON

M **KINGS COUNTY HISTORICAL SOCIETY AND MUSEUM,** General Delivery, Sussex Corner, E0E 1R0. Tel 506-433-3244. *Pres* J William Titus; *Treasurer* Muriel Sherwood; *Cur* W Harvey Dalling
Open 10 AM - 5 PM. Admis adults $.50, school age children $.25. Estab 1968 to preserve loyalist history and artifacts. Maintains small reference library. Average Annual Attendance: 2400. Mem: 297; dues $5; annual meeting fourth Fri in Nov
Income: $2500 (financed by provincial and student grant)
Collections: Coin; dairy; glass; 1854 brass measures; jewelry; quilts
Exhibitions: School exhibitions; Women's Institute; Special Quilt Fair
Publications: Newsletters
Activities: Lectures open to public; tours; sales shop sells books

MONCTON

M **GALERIE D'ART DE L'UNIVERSITE DE MONCTON,** E1A 3E9. Tel 506-858-4088. *Dir* Marc Pitre; *Secy* Carmelle Poirer
Open 2 - 4 PM Tues - Sun, Wed evening 7 - 9 PM, cl Mon. No admis. Estab 1965 to offer outstanding shows to the university students and to the public. 400 linear ft wall space, 3500 sq ft vinyl plywood walls, controlled light, temperature, humidity systems, security system. Average Annual Attendance: 13,000
Income: $30,000 (financed through university)
Collections: Artists represented in permanent collection: Bruno Bobak; Alex Colville; Francis Coutellier; Tom Forrestall; Georges Goguen; Hurtubise; Hilda Lavoie; Fernand Leduc; Rita Letendre; Toni Onley; Claude Roussel; Romeo Savoie; Pavel Skalnik; Gordon Smith
Exhibitions: Marie-Reine Chiasson-Ulmer; Francis Coutellier; Claude Gauvin; Jean-Marie Martin; Andre Michel; Peter Powning; Roger Savage; Gruppe Sieben German Artists; Pavel Skalnik; Survival Atlantic Style; Claude Theriault; Hermenegilde Chiasson; Ginette Gould; Soeur Annie Forest; Roesline Le Blanc; Anne Marie Sirois; Georges Goguen; Artistes Canadiens Contemporains; Ginette Pellerin; Robert Joanette; Moncton Collects; Marie-Reine Chiasson Ulmer; Lynn Bard & Magda Mujica; Louis Comeau; Etudiants finissants arts visuels; Yolande Desjardins; Denise Bourgeois & Jeannine Blanchard; Jean-Eudes Gionet; Arthur Warwick; Hanzel Hedley; Rick Burns; Pat Badani; Yvon Gallant; Bill Leeming; Photographes acadiens contemporains; Joanne Gallant; Maurice Richard; Therese Bujold/Pierre Gerin; Lucille Robichaud/Nora; Guy Duguay; Jean-Claude Roy; Pierre Landry; Claude Roussel; Jean-Charle Tremblay; Therese Bujold; Carol Taylor; Marguerite Ann Capper; Jean Bertheleme; Diane Goulet; Estampes/dessins Quebecois
Activities: Classes for children, dramatic programs; lectures open to public, 10 vis lectr per yr; concerts; gallery talks; tours; individual paintings & original objects of art lent to university personnel & art galleries & museums; lending collection contains 500 reproductions, 300 original art works, 180 original prints, 30 paintings, 20 sculpture

SACKVILLE

M **MOUNT ALLISON UNIVERSITY,** Owens Art Gallery, York St, E0A 3C0. Tel 506-536-2040, Ext 270, 291; Telex 014-2266. *Dir* T Keilor Bentley
Open Mon - Fri 10 AM - 5 PM, Thurs evenings 7 - 10 PM, Sat & Sun 2 - 5 PM, cl university holidays. No admis fee. Estab 1895, rebuilt 1972. Building includes five gallery areas; lecture hall; reading room; conservation laboratory. Average Annual Attendance: 11,000
Income: Financed by Mount Allison University, Government, Corporate and Private Assistance
Collections: Broad collection of graphics, paintings, sculpture; parts of collection on display throughout the campus; 19th & 20th century Canadian, European and American Art
Publications: Exhibition catalogs
Activities: Classes for adults and children; dramatic programs; docent training; lectures open to the public, 2 vis lectr per yr; concerts; gallery talks; tours; individual paintings lent to other galleries and museums; book traveling exhibitions, 10 - 12 per yr; originate traveling exhibitions; museum & sales shops

SAINT ANDREWS

O **SUNBURY SHORES ARTS AND NATURE CENTRE, INC,** 139 Water St, PO Box 100, E0G 2X0. Tel 506-529-3386. *Pres* J M Anderson; *Dir* Charles Grant; *Secy* Heather Brown; *Programme Coordr* Mary Blatherwick
Open Tues - Fri 9 AM - 4:30 PM, Sat & Sun 1:30 - 4 PM. No admis fee. Estab 1964, to function as a link for, and harmonize views of scientists, artists and industrialists. Gallery maintained, 200 running ft, fire and burglar protection, security during hours, controllable lighting and street frontage. Average Annual Attendance: 3000. Mem: 600; dues family $18, individual $12, students and senior citizens $6; annual meeting Sept
Income: Financed by endowment, membership and grants
Publications: Brochure, summer annually; Sunbury Notes, quarterly
Activities: Lect open to public, 10 - 15 visiting lectr per year; gallery talks; scholarships
L **Library,*** 139 Water St, PO Box 100, Saint Andrews, E0G 2X0. Tel 506-529-3386
Open to public
Library Holdings: Vols 700; Per subs 10

SAINT JOHN

M **NEW BRUNSWICK MUSEUM,** 277 Douglas Ave, E2K 1E5. Tel 506-693-1196. *Dir* Dr Alan McNairn; *Exec Asst* Margo Flewelling; *Exec Secy* Florence Whipple; *Business Mgr* Art Robinson; *Chief Cur* Gregg Finley; *Asst Cur Art* Regina Mantin; *Cur Decorative Arts* Valerie Simpson; *Actg Head Canadian History* Gary Hughes; *Actg Head Natural Sciences* Gayl Hipperson; *Design Chief* Edward Milota; *Education Officer* Barry King; *Maintenance Chief* Eldon Paisley; *Sales Mgr* Vivian Hachey
Open May - Sept daily 10 AM - 5 PM, Oct - April Sun - Fri 2 - 5 PM, Sat 10 AM - 5 PM. Admis adults $2, students $.50, families $4, senior citizens & children under 6 free. Estab 1842 to collect, conserve, exhibit and interpret the Human and Natural history of New Brunswick in relation to itself and to the outside world. Six major galleries for permanent exhibits, three galleries for changing temporary exhibits. Average Annual Attendance: 60,000. Mem: 375; dues $15 - $100; annual meeting June
Income: $900,000 (financed by membership. federal and provincial appropriations)
Purchases: $1000
Collections: New Brunswick and Maritime artists of the 19th and 20th centuries; contemporary prints; Japanese prints; decorative arts; maps; social history; dolls
Publications: The Beacon, six per year; Journal of the New Brunswick Museum, yearly; bi-monthly newsletter
Activities: Classes for children; docent training; lectures open to the public; concerts; gallery talks; tours; extension department serving New Brunswick; individual paintings and original objects of art lent to museums and galleries; book traveling exhibitions, 6 per yr; traveling exhibitions organized and circulated; sales shop sells books and gifts
L **Library,** 277 Douglas Ave, E2K 1E5. *Librn* Carol Rosevear
Open to the public for reference only
Library Holdings: Vols 3000; Per subs 20; Micro — Fiche; AV — A-tapes, slides; Other — Exhibition catalogs, photographs

NEWFOUNDLAND

SAINT JOHN'S

M **MEMORIAL UNIVERSITY OF NEWFOUNDLAND,** Art Gallery, Arts and Culture Centre, A1C 5S7. Tel 709-737-8209. *Cur* Patricia Grattan; *Coordr of Operations* Edward Cadigan; *Coordr of Exhibitions* Caroline Stone; *Secy* Gwendolyn Kerri
Open Tues - Sun Noon - 10 PM, cl Mon. No admis fee. Estab 1963 to display contemporary Canadian art; to promote contemporary Newfoundland work; to reflect the cultural history of the province. Three galleries with 130 running ft each. Average Annual Attendance: 70,000
Income: Financed through the university and federal funding
Collections: Canadian Art of the 1960's and 1970's
Exhibitions: Contemporary Canadian and Newfoundland Folk Art
Activities: Classes for adults and children; dramatic programs; workshops; lect open to public; concerts; gallery talks; tours; exten dept serves the province; individual paintings and original objects of art lent to other institutions; lending collection contains books, catalogues and 1500 slides; book traveling exhibitions 65 per year; originate traveling exhibitions; sales shop sells original prints, works on paper, original art and prints
L **Library,*** Arts and Culture Centre, A1C 5S7
Open to artists, docents and members

M **NEWFOUNDLAND MUSEUM,** 285 Duckworth St, A1C 1G9. Tel 709-737-2460. *Dir* Martin Bowe; *Asst Dir* David Mills; *Chief Cur* Victoria Dickenson; *Information Officer* Joanne Bieler; *Exhibits Officer* Allan Clarke
No admis fee. Estab 1878 as the Athenaeum for the preservation of Provincial Heritage. The Newfoundland Museum now houses collections & exhibitions reflecting the 7000 year history of Newfoundland & Labrador. Branches at The Murray Premises Museum, St John's & The Newfoundland Seamen's Museum at Grand Bank. Average Annual Attendance: 80,000
Income: Financed by federal and provincial appropriations
Collections: Beothuk, Thule, Maritime Archaic, pre-Dorset, Dorset, Naskapi, Montagnais and Micmac artifacts; history material; maps; naval and military; 19th century Newfoundland domestic artifacts, maritime, natural history, mercantile; 18th - 20th century Newfoundland material, outport furniture, textiles, navigational instruments, ship portraits, watercolors, prints, drawings
Exhibitions: Newfoundland Photography 1849-1949, modern contact prints taken from early glass plate negatives; Ted Drover, Ship Drawings; The Age of Shakespeare; The Newfoundland Postal Eshibition, reproductions of Newfoundland stamps
Publications: Museum Notes; exhibition catalogues; technical bulletins; Archeology in Newfoundland and Labrador, annual report
Activities: Classes for children; docent training; lectures open to public, 12 visiting lecturers per year; tours; book traveling exhibitions; originate traveling exhibitions; sales shop sells books, magazines, prints, slides, crafts
M **Murray Premises Branch,** Saint John's, A1C 1G9
Open Mon - Fri 9 AM - 5 PM, Sat, Sun & holidays 10 AM - 6 PM. No admis fee. This branch displays the marine history, natural history, and military history components of the Newfoundland Museum's collection
Activities: Educ Dept
L **Library,** Duckworth St, A1C 1G9. Tel 709-737-2460
Open to researchers for reference
Special Subjects: Military history
Collections: Mercury Series of National Museums in Archaeology, Ethnology, Restoration; National Historic Parks and Sites Reports

NOVA SCOTIA

DARTMOUTH

M **DARTMOUTH HERITAGE MUSEUM**, 1000 Wyse Rd, B3A 1M1. Tel 902-421-2300. *Dir* G S Gosley; *Secy* Mrs R Gargan; *Asst Art* John Tate
Open summer Mon - Sat 9 AM - 9 PM, Sun 2 - 5 PM, winter Mon - Sat 1 - 5 PM, Sun 2 - 5 PM. No admis fee. Estab 1968 to collect and preserve the story of the City of Dartmouth. Average Annual Attendance: 35,000. Mem: Annual meeting June
Income: Financed by city appropriation & provincial funds
Collections: †Nova Scotia Glass; aircraft models; †artifacts (local history); †works of art
Exhibitions: 16 exhibits
Activities: Classes for adults and children; gallery talks; tours; exten dept serves historic houses; book traveling exhibitions

HALIFAX

M **ART GALLERY OF NOVA SCOTIA**, 6152 Coburg Rd, PO Box 2262, B3J 3C8. Tel 902-424-7542. *Chmn Bd of Dir* Struan Robertson; *VChmn* Struan Robertson; *Cur & Dir* Bernard Riordon; *Asst Cur* Patrick Laurette; *Acting Registrar* Judy Dietz; *Education Officer* Alice Hoskins; *Traveling Exhib Officer* Deborah Young
Open Mon - Wed, Fri, Sat 10 AM - 5:30 PM, Thurs 10 AM - 9 PM, Sun Noon - 5:30 PM. No admis fee. Estab 1975 to replace the Nova Scotia Museum of Fine Arts; dedicated to the collection, preservation, display and interpretation of art. Three galleries: Main, Mezzanine and Permanent Collection. Average Annual Attendance: 40,000. Mem: 1000; dues family $20, individual $10, student $5; annual meeting April
Income: Financed by provincial and federal agencies, donations
Collections: †Nova Scotia Folk Art; †Nova Scotian, Canadian Collection (both historical and contemporary); drawings, paintings, prints and sculpture
Activities: Docent training; lectures open to the public; concerts; gallery talks; tours; scholarships; exten dept serves Canada; artmobile; individual paintings and original objects of art lent to Province and Government House; lending collection contains original art works, framed reproductions, original prints, paintings, phonorecords & sculpture; book traveling exhibitions, 6 - 8 per yr; originate traveling exhibitions, 10 - 15 per yr; museum and sales shop sells books, magazines, original art, prints, reproductions, slides and crafts and also rental service

M **DALHOUSIE UNIVERSITY**, Art Gallery, 6101 University Ave, B3H 3J5. Tel 902-424-2403, 424-2195. *Dir* Linda J Milrod; *Registrar* Mern O'Brien; *Public Relations* Semey Kelly
Open Tues - Fri 11 AM - 5 PM, Tues 7 - 10 PM, Sat & Sun 1 - 5 PM, cl Mon. No admis fee. Estab 1970 to collect, preserve, interpret & display works of art, primarily of Canadian origin. Dalhousie Art Gallery is located in the Dalhousie Arts Centre and open to university community and local area; it contains 400 running ft of wall space & 4000 sq ft floor space. Average Annual Attendance: 16,000
Income: Financed by university supplemented by government grants
Collections: †Canadian works on paper
Publications: Annual Report; Calendar of Events, 3 times per yr
Activities: Classes for children; docent training; lectures open to public, 12 vis lectr per yr; concerts; gallery talks; tours; exten dept serves regional & national area; individual paintings & original objects of art lent to professional galleries & campus areas; book traveling exhibitions; originate traveling exhibitions; sales shop sells gallery publications

M **MOUNT SAINT VINCENT UNIVERSITY**, Art Gallery, B3M 2J6. Tel 902-443-4450, Ext 160. *Dir Art Gallery* Mary Sparling; *Exhibition Officer* Sandy Miller; *Office Mgr* Debbie Cameron
Open Mon - Fri 9 AM - 5 PM, Sat, Sun & holidays Noon - 5 PM, Tues until 9 PM. No admis fee. Estab 1970 and operating throughout the year with continuously-changing exhibitions of local, regional, national and international origin in the area of fine arts and crafts. Gallery situated on the main floor and mezzanine. Average Annual Attendance: 16,000
Income: Financed by university funds
Purchases: Judith Mann; Peter Barss; Susanne MacKay, Herself; Felicity Redgrave, Peggy's Rocks; Carol Fraser, Nocturne
Collections: The Art Gallery is custodian of a collection of pictures, ceramics and pottery of the late Alice Egan Hagen of Mahone Bay, noted Nova Scotia potter and ceramist; †works by women
Exhibitions: Drawing, A Canadian Survey 1977-1982; Primary Flowers; Nova Scotia Crafts IV: Barry Wheaton, Wood Sculpture & Joleen Gordon, Basketry; Now Appearing; Correspondences; Nova Scotia Crafts V: Jane Donovan, Ceramics; Maxwell Bates: Landscapes 1948-1978; Nova Scotia Crafts VII: Rejene Stowe & Andrew Terris, Glass; Bruce Ferguson
Publications: Gallery News, 4 times per yr; exhibition catalogs
Activities: Classes for adults and children; workshops; lect open to public, 12 visiting lectr per year; concerts; gallery talks; tours; competitions; individual paintings and original objects of art lent to other galleries; lending collection contains videotapes; originate traveling exhibitions

O **NOVA SCOTIA ASSOCIATION OF ARCHITECTS**, 1361 Barrington St, B3J 1Y9. Tel 902-423-7607. *Exec Dir* Diane Scott
Estab 1932. Mem: 170; annual meeting Feb
Publications: Newsletter, monthly

M **NOVA SCOTIA COLLEGE OF ART AND DESIGN**, Anna Leonowens Gallery, 5163 Duke St, B3J 3J6. Tel 902-422-7381. *Pres* Garry Neill Kennedy; *Dean* Alan Barkley; *Dir* Vera Lemecha
Open Tues - Sat 11 AM - 5 PM, Thurs evenings 5 - 9 PM. Estab for educational purposes. One small and two large galleries
Income: Financed by city and state appropriations and tuition
Exhibitions: 30-40 exhibitions per year
Publications: Ten books; one periodical; exhibition catalogues
Activities: Lectures open to public; gallery talks; book travleing exhibitions

L **Library,*** 5163 Duke St, B3J 3J6. Tel 902-422-7381, Ext 181. *Dir* John Murchie; *Asst Dir* Mary Snyder
Open Mon - Fri 8:30 AM - 11 PM, Sat 9 AM - 6 PM, Sun 1 - 11 PM. Circ 30,000
Income: $239,000 (financed by state appropriation and student fees)
Purchases: $57,500
Library Holdings: Vols 20,000; Per subs 300; Micro — Fiche, reels; AV — A-tapes, cassettes, fs, rec, slides, v-tapes; Other — Exhibition catalogs, pamphlets
Special Subjects: Contemporary art

M **NOVA SCOTIA MUSEUM**, W D Lawrence House, 1747 Summer St, B3H 3A6. Tel 902-429-4610
Open May 15 - Oct 15 9:30 AM - 5:30 PM, Sun 1 - 5:30 PM. Estab 1967 as a historic building housing marine history. Average Annual Attendance: 7387
Income: Financed by state appropriations
Collections: Historical Marine Painting display; Lawrence Family memorabilia

M **ST MARY'S UNIVERSITY**, Art Gallery, Robie St, B3H 3C3. Tel 902-423-7727. *Dir & Cur* J R Leighton Davis; *Asst Dir & Cur* Laura Tsinman; *Performing Arts Coordr* Jennifer Fisher
Open Tues - Thurs 1 PM - 7 PM, Fri 1 - 5 PM, Sat & Sun 2 - 4 PM, cl Mon. Estab 1970 to present a variety of exhibitions and performances of both regional and national interest and by contemporary artists. Average Annual Attendance: 12,000
Income: Financed by provincial appropriation
Collections: Works on paper by contemporary Canadian artists
Activities: Lectures open to the public, 3 - 4 vis lectr per yr; concerts; gallery talks; tours; individual paintings & original objects of art lent; book traveling exhibitions, 2 - 3 per year

YARMOUTH

M **YARMOUTH COUNTY HISTORICAL SOCIETY**, Yarmouth County Museum, 22 Collins St, PO Box 39, B5A 4B1. Tel 902-742-5539. *Pres* Ray Corbett; *Secy* Eleanor Blackie; *Chmn of Trustees* Oscar Nauss; *Cur* Eric Ruff
Open May - June 14 & Oct 10 AM - 12, 2 - 5 PM, June 15 - Sept 9 AM - 5 PM, July & Aug Sun - Tues 7:30 - 9:30 PM, Sun 1 - 5 PM, Nov - April 2 - 5 PM, cl Mon. Admis adults $1, students $.50, children $.25. Estab 1958 to display artifacts and paintings relating to Yarmouth's past. Located in former Congregational Church built in 1893. Average Annual Attendance: 14,000. Mem: 300; dues $7; meetings first Fri each month
Income: $35,000 (financed by membership, admis and state appropriation)
Purchases: $500
Collections: General historial collection; paintings of and by Yarmouthians; collection of ship portraits of Yarmouth vessels and vessels commanded by Yarmouthians
Publications: Newsletter, monthly
Activities: Classes for children; lectures open to public, 12 vis lectr per yr; concerts; gallery talks; tours; museum shop sells books; Saturday morning club

ONTARIO

ALMONTE

M **MISSISSIPPI VALLEY CONSERVATION AUTHORITY**, R Tait McKenzie Memorial Museum, RR 1 (Mailing add: PO Box 268, Lanark, K0G 1K0). Tel 613-256-3610. *Cur* Dianna Carlisle; *Community Relations Coordr* Pamela McGrath
Open May 15 - Labour Day Weekend daily 10 AM - 6 PM, Labour Day Weedend - Oct 15 Mon - Fri 1 - 4:30 PM, Sat, Sun & holidays 10 AM - 4:30 PM. Admis family $2.50, adults $1, senior citizens & children $.50. Estab 1952 as a private museum, publicly owned since 1973 by Mississippi Valley Conservation Authority as a memorial to Dr R Tait McKenzie, Canadian sculptor, physical educator, surgeon and humanitarian. Average Annual Attendance: 7500
Income: Financed by provincial government grant
Collections: 70 Original Athletic, Memorial and Monumental Sculptures, nearly all in plaster; 600 Pioneer Artifacts, mostly collected by Dr McKenzie
Exhibitions: Athletic Sculpture Plaque exhibited in connection with Olympiad in Montreal 1976
Activities: Classes for children; docent training; lectures open to the public; gallery talks; tours; sales shop sells books and reproductions

L **Research Library,*** RR 1, K0A 1A0. Tel 613-256-3610
Special Subjects: Sculpture

BELLEVILLE

M **HASTINGS COUNTY MUSEUM**, 257 Bridge St E, K8N 1P4. Tel 613-962-2329. *Cur* Mrs M E Simonds; *Education* Nancy Mohan
Open summer Tues - Sun 10 AM - 4:30 PM, winter Tues - Sun 1 - 4:30 PM. Admis $1.25. Estab 1973. Historic House with art gallery dedicated to local artist Manley McDonald, also extensive collection of Victorian paintings, copies of Gainsborough, Constable, Uens & Wilkie. Average Annual Attendance: 11,500
Income: Financed by city and state appropriation
Exhibitions: Permanent Collection of Manley McDonald Originals and Beverley McDonald Originals; artists, photographers
Activities: Classes for children; gallery talks; tours; lending collection contains nature artifacts and slides; museum shop sells books and magazines

BRAMPTON

L CITY OF BRAMPTON PUBLIC LIBRARY, Art Gallery, 250 Central Park Dr (Mailing add: 65 Queen St E, L6W 3L6). Tel 416-453-2444. *Dir* G C Burgis
Open Mon - Thurs 10 AM - 9 PM, Fri 10 AM - 6 PM, Sat 10 AM - 5 PM, Sun 1 - 5 PM. No admis fee. Estab 1972 to encourage an interest in and knowledge of the arts through exhibits and related activities. Gallery is 2950 sq ft, 250 running ft and walls are stretch fabric over wood. Average Annual Attendance: 80,000
Income: $55,000 (financed by city and state appropriation)
Collections: Small permanent collection
Activities: Classes for children; dramatic programs; lect open to public; concerts; gallery talks

M REGION OF PEEL MUSEUM AND ART GALLERY, 3 Wellington St E, L6W 1Y1. Tel 416-451-9051. *Dir* William D Barber; *Asst to Dir* Janice Calvert
Open daily 1:30 - 4:30 PM. Admis adults $.75, sr citizens and students $.50, members free. Estab 1968. Average Annual Attendance: 10,000. Mem: 300; dues family $10, individual $8; annual meeting last Tues in Jan
Collections: Permanent art collection of Peel Artists: Artifacts of Peel 1850 to present
Exhibitions: 7 exhibits per year, all mediums: Annual Open Juried Show; Regional Artists
Activities: Classes for adults and children; docent training; workshops; lectures open to the public, 10 - 15 vis lectr per yr; gallery talks; tours; book traveling exhibitions, 2 per yr; sales shop sells books, reproductions & prints
L Library, Brampton, L6W 1Y1
Reference only
Library Holdings: Vols 100; Per subs 50; Other — Clipping files, exhibition catalogs

BRANTFORD

M ART GALLERY OF BRANT, INC, 76 Dalhousie St, PO Box 1747, N3T 5V7. Tel 519-753-7581. *Dir* Richard Pottruff; *Chmn* A Meens; *Secy* Edie Mountjoy
Open Tues - Fri 9 AM - 5 PM, Sat 10 AM - 5 PM, cl Sun & Mon. No admis fee. Estab 1971 as a non-profit public art gallery serving the citizens of Brantford and Brant County. Store-front gallery; one main gallery room. Average Annual Attendance: 20,000. Mem: 375; dues sustaining $25, family $10, individual $7, student and senior citizens $2; annual meeting Sept/Oct
Income: Financed by membership, municipal, provincial & federal appropriations & local foundations
Collections: †Original Prints and Drawings by Contemporary Canadian Artists; Original Prints by European and American Artists; Works of Historical Nature by local area Artist Robert Whale
Publications: Annual report; Calendar of Events, quarterly; catalogues for exhibitions throughout the year
Activities: Classes for adults and children; docent training; film series; lect open to public, 8 visiting lectr per year; gallery talks; competitions; individual paintings and original objects of art lent to galleries and businesses; originate traveling exhibitions
L Library, 76 Dalhousie St, N3T 5V7
Open to public for reference
Library Holdings: Vols 35

M BRANT HISTORICAL SOCIETY, Brant County Museum, 57 Charlotte St, N3T 2W6. Tel 519-752-2483. *Dir* Beth L Hanna
Open Sept - Apr Tues - Fri 9 AM - 5 PM, Sat 1 - 4 PM, May - Aug Tues - Fri 9 AM - 5 PM, Sat & Sun 1 - 4 PM. Admis adults $1, students $.50, children $.25, under 6 with parent free. Estab 1908 to preserve, interpret & display Brant County history. Average Annual Attendance: 8000. Mem: 150; dues patron $25, family $10, single $7
Income: Financed by memberships, provincial, county & city grants & fundraising
Collections: Early Indian history; historical figures; portraits & paintings; Brant County history
Publications: Annual brochure
Activities: Classes for children; docent training; lectures open to public; tours; museum shop sells books, reproductions & prints
L Library, 57 Charlotte St, N3T 2W6
Library Holdings: Vols 500
Collections: First editions of history and archaeology; old Bibles available for research on premises under supervision of curator; rare books

CAMBRIDGE

L CAMBRIDGE PUBLIC LIBRARY AND GALLERY, 20 Grand Ave N, N1S 2K6. Tel 519-621-0460. *Chief Librn* Greg Hayton; *Coordr Cultural Services* Eric Dewdney
Open Mon - Thurs 9:30 AM - 8:30 PM, Fri & Sat 9:30 AM - 5:30 PM. No admis fee. Estab 1969. Gallery on second floor mezzanine with 2000 sq ft, 250 linear ft. Average Annual Attendance: 25,000
Income: Financed by provincial appropriation, federal and private
Collections: Regional Artists
Publications: Bi-monthly newsletter
Activities: Classes for adults and children; lect open to public, 10 visiting lectr per year; concerts; gallery talks; tours; competitions; awards; individual paintings and original objects of art lent; book traveling exhibitions five per year; originate traveling exhibitions

CHATHAM

O CHATHAM CULTURAL CENTRE, 75 William St N, N7M 4L4. Tel 519-354-8338. *Dir* David K McNeil; *Programme-Publicity Officer* Karen Rickers
Open Tues - Sun 1 - 5 PM. No admis fee. Estab 1963 to operate as a regional arts centre, to advance knowledge and appreciation of, and to encourage, stimulate and promote interest in the study of culture and the visual and performing arts. Gallery maintained; designated National Exhibition Centre for the presentation of visual art works and museum related works, to the public of this country. Average Annual Attendance: 25,000. Mem: 600; dues family $18, single $10
Income: Financed by membership, city and state appropriation, and National Museum Grants
Collections: Local Artists; Historical Photographs
Publications: Chatham-Kent Events, quarterly; bi-monthly bulletin
Activities: Classes for adults and children; dramatic programs; docent training; workshops; theatre series; lect open to the public, 2-6 vis lectrs per year; concerts; gallery talks; tours; films; individual and original objects of art lent to accredited galleries and museums; lending collection contains 2100 slides; book traveling exhibitions; originate traveling exhibitions

DOWNSVIEW

M YORK UNIVERSITY, Art Gallery,* 4700 Keele St, Ross Bldg N145, M3T 1P3. Tel 416-667-3427, 667-2100. *Cur of Art* Michael Greenwood; *Cur Asst* Shelagh Keeley; *Asst* Louise Greenwood; *Secy* Maxine Burns
Open Mon - Fri 10 AM - 4:30 PM. No admis fee. Estab 1970 to maintain a program of exhibitions covering a broad spectrum of the visual arts and artifacts of mankind from diverse cultures. Gallery is 2115 sq ft, exhibition space only 1200 sq ft, program space only 420 sq ft and support space only 485 sq ft. Average Annual Attendance: 10,000
Income: Financed by university
Collections: Approx 750 works including ethnographical items and artifacts, approx 550 of the works are by Canadian artists
Exhibitions: Bill Featherston: Recent Paintings; Alan Reynolds: Recent Sculpture; Don Haluska: Paradise Lost and Found; Equipment for Eternity: Egyptian Arts and Crafts of the New Kingdon, 1570 to 1085 BC; Robert Bourdeau: 45 Photographic Images of Canada, Utah and Sri Lanka; Edward Curtis: 70 Photographs of Canadian West Coast Indian Life before the First World War; Joseph Beuys: Prints, Photographs and Drawings; Ernst Barlach (1870-1938): Graphic Work; The Drawings of Christiane Pflug (1936-1972); Emil Orlik: Drawings and Prints (1870-1932); Connections: Krizan, Mcaulay & Wright; National Print Show '80: Professional Photographers of Canada, Inc; 19th century drawings and prints; Slowly I Turned...Brian Condron
Publications: Human Images through the Ages from the Finlayson Collection; Douglas Bentham Enclosures and Opens 1975-76; The Rayfield Collection of Ethiopan Art; Historic Canadian Silver from The Henry Birks Collection; Slowly I Turned..Brian Condron; exhibition catalogs
Activities: Lectures; concerts; gallery talks; tours; competitions; awards; scholarships; individual paintings and original objects of art lent for major shows or retrospectives to other members of the University and faculty for their offices; originate traveling exhibitions
L Fine Arts Slide Library, 4700 Keele St, M3T 1P3. Tel 416-667-3749. *Cur* M Metraux; *Slide Librn* L Szczepaniak; *Asst Slide Librn* D MacFarlane
Income: Financed through university
Library Holdings: Vols 16,235; AV — A-tapes, cassettes, fs, Kodachromes, lantern slides, motion pictures, rec, slides 160,000, v-tapes; Other — Clipping files, exhibition catalogs, manuscripts
Collections: Bazin Library; T A Heinrich Collection; Rare Books Library

GANANOQUE

M GANANOQUE HISTORICAL MUSEUM, 10 King St, E, PO Box 158, K7G 2T8. Tel 613-382-4663. *Pres* Derrol Simpson; *Secy* Lorna Whyte; *Cur* Margaret Brennan
Open Mon - Sat Noon - 5 PM. Admis adults $.75, children under 12 $.25. Estab 1964 to house many local artifacts. Average Annual Attendance: 3600
Collections: China Collection; Military and Indian Artifacts; Victorian Dining Room, Parlour and Bedroom; glass; portraits and photographs pertaining to local history
Activities: Book traveling exhibitions

GUELPH

M MACDONALD STEWART ART CENTRE, 358 Gordon St, N1G 1Y1. Tel 519-837-0010. *Chmn* Charles C Ferguson; *VChmn* R Spencer; *Secy* Mrs V Myers; *Dir* Judith Nasby; *Cur* Lynn Barbeau; *Cur* Ingrid Jenkner; *Gallery Technician* Rob Freeman
Open Tues - Sun 12 - 5 PM. Estab 1978 by Univ of Guelph, city, county and board of education to collect and exhibit works of art; maintain and operate a gallery; and related facilities for this purpose fulfilling a public role in city and county. 30,000 sq ft building comprising galleries, lecture room, studio, meeting rooms, resource centre, gift shop and rental service. Restored and renovated in 1980. Average Annual Attendance: 25,000. Mem: 500; dues family $25, individual $15, student $5; annual meeting Sept-Oct
Income: Financed by university, city, county, board of education, provincial and federal grants, memberships and donations
Purchases: Canadian art
Collections: Decorative arts; †historical & contemporary Canadian art; †historical & contemporary international prints; †Inuit Collection; †contemporary sculpture
Exhibitions: (1982-83) Bridges: A Collaboration between Paul Fournier & Robert Daigneault; Posters from Lithuania; Michael Collins; Permanent Collection: A Survey; Inuit Art from the Permanent Collection; Outdoor Sculpture; Ed Zelenak & E Turvey; Ian McKay; Town & Cityscapes; World Print III; Canada in the Graphic Arts; A Tribute to David Milne; Permanent Collection; Eliyakota's

Birds; Circa 1800; Canada Packers' Collection; Paul Beau; Josef Drenters: Images of the Madonna; David H Kaye: Engaged Reliefs; James Kerr-Lawson: A Canadian Abroad; Contemporary Graphics from Permanent Collection; Regional Artists; Viewpoints; Paintings of Imperial & Princely India; Stephen Cruise; A Y Jackson: The Early Years

Publications: Catalogue of permanent collection of University of Guelph 1980; exhibition catalogues, 6 per yr; newsletter

Activities: Classes for adults & children; docent training; parent/child workshops; lectures open to public; gallery talks; tours; awards; exten dept serves Wellington County and other Canadian public galleries, also have circulated in US; individual paintings lent to institutions and public galleries; art rental to gallery members; lending collection contains original paintings, prints, photographs and sculpture; book traveling exhibitions seven per year; originate traveling exhibitions, 1 -2 per yr; sales shop sells books, magazines, reproductions, toys, pottery, textiles, jewelry and catalogues

HAMILTON

M **ART GALLERY OF HAMILTON,** 123 King St W, L8P 4S8. Tel 416-527-6610. *Dir* Glen E Cumming; *Asst to Dir* Bradford Gorman; *Education & Extension Officer* Sheila Greenspan; *Community Relations* Keith Courtney; *Preparator* Jim Morrison; *Registrar* David Somers
Open Tues - Sat 10 AM - 5 PM, Thurs evenings 7 - 9 PM, Sun 1 - 5 PM. No Admis fee. Estab Jan 1914 to develop and maintain a centre for the study and enjoyment of the visual arts; new gallery opened Oct 1977. Building is 76,000 sq ft, 24,000 sq ft of exhibition space. Average Annual Attendance: 85,000. Mem: 3395; dues family $30, single $20; annual meeting last Thurs in May
Income: Financed by endowment, membership, city and provincial appropriation and federal grants
Collections: Complete graphics of Karel Appel; †Canadian fine arts; †American, †British & †European fine arts
Exhibitions: 36 annually
Publications: Art Gallery of Hamilton Bulletin, bimonthly
Activities: Classes for adults and children; docent training; lect open to public, 18 visiting lectr per year; concerts; gallery talks; tours; exten dept; individual paintings and original objects of art lent to other galleries and museums; lending collection contains 1751 original prints, 1361 paintings, 135 sculpture, 461 drawings; originate traveling exhibitions; museum shop sells books, magazines and reproductions
L **Muriel Isabel Bostwick Library,*** 123 King St W, Hamilton, L8P 4S8. Tel 416-527-6610. *Cur History Coll* Andrew J Oko
Open to gallery members and researchers for reference
Library Holdings: Vols 3000; Per subs 14; Other — Clipping files, exhibition catalogs, photographs
Special Subjects: Good references on Canadian art history and large holding of exhibition catalogues relating to this field

M **DUNDURN CASTLE,** Dundurn Park, York Blvd, L8R 3H1. Tel 416-522-5313. *Cur* Marilynn Soules; *Head Historical Interpreter* Ania Latoszek; *Cur* Marilyn Saules
Open mid-June to Labor Day daily 11 AM - 4 PM, evening appointments for groups of 25 or more, Labor Day to mid-June booked tours mornings and evenings, open to public 1 - 4 PM, cl Christmas and New Year's Day. Admis adults $2.65, senior citizen $1.85, students $1.35, children $.80, family $6.35, group rates for over 25 people. Dundurn, the home of Sir Allan Napier MacNab; Hamilton's Centennial Project was the restoration of this historic house; built in 1832-35, it was tenured by MacNab until his death in 1862. The terminal date of the furnishings is 1855. Approximately 35 rooms are shown; three-room on-site museums. Average Annual Attendance: 82,000
Income: Financed by city of Hamilton, owner & operator
Activities: Classes for adults & children; docent training; lectures open to the public; tours; individual paintings & original objects of art lent; museum shop sells books, reproductions & prints

M **MCMASTER UNIVERSITY,** Art Gallery, 1280 Main St W, L8S 4M2. Tel 416-525-9140, Ext 4685. *Secy* Mrs S Waxman; *Dir* Hayden Maginnis; *Cur* Stephen Lamia
Open Tues - Fri 10 AM - 5 PM, Thurs evening 7 - 9 PM, Sun 1 - 5 PM. No admis fee. Estab 1967 to provide the university and public with historical and contemporary art from Canada and other countries. Three galleries 2136 sq ft and 447 sq ft & 260 sq ft; incandescent lighting throughout; display cases; sculpture stands. Average Annual Attendance: 7000
Income: $9800 (financed by university and private endowment)
Purchases: $15,000
Collections: †American and Canadian Art; European paintings, prints and drawings; †German Expressionist Prints
Exhibitions: (1983-84) Around American Pop; From Istanbul to Bokhara: Antique Carpets of the Near East; 100 Golden Years: Canadian Art 1830-1930; Wayne Boucher: Nova Scotia Painter; Arlone Berman: Multi-Media Artists From Toronto; Graham Todd & Judy Major: Studio Faculty Show; Animals in Art: Drawings From the National Gallery of Canada; Ontario at Work: Photographs
Activities: Classroom facilities; lect open to public; concerts; gallery talks; individual paintings and original objects of art lent to National Gallery of Canada, Art Gallery of Ontario; University of Minnesota Art Gallery
L **Library,*** McMaster University, 1280 Main St W, L8S 4M2. Tel 416-525-9140, Ext 4256. *Librn* Harold Siroonian
Open Mon - Thurs 10 AM - 5 PM, Thurs evenings 7 - 9 PM, Sun 1 - 5 PM. Houses reference materials on art gallery management, exhibition and sales catalogues
Library Holdings: Vols 100

JORDAN

M **JORDAN HISTORICAL MUSEUM OF THE TWENTY,** Vintage House, Main St, L0R 1S0. Tel 416-562-5242. *Cur* Sandra Overstrom
Open May - Oct daily 1 - 5 PM. Admis $1. Estab 1953 to preserve the material and folklore of the area known as The Twenty, Mile Creek vicinity. Average Annual Attendance: 10,000. Mem: 100; dues $5; annual meeting Feb
Income: Financed by admissions, provincial grants, municipal grants, internal fund raising activities & donations
Collections: Archives; furniture; historical material & textiles
Exhibitions: Special annual exhibits
Activities: Classes for children; Special displays as requested by the community; Pioneer Day first Sat after Canadian Thanksgiving holiday; lectures open to public, 1 vis lectr per yr; individual paintings & original objects of art lent; sales shop sells books, original art, prints, pottery, textiles & local craft items

KINGSTON

M **QUEEN'S UNIVERSITY,** Agnes Etherington Art Centre,* K7L 3N6. Tel 613-547-6551. *Dir* Robert F Swain; *Cur* Dorothy Farr; *Assoc Cur* William Muysson; *Educational Officer* Catherine Gold
Open Tues, Thurs 10 AM - 9 PM, Wed, Fri - Sun 10 AM - 5 PM. No admis fee. Estab 1957 to provide the services of a public art gallery and museum for the community and region. Gallery has approximately 8000 sq ft of display space, in four separate areas, showing a balanced program of exhibitions of the contemporary and historical, of national, international and regional art. Average Annual Attendance: 30,000. Mem: 850; dues $15 - $150; annual meeting May
Income: $550,000 (financed by endowment, city and state appropriation, University and Canada Council funds)
Purchases: $55,000
Collections: †Canadian Paintings, Prints, Sculpture, Historical and Contemporary; †European Graphics; Ethnological Collection; Old Master Paintings
Exhibitions: About 30 exhibitions mounted each year
Publications: Bulletin, bimonthly; exhibition publications and catalogues; studies
Activities: Classes for adults and children; docent training for school groups; studio classes; lect open to public, 10 visiting lectr per year; concerts; gallery talks; tours; individual paintings lent by Gallery Association Art Rental to private individuals and businesses; lending collection contains original prints and paintings; originate traveling exhibitions
L **Art & Music Library,*** Ontario Hall, Kingston, K7L 3L6. Tel 613-547-5999. *Librn* E Albrich
Open to students, researchers and the public for reference only
Purchases: $20,700
Library Holdings: Vols 21,500; Per subs 141; reference books; Micro — Fiche 600, reels 118; Other — Exhibition catalogs, pamphlets 240

KITCHENER

M **KITCHENER-WATERLOO ART GALLERY,** 101 Queen St N, N2H 6P7. Tel 519-579-5860. *Pres* Open; *Dir* Brad Blain; *Cur* Jennifer C Watson; *Extension Cur & Education Officer* Paul Blain; *Asst* Cindy Schaefer
Open Tues, Wed, Fri & Sat 10 AM - 5 PM, Thur 10 AM - 5 PM, 7 - 9 PM, Sun 1 - 5 PM, cl Mon. Admis contribution adults $1.50, student & sr citizens $.50. Estab 1956, the Kitchener-Waterloo Art Gallery is a public institution interested in stimulating an appreciation of the visual arts and dedicated to bringing to the community exhibitions, art classes, lectures, films, workshops and special events. Average Annual Attendance: 75,492. Mem: 904; dues business $50, family $20, individual $15, senior citizens and students $5
Income: Financed by government grants, foundation grants, corporate and individual donations, special events, membership dues, voluntary admissions & sales of publications
Collections: Canadian paintings, prints, drawings & sculpture; Homer Watson Collection; British 18th & 19th century painting; German 20th century prints; Ernst Fuchs prints
Exhibitions: A Provincial Elegance; Elizabeth Eastman: A Quiet Inner Authority; Albert H Robinson: The Mature Years; Heritage Waterloo: The Art of Woldemar Neufeld; Barry Hodgson: Landscapes; annual Artforms - work by artists of central Ontario; Kitchener-Waterloo/Stratford/Windsor Exchange; Gene Chu: The Printmaker's Eye; H Werner Zimmerman: Land Forms; Willen Verhulst
Publications: Calendar of events, 4 times a year; exhibition catalogs
Activities: Classes for adults and children; docent training; workshops; seminars; lectures open to public, 6 vis lectr per year; concerts; gallery talks; tours; films; free tuition awards; scholarships; extension dept serves Waterloo region; individual paintings and original objects of art lent to schools, malls, senior citizen homes, offices, other galleries and museums; lending collection contains cassettes, color reproductions, sculpture, slides, original prints & paintings; book traveling exhibitions; originate traveling exhibitions to galleries and museums through Canada; museum shop sells books, magazines, original art, reproductions, prints, sculpture, pottery, toys, jewelry, paper, cards, decorative items & glass
L **Eleanor Calvert Memorial Library,** 101 Queen St N, Kitchener, ON N2H 6P7. Tel 519-579-5860. *Librn* Nancy E Francis
Estab 1972 for public art reference & lending to memebers
Library Holdings: Vols 3500; Per subs 20; AV — Cassettes, slides; Other — Clipping files, exhibition catalogs, pamphlets, reproductions
Special Subjects: Canadian artists biographical material

KLEINBURG

M **MCMICHAEL CANADIAN COLLECTION,*** L0J 1C0. Tel 416-893-1121. *Dir* Dr Robert McMichael; *Chmn Board Turstees* J Allyn Taylor; *Vice Chmn Board Trustees* Warren E Jones
Open Tues - Sun Noon - 5:30 PM, school tours Mon - Fri mornings, by appointment. No admis fee. Estab 1965 to give better understanding of Canadian art to people of all ages. Average Annual Attendance: 281,000

Income: Operations financed by the Government of Ontario
Collections: Canadian Group of Seven and their contemporaries: Emily Carr, David Milne, Tom Thomson, etc; Canadian, Eskimo and Indian Art
Publications: Annual art calendar; The Group of Seven and Tom Thomson (book); The McMichael Canadian Collection (book)
Activities: Ext dept serves Ontario; individual paintings and original objects of art loaned; museum shop sells books, reproductions and prints
L **Library,*** L0J 1C0. *Librn & Archivist* Linda Barr
Library Holdings: Mainly archival material; AV — Cassettes, fs, motion pictures, slides; Other — Clipping files, exhibition catalogs, manuscripts, memorabilia, original art works, pamphlets, photographs, prints, reproductions
Special Subjects: Inuit, West Coast Indian, Woodland Indian

LONDON

M **LONDON REGIONAL ART GALLERY,*** 421 Ridout St N, N6A 5H4. Tel 519-672-4580. *Dir* Brenda Wallace; *Asst Dir & Cur* Paddy O'Brien; *Coordr Animation Servs* Open; *Registrar* Barry Fair; *Coordr Gallery Services & Mem Secy* Jan Delaney; *Financial Servs* Anne Paul; *Dir of Develop* Nancy Bigger Smith
Open Tues & Sun Noon - 6 PM, Wed, Thurs, Fri Noon - 9 PM, Sat 10 AM - 6 PM, restricted holiday hours. Admis adults $1, senior citizens & students $.50, under 12 free, no admin fee on Wed. Estab 1976. New bldg open 1980 containing 26,500 sq ft of exhibition space, 150 seat auditorium. Mem: 3300; dues $25, senior citizens and students $10; annual meeting in the Fall
Income: Financed by membership, city and province appropriation and federally funded
Collections: Permanent Collection stresses regional and local artists, who have become internationally and nationally recognized such as Jack Chambers, Greg Curnoe, Paul Kane and Paul Peel; Hamilton King Meek Memorial Collection of Artifacts; F B Housser Memorial Collection; The Moore Collection
Exhibitions: Works of art - international, national and regional; programmes of multi-media nature, including performing arts
Publications: Exhibition catalogues
Activities: Classes for children; docent training; lect open to public, some for members only; concerts; gallery talks; tours; exten dept serves the Region; individual paintings and original objects of art lent; book traveling exhibitions; originate traveling exhibitions; museum shop sells books, jewelry magazines, original art, prints and reproductions

M **UNIVERSITY OF WESTERN ONTARIO,** McIntosh Art Gallery, 1151 Richmond St, N6A 3K7. Tel 519-679-3181, 679-6027. *University Art Cur* Maurice Stubbs; *Exhib Coordr* Catherine Elliot; *Secy* Susan Skaith; *Installations Officer* David Falls
Open Sept - April Mon - Fri 11 AM - 5 PM, Sat & Sun 2 - 5 PM, Wed & Thurs evenings 7 - 9 PM, May - Aug Mon - Fri 11 AM - 4 PM, Sun 2 - 5 PM, cl Sat. No admis fee. Estab 1942. Three galleries with a total of 2960 sq ft. Average Annual Attendance: 14,000. Mem: 155
Income: Financed by endowment, membership, provincial appropriation, special grants and University funds
Purchases: $70,000
Collections: Canadian Art
Exhibitions: (1983-84) Indian Miniatures; New Acquisitions; Bryan Maycock and Michael Cochie: New Paintings; Doreen Lindsay Prints; Montreal Tapestry Biennial; Inuit Objects and Image: Shieky Browstone, photographs; Arctic Paintings: Kerry Ferris; Bridgetown Series: Ken Tolmie, paintings; Regionalism in London: Art in the 60s; Education of the Artist I: Eric Atkinson, drawings; The Lost Craft of Ornamented Architecture: Canadian Architectural Drawings 1850-1930; The Pilgrimage: Gerald Trottier's Easter Series; Manitoba juried photography exhibition; Pressure '83; The Rockies: Harris, Jackson, MacDonald, Johnston; New Accessions; The University of Western Ontario Visual Arts Department graduating exhibition; Fanshawe College Department of Fine Art graduating exhibition; The Winds of Western
Publications: Bulletin, bimonthly; catalogues for exhibition
Activities: Lect open to public, 4 - 6 visiting lectr per year; concerts; gallery talks; tours; individual paintings and original objects lent to galleries; originate traveling exhibitions
L **The D B Weldon Library,** 1151 Richmond St, N6A 3K7. Tel 519-679-2111. *Dir of Library* Dr Robert E Lee
Open to all university staff, faculty, and students for research and borrowing. Open to the public for in-house research
Library Holdings: Vols 47,504; Per subs 129; Micro — Fiche, reels; Other — Exhibition catalogs, pamphlets
Special Subjects: Decorative Arts, Applied Art, Canadian Art, Western Art

MISSISSAUGA

L **MISSISSAUGA LIBRARY SYSTEM,** 110 Dundas St W, L5B 1H3. Tel 416-279-7002. *Chief Librn* Noel Ryan; *Gallery Mgr* Keith Moreau
Hours vary according to branch. No admis fee. Outlet for local artists at branch galleries; present more widely recognised artists at Central and Burnhamthorp Galleries. Total of eleven galleries in system, 90 running ft each, often multi-purpose rooms
Collections: Permanent collection of 135 paintings and prints by Canadian artists, emphasis on prints (all framed)
Exhibitions: Annual Juried Art Show Open
Publications: Artifacts, monthly brochure; Link News Tabloid Format, every other month; Monthly Branch Brochure
Activities: Lectures open to public; competitions with cash prizes; lending collection contains books and 150 motion pictures; book traveling exhibitions
L **Central Library, Art Division,*** 110 Dundas St W, L5B 1H3. Tel 416-279-7002. *Librn* Diane Dineen
Open Mon - Fri Noon - 9 PM, Sat 9 AM - 5 PM, Sun 1 - 5 PM. Deposit library for Central Ontario Regional Library System
Library Holdings: Vols 22,700; Per subs 29; AV — Cassettes, fs, lantern slides, motion pictures, slides, v-tapes; Other — Clipping files, exhibition catalogs, framed reproductions, original art works, pamphlets, prints
Special Subjects: Canadian prints

L **SHERIDAN COLLEGE SCHOOL OF APPLIED ARTS AND TECHNOLOGY,** School of Crafts and Design Library, 1460 S Sheridan Way, L5L 1Z7. Tel 416-274-3685. *Head Librn* Cathy Zuraw; *Library Technician* Madeleine LaPointe
Estab 1970 to accommodate students on campus
Income: Financed by college
Purchases: $14,000
Library Holdings: Vols 5000; Per subs 100; AV — Cassettes, fs, slides, v-tapes; Other — Clipping files, exhibition catalogs
Special Subjects: Architecture, Ceramics, Metalwork, Sculpture, Textiles, Design, Glass-blowing, Wood
Activities: Classes for adults

M **UNIVERSITY OF TORONTO,** Erindale Campus Art Gallery, Mississauga Rd, L5L 1C6. Tel 416-828-5214. *Chmn* Arlene Leib; *Cur* Nancy Hazelgrove
Open Mon - Sun 1 - 7 PM, Thurs until 9 PM. No admis fee. Estab 1973 to educate the public & display artists works. Gallery has four walls with various dividers & floor space of 36 x 60 ft. Average Annual Attendance: 2000
Collections: Oils, sculpture, water colour, pen sketches & prints
Exhibitions: Cuba: Pintura Joven Young Painting, Cuba exhibition; Sally Gregson, paintings; Pat Martin Bates, prints
Publications: The Dale, monthly
Activities: Classes for adults & children; lectures open to public, 15 vis lectr per yr; competitions with awards; individual paintings & original objects of art lent; book traveling exhibitions

OAKVILLE

M **OAKVILLE GALLERIES,** 120 Navy St, L6J 2Z4. Tel 416-844-4402. *Chmn* R Mahler; *Dir* Margot Fisher-Page; *Asst Dir* Catherine Siddall; *Education Officer* Dianne Bos
Centennial open Mon - Fri 10 AM - 9 PM, Sat 10 AM - 5 PM, Sun 1 - 5 PM; Gairloch, located at 1306 Lakeshore Rd E, open Tue - Sun 1 - 5 PM, July - Aug Tue - Sun 1 - 8 PM. Estab Centennial 1967, Garloch 1972, to exhibit and to educate historical and contemporary visual arts. Centennial is the larger, more central gallery; Gairloch is a smaller, estate house-gallery in park setting. The two galleries now have been renamed as one organization - The Oakville Galleries. Average Annual Attendance: 31,000. Mem: 400
Income: $170,000 (financed by city and provincial appropriation)
Collections: Contemporary Canadian painting, †drawing and prints; Keene Collection of posters; North American Native Indian art and artifacts; contemporary outdoor sculpture
Exhibitions: (1981)Ivan Wheale; Masks & Weavings; The Heritage of Jack Bush; Art Rental; John Oslansky/Blake Fitzpatrick; Clay and Cloth; OSA Sculpture & Wall Hanging; Kunichika; (1982) Shell Employees Collect; Reflections of an Age; Art Sparks; For the Birds; Oakville Handweavers & Spinners; Spectrum; Susan Rome, Costume Design; Edward S Curtis; Leah Valian; Annual Art Auction; Shiela Maki; MOONYEEN Cormack; Photography Juried Show; Arthur Kendrick (photos); Stacey Spiegel (sculptor); Animal Symbolism; GRAPHEX 81; Fay Rooke/Gery Puley; Stephen Arthurs; Graham Cantieni PARERGON; Art Rental; Archaelogy and Art, John Wood; Clay & Cloth; Giant Worlds; Lila Irving (woodcuts); CAPE DORSET; OSA Juried Show
Activities: Classes for adults and children; docent training, volunteer committee; lect open to public, 12 - 15 visiting lectr per year; gallery talks; tours; competitions; individual paintings and original objects of art lent to qualified and controlled art galleries and museums in Canada; lending collection contains 100 original art works; originate traveling exhibitions; sales shop sells books, original art, reproductions, prints and locally produced pottery etc
L **Library,*** 1306 Lakeshore Rd E, L6J 1L6
Open Tue - Sun 1 - 5 PM, July & August 1 - 8 PM. Estab 1979, primarily art magazines from 1967-79 dealing with contemporary art. Reference library
Library Holdings: Magazines; AV — Slides, v-tapes
Special Subjects: Contemporary Canadian Art

M **TARAS H SCHEVCHENKO MUSEUM AND MEMORIAL PARK FOUNDATION,*** 1363 Dundas St W, L6J 4Z2. Tel 416-827-2651. *Pres & Cur* Peter Prokop; *Secy* Stanley Dobrowolsky
Open July & Aug Sun Noon - 5 PM, and by appointment. Admis by voluntary donation. Estab 1952, a 16.5 acre park, complete with monument and museum opened as a symbol of the unity and brother of Ukrainian Canadians with Canadians of all national origins. Toronto Office: 42 Roncesvalles Ave, Toronto M6R 2K3; Tel: 416-535-1063
Income: Financed by donations
Collections: Reproductions and copies in oil and watercolor of Taras H Schevchenko's own paintings and sketches, also paintings done by other artists and authors representing some aspects of T H Schevchenko's life. Display and handicrafts - ceramics from Ukraine, handicrafts made by Ukrainian Canadians and exhibits of Ukranian pioneer life in Western Canada

L **SHERIDAN COLLEGE OF APPLIED ARTS AND TECHNOLOGY,** Visual Arts Library,* 1430 Trafalgar Rd, L6H 2L1. Tel 416-823-9730. *Libr Tech* J Allen; *Library Technician* Jacqueline Payne
Open daily 9 AM - 5 PM. Estab 1970 to serve the students and faculty of the School of Visual Arts
Library Holdings: Vols 3500; Per subs 68
Special Subjects: Art History, Photography, Animation

OSHAWA

M **THE ROBERT MCLAUGHLIN GALLERY,** Civic Centre, L1H 3Z3. Tel 416-576-3000. *Dir* Joan Murray; *Business Administrator* Jack Leroux
Open Mon - Fri 10 AM - 6 PM, Tues evenings 7 - 9 PM, Sat Noon - 5 PM, Sun 2 - 5 PM. No admis fee. Estab Feb 1967 as The Art Gallery of Oshawa, in May 1969 as the Robert McLaughlin Gallery. Main Gallery 28 x 46 x 15 ft; North Gallery 24 x 31 x 10 ft; South Gallery 18 x 27 x 10 ft, with foyer and Director's office. Average Annual Attendance: 27,000. Mem: 700; dues family $20, single

$15, student & Sr citizen $5; annual meeting Feb
Income: Financed by membership, city appropriation, Canada Council, Ministry Culture & Recreation, Wintario & Ontario Arts Council
Collections: Canadian 19th & 20th century drawings, paintings, prints & sculpture; †major collection of works by Painters Eleven
Exhibitions: (1982) Ray Mead: Two Decades; Regina Five, Exhibition Two; permanent collection; American Water Colours: Cigar Box Top Designs; Mary Pratt; K - 13 - V; General Motors Employees Exhibition; Oshawa Art Association Exhibition; The Art of Quilting: Past & Present; Remember When; Louis Stokes; Six Artists: Two Points of View; Art Treasures; Canadians Look at Europe; Art Rental Exhibition; Appraisal Day; Art Mart; William Blair Bruce, 1859-1906; Foiling Around; (1983) Bridges: Fournier/Daigneault; Lawren Harris Drawings; Isabel McLaughlin: Recollections; Children's Art; General Motors Employees' Exhibition; Oshawa Art Association Exhibition; permanent collection; Kurelek's Vision of Canada; Canadian Fiesta; The Seeing Brain; Visual Arts Camp 1982; Bruno Bobak; Art Rental Exhibition; 5th Annual Durham Board of Education Employees' Exhibition; Art Mart '83; Pegi Nicol MacLeod: 1904-1949; Variations on a Christmas Theme
Publications: Annual Report; Bulletin, monthly; Calendar of Events, annually, Exhibition catalogs
Activities: Classes for adults and children; docent training; lect open to public, 6 visiting lectr per year; concerts; gallery talks; tours; competitions; exten dept; individual paintings and original objects of art lent to schools, institutions and industries; lending collection contains 300 cassettes, 300 color reproductions, framed reproductions, 10 original art works, 10,000 slides, 2000 books; originate traveling exhibitions; sales shop sells books, original art and local crafts

L **Library,** Civic Centre, L1H 3Z3. *Librn* Patricia Claxton-Oldfield
Open to gallery members
Library Holdings: Vols 2000; AV — A-tapes, cassettes, slides, v-tapes; Other — Clipping files, exhibition catalogs, manuscripts, pamphlets, photographs
Special Subjects: Research of Painters Eleven and 19th and 20th Century works
Collections: †Canadian contemporary art books

OTTAWA

M **CANADIANA SPORT ART COLLECTION,** National Sport and Recreation Centre Inc, 333 River Rd, K1L 8B9. *Dir Services* John P Restivo
Open Mon - Fri 8:30 AM - 4:30 PM. Estab 1970 to provide a vehicle through which recognition could be passed on to the many fine amateur athletes of Canada, by Canadian artists. Average Annual Attendance: 15,000
Exhibitions: Jack Bush: The Pass (painting); Ken Danby - Skates (and other watercolors); Paintings from Prudential Insurance Company of America's collection; Great Moments in Canadian Sport; Louis Phillipe Hebert (bronze sculpture); McKenzie Bronze Sculptures: Athlete, Boxer, The Competitor, The Relay, Sprinter, Supple Juggler; Allan de la Plante (photographs); Siggy Puchta Bronze Sculptures: Decisive Moment, Karate Player and Touchdown; Joe Rosenthal's Struggle with Time (bronze sculpture); Hanni Rothschild: Hockey Player, Ball Game (ceramics); Alan Sapp: Playing Hockey (painting); Esther Wertheimer: The Olympics (metal sculpture); William Winter's Street Hockey
Activities: Tours; artmobile; individual paintings and original objects of art lent to Canada's Sport Hall of Fame, Canada Games Society and Olympic Association; originate traveling exhibition; sales shop sells reporductions and prints

CANADIAN CONFERENCE OF THE ARTS
For further information, see National Organizations in Canada

CANADIAN CRAFTS COUNCIL, Canadien de l'Artisanat
For further information, see National Organizations in Canada

CANADIAN MUSEUMS ASSOCIATION, Association des Musees Canadiens
For further information, see National Organizations in Canada

M **NATIONAL FILM BOARD OF CANADA,** Still Photography Division, Tunney's Pasture, K1A 0N1. Tel 613-992-1920. *Executive Producer* Martha Langford; *Producer* Martha Hanna; *Producer* Pierre Dessureault; *Admin Officer* Lise Krueger
Estab 1939 to initiate and promote the production and distribution of still photographs designed to interpret Canada to Canadians and to other nations
Income: Financed by federal government agency
Collections: Collection of works by Contemporary Canadian Photographers
Exhibitions: Philip Bergerson; Robert Bourdeau; Randy Bradley; Corinne Bronfman; Edward Burtynsky; Michel Campeau; Fred Cattroll; Lawrence Chrismas; Donigan Cumming; Doug Curran; Walter Curtin; Nigel Dickson; Pierre Gaudard; Richard Holden; Stephen Livick; Chris Lund; David Miller; Pat Morrow; David McMillan; Claude Palardy; John Paskievich; Denis Plain; Michael Schreier; Volker Seding; Orest Semchishen; Tom Skudra; James Stadnick; Shin Sugin; Kryn Taconis; Sam Tata; Jeremy Taylor; Gary Wilson
Publications: B C Almanac; photography publications
Activities: Gallery talks on request; originate traveling exhibitions, across Canada and outside the country under the auspices of the Department of External Affairs

M **NATIONAL GALLERY OF CANADA,** Lorne Bldg, Elgin & Slater Sts, K1A 0M8. Tel 613-992-4636. *Dir* Joseph Martin; *Actg Asst Dir Public Programs* Gyde V Shepherd; *Asst Dir Coll & Research* Brydon Smith; *Asst Dir Finance & Admin* Kersti Krug; *Chief Department of Exhib* Willard Holmes; *Chief Information Servs & Public Relations* Janine Smiter; *Head Publications & Communications* Peter Smith; *Cur Canadian Art* Charles Hill; *Cur Drawings* Mimi Cazort; *Cur Prints* Douglas Druick; *Research Cur Canadian Art* Jean-Rene Ostiguy; *Cur European Art* Myron Laskin Jr; *Actg Head Restoration & Conservation Lab* Gregor Grant; *Registrar* Andre Fronton; *Asst Cur Contemporary Art* Jessica Bradley; *Asst Cur Contemporary Art* Diana Nemiroff
Open Tues - Sat 10 AM - 5 PM, Thur until 9 PM, Sun & holidays 10 AM - 5 PM, cl Christmas Day, Mon Oct - April. No admis fee. Founded 1880 under the patronage of the Governor-General, the Marquess of Lorne, and his wife the Princess Louise; first incorporated 1913 and charged with the development and care of the National Collections and the promotion of art in Canada. Since 1968, the National Gallery has been part of the National Museums of Canada, reporting to a Board of Trustees estab for the Corporation. The Gallery is housed (since 1960) in the Lorne Building with 8 floors devoted to exhibition space, auditorium, workshops, offices, laboratories and cafeteria. Average Annual Attendance: 350,000
Purchases: $1,500,000
Collections: 23,000 Canadian decorative arts, silver, painting and sculpture from 17th - 20th century; contemporary American art; diploma works of the Royal Canadian Academy of the Arts; European decorative arts, painting and sculpture from 14th - 20th Century; Far Eastern art; photography; prints and drawings of the five principal art schools; American painting and sculpture, including Calder (Jacaranda), Newman (the Way I); Canadian works by Brymner, Carr-Harris, Max Dean, Edson, FitzGerald, Fraser, Goodwin, Jacobi, Bill Jones, Lyman, Magor, Massey, Peel, D and R Rabinowitch, Snow, A Y Jackson, Homer Watson, John Hammond, George Reid, Louis-Philippe Hebert, Claude Tousignant, Charles Gagnon, William Ronald, Michael Snow, Robin Collyer, Joe Fafard, Betty Goodwin, Ulysse Comtois, Louise Gadbois, Dennis Burton, William von Mott Berczy, Paul-Emile Borduas, Daniel Gowler, Lucius O'Brien, Joyce Weiland, Adolph Vogt, Cornelius Krieghoff, J W Beatty, Otto Jacobi, Emanuel Hahn, Elizabeth Wyn Wood, John Lyman, Maurice Cullen, Henry Sandham, Charles Comfort, Paterson Ewen, David Bolduc, David Craven, Roland Poulin; Shirley Wutasalo, Paraskeva Clark, Graham Coughtry, Jack Humphrey, Greg Curnoe, J W G MacDonald, Carl Schaefer, Jean-Baptiste Cote, William Sawyer, Denis Juneau, Pierre Boogaerts; European painting and sculpture including Jan Both, Annibale Caracci, Courbet, A Cuyp, Philippe de Champaigne, Jean-Germain Drouais, Baron Gros, Klee Jean-Francois Millet, Murillo, Preti, Theodore Rousseau, Vernet, Carriera, James Ensor, Giovannit Battista, Foggini, Braque, Salvator Rosa, Bernardo Cavallino; prints and drawings by Cezanne, Degas, Fragonard, M Gandolfi, Kandinsky, Le Prince, A Milani, Pissaro, Rembrandt, Redon, Paul Klee, Edouard Manet, Honore Daumier, Henri Fantin-Latour, Edvard Munch, Mauro Gandoffi, Annibule Carracci, Jean-Baptiste Oudry, Salvador Dali, Camille Pissarro, Edgar Degas, J B C Corot, Mary Cassatt, Paul Signac Baron Gros (Bacchus and Ariadne), Klee (Angst), Jean-Francois Millet (The Pig Slaughter), Murillo (Portrait of a Vacalier), Preti (The Feast of Absalom), Theodore Rousseau (The Old Park at St Cloud); prints and drawings by Cezanne, Degas, Fragonard, M Gandolfi, Kandinsky, Le Prince, A Milani, Pissaro, Rembrandt, Redon
Exhibitions: Exhibitions from abroad, permanent collections, private and public sources are organized and circulated in Canada and abroad
Publications: Annual Bulletin (incorporating Annual Review, with current acquisition lists); Canadian Artists; catalogues of permanent collections (beginning Nov 1980); Documents in the History of Canadian Art; exhibition-related books and catalogues; Masterpieces in the National Gallery of Canada; National Gallery of Canada Journal
Activities: Lectures; films; gallery talks; guided tours at Gallery and lect tours throughout Canada; rents transparencies and colour separations and sells slides, catalogues and black and white prints, through sub-section Reproduction Rights and Sales; originate traveling exhibitions; specialized art bookstore with reproductions, postcards, etc

L **Library,*** K1A 0M8. Tel 613-995-6245. *Chief Librn* J Hunter; *Reference Librn* M Vilcins; *Art Documentalist* S Hasbury
Open Tues - Fri 10 AM - 6 PM. Estab 1918 to support the research and information requirements of gallery personnel; to make its collections of resource materials in the fine arts available to Canadian libraries and scholars; to serve as a source of information about Canadian art and art activities in Canada
Library Holdings: Vols 79,000; Per subs 980; Micro — Fiche, reels; Other — Clipping files, exhibition catalogs, pamphlets
Special Subjects: Canadian art, post-medieval Western art with special emphasis on drawings, painting, prints, photography and sculpture
Collections: Art Documentation; Canadiana
Publications: Artists in Canada; Files in National Gallery Library; Files of Fiche: Canadian Art Microdocuments
Activities: Library tours

M **NATIONAL MUSEUM OF MAN,** Victoria Memorial Museum Bldg, Metcalfe and McLeod Sts, K1A 0M8. *Dir* Dr George MacDonald; *Asst Dir Pub Prog* Frank Corcoran; *Asst Dir Operations* M Carroll; *Chief Archaeological Survey of Canada* Dr J V Wright; *Chief Canadian Ethnology Service* A McFadyen Clark; *Chief Canadian Centre for Folk Culture Studies* Dr Paul Carpentier; *Chief History Division* Dr F Thorpe; *Chief Cur Canadian War Museum* L Murray; *Chief Education & Cultural Affairs Div* Lorna Kee; *Chief Nat Prog Div* Sylvie Morel; *Senior Scientist Canadian Centre for Folk Culture Studies* Dr Carmen Roy; *Asst Dir Finance & Admin* C Laing
Victoria Memorial Museum Building open Tues - Sun 10 AM - 6 PM, summer Sun - Sat 10 AM - 6 PM. Canadian War Museum open Sun - Sat 9 AM - 5 PM. No admis fee. Estab 1968 as one of four components of the National Museums of Canada; to trace the development of Man from prehistoric times to the present, particularly Canadian development. The Victoria Memorial Museum Building, located at Metcalfe and McLeod Streets, houses on the first floor the development of early man and the technology of Canada's indigenous peoples and archaeological method of recovering such past; on the second floor an overview of the Plains Indians and Iroquois; on the third floor an overview of contemporary and traditional native art; on the fourth floor Canadian history to present and tracing the contribution made by ethnic peoples in Canada. The Canadian War Museum, located at 330 Sussex Drive, displays historical material relating to the military history of Canada and of other countries. Average Annual Attendance: Victoria Memorial Museum Building 450,000; Canadian War Museum 390,000
Collections: Archaeological Collection; Ethnological Collection; Folk Culture Collections; Historical Collection; Military History Collection
Publications: Several series of publications and periodicals, 500 titles published in-house in last six years
Activities: Classes for adults and children; dramatic programs; docent training; lect open to the public, several vis lectr per year; extension department; original artifacts and individual artifacts lent to museums and other institutions meeting specifications regarding security, environment, etc; originate traveling exhibitions; museum shop sells books, reproductions, magazines, prints

M NATIONAL MUSEUMS OF CANADA, Esplanade Laurier, 300 Laurier W, K1A 0M8. Tel 613-995-9832. *Secy General* Leo Dorais; *Dir, National Museum of Man* George F MacDonald
The beginnings of the National Gallery of Canada are associated with the founding of the Royal Canadian Academy of Arts in 1880. Until 1907 the National Gallery was under the direct control of a minister of the Crown but in that year, an Advisory Arts Council, consisting of three persons outside government, was appointed to administer grants to the National Gallery. In 1913 the National Gallery was incorporated by Act of Parliament and placed under the administration of a board of trustees appointed by the Governor General in Council. Since 1960, the National Gallery has occupied the Lorne Building in Ottawa. The National Museum of Man and the National Museum of Natural Sciences evolved from the collections of the Geological Survey of Canada in the nineteenth century. The collections were transferred to the newly built Victoria Memorial Museum Building in 1911. The National Museum of Canada was formally established in 1927. In 1957 this museum was divided into two branches: Human History and Natural History, with an additional branch, Science and Technology, being established in 1966.
In April 1968 a new act amalgamated these three branches, together with the National Gallery of Canada, under the aegis of one corporation known as the National Museums of Canada. The purposes of the Corporation are to demonstrate the products of nature and the works of man, with special but not exclusive reference to Canada, so as to promote interest therein throughout Canada and to disseminate knowledge therof. The individual museums of the National Museums of Canada are located in Ottawa. Average Annual Attendance: Exceeds two and one-half million for all museums
Publications: Over 100 publications in archaeology, general art, botany, Canadian art, children and young adults, folk culture, history, military history, native peoples, photography, song books and zoology
Activities: Conducted tours; talks and lectures; film and theatre presentations; boutiques sell prints, books, bulletins, recordings, models, artifacts, postcards and slides
L Library, 2086 Walkley Rd, K1A 0M8. *Dir, Library Servs* Valerie Monkhouse
Open Mon - Fri 8:30 AM - 4:30 PM. Estab 1845 to serve the staff of the Corporation of the National Museums of Canada & other workers in subject areas related to the disciplines of the Museums; other users may use collection for reference purposes or borrow through interlibrary loan
Library Holdings: Vols 200,000; Per subs 2500; Rare Book Collection; Micro — Cards, fiche, prints, reels; AV — A-tapes, cassettes, fs, lantern slides, slides; Other — Clipping files, manuscripts, memorabilia, pamphlets, photographs
Special Subjects: Archaeology, Ethnology, Folk Art, Conservation of art objects & restoration, Indian & Inuit art
Publications: Monthly list of accessions to the library
M National Gallery of Canada, Lorne Building, Elgin & Slater Sts, K1A 0M8. Tel 613-992-4636. *Dir* Joseph Martin
M National Museum of Man, Metcalfe & McLeod Sts, K1A 0M8. Tel 613-992-3497. *Dir* Dr W E Taylor Jr
M Canadian War Museum, 330 Sussex Dr, K1A 0M8. Tel 613-992-2774. *Cur* L F Murray
M National Museum of Natural Sciences, Metcalfe and McLeod Sts, K1A 0M8. Tel 613-996-3102. *Dir* Dr Alan R Emery
Open Sept - May Tues - Sun 10 AM - 5 PM, May - Sept Tues - Sun 10 AM - 5 PM, cl Mon, Christmas. No admis fee. Estab 1842 to disseminate knowledge about the natural sciences, with particular but not exclusive reference to Canada. Average Annual Attendance: 500,000
M National Museum of Science and Technology, 1867 Saint Laurent Blvd, K1A 0M8. Tel 613-998-4566. *Dir* William McGowan
Open Mon - Fri 9 AM - 9 PM
M National Aeronautical Collection, Rockcliffe Air Force Base, K1A 0M8. Tel 613-993-2010

L OTTAWA PUBLIC LIBRARY, Fine Arts Dept, 120 Metcalfe St, K1P 5M2. Tel 613-236-0301. *Dir* Gilles Frappier; *Asst Dir* Jean de Temple; *Admin Officer* Wilfred Blain
Open Mon - Thurs 10 AM - 9 PM, Fri 10 AM - 6 PM, Sat 9:30 AM - 5 PM, Sun 1 - 5 PM (summers). Estab 1906 to serve the community as a centre for general & reliable information; to select, preserve & administer books & related materials in organized collections; to provide opportunity for citizens of all ages to educate themselves continuously
Library Holdings: Micro — Fiche, reels; AV — Cassettes, fs; Other — Clipping files, pamphlets
Exhibitions: Monthly exhibits highlighting local artists, craftsmen, photographers and collectors
Activities: Lect open to public; library tours

PUBLIC ARCHIVES OF CANADA
L Picture Division, 395 Wellington St, K1A 0N3. Tel 613-995-1300, 996-6011. *Dominion Archivist* Dr W I Smith; *Collections Mgr* Jim Burant; *Special Collections* Auguste Vachon; *Documentary Art* Douglas Schoenherr; *Art Inventory Section* Raymond Vezina
Open daily 9 AM - 4:45 PM. Estab 1905 to acquire and preserve significant Canadian archival material in the area of visual non-photographic media, paintings, watercolours, drawings, prints, medals, heraldry, costume designs and posters, relating to all aspects of Canadian life and to the development of the country, and to provide suitable research services and facilities to make this documentation available to the public by means of exhibitions, publications and public catalogue
Income: Financed by federal appropriation
Purchases: $50,000
Library Holdings: Vols 1000
Collections: †2900 paintings; †18,000 watercolours & drawings; †80,000 prints; †13,000 posters; †10,000 medals; †7000 heraldic design & seals
Exhibitions: (1982) Printmaking in Canada; Daily Smile; Friendly Spies on the Northern Tour, 1815-1837; The Garrison Years: London, Canada West 1793-1853; 1931 Painters of Canada Series; Exhibition of Christmas Cards
Publications: Catalog of publications available on request

M Laurier House, 335 Laurier Ave E, K1N 6R4. Tel 613-992-8142. *Cur* Valerie Proctor; *Education Officer* Robert Ferris
Open Oct - Mar Tues - Sat 10 AM - 5 PM, Sun 2 - 5 PM, Apr - Sept Tues - Sat 9 AM - 5 PM, Sun 2 - 5 PM. No admis fee. Estab 1951. This is a historic house and former residence of two Prime Ministers, Sir Wilfrid Laurier and the Rt Honorable William Lyon Mackenzie King, and contains furniture and memorabilia belonging to a third Prime Minister, Lester Pearson. The house is primarily furnished in the style of its last occupant, the Rt Honorable William Lyon Mackenzie King, with space given to the Laurier Collection. In 1974 the Lester Pearson study was installed. Average Annual Attendance: 25,000
Income: Financed by endowment and federal government
Exhibitions: A Child's Best Friend (a doll display); Our Shared Responsibility (a photographic exhibit on the care and handling of artifacts)
Activities: Classes for children; Annual Christmas programme for children; Annual International Museums Day Event

ROYAL ARCHITECTURAL INSTITUTE OF CANADA
For further information, see National Organizations in Canada

OWEN SOUND

M TOM THOMSON MEMORIAL GALLERY AND MUSEUM OF FINE ART,* 840 First Ave W, Box 312, N4K 5P5. Tel 519-376-1932. *Dir* James Logan; *Asst Dir* Catherine R Harrison
Open Sept - June Tues - Thurs, Sat & Sun Noon - 5 PM, Wed & Fri Noon - 5 PM & 7 - 9 PM, July & Aug Mon, Tues, Thur - Sun Noon - 5 PM, Wed & Fri Noon - 5 PM & 7 - 9 PM. Admis $.50, students, sr citizens and members free. Estab 1967 to collect and display paintings by Tom Thomson, a native son of Canadas foremost landscape artist; to educate the public. Two galleries: paintings by Tom Thomson on permanent display; changing exhibitions in both galleries. Average Annual Attendance: 10,000. Mem: 395; dues benefactor $1000, life $100, family $15, individual $10
Income: Financed by city appropriation and provincial grants
Collections: Tom Thomson; 19th Century artists; †contemporary Canadian artists; Group of Seven
Publications: Bulletin, ten per year
Activities: Classes for children; docent training; lect open to public; gallery talks; tours; films; competitions; museum shop sells books, reproductions, prints and postcards
L Library,* 840 First Ave W, Box 312, N4K 5P5
Open for reference
Library Holdings: Vols 500; Per subs 300; Other — Exhibition catalogs
Collections: Files on Tom Thomson

PETERBOROUGH

M ART GALLERY OF PETERBOROUGH, 2 Crescent St, K9J 2G1. Tel 705-743-9179. *Board Pres* Margaret L Heideman; *VPres* Audrey Armstrong; *Secy* Lois Davis; *Dir* Illi-Maria Tamplin; *Education Officer* Jann Bailey; *Secy* Sally Wright
Open Tues - Sun 1 - 5 PM, Thurs 1 - 9 PM. No admis fee. Estab 1973. Gallery situated along a lake and in a park; new extension added and completed June 1979. Average Annual Attendance: 18,600. Mem: 1000; dues sustaining $25, family $18, individual $15, sr citizens $12, student $8; annual meeting June
Income: $140,292 (financed by membership, fund raising, grant, provincial grants, federal grants)
Collections: European and Canadian Works of Art
Publications: Catalogues on some exhibitions; Bulletin of Events, monthly; pamphlets on artists in exhibitions
Activities: Classes for adults and children; dramatic programs; docent training; workshops; art program to public schools; lectures open to public, 6 vis lectr per yr; concerts; gallery talks; tours; individual paintings & original objects of art lent to other galleries; lending collection contains 187 original art works; originate traveling exhibitions; sales shop sells books, magazines, original art & reproductions

SAINT CATHARINES

O RODMAN HALL ARTS CENTRE, 109 St Paul Crescent, L2S 1M3. Tel 416-684-2925. *Pres* R Prince; *VPres* M Zuberec; *Secy* A Pattemore; *Dir* A Peter Harris; *Executive Secy* Susan Dickinson; *Cur of Education* Debra Attenborough; *Chief Custodian* Charles Verworn
Open Tues, Thurs, Fri 9 AM - 5 PM, Wed 9 AM - 5 PM & 7 - 10 PM, Sat & Sun 1 - 5 PM, cl Mon. No admis fee. Estab 1960, art gallery, cultural centre and visual arts exhibitions. Four galleries in an 1853, 1960 and 1975 addition. 1975 - A1 - National Museums of Canada. Average Annual Attendance: 30,000. Mem: 850; dues $50, $25, $15, & $5; annual meeting in Sept
Income: Financed by membership, city, state and national appropriation
Collections: American graphics & drawings; †Canadian drawings, †paintings, †sculpture & †watercolours; international graphics & sculpture
Exhibitions: (1983-84) Rodman Hall Permanent Collection; The Hague - Collecting in Canada at the Turn of the Century; The St Catharines Art Association Annual Jury Show; Rodman Hall Autumn Happening - Women's Committee; Douglas Boutilier - One Man Show; 20th century drawings from the collection of Mr Tom LaPierre; Ontario at Work, photographs; Winnipeg West (1945-1970); Lorne Toews, one man exhibition; Canadian Society of Painters in Water Color; Alice Crawley, constructions; Sally Glanville, prints; Max Klinger; Cliches Verre; A Montreal Collector; Karoly Veress, sculpture; Anne-Marie Beneteau, one woman show; Rodman Hall 1984 Ontario Jury Show
Publications: Catalogue - Lord and Lady Head Watercolours; monthly calendar; Rodman Hall Arts Center (1960-1981)
Activities: Classes for adults and children; dramatic programs; docent training; lectures open to public, 5 vis lectr per year; concerts; gallery talks; tours; jury show competitions; jury and public awards given for best three works in exhibition; exten dept serves city of St Catharines; individual paintings and original objects of art lent to schools and gallery at City Hall; lending collection contains 10 original art works and 200 original prints; book traveling exhibitions, 16 per year; originate traveling exhibitions; sales shop sells books, crafts, magazines, paper things, prints, reproductions and weaving

L **Library,** 109 St Paul Crescent, Saint Catharines, L2S 1M3
Open Tues - Fri 9 AM - 5 PM. Estab 1960. Reference library
Library Holdings: Vols 1000; Per subs 300; Micro — Prints; AV — Lantern
slides, slides; Other — Clipping files, exhibition catalogs, memorabilia, pamphlets,
photographs, reproductions

SARNIA

L **SARNIA PUBLIC LIBRARY,** Art Gallery, 124 Christina St S, N7T 2M6. Tel
519-337-3291; Telex 064-76116. *Dir* Howard Ford; *Chmn* Mrs G Young; *Cur*
Megan Bice; *Asst Cur Education* Diana Lavelle
Open Mon - Fri 9 AM - 9 PM, Sat 9 AM - 5:30 PM, Sun Oct - May 2 - 5 PM.
No admis fee. Estab 1961, a collection of Canadian paintings instituted in 1919
and administered by the Women's Conservation Art Association of Sarnia. The
Collection was turned over to the Sarnia Library Board in 1956 and additions are
being made from time to time. Average Annual Attendance: 41,000
Collections: Canadian Paintings; Eskimo Carvings; a Collection of Old
Photographs of Sarnia and Lambton County; sculpture
Exhibitions: Twelve to fifteen shows a year, either traveling from other galleries
or initiated by the Sarnia Art Gallery
Publications: Exhibition catalogues
Activities: Classes for adults and children; lectures open to the public, 5 - 10;
gallery talks; tours; competitions; individual paintings & original objects of art
lent; book traveling exhibitions, 6 - 8 per yr; originate traveling exhibitions

SIMCOE

M **EVA BROOK DONLY MUSEUM,** 109 Norfolk St S, N3Y 2W3. Tel 519-426-
1583. *Managing Dir* Kenneth S McArthur; *Cur* William Yeager
Open Sept - May Wed - Sun 1 - 5 PM, May - Sept Mon - Fri 10 AM - 5 PM,
Sat & Sun 1 - 5 PM. Admis tours $5 per 35, $.10 each additional person, $3 per
year mem, children free with adult, adult $.50, student $.25, children under 12
free. Estab 1946 to display and aid research in the history of Norfolk County.
Average Annual Attendance: 7000. Mem: 600; dues $10; annual meeting Jan
Income: Financed by endowment, membership, city and provincial appropriation
Collections: Large Collection of important Early Documents and Newspapers,
370 Paintings of Historic Norfolk by W E Cantelon; Display of Artifacts of the
19th Century Norfolk County; Historical Material
Exhibitions: Concerned mainly with focusing new light on some aspects of the
permanent collection
Activities: Lectures open to the public, 15 vis lectrs per yr; tours; book traveling
exhibitions, 3 per yr; museum shop sells books, crafts & candy
L **Library,** 109 Norfolk St S, N3Y 2W3. Tel 519-426-1583
Reference and a photograph collection for display
Library Holdings: Vols 2000; Per subs 2; Micro — Fiche, reels; AV — Cassettes,
slides; Other — Clipping files, manuscripts, memorabilia, original art works,
photographs, prints

O **LYNNWOOD ARTS CENTRE,** 21 Lynnwood Ave, PO Box 67, N3Y 4Y1. Tel
519-428-0540. *Chmn* Hugh Brennian; *First Vice Chmn* Dave Muir; *Dir* Ellen
McIntosh; *Office Mgr* Julia Loncke; *Education Coordr* Beverly Goodhue
Open Tues - Fri 9 AM - 5 PM, Sat & Sun 1 - 5 PM. No admis fee. Estab 1973
to provide a focal point for the visual arts in the community. Built in 1851 -
Greek Revival Architecture; orange brick with ionic columns; and is a National
Historic Site. Average Annual Attendance: 20,000. Mem: 800, student & sr
citizen $5; dues family $15, individual $10; annual meeting Jan
Income: $100,000 (financed by membership, patrons - private and commerical,
Ministry of Culture and Recreation, Ontario Arts Council, Town of Simcoe,
Regional Municipality of Haldimand-Norfolk)
Collections: †Contemporary Canadian Art; Early Canadian Quilts and Mats
Exhibitions: (1983) Quilts & Decoys #3; The Best of Graphex; Prints of the
Great Kahuki; Actors, Original Watercolors by Elizabeth Simcoe; New
Watercolour Paintings of Birds; John Nold, paintings; Bennett Collection; From
Our Hands; Paul Fournier, recent works; Sigrid Lochner, 5 years; Cats in Art
Publications: Bi-monthly Newsletter
Activities: Classes for adults and children; docent training; lect open to public, 15
lectr per year; concerts; gallery talks; tours; seminars; juried art exhibitions (every
two years) with purchase awards; individual paintings and original objects of art
lent to members; book traveling exhibitions; originate traveling exhibitions;
museum shop sells books, hand-crafted items, original art, prints and
reproductions

STRATFORD

M **STRATFORD ART ASSOCIATION,** Gallery Stratford, 54 Romeo St N, N5A
4S9. Tel 519-271-5271. *Dir* Paul Bennett; *Pres Bd Trustees* Dr David Leaney
Open Sept - May Sun, Tues - Fri 1 - 5 PM, Sat 10 AM - 5 PM; Summer Hours
June - Sept Tues - Sun 10 AM - 8 PM, Mon 10 AM - 5 PM; business hours
Weekdays 9:30 AM - 5 PM. Admis $2, students $1, children under 12 free.
Estab 1967 as a non-profit permanent establishment open to the public and
administered in the public interest for the purpose of studying, interpreting,
assembling and exhibiting to the public. Average Annual Attendance: 50,000.
Mem: 800; annual meeting March
Income: $200,000 (financed by membership, city appropriation, provincial and
federal grants)
Collections: Works of art on paper
Exhibitions: Changing exhibits, monthly geared to create interest for visitors to
Stratford Shakespearean Festival; during winter months geared to local
municipality
Publications: Catalogs; calendar of events
Activities: Classes for adults and children; docent training; lectures open to the
public, 4 visiting lecturers each year; concerts; gallery talks; tours; competitions;
extension department serving art in the schools; traveling exhibitions organized
and circulated; sales shop sells books, prints and crafts

SUDBURY

LAURENTIAN UNIVERSITY

M **Museum and Arts Centre,** c/o Department Cultural Affairs, Laurentian
University, P3E 2C6. Tel 705-675-1151, Ext 400, 401. *Dir* Pamela Krueger
Open Tues - Sun Noon - 5 PM, cl Mon, mornings by appointment. No admis
fee. Estab 1968 to present a continuous program of exhibitions, concerts and
events for the people of Sudbury and the district. Gallery has two floors of space:
124 running ft in one and 131 running ft in the second gallery and 68.5 running
feet in third gallery. Average Annual Attendance: 23,000. Mem: 400; dues family
$13, single $8; annual meeting June
Income: Financed by endowment, membership, city and provincial appropriation,
government and local organizations
Collections: Canadian collection dating from the late 1800's & early 1900's to
contemporary. The Group of Seven, Eskimo sculptures & prints as well as works
of historical Canadian artists comprise the collection; †Indian works from
Northern Ontario
Exhibitions: (1982-83) Pop Art; Montreal 1900-1950; Reflections of an Age-19th
Century British Art; Westburne Collection; Michael Couchie; A Y Jackson -
Commemorative Exhibition; Jonathan King; Don Barton & John Haynes; White
on White; Judith Huntress-Allsopp; Mary Green; Jane Agnew; Fiction;
permanent collection; Strangers No More, a Sudbury centennial photographic
exhibition; Norart - 5th Annual Juried Exhibition of Northern Ontario Artists;
Eskimo Prints; Thomas Mower Martin; Prints of the Great Kabuki Actors;
Visions & Victories: Canadian Women Artists - 1914-1945; Ivan Wheale - Recent
Work; Italian Prints; The Hague School - Collecting in Canada at the Turn of the
Century; Doug Donley Roseisle, Manitoba - Photographs by Cal Bailey;
Ukrainian Exhibition; White Water on the Road to Nickel City; (1979) Lynn
Donoghue (paintings and drawings); Norart (first annual exhibition open to all
artists living and working in Northern Ontario); Sculpture in Canada; Sculpture
Ybes Trudeau; 10th Annual Secondary School Art Exhibition
Publications: Communique, every six weeks
Activities: Docent training; lect open to public, 10 visiting lectr per year;
concerts; gallery talks; tours; lending collection contains 40 framed reproductions,
500 original art works and 4000 slides; museum shop sells magazines, catalogues,
postcards, posters and prints
L **Art Center Library,** Department Cultural Affairs, Laurentian University, P3E
2C6. Tel 705-675-1151, Ext 400
Open winter daily 9 AM - 4:30 PM, summer daily 8:30 AM - 4 PM. Estab 1977
for reference
Library Holdings: Vols 3900; Per subs 78; Micro — Cards; AV — Cassettes,
lantern slides, slides 4000, v-tapes; Other — Clipping files, exhibition catalogs,
framed reproductions, pamphlets, photographs

TORONTO

M **ART GALLERY OF ONTARIO,** 317 Dundas St W, M5T 1G4. Tel 416-977-
0414. *Dir* W J Withrow; *Chief Cur* Dr Roald Nasgaard; *Chief of Admin* Norman
Walford; *Controller* Timothy Hopcraft; *Head Education Services* James
Williamson; *Mgr Marketing Public Relations* Elizabeth Addison; *Mgr
Development* Marie DunSeith
Open Tues - Sun 11 AM - 5:30 PM, Wed & Thurs evening until 9 PM, cl Mon.
Admis adults $3.50, students $1.50, sr citizens $1.50 & free on Thurs, members
& accompanied children under 12 free, Thurs evenings free. Estab 1900 to
cultivate and advance the cause of the visual arts in Ontario; to conduct
programmes of education in the origin, development, appreciation and techniques
of the visual arts; to collect and exhibit works of art and displays and to maintain
and operate a gallery and related facilities as required for this purpose; to
stimulate the interest of the public in matters undertaken by the Gallery. Average
Annual Attendance: 400,000. Mem: 30,000; dues supporting $100, family $40,
individual $30; annual meeting June
Income: Financed by membership, provincial, city and federal appropriations and
earned income
Purchases: $927,648
Collections: American and European Art (16th Century to present); Canadian
Historical and Contemporary Art; Henry Moore Sculpture Centre
Exhibitions: Artists with Their Work; Oscar Cahen Retrospective; The Canada
Packers Collection: Selected Oil Paintings & Works on Paper; The Cliches-Verre
of the Barbizon School; Alex Colville: A Retrospective; Contact 1983-84:
Christopher Broadhurst, Paintings, Simon Harwood, Still Life in Relief, Robert
Rauschenberg, Dante's Inferno, Rideau, Spirits & Transformation; Contemporary
International Prints: Selections from the Gift of Mr & Mrs Neville Burston;
Daumier & La Caricature; Early Jack Bush; Eden Revisited: Graphic Works by
German Romantic Artists; Murray Favro: A Retrospective Exhibition; An
Intimate Glimpse of van Gogh at Nuenen (as seen in a recently acquired
drawing); Grasp Tight the Old Ways: Selections from the Klamer Family
Collection of Inuit Art; The Hague School: Collecting in Canada at the Turn of
the Century; Italian Prints 1500-1800; John Baptist Jackson: The Venetian Set;
Max Klinger: Graphic Work; The Later Work of Lawren Harris; The Later Work
of Arthur Lismer; Henry Moore from the Collection of the Art Gallery of
Ontario: Sculpture, Drawings & Prints; Norval Morrisseau & the Emergence of
the Image Makers; The 1940's: A Decade of Painting & Drawing in Ontario;
William Norman's Staff & Studio; Painting in Toronto, 1984; Pictures for the
Parlour: The English Reproductive Print 1775-1900; Recollections: Ten Women
in Photography; Toronto Painting of the 1960's; W J Wood: Paintings &
Graphics
Publications: The Gallery, ten times per year; annual report; exhibition catalogs
Activities: Classes for adults & children; docent training; lectures open to public;
concerts; gallery talks; tours; exten dept organizes traveling exhibitions, circulated
throughout the Province, Canada and United States; individual paintings and
original objects of art loaned; originate traveling exhibitions; sales shop sells
books, magazines, reproductions, prints, slides and jewelry; art rental shop for
members to rent original works of art

L **Edward P Taylor Reference Library,** 317 Dundas St W, M5T 1G4. Tel 416-977-0414, Ext 339. *Chief Librn* Karen McKenzie; *Deputy Librn* Larry Pfaff; *Catalogue Librn* Carol Lowrey; *Library Technician* Gloria Marsh; *Documentalist* Randall Speller
Open Tues - Fri 11 AM - 4:45 PM. Estab 1933 to collect printed material for the documentation and interpretation of the works of art in the Gallery's collection; to provide research and informational support for the Gallery's programmes and activities; to document the art and artists of Ontario, Toronto, and Canada
Library Holdings: Vols 40,000; Per subs 350; original documents; Micro — Fiche, reels; Other — Clipping files, exhibition catalogs, manuscripts, pamphlets, photographs, reproductions
Special Subjects: Canadian, American and European Art from the Renaissance to the present, concentrating mainly on drawing, engraving, painting and sculpture
Collections: †Canadian Illustrated Books; Alan Garrow Collection of British Illustrated Books and Wood Engravings of the 1860's Canadian Book-Plates; †International Guide Books; Robert D McIntosh Collection of Books on Sepulchral Monuments
Publications: Selected Acquisitions List, quarterly

L **Edward P Taylor Audio-Visual Centre,*** 317 Dundas St W, M5T 1G4. Tel 416-977-0414, Ext 258. *Head* Catherine Jonasson
Media collection contains both circulating and archive material
Library Holdings: 48 media kits circulating coll; 315 reel-to-reel tapes archive coll; Micro — Reels 250; AV — A-tapes 247, cassettes 160, fs 3, lantern slides 2000, motion pictures 176, rec 5, slides 50,000, v-tapes 60

O **ART METROPOLE,** 217 Richmond St W, M5V 1W2. Tel 416-977-1685. *Dir* John Goodwin; *Head Publications* A A Bronson; *Video Cur* Christina Ritchie; *Cur* Tim Guest; *Bookstore Mgr* Ann McFarland; *Bookstore Mgr* David Buchan; *Video Distribution Mgr* Ara Rose Parker; *Permanent Collection* Paul Housego
Open Tues - Sat 1 - 6 PM. Estab 1974 to show & promote artist's video, bookworks & performances. Average Annual Attendance: 4000
Special Subjects: Books by artists, performance by artists, video by artists
Collections: Ongoing collection of Books by Artists
Exhibitions: Books by Artists
Publications: Catalog of available stock, semi-annually
Activities: Lect; lending collection contains 250 video-tape titles by 35 artists and research archive of information on contemporary art; originate traveling exhibitions; sales shop sells books, magazine and original art

L **Library,*** 217 Richmond St W, M5V 1W2. *Archivist* Tim Guest
Open Tues - Sat Noon - 6 PM. Estab 1974 to document work by artist internationally working in non-conventional and multiple media. For reference only
Library Holdings: AV — A-tapes, motion pictures, rec, v-tapes; Other — Exhibition catalogs, manuscripts, memorabilia, original art works, pamphlets, photographs, prints
Collections: Books, video and performances by artists

O **ARTS AND LETTERS CLUB OF TORONTO,*** 14 Elm St, M5G 1G7. Tel 416-597-0223. *Pres* Paul Fleck; *Secy* William Osler
Estab 1908. Mem: 450; annual meeting May
Collections: Club Collection - art by members and others; Heritage Collection art by members now deceased

L **Library,*** 14 Elm St, M5G 1G7
Open to club members and researchers for reference
Library Holdings: Vols 2000
Special Subjects: Architecture, Sculpture, Theatre Arts, Literature, Music, Paintings

ASSOCIATION OF CANADIAN INDUSTRIAL DESIGNERS, ONTARIO
For further information, see National and Regional Organizations

O **CANADIAN ARTISTS' REPRESENTATION,** Le Front Des Artistes Canadiens,* 67 Mowat Ave Rm 345, M6K 3E3. Tel 416-534-8218. *Dir* E Jane Condon; *Secy* Elizabeth Sharpe
Canadian Artists' Representation-Les Front des Artistes Canadiens is an association of professional artists whose mandate is the improvement of the financial and professional status of all Canadian artists. CARFAC is a national organization run by artists for artist, membership works on three levels: local, provincial and national. Average Annual Attendance: 1000 (open to practicing professional artists); dues $12 - $25; annual meeting May. Mem: Dues $20-$40; annual meeting May
Income: Financed by endowment and membership
Publications: CARFAC News, 3 issues per year; Canadian Visual Artist; Taxation Information for Canadian Visual Arts
Activities: Lobby Group, educational resource

CANADIAN SOCIETY OF PAINTERS IN WATERCOLOUR
For further information, see National and Regional Organizations

O **LYCEUM CLUB AND WOMEN'S ART ASSOCIATION OF CANADA,*** 23 Prince Arthur Ave, M5R 1B2. Tel 416-922-2060. *Pres* Mrs G H Rawson; *Recording Secy* Mrs H Macknight
Open Mon - Fri 8:30 AM - 2:30 PM, cl Sat & Sun. Estab 1885, branches in Ontario in Hamilton, Owen Sound, St Thomas and Peterborough. Mem: 250; annual meeting April
Activities: Special exhibitions; drawing, painting; study groups; awards Founder's memorial scholarships to art students annually; scholarships given to Ontario College of Art, Royal Conservatory of Music, National Ballet

L **Library,*** 12 Prince Arthur Ave, M5R 1B2
Library Holdings: Vols 500
Special Subjects: Extensive Canadiana

METROPOLITAN TORONTO LIBRARY BOARD
L **Fine Art Dept,*** 789 Yonge St, M4W 2G8. Tel 416-928-5214. *Library Bd Dir* Donald F Meadows; *Asst Dir Reference Division* Margery Allen
Open Mon - Fri 9 AM - 9 PM, Sat 9 AM - 5 PM, Sun Oct 15 - April 30 1:30 - 5 PM. Estab 1959 for public reference
Income: Financed by city appropriation
Library Holdings: Vols 47,458; Per subs 390; Micro — Fiche, reels; Other — Clipping files, exhibition catalogs
Special Subjects: Costume Design & Construction, Decorative Arts, Canadian fine arts, printing and printing design
Collections: Postcards, scenic and †greeting; †printed †ephemera; private presses with emphasis on Canadian; 676,500 picture clippings

L **Canadian History Dept,** 789 Yonge St, M4W 2G8. Tel 416-928-5275; Telex 06-22232. *Head Canadian History Department* David B Kotin
Open Mon - Fri 9 AM - 9 PM, Sat 9 AM - 5 PM, Sun Oct 15 - April 30 1:30 - 5 PM. Estab 1960 to house rare Canadiana and to support Canadian historical research
Library Holdings: Other — Original art works, photographs, prints
Collections: †60,000 paintings, prints and photographs

O **ONTARIO ASSOCIATION OF ART GALLERIES,** 38 Charles St E, M4Y 1T1. Tel 416-920-8378. *Pres* Brad Blain; *VPres* Ted Pietrezack; *Executive Dir* Rory O'Donal
Open 9 AM - 5 PM. Estab 1968 to encourage cooperation among member galleries and museums; to encourage cooperation between Ontario Asn of Art Galleries and the Arts Council and all similar agencies involved in the cause of the visual arts; to assist the development of visual arts centres in the Province of Ontario; to promote high standards of excellence and uniform methods in the care and presentation of art; to serve as an advisory body in matters of professional interest in the Province of Ontario. Gallery not maintained. Mem: 83; annual meeting June
Income: Financed by membership, Ontario Arts Council, Ontario Ministry of Citizenship and Culture and National Museums of Canada
Publications: Dateline, bimonthly newsletter
Activities: Training seminars under gallery development and professional development committees; job referral assistance; counseling to professional and galleries

L **Resource Centre,*** 38 Charles St E, M4Y 1T3. *Admin Asst* Charlene Morgan
Open 9 AM - 5 PM. Estab to provide information to estab and growing galleries pertinent to existance. Reference library
Library Holdings: Vols 300; Per subs 10; Other — Exhibition catalogs, framed reproductions, manuscripts, memorabilia, original art works, pamphlets, photographs, prints, reproductions
Special Subjects: Taxation and litagation pertaining to visual arts

M **ONTARIO COLLEGE OF ART,** Gallery 76,* 100 McCaul St, M5T 1W1. Tel 416-366-4977, Ext 62. *Dir* Dr Paul D Fleck
Open Mon - Fri 10 AM - 5 PM, Sat & Sun Noon - 5 PM. Estab 1970 for faculty and student exhibitions and to exhibit outside work to benefit the college. Average Annual Attendance: 15,000
Income: Financed by College
Collections: Small print collection
Publications: Invitations; small scale catalogs
Activities: Dramatic programs; Concerts; competitions; individual paintings and original objects of art lent; traveling exhibitions organized and circulated

L **Library-Audiovisual Centre,*** 100 McCaul St, M5T 1W1. Tel 416-977-5311, Ext 255. *Dir* Ian Carr-Harris
Open Mon - Thurs 9 AM - 9:30 PM, Fri 9 AM - 5 PM. Estab to support the curriculum
Income: Financed through the College
Purchases: $55,800
Library Holdings: Vols 19,535; Per subs 225; VF 43,000; Micro — Fiche, reels; AV — A-tapes 200, cassettes, fs, Kodachromes, lantern slides, motion pictures, rec, slides 43,000, v-tapes 350; Other — Clipping files, exhibition catalogs, pamphlets
Special Subjects: Contemporary art & design

O **ONTARIO CRAFTS COUNCIL,** 346 Dundas St W, M5T 1G5. Tel 416-977-3551. *Pres* Donald Stuart; *Exec Dir* Joan Foster; *Mgr Resource Centre* Ted Rickard
Open Tues - Sat 10 AM - 5 PM, Sun 2 - 5 PM. No admis fee. Estab 1976 to foster crafts & craftsmen in Ontario & is the largest craft organization in Canada. Has over 60 affiliated groups. Maintains an art gallery. Average Annual Attendance: 12,000. Mem: 3100; dues $25; annual meeting June
Income: Financed by membership and provincial appropriation, Guild shop, fund raising & publications
Collections: †Canadian Contemporary Crafts
Exhibitions: Ontario Crafts Regional Juried Exhibition; travelling exhibitions; monthly exhibitions in craft gallery
Publications: Craftnews, 8 times a yr; Craft Organizations in Canada; Ontario Craft, quarterly magazine
Activities: Lectures open to public; gallery talks; competitions with awards; scholarships; exten dept serves Ontario; original objects of art lent to galleries, libraries & alternate exhibition spaces; book traveling exhibitions; originate traveling exhibitions; sales shop sells books, original craft, prints, Innuit art, sculpture & prints

L **Craft Resource Centre,** 346 Dundas St W, M5T 1G5. *Mgr* Ted Rickard; *Information Services Officer* Sandra Dunn
Open Tues - Fri Noon - 5 PM. Estab 1976. A comprehensive, special library devoted exclusively to the field of crafts. It is a partly government-funded non-profit organization & is available as an information service to the general public & Ontario Crafts Council members. Has a registry of craft instructors
Library Holdings: Vols 600; Per subs 160; Portfolios of craftsmen, Slide kits 200, Vertical files; AV — Slides 16,000, v-tapes; Other — Exhibition catalogs, pamphlets, photographs
Special Subjects: Enamels, Glass, Metalwork, Pottery, Fibre, Leather, Wood
Publications: Crafts & Hazards to Health; Directory of Suppliers of Craft Materials; Ontario Crafts Directory; The Photography of Crafts; The Shows List
Activities: Outreach program; slide rental

PRINTING AND DRAWING COUNCIL OF CANADA
For further information, see National and Regional Organizations

PROFESSIONAL ART DEALERS ASSOCIATION OF CANADA
For further information, see National Organizations in Canada

C **ROTHMANS OF PALL MALL CANADA LIMITED,*** 75 Dufflaw Rd, M6A
2W4. Tel 416-449-5525. *Dir Rothmans Art Program* Alan R Hanlon
Open to public. No admis fee. Estab 1967. Collection displayed at head office
Collections: Contemporary Canadian art from last decade
Activities: Awards for Toronto Outdoor Art Exhibition each year; individual
objects of art lent to traveling or special exhibitions; originate traveling
exhibitions to all major public galleries in Canada

ROYAL CANADIAN ACADEMY OF ARTS
For further information, see National and Regional Organizations

M **ROYAL ONTARIO MUSEUM,*** 100 Queen's Park, M5S 2C6. Tel 416-978-
3692. *Chmn Board of Trustees* Sydney M Hermant; *Secy Board of Trustees*
Frank Dunbar; *Dir* Dr James E Cruise; *Assoc Dir* Barbara Stephen; *Asst Dir
Admin & Facilities* C Gordon G Bristowe; *Asst Dir Education & Communication*
R McCartney Samples; *Head, Programmes & Public Relations* David Young
Open June - mid-Aug Wed - Sun 2 - 9 PM, mid-Aug - Labour Day Mon - Sun
10 AM - 9 PM. No admis. Estab 1914 and includes 20 curatorial departments in
the fields of art, archaeology and the natural sciences. Average Annual
Attendance: 900,000. Mem: 7400; dues individual $25
Income: $10,498,134 (financed by federal grants, provincial grants, museum
income, memberships, bequests, grants and donations)
Publications: Numerous academic publications; gallery guides; exhibition
catalogs; publications in print
Activities: Classes for adults and children; throughout the school year, pre-
booked classes receive lessons in the Museum. Unconducted classes can also be
arranged with the Museum at a cost of $.50 per student; lect open to public with
visiting lectr, special lect for members only; concerts; gallery talks; tours;
competitions; extend dept serves Ontario; artmobile; individual paintings and
original objects of art lent to museums and galleries; originate traveling
exhibitions; museum shop sells books, magazines, reproductions, prints and slides
—**Library,*** 100 Queen's Park, M5S 2C6. *Librn* Isabella Guthrie-McNaughton
Estab 1960 for curatorial research
Library Holdings: Vols 80,000; Micro — Fiche
Special Subjects: Decorative Arts, Textiles

M **Canadiana Gallery,** 14 Queen's Park Crescent W, M5S 2C6. Tel 416-978-4179.
Cur Donald B Webster; *Asst Cur* Mrs M Allodi; *Secy* K Smith; *Cur Asst* Mrs H
dePencier; *Cur Asst* J Holmes
Open Mon - Sat 10 AM - 5 PM, Sun 1 - 5 PM. No admis fee. Estab 1951 to
collect, exhibit & publish material on Canadian historical paintings & Canadian
decorative arts. Canadiana Gallery has three galleries: first gallery has six rooms
showing English Colonial, French, Maritime, Ontario & German-Ontario
furniture, also silver, glass, woodenware; second gallery has ceramics, toys,
weathervanes, religious carving, early 19th century Quebec panelled room; third
is a picture gallery for changing exhibitions. Average Annual Attendance: 35,000
Collections: Canadian 18th & 19th century decorative arts - ceramics, coins &
medals books, †furniture, †glass, guns, silver, woodenware; 16th-18th century
†portraits of Canadians & military & administrative people connected with
Canada; 18th & 19th century topographic & historical Canadian views; 19th
century travels
Exhibitions: M Allodi - Printmaking in Canada: The Earliest Views & Portraits;
D B Webster: Canadian Georgian Furniture
Publications: M Allodi Canadian Watercolours & Drawings; The William Eby
Pottery, Congestogo, Ontario, 1855-1970; D B Webster Brantford Pottery
Activities: Classes for children; lectures; gallery talks; exten dept serves Ontario;
original objects of art lent to institutions

L **RYERSON POLYTECHNICAL INSTITUTE LIBRARY,** 50 Gould St, M5B
1E8. Tel 416-595-5398. *Dean Applied Arts* P Nowack; *Dean Art* N Siller; *Dir
Learning Resources Center* John North
Open during term Mon - Thurs 8:30 AM - 10:30 PM, Fri 8:30 AM - 5 PM, Sat
9 AM - 5 PM. Estab 1948 to meet the needs of the students
Income: Financed by provincial appropriation
Purchases: $27,200
Library Holdings: Vols 16,070; Per subs 141; Micro — Fiche, prints, reels;
AV — A-tapes, cassettes, fs, motion pictures, rec, slides, v-tapes; Other —
Clipping files, pamphlets
Special Subjects: Architecture, Fashion Arts, Interior Design, Photography,
Theatre Arts, Television Arts

SCULPTOR'S SOCIETY OF CANADA
For further information, see National and Regional Organizations

SOCIETY OF CANADIAN ARTISTS
For further information, see National and Regional Organizations

UNIVERSITY OF TORONTO
M **Justina M Barnicke Gallery,** 7 Hart House Circle, M5S 1A1. Tel 416-978-2453,
978-2436. *Warden* Richard Alway; *Dir* Judith Schwartz
Open Tues - Sat 11 AM - 6 PM. No admis fee. Estab 1919 to promote young
Canadian artists, as well as present a historical outlook on Canadian art. Gallery
has modern setting and total wall space of 350 running ft; outdoor quadrangle is
available for summer sculpture shows. Average Annual Attendance: 12,000
Income: Financed by Hart House
Collections: †Canadian Art (historical and contemporary)
Publications: The Hart House Collection of Canadian Paintings by Jeremy
Adamson
Activities: Classes for adults; docent training; lectures, 8 vis lectr per year;
concerts; gallery talks; tours; individual paintings and original objects of art lent;
originate traveling exhibitions

L **Fine Art Library,** Smith Hall, Room 6032B, 100 St George St, M5S 1A1. Tel
416-978-5006. *Librn* A Retfalvi
Open Mon - Fri 10 AM - 5 PM. Estab 1936 for reference only
Income: Financed by state appropriation and Department of Fine Art
Library Holdings: Vols 1000; Per subs 2; Other — Exhibition catalogs 20,000,
photographs 80,000
Special Subjects: Archaeology, Art History
Collections: Catalog materials including temporary, permanent, dealer and
†auction catalogs; photographic archives in various field of †Western art
Publications: Canadian Illustrated News (Montreal); Index to Illustrations,
quarterly

O **VISUAL ARTS ONTARIO,*** 417 Queen's Quay W, M5V 1A7. Tel 416-366-
1607. *Chmn Board* Alan Bakes; *VChmn Board* Robert Jekyll; *Secy* Jean Burke;
Treas John Morrow; *Exec Dir* William J S Boyle; *Exec Asst* Janni de Savoye;
Communications Officer Gail J Habst; *Secy* Laura Lerand
Open 9 AM - 5 PM. Estab 1974 to further the awareness and appreciation of the
visual arts. Mem: 6000
Income: $350,000 (financed by membership, provincial appropriation, and private
donations)
Collections: Archival Material from several major professional art societies;
Artists Registry; Slide System of Ontario Artists
Exhibitions: Traveling exhibits of member organizations
Publications: Artcards; Artviews, bimonthly; The Index of Ontario Artists; The
Visual Arts Handbook; Art in Architecture Index; Toronto Art and Artists
Guide; An Artist Guide for the Use of Native Communities
Activities: Workshops for professional artists; art rental program designed for
government offices and corporations called The Bare Facts; originate traveling
exhibitions
L **Library,*** 417 Queen's Quay W, M5V 1A7
Resource library open to public for reference
Library Holdings: Archival material and current art periodicals
Special Subjects: Archives for Society of Canadian Painters-Etchers and
Engravers, Canadian Society of Graphic Art, Canadian Society of Painters in
Watercolour, Ontario Society for Education Through Art, Ontario Society of
Artists, Sculptors Society of Canada, Society of Canadian Artists

WATERLOO

UNIVERSITY OF WATERLOO *
M **Arts Centre Gallery,** N2L 3G1. Tel 519-885-4281. *Adminr* Earl W Stieler;
Installations Officer & Designer Mark Ualeri
Open Mon - Fri 9 AM - 4 PM, Sun 2 - 5 PM, cl Sun June - Aug. No admis fee.
Estab 1962
Collections: Contemporary Canadian Art
Exhibitions: Political Cartoons; Art Forms In Silver; Sword Street Press Prints;
Clay Sculpture; UW Documentary Photograph Exhibition; Fantastic Drawings;
Alumni Art; Iniut, Eskimo Art
L **Dana Porter Arts Library,** University Ave, N2L 3G1. Tel 519-885-1211, Ext
2282; Telex 069-5259. *University Librn* Murray Shepherd; *Special Coll Librn*
Susan Bellingham; *Reference and Coll Development Librn - Fine Arts and
Architecture* Jo Beglo
Open Mon - Fri 8 AM - 12 AM, Sat 9 AM - 12 AM, Sun 1 PM - 12 AM. Estab
1958 to provide access to information appropriate to the needs of the academic
community
Income: $203,214
Library Holdings: Vols 17,500; Per subs 175; Micro — Cards, fiche, reels; AV —
Fs, motion pictures, rec; Other — Clipping files, exhibition catalogs
Special Subjects: Euclid's Elements and History of Mathematics
Collections: The Dance Collection (monographs, periodicals and pamphlets from
1535 to date relating to the history of dance-ballet); B R Davis Southy
Collection; Eric Gill Collection; Lady Aberdeen Library of Women; George
Santayana Collection; Private Collection
Publications: Library publishes four bibliographic series: Aids, Bibliography,
Focus, Research Guide, irregularly
Activities: Undergraduate curriculum in architecture, art history and studio

M **WILFRID LAURIER UNIVERSITY,** Concourse Gallery,* N2L 3C5. Tel 519-
884-1970. *Pres* Dr Neale Tayler; *VPres* Dr John Wier; *Chmn of Art Committee*
M Purses-Smith
Open 7 AM - 11 PM. No admis fee. Estas 1969 to exhibit for the students, staff
& faculty. The gallery forms part of the central concourse of the universtiy.
Average Annual Attendance: 30,000
Income: $16,000 (financed by grants)
Purchases: $10,000
Collections: 200 pieces of original art works
Exhibitions: The gallery mounts from 12-14 exhibitions each year, mostly shows
by artsits in local area
Activities: Lectures open to public; sponsors faculty-student exhibition annually;
book traveling exhibitions, 1-2 per yr

WINDSOR

M **ART GALLERY OF WINDSOR,** 445 Riverside Dr W, N9A 6T8. Tel 519-258-
7111. *Pres* Mignon Briggs; *VPres* Christopher DeWolfe; *Dir* Dr Kenneth
Saltmarche; *Business Mgr* Ken Ferguson; *Cur* Ted Fraser; *Education Cur* Terry
Graff; *Extension Cur* Michele Goulette
Open Tues, Thurs, Fri, Sat 10 AM - 5 PM, Wed 10 AM - 10 PM, Sun 1 - 5 PM,
cl Mon. No admis fee. Estab 1943 for collection and exhibition of works of art,
primarily Canadian, for the study and enjoyment of the Windsor-Detroit area.
Gallery contains 56,000 sq ft of space on three floors; it is environmentally-
controlled and highly fire resistant; outdoor sculpture terrace. Average Annual
Attendance: 120,000. Mem: 1800; dues patron $75, family $35, single $20, out-
of-town $10, student $10; annual meeting March
Income: $800,000 (financed by membership, city & county appropriation &

federal & provincial grants)
Collections: †Primarily Canadian drawings, paintings, prints and sculpture 18th century to present; †Inuit prints and sculpture; non-Canadian paintings and sculpture; decorative arts
Exhibitions: Approximately 35 exhibitions a year, besides installation of permanent collection, of mostly Canadian Historic and Contemporary Sculpture, Painting and Graphics
Publications: Projections bi-monthly bulletin and catalogues for exhibitions organized by this gallery, six times a year
Activities: Summer Arts Club classes for children; docent training; occasional workshops for adults and children; lect open to public, 20 visiting lectr per year; concerts; tours; exten dept serves Essex County; individual paintings and original objects of art lent; book traveling exhibitions approximately 20 per year; originate traveling exhibitions; museum shop sells Canadian handicrafts, original art, reproductions and prints; Children's Gallery
L **Reference Library,** 445 Riverside Dr W, N9A 6T8. Tel 519-258-7111. *Librn* Betty F Wilkinson
Open Tues, Thurs, Fri Sat 10 AM - 5 PM, Wed 10 AM - 10 PM, Sun 1 - 5 PM, cl Mon. Estab 1966. Reference for staff, members and public
Income: $2000
Library Holdings: Vols 700; Per subs 15; Catalogs and museum bulletins; Other — Clipping files, exhibition catalogs

WOODSTOCK

M **WOODSTOCK ART GALLERY,*** Woodstock Public Library, 445 Hunter St, N4S 4G7. Tel 519-539-6761. *Chief Librn* Carolyn Croke; *Cur* J T Henderson
Open Mon - Thurs Noon - 8:30 PM, Fri & Sat Noon - 5 PM, cl Sun. No admis fee. Estab 1966 as a community art gallery. Two galleries, 210 ft wall space, 1823 sq ft. Average Annual Attendance: 15,000. Mem: 275; dues family $7.50, individual $5
Income: Financed by membership, city and province appropriation, Ontario Arts Council and Ministry of Culture and Recreation
Collections: Small collection of Canadian Art, concentrating on Florence Carlyle
Exhibitions: (1982) Filipino Artists in North America; Vicki Easton McClung; Quilts by Anne LaRock; Canadian Embroiderer's Guild; High School Art; Cape Dorset Engravings; Oxford County Juried Exhibition; Charlene Tatham; Ramon Joyes; Joan McCann; Anne Harris; Marion Drysdale; Phil Walker
Publications: Bi-monthly newsletter
Activities: Classes for children; docent training; lect open to public, 4 visiting lectr per year; concerts; gallery talks; tours; individual paintings are lent to residents of Oxford County and business firms; lending collection contains 100 paintings; book traveling exhibitions 1 - 3 per year

PRINCE EDWARD ISLAND

CHARLOTTETOWN

M **CONFEDERATION CENTRE ART GALLERY AND MUSEUM,** PO Box 848, C1A 7L9. Tel 902-892-2464. *Chmn* Dr Collin McMillan; *Dir* David A Webber; *Executive Dir* William J Hancox; *Personal Asst & Secy* Debbie Youland; *Cur* Mark Holton; *Registrar* Judy MacDonald
Open Tues - Sat 10 AM - 5 PM, Sun 2 - 5 PM, cl Mon. No admis fee. Estab 1964 as a national collection devoted to Canadian art and fine crafts. Average Annual Attendance: 100,000. Mem: 600, family $12, individual $5
Income: Financed by federal, provincial, city and the private sector
Collections: †Canadian Art early and contemporary; †Canadian Fine Crafts; Robert Harris Paintings and Drawings
Exhibitions: An average of thirty exhibitions a year from own and circulation collections; special exhibitions each July and August to coincide with summer festival
Publications: ArtsAtlantic, quarterly subscription
Activities: Classes for adults and children; dramatic programs; contemporary dance; lect open to public; tours; concerts; exten dept serving province; lending collection contains paintings, 7000 Kodachromes, 12 motion pictures, 50 film strips, slides; originate traveling exhibitions; junior museum
L **Library,*** PO Box 848, Charlottetown, C1A 7L9. Tel 902-892-2464
Open for reference
Library Holdings: Vols 2000; Per subs 20; AV — A-tapes 20, fs 60, slides 2000; Other — Photographs

WEST ROYALTY

L **HOLLAND COLLEGE,** School of Visual Arts Library & Gallery, Burns Ave, C1A 7N8. Tel 902-566-2401. *Dir* Henry Purdy
Open Mon - Fri 8:30 AM - 5 PM and 6:30 - 10 PM, Sat & Sun 10 AM - 6 PM. Average Annual Attendance: 5000
Library Holdings: Vols 3000; Per subs 35; Micro — Cards; AV — A-tapes, cassettes; Other — Clipping files, exhibition catalogs, photographs
Exhibitions: (1983) Beginnings; Island Art Collection: Kings and Prince County; Island Art Collection: Queens County; Permanent Collection Works; My Energy: Elaine Harrison; Athol Buell Paintings and Christopher Phillis Sculptures; An Exhibition of Art Work by Nigel Roe; Photographs by The Monday Night Photography Club; Sister Joan MacNeil; annual exhibition by the students of the school; An Exhibition of Art Work by Maria Maryniak; Leather or Not; PEI Annual Handcraft Award Exhibition; Island Visual Artists '84
Activities: Classes for adults and children; workshops; summer courses; lectures open to the public, 8 vis lectr per yr; gallery talks; tours; competitions; scholarships; individual paintings & original objects of art lent to schools & public buildings; book traveling exhibitions, 3 - 6 per yr; originate traveling exhibitions; sales shop sells crafts

QUEBEC

CAHUGHNAWAGA

M **MUSEE KATERI TEKAKWITHA,*** Mission Saint Francois Xavier, CP 70, J0L 1B0. Tel 514-632-6030. *Dir* Leon Latoie
Open daily 9 AM - Noon and 1 - 5 PM. No admis fee. Estab as a mission in 1667
Collections: Archives, Canadian church silver, historic chapel, old paintings
Publications: Kateri

CHICOUTIMI

O **LA SOCIETE DES ARTS DE CHICOUTIMI,*** 534 est rue Jacques-Cartrin, PO Box 230, G7H 5B7. Tel 418-549-3618. *Pres* M Calude Dufour
Open Mon - Sat 1:30 - 5 PM & 7 - 10 PM. No admis fee. Estab 1963. Mem: Dues adults $10, students $3
Income: Financed by city appropriation and membership
Collections: Ceramics, graphics, paintings, sculpture
Publications: Monthly Journal
Activities: Gallery talks; films; traveling exhibitions organized and circulated

DORVAL

O **DORVAL CULTURAL CENTRE,*** 1401 Lakeshore Dr, H9S 2E5. Tel 514-636-4043. *Coordr* Danyelle Brodeur; *Animator* Linda Burdayron
Open Tues - Fri 2 - 5 PM & 7 - 9 PM, Sat & Sun 2 - 5 PM. No admis fee. Estab 1967 to promote culture and art. Maintains an art gallery
Income: Financed by city appropriation
Exhibitions: All Visual and Expression Arts
Publications: Calendar, biannually
Activities: Classes for adults and children; dramatic programs; lect open to public; gallery talks; tours

HULL

L **BIBLIOTHEQUE CENTRALE DE PRET DE L'OUTAOUAIS ET DES LAURENTIDES INC,*** 221 chemin Freeman, CP 3000, J8Z 1V7. Tel 819-771-7345. *Dir General* Jean-Pierre Germain
Open Mon - Fri 8:30 AM - 4:30 PM. No admis fee
Collections: Paintings, graphics, reproductions and sculpture
Activities: Lectures; films

JOLIETTE

M **MUSEE D'ART DE JOLIETTE,** 145 Wilfrid-Corbeil St, PO Box 132, J6E 3Z3. Tel 514-756-0311. *Pres* Raymond C Lapierre; *VPres* Me Serge Joyal; *VPres* Juge Jacques Dugas; *VPres* Ulric Laurin; *Dir* Bernard Schaller; *Animator* Carmen DeLorme; *Technician* Michel Forest; *Executive Secy* Ginette Tremblay
Open Tues & Thurs Noon - 5 PM, Sat & Sun Noon - 5 PM. Admis adults $1, students $.25. Estab 1961 for educational purposes; preservation of the collections; save local patrimony. Gallery Six - Contemporary Gallery, temporary exhibitions; Sacred Art Gallery; European Medieval Renaissance Gallery; Canadian Art Gallery; Permanent Collection. Average Annual Attendance: 15,000. Mem: 200; dues $10; annual meeting Sept
Income: $170,000 (financed by endowment, municipal & provincial government grants)
Collections: †Canadian art; European art; sacred art of Quebec; furniture, painting and sculpture
Exhibitions: 18 exhibitions per year
Publications: Catalog and pamphlet entitled Le Musee d'Art de Joliette
Activities: Classes for children; lectures open to public; concerts; gallery talks; tours; films; sales shop sells books, magazines, postcards & reproductions
L **Library,*** 145 Wilfrid-Corbeil St, PO Box 132, J6E 3Z3. Tel 514-756-0311. *In Charge* Carmen Delorme-toupin
Estab 1976. Open with reservations only for art reference
Purchases: $200-$250
Library Holdings: Vols 1000; Per subs 5; AV — Slides; Other — Exhibition catalogs, photographs, sculpture
Special Subjects: History of art, well-known artists
Collections: Art Journal; Great Masters; History of Painting; Larousse Mensuel

MONTREAL

C **ALCAN SMELTERS AND CHEMICALS LIMITED,** 1, Place Ville Marie, PO Box 6090, H3C 3H2. Tel 514-877-2270. *Chmn Art Committee* Linton Baudains
Estab 1979 to enhance the offices in which they are installed and enrich the lives of those who work there. Collection displayed in reception areas and private offices
Purchases: $250,000
Collections: Contemporary Canadian Art
Activities: Lect; individual objects of art lent for special exhibits upon request

C **BENSON & HEDGES (CANADA) INC,*** 1010 Lagauchetiere St W, H3B 2P4. Tel 514-878-3471. *Dir of Corporate Affairs* Cynthia Heide
Estab to assist arts in different areas of the Country. Annual amount of contributions and grants $30,000
Activities: Sponsors exhibitions, including an Eskimo Art Exhibition

O SAIDYE BRONFMAN CENTRE, 5170 Cote Ste Catherine Rd, H3W 1M7. Tel
514-739-2301. *Executive Dir* Harry Gulkin; *Dir Continuing Education & Jewish
Studies* Louise Roskies; *Dir Fine Arts* Alina Michaely; *Cur* Peter Thomas Krausz
Open Mon - Thurs 9 AM - 9 PM, Fri 9 AM - 3:30 PM, Sun 9 AM - 5 PM, cl
Sat. No admis fee. Estab 1967 as a non-profit cultural centre for the promotion
and dissemination of the arts. 3000 sq ft gallery. Average Annual Attendance:
90,000
Income: Financed by membership and government grant
Exhibitions: Twelve plus major exhibitions per yr, special interest in
contemporary art, local, national & international
Publications: Exhibition catalogs
Activities: Classes for adults & children; lectures open to public, 12 vis lectr per
yr; gallery talks; tours; competitions with awards; book traveling exhibitions;
originate traveling exhibitions; sales shop sells books & magazines

M CHATEAU DE RAMEZAY, Antiquarian and Numismatic Society of Montreal,
280 Notre-Dame E, H2Y 1C5. Tel 514-861-7182. *Dir* Pierre Brouillard
Open Tues - Sun 10 AM - 4 PM, cl Mon. Admis adults $1, students $.50. Estab
1895 in residence (1705) of Claude de Ramezay, governor of Montreal. Average
Annual Attendance: 60,000. Mem: 300; dues life $500, individual $10
Collections: Early Canadian portraits; Indian collection; furniture, handicrafts
and woodcarvings
Activities: Classes for children; docent training; lectures open to public & some
for members only, 6 vis lectr per yr; gallery talks; tours; sales shop sells books,
reproductions, prints & slides
L Library,* 280 Notre-Dame E, H2Y 1C5
Library Holdings: Vols 2200
Special Subjects: Canadian history

M CONCORDIA UNIVERSITY, Art Gallery, 1455 de Maisonneuve Blvd West,
H3G 1M8. Tel 514-879-5917. *Cur* Sandra Paikowsky
Open Mon - Fri 10 AM - 8 PM, Sat 10 AM - 5 PM. No admis fee. Estab 1962
to display in a scholarly fashion the University collection; provide a venue for a
variety of significant touring exhibitions chosen from within the region and
across Canada, all with the idea of providing an interesting cultural milieu both
for the university and public alike. Three galleries, 4000 sq ft with 521 running ft,
located in mezzanine area. Average Annual Attendance: 66,000
Income: Financed by university funds
Purchases: Historic, modern & contemporary Canadian art
Collections: †Modern and contemporary Canadian art
Exhibitions: (1982-84) Andrew Dutkewych: Cascade Series; Tom Gibson:
Selected Photographs 1965-1980; Lynn Donoghue: Portraits; Francoise Sullivan:
New Work; Women Painters of the Beaver Hall Group; The Heritage of Jack
Bush, A Tribute; Highlights of the Collection: 20th Anniversary Exhibition of the
Sir George Williams Art Galleries; Bruno Bobak: Selected Works 1943-1980;
Faculty of Fine Arts Biennale; Eugene Atget (1857-1927); Eric Fischl Paintings;
Shirley Ng: Prints; British Masters from the Collection of the National Gallery of
Canada; Carol Wainio: Paintings & Works on Paper; Images of Montreal; Andre
Fauteux: Ten Years 1972-1982; Correspondence; undergraduate student
exhibition; Drawings by Contemporary Sculptors; The Non-Figurative Artists'
Association of Montreal; The Inhabited Landscape: A Selection from the
Concordia University Collection of Art; Otto Rogers: A Survey 1973-1982;
Selections from the Westburne Collection; Edge and Image; Canadian
Contemporary Art; Stephen Livick: Rocks of Newfoundland; Jean McEwen:
New Paintings; Robert Bigelow: Paintings; David Milne: The New York Years
1903-1916; European Master Prints from Montreal Collections; Lynn Hughs:
Selected Work; Christian Knudsen: New Work; Caven Atkins Retrospective
1926-1944; Montreal Paintings Now; F W Hutchison 1971-1953; The New York
Connection
Publications: Exhibition catalogues
Activities: Lect open to public, 3 visiting lectr per year; originate traveling
exhibitions; bookstore

O GUILDE CANADIENNE DES METIERS D'ART, QUEBEC, Canadian Guild
of Crafts, Quebec, 2025 Peel St, H3A 1T6. Tel 514-849-6091. *Dir* Virginia J
Watt
Mem: dues $25 and up; annual meeting Mar/Apr
Collections: Permanent collection of Eskimo and Indian Arts and Crafts
Exhibitions: Craft exhibitions every 3 weeks except Jan & Feb
L Library, 2025 Peel St, H3A 1T6
Reference library for members only by appointment

O LA SOCIETE DES DECORATEURS-ENSEMBLIERS DU QUEBEC,
Interior Decorators' Society of Quebec, Studio G, 451 St Sulpice St, H2Y 2V9.
Tel 514-288-9046. *Pres* Claude Berube; *VPres* Denis Chouinard; *Secy* Raymonde
April; *Treas* Sylvie Legault
Open 9 AM - 5 PM. Estab 1935 as a nonprofit professional association. Mem:
476; dues $250
Income: $100,000 (financed by membership)
Exhibitions: Traveling exhibitions in the Province of Quebec
Publications: Journal magazine, monthly; News Bulletin, 10 issues per year
Activities: Education Committee to improve the level of teaching in interior
design; lect for members only, 5-8 visiting lecturers per year; book traveling
exhibitions

MCGILL UNIVERSITY
M McCord Museum, 690 Sherbrooke St W, H3A 1E9. Tel 514-392-4778. *Dir* Dr
Shirley Thomson; *Cur Photography* Stanley Triggs; *Cur Costume* Jacqueline
Beaudoin-Ross; *Exhib Coordr* Delphine Bourdius; *Registrar* Conrad Graham
Open Wed - Sun 11 AM - 5 PM, cl Mon & Tues. Admis $1. Estab 1919 as a
museum of Canadian Ethnology and Social History. Average Annual Attendance:
55,000
Income: $500,000 (financed by endowment, federal and provincial government
and university)
Collections: †Canadian ethnology; †decorative arts; †documentary photography;
†documentary prints, drawings, paintings - historical; †historical costume
Exhibitions: Approximately ten temporary exhibitions annually; semi-permanent

thematic displays
Publications: Exhibition catalogs and monographs; guides to collections for
children
Activities: Lect; exten dept; individual paintings and original objects of art lent to
international museum - art gallery exhibitions; book traveling exhibitions 3 per
year; originate traveling exhibitions
L Blackader-Lauterman Library of Architecture and Art, 3459 McTavish St,
Montreal, H3A 1Y1. Tel 514-392-5211, 392-4960. *Librn* Mrs I Murray; *Sr
Library Asst* Mrs M Berger
Open winter 9 AM - 9 PM, summer 9 AM - 6 PM. Estab 1922 to establish a
special collection of architectural material. Circ 68,000
Library Holdings: Vols 53,000; Per subs 255; Other — Exhibition catalogs,
pamphlets, photographs

M MONTREAL MUSEUM OF FINE ARTS,* 3400 Ave du Musee, H3G 1K3.
Tel 514-285-1600. *Dir* Jean Trudel; *Chief Conservator* Robin Ashton; *Cur
Decorative Arts* Robert Little; *Assoc Cur Dept Prints and Drawings* Dr
Micheline Moisan; *Research Cur* Dr Myra Nan Rosemfeld; *Cur Contemporary
Canadian Art* Normand Theriault; *Registrar* Elaine Tolmatch
Open Tues - Sun 11 AM - 5 PM, cl Mon. Admis adults $2, students $.75,
children under 12, handicapped, sr citizens & members free. Estab 1860 as an
art association for the exhibition of paintings; museum estab 1916. Average
Annual Attendance: 275,000. Mem: 11,000; dues $20 and up; annual meeting
Sept
Income: Financed by endowment, membership and provincial appropriation
Collections: Collection of African art by Fr Gagnon; Chinese, Near Eastern,
Peruvian, Inuit primitive art; Saidye and Samuel Bronfman Collection of
Contemporary Canadian art; European decorative arts; French, Spanish, Dutch,
British, Canadian and other schools; Japanese incense boxes; The Parker Lace
Collection; Harry T Norton Collection of ancient glass; Lucile Pillow Collection
of porcelain; decorative arts, painting, sculpture from 3000 BC to the present
Exhibitions: Art in Quebec in the Wake of the Conquest; Gold of the Gods;
Hundertwasser; Japanese Incense Boxes rediscovered; Leningrad; Master
paintings from The Hermitage and the State Russian Museum; Guido Molinari
Retrospective; Alfred Stevens
Publications: Collage (a calendar of events)
Activities: Docent training; lect open to public; concerts; gallery talks; tours;
exten dept serving Quebec and other provinces; individual paintings and original
objects of art lent to art galleries and cultural centers; museum shop selling
books, original art, reproductions, prints, slides
L Library,* 3400 Ave du Musee, H3G 1K3. *Librn* Juanita Toupin
Open 11 AM - 5 PM, cl Mon. Estab 1882 for a reference and research centre for
art students, specialists and visitors. Open for reference to students, scholars,
teachers, researchers
Income: Financed by endowment and membership
Library Holdings: Vols 49,710; Per subs 500; art sales catalogs; 6000 vertical
files; Micro — Fiche; AV — A-tapes, slides; Other — Clipping files, exhibition
catalogs, manuscripts, original art works, pamphlets, photographs
Collections: Canadiana; costumes

M MUSEE D'ART CONTEMPORAIN, Cite du Havre, H3C 3R4. Tel 514-873-
2878. *Dir* Andre Menard; *Admin Asst* Fernand Briand; *Dir of Exhib* Mrs France
Gascon; *Dir of Traveling Exhib* Real Lussier
Open Tues, Wed & Fri - Sun 10 AM - 6 PM, Thur 10 AM - 10 PM, cl New
Years. No admis fee. Estab 1964. Conservation and information about
contemporary art are the most important aspects of the museum; also to present
contemporary artists to the general public. Building is a medium-sized two-story
art museum, with an exhibition area of 2200 sq meters divided in four
galleries and a foyer. Average Annual Attendance: 80,000
Income: Financed by provincial grants
Collections: Contemporary Art - †Canadian, international and †Quebecois:
drawings, engravings, paintings, photographs and sculptures
Publications: Catalogs of exhibitions
Activities: Lect open to public, 15 visiting lectr per year; concerts; gallery talks;
tours; competitions; exten dept serving Quebec province; originate traveling
exhibitions; sales shop sells books, magazines, reproductions, prints and slides
L Bibliotheque, Cite du Havre, H3C 3R4. Tel 514-873-2878. *Librn* Isabelle
Montplaisir
Open Tues - Fri 10 AM - 5 PM, Sat & Sun Noon - 6 PM, except summer. Estab
1967. For reference only
Income: Financed by Quebec Government
Purchases: $22,000
Library Holdings: Vols 5700; Per subs 150; Micro — Fiche 1020; AV — A-tapes
65, Kodachromes 2790, slides 30,000, v-tapes 200; Other — Clipping files 3000,
exhibition catalogs 8715, photographs 20,000
Special Subjects: Contemporary art
Collections: Archives of Paul-Emile Borduas (Painter 1905-1960); about 12,500
items including writings, correspondence, exhibition catalogs, etc

M MUSEE DE LA BASILIQUE NOTRE-DAME, 424 St Sulpice St, H2Y 2V5.
Tel 514-842-2925. *Pastor & Dir* Fernand Lecavalier
Open Sat, Sun & Holidays 9 AM - 4:30 PM. Admis adults $1, students and
adults over 65 $.50. Estab 1937 as an historical and religious museum. Average
Annual Attendance: 10,000 - 15,000
Activities: Concerts; tours; individual paintings & original objects of art lent to
other museums; lending collection contains cassettes, film strips, framed
reproductions, nature artifacts, original art works, original prints & paintings

M PAVILION OF HUMOUR, Man and His World, H3C 1A0. Tel 514-872-6079.
Dir Robert LaPalme; *Secy* Jocelyne Gagne; *Cur* Olivier Charest
Open June 21 - Labor Day 10 AM - 8:30 PM. Estab 1968 to show graphic
humor from over 60 countries, plus humorous sculptures borrowed from all over.
Pavilion of Humour is part of Man and His World. Average Annual Attendance:
300,000
Income: $300,000 (financed by endowment and city and state appropriations)
Collections: Collection of American Editorial Cartoons from 1867 to present;
Collection of Panel Cartoons from 1860 to present; Drawings from Pulitzer Prize

Winners; Drawings from Reuben Award Winners; Drawings on International Salon of Cartoons Winners; Strip Cartoons

Publications: Catalogs for Cartoonist of the Year Exhibition and International Salon of Cartoons

Activities: Competitions; original books and money are awarded to winners in a junior cartoon exhibition; objects of art lent; material available to universities and museums; originate traveling exhibitions

L **Library,** H3C 1A0
Reference
Library Holdings: Vols 3000

M **POWERHOUSE GALLERY,** 3738 St Dominique, H2X 2X9. Tel 514-844-3489. *Coordr* Nell Tenhaaf; *Coordr* Susanne De Lotbinier-Harwood; *Asst Coordr* Mary Milne
Open Tues - Fri & Sun Noon - 5 PM, Sat 11 AM - 5 PM. No admis fee. Estab 1973 to promote and broadcast the work of women artists in all domains. Two gallery spaces. Mem: 35; annual meeting in June
Income: $30,000 (financed by membership, grants from federal, provincial and city governments and corporate and private donations)
Exhibitions: Twenty-four exhibitions per year; a mixture of local and other parts of the country, occasionally American
Activities: Lectures open to public, 2-3 vis lectr per year; book traveling exhibition, 1-2 per year; sales shop sells books and magazines

M **SAINT JOSEPH'S ORATORY,** 3800 Queen Mary Ch, H3V 1H6. Tel 514-733-8211. *Dir* Marcel Lalonde; *Artistic Cur* Paul LeDuc
Open daily 10 AM - 5 PM. Admis adults $.50, children $.25, special group rates. Shrine founded 1904, estab 1953 as art museum. St Joseph's Oratory is also a Montreal landmark, the highest point in this city (856 ft above sea level), a piece of art - architecture - with a history, style, etc of its own
Collections: Ancient and Contemporary Art
Exhibitions: (1980) Sculpture in Taille Directe (direct carving as opposed to modeling) by French and Canadian Sculptors Henri Charlier (1883-1975), Fernand Py (1887-1949) and Sylvia Daoust (comtemporary)
Activities: Concerts; films

L **Library,** 3800 Queen Mary Ch, H3V 1H6. Tel 514-733-8211, Ext 234
Open to public for use on the premises, and for inter-library loan
Library Holdings: Vols 80,000; Micro — Reels; Other — Photographs

M **SOCIETY OF THE MONTREAL MILITARY AND MARITIME MUSEUM,** Saint Helen's Island Museum, The Old Fort, St Helen's Island, PO Box 1024 Station A, H3C 2W9. Tel 514-861-6738. *Mgr* Bruce D Bolton; *Mgr* Guy P E Duchesneau; *Cur* Guy Vandeboncoeur
Open summer daily 10 AM - 5 PM, cl Mon, Sept - April. Admis mid-June to Labour Day adults $1.50, children and groups $1. Estab 1955 to exhibit artifacts relating to Canada's colonial history, with emphasis on military and maritime themes. Located in an old British Arsenal, built between 1820-24; galleries cover theme chronologically and by collection. Average Annual Attendance: 100,000. Mem: 100; dues $2; annual meeting May
Income: $650,000 (financed by endowment, membership, city and state appropriation, federal funds and donations)
Collections: Arms and Ammunition; Kitchen and Fireplace, dating from 16th century; prints
Activities: Lect open to public and some to members only, 10 visiting lectr per year; during summer months 18th century military parades by La Compagme Franche de la Marine and the 78th Fraser Highlanders; museum shop sells books, reproductions, prints and slides

L **MacDonald-Steward Library,** The Old Fort, St Helen's Island, PO Box 1024, Station A, H3C 2W9. Tel 514-861-6738. *Librn* Elizabeth F Hale
Open by appointment. Estab 1955 an an administrator's library. Library of rare books. Open to researchers and members for reference
Library Holdings: Vols 7000; Per subs 50; AV — Slides; Other — Original art works, photographs, reproductions
Special Subjects: Canadian history pre 1763
Activities: Classes for children; museum shop sells books, reproductions, prints and slides

L **UNIVERSITE DE MONTREAL,** Bibliotheque d'Amenagement, 5620 Darlington #1004, CP 6128, H3C 3J7. Tel 514-343-6009, 343-7177. *Chef de Bibliotheque* Jacqueline Pelletier
Estab 1964
Purchases: $38,000
Library Holdings: Vols 25,000; Per subs 545; AV — Slides; Other — Clipping files
Special Subjects: Architecture, Constructions, Design
Collections: Rare Books

POINTE CLAIRE

O **POINTE CLAIRE CULTURAL CENTRE,** Stewart Hall, 176 Lakeshore Rd, H9S 4J7. Tel 514-695-3312. *Chmn Stewart Hall* Henry Bolker; *Admin* Denise G O'Brien; *Art Gallery Dir* Helen Judkins; *Cultural Dir* Ruth Aversperg
Open fall & winter Mon & Wed 9 - 9 PM, Tues & Fri 2:30 - 4:30 PM, Sat 10 AM - 5 PM, summer Mon - Fri 9 AM - 5 PM, Wed 7:30 - 9:30 PM. No admis fee. Estab 1963. Gallery is 25 x 80 ft. Average Annual Attendance: 10,000.
Mem: Policy and Planning Board meets ten times per year
Income: Financed by endowment and city appropriation
Exhibitions: Approximately ten per year, local, provincial, national and international contest
Publications: Bulletins; schedules of classes, study series, social events, approximately 30 per year
Activities: Classes for adults and children; dramatic programs; resident workshops in pottery, weaving and photography; lect open to public, 10 visiting lectr per year; concerts; gallery talks; tours; individual paintings lent; lending collection contains framed reproductions, original prints and paintings; sells framed reproductions for young people and adults in Art Lending Service

QUEBEC

M **L'UNIVERSITE LAVAL,** Ecole des Arts Visuels de L'Universite Laval, Bureau 3412, Pavillon Cassult, Cite Universitaire, G1K 7P4. Tel 418-656-2131. *Dir* Pierre Larochelle
Open Mon - Fri 10 AM - 10 PM, cl holidays. No admis fee. Estab 1921
Collections: Art color slides, decorative arts, graphics, paintings, sculpture
Exhibitions: Temporary and traveling exhibitions, changing monthly
Activities: Traveling exhibitions organized and circulated

L **Library,** Pavillon de la Faculte des Arts, G1K 7P4
Open to the public for use on the premises; original prints and works of art available for study
Library Holdings: Vols 25,000

M **MUSEE DES AUGUSTINES DE L'HOTEL DIEU OF QUEBEC,** 32 rue Charlevoix, G1R 5C4. Tel 418-692-2492. *Conservator* Sr Claire Gagnon; *Guide* M Jeanne Morin; *Guide* Rachel Morin; *Guide* Heline Baucher
Open daily 9 - 11 AM & 2 - 5 PM, Sun 2 - 5 PM, other times by appointment, cl carnival time. No admis fee. Estab 1639 in the Monastere des Augustines (1695). The Hotel Dieu relives three centuries of history of the French Canadian people
Collections: Archives, medical history, paintings, sculpture

L **Library,** 32 rue Charlevoix, G1R 3R9
Religious and medical books available for research upon special request
Library Holdings: Vols 2000

M **MUSEE DU QUEBEC,** Parc des Champs de Bataille, G1S 1C8. Tel 418-643-2150. *Dir* Pierre Lochapelle; *Conservator Ancient Art* Claude Thibault; *Conservator Contemporary Art* Michel Martin; *Conservator & Ethnographer* Paul Carpentier; *Educatives Services* Guy Mercier; *Conservator Drawing* Guy Paradis; *Exec Asst* Lise Nantais-Picher; *Chief Cur* Andre Marchard
Open daily 9 AM - 5 PM, Sun & holidays 1 - 5 PM. Estab 1933 under Government of Province of Quebec. Branch Museums, Hotel Chevalier, 5 Champlain St: Old French Canadian Homestead
Purchases: $60,000
Collections: †Furniture by Quebec artists and carvers from the 17th century to present; †paintings; sculpture
Exhibitions: Rotating exhibitions

L **Bibliotheque des Art,** Parc des Champs de Bataille, 1 rue Wolfe, G1R 5H3. Tel 418-643-7134. *Chief Librn* F Lafortune; *Asst* Diane Aubry; *Asst* Luce Gariepy; *Asst* Philippe Trefry
Open 9 AM - Noon, 2 - 4 PM. Estab 1933
Income: $150,000 (financed by Quebec government appropriation)
Purchases: $35,000
Library Holdings: Vols 30,000; Per subs 325; Micro — Fiche, reels; AV — A-tapes, cassettes, lantern slides, motion pictures, rec, slides 58,000, v-tapes; Other — Clipping files, exhibition catalogs, pamphlets, photographs 18,000
Special Subjects: Ethnology, Qubecois art; Canadian art; American art; English art; French art

M **MUSEE DU SEMINAIRE DE QUEBEC,** CP 460, G1R 4R7. Tel 418-692-2843. *Dir* Carolle Gagnon; *Archivist* Marie-Monique Turgeon; *Cur* Magella Paradis; *Dir Exhibitions* Genevieve Auger; *Asst to Archivist* Jean-Pierre Pare
Admis groups up to 45 $10, adults $1, children and students free. Estab 1874. Average Annual Attendance: 5000
Income: Financed by Ministere des Affaires Culturelles, Gouvernement du Quebec Musees Nationaux du Canada, Gouvernement Federal Seminaire de Quebec
Collections: Canadian art XVIIIth and XIXth Centuries; European XVIIth and XVIIIth Centuries

RIMOUSKI

M **LE MUSEE REGIONAL DE RIMOUSKI,** 35 W St Germain, G5L 4B4. Tel 418-724-2272. *Dir Museum* Diane Paquin; *Pres Board Dir & Pres Executive Committee* Jean-Guy Cote
Open summer daily 10 AM - 10 PM, winter Wed - Sun 1:30 - 9:30 PM. Adults $1, students $.50, children and handicapped persons free. Estab 1972 for the diffusion of fine arts, painting, sculpture and tapestry; to present local, national and international exhibitions and organize itinerant exhibitions. An old church, built in 1823, now historical monument, completely restored inside with three floors of exhibitions. Average Annual Attendance: 60,000. Mem: 300; dues $5; annual meeting June
Income: $135,000 (financed by membership, city, provincial and federal appropriations, annual subscription campaign)
Collections: Canadian art, paintings, sculpture & silversmithing; European paintings
Exhibitions: L'Art du Vitrail; Artisanat 1978; Edward Curtis; Dessins et Surrealisme au Quebec; Une Famille au Musee: Famille Jomphe; Peinture d'Email de Jacqueline de Champlain; Philatelistes et Numismates; le Quebec au Jour le Jour de Lida Moser; la Revolution Automatiste; la Semaine Multiculturelle; Un Village au Musee: Trois-Pistoles
Activities: Classes for children; lectures open to public; concerts; book traveling exhibitions; originate traveling exhibitions; sales shop sells books, magazines, reproductions, prints and slides

L **Library,** 35 W St Germain, G5L 4B4
Open to public for reference
Library Holdings: Vols 2000; Per subs 100; Documents 600; Micro — Cards, fiche, prints, reels; AV — Cassettes, fs, slides 8000, v-tapes; Other — Clipping files, exhibition catalogs, original art works, pamphlets, photographs, prints, reproductions, sculpture

SAINT-LAURENT

M **MUSEE D'ART DE SAINT-LAURENT,** 615 Blvd Sainte-Croix, H4L 3X6. Tel 514-747-7367. *Pres* Mrs L Ethier; *VPres* G Lavallee; *Secy* Mrs R Barbeau; *Exhib & Research* Danielle Legentil; *Exhib & Research* Luc Gagnon
Open Sun & Tues - Fri 11 AM - 5 PM. No admis fee. Estab 1962 to didactic exhibitions of traditional arts and crafts of Quebec. Gallery situated in a Gothic chapel of the Victorian period, built in 1867 in Montreal and moved in Saint-Laurent in 1930. Besides its permanent collection, the Museum presents periodical modern art exhibitions
Collections: European and African prehistoric stones; Indian artifacts: artifacts, ceramics, costumes, prehistoric stones; traditional and folk art of French Canada from 17th - 19th century: artifacts, ceramics, furniture, metalworks, sculpture, silver, textiles, tools, wood-carving
Publications: Album: Images Taillees du Quebec; monthly calendar; La main et l'outil, catalogue
Activities: Lect open to public; concerts; gallery talks; tours

SHAWINIGAN

O **CENTRE CULTURAL DE SHAWINIGAN,*** 2100 rue Dessaules, CP 48, Station B, G9N 6V3. Tel 819-539-4822. *Dir* Henry J Blanchard; *Asst Dir* Jean-Luc Houde; *Tech Dir* Sylvain Goudreault
Open daily 2 - 5 PM & 7 - 9 PM. No admis fee. Estab 1967. Gallery is maintained. Average Annual Attendance: 100,000
Income: Financed by city appropriation
Collections: Oils; pastels; watercolors; polyesters; reproductions; copper enameling; inks; sculpture; tapestries
Activities: Classes for adults and children; dramatic programs; concerts; lending collection contains original art works, original prints, paintings, sculpture, slides; sales shop selling original art

SHERBROOKE

M **UNIVERSITY OF SHERBROOKE CULTURAL CENTER,** Art Gallery, J1K 2R1. Tel 819-565-5445. *Exhibition Staff* Johanne Brouillet
Open Mon - Fri 12:30 - 5 PM, Tues, Wed, Sat & Sun 8 - 10 PM. No admis fee. Estab 1964 to introduce public to the best art work being done in Canada and to place this work in an historical (European) and geographical (American) context. Gallery has three exhibition areas totalling 10,000 sq ft on university campus and serves the community. Average Annual Attendance: 18,000
Income: $250,000 (financed by city and state appropriation and university funds)
Collections: Contemporary Quebec Graphics and Paintings
Exhibitions: (1980)l'Art des Cantons de l'Est 1800-1950; (1981) Sherbrooke 81; Concours d'Estampe et de Dessin Quebecois (prints and drawings)
Publications: Bulletin, monthly, catalogues
Activities: Classes for adults and children; lect open to public, 20 visiting lectr per year; gallery talks; tours; competitions; cash awards; lending collection contains books, cassettes, color reproductions, Kodachromes, original prints, paintings, photographs, sculpture, slides and videos; book traveling exhibitions 3 per year; originate traveling exhibitions

TROIS RIVIERES

O **CENTRE CULTUREL DE TROIS RIVIERES,** 1425 Place de l'Hotel de Ville, G9A 4S7. Tel 418-374-3521, Ext 216. *Dir* Francois Lahaye
Open 9 AM - Noon, 1:30 - 5 PM and 7 - 10 PM. Estab 1967
Income: Financed by city appropriation
Activities: Classes for adults and children; dramatic programs

VAUDREUIL

M **MUSEE HISTORIQUE DE VAUDREUIL,** Vaudreuil Historical Museum,* 431 Blvd Roche, CP 121, Darion, J7V 2N3. Tel 514-455-2092. *Pres* Lucien Theriault; *VPres* Fernande Letourneau; *Secy* Pierre Edmond; *Dir* David Aird; *Mgr* Andree Boileau
Open Tues - Sun 11 AM - 5 PM. Admis adults $1.50, children $.50. Estab 1953, non-profit organization subsidized by the Direction des Musees et Centres d'Exposition of the Ministere des Affaires culturelles du Quebec. The collection consists of artifacts and artists production that have and still illustrate the traditional way of life in the counties of Vaudreuil and Soulanges, the surroundings and the Province of Quebec. Museum has four rooms for permanent collection and one for temporary and traveling exhibitions. A documentation centre is open for searchers and students and an animator will receive groups on reservation for a commented tour. Average Annual Attendance: 10,000. Mem: 100; dues $5; annual meeting May 26
Income: Financed by endowment
Collections: Edison Gramophone 1915; antique pottery; historic documents and material; farming; furniture, paintings, portraits, sculpture and woodworking
Publications: Musee de Vaudreuil Catalog (selectif); Vaudreuil Soulanges, Western Gateway of Quebec
Activities: Classes for children; concerts; original objects of art lent; book shop
L **Library,*** 431 Blvd Roche, J7V 2N3
Reference only
Library Holdings: AV cylinders 600; Other — Photographs

SASKATCHEWAN

ESTEVAN

M **ESTEVAN NATIONAL EXHIBITION CENTRE INC,** 118 4th St (Mailing add: 1102 4th St, S4A 0W7). Tel 306-634-7644. *Dir* Peter M J Tulumello, MFA; *Admin Asst* Doreen Stannard, SHK; *Education Coordr* Ethelwyn Dzuba, BED
Open Mon - Fri 9 AM - 5 PM, Sat & Sun 1 - 5 PM. No admis fee. Estab 1978 to receive, display and interpret objects and collections, that would increase the communities access to culture. Two galleries; one 20 x 30, the other 40 x 60. Average Annual Attendance: 30,000
Income: $100,000 (financed by federal, state & city appropriation & private sector fund raising)
Collections: Saskatchewan artists print series; Saskatchewan painting collection
Exhibitions: 7th Annual Regional Art Show; Night Wings; PPOC National Print Show; Treherne—Retrospective; Dreams of An Empire; Ann Newdigate Mills—Tapestries; Irene Roy—Variations of Albrechts Rhino in Fabric; Summer Resort Living; Douglas Walker—Rodeo Photographs; Weavings from the SAB Collection; Making Art in Saskatchewan, 5 approaches; Collecting our Natural Heritage; Archeology; Sweden Saves Energy; Water & Colour & Paper; Estevan History; Regional Art Show VIII; Roy Gunn—Lino Prints; In Praise of Wood & Men; Marconi; Regional Art Show IX; The Work of Craft; Whales—Fragile Giants of the Sea; Regional Art Show V; The Discovery, Captain Cook; Haida Art; Contemporary Quebec Prints; Australia Aboriginal Art; Fine Arts and Antiques Exhibition and Auction; Judith Friswell (weavings); Cycles; Understanding Clay; In Advance of the Landing; Bruce Hanks; Alberta Birds; Prairie Illustrators; Rodeo and Horse Brasses; Louise Walters (paintings & prints); Charlene Dee Stauffer (paintings & prints); Prairie Houses; Regional Art Show VI; Australian Aboriginal Art; Tangata II-Maori Carving (photo display); Equipment for Eternity
Publications: QU - Art Early Update, quarterly, annum; newsletter
Activities: Classes for adults and children; docent training; lectures open to public, 4 vis lectr per yr; children's and regional art show competitions; awards of merit; book traveling exhibitions, 13-18 per yr; originate traveling exhibitions

LLOYDMINSTER

O **LLOYDMINSTER BARR COLONY MUSEUM COMMITTEE,** c/o City Hall, 5011 49th Ave, S9V 0T8. Tel 403-825-6184, 825-3726. *Chmn* Richard Larsen; *Secy* Blaire L Bowsfield; *Cur* Mrs R Foster
Open May 1 to Sept 30 9 AM - 9 PM. Admis family $4, adults $1.50, senior citizens & students $1, children $.35. Estab 1965 to promote an interest in the history of our city. Mem: 5; dues donations
Income: Financed by donations
Collections: Antique Museum; Fuch's Wildlife; Imhoff Paintings

MOOSE JAW

M **MOOSE JAW ART MUSEUM AND NATIONAL EXHIBITION CENTRE,** History Museum, Crescent Park, S6H 0X6. Tel 306-692-4471. *Dir* Gerald Jessop; *Adminr Asst to Dir* Joan Goodnough; *Caretaker & Watchman* Gordon Ambrose
Open summer Noon - 5 PM & 7 - 9 PM, cl Mon; winter Tues - Sun Noon - 5 PM, Thurs & Fri 7 - 9 PM, cl Mon. No admis fee. Estab 1966 for preservation, education, collection and exhibitions. Museum is 150 running ft; Gallery I is 140 running ft; Gallery II is 90 running ft; walls are burlap, smoke retardant. Average Annual Attendance: 21,000. Mem: 167; dues $7
Income: $160,000 (financed by city, state and national appropriation)
Collections: †Canadian Traditional and Contemporary; Local and District Historical Artifacts 3000; Sioux and Cree Beadwork, Native Weapons and Tools
Activities: Classes for children; docent training; lect open to public, 6 visiting lectr per year; gallery talks; tours; individual paintings and original objects of art lent; lending collection contains 14 cassettes, 200 paintings, 400 slides; book traveling exhibitions 20 per year; originate traveling exhibitions

PRINCE ALBERT

M **JOHN M CUELENAERE LIBRARY,** Grace Campbell Gallery, 125 12th St E, S6V 1B7. Tel 306-763-8496. *Head Librn* Eleanor Acorn
Open Mon - Fri 9 AM - 8:30 PM, Sat 9 AM - 5 PM, Sun 1 - 5 PM. No admis fee. Estab 1973. Gallery is 100 linear ft
Income: Financed by city appropriation

REGINA

CANADIAN SOCIETY FOR EDUCATION THROUGH ART
For further information, see National and Regional Organizations

M **LEGISLATIVE BUILDING ART GALLERY,** 2405 Legislative Dr, S4S 0B3. Tel 306-565-5357. *Guide Supervisor* Dorothy Everett
Open winter daily 9 AM - 5 PM, summer daily 9 AM - 9 PM. No admis fee. Estab 1912. Average Annual Attendance: 35,000
Income: Financed by provincial government and donations
Collections: Howard Hatton, pencil sketchings; Edmund Morris Indian Paintings Collection; Fomer Premiers, Cabinets & Lieutenant-Governors of Province Picture Collection
Activities: Classes for adults; guided tours; exten dept serves advanced education dept; original objects of art lent to museums

L **REGINA PUBLIC LIBRARY,** Art Dept, PO Box 2311, S4P 3Z5. Tel 306-569-7576. *Chief Librn* Ronald Yeo
Open Mon - Fri 9:30 AM - 9 PM, Sat 9:30 AM - 6 PM, Sun 1:30 - 5 PM, cl holidays. No admis fee. Estab 1947. Also operate: Glen Elm Branch Gallery and Sherwood Village Branch Gallery
Library Holdings: Vols 10,230; Per subs 60; Micro — Fiche; AV — A-tapes, cassettes, fs, motion pictures, rec, slides, v-tapes; Other — Clipping files, exhibition catalogs 4000, framed reproductions, original art works, pamphlets, photographs, prints
Special Subjects: Saskatchewan Art and Artists; Folk Art

M **Dunlop Art Gallery,** 2311 12th Ave, Regina, S4P 0N3. *Dir & Cur* W P Morgan; *Asst Cur* Elise Stoesser; *Asst Cur* Linda Harvey; *Cur Asst* Suzanne Posyniak; *Technician* Jack Severson
No admis fee. Estab 1947. Average Annual Attendance: 120,000
Income: Financed by city appropriation, provincial & federal grants
Purchases: $10,000
Collections: †Permanent collection of Saskatchewan art; Inglis Sheldon-Williams Collection; †Art Rental Collection
Exhibitions: About 30 per year; local, regional, provincial, national and international art, artists, and themes in all media, both as loan exhibitions and self-organized
Publications: At the Dunlop, quarterly; exhibition catalogs
Activities: Classes for adults and children; lectures open to the public, 6 vis lectr per yr; gallery talks; tours; competitions; individual paintings & original objects of art lent through an art rental collection available to the public and works from permanent collection lent to other galleries; lending collection contains original art works, original print and drawings; book traveling exhibitions; originate traveling exhibitions; sales shop sells books, magazines, cards, catalogues & posters

SASKATCHEWAN ARTS BOARD
For further information, see National & Regional Associations

C **SASKATCHEWAN POWER CORPORATION,** Gallery on the Roof, 2025 Victoria Ave, S4P 0S1. Tel 306-566-3174. *Secy* Leanne Garratt; *Graphics Supv* R Bourassa; *Commercial Artist* D Kilbride
Open Mon - Fri 9 AM - 5 PM, Sun & holidays 2 - 9 PM. No admis fee. Estab 1963 to give local artists and art groups exposure. Gallery approx 100 ft of wall space adjoining the observation deck that overlooks the city. Average Annual Attendance: 100,000
Exhibitions: Changing monthly
Publications: Brochure, monthly; exhibition brochures

M **UNIVERSITY OF REGINA,** Mackenzie Art Gallery, College and Scarth Sts, S4S 0A2. Tel 306-352-5801. *Dir* Carol Phillips; *Coordr Education & Extension* Jane Turnbull Evans; *Business Mgr* Shirley Brocewell; *Cur Exhibitions* Michael Parke-Taylor; *Public Relations* Glenn Gordon; *Education Officer* Mary Jones; *Community Program Officer* Kevin Forrest
Open Tues - Sun Noon - 6 PM, Wed evenings till 10 PM. No admis fee. Estab 1953 to preserve and expand the collection left to the gallery by Norman Mackenzie and to offer exhibitions to the city of Regina; to offer works of art to rural areas through the Community Programme. There are five discreet galleries totalling approx 750 running ft of exhibition space. Average Annual Attendance: 80,000
Income: $1,000,000 (financed by federal and provincial governments, University of Regina and city of Regina and private funds)
Collections: Contemporary Canadian and American work; contemporary Saskatchewan work; 19th and early 20th century works on paper; a part of the collection is early 20th century replicas of Eastern and Oriental artifacts and art
Exhibitions: Changing exhibitions from the permanent collection and traveling exhibitions
Publications: Exhibition catalogues; staff publications of a professional nature; Tabloid, quarterly
Activities: Docent training; community programme of touring exhib in Saskatchewan; interpretive programs; lect open to public, 8 - 10 visiting lectr per year; concerts; gallery talks; tours; films; exten dept serves entire province; originate traveling exhibitions nation-wide; gallery shop sells cards and catalogues

L **Art Gallery Resource Centre,*** S4S 0A2. *Librn* Pat Roulston
Open Mon - Fri Noon - 5 PM, Sat & Sun 1 - 5 PM, Wed & Thurs 7 - 10 PM. Estab 1970 to offer the community a resource for art information, both historical and current. For reference only
Library Holdings: Vols 1000; Per subs 32; AV — Slides; Other — Clipping files, exhibition catalogs, original art works, pamphlets, sculpture
Special Subjects: Canadian art
Collections: Regional press clippings from 1925

L **Fine Arts Library,** College Ave, S4S 0A2. *Library Asst* L Eley
Open Mon - Fri 8:30 - 5 PM and 6:30 - 9:30 PM. Estab 1969 to service the students of music, drama and the visual arts
Library Holdings: Vols 23,700; Per subs 70; AV — Rec

L **Slide Library,** Visual Arts Department, S4S 0A2. Tel 306-584-4879. *Cur* Nancy Hillabold
Estab for the instruction of art history
Library Holdings: AV — Slides 75,000
Special Subjects: 20th century art
Collections: †Prehistoric - contemporary, Eastern & Western art

SAINT WALBURG

M **IMHOFF ART GALLERY,*** Box 36, S0M 2T0. Tel 306-248-3818
Open 8 AM - 6 PM. Admis adults $1, students $.50, children $.25. Estab to exhibit 200 paintings done by Berthold Imhoff, who died in 1939

SASKATOON

M **MENDEL ART GALLERY AND CIVIC CONSERVATORY** (Formerly Saskatoon Gallery and Conservatory Corporation), 950 Spadina Crescent E, PO Box 569, S7K 3L6. Tel 306-664-9610. *Pres* M F Mitchell; *Dir & Cur* Allan MacKay; *Asst Cur* G Moppett; *Extension Officer* J Goodwin; *Business Mgr* R Moldenhauer
Open daily 10 AM - 10 PM, cl holidays. No admis fee. Estab 1964 to exhibit, preserve, collect, works of art; to encourage the development of the visual arts in Saskatoon; to provide the opportunity for citizens to enjoy, understand and to gain a greater appreciation of the fine arts. Maintains an art gallery. Average Annual Attendance: 140,000. Mem: 700; dues $5 - $30
Income: $658,000 (financed by city and federal appropriations)
Purchases: $22,000
Collections: Regional, National and International Art
Exhibitions: (1981)Emily Carr: Oil on Paper Sketches; Watercolour Painting in Saskatchewan 1905-1980; Five California Clay Sculptors: Blackburn, Brady, Costanzo, Roloff, Vandenberge; Sylvain P Cousineau: Photographs and Paintings; Doug Haynes (paintings); Tim Zuck (paintings); The Bizarre Imagery of Yoshitoshi: The Herbert Cole Collection Ed Zelenak (wallworks and sculptures); Louis Comtois 1974-1979 (paintings); Banff Purchase; Giacomo Manzu 100 Works 1938-1980; Jeff Spalding (paintings); Saskatoon School Works: Young at Art; John Hall (paintings & constructions); Harvey McInnes (drawings); Selections from the Canada Council Art Bank; Noel Harding: Enclosure for Conventional Habit; Figure in Landscape, Denis Nokony (drawings); Barbara Astman Red; Don Foulds: Interiors; Goodrige Roberts; Floral Watercolours: Don McVeigh; Mary Pratt; William Perehudoff: Ten Years 1970-1980; Agnes Martin; Navajo Blankets; Roger Hilton: Works on Paper; Permanent Collection
Publications: Exhibition catalogues; Folio, monthly
Activities: Classes for adults & children; docent training; lectures open to public; concerts; gallery talks; tours; competitions; exten dept serves Western Canadian Provinces; individual paintings & original objects of art lent to other galleries; book traveling exhibitions; originate traveling exhibitions; gallery shop sells books, magazines, original art, reproductions, prints, slides & craft items

L **Reference Library,** 950 Spadina Crescent E, PO Box 569, S7K 3L6. Tel 306-664-9610. *Librn* Joan Steel
Open to public for reference
Library Holdings: Vols 6500; Per subs 45; AV — Cassettes, fs, rec, slides; Other — Clipping files, exhibition catalogs, pamphlets, photographs
Special Subjects: Canadian art, Saskatchewan art

L **NUTANA COLLEGIATE INSTITUTE,** Memorial Library and Art Gallery, 411 11th St E, S7N 0E9. Tel 304-653-1677. *Principal* L W Fast; *VPrincipal* Dennis Ens; *Cur* B Shewkenek
Open daily 8 AM - 4 PM, summer 9 AM - 3 PM. No admis fee. Estab 1919 to promote an appreciation for art; a memorial to students who lost their lives in the two world wars. Maintains an art gallery
Library Holdings: Vols 12,000; Per subs 100; Micro — Reels; AV — A-tapes, cassettes, fs, Kodachromes, motion pictures, rec, slides, v-tapes; Other — Clipping files, exhibition catalogs, original art works, pamphlets
Collections: Paintings & wood cuts by Canadian artists

M **PHOTOGRAPHERS GALLERY,** 236 Second Ave S, S7K 1K9. Tel 306-244-8018. *Dir* Daniel Thorburn
Open daily Noon - 5 PM. No admis fee. Estab 1970, incorporated 1973 to encourage the development of photography as a creative visual art. Main gallery is 500 sq ft, and workshop gallery is 250 sq ft. Average Annual Attendance: 6000. Mem: 150; dues $25 - $120; annual meeting first Sun in May
Income: $138,000 (financed by membership, province appropriation and federal grants)
Collections: Permanent Collection of Contemporary Photographs (emphasizes Canadian work)
Publications: Members monthly newsletter; Photographers Gallery Quarterly
Activities: Classes for adults and children; lect open to public, 10 visiting lectr per year; concerts; gallery talks; tours; competitions; extension department; original objects of art lent; workshops throughout the province; portable darkrooms travel with instructors; book traveling exhibitions; originate traveling exhibitions

L **Library,*** 236 Second Ave S, S7K 1K9. *Dir* Patrick Close
Open daily Noon - 5 PM. Estab 1970. Reference
Library Holdings: Vols 1500; Per subs 10; AV — A-tapes, cassettes, slides; Other — Clipping files, exhibition catalogs, manuscripts, pamphlets, reproductions

O **SASKATCHEWAN ASSOCIATION OF ARCHITECTS,** 101-107 Broadway, S7N 1B3. Tel 306-242-0733. *Pres* Bob Ellard; *Secy & Treas* David Thane
Estab 1911. Mem: 102; dues $275; annual meeting Feb
Publications: Newsletter, monthly
Activities: Book prize given to architectural technology student at Saskatchewan Technical Institute, Moose Jaw (4 twice a year); scholarships

M **UNIVERSITY OF SASKATCHEWAN,** Gordon Snelgrove Art Gallery,* S7N 0W0. Tel 306-343-4528. *Gallery Supv* Robert Christie
Open Mon, Wed & Fri 10 AM - 4 PM, Sun, Tues & Thurs 2 - 5 PM and 6 - 9 PM. No admis fee. Estab approx 1960 for the education of students and local public. Gallery covers approx 3000 sq ft of floor space, 300 running ft of wall space. Average Annual Attendance: 5000
Income: Financed by provincial and federal government appropriations and university funds
Exhibitions: Constantly changing exhibitions of art works; internationally organized and traveling shows
Publications: Show announcements, every three weeks
Activities: Originate traveling exhibitions on a limited basis

II ART SCHOOLS

Arrangement and Abbreviations

Art Schools in the U.S.

Art Schools in Canada

ARRANGEMENT AND ABBREVIATIONS
KEY TO ART SCHOOLS

ARRANGEMENT OF DATA

Name and address of institution; telephone number, including area code.
Name and title of the head of the school or department; names and titles
    of primary art faculty.
Date school or department was established.
Control of institution (denominational, private, public).
Scholarships and fellowships offered.
Enrollment for day and evening classes and for majors and non-majors.
Number of studio courses, lab courses, lecture courses, and graduate courses offered.
Number of classes held during the day and evening.
Entrance requirements.
Degrees granted and number of years required for graduation.
Tuition and statement of campus residence availability.
Adult hobby and children's classes offered.
Summer school enrollment, tuition, duration, and courses.

ABBREVIATIONS AND SYMBOLS

Acad — Academic	Enrl — Enrollment	Prof — Professor
Admis — Admission	Ent Req — Entrance Requirements	Prog — Program
AM — Morning	Estab — Established	PT — Part Time Instructor
Approx — Approximate, Approximately	Exam — Examination	Pts — Points
Assoc — Associate	Fel(s) — Fellowship(s)	Pub — Public
Asst — Assistant	FT — Full Time Instructor	Pvt — Private
Ave — Avenue	GC — Graduate Course	Qtr — Quarter
Blvd — Boulevard	Gen — General	Rd — Road
Bro — Brother	Grad — Graduate	Reg — Registration
c — circa	Hr — Hour	Req — Requirements
Cert — Certificate	HS — High School	Res — Residence, Resident
Chmn — Chairman	Hwy — Highway	S — South
Cl — Closed	Incl — Including	SC — Studio Course
Col — College	Instr — Instructor	Schol — Scholarship
Coordr — Coordinator	Jr — Junior	Sem — Semester
Cr — Credit	Lab C — Laboratory Course	Sr — Senior, Sister
D — Day	LC — Lecture Course	St — Street
Den — Denominational	Lect — Lecture(s)	Tui — Tuition
Dept — Department	Lectr — Lecturer	TV — Television
Dipl — Diploma	M — Men	Undergrad — Undergraduate
Dir — Director	Maj — Major in Art	Univ — University
Div — Division	N — North	W — West, Women
Dorm — Dormitory	Nonres — Nonresident	Wk — Week
Dr — Doctor, Drive	PM — Afternoon	Yr — Year(s)
E — East, Evening	Pres — President	
Educ — Education	Prin — Principal	

*No response to questionnaire
† Denotes subject field is offered as major

292

Art Schools In The United States

ALABAMA

AUBURN

AUBURN UNIVERSITY, Dept of Art,* School of Architecture and Fine Arts, 36849. Tel 205-826-4373. *Head* C J Hiers; *Dean* E Keith McPheeters
Estab 1928; pub; D; enrl 370
Ent Req: HS dipl, ACT, SAT
Degrees: BFA 4 yr, MFA 2 yr
Tuition: Res—$330 per quarter; nonres—$760 per quarter
Courses: Drawing, Graphic Design, Illustration, Painting, Printmaking, Sculpture
Adult Hobby Classes: Courses—Same as above
Summer School: Complete 10 wk program

BAY MINETTE

JAMES H FAULKNER STATE JR COLLEGE, PO Box 880, 36507. Tel 205-937-9581. *Div Chmn* Milton Jackson, MM; *Instr* Joseph Montgomery, MFA
Estab 1965; pub; D & E; scholarships; SC 4, LC 3; enrl D 35, E 40, non-maj 57, maj 18
Ent Req: HS dipl
Degrees: AA 2 yrs
Tuition: Res—undergrad $150 per quarter; nonres $300 per quarter; campus res—room & board $1215
Courses: Art History, †Drawing, History of Art & Archaeology, †Painting, †Printmaking, †Sculpture
Summer School: Dir, Milton Jackson. Courses—Art Appreciation

BIRMINGHAM

BIRMINGHAM-SOUTHERN COLLEGE, Art Dept,* 800 Eighth Ave W, 35254. Tel 205-328-5250. *Chmn Div Fine & Performing Arts* Thomas J Gibbs Jr. Instrs: FT 4
Estab 1946; den; D; financial aid awarded, some leadership scholarships available on variable basis; SC 22, LC 8, interim term courses of 4 or 8 wk, 4 req of each student in 4 yr period; enrl 500, maj 50
Ent Req: HS dipl, ACT, SAT scores, C average
Degrees: AB, BS, BFA, BM and BME 4 yr
Tuition: $2300 per term
Courses: Art Education, Art Education, Drawing, Graphic Design, Painting, Printmaking, Sculpture
Children's Classes: Enrl approx 20. Laboratory for training teachers
Summer School: 8 wk beginning June 11 and Aug 10. Courses—Advanced Painting, Art and Music, Graphics, Painting and Drawing, Problems in Composition, Sculpture

SAMFORD UNIVERSITY, Art Dept, 800 Lakeshore Dr, 35209. Tel 205-870-2840, 870-2849. *Chmn* Dr Lowell C Vann. Instrs: FT 3, PT 1
Estab 1841; pvt; D; scholarships; SC 24, LC 4
Ent Req: HS dipl, ent exam, ACT, SAT
Degrees: BA and BSEduc 4 yrs
Tuition: $107 per sem hr
Courses: Advertising Design, Art Education, Ceramics, Commercial Art, Costume Design & Construction, Drawing, Graphic Arts, Graphic Design, Handicrafts, History of Art & Archaeology, Interior Design, Painting, Photography, Sculpture, Stage Design, Teacher Training, Theatre Arts
Adult Hobby Classes: Enrl 45; tuition $169 for 3 hr cr. Courses—Appreciation, Studio Courses
Children's Classes: Enrl 10; 2 wk summer session. Courses—Introduction to Art
Summer School: Dir, Lowell Vann. Enrl 30, 2 six week terms. Courses—Appreciation, Studio Arts

UNIVERSITY OF ALABAMA IN BIRMINGHAM, Dept of Art, School of Humanities, Building 3, 35294. Tel 205-934-4941. *Chmn Dept* John M Schnorrenberg, PhD; *Prof* John Dillon, MFA; *Prof* Edith Frohock, MFA; *Asst Prof* James Alexander, MFA; *Asst Prof* Sonja Rieger, MFA; *Asst Prof* Cerise Camille, MFA; *Asst Prof* Janice Kluge, MFA; *Asst Prof* Heather McPhersom, PhD; *Instr* Ellen Elsas, MEd. Instrs: FT 9, PT 2
Estab 1966, dept estab 1974; pub; D & E; SC 27, LC 34, GC 10; enrl D 212, E 78, maj 100, grad 18
Ent Req: HS dipl, ACT, SAT
Degrees: BA
Tuition: Res—undergrad $1386 per yr, $462 per term, $42 per hr, grad $1470 per yr, $450 per term, $49 per hr; nonres—double res rate
Courses: Aesthetics, †Art History, †Ceramics, Drawing, †Graphic Design, †Painting, †Photography, †Printmaking, †Sculpture, †Teacher Training, Theatre Arts
Adult Hobby Classes: Enrl 208; tuition $35-$60. Courses—Calligraphy, Drawing & Sketching, Experience of Art, Painting
Children's Classes: Enrl 60; tuition $20-$30. Courses—Drawing & Sketching, Painting, Sculpture
Summer School: Enrl 107; tuition as above for term of 11 wks beginning June 7. Courses—range over all fields and are about one half regular offerings

BREWTON

JEFFERSON DAVIS STATE JUNIOR COLLEGE, Art Dept,* Alco Dr, 36426. Tel 205-867-4832. *Instructor* Larry Manning
Estab 1965; pub; D & E; SC 10, LC 1; enrl D 700, E 332, maj 25
Ent Req: HS dipl or equiv
Degrees: AA & AS
Tuition: Res—$125 per yr; nonres—$250 per yr
Courses: Ceramics, Drawing, Handicrafts, Painting, Photography, Basic Design, Introduction to Art
Summer School: Enrl 200. Courses—Ceramics, Drawing, Introduction to Art

DECATUR

JOHN C CALHOUN STATE COMMUNITY COLLEGE, Art Dept, Hwy 31 North, PO Box 2216, 35602. Tel 205-353-3102. *Head Dept* Arthur Bond, PhD; *Instr* Helen C Austin, PhD; *Instr* Richard Green, MFA; *Instr* Robert Stephens, MA
Estab 1963, dept estab 1963; pub; D & E; scholarships; SC 46, LC 8; enrl D 80, E 22, non-maj 29, maj 70, others 3
Ent Req: HS dipl, GED
Degrees: AS and AAS 2 yrs
Tuition: $450 per yr, $150 quarterly
Courses: Advertising Design, †Art Education, Art History, Ceramics, Commercial Art, Drawing, †Film, †Graphic Design, Illustration, Lettering, Museum Staff Training, Painting, †Photography, Printmaking, Sculpture, †Video
Summer School: Courses are selected from regular course offerings

FLORENCE

UNIVERSITY OF NORTH ALABAMA, Dept of Art,* Wesleyan Ave, PO Box 5252, 35632. Tel 205-766-4100, Ext 334. *Asst Prof* Albert Charles Hausmann, MFA; *Head* Fred Owen Hensley, MFA; *Assoc Prof* Thomas E Mims, MFA; *Asst Prof* Lawman F Palmer, MEd; *Asst Prof* Jacqueline Simone Campbell, MA; *Asst Prof* Helen C Austin, PhD; *Instructor* Ronald Rishady, MFA. Instrs: FT 8
Estab 1872, dept estab approx 1930; pub; D; SC 46, LC 6; enrl D 675, non-maj 475, maj 200, grad 20
Ent Req: HS dipl, or GED, ACT
Degrees: BS and BA 4 yr, MA 30 sem hr
Tuition: $470 per sem; campus res—room and board $1040
Courses: Art History, Ceramics, Commercial Art, Drawing, Handicrafts, Illustration, Lettering, Painting, †Photography, Printmaking, Sculpture
Summer School: Tui $188 for term of 8 wks beginning June 7. Courses—lect and studio areas

HUNTSVILLE

ALABAMA A & M UNIVERSITY, Art Education Dept, 35762. Tel 205-859-7354. *Head Dept* Clifton Pearson, EdD; *Assoc Prof* Robert Adams, PhD; *Assoc Prof* Jimmie Dawkins, MFA; *Asst Prof* William W Nance, MFA; *Asst Prof* William L Boyd, MA
Estab 1875, dept estab 1966; pub; D & E; SC 18, LC 3; enrl non-maj 430, maj 35, grad 10
Ent Req: HS dipl
Degrees: BS(Art Educ)
Courses: †Art Education, Art History, Ceramics, Design, Drawing, Handicrafts, Jewelry, Painting, Photography, Printmaking, Sculpture, Teacher Training, Fibers
Adult Hobby Classes: Courses offered
Children's Classes: Courses offered
Summer School: Courses—Various specialized workshops and art education offerings

UNIVERSITY OF ALABAMA IN HUNTSVILLE, School of Arts, Humanities & Science,* 4701 University Dr, PO Box 1247, 35899. Tel 205-895-6120. *Chmn Art & Art History Dept* Jeffrey J Bayer, MFA; *Assoc Prof* John P Dempsey, MA; *Assoc Prof* Richard C Pope, MFA; *Asst Prof* Michael G Crouse, MFA
Estab 1969 (as independent, autonomous campus), dept estab 1965; pub; D & E;

293

schol; SC 46, LC 14; enrl D 150
Ent Req: HS dipl, ACT
Degrees: BA, MA
Tuition: Res—$373; nonres—$746
Courses: Advertising Design, †Art Education, †Art History, Calligraphy, Collages, †Commercial Art, Drafting, Drawing, Film, Graphic Arts, Illustration, Industrial Design, Interior Design, Lettering, Mixed Media, Painting, Photography, †Printmaking, †Sculpture
Adult Hobby Classes: Courses—Calligraphy, Watercolor, other miscellaneous workshops offered through Division of Continuous Education
Summer School: Dir, Jeffrey J Bayer. Tui $322 for 9-12 hrs for term of 10 wk beginning mid-June. Courses—vary from summer to summer, part of the 46 studio classes and some art history offered

JACKSONVILLE

JACKSONVILLE STATE UNIVERSITY, Art Dept, 36265. Tel 205-435-9820, Ext 625, 626. *Head* Dr Emilie E Burn, EdD
Estab 1883; pub; D & E; SC 22, LC 8, GC 4; enrl D 7000, E 24, non-maj 70, maj 90, grad 11, others 15
Ent Req: HS dipl, ACT
Degrees: BS and BA 4 yr

LIVINGSTON

LIVINGSTON UNIVERSITY, Division of Fine Arts,* 35470. Tel 205-652-9661.
Chmn Dennis P Kudlawiec
Estab 1835; pub; scholarships; enrl 1800
Degrees: BA, BS, BMus, MEd, MSc
Tuition: $270 per qtr
Courses: Art Education, Art History, Ceramics, Display, Drawing, Graphic Arts, Industrial Design, Painting, Art Appreciation, Art for the Teacher, Crafts, Design, Mechanical Drawing, Metal Work, Woodworking

MARION

JUDSON COLLEGE, Division of Fine Arts,* 36756. Tel 205-683-6161. *Chmn* Laurence Brasey Campbell
Estab 1838; den; D & E; scholarships, loans, grants; SC 23, LC 6; enrl 450
Ent Req: HS grad, adequate HS grades and ACT scores
Degrees: BA 3-4 yr
Tuition: $2140 per yr
Courses: Commercial Art, Drawing, Painting, Crafts, Design, Watercolor, Special Courses
Adult Hobby Classes: Enrl 5. Courses—Studio Drawing, Painting
Children's Classes: Enrl 15. Courses—Studio Drawing

MOBILE

SPRING HILL COLLEGE, Fine Arts Dept, 36609. Tel 205-460-2383. *Chmn* Barbara Patten, MA; *Asst Prof* Ruth Belasco, MFA; *Asst Prof* Thomas Loehr, MFA
Estab 1830; dept estab 1965; den; D & E; SC 21, LC 3; enrl D 70, non-maj 50, maj 20
Ent Req: HS dipl, ACT, CEEB, SAT
Degrees: BA
Tuition: Undergrad $2375 per sem; campus res—room $625, board $600-$700 per sem
Courses: †Art Business, †Art Therapy, †Fine Arts

UNIVERSITY OF SOUTH ALABAMA, Dept of Art, 307 University Blvd, 36688. Tel 205-460-6335. *Chmn* James E Kennedy, MAT
Estab 1963, dept estab 1964; pub; D & E; SC 32, LC 25; enrl maj & 150
Ent Req: HS dipl, ACT
Degrees: BA, BFA and BA(Art History) 4 yrs
Courses: Advertising Design, Aesthetics, Architecture, Art Education, Art History, Ceramics, Commercial Art, Drawing, Graphic Arts, Painting, Photography, Printmaking, Sculpture
Summer School: Chmn, James E Kennedy. Courses—Drawing, Painting, Three-Dimensional Design

MONROEVILLE

PATRICK HENRY STATE JUNIOR COLLEGE, Art Dept, Frisco City Hwy, 36460. Tel 205-575-3156. *Instr* Betsy Gordon, MA
Sch estab 1965, dept estab 1971; pub; D & E; SC 6, LC 1; enrl D 25, E 8, non-maj 23, maj 3
Ent Req: HS dipl, GED
Tuition: Res—undergrad $450 per academic yr; non-res—undergrad $600 per academic yr
Courses: Art Appreciation, Drafting, †Drawing, †Painting, Stage Design, Theatre Arts

MONTEVALLO

UNIVERSITY OF MONTEVALLO, College of Fine Arts,* Art Department, 35115. Tel 205-665-2521, Ext 224. *Dean* John Stewart; *Chmn* L Frank McCoy
Estab 1896; pub; D & E; scholarships, Work Study; SC 35, LC 10, GC 7; enrl Maj 80, others 2800
Ent Req: ACT
Degrees: BA, BS, BFA, BM, MA, MM
Tuition: $490 per sem
Courses: Advertising Design, Art Education, Art History, Ceramics, Handicrafts, Painting, Photography, Printmaking, Sculpture
Summer School: Enrl 1000; two 5 wk sessions beginning June 5 and July 5

MONTGOMERY

ALABAMA STATE UNIVERSITY, Art Dept,* S Jackson St, 36111. Tel 205-832-6072. *Dir* Arthur L Britt Sr
Degrees: BA, BS
Tuition: Res—$600 per yr; nonres—$1200 per yr
Courses: Advertising Design, Art Appreciation, Art History, Calligraphy, Ceramics, Design, Drawing, Handicrafts, Printmaking, Photography, Printmaking, Stage Design

AUBURN UNIVERSITY AT MONTGOMERY, Art Dept,* 36109. Tel 205-279-9110, Ext 376. *Head Dept* Joseph Schwarz, PhD; *Dean School Liberal Arts* Marion Michaels; *Assoc Prof* Philip Coley, MFA; *Asst Prof* Richard Mills, MFA; *Instr Music* Gary Blackburn; *Adjunct Instructor* Nita Whetstone, MFA; *Adjunct Instructor* Reynolds Brown, MA; *Adjunct Instructor* Lizetta Collins, MFA. Instrs: FT 4, PT 3
Estab 1972; pub; D & E; SC 18, LC 5, GC 4; enrl D 400, nonmaj 200, maj 60
Ent Req: HS dipl
Degrees: BA
Tuition: Res—$265 per quarter; nonres—$610 per quarter; campus residence available
Courses: Art Education, Art History, Ceramics, Drawing, Graphic Arts, Painting, Photography, Sculpture
Adult Hobby Classes: Courses—Ceramics, Painting
Summer School: Head, Joseph Schwarz. Tui $265. Courses—same as above

HUNTINGDON COLLEGE, Dept of Visual and Performing Arts,* 1500 E Fairview Ave, 36106. Tel 205-265-0511, Ext 55. *Instr* L Dennis Sears
Estab 1973; E; enrl 119
Tuition: $2800 per yr
Courses: Drafting, Painting, Photography, Sculpture, Architectural Rendering, Creative Thinking, Graphics,
Adult Hobby Classes: Courses—non-credit offered through continuous educational programs

TROY

TROY STATE UNIVERSITY, Dept of Art,* 36082. Tel 205-566-3000, Ext 278.
Dean School of Fine Arts Dr John M Long. Instrs: FT 7
Estab 1957. University has 2 other campuses; pub; schol and fel; SC 23, LC 11
Ent Req: HS grad, ent exam
Degrees: BA and BS(Arts & Sciences), MS
Tuition: Res—$315 per yr; nonres—$472.40 per yr
Courses: †Art History, Commercial Art, Drawing, Graphic Arts, Handicrafts, Jewelry, Lettering, Painting, Photography, Silversmithing, Teacher Training, Museology, Pottery

TUSCALOOSA

STILLMAN COLLEGE, Stillman Art Gallery and Art Dept, 3601 15th St, PO Box 1430, 35403. Tel 205-752-2548, Ext 64. *Coordr of Art* Brenda C Lispcome, MS; *Assoc Prof* Raymond L Guffin, MFA
Estab 1876, dept estab 1951; pvt den; D; SC 8, LC 2; enrl D 73, non-maj 73
Ent Req: HS dipl, ent exam
Tuition: $550 per yr; campus res—room & board $2973 per yr
Courses: Art Education, Art History, Ceramics, Commercial Art, Design, Drawing, Mixed Media, Painting, Sculpture, Afro-American Art History
Summer School: Dir, Dr Eddie Johnson. Courses—Art Education, Painting

UNIVERSITY OF ALABAMA, Art Dept, PO Box F, 35486. Tel 205-348-5967.
Prof Virginia Pitts Rembert; *Prof* Angelo Granata, MFA; *Prof* Richard Brough; *Prof* Shirley Murgrave, PhD; *Prof* Joseph Bolt, PhD; *Prof* Alvin Sella; *Assoc Prof* Robert Mellown, PhD; *Assoc Prof* Eloise Angiola, PhD; *Assoc Prof* Arthur Oakes, MFA; *Assoc Prof* Gay Burke, MFA; *Assoc Prof* Henry Betak, MFA; *Asst Prof* Christopher Kakas, MFA; *Asst Prof* Thomas Barnes, MFA; *Asst Prof* Bruce Growe, MFA; *Asst Prof* James McNutt, MA
Scholarships
Children's Classes: Enrl 75; tuition $3.50 per class hr for 10 wks. Courses—Basic Skills, Ceramics, Figure Drawing, Photography, Printmaking

TUSKEGEE INSTITUTE

TUSKEGEE INSTITUTE, Art Dept, College of Arts and Sciences, 36088. Tel 205-727-8011. *Dept Chmn* Elaine Thomas. Instrs: FT 5
Estab 1881; pvt
Degrees: 4 yr
Courses: Art Education, Art History, Drawing, Handicrafts, Textile Design, Applied Art, Art Appreciation, Design, Mural Techniques, Weaving

UNIVERSITY

UNIVERSITY OF ALABAMA, Art Dept, Box F, 35486. Tel 205-348-5967. *Chmn Dept* Virginia Pitts Rembert, PhD
Estab 1831, dept estab 1919; pub; D & E; scholarships; SC 43, LC 12, GC 18; enrl D 750, maj 130, grad 8
Ent Req: HS dipl, ACT
Degrees: BA and BFA 4 yr, MFA 2 yr, MA 1 yr
Tuition: Res—undergrad & grad $574 per sem; nonres—undergrad & grad $1231.50 per sem; campus res available
Courses: †Art Education, †Art History, †Graphic Design, †Painting, †Photography, †Printmaking, †Sculpture, †Ceramics-Glass, Drawing and Design
Children's Classes: Enrl 60; tuition $3.50 per class hr for 10 wks
Summer School: Dir, Virginia Pitts Rembert. Enrl 300; tuition $44 per cr hr & $39.75 registration fee. Courses offered in all major areas

ALASKA

ANCHORAGE

UNIVERSITY OF ALASKA AT ANCHORAGE, Dept of Art, College of Arts and Sciences, 3221 Providence Ave, 99508. Tel 907-786-1783. *Chmn* Saradell Ard.
Instrs: FT 4, PT 3
Pub; D & E; schol; SC 22, LC 3-5; enrl College of Arts & Sciences FT 1256
Ent Req: Open enrl
Degrees: AA in art, BA in art, BFA 4 yr
Tuition: Res—$25 per cr, $300 for 12 or more cr; nonres—$65 per cr, $780, 12 or more cr
Courses: †Art Education, †Ceramics, †Drawing, †Graphic Arts, Jewelry, †Painting, †Photography, †Printmaking, †Sculpture, Teacher Training, Metalcraft
Adult Hobby Classes: Same as regular prog
Summer School: One term of 10 wks beginning May or two 5 wk sessions.
Courses—Native Art History, Art Appreciation, Photography, Art Education

FAIRBANKS

UNIVERSITY OF ALASKA, Dept of Art,* Fine Arts Complex, 99701. Tel 907-479-7530. *Dept Head* Ronald Senungetuk; *Prof* L Stanley Zielinski; *Prof* Terence T Choy; *Assoc Prof* Glen C Simpson; *Assoc Prof* Arthur W Brody; *Asst Prof* Barbara Alexander; *Asst Prof* Kessler Woodward; *Asst Prof* Catherine Zuelsdorf
Estab 1963; pub; D & E; scholarships; SC 28, LC 4; enrl D 293, E 50, maj 45
Ent Req: HS dipl
Degrees: BA, BFA
Tuition: Res—$200 per sem; nonres $780 per sem
Courses: Ceramics, Drawing, Graphic Arts, History of Art & Archaeology, Jewelry, Lettering, Painting, Sculpture, Textile Design
Adult Hobby Classes: Enrl 30; courses—Crafts, Drawing, Painting, under the direction of the community college
Children's Classes: Enrl 40; courses—Ceramics, Drawing & Painting, Sculpture, under the direction of the community college
Summer School: Dean, Donald R Theophilus. Term of 3 or 6 wk.
Courses—Drawing, Painting, Printmaking, Sculpture, Watercolor

ARIZONA

DOUGLAS

COCHISE COLLEGE, Art Dept,* 85607. Tel 602-364-7943. *Instructor* Don Johnson; *Instructor* Albert Kogel; *Instructor* Ray Levra; *Instructor* Manual Martinez.
Instrs: PT 11
Estab 1965, department estab 1965; pub; D & E; scholarships; SC 12, LC 2; enrl D 280, E 225, maj 20
Ent Req: HS dipl, GED
Degrees: AA
Tuition: Res—$100 registration & $6 per unit per sem; nonres—$1076 registration & $6 per unit per sem; campus res available
Courses: Advertising Design, Architecture, Art Education, Art History, Calligraphy, Ceramics, Collages, Commercial Art, Constructions, Costume Design & Construction, Display, Drafting, Drawing, Fashion Arts, Goldsmithing, Graphic Arts, Graphic Design, Handicrafts, History of Art & Archaeology, Illustration, Jewelry, Lettering, Mixed Media, Occupational Therapy, Painting, Photography, Printmaking, Sculpture, Silversmithing, Teacher Training
Adult Hobby Classes: Courses—Painting

FLAGSTAFF

NORTHERN ARIZONA UNIVERSITY, Art Dept, 86001. Tel 602-523-4612.
Head Dr D Bendel, EdD; *Prof* Richard Beasley, MFA; *Assoc Dir* Bruce Horn, MFA; *Assoc Prof* M Webster, MFA; *Assoc Prof* W Williams, MFA; *Assoc Prof* C Caldwell, MFA; *Assoc Prof* O Carley, MFA; *Assoc Prof* T Knights, MFA; *Assoc Prof* G Monthan, MA; *Asst Prof* A Bakovych, MA; *Asst Prof* J Cornett, MFA; *Asst Prof* S Peirce, PhD; *Asst Prof* P Veinus, PhD; *Asst Prof* C Mulunaux, PhD; *Instr* J O'Hara, MFA
Estab 1899; pub; D & E; scholarships; SC 56, LC 19, GC 8-10; enrl D 400, E 100, non-maj 250, maj 250, grad 20
Ent Req: HS dipl, ACT
Degrees: BFA, BA & BS 4 hr, MA(Art Education), MA(Studio) 1-2 yr
Tuition: Res—undergrad & grad $425 per sem; nonres—undergrad & grad $3195 yr, $1597.50 per sem; campus res available
Courses: Art History, Ceramics, Graphic Design, Illustration, Jewelry, Painting, Photography, Printmaking, Printmaking, Sculpture, Fibers, Metalsmithing
Adult Hobby Classes: Courses—Most of the above studio areas
Children's Classes: Enrl 80; tuition $5 for 5 Sat. Courses—Ceramics, Drawing, Painting, Puppetry
Summer School: Dir, Donald Bendel. Enrl 200; tuition $46 per cr. Courses—Most regular courses

HOLBROOK

NORTHLAND PIONEER COLLEGE, Art Dept, 1200 E Hermosa Dr, 86025. Tel 602-524-6111. *Coordr* Ortho R Fairbanks, MFA. Instrs: FT 1, PT 60
Estab 1974; pub; D & E; SC 26, LC 2
Degrees: AA, Assoc of Applied Sci 2 yr
Tuition: Full time res $12 per sem, full time out-of-state $900 per sem, full time out-of-county $850 per sem

Courses: Art History, Calligraphy, Ceramics, Commercial Art, Drawing, Graphic Arts, Jewelry, Painting, Photography, Printmaking, Sculpture, Silversmithing, Textile Design, Crafts
Adult Hobby Classes: Courses—Same as above

MESA

MESA COMMUNITY COLLEGE, Dept of Art & Photography, 1833 W Southern Ave, 85202. Tel 602-833-1261, Ext 321. *Chmn Dept Art* Darlene Swaim, MFA; *Instructor* Carole Drachler, PhD; *Instructor* Jim Garrison, MA; *Instructor* Ned Tuhey, MA; *Instructor* Bill Voss, MA
Estab 1965; pub; D & E; schol; SC 10, LC 8; enrl D 667, E 394
Ent Req: HS dipl or GED
Degrees: AA 2 yrs
Tuition: Res—$14 per cr hr, nonres—out of state $275 per cr hr, out of county $55 per cr hr, audit $20 per hr
Courses: †Advertising Design, Art Appreciation, Design, †Drawing, †Film, Interior Design, Jewelry, †Painting, †Photography, Weaving, Crafts

PHOENIX

GRAND CANYON COLLEGE, Art Dept, 3300 W Camelback Rd, 85061. Tel 602-249-3300, Ext 332. *Actg Chmn* Colleen E Scheck, MFA; *Assoc Prof* Cary Adkins, MFA; *Instructor* K Graves, MFA; *Artist in Residence* Dennis L Jones, MFA
Estab 1951; den; D & E; scholarships; SC 23, LC 10; enrl D 175, E 75, non-maj 75, maj 40
Ent Req: HS dipl
Degrees: BA and BS
Tuition: Res—undergrad $1664 per yr, $832 per sem, $78 per hr; nonres—undergrad $2958 per yr, $1479 per sem, $78 per hr; campus residency available
Courses: Aesthetics, †Art History, Ceramics, Drawing, Jewelry, Graphic Design, Mixed Media, Painting, Printmaking, Sculpture, Teacher Training, Professional Artist Workshop
Children's Classes: Enrl 100; tuition $25 for 5 weeks. Courses—Ceramics & Sculpture, Crafts, Dramatics, Drawing & Composition, Photography

PHOENIX COLLEGE, Dept of Art and Photography, 1202 W Thomas Rd, 85013. Tel 602-264-2492, Ext 471. *Chmn* Dr Gail Jamieson. Instrs: FT 5, PT 22
Estab 1948; pub; schol
Ent Req: HS dipl
Degrees: AA & AG 2 yrs
Tuition: $14 per sem hr
Courses: Ceramics, Commercial Art, Drawing, Handicrafts, Painting, Photography, Sculpture, Art Appreciation, Basic Design, Mexican Arts & Crafts, Oil Painting, Watercolor

PRESCOTT

YAVAPAI COLLEGE, Art Dept,* 86301. Tel 602-445-7300. *Chmn* Glen L Peterson; *Instr* Edward V Branson, MA; *Instr* Elaine W Farrar, MA; *Instr* Vincent N Kelly, EdD; *Instr* Richard B Marcusen, MFA
Estab 1966, dept estab 1969; pub; D & E; schol; SC 50, LC 50; enrl D 1650, E 1563
Ent Req: HS dipl
Degrees: AA 2 yr
Courses: Advertising Design, Art History, Ceramics, Commercial Art, Drafting, Drawing, Sculpture, Glass, Handicrafts (batik, crafts, dyeing, macrame, spinning, stitchery, weaving, wood), Indian art survey, Stained Glass, Watercolor, Welded Metal
Adult Hobby Classes: Enrl open; tuition per course. Courses offered through Retirement College
Children's Classes: Enrl open; tuition $15 per course. Courses—Ceramics, Drawing, Painting
Summer School: Dir, Donald D Hiserodt. Enrl open; tuition $12 per sem hr for term of 6 wks beginning June 4. Courses—Ceramics, Drawing, Jewelry, Painting, Photography, Printmaking

TEMPE

ARIZONA STATE UNIVERSITY
—School of Art, 85287. Tel 602-965-3468. *Dean College of Fine Arts* Jules Heller, PhD; *Dir* Leonard Lehrer, MFA
Estab 1885; pub; D & E; SC 80, LC 74, GC 84; enrl D 41,000, maj 1000, grad 175
Ent Req: HS dipl, ACT
Degrees: BA and BFA 4 yrs, MFA 3 yrs, MA 2 yrs, EdD 3 yrs
Tuition: Res—undergrad & grad $325 per sem; nonres—undergrad & grad $1475 per sem; campus res—room & board $2415
Courses: Art Education, Art History, Ceramics, Drawing, Graphic Design, Intermedia, Jewelry, Painting, Photography, Sculpture, Art Anatomy, Art Criticism, Fibers, Fine Art Typography, Intaglio, Lithography, Papermaking, Silkscreen, Wood Art, Woodburytype
Children's Classes: Tuition $25 for 5 wk term. Courses—Studio Art
Summer School: Dir, Dr Jon Sharer. Enrl 150; tuition $36 per sem hr for two 5 week sessions June through August. Courses—same as regular session
—College of Architecture, 85287. Tel 602-965-3216. *Dean* Gerald R McSheffrey; *Chmn Archit* Roger L Schluntz, MArchit; *Chmn Design Sciences* Tom Witt, MFA; *Chmn Planning* Elizabeth Burns, PhD
Estab 1885; college estab 1949; pub; D & E; enrl non-maj 650, maj 280, grad 65
Ent Req: HS dipl, SAT
Degrees: MArch 6 yrs, BS(Design) 4 yrs, MEP 2 yrs
Tuition: Res—undergrad $325 per sem, grad $325 per sem; non-res—undergrad $1475 per sem, grad $1475 per sem; PT $36 per hr; campus res—room & board $2415 per yr
Courses: Advertising Design, †Architecture, Drafting, Drawing, Film, Graphic Arts, Graphic Design, †Industrial Design, †Interior Design, †Landscape Architecture,

Lettering, Mixed Media, Photography, Restoration & Conservation, Video, Architectural History, †Housing and Urban Development, †Planning
Summer School: Courses—pre-professional courses primarily in Design, Graphics, History, Sketching and Rendering

THATCHER

EASTERN ARIZONA COLLEGE, * 626 Church St, 85552. Tel 602-428-1133, Ext 47. *Instr* Justin Fairbanks, MFA. Instrs: PT 9
Estab 1888, dept estab 1946; pub; D & E; scholarships; SC 25, LC 3; enrl D 105, E 202, maj 12
Ent Req: HS dipl or GED
Degrees: AA 2 yrs
Tuition: Res—$128 per sem; nonres—$1224 per sem
Courses: Photography, Sculpture, Silversmithing, Lapidary, Weaving

TUCSON

TUCSON MUSEUM OF ART SCHOOL, 140 N Main Ave, 85705. Tel 602-884-8673. *Dir* Pat Villeneuve. Instrs: PT 30
Estab 1924; pvt; D & E; schol; SC 42, LC 2; enrl D & E 1139
Ent Req: None
Tuition: Varies per course; no campus res
Courses: Art Appreciation, Art History, Ceramics, Drawing, Painting, Photography, Printmaking, Sculpture, Papermaking, Stained Glass
Adult Hobby Classes: Courses—Sculpture
Children's Classes: Courses—Ceramics, Drawing, Painting, Photography, Primary art
Summer School: Enrl 450

UNIVERSITY OF ARIZONA, Dept of Art, College of Fine Arts, 85721. Tel 602-621-1251. *Dept Head* Howard Conant, EdD; *Coordr Painting & Drawing* Chuch Hitner; *Coordr Three-Dimensional Areas* Michael Croft, MFA; *Coordr Photography* Harold Jones, MFA; *Coordr Art History* Sheldon Reich, PhD; *Coordr Art Educ* Dwaine Greer, PhD; *Coordr Graphic Design* Jackson Boelts, MFA; *Coordr Printmaking* Lynn Schroeder
Estab 1891, dept estab 1927; pub; D; scholarships; SC 30, LC 21, GC 32; enrl D 3094, maj 535, grad 70
Ent Req: HS dipl, ACT
Degrees: BFA(Studio), BFA(Art Educ) and BA(Art History) 4 yrs, MFA(Studio) and MA(Art History or Art Educ) 2-3 yrs
Tuition: Res $377.50 per sem; nonres $2665 per sem; campus res—room & board $1500 per sem
Courses: †Art Education, †Art History, †Ceramics, †Drawing, †Graphic Arts, †Painting, †Photography, †Printmaking, †Sculpture, †Silversmithing, Fibers, Metalwork
Summer School: Two sessions offered. Request catalog (available in April) by writing to: Summer Session Office, University of Arizona, Tucson, AZ 85721

ARKANSAS

ARKADELPHIA

OUACHITA BAPTIST UNIVERSITY, Dept of Art,* School of Arts and Sciences, 410 Ouachita St, 71923. Tel 501-246-4531, Ext 196. *Chmn* Betty Berry, MA; *Dean School Arts & Science* T J Turner; *Instructor* Ted Barnes, MFA
Estab 1886, dept estab 1934; den; D; scholarship; SC 11, LC 2
Ent Req: HS dipl, ACT
Degrees: BA, BSE, BS and BME 4 yr, MSE and MME 1 yr
Tuition: $1350 per sem
Courses: †Advertising Design, Aesthetics, †Art Education, Art History, Ceramics, Commercial Art, Costume Design & Construction, Drawing, Graphic Arts, Handicrafts, History of Art & Archaeology, Illustration, Interior Design, Jewelry, Lettering, Painting, Photography, Sculpture, Teacher Training, †Theatre Arts, Macrame, Tole, Weaving
Summer School: Dir, Jim Berryman. Enrl 550; tui $50 sem hr; two terms of 5 wks beginning June 1

CLARKSVILLE

COLLEGE OF THE OZARKS, Dept of Art,* Ward and College St, 72830. Tel 501-754-3431. *Head Dept* Lyle Ward, MFA
Estab 1836, dept estab 1952; den; D; schol; SC 9, LC 2; enrl D 83, nonmaj 8, maj 17
Ent Req: HS dipl, ACT
Degrees: BA and BS 4 yr
Tuition: $1425 per yr; campus res available
Courses: Art Education, Art History, Ceramics, Drawing, Painting, Art Appreciation
Summer School: Dir, Lyle Ward. Workshop in Art Education and(or) Painting

COLLEGE CITY

SOUTHERN BAPTIST COLLEGE, Dept of Art, 72476. Tel 501-886-6741. *Chmn* Jerry Gibbons, MS
Den; D & E; scholarships
Tuition: Res—$1850 per yr; campus residence available
Courses: Art Education, Ceramics, Conceptual Art, Drawing, Graphic Design, Painting, Theatre Arts
Summer School: Dir, Dr Jerrol Swaim. Tuition $925 for 12-16 hrs, $59 for less than 12 hrs, $59 for each additional hr over 16 hrs

CONWAY

UNIVERSITY OF CENTRAL ARKANSAS, Art Dept, 72032. Tel 501-450-3113. *Head Dept* Dr Jerry D Poole; *Assoc Prof* Patric Larsen; *Assoc Prof* Robert C Thompson; *Asst Prof* Gene Hatfield; *Asst Prof* Tim Morris; *Asst Prof* Helen Phillips. Instrs: FT 6
Estab 1908; pub; SC 14, LC 4
Ent Req: HS dipl
Degrees: 4 yr
Tuition: Res—$395 12 hrs & up; nonres—additional fee $790; summer terms res—$35 per cr hr; nonres—$70 per cr hr
Courses: Art Appreciation, Art Education, Art History, Ceramics, Design, Drawing, Illustration, Painting, Printmaking, Sculpture, Advanced Design, Figure, Watercolor, Crafts, Fiber, Enameling
Summer School: Dir, Jerry D Poole. Tuition $70 per sem hr. Courses—various

FAYETTEVILLE

UNIVERSITY OF ARKANSAS, Art Dept,* FA 116, 72701. Tel 501-575-5202. *Dept Chairperson* Kenneth Stout; *Prof Emeritus* Lothar Krueger, MS; *Assoc Prof* Thomas D Turpin, MFA; *Asst Prof* Walter D Curtis, MFA; *Asst Prof* Dominic Ricciotti, PhD; *Asst Prof* John W Smith, EdD. Instrs: FT 13, PT 1
Estab 1871; pub; D & E; scholarships; SC 34, LC 16, GC 20; enrl D 13,500, non-maj 650, maj 200, grad 20
Ent Req: HS dipl, ent exam, GED
Degrees: MFA 2 1/2 yrs and BA 4 yrs
Tuition: $360 per sem; campus res available
Courses: Art Education, Art History, Calligraphy, Ceramics, Constructions, Drawing, Graphic Arts, Jewelry, Painting, Photography, Printmaking, Sculpture
Adult Hobby Classes: Ceramics, Painting, Sculpture
Summer School: Courses offered

HARRISON

NORTH ARKANSAS COMMUNITY COLLEGE, Art Dept,* Pioneer Ridge, 72601. Tel 501-743-3000, Ext 48. *Chmn Div of Communications & Arts* Bill Skinner
Estab 1974, dept estab 1975; pub; D & E; SC 7, LC 1; enrl in art dept D 80, E 30-40, non-maj 45, maj 35
Ent Req: HS dipl
Degrees: AA 2 yrs
Tuition: County res—$210 per sem; non-county res—$270 per sem; nonres—$402 per sem
Courses: Advertising Design, Aesthetics, Architecture, Art Education, Art History, Calligraphy, Ceramics, Collages, Commercial Art, Constructions, Costume Design & Construction, Display, Drafting, Drawing, Fashion Arts, Film, Graphic Arts, Graphic Design, Handicrafts, History of Art & Archaeology
Adult Hobby Classes: Various courses offered each sem through Continuing Education Program
Summer School: Enrl 20-30; tuition $30-$35 for term of 6-8 wks beginning June 1. Courses—open; Art Workshop on Buffalo National River

HELENA

PHILLIPS COUNTY COMMUNITY COLLEGE, Dept of English and Fine Arts,* Box 785, 72342. Tel 501-338-6474. *Artist in Res* Larry Spakes, visual
Estab 1966; pub; D & E; scholarships; SC 8, LC 1; enrl 55
Ent Req: HS dipl, ent exam, GED
Degrees: AA and AAS 2 yr
Tuition: County res—$232 per sem; non-county res—$296 per sem; nonres—$438 per sem
Courses: Ceramics, Drafting, Drawing, History of Art & Archaeology, Painting
Summer School: Tui same. 5 wk term beginning May 28

LITTLE ROCK

ARKANSAS ARTS CENTER, PO Box 2137, 72203. Tel 501-372-4000. *Exec Dir* Townsend Wolfe; *Asst to Dir* Bill Atkins, MA; *Instr* David Anhalt, BS; *Instr* Jan Barger, BA; *Instr* Gayle Batson, BA; *Instr* Ming Wu Chow, PhD; *Instr* Tarrence Corbin, MFA; *Instr* Aimee Dixon, BA; *Instr* Park Fleming; *Instr* Charles Fogle; *Instr* Harvey Luber, BS; *Instr* Leslie Mangiamele, BA; *Instr* Debra Moseley, BFA; *Instr* B J Moses, BA; *Instr* Sheila Parsons, MA; *Instr* Susan Purvis, BA; *Instr* Fred Schmidt, MFA; *Instr* Aj Smith, MFA; *Instr* Marjorie Smith, MFA; *Instr* David Soos; *Instr* Richard Williams; *Instr* Nancy Wilson, MA; *Instr* Derek Wood, MFA. Instrs: FT 4, PT 27
Estab 1960, dept estab 1965; pub; D & E; schol; SC 62, LC 3; enrl D 350, E 300 children & adults
Ent Req: Open to anyone age 3 through adult
Tuition: 12 wk course for adults $60, 12 wk course for children $33, dance classes $25 per month
Courses: Art History, Calligraphy, Drawing, Jewelry, Painting, Photography, Printmaking, Sculpture, Theatre Arts, Enameling, Glassblowing, Pottery, Stained Glass, Woodworking
Adult Hobby Classes: Enrl 600; tuition $75. Courses—same as regular
Children's Classes: Enrl 150; tuition $45 per 12 wks. Courses—same as regular
Summer School: Dir, Bill Atkins. Enrl 600; tuition $60 per 8 wks. Courses—same as regular

UNIVERSITY OF ARKANSAS AT LITTLE ROCK, Dept of Art, 33rd and University Ave, 72204. Tel 501-565-3182. *Chmn* Dr Lloyd W Benjamin III. Instrs: FT 11, PT 5
Estab 1928; pub; D & E; schol; SC, LC; enrl 5000
Ent Req: HS grad
Degrees: BA 4 yr, MA(studio), MA(art history)

Tuition: $450 per yr
Courses: Art Education, Art History, †Commercial Art, †Drawing, Handicrafts, †Painting, †Photography, †Printmaking, †Sculpture, †Design, †Pottery
Summer School: Dir, Lloyd W Benjamin III. Enrl 200; tuition $270 per term. Courses—Art History, Studio Art

MAGNOLIA

SOUTHERN ARKANSAS UNIVERSITY, Dept of Art, Magnolia Branch, Jackson & Southern University, 71753. Tel 501-234-5120. *Chmn* Willard C Carpenter; *Asst Prof* Fred Henry, MFA; *Asst Prof* Dianne O'Hern, MA
Estab 1909; pub; D & E; scholarships; SC 18, LC 4; enrl D 240, non-maj 260, maj 40
Ent Req: HS dipl
Degrees: BA and BSE 4 yr
Tuition: Res—undergrad $780 per yr; nonres—undergrad $1250 per yr
Courses: †Art Education, Art History, Ceramics, Drawing, †Graphic Arts, †Painting, †Printmaking, †Sculpture, Architecture
Children's Classes: Enrl 30; tuition $30. Courses—Kinder Art
Summer School: Chmn, Willard C Carpenter. Enrl 80

MONTICELLO

UNIVERSITY OF ARKANSAS AT MONTICELLO, Fine Arts Dept,* 71665. Tel 501-367-6811. *Dept Chmn* John W Dougherty
Degrees: BA
Tuition: Res—$720 per yr; nonres—$1490 per yr
Courses: Art Education, Art History, Ceramics, Design, Drawing, Jewelry, Painting, Printmaking

PINE BLUFF

SOUTHEAST ARKANSAS ARTS AND SCIENCE CENTER, Little Firehouse Studio,* Civic Center, 200 E Eighth, 71601. Tel 501-536-3375, 536-2476
Estab 1966; pvt; D & E; SC 14, LC 1; enrl D 200, E 250
Degrees: No degrees granted
Tuition: $15-$75 per course; no campus res
Courses: Art Education, Art History, Ceramics, Drawing, Graphic Arts, Jewelry, Painting, Photography, Printmaking, Theatre Arts, Stained Glass
Children's Classes: Enrl 15; tui $15 per course. Courses—Crafts, Drawing, Mixed Media, Painting, Pottery, Weaving. Special workshops with guest artists

UNIVERSITY OF ARKANSAS AT PINE BLUFF, Art Dept,* UAPB Box 15, 71601. Tel 501-541-6500. *Acad Dean* Lawerence A Davis Jr
Scholarships offered
Degrees: BS
Tuition: Res—$600 per yr; nonres—$1230 per yr
Courses: Art Appreciation, Art Education, Art History, Calligraphy, Ceramics, Design, Drawing, Handicrafts, Jewelry, Painting, Printmaking, Sculpture, Textile Design, Weaving

RUSSELLVILLE

ARKANSAS TECH UNIVERSITY, Dept of Art, 72801. Tel 501-968-0244. *Head Dept* Ron Reynolds, MA; *Prof* Ed Wilwers, MFA; *Asst Prof* Gary Barnes, MA
Estab 1909; pub; D & E; schol; SC 28, LC 5, GC 1; enrl D 200, nonmaj 130, maj 90
Ent Req: HS dipl
Degrees: BA 4 yr
Tuition: Res—undergrad $360 per sem, $30 per cr hr, grad $36 per cr hr; nonres—undergrad $710 per sem, $59 per cr hr, grad $74 per cr hr; no campus res
Courses: Advertising Design, Architecture, †Art Education, Art History, Ceramics, †Commercial Art, Display, Drawing, Graphic Arts, Graphic Design, Illustration, Industrial Design, Lettering, Painting, Printmaking, Teacher Training, †Fine Arts, Intro to Art, Packaging Design
Adult Hobby Classes: Drawing, Oil Painting, Watercolor
Summer School: Head Dept, Ron Reynolds. Enrl 30-50; tuition res—$140, nonres—$285; term of 6 wk beginning June 7 and July 12. Courses—Art Education, Art History, Design, Drawing, Painting

SEARCY

HARDING UNIVERSITY, Dept of Art, Box 938, 72143. Tel 501-268-6161, Ext 426. *Chmn Dept* Don D Robinson, MA; *Prof* Elizabeth Mason, MA; *Assoc Prof* Faye Doran, EdD; *Assoc Prof* Paul Pitt, MA; *Asst Prof* John Keller, MA; *Instructor* Stanley Green, BSE
Estab 1924; pvt; D; schol; SC 27, LC 9, GC 7; enrl D 65, non-maj 15, maj 65
Ent Req: HS dipl, ACT
Degrees: BA, BS and BFA 4 yrs, MEd 5-6 yrs
Tuition: $92 per sem hr; campus res—room & board $1824 per yr
Courses: Advertising Design, Aesthetics, Art Education, Art History, Ceramics, Commercial Art, Constructions, Drafting, Drawing, Graphic Design, Graphic Arts, Handicrafts, History of Art & Archaeology, Illustration, Interior Design, Jewelry, Lettering, Mixed Media, Painting, Printmaking, Sculpture, Silversmithing, Weaving, 2-D Design, Color Theory
Summer School: Dir, Dr Larry Long. Enrl 1000; tuition $82 per sem hr for 10 wk term beginning June 9. Courses—vary depending upon the demand, usually Art History, Ceramics, Drawing, Painting, Art Education

SILOAM SPRINGS

JOHN BROWN UNIVERSITY, Art Dept, 72761. Tel 501-524-3131. *Head Dept* Doris I Brookhart, MFA
Estab 1919; pvt; D; SC 9, LC 3
Ent Req: HS grad
Degrees: AS(Art)
Tuition: $2700 yr, $1350 per sem, $112.50 per sem hr; campus res—room & board $2100
Courses: Art Education, Painting, Design and Color, Crafts (copper tooling, enameling, jewelry, macrame, mosaic, pottery, weaving)

STATE UNIVERSITY

ARKANSAS STATE UNIVERSITY, Dept of Art, PO Box 1920, 72467. Tel 501-972-3050. *Chmn Dept* William Allen, PhD; *Prof* Evan Lindquist, MFA; *Prof* Karl Richards, PhD; *Assoc Prof* T R Baker, DEd; *Assoc Prof* Tom Chaffee, MFA; *Asst Prof* Charlott Jones, PhD; *Asst Prof* John Keech, MFA; *Asst Prof* Roger Carlisle, MFA; *Asst Prof* Don Osborn, MFA; *Asst Prof* William Rowe, MFA; *Asst Prof* Curtis Sleele, MFA; *Asst Prof* Ronald Clayton, MFA. Instrs: FT 12
Estab 1909, dept estab 1938; pub; D & E; scholarships; SC 33, LC 10, GC 34; enrl D 300, E 100, non-maj 800, maj 192, grad 10
Ent Req: HS dipl
Degrees: BFA, BSE and BS 4 yrs, MA
Tuition: Res—$375 per sem, $32 per sem hr; nonres—$775 per sem, $66 per sem hr; campus res—room & board $820 per yr
Courses: Aesthetics, †Art Education, Art History, Calligraphy, †Ceramics, Constructions, Drawing, †Graphic Arts, †Graphic Design, History of Art & Archaeology, †Illustration, Lettering, †Painting, †Printmaking, †Teacher Training
Adult Hobby Classes: Enrl 50; tuition $32 per sem hr. Courses—Ceramics, Painting
Summer School: Tuition res—$182; nonres—$370 for term of 5 wks beginning June 1 & July 6. Courses—Art Appreciation, Art Education, Art History, Drawing, Painting, Sculpture

CALIFORNIA

ALTA LOMA

CHAFFEY COMMUNITY COLLEGE, Art Dept,* 5885 Haven Ave, 91701. Tel 714-987-1737
E; scholarships offered
Degrees: AA
Tuition: Nonres—$55 per unit
Courses: Advertising Design, Art History, Ceramics, Design, Drawing, Industrial Design, Interior Design, Jewelry, Painting, Photography, Printmaking, Stage Design, Weaving

ANGWIN

PACIFIC UNION COLLEGE, Art Dept, 94508. Tel 707-965-6011. *Chmn* Jon Carstens
Degrees: AS, BA, BS, cert
Courses: Advertising Design, Art Appreciation, Art History, Ceramics, Design, Illustration, Painting, Photography, Printmaking, Sculpture, Stained Glass

APTOS

CABRILLO COLLEGE, Visual Arts Division,* 6500 Soquel Dr, 95003. Tel 408-425-6464. *Chmn* David F McGuire. Instrs: FT 12, PT 8
Estab 1959; pub; D & E; SC 46, LC 7
Ent Req: HS dipl
Degrees: AA 2 yr
Courses: Ceramics, Drawing, Graphic Arts, Graphic Design, Handicrafts, History of Art & Archaeology, Jewelry, Painting, Photography, Sculpture, Textile Design
Summer School: Courses offered

ARCATA

HUMBOLDT STATE UNIVERSITY, College of Creative Arts & Humanities,* 95521. Tel 707-826-3625. *Chmn* W T Anderson; *Faculty* M D Benoon; *Faculty* M Bravo; *Faculty* C DiCostanza; *Faculty* M Isaacson; *Faculty* S Jacobson; *Faculty* R Johnson; *Faculty* T L Knight; *Faculty* E Land-Weber; *Faculty* D M LaPlantz; *Faculty* L B Marak; *Faculty* D Mitsanas; *Faculty* M Morgan; *Faculty* L Price; *Faculty* S Ross; *Faculty* E S Sundet; *Faculty* W H Thompson
Estab 1913; pub; D & E; scholarships; SC 35, LC 11, GC 11
Degrees: MA 1 yr, BA 4 yr, BA with credential 5 yr
Tuition: Res—$4200 per yr; campus residence available
Courses: Ceramics, Drawing, Graphic Design, Jewelry, Painting, Photography, Printmaking, Sculpture, Teacher Training
Children's Classes: Enrl 10, art 12
Summer School: Enrl 800; tui $25 per unit, 6 wk term beginning June

AZUSA

AZUSA PACIFIC UNIVERSITY, College of Liberal Arts, Art Dept,* Alosta at Citrus Ave, 91702. Tel 213-969-3434. *Chmn Dept* Robert S Bullock, MA; *Instr* Tom Dunn, MA; *Lectr* Steve Kunze, MS; *Lectr* Dixie Pieslak
Estab 1915, dept estab 1974; den; D & E; scholarships; SC 21, LC 3; enrl E 80,

non-maj 120, maj 22
Ent Req: HS dipl, state test
Degrees: BA(Art) 4 yrs
Tuition: $4312 per yr
Courses: Advertising Design, †Art Education, Art History, †Ceramics, Drawing, Graphic Arts, Illustration, †Painting, Printmaking, Teacher Training

CITRUS COLLEGE, Art Dept,* 18824 Foothill Blvd, Box RRR, 91348. Tel 213-335-0521. *Art Dept Chmn* Robert Hallett, MA
Estab 1915; pub; D & E; scholarships; SC 26, LC 7; enrl D 400, E 175, non-maj 400, maj 175
Ent Req: HS dipl
Degrees: AA and AS 2 yrs
Tuition: Nonres—$76 per unit
Courses: Advertising Design, Art History, Calligraphy, Ceramics, Collages, Commercial Art, Drawing, Graphic Arts, History of Art & Archaeology, Interior Design, Jewelry, Lettering, Mixed Media, Painting, Photography, Printmaking
Children's Classes: Courses—Ceramics, Painting
Summer School: Dir, Robert Hallet. Enrl 150; Term of 6 wks beginning June 20. Courses—Art History, Ceramics, Drawing, Painting

BAKERSFIELD

BAKERSFIELD COLLEGE, Art Dept, 1801 Panorama Dr, 93305. Tel 805-395-4011. *Chmn* Bertil Brink
Estab 1913; pub; D & E; SC 16, LC 4; enrl D 6000, maj 150-200
Ent Req: Ent exam, open door policy
Degrees: AA 2 yr
Courses: Glassblowing
Adult Hobby Classes: Enrl 100-150. Courses—Ceramics, Painting, Photography
Summer School: Dir, Ron McMasters. For term of 6 wks beginning June. Courses—Ceramics, Design, Drawing, Figure Drawing, Photography

CALIFORNIA STATE COLLEGE BAKERSFIELD, Fine Arts Dept,* 9001 Stockdale Hwy, 93309. Tel 805-833-2241. *Chmn* Jerome Kleinsasser. Instrs: FT 8
Scholarships offered
Degrees: BA
Tuition: Res—$152 per qtr; nonres $222 per qtr
Courses: Art Education, Art History, Design, Drawing, Painting, Photography, Printmaking, Weaving

BELMONT

COLLEGE OF NOTRE DAME, Dept of Art, 1400 Ralston Ave, 94002. Tel 415-593-1601. *Chmn* Robert David Ramsey. Instrs: FT 2, PT 6
Estab 1951; den; D & E; scholarships; SC 18, LC 12; enrl D 200, E 70, maj 50
Ent Req: HS dipl, ent exam
Degrees: BA 3 1/2-4 yrs, BFA, MAT
Courses: Advertising Design, Art Education, Ceramics, Drawing, History of Art & Archaeology, Interior Design, Painting, Photography, Sculpture, Anatomical Drawing, Color, Composition, Etching, Gallery Techniques, Lithography, Silk Screen, 2-D & 3-D Design
Summer School: Upper division courses as in regular program plus special art education workshops; 6 wk term

BERKELEY

PACIFIC BASIN SCHOOL OF TEXTILE ARTS, 1659 San Pablo Ave, 94702. Tel 415-526-9836. *Admin Dir* Gwen Jennings, BA; *Program Adminr* Inger Jensen, MA; *Program Dir* Pat McGaw, MFA; *Program Adminr* Kathleen Larisch, MFA
Estab 1972; SC 74, LC 13; enrl D 544, maj 21
Ent Req: Interview and portfolio
Degrees: Cert
Tuition: $4005 per yr; $85 - $94 per cr hr
Courses: Art History, Costume Design & Construction, Design, Drawing, Fashion Arts, Handicrafts, Interior Design, Photography, Sculpture, Textile Design, †Weaving, Surface Design
Summer School: Enrl 141; tuition $40 - $350 for term of 1 - 5 wks beginning June 20. Courses—Loom Weaving, Polychromatic Printing, Spinning, Papermaking, Computer Aided Pattern Design, Marketing, Professional Weaving, Katazome, Design

UNIVERSITY OF CALIFORNIA, BERKELEY
—**College of Letters & Sciences,** 201 Campbell Hall, 94720. Tel 415-642-2582. *Chmn* James S Melchert, MFA; *Prof* Elmer N Bischoff, MA; *Prof* Joan Brown, MFA; *Prof* Sidney Gordin; *Prof* Robert Hartman, MA; *Prof* David Simpson, MA; *Prof* Peter H Voulkos, MFA; *Prof* Brian Wall
Estab 1915; pub; D; scholarships
Degrees: AB
Courses: Art & Art History
—**College of Environmental Design,** 234 Wurster Hall, 94720. Tel 415-642-0832. *Dean Environmental Design* Richard Bender; *Chmn Architecture* Sanford Hirshen; *Chmn City & Regional Planning* Frederick Collingnon; *Chmn Landscape Archit* Robert Twiss
College encompasses Schools of Architecture, Landscape Architecture & City & Regional Planning. Maintains reference library of 150,000 vols; pub; D & E; scholarships
Degrees: AB, AB(Archit, Landscape), MArch, MCP, PhD
Courses: Design, Landscape Architecture, Photography, Environmental Design, History of Environment, Urban Planning, Visual Studies

CARMEL

CARMEL ART INSTITUTE, School of Painting,* 25800 Hatton Rd, PO Box 9, 93921. Tel 408-624-9951. *Pres* John Cunningham
Estab 1938, inc 1955; pvt; D; enrl D 20
Degrees: Certificate of Completion, 4 yr course for Fine Arts, objective painter
Courses: Aesthetics, Painting, Anatomy, Design, Etching, Lithography

CARSON

CALIFORNIA STATE UNIVERSITY, DOMINGUEZ HILLS, Art Dept, School of Humanities & Fine Arts, 1000 E Victoria St, 90747. Tel 213-516-3310. *Chmn* Bernard W Baker
Estab 1960; pub; D & E; SC 35, LC 25; enrl maj 130
Ent Req: 2.0 GPA
Degrees: BA 4 yr
Tuition: Res—undergrad fall quarter $141 for 5.9 units or less, $231 for 6 units or more, winter & spring quarter $130 for 5.9 units or less, $220 or 6 units or more; nonres—undergrad $72 per unit plus $240 reg per quarter
Courses: Art History, Design, Studio Art, Certificate in Graphic Production & Single Subject Credential in Art
Children's Classes: Tuition $36 - $55 per unit for 4 - 8 wk term. Courses - Crafts
Summer School: Dir Bernard W Baker. Enrl 40; tuition $36 - $55 per unit for 4 - 8 wk term. Courses—Crafts, Experiencing Creative Art

CHICO

CALIFORNIA STATE UNIVERSITY, CHICO, Art Dept, 95929. Tel 916-895-5331, 895-5218. *Chmn* Marion A Epting; *Graduate Advisor* Sharon Smith; *Undergraduate Advisor* Michael Monahan; *Instr* Michael Bishop, MFA; *Instr* James Crawford, EdD; *Instr* Marion Epting, MFA; *Instr* Paul Feldhaus, MA; *Instr* Thomas Griffith, MFA; *Instr* Richard Hornaday, MFA; *Instr* Sherry Karver, MFA; *Instr* Yoshio Kusaba, PhD; *Instr* Ira Latour, BA; *Instr* Fred Lucero, MA; *Instr* James McManus, MFA; *Instr* Winston Megorden, MA; *Instr* Dolores Mitchell, PhD; *Instr* Michael Monahan, MFA; *Instr* Ken Morrow, MA; *Instr* Vernon Patrick, MFA; *Instr* Ann Pierce, MFA; *Instr* Michael Simmons, EdD; *Instr* Sharon Smith, EdD; *Instr* Karen VanDerpool, MFA; *Instr* Stephen Wilson, MFA; *Instr* Jack Windsor, MA
Estab 1887; pvt; D & E; scholarships; SC 39, LC 29, GC 29; enrl nonmaj & maj 1704, grad 59
Ent Req: Ent exam and test scores
Degrees: BA 4 yr, MA 1 1/2 yr minimum
Tuition: Res—$190.50 per sem for less than 6 cr hrs, $205.50 per sem for over 6 cr hrs; nonres—$94.50 per unit
Courses: Aesthetics, Art History, †Ceramics, †Drawing, †Painting, †Printmaking, †Sculpture, †Glass, †Weaving
Summer School: Chmn, Marion A Epting. Courses—same as above

CLAREMONT

PITZER COLLEGE, Dept of Art, 1050 N Mills Ave, 91711. Tel 714-621-8129. *Prof Art* C H Hertel
Estab 1964; pvt; D; scholarships; SC 8, LC 6; enrl Sept-June maj 19, grad 10 (Claremont Grad School)
Ent Req: HS dipl, various criteria, apply Dir of Admis
Degrees: BA 4 yr
Tuition: Res—$7110 (including campus res)
Courses: Aesthetics, Ceramics, Drawing, Graphic Arts, History of Art & Archaeology, Painting, Photography, Sculpture, Environments, Weaving

POMONA COLLEGE, Art Dept, College & E Bonita Ave, 91711. Tel 714-621-8000, Ext 2221. *Chmn Dept* Judon Emerick, PhD; *Prof* Carl Benjamin, MFA; *Prof* Gerald Ackerman, PhD; *Assoc Prof* Norman Hines, MFA; *Assoc Prof* Charles Daugherty, MFA; *Asst Prof* Rita Dibert, MFA; *Asst Prof* George Gorse, PhD
Estab 1889; pvt; D; schol; SC 15, LC 25; enrl D 330 maj 37
Ent Req: HS dipl
Degrees: BA 4 yrs
Tuition: Res—undergrad $2500 per sem, $3500 with room & board
Courses: †Art History, Ceramics, Drawing, Graphic Design, Painting, Photography, Sculpture, †Practice of Art

SCRIPPS COLLEGE, Art Dept, Lang Art Bldg, Ninth at Columbia, 91711. Tel 714-621-8000, Ext 2973. *Chmn Dept* Neda Alhilali
Estab 1928, dept estab 1933; pub; D; scholarships; enrl D 580, non-maj 480, maj 100
Ent Req: HS dipl
Degrees: BA
Courses: †Architecture, †Art History, †Ceramics, †Drawing, †Film, †History of Art & Archaeology, Mixed Media, †Painting, †Photography, †Printmaking, †Sculpture, Fiber Arts, Typography

COALINGA

WEST HILLS COLLEGE, Fine Arts Dept, 300 Cherry Lane, 93210. Tel 209-935-1686. *Instr* Ronald T Mitchell, MA; *Instr* Arnold Walter, MA
Estab 1935; pub; D & E; SC 15, LC 2; enrl D 625, E 1250, non-maj 25, maj 10
Degrees: AA 2 yrs
Tuition: Campus res available
Courses: †Advertising Design, †Art History, †Ceramics, †Commercial Art, †Drawing, Fashion Arts, †Graphic Design, †Illustration, Lettering, †Museum Staff Training, †Painting, Sculpture

COLUMBIA

COLUMBIA COLLEGE, Dept of Physical Creative and Performing Arts,* PO Box 1849, 95310. Tel 209-532-3141. *Faculty* Jall Barber; *Faculty* Dale L Bunse
Estab 1968; pub; D & E; SC 50, LC 4; enrl D 100, E 75, non-maj 90, maj 10
Ent Req: HS dipl or over 18 yrs old
Degrees: AA 2 yrs
Tuition: Nonres—$58 per unit; no campus res
Courses: Art History, Calligraphy, Ceramics, Costume Design & Construction, Design, Drawing, Jewelry, Lettering, Painting, Photography, Printmaking, Sculpture, Silversmithing
Summer School: Dir, C H Palmer. Courses—Ceramics, Watercolor

COMPTON

COMPTON COMMUNITY COLLEGE, Art Department, 1111 E Artesia Blvd, 90221. . *Prof* Van E Slater; *Assoc Prof* Roberto Gomez. Instrs: FT 2
Estab 1929; pub; D & E; schol; SC 16, LC 6; enrl D 3500, E 2000, maj 18
Ent Req: HS dipl, 18 yrs of age
Degrees: AA 2 yr
Tuition: None for state residents
Courses: Advertising Design, Drafting, Drawing, History of Art & Archaeology, Lettering, Painting, Photography, Theatre Arts, Afro-American Art, Art Appreciation, Showcard Writing
Summer School: Courses—Art Appreciation

CORONA DEL MAR

BRANDT PAINTING WORKSHOPS, 405 Goldenrod Ave, 92625. Tel 714-675-0093. *Co-Dir* Rex Brandt, BA; *Co-Dir* Joan Irving
Estab 1946; pvt; D; schol; SC 3; enrl D 145
Ent Req: Grad degree in art or equivalent
Tuition: 5 day session $110; no campus res. Summer school only
Courses: Painting

CORONADO

CORONADO SCHOOL OF FINE ARTS, 176 C Ave, PO Box 156, 92118. *Dir* Monty Lewis. Instrs: FT D 2, E 1, PT 6
Estab 1944; pvt; SC, LC; enrl D 50, E 25
Degrees: Dipl 3-4 yrs
Tuition: $160 per 4 wks, PT $109 per 4 wks. Approved for veterans and foreign students
Courses: Advertising Design, Art History, Commercial Art, Graphic Arts, Illustration, Painting, Sculpture, Fine Arts, Mural Decoration
Children's Classes: Enrl 15; tuition $25 for Sat morning classes
Summer School: Dir, Monty Lewis. Enrl 75; tuition $160 per 4 wk; watercolor seminar $95 per 4 wk, $160 per 8 wk

COSTA MESA

ORANGE COAST COLLEGE, Division of Fine Arts, 2701 Fairview, 92626. Tel 714-432-5629. *Division Dean* Edward R Baker. Instrs: FT 33, Adjunct 107
Estab 1946; pub; D & E; scholarships; SC 225, LC 25; enrl D 4000, E 3000, maj 750
Ent Req: Ent exam
Degrees: AA 2 yr
Tuition: None; no campus res
Courses: Photography, Theatre Arts, Basic Exhibition Design, Weaving Fibers
Summer School: Eight wk session. Courses—same as regular session

CUPERTINO

DE ANZA COLLEGE, Art Dept, Fine Arts Division, 21250 Stevens Creek Blvd, 95014. Tel 408-996-4832. *Dean of Fine Arts* George Beers; *Instructor* Gerald Eknoian; *Instructor* William Geisinger; *Instructor* Sal Pecoraro; *Instructor* Lillian Quirke; *Instructor* Lee Tacang; *Instructor* Charles Walker; *Instructor* Michael Cooper; *Instructor* Charles Jascob
Estab 1967, dept estab 1967; pub; D & E; scholarships
Ent Req: 16 yrs of age
Degrees: Certificates of Proficiency, AA 2 yrs
Courses: Aesthetics, Art History, Ceramics, Drafting, Drawing, Film, Graphic Arts, Graphic Design, Lettering, Painting, Photography, Printmaking, Sculpture, Textile Design, Theatre Arts, Video, Weaving, Stage Design, Textile Design, Theatre Arts, Video, Dye, Spinning
Adult Hobby Classes: Tuition varies per class. Courses—Bronze Casting, Calligraphy, Museum Tours, Stained Glass
Children's Classes: Computer art camp
Summer School: Dean, George Beers. Courses—Drawing, Jewelry, Painting, Printmaking, Textile Class

CYPRESS

CYPRESS COLLEGE, Fine Arts Division, 9200 Valley View St, 90630. Tel 714-826-2220, Ext 142. *Chairperson* Lester Johnson, MA
Estab 1966; pub; D & E; scholarships; enrl D 15,200
Ent Req: HS dipl
Degrees: AA 2 yrs
Tuition: $47.50 per unit; no campus res
Courses: Advertising Design, Art History, Ceramics, Drawing, Film, Jewelry, Painting, Printmaking, Sculpture, Stage Design, Textile Design, Theatre Arts
Adult Hobby Classes: Adults may take any classes offered both day and extended; also offer adult education classes
Summer School: Extended Day Coordinator, Dr Bonnie Fouste

DAVIS

UNIVERSITY OF CALIFORNIA, DAVIS, Art Dept, 95616. Tel 916-752-0105. *Dept Chmn* Open. Instrs: FT 17
Estab 1952; pub; D; scholarships; SC 28, LC 35; enrl maj 130, others 1000
Degrees: BA 4 yrs, MA(Art History), MFA(Art Studio)
Tuition: Res—$451; nonres—$1582 per quarter
Courses: †Art History, Ceramics, Drawing, Film, Painting, Photography, Printmaking, Sculpture, †Art Practice

EL CAJON

GROSSMONT COLLEGE, Art Dept, Div of Fine Arts, 8800 Grossmont College Dr, 92020. Tel 619-465-1700. Instrs: FT 9
Estab 1961; pub; D & E; schol; SC 22, LC 1; enrl total 1000
Ent Req: None
Degrees: AA
Courses: Ceramics, Drawing, Painting, Photography, Sculpture, Art History, Composition
Summer School: Dir, Suda House. Enrl 100. Courses—Art History, Photography

EUREKA

COLLEGE OF THE REDWOODS, Art Dept,* 7351 Tompkins Hill Rd, 95501. Tel 707-443-8411. Instrs: FT 5 PT 8
Estab 1964; pub; D & E; scholarships; SC 15, LC 3 per quarter; enrl 8330, maj 160
Ent Req: HS grad
Degrees: AA 2 yrs
Tuition: Nonres—$50 per unit
Courses: Art Fundamentals, Fabrics
Summer School: Tuition free. Courses to be announced

FRESNO

CALIFORNIA STATE UNIVERSITY, FRESNO, Art Dept,* Maple & Shaw Aves, 93740. Tel 209-294-4240. *Chmn* Ara H Dolarian. Instrs: FT 18
Estab 1911, dept estab 1915; pub; D; schol; SC 45, LC 9, GC 4; enrl 1000
Ent Req: HS dipl, SAT or ACT
Degrees: BA 4 yrs, MA 2 yrs
Tuition: Res—$138 per yr; nonres—$243 per yr; campus res available
Courses: Art Education, Art History, Calligraphy, Ceramics, Drawing, Film, Goldsmithing, Graphic Design, Handicrafts, Jewelry, Museum Staff Training, Painting, Photography, Printmaking, Sculpture, Silversmithing, Teacher Training, Textile Design
Adult Hobby Classes: Tuition $35 unit. Courses—various
Summer School: Courses—Ceramics

FRESNO CITY COLLEGE, Art Dept, 1101 E University Ave, 93741. Tel 209-442-4600. *Dean* Carl Waddel, PhD
Estab 1910, dept estab 1955; pub; D & E; SC 13, LC 3; enrl D 705, E 340
Ent Req: None, open door policy
Degrees: AA 2 yrs
Tuition: $6 membership fee per sem (6 units or more); nonres $685 per sem (16 units or more)
Courses: Art History, Ceramics, Drawing, Handicrafts, Painting, Printmaking, Sculpture, Art Appreciation

FULLERTON

CALIFORNIA STATE UNIVERSITY, FULLERTON, Art Dept, 92634. Tel 714-773-3471. *Dean Sch Arts* Jerry Samuelson, MA; *Chmn Dept* George James
Estab 1957, dept estab 1959; pub; D & E; SC 62, LC 27, GC 12; enrl grad 85, undergrad 700
Ent Req: HS dipl, SAT or ACT
Degrees: BA, BFA, MA, MFA
Tuition: Res—undergrad & grad $212 for 0-6 units, $347 for 7 or more units; nonres—undergrad & grad $108 per units plus $230 or $365; no campus res
Courses: Art Education, Art History, Ceramics, Design, Drawing, Graphic Design, Illustration, Jewelry, Painting, Photography, Printmaking, Sculpture, Fibers, Museum Studies, Wood
Summer School: Tuition $175 per 3 unit lecture class of 6 wks. Courses—Art History, Introduction to Art

FULLERTON COLLEGE, Division of Fine Arts,* Art Dept, 321 E Chapman Ave, 92634. Tel 714-871-8000. *Chmn Division Fine Arts* Terrence Blackley
Estab 1913; pub; D & E; scholarships
Ent Req: HS dipl, ent exam
Degrees: AA 2 yr
Tuition: Nonres—$72 per unit; no campus res
Courses: Art Education, Art History, Ceramics, Display, Drawing, Graphic Arts, Graphic Design, Illustration, Jewelry, Museum Staff Training, Painting, Photography, Printmaking, Sculpture, Teacher Training, Textile Design, Weaving, Woodworking

GILROY

GAVILAN COLLEGE, Art Dept, 5055 Santa Therese Blvd, 95020. Tel 408-847-1400. *Fine Arts Dept Chmn* Kent Child. Instrs: FT 2, PT 3
Estab 1919; pub; D & E; SC 12, LC 2; enrl D 150, E 75, maj 30
Ent Req: HS dipl or 18 yrs of age
Degrees: AA 2 yrs
Tuition: None to res; no campus res
Courses: Ceramics, Drafting, Drawing, Painting, Photography, Sculpture, Teacher Training, Theatre Arts, History of Art & Architecture
Summer School: Courses—Ceramics, Drawing, Painting

GLENDALE

GLENDALE COLLEGE, Dept of Fine Arts, 1500 N Verdugo Rd, 91208. Tel 213-240-1000. *Chmn Dept* Veloris Lang, EdD; *Prof* Robert W Brown, MFA; *Prof* Leonard de Grassi, MA; *Prof* Louis Gross, MA; *Prof* Martin Mondrus, MFA; *Prof* Robert E Thomsen, MA; *Assoc Prof* Andrew Georgias, MFA; *Asst Prof* Robert Kibler, MA; *Instr* Susan Sing, MA; *Instr* Carol Arutian, MFA; *Instr* Janet Olenik, MA
Estab 1927; pub; D & E; SC 25, LC 7; enrl D 4100, E 3900, nonmaj 800, maj 200
Ent Req: HS dipl, ent exam
Degrees: AA 2 yrs
Tuition: None
Courses: Advertising Design, Architecture, Art History, Ceramics, Commercial Art, Design, Drafting, Drawing, Film, Graphic Arts, Graphic Design, Lettering, Painting, Photography, Printmaking, Sculpture, Crafts, Serigraphy
Summer School: Dir, Dr John Davitt. Term of 8 wk beginning end of June.
Courses—Art History, Ceramics, Design, Drawing, Photography

HAYWARD

CALIFORNIA STATE UNIVERSITY, HAYWARD, Art Dept, 94542. Tel 415-881-3111
Estab 1960; pub; D & E; scholarships; SC 30, LC 12; enrl 9000
Ent Req: HS dipl, ent exam, ACT
Degrees: BA 4 yr
Tuition: Res—undergrad $285 per yr; nonres—undergrad $2160 per yr
Adult Hobby Classes: Courses offered through Continuing Education Dept

CHABOT COLLEGE, Humanities Division, 25555 Hesperian Blvd, 94545. Tel 415-782-3000, Ext 287. *Chmn* Elliott Charnow. Instrs: FT 240, PT 400
Estab 1961; pub; D & E; schol; SC 27, LC 5
Ent Req: HS dipl
Degrees: AA 2 yr
Tuition: None to res; nonres—$24.49 per quarter unit, 15 units or more, $367.35 per yr; no campus res
Courses: Advertising Design, Ceramics, Costume Design & Construction, Drafting, Drawing, History of Art & Archaeology, Illustration, Lettering, Painting, Sculpture, Stage Design, Theatre Arts, Cartooning
Summer School: Dir, Robert Hunter. Enrl 72 - 100; tuition $2 - $100 per 6 wks.
Courses—Art History, Drawing, Introduction to Art, Sculpture, Watercolor

HOLLYWOOD

HOLLYWOOD ART CENTER SCHOOL, * 2027 N Highland Ave, 90028. Tel 213-851-1103
Estab 1912; pvt; D & E; SC 6; enrl D 40, E 12
Ent Req: HS dipl, submission of art work
Degrees: 3 yr cert
Courses: Cartooning, Fabric Design, Furniture

HUNTINGTON BEACH

GOLDEN WEST COLLEGE, Arts, Humanities and Social Sciences Institute,* 15744 Golden West St, 92647. Tel 714-892-7711, Ext 405 and 406. *Dean* Thomas A Chambers, PhD; *Assoc Dean* Donna E Willoughby, MA; *Instructor* R Camp, MFA; *Instructor* H Clemans, MA; *Instructor* B Conley, MA; *Instructor* P Donaldson, MFA; *Instructor* D Ebert, MA; *Instructor* J Heard, MA; *Instructor* R Huber, MA; *Instructor* A Jackson, MA; *Instructor* C Mitchell, MA; *Instructor* K Mortenson, MFA; *Instructor* R Schiffner, MA; *Instructor* P Sopocko, MA; *Instructor* N Tornheim, MA; *Instructor* H Warner, MA; *Instructor* R Alderette, MFA; *Instructor* S Rogers, MA. Instrs: PT 26
Estab 1966; pub; D & E; SC 12, LC 6; enrl D 13,820, E 9339
Ent Req: HS dipl
Degrees: AA 2 yrs
Tuition: Nonres—undergrad $73 per unit
Courses: †Advertising Design, Art History, Calligraphy, Ceramics, Costume Design & Construction, Display, Drafting, Drawing, Illustration, Interior Design, Jewelry, Lettering, Mixed Media, Painting, Photography, Printmaking, Sculpture, Silversmithing, Stage Design, Textile Design, Theatre Arts, Video
Summer School: Classes offered

IDYLLWILD

UNIVERSITY OF SOUTHERN CALIFORNIA, Idyllwild School of Music and the Arts,* PO Box 38, 92349. Tel 714-659-2171. *Chmn Painting & Drawing Workshops* Francoise Gilot; *Instructor* Lucy Lewis; *Instructor* Joseph Mugnaini; *Instructor* Susan Peterson; *Instructor* Harry Sternberg; *Instructor* Cornelia Von Mengershansen; *Instructor* Norman Corwin; *Instructor* Bella Lewitzky
Estab 1950; pvt; Idyllwild School of Music and the Arts is a 14 wk summer program beginning in mid-June with courses in the arts for all ages; schol
Degrees: Not granted by the Idyllwild Campus, university credits earned through USC-LA Campus; documentation provided to high schools for credit
Tuition: Ranges from $145-170 wk; campus res available
Courses: Ceramics, Painting, Sculpture, Etching, Stained Glass
Adult Hobby Classes: Enrl open; tui $165 per wk
Children's Classes: Enrl open; tui $90 - $120 per wk, $65 for half day program. Day and Residential Children's Arts Program; also Youth Ceramics

IMPERIAL

IMPERIAL VALLEY COLLEGE, Art Dept, PO Box 158, 92251. Tel 714-352-8320. Instrs: FT 2
Scholarships offered
Degrees: AA
Courses: Art Appreciation, Art History, Design, Drawing, Painting, Sculpture

IRVINE

UNIVERSITY OF CALIFORNIA, IRVINE, Studio Art Dept, School of Fine Arts, 92717. Tel 714-856-6648. *Dean* Dr Robert Garfius; *Chmn* Jerry Anderson
Estab 1965; pub; D; scholarships; SC 24, LC 2, GC 4
Ent Req: HS dipl
Degrees: BA(Studio Art) 4 yr, MFA(Art)
Tuition: Nonres—$1200 per quarter, $67 per unit less than 12 units
Courses: Architecture, Ceramics, Costume Design & Construction, Design, Drawing, Film, History of Art & Archaeology, Painting, Printmaking, Sculpture, Stage Design, Theatre Arts
Summer School: Ceramics, Drawing, Painting, Printmaking

KENTFIELD

COLLEGE OF MARIN, Dept of Art, 94904. Tel 415-485-9480. *Chmn Dept* Gilbert C Wheat; *Instructor* Rick Hall, MFA
Estab 1926; pub; D & E; SC 48, LC 8; enrl D 5000
Ent Req: HS dipl, ent exam
Degrees: AA, AS 2 yrs
Courses: Advertising Design, Architecture, Art History, Ceramics, Drawing, Interior Design, Jewelry, Museum Staff Training, Painting, Photography, Printmaking, Sculpture, Textile Design, Architectural Design, History of Art & Architecture
Adult Hobby Classes: Enrl 400. Courses—Calligraphy, Ceramics, Drawing, Illustration, Jewelry, Painting, Printing
Children's Classes: College for Kids

LAGUNA BEACH

LAGUNA BEACH SCHOOL OF ART, 2222 Laguna Canyon Rd, 92651. Tel 714-497-3309. *Admin Dir* Ruth Osgood Salyer
Estab 1962; pvt; D & E; schol; SC 20, LC 1
Ent Req: HS dipl or desire to learn at any age beyond high school
Degrees: Cert of completion 3 yrs
Tuition: Res—$160 each 6 hr class per quarter
Courses: Art History, †Ceramics, Collages, Drawing, Graphic Arts, Graphic Design, Jewelry, Mixed Media, †Painting, Photography, †Printmaking, Sculpture, Silversmithing, †Fine Arts
Children's Classes: Enrl 15; tuition $55 per quarter. A 2 hr class on Sat

LA JOLLA

UNIVERSITY OF CALIFORNIA, SAN DIEGO, Visual Arts Dept, B-027, 92093. Tel 619-452-2860. *Dept Chmn* David Antin
Estab 1967; pub; D & E; scholarships; SC 55, LC 30, GC 15; enrl D 3600, maj 250, grad 40
Ent Req: HS dipl
Degrees: BA(Studio Art, Art History/Criticism, & Communications/Visual Arts) 4 yrs, MFA(Studio or Art Criticism) 2-3 yrs
Courses: Art Criticism/Film Criticism
Summer School: Dir, Tom Hull

LA MIRADA

BIOLA UNIVERSITY, Art Dept, 13800 Biola Ave, 90639. Tel 213-944-0351, Ext 3268. *Chmn Dept* Craig Steketee, MFA; *Assoc Prof* Frank Zamora, MFA; *Instructor* Barry Krammers, MFA
Estab 1908, dept estab 1971; pvt; D & E; scholarships; SC 17, LC 4; enrl D 55, maj 55
Ent Req: HS dipl, SAT or ACT
Degrees: BA 4 yrs
Tuition: $3634 per yr, $1817 per sem, PT $152; campus res—room & board $2148 per yr
Courses: †Advertising Design, †Art History, †Ceramics, Design, †Drawing, Lettering, †Painting, †Printmaking, †Sculpture
Summer School: Dir, Craig Stekette. Six week courses. Courses—vary

LANCASTER

ANTELOPE VALLEY COLLEGE, Art Dept, Division of Fine Arts, 3041 W Ave K, 93534. Tel 805-943-3241. *Fine Arts Coordr* Patricia Hinds, MFA; *Prof* Robert McMahan, MFA; *Prof* Richard Sim, MFA
Estab 1929; pub; D & E
Degrees: AA 2 yrs
Tuition: Nonres—undergrad $1170 yr; no campus res
Courses: Art History, Ceramics, Drawing, Graphic Arts, Jewelry, Painting, Photography, Sculpture, Color & Design

LA VERNE

UNIVERSITY OF LA VERNE (Formerly La Verne College), Division of
Humanities, 1950 Third St, 91750. Tel 714-593-3511. *Chmn* John Gingrich
Estab 1891; pvt; D & E; scholarships; SC 12, LC 4; enrl D 125, E 60, maj 6
Ent Req: HS dipl
Degrees: BA(Art) 4 yrs
Tuition: $2775 per sem; campus res—room and board $1375 per sem
Courses: Ceramics, Drawing, History of Art & Archaeology, Painting, Photography,
Sculpture, Theatre Arts, Batik, Quilt & Patch Work, Stained Glass
Summer School: Terms of 3 and 4 wks

LONG BEACH

CALIFORNIA STATE UNIVERSITY, LONG BEACH
—**Art Dept**, 1250 Bellflower Blvd, 90840. Tel 213-498-4376. *Actg Chmn* Robert W
Ramsey. Instrs: FT 42, PT 37
Estab 1949; pub; scholarships; SC 164, LC 26, GC 23, for both locations; enrl 5356
for both locations
Ent Req: HS grad, ent exam
Degrees: BA, BFA 4 yrs, MA, MFA
Tuition: Res— $343.50 per sem for 12 units, $105 each additional; nonres—$1506
per sem for 12 units, $105 each additional; campus res $2200-$2400 per yr
Courses: †Art Education, †Art History, †Ceramics, †Drawing, Handicrafts,
†Illustration, †Jewelry, †Painting, †Printmaking, †Sculpture, †Textile Design,
†General Art, †Metalsmithing
Summer School: Dean, Dr Donna George. Tuition $54 per unit for two 6 wk
sessions beginning June 22. Courses—Drawing, Painting
—**Design Dept**, 1250 Bellflower Blvd, 90840. Tel 213-498-5089. *Chmn* Michael J
Kammermeyer. Instrs: FT 10, PT 9
Estab 1949; pub; SC 164, LC 26, GC 23 for both locations; enrl 5356 for both
locations
Ent Req: HS grad, ent exam
Degrees: BA, BFA 4 yrs, MA, MFA
Tuition: Res—$343.50 per sem for 12 units, $105 each additional; nonres—$1506
per sem for 12 units, $105 each additional; campus res $2200-$2400 per yr
Courses: †Display, †Graphic Arts, †Industrial Design, †Interior Design
Summer School: Dean, Dr Donna George

LONG BEACH CITY COLLEGE, Dept of Art, 4901 E Carson St, 90808. Tel 213-
420-4319. *Head Dept Art* Richard D Keyes, MA; *Instructor* Joseph Hooten, MA;
Instructor Marcia Lewis, MA; *Instructor* Robert McMenomy, MA; *Instructor*
Richard Keyes, MA; *Instructor* James Simpson, MA; *Instructor* Carol Roemer, MA
Pub; D & E; SC 13, LC 2; enrl D 400, E 200, non-maj 450, maj 150
Ent Req: HS dipl, ent exam
Degrees: AA and cert 2 yrs
Tuition: None
Courses: Art History, Ceramics, Collages, Commercial Art, Drawing, Illustration,
Jewelry, Lettering, Mixed Media, Painting, Photography, Printmaking, Sculpture,
Video, Studio Crafts, Weaving
Adult Hobby Classes: Enrl 800; tui none. Courses—Crafts, Drawing, Painting
Summer School: Tuition none. Courses—same as above

LOS ALTOS HILLS

FOOTHILL COLLEGE, Fine Arts Division,* 12345 El Monte Rd, 94022. Tel 415-
948-8590. *Dean* John Mortarotti, MA
College has three campuses; scholarships
Degrees: AA, cert
Courses: Advertising Design, Art Appreciation, Art History, Calligraphy, Ceramics,
Design, Drawing, Fashion Arts, Film, Illustration, Interior Design, Jewelry, Painting,
Photography, Printmaking, Sculpture, Stage Design, Textile Design, Weaving

LOS ANGELES

ART IN ARCHITECTURE, 7917 1/2 W Norton Ave, 90046. Tel 213-654-0990,
656-2286. *Dir* Joseph L Young
Estab 1955; pvt; D; scholarships; SC 4, LC 4, GC 4; enrl D 6, E 7, non-maj 2, maj
8, grad 3
Ent Req: HS dipl, ent exam
Tuition: $1500 for annual nine month program
Courses: Architecture, Art History, Conceptual Art, Drawing, †History of Art &
Archaeology, Mixed Media, Painting, Sculpture

BRENTWOOD ART CENTER, 13031 Montana Ave, 90049. Tel 213-451-5657.
Dir Edward Buttwinick, BA
Estab 1971; D & E; SC 40; enrl D 300, E 100
Tuition: $85
Courses: Collages, Drawing, Mixed Media, Painting, Sculpture
Adult Hobby Classes: Enrl 200; tuition $80 - $90 per month. Courses—Life
Drawing, Basic Drawing, Painting, Sculpture, Design
Children's Classes: Enrl 200; tuition $80 per month. Courses—Cartooning,
Drawing, Mixed Media, Painting

CALIFORNIA STATE UNIVERSITY, LOS ANGELES, Art Dept, 5151 State
University Dr, 90032. Tel 213-224-3521. *Chmn* E C Forde, MFA; *Assoc Chmn*
Charles Borman, MA
Estab 1947; pub; D & E; SC 85, LC 12, GC 9; enrl D 2500 (Art), non-maj 45, maj
55, grad 180 (per quarter)
Ent Req: HS dipl, ent exam
Degrees: BA(Art), MA(Art), MFA(Art)
Tuition: Res—grad $236, undergrad $224 per quarter; nonres—undergrad & grad
$72 per hr; no campus res
Courses: Advertising Design, Art Education, Art History, Ceramics, Drawing,
Graphic Arts, Graphic Design, Illustration, Interior Design, Jewelry, Lettering,
Painting, Photography, Printmaking, Sculpture, Teacher Training, Video, Textile
Design, Art Therapy, Costume Design, Design Theory, Enameling, Exhibition
Design, Fashion Illustration, Textiles, Weaving, Computer Graphics
Children's Classes: Tuition $5 per 6 wks. Courses—Painting, Drawing, Design
Summer School: Same as any academic quarter

EL CAMINO COLLEGE, Division of Fine Arts, 16007 Crenshaw Blvd, 90506. Tel
213-532-3670, Ext 526. *Dean Div* Lewis E Hiigel, EdD. Instrs: FT 19, PT 13
Estab 1947; pub; D & E; scholarships; SC 46, LC 6; enrl D 1700, E 900, non-maj
2378, maj 222
Ent Req: HS dipl
Degrees: AA 2 yrs
Tuition: None; no campus res
Courses: †Advertising Design, Architecture, Art History, Calligraphy, Ceramics,
Costume Design & Construction, Display, Stage Design, Textile Design, †Theatre
Arts, Stage Design, Textile Design, Theatre Arts
Children's Classes: Enrl 30. Courses—Exploration of Children's Art

LOS ANGELES CITY COLLEGE, Dept of Art,* 855 N Vermont Ave, 90029. Tel
213-663-9141, Ext 240. *Chmn* Russell Cangialosi, PhD; *Prof* Clyde Kelly, MA;
Assoc Prof Raoul De Sota, MA; *Asst Prof* Phyllis Muldavin-Smirle, MA; *Asst Prof*
Lee Whitten, MA. Instrs: PT 11
Estab 1929; pub; D & E; schol; SC 48, LC 8; enrl D 450, E 150, non-maj approx
2/3, maj approx 1/3
Ent Req: HS dipl and over 18 yrs of age
Degrees: AA 2 yr
Tuition: Nonres—$97 per sem unit
Courses: †Advertising Design, Aesthetics, Architecture, †Art History, Ceramics,
†Commercial Art, Display, Drawing, †Graphic Design, Handicrafts, History of Art
& Archaeology, †Painting, Printmaking, Sculpture
Adult Hobby Classes: Enrl 2090; tui approx $20 per class of 8 wks
Children's Classes: Tui approx $20 per class for 8 wks
Summer School: Chmn, Russell Cangialosi. Enrl 250; tui none, term of 6 wks
beginning mid-June. Courses—basic courses only

LOYOLA MARYMOUNT UNIVERSITY, Dept of Art & Art Hist,* College of
Fine and Communication Arts, Loyola Blvd & W 80th St, 90045. Tel 213-642-3128.
Chmn Susan Robinson, PhD; *Prof* Regina Buchholz, PhD; *Prof* Pauline Majoli,
MFA; *Prof* Genevieve Underwood, MFA; *Assoc Prof* Teresa Munoz, MA; *Asst Prof*
Rudolf Fleck, MA; *Asst Prof* Katherine Harper Lorenzana, PhD; *Asst Prof* Patrick
Nagatzni, MFA. Instrs: FT 6, PT 2
Estab as Marymount Col in 1940, merged with Loyola Univ 1968. University has 2
campuses; pvt; D; scholarships; SC 37, LC 21
Ent Req: HS dipl
Degrees: BA 4 yrs
Tuition: $5580 annual tuition; campus res available
Courses: Advertising Design, Art Education, Art History, Ceramics, Design,
Drawing, Jewelry, Lettering, Mixed Media, Painting, Photography, Printmaking,
Sculpture, Silversmithing
Adult Hobby Classes: Continuing Education
Children's Classes: Summer Arts Conservatory
Summer School: Dean Continuing Educ & Summer Session, Dr Alex Aloin

MOUNT SAINT MARY'S COLLEGE, Art Dept,* 12001 Chalon Rd, 90049. Tel
213-476-2237, Ext 250. *Chmn* Jake Gilson, MFA; *Assoc Prof* James Murray, BS,
MS; *Assoc Prof* Norman W Schwab, BA, MA; *Asst Prof* Leonard Esbensen, MFA;
Lectr P Israel Schellin, BFA, MA & PhD
Chalon Campus estab 1925, also maintains Doheny Campus estab 1962; den; D & E;
scholarships; enrl D 60, non-maj 31, maj 29
Ent Req: HS dipl
Degrees: BA and BFA 4 yrs
Tuition: $4420 per yr; $2210 per sem; campus res—room & board available
Courses: †Aesthetics, †Art Education, †Art History, †Calligraphy, †Ceramics,
†Collages, †Commercial Art, †Conceptual Art, †Constructions, †Drawing, †Graphic
Arts, †Graphic Design, †Illustration, †Intermedia, †Mixed Media, Museum Staff
Training, †Painting, †Photography, †Printmaking, †Sculpture, †Textile Design, Video
Summer School: Dir, Sr Paulette Gladis. Enrl 30-50; tuition $300 per unit.
Courses—Ceramics, Drawing, History, Painting, Printmaking

OCCIDENTAL COLLEGE, Art Dept, 1600 Campus Rd, 90041. Tel 213-259-2749.
Chmn Louise Yuhas. Instrs: FT 5, PT 1
Estab 1887; pvt; D; schol & grants according to need; SC 19, LC 25, GC 5; enrl maj
50, others 300
Ent Req: HS dipl, col transcript, SAT, recommendations
Degrees: BA 4 yr
Tuition: $2584; campus res—room & board $988-$1100 per term
Courses: Art Education, †Art History, Drawing, Painting, Sculpture, Graphics,
Theory & Criticism
Summer School: Dir, Louise Yuhas. Enrl 25; two 5 week terms. Courses—Ceramics,
Drawing, Sculpture

OTIS ART INSTITUTE OF PARSONS SCHOOL OF DESIGN, 2401 Wilshire
Blvd, 90057. Tel 213-387-5288
Estab 1918; pvt(see also Parsons School of Design, New York, New York);
scholarships; SC 150, LC 48, GC 9; enrl D 618, E 209, maj 122, grad 26, others 581
Degrees: BFA 4 yrs, MFA 2 yrs
Courses: †Ceramics, †Drawing, †Illustration, †Interior Design, †Painting,
†Photography, †Printmaking, †Sculpture, Architecture Design, Communication
Design, †Fashion Design
Adult Hobby Classes: AAS degree offered through Continuing Education. Enrl 141;
tuition $160 per cr. Courses—Advertising Design, Environmental & Interior Design,
Fashion Design, Fine Arts, Graphic Design, Illustration, Photography
Summer School: Continuing education and pre-college programs

UNIVERSITY OF CALIFORNIA, LOS ANGELES, Dept of Art, Design & Art History,* College of Fine Arts, 405 Hilgard Ave, 90024. Tel 213-825-4321. *Chmn* Raymond B Brown. Instrs: FT 32, PT 2
Estab 1919; enrl maj 700
Degrees: BA, MA, MFA, PhD(Art Hist)
Tuition: Nonres—$1120 per qtr
Courses: Ceramics Design, Glass Design, New Forms & Concepts

UNIVERSITY OF JUDAISM, Dept of Continuing Education, 15600 Mulholland Dr, 90077. Tel 213-879-4114. *Dir* Jack Schecter, MA; *Chmn* Mary Ann Devine, BA; *Instr* Linda Steinberg, MA; *Instr* Ora Cooper, MFA
Sch estab 1947; den; SC 14, LC 6
Degrees: Units in continuing education only
Tuition: $89 per sem
Courses: Art History, Calligraphy, Drawing, Interior Design, Painting, Sculpture
Adult Hobby Classes: Enrl 8; tuition $89 per sem
Summer School: Courses offered

UNIVERSITY OF SOUTHERN CALIFORNIA, School of Fine Arts, Watt Hall 104, University Ave, 90089. Tel 213-743-2311. *Dean* John S Gordon; *Dir Museum Studies & University Art Galleries* Dr Selma Holo; *Prof* Ruth Weisberg; *Assoc Prof* Robert Flick; *Assoc Prof* Margit Omar; *Assoc Prof* Gerald Purdy; *Assoc Prof* Ronald Rizk; *Assoc Prof* Jay Willis; *Assoc Prof* Dr Susan Larsen-Martin; *Assoc Prof* Dr Lynn Matteson; *Asst Prof* Jud Fine; *Asst Prof* Joyce Kohl; *Asst Prof* Stephen Meltzer; *Asst Prof* David Schirm; *Asst Prof* Dr Kenneth Hamma; *Asst Prof* Dr Eunice Howe; *Asst Prof* Dr Carolyn Malone; *Asst Prof* Dr Richard Vinograd; *Adjunct Prof* Dr Jiri Frel; *Adjunct Prof* Dr Pratapaditya Pal; *Adjunct Asst Prof* Joe Fay; *Vis Asst Prof* Amy Goldman; *Vis Asst Prof* Dennis Grady
Estab 1887, dept estab 1979; pvt; D & E; scholarships; SC 78, LC 11, GC 23; enrl non-maj 600, maj 300, grad 33
Ent Req: HS dipl, SAT, GRE
Degrees: BA 4 yrs, BFA 4 yrs, MFA 2-3 yrs, MA 2 yrs, MA with Museum Studies Option 3 yrs, PhD 4 yrs minimum
Tuition: $290 per unit
Courses: Art History, Ceramics, Design, Drawing, Painting, Photography, Printmaking, Sculpture, Teacher Training
Children's Classes: Enrl 25; tuition $35 per sem unit. Courses—Airbrush, Printmaking, Drawing
Summer School: Enrl 100; tuition $290 per unit for 7 wks. Courses—regular courses

WOODBURY UNIVERSITY, Professional Arts Division,* 1027 Wilshire Blvd, PO Box 17962, 90017. Tel 213-482-8491. *Chmn Div* Rosalie Utterbach, MA; *Chmn Dept Fashion Design* Betty Bixenman, BS; *Chmn Dept Interior Design* Don Conway, MA; *Instr* Joan A Greenfield; *Instr* Marguerite H Hossler; *Instr* Dollie Chapman; *Instr* Werner Schier; *Instr* Pat Stone; *Instr* Raymond Wark; *Instr* Art Weiss; *Instr* Rosalind Wilcox
Estab 1884; pvt; D & E; SC 56, LC 18; enrl 1341
Ent Req: HS dipl
Degrees: BS 3-4 yrs, MBS 2 yrs
Tuition: $1243 per quarter, 12-16 units; $85 per unit per quarter for 11 or less units; campus residency available
Courses: †Art History, †Costume Design & Construction, †Drawing, †Film, †Graphic Design, †Illustration, †Industrial Design, †Lettering, †Photography, †Textile Design, Film, Graphic Arts, Graphic Design, History of Art & Archaeology, Illustration, †Interior Design, Lettering, Photography, Textile Design, Fashion Merchandising
Summer School: Regular session

MALIBU

PEPPERDINE UNIVERSITY, SEAVER COLLEGE, Dept of Art, 24255 Pacific Coast Highway, 90265. Tel 213-456-4155. *Instr* Avery Falkner; *Instr* Bob Privitt; *Instr* Joe Plasentin. Instrs: PT 2
Scholarships
Tuition: $235 per unit; campus res—room & board per trimester $1700
Courses: Art Appreciation, Art Education, Art History, Ceramics, Design, Drawing, Jewelry, Painting, Sculpture, Monotypes
Summer School: Enrl 20; tuition $235 per unit. Courses—Jewelry, Monotypes, Mixed Media, Painting

MARYSVILLE

YUBA COLLEGE, Fine Arts Division,* Beale Rd at Linda Ave, 2088 N Beale Rd, 95901. Tel 916-742-7351. Instrs: FT 2
Estab 1927; pub; D & E; scholarships; SC 23, LC 2; enrl total 1437, maj 493
Ent Req: HS grad or 18 yrs of age
Degrees: AA 2 yr
Tuition: Res—$14 per sem; nonres—$72 per unit
Summer School: Dean & Assoc Dean Community Educ, Rex McDougal. Term of 6 wks beginning mid-June. Courses—Full Curriculum, plus Home Decorative Arts, Lapidary, Navajo Silversmithing, Non-Loom Weaving

MENDOCINO

MENDOCINO ART CENTER, INC, 45200 Little Lake St, PO Box 765, 95460. Tel 707-937-5818. *Executive Dir* Karen A Kesler, MFA; *Dir Textile Arts* Lolli Jacobsen, MFA
Estab 1959, inc 1974; pvt; D & E; SC 24, LC 6; enrl D 18, maj 18
Ent Req: Mutual interview, textile arts 3 yr program
Tuition: $1800
Courses: Art Education, Art History, Calligraphy, Ceramics, Collages, Conceptual Art, Constructions, Display, Drawing, Graphic Arts, Painting, Photography, Sculpture, Textile Design, Silkscreen
Summer School: Tuition $70 per each one week workshop offered between June 23 and Aug 22. Courses—over 50 week long classes in all media

MERCED

MERCED COLLEGE, Arts Division, 3600 M St, 95340. Tel 209-384-6000. *Head* Dr Ron Williams, PhD; *Chmn* Allan Beymer
Estab 1964; pub; D & E; scholarships; SC 50, LC 10; enrl D 4741, E 3187, non-maj 3700, maj 4228
Ent Req: 18 yrs & older
Degrees: AA & AS 2 yr
Tuition: Res—undergrad $13 per sem; non-res—undergrad $75 per hr
Courses: Art History, Ceramics, Constructions, Costume Design & Construction, Drawing, Handicrafts, Illustration, Lettering, Painting, Photography, Sculpture, Theatre Arts
Summer School: Dir, Dr Ron Williams, Dean of Arts & Sciences. Tuition res—undergrad $13 for 7 wk term beginning June 21

MODESTO

MODESTO JUNIOR COLLEGE, Arts Humanities and Speech Division, College Ave, 95350. Tel 209-575-6081. *Chairperson Div* J Stephen Collins, MA; *Instructor* Paul J Corrigan, MA; *Instructor* Robert G Gauvreau, MFA; *Instructor* Terry L Hartman, MA; *Instructor* Walter F Lab, MAA; *Instructor* Daniel W Petersen, MA; *Instructor* Jerry M Reilly, MFA; *Instructor* Joseph G Remsing, MA. Instrs: FT 259, PT 385
Estab 1921, div estab 1964; pub; D & E; schol; enrl 16,024 total
Ent Req: Grad of accredited high school, minor with California High School Proficiency Cert and parental permission, 11th and 12th graders with principal's permission, persons 18 or older who are able to profit from the instruction
Degrees: AA and AS 2 yrs
Tuition: Res—$6 health fee; non-res—$87 per sem unit to maximum of $1044 per sem plus health fee; no campus res
Courses: Advertising Design, Architecture, Art History, Ceramics, Display, Drafting, Drawing, Film, Jewelry, Lettering, Painting, †Photography, Printmaking, Sculpture, Silversmithing, Theatre Arts, Enameling, Lapidary
Adult Hobby Classes: Courses—Arts & Crafts, Lapidary
Summer School: Dir, Dudley Roach. Tuition $6 health fee. Courses—a wide variety offered

MONTEREY

MONTEREY PENINSULA COLLEGE, Art Dept, Div of Creative Arts, 980 Fremont St, 93940. Tel 408-646-4200. *Chairperson Div Creative Arts* Don Chamber, MA; *Chairperson Dept Art* Pat Boles, BA; *Instructor* Richard Bibler, MA; *Instructor* Richard Janick, MA; *Instructor* Alex Gonzales, MFA; *Instructor* Joe Hysong, MA; *Instructor* Peter Pilat, MA; *Instructor* Anita Benson, MA
Estab 1947; pub; D & E; schol; SC 17, LC 8; enrl D 1343, E 623, maj 160
Ent Req: HS dipl, 18 yrs or older
Degrees: AA and AS 2 yrs
Tuition: None to res; nonres—$28 per unit; no campus res
Courses: †Art History, Design, Drawing, Painting, Photography, Weaving, Commercial Graphics, Studio Art
Summer School: Dir, Keith Merrill. Term of 6 wks beginning June. Courses are limited

MONTEREY PARK

EAST LOS ANGELES COLLEGE, Art Dept, 1301 E Brooklyn Ave, 91754. Tel 213-265-8650. *Dept Chmn* Ruth Schwimmer. Instrs: FT 7, PT 4
Estab 1949; pub; D & E; SC 35, LC 10; enrl D 350, E 310, maj 660
Degrees: AA 2 yr
Courses: Advertising Design, Art History, Ceramics, Design, Drawing, Lettering, Painting, Printmaking, Sculpture, Art Fundamentals; Life Drawing
Children's Classes: Enrl 60. Courses—Ceramics, Direct Printing Methods, Drawing, Painting
Summer School: Dir, Ruth Schwimmer

NAPA

NAPA COLLEGE, Art Dept, 2277 Napa Vallejo Hwy, 94558. Tel 707-255-2100; TTY 253-7831. *Dir* Michael Tausig; *Prof* Frank Akamura; *Prof* Caroyln Broodwell; *Prof* Ralph Hunter
Courses: Art Appreciation, Art History, Ceramics, Design, Drawing, Painting, Photography, Printmaking, Sculpture
Adult Hobby Classes: Courses offered
Children's Classes: Courses offered
Summer School: Courses—Painting, Ceramics

NORTHRIDGE

CALIFORNIA STATE UNIVERSITY, NORTHRIDGE, Dept of Art-Two Dimensional Media, School of the Arts, 18111 Nordhoff St, 91330. Tel 213-885-2348. *Dept Chmn* Art Weiss, MFA; *Chmn General Studies* Anne Heath; *Chmn Art 3-D Media* Gilbert Rios. Instrs: 31
Estab 1956; pub; D & E; SC 13, GC 5; enrl D & E 2231, grad 101
Ent Req: HS dipl, GRE, SAT
Degrees: BA 4-5 yrs, MA
Tuition: Nonres—$105 per unit
Courses: †Advertising Design, Calligraphy, †Drawing, †Graphic Design, Illustration, Lettering, †Painting, †Photography, †Printmaking, Airbrush, Animation, Typography, Packaging Graphics, Reproduction Graphics
Summer School: Dir, Art Weiss. Tui $50 per unit for 8 wks beginning June 1. Courses—Advertising Graphics, Beginning Design, Drawing, Illustration, Painting, Photography, Reprographics

—**Art History Dept**, 18111 Nordhoff St, 91324. Tel 213-885-2192. *Chmn* Dr Dolores M Yonker
Estab 1958, dept estab 1971; pub; D & E; SC 1, LC 30, grad 10; enrl grad 50, undergrad 850
Ent Req: HS dipl, SAT, subject to GPA
Degrees: BA(Art) 4 yrs, MA(Art History) 5 yrs
Courses: Art History, Drawing, 2-D Design, 3-D Design, Survey of Non-Western Arts
Adult Hobby Classes: Courses available through Continuing Educ Extension Prog
Summer School: Courses—survey courses only

NORWALK

CERRITOS COLLEGE, Art Dept,* 11110 Alondra Blvd, 90650. Tel 213-860-2451. *Assoc Dean Fine Arts & Communication* Charles Tilghman
Estab 1956; pub; D & E; scholarships; SC 36, LC 6
Ent Req: HS dipl or 18 yrs of age
Degrees: AA 2 yrs
Tuition: Res—None; nonres—$72 per unit
Courses: Calligraphy, Ceramics, Commercial Art, Display, Drawing, Graphic Arts, Graphic Design, History of Art & Archaeology, Jewelry, Museum Staff Training, Printmaking, Sculpture, 2-D & 3-D Design
Summer School: Drawing, Painting, History, Design, Ceramics, Calligraphy

OAKLAND

CALIFORNIA COLLEGE OF ARTS AND CRAFTS, 5212 Broadway, 94618. Tel 415-653-8118. *Pres* Harry X Ford, MA; *Interior Architecture Design* Hank Dunlop; *Wood Design* Skip Benson; *Textiles* Dr Ruth Boyer; *Photography* Chris Johnson; *Ceramics* Art Nelson; *Printmaking* Charles Gill; *General Studies* Sandra Roos; *Film-Video* David Heintz; *Sculpture* Dennis Leon; *Graduate Studies* Philip Linhares; *Glass* Marvin Lipofsky; *Drawing* Larry McClary; *Art History* Marc LeSueur; *Graphic Design* Steve Reoutt; *Metal Arts* Florence Resnikoff; *Art Education* Dr Piroja Shroff; *Painting* Phil Hocking; *General Design* Dean Snyder; *Ethnic Art Studies* Malaquias Montoya
Estab 1907; pvt; D & E; scholarships; SC 24, LC 58, GC 5; enrl D 1000, non-maj 147, maj 773, grad 79, exten school 310
Ent Req: HS dipl, SAT or ACT requested not required, C grade-point average, 2 letters of recommendation
Degrees: 3 yr cert, BFA 4 yrs, MFA 3 yrs, MAEd 2 yrs
Tuition: Per trimester $2595; campus residency available
Courses: Advertising Design, Aesthetics, Art History, Calligraphy, †Ceramics, Conceptual Art, Drafting, †Drawing, †Film, Goldsmithing, Graphic Arts, Handicrafts, Illustration, †Interior Design, †Jewelry, Lettering, Mixed Media, †Painting, †Photography, †Printmaking, †Sculpture, Silversmithing, †Teacher Training, †Textile Design, †Video, †Ethnic Studies, †Fine Arts, †General Design, †General Crafts, †Glass, †Interior Architectural Design, †Textiles, TV, †Wood Design
Adult Hobby Classes: Courses—Art Therapy, Artists' Business, Design, Drawing, Film & TV, Graphic Design, Jewelry, Painting, Papermaking, Photography, Printmaking, Sculpture, Textiles
Children's Classes: Courses—Crafts, Drawing, Printmaking
Summer School: Dean, Ellen Jouret. Enrl 150-250 per session; tuition $226 per unit for term of 5 wks beginning mid May, June, July. Courses—Full range

HOLY NAMES COLLEGE, Art Dept, 3500 Mountain Blvd, 94619. Tel 415-436-0111. Instrs: FT 2, PT 4
Estab 1917; pvt; D & E; schol; SC 24, LC 4
Ent Req: HS dipl
Degrees: BA and BFA 4 yrs
Tuition: $165 per unit, $2475 per sem
Courses: Art History, Calligraphy, Ceramics, Drawing, Jewelry, Painting, Photography, Printmaking, Sculpture, Weaving, Stained Glass

LANEY COLLEGE, Art Dept, 900 Fallon St, 94607. Tel 415-834-5740. *Chmn* Lucille Margosian. Instrs: FT 8, PT 9
Estab 1962; pub; D & E; SC 52, LC 8; enrl D 1400, E 450
Ent Req: HS dipl
Degrees: AA 2 yrs
Courses: †Ceramics, †Commercial Art, Design, Drawing, †Graphic Arts, Graphic Design, Handicrafts, History of Art & Archaeology, Lettering, †Painting, †Sculpture, Illustration, Cartooning, Color & Design, Etching, Lithography, Portraiture, Relief Printing, Silkscreen, Advertising Design and Architectural Design Courses available through the Architectural Design Dept; Photography Courses available through the Photography Dept
Summer School: Chmn, Lucille Margosian. Enrl 250; tuition $2 for 6 weeks

MERRITT COLLEGE, Art Dept, 12500 Campus Dr, 94619. Tel 415-531-4911. *Dir* Helmut Schmitt
Degrees: AA
Courses: Art History, Ceramics, Design, Illustration, Painting, Photography, Sculpture, Life Drawing
Adult Hobby Classes: Dir, Helmut Schmitt
Summer School: Dir, Helmut Schmitt; six week courses. Courses—Life Drawing

MILLS COLLEGE, Art Dept, 5000 MacArthur Blvd, PO Box 9975, 94613. Tel 415-430-2117. *Prof Art & Chmn Dept* JoAnne G Bernstein, PhD; *Prof* Robert Dhaemers, MFA; *Asst Prof* Jay DeFeo, MFA; *Asst Prof* Ron Nagle; *Asst Prof* Susan Platt, PhD; *Asst Prof* Mary Ann Lutzker, PhD; *Lecturer* John Roloff, MFA; *Lecturer* Catherine Wagner, MFA
Estab 1852; pvt; D; scholarships; SC 23, LC 22, GC 20; enrl grad 16-20
Ent Req: HS dipl, SAT, Advanced Placement Exam
Degrees: BA, MA, MFA 2 yrs
Tuition: Res—undergrad $10,720 yr, grad $5360 per sem, $3450 yr, grad $800 per course, undergrad $825 per course, $412.50 per half course; nonres—undergrad $7000 yr, other $412.50 per course to audit; campus res—room & board $3500 per yr
Courses: Aesthetics, Art History, Ceramics, Drawing, Film, Mixed Media, Painting, Photography, Printmaking, Sculpture, Video, Hand Bookbinding; 3-D Design

OCEANSIDE

MIRACOSTA COLLEGE, Art Dept, 1 Barnard Dr, 92054. Tel 714-757-2121. *Chmn* Kristina Rice Nugent, MFA
Estab 1934; pub; D & E; scholarships; SC 12, LC 4; enrl maj 200
Ent Req: HS dipl
Degrees: AA and AS normally 2 yrs
Tuition: Res—no fee; nonres—$1272 per yr; no campus res
Courses: Art History, Ceramics, Design, Drawing, Painting, Photography, Printmaking, Sculpture, Computer Art, Woodworking and Furniture Design
Summer School: Enrl 250; 6 wk session. Courses—Ceramics, Painting, Photography, Drawing

ORANGE

CHAPMAN COLLEGE, Art Dept, 333 N Glassell, 92666. Tel 714-997-6729. *Chairperson* Richard Turner, MFA; *Instructor* William Boaz, MA; *Instructor* R Bret Price, MFA; *Instructor* Jane Sinclair, MFA; *Instructor* Susan Rankaitis, MFA
Estab 1918, branch estab 1954; den; D & E; scholarships; SC 20, LC 15; enrl D 245, non-maj 200, maj 35
Ent Req: HS dipl, ACT, SAT or CLEP
Tuition: $190 per unit; campus res—room & board $2700 per yr
Courses: Advertising Design, Art Education, Art History, Ceramics, Drawing, Film, Graphic Arts, Illustration, Painting, Photography, Printmaking, Sculpture, Teacher Training
Children's Classes: Courses—workshops in connection with art education classes

OROVILLE

BUTTE COLLEGE, Dept of Fine & Performing Arts,* 3536 Butte Campus Dr, Pentz & Clark Rds, 95965. Tel 916-895-2404. *Assoc Dean* Frederick E Allen, MFA; *Coordr Fine & Performing Arts* Albert J Walsh Jr, MA; *Ceramic Coordr* Idie Adams, MA; *Prof* Jeffrey Nelson, MA; *Prof* John R Wilson, MA; *Vis Prof* Ruben Heredia, commercial art
Estab 1968; pub; D & E; schol; SC 21, LC 4; enrl D 3988, E 4194
Ent Req: HS dipl or 18 yrs or older
Degrees: AA 2 yrs
Tuition: Nonres—$48 per unit; no campus residence
Courses: Ceramics, Commercial Art, Costume Design & Construction, Drafting, Fashion Arts, Photography, Video
Adult Hobby Classes: Courses—Macrame, Stained Glass
Summer School: Dean of Evening College, Tom O'Conner. Regular fee $9-$17 per quarter

PALM DESERT

COLLEGE OF THE DESERT, Art Dept,* 43-500 Monterey Ave, 92260. Tel 714-346-8041. *Chmn* Hovak Najarian. Instrs: FT 4, PT 14
Estab 1962; pub; D & E; schol; SC 10, LC 3; enrl D 150, E 150, maj 15
Ent Req: HS dipl, ent exam
Degrees: AA 2 yrs
Tuition: None; no campus res
Courses: Art History, Ceramics, Design, Drawing, Painting, Photography, Printmaking, Sculpture, Advertising Art, Introduction to Art, Oriental Brush Painting

PASADENA

ART CENTER COLLEGE OF DESIGN,* 1700 Lida St, 91103. Tel 213-577-1700. *Pres & Dir* Don Kubly, BA; *Asst Dir & VPres* Joseph Henry; *Communication Design Chmn* Paul Hauge, BFA; *Fine Arts Dept Chmn* Laurence Drieband, MFA; *Film Dept Chmn* Jim Jordan, BFA; *Photography Dept Chmn* Charles Potts, BPA; *Industrial Design Chmn* Keith Teter, BS; *Academic Studies Dept Chmn* Richard Hertz, PhD
Estab 1930; pvt; D & E; scholarships; SC 168, LC 82, GC 22; enrl D 1150, E 200, non-maj 200, maj 1130, grad 20
Ent Req: HS dipl, ACT, SAT if no col background, portfolio required, at least 12 samples of work in proposed maj
Degrees: BFA, BS, MFA, MS
Tuition: Res—$1790 for 14 wk sem (trimester); no campus res
Courses: †Advertising Design, Art History, Display, Drawing, †Film, †Graphic Design, †Illustration, †Industrial Design, Lettering, Painting, †Photography, , †Advertising Illustration, †Environmental Design, †Fashion Illustration, †Graphic Packaging, †Product Design, †Transportation Design
Adult Hobby Classes: Evening classes for adults
Children's Classes: Evening classes; Saturday classes for high school students

PASADENA CITY COLLEGE, Art Dept, 1570 E Colorado St, 91106. Tel 213-578-7238. *Chmn Dept* David J Schnabel; *Area Chmn Design* Bob Rahm, MA; *Area Chmn Studio Art* Ben Sakaguchi, MA; *Area Chmn Photography* Roland Percey, MA; *Area Chmn Art History* Vern Wells, MA; *Area Chairperson Apparel Arts* Karlene Cunningham, MA; *Area Chmn Crafts* John Dickenhof, MA; *Area Chmn Ceramics* Phil Cornelius, MA
Estab 1902; dept estab 1916; pub; D & E; SC 50; enrl D 2000, E 1200, non-maj 3200, maj 400
Ent Req: HS dipl
Degrees: AA 2 yrs
Courses: Advertising Design, Architecture, Art History, Ceramics, Commercial Art,

Costume Design & Construction, Display, Drafting, Drawing, Fashion Arts, Film, Graphic Arts, Graphic Design, Handicrafts, History of Art & Archaeology, Illustration, Interior Design, Jewelry, Lettering, Museum Staff Training, Painting, Photography, Printmaking, Sculpture, Silversmithing, Stage Design, Textile Design, Video
Summer School: Six wk term. Courses—Beginning Drawing, Design, Ceramics, Painting, Photography

POMONA

CALIFORNIA STATE POLYTECHNIC UNIVERSITY, POMONA, Art Dept, School of Arts, 3801 Temple Blvd, 91768. Tel 714-598-4567. *Chmn* Joe Hannibal, MFA; *Prof* Diane Divelbess, MFA; *Prof* Walter Glaser, MFA; *Prof* Stanley Wilson, MFA; *Prof* Yoram Makow, MA; *Assoc Prof* Maren Henderson, MA; *Assoc Prof* Charles Fredrick, MA; *Asst Prof* Eileen Fears, MFA; *Lectr* Jim Dobbs, PhD; *Lectr* William Armstrong, MA; *Lectr* David Authier, MFA; *Lectr* Sandra Rowe, MFA; *Lectr* Deborah Gray, MFA
Estab 1966; pub; D & E; SC 66, LC 15; enrl D approx 300, E approx 50, non-maj 470, maj 175
Ent Req: HS dipl, plus testing
Degrees: BA 4 yrs
Tuition: Res—undergrad (commuting) $153 quarterly, (living in dorms) $603 quarterly; campus res $1809 yr
Courses: Advertising Design, Aesthetics, Art Education, Art History, Ceramics, Drafting, Drawing, Graphic Arts, History of Art & Archaeology, Illustration, Lettering, Museum Staff Training, Painting, Teacher Training, Textile Design, Studio Crafts
Summer School: Regular 10 wk quarter

PORTERVILLE

PORTERVILLE COLLEGE, Dept of Fine Arts,* 900 S Main St, 93257. Tel 209-781-3130, Ext 66. *Chmn Applied & Fine Arts* Michael Rost. Instrs: FT 50, PT 80
Estab 1927; pub; D & E; SC 18, LC 3; enrl D 300, E 78, non-maj 320, maj 58
Ent Req: HS dipl or over 18 yrs of age
Degrees: AA and AS 2 yrs
Tuition: Nonres—$1080 per sem
Courses: Art History, Ceramics, Drawing, Goldsmithing, Handicrafts, Jewelry, Painting, Photography, Sculpture, Silversmithing, Textile Design, Theatre Arts, Weaving
Adult Hobby Classes: Courses—Jewelry, Weaving
Summer School: Dir, Nero Pruitt. Enrl 700 Term of 6 wks beginning June 13. Courses—Ceramics, Jewelry, Weaving

QUINCY

FEATHER RIVER COMMUNITY COLLEGE, Art Dept, PO Box 1110, 95971. Tel 916-283-0202. *Dir* Marvin Schmidt
Scholarships
Courses: Art Appreciation, Art History, Ceramics, Design, Drawing, Painting, Sculpture, Textile Design, Weaving

REDDING

SHASTA COMMUNITY COLLEGE, Art Dept, Fine Arts Division, PO Box 6006, 96099. Tel 916-241-3523, Ext 361. *Dir Div Fine Arts* Robert Davis, MBA; *Art Dept Chmn* Bert Oldham, MA
Estab 1950; pub; D & E
Ent Req: HS dipl
Degrees: AA 2 yr
Tuition: Nonres--$73 per cr hr
Courses: Art History, Ceramics, Commercial Art, Drawing, Film, Painting, Photography, Printmaking, Sculpture

REDLANDS

UNIVERSITY OF REDLANDS, Dept of Art,* Peppers Art Center, 1200 E Colton Ave, 92373. Tel 714-793-2121. *Assoc Prof Art* John R Nava
Estab 1909; pvt; D & E; scholarships and fels; SC 18, LC 12; enrl 1500
Ent Req: HS grad, ent exam
Degrees: BA and BS 4 yr, MA, ME, MAT
Tuition: $6750 per yr; campus res available
Courses: Art History, Ceramics, Drawing, Graphic Arts, Painting, Teacher Training, Ethnic Art

RIVERSIDE

CALIFORNIA BAPTIST COLLEGE, Art Dept,* 8432 Magnolia Ave, 92504. Tel 714-689-5771
Scholarships
Degrees: BA
Tuition: $1515 per sem
Courses: Art Appreciation, Art History, Ceramics, Design, Drawing, Painting, Printmaking, Sculpture

LOMA LINDA UNIVERSITY, LA SIERRA CAMPUS, Art Dept, 4700 Pierce, 92515. Tel 714-785-2170. *Chmn* Prof Roger Churches, MFA; *Prof* Alan Collins; *Asst Prof* Susan Davis Patt, MEd
Estab 1905; den; D & E; SC 29, LC 8, GC 1; enrl D 2354
Ent Req: HS dipl, SAT
Degrees: BA, BS 4 yr
Tuition: Campus Res—$2647 per quarter; off campus res—$1830 per quarter

Courses: Art History, Calligraphy, †Ceramics, Drawing, †Graphic Design, Illustration, Lettering, Occupational Therapy, †Painting, †Photography, †Printmaking, †Sculpture, Stained Glass
Adult Hobby Classes: Enrl 35 per wk; tuition $330 per wk for 4 wk term. Courses—Watercolor Workshop
Summer School: Chmn, Roger Churches. 6 wk, 2-4 units. Courses—Art in the Elementary & Secondary School

RIVERSIDE CITY COLLEGE, Dept of Art, Arts & Letters Division, 4800 Magnolia Ave, 92506. Tel 714-684-3240. *Division Dean* Richard Stover
Estab 1917; pub; D & E; SC 20, LC 3; enrl D 910, E 175
Ent Req: HS dipl or over 18 yrs of age
Degrees: AA 2 yrs
Summer School: Term of 6 wks beginning June 21. Courses—Art for Elementary Teachers, Art History, Ceramics, Drawing, Painting, Sculpture

UNIVERSITY OF CALIFORNIA, RIVERSIDE
—Art History Dept, 92521. Tel 714-787-4627. *Chmn* Dericksen M Brinkerhoff, PhD; *Prof* Richard G Carrott, PhD; *Prof* Francoise Forster-Hahn, PhD; *Assoc Prof* Thomas O Pelzel, PhD
Estab 1954; pub; D; LC 18, GC 5; enrl maj 20, grad 15
Ent Req: HS dipl, res grad-point average 3.1, nonres grade-point average 3.4
Degrees: BA 4 yrs, MA 2 yrs
Tuition: Res—undergrad $486 per quarter, grad $471 per quarter; nonres—$1120 per quarter; campus res—room & board $905 per fall quarter, $870 per winter & spring quarters
Courses: Art History, History of Photography
—Program in Art,* 92521. Tel 714-787-4634. *Chmn* William T Bradshaw, MA; *Prof* James S Strombotne, MFA; *Asst Prof* Joe M Deal, MFA; *Lectr* Kenda North, MFA; *Lectr* Gordon L Thorpe, MA
Estab 1954; pub; D; SC 14, LC 2; enrl maj 60
Ent Req: HS dipl
Degrees: BA 4 yrs
Tuition: Nonres—$1120 per qtr
Courses: Drawing, Painting, Photography, Graphics

ROCKLIN

SIERRA COLLEGE, Art Dept,* Humanities Division, 5000 Rocklin Rd, 95677. Tel 916-624-3333. *Chmn Division* Dr Robert Meyer; *Instructor* Jim Adamson, MA; *Instructor* Pam Johnson
Estab 1914; pub; D & E; SC 18, LC 4; enrl D & E approx 9000
Ent Req: English Placement Test
Degrees: AA and AS
Tuition: Nonres—$72 per unit; campus res available
Courses: Art Education, Art History, Ceramics, Collages, Conceptual Art, Drawing, Painting, Photography, Printmaking, Sculpture
Summer School: Courses—Ceramics, Painting

ROHNERT PARK

SONOMA STATE UNIVERSITY, Art Dept, 1801 East Cotati Ave, 94928. Tel 707-664-2151, 664-2364. *Art Chmn* Dr Susan Moulton, PhD
Estab 1961; dept estab 1961; pub; D & E; SC 38, LC 17; enrl D 5000
Ent Req: HS dipl, SAT, eligibility req must be met
Degrees: BA and BS
Tuition: Res—$355 per sem, nonres—$292 per sem plus $108 per unit; campus residence available
Courses: Art Education, Art History, Ceramics, Collages, Conceptual Art, Display, Drawing, Film, Mixed Media, Painting, Photography, Printmaking, Sculpture, Teacher Training, Papermaking
Adult Hobby Classes: Various classes offered through Extended Education
Children's Classes: Courses—Art Education, Basic Arts & Crafts
Summer School: Various classes offered through Extended Education

SACRAMENTO

AMERICAN RIVER COLLEGE, Dept of Art, 4700 College Oak Dr, 95841. Tel 916-484-8011. *Chmn* James S Kaneko, MA; *Instr* Phyllis Y Robbins, MA; *Instr* Joe Patitucci, BA; *Instr* Jean A Pratt, MA; *Instr* Gary L Pruner, MA; *Instr* John H Kaneko, MA; *Instr* Tom J Brozovich, MA; *Instr* William C MacArthur, MFA
Estab 1954; pub; D & E; scholarships; SC 50, LC 12; enrl D 10,000, E 10,000, non-maj 5000, maj 5000
Ent Req: HS dipl
Degrees: AA 2 yrs or more
Tuition: Nonres—$600 per sem or $40 per unit
Courses: Advertising Design, Art Education, Art History, Calligraphy, Ceramics, Commercial Art, Conceptual Art, Constructions, Costume Design & Construction, Display, Drawing, Fashion Arts, Film, Graphic Arts, Graphic Design, Handicrafts, History of Art & Archaeology, Interior Design, Jewelry, Lettering, Mixed Media, Painting, Photography, Printmaking, Sculpture, Silversmithing, Teacher Training, Theatre Arts, Textile Design
Summer School: Tuition none. Courses—same as above

CALIFORNIA STATE UNIVERSITY, SACRAMENTO, Dept of Art,* 6000 J St, 95819. Tel 916-454-6166. *Chmn* P Hitchcock. Instrs: FT 30
Estab 1950; pub; D; schol; SC 40, LC 18, GC 12; enrl major 606
Ent Req: HS dipl, ent exam
Degrees: BA 4 yr, MA
Tuition: Nonres—$105 per unit
Courses: Art Education, Art History, Ceramics, Drawing, Handicrafts, Jewelry, Painting, Printmaking, Sculpture, Cinematography
Summer School: Enrl 225; 1 wk pre-session, 6 wks

SACRAMENTO CITY COLLEGE, Art Dept,* 3835 Freeport Blvd, 95822. Tel 916-449-7551. *Instructor* George A Esquibel, MA; *Instructor* Al Byrd, MFA; *Instructor* Laureen Landau, MFA; *Instructor* Willard Melton, MFA; *Instructor* Larry Welden, MAEd; *Staff* Fred Dalkey, MA
Estab 1927, dept estab 1929; pub; D & E; SC 17, LC 9; enrl D 880, E 389
Ent Req: HS dipl
Degrees: AA 2 yr
Tuition: None; no campus res
Courses: Art Education, Art History, Ceramics, Commercial Art, Costume Design & Construction, Drafting, Drawing, Film, Painting, Photography, Printmaking, Sculpture, Stage Design, Theatre Arts, Video
Summer School: Dir, George A Esquibel. Courses—Art History, Design, Drawing, Oil-Acrylic, Watercolor

SALINAS

HARTNELL COLLEGE, Art and Photography Dept, 156 Homestead Ave, 93901. Tel 408-758-8211. *Chmn Fine Arts* Manuel Rivera. Instrs: FT 3, PT 10
Estab 1922; pub; D & E; SC 14, LC 3; enrl D 350 E 160, major 30
Ent Req: HS dipl
Degrees: AA 2 yr
Tuition: None; no campus res
Courses: Ceramics, Drafting, Drawing, Graphic Arts, History of Art & Archaeology, Jewelry, Painting, Photography, Sculpture, Stage Design, Theatre Arts, Video, Foundry, Gallery Management, Glassblowing, Metalsmithing
Summer School: Enrl 150; tuition free; begins approx June 15. Courses—Art Appreciation, Ceramics, Drawing, Film Making, Photography

SAN BERNARDINO

CALIFORNIA STATE COLLEGE, SAN BERNARDINO, Art Dept, 5500 State College Parkway, 92407. Tel 714-887-7459. *Chmn Dept* Julius Kaplan, PhD; *Instructor* Leo Doyle, MFA; *Instructor* Roger Lintault, MFA; *Instructor* Jose Moran, MFA; *Instructor* Bill Warehall, MFA; *Instructor* Don Woodford, MFA
Estab 1965; pub; D & E; schol; enrl D 5000, maj 100
Ent Req: HS dipl, SAT
Degrees: BA 4 yrs
Tuition: Res—undergrad $150 per 15 units; nonres—undergrad $72 per unit; campus res—room & board $2191 per yr
Courses: †Advertising Design, Art Education, †Art History, †Ceramics, Drawing, †Jewelry, †Painting, †Printmaking, †Sculpture, †Furniture Design, †Glassblowing

SAN BERNARDINO VALLEY COLLEGE, Art Dept,* 701 S Mount Vernon Ave, 92403. Tel 714-888-6511. *Head Dept* David Lawrence; *Humanities Div Chmn* Judith R Hert. Instrs: FT 224, PT 510
Estab 1926; pub; D & E; schol; enrl D 750, E 400, maj 230
Ent Req: HS dipl or 18 yrs of age
Degrees: AA and AS 2 yrs
Tuition: Nonres—$75 per unit
Courses: Advertising Design, Architecture, Art Education, Art History, Ceramics, Drafting, Drawing, Film, Jewelry, Landscape Architecture, Lettering, Painting, Photography, Sculpture, Theatre Arts, Artistic Weaving, Glass Blowing, Life Drawing

SAN DIEGO

ALEXANDER SCHOOL OF PAINTING, 2068 Front St, 92101. Tel 619-234-7356
Degrees: Cert
Courses: Advertising Design, Art Education, Design, Drawing, Painting

SAN DIEGO MESA COLLEGE, Fine Arts Dept,* 7250 Mesa College Drive, 92111. Tel 714-230-6895. *Instructor* John Conrad, PhD; *Instructor* Barbara Blackmun, PhD; *Instructor* Ross Stockwell, MA; *Instructor* Albert J Lewis, MA; *Instructor* Hiroshi Miyazaki, MA; *Instructor* Malcolm Nichols, MA
Estab 1964; pub; D & E; scholarships; enrl in col D 10,000, E 10,000, maj 300
Ent Req: HS dipl or age 18
Degrees: AA 2 yrs
Tuition: Nonres—$62 per unit; no campus residence
Courses: Architecture, †Art History, †Ceramics, Drafting, †Drawing, Jewelry, Lettering, †Painting, Photography, †Sculpture, †Crafts, Fibers
Summer School: Tui $38 per unit. Courses—all basic, varied advanced

SAN DIEGO STATE UNIVERSITY, Dept of Art, 92182. Tel 619-265-6511. *Chmn* Fredrick Orth, MFA; *Grad Coordr* Lawrence B Hunter, MFA
Estab 1897; pub; D & E; schol; SC 140, LC 35, GC 30; enrl maj 1044
Ent Req: HS dipl
Degrees: BA 4 yrs, MA, MFA
Tuition: Campus res—room & board
Courses: †Advertising Design, Aesthetics, Architecture, †Art Education, †Art History, †Ceramics, †Commercial Art, Conceptual Art, †Drawing, Fashion Arts, Goldsmithing, †Graphic Arts, †Graphic Design, Handicrafts, History of Art & Archaeology, †Interior Design, †Jewelry, Mixed Media, †Painting, †Printmaking, †Sculpture, †Silversmithing, Teacher Training, †Textile Design, †Enameling, †Environmental Design, †Furniture Design †Gallery Design, †Weaving
Summer School: Chmn, Fredrick Orth, MFA

UNITED STATES INTERNATIONAL UNIVERSITY, School of Performing and Visual Arts, 10455 Pomerado Rd, 92131. Tel 714-569-4630. *Dir* Gordon Hilker
Estab 1966; pvt; D; scholarships; SC 27, LC 4; enrl D 300
Ent Req: HS dipl, interview, portfolio, letters of recommendation
Degrees: BA(Comprehensive Design), BA(Art Teaching), BFA(Advertising Design), BFA(Design for Stage), BFA(TV & TV Production) 4 yrs, MFA(Advertising Design), MFA(Design for Stage & TV) 2 yrs
Tuition: $1770 per qt; $118 per unit; campus res available

Courses: Advertising Design, Art Education, Ceramics, Commercial Art, Costume Design & Construction, Drafting, Drawing, Graphic Design, Graphic Design, History of Art & Archaeology, Illustration, Interior Design, Painting, Photography, Printmaking, Stage Design, Teacher Training, Theatre Arts, Lighting Design
Children's Classes: Conservatory of the Arts for children
Summer School: Two 5 wk terms

UNIVERSITY OF SAN DIEGO, Art Dept,* Alcala Park, 92110. Tel 619-291-6480. *Dean College Arts & Science* C Joseph Pustari. Instrs: FT 3
Estab 1952; pvt; D & E; schol; SC 19, LC 7; enrl univ 5000, maj 50
Ent Req: HS dipl, SAT
Degrees: BA 4 yrs
Tuition: $2550 per sem; campus res—room and board $900-$1500 per sem
Courses: Art History, Ceramics, Drawing, Painting, Photography, Printmaking, Sculpture, Art in Elementary Education, Art Management, Design, Enameling, Exhibition Design, Museum Internship, Weaving
Summer School: Tui $135 per unit for terms of 3 wk, 6 wk beginning June 1; 2 courses offered

SAN FRANCISCO

ACADEMY OF ART COLLEGE,* 540 Powell, 94102. Tel 415-673-4200. *Pres* Donald A Haight, MFA; *Dir Advertising/Graphic Design* Michael Dattel, BFA; *Dir Illustration* Barbara Bradley, BFA; *Dir Fine Art* Michael Woods, MFA; *Dir Photography* Paul Raedeke; *Dir of Interior Design* Martha Miller. Instrs: FT 2, PT 8
Estab 1929; pvt; D & E; scholarships; SC 100, LC 50; enrl D 1050, E 150, grad 20
Ent Req: HS dipl
Degrees: BFA 4 yrs, MA 2 yrs
Tuition: Res—undergrad $2720 per yr, $1360 per sem, $110 per unit, grad $2240 per yr, $1120 per sem, $110 per unit; campus res available
Courses: Advertising Design, Aesthetics, Art Education, Art History, Calligraphy, Ceramics, Collages, Commercial Art, Conceptual Art, Display, †Drawing, †Fashion Arts, Film, Goldsmithing, †Graphic Arts, †Graphic Design, Handicrafts, †Illustration, Interior Design, Jewelry, Lettering, †Painting, †Photography, †Printmaking, †Sculpture, Theatre Arts
Adult Hobby Classes: Enrl 75; tuition $110 per unit. Courses—Basic Painting, Ceramics, Portrait Painting, Pottery
Summer School: Tuition $880 for term of 6 wks beginning June 23. Courses—Commercial and Fine Art

CITY COLLEGE OF SAN FRANCISCO, Art Dept, 50 Phelan Ave, 94112. Tel 415-239-3252. *Chairperson* Jesse Hover, MA; *Coordr Fine Arts* Richard Rodrigues, MA; *Coordr Professional Art* Arthur Irwin, MA
Estab 1935; pub; D & E; SC 45, LC 10; enrl col D 15,000, E 11,000
Degrees: AA 2 yrs
Tuition: None
Courses: Art History, Ceramics, Drawing, Graphic Design, Illustration, Industrial Design, Jewelry, Lettering, Painting, Sculpture, Basic Design, Metal Arts, Visual Communication
Summer School: Courses—same as regular yr

DE YOUNG MUSEUM ART SCHOOL,* Golden Gate Park, 94118. Tel 415-750-3656. *Dir* Jim Stevenson; *Chmn Drawing & Painting* John DiPaolo; *Chmn Photography* John Friedman; *Chmn Textiles* Kay Russell; *Chmn Metal Arts* Janet Tyne; *Chmn Art History* Tom Gates; *Chmn Children's Classes* Eileen Lew
Estab 1966; pub; D & E; scholarships; SC 96, LC 7; enrl D 750, E 1750
Courses: Art History, Ceramics, Drawing, Graphic Arts, Painting, Printmaking, Sculpture, Textile Design, Metal Arts
Adult Hobby Classes: Same as regular session
Children's Classes: Children 4-12 yrs old. Tui $31-$35. Courses—Ceramics, Clay and Building, Color, Line & Media, Drawing, Illustrations, Mixed Media, Painting, Sketching, Wood Construction. Young adults 12-16 yrs old. Tui $40-$48. Courses—Ceramics, Design, Drawing, Painting, Photography, Watercolor

SAN FRANCISCO ART INSTITUTE, Admissions Office, 800 Chestnut St, 94133. Tel 415-771-7020. *Chmn Filmmaking Dept* Phil Green; *Chmn Painting Dept* Sam Tchakalian; *Chmn Printmaking Dept* Gordon Kluge; *Chmn Photography Dept* Jack Fulton; *Chmn Sculpture Dept* Richard Berger; *Chmn Performance & Video Dept* Howard Fried
Estab 1871; pvt; D & E; schol; SC 80, LC 22, GC 11; enrl non-maj 49, maj 523, grad 105
Ent Req: HS dipl or GED
Degrees: BFA 4 yrs, MFA 2 yrs
Tuition: $5110 per yr, $2555 per sem, $742 per course; no campus res
Courses: Art History, Ceramics, Drawing, †Film, †Painting, †Photography, †Printmaking, †Sculpture, †Performance/Video
Summer School: Tuition $742 for term of 6 wks beginning June 1 and July 2. Courses—above areas

SAN FRANCISCO STATE UNIVERSITY, Art Dept,* 1600 Holloway, 94132. Tel 415-469-2176. *Chmn* Margery Livingston, BA; *Faculty* Wesley Chamberlin, MA; *Dean* A James Braunr. Instrs: FT 28, PT 8-15
Estab 1899; pub; D; SC 80, LC 20, GC 15; enrl D 450, maj 450, grad 80
Ent Req: HS dipl
Degrees: BA 4 yrs, MA 2 yrs
Tuition: Nonres—$105 per unit; campus residence available
Courses: Art Education, Art History, Ceramics, Jewelry, Painting, Photography, Printmaking, Sculpture, Textile Design, Conceptual Design, Metal Arts
Summer School: Not regular session. Self-supporting classes in Ceramics, Photography and Printmaking

RUDOLPH SCHAEFFER SCHOOL OF DESIGN, 2255 Mariposa St, 94110. Tel 415-863-0715. *Dir* Lennox Tierney; *Deputy Dir* Tom Kass; *Dir Emeritus* Rudolph Schaeffer; *Actg Administrator* Jimmie Beardsley; *Instructor* Laverne Edwards; *Instructor* Jeff Berner; *Instructor* Agnes Bourne; *Instructor* Dale Carlton; *Instructor* Leslie Clark; *Instructor* Jeff Degen; *Instructor* Renee L Hilpert; *Instructor* Robert

Jensen; *Instructor* Janice Langdon; *Instructor* Shuko Robayashi; *Instructor* Joy Stocksdale; *Instructor* Susie Taylor; *Instructor* Marcia Teitgen
Estab 1926; pvt; D & E; schol; SC all, LC 3; enrl D 100, E 40, grad 22
Degrees: Dipl 3 yr prog
Tuition: Res—undergrad $3880 yr
Courses: Drafting, Drawing, Interior Design
Summer School: Enrl 25; tuition $425 for term of 6 wks beginning June. Courses—Architectural Graphics, Color, Design

SAN JACINTO

MOUNT SAN JACINTO COLLEGE, Art Dept, 1499 N State St, 92383. Tel 714-654-7321. *Instr* John Christenson, MFA; *Instr* Frederick L Olsen, MFA; *Instr* Max DeMoss, MFA; *Instr* Bruce Wride, MFA; *Instr* David Weirich, BA; *Instr* Dan Martinez, BFA; *Instr* Elanie Moore, MFA; *Instr* Carolyn Kaneshiro, MFA
Estab 1964; pub; D & E; SC 8, LC 2; enrl D 250, E 420, non-maj 400, maj 50
Ent Req: HS dipl
Degrees: AA and AS
Tuition: $20
Courses: †Art History, †Ceramics, History of Art & Archaeology, †Interior Design, †Jewelry, †Painting, Printmaking, †Sculpture, Silversmithing, †Theatre Arts
Children's Classes: Courses offered

SAN JOSE

SAN JOSE CITY COLLEGE, School of Fine Arts,* 2100 Moorpark Ave, 95128. Tel 408-298-2181. *Dir School Fine Arts* Edwin L Stover, PhD
Estab 1921; pub; D & E; SC 7, LC 2; enrl D 320, E 65
Ent Req: HS dipl or 18 yrs of age or older
Degrees: AA 2 yrs
Tuition: Res—$10 per unit; nonres—$57 per unit
Courses: Art History, Ceramics, Commercial Art, Drawing, Jewelry, Painting, Printmaking, Theatre Arts

SAN JOSE STATE UNIVERSITY, Art Dept, 125 S Seventh St, 95192. Tel 408-277-2542. *Chmn* Frederick Spratt, MA; *Art Educ Coordr* Jose Colchado, EdD; *Assoc Chair, Art History* William Gaugler, LittD; *Assoc Chair, Studio* Stephen French, MFA; *Assoc Chair, Design* Ralf Schubert, BPA; *Graduate Program Coordr* Kenneth Auvil, MFA
Estab 1857, dept estab 1911; pub; D & E; SC 90, LC 28, GC 25; enrl D 4529, maj 1223, grad 94
Ent Req: ACT and grade point average, SAT
Degrees: BA(Art), BA(Art History) 4 yrs, BS(Graphic Design), BS(Industrial Design), BS(Interior Design) and BFA 4 1/2 yrs, MA 1 yr, MFA 2 yrs
Tuition: Res $220-$355 per sem; non-res $220-$355 per sem plus $94.50 per unit
Courses: †Art Education, †Art History, †Ceramics, Drawing, †Graphic Design, †Handicrafts, Illustration, †Industrial Design, †Interior Design, Jewelry, †Painting, Photography, †Printmaking, †Sculpture, Teacher Training, Textile Design
Summer School: Dean Continuing Educ, Ralph C Bohn. Tuition $68 per unit for three summer sessions of 3, 3 and 6 wks; 3 wk January session. Courses—vary according to professors available and projected demand

SAN LUIS OBISPO

CALIFORNIA POLYTECHNIC STATE UNIVERSITY AT SAN LUIS OBISPO, Art Dept, 93407. Tel 805-546-1148. *Prof* Barbara Young, PhD; *Prof* Helen Kelley, MS; *Prof* Bernard W Dusek, MA; *Prof* Robert Reynolds, MAE; *Assoc Prof* Robert Densham, MFA; *Assoc Prof* Clarissa Hewitt, MFA; *Assoc Prof* Robert D Howell, MA; *Assoc Prof* Charles W Jennings, MFA; *Assoc Prof* Henry Wessels, MFA; *Assoc Prof* John Mendenhall, MA; *Assoc Prof* Dan Piel, MS; *Assoc Prof* Keith Dills, PhD; *Asst Prof* Eric Johnson, MFA. Instrs: FT 14
Estab 1901, dept estab 1969; pub; D & E; SC 40, LC 12; enrl D 1000, E 100, non-maj 1100, maj 220
Ent Req: HS dipl, portfolio review
Degrees: BS(Applied Art & Design) 4 yrs
Tuition: Res—undergrad $300 yr; nonres—undergrad $1380; campus res—room & board $560 yr
Courses: Advertising Design, Art History, Ceramics, Drawing, Graphic Arts, Painting, Photography, Printmaking, Sculpture, Design History, Metalsmithing
Summer School: Dir, Barbara Young, PhD. Enrl 90; tuition $200 for term June 20-Sept 2. Courses—Fundamentals of Drawing, Basic B/W Photography, Intermediate Drawing, Ceramics

CUESTA COLLEGE, Art Dept,* PO Box J, 93403. Tel 805-544-2943, Ext 267. *Chmn Fine Arts Div* Barry Frantz, MA; *Instructor* Cuet Amyx, MA; *Instructor* Rupert Deese, MFA; *Instructor* Robert Pelfrey, MA
Estab 1964; pub; D & E; schol; enrl in col D 3200, E 3082
Ent Req: HS dipl or Calif HS Proficiency Exam
Degrees: AA and AS
Tuition: Nonres—$75 per unit
Courses: Art History, Ceramics, Display, Drawing, Graphic Design, Jewelry, Painting, Printmaking, Sculpture, Stage Design, Theatre Arts, Video, Camera Art
Summer School: Chmn Div Fine Arts, Barry Frantz

SAN MATEO

COLLEGE OF SAN MATEO, Art, Commercial Art & Photo Art,* 1700 W Hillsdale Blvd, 94402. Tel 415-574-6288. *Dir Fine Arts* Leo N Bardes
Pub; D & E
Ent Req: HS dipl
Tuition: Nonres—$77 per unit; no campus res
Courses: Architecture, Art History, Ceramics, Commercial Art, Drafting, Drawing, Film, History of Art & Archaeology, Interior Design, Lettering, Painting, Photography, Printmaking, Sculpture, Theatre Arts, Stained Glass

SAN PABLO

CONTRA COSTA COLLEGE, Dept of Art,* 2600 Mission Bell Dr, 94806. Tel 415-235-7800. *Dept Head* Paul Pernish, MFA
Estab 1950; pub; D & E; SC 10, LC 16; enrl D 468, E 200
Ent Req: HS dipl or 18 yrs old
Degrees: Cert of Achievement 1 yr, AA and AS 2 yrs
Tuition: Nonres—$76 per unit; no campus res
Courses: Art History, Ceramics, Graphic Arts, Painting, Photography, Sculpture
Summer School: Assoc Dean Continuing Educ, William Vega. Enrl 50; tuition free for term of 8 wks beginning June 26. Courses—Art, Art Appreciation

SAN RAFAEL

DOMINICAN COLLEGE OF SAN RAFAEL, Art Dept,* 1520 Grand Ave, 94901. Tel 415-457-4440. *Asst Prof* Mary Joanne Cullimore
Scholarships
Degrees: BA
Tuition: $4500 annual tuition
Courses: Advertising Design, Art Appreciation, Art Education, Art History, Calligraphy, Ceramics, Design, Drawing, Handicrafts, Jewelry, Museum Staff Training, Painting, Photography, Printmaking, Sculpture, Stage Design, Textile Design, Theatre Arts, Weaving

SANTA ANA

SANTA ANA COLLEGE, Art Dept,* 17th at Bristol, 92706. Tel 714-667-3000. *Dean of Fine & Performing Arts* Burt Peachy, MA; *Asst Supt & VPres Acad Affairs* Gene Isaacson; *Instructor* Estelle Friedman, MFA; *Instructor* George E Geyer, MA; *Instructor* Patrick Crabb, MA; *Instructor* Frank Molner, MA; *Instructor* Sharon Ford, MA
Estab 1915, dept estab 1960; pub; D & E; schol; SC 21, LC 5; enrl D 280, E 160, maj 57
Ent Req: HS dipl
Degrees: AA 2 yrs
Tuition: Nonres—$72 per unit
Courses: Advertising Design, Architecture, Art History, Ceramics, Commercial Art, Display, Drawing, Graphic Arts, Graphic Design, Handicrafts, Interior Design, Jewelry, Museum Staff Training, Painting, Printmaking, Sculpture
Adult Hobby Classes: Ceramics, Stained Glass
Summer School: Dir, Dean Burt Peachy. Enrl 3000; tui free for term of 8 wks beginning late June. Courses—Ceramics, Design, Drawing, Painting

SANTA BARBARA

SANTA BARBARA CITY COLLEGE, Fine Arts Dept, 721 Cliff Dr, 93109. Tel 805-965-0581. *Dir* O Bucher
Scholarships
Degrees: AA
Courses: Advertising Design, Architecture, Art Appreciation, Art History, Calligraphy, Ceramics, Design, Drawing, Fashion Arts, Film, Handicrafts, Industrial Design, Interior Design, Jewelry, Painting, Printmaking, Sculpture, Stage Design, Textile Design, Textile Design, Weaving, Cartooning, Glassblowing

UNIVERSITY OF CALIFORNIA, SANTA BARBARA, Dept of Art Studio, 93106. Tel 805-961-3138. *Chmn Dept* Michael Arntz, MFA
Estab 1868, dept estab 1950; pub; D; schol; SC 32, LC 17, GC 7; enrl D 431, grad 60
Ent Req: HS dipl
Degrees: BA 4 yrs, MFA 2 yrs, MA 2 yrs, PhD 7 yrs
Courses: Art Education, Ceramics, Drawing, Painting, Printmaking, Sculpture

SANTA CLARA

UNIVERSITY OF SANTA CLARA, Fine Arts Dept, Alameda & Bellomy, 95053. Tel 408-984-4008. *Chmn* San R Hernandez, MFA; *Asst Prof* Dr Brigid S Barton, PhD; *Asst Prof* Kelly Detweiler, MFA; *Asst Prof* Susan Felter, MFA; *Asst Prof* Sam Hernandez, MFA; *Lectr* Dr Jan Thompson, PhD; *Lectr* Gerald P Sullivan
Estab 1850, dept estab 1972; pvt; D; SC 9, LC 14; enrl D 270, non-maj 245, maj 25
Ent Req: HS dipl
Degrees: BA(Fine Arts)
Tuition: $1869 per qtr; campus res room & board $1010 per qtr
Courses: †Art History, Ceramics, Drawing, Museum Staff Training, Painting, Photography, Printmaking, Sculpture, Etching, Intro to Studio Art, Lithography, Silkscreen

SANTA CRUZ

UNIVERSITY OF CALIFORNIA, SANTA CRUZ, Board of Studies in Art,* Performing Arts Bldg, 95064. Tel 408-429-2272. *Prof* Hardy Hanson
Pub; D; SC per quarter 11, LC per quarter 3; enrl D approx 7000, maj 80
Ent Req: HS dipl
Degrees: BA 4 yrs
Tuition: Res—$1120 per qtr; nonres—$486 per qtr
Courses: Aesthetics, Ceramics, Drawing, Graphic Arts, History of Art & Archaeology, Painting, Photography, Sculpture, Stage Design, Theatre Arts

SANTA MARIA

ALLAN HANCOCK COLLEGE, Fine Arts Dept,* 800 South College Drive, 93454. *Head* George Muro. Instrs: FT 11, PT 7
Estab 1920. College has three other locations; pub; D & E; SC 24, LC 4; enrl D 800, E 220, maj 115
Ent Req: HS dipl, over 18 and educable
Degrees: AA 2 yrs
Tuition: Nonres—$75 per unit
Courses: Art History, Ceramics, Drawing, Film, Graphic Design, Handicrafts, Jewelry, Lettering, Painting, Photography, Sculpture, Theatre Arts, Art Appreciation, Design, Life Drawing, Silk Screen
Adult Hobby Classes: Tui varied; classes offered upon need
Summer School: Enrl 230; term of 6 - 8 wks beginning June. Courses—Ceramics, Crafts, Drawing, Opera Workshop, Repertory Theatre, Watercolor

SANTA MONICA

SOUTHERN CALIFORNIA INSTITUTE OF ARCHITECTURE,* 1800 Berkeley St, 90404. Tel 213-829-3482
Degrees: BArch
Tuition: $3350 per yr
Courses: Architecture

SANTA ROSA

SANTA ROSA JUNIOR COLLEGE, Art Dept, 1501 Mendocino Ave, 95401. Tel 707-527-4259. *Chmn Dept* John LeBaron; *Instr* Sarah Gill, PhD; *Instr* Max Hein, MFA; *Instr* Maurice Lapp, MA; *Instr* James M Rosen, MFA; *Instr* John Watrous, MFA; *Instr* Jean Yates, MA; *Instr* Will Collier, MA
Estab 1918, dept estab 1935; pub; D & E; schol; SC 40, LC 8; enrl D approx 800, E approx 1000
Ent Req: HS dipl
Degrees: AA 2 yrs
Tuition: Res—undergrad none; nonres—undergrad $510 per sem, $73 per unit; campus res available
Courses: Art Appreciation, Art History, Ceramics, Drawing, Graphic Design, Jewelry, Lettering, Painting, Photography, Printmaking, Sculpture, Weaving, Bronze Casting, Etching, Layout, Poster Design, Pottery, Principles of Color, Silkscreen, 3-D Design, Watercolor
Summer School: Chmn Dept, John LeBaron. Term of 6 wks beginning June 20.
Courses—Art History, Ceramics, Design, Drawing, Jewelry, Painting, Printmaking, Sculpture, Watercolor

SARATOGA

WEST VALLEY COLLEGE, Art Dept, 14000 Fruitvale Ave, 95070. Tel 408-867-2200. *Chmn* Charles Escott. Instrs: FT 9, PT 2
Estab 1964; pub; D & E; SC 51, LC 12; enrl D 1260, E 801
Ent Req: HS dipl or 18 yrs of age
Degrees: 8, 2 yrs
Tuition: Res fee under $10; no campus res
Courses: Aesthetics, †Ceramics, Commercial Art, Costume Design & Construction, †Drawing, †Graphic Arts, †History of Art & Archaeology, †Jewelry, †Lettering, Museum Staff Training, †Painting, †Sculpture, Stage Design, Theatre Arts, †Design, †Furniture Design, †Occupational Work Experience, †Metal Casting, Stained Glass, Weaving
Adult Hobby Classes: Tuition varies. Courses—many classes offered by Community Services Dept
Summer School: Tuition under $10 for term of 6 wks beginning mid-June.
Courses—Ceramics, Design, Drawing, Jewelry, Sculpture

SOUTH LAKE TAHOE

LAKE TAHOE COMMUNITY COLLEGE, Art Dept, PO Box 14445, 95702. Tel 916-541-4660, Ext 45. *Chmn Art Dept* David Foster, MA
Estab 1975; pub; D & E; schol; SC 22, LC 6; enrl D 375, E 150, non-maj 300, maj 75
Ent Req: HS dipl
Degrees: AA 2 yrs
Tuition: $6 per quarter
Courses: Art History, Ceramics, Drawing, Graphic Arts, Photography, Painting, Printmaking, Sculpture, Color, Design
Summer School: Dir, David Foster. Enrl 100; tuition $6 for six week session.
Courses—Graphic Design, Pottery, Landscape Drawing

STANFORD

STANFORD UNIVERSITY, Dept of Art, Cummings Art Building, 94305. Tel 415-497-3404. *Chmn Dept Art* Lorenz Eitner, PhD. Instrs: FT 18, PT 1
Estab 1891; pvt; D; schol; SC 38, LC 55, GC 19 (seminars); enrl 2850, maj 120, grad 35
Ent Req: HS dipl
Degrees: BA 4 yrs, MA 1 yr, MFA 2 yrs, PhD 5 yrs
Tuition: $9027 per yr; campus res—room and board $3307 per yr
Courses: Art Education, †Art History, †Drawing, †Graphic Design, †Painting, †Photography, †Printmaking, †Sculpture, †Textile Design
Summer School: Dir, Lorenz Eitner. Enrl 115; tuition $2740 for 8 week term.
Courses—Art History, Drawing, Monotype, Painting, Photography

STOCKTON

SAN JOAQUIN DELTA COLLEGE, Art Dept, 5151 Pacific Ave, 95207. Tel 209-474-5209. *Chmn* Dr Don Bennett
Estab 1935; pub; D & E; SC 12, LC 2; enrl D 7000, E 6000, Maj 100
Ent Req: HS dipl
Degrees: AA 2 yrs
Tuition: Non-res—$1728 per yr; no campus res
Courses: Art History, Ceramics, Drafting, Drawing, Graphic Arts, Lettering, Painting, Photography, Sculpture, Stage Design, Theatre Arts
Summer School: Dir, Dr Merrilee R Lewis. Enrl 8000; five week session.
Courses—Same as regular sessions

UNIVERSITY OF THE PACIFIC, Dept of Art, 3600 Pacific Ave, 95211. Tel 209-946-2242. *Chmn* J Ronald Pecchenino. Instrs: FT 8
Estab 1851; pvt; 37 (3 unit) courses & 13 (4 unit) courses available over 4 yrs, independent study; enrl maj 45-50
Ent Req: HS grad with 20 sem grades of recommending quality earned in the 10th, 11th and 12th years in traditional subjects, twelve of these grades must be in acad subj
Degrees: BA & BFA
Tuition: $7680 per yr, $338 per unit (6 1/2 - 11 1/2 units), $266 per unit (1/2 - 6 units); campus res—$3280
Courses: Art Education, †Art History, Ceramics, Design, †Graphic Design, †Painting, Photography, Sculpture, Commercial Design, †Studio Art, †Visual Arts Management
Summer School: Two 5 wk sessions

SUISUN CITY

SOLANO COMMUNITY COLLEGE, Dept of Fine & Applied Art, Suisun Valley Rd, PO Box 246, 94585. Tel 707-864-7000. *Div Chmn Fine & Applied Art* Carol Bishop; *Instructor* Jan Eldridge; *Instructor* Susan Knopka; *Instructor* Dorothy Herger; *Instructor* Emi Luptak; *Instructor* Ray Salmon; *Instructor* Jack Vickers; *Instructor* Jake Lovejoy
Estab 1945; pub; D & E; SC 16, LC 5; enrl D 255, E 174
Ent Req: HS dipl
Degrees: AA 2 yrs
Tuition: Nonres—$47.65 per unit; no campus res
Courses: Art History, Ceramics, Commercial Art, Drawing, Lettering, Painting, Printmaking, Sculpture, Form & Composition, Fundamentals of Art, Survey of Modern Art
Adult Hobby Classes: Tuition varies per class. Courses—Cartooning, Jewelry Design, Stained Glass
Summer School: Dean summer session, Dr Marjorie Blaha

TAFT

TAFT COLLEGE, Division of Performing Arts,* 29 Emmons Park Dr, 93268. Tel 805-765-4191. *Chmn Div* Jack Mettier, MA; *Instr* John Christensen, MA; *Instr* Konrad McMillan, MA
Estab 1922; pub; D & E; scholarships; SC 67, LC 6; enrl 1500 total
Ent Req: HS grad or 18 yrs old
Degrees: AA 2 yrs
Tuition: Nonres—$72 per unit under 7, 7 - 14 units $1080
Courses: Architecture, †Art History, Ceramics, Commercial Art, Conceptual Art, †Drafting, Drawing, Fashion Arts, Graphic Arts, Graphic Design, Handicrafts, †History of Art & Archaeology, Illustration, Interior Design, Jewelry, Painting, †Photography, Sculpture, Textile Design, †Theatre Arts
Adult Hobby Classes: Courses—Ceramics, Graphic Arts, Jewelry, Painting, Photography
Summer School: Dean, Mr Don Zumbro. Term of 6-8 wks. Courses—vary

THOUSAND OAKS

CALIFORNIA LUTHERAN COLLEGE, Art Dept, 60 Olson Rd, 91360. Tel 805-492-2411, Ext 254. *Chmn Dept* Jerry Slattum, PhD; *Assoc Prof* John Solem, MA; *Vis Prof* B M A Weber
Estab 1961; pvt; D & E; scholarships; SC 12, LC 7; enrl D 110, non-maj 46, maj 64
Ent Req: HS dipl, SAT or ACT, portfolio suggested
Degrees: BA 4 yr; MA(Educ) 1 - 2 yr
Tuition: Res—undergrad $4900 per yr, $2450 per sem, $160 per unit; campus res—room & board $2400 per year
Courses: Advertising Design, Art Education, Art History, Calligraphy, Ceramics, Collages, Commercial Art, Costume Design & Construction, Drawing, Fashion Arts, Graphic Arts, Graphic Design, History of Art & Archaeology, Illustration, Mixed Media, Painting, Photography, Printmaking, Sculpture, Stage Design, Teacher Training, Theatre Arts
Summer School: Dir, James Jackson. Tuition $130 per unit for term June-July, July-Aug. Courses—Art Education, Design, Drawing, Painting, Pottery, Sculpture

TUJUNGA

MCGROARTY CULTURAL ART CENTER, Cultural Affairs Dept, City of Los Angeles, 7570 McGroarty Terrace, 91042. Tel 213-352-5285, 352-6275. *Dir* Audrey L Davis, MA. Instrs: PT 24
Estab 1953; pub; D & E; scholarships; SC 40, LC 1; enrl D 600, E 200
Tuition: Fees for adults $15-$50 per 10 wk session; fees for children and teens $5 per 10 wk session
Courses: Aesthetics, Art Education, Art History, Calligraphy, Ceramics, Collages, Costume Design & Construction, Drawing, Graphic Arts, Handicrafts, Sculpture, Weaving, Mixed Media, Painting, Textile Design, Chinese Brush Painting, Lace Making & Embroidery, Quiltmaking, Stained Glass, Tai Chi Chuan, Water Colors
Adult Hobby Classes: Clothing Construction
Children's Classes: Arts & Crafts, Ceramics, Maskmaking, Painting, Sculpture
Summer School: Classes held year-round

TURLOCK

CALIFORNIA STATE COLLEGE, STANISLAUS, Art Dept, 800 Monte Vista Ave, 95380. Tel 209-667-3431. *Chmn Dept & Gallery Dir* Hope B Werness, PhD; *Prof* Martin Camarata, MA; *Prof* Ralf Parton, MA; *Prof* James Piskoti, MFA; *Prof* Winston McGee, MA; *Vis Lectr* Richard Savini, MFA; *Vis Lectr* Eric Adfelstadt, MFA
Estab 1963, dept estab 1967; pub; D & E; scholarships; SC 27, LC 6, GC 4; enrl D 400, E 50, non-maj 350, maj 85, grad 20
Ent Req: HS dipl
Degrees: BA 4 yrs; Printmaking Cert Prog, Special Masters Degree Prog
Tuition: Res—undergrad $668, grad $704 per yr, $50 winter terms; nonres—undergrad & grad are same as res plus $108 per unit; limited campus residence
Courses: Art History, Ceramics, Drawing, Film, Graphic Arts, Painting, Photography, Printmaking, Sculpture, Teacher Training, Gallery Management
Summer School: Enrl 50. Courses—Ceramics

VALENCIA

CALIFORNIA INSTITUTE OF THE ARTS, School of Art, 24700 McBean Pkwy, 91355. Tel 805-255-1050. *Pres* Robert Fitzpatrick; *Dean* Catherine Lord. Instrs: FT 15
Estab 1970; pvt; scholarships; enrl D 130 first yr, 260 in 1983
Ent Req: Portfolio, health cert
Degrees: BFA 4 yrs, MFA
Tuition: Campus res available
Courses: Drawing, Film, Graphic Arts, Painting, Photography, Sculpture, Video, Post Studio, Visual Communication, Critical Theory

COLLEGE OF THE CANYONS, Art Dept,* 26455 Rockwell Canyon Rd, 91356. Tel 805-259-7800, Ext 308. *Head Dept* Joanne Julian, MFA
Estab 1970, dept estab 1974; pub; D & E; SC 11, LC 4; enrl D 300, E 300, maj 50
Ent Req: Must be 18 yrs of age
Degrees: AA and AS 2 yrs
Tuition: Student fee $10
Courses: Advertising Design, Art History, Ceramics, Drafting, Drawing, Painting, Photography, Printmaking, Sculpture
Adult Hobby Classes: Tui $10 plus lab fees usually another $10 per sem
Children's Classes: Classes offered in continuing education under child development

VAN NUYS

LOS ANGELES VALLEY COLLEGE, Art Dept, 5800 Fulton Ave, 91401. Tel 213-781-1200, Ext 356. *Chmn* Henry Klein
E
Degrees: AA, cert
Courses: Advertising Design, Art History, Ceramics, Design, Drawing, Handicrafts, Jewelry, Painting, Photography, Printmaking, Sculpture, Textile Design

VENICE

VENICE SCULPTURE STUDIO, INC, 346 Sunset Ave, 90291. Tel 213-399-9653. *Chmn Painting Dept* Jan Saether
Estab 1976; pvt; D & E; SC 22; enrl D 50, E 50
Ent Req: Portfolio
Degrees: None
Tuition: $55-$70 monthly; no campus res
Courses: Drawing, Painting, Sculpture
Summer School: Dir, Martine Olga Vaugel. Courses—same as regular offerings

VENTURA

VENTURA COLLEGE, Fine Arts Division, 4667 Telegraph Rd, 93003. Tel 805-642-3211, Ext 229. Instrs: FT 13, PT 15
Estab 1925; pub; D & E; scholarships; SC 50, LC 15; enrl D 500, E 500, maj 300
Ent Req: HS dipl or 18 yrs of age
Degrees: AA and AS
Tuition: None to res; no campus residence
Courses: Advertising Design, Art Appreciation, Art History, Ceramics, Commercial Art, †Display, Drawing, Fashion Arts, Graphic Arts, Graphic Design, Handicrafts, Illustration, Painting, †Photography, Sculpture, Textile Design, Fiber Design
Summer School: Assoc Dean, Yvonne Bodle. Many of the regular session courses are offered

VICTORVILLE

VICTOR VALLEY COLLEGE, Art Dept, 18422 Bear Valley Rd, 92392. Tel 714-245-4271. *Chmn Dept* Gene Kleinsmith, MFA; *Instr* Molly Haines Kohlschreiber, MFA; *Instr* Ruth Rutledge, AA; *Ceramics Technician* Brent Taylor, BA; *Vis Prof* Bruce Howdle, ceramics; *Vis Prof* Futzie Nutzle, cartooning; *Vis Prof* William C Alexander, ceramics; *Vis Prof* Ken Ferguson, ceramics; *Vis Prof* Don Bendel, ceramics
Estab 1961, dept estab 1971; pub; D & E; scholarships; SC 20, LC 5; enrl D 125, E 125, non-maj 200, maj 50
Ent Req: HS dipl
Degrees: AA 2 yrs
Courses: Advertising Design, Aesthetics, Art History, Calligraphy, Ceramics, Commercial Art, Conceptual Art, Drawing, Graphic Arts, Graphic Design, History of Art & Archaeology, Interior Design, Painting, Photography, Printmaking, Sculpture
Adult Hobby Classes: Enrl 100; tuition $10 per 6 wks. Courses · Interior Design
Summer School: Enrl 60. Courses—Art History, Art Concepts

VISALIA

COLLEGE OF THE SEQUOIAS, Art Dept, Fine Arts Division, Mooney Blvd, 93277. Tel 209-733-2050. *Chmn* George C Pappas, MA; *Instructor* Ralph Homan, MA; *Instructor* Gene Maddox, MA; *Instructor* Alfred Pietroforte, MA; *Instructor* Barbara Strong, MA; *Instructor* Robert Marcellus, MA
Estab 1925, dept estab 1940; pub; D & E; scholarships; SC 12, LC 4; enrl D 60, E37, maj 10
Ent Req: HS dipl, must be 18 yr of age
Degrees: AA 2 yr
Tuition: None; no campus res
Courses: Aesthetics, Art Education, Art History, Ceramics, Commercial Art, Drawing, Film, Graphic Arts, History of Art & Archaeology, Lettering, Museum Staff Training, Painting, Printmaking, Sculpture, Stage Design, Theatre Arts
Adult Hobby Classes: Ceramics, China Painting, Jewelry, Stained Glass
Summer School: Dir, George C Pappas. Courses—Drawing, Painting, Stained Glass

WALNUT

MOUNT SAN ANTONIO COLLEGE, Art Dept,* 1100 N Grand Ave, 91789. Tel 714-594-5611, Ext 319. *Chmn* Ronald B Ownbey. Instrs: FT 14, PT 3
Estab 1945; pub; D & E; SC 24, LC 5; enrl D 2254, E 852, maj 500
Ent Req: Over 18 yrs of age
Degrees: AA and AS 2 yrs
Tuition: Non-district res—$80 per unit
Courses: Advertising Design, Ceramics, Commercial Art, Drafting, Drawing, Graphic Arts, Art History, Illustration, Lettering, Painting, Photography, Printmaking, Sculpture, Theatre Arts, Fibers, Life Drawing, Metals & Enamels, Watercolor, Woodworking
Summer School: Enrl art 50; term of 6 wks beginning June 16. Courses—Ceramics, Drawing

WEED

COLLEGE OF THE SISKIYOUS, Art Dept, 800 College Ave, 96094. Tel 916-938-4463, Ext 239. *Head Dept* Barry R Barnes, MA
Estab 1957; pub; D & E; scholarships; SC 15, LC 2; enrl D 1200, maj 20
Ent Req: HS dipl
Degrees: AA 2 yrs
Tuition: None to res; campus residence available
Courses: Art History, Ceramics, Collages, Constructions, Drafting, Drawing, Graphic Arts, History of Art & Archaeology, Painting, Photography, Printmaking, Sculpture

WHITTIER

RIO HONDO COLLEGE, Fine Arts Dept, 3600 Workman Mill Rd, 90608. Tel 213-692-0921, Ext 361. *Chmn Dept* John R Jacobs, MA. Instrs: FT 21, PT 14
Estab 1962; pub; D & E; SC 18, LC 3; enrl D & E 2178, non-maj 2000, maj 178
Ent Req: HS dipl
Degrees: AA 2 yrs
Tuition: None; no campus residence
Courses: Advertising Design, Art History, Ceramics, †Commercial Art, Costume Design & Construction, Display, Drawing, Film, Graphic Arts, History of Art & Archaeology, Illustration, Jewelry, Lettering, Painting, Photography, Printmaking, Sculpture, Stage Design, Theatre Arts, Video
Summer School: Enrl approx 396; tuition free for term of 6 wks beginning June 25

WHITTIER COLLEGE, Dept of Art, 13406 Philadelphia St, 90608. Tel 213-693-0771, Ext 309. *Chmn* Robert W Speier. Instrs: FT 2, PT 2
Estab 1901; pvt; D & E; scholarships and fels; SC 12, LC 12; enrl 552-560 per sem
Ent Req: HS dipl, accept credit by exam CLEP, CEEBA
Degrees: BA 4 yrs
Tuition: $6675; $7165 total per year live off campus, $9871 total per year live on campus
Courses: Art Education, Art History, Ceramics, Drawing, Painting, Printmaking, Adult and children's classes for special students; tui $5
Summer School: Dir, Robert W Speier. Enrl 25; tui $140 per credit 1-7 credits, $125 per credit 7-up credits, May 31-June 17, June 20-July 29, Aug 1-Aug 19. Courses—Water Soluble Painting, Color & Basic Drawing

WILMINGTON

LOS ANGELES HARBOR COLLEGE, Art Dept, 1111 Figueroa Place, 90744. Tel 213-518-1000. *Humanities & Fine Arts Chmn* Robert H Billings, MA; *Assoc Prof* John Cassone, MA; *Asst Prof* Nancy E Webber, MFA; *Instructor* DeAnn Jennings, MA; *Instructor* Jay McCafferty, MA
Estab 1949; pub; D & E; SC 48, LC 11; enrl D 10,000, E 4200
Ent Req: HS dipl
Degrees: AA 2 yrs
Tuition: Non-res—$1116 per yr
Courses: Architecture, Art History, Ceramics, Drawing, Fashion Arts, Painting, Photography, Printmaking, Stage Design, Theatre Arts
Summer School: Art Dept Chmn, DeAnn Jennings. Courses—Art Fundamentals, Art History and Photography

WOODLAND HILLS

PIERCE COLLEGE, Art Dept, 6201 Winnetka, 91371. Tel 213-347-0551. *Art Dept Chmn & Prof* John D Kuczynski; *Prof* Alfred Van Auker, MFA; *Prof* James Crandall; *Prof* Milton Hirschl, MA; *Prof* Walter Smith, MFA; *Assoc Prof* Roberta Barrager, MFA; *Assoc Prof* John W Corbeil, MA; *Asst Prof* Alfred Carrillo, MFA; *Asst Prof* A Nancy Snooks, MFA; *Instr* Paul C Nordberg, AA
Estab 1947, dept estab 1956; pub; D & E; scholarships; SC 35, LC 3;

enrl D & E 23,000
Ent Req: HS dipl 18 yrs and over
Degrees: AA 60 units
Tuition: Nonres—$97 per unit; no campus res
Courses: †Advertising Design, Art History, Ceramics, †Commercial Art, Display, Drawing, Film, Graphic Arts, Graphic Design, Illustration, Interior Design, Jewelry, Lettering, Painting, †Photography, Printmaking, Sculpture
Adult Hobby Classes: Offered through Community Services Dept
Summer School: Dir, Robert D Chase

COLORADO

ALAMOSA

ADAMS STATE COLLEGE, Dept of Visual Arts, 81102. Tel 303-589-7823. *Prof* Cloyde E Snook, MFA; *Prof* Paul H Williams, MFA; *Prof* Edwin L Clemmer, MFA; *Adjunct Prof* Mary Lavey, MA; *Visiting Prof* Gene Daniels, MA; *Visiting Prof* Stephen Quiller
Estab 1924; pub; D & E; scholarships; SC 43, LC 6, GC 5; enrl D 450, non-maj 200, maj 40, grad 7
Ent Req: HS dipl, ACT & SAT
Degrees: BA 4 yrs, MA 1-1/2 yrs
Tuition: Res—undergrad $493 per sem, grad $510 per sem; nonres—$1526 per sem, grad $1596 per sem; campus res—room & board $395-$755
Courses: Art Education, Art History, Ceramics, Drawing, Jewelry, Painting, Photography, Printmaking, Sculpture, Teacher Training
Adult Hobby Classes: Tuition $32 per sem hr. Courses—Design, Photography, Sculpture, Stained Glass
Summer School: Dir, Dr Lloyd Swenson. Tuition $32 per credit hour. Courses—Art for Teachers, Ceramics, Metal Casting, Painting, Photography

BLACK HAWK

BLACKHAWK MOUNTAIN SCHOOL OF ART,* Box 258, 251 Main St, 80422. Tel 303-582-5235. *Pres* Michael S Parfenoff, MFA; *Instr* Ken Bowman, BFA; *Instr* Jordan Krimstein, BFA; *Instr* Robert Lockart, MFA; *Instr* David Schnieder, MFA; *Instr* Janau Noerdlinger, MFA; *Instr* Dixie Glenn, MFA
Estab 1963; pub; SC 6, LC 3; enrl D 25-35
Ent Req: Letter of recommendation and a personal contract
Degrees: None
Tuition: $1700 for 7 wks, $1000 for 4 wks, $759 for 3 wks. Terms begin June 16 through August 4; campus res room and board included in total cost
Courses: Ceramics, Drawing, Film, Graphic Arts, Mixed Media, Painting, Photography, Printmaking, Sculpture

BOULDER

UNIVERSITY OF COLORADO, BOULDER, Dept of Fine Arts, Sibell-Wolle Fine Arts Bldg N196A, Campus Box 318, 80309. Tel 303-492-6504. *Chmn* Jerry W Kunkel; *Assoc Chmn* Luis E Eades. Instrs: FT 28
Estab 1861; pub; D & E; scholarships; SC 55, LC 53, GC 67; enrl D 2000, E 150, non-maj 400, maj 325, grad 84, others 100
Ent Req: HS dipl
Degrees: BA or BFA(Art Educ, Art History and Studio Arts) 4 yrs, MA(Art Educ and Art Hist) 3-5 yrs, MFA(Studio Arts) 2-3 yrs
Tuition: Res—undergrad $535 per sem plus $123 fees; grad $572 per sem for 9-15 hrs plus $123 fees; nonres—undergrad $2425 per sem plus $123 fees; grad $2395 per sem plus $123 fees; campus res—room & board $1223-$1408 per sem, $2446-$2816 per yr
Courses: †Art Education, †Art History, Ceramics, Drawing, Jewelry, Painting, Photography, Printmaking, Sculpture, Video, Watermedia
Summer School: Enrl 20-25 per course; tuition $540 res, $1920 nonres for term of 5 weeks beginning in June. Courses—Art History, Drawing, Painting, Photography, Printmaking, Sculpture, Special Topics, Watermedia

COLORADO SPRINGS

COLORADO COLLEGE, Dept of Art, 80903. Tel 303-473-2233, Ext 365. *Chmn & Asst Prof* Carl Reed, MFA; *Prof* James Trissel, MFA; *Assoc Prof* Louise LaFond, MFA; *Asst Prof* Gale Murray, PhD; *Asst Prof* Ruth Kolarik, PhD; *Asst Prof* Bogdan Swider, MFA; *Asst Prof* Edith Kirsch, PhD
Estab 1874; pvt; D; schol; SC 20, LC 20; enrl D 1800, maj 40
Ent Req: HS dipl or equivalent and selection by admissions committee
Degrees: BA and MAT 4 yr
Tuition: Res—undergrad $7000 per yr; campus res—room and board $2400
Courses: Art Education, Art History, Drawing, Graphic Design, Painting, Photography, Printmaking, Sculpture, 3-D Design, Art Studio
Summer School: Dean, Elmer R Peterson. Tuition $260 per unit for term of 8 wks beginning June 19. Courses—Architecture, Art Education, Photography

DENVER

COLORADO INSTITUTE OF ART, 200 E Ninth Ave, 80203. Tel 303-837-0825. *Pres* Cheryl Murphy; *Dir of Educ* James Graft
Estab 1952; pvt; D & E; schol; SC all; enrl D 950, E 200 non-maj 200, maj 725
Ent Req: HS dipl
Degrees: Assoc 2 yr
Tuition: Undergrad—$1290 per quarter; photography $1390; campus res $1190 - $1475 per quarter

Courses: †Advertising Design, Commercial Art, Drawing, †Fashion Arts, Graphic Design, Illustration, †Interior Design, Lettering, Mixed Media, Painting, †Fashion Illustration, †Fashion Merchandising
Adult Hobby Classes: Evening career training; 1 yr diploma. Courses—Commercial Art, Technician Interior Planning-Decorating, Photo Technician. Nine week avocational workshops in fine arts and photography
Children's Classes: Sat teen workshops, grades 7-12; monthly tuition $24
Summer School: Commercial art prep school for post-secondary students only

COLORADO WOMEN'S COLLEGE, Dept of Art,* Montview Blvd & Quebec, 80220. Tel 303-394-6012. *Instr* Joyce Eakins, MFA; *Instr* Steve Hutchner, PhD; *Instr* Tom MacCluskey, MMus
Estab 1898; pvt; D; scholarships; SC 30, LC 15; enrl D 158, maj 45
Ent Req: HS dipl
Degrees: BA 4 yr, BFA 5 yr
Tuition: $110 per cr hr
Courses: †Art Education, †Art History, Ceramics, Conceptual Art, Drawing, Jewelry, †Mixed Media, Painting, Photography, Printmaking, Sculpture, Stage Design, Teacher Training, Textile Design, Theatre Arts
Summer School: Dir, James Polt. Enrl 15 per class; Term of 3 wks beginning May and July. Courses—Jewelry, Painting, Photography, Primitive Pottery, Printmaking

LORETTO HEIGHTS COLLEGE, Dept of Art, 3001 S Federal Blvd, 80236. Tel 303-922-4011. *Prog Dir* Max Di Julio. Instrs: FT 2, PT 3
Estab 1880; pvt; D & E; SC 8, LC 4
Ent Req: HS dipl, ent exam
Degrees: BA, BS and BFA 4 yrs
Courses: Art Education, Ceramics, Drawing, Graphic Arts, History of Art & Archaeology, Jewelry, Lettering, Painting, Sculpture, Weaving
Summer School: Courses—Ceramics, Glass, Jewelry, Printmaking, Weaving

METROPOLITAN STATE COLLEGE, Art Dept, 1006 11th St, 80204. Tel 303-629-3090. *Chmn* J Thomas Logan, MFA
Estab 1963, dept estab 1963; pub; D & E; SC 52, LC 8; enrl D 650, E 325, maj 465
Ent Req: HS dipl or GED
Degrees: BA 4 yrs
Courses: Advertising Design, Art Education, Art History, Ceramics, Commercial Art, Drawing, Graphic Arts, Graphic Design, Industrial Design, Jewelry, Painting, Photography, Printmaking, Sculpture, Silversmithing, Design in Wood, Product Design
Summer School: Same as regular session

ROCKY MOUNTAIN SCHOOL OF ART, 1441 Ogden St, 80218. Tel 303-832-1557. *Dir* Philip J Steele; *Asst Dir* Steven Steele; *Financial Aid* Craig Steele; *Student Servs* Lisa Steele; *Adminr* Kristi Allen. Instrs: PT 25
Estab 1963; pvt; D & E; scholarships; enrl D 250
Ent Req: Portfolio
Degrees: AA
Tuition: $825 per quarter; no campus res
Courses: Advertising Design, Art History, †Commercial Art, Drawing, Fashion Arts, Graphic Design, Illustration, Lettering, †Painting, Printmaking, Sculpture, †Sign Painting

UNIVERSITY OF COLORADO AT DENVER, Dept of Fine Arts, 1100 14th St, Box 103, 80202. Tel 303-629-2626. *Chmn* John R Fudge, MFA; *Prof* Ludwik Turzanski, MFA; *Prof* Charles L Moone, MFA; *Assoc Prof* Ernest O Porps, MFA; *Assoc Prof* Gerald C Johnson, MFA; *Asst Prof* Celia Rabinovitch, PhD; *Asst Prof* Ruth Thorne-Thomsen, MFA; *Adjunct Prof* Jane Comstock, MA
Estab 1876, dept estab 1955; pub; D & E; schol; SC 21, LC 13, GC 11; enrl maj 114
Ent Req: HS dipl, ACT or SAT, previous academic ability and accomplishment
Degrees: BA and BFA 4 yrs
Tuition: Res—undergrad & grad $261 per sem, $23 per cr hr; nonres—undergrad & grad $1146 per sem, $77 per cr hr; no campus res available
Courses: †Art History, †Drawing, Film, †Painting, †Photography, †Printmaking, †Sculpture
Summer School: Tuition same as regular sem, term of 10 wk beginning June 12. Courses—Art History, Studio Workshops

UNIVERSITY OF DENVER, School of Art, 2121 E Asbury, 80208. Tel 303-753-2846. *Dir* Mel Strawn, MFA
Estab 1880; pvt; D; scholarships; SC 44, LC 33, GC 50; enrl D 450, non-maj 170-200, maj 176, grad 40
Ent Req: HS dipl
Degrees: BA and BFA 4 yrs, MFA 2 yrs, MA 4 quarters; honors program
Tuition: $2112 per qtr, $176 per qtr hr; campus residency available
Courses: Art Education, †Art History, †Ceramics, †Drawing, Graphic Arts, Graphic Design, †Museum Staff Training, †Painting, †Photography, †Printmaking, †Sculpture, Fabric Dyeing, †Visual Communications Design, Off-loom Weaving
Adult Hobby Classes: Enrl 25; tuition $35-$60 per course. Courses—Ceramics, Drawing, Painting, Photography, Printmaking
Summer School: Dir, Mel Strawn. Enrl 100; tuition $143 per quarter hr for sem of 8 wks beginning June 16. Courses—Art History, Ceramics, Photography and Design, Workshop-Seminar in conjunction with Aspen Design Conference

DURANGO

FORT LEWIS COLLEGE, Art Dept, 81301. Tel 303-247-7152. *Chmn* Mick Reber, MFA; *Prof* Stanton Englehart, MFA; *Assoc Prof* Gerald Wells, MFA; *Assoc Prof* Laurel Covington-Vogl, MFA; *Assoc Prof* David Hunt, MA; *Instr* Ellen Cargile; *Artist in Residence* Bruce Lowney
Estab 1956; pub; D & E; scholarships; SC 30, LC 6; enrl D 600, non-maj 450, maj 150
Ent Req: HS dipl, SAT
Degrees: BA & BS
Tuition: Campus res available
Courses: Advertising Design, Aesthetics, Art Education, Art History, Ceramics,

Commercial Art, Drawing, Handicrafts, Illustration, Industrial Design, Intermedia, Jewelry, Mixed Media, Painting, Printmaking, Sculpture, Silversmithing, Teacher Training
Summer School: Dean, Ed Angus. Enrl 1000. Courses—Art Education, Ceramics, Drawing, Mural Design, Painting

FORT COLLINS

COLORADO STATE UNIVERSITY, Dept of Art, 80523. Tel 303-491-6774. *Chmn* Peter A Jacobs, EdD; *Asst Chmn* Lawrence Von Bamford; *Coordr Teacher Cert* Perry Ragouzis; *Prof* John Curfman, MS; *Prof* Richard DeVore, MFA; *Prof* Nilda C Getty, MFA; *Prof* John Sorbie, MSA Ed; *Prof* Leroy Twarogowski, MFA; *Prof* John Berland, MFA. Instrs: FT 30, PT 5
Estab 1870, dept estab 1956; pub; D; SC 55, LC 13, GC 5; enrl D 547, non-maj 860, maj 547, grad 19
Ent Req: HS dipl, portfolio if by transfer
Degrees: BA(Art History & Art Education) and BFA 4 yr, MFA 70 hrs
Tuition: Res—undergrad $1274.84 per yr, $637.42 per sem, $55 per cr up to 8 cr; grad $1426.84 per yr, $713.42 per sem; nonres—undergrad $4641.84 per yr, $2320.92 per sem; grad $4866.84 per yr, $2433.42 per sem; campus residence available $4000
Courses: †Art Education, †Art History, †Ceramics, †Drawing, †Graphic Design, †Interior Design, †Jewelry, †Painting, †Photography, †Printmaking, †Sculpture, †Fibers
Children's Classes: Continuing education art offerings not on regular basis
Summer School: 4 wk and 8 wk sessions beginning May 17 and June 14

GOLDEN

FOOTHILLS ART CENTER, INC, 809 15th St, 80401. Tel 303-279-3922. *Exec Dir* Marian J Metsopoulos, MA. Instrs: PT 10
Estab 1968; pvt; D & E (winter and spring)
Ent Req: None
Tuition: $20-$54 for 6-10 wk class
Courses: Calligraphy, Drawing, Jewelry, Painting, Printmaking, Watercolor
Adult Hobby Classes: Enrl limited; tuition $30-$45 for 8-10 wk class.
Courses—Pottery, Printmaking
Summer School: Exec Dir, Marian J Metsopoulos. Workshops for adults and classes for children beginning in June

RED ROCKS COMMUNITY COLLEGE, Human Resources & Services Division, 12600 W Sixth Ave, 80401. Tel 303-988-6160. *Instr Pottery* Thomas L Nielsen. Instrs: FT 4
Tuition: $28 per sem cr hr
Courses: Art Appreciation, Art History, Ceramics, Design, Drawing, Painting, Textile Design, Weaving
Adult Hobby Classes: Courses—Stained Glass Design, Drawing from the Right Side of the Brain
Children's Classes: Courses—Drawing, Printmaking Without a Press
Summer School: Enrl 80; tuition $84 per 3 cr course per 10 wks.
Courses—Ceramics, Drawing, Design, Watercolor

GRAND JUNCTION

MESA COLLEGE, Art Dept, 81501. Tel 303-248-1020. *Dean* Bruce Crowell
Estab 1925; pub; D & E; scholarships; SC 23, LC 5; enrl D 538, E 103
Ent Req: HS dipl, GED
Degrees: AA, BA
Courses: Art Education, Art History, Ceramics, Drawing, Painting, Printmaking, Sculpture, Exhibitions & Management, Metalsmithing
Children's Classes: Enrl 50. Courses-Ceramics, Dance, Drawing, Music, Theatre

GREELEY

AIMS COMMUNITY COLLEGE, Program for Design & Creative Studies, PO Box 69, 80632. Tel 303-330-8008. *Chmn Div Communication & Humanities* Ester Sims; *Design & Creative Studies Program Coordr* Tedd Runge
Tuition: Res—$11 per cr hr; $18.50 per cr hr for in-state, out of district; nonres—$65 per cr hr
Courses: Architecture, Art Appreciation, Art History, Ceramics, Design, Drawing, Fashion Arts, Interior Design, Jewelry, Painting, Photography, Sculpture, Textile Design, Weaving
Children's Classes: Courses offered
Summer School: Courses offered

UNIVERSITY OF NORTHERN COLORADO, Dept of Visual Arts,* 80639. Tel 303-351-2143, 351-2477. *Chmn* Richard Munson. Instrs: FT 7
Estab 1889; pub; D & E
Ent Req: HS dipl
Degrees: BA
Tuition: Res—$309 per qtr; nonres—$1317 per qtr
Summer School: Courses—Comparative Arts Program in Florence, Italy, Study of the Indian Arts of Mesa Verde, Mesa Verde workshop and on campus courses, Workshops in Weaving & Ceramics in Steamboat Springs, Colorado

GUNNISON

WESTERN STATE COLLEGE OF COLORADO, Dept of Art,* 81230. Tel 303-943-3083. *Chmn Arts & Human* Theodore C Johnson. Instrs: FT 7, PT 1
Estab 1911; pub; D & E; SC 29, LC 7, GC 8; enrl 850
Ent Req: HS dipl, special exam
Degrees: 4 yr
Tuition: Res—$380 per sem; nonres—$1652 per sem

Courses: Art Education, Calligraphy, Ceramics, Drawing, Jewelry, Painting, Printmaking, Sculpture, Design, Indian Art, Introduction to Art, Studio Art, Weaving
Summer School: Dir, Dr Edwin H Randall. 2, 4 and 8 wk courses

LA JUNTA

OTERO JUNIOR COLLEGE, Art Dept, 18th & Colorado Ave, 81050. Tel 303-384-8721. *Head Dept* Mignon Hively
Estab 1941; pub; D & E; scholarships; SC 12, LC 3; enrl 776
Ent Req: HS grad
Degrees: AA and AAS 2 yr
Courses: Art History, Ceramics, Drawing, Painting, Creative Design, Metal Sculpture, Watercolor
Adult Hobby Classes: Enrl 60; tuition $45 per quarter. Courses—Art, Drawing, Painting

PUEBLO

UNIVERSITY OF SOUTHERN COLORADO, BELMONT CAMPUS, Dept of Art, 2200 Bonforte Blvd, 81001. Tel 303-549-2817. *Chmn* Edward R Sajbel, MA; *Prof* Jo Ann Brassill, MFA; *Prof* Lewis Tilley, MFA; *Assoc Prof* Robert Hench, MA; *Assoc Prof* Dr Mildred Montverde, PhD; *Asst Prof* Carl Jensen, MFA; *Asst Prof* Robert Wands, MA; *Instructor* Nick Latka, MFA
Estab 1933; pub; D & E; scholarships; SC 66, LC 19, GC 2; enrl D 700, E 50, non-maj 600, maj 150
Ent Req: HS dipl, GED, Open Door Policy
Degrees: BA and BS 4 yrs
Tuition: Res—undergrad $533 18 hr sem; nonres—$1972 18 hr sem; campus residency available
Courses: Advertising Design, Art History, Ceramics, Collages, Commercial Art, Drawing, Film, Graphic Design, Illustration, Jewelry, Museum Staff Training, Painting, Photography, Printmaking, Sculpture, Silversmithing, Teacher Training
Summer School: Dir, Ed Sajbel. Enrl 125; tuition resident $40 per cr hr, nonres $150 per cr hr. Courses—Art Education, Art History, Ceramics, Introduction to Art, Painting

STERLING

NORTHEASTERN JUNIOR COLLEGE, Dept of Art,* 80751. Tel 303-522-6600, Ext 671. *Head Dept* Peter L Youngers, MFA; *Div Chmn Humanities* Dorothy Corsberg
Estab 1941; pub; D & E; schol; SC 16, LC 2; enrl D 103, E 23, non-maj 73, maj 30, others 23
Ent Req: HS dipl, GED
Degrees: AA 2 yr
Tuition: Res—$783 per yr; nonres—$1998 per yr
Courses: Art Education, Art History, Ceramics, Display, Drawing, Handicrafts, Lettering, Mixed Media, Painting, Printmaking, Sculpture, Teacher Training
Adult Hobby Classes: Enrl 100; tuition $8 per cr hr. Courses—Basic Crafts, Ceramics, Drawing, Macrame, Painting, Stained Glass
Summer School: Dir, Dick Gritz. Courses—vary each yr

VAIL

COLORADO MOUNTAIN COLLEGE, Summervail Workshop for Art & Critical Studies, PO Box 1114, 81657. Tel 303-827-5703. *Dir* Randy Milhoan, BFA
Estab 1971 for summers only; enrl 1500 per summer
Tuition: Res room & board approx $150 per week
Courses: Ceramics, Drawing, Painting, Photography, Printmaking, Sculpture, Blacksmithing, Children's Art, Enameling, Foundry Fibers & Surface Design, Flat & Hot Glass, Metalsmithing, Watercolor, Woodworking

CONNECTICUT

BRIDGEPORT

HOUSATONIC COMMUNITY COLLEGE, Art Dept,* 510 Barnum Ave, 06680. Tel 203-579-6440, 579-6400. *Chmn* David Kintzler, MFA; *Faculty* Ronald Abbe, MFA; *Faculty* Burt Chernow, MA; *Faculty* Michael Stein, MFA
Estab 1967, dept estab 1968; pub; D & E; SC 15, LC 5; enrl maj 100
Ent Req: HS dipl
Degrees: AA 2 yr
Tuition: Res—$165 per sem; nonres—$625 per sem
Courses: Art Education, Art History, Ceramics, Collages, Constructions, Drafting, Drawing, Film, †Graphic Design, Mixed Media, Painting, Photography, Sculpture, Teacher Training
Adult Hobby Classes: Varied
Summer School: Dir, Dr Joseph Shive. Courses—Same as regular session

SACRED HEART UNIVERSITY, Dept of Art, PO Box 6460, 06606. Tel 203-371-7737. *Chmn* Virginia F Zic, MFA. Instrs: 18
Estab 1963, dept estab 1977; pvt; D & E; SC 26, LC 5; enrl D 300, E 100, non-maj 225, maj 79
Ent Req: HS dipl
Degrees: BA 4 yrs
Tuition: $1750 per sem; no campus res
Courses: Art History, †Drawing, †Graphic Design, †Illustration, †Painting, Design
Summer School: Dir, Virginia Zil. Tuition $330 per 5 wk term. Courses—Art History, Drawing, Design

UNIVERSITY OF BRIDGEPORT, Art Dept, College of Fine Arts, University and Iranistan Ave, 06602. Tel 203-576-4436. *Chmn* Robert H Brennan, MA; *Prof* Eileen Lord, PhD; *Prof* August Madrigal, MA; *Prof* Robert Morris, MFA; *Prof* Bruce Glaser, MA; *Prof* Donal J O'Hara; *Prof* Paul Vazquez, MFA; *Assoc Prof* Arthur Nager, MFA; *Assoc Prof* Robert Cuneo, MFA; *Assoc Prof* Susan Reinhart, MFA; *Assoc Prof* Peter Schier, MA; *Asst Prof* Adele Shtern, MFA
Estab 1927, dept estab 1947; pvt; D & E; scholarships; SC 38, LC 24, GC 15; enrl D 1150, E 200, non-maj 1070, maj 260, GS 22
Ent Req: Portfolio for BFA candidates only, college boards
Degrees: Certificate 1 yr, AA 2 yr, BA, BS and BFA 4 yr, MS 1 yr
Tuition: Res—undergrad $3130 per sem, grad $155 per cr hr; nonres—undergrad $145 per cr hr, grad $155 per cr hr; campus residence available
Courses: †Ceramics, Drafting, Drawing, †Film, Graphic Arts, †Graphic Design, Handicrafts, †Illustration, †Industrial Design, Jewelry, Lettering, †Painting, †Photography, †Printmaking, †Sculpture, Stage Design, Teacher Training, Textile Design, †Theatre Arts, Video, †Art Therapy, †Pre-Architecture, Weaving
Adult Hobby Classes: Enrl open; Courses—most crafts
Summer School: Chmn, Robert H Brennan. Tuition $145 per hr for term of 5 wks beginning May or June. Courses—Art History, Color, Design, Drawing, Graphic Design, Painting, Photography, Photo Graphics, Photo History

DANBURY

WESTERN CONNECTICUT STATE UNIVERSITY, School of Arts & Sciences,* 181 White St, 06810. Tel 203-797-4336. *Dean* James Pegolotti; *Dept Chmn* W Boelke. Instrs: FT 6
Estab 1800; pub; D & E; scholarships; SC 30, LC 3-6, GC 5; enrl D 25
Ent Req: HS dipl
Degrees: BA (graphic communications) 4 yr
Tuition: Res—$582 per yr; nonres—$1362 per yr
Courses: Cloth as an art form
Summer School: Dir, Dr Jack Rudner. Courses—same as regular session

FAIRFIELD

FAIRFIELD UNIVERSITY, Fine Arts Dept, N Benson Rd, 06430. Tel 203-255-5411. *Chmn* Dr Joanna Nicholson
Scholarships offered
Tuition: $2500 per sem
Courses: Art History, Design, Drawing, Video, Painting, Photography, Printmaking, Sculpture, Film Production, History of Film, Visual Communications
Adult Hobby Classes: Enrl 500; tuition $330 per 3 cr course
Summer School: Dir, Dr Joanna Nicholson. Enrl 500; tuition $330 per 3 cr course

FARMINGTON

TUNXIS COMMUNITY COLLEGE, Graphic Design Dept,* Junction Route 6 & 177, 06032. Tel 203-677-7701. *Actg Acad Dean* Del P Higham; *Graphic Design Coordr* Anna Lafferty, MFA & MAEd; *Fine Arts Coordr* George Fitch, MFA; *Lectr* Nathan Poellnitz, MFA; *Lectr* Marie Bavolack, BFA; *Lectr* Margaret Bliss, MA; *Lectr* Ellen Childs, BA; *Lectr* Isabel Compasso, BA; *Lectr* Barbara Grossman, BFA; *Lectr* William Kluba, MFA; *Lectr* Sanford Rich, MA
Estab 1970, dept estab 1973; pub; D & E; SC 15, LC 4; enrl non-maj 40, maj 90
Ent Req: HS dipl
Degrees: AS, AA(Graphic Design, Visual Fine Arts)
Tuition: $165 per sem
Courses: Advertising Design, Art History, Commercial Art, Conceptual Art, Drawing, †Graphic Design, History of Art & Archaeology, Illustration, Lettering, Painting, Photography
Adult Hobby Classes: Tuition $9 per cr. Courses—Design, Drawing, Painting, Watercolor
Summer School: Dir Community Services, Dr Kyle. Courses—Drawing, Painting

GREENWICH

PROPERSI GALLERIES AND SCHOOL OF ART INC, 44 W Putnam Ave, 06830. Tel 203-869-4430. *Dir* August Propersi; *VPres* Joann Propersi; *Office Mgr* Michael Propersi; *Administrative Asst* Linda Propersi; *Chmn Dept* Dan Loizeaux
Estab 1954; pvt; D & E; scholarships; SC 7, LC 2; enrl D 60, E 40
Ent Req: HS dipl, portfolio, interview
Degrees: Dipl, 3 yrs
Tuition: $3600 per yr; no campus res
Courses: Advertising Design, Commercial Art, Conceptual Art, Drawing, Graphic Design, Illustration, Lettering, Mixed Media, Mixed Media, Painting, Fine Art, Production, Studio Skills

HAMDEN

PAIER COLLEGE OF ART, INC, 6 Prospect Court, 06511. Tel 203-777-7319. *Pres* Edward T Paier. Instrs: FT 8, PT 45
Estab 1946; pvt; D & E; SC 10, LC 6 GC 1; enrl D 285, E 150
Ent Req: HS grad, presentation of portfolio, transcript of records, recommendation
Degrees: BFA & AFA programs offered
Tuition: 5544 per yr
Courses: Graphic Design, Illustration, Interior Design, Photography, Fine Arts
Summer School: Dir E T Paier. Enrl 100; $168 per term, two terms of 5 beginning May. Courses—Fine Arts, Graphic Design, Illustration, Photography

HARTFORD

GREATER HARTFORD COMMUNITY COLLEGE, Humanities Division & Art Dept, 61 Woodland St, 06105. Tel 203-549-4200. *Asst Prof* Ronald Buksbaum; *Asst Prof* Thomas Werle
Degrees: Cert
Tuition: $250 per sem
Courses: Art History, Ceramics, Design, Drawing, Painting, Printmaking, Sculpture, Figure Drawing
Summer School: Courses offered

TRINITY COLLEGE, Dept of Fine Arts, Summit St, 06106. Tel 203-527-3151. *Chmn* Michael R T Mahoney, PhD; *Dir* George Chaplin, MFA; *Prof* Thomas P Baird, MFA; *Asst Prof* Mardges Bacon, PhD; *Asst Prof* Alden R Gordon, PhD; *Artist-in-Residence* John Smith, MFA; *Artist-in-Residence* Elizabeth Tracy, MFA
Estab 1823, dept estab 1939; pvt; D; scholarships; SC 20, LC 22; enrl D 400, non-maj 350, major 50
Ent Req: HS dipl
Degrees: MA
Tuition: Res—undergrad $7800 per yr; campus res—room $1650, board $1400
Courses: Aesthetics, Architecture, †Art History, Drawing, Painting, Printmaking, †Studio Arts

MANCHESTER

MANCHESTER COMMUNITY COLLEGE, Fine Arts Dept,* 60 Bidwell St, PO Box 1046, 06040. Tel 203-646-4900. *Prof* Robert F Manning, MAEd. Instrs: PT 5
Estab 1963, dept estab 1968; pub; D & E; enrl D & E 300, non-maj 240, maj 60
Ent Req: HS dipl, portfolio for visual fine arts prog
Degrees: AA and AS 2 yrs
Tuition: Res—$150 per sem; nonres—$570 per sem
Courses: Art History, Calligraphy, Ceramics, Drawing, Film, Lettering, Painting, Photography, Printmaking, Sculpture, Basic Design, History of Film, Sign Painting

MIDDLETOWN

MIDDLESEX COMMUNITY COLLEGE, Fine Arts Dept,* 100 Training Hill Rd, 06457. Tel 203-344-3011. *Instr* Pattsy L L Bates, MFA
Degrees: AS
Tuition: Res—$165 per sem; nonres—$625 per sem
Courses: Art History, Ceramics, Design, Drawing, Jewelry, Painting, Sculpture

WESLEYAN UNIVERSITY, Art Dept, Center for the Arts, Wesleyan Station, 06457. Tel 203-347-9411, Ext 2253. *Chmn* John Frazer; *Prof* John Martin, MFA; *Prof* John T Paoletti, PhD; *Prof* David Schorr, MFA; *Prof* John Risley, MFA; *Assoc Prof* Clark Maines, PhD; *Assoc Prof* J Seeley, MFA; *Assoc Prof* Jonathan Best, PhD; *Asst Prof* Judith Rohrer, MA; *Asst Prof* Jacqueline Gourentech, MFA; *Adjunct Prof* Ellen D'Oench, PhD; *Adjunct Prof* Mary Risley, MFA
Estab 1831, dept estab 1928; pvt; D; SC 30, LC 25; enrl in school D 2686, maj 95, grad 15
Ent Req: HS dipl, SAT
Degrees: BA 4 yrs
Tuition: Campus res available
Courses: Architecture, Ceramics, Drawing, Graphic Arts, Graphic Design, History of Art & Archaeology, Mixed Media, Painting, Photography, Printmaking, Sculpture, Silversmithing, Film History, Film Production, History of Prints, Printroom Methods & Techniques
Summer School: Dir, Barbara MacEachern. Enrl 576; Term of 6 wks beginning July 5. Courses—grad courses in all areas

NEW BRITAIN

CENTRAL CONNECTICUT STATE UNIVERSITY, Dept of Art, 1615 Stanley St, 06050. Tel 203-827-7326. *Chmn Dept* Frank Casa. Instrs: FT 14, PT 15
Estab 1849; pub; D & E; SC 36, LC 8, GC 20; enrl D 200, E 150, non-maj 1000, maj 200, grad 500
Ent Req: HS dipl
Degrees: BA(Special Studies) and BS(Art Educ) 4 yrs
Courses: Advertising Design, Art Education, Art History, Ceramics, Display, Drawing, Graphic Arts, Handicrafts, Jewelry, Lettering, Painting, Photography, Printmaking, Sculpture, Teacher Training, Ceramic Sculpture, Color Theory, Fibre Sculpture, Serigraphy (Silk Screen), Stained Glass
Children's Classes: Enrl 5-17 yr olds; tuition $10. Courses—vary
Summer School: Dean Exten Col, R Tupper. Tuition $48 per cr hr for term of 5 wks. Courses—varied and comprehensive

NEW CANAAN

SILVERMINE GUILD SCHOOL OF THE ARTS, 1037 Silvermine Rd, 06840. Tel 203-866-0411. *Dir* Michael J Costello
Estab 1949; pvt; D & E; SC 60, LC 1; enrl 560
Ent Req: None
Degrees: None
Tuition: No campus res
Courses: Advertising Design, Art History, Ceramics, Collages, Drawing, Illustration, Jewelry, Painting, Photography, Printmaking, Sculpture, Weaving, Stained Glass, Acting Studio, Sogetsu Ikebana, Papermaking
Children's Classes: Courses—Acting Studio, Art Workshops, Ceramics
Summer School: Dir, Michael J Costello. 8 wk prog. Courses—same as above

NEW HAVEN

ALBERTUS MAGNUS COLLEGE, Art Dept, 700 Prospect St, 06511. Tel 203-777-6631. *Chmn* Sr Thoma Swanson, MFA; *Prof* Jerome Nevins, MFA; *Prof* Juliana D'Amato, PhD; *Instructor* Jongsoon P Chung, MFA; *Instructor* Beverly Chieffo, MA
Estab 1925, dept estab 1970; pvt; D & E; schol; SC 20, LC 9; enrl D 120, non-maj 60, maj 40
Ent Req: HS dipl, SAT, CEEB
Degrees: BA, BFA 8 sem
Tuition: Res—undergrad $5000 per yr, part-time $98 per cr; non-res—undergrad $4050 per yr; campus res—room & board $2530 per yr
Courses: Aesthetics, Art Education, Art History, Ceramics, Collages, Drawing, Graphic Design, History of Art & Archaeology, Lettering, Mixed Media, Painting, Photography, Printmaking, Sculpture, Stage Design, Teacher Training, Art Therapy, Weaving, Batik
Adult Hobby Classes: Courses offered
Summer School: Dir, Sister Jane McDermott. Courses—vary

SOUTHERN CONNECTICUT STATE COLLEGE, Dept of Art, 501 Crescent St, 06515. Tel 203-397-4279. *Dept Head* Jack R Smith, MFA. Instrs: FT 21, PT 8
Estab 1893; pub; D & E; SC 40, LC 18, GC 20; enrl D 350, GS 100
Ent Req: HS dipl, SAT
Degrees: BS, MS(Art Educ), BA(Art History) and BA, BS, MA(Studio Art) 4 yrs
Tuition: Res—$1006 yr, $63 per cr hr; nonres—$2200 yr, $75 per cr hr; campus residence available
Courses: Art Education, Art History, Ceramics, Drawing, Graphic Design, Illustration, Jewelry, Painting, Photography, Printmaking, Sculpture, Eastern Art Histories, Glassblowing, Graphic Processes, Metalsmithing, Weaving
Summer School: Dir, Jack R Smith. Enrl 230; tuition undergrad $63 per cr hr, grad $75 per cr hr for 2 - 5 wk term. Courses—Photography, Drawing, Painting, Printmaking, Graphic Design, Art History

YALE UNIVERSITY
—School of Art, 180 York St, 06520. Tel 203-436-0308. *Dean* David Pease, MFA; *Prof* Andrew Forge, MA; *Prof* Alvin Eisenman, MA; *Prof* Tod Papageorge, BA; *Prof* Gabor Peterdi, MA; *Assoc Prof* David vonSchlegell; *Prof* Richard Lytle, MFA; *Assoc Prof* Robert Reed, MFA
Estab 1868; pvt; D; scholarships; GC 106
Ent Req: BFA, BA, BS or dipl from four year professional art school and portfolio
Degrees: MFA 2 yrs
Tuition: $7000 per yr
Courses: Drawing, Graphic Design, Painting, Photography, Printmaking, Sculpture
Summer School: Four undergrad eight wk courses, 3 credits
—Dept of the History of Art, Box 2009, 56 High St, 06520. Tel 203-436-8853. *Dir Undergrad Studies* Diana Kleiner; *Dir Grad Studies* Vincent Scully; *Chmn* Jerome J Pollitt; *Admin Asst* Paula Saddler. Instrs: FT 27, PT 2
Estab 1940; pvt; D; scholarships, fels and assistantships
Ent Req: For grad prog—BA and foreign language
Degrees: BA, MA, PhD
Tuition: $8720
Courses: †Art History
—School of Architecture, 06520. Tel 203-436-0550. *Dean* Cesar Pelli
Estab 1869; pvt; enrl 142 maximum
Ent Req: Bachelor's degree, grad record exam
Degrees: MArchit 3 yrs, MEnviron Design 2 yrs
Tuition: $8450

NEW LONDON

CONNECTICUT COLLEGE
—Dept of Art, Mohegan Ave, 06320. Tel 203-447-1911. *Chmn* Peter Leibert; *Prof* Richard Lukosius; *Prof* David Smalley; *Assoc Prof* Barkley L Hendricks; *Assoc Prof* Maureen McCabe; *Asst Prof* Tim McDowell; *Asst Prof* Cynthia Rubin; *Instructor* Ted Hendrickson
Estab 1911; pvt; D; scholarships; SC 20, LC 34
Ent Req: HS dipl, ent exam
Degrees: BA 4 yrs
Tuition: $8750 per yr; campus res—room & board $2700
Adult Hobby Classes: Chmn, Peter Leibert
Summer School: Dir, Peter Leibert. Courses—Ceramics, Drawing, Painting, Photography, Printmaking, Sculpture
—Dept of Art History, 270 Mohegan Ave, 06320. Tel 203-447-1911. *Chmn* Nancy Rash; *Prof* Edgar Mayhew, PhD; *Prof* Charles Price, PhD; *Assoc Prof* Barbara B Zabel, PhD; *Asst Prof* Richard Chafee, MA
Estab 1911, dept estab 1972; pvt; D & E
Ent Req: HS dipl, SAT
Degrees: BA 4 yrs
Courses: †Art History

STORRS

UNIVERSITY OF CONNECTICUT, Art Dept, 06268. Tel 203-429-3930. *Head Dept* Richard Thornton. Instrs: FT 30, PT 8
Estab 1882, dept estab 1950; pub; D; SC 32, LC 20; enrl D 1700, maj 340
Ent Req: HS dipl, SAT
Degrees: BA(Art History), BFA(Studio) 4 yrs
Tuition: Res—undergrad $438, nonres—undergrad $1640; campus residency available
Courses: Architecture, †Art History, †Ceramics, Drawing, †Graphic Design, Illustration, †Painting, †Photography, †Printmaking, †Sculpture
Summer School: Tuition $55 per cr hr; three week workshops beginning May 19. Courses—Drawing, Graphic Design, Lithography, Painting, Sculpture

VOLUNTOWN

FOSTER CADDELL'S ART SCHOOL, Northlight, Rt 49, RFD 1, 06384. Tel 201-376 9583. *Head Dept* Foster Caddell
Estab 1958; D & E; enrl D 75, E 50
Tuition: $400 per course; no campus res
Courses: †Drawing, †Painting, †Teacher Training, †Pastel
Summer School: Tuition $175 per wk. Courses—Painting Demonstrations and Lecture; Summer Workshops and Seminars

WEST HARTFORD

HARTFORD ART SCHOOL OF THE UNIVERSITY OF HARTFORD, 200 Bloomfield Ave, 06117. Tel 203-243-4391, 243-4393. *Dean* Alfred E Hammer, MFA; *Asst Dean* Doris Kinsella, MA; *Asst Dean* Steven Keller, MA; *Prof* Wolfgang Behl; *Prof* Rudolph Zallinger, MFA; *Prof* Paul Zimmerman, BFA; *Assoc Prof* Robert Cumming, MFA; *Assoc Prof* Lloyd Glasson, MFA; *Assoc Prof* Gilles Giuntini, MFA; *Assoc Prof* Christopher Horton, MAT; *Assoc Prof* Peter McLean, MFA; *Assoc Prof* Frederick Wessel, MFA; *Assoc Prof* Marvin Kendrick, PhD; *Asst Prof* Walter Hall, MFA; *Asst Prof* Bruce Ostwald, MFA; *Asst Prof* Brenda Huffman, MFA; *Asst Prof* Margia Kramer, MFA; *Asst Prof* Patricia Sutton, MA; *Instructor* Mary Frey, MFA
Estab 1877; pvt; D & E; schol; SC 70, LC 5, GC 32; enrl D 275, E 100, non-maj 125, maj 275, grad 50
Ent Req: HS dipl, SAT
Degrees: BFA and BFA(Art Ed) 4 yr, MA Ed 2 yr
Tuition: Undergrad $6660 yr, $3336 per sem, $160 per cr hr; $160 evenings; campus res room and board $1250-$2550
Courses: Art Education, Ceramics, Design, Drawing, Film, Painting, Photography, Printmaking, Sculpture, Video
Adult Hobby Classes: Day and evening classes
Children's Classes: Summer only
Summer School: Tuition same for term of 4-6 wks beginning July

SAINT JOSEPH COLLEGE, Dept of Fine Arts, 1678 Asylum Ave, 06117. Tel 203-232-4571. *Chmn Dept* Vincenza Uccello. Instrs: FT 2, PT 1
Estab 1932; pvt; W; D & E; schol; SC 5, LC 7; enrl D 104
Ent Req: HS dipl, CEEB
Degrees: BA, BS and MA 4 yr
Courses: Art Education, Drawing, †Art History, Graphic Arts, Painting, Batik, Enameling, Mosaic, Creative Crafts, Fundamental of Design, Pre-Art Therapy

WEST HAVEN

UNIVERSITY OF NEW HAVEN, Dept of Humanities, Fine & Performing Arts, School of Arts & Sciences, 300 Orange Ave, 06516. Tel 203-932-7101. *Coordr of Art* Beth Moffitt. Instrs: FT 2, PT 8
Estab 1927, dept estab 1972; pvt; D & E; SC 30, LC 5; enrl D 350, E 110
Ent Req: HS dipl
Degrees: BA & BS 4 yrs, AS 2 yrs
Courses: †Advertising Design, Art History, Calligraphy, Ceramics, Collages, †Commercial Art, Constructions, Drawing, Fashion Arts, Graphic Arts, †Graphic Design, History of Art & Archaeology, Illustration, †Interior Design, Lettering, Mixed Media, †Painting, †Photography, Printmaking, †Sculpture, Textile Design, Dimensional Design, Film Animation, Interaction of Color, Weaving
Summer School: June 12th - July 20th. Courses—Ceramics, Drawing, History of Art, Painting, Photography, Sculpture

WILLIMANTIC

EASTERN CONNECTICUT STATE COLLEGE, Art Dept,* 83 Windham St, 06226. Tel 203-456-2331, Ext 507. *Chmn* Richard Wolf. Instrs: FT 3, PT 4
Estab 1881; pub; D & E; scholarships; enrl D 300, E 75, maj 40
Ent Req: HS dipl
Degrees: BA(Fine Arts) & BS(Art) 4 yrs
Tuition: Res—$220 per sem; nonres—$515 per sem
Courses: Art History, Ceramics, Drawing, Graphic Arts, Interior Design, Jewelry, Painting, Sculpture, Textile Design, Enameling, Weaving
Summer School: Dir, Owen Peagler. Courses—Art & Craft Workshop

WINSTED

NORTHWESTERN CONNECTICUT COMMUNITY COLLEGE, Fine Arts Dept, Park Place, 06098. Tel 203-379-8543
Courses: Advertising Design, Art Appreciation, Art History, Calligraphy, Ceramics, Design, Drawing, Painting, Photography, Printmaking, Sculpture

DELAWARE

DOVER

DELAWARE STATE COLLEGE, Dept of Art and Art Education, 19901. Tel 302-736-5182. Instrs: FT 4
Estab 1960; pub; D & E; scholarships; SC 13, LC 9; enrl 50-60 maj
Ent Req: HS dipl or GED, SAT or ACT
Degrees: BS(Art Educ), BS(General Art) & BS(Art Business)
Courses: Advertising Design, Aesthetics, †Art Education, Ceramics, Commercial Art, Drawing, History of Art & Archaeology, Interior Design, Lettering, Painting, Photography, Printmaking, Sculpture, Teacher Training, Design, Fibers, Independent Study
Adult Hobby Classes: Courses—same as above
Summer School: Courses—same as above

NEWARK

UNIVERSITY OF DELAWARE, Dept of Art, 19711. *Chmn* Larry Holmes, MFA;
Coordr Art Educ Norman Sasowsky, EdD; *Coordr Sculpture* Joe Moss, MA; *Coordr
Photography* John Weiss, MFA; *Coordr Ceramics* Victor Spinski, MFA; *Coordr
Printmaking* Rosemary Hooper, MFA; *Coordr Jewelry* Anne Graham, MFA; *Coordr
Drawing & Painting* Steven Tanis, MFA; *Coordr Foundations* Robert Straight,
MFA; *Coordr Fibers* Vera Kaminsky, MFA; *Coordr Graphic Design* Ray Nichols,
MFA
Estab 1833; pub; D & E; SC 62, LC 2, GC 12, non-maj 600, maj 400, grad 30
Ent Req: Portfolio, BFA prog and graphic design prog (both sophomore yr)
Degrees: BA, BS and BFA 4 yrs, MFA 2 yrs, MA 1 yr
Tuition: Res—undergrad $1590 per yr, grad $89 per cr hr, res grad $795 per sem;
nonres—undergrad $3900, grad $217 per cr hr, nonres grad $1950 per sem; campus
res—room & board $2254, nonres room & board $2354
Courses: †Art Education, †Ceramics, †Drawing, †Graphic Design, †Jewelry,
†Painting, †Photography, †Printmaking, †Sculpture, Fibers
Adult Hobby Classes: Courses—various

REHOBOTH BEACH

REHOBOTH ART LEAGUE, INC, PO Box 84, 19971. Tel 302-227-8408. *Head
Dept* Mary L Pearce
Estab 1938; pvt; D; SC 7; enrl D 400, others 400
Ent Req: Interest in art
Courses: Ceramics, Drawing, Graphic Arts, Painting, Printmaking
Adult Hobby Classes: Enrl 150. Courses—Ceramics, Drawing, Painting,
Printmaking, Pottery, Weaving
Children's Classes: Courses—Art Forms
Summer School: Dir, Mary L Pearce

DISTRICT OF COLUMBIA

WASHINGTON

AMERICAN UNIVERSITY, Dept of Art,* 4400 Massachusetts Ave NW, 20016.
Tel 202-686-2114. *Chmn Dept* Michael Tom Graham; *Prof* Mary D Garrard, PhD;
Prof Helene M Herzbrun; *Prof* Ben L Summerford; *Assoc Prof* Norma Broude, PhD;
Assoc Prof Stephen Pace; *Assoc Prof* Lucinao J Penay, MA; *Assoc Prof* A E Feltus;
Assoc Prof M Hirano; *Assoc Prof* M Oxman; *Assoc Prof* C Ravence; *Assoc Prof* R
Shaffer; *Assoc Prof* T Turak; *Asst Prof* Robert D'Arista
Estab 1893, dept estab 1945; pvt; D & E; scholarships; SC 19, LC 14, GC 26; enrl D
& E 1520, maj 191, grad 65
Ent Req: HS dipl
Degrees: BA, BFA(Studio Art), BA(Design), BA(Art History) & BS(Art Educ) 4
yrs, MA(Art History) 18 months, MFA(Painting, Sculpture, Printmaking) 2 yrs
Tuition: $3500 per sem
Courses: Advertising Design, Art Education, Ceramics, Drawing, Graphic Arts,
Graphic Design, History of Art & Archaeology, Illustration, Lettering, Painting,
Printmaking, Sculpture
Summer School: Dir, Ben L Summerford. Tui $175-$184 per cr hr.
Courses—Design, Studio & Art History

CATHOLIC UNIVERSITY OF AMERICA
—Dept of Architecture and Planning, 20064. Tel 202-635-5188. *Chmn* Peter Flake,
BArch; *Asst Chmn & Dir Undergrad Studies* James O'Hear III, MArch; *Dir
Grad Studies* Joseph Miller, BArch; *Prof* Seymour Auerbach, MArch; *Prof*
William Loerke, PhD; *Prof* Forrest Wilson, PhD; *Prof* W Dodd Ramberg, BArch;
Assoc Prof Julius S Levine, MCP; *Assoc Prof* George T Marcou, MArch; *Assoc
Prof* Theodore Naos, MArch; *Assoc Prof* John V Yanik, MArch; *Asst Prof* Judith
Capen, MArch; *Asst Prof* Peter Hetzel, MArch; *Asst Prof* J Ronald Kabriel,
MArch; *Asst Prof* Dhiru Thadani, MArch; *Asst Prof* Thomas Walton, PhD
Estab 1887, dept estab 1930; den; D & E; SC 6, LC 12 per sem, GC 39 per sem;
enrl D 260, maj 260, grad 80
Ent Req: HS dipl and SAT for undergrad, BS or BA in Archit or equivalent plus
GPA of 2.5 in undergrad studies for grad
Degrees: BS(Archit) 4 yrs, MArch 2 yrs, MArch & PhDArch 4 yrs
Tuition: Undergrad—$6350 per yr, PT (10 hrs or less) $184 per hr; grad—$6350 per
yr, PT (7 hrs or less) $240 per sem hr; campus res—room $810-$1230 per sem, bd
$620-$782 per sem
Courses: †Architecture, Photography, Rendering, History and Theory of
Architecture, Urban Design
Children's Classes: Session of 2 wks. Courses—Experiences in Architecture
Summer School: Dirs, Steven Hurtt & Steven Sachs. Enrl 150; term of 5-9 wks
May-June. Courses—Design Studio, History & Theory of Architecture, Mechanical
Equipment, Photography, Structures, Theory of Architecture, Working Drawings
—Dept of Art,* 20064. *Chmn Dept* John R Winslow; *Assoc Prof* Thomas Rooney;
Asst Prof Robert Ross
Estab 1930; den; D & E; scholarships; SC 17, LC 9, GC 20; enrl D 48, maj 38, grad
10
Ent Req: HS dipl and SAT for undergrad, BA-BFA; MAT, GRE for grad
Degrees: MFA
Tuition: FT—$2450 per sem; PT—$184 per cr hr
Courses: Art Education, Art History, Ceramics, Drawing, History of Art &
Archaeology, Jewelry, Painting, Printmaking, Sculpture
Summer School: Chmn, Thomas P Rooney. Term of 8 wks beginning June.
Courses—Drawing, Jewelry, Painting, Special Independent Courses

CORCORAN SCHOOL OF ART, 17th St & New York Ave NW, 20006. Tel 202-
628-9484. *Dean* William O Barrett, MA; *Asst Dean* Rona Slade, BA; *Chmn Fine
Arts* Robert Stackhouse, MFA; *Chmn Academic Studies* Doug Lang; *Chmn
Ceramics* Robert Epstein, MFA; *Chmn Printmaking* Gene Fredrick; *Chmn Sculpture*

Berthold Schmutzhart; *Chmn Photography* Steve Szabo; *Chmn Graphic Design* Paul
Levy, MFA
Estab 1890; pvt; D & E; scholarships; SC 120 LC 23; enrl D 235 major, E 600 non
major
Ent Req: HS dipl, SAT or ACT, portfolio and interview
Degrees: BFA 4 yrs
Tuition: $4470 per yr, $2235 per sem, $375 per 3 cr hr course; campus res dorm
$2200 per yr
Courses: Art History, Aesthetics, Calligraphy, †Ceramics, †Commercial Art,
†Drawing, †Graphic Design, Illustration, †Painting, †Photography, †Printmaking,
†Sculpture, Animation, Business & Law for the Artist, Color, Fine Arts, Furniture,
History of Photography, Philosophy, Typography, Watercolor
Adult Hobby Classes: Enrl 550 per sem; tuition $325 - $375 for 15 wks.
Courses—Art History, Photography, Drawing, Painting, Printmaking, Ceramics,
Sculpture, Furniture, Calligraphy, Graphic Design, Illustration, Commercial Art,
Color & Design
Children's Classes: Enrl 50; tuition $175 per sem. Saturday. Ages 11 - 14.
Courses—General Studio. Ages 15 - 18. Courses—Drawing,Painting, Portfolio Prep
Workshop
Summer School: Dean, William O Barrett. Enrl 350. Adult—Tuition $250 for 6 wks
beginning June. Courses—Animation, Calligraphy, Ceramics, Drawing, Graphic
Design, Illustration, Painting, Photography, Printmaking, Sculpture, Watercolor.
High School (15 - 18)—Tuition $175 for 5 wks beginning June.
Courses—Pre-College Workshop, Portfolio Prep, Ceramics, Drawing, Painting,
Photography, Graphic Design, Printmaking. Junior High (11 - 14)—Tuition $175 for
5 wks beginning June

GEORGETOWN UNIVERSITY, Dept of Fine Arts, 20057. Tel 202-625-4085. *Prof*
Carra Ferguson, PhD; *Prof* Clifford Chieffo, MA; *Prof* Donn Murphy, PhD; *Fac*
Peter Charles, MFA; *Fac* Alison Hilton, PhD; *Fac* Margaret Himel, MFA;
Instructor Paul McCarren
Estab 1789, dept estab 1960; pvt; D; SC 8, LC 6; enrl D 600 (includes non-maj), maj
12 per yr
Ent Req: HS dipl
Degrees: BA 4 yrs
Tuition: $7650 yr; campus residence available
Courses: †Art History, †Drawing, Graphic Arts, †Painting, †Printmaking,
†Sculpture, Theatre Arts, Music History
Adult Hobby Classes: Continuing Education Dir, Phyllis O'Callaghan
Summer School: Dir, Gerald Sullivan. Courses offered

GEORGE WASHINGTON UNIVERSITY, Dept of Art, 2000 G St, NW, 20052.
Tel 202-676-6086. *Chmn* Lilien F Robinson, PhD; *Prof* Francis S Grubar, PhD; *Prof*
Douglas H Teller, MFA; *Prof* J Franklin Wright Jr, MFA; *Assoc Prof* H I Gates,
MFA; *Assoc Prof* D Michael Hitchcock, PhD; *Assoc Prof* Jerry L Lake, MFA;
Assoc Prof Turker Ozdogan, MFA; *Assoc Prof* Arthur Hall-Smith, MFA; *Assoc
Prof* Barbara Von Barghahn, PhD; *Asst Prof* Jeffrey C Anderson, PhD; *Asst Prof*
Constance C Costigan, MFA; *Asst Prof* Samuel B Molina, MMFA; *Asst Prof* Jeffrey
L Stephanic, MFA; *Asst Prof* Fuller O Griffith, MFA; *Asst Prof* Ellen R Williams,
PhD; *Asst Prof* W T Woodward, MFA; *Asst Prof* Melvin P Lader, PhD
Estab 1821, dept estab 1893; pvt; D & E; scholarships; SC 103, LC 74, GC 68; enrl
D 1350, GS 196
Ent Req: HS dipl, ent exam
Degrees: BA 4 yr, MA 2-2 1/2 yr, MFA 2 yr
Tuition: Res—$6100 per yr; campus res—room and board $3570 - $3700
Courses: †Art History, †Ceramics, †Drawing, †Design, †Graphic Arts, †Painting,
†Photography, †Sculpture, †American Art, †Classical Art & Archaeology,
†Contemporary Art, †Medieval Art, †Renaissance & Baroque Art, †Visual
Communications
Summer School: Dean, William F Long. Tuition $134 per hr for term of 3 separate
terms beginning May 15

HOWARD UNIVERSITY, Art Dept,* College of Fine Arts, 2455 6th St NW,
20001. Tel 202-636-7047, 636-6100. *Dean* Thomas J Flagg; *Head Dept* Starmanda
Bullock. Instrs: FT 16
Estab 1921; pvt; D & E; scholarships and fels; enrl 200, others 450
Degrees: BFA, MA(History of Art and Art Educ) and MFA 2 yrs
Tuition: $2000 per yr; campus residency available
Courses: Art Education, Art History, Ceramics, Painting, Photography, Printmaking,
Sculpture, Design

MOUNT VERNON COLLEGE, Art Dept, 2100 Foxhall Rd NW, 20007. Tel 202-
331-3416, 331-3495. *Dept Chmn* James Burford
Estab 1875; pvt; D & E; scholarships; SC 16
Degrees: AA and BA
Courses: Teacher Training, Theatre Arts, Video

TRINITY COLLEGE, Art Dept, 20017. Tel 202-244-2272. *Head Dept & Prof* Dr
Liliana Gramberg; *Asst Prof* Dr Yvonne Dixon; *Lectr* Robert Fergerson; *Lectr* Janis
Goodman; *Lectr* Judith Andraka; *Lectr* Claudia Smigrod
Estab 1897; den; D & E; scholarships; SC 8, LC 2-3; enrl D 120, maj 34
Ent Req: HS dipl, SAT or ACT, recommendation
Degrees: BA, BS & BFA 4 yrs, MA 2 yrs
Tuition: $5700 per yr, $183 per cr hr; campus res room & board available
Courses: Aesthetics, †Art History, Calligraphy, Design, Drawing, Graphic Arts,
Graphic Design, Lettering, †Painting, †Photography, †Printmaking, †Sculpture,
Textile Design, Documentary Photography, Photojournalism, Techniques of Etching,
Serigraphy
Summer School: Courses vary

UNIVERSITY OF THE DISTRICT OF COLUMBIA, Art Dept, 916 G Street
NW, 20001. Tel 202-727-2662. *Head Dept* Charles A Young, MA; *Prof* Mavera
Morgan, PhD; *Prof* Meredith Rode, MFA; *Prof* Manon Cleary, MFA; *Prof* David
Lanier, MFA; *Prof* Frederick Ropko, PhD; *Assoc Prof* Yvonne Carter, MFA; *Assoc
Prof* Zeki Findkoglu, MFA; *Asst Prof* Walter Lattimore, BFA; *Asst Prof* George
Smith, MS; *Asst Prof* William Taylor, Cert; *Asst Prof* Paula Weaver, MS; *Asst Prof*
Rufus Wells, BFA

Estab 1969, dept estab 1969; pub; D & E; SC 65, LC 21; enrl D 708, E 142, non-maj 605, maj 150
Ent Req: HS dipl, GED
Degrees: AA(Advertising Design) 2 yrs, BA(Studio Art) and BA(Art Educ) 4 yrs
Tuition: Res—undergrad $364 per yr, $182 per sem; non-res—undergrad $87 per sem; no campus res
Courses: Advertising Design, Art Education, Art History, Ceramics, Commercial Art, Conceptual Art, Drawing, Graphic Arts, Graphic Design, Handicrafts, Illustration, Interior Design, Lettering, Mixed Media, Museum Staff Training, Painting, Photography, Painting, †Sculpture, Textile Design
Summer School: Chmn Art Dept, C A Young. Enrl 200. Courses—Art History, Ceramics, Drawings, Painting, Photography

FLORIDA

BOCA RATON

COLLEGE OF BOCA RATON, Art & Commercial Art Dept,* Military Trail, 33431. Tel 305-994-0770. *Faculty* Ernest Ranspach, MFA
Scholarships offered
Degrees: AA
Tuition: $4400 per yr
Courses: Advertising Design, Art Appreciation, Art History, Ceramics, Design, Drawing, Fashion Arts, Handicrafts, Interior Design, Painting, Photography, Printmaking, Stage Design, Textile Design

FLORIDA ATLANTIC UNIVERSITY, Art Dept, 33431. Tel 305-393-3000, Ext 3870. *Chairperson* C V Dorst. Instrs: FT 8
Estab 1964; pub; D & E; SC 37, LC 14, GC 1; enrl D 1600, maj 150, grad 8, special students 7
Ent Req: AA
Degrees: BFA and BA 2 yrs
Tuition: Res—$28.10 per cr hr; nonres—$78 per cr hr; campus res—$382.50 per sem
Courses: Aesthetics, Art History, Ceramics, Drawing, Jewelry, Lettering, Museum Staff Training, Painting, Photography, Sculpture, Applied Art, History of Architecture, Silkscreen & Etching, Studio Crafts, Weaving
Adult Hobby Classes: Courses offered through continuing education
Summer School: Courses offered

BRADENTON

MANATEE JUNIOR COLLEGE, Dept of Art, PO Box 1849, 33506. Tel 813-755-1511, Ext 251. *Chmn* Cortez Francis, MA; *Prof* Edward Camp, MFA; *Prof* James McMahon, MFA; *Prof* Priscilla Stewart, MA. Instrs: FT 4, PT 1
Estab 1958; pub; D & E; scholarships; SC 22, LC 5; enrl D 310, E 90, maj 75
Ent Req: HS dipl, SAT
Degrees: AA & AS 2 yrs
Tuition: Res—undergrad $19 per cr hr; nonres—undergrad $38 per cr hr
Courses: Art History, Ceramics, Drawing, Interior Design, Lettering, Painting, Photography, Printmaking, Sculpture, Art Appreciation, 2-D & 3-D Design, Color Fundamentals, Fabric Design, Figure Drawing, Studio Crafts, Movie Making
Adult Hobby Classes: Enrl 200; average tuition $20 per class. Courses—Calligraphy, Color Theory, Drawing, Flower Arranging, Frame Making, Oil Painting, Photography, Portraiture Painting, Stained Glass, Studio Design, Studio Painting, Cartoon & Illustration
Children's Classes: Enrl 21; tuition $75 per 6 wks. Courses—Creative Dramatics
Summer School: Pres, Stephen Korcheck. Enrl 100; tuition $19 per cr hr for term of 6 wks. Courses—Ceramics, Photography, Art Appreciation, Drawing

CLEARWATER

FLORIDA GULF COAST ART CENTER, INC, 222 Ponce de Leon Blvd, 33516. Tel 813-584-8634. *Managing Dir* Judith Boodon Powers
Estab 1949; pvt; D & E; enrl D 315
Ent Req: None
Degrees: None
Courses: Ceramics, Drafting, Drawing, Handicrafts, History of Art & Archaeology, Jewelry, Painting, Photography, Sculpture, Creative Writing, Crewel, Weaving, Wood Carving

CORAL GABLES

UNIVERSITY OF MIAMI, Dept of Art & Art History, PO Box 248106, 33124. Tel 305-284-2542. *Chmn* William E Betsch, PhD; *Prof* Eugene Massin, MFA; *Prof* Andrew Morgan, MFA; *Prof* Ken Uyemura, MFA; *Prof* Bill Ward, MFA; *Prof* Gerald G Winter, MFA; *Assoc Prof* Paula Harper, PhD; *Assoc Prof* R W Downs, MFA; *Assoc Prof* Christine Federighi, MFA; *Assoc Prof* Edward Ghannam, MFA; *Assoc Prof* Marilyn Schmitt, PhD; *Assoc Prof* Marcilene Wittmer, PhD; *Assoc Prof* Peter Zorn, MFA; *Asst Prof* Ron Fondaw; *Instr* Tom Gormley
Estab 1925, dept estab 1960; pvt; D & E; scholarships; SC 81, LC 15, GC 25; enrl D 975, non-maj 800, maj 175, grad 10
Ent Req: HS dipl, SAT
Degrees: BA and BFA 4 yrs
Tuition: Res & nonres—undergrad $6350 per yr, $3175 per sem, $211 per cr hr
Courses: †Art History, Ceramics, †Graphic Arts, Illustration, †Painting, †Photography, †Printmaking, †Sculpture, †Weaving
Adult Hobby Classes: Courses offered
Summer School: Enrl 80. Courses— 20th Century Art History, Introduction to Art History, Drawing, Photography

DAYTONA BEACH

DAYTONA BEACH COMMUNITY COLLEGE, Dept of Performing and Visual Arts, PO Box 1111, 32015. Tel 904-255-8131, 362-3011. *Chairperson* H Kenneth Walker III, PhD; *Instructor* Shizuko Alexander, MFA; *Instructor* Pamela Greisinger, MFA; *Instructor* Stephen Marsh, MA; *Instructor* James Smiley, MS
Estab 1958; pub; D & E; scholarships; SC 15, LC 3; enrl D 250, E 50, maj 30
Ent Req: HS dipl or GED
Degrees: 2 year program offered
Tuition: Res—$19.95 per sem hr; nonres—$43.05 per sem hr
Courses: Ceramics, Design, Drawing, Jewelry, Painting, Sculpture, Cinematography, Papermaking
Summer School: Courses offered

DE LAND

STETSON UNIVERSITY, Art Dept, 32720. Tel 904-734-4121, Ext 208. *Head Dept* Fred Messersmith. Instrs: FT 2, PT 1
Estab 1880; den; scholarships; SC 5, LC 5; enrl 200
Ent Req: Col boards
Degrees: 4 yr
Tuition: $4540
Courses: Art Education, Art History, Ceramics, Commercial Art, Drawing, Graphic Arts, Painting, Sculpture, Design, Watercolor
Summer School: Dir, Fred Messersmith

DUNEDIN

DUNEDIN FINE ARTS AND CULTURAL CENTER, 1143 Michigan Blvd, 33528. Tel 813-734-5371, 736-6731. *Dir* Paul E Kavin; *Instructor* Bede Clark; *Instructor* John Houglum; *Instructor* Sue Holt; *Instructor* Kitty Johnson; *Instructor* Jim Nordmeyer; *Instructor* Dave Pierson; *Instructor* Lois Rector; *Instructor* Susan Huskey; *Instructor* Mary Lowe; *Instructor* Rolf Holmquist; *Instructor* Ira Burhans; *Instructor* Lois Barlow
Estab 1975; pub; D & E and weekends; scholarships; SC 20-25, LC 5-10; enrl approx 900
Tuition: Members $20-$50; nonmembers $28-$60; no campus res
Courses: Aesthetics, Art History, Ceramics, Collages, Drawing, Handicrafts, Landscape Architecture, Painting, Photography, Printmaking, Sculpture, Textile Design, Theatre Arts, Antiques, Arts for Handicapped, Batik, Etching, Papermaking, Performing Arts, Weaving, Scrimshaw
Children's Classes: Tuition $15-$25 per quarter. Courses—Fine Arts, Drama
Summer School: Dir, Deborah K Eckstein; enrl approx 250; tuition $15-$45 for two 5 wk sessions beginning June. Courses—Visual Arts

FORT LAUDERDALE

ART INSTITUTE OF FORT LAUDERDALE, 3000 E Las Olas Blvd, 33316. Tel 305-463-3000. *Pres* Mark Wheeler, BA; *VPres & Dir Admissions* Robert S Peterson, BBA; *VPres & Dir Education* Frank Raia, MA; *Dir Advertising Design* Nevin Meinhardt, BS; *Dir Photography* James Boyd, BA; *Dir Fashion* Jack Rose, BA; *Dir Interior Design* Bill Kobrynich, AA; *Dir Fashion Illustration* John Miele; *Asst Chmn Advertising Design* Paul Wullschleger, BFA; *Asst Chmn Photography* Sterling Clark; *Asst Chmn Fashion* June Fisher, BA
Estab 1968; pvt; D & E; scholarships; enrl D 1300, maj 1300
Ent Req: HS dipl
Degrees: AS(technology)
Tuition: Varies with major; campus res available, rates vary with dorm
Courses: †Advertising Design, Art History, †Commercial Art, Conceptual Art, Display, Drafting, Drawing, †Fashion Arts, Graphic Arts, Graphic Design, Illustration, †Interior Design, Lettering, Mixed Media, Painting, †Photography, Video, †Fashion Illustration, †Fashion Merchandising
Children's Classes: Tuition $100 for 4 wks during the summer
Summer School: Same as regular semester

FORT MYERS

EDISON COMMUNITY COLLEGE, Dept of Fine and Performing Arts, College Parkway, 33907. Instrs: FT 1, PT 5
Estab 1962; pub; D & E; scholarships
Ent Req: HS dipl
Degrees: AA & AS 2 yrs
Tuition: Res—$19 per cr hr; nonres—$34 per cr hr
Courses: Art History, Ceramics, Commercial Art, Drawing, Jewelry, Painting, Photography, Printmaking, Sculpture, Design
Adult Hobby Classes: Enrl 20. Courses—any non-cr activity of interest for which a teacher is available

FORT PIERCE

INDIAN RIVER COMMUNITY COLLEGE, Fine Art Dept, Virginia Ave, 33450. Tel 305-464-2000. *Asst Prof* Tony Allo, MA; *Asst Prof* Jane B Howard, MA; *Asst Prof* Jack Biedenharn, MA & MFA; *Div Dir of Art & Sci* Ray C Lunceford, EDDS
Estab 1960; pub; D & E; scholarships; SC 10, LC 10
Ent Req: HS dipl
Degrees: AA & AS 2 yrs
Tuition: $15 per credit hr plus some lab fees
Courses: Advertising Design, Art Education, Art History, Ceramics, Display, Drafting, Drawing, Graphic Arts, Painting, Printmaking, Sculpture, General Art, Landscape, Portrait
Summer School: Dir, Jane Howard. Enrl 80. Courses—Gifted students in the arts

GAINESVILLE

UNIVERSITY OF FLORIDA, Dept of Art, 302, FAC Complex, 32611. Tel 904-392-0211. *Chmn* Robert H Westin, PhD; *Prof* Eugene E Grissom, MFA; *Prof* Kenneth A Kerslake, MFA; *Prof* Geoffrey J Naylor, MFA; *Prof* Jack C Nichelson, MFA; *Prof* Robert C Skelley, MFA; *Prof* Phillip A Ward, MFA; *Graduate Research Prof* Jerry N Uelsmann, MFA; *Assoc Prof* Don E Murray, MFA; *Assoc Prof* John A O'Connor, MFA; *Assoc Prof* Evon Streetman, MFA; *Assoc Prof* John L Ward, MFA; *Assoc Prof* Wallace Wilson, MFA; *Asst Prof* Barbara Barletta, PhD; *Asst Prof* Jerry Cutler, MFA; *Asst Prof* Richard Heipp, MFA; *Asst Prof* Marcia Isaacson, MFA; *Asst Prof* David Kremgold, MFA; *Asst Prof* Robin Poynor, PhD; *Asst Prof* John Scott, PhD; *Asst Prof* Nan Smith, MFA; *Asst Prof* David Stanley, PhD. Instrs: FT 21
Estab 1925; pub; D & E; scholarships; SC 40, LC 26, GC 11; enrl maj 200 upper div, grad 16
Ent Req: HS dipl, SAT, ACT, TOEFL, SCAT or AA degree (transfers must have 2.0 average) GRE
Degrees: BAA and BFA 4 yrs, MFA 2 yrs
Tuition: Res—undergrad $15-$22 per cr hr, grad $17-$24 per cr hr; nonres—undergrad $38-$62 per cr hr, grad $52-$64 per cr hr; campus res $570 per yr without air conditioning, $735 per yr with air conditioning
Courses: †Art Education, †Art History, †Ceramics, †Drawing, †Graphic Design, Lettering, †Painting, †Photography, †Printmaking, †Sculpture, Typography
Summer School: Limited classes

HOLLYWOOD

SOUTH FLORIDA ART INSTITUTE OF HOLLYWOOD, 1301 S Ocean Dr, 33019. Tel 305-923-6490. *Dir* Elwin Porter
Estab 1958; pvt; D & E; scholarships; SC 30, LC 2, GC 2; enrl D 230, E 20
Ent Req: Portfolio
Degrees: Cert fine arts and cert graphic art 2 and 4 yrs
Tuition: $1180 per yr, $640 per sem; no campus res
Courses: Design, Drawing, Graphic Design, Painting, Sculpture, Abstraction, Anatomy, Clay Modeling, Color Theory, Composition, Life Sketching
Adult Hobby Classes: Enrl 100. Courses—Fine Arts, Graphic Design
Children's Classes: Enrl 30; tuition $45 per 8 wks. Courses—Painting, Drawing, Sculpture
Summer School: Dir, Elwin Porter. Courses—Most of above

JACKSONVILLE

FLORIDA JUNIOR COLLEGE AT JACKSONVILLE, SOUTH CAMPUS, Art Dept, 11901 Beach Blvd, 32216. Tel 904-646-2150. *Chmn Div Fine Arts & Humanities* Dr John G Stanley. Instrs: FT 5
Estab 1966; pub; D & E; scholarships; SC 14, LC 6; enrl D 150, E 75
Ent Req: HS dipl
Degrees: AA & AS 2 yrs
Tuition: Res—$18 per cr hr; nonres—$36 per cr hr; no campus res
Courses: Ceramics, Drawing, Graphic Design, Handicrafts, History of Art & Archaeology, Painting, Photography, Sculpture, Batik, Blockprinting, Glaze Techniques, Macrame, Weaving
Adult Hobby Classes: Enrl 75-80; for term of 6 wks beginning June. Courses—Art Appreciation, Crafts, Drawing, Painting, Photography
Summer School: Courses—Ceramics, Design, Drawing, Painting, Printmaking, Sculpture

JACKSONVILLE UNIVERSITY, Dept of Art, College of Fine Arts, 2800 University Blvd N, 32211. Tel 904-744-3950. *Dean* Dr Thomas G Owen; *Chmn Div* Dr J Davis Sikes
Estab 1932; pvt; D & E; scholarships; SC 47, LC 13; enrl D 403, maj 80
Ent Req: HS dipl, ent exam
Degrees: BFA (studio art, art history, commercial art) and BA Ed 4 yr
Tuition: $2100 per sem
Adult Hobby Classes: Enrl 10; tuition $1260. Courses vary
Children's Classes: Courses offered June-July
Summer School: Tuition $90 per sem hr. Courses—Basic Art

UNIVERSITY OF NORTH FLORIDA, Dept of Fine Arts, 4567 St Johns Bluff Rd S, 32216. Tel 904-646-2960. *Chmn* Merrill J Palmer; *Assoc Prof* Charles Charles, MA; *Assoc Prof* Kenneth L McMillan, MFA; *Assoc Prof* David S Porter, MFA; *Assoc Prof* Robert L Cocaougher, MFA; *Asst Prof* Ted Reynolds, PhD; *Instr* Paul Ladnier
Estab 1970; pub; D & E; enrl maj 95
Ent Req: AA
Degrees: BA 2 yr, BFA
Tuition: Res—undergrad $16.50 per sem hr, grad $22 per qtr hr; nonres—undergrad $51.50 per qtr hr, grad $62 per qtr hr
Courses: Art Education, Art History, Ceramics, Drawing, Graphic Design, Painting, Photography, Printmaking, Sculpture, Teacher Training

KEY WEST

FLORIDA KEYS COMMUNITY COLLEGE, Art Dept,* 33040. Tel 305-296-9081. *Chmn Fine Arts Div* Richard F Fitzgerald
Scholarships offered
Degrees: AA, AS
Tuition: Res—$19 per cr hr; nonres—$41 per cr hr
Courses: Art Appreciation, Art History, Ceramics, Design, Drawing, Handicrafts, Painting, Photography, Printmaking, Sculpture, Stage Design

LAKE CITY

LAKE CITY COMMUNITY COLLEGE, Art Dept, 32055. Tel 904-752-1822, Ext 256. Instrs: FT 1, PT 2
Estab 1962; pub; D & E; SC 9, LC 2; enrl D 160, maj 10
Ent Req: HS dipl
Degrees: AA 2 yrs
Courses: Ceramics, Drawing, Handicrafts, Jewelry, Painting, Sculpture, Composition, Weaving

LAKELAND

FLORIDA SOUTHERN COLLEGE, Art Dept, 33802. Tel 813-683-5521, Ext 431, 244. *Coordr Dept* Downing Barnitz, MFA; *Assoc Prof* Banton S Doak, EdS; *Asst Prof* Gale L Doak, MA; *Instructor* Beth M Ford, MA; *Instructor* Joyce Davis, PhD
Estab 1885; den; D; scholarships; SC 20, LC 6, maj 34
Ent Req: HS dipl
Degrees: AB & BS 128 hr
Courses: Art Education, Art History, Ceramics, Drawing, Graphic Arts, Handicrafts, Jewelry, Lettering, Painting, Photography, Sculpture, Silversmithing, Teacher Training, Theatre Arts, Advertising Design, Ancient & Medieval Art, †Art Communication, †Art Therapy, Design (19th & 20th century art), Graphic Illustration, Renaissance & Baroque Art, †Studio Art, Watercolor
Adult Hobby Classes: Courses—Graphics, Interior Design, Oil Painting
Summer School: Dean, Dr Mobberley. Tuition $100 per hr, two terms of 4 wks beginning June and July. Courses—Painting, Ceramics, Drawing

LAKE WORTH

PALM BEACH JUNIOR COLLEGE, Dept of Art, 4200 South Congress Ave, 33461. Tel 305-439-8000; Cable FLASUNCOM. *Chmn* Reuben Hale
Estab 1935; pub; D & E; SC 20, LC 5; enrl D 15,000 maj 400
Ent Req: HS dipl or over 25
Degrees: AA and AS 2 yr
Tuition: $19 per cr hr
Courses: †Advertising Design, Ceramics, †Commercial Art, †Drawing, †Graphic Design, †History of Art & Archaeology, †Interior Design, †Jewelry, †Lettering, †Painting, †Photography, †Sculpture, †Architectural Drawing, †Basic Design, Enameling, †Etching, †Lithography, †Screen Printing, †Technical Photo Courses, †Typography
Adult Hobby Classes: Courses—Floral Design, Jewelry, Picture Frame Making, Weaving, Photography, Painting, Printmaking
Summer School: Courses—Art Appreciation, Design, Drawing, History of Art, Photography

MADISON

NORTH FLORIDA JUNIOR COLLEGE, Dept Humanities & Art,* Turner Davis Dr, 32340. Tel 904-973-2288. *Chmn* Edith H Day; *Faculty* Jules de R Bacot; *Faculty* William F Gardner Jr
Scholarships
Degrees: AA
Tuition: Res—$14 per sem hr; nonres—$28 per sem hr
Courses: Art History, Ceramics, Design, Drawing, Handicrafts, Painting, Printmaking, Sculpture, Cartooning

MARIANNA

CHIPOLA JUNIOR COLLEGE, Division of Fine Arts and Humanities, 32446. Tel 904-526-2761. *Coordr Fine & Performing Arts* Lawrence R Nelson
Estab 1947; pub; D & E; scholarships; SC 14, LC 2; enrl D 60
Ent Req: HS dipl
Degrees: AA 2 yr
Tuition: Res—$18 per sem hr; nonres—$39 per sem hr
Courses: Art History, Ceramics, Drawing, Jewelry, Painting, Sculpture, Stage Design, †Theatre Arts, 2-D & 3-D Design
Summer School: Dir, Dr Donald A Dellow. Enrl 300; tuition res—$18 per sem hr, nonres—$39 per sem hr. Courses—varied

MIAMI

FLORIDA INTERNATIONAL UNIVERSITY, Visual Arts Dept, Tamiami Trail, 33199. Tel 305-554-2897. *Chairperson* Francis Wyroba; *Assoc Prof* William J Burke; *Assoc Prof* James M Couper; *Assoc Prof* Ellen Jacobs; *Assoc Prof* R F Buckley; *Assoc Prof* Richard Duncan; *Assoc Prof* William Maguire; *Gallery Dir & Lecturer* Dahlia Morgan
Estab 1972, dept estab 1972; pub; D & E; scholarships; SC 20, LC 12, GC 18; enrl D 320, E 100, non-maj 225, maj 175, grad 20
Ent Req: 1000 on SAT, 3.0 HS grade point average
Degrees: BFA, BS(Art Educ) and MS(Art Educ)
Tuition: Res—undergrad $750 per yr, grad $990 per yr; non-res—undergrad $2640 per yr, grad $3150 per yr; no campus res
Courses: Art Education, Art History, Ceramics, Drawing, Jewelry, Painting, Photography, Printmaking, Sculpture, Teacher Training, Fabrics & Fibers, Glass
Summer School: Dir, Francis Wyroba. Enrl 160; tuition $250 for term of 6.5 wks beginning May 13 & June 28

INTERNATIONAL FINE ARTS COLLEGE,* 1737 N Bayshore Dr, 33132. Tel 305-373-4684. *Chmn* Gregory Hoffman; *Pres College* Edward Porter; *Dean* Danial M Stack
Estab 1965, dept estab 1966; pvt; D; SC 6; enrl D 180, maj 180
Ent Req: HS dipl
Degrees: AA
Courses: Art History, Costume Design & Construction, Display, Drawing, Fashion Arts, History of Art & Archaeology, Illustration, Interior Design, Painting

MIAMI-DADE COMMUNITY COLLEGE CAMPUSES, Art Dept, 11011 SW 104 St, 33176. Tel 305-596-1281. *Chmn Dept* Robert Huff
Estab 1960, dept estab 1967; pub; D & E; scholarships; SC 14, LC 4; enrl E 300, non-maj 150, maj 150
Ent Req: Open door
Degrees: AA and AS 2 yr
Tuition: Res—$20 per cr; nonres—$43 per cr
Courses: Ceramics, Design, Drawing, Jewelry, Painting, Photography, Printmaking, Sculpture, Metals
Adult Hobby Classes: Courses by demand
Summer School: Dir, Robert Huff. Courses vary

MIAMI SHORES

BARRY UNIVERSITY, Dept of Art,* 11300 NE Second Ave, 33161. Tel 305-758-3392. *Chmn Fine Arts Dept* Patricia Minnaugh, MFA; *Dean* Dr Andre Cote; *Assoc Dean* Eileen McDonough. Instrs: FT 4, PT 3
Estab 1940; pvt; D & E; scholarships; SC 8, LC 2; enrl D 300, E 60, maj 40
Ent Req: HS dipl, portfolio for BFA
Degrees: BA, BFA, BA(Educ) 4 yrs
Tuition: $2200 per sem
Courses: Advertising Design, Art Education, Ceramics, Commercial Art, Costume Design & Construction, Drawing, Fashion Arts, Graphic Arts, Graphic Design, History of Art & Archaeology, Illustration, Jewelry, Painting, Photography, Sculpture, Stage Design, Teacher Training, Textile Design, Theatre Arts

NICEVILLE

OKALOOSA-WALTON JUNIOR COLLEGE, Dept of Fine and Performing Arts,* 100 College Blvd, 32578. Tel 904-678-5111. *Instr* Richard J Warren, PhD; *Instr* Walter B Shipley, MA
Estab 1964, dept estab 1964; pub; D & E; scholarships; SC 26, LC 3; enrl D 2000, E 1000, maj 80
Ent Req: HS dipl
Degrees: AA 2 yrs
Tuition: Res—$15 per cr hr; nonres—$34.50 per cr hr; campus res available
Courses: Architecture, Art History, Ceramics, Costume Design & Construction, Drafting, Drawing, Graphic Arts, Graphic Design, Handicrafts, History of Art & Archaeology, Interior Design, Jewelry, Painting, Photography, Printmaking, Sculpture, Silversmithing, Stage Design, Teacher Training, Theatre Arts, Weaving
Adult Hobby Classes: Enrl 15 per class. Courses—Antiques, Interior Decorating, Painting, Photography, Pottery, Vase Painting, others as needed
Summer School: Dir, Dr James Durham. Term of 6 or 12 wks beginning May 2 and June 18. Courses—same as regular sessions

OCALA

CENTRAL FLORIDA COMMUNITY COLLEGE, Humanities Dept,* 3001 SW College Rd, PO Box 1388, 32678. Tel 904-237-2111. *Chmn Dept* Charles Adams, MA
Estab 1957; pub; D & E; SC 5, LC 1; enrl 2015, non-maj 85, maj 15
Ent Req: HS dipl
Degrees: AA and AS 2 yr
Tuition: Res—$19 per cr hr; nonres—$41 per cr hr
Courses: Art History, Ceramics, Design, Drawing, Painting, Printmaking
Adult Hobby Classes: Ceramics, Drawing, Painting, Commercial Art; Design
Summer School: Two 6 week terms

ORLANDO

UNIVERSITY OF CENTRAL FLORIDA, Art Dept, PO Box 25000, 32816. Tel 305-275-2676. *Chmn* Charles W Wellman
Scholarships
Degrees: BA, BFA, cert
Courses: Advertising Design, Art History, Ceramics, Design, Drawing, Painting, Photography, Printmaking, Sculpture, Weaving
Summer School: Dir, Charles Wellman. Tuition same as above. Courses—various

VALENCIA COMMUNITY COLLEGE, Art Dept, 1800 S Kirkman Rd, PO Box 3028, 32802. Tel 305-299-5000, Ext 2-337. *Dept Chmn* Qurentia P Throm, MA
Estab 1967, dept estab 1974; pub; D & E; scholarships; SC 16, LC 5; enrl D 6858
Ent Req: HS dipl
Degrees: AA and AS 2 yrs
Courses: Art History, Ceramics, Drawing, History of Art & Archaeology, Painting, Photography, Printmaking, Sculpture
Summer School: Same as for regular academic yr

PALATKA

FLORIDA SCHOOL OF THE ARTS, Visual Arts, 5001 Saint John Ave, 32077. Tel 904-328-1571. *Dean* David R Humphrey, PhD; *Coordr Fine Art* Gene Roberds, MFA; *Coordr Graphic Design* Steven Lebeck, MA; *Dir Galleries* David Ovellette, MFA
Estab 1974, dept estab 1974; pub; D; scholarships; SC 35, LC 10; enrl D 85, maj 85
Ent Req: HS dipl, recommendation, review, interview
Degrees: AA 2 yrs, AS 2 1/2 yrs
Tuition: Res—$18 per hr; nonres—$35 per hr
Courses: Advertising Design, Art History, Ceramics, Commercial Art, Display, Drafting, Drawing, Graphic Arts, †Graphic Design, Illustration, Intermedia, Lettering, Mixed Media, Museum Staff Training, †Painting, Photography, †Printmaking, †Stage Design, †Theatre Arts

PANAMA CITY

GULF COAST COMMUNITY COLLEGE, Division of Fine Arts, 5230 W Highway 98, 32401. Tel 904-769-1551. *Chmn* Norman J Hair, MM; *Assoc Prof* Sharron Barnes, MA; *Assoc Prof* Roland L Hockett, MS; *Assoc Prof* Louise L Lewis, MA
Estab 1957; pub; D & E; SC 5, LC 2; enrl D 300, E 70, non-maj 330, maj 40
Ent Req: HS dipl
Degrees: AA 2 yrs
Tuition: Res—undergrad $18 per cr hr; nonres—undergrad $36 per cr hr
Courses: Advertising Design, Art History, Ceramics, Commercial Art, Design, Drawing, Graphic Arts, History of Art & Archaeology, Graphic Design, Illustration, Lettering, Photography, Printmaking, African Design
Adult Hobby Classes: Courses—Macrame, Painting

PENSACOLA

PENSACOLA JUNIOR COLLEGE, Dept of Visual Arts, 1000 College Blvd, 32504. Tel 904-476-5410, Ext 2250. *Head Dept* Carl F Duke. Instrs: FT 11, PT 5
Estab 1948; pub; D & E; scholarships; enrl maj 100
Ent ReqD HS dipl
Degrees: AS & AA 2 yrs
Tuition: Res—$20 per cr hr; nonres—$40 per cr hr; no campus res
Courses: Art History, Ceramics, Drawing, Graphic Arts, Illustration, Painting, Photography, Printmaking, Sculpture, Crafts, Design, Pottery
Adult Hobby Classes: Enrl 600; tuition none. Courses—Drawing, Painting
Summer School: Dir, Carl F Duke. Enrl 80; tuition $20. Courses same as regular session

UNIVERSITY OF WEST FLORIDA, Faculty of Art, College of Arts & Sciences, 32514. Tel 904-474-2671. *Chmn* Robert L Armstrong, PhD; *Prof Emeritus* John T Carey, PhD; *Assoc Prof* Henry J Heuler, MFA; *Assoc Prof* Robert B Marshman, MFA; *Assoc Prof* William A Silhan, EdD; *Assoc Prof* Duncan E Stewart, MA; *Asst Prof* Judith A Heuler, MFA; *Asst Prof* Stephen K Haworth, MFA; *Asst Prof* Suzette J Doyon-Bernard, PhD
Estab 1967; pub; D & E; SC 20, LC 10; enrl D 50, E 10, non-maj 40, maj 50
Ent Req: AA degree or 60 sem hrs credit
Degrees: BA & BFA 2 yr
Tuition: Res—undergrad $29 per sem hr, grad $39 per sem hr; nonres—undergrad $92 per sem hr, grad $111 per sem hr; campus res—room and board $2000 two sem
Courses: †Art Education, †Art History, Ceramics, Commercial Art, Drawing, Graphic Arts, Jewelry, Lettering, Painting, Photography, Printmaking, Sculpture, Silversmithing, Teacher Training
Summer School: Same as above

SAINT AUGUSTINE

FLAGLER COLLEGE, Visual Arts Dept, King St, 32084. Tel 904-829-6481. *Chmn* Robert Hall; *Assoc Prof* Enzo Torcoletti, MFA; *Asst Prof* Don Martin
Estab 1968; pvt; D & E; scholarships; SC 29, LC 7; enrl D 50, maj 45
Ent Req: HS dipl
Degrees: BA 4 yr
Tuition: Res—$4350 per yr; campus res available
Courses: Advertising Design, Art Education, Art History, †Commercial Art, Illustration, Drawing, Graphic Design, Jewelry, Painting, Printmaking, Sculpture, †Teacher Training, †Visual Arts
Summer School: Dir, Robert Carberry. Tui $60 per hr for term of 4 or 6 wks beginning May. Courses—Ceramics, Creative Photography, Landscape Drawing

SAINT PETERSBURG

ECKERD COLLEGE, Art Dept, PO Box 12560, 33733. Tel 813-867-1166. *Prof* James Crane; *Assoc Prof* Margaret Rigg; *Asst Prof* Arthur Skinner; *Asst Prof* John Eckert
Scholarships
Degrees: BA
Tuition: $5990 full time
Courses: Art Education, Art History, Calligraphy, Ceramics, Design, Drawing, Painting, Photography, Printmaking
Adult Hobby Classes: Enrl 25. Courses—Ceramics, Drawing, Painting
Summer School: Dir, Cheryl Gold. Enrl 150

SAINT PETERSBURG JUNIOR COLLEGE, Humanities Dept,* 6605 Fifth Ave N, PO Box 13489, 33733. Tel 813-381-0681
Estab 1927. College has four campuses; pub; D & E; scholarships; SC 13, LC 3; enrl D 7031, E 2478
Ent Req: HS dipl
Degrees: AA and AS 2 yr
Tuition: Res—$19 per cr hr; nonres—$41 per cr hr; no campus residence
Courses: Advertising Design, Aesthetics, Ceramics, Design, Drafting, Drawing, Painting, Photography, Sculpture, Stage Design, Theatre Arts, Art History Survey, Survey in Crafts
Summer School: Courses—Same as regular session

SARASOTA

FRIENDS OF THE ARTS AND SCIENCES, HILTON LEECH STUDIO, 4433 Riverwood, PO Box 15766, 33579. Tel 813-923-3031. *Consultant Special Projects* Katherine L Rowland
Estab 1946, dept estab 1963; pvt; SC 16; enrl D 200, E 10
Courses: Drawing, Painting, Photography
Adult Hobby Classes: Enrl 200. Courses—Drawing, Painting, Photography
Summer School: Dir, Katherine L Rowland. Enrl 80. Courses—Photography, Watercolor

NEW COLLEGE OF THE UNIVERSITY OF SOUTH FLORIDA, Fine Arts Dept, Humanities Division, Humanities Division, 5700 N Tamiami Trail, 33580. Tel 813-355-7671. Instrs: FT 4
Estab 1963; D; SC 6, LC 5; enrl D 150-200, maj 15
Ent Req: Ent exam, SAT
Degrees: BA(Fine Arts) 3 yrs
Tuition: Res—$391 per sem; non-res—$1047 per sem
Courses: †Aesthetics, †Art History, Ceramics, †Drawing, †Painting, †Printmaking, †Sculpture, †Color Theory, Design, Life Drawing, Stained Glass

RINGLING SCHOOL OF ART AND DESIGN, 1111 27th St, 33580. Tel 813-351-4614. *Pres* Herbert Burgart, DEd; *Dir Admissions* Rebecca McConville. Instrs: 31
Estab 1931; pvt; scholarships; enrl 430
Ent Req: HS dipl or equivalency, portfolio
Degrees: 3-year certificate, BFA, 4 yrs
Tuition: $3600; campus res—room & board $2500
Courses: Advertising Design, Art History, Graphic Design, †Illustration, Lettering, Painting, Photography, Sculpture, †Fine Arts, †Interior Design & Space Planning
Adult Hobby Classes: Enrl 150; tuition $40 per 7 wk session

TALLAHASSEE

FLORIDA A & M UNIVERSITY, Dept of Visual Arts and Humanities,* 32307. Tel 904-599-3000. *Prof* H L Williams, EdD
Estab 1887; pub; D & E; enrl D 5887, non-maj 5800, maj 87
Ent Req: HS dipl, ent exam
Degrees: BS and BA with Fine Arts Cert
Tuition: Res—$25 per sem hr; nonres—$66 per sem hr
Summer School: Enrl 125; tui same as regular session for term of 9 and 7 wks beginning June. Courses—Ceramics, Design, Drawing, Arts, Textile Design, Wood, Metal & Plastics

FLORIDA STATE UNIVERSITY
—**Art Dept,*** 236 Fine Arts Bldg, 32306. Tel 904-644-6474. *Chairperson Studio Art* James J Murphy; *Prof* Trevor Bell; *Prof* Arthur E Deshaies, MFA; *Assoc Prof* George Bocz, MEd; *Assoc Prof* Ray Burggraf, MFA; *Assoc Prof* Robert W Fichter, MFA; *Assoc Prof* Grazyna Gindvainis, MFA; *Assoc Prof* William C Harper, MS; *Assoc Prof* Janice E Hartwell, MFA; *Asst Prof* Joan Ballon, MFA; *Asst Prof* George C Blakely, MFA; *Asst Prof* Henry Chotowski, MFA; *Asst Prof* James Cogswell, MFA; *Asst Prof* Charles E Hook, MFA; *Asst Prof* Paul Rutkowsky, MFA; *Asst Prof* E Thomas Thompson, BA; *Asst Prof* Judith West, MFA
Estab 1857, dept estab 1911; pub; D & E; scholarships
Ent Req: HS dipl, C average and upper 40 percent of graduating class, SAT
Degrees: BA, BFA, MFA, MA, PhD
Tuition: Res—undergrad $25 per cr hr; nonres—undergrad $66 per cr hr; res—grad $38 per cr hr; nonres—grad $110 per cr hr; campus res—$499 per term
Courses: Advertising Design, Commercial Art, Conceptual Art, Constructions, Drawing, Fashion Arts, Film, Graphic Arts, Graphic Design, History of Art & Archaeology, Illustration, Interior Design, Lettering, Painting, Photography, Printmaking, Sculpture, †Studio Art
Summer School: Term of 8 wks beginning June
—**Art Education Dept,*** 32306. Tel 904-644-6573. *Chmn* Marylou Kuhn, PhD; *Prof* Jessie Lovano-Kerr, PhD; *Asst Prof* James R Anderson, MA; *Asst Prof* Linda S Bradley, PhD; *Asst Prof* Betty J Troeger, PhD
Estab 1857, dept estab 1948; pub; D & E; scholarships
Ent Req: HS dipl
Degrees: BS, BA, MA & MS(all in art education)
Courses: †Art Education, Teacher Training
Summer School: Same as regular session
—**Art History Dept,** 32306. *Chmn* Patricia Rose, PhD; *Dean School Visual Arts* Jenny L Draper, PhD; *Prof* Francois Bucher, PhD; *Prof* Penelope E Mason, PhD; *Prof* M Von Hennenburg; *Asst Prof* Craig Adcoch, PhD; *Asst Prof* Cynthia J Hahn, PhD; *Asst Prof* Robert M Neuman, PhD; *Asst Prof* Timothy Verdon, PhD
Estab 1857, dept estab 1948; pub; D & E; scholarships
Ent Req: HS dipl
Degrees: BA, MA & PhD(all in art history)
Courses: Art Appreciation, Art History, History of Art & Archaeology

TALLAHASSEE COMMUNITY COLLEGE, Art Dept, 32304. Tel 904-576-5181. *Chmn Art Prog* Ruth Dryden Deshaies, MA
Estab 1966; pub; D & E; SC 8, LC 2; enrl D 130, E 40
Ent Req: HS dipl
Degrees: AA 2 yrs
Tuition: $16 per sem hr
Courses: Art History, Design, Drawing, Painting, Photography, Color Theory, History & Appreciation of Cinema, Silk Screen
Summer School: Chmn Art Program, Ruth Dryden Deshaies, MA. Enrl 50; 10 wk term. Courses—Silkscreen, Art History

TAMPA

HILLSBOROUGH COMMUNITY COLLEGE, Fine Arts Dept,* PO Box 22127, 33622. Tel 813-879-7222. *Assoc Prof* Steve Holm
Scholarships
Degrees: AA
Tuition: Res—$19 per cr hr; nonres—$42 per cr hr
Courses: Art Appreciation, Art History, Ceramics, Design, Drawing, Painting, Photography, Printmaking, Sculpture, Weaving

UNIVERSITY OF SOUTH FLORIDA, Art Dept, College of Fine Arts, 4202 Fowler Ave, 33620. Tel 813-974-2360. *Chmn* David Yager. Instrs: FT D 26
Estab 1956; pub
Ent Req: HS grad, 14 units cert by HS, ent exam
Degrees: BA(Art) minimum 120 sem hrs and MFA 60 sem hrs
Tuition: Res—undergrad $25 per cr hr, grad $38 per cr hr; nonres—undergrad $66 per cr hr, grad $110 per cr hr
Courses: Art History, Ceramics, Drawing, Painting, Photography, Sculpture, Printmaking, Cinematography
Adult Hobby Classes: Chmn, David Yager
Summer School: 7 - 14 wks

UNIVERSITY OF TAMPA, Dept of Art, Fine Arts Division, 401 W Kennedy Blvd, 33606. Tel 813-253-8861. *Dir* Dorothy Cowden. Instrs: FT 5
Estab 1930; pvt; D & E; SC 17, LC 8
Degrees: 4 yrs
Courses: Art Education, Art History, Ceramics, Drawing, Painting, Photography, Printmaking, Sculpture, Design, Arts Management
Adult Hobby Classes: Enrl 35; tuition $45 per 8 wks. Courses—Jewelry Making, Silver Smithing, Fabric Dyeing
Summer School: Courses offered

TEMPLE TERRACE

FLORIDA COLLEGE, Division of Art,* 33617. Tel 813-988-5131. *Faculty* H D Vann, MA
Scholarships offered
Degrees: BA
Tuition: $1200 per sem
Courses: Advertising Design, Art Appreciation, Art Education, Art History, Ceramics, Design, Drawing, Handicrafts, Jewelry, Painting, Photography, Sculpture

WINTER HAVEN

POLK COMMUNITY COLLEGE, Division of Communications and Fine Arts, 33880. *Dir* Dion K Brown, EdS; *Prof* Gary Baker, MFA; *Prof* Jane Jaskevich, MEd; *Prof* Bob Morrisey, MFA
Estab 1964; pub; D & E; scholarships; SC 10, LC 1; enrl D 175, E 50
Ent Req: HS dipl
Degrees: AA & AS 2 yrs
Tuition: Res—undergrad $19 per cr hr; nonres—undergrad $41 per cr hr; no campus res
Courses: Advertising Design, Art History, Ceramics, Drafting, Drawing, Film, Graphic Arts, Interior Design, Printmaking, Painting, Photography, Sculpture, Video
Adult Hobby Classes: Enrl 60; tuition $1.60 per class hr. Courses—Calligraphy, Ceramics, Christmas Crafts, Drawing, Interior Design, Jewelry, Painting

WINTER PARK

ROLLINS COLLEGE, Dept of Art, Main Campus, 32789. Tel 305-646-2000. *Chmn* Robert Lemon
Estab 1885; pvt; D & E; scholarships; SC 11, LC 10; enrl D & E 250
Degrees: 4 yrs
Tuition: Res—$4,990
Courses: Aesthetics, Art History, Drawing, Painting, Sculpture, Art History Survey, Design, Humanities Foundation, Principles of Art
Adult Hobby Classes: Courses—selected studio and history courses
Summer School: Courses—selected art history and appreciation courses

GEORGIA

AMERICUS

GEORGIA SOUTHWESTERN COLLEGE, Art Dept,* Wheatley St, 31709. Tel 912-928-1279. *Chmn* Steve Gurr
Scholarships
Degrees: BA, BSEd, cert
Tuition: Res—$278 per quarter; nonres—$708 per quarter
Courses: Drawing, Fashion Arts, Jewelry, Painting, Photography, Sculpture, Textile Design, Weaving, Bookbinding, Glassblowing, Papermaking

ATHENS

UNIVERSITY OF GEORGIA, FRANKLIN COLLEGE OF ARTS AND SCIENCES, Dept of Art, 30602. Tel 404-542-1511. *Dean* William J Payne; *Head Dept* Francis A Ruzicka; *Undergrad Coordr* Oliver Coleman; *Grad Coordr* Paul Edmonston; *Art Appreciation* William Squires; *Art Education* W Robert Nix; *Art History* Michael Jacobsen; *Ceramics* Ronald Meyers; *Drawing & Painting* Arthur Rosenbaum; *Fabric Design* Glen Kaufman; *Foundation* William Marriott; *Graphic Design* Kenneth Williams; *Interior Design* John Huff; *Jewelry & Metalwork* Gary Noffke; *Photographic Design* Wiley Sanderson; *Printmaking* Charles Morgan; *Sculpture* William Thompson
Opened 1801, chartered 1875; scholarships & grad assistantships
Ent Req: HS dipl, SAT
Degrees: BA, BFA, BSEd, MA, MFA, MAE, EdS, EdD, PhD
Tuition: Res—undergrad $414 per qtr, grad $369 per qtr; nonres—undergrad $1070 per qtr, grad $939 per qtr
Courses: Art Appreciation, Art Education, Art History, Ceramics, Drawing, Graphic Design, Interior Design, Jewelry, Painting, Photography, Printmaking, Sculpture, Fabrics, Foundation, Metalwork
Summer School: Dept Head, Francis A Ruzicka

ATLANTA

ART INSTITUTE OF ATLANTA,* 3376 Peachtree Rd NE, 30326. Tel 404-266-1341
The Institute has the following departments: Visual Communications, Photography, Interior Design, Fashion Illustration & Fashion Merchandising; scholarships offered
Degrees: AA
Courses: Advertising Design, Commercial Art, Art History, Calligraphy, Design, Drawing, Fashion Arts, Graphic Design, Illustration, Interior Design, Photography, Cartooning, Fashion, Photo Design, Portrait

ATLANTA AREA TECHNICAL SCHOOL, Dept of Commercial Art, 1560 Stewart Ave SW, 30310. Tel 404-758-9451. *Head Dept* Don M Ballentine
Estab 1967; pub; D & E; SC 13; enrl D 25, E 25
Ent Req: HS dipl, ent exam
Degrees: AA in conjunction with The Atlanta Jr Col
Tuition: $50 per quarter plus testing fees
Courses: Advertising Design, Commercial Art, Graphic Arts, Photography, Video, Print Production Art

ATLANTA COLLEGE OF ART, 1280 Peachtree St NE, 30309. Tel 404-892-3600.
Pres William J Voos, MFA; *Academic Dean* James C Striby, MFA; *Dir Student Servs* Elizabeth Shackelford; *Foundation Chmn* William Nolan; *Video Chmn* Ben Davis; *Academic Chmn* Barbara DeConcini; *Painting Chmn* Tom Francis; *Drawing Chmn* Richard Hill; *Sculpture Chmn* Curtis Patterson; *Printmaking Chmn* Norman Wagner; *Visual Communication Chmn* Girish Patel; *Photography Chmn* Robert Stewart; *Instructor* Diane Benoit, MA; *Instructor* Michael Brekke, MFA; *Instructor* Scott Gilliam, MFA; *Instructor* Fred Gregory, MFA; *Instructor* Corrine Colarusso, MFA; *Instructor* Keith Rasmussen, MFA; *Instructor* Ann Crowe, MA; *Instructor* Daniel Zins, PhD; *Instructor* Marcia Cohen, MA; *Instructor* Martin Emanuel, MFA
Estab 1928; pvt; D & E; scholarships; SC 96, LC 48; enrl D 270, E 350, non-maj 350, maj 270
Ent Req: HS dipl, ent exam, SAT, portfolio of art work
Degrees: BFA 4 yrs
Tuition: $4330 yr
Courses: Drawing, Graphic Arts, Graphic Design, Illustration, Intermedia, Mixed Media, Painting, Photography, Printmaking, Sculpture, Video
Adult Hobby Classes: Dir, Susan Erck. Enrl 650 - 800; tuition $140 for 15 wk term
Children's Classes: Enrl 20 - 30; tuition $80 for 12 wk term. High School (15 - 18) - Enrl 40; tuition $100 for 12 wk term
Summer School: Dir, Susan Erck. Enrl 240; tuition $90 for term of 6 wks.
Children's Classes - Enrl 20; tuition $60 for 12 wks. Courses—Crafts, Drawing, Painting. High School Summer Program Enrl 20; tuition $140 for 5 wk term

CLARK COLLEGE, Dept of Art, 240 Chestnut St SW, 30314. Tel 404-681-3080, Ext 275. *Chmn Dept* Emmanuel V Asihene, PhD
Estab 1869; dept estab 1964; pvt; D; SC 8, LC 8; enrl D 300, non-maj 242, maj 32
Ent Req: HS dipl
Degrees: BA(Art) and BA(Art Educ) 4 yrs, Honors Program
Tuition: Res—undergrad $3940 yr; nonres—undergrad $2080 yr; campus res—$1450
Courses: Art Education, Art History, Drawing, Painting, Photography, Printmaking, Sculpture, Design

EMORY UNIVERSITY, Art History Dept, 30322. Tel 404-329-6282. *Chmn & Prof* John Howett, PhD; *Prof* William R Crelly, PhD; *Prof* Thomas W Lyman, PhD; *Assoc Prof* Clark V Poling, PhD; *Asst Prof* Dorinda Evans, PhD; *Asst Prof* Bonna Westcoat, PhD; *Asst Prof* Jontyle Robinson, PhD; *Lecturer* William Archie Brown, MFA; *Lecturer* Mollie Michala, MFA; *Lecturer* Eycke Strickland; *Lecturer* Monique Seefried, PhD
Estab 1847; pvt; D; scholarships; SC 4, LC 29, GC 18; enrl non-maj 600, maj 26, grad 40
Ent Req: HS dipl, ent exam, SAT
Degrees: MA(Art History) and PhD through Institute of Liberal Arts
Tuition: $6850 per yr; campus residency available
Courses: †Art History, Ceramics, Drawing, Film, †History of Art & Archaeology, Photography, Video
Summer School: Enrl 15; tuition $2569 for term of 6 wks beginning June 15.
Courses—Seminars in Europe (variable) 10 cr hrs

GEORGIA INSTITUTE OF TECHNOLOGY, College of Architecture, 225 North Avenue NW, 30332. Tel 404-894-3880. *Dean* William L Fash, MA
Estab 1885, dept estab 1908; pub; D; schol; SC 41; enrl D 904, maj 904, grad 165
Ent Req: HS dipl, CEEB
Degrees: BS(Architecture), BS(Industrial Design) and BS(Building Construction) 4 yr, M(Architecture) and MCP 2 yr
Tuition: Res—$285; nonres—$981
Courses: Architecture, Industrial Design, Building Construction, City Planning
Summer School: Dir, Alan Balfour. Enrl 100; tuition same. Courses—vary

GEORGIA STATE UNIVERSITY, Dept of Art, 33 Gilmer St SE, 30303. Tel 404-658-2257. *Head Dept* Larry Walker. Instrs: FT 25, PT 4
Estab 1914; pub; schol; SC 80, LC 16; enrl maj 360, others 20
Ent Req: HS dipl, ent exam, college board, interview
Degrees: BVA, AB(Art) and BA(Art History) 4 yrs, MA(Art History), MVA
Courses: Advertising Design, Art History, Ceramics, Drawing, Graphic Arts, Graphic Design, Handicrafts, Illustration, Interior Design, Jewelry, Lettering, Painting, Sculpture, Teacher Training, Textile Design, Metalwork, Weaving
Summer School: Dir, Larry Walker. Enrl 450; term of 9 wks beginning June

AUGUSTA

AUGUSTA COLLEGE, Dept of Fine Arts, 2500 Walton Way, 30904. Tel 404-737-1453. *Head Dept* Alan Drake; *Assoc Prof* Jack King, MFA; *Assoc Prof* Eugenia Comer; *Asst Prof* Janice Williams, MFA; *Asst Prof* Steven Greenquist, MFA
Estab 1925, dept estab 1965; pub; D & E; scholarships; SC 46, LC 4, GC 1; enrl D 150, E 30, non-maj 10, maj 140, GS 5

Ent Req: HS dipl, SAT
Degrees: AA, BA & BFA
Tuition: Res—undergrad $247 per quarter, $21 per quarter hr; nonres—undergrad $742 per quarter, $62 per quarter hr; no campus res
Courses: †Art Education, Art History, †Ceramics, †Drawing, †Photography, †Mixed Media, †Painting, †Printmaking, †Sculpture
Adult Hobby Classes: Enrl 25; tuition $30-$60 per 10 sessions. Courses—Painting

BARNESVILLE

GORDON JUNIOR COLLEGE, Art Dept,* College Dr, 30204. Tel 404-358-1700
Scholarships offered
Degrees: AA
Tuition: Res—$187 per quarter; nonres—$562 per quarter
Courses: Art Appreciation, Ceramics, Design, Drawing, Painting, Printmaking

CARROLLTON

WEST GEORGIA COLLEGE, Art Dept, 30017. Tel 404-834-1235. *Chmn* Bruce Bobick
Estab 1975; pub; D; schol; SC 24, LC 10, GC 1; enrl maj 124
Ent Req: HS dipl, ent exam
Degrees: AB(Studio, Art Educ) 4 yr
Tuition: Res—$966 per yr, PT $21 per quarter hr; nonres—$817 per quarter, PT $62 per quarter hr; campus res—$222 - $237 per quarter
Courses: †Art Education, Art History, Ceramics, Graphic Arts, Graphic Design, Painting, Photography, Sculpture, Textile Design, Art Appreciation, Weaving
Children's Classes: Enrl 10-20; Sat school. Creative studio experiences in fine arts & crafts
Summer School: Courses—Art Education, Art History, Ceramics, Design, Drawing, Graphics Painting, Sculpture

CLEVELAND

TRUETT-MCCONNELL COLLEGE, Arts Dept,* 30528. Tel 404-865-5688.
Faculty B Caldwell, MA
Estab 1946; den; D & E; SC 10, LC 2; enrl D 700, non-maj 98, maj 15
Ent Req: HS dipl, SAT
Degrees: AA and AS 2 yr
Tuition: $670 per quarter
Courses: Aesthetics, Art History, Ceramics, Drawing, Graphic Design, Handicrafts, Painting, Sculpture, Three Dimensional Design
Children's Classes: Enrl 21; tuition $20. Courses—Children's Art

COCHRAN

MIDDLE GEORGIA COLLEGE, Dept of Art, 31014. Tel 912-934-6221, Ext 288.
Instrs: FT 2
Estab as Junior College Unit of University of Georgia; Pub; D & E; SC 6; enrl D 270, E 45
Ent Req: HS dipl, GED
Degrees: AA 2 yr
Tuition: $163 per quarter; campus res—$225 to $325 per quarter; board (5 day) $275, (7 day) $300 per quarter
Courses: Art Education, Commercial Art, Drawing, Handicrafts, Lettering, Painting

COLUMBUS

COLUMBUS COLLEGE, Dept of Art Fine Arts Hall, Algonquin Dr, 31993. Tel 404-568-2047. *Chair* Dr Donna L Maddox
Estab 1949; pub; D & E; scholarships; SC 30, LC 7, GC 28; enrl D 300, E 50, maj 130, grad 20
Ent Req: HS dipl, ent exam
Degrees: BS (Art Educ), BA (Art) and MEd (Art Educ) 4 yr
Courses: Fibers
Adult Hobby Classes: Enrl 200. Courses—various subjects
Children's Classes: Enrl 200. Courses—various subjects
Summer School: Enrl 200; term of one quarter. Courses—various

DAHLONEGA

NORTH GEORGIA COLLEGE, Fine Arts Dept, 30533. Tel 404-864-3391. *Chmn* Robert L Owens
Scholarships
Degrees: BA, BS, MEd
Courses: Art Appreciation, †Art Education, Art History, Calligraphy, †Ceramics, Design, Drawing, Handicrafts, †Painting, Photography, †Printmaking, Sculpture, †Textile Design, †Weaving
Adult Hobby Classes: Enrl 15; tuition varies. Courses—Drawing, Pottery, Weaving
Children's Classes: Enrl 20; tuition varies. Courses—Art Education
Summer School: Dir, Robert L Owens. Enrl 15; tuition varies. Courses—Pottery

DECATUR

AGNES SCOTT COLLEGE, Dept of Art, East College Ave, 30030. Tel 404-373-2571. *Chmn* Marie Huper Pepe, PhD; *Assoc Prof* Leland Steven, MFA; *Asst Prof* Terry McGehee, MFA; *Instr* Anthony J Bucek, MFA
Estab 1889; pvt; D; scholarships; SC 13, LC 15; enrl non-maj 200, maj 23
Degrees: BA 4 yr
Tuition: Res—undergrad $5500 yr; nonres—undergrad $5500 yr; room & board $2250 per yr
Courses: Aesthetics, Art History, Ceramics, Drawing, Graphic Arts, History of Art & Archaeology, Painting, Printmaking, History of Architecture

DEMOREST

PIEDMONT COLLEGE, Art Dept, 30535. Tel 404-778-8033. *Dept Head* Dianne Mize
Scholarships offered
Degrees: BA
Tuition: $189 per cr
Courses: Art Appreciation, Art Education, Art History, Ceramics, Design, Drawing, Handicrafts, Jewelry, Painting, Photography, Printmaking

DOUGLAS

SOUTH GEORGIA COLLEGE, Art Dept,* 31533. Tel 912-384-1100
Scholarships offered
Degrees: AA
Tuition: Res—$163 per quarter; nonres—$489 per quarter
Courses: Art Appreciation, Art Education, Art History, Ceramics, Design, Drawing, Handicrafts, Photography, Printmaking

FORSYTH

TIFT COLLEGE, Dept of Art, 31029. Tel 912-994-6689. *Assoc Prof* Alan Parker, MFA
Estab 1849, dept estab 1976; den, D - W, E & off campus - M & W; D & E; scholarships; SC 6, LC 3; enrl D 5, non-maj 50, maj 10, others 1
Ent Req: HS dipl, SAT
Degrees: BA and BS 4 yr
Tuition: Res—undergrad $1455 yr; nonres—undergrad $2835 yr; campus res—room and board $1440
Courses: Art History, †Drawing, †Illustration, †Painting, Photography, Printmaking, Teacher Training, Advertising, Art Survey, †Design

GAINESVILLE

BRENAU COLLEGE, Art Dept, 204 Boulevard, 30501. Tel 404-534-6240, Ext 6242. *Dir* Mary Jane Taylor, MAEd
Estab 1878; pvt; D & E; Schol; enrl maj 45
Ent Req: HS dipl
Degrees: BA & BS 4 yrs
Courses: Advertising Design, †Art Education, Art History, Ceramics, †Commercial Art, Drawing, Graphic Design, †Handicrafts, †Interior Design, Jewelry, Lettering, Painting, Photography, Printmaking, Sculpture, Textile Design, Silkscreen, †Studio, Quilting

LA GRANGE

LA GRANGE COLLEGE, Lamar Dudd Art Center, 30240. Tel 404-882-1040. *Head Dept* John D Lawrence. Instrs: FT 3, PT 1
Estab 1831; pvt; D & E; scholarships; SC 11, LC 2; enrl maj 40
Ent Req: HS dipl, ent exam
Degrees: BA 4 yr
Tuition: $855 per qtr
Courses: Art Education, Art History, Ceramics, Commercial Art, Drawing, Painting, Photography, Printmaking, Sculpture, Textile Design, Art History Survey, Batik, Weaving
Summer School: Dir, Luke Gill. Enrl 200; tuition $250 per course. Courses—Art History, Ceramics, Drawing, Photography

MACON

MERCER UNIVERSITY, Art Dept, 1400 Coleman Ave, 31207. Tel 912-744-2591. *Chmn* Marshall Daugherty. Instrs: FT 4
Estab 1945; den; D; SC 9, LC 7, GC 2; enrl maj 25
Ent Req: HS dipl
Degrees: BA 4 yr
Tuition: $4530 per yr; campus res—room and board $2196
Courses: Art Education, Art History, Ceramics, Drawing, Graphic Arts, Sculpture
Adult Hobby Classes: Chmn, Marshall Daugherty. Evening classes
Summer School: Dir, JoAnna Watson. 2 terms, 5 wks each beginning June 15. Courses—Ceramics, Crafts, Drawing, Painting, Photography, Sculpture

WESLEYAN COLLEGE, Art Dept, Forsyth Rd, 31201. Tel 912-477-1110. *Head of Dept* Anthony Rice, MFA; *Asst Prof* Scott Duce, MFA; *Asst Prof* Art Werger, MFA
Estab 1836; den; D & E; schol; SC 38, LC 10; enrl D 159, non-maj 13, maj 45, others 12
Ent Req: HS dipl, SAT, GPA
Degrees: BFA 4 yrs
Tuition: $3600 per yr, $50 per course; $5520 per yr incl room & board
Courses: †Advertising Design, Aesthetics, Art History, †Art Education, Calligraphy, †Ceramics, †Commercial Art, †Drawing, Graphic Arts, †Graphic Design, History of Art & Archaeology, Illustration, Jewelry, Lettering, †Painting, Photography, †Printmaking, †Sculpture, Stage Design, Teacher Training, Theatre Arts
Summer School: Dir, Dr Karyon McMinn. Courses—Art Appreciation, Cartooning, Ceramics, Graphic Design, Illustration, Printmaking, Watercolour

MILLEDGEVILLE

GEORGIA COLLEGE, Art Dept, 31061. Tel 912-453-4444. *Chmn* George H Gaines
Scholarships
Courses: Art Appreciation, Art Education, Art History, Ceramics, Design, Drawing, Handicrafts, Jewelry, Printmaking, Sculpture, Textile Design, Weaving, Watercolor
Adult Hobby Classes: Courses offered
Summer School: Courses offered

MOUNT BERRY

BERRY COLLEGE, Art Dept, 30149. Tel 404-232-5374, Ext 2219. *Chmn* T J Mew, PhD; *Asst Prof* Jere Lykins, MEd
Estab 1902, dept estab 1942; pvt; D & E; scholarships; SC 24, LC 9; enrl D 122, non-maj 38, maj 84, others 7
Ent Req: HS dipl, SAT, CEEB, ACT
Degrees: BA, BS 4 yrs
Tuition: Res—undergrad $3150 yr; nonres—undergrad $3630 yr; campus residency available
Courses: Aesthetics, Art Education, Art History, Calligraphy, †Ceramics, Collages, Conceptual Art, Constructions, Drawing, Film, Graphic Arts, Handicrafts, †History of Art & Archaeology, Printmaking, Sculpture, Teacher Training, Video, Weaving, Sculpture, Teacher Training, Video, Ecological Art
Summer School: Dir, Dr T J Mew. Courses—Same as above

MOUNT VERNON

BREWTON-PARKER COLLEGE, Visual Arts, Hwy 280, 30445. Tel 912-583-2241, Ext 44. *Visual Arts Dir* Steve Coffey, MEd
Estab 1906, dept re-estab 1976; pvt, den; D & E; SC 10, LC 4; enrl in dept D 19, non-maj 4, maj 15
Ent Req: HS dipl
Degrees: AA(Visual Arts) 2 yrs
Tuition: $1900 per yr, $633 per quarter, $40 per hr; campus res—room $235 per quarter & board $185 per quarter
Courses: Art History, Drawing, Painting, Photography, Printmaking, Printmaking, Sculpture, Art Media & Theory, 2-D & 3-D Design
Adult Hobby Classes: Same courses as above, on and off campus classes
Summer School: Same courses as above

ROME

SHORTER COLLEGE, Art Dept,* Shorter Ave, 30161. Tel 404-291-2121. *Prof* Ralph Cook; *Asst Prof* George M Hayes, MFA
Estab 1873, dept estab 1900; den; D; schol; SC 5; enrl D 140, non-maj 115, maj 25
Ent Req: HS dipl
Degrees: AB(Art) and BS(Art Ed) 4 yr
Tuition: $2950
Courses: †Art Education, Art History, Ceramics, Commercial Art, Drawing, Handicrafts, Painting, Photography, Sculpture, Teacher Training, Textile Design, Enameling

SAVANNAH

ARMSTRONG STATE COLLEGE, Fine Arts Dept, 11935 Abercorn St, 31406. Tel 912-927-5275. *Chmn* Dr Stephen Brandon
Tuition: Res—$282 per quarter; nonres—$777 per quarter
Courses: Art Appreciation, Art Education, Art History, Ceramics, Design, Drawing, Handicrafts, Painting, Photography, Printmaking, Sculpture, Weaving
Adult Hobby Classes: Courses—Ceramics, Painting, Watercolors

SAVANNAH STATE COLLEGE, Dept of Fine Arts, Box 20059, 31404. Tel 912-356-2208. *Fine Arts Coordr* Dr R L Stevenson, PhD; *Asst Prof* Farnese Lumpkin, MA; *Asst Prof* Clara Aquero, MA
Estab 1880s, dept estab 1950s; pub; D; SC 13, LC 3
Ent Req: HS dipl
Tuition: Res $540, nonres $238; campus residence available
Summer School: Dir, Dr Luetta Milledge. Enrl 60; tuition $180. Courses—on demand

STATESBORO

GEORGIA SOUTHERN COLLEGE, Dept of Art, 30458. *Head Dept* Richard Tichich, MFA; *Prof* Stephen Bayless, EdD; *Prof* Henry Iler, MFA; *Prof* Joseph Olson Jr, EdD; *Assoc Prof* Bernard Solomon, MFA; *Asst Prof* Diane Massey, MFA; *Asst Prof* Thomas Steadman, MFA; *Asst Prof* David Posner, MFA; *Instr* Gary Bodenhousen, MFA
Pub; D & E
Ent Req: HS dipl
Degrees: AB and BSEd 4 yr
Tuition: Res—undergrad $145 per quarter; nonres—undergrad $383 per quarter; campus res—room and board $885
Courses: Art Education, Art History, Ceramics, Commercial Art, Constructions, Drawing, Graphic Arts, Graphic Design, Lettering, Mixed Media, Painting, Photography, Printmaking, Sculpture, Teacher Training
Adult Hobby Classes: Enrl 40; tuition $35 per 10 wks. Courses—Painting, Photography
Children's Classes: Offered in Laboratory School & Sat Program

THOMASVILLE

THOMAS COUNTY COMMUNITY COLLEGE, Humanities Division,* 31792.
Tel 912-226-1621. *Division Chmn* Peter Johnston, MEd
Scholarships offered
Degrees: AA
Tuition: $35 per quarter cr hr
Courses: Architecture, Art Appreciation, Art Education, Art History, Drawing,
Painting

TIFTON

ABRAHAM BALDWIN AGRICULTURAL COLLEGE, Art & Humanities Dept,
ABAC Sta, 31793. Tel 912-386-3236
Degrees: Certificate
Courses: Art Appreciation, Art History, Design, Drawing, Painting

VALDOSTA

VALDOSTA STATE COLLEGE, Dept of Art, Patterson St, 31601. Tel 912-333-
5835. *Head Dept* R G McRae. Instrs: FT 7
Estab 1911; pub; D; Scholarships; SC 25, LC 10, GC 9; enrl 400, maj 90, total 5900
Ent Req: SAT
Degrees: AB, BFA and BFA(Art Ed) 4 yr
Tuition: Res—$315 or more per quarter, $21 per hr; nonres—$810 12 hrs or more,
$62 per hr; plus other fees
Courses: Advertising Design, Art Education, Art History, Ceramics, Commercial
Art, Drawing, Graphic Arts, Graphic Design, Illustration, Painting, Photography,
Sculpture, Teacher Training, Museum Tour, Weaving
Adult Hobby Classes: Enrl 60; tuition $15 - $20 per 6 wks. Courses—Painting,
Basket Weaving
Children's Classes: Enrl 120; tuition $15 - $30 per cr for 1 - 6 wks.
Courses—Drawing, Painting, Macrame
Summer School: Dir, R G McRae. Enrl 45; tuition $105 per 4 - 6 wks.
Courses—Advertising Layout, Teacher Education, Enjoyment of Art

YOUNG HARRIS

YOUNG HARRIS COLLEGE, Dept of Art, 30582. Tel 404-379-3112. *Chmn*
Richard Aunspaugh; *Instructor* Marcia Langham. Instrs: FT 2
Estab 1886; den; D; schol; SC 6, LC 4; enrl D 500, maj 30
Ent Req: HS dipl
Degrees: AFA 2 yr
Tuition: $2000 per yr
Courses: †Art History, †Drawing, †Painting, †Sculpture, Design

HAWAII

HONOLULU

HONOLULU ACADEMY OF ARTS, Studio Program,* 900 S Beretania St, 96814.
Tel 808-538-3693. *Cur* Joseph Feher. Instrs: FT 3, PT 1
Estab 1946; pvt
Ent Req: 16 yrs of age with talent
Courses: Drawing, Painting, Printmaking, Etching, Lithography

HONOLULU COMMUNITY COLLEGE,* 874 Dillingham Blvd, 96817. Tel 808-
845-9211. *Dept Head* Kit Kowalke, MFA; *Instr Commercial Art* Jerome Hock; *Instr
Commercial Art* Michael Kaiser; *Instr Graphic Arts* Romolo Valencia, BA
College maintains three art departments: Commercial Art, Art & Graphic Arts; pub;
D & E; SC 20, LC 2; enrl D 150 majors
Ent Req: 18 yrs of age, English & math requirements, motivation, interest in
learning, willingness to work
Degrees: AS 2 yr
Tuition: Res—$80 fee plus $12 per cr hr; nonres—$650 fee plus $12 per cr hr
Courses: Advertising Design, Commercial Art, Drafting, Drawing, Graphic Arts,
Graphic Design, Illustration, Lettering, Painting, Photography, Printmaking, Textile
Design

KAPIOLANI COMMUNITY COLLEGE, Diamond Head Campus, 4303 Diamond
Head Rd, 96816. Tel 808-735-3511. Instrs: FT 2, PT 3
Estab 1965; pub; D & E; scholarships; SC 11, LC 5; enrl D 4800, E 500
Ent Req: Ent exam
Degrees: AA and AS 1-2 yr
Tuition: No campus res
Courses: Art History, Ceramics, Design, Drawing, Painting, Photography, Textile
Design, Art Appreciation, Light and Color, Perception, Screen Printing Crafts, 3-D
Design, Visual Arts
Adult Hobby Classes: Enrl 25 per class; tuition depends on number of units.
Courses—Drawing, Intro to Visual Arts; Painting
Summer School: Enrl 700; tuition depends on number of units taken for term of 6
wks. Courses—vary each summer

UNIVERSITY OF HAWAII AT MANOA, Dept of Art, 2535 The Mall, 96822.
Tel 808-948-8251. *Chmn* John Wisnosky, MFA. Instrs: FT 30, PT 30
Estab 1907; pub; D & E; schol; SC 64, LC 34; enrl maj 600, grad 60
Ent Req: HS dipl or GED and SAT or ACT
Degrees: BA(Art History), BA(Studio) and BFA 4 yr
Tuition: Res—undergrad $325 per sem, $28 per cr hr; grad $390 sem, $33 per cr hr;
nonres—undergrad $1045 per sem, $88 per cr hr; grad $1260 per sem, $105 per cr

hr; plus fees; campus res available
Courses: Art History, Ceramics, Drawing, Graphic Arts, Graphic Design, Painting,
Photography, Printmaking, Sculpture, Fiber, Screen Printing
Adult Hobby Classes: Evenings only. Courses—Chinese Brush Painting, Drawing,
Painting, Sculpture
Summer School: Head, Dean Robert Sakai, PhD. Tuition res $50 per cr hr, nonres
$100 per cr hr, plus fees. Courses—Art History (Western and Pacific), Ceramics,
Drawing, Design, Painting, Printmaking, Sculpture

KAHULUI

MAUI COMMUNITY COLLEGE, Art Dept,* 310 Kaahumanu Ave, 96732. Tel
808-244-9181. *Chmn* Barbara Miller. Instrs: FT 1, PT 3
Estab 1967; pub; D & E; schol; SC 8, LC 2; enrl D 1400, E 400
Ent Req: Ent exam
Degrees: AS 2 yr
Tuition: Res—$80; nonres—$650
Courses: Advertising Design, Architecture, Ceramics, Display, Drawing, Graphic
Arts, Graphic Design, History of Art & Archaeology, Jewelry, Painting,
Photography, Sculpture, Textile Design, Batik, Copper Enameling, History of
Architecture, Welding, Weaving
Adult Hobby Classes: Enrl 60; tuition $10.50-$45. Courses—Batik, Jewelry, Silk
Screen
Summer School: Enrl 40; term of 6 wk beginning June. Courses—Introduction to
the Visual Arts

LAIE

BRIGHAM YOUNG UNIVERSITY, HAWAII CAMPUS, Division of Fine Arts,
55 220 Kulanui, 96762. Tel 808-293-3211. *Chmn* A La Moyne Garside
Scholarships
Degrees: BA
Tuition: $575 per sem
Courses: †Ceramics, Illustration, †Painting, †Printmaking, †Sculpture, Polynesian
Handicrafts
Adult Hobby Classes: Tuition $30. Courses—Batik, Ceramics, Silkscreening
Children's Classes: Tuition $30. Courses—Ceramics, Drawing
Summer School: Dir, V Napua Tengaio. Tuition $60 per cr, 2 four wk blocks.
Courses—Ceramics, Polynesian Handicrafts

LIHUE

KAUAI COMMUNITY COLLEGE, Dept of Art,* RR 1, Box 216, 96766. Tel 808-
245-8311. *Faculty* Wayne A Miyata, MFA; *Faculty* Waihang Lai, MA. Instrs: FT 2,
PT 1
Estab 1965; pub; D & E; schol; SC 6, LC 2; enrl D 965, E 468
Ent Req: HS dipl
Degrees: AA and AS 2 yr
Tuition: Res—$7 per cr hr; nonres—$55 per cr hr
Courses: Ceramics, Drafting, Drawing, Graphic Arts, History of Art & Archaeology,
Painting, Photography, Oriental Brush Painting, Watercolor
Summer School: Term of 6 wk beginning June and July. Courses—Ceramics,
Photography

PEARL CITY

LEEWARD COMMUNITY COLLEGE, Arts and Humanities Division,* 96-045
Ala Ike, 96782. Tel 808-455-0350. *Instr* Douglas Kaya
Estab 1968; pub; D & E; schol; SC 11, LC 3; enrl D 400, E 100
Ent Req: Over 18 yrs of age
Degrees: AA and AS 2 yrs
Tuition: Res—$7 per cr hr; nonres—$55 per cr hr
Courses: Art History, Ceramics, Costume Design & Construction, Drawing, Graphic
Arts, Painting, Photography, Printmaking, Sculpture, Theatre Arts, Aspects of Asian
Art, Two Dimensional Design, Three Dimensional Design
Summer School: Enrl 100; Term of 7 wks beginning June 12th. Courses—vary

IDAHO

BOISE

BOISE STATE UNIVERSITY, Art Dept, 1910 University Blvd, 83725. Tel 208-
385-1011. *Chmn* Louis A Peck
Estab 1932; pub; D & E; scholarships; SC 51, LC 8, GC 4; enrl D 2539, maj 441,
GS 14
Ent Req: HS dipl
Degrees: BA, BFA, BA(Educ), BFA(Educ), BA(Advertising Design) and
BFA(Advertising Design) 4 yr
Courses: Metal

COEUR D'ALENE

NORTH IDAHO COLLEGE, Art Dept,* 1000 W Garden Ave, 83814. Tel 208-
667-7422. *Faculty* Lisa Daboll, MA
Tuition: Res—$584 per yr; nonres—$1292 per yr
Courses: Advertising Design, Art Education, Art History, Calligraphy, Ceramics,
Design, Drawing, Fashion Arts, Fashion Arts, Illustration, Interior Design, Painting,
Photography, Printmaking, Stage Design, Weaving, Animation, Cartooning

LEWISTON

LEWIS-CLARK STATE COLLEGE, Art Dept, 83501. Tel 208-746-2341.
Discipline Coordr Robert Almquist, MFA. Instrs: FT 1
Estab 1893; pub; D & E; schol; SC 10, LC 1; enrl D 89, E 43
Ent Req: HS dipl or GED, ACT
Degrees: BA and BS 4 yrs
Tuition: Res—undergrad $600 per yr; nonres—undergrad $2300 per yr; PT (up to 7 cr) $40 per cr; campus res—room and board $1870 double room, $2070 single room
Courses: Art Education, Drawing, Graphic Arts, Painting, Stage Design, Teacher Training, Theatre Arts, Video, Composition, Independent Study, Watercolor
Adult Hobby Classes: Discipline Coordr, Robert Almquist, MFA

MOSCOW

UNIVERSITY OF IDAHO, College of Art & Architecture, 83843. Tel 208-885-6111. *Dept Chmn* Frank A Cronk; *Prof* George T Wray
Estab 1923; pub; D & E; scholarships; SC 30, LC 6, GC 8; enrl D 450 (Art and Architecture), non-maj 345 (Architecture), maj 85 (Art), GS 18 (Art)
Ent Req: HS dipl
Degrees: BA, BS, BFA, MFA, MA, MAT
Tuition: Campus res available
Summer School: Dir, Frank Cronk. Enrl 40; tuition $43 per cr hr per 8 wks.
Courses—vary

NAMPA

NORTHWEST NAZARENE COLLEGE, Art Dept, Holly at Dewey, 83651. Tel 208-467-8412. *Art Head* Dr Mary Shaffer. Instrs: FT 3
Den; D & E; schol; SC 12, LC 5; enrl D 200, E 40, maj 24
Ent Req: HS dipl
Degrees: AA and AB 4 yrs
Courses: Advertising Design, Art Education, Ceramics, Commercial Art, Drafting, Drawing, Graphic Arts, History of Art & Archaeology, Illustration, Lettering, Painting, Sculpture, Teacher Training, Crafts for Teachers
Adult Hobby Classes: Crafts
Summer School: Courses—Art Education

POCATELLO

IDAHO STATE UNIVERSITY, Dept of Art,* 741 South Seventh Ave, PO Box 8004, 83209. Tel 208-236-0211. *Head Dept* Paul L Blanton; *Faculty* Frank A Cronk, MFA; *Chmn* Nelson Curtis, MFA; *Faculty* Jas A Englehardt, BFA; *Faculty* David F Grese, MFA; *Faculty* H Lynne Hargensen, MFA; *Faculty* David L Moreland, MFA; *Faculty* George H Roberts, MS; *Faculty* George T Wray, MFA
Estab 1901; pub; D & E; SC 32, LC 6, GS 22; enrl maj 75, GS 15, total 500
Ent Req: HS dipl, GED, ACT
Degrees: BA, BFA and MFA 4 yr
Tuition: Nonres—$850 per yr; campus residence $1260 per yr
Courses: Art Education, Art History, Ceramics, Drawing, Painting, Printmaking, Sculpture, Design, Metals, Weaving
Summer School: 4 wk and 8 wk sessions

REXBURG

RICKS COLLEGE, Dept of Art, 83440. Tel 208-356-2339. *Chmn* Robert Worrell
Estab 1888; pvt; D & E; schol; SC 23, LC 1; enrl D 123, maj 123
Ent Req: HS dipl
Degrees: AAS, AAdv Design and AFA 2 yrs
Courses: †Advertising Design, Art Education, Art History, Ceramics, †Commercial Art, †Drawing, Graphic Design, History of Art & Archaeology, Illustration, Interior Design, Lettering, †Painting, †Sculpture, Teacher Training

SUN VALLEY

SUN VALLEY CENTER FOR THE ARTS AND HUMANITIES, Dept of Fine Art, PO Box 656, 83353. Tel 208-622-9371. *Head Dept* Greer Markle
Estab 1970, dept estab 1977; den; D & E; scholarships; SC 25, LC 5, GC 5; enrl D 20, E 15, grad 5
Ent Req: Portfolio
Courses: Aesthetics, Art Education, Art History, Ceramics, Conceptual Art, Drawing, Film, Graphic Arts, Illustration, Mixed Media, Painting, Photography, Printmaking, Theatre Arts, Video
Adult Hobby Classes: Courses—Ceramics, Photography
Children's Classes: Courses—Ceramics, Photography, Theatre Arts

TWIN FALLS

COLLEGE OF SOUTHERN IDAHO, Art Dept, PO Box 1238, 83301. Tel 208-733-9554, Ext 260. *Chmn* LaVar Steel, MS; *Assoc Prof* Michael Green, MFA; *Assoc Prof* Wes Wada
Estab 1965; pub; D & E; schol; SC 26, LC 2; enrl D 3000, E 2000, non-maj 50, maj 45
Ent Req: HS dipl, ACT
Degrees: Dipl or AA
Tuition: Res—undergrad $300 per yr, $150 per sem, $32 per sem hr; nonres—undergrad $950 per yr, $475 per sem, $32 per cr hr; campus res room and board
Courses: Art History, Ceramics, Drawing, Handicrafts, Jewelry, Lettering, Mixed Media, Painting, Photography, Sculpture, Silversmithing, Theatre Arts, Acrylic Painting, Design, Weaving, Watercolor
Adult Hobby Classes: Enrl 15 per class; tuition $40 per sem. Courses—Jewelry,

Photography, Pottery, Weaving
Children's Classes: Enrl 30 per class; tuition $20 per 10 wks. Courses—Ceramics, Drawing, Painting, Puppets
Summer School: Dir, Lavar Steel. Tuition $44 per class beginning June 5th.
Courses—Art History, Ceramics, Drawing, Painting, Photography

ILLINOIS

AURORA

AURORA COLLEGE, Art Dept,* 347 S Gladstone Ave, 60507. Tel 312-892-6431, Ext 64. *Assoc Prof* John L Rogers, MFA; *Instructor* J Cosgrove, MA; *Instructor* Stephen Lowrey, MFA; *Instructor* Brent Wall, MFA
Estab 1893, dept estab 1979; pvt; D & E; SC 12, LC 5; enrl D 80, E 40, non-maj 120, maj 8
Ent Req: HS dipl
Degrees: BA 4 yrs
Tuition: $3000 per yr, $900-$1050 per trimester; campus res $1785 per yr
Courses: Advertising Design, Aesthetics, †Art Education, †Art History, Collages, Costume Design & Construction, †Drawing, Graphic Design, History of Art & Archaeology, Intermedia, †Painting, †Printmaking, Sculpture, Stage Design, †Teacher Training, †Theatre Arts
Summer School: Tui $360 for term of 6 wks. Courses—Design, Drawing or Painting

BELLEVILLE

BELLEVILLE AREA COLLEGE, Art Dept,* 2500 Carlyle Rd, 62221. Tel 618-239-2700. *Dept Head* Vito Benivegna; *Faculty* Dan Lowery; *Faculty* Wayne Shaw; *Faculty* Dale Threlkeld
Estab 1948; pub; D & E; scholarships; SC 36, LC 9; enrl D 4000, E 3500, maj 200
Ent Req: HS dipl
Degrees: AA and AS 2 yrs

BLOOMINGTON

ILLINOIS WESLEYAN UNIVERSITY, School of Art, 61701. Tel 309-556-3077.
Dir Miles Bair, MA; *Instructor* Fred Brian, MFA; *Instructor* Anna Holcombe, MFA; *Instructor* Timothy Garvey, PhD; *Instructor* Kevin Strandberg, MFA
Estab 1855, school estab 1946; pvt; D; enrl non-maj 150, maj 60
Ent Req: HS dipl, SAT or ACT
Degrees: BA, BFA and BFA with Teaching Cert 4 yrs
Courses: Art Education, Art History, Ceramics, Conceptual Art, Drawing, Film, Graphic Arts, History of Art & Archaeology, Painting, Photography, Printmaking, Sculpture, Teacher Training

CANTON

SPOON RIVER COLLEGE, Art Dept,* 61520. Tel 309-647-4645. *Dir* Janet Gardner, PhD; *Faculty* Betty J Starasta, MA
College maintains three campuses; scholarships offered
Degrees: AA
Tuition: $14 per cr hr
Courses: Art Appreciation, Art Education, Art History, Calligraphy, Ceramics, Design, Drawing, Painting, Sculpture

CARBONDALE

SOUTHERN ILLINOIS UNIVERSITY, School of Art, 62902. Tel 618-453-4315.
Dir L Brent Kington, MFA; *Undergrad Admissions* Patricia B Covinton, PhD; *Grad Studies* Michael O Onken, MA; *Two-Dimensional Area Head* Robert Paulson, MFA; *Sculpture Area Head* Thomas Walsh, MFA; *Crafts Area Head* Bill H Boysen, MFA; *Academic Area Head* Roy E Abrahamson, EdD; *Prof* Herbert L Fink, MFA; *Prof* Milton F Sullivan, MA; *Assoc Prof* Lawrence A Bernstein, MFA; *Assoc Prof* Harris Deller, MFA; *Assoc Prof* Sylvia R Greenfield, MFA; *Assoc Prof* George Mavigliano, MFA; *Assoc Prof* Richard Mawdsley, MFA; *Assoc Prof* Edward H Shay, MFA; *Assoc Prof* James E Sullivan, MA; *Assoc Prof* Dan D Wood, MA; *Assoc Prof* M Joan Lintault, MFA; *Assoc Prof* Aldon Addington, MFA; *Asst Prof* Joel B Feldman, MFA; *Asst Prof* F Lee Littlefield, MA; *Asst Prof* Michael S Youngblood, PhD
Estab 1874; pub; D & E; scholarships; SC 100, LC 24, GS 28; enrl D 1304, E 338, non-maj 672, maj 350, grad 60, others 400
Ent Req: HS dipl, upper 50 percent of class, ACT
Degrees: BA, BFA and BS 4 yrs, MFA 3 yrs
Tuition: Res—undergrad and grad $447 per sem, $37.25 per cr hr; nonres—undergrad and grad $1341 per sem, $111.75 per cr hr; campus res available
Courses: Advertising Design, Aesthetics, †Architecture, †Art History, †Art Education, †Ceramics, †Commercial Art, Conceptual Art, Constructions, Drafting, †Drawing, Fashion Arts, †Film, †Goldsmithing, Graphic Arts, †Graphic Design, †History of Art & Archaeology, †Illustration, †Industrial Design, †Jewelry, Lettering, Mixed Media, Museum Staff Training, †Painting, †Photography, †Printmaking, †Sculpture, †Silversmithing, Stage Design, †Teacher Training, Textile Design, Art for Elementary Education, †Blacksmithing, †Fibers, †Foundry, †Glassblowing, †Weaving
Adult Hobby Classes: Courses—Drawing, Jewelry, Painting
Children's Classes: Enrl 120; tuition $10 per 6 wk term. Courses—Drawing, Painting, Ceramics, 3-D Design
Summer School: Enrl 500; tuition $37.25 per hr for term of 8 wks beginning June. Courses—selection from regular courses and two wk workshops

CARLINVILLE

BLACKBURN COLLEGE, Dept of Art,* 62626. Tel 217-854-3231. *Chmn* James M Clark, MFA; *Faculty* Peter J Slavish, MFA. Instrs: FT 2, PT 2
Estab 1949; pvt; D & E; scholarships; SC 14, LC 7; enrl maj 40
Ent Req: HS grad
Degrees: BA 4 yrs
Tuition: 1580 per sem; room & board $310
Courses: Art History, Ceramics, Drawing, Painting, Printmaking, Teacher Training, Theatre Arts

CHAMPAIGN

UNIVERSITY OF ILLINOIS, URBANA-CHAMPAIGN, College of Fine and Applied Arts, 61820. Tel 217-333-1661. *Dean* Jack H McKenzie. Instrs: FT 268, PT 150
Estab 1931; pub; D; scholarships, fels and assistantships; enrl undergrad 2003, grad 796
Ent Req: HS grad, ent exam
Degrees: Bachelors 4 yrs, masters, doctors
Tuition: Res—undergrad $1532, grad $1742; nonres—undergrad $3740, grad $4370
Adult Hobby Classes: Scheduled through University Extension
Children's Classes: Sat; summer youth classes
Summer School: courses offered
—School of Art and Design, 143 Art and Design Bldg, Fourth and Peabody Dr, 61820. Tel 217-333-0855. *Dir School* Eugene C Wicks, MFA; *In Charge Art Educ* George W Hardiman, EdD; *In Charge Art History* Jerrold Ziff, PhD; *In Charge Ceramics, Glass & Metal* Don Frith, MFA; *In Charge Graphic Design* Doyle Moore, MFA; *In Charge Industrial Design* Edward J Zagorski, MFA; *In Charge Painting* Frank Gunter, MFA; *In Charge Photography* Barbara DeGenevieve, MFA; *In Charge Printmaking* Dan Socha, MFA; *In Charge Sculpture* Frank Gallo, MFA
Estab 1867, dept estab 1877; pub; D & E; scholarships; SC 119, LC 72, GC 77; enrl maj 563, grad 137, others 15
Ent Req: HS dipl, ACT, SAT, CLEP
Degrees: BFA 4 yrs, MA 1 yr, MFA 2 yrs, EdD and PhD 5 yrs
Tuition: Res—undergrad $1314 per yr, $657 per sem, part time $443 per sem, grad $1458 per yr, $729 per sem, part time $491 per sem; nonres—undergrad $3942 per yr, $1971 per sem, part time $1329 per sem, grad $4375 per yr, $2187 per sem, part time $1473 per sem; campus res—room & board $2770 per sem
Courses: †Art Education, †Art History, †Ceramics, Drawing, Film, †Graphic Design, †History of Art & Archaeology, †Industrial Design, Jewelry, Museum Staff Training, †Painting, †Photography, †Printmaking, †Sculpture, Silversmithing, Teacher Training, †Cinematography, Glassmaking
Children's Classes: Enrl 220; tuition $30 per sem. Courses—Creative Arts for Children
Summer School: Dir, Eugene C Wicks. Courses—foundation and lower division courses with some limited offerings and independent study at upper division and graduate levels

CHARLESTON

EASTERN ILLINOIS UNIVERSITY, School of Fine Arts,* FAA 216, 61920. Tel 217-581-3410. *Dept Chmn* James K Johnson, MFA; *Dean* Vaughn Jaenike; *Prof* Bill Heyduck, DEd; *Prof* June Krutza, PhD; *Prof* Carl Shull, PhD; *Prof* Walter Sorge, DEd; *Prof* Lynn Trank, PhD; *Prof* Ben Watkins, PhD; *Prof* Garret DeRuiter, MFA; *Prof* Cary Knoop, MFA; *Prof* Carl Emmerich, DEd; *Assoc Prof* Al Moldroski, MA; *Assoc Prof* Carl Wilen, MFA; *Assoc Prof* Jerry McRoberts, PhD; *Assoc Prof* Suzan Braun, MFA; *Asst Prof* Hannah Eads, MSE; *Asst Prof* Paul Bodine, MA; *Asst Prof* Janina Darling, PhD; *Asst Prof* Terry Roller, MFA; *Asst Prof* Rod Buffington, MA; *Instr* Melinda Hegarty, MA. Instrs: FT 22, PT 6
Estab 1895, dept estab 1930; pub; D & E; scholarships; enrl 1930, non-maj 1700, maj 230, grad 20
Ent Req: HS dipl, grad - MAT or GRE
Degrees: BA 4 yrs, MA 1 yr, Specialist Educ 2 yrs
Tuition: Res—$387 per sem; nonres—$1161 per sem
Courses: Art Education, Art History, Ceramics, Drawing, Painting, Printmaking, Sculpture, Silversmithing, Design, Visual Communications, Watercolor, Weaving
Summer School: Dept Chmn, James K Johnson, MFA; intersession 3 1/2 weeks, one 5 wk session, one 8 wk session. Tui res—undergrad $319.10, $38.55 per hr, grad $337.10, $40.80 per hr; non-res—undergrad $763.10, $94.05 per hr, grad $817.10, $100.80 per hr. Courses—same as Fall and Spring semesters

CHICAGO

AMERICAN ACADEMY OF ART, 220 S State St, 60604. Tel 312-939-3883. *Dir* Irving Shapiro. Instrs: FT 16, PT 11
Estab 1923; pvt; D & E; scholarships; SC 10; enrl D 450, E 525
Ent Req: HS dipl, portfolio
Degrees: AA 2-3 yrs
Tuition: $3880 per yr; no campus res
Courses: Advertising Design, Commercial Art, Drawing, Graphic Arts, Graphic Design, Illustration, Lettering, Painting, Photography, Cartooning
Adult Hobby Classes: Enrl 420; tuition $1940 per semester, $3880 per school year. Courses—Advertising Design, Illustration, Photography, Basics of Fine Arts
Children's Classes: Enrl 20; tuition $75 for 10 Saturdays. Courses - Design & Experimental Drawing
Summer School: Dir, Irving Shapiro. Enrl 600; tuition $370 for term of 8 wks beginning June 26. Courses—general

CITY COLLEGES OF CHICAGO
—Daley College,* Art and Architecture Dept, 7500 S Pulaski Rd, 60652. Tel 312-735-3000. *Chmn Art* Nancy Lapaglia; *Chmn Architecture* Michael Rosen
Estab 1960; enrl 4700
Tuition: Undergrad—$600
Courses: Weaving

—Kennedy-King College,* Art and Humanities Dept, 6800 S Wentworth Ave, 60621. Tel 312-962-3200. *Chmn* Dr Sondra Rosenberg
Estab 1935; enrl 9010
Tuition: Undergrad—$400
Courses: Art Education, Drafting, Drawing, History of Art & Archaeology, Industrial Design, Painting, Photography, Theatre Arts, Radio-TV
—Loop College,* Art and Humanities Dept, 30 E Lake St, 60601. Tel 312-781-9430. *Chmn Humanities* James Mack
Estab 1962; enrl 5000
Tuition: Undergrad—$340
Courses: Art Education, Drafting, Drawing, History of Art & Archaeology, Industrial Design, Painting, Theatre Arts
—Malcolm X College,* Art and Humanities Dept, 1900 W Van Buren St, 60612. Tel 312-942-3000. *Asst Prof* Barbara J Hogu; *Asst Prof* Robert Witter
Estab 1911; enrl 5000
Tuition: District res—$408 per yr; state res—$735.84 per yr; nonres—$1130.16 per yr
Courses: Art Appreciation, Art Education, Art History, Ceramics, Design, Drawing, Painting, Sculpture, Theatre Arts, Photography, Radio-TV
—Olive-Harvey College,* Art and Humanities Dept, 10001 S Woodlawn Ave, 60628. Tel 312-568-3700
Estab 1957; enrl 4700
Tuition: Undergrad—$510
Courses: Art Education, Drafting, Drawing, History of Art & Archaeology, Industrial Design, Painting, Theatre Arts
—Truman College,* Art and Humanities Dept, 1145 W Wilson Ave, 60640. Tel 312-878-1700
Estab 1956; enrl 3800
Tuition: Undergrad—$510
Courses: Art Education, Ceramics, Drafting, Drawing, History of Art & Archaeology, Industrial Design, Painting, Photography, Theatre Arts
—Wright College,* Art and Humanities Dept, 3400 N Austin Ave, 60634. Tel 312-777-7900. Instrs: FT 3
Estab 1934; pub; D & E; SC 15, LC 5; enrl D 3000, E 2500
Ent Req: HS dipl
Degrees: AA 2 yrs
Tuition: Res—$23 per cr hr; nonres out of district $36.39 per cr hr; nonres out of state $50.33 per cr hr
Courses: Advertising Design, Architecture, Art Appreciation, Commercial Art, Drafting, Drawing, Graphic Design, History of Art & Archaeology, Lettering, Painting, Sculpture, Theatre Arts
Adult Hobby Classes: Enrl 3500; 6 & 8 wks courses. Courses—vary
Children's Classes: Enrl 1000; tuition $15 per class per 6 wks. Courses—vary
Summer School: Dir, E V Clements. Enrl 1500; tuition $15 per class per 8 wks. Courses—vary

COLUMBIA COLLEGE, Art Dept, 600 S Michigan Ave, 60605. Tel 312-663-1600. *Chairperson Art & Photography Depts* John Mulvany, MFA; *Coordr Graphics* Marlene Lipinski, MFA; *Coordr Interior Design* Tony Patano, BFA; *Coordr Fine Arts* Tom Taylor, BFA
Estab 1893; pvt; D & E; scholarships; SC 43, LC 17
Ent Req: HS dipl
Tuition: Non-res—undergrad $1485 per sem, $103 per cr hr; no campus res
Courses: †Advertising Design, Architecture, Art Education, Art History, Calligraphy, Ceramics, Commercial Art, Costume Design & Construction, Drafting, Drawing, Fashion Arts, Film, Goldsmithing, Graphic Arts, Graphic Design, Handicrafts, Illustration, Industrial Design, Interior Design, Jewelry, Mixed Media, Museum Staff Training, Painting, Printmaking, Sculpture, Silversmithing, Silk Screen, Typography, Weaving, Fine Arts & Professional Photography, Photojournalism
Summer School: Dir, John Mulvany

CONTEMPORARY ART WORKSHOP, 542 W Grant Place, 60614. Tel 312-525-9624. *Dir* John W Kearney, BA; *Admin Dir* Lynn Kearney, BA; *Sculpture* Paul Zakoian, MA
Estab 1950; D & E
Ent Req: No entrance requirements for classes. Studio artists are juried
Degrees: None, we offer an apprentice program in sculpture
Tuition: $80 for 10 wks
Courses: Painting, Sculpture
Adult Hobby Classes: Tuition $80 for 10 wks. Courses—Sculpture
Summer School: Summer courses—Painting, Sculpture

DEPAUL UNIVERSITY, Dept of Art, College of Liberal Arts and Sciences, 2323 N Seminary, 60614. Tel 312-321-8194. *Chmn Dept & Prof* William Conger, MFA; *Prof* Sally Kitt Chappell, PhD; *Assoc Prof* Robert Donley, MFA; *Assoc Prof* Stephen Luecking, MFA; *Asst Prof* Simone Zurawski, PhD
Estab 1897, dept estab 1965; pvt; D; SC 20, LC 12; enrl D 30 art maj
Ent Req: HS dipl, SAT or ACT
Degrees: BA(Art) 4 yrs
Tuition: All tuition fees are subject to change, contact admissions office for current fees; campus residency available
Courses: †Art History, Design, Drawing, Painting, Photography, Printmaking, Sculpture, †Studio Art
Adult Hobby Classes: Evening courses, Studio and Art History
Summer School: Chmn, William Conger

FELICIAN COLLEGE, Art Dept, 3800 W Peterson Ave, 60659. Tel 312-539-1919. *Art Dir* Sister Mary Lauriana, MFA
Estab 1953; pvt; D & E; scholarships; enrl D 167, E 240
Ent Req: HS dipl
Degrees: AA 2 yrs
Tuition: $2000 per yr, $1000 per sem
Courses: Art Education, Art History, Drawing, Mixed Media, Painting
Adult Hobby Classes: Enrl 30; tuition $55 for 15 sessions. Courses—Calligraphy, Painting
Children's Classes: Enrl 30; tuition $50 for 3 weeks. Courses—Adventures in Art
Summer School: Dir, Sister Mary Lauriana. Enrl 20; tuition $100 for 5 weeks. Courses—Design, Drawing, Painting

HARRINGTON INSTITUTE OF INTERIOR DESIGN, 410 S Michigan, 60605.
Tel 312-939-4975. *Dean* Robert C Marks
Estab 1931; pvt; D & E; enrl D 228, E 220
Ent Req: HS dipl, interview
Degrees: AA & BA(interior design)
Tuition: $4350 per yr, $2175 per sem; campus res—room & board $3000
Courses: Interior Design
Adult Hobby Classes: Enrl 220; tuition $1020 per sem. Courses—Interior Design

ILLINOIS INSTITUTE OF TECHNOLOGY
—College of Architecture, Planning and Design, Dept of Architecture, * Crown Hall
Bldg, 3300 S Federal St, 60616. Tel 312-567-3262. *Chmn Architecture* George
Schipporeit; *Dean* Arthur S Takeuchi. Instrs: FT 15
Estab 1895 as Armour Institute, consolidated with Lewis Institute of Arts and
Sciences 1940; pvt; enrl 200
Degrees: BArchit, MSArchit, MSCity and Regional Planning 5 yrs
Tuition: $6390 per yr
Courses: Architecture
Summer School: Term June 15 through August 8
—Institute of Design, 3360 S State St, 60616. Tel 312-567-3250, Ext 3250. *Chmn*
Dale E Fahnstrom. Instrs: FT 12, PT 5
Estab 1937; pvt; D; scholarships; enrl D 150
Degrees: BS(Design) 4 yrs, MS(Visual Design, Product Design, Photography)
Tuition: Res—undergrad and grad $3195 per sem
Courses: Industrial Design, Photography, Visual Communications

INSTITUTE OF LETTERING AND DESIGN, 428 S Wabash Ave, Box A-3380,
60605. Tel 312-341-1300. *Dir* Sidney Borden
Estab 1948; pvt; D & E; enrl D 49, E 30
Ent Req: HS dipl, waived if student is interviewed
Courses: Advertising Design, Calligraphy, Commercial Art, Graphic Arts, Graphic
Design, Lettering, Photography, Sign Painting, Photolithography

LOYOLA UNIVERSITY OF CHICAGO, Fine Arts Dept, 6525 N Sheridan Rd,
60626. Tel 312-274-3000, Ext 2820. *Chmn Fine Arts Dept* Mary S Lawton, PhD;
Prof Jean Unsworth, MFA; *Prof* Ralph Arnold, MFA; *Prof* Juliet Rago, MFA;
Assoc Prof Ralph Schaller, MFA; *Assoc Prof* Justine Wantz, MFA; *Asst Prof*
Roberta Kozuch; *Asst Prof* James Jensen, MFA; *Asst Prof* Timothy Standring,
MFA; *Asst Prof* Eugene Geimzer, MFA. Instrs: PT 20
Estab 1870, dept estab 1970; den; D & E; SC 25, LC 17
Degrees: BA & BS 4 yrs
Tuition: $4620 per yr, $2310 per sem, $123 per hr; campus res—room & board
$1460-$1540 per sem
Courses: Art Education, Art History, Calligraphy, Ceramics, Drawing, Jewelry,
Painting, Photography, Printmaking, Sculpture, Art Therapy, Communications
Design, Medical Illustration
Summer School: Dir, Dr Mark Wolff. Courses—Art Appreciation, Art History,
Communications Design, Ceramics, Design, Drawing, Painting, Photography

NORTHEASTERN ILLINOIS UNIVERSITY, Art Dept, St Louis at Bryn Mawr
Ave, 60625. Tel 312-583-4050, Ext 580. *Chmn* Jean Gillies
Estab 1869; pub; D & E; scholarships; SC 44, LC 22; enrl total 10,200, maj 175,
grad 1583, others 798
Ent Req: HS dipl, GED, upper half high school class or higher ACT
Degrees: BA 4 yrs
Courses: Art Education, Art History, Ceramics, Drawing, Graphic Arts, Jewelry,
Lettering, Painting, Photography, Printmaking, Sculpture, Teacher Training, Metal
Enameling

NORTH PARK COLLEGE, Art Dept, 5125 N Spaulding, 60625. Tel 312-583-
2700, Ext 296. *Chmn Dept* Neale Murray, MA; *Prof* Gayle V Bradley-Johnson,
MA; *Prof* Peter Fikaris; *Prof* Lars Sponberg
Estab 1957; den; D & E; scholarships; SC 18, LC 5; enrl D 40
Ent Req: HS dipl
Degrees: BA 4 yrs
Tuition: Res—undergrad $5190 per yr; nonres—undergrad $7953; campus res
available
Courses: Advertising Design, Aesthetics, Art Education, Art History, Calligraphy,
Ceramics, Commercial Art, Drawing, Illustration, Painting, Photography,
Printmaking, Sculpture, Teacher Training
Adult Hobby Classes: Tuition $35 per term. Courses—Calligraphy, Painting
Summer School: Enrl 25; tuition $200 course for term of 8 wks beginning June 12.
Courses—Ceramics, Drawing, Painting, Sculpture

RAY-VOGUE COLLEGE OF DESIGN, 664 N Michigan Ave, 60611. Tel 312-280-
3500. *Dir* Wade Ray; *Dept Head* Ellen Long; *Dept Head* Bernie Dennett; *Dept
Head* John Goehlich; *Dept Head* Norman Mier; *Dept Head* Robert Miller; *Dept
Head* Jeanne Radysh; *Dept Head* Cheryl Zuhn
Estab 1916; pvt; D & E; SC 7; enrl D 450, E 125
Ent Req: HS dipl, portfolio review
Degrees: Dipl 1 or 2 yr courses
Tuition: $3960 per yr, $1980 per sem; no campus res
Courses: Commercial Art, Display, Fashion Arts, Illustration, Interior Design,
Photography, Fashion Merchandising, Fashion Design
Adult Hobby Classes: Enrl 125; tuition $270 for 18 eve. Courses—Dress Design,
Interior Design, Photography
Summer School: Dir, Wade Ray. Enrl 190; tuition $760 for 10 wks beginning June
21. Courses—Commercial Art, Dress Design, Fashion Illustration, Interior Design,
Photography, Fashion Merchandising

SAINT XAVIER COLLEGE, Dept of Art, 3700 W 103rd St, 60655. Tel 312-779-
3300. *Chairperson* Gretchen Garner, MFA; *Assoc Prof* Brent Wall, MFA; *Assoc
Prof* Mary Ann Bergfeld, MFA; *Asst Prof* Jayne Hileman, MFA; *Asst Prof* Michael
Rabe, MA; *Asst Prof* Cathie Ruggie, MFA; *Instructor* Gail Sellers, MFA
Estab 1847, dept estab 1917; pvt; D & E; scholarships; SC 35, LC 15; enrl D 50, E
5, maj 55, others 250
Ent Req: HS dipl

Degrees: BA & BS 4 yrs
Tuition: $147 per cr hr; campus res—room & board $2500
Courses: Art Education, Art History, Ceramics, Drawing, Film, Graphic Design,
Illustration, Painting, Photography, Printmaking, Sculpture, Teacher Training, Video,
Art Business
Adult Hobby Classes: Enrl 15-20; tuition $20-$40 per course. Courses—Drawing,
Calligraphy, Painting, Photography
Summer School: Dir, Gretchen Garner. Enrl 20 per class; tuition $441 for term of 6
weeks beginning June 1. Courses—various studio courses

SCHOOL OF THE ART INSTITUTE OF CHICAGO, Jackson Blvd and
Columbus Dr, 60603. Tel 312-443-3700. *Pres* Neil J Hoffman; *Dean* Roger Gilmore;
Undergrad Division Chmn Martin Prekop; *Grad Division Chair* Mary McCarty; *Dir
of Admissions* Jana Wright; *Prof* Leah Bowman; *Prof* Barbara Crane; *Prof* Theodore
Halkin; *Prof* Ken Josephson; *Prof* Richard Keane; *Prof* Robert Loescher; *Prof*
Richard Loving; *Prof* Ray Martin; *Prof* Bill Farrell; *Prof* Ray Yoshida; *Prof* John
Kurtich; *Prof* Roxie Tremonto; *Prof* James Zanzi. Instrs: FT 75, PT 95
Estab 1866; pvt; D 215; E 45; scholarships; SC 240, LC 60, GC 35; enrl maj 1150,
non-maj 550
Ent Req: Portfolio; recommendations
Degrees: BFA 4 yrs, MFA 2 yrs, Grad Certificate in Art History 1 yr, Advanced
Certificate in Art Therapy 1 yr
Tuition: $5550 academic year
Courses: †Art Education, Art History, †Ceramics, †Drawing, †Film, †Painting,
†Photography, †Printmaking, †Sculpture, †Video, †Art & Technology, Art Therapy,
†Fashion Design, †Fiber, †Interior Architecture† Time Arts, †Visual
Communication, Scientific Illustration, Holography-Laser Sculpture, Computer
Graphics
Adult Hobby Classes: Enrl 500; tuition $555 per 15 wk 3 cr course.
Courses—various
Children's Classes: Tuition $125 per 14 wk sem or 6 wk summer course.
Courses—Visual Arts, Studio Courses
Summer School: Dean, Roger Gilmore. Enrl 500; tuition $555 per 8 wk 3 cr course.
Courses—Visual Art Studio Areas, Art Education, Art History, Art Therapy

UNIVERSITY OF CHICAGO, Dept of Art History and Committee on Art and
Design, 5540 S Greenwood, 60637. Tel 312-753-1234. *Chmn* Reinhold Heller, PhD
Estab 1892; pvt; D; scholarships; SC, LC and GC vary; enrl maj 11, grad 104, others
3
Ent Req: Through college of admissions
Degrees: BA 4 yrs, MA 1 yr, PhD 4-6 yrs

UNIVERSITY OF ILLINOIS AT CHICAGO, College of Architecture, Art and
Urban Planning, PO Box 4348, 60680. Tel 312-996-3351, Art & Design 996-3337.
Dean Richard R Whitaker Jr; *Dir School Architecture* Tom Beeby; *Dir School Art
& Design* Martin Hurtig; *Chmn Dept Hist of Architecture & Art* David Sokol; *Dir
School Urban Planning* George Hemmens. Instrs: FT 80, PT 28
Estab 1946; pub; D; scholarships; SC 79, LC 10, GC 3; enrl D 579, non-maj 325,
maj 579, grad 17
Ent Req: 3 units of English plus 13 additional units, rank in top one-half of HS class
for beginning freshman, transfer students 3.25 grad point average
Degrees: BA(Design), BA(Studio Arts), BA(Art Educ), BA(History of Archit and
Art), BArchi, MFA(Studio Art or Design), MArchit
Tuition: Res—undergrad freshmen & sophomores $1350 yr, juniors & seniors $1506
yr, grad $1608 yr; nonres—undergrad freshmen & sophomores $3294, juniors &
seniors $3762, grad $4068; no campus res
Courses: †Architecture, †Art Education, Ceramics, Drawing, †Film,
†Industrial Design, †Painting, †Photography, †Printmaking, †Sculpture, †Video,
†Communications Design, †Comprehensive Design, †Studio Arts, †Urban Planning
& Policy
Children's Classes: Enrl 50; tuition $5. Courses—Saturday school in connection
with art education classes
Summer School: Dir, Morris Barazani. Tuition res undergad $229, nonres undergrad
$547 for term of 8 wks beginning June

UNIVERSITY OF ILLINOIS, CHICAGO, HEALTH SCIENCE CENTER, Dept
of Biocommunication Arts, College of Associated Health Professions, Room 211,
1919 Taylor St, 60612. Tel 312-996-7337. *Head* Alice M Katz, MEd; *Assoc Prof*
Robert Parshall, BS; *Assoc Prof* William Schwarz, BS; *Assoc Prof* Alfred Teoli,
MFA; *Asst Prof* Susan Zimmerman, MEd; *Instructor* Deirdre McConathy, MA
Estab 1963; pub; D
Ent Req: Bachelors degree
Degrees: Master of Associated Medical Sciences in Biocommunication Arts
Tuition: Res—$486 per quarter; nonres—$1458 per quarter
Courses: Medical Illustration

CHICAGO HEIGHTS

PRAIRIE STATE COLLEGE, Art Dept, 197th & Halsted, 60411. Tel 312-756-
3110. *Chmn & Prof* Michael Henry. Instrs: FT 6, PT 19
Estab 1958; pub; D & E; SC 24, LC 6; enrl dept 600, maj 200
Ent Req: HS dipl, ACT
Degrees: AA 2 yrs
Tuition: $27 per cr hr, out of district $76 per cr hr, out of state $103 per cr hr
Courses: Art History, Design, Drawing, Graphic Design, Illustration, †Interior
Design, Painting, †Photography, Printmaking, Weaving, Airbrush, Computer
Graphics, Life Drawing, Materials Workshop, Package Design, Production
Processes, Sign Painting, Stained Glass, Typography, Video Graphics, Watercolor
Summer School: Dir, Michael Henry. Tuition $27 per cr hr for term of 8 wks.
Courses—Art History, Design, Drawing, Materials Workshop, Painting, Photography

DECATUR

MILLIKIN UNIVERSITY, Art Dept, 1184 W Main St, 62522. Tel 217-424-6227. *Chmn Art Dept* Marvin L Klaven, MFA. Instrs: FT 3, PT 1
Estab 1901, dept estab 1904; pvt; D & E; scholarships; SC 47, LC 3; enrl D 1500, non-maj 25, maj 40
Ent Req: HS dipl, ACT
Degrees: BA & BFA 4 yrs
Tuition: $5000 per yr; campus res—room & board $2200 yr
Courses: Art Education, Art History, Ceramics, Commercial Art, Drawing, Graphic Arts, History of Art & Archaeology, Jewelry, Mixed Media, Painting, Printmaking, Sculpture, Theatre Arts, Art Management, Art Therapy
Summer School: Dir Special Prog, William Lewis. Enrl 25; tuition $100 cr hr for term of 7 wks beginning June 13. Courses—Studio Painting, Drawing & Printmaking

DE KALB

NORTHERN ILLINOIS UNIVERSITY, Dept of Art, College of Visual and Performing Arts, 60115. Tel 815-753-1473. *Chmn Dept Art* Robert L Even, PhD; *Asst Chairperson Dept* Vesta Daniel, EdD; *Grad Coordr* Carl Hayano, MAE; *Area Coordr* Elisabeth Bond, MSEd; *Area Coordr* Robert Bornhuetter, MFA; *Area Coordr* William Brown, EdD; *Area Coordr* J Dimitri Liakos
Estab 1895; pub; D & E; scholarships; SC 140, LC 606, GC 70; enrl D 5000, maj 1000, grad 195
Ent Req: HS dipl
Degrees: BA, BFA, BSEd 4 yrs, MA, MSEd 2 yrs, MFA 3 yrs, EdD 3 yrs
Tuition: Res—$985 per yr; nonres—$3982 per yr; campus residency available
Courses: †Art Education, †Art History, †Ceramics, Commercial Art, Display, Drafting, Drawing, Film, Graphic Arts, Graphic Design, Jewelry, History of Art & Archaeology, Illustration, Intermedia, Interior Design, Lettering, Mixed Media, Museum Staff Training, Painting, Photography, Printmaking, Sculpture, Silversmithing, Stage Design, Teacher Training, Textile Design, Theatre Arts, Video, Art Therapy, Visual Communication
Summer School: Dir, Robert L Even. Tuition res $185, nonres $459. Courses—vary

DES PLAINS

OAKTON COMMUNITY COLLEGE, Art & Architecture Dept,* 1600 E Golf Rd, 60016. Tel 312-635-1600. *Prof & Discipline Coordr* Robert A Stanley, MS; *Assoc Prof* James A Krauss, MA; *Assoc Prof* Bernard K Krule, MS
Degrees: AA
Tuition: Res district—$16 per sem hr; nonres district—$55 per sem hr; nonres—$75 per sem hr
Courses: Architecture, Art Appreciation, Art History, Ceramics, Drawing, Fashion Arts, Jewelry, Painting, Photography, Printmaking, Textile Design, Weaving

EAST PEORIA

ILLINOIS CENTRAL COLLEGE, Fine Arts Dept, 61635. Tel 309-694-5113. *Chmn* Dr Kenneth Camp; *Instr* Shelby Adams, MA; *Instr* Wayne Forbes, MFA; *Instr* Fred Hentchel, MFA; *Instr* Robert Majeske, MFA; *Instr* Marlene Miller, MFA; *Instr* Peg Creasy; *Instr* Stan Adams, MA; *Instr* Norman Hines, MA
Estab 1967, dept estab 1967; pub; D & E; SC 27, LC 3; enrl D 800, E 400, maj 272
Ent Req: HS dipl
Degrees: Associate in Arts and Science 2 yrs, Associate in Applied Science
Tuition: $16 per sem hr; no campus res
Courses: †Advertising Design, Art Education, Art History, Ceramics, †Commercial Art, Drawing, †Graphic Arts, †Graphic Design, Illustration, Interior Design, Jewelry, Lettering, Painting, Photography, Printmaking, Sculpture, Color, Design
Adult Hobby Classes: Tuition $16 per cr hr. Courses—Drawing & Painting
Summer School: Chmn Fine Arts, Kenneth Camp. Tuition $16 per cr hr. Courses—Photography, Introduction to Art, Sculpture

EDWARDSVILLE

SOUTHERN ILLINOIS UNIVERSITY AT EDWARDSVILLE, Dept of Art and Design, 62026. Tel 618-692-3071. *Chmn Dept* Don F Davis, MA; *Asst Chmn Dept* Michael J Smith, MFA; *Head Art History* John A Richardson, EdD; *Head Printmaking* Robert R Malone, MFA; *Head Drawing & Painting* Dennis L Ringering; *Head Sculpture* Thomas D Gipe, MFA; *Head Fiber & Fabric* Tracy B Colby; *Head Ceramic* Daniel J Anderson; *Art Education* Joseph A Weber, PhD; *Photography & Graphic Design* Robert C Weaver, MFA
Estab 1869, dept estab 1959; pub; D & E; scholarships; SC 65, LC 26, GC 45; enrl D 325, E 75, maj 200, grad 40
Ent Req: HS dipl, ACT, portfolio req for BFA and MFA
Degrees: BA, BS and BFA 4 yrs, MFA 3 yrs, MS 2 yrs
Tuition: Res—undergrad & grad $798 per yr, $266 per quarter, $148 for 5 hrs, $261 for 6-11 hrs, $364 for 12 hrs or more; non-res for 12-up hours—undergrad & grad $2394 per yr, $896 per quarter, $326 for 5 hrs, $616 for 6-11 hrs, $896 for 12 hrs or more; campus res available
Courses: Aesthetics, †Art Education, Art History, †Ceramics, †Drawing, †Graphic Design, History of Art & Archaeology, Jewelry, Mixed Media, †Painting, Photography, †Printmaking, †Sculpture, Silversmithing, †Teacher Training, Fiber Art
Summer School: Chmn, Don F Davis. Term of 8 weeks beginning June 21. Courses—full curriculum

ELGIN

ELGIN COMMUNITY COLLEGE, Fine Arts Dept,* 1700 Spartan Dr, 60120. Tel 312-697-1000. *Chmn* Gail Shadwell
Scholarships offered
Degrees: AA
Tuition: In district—$16 per cr hr; res—$64 per cr hr; nonres—$96 per cr hr
Courses: Advertising Design, Art Appreciation, Art Education, Art History, Calligraphy, Ceramics, Design, Drawing, Jewelry, Painting, Photography, Printmaking, Sculpture

JUDSON COLLEGE

JUDSON COLLEGE, Division of Fine Arts, 1151 N State, 60120. Tel 312-695-2500. *Chmn* Jeffrey Thompson, MFA; *Vis Instr* Gail Kushnir, BFA
Pvt; D; scholarships; SC 15, LC 10; enrl D 450
Ent Req: HS dipl, ent exam, ACT, or SAT
Degrees: BA 4 yrs
Tuition: $2325 per sem; campus res—room & board $2290 per yr
Courses: Aesthetics, Art Education, Art History, Ceramics, Drawing, Graphic Arts, Graphic Design, History of Art & Archaeology, Painting, Printmaking, Stage Design, Teacher Training, Textile Design, Theatre Arts

ELMHURST

ELMHURST COLLEGE, Art Dept, 190 Prospect, 60126. Tel 312-279-4100. *Chairperson Art Dept* Sandra Jorgensen, MFA; *Assoc Prof* John Weber, MFA; *Asst Prof* Carole R Brown, MFA; *Asst Prof* Richard Paulsen, MFA. Instrs: FT 95
Estab 1871; den; D & E; scholarships; SC 13, LC 8; enrl D 1927, E 1294, maj 33
Ent Req: HS dipl, ACT or SAT
Degrees: BS, BA and BM 4 yrs
Tuition: $6300 per yr including room and board, $4040 per yr without room and board
Courses: Architecture, †Art Education, Art History, Collages, Conceptual Art, Constructions, Drawing
Summer School: Dir, Tom Fauquet. Enrl 1379; tuition $440 per course, $110 per cr hr for courses of 4, 6 & 8 weeks. Courses in selected program

EVANSTON

NORTHWESTERN UNIVERSITY, EVANSTON
—**Dept of Art,** 1859 Sheridan Rd, 60201. Tel 312-492-7346. *Chmn Art Dept* Edward F Paschke. Instrs: FT 5, PT 3
Estab 1851; pvt; assistantships; SC 15, LC 8, GC 5; enrl 300-500
Degrees: AB 4 yrs, MFA
Courses: Practice of Art, Teaching of Art
Summer School: Courses—Beginning Drawing & Painting
—**Dept of Art History,** 255 Kresge Hall, 60201. Tel 312-492-3230. *Chmn Dept* Larry Silver, PhD; *Asst Prof* Nancy Troy, PhD; *Assoc Prof* Betty Iverson Monroe, PhD; *Assoc Prof* David van Zanten, PhD; *Asst Prof* Hollis Clayson, PhD; *Asst Prof* Olan A Rand Jr, PhD; *Asst Prof* Susan Siegfried, PhD; *Asst Prof* Marcia Kupfer, PhD
Estab 1851; pvt; D; scholarships; LC 36, GC 15; enrl maj 29, grad 20
Ent Req: HS dipl, SAT or ACT
Degrees: BA 4 yrs, MA 1 yr, PhD 3 yrs
Tuition: $8895 per yr, $2965 per quarter; PT $820 per course; campus res available
Courses: Architecture, †Art History

FREEPORT

HIGHLAND COMMUNITY COLLEGE, RFD 2, Pearl City Rd, 61032. Tel 815-235-6121. *Instr* Kris Kolinski. Instrs: FT 1, PT 5
Estab 1962; pub; D & E; scholarships; SC 6, LC 1; enrl 126
Ent Req: HS dipl, ent exam
Degrees: AS, AA, ABA, AAS 2 yrs
Tuition: $18 per cr hr
Courses: Art History, Design, Drawing, Graphic Design, Painting, Printmaking, Sculpture, Art Materials & Processes, Fabrics, History of Modern Art, Introduction to Art, Pottery, Metals & Jewelry
Adult Hobby Classes: Enrl 278. Courses—Basic Drawing, Oil, Charcoal, Printmaking, Sculpture, Pottery, Handweaving & Related Crafts, Rosemaking, Macrame, Needlepoint
Children's Classes: Occasional summer workshops for high school and elementary school students
Summer School: Courses same as above

GALESBURG

KNOX COLLEGE, Dept of Art,* 61401. Tel 309-343-0112. *Chmn* Harland J Goudie, MFA; *Assoc Prof* Stephen Fineberg, PhD; *Actg Chmn & Assoc Prof* Henry Joe, MFA; *Asst Prof* Frederick Ortner, MA
Tuition: $6909 per yr
Courses: Art Education, Art History, Ceramics, Illustration, Painting, Photography

GLEN ELLYN

COLLEGE OF DUPAGE, Humanities Division, Lambert Rd at 22nd St, 60137. Tel 312-858-2800. *Instructor* Patricia Kurriger, PhD; *Instructor* Adnan Ertas, MFA; *Instructor* Pamela B Lowrie, MS-MA; *Instructor* Richard Lund, MFA; *Instructor* Willard Smith, MS; *Instructor* John A Wantz, MA
Estab 1966; pub; D & E; SC 24, LC 5
Ent Req: Completion of application
Degrees: AA(Art) & AAS(Interior Design, Fashion Design, Commercial Art) 2 yrs
Tuition: $17 per cr hr; no campus res
Courses: Aesthetics, Architecture, Art History, Ceramics, Commercial Art, Costume Design & Construction, Design, Drafting, Drawing, Fashion Arts, Graphic Arts, Illustration, Interior Design, Jewelry, Landscape Architecture, Painting, Photography, Printmaking, Sculpture, Textile Design, Theatre Arts
Children's Classes: Courses—Ceramics
Summer School: Tuition $17 per hr for term of 3, 5 or 10 wks. Courses vary

GODFREY

LEWIS AND CLARK COMMUNITY COLLEGE, Art Dept, 5800 Godfrey Rd, 62035. Tel 618-466-3411, Ext 279. *Chmn Div Communications & Humanities* Edna Hollis. Instrs: FT 2, PT 3
Estab 1970, formerly Monticello College; pub; D & E; scholarships; SC 13, LC 2; enrl D 1800, E 600, maj 40
Ent Req: HS dipl, ent exam, open door policy
Degrees: AA 2 yrs
Tuition: $17 per sem hr; no campus res
Courses: Art History, Ceramics, Drafting, Drawing, Handicrafts, Painting, Sculpture, Basic Design, Weaving
Adult Hobby Classes: Enrl 30; tuition variable. Courses—Antiques, Interior Design, Introduction to Drawing & Painting
Summer School: Enrl 15; tuition $17 per sem hr for 8 wks. Courses—Introduction to Visual Arts

GRAYSLAKE

COLLEGE OF LAKE COUNTY, Art Dept,* 19351 W Washington St, 60030. Tel 312-223-6601, Ext 377. *Chmn* Russ Hamm, MA; *Assoc Dean* Russell D Peterson
Estab 1969, dept estab 1969; pub; D & E; SC 22, LC 5; enrl D 250, E 250, non-maj 500, maj 100
Ent Req: HS dipl, SAT
Degrees: AA and AS 2 yrs
Tuition: In-district—$17.25 per sem hr; out-of-district—$56.27 per sem hr; nonres—$83.23 per sem hr
Courses: Art Education, Art History, Ceramics, Costume Design & Construction, Drafting, Drawing, Fashion Arts, Landscape Architecture, Mixed Media, Painting, Photography, Printmaking, Sculpture, Stage Design, Theatre Arts
Adult Hobby Classes: Advertising, Ceramics, Drawing, Lettering, Mixed Media, Portrait, Stained Glass
Summer School: Dir, Russ Hamm. Courses—same as above

GREENVILLE

GREENVILLE COLLEGE, Division of Language, Literature & Fine Arts,* Dept of Art, 62246. Tel 618-664-1840, Ext 311. *Chmn* Kenneth G Ryden, MFA; *Asst Prof* Guy M Chase, MFA; *Instructor* Susan I Crotchett, MA
Estab 1892, dept estab 1965; pvt; D & E; SC 16, LC 4; enrl D 135, non-maj 105, maj 30
Ent Req: HS dipl
Degrees: BA 4 yrs, BS 4 1/2 yrs
Tuition: $4026 per yr; campus res—room & board $1592 per yr
Courses: †Art Education, Art History, Calligraphy, †Ceramics, †Drawing, †Graphic Arts, †Graphic Design, Handicrafts, History of Art & Archaeology, Lettering, †Painting, Photography, †Sculpture, †Teacher Training
Summer School: Registrar, Tom Morgan. Tuition $424 or $848 for term of 8 wks beginning June. Courses—Introduction to Fine Arts

JACKSONVILLE

MACMURRAY COLLEGE, Art Dept, 447 East College, 62650. Tel 217-245-6151. *Chmn Art Dept* Larry Calhoun; *Instructor* Howard F Sidman; *Instructor* Mark Hall
Estab 1846; den; scholarships; SC 29, LC 6
Degrees: 4 yr degrees
Tuition: Res—$3160 per yr
Courses: Advertising Design, Ceramics, Drawing, Painting, Teacher Training, Printmaking, Photography, Sculpture, Offset Processes

JOLIET

COLLEGE OF SAINT FRANCIS, Creative Art Dept, Division of Humanities and Fine Arts, 500 Wilcox, 60435. Tel 815-740-3400. *Dept Head* Dr K M Kietzman
Estab 1950; pvt; D & E; SC 6, LC 3; enrl D 150, maj 25
Ent Req: HS grad, ent exam
Degrees: BA(Creative Arts with Art Specialization or Art Educ)
Children's Classes: Courses—Art in variety of media
Summer School: Term of 6 wks beginning June

JOLIET JUNIOR COLLEGE, Fine Arts Dept, 1216 Houbolt Ave, 60436. Tel 815-729-9020, Ext 297. *Chmn Dept* Jerry Lewis, MM; *Instructor* James Dugdale, MA; *Instructor* Sharlene Kassiday; *Instructor* Joe Milosevich, MFA; *Instructor* William Fabrycki, MA
Estab 1901, dept estab 1920; pub; D & E; scholarships; SC 15, LC 4; enrl D 10,000, maj 120
Ent Req: HS dipl, ent exam
Degrees: AA 2 yrs
Tuition: $18 per sem cr for res of Ill Dist 525; $52.30 per sem cr for res outside Ill Dist 525; no campus res
Courses: Art Education, Art History, Ceramics, Drawing, Interior Design, Jewelry, Painting, Silversmithing, Weaving, Two & Three Dimensional Design
Summer School: Dir, Jerry Lewis, MM. Courses—Same as winter school

KANKAKEE

OLIVET NAZARENE COLLEGE, Dept of Art, 60901. Tel 815-939-5229. *Chmn Dept* Harvey A Collins, MFA; *Asst Prof* J Paul Thompson, MA. Instrs: PT 2
Estab 1907, dept estab 1953; den; D & E; scholarships; SC 14, LC 4; enrl D 100, non-maj 80, maj 21
Ent Req: HS dipl
Degrees: BS & BA 4 yrs, MEd & MTheol 2 yrs
Tuition: $1940 per yr, $970 per sem, $81 per sem hr; campus res—room & board

Courses: †Art Education, Art History, †Ceramics, Drawing, Film, Graphic Arts, Graphic Design, Lettering, †Painting, Photography, Printmaking, Sculpture, Teacher Training, Textile Design
Summer School: Dir, Harvey A Collins. Term of 5 wks beginning June 26.
Courses—Ceramics, Introduction to Fine Arts, Painting

LAKE FOREST

BARAT COLLEGE, Dept of Art, 700 E Westleigh Rd, 60045. Tel 312-234-3000, Ext 353. *Chmn Art Dept* Irmfriede Hogan. Instrs: FT 6, PT 4
Estab 1858; den, W; D; scholarships; SC 32, LC 16; enrl maj 58
Ent Req: HS dipl, ent exam
Degrees: BA & BFA 4 yrs
Courses: Ceramics, Drawing, History of Art & Archaeology, Illustration, Painting, Photography, Printmaking, Sculpture, Theatre Arts, Fibers, Three Dimensional Design, Weaving
Summer School: Courses—Ceramics, Fibers, History of Art, Painting, Photography, Two Dimensional Design

LAKE FOREST COLLEGE, Dept of Art, Sheridan Rd, 60045. Tel 312-234-3100, Ext 324. *Chmn Dept* Alex F Mitchell, DA; *Prof* Michael Croydon, ARCA; *Prof* Franz Schulze, MFA; *Instructor* Amelia Carr, BA; *Lectr* Arthur Lazar, MFA; *Lectr* Ramona Mitchell, Staatsexamen; *Lectr* Nicholas Prokos, MFA
Estab 1857; pvt; D & E; SC 8, LC 21; enrl D 1050 (sch total), maj 38
Ent Req: HS dipl, SAT, CEEB or ACT
Degrees: BA 4 yrs
Tuition: Res—undergrad $10,112 per yr, $5167-$4945 per sem; nonres—undergrad $7710 per yr, $3920-$3790 per sem; $947.50 per course; campus res—room & board $2310 per yr
Courses: Aesthetics, Architecture, Art Education, Art History, Ceramics, Design, Drawing, Painting, Photography, Sculpture
Adult Hobby Classes: Enrl 5-15. Courses—Photography
Summer School: Dir, Carol Gayle. Enrl 200; tuition $725 per 4 sem hrs for 7 wks. Courses—Photography

LINCOLN

LINCOLN COLLEGE, Art Dept, 300 Keokuk St, 62656. Tel 217-732-3155. *Division Chair* Connie DiLillo, PhD; *Assoc Prof* David Schroder, MS; *Assoc Prof* Leola Dowling, MA; *Assoc Prof* Marty Hargett, EdD; *Asst Prof* A Y Wong, MFA
Estab 1865; pvt; D & E; scholarships; SC 35, LC 5; enrl maj 200
Ent Req: HS dipl
Degrees: AA
Tuition: $4000 per yr; campus res—$3000 per yr
Courses: Advertising Design, Art Education, Art History, Ceramics, Commercial Art, Drawing, Graphic Design, Illustration, Painting, Photography, Stage Design, Textile Design, Theatre Arts
Children's Classes: Courses offered through summer
Summer School: Dir, Dr Joe DiLillo. Courses—Art of France, Theatre of England, Introduction to Fine Arts (New York)

LISLE

ILLINOIS BENEDICTINE COLLEGE, Fine Arts Dept, 5700 College Rd, 60532. Tel 312-960-1500. *Head* Michael E Komechak, MA
Estab 1887, dept estab 1978; den; D & E; LC 5; enrl Full time 2060, grad 400
Ent Req: HS dipl, ACT, SAT
Degrees: BA, BS & BMA 4 yrs
Tuition: Res—undergrad 7050 per year; nonres—undergrad $4500 per year; campus res available
Summer School: Dir, Philip Bean, PhD

MACOMB

WESTERN ILLINOIS UNIVERSITY, College of Fine Arts,* 61455. Tel 309-298-1549. *Chmn Dept* Daniel L Kuruna, DEd; *Faculty* D E Crouch, MFA; *Faculty* P Jackson, MFA; *Faculty* F G Jones, MFA; *Faculty* T M Karlowicz, PhD; *Faculty* J Kelly, MFA; *Faculty* R B Law, EdD; *Faculty* W L Moffett, MFA; *Faculty* A G Mullin, MFA; *Faculty* J E Neumann, MFA; *Faculty* S M Parker, MFA; *Faculty* G W Potter, MFA; *Faculty* D Raizman, PhD; *Faculty* J Sanders, MFA; *Faculty* D F Scharfenberg, EdD; *Faculty* A Schindle, MFA; *Faculty* L C Schwartz, PhD; *Faculty* J Smith, MA; *Faculty* E V Solot, MFA
Estab 1900, dept estab 1968; pub; D & E; scholarships; SC 40, LC 30, GC 50; enrl maj 200
Ent Req: HS dipl
Degrees: BA 4 yrs, MA 2 yrs
Tuition: $774 per yr; campus residence available
Courses: Advertising Design, †Art Education, Art History, †Ceramics, †Commercial Art, Conceptual Art, Costume Design & Construction, Drafting, †Drawing, Fashion Arts, †Graphic Design, †Handicrafts, Illustration, Interior Design, †Jewelry, †Painting, †Printmaking, †Sculpture, Stage Design, Foundry Casting, Metal Working, Weaving
Children's Classes: Dir, R Law, EdD. High School Summer Arts Prog

MOLINE

BLACK HAWK COLLEGE, Art Dept, 6600 34th Ave, 61265. Tel 309-796-1311, Ext 233. *Chmn Dept* Philip H Johnson, MS; *Assoc Prof* Joseph Ramsauer, MFA; *Assoc Prof* William Hannan; *Assoc Prof* Jan Rorem, MFA
Estab 1962; pub; D & E; SC 17, LC 4; enrl D 300, E 100, non-maj 300, maj 50
Ent Req: HS dipl
Degrees: AA 2 yrs
Tuition: Res—undergrad $27.50 per cr hr; non-res—undergrad $71 per cr hr; outside

dist res—undergrad $45.50 per cr hr; no campus res
Courses: Advertising Design, Art History, Calligraphy, Ceramics, Drawing, Graphic Design, Jewelry, Painting, Photography, Printmaking, Sculpture, Art Appreciation
Adult Hobby Classes: Courses—Calligraphy, Drawing, Painting, Stained Glass
Summer School: Chmn, Philip H Johnson. Enrl 20; tuition $27.50 per cr hr for term of 6 wks beginning June 7. Courses—Art Appreciation, Ceramics, Photography

MONMOUTH

MONMOUTH COLLEGE, Dept of Art,* Art Center, N Ninth St, 61462. Tel 309-457-2105. *Chmn Dept* George L Waltershausen. Instrs: FT 2, PT 1
College estab 1853; pvt; D; scholarships, grants; SC 16, LC 4
Ent Req: 15 units incl English, history, social science, foreign language, mathematics & science, SAT or ACT
Degrees: BA
Tuition: $5335 per yr
Courses: Art History, Drawing, Painting, Photography, Printmaking, Sculpture, Advanced Special Topics, Contemporary Art, Independent Study, Secondary Art Methods, Senior Art Seminar, Studio A & B

NAPERVILLE

NORTH CENTRAL COLLEGE, Dept of Art, 30 N Brainard St, 60566. Tel 312-420-3429. *Chmn* Barry Skurkis, MA; *Prof Emeritus* Diane Duvigneaud, MFA; *Vis Lecturer* Bruce Feddema, MFA; *Vis Lecturer* Diane Gaskill, MS Ed; *Vis Lecturer* Helen Naumann, BA; *Vis Lecturer* Bill Vose, BA; *Vis Lecturer* Dale Wisniewski, MA; *Vis Lecturer* Robert Cosgrove, PhD; *Vis Lecturer* Paul Eshelman, MFA
Estab 1861; pvt; D & E; SC 16, LC 5; enrl non-maj 365, maj 20
Ent Req: HS dipl, SAT or ACT
Degrees: BA 4 yrs
Tuition: Res & nonres—undergrad $5112 per yr, $1704 per term, $114-$1364 part time per term; non-degree—$88-$1575 per term; campus res—room & board $2442 per yr
Courses: Art Education, Art History, Ceramics, Drawing, Jewelry, Mixed Media, Painting, Photography, Printmaking, Teacher Training, Figure Drawing
Children's Classes: Enrl 48; tuition $30 per term of 10 weeks. Courses—Art, Beginning Art
Summer School: Dir, Christine Gumm. Enrl 50; tuition $425 per course. Courses—Art History, Ceramics, Drawing, Painting

NORMAL

ILLINOIS STATE UNIVERSITY, Art Dept, Center for the Visual Arts, 61761. Tel 309-438-5621. *Chmn Art Dept* Fred V Mills, EdD. Instrs: FT 50; 6 vis profs per sem
Estab 1857; pub; D & E; scholarships; SC 50, LC 35, GC 40; enrl D 5000, E 300, non-maj 1972, maj 3076, grad 452
Ent Req: HS dipl
Degrees: BA & BS 4 yrs, BFA 5 yrs, MA, MS, MFA, EdD
Tuition: Res—undergrad & grad $548 per yr, $274 per sem, $18 per hr; nonres—undergrad $1644 per yr, $822 per sem, $45 per hr, grad $1064 per yr, $532 per sem
Courses: †Advertising Design, †Art Education, †Ceramics, †Commercial Art, Constructions, Display, †Drawing, †Film, †Goldsmithing, †Graphic Arts, †Graphic Design, †History of Art & Archaeology, Illustration, †Jewelry, Lettering, Mixed Media, Museum Staff Training, Occupational Therapy, †Painting, †Photography, †Teacher Training, †Textile Design
Summer School: Tuition res $149.75, nonres $266.25 for term of 8 wks beginning June 20

OGLESBY

ILLINOIS VALLEY COMMUNITY COLLEGE, Div of Humanities and Fine Arts,* RR No 1, 61348. Tel 815-224-2720. *Chmn* Dr John H Knight, PhD; *Instr* Jean Church, MA; *Instr* Dana Collins, MFA
Estab 1924; pub; D & E; scholarships offered; SC 14, LC 2; enrl D 120, E 44, non-maj 156, maj 8
Degrees: AA 2 yrs
Tuition: $10 per sem hr
Courses: Art Education, Art History, Ceramics, Drawing, Graphic Design, Painting, Photography, Sculpture, Weaving
Summer School: Dir, Dr John H Knight. Tuition $10 per hr

PARK FOREST SOUTH

GOVERNORS STATE UNIVERSITY, College of Arts & Science, Art Dept,* 60466. *Chmn* Warrick Carter, PhD
Scholarships offered
Degrees: BA, MA
Tuition: Res—$453; nonres—$1359
Courses: Art History, Ceramics, Drawing, Film, Handicrafts, Jewelry, Painting, Photography, Printmaking, Sculpture, Stage Design

PEORIA

BRADLEY UNIVERSITY, Division of Art, 1501 W Bradley Ave, 61625. Tel 309-676-7611, Ext 496. *Dir* Charles E Meyer. Instrs: FT 9
Pvt; scholarships; enrl maj 91, others 400
Ent Req: HS grad
Degrees: AB, BS, BFA 4 yrs, MA, MFA
Courses: †Art History, †Ceramics, †Drawing, †Graphic Design, †Jewelry, †Painting, †Photography, †Printmaking, †Sculpture, †Art Metal
Summer School: Dir, Dr Charles E Meyer. Enrl 60 - 90; tuition $118 per cr hr for courses June - Aug. Courses—Drawing, Painting, Graphic Design, Ceramics

QUINCY

QUINCY COLLEGE, Dept of Art, 62301. Tel 217-222-8020. *Chmn* Thomas Brown. Instrs: FT 3
Estab 1860, dept estab 1953; SC 21, LC 13; enrl maj 35, total enrl 1715, E 150
Ent Req: HS grad, ACT or SAT ent exam
Degrees: BA, BS & BFA 4 yrs
Tuition: $2100 per sem; campus res $440-$495 per sem
Courses: Aesthetics, Art History, Ceramics, Commercial Art, Drawing, Illustration, Jewelry, Mixed Media, Painting, Photography, Printmaking, Sculpture, Art Seminars, Modern Art, Non-Western Art, 2-D & 3-D Design, Watercolor, Weaving
Adult Hobby Classes: Tuition $360 per sem. Courses—Secondary Art Methods
Summer School: Dir, Thomas Brown. Tuition $120 per sem hr for 4 wks beginning June 9 or 4 wks beginning June 7 or July 6. Summer Seminar in Europe; Optional junior year abroad. Courses—Ceramics, Watercolors

RIVER GROVE

TRITON COLLEGE, School of Arts & Sciences, 2000 Fifth Ave, 60171. Tel 312-456-0300, Ext 467. Instrs: FT 5, PT 6
Estab 1965; pub; D & E; SC 17, LC 3; enrl D 650, E 150, maj 138, adults and non-cr courses
Ent Req: HS dipl, some adult students are admitted without HS dipl, but with test scores indicating promise
Degrees: AA 2 yrs
Tuition: No campus res
Courses: Advertising Design, Art History, Ceramics, Commercial Art, Drawing, Graphic Arts, Graphic Design, Illustration, Lettering, Painting, Printmaking, Sculpture, Theatre Arts, Recreational Arts & Crafts
Adult Hobby Classes: Enrl 550. Courses—Candle Making, Continuing Education Classes, Crafts, Drawing, Ceramics, Jewelry, Quilting, Painting, Plastics, Stained Glass, Sculpture, Theatre Arts
Summer School: Term of 8 wks beginning June. Courses—Most of above courses are offered

ROCKFORD

ROCKFORD COLLEGE, Dept of Fine Arts,* Clark Arts Center, 5050 E State St, 61101. Tel 815-226-4000. *Chmn Dept Fine Arts* Philip Dedrick, MA. Instrs: FT 4
Estab 1847, dept estab 1848; pvt; D & E; scholarships; SC 20, LC 3-4; enrl D 600, E 600, non-maj 24, maj 16
Ent Req: HS dipl, SAT or ACT
Degrees: BA, BFA and BS 4 yrs, MAT and MLS 2 yrs
Tuition: $4890 per yr
Courses: Papermaking
Summer School: Dir, Dr Curtis Moore. Courses—Art History, Fine Arts (Studio), Stage Design

ROCK VALLEY COLLEGE, Dept of Art, 3301 N Mulford Rd, 61101. Tel 815-654-4265. *Chmn* R David Gustafson, MS. Instrs: FT 2, PT 1
Estab 1964, dept estab 1965; pub; D & E; SC 10, LC 4; enrl D 158, non-maj 70, maj 27
Degrees: AA, AS & AAS 2 yrs
Courses: Art Education, Art History, Drawing, Painting, Printmaking, Color Theory, Design

ROCK ISLAND

AUGUSTANA COLLEGE, Art Dept, 61201. Tel 309-794-7234. *Chmn Dept* Mary Em Kirn. Instrs: FT 4, PT 4
Estab 1860; den; D & E; scholarships & fels; SC 8, LC 9, LabC 3; enrl 2000
Ent Req: HS grad plus exam
Degrees: 4 yr degree
Tuition: $1718 per quarter
Courses: Art Education, Art History, Ceramics, Design, Drawing, Painting, Photography, Sculpture, Fibers
Adult Hobby Classes: Tuition $30-$45 for 8 week session. Courses—Calligraphy, Drawing, Painting, Textiles
Children's Classes: Tuition $20-$30 for 8 week session. Course—Drawing, Multimedia, Painting, Sculpture
Summer School: Chmn Mary Em Kirn

SOUTH HOLLAND

THORNTON COMMUNITY COLLEGE, Art Dept, 15800 S State St, 60473. Tel 312-596-2000. *Chmn* Dr Fred L Hanzelin
Degrees: AA, AAS
Tuition: $24 per cr hr
Courses: †Advertising Design, Art Appreciation, Art History, Calligraphy, Ceramics, Design, Drawing, Illustration, Jewelry, Painting, Printmaking, Sculpture, Illustration
Summer School: Dir, Dr Fred Nanzelin. Enrl 65; tuition $24 per academic hr. Courses—Art History, Ceramics, Design, Drawing, Nature of Art

SPRINGFIELD

SANGAMON STATE UNIVERSITY, Creative Arts Program, Shepherd Rd, 62708. Tel 217-786-6790. *Asst Prof* Bob Dixon, MFA & MS; *Asst Prof* Karen Gilg, MFA; *Asst Prof* Anne Devaney, MFA
Estab 1969, dept estab 1974; pub; D & E; scholarships; SC 24, LC 10
Ent Req: 2 yrs col educ
Degrees: BA(Creative Arts) 2 yrs
Tuition: Res—$390 per sem, $33 per hr PT; nonres—undergrad $1170 per sem, $99 per hr PT; campus res
Courses: †Advertising Design, Aesthetics, †Art History, †Ceramics, Constructions, †Drawing, †Painting, †Photography, †Printmaking, †Sculpture, Theatre Arts, Video

SPRINGFIELD COLLEGE IN ILLINOIS, Dept of Art, 1500 N Fifth, 62702. Tel 217-525-1420. *Head Dept* Regina Marie Fronmuller, MA; *Instructor* Jeannie Mitchell, BA; *Instructor* John Seiz, MA; *Instructor* Terrance Farmer, BA
Estab 1929, dept estab 1968; pvt; D & E; SC 12, LC 4; enrl D 27, E 6, non-maj 11, maj 16
Ent Req: HS dipl, ACT
Degrees: AA 2 yrs
Tuition: $1425 per sem
Courses: Art History, Ceramics, Drawing, Mixed Media, Painting, Photography, Printmaking, Sculpture, Two & Three Dimensional Design, Weaving
Adult Hobby Classes: Courses—Pottery, Weaving, Drawing, Design
Children's Classes: Enrl 20; tuition $30 for 2 wks in summer. Courses—Art for Children 6-9 yrs, 10-14 yrs
Summer School: Dir, Regina Marie Fronmuller. Term of 6 wks beginning June 2 & July 14. Courses—Ceramics, Photographic Serigraphy

SUGAR GROVE

WAUBONSEE COMMUNITY COLLEGE, Fine Arts Dept, Route 47 at Harter Rd, 60554. Tel 312-466-4811. *Chairperson* Robert Gage
Estab 1967; pub; D & E; scholarships; SC 8, LC 3; enrl D approx 275, E approx 200, maj 25
Ent Req: HS dipl, open door policy for adults without HS dipl
Degrees: AA, AS and AAS 2 yrs
Tuition: $20.50 per sem hr
Courses: Art Education, Art History, Ceramics, Drawing, Jewelry, Painting, Teacher Training, Theatre Arts, Video
Adult Hobby Classes: Enrl 250; tuition $20.50 per sem hr. Courses—Ceramics, Interior Design, Oil Painting
Children's Classes: Enrl 50; tuition $30 per course. Courses—Dramatics, Experience in Art, Photography
Summer School: Asst Dean Instrs, Carol J Viola. Enrl 50; tuition $20.50 per sem hr for term of 8 wks beginning June 6. Courses—Per regular session

WHEATON

WHEATON COLLEGE, Dept of Art, 501 E Seminary, 60187. Tel 312-260-5050. *Chmn* Dr E John Walford. Instrs: FT 4, PT 1
Estab 1861; pvt; D & E; scholarships; SC 20, LC 5; enrl 2985, maj 30
Ent Req: HS dipl
Degrees: BA 4 yrs
Tuition: $2640 per sem; room and board $1330 per sem
Courses: Advertising Design, Aesthetics, Art Education, Ceramics, Drawing, Film, Graphic Arts, Graphic Design, History of Art & Archaeology, Painting, Photography, Printmaking, Sculpture, Textile Design, Video, Theory & Techniques
Summer School: Biannual travel to Europe

WINNETKA

NORTH SHORE ART LEAGUE, 620 Lincoln, 60093. Tel 312-446-2870. *Pres* Peg Spengler
Estab 1924; pvt; D & E; SC 28; enrl D 310, E 84
Tuition: 16 wks, 3 hrs a session; no campus res
Courses: Drawing, Graphic Arts, Graphic Design, Jewelry, Painting, Sculpture, Critique, Pottery, Stitchery

INDIANA

ANDERSON

ANDERSON COLLEGE, Art Dept, 1100 E Fifth & College, 46011. Tel 317-644-0951, Ext 458. *Chmn* Raymond A Freer, MFA. Instrs: FT 4, PT 4
Estab 1928; pvt; D & E; scholarships; SC 30, LC 3; enrl non-maj 15, maj 60
Ent Req: HS dipl, ent exam plus recommendation
Degrees: BA 4 yrs
Courses: Advertising Design, Art Education, †Art History, Ceramics, Commercial Art, Drawing, †Graphic Arts, Graphic Design, History of Art & Archaeology, Illustration, Jewelry, Lettering, Museum Staff Training, †Painting, †Photography, Printmaking, Sculpture, †Stage Design, Teacher Training, †Air Brush & Watercolor Painting
Summer School: Dir, Robert Smith

BLOOMINGTON

INDIANA UNIVERSITY, BLOOMINGTON, School of Fine Arts, 47405. Tel 812-335-7766. *Dir* Stephen Murray; *Prof* Robert Barnes; *Prof* Bruce Cole; *Prof* Thomas Coleman; *Prof* John Goodheart; *Prof* Louis Hawes; *Prof* William Itter; *Prof* Jerry Jacquard; *Prof* Eugene Kleinbauer; *Prof* Marvin Lowe; *Prof* Ronald Markman; *Prof* Rudy Pozzatti; *Prof* Roy Sieber; *Prof* Budd Stalnaker; *Prof* Joan Sterrenburg; *Assoc Prof* Wendy Calman; *Assoc Prof* Kent Dawalt; *Assoc Prof* Jean-Paul Darriau; *Assoc Prof* Molly Faries; *Assoc Prof* Barry Gealt; *Assoc Prof* Reginald Heron; *Assoc Prof* Patrick McNaughton; *Assoc Prof* Wolf Rudolph; *Asst Prof* L Philip Ayers; *Asst Prof* Sarah Burns; *Asst Prof* Eric Hostetter; *Asst Prof* Deborah Kahn; *Asst Prof* Janet Kennedy; *Asst Prof* Randy Long; *Asst Prof* Susan Nelson; *Asst Prof* James Reidhaar; *Asst Prof* Frances Whitehead; *Asst Prof* Jeffrey Wolin; *Lectr* Shehira Davezac; *Lectr* Mazelle Van Buskirk
Estab 1911; pub; D; scholarships; SC 55, LC 100, GC 110; enrl maj undergrad 350, grad 150 (45 Art History, 90 Studio), others 5600
Ent Req: Admis to the Univ

Degrees: AB, BFA, 4 yrs, MA, MFA, PhD
Tuition: Grad res—$1500 per yr, undergrad res—$1450 per yr; nonres—grad $4500 per yr, undergrad $4000 per yr
Courses: Art History, Ceramics, Graphic Design, Jewelry, Photography, Printmaking, Sculpture, Painting & Drawing, Printed Textiles, Woven Textiles
Summer School: Dir, Stephen Murray. Tuition res grad—$61.50 per cr hr, undergrad—$47.25 per cr hr; nonres grad—$168.50 per cr hr, undergrad $133.25 per cr hr. Courses—Art History, Drawing, Painting, Ceramics, Photography, Printmaking, Textiles, Sculpture, Graphic Design

CRAWFORDSVILLE

WABASH COLLEGE, Art Dept, 47933. Tel 317-362-1400, Ext 386. *Chmn* Gregory Huebner, MFA; *Asst Prof* Douglas Calisch, MFA
Estab 1832, dept estab 1950; pvt; D; SC 19, LC 6; enrl D 80, non-maj 80
Ent Req: HS dipl, SAT
Degrees: BA 4 yrs
Tuition: $5700 per yr, $2850 per sem; campus res—room & board $2500
Courses: Aesthetics, Art History, †Ceramics, Display, †Drawing, History of Art & Archaeology, †Painting, †Photography, Printmaking, †Sculpture, 2-D & 3-D Design

DONALDSON

ANCILLA COLLEGE, Art Dept,* Box 1, 46513. Tel 219-936-8898. *Head Dept* Sr M Angelene Bilicke, MA; *Instructor* Sr M Consilia Danyi, MFA
Estab 1936, dept estab 1965; pvt; D & E; SC 9-12, LC 2
Ent Req: HS dipl
Degrees: AA, AAA(Applied Arts) 2 yrs
Tuition: $36 per sem hr, $15 applied fee
Courses: Aesthetics, Art Appreciation, Art Education, Calligraphy, Ceramics, Design, Drawing, Graphic Design, Handicrafts, Lettering, Painting, Enameling
Children's Classes: Enrl 12; tui $40 for 6 sessions; Courses—Crafts for Childen, Drawing and Painting for Children. Classes on Saturday

EVANSVILLE

INDIANA STATE UNIVERSITY, EVANSVILLE, Art Dept,* 8600 University Blvd, 47712. Tel 812-864-8600. *Chmn* Dr James R Blevins; *Prof* James W McNaughton, MFA; *Asst Prof* Michael Aakhus, MFA; *Asst Prof* Leonard Dowhie Jr, MFA; *Asst Prof* Kathryn M Waters, MFA. Instrs: FT 5, PT 1
Estab 1969; pub; D & E; scholarships; SC 27, LC 4; enrl D 150, E 30, maj 90
Ent Req: HS dipl
Degrees: BS (Art Educ), BA (Art) 4 yrs
Tuition: Res—$36 per sem hr; nonres—$84 per sem hr
Courses: Furniture Design, Stained Glass
Adult Hobby Classes: Enrl 25. Courses—Silkscreen

UNIVERSITY OF EVANSVILLE, Art Dept, PO Box 329, 47702. Tel 812-479-2043. *Dept Head* Leslie Miley Jr, MFA; *Prof* Howard Oagley, MA; *Asst Prof* Susan Harris, MFA; *Asst Prof* William Brown, MFA; *Asst Prof* William Richmond, MFA; *Lectr* Jeff Bender, MFA; *Lectr* James Goodridge, MA
Estab 1854; pvt; D & E; scholarships; SC 22, LC 11, GC 11; enrl D 800, E 400, maj 72, grad 21
Ent Req: HS dipl
Degrees: BA(Educ), BS(Art), BFA 4 yrs, MA 1 yr
Tuition: Campus res available
Courses: Aesthetics, Art Education, Art History, Ceramics, Drawing, History of Art & Archaeology, Jewelry, Lettering, Painting, Printmaking, Sculpture, Teacher Training, Art Therapy
Summer School: Dir, Les Miley. 5 wk sessions. Courses—Painting, Ceramics, Weaving, Art Education

FORT WAYNE

INDIANA UNIVERSITY-PURDUE UNIVERSITY, Dept of Fine Arts, 1026 W Berry St, 46804. Tel 219-482-5201. *Chmn Dept* Russell L Oettel, MFA; *Prof* Noel Dusendschon, MFA; *Assoc Prof* Hector Garcia, MFA; *Assoc Prof* Donald Kruse, BS; *Assoc Prof* Leslie Motz, MFA; *Asst Prof* Nancy McCroskey; *Lectr* Dr J David McGee
Estab 1920, dept estab 1976; pub; D & E; scholarships; SC 96, LC 5; enrl non-maj 85, maj 167, others 10
Degrees: AB and BFA 4 yrs
Tuition: Res—$52 per cr hr; nonres—$98 per cr hr; no campus res
Courses: †Advertising Design, Art History, †Ceramics, †Drawing, Film, †Graphic Arts, Graphic Design, †History of Art & Archaeology, Illustration, †Jewelry, †Painting, Photography, †Printmaking, †Sculpture, Silversmithing, Weaving
Children's Classes: Enrl 150; tuition $44 for 11 wks. Courses—Ceramics, Painting, Sculpture
Summer School: Chmn, Russell L Oettel

SAINT FRANCIS COLLEGE, Art Dept, 2701 Spring St, 46808. Tel 219-432-3551, Ext 236. *Head Dept* Maurice A Papier, MS & MA; *Assoc Prof* Sufi Ahmad, MFA; *Asst Prof* Rick Cartwright, MFA; *Asst Prof* Robert Barnum, MFA; *Instr* Stephan Perfect; *Instr* Robert Johnson, MA; *Instr* Lawrence Endress, MAT; *Instr* Donald Lutz
Estab 1890; den; D & E; scholarships; SC 22, LC 6, GC 14; enrl D 105, maj 105
Ent Req: HS dipl, class rank in HS, SAT
Degrees: AA(Commercial Art) 2 yrs, BA and BS(Art or Art Educ) 4 yrs, MA(Art Educ) 1 yr
Tuition: Undergrad $104 per sem hr, grad $107 per sem hr; campus res—room & board $2100 yr
Courses: Advertising Design, †Art Education, Art History, Calligraphy, Ceramics, †Commercial Art, Display, Drawing, Fashion Arts, Graphic Arts, Graphic Design, Illustration, Interior Design, Jewelry, Lettering, Painting, Photography, Printmaking,

Sculpture, †Teacher Training
Children's Classes: Enrl 60; tuition $40 per sem. Courses—Arts & Crafts
Summer School: Dir, M Papier. 3 wk session begins June, 5 wk session begins July. Courses—Art History, Ceramics, Commercial Art, Drawing, Painting, Photography, Sculpture, Weaving

FRANKLIN

FRANKLIN COLLEGE, Art Dept, 46131. Tel 317-736-8441. *Chmn Dept* Luigi Crispino. Instrs: FT 1, PT 1
Estab 1834; den; D; SC 9, LC 4; enrl 650
Ent Req: HS grad
Degrees: BA 4 yrs
Tuition: $7210 per yr includes room & board & fees
Courses: Art Education, Ceramics, Drawing, Painting, Sculpture, Basic Design, Print Shop

GOSHEN

GOSHEN COLLEGE, Art Dept, 1600 S Main St, 46526. Tel 219-533-3161, Ext 354; WATS 800-348-7422. *Chmn* Abner Hershberger, MFA; *Prof* Marvin Bartel, EdD; *Asst Prof* Judy Wenig-Horswell, MFA
Estab 1950; den; D & E; scholarships; enrl D 145, E 25, non-maj 60, maj 40
Ent Req: HS dipl, top half of class
Degrees: AB(Art) and AB(Art) with Indiana Teaching Cert
Tuition: $3420 per yr, $1720 per trimester, $150 per hr; campus res—room & board $1590 yr
Courses: Art Education, Art History, Ceramics, Drawing, Graphic Design, Jewelry, Painting, Photography, Printmaking, Sculpture, Teacher Training
Children's Classes: Courses—Art, Ceramics, Drawing, Jewelry, Printmaking
Summer School: Acad Dean, Victor Stoltzfus. Tui $265 for term of 3 1/2 wks beginning end of Apr, ending in late July. Courses—Drawing, New York Art Study, Raku, Screenprinting, Watercolor; Florence, Italy Tour

GREENCASTLE

DEPAUW UNIVERSITY, Art Dept, 46135. Tel 317-658-4633. *Chmn* William Meehan, MFA; *Asst Prof* David Herrold, MFA; *Asst Prof* Robert Kingsley, MFA
Estab 1837, dept estab 1877; pvt den; D; SC 14, LC 9, GC 18; enrl D 300, E 20 (Art Dept), non-maj 25%, maj 75%, grad 20
Ent Req: HS dipl, upper half of high school graduating class
Degrees: BA & BM 4 yrs, MAEd, MAT
Tuition: $3350 per sem; campus res—room & board $1400 per sem
Courses: Art Education, †Art History, Ceramics, Commercial Art, Drawing, Graphic Arts, Illustration, Painting, Photography, Printmaking, Studio Arts

HAMMOND

PURDUE UNIVERSITY CALUMET CAMPUS, Dept of Creative Arts,* 46323. Tel 219-844-0520, Ext 422. *Head* Michael R Moore
Estab 1946; pub; D & E; scholarships; SC 1-4, LC 1-2, GC 1
Ent Req: HS dipl
Tuition: Res—$39.50; nonres—$99.75
Courses: Architecture, Art Education, Ceramics, Drawing, Film, Painting, Teacher Training, Theatre Arts, Video, Watercolor

HANOVER

HANOVER COLLEGE, Dept of Art,* 47243. Tel 812-866-2151. *Assoc Prof* James W Shaffstall, MFA; *Assoc Prof* John Thomas, MFA
Estab 1827, dept estab 1967; pvt; D; schol; SC 16, LC 4; enrl D 960
Ent Req: HS dipl
Degrees: BS and BA 4 yrs
Tuition: $3640 per yr
Courses: Advertising Design, Aesthetics, Art Education, Art History, Ceramics, Collages, Commercial Art, Constructions, Drawing, Film, Graphic Arts, Graphic Design, Jewelry, Painting, Photography, Printmaking, Sculpture, Stage Design, Teacher Training, Textile Design, Theatre Arts, Video

HUNTINGTON

HUNTINGTON COLLEGE, Art Dept, 2303 College Ave, 46750. Tel 219-356-6000. *Dean* Gerald D Smith; *Instr* Angela Gohman; *Instr* Diane Sowder
Estab 1897; den; D & E; SC 5, LC 3
Ent Req: HS dipl, SAT & two recomendations
Tuition: $4375 per year; campus res available
Courses: Art Appreciation, Art History, Ceramics, Drawing, Graphic Design, Painting, Photography, 3-D Arts & Crafts
Summer School: Dean, Dr G D Smith. Enrl 30; tuition $115 per sem hr beginning June 1. Courses—same as above

INDIANAPOLIS

HERRON SCHOOL OF ART, Indiana University-Purdue University, Indianapolis, 1701 N Pennsylvania St, 46202. Tel 317-923-3651. *Dean* Arthur Weber; *Chmn Visual Communications* Aaron Law; *Chmn Art Educ* Lance Baber, MS; *Chmn Printmaking, Painting and Drawing* Margaret Fierke, MFA; *Chmn Sculpture* Gary Freeman, MFA; *Chmn Found Prog* Sarah Burns, MFA; *Chmn Art History* A Ian Fraser, PhD; *Chmn Art Ceramics, Photography, Woodworking & Design* Phillip Tennant
Estab 1902; pub; D & E; scholarships; SC 112, LC 16, GC 20; enrl D 385, non-maj

300, grad 20
Ent Req: Portfolio
Degrees: BFA and BAE 4 yrs, MAE 5 yrs
Tuition: Res—undergrad $43.25 per cr hr, grad $61.50 per cr hr; nonres—undergrad $114.25 per cr hr; grad $168.50 per cr hr; no campus res
Courses: †Art Education, †Art History, Ceramics, Drawing, Graphic Arts, Graphic Design, Illustration, Mixed Media, †Painting, Photography, †Printmaking, †Sculpture, Teacher Training, †Fine Arts, Furniture Design, †Visual Communications
Children's Classes: Saturday classes for junior high and high school students
Summer School: Enrl 200; tuition $43.25 per cr hr, two 6 wk sessions available. Courses—Art Education, Art History, Design, Drawing, Painting, Photography, Sculpture, Three-Dimensional Design

INDIANA CENTRAL UNIVERSITY, Fine Arts Dept, 1400 E Hanna Ave, 46227. Tel 317-788-3253. *Chmn Dept* Gerald G Boyce, MFA; *Assoc Prof* Earl Snellenberger, MFA; *Asst Prof* Dee Schaad, MFA
Estab 1902; den; D & E; scholarships; SC 24, LC 7, GC 7; enrl D 360, E 150, maj 36, grad 60
Ent Req: HS dipl, SAT, upper half of HS class
Degrees: BA and BS 4 yrs
Tuition: Commuter $2230 per yr; campus res—room & board $3500 per yr
Courses: Architecture, †Art Education, Art History, Ceramics, Commercial Art, Drawing, Graphic Arts, History of Art & Archaeology, Jewelry, Lettering, Painting, Photography, Printmaking, Sculpture, Silversmithing, Textile Design, †Art Therapy
Adult Hobby Classes: Enrl 20; tuition same as regular sem
Summer School: Dir Gerald G Boyce. Enrl 60; tuition $63 per cr hr. Courses—Art Introduction, Photography

MARIAN COLLEGE, Art Dept, 3200 Cold Spring Rd, 46222. Tel 317-924-3291. *Chairperson* Sr Sandra Schweitzer, MEd; *Instr* Clarence Hawkins, BA; *Instr* Peggy Lovett, MA; *Instr* Katie Hamilton, MS; *Instr* Onoosh Kowalski, MA; *Instr* Maureen Suelzer, BA; *Instr* Karen Wolf, MA; *Instr* Joseph Fischer, AIA
Estab 1851, dept estab 1938; den; D & E; scholarships; SC 21, LC 6; enrl D 60, E 30, non-maj 20, maj 30
Ent Req: HS dipl, SAT
Degrees: AA 2 yrs, BA and BS 4 yrs
Tuition: Undergrad—$3500 per yr; campus res—room & board $2000 per yr
Courses: Art Education, Art History, Ceramics, Costume Design & Construction, Drawing, Graphic Arts, Handicrafts, Interior Design, Painting, Sculpture, Stage Design, Teacher Training, Theatre Arts, Art therapy

MARION

MARION COLLEGE, Art Dept, 4201 S Washington, 46953. Tel 317-674-6901. *Head Dept* Ardelia Williams, MA; *Instr* Rodney Crossman, BS Ed; *Vis Prof* Robert Curfman, ceramics & photography
Estab 1890, dept estab 1969; den; D & E; SC 20, LC 4; enrl D 35, non-maj 5, maj 30
Ent Req: HS dipl
Degrees: BS(Art Educ)
Tuition: $3900 per yr; campus res available
Courses: †Art Education, Art History, Ceramics, Commercial Art, Drawing, Graphic Arts, Graphic Design, Jewelry, Painting, Photography, Sculpture, Silversmithing, †Teacher Training, Weaving, Batik, Fibers, Stained Glass, Studio Administration, Studio Practicum, †Visual Arts Education

MUNCIE

BALL STATE UNIVERSITY, Art Dept, 2000 University Ave, 47306. Tel 317-285-5638. *Head Art Dept* Rex Dorethy, EdD; *Vis Prof* Manfred Maier, design - 1979. Instrs: FT 26
Estab 1918; pub; D & E; SC 28, LC 21, GC 40; enrl non-maj 633, maj 650, grad 35
Ent Req: HS dipl
Degrees: BS & BFA 4 yrs, MA 1 yr, DEd 2 yrs or more
Tuition: Res—undergrad $280 per quarter, grad $300 per quarter; non-res—undergrad $600 per quarter, grad $645 per quarter; campus residency available
Courses: Aesthetics, †Art Education, Art History, Ceramics, †Drawing, †Graphic Design, †Interior Design, †Painting, †Photography, †Printmaking, †Sculpture, †Metals, †Visual Communications, Typography
Adult Hobby Classes: Enrl 20; tuition $35 per person. Courses—Painting, Drawing
Children's Classes: Enrl 75; tuition $5 per child. Courses—General Art Activities
Summer School: Enrl 7000; tuition $180 for term of 5 wks beginning June. Courses—Art Education, Art History, Studio, Graphic Design

NEW ALBANY

INDIANA UNIVERSITY SOUTHEAST, Fine Arts Dept,* 4201 Grantline Rd, 47150. Tel 812-945-2731, Ext 313. *Coordr & Prof* Jonas A Howard, MA; *Assoc Prof* John R Guenthler, MFA; *Asst Prof* Brian H Jones, MFA; *Asst Prof* Susan M Matthias, MFA
Estab 1945, dept estab 1966; pub; D & E; SC 25, LC 2; enrl D 150, E 35, non-maj 100, maj 50
Ent Req: HS dipl
Degrees: BA 4 yrs
Tuition: $1200 per sem; no campus residence
Courses: Art Education, Art History, Ceramics, Drawing, Painting, Printmaking, Teacher Training
Adult Hobby Classes: Enrl 35; tuition $25 per sem. Courses—Crafts, Watercolor
Summer School: Enrl 60; term of two 6 wk sessions beginning May 15 and July 5. Courses—same as above

NORTH MANCHESTER

MANCHESTER COLLEGE, Art Dept, College Ave, 46962. Tel 219-982-2141.
Head Dept James R C Adams, MFA; *Assoc Prof* Stephen Batzka, BA
Estab 1889; den; D & E; scholarships; SC 15, LC 3; enrl D 45, maj 15
Ent Req: HS dipl
Degrees: AA 2 yrs, BA and BS 4 yrs
Tuition: Res—undergrad $6500 per yr, including room & board
Courses: Advertising Design, Art Education, †Art History, Ceramics, Drawing,
Film, Graphic Arts, Handicrafts, History of Art & Archaeology, Lettering, Painting,
Photography, Printmaking, Sculpture, Teacher Training, Textile Design, Camera
Techniques
Adult Hobby Classes: Tuition $38 per sem. Courses—Camera Techniques, Sculpture

NOTRE DAME

SAINT MARY'S COLLEGE, Dept of Art,* 46556. Tel 219-232-3031. *Chmn* H
James Paradis, BS & MAT
Estab 1855; pvt, W; D & E; scholarships, fels; SC 21, LC 10; enrl maj 117, others
418
Ent Req: CEEB, standing, recommendations, others
Degrees: BA and BFA 3 1/2-5 yrs
Tuition: $2735 per sem
Courses: Art Education, Ceramics, Drawing, Jewelry, Painting, Photography,
Printmaking, Sculpture, Design, Photo Silkscreen, Weaving. Rome Program:
Courses—Art History, Design, Drawing

UNIVERSITY OF NOTRE DAME, Dept of Art, Art History & Design, 46556.
Tel 219-239-7602. *Chmn* Frederick S Beckman. Instrs: FT 14, PT 4
Estab 1855; pvt; D; fels; SC 38, LC 8, GC 20; enrl maj 100
Ent Req: Upper third HS class, ent exam
Degrees: AB, BFA 4 yrs, MA, MFA
Tuition: Undergrad $6450, grad $6270 per yr; campus res available
Courses: Advertising Design, Art History, Ceramics, Industrial Design, Painting,
Photography, Printmaking, Sculpture, Fibers
Summer School: Chmn, Frederick S Beckman. Special workshops and regular
undergraduate and advanced degree programs

OAKLAND CITY

OAKLAND CITY COLLEGE, Division of Fine Arts,* 47660. Tel 812-749-4781,
Ext 53. *Fine Arts Chmn* Paul Olson; *Prof* Marie M McCord, EdD; *Asst Prof* Joseph
E Smith, MS. Instrs: FT 4, PT 1
Estab 1961; den; D & E; scholarships; SC 10, LC 5; enrl maj 35
Ent Req: HS dipl, SAT
Degrees: AA 2 yrs, BA and BS 4 yrs
Tuition: $1100 per quarter
Courses: Advertising Design, Art Education, Ceramics, Drawing, History of Art &
Archaeology, Lettering, Painting, Sculpture, Teacher Training, Macrame, Pottery,
Weaving
Summer School: Two 5 wk terms. Courses—Painting, Pottery, plus others

RICHMOND

EARLHAM COLLEGE, Art Dept, National Rd W, 47374. Tel 317-962-6561, Ext
410. *Chmn Dept* JoAnne D Sieger, PhD
Estab 1847; den; D; scholarships; SC 10, LC 7; enrl maj 10
Ent Req: HS dipl
Degrees: BA 4 yrs
Courses: Aesthetics, Art History, Ceramics, Drawing, Film, Graphic Arts, Graphic
Design, Lettering, Mixed Media, Museum Staff Training, Painting, Photography,
Printmaking, Sculpture, Stage Design, Theatre Arts, Video

INDIANA UNIVERSITY EAST, Arts & Science Dept,* Chester Blvd, 47374. Tel
317-966-8261
Tuition: Res—$37.25 per cr hr; nonres—$91 per cr hr
Courses: Art Appreciation, Art Education, Art History, Drawing, Handicrafts,
Painting, Photography, Sculpture

SAINT MARY-OF-THE-WOODS

SAINT MARY-OF-THE-WOODS COLLEGE, Art Dept, 47876. Tel 812-535-
4141. *Chmn* Jacquelin Ruttinger; *Chmn* Steve Glazer. Instrs: FT 2, PT 1
Estab 1840; den; D; scholarships; SC 15, LC 4; enrl maj 15
Ent Req: HS dipl, SAT or ACT
Degrees: BA and BS 4 yrs
Tuition: Campus res available
Courses: †Art Education, Art History, †Ceramics, Drawing, †Graphic Design,
†Painting, Photography, †Printmaking, Teacher Training, Fiber Arts

SAINT MEINRAD

SAINT MEINRAD COLLEGE, Dept of Art,* 47577. Tel 812-357-6528. *Chmn*
Steven S Scheer, PhD; *Assoc Prof* Donald Walpole
Estab 1854; pvt; D & E; SC 3, LC 3; enrl D 36, E 30
Ent Req: Admis and reg in the school
Tuition: $1235 per sem
Courses: Advertising Design, Aesthetics, Ceramics, Drawing, Graphic Design,
History of Art & Archaeology, Painting, Theatre Arts
Adult Hobby Classes: Enrl 30. Courses—Ceramics, Painting

SOUTH BEND

INDIANA UNIVERSITY AT SOUTH BEND, Fine Arts Dept, 1700 Mishawaka
Ave, 46615. Tel 219-237-4278. *Chmn* Harold Zisla, AM; *Prof* Anthony Droege,
MFA; *Prof* Harold Langland, MFA; *Assoc Prof* Alan Larkin, MFA; *Asst Prof*
Stephanie Spencer, PhD; *Adjunct Lectr* David Blodgett, MFA; *Adjunct Lectr* Linda
Crimson, MFA
Estab 1964; pub; D & E; SC 18, LC 6; enrl non-maj 300, maj 80
Ent Req: HS dipl
Degrees: BA(Fine Arts) 4 yrs
Tuition: Res—undergrad $26 cr hr, grad $34 cr hr; nonres—undergrad $59 cr hr,
grad $70 cr hr
Courses: Art Education, Art History, Drawing, Graphic Design, Painting,
Printmaking, Sculpture
Summer School: Chmn, Harold Zisla. Tuition same as regular session; two 6 wk
summer sessions. Courses—Art Appreciation, Drawing, Painting

TERRE HAUTE

INDIANA STATE UNIVERSITY
—Dept of Art, 47809. Tel 812-232-6311, Ext 2222. *Chmn* Fredrick W Bunce, PhD.
Instrs: FT 19, PT 6
Estab 1870; pub; D & E; SC 67, LC 47, GC 65; enrl D 2350, E 250, maj 200, grad
30
Ent Req: HS dipl
Degrees: BS and BFA 4 yrs, MS, MA and MFA 2 yrs
Tuition: Res—undergrad & grad $48 per cr hr; nonres—undergrad & grad $79 per cr
hr; campus res—room and board $375 for halls, except Lincoln Guard which is $391
Courses: Art Education, Art History, Ceramics, Drawing, Goldsmithing, Graphic
Design, Jewelry, Mixed Media, Painting, Photography, Printmaking, Sculpture,
Silversmithing, Woodworking & Furniture Design
Summer School: Dir, Dr Harriett Darrow. Tuition res $28, nonres $56 for term of
two 5 wks beginning June. Courses—same as above
—Dept of Humanities,* Parsons Hall, 47809. Tel 812-232-6311. *Chairperson* David
Johnson, PhD; *Prof* Harriet Caplow, PhD; *Prof* Roslyn Erbes, PhD; *Asst Prof*
Charles Mayer, PhD
Dept estab 1964; pub; D & E; scholarships; LC 12, GC 12; enrl in dept D 1250, E
50, maj 10, grad 10
Degrees: BA(Art History) 4 yrs, MA in Humanities with Art History concentration
1 1/2-2 yrs
Tuition: Res—$47 per yr; nonres—$85 per yr
Courses: Architecture, Art History
Summer School: Dean, Harriet Darrow

UPLAND

TAYLOR UNIVERSITY, Art Dept, 46989. Tel 317-998-2751, Ext 322. *Chmn* Ray
E Bullock, EdD; *Prof* Craig Moore, MFA
Estab 1846, dept estab 1968; pvt; D & E; SC 12, LC 7; enrl D 175, E 16, non-maj
125, maj 35
Ent Req: HS dipl, SAT, recommendations
Degrees: BA and BS 4 yrs
Tuition: Campus res—room & board $6640 per yr
Courses: Advertising Design, Aesthetics, †Art Education, Art History, Ceramics,
Collages, Drawing, Graphic Arts, †Jewelry, Lettering, Mixed Media, Painting,
Photography, Printmaking, Sculpture, Silversmithing, Stage Design, †Teacher
Training
Children's Classes: Enrl 40; tuition free. Courses—Design, Drawing, Jewelry,
Painting, Pottery
Summer School: Dir, Dr Ray E Bullock. Courses—Photography, Survey of Fine
Arts, Art for Teachers

VINCENNES

VINCENNES UNIVERSITY, Art Dept, 1002 N First St, 47591. Tel 812-885-
4318. *Chmn & Assoc Prof* Andrew Jendrzejewski, MFA; *Assoc Prof* Amy Delap
Jendrzejewski, MFA; *Assoc Prof* Jim Pearson, MFA; *Assoc Prof* James Gorman,
MFA; *Instructor* Jenny Vinzani. Instrs: PT 1
Estab 1801; pub; D & E; scholarships; SC 20, LC 4; enrl maj 45
Ent Req: HS dipl or GED
Degrees: AA and AS 2 yrs
Tuition: Res—undergrad $1014 per yr, $507 per sem, $35 per hr; nonres—undergrad
$2954 per yr, $1477 per sem, $100 per hr; campus res—room & board $1930 per yr
Courses: Art History, Art Appreciation, Ceramics, Drawing, †Graphic Design,
Painting, Photography, Printmaking, Sculpture, Figure Drawing, Typography
Adult Hobby Classes: Enrl 20-40; tuition $35 per hr for 15 wks. Courses—Art
Appreciatioon, Photography, Drawing, Ceramics
Summer School: Chmn, Andrew J Jendrzejewski. Enrl 15-20; tuition $36 per hr for
term of 5 wks beginning May 30 and July 5. Courses—Ceramics, Drawing, Painting,
Photography, Printmaking

VINCENNES UNIVERSITY JUNIOR COLLEGE, Art Dept, Second & Harrison
Sts, 47591. Tel 812-882-3350. *Chmn* Andrew Jendrzejewski; *Instr* Amy DeLap;
Instr Jim Borman; *Instr* Jim Pearson; *Instr* Starla Stunsaas; *Instr* Jeannie LaCosta
Burke
Scholarships offered
Degrees: AA, AS
Tuition: Knox county res—$507, other Ind & nearby Ill counties—$537, state
nonres—$1477; campus res $1930 per yr
Courses: Art Appreciation, Art Education, Art History, Calligraphy, Ceramics,
Design, Drawing, Graphic Design, Illustration, Interior Design, Painting,
Photography, Printmaking, Sculpture, Design & Materials, Portfolio Development &
Review, Typographic Design
Adult Hobby Classes: Enrl 10; tuition $35 per cr hr for 15 wks. Courses—Ceramics,
Photography
Summer School: Dir, Andrew Jendrzejewski. Enrl 6, tuition $35 per cr hr for 5 wks.
Courses—Ceramics

WEST LAFAYETTE

PURDUE UNIVERSITY, LAFAYETTE, Dept of Creative Arts, Art & Design Section, School of Humanities, 47907. Tel 317-494-3056. *Head Dept* G R Sudano; *Chmn Dept* M B Levy Instrs: FT 33
Estab 1925; pub; D & E; scholarships; SC 50, LC 22, GC 22; enrl maj 394, others 1746
Ent Req: BA 4 yrs, MA
Tuition: Nonres—$1414 per sem
Courses: Art History, Ceramics, Graphic Arts, Industrial Design, Interior Design, Jewelry, Painting, Photography, Sculpture, Teacher Training, Visual Communication Desgin
Summer School: Courses offered

WINONA LAKE

GRACE COLLEGE, Dept of Art, 200 Seminary Dr, 46590. Tel 219-267-8191, Ext 241. *Head Dept* Jean L Coverstone, MA; *Asst Prof* Art Davis, MA
Estab 1952, dept estab 1971; pvt; D & E; SC 12, LC 3; enrl maj 40, non-maj 80
Ent Req: HS dipl, SAT
Degrees: 4 yr Art Major, 4 yr Art Educ Major, and 2 yr cert
Tuition: $105 per hr; campus res available
Courses: †Art Education, Art History, Ceramics, Drawing, Graphic Design, Handicrafts, Painting, Photography, Printmaking, Sculpture, Teacher Training
Children's Classes: Sponsors competitions with awards
Summer School: scholarships

IOWA

AMES

IOWA STATE UNIVERSITY, Dept of Art and Design, 158 College of Design Bldg, 50011. Tel 515-294-6724. *Chmn Dept* Evan R Firestone, PhD; *Coordr Drawing & Painting* Robert Lorr, MFA; *Coordr Interior Design* Fred Maluen, PhD; *Coordr Crafts* Shirley Held, MS; *Coordr Graphic Design* Roger Baer, MFA; *Coordr Art Educ* Dennis Dake, MA
Estab 1858, dept estab 1920; pub; D & E; scholarships; SC 45, LC 15, GC 6; enrl non-maj 1500, maj 800, grad 16
Ent Req: HS dipl
Degrees: BA, BFA(Graphic Design, Art Educ, Craft Design, Interior Design, Drawing, Painting & Printmaking)
Tuition: Res—undergrad $621 per sem; nonres—undergrad $1725 per sem; campus res available
Courses: †Art Education, Art History, Calligraphy, Ceramics, Design, Drawing, Graphic Design, Interior Design, Jewelry, Painting, Printmaking, Sculpture, Weaving, Batik, Dyeing, Fashion Illustration, Surface Design, Wood Design
Summer School: Dir, Dr Evan R Firestone. Terms of 8 wks. Courses—Graphic Design, Drawing, Interior Design, Painting, Wood Design, Art History, Workshops: Art Education, Ceramics, Jewelry, Weaving

BOONE

DES MOINES AREA COMMUNITY COLLEGE, Art Dept,* Boone Campus, 1125 Hancock Dr, 50036. Tel 515-964-6200
Estab 1927, dept estab 1970; pub; D & E; SC 3, LC 2; enrl D 100, E 60
Ent Req: HS dipl
Degrees: AA 2 yrs
Tuition: Res—$405 per sem; nonres—$810 per sem
Courses: Art History, Painting, Stage Design, Teacher Training, Theatre Arts, Life Drawing

CEDAR FALLS

UNIVERSITY OF NORTHERN IOWA, Dept of Art, Col of Humanities and Fine Arts, 50613. Tel 319-273-2077. *Head Dept* Joseph M Ruffo, MFA; *Prof* Don Finegan, MFA; *Prof* Ken Gogel, MA; *Prof* Shirley Haupt, MFA; *Prof* John Page, MFA; *Assoc Prof* Reed Estabrook, MFA; *Assoc Prof* Steve Bigler, MFA; *Assoc Prof* Barbara Cassino, MFA; *Assoc Prof* Felipe Echeverria, MFA; *Asst Prof* Hale Danderson, MFA; *Asst Prof* Allan Shickman, MA; *Asst Prof* Vera Jo Siddens, MFA; *Asst Prof* Maynard Gunter, PhD; *Asst Prof* Dan Powell, MFA; *Asst Prof* Charles Adelman, PhD; *Asst Prof* Richard Bigus, MFA; *Asst Prof* Fred Burton, MFA; *Asst Prof* Richard Colburn, MFA; *Asst Prof* Sheery Leedy, MFA; *Asst Prof* Sidney VanderWerf, MFA; *Instr* Onyile Onyile, MFA; *Adjunct Instr* Kay Anderson, MA; *Adjunct Instr* Kim Behm, MA; *Adjunct Instr* Paula Hanes, Ba; *Adjunct Instr* Ardith Hoff, MA; *Adjunct Instr* Nina Ward, MFA; *Emeritus Prof* David Delafield, PhD; *Emeritus Prof* Harry Guillaume, EdD
Estab 1876, dept estab 1945; pub; D & E; scholarships; SC 32, LC 9, GC 10; enrl D 933, E 106, non-maj 150, maj 250, grad 3
Ent Req: HS dipl, ACT
Degrees: BA and BFA 4 yrs, MA 1 yr
Tuition: Res—undergrad $1050 per yr, $525 per sem, grad $1140 per yr, $570 per sem; nonres—undergrad $2174 per yr, $1087 per sem, grad $2484 per yr, $1242 per sem; campus res—room and board $1700 per yr
Courses: Art Education, Art History, Ceramics, Commercial Art, Drawing, Graphic Design, Painting, Photography, Printmaking, Sculpture, Metalwork
Summer School: Head Dept, Jospeh M Ruffo. Enrl 82; tuition $525 for term of 8 wks beginning June 8. Courses—same curriculum as acad yr, but limited

CEDAR RAPIDS

COE COLLEGE, Dept of Art, 52402. Tel 319-399-8564. *Prof* Robert Kocher, MA; *Chmn* John Beckelman, MFA; *Asst Prof* David Goodwin, MFA; *Asst Prof* Paul Howard, MFA; *Asst Prof* Steve Whitney; *Lectr* Will Valk
Estab 1851; pvt; D & E; scholarships; SC 15, LC 8; enrl D 1200
Ent Req: HS dipl, SAT, ACT or portfolio
Degrees: BA 4 yr
Tuition: Campus res—room & board $7920 per yr
Courses: Art Education, Art History, Ceramics, Drawing, Illustration, Painting, Photography, Printmaking, Sculpture, Teacher Training, Textile Design, Theatre Arts
Summer School: Chmn Dept, John Beckelman. Enrl average 80; tuition $290 per course for term of 5 wks beginning in June and mid-July. Courses—American Art History, Ceramics, Drawing, Painting, Photography

KIRKWOOD COMMUNITY COLLEGE, Dept of Fine Arts, 6301 Kirkwood Blvd SW, 52406. Tel 319-398-5537. *Head Dept* Doreen Maronde, MS; *Instructor* Doug Hall, MFA; *Instructor* Ray Mullen, MFA
Estab 1966; pub; D & E; SC 18, LC 6; enrl D 180, E 50
Ent Req: HS dipl
Degrees: AA 2 yr
Tuition: $20 per cr hr or $240 per quarter; no campus res
Summer School: Tuition $20 per cr hr or $240 per quarter. Courses—Art History, Art Appreciation, Ceramics, Design, Drawing, Lettering, Painting, Photography, Printmaking, Sculpture

MOUNT MERCY COLLEGE, Art Dept, 1330 Elmhurst Dr NE, 52402. Tel 319-363-8213, Ext 256. *Chmn Dept* Jane Gilmor, MFA; *Prof* Charles Barth, PhD; *Asst Prof* Robert Naujoks, MFA
Estab 1928, dept estab 1960; pvt; D & E; scholarships; SC 20, LC 6; enrl D 150, E 35, non-maj 150, maj 35
Ent Req: HS dipl, ACT
Degrees: BA 4 yr
Tuition: $2830 per yr, $1415 per sem, $195 per course; campus res—room & board $945
Courses: †Art Education, Art History, Drawing, Graphic Design, Mixed Media, Painting, Photography, Printmaking, Sculpture, Textile Design
Summer School: Dir, Judy Fuller. Enrl 500, tuition $210 per 3 hr course, two five week sessions. Courses—Art Appreciation, Ceramics, Drawing, Painting, Photography

CENTERVILLE

INDIAN HILLS COMMUNITY COLLEGE, Dept of Art, Centerville Campus, N First St, 52544. Tel 515-856-2143, Ext 27. *Head Dept* Richard H Dutton, MA; *Instructor* Mark McWhorter, MA
Estab 1932, dept estab 1967; pub; D & E; scholarships; SC 10; enrl D 70, E 30, non-maj 50, maj 14
Ent Req: HS dipl or equal, open door
Degrees: AA 2 yr
Tuition: Res—$480 per yr; nonres—$720 per yr
Courses: Art History, Ceramics, Drawing, Painting, Sculpture, Art Appreciation, Arts & Crafts, Design, Watercolor
Adult Hobby Classes: Enrl 20; tuition $54 for 12 wks. Courses—Ceramics, Design, Drawing, Painting, Watercolor
Summer School: Dir, Dick Sharp. Courses—Art Appreciation, Ceramics, Design, European Art Tours, Painting

CLINTON

EASTERN IOWA COMMUNITY COLLEGE, Art Dept,* 100 Lincoln Blvd, 52732. Tel 319-242-6841
Degrees: AA
Courses: Art Appreciation, Design, Drawing, Painting

MOUNT SAINT CLARE COLLEGE, Art Dept, 400 N Bluff, 52732. Tel 319-242-4023. *Head Dept* Sr Carmel Jacobs
Estab 1928, dept estab 1940; den; D & E; scholarships; SC 5, LC 1; enrl non-maj 80, maj 8
Ent Req: HS dipl
Degrees: AA 2 yr
Tuition: $1495 per sem; campus res—room & board $1000 per sem, $2000 per yr
Courses: Calligraphy, Ceramics, Drawing, Painting, Art Appreciation, 2-D Design, 3-D Design
Summer School: Courses—Art Appreciation, Calligraphy, Painting

COUNCIL BLUFFS

IOWA WESTERN COMMUNITY COLLEGE, Art Dept, 2700 College Rd, 51502. Tel 712-325-3200. *Chmn* Charles C Crandall
Enrl 2000
Courses: Art Appreciation, Art History, Ceramics, Design, Drawing, Painting, Sculpture

CRESTON

SOUTHWESTERN COMMUNITY COLLEGE, Art Dept, 1501 W Townline Rd, 50801. Tel 515-782-7081. *Dir Arts Dept* Mirle E Freel Jr, MFA
Estab 1966; pub; D & E; SC 6, LC 3; enrl D 550, E 200, non-maj 40, maj 15, others 15
Ent Req: HS dipl
Degrees: AA 2 yrs
Courses: Art Education, Art History, Ceramics, Design, Drawing, Painting, Photography, Teacher Training
Adult Hobby Classes: Enrl 10-30; tuition $30 per sem. Courses—Per regular session
Summer School: Workshops in arts science

DAVENPORT

MARYCREST COLLEGE, Art Dept, 1607 W 12th St, 52804. Tel 319-326-9512.
Chmn Dr Alan Garfield; *Asst Prof* Robert Lipnick; *Lecturer* Ingrid Bogdanowicz;
Lecturer David Rossi; *Prof Emeritus* Sr Clarice Eberdt
Estab 1939; den; D & E; scholarships; SC 35, LC 15, GC 13; enrl D 446, E 129, maj
68, grad 56
Ent Req: HS dipl
Degrees: BA 3-4 yrs, MA
Tuition: Tuition $2070 per sem; campus res—room & board $995 per sem
Courses: Advertising Design, Aesthetics, Art Education, Ceramics, Commercial Art,
Costume Design & Construction, Drafting, Drawing, Fashion Arts, Graphic Design,
History of Art & Archaeology, Illustration, Jewelry, Lettering, Museum Staff
Training, Painting, Photography, Sculpture, Stage Design, Teacher Training, Theatre
Arts, †Computer Graphics
Adult Hobby Classes: Tuition $125 per cr hr; Weekend College Courses—Art
Appreciation, Drawing, Composition, Masterpieces of Art, Painting
Summer School: Dir, Dr J Lawrence. Tuition $145 per cr hr per 6 wks session.
Courses—Independent Study, Painting, Readings

SAINT AMBROSE COLLEGE, Art Dept,* 518 W Locust St, 52803. Tel 319-324-
1681. *Assoc Prof* Leslie B Bell; *Faculty* James P Anderson, EdD; *Faculty* Thomas F
Chouteau, MA; *Faculty* John W Schmits, BA
Estab 1892; den; D & E; scholarships; SC 17, LC 12; enrl D 450, E 40, maj 55
Ent Req: HS dipl
Degrees: BA 4 yrs
Tuition: 160 per sem cr; campus residence available
Courses: Advertising Design, Art Education, Calligraphy, Ceramics, Commercial
Art, Drafting, Drawing, Graphic Arts, Graphic Design, History of Art &
Archaeology, Illustration, Lettering, Painting, Photography, Sculpture, Teacher
Training
Summer School: Courses—Painting, Photography

DECORAH

LUTHER COLLEGE, Art Dept, 52101. Tel 319-387-1113. *Head Dept* Dean
Schwarz. Instrs: FT 3, PT 4
Estab 1861; den; D; scholarships; SC 13, LC 5; enrl D 160
Ent Req: HS dipl or ent exam
Degrees: BA 4 yr
Courses: †Aesthetics, †Art Education, †Ceramics, †Drawing, Graphic Arts, †History
of Art & Archaeology, †Lettering, †Painting, †Printmaking, †Stage Design, †Teacher
Training, †Theatre Arts, †Weaving
Summer School: Courses—Drawing, Painting

DES MOINES

DRAKE UNIVERSITY, Art Dept,* 25th & University Ave, 50311. Tel 515-271-
2863. *Chairperson Dept* Condon Kuhl, MFA. Instrs: FT 17, PT 2
Estab 1881; pvt; D & E; scholarships; SC 64, LC 15, GC 33; enrl D 275, maj 275,
grad 15
Ent Req: 2 pt average in HS or previous col
Degrees: BA, BFA, MFA
Tuition: $2615 per sem
Courses: †Advertising Design, Aesthetics, †Art Education, †Ceramics, †Commercial
Art, Constructions, Costume Design & Construction, †Drawing, Film,
†Goldsmithing, †Graphic Arts, †Graphic Design, Handicrafts, History of Art &
Archaeology, Illustration, †Interior Design, †Jewelry, Lettering, †Painting,
Photography, †Printmaking, †Sculpture, †Silversmithing, Stage Design, Teacher
Training, Textile Design, †Theatre Arts, Video, Creative Arts Therapy
Summer School: Dir, Lewis Hainlin. Courses—Art Education, Art History,
Ceramics, Drawing, Jewelry, Painting, Sculpture

GRAND VIEW COLLEGE, Art Dept,* 1200 Grandview Ave, 50322. Tel 515-263-
2800. *Assoc Prof* Dennis Kaven
Scholarships offered
Degrees: BA, cert
Tuition: $1695 per sem
Courses: Advertising Design, Art Appreciation, Art Education, Art History,
Calligraphy, Design, Jewelry, Photography, Printmaking, Textile Design, Theatre
Arts

DUBUQUE

CLARKE COLLEGE, Dept of Art, 1550 Clarke Dr, 52001. Tel 319-588-6300.
Chmn Sr Joan Lingen
Estab 1843; den; D & E; SC 15, LC 4; enrl maj 50, others 200
Ent Req: HS grad, 16 units and Col Ent Board
Degrees: BFA(studio) & BA(studio & art history)
Courses: †Art History, †Ceramics, †Drawing, Jewelry, Lettering, †Painting,
†Printmaking, †Sculpture, †Teacher Training, †Adult Continuing Educ Program: D
& E
Adult Hobby Classes: Courses offered
Summer School: Enrl art 50; three 3 wk sessions

LORAS COLLEGE, Dept of Art,* 1450 Alta Vista, 52001. Tel 319-588-7100.
Chmn Thomas Jewell-Vitale
Tuition: $2000 per sem
Courses: Art Appreciation, Art Education, Art History, Design, Drawing, Jewelry,
Painting, Photography, Printmaking, Sculpture, Weaving

ESTHERVILLE

IOWA LAKES COMMUNITY COLLEGE, Dept of Art, 300 S 18th, 51334. Tel
712-362-4865. *Dept Head* Dallas Freeman, MA; *Instructor* Ken Nordstom, MA;
Instructor David Goughnour, MA; *Instructor* Dick Williams, MA
Estab 1967; pub; D & E; scholarships; SC 26, LC 1
Ent Req: HS dipl
Degrees: AA, AS(Commercial Art) 2 yrs
Tuition: Res—undergrad $230 per quarter; nonres—undergrad $345 per quarter;
campus res available
Courses: Advertising Design, Art History, Calligraphy, Ceramics, Commercial Art,
Drawing, Graphic Arts, Graphic Design, Illustration, Mixed Media, Painting,
Photography
Summer School: Courses—Internships in Commercial Art

FOREST CITY

WALDORF COLLEGE, Art Dept, 50436. *Chmn Dept* Ruth Ann Kovach. Instrs:
FT 1, PT 1
Estab 1903; den; D; scholarships; SC 4; enrl D 80, maj 15
Ent Req: HS dipl, ACT or SAT
Degrees: AA, AC and AAS 2 yr
Tuition: $2137 per sem
Courses: Design, Photography, Printmaking, Art History, Ceramics, Drafting,
Drawing, Painting, Woodcrafts

FORT DODGE

IOWA CENTRAL COMMUNITY COLLEGE, Dept of Art, 330 Ave M, 50501.
Tel 515-576-3103; WATS 800-362-2793. *Assoc Prof* Robert J Halm, MFA;
Instructor Raymond R Atwood, MA
Pub; D & E; SC 4, LC 2; enrl D 120, E 15, non-maj 153, maj 20
Ent Req: HS dipl
Degrees: AA 2 yr
Tuition: Res—$310 per sem, $26 per hr; nonres—$465 per sem, $39 per hr; campus
res—room & board $1475 per yr
Courses: Art History, Painting, Studio Art

GRINNELL

GRINNELL COLLEGE, Dept of Art,* 1202 Park St, 50112. Tel 515-236-7545.
Chmn Dept Louis G Zirkle, MFA; *Chmn Dept* Robert McKibbin; *Prof* Richard
Cervene, MFA; *Assoc Prof* Merle Waller Zirkle, MFA; *Asst Prof* Timothy R
Chasson, PhD; *Faculty* Susan Strauber
Estab 1846, dept estab 1930; pvt; D; scholarships; SC 9, LC 9; enrl D 150, non-maj
125, maj 25
Ent Req: HS dipl, SAT or ACT
Degrees: BA 4 yrs
Tuition: Res—undergrad $6522 per yr; campus res—room and board
Courses: Art Education, Art History, Ceramics, Drawing, Graphic Arts, Jewelry,
Painting, Printmaking, Sculpture, Silversmithing, Design, Watercolor

INDIANOLA

SIMPSON COLLEGE, Art Dept, 50125. Tel 515-961-1561. *Chairperson Dept*
Janet Heinicke
Estab 1860, dept estab 1965; pvt; D & E; scholarships; SC 3, LC 3; enrl D 67, maj 6
Ent Req: HS dipl, ACT or SAT
Degrees: BA and BM 4 yrs
Tuition: Res—undergrad $4480 per yr; campus res—room $720 and board $910
Courses: Art Education, Art History, Ceramics, Drawing, History of Art &
Archaeology, Jewelry, Mixed Media, Painting, Photography, Printmaking, Sculpture,
Stage Design, Teacher Training, 3-D Design, Color Theory, Design History,
Etching, Relief, Silkscreen
Summer School: Dir, Tom Westbrook; enrl 350; tuition $90 per cr hr for 2 wk
sessions

IOWA CITY

UNIVERSITY OF IOWA, School of Art and Art History, N Riverside Dr, 52242.
Tel 319-353-4550. *Dir* Wallace J Tomasini, PhD. Instrs: FT 40, PT 2
Estab 1847, school estab 1911; pub; D & E; scholarships; SC 60, LC 55, GC 55; enrl
D 590 maj 400, grad 190
Ent Req: HS dipl, ACT or SAT, upper rank in HS
Degrees: BA and BFA 4 yr, MA, MFA, PhD
Tuition: Res—undergrad $552 per sem, grad $640 per sem; nonres—undergrad
$1325 per sem, grad $1492 per sem; campus res—room and board $2050 per yr
Courses: Aesthetics, †Art Education, †Art History, †Ceramics, †Drawing, †Graphic
Design, †Industrial Design, †Intermedia, †Interior Design, †Jewelry, Lettering,
†Painting, †Photography, †Printmaking, †Sculpture, †Silversmithing, †Teacher
Training, †Video, †Multimedia
Summer School: Dir, Wallace J Tomasini. Enrl undergrad 160, grad 135; tui
res—undergrad $460, grad $576; nonres—undergrad $1160, grad $1328 for term of
8 wks, beginning June 11. Courses—full range of art education, art history and
studio courses

IOWA FALLS

ELLSWORTH COMMUNITY COLLEGE, Dept of Fine Arts, 1100 College Ave, 50126. Tel 515-648-4611. *Chmn* Craig Knudson, MA; *Instr* Robert Myers, MA; *Instr* Steve Kramer, MA
Estab 1890, dept estab 1890; pub; D & E; SC 10, LC 1; enrl in dept D 20-25
Ent Req: HS dipl, ACT
Degrees: AA 2 yrs
Tuition: Res $620 per yr; nonres undergrad $1240; campus res—room & board $1670
Courses: †Advertising Design, Art Education, Art History, Calligraphy, Ceramics, Commercial Art, Conceptual Art, Drawing, Handicrafts, Illustration, Lettering, Mixed Media, Painting, Photography, Sculpture, Teacher Training, Theatre Arts, Weaving
Adult Hobby Classes: Enrl 12; tuition $20 per 20 hrs. Courses—Pottery
Children's Classes: Enrl 20; tuition $30 for one week summer art camp
Summer School: Dir, Dr Thomas Seymour. Enrl 14; tuition $26 per sem hr for 4 weeks. Courses—Art Interpretatione

LAMONI

GRACELAND COLLEGE, Art Dept,* College Ave, 50140. Tel 515-784-3311. *Chmn Fine Arts* Oliver C Houston; *Instr* Daniel T Keegan; *Instr* Brent E Pulsipher; *Instr* Lester D Wright
Estab 1895, dept estab 1961; pvt den; D; scholarships; SC 30, LC 10; enrl D 180, maj 52, others 4
Ent Req: HS dipl
Degrees: BA and BS 4 yrs
Tuition: $2205 per sem
Courses: Advertising Design, †Art Education, Art History, Ceramics, Commercial Art, Constructions, Drawing, Graphic Arts, History of Art & Archaeology, Intermedia, Lettering, Painting, Photography, Printmaking, Sculpture, Teacher Training
Summer School: Dir, Dr Velma Ruch

LEMARS

WESTMAR COLLEGE, Art Dept,* 1002 Third Ave SE, 51031. Tel 712-546-7081, Ext 231. *Dir* Dr Ruth E Monroe; *Assoc Prof* Gary R Bowling. Instrs: FT 1, PT 2
Estab 1890; pvt; D; enrl 700, maj 22
Ent Req: ACT, SAT or PSAT
Degrees: BA, BMEd and BAS 4 yr
Tuition: $4060 per yr
Courses: Art Education, Art History, Ceramics, Commercial Art, Drawing, Graphic Arts, Handicrafts, Painting, Sculpture, Art Philosophy & Criticism, Business World of Art, Design, Foundations of Art, Synthetic Media & Color, Watercolor
Adult Hobby Classes: JANUS Continuing Education for Retired Persons

MASON CITY

NORTH IOWA AREA COMMUNITY COLLEGE, Dept of Art, 500 College Dr, 50401. Tel 515-423-1264, Ext 242. Instrs: FT 1
Estab 1964; pub; D & E; scholarships; SC 4, LC 2; enrl D 198, E 25, maj 30
Ent Req: HS dipl
Degrees: AA 2 yr
Tuition: $330 per sem
Courses: Art Education, Art History, Ceramics, Drawing, Painting, Basic Design
Adult Hobby Classes: Enrl 30. Courses—Crafts, Painting
Summer School: Term of 5 wks beginning early June. Courses—Art Essentials, Painting

MOUNT PLEASANT

IOWA WESLEYAN COLLEGE, Art Dept,* 601 North Main, 52641. Tel 319-385-8021. *Head Dept Art* Don Jones
Estab 1842; den; scholarships; SC 10, LC 4; enrl maj 32
Degrees: 4 yr degrees
Tuition: 2450 per sem
Courses: Art Education, Art History, Ceramics, Drawing, Graphic Arts, Painting, Sculpture, Introduction to Art, Secondary Art, Special Problems, Twentieth Century Art History

MOUNT VERNON

CORNELL COLLEGE, Art Dept, Armstrong Hall, Fine Arts, 52314. Tel 319-895-8811, Ext 128. *Head Dept* Hugh Lifson. Instrs: FT 3
Estab 1853; den; D; scholarships; SC 30, LC 3; enrl 900
Ent Req: HS dipl
Degrees: BA, BSS and BPhil 4 yr
Tuition: 5710
Courses: Art History, Ceramics, Drawing, Painting, Photography, Sculpture, Batik, Design, Metal & Fiber Design, Weaving

ORANGE CITY

NORTHWESTERN COLLEGE, Art Dept, 51041. Tel 712-737-4821. *Chmn Dept* John Kaericher, MFA; *Asst Prof* Rein Vanderhill, MFA
Estab 1882, dept estab 1965; den; D & E; scholarships; SC 25, LC 3-4; enrl D 200, non-maj 175, maj 23-25
Ent Req: HS dipl
Degrees: BA 4 yr
Tuition: Campus residency available

Courses: †Art Education, Art History, Ceramics, Drawing, Graphic Arts, Graphic Design, Mixed Media, Painting, Photography, Printmaking, Sculpture, Stage Design, Art Therapy
Adult Hobby Classes: Courses—Photography, Watercolor

OSKALOOSA

WILLIAM PENN COLLEGE, Art Dept, 52577. Tel 515-673-8311. *Chairperson* Dr David Evans, PhD
Estab 1876; pvt; D & E; scholarships; SC 5, LC 5; enrl D 120
Ent Req: HS dipl, ACT, PSAT or SAT
Degrees: BA
Courses: Art Education, Ceramics, Costume Design & Construction, Drafting, Drawing, History of Art & Archaeology, Industrial Design, Interior Design, Teacher Training
Adult Hobby Classes: Enrl 500; tuition $120 per hr. Courses—Crafts
Summer School: Dir, Dr Howard Reitz. Tuition $120. Courses—Ceramics, Elementary Art Methods

OTTUMWA

INDIAN HILLS COMMUNITY COLLEGE, OTTUMWA CAMPUS, Dept of Art, Grandview at Elm, 52501. Tel 515-682-4551. *Dept Head* Richard Dutton; *Dir of Arts & Sciences* Bob Thomas; *Instructor* Mark McWhorter
Estab 1925; pvt; D & E; scholarships; SC 3, LC 2; enrl D 73, E 5
Ent Req: HS dipl, GED, ACT or SAT
Degrees: AA, AAS and AAA 2 yrs
Tuition: In-state $160 per quarter; out-of-state $240 (res acquired after 90 days)
Courses: Ceramics, Design, Drawing, Painting, Crafts, Watercolors
Adult Hobby Classes: Enrl 10-20; tuition $55 per quarter. Courses—Painting, Ceramics, Watercolor
Children's Classes: Enrl 15-20. Courses—General Workshops, Painting, Ceramics
Summer School: Dir, Bob Thomas. Enrl 120; six wk session. Courses—Liberal Arts

PELLA

CENTRAL COLLEGE, Art Dept,* 812 University, 50219. Tel 515-628-4151. *Chmn* Lawrence Mills, PhD; *Prof* J D DeJong, PhD; *Assoc Prof* J Vruwink, MFA
Estab 1853; pvt; D & E; scholarships; SC 20, LC 6; enrl D 180, non-maj 140, maj 40
Ent Req: HS dipl, ACT
Degrees: BA 4 yrs
Tuition: $1550 per term
Children's Classes: Enrl 40; part of Elementary School Art Program

SIOUX CITY

BRIAR CLIFF COLLEGE, Art Dept, 3303 Rebecca St, 57038. Tel 712-279-5321, Ext 452. *Chairperson* William J Welu, MFA; *Instructor* Mary Ann Lonergan, MA
Estab 1930; den; D & E; scholarships; SC 7, LC 7; enrl D 250, non-maj 150, maj 30
Ent Req: HS dipl, ACT
Degrees: BA and BS 4 yr
Tuition: $1200 per term, $120 per hr; campus res—room & board $1860 per yr
Courses: Art Education, Art History, Drawing, Teacher Training, Art 1, 2, 3 & 4 (major studio areas & independent study), Critical Seminar, Design
Summer School: Tuition $90 per cr hr; term of 6 wks beginning June 12. Courses—Art Appreciation, Contemporary Art, Drawing, Elementary Art Education, Independent Studio Courses, Pottery

MORNINGSIDE COLLEGE, Art Dept, 1501 Morningside Ave, 51106. Tel 712-274-5212. Instrs: FT 3
Pvt; D & E; SC 17, LC 4; enrl D 161, maj 35
Ent Req: HS dipl
Degrees: BA and BS (Art Educ) 4 yr
Tuition: $4038 per yr; campus res—$1470 per yr
Courses: Art Appreciation, Art Education, Art History, Ceramics, Drawing, Graphic Design, Painting, Photography, Sculpture, Teacher Training, Textile Design, Jewelry, Printmaking
Children's Classes: Enrl 50
Summer School: Tuition $100 per hr for two 5 wk sessions, beginning June 4 and July 9. Courses—Art Education, Art History, Ceramics

SIOUX CITY ART CENTER, 513 Nebraska St, 51101. Tel 712-279-6272. *Asst Dir* Tom Butler; *Educ Coordr* Dianne Mumm; *Instructor* Gary Bowling, MA; *Instructor* Marvel Cox, BA; *Instructor* John Gordon, MFA; *Instructor* Peggy Parris, BA; *Instructor* Ernest Ricehill, BA; *Instructor* David Wost, BFA
Estab 1938; pvt; D & E; SC 14-20, LC 1-2; enrl D 100, E 400
Tuition: None
Courses: Art Education, Art History, Ceramics, Drawing, Interior Design, Jewelry, Mixed Media, Painting, Photography, Printmaking, Sculpture, Silversmithing, Teacher Training

WAVERLY

WARTBURG COLLEGE, Dept of Art, 222 9th St NW, 50677. Tel 319-352-1200; WATS 800-553-1797. *Dept Head* Arthur C Frick, MS; *Prof* Maynard Anderson, PhD
Estab 1852; den; D & E; SC 18, LC 4; enrl D 135, non-maj 110, maj 25
Ent Req: HS dipl, PSAT, ACT & SAT, foreign students TOEFL and upper 50 percent of class
Degrees: BA(Art), BA(Art Education) 4 yrs
Tuition: Res—undergrad $5054 per year, $845 part time; campus res—room $840, board $1150
Courses: †Art Education, Art History, Ceramics, Commercial Art, Drawing, Graphic

Arts, Jewelry, Painting, Photography, Printmaking, Sculpture, Teacher Training, †Studio Art
Summer School: Dir, Dr Ann L Henninger. Tuition $495 per course.
Courses—Drawing, Independent Study, Painting

KANSAS

ATCHISON

BENEDICTINE COLLEGE, Art Dept,* 66002. Tel 913-367-6110. *Prof* Dennis McCarthy, MFA; *Chmn* Sr Helen Buening, MFA. Instrs: FT 1
Estab 1971; den; D; SC 15, LC 3; enrl D 145, non-maj 123, maj 22
Ent Req: HS dipl, ent exam
Tuition: Campus res—room and board $3800
Courses: Art Education, Art History, Calligraphy, Ceramics, Drawing, Graphic Arts, Interior Design, Painting, Photography, Printmaking, Sculpture, Teacher Training, Textile Design

BALDWIN CITY

BAKER UNIVERSITY, Dept of Art,* 606 Eighth St, 66006. Tel 913-594-6451.
Chmn Walter J Bailey; *Prof* Thomas L Russell; *Instr* Leni Salkind
Estab 1858; pvt; D; scholarships; SC 11, LC 3; enrl D 105, maj 28
Ent Req: HS dipl, provision made for entrance without HS dipl by interview and committee action
Degrees: AB (Art) 4 yrs
Tuition: $33 annual tuition
Courses: Art Education, Ceramics, Drawing, Graphic Arts, History of Art & Archaeology, Painting, Sculpture, Teacher Training, Textile Design

COFFEYVILLE

COFFEYVILLE COMMUNITY COLLEGE, Art Dept, 67337. Tel 316-251-7700, Ext 47. *Head Dept* Douglas Keller, MA
Estab 1923, dept estab 1969; pub; D & E; scholarships; SC 8, LC 2; enrl D 75, E 60, non-maj 25, maj 110
Ent Req: HS dipl
Degrees: AA
Tuition: Res—undergrad approx $375 per yr (includes $41.50 fees); nonres—undergrad $33.50 per cr hr (includes $41.50 fees); campus res $1100
Courses: Art History, Ceramics, Drawing, Handicrafts, Painting, Photography, Printmaking, Sculpture
Adult Hobby Classes: Crafts

COLBY

COLBY COMMUNITY COLLEGE, Visual Arts Dept, 1255 South Range, 67701. Tel 913-462-3984. *Head Dept* Kenneth Eugene Mitchell, MA
Estab 1965, dept estab 1966; pub; D & E; scholarships; SC 18, LC 8; enrl D 141, E 210, maj 18
Ent Req: HS dipl
Degrees: AA 2 yrs
Courses: Color Structure and Design, Figure Drawing: Advanced, Problems in Drawing, Problems in Painting, Watercolor I & II
Adult Hobby Classes: Enrl 10-20; tui $15 per hr
Summer School: Enrl 5-20; Term of 4 wks beginning June 1. Courses—Drawing, Jewelry, Watercolor

EL DORADO

BUTLER COUNTY COMMUNITY COLLEGE, Art Dept, Route 1, PO Box 888, 67042. Tel 316-321-5083. *Instr* Robert H Chism, MA; *Instr* Lynn B Havel, MFA; *Instr* Peter Johnson, MFA
Estab 1927, dept estab 1964; pub; D & E; scholarships; SC 13, LC 1; enrl D 168, E 57
Ent Req: HS dipl, ACT, EED
Degrees: AA 2 yr
Tuition: Res—$280 per yr; nonres—$800 per yr
Courses: Art History, Ceramics, Drawing, Interior Design, Painting, Printmaking, Silversmithing

EMPORIA

EMPORIA STATE UNIVERSITY, Dept of Art, 66801. Tel 316-343-1200, Ext 246. *Chmn* Donald Perry, MFA
Estab 1863, dept estab early 1900's; pub; D & E; scholarships; SC 42, LC 15, GC 30; enrl D 700, E 25, maj 120, grad 25
Ent Req: HS dipl, HS seniors may enroll in regular classes
Degrees: BFA, BSEd, BS(Art Therapy) 4 yr, MA(Studio & Art Educ), MS(ArtTherapy)
Tuition: Res—undergrad and grad $432 per sem; nonres—undergrad and grad $908 per sem; campus res—room & board $1565
Courses: †Art Education, Art History, †Ceramics, Commercial Art, Costume Design & Construction, Display, Drafting, Drawing, Fashion Arts, Goldsmithing, Graphic Arts, Handicrafts, History of Art & Archaeology, Illustration, Interior Design, †Jewelry, Mixed Media, †Painting, Photography, †Printmaking, †Sculpture, †Silversmithing, Stage Design, †Teacher Training, Textile Design, Theatre Arts, Weaving, †Art Therapy
Summer School: Dir, J W Brinkman. Enrl 150; tuition res $24 per hr, nonres $37 per hr for term beginning June 11. Courses—most of the regular classes

GARDEN CITY

GARDEN CITY COMMUNITY JUNIOR COLLEGE, Art Dept,* 801 Campus Dr, PO Box 977, 67846. Tel 316-276-7611. *Chmn Human & Fine Arts* Max R Goldsberry
Degrees: AA
Courses: Art Appreciation, Art History, Calligraphy, Ceramics, Design, Drawing, Handicrafts, Interior Design, Jewelry, Painting, Photography, Printmaking, Stage Design, Stained Glass

HAYS

FORT HAYS STATE UNIVERSITY, Dept of Art, Visual Arts Center, 600 Park St, 67601. Tel 913-628-4247. *Chmn* John C Thorns Jr, MFA; *Prof* Jim Hinkhouse, MFA; *Prof* Kathleen Kuchar; *Prof* Darrell McGinnis, MA; *Assoc Prof* Dale Ficken, MA; *Assoc Prof* Joanne Harwick, MFA; *Assoc Prof* Frank Nichols, MFA; *Assoc Prof* Zoran Stevanov, MFA; *Asst Prof* Martha Holmes, MA; *Asst Prof* Michael Jile, MFA; *Instr* Chaiwat Thumsujarit, MFA
Estab 1902, dept estab 1930; pub; D & E; scholarships; SC 66, LC 19, GC 28; enrl D 850, non-maj 665, maj 148, grad 37, others 7
Ent Req: HS dipl
Degrees: BA and BFA 4 yrs, AA and MA 2 yrs, MFA 2-3 yrs
Tuition: Res—undergrad and grad $31.50 per cr hr; nonres—undergrad and grad $63.25 per cr hr; campus res—room & board $499 and up
Courses: †Advertising Design, †Art Education, †Art History, †Ceramics, †Commercial Art, †Drawing, †Graphic Design, †Handicrafts, †History of Art & Archaeology, †Illustration, †Jewelry, †Mixed Media, †Painting, †Photography, †Printmaking, †Sculpture, †Silversmithing, †Teacher Training, †Art Therapy
Summer School: Enrl 145; tuition $31.50 per cr hr for term of 8 wks beginning June 4. Courses—Studio Courses & Workshops

HESSTON

HESSTON COLLEGE,* Box 3000, 67062. Tel 316-327-4221, Ext 240. *Head Dept* John Blosser, MA
Estab 1915; den; D & E; SC 9, SC 1; enrl non-maj 50, maj 5
Ent Req: HS dipl
Degrees: AA 2 yr
Tuition: $3400 annual tuition; campus res available
Courses: Art History, Ceramics, Drafting, Drawing, Painting, Photography, Sculpture, Design

HUTCHINSON

HUTCHINSON COMMUNITY JUNIOR COLLEGE, Art Dept,* 1300 N Plum St, 67501. Tel 316-665-3500, Ext 3518. *Prof* Dennis Chegwidden, MFA; *Prof* Jane Dronberger, MA; *Prof* Roy Swanson, MFA
Estab 1928; pub; D & E; scholarships; SC 17, LC 4; enrl D 215, E 41, non-maj 180, maj 29
Ent Req: HS dipl
Degrees: AA 2 yrs
Tuition: $14 per cr hr; campus res—room & board $1060 per yr
Courses: †Art Education, †Art History, †Ceramics, †Drawing, †Graphic Design, †History of Art & Archaeology, †Jewelry, †Painting, †Printmaking, †Sculpture, †Silversmithing, †Theatre Arts
Summer School: Tui $9 per course

IOLA

ALLEN COUNTY COMMUNITY COLLEGE, Art Dept,* 1801 N Cottonwood, 66749. Tel 316-365-5116. *Dept Head* Ronald Medley, MFA
Estab 1965; pub; D & E; scholarships; SC 5, LC 2; enrl D 400, E 435, non-maj 40, maj 6
Ent Req: HS dipl or GED
Degrees: AA 2 yr
Tuition: Res—$10 per cr hr; nonres—$44.50 per cr hr
Courses: Art History, Ceramics, Commercial Art, Drawing, Handicrafts, Painting, Photography, Printmaking, Sculpture, Art Appreciation, Art Fundamentals, Design (2nd and 3rd dimensional)
Summer School: Courses—all courses

LAWRENCE

HASKELL INDIAN JUNIOR COLLEGE, Art Dept, 66044. Tel 913-749-8458. *Instr* Jean S Allen, MFA; *Instr* Clinton J Leon, MS; *Instr* Danny Miller, AA
Estab 1884, dept estab 1970; pub; D; SC 14, LC 1; enrl in dept D, non-maj 90, maj 10
Ent Req: HS dipl or GED, at least 1/4 Indian, Eskimo or Aleut and receive agency approval
Degrees: AA and AAS 2 yrs
Tuition: Campus residence available
Courses: Art Appreciation, Ceramics, Design, Drawing, Jewelry, Painting, Sculpture, Textile Design

UNIVERSITY OF KANSAS, School of Fine Arts, 66045. Tel 913-864-4401. *Dean* James Moeser; *Assoc Dean* Jerry C Moore
Pub; scholarships and fels; enrl 250
Degrees: BFA, BAE, BS, MFA 4-5 yrs
—**Dept of Art,** 66045. Tel 913-864-4401. *Chmn* Phillip Blackhurst. Instrs: FT 19
Estab 1885; SC 50, GC 25; enrl maj 150
Tuition: Res—$520 per sem; nonres—$1310 per sem
Courses: Drawing, Painting, Printmaking, Sculpture
Summer School: Term of eight weeks beginning June

—**Dept of Design,** 66045. Tel 913-864-4401. *Chmn* S Lee Mann. Instrs: FT 25, PT 5
Estab 1921; SC 83, LC 32, GC 26; enrl maj 450, grad 30
Tuition: Res—$459; nonres—$1117 per sem
Courses: Art Education, Art History, Ceramics, Industrial Design, Interior Design, Jewelry, Teacher Training, Textile Design, Design, Weaving, Textile Printing & Dyeing, Visual Communications
Summer School: Term of eight weeks beginning June
—**Kress Foundation Dept of Art History,** Spencer Museum of Art, 66045. Tel 913-864-4713. *Chairperson* Jeanne Stump, PhD; *Grad Advisor* Stephen Addiss, PhD; *Prof* Chu-tsing Li, PhD; *Prof* Marilyn Stokstad, PhD; *Assoc Prof* Edmund Eglinski, PhD; *Assoc Prof* James L Connelly, PhD; *Assoc Prof* Thomas Southall, MA; *Assoc Prof* Timothy Mitchell, PhD; *Asst Prof* Linda Stone-Ferrier, PhD; *Lectr* Ross Taggart; *Lectr* Marc Wilson; *Lectr* Roger Ward; *Lectr* Laurence Sickman
Estab 1866, dept estab 1953; pub; D & E; scholarships; LC 30, GC 10; enrl D 900, E 49, maj 50, grad 70
Ent Req: HS dipl
Degrees: BA, BGS, MFA, MA, PhD
Tuition: Campus res available
Courses: Art History, Chinese and Japanese Art, North American Art, Western European Art
Summer School: Enrl 25; tuition varies. Courses—Art History, History, Literature. Classes in Great Britain
—**Dept of Art, Music Education and Music Therapy,** 311 Bailey Hall, 66045. Tel 913-864-4784. *Chmn Dept* George L Duerksen, PhD; *Prof* Philip H Rueschhoff, EdD; *Asst Prof* Ann Sherman, PhD; *Instr* Dixie Glenn, MA
Estab 1865, dept estab 1969; pub; D & E; scholarships; GC 12; enrl D 535, maj 123, grad 123, others 289
Ent Req: HS dipl, ent exam
Degrees: BAE 4 yrs, MA 1-6 yrs, EdD and PhD 3-6 yrs
Tuition: Res—$520 per sem, $43 per cr hr; nonres—$1310 per sem, $96 per cr hr; campus res available
Courses: Visual Arts Education
Summer School: Term of 8 wks beginning June

LEAVENWORTH

SAINT MARY COLLEGE, Art Dept,* 4100 S Forth St, 66048. Tel 913-682-5151. *Assoc Prof* Mary Rebecca Conner, MA; *Asst Prof* Carmen Echevarria, MA; *Lectr* David Melby, MFA
Estab 1923; pvt; D & E; scholarships; SC 25, LC 5; enrl non-maj 80, maj 10
Ent Req: HS dipl
Degrees: BA, BS, BM and BME 4 yr
Courses: Art Education, Art History, Calligraphy, Ceramics, Commercial Art, Drawing, Graphic Arts, Handicrafts, History of Art & Archaeology, Interior Design, Jewelry, Lettering, Mixed Media, Painting, Photography, Printmaking, Sculpture, Teacher Training, Textile Design, Stitchery, Weaving
Children's Classes: Enrl 30; Courses—Crafts Camp; Painting (Saturday)
Summer School: Courses—variable 3 wk workshop

LIBERAL

SEWARD COUNTY COMMUNITY COLLEGE, Art Dept,* North Hwy 83, Box 1137, 67901. Tel 913-624-1951. *Chmn Fine Arts & Communication* Steve Heckman, MFA
Estab 1969; pub; D & E; scholarships; SC 13, LC 6; enrl D 650, E 350
Ent Req: HS dipl
Degrees: AA 2 yrs
Tuition: Res—$420 per yr; nonres—$1220 per yr
Courses: Art Education, Art History, Ceramics, Costume Design & Construction, Drawing, History of Art & Archaeology, Painting, Photography, Sculpture, Stage Design
Summer School: Dir, Steve Heckman. Term of 6 wks beginning June 4. Courses—Varied and subject to change

LINDSBORG

BETHANY COLLEGE, Art Dept, Box 111, 67456. Tel 913-227-3311, Ext 147. *Head Art Dept* Nicholas Hill, MFA; *Prof* Ray Kahmeyer, MA; *Instructor* Vicky Randall, MFA; *Instr* Sharon Stockwell, MFA
Den; D; scholarships; SC 19, LC 3; enrl D 195, non-maj 200, maj 40
Ent Req: HS dipl
Degrees: BA 3-4 yr
Courses: †Art Education, Art History, †Ceramics, Design, †Drawing, Graphic Design, †Painting, †Photography, †Printmaking, †Sculpture, Metalsmithing, Studio Concentration
Summer School: Acad Dean, Dr Alan Steinbach

MANHATTAN

KANSAS STATE UNIVERSITY
—**Art Dept,** 66506. Tel 913-532-6605. *Head Dept* Charles Stroh, MFA; *Prof* Angelo Garzio, MFA; *Prof* Oscar V Larmer, MFA; *Prof* Elliott Pujol, MFA; *Assoc Prof* James C Munce; *Assoc Prof* Rex Replogle, MFA; *Assoc Prof* John Vogt, MFA; *Assoc Prof* Gary Woodward, MFA; *Assoc Prof* Lou Ann Culley, PhD; *Assoc Prof* Ed Sturr, DEd; *Assoc Prof* Yoshiro Ikeda, MFA. Instrs: FT 23, PT 2, 13 Area Coordrs
Estab 1863, dept estab 1965; pub; D & E; scholarships; SC 45, LC 19, GC 7; enrl D 1940, E 60, non-maj 1800, maj 200, grad 15
Ent Req: HS dipl
Degrees: BS(Art Educ) jointly with Col Educ, BA and BFA 4 yrs, MFA 60 sem cr
Tuition: Res—$449 per sem; nonres—$1107 per sem; campus res available
Courses: Art Education, Art History, Ceramics, Drawing, Graphic Design, Jewelry, Lettering, Painting, Printmaking, Sculpture, Fibers, Pre-Art Therapy
Summer School: Dir, Charles Stroh. Enrl 150; tuition res $31 per cr hr, nonres $75 per cr hr for term of 4 to 8 wks beginning June 5. Courses—most of above, varies from summer to summer

—**College of Architecture and Design,** Seaton Hall, 66506. Tel 913-532-5950. *Asst Dean* R Foreyta. Instrs: FT 53
Estab 1904; enrl 950
Degrees: BArchit, BInterior Archit and BLandscape Archit 5 yrs, MArchit, MLandscape Archit, MRegional and Community Planning
Tuition: Nonres—$1747 per sem
Courses: †Architecture, †Landscape Architecture, †Interior Architecture, †Regional and Community Planning
Adult Hobby Classes: Dean, Bernd Foerster
Children's Classes: Courses—Special Design Program in June
Summer School: Dean, Bernd Foerster. 8 wks from June 4

MCPHERSON

MCPHERSON COLLEGE, Art Dept, 1600 E Euclid, PO Box 1402, 67460. Tel 316-241-0731, Ext 234. *Chmn* Mary Ann Robinson, MA; *Instructor* Wayne Conyers, MA
Estab 1887; den; D & E; scholarships; SC 14, LC 5; enrl D 150, maj 10, others 140
Ent Req: HS dipl, ACT
Degrees: AB 4 yr
Tuition: Res—undergrad $4000 per yr, $125 per cr hr; campus res—room and board $2100
Courses: †Art Education, Art History, Ceramics, Drawing, †Interior Design, Lettering, Museum Staff Training, Painting, Printmaking, Teacher Training, Textile Design
Summer School: Dir, Dr Dayton Rothrock. Term of 10 wks beginning end of May, Courses—Varied Liberal Arts

NORTH NEWTON

BETHEL COLLEGE, Dept of Art, 67117. Tel 316-283-2500. *Chmn* Robert W Regier, MFA; *Assoc Prof* Paul Friesen, MA; *Asst Prof* Gail Lutsch, MFA
Estab 1888, dept estab 1959; den; D; scholarships; SC 11, LC 3; enrl D 240, non-maj 25
Ent Req: HS, ACT
Degrees: BA(Art) 4 yrs
Tuition: $3700 per yr, $1850 per sem, $132 per hr; campus res—room & board $2150 per yr
Courses: Art Education, Art History, Ceramics, Drawing, Graphic Arts, Graphic Design, Painting, Photography, Printmaking, Sculpture, Crafts
Adult Hobby Classes: Enrl 15; tuition $40 per 6 wk session. Courses—Ceramics, Drawing, Painting
Summer School: Courses—Drawing, Painting

OTTAWA

OTTAWA UNIVERSITY, Dept of Art, Tenth & Cedar Sts, 66067. Tel 913-242-5200. *Dir* Frank J Lemp. Instrs: FT 1
Estab 1865; pvt; D; scholarships; SC 16, LC 5; enrl D 35, maj 5
Ent Req: HS grad, SAT, ACT
Degrees: BA 4 yrs
Courses: Art Education, Art History, Ceramics, Drawing, Graphic Arts, Painting, Photography, Arts Management
Children's Classes: Enrl 15. Courses—Art Foundation, Ceramics
Summer School: Dir, Dr Ed Morrissey. Tuition $73 for 8 wk session. Courses—Continental Art History, Art In Western World

OVERLAND PARK

JOHNSON COUNTY COMMUNITY COLLEGE, Humanities Division,* 12345 Col at Quivira Rd, 66210. Tel 913-888-8500, Ext 690. *Dir* Landon Kitchner, PhD; *Instructor* Stuart Beals, BA; *Instructor* Judy Brazil, BA; *Instructor* Ron Hicks, MS; *Instructor* Jean Howard, EdD; *Instructor* Karen Schory, MFA; *Instructor* Thomas Tarnowski, MFA; *Instructor* Dorothy Wadsworth, MFA
Estab 1969; pub; D & E; SC 30, LC 4; enrl D 200, E 100
Ent Req: HS dipl or equivalent
Degrees: AA 2 yr
Tuition: Res—$15 per sem cr hr; nonres—$55 per sem cr hr; no campus residence
Courses: Art Education, Art History, Ceramics, Commercial Art, Illustration, Lettering, Painting, Photography, Printmaking, Sculpture, Silversmithing, Design (2-dimensional, 3-dimensional & color), Layout, Preparation of Portfolio, Silkscreen, Weaving, Visual Communications, Visual Technology
Summer School: Enrl 100; tui $17.50 per cr hr for term of 8 wks beginning June 5

PITTSBURG

PITTSBURG STATE UNIVERSITY (Formerly Kansas State College), Art Dept, 1701 S Broadway St, 66762. *Chairperson & Prof* Harry E Krug, MS; *Prof* Robert Blunk Jr, MS; *Assoc Prof* Alex Barde, MFA; *Assoc Prof* Robert Russell, MFA; *Assoc Prof* Marjorie Schick, MFA; *Assoc Prof* Laurence Wooster, MA
Estab 1903, dept estab 1921; pub; D & E; SC 48, LC 12, GC 14; enrl D 600, E 50, non-maj 300, maj 80, grad 30
Ent Req: HS dipl
Degrees: BFA & BSEd 4 yr, MA & MS 33 hr
Tuition: Res—undergrad and grad $421 per sem, $21.50 per sem hr; nonres—undergrad and grad $897 per sem, $53.25 per sem hr; campus res—room and board $2038 per yr
Courses: †Art Education, Art History, †Ceramics, †Drawing, Film, †Jewelry, †Painting, †Photography, †Printmaking, †Sculpture, †Silversmithing, †Teacher Training, †Art Therapy
Summer School: Enrl 200; tuition res $24 per cr hr, nonres $50.50 per cr hr for term of 8 wks beginning June 5th. Courses—as above

PRATT

PRATT COMMUNITY COLLEGE, Art Dept, Highway 61, 67124. Tel 316-672-5641. *Chmn* Gene Wineland, MA
D & E; scholarships; SC 12, LC 1
Ent Req: HS dipl
Degrees: AA and AS
Tuition: Res—$273 per sem total fees; nonres $863 per sem, $1726 per yr total fees
Courses: Ceramics, Commercial Art, Drawing, Jewelry, Painting, Photography, Printmaking, Elementary School Arts, Introduction to Art
Adult Hobby Classes: Variety per sem
Summer School: Small selection of courses

SALINA

KANSAS WESLEYAN UNIVERSITY, Art Dept,* Santa Fe & Clafin St, 67401. Tel 913-827-5541. *Chmn* George F Chlebak
Estab 1886; den; scholarships; SC 8, LC 3; enrl maj 15, others 500 for two sem
Degrees: AB 4 yr
Courses: Art History, Drawing, Painting, Design
Summer School: Enrl 125; for term of 8 wks beginning June

MARYMOUNT COLLEGE, Art Dept,* E Iron & Marymount Rd, 67401. Tel 913-825-2101. *Chmn* Dennis Denning, PhD
Tuition: $1775 per sem
Courses: Advertising Design, Art Appreciation, Art Education, Art History, Calligraphy, Ceramics, Design, Drawing, Film, Illustration, Painting, Photography, Printmaking

STERLING

STERLING COLLEGE, Art Dept, 540 E Main, 67579. Tel 316-278-3609, Ext 245. *Head Dept* Gordon Zahradnik, MFA
Estab 1876; den; D & E; scholarships; SC 16, LC 2; enrl D 410
Ent Req: HS dipl
Degrees: AB and BS
Tuition: Campus residency available
Courses: Advertising Design, Art Education, Art History, Calligraphy, Ceramics, Collages, Commercial Art, Costume Design & Construction, Drawing, Graphic Arts, Graphic Design, Handicrafts, Interior Design, Jewelry, Lettering, Painting, Photography, Printmaking, Textile Design, Theatre Arts, Copper Enameling, Fibers
Adult Hobby Classes: Enrl 25; tuition $20. Courses—all areas
Children's Classes: Courses—Art Education

TOPEKA

WASHBURN UNIVERSITY OF TOPEKA, Dept of Art,* Mulvane Art Center, 17th and Jewell Sts, 66621. Tel 913-295-6324. *Head Dept* James Hunt; *Art & Theatre Arts Chmn* John Hunter. Instrs: FT 6
Estab 1900; pub; SC 11, LC 5; enrl maj 60, others 280
Ent Req: HS dipl
Degrees: AB and BFA 4 yr
Tuition: Res—$857 per yr; nonres—$1570 per yr
Courses: Art History, Ceramics, Drawing, Painting, Photography, Sculpture, Art Appreciation, Design
Adult Hobby Classes: Tuition $35 for eight 3 hr sessions
Children's Classes: Tuition $30 for ten 1 1/2 hr sessions

WICHITA

FRIENDS UNIVERSITY, Art Dept, 2100 University Ave, 67213. Tel 316-261-5800. *Chairperson & Assoc Prof* Dee M Connett, MA; *Asst Prof* Michael Oliver, MFA
Estab 1898; den; D & E; scholarships; SC 18, LC 4; enrl D 329, E 37
Ent Req: HS dipl
Degrees: BA and BS 4 yr
Tuition: Res—undergrad $3890 per yr or $1945 per sem; campus res—room & board $1790 per yr, $895 per sem
Courses: †Art Education, Art History, Ceramics, †Commercial Art, Drawing, Graphic Arts, Graphic Design, Jewelry, Painting, Photography, Printmaking, Sculpture, Silversmithing, Teacher Training, †2-D Art, †3-D Art, †Art Business
Adult Hobby Classes: Courses—Drawing, Jewelry, Painting
Summer School: Courses of 6 wks beginning June 5th

SCHOOL OF THE WICHITA ART ASSOCIATION, 9112 E Central, 67206. Tel 316-686-6687. *Dir* Glenice L Matthews. Instrs: 20
Estab 1920; pvt; D & E; scholarships; enrl 300
Courses: Art History, Ceramics, Commercial Art, Drawing, Painting, Photography, Printmaking, Sculpture, Silversmithing, Enameling, Pottery, Weaving
Summer School: 6 wk June-July

WICHITA STATE UNIVERSITY, Division of Art, College of Fine Arts, 67208. Tel 316-689-3555. *Asst Dean & Grad Coordr* Robert M Kiskadden; *Chmn Art Educ* Mary Sue Foster, MA; *Chmn Art History* Stockton Garver, PhD; *Chmn Graphic Design* Clark Britton, MAA; *Chmn Studio Arts* Richard St John, MFA
Estab 1895, dept estab 1901; pub; D & E; scholarships; enrl D 1149, E 194, non-maj 78, maj 285, grad 51, others 2
Ent Req: HS dipl
Degrees: BAE and BFA 4 yr, MFA 2 yr, MA 1 yr
Tuition: Res—undergrad and grad $410.25 per sem, $27.35 per hr; nonres—undergrad and grad $1200 per sem, $80 per hr; no campus res
Courses: †Art Education, †Art History, †Ceramics, Drawing, †Graphic Design, Illustration, Lettering, †Painting, Photography, †Printmaking, †Sculpture, Teacher Training
Summer School: Tuition as above for term of 8 wks

WINFIELD

SOUTHWESTERN COLLEGE, Art Dept,* 67156. Tel 316-221-4150, Ext 270. *Asst Dean Faculty & Assoc Prof* Warren D Brown, MA; *Instructor* Benton Peugh, MFA
Estab 1885; pvt & den; D & E; scholarships; SC 12, LC 4
Ent Req: HS dipl
Degrees: BA 4 yr
Tuition: $1480 per term
Courses: †Art Education

KENTUCKY

BARBOURVILLE

UNION COLLEGE, Art Dept,* College St, 40906. Tel 606-546-4151. *Dept Head* Allan Green
Den; D & E
Ent Req: HS dipl
Degrees: BA, BS and MA (Educ) 4 yr
Tuition: $1950 per sem
Courses: Art Education, Art History, Drawing, Painting, Teacher Training, Theatre Arts, Art Appreciation, Art Fundamentals, Recreational Arts and Crafts

BEREA

BEREA COLLEGE, Art Dept, 40404. Tel 606-986-9341, Ext 292. *Chmn* Lester F Pross, MA; *Prof* Dorothy Tredennick, MA; *Prof* Neil DiTeresa, AM; *Prof* Sally Wilkerson, MFA; *Assoc Prof* Walter Hyleck, MFA; *Asst Prof* Christopher Pierce, MFA; *Asst Prof* William Morningstar, MFA; *Asst Prof* Robert Boyce
Estab 1855, dept estab 1936; pvt; D; scholarships; SC 14, LC 8; enrl C 1500, D 324, maj 71
Ent Req: HS dipl (preference given to students from Southern Appalachian region)
Degrees: BA 4 yr
Tuition: None; campus res—room and board $1812
Courses: †Art Education, †Art History, †Ceramics, †Drawing, †Painting, †Printmaking, †Sculpture, †Textile Design

BOWLING GREEN

WESTERN KENTUCKY UNIVERSITY, Art Dept, Ivan Wilson Center for Fine Arts, Room 441, 42101. Tel 502-745-3940. *Head Dept* Dr Joseph W Gluhman. Instrs: FT 13
Pub; D; SC 46, LC 19; enrl maj 200
Ent Req: HS dipl
Degrees: BA and BFA 4 yrs, MA(Art Educ)
Tuition: $391 per sem; nonres—$1132; campus res $335-$350 per sem
Courses: †Art Education, Art History, Ceramics, †Commercial Art, Drawing, Graphic Design, †Painting, Photography, Printmaking, Design, Weaving
Summer School: Tuition $396, nonres $1134 for term of 8 wks beginning June 7. Courses—Art Education, Art History, Ceramics, Design, Drawing, Painting

CAMPBELLSVILLE

CAMPBELLSVILLE COLLEGE, Fine Arts Division, 42718. Tel 502-465-8158. *Div Head* James Moore
Estab 1906, dept estab 1967; den; D & E; scholarships; SC 28, LC 5; enrl D 35, E 10, non-maj 12, maj 22, others 8 minors
Ent Req: HS dipl, ACT
Degrees: BA, BS, BS(Med Tech), BM and BChM 4 yr, AA, AS and ASSW 2 yr
Courses: Advertising Design, Architecture, Art Education, Art History, Ceramics, Commercial Art, Conceptual Art, Display, Drafting, Drawing, Graphic Arts, Graphic Design, Handicrafts, Jewelry, Painting, Photography, Printmaking, Sculpture, Silversmithing, Stage Design, Teacher Training, Theatre Arts
Summer School: Term of 8 wks beginning June 9, 1980. Courses—Art Education, Art Appreciation, Drawing, Painting

FORT MITCHELL

THOMAS MORE COLLEGE, Art Dept, 2771 Turkeyfoot Rd, 41017. Tel 606-341-5800. *Chmn* Darrell W Brothers, MFA; *Assoc Prof* Sr M De Rauf, MFA
Estab 1921; pvt; D & E; SC 9, LC 4; enrl D 12, E 5, maj 17
Ent Req: HS dipl
Degrees: BA, BES, BS, AA and AES
Tuition: $125 per sem hr; campus res—room and board $1135 per sem
Courses: Aesthetics, Art Education, Art History, Ceramics, Design, Drawing, Painting, Photography, Printmaking, Sculpture, Teacher Training, Theatre Arts, Arts Management, Figure Drawing, Anatomy, Perspective, Color
Summer School: Dir, Dr Raymond Hebert. Courses—various

GEORGETOWN

GEORGETOWN COLLEGE, Art Dept, Fine Arts Division, 40324. Tel 502-863-8351. *Chmn* Charles James McCormick. Instrs: FT 2
Estab 1829; den; D; scholarships and grants; SC 14, LC 6; enrl 1150
Ent Req: HS transcript, ACT
Degrees: BA 4 yrs
Tuition: Res—$1480 per term; nonres—$1525 per term; sem curriculum;

May interterm
Courses: Art History, Ceramics, Graphic Arts, Painting, Photography, Sculpture, Art Appreciation, Art Careers, Art Survey, Graphic Design Internship, Public School Art, Secondary Art, Three-Dimensional Design, Travel Classes, Two-Dimensional Design
Summer School: Two 4 1/2 wk sem 6-7 hrs each. Courses—Art Education, Art Humanities, Studio Classes

HIGHLAND HEIGHTS

NORTHERN KENTUCKY UNIVERSITY, Fine Arts Dept,* 41076. Tel 606-372-5420. *Chmn* Rosemary I Strauss. Instrs: FT 23, PT 5
Estab 1968; pub; D & E; SC 31, LC 10
Ent Req: HS grad, ACT scores
Degrees: BA(Art Educ) BA(Art History), BA(Graphic Design)
Tuition: Res—$408 per yr; nonres—$1183 per yr
Courses: Art Education, Art History, Ceramics, Drawing, Graphic Design, Painting, Photography, Printmaking, Sculpture

LEXINGTON

TRANSYLVANIA UNIVERSITY, Studio Arts Dept, 300 N Broadway, 40508. Tel 606-233-8111, 233-8246. *Prof & Program Dir* Dan Selter, MFA; *Prof* Jack Girard, MFA; *Instr* Nancy Wolsk, MA; *Instr* Anne Binford, AB
Estab 1780; pvt; D & E; scholarships; SC 20, LC 3; enrl D 105, E 14, maj 18
Ent Req: HS dipl
Degrees: BA and BS
Tuition: $7500
Adult Hobby Classes: Enrl 5 - 10; tuition $40 - $80 per 3 - 5 wk sessions
Children's Classes: Enrl 5 - 10; tuition $40 - $60 per 3 - 5 wk sessions
Summer School: Dir, Dan Selter. Enrl 5 -20; tuition $400 per course.
Courses—Ceramics, Painting, Printing

UNIVERSITY OF KENTUCKY, Dept of Art, College of Fine Arts, 40506. Tel 606-251-8151. *Dean* Richard C Domek; *Chmn* Marilyn Hamann. Instrs: FT 20, PT 4
Estab 1918; pub; scholarships and grad assistantships; SC 23, LC 19, GC 6; enrl maj 200, others 800
Degrees: BA, BFA, MA and MFA 4 yr
Tuition: Res—undergrad $509, grad $556; nonres—undergrad $1443, grad $1583
Courses: Art Education, †Art History, †Ceramics, Drawing, Graphic Design, Painting, Photography, Printmaking, Sculpture, Studio Art
Summer School: Dir, Marilyn Hamann. Tuition res $41 per cr hr, nonres $119 per cr hr. Courses vary

LOUISVILLE

JEFFERSON COMMUNITY COLLEGE, Fine Arts, First & Broadway, PO Box 1036, 40201. Tel 502-584-0181, Ext 289. *Coordr Fine Arts & Assoc Prof* R M Crask; *Assoc Prof* Ann Hemdahl-Owen. Instrs: PT 6
Estab 1964; pub; D & E; scholarships; SC 11, LC 6; enrl D 4774, E 4172
Ent Req: HS dipl
Degrees: AFA, AAA and Assoc in Photography 2 yrs
Tuition: $207 per yr, $18 per hr
Courses: †Advertising Design, Aesthetics, Art Education, Art History, †Commercial Art, Display, Drawing, Graphic Arts, Graphic Design, History of Art & Archaeology, Mixed Media, Painting, †Photography, Sculpture, †Theatre Arts
Summer School: Dir, Dr Ronald Horvath. Courses—Drawing, Photography

UNIVERSITY OF LOUISVILLE, Allen R Hite Art Institute,* Department of Fine Arts, Belknap Campus, 40208. Tel 502-588-6794. *Dir* Donald R Anderson, MFA; *Prof* Henry J Chodkowski, MFA; *Prof* E Thomas Marsh, MAT. Instrs: FT 16, PT 6
Estab 1846; dept estab 1935; pub; D & E; scholarships; SC 35, LC 71, GC 26; enrl D 1000, E 90, non-maj 800, maj 264, grad 29
Ent Req: HS dipl, CEEB
Degrees: BA 4 yr, MA 1 to 2 yrs
Tuition: Res—undergrad $570 per yr, $285 per sem, $24 per hr, grad $648 per yr, $324 per sem, $27 per hr; nonres—undergrad $2000 per yr, $1000 per sem, $84 per hr, grad $1992 per yr, $996 per sem, $83 per hr; campus res—room & board $1380
Courses: Art Education, Art History, †Ceramics, Drawing, †Graphic Design, Handicrafts, †History of Art & Archaeology, †Painting, †Photography, †Printmaking, †Sculpture, Teacher Training, Textile Design
Summer School: Tuition res $24 pr hr, nonres $84 per hr for term of 5 wks, beginning early June. Courses—3 or 4 of above courses

MIDWAY

MIDWAY COLLEGE, Art Dept,* Stephens St, 40347. Tel 606-846-4423, Ext 27. *Chmn* Virginia Hutton; *Faculty* Wayne Gebb, BM; *Faculty* Linda MacKellar, MFA; *Faculty* Linda Vore, MA. Instrs: FT 1
Den; D, W; scholarships; SC 7, LC 3; enrl 55
Ent Req: HS dipl, ACT
Degrees: 2 yr
Tuition: $1500 per sem
Courses: Art Education, Ceramics, Drawing, Painting, Sculpture, Textile Design, Basic Design, Historical Furniture

MOREHEAD

MOREHEAD STATE UNIVERSITY, Art Dept,* Claypool-Young Art Bldg, UPO Box 714, 40351. Tel 606-783-2221
Estab 1922; pub; D & E; scholarships; SC 40, LC 16, GC 28; enrl D 900, E 20, non-maj 180, maj 180, GS 55, others 145
Ent Req: HS dipl, ACT
Degrees: BA 4 yr, MA 1 yr
Tuition: Res—$413 per sem; nonres—$1188 per sem
Courses: Weaving
Adult Hobby Classes: Courses—Ceramics, Crafts, Oil Painting, Watercolor Painting, Weaving
Summer School: Courses—same as above on demand

MURRAY

MURRAY STATE UNIVERSITY, Art Dept, College of Creative Expression, 42071. Tel 502-762-3784. *Chmn* Robert W Head, MFA; *Prof* Karen W Boyd, MFA; *Prof* Fred Shepard, MFA; *Assoc Prof* Harry Furches, MFA; *Assoc Prof* Michael Johnson, MFA; *Assoc Prof* Melody Weiler, MFA; *Assoc Prof* Dale Leys, MFA; *Asst Prof* Michael Watts, MFA; *Asst Prof* Joe Rigsby, BFA; *Asst Prof* Steve Bishop, MFA; *Asst Prof* Jerry Speight, MA; *Asst Prof* Paul Sasso, MFA; *Asst Prof* Mary Jane Timmerman, MFA; *Asst Prof* Nadya Brown, MFA; *Asst Prof* Martha Ehrlich, PhD; *Asst Prof* Diane Gregory, PhD
Estab 1925, dept estab 1931; pub; D & E; scholarships; SC 329, LC 151, GS 20; enrl D 801, E 35, non-maj 316, maj 150, grad 13
Ent Req: HS dipl from accredited Kentucky HS, out of state must rank in the upper third of their HS and(or) ACT test score of 20 or above
Degrees: BA, BS and BFA 4 yr, MAEd, MACT and MA(Studio) approx 1 1/2 yrs
Tuition: Res—undergrad $836 per yr, $418 per sem, $35 per hr, grad $914 per yr, $457 per sem, $51 per hr; nonres—undergrad $2386 per yr, $1193 per sem, $100 per hr, grad $2610 per yr, $1305 per sem, $145 per hr; campus res—room and board $640 per yr
Courses: Advertising Design, Art Education, Art History, †Ceramics, †Commercial Art, †Drawing, Graphic Design, †Jewelry, †Painting, †Photography, †Printmaking, †Sculpture, †Silversmithing, †Teacher Training, †Weaving, †Functional Design, †Surface Design
Children's Classes: Special program for advanced students; summer workshop for HS students (they stay on campus, $165 per 1 wk)
Summer School: Enrl 52; tuition res undergrad $35 per hr, grad $51 per hr; nonres undergrad $100 per hr, grad $145 per hr for one eight wk session

OWENSBORO

BRESCIA COLLEGE, Dept of Art, 120 W Seventh St, 42301. Tel 502-685-3131. *Chmn* Gerald A Matlick. Instrs: FT 4
Estab 1950; den; D & E; scholarships; SC 47, LC 10; enrl 960, maj 50
Ent Req: HS dipl, placement exam, ACT, GED
Degrees: AA(Photograph) 2 yr in art and art education 4 yr
Tuition: $96.50 per cr hr; campus res—$500 - $560 per yr room, $1295 yr board
Courses: Art Education, †Art History, Calligraphy, †Ceramics, †Drawing, †Painting, †Printmaking, †Black & White Photography, †Color Photography, Flatglass, 2-D & 3-D Design, Museology
Adult Hobby Classes: Tuition $96.50 per cr hr, sr citizens free. All regular courses offered
Summer School: Dir Gerald A Matlick. Tuition $96.50 per cr hr for 6 week term. Courses according to demand

KENTUCKY WESLEYAN COLLEGE, Dept Art,* 3000 Frederica St, 42301. Tel 502-926-3111. *Chmn* Robert Pevitts; *Asst Prof* William Kolok Jr, MFA; *Asst Prof* Georgia Tangi, PhD
Dept estab 1950; den; scholarships; SC 11, LC 4; enrl maj 40
Degrees: BA 4 yr
Courses: Art Appreciation, Arts and Crafts, Design, Watercolor
Summer School: Enrl 60. Courses—Art for the Elementary Schools, Art Survey

PIKEVILLE

PIKEVILLE COLLEGE, Fine Arts Dept,* Sycamore St, 41501. Tel 606-432-9200. *Dir* Russell Patterson
Estab 1889; pvt den; D & E; SC 16, LC 5
Ent Req: SAT, ACT
Degrees: BA and BS 4 yrs
Tuition: $2825 annual tuition
Courses: †Art Education, Art History, Ceramics, Drawing, History of Art & Archaeology, Painting, Printmaking, Sculpture, †Teacher Training
Summer School: Courses—vary

PIPPA PASSES

ALICE LLOYD COLLEGE, Art Dept,* 41844. Tel 606-368-2101. *Instr* Wendell Barry Stevens, BFA. Instrs: FT 1, PT 1
Estab 1922; pvt; D & E; scholarships; SC 6, LC 1
Ent Req: HS dipl, ent exam
Degrees: AA and CA 2 yr
Tuition: $2245 per yr
Courses: Drawing, Painting, Photography
Children's Classes: Enrl 10-20; tui free. Courses—Drawing, Painting, Sculpture

RICHMOND

EASTERN KENTUCKY UNIVERSITY, Art Dept, Campbell 309, Lancaster Ave, 40475. Tel 606-622-1629. *Chmn* Daniel N Shindelbower
Estab 1910; pub; D; SC 30, LC 6, GC 6
Ent Req: HS grad
Degrees: BA, BFA and MA (Educ) 4 yrs
Tuition: Res—$626 per yr; nonres—$1780 per yr
Courses: Painting, Sculpture, Drawing Media, Figure Drawing, Figure Painting, Graphics II, Greek & Roman Art, Metal Casting, Synthetic Media, Senior Exhibition, Twentieth Century Painting
Summer School: Tuition varies; campus res available beginning June

WILLIAMSBURG

CUMBERLAND COLLEGE, Dept of Art,* Walnut St, College Station Box 523, 40769. Tel 606-549-2082. *Chmn* Harold R Wortman, PhD; *Assoc Prof* Russell A Parker, MA
Estab 1959; den; D & E; scholarships; SC 26, LC 12; enrl D 720, E 90, maj 38
Ent Req: HS dipl, special approval may be granted for admission
Degrees: BA and BS 4 yr
Tuition: $1190 per sem
Courses: Basketry, Batik, Enameling, Weaving
Summer School: Enrl 110; term of 5 wks beginning June. Courses—Art Appreciation, Art History, Two and Three Dimensional Studio

WILMORE

ASBURY COLLEGE, Art Dept,* 201 N Lexington Ave, 40390. Tel 606-858-3511. *Chmn Fine Arts* Dr Gilbert Roller. Instrs: FT 13
Estab 1892; pvt; D & E; scholarships; SC 30, LC 6; enrl D 1250, maj 65, others 250
Ent Req: HS dipl
Degrees: AB & BS 4 yr
Tuition: $986 per qtr
Courses: Aesthetics, Art Education, Art History, Ceramics, Drawing, Handicrafts, Lettering, Mixed Media, Painting, Photography, Printmaking, Sculpture, Teacher Training, Batik, Weaving
Summer School: Enrl 12 each for term of 4 - 8 wks beginning June 9th. Courses—Crafts, Drawing, Painting

LOUISIANA

BATON ROUGE

LOUISIANA STATE UNIVERSITY, School of Art, 110 Foster Hall, 70803. Tel 504-388-5402, 388-2166. *Head Dept* Dr Walter E Rutkowski, EdD; *Prof* Ruth Millward, MFA; *Prof* James Burke, MFA; *Prof* Joe Bova, MA; *Prof* Paul Dufour, BFA; *Prof* Michael Daugherty, MFA; *Assoc Prof* Mark Zucker, PhD; *Assoc Prof* Michael Crespo, MFA; *Assoc Prof* Bill Detmers, EdD; *Assoc Prof* Gerald Bower, MFA; *Assoc Prof* A J Meek, MFA; *Assoc Prof* Christopher Hentz, MFA
Estab 1874, dept estab 1935; pub; D & E; scholarships
Ent Req: HS dipl, ACT scores
Degrees: BFA 4 yr, MFA 2
Tuition: Res—undergrad and grad $484 per sem; nonres—undergrad $1234 per sem, grad $1009 per sem; campus res—room $357-$663, board $369-$389 per sem
Courses: Art Education, Art History, Ceramics, Drawing, Graphic Design, Jewelry, Painting, Photography, Printmaking, Sculpture, Glassblowing, Stained Glass
Summer School: Tuition—res $268, nonres $648 per 9 wk term. Courses—same as above

SOUTHERN UNIVERSITY A & M COLLEGE, Division of Architecture, Southern Branch PO, 70813. Tel 504-771-3015. *Dir* Arthur L Symes, DArch
Estab 1956; pub; D & E; scholarships; SC 14; enrl D 250, non-maj 7, maj 162
Ent Req: HS dipl
Degrees: BA 5 yrs
Tuition: Res—undergrad $325 per sem, grad $335 per sem; nonres undergrad $640 per sem, grad $650
Courses: Architecture, Art Education
Summer School: Dir, Arthur L Symes. Tuition $164 for term of 8 wks beginning June. Courses—Architectural Design, Construction Materials & Systems, Graphic Presentation, Structures

GRAMBLING

GRAMBLING STATE UNIVERSITY, Art Dept,* 71245. Tel 318-247-6941. *Chmn* Dr Thomas L Richardson, EdD
Scholarships offered
Tuition: Res—$234 per sem; nonres—$549 per sem
Courses: Art Appreciation, Art Education, Art History, Ceramics, Design, Drawing, Handicrafts, Jewelry, Painting, Printmaking, Sculpture, Weaving

HAMMOND

SOUTHEASTERN LOUISIANA UNIVERSITY, Dept of Visual Arts, 70402. Tel 504-549-2193. *Chmn* Barbara C Walker, PhD; *Prof* Hymel G Falgoust, MA; *Assoc Prof* Barbara Tardo, MA; *Assoc Prof* Ronald Kennedy, MFA; *Asst Prof* C Roy Blackwood, MFA; *Instructor* Gail Hood, MFA; *Instructor* Erica Spindler, MFA; *Instructor* Benny Burts, MFA; *Instructor* Dorothy Furlong-Gardner, MFA
Estab 1925; pub; D & E; SC 25, LC 4, GC 2; enrl D 109, E 75, maj 122

Ent Req: HS dipl, ACT
Degrees: BA(Educ) & BA(Humanities) 4 yrs
Courses: Art Education, Art History, Ceramics, Drawing, Goldsmithing, Jewelry, Painting, Photography, Printmaking, Sculpture, Teacher Training
Adult Hobby Classes: Courses—Art Education, Drawing, Painting
Summer School: Art Education, Art History, Drawing

LAFAYETTE

UNIVERSITY OF SOUTHWESTERN LOUISIANA, School of Art and Architecture, 70504. Tel 318-231-6224. *Dir* G C Carner. Instrs: FT 40, PT 5
Estab 1900; pub; enrl univ 16,000
Degrees: BArchit & BFA 4-5 yrs
Tuition: $300 per sem
Courses: †Advertising Design, †Architecture, †Art Education, †Ceramics, †Photography, †Choreographic Design, †Fine Arts, †Interior Architecture
Children's Classes: Courses for gifted children—Design, Drawing, Photography
Summer School: Courses—Ceramics, Design, Drawing, Painting, Photography

LAKE CHARLES

MCNEESE STATE UNIVERSITY, Dept of Visual Arts,* Ryan St, 70609. Tel 318-477-2520. *Chmn* Bill R Iles. Instrs: FT 4
Estab 1950, dept estab 1953; pub; D & E; scholarships; SC 24, LC 4, GC 1; enrl D 85, E 15, non-maj 215, maj 85
Ent Req: HS dipl
Degrees: BA (Art Educ) and BA (Studio Arts) 4 yrs
Tuition: $330.50 per sem
Courses: Survey crafts course
Adult Hobby Classes: Enrl 15; Courses—Drawing and Composition, Painting
Summer School: Courses—per regular session

MONROE

NORTHEAST LOUISIANA UNIVERSITY, Dept of Art, College of Liberal Arts, 71209. Tel 318-342-3110. *Head Dept* Ronald J Alexander, MFA
Estab 1931, dept estab 1956; pub; D & E; SC 28, LC 4, GC 9; enrl non-maj 300, maj 125, GS 3
Ent Req: HS dipl
Degrees: AA & BFA 4 yrs, MEd
Tuition: Res—$125, nonres—$315
Courses: Advertising Design, Ceramics, Painting, Photography, Printmaking, Weaving, Fiber Art
Adult Hobby Classes: Courses offered
Children's Classes: Courses offered
Summer School: Courses offered

NATCHITOCHES

NORTHWESTERN STATE UNIVERSITY OF LOUISIANA, Dept of Art, 71497. Tel 318-357-4544. *Head Dept* Billy J Bryant, DEd; *Prof* Grady Harper, PhD; *Prof* Rivers C Murphy, MFA; *Assoc Prof* Charles V Coke, MA; *Assoc Prof* Mary C Roberts, DEd; *Assoc Prof* James C Thorn, MFA; *Asst Prof* Bryan Jowers, MFA; *Asst Prof* Nolan Bailey, MA
Estab 1885; pub; D & E; SC 67, LC 17, GC 36; enrl maj 93, grad 9
Degrees: BA & BS 4 yrs, MA 2 yrs, special prog for advanced students MA in Art
Courses: †Advertising Design, †Art Education, Art History, Ceramics, Commercial Art, Drawing, Painting, Printmaking, Sculpture, Fiber Arts, Stained Glass, Stringed Instrument Construction
Adult Hobby Classes: Courses—Most of above

NEW ORLEANS

DELGADO COLLEGE, Dept of Fine Arts,* 615 City Park Ave, 70119. Tel 504-483-4114. *Chmn Fine Arts* Dr Marvin E Thames
Dept estab 1967. College has 2 campuses; pub; D & E; scholarships; SC 12-20, LC 12-20; enrl D 150, E 65, maj 60
Ent Req: HS dipl, 18 yr old
Degrees: AA and AS 2 yrs
Tuition: Res—$229.75 per sem; nonres—$544.75 per sem
Courses: Drawing, History of Art & Archaeology, Painting, Art Appreciation

LOYOLA UNIVERSITY OF NEW ORLEANS, Dept of Visual Arts, 6363 Saint Charles Ave, 70118. Tel 504-865-2780. *Chmn* Mark Grote
Den; D & E; scholarships; SC 9, LC 3; enrl D 150, E 45, maj 28
Ent Req: HS dipl, ent exam
Degrees: BA Visual Arts 4 yrs
Tuition: $3200 per yr
Courses: Ceramics, Drawing, Painting, Sculpture, Teacher Training
Summer School: Chmn, John Sears. Enrl 40; term of 6 wks beginning in June. Courses—Drawing, Painting, Printmaking, Sculpture

SOUTHERN UNIVERSITY IN NEW ORLEANS, Art Dept, 6400 Press Dr, 70126. Tel 504-282-4401, Ext 267. *Head Dept* Dr Jack Jordan; *Assoc Prof* Dr Roscoe Reddix, MA; *Prof* Sara Dickenson, MA; *Asst Prof* Rodney Ferguson, MFA
Estab 1951, dept estab 1960; pub; D & E; BA 4 yrs; enrl D 21, E 26, non-maj 700, maj 47
Ent Req: HS dipl
Courses: †Art Education, Art History, Ceramics, Commercial Art, Drawing, Fashion Arts, Graphic Arts, Handicrafts, Painting, Photography, Printmaking, Sculpture, Teacher Training, Design, †Fine Arts
Adult Hobby Classes: Courses offered
Summer School: Courses offered

TULANE UNIVERSITY
—**School of Architecture,** 70118. Tel 504-865-6472. *Dean* Ronald C Filson; *Assoc Dean* Stephen P Jacobs; *Asst Dean* Mark L Denton. Instrs: FT 24, PT 2
School estab 1907; pvt; enrl 320
Degrees: BArchit 3 yrs and 5 yrs, MArchit 1 yr
Tuition: $3275 per yr
Courses: †Architecture
—**Sophie H Newcomb Memorial College,** Art Department, 119 Newcomb Art Bldg, 70118. Tel 504-865-4631. *Chmn* John Clemmer; *Prof* Norman B Boothly; *Prof* Jessie J Poesch; *Prof* Donald Robertson; *Prof* James L Stey; *Prof* Pat Trivigno; *Assoc Prof* J Franklin Adams; *Assoc Prof* Harold E Carney; *Assoc Prof* Caecilia W Davis; *Assoc Prof* Authur E Kun; *Assoc Prof* Gene H Koss; *Assoc Prof* Richard J Tuttie; *Asst Prof* Marilyn R Brown; *Asst Prof* Molly Mason
Estab 1886; pvt; D & E; scholarships; SC 33, LC 25, GC 29; enrl D 817 per sem, E 37 per sem
Ent Req: HS dipl, CEEB, interview, review of work by chairman and/or faculty (optional)
Degrees: BA and BFA 4 yrs, MA, MFA and MAT 2 yrs
Courses: †Art Education, †Art History, †Ceramics, †Drawing, †History of Art & Archaeology, †Painting, †Photography, †Printmaking, †Sculpture, Glass
Adult Hobby Classes: Courses—Ceramics, Drawing, Painting, Photography, Printmaking, Sculpture
Summer School: Acting Dean, Wayne S Woody. Courses—Art History, Ceramics, Drawing, Glass, Painting, Sculpture

UNIVERSITY OF NEW ORLEANS, Dept of Fine Arts, 70148. Tel 504-286-6493. *Chmn* Doyle Gertjejansen, MFA; *Prof* William Thomas Young, EdD; *Prof* Howard Jones, MFA; *Prof* Jim Richard, MFA; *Assoc Prof* Richard A Johnson, MFA; *Assoc Prof* Peggy McDowell, MA; *Assoc Prof* George Rowan, MFA; *Asst Prof* Carolyn K Lewis, PhD; *Asst Prof* Ron Todd, MFA
Estab 1958, dept estab 1968; pub; D & E; SC 29, LC 24, GC 34; enrl D 16,000 (university), non-maj 3000, maj 150, grad 14
Ent Req: HS dipl
Degrees: BA 4 yrs, MFA 2 yrs
Tuition: Res—undergrad $984 yr, $492 per sem, $194-$416 PT, grad $984 per yr, $492 per sem, $194-$416 PT; nonres—undergrad $1147 per sem, $443-$992 PT, grad $932 per sem, $443-$707 PT; campus residence available
Courses: Art Education, †Art History, Drawing, †Graphic Arts, †Painting, †Photography, †Printmaking, †Sculpture
Summer School: Tuition $205 for term of 6 wks beginning June. Courses—Art History, Art Structure, Drawing, Graphics, Painting

XAVIER UNIVERSITY OF LOUISIANA, Dept of Fine Arts,* 7325 Palmetto St, 70125. Tel 504-486-7411. *Chmn* Martin F Payton, MFA; *Prof* John T Scott, MFA
Estab 1926, dept estab 1935; den; D & E; scholarships; SC 48, LC 10; enrl D 50, E 12, non-maj 10, maj 52
Ent Req: HS dipl, SAT or ACT, health cert, C average at least
Degrees: BA, BA(Art Ed), BFA, BS and MA
Tuition: $1500 per sem
Adult Hobby Classes: Courses—Creative Crafts

PINEVILLE

LOUISIANA COLLEGE, Dept of Art, 71359. Tel 318-487-7262. *Chmn* John T Suddith; *Assoc Prof* Charles Jeffress
Den; scholarships; LC, Lab C; enrl maj 35
Ent Req: HS grad
Degrees: BA & BS 4 yrs, 49 hrs of art req plus 78 hrs acad for degree
Tuition: Res—$59 per sem hr
Courses: Advertising Design, Art Education, Studio Arts
Summer School: Limited courses

RUSTON

LOUISIANA TECH UNIVERSITY, School of Art and Architecture, PO Box 6277 Tech Station, 71270. Tel 318-257-3909. *Dir* Joseph W Strother. Instrs: FT 28, PT 14
Estab 1904; pub; D; scholarships; SC 98, LC 8, GC 87; enrl maj 652, others 538
Ent Req: HS dipl
Degrees: BA, BFA, MA & MFA 4 yrs, BArchit 5 yrs
Courses: †Architecture, Ceramics, †Drawing, †Graphic Design, †Interior Design, †Painting, †Photography, Printmaking, †Sculpture
Summer School: Summer program in Rome & on campus

SHREVEPORT

CENTENARY COLLEGE OF LOUISIANA, Dept of Art, Centenary Blvd, 71104. Tel 318-869-5261. *Chmn Dept & Prof* Willard Cooper, MFA; *Asst Prof* Bruce Allen, MFA; *Lectr* Neil Johnson, BA; *Lectr* B Lee Sutton, BID; *Lectr* Barbara Dupree, BA
Estab 1825, dept estab 1935; den; D & E; scholarships; SC 22, LC 8; enrl D 125 per sem
Ent Req: HS dipl, SAT or ACT
Degrees: BA 4 yrs
Tuition: $3450 per yr, $130 per hr; campus res—room & board $2330 per yr
Courses: Aesthetics, Art Education, Art History, Ceramics, Drafting, Drawing, Graphic Arts, Handicrafts, †Painting, Printmaking, Sculpture, Teacher Training, Weaving
Adult Hobby Classes: Enrl 800 (for people over 60); no tuition. Courses—Studio Art & Appreciation
Summer School: Dir, Willard Cooper. Tuition $100 per hr for term of 8 wks beginning June 10. Courses—Art Education, Art History, Drawing, Painting

THIBODAUX

NICHOLLS STATE UNIVERSITY, Dept of Art,* PO Box 2025, 70310. Tel 504-446-8111. *Art Dept Head* Armando Garzon-Blanco, PhD. Instrs: FT 5
Estab 1948; pub; D & SC 73, LC 6; enrl D 100, non-maj 20, maj 80, others 20
Ent Req: HS dipl, ACT
Degrees: BA 4 yrs
Tuition: Res—$326.05 per sem; nonres—$641.05 per sem
Courses: †Advertising Design, Art Education, Art History, †Ceramics, Commercial Art, Conceptual Art, †Drawing, Graphic Arts, Graphic Design, Illustration, Mixed Media, †Painting, Photography, †Printmaking, †Sculpture, Teacher Training, Applied Design, Rendering, Water Media

MAINE

AUGUSTA

UNIVERSITY OF MAINE AT AUGUSTA, Division of Arts and Humanities, University Heights, 04330. Tel 207-622-7131. *Chmn Div* Charles D Danforth, MM; *Prof* Joshua Nadel, MFA; *Prof* Rhoda Oakley, MA; *Prof* Philip Paratore, MFA; *Prof* Robert Katz, MFA
Estab 1965, dept estab 1970; pub; D & E; SC 20, LC 8; enrl D 50, E 40, non-maj 40, maj 50
Ent Req: HS dipl
Degrees: AA 2 yrs
Tuition: Res—$1410 per yr, $47 per cr hr; nonres—$3630 per yr, $121 per cr hr
Courses: Advertising Design, Aesthetics, Art History, Ceramics, Drawing, Museum Staff Training, Graphic Arts, Mixed Media, Painting, Photography, Printmaking, Sculpture, Video, Paper Making
Summer School: Assoc Dean Acad Affairs, Tom Abbott. Enrl 30-50; tuition $47 per cr hr for term of 7 wks beginning last wk in June. Courses—Art History, Drawing, Painting

BRUNSWICK

BOWDOIN COLLEGE, Art Dept, Visual Art Center, 04011. Tel 207-725-8731, Ext 697. *Chmn* Larry D Lutchmansingh, PhD; *Dir Visual Arts Program* Gerard Haggerty, MFA; *Emeritus Prof* Philip C Beam, PhD; *Prof* C C Olds, PhD; *Prof* Susan Wegner, PhD; *Prof* Thomas B Cornell, AB; *Prof* Kevin Donahue, MFA; *Lecturer* John McKee, MA
Estab 1794; pvt; D & E; scholarships; SC 15, LC 18; enrl D 655, maj 47
Ent Req: HS dipl
Degrees: BA 4 yrs
Tuition: $8635 per yr, campus res—room & board $3155
Courses: †Art History, Visual Arts

DEER ISLE

HAYSTACK MOUNTAIN SCHOOL OF CRAFTS, 04627. Tel 207-348-6946. *Dir* Howard M Evans. Instrs: FT 28
Estab 1951; pvt; D, Summer school; enrl D 75
Ent Req: HS dipl
Tuition: $110 per wk plus shop fees
Courses: Ceramics, Graphic Arts, Photography, Fabric, Glassblowing, Metalsmithing, Stained Glass, Woodworking, Weaving

GORHAM

UNIVERSITY OF SOUTHERN MAINE, Art Dept, College Ave, 04038. Tel 207-780-5460. *Chmn* Duncan A Hewitt, MFA
Estab 1878, dept estab 1956; pub; D & E; SC 9, LC 2; enrl maj 120
Ent Req: HS dipl, portfolio
Degrees: BA, BFA, BS
Tuition: Res—undergrad $820 per yr, $410 per sem, $30 per cr hr; nonres—undergrad $2625 per yr, $97 per cr hr; campus residence available
Courses: Art Education, Art History, Ceramics, Design, Drawing, Film, Museum Staff Training, Painting, Photography, Printmaking, Sculpture, Textile Design, Philiosophy of Art; Problems in Art
Summer School: Courses—Art History, Ceramics, Design, Drawing, Photography, Painting, Sculpture

LEWISTON

BATES COLLEGE, Art Dept,* Liberal Arts College, 04240. Tel 207-783-3941. *Chmn* Donald Lent. Instrs: FT 3, PT 1
Estab 1864, dept estab 1964; pvt; D; SC 9, LC 13; enrl 1200 total
Degrees: BA 4 yr
Tuition: $8100 per yr
Courses: Art History, Ceramics, Drawing, Painting, Printmaking

ORONO

UNIVERSITY OF MAINE, Art Dept, 04469. Tel 207-581-3245. *Chmn* Ronald Ghiz, MFA; *Emeritus Prof* Vincent A Hartgen, MFA; *Prof* Michael Lewis, MFA; *Assoc Prof* David O Decker, MA; *Asst Prof* James Linehan, MFA; *Asst Prof* David Ebitz, PhD; *Asst Prof* Deborah DeMoulpied, MFA; *Asst Prof* Mary Ann Stankiewicz, PhD; *Asst Prof* Susan Groce, MFA; *Asst Prof* Diana Hulick, PhD
Estab 1862, dept estab 1946; pub; D & E; scholarships; SC 24, LC 24;

enrl D 135, maj 135
Ent Req: HS dipl, 3 CEEB tests
Degrees: BA and BS 4 yrs
Tuition: Res—undergrad $1509 per yr, $754.50 per sem; nonres—undergrad $4560 per yr, $2280 per sem; campus res—room & board $2775 per yr
Courses: †Art Education, †Art History, †Drawing, †Painting, †Printmaking, †Sculpture, †Teacher Training
Children's Classes: Chmn, Ronald Ghiz, MFA
Summer School: Dir, Edward W Hackett. Tuition $66 per cr hr. Courses—Basic Drawing, Basic Painting, Fundamentals of Painting, Principles of Art, Problems in Art, Teaching of Art

PORTLAND

PORTLAND SCHOOL OF ART, 04101. Tel 207-775-3052. *Pres* James B Goodbody; *Instructor* Richard A Butz, MFA; *Instructor* Edwin P Douglas, MFA; *Instructor* John Eide, MFA; *Instructor* Allan R Gardner; *Instructor* Joseph Guertin, BFA; *Instructor* Regina Kelley, MFA; *Instructor* John T Ventimiglia, MFA; *Instructor* Harold Schremmer; *Instructor* Lisa Allen, MFA; *Instructor* Johnnie Ross, MFA; *Instructor* Margot Trout, MFA; *Instructor* Joan Uraneck, MFA; *Instructor* Jonathan Aldrich, MA; *Instructor* Veronica Benning, MFA
Estab 1882; pvt; D & E; SC 37, LC 9; enrl D 230, E 200, maj 193, others 140 PT
Ent Req: HS dipl, portfolio
Degrees: BFA 4 yr (under Maine law, an academically advanced high school senior may take the freshman yr at Portland School of Art for both HS and Portland School of Art credit)
Tuition: $4950 per yr; no campus res
Courses: Art History, †Ceramics, Drawing, †Graphic Design, †Jewelry, †Painting, †Photography, †Printmaking, †Sculpture, †Silversmithing
Adult Hobby Classes: Enrl 200, tuition $100 per 1 credit course plus lab fee $10-$25. Courses—Ceramics, Design, Drawing, Jewelry, Painting, Photography, Printmaking, Sculpture, Silversmithing
Children's Classes: Enrl 80; tuition $100 per class. Courses—Ceramics, Drawing, Graphic Design, Photography, Printmaking, Sculpture, Silversmithing
Summer School: Enrl 100; tuition $100 per cr for term of 6 wks beginning June 25, 1984. Courses—Art History, Ceramics, Drawing, Graphic Design, Jewelry & Silversmithing, Painting, Photography, Printmaking, Sculpture, 2 & 3-D Design, Watercolor

ROCKPORT

MAINE PHOTOGRAPHIC WORKSHOPS, * Two Central St, 04856. Tel 207-236-8581. *Founder & Dir* David H Lyman
Enrl 1200
Degrees: AA
Tuition: Workshops $250-$600
Courses: Photography
Adult Hobby Classes: Programs abroad
Summer School: 100 summer workshops

SKOWHEGAN

SKOWHEGAN SCHOOL OF PAINTING AND SCULPTURE, Box 449 (Mailing add: Winter Office, 329 E 68th St, New York, NY 10021). Tel 212-861-9270; 207-474-9345. *Exec Dir* Roy Leaf; *Academic Dir* Sidney Simon. Instrs: Six res; 6 visiting artists
Estab 1946; pvt nine wk summer residency program for independent work; enrl 65
Ent Req: Presentation of slide portfolio
Degrees: Credits recognized for transfer, no degrees
Tuition: Summer only $3000 includes room & board (residency required)
Courses: Drawing, Painting, Sculpture, Fresco Technique

WATERVILLE

COLBY COLLEGE, Art Dept, 04901. Tel 207-873-1131, Ext 2231. *Chmn Dept* David L Simon, PhD; *Assoc Prof* Harriett Matthews, MFA; *Asst Prof* Gina Werfel, MFA; *Asst Prof* Sonia C Simon, PhD; *Asst Prof* Hearne Pardee, MFA; *Asst Prof* David Lubin, PhD; *Instr* Michael Marlais, MA
Estab 1813, dept estab 1944; pvt; D & E; scholarships; SC 12, LC 17; enrl D 350, non-maj 305, maj 45
Ent Req: HS dipl
Degrees: BA 4 yrs
Tuition: $6200 per yr; campus res available
Courses: History of Art & Archaeology, Painting, Sculpture

MARYLAND

BALTIMORE

COLLEGE OF NOTRE DAME OF MARYLAND, Art Dept, 4701 N Charles St, 21210. Tel 301-435-0100. *Chmn* Dr John Connolly, Jr, PhD; *Prof* Linelle LaBante, MFA; *Prof* Kevin Raines, MFA; *Prof* Ruth Watkins, ME; *Asst Prof* Veberly Witgus, MFA
Pvt den; D & E; scholarships; SC 16, LC 8; enrl D 285, non-maj 250, maj 35
Ent Req: HS dipl, SAT
Degrees: BA 4 yrs
Tuition: Res—undergrad $6200 yr, $3100 per sem; nonres—undergrad $3800 per yr, $1900 per sem; campus res—room & board $2500
Courses: Advertising Design, Aesthetics, Art History, Ceramics, Collages,

Commercial Art, Drawing, Film, Graphic Arts, Graphic Design, Handicrafts, History of Art & Archaeology, Interior Design, Painting, Photography, Printmaking, Sculpture, Stage Design, Teacher Training
Adult Hobby Classes: Classes offered in Weekend College and Continuing Education Programs. Tuition $75 per cr
Summer School: Dir, Edi Donahue. Tuition $75 per cr. Courses—Advanced Painting

COMMUNITY COLLEGE OF BALTIMORE, Dept of Fine & Applied Arts, Liberty Campus, 2901 Liberty Heights Ave, 21215. Tel 301-396-7980. *Chmn & Prof* Bennard B Perlman, MA; *Prof* Nelson Adlin, MA; *Prof* Allyn O Harris, MFA; *Prof* Frank Holston; *Assoc Prof* Carlton Leverette, MFA; *Assoc Prof* David Bahr, MFA; *Assoc Prof* Estelle Brenner; *Assoc Prof* Halina Zytkiewicz; *Instr* Sally Monteferrante, MEd; *Instr* Robert Goald; *Instr* Beverly Brown; *Instr* Thresa Rogers. Instrs: FT 12, PT 13
Estab 1947; pub; D & E; scholarships; SC 17, LC 2; enrl D & E 9400, non-maj 480, maj 435
Ent Req: HS dipl or HS equivalency, ent exam
Degrees: AA 2 yrs
Tuition: City res—$528 per yr, $264 per sem, $20 per cr hr; state res—$1003 per yr, $501.50 per sem, $40 per cr hr; non-res—$1853 per yr, $926.50 per sem; no campus res
Courses: Advertising Design, Art Education, Art History, Ceramics, †Commercial Art, Drawing, Graphic Arts, Graphic Design, Jewelry, Painting, †Photography, Printmaking, Sculpture, Textile Design, Fashion Design
Adult Hobby Classes: Tuition county res $23 per cr; state res $46 per cr; nonres $69 per cr. Courses—same as above
Summer School: Dir, Dr Jerry Cohen. Enrl 54. Courses—Drawing, Design, Ceramics, Crafts, Fashion Design

COPPIN STATE COLLEGE, Art Dept,* 2500 W North Ave, 21216. Tel 301-448-5925, 448-5929. *Assoc Prof* Luke A Shaw. Instrs: FT 1, PT 2
Scholarships; SC 6, LC 7; enrl D 350, E 45
Degrees: BS, MA & Doc in Art Education
Tuition: Res—$1030 per yr; nonres—$2140 per yr
Courses: Advertising Design, Art Education, Art History, Calligraphy, Ceramics, Drawing, Film, Graphic Design, Lettering, Painting, Photography, Printmaking, Sculpture, Teacher Training, Theatre Arts

JOHNS HOPKINS UNIVERSITY
—**Dept of the History of Art,** * 3400 N Charles St, 21218. Tel 301-338-7117. *Chmn* Herbert L Kessler. Instrs: FT 5, PT 3
Estab 1947; pvt; D & E; scholarships; LC; enrl 10-30 in advanced courses, 200 in introductory courses
Degrees: BA, MA & PhD
Tuition: $7600 per yr; $253 per cr hr
Courses: Art History
—**School of Medicine, Dept of Art as Applied to Medicine,** 624 N Broadway, 21205. Tel 301-955-3213. *Dir Dept & Assoc Prof* Gary P Lees, MS; *Dir Emeritus* Ranice W Crosby, MLA; *Asst Prof* Leon Schlossberg; *Asst Prof* J Lindsey Burch; *Asst Prof* Marjorie Gregerman, BA; *Asst Prof* Timothy Hengst, MA; *Instr* Howard C Bartner, MA; *Instr* Elizabeth Blumenthal; *Lectr* Joseph Dieter Jr
Univ estab 1876, School Medicine estab 1893, dept estab 1911; pvt; D; scholarships; SC 13, LC 5, GC 18; enrl 12, grad 6
Ent Req: Baccalaureate degree
Degrees: MA 2 yrs
Tuition: $7600 per yr; campus res—room $1890 & board $1750 per 9 months
Courses: Display, Drawing, Graphic Design, Illustration, Intermedia, Mixed Media, Painting, Photography, Sculpture, Video

MARYLAND INSTITUTE, College of Art, 1300 W Mt Royal Ave, 21217. Tel 301-669-9200. *Pres* Fred Lazarus IV. Instrs: FT 45, PT 55
Estab 1826; pvt; D & E; scholarships; enrl D 1107, E 554, Sat 280
Ent Req: HS grad, exam
Degrees: BFA and MFA 4 yrs
Tuition: $5300 per yr; campus res—$2750
Courses: Ceramics, Drawing, Graphic Design, Handicrafts, Illustration, Interior Design, Painting, Photography, Printmaking, Sculpture, Teacher Training, Foundation
Adult Hobby Classes: Evenings and Saturdays, credit-non credit classes
Children's Classes: Saturdays and Summer classes
Summer School: Dir Continuing Studies, Barbara Miller. Enrl 850; tuition $3000 per yr for Continuing Studies
—**Hoffberger School of Painting,** * 21217. Tel 301-669-9200. *Dir* Grace Hartigan; *Artist-in-Residence* Salvatore Scarpitta
Fel awarded annually for study at the grad level; enrl limited to 20
—**Rinehart School of Sculpture,** * 21217. *Dir* Norman Carlberg
—**Mount Royal Graduate School of Painting,** * 21217. Tel 301-669-9200. *Dir* Babe Shapiro, MA
Enrl 30
Degrees: MFA programs
Tuition: $4000 per year

MORGAN STATE UNIVERSITY, Dept of Art,* Hillen Road at Coldspring Lane, 21239. Tel 301-444-3333. *Dir* James Edward Lewis, MFA; *Asst Prof* Oliver Patrick Scott, MA. Instrs: FT 6
Estab 1867, dept estab 1950; pub; D & E; scholarships; SC 28, LC 11, GC 17; enrl D 340, E 50, non-maj 250, maj 140, GS 11
Ent Req: HS dipl
Degrees: BA (Art) and BS (Art Educ) 4 yr, MA (Art History & Museology) and MA (Art Studio) 2 yr
Tuition: Res—$372.50 per sem; nonres—$890 per sem
Courses: Art Appreciation, Weaving
Children's Classes: Enrl 20; tuition $10 per sem. Courses—Painting, Printmaking, Sculpture
Summer School: Dir, Dr Beryl W Williams. Term of 6 wks beginning June and July. Courses—Art Appreciation, Art Education, Basic Design, Photography

SCHULER SCHOOL OF FINE ARTS, 5 E Lafayette Ave, 21202. Tel 301-685-3568. *Dir* Hans C Schuler
Estab 1959; pvt; D & E; SC 9, GC 3; enrl D 50, E 30, grad 2
Degrees: 4 yrs
Tuition: $1700 per yr, part-time students pay by schedule for sem
Courses: Drawing, Painting, Sculpture
Children's Classes: Tuition $400-$550 (summer - ages 14 and over).
Courses—Drawing, Painting, Sculpture
Summer School: Dir, Hans C Schuler. Enrl 30; tuition $400 for term of 6 wks
beginning June, $550 for 6 hrs per day, 6 wks. Courses—Drawing, Oil Painting,
Sculpture, Watercolor

TOWSON STATE UNIVERSITY, Dept of Art, 21204. Tel 301-321-2808. *Dept
Chmn* James W Flood. Instrs: FT 22, PT 12
Estab 1866; pub; D & E
Ent Req: HS grad
Degrees: BA, BS, MEd(Art Educ) 4 yr & MFA; spring sem Florence, Italy, Feb-May
Courses: Art Education, Art History, Ceramics, Drawing, Graphic Arts, Jewelry,
Painting, Sculpture, Textile Design, Enameling, Weaving, Wood & Metal
Summer School: Dir, Jim Flood. Enrl 25; 2 five wk sessions. Courses—Art History,
Studio

BEL AIR

HARFORD COMMUNITY COLLEGE, Humanities Division, 401 Thomas Run
Rd, 21014. Tel 301-879-8920. *Assoc Dean* Homer Morris. Instrs: FT 4, PT 5
Estab 1957; pub; D & E; scholarships; SC 17, LC 4; enrl FT 1000, PT 1000
Ent Req: HS dipl
Degrees: AA 2 yrs
Tuition: No campus res
Courses: Ceramics, Drawing, Graphic Arts, History of Art & Archaeology, Interior
Design, Painting, †Photography, Sculpture, Architectural Drawing, Design
Summer School: Assoc Dean, Homer Morris

BOWIE

BOWIE STATE COLLEGE, Dept of Fine and Performing Arts,* Jericho Park Rd,
20715. Tel 301-464-3000. *Chairperson Dept* Dr H D Flowers II. Instrs: FT 12
Estab 1865, dept estab 1968; pub; D; SC 7, LC 3; enrl D 1600, E 350, non-maj 180,
maj 45
Ent Req: HS dipl
Degrees: BA (Art) and BS (Art Educ)
Tuition: Res—$480 per sem; nonres—$1000 per sem
Summer School: Dir, Dr Ida Brandon. Courses—Ceramics, Media Workshop

CATONSVILLE

CATONSVILLE COMMUNITY COLLEGE, Art Dept, 21228. Tel 301-455-4326.
Chmn Dept Dr Dian Fetter
Estab 1957; pub; D & E; scholarships; SC 26, LC 6; enrl D 600, E 400, non-maj
200, maj 300, applied arts maj 350
Ent Req: HS dipl
Degrees: Cert & AA 2 yrs
Tuition: $20 per cr
Courses: †Advertising Design, Art Education, Art History, Ceramics, Commercial
Art, Drawing, Graphic Design, Illustration, Interior Design, Painting, †Photography,
Sculpture
Adult Hobby Classes: Chmn Dept, Dr Dian Fetter
Summer School: Same as above

UNIVERSITY OF MARYLAND BALTIMORE COUNTY, Visual Arts Dept,*
5401 Wilkens Ave, 21228. Tel 301-455-2150. *Chmn* E Stanley Van Der Beck; *Assoc
Prof* LeRoy Morais, MFA. Instrs: FT 5
Estab 1966, dept estab 1966; pub; D & E; SC 27, LC 12, GC 4; enrl in dept D 485,
non-maj 375, maj 110
Ent Req: HS dipl, SAT
Degrees: BA 4 yrs
Tuition: Res—$681 per sem; nonres—$1879 per sem
Courses: Advertising Design, Aesthetics, †Art History, Calligraphy, Ceramics,
Collages, Commercial Art, Conceptual Art, †Drawing, †Film, †Graphic Arts,
†Graphic Design, †History of Art & Archaeology, Intermedia, Lettering, Mixed
Media, †Painting, †Photography, Printmaking, †Video

COLLEGE PARK

UNIVERSITY OF MARYLAND, Art Dept, Art-Sociology Bldg, 20742. Tel 301-
454-3431. *Chmn* Jack W Burnham. Instrs: FT 44, PT 3
Estab 1944; pub; D; SC 39, LC 37, GC 22; enrl 3200 per sem, maj 600, grad 100
Ent Req: 3.0 grad average
Degrees: BA, MA, MFA, PhD 4 yrs
Courses: Art Education, Art History, Drawing, Museum Staff Training, Painting,
Printmaking, Sculpture, Design
Adult Hobby Classes: Enrl 5400 per yr. Courses—Art Studio, Art History,
Elementary Art Education
Summer School: Dir, Dr Melvin Bernstein. Enrl 350; tuition $56 per cr hr for term
of 6 wks. Courses—Basic Art History, Studio Art

CUMBERLAND

ALLEGANY COMMUNITY COLLEGE, Willow Brook Rd, PO Box 1695, 21502.
Tel 301-724-7700. *Head Dept* Wini Clayton
Estab 1966; pub; D & E; scholarship; SC 6, LC 1; enrl Enrl D 30, E 9
Ent Req: HS dipl
Degrees: AA 2 yrs
Courses: Ceramics, Drawing, Painting, Survey of Art History, Two & Three
Dimensional Design
Summer School: Term of 6 wks beginning July. Courses—Painting, Two
Dimensional Design

EMMITSBURG

MOUNT SAINT MARY'S COLLEGE, Fine Arts Dept, 21727. Tel 301-447-6122.
Chmn Daniel C Nusbaum, PhD; *Prof* Helen-Lee Jones, MFA; *Prof* Walter Nichols,
MA; *Prof* Pamela Wegner, MA
Estab 1808; pvt; D & E; scholarships; SC 9, LC 10; enrl D 1200, maj 12
Ent Req: HS dipl, SAT
Degrees: BA and BS 4 yrs
Tuition: $3650 per yr, $1825 per sem; campus res available
Courses: Art History, Drawing, Painting, Sculpture, Theatre Arts

FREDERICK

HOOD COLLEGE, Dept of Art, 21701. Tel 301-663-3131. *Chairperson* Alexander
Russo, DA; *Assoc Prof* Elaine Gates, MFA; *Assoc Prof* Mary Ellen Randolph, MA;
Asst Prof Anne Derbes, PhD
Estab 1893; pvt, W; D; SC 18, LC 16; enrl D 700, maj 60
Ent Req: HS dipl
Degrees: BA 4 yrs
Tuition: Res—undergrad $5500 per yr; nonres—undergrad $3800 per yr; campus
res—room & board $2000
Courses: Five Areas of Concentration: Studio Arts, Art History, Art Therapy,
Secondary Art Eduction, Visual Communications
Summer School: Dir, Dr Patricia Bartlett. Tuition by course for term of 6 wks, June-
Aug. Courses—Internships and Independent Studies, Photography, Watercolor and
Sketching, Woodcut

FROSTBURG

FROSTBURG STATE COLLEGE, Dept of Art and Art Education, East College
Ave, 21532. Tel 301-689-4109. *Head Dept* Dustin P Davis
Estab 1898; pub; D; SC 25, LC 5; enrl D 230, maj 150, GS 13
Ent Req: HS dipl
Degrees: BA (Art, Art Educ), BS and MEd (Art Educ) 4 yrs
Tuition: Res—$310 per sem; nonres—$760 per sem; campus res—room and board
$1330-$1502 per yr
Courses: Advertising Design, Art Education, Art History, Ceramics, Drawing,
Graphic Design, Jewelry, Painting, Photography, Printmaking, Sculpture, Teacher
Training, Textile Design, Art Therapy, Art Awareness, Crafts, 2-D & 3-D Design
Children's Classes: Tuition $5. Sat school program
Summer School: Dir, David Sanford. Tuition $25 per cr hr for term of 4 1/2 wks
beginning May

HAGERSTOWN

HAGERSTOWN JUNIOR COLLEGE, Art Dept,* 751 Robinwood Dr, 21740. Tel
301-790-2800. *Coordr* G Roslyn Rutsten, MA
Sch estab 1946; pub; D & E; SC 10, LC 4; enrl D 110, E 66
Degrees: AA, 2 yrs
Tuition: Washington County Res—$21 per cr hr; out of county—$45 per cr hr;
nonres—$70 per cr hr
Courses: Art History, Ceramics, Drawing, Painting, Photography, Sculpture, Video,
Basic Design
Summer School: Courses—Basic Drawing, Painting, Photography, Special Studies in
Ceramics

LARGO

PRINCE GEORGE'S COMMUNITY COLLEGE, Art Dept, Humanities Division,
301 Largo Rd, 20870. Tel 301-336-6000, Ext 324. *Chmn* Caroline Huff, MFA
Estab 1958, dept estab 1967; pub; D & E; scholarships; SC 18, LC 2; enrl D 220, E
140, maj 11
Ent Req: HS dipl, CGP test
Degrees: AA
Courses: Advertising Design, Ceramics, Drawing, Jewelry, Lettering, Painting,
Photography, Printmaking, Sculpture, Advertising Illustration, Art Survey
Summer School: Dir, Dr John Handley. Courses—Drawing, Intro to Art, Painting,
Photography

PRINCESS ANNE

UNIVERSITY OF MARYLAND EASTERN SHORE, Art Education Dept,
21853. Tel 301-651-2200. *Chmn* Ernest P Satchell
Tuition: $1128
Courses: Art Appreciation, Art Education, Art History, Calligraphy, Ceramics,
Drawing, Handicrafts, Jewelry, Painting, Photography, Printmaking, Sculpture

ROCKVILLE

MONTGOMERY COLLEGE, Dept of Art, 51 Manakee St, 20805. Tel 301-279-5115. *Chmn* Allan Thomas Marsh, PhD
Estab 1946, dept estab 1966; pub; D & E; scholarships; SC 25, LC 7
Ent Req: HS dipl
Degrees: AA 2 yrs
Tuition: Res—$900 per yr, $450 per sem, $30 per sem hr; nonres—$2430 per yr, $81 per sem hr
Courses: †Advertising Design, †Architecture, Art Appreciation, †Art Education, †Art History, Ceramics, †Commercial Art, Design, Drawing, Film, Goldsmithing, †Illustration, †Interior Design, Jewelry, Lettering, Painting, †Photography, Printmaking, Sculpture, Video, Color, Enameling, Watercolor, Crafts, Computer Graphics, Metalsmith
Summer School: Dir Allan T Marsh. Tuition $30 per sem hr. Courses—Ceramics, Color, Crafts, Design, Drawing, Painting, Printmaking, Watercolor

SAINT MARY'S CITY

SAINT MARY'S COLLEGE OF MARYLAND, Arts and Letters Division, 20686. Tel 301-994-1600, Ext 387. *Chmn* Elinor S Miller, PhD; *Asst Prof* Jonathan Ingersoll, MS; *Assoc Prof* William Thomas Rowe, MFA; *Asst Prof* Joseph B Ross, MA; *Asst Prof* Sandra L Underwood, PhD; *Instructor* Lisa Scheer, MFA
Estab 1964; pub; D & E; scholarships; SC 14, LC 16; enrl D 155, E 43, non-maj 128, maj 70
Ent Req: HS dipl, SAT scores
Degrees: BA
Tuition: Res—undergrad $1220 per yr; nonres—undergrad $2220 per yr; campus res—room & board $3780
Courses: Art Education, Art History, Ceramics, Drawing, Graphic Arts, Jewelry, Museum Staff Training, Painting, Photography, Printmaking, Sculpture, Weaving
Adult Hobby Classes: Courses—Drawing, Ceramics, Painting, Sculpture
Summer School: Courses—Watercolor, Painting, Sculpture

SALISBURY

SALISBURY STATE COLLEGE, Art Dept, College & Camden Ave, 21801. Tel 301-543-6270. *Chmn & Assoc Prof* James L Burgess, MA; *Assoc Prof* Kent N Kimmel, MA; *Assoc Prof* Marie A Tator, MA; *Asst Prof* Ursula M Ehrhardt, MA; *Asst Prof* John R Cleary, MFA; *Instructor* Janice Golojuch, MFA
Estab 1925, dept estab 1970; pub; D & E; SC 26, LC 7, GC 1; enrl non-maj 500, maj 111, grad 2
Ent Req: HS dipl, SAT verbal & math
Degrees: BA, BS & BSW 4 yrs, MA & MEd 1 yr
Tuition: Res—undergrad $900 per yr, $452.50 per sem, $25 per cr hr, other $20 reg-col ctr; nonres—undergrad $1605 per yr, $802.50 per sem, $35 per cr hr, other $20 reg-col ctr, grad $48 per cr hr, $20 reg-col ctr; campus res—room and board $1300
Courses: Aesthetics, †Art Education, †Ceramics, †Commercial Art, Costume Design & Construction, Drawing, Film, †Graphic Design, †Handicrafts, †History of Art & Archaeology, Museum Staff Training, †Painting, †Photography, †Printmaking, †Sculpture, Stage Design, †Teacher Training, †European Field Study, †Independent Study, †Principles of Color
Summer School: Dean, Dr Darrel Hagar. Courses—various art education & studio courses

SILVER SPRING

MARYLAND COLLEGE OF ART AND DESIGN, 10500 Georgia Ave, 20902. Tel 301-649-4454. *Pres* Richard Weikart; *Academic Dean* Ellen Vincent; *Prof* Christopher Bartlett, MFA; *Assoc Prof* Oscar Chelimsky, BA; *Asst Prof* Lewis Hawkins, MFA; *Instr* Ruth Bolduan, MFA; *Instr* Jack Hammond, MEd; *Instr* Charles Mendez, BA; *Instr* Deane Nesgih, BA; *Instr* Gary Shankman, MFA
Estab 1955; pvt; D & E; scholarships; SC 30, LC 12; enrl D 125, E 50, non-maj 135, maj 55
Ent Req: HS dipl, portfolio interview
Degrees: AA 2 yrs
Tuition: $3800 per yr, $1267 per quarter, $90 per cr hr; no campus res
Courses: †Commercial Art, Graphic Design, Illustration, †Painting, Photography, Printmaking, Sculpture, †Fine Art
Adult Hobby Classes: Enrl 25; tuition $50 per course per 10 wks. Courses—Portrait, Drawing, Painting, Watercolor
Children's Classes: Enrl 25; tuition $50 per course per 10 wks. Courses—Commercial Art, Drawing, Painting
Summer School: Dir, Ellen Vincent. Enrl 50; tuition same as regular quarter divided into 2 5-wk sessions. Courses—same as regular

TOWSON

GOUCHER COLLEGE, Art Dept,* 1021 Dulaney Valley Rd, 21204. Tel 301-825-3300. *Chmn* Lincoln F Johnson, Jr
Estab 1885; pvt; D; scholarships; SC 38, LC 18; enrl D 970, non-maj 558, maj (art) 29
Ent Req: HS dipl, SAT achievement tests (CEEB), American College Testing Program
Degrees: MA 4 yrs, MA (Dance Movement Therapy) 2 yrs
Tuition: $3500 per sem
Summer School: Dir, Fontaine M Belford. Enrl 160; Term of 4 wks beginning June 12 and July 10. Courses—(Art) Dance, Fibers Workshop, Nature Drawing Workshop, Photography, Pottery Workshop, Theatre

WESTMINSTER

WESTERN MARYLAND COLLEGE, Art Dept, 21157. Tel 301-848-7000, Ext 596. *Head Dept* Wasyl Palijczuk; *Prof* Roy Fender; *Assoc Prof* Dr Julie O Badier. Instrs: FT 3, PT 1
Estab 1867; independent; D & E; SC 15, LC 12, GC 6; enrl D 1213, maj 35-50, grad 13
Ent Req: HS dipl, ent exam, SAT
Degrees: BA, BS & MEd 4 yrs
Tuition: $4500 per yr; campus res $1200
Courses: Aesthetics, Art Education, Ceramics, Drawing, History of Art & Archaeology, Jewelry, Lettering, Painting, Photography, Printmaking, Sculpture, Teacher Training, Design, Watercolor, Commercial Art
Children's Classes: Enrl over 120 Sat AM conducted by col students
Summer School: Two 5 wk terms beginning June 21. Courses—Ceramics, Painting, Printmaking, Sculpture, Weaving

MASSACHUSETTS

AMHERST

AMHERST COLLEGE, Dept of Fine Arts, Fayerweather Hall, 01002. Tel 413-542-2365. *Chmn* Robert T Sweeney. Instrs: FT 7
Estab 1822; pvt; D; scholarships; SC 15, LC 15
Ent Req: HS dipl
Degrees: BA 4 yrs
Tuition: $11,700 comprehensive fee for yr
Courses: Aesthetics, Art History, Drawing, Painting, Sculpture, Anatomy, 3-D Design, Serigraphy

UNIVERSITY OF MASSACHUSETTS, AMHERST
—College of Arts and Sciences, Department of Art, 01002. Tel 413-545-1902.
Chmn Dept George Wardlaw. Instrs: FT 36
Dept estab 1958; pub; scholarships; SC 50, LC 19, GC 20; enrl maj undergrad 430, grad 85
Ent Req: HS grad, portfolio required, 15 units HS, ent exam
Degrees: BA(Studio, Art History) and BFA (Studio, Interior Design, Art Educ) 4 yrs, MA(Art History), MFA(Ceramics, Painting, Printmaking, Sculpture), MS(Interior Design), MAT
Courses: Computer Graphics, 2-D Design, 3-D Design
Adult Hobby Classes: Enrl 75-125; tuition $175 per 3 cr course of 14 wks. Courses—Architectural Drawing, Drawing, Painting
Summer School: Dir, Angel Ramirez. Enrl 150-250; tuition $175 per 3 cr course, 2 six wk sessions. Courses—Architectural Drawing, Design, Drawing, Painting
—Art History Program,* 317 Bartlett Hall, 01003. Tel 413-545-3595. *Prof* Jack Benson, PhD; *Prof* Iris Cheney, PhD; *Prof* Paul Norton, PhD; *Prof* Mark Roskill, PhD; *Assoc Prof* Walter B Denny, PhD; *Asst Prof* Kristine Edmondson-Haney, PhD
Estab 1947, prog estab 1958; pub; D & E; scholarships; LC 36, GC 8; enrl D 1400, non-maj 600, maj 55, grad 35
Ent Req: HS dipl and transcript, SAT
Degrees: BA(Art History) 4 yrs, MA(Art History) 2 yrs
Tuition: $1129 annual tuition; room & board available
Courses: Aesthetics, Architecture, †Art History, History of Art & Archaeology, Museum Staff Training
Summer School: Enrl 15 per course. Tuition $30 per cr and $42 service fee for term of 6 wks beginning June 2 and July 14. Courses—American Art and Modern Art
—Dept Landscape Architecture & Regional Planning, Hills North 109, Landscape Archit Prog, 01003. Tel 413-545-2255. *Head* E Bruce MacDougall, PhD; *Dir MLA Prog* Nicholas Dines, MLA
Estab 1903; pub; D; SC 6, LC 5; enrl 35
Ent Req: Bachelor's degree, grad rec, exams, portfolio
Degrees: MLA 2-3 yrs
Tuition: Res—$558 per sem, $46.50 per cr hr; nonres—$1675 per sem, $140 per cr hr; campus res—room & board $4000 per yr
Courses: Drafting, Drawing, Landscape Architecture
Summer School: Planning and design short courses

AUBURNDALE

LASELL JUNIOR COLLEGE, Art Dept,* 1844 Commonwealth Ave, 02166. Tel 617-243-2206. *Head* Leonie S Bennett
Estab 1851; pvt; W; D & E; scholarships
Ent Req: HS dipl, portfolio in Art Dept
Degrees: AA and AS 2 yrs
Tuition: Res—undergrad $4895 per yr
Courses: Advertising Design, Ceramics, Drawing, Interior Design, Jewelry, Painting, Photography, Printmaking, Art for Child Study, Design & Color, Three-Dimensional Design, Portfolio

BEVERLY

ENDICOTT COLLEGE, Art Dept, 376 Hale St, 01915. Tel 617-927-0585. *Head Dept* J David Broudo, EdM
Estab 1939; pvt; W; D; scholarships; enrl 205, non-maj 13, maj 192
Ent Req: HS dipl
Degrees: AA & As 2 yrs
Tuition: Res—$8200 per yr (incl tuition, room & board); nonres—$4000 per yr
Courses: Advertising Design, Art History, †Ceramics, †Commercial Art, Drafting, Drawing, Fashion Arts, Graphic Arts, Illustration, †Interior Design, Jewelry, Painting, †Photography, Printmaking, Sculpture, Silversmithing, Weaving, †Apparel Design, †Fibers, †Metal
Adult Hobby Classes: Dir, J Jaffee. Courses—Drawing, Graphics Illustration, Interior Design, Metal, Painting, Understanding Art
Summer School: Dir, Elder Hostel

MONTSERRAT SCHOOL OF VISUAL ART, Dunham Rd, Box 62, 01915. Tel 617-922-8222. *Pres* Tames Davies; *Dean* Kenton Sharp; *Foundation Project* Barbara Moody; *Art History* Thorp Feidt; *Gallery Dir* Ethan Berry; *Painting* Oliver Balf; *Painting* James Sweeney; *Design* Roger Martin; *Illustration* Alissa Della-Piana
Estab 1970; pvt; D & E; scholarships; SC 53, LC 3; enrl D 112, E 207
Ent Req: Personal interview and portfolio review
Degrees: 4 yr dipl granted
Tuition: $3200 per yr, $1600 per sem, $360 per yr per course; no campus res
Courses: Advertising Design, Art Appreciation, Art History, Commercial Art, Conceptual Art, Design, Drawing, †Graphic Arts, Graphic Design, †Illustration, †Painting, Photography, †Printmaking, Sculpture
Adult Hobby Classes: Enrl 197; tuition $85 per 9 wks. Courses—Painting, Drawing, Printmaking, Monoprinting, Graphic Design, Photography, Watercolor
Children's Classes: Enrl 10; tuition $55 per sem. Courses—Painting & Drawing
Summer School: Dir, Rose Olson. Enrl 200; tuition $65 - $85 per 8 wks beginning July. Courses—same as above

BOSTON

ART INSTITUTE OF BOSTON, 700 Beacon St, 02215. Tel 617-262-1223, 262-2844. *Pres* William H Willis Jr, MFA; *Chmn Design Dept* Sue Morrison, MFA; *Chmn Illustration Dept* Annie Gusman; *Chmn Fine Arts Dept* John Bageris, MFA; *Co-Chmn Photography Dept* Bruce Kinch, MFA; *Co-Chmn Photography Dept* David Ulrich, MFA; *Chmn Found Dept* Nathan Goldstein, MFA; *Chmn Acadamic Studies* Robert Simon, MFA
Estab 1912; pvt; D & E; scholarships; SC 80, LC 20; enrl D 400, E 250
Ent Req: HS dipl, portfolio and interview
Degrees: (with Northeastern University) BS(Art) and BFA yrs vary
Tuition: Res—$3000 per yr, $1500 per sem
Courses: †Advertising Design, Art History, Calligraphy, †Ceramics, Collages, †Commercial Art, Drawing, Film, Graphic Arts, †Graphic Design, History of Art & Archaeology, †Illustration, Interior Design, Lettering, Mixed Media, †Painting, †Photography, †Printmaking, †Sculpture
Adult Hobby Classes: Enrl 200; tuition $70 per cr. Courses—Continuing education offers most of the above typically 2-3 cr each
Summer School: Dir, Mary Kaye. Enrl 250; tuition $70 per cr for 2 term of 8 wks beginning July 15. Courses—most of above

BOSTON CENTER FOR ADULT EDUCATION,* 5 Commonwealth Ave, 02116. Tel 617-267-4430. *Exec Dir* Harriet McLean; *Instructor* Alexander Farquharson, BFA; *Instructor* Shirley Pransky, Dipl; *Instructor* Barbara Newman, BFA; *Instructor* Ellen Stutman, MFA; *Instructor* Rubin Gold, Dipl; *Instructor* Amanda Annis, MFA; *Instructor* Ellen Maurie Rusinow, MA; *Instructor* Kelly Burke, MFA; *Instructor* Maria Fana, BFA
Estab 1933; pvt; D & E; scholarships; SC 26, LC 2; enrl D 2300, E 14,000
Ent Req: Open to all over 17
Tuition: $57 for 2 hr art or craft studio course; no campus res
Courses: Advertising Design, Architecture, Art Appreciation, Art History, Calligraphy, Ceramics, Display, Drawing, Graphic Design, History of Art & Archaeology, Interior Design, Lettering, Painting, Photography, Printmaking, Video, Weaving, Printmaking, Sculpture, Theatre Arts, Crafts, Studio Crafts, Chinese Brush Painting, Stained Glass, Stone Carving, Wood Carving
Children's Classes: Program for 14-17 year olds in art, writing and dance
Summer School: Same as winter program

BOSTON UNIVERSITY, School of Visual Arts, 855 Commonwealth Ave, 02215. Tel 617-353-3371. *Dir* Edward F Leary, EdM; *Prof* David Aronson; *Prof* Harold Tovish; *Prof* James Weeks; *Assoc Prof* Alston Purvis
Estab 1869, school estab 1954; pvt; D; scholarships; SC 38, LC 12, GC 15; enrl 395, non-maj 75, maj 260, grad 60
Ent Req: HS dipl, portfolio and SAT or ACT
Degrees: BFA 4 yrs, MFA 2 yrs
Tuition: $8300 per yr, $260 per cr; campus res—room & board $3650 per yr
Courses: †Art Education, Art History, Design, Drawing, †Graphic Design, †Painting, Photography, Printmaking, †Sculpture, Teacher Training, †Studio Teaching (grad level), Typographic Design
Adult Hobby Classes: Courses—High School Drawing Class
Summer School: Dir, Edward F Leary. Tuition $120 per cr for terms of 6 weeks each. Courses—Drawing, Graphic Design, Painting
—Program in Artisanry, 620 Commonwealth Ave, 02215. Tel 617-353-3022. *Dir* Robert L Cardinale, EdD; *Asst Dir* Patricia Doran, MBA
Estab 1975; D & E; scholarships; SC 60, GC 10; enrl D 97, E 30, maj 97, grad 40
Ent Req: HS dipl
Degrees: Certificate of Mastery, AA, BFA, MFA
Tuition: $8300 per yr, $260 per sem hr; campus res $3780
Courses: Ceramics, Design, Drawing, Goldsmithing, Jewelry, Silversmithing, Textile Design, Weaving, Craft History, Enameling, Glass, Historic Stringed Instruments, Textile Printing, Wood Working & Furniture Design

BUTERA SCHOOL OF ART, 111 Beacon St, 02116. Tel 617-536-4623. *Dir* Joseph L Butera, MFA; *Head Commercial Art* Hal Trafford; *Head Sign Painting* Jim Garballey
Estab 1932; pvt; D & E; enrl D 100, E 60
Ent Req: HS dipl, portfolio
Degrees: 2 yr and 3 yr dipl progs
Tuition: $3700-$3850 per yr; independent dormitories available
Courses: Advertising Design, Art Education, Art History, Calligraphy, Commercial Art, Drawing, Fashion Arts, Graphic Arts, Graphic Design, Illustration, Lettering, Painting, Sign Painting

CHAMBERLAYNE JUNIOR COLLEGE, Dept of Applied Arts,* 128 Commonwealth Ave, 02116. Tel 617-536-4500. *Chmn Dept* J M Vascovitch; *Assoc Prof* M Vitagliano; *Instr* T Bowling, MA; *Instr* Z Girard, AAS; *Instr* P Magri, BS; *Lectr* M Crowe, MFA; *Lectr* M Enos, cert; *Lectr* D Hurley, BSEd
Estab 1892, dept estab 1952; pvt; D & E; SC 23, LC 11; enrl D 253, E 38, maj 253
Ent Req: HS dipl
Degrees: AAS 2 yrs, Interior Design 3 yrs

Tuition: $3660 per yr; campus res—room & board $2750
Courses: Architecture, Art History, †Commercial Art, †Costume Design & Construction, Drafting, Drawing, Fashion Arts, †Graphic Arts, †Illustration, †Interior Design, Jewelry, Painting, Sculpture, Textile Design, †Landscape Architecture
Summer School: 12 wks beginning June 1. Courses same as regular academic yr

EMMANUEL COLLEGE, Art Dept, 400 The Fenway, 02115. Tel 617-277-9340, Ext 194. *Chairperson Dept* Ellen Marie Glavin; *Prof* Donald Procaccini, PhD; *Assoc Prof* Michael Jacques, MFA; *Assoc Prof* Theresa Monaco, MFA; *Asst Prof* C David Thomas, MFA
Estab 1919, dept estab 1950; pvt; D & E; scholarships; SC 30, LC 11; enrl D 300, E 50, non-maj 200, maj 80, grad 15
Ent Req: HS dipl, SAT
Degrees: BA 4 yrs, BFA 4-5 yrs
Tuition: $5300 full time or $664 per course; campus res—room & board $2900 per yr
Courses: Aesthetics, †Art Education, Art History, Ceramics, Commercial Art, Drawing, Graphic Arts, Graphic Design, Handicrafts, Mixed Media, †Painting, †Printmaking, Sculpture, Teacher Training, †Art Therapy
Adult Hobby Classes: Tuition $93 per credit. Courses—all courses offered
Summer School: Dir, Sr Mary Ellen O'Keefe. Enrl 100; tuition $93 per cr hr for term of 1 wk beginning July. Courses—Art Education, Printmaking, Art Therapy

MASSACHUSETTS COLLEGE OF ART, 364 Brookline Ave, 02215. Tel 617-731-2340. *Pres* John F Nolan, MS; *Academy VPres* Jerome J Hausman, EdD; *Dean Undergrad* Edward D Movitz, MAT; *Dean Grad & Continuing Educ* Theodore C Landsmark, JD; *Chmn Fine Arts, 2D* Jeremy Foss, MFA; *Chmn Fine Arts, 3D* Marilyn Pappas, EdD; *Chmn Design* Margaret Hickey, BArch; *Chmn Art Educ* Diana Korzenik, DEd; *Chmn Media* Johanna Gill, MFA; *Chmn Critical Studies* Marjorie Hellerstine, PhD
Estab 1873; pub; D & E; SC 400, LC 250, GC 50; enrl D 1094, E 1900, maj 1058, grad 90, others 1800
Ent Req: HS dipl, SAT and Portfolio
Degrees: BFA 4 yrs, MFA 2 yrs, MSAE 1 yr
Tuition: Res—$845 per yr; nonres—$2792 per yr; no campus res
Courses: Architecture, Art Education, Art History, Ceramics, Fashion Arts, Film, Graphic Design, Illustration, Industrial Design, Museum Staff Training, Painting, Photography, Printmaking, Sculpture, Art Certification, Fibers, Glass, Metals, Studio Education
Adult Hobby Classes: Tuition $25 per cr hr. Courses—All areas
Children's Classes: Enrl 750; tuition $10. Courses—All areas
Summer School: Dir Continuing Educ, Dr Donald Lettis. Enrl 900; tuition $25 per cr hr. Courses—all areas

NEW ENGLAND SCHOOL OF ART & DESIGN, 28 Newbury St, 02116. Tel 617-536-0383. *Pres* Christy R Rufo; *VPres* W M Davis; *Chmn Dept of Graphic Design* Robert Linsky; *Chmn Dept of Interior Design* Barbara Kingsbury; *Chmn Dept of Interior Design* Linda Briggs; *Chmn Fashion Illustration* Frank Raneo; *Chmn Fine Arts* William Maynard
Estab 1923; pvt; D & E; enrl D 230, E 250, maj 200
Ent Req: HS dipl, portfolio
Degrees: 3 yr dipl
Tuition: $3650 per yr, $1825 per sem, $190 per cr for PT; no campus res
Courses: †Advertising Design, Art History, Calligraphy, Commercial Art, Drafting, Drawing, Film, Graphic Arts, †Graphic Design, Illustration, †Interior Design, Lettering, Painting, Photography, Printmaking, †Fashion Illustration, †Fine Arts, Landscape Architecture
Summer School: Dir of Admis, Sara Chadwick. Enrl approx 250; tuition $190 per cr for term beginning early June. Courses—those above

NORTHEASTERN UNIVERSITY, Dept of Art, 360 Huntington Ave, 02115. Tel 617-437-2347. *Chmn* Peter Serenyi, PhD; *Prof* Robert Wells, MA; *Assoc Prof* Samuel Bishop, MFA; *Assoc Prof* Wheaton Holden, PhD; *Asst Prof* Talbot N Rantoul, MFA
Estab 1898, dept estab 1952; pvt; D & E; scholarships; enrl D 1200, E 260, non-maj 1400, maj 60
Ent Req: HS dipl
Degrees: BA & BS 4 yrs
Tuition: Freshmen $5325 per academic year; upperclassmen $4958 per academic year, $620 per course; campus res available
Courses: †Art History, Drafting, Drawing, Film, Graphic Arts, Graphic Design, Painting, Photography, Printmaking, †History of Architecture
Summer School: Chmn, Peter Serenyi. Enrl 150. Courses—same as above

THE SCHOOL OF FASHION DESIGN, 136 Newbury St, 02116. Tel 617-536-9343. *Head Art Dept* Rita Berkowitz, BA; *Instr* Elzino O'Brien, BA
Estab 1934; pvt; D & E; scholarships; enrl D approx 100, E approx 200
Ent Req: HS dipl
Degrees: No degrees, 2 yr cert or 3 yr dipl
Tuition: Res—$2500 per yr; no campus res
Courses: Costume Design & Construction, Drawing, Fashion Arts, Illustration, Textile Design, Theatre Arts
Adult Hobby Classes: Enrl 100; tuition $250 per 3 cr course. Courses—Fashion Design
Summer School: Dir, R F Alantosky. Enrl 100; tuition $250 per 3 cr course of 15 wks. Courses—Fashion Design

SCHOOL OF THE MUSEUM OF FINE ARTS, 230 The Fenway, 02115. Tel 617-267-9300. *Dean* Bruce K MacDonald, PhD
Estab 1876; pvt; D & E; scholarships; SC 139, LC 16; enrl D 569, E 305, grad 32, others 25
Ent Req: HS dipl, HS and col transcripts, portfolio
Degrees: BFA, BFA plus BA or BS, BSEd, MFA, dipl (all degrees in affiliation with Tufts University)
Tuition: Dipl $5300 per yr; BFA $5864 per yr; MFA $8534 first yr, none second yr; E $300 per course; no campus res

Courses: Art Education, Ceramics, Drawing, Film, Graphic Design, Intermedia, Jewelry, Painting, Photography, Printmaking, Sculpture, Video, Metalsmithing, Stained Glass
Adult Hobby Classes: Evening classes; enrl 305; tuition $300 per 15 wk sem, 3 cr per course; Saturday classes; tuition $160 per course
Summer School: Dir, Donald Grey. Enrl 360; term of 6 wks beginning last wk in June

UNIVERSITY OF MASSACHUSETTS AT BOSTON, Art Dept,* Morrissey Blvd, Harbor Campus, 02125. Tel 617-287-1900, 929-7000. *Chmn & Prof* Harold Thurman, MA; *Prof* Ruth Butler, PhD; *Assoc Prof* Renee Arb, PhD; *Assoc Prof* Roslyn Barron, BFA; *Assoc Prof* Frances Fergusson, PhD; *Assoc Prof* William Hansard, BA; *Assoc Prof* Robert Risse, PhD; *Assoc Prof* Richard Yarde, MFA
Sch estab 1965, dept estab 1966; pub; D & E; SC 18, LC 32; enrl D 900, E 100, maj 200
Ent Req: Entrance exam
Degrees: BA
Tuition: Res—$952 per yr; nonres—$3350 per yr
Courses: Aesthetics, Art History, Conceptual Art, Constructions, Drawing, Film, Intermedia, Painting, Photography, Printmaking, Video

GEORGE VESPER SCHOOL OF ART,* 44 St Botolph St, 02116. Tel 617-267-2045. *Dir* Fletcher Adams
Estab 1924; pvt; scholarships
Degrees: 3 yrs
Courses: Illustration, Interior Design, Advertising Art, Design, Fashion Illustration, Fine Arts
Children's Classes: Sat

BRADFORD

BRADFORD COLLEGE, Creative Arts Division, 320 S Main St, 01830. Tel 617-372-7161. *Chmn* Richard Newman, MFA; *Asst Prof* Kathy Hoffman, PhD; *Asst Prof* Marc Mannheimer, MFA; *Asst Prof* David Powell, BFA; *Asst Prof* Kay Rosenberg, MFA; *Asst Prof* Jan Watson, MA
Estab 1803; pvt; D & E; scholarships; SC 20, LC 12; enrl D 300
Ent Req: HS dipl
Degrees: AA 2 yrs, BA(Creative Arts) 4 yrs
Tuition: Res $9625 per yr, nonres $6235; campus res—room $3390 per yr
Courses: Aesthetics, Art History, Ceramics, Collages, Constructions, Drawing, Film, History of Art & Archaeology, Jewelry, Painting, Photography, Printmaking, Sculpture, Silversmithing, Stage Design, Textile Design, Theatre Arts, Weaving

BRIDGEWATER

BRIDGEWATER STATE COLLEGE, Art Dept, School and Summer Sts, 02324. Tel 617-697-8321, Ext 249 & 486. *Chmn* Stephen Smalley, EdD; *Assoc Prof* John Droege, MFA; *Prof* John Heller, MFA; *Prof* Joan Hausrath, MFA; *Asst Prof* William Kendall, MFA; *Asst Prof* Roger Dunn, PhD; *Asst Prof* Dorothy Pulsifer, MA
Estab 1840, dept estab 1840; pub; D & E; SC 35, LC 10, GC 35; enrl D 500, E 100, non-maj 440, maj 150, grad 10
Ent Req: HS dipl, SAT
Degrees: BA 4 yrs
Tuition: $35.50 per cr, $950 per yr; campus residence available
Courses: †Art Education, Art History, Ceramics, Drawing, Goldsmithing, Graphic Arts, History of Art & Archaeology, Jewelry, Painting, Printmaking, Sculpture, Silversmithing, Stage Design, Textile Design, Theatre Arts, Glass, Weaving
Summer School: Art History Study Tour of Europe; Coastal Maine Drawing & Painting Workshop

CAMBRIDGE

HARVARD UNIVERSITY, Dept of Fine Arts,* 02138. Tel 617-495-2377. *Chmn Dept* James S Ackerman; *Aga Khan Prof Islamic Art* Oileg Graber. Instrs: FT 23
Estab 1874; pvt; Scholarships; LC 26 incl GC 12; enrl undergrad 88, grad 100
Courses: Art History

LESLEY COLLEGE, Arts Institute,* 29 Everett St, 02238. Tel 617-868-9600
Tuition: $5400 annual tuition
Courses: Art Appreciation, Art Education, Art History, Ceramics, Design, Drawing, Handicrafts, Painting, Photography, Printmaking

MASSACHUSETTS INSTITUTE OF TECHNOLOGY
—School of Architecture and Planning,* 77 Massachusetts Ave, 02139. Tel 617-253-4401. *Dean* John de Monchaux; *Assoc Dean* Lois A Craig; *Head Dept* John Randolph Myer. Instrs: FT 37
Estab 1865; pvt; SC, LC, GC; enrl 544
Degrees: SB(Art and Design), SB(Urban Studies), MArchit, AS(Advanced Studies), MCP, PhD(City Planning), PhD(Archit, Art Environmental Studies) 2, 4 and 6 yrs
—Center for Advanced Visual Studies, 40 Massachusetts Ave, W11, 02139. Tel 617-253-4415; Telex 92-1473; TWX 710-320-0058. *Dir* Otto Piene
Estab dept 1967; pvt; D & E; SC 9, LC 1, GC 5; enrl D & E 250, non-maj 240, grad 10
Ent Req: BA degree
Degrees: MS 2 yrs
Tuition: Same as Institute
Courses: Architecture, Art History, Film, Graphic Arts, Graphic Design, Mixed Media, Photography, Printmaking, Video, Celebrations, Concepts, Developmental Media, Environmental Art, History of Architecture, Holography, Laser

CHESTNUT HILL

PINE MANOR COLLEGE, Visual Arts Dept, 400 Heath St, 02167. Tel 617-731-7000. *Head* Iso Papo, MS
Estab 1911; pvt; D; SC 25, LC 25; enrl D 80
Ent Req: HS dipl
Degrees: AA & AS 2 yrs, BA 4 yrs
Tuition: Res—undergrad $7200 per academic yr; campus res—room & board $4200 per academic yr
Courses: Architecture, †Art History, Costume Design & Construction, Drafting, Drawing, Graphic Arts, Interior Design, Museum Staff Training, Painting, Printmaking, Sculpture, Stage Design, Theatre Arts, Visual Arts
Adult Hobby Classes: Studio courses 25, lecture courses 25
Summer School: Dir, Dr Eva I Kampits

CHICOPEE

ELMS COLLEGE (Formerly College of Our Lady of the Elms), Dept of Fine Arts, 291 Springfield St, 01013. Tel 413-598-8351, Ext 255. *Chmn Dept* Theresa Amiot; *Assoc* James McDowell; *Assoc* Nancy Costanzo
Estab 1928, dept estab 1950; pvt; D & E; scholarships; SC 14, LC 6; enrl D 210, non-maj 193, maj 17
Ent Req: HS dipl, Col Ent Exam (Verbal and Math)
Degrees: BA 4 yrs
Tuition: Res—$6850 per yr; nonres—$4350 per yr
Courses: Art Education, Photography, Art History, Calligraphy, Ceramics, Drawing, Painting, Printmaking, Sculpture

DOVER

CHARLES RIVER CREATIVE ARTS PROGRAM, 56 Centre St, 02030. Tel 617-785-0068, 785-1260. *Dir* Priscilla B Dewey; *Dir* Talbot Dewey Jr
Estab 1969; pvt summer school; D
Ent Req: None
Tuition: $425
Courses: Ceramics, Costume Design & Construction, Drawing, Film, Mixed Media, Painting, Photography, Printmaking, Silversmithing, Stage Design, Theatre Arts, Video
Children's Classes: Enrl 210; tuition $425 for 4 weeks
Summer School: Dir, Priscilla B Dewey & Talbot Dewey Jr. Tuition $425 for 2 - 4 week sessions. Courses—same as regular session

FRAMINGHAM

DANFORTH MUSEUM SCHOOL, 123 Union Ave, 01701. Tel 617-872-0858, 620-0050. *School Dir* Marcia Rosenberg; *Instr* Gaetano Alibrandi, MA; *Instr* Elizabeth Bryant, MA; *Instr* James Eng, MFA; *Instr* Anne Forbes, BA; *Instr* Alston Stoney Conley, BFA; *Instr* Nan Feldman, BFA; *Instr* Lila Green, BA; *Instr* Gillian Frazier, BS; *Instr* Anna Lochiatto, BFA; *Instr* Dominic Malizia, MFA; *Instr* Mary Mead-Desehenes, BFA; *Instr* Candida Poor-Monteith, BFA; *Instr* Elli Crocker, MFA; *Instr* Michael Dowling, MFA; *Instr* Rhoda Rosenberg, BFA; *Instr* Patricia Walker, MA; *Instr* Chriss Holderness, MFA; *Instr* Karolina Illigen, MA; *Instr* Rose Marston, BS; *Instr* Leslie Starobin, MFA
Pub; scholarships
Ent Req: None
Tuition: Varies per course; museum members receive a tuition reduction
Courses: Art History, Calligraphy, Ceramics, Drawing, Graphic Arts, Jewelry, Painting, Photography, Printmaking, Sculpture, Weaving, Stained Glass, Watercolor
Adult Hobby Classes: Enrl 100-200; tuition varies per 10 wk sessions.
Courses—Arts, Crafts, Photography
Children's Classes: Enrl 50-100; tuition varies per 10 wk session. Courses—Art Multi-Media, Ceramics
Summer School: Enrl 100-150; tuition varies per 3-8 wk courses. Courses—same as above

FRAMINGHAM STATE COLLEGE, Art Dept, State St, 01701. Tel 617-620-1220. *Chmn* Gene Sullivan, MFA; *Prof* Stephen Durkee, MS; *Assoc Prof* Dr Brucia Witthoft, PhD; *Asst Prof* James Eng, MFA; *Asst Prof* Fred Fiandaca, MA; *Instr* Richard Fisher, MFA
Estab 1839, dept estab 1920; pub; D & E; scholarships; SC 20, LC 10, GC 10; enrl D 3000, E 2500, maj 124
Ent Req: HS dipl, portfolio review
Degrees: BA 4 yrs
Tuition: Res $845 per yr, nonres $2957; campus res—room & board $1800 per yr
Courses: †Art History, Museum Studies, †Studio Art
Adult Hobby Classes: Art History, Studio Art
Summer School: Dir, Dr Joseph Palladino. Tuition $170 per course for term of 8 wks. Courses—Art History, Studio

FRANKLIN

DEAN JUNIOR COLLEGE, Visual and Performing Art Dept, 99 Main St, 02038. Tel 617-528-9100. *Chairperson Dept* Lawry Reid, MFA; *Assoc Prof* Stanley Sobocinski, MFA; *Asst Prof* Richard Dean, MFA; *Asst Prof* Myron Schmidt, MA; *Instructor* Theodore P Casher, MM
Estab 1865, dept estab 1960; pvt; D & E; scholarships; SC 12, LC 4; enrl D 220, E 30, non-maj 180, maj 40
Ent Req: HS dipl
Degrees: AA, AS 2 yrs
Tuition: $5145 per yr; campus res—room and board $2460
Courses: Art History, Ceramics, Drawing, Graphic Arts, Painting, Photography, †Theatre Arts, Fashion Merchandising, †Interior Merchandising, 3-D Design, Visual Arts, Visual Art

GREAT BARRINGTON

SIMON'S ROCK OF BARD COLLEGE, Studio Arts Dept, Fine Arts Division, Alford Rd, 01230. Tel 413-528-0771. *Chairperson Studio Arts Dept* William Jackson, MFA; *Instructor* Arthur Hillman, MFA. Instrs: PT 2
Estab 1966; pvt; D & E; scholarships; SC 14, LC 4
Ent Req: Personal interview
Degrees: AA 2-3 yrs, BA 4 yrs
Tuition: $8100 per yr, room & board $2800
Courses: Aesthetics, Art History, Ceramics, Drawing, Graphic Design, Jewelry, Painting, Photography, Printmaking, Sculpture, Artist and the Book, Introduction to the Arts, 3-D Design

GREENFIELD

GREENFIELD COMMUNITY COLLEGE, Art Dept, One College Dr, 01301. Tel 413-774-3131. *Head Art Dept* T Budge Hyde, MFA; *Instructor* John Bross, MFA; *Instructor* Peter Dudley, MFA; *Instructor* Pamela Sacher, MA; *Instructor* Margaret Stein, MFA; *Instructor* Tom Young, MFA; *Art Historian* Joan Rising, MFA
Estab 1962; maintains a small student gallery; pub; D & E; scholarships; SC 16; enrl in school D 1400, E 400, maj 110
Ent Req: HS dipl
Degrees: AA, AS 2 yrs
Tuition: Res—$600 per yr, $300 per sem; nonres—$1100 per yr, $550 per sem
Courses: †Advertising Design, †Art History, †Commercial Art, Constructions, Display, †Drawing, Graphic Arts, †Graphic Design, History of Art & Archaeology, Illustration, †Painting, †Photography, †Printmaking
Adult Hobby Classes: Enrl 85. Courses—Photography, Drawing, Painting, Printmaking & Art History
Children's Classes: Enrl 50. Courses—Introduction to Drawing & Studio Art
Summer School: Dir, T Budge Hyde, MFA. Tuition $20-$30 per hr for term of 6 wks beginning June. Courses—Art History, Drawing, Painting, Photography & Printmaking

HOLYOKE

HOLYOKE COMMUNITY COLLEGE, Dept of Art,* 303 Homestead Ave, 01040. Tel 413-538-7000. *Chmn* Gerhard M Wilke, MFA
Estab 1946; pub; D & E; scholarships; SC 7, LC 4; enrl D 115, E 20, maj 50
Ent Req: HS dipl, portfolio
Degrees: AA 2 yrs
Tuition: Res—$228 per sem; nonres—$1008 per sem
Courses: Art Education, Drawing, Graphic Arts, Graphic Design, History of Art & Archaeology, Painting, Photography
Summer School: Dir, William Murphy. Courses—Per regular session, on demand

LONGMEADOW

BAY PATH JUNIOR COLLEGE, Dept of Art, 588 Longmeadow St, 01106. Tel 413-567-0621. *Chmn* Muriel Mitchell. Instrs: FT 2, PT 10
Estab 1947; pvt; W; D & E; scholarships; SC 18, LC 2; enrl D 660, E 400, maj 10
Ent Req: HS dipl
Degrees: AFA 2 yr
Tuition: $133 per cr, $7600 comprehensive tuition, room & board
Courses: Ceramics, Drawing, Graphic Arts, Handicrafts, History of Art & Archaeology, Painting, Photography, Sculpture, Foundation Art
Adult Hobby Classes: Enrl 100; tuition varies, Courses—Ceramics, Painting, Watercolor

LOWELL

UNIVERSITY OF LOWELL, Dept of Art, South Campus, 01854. Tel 617-452-5000, Ext 2872. *Chairperson Dept* Dr Liana Cheney; *Prof* Carlton Plummer, MFA; *Prof* Brenda Pinardi, MFA; *Assoc Prof* Leo Panas, EdM; *Assoc Prof* Fred Faudie, MFA; *Asst Prof* Robert Griffith, MFA; *Asst Prof* James Coates, MFA
Estab 1975 (merger of Lowell State College and Lowell Technological Institute); pub; D & E; enrl D 1200, E 25, non-maj 450, maj 150
Ent Req: HS dipl, SAT
Degrees: BA(Art), BFA 4 yrs
Tuition: Res—undergrad $986 per yr, $493 per sem; nonres—undergrad $3242 per yr, $1621 per sem; campus res—room & board $2366 per yr
Courses: Art History, Studio Art
Adult Hobby Classes: Enrl 15-20 per course; tuition $35 per cr. Courses—Art Appreciation, Drawing, Painting, Survey of Art
Summer School: Dir, Ed James. Enrl 10-15; tuition $35 per cr for three weeks. Courses—Appreciation of the Visual Arts, Art History, Drawing, Photography, Survey of Art, Seminars in Italy

MEDFORD

TUFTS UNIVERSITY, Fine Arts Dept, 11 Talbot Ave, 02155. Tel 617-628-5000, Ext 396. *Chmn Fine Arts Dept* Margaret Floyd, PhD; *Prof* Madeline H Caviness, PhD; *Prof* Anne vanBuren, PhD; *Assoc Prof* Ivan Galantic, PhD; *Asst Prof* Pamela Allara, PhD; *Asst Prof* Barbara White, PhD; *Asst Prof* Elizabeth Swinton; *Asst Prof* Mary CrawfordVolk; *Asst Prof* Anne Mochon; *Vis Lectr* Bruce MacDonald; *Vis Lectr* William Young
Pvt; D; scholarships
Ent Req: HS dipl
Degrees: BA, BS, BEd, BFA, MA, MFA
Tuition: $6725 per yr; campus res—room & board $1830 per yr
Courses: Ceramics, Drawing, Graphic Arts, History of Art & Archaeology, Jewelry, Occupational Therapy, Painting, Photography, Sculpture, History of Architecture
Adult Hobby Classes: Courses offered
Summer School: Dir, Bonnie J Newman. Enrl 75; 2 sessions. Courses vary

NEW BEDFORD

SWAIN SCHOOL OF DESIGN, 19 Hawthorn St, 02740. Tel 617-997-7831. *Pres* Bruce H Yenawine
Estab 1881; pvt; D; Scholarships; SC 16, LC 16; enrl D 144, maj 21
Ent Req: HS dipl, portfolio
Degrees: BFA 4 yr
Tuition: $4300
Courses: †Graphic Design, †Painting, †Printmaking, †Sculpture

NEWTON

BOSTON COLLEGE, Fine Arts Dept, 885 Centre St, 02159. Tel 617-552-8000
Degrees: BA offered
Courses: Art History, Ceramics, Drawing, Film, Painting, Photography, Printmaking, Sculpture, Animation

NEWTON CENTER

MOUNT IDA JUNIOR COLLEGE, Art Dept,* 777 Dedham St, 02159. Tel 617-969-7000. *Chmn* John Avakian, MFA
Scholarships offered
Degrees: AA
Tuition: $4290 per sem
Courses: Design, Drawing, Fashion Arts, Interior Design, Photography, Printmaking

NORTHAMPTON

SMITH COLLEGE, Art Dept, 01063. Tel 413-584-2700. *Chairperson Art Dept* Gary Niswonger, MFA; *Prof* James Holderbaum; *Prof* Robert Harris; *Prof* Helen Searing; *Prof* Charles Talbot, PhD; *Prof* Elliot Offner, MFA; *Assoc Prof* John Pinto; *Assoc Prof* Jaroslaw Leshko; *Assoc Prof* Chester Michalik, MFA; *Asst Prof* Caroline Houser; *Asst Prof* Nicholas vonBujdoss, MFA; *Asst Prof* Susan Heidman, MFA; *Asst Prof* Dwight Pogue, MFA; *Asst Prof* A Lee Burns, MFA; *Asst Prof* Barbara Kellum; *Lectr* Marylin Rhie, PhD; *Lectr* Andrus Burr, MArch. Instrs: FT 17
Estab 1875, dept estab 1877; pvt; W; D; scholarships; SC 24, LC 34; enrl maj 170
Ent Req: HS dipl, col board exam
Degrees: BA 4 yr
Tuition: $11,830 per yr incl room & board
Courses: Aesthetics, Architecture, Art Education, Art History, Calligraphy, Constructions, Costume Design & Construction, Drafting, Drawing, Graphic Arts, Graphic Design, History of Art & Archaeology, Intermedia, Landscape Architecture, Mixed Media, Museum Staff Training, Painting, Photography, Printmaking, Sculpture, Stage Design

NORTH DARTMOUTH

SOUTHEASTERN MASSACHUSETTS UNIVERSITY, College of Visual and Performing Arts, Old Westport Rd, 02747. Tel 617-999-8564. *Dean* Col Barbara H Noel; *Chairperson Music Dept* Eleanor Carlson, DMA; *Chairperson Art Educ* Dante Vena, PhD; *Chairperson Fine Art* Anthony J Miraglia, MFA; *Chairperson Design* Howard Windham, MFA; *Chairperson Art History* Thomas Puryear, PhD; *Coordr Gallery* Harvey Goldman, MFA. Instrs: FT 28, PT 12
Estab 1895, col estab 1948; pub; D & E; SC 75, LC 41, GC 7; enrl D 450
Ent Req: HS dipl, SAT, open admis to qualified freshmen
Degrees: BFA and BA 4 yr, MFA and MAE 2-5 yrs
Tuition: Res—undergrad $802 per yr, grad $883 per yr; nonres—undergrad $2808 per yr, grad $2887 per yr; campus res room & board $2836 per yr
Courses: Advertising Design, Aesthetics, Art Education, Art History, Calligraphy, Ceramics, Commercial Art, Conceptual Art, Drawing, Film, Goldsmithing, Graphic Arts, Graphic Design, History of Art & Archaeology, Illustration, Intermedia, Jewelry, Lettering, Mixed Media, Painting, Photography, Printmaking, Sculpture, Silversmithing, Teacher Training, Textile Design, Theatre Arts, Video
Summer School: Dean, Dr Robert E Piper

NORTON

WHEATON COLLEGE, Art Dept, 02766. Tel 617-285-7722. *Chmn Dept* Ann H Murray. Instrs: FT 6, PT 3
Estab 1834; pvt; W; scholarships; SC 6, LC 18; enrl 1384
Degrees: AB 4 yr
Tuition: $11,885 incl room and board
Courses: †Art History, Drawing, Painting, Photography, Printmaking, Sculpture, 2-D & 3-D Design

PAXTON

ANNA MARIA COLLEGE, Dept of Art, Sunset Lane, 01612. Tel 617-757-4586. *Chmn Dept* Ralph Parente. Instrs: FT 1, PT 3
Estab 1948; pvt; D & E; scholarships; SC 15, LC 12; enrl D 397, maj 32
Ent Req: HS dipl, ent exam
Degrees: 4 yr
Courses: †Advertising Design, Aesthetics, †Art Education, Art History, Ceramics, Drawing, Lettering, Painting, Photography, Sculpture, †Teacher Training, Art Therapy, Enameling, Macrame, Modeling, Rug Design, Silk Screen, Stitchery, Weaving, †Studio Art
Adult Hobby Classes: Enrl 10; one sem. Courses—Art that Works
Summer School: Dir, Richard Connors. Two sessions beginning May. Courses—Crafts for the Retarded, Lettering, Oil Painting, Watercolor Techniques

PITTSFIELD

BERKSHIRE COMMUNITY COLLEGE, Dept Fine Arts, West St, 01201. Tel 413-499-4660. *Chmn Dept* Robert M Boland, MFA; *Assoc Prof* Nancy Delaiti, MA; *Asst Prof* Julio Granda, MFA; *Instr* Benigna Chilla, MFA; *Instr* Pleter Lips, MFA; *Instr* Mark Milloff, MFA; *Instr* Lyn Newell, MFA
Estab 1960, dept estab 1961; pub; D & E; scholarships; SC 16, LC 4; enrl D 72, E 75, non-maj 12, maj 72
Ent Req: HS dipl
Degrees: AA 2 yrs
Tuition: Res—$288 per sem; nonres—$1008 per sem; no campus res
Courses: Art History, Calligraphy, Costume Design & Construction, Drawing, Mixed Media, Painting, Photography, Printmaking, Stage Design, Theatre Arts, Applied Graphics, 2-D Design, 3-D Design, Primitive Art, 20th Century Art
Adult Hobby Classes: Continuing education evening classes, some may be applied to degree program
Summer School: Enrl 75; tuition $35 per cr hr for term of 7 wks beginning June.
Courses—Design, Drawing, Painting, Photography

PROVINCETOWN

CAPE SCHOOL OF ART, Conwell St, 02657. Tel 617-487-0703. *Dir* Henry Hensche
Estab 1930; pvt summer school; D
Ent Req: None
Tuition: $300 for 2 months, July-August
Courses: Art History, Drawing, Painting

QUINCY

QUINCY JUNIOR COLLEGE, Fine Arts Dept,* 34 Coddington St, 02169. Tel 617-786-8777
Degrees: AA, AS and Certificate offered
Tuition: $712.50 per sem
Courses: Art Appreciation, Drawing

SALEM

SALEM STATE COLLEGE, Art Dept, 352 LaFayette St, 01970. Tel 617-745-0556. *Chmn Dept* Thomas Leary, MFA; *Prof* Elissa Ananian, MAT; *Prof* N E Wagman, ME; *Prof* Ingrida Mangulis; *Assoc Prof* Marion G Miller, MEd; *Prof* Mark Raudzens, MFA; *Prof* Arthur Smith, MEd; *Prof* Frank Quimby, MEd
Estab 1854; pub; D & E; scholarships; SC 19, LC 8, GC 5; enrl maj 102
Ent Req: HS dipl
Degrees: BA 4 yrs, internships
Tuition: Res—$645 per yr; nonres—$1465 per yr; campus res available
Courses: Art Education, Art History, Ceramics, Drawing, Film, Graphic Design, Jewelry, Painting, Photography, Printmaking, Sculpture, Stage Design, Teacher Training
Adult Hobby Classes: Enrl 80; tuition $150 per 15 wks. Courses—varied
Summer School: Dir, Dr Nancy D Harrington. Enrl 120; tuition $137.50 per two 5 wk sessions. Courses—varied

SOUTH HADLEY

MOUNT HOLYOKE COLLEGE, Art Dept, College St, 01075. Tel 413-538-2000. *Chmn* John L Varriano, PhD; *Prof* Leonard De Longa, MFA; *Prof* Jean C Harris, PhD; *Prof* Martha Leeb Hadzi, PhD; *Assoc Prof* Marion G Miller, MFA; *Asst Prof* E James Mundy, PhD; *Asst Prof* Nancy Campbell; *Asst Prof* Paul J Staiti, PhD; *Asst Prof* Louisa McDonald Kodera, PhD; *Visiting Artists* George Creamer, MFA
Estab 1858; pvt, W; D & E; scholarships; SC 13, LC 32; enrl D 409, maj 52
Ent Req: SAT, college boards
Degrees: BA
Tuition: $8650 per yr; campus res—room & board $3050
Courses: †Art History, †Graphic Arts, †History of Art & Archaeology, Museum Staff Training, †Painting, Photography, †Printmaking, †Sculpture
Adult Hobby Classes: Continuing education program leading to BA

SPRINGFIELD

SPRINGFIELD COLLEGE, Dept of Visual and Performing Arts, 263 Alden St, 01109. Tel 413-788-3300. *Chmn Dept* William Blizard, MA; *Prof* Carl Bartels, MA; *Adjunct Prof* Emil Schnorr, MA; *Instructor* Robert Funk, MFA; *Instructor* Judy Bowerman, MFA; *Instructor* Ron Maggio, MFA; *Instructor* Marge Paar, MA; *Instructor* Gene La Ford, MFA
Estab 1885, dept estab 1971; pvt; D & E; scholarships; SC 30, LC 6; enrl D 335, E 10, non-maj 300, maj 35
Ent Req: HS dipl, SAT, portfolio
Degrees: BA, BS 4 yr
Tuition: $4500 per yr, $130 per hr; campus res—room and board $2380; $7135 total
Courses: Advertising Design, Art History, †Ceramics, Collages, Conceptual Art, Constructions, Drawing, Graphic Arts, †Illustration, Intermedia, Mixed Media, †Museum Staff Training, Occupational Therapy, †Painting, Photography, †Printmaking, Restoration & Conservation, †Sculpture, Stage Design, Theatre Arts, Video, †Art Therapy, †Computer Graphics, †Creative Arts Therapy, †Environmental Design
Adult Hobby Classes: Enrl 25; tuition $130 per credit hour for 15 weeks. Courses—Crafts
Summer School: Dir, Dr Mark Ehman. Enrl 200; tuition $131 per hr for term of 3 or 6 wks beginning May 30. Courses—Ceramics, Crafts, Painting, Printmaking

TRURO

TRURO CENTER FOR THE ARTS AT CASTLE HILL, INC,* Castle Rd, Box 756, 02666. Tel 617-349-3714. *Dir* Joyce Johnson; *Instructor* Alan Dugan; *Instructor* Xavier Gonzalez; *Instructor* Charles LeClair; *Instructor* Bruce Hoadley, PhD; *Instructor* Mikhail Zakin. Instrs: over 45 other nationally known instructors
Estab 1972; pvt summer school; D & E; scholarships; SC 50, LC 3, GC 30; enrl 340
Ent Req: None
Degrees: None, credits granted through Massachusetts College of Art
Tuition: $72 for one wk; no campus res
Courses: Ceramics, Drawing, Painting, Sculpture, Bronze Foundry, Cartooning, Fresco Painting, Weaving

WALTHAM

BRANDEIS UNIVERSITY, Dept of Fine Arts, 02254. Tel 617-647-2555. *Chmn* R Maeda. Instrs: FT 11, PT 1
Estab 1948; pvt; D; scholarships; SC 10, LC 28; enrl 2800
Ent Req: HS dipl, college board ent exam
Degrees: BS 4 yr
Tuition: $6700; campus res available
Courses: Art History, Drawing, Graphic Arts, Painting, Sculpture, Design

WELLESLEY

WELLESLEY COLLEGE, Art Dept, 02181. Tel 617-235-0320, Ext 2044. *Chmn* Anne de C Clapp; *Prof* Lilian Armstrong, PhD; *Prof* Peter J Fergusson, PhD; *Prof* James F O'Gorman, PhD; *Prof* James W Rayen, MFA; *Prof* Richard W Wallace, PhD; *Prof* Eugenia P Janis, PhD; *Assoc Prof* Miranda C Marvin, PhD; *Asst Prof* Nan B Freeman, PhD; *Asst Prof* Bunny Harvey, MFA; *Asst Prof* Wendy S MacNeil, AB; *Asst Prof* Margaret D Carroll, PhD; *Asst Prof* William A Drew, MFA; *Asst Prof* Alice T Friedman, PhD; *Asst Prof* Judith Davies, MFA; *Lecturer* Ann R Gabhart, AM
Estab 1875, dept estab 1897; pvt; D; SC 15, LC 49; enrl D 2168
Ent Req: HS dipl
Degrees: BA
Tuition: $8550 per yr; campus res—room & board $3340
Courses: †Art History, Drawing, Film, Graphic Arts, Painting, Photography, Printmaking, Sculpture, Theatre Arts, †Studio Art

WEST BARNSTABLE

CAPE COD COMMUNITY COLLEGE, Art Dept, Humanities Division, 02668. Tel 617-362-2131. *Coordr Art* Robert McDonald, MFA; *Prof* David Laakso, MFA; *Prof* Douglas Mitchell, MFA; *Prof* Joseph Fiorello, MA
Estab 1963, dept estab 1973; pub; D & E; SC 14, LC 7; enrl in school D 2000, E 3000, maj 60
Ent Req: HS dipl
Degrees: AA and AS 2 yrs
Tuition: Res—$634 per yr, nonres—$2098 per yr
Courses: Art History, Drafting, Drawing, Film, Graphic Design, Illustration, Mixed Media, Painting, Sculpture, Stage Design, Theatre Arts, Video, Visual Fundamentals
Adult Hobby Classes: Calligraphy, Interior Design, Photography, Stained Glass, Toy Making
Summer School: Dean Continuing Educ, Peter Birkel. Tuition $124 per 3 cr courses for term of 8 wks beginning June. Courses—Drawing, Graphic Design, Painting, Watercolor

WESTFIELD

WESTFIELD STATE COLLEGE, Art Dept, Western Ave, 01085. Tel 413-568-3311, Ext 256. *Chmn Dept* Arno Maris, MFA
Estab 1972; pub; D & E
Ent Req: HS dipl
Degrees: BA (Fine Arts) 4 yrs
Courses: Advertising Design, Art Education, Art History, Ceramics, Commercial Art, Drawing, Graphic Arts, Illustration, Lettering, Mixed Media, Printmaking, Sculpture, Teacher Training, Anatomy for artist practicum
Summer School: Dir, Dr Richard E Greene. Courses—Visual Communication, Watercolor Paintings

WESTON

REGIS COLLEGE, Dept of Art,* 235 Wellesley St, 02193. Tel 617-893-1820. *Prof* Sr Louisella Walters, MFA; *Assoc Prof* Marie de Sales Dinneen, PhD
Estab 1927, dept estab 1944; den; D & E; scholarships; SC 12, LC 12; enrl D 250, non-maj 200, maj 50
Ent Req: HS dipl, SAT, various tests
Degrees: AB 4 yr
Tuition: $5150 annual tuition
Courses: Art Therapy, Collograph, Enameling, Etching, Silk Screen, Stained Glass, Weaving, Woodcut

WILLIAMSTOWN

WILLIAMS COLLEGE, Dept of Art, 01267. Tel 413-597-2377. *Chmn Dept* Zirka Z Filipczak, PhD; *Dir Grad Program* Samuel Y Edgerton, PhD; *Vis Prof* Robert Sterling Clark. Instrs: FT 10, PT 13
Estab 1793, dept estab 1903; pvt; D; scholarships; SC 14, LC 40, GC 10; enrl 1975, maj 64, grad 22
Ent Req: HS dipl
Degrees: BA 4 yrs, MA(History of Art) 2 yrs
Tuition: $8550 per yr; campus res—room & board $2955 per yr
Courses: Architecture, Art History, Drawing, History of Art & Archaeology, Painting, Photography, Printmaking, Sculpture

WORCESTER

ASSUMPTION COLLEGE, Dept of Fine Arts and Music,* 500 Salisbury St, 01609. Tel 617-752-5615, Ext 259. *Chmn* Donal Lamothe, PhD; *Prof* Richard Richards, MA; *Asst Prof* Richard E Lamoureux, PhD; *Asst Prof* William Harsh, MFA
Estab 1904, dept estab 1976; den; D & E; scholarships; enrl D 600, E 25, grad 25
Ent Req: HS dipl
Degrees: BA 4 yr, MAT, MA, Cert Advanced Grad Study
Tuition: $4830 per yr; campus res available
Courses: Aesthetics, Architecture, Art Education, Art History, Drawing, Graphic Arts, History of Art & Archaeology, Painting, Printmaking, Theatre Arts
Summer School: Dir, Dr Marjorie Nickel. Tui $86 per cr hr

CLARK UNIVERSITY, Dept of Visual & Performing Arts, 55 Salisbury St, 01608. Tel 617-793-7113. *Chmn Dept* Albert A Anderson, PhD; *Dir Studio Art Program* Donald W Krueger, MFA; *Dean of Admis* Richard Pierson. Instrs: FT 4, PT 10
University estab 1887; pvt; D & E; scholarships; SC 50, LC 24; enrl Maj 100, non-maj 450, other 20
Ent Req: HS dipl, portfolio, CEEB, achievement tests, SAT & ACH
Tuition: BFA & BA $7906 per yr, diploma $4000 per yr; campus res room & board $2610 per yr
Courses: Aesthetics, Ceramics, Drawing, †Graphic Design, †Illustration, †Painting, †Photography, Printmaking, Arts Management, Art Therapy, Environmental Art, †History of Art & Architecture, Visual Design, Visual Studies
Adult Hobby Classes: Offered through Clark University College of Professional and Continuing Education
Summer School: Offered through Clark University College of Professional and Continuing Education

COLLEGE OF THE HOLY CROSS, Dept Visual Arts,* 01610. Tel 617-793-2237. *Chmn & Assoc Prof* John P Reboli, MA; *Assoc Prof* J N Italiano, MFA; *Assoc Prof* J C Raguin, PhD; *Assoc Prof* J P Reardon, MFA; *Asst Prof* T Priest, MFA; *Asst Prof* J S Scannell, MA
Estab 1843, dept estab 1954; pvt; D; SC 12, LC 15; enrl D 485, maj 40
Ent Req: HS dipl, SAT, ATS
Degrees: BA 4 yr
Tuition: Res—undergrad $8050 per yr; non-res—undergrad $5400; campus residence available
Courses: Aesthetics, Architecture, †Art History, Ceramics, Drawing, Graphic Arts, Graphic Design, History of Art & Archaeology, Painting, Printmaking, Sculpture

WORCESTER CRAFT CENTER, 25 Sagamore Rd, 01605. Tel 617-753-8183. *Exec Dir* Cyrus D Lipsitt, BFA
Estab 1856; pvt; D & E; scholarships; SC 33, LC varies; enrl D & E 280, non-maj 30, maj 12
Ent Req: Portfolio review for professional prog, no req for adult educ
Tuition: $1400 per sem; adult educ $75 per sem; no campus res
Courses: Calligraphy, †Ceramics, †Goldsmithing, †Jewelry, Photography, Restoration & Conservation, †Silversmithing, †Fibre, †Wood Working
Adult Hobby Classes: Enrl 1300; four 10 wk sessions. Courses—Ceramics, Enamel, Furniture Refinishing, Photography, Quilting, Stained Glass, Weaving & Fibre, Wood Working, Metal Working
Children's Classes: Enrl 120 - 200; tuition $50 per 10 wks. Courses—Clay, Wood, Photography, Fibre, Metal, Printmaking
Summer School: Exec Dir, Cyrus D Lipsitt. Enrl 100

WORCESTER STATE COLLEGE, Arts & Humanities, 486 Chandler, 01602. Tel 617-793-8000. *Chmn* Dion Schaff
Estab 1874; pub; D & E; SC 18, LC 9; enrl D & E 725
Ent Req: HS dipl, col board exams, completion of systems application form
Degrees: BA and BS 4 yrs
Courses: Art Education, Art History, Collages, Drafting, Drawing, Graphic Design, Handicrafts, Intermedia, Mixed Media, Painting, Printmaking, Sculpture, Environmental Design, History of Urban Form
Summer School: Usually 5-8 courses and workshops

MICHIGAN

ADRIAN

ADRIAN COLLEGE, Art Dept, 110 S Madison, 49221. Tel 517-265-5161, Ext 246. *Chmn Art Dept* Norman Knutson, MFA; *Prof* Michael Cassino, MFA; *Instructor* Pauleve Benio, MFA
Estab 1859, dept estab 1962; den; D & E; scholarships; enrl in dept D 250, E 50, non-maj 200, maj 30
Ent Req: HS dipl
Degrees: BA, BA with teaching cert and BFA 4 yr
Tuition: $2688 per sem, $120 per sem hr; $806 per yr for room, $1216 per yr for board
Courses: Art Education, Art History, †Ceramics, Drawing, †Painting, Photography, †Printmaking, Silversmithing, Fibers, Two & Three-Dimensional Design, Weaving

SIENA HEIGHTS COLLEGE, Studio Angelico Art Dept, 1247 Siena Heights Dr, 49221. Tel 517-263-0731, Ext 272. *Chairperson Dept* Jeannine Klemm, EdD; *Prof* David Van Horn, MFA; *Assoc Prof* Hennie Reimer, MFA; *Assoc Prof* Joseph Bergman, MFA; *Assoc Prof* Sr Jean Agnes Klemm, PhD; *Asst Prof* Tom Venner, MFA; *Asst Prof* John Wittershiem; *Instructor* Lois DeMots, MFA
Estab 1919; pvt; D & E; scholarships; SC 56; enrl D 200, maj 96, grad 25
Ent Req: HS dipl
Degrees: AFA 2 yrs, BFA and BA 4 yrs
Tuition: Undergrad $124 per cr hr, grad $129 per cr hr; campus res—room & board $2200 per yr

Courses: Advertising Design, Aesthetics, Art Education, Art History, Calligraphy, Ceramics, Costume Design & Construction, Drawing, Fashion Arts, Goldsmithing, Graphic Arts, Jewelry, Painting, Photography, Printmaking, Sculpture, Silversmithing, Stage Design, Teacher Training, Textile Design, Theatre Arts, Fibers
Summer School: Dir, Jeannine Klemm. Enrl 60; tuition $124 per cr hr, June 30-July 30. Courses—Ceramics, Photography, Calligraphy & 2-D Design

ALBION

ALBION COLLEGE, Dept of Visual Arts, 49224. Tel 517-629-5511, Ext 246. *Chmn Dept Visual Arts* Frank Machek, MFA; *Prof* Richard Leach, MFA; *Assoc Prof* Richard Brunkus, MFA; *Asst Prof* Craig Hoernschemeyer, MFA; *Asst Prof* Peter Kaniaris, MFA
Estab 1835; den; D & E; SC 32, LC 8
Ent Req: HS dipl
Degrees: BA and BFA 4 yrs
Tuition: $2718 per sem; campus res—room & board $1315 per sem
Courses: Art History, Ceramics, Drawing, Film, Painting, Photography, Printmaking, Sculpture, Stage Design, Teacher Training, Theatre Arts
Summer School: Acad Dean, Dr Russel Acito. Tui $105.50 per sem hr for term of 7 wks beginning May 15

ALLENDALE

GRAND VALLEY STATE COLLEGES, Art Dept, College Landing, 49401. Tel 616-895-6611, Ext 486. *Chmn Dept* Donald Kerr, MFA; *Prof* Chester Alkema, MFA; *Assoc Prof* Beverly Seley, MFA; *Assoc Prof* Gray Sweeney, PhD; *Assoc Prof* Takeshi Takahara, MFA
Estab 1960; pub; D & E; SC 15, LC 12, GC 1; enrl D 80, E 40
Ent Req: HS dipl or equivalent, ent exam
Degrees: BA(Art History), BS(Studio) and BFA 4 yrs
Tuition: Res—undergrad $4220 per yr, $45 per hr; nonres—undergrad $2730 per yr, $91 per hr; campus res—room & board $2600 per yr
Courses: Art Education, Art History, Ceramics, Drawing, Goldsmithing, Jewelry, Painting, Printmaking, Silversmithing, Teacher Training
Summer School: Courses—Introduction to Art, Introduction to Studio, Workshops; Drawing and Painting at Slade School, London, England

ALMA

ALMA COLLEGE, Dept of Art and Design, 614 W Superior, 48801. Tel 517-463-7220, 463-7111. *Chmn* Kent Kirby, MFA; *Asst Prof* Carie Parks-Kirby, MFA; *Asst Prof* Robert Rozier, MFA
Estab 1886; pvt; D & E; scholarships; SC 10, LC 3; enrl D 200, maj 15
Degrees: BA, BFA
Tuition: Res—$5980; campus res—room and board $2516
Courses: Ceramics, Drawing, Graphic Design, History of Art & Archaeology, Museum Staff Training, Painting, Photography, Printmaking, Sculpture, Weaving, Computer Graphics, Foreign Study

ANN ARBOR

UNIVERSITY OF MICHIGAN, ANN ARBOR
—**School of Art,** 2000 Bonisteel Blvd, 48109. Tel 313-764-0397. *Dean School* George V Bayliss, MFA
Estab 1817, school estab 1974; pub; D & E; scholarships; SC 50, LC 6, GC 12; enrl D 430, E 25, non-maj 300, maj 555, grad 35, special students 6
Ent Req: HS dipl, portfolio exam
Degrees: BFA 4 yrs, MA 1 yr, MFA 2 yrs, MS(Med Illustration) 2 1/2 yrs
Tuition: Res—undergrad $1084 per sem, grad $1598 per sem; nonres—undergrad $3148 per sem, grad $3428 per sem; campus res available
Courses: Art Education, Ceramics, Drawing, Graphic Design, Illustration, Industrial Design, Interior Design, Jewelry, Lettering, Mixed Media, Painting, Photography, Printmaking, Sculpture, Silversmithing, Textile Design
Summer School: Dean, George V Bayliss. Enrl varies; tuition res $542, nonres $1574 for term of spring or summer, spring May 1 to June 30, summer July 1 to Aug 30. Courses—vary from year to year
—**Dept of History of Art,** 48109. Tel 313-764-5400. *Chmn* Joel Isaacson. Instrs: FT 15
Dept estab 1910; pub; scholarships and fels; enrl maj 75, grad 60
Degrees: BA, MA, PhD
Courses: †Art History, Museology
Summer School: Chairman, Joel Isaacson. Enrl 77; tuition $182 per cr res, $368 per cr nonres

BATTLE CREEK

KELLOGG COMMUNITY COLLEGE, Arts Dept, 49016. Instrs: FT 3, PT 9
Estab 1962; pub; D & E; scholarships; enrl D 2200, E 2000, maj 50
Ent Req: None
Degrees: AA 2-4 yr
Courses: Advertising Design, †Architecture, †Art Education, †Art History, †Ceramics, †Commercial Art, Costume Design & Construction, †Drafting, †Drawing, †Graphic Arts, †Graphic Design, †Illustration, Industrial Design, Jewelry, Lettering, †Painting, †Photography, Sculpture, Stage Design, †Teacher Training, Textile Design
Adult Hobby Classes: Courses—all areas
Summer School: Courses—Basic Art & Appreciation

BENTON HARBOR

LAKE MICHIGAN COLLEGE, Dept of Art, 2755 E Napier Ave, 49022. Tel 616-927-3571. *Assoc Prof* Ken Schaber, MFA
Estab 1943; pub; D & E; scholarships; SC 10, LC 5; enrl 3377 total
Ent Req: Open door policy
Degrees: AA 2 yrs
Tuition: Res—$23 per sem hr; nonres—out of district $31 per sem hr, out of state $39 per sem hr; no campus res
Courses: Art Appreciation, Art Education, Art History, Ceramics, Drawing, Jewelry, Painting, Printmaking, Sculpture, Textile Design, 2-D & 3-D Design

BERRIEN SPRINGS

ANDREWS UNIVERSITY, Art Dept,* 49104. Tel 616-471-7771. *Prof* Greg Constantine; *Faculty* P D Erhard; *Faculty* W E Hazen; *Faculty* D L May. Instrs: FT 4
Estab 1952; den; D & E; SC 18, LC 5; enrl 130, maj 35
Ent Req: HS grad
Degrees: BS(Art Educ), BA 4 yrs, MAT
Tuition: Tuition, room & board $2540 per quarter
Courses: Advertising Design, †Art Education, †Ceramics, Drawing, †Painting, †Photography, Printmaking, Sculpture, †Design, European Study
Summer School: Classes June 14-Aug 6

BIG RAPIDS

FERRIS STATE COLLEGE, Commercial Art Dept, 901 S State St, 49307. Tel 616-796-0461. Instrs: 10
Scholarships offered
Degrees: AAS and BS offered
Tuition: $557 per qtr
Courses: Advertising Design, Art Education, Art History, Calligraphy, Ceramics, Design, Drawing, Film, Painting
Adult Hobby Classes: Enrl 400; tuition $46.50 per cr hr
Summer School: Dir, Karl Walker. Enrl 3195, tuition $557 per qtr

BIRMINGHAM

BIRMINGHAM-BLOOMFIELD ART ASSOCIATION, 1516 S Cranbrook Rd, 48099. Tel 313-644-0866. *Executive Dir* Kenneth R Gross, MFA
Estab 1956; pub; D & E; SC 90-100, LC 4; enrl 3000 total
Tuition: No campus residence
Courses: Aesthetics, Art History, Calligraphy, Ceramics, Collages, Commercial Art, Drawing, Goldsmithing, Graphic Arts, Graphic Design, Handicrafts, Illustration, Intermedia, Jewelry, Mixed Media, Painting, Sculpture, Silversmithing, Textile Design, Design, Glass, Surface Design
Adult Hobby Classes: Exec Dir, Kenneth R Gross, MFA. Courses—Same as above
Children's Classes: Courses—Crafts, Drawing, Painting, Pottery, Sketching
Summer School: Same program on abbreviated basis

BLOOMFIELD HILLS

CRANBROOK ACADEMY OF ART, 500 Lone Pine Rd, PO Box 801, 48013. Tel 313-645-3300. *Pres* Roy Slade; *Dean* Beatrice Rivas Sanchez; *Assoc Head Design Dept* Michael McCoy; *Assoc Head Design Dept* Katherine McCoy; *Head Fiber Dept* Gerhardt Knodel; *Head Metalsmithing Dept* Richard C Thomas; *Head Painting Dept* George Ortman; *Head Photography Dept* Carl Toth; *Head Ceramics Dept* Jun Kaneko; *Head Architecture Dept* Daniel Libeskind; *Head Sculpture Dept* Michael D Hall; *Head Printmaking Dept* Steve Murakishi
Estab 1932; pvt; scholarships; enrl 150
Ent Req: Portfolio
Degrees: MFA & MArchit 2 yrs
Tuition: $5500 per yr; campus res—room & board $2600
Courses: Architecture, Ceramics, Painting, Photography, Printmaking, Sculpture, Design, Fiber, Metalsmithing

DEARBORN

HENRY FORD COMMUNITY COLLEGE, Art Dept, 5101 Evergreen Rd, 48128. Tel 313-271-2750, Ext 489. *Chmn Dept* Robert A Cadez. Instrs: FT 5, PT 25
Estab 1938; pub; D & E; scholarships; SC 25, LC 9; enrl D 3500, E 7500, maj 600
Ent Req: HS dipl
Degrees: AA 2 yrs
Tuition: Res—$28 per cr hr; nonres—$40 per cr hr, plus lab fees; drive in campus
Courses: Advertising Design, Art Appreciation, Art History, Ceramics, Commercial Art, Drawing, Graphic Arts, History of Art & Archaeology, †Interior Design, Jewelry, Painting, Photography, Sculpture, Textile Design, 2-D Design, 3-D Design, Weaving
Summer School: Dir, Robert A Cadez. Tuition $28 per cr hr, nonres $40. Courses—Art Appreciation, Art History, Ceramics, Directed Study, Drawing, Black & White Photography, 2-D Design

DETROIT

CENTER FOR CREATIVE STUDIES—COLLEGE OF ART AND DESIGN, 245 E Kirby, 48202. Tel 313-872-3118. *Pres* Jerome L Grove; *Chmn Graphic Communication* Powell Tripp; *Actg Chmn Industrial Design* William House; *Chmn Photography* Robert Vigiletti; *Chmn Fine Arts* Aris Koutroulis; *Chmn Crafts* Susan Aaron Taylor; *Chmn General Studies* Harry Smallenberg
Estab 1926; pvt; D & E; scholarships; enrl D 900, E 223, others 60
Ent Req: HS dipl & portfolio

Degrees: BFA 4 yrs
Tuition: $3900 yr, $1950 per sem
Courses: †Advertising Design, †Ceramics, †Illustration, †Industrial Design, †Jewelry, Lettering, †Painting, †Photography, †Printmaking, †Sculpture, †Printmaking, Sculpture, Textile Design, Art Direction, Environmental/Interior Design, Fiber Design, †Glass, Product Design, Transportation Design, Wood, Computer Graphics, Art Therapy
Adult Hobby Classes: Tuition $165 per cr hr. Courses—Most of the above
Children's Classes: Youth, high school and pre-college programs
Summer School: Dean, Arthur Greenblatt. Enrl 250; tuition $165 per cr hr for term of 8 wks beginning June 16. Courses—Advertising Design, Crafts, Fine Arts, Industrial Design, Photography

MARYGROVE COLLEGE, Dept of Art and Art History, 8425 W McNichols Rd, 48221. Tel 313-862-8000. *Chmn Dept* Sr Edith Kenny; *Assoc Prof* Rose E Desloover, MFA; *Assoc Prof* Sr John Louise Leahy, DEd; *Assoc Prof* Helen Sherman, PhD; *Assoc Prof* David Vandegrift, MFA; *Instr* James Lutomski, MFA; *Instr* Jerry Sadowski, MFA
Estab 1910; pvt; D & E; SC 37, LC 20, GC 5; enrl D 150, E 25, non-maj 60, maj 50, grad 5
Ent Req: Interview with portfolio
Degrees: BA & BFA 4 yrs
Tuition: Undergrad $124 per cr hr; grad $105 per cr hr; campus residence available
Courses: Advertising Design, Aesthetics, Art Education, Art History, †Ceramics, Collages, Commercial Art, Conceptual Art, Constructions, †Drawing, †Graphic Arts, Graphic Design, †History of Art & Archaeology, Lettering, Mixed Media, †Painting, Photography, †Printmaking, †Teacher Training
Adult Hobby Classes: Enrl 65; tuition $35-$90 per course. Courses—Drawing, Painting, Photography
Children's Classes: Enrl 100; tuition $20-$50 per course. Courses—Ceramics, Painting, Photography
Summer School: Dean Continuing Educ, Sr Andrea Lee, PhD. Enrl 40, tuition $86 per cr hr for term of two 6 wk terms. Courses—Basic courses, graduate and undergraduate

MERCY COLLEGE OF DETROIT, Art Dept,* 8200 W Outer Dr, 48219. Tel 313-592-6000. *Chmn* Lloyd Radell; *Acad Ctr Dir* Daniel Hoeber
Scholarships offered
Tuition: $1570 per sem
Courses: Art Education, Design, Drawing, Fashion Arts, Jewelry, Painting, Sculpture, Textile Design, Weaving

UNIVERSITY OF DETROIT, School of Architecture, 4001 W McNichols, 48221. Tel 313-927-1149. *Dean* Bruno Leon, B Arch
Univ estab 1877, school estab 1964; pvt; D & E; scholarships; SC 14, LC 36; enrl D 220, maj 220
Ent Req: HS dipl, B average
Degrees: B Arch 5 yrs
Tuition: $2715 per sem, $181 per credit hour; campus res—room $496-$880, board $688 per term
Courses: Aesthetics, †Architecture, Art History, Drawing, Landscape Architecture

WAYNE STATE UNIVERSITY, Dept of Art and Art History, College of Liberal Arts, 450 Reuther Mall, 48202. Tel 313-577-2980. *Chmn* Richard J Bilaitis, MFA. Instrs: FT 25, PT 20
Tuition: Res—undergrad $712 for 12 cr hrs, grad $696 for 8 cr hrs; nonres—undergrad $1552, grad $1464 for 8 cr hrs
Courses: Advertising Design, Art History, Ceramics, Design, Drawing, Jewelry, Industrial Design, Painting, Photography, Printmaking, Sculpture, Weaving, Fibers, Lithography, Metal Arts, Papermaking, Serigraphy, 3-D Design

DOWAGIAC

SOUTHWESTERN MICHIGAN COLLEGE, Communications-Humanities Dept, Cherry Grove Rd, 49047. Tel 616-782-5113. *Chmn* Will Tomory, PhD; *Instr* David R Baker, MFA; *Instr* Jeff Burden, MFA; *Instr* Mary Biek, MA
Estab 1964; pub; D & E; scholarships; SC 13, LC 3; enrl D 200, E 100, non-maj 200, maj 100
Ent Req: HS dipl
Degrees: AA & AS
Tuition: Res—undergrad $26 per hour; nonres—undergrad $31 per hour; out of state $35 per hour
Courses: Advertising Design, Architecture, Ceramics, †Commercial Art, Drafting, Drawing, Fashion Arts, Graphic Arts, Lettering, Painting, Photography, Printmaking
Adult Hobby Classes: Art Appreciation, Ceramics, Painting, Photography
Summer School: Dir, William Spencer. Enrl 1000; 6-8 week terms. Courses—Ceramics, Design, Painting, Printmaking

EAST LANSING

MICHIGAN STATE UNIVERSITY, Dept of Art,* College of Arts & Letters, 113 Kresge Art Center, 48824. Tel 517-355-7610. *Chmn Dept* Paul W Deussen. Instrs: FT 26, PT 1
Estab 1855; pub; D & E; scholarships; SC 76, LC 49, GC 88; enrl D 2000, non-maj 1000, maj 550, grad 70
Ent Req: HS dipl
Degrees: BA & BFA 4 yrs, MA 1 yr, MFA 2 yrs
Tuition: Res—undergrad $35.50 per cr hr, grad $41.50 per cr hr; nonres—undergrad $82.50 per cr hr, grad $85 per cr hr; campus res—room & board $711.25 - $841.25
Courses: †Art Education, †Art History, †Ceramics, †Commercial Art, †Drawing, †Film, †Graphic Design, †Industrial Design, Jewelry, †Painting, †Photography, †Printmaking, †Sculpture, †Silversmithing, †Teacher Training, Metalsmithing
Adult Hobby Classes: Tui $30-$40 per class, these meet once per wk. Courses—Ceramics, Drawing, Painting, Photography, Sculpture
Children's Classes: Saturday Art Program $10 per quarter. Courses—Fabrics & Fibers, Drawing, Painting, Photography, Printmaking, Two & Three Dimensional Media
Summer School: See Leland, Michigan

ESCANABA

BAY DE NOC COMMUNITY COLLEGE, Art Dept,* Danforth Rd, 49829. Tel 906-786-5802
Scholarships offered
Tuition: County res—$25 per sem cr hr; non-county res—$34 per sem cr hr; non-state res—$49 per sem cr hr
Courses: Art History, Design, Drawing, Painting, Printmaking, Sculpture

FARMINGTON HILLS

OAKLAND COMMUNITY COLLEGE, Humanities Dept,* Orchard Ridge Campus, 27055 Orchard Lake Rd, 48018. Tel 313-471-7500
Degrees: AA and ASA offered
Tuition: District res—$21.50 per cr hr; non-district—$33.50 per cr hr; non-state—$45.50 per cr hr
Courses: Advertising Design, Art Appreciation, Art History, Calligraphy, Ceramics, Design, Drawing, Fashion Arts, Film, Handicrafts, Jewelry, Photography, Printmaking, Sculpture, Weaving

FLINT

CHARLES STEWART MOTT COMMUNITY COLLEGE, Fine Arts Division, 1401 E Court St, 48503. Tel 313-762-0443. *Chmn Dept* Samuel E Morello, MFA; *Instructor* Dorothy Bates, MA; *Instructor* Thomas Bohnert, MFA; *Instructor* Robert Caskey, MFA; *Instructor* Thomas Nuzum, MFA; *Instructor* William O'Malley, MAEd; *Instructor* Douglas Warner, MSDes; *Instructor* Barbara White, MFA
Estab 1923; pub; D & E; scholarships; enrl D & E 250, maj 250
Ent Req: HS dipl or 19 yrs old
Degrees: AA 2 yrs
Tuition: Dist res—$29 per cr hr; state res—$39 per cr hr; nonres—$51 per cr hr; no campus res
Courses: Art Education, Art History, Ceramics, Drafting, Drawing, Film, Jewelry, Painting, Photography, Printmaking, Sculpture, Stage Design, Teacher Training, Theatre Arts, Video
Adult Hobby Classes: Classes offered through cont education division
Summer School: Chmn, Samuel E Morello. Tuition same as above; 8 wk sessions, first May 15-July 1, second July 1-Aug 15. Courses—vary

GRAND RAPIDS

AQUINAS COLLEGE, Art Dept, 1607 Robinson Rd SE, 49506. Tel 614-459-8281. *Chmn Dept* Ronald Pederson, MFA; *Assoc Prof* Larry Blovits, MFA; *Assoc Prof* James Karsina, MFA; *Vis Assoc Prof* Sr Marie Celeste Miller, MA, PhD; *Lectr* Ferdinand Martinez, MFA; *Vis Lectr* Stephen Schousen, MFA
Estab 1940; dept estab 1965; pvt; D & E; scholarships; SC 28, LC 9; enrl D 250, non-maj 210, maj 40
Ent Req: HS dipl
Degrees: BA and BFA 4 yrs
Tuition: $4790 per yr; campus res—room & board $2436 per yr
Courses: Art Education, Art History, †Drawing, †Painting, †Printmaking, †Sculpture, Teacher Training, Photography, Basic Design
Adult Hobby Classes: Courses—Drawing, Painting

CALVIN COLLEGE, Art Dept, 49506. Tel 616-949-4000, Ext 326. *Assoc Prof* Chris Stoffel Overvoorde, MFA; *Assoc Prof* Edgar G Boeve, MSD; *Assoc Prof* Carl J Huisman, MFA; *Dir & Assoc Prof* Robert A Jensen, MFA; *Asst Prof* Helen Bonzelaar, MA; *Asst Prof* Charles Young, PhD; *Instructor* Macyn Bolt, MFA
Estab 1876; dept estab 1965; den; D & E; scholarships; SC 16, LC 4, GC 5; enrl maj 130, grad 4, others 4
Ent Req: HS dipl, SAT or ACT
Degrees: BA(Art, Art Educ, Art History) & BFA(Art), MAT
Tuition: $2140 per sem, $575 per class; campus res—room & board $1980 per yr
Courses: Aesthetics, Architecture, †Art Education, †Art History, Ceramics, Collages, Conceptual Art, Drawing, Film, Graphic Arts, Jewelry, Painting, Photography, Printmaking, Sculpture, †Teacher Training, Art Therapy
Summer School: Chmn Art Dept, Robert Jensen. Enrl varies; tuition $400 for term of 3 1/2 wks beginning May. Courses vary

GRAND RAPIDS JUNIOR COLLEGE, Art Dept,* 143 Bostwock NE, 49502. Tel 616-456-4572. *Prof* Glenn T Raymond. Instrs: FT 6, PT 4
Estab c 1920; pub; D & E; scholarships; SC 17, LC 2; enrl D 250, E 75, maj 60
Ent Req: HS dipl or ent exam
Degrees: AA 2 yrs
Tuition: $700 per yr; no campus res
Courses: Art Education, Ceramics, Drafting, Drawing, Graphic Arts, Graphic Design, History of Art & Archaeology, Jewelry, Painting, Printmaking, Sculpture, Teacher Training, Fiber & Fabric Art, Watercolor
Summer School: Term of 8 wks beginning June. Courses—Art History & Appreciation, Drawing, Teacher Training

KENDALL SCHOOL OF DESIGN,* 1110 College NE, 49503. Tel 616-451-2787. *Pres* Phyllis I Danielson, EdD; *Academic Dean* Constance Phillips, BFA; *Chmn-Foundation* Thomas Gondek, MFA; *Asst Prof Interior Design* Erli Gronberg, BA; *Instr Visual Communications* Donald Williamson, BFA. Instrs: FT 21, PT 28
Estab 1928; pvt; D; scholarships; SC 64, LC 9; enrl 510
Ent Req: HS dipl, ACT, SAT, portfolio
Degrees: 3 yr cert, AFA, BFA 4 yrs
Tuition: $110 per cr hr
Courses: †Advertising Design, †Graphic Design, †Illustration, †Industrial Design, †Environmental Design, †Furniture Design, †Fine Arts, †Television Communications
Adult Hobby Classes: Courses—Drawing, Painting, Calligraphy, Photography (Airbrush), Trapunto, Interiors, Advertising, Furniture Detailing
Children's Classes: Courses—Drawing, Painting, Commercial Art, Calligraphy
Summer School: Full semester, May - July; same program as regular session

HANCOCK

SUOMI COLLEGE, Fine Arts Dept, Quincy St, 49930. Tel 906-482-5300. *Chairperson Dept* Jon Brookhouse, MA; *Instr* Elizabeth Leifer, MA; *Instr* Rob Roy, BA
Estab 1896, dept estab 1974; pvt; D & E; SC 5; enrl D 24, E 30, non-maj 18, maj 12
Ent Req: HS dipl, open door policy
Degrees: AA 2 yrs
Tuition: $4900 per yr, $2450 per sem; campus residence available
Courses: Ceramics, Drawing, Graphic Arts, Painting, Photography, Printmaking, Weaving

HILLSDALE

HILLSDALE COLLEGE, Art Dept, 49242. Tel 517-437-7341, Ext 309. *Acting Dir* Samuel Knecht, MFA; *Assoc Prof* Bertram Fink, MFA
Estab 1844; pvt; SC 12, LC 5; enrl D 1000, non-maj 150, maj 10
Ent Req: HS dipl, SAT
Degrees: BA, BS & BLS 4 yrs
Tuition: $3690 per yr, $1845 per sem; campus residence available
Courses: Art Education, Art History, Ceramics, Drawing, Painting, Printmaking, Sculpture, Teacher Training
Summer School: Dir, Dr Jerome Fallon. Courses vary

HOLLAND

CRAFTS GUILD ART SCHOOL FOR THE DEAF, 0-380 S 168th Ave, 49423. Tel 616-399-4885. *Dir* Alleene Lowery Fisher
Estab Detroit 1927, Holland 1948 as a year round resident art center for the deaf; pvt; enrl limited to 100
Tuition: $975 per qtr; housing $650 per qtr
Courses: Design, Clay, Color, Oil Painting Fundamentals, Still Life, Portraiture, Landscape

HOPE COLLEGE, Art Dept,* 49423. Tel 616-392-5111. *Asst Prof* Bruce McCombs, MFA; *Chmn* Delbert Michel, MFA; *Prof* Robert Vickers, MA; *Instr* William Mayer, BFA; *Instr* John M Wilson, PhD
Estab 1866, dept estab 1962; den; D & E; scholarships; SC 18, LC 12; enrl D 185, E 61, non-maj 228, maj 18
Ent Req: HS dipl, CEEB-SAT or ACT
Degrees: BA and BM 4 yrs
Tuition: $2690 per sem
Courses: Architecture, Art Education, Art History, Drawing, History of Art & Archaeology, Painting, Photography, Printmaking, Sculpture, Teacher Training, Silkscreen, Two-Dimensional & Three-Dimensional Design
Summer School: Dir, Dr Donald Williams. Tuition $55 per cr hr. Courses—Vary from year to year

INTERLOCHEN

INTERLOCHEN ARTS ACADEMY, Dept of Visual Art,* 49643. Tel 616-276-9221, Ext 272. *Chairperson Dept* Lary Lien, MFA; *Instructor* James Alley, MFA; *Instructor* Wayne Brill, BS; *Instructor* John Church, MFA; *Instructor* Lina Dean, BFA; *Instructor* Jean Parsons, MFA
Pvt; D; scholarships; enrl 70, non-maj 40, maj 30
Ent Req: Portfolio, HS dipl
Tuition: $6850 per yr, includes room and board
Courses: Ceramics, Drawing, Painting, Photography, Printmaking, Sculpture, Metalsmithing, Weaving
Summer School: National Music Camp

IRONWOOD

GOGEBIC COMMUNITY COLLEGE, Art Dept, Jackson Rd & Greenbush St, 49938. Tel 906-932-4231. *Asst Prof* James A Wing, MA
Estab 1932; pub; D & E; scholarships; SC 14, LC 3; enrl D 37, E 32, non-maj 65, maj 4
Ent Req: HS dipl or equivalent
Degrees: AA 2 yrs
Adult Hobby Classes: Courses—Painting, Rock Polishing
Summer School: Dean Instruction, Gene Danlin. Courses—Ceramics, Ceramic Sculpture, Drawing, Painting

KALAMAZOO

KALAMAZOO COLLEGE, Art Dept, 1200 Academy St, 49007. Tel 616-383-8400. *Chmn Dept* Bernard S Palchick, MFA; *Instr* Marcia J Wood, MFA; *Instr* Billie Fischer, PhD
Estab 1833, dept estab approx 1940; pvt; D; scholarships; SC 14, LC 10; enrl (school) 1200, non-maj 250 (dept), maj 20, others 5
Ent Req: HS dipl, SAT, ACT, class rank
Degrees: BA 4 yrs
Tuition: $4800 per yr; campus res available
Courses: Art Education, †Art History, †Ceramics, Drawing, †Painting, Printmaking, †Sculpture

KALAMAZOO INSTITUTE OF ARTS, Artcenter School, 314 S Park St, 49007. Tel 616-349-7775. *Asst Dir Art Center School* Thomas Kendall, MA; *Head Sculpture Dept* William Tye, MFA; *Head Photography Dept* Gary Cialdella, MA; *Head Printmaking Dept* Denise Lisiecki Freed, MA
Estab 1924; pvt; D & E; SC 29; enrl D 530, E 490
Tuition: $75-$80 depending upon membership; no campus res
Courses: Ceramics, Drawing, Jewelry, Painting, Photography, Sculpture, Weaving

Adult Hobby Classes: Enrl 275; tuition $75 per 15 wks. Courses—Painting, Sculpture, Drawing, Printmaking, Ceramics, Studio classes in media photography
Children's Classes: Enrl 120; tuition $45 per 15 wks. Courses—Ceramics, Painting, Jewelry, Photography
Summer School: Dir, Tom Kayser. Enrl 130; tuition $60 per 12 sessions per 6 wks. Courses—same as adult

KALAMAZOO VALLEY COMMUNITY COLLEGE, Dept of Art,* 6767 West O Ave, 49009. Tel 616-372-5000. *Instr* Arleigh Smyrnios, MA
Estab 1968; pub; E; SC 12; enrl D & E 500
Degrees: AA and AS
Tuition: In-county—$20 per cr hr; out-of-county—$40 per cr hr; nonres—$60 per cr hr
Courses: Ceramics, Drafting, Drawing, Graphic Design, Jewelry, Painting, Photography, Sculpture, Textile Design, 2-D Design
Summer School: Alternate regular art offerings

WESTERN MICHIGAN UNIVERSITY, Dept of Art, 49008. Tel 616-383-0407. *Chairperson Dept* John Link, MFA. Instrs: FT 20
Estab 1904, dept estab 1939; pub; D & E; scholarships; SC 60, LC 9, GC 8; enrl non-maj 200, maj 350, grad 20
Ent Req: HS dipl, ACT
Degrees: BA and BFA 4 yrs, MA 1 yr, MFA 2 yrs
Tuition: Res—undergrad $50 per cr hr, grad $55 per cr hr; nonres—undergrad $140 per cr hr, grad $150 per cr hr; campus res—room & board $1900 per yr
Courses: Art Education, Art History, Ceramics, Drawing, Graphic Design, Jewelry, Mixed Media, Painting, Sculpture, Textile Design, Metalsmithing, Printmaking
Adult Hobby Classes: Chairperson Dept, John Link
Summer School: Chairperson Dept, John Link. Enrl 250; tuition same per hr as acad yr for one 8 wk term beginning May. Courses—same as above

LANSING

LANSING COMMUNITY COLLEGE, Performing and Creative Arts Dept, 419 N Capital Ave, PO Box 40010, 48901. Tel 517-483-1476. *Prog Dir Art* Nancy Lombardi. Instrs: FT & PT 60
Estab 1957, dept estab 1967; pub; D & E; scholarships; SC 80, LC 10; enrl D 758, E 506, non-maj 460, maj 504, others 300
Ent Req: HS dipl
Degrees: AA 2 yrs
Tuition: Res—$16 per cr hr; nonres—$23 per cr hr; out-of-state—$33.50 per cr hr; no campus res
Courses: †Ceramics, †Commercial Art, †Drawing, †Illustration, †Interior Design, †Jewelry, †Painting, †Printmaking, †Scenic Design
Summer School: Prog Dir Art, Nancy Lombardi

LELAND

MICHIGAN STATE UNIVERSITY, Leland Summer Art School, 49654. Tel 616-355-7612. *Instructor* Clif McChesney; *Instructor* Jim Lawton; *Instructor* Peter Glendinning
Estab 1939; (Sponsored by Michigan State University Art Dept)
Tuition: $50 per cr hr
Courses: Drawing, Painting, Photography, Sculpture

LIVONIA

MADONNA COLLEGE, Art Dept, 36600 Schoolcraft Rd, 48150. Tel 313-591-51187. *Chairperson Art Dept* Sr M Angeline, PhD; *Instructor* Anthony Balogh, MA; *Instructor* Gerry Panyard; *Instructor* Loretta Hubley, MA; *Instructor* Nelson Smith; *Instructor* Marjorie Chellstrop; *Instructor* Ralph Glenn
Estab 1947; pvt; D & E; SC 17, LC 3; enrl D 43, E 22, maj 17
Ent Req: HS dipl, portfolio
Degrees: AA 2 yrs, AB 4 yrs
Tuition: $58 per cr hr; campus residence available
Courses: Advertising Design, Art History, Calligraphy, Ceramics, Commercial Art, Drawing, Jewelry, Lettering, Mixed Media, Painting, Photography, Printmaking, Sculpture, Teacher Training
Adult Hobby Classes: Enrl 35; tuition $50 per 10 wk course. Courses—Painting
Summer School: Dir, Sr Mary Angeline

SCHOOLCRAFT COLLEGE, Dept of Art, 18600 Haggerty Rd, 48152. Tel 313-591-6400. *Chairperson Dept Art* Lincoln Lao, MFA; *Instr* James R Black, MFA; *Instr* Cecilia Kelley, MA; *Instr* Robert DuFort, MFA
Estab 1964; pub; D & E; SC 13, LC 4; enrl D 200, E 60, maj 48
Ent Req: Ent exam
Degrees: AA 2 yrs
Tuition: Res—In District $510 per yr, In State $825 per yr; nonres—$1215 per yr; no campus res
Courses: Ceramics, Design, Drawing, Film, Graphic Arts, Jewelry, Painting, Photography, Printmaking, Sculpture, History of Art & Design
Adult Hobby Classes: Courses—Acrylic Painting, Cermics, Drawing, Jewelry, Macrame, Photography, Stained Glass
Summer School: Courses—Drawing, Design, Printmaking, Watercolor

MARQUETTE

NORTHERN MICHIGAN UNIVERSITY, Dept of Art and Design, 49855. Tel 906-227-2194, 227-2279. *Head Dept* Michael J Cinelli; *Prof* Thomas Cappuccio; *Prof* John D Hubbard; *Prof* John V Rauch; *Prof* Marvin Zehnder; *Assoc Prof* William C Leete; *Assoc Prof* James Quirk; *Assoc Prof* Diane D Kordich; *Asst Prof* Dennis Staffne; *Instructor* Dale Wedig
Estab 1899, dept estab 1964; pub; D & E; scholarships; SC 30, LC 20, GC 18
Ent Req: HS dipl, ACT

Degrees: BS, BFA, BA 4 yrs, MAE
Tuition: Res—undergrad $46 per cr hr, grad $60.50 per cr hr; nonres—undergrad $106 per cr hr, grad $106 per cr hr; campus res—room & board $2316 per yr
Courses: †Art Education, †Art History, †Ceramics, †Drawing, †Film, †Graphic Design, †Illustration, †Industrial Design, †Jewelry, †Painting, Video, †Photography, †Printmaking, †Sculpture, †Environmental, †Furniture & Package Design, †Metalworking, †Weaving, †Woodworking

MIDLAND

MIDLAND CENTER FOR THE ARTS, Midland Art Council, 1801 W St Andrews, 48640. Tel 517-631-3250. *Dir Midland Art Council* Hilary D Bassett. Instrs: FT 15
Estab 1971; pvt; D & E; SC 12-20, LC 2; enrl D & E 250
Tuition: $35-$80 member-nonmember status
Courses: Calligraphy, Ceramics, Mixed Media, Painting, Photography, Printmaking, Sculpture, Design, Metalsmithing, Papermaking, Stained Glass, Weaving
Adult Hobby Classes: Enrl 200; tuition $35-$80 per sem
Children's Classes: Enrl 50; tuition $25-$30 per sem

NORTHWOOD INSTITUTE, Alden B Dow Creativity Center, 48640. Tel 517-631-1600, Ext 403. *Exec Dir* Carol B Coppage
Available to those with innovative ideas or specific projects

MONROE

MONROE COUNTY COMMUNITY COLLEGE, Humanities Division,* 1555 S Raisinville Rd, 48161. Tel 313-242-7300. *Chmn* David R McKay. Instrs: FT 8
Degrees: AFA offered
Tuition: Res—$18.50 per sem cr hr; nonres—$27.50 per sem cr hr
Courses: Art Appreciation, Art History, Ceramics, Design, Drawing, Painting, Printmaking, Sculpture

MOUNT PLEASANT

CENTRAL MICHIGAN UNIVERSITY, Dept of Art, 48859. Tel 517-774-3025. *Chmn Dept* Richard Kline, MFA. Instrs: FT 19, PT 4
Estab 1892; pub; D & E; SC 50, LC 9; enrl for univ 16,300
Ent Req: HS dipl
Degrees: BA, BFA & AB 4 yrs, MA, MFA
Tuition: Res—undergrad $47 per cr hr, grad $63.50 per cr hr; nonres—undergrad $120 per cr hr, grad $138 per cr hr
Courses: Aesthetics, Art Education, Art History, Ceramics, Commercial Art, Conceptual Art, Drawing, Jewelry, Painting, Photography, Printmaking, Sculpture, Weaving, Art Appreciation

MUSKEGON

BLUE LAKE COMMUNITY SCHOOL OF ARTS, Visual Arts Dept, 136 W Webster, 49440. Tel 616-894-9026, 728-0440. *Instr* Marilyn Swider; *Instr* Douglas Fairfield
Courses: Drawing, Illustration, Painting, Photography
Adult Hobby Classes: Courses—Drawing, Painting, Photography, Watercolor
Children's Classes: Courses—Drawing, Painting

MUSKEGON COMMUNITY COLLEGE, Dept of Creative and Performing Arts,* 221 S Quarterline, 49443. Tel 616-773-9131, Ext 324
Estab 1926; pub; D & E; scholarships; SC 18, LC 6; enrl D 280, E 60
Ent Req: HS dipl
Degrees: AA 2 yrs
Tuition: County res—$23 per cr hr; state res—$32 per cr hr; nonres—$44 per cr hr
Courses: Art Education, Art History, Ceramics, Costume Design & Construction, Drawing, Film, Interior Design, Painting, Printmaking, Sculpture, Stage Design, Teacher Training, Theatre Arts
Adult Hobby Classes: Tuition $15 or $21 per hr. Courses—Ceramics, Interior Design, Painting

OLIVET

OLIVET COLLEGE, Art Dept, 49076. Tel 616-749-7661. *Chmn* Donald Rowe, MFA; *Asst Prof* Dale Johnson, MFA; *Instructor* Susan Rowe, MFA
Estab 1844, dept estab 1870; pvt; D & E; scholarships; SC 17, LC 8, GC 10; enrl D 610, non-maj 50, maj 20, grad 2
Ent Req: HS dipl
Degrees: BS and BM 4 yrs, MA 1 yr
Tuition: $3390 per yr, part-time $110 per hr; campus res—room & board $1700 per yr
Courses: Art History, †Commercial Art, †Design, †Drawing, †Painting, †Printmaking, †Sculpture

PETOSKEY

NORTH CENTRAL MICHIGAN COLLEGE, Art Dept,* Howard St, 49770. Tel 616-347-3973. *Faculty* Douglas Melvin, AB
Degrees: AA offered
Tuition: Res—$22 per cr hr; nonres—$28 per cr hr
Courses: Art Education, Art History, Drawing, Industrial Design, Painting, Photography, Printmaking, Sculpture

PONTIAC

PONTIAC ART CENTER, 47 Williams St, 48053. Tel 313-333-7849. *Exec Dir* Mary C Lilley
Estab 1968; pub, D & E; scholarships; SC 15; enrl 200
Ent Req: Open enrollment
Tuition: Varies; no campus res
Courses: Ceramics, Drawing, Jewelry, Painting, Photography, Sculpture, Metalsmithing, Watercolor, Weaving
Children's Classes: Tuition $25 per class. Courses—Drawing, Painting, Sculpture
Summer School: Term of 10 wks beginning June. Courses—Drawing, Jewelry, Metalsmithing, Painting, Photography, Sculpture, Weaving

PORT HURON

SAINT CLAIR COUNTY COMMUNITY COLLEGE, Art Dept, 323 Erie St, 48060. Tel 313-984-3881. *Chmn Fine Art Dept* Albert Dale Northup
Estab 1923; pub; D & E; scholarships; SC 30, LC 5; enrl D 60
Ent Req: HS dipl
Degrees: AA and AAS 2 yrs
Tuition: In-county—$23.50 per cr hr; out-of-county—$38 per cr hr; nonres—$54 per cr hr
Courses: †Advertising Design, Drawing, Graphic Arts, Graphic Design, Illustration, †Interior Design, Lettering, Painting, Photography, Sculpture, Theatre Arts, Pottery
Adult Hobby Classes: Courses—Drawing, Painting, Pottery
Summer School: Dir Albert D Northup

ROCHESTER

OAKLAND UNIVERSITY, Dept of Art and Art History, 48063. Tel 313-377-3375. *Chmn Dept* John B Cameron, PhD; *Prof* Carl F Barnes Jr, PhD; *Assoc Prof* John Beardman, MFA & MA; *Asst Prof* C Franklin Sayre, PhD; *Asst Prof* Charlotte Stokes, PhD; *Asst Prof* Janice C Schimmelman, PhD; *Lectr* Lisa Brantigan, MA; *Lectr* Judith Toth, MFA; *Lectr* Paul Webster, MFA
Estab 1957, dept estab 1960; pub; D & E; scholarships; SC 3, LC 9
Ent Req: HS dipl
Degrees: BA 4 yrs
Tuition: Res—on campus $36 Freshman & Sophmore, $40 Junior & Senior, off campus $41 Freshman & Sophmore, $44.50 Junior & Senior per cr hr; nonres—undergrad $95 Freshman & Sophmore, $102 Junior & Senior per cr hr, grad on campus $60 per cr hr, off campus $62 per cr hr; campus res room & board $1067.70 fall & winter sems, $560 spring & summer sems
Courses: Art History, History of Art & Archaeology, Studio Art

SAUGATUCK

OXBOW CENTER FOR THE ARTS, Ox Bow Office, Box 5809, Chicago, IL 60680. Tel 616-857-5811. *Program Dir* David Greenwood; *Instr* Timothy Barrett; *Instr* Leslie Bellavance; *Instr* Phil Chen; *Instr* Howard Clark; *Instr* Kathryn Clark; *Instr* Jennifer Hilton; *Instr* Dennis Kowalski; *Instr* Paul Krainak; *Instr* Winifred Lutz; *Instr* Will Petersen; *Instr* Paul Robbert; *Instr* Dean Snyder
Estab 1910; pvt; D & E; scholarships; enrl 55 per session, 2 sessions per summer
Ent Req: Over 18 yrs, slides must be submitted
Degrees: Credit toward graduation recognized by most schools
Tuition: $800 for 3 wk session, incl room & board
Courses: Drawing, Mixed Media, Painting, Photography, Printmaking, Sculpture, Papermaking

SCOTTVILLE

WEST SHORE COMMUNITY COLLEGE, Division of Humanities and Fine Arts, 3000 N Stiles Rd, 49454. Tel 616-845-6211. *Head Dept* Leo Teholiz, MA; *Prof* Joseph Jurkowski, MA; *Instr* Susan Johnson, MA; *Instr* Paul Flickenger; *Instr* David Masten, BA. Instrs: PT 4
Pub; D & E; scholarships; SC 18, LC 10; enrl non-maj 273, maj 10
Ent Req: HS dipl
Degrees: AA 2 yrs
Tuition: Res—$350 per sem, $23 per cr hr; non-res—$525 per sem, $35 per cr hr; no campus res
Courses: †Art History, Calligraphy, Ceramics, Drafting, Drawing, Graphic Design, Lettering, Mixed Media, Painting, Photography, Printmaking, Sculpture, Stage Design, Teacher Training, Theatre Arts
Adult Hobby Classes: Enrl approx 23 per class; tuition $14 for 5 week classes; directed by Community Services. Classes—Art workshops, Crafts, Photography
Summer School: Dir, Leo Teholiz. Enrl 15-20; tuition $5 per non-cr class, $21 per cr hr for term of 8 wks beginning mid-June. Summer Art Workshop (Outdoor Off-Campus Classes). Courses—Clay Modeling, Pottery

SOUTHFIELD

LAWRENCE INSTITUTE OF TECHNOLOGY, School of Architecture,* 21000 W Ten Mile Rd, 48075. *Dean* Karl H Greimel
Degrees: BArch
Tuition: $750 per term
Courses: Architecture

SPRING ARBOR

SPRING ARBOR COLLEGE, Art Dept, 49283. Tel 517-750-1200. *Dir* Bill Bippes, MFA; *Prof* Rhoda Knisley, MA; *Prof* Paul Wolber, MA; *Instr* Marta Tanenbaum, MFA
Estab 1873, dept estab 1971; pvt den; D & E; scholarships; SC 17, LC 6; enrl D 200, E 20, non-maj 20, maj 32
Ent Req: HS dipl
Degrees: AA(Commercial) 2 yrs, BA 4 yrs
Tuition: $4590 per yr, $2295 per sem, $95 per hr; campus res—room & board $2108 per yr
Courses: †Advertising Design, Commercial Art, †Drawing, †Graphic Arts, †Illustration, †Painting, †Printmaking, †Sculpture, †Teacher Training
Children's Classes: Summer programs. Enrl 15-20; tuition $25
Summer School: Dir, Dr Charles Campbell. Courses—Crafts, Drawing, Ceramics

TRAVERSE CITY

NORTHWESTERN MICHIGAN COLLEGE, Art Dept, 1701 E Front St, 49684. Tel 616-946-5650, Ext 525. *Chmn Dept* Paul Welch, MA; *Instr* Norman Averill, MA; *Instructor* Stephen Ballance, MA; *Instructor* Jack Ozegovic, MFA; *Instructor* Jill Averill
Estab 1951, dept estab 1957; pub; D & E; scholarships; SC 40, LC 4; enrl non-maj 400, maj 75
Ent Req: HS dipl
Degrees: AA 2 yrs
Tuition: $11.50 per cr hr per term In-Dist, $19 per cr hr per term In-Serv Area, $21 per cr hr per term In-State, $23 per cr hr per term Out-of-State; campus res room & board
Courses: Advertising Design, Art Education, Art History, Ceramics, †Commercial Art, Drawing, Film, Goldsmithing, Graphic Arts, Graphic Design, Illustration, Jewelry, Lettering, Painting, Photography, Printmaking, Sculpture, Silversmithing, Textile Design
Summer School: Dir, Paul Welch. Tuition same as regular session

UNIVERSITY CENTER

DELTA COLLEGE, Art Dept, Humanities Division, 48710. Tel 517-686-9000. *Chmn Dept* Larry Butcher, MA; *Prof* Charles A Breed, MA; *Assoc Prof* Larry Oughton, MFA; *Assoc Prof* John McCormick, MFA; *Assoc Prof* Russell Thayer, MFA; *Asst Prof* Linda Menger, MA
Estab 1960; pub; D & E; scholarships; SC 21, LC 5; enrl D 550, E 100, maj 190
Ent Req: Open door policy
Degrees: AA 2 yrs
Tuition: Res—in district $850 per yr, out of district $1350 per yr; nonres—$1800 per yr; campus res—room and board $1067.50 per sem
Courses: Art Education, Art History, Ceramics, Commercial Art, Drawing, Graphic Design, Interior Design, Painting, Photography, Printmaking, Sculpture

SAGINAW VALLEY STATE COLLEGE, Dept of Art and Design, Pierce Rd, 48710. Tel 517-790-4390. *Chmn Dept* Barron Hirsch, MFA; *Prof* Matthew Zivich, MFA; *Instructor* Paul Davis, MA; *Instructor* Curtis Leece, BFA; *Instructor* Lindy Babcock, MA; *Instructor* Gary Laatsch, MFA; *Instructor* Marlene Pellerito
Estab 1960, dept estab 1968; pub; D & E; scholarships; SC approx 20, LC approx 15; enrl D 200, E 50, maj 47
Ent Req: HS dipl
Degrees: BA(Art) 4 yrs or less
Tuition: $49 per cr hr; campus residence available
Courses: †Advertising Design, †Art Education, †Art History, Ceramics, †Collages, †Commercial Art, †Constructions, †Drawing, †Graphic Arts, †Graphic Design, †Handicrafts, †Illustration, †Intermedia, †Painting, †Photography, †Printmaking, †Sculpture, †Teacher Training, †Textile Design
Summer School: Courses vary

WARREN

MACOMB COUNTY COMMUNITY COLLEGE, Art Dept, Division of Humanities, 14500 Twelve Mile Rd, 48093. Tel 313-779-7000. *Prof* David Barr, MA; *Prof* Al Hebert, MA; *Prof* James Johnston, MA; *Prof* James Pallas, MFA
Estab 1960, dept estab 1965; pub; D & E; scholarships; SC 14, LC 6
Ent Req: HS dipl, ent exam
Degrees: AA 2 yrs
Tuition: Res—In County $15 per hr, In State $28 per hr; nonres—$38 per hr
Courses: Art History, Ceramics, Design, Drawing, Graphic Design, Illustration, Jewelry, Painting, Photography, Sculpture, Painting, Photography, Sculpture

YPSILANTI

EASTERN MICHIGAN UNIVERSITY, Dept of Art, 48197. Tel 313-487-1268. *Head Dept* John E Van Haren, MS
Estab 1849, dept estab 1901; pub; D & E; scholarships; SC 55, LC 18; enrl undergrad maj 300, non-maj 800, grad 100
Ent Req: HS dipl
Degrees: BA, BS & BA(Art Educ) 4 yrs, MA(Art Educ), MA(Studio) & MFA 2 yrs
Courses: Advertising Design, †Art Education, Art History, Ceramics, Conceptual Art, Drawing, Goldsmithing, Graphic Arts, Graphic Design, Illustration, Intermedia, Jewelry, Lettering, Mixed Media, Painting, Photography, Printmaking, Sculpture, Textile Design
Children's Classes: Enrl 50; tuition $25 for 8-10 classes offered on Sat
Summer School: Head Dept, John E Van Haren, MS. Term of 6 wks beginning June 23

MINNESOTA

BEMIDJI

BEMIDJI STATE UNIVERSITY, Art Dept, 56601. Tel 218-755-3939. *Chmn* Sally James, BFA; *Prof* Eugene Dalzotto, MFA; *Prof* A Keith Malmquist, MFA; *Prof* Marlin Kaul, MFA; *Assoc Prof* William Kelly, MFA; *Asst Prof* John Holden, MFA
Estab 1918; pub; D & E; SC 54, LC 17, GC individual study
Ent Req: HS dipl, ACT, SAT, PSAT, or SCAT
Degrees: BA, BS(Teaching) and BS(Tech Illustration, Commercial Design), BFA
Tuition: Res—undergrad $23.35 per quarter hr, grad $14 per quarter hr; nonres—undergrad $23.35 per quarter hr, grad $25 per quarter hr; campus residency available
Courses: †Art Education, Art History, Ceramics, †Commercial Art, Conceptual Art, Design, Drawing, †Graphic Arts, †Graphic Design, Handicrafts, History of Art & Archaeology, Illustration, Industrial Design, Jewelry, Lettering, Painting, Printmaking, Sculpture, Teacher Training, Textile Design, Theatre Arts, Video
Children's Classes: Enrl 20; tuition free. Courses—Art, preschool classes offered each fall
Summer School: Dir, Ed Gersich. Tuition as above for term of two 5 wk sessions beginning June. Courses—most of regular courses plus special summer session only courses

BLOOMINGTON

NORMANDALE COMMUNITY COLLEGE, Art Dept,* 9700 France Ave S, 55431. Tel 612-830-9300. *Instr* E L Gleeman, MA; *Instr* D R Peterson, BFA; *Instr* Mary Strother, BFA; *Instr* Marilyn Wood, MFA
Courses: Art Appreciation, Art Education, Art History, Ceramics, Design, Drawing, Film, Handicrafts, Jewelry, Painting, Photography, Stage Design, Weaving

COLLEGEVILLE

SAINT JOHN'S UNIVERSITY, Art Dept, 56321. *Head Dept* Hugh Witzmann, MFA; *Assoc Prof* Bela Petheo, MFA; *Asst Prof* Jim Hendershot, MFA; *Instructor* Bro Alan Reed, MFA
Estab 1856; pvt; D; scholarships; SC 33, LC 10
Ent Req: HS dipl
Degrees: BA, BS
Tuition: $3475 per yr; campus res—room & board $500-$900
Courses: Aesthetics, †Art Education, †Art History, †Ceramics, †Drawing, Graphic Arts, Jewelry, Mixed Media, †Painting, †Photography, †Printmaking, †Sculpture, †Teacher Training

COON RAPIDS

ANOKA RAMSEY COMMUNITY COLLEGE, Art Dept,* 11200 Mississippi St, 55433. Tel 612-427-2600. *Instr* Robert E Toensing, MFA
Scholarships offered
Degrees: AA offered
Tuition: $18.25 per cr hr
Courses: Advertising Design, Art Appreciation, Art Education, Ceramics, Design, Drawing, Film, Jewelry, Painting, Photography, Sculpture, Glassblowing

DULUTH

UNIVERSITY OF MINNESOTA, DULUTH, Art Dept, 55812. Tel 218-726-8224. *Prof* Rudolph Schauer, MS; *Assoc Prof* Phillip Meany, MFA; *Prof* Dean R Lettenstrom, MFA; *Assoc Prof* Leif Brush, MFA; *Assoc Prof* James H Brutger, MA; *Assoc Prof* Alyce Coker, MFA; *Assoc Prof* Phillip Meany, MFA; *Assoc Prof* Thomas F Hedin, PhD; *Asst Prof* Gloria Brush, MFA; *Asst Prof* Edna J Garte, PhD; *Asst Prof* Frederick Burkett, EDd; *Asst Prof* Chen-Khee Chee, MA; *Teaching Specialist* Avis Mattson
Pub; D & E; scholarships; SC 30, LC 6, GC 10; enrl D 200, E 50, maj 200, grad 12
Ent Req: HS dipl
Degrees: BFA, BA 4 yrs, MA
Tuition: Averages $20 per cr hr; campus residence available
Courses: Advertising Design, Art Education, Ceramics, Commercial Art, Constructions, Drawing, Film, Graphic Arts, Graphic Design, History of Art & Archaeology, Jewelry, Lettering, Mixed Media, Museum Staff Training, Painting, Photography, Printmaking, Sculpture, Silversmithing, Teacher Training, Textile Design, Fibers
Adult Hobby Classes: 10 wk course
Children's Classes: Courses—Ceramics, Photography, Graphic Design, Commercial Art
Summer School: Dir, James H Brutger. Courses—Painting, Drawing, Art Education, Photography, Prints, Fibers

ELY

VERMILION COMMUNITY COLLEGE, Art Dept, 1900 East Camp St, 55731. Tel 218-365-3256. *Dept Head* Dan Wood, MAE
Estab 1922, dept estab 1964; pub; D & E; SC 13, LC 5; enrl D 63, E 15, non-maj 65, maj 13
Ent Req: HS dipl
Degrees: AA 2 yr
Adult Hobby Classes: Tuition $10 per class. Courses—Ceramics, Crafts, Enameling, Stained Glass
Children's Classes: Tuition $10 per class. Courses—Crafts, Drawing, Painting
Summer School: Dir, Lisa Borelli. Enrl 20; term of 2 weeks June 8 - June 30. Courses—Art for Kids, Ceramics, Life Drawing

FERGUS FALLS

LUTHERAN BRETHREN SCHOOLS, 56537. Tel 218-739-3371. *Head Dept* Joel Lunde, BA
Estab 1900; den; D & E; SC 1, LC 1; enrl D 20
Ent Req: HS dipl, questionnaire
Tuition: $900 per sem; campus res—room & board $770 per sem
Courses: Drawing, Painting

GRAND MARAIS

GRAND MARAIS ART COLONY, 55604. Tel 218-387-1541. *Co-owner* Marion Quick
Estab 1947; pvt; D & E; scholarships; SC 4; enrl D 125
Ent Req: Open
Courses: Drawing, Painting, Printmaking, Sculpture
Adult Hobby Classes: Courses—Drawing, Painting, Sculpture

HIBBING

HIBBING COMMUNITY COLLEGE, Art Dept,* 1515 E 25th St, 55746. Tel 218-262-3877
Scholarships offered
Degrees: AA and Certificate offered
Tuition: Res—$675 per yr; nonres—$1200 per yr
Courses: Art Appreciation, Ceramics, Design, Drawing, Painting, Photography, Sculpture, Stage Design

MANKATO

BETHANY LUTHERAN COLLEGE, Art Dept, 734 Marsh St, 56001. Tel 507-625-2977. *Head of Dept* William Bukowski
Estab 1927, dept estab 1960; den; D; scholarships; SC 2, LC 2; enrl D 36, non-maj 26, maj 10
Ent Req: HS dipl, ACT
Degrees: AA 2 yr, dipl
Tuition: $2970
Courses: Art History, Ceramics, Design, Drawing, Painting, Art Structure

MANKATO STATE UNIVERSITY, Art Dept, 56001. Tel 507-389-6412. *Chmn* John E Spurgin, MFA. Instrs: FT 15
Estab 1868, dept estab 1938; pub; D & E; SC 42, LC 28, GC 54; enrl D 3000 (total), E 500, non-maj 1000, maj 200, grad 50
Ent Req: HS dipl
Degrees: BA, BFA and BS 4 yr, MA and MS 1-1 1/2 yr
Tuition: Res—undergrad $847 per yr, $17.65 per quarter hr, grad $1012 per yr, $22.60 per quarter hr; nonres—undergrad $1687 per yr, $35.15 per quarter hr, grad $2045 per yr, $45.45 per quarter hr
Courses: Advertising Design, Art Education, Art History, Calligraphy, Ceramics, Commercial Art, Drawing, Graphic Arts, Graphic Design, Illustration, Jewelry, Lettering, Painting, Photography, Printmaking, Sculpture
Summer School: Tuition same as above

MINNEAPOLIS

ART INSTRUCTION SCHOOLS, 500 S 4th St, 55415. Tel 612-339-8721. *Dir* A Conrad Posz, EdD; *Assoc Dir* Don Jardine, PhD
Estab 1914; pvt
Courses: Fundamentals of Art and Specialized Art

AUGSBURG COLLEGE, Art Dept, 731 21st Ave W, 55454. Tel 612-330-1233. *Chmn* Philip Thompson. Instrs: FT 2, PT 5
Estab 1869, dept estab 1960; den; D & E; scholarships; SC 15, LC 4; enrl D 200, maj 60, others 1500
Ent Req: HS dipl
Degrees: BA 4 yrs
Tuition: $5160 per yr; campus res—room & board $2335
Courses: Aesthetics, Art Education, Art History, Ceramics, Drawing, Graphic Design, Handicrafts, History of Art & Archaeology, Jewelry, Lettering, Museum Staff Training, Painting, Photography, Sculpture, Stage Design, Teacher Training, Theatre Arts, Weaving
Summer School: Enrl 250; term of six or four wks beginning end of May

**MINNEAPOLIS COLLEGE OF ART AND DESIGN,* 133 E 25th St, 55404. Tel 612-870-3346. *Pres* G Richard Slade, BA; *Chmn Fine Arts* Ronald Dahl, MFA; *Chmn Design* Patrick Whitney, MFA; *Basic Studies* Gerald Allan, MA; *Liberal Arts* Raymond Merritt, PhD; *Vis Prof* John Miller, painting 1982; *Vis Prof* Michael Kelley, performing artist 1982. Instrs: FT 40, PT 20
Estab 1886; pvt; D & E; scholarships; SC 78, LC 23; enrl D 650, E 480
Ent Req: HS dipl or GED
Degrees: BFA 4 yr
Tuition: $4070 annual tuition; campus res available
Courses: Art History, Calligraphy, Drawing, Fashion Arts, Film, Graphic Arts, Illustration, Painting, Photography, Printmaking, Sculpture, Video, Critical Studies, Design Theory and Methods, Environmental Design, Liberal Arts, Packaging and Product Design
Adult Hobby Classes: Extension Division
Children's Classes: Courses offered
Summer School: Dir of Extension Prog, Ellen Meyer. Courses—Drawing, Graphic Design, History of Art and Design, Liberal Arts, Painting, Papermaking, Photography, Printmaking, Sculpture, Video

NORTH HENNEPIN COMMUNITY COLLEGE, Art Dept, 7411 85th Ave N, 55445. Tel 612-425-4541. Instrs: FT 6
Estab 1964; pub; D & E; scholarships; SC 15, LC 4; enrl D 500, E 100, maj 200, others 100
Ent Req: HS dipl. ent exam
Degrees: AA & AAS 2 yr
Tuition: In-state $22.50 per hr; out-of-state $45 per hr
Courses: Art History, Drawing, Graphic Design, Illustration, Jewelry, Painting, Photography, Printmaking, Contemporary Crafts, Exhibition Design, Introduction to Art, Metalsmithing, 2-D & 3-D Design, Typography, Visual Communications
Adult Hobby Classes: Enrl 30-100. Courses—Painting, Photography, Video
Summer School: Two 5 week sessions. Enrl 700; Courses—Drawing, Introduction of Art, Photography, Fundamentals of Color, Painting

UNIVERSITY OF MINNESOTA, MINNEAPOLIS
—**Art History,** 27 Pleasant St SE, 108 Jones Hall, 55455. Tel 612-373-3057. *Chmn* Karal Ann Marling; *Prof* Frederick Asher, PhD; *Prof* Norman Canedy, PhD; *Prof* Sheila McNally, PhD; *Prof* Marion Nelson, PhD; *Prof* Robert Poor, PhD; *Prof* Sidney Simon, PhD; *Prof* Melvin Waldfogel, PhD; *Assoc Prof* John Steyaert, PhD; *Assoc Prof* Michael Stoughton, PhD; *Asst Prof* Fred T Smith, PhD
Pub; D & E; scholarships; LC 28, GC 59; enrl Res 71 per cr per quarter, nonres 142 per quarter, maj 65, grad 70
Ent Req: HS dipl, ent exam, GRE required for grad school
Degrees: BA 4 yrs, MA 2 yrs
Courses: †Art History, History of Art & Archaeology, Museology
—**Dept of Studio Art,*** 216 21st Ave S (Mailing add: 210 Art Bldg, West Bank, 55455). Tel 612-373-3663. *Chmn Dept* Warren MacKenzie
Estab 1851, fine arts estab 1939; pub; D & E; scholarships; SC 39, LC 7; enrl D 1630, E approx 1000, maj 537, grad 53
Ent Req: HS dipl, PSAT, ACT
Degrees: BA and BFA 4 yrs, MFA 2-3 yrs
Tuition: $1680 annual tuition
Courses: †Ceramics, †Drawing, †Painting, †Photography, †Printmaking, †Sculpture, †Glassworking
Summer School: Dir, Willard Thompson. Tuition $20.75 per cr hr for term of 5 wks beginning June 12 and July 17. Courses—Ceramics, Drawing, Glassworking, Painting, Photography, Printmaking, Sculpture

MOORHEAD

CONCORDIA COLLEGE, Art Dept, 920 S Eighth, 56560. Tel 218-299-4623. *Chmn* Barbara Glasrud, MA; *Prof* Elizabeth Strand, MFA; *Assoc Prof* Orland J Rourke, MA; *Asst Prof* Paul F Allen, MFA; *Instr* Duane Mickelson; *Instr* Suzanne Smemo
Estab 1891; pvt; D; scholarships; SC 10, LC 5; enrl D 150, maj 40, total 2600
Ent Req: HS dipl, character references
Degrees: BA and BM 4 yrs, independent studio work, work-study prog and special studies
Tuition: $5260 per yr, $875 per course, student association dues $45; campus res—room $775 & board $1020
Courses: †Art Education, †Art History, Ceramics, Drawing, Lettering, Painting, Printmaking, Sculpture, Teacher Training, Weaving, Figure Drawing, Visual Studies, †Studio Art
Summer School: Dir, Donald Dale. Enrl 40; tuition $695 for term of 4 wks beginning May 15 and June 12. Courses—Art History Travel Seminar, Drawing, Painting, Printmaking

MOORHEAD STATE UNIVERSITY, Dept of Art, 56560. Tel 218-236-2151. *Chmn* P R Szeitz, MFA; *Prof* Lyle Laske, MFA; *Prof* Dr John Boyd Hollad, PhD; *Prof* P J Mousseau, MFA; *Prof* Dr Virginia Barsch, PhD; *Assoc Prof* Donald B McRaven Jr, MFA; *Assoc Prof* Timothy Ray; *Assoc Prof* Marcel C Stratton, MA; *Asst Prof* Carl Oltvedt, MFA; *Asst Prof* Deborah Broad, MFA
Estab 1887; pub; D & E; scholarships; SC 47, LC 20, GC 11; enrl D 4520, maj 175, grad 2
Ent Req: HS dipl
Degrees: BA, BS 4 yr, BFA 5 yr, MS additional 1 1/4 yr
Tuition: Res—undergrad $26.85 per cr hr, grad $34.40 per cr hr; nonres—undergrad $28.20 per cr hr, grad $36.10 per cr hr; campus res—room & board $1491 per yr
Courses: Advertising Design, Art Education, Art History, Ceramics, Collages, Conceptual Art, Constructions, Drawing, Graphic Arts, Graphic Design, Illustration, Mixed Media, Painting, Photography, Printmaking, Sculpture, Stage Design, Teacher Training, Theatre Arts
Summer School: Tuition per cr hr for term of 5 wks beginning June. Courses—Basic Drawing, Ceramics, Elements of Art Design, Graphic Design, Painting, Photography, Printmaking

MORRIS

UNIVERSITY OF MINNESOTA, MORRIS, Humanities Division, 56267. Tel 612-589-2211. *Chmn* Nathaniel Hart; *Coordr* Lois Hodgell, MFA; *Coordr* Frederick Peterson, PhD
Estab 1960, dept estab 1963; pub; D; scholarships; SC 16, LC 8; enrl D 195, non-maj 150, maj 45
Ent Req: Top 50% in HS, ACT or PSAT
Degrees: BA 4 yrs
Tuition: Res—undergrad $471.38 per quarter; nonres—undergrad $1388.85 per quarter; campus res—room and board $712
Courses: †Art History, Teacher Training, †Studio Art

NORTHFIELD

CARLETON COLLEGE, Dept of Art & Art History, 55057. Tel 507-663-4000. *Chmn* Timothy L Lloyd
Estab 1921; pvt; scholarships; SC 30, LC 20; enrl maj 30, others 550
Degrees: 4 yr
Tuition: $10,200, campus res available
Courses: Art History, Studio Art

SAINT OLAF COLLEGE, Art Dept, 55057. Tel 507-663-3248. *Chmn* Wendell Arneson, MFA; *Prof* John Maakestad, MFA; *Prof* Edward Sovik; *Prof* Reidar Dittman, PhD; *Assoc Prof* Dorothy Divers, MFA; *Assoc Prof* Malcolm Gimse, MFA; *Assoc Prof* Arch Leean, MA
Estab 1875, dept estab 1932; den; D & E; scholarships
Ent Req: HS dipl, SAT
Degrees: BA 4 yr
Tuition: Campus residency available
Courses: Aesthetics, Architecture, †Art Education, †Art History, Calligraphy, Ceramics, Commercial Art, Drafting, Drawing, Film, Graphic Arts, Graphic Design, History of Art & Archaeology, Interior Design, Lettering, Painting, Photography, Printmaking, Sculpture, Stage Design, Teacher Training, Theatre Arts, †Art Studio
Adult Hobby Classes: Dir, Lydia Quanbeck
Summer School: Dir, Lydia Quanbeck. Courses—Production Art, 20th Century Art

NORTH MANKATO

MANKATO AREA VOCATIONAL-TECHNICAL INSTITUTE, Commercial and Technical Art Dept, 1920 Lee Blvd, 56001. Tel 502-615-3441. *Instr* Robert Williams
Estab 1969; pub; D; scholarships; enrl D 20
Ent Req: Portfolio
Degrees: 2 yr certificate of graduation
Courses: Advertising Design, Calligraphy, Commercial Art, Conceptual Art, Drafting, Drawing, Fashion Arts, Graphic Arts, Graphic Design, Illustration, Lettering, Mixed Media, Cartooning, Package Design

ROCHESTER

ROCHESTER COMMUNITY COLLEGE, Art Dept, 55904. Tel 507-285-7236. *Instructor* Terry Dennis, MFA; *Instructor* Pat Kraemer, BA; *Instructor* James Prom, MS; *Instructor* Flo Sandok, MA
Estab 1920s; pub; D & E; SC 17, LC 4; enrl D & E 3200, maj 50
Ent Req: State req
Degrees: AA
Tuition: Res-$22.50 per cr; nonres—$45 except in reciprocal states
Courses: Advertising Design, Art History, Ceramics, Drawing, Handicrafts, Jewelry, Painting, Photography, Printmaking, Sculpture, Photography, Printmaking, Sculpture, Stage Design, Fibers
Adult Hobby Classes: Tuition variable. Courses—Embroidery, Stained Glass, Wood Carving, Cartooning, others on less regular basis
Summer School: Dir, A Olson. Art workshops are offered for at least one session each summer

SAINT CLOUD

SAINT CLOUD STATE UNIVERSITY, Dept of Art,* 56301. Tel 612-255-4283, 255-0121. *Chmn* Dr James Roy. Instrs: FT 15, PT 4
Pub; D & E; SC 65, LC 15, GC 20; enrl maj 400, grad 60
Ent Req: HS dipl
Degrees: BA, BFA, BS MA(Studio Art) and MS 4 yrs
Tuition: Res—$633.60 per yr; nonres—$1212 per yr
Courses: Advertising Design, Aesthetics, Art Education, Ceramics, Commercial Art, Display, Drawing, Graphic Arts, Graphic Design, History of Art & Archaeology, Illustration, Jewelry, Lettering, Museum Staff Training, Painting, Photography, Sculpture, Teacher Training, Textile Design, Glass Blowing, Weaving

SAINT JOSEPH

COLLEGE OF SAINT BENEDICT, Art Dept, 56374. Tel 612-363-5785. *Chmn* S Johanna Becker, PhD; *Prof* Gordon Goetemann, MFA; *Assoc Prof* Stan Shafer, MFA; *Assoc Prof* Sr Baulu Kuan, MA; *Asst Prof* Sr Dennis Frandrup, MFA; *Instr* Marjorie Masel, MFA
Estab 1913; pvt; D & E; scholarships; SC 21, LC 15; enrl D 1726, maj 60
Ent Req: HS dipl, SAT, PSAT, ACT
Degrees: BA(Art Educ), BA(Art) and BA(Art History) 4 yr, internships and open studio
Tuition: $4390 per year; campus res—room and board $1625 per year
Courses: †Art Education, †Art History, †Ceramics, Commercial Art, Drawing, Graphic Arts, Graphic Design, Jewelry, Mixed Media, †Painting, †Photography, †Printmaking, †Sculpture, †Teacher Training
Children's Classes: Enrl 30; tuition $25 per term. Courses—mixed and various media

SAINT PAUL

BETHEL COLLEGE, Dept of Art, 3900 Bethel Dr, 55112. Tel 612-638-6400, Ext 6263 . *Prof* Dale R Johnson, MFA; *Prof* Stewart Luckman, MFA; *Prof* George Robinson, BFA; *Assoc Prof* Tom R Toperzer, MFA; *Assoc Prof* Barbara Glenn, MA; *Asst Prof* Wayne Roosa, MA; *Instructor* John Turula, BS
Estab 1871; den; D & E; scholarships; SC 20, LC 12; enrl non-maj 100, maj 100
Ent Req: HS dipl, SAT, ACT, PSAT or NMSQT, evidence of a standard of faith and practice that is compatible to Bethel lifestyle
Degrees: BA(Art Educ) and BA(Studio Arts) 4 yr
Tuition: $2475 per sem; campus res—room ($675) and board ($500)

Courses: Art Education, Art History, Ceramics, Drawing, Graphic Design, Painting, Photography, Printmaking, Sculpture, Three Dimensional Design, Two Dimensional Design, Visual Awareness
Summer School: Dir, Tricia Brownlee. Two sessions offered

COLLEGE OF SAINT CATHERINE, Visual Arts Dept, 2004 Randolph, 55105. Tel 612-690-6636. *Chmn* M Wilson. Instrs: FT 4, PT 8
Pvt, W; D; scholarships
Ent Req: HS dipl
Degrees: BA(Art) 4 yr
Courses: Art Education, Art History, Calligraphy, Ceramics, Drawing, Jewelry, Lettering, Painting, Printmaking, Photography, Sculpture, Pottery, Publication Design, Typography
Adult Hobby Classes: Special Workshops
Summer School: Summer high school workshop

COLLEGE OF SAINT THOMAS, Dept of Art History, 2115 Summit Ave, 55108. Tel 612-647-5789. *Div Dir Fine Arts* George Poletes
Estab 1885, dept estab 1978; den; D & E; scholarships; SC 25, LC 8; enrl D 2847, E 275, maj 40
Ent Req: HS dipl
Degrees: BA 4 yrs
Courses: Art Education, †Art History, Calligraphy, Ceramics, Drawing, Graphic Arts, Graphic Design, Jewelry, Painting, Photography, Printmaking, Sculpture, Teacher Training
Summer School: Dir, Dr Verome Halverson. Courses—Introduction to Art History

CONCORDIA COLLEGE, Art Dept,* Fine Arts Division, Hamline - Marshall, 55104. Tel 612-641-8494. *Chmn Div* Fred Brauer, MA; *Prof* Robert E Rickels, MA; *Assoc Prof* Benjamin W Marxhausen, MA
Estab 1897, dept estab 1967; den; D & E; scholarships; SC 14, LC 3; enrl D 84, E 20, others 35
Ent Req: HS dipl
Degrees: BS and BA 4 yrs
Tuition: $1150 per qtr
Courses: Aesthetics, Art Education, Art History, Ceramics, Drawing, Jewelry, Painting, Photography, Printmaking, Sculpture, Teacher Training, Theatre Arts
Summer School: Dean of Faculty, David Schmiel. Courses—Art Educ Methods, Art Fundamentals

HAMLINE UNIVERSITY, Art Dept, 55104. Tel 612-641-2296, Ext 2415. *Head Dept* Michael Price, MFA; *Prof* James Conaway, MFA; *Prof* Leonardo Lasansky, MFA; *Prof* Frederick D Leach, PhD; *Instructor* Clifford Garten, MFA
Estab 1854; pvt; D & E; scholarships; SC 13, LC 13; enrl non-maj 70, maj 35
Ent Req: HS dipl
Degrees: BA 4 yrs
Tuition: $5975 per yr; campus res—room & board $2400 per yr
Courses: Art Education, Art History, Ceramics, Drawing, History of Art & Archaeology, Museum Staff Training, Painting, Photography, Printmaking, Sculpture
Summer School: Dean, Jack Johnson

MACALESTER COLLEGE, Dept of Art, 1600 Grand Ave, 55105. Tel 612-696-6279. *Head Dept* Anthony Caponi
Estab 1946; den; D; scholarships; SC 9, LC 8; enrl 20
Degrees: 4 yr
Tuition: Average yr $5425; campus residence available
Courses: Art History, Ceramics, Design, Drawing, Painting, Printmaking, Sculpture, American Art, Art of the Last Decade, Classical Art, Fibers, Principles of Art, Primitive Art, Senior Seminar
Summer School: Dir, W Harley Henry. Two 4 wk sessions June and July

SCHOOL OF THE ASSOCIATED ARTS, 344 Summit Ave, 55102. Tel 612-224-3416. *Dir* Virginia Rahja, MFA; *Dean* Ronald Swenson, MFA; *Instructor* Elaine Pelosini, MFA; *Instructor* John Lenertz, BFA; *Instructor* Philip Ogle, MFA
Estab 1924; pvt; D; scholarships; SC 30, LC 8; enrl D 109, maj 109
Ent Req: HS dipl
Degrees: BFA 4 yr
Tuition: $2950 per yr; campus res—room & board $3700
Courses: Advertising Design, †Art History, Commercial Art, †Drawing, Graphic Design, †Illustration, Lettering, †Painting, †Photography, †Sculpture, Mass Communications

UNIVERSITY OF MINNESOTA, Dept of Design, Housing & Apparel, 1985 Buford Ave (Mailing add: 240 McNeal Hall, 55108). Tel 612-373-1032. *Head Dept* Joanne B Eicher
Pub; D & E; SC 31, LC 15, GC 33; enrl D 1012 (winter quarter 78), non-maj 265, maj 747, grad 39, others 21 adult specials
Ent Req: HS dipl
Degrees: BS, MS and PhD 4 yr, evening extension 2 yr cert
Courses: Art History, †Costume Design & Construction, Drawing, Goldsmithing, Handicrafts, †Interior Design, Jewelry, †Silversmithing, Textile Design, †Applied Design, Costume History, Decorative Arts, Housing, †Textiles Clothing, Weaving Off-Loom
Summer School: Dir, Gertrude Strinden. Courses—vary each yr

SAINT PETER

GUSTAVUS ADOLPHUS COLLEGE, Art Dept, Schaefer Fine Arts Center, 56082. Tel 507-931-4300, Ext 462. *Chmn* Bruce A McClain. Instrs: FT 5 PT 2
Estab 1876; den; D; scholarships; SC 27; enrl 2300 total, 750 art, maj 50
Ent Req: HS grad, ent exam
Degrees: BA 4 yrs
Tuition: $8150 per yr (comprehensive fee); PT $700 per course
Courses: †Art Education, †Art History, Ceramics, Drawing, Painting, Photography, Printmaking, Sculpture, Textile Design, Theatre Arts, Basic Design, Bronze Casting, Weaving, †Studio Art
Summer School: Enrl approx 25; one 4 wk term from June to July

WHITE BEAR LAKE

LAKEWOOD COMMUNITY COLLEGE, Humanities Dept, 3401 Century Ave, 55110. Tel 612-770-1331
Courses: Art Appreciation, Art History, Calligraphy, Ceramics, Design, Drawing, Painting, Photography, Printmaking, Sculpture, Stage Design

WILLMAR

WILLMAR COMMUNITY COLLEGE,* 56201. Tel 612-231-5102. *Staff* Robert Mattson. Instrs: FT 1, PT 1
Estab 1962-63; pub; D & E; SC 8, LC 3; enrl D 50, maj 15
Ent Req: HS dipl
Degrees: AA and AS 2 yrs
Tuition: Res—$18.25 per cr hr; nonres—$36.50 per cr hr
Courses: Art Education, Ceramics, Display, Drawing, Graphic Arts, Graphic Design, History of Art & Archaeology, Painting, Teacher Training, Introduction to Studio Practices, Structure
Adult Hobby Classes: Courses—Design, History of Art, Painting

WINONA

COLLEGE OF SAINT TERESA, Art Dept, 55987. Tel 507-454-2930. *Chairperson* Anna Poulos, MFA; *Asst Prof* John DeFrancesco, MS; *Instr* Betty Ann Mocek, MFA; *Instr* Dr Wallace Johnson
Estab 1904, dept estab 1964; pvt; D; scholarships; SC 28, LC 10; enrl D 450, non-maj 10, maj 30
Ent Req: HS dipl, SAT
Degrees: BA 4 yrs
Tuition: $4995
Courses: Art Appreciation, Art History, Ceramics, Commercial Art, Design, Drawing, Graphic Arts, Handicrafts, Jewelry, Painting, Sculpture, Teacher Training, Textile Design, Art in Elementary School, Art Therapy, Etchings, Exhibition, Silkscreen, 3-D Design, Visual Analysis
Summer School: Elder Hostel Program; Courses—vary

SAINT MARY'S COLLEGE, Art Dept, Terrace Heights, 55987. Tel 507-452-4430. *Head Dept & Assoc Prof* Karen Kryzsko, MFA; *Assoc Prof* Helen Galloway, PhD; *Asst Prof* Margaret Mear, MFA; *Asst Prof* Roderick Robertson, MFA
Estab 1912, dept estab 1970; den; D; SC 20, LC 6; enrl in school D 1240
Ent Req: HS dipl
Degrees: BA 4 yrs
Tuition: $4700 per yr; campus res—room & board $2200 per yr
Courses: Aesthetics, Art History, Ceramics, Drawing, Graphic Design, Handicrafts, Jewelry, Painting, Photography, Printmaking, Sculpture, Copper Enameling

WINONA STATE UNIVERSITY, Art Dept, Johnson and Sanborn Sts, 55987. Tel 507-457-5395. *Chairperson* Thomas Sternal, MFA; *Prof* Virginia H Vint, EdD; *Asst Prof* Donald Schnidlapp, MFA; *Asst Prof* Wilfred McKenzie, MFA; *Asst Prof* Judy Schlawin, MS
Estab 1860; pub; D & E; scholarships
Degrees: BA and BS
Tuition: Res—undergrad $23.35 per cr hr, grad $29.90 per cr hr; nonres—undergrad $46.70 per cr hr, grad $59.80 per cr hr; plus student fees; campus res—$556 per yr single occupancy, double occupancy $499
Courses: Art Education, Art History, Ceramics, Commercial Art, Drawing, Graphic Arts, Interior Design, Jewelry, Lettering, Painting, Printmaking, Sculpture, Weaving
Adult Hobby Classes: Chairperson, Thomas Sternal
Summer School: Courses offered

MISSISSIPPI

BLUE MOUNTAIN

BLUE MOUNTAIN COLLEGE, Art Dept,* Box 338, 38610. Tel 601-685-5711, 685-4771, Ext 62. *Chmn Dept* William Dowdy, MA
Estab 1873, dept estab 1875; den; D & E; scholarships; SC 16, LC 2; enrl D 28, E 12, non-maj 20, maj 8, others 12
Ent Req: HS dipl
Degrees: BA and BS(Educ) 4 yr
Tuition: $1920 per yr
Courses: Art Education, Art History, Commercial Art, †Drawing, †Painting
Adult Hobby Classes: Enrl 12; tuition $42 per sem hr. Courses—Drawing, Painting
Summer School: Dir, William Dowdy. Enrl 20

BOONEVILLE

NORTHEAST MISSISSIPPI JUNIOR COLLEGE, Art Dept, 38829. Tel 601-728-7751, Ext 229. *Chmn* Marty McLendon. Instrs: FT 1, PT 2
Estab 1948; pub; D & E; scholarships; SC 6, LC 3; enrl D 2300, maj 30
Ent Req: HS dipl, ent exam
Degrees: 2 yr Associate degrees in art educ, fine arts and interior design
Tuition: $240 per sem
Courses: Advertising Design, Aesthetics, †Art Education, †Art History, †Ceramics, †Design, Drafting, †Drawing, †Painting, Teacher Training, Theatre Arts
Adult Hobby Classes: Watercolor

CLARKSDALE

COAHOMA JUNIOR COLLEGE, Art Education & Fine Arts Dept,* Box 616, Rte 1, 38614. Tel 601-627-1161, 627-2571. *Chmn* Thomas Richardson
Degrees: AA
Tuition: In district—$516 per yr; res—$816 per yr; nonres—$1416 per yr
Courses: Art Appreciation, Art Education, Art History, Ceramics, Design, Drawing, Handicrafts, Painting

CLEVELAND

DELTA STATE UNIVERSITY, Dept of Art, Box D-2, 38733. Tel 601-843-2151. *Chmn* Malcolm M Norwood, MA; *Prof* Carolyn Rea Stone, PhD; *Assoc Prof* Sam Glenn Britt, MFA; *Assoc Prof* Terry K Simmons, MA; *Assoc Prof* William Carey Lester Jr, MFA; *Asst Prof* Lallah M Perry, MEd; *Instructor* Larry Hirst; *Instructor* Mary Jane Baird, ASID; *Instructor* Mary Anne Ross, BFA; *Instructor* Nan Goggin, MFA; *Instructor* William Powell, MA; *Vis Artist* Andrew Bucci, MFA
Estab 1924; pub; D & E; scholarships; SC 42, LC 10, GC 30; enrl maj 116
Ent Req: HS dipl
Degrees: BA, BFA and BSE 4 yr, MEd(Art Educ) 1 yr
Tuition: Res—undergrad & grad $1976 per yr, $988 per sem; non-res—undergrad & grad $2902 per yr, $1451 per sem
Courses: †Advertising Design, Aesthetics, †Art Education, Art History, Calligraphy, Ceramics, †Commercial Art, Costume Design & Construction, Drawing, Fashion Arts, Graphic Arts, Graphic Design, Handicrafts, Illustration, †Interior Design, Lettering, Mixed Media, †Painting, Printmaking, †Sculpture, Teacher Training, Textile Design, Clay, Fibers
Children's Classes: Enrl 15 per class; tuition $25 per sem. Two classes ages 6-8 and 9-12
Summer School: Tuition $318 per term, June 2 - July 3 or July 7 - August 8. Courses—Art for Elementary, Ceramics, Drawing, Internship in Commercial Design, Introduction to Art, Painting, Sculpture

CLINTON

MISSISSIPPI COLLEGE, Art Dept, PO Box 4186, 39056. Tel 601-924-5131. *Head Dept* Dr Sam Gore. Instrs: FT 3, PT 4
Estab 1825, dept estab 1950; den; HS grad; scholarships and student assistantships; SC 22, LC 3; enrl maj 80, others 300
Ent Req: BA, BE(Art) and ME(Art) 4 yr, Freshman Art merit
Courses: †Art Education, Art History, Ceramics, Drawing, †Graphic Design, †Interior Design, †Painting, †Sculpture, Foundry Casting
Adult Hobby Classes: Enrl 50; tuition $35 for 5 weeks. Courses—Calligraphy, Drawing, Flower Arranging, Painting
Summer School: Dir, Dr Sam Gore. Tuition $1200 for 2 6 week terms. Courses—Ceramics, Drawing, Painting, Printmaking

COLUMBUS

MISSISSIPPI UNIVERSITY FOR WOMEN, Division of Fine & Performing Arts, PO Box W-70 MUW, 39701. Tel 601-329-4750 Ext 341. *Head Dept & Prof* Eugenia Summer, MA; *Prof* Mary Evelyn Stringer, PhD; *Prof* David Frank, MFA; *Prof* Thomas Nawrocki, MFA; *Assoc Prof* Lawrence Feeny, MFA; *Asst Prof* Janice Hathaway, MFA; *Asst Prof* Paul Olsen, MFA
Estab 1884; pub; D & E; scholarships; SC 49, LC 8; enrl D 263, E 39, non-maj 45, maj 72
Ent Req: HS dipl, ACT, SAT
Degrees: BA, BS and BFA 4 yrs
Tuition: Res—undergrad $412.50 per sem; nonres—undergrad $1242.50 per sem; $34.50 per sem hr
Courses: †Advertising Design, †Art Education, †Art History, Calligraphy, Ceramics, Collages, †Commercial Art, Conceptual Art, †Interior Design, Jewelry, Illustration, Lettering, Mixed Media, †Painting, Photography, †Printmaking, Sculpture, Stage Design, Teacher Training, Textile Design, †Theatre Arts, Weaving, Glassblowing, Metalcrafts
Adult Hobby Classes: Enrl 45; tuition $23 per hr. Courses—Calligraphy, Ceramics, Drawing, Interior Design, Painting, Weaving
Summer School: Tuition $34.50 per hr for term of 5 wks beginning June 1 & July 6. Courses—vary according to demand

DECATUR

EAST CENTRAL JUNIOR COLLEGE, Art Dept, Box 27, 39327. Tel 601-635-2121. *Head Dept* J Bruce Guraedy, MEd
Estab 1928, dept estab 1965; pub; D & E; SC 10, LC 4; enrl in dept D 120, E 52, non-maj 58, maj 10
Ent Req: HS dipl, GED
Degrees: AA and AS 2 yrs
Tuition: Res—$1200 per yr, $600 per sem; nonres—$1400 per yr, $700 per sem; campus residence available
Courses: Art Education, Art History, Ceramics, Drafting, Drawing, Fashion Arts, Industrial Design, Painting, Sculpture, Teacher Training, Theatre Arts
Adult Hobby Classes: Enrl 48; tuition $30 per sem. Courses—Painting
Children's Classes: Pvt lessons available
Summer School: Acad Dean, Dr B J Tucker. Enrl 200-300; tuition $18 per sem hr for term of 10 wks. Courses—vary according to student demand

ELLISVILLE

JONES COUNTY JUNIOR COLLEGE, Art Dept,* Court St, 39437. Tel 601-477-9311. *Chmn* Mlifred Valentine, PhD
Estab 1927; pub; D; scholarships; SC 12, LC 4; enrl D 100, E 12, maj 15, others 12
Ent Req: HS dipl
Degrees: AA 2 yrs
Tuition: District res—$400 per yr; non-district res—$440 per yr; non-state res—$1000 per yr
Adult Hobby Classes: Enrl 20. Courses—Painting
Summer School: Dir, B F Ogletree. Term of 4 wks beginning June. Courses—same as regular session

GAUTIER

JACKSON COUNTY JUNIOR COLLEGE, Art Dept, Highway 90, Jackson County Campus, 39533. Tel 601-497-9602. *Head* Patt Odom, Masters; *Fine Arts Dept Head* Martha Richardson, Masters
Pub; D & E; scholarships; SC 9, LC 2; enrl D 40, E 8, non-maj 25, maj 5
Degrees: AA, 2 yrs
Courses: Aesthetics, Art Appreciation, Art Education, Art History, Ceramics, Design, Display, Drafting, Drawing, Fashion Arts, Lettering, Mixed Media, Occupational Therapy, Painting, Photography, Sculpture, Theatre Arts, Video
Adult Hobby Classes: Courses—Ceramics, Art Appreciation, Drawing, Painting
Children's Classes: Enrl 25. Courses—Drawing, Painting
Summer School: Dir, Patt Odom. Courses—Art Appreciation, Ceramics, Introductory Art

HATTIESBURG

UNIVERSITY OF SOUTHERN MISSISSIPPI, Dept of Art, College of Fine Arts, 39401. Tel 601-266-4972. *Chmn* William C Baggett Jr. Instrs: FT 10, PT 4
Estab 1910; pub; D & E; scholarships; SC 64, LC 41, GC 34; enrl non-maj 35, maj 110, grad 7
Ent Req: HS dipl
Degrees: BA, BFA, MAE, MFA
Tuition: Campus residency available
Courses: Aesthetics, †Art Education, Art History, Ceramics, Commercial Art, Display, Drawing, Goldsmithing, Graphic Arts, †Graphic Design, Handicrafts, Illustration, Jewelry, Lettering, †Painting, Printmaking, †Sculpture, Silversmithing, Teacher Training, Textile Design, Weaving
Adult Hobby Classes: Courses—Ceramics, Drawing, Painting
Summer School: Dir, William C Baggett Jr. Courses—as above

WILLIAM CAREY COLLEGE, Art Dept,* 39401. Tel 601-582-5051, Ext 237. *Chmn* Lucile Parker, MFA
Estab 1906, dept estab 1974; den; D & E; scholarships; enrl D 75, E 25, non-maj 86, maj 14
Ent Req: HS dipl, qualifications
Degrees: BA, BS, BM, MM and MEd 4 yr
Tuition: $73 per sem hr
Courses: Advertising Design, Art Education, Art History, Ceramics, Drawing, Graphic Arts, Graphic Design, Lettering, Painting, Photography, Printmaking
Adult Hobby Classes: Courses—Drawing, Painting

ITTA BENA

MISSISSIPPI VALLEY STATE UNIVERSITY, Fine Arts Dept, PO Box 1301, 38941. Tel 601-254-9041, Ext 6261. *Head* Dr Herbert Coleman, DMA
Estab 1952; pub; D & E
Ent Req: HS dipl
Degrees: BA & BS
Tuition: Res—$1221 per sem; nonres—undergrad $400; campus res—room & board $2443 per yr
Courses: Advertising Design, †Art Education, Art History, Ceramics, †Commercial Art, Drawing, Graphic Arts, Graphic Design, Handicrafts, Illustration, Lettering, Painting, Photography, Printmaking, Teacher Training, Art Appreciation, Public School Art
Summer School: Art Appreciation, Public School Art

JACKSON

BELHAVEN COLLEGE, Art Dept, 1500 Peachtree, 39202. Tel 601-355-6893. *Chmn* Jon Whittington, MA
Estab 1883, dept estab 1889; den; D & E; scholarships; LC 3; enrl D 650, E 200, maj 30
Ent Req: HS dipl
Degrees: BA
Courses: Art History, Drawing, Graphic Arts, Painting, Photography, Printmaking
Summer School: Dir, Dr Dewey Buckley

JACKSON STATE UNIVERSITY, Dept of Art, Lynch at Dalton St, 39207. Tel 601-968-2040. *Chmn* Grace Hampton
Estab 1949; pub; D; scholarships; SC 16, LC 7, GC 1; enrl D 486, maj 112
Ent Req: HS dipl
Degrees: BS(maj in Art) 4 yrs
Tuition: Res—$832 per yr; non-res—$926 per yr; campus res available
Courses: †Art Education, Art History, Ceramics, †Commercial Art, †Drawing, †Graphic Arts, †Painting, Teacher Training, Studio Crafts
Adult Hobby Classes: Athenian Art Club activities
Summer School: Dir, Dr Grace Hampton. Courses—same as regular session

LORMAN

ALCORN STATE UNIVERSITY, Dept of Fine Arts, 39096. Tel 601-877-6271. *Chmn* Joyce Bolden, PhD; *Asst Prof* Constance Alford, MFA; *Instr* Brenda Rodgers, MA
Estab 1871, dept estab 1973; pub; D & E; SC 9, LC 3
Ent Req: HS dipl, ACT
Tuition: In-state $628 per yr; out-of-state $1428
Courses: Art Education, Art History, Ceramics, Drawing, Painting
Adult Hobby Classes: Enrl 20. Courses—Drawing, Painting, Graduate Level Art Education
Summer School: Enrl 40 for term of 10 wks beginning May 28. Courses—Art Education, Fine Arts

MISSISSIPPI STATE

MISSISSIPPI STATE UNIVERSITY, Art Dept, PO Box 5182, 39762. Tel 601-325-2970. *Head* Jack Bartlett, MFA; *Prof* Authur Leonard Farley, MA; *Assoc Prof* Kenneth Clifford, MFA; *Assoc Prof* Larry Jan Webber, BFA; *Assoc Prof* DeAnna Douglas, MFA; *Asst Prof* Paul Grootkerk, PhD; *Assoc Prof* Robie Scucchi, MFA; *Instructor* Julie Schnell, MFA; *Lecturer* Brent Funder Furk
Estab 1879, dept estab 1971; pub; D; SC 23, LC 6; enrl D 750, non-maj 650, maj 100
Ent Req: HS dipl
Degrees: BA & BS 4 yrs
Tuition: Campus res—room & board $1700 per yr
Courses: Art Education, Art History, Ceramics, Commercial Art, Drawing, Painting, Photography, Printmaking, Sculpture
Adult Hobby Classes: Enrl 80; tuition $1700 per yr. Courses—Basic Fundamentals; Painting; Watercolor
Summer School: Dir, Michael Dorsey. Enrl 145. Courses—Art Appreciation, Art History, Ceramics, Drawing, Painting, Photography, Printmaking

MOORHEAD

MISSISSIPPI DELTA JUNIOR COLLEGE, Dept of Fine Arts,* 38761. Tel 601-246-5311. *Chmn* Joseph R Abrams III; *Instr* Jean Abrams
Estab 1926; pub; D & E; SC 11, LC 2; enrl D 68, E 29, maj 28
Ent Req: HS dipl, ent exam
Degrees: AA and AS(Commercial Art) 2 yrs
Courses: Advertising Design, Ceramics, Commercial Art, Drawing, Graphic Arts, Painting, Art Appreciation
Adult Hobby Classes: Enrl 29. Courses—Ceramics, Painting

POPLARVILLE

PEARL RIVER JUNIOR COLLEGE, Fine Arts Dept, Station A, 39470. Tel 601-795-4931. *Chmn* Dr Larry Newell
Estab 1921; pub; D; enrl D 20, non-maj 20
Ent Req: HS dipl
Tuition: Campus residence available
Courses: Art Education, Drafting, Photography

RAYMOND

HINDS JUNIOR COLLEGE, Dept of Art, 39154. Tel 601-857-5261, Ext 302. *Chmn* Bob A Dunaway. Instrs: FT 4
Estab 1917; pub; D & E; SC 5, LC 2; enrl D 400, E 75, maj 60
Ent Req: Ent exam
Degrees: AA 2 yr
Courses: Advertising Design, Ceramics, Commercial Art, Display, Drawing, Graphic Design, Lettering, Painting
Adult Hobby Classes: Courses offered
Children's Classes: Courses offered
Summer School: Courses offered

SCOOBA

EAST MISSISSIPPI JUNIOR COLLEGE, Art Dept,* Box 176, 39358. Tel 601-476-5669. *Staff* Terry Cherry, MA
Estab 1927. College maintains two campuses; pub; D; scholarships; SC 5, LC 1; enrl D 650 total, non-maj 7, maj 9
Ent Req: HS dipl, ACT
Degrees: AA 2 yr
Tuition: Out-of-state—$225; out-of-district—$45; campus res available
Courses: Advertising Design, Commercial Art, Drawing, Painting, Photography, Printmaking

TOUGALOO

TOUGALOO COLLEGE, Art Dept, 39174. Tel 601-956-4941. *Chmn Dept* Ronald Schnell, MFA; *Asst Prof* Bruce O'Hara, MFA
Estab 1869, dept estab 1968; pvt; D; scholarships; SC 14, LC 4; enrl D 800, non-maj 420, maj 28
Ent Req: HS dipl
Degrees: BA and BS 4 yrs
Tuition: Res—undergrad average $2800 per yr
Courses: Art Appreciation, Art Education, Art History, Commercial Art, Drawing, Graphic Arts, History of Art & Archaeology, Painting, Photography, Printmaking, Sculpture, Career Internship, Independant Study, Photo Journalism

UNIVERSITY

UNIVERSITY OF MISSISSIPPI, Dept of Art, 38677. Tel 601-232-7193. *Chmn* Margaret Gorove, MFA; *Prof* Robert L Tettleton, MEd; *Prof* Charles M Gross, MFA; *Prof* Lucy Turnbull, PhD; *Assoc Prof* John L Winters, MFA; *Assoc Prof* Jere H Allen, MFA; *Assoc Prof* Tom Dewey II, PhD; *Asst Prof* Mike Hodges, MFA; *Asst Prof* Maude Wahlman, PhD; *Asst Prof* Ron Dale, MFA; *Asst Prof* Betty Pate, MFA. Instrs: FT 11, PT 4
Dept estab 1949; pub; D; merit scholarships and out-of-state tuition waivers; SC 73, LC 36, GC 46; enrl D 612, non-maj 250, maj 120, grad 15
Ent Req: HS dipl
Degrees: BA 4 yr, BFA 4.5 yr, MFA 2 yr, MA 1 yr
Tuition: Res—undergrad $583.50 per sem, $42 per cr hr, grad $583.50 per sem, $55 per cr hr; nonres—undergrad $1046.50 per sem $81 per cr hr, grad $1046.50 per sem, $91 per cr hr; campus res—room $425
Courses: Advertising Design, Aesthetics, †Art Education, †Art History, †Ceramics, Drawing, Graphic Arts, †Graphic Design, Illustration, †Interior Design, †Painting, †Printmaking, †Sculpture, Watercolor
Summer School: Dr, G Walton. Two 5 wk sessions beginning June. Courses—Art Education, Art History, Ceramics, Design, Drawing, Painting, Printmaking, Sculpture

UTICA

UTICA JUNIOR COLLEGE, Humanities Division,* 39175. Tel 601-885-6062. *Div Head* Dr Bobby Cooper, EdD; *Instructor* Michael McCarty, MFA
Estab 1903, dept estab 1976-77; pub; D & E; SC 9, LC 1; enrl in col 600, non-maj 30, maj 2
Ent Req: HS dipl
Degrees: AA 2 yr
Tuition: $330 per yr
Adult Hobby Classes: Dir, Bobby Cooper
Children's Classes: Dir, Bobby Cooper

MISSOURI

BOLIVAR

SOUTHWEST BAPTIST UNIVERSITY, Art Dept, 623 S Pike, 65613. Tel 417-326-2208. *Chmn* Wesley A Gott, MFA; *Asst Prof* Sandra Brown, MFA; *Spec Instr* Diane Callahan, BFA
Sch estab 1876, dept estab 1974; den; D & E; scholarships offered; SC 30, LC 3; enrl D 150, E 20, maj 35
Ent Req: HS dipl
Degrees: BS & BA
Tuition: Res—undergrad $75 per hr; nonres—undergrad $3500; campus res—room & board $2400 per academic yr
Courses: †Art Education, Art History, †Ceramics, Commercial Art, Costume Design & Construction, †Drawing, Graphic Arts, Graphic Design, Interior Design, †Painting, Photography, Printmaking, †Sculpture, Stage Design, †Teacher Training, Theatre Arts
Summer School: Enrl 600; tuition $75 per hour for 4 wk term beginning in June, also a 4 wk term beginning in July. Courses—Drawing, Painting, Photography

CANTON

CULVER-STOCKTON COLLEGE, Division of Fine Arts, 63435. Tel 314-288-5221. *Head Division* John H Gerber
Estab 1853; pvt; D; scholarships; SC 16, LC 6; enrl 844, maj 30
Ent Req: HS dipl, ACT or Col Board Ent Exam
Degrees: BA(Visual Arts), BS(Art Educ) and BS(Arts Management) 4 yrs
Tuition: $3270 per yr; campus res—room & board $1750
Courses: Aesthetics, Art Education, Ceramics, Costume Design & Construction, Drawing, Film, Graphic Arts, History of Art & Archaeology, Illustration, Jewelry, Museum Staff Training, Painting, Photography, Sculpture, Stage Design, Teacher Training, Theatre Arts
Summer School: Reg, Olga Bays. Tuition $800 for 5 wks, $1600 for 10 wks. Courses—Art Appreciation, Art Education, Ceramics

CAPE GIRARDEAU

SOUTHEAST MISSOURI STATE UNIVERSITY, Dept of Art, Normal Ave, 63701. Tel 314-651-2527. *Chairperson* Bill Needle
Estab 1873, dept estab 1920; pub; D & E; scholarships; SC 28, LC 10, GC 18; enrl D 1300
Ent Req: HS dipl
Degrees: BS, BS(Educ) and BA 4 yrs, MAT
Tuition: Res—$300 per sem; nonres—$590 per sem
Courses: Advertising Design, Art Education, Art History, Ceramics, Commercial Art, Drawing, Handicrafts, History of Art & Archaeology, Illustration, Jewelry, Lettering, Painting, Photography, Printmaking, Sculpture, Silversmithing, Teacher Training
Summer School: Chairperson, Bill Needle. Enrl 164 undergrad, 60 grad; tuition $160 for res, $375 for nonres

COLUMBIA

COLUMBIA COLLEGE, Art Dept,* Christian College Ave, 65216. Tel 314-449-0531. *Assoc Prof* Ben Cameron; *Instructor* Sidney Larson, MA; *Instructor* John Lynch, BS; *Instructor* William J Williams, MFA; *Instructor* Thomas Watson, MFA; *Instructor* Walter Berry, MFA; *Instructor* Kathleen Shanahan, MFA; *Vis Prof* Carl Slaughter, Design. Instrs: FT 8, PT 3
Estab 1851; den; D; scholarships; SC 55, LC 13; enrl D 180, non-maj 80, maj 115
Ent Req: HS dipl or equivalent, ACT or SAT, also accept transfer students
Degrees: AA 2 yrs, BA, BS and BFA 4 yrs
Tuition: $4425 per yr
Courses: †Advertising Design, †Art Education, †Art History, Ceramics, Collages, †Commercial Art, Drawing, †Fashion Arts, Graphic Arts, †Graphic Design, History of Art & Archaeology, Illustration, †Jewelry, Lettering, †Painting, †Photography, †Printmaking, Restoration & Conservation, †Sculpture
Adult Hobby Classes: Enrl 15; tui $75 per cr. Courses—Arts & Crafts, Photography
Summer School: Evening Studies Dir, Dr John Hendricks. Enrl 20; tui $75 per cr hr

STEPHENS COLLEGE, Art Dept,* 65215. Tel 314-442-2211, Ext 302. *Head Dept* Ralph Komives, MFA; *Faculty* L L Luthi, MFA; *Faculty* R Moulton, MFA; *Faculty* M Sleadd, BA; *Faculty* N Stanske, BA; *Faculty* G Williams, MA & MPhil. Instrs: FT 7
Estab 1833, dept estab 1850; pvt; D & E; scholarships; SC 25, LC 6; enrl D 800, maj 100, others 10
Ent Req: SAT or ACT, recommendations, interview
Degrees: BA 3-4 yrs, BFA 3 1/2-4 yrs
Tuition: $7500 per yr; Stephens Col Without Walls $265 per course; campus res—room & board incl in tui
Courses: Advertising Design, Architecture, †Art Education, †Art History, †Ceramics, Commercial Art, Costume Design & Construction, Drafting, Drawing, †Fashion Arts, †Film, Graphic Arts, †Graphic Design, Illustration, †Interior Design, Museum Staff Training, Occupational Therapy, †Painting, †Photography, †Printmaking, †Sculpture, †Stage Design, Teacher Training, †Theatre Arts, †Video
Children's Classes: Tui $900 per yr; Stephens Child Study Center, grades K-3, preschool; includes special creative arts emphasis
Summer School: Dir, Barbara Losty. Tui $1225 for term of 7 wks beginning May 17. Courses—Ceramics, Sculpture, Color, Drawing & Painting, Graphic Design

UNIVERSITY OF MISSOURI
—Art Dept, A 126 Fine Arts, 65201. Tel 314-882-3555. *Chmn* Brooke Cameron, MA. Instrs: FT 12, PT 5
Estab 1901, dept estab 1912; pub; D & E; SC 76, LC 1, GC 53; enrl non-maj 1600 per sem, maj 250, grad 25
Ent Req: HS dipl
Degrees: BFA, BS(Art Educ), MFA(Educ), MEd, DEd, PhD and Educ Specialist
Tuition: Res—$435 per sem; nonres—$870 per sem
Courses: Art Education, Calligraphy, Ceramics, Drawing, Graphic Design, Illustration, Jewelry, Lettering, Painting, Photography, Printmaking, Sculpture, Fibers, Serigraphy, Watercolor
Summer School: Dir, Frank Stack. Enrl 175, tuition $161 for term of 8 wks beginning June 12. Courses—Art Education, Ceramics, Design, Drawing, Jewelry, Printmaking, Sculpture, Watercolor
—Art History and Archaeology Dept, 109 Pickard Hall, 65211. Tel 314-882-6711. *Chmn* Vera Townsend, PhD; *Prof* Osmund Overby, PhD; *Prof* Homer Thomas, PhD; *Prof* William R Biers, PhD; *Assoc Prof* Edward Baumann, PhD; *Assoc Prof* Norman Land, PhD; *Assoc Prof* Albert Leonard, PhD; *Assoc Prof* Patricia Crown, PhD; *Asst Prof* Kathleen Slane, PhD; *Adj Prof* Howard Marshall, PhD
Estab 1839, dept estab 1915; pub; D; scholarships; LC 32, GC 16; enrl D 1071
Ent Req: HS dipl, SAT, GRE for grad students
Degrees: BA 4 yrs, MA 2-3 yrs, PhD 4 yrs
Tuition: Res—grad $162 per course; nonres—grad $1288; campus res available
Courses: †Art History, History of Art & Archaeology, Museum Staff Training, Historic Preservation, Humanities
Summer School: Courses offered

FERGUSON

SAINT LOUIS COMMUNITY COLLEGE AT FLORISSANT VALLEY, Dept of Art, 3400 Pershall Rd, 63135. Tel 314-595-4365. *Chairperson Dept* Richard Buckman, MA; *Prof* Edward Menges, MFA; *Prof* Frank Stanton, MFA; *Prof* Charles J Jones, MFA; *Prof* Larry Kozuszek, MFA; *Assoc Prof* George Bartko, MFA; *Asst Prof* Kim Mosley, MFA; *Asst Prof* John Ortbals, MFA; *Asst Prof* Kermit Ruyle, BA; *Asst Prof* Michael Aehle, MAT
Estab 1962; pub; D & E; SC 36, LC 4; enrl maj 70
Ent Req: HS dipl, ent exam
Degrees: AA, AAS 2 yr
Tuition: Res—$20.50 per cr hr; nonres—$38.50 per cr hr; no campus res
Courses: †Advertising Design, Art History, Ceramics, Commercial Art, Drawing, History of Art & Archaeology, Illustration, Lettering, Painting, Photography, Printmaking, Sculpture, Technical Illustration
Summer School: Dir, Richard Buckman. Enrl 270; tuition $20.50 per cr hr for term of 8 wks beginning June 9. Courses—Design, Drawing, Figure Drawing, Lettering, Painting

FULTON

WILLIAM WOODS-WESTMINSTER COLLEGES, Art Dept, William Woods College, 65251. Tel 314-642-2251, Ext 323. *Chmn Div Fine Arts & Head Art Dept* George E Tutt, MA; *Assoc Prof* Paul Clervi, MA; *Asst Prof* Roger Bowman; *Instructor* Rodney Casebier, MA; *Emeritus Prof* George Latta, MFA; *Artist-in-Residence* Wayne Sullivant, MFA
Estab 1870; pvt; D; scholarships; SC 54, LC 6; enrl maj 71
Ent Req: HS dipl, SAT or ACT
Degrees: BA, BS and BFA 4 yr
Tuition: Res—$6100 per yr (incl room and board); nonres—$4160 per yr; campus

res—room and board $1790
Courses: Aesthetics, Art Education, Art History, Ceramics, Collages, Commercial Art, Costume Design & Construction, Drawing, Handicrafts, History of Art & Archaeology, Illustration, Interior Design, Jewelry, Painting, Photography, Printmaking, Sculpture, Silversmithing, Stage Design, Teacher Training, Theatre Arts, Weaving, Art Therapy

HANNIBAL

HANNIBAL LA GRANGE COLLEGE, Art Dept,* College Heights, 63401. Tel 314-221-3675. *Chmn* Mary Wiehe; *Instr* Robert L Skaggs, MSE
Scholarships offered
Degrees: AA
Tuition: $1390 per sem
Courses: Advertising Design, Art Appreciation, Art Education, Art History, Calligraphy, Ceramics, Design, Drawing, Fashion Arts, Handicrafts, Jewelry, Painting, Printmaking, Sculpture, Textile Design, Cartooning

JEFFERSON CITY

LINCOLN UNIVERSITY, Dept Fine Arts,* 820 Chestnut St, 65102. Tel 314-751-2325, Ext 333. *Fine Arts Chmn* John A Taylor; *Asst Prof* Jas Tatum; *Instr* John S Bator. Instrs: FT 2, PT 1
Estab 1927; pub; enrl maj 35, others 100
Degrees: BS(Art) and BS(Art Educ) 4 yr
Tuition: Res—$300; nonres—$600
Courses: Teacher Training, Applied Art
Summer School: Courses—same as above

JOPLIN

MISSOURI SOUTHERN STATE COLLEGE, Dept Fine Art,* Newman & Duquesne Rds, 64801. Tel 417-624-8100, Ext 263. *Dir Dept* Jon H Fowler, MFA. Instrs: FT 4
Estab 1937; pub; D & E; scholarships; SC 22, LC 3; enrl D 425, E 83, non-maj 360, maj 105, others 10 (over sixty)
Ent Req: HS dipl
Degrees: BA & BSE 4 yrs
Tuition: Res—$235 for 8 cr hrs or more, $21 per cr hr; nonres—$470 for 8 cr hrs or more, $37 per cr hr
Courses: Art Education, Art History, Ceramics, Drawing, Jewelry, Painting, Printmaking, Sculpture, Metal Casting, Studio Crafts
Adult Hobby Classes: Enrl approx 30; tui $1 per hr. Courses—Photography, Tole, plus others. Offered by Continuing Educ Div
Summer School: Dir Art, Darral A Dishman. Enrl 15-20 per workshop; tui res $17 per cr hr, nonres $27 per cr hr for term of 2 wks beginning June. Courses—Arts & Crafts, Drawing, Jewelry, Pottery, Printmaking, Watercolor, and others

KANSAS CITY

AVILA COLLEGE, Art Division, Dept of Performing and Visual Art, 11901 Wornall Rd, 64145. Tel 816-942-8400. *Coordr* Myron Brody, MFA; *Assoc Prof* Sr Colette Doering, MA; *Instructor* Peter Perdairs, PhD; *Instructor* Diane Covert, MPA; *Instructor* Joel Vogt, MA; *Instructor* Carol Zastoupil, MFA; *Instructor* Steven Hill, BFA
Estab 1963; den; D & E; scholarships; SC 35, LC 4; enrl D 140, E 20, non-maj 120, maj 40
Ent Req: HS dipl, SAT and PSAT
Degrees: BA 4 yrs
Tuition: $4200 per yr; D $130 per cr hr, E $75 per cr hr
Courses: Art Education, Ceramics, Drawing, Painting, Photography
Adult Hobby Classes: Courses offered

KANSAS CITY ART INSTITUTE, 4415 Warwick Blvd, 64111. Tel 816-561-4852. *Interim Pres* Richard W Dodderidge; *Chmn Crafts* Kenneth Ferguson, MFA; *Chmn Design* Roger Funk; *Chmn Painting & Printmaking* Wilbur Niewald, MFA; *Chmn Photography* Reed Estabrook, MFA; *Chmn Sculpture* Dale Eldred, MFA; *Chmn Found* Steven Whitacre, MFA; *Chmn Liberal Arts* George Burris, MA
Estab 1885; D & E; scholarships; maj areas 7, LC 104 in liberal arts; enrl D 450, maj 450
Ent Req: HS dipl, portfolio interview
Degrees: BFA 4 yr
Tuition: $5100 per yr, $3075 per sem, $240 per cr hr; campus res—room $1255 per yr (double occupancy)
Courses: Art History, †Ceramics, Commercial Art, †Design, †Drawing, Film, Graphic Arts, †Graphic Design, †Illustration, †Industrial Design, Interior Design, Mixed Media, †Painting, †Photography, †Printmaking, †Sculpture, †Video, †Textile
Adult Hobby Classes: Enrl 250; tuition $185 per cr hr for 14 wk term. Courses—Ceramics, Design, Fiber, Liberal Arts, Painting, Printmaking, Photography
Children's Classes: Enrl 150; tuition $75 per 12 wk term. Courses—Ceramics, Design, Drawing, Fiber, Painting, Photography
Summer School: Dir, Allen Jenks. Enrl 120; tuition $185 per cr hr for 4 wk session. Courses—various

MAPLE WOODS COMMUNITY COLLEGE, Dept of Art and Art History, 2601 NE Barry Rd, 64156. Tel 816-436-6500, Ext 179. *Head Dept* Helen Mary Turner, MSecEd. Instrs: PT 6
Estab 1969; pub; D & E; scholarships; SC 12, LC 2; enrl D 125, E & Sat 80
Ent Req: HS dipl or GED
Degrees: AA 2 yrs
Tuition: District res—$20 per cr hr, max $300 per sem; nonres district—$27 per cr hr, max $405 per sem; nonres state—$47 per cr hr, max $705 per sem
Courses: Art History, Ceramics, Commercial Art, Drawing, Painting, Photography, Printmaking, Sculpture, Art Fundamentals, Stained Glass

Adult Hobby Classes: Enrl 30; tuition same as above. Courses same as above
Children's Classes: Summer classes; enrl 30; tuition $30 for 6 wks
Summer School: Dir, Helen Mary Turner. Tuition same as above for 8 wks beginning June 1. Courses—Drawing, Painting, Ceramics

PENN VALLEY COMMUNITY COLLEGE, Art Dept,* 3201 SW Trafficway, 64111. Tel 816-932-7600. *Chmn* Carder Manning
Scholarships offered
Degrees: AA
Tuition: District res—$19 per sem hr; non-district res—$26 per sem hr; non-state res—$36 per sem hr
Courses: Advertising Design, Art Appreciation, Art History, Calligraphy, Ceramics, Design, Drawing, Fashion Arts, Film, Painting, Photography, Printmaking, Sculpture, Video, Animation, Cartooning

UNIVERSITY OF MISSOURI-KANSAS CITY, Dept of Art and Art History, 5100 Rockhill Rd, 64110. Tel 816-276-1501. *Chmn* Louis M Cicotello. Instrs: FT 13, PT 2
Estab 1933; pub; D & E; enrl maj 210
Ent Req: Contact Admis Office
Tuition: Res—undergrad $647, grad $801; nonres—undergrad $1823, grad $2089
Courses: Art Education, Art History, Drawing, Graphic Design, Painting, Photography, Printmaking, Sculpture, Video, Computer Graphics
Summer School: Chmn, Louis M Cicotello

KIRKSVILLE

NORTHEAST MISSOURI STATE UNIVERSITY, Art Dept,* Division of Fine Arts, 63501. Tel 816-665-5121, Ext 7196. *Head Div Fine Arts* Dean Dale Jorgenson
Estab 1867; pub; D & E; scholarships; SC 27, LC 8, GC 8; enrl D 220, non-maj 45, maj 175, grad 12
Ent Req: HS dipl, portfolio
Degrees: BSE(Art Educ) and BA(Commercial, Studio) 4 yrs, MA(Art Educ) 5 yrs
Tuition: Res—$20 per sem hr; nonres—$40 per sem hr
Courses: Advertising Design, Aesthetics, †Art Education, Art History, Ceramics, †Commercial Art, Constructions, Drawing, †Graphic Arts, Graphic Design, Handicrafts, Illustration, Lettering, Museum Staff Training, †Painting, Photography, †Printmaking, †Sculpture, †Teacher Training, Textile Design, Macrame
Adult Hobby Classes: Enrl 35; tui free. Courses—Art Appreciation for Sr Citizens
Summer School: Enrl 80-100; Term of two 5 wk sessions beginning June & July

LIBERTY

WILLIAM JEWELL COLLEGE, Art Dept, College Hill, 64068. Tel 816-781-3806. *Chmn* David B Johnson, MFA; *Instructor* Phil Masin, BFA; *Instructor* Marilyn Jones, MFA; *Instructor* Rebecca Koop, BFA
Estab 1849, dept estab 1966; pvt (cooperates with the Missouri Baptist Convention); D & E; enrl D 120, E 35-40, maj 20
Degrees: BA & BS 4 yrs
Tuition: $5600 (incl room & board)
Courses: Art Education, Art History, Calligraphy, Ceramics, Drawing, Jewelry, Painting, Photography, Printmaking
Adult Hobby Classes: Courses—Calligraphy, Drawing & Painting, Photography
Children's Classes: Courses—Ceramics, Drawing & Painting, Printmaking
Summer School: Courses vary

MARYVILLE

NORTHWEST MISSOURI STATE UNIVERSITY, Dept of Art, 64468. Tel 816-582-7141, Ext 1314. *Chmn Dept* Lee Hageman, MFA; *Assoc Prof* Donald Robertson, MA; *Assoc Prof* Robert Sunkel, MFA; *Assoc Prof* Philip VanVoorst, MFA; *Asst Prof* Kenneth Nelsen, MFA; *Asst Prof* Russell Schmaljohn, MS; *Asst Prof* Norman Weil, MFA; *Asst Prof* Philip Laker, MFA
Estab 1905, dept estab 1915; pub; D & E; scholarships; SC 74, LC 19; enrl D 450, E 50, non-maj 350, maj 150
Ent Req: HS dipl
Degrees: BFA, BSE & BA 4 yrs
Tuition: Res—$275 per sem, $31 per hr; nonres—$465 per sem, $52 per hr; campus res $250 (room only)
Courses: †Art Education, Art History, Ceramics, Drawing, Goldsmithing, Jewelry, Painting, Photography, Printmaking, Sculpture, Silversmithing, Teacher Training, Fibers, Metalsmithing, Pewtersmithing
Summer School: Chmn Dept Art, Lee Hageman. Two week short courses varying from summer to summer; cost is hourly rate listed above. Courses—Ceramics, Photography, Watercolor, Weaving

NEOSHO

CROWDER COLLEGE, Dept of Art, 64850. Tel 417-451-3223. *Instructor* Richard Boyt. Instrs: FT 1, PT 7
Estab 1964; Pub; D & E; scholarships; enrl D 1000, E 300, maj 15, others 100
Ent Req: HS grad or equivalent
Degrees: AA & AAS 2 yrs
Courses: Art History, Ceramics, Commercial Art, Drawing, Jewelry, Painting, Photography, Sculpture, Design, Foundry, Introduction to Visual Arts, Quilting, Weaving
Summer School: Dean of Col, J Cavanough. Term of 8 wks beginning in June. Courses—Varied academic courses

NEVADA

COTTEY COLLEGE, Fine Arts Division,* 64772. Tel 417-667-8181. *Dean of Col* Earl M Tinsley; *Instr* James Hurt, MFA; *Instr* Robert S Lawrence, MS; *Instr* Donna Lynde, MFA. Instrs: FT 3
Estab 1884; pvt, W; D; SC 15, LC 4; enrl maj 12-15, total 369
Ent Req: HS grad, AC Board
Degrees: AA 2 yrs
Tuition: $1100 annual tuition
Courses: Art History, Ceramics, Drawing, Graphic Arts, Handicrafts, Jewelry, Painting, Photography, Printmaking, Design, Metals, Weaving

PARKVILLE

PARK COLLEGE, Dept of Art, 64152. Tel 816-741-2000, Ext 158. *Assoc Prof* Mel Kauila Clark, MEA
Estab 1875; pvt; D & E; SC 13, LC 4; enrl D 50, non-maj 40, maj 11
Ent Req: HS dipl, ACT
Degrees: BA, 4 yrs
Tuition: Res—undergrad $60 per hr; campus res—room & board
Courses: Advertising Design, Art Appreciation, Art History, Ceramics, Costume Design & Construction, Drawing, History of Art & Archaeology, Lettering, Painting, Photography, Sculpture, Teacher Training, Theatre Arts, 3-D Design
Adult Hobby Classes: Tuition $60 per hr
Summer School: Dir, Mel Kauila Clark. Tuition $60 per hr

POINT LOOKOUT

SCHOOL OF THE OZARKS, Dept of Art, 65726. Tel 417-334-6411, Ext 253. *Prof & Chmn* Kenneth E Burchett, PhD; *Assoc Prof* Donald Barr, MA; *Assoc Prof* Jayme Burchett, MFA; *Asst Prof* Anne Allman, PhD; *Asst Prof* Jeff Johnston, MFA
Estab 1906, dept estab 1962; pvt; D & E; scholarships; SC 22, LC 4; enrl D 200, E 25, non-maj 180, maj 40
Ent Req: HS dipl, ACT
Degrees: BA & BS 4 yr
Tuition: No fees are charged; each student works 960 hrs in on-campus employment
Courses: †Art Education, Art History, †Ceramics, †Drawing, †Painting, †Printmaking, †Sculpture, Textile Design, †Teacher Training, Color, †Fibers, Glass

SAINT CHARLES

LINDENWOOD COLLEGES, Art Dept, 63301. Tel 314-946-6912, Ext 240. *Chmn Dept* W Dean Eckert. Instrs: FT 3, PT 2
Estab 1827; pvt; D & E; scholarships; SC 24, LC 16; enrl D 200, E 30, maj 30
Ent Req: HS dipl, ent exam
Degrees: BA, BS, BFA 4 yrs, MA
Courses: Art Education, Art History, Ceramics, Design, Drawing, Painting, Photography, Printmaking, Teacher Training

SAINT JOSEPH

MISSOURI WESTERN STATE COLLEGE, Art Dept,* 4525 Downs Dr, 64507. Tel 816-271-4200, Ext 422. *Chmn Dept* Jane Nelson, MFA; *Assoc Prof* John Hughes, MFA; *Assoc Prof* Jim Estes, MFA; *Asst Prof* Jean Harmon, MFA; *Asst Prof* William Eickhorst, EdD
Estab 1969; pub; D & E; scholarships; SC 25, LC 8; enrl D 355, E 100, non-maj 120, maj 70
Ent Req: HS dipl, GED, ACT
Degrees: BS(Art Educ) and BA 4 yrs
Tuition: Res—$440 per sem; nonres—$835 per sem; campus residence available
Courses: Art Education, Art History, Ceramics, Drawing, Jewelry, Mixed Media, Painting, Photography, Printmaking, Sculpture, Art Appreciation, Design, Tools and Techniques
Summer School: Chmn, Art Dept, John T Hughes. Tui res—$130 for 5 or more cr hrs, non-res—$240 for 5 or more cr hrs; term of 8 wks beginning June 1. Courses—Art Education, Ceramics, Introduction to Art, Photomedia, Painting

SAINT LOUIS

FONTBONNE COLLEGE, Art Dept, 6800 Wydown Blvd, Clayton, 63105. Tel 314-862-3456, Ext 296. *Chmn Dept* Rudolph E Torrini, MFA
Estab 1923; pvt; D & E; scholarships; SC 10, LC 2, GC 6; enrl non-maj 10, maj 46, grad 12, others 5
Ent Req: HS dipl, portfolio
Degrees: BA and BFA 4 yrs, MA 1 yr, MFA 2 yrs
Courses: Aesthetics, Art Education, Art History, †Ceramics, Drawing, Interior Design, Mixed Media, †Painting, Photography, Printmaking, †Sculpture

MARYVILLE COLLEGE, ST LOUIS, Art Division, 13550 Conway Rd, 63141. Tel 314-576-9300, Ext 413. *Art Division Chmn* Steven Teczar, MA; *Prof* B Kent Addison, MA; *Prof* Rodney M Winfield; *Prof* Charles F Jamieson, MFA; *Assoc Prof* Virginia O'Meara, MA; *Assoc Prof* Nancy Rice, MFA; *Adjunct Instr* Catherine Waymeyer; *Adjunct Instr* Jerry Pruce; *Adjunct Instr* Clay Pursell; *Adjunct Instr* Roy Zingrich, AIA; *Adjunct Instr* Mark Weber; *Adjunct Instr* Esley Hamilton; *Adjunct Instr* Elizabeth Metcalfe; *Adjunct Instr* Randall Choate, ASID; *Adjunct Instr* Cynthia Kistner, ASID; *Adjunct Instr* Muriel Eulich; *Adjunct Instr* Lorraine Briggs
Estab 1872, dept estab 1961; pvt; D & E; scholarships; SC 74, LC 6; enrl D 150, E 30, non-maj 60, maj 120
Ent Req: HS dipl, ACT or SAT
Degrees: BA, BFA, cert(Interior Design), MA, MS
Tuition: $4500 per yr, $2250 per sem, $150 per cr hr; campus res—room & board $2310 per yr
Courses: Art History, Calligraphy, †Ceramics, Drafting, †Drawing, Graphic Arts,

Graphic Design, †Interior Design, †Painting, Photography, †Printmaking, †Sculpture, Art Therapy, Art Studio, Color Theory, Furniture Design, †Therapeutic Art, 2-D Design, 3-D Design
Adult Hobby Classes: Enrl 30. Courses—Photography, Art and Architectural History, Interior Design
Summer School: Assoc Dean, Joe Dyer. Enrl 60; tuition same as regular year. Courses—Photography, Art Appreciation, Drawing, 2-D Design, Design & Color Theory

SAINT LOUIS COMMUNITY COLLEGE AT FOREST PARK, Fine Arts Dept,* 5600 Oakland, 63110. Tel 314-644-9350. *Chmn* James Hogan; *Assoc Prof* Leon Anderson, MFA; *Assoc Prof* Mary L Fifield, MFA; *Asst Prof* Katie Knight, MAEd. Instrs: PT 12
Estab 1962, dept estab 1963. College maintains three campuses; pub; D & E; scholarships; SC 36, LC 6; enrl D 200, E 100, non-maj 75, maj 75
Ent Req: HS dipl
Degrees: AA & AAS 2 yrs
Tuition: College area—$20.50 per cr hr; out of area—$28.50 per cr hr; nonres—$38.50 per cr hr
Courses: Advertising Design, Art History, Ceramics, †Commercial Art, Drawing, Graphic Design, Illustration, Lettering, Painting, Photography, Printmaking, Color, Design
Adult Hobby Classes: Courses—Drawing, Painting, Photgraphy
Summer School: Dir, Mary L Fifield. Enrl 100; tuition $20.50 per cr hr. Courses—Same as those above

SAINT LOUIS COMMUNITY COLLEGE AT MERAMEC, Art Dept, 11333 Big Bend Blvd, 63122. Tel 314-966-7632. *Chmn Dept* David Durham, BFA; *Instructor* F Robert Allen, MFA; *Instructor* John Ferguson; *Instructor* Kay Hagan, MA; *Instructor* Ruth Hensler, MFA; *Instructor* Peter Hoell, BFA; *Instructor* John Nagel, BA; *Instructor* Patrick Shuck, MFA; *Instructor* Mary Sprague, AM; *Instructor* Ronald Thomas, MFA; *Instructor* Sam Wayne, MA; *Instructor* Yvette Woods, BFA; *Instructor* Patrick Morain
Estab 1964; D & E; scholarships; SC 15, LC 2
Ent Req: HS dipl
Degrees: AA 2 yrs
Tuition: $22.50 per cr hr; no campus res
Courses: Advertising Design, Art History, Ceramics, Commercial Art, Drawing, Illustration, Interior Design, Painting, Photography, Printmaking, Sculpture
Summer School: Chmn Dept, David Durham. Tuition $22.50 per cr hr for term of 8 wks beginning June 11. Courses—Art Appreciation, Ceramics, Drawing, Design, Photography

SAINT LOUIS UNIVERSITY, Art & Art History Dept, 221 N Grand, 63103. Tel 314-658-3030. *Chmn* Mary Gutenschwager
Scholarships offered
Degrees: BA, MA
Tuition: Undergrad $2,495 full-time per term, $187 part-time per hr; grad $187 per hr
Courses: Art Appreciation, Art Education, †Art History, Design, Drawing, Painting, †Studio Art
Summer School: Courses—Studio Art, Drawings, Painting

UNIVERSITY OF MISSOURI-SAINT LOUIS, Art Dept, 8001 Natural Bridge, 63121. Tel 314-453-5975. *Chairperson Dept* Michael D Taylor, PhD; *Assoc Prof* Sylvia Solochek Walters, MFA; *Assoc Prof* Janet Berlo; *Asst Prof* Thomas Patton; *Asst Prof* Thomas Pickrel; *Asst Prof* Ruth Bohar
Estab 1963; pub; D & E; Scholarships; SC 7, LC 20; enrl maj 40
Ent Req: HS dipl
Degrees: BA(Art Hist)
Tuition: $380 per sem; no campus res
Courses: Art History, Graphic Design, History of Art & Archaeology, Painting, Printmaking
Adult Hobby Classes: Courses—Photography
Summer School: Courses—Introduction to Art, Primitive Art

WASHINGTON UNIVERSITY
—**School of Fine Arts,** Lindell and Skinker, 63130. Tel 314-889-6500. *Dean School* Roger DesRosiers, MFA; *Assoc Dean School* Kim Strommen, MFA; *Chairperson 3-D Dept* James Sterritt, MA; *Chairperson Two-Dimensional Dept* Peter Marcus, MFA; *Chairperson Design Dept* Robert Smith, BFA
Estab 1853; pvt; D; scholarships; SC 62, LC 10, GC 31; enrl 390, non-maj 50, maj 300, grad 40
Ent Req: HS dipl, SAT or ACT, portfolio
Degrees: BFA 4 yrs, MFA 2 yrs
Tuition: $7900 per yr, $3950 per sem, $330 per cr hr; campus res—room & board $3224 per yr
Courses: †Advertising Design, Aesthetics, Architecture, Art Education, Art History, Calligraphy, †Ceramics, Commercial Art, †Conceptual Art, Costume Design & Construction, Drawing, †Fashion Arts, Goldsmithing, Graphic Arts, †Graphic Design, History of Art & Archaeology, †Illustration, Intermedia, †Jewelry, Lettering, Mixed Media, †Painting, †Photography, †Printmaking, †Sculpture, †Silversmithing, Teacher Training, Textile Design, Theatre Arts, Video, Glassblowing
Adult Hobby Classes: Courses—Basic Design, Drawing, Calligraphy, Graphic Design, Painting, Metalsmithing
Children's Classes: Sat and summer classes for high school students
Summer School: Assoc Dean, Kim Strommen. Courses—Drawing, Graphic Communications
—**School of Architecture,** Box 1079, 63130. Tel 314-889-6200. *Dean School* C Michaelides, MArch
Estab 1910; pvt; D; scholarships; SC 28, LC 58, GC 42; enrl 330, maj 210, grad 120
Degrees: BA(Arch), MArch & Urban Design, MArch
Tuition: $7900 per yr; campus res—room & board tui varies
Courses: †Architecture
Adult Hobby Classes: Enrl 77; tuition $90 per unit. University College certificate program, Bachelor of Technology in Architecture
Summer School: Tuition varies. Courses—Advanced Architectural Design, Fundamentals of Design, Structural Principles

SPRINGFIELD

DRURY COLLEGE, Art, Art History and Architecture Dept, 65802. Tel 417-865-8731, Ext 263. *Chmn Dept* Thomas Parker. Instrs: FT 6, PT 9
Estab 1873; den; scholarships; SC 12, LC 5; enrl 2246
Degrees: 4 yrs
Tuition: $3875
Courses: Architecture, Art History, Commercial Art, Photography, Teacher Training, Studio Arts
Adult Hobby Classes: Courses offered
Summer School: Dir, Thomas Parker. Enrl 206; term of 8 weeks. Courses same as regular session

SOUTHWEST MISSOURI STATE UNIVERSITY, Dept of Art, 901 S National, 65804. Tel 417-836-5110. *Head Dept* Norman Annis. Instrs: FT 23, PT 5
Estab 1901; D & E; scholarships; SC 31, LC 14; enrl maj 325, others 1700
Ent Req: HS dipl, ent exam
Degrees: BFA, BS(Educ, Educ Comprehensive) & BA 4 yrs
Tuition: Res—$432; nonres—$792; campus res—$670 or $775 per sem
Courses: Art Education, Art History, Ceramics, Drawing, Graphic Design, Jewelry, Painting, Photography, Printmaking, Sculpture, Silversmithing, Fibers, Bronze Casting
Adult Hobby Classes: Drawing, Painting, Photography
Summer School: Dir, Dean Russell Keeling. Enr 3500; special workshops available during summer session; tuition $36 per cr hr for 5 & 8 wk sessions. Courses—Selected from above curriculum

UNION

EAST CENTRAL JUNIOR COLLEGE, Art Dept,* PO Box 529, 63084. Tel 314-583-5193. *Chmn* Larry Pogue, BFA & MS. Instrs: FT 1, PT 6
Estab 1968; pub; D & E; scholarships; SC 8, LC 8; enrl D 370, E 120, maj 37
Ent Req: HS dipl, ent exam
Degrees: AA & AAS 2 yrs
Tuition: In-district—$16 per cr hr; out-of-district—$26 per cr hr; nonres—$38 per cr hr
Courses: Art Education, Design, Drawing, Handicrafts, Lettering, Painting, Photography, Printmaking, Sculpture, Art Appreciation, Figure Drawing, Layout, Watercolor
Adult Hobby Classes: Courses—Painting
Children's Classes: Childrens Summer Art Program
Summer School: Courses—Art Appreciation, Painting

WARRENSBURG

CENTRAL MISSOURI STATE UNIVERSITY, Art Dept, 64093. Tel 816-429-4480. *Chair Dept* Richard D Monson, MFA; *Asst Prof* John R Haydu, MFA; *Asst Prof* Margaret Peterson, MFA; *Asst Prof* Harold M Reynolds, EdD; *Asst Prof* George Sample, MSEd; *Asst Prof* Stephen Phillips, MFA; *Asst Prof* Andrew Katsourides, MFA; *Asst Prof* Lillian Sung, MFA; *Instr* Raeford W Lewis, MA
Estab 1871; pub; D & E; scholarships; SC 40, LC 14, GC 7; enrl D 272, maj 272
Ent Req: HS dipl, Missouri School & Col Ability Test, ACT
Degrees: BA, BSE, and BFA 4 yrs, MSE & MA 1 yr
Tuition: Res—$210 per quarter; nonres—$435 per quarter; campus res—room & board $582
Courses: †Art Education, †Art History, Calligraphy, †Commercial Art, Drawing, Graphic Arts, Illustration, †Interior Design, †Painting, †Printmaking, †Sculpture, Teacher Training
Summer School: Chair Dept, Richard D Monson. Term of 8 wks beginning first wk in June. Courses—Ceramics, Drawing, Grad Studio Courses, Painting

WEBSTER GROVES

WEBSTER COLLEGE, Art Dept,* 470 E Lockwood Blvd, 63119. Tel 314-968-7000, 968-6900. *Chairperson Dept* Kathleen J Regier, PhD; *Assoc Prof* Jack Canepa, MA; *Assoc Prof* Leon Hicks, MFA; *Assoc Prof* Sr Gabriel Mary Hoare, MA; *Assoc Prof* Thomas Lang, MFA; *Assoc Prof* Phil Sultz, BFA; *Asst Prof* Susan Hacker, MFA; *Instructor* John Ruppert, MFA; *Lectr* Jan Sultz, MFA
Estab 1915, dept estab 1946; pvt; D & E; scholarships; SC 60, LC 15; enrl 424, non-maj 318, maj 100
Ent Req: HS dipl, SAT or ACT
Degrees: BA & BFA 4 yrs
Tuition: $3900 per yr; campus res available
Courses: †Art Education, †Art History, †Ceramics, Collages, Conceptual Art, †Drawing, Film, †Painting, †Photography, †Printmaking, †Sculpture, Teacher Training, Papermaking
Summer School: Undergrad Dean, Charles Madden. Tuition $112 per cr hr for term of 6 or 8 wks beginning June 19. Courses vary each summer

MONTANA

BILLINGS

EASTERN MONTANA COLLEGE, Art Dept,* 1500 N 30th St, 59101. Tel 406-657-2324. *Head* Alan K Newberg. Instrs: FT 6, PT 8
Estab 1927; pub
Ent Req: HS dipl
Degrees: AA, BS(Educ), BSEd(Art), BA(Lib Arts), BA(Art Therapy)
Tuition: Res—$13.50 per cr hr; nonres—$33 per cr hr
Courses: Art History, Ceramics, Commercial Art, Drawing, Graphic Arts, Jewelry, Lettering, Painting, Photography, Sculpture, Crafts, Design, Fibers, Metalwork
Summer School: Usually 6 courses with emphasis on studio courses and teacher training

ROCKY MOUNTAIN COLLEGE, Art Dept, 1511 Poly Dr, 59102. Tel 406-657-1094. *Chmn Dept* Robert Morrison, MA; *Assoc Prof* Kathleen Joyce, PhD
Estab 1878, dept estab 1957; pvt; D; scholarships; SC 12, LC 5; enrl 112, non-maj 40, maj 30, others 5
Ent Req: HS dipl, ACT
Degrees: BA & BS 4 yrs
Tuition: $2900 per yr, $1450 per sem, $105 per sem hr; campus res—room & board $1750 per yr
Courses: Art Education, Art History, Ceramics, Drawing, Graphic Arts, Graphic Design, Illustration, Painting, Photography, Printmaking, Sculpture, Stage Design, Teacher Training
Adult Hobby Classes: Enrl 100; tuition $20 for 5 wks. Courses—Crafts, Painting, Picture Framing

BOZEMAN

MONTANA STATE UNIVERSITY
—**School of Art,*** Haynes Hall, 59717. Tel 406-994-4501. *Dir Art* John Catterall, MFA
Estab 1893; pub; D; SC 38, LC 19, GC 13; enrl maj 300, grad 19
Ent Req: HS dipl
Degrees: BA 4 yrs, MFA 2 yrs
Tuition: Res—$674 per qtr; nonres—$2042 per qtr
Courses: †Art Education, †Art History, †Ceramics, Drawing, †Graphic Design, Interior Design, Jewelry, Painting
Summer School: Dir, Dr Rex Dayl. Courses—vary each summer according to demand
—**School of Architecture,*** Creative Arts Complex, 59717. Tel 406-994-4255. *Dir Architecture* Robert C Utzinger. Instrs: FT 14, PT 1
Pub; LabC 15, LC 14; enrl maj 374
Degrees: BArchit 5 yrs
Tuition: Res—$674 per qtr; nonres—$2042 per qtr; campus res available
Courses: Architecture
Summer School: Dir, Robert C Utzinger

DILLON

WESTERN MONTANA COLLEGE, Art Dept, 710 S Atlantic, 59725. Tel 406-683-7312. *Chmn Dept* Don Walters. Instrs: FT 3
Estab 1897; pub; D & E; scholarships; SC 15, LC 6, GC 21
Ent Req: HS dipl
Degrees: BS 4 yrs, MA
Courses: Art Education, Art History, Ceramics, Commercial Art, Drawing, Graphic Arts, Handicrafts, Jewelry, Lettering, Painting, Photography, Sculpture, Design, Glass Blowing, Stained Glass, Weaving
Summer School: Dir, Dr Lee Spuhler. Tuition res $366.50, nonres $966 per 15 wk term

GREAT FALLS

COLLEGE OF GREAT FALLS, Dept of Art,* 1301 20th St S, 59405. Tel 406-452-9584, 761-8210. *Dean of Studies* Dr Charles M Hepburn; *Div Chmn* Dr Timothy O'Hare. Instrs: FT 2, PT 2
Estab 1933; den; D & E; SC, Lab C, LC; enrl approx 1250
Degrees: 4 yrs
Tuition: $2850 per yr
Courses: Art Education, Ceramics, Drawing, Handicrafts, Jewelry, Painting, Photography, Printmaking, Sculpture, Silversmithing, Textile Design, Design
Summer School: Dir, Richard Gretch; 6 wks

HAVRE

NORTHERN MONTANA COLLEGE, Dept of Art and Languages,* 59501. Tel 406-265-7821. *Art Dept Chairperson* Mary Engle, PhD
Estab 1929; pub; D & E; scholarships; SC 15, LC 5, GC 9; enrl D 425, grad 7
Ent Req: HS dipl
Degrees: AA 2 yrs, BS(Educ) and BA 4 yrs, MSc(Educ)
Tuition: Res—$209 per quarter; nonres—$569 per quarter
Courses: Art Education, Ceramics, Commercial Art, Drafting, Drawing, Graphic Arts, Painting, Sculpture, Teacher Training
Summer School: Dir, Dr J Callahan. Enrl 900 col, 47 art classes; term of 8 wks. Courses—Art Appreciation, Art Therapy, Art Education, Ceramics

MILES CITY

MILES COMMUNITY COLLEGE, Dept of Fine Arts and Humanities, 2715 Dickinson St, 59301. Tel 406-232-3031. *Head Dept* Sydney R Sonneborn, MA; *Instructor* Fred McKee, MFA
Estab 1937, dept estab 1967; pub; D & E; scholarships; SC 17, LC 1; enrl D 36, E 23, non-maj 55, maj 4
Ent Req: HS dipl, ACT
Degrees: AA 2 yrs, cert
Tuition: Res—$420 per yr; nonres—$870 per yr; campus res available
Courses: Advertising Design, Ceramics, Drawing, Jewelry, Painting, Photography, Stage Design, Teacher Training, Theatre Arts
Adult Hobby Classes: Enrl 39; tuition $33 per cr hr. Courses—Crafts, Jewelry Making, Painting, Photography, Pottery

MISSOULA

UNIVERSITY OF MONTANA, Dept of Art, 59812. Tel 406-243-4181. *Chmn Dept* James Todd, MFA; *Prof* Rudy Autio, MFA; *Prof* Don Bunse, MFA; *Prof* James Dew, MA; *Assoc Prof* Stephen Connell, MA; *Assoc Prof* Richard Reinholtz, MEd; *Asst Prof* Julie F Codell, PhD; *Asst Prof* Marilyn Bruya, MA; *Asst Prof* Dennis Voss, MFA
Pub; D & E; SC 28, LC 20, GC 10; enrl D 850, E 30
Ent Req: HS dipl
Degrees: BA & BFA 4 yrs, MA & MFA
Tuition: Res—$317 per quarter (12-18 cr hrs); nonres—$833 per quarter (12-18 cr hrs)
Courses: †Art Education, Art History, †Ceramics, †Drawing, Jewelry, Lettering, †Painting, Photography, †Printmaking, †Sculpture, Art Criticism and Social History of Art
Summer School: Chmn, James Todd. Tuition same as above for 4 wk term. Courses—Art Education, Art History, Ceramics, Drawing, Painting, Photography, Sculpture

NEBRASKA

BELLEVUE

BELLEVUE COLLEGE, Art Dept,* Wright Way at Galvin Rd, 68005. Tel 402-291-8100. *Chmn* Joyce Wilson, MA
Scholarships offered
Degrees: BA and BFA offered
Tuition: $45 per cr hr
Courses: Advertising Design, Art History, Ceramics, Design, Drawing, Painting, Photography, Printmaking, Sculpture

BLAIR

DANA COLLEGE, Art Dept,* College Dr, 68008. Tel 402-426-4101. *Asst Prof* James T Olsen
Scholarships offered
Degrees: BA, BS
Tuition: $2140 per sem
Courses: Advertising Design, Art History, Ceramics, Design, Drawing, Jewelry, Painting, Photography, Printmaking, Sculpture

CHADRON

CHADRON STATE COLLEGE, Division of Fine Arts, Tenth & Main Sts, 69337. Tel 308-432-6317. *Chmn Div* Charles J Harrington, PhD; *Prof* Noel Gray, EdD; *Asst Prof* John Dillon, MFA; *Asst Prof* Paul Pfrehm, MFA
Estab 1911, div estab 1935; pub; D & E; scholarships; SC 20, LC 4, GC 2; enrl D 280, non-maj 200, maj 30
Ent Req: HS dipl
Degrees: BSE & BA 4 yrs
Tuition: Res—$25 per hr; nonres—$42 per hr; campus res—room & board $850
Courses: Aesthetics, Art Education, Art History, Ceramics, Commercial Art, Drawing, Graphic Arts, Jewelry, Lettering, Painting, Photography, Sculpture, Teacher Training, Theatre Arts, Glass Blowing, Weaving
Adult Hobby Classes: Enrl 30. Tuition varies. Courses vary
Summer School: Dir, Charles J Harington. Enrl 30; tuition same as above. Courses—usually 2-4 courses on semi-rotation basis

COLUMBUS

CENTRAL COMMUNITY COLLEGE - PLATTE CAMPUS, Creative and Social Cluster, Mason Rd, 68601. Tel 402-564-7132. *Head Dept* Roger Augspurger, EdD; *Instructor* Richard Abraham, MA
Estab 1969, dept estab 1971; pub; D & E; scholarships; SC 8, LC 1; enrl D 100, E 20, non-maj 77, maj 43
Ent Req: HS dipl
Degrees: AA 2 yrs
Tuition: Res $576 per yr, $288 per sem, $24 per hr; campus res
Courses: Art History, Ceramics, Commercial Art, Design, Drafting, Drawing, Graphic Arts, Handicrafts, Interior Design, Mixed Media, Photography, Stage Design, Textile Design, Theatre Arts, Oil, Acrylic & Watercolor Painting
Summer School: Dir, Richard D Abraham. Enrl 40; tuition $24 per hr for term of 5 wks beginning June. Courses—Drawing, Painting

CRETE

DOANE COLLEGE, Dept of Art,* 68333. Tel 402-826-2161, Ext 273. *Head Dept* Mary C Taylor; *Chmn Human & Fine Arts* C D Peterson
Estab 1872, dept estab 1958; pvt; D; scholarships; SC 6, LC 5; enrl 150, non-maj 140, maj 10
Ent Req: HS dipl
Degrees: BA 4 yrs
Tuition: $3750 per yr; campus res available
Courses: Art Education, Art History, Ceramics, Drawing, Film, Graphic Design, Jewelry, Painting, Printmaking, Sculpture, Stage Design

HASTINGS

HASTINGS COLLEGE, Art Dept, 68901. Tel 402-463-2402. *Chmn Dept* Richard L Brink. Instrs: FT 3
Estab 1925; den; scholarships; SC 16, LC 5; enrl maj 50, others 350
Ent Req: HS grad
Degrees: BA 4 yrs
Tuition: $4000; campus res—room & board $2250
Courses: Art Education, Art History, Ceramics, Design, Drawing, Painting, Printmaking, Sculpture, Color, Glass Blowing
Adult Hobby Classes: Enrl 15; tuition $140 per cr hr, per sem
Children's Classes: Enrl 200; tuition $25 for 3 week workshop
Summer School: Actg Dean, Duagne Strasheim. Enrl 25; tuition $140 per cr hr for 6 weeks beginning June

KEARNEY

KEARNEY STATE COLLEGE, Dept of Art, 68849. Tel 308-236-4221. *Chmn Dept* Jack Karraker, MFA; *Prof* Keith Lowry, MFA; *Prof* Larry D Peterson, EdD; *Prof* Raymond W Schultze, MFA; *Prof* Gary E Zaruba, EdD; *Prof* John N Dinsmore, EdD; *Prof* Elmer Holzrichter, MA; *Asst Prof* Mary Lierley, Phd; *Asst Prof* James M May, MA; *Asst Prof* M Kinsella, MFA; *Asst Prof* M Cleveland, MFA. Instrs: PT 11, PT 8
Estab 1903; pub; D & E; scholarships; SC 20, LC 12, GC 18; enrl D 870, E 22, non-maj 1400, maj 200, grad 25
Ent Req: HS dipl, SAT or ACT recommended
Degrees: BFA, BA, BA(Educ), BFA(Educ) 4 yrs, MA(Educ-Art)
Tuition: Res—$25 per cr hr; nonres—$42 per cr hr; campus res—$728 per yr
Courses: Aesthetics, †Art Education, †Art History, †Ceramics, Commercial Art, †Drawing, †Painting, Photography, †Printmaking, †Sculpture, †Teacher Training, †Textile Design, Color Theory, Design, Glass Blowing, Weaving
Adult Hobby Classes: Off-campus classes offered
Summer School: Second summer session 8 wks; tuition $25 per cr hr.
Courses—Basic art curriculum, two week workshops

LINCOLN

NEBRASKA WESLEYAN UNIVERSITY, Art Dept, 50th & St Paul, 68504. Tel 402-466-2371. *Head Dept* Betty Wallace, MFA; *Asst Prof* John Clabaugh; *Vis Prof* Lynn Soloway; *Vis Prof* Margaret MacKichan; *Vis Prof* Dan Funk
Estab 1888, dept estab 1890; pvt; D & E; scholarships; SC 22, LC 4; enrl non-maj 300, maj 50
Ent Req: HS dipl, ent exam
Degrees: AA 2 yrs, BA & BS 4 yrs
Tuition: $2100 per sem
Courses: Advertising Design, Art Education, Art History, Ceramics, Commercial Art, Drawing, Jewelry, Museum Staff Training, Painting, Photography, Printmaking, Sculpture, Silversmithing, Design
Adult Hobby Classes: Enrl 30; tuition $80 per sem hr. Degree Program
Children's Classes: Enrl 20; tuition $25 per 4 wks. Courses—Ceramics, Sculpture, Drawing, Painting
Summer School: Head, Betty Wallace. Enrl 30; tuition $80 per sem hr per 8 wks. Courses—Painting, Paste-up, Special Projects

UNIVERSITY OF NEBRASKA AT LINCOLN, Dept of Art, 207 Nelle Cochrane Woods Hall, 68588. Tel 402-472-2631. *Actg Chmn Dept* Larry Lusk; *ViceChmn Dept* James Eisentrager, MFA; *Chmn Graduate Committee* Douglas Ross, MFA; *Chief Acad Advisor* Peter Worth, ARCA. Instrs: FT 20, PT 20
Estab 1869, dept 1912; pub; D & E; scholarships; SC 71, LC 27, GC 45; enrl D 1950, E 175, non-maj 600, maj 400, grad 25
Ent Req: HS dipl
Degrees: BA, BFA and BFA(Educ) 4 yrs, MFA 3 yrs
Tuition: Res—$525 per sem for 15 hrs, $35 per cr hr; nonres—$1395 per sem for 15 sem hrs, $93 per cr hr; campus res—room & board $2205 per yr (single), $1860 (double)
Courses: Advertising Design, †Art Education, †Art History, †Ceramics, Commercial Art, †Drawing, Film, †Graphic Design, Handicrafts, Illustration, Lettering, Mixed Media, †Painting, †Photography, †Printmaking, †Sculpture, Teacher Training, 2-D & 3-D Design, Weaving
Summer School: Dir, Robert Patterson. Enrl 250; two 5 wk sessions beginning June and Aug. Courses—Art History, Ceramics, Design, Drawing, Painting, Photogaphy, Printmaking, Special Problems & Topics

NORFOLK

NORTHEAST TECHNICAL COMMUNITY COLLEGE, Dept of Art, 801 E Benjamin Ave, 68701. Tel 402-371-2020, Ext 245. *Chmn Dept* Patrick Keating, PhD; *Instructor* LeRoy VonGlan; *Instructor* Harry Lindner; *Instructor* Karen Harrington; *Instructor* Donna Faster, BFA
Estab 1928; pub; D & E; scholarships; SC 5, LC 5; enrl D 150, E 50, non-maj 100, maj 50
Ent Req: HS dipl
Degrees: AA 2 yrs
Tuition: Res—$225 per sem, $15 per cr hr; non-res—$360 per sem, $24 per cr hr; campus res—room & board $1500 per yr
Courses: Art Education, Art History, Drawing, Graphic Design, Painting, Photography
Adult Hobby Classes: Oil Painting
Summer School: Chmn Dept, Patrick Keating. Tuition same as regular yr. Courses—Photography

OMAHA

COLLEGE OF SAINT MARY, Art Dept, 1901 S 72nd St, 68124. Tel 402-399-2400. *Chmn Dept* Tom Schlosser
Estab 1923; pvt, W; D & E; scholarships; SC 11, LC 5; enrl D 620, maj 18, special 2
Ent Req: HS dipl
Degrees: BA and BS 4 yrs
Tuition: $133 per cr hr
Courses: Art History, Ceramics, Painting, Photography, Sculpture, Teacher Training, Design, Women in Art
Adult Hobby Classes: Enrl 587; tuition $133 per cr hr. Evening & weekend college offer full range of general education classes
Summer School: Dir, Dr Vernon Lestrud. Enrl 572; tuition $133 per cr hr. Full range of studio & history general education classes

CREIGHTON UNIVERSITY, Fine and Performing Arts Dept, 2500 California St, 68178. Tel 402-280-2509. *Chmn Dept* Donald A Doll; *Asst Prof* Michael Flecky, MFA; *Instr* Suzanne Dieckman, PhD; *Instr* Roger Aikin, PhD; *Instr* Bill Hutson, PhD; *Instr* Lee Lubbers, PhD; *Instr* Jill Lile, MFA; *Instr* Valerie Roche, ARAD; *Instr* John Thein, MFA; *Instr* Tom Moazur, MA; *Instr* Jerome Horning, MFA; *Instr* Carole Bean, B Mus Ed; *Instr* Bob Bosco, MFA; *Artist-in-Res* Jonathan Haschka, MFA
Estab 1878, dept estab 1966; den; D & E; scholarships; SC 87, LC 16; enrl 888, non-maj 850, maj 38, cert prog 24
Ent Req: HS dipl, regular col admis exam
Degrees: BA and BFA 4 yrs
Tuition: $4200 average per yr; campus res available
Courses: Advertising Design, Art Education, Art History, Ceramics, Costume Design & Construction, Drawing, History of Art & Archaeology, Painting, Photography, Printmaking, Sculpture, Theatre Arts, Design, Intaglio, Lithography, Pottery, Studio Fundamentals
Adult Hobby Classes: Life Drawing

STUDIO ACADEMY SCHOOL OF ADVERTISING ART AND DESIGN INC,* 1021 N 46th St, 68132. Tel 402-553-1733
Degrees: Certificate offered
Courses: Art Appreciation, Art History, Calligraphy, Design, Drawing, Fashion Arts, Cartooning

UNIVERSITY OF NEBRASKA AT OMAHA, Dept of Art, 60th & Dodge Sts, 68182. Tel 402-554-2420. *Chmn Dept* Dr James G Czarnecki; *Prof* Dr J V Blackwell; *Prof* Sidney Buchanan, MA; *Prof* Peter Hill, MFA; *Prof* Thomas H Majeski, MFA; *Assoc Prof* Larry Bradshaw, MFA; *Assoc Prof* Henry Serenco, MFA; *Asst Prof* Frances T Keuz, MA; *Asst Prof* Gary Day, MFA
Estab 1908, dept estab 1910; pub; D & E; scholarships; SC 32, LC 22, GC 10; enrl D 550, E 100
Ent Req: HS dipl
Degrees: BA & BFA 4 yrs
Tuition: Res—undergrad $34.50 per cr hr, grad $41 per cr hr; nonres—undergrad $93.50 per cr hr, grad $100 per cr hr; no campus res
Courses: †Art Education, †Art History, †Ceramics, †Drawing, †Painting, †Printmaking, †Sculpture
Summer School: Chmn Dept, James G Czarnecki. Tuition same as above for term of 5 wks. Courses vary

PERU

PERU STATE COLLEGE, Art Dept,* 68421. Tel 402-872-3815. *Chmn Applied Arts* Lester Russell
Scholarships offered
Degrees: BA, BAEd, BS
Tuition: Res—$375 per sem; nonres—$630 per sem
Courses: Art Appreciation, Art Education, Art History, Ceramics, Design, Drawing, Painting, Photography, Printmaking, Sculpture, Stage Design, Cartooning

SCOTTSBLUFF

NEBRASKA WESTERN COLLEGE, Division of Language and Arts,* 1601 E 27th St NE, 69361. Tel 308-635-3603, Ext 285. *Chairperson Division Language & Arts* Dan Steadman, DA; *Instructor* Roy D Doerfler, MA
Estab 1926; pub; D & E; scholarships; SC 8, LC 3; enrl D 60, E 150, non-maj 50, maj 10
Ent Req: HS dipl
Degrees: AA & AS 2 yrs
Tuition: Res—$289.50; nonres—$405; campus res available
Courses: Art Education, Art History, Drawing, Painting, Photography, Theatre Arts, Music Education
Adult Hobby Classes: Enrl 150; tui $15 per course. Courses—Carving, Drawing, Macrame, Pottery, Sculpture, Stained Glass, Watercolor & Oil Painting, Weaving

SEWARD

CONCORDIA COLLEGE, Art Dept,* 800 N Columbia, 68434. Tel 402-643-3651. *Head Dept* William R Wolfram, MFA; *Prof* Donald Dynneson, MFA; *Prof* Reinhold P Marxhausen, MFA; *Prof* Richard Wiegmann, MFA
Estab 1894; den; D & E; scholarships; SC 8, LC 4; enrl non-maj 30, maj 40
Ent Req: HS dipl
Degrees: BS, BA 4 yr
Tuition: $110 per cr hr; campus res available
Courses: Art Education, Art History, Ceramics, Drawing, Handicrafts, History of Art & Archaeology, Painting, Photography, Printmaking, Sculpture, Teacher Training
Summer School: Tui $80 per cr hr for term of 2 1/2 wks beginning June 6. Courses—Fundamentals of Art

WAYNE

WAYNE STATE COLLEGE, Art Dept, 68787. Tel 402-375-2200, Ext 360. *Div Chmn* Dr Jay O'Leary. Instrs: FT 4
Estab 1910; pub; scholarships; SC 21, LC 8; enrl maj 51, others 700, total 2100
Ent Req: HS grad
Degrees: BA, BFA
Tuition: Res—$18 per cr hr; nonres—$32 per cr hr
Courses: Art History, Ceramics, Drafting, Drawing, Graphic Arts, Handicrafts, Jewelry, Painting, Sculpture, †Teacher Training, Design
Summer School: Pres, Ed Elliott. Three sessions

YORK

YORK COLLEGE, Art Dept, 9th & Kiplinger St, Box 246, 68467. Tel 402-362-4441, Ext 268; WATS 800-228-4342. *Assoc Prof* Michael Fowler, MFA
Sch estab 1956; dept estab 1962; pvt; D; scholarships; SC 6, LC 1; enrl D 26, non-maj 20, maj 6
Ent Req: HS dipl, ACT
Degrees: AA 2 yrs
Tuition: Res—undergrad $1150 per sem
Courses: Aesthetics, Design, Drawing, Painting

NEVADA

LAS VEGAS

UNIVERSITY OF NEVADA, LAS VEGAS, Dept of Art, 4505 Maryland Parkway, 89154. Tel 702-739-3011. *Chmn Dept* Thomas J Holder, MFA; *Prof* Rita Deanin Abbey, MFA; *Assoc Prof* Michael L McCollum, MFA; *Assoc Prof* Lee T Sido; *Asst Prof* Cathie Kelly
Estab 1955; pub; D & E; scholarships; SC 32, LC 18; enrl all courses 551, maj 95
Ent Req: HS dipl, ACT
Degrees: BA and BFA 4 yrs
Tuition: Out-of-state $1100 per sem, $36 per hr; campus res—room & board $1000-$1200 per sem
Courses: Art History, Ceramics, Conceptual Art, Drawing, Film, Intermedia, Painting, Photography, Printmaking, Sculpture
Summer School: Dir, W Hubert Johnson; tuition $30 per cr hr for 5 wks beginning June 12 and July 17. Courses—vary with each session

RENO

UNIVERSITY OF NEVADA, RENO, Art Dept, 89557. Tel 702-784-6682. *Chmn Dept* Edward W Martinez. Instrs: FT 10
Estab 1940; pub; scholarship; SC 20, LC 6, GC 5; enrl maj 120, others 800
Ent Req: HS grad and 16 units
Degrees: BA 4 yr
Courses: †Art Education, Art History, †Ceramics, †Drawing, Graphic Design, †Painting, †Photography, †Printmaking, †Sculpture
Adult Hobby Classes: Evening division in all areas
Summer School: Courses in all studio areas

NEW HAMPSHIRE

DURHAM

UNIVERSITY OF NEW HAMPSHIRE, Dept of the Arts, Paul Creative Arts Center, 03824. Tel 603-862-2190. *Chmn* David S Andrew, PhD; *Prof* Sigmund Abeles, MFA; *Prof* John Hatch, MFA; *Prof* John Laurent, MFA; *Prof* Melvin Zabarsky, MFA; *Assoc Prof* Conley Harris, MFA; *Assoc Prof* Arthur Balderacchi, MFA; *Assoc Prof* Margot Clark, PhD; *Assoc Prof* Michael McConnell, MFA; *Assoc Prof* Richard Merritt, MFA; *Assoc Prof* Maryse Searls, MFA; *Assoc Prof* Winifred Shaw, MFA; *Assoc Prof* Dan Valenza, MFA; *Assoc Prof* Mara Witzling, PhD; *Asst Prof* Carol Aronson, MFA; *Asst Prof* David Smith, PhD
Estab 1928, dept estab 1941; pub; D & E; scholarships; SC 60, LC 20; enrl non-maj 1000, maj 175, grad 5, others 60
Ent Req: HS dipl, portfolio
Degrees: BA, BFA and BA(Art History) 4 yrs, MAT 5 yrs
Tuition: Campus res available
Courses: Architecture, Art Education, Art History, Ceramics, Drawing, Jewelry, Painting, Photography, Printmaking, Sculpture, Silversmithing, Teacher Training
Summer School: Dir, Edward J Durnall. Courses—varied

HANOVER

DARTMOUTH COLLEGE, Dept of Art, 03755. Tel 603-646-2306. *Chmn* Jim M Jordan. Instrs: FT 12, PT 2
Estab 1906; pvt; scholarship and fel; SC 16, LC 26; enrl in col 4000, maj 46
Degrees: AB 4 yr
Tuition: Incl campus res fee, $3030 per term; operating 4 terms on yr-round basis
Courses: Architecture, Art History, Design, Drawing, Graphic Arts, Painting, Photography, 3-D Design

HENNIKER

NEW ENGLAND COLLEGE, Visual Arts Dept,* Proctor Square, 03242. Tel 603-428-2211. *Assoc Prof* David F MacEachran, MFA; *Asst Prof* Farid A Haddah, MFA; *Asst Prof* Doris A Birmingham, PhD; *Asst Prof* Graham O Tite, MSc; *Asst Prof* Marguerite Walsh, MFA
Also has campuses in England
Degrees: BA
Courses: Art Appreciation, Art History, Ceramics, Design, Drawing, Film, Painting, Photography, Printmaking, Stage Design, Video

MANCHESTER

MANCHESTER INSTITUTE OF ARTS AND SCIENCES, 148 Concord St, 03104. Tel 603-623-0313. *Exec Dir* Angelo Randazzo; *Program Coordr* Andrienne Lavallee; *Registrar* Nina Gardner. Instrs: PT 30
Estab 1898; pvt; credit and adult educ courses; SC 16; enrl 1000
Ent Req: None
Courses: Calligraphy, Ceramics, Drawing, Graphic Design, Jewelry, Painting, Photography, Silversmithing, Stained Glass, Weaving
Adult Hobby Classes: Enrl 340; tuition $70 - $80

NOTRE DAME COLLEGE, Art Dept, 2321 Elm St, 03104. Tel 603-669-4298. *Assoc Prof* Sr Liliosa Shea, MFA; *Asst Prof* Frank Oehlschlaeger, MA; *Asst Prof* Harry Umen, MFA; *Asst Prof* William Dobe, MEd; *Asst Prof* Sandra Adams, MFA; *Lectr* Fred Dobrowolski, Med; *Lectr* Charles Lemay, AB; *Lectr* Gloria Martin, PhD; *Lectr* John Bowers; *Lectr* Jean Nelson, AB; *Lectr* Jean Bourassa, MAT; *Lectr* Ruthanne Harrington, Med; *Lectr* Blanche Lamarre, MFA. Instrs: 2
Estab 1950, dept estab 1965; pvt; D & E; scholarship; SC 20, LC 6; enrl non-maj 15, maj 125
Ent Req: HS dipl
Degrees: BA(Fine Arts), BA(Commercial Art & Art Educ) 4 yr
Tuition: Undergrad $3520 yr, $1760 sem, $270 PT, grad $225 PT; campus res—room and board $2420 yr
Courses: Advertising Design, †Art Education, Art History, Calligraphy, Ceramics, †Commercial Art, Display, Drafting, Drawing, Graphic Arts, Graphic Design, Illustration, Lettering, Painting, Printmaking, Sculpture, Teacher Training, Art Therapy, Visual Arts

SAINT ANSELM COLLEGE, Dept of Fine Arts,* 03102. Tel 603-669-1030, Ext 256. *Chmn* Joseph E Scannell. Instrs: FT 2
Estab 1889; pvt; D & E; SC 2, LC 9; enrl 1500
Ent Req: HS dipl, relative standing, SAT, interview
Degrees: BA 4 yr
Tuition: $2600 annual tuition
Courses: Art History, Photography, Studio
Summer School: Courses—History of American Art Seminar, Still Photography

NASHUA

ARTS AND SCIENCE CENTER, 14 Court St, 03060. Tel 603-882-1506. Instrs: PT 35-40
Estab 1958; pub; D & E; SC, LC
Ent Req: None
Degrees: None, noncredited
Courses: Ceramics, Drawing, Jewelry, Painting, Photography, Sculpture, Theatre Arts, Enameling, Macrame, Weaving
Adult Hobby Classes: Tuition varied. Courses—all of the above
Children's Classes: Tuition varied. Courses—Drawing, Jewelry, Painting, Pottery, Preschool Art, Puppet Making, Sculpture
Summer School: Tuition varied; 5 wk terms from June to July

RIVIER COLLEGE, Art Dept, 410 S Main St, 03060. Tel 603-888-1311, Ext 75. *Chmn Dept* Sr Marie Couture, MA
Estab 1933, dept estab 1940; pvt; D & E; scholarships; SC 80, LC 11; enrl D 221, E 57, non-maj 12, maj 266
Ent Req: HS dipl, SAT, certain HS equivalencies, preliminary evidence of artistic ability, slide portfolio
Degrees: AA 2 yrs, BA, BS and BFA 4 yrs
Tuition: Campus residence available
Courses: Aesthetics, †Art Education, Art History, Calligraphy, †Ceramics, Conceptual Art, Constructions, Display, Drawing, Film, †Graphic Design, Illustration, Jewelry, Lettering, Mixed Media, †Painting, Photography, Printmaking, †Sculpture, Teacher Training, Textile Design, Art Therapy, Loom Weaving, Stitchery
Adult Hobby Classes: Courses—Commercial Graphics, various non cr courses
Summer School: Dir, Dr Maryanne Civitello. 10 day workshops

NEW LONDON

COLBY-SAWYER COLLEGE, Art Dept, 03257. Tel 603-526-2010, Ext 229. *Chairperson* John Bott, MFA; *Instructor* Donald Campbell, MFA; *Instr* Loretta Barnett, MFA; *Instr* Martha Andrea, MFA; *Instr* David Hale. Instrs: FT 5
Estab 1837; pvt; W; D; scholarship; SC 22, LC 7; enrl 500
Degrees: BA & BFA 4 yrs
Tuition: Res—undergrad $9800 per yr, $4900 per sem; nonres—undergrad $6960 per yr, $3480 per sem; campus res available
Courses: †Ceramics, †Drawing, †Painting, †Photography, †Printmaking, †Sculpture, Design, Watercolor
Adult Hobby Classes: Chairperson, John Bott, MFA

PETERBOROUGH

SHARON ARTS CENTER, RFD 2, Box 361, 03458. Tel 603-924-7256. *Dir* Alan Erdossy. Instrs: PT 10
Estab 1947; pvt; D & E; scholarship; SC 20; classes yr round
Ent Req: None
Tuition: $50 members, $60 non-members
Courses: Calligraphy, Ceramics, Drawing, Fashion Arts, Graphic Arts, Jewelry, Lettering, Painting, Photography, Printmaking, Textile Design, Batik, Patchwork & Applique, Pottery, Stained Glass, T'ai Chi Ch'uan, Weaving
Adult Hobby Classes: Enrl 500. Courses—Visual & Tactile Arts
Children's Classes: Enrl 100. Courses—Visual & Tactile Arts
Summer School: Dir, Alan Erdassy. Enrl 200; tuition $60 per 8 wks. Courses—Visual & Tactile Arts

PLYMOUTH

PLYMOUTH STATE COLLEGE, Art Dept, 03264. Tel 603-536-1550, Ext 201. *Head Dept* Ellwyn Hayslip. Instrs: FT 9
Estab 1871; pub; D & E; scholarships; SC 17, LC 8; enrl D 3000, maj 170
Ent Req: HS grad, references, health record, transcript, SAT, CEEB, ACT
Degrees: BS, BFA & BA 4 yrs
Courses: Art Education, Art History, Ceramics, Drawing, Museum Staff Training, Painting, Photography, Printmaking, Sculpture, Design
Adult Hobby Classes: Courses available
Children's Classes: Courses available
Summer School: Dir, Dr Julian Shlager. Courses—varied

RINDGE

FRANKLIN PIERCE COLLEGE, Art Dept, 03461. Tel 603-899-5111
Estab 1962; pvt; D & E; scholarships; SC 20, LC 2
Ent Req: HS dipl
Degrees: BA(Fine Arts), BA(Commercial Art)
Tuition: $5850; campus res—room & board $2640
Courses: Art History, Ceramics, Design, Drawing, Graphic Arts, Painting, Photography, Printmaking, Sculpture, Stage Design, Glassblowing, Stained Glass
Summer School: Courses—Ceramics, Glassblowing, Painting, Photography

NEW JERSEY

BLACKWOOD

CAMDEN COUNTY COLLEGE, Dept of Art,* PO Box 200, 08012. Tel 609-227-7200. *Chmn Dept* William Marlin, EdD; *Acad Dean* Michael Donahue
Estab 1966; SC 12, LC 10; enrl 100
Ent Req: HS dipl or equivalent
Degrees: AA 2 yrs
Tuition: In county—$17 per cr hr; res—$19 per cr hr; nonres—$65 per cr hr
Courses: Art History, Calligraphy, Drawing, Lettering, Painting, Sculpture, Art Therapy, Design

CALDWELL

CALDWELL COLLEGE, Art Dept,* Ryerson Ave, 07006. Tel 201-228-4424. *Chmn Dept* Mary Costantini. Instrs: FT 3, PT 6
Estab 1964; pvt; W; D; scholarship; SC 24, LC 12; enrl maj 76, dept 90
Ent Req: HS grad, ent exam, art portfolio
Degrees: BA 3-4 yr, BFA 4-5 yr
Tuition: $95 per cr hr
Courses: Advertising Design, Aesthetics, Art Education, Ceramics, Commercial Art, Drawing, Graphic Arts, Handicrafts, History of Art & Archaeology, Jewelry, Lettering, Painting, Photography, Sculpture, Teacher Training, Batik, Chip Carving, Enameling, Leather Carving, Metal Workshop, Weaving
Summer School: Dir, Sr Mary Daniel. Three terms of 3 wks each beginning June. Courses—Crafts, Drawing, Painting, Sculpture

CAMDEN

RUTGERS UNIVERSITY, CAMDEN, Art Dept, Camden College of Arts and Sciences, 311 N Fifth St, 08102. Tel 609-757-6244. *Chmn* Olga Moore. Instrs: FT 5, PT 8
Pub; D; SC 24, LC 13; enrl art D 450, maj 75
Ent Req: HS dipl, must qualify for regular col admis, portfolio
Degrees: BA(Art) 4 yrs
Courses: †Art History, †Graphic Arts, †Painting, †Printmaking, †Sculpture, Environmental Design, †Gallery Operations
Summer School: Dir, Helen Weber. Three sessions beginning May 20. Courses—Photography

CONVENT STATION

COLLEGE OF SAINT ELIZABETH, Art Dept,* 07961. Tel 201-539-1600. *Chmn Dept* Sr Ann Haarer
Estab 1899, dept 1956; den, W; D & E; scholarships; SC 17, LC 4; enrl D 250, maj 27
Ent Req: HS dipl, ent exam
Degrees: BA 4 yrs
Tuition: $4000 per yr; campus residence available
Courses: Sculpture, Teacher Training, Color and Design, Leather Work, Sand Casting, Stitchery
Summer School: Dir, Sr Mary Kathleen. Courses—Art Education, Painting

DOVER

JOE KUBERT SCHOOL OF CARTOON AND GRAPHIC ART INC, 45 Lehigh St, 07801. Tel 201-361-1327. *Pres* Joe Kubert; *Instr* John Belfi; *Instr* Phillip Blaisdell; *Instr* Hy Eisman; *Instr* Irwin Hasen; *Instr* Milton Neil; *Instr* Ben Ruiz; *Instr* Sal Amendola; *Instr* Jose Delbo; *Instr* Stan Kay; *Instr* Greg Hildebrandt; *Instr* Denton Lund; *Instr* Bruce Wands; *Instr* Louis Scarborough; *Vis Lectr* Sergio Aragones, cartoons; *Vis Lectr* Frank Throne, cartoons
Estab 1976; pvt; D & E; SC all, LC all; enrl D 200, E 50
Ent Req: HS dipl, interview, portfolio
Degrees: 3 yr dipl
Tuition: $3800 per yr; PT $600; campus res—room $1485 per yr
Courses: Advertising Design, Commercial Art, Graphic Arts, Cartoon Graphics, Cinematic Animation
Adult Hobby Classes: Enrl 25, tuition $325 per sem. Courses—Basic and Advanced Paste-Ups and Mechanicals, Saturday Cartoon Sketch Class
Children's Classes: Enrl 25; tuition $48 per month. Courses—Saturday Cartoon Sketch Class

EAST ORANGE

ART CENTRE OF NEW JERSEY, Upsala College, Art Bldg, 07019. Tel 201-674-8445. *Pres* John Richeter Jr; *VPres* Nissan Gallant; *Second VPres* Fern Relkin; *Recording Secy* Cecelia VanDuyne
Estab 1924 as an art school and as a venue for art events, lectures, etc;
Adult Hobby Classes: Workshops
Children's Classes: lect open to public; gallery talks; competitions with awards

EDISON

MIDDLESEX COUNTY COLLEGE, Visual Arts Dept, Woodbridge Ave & Mill Road, 08817. Tel 201-548-6000. *Chmn* Dr Stephen Wyman
Degrees: AA
Courses: Art Appreciation, Art Education, Art History, Ceramics, Design, Drawing, Painting, Sculpture, Stage Design, Video

GLASSBORO

GLASSBORO STATE COLLEGE, Dept of Art,* Route 322, 08028. Tel 609-445-5000. *Chmn Dept* George Neff
EStab 1925; pub; D & E; enrl D 6100, E 5000, maj 300, grad 100
Ent Req: HS dipl, ent exam, portfolio and SAT
Degrees: BA 4 yrs, MA
Tuition: Res—$27 per cr hr; nonres—$47 per cr hr
Courses: Sculpture, Stage Design, Teacher Training, Textile Design, Theatre Arts, Batik, Enameling

HACKETTSTOWN

CENTENARY COLLEGE, Art Dept, Fine Arts Division, 07840. Tel 201-852-1400. *Assoc Prof* Barbara J Buley. Instrs: FT 4, PT 4
Estab 1874; pvt, W; scholarships; SC 11, LC 2; enrl maj 70, others 367, total 678
Degrees: AA(Fine Art), AA(Graphic Design), AA(Interior Design) and BFA(Fine Art), BFA(Interior Design), BFA(Graphic Design)
Tuition: Res—$3750; nonres—$6700
Adult Hobby Classes: Tuition $98 per cr. Courses—Interior Design, Graphic Arts
Summer School: Dir, Larry Friedman. Tuition $98 per cr. Courses—Graphic Art, Interior Design

JERSEY CITY

JERSEY CITY STATE COLLEGE, Art Dept, 2039 Kennedy Blvd, 07305. Tel 201-547-3214, Ext 3241 or 3242. *Chairperson* Dorothy Harris, BFA & MA; *Prof* Dr Elaine Foster, EdD; *Prof* Harold Lemmerman, EdD; *Prof* Anneke Prins Simons, PhD; *Prof* Dr Raymond Walker, EdD; *Prof* Dr Jean Lane, EdD; *Assoc Prof* Charles Boyens, MFA; *Assoc Prof* Dr Robert Russell, EdD; *Assoc Prof* Dr Eleanor Campolli, EdD; *Assoc Prof* Marguarite LaBelle, MA; *Assoc Prof* Dr Esther Barrish, EdD; *Asst Prof* Doris Muller, MA; *Asst Prof* Charles Plosky, MFA; *Asst Prof* Herbert Rosenberg, MFA; *Asst Prof* Raymond Statlander, MFA; *Asst Prof* Sr Joan Steans, MFA; *Asst Prof* William White, MFA; *Asst Prof* Mary Campbell, MFA. Instrs: PT 12
Estab 1927, dept estab 1961; pub; D & E; SC 61, LC 19, GC 31; enrl D 250, E 60, GS 60
Ent Req: HS dipl or equivalent
Degrees: BA 128 sem hrs, MA
Tuition: Res—undergrad $22 per cr, grad $45 per cr; nonres—undergrad $44 per cr, grad $65 per cr; campus residence available
Courses: Art History, Design, Photography, Photography, Printmaking, Sculpture, Teacher Training, †Art Therapy, Commercial Design, Design & Crafts, Fabric Design, Fibers, Crafts, Communication Design & Technology
Summer School: Dir, Dr Jean C Lane. Tuition $22 per sem hr for two terms beginning May 27 and June 23. Courses—Air Brush & Other Rendering Techniques, Art & Society, Ceramics, Contemporary Art, Cultural Resources, Drawing & Composition, Gothic to Modern, Painting, Photography, Two-Dimensional Design

SAINT PETER'S COLLEGE, Fine Arts Dept,* 2641 Kennedy Blvd, 07306. Tel 201-333-4400, Ext 330. *Chmn* Oscar G Magnan
Estab 1963; den; D & E; scholarships; SC 4, LC 13; enrl D 650, E 250, maj 20
Ent Req: HS dipl
Degrees: BA, BA in Cursu Classico, BS 4 yrs
Tuition: $116 per cr hr
Courses: Art History, Drawing, Film, Painting, Sculpture
Summer School: Two 5 wk sessions. Courses—Drawing, Film History, Introduction to Visual Arts, Painting, Visual Arts in America

LAKEWOOD

GEORGIAN COURT COLLEGE, Dept of Art, Lakewood Ave, 08701. Tel 201-364-2200, Ext 48. *Head Dept* Sr Mary Christina Geis, MFA; *Assoc Prof* Douglas L McIlvain, MA; *Asst Prof* Geraldine Velasquez, MA; *Instr* Sr Joyce Jacobs, MA; *Instr* Suzanne Pilgram, MA; *Lectr* Vincent Hart
Estab 1908, dept estab 1924; pvt; D; scholarships; SC 18, LC 11; enrl in dept 200, non-maj 150, maj 50
Ent Req: HS dipl, col board scores, portfolio
Degrees: BA 4 yr
Tuition: Undergrad $3400, $95 per cr; campus res—room & board 7 day $2200, 5 day $2050
Courses: Advertising Design, †Art Education, †Art History, Ceramics, Commercial Art, Drafting, Drawing, Fashion Arts, Handicrafts, History of Art & Archaeology, Illustration, Jewelry, Painting, Photography, Printmaking, Sculpture, Teacher Training, Textile Design, Weaving, Basic Design
Summer School: Dir, Sr Mary Catharine Sullivan. Enrl 30; tuition $95 per cr for term of 6 wks beginning June 27. Courses—Art History, Ceramics, Painting, Sculpture

LAWRENCEVILLE

RIDER COLLEGE, Dept of Fine Arts,* 2083 Lawrenceville, 08648. Tel 609-896-5168. *Chmn* Patrick Chmel. Instrs: FT 3
Estab 1966; pvt; D & E; SC 9, LC 4; enrl D 3500, E 5169, maj 100
Ent Req: HS dipl
Degrees: BA(Fine Arts) 4 yrs
Tuition: $4000 per yr; campus res available
Courses: Ceramics, Drawing, Graphic Arts, Graphic Design, Painting, Stage Design

LINCROFT

BROOKDALE COMMUNITY COLLEGE, Art Dept,* Newman Springs Rd, 07738. Tel 201-842-1900
Degrees: AA
Tuition: County res—$23 per cr hr; non-county res—$46 per cr hr; non-state res—$92 per cr hr
Courses: Calligraphy, Ceramics, Design, Drawing, Film, Handicrafts, Jewelry, Painting, Photography, Printmaking, Sculpture, Stage Design, Weaving

MADISON

DREW UNIVERSITY, Art Dept,* College of Liberal Arts, 36 Madison Ave, 07940. Tel 201-377-3204, Ext 330. *Chmn Dept* Martyvonne Dehoney, EdD; *Asst Prof* Sara Henry, PhD; *Asst Prof* Livio Sagonic, PhD; *Vis Prof* Nick Foster, Photography; *Vis Assoc Prof* Sally Roberts, PhD; *Vis Instr* David Rohn, MFA Watercolor
Estab 1928; pvt; D & E; scholarships; SC 17, LC 10; enrl D 275, E 12, maj 42, minors 4
Ent Req: HS dipl
Degrees: BA 4 yrs
Tuition: $3865 per yr
Courses: Aesthetics, †Art History, Ceramics, Drawing, History of Art & Archaeology, Painting, Photography, Printmaking, Sculpture
Summer School: Dir, Vivian Bull. Term of 3 1/2 wks beginning June. Courses—Studios

MAHWAH

RAMAPO COLLEGE OF NEW JERSEY, School of Contemporary Arts, 505 Ramapo Valley Rd, 07430. Tel 201-825-2800, Ext 501. *Prof Art History* Carol Duncan, PhD; *Assoc Prof Photography* David Freund, MFA; *Assoc Prof Architecture* Newton LeVine, MCRP; *Assoc Prof* Jay Wholley, MFA; *Asst Prof* Judith Peck, EdD; *Asst Prof Painting* Warner W Wada, MFA
Estab 1968; pub; D & E; SC 53, LC 15; enrl D 800, E 50, non-maj 750, maj 100
Ent Req: HS dipl, SAT
Degrees: BA
Tuition: Res—undergrad $32 per cr hr; nonres—undergrad $50 per cr hr; campus res available
Courses: Architecture, Art Appreciation, Art Education, Art History, Commercial Art, Conceptual Art, Design, Drawing, Film, Graphic Arts, Graphic Design, Intermedia, Painting, Photography, Printmaking, Sculpture, Stage Design, Teacher Training, Video

MERCERVILLE

JOHNSON ATELIER TECHNICAL INSTITUTE OF SCULPTURE, 60 Ward Ave Extension, 08619. Tel 609-890-7777. *Exec Dir* Herk Van Tongeren, MFA; *Asst Dir* James Barton, MFA; *Asst Dir* Linda Levin; *Acad Dir* Brooke Barrie, MFA
Estab 1974; pvt; D & E; scholarships; SC 12; enrl D 50, maj 45, grad 5
Ent Req: BFA or MFA in sculpture
Degrees: The Atelier is a non degree granting institution with a two year

apprenticeship program in sculpture
Tuition: $4800 per academic yr, $400 monthly
Summer School: Acad Dir, Brooke Barrie. Enrl 5-8; tuition $1200 per 3 months. Courses—various

MONTCLAIR

MONTCLAIR ART MUSEUM, Museum Art Classes, 3 S Mountain Ave, PO Box 1582, 07042. Tel 201-746-5555. *Dir* Robert J Kpenig; *Registrar* Patricia P Barnes; *Instructor* Bill Greh; *Instructor* Kirsten Kree; *Instructor* Michael Burben; *Instructor* Janet Cooke; *Instructor* Tim Gaydos; *Instructor* Edwin Havas; *Instructor* Frances McQuillan; *Instructor* Diana Naspo; *Children's Instructor* Lesley Dill; *Children's Instructor* Anne Burg
Art school estab 1924; pvt; D & E; scholarships; SC 17; enrl D 300 per term, E 100 per term
Tuition: Young people $50 for 12 sessions; adults $80 for 12 sessions
Courses: Aesthetics, Art Education, Collages, Constructions, Drawing, Mixed Media, Painting, Portraiture, Watercolor

MONTCLAIR STATE COLLEGE, Fine Arts Dept, School of Fine & Performing Arts, 07043. Tel 201-893-4308. *Dean* Donald A Mattran; *Chmn* Helene Ross. Instrs: FT 26, PT 8
Estab 1908; pub; scholarship; SC 35, LC 18; enrl maj 250, grad maj 200
Ent Req: HS grad and exam, interview, portfolio
Degrees: BA 4 yr, BFA 4 yr, MA
Courses: Art Education, Art History, Ceramics, Drawing, Film, Jewelry, Painting, Photography, Printmaking, Sculpture, Textile Design, Theatre Arts, Communications Design, Metalwork, TV as Art
Summer School: Courses—Life drawing, painting, photography, sculpture

YARD SCHOOL OF ART, 99 S Fullerton Ave, 07042. Tel 201-746-6106. *Dean* Beatrice Harris
Estab 1927; pvt; D & E; scholarships available to handicapped students & worthy talented students; enrl D 130, E 6
Courses: Calligraphy, Collages, Drawing, Painting, Portraiture
Adult Hobby Classes: Courses offered
Children's Classes: Tuition $28 per month

NEWARK

NEWARK SCHOOL OF FINE AND INDUSTRIAL ART, 550 M L King Blvd, 07102. Tel 201-733-7390. *Dir* Edward John Stevens Jr. Instrs: D PT 42, E PT 28
Estab 1882; pub; enrl D 300, E 300
Tuition: City res—$300 per yr; nonres—$850 per yr
Courses: †Advertising Design, Ceramics, †Fashion Arts, †Illustration, †Interior Design, †Painting, †Sculpture, †Textile Design, Fine Arts
Adult Hobby Classes: Enrl 150; tuition res—$300, nonres—$850.
Courses—Advanced Illustration, Fashion Textile, Interior Design
Children's Classes: Enrl 150. Courses—General Art
Summer School: Dir, E J Stevens

RUTGERS UNIVERSITY, NEWARK, Art Dept, Newark Col of Arts & Sciences, 392 High St, Bradley Hall, 07102. *Chmn Dept* Hildreth York. Instrs: FT 5, PT 5
Pub; D; scholarship; enrl D 486, maj 100
Ent Req: HS dipl, or as specified by col and univ
Degrees: BA 4 yr
Courses: Art Education, Ceramics, Drawing, Graphic Design, History of Art & Archaeology, Illustration, Museum Staff Training, Painting, Photography, Printmaking, Sculpture, Weaving
Children's Classes: Enrl 50. Courses—Art & Design, Graphic Design
Summer School: Dir, Hildreth York. Courses—Drawing, Photography

NEW BRUNSWICK

RUTGERS, THE STATE UNIVERSITY OF NEW JERSEY
—Mason Gross School of the Arts, Visual Arts Dept, Downtown Arts Bldg, 358 George St, 08903. Tel 201-932-9078, 932-9093. *Dean* John Bettenbender, MFA; *Dir Visual Arts* B Pickard-Pritchard, PhD; *Actg Dean* Leon Golub, MFA; *Assoc Dean* Dr Charles Woolfolk; *Prof* Berger Mark, MA; *Prof* Edwards Melvin, BFA; *Prof* John Goodyear, MDesign; *Prof* Daniel Newman, BA; *Prof* Peter Stroud, MFA; *Prof* Robert Watts, BME; *Assoc Prof* Paul Bruner, MFA; *Assoc Prof* Robert T Cooke, MFA; *Assoc Prof* Lauren Ewing, MFA; *Assoc Prof* Gary Kuehn, MFA; *Assoc Prof* Phil Orenstein, MFA; *Assoc Prof* Rafael Ortiz, EdD; *Assoc Prof* Ka Kwong Hui, MFA; *Assoc Prof* Lloyd McNeill, MFA; *Assoc Prof* Joan Semmel, MFA; *Assoc Prof* Joyce Sills, MFA; *Assoc Prof* Samuel Weiner, MA; *Asst Prof* Sandi Fellman, MFA; *Asst Prof* Amy Stromsten, MFA; *Asst Prof* Emma Amos, MA; *Asst Prof* Martha Rosler, MFA
Estab 1766, school estab 1976; pub; D; scholarships; SC 24, LC 9, GC 33; enrl MFA program 450, BFA program 60
Ent Req: HS dipl, portfolio
Degrees: BFA, MFA
Tuition: Res—undergrad $1490 per sem, grad $1060 per sem; nonres—undergrad $2980 per sem, grad $1527 per sem
Courses: Ceramics, Film, Mixed Media, Painting, Photography, Printmaking, Sculpture, Video, Computer Arts, Critical Studies, Event and Performance, Seminars and Museum Internship
Summer School: Dir, Dr B Pickard-Pritchard. Four weeks courses.
Courses—Computer Art, Drawing Fundamentals, Figure Drawing, Painting Studio, Seminar on Contemporary Art, Studio Fundamentals
—Graduate Program in Art History, Voorhees Hall, Hamilton St, 08903. Tel 201-932-7041. *Dir Prog* Olga Berendsen, PhD; *Prof* Matthew Baigell, PhD; *Prof* Elizabeth McLachlan, PhD; *Prof* Jack J Spector, PhD; *Prof* James H Stubblebine, PhD; *Prof* Martin Eidelberg, PhD; *Assoc Prof* Hildreth York, PhD; *Assoc Prof* John F Kenfield, PhD; *Asst Prof* Sarah Wilk, PhD; *Asst Prof* Thomas M Shaw, PhD; *Asst Prof* Cynthia Lawrence, PhD; *Asst Prof* Joan Marter, PhD; *Asst Prof* Tod Marder,

PhD; *Asst Prof* Archer St Clair Harvey, PhD
Estab 1766, grad prog estab 1971; pub; D; scholarships; grad courses 15; enrl grad students 80
Ent Req: BA
Degrees: MA 2 yrs, PhD 4 yrs
Tuition: Res—grad $88 per cr; nonres—grad $128 per cr plus student fee; campus res—room $1156 per yr maximum & board $424
Courses: †Art History
Summer School: Dir, Albert A Austen. Courses—Intro to Art Hist, 19th & 20th century Art

OCEAN CITY

OCEAN CITY ARTS CENTER, 409 Wesley Ave, 08226. Tel 609-399-7628 or 399-6111, Ext 280. *Head Teaching Staff* Edward Wismer; *Instr* Florence Deeley; *Instr* Lance Balderson, BA; *Instr* Susan Hopkins, BA; *Instr* Lorraine Watson; *Instr* Susan Brooks, BAED; *Instr* Kathleen Fell, BS; *Instr* Ruth Veasey; *Instr* Scott Griswold; *Instr* Robin Conovey; *Instr* Matilda Phifer; *Instr* Leslie Fontana; *Instr* Robin McCoy; *Instr* Anita Collings; *Instr* Mary Deltry; *Instr* Bruce Hippel
Estab 1974; pvt; D & E; scholarship; SC 14, LC 1; enrl D 1, E 8
Ent Req: None
Tuition: Varies
Courses: Calligraphy, Ceramics, Drawing, Mixed Media, Painting, Photography, Sculpture, Pottery
Summer School: Courses—Same classes offered during summer plus workshops and demonstrations

PARAMUS

BERGEN COMMUNITY COLLEGE, Fine Arts Dept,* 400 Paramus Rd, 07652. Tel 201-447-1500
Scholarships offered
Degrees: AA
Tuition: In county—$600 per yr; res—$1200 per yr; nonres—$2400 per yr
Courses: Art Appreciation, Calligraphy, Ceramics, Design, Drawing, Fashion Arts, Handicrafts, Painting, Photography, Sculpture

PATERSON

PASSAIC COUNTY COMMUNITY COLLEGE, Division of Humanities,* College Blvd, 07509. Tel 201-279-5000
Estab 1969, dept estab 1969; pub; D & E; SC 4, LC 3; enrl D 100, E 25
Ent Req: HS dipl, New Jersey basic skills exam
Degrees: AA 2 yrs
Tuition: $920 annual tuition
Courses: Advertising Design, Aesthetics, Art History, Drawing

PEMBERTON

BURLINGTON COUNTY COLLEGE, Fine Arts Dept,* Pemberton & Browns Mills Rd, 08068. Tel 609-894-9311. *Chmn* Robert Welsh
Degrees: AA
Tuition: County res—$29 per cr hr; non-county res—$31 per cr hr; non-state res—$77 per cr hr
Courses: Art Appreciation, Art Education, Art History, Calligraphy, Ceramics, Design, Drawing, Film, Handicrafts, Painting, Photography, Sculpture, Theatre Arts, Video

PRINCETON

PRINCETON UNIVERSITY
—**Dept of Art and Archaeology,** 104 McCormick Hall, 08540. Tel 609-452-3781. *Chmn Dept* John Shearman, PhD; *Chmn Prog Chinese and Japanese Art and Archaeology* Wen Fong, PhD; *Chmn Prog in Classical Archaeology* T Leslie Shear Jr, PhD; *Prof* David R Coffin, PhD; *Prof* Sam Hunter, MFA; *Prof* Robert Koch, PhD; *Prof* John R Martin, PhD; *Prof* John Plummer, PhD
Estab 1783; pvt; scholarships; LC 14, GC 9; enrl 761, maj 35, grad 50
Degrees: AB, MA, MFA, PhD
Tuition: Res—undergrad $9450 per yr, grad $9950 per yr; campus res room & board $3460 per yr
Courses: Art History, History of Art & Archaeology, Architecture History, History of Photography, Visual Arts
—**School of Architecture,** * Architecture Bldg, 08540. *Dean* Robert M Maxwell. Instrs: FT 14
Estab 1919; pvt; D; scholarships and fels; SC 6, LC 13, GC 6, seminars 17; enrl undergrad 120, grad 50
Ent Req: High
Degrees: AB 4 yr, MArchit, MArchit Art in Urban Design, PhD(Archit)
Tuition: $8480 annual tuition

RANDOLPH

COUNTY COLLEGE OF MORRIS, Art Dept, Route 10, Center Grove Rd, 07869. Tel 201-361-5000. *Chmn & Prof* Edyth Skinner
Estab 1970; pub; D & E; SC 15, LC 3; enrl maj 263
Ent Req: HS dipl
Degrees: AA(Humanities/Art) 2 yrs, AAS(Photography Technology) 2 yrs
Tuition: In-county $800 per yr; in-state $1764 per yr
Courses: Advertising Design, Art History, Ceramics, Drawing, Painting, Photography, Printmaking, Sculpture, Color & Design, Major Styles & Historical Periods, Modern Art
Summer School: Two 5 week day sessions, one evening session

RIDGEWOOD

RIDGEWOOD SCHOOL OF ART AND DESIGN, * 83 Chestnut St, 07450. Tel 201-444-7100. *Dir* Robert Crawford
Estab 1961; pvt; D & E; SC 35, LC 2; enrl D 150, E 50
Ent Req: HS dipl
Tuition: $2100 per yr; no campus res
Courses: Advertising Design, Art History, Ceramics, Commercial Art, Drawing, Fashion Arts, Graphic Design, Illustration, Lettering, Painting, Photography, Printmaking, Sculpture

SEWELL

GLOUCESTER COUNTY COLLEGE, Liberal Arts Dept,* Tanyard Rd, 08080. Tel 609-468-5000. *Head* Dr Ross Beitzel
Estab 1967; pub; D & E; scholarships; SC 6, LC 6
Ent Req: HS dipl
Tuition: In-county—$550 per yr; in-state—$19 per cr hr; nonres—$2560 per yr
Courses: Art History, Ceramics, Drawing, Graphic Arts, Jewelry, Mixed Media, Painting, Sculpture, arts & crafts for handicapped, general design
Summer School: Dir, Dr Mossman

SHREWSBURY

GUILD OF CREATIVE ART, * 620 Broad St, 07701. Tel 201-741-1441
Courses: Design, Drawing, Handicrafts, Painting, Stage Design

SOUTH ORANGE

SETON HALL UNIVERSITY, Dept of Art and Music,* South Orange Ave, 07079. Tel 201-762-9000. *Chmn* Petra Ten-Doesschate Chu, PhD; *Prof* Louis de Crenascol, LDD; *Prof* Julius Zsako, PhD; *Assoc Prof* F Ming Chang, MA; *Asst Prof* Edwin Havas; *Asst Prof* Barbara Kaufman, MA; *Asst Prof* Anthony Triano; *Asst Prof* William K Burns, MA; *Asst Prof* Jeanette Hile, MA; *Asst Prof* Joseph Wozniak, MA. Instrs: FT 10, PT 9
Estab dept 1968; pvt; D & E; SC 8
Degrees: BA 4 yr
Tuition: $2048 per sem
Courses: Architecture, Art Education, Art History, Commercial Art, Design, Drawing, Illustration, Mixed Media, Painting, Printmaking, Sculpture, Chinese Brush Painting, Music Art

TEANECK

FAIRLEIGH DICKINSON UNIVERSITY, Fine Arts Dept, 900 River Rd, 07666. Tel 201-692-2254. *Chairwoman* Mary Anne Farese, MEd; *Prof* A William Clark, MA; *Prof* Harold Keller, MA; *Prof* Robert Nunnelley, MFA; *Assoc Prof* Joan Taylor, MA; *Asst Prof* Jacqueline Rettig, MA
Estab 1942, dept estab 1965; pvt; D & E; scholarships offered; SC 37, LC 9; enrl D 367, E 139, non-maj 466, maj 40
Ent Req: HS dipl, SAT
Degrees: BA(Fine Arts)
Tuition: Res undergrad—$8197 per yr; nonres undergrad $157 per cr hr; campus res available
Courses: Advertising Design, Art Appreciation, Art History, Calligraphy, Ceramics, Commercial Art, Constructions, Design, Display, Drafting, Drawing, Graphic Arts, History of Art & Archaeology, Illustration, Lettering, Mixed Media, Painting, Photography, Printmaking, Sculpture

TOMS RIVER

OCEAN COUNTY COLLEGE, Humanities Dept, College Drive, 08753. Tel 201-255-4000, Ext 333 or 255-1131. *Chmn Dept* Dr James Doran, EdD; *Asst to Chmn Fine and Performing Arts* Robert L Huber, MA; *Prof* Tom Funk, MFA; *Prof* William Schoenfeld, MA; *Prof* Howard Unger, EdD
Estab 1964, dept estab 1964; pub; D & E; SC 19, LC 3; enrl D 1500, E 1500, maj 67
Ent Req: HS dipl
Degrees: AA in Liberal Arts with concentration in Fine Art & AAS(Visual Communication Technology) 2 yrs
Tuition: Res—undergrad $700 per yr, $350 per sem, PT $29; nonres—undergrad $820 per yr, $410 per sem, PT $34; no campus res
Courses: †Advertising Design, Aesthetics, †Art History, Calligraphy, †Ceramics, †Commercial Art, †Conceptual Art, Costume Design & Construction, †Drawing, †Film, †Graphic Arts, †Graphic Design, †Handicrafts, †Lettering, †Painting, †Photography, †Printmaking, †Sculpture, †Stage Design, †Theatre Arts
Summer School: Dir, Dr James Doran. Enrl 175; tuition $29 for term of 5 wks or 6 wks beginning June. Courses—Arts and Humanities, Basic Drawing, Ceramics, Crafts

TRENTON

TRENTON STATE COLLEGE, Art Dept, Pennington Rd, 08625. Tel 609-771-2652. *Chmn Dept* Dr Howard Goldstein; *Prof* Ilse Johnson, MA; *Prof* Norval C Kern, EdD; *Prof* Joseph Shannon, EdD; *Assoc Prof* Hiroshi Murata, MFA; *Asst Prof* Robert Bird, MA; *Asst Prof* Wendell Brooks, MFA; *Asst Prof* Saundra De Geneste, MFA; *Asst Prof* Christina Craig, MA; *Asst Prof* Lois Fichner-Rathus, PhD; *Asst Prof* Sylvia Honig, MAATR; *Asst Prof* Charles Kumnick, MFA; *Asst Prof* Mark Lehman, MFA; *Asst Prof* Joan Wadleigh Curran, MFA; *Asst Prof* Bruce Rigby, MFA; *Asst Prof* Louis Ross, MA; *Asst Prof* Marcia Taylor, PhD, MAATR; *Asst Prof* Jacqueline Gikow, MFA; *Asst Prof* Marilyn Hochhouser, MA; *Asst Prof* Kenneth Kaplowitz, MFA. Instrs: FT 20, PT 9

Estab 1855; pub; D & E; scholarship; SC approx 40, LC 10, GC 11; enrl non-maj 300, maj 600
Ent Req: HS dipl
Degrees: BA 4 yr
Tuition: Res—$1257.60; nonres—$1897.60
Courses: †Advertising Design, †Art Education, †Art History, Calligraphy, Ceramics, Drawing, Fashion Arts, Graphic Arts, Illustration, †Interior Design, Jewelry, Lettering, Painting, Photography, Printmaking, , Sculpture, Silversmithing, Teacher Training, Textile Design, †Art Therapy, Crafts, †Fine Arts
Children's Classes: Sat mornings, fall sem
Summer School: June & July five wk sessions

UNION

KEAN COLLEGE OF NEW JERSEY, Fine Arts Dept,* Morris Ave, 07083. Tel 201-527-2307. *Chmn Fine Arts Dept* James Howe, MA; *Instr Interior Design* H Bernard Lipscomb III, MA; *Instr Art Educ* Pearl Greenbert, EdD; *Instr Visual Commun* W Martin Holloway, MFA; *Instr Specialized Studio* Leonard Pierro, MA; *Instr Art History* Virginia Stotz, MA. Instrs: FT 31
Estab 1855; pub; D & E; scholarships; SC 58, LC 37, GC 24; enrl FT 383, PT 236, maj 656, grad 37
Ent Req: HS dipl, portfolio interview for art maj
Degrees: BA 4 yr
Tuition: Res—$27 per sem hr; nonres—$47 per sem hr; campus res available
Courses: Advertising Design, Aesthetics, †Art Education, †Art History, Ceramics, †Commercial Art, Display, Drafting, Drawing, Film, Graphic Arts, Graphic Design, Illustration, †Interior Design, Jewelry, Lettering, Museum Staff Training, Occupational Therapy, Painting, Photography, Painting, Printmaking, Sculpture, Textile Design, Furniture Making
Summer School: Asst Dir, Mrs Madsen. Tui $25 per cr for term of 6 wks beginning June 26. Courses—Art History, Art in Education, Ceramics, Drawing, Introduction to Art, Introduction to Interior Design, Jewelry, Life Drawing, Painting, Printmaking, Sculpture, Watercolor

VINELAND

CUMBERLAND COUNTY COLLEGE, Humanities Dept, College Dr & Sherman Ave, 08360. Tel 609-691-8600. *Prof* C Frederick Horbach, PhD
Tuition: County res—$350 per sem; out of county res—$700 per sem; out of state res—$1400 per sem
Courses: Art Appreciation, Art History, Drawing, Painting, Photography, Video

WAYNE

WILLIAM PATERSON COLLEGE, Art Dept, Div of Fine and Performing Arts, 300 Pompton Rd, 07470. Tel 201-881-2402. *Chmn* Alan H Lazarus. Instrs: FT 24, PT 8
Dept estab 1958; pub; scholarships; SC 9, LC 9; enrl maj 420, grad 105, E non-maj 170
Degrees: BA 4 yr, BFA, MA
Tuition: Res—$70.75, undergrad $34
Courses: Art History, Graphic Design, Painting, Sculpture, Enameling, Furniture Design, Gallery Workshop & Design, Lapidary, Metal
Summer School: Enrl 80-100; tuition $34 per cr. Courses—Art History, Drawing, Painting

WEST LONG BRANCH

MONMOUTH COLLEGE, Dept of Art, Norwood & Cedar Aves, 07764. Tel 201-222-6600, Ext 346. *Chmn* Alfred Provencher, MA; *Assoc Prof* Vincent DiMattio, MFA; *Assoc Prof* Arie van Everdingen, MFA; *Assoc Prof* Martin Ryan, MA; *Asst Prof* Edward Jankowski, MFA; *Instructor* Hedy daCosta-Nunes, MA
Estab 1933; pvt; D & E; scholarship; SC 25, LC 8; enrl in dept D 108, E 6, non-maj 80, maj 108, audits 6
Ent Req: HS dipl, portfolio for transfer students
Degrees: BA(Art), BFA and BA(Art Educ) 4 yr
Tuition: $3480 per yr, $740 per sem, $105 per cr hr; campus res—room and board $900
Courses: †Art Education, Art History, †Ceramics, Drawing, Graphic Arts, Handicrafts, History of Art & Archaeology, †Painting, Photography, Printmaking, †Sculpture, Teacher Training, Appreciation of Art, Metalsmithing
Adult Hobby Classes: Courses—Painting
Summer School: Dean, Kenneth C Stunkel. Enrl approx 80; tuition $89 per cr hr for 3 or 6 wk courses beginning June 2. Courses—Art Appreciation, Ceramics, Independent Study, Painting, Sculpture

NEW MEXICO

ALBUQUERQUE

AMERICAN CLASSICAL COLLEGE, 614 Indian School Rd NW, 87102. Tel 505-843-7749. *Dir* Dr C M Flumiani. Instrs: FT 2
Estab 1970; pvt; D; scholarship
Ent Req: Ent exam
Degrees: None
Tuition: FT $100 mo
Courses: Advertising Design, Aesthetics, Art Education, Commercial Art, Drawing, History of Art & Archaeology, Painting, Sculpture

SOUTHWESTERN SCHOOL OF ART, 10301 Comanche NE, 87111. Tel 505-299-0316. *Dir* Ted C Hogsett, BS; *Asst Dir* Doug Dean; *Instructor* Cherie Kelly; *Instructor* Lucille Kologie; *Instructor* Margaret Smithers
Estab 1972; pvt; D & E; SC 7, LC 8; enrl D 20, E 46
Degrees: Cert
Tuition: Adults $48 per 8 week session, children $45 per 8 week session; no campus res
Courses: Art History, Drawing, Painting
Adult Hobby Classes: Enrl $350 per yr; tuition $48 per course of 8 wks.
Courses—Drawing, Figure Workshops, Oil Painting, Portraiture, Watercolor
Children's Classes: Enrl 150; tuition $45 per course fo 8 wks. Courses—Drawing, Oil Painting
Summer School: Dir, Ted Hogsett. Enrl 125, tuition $48 per course of 8 wks. Courses—Figure Workshops, Drawing, Oil Painting, Portraiture, Watercolor

UNIVERSITY OF ALBUQUERQUE, Art Dept, Saint Joseph Place NW, 87140. Tel 505-831-1111. *Dept Head* Ed Vega
Estab 1920; den; D & E; SC 30, LC 12; enrl maj 32
Ent Req: HS dipl
Degrees: AA(Advertising Art) 2 yrs, BA and BFA 4 yrs
Courses: †Advertising Design, Art Education, Art History, †Ceramics, Commercial Art, Costume Design & Construction, †Drawing, Fashion Arts, Graphic Arts, Graphic Design, Illustration, Industrial Design, Jewelry, Lettering, †Painting, †Photography, Printmaking, Sculpture, Silversmithing, Stage Design
Summer School: Dean, Sister Flora. Tuition $115 per cr hr for term of 5 wks beginning May 26-June 30. Courses—Bronze Casting, Ceramics, Drawing, Watercolor

UNIVERSITY OF NEW MEXICO
—College of Fine Arts,* Fine Arts Ctr, 87131. Tel 505-277-2111. *Dean Col* Donald C McRae, MA
Estab 1935; pub
Tuition: Res—$384 per yr; nonres—$1224 per yr
—Dept of Art, 87131. Tel 505-277-5861. *Chmn* Garo Z Antreasian, BFA
Estab 1889; pub; D & E; scholarships; SC 190, LC 43, GC 73; enrl E 511, non-maj 230, maj 227, grad 116
Ent Req: HS dipl
Degrees: BA and BFA 4 yrs, MA 2 yrs, MFA 3 yrs, PhD 3 yrs
Tuition: Res—undergrad $774 per yr, $387 per sem, grad $776 per yr, $388 per sem; nonres—undergrad $2568 per yr, $1284 per sem, grad $2570 per yr, $1285 per sem
Courses: Art History, Ceramics, Drawing, Jewelry, Painting, Photography, Printmaking, Sculpture
Children's Classes: Offered through Art Educ Dept
Summer School: Tuition res $32.25 per cr hr, 6 - 9 hrs $100. Eight week term beginning June 7. Courses—same as above
—Tamarind Institute, 108 Cornell Ave SE, 87131. Tel 505-277-3901. *Dir* Clinton Adams; *Asst Dir* Marjorie Devon; *Tamarind Master Printer & Studio Mgr* Lynne Allen Haberman
Fellowships offered
Degrees: Two yr prog leading to cert as Tamarind Master Printer
Tuition: Res—$30 per cr hr; non-res—$93 per cr hr
Courses: †Lithography
Summer School: Intensive summer study program leading to acceptance into regular programs. Dues regular university fees plus approx $500 - on campus res available

FARMINGTON

SAN JUAN COMMUNITY COLLEGE, Art Dept, 4601 College Blvd, 87401. Tel 505-326-3311. Instrs: FT 1, PT 2
Scholarships offered
Degrees: AA
Tuition: Res—$180; nonres—$504
Courses: Art Appreciation, Art Education, Art History, Calligraphy, Ceramics, Design, Drawing, Film, Graphic Design, Jewelry, Painting, Photography, Printmaking, Sculpture
Summer School: Dir, Jay B Zelber. Enrl 50; tuition $15 per cr hr. Courses—Motion Picture as Art, Painting, Drawing, Ceramics

HOBBS

NEW MEXICO JUNIOR COLLEGE, Arts, Business & Humanities Division, Lovington Hwy, 88240. Tel 505-392-6526. *Chmn* Joe Walker, MA; *Instr* Terry Bumpass, MFA; *Instr* Lawrence Wilcox, MFA
Estab 1965; dept estab 1965; pub; D & E; scholarships; SC 5, LC 1; enrl D 75, E 25, non-maj 95, maj 5
Ent Req: HS dipl, GED or special approval
Degrees: AA 2 yrs
Courses: Advertising Design, Ceramics, Drawing, Goldsmithing, Interior Design, Jewelry, Painting, Photography, Printmaking, Color & Design
Summer School: Div Chmn, Joe Walker. Enrl 30; term of 8 wks beginning June 10. Courses—Ceramics, Printmaking

LAS CRUCES

NEW MEXICO STATE UNIVERSITY, Art Dept, Box 3572, 88003. Tel 505-646-1705. *Dept Head & Prof* John Catterall, MFA; *Prof* Ken Barrick, MA; *Prof* William Charland, MFA; *Prof* Spencer Fidler, MFA; *Prof* John Moffitt, PhD; *Prof* Lee Richards, EdD; *Prof* Kate Wagle, MFA; *Prof* Peter Voris, MFA; *Prof* Christiane L Joost-Gaugier, PhD
Estab 1975; pub; D & E; SC 52, LC 25, GC 53; enrl maj 100, grad 24
Ent Req: HS dipl
Degrees: BA, BFA & BS(Art Educ) 4 yrs, MA(Studio), MA(Art Hist) & MS(Art Educ) 2 yrs
Tuition: Res—$798 per yr, $399 per sem; nonres—$2586 per yr, $1293 per sem

Courses: Architecture, †Art Education, †Art History, †Ceramics, Conceptual Art, †Drawing, Graphic Arts, Handicrafts, History of Art & Archaeology, Jewelry, Museum Staff Training, †Painting, Photography, †Printmaking, †Sculpture, †Design, †Metal Arts, Weaving
Summer School: Tuition $186 for term of 6 wks. Courses—Art Appreciation, Ceramics, Drawing, Painting, Sculpture

LAS VEGAS

NEW MEXICO HIGHLANDS UNIVERSITY, Division of Fine Arts,* 87701. Tel 505-425-7111, Ext 359. *Chmn* Dr Loren E Wise, DMA; *Prof* Harry M Leippe, MA; *Asst Prof* Helen Thompson, MFA; *Asst Prof* Carolyn Powers, MA; *Asst Prof* Nancy Rosnow, MFA
Estab 1898; pub; D & E; scholarships; SC 24, LC 8, GC 12; enrl non-maj 55, maj 51, grad 4
Ent Req: HS dipl, ACT, Early Admis Prog, GED
Degrees: BA 4 yrs, MA 1 yr
Tuition: Res—$255 per sem; nonres—$898 per sem; campus res available
Courses: Art Education, Art History, Calligraphy, Ceramics, Constructions, Drawing, Graphic Arts, Jewelry, Lettering, Painting, Photography, Printmaking, Sculpture, Silversmithing, Stage Design, Teacher Training, Theatre Arts
Adult Hobby Classes: Courses—Ceramics, Painting, Weaving
Summer School: Dean, Jessie Querry. Tuition same as above. Courses—Mainly studio plus core curriculum, depending upon staffing

PILAR

PLUM TREE FINE ARTS PROGRAM, Box 1-A, 87571. Tel 505-758-4696. *Coordr* Dick Thibodeau, BFA; *Dir* John Patrick Lamkin
Estab 1982; pvt; D; scholarships; SC 26; enrl D 105
Tuition: Campus res available
Courses: Advertising Design, Ceramics, Drawing, Graphic Arts, Lettering, Mixed Media, Painting, Photography, Printmaking, Sculpture
Summer School: Enrl 105; tuition $50-$250

PORTALES

EASTERN NEW MEXICO UNIVERSITY, Dept of Art,* 88130. Tel 505-562-2652. *Chmn* Chris Gikas, MFA; *Prof* Vernon Acker, MFA; *Prof* Charles Wiley, PhD; *Assoc Prof* Dale Hamlett, MA
Estab 1932; pub; D & E; scholarships; SC 44, LC 6, GC 25; enrl D 550, E 220, maj 105, grad 20
Ent Req: HS dipl, GED, ACT
Degrees: AA 2 yrs, BS, BA & BFA 4 yrs
Courses: †Advertising Design, Art Education, Art History, Calligraphy, †Ceramics, †Commercial Art, Drafting, †Drawing, †Graphic Arts, Graphic Design, History of Art & Archaeology, Illustration, †Jewelry, Lettering, †Painting, Photography, †Sculpture, Silversmithing, †Teacher Training, Theatre Arts, Video
Summer School: Chmn, Chris Gikas. Term of 8 wks beginning June 4. Courses—Ceramics, Commercial Art, Crafts, Drawing, Lettering, Photography

RUIDOSO

CARRIZO ART AND CRAFT WORKSHOPS, Carrizo Canyon Rd, PO Drawer A, 88345. Tel 505-257-9131. *Art Dir* Ken Hosmer. Instrs: PT 75
Estab 1956; pvt; D; SC 150; enrl 700 summer school; 300 fall school; 300 spring school
Ent Req: Art interest
Tuition: $100 to $185 for 1 wk workshop; campus res—room & board $200-$500 for 1 wk
Courses: Calligraphy, Mixed Media, Painting, Photography, Sculpture, Weaving, Creative Writing, Stained Glass

SANTA FE

COLLEGE OF SANTA FE, Visual Art Division, Humanities Dept, Saint Michael's Dr, 87501. Tel 505-473-6557. *Assoc Prof* Ronald Picco, MFA; *Asst Prof* Linda Nestor, MFA; *Instructor* Ralph Pardington, MFA; *Instructor* David Schienbaum, MFA
Estab 1947, dept estab 1974; pvt; D & E; scholarships; SC 26, LC 20; enrl D 200, E 50, non-maj 50, maj 70, others 20 (sr citizens)
Ent Req: HS dipl or GED
Degrees: BFA(Visual Arts)
Tuition: $110 per sem hr; campus res—room & board $1800 per yr
Courses: †Art Education, Ceramics, Drawing, Painting, Photography, Printmaking, Sculpture, Primitive Pottery, Southwestern Art History, †Studio Arts, 2-D & 3-D Design
Adult Hobby Classes: Photo Silkscreening
Summer School: Dir, Ron Picco. Tuition $110 per sem hr for term of 4-12 wks beginning May 15. Courses—Art History, Drawing, Outdoor Sketching, Landscape Painting, Photography, Printmaking, Primitive Pottery

INSTITUTE OF AMERICAN INDIAN ARTS, 1369 Cerrillos Rd, 87501. Tel 505-988-6281. *Dir* Charles A Dailey
Estab 1962; pvt; D; scholarships; SC 18, LC 11; enrl 263
Ent Req: HS dipl
Degrees: AA (Fine Arts) 2 yrs
Tuition: $60 per hr non-Indian, free to native Americans
Courses: Museum Staff Training, Traditional Indian Techniques, Two & Three-Dimensional Design
Summer School: Dir, Jon Wade. Enrl 150; tuition $60 per cr hr, free to Native Americans. Courses—Arts, Creative Writing, Museum Training

SANTA FE WORKSHOPS OF CONTEMPORARY ART,* PO Box 1344, 87501. Tel 505-983-5573. *Adv Dir* Geraldine Price
Estab 1959, Santa Fe 1971; pvt; D; scholarships; enrl limited
Ent Req: Age 18 or over
Degrees: Certificate
Courses: Drawing, Painting, Art Therapy

SOUTHWEST ART LEAGUE SEMINARS, Art Horizons Ltd (Mailing add: PO Box 4605, 87502). Tel 505-982-9981, 983-4825. *Head Dept* Maurice Loriaux, PhD; *Instr* James Whitlow
Estab 1971; D & E; enrl all seminars are limited to 16 delegates
Ent Req: Intermediate proficiency in painting—watercolor, oil, acrylics, all styles
Tuition: $525 per 10 day seminar includes room & board
Courses: All media

SILVER CITY

WESTERN NEW MEXICO UNIVERSITY, College of Arts and Letters, Art Dept, 88061. Tel 505-538-6517. *Dean* James Waddell; *Prof* Susan Eigenbrodt, MFA; *Prof* Cecil Howard, MFA; *Prof* Polly Hughes, MA; *Prof* Tom Hollenderr, MA; *Prof* Claude Smith, MFA
Pub; D & E; SC 10, LC 7; enrl D 200, non-maj 160, maj 40
Ent Req: HS dipl
Degrees: BA, 4yrs
Tuition: Campus residence available
Courses: Art Education, Art History, †Ceramics, Collages, Constructions, Drawing, Graphic Design, †Jewelry, Mixed Media, †Painting, †Printmaking, †Sculpture, Silversmithing, Teacher Training, Textile Design, Fiber Arts
Adult Hobby Classes: Courses—Ceramics, Lapidary, Silversmithing, Stained Glass
Summer School: Dir Summer Sessions, John Batler. Courses—Art Appreciation, Ceramics, Drawing, Painting, Special Workshops

NEW YORK

ALBANY

COLLEGE OF SAINT ROSE, Division of Art,* 432 Western Ave, 12203. Tel 518-454-5111. *Assoc Prof* Patricia Clahassey, EdD; *Assoc Prof* Karene Faul, MFA; *Asst Prof* Leonard LaRoux, MFA; *Asst Prof* Paul Mauren, MFA; *Asst Prof* Judith Lodge, MFA; *Instr* Dean Peterson, MA
Estab 1920, dept estab 1970; pvt; D & E; scholarships; SC 21, LC 7, GC 8; enrl non-maj 200, maj 111, GS 14
Ent Req: HS dipl, SAT or ACT, rank in top 2/5 of class
Degrees: BS(Art, Art Educ, Advertising & Graphic Design, Studio Art), MS(Art Educ)
Tuition: $2200 per sem
Courses: †Advertising Design, Aesthetics, †Art Education, Art History, Calligraphy, Ceramics, †Drawing, Graphic Arts, Handicrafts, Illustration, Jewelry, †Painting, Photography, †Printmaking, Sculpture, Teacher Training, Weaving, Fibers, Studio Art
Adult Hobby Classes: Enrl 20; tui $57.50 per cr hr. Courses—Some continuing education courses each semester

JUNIOR COLLEGE OF ALBANY, Fine Arts Division, 12208. Tel 518-445-1778. *Chairperson* Nance Goren
Estab 1957, dept estab 1970; pvt; D & E; scholarships; SC 43, LC 16 (Art); enrl D 1000 (total), 200 (art), E 823 (total)
Ent Req: HS dipl, references, records, SAT
Degrees: AA, AS and AAS 2 yrs
Courses: Advertising Design, Art Education, Art History, Ceramics, Commercial Art, Drawing, Graphic Arts, Graphic Design, Handicrafts, Illustration, Interior Design, Jewelry, Mixed Media, Painting, Photography, Printmaking, Sculpture, Theatre Arts, Serigraphy, Special Education, State Design
Children's Classes: Summer courses for High School students
Summer School: Dir, Robert Pennock. Courses—vary

STATE UNIVERSITY OF NEW YORK AT ALBANY, Art Dept, 1400 Washington Ave, 12222. Tel 518-457-8487. *Chair Dept* Dennis Byng, MS; *Prof* Edward Mayer, MFA; *Prof* Edward Cowley, MA; *Prof* Mojimir Frinta, PhD; *Prof* Thom O'Connor, MFA; *Prof* William Wilson, MFA; *Prof* Richard Callner, MAFA; *Assoc Prof* Mark Greenwold; *Assoc Prof* Arthur Lennig; *Assoc Prof* Robert Cartmell, MFA; *Assoc Prof* Phyllis Galembo; *Asst Prof* Roberta Bernstein, PhD; *Asst Prof* Marja Vallila, MFA
Estab 1848; pub; D & E; scholarships; SC 43, LC 20, GC 33; enrl D 750, E 400, non-maj 600, maj 150, grad 45
Ent Req: HS dipl and portfolio
Degrees: BA 4 yr, MA 1.5 yr, MFA 2 yr
Tuition: Res—Undergrad $4600 yr, $35 cr, $2455 for commuter, grad $5130 per sem, $71 hr; Nonres—Undergrad $5300 yr, $40 cr hr, grad $1500 per sem, $90 hr; campus residence room and board $2280 per yr
Courses: Aesthetics, Art History, Calligraphy, Collages, Constructions, †Drafting, History of Art & Archaeology, Intermedia, Mixed Media, †Painting, †Photography, †Printmaking, †Sculpture, Theatre Arts, Plastics
Adult Hobby Classes: Courses in all studio areas
Summer School: Asst Dean Grad Studies, Paul Saimond. Enrl 350; term of 3 - 6 wks beginning July 1

ALFRED

NEW YORK STATE COLLEGE OF CERAMICS AT ALFRED UNIVERSITY, Division of Art & Design, 14802. Tel 607-871-2442. *Head Dept* Tony Hepburn.
Instrs: FT 20
Estab 1900; enrl maj undergrad 280, grad 25, others 250. Two yrs of foundation study and two yrs of upper level study
Degrees: BFA and MFA 4 yrs
Tuition: Res—undergrad $2250, grad $2750; nonres—undergrad $3350, grad $3550; campus res—room & board $2660
Courses: Art Education, Ceramics, Painting, Photography, Printmaking, Sculpture, Video, Design, Glass
Summer School: Dean, Lewis Butler

AMHERST

DAEMEN COLLEGE, Art Dept, 14226. Tel 716-839-3600, Ext 241. *Chmn Dept* Carol A Townsend, MFA; *Prof* Sr M Jeanne File, PhD; *Prof* James K Y Kuo, MA; *Prof* James A Allen, MFA; *Assoc Prof* Margaret Bacon, EdD; *Assoc Prof* Dennis Barraclough, MFA; *Assoc Prof* Bruce Marzahn, MFA; *Asst Prof* Elizabeth Simon, MFA
Estab 1947; pvt; D & E; SC 55; enrl D 1400, non-maj 1100, maj 100
Ent Req: HS dipl, art portfolio
Degrees: BFA(Ceramics, Graphic Design, Painting, Printmaking, Sculpture), BS(Art) and BS(Art Educ) 4 yrs
Tuition: Undergrad—$2230, per sem, $147 per cr hr; campus res—room & board $1500
Courses: Aesthetics, Art Education, Art History, Calligraphy, Ceramics, Drawing, †Graphic Design, Illustration, Painting, Photography, Printmaking, Sculpture, Silversmithing, Teacher Training, Theatre Arts
Summer School: Dean, Mary Anne Rehnke

ANNANDALE-ON-HUDSON

BARD COLLEGE, Milton Avery Graduate School of the Arts, Division of Art, Music, Drama, 12504. Tel 914-758-6822, Ext 133. *Dir Program* Adolfas Mekas; *Instructor* Benjamin Boretz; *Instructor* Robert Kelly; *Instructor* Alan Cote; *Instructor* Jacob Grossberg; *Instructor* Elie Yarden; *Instructor* Joan Tower; *Instructor* David Diao; *Instructor* Elaine Mayes; *Instructor* Regina Granne
Estab 1981; pvt; scholarships; enrl 43
Degrees: MFA
Tuition: $3055
Courses: †Painting, †Photography
Summer School: A student will normally be in residence for four summers terms, earning 13 credits per term; eight credits are awarded for the Master's project, for a total of 60. When advisable, student can undertake independent work for credit, over two winters away from Bard, in lieu of attendance at one of the summer sessions

AURORA

WELLS COLLEGE, Dept of Art & Art History, 13026. Tel 315-364-3281. *Division Chmn* Sheila Edmunds
Estab 1868; pvt, W; D; SC 19, LC 20; enrl D 500(total), non-maj 122, maj 18
Ent Req: HS dipl, credit by examination programs
Degrees: BA 4 yrs
Tuition: Res—undergrad $6,500 per yr; campus res available
Courses: Aesthetics, †Art History, †Ceramics, †Drawing, †Painting, Photography, Printmaking, Teacher Training, †Theatre Arts

BAYSIDE

QUEENSBOROUGH COMMUNITY COLLEGE, Dept of Art and Design, 11364. Tel 212-631-6395. *Chmn & Prof* John Hawkins, MFA; *Prof* Lola B Gellman, PhD; *Assoc Prof* Paul Tschinkel, MFA; *Assoc Prof* Kenneth Walpuck, PhD; *Asst Prof* Robert Rogers, MFA; *Asst Prof* Heina Wipfler, MA; *Lectr* Jules Allen
Estab 1958, dept estab 1968; pub; D & E; scholarships; SC 21, LC 14; enrl D 9000, E 4000
Ent Req: HS dipl, placement exams
Degrees: AA, AS and AAS
Tuition: Res—undergrad $612.50 per sem, $40 per cr; nonres—undergrad $1012.50 per sem, $76 per cr; no campus res
Courses: Advertising Design, Art History, Ceramics, Drawing, Painting, Photography, Printmaking, Sculpture, Video, Arts Internships, Color Theory, Design
Adult Hobby Classes: Enrl 18; tuition $65 - $90 per course. Courses—Antiques, Calligraphy, Interior Design, Jewelry, Photography, Stained Glass, Ceramics, Cabinetmaking, Drawing Techniques
Summer School: Dir, Will Valk. Tuition $40 per cr for term of 7 wks beginning mid-June. Courses—Ceramics, Drawing, Photography, Watercolor

BEDFORD HILLS

GOETZ ART SCHOOL, 535 Bedford Center Rd, 10507. Tel 914-234-9417. *Dir* Richard V Goetz; *Instructor* Edith Goetz
Estab 1946; pvt; D & E; SC 6, LC 2; enrl D 70, E50
Tuition: Monthly; no campus residence
Courses: Aesthetics, Drawing, Mixed Media, Painting, Painting (figure, landscape, portrait, still life)
Summer School: Enrl 50-70; tuition $75 per wk for term of 4 wks beginning June 1

BINGHAMTON

STATE UNIVERSITY OF NEW YORK AT BINGHAMTON, Dept Of Art & Art History, Vestal Parkway East, 13901. Tel 607-798-2000. *Chmn Dept* Ed Wilson
Estab 1950; pub; D; scholarships; SC 18, LC 32, GC 63; enrl 679, non-maj 400, maj 82, grad 45
Ent Req: HS dipl, Regents Scholarship, ACT or SAT
Degrees: BA 4 yrs, MA 1-2 yrs, PhD varies

BROCKPORT

STATE UNIVERSITY OF NEW YORK COLLEGE AT BROCKPORT, Dept of Art, Fine Arts Bldg, 14220. Tel 716-395-2209. *Chmn* Wolodymyr Pylyshenko.
Instrs: FT 15
Pub; D; scholarships; SC 23, LC 29(Art History); enrl 8188, maj 200, grad 2000
Ent Req: HS dipl, ent exam
Degrees: BA & BS 4 yrs
Tuition: Res—$1050; nonres—$1750
Courses: Ceramics, Drawing, Graphic Design, History of Art & Archaeology, Jewelry, Painting, Photography, Printmaking, Sculpture
Children's Classes: Saturday morning classes; Courses—Ceramics
Summer School: Two five-week sessions per year

BRONX

BRONX COMMUNITY COLLEGE, Music & Art Dept, 180 St & University Ave, 10453. Tel 212-220-6213, 220-6240. *Chmn* Dr Marvin Salzberg; *Deputy Chmn* Peter Schira
Degrees: Cert
Courses: Art Appreciation, Art History, Ceramics, Commercial Art, Design, Drawing, Painting, Photography, Printmaking, Modern Art, Oriental Art
Adult Hobby Classes: Enrl 25; tuition $45 for 7 weeks. Courses—Calligraphy, Drawing

HERBERT H LEHMAN COLLEGE, Art Dept, 2 Van Cortlandt Ave E (Mailing add: Bedford Park Blvd, 10468). Tel 212-960-8256. *Chmn* George Corbin, PhD; *Prof* William McGee, MAT; *Prof* Richard Ziemann, MFA; *Prof Emeritus* Ursula Meyer, MA; *Assoc Prof* Theo Stavropoulos, BFA; *Assoc Prof* Arvn Bose; *Asst Prof* Salvatore Romano; *Asst Prof* Herbert Broderick, PhD; *Asst Prof* David Gillison, MFA; *Asst Prof* Perri Hale, MFA
Dept estab 1968; pub; D & E; scholarship; SC 18, LC 29, GC 31; enrl non-maj 100, major 50, grad 15
Ent Req: HS dipl, ent exam
Degrees: BA & BFA 4 yrs, MA, MFA & MA 2 yrs
Tuition: Res—undergrad $462.50 per sem, $35 & $40 per cr, grad $750 per sem, $75 per cr; nonres—undergrad $712.50 per sem, $55 per cr, grad $1000 per sem, $95 per cr; no campus res available
Courses: †Art History, †Graphic Arts, †Painting, †Sculpture
Summer School: Dean, Chester Robinson. Enrl 45; tuition $35 & $40 per cr for 6 wk term beginning June 28. Courses—Art History, Drawing, Painting

MANHATTAN COLLEGE, School of Arts and Sciences, Manhattan College Parkway, 10471. Tel 212-548-1400. *Chmn Fine Arts Dept* George L McGeary, EdD; *Asst Prof* John F Omelia, PhD; *Adjunct Lectr* Charles Porter; *Adjunct Lectr* Kavin Frederick
Estab 1853; pvt den; D & E; scholarships; LC 8; enrl D 4000
Ent Req: HS dipl
Degrees: BA 4 yrs
Tuition: Res—undergrad $6320 per yr, $135 per cr; nonres—undergrad $3820 per yr; campus res—room & board $2500 per yr
Courses: Aesthetics, Art Education, Art History, Ceramics, Drawing, Film, †Graphic Arts, Graphic Design, History of Art & Archaeology, †Painting, Photography, Printmaking, Sculpture, Video
Adult Hobby Classes: Enrl 40; tuition $135 per cr hr per sem
Summer School: Dean General Studies, Tom C Chambers. Tuition $135 per cr hr for 4 terms of 3-4 weeks beginning May 15. Courses—vary

BRONXVILLE

CONCORDIA COLLEGE, * 171 White Plains Rd, 10708. Tel 914-337-9300. *Assoc Prof* James Brauer; *Asst Prof* Ellen F Halter, MA
Estab 1881; pvt; D; scholarships; SC 4, LC 2
Ent Req: HS dipl, SAT or ACT
Degrees: BA and BS 4 yrs
Tuition: $3490 per sem
Courses: Art Education, Art History, Ceramics, Drawing, Handicrafts, History of Art & Archaeology, Painting, Photography, Sculpture, Teacher Training
Adult Hobby Classes: Courses—Painting

SARAH LAWRENCE COLLEGE, Dept of Art,* 10708. Tel 914-337-0700, Ext 394. *Staff* M Zakin; *Faculty* Frances Barth, MA; *Faculty* Douglas Baz, MBA & MS; *Faculty* Gary Burnley, MFA; *Faculty* Mary Dela Loyd, MA; *Faculty* Joseph C Forte, MA & MPhil; *Faculty* Philip Gould, BA; *Faculty* Marcia Hafif, MFA; *Faculty* Barbara Jaroche, MA; *Faculty* Mary Miss, MFA; *Faculty* John Newman, MFA; *Faculty* Christopher Sanderson, MFA; *Faculty* Ansei Uchima; *Faculty* Jerry Zeniuk, MFA. Instrs: FT 1, PT 9
Estab 1926; pvt; D; scholarships
Ent Req: HS dipl
Degrees: AB 4 yrs
Tuition: $8150 per yr
Courses: Ceramics, Drawing, Graphic Arts, Painting, Art History, Photography, Sculpture, Theatre Arts, Filmmaking
Summer School: Center for Continuing Education

BROOKLYN

BROOKLYN COLLEGE, Art & Art History Dept, Bedford Ave & Ave H, 11210.
Tel 212-780-5181. *Chmn* Morris Dorsky
Scholarships offered
Degrees: BA, BFA, MA, MFA
Courses: Architecture, Art History, Ceramics, Design, Drawing, Interior Design,
Painting, Photography, Printmaking, Sculpture

BROOKLYN MUSEUM ART SCHOOL,* Eastern Pkwy & Washington Ave,
11238. Tel 212-638-4486. *Asst Dir Education & Program Development* G
LeFrancois; *Registrar* Marjorie Stephens. Instrs: FT 1, PT 8
Estab 1841; pub; D & E; scholarships; enrl approx 300
Courses: Drawing, Painting, Photography, Printmaking, Sculpture
Children's Classes: Enrl 75, July-August. Courses—Drawing, Printmaking,
Sculpture, Painting
Summer School: Courses—Drawing, Graphics, Painting, Sculpture, Photography

KINGSBOROUGH COMMUNITY COLLEGE, Dept of Art, 2001 Oriental Blvd,
11235. Tel 212-394-5718. *Chmn* Thomas I Nonn, PhD
Estab 1965, dept estab 1972; pub; D & E; SC 10, LC 8; enrl maj 135
Ent Req: HS dipl
Degrees: AS 2 yrs
Courses: Art History, Ceramics, Drawing, Graphic Arts, Graphic Design, History of
Art & Archaeology, Intermedia, Mixed Media, Painting, Printmaking, Sculpture,
Theatre Arts
Summer School: Courses—Art

LONG ISLAND UNIVERSITY, Brooklyn Center Art Dept, University Plaza,
11201. Tel 212-403-1051. *Chmn* Cynthia Dantzic. Instrs: FT 2, PT 15
Pvt; D & E; scholarships; SC 5, LC 3
Ent Req: HS dipl, ent exam
Degrees: BA & BS 4 yrs
Tuition: $167 per cr
Courses: Art History, Calligraphy, Ceramics, Drawing, Painting, Printmaking,
Sculpture, Arts Management, Media Arts, Medical-Scientific Illustration, Teaching
Art to Children, Visual Experience
Adult Hobby Classes: Courses same as regular curriculum
Summer School: Term of two 6 wk sessions beginning June and July.
Courses—Drawing, History of Art, Painting, Workshop, Ceramics

**NEW YORK CITY TECHNICAL COLLEGE OF THE CITY UNIVERSITY OF
NEW YORK,** Dept of Art and Advertising Design, 300 Jay St, 11210. Tel 212-643-
8378. *Chairperson* Benjamin Einhorn, MA
Estab 1949, dept estab 1949; pub; D & E; SC 16, LC 3; enrl D 350, E 125
Ent Req: HS dipl
Degrees: AAS 2 yrs
Courses: †Advertising Design, Commercial Art, Drawing, Graphic Design,
Illustration, Lettering, Painting, Printmaking, Packaging, Paste-ups, Type Spacing
Summer School: Dir, B Einhorn. Enrl 50. Courses—Design, Lettering, Life
Drawing, Paste-up

PRATT INSTITUTE
—**School of Art and Design,*** 200 Willoughby Ave, 11205. Tel 212-636-3600, 636-
3619. *Actg Dean* Andrew Phelan
Pub; enrl 4400
Tuition: $2600 per sem
Courses: Art Education, Ceramics, Drawing, Fashion Arts, Film, Industrial Design,
Interior Design, Painting, Photography, Printmaking, Sculpture, Theatre Arts,
Illustration, Art Therapy, Communication Design
Adult Hobby Classes: Dean, Bruce Sharpe
Children's Classes: Morning classes
Summer School: Dean, Bruce Sharpe
—**School of Architecture,*** 200 Willoghby Ave, 11205. Tel 212-636-3405. *Dean*
Paul Herper
Degrees: BS and BProf Studies 4 yrs, BArchit 5 yrs, MArchit, MS(Urban Design),
MS(Planning), BArchit/MS(Urban Design) and BArchit/MS(Planning)
Tuition: Res—undergrad $138 per cr, grad $157 per cr
Courses: Architecture, Art History, Landscape Architecture, Design, History of
Architecture, Materials, Structures

BUFFALO

STATE UNIVERSITY OF NEW YORK, BUFFALO, Dept of Art and Art History,
2917 Main St, 14214. Tel 716-831-3477. *Chmn* Tyrone Georgion; *VChmn Art Hist*
L Vance Watrous
Estab 1894; pub; D & E; scholarships, fellowships; SC, LC, GC; enrl D 250, E 150,
grad 35
Ent Req: HS dipl, portfolio, for transfer students only
Degrees: BA and BFA 4 yrs, MFA 2 yrs, MAH 1 yr
Tuition: Res—undergrad $675 per sem, grad $45 per cr hr, grad $1075 per sem, $90 per
cr hr; nonres—undergrad $1325 per sem, $88.50 per cr hr, grad $1592 per sem,
$133 per cr hr; campus res—single $800 per sem, double $700 per sem, three-person
$625 per sem
Courses: Art Education, Art History, Drawing, Painting, Photography, Sculpture,
Communications Design, Design, Intaglio, Lithography, Serigraphy
Summer School: Actg Dean, Eric Streiff. Courses—Design Workshops, Drawing,
Painting, Photo & Film Workshops, Printmaking Workshops, Sculpture

STATE UNIVERSITY OF NEW YORK COLLEGE AT BUFFALO, Fine Arts
Dept, 1300 Elmwood Ave, 14222. Tel 716-878-6014. *Chmn* Robert W Brock. Instrs:
FT 16
Estab 1875, dept estab 1969; pub; D & E; SC 34, LC 17, GC 6; enrl maj 300 (art)
50 (BFA) 12 (art history)
Ent Req: HS dipl
Degrees: BA(Art), BA(Art History) & BFA 4 yrs

Tuition: Res—undergrad $675 per sem, $30 per cr hr; nonres undergrad—$1325 per
sem, $88.50 per cr hr; campus res available double $700 per sem
Courses: †Art History, Drawing, †Painting, †Photography, †Printmaking, †Sculpture,
Papermaking
Summer School: Limited course work; special workshops

VILLA MARIA COLLEGE OF BUFFALO, Art Dept,* 240 Pine Ridge Rd, 14225.
Tel 716-896-0700, Ext 324. *Assoc Prof* James W Jipson, MFA; *Instr* Brian R Duffy,
MFA; *Instr* Carol B Wells, MS; *Instr* Carole C Gates, MS
Estab 1961; pvt; D & E; scholarships; SC 27, LC 3; enrl D 450, E 100, maj 170
Ent Req: HS dipl of equivalency
Degrees: AA, AAS & AS 2 yrs
Tuition: $1125 per sem
Courses: Advertising Design, Art History, Ceramics, Commercial Art, Drafting,
Drawing, Graphic Arts, †Graphic Design, †Interior Design, Lettering, Painting,
†Photography, Printmaking, Sculpture, Textile Design
Adult Hobby Classes: Courses—Arts & Crafts, drawing, painting, photography,
quilting
Summer School: Enrl 10-20. courses—a variety of interest courses, including
drawing, painting and photography

CANANDAIGUA

COMMUNITY COLLEGE OF THE FINGER LAKES, Visual & Performing Arts
Dept,* Lincoln Hill Campus, 14424. *Chmn* John Walker, MFA; *Assoc Prof* Thomas
F Insalaco, MFA; *Asst Prof* John Fox, MFA. Instrs: FT 5
Estab 1966; pub; D & E; SC 14, LC 2; enrl D 60, non-maj 700, maj 50
Ent Req: HS dipl
Degrees: AA 2 yrs
Tuition: Res—$550 per sem; nonres—$1100 per sem
Courses: Advertising Design, Art History, Ceramics, Commercial Art, Drawing,
Graphic Arts, Graphic Design, Illustration, Painting, Photography, Printmaking,
Sculpture, Stage Design, Theatre Arts
Summer School: Courses—Per regular session

CANTON

SAINT LAWRENCE UNIVERSITY, Dept of Fine Arts, 13617. Tel 315-379-5192.
Chmn & Prof J Michael Lowe, MFA; *Prof* Harlan H Holladay, PhD; *Prof* Guy
Berard, MFA; *Assoc Prof* Roger Bailey, MFA; *Asst Prof* Elizabeth Kahn, PhD;
Instructor Betsy C Rezelman, MA
Estab 1856; pvt; D; SC 16, LC 13; enrl maj 30
Ent Req: HS dipl
Degrees: BA
Tuition: $7800 per yr; campus res—room & board $2710
Courses: Art History, Ceramics, Drawing, Painting, Photography, Printmaking,
Sculpture, Teacher Training
Summer School: Dir, P J Angelo

CAZENOVIA

CAZENOVIA COLLEGE, Center for Art & Design Studies, 13035. Tel 315-655-
9446, Ext 246. *Chmn* John Aistars, MFA; *Instructor* Laurel Long, MFA; *Instructor*
Jeanne King, BFA; *Instructor* Josef Ritter, BFA; *Instructor* Anita Fitzgerald, MFA;
Instructor Scotty Ottaviano, BFA
Estab 1824; pvt; D & E; scholarships; SC 21, LC 3
Ent Req: HS dipl
Degrees: AA, AS & AAS 2 yrs
Tuition: Res $4780 per yr, $120 per cr hr; campus res—room & board $2500
Courses: †Advertising Design, Ceramics, Drawing, Drafting, †Fashion Arts,
Illustration, †Interior Design, Landscape Architecture, Lettering, Painting,
Photography, Printmaking, Advertising Layout, Advanced Studio Art, Basic Design,
Typography, Rendering Residential Interiors, Office & Mercantile Interiors

CHAUTAUQUA

CHAUTAUQUA INSTITUTION, The Art Center, Box 1098, 14722. Tel 716-357-
4411, 357-6200, Ext 234. *Painting & Drawing* Revington Arthur; *Ceramics* Paul
Sires; *Head Sculpture* H Richard Duhme Jr; *Head Photography* Robert Gilson; *Head
Fibers* Kristin Rowley; *Painting & Drawing* Suzanne Roth; *Painting & Drawing*
Warren Taylor; *Ceramics* Linda Heckenkamp
Estab 1874; pub; D (summers only); scholarships; SC 40, LC 20; enrl D 500
Tuition: $50 per week; $520 per 8 wk term
Courses: Calligraphy, Ceramics, Drawing, Handicrafts, Interior Design, Jewelry,
Painting, Photography, Sculpture, Porcelain, Paper Sculpture, Stained Glass
Adult Hobby Classes: Courses—same as above
Children's Classes: Young artists programs, ages 6 - 15
Summer School: June 23 - Aug 25

CLAYTON

THOUSAND ISLANDS CRAFT SCHOOL & TEXTILE MUSEUM, 314 John St,
13624. Tel 315-686-4123. *Admin* Jane Gillett. Instrs: PT 27
Estab 1964; D & E; scholarships; SC 21; enrl D 210, E 10
Degrees: No degrees but transfer credit
Tuition: $50 plus $25 registration fee for each week course
Courses: Ceramics, Drawing, Jewelry, Photography, Weaving, Basketry, Bird
Carving, Country Painting, Decoy Carving, Manuscript Illumination, Pottery, Quilt
Making, Spinning, Stained Glass, Watercolor
Children's Classes: Courses—Drawing, Pottery, Weaving
Summer School: July 3 - August 25. Courses—Country Painting, Creative Stitchery,
Decoy Carving, Enameling, Pattern Weaving, Photography, Pottery, Reverse
Painting on Glass, Watercolor Painting, Weaving

CLINTON

HAMILTON COLLEGE, Art Dept, 13323. Tel 315-859-7468. *Chmn* Rand Carter, PhD; *Instr* Deborah Pokinski, PhD; *Instr* Steven Liebman, MFA; *Instr* Robert Palusky, MFA; *Instr* William Salzillo, MFA; *Instr* Robert Muirhead, MFA; *Instr* Michael Aurbach, MFA; *Instr* John McEnroe, PhD
Pvt; D; enrl non-maj 850, maj 50
Ent Req: HS dipl, SAT
Degrees: AB
Courses: Art History, Ceramics, Drawing, Painting, Photography, Printmaking, Video

COBLESKILL

STATE UNIVERSITY OF NEW YORK, AGRICULTURAL AND TECHNICAL COLLEGE, Art Dept, 12043. Tel 518-234-6694. *Art Dept* Charles C Matteson, MA
Estab 1950; pub; D & E; SC 2, LC 2; enrl D 95
Ent Req: HS dipl
Degrees: AA and AS 2 yrs
Tuition: Res—undergrad $675 per sem; nonres—undergrad $600 per sem; campus res—room & board $1260 per yr
Courses: Art Education, Art History, Drawing, Painting, Sculpture, Teacher Training, Theatre Arts
Adult Hobby Classes: Enrl 4000 per yr; tui $9 per course. Courses—large variety of mini-courses

CORNING

CORNING COMMUNITY COLLEGE, Division of Humanities, 14830. Tel 607-962-9238. *Chmn & Prof* John M Runyon, MFA; *Prof* Margaret Brill, MA; *Assoc Prof* Horst Werk, MFA. Instrs: FT 3
Estab 1958, dept estab 1963; pub; D & E; SC 8, LC 6
Ent Req: HS dipl, SAT
Degrees: AA, AS, AAS 2 yrs
Tuition: $550 per sem
Courses: Art History, Lettering, Ceramics, Drawing, Handicrafts, Jewelry, Painting, Silversmithing, Airbrush, 2-D & 3-D Design, Layout
Summer School: Dir, Nan Lanning

CORTLAND

STATE UNIVERSITY OF NEW YORK COLLEGE AT CORTLAND, Art Dept, 13045. Tel 607-753-4316. *Chmn* Bard Prentiss, MA; *Asst Prof* Steven Barbash, MFA; *Prof* Gerald DiGiusto, BFA; *Prof* John Jessiman, MFA; *Prof* Libby Kowalski, MFA; *Assoc Prof* George Dugan, MFA; *Assoc Prof* James Thorpe, MFA; *Assoc Prof* Frederick Zimmerman, PhD; *Asst Prof* David Craven, PhD; *Asst Prof* J Catherine Gibian, MFA; *Asst Prof* Charles Heasley; *Instructor* Mark Graham, MA
Estab 1868, dept estab 1948; pub; D & E; scholarships; SC 40, LC 10; enrl D 5300 (total), 1200 (art), maj 80
Ent Req: HS dipl, all college admissions standards based on high school average or scores from SAT, ACTP or Regent's tests
Degrees: BA 4 yrs
Tuition: Res—undergrad $1450 per yr; nonres—undergrad $3100 per yr; other college fee & activity assessment $87 per yr; campus res—$1400 per yr(room) and $972 per yr(board)
Courses: Aesthetics, Art Education, Art History, Ceramics, Drawing, Film, Graphic Arts, History of Art & Archaeology, Painting, Photography, Printmaking, Sculpture, Textile Design, Arts Management, Design, Lithography, Weaving
Summer School: Dir, William Lowe. Enrl approx 40; term of 6 wks beginning June 26. Courses—Art History, Studio

ELMIRA

ELMIRA COLLEGE, Art Dept,* 14901. Tel 607-734-3911, Ext 354. *Chmn* Dr Roger Held; *Asst Prof* Peter Chamberlain, MFA; *Asst Prof* Douglas Holtgrewe, MFA; *Instructor* Leslie Kramer, MFA
Estab 1855; pvt; D & E; scholarships; SC 26, LC 15, GC 8; enrl D 250, E 125, maj 35, grad 6
Ent Req: HS dipl
Degrees: AA, AS, BA, BS and MEduc
Tuition: $5990 per yr; campus res available
Courses: †Art Education, †Art History, †Ceramics, †Drawing, †Jewelry, †Painting, †Photography, †Printmaking, †Sculpture, †Silversmithing
Adult Hobby Classes: Art History, Ceramics, Graphics, Jewelry, Photography
Summer School: Art History, Ceramics, Raku

FARMINGDALE

STATE UNIVERSITY OF NEW YORK AT FARMINGDALE, Advertising Art Design Dept, Melville Rd, 11735. Tel 516-420-2000. *Dept Chmn* Francis N Pellegrini
Degrees: AAS
Courses: Advertising Design, Calligraphy, Design, Drawing, Illustration, Painting, Photography, Printmaking

FLUSHING

QUEENS COLLEGE, Art Dept, 11367. Tel 212-520-7000. *Chmn* Harold J Bruder
Degrees: BA, BFA, MA, MFA, MSEd
Courses: Advertising Design, Architecture, Art Appreciation, Art Education, Art History, Calligraphy, Ceramics, Design, Drawing, Illustration, Painting, Photography, Printmaking, Sculpture
Summer School: Courses held at Caumsett State Park

FOREST HILLS

CATAN-ROSE INSTITUTE OF ART, 72-72 112th St, 11375. Tel 212-263-1962. *Dir* Richard Catan-Rose
Estab 1943; pvt; D & E; scholarships
Ent Req: HS grad, no ent req for adult or children's classes
Degrees: Assoc Cert 2 yrs, Cert 4 yrs
Courses: Graphic Arts, Illustration, Fine Arts, Exterior Design, Research Projects
Summer School: 7 and 11 wks. Foundation courses—Fine Arts, Graphic Arts, Indoor and Outdoor, Interiors

FOREST HILLS ADULT EDUCATION SYSTEM, 6701 110th St, 11375. Tel 212-263-8066
Degrees: Cert
Courses: Art Appreciation, Art History, Calligraphy, Ceramics, Drawing, Handicrafts, Jewelry, Painting, Photography, Cartooning

FREDONIA

STATE UNIVERSITY COLLEGE, Dept of Art, 14063. Tel 716-673-3537. *Chmn* John Hughson, MFA
Estab 1867, dept estab 1948; pub; D & E; scholarships; SC 30, LC 18, GC 4; enrl D 650, E 70, non-maj 610, major 110
Ent Req: HS dipl, GRE, SAT, portfolio review (transfer students only)
Degrees: BA 4 yrs
Courses: †Art History, †Ceramics, †Commercial Art, †Drawing, †Graphic Arts, †Graphic Design, Illustration, Intermedia, Lettering, Mixed Media, †Painting, †Photography, †Printmaking, †Sculpture, Video

GARDEN CITY

ADELPHI UNIVERSITY, Dept of Art and Art History,* 11530. Tel 516-294-8700, Ext 7387. *Chmn* Harry Davies; *Prof* Grace Cantone, MA; *Prof* Milton Goldstein, MA; *Prof* W P Jennerjahn, MFA; *Assoc Prof* Yvonne Korshak; *Assoc Prof* Richard Vaux, MFA; *Asst Prof* Harvey Weiss, MA. Instrs: FT 8, PT 18
Estab 1896; pvt; D & E; scholarships; SC 40, LC 20, GC 20; enrl D 700, E 100, maj 130, grad 60
Ent Req: HS dipl; portfolio recommended for undergrad admission, required for grad
Degrees: BA 4 yrs, MA 1 1/2 yrs
Tuition: $2325 per sem; campus res available
Courses: Advertising Design, †Art Education, †Art History, Calligraphy, Ceramics, †Commercial Art, Drawing, Fashion Arts, Graphic Arts, Graphic Design, Jewelry, Painting, Photography, †Printmaking, †Sculpture, Weaving, Costume Design & Illustration, Enameling, Oriental Brush Painting, Stained Glass, Tapestry
Summer School: Dean, Gerald Heeger. Tui same as regular session; two 5 wk summer terms. Courses—Art Therapy, Creative Crafts, Drawing, Painting, Photography

NASSAU COMMUNITY COLLEGE, Art Dept,* Stewart Ave, 11530. Tel 516-222-7163. *Chmn & Prof* Robert Lawn; *Prof* Dr Stella Russell, PhD; *Prof* Jack Fink, MA; *Prof* Russell Housman, PhD; *Prof* Stanley Kaplan, MA; *Prof* Helen Muller, MA; *Prof* Leon Frankston, EDD; *Assoc Prof* Salli Zimmerman, MA; *Asst Prof* Charles Reina, MA; *Asst Prof* Helen Sisserson, MA
Estab 1959, dept estab 1960; pub; D & E; scholarships; SC 22, LC 5; enrl D 1213, E 712, non-maj 900-1000, maj 300
Ent Req: HS dipl
Degrees: AA, AS and AAS 2 yrs
Tuition: Res—$900 per yr; nonres—$1800 per yr
Courses: Advertising Design, Art History, Ceramics, Costume Design & Construction, Drafting, Drawing, Fashion Arts, Graphic Design, History of Art & Archaeology, Painting, Photography, Printmaking, Sculpture, Arts and Crafts (including macrame, jewelry, wood, paper, leather)
Summer School: Two 5 wk terms. Courses—By popular demand

GENESEO

STATE UNIVERSITY OF NEW YORK COLLEGE AT GENESEO, Dept of Art,* College of Arts & Science, 14454. Tel 716-245-5814. *Chmn* Paul Hepler. Instrs: FT 10, PT 2
Estab 1871; pub; D & E; SC 35, LC 7; enrl D 1000, E 1150, maj 115
Ent Req: HS dipl, ent exam
Degrees: BA(Art) 3-4 yrs
Tuition: $1050 per yr
Courses: Art Education, Art History, Ceramics, Drawing, Graphic Arts, Jewelry, Museum Staff Training, Painting, Photography, Sculpture, Textile Design, Photolithography, Wood Design
Summer School: Courses vary

GENEVA

HOBART AND WILLIAM SMITH COLLEGES, Art Dept, Houghton House, 14456. Tel 315-789-5500. *Chmn Dept* Dan Ewing. Instrs: FT 7
Estab approx 1822; pvt; D; scholarships; SC 15, LC 8; enrl D 1800
Ent Req: HS dipl, ent exam
Degrees: BA and BS 4 yrs
Courses: Aesthetics, Architecture, Drawing, Graphic Arts, History of Art & Archaeology, Painting, Sculpture

GREAT NECK

NORTH SHORE COMMUNITY ARTS CENTER,* Three St Pauls Place, 12123.
Tel 516-466-3636
Scholarships offered
Courses: Ceramics, Drawing, Jewelry, Painting, Printmaking, Sculpture

GREENVALE

C W POST CENTER OF LONG ISLAND UNIVERSITY, School of the Arts,*
11548. Tel 516-299-2464. *Chmn* Joyce Rosa; *Prof* Stanley Brodsky; *Prof* Arthur
Leipzig; *Prof* Arthur Silver; *Prof* Alfred VanLoen; *Prof* Donald Yacoe; *Prof* Jerome
Zimmerman; *Assoc Prof* Roger Goldstein; *Assoc Prof* Rose Krebs; *Assoc
Prof* Robert Yasuda; *Asst Prof* Lynn Croton; *Asst Prof* Gail Davidson; *Asst Prof*
William Hogarth; *Asst Prof* JoAnn Powers; *Asst Prof* Jack Stuck; *Asst Prof* Vincent
Wright
Dept estab 1957; pvt; D & E; scholarships; SC 70, LC 15, GC 40; enrl D 2000, E
450, non-maj 2000, maj 250, grad 150, others 50
Ent Req: HS dipl, portfolio
Degrees: BA(Art Educ), BA(Art Hist) and BA(Studio) and BS(Art Therapy) and
BFA 4 yrs, MA(Photography), MA(Studio), MS(Art Educ) and MFA(Art, Design
or Photography) 2 yrs
Tuition: $2368 per yr; campus residency available
Courses: †Advertising Design, Aesthetics, †Art Education, †Art History, Ceramics,
Collages, Commercial Art, Conceptual Art, Constructions, Drawing, Film, Graphic
Arts, Graphic Design, Handicrafts, Illustration, Intermedia, Jewelry, Lettering,
Mixed Media, Painting, Photography, Printmaking, Sculpture, Stage Design, Teacher
Training, Theatre Arts, Video, Enameling, †Fine Arts, Weaving
Summer School: Dir, Joyce Rosa. Tui undergrad $105 per cr, grad $114 per cr for 3
summer sessions from May 19 to June 20, June 23 to July 25 and July 28 to August
29

HAMILTON

COLGATE UNIVERSITY, Dept of Fine Arts, 13346. Tel 315-824-1000, Ext 633.
Chmn Eric Van Schaack, PhD; *Prof* Jim Loveless, MFA; *Asst Prof* Roni Horn,
MFA; *Asst Prof* Kathryn Horste, PhD; *Asst Prof* Robert McVaugh, PhD; *Asst Prof*
John Knecht, MFA; *Asst Prof* Karen Vournakis, MFA; *Asst Prof* Lynn Schwarzer,
MFA; *Lecturer* Carol Kinne, MFA
Estab 1819, dept estab 1905; pvt; D; scholarships; SC 16, LC 23; enrl D 941, maj 50
Ent Req: HS dipl, CEEB or ACT
Degrees: BA 4 yrs
Tuition: $8300 per yr; campus res—room & board $3020
Courses: Art History, Drawing, Film, Graphic Arts, Painting, Photography,
Printmaking, Sculpture

HEMPSTEAD

HOFSTRA UNIVERSITY
—**Dept of Fine Arts,** 11550. Tel 516-560-5474. *Chmn* David Jacobs. Instrs: FT 11,
PT 3
Estab 1935; pvt; D & E; scholarships; SC 32, LC 1, GC 3
Ent Req: Good secondary school record, col ent board exam
Degrees: BA & BS(Art Educ), BS(Design), BS(Painting), BS(Sculpture & Jewelry),
BS(Ceramics)
Courses: Drawing, †Painting, †Photography, †Sculpture, †Applied Design, Color &
Design, Etching, Figure Drawing, Graphic Expression, Metalsmithing, †Pottery, 3-D
Design, 2-D Representation, Woodcut
Adult Hobby Classes: Courses offered
Summer School: Courses offered
—**Dept of Art History,*** 11550. Tel 516-560-3528, 560-3529. *Chmn* Dr Robert
Myron, PhD. Instrs: FT 3
Estab 1935, dept estab 1972; pvt; D & E; scholarships; LC 20, GC 16; enrl D 1610,
maj 40, grad 35
Ent Req: HS dipl
Degrees: BA 4 yrs, MA 1-2 yrs
Courses: Advertising Design, Art Education, Art History, Ceramics, Commercial
Art, Drawing, Graphic Arts, History of Art & Archaeology, Painting, Sculpture,
Appraisal of Art and Antiques
Summer School: Dir, Dr Harold Yuker. Courses—Art History, Fine Arts

HERKIMER

HERKIMER COUNTY COMMUNITY COLLEGE, Humanities Division, 13350.
Tel 315-866-0300, Ext 200. *Chmn* Dr William Delz; *Prof* Guido Correro, MA;
Instructor James Bruce Schwabach, MFA
Estab 1966; pub; D & E; SC 8, LC 4; enrl D 329 (total), maj 16
Ent Req: HS dipl, SAT or ACT
Degrees: AA, AS & AAS 2 yrs
Tuition: Res—undergrad $390 per sem, $33 per cr hr; nonres—undergrad $780 per
sem; no campus res
Courses: Art Appreciation, Art History, Drawing, Museum Staff Training, Painting,
Photography, Sculpture, Theatre Arts, Video
Adult Hobby Classes: Enrl 40 credit, 100 non-credit; tuition $33 per cr hr.
Courses—Art Appreciation, Calligraphy, Pastels, Portraits, Photography
Children's Classes: Enrl 40; tuition varies. Courses—Cartooning Workshop,
Introduction to Drawing
Summer School: Dir, John Ribnikac. Enrl 40. Courses—Same as regular session

HOUGHTON

HOUGHTON COLLEGE, Art Dept, 14744. Tel 716-567-2211. *Head Art Dept*
Bruce Wenger
Estab 1883; den; D & E; scholarship; SC 8, LC 6
Tuition: $2085 per sem
Courses: Art History, Ceramics, Drawing, Graphic Arts, Graphic Design, History of
Art & Archaeology, Painting, Printmaking

ITHACA

CORNELL UNIVERSITY
—**Dept of Art,** College of Architecture, Art and Planning, 14853. Tel 607-256-3558.
Dean Colllege Jan Stewart; *Chmn Dept* Stanley Bowman, MFA; *Prof* Steve Poleskie,
BS; *Prof* Arnold Singer; *Prof* Jack L Squier, MFA; *Assoc Prof* Zevi Blum, BArch;
Assoc Prof Eleanore Mikus, MA; *Asst Prof* Langdon Quin, MFA; *Asst Prof* Roberto
Bertoia; *Asst Prof* Jean Locey, MFA; *Asst Prof* Elisabeth Meyer, MFA; *Asst Prof*
Greg Page, MFA; *Asst Prof* Robert Jessup, MFA
Estab 1868, dept estab 1921; pvt; D; scholarships; SC 25, LC 1, GC 4; enrl maj 118,
grad 13
Ent Req: HS dipl, portfolio interview, HS transcript, SAT
Degrees: BFA 4 yrs, MFA 2 yrs
Tuition: $9000 per yr, campus res
Courses: Aesthetics, Drawing, †Painting, †Photography, †Printmaking, †Sculpture
Summer School: Dir, Roberto Bertoia. Term of 3 wks beginning June 27.
Courses—Drawing, Painting, Photography, Printmaking, Sculpture
—**Dept of the History of Art,** College of Arts and Sciences, 35 Goldwin Smith Hall,
14853. Tel 607-256-4905. *Chmn & Assoc Prof* Andrew Ramage, PhD; *Prof*
Theodore M Brown, PhD; *Prof* Robert G Calkins, PhD; *Prof* H Peter Kahn, MFA;
Prof Thomas W Leavitt, PhD; *Prof* Stanley J O'Connor, PhD; *Prof* Albert S Roe,
PhD; *Prof* Martie W Young, PhD; *Assoc Prof* Esther G Dotson, PhD; *Asst Prof*
Laura Meixner, PhD; *Asst Prof* Claudia Lazzaro, PhD; *Vis Asst Prof* Nancy C
Neaher, PhD; *Vis Asst Prof* Judith Bernstock, PhD
Estab 1939; pvt; D; scholarships; LC 64, GC 12; enrl D 1300, maj 25, grad 15,
others 5
Ent Req: HS dipl, SAT, grad admission requires GRE
Degrees: BA, MA, PhD
Tuition: $8900 per yr; campus res—room & board $2250 per yr
Courses: Architecture, Art History, †History of Art & Archaeology, Museum Staff
Training, Archaeology, Art Criticism, Techniques and Materials
Summer School: Dir, Robert D MacDougall. Tuition $180 per cr hr.
Courses—introductory
—**New York State College of Human Ecology,** Dept of Design and Environmental
Analysis, 14853. Tel 607-256-2168. *Chmn Dept* William R Sims. Instrs: FT 24
Scholarships
Degrees: BS, MA, MS
Tuition: Undergrad res $3740, grad res $4310, nonres $6050
Courses: †Interior Design, †Apparel Design, †Human Environment Relations,
†Textile Science
Adult Hobby Classes: Courses offered
Summer School: Courses offered

ITHACA COLLEGE, Fine Art Dept,* Danby Road, 14850. Tel 607-274-3011, Ext
3330. *Chmn* Harry McCue, MFA; *Prof* Salvatore Grippi; *Prof* Robert Richenburg;
Asst Prof Gary Wojcik, MFA; *Lecturer* David Smyth, MFA; *Lecturer* Kumi Korf
Estab 1892, dept estab 1968; pvt; D & E; scholarship; SC 10; enrl non-maj 200, maj 40
Ent Req: HS dipl, SAT scores, review of portfolio
Degrees: BA and BFA 4 yrs
Tuition: $6026 per yr; campus res available
Courses: Drawing, Film, Painting, Printmaking, Sculpture, Printmaking, Sculpture,
Stage Design, Theatre Arts, Video, 2-D Design, 3-D Design, Book Design

JAMAICA

SAINT JOHN'S UNIVERSITY, Dept of Fine Arts, Grand Central & Utopia
Parkways, 11439. Tel 212-990-6161. *Chmn* Edward Manetta
Pvt; D; scholarships; SC 24, LC 9; enrl D 1300, maj 100
Ent Req: HS dipl, ent exam, portfolio review
Degrees: BFA and BS 4 yrs
Courses: Saturday Scholarship Program
Summer School: Dean, Dr George Ansalone

YORK COLLEGE OF THE CITY UNIVERSITY OF NEW YORK, Fine and
Performing Arts, 150-91 87th Rd, 11451. Tel 212-969-4062. *Coordr Fine Arts &
Asst Prof* Jane Schuyler, PhD; *Assoc Prof* Arthur Anderson, MFA; *Assoc Prof*
Phillips Simkin, MFA; *Asst Prof* Elena Borstein, MFA; *Asst Prof* Ernest Garthwaite,
MA
Estab 1968, dept estab 1968; pub; D & E; enrl 4303
Ent Req: HS dipl
Degrees: BA 4 yrs
Tuition: Nonres—undergrad $40 per cr, max $537.50 per sem; no campus res
Courses: Art Education, Art History, Drawing, Graphic Arts, Painting, Photography,
Printmaking, Sculpture
Summer School: Dean, Wallace Schoenberg. Enrl $20 per course; tuition $40 per cr
for term of 6 wks beginning late June. Courses—Art History, Drawing, Painting

JAMESTOWN

JAMESTOWN COMMUNITY COLLEGE, Art Dept, 525 Falconer St, 14701. Tel
716-665-5220. *Chmn* Virginia Yeager. Instrs: FT 3, PT 5
Estab 1950, dept estab 1970; pub; D & E; scholarships; SC 11, LC 1; enrl D 310, E
254
Ent Req: Open
Degrees: AA 60 cr hrs
Tuition: $35 per cr hr

Courses: Calligraphy, Ceramics, Drawing, Film, Painting, Photography, Printmaking, Sculpture, Stage Design, Theatre Arts, Video, Design, Fine Woodworking, Survey of Visual Arts, Wood Sculpture
Summer School: Dir, Virginia Yeager. Enrl 50- 75; tuition $35 per cr hr, 2 terms of 6 wks beginning May. Courses—Ceramics, Photography, Painting, Drawing

LARCHMONT

ADAMY'S PLASTICS AND MOLD-MAKING WORKSHOPS, 10538. Tel 914-834-6276. *Dir* George E Adamy, MBA. Instrs: FT 1, PT 1
Estab 1968; pvt; D & E; SC 13, LC 13; enrl D 20, E 30
Tuition: From $25 for 3 hr open-ended sessions to $225 for 10 sessions advanced courses. Individual arrangements for special projects or commissions, and for lectures and demonstrations at other schools, museums, art organizations; no campus res
Courses: Collages, Constructions, Museum Staff Training, Sculpture, Teacher Training, Bonded Bronze & other Metals, Fiberglass Lay-up, Mold-Making of Human Form and Objects, Plastics
Adult Hobby Classes: Courses offered
Children's Classes: Courses offered
Summer School: Courses offered

LOCH SHELDRAKE

SULLIVAN COUNTY COMMUNITY COLLEGE, Division of Commercial Art and Photography, Leroy Rd, 12759. Tel 914-434-5750, Ext 215. *Chmn* Joe Hopkins, MFA; *Prof* L Jack Agnew, MEd; *Asst Prof* Earl Wertheim, BS; *Instructor* Thomas Ambrosino, BPS; *Instructional Asst* Bernie Kroop
Estab 1962, dept estab 1965; pub; D & E; SC 24; enrl D 200, maj 180
Ent Req: HS dipl or equivalent
Degrees: AAS 2 yrs
Tuition: Res - undergrad $525 per sem, $43 per cr; nonres - undergrad $1187 per sem, $129 per cr
Courses: Advertising Design, Art History, Calligraphy, †Commercial Art, Conceptual Art, Display, Drawing, Film, Graphic Arts, Graphic Design, Illustration, Lettering, Mixed Media, †Photography, Video
Summer School: Assoc Dean of Faculty for Community Services, Allan Dampman

LONDONVILLE

SIENA COLLEGE, Fine Arts Dept, 12211. Tel 518-783-2300. *Chmn* Mark Heckler
Courses: Art Appreciation, Art History, Design, Drawing, Printmaking

MALDEN BRIDGE

MALDEN BRIDGE SCHOOL OF ART, 12115. Tel 518-766-3666. *Dir* Betty Warren. Instrs: FT 2, PT 5
Estab 1965; pvt; D; scholarships; SC 6; enrl D 55
Ent Req: Students who are seriously interested in developing their skills and knowledge
Courses: Ceramics, Drawing, Painting, Sculpture
Summer School: Dir, Betty Warren. Three 2 wk workshops. Courses—Drawing, Oil Painting

MIDDLETOWN

ORANGE COUNTY COMMUNITY COLLEGE, Art Dept, 115 South St, 10940. Tel 914-343-1121. *Chmn Dept* Leonard R Wallace, MFA; *Instr* Patrick Kennedy, BFA; *Instr* Ivan R Miseho, Dipl; *Instr* Claude Seward, MFA
Estab 1950, dept estab 1950; pub; D & E; SC 10, LC 4; enrl D 135, maj 135
Ent Req: HS dipl
Degrees: AA 2 yrs
Tuition: Res—undergrad $576 per sem; nonres—undergrad $1152 per sem; no campus res
Courses: Art History, Ceramics, Drawing, Painting, Photography, Sculpture, Color, Design

NEW PALTZ

STATE UNIVERSITY OF NEW YORK COLLEGE AT NEW PALTZ
—Art Studio Dept, SAB 106, 12561. Tel 914-257-2430. *Chmn* Michael Zadro. Instrs: 25
Pub
Degrees: BFA, BA, BS and MFA
Courses: †Ceramics, †Goldsmithing, †Graphic Design, †Painting, †Photography, †Printmaking, †Sculpture, †Silversmithing, Wood Design
Summer School: Chmn Michael Zadro
—Art Education Dept,* 12561. Tel 914-257-2435. *Chmn* Richard Ciganko. Instrs: 3
Degrees: BS(Art Educ) and MS(Art Educ)
Summer School: Dir, Robert Davidson. 8 wk sem

NEW ROCHELLE

COLLEGE OF NEW ROCHELLE SCHOOL OF ARTS AND SCIENCES, Undergraduate Art Dept, School of Arts and Sciences, 10801. Tel 914-632-5300, Ext 274. *Chmn* JoAnn O'Brien, MA; *Prof* Douglas Craft, MFA; *Prof* Dr Charles Daly, EdD; *Assoc Prof* Irene Kutsky, MFA; *Assoc Prof* Dr William Maxwell, EdD; *Assoc Prof* Mary Jane Robertshaw, MFA; *Assoc Prof* Jack Bosson, MFA; *Assoc Prof* Anne Terhune, PhD; *Asst Prof* Theresa Eppridge, MFA
Estab 1904, dept estab 1929; pvt; scholarships; SC 52, LC 14, GC 21; enrl D 340, non-maj 35, maj 207, grad 98

Ent Req: HS dipl, SAT or ACT scores, college preparatory program in high school
Degrees: BA, BFA and BS 4 yrs
Tuition: $4800 per yr; campus res—room and board $4500 per yr
Courses: Art Education, †Art History, Calligraphy, Ceramics, Design, Drafting, Drawing, Graphic Arts, Graphic Design, Illustration, Jewelry, Painting, Photography, Printmaking, Sculpture, Weaving, †Art Therapy, †Studio Arts, 2 & 3-D Design, Weaving
Summer School: Dir, Cathy Giles. Enrl 300; tuition $160 per cr for two terms of 5 wks beginning June. Courses—vary, 2 each semester

NEW YORK

AMERICAN ACADEMY IN ROME, 41 E 65th St, 10021. Tel 212-535-4250. *Chmn* John W Hyland Jr; *Pres* Sophie Consagra; *Deputy Dir-NY* Joan Nicholson
Estab 1894, chartered by Congress 1905; consolidated with School of Classical Studies 1913; Dept of Musical Composition estab 1921
Summer School: 28 fellowships

ARTIST STUDIO CENTERS, INC, 1651 Third Ave, 10028. Tel 212-348-3102. *Head Dept* James E Youngman
Estab 1956; pvt; D & E
Tuition: 2100 per yr
Courses: Drawing, Painting, Sculpture
Adult Hobby Classes: Tuition $48 per month E class, $70 per month D. Courses—Painting, Sculpture
Summer School: Summer workshops

ART LIFE STUDIOS, 1384 Third Ave, 10021. Tel 212-535-0840. *Dir* Ronald Mineo. Instrs: FT 5
Tuition: $170 per 3 month period
Courses: Art Appreciation, †Ceramics, †Drawing, †Painting, †Sculpture
Adult Hobby Classes: Enrl 200; tuition $170 for 3 months, $520 per yr. Courses—Ceramics, Drawing, Painting, Sculpture
Summer School: Dir, Ron Mineo. Enrl 100; tuition & courses same as regular session

ART RESTORATION TECHNICAL INST,* Second floor, 71 W 23rd St, 10010. Tel 212-691-9767
Degrees: Cert
Courses: Museum Staff Training, Painting, Sculpture, Theatre Arts, Bookbinding, Conservation-Restoration, Papermaking

ART STUDENTS LEAGUE OF NEW YORK, 215 W 57th St, 10019. Tel 212-247-4510. *Exec Dir* R A Florio. Instrs: FT 65
Estab 1875; pvt; schol; LC; enrl D 1200, E 600, Sat 500 (adults and children)
Ent Req: None
Courses: Drawing, Graphic Arts, Illustration, Painting, Sculpture
Children's Classes: Classes on Saturday
Summer School: Enrl 800, beginning June

BERNARD M BARUCH COLLEGE OF THE CITY UNIVERSITY OF NEW YORK, Art Dept, 46 E 26th St (Mailing add: 17 Lexington Ave, Box 281, New York, NY 10010). Tel 212-725-3240. *Chmn* Pamela Sheingorn, PhD
Estab 1968, dept estab 1968; pub; D & E; SC 26, LC 16; enrl D 2000, E 500
Ent Req: HS dipl
Degrees: BA, BBA and BSEd 4 yrs, MBA 5 yrs, PhD
Courses: Advertising Design, Art History, Ceramics, Drawing, Graphic Arts, Graphic Design, Industrial Design, Painting, Photography, Printmaking, Sculpture
Summer School: Dir, Katherine Crum. Courses—Art History Survey, Ceramics, Crafts, Drawing, Painting, Photography

THE CHILDREN'S AID SOCIETY, Lower Westside Center, Visual Arts Program, 209 Sullivan St, 10012. Tel 212-254-3075. *Dir* Allen M Hart
Extab 1854, dept estab 1968; D & E; scholarships; SC 7; enrl D 200, E 175
Tuition: Adults $60-$75 per sem; children $40-$50 per sem; no campus res
Courses: Aesthetics, Art Education, Art History, Ceramics, Collages, Constructions, Drawing, Handicrafts, Jewelry, Mixed Media, Painting, Photography, Silversmithing, Teacher Training, Cabinet Making, Enameling, Pottery, Puppet Making
Adult Hobby Classes: Enrl 95; tuition $60-$75 per sem. Courses—Cabinetmaking, Ceramics, Drawing, Enameling, Painting, Photography, Pottery
Children's Classes: Enrl 325; tuition $32-$42 per sem. Courses—Dance, Drawing, Enameling, Mixed Media, Painting, Photography, Puppet Making, Woodwork, Theatre & Mime
Summer School: Dir, H Zaremben & Allen M Hart

CITY COLLEGE OF NEW YORK, Art Dept, Eisner Hall, 10031. Tel 212-690-4201. *Chmn* Jacob Rothenberg, PhD; *Deputy Chair* Elizabeth O'Connor, PhD; *Dir Grad Studies* Irving Kaufman, MA; *Supervisor Art Education* Joan Price, EdD; *Dir Evening Session* Stanley Wyatt, MA
Estab 1847; pub; D & E; scholarships; SC 45, LC 29; enrl D 1043, E 133, maj 100, grad 122
Ent Req: HS dipl, entrance placement exams
Degrees: BA, MA, MFA
Tuition: Res—undergrad $612.50 per sem, $46 per cr hr, grad $1012.50 per sem, $81 per cr hr; nonres—undergrad $937.50 per sem, $76 per cr hr, grad $1337.50 per sem, $116 per cr hr
Courses: †Advertising Design, Art Appreciation, †Art Education, †Art History, Calligraphy, †Ceramics, Collages, Constructions, †Design, Drawing, †Graphic Arts, Illustration, †Interior Design, Mixed Media, Museum Staff Training, †Painting, †Photography, †Printmaking, †Sculpture, Teacher Training
Adult Hobby Classes: Courses—Drawing, Painting, Photography, Sculpture, Textile Design
Summer School: Dir, Stanley Wyatt. Courses—Introduction to Studio, Principles of Art, Drawing, Design, Painting, Photography, Art Education

CITY UNIVERSITY OF NEW YORK, PhD Program in Art History, Grad School & University Center, 33 West 42nd St, 10036. Tel 212-790-4451. *Chmn Exec Committee* William H Gerdts, PhD; *Distinguished Prof* John Rewald, PhD; *Distinguished Prof* Linda Nichlin-Pommer; *Prof* Marcia E Allentuck, PhD; *Prof* Eugene C Goossen, PhD; *Prof* Diane Kelder, PhD; *Prof* Rosalind Krauss, PhD; *Prof* Robert Pincus-Witten, PhD; *Prof* Jack Flam, PhD; *Prof* Rose-Carol Long, PhD; *Res Prof* Milton W Brown, PhD; *Assoc Prof* H Barbara Weinberg, PhD; *Assoc Prof* Eugene A Santomasso, PhD
Estab 1961, prog estab 1971; pub; D; scholarships; LC 6, GC 6; enrl D 95, grad 95
Ent Req: BA or MA in Art History
Degrees: PhD
Courses: †Art History

COLUMBIA UNIVERSITY
—**Graduate School of Architecture and Planning,*** Avery Hall, Broadway & 116th St, 10027. Tel 212-280-2783. *Dean Architectural Planning* James Stewart Polshek; *Chmn Div Architecture* J Max Bond Jr; *Chmn Div Urban Design* David G DeLong. Instrs: FT 31, PT 32
Estab 1881; pvt; scholarships and fels; enrl 400
Ent Req: Bachelor's degree in appropriate area of study
Degrees: MArchit 3 yrs, MSArchit & Urban Design 1 yr, MSPlanning 2 yrs, MSHistoric Preservation 1 1/2 yrs
Tuition: $7030 per yr; campus res available
Courses: Architecture, Architecture and Urban Design, Historic Preservation, Urban Planning
—**Dept of Art History and Archaeology,** 815 Schermerhorn Hall, 10027. Tel 212-280-4505. *Chmn* David Rosand; *Dir Grad Studies* Allen Staley
Pvt
Degrees: MA 2 yrs, MPhil 4 yrs, PhD 7 yrs
Tuition: $4410 per term
Courses: Classical Art & Archaeology, Far Eastern Art & Archaeology, History of Architecture, History of Western Art, Near Eastern Art & Archeology, Primitive & Pre-Columbian Art & Archaeology
Summer School: Dir, Howard McP Davis. Tuition $705 per course
—**Columbia College,** 10027
Pvt, M; scholarships and fels
Degrees: BA, MA, MPhil, PhD
Tuition: $2560 per yr (FT 15 or more cr); $170 (PT under 15 cr)
Courses: Art and Archaeology of South Eastern Asia, Asian Art and Archaeology, Classical Art and Archaeology, History of Western Art, Near Eastern Art and Archaeology, Primitive and Pre-Columbian Art and Archaeology
—**School of the Arts, Division of Painting & Sculpture,** 305 Dodge Hall, 116th St & Broadway, 10027. Tel 212-280-2829, 280-4065. *Chmn* Luise Kaish, MFA; *Prof* Leon Goldin, MFA; *Sr Lecturer* Anthony Harrison, BA; *Adjunct Prof* Roy Gussow, BS; *Adjunct Prof* John Ross, BFA; *Adjunct Prof* Jane Wilson, MA; *Adjunct Assoc Prof* Robert Blackburn; *Adjunct Assoc Prof* Jenny Snider, MFA; *Adjunct Assoc Prof* Paul Suttman, MFA; *Adjunct Asst Prof* Paul Brown, MFA; *Adjunct Asst Prof* Ray Ciarrochi, MFA; *Adjunct Asst Prof* Louise Fishman, MFA; *Adjunct Asst Prof* Reeva Potoff, MFA; *Lecturer* William Barrett, MFA; *Lecturer* Howard Buchwald, MA; *Lecturer* Donald Hazlitt, MA; *Lecturer* Susan Wilmarth, BFA
Estab 1754, div estab 1945; pvt; D & E; scholarships; SC 21, LC 1, GC 13; enrl non-maj 656, maj 8, grad 37
Ent Req: BA, BFA or other bachelor's degree from accredited undergrad institution, slide folio; special students: required to have completed two years of study at accredited institution of higher learning, admitted students must obtain written permission from Chmn of Div for courses in which they intend to register
Degrees: BA(Visual Arts), MFA(Painting), MFA(Printmaking), MFA(Sculpture)
Tuition: $306 per cr; campus res available
Courses: Drawing, Painting, Printmaking, Sculpture
Adult Hobby Classes: Tuition $267 per cr for 12 wk sem. Courses—Undergrad studio courses
Summer School: Dir, Peter Shamonsey. Enrl 20; tuition $267 per cr for term of 6 wks. Courses—Drawing, Painting
—**Barnard College,*** Dept of Art History, 10027. Tel 212-280-2014. *Chmn* Jane Rosenthal, PhD
Estab 1923; pvt; W; scholarships; enrl maj 29, total 1930
Degrees: 4 yrs
Tuition: $8590 per yr; campus res available
Courses: Art History, Painting
—**Teachers Col Program in Art & Education,** Teachers College, 525-W 120th St, 10027. Tel 212-678-3360, 678-3361. *Dean* P Michael Timpane; *Dir* William Mahoney
Estab 1888; pvt; scholarships and fels; GC; enrl 225
Ent Req: Bachelor's degree
Degrees: MA, MEduc, EdD
Tuition: $240 per cr
Courses: Graphic Arts, Painting, Sculpture, Art Appreciation, Design, Teacher Education, Crafts
Adult Hobby Classes: Enrl 35; tuition $150 per 10 wk session. Courses—Woodworking, Ceramics, Paper Making
Summer School: Enrl 130; tuition $240 per cr beginning mid May

COOPER UNION SCHOOL OF ART, Cooper Square, 10003. Tel 212-254-6300, Ext 286. *Dean* Lee Anne Miller, MFA
Estab 1859; pvt; D & E; schol
Ent Req: HS dipl, ent exam
Degrees: BFA 4 yr
Tuition: No tuition

EDUCATION ALLIANCE ART SCHOOL, 197 E Broadway, 10002. Tel 212-475-6200
Scholarships offered
Degrees: Cert
Courses: Ceramics, Drawing, Painting, Photography, Printmaking, Sculpture

FASHION INSTITUTE OF TECHNOLOGY, Art & Design Division, 227 W 27th St, 10001. Tel 212-760-7700. *Dean* Hilde W Jaffe, BA; *Chmn Interior Design* Martin Zelnik, MArch; *Chmn Fashion Design* B Zamkoff, BFA; *Chmn Advertising Design* T Giaccone, BFA; *Chmn Fine Arts* C Brown, MA; *Chmn Illustration* Elinore Brandon, BA; *Chmn Photography* I Schild, BFA; *Chmn Display Design* H Christie, AAS; *Chmn Jewelry Design* M Strump, AAS
Estab 1951; pub; D & E; schol; SC 317, LC 26; enrl D 3468, E 7004
Ent Req: HS dipl, ent exam
Degrees: AAS 2 yr, BFA 4 yr
Tuition: Res—undergrad $600 per sem; nonres—undergrad $1200 per sem; campus res—room and board $2800 per yr
Courses: †Advertising Design, Aesthetics, Art History, Calligraphy, †Costume Design & Construction, †Display, Drafting, Drawing, Fashion Arts, Goldsmithing, Graphic Arts, Graphic Design, History of Art & Archaeology, Illustration, †Interior Design, †Jewelry, Lettering, Mixed Media, Painting, †Photography, Printmaking, Restoration & Conservation, Sculpture, Silversmithing, Stage Design, †Textile Design, Theatre Arts, Video
Summer School: Dean, Richard Meagher. Enrl 2900; tuition $58 - $116 per course for term of 3, 5 & 7 wks beginning June. Courses—as above

HARRIET FEBLAND ART WORKSHOP, 245 E 63rd St, Suite 408, 10021. Tel 212-759-2215. *Dir* Harriet FeBland; *Instructor* Bernard Kassoy; *Instructor* Hortense Kassoy
Estab 1962; pvt; D & E; schol; SC 6, LC 1, GC 4; enrl D 115, E 35, grad 115, others 35
Ent Req: Review of previous work, paintings or sculpture
Tuition: Varies from $170-$200 per 15 wk class, $80 for 5 wk lect and critiques
Courses: Collages, Constructions, Drawing, Painting, Sculpture, Wood Carving
Adult Hobby Classes: Tuition varies from $170-$200. Courses—(all advanced) Painting, Drawing, Assemblage, Sculpture, Wood Carving

FORDHAM UNIVERSITY, Art Dept,* Arts Division, Lincoln Center, 10023. Tel 212-841-5210. *Division Chmn* David Davis. Instrs: FT 7
Estab 1968; pvt; D & E; scholarships; SC 18, LC 25; enrl D 900, E 1750, maj 56
Ent Req: HS dipl
Degrees: BA 4 yrs
Tuition: $154 per cr hr; campus res available
Courses: Aesthetics, Costume Design & Construction, Drawing, Graphic Arts, History of Art & Archaeology, Painting, Photography, Sculpture, Stage Design, Teacher Training, Theatre Arts, New Media and Concepts
Summer School: Dir, Dr Levak. Four terms per summer for 5 wks each

GREENWICH HOUSE POTTERY, School of Ceramics, 16 Jones St, 10014. Tel 212-242-4106. *Dir* Susan B Wood, MFA. Instrs: 19
Estab 1902, dept estab 1948; pvt; D & E; schol; SC 32; enrl D 200, E 94
Ent Req: None
Degrees: None
Tuition: $140 per sem; no campus res
Courses: Ceramics, Sculpture, Glazing Chemistry
Children's Classes: Enrl 94; tuition $45 and $55 per sem
Summer School: Dir, Susan B Wood. Invited fac in res—special prog per 4 wks

HENRY STREET SETTLEMENT ARTS FOR LIVING CENTER, 466 Grand St, 10002. Tel 212-598-0400. *Dir* Susan Fleminger
Estab 1895; pvt; D; scholarships; enrl D 60, E 60
Ent Req: None
Tuition: $30-$120 per course
Courses: Calligraphy, Ceramics, Drawing, Graphic Arts, Mixed Media, Painting, Printmaking, Sculpture
Adult Hobby Classes: Courses—Crafts, Drawing, Painting, Pottery
Children's Classes: Courses—Arts & Crafts, Cartooning, Drawing, Experimental Art, Painting, Pottery, Printmaking

HUNTER COLLEGE, Art Dept,* 695 Park Ave, 10021. Tel 212-860-1131. *Chmn Art Dept* Sanford Wurmfeld; *Dean* James N Settle, PhD. Instrs: FT 29
Estab 1890, dept estab 1935; pub; D & E; SC 20-25, LC 10, GC 14-20; enrl D 250 (including evening), maj 250, GS 250
Ent Req: HS dipl
Degrees: BA and BFA 4 yrs
Tuition: Res—$537.50 per sem; nonres—$787.50 per sem

JOHN JAY COLLEGE OF CRIMINAL JUSTICE, Dept of Art, Music and Philosophy, 10019. Tel 212-489-3557. *Chmn* Robert P Montgomery, ThD; *Prof* Marlene Park, PhD; *Prof* Laurie Schneider, PhD; *Assoc Prof* John Dobbs, BFA; *Assoc Prof* Helen Ramsaran, MFA; *Lectr* Irene Gordon, AB; *Lectr* John I Russell, BFA. Instrs: FT 6, PT 4
Estab 1964, dept estab 1971; pub; D & E; SC 5, LC 6; enrl D 180, E 180
Ent Req: HS dipl
Degrees: BA and BS 4 yr
Tuition: Res—undergrad $612 per sem, $35 per cr (lower division), $40 per cr (upper division); nonres—undergrad $712 per sem, $55 per cr; no campus res
Courses: Art History, Drawing, Film, Painting, Photography, Sculpture

MARYMOUNT MANHATTAN COLLEGE, Fine Arts Dept,* 221 E 71st St, 10021. Tel 212-472-3800. *Chmn Fine & Performing Arts Dept* Patricia Elliott. Instrs: FT 12
Tuition: $1995 per term
Courses: Advertising Design, Art Appreciation, Ceramics, Design, Drawing, Illustration, Museum Staff Training, Painting, Photography, Printmaking, Conservation-Restoration

MAYER SCHOOL OF FASHION DESIGN, Art Dept,* 64 W 36th St, 10018. Tel 212-563-3636. *Dir* Richard J Mayer
Estab 1931; pvt; D & E; SC 11; enrl D 110, E 350
Ent Req: Ent exam
Degrees: 9 month Cert in designing, patternmaking, draping, fashion drawing, dressmaking, grading
Tuition: 3105
Courses: Drawing, Fashion Arts, Dressmaking, Fashion Design, Fashion Draping, Patternmaking

NATIONAL ACADEMY SCHOOL OF FINE ARTS, 5 E 89th St, 10028. Tel 212-369-4880. *Dir* John Dobkin. Instrs: 25
Estab 1826; pvt; D & E; schol; SC 12; enrl 275
Ent Req: None
Tuition: $1300
Courses: Drawing, Graphic Arts, Painting, Sculpture, Architectural Drafting, Composition-Portraiture, Life Sketch Class, Perspective, Anatomy
Adult Hobby Classes: Enrl 275. Courses vary
Summer School: Dir, John H Dobkin. Enrl 175; tuition $400. Courses same as above

NEW SCHOOL FOR SOCIAL RESEARCH, Adult Education Division, 66 W 12th St, 10011. Tel 212-741-5600
Courses: Advertising Design, Art Appreciation, Art History, Calligraphy, Ceramics, Design, Drawing, Fashion Arts, Film, Handicrafts, Jewelry, Painting, Photography, Printmaking, Sculpture, Textile Design, Weaving, Cartooning, Glassblowing
Adult Hobby Classes: Enrl 1000; tuition $175 per course
Summer School: Dir, Wallie Heuholz; enrl 500

NEW YORK ACADEMY OF ART (Formerly New Brooklyn School), 13-15 Laight St 2nd Floor, 10013. Tel 212-966-6670. *Co-Dir* Francis Cunningham; *Co-Dir* Barney Hodes; *Instr* Xavier de Callatay; *Instr* Milet Andrejevic; *Instr* Eliot Goldfinger; *Instr* Anthony Panzera; *Instr* Salvatore Montano; *Instr* Jon Zahourek; *Instr* Alfonse Solimene, PhD; *Instr* Joan Root; *Instr* Israel Hershberg
Tuition: $375 - $475 for five classes per wk
Courses: Drawing, Painting, Sculpture, Anatomy
Summer School: Courses offered

NEW YORK INSTITUTE OF PHOTOGRAPHY, 211 E 43rd St, 10017. Tel 212-255-5150. *Dir* Donald Sheff; *Dean* T J Marino
Estab 1910; Correspondence course in photography approved by New York State and approved for veterans; accredited by Accrediting Commission of National Home Study Council; enrl 10,000
Tuition: $498
Courses: Photography

NEW YORK SCHOOL OF INTERIOR DESIGN, 155 E 56th St, 10022. Tel 212-753-5365. *Pres* Arthur Satz, MFA; *Academic Dean* Kerwin E Kettler, MS; *Dir Development* D L Wyckoff
Estab 1916; pvt; D & E; schol; SC 25, LC 8; enrl D 700, E 300, non-maj 865, maj 135
Ent Req: HS dipl, portfolio and interview
Degrees: 3 yr design program, AAS, BFA
Tuition: $3890 per yr, $1945 per sem, $160 per cr; no campus res
Courses: Architecture, Art History, Drafting, Drawing, Graphic Design, †Interior Design, Photography
Adult Hobby Classes: Enrl 300; tuition $160 per cr. Courses—lower division courses offered
Summer School: Dean, Kerwin Katler. Enrl 400; tuition $160 per cr per 6 wks. Courses—various

NEW YORK STUDIO SCHOOL OF DRAWING, PAINTING AND SCULPTURE, 8 West Eighth St, 10011. Tel 212-673-6466. *Dean* Bruce Gagnier; *Program Dir* Don Kimes; *Instr* Robert Bordo; *Instr* Gretna Campbell; *Instr* Jean Detheux; *Instr* Stanley Lewis; *Instr* Michael Loew; *Instr* Mercedes Matter; *Instr* Ruth Miller; *Instr* David Reed; *Instr* Frederic Thursz; *Instr* Norman Turner; *Instr* Esteban Vicente; *Instr* Peter Agostini; *Instr* Ronald Bladen; *Instr* Sidney Geist; *Instr* Jonathan Silver; *Instr* William Tucker; *Instr* Isaac Witkin. Instrs: PT 4
Estab 1964; pvt; D; scholarships; SC 13, LC 2; enrl D 80, grad 40
Ent Req: HS dipl, portfolio of recent work
Tuition: $1800 per sem; campus res available in summer only
Courses: Art History, †Drawing, †Painting, †Sculpture
Adult Hobby Classes: Enrl 40; tuition $150 per 12 wks. Courses—Drawing
Summer School: Program Dir, Don Kimes. Enrl 60; tuition $1000 for term of 8 wks beginning June 18th. Courses—Art History, Drawing, Painting, Sculpture

NEW YORK UNIVERSITY, Institute of Fine Arts, 1 E 78th St, 10021. Tel 212-772-5800. *Dir* James R McCredie
Pvt; D & E; scholarships and fels; enrl grad 400
Courses: History of Art & Archaeology, Conservation and Technology of Works of Art; Curatorial Staff Training
—Dept of Art Education & Division of Creative Arts,* School of Education, 239 Greene St, Rm 735, 10003. Tel 212-598-3481. *Chmn* Dr Angiola Churchill. Instrs: FT 14, PT 25
Pvt; D & E; scholarships and fels; undergrad SC 26, LC 13, grad SC 11, LC 15; enrl maj undergrad 115, grad 130
Ent Req: Col board ent exam, 85 HS average, portfolio, interview
Degrees: BS, EdD, MA and PhD
Tuition: $165 per credit
Courses: Aesthetics, Art History, Drawing, Graphic Arts, Painting, Printmaking, Sculpture, Teacher Training, Arts Administration, Art Therapy, Costume History and Design, Folk Art Studies; International Center for Advanced Studies in Art, Internships, Lithography
Summer School: Four summer sessions 3-week period, four days a week; International Overseas Program in Studio Arts in Venice, Italy. Three summer program, two summers abroad and one in New York (8 weeks each summer)

PACE UNIVERSITY, Art and Music Dept, Pace Plaza, 10038. *Chmn* Peter Fingesten
Estab 1950; pvt; D & E; SC 4, LC 20; enrl D 200, E 150, 700-800 per yr art only
Ent Req: HS dipl, ent exam
Degrees: 4 yr, no art major
Tuition: $135 per cr hr; campus res available
Courses: Drawing, Graphic Design, Leather, Macrame, Modern Art, Oriental Art, Studio Art
Adult Hobby Classes: Courses same as above
Summer School: Three summer sessions. Courses—History of Art and Architecture, Studio Art

PARSONS SCHOOL OF DESIGN, 66 Fifth Ave, 11215. Tel 212-741-8910. *Executive Dean* David C Levy, PhD
Estab 1896; pvt (see also Otis Art Institute of Parsons School of Design, Los Angeles, California); D & E; scholarships; SC 200, LC 400, GC 25; enrl D 1500, E 5000, GS 25, others 40
Ent Req: HS dipl, portfolio
Degrees: AAS, BFA, MA and MFA 2 yr
Tuition: 6320 per yr, $208 per cr; campus res—room & board $2300
Courses: †Advertising Design, Aesthetics, Architecture, †Art Education, Art History, Calligraphy, †Ceramics, †Commercial Art, Fashion Arts, †Graphic Design, History of Art & Archaeology, †Illustration, †Industrial Design, †Interior Design, †Jewelry, Landscape Architecture, Sculpture, †Silversmithing, †Textile Design, Weaving, †Environmental Design, †Fine Arts, †History of Decorative Arts
Adult Hobby Classes: Enrl 1500; tuition $190 per course. Courses—varied
Summer School: Dir, Francine Goldenhar. Enrl 500; tuition $450 for term of 4 wks, beginning July 1. Courses—same as regular session special program for high school students

PRATT INSTITUTE, Pratt-Phoenix School of Design, 160 Lexington Ave, 10016. Tel 212-685-2973. *Actg Chmn* Peter E Kelley
Estab 1892; pvt; D; scholarships
Ent Req: HS dipl, portfolio, interview
Degrees: Assoc 2 yrs
Tuition: $185 per cr, no campus res
Courses: †Advertising Design, †Graphic Design, †Illustration, †Batik, †Typography, †Weaving

SCHOOL OF VISUAL ARTS, 209 E 23rd St, 10010. Tel 212-679-7350, Div Continuing Educ 683-0600. *Chmn* Silas H Rhodes; *Pres* David Rhodes
Estab 1947; pvt; scholarships; enrl FT 2400, PT 3000
Ent Req: HS transcript, portfolio review, interview, 2 letters of recommendation
Degrees: BFA, MFA, provisional teachers' cert (K-12) in Art Educ
Tuition: $4200 plus fees per yr
Courses: †Advertising Design, †Film, †Graphic Design, †Illustration, †Photography, †Video, Art History & Criticism, Art Therapy, †Cartooning, Computer Graphics, †Fine Arts
Adult Hobby Classes: Tuition $95 per cr. Courses—same as above
Summer School: Courses—Fine Arts, Design & Photography in Tangier, Morocco, other courses same as above

SCULPTURE CENTER GALLERY & SCHOOL, 167 E 69th St, 10021. Tel 212-737-9870, 879-0430. *Dir* Gary Sussman; *Gallery Dir* Marion Griffith
Estab 1933; pvt; D & E; scholarships
Tuition: $36 per month, $245 per sem
Courses: Drawing, Sculpture (stone, wood, welding, plaster molds, bronze casting)
Adult Hobby Classes: Enrl 200; tuition $30 monthly of $240 per sem. Courses same as reg session
Children's Classes: Enrl 15; tuition $36 per month. Courses—Sculpture (clay, wood, stone & plaster)
Summer School: Dir, G L Sussman. Enrl 100; tuition $50 - $400. Courses—Same as reg session plus special seminars

TOBE-COBURN SCHOOL FOR FASHION CAREERS, 686 Broadway, 10012. Tel 212-460-9600. *Pres* Ann Z Wareham. Instrs: FT 9, PT 25
Estab 1937; pvt; D; scholarships; 2 yr course, 16 months, for HS grad; 1 yr course, 9-12 months, for those with 15 or more transferable college sem cr, classroom study alternates with periods of work in stores or projects in fashion field; enrl 425
Degrees: AOS(Occupational Studies)
Tuition: $6350 per yr
Courses: Display, Fashion Arts, Fabrics, Fashion Merchandising, Marketing and Management

TRAPHAGEN SCHOOL OF FASHION, 257 Park Ave S, 10010. Tel 212-673-0300. *Dir* Dorothy E Hellman; *Chmn Design Dept* Marion Roller, BA; *Chmn Fashion Illustration* Carol Loebelsohn; *Chmn Interior Design & Dec* Hal Hunt; *Clothing Chmn* Emilia Sierra
Estab 1923; pub; D & E; schol; enrl D 300 max, E 150
Ent Req: HS dipl, personal interview
Degrees: Cert 2 yr, co-op BA prog with NY Institute of Technology issuing degrees
Tuition: $2915 per yr; no campus res
Courses: Interior Design, Clothing Construction, Fashion Design, Fashion Illustration
Adult Hobby Classes: Courses—Dressmaking, Draping, Fashion Art, Finishing, Interior Design, Patternmaking
Summer School: Enrl 15 per class; tui $500 per term of 6 wk. Courses—Draping, Dressmaking, Fashion Art, Interior Design, Patternmaking, Samplemaking

UMBERTO ROMANO SCHOOL OF CREATIVE ART,* 162 E 83rd St, 10028. Tel 212-288-9621. *Dir* Umberto Romano
Estab 1933; pvt; D
Courses: Drawing, Graphic Arts, Painting, Sculpture

WOODSTOCK SCHOOL OF ART, INC, Rte 212, PO Box 338, 12498. Tel 914-679-2388. *Dir* Robert Angeloch; *Instructor* Vladimir Bachinsky; *Instructor* Nicholas Buhalis; *Instructor* Anna Contes; *Instructor* William Greenwood; *Instructor* F Tor Gudmundsen; *Instructor* Richard Segalman; *Instructor* Dan Gelfand
Estab 1968, dept estab 1981; pvt; D & E; scholarships; SC 14, LC 10; enrl D 110, E 15
Tuition: $35-$160
Courses: Drawing, Painting, Printmaking, Sculpture
Children's Classes: Instr, Jean Wrolsen. Summer classes in July & August
Summer School: Dir, Robert Angeloch

NIAGARA FALLS

NIAGARA UNIVERSITY, Fine Arts Dept,* De Veaux Campus, 14109. Tel 716-285-1212. *Assoc Prof* Louis M Centofanti
Degrees: Cert
Tuition: $2085 per sem
Courses: Art Appreciation, Art History, Ceramics, Drawing, Painting, Textile Design

OAKDALE

DOWLING COLLEGE, Dept of Art,* Idle Hour Blvd, 11769. Tel 516-589-6100, Ext 246. *Assoc Prof* Sara Hornstein; *Assoc Prof* Anthony J Giordano
Pvt; D & E; scholarships; enrl D 1100, E 500
Ent Req: HS dipl
Degrees: BA (Visual Art & Speech, Drama), BS and BBA 4 yrs
Tuition: $145 per cr hr
Adult Hobby Classes: Courses—Composition, Drawing, Painting

OLD WESTBURY

NEW YORK INSTITUTE OF TECHNOLOGY, Fine Arts Dept, Wheatley Rd, 11568. Tel 516-686-7543. *Chmn* John Murray, MFA; *Assoc Prof* Marvin Horowitz, MFA; *Assoc Prof* Valdes Kubris, MFA; *Assoc Prof* Shirley Marein, MFA; *Asst Prof* Janet de Cecilia, MA; *Asst Prof* Thomas Martin, MFA; *Asst Prof* Anthony Clementi, MA; *Instr* Peter Voci, MFA; *Adjunct Assoc Prof* Steven Woodburn, MFA; *Adjunct Asst Prof* Krystov Wodiczko; *Adjunct Instr* Janet Cohen, MA; *Adjunct Instr* Cynthia Gallagher, MFA; *Adjunct Instr* Domenic Alfano; *Master Printer* Roni Henning; *Photographer in Residence* Neil Scholl
Estab 1910, dept estab 1963; pvt; D; scholarships; SC 11, LC 85; enrl D 427, non-maj 100, maj 327
Ent Req: HS dipl, portfolio review
Degrees: BFA 4 yr
Tuition: $3680 per yr, $115 per cr; no campus res
Courses: Art History, Calligraphy, Drawing, Graphic Arts, †Graphic Design, Illustration, †Interior Design, Lettering, †Painting, Photography, †Printmaking, †Sculpture, Stage Design, †Teacher Training, Textile Design
Summer School: Tuition $80 per cr for term of 8 wks. Courses—Drawing, Interior Design, Painting, Sculpture

STATE UNIVERSITY OF NEW YORK COLLEGE AT OLD WESTBURY, Fine Arts Dept, Box 210, 11568. Tel 516-876-3000, 876-3056
Estab 1968, Dept estab 1969; pub; D & E; SC 10, LC 10; enrl D & E 277
Ent Req: HS dipl, skills proficiency exam, GED, special exception - inquire through admissions
Degrees: BA(Communicative & Creative Arts) 4 yr
Tuition: Res—$705 per sem
Courses: Art History, Ceramics, Conceptual Art, Drawing, Graphic Arts, †Intermedia, †Mixed Media, Painting, Photography, Printmaking, Sculpture

ONEONTA

HARTWICK COLLEGE, Art Dept, 13820. Tel 607-432-4200, Ext 520. *Chmn* Roberta Griffith, MFA. Instrs: FT 6, PT 8
Estab 1927; pvt; D; enrl 1387, non-maj 1334, maj 50
Ent Req: HS dipl, SAT of ACT, recommendation from teacher or counselor & personal essay, $25 fee
Tuition: $6800 per yr; campus res $2600
Courses: Art History, Ceramics, Drawing, Jewelry, Painting, Photography, Printmaking, Sculpture, Silversmithing, Teacher Training, Video, Fiber, Glassblowing, Papermaking, Weaving
Summer School: High school arts workshop, 2 wks in July

STATE UNIVERSITY OF NEW YORK COLLEGE AT ONEONTA, Dept of Art, 13820. Tel 607-431-3717, 431-3718. *Chmn* Daniel Young
Estab 1889; pub; D & E; SC 31, LC 22; enrl D 660, E 35, maj 123, approx 25-30 at Cooperstown Center
Ent Req: HS dipl, regents scholarship exam, SAT and ACT
Degrees: BA(Studio Art, Art History) other programs include: one leading to MA(Museum History, Folk Art, Conservation & Restoration of Works of Art) in conjunction with the New York State Historical Association at Cooperstown, NY 13326 (Dr Bruce R Buckley, SUNY Dir); a 3-1 program in conjunction with the Fashion Institute of Technology in New York City, with 3 years at Oneonta as a Studio Art major leading to a BS degree and/or 1 year at FIT leading to a AAS(Advertising and Communications, Advertising Design, Apparel Production and Management, Fashion Buying and Merchandising, Fashion Design, Textile Design, and/or Textile Technology)
Adult Hobby Classes: Offered only on a subscription basis at normal tuition rates through the Office of Continuing Education
Children's Classes: Dir, Dr Robert Porter. Enrl varies between 20-40 per yr. Offered only through the Upper Catskill Study Council
Summer School: Dir, Dr Robert Nichols. Tuition same as in regular session for two 6 wk terms beginning June and July. Courses—Art Criticism, Art History, Studio Courses (depending on demand)

ORANGEBURG

DOMINICAN COLLEGE OF BLAUVEIT, Art Dept, Western Hwy, 10962. Tel 914-359-7800. *Chmn* Margaret J Gillis
Tuition: $95 per cr hr
Courses: Art Appreciation, Art Education, Art History, Handicrafts, Painting
Summer School: Dir, Sr Florence Dwyer. Enrl 500; tuition $95 per cr for two 5 wk sessions. Courses—History of Art, Watercolors

OSWEGO

STATE UNIVERSITY OF NEW YORK COLLEGE AT OSWEGO, Art Dept, Tyler Hall, 13126. Tel 315-341-2111. *Chmn* T C Eckersley, MFA. Instrs: FT 18
Estab 1861; pub; D & E; SC 31, LC 9; enrl maj 150, grad 10
Ent Req: HS dipl, SAT or NYS regents scholarship exam
Degrees: BA 4 yr, BFA 4 yr, MA 2 yr
Tuition: Res—$525 per sem; nonres—$875 per sem; campus res room $625 per sem and board $446 per sem
Courses: Aesthetics, †Art History, †Ceramics, †Drawing, Graphic Arts, †Graphic Design, †Jewelry, Jewelry, Museum Staff Training, †Painting, †Photography, †Printmaking, Environmental Design
Adult Hobby Classes: Tui $25 per person. Courses—Glass Media, Painting
Summer School: Dir, Lewis C Popham III. Tuition state grad res $71 per cr hr, non-grad res $35 per cr hr, grad nonres $91.50 per cr hr, non-grad nonres $58 per cr hr

PLATTSBURGH

CLINTON COMMUNITY COLLEGE, Humanities Art Dept,* 12901. Tel 518-561-6650. *Assoc Prof* Ellen H Heyman
Courses: Art Appreciation, Design, Drawing, Painting, Photography, Sculpture

PLEASANTVILLE

PACE UNIVERSITY, Dept of Art & Design, 10603. Tel 914-769-3200. *Chmn* Brenda Bettinson; *Prof* John Mulgrew, MA; *Instructor* Beth Treadway, MA; *Instructor* Martha Bartsch, BFA. Instrs: FT 16
Estab 1906, dept estab 1978; pvt; D & E; scholarships
Ent Req: HS dipl, SAT scores, review by admissions committee and dept interview
Degrees: BS(Fine Arts) 4 yrs
Tuition: Campus residency available
Courses: Art History, Ceramics, Drawing, Graphic Arts, Graphic Design, Illustration, Interior Design, Painting, Photography, Printmaking, Sculpture, Scientific & Medical Illustration, Typography
Summer School: Dir, Brenda Bettinson

POTSDAM

STATE UNIVERSITY OF NEW YORK COLLEGE AT POTSDAM, Dept of Fine Arts, 13676. Tel 315-267-2251. *Chmn* Arthur Sennett, MFA; *Prof* John Riordan, PhD; *Prof* James Sutter, MFA; *Prof* Steven Sumner, MFA; *Assoc Prof* Joseph Hildreth, MFA; *Asst Prof* Julia Miller, PhD; *Instructor* Joy Adams, MFA
Estab 1948; pub; D & E
Ent Req: HS dipl, SAT, portfolio review recommended
Degrees: BA 4 yrs, special program Empire State studio sem in New York City
Tuition: Res undergrad lower div $1155 per yr, $525 per sem, $35.85 per cr hr; nonres—undergrad lower div $1855 per yr; no grad students; campus res $550 room & $470 (10 meals per wk) per sem
Courses: †Art History, †Ceramics, Drawing, †Painting, †Photography, †Printmaking, †Sculpture
Adult Hobby Classes: Enrl 15; tuition $30 for 10 weeks. Courses—Pottery
Children's Classes: Enrl 30; tuition $20 for 6 weeks. Courses—General Art Workshop
Summer School: Dir, Dr B Williams. Enrl 50-60; tuition $180 for 4 cr class of 3-4 weeks. Courses—Landscape, Painting, Photography, Pottery

POUGHKEEPSIE

DUTCHESS COMMUNITY COLLEGE, Dept of Visual Arts,* Pendell Rd, 12601. Tel 914-471-4500, Ext 339. *Head Dept* J Frankel; *Chmn Visual Art* Jerome Frankel
Estab 1957; pub; D & E; scholarships; SC 24, LC 22; enrl D 660, E 340, maj 100
Ent Req: HS dipl
Degrees: AAS (Commercial Art)
Tuition: Res—$850 per yr; nonres—$1700 per yr
Courses: Glass, Leather, Metal, Plastic, Weaving, Wood

VASSAR COLLEGE, Art Dept, 12601. Tel 914-452-7000, Ext 2642. *Chmn Art Dept* Susan D Kuretsky. Instrs: FT 10, PT 7
Estab 1861; pvt; D; scholarships; SC 8, LC; enrl maj 90, others 2400
Ent Req: HS grad, ent exam
Degrees: BA(Art History) 4 yr
Courses: Architecture, †Art History, Drafting, Drawing, Painting, Printmaking, Sculpture

PURCHASE

MANHATTANVILLE COLLEGE, Art Dept,* 10577. Tel 914-946-9600, 694-2200. *Head Dept* Louis Trakis
Estab 1841; pvt; D & E; scholarships; SC 25, LC 10, GC 7; enrl D 180, non-maj 90, maj 90, grad 10
Ent Req: HS dipl, portfolio, interview
Degrees: BA and BFA 4 yrs, MAT 1 yr, special prog MATA (Masters of Art in Teaching Art)
Tuition: $7040 per yr
Courses: Book Design, Design, Metal Sculpture
Summer School: Dir, Mary Thompson. Courses—Art History, Ceramics, Drawing, Painting, Photography, Sculpture

STATE UNIVERSITY OF NEW YORK COLLEGE AT PURCHASE
—Division of Visual Arts, 10577. Tel 914-253-5140. *Dean* Ed Colker. Instrs: FT 18, PT 18
Estab 1974; pub; scholarships; enrl 3600, maj 400
Degrees: BFA(Visual Arts)

Tuition: Res—undergrad $1050 per yr; non-res—undergrad $1750 per yr; campus res—room $1100 per yr, apartment $1240-$1350 per yr, board $794-$924.60 per yr
Courses: Art History, Drawing, Graphic Design, Painting, Printmaking, Photography, Arts of the Book, Design in Wood, Media, 3-D Design
Adult Hobby Classes: Enrl 450-500
Children's Classes: Enrl 50; summer session art program
Summer School: Dir, Laura Evans. Enrl 400; 6 wk sessions
—**Dept of Art History,*** 10577. Tel 914-253-5025. *Coordr* Eric Carlson, PhD; *Assoc Prof* Irving Sandler, PhD; *Asst Prof* Eleanor Saunders, PhD
Estab 1971, dept estab 1977; pub; D & E; scholarships; enrl total 2000, maj 25
Ent Req: HS dipl, essay on application, grades, test scores
Degrees: BA and BALA 4 yrs
Tuition: Res—$1050 per yr; nonres—$1750 per yr
Courses: Art History

RIVERDALE

COLLEGE OF MOUNT SAINT VINCENT, Fine Arts Dept,* West 263rd St and Riverdale Ave, 10471. Tel 212-549-8000. *Chmn* Enrico Giordano, BFA; *Assoc Prof* Christine Marie Murphy, MFA; *Lectr* Diane Lamb-Wanacha, MSAE
Estab 1911; pvt; D & E; scholarships; SC 22, LC 10; enrl D 950, E 50
Ent Req: HS dipl and SAT
Degrees: BA, BS and BS(Art Educ) 4 yrs
Tuition: $2275
Courses: Design
Summer School: Dir Continuing Education, Dr Marjorie Connelly. Courses—vary each summer

ROCHESTER

MONROE COMMUNITY COLLEGE, Art Dept,* 1000 E Henrietta Rd, 14623. Tel 716-442-9950, Ext 3373. *Faculty Prof* George C McDade, MA; *Assoc Prof* Bruce R Brown, MFA; *Assoc Prof* Douglas S Bull, BA; *Asst Prof* Charles W Haas, MFA
Estab 1961; pub; D & E; SC 16, LC 4
Ent Req: HS dipl
Degrees: Assoc in Arts 2 yrs, Assoc in Science 2 yrs, Assoc in Applied Science 2 yrs
Tuition: $1150 per nine months
Courses: Art History, Ceramics, †Commercial Art, Drafting, Drawing, Graphic Arts, Graphic Design, Handicrafts, Illustration, Jewelry, Lettering, Painting, Printmaking, Sculpture, Textile Design, Theatre Arts, Video, Weaving
Adult Hobby Classes: Tuition $36 per hr. Courses—Batik, Ceramics, Jewelry, Leatherwork, Macrame, Rugmaking, Soft Sculpture, Weaving
Summer School: Dir, George C McDade

NAZARETH COLLEGE OF ROCHESTER, Art Dept, 14610. Tel 716-586-2525, Ext 521. *Head Dept* Roger J Adams, PhD; *Prof* Sr Magdalen Larow, PhD; *Assoc Prof* Mary Jane Edwards, MFA; *Assoc Prof* Kathy Calderwood, BFA; *Asst Prof* Ron Netsky, MFA; *Asst Prof* Lynn Duggan, MFA; *Asst Prof* Susan Rowley, MFA; *Lectr* Karen Trickey, MSEd; *Lectr* Lawrence Merrill, MFA
Estab 1924, dept estab 1936; pvt; D & E; scholarships; SC 40, LC 15, GC 6; enrl D 180, E 74, non-maj 50, maj 200, grad 48
Ent Req: HS dipl
Degrees: BA and BS 4 yrs
Tuition: Undergrad $1890 per sem, $109 per cr hr; non-res—grad $121 per cr hr; campus res—room & board $2250 per yr
Courses: †Art Education, †Art History, Ceramics, Drawing, †Graphic Arts, Jewelry, Painting, Photography, Printmaking, Sculpture, Textile Design, Weaving, Art Therapy
Summer School: Dir, Elaine Hayden. Enrl 60; tuition $121 per cr hr for term of 6 wks beginning July 5th. Courses—grad and undergrad

ROBERTS WESLEYAN COLLEGE, Fine Arts Division, Art Dept, 2301 West Side Dr, 14624. Tel 716-594-9471. *Chmn* Robert Shewan; *Instr* Loren Baker; *Instr* Douglas Giebel; *Instr* Willard Peterson
Scholarships
Degrees: BA(Fine Art), BA(Studio Art), BS(Studio Art)
Tuition: $2200 per sem
Courses: Art Appreciation, Art History, Ceramics, Design, Drawing, Graphic Design, Jewelry, Lettering, Painting, Photography, Printmaking, Sculpture, Weaving
Adult Hobby Classes: Enrl 16; tuition $30 for 5 wks. Courses—Photography, Weaving
Summer School: Dir, Dr Oscar Lenning. Enrl 24; tuition $79 per cr for 5 wks. Courses—Ceramics, Visual Awareness

ROCHESTER INSTITUTE OF TECHNOLOGY
—**College of Fine and Applied Arts,** One Lomb Memorial Dr, 14623. Tel 716-475-2646. *Dean College* Dr Robert H Johnston; *Assoc Dean College* Dr Peter Giopulos; *Asst Dean* Robert Kerr; *Asst Dean Admin* Rose Marie Deorr
Tuition: Undergrad—$5559
Adult Hobby Classes: Courses offered
Children's Classes: One wk summer workshop for juniors in HS
Summer School: Two 5 wk sessions & special one wk workshops
—**School of Art and Design,** 14623. *Chmn* Bernadette Merkel, MFA; *Chmn Fine Arts* Ronald E Padgham, BFA; *Prof* Kener E Bond Jr, BEd; *Prof* Frederick Lipp, BFE; *Prof* Fred Meyer, MFA; *Prof* R Roger Remington, BFA; *Prof* Joanne Szabla, BFA; *Prof* James E Thomas; *Prof* Toby Thompson, BID; *Prof* Sheila Wells, BA; *Prof* Lawrence Williams, BFA; *Prof* Philip W Bornath, MAE; *Prof* Craig J McArt, BID; *Assoc Prof* Robert A Cole, MS; *Assoc Prof* Robert Heischman, BFA; *Assoc Prof* Barbara Hodik, BS; *Assoc Prof* Edward C Miller, BFA; *Assoc Prof* Bruce Sodervick, BS; *Assoc Prof* James Ver Hague, BS; *Assoc Prof* Joseph A Watson, BFA; *Assoc Prof* Norman Williams, MS; *Assoc Prof* Mary Ann Begland, BS; *Asst Prof* David Dickinson, MFA; *Asst Prof* Robert M Kahute, BFA; *Asst Prof* Steve Loar, BS; *Asst Prof* Robert C Morgan, BA; *Asst Prof* Joyce Shikowitz, BFA; *Asst Prof* James H Sias, MA; *Asst Prof* Robert Wabnitz, dipl & cert; *Vis Asst Prof* Heinz Klinkon,

BFA; *Vis Asst Prof* Mark Foster, MFA; *Lectr* Eric Beilmann, BS; *Instr* Luvon Sheppard, MST. Instrs: FT 43, PT 14
Estab 1829; pvt; enrl 550
Ent Req: HS grad, ent exam, portfolio
Degrees: AAS, BS, BFA, MFA
Tuition: Undergrad—$5559; campus res available
Courses: †Art Education, †Graphic Design, †Painting, †Printmaking, †Environmental Design, †Medical Illustration, †Packaging Design
Summer School: Two 5 wk sessions; one wk workshop. Courses—Painting, Printmaking, Graphic Design, Industrial & Interior Design, Computer Graphics
—**School for American Craftsmen,** 14623. *Crafts Chmn* William A Keyser Jr, BS; *Prof* Donald G Bujnowski, BS; *Prof* Robert D Schmitz, BS; *Assoc Prof* Gary Griffin, BA; *Assoc Prof* Max L Lenderman, BS & MS; *Assoc Prof* Douglas E Sigler, MFA; *Asst Prof* Graham Marks, BFA; *Asst Prof* Michael Taylor, BS; *Asst Prof* Leonard A Urso, BFA & MFA. Instrs: FT 9, PT 1
Estab 1946; pvt; enrl 150
Ent Req: HS grad, ent exam, portfolio
Degrees: AAS, BFA, MFA, MST 4-5 yrs
Tuition: Undergrad—$5559; campus res available
Courses: †Ceramics, †Jewelry, †Textile Design, †Weaving, Ceramic Sculpture, †Furniture Design, †Glass, Metalcrafts, †Woodworking
Adult Hobby Classes: Courses offered
Children's Classes: One wk summer crafts workshop for juniors in HS
Summer School: Two 5 wk terms and special one wk workshops. Courses—Ceramics, Sculpture, Weaving, Textile Design, Metalcrafts, Jewelry, Woodworking, Furniture Design
—**College of Graphic Arts and Photography,** 14623. *Dean* Mark F Guldin, PhD; *Assoc Dean* John L Kronenberg, BS
Tuition: $5559 per 3 quarter academic year
Adult Hobby Classes: Extensive seminar schedule
Summer School: scholarships
—**School of Photographic Arts & Sciences,** Rochester, 14623. *Dir* Russell C Kraus, BA & EdD; *Chmn Applied Photography* Thomas Iten, BFA & MS; *Chmn Imaging & Photographic Sciences* Ronald Francis, AB & PhD; *Chmn Photographic Technology* Leslie Stroebel, BS & MEd; *Chmn Fine Arts Photography* Richard D Zakia, BS & EdD; *Richard S Hunter Prof* Franc Grum, PhD; *Prof* Charles A Arnold Jr, BFA; *Prof* David A Engdahl, BS & MEd; *Prof* Lothar K Engleman, PhD; *Prof* James E McMillion Jr, BFA & MFA; *Prof* Martin A Rennalls, prof cert; *Prof* David J Robertson, BFA; *Prof* William S Shoemaker, BS; *Assoc Prof* John C Compton, BS & MS; *Assoc Prof* Ira B Current, BA; *Assoc Prof* Andrew Davidhazy, BFA & MFA; *Assoc Prof* Richard Floberg, BA; *Assoc Prof* Bradley T Hindson, BA; *Assoc Prof* John E Karpen, BS & MFA; *Assoc Prof* Weston D Kemp, MFA; *Assoc Prof* Robert B Kushner, MS; *Assoc Prof* Beatrice Nettles, BFA; *Assoc Prof* Nile R Root, MS; *Assoc Prof* Elliott Rubenstein, BA & MA; *Assoc Prof* Donald L Smith, BS; *Assoc Prof* John F Trauger, AB; *Assoc Prof* Charles C Werberig, BFA & MS; *Assoc Prof* Tom Muir Wilson, BFA; *Asst Prof* Terry L Bollman, AB; *Asst Prof* Owen Butler, BFA; *Asst Prof* Guenther Cartwright, BFA; *Asst Prof* Kathleen Collins, AB; *Asst Prof* William W DuBois, BFA; *Asst Prof* Michael A Geissinger, BFA & MST; *Asst Prof* John Head, MFA; *Asst Prof* Robert Kayser, BS; *Asst Prof* Hadrian Lechner, MS; *Asst Prof* Howard LeVant, BS; *Asst Prof* John Schott, BS; *Asst Prof* Michael Soluri, BS; *Asst Prof* Malcolm Spaull, BS; *Asst Prof* Erik Timmerman, BS; *Vis Assoc Prof* Peter Anderson
Enrl 1000
Degrees: BS, MS, MFA
Courses: †Biomedical Photographic Communication; †Film & Television; †Photographic Illustration; †Photographic Marketing Management; †Photographic Processing & Finishing; †Photographic Science & Instrumentation; †Technical Photography
—**School of Printing,** Rochester, 14623. *Dir* William A Pakan, BS, MS & PhD; *Chmn Management Division* W Frederick Craig, BS & MEd; *Chmn Photography Plates & Press Division* Walter G Horne, BS & MEd; *Chmn Design Composition Division* Emery E Schneider, BS & MEd; *Coordr Grad Program* Joseph L Noga, MS; *Paul & Louise Miller Prof* Robert G Hacker, BS; *Prof* Edward A Brabant, BS; *Prof* Walter A Campbell, BA; *Prof* Anthony R Sears, BS; *Prof* Julius L Silver, BS; *Prof* Miles F Southworth, BS; *Assoc Prof* Bekir E Arpag, BS; *Assoc Prof* William H Birkett, BS; *Assoc Prof* Joseph E Brown, BS; *Assoc Prof* Clifton T Frazier, BS; *Assoc Prof* Alfred F Horton, AAS; *Assoc Prof* James I Horton, BS; *Assoc Prof* Herbert H Johnson, BS; *Assoc Prof* Archibald D Provan, BS; *Assoc Prof* Werner Rebsamen, dipl; *Assoc Prof* Robert J Webster, BS; *Assoc Prof* Charles J Weigand, BS, MS & SUC; *Asst Prof* Robert Y Chung, BA; *Asst Prof* Hugh R Fox, AB & JD; *Asst Prof* Jack Jenkins, BS; *Asst Prof* David P Pankow, BA & MA; *Asst Prof* Harry Rab, BSME & MSME; *Asst Prof* Robert S Tompkins
School has 25 laboratories, occupying 125,000 sq ft. More than 70 courses are offered; enrl 700
Degrees: BS, MS, MST
—**Technical & Education Center of the Graphic Arts,** Rochester, 14623. *Dir* Herbert E Phillips, AAS; *Dir Technical Services* William S Eisner, BS; *Asst to the Dir* Sven Ahrenkilde; *Senior Technologist* Chester J Daniels, BS & MS; *Senior Technologist* Zenon A Elyjiw; *Research Assoc* Franz Sigg
Has its own full-time staff to render services to various fields of the graphic arts; conducts short, highly specialized courses for these engaged professionally in the graphic arts. Includes the Physical Testing Laboratory

UNIVERSITY OF ROCHESTER, Dept of Fine Arts, Morey Hall, 424, 14627. Tel 716-275-4284. *Chmn* Arch M Miller. Instrs: FT 10, PT 8
Estab 1902; scholarships; SC 25, LC 45; enrl Maj 45, others 900
Degrees: 4 yrs
Tuition: $7560 per yr
Courses: Art History, Painting, Photography, Sculpture

ROSLYN

HABER SCHOOL OF SCULPTURE,* 1170 Old Northern Blvd, 11576. Tel 516-484-9322. *Dir* Mortimer N Haber
Estab 1965; pvt; D & E; SC 5, LC integrated into prog; enrl D 60, E 13
Ent Req: Based on availability of openings
Degrees: None
Courses: Sculpture, Stone Carving
Summer School: Enrl 39-48; term of 8 wks beginning July. Courses—same as regular session

SANBORN

NIAGARA COUNTY COMMUNITY COLLEGE, Fine Arts Division,* 3111 Saunders Settlement Rd, 14303. Tel 716-731-3271, 731-4101, Ext 158. *Chmn* Donald Sleight. Instrs: FT 6, PT 6
Estab 1965; pub; D & E; SC 12, LC 4; enrl D 400, E 120, maj 140
Ent Req: HS dipl
Degrees: AS(Fine Arts) 2 yrs
Tuition: Res—$800 per yr; nonres—$1600
Courses: Art Education, Drawing, Fashion Arts, Graphic Design, History of Art & Archaeology, Illustration, Interior Design, Painting, Photography, Printmaking, Sculpture
Summer School: Dir, Judith Shipengrover. Enrl 30; term of 6-7 wks beginning June. Courses—Same as regular yr

SARATOGA SPRINGS

SKIDMORE COLLEGE, Dept of Art,* 12866. Tel 518-584-5000. *Chmn* Peter B Baruzzi. Instrs: FT 22
Estab 1911; pvt; scholarships; SC 32, LC 18; enrl maj 350, 2000 total
Ent Req: HS grad, 16 cr, ent exam, portfolio
Degrees: BA and BS 4 yrs
Tuition: $8050 per yr
Courses: Art Education, Art History, Drawing, Film, Graphic Design, Jewelry, Lettering, Painting, Photography, Printmaking, Sculpture, Design, Enameling, Pottery, Screen Printing, Weaving
Summer School: Dir, Regis Brodie. Enrl 194 for two 6 wk sessions. Courses—Advanced Studio & Independent Study, Art History, Ceramics, Drawing, Etching, Film Making, Jewelry, Lettering, Painting, Photography, Sculpture, Two-Dimensional Design, Watercolor, Weaving

YADDO, Box 395, 12866. Tel 518-584-0746. *Pres* Newman E Wait Jr; *Exec Dir* Curtis Harnack
Yaddo is a working retreat for writers, composers, and visual artists. The country estate of the late Mr & Mrs Spencer Trask was estab 1926 and opened to all who have achieved some measure of professional accomplishment. Applications must be received by Jan 15; work must be shown to an admission committee; invitations are issued by April 15 for periods up to 2 months; room, board and studio space for limited number; enrl limited number

SCHENECTADY

UNION COLLEGE, Dept of the Arts, Union St, 12308. Tel 518-370-6201. *Chmn* Daniel Robbins. Instrs: FT 9
Estab 1795; pvt; D; schol; SC 14, LC 4; enrl maj 35
Ent Req: HS dipl, ent exam
Degrees: BA with emphasis in music, art or theatre arts 4 yr
Tuition: $8050 per yr
Courses: Art History, Drawing, Graphic Arts, Graphic Design, Intermedia, Painting, Photography, Sculpture, Stage Design, Theatre Arts, History of Architecture, Improvisation, 2-D Design, 3-D Design
Adult Hobby Classes: Art History, Figure Drawing, Graphics, Relief Printmaking, 3-D Design Fundamentals, Photography
Summer School: Courses—Art History, Figure Drawing, Graphics, Relief Printmaking, 3-D Design Fundamentals, Photography

SEA CLIFF

STEVENSON ACADEMY OF TRADITIONAL PAINTING,* 361 Glen Ave, 11579. Tel 516-676-6611. *Head Dept* Harold Ransom Stevenson; *Asst Instr* Alma Gallanos. Instrs: FT 2
Estab 1960; pvt; E; SC 3, LC 5; enrl 95
Ent Req: Interview
Tuition: $100 per 10 wk sem, one evening per wk; $500 per 10 wk sem, five evenings per wk; no campus res
Courses: Drawing, Illustration, Painting, Artistic Anatomy, Basic Form
Summer School: Enrl 57; tui $80-$230 per term of 8 wks beginning June 1. Courses—Artistic Anatomy, Drawing, Painting

SELDEN

SUFFOLK COUNTY COMMUNITY COLLEGE, Art Dept, 533 College Rd, 11784. Tel 516-451-4352. Instrs: FT 8, PT 6
Degrees: AFA
Tuition: Res $39 per cr; nonres $78 per cr
Courses: Art Appreciation, Art History, Ceramics, Design, Drawing, Painting, Printmaking
Adult Hobby Classes: Enrl 200; tuition $15 per hr. Courses—Photography, Interior Design
Summer School: Dir, Maurice Flecker. Tuition res $39 per cr, nonres $78 per cr, for 6 - 8 wks sessions. Courses—Painting, Sculpture, 2-D Design, Life Drawing, Printmaking and Ceramics

SOUTHAMPTON

SOUTHAMPTON COLLEGE OF LONG ISLAND UNIVERSITY, C W Post Center Fine Arts Division, 11968. Tel 516-283-4000 Ext 191 & 192. *Division Dir & Assoc Prof* Yolanda Trincere; *Prof* Colonius Davis, PhD; *Prof* Robert Shaughnessy, PhD; *Prof* Robert Skinner, PhD; *Assoc Prof* William Phelan; *Assoc Prof* Constance Evans, MFA; *Assoc Prof* Yosh Higa, MGA; *Assoc Prof* Robert Munford
Estab 1963; pvt; D & E; schol; SC 36, LC 17, GC 11; enrl D 398, E 20, non-maj 100, maj 280, grad 20, others 18
Ent Req: HS dipl and portfolio review

Degrees: BFA, BS(Art Educ), BA(Fine Arts), 4 yrs, MA Educ
Tuition: $2270 sem; campus res—room and board $1330 sem
Courses: †Advertising Design, †Art Education, †Art History, Calligraphy, †Ceramics, Collages, †Commercial Art, Constructions, Drafting, †Drawing, †Graphic Arts, Handicrafts, History of Art & Archaeology, †Illustration, Jewelry, Lettering, Museum Staff Training, †Painting, †Photography, †Printmaking, †Sculpture, Silversmithing, Stage Design, Teacher Training, Textile Design, Theatre Arts, Art Therapy, Basketry, Enameling, †Weaving
Adult Hobby Classes: Courses—Drawing, Painting, Photography, Various Crafts
Children's Classes: 8 wk summer children's prog
Summer School: Dir, Yolanda Trincere. Tuition $144 per cr hr for term of 5 wks beginning July. Courses—various

SPARKHILL

SAINT THOMAS AQUINAS COLLEGE, Art Dept,* Route 340, 10976. Tel 914-359-9500, Ext 211. *Assoc Prof* Carl Rattner, MFA; *Instr* Roger Howrigan, MFA; *Instr* Sr Adele Myers, MFA; *Instr* Sr Elizabeth Slenker, MFA
Estab 1952, dept estab 1969; pvt; D & E; scholarships; enrl D 1100, maj 50
Ent Req: HS dipl
Degrees: BA and BS 4 yrs
Tuition: $3000 per yr; campus res available
Courses: Advertising Design, Art Education, Art History, Calligraphy, Commercial Art, Drawing, Handicrafts, Jewelry, Painting, Photography, Printmaking, Sculpture, Teacher Training, Textile Design, Theatre Arts, Video
Summer School: Dir, Dr Joseph Keane. Tui $210 for 3 cr course. Courses—Varies 3-6 art courses including Ceramics, Painting, Photography

STATEN ISLAND

COLLEGE OF STATEN ISLAND, Performing & Creative Arts Dept, 120 Stuyvesant Pl, 10301. Tel 212-390-7992. *Chmn* Dr Diane Kelder
Degrees: BA(Cinema Studies), BS(Art), BS(Photography)
Tuition: $900 per sem
Courses: Advertising Design, Architecture, †Art Appreciation, Art Education, †Art History, †Design, †Drawing, †Film, †Museum Staff Training, †Painting, †Photography, †Printmaking, Video
Summer School: Courses offered

WAGNER COLLEGE, Dept of Art, 631 Howard Ave, 10301. Tel 212-390-3000. *Chmn* Richard W Gaffney
Estab 1948; den; D & E; SC 20, LC 6; enrl maj 35, others 2500
Ent Req: HS grad
Degrees: BA(Art)
Tuition: Res—undergrad campus res $8200 per yr
Courses: Art History, Ceramics, Drawing, Mixed Media, Painting, Photography, Printmaking, Sculpture, Black Art History, Crafts Design, Three Dimensional Design, Two Dimensional Design
Summer School: Two sessions of 4 wks

STONE RIDGE

ULSTER COUNTY COMMUNITY COLLEGE, Dept of Visual Arts, 12484. Tel 914-687-7621, Ext 76. *Head Dept* Allan Cohen, MFA; *Asst Prof* John A Locke III, MFA; *Asst Prof* Peter Correia, MS. Instrs: PT 3
Estab 1963; pub; D & E; SC 17, LC 6; enrl D 500, E 100, non-maj 440, maj 60
Ent Req: HS dipl
Degrees: AA 2 yrs
Tuition: Res—undergrad $1150 per yr; nonres—undergrad $3450 per yr; no campus res
Courses: Advertising Design, Aesthetics, Art History, Drawing, †Graphic Arts, Painting, Photography, Theatre Arts, Life Drawing & Anatomy, Three Dimensional Design, Two Dimensional Design
Summer School: Dir, Allan Cohen. Enrl 60; tuition $40 per 6 - 8 wks. Courses—Drawing, Painting, Photography

STONY BROOK

STATE UNIVERSITY OF NEW YORK AT STONY BROOK, Art Dept, 11794. Tel 516-246-7070. *Chmn* Aldona Jonitis, PhD; *Prof* Jacques Guilmain, PhD; *Prof* George Koras; *Prof* Donald Kuspit; *Assoc Prof* Howardena Pindell, MFA; *Assoc Prof* Nina Mallory, PhD; *Assoc Prof* Mel Pekarsky, MA; *Assoc Prof* James H Rubin, PhD
Estab 1957; pub; D; SC 33, LC 39; enrl D 1850
Ent Req: HS dipl, SAT
Degrees: BA(Art History) & BA(Studio Art), MA(Art Criticism)
Tuition: Res—undergrad $1050 per yr, $525 per sem, $35 per cr hr; nonres—undergrad $1750 per yr, $875 sem, $58.50 per cr hr; campus res room $1250 per yr
Courses: †Art History, Drawing, Painting, Photography, Printmaking, Sculpture, 2-D Design, 3-D Design, †Studio Ceramics
Summer School: Tuition res—undergrad $35 per cr hr, grad $71 per cr hr; nonres—undergrad $58.50 per cr hr, grad $91.50 per cr hr for term of 5 1/2 wks (two sessions). Courses vary

SUFFERN

ROCKLAND COMMUNITY COLLEGE, Graphic Arts & Advertising Tech Dept,* 145 College Rd, 10901. Tel 914-356-4650, Ext 285. *Chmn* J P Murphy
Estab 1965; pub; D & E; SC plus apprenticeships; enrl D 900, E 300, maj 200
Ent Req: Open
Degrees: AAS 2 yrs
Tuition: Res—$46 per sem hr; nonres—$92 per sem hr

Courses: Advertising Design, Art History, Drawing, Graphic Arts, Graphic Design, Lettering, Painting, Photography, Sculpture, Art Appreciation, Art Therapy, Color Production, Electric Art
Adult Hobby Classes: Tui depends on enrl. Courses—varied
Children's Classes: Courses—Overseas programs
Summer School: Courses—Art History, Drawing, Graphic Techniques, Painting, Sculpture

SYRACUSE

LE MOYNE COLLEGE, Art Dept, Le Moyne Heights, 13214. Tel 315-446-2882. *Dir* Jacqueline Belfort-Chalat, member Royal Acad, DK; *Adjunct Asst Prof* Ronald Depentu, BFA; *Adjunct Asst Prof* Charles Wollowitz, MFA; *Adjunct Instr* Charles Aho, MA; *Adjunct Asst Prof* Barbara Perry, PhD
Pvt; D; SC 4, LC 1; enrl non-maj 300
Ent Req: HS dipl, SAT or ACT
Degrees: BS and BA 4 yrs
Tuition: $4700 per yr, $2350 per sem, $110 per hr; campus residence—room & board $2370 per yr
Courses: Art History, Drawing, Graphic Arts, Painting, Sculpture
Adult Hobby Classes: Dir Continuing Learning, James Fratto, PhD
Summer School: Dir Continuing Learning, James Fratto, PhD

SYRACUSE UNIVERSITY
—College of Visual and Performing Arts, School of Art, 203 Crouse College, 13210. Tel 315-423-2507. *Dean* Donald M Lantzy, MFA; *Dir* Rodger Mack, MFA. Instrs: FT 63, PT 19
Estab 1873; pvt; D & E; scholarships; SC 200, LC 25, GC 100; enrl D 1039, E 250, maj 1039, grad 108
Ent Req: HS dipl, portfolio review
Degrees: BID 5 yrs, BFA 4 yrs, MFA, MID and MS 2 yrs
Tuition: Undergrad $7600 per yr; grad $203 per cr; campus res available
Courses: †Advertising Design, Aesthetics, †Architecture, †Art Education, †Art History, †Ceramics, Drawing, †Film, †Illustration, †Industrial Design, †Interior Design, †Painting, †Printmaking, †Sculpture, †Video, †Art Photo Process, †Computer Graphics, †Editorial Design, †Experimental Studios, †Fashion Illustration, †Fiber Structure & Interlocking, †Metalsmithing, †Museology, Papermaking, †Selected Studies, †Surface Pattern Design, †Theatre Design
Adult Hobby Classes: Dean, Frank Funk. Enrl 250; tuition undergrad $128 per cr. Courses—same as above
Children's Classes: Enrl 65; tuition $30 per sem. Courses—general art
Summer School: Dean, Thomas O'Shea. Tuition undergrad $182 per cr, grad $203 per cr per 6 wk session. Courses—same as above
—Dept of Fine Arts, 441 Hall of Languages, 13210. Tel 315-423-4184. *Chmn* David Tatham, PhD; *Prof* Gary Radke, PhD; *Prof* Meredith Lillich, PhD; *Prof* Ellen Oppler, PhD; *Prof* Sidney Thomas, PhD; *Prof* Laurinda Dixon, PhD
Estab 1870, dept estab 1946; pvt; D & E; scholarships; LC 25, GC 12; enrl non-maj 900, maj 30, grad 20
Ent Req: HS dipl, SAT
Degrees: BA 4 yrs, MA 1-2 yrs, PhD 3-6 yrs
Tuition: Res—undergrad $9000 per yr, $4500 per sem, grad $203 per cr; campus res available
Courses: †History of Art & Archaeology

TARRYTOWN

MARYMOUNT COLLEGE, Art Dept, 10591. Tel 914-631-3200. *Chmn* Marilyn Picaidma; *Prof* John Lochtefeld, MFA; *Prof* Bianca Haglich, RSHM & MA; *Assoc Prof* Robert J Lee; *Asst Prof* Rebecca Conviser, MA
Estab 1918; pvt; D & E; schol; SC 42, LC 15; enrl D 806, Weekends 337
Ent Req: HS dipl, CEEB
Degrees: BA and BS 4 yrs
Tuition: Res—undergrad $9000 per yr; nonres—undergrad $5175 per yr; PT student $165 per hr; campus res—room board $3340 per yr
Courses: Advertising Design, Art Education, Art History, Ceramics, Drawing, Fashion Arts, Film, Handicrafts, Illustration, Interior Design, Mixed Media, Painting, Photography, Printmaking, Sculpture, Stage Design, Teacher Training, Textile Design, Theatre Arts, Weaving, Stitchery
Summer School: Dir, Dr Ellen Campbell. Tuition $165 per cr. Courses—American Architecture, Mixed Media (Art, Vision and Form), Raku - Japanese Ceramics

TROY

EMMA WILLARD SCHOOL ARTS DIVISION, Pawling Avenue, 12180. Tel 518-274-4440, Ext 231. *Div Chmn* Christine Leith
Estab 1814, dept estab 1969; pvt; D & E; scholarships
Courses: Art Appreciation, Art History, Ceramics, Drawing, Jewelry, Photography, Printmaking, Theatre Arts, Advanced Studio Art, Dance, Music, Visual Arts Foundation, Weaving

RENSSELAER POLYTECHNIC INSTITUTE
—School of Architecture, 12181. Tel 518-270-6460. *Dean* David S Haviland. Instrs: FT 17, PT 14
EStab 1929; pvt; D; scholarships; enrl 245
Degrees: BArchit, BS, MArchit and MS 4-5 yrs
Tuition: $8600 per yr; campus res
Courses: Architecture, Building Science
Summer School: Architectural Design
—Dept of Art, School of Humanities and Social Science, 12181. Tel 518-266-6668. *Chmn* Larry Kagan
Tuition: $8300 per yr
Courses: Ceramics, Drawing, Painting, Sculpture

RUSSELL SAGE COLLEGE, Visual and Performing Arts Dept, 203 Second St, 12180. Tel 518-270-2000. *Chmn* Richard L Jones
Pvt; W; enrl 20-40 per class
Ent Req: HS grad
Degrees: Fine arts and divisional maj in Music, Art and Drama 4 yrs

UTICA

MOHAWK VALLEY COMMUNITY COLLEGE, Advertising Design and Production, 1101 Sherman Dr, 13510. Tel 315-797-9530. *Pres* Michael L Schafer, PhD; *Head Dept* Milton Richards, PhD; *Assoc Prof* Virginia Juergensen, MFA; *Asst Prof* James O'Looney, BS; *Asst Prof* Henry Godlewski, BS; *Instructor* Karen Faryniak, BFA; *Instructor* Kathleen Partridge, BFA; *Instructor* Ronald La Buz, MA; *Instructor* John Rowntree, MA; *Instructor* Kenneth Murphy, BA; *Instructor* Robert Duffek, BA; *Instructor* Robert Clarke, BFA. Instrs: FT 9, PT 2
Estab 1947, dept estab 1955; pub; D & E; SC 18 (over 2 yr period), LC 6 (over 2 yr period); enrl D 280, E varies, maj 280
Ent Req: HS dipl
Degrees: AAS 2 yrs
Tuition: $1050 per yr; campus residency available
Courses: †Advertising Design, †Drawing, †Graphic Arts
Adult Hobby Classes: Tuition varies per quarter. Courses—Air Brush, Painting, Photography, Sketching, Watercolor
Summer School: Courses—vary

MUNSON-WILLIAMS-PROCTOR INSTITUTE, School of Art, 310 Genesee St, 13502. Tel 315-797-000. *Dir* Clyde E McCulley, PhD; *Instr* Everett Adelman, MFA; *Instr* Vincent Clemente, MS; *Instr* Georgia Deal, MFA; *Instr* Francis Fiorentino, MFA; *Instr* John Loy, MFA; *Instr* Marjorie Salzillo, MFA; *Instr* Keith Sandman, MFA; *Instr* John vonBergen, MFA; *Instr* Alfred Wardle, BS; *Vis Instr* Raymond George, MA. Instrs: FT 14, PT 20
Estab 1941; pvt; enrl adults 1480, children 533
Degrees: AA 2 yrs, Diploma 2 yrs
Tuition: Nonres undergrad—$75 per cr hr
Courses: Art Education, Ceramics, Drawing, Graphic Arts, Painting, Photography, Sculpture, Dance, Fine Arts Studio Series, Metal Arts, Pottery
Adult Hobby Classes: Courses—Ceramics, Dance, Drawing, Metal Arts, Painting, Printmaking, Photography, Quiltmaking, Sculpture, 2-D & 3-D Design
Children's Classes: Courses—Dance, Drawing, Painting, Pottery
Summer School: Courses—four morning classes per wk for 4 wks, classes on Tues & Thurs afternoon or evenings for 4 wks. High school courses—Ceramics, Dramatics, Drawing, Painting, Printmaking

UTICA COLLEGE OF SYRACUSE UNIVERSITY, Division of Humanities, Burrstone Rd, 13502. Tel 315-792-3057. *Chairperson Div* Robert W Millett, PhD
Estab 1946, school of art estab 1973; pvt; D; SC 20, LC 7; enrl School of Art D 94, Utica College maj 14
Degrees: BA(Fine Arts) 4 yrs
Courses: Art History, †Ceramics, Drafting, Drawing, Film, Graphic Arts, Occupational Therapy, †Painting, Photography, †Sculpture, Stage Design, Theatre Arts, Video, Design

WATERTOWN

JEFFERSON COMMUNITY COLLEGE, Art Dept,* PO Box 473, 13601. Tel 315-782-5250. *Pres* John T Henderson; *Prof* Klaus Ebeling. Instrs: FT 1
Estab 1963; pub; D & E; SC 2, LC 1; enrl 850 college total
Degrees: 2 yr
Tuition: $490 per sem
Courses: Art Appreciation, Art History, Photography, Sculpture, Film Appreciation, Two-Dimensional Studio
Summer School: Pres, John T Henderson

WHITE PLAINS

PACE UNIVERSITY, Dyson College Arts & Science,* Dept Art & Design, 78 N Broadway, 10603. Tel 914-682-7070. *Chmn* Brenda Bettinson; *Dean* Joseph E Houk. Instrs: PT 2
Pvt; D & E; SC 4, LC 4
Ent Req: HS dipl
Tuition: $140 per sem
Courses: Art Education, Drawing, Graphic Arts, History of Art & Archaeology, Painting, Photography, Stage Design, Theatre Arts
Summer School: Dir, Sister M Berchmanns Coyle. Courses—Painting

WESTCHESTER COMMUNITY COLLEGE, Westchester Art Workshop, County Center, 10607. Tel 914-683-3986. *Dir* Wayne Kartzinel
Estab 1926; pub; D & E; SC 60 per sem, 3 sem per yr; enrl D 450, E 250, others 700 (no credits given for courses)
Ent Req: No special req
Degrees: AAS
Tuition: $41.50 per credit; no campus res
Courses: Calligraphy, Ceramics, Drawing, Jewelry, Painting, Photography, Sculpture, Silversmithing, Weaving, Stained Glass
Children's Classes: Courses—Ceramics, Jewelry, Painting
Summer School: 700; tuition $41.50 per credit. Courses—same

YONKERS

ELIZABETH SETON COLLEGE, Art Dept,* 10701. Tel 914-969-4000. *Chmn* Robin Landa, MFA; *Assoc Prof* Sr Regina Kraft, MFA; *Assoc Prof* Sr Margaret Beaudette, MFA; *Instructor* Barbara Dodsworth, MA
Estab 1960; pvt; D, E & weekends; schol; SC 15, LC 3; enrl D 30, E 20, maj 25
Ent Req: HS dipl

Degrees: AS, AAS and AOS
Tuition: $3100 per yr; campus residency available
Courses: †Advertising Design, Art History, Calligraphy, Ceramics, Drawing, Illustration, Film, Interior Design, Jewelry, Lettering, Painting, Photography, Printmaking, Sculpture, Video, †Art Therapy
Adult Hobby Classes: Enrl 60. Courses—Art History, Calligraphy, Chinese Painting, Etching, Painting, Photography
Summer School: Courses in Fine and Commercial Art

NORTH CAROLINA

ASHEVILLE

UNIVERSITY OF NORTH CAROLINA AT ASHEVILLE, Dept of Art and Music,* University Heights, 28801. Tel 704-258-0200. *Chmn* S Tucker Cooke, MFA Estab 1927, dept estab 1965; pub; D & E; scholarships; SC 20, LC 5; enrl D 1280, E 300, non-maj 50, maj 40
Ent Req: HS dipl, ent exam
Degrees: BA 4-5 yrs
Tuition: Res—$314 per sem; nonres—$1105 per sem; campus res available
Courses: Art Education, Art History, Ceramics, Commercial Art, Costume Design & Construction, Drawing, Graphic Arts, Intermedia, Jewelry, Mixed Media, Painting, Photography, Printmaking, Sculpture, Stage Design, Theatre Arts
Summer School: Dir, S Tucker Cooke. Courses vary

BELMONT

SACRED HEART COLLEGE, Dept of Art,* Main St, 28012. Tel 704-825-5146. *Chmn* Sr M Theophane Field, MFA
Estab 1935, dept estab 1966; pvt & den; D; SC 30, LC 3; enrl maj 27, others 50
Ent Req: HS dipl, ent exam
Degrees: BA and BS 4 yrs, AA 2 yrs
Tuition: $2900 per yr; campus res available
Courses: Art History, Ceramics, Drawing, Graphic Arts, Graphic Design, Jewelry, Mixed Media, Painting, Photography, Printmaking, Sculpture, Teacher Training, Textile Design

BOONE

APPALACHIAN STATE UNIVERSITY, Dept of Art,* 28608. Tel 704-262-2000. *Chmn* Warren C Dennis; *Asst Dean* Noyes C Long
Estab 1960; pub; D; scholarships; SC 38, LC 10, GC 12; enrl D 1000, maj 236, grad 5
Ent Req: HS dipl, ent exam
Degrees: BA and BS (commercial design, art educ, studio art) 4 yrs
Tuition: Res—$366.25 per sem; nonres—$1260.25 per sem
Courses: Art Appreciation, Fabric Design
Summer School: Dir, L F Edwards. Enrl 300; term of 2, 4 & 6 wks beginning May-Aug. Courses—per regular session

BREVARD

BREVARD COLLEGE, Division of Fine Arts, 28712. Tel 704-883-8292. *Chmn* Virginia Tilotson; *Prof* Timothy G Murray, MACA; *Asst Prof* Cheryl Harrison. Instrs: PT 2
Estab 1853; den; D & E; scholarships; SC 12, LC 2
Ent Req: HS dipl
Degrees: AFA 2 yrs
Tuition: Res—undergrad $2600 per yr; nonres—undergrad $3200 per yr
Courses: Art History, Ceramics, Drawing, Film, Graphic Arts, Graphic Design, Painting, Photography, Printmaking, Sculpture, Theatre Arts
Summer School: Courses vary

CHAPEL HILL

UNIVERSITY OF NORTH CAROLINA AT CHAPEL HILL, Art Dept, 101 Art Classroom Studio Bldg 079A, 27514. Tel 919-962-2015. *Chmn* Jaroslav Folda, PhD; *Asst Chmn Art Hist* Mary C Sturgeon, PhD; *Asst Chmn Studio Art* Dennis Zaborowski, MFA; *Prof* Robert Barnard, MA; *Prof* John W Dixon, Jr, PhD; *Prof* Robert Howard, MA; *Prof* Frances Huemer, PhD; *Prof* Richard Kinnarid, MFA; *Prof* Marvin Saltzman, MFA; *Prof* J Richard Judson, PhD; *Prof* Arthur Marks, PhD; *Prof* Peter Plagens, MFA; *Assoc Prof* C Edson Armi, PhD; *Assoc Prof* Richard Shiff, PhD; *Assoc Prof* Dennis Zaborowski, MFA; *Assoc Prof* James Gadson, MFA; *Assoc Prof* Jerry Noe, MFA; *Asst Prof* Mary Sheriff, PhD; *Asst Prof* Sarah Bapst, MFA; *Lectr* Carolyn Bloomer, MA; *Lectr* Xavier Toubes, MA; *Vis Artist* Caspar Henselmann; *Vis Artist* Louise Stanley; *Vis Artist* Eugene Brodsky
Estab 1793, dept estab 1936; pub; D; scholarships; SC 15, LC 15, GC 10; enrl D 200 undergrad, 65 grad
Ent Req: HS dipl, SAT
Degrees: BA, BS and BFA 4 yrs, MFA and MA(Art History) 2 yrs, PhD(Art History) to 8 yrs
Tuition: Res—undergrad $382.75 per sem, grad $380.75 per sem; nonres—undergrad $1563.75 per sem, grad $1561.75 per sem
Courses: †Art History, †Ceramics, †Drawing, †Painting, †Printmaking, †Sculpture
Summer School: Chmn, Dennis Zoborowski. 2 terms of 5 wks beginning May 24 & July 3. Courses—various art history and studio courses

CHARLOTTE

CENTRAL PIEDMONT COMMUNITY COLLEGE, Art Division, PO Box 4009, 28204. Tel 704-373-6633. *Chmn* Louis Freeman
Tuition: Res—$4.25 per cr hr; nonres—$21.25 per cr hr
Courses: Advertising Design, Architecture, Art Appreciation, Art History, Calligraphy, Ceramics, Design, Drawing, Fashion Arts, Handicrafts, Interior Design, Jewelry, Painting, Photography, Printmaking, Sculpture, Stage Design, Weaving, Cartooning, Stained Glass

QUEENS COLLEGE, Art Dept,* 1900 Selwyn Ave, 28274. Tel 704-332-7121. *Fine Arts Chmn* George A Stegner; *Artists-in-Res* Paul Arlyn Nitsch. Instrs: FT 3, PT 1
Estab 1857; den; W; scholarships; SC 19, LC 7
Degrees: Granted
Tuition: $4600 annual tuition
Courses: Art History, Ceramics, Commercial Art

UNIVERSITY OF NORTH CAROLINA-CHARLOTTE, Creative Arts Dept, UNCC Station, 28223. Tel 704-597-2471. *Chmn* Donald R Byrum, MFA; *Faculty* Eric Anderson; *Faculty* Edwina Bringle; *Faculty* Esther Hill; *Faculty* Mike Kampen; *Faculty* Rod MacKillop; *Faculty* Joseph Spence; *Faculty* Martha Strawn; *Faculty* Winston Tite; *Faculty* Joan Tweedy
Estab 1965, dept estab 1971; pub; D & E; SC 25, LC 3; enrl D 670, non-maj 500, maj 185
Ent Req: HS dipl, SAT, Col Boards
Degrees: BCA 4 yrs
Tuition: Res—$324; nonres—$1218; room & board per sem $994 - $1183
Courses: Art Education, Ceramics, Costume Design & Construction, Drawing, Jewelry, Painting, Photography, Printmaking, Sculpture, Silversmithing, Stage Design, Fibers, Metalsmithing, Performing Arts, Weaving, Visual Communications & Design
Summer School: Dir, Donald Byrum. Enrl 60; tuition res—$122, nonres—$569; two 5 wk sessions. Courses—Art Appreciation, Freshmen Studio

CONCORD

BARBER-SCOTIA COLLEGE, Art Dept,* 145 Cabarrus Ave, 28025. Tel 704-786-5171. *Chmn Division Art, Science, Business* Dr Julian Pyles; *Prof* Grady Garfield Miles, MA
Estab 1867; pvt den; D & E; SC 10, LC 5; enrl non-maj 100, maj 1
Ent Req: HS dipl, contact admissions office for other req
Degrees: BA and BS
Tuition: $2000 per yr
Courses: Aesthetics, Art Education, Art History, Ceramics, Collages, Commercial Art, Constructions, Display, Drawing, Film, Graphic Arts, Graphic Design, Handicrafts, History of Art & Archaeology, Illustration, Intermedia, Interior Design, Lettering, Mixed Media, Occupational Therapy, Painting, Photography, Printmaking, Sculpture, Teacher Training, African Art, Afro-American Art

CULLOWHEE

WESTERN CAROLINA UNIVERSITY, Dept of Art, Belk Bldg, 28723. Tel 704-227-7210. *Actg Head Dept* Joan F Byrd; *Assoc Prof* Lee P Budahl, PhD; *Assoc Prof* Perry Kelly, EdD; *Assoc Prof* James E Smith, MFA; *Assoc Prof* William R Lidh, MFA; *Asst Prof* William C Buchanan, MFA; *Asst Prof* Lucy Puls, MFA; *Asst Prof* F Duane Oliver, MA; *Asst Prof* Wade Hobgood, MFA; *Artist-In-Res* David Nichols, MFA
Estab 1889, dept estab 1968; pub; D & E; SC 51, LC 12; enrl non-maj 1200 per sem, maj 150
Ent Req: HS dipl, SAT & C average in HS
Degrees: BFA, BA & BSE 4 yrs, art honors studio
Tuition: Res—undergrad and grad $783 per yr, $391.50 per sem; nonres—undergrad and grad $2571 per yr, $1285.50 per sem; campus res—room & board $1600 per yr
Courses: Art Education, Art History, Ceramics, Commercial Art, Drawing, Graphic Design, Illustration, Jewelry, Lettering, Interior Design, Painting, Photography, Printmaking, Sculpture, Teacher Training, Fibers, Glassblowing, Metalsmithing
Summer School: Dir, Dr Jerry Rice. Tuition $14 per sem hr for summer beginning June 19. Courses—Glassblowing, Introductory Studio Courses, Workshops in Primitive Pottery, Wheel Throwing & Techniques & Raku

DALLAS

GASTON COLLEGE, Art Dept,* New Dallas Highway, 28034. Tel 704-922-3136. *Dept Chmn* D Keithlambert
Estab 1965; pub; D & E; SC 22, LC 3; enrl D 140, E 50, maj 50
Ent Req: HS dipl
Degrees: AA and AFA 2 yrs
Tuition: Res—$3.25 per qtr cr hr; nonres—$16.50 per qtr cr hr
Adult Hobby Classes: Courses—Ceramics, Jewelry, Macrame, Weaving
Summer School: Dir, Franklin U Creech. Enrl 20; term of 11 wks beginning June. Courses—Design, Drawing, Painting, Pottery, Sculpture

DAVIDSON

DAVIDSON COLLEGE, Art Dept, Main St, 28036. Tel 704-892-2000. *Chmn* Herb Jackson, MFA; *Assoc Prof* Larry L Ligo, PhD; *Asst Prof* Linda Pellecchia, PhD; *Asst Prof* Russell Warren, MFA
Estab 1837, dept estab 1950; pvt & den; D; scholarships; SC 12, LC 9; enrl non-maj 300, maj 18
Ent Req: Col Boards, HS transcripts
Degrees: BA & BS 4 yrs
Tuition: $8000 per yr (comprehensive fee); campus res—room & board fee included in tuition
Courses: Aesthetics, Art History, Collages, Conceptual Art, Drawing, Graphic Design, History of Art & Archaeology, Painting, Printmaking, Theatre Arts

DOBSON

SURRY COMMUNITY COLLEGE, Art Dept,* PO Box 304, 27017. Tel 919-386-8121. *Instr* Abbe Rose Cox, MA; *Instr* Archie Bennett
Tuition: Res—$3.25 per qtr cr hr; nonres—$16.50 per qtr cr hr
Courses: Art Appreciation, Art Education, Art History, Ceramics, Design, Handicrafts, Painting, Printmaking, Sculpture

DURHAM

DUKE UNIVERSITY, Dept of Art, 112 East Duke Bldg, 27708. *Chmn Dept* John R Spencer, PhD; *Assoc Prof* W K Stars, MA; *Assoc Prof* Rona Goffen, PhD; *Asst Prof* Ann Epstein, PhD; *Asst Prof* Walter Melion, PhD; *Asst Prof* Vernon Pratt, MFA; *Asst Prof* Michael Shapiro, PhD; *Asst Prof* Caroline Bruzelius, PhD; *Asst Prof* Elizabeth Higdon, PhD; *Instr* Frank Smullin, MFA
Pvt; D; SC 7, LC 30, GC 10; enrl D 496, non-maj 467, maj 29
Ent Req: HS dipl & ent exam
Degrees: MA 4 yrs
Tuition: Campus residency available
Courses: Art Education, †Art History, Ceramics, Conceptual Art, Design, Drawing, Painting, Photography, Printmaking, Sculpture

NORTH CAROLINA CENTRAL UNIVERSITY, Art Dept, Fayetteville St, 27707. Tel 919-683-6391, 683-6062. *Chmn* Lana T Henderson, PhD; *Prof* Melvin Carver, MPD; *Prof* Mohinder Gill, EdD; *Prof* Michael Helton, MFA; *Prof* Robert Kennedy, MFA; *Prof* Isabell Levitt, MFA; *Prof* Norman Pendergraft, MA; *Prof* Mercedes Thompson, MA; *Prof* Michelle Patterson
Estab 1910, dept estab 1944; pub; D & E; SC 30, LC 11; enrl D 120, E 30, non-maj 1678, maj 120
Ent Req: HS dipl, SAT
Degrees: In Art Educ, Visual Communications & Studio Art 4 yrs
Tuition: Res—undergrad $421.50 yr; nonres—undergrad $1800 yr; campus res $2041.50-$2854.50 per yr
Courses: †Advertising Design, †Art Education, Art History, Calligraphy, Ceramics, Commercial Art, Drawing, Graphic Arts, Handicrafts, Illustration, Jewelry, Lettering, Painting, Printmaking, Sculpture, Teacher Training, Engineering Graphics, Stained Glass, Studio Arts
Children's Classes: Saturday school
Summer School: Dir, Dr W Maynor. Tuition $225 for term of 9 wks. Courses—Art Appreciation, Design, Drawing, Painting

ELIZABETH CITY

ELIZABETH CITY STATE UNIVERSITY, Dept of Art,* Parkview Dr, 27909. Tel 919-335-0551. *Art Dept Chmn* Dr Josiah Baird
Estab 1891, dept 1961; pub; D & E; SC 27, LC 18, advance courses in Studio and History of Art; enrl D 1650, E 455, non-maj 1500, maj 55
Ent Req: HS dipl, portfolio
Degrees: BS 4 yrs
Tuition: Res—$318 per yr; nonres—$1900 per yr
Courses: Sculpture, Teacher Training
Summer School: Dir, Edyth B Cole. Enrl 950. Courses—same as regular session

FAYETTEVILLE

FAYETTEVILLE STATE UNIVERSITY, Division of Humanitites and Fine Arts,* 1200 Murchison Rd, 28301. Tel 919-486-1111. *Head Division Humanities & Fine Arts* John T Wolfe
Estab 1877; pub; D & E; enrl D 60, E 20
Ent Req: HS dipl, ent exam
Tuition: Res—$616; nonres—$2198
Courses: Advertising Design, Aesthetics, Art Education, Ceramics, Drawing, Graphic Arts, Handicrafts, History of Art & Archaeology, Lettering, Painting, Photography, Sculpture, Weaving, Leather Craft
Summer School: Dir, Dr Beeman C Patterson. Courses—Art in Childhood Education, Arts & Crafts, Drawing, Photography, Survey of Art

METHODIST COLLEGE, Art Dept,* Raleigh Rd, 28301. Tel 919-488-7110, Ext 257. *Asst Prof* Silvana Foti, MFA. Instrs: FT 2, PT 1
Estab 1960; den; D & E; scholarships; SC 6, LC 4; enrl D 650, maj 22
Ent Req: HS dipl, SAT
Degrees: BA & BS 4 yrs
Tuition: $3550 annual tuition
Courses: Art Education, Art History, Drawing, Graphic Arts, Handicrafts, Painting, Photography, Sculpture, Weaving
Summer School: 3 terms, 3 wk early session, 5 wk main session, 6 wk directed study. Courses—Art Appreciation, Painting, Sculpture, others as needed

GOLDSBORO

GOLDSBORO ART CENTER, Community Arts Council, 901-A E Ash St, 27530. Tel 919-736-3335, 736-3300. *Instructor* Gloria Hasselbach, BA; *Instructor* Jim Morgan, BFA; *Instructor* Sara Paddison, BFA. Instrs: PT 14
Estab 1971; pub; D & E; scholarships; SC 25; enrl D 150, E 60, others 210
Tuition: $8 for adults, $18 for children per quarter
Courses: Art History, Calligraphy, Drawing, Handicrafts, Painting, Advanced Studio, Pottery, Spinning, Watercolor
Adult Hobby Classes: Enrl 180 per quarter; tui $8 per quarter. Courses—Calligraphy, Drawing, Interior Design, Painting, Pottery, Printmaking, Watercolor, Woodcarving
Children's Classes: Enrl 30 per quarter; tui $18 per quarter. Courses—Discovering Art, Drawing, Painting, Pottery

WAYNE COMMUNITY COLLEGE, Liberal Arts Dept, Caller Box 8002, 27530. Tel 919-735-5151
Degrees: AA
Tuition: Res—$57 per qtr; nonres—$261 per qtr
Courses: Art Appreciation, Art History, Design, Drawing
Adult Hobby Classes: Courses offered
Children's Classes: Courses offered in conjunction with Arts Council

GREENSBORO

GREENSBORO COLLEGE, Dept of Art, Division of Fine Arts, 815 W Market St, 27401. Tel 919-272-7102. *Chmn Dept* Robert Kowski, MFA; *Instr* Gretchen Williams, MFA
Estab 1838; pvt den; D; scholarships; SC 15, LC 4; enrl D 50, non-maj 30, maj 15
Ent Req: HS dipl
Degrees: BA 4 yrs
Tuition: Res and nonres—undergrad $3200 per yr; campus res—room & board $1960 per yr
Courses: Art History, Ceramics, Drawing, †Painting, †Sculpture
Summer School: Greensboro Regional Consortium Dir, Dr William Lanier. Tuition $95 per hr for term of 5 wks beginning May 12. Courses—Art Appreciation, Art History

NORTH CAROLINA AGRICULTURAL AND TECHNICAL STATE UNIVERSITY, Art Dept, 312 N Dudley St, 27411. Tel 919-379-7993. *Chmn* LeRoy F Holmes. Instrs: FT 4, PT 1
Estab 1930; pub; SC 29, LC 7; enrl maj 100
Courses: †Art Education, Art History, Ceramics, Commercial Art, Drawing, Graphic Arts, Handicrafts, †Painting, †Art Design, 3-D Design, 2-D Design
Summer School: Dir, Dr Ronald Smith. Courses—Crafts, Public School Art

UNIVERSITY OF NORTH CAROLINA AT GREENSBORO, Art Dept, 1000 Spring Garden St, 27412. Tel 919-379-5248. *Head* Dr Joan Gregory, EdD. Instrs: FT 20, PT 2
Dept estab 1935; pub; SC 22, LC 6, GC 8; enrl D 1000, non-maj 750, maj 200, grad 63
Ent Req: HS grad, ent exam
Degrees: BA, BFA, MEd & MFA 4 yrs
Courses: Art History, Ceramics, Drawing, Graphic Arts, Lettering, Painting, Photography, Printmaking, Sculpture, Teacher Training, Fibers
Summer School: Dir, Dr John Young. Enrl 225; beginning May - June and July - Aug. Courses—Art History, Drawing, Etching, Fibers, Jewelry, Moldmaking-Metal Casting, Painting, Photography, Picture Composition, Sculpture, Watercolor

GREENVILLE

EAST CAROLINA UNIVERSITY, School of Art, E Fifth St, 27834. Tel 919-757-6665. *Dean* Dr Edward M Levine. Instrs: FT 37, PT 3
Estab 1907; pub; SC 131, LC 29, GC 112; enrl maj 736
Ent Req: HS dipl, 15 units, Col Board Exam
Degrees: BA, BS, BFA, MA & MFA, MAEd
Tuition: Campus residence available
Courses: †Art Education, †Art History, †Ceramics, †Interior Design, †Painting, †Printmaking, †Sculpture, †Communication Arts, †Design
Summer School: Dir, Dr Susan McDaniel; Art Dir, Dr Edward M Levine. Enrl 13,800 for 10 wks beginning June

HICKORY

LENOIR RHYNE COLLEGE, Dept of Art, 28603. Tel 704-328-1741. *Head Dept* Dr Marion Love, PhD; *Asst Prof* Douglas Burton, MA; *Instr* Robert Winter, PhD
Estab 1892, dept estab 1976; den; D & E; scholarships; SC 5; enrl D 1200, E 350
Ent Req: HS dipl
Degrees: AB and BS 4 yrs
Tuition: Res—undergrad $3895 per yr; campus res—room & board $1650 per yr
Courses: Aesthetics, Art Appreciation, Art Education, Art History, Ceramics, Drawing, Painting, Photography, Printmaking, Sculpture
Adult Hobby Classes: Courses on Tues & Thurs evenings
Children's Classes: Summer courses for gifted & talented
Summer School: Dir, Dr James Lichtenstein. Enrl 900; tuition 70 per sem hr for 2-5 wk terms beginning June. Courses—Art Appreciation, Art Education, Ceramics, Painting

HIGH POINT

HIGH POINT COLLEGE, Fine Arts Dept, Montlieu Ave, 27262. Tel 919-885-5101. *Chmn* Paul J Lundrigan
Estab 1924, dept estab 1956; pvt den; D & E; scholarships; SC 16, LC 6; enrl non-maj 950, maj 10
Ent Req: HS dipl, SAT
Degrees: AB and BS 4 yrs
Tuition: Res—undergrad $3300 per yr, $1650 per sem; nonres—undergrad $3300 per yr, $1650 per sem; campus residence available
Courses: Advertising Design, Aesthetics, †Art Education, Art History, Ceramics, Costume Design & Construction, Drawing, Film, History of Art & Archaeology, Painting, Printmaking, Sculpture, Stage Design, Teacher Training, †Theatre Arts
Summer School: Dean, E Roy Epperson. Courses—general college courses

JAMESTOWN

GUILFORD TECHNICAL COMMUNITY COLLEGE, Commercial Art Dept, PO Box 309, 27260. Tel 919-454-1126, Ext 224. *Head* Norman D Faircloth, MEd Art; *Instructor* Ralph E Calhoun, MEd Art; *Instructor* Frederick N Jones, BFA; *Instructor* Jerry E Painter, BA; *Instructor* F Eugene Stafford, BFA; *Instructor* Matilda Curtis, MA
Estab 1964; pub; D & E; scholarships; SC 20, LC 4; enrl D 130, E 60
Ent Req: HS dipl, English & math placement
Degrees: AAS 2 yrs
Tuition: Res—undergrad $4.25 hr up to $57.50 per quarter; nonres—undergrad $21.25 hr up to $255 per quarter; no campus res available
Courses: Advertising Design, Art History, Commercial Art, Drafting, Drawing, Graphic Arts, Illustration, Lettering, Photography
Adult Hobby Classes: Tuition $.75 per contact hr. Courses—Variety of subjects
Summer School: Tuition $.75 per contact hr per 9 wk term. Courses—Various

KINSTON

LENOIR COMMUNITY COLLEGE, Art Dept, PO Box 188, 28501. Tel 919-527-6223. *Dept Head* Gerald A Elliott
Degrees: AFA
Tuition: Res—$51
Courses: Art Appreciation, Art History, Calligraphy, Ceramics, Design, Drawing, Handicrafts, Illustration, Painting, Photography, Printmaking
Summer School: Dir, Gerald A Elliott. Enrl 32; tuition $51 for 12 cr hrs. Courses—Lecture & Studio Art

LAURINBURG

SAINT ANDREWS PRESBYTERIAN COLLEGE, Art Program,* 28352. Tel 919-276-3652, Ext 235. *Chmn Dept Humanities & Fine Arts* Carl D Bennett; *Chmn Art Dept & Prof* B A Woodson; *Asst Prof* J E Linehan. Instrs: FT 2
Estab 1960; den; D; scholarships; SC 14, LC 2; enrl D 852, maj 15-20
Ent Req: HS dipl, SAT, 2.6 grade point average, 12 academic units
Degrees: BA, MS & BM 4 yrs or 32 courses
Tuition: $4650 per yr
Courses: Aesthetics, Art Education, Art History, Drawing, Painting, Sculpture
Summer School: Studio courses offered

LEXINGTON

DAVIDSON COUNTY COMMUNITY COLLEGE, Language-Fine Arts Dept, Old Greensboro Rd, PO Box 1287, 27292. Tel 704-249-8186, Ext 247. *Chmn* Katherine Montgomery, MFA; *Instructor* Camille Lawrence, MA. Instrs: FT 2, PT 3
Estab 1963, dept estab 1966; pub; D & E; scholarships; SC 14, LC 4; enrl D 100, E 30, non-maj 195, maj 35
Ent Req: HS dipl
Degrees: AFA & AA 2 yrs
Tuition: Res—undergrad $51 per quarter; no campus res available
Courses: Art Education, Art History, Ceramics, Drafting, Handicrafts, Painting, Printmaking, Sculpture, Design, Independent Studio
Adult Hobby Classes: Courses—Variety taught through continuing education

MARS HILL

MARS HILL COLLEGE, Art Dept, 28754. Tel 704-689-1200. *Chmn* Joe Chris Robertson, MFA; *Prof* Stephen Wing, MA; *Assoc Prof* Gordon Mahy, MFA
Estab 1856, dept estab 1932; pvt and den; D & E; scholarships; SC 9, LC 6; enrl D 130, non-maj 70, maj 36
Ent Req: HS dipl, ent exam
Degrees: BA 4 yrs
Tuition: Undergrad $3300 yr, $1650 per sem incl room & board
Courses: †Advertising Design, Aesthetics, †Art Education, †Art History, Ceramics, †Graphic Arts, †Painting, Photography, †Printmaking, Sculpture, †Teacher Training, †Theatre Arts
Summer School: Dir of Admissions, Dr John Hough. Enrl 400; tuition $450 for term of 6 wks beginning May 31. Courses—Aesthetics, Art Education, Photography, Pottery

MISENHEIMER

PFEIFFER COLLEGE, Art Program, 28109. Tel 704-463-7343. *Dir* James Haymaker. Instrs: FT 1
Estab 1965; den; D; scholarships; SC 4, LC 4; enrl D 100
Ent Req: HS dipl
Courses: Art Education, Art History, Ceramics, Drawing, Painting, Sculpture

MOUNT OLIVE

MOUNT OLIVE COLLEGE, Dept of Art, Breazeale Ave, 28365. Tel 919-658-2502
Estab 1951; den; D & E; scholarships; SC 5, LC 3
Degrees: AA and AS
Tuition: Res—undergrad $4600 per yr; campus residence available
Courses: Art History, Ceramics, Drawing, Painting, Art Appreciation, Color and Color Design, 3-D Design

MURFREESBORO

CHOWAN COLLEGE, Division of Art, Jones Dr, 27855. Tel 919-398-4101, Ext 267. *Head Div* David W Parker, MFA; *Prof* Douglas E Eubank, MHE; *Prof* Stanley A Mitchell, MA
Estab 1848, dept estab 1970; den; D; scholarships; SC 10, LC 2; enrl D 90, maj 60
Ent Req: HS dipl, SAT recommended
Degrees: AA 2 yrs
Tuition: Res—undergrad $4890 per year, room & board $2080 per year; commuter—$2180 per year, $1090 per sem
Courses: Advertising Design, †Art Education, Art History, Ceramics, †Commercial Art, Drafting, Drawing, Graphic Arts, Illustration, Lettering, Painting, Printmaking, Color & Design, †Studio Art
Summer School: Dean, Dr Franklin B Lowe. Enrl approx 20; tuition $60 per sem hr for term of 5 wks beginning June 4. Courses—Ceramics, Drawing, Painting

PEMBROKE

PEMBROKE STATE UNIVERSITY, Art Dept, Box 64, 28372. Tel 919-521-4214, Ext 216. *Chmn Dept* Paul VanZandt. Instrs: FT 3, PT 3
Estab 1887; pub; SC 30, LC 12; enrl maj 50
Ent Req: CEEB scores, HS record, scholastic standing in HS grad class, recommendation of HS guidance counselor & principal
Degrees: BA & BS 4 yrs
Courses: †Art Education, Art History, †Ceramics, Commercial Art, Drawing, †Graphic Arts, Handicrafts, Jewelry, †Painting, Photography, †Sculpture, Design
Summer School: Variety of courses

PENLAND

PENLAND SCHOOL OF CRAFTS, Penland Rd, 28765. Tel 704-765-2359
Estab 1929; pvt; D (summer only); scholarships; SC 10-20; enrl D approx 100
Ent Req: Age 18, special fall and spring sessions require portfolio and resume
Degrees: None granted but credit may be obtained through agreement with East Tennessee State Univ
Tuition: $70 per wk for term of 2-3 wks; campus res—room & board $80 per wk
Courses: Ceramics, Photography, Printmaking, Sculpture, Blacksmithing, Woodworking, Metalsmithing, Glass, Fibers, Enameling
Summer School: Dir, William J Brown. 2 & 3 week courses in June & Sept

RALEIGH

MEREDITH COLLEGE, Art Dept,* Hillsborough St, 27611. Tel 919-833-6461. *Chmn* J Craig Greene
Estab 1898; den; W; D & E; scholarships; SC 15, LC 5; enrl D 250, E 40, maj 50, others 10
Ent Req: HS dipl
Degrees: AB 4 yrs
Tuition: $1525 per sem
Adult Hobby Classes: Courses—Art History, Painting, Sculpture
Summer School: Dir, John Hiott. Courses—vary

NORTH CAROLINA STATE UNIVERSITY AT RALEIGH, School of Design, 27650. Tel 919-737-2201. *Dean* Claude E McKinney; *Dir Landscape Architecture* Arthur L Sullivan; *Actg Dir Architecture* Robert P Burns; *Dir Product Design Prog* Vincent M Foote; *Dir Design Fundamentals* Charles Joyner. Instrs: FT 38, PT 5
Estab 1948; pub; enrl Architecture 303, Landscape Architecture 119, Product Design 174
Ent Req: Col board, ent exam
Degrees: BEnvDesign (in Architecture, Landscape Architecture, Product Design & Visual Design Option), MArch, MLandscape Arch, MUrb Design, MProduct Design 4-6 yrs
Tuition: Res—$726; non-res—$3088

PEACE COLLEGE, Art Dept,* 15 E Peace St, 27604. Tel 919-832-2881. *Head Dept* C J Parker, MFA; *Chmn Division Fine Arts, Language, Literature* Dr E P deLuca; *Instr* Rebecca Bailey, PhD
Estab 1857; pvt; D; SC 8, LC 2; enrl D 500
Ent Req: HS dipl, SAT
Degrees: AA and AFA 2 yrs
Tuition: Res—$1950 per yr; nonres—$4850 per yr
Courses: Art Education, Art History, Ceramics, Drawing, Fashion Arts, History of Art & Archaeology, Painting, Sculpture, Theatre Arts, Color & Design

SAINT MARY'S COLLEGE, Art Dept, 900 Hillsborough St, 27611. Tel 919-828-2521. *Chmn Dept* Margaret Click Williams, EdD; *Asst Prof* Betty Adams, MAT; *Instructor* Ellen Anderson, MPD
Estab 1842; pvt den; D; scholarships; SC 11, LC 2; enrl D 150
Ent Req: HS dipl, SAT or PSAT
Degrees: AA
Tuition: Res—undergrad $3830 per yr; campus res available
Courses: Art History, Ceramics, Drawing, Graphic Arts, Painting, Printmaking, Stage Design, Theatre Arts
Adult Hobby Classes: Tuition $25-$50 for 6 week courses. Courses - Drawing, Painting
Summer School: Dean of the College, Robert J Miller. Enrl varies; tui $250 for term of 3-5 wks beginning May or June

ROCKY MOUNT

NORTH CAROLINA WESLEYAN, Dept of Art, College Station, 27801. Tel 919-442-7121. *Chair Dept* Daisy Thorp; *Faculty* Elise Smith; *Faculty* Bunny Ryals
Courses: Advertising Design, Architecture, Art Appreciation, Art Education, Art History, Design, Drawing, Photography
Adult Hobby Classes: Enrl 125; tuition $55 per sem hr. Courses—Art Appreciation

STATESVILLE

MITCHELL COMMUNITY COLLEGE, Visual Art Dept, E Broad St, 28677. Tel 704-873-2201, Ext 202. *Acting Chmn* Donald Everett Moore, MA. Instrs: FT 2, PT 1
Estab 1852, dept estab 1974; pub; D & E; scholarships; SC 12-15, LC 5; enrl D 85, E 25, non-maj 100, maj 30-35
Ent Req: HS dipl, HS transcripts, Placement Test
Degrees: AA & AFA 2 yrs
Tuition: Nonres—undergrad $150 yr, $50 per sem, $8 per course part-time; no campus res available
Courses: Art History, †Ceramics, Drawing, Intermedia, Mixed Media, †Painting, Photography, Printmaking, †Sculpture
Adult Hobby Classes: Tui $8 per 10 wks. Courses—Continuing education courses in art & crafts available
Summer School: Acting Chmn, Donald Everett Moore. Enrl 50; tui $50 for term of 10 wks beginning June 6. Courses—Varies, but same as courses listed above

SYLVA

SOUTHWESTERN TECHNICAL COLLEGE, Commercial Art and Advertising Design Dept, Webster Rd, PO Box 67, 28779. Tel 704-586-4091, Ext 233. *Head Dept* Bob Clark, MS; *Instructor* Sally Moore, BS. Instrs: FT 2, PT 3
Estab 1964, dept estab 1967; pub; D; scholarships; SC 19, LC 14; enrl D 40, maj 40
Ent Req: HS dipl
Degrees: AAS
Tuition: Res—undergrad $51 quarterly; nonres—undergrad $255 quarterly; no campus res
Courses: †Advertising Design, Art History, Calligraphy, †Commercial Art, Display, Drafting, Drawing, Fashion Arts, Graphic Arts, Graphic Design, Illustration, Lettering, Painting, Photography
Adult Hobby Classes: Enrl 30; tuition $4.25 per quarter hr. Courses—Painting

WHITEVILLE

SOUTHEASTERN COMMUNITY COLLEGE, Dept of Fine and Performing Arts, PO Box 151, 28472. Tel 919-642-7141, Ext 221. *Chmn* Richard F Burkhardt, MM; *Instr* Christa Balogh, MFA
Estab 1965; pub; D & E; scholarships offered; SC 18, LC 7
Ent Req: HS dipl or 18 yrs old
Degrees: AFA 2 yrs
Tuition: Res—undergrad $51 per qtr, part time $4.25 per hr; nonres—undergrad $198 per qtr, part time $21.25 per hr
Courses: Art History, Ceramics, Drawing, Painting, Printmaking, Sculpture, Pottery
Adult Hobby Classes: Tuition res—$10 per course
Summer School: Dir, R F Burkhardt

WILKESBORO

WILKES COMMUNITY COLLEGE, Arts and Science Division, Drawer 120, 28697. Tel 919-667-7136, Ext 51 or 52. *Dir* Bud Mayes; *Instr* William Moffett; *Instr* William Nichols; *Instr* Jack Young; *Instr* David Briggs
Estab 1965, dept estab 1967; pub; D & E; scholarships; SC 2, LC 2; enrl D 1600, E 800
Ent Req: HS dipl
Degrees: AA, AFA
Tuition: $39 per quarter; no campus res
Courses: Art History, Costume Design & Construction, Drafting, Drawing, Painting, Sculpture, †Theatre Arts, Art Travel Courses
Summer School: Dir, Bud Mayes

WILMINGTON

UNIVERSITY OF NORTH CAROLINA AT WILMINGTON, Dept of Creative Arts - Division of Art, PO Box 3725, 28406. Tel 919-791-4330. *Chmn* Dennis J Sporre; *Assoc Prof* Ann Louise Conner, MFA; *Asst Prof* John Myers, PhD; *Asst Prof* Stephen Lequire, MFA; *Instructor* Constance Hobbs, MFA; *Lectr* Gayla Sanders, MA
Estab 1789, dept estab 1952; pub; D & E; scholarships
Ent Req: HS dipl, ent exam
Degrees: BCA 4 yrs
Tuition: Res $235; nonres $1113; campus res—room & board $675-$700
Courses: Art Appreciation, Art History, Ceramics, Drawing, History of Art & Archaeology, Painting, Printmaking, Sculpture
Adult Hobby Classes: Courses—Drawing, Painting
Children's Classes: Courses—Painting
Summer School: Two sessions. Courses—varied

WILSON

ATLANTIC CHRISTIAN COLLEGE, Art Dept, 27893. Tel 919-237-3161. *Chmn* Edward Brown, MFA; *Assoc Prof* Norbert Irving, MFA; *Assoc Prof* Thomas Marshall, MA; *Assoc Prof* Chris Wilson, MFA
Estab 1903, dept estab 1950; pvt; D & E; SC 13, LC 8; enrl D 68, E 5, non-maj 68, others 8 (PT)
Ent Req: HS dipl, ent exam
Degrees: BS, BA & BFA 4 yrs
Tuition: Undergrad $3150 yr, $1575 per sem; campus res—room & board $1600 yr
Courses: Advertising Design, Art Education, Art History, Ceramics, Commercial Art, Display, Drawing, Graphic Arts, Graphic Design, Handicrafts, History of Art & Archaeology, Illustration, Museum Staff Training, Painting, Photography, Printmaking, Sculpture, Teacher Training, Textile Design, Theatre Arts
Adult Hobby Classes: Tuition $75 (audit) per term. Courses—any adult can audit any studio class
Summer School: Dir, Edward Brown. Courses—Art Education, Art Survey, Drawing, Lab

WINGATE

WINGATE COLLEGE, Division of Fine Arts, 28174. Tel 704-233-4061; WATS 800-222-4281 (in-state), 800-438-4203 (outside state). *Chmn Div* Ronald Bostic
Estab 1896, dept estab 1958; den; D & E; scholarships; enrl D & E 1500
Ent Req: HS grad
Degrees: BA(Art), BS(Art Education) 4 yrs
Tuition: $2580 average per yr, campus residency available
Courses: Art History, Ceramics, Drawing, Film, Painting, Photography, Printmaking, Sculpture, Art Appreciation, Art Methods, Composition, Gallery Tours, Metalsmithing, Sketching, 3-D Design
Summer School: Pres, Dr Paul R Corts. Term of 4 wks beginning first wk in June. Courses—all regular class work available if demand warrants

WINSTON-SALEM

SALEM COLLEGE, Art Dept, 27108. Tel 919-721-2600. *Prof* William Mangum; *Prof* Edwin Shewmake; *Asst Prof* Penny Griffin; *Instructor* Lea Lackey; *Instructor* Rick Flanery
Den, W; D; scholarships; enrl D 642, maj 44
Ent Req: HS Dipl
Degrees: BA 4 yrs
Tuition: Res—$7500 per yr, includes room and board
Courses: Art Education, Art History, Ceramics, Drawing, Graphic Arts, Painting, Sculpture

SAWTOOTH CENTER FOR VISUAL DESIGN (Formerly Arts and Crafts Association, Inc), 226 North Marshall St, 27101. Tel 919-723-7395. *Exec Dir* Ray Pierotti. Instrs: PT 75
Estab 1953
Tuition: $25-$65 per 10 wk course
Courses: Ceramics, Graphic Arts, Painting, Photography, Printmaking, Video, All visual arts media including advertising, interior architectural design, fibers, metals
Children's Classes: Three-17 yrs old; tuition $19-$35 per 4-6 wks. Courses—same as adult
Summer School: Courses offered

WAKE FOREST UNIVERSITY, Dept of Art, Box 7232, 27109. Tel 919-761-5310. *Gallery Dir* Victor Faccinto; *Chairwoman* Margaret Supplee Smith; *Prof* Robert Knott, PhD; *Asst Prof* Gary A Cook, MFA; *Asst Prof* Andrew Polk III, MFA; *Asst Prof* Paul H D Kaplan; *Instructor* Harry B Titus Jr; *Instructor* Deborah Fanelli
Estab 1834, dept estab 1968; pvt; D; scholarships; SC 14, LC 28; enrl D 250, non-maj 200, maj 50
Ent Req: HS dipl, SAT
Degrees: BA 4 yrs
Tuition: Res—undergrad $3970 yr, $1985 per sem, $85 per cr, grad $2750 yr, $90 per cr; nonres—undergrad $2750 yr, $85 per cr; campus res—room & board $1220 (no dormitory facilities are available on campus for grad students)
Courses: Art History, Drawing, Graphic Arts, Graphic Design, History of Art & Archaeology, Painting, Printmaking, Sculpture
Summer School: Dir Percival Perry. Enrl 25; tuition $125 per cr

WINSTON-SALEM STATE UNIVERSITY, Art Dept, 27102. Tel 919-761-2090. *Chmn* Roland S Watts, MFA
Estab, 1892, dept estab 1970; pub; D & E; SC 10, LC 7; enrl D 65, nonmaj 275, maj 65
Ent Req: HS Dipl
Degrees: BA 4 yr
Tuition: Campus residence available
Courses: Art Education, Art History, Drawing, Graphic Arts, Painting, Sculpture
Summer School: Courses offered

NORTH DAKOTA

BISMARCK

BISMARCK JUNIOR COLLEGE, Art Dept, Schafer Ave, 58501. Tel 701-223-4500. *Instructor* Ardyce L Miller; *Instructor* Richard Sammons
Degrees: AA
Courses: Art Appreciation, Art Education, Art History, Calligraphy, Ceramics, Design, Handicrafts, Photography

DICKINSON

DICKINSON STATE COLLEGE, Dept of Art, Div of Fine Arts and Humanities, 58601. Tel 701-227-2312. *Chmn* Frank C Pearson, PhD; *Prof* Dennis Edward Navrat, MFA; *Instructor* David Huether
Estab 1918, dept estab 1959; pub; D & E; scholarship; SC 36, LC 8; enrl D approx 150 per quarter, non-maj 130, maj 20
Ent Req: HS dipl, out-of-state, ACT, minimum score 18 or upper-half of class
Degrees: BA, BS and BCS 4 yr
Tuition: Res—undergrad $570 yr, $190 per quarter, $20.42 per quarter hr, $20 extension per quarter hr; nonres—undergrad $1131 yr, $377 per quarter, $32 per quarter hr, $32 extension per quarter hr; campus res—room & board $1494 yr
Courses: Advertising Design, †Art Education, Art History, †Ceramics, Costume Design & Construction, Display, Drawing, Graphic Design, Handicrafts, Intermedia, †Jewelry, Lettering, †Painting, Photography, †Printmaking, †Sculpture, Stage Design, Teacher Training, †Theatre Arts, Color, Leather, Serigraphy
Adult Hobby Classes: Above classes available for credit or audit
Summer School: VPres for Academic Affairs, Dr David Barry. Enrl approx 200; tuition same as above for term of 2, 4 wks beginning June 4. Courses—Basic Art, Photography, Watercolor, other division offerings

GRAND FORKS

UNIVERSITY OF NORTH DAKOTA, Visual Arts Dept, College of Fine Art, 58202. Tel 701-777-2257. *Chmn* Ronald Schaefer. Instrs: D FT 11
Estab 1883; pub; SC 30, LC 4, GC 14; enrl maj 90, others 1000
Degrees: BFA, BA, BSEd, MFA
Tuition: Campus residency available
Courses: Art History, †Ceramics, Design, †Drawing, †Jewelry, †Painting, †Printmaking, †Sculpture, Teacher Training, †Fibers
Summer School: Chmn, Ronald Schaefer

JAMESTOWN

JAMESTOWN COLLEGE, Art Dept,* 58401. Tel 701-253-2517. *Chmn* Robert Carter. Instrs: FT 1, PT 2
Pvt; D; scholarship; SC 13, LC 4; enrl 146, maj 14
Ent Req: HS dipl
Degrees: BA and BS 4 yr, directed study and individual study in advanced studio areas, private studios
Tuition: $4300 per yr; campus res available
Courses: Art Education, Art History, Ceramics, Drawing, Painting, Photography, Printmaking, 2-D Design
Summer School: Dir, Dr Andersen. Term of 6 wks beginning June

MINOT

MINOT STATE COLLEGE, Dept of Art, Division of Humanities, 58701. Tel 701-857-3108. *Art Coordr* C R Schwieger. Instrs: FT 3, PT 1
Estab 1913; pub; SC 30; enrl per quarter 250, maj 50
Degrees: BA and BS 4 yr
Tuition: Res—$279; nonres—$494; campus residency available
Courses: Advertising Design, Art History, Ceramics, Drawing, Handicrafts, Jewelry, Painting, Photography, Printmaking, Sculpture, Design, Silk Screen, Weaving
Summer School: Courses—same as above

VALLEY CITY

VALLEY CITY STATE COLLEGE, Art Dept, College St, 58072. Tel 701-845-7561. *Fine Arts Chairperson* Jeff Mongrain. Instrs: FT 2
Estab 1890, dept estab 1921; pub; D & E; scholarship; SC 20, LC 3; enrl D 1300, E 200, non-maj 120, maj 30
Ent Req: HS dipl, ACT
Degrees: AA 2yr, BS and BA 4 yr
Courses: Art Education, Art History, Ceramics, Commercial Art, Drawing, Painting, Printmaking, Sculpture, Teacher Training
Adult Hobby Classes: Enrl 20; tuition $21 per quarter. Courses—Drawing, Watercolor, Stained Glass

WAHPETON

NORTH DAKOTA STATE SCHOOL OF SCIENCE, Dept of Art,* 800 N Sixth St, 58075. Tel 701-671-1130. *Dean* Vernon E Hektner
Estab 1903, dept estab 1970; pub; D & E
Tuition: Res—$190 per qtr; nonres—$377 per qtr
Courses: Art Education, Drawing, Graphic Design, Handicrafts, Lettering, Occupational Therapy, Painting
Adult Hobby Classes: Enrl 15; tuition $30. Courses—Calligraphy, Drawing, Painting
Summer School: Dir, Mary Sand. 2 wk term, 3 hrs per day. Courses—Teacher's Art Workshop

WILLISTON

UNIVERSITY OF NORTH DAKOTA-WILLISTON CENTER, Interior Design Dept, PO Box 1376, 58801. Tel 701-572-6736. *Instr* Jan D Gathman; *Instr* Marlaine Slaaen
Scholarships offered
Degrees: Certificate offered
Tuition: $600 per sem
Courses: Advertising Design, Architecture, Art Appreciation, Art History, Calligraphy, Fashion Arts, Textile Design
Adult Hobby Classes: Enrl 18; tuition $1000 per yr. Courses—Interior Design Program

OHIO

ADA

OHIO NORTHERN UNIVERSITY, Dept of Art, 500 S Main St, 45810. Tel 419-634-9921. *Chmn* James DeVore
Pvt; D; scholarships; SC 30, LC 8; enrl maj 30
Ent Req: HS dipl, ent exam
Degrees: BA and BFA 4 yrs
Tuition: $7926
Courses: Art Education, Art History, Ceramics, Drawing, Graphic Arts, Jewelry, Lettering, Painting, Sculpture, Teacher Training
Adult Hobby Classes: Enrl 10-15; tuition $48 for 6 wks. Courses—Ceramics, Watercolor Painting
Summer School: Dir, James DeVore. Enrl 10. Courses—Ceramics, Drawing, Watercolor Painting

AKRON

UNIVERSITY OF AKRON, Dept of Art, 44325. Tel 216-375-7010. *Dept Head* Earl L Ertman, MA
Estab 1926; pub; D & E; scholarships; SC 25, LC 7, GC 8; enrl D 943, E 129, non-maj 429, maj 538
Ent Req: HS dipl
Degrees: AA 2 yr, BA, BS and BFA 4 yr
Tuition: Res—undergrad $1560 yr, grad $64 per credit; nonres—undergrad $3352 yr, grad $111 per cr; campus residency available
Courses: †Art History, †Ceramics, Commercial Art, †Drawing, Goldsmithing, †Graphic Design, Handicrafts, Illustration, Interior Design, †Jewelry, †Painting, †Photography, †Printmaking, †Sculpture, Silversmithing, Textile Design, Weaving
Summer School: Dir, Dr Carrino. Enrl 400; tuition by credit for term of 5 wks. Courses—all of the above

ALLIANCE

MOUNT UNION COLLEGE, Dept of Art, 44601. Tel 216-821-5320. *Chmn* James Hopper, MFA; *Asst Prof* Joel Collins, MFA
Estab 1846; pvt; D; scholarships; SC 27, LC 6; enrl D 150, non-maj 125, maj 25
Ent Req: HS dipl, SAT
Degrees: BA
Tuition: Res—undergrad $5000 per yr; campus residence available
Courses: Aesthetics, Art Education, Art History, Drawing, Lettering, Painting, Printmaking, Sculpture, Teacher Training

ASHLAND

ASHLAND COLLEGE, Art Dept,* College Ave, 44805. Tel 419-289-4005. *Chmn* Albert W Goad. Instrs: FT 4
Estab 1878; den; D & E; scholarship; enrl D 1460, maj 32, minors 12
Ent Req: HS dipl
Degrees: BA, BS 4 yr
Tuition: $5586 per yr
Courses: Teacher Training, Theatre Arts, Available through affiliation with the Art Institute of Pittsburgh: Fashion Design, Interior Design, Photography/Multi-media, Visual Communication

ATHENS

OHIO UNIVERSITY, School of Art, College of Fine Arts, 45701. Tel 614-594-5667. *Dean* Henry H Lin; *Assoc Dean* David Klahn. Instrs: FT 28, PT 9
Estab 1936; pub; D & E; scholarships and fel; SC 88, LC 30, LGC 29, SGC 50; enrl maj 573, others 1718
Ent Req: Secondary school dipl, portfolio
Degrees: BFA, MA and MFA 4-5 yr
Tuition: Res—undergrad $594 per quarter, grad $660 per quarter; nonres—undergrad $1211 per quarter, grad $1277 per quarter
Courses: †Art Education, †Art History, †Ceramics, †Drawing, †Graphic Design, †Illustration, †Painting, †Photography, †Printmaking, †Sculpture, †Art Therapy, Fibers, Glass, †Studio Arts, †Visual Communication
Summer School: Two - 5 wk sessions June-July and July-August; 18 quarter hr maximum per session; SC, LC, GC

BEREA

BALDWIN-WALLACE COLLEGE, Dept of Art, 95 E Bagley Rd, 44017. Tel 216-826-2900. *Chmn Div* Ted Marakas; *Head Dept* Dean Drahos
Estab 1845; den; D & E; SC 23, LC 12; enrl 1900, maj 65
Degrees: AB 4 yrs
Tuition: $5349 per yr; campus residence available
Courses: Art Education, Art History, Ceramics, Drawing, Painting, Photography, Printmaking, Sculpture, Design & Color
Summer School: Tuition $51 per cr hr

BETHANY

BETHANY NAZARENE COLLEGE, Art Dept, 6729 NW 39th Expressway, 73008. Tel 405-789-6400. *Head Dept* Nila West Murrow
Estab 1920; den; D & E; SC 13, LC 7; enrl D 51, E 6, non-maj 38, maj 13
Ent Req: HS dipl, ACT
Tuition: $80 per hr; campus residence available
Courses: Aesthetics, Art Education, Art History, Commercial Art, Drawing, Handicrafts, Painting, Sculpture, †Teacher Training, Pottery

BOWLING GREEN

BOWLING GREEN STATE UNIVERSITY, School of Art, Fine Arts Bldg, 43403. Tel 419-372-2787. *Dir* Maurice J Sevigny, PhD; *Asst Dir* Dawn Glanz, PhD; *Asst to Dir* Adrian R Tio, MFA; *Dir Grad Studies* Thomas Hilty, MFA; *Chmn Design Studies* Thomas Davenport; *Chmn Three-Dimensional Studies* Donald Ehrlichman, MFA; *Chmn Two-Dimensional Studies* Ronald Bandy, MFA; *Chmn Art Educ* Douglas Blandy, PhD; *Chmn Art History* Willard Misfeldt, PhD; *Gallery Dir* Ralph Warren, MA
Estab 1910, dept estab 1946; pub; D & E; scholarships and fels; SC 53, LC 14, GC 33; enrl D 2460, E 150, non-maj 995, grad 33, others 40
Ent Req: ACT (undergrad), GRE (grad)
Degrees: BA, BS & BFA 4 yrs, MA 1 yr, MFA 2 yrs
Tuition: Res—undergrad $647 per sem, housing $514 per sem, grad $40 per cr hr, FT $821 per sem; nonres—undergrad $945 per qtr, grad $1823 per sem
Courses: †Art Education, †Art History, †Ceramics, †Drawing, †Graphic Arts, †Graphic Design, †Handicrafts, †Jewelry, †Mixed Media, †Painting, †Photography, †Printmaking, †Sculpture, †Teacher Training, †Weaving, †Art Therapy, †Environmental Design, †Fibers, †Glass Working, †Product Design
Children's Classes: Enrl 120; tuition $40 per 10 wk sem of Sat mornings
Summer School: Dir, Dr Maurice Sevigny. Enrl 300; tuition $647 for 8 wk & 5 wk session. Courses—Art History, Drawing, Jewelry, Photography, Printmaking, Sculpture, Special Workshops, Watercolor, Guest Artists

CANTON

CANTON ART INSTITUTE, 1001 Market Ave North, 44702. Tel 216-453-7666. *Dir* Joseph R Hertzi; *Assoc Dir* Manuel J Albacete; *Business Mgr* Bebo Adams; *Registrar* Thelma Dittmar; *Administrative Secy* Verna R Blyer
Pub; D & E; SC 28; enrl D 322, E 984, others 1306
Tuition: Pre-school $38; Children $20; Adults $30-$39
Courses: Ceramics, Drawing, Mixed Media, Painting, Photography, Sculpture, Textile Design
Adult Hobby Classes: Courses—Calligraphy, Ceramics, Drawing, Oils, Photography, Portraits, Watercolor, Weaving
Children's Classes: Courses—Pre-school art, clay, creative workshop, drawing, painting
Summer School: Courses—same as above

KENT STATE UNIVERSITY, STARK CAMPUS, School of Art, 6000 Frank Ave NW, 44720. Tel 216-499-9600. *Prof* Joseph Wagner, MA; *Asst Prof* Robert Austin, MA; *Asst Prof* Emily Bokovec, MA; *Vis Prof* Elmer Day, Art Hist
Estab 1946, dept estab 1967; pub; D & E; scholarships; SC 20, LC 6; enrl D 174, E 13, non-maj 50, maj 40
Ent Req: HS dipl, ACT
Degrees: AA
Tuition: Res—undergrad $747 per sem, $61 per hr; nonres—$1228 per sem
Courses: †Advertising Design, †Art Education, †Art History, Calligraphy, Ceramics, Conceptual Art, Drawing, Film, †Graphic Design, †Industrial Design, †Painting, Photography, †Printmaking, †Sculpture, Weaving, Stained Glass
Adult Hobby Classes: Enrl 20. Courses—Art Education for Elementary Teachers

MALONE COLLEGE, Dept of Art,* Division of Fine Arts, 515 25th St NW, 44709. Tel 216-489-0800. *Chmn Fine Arts* Richard D Mountford; *Assoc Prof* Donald R Murray; *Instr* Vivian Gladden
Estab 1956; den; D & E; scholarships; SC 20, LC 2; enrl D 75, maj 30
Ent Req: HS dipl, ent exam
Degrees: BA and BS(Educ) 4 yrs
Tuition: $124 per sem hr; campus res available
Courses: †Art Education, †Ceramics, †Drawing, Lettering, †Painting, Printmaking, †Photography, †Printmaking, †Sculpture, Teacher Training, Applied Design, Graphic Communications, History and Criticism of Art
Summer School: Enrl 400; tui $124 cr for term of 5 wks beginning June 15 and July 15

CHILLICOTHE

OHIO UNIVERSITY-CHILLICOTHE CAMPUS, Fine Arts & Humanities Division,* 571 W Fifth St, PO Box 629, 45601. Tel 614-775-4500, 775-9500. *Coordr Human* Patricia Scott; *Asst Prof* Richard Ohman, MFA
Estab 1946; D & E; scholarships
Ent Req: HS dipl, ACT or SAT
Tuition: Res—$39 per hr; nonres—$91 per hr
Courses: Art Education, Art History, Commercial Art, Drawing, History of Art & Archaeology, Painting, Photography, Printmaking, Textile Design

CINCINNATI

ART ACADEMY OF CINCINNATI, Eden Park, 45202. Tel 513-721-5205. *Dir* Roger Williams, MFA; *Chmn* Anthony Batchelor, dipl; *Chmn* Stewart Goldman, BFA; *Chmn* Greg Wolfe, MS; *Instructor* April Foster, MFA; *Instructor* Laurence W Goodridge, MA; *Instructor* Kenn Knowlton, MS; *Instructor* Calvin Kowal, MS; *Instructor* Larry May, MFA; *Instructor* Anne Miotke, MFA; *Instructor* Diane Smith-Hurd, MA; *Instructor* Mark Barensfeld, BFA; *Instructor* Julio Zumeta, MA; *Instructor* Gary Gaffney, MFA
Estab 1887; pvt; D & E; scholarships; enrl 220
Ent Req: HS grad
Degrees: Cert, BS collaboration with Univ of Cincinnati, BFA offered at the academy, 4-5 yr
Tuition: $3950 per yr, $100 per cr hr; plus other fees
Courses: Art History, Drawing, Graphic Arts, Graphic Design, Illustration, †Painting, †Photography, †Printmaking, †Sculpture, †Communication Design
Adult Hobby Classes: Courses—Ceramics, Drawing, Painting, Sculpture, Photography
Children's Classes: Drawing, Introductory Studies Experience
Summer School: Supvr, Roger Williams. Enrl 64; tuition $90 per cr hr for term of 6 wks beginning June 17

CENTRAL ACADEMY OF COMMERCIAL ART, 2326 Upland Pl, 45206. Tel 513-961-2484. *Pres* Mrs Jackson Grey Storey; *Dean of Educ* Michael C McGuire; *Instructor* Samuel B McCausland; *Instructor* Robert A Trau; *Registrar* Jean Crontz
Tuition: $2500 yr, $1250 per sem
Courses: Advertising Design, Calligraphy, Commercial Art, Drawing, Fashion Arts, Illustration, Lettering, Painting, Color Composition, Finished Art, Keyline, Layout, Letterhead, Life Class Mediums, Logotype, Magic Marker, Mediums, Package Design, Perspective, TV Storyboard, others
Adult Hobby Classes: Enrl 90; tuition $2500 per yr

ANTON ELLI (Formerly Ohio Visual Art Institute), 124 E Seventh St, 45202. Tel 513-241-4338. *Dir* Ron French; *Dir Education* Jim Slouffman; *Instructor* Terry Harrob; *Instructor* Bart Inwood; *Instructor* Jon Keeling; *Instructor* Kelly Towe; *Instructor* Bob Wilson; *Instructor* Sharon Shaffer; *Instructor* Cris Taggert; *Instructor* DiAnn Cox; *Instructor* Judith Krekler. Instrs: FT 4, PT 5
Estab 1947; pvt; D & E; enrl D 160, E 10
Ent Req: HS dipl, review of portfolio
Tuition: Undergrad $875 Commercial Art & Interior Design, $975 Photography
Courses: Commercial Art, †Interior Design, †Photography

CLEVELAND

CASE WESTERN RESERVE UNIVERSITY, Dept of Art,* Wickenden Building, Mather House, 44106. Tel 216-368-2000. *Chmn* D Harvey Buchanan, PhD; *Prof* Walter Gibson, PhD; *Prof* Anita Rogoff, PhD; *Assoc Prof* Edward J Olszewski, PhD; *Asst Prof* Ellen G Landau, PhD; *Asst Prof* Hilliard Goldfarb, PhD; *Asst Prof* Jenifer Neils, PhD
Estab 1875; pvt; D; scholarships; SC 24, LC 55, GC 73; enrl D 644, grad 75
Ent Req: HS transcript, SAT or ACT, TOEFL for foreign students
Degrees: BA, BS, MA and PhD
Tuition: $3500 per sem; campus res available
Courses: †Architecture, †Art Education, Ceramics, Drawing, †History of Art & Archaeology, Jewelry, †Museum Staff Training, Painting, Photography, Textile Design, Enameling
Adult Hobby Classes: Chmn, D Harvey Buchanan
Summer School: An occasional introductory course in Art History

CLEVELAND INSTITUTE OF ART, 11141 E Blvd, 44106. Tel 216-421-4322. *Pres* Joseph McCullough, MFA; *Prof* Jerome Aidlin; *Prof* Sandra August; *Prof* Carroll Cassill; *Prof* Francis Meyers; *Prof* Mary Ellen McDermott; *Prof* Viktor Schreckengost; *Prof* Julian Stanczak; *Prof* Robert Jergens; *Prof* Lawrence Krause; *Assoc Prof* Robert Palmer; *Assoc Prof* James Mazurkewicz; *Assoc Prof* Brent Young; *Assoc Prof* Judith Salomon; *Lectr* Raphael Poritsky; *Vis Prof* Robert Carroll
Estab 1882; pvt; D & E; scholarships; SC 90, LC 38; enrl D 557, E 175, non-maj 248, maj 309, others 25
Ent Req: HS dipl SAT, ACT and transcript, portfolio
Degrees: BFA 5 yrs, BS & MEd (educ with Case Western Reserve Univ) 4 yrs
Tuition: Undergrad $4400 per year; campus res—room and board $2870
Courses: Aesthetics, Art Education, Art History, Calligraphy, †Ceramics, †Drawing, Film, †Graphic Arts, †Illustration, †Industrial Design, †Jewelry, †Painting, †Photography, †Printmaking, †Sculpture, †Silversmithing, †Enameling, †Fiber, †Glass, †Medical Illustration, †Surface Design
Adult Hobby Classes: Enrl 175; tuition $160 per course. Courses—Calligraphy, Ceramic, Crafts, Design, Drawing, Fiber and Surface Design, Graphic Design, Painting, Printmaking, Sculpture, Silversmithing, Watercolor
Children's Classes: Enrl 183; tuition $40 per course. Courses—Art Basics, Ceramic Sculpture, Crafts, Design, Drawing, Painting, Portfolio Preparation, Printmaking, Photography
Summer School: Dean of Faculty, Robert D Weitzel, Jr. Courses—Ceramics, Design, Drawing, Jewelry and Metalsmithing, Photography, Printmaking, Sculpture, Watercolor

CLEVELAND STATE UNIVERSITY, Art Dept, 2307 Chester Ave (Mailing add: 1983 E 24th St, Cleveland, OH 44115). Tel 216-687-2090, 687-2089. *Chmn* Henry Drewal, PhD; *Prof* Thomas E Donaldson, PhD; *Assoc Prof* June E Hargrove, PhD; *Assoc Prof* Marvin H Jones, MA; *Assoc Prof* Gene Kangas, MFA; *Assoc Prof* Walter C Leedy Jr, PhD; *Assoc Prof* Richard D Schneider, MA; *Assoc Prof* Kenneth Nevadomi, MFA; *Asst Prof* Masumi Hayashi, MFA; *Asst Prof* Mary Lou Stokrocki, DEd; *Asst Prof* John Hunter, PhD
Dept estab 1972; pub; D & E; scholarships; SC 26, LC 32
Ent Req: HS dipl
Degrees: BA 4 yr
Tuition: 1-11 hrs $45 per quarter per cr hr; 12-18 hrs $545 per quarter
Courses: †Art Education, †Art History, †Ceramics, †Drawing, †Painting, †Photography, †Printmaking, †Sculpture, †Fiber Arts, †Glass, Introduction to Art and Design
Summer School: Chmn, Henry Drewal. Tuition & courses same as regular schedule

CUYAHOGA COMMUNITY COLLEGE, Dept of Art,* 2900 Community College Ave, 44115. Tel 216-241-5966. *Prof* Richard Karberg, MA; *Assoc Prof* David Haberman, MFA; *Assoc Prof* Gerald Kramer, MFA; *Asst Prof* Bette Drake, MFA
Estab 1963. College maintains four campuses; pub; D & E; scholarships; SC 15, LC 4; enrl D 150, E 80, maj 50
Ent Req: HS dipl
Degrees: AA
Tuition: County res—$14 per cr hr; out-of-county—$16 per cr hr; nonres—$28 per cr hr
Courses: Art Education, Art History, Calligraphy, Ceramics, Graphic Design, Occupational Therapy, Painting, Photography, Printmaking, Sculpture, Stage Design, Teacher Training, Theatre Arts, Video
Summer School: Courses—various

JOHN CARROLL UNIVERSITY, Dept of Fine Arts,* University Heights, 44118. Tel 216-491-4388. *Chmn* Dr Roger A Welchans, PhD
Sch estab 1886, dept estab 1965; pvt; D & E; SC 3, LC 30; enrl D 400, non-maj 350, maj-humanities 30, art hist 14

Ent Req: HS dipl, SAT
Degrees: BA Art History 4 yrs, BA Humanities 4 yrs
Tuition: $136 per cr hr; campus res available
Courses: Aesthetics, Architecture, †Art History, Drawing, Film
Summer School: Dir, Dr Roger A Welchans. Tuition $111 per credit hr for 5 wk term beginning June 15. Courses—Art History, Musicology

COLUMBUS

CAPITAL UNIVERSITY, Art Dept,* 2199 E Main St, 43209. Tel 614-236-6011. *Chmn* Richard Phipps. Instrs: FT 3
Degrees: BA, BFA
Tuition: $5870 per yr
Courses: Advertising Design, Art Education, Art History, Ceramics, Design, Drawing, Jewelry, Painting, Photography, Sculpture, Theatre Arts, Weaving, Stained Glass

COLUMBUS COLLEGE OF ART AND DESIGN,* 47 N Washington Ave, 43215. Tel 614-224-9101. *Pres* Joseph V Canzani; *Dean* Mary T Kinney. Instrs: 68
Estab 1879; pvt; approved for Veterans; D & E; scholarships
Ent Req: HS grad, art portfolio
Degrees: BFA 4 yr
Courses: Advertising Design, Fashion Arts, Graphic Arts, Illustration, Industrial Design, Interior Design, Painting, Sculpture, Fine Arts, Packaging Design, Retail Advertising
Children's Classes: Saturday sessions 9 - 11:30 AM
Summer School: Dean, Mary T Kinney

OHIO DOMINICAN COLLEGE, Art Dept,* 1216 Sunbury Rd, 43219. Tel 614-253-2741. *Asst Prof* Juris Kakis, MA
Estab 1911; den; D & E; scholarships; SC and LC 709 per sem; enrl D 139, E 105, maj 17
Ent Req: HS dipl
Degrees: BA 4 yrs, also secondary educ cert or special training cert, K-12
Tuition: Campus res available
Courses: Textile Design, Theatre Arts, Video
Summer School: Dir, Joe Stotski. Term of 7 wks beginning June

OHIO STATE UNIVERSITY
—**School of Architecture,** 190 W 17th Ave, 43210. *Dir* Jerrold Voss, AIP. Instrs: FT 41, PT 6
Estab 1899; pub; enrl Archit 480, Landscape Archit 205, City and Regional Planning 100
Degrees: BSArchit, BSLand Archit, MArchit, MLA, MCRP
Courses: Architecture, Landscape Architecture, City and Regional Planning
—**College of the Arts,** 305 Mershon Auditorium, 30 W 15th Ave, 43210. Tel 614-422-5171. *Dean Col* Andrew J Broekema, PhD
Univ estab 1870, col estab 1968; pub; D & E; scholarships; SC 106, LC 192, GC 208; enrl D 3678, E varies, non-maj 2300, maj 893, grad 150
Ent Req: HS dipl
Degrees: BA, BAEd, BFA, BSID 4 yrs, MA, MFA, PhD
Tuition: Res—undergrad $1557 per yr, $519 per quarter, grad $2010 per yr, $670 per quarter; nonres—undergrad $3984 per yr, $1328 per quarter, grad $4830 per yr, $1610 per quarter; campus res—room & board $2625 per yr
Courses: †Art Education, †Art History, †Ceramics, †Drawing, †History of Art & Archaeology, †Industrial Design, Mixed Media, †Painting, Printmaking, †Sculpture, †Stage Design, †Teacher Training, †Theatre Arts, †Weaving, Glass, Graphics of Communication, Interior Space Design, Product Design
Adult Hobby Classes: Courses—art experiences in all media for local adults
Children's Classes: Enrl 300 per quarter; tuition $16 per quarter; Saturday School. Courses—art experiences in all media for local children
Summer School: Same as regular session
—**Dept of Art,*** 146 Hopkins, 128 N Oval Mall, 43210. Tel 614-422-5072. *Actg Chmn* Gilbert W Hall. Instrs: FT 36, PT 34
SC 56, LC 6, GC 30
Degrees: BA, BFA, MA, MFA
Tuition: Res—$470 per yr; nonres—$925 per yr
Courses: Ceramics, Drawing, Graphic Arts, Painting, Sculpture, Weaving, Fine Arts, Glass
Adult Hobby Classes: Offered through CAP (Creative Art Program)
—**Dept of Art Education,** Hopkins Hall 340, 43210. Tel 614-422-7183. *Chmn Dept* Kenneth A Marantz, EdD; *Prof* Arthur Efland, PhD; *Prof* Charles Csyri, MFA; *Assoc Prof* Robert Arnold, EdD; *Assoc Prof* Donald Duncan, MFA; *Assoc Prof* Nancy MacGregor, PhD; *Asst Prof* Barbara Boyer, PhD; *Asst Prof* James Hutchens, PhD; *Asst Prof* Judith Koroscik, PhD; *Asst Prof* Louis Lankford, PhD; *Asst Prof* Kathleen Desmond, PhD; *Asst Prof* Terry Barrett, PhD; *Asst Prof* Thomas Linehan, PhD
Estab 1907; pub; D & E; scholarships; SC 6, LC 10, GC 16; enrl maj 95, grad 115
Ent Req: HS dipl
Degrees: BAEd, MA, PhD
Courses: Art Education, Film, Goldsmithing, Graphic Arts, Jewelry, Mixed Media, Silversmithing, Teacher Training, Art Appreciation, Art Criticism, Art for Special Audiences, Bookmaking, Computer Graphics, Museum Art Administration, Photo Criticism
Children's Classes: Chmn Dept, Kenneth A Marantz, EdD
Summer School: Chmn Dept, Kenneth A Marantz, EdD
—**Dept of Industrial Design,** 380 Hopkins Hall, 128 N Oval Mall, 43210. Tel 614-422-6746. *Chmn Dept* Charles A Wallschlaeger, MFA. Instrs: FT 11, PT 5
Scholarships; SC 35, LC 10, GC 10
Degrees: BSID, MA
Tuition: Res-undergrad $486 per quarter, grad $627 per quarter; non-res-undergrad $1242 per quarter, grad $1506 per quarter
Courses: Interior Space Design, Product Design, Visual Communication Design
—**Dept of the History of Art,** 100 Hayes Hall, 108 N Oval Mall, 43210. Tel 614-422-7481. *Actg Chmn Dept* Anne M Morganstern, PhD
Estab 1871, dept estab 1968; pub; D & E; scholarships; LC 56, GC 29; enrl D 854, non-maj 700, maj 60, grad 56
Ent Req: HS dipl

Degrees: BA, BFA 4 yrs, MA 2 yrs, PhD 4-6 yrs
Courses: †Art History, History of Art & Archaeology
Summer School: Chmn, Howard Crane. Enrl 250; tuition same as regular session for term of 10 wks beginning June. Courses—vary each yr

CUYAHOGA FALLS

CUYAHOGA VALLEY ART CENTER, 1886 Front St, 44221. Tel 216-928-8092. *Pres* Pat Selby; *Instr* Eugene Bell; *Instr* Robert Putka; *Instr* Jean Deemer; *Instr* Dino Massaroni; *Instr* Leroy Cross; *Instr* Claudia Zeber
Estab 1942; pub; D & E; SC 23; enrl 200
Ent Req: None, interest in art
Degrees: None
Tuition: $65 for 10 wks; no campus res
Courses: Calligraphy, Ceramics, Collages, Drawing, Painting, Textile Design, Acrylic Painting, Oil Painting, Watercolor
Children's Classes: Tuition $35 per 10 wks. Courses—Ceramics, Painting
Summer School: Courses—same as regular session

STUDIOS OF JACK RICHARD CREATIVE SCHOOL OF DESIGN, 2250 Front St, 44221. Tel 216-929-1575. *Dir* Jack Richard. Instrs: FT 3
Estab 1960; pvt; D & E; scholarships; SC 4, LC 10; enrl D 50-60, E 50-60
Courses: Aesthetics, Art Education, Drawing, Illustration, Occupational Therapy, Painting, Photography, Sculpture, Color, Design, Mural
Adult Hobby Classes: Enrl 200 - 300 per session; tuition $11 per class. Courses—Drawing, Painting, Design
Children's Classes: Saturday mornings
Summer School: Dir, Jane Williams. Enrl 90; tuition $10 - $12 per class for term of 8 wks beginning June. Courses—Design, Drawing, Painting

DAYTON

SINCLAIR COMMUNITY COLLEGE, Dept of Art,* 444 W Third St, 45402. Tel 513-226-2500. *Chmn Fine Arts* John Polston
Estab 1973; pub; D & E
Ent Req: HS dipl, ent exam
Degrees: AA 2 yrs
Tuition: County res—$20 per cr hr; non-county res—$27 per cr hr; non-state res—$34 per cr hr; no campus res
Courses: Advertising Design, Ceramics, Commercial Art, Drawing, Graphic Arts, Painting, Sculpture, Theatre Arts
Summer School: Ten week term

UNIVERSITY OF DAYTON, Fine Arts Division,* 300 College Park, 45469. Tel 513-229-3237. *Chmn Performing & Visual Arts* Patrick S Gilvary, PhD; *Assoc Prof* Dr Berward Plogman, DEd; *Assoc Prof* Louis Weber, MA; *Asst Prof* A Jos Barrish, MA; *Asst Prof* Gordon Richardson, MFA; *Asst Prof* Mary Zahner, MA; *Asst Prof* Joann E Fiehler, MA; *Instr* Thomas Strohmaier, MFA
Estab 1850; pvt; D & E; SC 15, LC 8; enrl D 225, E 75-100, non-maj 100, maj 200
Ent Req: HS dipl
Degrees: BA, BFA
Tuition: $2050 per term; campus res available
Courses: Advertising Design, †Art Education, Art History, Calligraphy, Ceramics, Collages, †Commercial Art, Drawing, Graphic Arts, Graphic Design, Illustration, Jewelry, Lettering, Mixed Media, †Painting, †Photography, †Printmaking, †Sculpture, Silversmithing, Teacher Training
Children's Classes: Enrl 12-15; tuition $20 per 8 wks. Courses—Crafts, Drawing, Painting; special program offered for advanced high school seniors
Summer School: Dir, Joann E Fiehler. Tuition same as regular semester

WRIGHT STATE UNIVERSITY, Dept of Art & Art History, Colonel Glenn Hwy, 45435. Tel 513-873-2896. *Assoc Prof & Chmn* Jerry McDowell, MA; *Assoc Prof* Martha Dunkelman, PhD; *Assoc Prof* Ernest Koerlin, MFA; *Assoc Prof* David Leach, MFA; *Assoc Prof* Thomas Macaulay, MFA; *Assoc Prof* Raymond Must, MA; *Assoc Prof* Carol Nathanson, PhD; *Adjunct Assoc* John Dixon, MFA; *Asst Prof* Tim Bruce, MFA; *Asst Prof* Diane Fitch, MFA; *Asst Prof* Ron Geibert, MFA; *Asst Prof* Kimmerly Kiser, MFA
Estab 1964, dept estab 1965; pub; D & E; scholarships; SC 67, LC 16, GC 8; enrl D 516, E 43, non-maj 80, maj 150
Ent Req: HS dipl
Degrees: BA(Studio Art), BA(Art History), BFA 4 yr
Tuition: Res—undergrad $541 per quarter; nonres—undergrad $1082 per quarter; campus res—double room $343 per quarter, two bedroom apartment $375 per quarter, light food service $190 per quarter, heavy food service $250 per quarter
Courses: Art History, Drawing, Film, Painting, Photography, Printmaking, Sculpture, Video, Gallery Management, Museology, Visual Communication
Summer School: Dir, Jerry McDowell. Enrl 65; tuition $541 per 2-5 wk sessions. Courses—Painting, Drawing, Photography

DELAWARE

OHIO WESLEYAN UNIVERSITY, Fine Arts Dept, S Sandusky St, 43015. Tel 614-369-4431. *Chmn* Marty J Kalb, MA; *Prof* Everett Haycock, MA; *Prof* Justin Kronewetter, MFA; *Assoc Prof* Betty Heald, MFA; *Asst Prof* Joseph Rushton, PhD; *Asst Prof* Rinda Metz, MFA
Estab 1841, dept estab 1864; pvt; D & E; enrl D 1550, non-maj 1490, maj 60
Ent Req: HS dipl, SAT or ACT
Degrees: BA and BFA 4 yrs
Tuition: Res $6785 per yr; campus res—room & board $2715 per yr
Courses: Aesthetics, Art Education, Art History, Ceramics, Drawing, Graphic Design, Jewelry, Painting, Photography, Printmaking, Sculpture, Teacher Training, Fiber Arts
Children's Classes: Enrl 55; tuition $5 per 5 wks. Courses—various media
Summer School: Dean, L Wilson. Tuition $585 per unit, 6 & 8 wk courses offered. Courses—Varied

ELYRIA

LORAIN COUNTY COMMUNITY COLLEGE, Art Dept, 1005 N Abbe Rd, 44035. Tel 216-365-4191
Courses: Art Appreciation, Ceramics, Design, Drawing, Painting, Photography, Printmaking, Sculpture, Textile Design

FINDLAY

FINDLAY COLLEGE, Art Dept, 1000 N Main St, 45840. Tel 419-422-8313, Ext 277. Instrs: FT 2, PT 1
Estab 1882; pub; D & E; scholarships; SC 21, LC 4; enrl maj 30
Ent Req: HS dipl
Degrees: AA 2 yr, BA and BS 4 yr
Courses: Advertising Design, Aesthetics, Art Education, Art History, Ceramics, Collages, Drawing, Graphic Design, History of Art & Archaeology, Illustration, Lettering, Painting, Photography, Printmaking, Sculpture, Teacher Training
Adult Hobby Classes: Enrl 10-20. Courses—Ceramics
Children's Classes: Courses—Ceramics, Drawing
Summer School: Dir, Ed Erner

GAMBIER

KENYON COLLEGE, Art Dept, 43022. Tel 614-427-2244. *Chmn* Barry Gunderson, MFA; *Prof* Joseph Slate, BFA; *Assoc Prof* Martin Garhart, MFA; *Asst Prof* Eugene J Dwyer, PhD; *Asst Prof* Gregory P Spaid, MFA; *Asst Prof* Janis Bell, PhD
Estab 1824, dept estab 1965; pvt; D; scholarships; SC 15, LC 10; enrl D 450, non-maj 250, maj 60
Ent Req: HS dipl
Degrees: BA and BFA
Tuition: Res—undergrad $7600 yr; campus residency required
Courses: †Art History, Drawing, History of Art & Archaeology, Painting, Photography, Printmaking, Sculpture

GRANVILLE

DENISON UNIVERSITY, Dept of Art, Box M, 43023. Tel 614-587-0810. *Chmn Dept* Michael Jung, MFA; *Prof* George Bogdanovitch, MFA; *Prof* Eric E Hirshler, PhD; *Asst Prof* Claudia Esslinger, MFA; *Asst Prof* Peter Aberle, MFA; *Vis Prof* Janice Leoshko, Oriental art
Estab 1831, dept estab 1931; pvt; D; scholarships; SC 24, LC 16; enrl D 800, maj 65, double maj 35
Ent Req: HS
Degrees: BA, BFA, BS 4 yr
Tuition: Res—undergrad $7140 per yr; campus res—double room & board $1320 per yr
Courses: Aesthetics, Architecture, †Art History, †Ceramics, Conceptual Art, Constructions, Costume Design & Construction, Drawing, Film, Graphic Arts, Graphic Design, History of Art & Archaeology, Mixed Media, Museum Staff Training, †Painting, Photography, †Printmaking, Restoration & Conservation, †Sculpture, Stage Design, †Theatre Arts

HAMILTON

MIAMI UNIVERSITY, Art Dept, 1601 Peck Blvd, 45011. Tel 513-863-8833. *Chmn* Philip Joseph
Scholarships offered
Tuition: $67 per cr hr
Courses: Advertising Design, Art Appreciation, Art Education, Art History, Calligraphy, Design, Drawing, Industrial Design, Painting, Printmaking, Sculpture
Adult Hobby Classes: Enrl 25-30. Courses—Painting, Printmaking
Summer School: Courses—Drawing

HIRAM

HIRAM COLLEGE, Art Dept, Dean St, 44234. Tel 216-569-3211, Ext 304. *Chmn* Dennis Kievets. Instrs: FT 3, PT 2
Estab 1850; pvt; D; scholarships; SC 20, LC 14; enrl D 400
Ent Req: HS dipl
Degrees: AB 4 yr
Tuition: $6424 per acad year, $2142 per 10 wk term
Courses: Aesthetics, Art Education, †Art History, Ceramics, Drawing, Handicrafts, Lettering, †Painting, †Photography, Printmaking, Sculpture, Teacher Training, Textile Design, Dyeing, Spinning, Weaving
Summer School: Enrl 180. Courses—vary

HURON

BOWLING GREEN STATE UNIVERSITY, Art Dept,* Firelands Col, Div of Humanities, 901 Rye Beach Rd, 44839. Tel 419-433-5560. *Assoc Prof* Julius T Kosan, MFA. Instrs: FT 1, PT 3
Estab 1907, col estab 1966; pub; D & E; scholarships; SC 12, LC 3; enrl D 1200
Ent Req: HS dipl, SAT
Degrees: AA 2 yr
Tuition: $1294 per yr
Courses: Art Education, Art History, Drawing, History of Art & Archaeology, Painting, Photography, Teacher Training, Theatre Arts, Enameling
Summer School: Term of 5 wks beginning June 18. Courses—Art Education, Studio Courses

KENT

KENT STATE UNIVERSITY, School of Art, Col of Fine & Professional Art, 44242. Tel 216-672-2192. *Actg Dir* William Quinn; *Div Coordr Design* J Charles Walker, MFA; *Div Coordr Painting* J Noel Reifel; *Div Coordr Art History* Ben Bassham, PhD; *Div Coordr Art Educ* William Lewis, PhD; *Div Coordr Crafts* Jack Smith, MA; *Grad Coordr* Henry Halem. Instrs: FT 43, PT 6
Estab 1910; pub; D & E; scholarships; SC 105, LC 35, GC 50; enrl non-maj 600, maj 800, grad 125
Ent Req: HS dipl, ACT
Degrees: BFA, BA, BS 4 yrs, MA 1-2 yrs, MFA 2-3 yrs
Tuition: Res—undergrad $856 per sem, grad $1011 per sem; nonres—undergrad $1456 per sem, $190 per sem hr, grad $1611 per sem, $157 per sem hr; campus res—room & board $1500-$1700
Courses: †Art Education, †Art History, Calligraphy, †Ceramics, †Drawing, †Film, Goldsmithing, †Graphic Design, †Illustration, †Industrial Design, †Jewelry, Lettering, Mixed Media, Museum Staff Training, †Painting, †Printmaking, †Sculpture, Silversmithing, Teacher Training, Textile Design, Arts Therapy, Enameling
Adult Hobby Classes: Enrl 50; tuition $25 per class. Courses—Ceramics, Drawing, Fiber, Painting
Children's Classes: Enrl 20; tuition $5 per class. Courses—Art for Elementary School Students
Summer School: Actg Dir, William Quinn. Enrl 300-400; tuition undergrad $433 and grad $471 for term of 5 wks beginning June 11 and July 16. Courses—Art Education, Art History, Crafts, Drawing, Graphic Design, Painting, Printmaking, Sculpture

MARIETTA

MARIETTA COLLEGE, Art Dept,* 45750. Tel 614-373-4643. *Asst Prof* Valdis Garoza. Instrs: FT 2
Estab 1835; pvt; grants in aid and student loans; SC 20, LC 7; enrl maj 75, total col 1600
Degrees: AB, BFA 4 yr
Tuition: $3250 per sem
Courses: Calligraphy, Ceramics, Costume Design & Construction, Drawing, Graphic Arts, Painting, Sculpture, Teacher Training, Theatre Arts, Television

MENTOR

LAKELAND COMMUNITY COLLEGE, Visual Arts Dept, Rt 306 at I-90, 44060. Tel 216-953-7028. *Chmn & Prof* George J Somogyi, MA; *Prof* Thomas W Betts, MA; *Prof* Richard Parsons, MA; *Asst Prof* Walter Swyrydenko, MA; *Asst Prof* John Spriri, BA; *Instr* John Merchant, BA
Sch estab 1967, dept estab 1968; D & E; scholarships; enrl D & E 350
Ent Req: HS dipl
Degrees: AA with concentration in Art 2 yrs, AA Technology degree in Graphic Arts
Tuition: Res—undergrad $1000 per academic yr
Courses: Advertising Design, Art Appreciation, Art History, Calligraphy, Ceramics, Commercial Art, Conceptual Art, Drawing, †Graphic Arts, Graphic Design, Illustration, Intermedia, Jewelry, Lettering, Painting, Photography, Printmaking, Sculpture
Summer School: Courses—Ceramics, Drawing, Jewelry, Painting, Sculpture

MOUNT SAINT JOSEPH

COLLEGE OF MOUNT SAINT JOSEPH, Art Dept, Delhi and Neeb Roads, 45051. Tel 513-244-4309. *Prof & Chairperson* Betty Brothers, MAT; *Prof* John Nartker, MFA; *Prof* Daniel Mader, MA; *Asst Prof* Sharon Kesterson-Bollen, MA
Estab 1920; den; D & E; scholarships; SC 35, LC 4; enrl D 80, non-maj 35, maj 80
Ent Req: HS dipl, national testing scores
Degrees: AA 2 yr, BA and BFA 4 yr
Tuition: Res—undergrad $3936 per yr; campus res—room & board $1219 per sem
Courses: †Art Education, Art History, †Ceramics, †Drawing, †Graphic Design, Handicrafts, †Interior Design, †Jewelry, Lettering, †Painting, †Photography, †Printmaking, †Sculpture, †Silversmithing, Batik, Enameling, †Pre-Art Therapy
Summer School: Chairperson, Betty Brothers, MAT

MOUNT VERNON

MOUNT VERNON NAZARENE COLLEGE, Art Dept, Martinsburg Rd, 43050. Tel 614-397-1244. *Chmn* James Hendricks, MFA; *Instr* Nicholas Blosser, MFA
Estab 1968, dept estab 1970; den; D & E; scholarships; SC 20, LC 5; enrl D 1052, non-maj 1032, maj 20
Ent Req: HS dipl and grad of upper 2/3, ACT
Degrees: BA; Sr project required for graduation
Tuition: Res and nonres—undergrad $3576 per yr; campus res $2030
Courses: Aesthetics, Art History, Ceramics, Design, Drafting, Drawing, Painting, Photography, Printmaking, Sculpture, Graphic Communication, Studio Crafts

NEW CONCORD

MUSKINGUM COLLEGE, Creative & Performing Arts Dept,* 43762. Tel 614-826-8315. *Chmn* Richard Probert. Instrs: FT 2
Estab 1837; pvt; D; scholarships; SC 13, LC 6; enrl D 300, maj 15
Ent Req: HS dipl, ent exam, specific school standards
Degrees: BA and BS 4 yr
Tuition: $5444 per yr
Courses: Art History, Art Education, Ceramics, Drawing, Graphic Arts, Jewelry, Painting, Sculpture, Teacher Training, Theatre Arts

OBERLIN

OBERLIN COLLEGE, Dept of Art, 44074. Tel 216-775-8181. *Chmn* John Pearson, MFA; *Prof* Paul B Arnold, MFA; *Prof* Richard Spear, PhD; *Prof* Forbes Whitside, MFA; *Prof* Athena Tacha, D Univ Paris; *Assoc Prof* William Hood, PhD; *Asst Prof* Susan Kane, PhD; *Asst Prof* Joanna Frueh, PhD; *Asst Prof* Marsha Weidner, PhD; *Asst Prof* Arnold Klukas, PhD; *Asst Prof* John Glascock, MFA Estab 1833, dept estab 1917; pvt; D; scholarships; SC 28, LC 38, advanced undergrad and grad courses 13; enrl D approx 1200, non-maj 500, maj 100, grad 5
Ent Req: HS dipl, SAT
Degrees: BA 4 yr, MA(Art Hist) 2 yr
Tuition: Undergrad and grad $8375 yr; campus res—room and board $3050
Courses: Art History, Drawing, History of Art & Archaeology, Painting, Photography, Printmaking, Sculpture

OXFORD

MIAMI UNIVERSITY, Art Dept,* School of Fine Arts, 113 Heistand Hall, 45056. Tel 513-529-6010. *Dean School Fine Arts* Charles L Spohn, PhD; *Assoc Dean* Harold A Truax, EdD
Estab 1809, dept estab 1929; pub; D & E; scholarships; SC 49, LC 35, GC 20; enrl D 2309, non-maj 1890, maj 419, grad 32
Ent Req: HS dipl, class rank, ACT or SAT
Degrees: BFA and BS(Art) 4 yrs, MFA 2 yrs, MA(Art or Art Educ) and Med(Art Educ) 1 yr
Tuition: $835 per sem; campus res available
Courses: †Advertising Design, Architecture, †Art Education, Art History, Calligraphy, †Ceramics, Collages, Commercial Art, Display, †Drawing, Graphic Arts, †Graphic Design, History of Art & Archaeology, Illustration, †Jewelry, Lettering, Museum Staff Training, †Painting, Photography, †Printmaking, †Sculpture, †Silversmithing, †Teacher Training, †Textile Design, Stitchery, Weaving
Children's Classes: Enrl 70; tuition $5 per sem. Courses—General Art
Summer School: Dir, Peter Dahoda. Courses—varied workshops

PAINESVILLE

LAKE ERIE COLLEGE-GARFIELD SENIOR COLLEGE, Art Dept, 44077. Tel 216-352-3361, Ext 416. *Asst Prof* Jane Palmer. Instrs: FT 3, PT 1
Estab 1856; pvt; SC 20, LC 7; enrl 800 total
Ent Req: Col board exam
Degrees: BA and BFA 4 yrs
Tuition: Lake Erie, res—$8600; Garfield Sr, res—$120 per cr hr
Courses: Art Education, Art History, †Ceramics, †Painting, †Photography, †Printmaking, Sculpture, Design, Introductory Art

SAINT CLAIRSVILLE

OHIO UNIVERSITY BELMONT COUNTY CAMPUS, Art Dept,* National Rd W, 43950. Tel 614-695-2730. *Faculty* David Miles
Tuition: Res—$470; nonres—$1087
Courses: Art Appreciation, Art Education, Design, Drawing, Photography

SPRINGFIELD

SPRINGFIELD ART CENTER, 107 Cliff Park Rd, 45501. Tel 513-325-4673. *Dir* Patricia D'Arcy Catron. Instrs: PT 20
Estab 1951; pvt; D & E; scholarships; D 600
Tuition: No campus res
Courses: Ceramics, Drawing, Jewelry, Painting, Photography, Sculpture
Adult Hobby Classes: Enrl 287; tuition $55 per quarter
Children's Classes: Enrl 286; tuition $30 per quarter. Courses—Art Experiences, Drawing, Pottery and Sculpture

WITTENBERG UNIVERSITY, Art Dept, Koch Hall, PO Box 720, 45501. Tel 513-327-6311. *Chmn & Prof* George Ramsay, MFA; *Prof* Don Dunifon, MFA; *Prof* John Schlump, MA; *Assoc Prof* Richard Hagelberger, MFA; *Assoc Prof* Jack Osbun, MFA; *Asst Prof* Jack Mann, MA
Estab 1842; pvt den; D & E; scholarships; enrl D 350, non-maj 270, maj 80
Ent Req: HS dipl, class rank, transcript, SAT or ACT test results, recommendations and if possible, a personal interview
Degrees: AB and BFA 4 yr
Tuition: Non-res—undergrad $5895 yr; campus res—room & board $2385 yr
Courses: Advertising Design, Aesthetics, †Art Education, Art History, †Ceramics, Drawing, †Graphic Arts, Graphic Design, †Illustration, Interior Design, Jewelry, †Painting, Photography, †Printmaking, †Sculpture, †Teacher Training
Summer School: Provost, William Wiebenga. Enrl 400; tuition $250 for term of 7 wks beginning June 14. Courses—Art in the Elementary School, Fundamental of Art, Painting

SYLVANIA

LOURDES COLLEGE, Art Dept, 6832 Convent Blvd, 43560. Tel 419-882-2016. *Chmn Fine Arts* Sr Helen Chmura
Estab 1958; pvt, den; D & E; SC 11, LC 6; enrl D 55, E 26, non-maj 65, maj 16
Ent Req: HS dipl, ACT or SAT
Degrees: AA, BIS
Tuition: No campus res available
Courses: Art History, Calligraphy, Ceramics, Design, Drawing, Mixed Media, Occupational Therapy, Painting, Printmaking, Sculpture, Copper Enameling, Weaving, Watercolor
Adult Hobby Classes: Enrl 20. Courses—Calligraphy, Ceramics, Copper Enameling, Painting, Weaving, Art History

Children's Classes: Enrl 35; tuition $40 per 10 classes. Courses—Ceramics, Drawing, Painting
Summer School: Dir, Sr Helen Chmura. Enrl 35; tuition $65 per cr hr. Courses—Art History, Fiber Arts, Watercolor

TIFFIN

HEIDELBERG COLLEGE, Dept of Art,* 44883. Tel 419-448-2000. *Instr* Janis McConahay
Estab 1850; pvt; D; scholarships; SC 22, LC 9; enrl 200, maj 24
Ent Req: HS dipl, each applicant's qualifications are considered individually
Degrees: AB 4 yrs, independent study, honors work available
Tuition: $2780 per yr
Courses: Advertising Design, Aesthetics, Art Education, Ceramics, Commercial Art, Display, Drawing, Graphic Arts, Graphic Design, History of Art & Archaeology, Illustration, Jewelry, Lettering, Museum Staff Training, Painting, Sculpture, Stage Design, Teacher Training, Textile Design, Chip Carving, Copper Enameling, Metal Tooling, Mosaic
Summer School: Dir, Dr Roy M Bacon. Term of 6 wks beginning June. Courses—Materials and Methods in Teaching, Practical Arts

TOLEDO

TOLEDO MUSEUM OF ART, School of Design, Box 1013, 43697. Tel 419-255-8000. *Asst Dir* Charles F Gunther. Instrs: FT 13, PT 5
Estab 1919; pvt; D & E; scholarships
Degrees: In cooperation with Univ of Toledo 4 yr
Courses: Art History, Ceramics, Drawing, Painting, Printmaking, Sculpture, Design, Glass, Metalsmithing
Adult Hobby Classes: Enrl 300 per quarter
Children's Classes: Enrl 1100 per quarter. Free classes for children on Sat in art and music

UNIVERSITY OF TOLEDO, Dept of Art, Art Education and Art History,* 43606. Tel 419-537-2696. *Faculty* Duane Bastian, MEd; *Faculty* Elizabeth Cole, MEd; *Faculty* David Guip, EdD
Same as regular session
Ent Req: HS dipl
Degrees: BA, BA(Art History), BFA, MA(Art Educ)
Courses: Advertising Design, Art History, Ceramics, Drawing, Painting, Printmaking, Sculpture, Design, Glass, Metals

WARREN

KENT STATE UNIVERSITY, Art Dept,* 4314 Mahoning Ave NW, 44481. Tel 216-847-0571. *Chmn & Prof* Dr Stuart Schar, PhD; *Assoc Prof* Eric May Dept estab 1954; pub; D & E; SC 2-3, LC 2; enrl maj 10
Ent Req: HS dipl or GED
Degrees: AA, BA, BS, BFA
Tuition: Res—$841 per sem; nonres—$1441 per sem
Courses: †Art Education, Art History, Drawing, Painting, Printmaking
Adult Hobby Classes: Watercolor, oil
Summer School: Dr Dennis Smith, Acting Dir. Tuition $53 per credit hr. Courses—Art Survey

WESTERVILLE

OTTERBEIN COLLEGE, Dept of Visual Arts, 43081. Tel 614-890-3000. *Chmn* Earl Hassenpflug
Pvt; scholarships; SC 11, LC 4; enrl D 1400, maj 32
Ent Req: HS dipl
Degrees: BA 4 yrs
Courses: Architecture, Art Education, Ceramics, Drawing, Graphic Design, Handicrafts, History of Art & Archaeology, Painting, Photography, Sculpture, Stage Design, Teacher Training, Theatre Arts, Art Psychotherapy, Crafts

WILBERFORCE

CENTRAL STATE UNIVERSITY, Dept of Art, 45384. Tel 513-376-6610. *Chmn* Willis Bing Davis. Instrs: FT 6
Estab 1856; D; SC 20, LC 8; enrl D 175, maj 50, others 130
Ent Req: HS dipl
Degrees: BA and BS 4 yr
Courses: Advertising Design, Art Education, Art History, Ceramics, Drawing, Graphic Arts, Lettering, Painting, Sculpture, Teacher Training
Summer School: Chmn, Willis Bing Davis. Enrl maj 50, others 200; term of 12 wks beginning June 16, two sessions. Courses—Art for the Elementary Teacher, Art History, Black Artists, Ceramics, Introduction to Art, Painting, Sculpture

WILBERFORCE UNIVERSITY, Art Dept, 45384. Tel 513-376-2911. *Advisor* James Padgett, MFA
Estab 1856, dept estab 1973; pvt; D; scholarships; SC 22, LC 5
Ent Req: HS dipl
Degrees: BA, BS and BS(Educ) 4 yrs
Courses: Commercial Art, Printmaking, Sculpture, Teacher Training, Fine Arts
Summer School: Courses offered

WILLOUGHBY

SCHOOL OF FINE ARTS, Visual Arts Dept, 38660 Mentor Ave, 44094. Tel 216-951-7500. *Dir* James Savage, BM; *Visual Arts Coordr & Gallery Dir* Doris Foster, BFA
Estab 1957; pvt; D & E; scholarships; enrl D 120, E 200
Tuition: $$40-$85 per class; no campus res
Courses: Ceramics, Drawing, Intermedia, Mixed Media, Painting, Photography
Adult Hobby Classes: Enrl 130; tuition $61-$85. Courses—Drawing, Painting, Photography, Pottery
Children's Classes: Enrl 235; tuition $49-$51 for 16 wks. Courses—Drawing, Painting, Pottery
Summer School: Dir, James Savage. Enrl 200; tuition $38-$71 for term of 6 wks beginning mid-June. Courses—same as above

WILMINGTON

WILMINGTON COLLEGE, Art Dept,* 45177. Tel 513-386-6661. *Prof* Phillip Hidge, MA; *Asst Prof* Terry Inlow, MFA
Scholarships offered
Degrees: BA
Tuition: $1395 per yr
Courses: Art Appreciation, Art Education, Art History, Ceramics, Design, Drawing, Handicrafts, Painting, Photography, Printmaking, Sculpture, Stage Design

WOOSTER

COLLEGE OF WOOSTER, Dept of Art, University St, 44691. Tel 216-263-2388; WATS 800-321-9885. *Chmn* Arnold Lewis, PhD; *Prof* Thalia Gouma-Peterson, PhD; *Prof* George Olson, MFA; *Asst Prof* Walter Luiko, MFA; *Asst Prof* Catherine Fruhan, PhD
Estab 1866; pvt; D & E; SC 13, LC 19; enrl D 1000, maj 40
Ent Req: HS dipl
Degrees: BA 4 yr
Tuition: $9800 per yr (board & room included)
Courses: Architecture, Art Education, †Art History, Ceramics, Drawing, Graphic Arts, History of Art & Archaeology, Painting, Photography, Printmaking, Sculpture
Adult Hobby Classes: Available through student activities board. Enrl 12-20; tuition varies
Children's Classes: Available through Community Art Center. Enrl 10-20; tuition varies
Summer School: Dir, Dr Raymond McCall

YELLOW SPRINGS

ANTIOCH COLLEGE, Dept of Art, 45387. Tel 513-767-7331, Ext 464. *Chmn* Allan L Jones, MFA; *Prof* Karen Shirley, MFA
Estab 1853; pvt; D & E; SC 48, LC 10; enrl D 665 per quarter, non-maj 100, maj 50
Ent Req: HS dipl
Degrees: BA and BFA 5 yrs
Tuition: $9900 per year (tuition, fees, room & board)
Courses: Art Education, †Ceramics, Conceptual Art, Constructions, †Drawing, †Film, †Painting, †Photography, †Printmaking, †Sculpture
Adult Hobby Classes: Chmn, Allan L Jones

YOUNGSTOWN

YOUNGSTOWN STATE UNIVERSITY, Art Dept, 410 Wick Ave, 44555. Tel 216-742-3627. *Chmn Dept* Richard Mitchell
Estab 1908, dept estab 1952; pub; D & E; SC 44, LC 26, GC 8; enrl D & E 1250, maj 300, grad 15
Ent Req: HS dipl
Degrees: AB, BFA and BS 4 yrs
Courses: †Art Education, †Art History, †Ceramics, †Commercial Art, Drawing, Graphic Arts, †Graphic Design, Illustration, Interior Design, Jewelry, Lettering, Museum Staff Training, †Painting, Photography, †Printmaking, †Sculpture, †Teacher Training
Adult Hobby Classes: Courses—Calligraphy, Ceramics, Drawing, Painting, Photography, Weaving
Summer School: Two 5 wk sessions beginning June. Courses—same as above

OKLAHOMA

ADA

EAST CENTRAL UNIVERSITY, Art Dept, 74820. Tel 405-332-8000, Ext 353. *Chmn* Dee J Lafon, MFA; *Instructor* Robert Sieg, MFA; *Instructor* Grant Thorp, MFA; *Vis Prof* Marc Etier, MFA
EStab 1909; pub; D & E; scholarships; SC 22, LC 10, GC 8; enrl D 222, E 105, non-maj 103, maj 80, grad 3, others 36
Ent Req: HS dipl, ATC
Degrees: BA and BA(Educ) 4 yr, MEd 33 hrs, post graduate work, public service program
Tuition: Res—1000-2000 level courses $12, 3000-4000 level courses $13, 5000 level courses $15; nonres—1000-2000 level courses $31, 3000-4000 level courses $34, 5000 level courses $39
Courses: †Art Education, Art History, †Ceramics, Conceptual Art, †Drawing, Film, Graphic Arts, Jewelry, Mixed Media, †Painting, Photography, †Printmaking, †Sculpture, Silversmithing, †Teacher Training, Wood Design

Adult Hobby Classes: Enrl 25 average; tuition $30. Courses—Drawing, Painting, Silk Screen
Summer School: Dir, Dr Stephenson. Courses—Ceramics, Drawing, Painting, Printmaking

ALTUS

WESTERN OKLAHOMA STATE COLLEGE, Art Dept, 2801 N Main, 73521. Tel 405-477-2000. *Chmn* Lloyd C English
Scholarships offered
Degrees: AA, AS, AT
Courses: Advertising Design, Art Appreciation, Art History, Ceramics, Design, Drawing, Handicrafts, Jewelry, Painting, Photography, Printmaking, Sculpture, Stage Design, Video, Weaving

ALVA

NORTHWESTERN OKLAHOMA STATE UNIVERSITY, Art Dept, 73717. Tel 405-327-1700, Ext 243. *Chmn* Don Bellah, BFA
Estab 1897; pub; D; SC 28, LC 6, GC 3; enrl D 50-80, non-maj 50, maj 30, grad 3
Ent Req: HS dipl
Degrees: BA(Art), BA(Educ) and standard cert 4 yr, grad study for master of teaching degree 18 grad hrs available
Tuition: Res—undergrad lower division $17.40 hr, upper division $18.65 hr, grad $21.05 hr; nonres—undergrad lower division $45.85 hr, upper division $50.05 hr, grad $57.45 hr; other—correspondence $16.50, extension $20; campus res—room and board $1360 per yr
Courses: Advertising Design, Art Appreciation, †Art Education, Art History, Ceramics, Commercial Art, Drawing, Graphic Arts, History of Art & Archaeology, Painting, Printmaking, Sculpture
Adult Hobby Classes: Chmn, Don Bellah, BFA
Summer School: Enrl 40; tuition same as regular sem; class length & course offerings vary each summer

CHICKASHA

UNIVERSITY OF SCIENCE AND ARTS OF OKLAHOMA, Arts Dept, 73018. Tel 405-224-3140, Ext 301. Instrs: FT 3, PT 3
Estab 1909; pub; D; SC 26, LC 3; enrl maj 84, others 180
Degrees: 124 hr req for grad
Courses: Ceramics, Drawing, Jewelry, Painting, Sculpture, Teacher Training, Design, Pottery & Modeling, Watercolor
Adult Hobby Classes: Enrl 30; tuition $15 per hr. Courses—Ceramics, Stained Glass, Graphics Design, Drawing
Summer School: Enrl 60; tuition $15 per hr for 10 wk course. Courses—Painting, Sculpture, Ceramics

CLAREMORE

CLAREMORE COLLEGE, Art Dept,* College Hill, 74017. Tel 918-341-7510. *Dir* Gary E Moeller, MFA; *Instr* Barbara Cohenour, MT; *Instructor* Julana Hull, MFA; *Instructor* Martha Spielman, MFA; *Instructor* Brian Somers, MA
Estab 1971; pub; D & E; scholarships; SC 22, LC 3; enrl D 126, E 60, non-maj 146, maj 40
Ent Req: HS dipl, ACT
Degrees: AA and AS 2 yr
Tuition: Campus res available
Courses: Art History, Ceramics, Drawing, †Interior Design, Lettering, Painting, Photography, Printmaking, Sculpture, †Fine Arts, †Graphic Technology
Children's Classes: Tui $11.50 per hr. Courses—Children's Art
Summer School: Tui $11.50 per hr for term of 8 wks beginning June 5th. Courses—Advanced Ceramics, Art Appreciation, Drawing, Painting

DURANT

SOUTHEASTERN OKLAHOMA STATE COLLEGE, Art Dept,* 74701. Tel 405-924-0121. *Head* Dr Allen Platter; *Instructor* Max McClendon; *Instructor* James Barnette; *Instructor* Susan Brown
Estab 1909; pub; enrl 330
Ent Req: HS dipl, col exam
Degrees: BA, BS and BAEduc 4-5 yrs
Tuition: Res—$16.65 per yr; nonres—$41.40 per yr
Courses: Art Appreciation, Art History, Ceramics, Handicrafts, Painting, Sculpture, Applied Design, Design, Modeling (Clay), Perspective Drawing, Pictorial Composition, Watercolor
Adult Hobby Classes: Head, Dr Allen Platter
Summer School: Head, Dr Allen Platter

EDMOND

CENTRAL STATE UNIVERSITY, Art Dept, 100 North University Dr, 73034. Tel 405-341-2980. *Chmn* Kathryn Alcorn-Kunc
Estab 1890; pub; D & E; scholarships; enrl maj 280, grad 20, dept 1168, school 13,086
Ent Req: HS dipl, health exams, IQ test, scholarship tests
Degrees: BA, BS and MEduc 3-4 yrs
Courses: Advertising Design, Art Education, Art History, Ceramics, Commercial Art, Jewelry, Painting, Sculpture, Art Appreciation, Art in America, Arts & Crafts, Design, Etching & Lithography, Figure Drawing, Metal Design, Studio Art, Watercolor, Weaving
Summer School: Chmn, Kathryn/Alcorn-Kunc

ENID

PHILLIPS UNIVERSITY, Dept of Art, University Place, 73701. Tel 405-237-4433. *Chmn* John Randolph, MFA; *Prof* Jim Bray, MA; *Prof* Paul Denny Jr, MFA; *Assoc Prof* Pricilla Bain-Smith, PhD
Estab 1907, dept estab 1909; den; D & E; scholarships; SC 20, LC 6; enrl D 45, E 18, non-maj 20, maj 25, others 18
Ent Req: HS dipl
Degrees: MBA and ME 5 yrs, BA, BS and BFA 4 yrs
Tuition: Res & nonres—undergrad $100 per hr; campus res—room and board $3000
Courses: Advertising Design, †Art Education, †Art History, †Ceramics, Commercial Art, Constructions, Drawing, Graphic Arts, Graphic Design, Handicrafts, History of Art & Archaeology, Lettering, †Painting, †Sculpture, Teacher Training, Preart Therapy
Adult Hobby Classes: Enrl 18; tuition $85 per course. Course—Ceramics
Summer School: Enrl 15; tuition $100 for term of one cr hr. Courses vary

LANGSTON

LANGSTON UNIVERSITY, Art Dept,* General Delivery, PO Box 907, 73050. Tel 405-466-2231. *Chmn* Dr Reuben Manning
Estab 1897, dept estab 1928; pub; D & E; enrl D 51, non-maj 20, maj 31
Ent Req: HS dipl
Degrees: BA(Art Educ) and BA(Arts & Science)
Tuition: Res—$450 per yr; nonres—$685 per yr
Courses: Art Education, Art History, Ceramics, Commercial Art, Drawing, Graphic Arts, History of Art & Archaeology, Jewelry, Lettering, Mixed Media, Painting, Photography, Printmaking, Sculpture, Silversmithing, Teacher Training, Theatre Arts
Summer School: Term of 8 wks beginning June 5th. Courses—Drawing, Painting, Public School Art

LAWTON

CAMERON UNIVERSITY, Art Dept, 2800 Gore Blvd, 73505. Tel 405-248-2200. *Chmn* Jack Bryan
Estab 1970; pub; D & E; scholarships; SC 22, LC 5; enrl D 417, E 90, maj 60
Ent Req: HS dipl
Degrees: BA 4 yrs
Tuition: $13-$34 per sem hr; campus res—room and board $643 per sem
Courses: Art Appreciation, Art Education, †Art History, Ceramics, Drawing, Design, Graphic Arts, Graphic Design, Jewelry, †Mixed Media, Painting, Photography, †Printmaking, †Sculpture, Color, Crafts
Summer School: Courses—Art Education, Ceramics, Graphics, Jewelry, Painting, Photography

MIAMI

NORTHEASTERN OKLAHOMA A & M COLLEGE, Art Dept, 74354. Tel 918-542-8441, Ext 263. *Chmn* Nick Calcagno. Instrs: FT 2, PT 1
Estab 1919; pub; D & E; scholarships; SC 11, LC 1
Ent Req: HS dipl
Degrees: AA 2 yr
Tuition: Campus residency available
Courses: Art Education, Calligraphy, Costume Design & Construction, Drafting, Drawing, History of Art & Archaeology, Lettering, Mixed Media, Painting, Sculpture, Stage Design, Theatre Arts

NORMAN

UNIVERSITY OF OKLAHOMA, School of Art, 73019. Tel 405-352-2691. *Dir* Joe F Hobbs
Estab 1911; pub; scholarships; SC 27, LC 22, GC 12; enrl maj 300, others 1200
Degrees: BFA, MA(Art History) and MFA
Courses: Advertising Design, Art History, Ceramics, Drawing, Film, Graphic Arts, Painting, Photography, Sculpture, Video, Metal Design, Product Design

OKLAHOMA CITY

OKLAHOMA ART CENTER ANNEX AND ART SCHOOL, 3000 Pershing Blvd, 73107. Tel 405-946-5566. *School Coordr* Patti Bata-Hyde
Adult Hobby Classes: Enrl 172. Courses—Adult Basic Drawing, Watercolor, Oil & Acrylic, Sculpture, Silkscreen, Ceramics, Photography, Dance
Children's Classes: Enrl 100. Courses—Ceramics, Multi-media, Painting, Drawing, Creative Writing

OKLAHOMA CHRISTIAN COLLEGE, Art Dept,* Eastern at Memorial Rd, 73111. Tel 405-478-1661. *Asst Prof* Michael O'Keefe, MFA
Scholarships offered
Tuition: $1125 per trimester
Courses: Drawing, Handicrafts, Jewelry, Painting, Photography, Printmaking, Sculpture, Stage Design, Weaving, Bookbinding

OKLAHOMA CITY UNIVERSITY, Art Dept, 73106. Tel 405-521-5014. *Chmn* Jack R Davis. Instrs: FT 2, PT
Estab 1904; den; D & E; scholarships; LC 2; enrl maj 40
Degrees: 4 yr
Tuition: $5372 per year including room & board
Courses: Advertising Design, Art History, Ceramics, Drawing, Graphic Arts, Jewelry, Painting, Sculpture, Teacher Training, Art Marketing, Design, Native American Art, Watercolor
Adult Hobby Classes: Weekend classes available
Children's Classes: Enrl 10-15; tuition $35 per child. Courses—Christmas crafts, summer workshops
Summer School: Dir, Jack Davis. Enrl 300; tuition $97 per cr hr for two 6 wk sessions June to July, July to August

OKMULGEE

OKLAHOMA STATE UNIVERSITY, Graphic Arts Dept,* 4th and Mission, 74447. Tel 918-756-6211. *Head Dept* Forrest L Johns, BArch; *Instructor* Gary Borchert, BA; *Instructor* Paul A Gresham, MFA; *Instructor* Larry Rose; *Instructor* H Allen Shaw Jr, BFA; *Instructor* Bill Welch, BS. Instrs: FT 5, PT 1
Estab 1946, dept estab 1970; pub; D & E; scholarships; SC 12, LC 1; enrl D 130, E 18
Ent Req: HS dipl or 18 yrs of age
Degrees: 2 yr Associate, degree granting technical school, 2 yr associate degree
Tuition: Res—undergrad $735 per yr, $245 per trimester; nonres—undergrad $444 per trimester; campus res $1100 per yr
Courses: Advertising Design, Commercial Art, Drafting, Drawing, Graphic Arts, Graphic Design, Illustration, Jewelry, Lettering, Photography
Summer School: Tuition same as above per trimester beginning June 1st to last of Sept

SHAWNEE

OKLAHOMA BAPTIST UNIVERSITY, Art Dept, 500 W University, 74801. Tel 405-275-6611. *Chmn* Steve Hicks, MFA; *Asst Prof* Janie Wester, MA
Estab 1910; den; D; scholarships offered; SC 7, LC 3, grad 2; enrl D 100, non-maj 75, maj 25, grad 2
Ent Req: HS dipl, SAT-ACT
Degrees: BA & BFA 4 yrs
Tuition: Res—undergrad $1195 per sem, $85 per hr; nonres—undergrad $1200; campus res—room and board $690 per academic yr
Courses: Advertising Design, †Art Education, Art History, Calligraphy, †Ceramics, Drawing, Jewelry, †Painting, †Printmaking, Teacher Training, Fibers
Summer School: Dir, Steve Hicks. Tuition $170 for 8 wk term beginning May 30. Studio courses offered

SAINT GREGORY'S COLLEGE, Dept of Art,* 1900 MacArthur, 74801. Tel 405-273-9870. *Faculty* Augustine Horn; *Chmn* Marian Salwierak, MEd; *Faculty* Shirlie A Bowers, BFA
Estab 1898, dept estab 1960; den; D & E; SC 6; enrl D 325
Ent Req: HS dipl, ACT or SAT
Degrees: AA 2 yrs
Tuition: $1087.50 per scm
Courses: Art History, Ceramics, Commercial Art, Drawing, Mixed Media, Sculpture
Adult Hobby Classes: Courses—Ceramics, Drawing, Sculpture

STILLWATER

OKLAHOMA STATE UNIVERSITY, Art Dept, Bartlett Center for the Studio Arts, 74078. Tel 405-624-6016. *Dept Head* Richard A Bivins, MFA
Estab 1890, dept estab 1928; pub; D & E; SC 20, LC 4; enrl D 850, E 60, non-maj 810, maj 210
Ent Req: HS dipl
Degrees: BA, BA(Art Hist), BFA, 4 yr
Courses: Art History, Ceramics, Drawing, Graphic Design, Jewelry, Lettering, Painting, Printmaking, Sculpture
Summer School: Dept Head, Richard Bivins, MFA

TAHLEQUAH

NORTHEASTERN OKLAHOMA STATE UNIVERSITY, 74464. Tel 918-456-5511, Ext 405. *Chmn* Bruce Tibbetts, EdD; *Instructor* Jerry Choate, MFA; *Instructor* R C Coones, MFA; *Instructor* Dr Kathleen Schmidt, EdD
Estab 1889; pub; D & E; scholarships; enrl non-maj 50, maj 30, grad 10
Ent Req: HS dipl
Degrees: BA and BA(Educ) 4 yr
Tuition: Campus residency available
Courses: Art Education, Art History, Ceramics, Commercial Art, Costume Design & Construction, Drafting, Drawing, Graphic Arts, Jewelry, Lettering, Painting, Photography, Printmaking, Sculpture, Silversmithing, Stage Design, Teacher Training, Theatre Arts
Adult Hobby Classes: Courses— Indian Art, Silversmithing
Summer School: Regular summer session

TULSA

ORAL ROBERTS UNIVERSITY, Fine Arts Dept, 7777 S Lewis, 74171. Tel 918-495-6611. *Head Dept* Dr Leon Kroeker; *Assoc Prof* Sue B Montgomery, MFA; *Instr* Marsha Bush, MFA; *Instr* Charles Ramsay Sr, BS; *Vis Prof* Dorothea Heit, photography; *Vis Prof* Carol Kiper, printmaking; *Vis Prof* Stan Weir, commercial & studio art; *Vis Prof* Don Wilson, photography; *Vis Prof* Mike Kelly, commercial art
Estab 1965; pvt; D & E; scholarships; SC 22, LC 3; enrl D 65, non-maj 40, maj 65, others 10
Ent Req: HS dipl, SAT
Degrees: BA(Art Educ), BA(Commercial Art) and BA(Studio Art) 4 yrs
Tuition: Res and nonres—undergrad $145 per hr; campus res—room & board $1100 per sem
Courses: Advertising Design, †Art Education, Ceramics, †Commercial Art, Constructions, Drawing, Film, Graphic Arts, Graphic Design, Handicrafts, History of Art & Archaeology, Illustration, Intermedia, Interior Design, Lettering, Mixed Media, Painting, Photography, Printmaking, Sculpture, Teacher Training, Video, †Studio Art

TULSA JUNIOR COLLEGE, Art Dept, 909 S Boston, 74119. Tel 918-587-6561. *Instr* William Derrevere, MA; *Instr* Nota Johnson, MA. Instrs: PT 8
Estab 1970; pub; D & E; scholarships; SC 16, LC 7; enrl non-maj 40, maj 160
Ent Req: HS dipl
Degrees: AA 2 yrs

Tuition: Campus residency available
Courses: Art History, Drawing, Goldsmithing, Jewelry, Painting, Printmaking, Silversmithing, Art Appreciation, 2-D & 3-D Design, Health & Safety in the Arts & Crafts, Life Drawing
Adult Hobby Classes: Special prog of art courses and crafts courses
Summer School: Courses—Art Appreciation, 2-D Design, Drawing

UNIVERSITY OF TULSA, Dept of Art, 600 S College Ave, 74104. Tel 918-592-6000, Ext 2202. *Head Dept* Bradley E Place
Estab 1898; pvt; scholarships; SC 20, LC 13, GC 22; enrl maj 160, others 400
Degrees: BA, BFA, MA, MFA and MTA 4 yrs
Tuition: Res—$3700 per yr; campus res available
Courses: Art Education, Ceramics, Commercial Art, Painting, Printmaking, Sculpture
Summer School: Dir, Bradley Place. Enrl 100; tuition $130 per sem hr.
Courses—Art Education, Art History, Graphic Design, Painting

WEATHERFORD

SOUTHWESTERN OKLAHOMA STATE UNIVERSITY, Art Dept, 73096. Tel 405-772-6611, Ext 5000. *Chmn* James A Terrell
Estab 1901; dept estab 1941; pub; D & E; SC 35, LC 8, GC 43; enrl D 5000
Ent Req: HS dipl
Degrees: BA(Art), BA(Art Educ) and BA(Commercial Art) 4 yr
Tuition: Varies; campus residency available
Courses: Advertising Design, Art Education, Art History, Ceramics, Commercial Art, Drawing, Graphic Arts, Graphic Design, Illustration, Jewelry, Lettering, Mixed Media, Painting, Sculpture, Teacher Training
Summer School: Courses—Ceramics, Drawing, Elements of Art, Fundamentals of Art, Introduction to Clay, Jewelry, Metal, Painting

OREGON

ALBANY

LINN BENTON COMMUNITY COLLEGE, Fine & Applied Art Dept, 6500 SW Pacific Blvd, 97321. Tel 503-928-2361. *Chmn Dept* James A Tolbert; *Instructor* John Aikman; *Instructor* Rich Bergeman; *Instructor* Judith Rogers; *Instructor* Carlis Nixon; *Instructor* Gene Tobey; *Instructor* Sandra Zimmer
Estab 1968; pub; D & E; SC 14, LC 2; enrl D 2000, E 4000
Ent Req: Open entry
Degrees: AA, AS and AGS 2 yrs
Tuition: Res—$504 per yr
Courses: †Advertising Design, Art History, Ceramics, Display, Drafting, Drawing, †Graphic Arts, †Graphic Design, Handicrafts, Illustration, Jewelry, Lettering, Painting, Photography, Sculpture, †Textile Design, Theatre Arts, Weaving
Adult Hobby Classes: Courses—Painting, Tole Painting, Watercolor

ASHLAND

OREGON COLLEGE OF ART, * 30 S First St, 97520. Tel 503-482-0113. *Pres* Dr Richard K Walsh. Instrs: FT 2, PT 5
Estab 1971; pvt; D; scholarships; SC 24, LC 5; enrl D 40
Ent Req: HS dipl, portfolio
Degrees: Bachelor of Professional Arts or cr transfer for AA or BA at adjacent Southern Oregon State Col 4 yrs
Tuition: 2000 per year
Courses: Advertising Design, Commercial Art, Drawing, Graphic Arts, Graphic Design, Illustration, Lettering, Painting, Sign Painting

SOUTHERN OREGON STATE COLLEGE, Dept of Art, 1250 Siskiyou Blvd, 97520. Tel 503-482-6386. *Chmn Dept Art* Robert Alston
Estab 1926; pub; D & E; scholarships; SC 48, LC 11, GC 1; enrl D 120, E 30, non-maj 700, maj 100
Ent Req: HS dipl
Degrees: BFA, BA or BS(Art Educ), BA or BS(Art) 4 yrs
Tuition: Res—undergrad $1425 per yr; nonres—undergrad $4737 per yr; campus res available
Courses: Advertising Design, Art Appreciation, †Art History, Calligraphy, †Ceramics, †Drawing, Graphic Design, †Jewelry, †Painting, †Printmaking, †Sculpture, †Teacher Training, †Weaving
Adult Hobby Classes: Various courses
Children's Classes: Summer classes
Summer School: Dir, Larry Helms. Enrl 210; 8 wk term. Courses—various

BEND

CENTRAL OREGON COMMUNITY COLLEGE, Dept of Art,* College Way, 97701. *Assoc Prof* Douglas Campbell Smith, MA; *Assoc Prof* Tom Temple, MA
Estab 1949; pub; D & E; scholarships; enrl in col D 2025, E 2000
Ent Req: HS dipl
Degrees: AA, AS, Cert
Tuition: In-district—$180 per term; out-of-district—$300 per term; out-of-state—$984 per term; campus res available
Courses: Calligraphy, Ceramics, Drawing, Painting, Photography, Printmaking, Stage Design, Theatre Arts
Summer School: Dir, Forrest Daniel. Enrl 374; term of 8 wks beginning June 21; additional workshop formats

COOS BAY

COOS ART MUSEUM, * 515 Market Ave, 97420. Tel 503-267-3901. *Instr* Sylvia Duke; *Instr* Ruth Barnhart; *Instr* Judith Hedberg-Duff; *Instr* Lorraine Schneider; *Instr* Sara Spaugh. Instrs: PT 8
Estab 1966; pvt; D & E; SC 7; enrl D 15, E 100
Courses: Calligraphy, Drawing, Jewelry, Painting, Sculpture, Children's Craft & Stitchery, Spinning, Stitchery, Weaving
Adult Hobby Classes: Enrl 100; tui for 10 wks, non-mem $23, mem $20
Children's Classes: Tui $38 depending on course and membership status
Summer School: Tui same as above

SOUTHWESTERN OREGON COMMUNITY COLLEGE, Visual Arts Dept, Empire Lakes, 97420. Tel 503-888-2525. *Div Chmn* Nathan Douthit, PhD; *Assoc Prof* Howard A Hall, MFA; *Assoc Prof* Carol Vernon, MA
Estab 1962, dept estab 1964; pub; D & E; scholarships; SC 11, LC 1; enrl D 420, E 300, non-maj 250, maj 170
Degrees: AA 2 yrs
Tuition: Res—undergrad $180 per quarter, nonres grad—540 per quarter; nonres—undergrad $360 per quarter; no campus res
Courses: Art Education, Art History, Ceramics, Commercial Art, Drawing, Graphic Design, Painting, Photography, Printmaking, Sculpture, Theatre Arts, Video
Adult Hobby Classes: Tuition $150 per quarter. Courses—Art Appreciation, Ceramics, Painting, Tole Painting, Wood Carving
Children's Classes: Only as occasional workshops
Summer School: Dean Instruction, John Rulifson. Tuition varies. Courses—Ceramics, Painting and Composition, Watercolor

CORVALLIS

OREGON STATE UNIVERSITY, Dept of Art, 97331. *Chmn* Mark Sponenburgh, DFA; *Prof* John Rock, MFA; *Prof* William Crozier, MFA; *Assoc Prof* Raymond Masters. Instrs: FT 22, PT 2
School estab 1868, dept 1908; pub; D & E; scholarships; SC 38, LC 5, GC 21; enrl Non-maj 1500, maj 210, grad 10
Ent Req: HS dipl
Degrees: BA, BS, BFA & MAIS
Tuition: Res undergrad—$452 per quarter; res grad—$673 per quarter; nonres undergrad—$1327 per quarter; nonres grad—$1089 per quarter; campus res available
Courses: †Advertising Design, Calligraphy, Ceramics, Drawing, Graphic Arts, Graphic Design, History of Art & Archaeology, Illustration, Jewelry, Lettering, Mixed Media, Painting, Photography, Printmaking, Sculpture, Silversmithing, Textile Design
Summer School: Tuition $347 for term of 8 wks beginning June. Courses—same as above

EUGENE

LANE COMMUNITY COLLEGE, Art and Applied Design Dept, 4000 E 30th Ave, 97405. Tel 503-747-4501, Ext 2409. *Chmn Dept* Roger Cornell McAlister, MFA
Estab 1964, dept estab 1967; pub; D & E; SC 42, LC 4; enrl D 300, E 75, non-maj 240, maj 60
Ent Req: HS dipl
Degrees: AA, AS 2 yrs
Tuition: Res—$198 per term; nonres—$330 per term, out-of-state $825 per term
Courses: Metal Casting, 2-D & 3-D Design
Adult Hobby Classes: Varied courses
Summer School: Dir, Roger Cornell McAlister. Courses—Drawing, Painting

MAUDE KERNS ART CENTER SCHOOL, * 1910 E 15th Ave, 97403. Tel 503-345-1571. *Dir* Leslie Copland
Estab 1951; pvt; D & E; scholarships; SC 45; enrl D & E 450
Tuition: $38-$45 per class per quarter
Courses: Calligraphy, Ceramics, Graphic Arts, Handicrafts, Jewelry, Painting, Photography, Printmaking, Fiber Arts
Adult Hobby Classes: Enrl 100. Courses—Per regular session
Children's Classes: Enrl 50; tuition $30. Courses—Ceramics, Drawing and other special workshops
Summer School: Courses varied

UNIVERSITY OF OREGON, Dept of Fine & Applied Arts,* School of Architecture and Allied Arts, 97403. Tel 503-686-3610. *Prof* Kenneth R O'Connell, MFA. Instrs: FT 19
Pub; D; scholarships; enrl D 1400, non-maj 350, maj 1050
Degrees: BA, BS 4 yrs, BFA 5 yrs, MFA 2 yrs minimum after BFA or equivalent
Tuition: Res—$460 per term; nonres—$1335 per term; campus res available
Courses: Ceramics, Drawing, Painting, Photography, Printmaking, Sculpture, Weaving, Metalsmithing, Visual Design, Weaving
Summer School: Dir, C W Schminke. Tuition grad-$559, undergrad-$367 for term of 8 wks beginning June

FOREST GROVE

PACIFIC UNIVERSITY IN OREGON, Dept of Fine Arts,* Division of Humanities, 2043 College Way, 97116. Tel 503-357-6151. *Chmn Div* Kenneth I Combs; *Prof* Miles Shishido; *Asst Prof* Jan G Shield, MFA; *Asst Prof* Gary V Mueller, MS & MFA
Estab 1849; D & E; scholarships
Ent Req: HS dipl, SAT or ACT, counselor recommendation, transcript of acad work
Degrees: BA, MA(Teaching)
Tuition: $5400
Courses: Art History, Ceramics, Drawing, Graphic Design, Jewelry, Painting, Printmaking, Sculpture, Stained Glass
Summer School: Dir, John L Parker

GRESHAM

MOUNT HOOD COMMUNITY COLLEGE, Art Dept, 26000 SE Stark St, 97030. Tel 503-667-6422. *Chmn* Dave Spooner
Degrees: AA
Courses: Art Education, Art History, Calligraphy, Ceramics, Design, Drawing, Film, Graphic Design, Illustration, Jewelry, Painting, Printmaking, Sculpture, Stage Design, Weaving, Art Metal, Enamelling
Adult Hobby Classes: Eleven wk sessions. Courses—Calligraphy, Painting, Pottery, Drawing, Watercolor
Summer School: Dir, Dave Spooner. Enrl 60-90; two 5 wk sessions.
Courses—Ceramics, Drawing, Calligraphy, Watercolor, Molten Glass

LA GRANDE

EASTERN OREGON STATE COLLEGE, Arts & Humanities Dept,* Division of Humanities and Fine Arts, Eighth and K Sts, 97850. Tel 503-963-2171. *Dean Art* G E Young; *Assoc Prof Art* Ian Gatley, MA; *Assoc Prof Art* Thomas Morandi, MFA; *Assoc Prof Art* Thomas Dimond, MFA
Estab 1929; pub; D & E; SC 32, LC 8, GC 2
Ent Req: HS dipl
Degrees: BA & BS in Art, BA & BS in Secondary Educ with Endorsement in Art, BA & BS in Elementary Educ with Specialization in Art 4 yrs
Tuition: Res—$947 per yr; campus res available
Courses: Aesthetics, Art Education, Art History, Calligraphy, Ceramics, Design, Drawing, Lettering, Painting, Photography, Printmaking, Sculpture, Teacher Training, Textile Design, Theatre Arts, Glassblowing, Life Drawings
Adult Hobby Classes: Dir, Dr Werner Bruecher
Summer School: Dir, Dr Katsuyki Sakamoto. Term of 4-8 wks. Courses—Two or three a summer, beginning level

MARYLHURST

MARYLHURST COLLEGE, Art Dept, 97036. Tel 503-636-8141. *Chairperson* Kay Slusarenko; *Program Asst* Paul Sutinen; *Instructor* Marlene Bauer; *Instructor* Jennifer Guske; *Instructor* Dale Jones; *Instructor* Helen Lessick; *Instructor* Nancy McKimens; *Instructor* Steven Nance-Sasser; *Instructor* Christopher Rauschenberg; *Instructor* Tad Savinar; *Instructor* Margaret Shirley; *Instructor* Sr Patricia Stebinger; *Instructor* Valerie Willson
Scholarships; enrl 110
Ent Req: HS dipl or equivalent
Degrees: BA
Courses: Art Appreciation, Art History, Design, Drawing, Painting, Photography, Printmaking, Sculpture, History of Photography
Summer School: Chairperson, Kay Slusarenko

MCMINNVILLE

LINFIELD COLLEGE, Art Dept,* 97128. Tel 503-472-4121, Ext 274. *Chmn Dept* Steven Karatzas, MFA
Estab 1849, dept estab 1964; pvt; D; scholarships; SC 16, LC 2; enrl non-maj 150, maj 20
Ent Req: HS dipl
Degrees: BA 4 yr, ME 2 yr
Tuition: $4410 per yr
Courses: Advertising Design, Art Education, Art History, Calligraphy, Ceramics, Commercial Art, Constructions, Costume Design & Construction, Drawing, Film, Graphic Arts, Graphic Design, Interior Design, Lettering, Mixed Media, Painting, Photography, Printmaking, Sculpture, Stage Design, Teacher Training, Textile Design, Theatre Arts, Video

MONMOUTH

WESTERN OREGON STATE COLLEGE, Creative Arts Dept, Visual Arts,* 97361. Tel 503-838-1220, Ext 340. *Chmn Creative Arts* Ronald Wynn; *Prof* James T Mattingly. Instrs: FT 9, PT 1
Estab 1856; pub; D & E; SC 72, LC 21, GC 27; enrl total 2800
Degrees: BA and BS 4 yr
Tuition: Res—undergrad $307 per term, grad $464 per term; nonres—undergrad $975 per term, grad $795 per term
Courses: Art Education, Art History, Ceramics, Drawing, Graphic Arts, Jewelry, Lettering, Mixed Media, Painting, Photography, Printmaking, Sculpture, Art Theory, Design, Individual Studies, The Art Idea: Visual Thinking, Watercolor
Summer School: Tuition res—undergrad $323 for 12-21 hrs, grad $498 for 9-16 hrs. Courses—as above

ONTARIO

TREASURE VALLEY COMMUNITY COLLEGE, Art Dept, 650 College Blvd, 97914. Tel 503-889-6493, Ext 53. *Dept Chmn* Robert M Jackson, MFA; *Prof* Alan Stark, MFA; *Instructor* Carolyn A Jackson; *Vis Instructor* Erik Sandgren, painting 1982-1983
Estab 1961; pub; D & E; scholarships; SC 14, LC 1; enrl D 50, E 35, non-maj 10, maj 15
Ent Req: Placement testing
Degrees: AS & AA 2 yrs
Tuition: Res—$190 per quarter; out-of-county—$200 per quarter; out-of-state—$380 per quarter; out-of-country—$900 per quarter; campus res available
Courses: Art History, Drawing, Painting, Sculpture
Summer School: Chmn, Robert M Jackson. Tui $190 for term of 8 weeks beginning June 22. Courses—Ceramics, Drawing, Painting

OREGON CITY

CLACKAMAS COMMUNITY COLLEGE, Art Dept, 19600 S Molalla, 97045. Tel 503-657-8400 Ext 386. *Chmn* Norman Bursheim
Tuition: Res $20 per cr hr, nonres $73 per cr hr
Courses: Advertising Design, Art History, Calligraphy, Ceramics, Design, Drawing, Jewelry, Painting, Sculpture

PENDLETON

BLUE MOUNTAIN COMMUNITY COLLEGE, Fine Arts Dept, 2411 NW Carden Ave, PO Box 100, 97801. Tel 503-276-1260. *Chmn* William J Hughes, MFA; *Instruct* Bruce Guiwits, MA
Estab 1962, dept estab 1964; pub; D & E; SC 8, LC 2; enrl D 255, E 72
Degrees: AA, 2 yrs
Tuition: Res—undergrad $540 per yr; non-res—undergrad $792 per yr
Courses: Art History, Ceramics, Drawing, Jewelry, Lettering, Painting

PORTLAND

LEWIS AND CLARK COLLEGE, Dept of Art, 0615 SW Palatine Hill Rd, 97219. Tel 503-244-6161, Ext 305. *Chmn of Dept* Stewart Buettner; *Prof* Ken Shores, MFA; *Assoc Prof* Norman Paasche; *Asst Prof* Phyllis A Yes; *Lectr* Judith Fawkes; *Lectr* Jack Portland; *Lectr* Bruce West
Dept estab 1946; pvt; D; scholarships; SC 10, LC 2
Ent Req: HS dipl
Degrees: BS and BA 4 yr
Tuition: $624 per studio course per term, $935 per other course per term
Courses: Art History, Calligraphy, Ceramics, Drawing, Graphic Arts, History of Art & Archaeology, Jewelry, Painting, Printmaking, Sculpture, Weaving
Summer School: Dir, Sid Eiders

OREGON SCHOOL OF ARTS AND CRAFTS, 8245 SW Barnes Rd, 97225. Tel 503-297-5544. *Dir* Mary Greeley. Instrs: PT 30
Estab 1906; pvt; D & E; scholarships; SC and LC 50; enrl D 225-250, E 200-225
Ent Req: None
Degrees: None; college credit available on request through affiliate university
Tuition: All courses cost $116 per ten wk period; classes vary in laboratory fees; no campus res
Courses: Calligraphy, Ceramics, Drawing, Jewelry, Photography, Printmaking, Silversmithing, Textile Design, Design, Weaving, Woodworking, Arts & Crafts History
Children's Classes: Courses offered
Summer School: Courses—same as above; special workshops in all areas

PACIFIC NORTHWEST COLLEGE OF ART (Formerly Portland Art Museum, Museum Art School), 1219 SW Park Ave, 97205. Tel 503-226-4391. *Actg Dir* Sally Lawrence; *Instr* Frank Irby; *Instr* Terry Toedetemeir; *Instr* Manuel Izquierdo; *Instr* Robert Hanson; *Instr* Betsey Lindsay; *Instr* Harry Widman; *Instr* Jack Myers. Instrs: FT 17, PT 15
Estab 1909; pvt; D & E; scholarships; SC 24, LC 9; enrl D FT 166, PT 25, E 249
Ent Req: HS dipl, portfolio or drawing test
Degrees: BFA 4 yr
Tuition: $3550 per yr, $1775 per sem; no campus res
Courses: †Ceramics, †Drawing, †Graphic Design, †Illustration, †Painting, †Photography, Printmaking, †Sculpture, Etching, Lithography, Silkscreen
Adult Hobby Classes: Enrl 245; tuition $100-$120 per 10 week course. Courses—Calligraphy, Ceramics, Graphic Design, Illustration, Life Drawing, Painting, Photography, Printmaking, Sculpture
Children's Classes: Enrl 87; tuition $85 per sem. Courses—General Art
Summer School: Dir, Mirra Meyer. Enrl 150; tuition $100-$125

PORTLAND COMMUNITY COLLEGE, Visual & Performing Arts Dept, 12000 SW 49th, 97219. Tel 503-244-6111. *Dept Chmn* Owen Chamberlain, MFA
Estab 1961, dept estab 1963; pub; D & E; SC 40, LC 5; enrl D 864, E 282
Ent Req: None
Degrees: AA 2 yrs
Tuition: No campus res
Courses: Advertising Design, Art Education, Art History, Calligraphy, Ceramics, †Drawing, Fashion Design, Graphic Arts, Graphic Design, Illustration, Jewelry, Lettering, Painting, Photography, Sculpture, Silversmithing, Stage Design, Theatre Arts, Video
Adult Hobby Classes: Tuition varies per quarter. Courses—various
Children's Classes: Courses offered
Summer School: Dept Chmn, Owen Chamberlain. Enrl 400; Term of 8 wks beginning June. Courses—same as regular session

PORTLAND STATE UNIVERSITY, Dept of Art and Architecture, PO Box 751, 97207. Tel 503-229-3515. *Head Dept* Robert Kasal, MA; *Prof* Byron Gardner, Cert; *Prof* Jean Glazer, MA; *Prof* Raymond Grimm, MA; *Prof* James L Hansen, Dipl; *Prof* Frederick H Heidel, MFA; *Prof* James Hibbard, MFA; *Prof* Mary Constans, MA; *Prof* Melvin Katz, Cert; *Prof* Robert Morton, MA; *Prof* Leonard B Kimbrell, PhD; *Prof* Craig Cheshire, MFA; *Prof* Richard Muller, MFA; *Prof* Richard Prasch, MFA; *Assoc Prof* Jane Kristof, PhD; *Assoc Prof* Andrea Joseph, MA; *Assoc Prof* Michihiro Kosuge, MFA; *Asst Prof* Claire Kelly, MA; *Asst Prof* George Ivan Smith, MA; *Asst Prof* Lisa Audrus, PhD
Estab 1955; pub; D & E; scholarships; enrl E 2000, non-maj 1300, maj 600, grad 30, others 70
Ent Req: HS dipl
Degrees: BS and BA(Art) 4 yr, MFA(Painting, Ceramics, Sculpture) 2 yr
Tuition: Res—undergrad $452 per term, grad $673 per term; nonres—undergrad $1327 per term; campus residency available
Courses: Architecture, Art History, †Ceramics, †Drawing, †Graphic Design, †Painting, Printmaking, †Sculpture, †Applied Design, †Metalsmithing
Summer School: Enrl 4-500; term of 8-12 wks beginning June 28. Courses—vary. Two centers, one in Portland and one at Cannon Beach: The Haystack Program

REED COLLEGE, Dept of Art,* 3203 S E Woodstock Blvd, 97202. Tel 503-771-1112. Instrs: FT 6
Estab 1911; pvt; D; scholarships; SC 7, LC 5; enrl D 1150, E 15
Degrees: BA 3-5 yr
Tuition: $7430 annual tuition; campus res available
Courses: Aesthetics, Calligraphy, Drawing, Painting, Sculpture, History of Art & Architecture, Paleography

ROSEBURG

UMPQUA COMMUNITY COLLEGE, Fine & Performing Arts Dept, PO Box 967, 97470. Tel 503-440-4600, Ext 691. *Coordr* Joel Lynn Boyce Jr, MFA; *Instructor* Marie Rasmussen; *Instructor* Tina Daily; *Instructor* Susan Comerford; *Instructor* Douglas Beauchamp; *Instructor* Huff Jones; *Instructor* Ellen Perlis; *Instructor* Pat Harris; *Instructor* Billie Sheets; *Instructor* Donna Watson; *Instructor* Robert Bell; *Instructor* Lillian Douglas
Estab 1964; pub; D & E; scholarships; SC 5, LC 2; enrl D 190, E 90, maj 18
Ent Req: HS dipl
Degrees: AA 2 yr
Courses: Art History, Calligraphy, Ceramics, Drawing, Painting, Photography, Printmaking, Sculpture, Theatre Arts, Jewelry, Basic Design, Lapidary, Music Arts, Weaving
Adult Hobby Classes: Enrl 150; tuition $29 & lab fee for 10 weeks.
Courses—Calligraphy, Ceramics, Drawing, Painting, Photography, Printmaking, Sculpture

SALEM

CHEMEKETA COMMUNITY COLLEGE, Dept of Humanities & Communications, 4000 Lancaster Dr NE, PO Box 14007, 97309. Tel 503-399-5000. *Dir* Thomas Gill, MFA; *Instructor* Robert Bibler, MFA; *Instructor* Lee Jacobson, MFA; *Instructor* Donna Reid, PhD
Estab 1969, dept estab 1975; pub; D & E; scholarships; SC 9, LC 3; enrl D 125, E 75
Ent Req: None
Degrees: AA 2 yr
Tuition: Res—$15 per cr hr, $150 quarterly; nonres—$20-$50 per cr hr, $195-$485 quarterly; no campus res
Courses: Art History, Calligraphy, Ceramics, Drafting, Drawing, Film, Painting, Photography, Printmaking, Sculpture, Theatre Arts
Adult Hobby Classes: Enrl 150-200; tuition $.75 per contact hr
Summer School: Dir, Thomas Gill. Term of 8 wks

SHERIDAN

DELPHIAN SCHOOL, Box 195, Rte 2, 97378. Tel 503-843-3521
Degrees: Cert
Courses: Art Education, Calligraphy, Design, Drawing, Handicrafts, Jewelry, Painting, Printmaking, Sculpture

PENNSYLVANIA

ALLENTOWN

CEDAR CREST COLLEGE, Art Dept,* 18104. Tel 215-437-4471. *Prof* Ryland W Greene; *Chmn* Nelson R Maniscalco, MFA. Instrs: FT 3, PT 2
Estab 1867; pvt; D & E; scholarships; SC 11, LC 4; enrl 750
Ent Req: HS dipl, CEEB
Degrees: BA, BS, Interdisciplinary Fine Arts Maj (art, theatre, music, dance, creative writing), 4 yr
Tuition: Res—$8200 per yr; nonres—$5600 per yr
Courses: Aesthetics, Art Education, Art History, Ceramics, Drawing, Jewelry, Painting, Sculpture, Theatre Arts, Comparative Study of Art, Metal Forming
Summer School: Courses—Ceramics, Jewelry-Metalsmithing

MUHLENBERG COLLEGE, Dept of Art, Chew St, 18104. Tel 215-433-3191. *Prof* Ellen Callmann, PhD; *Asst Prof* Raymond S Barnes, MFA; *Asst Prof* Carol Parker, MFA; *Asst Prof* Joseph Elliott, MFA
Estab 1848; den; D & E; SC 16, LC 12; enrl D 320, non-maj 284, maj 36
Ent Req: HS dipl, SAT, 3 achievement tests and English Composition Achievement required
Degrees: BA 4 yrs
Tuition: $5150; campus res—room & board $1675
Courses: Art Education, †Art History, Ceramics, Drawing, Graphic Arts, History of Art & Archaeology, Painting, Photography, Printmaking, Sculpture, †Studio Arts

BETHLEHEM

LEHIGH UNIVERSITY, Dept of Art and Architecture, Chandler-Ullmann Hall, Bldg 17, 18015. Tel 215-861-3610. *Chmn Dept* Nicholas Adams, PhD; *Prof* Richard J Redd, MFA; *Prof* Carlos J Alvare, MArch; *Assoc Prof* Ricardo Viera, MFA; *Asst Prof* Lucy Gans, MFA; *Asst Prof* Paul Felder, MSArch. Instrs: PT 1
Estab 1925; pvt; D & E; SC 22, LC 16; enrl D & E 700
Ent Req: HS dipl, SAT, CEEB
Degrees: BA 4 yrs
Tuition: $8000 per yr, $4000 per sem; campus residency available
Courses: †Architecture, †Art History, Drawing, Mixed Media, Painting, Photography, Printmaking, †Studio Art
Summer School: Dir, Dr Norman Sam. Courses—Teacher Training

MORAVIAN COLLEGE, Dept of Art, Church Street Campus, 18018. Tel 215-861-1480. *Chmn Dept* Rudy S Ackerman, DEd; *Assoc Prof* Daniel Tereshko, MFA; *Asst Prof* Charlene Engel, PhD; *Asst Prof* Judy Ross, MA; *Instr* Dennis Johnson, MA; *Ceramist-in-Residence* Renzo Faggioli, Master Craftsman
Estab 1807, dept estab 1963; pvt; D & E; scholarships; SC 15, LC 8; enrl D 350, E 15, non-maj 1200, maj 50
Ent Req: HS dipl
Degrees: BA and BS 4 yrs
Tuition: $5660 per yr
Courses: †Art History, †Ceramics, †Drawing, Film, Jewelry, †Painting, †Photography, Printmaking, Sculpture, Silversmithing, Textile Design
Adult Hobby Classes: Enrl 15; tuition $340 per course. Courses—Design, Drawing, Painting, Sculpture
Summer School: Dir, Susan Schuehler. Enrl 75; tuition $340 per course, term of 6 weeks. Courses—Art History, Ceramics, Metalsmithing, Painting

NORTHAMPTON COUNTY AREA COMMUNITY COLLEGE, Art Dept, 3835 Green Pond Rd, 18017. Tel 215-865-5351. *Prog Coordr* Gerald Rowan; *Asst Prof* Andrew Szoke; *Asst Prof* Tom Short
Estab 1967; pub; D & E; scholarships; SC 12, LC 8; enrl D 100, E 350
Ent Req: HS dipl, portfolio
Degrees: AAS(Advertising), cert in photography
Tuition: $32 per sem hr
Courses: Advertising Design, Architecture, Art History, Ceramics, Commercial Art, Drafting, Drawing, Fashion Arts, Graphic Arts, Graphic Design, Handicrafts, History of Art & Archaeology, Illustration, Interior Design, Lettering, Painting, Photography, Printmaking, Sculpture, Pottery
Adult Hobby Classes: Courses—Art, Photography

BLOOMSBURG

BLOOMSBURG UNIVERSITY, Dept of Art, Blakeless Center for the Humanities, 17815. Tel 717-389-4184. *Chmn Dept* Barbara J Strohman, MFA; *Prof* Percival R Roberts III, EdD; *Assoc Prof* Stewart Nagel, MFA; *Assoc Prof* Robert Koslosky, MA; *Assoc Prof* Kenneth T Wilson, MA; *Asst Prof* Karl Beamer, MFA; *Asst Prof* Gary F Clark, MA; *Asst Prof* John Cook, MA; *Asst Prof* Charles Thomas Walter, PhD
Estab 1839, dept estab 1940; pub; D & E; scholarships; SC 7, LC 12; enrl D 1800, E 200, maj 75
Ent Req: HS dipl
Degrees: BA(Art Studio) and BA(Art History) 4 yrs, MA(Art Studio)
Tuition: Res—$740 per sem; nonres—$1295 per sem; campus residency available
Courses: Aesthetics, Art Education, Art History, Ceramics, Drawing, History of Art & Archaeology, Jewelry, Painting, Printmaking, Sculpture, Stage Design, Textile Design, Theatre Arts, Crafts, General Design, Weaving
Adult Hobby Classes: Creative arts & crafts mini-courses offered
Children's Classes: Enrl 20; tuition $30 per 8 sessions
Summer School: Dean, Daniel Pantaleo. Enrl 200-300; tuition $62 per cr hr. Courses—vary

BLUE BELL

MONTGOMERY COUNTY COMMUNITY COLLEGE, Communicating Arts Dept, 340 De Kalb Pike, 19422. Tel 215-641-6327. *Chmn* Dr Albert Rauer; *Coordr & Assoc Prof* Mike Smyser, MFA; *Assoc Prof* Dorothy Zimmer, MED; *Assoc Prof* Roger Cairns, MFA; *Assoc Prof* Tony Kinkay, MFA; *Instr* Frank Short, MFA. Instrs: FT 6, PT 8
Pub; D & E; scholarships; LC 3; enrl D 250
Ent Req: HS dipl
Degrees: AA Fine Arts, AAS Commercial Art
Tuition: County res—undergrad $494 per sem, $41 per credit hr; nonres—undergrad $988 per sem, $82 per credit hr
Courses: Advertising Design, Art Education, Art History, Ceramics, †Commercial Art, Drawing, Film, Graphic Arts, Graphic Design, Illustration, Painting, Photography, Printmaking, Sculpture, Teacher Training, Theatre Arts, Video, †Fine Art
Summer School: Dir, Albert Rauer. Enrl 200; tuition $41 per cr, 2 six wk sem. Courses—Most classes offered on rotating basis

BRYN MAWR

BRYN MAWR COLLEGE, Dept of the History of Art,* 19010. Tel 215-645-5334. *Chmn Dept & Assoc Prof* Dale Kinney, PhD; *Prof* James E Snyder, PhD; *Prof* Phyllis B Bober, PhD; *Assoc Prof* David Cast, PhD; *Assoc Prof* Steven Levine, PhD; *Asst Prof* Gridley McKim-Smith, PhD; *Asst Prof* Kim Orr-McMahon, MA. Instrs: FT 4, PT 2
Estab 1913; pvt; W (men in grad school); scholarships and fel; LC 10, GC 8; enrl maj 15, grad 30, others 250
Degrees: BA 4 yr, MA, PhD
Tuition: $8345 per yr; campus res available
Courses: Art History

HARCUM JUNIOR COLLEGE, Dept of Fine Arts,* 19010. Tel 215-525-4100, Ext 215. *Prof* Martin Zipin. Instrs: FT 1, PT 5
Estab 1915; pvt; W; D & E; scholarships; SC 7, LC 1; enrl D 40, E 8, maj 10
Ent Req: HS dipl
Degrees: AA 2 yr
Tuition: $2500 per yr
Courses: Commercial Art, Drawing, Fashion Arts, Graphic Design, History of Art & Archaeology, Lettering, Painting, Sculpture

CALIFORNIA

CALIFORNIA UNIVERSITY OF PENNSYLVANIA, Dept of Art, 15419. Tel 412-938-4000. *Dept Chmn* Raymond Dunlevy
Estab 1852, dept estab 1968; pub; D & E; SC 20, LC 5; enrl maj 64
Ent Req: SAT
Degrees: BA 4 yrs
Courses: Advertising Design, Architecture, Art History, Calligraphy, Ceramics, Drafting, Drawing, Graphic Arts, Graphic Design, Industrial Design, Intermedia, Jewelry, Painting, Photography, Printmaking, Sculpture, Teacher Training
Adult Hobby Classes: Enrl 25 per class. Courses—Pottery, Stained Glass
Summer School: Chmn, Raymond E Dunlevy. Term of 5 or 10 wks beginning June

CARLISLE

DICKINSON COLLEGE, Fine Arts Dept, High St, 17013. Tel 717-243-5121. *Chairperson & Assoc Prof* Sharon Hirsh, PhD; *Prof* Dennis Akin, MFA; *Assoc Prof* Harry Krebs, PhD; *Asst Prof* Barbara Diduk, MFA; *Instructor* Mary Pardo, MA
Estab 1773, dept estab 1940; pvt; D; SC 7, LC 11; enrl 250, non-maj 200, maj 50
Ent Req: HS dipl, SAT
Degrees: BA and BS 4 yrs
Tuition: Res—undergrad $8995 per yr; campus res available
Courses: †Art History, Ceramics, Drawing, Mixed Media, Painting, Photography, Printmaking, Sculpture
Summer School: Dir, Peggy Garrett. Tuition $125 per course for term of 5 1/2 wks beginning May. Courses—per regular session

CHELTENHAM

CHELTENHAM ART CENTRE, 439 Ashbourne Rd, 19012. Tel 215-379-4660. *Pres* Lorraine Alexander; *Exec Dir* Marie Rennich
Estab 1940; enrl 3600
Courses: Drawing, Jewelry, Mixed Media, Painting, Photography, Sculpture, Pottery, Stained Glass, Theatre Class

CHEYNEY

CHEYNEY UNIVERSITY OF PENNSYLVANIA, Dept of Art,* 19319. Tel 215-758-2286. *Prof* Samuel L Curtis, PhD
Estab 1937; pub; D & E; scholarships; SC 16, LC 4
Ent Req: HS dipl, ent exam
Degrees: BA 4 yrs
Tuition: Res—$740 per sem; nonres—$1295 per sem
Courses: Aesthetics, Ceramics, Drawing, Graphic Arts, Handicrafts, History of Art & Archaeology, Painting, Sculpture, †Art Therapy

CLARION

CLARION UNIVERSITY OF PENNSYLVANIA, Dept of Art, 16214. Tel 814-226-2291. *Chmn* Eugene A Seelye, MA; *Prof* Francis C Baptist, EdD; *Prof* Robert D Hobbs, EdD; *Assoc Prof* William T Edwards Jr, EdD; *Assoc Prof* William E Grosch, MEd; *Assoc Prof* Alfred B Charley, MFA; *Assoc Prof* Andor S P-Jobb, MA; *Asst Prof* Cathie Joslyn, MFA
Estab 1867; pub; D & E; SC 12, LC 7; enrl D & E 925 per sem, maj 25
Ent Req: HS dipl
Degrees: BFA(Art)
Tuition: Campus residency available
Courses: Art Education, Art History, †Ceramics, Drawing, Graphic Arts, Graphic Design, Handicrafts, Jewelry, †Painting, †Sculpture, Calligraphy, †Fabric—Fiber, 3-D Design
Adult Hobby Classes: Enrl 20; tuition $55-$65 for 9-12 wk course. Courses—Calligraphy, Ceramics, Drawing, Painting
Summer School: Dir, Dr Charles Shontz. Tuition $62 per cr hr for 2-5 wk sessions. Courses—various

CRESSON

MOUNT ALOYSIUS JUNIOR COLLEGE, Art Dept,* Rte 22, 16630. Tel 814-886-4131, Ext 40. *Chmn* Vivian Wilkinson, MEd. Instrs: FT 2
Estab 1939; den; D & E; scholarships; SC 10, LC 12; enrl D 212, E 8, maj 27
Ent Req: HS dipl, SAT, ACT, health record, art portfolio and interview
Degrees: AA 2 yr
Tuition: $3750 annual tuition; campus res available
Courses: Advertising Design, Art Education, Art History, Calligraphy, Ceramics, Commercial Art, Display, Drawing, Graphic Design, Painting, Photography, Printmaking, Sculpture, Teacher Training, Art Therapy, Bio-Medical Communications, Fabrics, Two & Three-Dimensional Design, Typography

DALLAS

COLLEGE MISERICORDIA, Art Dept,* 18612. Tel 717-675-2181, Ext 234. *Art Program Dir* Maxine Watter Silva, MFA; *Asst Prof* Denise Faleski, MA; *Instructor* Cora Artim, MA; *Instructor* Brian Benedetti, MA; *Instructor* Sr Elaine Tulanowski, MA
Estab 1924, dept estab 1965; pvt; D & E; scholarships; SC 35, LC 10; enrl D 40, non-maj 25, maj 40, others 4 extension
Ent Req: HS dipl
Degrees: AAS, BA, BS, BM
Tuition: Campus residency available
Courses: Aesthetics, †Art Education, Art History, Calligraphy, Ceramics, Drawing, Painting, Photography, Printmaking, Sculpture, Teacher Training, Theatre Arts
Summer School: Dir, Sr Mary Glennon. Courses—vary

EASTON

LAFAYETTE COLLEGE, Dept of Art, 18042. Tel 215-250-5356, 5357, 5358, 5358 & 5360. *Dept Head* Ed Kerns. Instrs: FT 4
Estab 1827; pvt; D & E; scholarships; SC 8, LC 12; enrl D 300, E 250, non-maj 1, maj 17
Ent Req: HS dipl, ent exam, selective admis
Degrees: BS and AB 4 yr
Tuition: $7725 per yr
Courses: Art History, Drawing, Painting, Printmaking, Sculpture, History of Architecture, Two & Three-Dimensional Design

EAST STROUDSBURG

EAST STROUDSBURG STATE COLLEGE, Art Dept,* Fine Arts Bldg, 18301. Tel 717-424-3254. *Prof* Dr Irene Mitchel, EdD; *Assoc Prof* Angelo Carniel, MFA; *Assoc Prof* Daniel Luongo, MEd; *Assoc Prof* John McIntyre, MA; *Asst Prof* Edward Demansky, MEd
Estab 1894; pub; D & E; scholarships offered; SC 17, LC 6, grad 1; enrl D 45
Ent Req: HS dipl, HS equivalency
Degrees: BA in Fine Arts
Tuition: $740 per sem; campus res available
Courses: Aesthetics, Art Education, Art History, Calligraphy, Ceramics, Drawing, Film, Graphic Arts, Graphic Design, Landscape Architecture, Lettering, Mixed Media, Painting, Photography, Printmaking, Sculpture, Silversmithing, Stage Design, Theatre Arts, Video
Summer School: Dir, Susan R Hicks. Tuition res—undergrad $158 per cr hr, grad $78 per cr hr; nonres—undergrad $102 per cr hr, grad $78 per cr hr for 3 wk pre & post session & 6 week main session

EDINBORO

EDINBORO UNIVERSITY OF PENNSYLVANIA, Art Dept, 16444. Tel 814-732-2406. *Chmn Art Dept* Robert W Milnes, MFA; *Chmn 2-D Area* Anthony Ko, MA; *Chmn 3-D Area* Charles McClecny, MFA; *Chmn Crafts* Eugene Bahling, MEd; *Chmn Art History* Barthwell Farmer, MA; *Chmn Art Educ* Dorn Howlett, MA; *Cur Coll* L Rosenfeld, MA. Instrs: FT 36
Estab 1857; pub; D & E; scholarships; SC 86, LC 30, GC 20; enrl D 400 art maj, non-maj 6000, grad 30
Ent Req: HS dipl, SAT
Degrees: BSEd, BFA and BA 4 yrs, MEd 1 yr, MFA 2 yrs
Tuition: Res—undergrad $1480 per yr, $740 per sem, grad $740 per sem, $82 per cr hr; nonres—undergrad $2590 per yr, $1295 per sem, grad $740 per sem, $82 per cr hr; campus residency available
Courses: Aesthetics, †Art Education, †Art History, †Ceramics, †Conceptual Art, †Drawing, †Film, Graphic Design, Illustration, †Jewelry, Lettering, Mixed Media, †Painting, †Photography, †Printmaking, †Sculpture, †Silversmithing, Teacher Training, †Textile Design, †Communications Graphics, †Weaving
Adult Hobby Classes: Various studio, art library classes
Summer School: Dir, Robert Milnes. Courses—Drawing, Jewelry, Painting, Printmaking, Sculpture, Textile Design, Weaving

ERIE

MERCYHURST COLLEGE, Dept of Art, 501 E 38th St, 16501. Tel 814-864-0681. *Dept Chmn* Dan Burke. Instrs: PT 4
Estab 1926, dept estab 1950; pvt; D & E; scholarships; SC 45, LC 12; enrl D 100, E 30, maj 100
Ent Req: HS dipl, col boards, portfolio review
Degrees: BA 4 yr
Courses: Advertising Design, Art Education, Art History, Ceramics, Commercial Art, Drawing, Jewelry, Painting, Photography, Printmaking, Sculpture, Art Appreciation, Art Foundations, Art Therapy, Child Art, Contemporary Art Theories, Creative Arts for Adolescents and Children, Creativity, Fabrics, Fibers, Independent Study, Individualized Studio, Senior Seminar, Teaching Internship, Television Internship
Adult Hobby Classes: 6-8 wks. Courses—Crafts, Drawing, Painting
Summer School: Dir, Daniel Burke. Term of 5-6 wks beginning June/July. Courses—vary

FACTORYVILLE

KEYSTONE JUNIOR COLLEGE, Fine Arts Dept, College Avenue (Mailing add: LaPlume, PA 18440). Tel 717-945-5141. *Chmn Fine Arts* Karl O Neuroth, MEd; *Assoc Prof* William Tersteeg, MFA; *Assoc Prof* Clifton A Prokop, MFA; *Instr* Renee Foulks, MFA
Estab 1868, dept estab 1965; pvt; D & weekends; scholarships; SC 15, LC 2; enrl D 155, weekenders 15, non-maj 100, maj 55
Ent Req: HS dipl, SAT
Degrees: AFA 2 yrs
Tuition: Res—$3780 per yr; campus res—room & board $2400
Courses: Art History, Ceramics, Drawing, Handicrafts, Painting, Photography, Printmaking, Sculpture, Color, Intro to Commercial Design, Life Drawing, Three-Dimensional Design, Two-Dimensional Design
Summer School: Dean of College, William Messner. Enrl limited to 18; tuition $100 per cr for term of 5 wks beginning June. Courses—Ceramics, Photography

GETTYSBURG

GETTYSBURG COLLEGE, Dept of Art,* 17325. Tel 717-334-3131, Ext 220.
Chmn James Agard, MFA; *Asst Prof* Alan Paulson; *Instr* Carol Small
Estab 1832, dept estab 1956; pvt; D; scholarships; SC 10, LC 15; enrl D 300
Ent Req: HS dipl, ent exam
Degrees: BA 4 yrs
Tuition: $7060 annual tuition; campus res available
Courses: Aesthetics, †Art History, †Drawing, †Painting, †Printmaking, †Sculpture, Basic Design, Figure Drawing

GLENSIDE

BEAVER COLLEGE, Dept of Fine Arts, Easton & Church Rds, 19038. Tel 215-572-2900. *Chmn* Jack Davis, MA; *Asst Prof* Bonnie Hayes, MA, ABD; *Asst Prof* Robert Mauro, MFA; *Asst Prof* Dennis Kuronen, MFA; *Asst Prof* Ann Williams, MFA. Instrs: PT 7
Estab 1853; pvt; D & E; scholarships; SC 43, LC 14; enrl in Col D FT 639, PT 133, non-maj in dept 30, maj in dept 140
Ent Req: HS dipl, SAT, ACT, optional portfolio review
Degrees: BA and BFA 4 yrs, MA(Educ) 1 yr
Tuition: $5800 per year, $2900 per sem, $676 per 4 cr course; campus res—room & board $2600
Courses: Advertising Design, Aesthetics, †Art Education, †Art History, †Ceramics, †Commercial Art, Drawing, †Graphic Design, †Illustration, †Interior Design, †Jewelry, †Painting, †Photography, †Printmaking, Teacher Training
Summer School: Chmn, Jack Davis. Enrl approx 200; tuition $100 per cr hr for term of 7 wks beginning June 8. Courses—Painting, Printmaking

GREENSBURG

SETON HILL COLLEGE, Dept of Art, 15601. Tel 412-834-2200, Ext 393.
Chairperson Josefa Filkosky, MFA; *Assoc Prof* Suzanne Hardeny, PhD; *Assoc Prof* Raymond DeFazio, MEd; *Asst Prof* Laura Bench, MFA; *Instr* Maureen McDonnell
Estab 1918, dept estab 1950; den; D & E; scholarships; SC 40, LC 8; enrl D 200, maj 65, minor 10, PT 20, art therapy 10, art management 12
Ent Req: HS dipl, review portfolio
Degrees: BFA 4 yr
Tuition: $4500 per yr; campus res—room and board $2400 per yr
Courses: †Art Education, Calligraphy, †Ceramics, †Drawing, Film, Goldsmithing, †Graphic Design, Handicrafts, †Jewelry, Lettering, †Painting, †Photography, †Printmaking, †Sculpture, †Silversmithing, †Teacher Training, Fabrics
Adult Hobby Classes: Enrl 10-15; tuition $12 per cr. Courses—Calligraphy, Illustration
Summer School: Dir, Jan Orsis. Enrl 20-30. Courses—Art in Elementary Schools, Ceramics, Photography

GREENVILLE

THIEL COLLEGE, Dept of Art, College Ave, 16125. Tel 412-588-7700, Ext 265.
Chmn Dept Ronald A Pivovar, MFA
Estab 1866, dept estab 1965; pvt; D & E; scholarships; SC 14, LC 11; enrl D 105, non-maj 65, maj 40
Ent Req: HS dipl, interviews
Degrees: BA 4 yrs
Courses: Art History, Ceramics, Drawing, Graphic Arts, Jewelry, Painting, Printmaking, Sculpture, Stage Design, Theatre Arts
Summer School: Asst Acad Dean, Richard Houpt. Term of 4 wks beginning June 3. Courses—Art History, Extended Studies

HARRISBURG

HARRISBURG AREA COMMUNITY COLLEGE, Division of Communication and the Arts, 3300 Cameron Street Rd, 17110. Tel 717-236-9533. *Chairperson* Paul Hurley, PhD; *Prof* Robert Wicks, MA; *Assoc Prof* Edith Socolow, MA; *Instr* Ronald Talbott, MFA; *Vis Prof* George Rey; *Vis Prof* Lawrence von Barann
Estab 1964; pub; D & E; SC 15, LC 5; enrl D 500, E 100, maj 100
Ent Req: HS dipl
Degrees: AA 2 yrs
Tuition: Res—undergrad $700 per yr, $350 per sem, $29 per cr hr; out of district—undergrad $1400 per yr, $700 per sem, $58 per cr hr; out-of-state $2100 per yr, $1050 per sem, $87 per cr hr; no campus res
Courses: Art History, Ceramics, Commercial Art, Drafting, Drawing, Film, Graphic Arts, Handicrafts, Jewelry, Painting, Photography, Printmaking, Sculpture, Stage Design, Theatre Arts
Adult Hobby Classes: Courses—Calligraphy, Drawing, Painting, Photography, Pottery
Children's Classes: Courses—Creative Dramatics, Calligraphy
Summer School: Dir, Paul Hurley. Courses—vary

HAVERFORD

HAVERFORD COLLEGE, Fine Arts Dept,* 19041. Tel 215-896-1266. *Chmn* R Christopher Cairns; *Prof* Charles Stegeman; *Asst Prof* William E Williams, MFA
Estab 1833, dept estab 1969; pvt; D, M; scholarships; enrl maj 15
Ent Req: HS dipl, programs in cooperation with Bryn Mawr College, Fine Arts Department
Degrees: BA 4 yrs
Tuition: $8000 annual yr; campus res available
Courses: Drawing, Graphic Arts, History of Art & Archaeology, Painting, Photography, Sculpture

MAINLINE CENTER OF THE ARTS, Old Buck Rd & Lancaster Ave, 19041. Tel 215-LA5-0272. *Admin Exec Dir* Eleanor Daitzman; *Instr* Jerilyn Arnon, MB; *Instr* Pandy Bevans; *Instr* Joyce Borden; *Instr* Janet Cebular; *Instr* Nancy Cohen; *Instr* Jacqueline Cotter, BFA; *Instr* Eugene Daub, BFA; *Instr* Ruth Elgart, BFA; *Instr* Bruce Feldman; *Instr* Robert Finch, BFA; *Instr* J Dustin Rode-Finch, BFA; *Instr* Joanne Fink, MBA; *Instr* Rose Brein Finkel, EFA; *Instr* Arlene Renee Finston, BFA; *Instr* Cyril Gardner, BFA; *Instr* Albert Gury, BFA; *Instr* John Gwinn, MFA; *Instr* Julia Hogan, BS; *Instr* Marilynn Briggs Juliano, BFA; *Instr* Sandra Kohler, PhD; *Instr* Maxine Krinsky, MBA; *Instr* Ronald F Linder, MBA; *Instr* Kathleen B Logue; *Instr* Jane Milner; *Instr* Charles L Reeder, MEd; *Instr* Salee Rush, MBA; *Instr* Amy Sarner, BA; *Instr* Itzhak Sankowsky, MA; *Instr* Marcia Wohl, BFA; *Instr* Marianne Tebbens, BA; *Instr* Ezio Zuccarini
Estab 1937; pvt; D & E; SC 45; enrl D 300, E 250
Ent Req: Must be member of the Arts Center
Tuition: $40 to $100 for 8-14 wks; no campus res
Courses: Art History, Calligraphy, Ceramics, Collages, Commercial Art, Conceptual Art, Constructions, Drawing, Film, Goldsmithing, Graphic Arts, Graphic Design, Handicrafts, Illustration, Jewelry, Lettering, Mixed Media, Painting, Photography, Printmaking, Sculpture, Silversmithing, Theatre Arts, Basketry, Batik, Cartoon & Caricature, China Painting, Deocrative Arts, Tie-dyeing, Weaving
Children's Classes: Enrl 150; tuition $50 for 14 wks. Courses—General Arts, Pottery
Summer School: Admin Dir, Eleanor Daitzman. Tuition varies, classes begin mid-June. Courses—same as above

HUNTINGDON

JUNIATA COLLEGE, Dept of Art, Moore St, 16652. Tel 814-643-4310. *Chmn Dept* Alexander T McBride. Instrs: FT 1, PT 1
Estab 1876; pvt; D; scholarships; SC 12, LC 3; enrl 300, maj 10
Ent Req: HS dipl
Degrees: BA 4 yrs
Tuition: Campus res
Courses: Aesthetics, Ceramics, Drawing, Graphic Arts, History of Art & Archaeology, Painting, Photography, Teacher Training, Theatre Arts
Summer School: Dir, Dr James D Westwater. Courses—Art History, Ceramics, Studio Art

INDIANA

INDIANA UNIVERSITY OF PENNSYLVANIA, Dept of Art and Art Education, Sprowls Hall, 15705. Tel 412-357-2530. *Chairperson* Joanne P Lovette, DA; *Instructor* Dr B Balsiger, PhD; *Instructor* Thomas Dongilla, MEd; *Instructor* Dr H Russell, DA; *Instructor* Dr R C Seelhorst, EdD; *Instructor* Dr R J Vislosky, EdD
Estab 1875, dept estab 1875; pub; D & E; scholarships; SC 26, LC 21, GC 30; enrl D 315, non-maj 850, maj 315, grad 50
Ent Req: HS dipl, SAT, portfolio review
Degrees: BS(Art Educ), BA(Humanities with Art Concentration), BFA 4 yr, MEd, MA 2 yr
Tuition: Res—undergrad $900 per yr, grad $1750 per yr; nonres—undergrad $1700 per yr, grad $1750 per yr; campus res—room & board $1200 per yr
Courses: Aesthetics, †Art Education, Art History, Ceramics, Collages, Conceptual Art, Constructions, Drawing, Goldsmithing, Graphic Arts, Graphic Design, Jewelry, Lettering, Mixed Media, Museum Staff Training, Painting, Printmaking, Restoration & Conservation, Sculpture, Silversmithing, Teacher Training, Textile Design, Art Therapy
Adult Hobby Classes: Enrl 60; tuition $20 - $30 per sem. Courses—Drawing, Art Appreciation
Children's Classes: Enrl 150; Courses—all studio areas
Summer School: Dir, J P Lovette. Enrl 200; tuition regular acad sem cr cost. Courses—Studios, Art History

JOHNSTOWN

UNIVERSITY OF PITTSBURGH AT JOHNSTOWN, Dept of Fine Arts, 15904. Tel 814-266-9661. *Assoc Prof* Richard Channin, PhD
Estab 1968; pub, pvt; D & E; SC 4, LC 10; enrl D 120, maj 3
Ent Req: HS dipl, SAT
Degrees: BA 4 yrs
Tuition: Campus res available
Courses: Aesthetics, Art Education, Art History, †Commercial Art, Drawing, Film, History of Art & Archaeology, Painting, Photography, Stage Design, Theatre Arts
Summer School: Enrl 30. Courses—Contemporary Art

LANCASTER

FRANKLIN AND MARSHALL COLLEGE, Art Dept, 17604. Tel 717-291-4199.
Chmn Dept Linda Cunningham, MFA; *Assoc Prof* Folke T Kihlstedt; *Asst Prof* Diana Galis, PhD; *Asst Prof* James Peterson, MFA; *Adjunct Instr* Jeanette Cole, MFA
Estab 1966; pvt; D & E; scholarships; SC 10, LC 20; enrl in col D 2011, E 605
Ent Req: HS dipl, SAT
Degrees: BA 4 yr
Tuition: Res—$7530 per yr
Courses: Architecture, Art History, Drawing, History of Art & Archaeology, Painting, Printmaking, Sculpture, Basic Design
Summer School: Dir, Russ Burke. Tuition $460 for course, two 5 wk sessions beginning June 6. Courses—Architecture, Drawing, Painting

LEWISBURG

BUCKNELL UNIVERSITY, Dept of Art, 17837. Tel 717-524-1307. *Head Dept* William Lasansky, MFA; *Prof* Neil Anderson, MFA; *Prof* James Turnure, PhD; *Prof* Gerald Eager, PhD; *Prof* Rosalyn Richards, MFA; *Lectr* John McCluskey
Estab 1846; pvt; D; scholarships; SC 19, LC 20, GC 30; enrl D 500, non-maj 450, maj 50, grad 2
Ent Req: HS dipl
Degrees: BA 4 yrs
Tuition: $8250 per yr; campus residency available
Courses: Art History, Drawing, Graphic Arts, History of Art & Archaeology, Painting, Printmaking, Sculpture
Summer School: Dir Summer Session, Hugh McKeegan. Enrl 426; term of 3 or 6 wks beginning June 4. Courses—Lectures, Studio

LOCK HAVEN

LOCK HAVEN STATE COLLEGE, Art Dept,* 17745. Tel 717-893-2000. *Chmn* E May Dyer. Instrs: FT 4
Scholarships offered
Degrees: BA
Tuition: $700 per sem
Courses: Art Appreciation, Art Education, Art History, Ceramics, Drawing, Jewelry, Jewelry, Painting, Photography, Printmaking, Sculpture, Stage Design, Textile Design, Weaving

LORETTO

ST FRANCIS COLLEGE, Fine Arts Dept,* 15940. Tel 814-472-7000. *Chmn* Micheal Strueber
Scholarships offered
Tuition: $120 per cr hr
Courses: Art Appreciation, Art History, Ceramics, Design, Drawing, Handicrafts, Jewelry, Painting, Photography, Printmaking, Sculpture, Textile Design, Weaving

MANSFIELD

MANSFIELD STATE COLLEGE, Art Dept, School of Professional Studies, 16933. Tel 717-662-4092. *Chmn Dept* James G Cecere, DEd; *Prof* Steve Bencetic, DEd; *Assoc Prof* Dale Witherow, MFA; *Prof* Ernest Frombach, MEd; *Assoc Prof* Tom Loomis, MA; *Asst Prof* Sam Thomas, MEd; *Asst Prof* Stan Zujkowski, MS
Estab 1857; pub; D; SC 26, LC 18; enrl D 700, maj 90
Ent Req: HS dipl, SAT, portfolio and interview
Degrees: BA(Studio Art), BA(Art History) and BSE(Art Educ) 4 yr, MEd(Art Educ)
Tuition: Res—$950 per yr, $475 per sem; nonres—$1780 per yr, $890 per sem; campus residency available
Courses: Aesthetics, Art Education, Art History, Ceramics, Drawing, Jewelry, Painting, Photography, Printmaking, Sculpture, Fibers, Studio Crafts
Children's Classes: Tuition $10 per sem for Sat classes
Summer School: Term of 5-6 wks beginning June 9. Courses—Ceramics, Drawing, Fibers, Graduate Courses, Painting, Printmaking, Sculpture, Studio Courses

MEADVILLE

ALLEGHENY COLLEGE, Art Dept, 16335. Tel 814-724-3371. *Head Dept* Richard Kleeman, MFA
Estab 1815, dept estab 1930; pvt; D; scholarships; SC 17, LC 7; enrl 450, maj 15
Ent Req: HS dipl, ent exam
Degrees: BA and BS 4 yr
Courses: Art History, Ceramics, Drawing, Graphic Arts, Lettering, Painting, Photography, Printmaking, Sculpture
Summer School: Dir, R Kleeman. Enrl 40. Courses—Art History, Studio Art

MEDIA

DELAWARE COUNTY COMMUNITY COLLEGE, Communications and Humanities House,* Route 252 & Media Line Rd, 19063. Tel 215-353-5400. *Assoc Dean Instruction* D James Donald; *Prof* John Botkin, MFA; *Prof* Alf Svendsen, MFA; *Prof* Al DeProspero, EdM
Estab 1967; pub; D & E
Degrees: AS, AA and AAS 2 yrs
Tuition: District res—$348 per sem; non-distrcit res—$696 per sem; non-state res—$1044 per sem; no campus res
Courses: Art Education, Art History, Drawing, Graphic Design, Painting, Photography, Printmaking, Theatre Arts
Adult Hobby Classes: Enrl varies; tuition varies. Courses—Calligraphy, Crafts, Drawing, Graphic Design, Interior Design, Needlepoint, Photography, Stained Glass, Sketching, Woodcarving
Summer School: Tuition res $27 per cr hr, nonres $81 per cr hr for term of 6 wks. Courses—Drawing, Painting

MIDDLETOWN

PENNSYLVANIA STATE UNIVERSITY, CAPITOL CAMPUS, Dept of Humanities, 17057. Tel 717-948-6189. *Prof* Irwin Richman, PhD; *Asst Prof* Troy Thomas, MFA & PhD; *Instr* Linda Ross, MA. Instrs: PT 10
Estab 1965; pub; D & E; scholarships; SC 7, LC 15; enrl D & E 60, grad 40
Ent Req: 2 yrs of col or CLEP
Degrees: BHumanities 2 yrs, MA
Tuition: Res—$2312 per yr; nonres—$4644 per yr; campus res—room & board $2464 per yr
Courses: Aesthetics, Architecture, Art Education, Art History, Drawing, Graphic Design, History of Art & Archaeology, Mixed Media, Painting, Photography, Theatre Arts, Video

MILLERSVILLE

MILLERSVILLE UNIVERSITY, Art Dept, 17551. Tel 717-872-3298. *Dir* R Gordon Wise, EdD
Estab 1855, dept estab 1965; pub; D & E; SC 65, LC 10, GC 64; enrl maj 210, grad 20
Ent Req: HS dipl
Degrees: BS(Art Educ), BA(Art), BFA 4 yr, MEd(Art Educ) 1 yr
Tuition: $750 per sem
Courses: Art Education, Art History, Ceramics, Drawing, Film, Graphic Arts, Illustration, Jewelry, Lettering, Painting, Photography, Printmaking, Sculpture, Silversmithing, Teacher Training, Weaving, Fabrics, Visual Communication
Summer School: Dir, Gordon Wise. Enrl 300; terms of 5 wks, two sessions beginning June and July. Studio courses offered

MONROEVILLE

COMMUNITY COLLEGE OF ALLEGHENY COUNTY, BOYCE CAMPUS, Art Dept, Beatty Rd, 15146. Tel 412-327-1327. *Assoc Prof* Bruno Sorento, MFA; *Assoc Prof* Jeanne Connors, MEd
Pub; D & E; SC 13, LC 1; enrl D 200, E 40, non-maj 140, maj 60
Ent Req: HS dipl
Degrees: AS 2 yrs
Tuition: Nonres—undergrad $795 per yr, $400 per sem; PT $33 per cr; no campus res
Courses: Art History, Ceramics, Collages, Constructions, Drawing, Graphic Arts, Mixed Media, Painting, Photography, Printmaking, Sculpture
Adult Hobby Classes: Courses—Calligraphy, Drawing, Painting, Photography
Children's Classes: Enrl varies. Tuition $17 per course. Courses—Drawing, Painting
Summer School: Tuition $25 per cr. Courses vary

NANTICOKE

LUZERNE COUNTY COMMUNITY COLLEGE, Commercial Art Dept,* Prospect St, 18634. Tel 717-735-8300. *Coordr* Susan Sponenberg, BFA; *Asst Prof* Robert Kray; *Asst Instr* George Schelling
Estab 1967; pub; D & E; SC 20, LC 7; enrl D 65, E 10, non-maj 5, maj 60
Ent Req: HS dipl
Degrees: 2 year programs offered
Courses: Art History, Drawing, Graphic Arts, Graphic Design, Illustration, Lettering, Mixed Media, Painting, Photography, Color & Design, Life Drawing

NEW KENSINGTON

PENNSYLVANIA STATE UNIVERSITY AT NEW KENSINGTON, Depts of Art & Architecture, 3550 Seventh St, 15068. Tel 412-339-7561. *Chief Exec Officer* Robert Arbuckle. Instrs: FT 2
Estab 1968; pub; D; scholarships; SC 3-4, LC 1 per sem
Ent Req: Col boards
Degrees: 2 yr (option for 4 yr at main campus at University Park)
Tuition: No campus res
Courses: Art Education, Art History, Ceramics, Drawing, Painting, Theatre Arts, Design, Music, Watercolor
Adult Hobby Classes: Enrl 250; tuition $75 per cr hr. Courses—Theater for Children, Ceramics, Painting
Children's Classes: Enrl 100; tuition $75 per cr hr. Courses—Drama, Art, Music Workshops
Summer School: Dir, Joseph Ferrino. Enrl 100; 8 wk term. Courses—Drama, Art, Music Workshops

NEWTON

BUCKS COUNTY COMMUNITY COLLEGE, Fine Arts Dept, Swamp Rd, 18940. Tel 215-968-8421. *Chairperson Dept* Bruce Katsiff, MFA; *Instructor* Jon Alley; *Instructor* Selma Bortner; *Instructor* Robert Dodge; *Instructor* Frank Dominguez; *Instructor* Jack Gevins; *Instructor* Alan Goldstein; *Instructor* Nancy Hellebrand; *Instructor* Catherine Jansen; *Instructor* Paul Keene; *Instructor* Diane Lindenheim; *Instructor* Marlene Miller; *Instructor* Bernarnd Mangiaracina; *Instructor* Charlotte Schatz; *Instructor* Helen Weisz; *Instructor* Mark Sfirri
Estab 1965; pub; D & E; enrl D & E 9200 (school)
Ent Req: HS dipl
Degrees: AA
Courses: Art History, Ceramics, Drawing, Graphic Design, Jewelry, Painting, Photography, Printmaking, Sculpture, Design, Glass, Woodworking

NEW WILMINGTON

WESTMINSTER COLLEGE, Art Dept, 16172. Tel 412-946-8761, Ext 1361. *Head Dept* Dr Robert Hild. Instrs: 3
Estab 1852; den; D; enrl maj 50, total 1500
Degrees: BS and BA(Fine Arts, Educ) 4 yrs

PHILADELPHIA

ART INSTITUTE OF PHILADELPHIA, 1622 Chestnut St, 19103. Tel 215-567-7080; TWX 222-2787; WATS 800-235-2787. *Pres* Philip Trachtman, BFA; *VPres & Dir Education* Charles Hamilton; *Dir Admissions* Richard Vallari; *Registrar* Dianne Saridakis. Instrs: FT 31, PT 35
Estab 1966; pvt; D & E; scholarships; SC 30, LC 8; enrl D 1125, E 72
Ent Req: HS dipl, portfolio
Degrees: AST 2 yr
Tuition: Res—$1390 per qtr hr; nonres—$1490 per qtr hr

Courses: Advertising Design, Art History, †Commercial Art, Design, †Fashion Arts, Graphic Design, Illustration, †Interior Design, Lettering, Mixed Media, †Photography, Computer Graphics
Children's Classes: Enrl 60; tuition $20 per month
Summer School: Dir, Philip Trachtman. Courses—as above

DREXEL UNIVERSITY, Dept of Design, Nesbitt Col, Nesbitt Hall, 33rd & Market Sts, 19104. Tel 215-895-2390. *Dean* Marjorie E Rankin; *Head Dept* Sylvia Clark. Instrs: FT 10, PT 20
Estab 1891; pvt; scholarships; SC 39, LC 9; enrl undergrad 480, grad 45
Ent Req: Col board exam
Degrees: BS 4 yr, MS and cooperative plan
Tuition: Freshmen $4882; Sophomore - Senior $5807; plus $343 general fee
Courses: Fashion Arts, Interior Design, Design & Merchandising
Summer School: Dean, Marjorie E Rankin. Enrl 159; term of 12 wks

SAMUEL S FLEISHER ART MEMORIAL, 709-721 Catharine St, 19147. Tel 215-922-3456. *Dir* Thora E Jacobson; *Instructor* Filomena Dellaripa; *Instructor* Mac Fisher; *Instructor* Frank Gasparro; *Instructor* Tom Gaughan; *Instructor* Martin Jackson
Estab 1898; administered by the Philadelphia Museum of Art; pvt; E; LC 1; enrl E 2000
Ent Req: None
Degrees: None
Courses: Ceramics, Drawing, Painting, Photography, Printmaking, Sculpture
Adult Hobby Classes: Enrl 2800
Children's Classes: Enrl 1450; no tuition. Courses—Drawing, Painting, Sculpture
Summer School: Courses—Ceramics, Drawing, Landscape Painting, Painting, Photography, Printmaking, Sculpture

HUSSIAN SCHOOL OF ART, INC, Commercial Art Dept, 1010 Arch St, 19107. Tel 215-238-9000. *Pres* Ronald Dove. Instrs: FT 4, PT 22
Estab 1946; pvt; D; enrl 225
Ent Req: HS dipl, portfolio interview
Degrees: AST
Tuition: No campus res
Courses: Advertising Design, Art History, Commercial Art, Drawing, Graphic Arts, Graphic Design, Illustration, Lettering, Painting, Photography
Adult Hobby Classes: Courses offered
Summer School: Five week summer workshop in Advertising Design, Illustration, Drawing & Painting

LA SALLE COLLEGE, Dept of Fine Arts, 20th St & Olney Ave, 19141. Tel 215-951-1000. *Chmn Dept Fine Arts* George K Diehl, PhD; *Asst Prof* James Hanes; *Asst Prof* Thomas Ridington, MFA; *Asst Prof* James Lang, MFA
Estab 1865, dept estab 1972; den; D & E; SC 2; enrl D 15, maj 15
Ent Req: HS dipl
Degrees: BA 4 yr
Tuition: $4800 per yr; campus residency available
Courses: Art History, Painting, Printmaking

MOORE COLLEGE OF ART, 20th & The Parkway, 19103. Tel 215-568-4515. *Pres* Edward C McGuire, PhD; *Dean* Julie Rerch, PhD; *Chmn Advertising Design* Carol Gangemi; *Chmn Fine Arts* Gerald Crimmings, MFA; *Chmn Fashion Design* Nancy McGee, MFA; *Chmn Fashion Illustration* Mildred Ivins, Dipl; *Chmn Academics* Joan Stevens, PhD; *Chmn Illustration* Beth Krush, Dipl; *Chmn Interior Design* Harriet Roberts, MFA; *Chmn Fine Arts* Wayne Morris, MFA; *Chmn Photography* Charles Gardner, Dipl; *Chmn Textile Design* Michael Olszewski, MFA; *Chmn Basic Arts* David Bowman, MFA
Estab 1844; pvt; D; scholarships; enrl in col D 535, non-maj 19, maj 516
Ent Req: HS dipl, portfolio, SAT
Degrees: BFA 4 yr, Certification in Art Education
Tuition: $5500 per yr; PT students $220 per cr; campus res room & board $2925 per yr
Courses: †Advertising Design, Art History, †Ceramics, Drawing, †Fashion Arts, Film, †Illustration, †Interior Design, †Jewelry, Lettering, Mixed Media, †Painting, †Photography, †Printmaking, †Sculpture, †Textile Design, †Fashion Design, †Fashion Illustration
Children's Classes: Enrl 161; tuition $95 per sem. Courses—General Art
Summer School: Dir, Julie Reich

PENNSYLVANIA ACADEMY OF THE FINE ARTS, Broad & Cherry Sts, 19102. Tel 215-972-7624. *Dir* Ephraim Weinberg, MAE
Estab 1805; pvt; D & E; scholarships; SC 15, LC 4
Ent Req: HS dipl, portfolio & recommendations
Degrees: Certificate, 4 yrs; BFA coordinated program with Univ of Pennsylvania or Philadelphia Col Art, 5 yr
Tuition: Nonres—undergrad $2600 per yr, $1300 per sem; no campus res
Courses: Art History, Drawing, Painting, Printmaking, Sculpture, Anatomy, Perspective
Adult Hobby Classes: Enrl 170. Courses—Clay Modeling, Wood & Stone Carving, Life Drawing & Painting, Portrait, Still Life
Summer School: Dir, Gail Kemner. Enrl 200; term of 6 wks. Courses—Life Drawing & Painting, Still Life & Landscape Drawing, Portrait, Sculpture

PHILADELPHIA COLLEGE OF ART, Broad & Spruce Sts, 19102. Tel 215-893-3100. *Pres* Peter Solmssen, JD; *Dean Academic Affairs* Joanne Ryan, PhD; *Assoc Dean Academic Affairs* Martin Novelli, PhD; *Chairperson Crafts* Richard Reinhardt, BA; *Chairperson Crafts* Petras Vaskys, Dipl; *Chairperson Educ* Arlene Gostin, MA; *Chairperson Architectural Studies* Larry Mitnic, MA; *Chairperson Graphic Design* Kenneth Hiebert, BA; *Chairperson Illustration* Ruth Lozner, MFA; *Chairperson Industrial Design* Noel Mayo; *Co-Chairperson Painting & Drawing* Steven Jaffe, MFA; *Co-Chairperson Painting & Drawing* David Kettner, MFA; *Chairperson Photography & Film* Gerald Greenfield, MFA; *Chairperson Printmaking* Jerome Kaplan, MFA; *Chairperson Sculpture* Barry Parker, MFA; *Co-Chairperson Foundation Program* Robert McGovern, Dipl; *Co-Chairperson Foundation Program* Karen Saler, MFA

Estab 1876; pvt; D & E; scholarships; SC 339, LC 74, GC 5; enrl D 1225, E 900, grad 25
Ent Req: HS dipl, portfolio, SAT
Degrees: BFA 4 yrs, MA 5 yrs
Tuition: $6375 per yr, $225 per cr; campus res—room & board $2475 per yr
Courses: †Advertising Design, †Architecture, †Art Education, Art History, Calligraphy, †Ceramics, Drafting, Drawing, †Film, †Graphic Arts, †Graphic Design, †Illustration, †Industrial Design, †Jewelry, Landscape Architecture, †Painting, †Photography, †Printmaking, †Sculpture, †Silversmithing, †Teacher Training, Textile Design, †Weaving, Art Therapy, Environmental Design, Furniture Design, Glassblowing, Liberal Arts, Typography, Woodworking
Adult Hobby Classes: Evening program; Enrl 2000; tuition $200 per cr.
Courses—Advertising/Design, Fine Arts, Illustration, Interior Design; Photography
Children's Classes: Saturday school; enrl 270; tuition $95 per course.
Courses—Ceramics, Design, Drawing, Jewelry, Painting, Photography and Film, Printmaking, Illustration
Summer School: Dir, Fred Osborne. Pre-College Program: Enrl 125; tuition $650; term of 5 wks beginning July. Summer Session: Enrl 125; tuition $225 per cr

PHILADELPHIA COLLEGE OF TEXTILES AND SCIENCE, School of Textiles,* School House Lane & Henry Ave, 19144. Tel 215-843-9700, 951-2950. *Pres* Donald B Partridge
Estab 1884; pvt; scholarships; enrl D 1600, E 1100
Degrees: BS 4 yrs
Tuition: $4700 per yr
Courses: Drawing, Apparel Design, Apparel Management, Basic Design, Chemistry & Dyeing, Fabric Design, Fashion Textile Retailing, Knitted Design, Print Design, Textile Engineering, Textile Quality Control & Testing, Weaving Design
Summer School: Dir, Peter Mills

PHILADELPHIA COMMUNITY COLLEGE, Dept of Fine Arts, 1700 Spring Garden St, 19130. Tel 215-751-8771. *Dir Div Humanities* William Baker, MA; *Assoc Prof* Wallace Peters, MA; *Assoc Prof* Valerie Seligsohn, MFA; *Assoc Prof* Diane Burko, MFA; *Assoc Prof* Robert Paige, MFA; *Assoc Prof* Kyung Lee, MFA
Estab 1967; pub; D & E; SC 10, LC 6; enrl D 80 art maj
Ent Req: HS dipl, portfolio
Degrees: AA 2 yr
Tuition: $950 per yr; no campus res
Courses: Art History, Ceramics, Drawing, Graphic Design, Painting, Photography, Design, Transfer Foundation Program
Summer School: Courses offered

SAINT JOSEPH'S UNIVERSITY, Fine Arts Dept, 5600 City Ave, 19131. Tel 215-879-7604. *Dir* Dennis W Weeks, MFA; *Asst Prof* Dennis McNally, MA; *Asst Prof* Lewis Gordon, DMA; *Asst Prof* Betsy Anderson, MA; *Lectr* Peg Schofield, MFA; *Lectr* Lynn Denton, MFA; *Lectr* Theresa Donahue, MFA; *Lectr* Dennis Kerr, PhD
Estab 1851, prog estab 1975; den; D & E; SC 15, LC 4; enrl D 150, E 30
Ent Req: HS dipl
Tuition: $95 per cr hr; campus res available
Courses: Aesthetics, Art Education, Art History, Ceramics, Drawing, Film, Painting, Photography, Printmaking, Stage Design, Theatre Arts

STUDIO SCHOOL OF ART AND DESIGN, 117 Chestnut St, 19106. Tel 215-735-0908. *Dir* Maggie De Baecke, Dipl; *Asst Dir* Colleen Bronstien; *Instr* Rita Smith; *Instr* Chris Rykowski; *Instr* Andrew Theis; *Instr* Ira Hokanson; *Instr* Bryn Thomas; *Instr* Jim Souder; *Instr* Mary Nomecos; *Instr* Chris Hodges; *Instr* Carmen Console
Estab 1959; pvt; D; SC 8, LC 4; enrl 41
Ent Req: HS dipl, interview, portfolio
Tuition: Res—$2670 per yr, $1335 per sem, $281.05 monthly; no campus res
Courses: †Advertising Design, Art History, †Commercial Art, †Graphic Arts, †Graphic Design, †Illustration, Lettering, Mixed Media, Painting, Photography, Three-Dimensional Design, Two-Dimensional Design
Adult Hobby Classes: Enrl 45; tuition $26.70 per hr. Courses—Illustration & Advertising Art

TEMPLE UNIVERSITY, Tyler School of Art, Beech & Penrose Ave, Elkins Park, 19126. Tel 215-224-7575. *Actg Dean* Philip Betancourt, PhD; *Prof* Stephen Greene, MA; *Prof* John Moore, MFA; *Prof* Stanley Lechtzin, MFA; *Prof* Stanislaw Zagorski; *Prof* Romas Viesulas; *Prof* Adela Akers; *Prof* William Larson, MS; *Asst Prof* Winifred Lutz, MFA; *Vis Artist* John O'Leary, Graphic Design
Dept estab 1935; pvt; D & E; scholarships; enrl D 679, grad 85
Ent Req: HS dipl, SAT, portfolio
Degrees: BA(Art History) & BFA, BFA(Teaching), MA(Art History), MEd
Tuition: Res—undergrad $2882 per yr, $95 per sem hr, grad $3048 per yr, $127 per sem hr; nonres—undergrad $5068 per yr, $131 per sem hr, grad $4044 per yr, $161 per sem hr; campus res available
Courses: Art Education, †Art History, †Ceramics, Collages, Drawing, Film, Goldsmithing, †Graphic Design, History of Art & Archaeology, Illustration, †Jewelry, Lettering, †Painting, †Photography, †Printmaking, †Sculpture, Silversmithing, Teacher Training, Textile Design, Video, †Weaving, Foundry, Handmade Cameras, Papermaking, Performance Art, Photo Etching in Jewelry
Children's Classes: Enrl 40; tuition $175 for 12 wks. Courses—Ceramics, Glass, Jewelry, Weaving

TRACEY-WARNER SCHOOL, 401 N Broad St, 19108. Tel 215-574-0402. *Pres* Lewis H Warner
Estab 1956; pvt; D; enrl D 125
Ent Req: HS dipl
Degrees: AA 2 yrs, dipl or cert
Tuition: $4950
Courses: Advertising Design, Art Education, Art History, †Costume Design & Construction, Fashion Arts, Handicrafts, †Illustration, Jewelry, Textile Design, †Draping Design, Pattern Drafting, Pattern Grading
Adult Hobby Classes: Enrl 75; tuition $4950 per 2 yr course. Courses—Fasion Technology, Fashion Merchandising & Retailing, Men's & Women's Tailoring

UNIVERSITY OF PENNSYLVANIA, Graduate School of Fine Arts, 19104. Tel 215-243-8321. *Dean* Lee G Copeland, MArchit & MCP
Estab 1874; pvt; scholarships and fels; GC
Ent Req: Ent exam
Tuition: Campus res available
Summer School: Dir, Adele Santos. Tuition $2500 per 6 wks. Studio courses in Paris, Venice & India
—**Dept of Architecture,** 110 Meyerson Hall, 19104. Tel 215-898-5728. *Chmn* Adele Santos; *Chmn Grad Group* Peter McCleary. Instrs: FT 7, PT 25
Enrl 180
Degrees: MArchit, PhD
Tuition: $8850 per yr
Courses: Architectural Design and Construction
Summer School: Enrl 60; tuition $3000 per 6-12 wk term. Courses—Summer studios (only upper level students)
—**Dept of Landscape Architecture and Regional Planning,*** 19104. Tel 215-243-6591. Instrs: FT 8, PT 5
LC 7, Design Courses 4; enrl 113
Degrees: MLA, MRP
Courses: Graduate program only; no majors declared
—**College Arts & Science,*** Dept of Fine Arts, 19104. *Prof* Robert M Engman; *Prof* Neil G Welliver; *Assoc Prof* Maurice C Lowe; *Asst Prof* Michael Eisenman; *Asst Prof* Hitoshi Nakazato; *Lectr* Rudy Burckhardt; *Lectr* Hugh M Hall; *Lectr* Martin Ingram; *Lectr* Susan Lettes; *Lectr* Nick Vidnovic; *Lectr* Becky Young. Instrs: FT 7, PT 4
SC 21, LC 5, GC; enrl 60
Degrees: BFA, MFA
Tuition: $4440 per sem
Courses: Art History, Drawing, Painting, Printmaking, Sculpture, Color

WILLET STAINED GLASS STUDIOS, 10 East Moreland Ave, 19118. Tel 215-247-5721. *Pres* E Crosby Willet; *General Manager* William G Stewart
Estab 1890 as the largest stained glass studio in the United States

PITTSBURGH

ART INSTITUTE OF PITTSBURGH, 526 Penn Ave, 15222. Tel 412-263-6600. *Pres* John R Knepper
Estab 1921; pvt; scholarships; enrl D 1700, E 200
Ent Req: HS grad
Degrees: AA 2 yrs, dipl
Tuition: $1270 per qtr
Courses: †Interior Design, Photography, Airbrush Technique, †Fashion Illustration, †Photography-Audiovisual-Multimedia, †Visual Communications
Adult Hobby Classes: Tuition $635 for 4 qtr. Courses—Commercial Art Technician, Interior Planning, Photography

CARLOW COLLEGE, Art Dept,* 3333 Fifth Ave, 15213. Tel 412-578-6028, 578-6033. *Chmn Dept* Richard Devlin; *Assoc Chmn* Suzanne Steiner; *Lectr* Carole Kunkle-Miller. Instrs: FT 1, PT 3
Estab 1945; den; D & E; scholarships; SC 17, LC 6; enrl 800, maj 35
Ent Req: HS dipl and transcript, col boards
Degrees: BA, Certificate Art Education
Tuition: $2070 per sem
Courses: Art Education, Ceramics, Drawing, Painting, Printmaking, Sculpture, Teacher Training, American Art, Art Therapy, Fiber Arts, Survey of Art, Twentieth Century Art, 2-D Design
Summer School: Acad Dean, Sr Elizabeth McMillan. Enrl approx 40; two summer sessions 4 wks each. Courses—Fiber Arts, Ceramics

CARNEGIE-MELLON UNIVERSITY, College of Fine Arts, 5000 Forbes Ave, 15213. Tel 412-578-2000, Ext 2354. *Dean* Akram Midani
Estab 1905; pvt; scholarships and fels
Ent Req: Col board ent exam plus auditions or portfolio
Degrees: 4-5 yr, MFA in Stage Design available in Dept of Drama
Tuition: $6300 per yr; campus res available
Summer School: Term of 6 wks. Courses—includes some pre-college courses
—**Dept of Architecture,** 15213. Tel 412-578-2355. *Head* Omer Akin. Instrs: FT 17, PT 15
Enrl 295
Degrees: BArch, MArch, PhD
Tuition: Undergrad $7500, grad $8200
Courses: Architecture
Summer School: Dir, Jay Garrott. Tuition $1296 per 6 wks
—**Dept of Design,** Baker Hall 35A, 15213. *Head* Joseph Ballay. Instrs: FT 11, PT 6
Enrl 162
Degrees: BFA(design), MFA(computer aided design)
Courses: Graphic Design, Industrial Design, Computer Aided Design, Design Theory, Interior Environments
Adult Hobby Classes: Courses—Calligraphy
Summer School: Courses—Design Studio
—**Dept of Art,*** 15213. *Head* Orvill Winsand. Instrs: FT 20, PT 2
Enrl 235
Degrees: MFA, DA
Tuition: $6300 per yr
Courses: Art Education, Handicrafts, Painting, Printmaking, Sculpture

CHATHAM COLLEGE, Dept of Art, Woodland Rd, 15232. Tel 412-441-8200. *Chmn* Jerry Caplan. Instrs: FT 3, PT 1
Estab 1869; pvt; W; SC 17, LC 7
Ent Req: HS grad
Degrees: BA 4 yrs
Tuition: $5250 incl res fees
Courses: Art History, Ceramics, Drawing, Graphic Arts, Painting, Photography, Sculpture, Design, Independent Study

LA ROCHE COLLEGE, Division of Graphics, Design,* 9000 Babcock Blvd, 15237. Tel 412-367-9300. *Chairperson* Harvey R Levenson, Phd; *Instructor* Wendy Bockwith, MArchitecture; *Instructor* Grant Dinsmore, MFA; *Instructor* Sally McCoy, MA; *Instructor* Martha Shepler, MFA; *Instructor* Mack Taylor, BFA. Instrs: PT 15
Estab 1963, dept estab 1965; pvt; D & E; SC 25, LC 15; enrl D & E 200, non-maj 20, maj 180
Ent Req: HS dipl
Degrees: BA and BS 4 yr
Tuition: $1375 per yr; campus res available
Courses: Advertising Design, Aesthetics, Art History, Ceramics, Commercial Art, Display, Fashion Arts, †Graphic Arts, †Graphic Design, Illustration, Industrial Design, Interior Design, Lettering, Painting, Photography, Sculpture, Platemaking, Presswork—Lithography, Reproduction Processes, Typesetting
Summer School: Dir, Betsey Devon. Tuition $70 cr

POINT PARK COLLEGE, Performing Arts Dept, Wood St & Blvd of Allies, 15222. Tel 412-391-4100. *Chmn* Mark Lewis
Degrees: BA
Tuition: $4300
Courses: Advertising Design, †Architecture, Art Appreciation, †Art History, Calligraphy, †Design, Drawing, Fashion Arts, Film, Interior Design, Painting, Photography, Stage Design, Cartooning

UNIVERSITY OF PITTSBURGH 15260
—**Henry Clay Frick Fine Arts Dept,** 15260. Tel 412-624-4121. *Chmn* John Williams, PhD
Estab 1787, dept estab 1927; pvt; D & E; scholarships; LC 35, GC 20; enrl D 600, E 200, grad 30
Ent Req: HS dipl, BA, GRE for grad work
Degrees: BA 4 yrs, MA 2 yrs, PhD
Tuition: Res—grad $1445; nonres—grad $2890
Courses: †Art History
Summer School: Courses offered
—**Dept of Studio Arts,** 15260. Tel 412-624-4118. *Chmn* Virgil D Cantini. Instrs: FT 6, PT 1
Estab 1968; pub; D; LC 29; enrl 1500
Degrees: BA, undergrad maj in Studio Arts
Tuition: Res—$1210 per term; nonres—$2420 per term
Courses: Graphic Arts, Painting, Sculpture
Adult Hobby Classes: Enrl 10; tuition res—$80 per cr, nonres—$160 per cr for 15 wk term. Courses—Design, Color, Drawing, Sculpture
Summer School: Dir, Edward Powell & Girts Purins. Enrl 60; tuition res—$80 per cr, nonres—$160 per cr, 7 1/2 wks each. Courses—Design, Color, Drawing, Sculpture

PLYMOUTH MEETING

ANTONELLI INSTITUTE OF ART & PHOTOGRAPHY, Professional Photography, Commercial Art & Interior Design, 2910 Jolly Rd, PO Box 570, 19462. Tel 215-275-3040. *Pres* Joseph B Thompson; *VPres* Harry W Hollingsworth; *Dir* Gilbert H Weiss, BS; *Instructor* Robert D Golding, BFA; *Instructor* James Doanto, MBA
Estab 1938; pvt; D & E; enrl D 350, E 75
Ent Req: HS dipl
Tuition: No campus res
Courses: Commercial Art, Interior Design, Professional Photography
Adult Hobby Classes: Workshops as scheduled

RADNOR

CABRINI COLLEGE, Dept of Fine Arts, Eagle & King of Prussia Rds, 19087. Tel 215-687-2100, Ext 53. *Chmn Dept* Adeline Bethany. Instrs: FT 2, PT 3
Estab 1957; den; D & E; scholarships; SC 11, LC 4
Ent Req: HS dipl, satisfactory average and rank in secondary school class, SAT, recommendations
Degrees: BA(studio art), BS & BSEd
Tuition: $4130
Courses: Art Education, Ceramics, Drawing, History of Art & Archaeology, Painting, Teacher Training, Design & Composition
Adult Hobby Classes: Courses offered
Summer School: Dir, Midge Leahy. Term of 6 wks beginning May and July. Courses—Drawing, Painting, Mixed Media, Calligraphy, Color Theory, Elem Art Methods

READING

ALBRIGHT COLLEGE, Dept of Art,* 13th & Exeter Sts, 19604. Tel 215-921-2381. *Head Dept* Thomas C Watcke, MFA; *Assoc Prof* Harry G Koursaros, MA
Estab 1856, dept estab 1964; SC 14, LC 7; enrl D 322, E 41, non-maj 340, maj 8, others 15
Ent Req: HS dipl, SAT
Degrees: BA 4 yrs
Tuition: $6220 annual tuition; campus res available
Courses: †Art History, Ceramics, Constructions, Drafting, Drawing, Fashion Arts, Film, Graphic Arts, History of Art & Archaeology, Interior Design, Mixed Media, †Painting, Photography, Printmaking, †Sculpture, Theatre Arts
Summer School: Chairperson Art Dept, Thomas Watcke. Enrl 35; term of 4 wks beginning June. Courses—Drawing, Photography

ROSEMONT

ROSEMONT COLLEGE, Division of the Arts,* 19010. Tel 215-527-0200. *Chmn Div* Michael D Willse, MFA; *Instr* Rosalind Bloom, MA; *Instr* Thomas L Davies, MA; *Instr* John Furmicola; *Instr* Ronald F Linder, MFA; *Instr* Peter Lister; *Instr* Janice Merendino, BFA; *Instr* Patricia Nugent, MFA; *Instr* George Radan, PhD; *Instr* Hilda SaVar, BS; *Instr* Joan F Smith, MFA; *Instr* Theresa Stamm, PhD; *Instr* David Tafler, MFA; *Instr* James Victor; *Instr* Brian Wagner, MFA; *Instr* Irwin Weiss, MFA. Instrs: FT 3, PT 19
Estab 1921; pvt, W (exchange with Villanova Univ); D; scholarships; enrl total col 703, art 383, grad approx 24, 58 theatre
Ent Req: HS dipl, SAT
Degrees: BA(Art History, Studio Art), Teacher certificate
Tuition: $4550 annual tuition; campus residence available
Courses: Aesthetics, Art Education, Ceramics, Drawing, Graphic Arts, History of Art & Archaeology, Painting, Photography, Sculpture, Teacher Training, Theatre Arts, Fibres, Watercolor
Summer School: Summer Program with Villanova in Siena, Italy

SCRANTON

INTERNATIONAL CORRESPONDENCE SCHOOLS
School of Interior Design, Oak St, Scranton, 18515. Tel 717-342-7701, Ext 341. Instrs: FT 1, PT 1
Estab 1891; dept estab 1969; pvt; enrl 1800
Ent Req: 8th grade
Tuition: $689
Courses: Interior Design
School of Art, Oak St, Scranton, 18515. Tel 717-342-7701, Ext 341. *VPres Educ* Leonard Valore; *Dir* Elaine G Thomas, MS. Instrs: FT 1, PT 1
Estab 1891; pvt; enrl 1000
Ent Req: 8th grade
Tuition: $589
Courses: Drawing, Painting

LACKAWANNA JUNIOR COLLEGE, Graphic Arts Dept,* 901 Prospect Ave, 18503. Tel 717-961-7827
Degrees: AA
Courses: Art Appreciation, Art History, Calligraphy, Design, Drawing, Painting, Photography, Printmaking

MARYWOOD COLLEGE, Art Dept, 2300 Adams Ave, 18509. Tel 717-343-6521, Ext 339. *Chairperson Dept* Sr Cor Immaculatium. Instrs: FT 5, PT 4
Estab 1926; pvt; D & E; scholarships; SC 28, LC 7, GC 12; enrl maj 150, grad 31
Ent Req: HS dipl, portfolio and interview
Degrees: BA(Art Educ), BS(Educ with concentration in Art), BFA(Drawing & Painting, Illustration, Printmaking, Advertising Graphics, Photography, Ceramics, Sculpture, Textile Art, Weaving, Interior Design), MA(Studio Art, Art Educ, Art Therapy), MFA(Painting, Ceramics, Weaving)
Tuition: Grad $107 per cr, undergrad $100 per cr
Courses: Advertising Design, Art Education, Art History, Calligraphy, Ceramics, Drawing, Fashion Arts, Graphic Arts, Illustration, Interior Design, Jewelry, Mixed Media, Painting, Photography, Printmaking, Sculpture, Textile Design, Theatre Arts, Art Therapy, Contemporary Learning Theories, Fabrics, Metalcraft, Serigraphy, Tapestry, Weaving
Adult Hobby Classes: Program for Adult Continuing Education (Pace)
Children's Classes: College for Kids, Young Peoples' Art Workshop, 4 wk term beginning June 1
Summer School: 6 wk term beginning in June. Courses—both graduate and undergraduate levels

SHIPPENSBURG

SHIPPENSBURG STATE COLLEGE, Art Dept, Prince St, 17257. Tel 717-532-1530. *Chmn Art Dept* Harry D Bentz, EdD; *Instructor* Betsy Farmer, PhD; *Instructor* William Hynes, MEd; *Instructor* Vida Hull, PhD; *Instructor* George Waricher, MEd
Estab 1871; dept estab 1920; pub; D & E; scholarships; SC 13, LC 4; enrl D 400, E 100, non-maj 600, grad 15, others 20 continuing educ
Ent Req: HS dipl
Degrees: BA(Art), BS(Elementary Educ)
Tuition: $843 per sem; PT $62 per cr hr; campus res—room & board $855 per sem
Courses: Art History, Ceramics, Drawing, Graphic Arts, Handicrafts, Lettering, Painting, Printmaking, Sculpture, Teacher Training, Textile Design
Adult Hobby Classes: Enrl 25; tuition $15 per course. Courses—Basic Watercolor, Ceramics, Quilting, Calligraphy
Summer School: Dir, Dr Harry D Bentz. Tuition $62 per cr hr for term of 3-5 wks beginning May 27. Courses—Arts & Crafts, Introduction to Art, Ceramics, Creative Experiences in Art, Enameling

SLIPPERY ROCK

SLIPPERY ROCK UNIVERSITY OF PENNSYLVANIA, Dept of Art,* 16057. Tel 412-794-7271. *Chmn Dept* J Robert Crayne. Instrs: FT 9
Pub; D & E; SC 27, LC 3; enrl maj 70
Ent Req: HS dipl
Degrees: BA(Art), BFA(Art) 4 yr
Tuition: $1000 per yr; campus res $1008 per yr
Courses: Art Education, Ceramics, Drawing, History of Art & Archaeology, Painting, Photography, Printmaking, Sculpture, Textile Design, Metalsmithing
Summer School: Tui $52 per cr hr

SWARTHMORE

SWARTHMORE COLLEGE, Dept of Art, 19081. Tel 215-447-7116. *Chairperson Dept Art* Constance Cain Hungerford, PhD; *Prof* T Kaori Kitao, PhD; *Asst Prof* Michael Cothren, PhD; *Asst Prof* Curtis Brizendine, PhD; *Asst Prof* Randall L Exon, MFA; *Asst Prof* Brian A Meunier, MFA
Estab 1864, dept estab 1925; pvt; D; scholarships; SC 14, LC 33; enrl non-maj 500, maj 25
Ent Req: HS dipl, SAT, CEEB
Degrees: BA 4 yrs
Tuition: $8430 per yr; campus res—room & board $3260 per yr
Courses: Art History, Ceramics, Drawing, Painting, Photography, Printmaking, Sculpture, History of Architecture, History of Cinema, Urban History

UNIONTOWN

PENNSYLVANIA STATE UNIVERSITY, FAYETTE CAMPUS, Dept of Art, Col of Arts & Architecture, Hwy 119 N, 15401. Tel 412-437-2801, Ext 29. *Instr* David A Dipietro, MFA
Estab 1968; pub; D & E
Ent Req: HS dipl
Tuition: $998 per sem
Courses: Architecture, Art History, Ceramics, Drafting, Drawing, Painting, Sculpture, Watercolor, 2-D & 3-D Design
Adult Hobby Classes: Courses—Watercolor, Ceramics, Drawing

UNIVERSITY PARK

PENNSYLVANIA STATE UNIVERSITY, UNIVERSITY PARK
—College of Arts and Architecture, 111 Arts Building, 16802. Tel 814-865-2591. *Dean* Robert W Holmes, PhD; *Head Dept Archit* Raniero Corbelletti, MS; *Dir School Visual Arts* Jerrold Maddox, MFA; *Head Dept Art History* Hellmut Hager, Dr Phil; *Head Dept Landscape Archit* David Young, MLA; *Head Dept Theatre and Film* Douglas Cook, MA
Estab 1855, col estab 1963; pub; D & E; scholarships; SC 282, LC 99, GC 104; enrl D 27,848, maj 1148, grad 172
Ent Req: HS dipl and GPA, SAT
Degrees: BA, BS, BM and BFA 4 yrs, Bachelor of Archit 5 yrs, MS, MArchit, MFA, MEd, DEd, PhD
Tuition: Res—undergrad $2118 per yr, $1059 per sem, $89 per cr, grad $2256 per yr, $1128 per sem, $94 per cr; nonres—undergrad $4254 per yr, $2127 per sem, $178 per cr, grad $4512 per yr, $2256 per sem, $188 per cr; campus res—room & board $2274
Courses: Aesthetics, †Architecture, †Art Education, †Art History, Ceramics, Constructions, Costume Design & Construction, Drafting, Drawing, †Film, Graphic Arts, Graphic Design, History of Art & Archaeology, Jewelry, †Landscape Architecture, Mixed Media, Painting, Photography, Printmaking, Restoration & Conservation, Sculpture, Silversmithing, Stage Design, Textile Design, †Teacher Training, †Theatre Arts, Weaving
Adult Hobby Classes: Tuition varies. Courses—informal, vary with demand
Children's Classes: Enrl 60; tuition $12 for 8 wks. Courses—Ceramics, Drawing, Fibers, Jewelry, Painting, Photography, Printmaking, Sculpture
Summer School: Dean, Robert W Holmes. Enrl 1565; tuition same. Courses—regular session
—Dept of Art History, 229 Arts II Bldg, 16802. Tel 814-865-6326. *Evan Pugh Prof* Eugenio Battisti, PhD; *Prof* Anthony Cutler, PhD; *Prof* Roland E Fleischer, PhD; *Prof* George L Mauner, PhD; *Assoc Prof* Heinz Henisch, PhD; *Assoc Prof* Jeanne Chenault Porter, PhD; *Asst Prof* Elizabeth B Smith, PhD; *Asst Prof* Elizabeth J Walters, PhD; *Asst Prof* Mary N Woods, PhD
Estab 1855, dept estab 1963; pub; D & E; scholarships; LC 50, GC 36; enrl D 56, maj 20, grad 26, others 10
Ent Req: HS dipl
Degrees: BA 4 yrs, MA 2-3 yrs, PhD approx 4 yrs
Tuition: Res—undergrad $1156 per sem, grad $1232 per sem; nonres—undergrad $2322 per sem, grad $2463 per sem; campus res—room & board $1232
Courses: Aesthetics, †Art History, History of Art & Archaeology, Connoisseurship, History of Photography, Historiography
Adult Hobby Classes: Classes offered through Continuing Education
Summer School: Courses same as regular session, but limited

VILLANOVA

VILLANOVA UNIVERSITY, Dept of Art and Art History, 19085. Tel 215-645-4610. *Prof* George Radan; *Instructor* Richard Cannuli; *Instructor* Henry Syvinski; *Instructor* Thomas Johnston
Estab 1842, dept estab 1971; pvt; D & E; SC 25, LC 6; enrl D 35, maj 35
Ent Req: HS dipl, SAT
Degrees: BFA 4 yrs; courses taught in conjunction with Rosemont College
Tuition: Res—undergrad $3500 per yr; campus res—room & board $2200 per yr
Courses: Aesthetics, Art Education, Art History, Ceramics, Drawing, Film, Graphic Arts, Graphic Design, History of Art & Archaeology, Painting, Photography, Printmaking, Restoration & Conservation, Sculpture, Teacher Training, Theatre Arts, Watercolor
Adult Hobby Classes: Enrl 20-30; tuition $336 per course in 14 wk sem. Courses—Drawing, Calligraphy
Summer School: Held in Siena, Italy. Courses—Art History, Studio Art, Language

WASHINGTON

WASHINGTON AND JEFFERSON COLLEGE, Art Dept, Olin Art Center, 15301. Tel 412-222-4400. *Chmn Art Dept* Paul B Edwards, MA; *Prof* Hugh H Taylor, MA; *Asst Prof* Patricia Maloney, MFA; *Adj Prof* Gerald Chambers, MA
Estab 1787, dept estab 1959; pvt; D & E; scholarships; SC 14, LC 8; enrl D 162, E 18, non-maj 139, maj 23, others 15

Ent Req: HS dipl, SAT, achievement tests
Degrees: BA 4 yr, MA
Tuition: $6450 per yr; campus res—room & board $2280 per yr
Courses: †Art Education, Art History, Ceramics, Drawing, Graphic Arts, Painting, Printmaking, Restoration & Conservation, Sculpture, Gallery Management
Adult Hobby Classes: Enrl 24; tuition $110 per 13 wks. Courses—Art Education, Drawing, Matting & Framing
Summer School: Dir, Dr William W Leake. Enrl 15; tuition $100 per cr hr for term of 6 wks beginning mid June. Courses—full range

WAYNE

WAYNE ART CENTER, 413 Maplewood Ave, 19087. Tel 215-688-3553. *Pres* Linda Rodgers; *Exec Dir* Meg Miller; *Instr* Jack Abrams; *Instr* Fred Danziger; *Instr* Zenos Frudakis; *Instr* Greta Garr; *Instr* Bette Greenwood; *Instr* William Greenwood; *Instr* Edward Lis; *Instr* Elizabeth Kempf; *Instr* Maxine Krinsky; *Instr* Sandy Slaymaker; *Instr* Maxine Sperling; *Instr* Marianne Tebbens; *Instr* Maevernon Varnum
Estab 1930; pvt; D & E; SC 15; enrl D 130, E 50, others 40
Ent Req: None; free program for senior citizens
Courses: Drawing, Mixed Media, Painting, Sculpture, Pottery, Woodcarving
Adult Hobby Classes: Tuition $84 for 12 wk sem, yearly dues $20. Courses—as above
Children's Classes: Tui $35 for 10 wk sem, yearly dues $6. Courses—Drawing, Painting, Sculpture
Summer School: Exec Dir, Meg Miller. Courses—same as above plus Landscape Painting

WAYNESBURG

WAYNESBURG COLLEGE, Dept of Fine Arts, 15370. Tel 412-627-8191. *Chmn* Daniel Morris, MA; *Asst Prof* Susan Howsare, MFA; *Instr* Robert Gay, BSJ
Estab 1849, dept estab 1971; pvt; D & E; scholarships; SC 25, LC 6; enrl D 131, E 3, maj 17
Ent Req: HS dipl
Degrees: BA(Visual Communication) 4 yrs
Tuition: Res—undergrad $6300 per yr; nonres—undergrad $4200 per yr; campus residence available
Courses: Aesthetics, Art Education, Art History, Design, Drawing, Graphic Arts, Painting, Photography, Printmaking, Theatre Arts, Layout & Photography for Media, Media Presentation, Television, Typography
Adult Hobby Classes: Courses—Art History, Graphic Design, Photography
Summer School: Dept Chmn, Daniel Morris. Tuition $270 for term of 5 wks beginning June 2 and July 7

WEST MIFFLIN

COMMUNITY COLLEGE OF ALLEGHENY COUNTY, Fine Arts Dept,* 1750 Clairton Rd, 15122. Tel 412-469-1100. *Chmn Arts Dept* Micheal Stefanko
Degrees: AA, AS
Tuition: $700 per yr
Courses: Advertising Design, Art Appreciation, Art Education, Art History, Calligraphy, Ceramics, Design, Drawing, Film, Handicrafts, Jewelry, Painting, Photography, Printmaking

WILKES-BARRE

WILKES COLLEGE, Dept of Art, S River St, 18766. Tel 717-824-4651, Ext 385. *Chmn* William H Sterling, PhD; *Prof* Chester Colson, MS; *Assoc Prof* Berenice D'Vorzon, MA; *Assoc Prof* Richard Fuller, MA; *Assoc Prof* Herbert Simon, MA; *Adjunct Prof* Mark Cohen, BA
Estab 1947; pvt; D & E; scholarships; SC 20, LC 7; enrl D 115, E 40, non-maj 80, maj 45
Ent Req: HS dipl, SAT
Degrees: BA & BFA 4 yr
Tuition: Undergrad $5050 per yr, $2525 per sem, pt $105 per cr hr; campus res—room & board $2540 per yr
Courses: Advertising Design, Aesthetics, †Art Education, †Art History, †Ceramics, Drawing, Handicrafts, †Painting, †Photography, †Printmaking, †Sculpture, Stage Design, Teacher Training, Theatre Arts, Batik, †Fiber Design, Weaving
Adult Hobby Classes: Courses variable
Summer School: Dir, John Meyers. Enrl variable; tuition $105 per cr hr for term of 5-8 wks beginning June 8. Courses—variable

WILLIAMSPORT

LYCOMING COLLEGE, Art Dept, 17701. Tel 717-326-1951, Ext 262, 263. *Chmn Dept* Jon Robert Bogle, MFA; *Assoc Prof* Roger Douglas Shipley, MFA; *Asst Prof* Diane M Lesko, PhD; *Instructor* Rome Hanks, MFA
Estab 1812; pvt; D & E; scholarships; SC 20, LC 7; enrl College 1200, Dept 500, maj 15
Ent Req: HS dipl, ACT or SAT
Degrees: BA 4 yr, BFA(Sculpture) 4 yr
Tuition: $5580 per yr; campus res—room & board $2380 per yr
Courses: Art History, †Advertising Design, Art History, Ceramics, Drawing, Graphic Arts, †Painting, Photography, †Printmaking, †Sculpture
Summer School: Tuition $460 for 6 wks course. Courses—Photography

WILLIAMSPORT AREA COMMUNITY COLLEGE, Dept of Engineering and Design,* 1005 W Third St, 17701. Tel 717-326-3761. *Dir Dept* Dr Paul L McQuay; *Prof* Dale Straub, MEd; *Assoc Prof* Chalmer Van Horn, BS; *Asst Prof* Lloyd Cotner; *Asst Prof* William Ealer, BS & BArchitecture; *Asst Prof* Dale Metzker; *Asst Prof* Patrick Murphy, BA; *Instructor* Joseph Mark, BArchitecture; *Instructor* Harold

Newton; *Instructor* Fred Schaefer Jr; *Instructor* Jackie Welliver, CET
Estab 1965; pub; D & E; scholarships; enrl D 2903, E 2909
Ent Req: HS dipl, placement test
Degrees: AA 2 yr
Tuition: District res—$495 per yr; non-district res—$1091.50 per yr; non-state res—$1485 per yr
Courses: †Advertising Design, †Architecture, Commercial Art, Constructions, †Drafting, Drawing, †Graphic Arts, Landscape Architecture, Lettering, Restoration & Conservation, Technical Illustration
Summer School: Coordr, Thomas E Vargo

YORK

YORK COLLEGE OF PENNSYLVANIA, Dept of Humanities and Fine Arts,* Country Club Rd, 17405. Tel 717-846-7788. *Chmn Fine Arts* Paul W Diener
Estab 1941; pvt; D & E; SC 17, LC 7
Ent Req: HS dipl, SAT or ACT
Degrees: BA 4 yrs and AA 2 yrs
Tuition: $1335 per sem; campus res available
Courses: Art Education, Art History, Commercial Art, Drawing, Painting, Photography, Sculpture
Adult Hobby Classes: Enrl 40; Courses—per regular session
Summer School: Dir, Thomas Michalski. Enrl 15; Term of three weeks beginning May 19 and two 5 week sessions beginning June and July

RHODE ISLAND

BRISTOL

ROGER WILLIAMS COLLEGE, Art Dept, Old Ferry Road, 02809. Tel 401-255-1000. *Coordr* Carol J Hathaway, MA; *Instructor* Mary Dondero, MAT; *Instructor* Richard Carbotti, MFA; *Instructor* Michele McRoberts; *Instructor* Thomas Russell, MFA; *Instructor* Robin Wiseman, MA; *Instructor* Elizabeth Hull, MFA
Estab 1948, dept estab 1967; pvt; D & E; SC 18, LC 8; enrl D 1800, E 1500, maj 42
Ent Req: HS dipl
Degrees: AA 2 yr, BA 4 yr, apprenticeship and senior teaching
Tuition: Res $5012 per yr; campus res—room & board $3130 per yr
Courses: Aesthetics, Architecture, Art Education, Art History, Ceramics, Costume Design & Construction, Drafting, Drawing, Film, Graphic Arts, Graphic Design, Handicrafts, History of Art & Archaeology, Museum Staff Training, Painting, Photography, Printmaking, Restoration & Conservation, Sculpture, Stage Design, Teacher Training, Theatre Arts, Weaving, Gallery Mgmt, Leather, Macrame, Two and Three Dimensional Design
Summer School: Dean, Bart Schiaro. Courses—Ceramics, Design, Drawing, Painting, Weaving

KINGSTON

UNIVERSITY OF RHODE ISLAND, Dept of Art, Fine Arts Center, 02881. Tel 401-792-2131, 792-5821. *Chmn* Ronald Onorato, PhD; *Prof* William Klenk, PhD; *Prof* William Leete, MFA; *Prof* Bart Parker, MFA; *Prof* Robert H Rohm, MFA; *Prof* Richard Calabro, MFA; *Prof* David Ketner, PhD; *Prof* Richard Fraenkel, PhD; *Assoc Prof* Wendy Holmes, PhD; *Assoc Prof* Natalie Kampen, PhD; *Assoc Prof* Marjorie Keller, MFA; *Assoc Prof* Gary Richman, MFA; *Assoc Prof* Wendy Roworth, PhD; *Assoc Prof* Christopher Cordes, MFA & TMP. Instrs: FT 14, PT 3
Estab 1892; pub; D & E; scholarships; SC 21, studio seminars 24, LC 23; enrl D 900, E30, non-maj 725, maj 175, others 10-20
Ent Req: Same as required for Col of Arts & Sciences
Degrees: BA(Studio), BA(Art History) and BFA(Art Studio) 4 yrs
Tuition: In-state—undergrad $2785 per yr, $1392 per sem, $397 per month, $974 PT, $42 per cr hr; out-of-state—undergrad $4595 per yr, $2297 per sem, $656 per month, $2288 PT, $104 per cr hr; campus res
Courses: Art History, Drawing, Film, Graphic Design, Painting, Photography, Printmaking, Sculpture
Summer School: Chairperson Dept Art, Ronald J Onorato. Enrl 45-50; tuition $44 per undergrad cr for term of 5 wks beginning June 16. Courses—Art History, Drawing, Photography

NEWPORT

NEWPORT ART MUSEUM SCHOOL, 76 Bellevue Ave, 02840. Tel 401-847-0179. *Secretary* Judith Tucker
Estab 1913; D & E; scholarships; SC 14, LC 3; enrl D 200 (total)
Ent Req: None
Degrees: None; col cr given through Roger Williams Col
Tuition: $78-$94 per course per 12 wk sem; classes meet 3 hr per wk
Courses: Drawing, Painting, Photography, Printmaking, Sculpture, Etching, Pastels, Pottery
Adult Hobby Classes: Enrl 140; tuition $75 per 10 wks. Courses—Drawing, Painting, Pottery, Etching, Papermaking
Children's Classes: Enrl 50 per term; tuition $65 per 10 wks. Courses—Multimedia, Drawing, Painting, Pottery
Summer School: Dir, Susan Lacouture. Enrl 160; tuition $45 per 8 wks. Courses—Painting, Drawing, Workshops, Children's Art Day Camp

SALVE REGINA - THE NEWPORT COLLEGE, Art Dept, Ochre Point Ave, 02840. Tel 401-847-6650, Ext 379. *Chairperson* Jay Lacouture, MFA; *Asst Prof* Angelo Marinosci, MA; *Asst Prof* Sr Arlene Woods, MFA; *Instr* William Reis; *Instr* Richard Carbotti; *Instr* Belynda Gabryl
Estab 1947; den; D & E; SC 28, LC 8; enrl D 180 per sem (dept),

non-maj 95, maj 38
Ent Req: HS dipl, ent exam
Degrees: BA 4 yr
Tuition: Res—undergrad $2400 per sem, $150 per sem hr, $100 per cr (night), grad $90 per cr; nonres—undergrad $1975 per sem, $90 per cr (day), $45 per cr (night), grad $90 per cr; campus res—room & board $1100 per sem
Courses: †Art Education, Calligraphy, †Ceramics, Drawing, †Graphic Design, †Painting, Printmaking, Aesthetics, Anatomy, Environmental Design, 2 & 3-D Design
Summer School: Dir, Jay Lacouture

PROVIDENCE

BROWN UNIVERSITY, Dept of Art, 02912. Tel 401-863-2421. *Chmn* Roger Mayer
Pvt; D; SC 19-21, LC 13-15, GC 10-12; enrl maj 70, GS 40
Degrees: BA 4 yrs, MA & PhD in Art History
Tuition: undergrad $12,495 per sem, $6247 per sem, $1144 per unit, grad depends on boarding arrangements; nonres—undergrad & grad $9150 per yr; campus res available
Courses: Art History, Drawing, Painting, Printmaking, Sculpture, Foundation Design

PROVIDENCE COLLEGE, Art and Art History Dept, River Ave & Eaton St, 02918. Tel 401-865-2401, 865-1000. *Chmn* Richard N Elkington, MFA; *Assoc Prof* James Baker, MFA; *Assoc Prof* Adrian G Dabash, MFA; *Assoc Prof* Richard A McAlister, MFA; *Asst Prof* John DiCicco, MFAEd; *Asst Prof* Alice H Hauck, PhD; *Asst Prof* Suzanne H D'Avanzo, MA; *Instructor* Nancy E Hampshire, MA
Estab 1917, dept estab 1969; pvt; D & E; SC 49, LC 8; enrl D 254, E 250, non-maj 209, maj 45
Ent Req: HS dipl, portfolio needed for transfer students
Degrees: BA 4 yr
Tuition: Res & nonres—undergrad $5828 per yr; campus res—room & board $3350 per yr
Courses: †Art History, †Ceramics, †Drawing, †Painting, †Photography, †Printmaking, †Sculpture, Architecture History, †Studio Art
Adult Hobby Classes: Dean, Dr Roger L Pearson. Courses—History of Architecture, Art History, Calligraphy, Ceramics, Drafting, Drawing, Handicrafts, Lettering, Painting, Photography, Printmaking, Sculpture, Studio Art, Watercolor
Summer School: Dir, James M Murphy. Tuition $159 & $40 lab fee for three credit course beginning mid-June through July. Courses—Art History, Calligraphy, Ceramics, Drawing, Painting, Photography, Printmaking, Soft and Hard Crafts. A summer program is offered at Pietrasanta, Italy: Dir, Richard A McAlister, MFA. Courses—Art History, Languages, Literature, Religious Studies, Studio Art, Drawing, Painting, Sculpture

RHODE ISLAND COLLEGE, Art Dept, 02908. Tel 401-456-8054. *Chmn* Richard A Kenyon, EdD; *Prof* John DeMelim, MFA; *Prof* Angelo V Rosati, MA; *Prof* Donald C Smith, MA; *Prof* Ronald M Steinberg, PhD; *Prof* Lawrence F Sykes, MS; *Prof* David M Hysell, PhD; *Prof* Enrico Pinardi, MFA; *Assoc Prof* Curtis K LaFollette, MFA; *Asst Prof* Samuel B Ames, MFA; *Asst Prof* Krisjohn O Horvat, MFA; *Asst Prof* Mary Ball Howkins, PhD; *Asst Prof* Betty E Ohlin, EdD; *Instructor* Roberta Houllahan, MFA; *Instructor* Cheryl Goldman, MA
Estab 1854, dept estab 1969; pub; D & E; SC 31, LC 10, GC 5; enrl D 443, E approx 50, non-maj approx 228, maj 357, grad 30
Ent Req: HS dipl, CEEB and SAT
Degrees: BA(Art History), BA & MA(Studio) and BS(Art Educ) 4 yr, MAT 1 yr
Tuition: Res—$910 plus fees $160, grad $60 per cr; nonres—$3174 plus fees $160, grad $125 per cr; campus res—room & board $1345 - $1396
Courses: †Art Education, †Art History, Ceramics, Drawing, Film, Graphic Design, Painting, Photography, Printmaking, Sculpture, Teacher Training, †Art Studio, Fiber, Metal
Adult Hobby Classes: Visual Arts in Society, Drawing, Design, Photography
Children's Classes: Enrl 165; tuition $85 per 20 wks. Courses—Ceramics, Drawing, Life Drawing, Painting, Printmaking
Summer School: Dir, Richard A Kenyon. Enrl approx 150; tuition $54 per cr, nonres $90 per cr for term of 6 wks beginning June 26th. Courses—Ceramics, Drawing, Fiber, Painting, Photography

RHODE ISLAND SCHOOL OF DESIGN, 2 College St, 02903. Tel 401-331-3507. *Pres* Thomas F Schutte
Estab 1877; pvt; endowed; scholarships, grants-in-aid to res, student loans, fels; enrl D 1700, E 650
Ent Req: HS grad
Degrees: BArch, BID, BFA, BLandscape Arch, MA(Art Educ), MAT, MFA and MID 4-5 yrs
Tuition: $7500
Courses: †Architecture, †Ceramics, †Film, †Graphic Design, †Illustration, †Industrial Design, †Jewelry, †Landscape Architecture, †Painting, †Photography, †Printmaking, †Sculpture, †Teacher Training, †Textile Design, †Apparel Design, †Glass, †Interior Architecture, †Metalsmithing, †Television Studies, †Wood & Furniture Design
Adult Hobby Classes: Enrl 2000; tuition $190 for 1.5 cr of 14 wks. Courses—Fine & Applied Arts
Children's Classes: Enrl 330; tuition $175 per sem. Courses—Young Artists Paint Box
Summer School: Dir, Dana Prescott. Enrl 800; tuition varies. Courses—Fine & Applied Arts

WARWICK

COMMUNITY COLLEGE OF RHODE ISLAND, Dept of Art, 400 East Ave, 02886. Tel 401-825-2267. *Chmn* Donald F Gray. Instrs: FT 10, PT 15
Estab 1964; pub; D & E; scholarships; SC 16, LC 3, seminar 1; enrl D 4600
Ent Req: HS dipl, ent exam, equivalency exam
Degrees: AA, AFA, AS & AAS 2 yr
Courses: Ceramics, Commercial Art, Drafting, Drawing, Graphic Arts, Graphic Design, Handicrafts, History of Art & Archaeology, Interior Design, Painting, Photography, Sculpture

SOUTH CAROLINA

AIKEN

UNIVERSITY OF SOUTH CAROLINA AT AIKEN, Arts & Letters, 171 University Parkway, 29801. Tel 803-648-6851. *Head Dept* Sandra Hochel
Estab 1961, dept estab 1970; pub; D & E; SC 15, LC 5; enrl D 100, E 25, non-maj 80, maj 25
Ent Req: HS dipl, GED, SAT
Summer School: Tuition varies; 2 terms of 5 wks. Courses vary

CHARLESTON

BAPTIST COLLEGE AT CHARLESTON, Dept of Art,* Hwy 78 at I-26, 29411. Tel 803-797-4303. *Chmn* Joseph Ward
Estab 1960; den; D & E; scholarships; SC 14, LC 2; enrl D 80, E 71, maj 15
Ent Req: GED or HS dipl
Degrees: BA and BS 4 yrs
Tuition: $1975 per sem; campus res available
Courses: †Art Education, Ceramics, Drawing, Graphic Arts, History of Art & Archaeology, Painting, Sculpture, Teacher Training
Summer School: Enrl 1500; tui $45 per sem hr; campus res—room and board $240 per sem; two 5 wk sessions beginning June. Courses—same as regular session

COLLEGE OF CHARLESTON, Fine Arts Dept, 66 George St, 29401. Tel 803-792-5600. *Chmn* Arthur W McDonald
Estab 1966; pub; D & E; SC 36, LC 24
Ent Req: HS dipl
Degrees: BA(Fine Arts) 4 yrs
Tuition: Res—$1470 per yr; nonres—$2670 per yr
Courses: Art History, Drawing, †Painting, †Sculpture, †Stage Design, †Theatre Arts

GIBBES ART GALLERY SCHOOL,* 76 Queen St, 29401. Tel 803-577-7275. *Dir* Valerie Miller. Instrs: PT 20
Estab 1969; pub; D & E; scholarships; SC 18; enrl D 150, E 150
Ent Req: None
Tuition: $55 per course, materials fee $10
Courses: Calligraphy, Drawing, Graphic Design, Handicrafts, Interior Design, Photography, Printmaking, Pottery, Weaving
Children's Classes: Enrl 15 per course; tuition $37 per course per sem. Courses—Mixed Media (ages 4-7)
Summer School: Dir, Valerie Miller. Courses—same as regular session

CLEMSON

CLEMSON UNIVERSITY, College of Liberal Arts,* College of Architecture, Lee Hall, 29631. Tel 803-656-3311. *Head Dept* John Thomson Acorn
Estab 1967; pub; D; GC 24, SC 40, LC 29 (undergrad courses for service to pre-architecture and other Univ requirements); enrl approx 1500 annually, grad maj 10
Ent Req: Available on request
Degrees: MFA 60 hrs
Tuition: Res—$25 per sem; nonres—$100 per sem
Courses: Architecture, Art History, Ceramics, Drawing, Graphic Design, Painting, Photography, Printmaking, Sculpture

CLINTON

PRESBYTERIAN COLLEGE, Fine Arts Dept,* 29325. Tel 803-833-2820, Ext 296. *Chmn* Stephen G Schneffer; *Prof* C T Gaines; *Assoc Prof* D O Raines; *Asst Prof* N N Noble; *Instr* K Y Mahnke
Estab 1880, Dept estab 1966; den; D & E; scholarships; SC 8, LC 5; enrl D 200, non-maj 190, maj 10
Ent Req: HS dipl with C average, SAT
Degrees: BA 4 yr
Tuition: $4580 annual tuition; campus res available
Courses: †Art Education, Art History, Drawing, †Painting, Printmaking, Sculpture
Summer School: Dean, Dr Don King. Enrl 150; tuition $75 per cr hr for term of 5 wks beginning June 5. Courses—Art Appreciation, Painting

COLUMBIA

BENEDICT COLLEGE, Visual Art Studies, Taylor and Harden Sts, 29204. Tel 803-256-4220. *Asst Cur* Dr Lynne De Bauche; *Cur* Thomas Mac Pherson; *Staff* David Johnson Sr; *Staff* Wilma King
Estab 1870; pvt; D; scholarships; SC 11, LC 6
Ent Req: HS dipl
Degrees: BA(Teaching of Art), BA(Commercial Art)
Courses: Commercial Art, Teacher Training
Summer School: Term of two 5 wk sessions beginning June. Courses—Art Appreciation, Arts & Crafts

COLUMBIA COLLEGE, Dept of Art, 29203. Tel 803-786-3012. *Chmn* Vicki Pullen
Scholarships
Degrees: BA, cert
Tuition: $6500
Courses: Advertising Design, Art Appreciation, Art History, Calligraphy, Ceramics, Design, Drawing, Illustration, Painting, Photography, Printmaking, Fibers, Papermaking
Adult Hobby Classes: Enrl 20 per class. Courses—Art Appreciation, Art History, Drawing, Photography
Summer School: Dir, Becky Hulion. Enrl 20 per class. Courses—Art Appreciation, Art History, Art Education, Drawing, Photography, Printmaking

RICHLAND ART WORKSHOP,* 1500 Gervais St, 29206. Tel 803-799-2810.
Supervisor Jean McWhorter. Instrs: PT 4
Estab 1950 (operates as service of the Columbia Museum of Art); D & E
Ent Req: None; classes for youths and adults
Courses: Drawing, Painting

UNIVERSITY OF SOUTH CAROLINA, Dept of Art, Sloan College, 29208. Tel
803-777-4236. *Chmn* John Oneil, PhD; *Chmn Studio* Boyd Saunders, MFA; *Chmn
Art Educ* Jim Cromer, EdD; *Chmn Art History* Annie Paul Quinsac, PhD; *Instr*
Philip Mullen, PhD; *Instr* Howard Woody, MA
Estab 1801, dept estab 1924; pub; D & E; scholarships; SC 89, LC 57, GC 73; enrl
D 1620, E 174, non-maj 1000, maj 620, grad 82
Ent Req: HS dipl
Degrees: BA, BFA and BS 4 yrs, MA and MAT 1 yr, MFA 2 yrs
Tuition: Res—undergrad $740 per yr, $370 per sem, PT $30 per cr, grad $980 per
yr, $490 per sem; nonres—undergrad $1700 per yr, $850 per sem, PT $70 per cr,
grad $980 per yr, $490 per sem; campus res—room $620 & board $900 per yr
Courses: †Advertising Design, †Art Education, †Art History, †Ceramics,
†Commercial Art, Conceptual Art, †Drawing, Film, Goldsmithing, †Graphic Arts,
†Graphic Design, Illustration, †Interior Design, Jewelry, Mixed Media, Museum
Staff Training, †Painting, Photography, †Printmaking, Restoration & Conservation
Adult Hobby Classes: Tuition $30 per cr. Courses—Ceramics, Painting,
Printmaking, Sculpture
Children's Classes: Enrl 60; tuition $20 per sem. Courses—Crafts, Drawing,
Painting
Summer School: Dir, John Oneil. Enrl 400; tuition res $30 per cr, nonres $70 per cr
for term of 5 wks. Courses—same as regular session

DUE WEST

ERSKINE COLLEGE, Dept of Art, 29639. Tel 803-379-8887. *Head Dept* Mary E
Carmichael, MFA
Estab 1839; den; D; SC 3, LC 1; enrl 60-80 per sem
Degrees: None
Courses: Drawing, Painting, Art Appreciation, Art for Teachers, K-6, Color &
Design, Studio
Summer School: Courses—Art Appreciation, Art for Teachers, K-6

FLORENCE

FRANCIS MARION COLLEGE, Fine & Applied Arts Dept,* PO Box F7500,
29501. Tel 803-669-4121. *Chmn* John W Baker
Scholarships offered
Degrees: BA, BS
Tuition: Res—$940 per yr; nonres—$1880 per yr
Courses: Art Appreciation, Art Education, Art History, Design, Drawing,
Handicrafts, Painting, Sculpture, Stage Design

GAFFNEY

LIMESTONE COLLEGE, Art Dept, Division of Fine Arts, 29340. Tel 803-489-
7151. *Chmn* Robert B Welch
Estab 1845; pvt; D & E; scholarships; SC 19, LC 9; enrl D 112, maj 42, others 3
Ent Req: HS dipl, ent exam
Degrees: BS(Educ, Studio) 4 yrs
Courses: Silk-Screen, Wood-Block

GREENVILLE

BOB JONES UNIVERSITY, School of Fine Arts, 29614. Tel 803-242-5011, Ext
2700. *Dean* Dwight Gustafson, DMus; *Chmn Division of Art* Emery Bopp, MFA;
Instructor David Appleman, MA; *Instructor* Kathy Bell, MA; *Instructor* Carl Blair,
MFA; *Instructor* James Brooks, BA; *Instructor* Karen Keen, BA; *Instructor* Darrel
Koons, MA; *Instructor* Harrell Whittington, MA
Estab 1927, dept estab 1945; pvt; D; SC 29, LC 12, GC 10; enrl D 235,
non-maj 108
Ent Req: HS dipl, letters of recommendation
Degrees: BA & BS 4 yrs, MA 1-2 yrs
Tuition: $1998 per yr, $999 per sem; campur res—room & board $2430
Courses: Advertising Design, Aesthetics, †Art Education, Art History, Calligraphy,
Ceramics, Collages, †Commercial Art, Conceptual Art, Costume Design &
Construction, †Drawing, †Film, †Graphic Arts, Graphic Design, Handicrafts,
History of Art & Archaeology, Illustration, Lettering, †Painting, †Photography,
Printmaking, Restoration & Conservation, Sculpture, †Stage Design, Teacher
Training, †Theatre Arts, Elective courses available from the Division of Cinema and
the Dept of Dramatic Production

FURMAN UNIVERSITY, Dept of Art, 29613. Tel 803-294-2074. *Chmn* Thomas E
Flowers
Estab 1826; pvt den; D & E; scholarships; SC 19, LC 7; enrl D 80, non-maj 40,
maj 40
Ent Req: HS dipl, SAT
Degrees: BA 4 yr
Courses: Advertising Design, Aesthetics, Art Education, Art History, Calligraphy,
Ceramics, Drawing, Graphic Design, Handicrafts, History of Art & Archaeology,
Lettering, Museum Staff Training, Painting, Printmaking, Sculpture, Teacher
Training, Book Arts, Watercolor

GREENVILLE COUNTY MUSEUM OF ART, Museum School of Art,* 420
College St, 29601. Tel 803-271-7570. *Dir* Sharon W Campbell. Instrs: FT 1, PT 31
Estab 1960; pub; D & E; scholarships; SC 12, LC 2, GC 6; enrl D 250, E 170
Degrees: AAA and AFA 2-3 yr
Tuition: $25 registration fee, cost on per class basis
Courses: †Advertising Design, Art History, †Drawing, Film, Handicrafts, †Painting,

†Photography, †Printmaking, †Sculpture, Video, Museology, Philosophy of Art,
†Pottery, Weaving
Adult Hobby Classes: Classes offered each semester
Children's Classes: Enrl 15 per course, ages 4-12. Courses—Mixed-media
Summer School: Enrl approx 300 per sem; 8 wk term. Courses—same as regular sem

GREENVILLE TECHNICAL COLLEGE, Art History Dept, Station B, PO Box
5616, 29609. Tel 803-242-3170. *Chmn* Dr David S Trask
Degrees: AA
Tuition: $175 per qtr
Courses: Art Appreciation, Art History, Film
Adult Hobby Classes: Courses offered
Summer School: Dir, Dr David S Trask. Enrl 20. Courses—Art Appreciation

GREENWOOD

LANDER COLLEGE, Dept of Fine Arts, 29646. Tel 803-229-8231, 229-8323, 229-
8362. *Chmn* Alan MacTaggart. Instrs: FT 3, PT 2
Estab 1872; pub; D & E; scholarships; SC 25, LC 5; enrl D 235, E 60, maj 45
Ent Req: HS dipl
Degrees: BA(Art) 4 yrs
Tuition: 700 per yr; nonres $1300 per yr; campus res $1300-$1500
Courses: Advertising Design, Aesthetics, Art Education, Ceramics, Commercial Art,
Drawing, Graphic Arts, Graphic Design, History of Art & Archaeology, Illustration,
Painting, Photography, Sculpture, Teacher Training
Adult Hobby Classes: Ceramics, Enameling
Children's Classes: General Studio Skills
Summer School: Art Appreciation, Art Education, Ceramics, Photography,
Printmaking

HARTSVILLE

COKER COLLEGE, Art Dept, 29550. Tel 803-332-1381, Ext 512. *Head Dept* R
Nickey Brumbaugh. Instrs: FT 3
Estab 1908; pvt; D & E; scholarships; SC 26, LC 9; enrl 355, art maj 19
Ent Req: HS dipl, ent exam
Degrees: AB and BS 4 yrs
Tuition: $4135 per yr; campus res—room & board $1840 per yr
Courses: †Art Education, †Art History, Ceramics, Design, Drawing, †Graphic
Design, Handicrafts, †Painting, †Photography, Sculpture
Summer School: Tuition $180 per sem hr for 5 wk term. Courses—Introduction
level art

NEWBERRY

NEWBERRY COLLEGE, Dept of Art, College St, 29108. Tel 803-276-5010. *Head
Dept* Kenneth David Brown, MA
Estab 1856, dept estab 1973; den; D & E; SC 35, LC 2; enrl D 114, non-maj 106,
maj 15
Ent Req: HS dipl, SAT
Degrees: AB(Art) 4 yrs, BS(Arts Mgt), two courses in independent study, financial
aid available
Courses: Art History, †Ceramics, Costume Design & Construction, †Drawing, Mixed
Media, †Painting, †Printmaking, †Sculpture, Stage Design, Theatre Arts

ORANGEBURG

CLAFLIN COLLEGE, Dept of Art, College Ave, 29115. Tel 803-534-2701. *Chmn*
Karen Woodfaulk, MFA; *Assoc Prof* Earnest McNealy, PhD
School estab 1869, dept estab 1888; pvt; D; scholarships; SC 10, LC 2; enrl D 20
Ent Req: HS dipl, SAT
Degrees: BA 4 years, BA Teacher Educ 4 years
Tuition: Res—undergrad $2200 per academic year; nonres—undergrad $2200 per
academic year; campus res available
Courses: †Advertising Design, Aesthetics, †Art Education, Art History, Ceramics,
Drawing, Film, Graphic Arts, Handicrafts, Lettering, Mixed Media, Painting,
Photography, Printmaking, Sculpture, Video, Art Tech
Summer School: Dir, Karen Woodfaulk. Enrl 10-12, 6 wk term beginning June.
Course—Art Appreciation, Art-Elem School Crafts, Advertising Art, Textile Design

SOUTH CAROLINA STATE COLLEGE, Art Program, 29117. Tel 803-536-7174.
Dir Leo F Twiggs, EdD; *Assoc Prof* Henry G Michaux, EdD; *Asst Prof* James L
McFadden, MFA; *Instructor* Terry K Hunter, MFA
Dept estab 1972; D & E; SC 15, LC 7; enrl D 73, nonmaj 8, maj 73
Ent Req: HS dipl
Degrees: BA & BS 4 yrs, MA & MS approx 2 yrs
Tuition: Res $450 per sem, nonres $900 per sem; campus residence available
Courses: Art Education
Adult Hobby Classes: Courses—Ceramics, Sculpture
Summer School: Dir, Dr Carl A Carpenter. Tuition $34 per cr hr. Courses—Art
Appreciation, Arts & Crafts for Children

ROCK HILL

WINTHROP COLLEGE, Dept of Art, 29733. Tel 803-323-2126. *Chmn* Edmund D
Lewandowski, Dipl; *Assoc Prof* David Freeman, MFA; *Assoc Prof* Mary Mintich,
MFA; *Asst Prof* Jean McFarland, MFA; *Asst Prof* Lary Pierce, MA; *Asst Prof* Rex
Stambaugh, MFA
Estab 1886; pub; D & E; SC 42, LC 10; enrl in college D 4983, non-maj 360, maj
147, grad 6
Ent Req: HS dipl, SAT, CEEB
Degrees: BA and BVA 4 yrs
Tuition: Res—undergrad $1201 per yr, $601 per sem, grad $605 ;

nonres—undergrad $2100 per yr, $1050 per sem, grad $693; campus residence available
Courses: †Advertising Design, Art Education, Art History, Calligraphy, †Ceramics, Collages, †Commercial Art, Conceptual Art, †Drawing, Fashion Arts, †Graphic Arts, †Graphic Design, Handicrafts, †Illustration, Interior Design, Jewelry, Lettering, Mixed Media, †Painting, †Photography, †Printmaking, †Sculpture, Silversmithing, Teacher Training, Textile Design
Summer School: Dir, Edmund D Lewandowski. Enrl 60. Courses—Art Appreciation, Creative Art for Children, Design, Drawing, Graphic Design, Painting

SPARTANBURG

ART ASSOCIATION SCHOOL, 385 S Spring St, 29301. Tel 803-583-1399. *Educ Chmn* Glenda Smart; *Dir* Anne Greene
Estab 1970; D & E; SC 25; enrl 300-400
Ent Req: None
Tuition: $45-$62 for 10 wks
Courses: Calligraphy, Commercial Art, Drawing, Interior Design, Mixed Media, Painting, Photography, Sculpture, Weaving, Pottery, Stained Glass
Children's Classes: Tuition $48 for 8-10 wk term. Courses—Drawing, Painting, Pottery

CONVERSE COLLEGE, Art Dept,* PO Box 29, 29301. Tel 803-585-6421, Ext 251. *Chmn Dept* Henry Fagen Jr, EdD; *Assoc Prof* David Harrison, MA; *Assoc Prof* Melba LeGrande Long, MFA; *Assoc Prof* Mayo McBoggs, MFA; *Asst Prof* Judy Voss Jones, MFA
Col estab 1889; pvt; D; SC 40, LC 17; enrl D 290, non-maj 240, maj 50, others 12
Ent Req: HS dipl, SAT, CEEB, ACT, Advanced placement in Art & Art History
Degrees: BA & BFA 4 yrs
Tuition: Res—$6920 comprehensive fees; nonres—$9000 comprehensive fees
Courses: Art Education, †Art History, Ceramics, †Drawing, Film, †Interior Design, Museum Staff Training, †Painting, Photography, †Printmaking, †Sculpture, Teacher Training

SOUTH DAKOTA

ABERDEEN

NORTHERN STATE COLLEGE, Art Dept, 57401. Tel 605-622-2514. *Chmn* Lonn M Sweet; *Prof* Jim Gibson, MFA; *Prof* Mark Shekore, MFA; *Assoc Prof* Mark McGinnis, MFA; *Asst Prof* James Lauver, MS; *Asst Prof* Bill Hoar, PhD; *Asst Prof* Lynn Carlsgaard, MA. Instrs: Estab 1901, dept estab 1920
Pub; D & E; scholarships; SC 40, LC 14, GC 6; enrl D 385, non-maj 300, maj 85
Ent Req: HS dipl
Degrees: AA 2 yrs, BA, BS, BSEd 4 yrs
Tuition: Res—undergrad $27.29 per cr, grad $40.93 per cr; nonres—undergrad $56.44 per cr, grad $74.37 per cr; campus res—room $330 per sem
Courses: Advertising Design, Aesthetics, †Art Education, †Ceramics, †Commercial Art, †Drawing, Goldsmithing, Handicrafts, History of Art & Archaeology, Illustration, Interior Design, Jewelry, Mixed Media, †Painting, Photography, †Printmaking, †Sculpture, Silversmithing, †Teacher Training, Textile Design
Adult Hobby Classes: Enrl 30; tuition $27.29 per cr
Summer School: Dir, Lonn M Sweet. Enrl 35; tuition $27.29 per cr for term of 4 wks beginning June 4

BROOKINGS

SOUTH DAKOTA STATE UNIVERSITY, Dept of Visual Arts, Solberg Hall, 57007. Tel 605-688-4103. *Head Dept* Jim Jordan, PhD; *Prof* Richard Edie, MFA; *Prof* Joseph Stuart, MA; *Assoc Prof* Melvin Spinar, MFA; *Assoc Prof* Helen Morgan, MAE; *Assoc Prof* Gerald Kruse, MFA; *Asst Prof* Don Boyd, MFA; *Asst Prof* Mark Lazarus, MFA; *Asst Prof* Signe Stuart, MA
Estab 1881; pub; D & E; scholarships; SC 28, LC 8
Ent Req: HS dipl, ent ACT
Degrees: BA & BS 136 sem cr
Tuition: Res—$19.50 per sem; nonres—$44.50 per sem
Courses: †Art Education, Calligraphy, †Ceramics, Drawing, Film, †Graphic Arts, †Graphic Design, History of Art & Archaeology, Intermedia, Lettering, Museum Staff Training, †Painting, Photography, Printmaking, †Sculpture, Textile Design, †Applied Design, Art Criticism, Design, Watercolor, Weaving
Adult Hobby Classes: Head Dept, Jim Jordan
Summer School: Head Dept, Jim Jordan. Regular tuition per credit hour. Courses-Art History, Design, Drawing

HURON

HURON COLLEGE, Art Dept,* 57350. Tel 605-352-8721. *Head Div* James Sperry
Pub; D; scholarships; SC 9, LC 2; enrl D 580
Ent Req: HS dipl, ent exam
Degrees: BA and BS 4 yrs
Tuition: $3200 per yr
Courses: Art Education, Drawing, Graphic Arts, Graphic Design, History of Art & Archaeology, Painting, Photography, Sculpture, Teacher Training

MADISON

DAKOTA STATE COLLEGE, Division of Fine and Applied Art,* 57042. Tel 605-256-3551, Ext 219. *Chmn* Orval Van Deest. Instrs: FT 1, PT 1
Estab 1881; pub; D; scholarships; SC 16, LC 5; enrl D 120, maj 20
Ent Req: HS dipl, ACT
Degrees: BS 4 yrs
Tuition: $1025 per yr
Courses: Art Education, Art History, Ceramics, Drawing, Jewelry, Painting, Sculpture, Teacher Training
Summer School: Term of 8 wks beginning June

SIOUX FALLS

AUGUSTANA COLLEGE, Art Dept, 57197. Tel 605-336-0770. *Chmn* Robert J Aldern, BFA; *Assoc Prof* Carl A Grupp, MFA; *Asst Prof* Paul J Koehler, MFA
Estab 1860; den; D & E; scholarships; SC 14, LC 3; enrl total 1861
Ent Req: HS dipl, ent exam
Degrees: BA and MAT
Tuition: $4100 annual tuition; campus res available
Courses: †Art Education, †Art History, †Ceramics, †Drawing, Graphic Design, †Painting, Photography, Printmaking, †Sculpture, Etching, Lithography
Summer School: Dir, Dr Gary D Olson. Term of 7 wks beginning June. Courses—Arts, Crafts, Drawing

SIOUX FALLS COLLEGE, Dept of Art,* Division of Fine Arts, 1501 S Prairie St, 57101. Tel 605-331-5000. *Chmn* Edgar Harvey, PhD
Estab 1883; pub; scholarships; SC, LC; enrl 1000
Degrees: BA with maj in Art or Art Educ 4 yrs
Tuition: $3900 per yr
Courses: Art Education, Art History, Drawing, Handicrafts, Painting, Design & Illustration
Summer School: Terms one 3 wk session, two 4 wk sessions. Courses—Crafts, Design, Drawing, Education

SPEARFISH

BLACK HILLS STATE COLLEGE, Art Dept,* 57783. Tel 605-642-6272. *Chmn* Dr Victor Weidensee. Instrs: FT 13
Estab 1883; pub; D; scholarships; SC 15, LC 4; enrl maj 50
Ent Req: HS dipl, transcripts, ACT, physical exam
Degrees: BA 4 yrs
Tuition: $816.64 per yr
Courses: Art Education, Calligraphy, Ceramics, Commercial Art, Drafting, Drawing, Painting, Photography, Sculpture
Summer School: Courses—Art in our Lives, Ceramics, Drawing, Painting, School Arts & Crafts

SPRINGFIELD

UNIVERSITY OF SOUTH DAKOTA, SPRINGFIELD, 57062. Tel 605-369-2201. *Head Dept* Ed Gettinger
Estab 1881; pub; D; scholarships; SC 12, LC 2; enrl D 70, maj 14, grad 70
Ent Req: HS dipl
Degrees: AA, AS and AAS 2 yrs
Tuition: Res—$1225 per sem; nonres—$1625 per sem
Courses: Art Appreciation, Ceramics, Design, Drawing, Lettering, Painting, Sculpture
Adult Hobby Classes: Enrl 15. Courses—Ceramics, Painting

VERMILLION

UNIVERSITY OF SOUTH DAKOTA, Dept of Art, 57069. Tel 605-677-5636. *Dean* John A Day, MFA; *Chmn Dept* Richard Zauft, MFA; *Prof* Daniel Packard, MFA; *Prof* Kenneth Grizzell, MFA; *Prof* Lloyd Menard, MFA; *Assoc Prof* William Wold, MA; *Asst Prof* Wu Chien Lem, MFA; *Assoc Prof* Martin Wanserski, MFA; *Asst Prof* Jeff Freeman, MFA; *Asst Prof* John Banasiak, MFA; *Instr* Ann Balakier, MFA
Estab 1862, dept estab 1931; pub; D & E; scholarships; SC 32, LC 9, GC 9; enrl non-maj 50, maj 100, grad 10
Ent Req: HS dipl, ACT
Degrees: BFA, BS, BFA with Teacher Cert
Tuition: Res—undergrad $28.57 per cr hr, grad $42.89 per cr hr; nonres—undergrad $64.78 per cr hr, grad $83.13 per cr hr; campus res—room & board $1500
Courses: Aesthetics, †Art Education, Calligraphy, †Ceramics, Drawing, †Graphic Arts, Graphic Design, History of Art & Archaeology, Museum Staff Training, †Painting, †Photography, †Printmaking, †Sculpture, Weaving
Summer School: Chmn, Richard Zauft. Tuition $28.57 per cr hr for term of 8 wks beginning June

YANKTON

MOUNT MARTY COLLEGE, Art Dept,* 57078. Tel 605-668-1011, 668-1574. *Prof Emeritus* Sr Leonarda Longen, MFA; *Instr* Sr Mary Kay Banowicz, MSS; *Lectr* Sr Kathleen Courtney, MA; *Lectr* Edmond Gettinger; *Lectr* Kathleen Hickenbotham
Estab 1936; den; D; scholarships; SC 17, LC 5; enrl 9
Ent Req: HS dipl
Degrees: BA 4 yrs
Tuition: $3400 annual tuition; campus res available
Courses: Art Education, Art History, Calligraphy, Ceramics, Drawing, Handicrafts, Painting, Photography, Printmaking, Sculpture
Adult Hobby Classes: Courses—Calligraphy
Summer School: Dir, Sr Consuelo Chavez. Tuition $90 per cr hr for term of 4 wks beginning June and July

YANKTON COLLEGE, Dept of Art, 57078. Tel 605-665-3661. *Head Dept* Randy Norris. Instrs: PT 3
Estab 1881; pvt, den; scholarships
Ent Req: HS grad
Degrees: 4 yr
Courses: Art Education, Art History, Ceramics, Drawing, Jewelry, Painting, Photography, Sculpture, Art Appreciation, Foundations, Philosophy of Art, Weaving

TENNESSEE

ATHENS

TENNESSEE WESLEYAN COLLEGE, Dept of Art,* PO Box 40, 37303. Tel 615-745-5872
Estab 1857, dept estab 1966; den; D & E; SC 7, LC 5; enrl total 500, maj 10
Ent Req: HS dipl
Degrees: BA and BS 4 yrs
Tuition: $1000 per quarter
Courses: Art Education, Art History, Drawing, Painting, Sculpture, Design

CHATTANOOGA

CHATTANOOGA STATE TECHNICAL COMMUNITY COLLEGE, Advertising Arts Dept,* 4501 Amnicola Hwy, 37406. Tel 615-622-6262. *Asst Prof* Bill Ransom, MFA; *Asst Prof* Denise Frank; *Instr* William Helseth
Pub; D & E; scholarships; SC 30, LC 5; enrl D 3000, E 2000
Ent Req: HS dipl
Degrees: Certificate, AA(Advertising Art)
Tuition: Res—$13 per qtr hr; nonres—$64 per qtr hr
Courses: Advertising Design, Art Education, Art History, Ceramics, Commercial Art, Display, Drafting, Drawing, Graphic Arts, Graphic Design, Illustration, Lettering, Mixed Media, Painting, Photography, Printmaking, Sculpture, Teacher Training
Adult Hobby Classes: Tuition $45 per course. Courses—Painting, Photography
Children's Classes: Tuition $20 per course. Courses—Arts & Crafts, Ceramics & Sculpture
Summer School: Tuition $140 per term of 10 weeks

UNIVERSITY OF TENNESSEE AT CHATTANOOGA, Dept of Art, 615 McCallie Ave, 37402. Tel 615-755-4178. *Head* George Cress, MFA; *Assoc Prof* E Alan White, MFA; *Assoc Prof* Anne Lindsey, PhD; *Assoc Prof* Bruce Wallace, MFA; *Asst Prof* Jean Gallagher, MFA; *Asst Prof* Stephen S LeWinter, MA; *Asst Prof* Marilyn Morton; *Asst Prof* Richard Lizza
Estab 1928; pub; D & E; SC 11, LC 13, GC 1; enrl D 420, E 80, non-maj 500, maj 130, grad 6, others 14
Ent Req: HS dipl, ACT or SAT, health exam
Degrees: BA and BFA 4 yrs
Tuition: Res—undergrad $394 per sem, grad $512 per sem; nonres—undergrad $1272 per sem, grad $1391 per sem; campus res—room and board $450 per sem
Courses: Art Education, Art History, Ceramics, Commercial Art, Drawing, Graphic Design, Painting, Printmaking, Sculpture
Summer School: Tuition $38 per sem hr

CLARKSVILLE

AUSTIN PEAY STATE UNIVERSITY, Dept of Art, Box 4677, 37040. Tel 615-648-7011. *Chmn Dept* James T Diehr, PhD; *Instructor* Olen Bryant, MFA; *Instructor* Charles Young, MA; *Instructor* Bruce Childs, MFA; *Instructor* T Max Hochstetler, MFA; *Instructor* Larry Hortenburg, MFA; *Instructor* Philancy Holder, PhD; *Instructor* Susan Bryant
Estab 1927, dept estab 1930; pub; D & E; scholarships; GC 3; enrl D 615, E 75, non-maj 475, maj 140
Ent Req: HS dipl
Degrees: AA 2 yrs, BFA, BA & BS 4 yrs
Tuition: Res—$625 per yr; nonres—$1625 per yr; campus res—room & board $1450 per yr
Courses: †Advertising Design, †Art Education, Art History, Calligraphy, Ceramics, Commercial Art, Drafting, Drawing, †Graphic Arts, Graphic Design, Handicrafts, Illustration, Lettering, Mixed Media, †Painting, †Photography, Printmaking, †Sculpture, Stage Design, Teacher Training, Textile Design
Summer School: Dir, Dr Diehr. Enrl 100; 8 wk sessions. Courses—Art Appreciation, Drawing, Photography

CLEVELAND

CLEVELAND STATE COMMUNITY COLLEGE, Dept of Art,* Adkisson Dr, PO Box 1205, 37311. Tel 615-472-7141. *Assoc Dean* Mary Baker; *Assoc Prof* Jere Chumley, MA; *Instr* Floyd Dockery, AA; *Instr* Catherine Smith, MS
Estab 1967; pub; D & E; SC 6, LC 5; enrl D 107, E 28, non-maj 76, maj 59
Ent Req: HS dipl or GED
Degrees: AA and AS 2 yrs
Tuition: Res—$154 per quarter; nonres—$740 per quarter
Courses: Art Education, Art History, Ceramics, Commercial Art, Drawing, Handicrafts, Painting, Printmaking, Sculpture, Art Appreciation, Design, Weaving

LEE COLLEGE, Dept of Music & Fine Arts,* North Ocoee St, 37311. Tel 615-472-2111. *Prof* Jimmy W Burns; *Asst Prof* John W Simmons, MA. Instrs: FT 7
Tuition: $1140 per sem
Courses: Art Appreciation, Art Education, Design, Drawing, Painting

COLLEGEDALE

SOUTHERN MISSIONARY COLLEGE, Art Dept,* 37315. Tel 615-396-2111. *Chmn Arts & Letters* Floyd Greenleaf
Estab 1969; den; D & E; LC 3; enrl maj 34
Ent Req: HS dipl, ent exam
Degrees: BA(Art) and BA(Art Educ) 4 yrs
Tuition: $2880 per yr

COLUMBIA

COLUMBIA STATE COMMUNITY COLLEGE, Dept of Art, PO Box 670, 38401. Tel 615-388-0120. *Head Dept* Fred Behrens, MFA
Estab 1966; pub; D & E; scholarships; SC 17, LC 4; enrl D 230, non-maj 215, maj 12-15
Ent Req: Open door institution
Degrees: AA & AS 2 yrs
Tuition: $154 per qtr
Courses: †Art Education, Ceramics, Drawing, Film, History of Art & Archaeology, Painting, Photography, Printmaking, †Art Studio
Children's Classes: Enrl 18-20, tuition $30 per session

FRANKLIN

HARRIS SCHOOL OF ART, INC,* 1109 Battlewood St, Battlewood Estates, 37064. Tel 615-790-0407, 794-8544
Estab 1932; pvt; D; SC, LC; enrl 75
Ent Req: HS dipl
Degrees: 2, 3 and 4 yr cert in advertising art
Courses: Advertising Layout, Advertising and Fiction Illustration, Airbrush Rendering, Artistic Anatomy, Composition and Design, Figure Drawing and Painting, Head Drawing and Painting, Lettering and Typography, Lithography, Mechanical Art and Paste-Up, Perspective Drawing, Photoengraving, Printing Processes, Still Life Painting

GATLINBURG

ARROWMONT SCHOOL OF ARTS AND CRAFTS, 4590 Parkway, Box 567, 37738. Tel 615-436-5860. *Dir* Sandra J Blain; *Prog Coordr* Clare Verstegen
Estab 1945; pvt; D & E (operate mostly in spring & summer with special programs for fall & winter); scholarships; SC 44-50, GC 30; enrl D 1000
Degrees: None granted, though credit is offered for courses through the Univ of Tennessee, Knoxville & other similar institutions
Tuition: $110 per wk, 1 and 2 wk sessions; campus res—room & board $95-$145 per wk
Courses: Ceramics, Drawing, Graphic Arts, Weaving, Jewelry, Painting, Photography, Textile Design, Basketry, Blacksmithing, Bookbinding, Enamel, Leather, Papermaking, Stained Glass, Wood

GREENEVILLE

TUSCULUM COLLEGE, Fine Arts Dept,* Division of Creative Arts & Humanities, Box 48, 37743. Tel 615-639-2861. *Prof* Clement Allison, MFA
Estab 1794; den; D; scholarships; SC 25, LC 3; enrl D 445, maj 18
Ent Req: HS dipl
Degrees: BA and BS 4 yrs
Tuition: $1500 per sem
Courses: Art Education, Ceramics, Drawing, History of Art & Archaeology, Painting, Printmaking, Sculpture, Glassblowing, Life Drawing, Two & Three-Dimensional Design
Adult Hobby Classes: Enrl 14. Courses—Painting

HARROGATE

LINCOLN MEMORIAL UNIVERSITY, Division of Fine Arts,* Box 670, 37752. Tel 615-869-3611. *Chmn* Robert Brown, EdD
Estab 1897, dept estab 1974; pvt; D & E; SC 30, LC 3; enrl D 120, E 75, non-maj 97, maj 98
Ent Req: HS dipl
Degrees: BA 4 yrs
Tuition: $2400 per yr
Courses: Aesthetics, †Art Education, Art History, †Ceramics, †Commercial Art, †Drawing, Film, Goldsmithing, Graphic Arts, †Jewelry, Lettering, Museum Staff Training, †Painting, †Photography, †Sculpture, Silversmithing, †Teacher Training, †Textile Design, †Theatre Arts, Weaving

JACKSON

LAMBUTH COLLEGE, Dept of Art,* 38301. Tel 901-427-6743. *Chmn* Russell McIntire, PhD; *Assoc Prof* Lawrence A Ray, MA
Estab 1843, dept estab 1950; den; D & E; SC 21, LC 10
Ent Req: HS dipl
Degrees: BA and BS 4 yrs
Tuition: $1675 per sem
Courses: Advertising Design, Aesthetics, Architecture, †Art Education, †Art History, †Commercial Art, Drawing, Fashion Arts, Graphic Design, †History of Art & Archaeology, †Interior Design, †Painting, Photography, †Printmaking, †Sculpture, Stage Design, Teacher Training, Theatre Arts, Stained Glass

UNION UNIVERSITY, Dept of Art, Hwy 45 Bypass, Union University Box 1845, 38301. Tel 901-668-1818. *Chmn Dept Art* Grove Robinson, MFA
Estab 1824, dept estab 1958; den; D & E; scholarships; SC 20, LC 5; enrl D 200, E 40, maj 28
Ent Req: HS dipl, ACT
Degrees: BA and BS 4 yrs
Tuition: $1225
Courses: Advertising Design, Art Education, Art History, †Ceramics, Commercial Art, Drawing, Handicrafts, Jewelry, Lettering, †Painting, Photography, Printmaking, Sculpture, Silversmithing, Teacher Training, Art Appreciation
Children's Classes: Enrl 20; 5 wk session. Courses—Drawing
Summer School: Assoc Acad VPres, Dr Pat Taylor. Enrl 423. Courses—various

JEFFERSON CITY

CARSON-NEWMAN COLLEGE, Art Dept, 37760. Tel 615-475-9061, Ext 332. *Chmn Dept* R Earl Cleveland. Instrs: FT 3
Col estab 1851; den; D & E; scholarships; SC 26, LC 7; enrl maj 36
Ent Req: HS dipl
Degrees: BA(Art & Photography) 4 yrs
Tuition: $3300 per yr, studio fees $5-$100; campus res $1800
Courses: Aesthetics, Art Education, Art History, Ceramics, Drawing, Handicrafts, Lettering, Painting, Photography, Printmaking, Sculpture, Stage Design, Teacher Training, Theatre Arts
Summer School: Chmn, R Earl Cleveland. Courses—Art Appreciation, Photography, Teacher Workshops; Travel Study in Europe

JOHNSON CITY

EAST TENNESSEE STATE UNIVERSITY, Fine Arts Dept, Box 23740A, 37601. Tel 615-929-4247. *Chmn Dept* John E Schrader, MFA; *Prof* John Pav, PhD; *Assoc Prof* Gerald Edmundson, MA; *Assoc Prof* David Logan, MFA; *Assoc Prof* James Mills, PhD; *Assoc Prof* George Moldovan, MA; *Assoc Prof* John Steele, MA; *Assoc Prof* Charles Thompson, MFA; *Asst Prof* Vickie Francoeur, MFA; *Asst Prof* Jonathan Donehoo, MFA; *Asst Prof* Michael Smith, MFA; *Asst Prof* M Wayne Dyer, MFA
Estab 1909, dept estab 1949; pub; D & E; scholarships; SC 102, LC 30, GC 46; enrl D approx 1400
Ent Req: HS dipl, ACT or SAT
Degrees: BA, BS & BFA 4 yrs, MA, MFA
Tuition: Res—undergrad $37 per semester hr, $393 per semester, grad $50 per semester hr, $507 per semester; nonres—undergrad $76 per semester hr, $879 per semester; campus res—room & board approx $600 per semester
Courses: †Art Education, †Art History, †Ceramics, †Drawing, †Graphic Design, †Jewelry, Lettering, †Painting, †Photography, Printmaking, †Sculpture, †Metalsmithing, †Weaving
Adult Hobby Classes: Credit/no credit classes at night. Courses—Art History, Drawing, Photography
Children's Classes: Saturdays
Summer School: Two semesters of 5 wks each and a 3 wk intersession beginning May 16 and June 6. Courses—Same as above

KNOXVILLE

UNIVERSITY OF TENNESSEE, KNOXVILLE, Dept of Art, 1715 Volunteer Blvd, 37996. Tel 615-974-3408. *Head Art Dept* Donald F Kurka, PhD. Instrs: FT 31
Estab 1794, dept estab 1951; pub; D & E; scholarships; SC 51, LC 23, GC 50; enrl D 1500, E 250, non-maj 300, maj 350, grad 25
Ent Req: HS dipl
Degrees: BA & BFA, MFA; both undergraduate & graduate credit may be earned through the affiliated program at Arrowmont School of Arts & Crafts, Gatlinburg, TN
Tuition: Res—undergrad $25 per qtr hr, grad $38 per qtr hr; nonres—undergrad $61 per qtr hr, grad $88 per qtr hr; campus res—room & board $2000 per yr
Courses: Advertising Design, †Art History, Ceramics, Commercial Art, Constructions, †Drawing, Film, Graphic Arts, †Graphic Design, Jewelry, Lettering, †Painting, †Photography, †Printmaking, †Sculpture, †Fiber-Fabric, †Watercolor
Summer School: Prof, William Kennedy. Enrl 400; term of 2 sessions beginning June & Aug. Courses—same as above

MARYVILLE

MARYVILLE COLLEGE, Division of Fine Arts, Art Section,* 37801. Tel 615-982-6412. *Chmn* Dr James Bloy. Instrs: FT 2, PT 1
Estab 1937; den; scholarships; SC 10, LC 5
Degrees: 4 yr
Tuition: $1176 per term
Courses: Art Education, Art History, Ceramics, Drawing, Jewelry, Painting, Photography, Printmaking, Enameling, Fabric Design, Visual Theory & Design, Weaving
Children's Classes: Art Education, Crafts

MEMPHIS

MEMPHIS ACADEMY OF ARTS, Overton Park, 38112. Tel 901-726-4085. *Dean* Phillip S Morris, MFA. Instrs: FT 14, PT 10
Estab 1936; pvt; D & E; scholarships; enrl D 200, E 300
Ent Req: HS dipl
Degrees: BFA 4 yrs
Tuition: $1550 per sem; no campus res
Courses: †Advertising Design, Aesthetics, Art History, Calligraphy, †Ceramics, Commercial Art, Drawing, Illustration, †Jewelry, Lettering, †Painting, †Photography, †Printmaking, †Sculpture, †Silversmithing, †Textile Design, †Enameling
Adult Hobby Classes: Enrl 200; term of 16 wks. Courses—Drawing, Metal Arts, Painting, Photography, Pottery, Sculpture, Watercolor
Children's Classes: Enrl 250; tuition $80 for 25 wks. Courses—Drawing, Jewelry, Painting, Photography, Pottery, Sculpture
Summer School: Enrl 500; tuition $130 per cr hr for term of 6 wks beginning early June. Courses—Drawing, Metal Arts, Painting, Photography, Printing & Dyeing, Sculpture, Watercolor

MEMPHIS STATE UNIVERSITY, Dept of Art, 38152. Tel 901-454-2216. *Chmn Dept* Carol Crown, PhD
Estab 1912; pub; D & E; SC 100, LC 40, GC 30; enrl D 2200, maj 400, grad 80
Ent Req: HS dipl, SAT
Degrees: BA & BFA 4 yrs, MA & MAT 1 yr, MFA 2 yrs
Tuition: Campus residence available
Courses: Advertising Design, Art Education, Art History, Ceramics, Display, Drawing, Graphic Design, History of Art & Archaeology, Illustration, Intermedia, Interior Design, Jewelry, Museum Staff Training, Painting, Photography, Printmaking, Sculpture, Teacher Training
Summer School: Dir, Carol Crown

SOUTHWESTERN AT MEMPHIS, Dept of Art, 2000 N Parkway, 38112. Tel 901-180-0321. *Chmn Dept* Lawrence K Anthony, MFA; *Asst Prof* Alice M Hyland, PhD; *Asst Prof* Christine Hyland, PhD; *Asst Prof* Murray Riss, MFA; *Instr* Betty Gilow, BFA; *Instr* Martha Christian, BFA; *Instr* William Womack, BFA; *Lectr* Jean Sizemore, PhD; *Lectr* Richard Gruber, PhD
Estab 1848, dept estab 1940; pvt; D & E; SC 17, LC 12; enrl D 250, non-maj 240, maj 10
Ent Req: SAT or ACT, 13 acad credits, 16 overall
Degrees: BA 4 yrs
Tuition: $4500 per yr; campus res—room & board $2712 per yr
Courses: Aesthetics, Architecture, Art History, Calligraphy, Drawing, Film, History of Art & Archaeology, Museum Staff Training, Painting, Photography, Printmaking, Sculpture, Textile Design, Theatre Arts

MURFREESBORO

MIDDLE TENNESSEE STATE UNIVERSITY, Art Dept, Box 25, 37132. Tel 615-898-2455. *Chmn Art Dept* Phillip VanderWeg
Estab 1911, dept estab 1952; pub; D & E; scholarships; SC 62, LC 10, GC 35; enrl non-maj 900, maj 200, grad 5
Ent Req: HS dipl
Degrees: BS(Art Educ), BA & BFA 4 yrs
Courses: †Advertising Design, †Art Education, †Ceramics, †Commercial Art, Drawing, Goldsmithing, †Jewelry, †Painting, †Printmaking, †Sculpture, †Silversmithing, Textile Design
Children's Classes: Creative Art Clinic for Children; enrl 45; tuition $25 per term

NASHVILLE

FISK UNIVERSITY, Division of Humanities & Fine Arts,* PO Box 2, 37203. Tel 615-329-8685. *Dir* Arlene L Clifr; *Cur* Robert Hall, MA; *Assoc Prof* Gregory Ridley, MA; *Instructor* Jerry Waters, MA
Estab 1867, dept estab 1937; pvt; D; SC 10, LC 3; enrl 120, non-maj 90, maj 30
Ent Req: HS dipl, SAT
Degrees: BS & BA 4 yrs
Tuition: $2275 per sem; campus res available
Courses: Aesthetics, Art History, Ceramics, Drawing, Painting, Photography, Printmaking, Sculpture

TENNESSEE BOTANICAL GARDENS AND FINE ARTS CENTER, Education Dept, Cheekwood, Forrest Park Dr, 37205. Tel 615-352-8632. *Dir Fine Arts Ctr* Kevin Grogan; *Dir Botanical Gardens* Richard C Page; *Program Coordr Educ* Carol A Mode
Estab 1960; pvt; D & E; SC 10-15, LC 5-10
Courses: Art History, Commercial Art, Drawing, Graphic Arts, Painting, Printmaking, Sculpture, Textile Design, Landscape Design
Adult Hobby Classes: Courses—Calligraphy, Design, Life Drawing, Painting, Photography, Printmaking, Watercolor
Children's Classes: Jr Studio Courses—Art Start, Exploring Art

VANDERBILT UNIVERSITY, Dept of Fine Arts, West End Ave at 23rd St, Box 1801 Station B, 37235. Tel 615-322-2831. *Chmn* F Hamilton Hazlehurst, PhD; *Prof* Thomas B Brumbaugh, PhD; *Assoc Prof* Robert A Baldwin, MFA; *Assoc Prof* Donald Evans, MFA; *Assoc Prof* Christine Colley, PhD; *Assoc Prof* Milan Mihal, PhD; *Assoc Prof* Robert L Mode, PhD; *Assoc Prof* Ljubica D Popovich, PhD; *Assoc Prof* Ned Nabers, PhD; *Asst Prof* Leonard Folgarait, PhD; *Asst Prof* Marilyn Murphy, MFA; *Asst Prof* Gloria DeArcangelis, MFA; *Asst Prof* Andrew Ladis, PhD
Estab 1873, dept estab 1944; pvt; D; scholarships; SC 8, LC 35, GC 30; enrl non-maj 2000, maj 75, grad 6
Ent Req: HS dipl, ent exam
Degrees: BA 4 yrs, MA(Art Hist) 1-2 yrs
Tuition: $6800 per yr, $3400 per sem; campus res—room & board $3100 per yr
Courses: †Art History, Drawing, Film, Printmaking, Sculpture, Painting, Photography, Multimedia Design
Summer School: Dean, John Venable. Tuition $152 per sem hr for two 4 wk terms beginning June 4. Courses vary

WATKINS INSTITUTE, School for Adults, 601 Church, 37219. Tel 615-242-1851. Instrs: PT 7
Estab 1885; pvt; D & E; SC 10, LC 1; enrl D 125, E 200
Ent Req: Noncredit adult educ program, must be 17 yrs of age or older
Degrees: AA in Art, approved by Tennessee Dept of Education, 2 yr
Tuition: $50 per course
Courses: Art History, Drawing, Painting, Photography, Printmaking, Sculpture, Art

Essentials, Composition & Design, Landscape Painting
Adult Hobby Classes: Enrl 325; tuition $50 per course for 3-10 wks. Lecture & studio courses
Children's Classes: Enrl 60; tuition $35 for 8 wks. Courses—Basic Drawing
Summer School: Enrl 1000. Tuition $50 per course for 8 wks

SEWANEE

UNIVERSITY OF THE SOUTH, Dept of Fine Arts,* Carnegie Hall, 37375. Tel 615-598-5931, Ext 256, 223. *Chmn Dept* William Bert Wadley, MA. Instrs: FT 4
Pvt, den; D; scholarships; SC 20, LC 20; enrl D 250, non-maj 225, maj 30
Degrees: BS & BA, MDivinity
Tuition: $7100 per yr
Courses: Aesthetics, Art Education, Conceptual Art, Costume Design & Construction, Drawing, Film, Graphic Arts, History of Art & Archaeology, Mixed Media, Painting, Photography, Printmaking, Sculpture, Stage Design, Teacher Training, Theatre Arts
Children's Classes: Enrl 30-60; tuition $15 per 6 wk session. Art classes in conjunction with art education classes
Summer School: Dir, Dr William Cocke. Enrl 150 for term of 6 wks beginning June. Courses—Regular university curriculum

TULLAHOMA

MOTLOW STATE COMMUNITY COLLEGE, Art Dept,* Ledford Mill Rd, 37388. Tel 615-455-8511. *Assoc Prof* Jack L Moore, MA
Scholarships offered
Tuition: Res—$154 per quarter; nonres—$740 per quarter
Courses: Art Appreciation, Calligraphy, Ceramics, Design, Drawing, Painting, Photography

TEXAS

ABILENE

ABILENE CHRISTIAN UNIVERSITY, Art Dept, 79699. Tel 915-677-1911, Ext 2085. *Head Dept* Brent Green. Instrs: FT 6, PT 2
Estab 1906; den; D & E; SC 29, LC 8; enrl maj 79
Ent Req: Upper 3/4 HS grad class or at 15 standard score ACT composite
Degrees: BA, BFA & BS(Educ) 4 yrs
Courses: Art History, Commercial Art, Drawing, Painting, Sculpture, Teacher Training, Design, Pottery
Summer School: 5 1/2 wks beginning June

HARDIN-SIMMONS UNIVERSITY, Art Dept, Hickory at Ambler St, Box 837 Univ Station, 79698. Tel 915-677-7281. *Chmn* Ira M Taylor, MFA; *Instructor* Martha Kiel, MEd; *Assoc Prof* Bob Howell, MFA; *Instructor* Linda Fawcett, MFA
Univ estab 1891; den; D & E; SC 27, LC 5; enrl D 130, E 25, non-maj 65, maj 65
Ent Req: HS dipl, SAT, ACT
Degrees: BFA, BEd & BA 4 yrs
Tuition: $92 per cr hr; campus res—room and board $895-$1050
Courses: †Art Education, †Art History, †Ceramics, †Painting, †Printmaking, Sculpture, †Stage Design, †Teacher Training, †Theatre Arts
Summer School: Dir, Ira M Taylor. Enrl 50; tuition $92 per cr hr for term of 15 wks beginning June 2. Courses vary

MCMURRY COLLEGE, Art Dept, Box 8 McMurry Station, 79697. Tel 915-692-4130, Ext 307. *Head Dept* Sherwood E Suter, MFA; *Asst Prof* George Holland; *Lectr* J Robert Miller, BS; *Lectr* Kathryn Benson, MFA; *Lectr* Marsha Murray, BA; *Lectr* Vic Behrens Jr, BA
Estab 1923; pvt; D & E; scholarships; SC 19, LC 1; enrl D 80, E 8, non-maj 18, maj 15
Ent Req: HS dipl
Degrees: BA, BFA & BS 4 yrs
Tuition: Res—undergrad $4848 per yr, $2365 per sem (incl room & board), $90 per sem hr; nonres—same as resident fees
Courses: Advertising Design, Art Education, Art History, Ceramics, Drawing, Jewelry, Lettering, Painting, Printmaking, Teacher Training, Design, Stone Sculpture
Summer School: Dir, Dr Paul Jungmeyer. Enrl 25; tuition $90 per sem hr for term of 6 wks beginning June into first wk of July. Courses—Ceramics, Design, Painting

ALPINE

SUL ROSS STATE UNIVERSITY, Dept of Art, Division of Fine Arts, 79830. Tel 915-837-3461. *Head Dept* Miriam A Lowrance, MA
Estab 1920, dept estab 1922; pub; D & E; scholarships; SC 21, LC 3, GC 19; enrl D 183, E 32, non-maj 170, maj 45-60, GS 32
Ent Req: HS dipl, ACT or SAT
Degrees: BA and BFA 4 yrs, MEd(Art) 1 1/2 yrs
Tuition: Res 12 hr $202 per sem; nonres 12 hr $632 per sem
Courses: Art Appreciation, Art Education, Art History, Ceramics, Design, Drawing, Jewelry, Painting, Printmaking, Advertising Art
Summer School: Res 6 hr $101 per term; nonres 6 hr $316 per term

ALVIN

ALVIN COMMUNITY COLLEGE, Art Dept,* 3110 Mustang Rd, 77511. Tel 713-331-6111. *Chmn* Ziya Sever, MA
Estab 1949; D & E
Ent Req: HS dipl
Degrees: AA 2 yrs
Tuition: In district—$60; res—$105; nonres—$257
Courses: Ceramics, Commercial Art, Drawing, Graphic Design, Painting, Art Appreciation, Watercolor

AMARILLO

AMARILLO COLLEGE, Art Dept, 2200 S Washington, PO Box 447, 79178. Tel 806-376-5111, Ext 397. *Chmn* Denny Fraze, MFA; *Assoc Prof* David Cale, MFA; *Asst Prof* Tom Glover, MFA; *Instructor* Bill Burrell, MFA
Estab 1926; pub; D & E; scholarships; SC 18, LC 2; enrl D 142, E 60
Ent Req: HS dipl, CEEB
Degrees: AA 2 yrs
Tuition: Res—undergrad $125 per sem; nonres—undergrad $200 per sem; no campus res
Courses: †Art History, †Ceramics, †Commercial Art, †Drawing, †Jewelry, †Painting, †Sculpture
Summer School: Chmn, Denny Fraze, MFA

TEXAS STATE TECHNICAL INSTITUTE, Dept of Commercial Art, PO Box 11016, 79111. Tel 806-335-2316, Ext 403. *Program Chmn* Lloyd Cook
Estab 1970; pub; D; scholarships; SC 32, LC 2; enrl D 42, non-maj 1, maj 47
Ent Req: HS dipl, GED
Degrees: AAA 1 1/2 yrs
Tuition: Res—$85 per qtr, nonres—$265 per qtr
Courses: Advertising Design, Commercial Art, Drafting, Graphic Arts, Graphic Design, Illustration, Lettering, Mixed Media, Painting, Photography, Air Brush, Corporate Design, Delineation, Figure Drawing, Screen Printing
Summer School: Same as regular session

ARLINGTON

UNIVERSITY OF TEXAS AT ARLINGTON, Dept of Art, 144 Fine Arts Bldg, Box 19089, 76019. Tel 817-273-2891. *Chmn* Vincent J Bruno, PhD
Estab 1895, dept estab 1933; pub; D & E; SC 46, LC 39, maj 340
Ent Req: HS dipl, SAT of ACT
Degrees: BA 4 yrs, BFA 4 yrs, MFA 2 yrs
Tuition: Res—$233 for 15 cr hrs; nonres—$773 for 15 cr hrs
Courses: †Art Education, †Art History, †Ceramics, †Commercial Art, Drawing, †Fashion Arts, †Film, †Painting, †Photography, †Printmaking, †Sculpture, Metalsmithing
Adult Hobby Classes: Continuing Education division of university
Children's Classes: Continuing Education division of university
Summer School: Chmn Vincent J Bruno, PhD

AUSTIN

AUSTIN COMMUNITY COLLEGE, Dept of Commercial Art & Fine Arts, RDV Campus, PO Box 2285, 78768. Tel 512-495-7427. *Head Dept* Ro Thompson, BFA. Instrs: FT 28
Estab 1974; pub; D & E; enrl 300 per sem
Ent Req: HS dipl or GED
Degrees: AA 2 yrs
Tuition: Res—undergrad $13 per cr hr; nonres—undergrad $33 per cr hr; other adult continuing education noncr courses $1 per hr
Courses: †Advertising Design, †Art History, †Calligraphy, †Ceramics, †Commercial Art, †Drafting, †Drawing, †Film, †Graphic Arts, †Graphic Design, †Illustration, †Lettering, †Mixed Media, †Painting, †Photography, †Printmaking, †Sculpture, †Video, †Animation, †Commercial Art History, †Computer Graphics, †Design, †Environmental Graphics, †Figure Drawing, †Illustrative Techniques, †Intaglio, †Production Art, †Printing & Desing, †Sign Painting, †Silkscreen Printing, †Typography, Special Problems course which allows students to specialize, Graphics Practicum to allow college credit for free-lancing or live job situations
Adult Hobby Classes: Tuition $1 per hr. Courses—Calligraphy, Drawing, Handicrafts, Macrame, Painting, Photography, Pottery, Stained Glass, Weaving, Woodworking

CONCORDIA LUTHERAN COLLEGE, Dept of Fine Arts,* 3400 Interstate 35 North, 78705. Tel 512-452-7661. *Chmn* Richard Dinda. Instrs: PT 1
Estab 1925; den; D; scholarships; SC 1, LC 1; enrl D 350
Ent Req: HS dipl
Degrees: AA 2 yrs
Tuition: $105 per sem hr; campus res available
Courses: Drawing, Painting, , Art Fundamentals

UNIVERSITY OF TEXAS
—School of Architecture,* PO Box 7908, 78712. Tel 512-471-1922. *Dean* Harold Box. Instrs: FT 38, PT 9
Estab 1909; pub; scholarships; enrl undergrad 450, grad 210
Ent Req: Reasonable HS scholastic achievement, SAT, ACT
Degrees: BS 4 yr, BArch 5 yr, BS(archit eng) 6 yr, MArch 1-3.5 yr
Courses: †Architecture
Adult Hobby Classes: Courses through Division of Continuing Education
Children's Classes: Six week summer program for high school
Summer School: Dir, Harold Box
—Dept of Art, 78712. Tel 512-471-3365. *Dean* J Robert Wills. Instrs: FT 66, PT 8
Estab 1938; scholarships; enrl maj 700, others 900
Degrees: BA, BFA, MA, PhD
Courses: †Art History, †Ceramics, †Commercial Art, †Drawing, †Graphic Arts, †Handicrafts, †Illustration, †Painting, †Printmaking, †Sculpture, †Teacher Training, †Weaving, †Criticism of Art, Design, Pictorial Composition
Summer School: Two 6 wk terms

BEAUMONT

LAMAR UNIVERSITY, Art Dept, PO Box 10027, 77710. Tel 409-838-8141. *Head Dept* Robert C Rogan, DEd; *Prof* J Robert Madden, MFA; *Prof* Jerry Newman, MFA; *Prof* Robert O'Neili, MFA; *Prof* Meredith M Jack, MFA; *Instructor* Philip Fitzpatrick, MFA; *Instructor* Lynn Lokensgard, MA; *Instructor* John F Sommerfeld, MS; *Adjunct Instructor* Clem Webb
Estab 1923, dept estab 1951; pub; D & E; scholarships; SC 50, LC 10; enrl D 607, E 62, non-maj 214, maj 192
Ent Req: HS dipl
Degrees: BA, BFA & BS 4 yr
Tuition: Res—undergrad $102 for 3 sem hrs; nonres—undergrad $220 for 3 sem hrs; campus residency available
Courses: Advertising Design, †Art Education, Art History, Ceramics, †Commercial Art, Drawing, Fashion Arts, Film, Graphic Arts, Handicrafts, History of Art & Archaeology, Illustration, Jewelry, †Painting, Photography, Printmaking, Sculpture, Weaving
Children's Classes: Enrl 77; tuition $13 per 2 wks. Courses—Children's Workshop
Summer School: Dir, Dr Robert C Rogan. Enrl 266; two six-wk sessions, res $84 per 3 sem hr; nonres $219 per 3 sem hr. Courses—Drawing, Photography, Ceramics, Sculpture, Painting, Design, Art Education, Printmaking, Crafts

BELTON

UNIVERSITY OF MARY HARDIN-BAYLOR, Dept of Fine Arts,* 76513. Tel 817-939-5811. *Chmn* George Stansbury; *Head Art Dept* Ted L Austin
Estab 1845; den; D & E; scholarships; SC 6, LC 1 and one independent learning course per sem
Ent Req: Upper half of HS grad class
Degrees: BA, BFA and BS 4 yr
Tuition: $2400 annual tuition
Courses: Art Education, Art History, Ceramics, Drawing, Graphic Arts, Jewelry, Painting, Design
Summer School: Dir, Ted L Austin. Sem of 5 wks, from 1 to 4 cr hrs. Courses—Crafts, Independent Learning

BIG SPRING

HOWARD COLLEGE, Art Dept,* Division of Fine Arts, 100 Birdwell Lane, 79720. Tel 915-267-6311. *Chmn* Mary L Barley; *Faculty* Becky Smiley, MEd
Estab 1948, dept estab 1972; pub; D & E; scholarships; SC 5, LC 1; enrl D 70, E 20, non-maj 60, maj 10
Ent Req: HS dipl, ACT
Degrees: AA
Tuition: Res—$4 per sem cr hr; nonres—$20 per sem cr hr

BORGER

FRANK PHILLIPS COLLEGE, Art Dept, Fine Arts Division, Box 5118, 79007. Tel 806-274-5311. *Chmn Div* R K Palmer, MA
Estab 1948; pub; D & E; scholarships; SC 14, LC 3; enrl D 60, E 10, non-maj 20, maj 40
Ent Req: HS dipl, GED or transfer from another college
Degrees: AA, AS and AAS 2 yrs
Courses: Advertising Design, Art Appreciation, Art Education, Art History, Calligraphy, Ceramics, Commercial Art, Design, Drawing, Graphic Arts, Painting, Photography, Sculpture, Pottery
Adult Hobby Classes: Enrl 100; tuition $30 & up. Courses—Community Services classes, Calligraphy, Ceramics, Drawing, Painting, Photography, others on demand
Children's Classes: Enrl 90; tuition $10 & up. Courses—Drawing, Painting
Summer School: Dir, R K Palmer. Courses—Painting, others on demand

BROWNSVILLE

TEXAS SOUTHMOST COLLEGE, Fine Arts Dept,* 83 Fort Brown, 78521. Tel 512-541-1241, 546-7121. *Chmn* Robert H Shaw; *Chmn Art Dept* George Truan
Estab 1973; pub; D & E; scholarships; SC 10, LC 10; enrl D 300, E 100
Ent Req: HS dipl
Degrees: AA(Fine Arts) 2-3 yrs
Tuition: In district—$256 per yr; res—$308 per yr; nonres—$1118 per yr
Courses: Art Education, Ceramics, Drawing, Graphic Design, History of Art & Archaeology, Painting, Sculpture, Design I and II
Adult Hobby Classes: Courses—Ceramics, Drawing
Summer School: Term of 16 wks. Courses—Art Appreciation

BROWNWOOD

HOWARD PAYNE UNIVERSITY, Dept of Art,* School of Fine and Applied Arts, Howard Payne Station, 76801. Tel 915-646-2502. *Dean* Don Jackson, MS; *Chmn Div Fine Arts* Henry Lindsay, PhD; *Chmn Dept Art* Maurine Stewart, MEd. Instrs: FT 2
Estab 1889; den; D & E; SC 18, LC 12; enrl D 200, E 69, maj 3
Ent Req: HS dipl, ent exam
Degrees: BA, BFA(Studio or Art Educ) and BS 4-5 yrs
Tuition: $70 per sem hr
Courses: Metalcrafts
Adult Hobby Classes: Enrl 30; tuition $35 per course. Courses—Metalcrafts, Painting, Weaving
Summer School: Enrl 75; tuition term of 6 wks beginning June. Courses—Art Education, Crafts, Painting

CANYON

WEST TEXAS STATE UNIVERSITY, Art Dept, 79016. Tel 806-656-2291. *Head Dept* Steven L Mayes, MFA; *Assoc Prof* Darold Smith, MFA; *Asst Prof* David Rindlisbacher, MFA; *Asst Prof* Eleann Ann Gregory; *Instructor* Hunter Ingalls; *Instructor* Bill Shires
Estab 1910; pub; D & E; scholarships; SC 70, LC 23, GC 50; enrl maj 120, grad 23
Ent Req: HS dipl
Degrees: BA, BS, BFA, MA and MFA
Tuition: Res $64 per sem, $50 PT; non-res $640 per sem, $360 PT; foreign students $640 per sem; campus res $1000
Courses: †Advertising Design, Aesthetics, †Art Education, Art History, †Ceramics, Commercial Art, †Drawing, †Goldsmithing, Graphic Arts, †Graphic Design, Handicrafts, Illustration, †Jewelry, †Painting, †Printmaking, †Sculpture, †Silversmithing, Teacher Training, Textile Design, Macrame, Rugs
Children's Classes: Head Dept, Steven L Mayes, MFA
Summer School: Courses—as above

COLLEGE STATION

TEXAS A & M UNIVERSITY, College of Architecture and Environmental Design, 77843. Tel 409-845-1221. *Dean* Dr Charles Hix Jr. Instrs: FT 92
Estab 1905; pub; D; enrl maj Ed 800, total 1750
Ent Req: SAT; Achievement, HS rank
Degrees: BEnviron Design, BS(Building Construction), BS(Landscape Arch), DEnviron Design, MArch, M Landscape, M Planning, PhD(Urban Science) 4 yr
Tuition: Res $4 per sem cr hr; nonres $40 per sem cr hr; fees approx $652
Summer School: Dir Dr Charles Hix Jr. Enrl 1000; tuition same as above per 2-5 wk sessions. Courses—same as above

COMMERCE

EAST TEXAS STATE UNIVERSITY, Dept of Art, 75428. Tel 214-886-5208. *Head Dept* Jim Davis, MFA; *Chmn Painting* Bruce Tibbetts, MFA; *Chmn Ceramics* Barbara Frem, MFA; *Chmn Graphics* Lee Baxter Davis, MFA; *Chmn Sculpture* Jerry Dodd, MFA; *Chmn Art Ed* Dr James Allumbaugh; *Chmn Advertising Art* Charles McGough; *Coordr Grad Programs* Gerard Huber, MFA
Pub; D & E; scholarships; SC 64, LC 29, GC 19; enrl maj 300, GS 34
Ent Req: HS dipl, ACT or SAT
Degrees: BA, BS and BFA 4 yrs, MFA 2 yrs, MA and MS 1 1/2 yrs. There is a special program called the Post Masters-MFA which is worked out on an individual basis
Tuition: campus res available
Courses: †Advertising Design, Aesthetics, †Art Education, Art History, †Ceramics, Collages, †Commercial Art, Constructions, Drafting, Drawing, †Graphic Arts, †Graphic Design, History of Art & Archaeology, †Illustration, Intermedia, Industrial Design, Jewelry, Lettering, Mixed Media, Painting, Photography, †Printmaking, †Sculpture, Silversmithing, †Teacher Training, Video, Intoglio Printmaking, Lithography, Papermaking and Casting
Adult Hobby Classes: Enrl 15; tuition $77 per sem. Courses—Bonzai, Ceramics, Drawing, Painting, Watercolor
Summer School: Enrl 15; tuition res—$37-$187; nonres—$52-$727, for 2 terms of 2 to 6 wks beginning June. Courses—Art Education, Ceramics, Design, Drawing, Graphics, Painting

CORPUS CHRISTI

DEL MAR COLLEGE, Dept of Art, Ayers at Baldwin, 78404. Tel 512-881-6216. *Chmn* William E Lambert, MFA; *Assoc Prof* Ronald Dee Sullivan, MA; *Assoc Prof* Jan R Ward, MA; *Instructor* Randolph Flowers; *Instructor* Kitty Dudics
Estab 1941, dept estab 1965; pub; D & E; scholarships; SC 21, LC 3; enrl D 500, E 100, non-maj 400, maj 139
Ent Req: HS dipl, SAT score or any accepted test including GED
Degrees: AA 2 yr in studio, art educ and art history
Tuition: Res $4 per sem hr, $25 minimum; nonres—$5 per sem hr, $60 maximum; foreign students $14 per sem hr, $200 minimum; plus other fees; no campus res
Courses: Advertising Design, Aesthetics, Art Education, Art History, Collages, Commercial Art, Display, Drawing, Graphic Arts, Graphic Design, History of Art & Archaeology, Lettering, Painting, Photography, Printmaking, Sculpture, Teacher Training
Adult Hobby Classes: Tuition varies according to classes. Courses—as above
Summer School: Chmn, W E Lambert, MFA. Tuition same. Courses—as above

CORSICANA

NAVARRO COLLEGE, Art Dept, Box 1170, 75110. Tel 214-874-6501. *Dir* Margaret Hicks. Instrs: FT 1, PT 25
Estab 1946; pub; D & E; scholarships; SC 11, LC 1; enrl D 300, maj 30
Ent Req: HS dipl, ent exam, special permission
Degrees: AA, AS, A Gen Educ and A Appl Sci 60 sem hr
Courses: Advertising Design, Art Appreciation, Commercial Art, Drawing, Illustration, Painting, Photography, Sculpture
Adult Hobby Classes: Enrl 300; tuition $250 per 15 wks. Courses—Drawing, Design, Crafts, Art Appreciation, Photography, Painting, Sculpture

DALLAS

DALLAS BAPTIST COLLEGE, Dept of Art, 7777 W Kiest, PO Box 21206, 75211. Tel 214-331-8311. *Asst Prof* Dawna Hamm Walsh, MA & MFA; *Asst Prof* James Rice, MFA; *Artists-in-Residence* Jack Hamm
Estab 1965; pvt den; D & E; scholarships; enrl D 75, E 25, non-maj 75, maj 25
Ent Req: HS dipl
Degrees: BA and BS 4 yrs, Bachelor of Career Arts 2-4 yrs

Tuition: $90 per sem hr
Courses: Art Education, Art History, Ceramics, Commercial Art, Drawing, Graphic Design, Handicrafts, Interior Design, Jewelry, Painting, Photography, Sculpture, Teacher Training, Theatre Arts
Adult Hobby Classes: Courses—Batik, Candle Making, Crafts, Macrame, Raku
Children's Classes: Enrl 30; tuition $10 per 2 wks. Courses—Arts for Summer
Summer School: Dir, James Rice. Tuition—$90 per sem hr. Courses vary

FASHION & ART INSTITUTE OF DALLAS, 2829 W Northwest Hwy, 75220. Tel 214-350-8874
Scholarships offered
Degrees: AA
Tuition: $4200 per year
Courses: Advertising Design, Architecture, Art History, Calligraphy, Design, Drawing, †Fashion Arts, Film, †Graphic Arts, Handicrafts, †Interior Design, Animation, Bookbinding, Cartooning, Glassblowing
Adult Hobby Classes: Tuition $850 for 6 weeks. Courses—Computer Graphics

SOUTHERN METHODIST UNIVERSITY, Division of Art and Art History, 75275. Tel 214-692-2489, 692-2698. *Chmn Art* Laurence Scholder, MA; *Chmn Art History* Karl Kilinski II, PhD
Estab 1911, Meadows School of Arts estab 1964; pvt; D & E; scholarships; enrl maj 142, grad 41
Ent Req: Selective admission
Degrees: BFA(Art), BFA(Art History), BA(Art History) 4 yr, MFA(Art) 2 yr, MA(Art History) 1 1/2 yr
Tuition: $2800 per sem, $235 per cr hr, $358 fee per sem; campus res—room & board $1699
Courses: †Art History, †Ceramics, Drawing, †Painting, †Photography, †Printmaking, †Sculpture, Museum Education Training
Summer School: Tuition $570 per course for term of 5 wks beginning June 4. Selected courses in art and art history

DENISON

GRAYSON COUNTY COLLEGE, Art Dept, 6101 Hwy 691, 25020. Tel 214-465-6030. *Dept Head* David Petrash
Estab 1965; pub; D & E; scholarships; LC 3; enrl D 63, E 35
Ent Req: HS dipl
Degrees: AA 2 yrs
Courses: Art Education, Art History, Ceramics, Drawing, Graphic Design, Painting, Photography, Appreciation, Watercolor
Adult Hobby Classes: Courses—Ceramics, Crafts, Drawing, Painting
Summer School: Dir, Mary Lois O'Neal. Courses—Drawing, Painting, Watercolor

DENTON

NORTH TEXAS STATE UNIVERSITY, Art Dept, PO Box 5098, 76203. Tel 817-565-2855. *Chair* Margaret Lucas, PhD; *Grad Studies Coordr* Scott A Sullivan, PhD; *Undergrad Coordr* Henry Swartz, MFA; *Interior Design Coordr* John Olvera, MA; *Advertising Design Coordr* David Blow, MFA; *Printmaking Coordr* Judy Youngblood, MFA; *Photography Coordr* Brent Phelps, MFA; *Painting and Drawing Coordr* Robert Erdle, MFA; *Asst Prof* Richard Davis, MA; *Art History Coordr* Larry Gleeson, PhD; *Fashion Design Coordr* Alberta Mattil, MA; *Weaving & Fabric Design Coordr* Roger Thomason, MFA; *Ceramics Coordr* Elmer Taylor, MFA; *Jewelry & Metalsmithing Coordr* Harlan Butt, MFA; *Basic Drawing Coordr* Claudia Betti, MFA; *Basic Design Coordr* William Evans, MFA
Estab 1897, dept estab 1901; pub; D & E; scholarships; SC 92, LC 54, GC 83; enrl non-maj 230, maj 932, grad 78, others 15
Ent Req: HS dipl, SAT, GRE, portfolio for MFA, letters of recommendation for PhD
Degrees: BFA 4 yrs, MFA, MA, PhD
Tuition: Res—undergrad and grad $4 per sem hr, minimum of $50 plus fees; non-res—undergrad, grad and foreign $40 per sem hr; campus res—room & board $970.50-$1531.88 per sem
Courses: †Advertising Design, Aesthetics, †Art Education, †Art History, †Ceramics, Commercial Art, Conceptual Art, Drafting, †Drawing, Fashion Arts, Graphic Arts, Graphic Design, †Handicrafts, †Interior Design, †Jewelry, Museum Staff Training, †Painting, †Photography, †Printmaking, Restoration & Conservation, †Sculpture, Silversmithing, Teacher Training, Textile Design, Video, Weaving
Adult Hobby Classes: Tuition determined by class. Courses—Mini-classes in arts and craft related areas
Children's Classes: Courses—Mini-classes in arts and crafts related areas; special prog for advanced students
Summer School: Dir, Margaret Lucas. Enrl approx 275 per session; tuition $4 per sem hr for term of 6 wks; 2 summer sessions. Courses—all studio and lecture courses as needed

TEXAS WOMAN'S UNIVERSITY, Dept of Art, Box 22995, TWU Station, 76204. Tel 817-382-8923. *Chmn* Betty D Copeland, EEd; *Prof* J Brough Miller, MFA; *Prof* Dr John Rios, MFA; *Assoc Prof* Winifred S Williams, MS; *Assoc Prof* Alfred E Green, MFA; *Asst Prof* Mark S Smith, MFA; *Asst Prof* Linda Stuckenbruck-Smith, MFA; *Asst Prof* John A Calabrese, PhD; *Asst Prof* Nancy K Davis, MFA; *Instructor* Susan K Grant, MFA; *Adjunct Instructor* Gina Rogers, MA; *Visiting Lecturer* Kathleen Mitchell, MFA
Estab 1901; pub; D & E; scholarships; SC 21, LC 34, GC 17; enrl non-maj 303, maj 70, undergrad 100, total 505
Ent Req: HS dipl, MA and MFA portfolio review required
Degrees: BA, BS and BFA 4 yrs, MA 1 yr, MFA 2 yrs
Tuition: Res $4 per sem hr, $50 minimum; nonres $40 per sem hr, campus res $470-$1000 for room only, meal plan available at extra charge
Courses: Art Education, Art History, Ceramics, Interior Design, Jewelry, Painting, Photography, Sculpture, Textile Design, Advertising Art, Fibers, Fashion Illustration & Costume Design, Metalsmithing, Premedical Illustration
Adult Hobby Classes: Courses through Office of Continuing Education
Children's Classes: Courses through Office of Continuing Education
Summer School: Enrl 137; tuition same as above for term of 6 wks beginning June 7. Courses—as above

EDINBURG

PAN AMERICAN UNIVERSITY, Art Dept, 78539. Tel 512-381-3141. *Chmn Dept* Richard Hyslin, MA; *Chmn Elem Art Educ* Dr Norman Browne, EdD; *Chmn Painting* E E Nichols, MFA; *Chmn Printmaking* Philip Field, MFA; *Chmn Advertising Design* Frank Manuella, MS; *Chmn Art History* Sandra Swenson, MA; *Chmn Secondary Art & Jewelry Education* Dr Nancy Moyer-Prince
Estab 1927, dept estab 1972; pub; D & E; scholarships; SC 43, LC 14; enrl D 1200, E 150, non-maj 650, maj 209
Ent Req: Open, immunization
Degrees: BA and BFA 4 yrs
Tuition: Res—$59-$204; nonres—$49-$852; foreign $206-$367; campus res—room & board $990-$1040 per sem
Courses: †Advertising Design, †Art Education, Art History, †Ceramics, Drawing, Graphic Arts, Graphic Design, Illustration, †Jewelry, Lettering, †Painting, Photography, †Printmaking, †Sculpture, †Silversmithing
Summer School: Dir, Richard Hyslin. Enrl 23 per class; tuition $31-$78 for term of 5 wks beginning June 2 and July 9. Courses—Art Education, Art Appreciation, Beginning & Advanced Painting, Ceramics, Drawing, Elementary Art Educ, Metals, Photography, Sculpture

EL PASO

UNIVERSITY OF TEXAS AT EL PASO, Dept of Art, 79968. Tel 915-747-5181. *Head Dept* Charles Fensch. Instrs: FT 9
Estab 1939; pub; D & E; scholarships; SC 24, GC 8; enrl 200
Degrees: BA & BFA 4 yrs
Tuition: $200 per sem
Courses: Art Education, Art History, Ceramics, Design, Drawing, Graphic Design, Painting, Printmaking, Sculpture, Metals
Adult Hobby Classes: Tuition varies from class to class. Courses—offered through Extension Division
Children's Classes: Enrl 60; tuition $50 for 8 week class. Courses—Kidzart
Summer School: Chmn, Charles Fensch. Enrl 100; tuition $55 for hr course. Courses—Selected studio & art education

FORT WORTH

TEXAS CHRISTIAN UNIVERSITY, Art & Art History Dept, School of Fine Arts, Box 30793, 76129. *Dean* George T Tade. Instrs: FT 10, PT 9
Estab 1909; pvt; scholarships and grad fels; SC 35, LC 10, GC; enrl maj 150, others 450
Tuition: $140 per sem hr
Courses: †Art Education, †Art History, †Ceramics, †Commercial Art, †Design, Drawing, †Painting, †Photography, †Printmaking, †Sculpture, †Metals
Summer School: Dir, Dr Charles F Falk. Enrl 100; tuition $140 per sem hr. Courses-Art History, Design, Drawing, Graphic Design, Photography

TEXAS WESLEYAN COLLEGE, Dept of Art,* PO Box 50010, 76105. Tel 817-534-0251. *Dean* Karen J Waters; *Assoc Prof* Mary Apple
Den; D & E; scholarships; SC, LC
Ent Req: HS dipl
Degrees: BA 4 yrs
Tuition: $1700 per sem
Courses: Art Education, Ceramics, Drawing, History of Art & Archaeology, Painting, Printmaking, Teacher Training

GAINESVILLE

COOKE COUNTY COLLEGE, Fine Arts Dept, Hwy 51, PO Box 240, 76240. Tel 817-668-7731. *Chairperson Dept* Vera Speece, MA
Estab 1924; pub; D & E; scholarships; SC 14, LC 1; enrl D 50
Ent Req: HS dipl, SAT or ACT, individual approval
Degrees: AA and AFA 2 yrs
Tuition: Res—undergrad $98 per sem; nonres—undergrad $210 per sem; Texas res $126 per sem; campus res $200 per sem
Courses: Art Education, Ceramics, Drafting, Drawing, Graphic Design, Painting, Photography, Sculpture, Teacher Training, Textile Design, Weaving
Adult Hobby Classes: Courses—Drawing, Painting, Weaving

GEORGETOWN

SOUTHWESTERN UNIVERSITY, Art Dept, 78626. Tel 512-863-6511. *Chmn* Patrick Veerkamp, MFA; *Assoc Prof* Clande L Kennard, MA; *Adjunct Instr* Peter Nickel, MFA; *Adjunct Instr* Mary Visser, MFA; *Visiting Artist* Kathleen Raymond, MFA
Estab 1840, dept estab 1940; pvt; D; scholarships; SC 28, LC 9; enrl D 160, maj 35
Ent Req: HS dipl, SAT, portfolio
Degrees: BA and BFA 4 yrs
Courses: Art History, Ceramics, Design, †Painting, Printmaking, Sculpture
Summer School: Courses—various

HILLSBORO

HILL JUNIOR COLLEGE, Fine Arts Dept,* PO Box 619, 76645. Tel 817-582-2555. *Music & Art Program Coordr* Leland Lundgren
Scholarships offered
Degrees: AA, cert
Tuition: In district—$30.50 per sem hr; res—$33 per sem hr; nonres—$76 per sem hr
Courses: Art Appreciation, Art Education, Art History, Ceramics, Design, Drawing, Painting, Weaving, Stained Glass

HOUSTON

THE DESIGN SCHOOLS, Art Institute of Houston, 3600 Yoakum Blvd, 77006. Tel 713-523-2564. *Dir Education* David Anderson; *Dept Head, Interior Design* Pam Mendenhall; *Dept Head, Photography* Wally Lewis; *Dept Head, Advertising Design* David Bennett. Instrs: FT 25, PT 15
Estab 1964; pvt; D & E; scholarships; enrl D 550, E 150
Ent Req: HS transcripts and graduation or GED, interview
Tuition: $1330 per quarter
Courses: Advertising Design, Interior Design, Photography, Fashion Illustration
Adult Hobby Classes: Enrl 150; tuition $2860 per yr. Courses—Commercial Art Technician, Interior Planning & Decorating, Photography Technician
Children's Classes: Enrl 20; tuition $30 for 6 weeks. Courses—Commercial art
Summer School: Dir, Eric Gearhart. Enrl 25; tuition $100 for two weeks. Courses—Commercial Art Survey

ALFRED C GLASSELL SCHOOL OF ART,* The Museum of Fine Arts, 5101 Montrose, 77005. Tel 713-529-7659. *Admin Dean* Clem Barron; *Dean Junior School* Norma R Ory, BFA; *Art Historian* David Brauer, MFA equivalent; *Instr* William Dennard, MFA; *Instr* Suzanne Manns, BFA; *Instr* Arthur Turner, MFA; *Instr* Robert Weimerskirch, MFA equivalent; *Instr* James Estes, MFA; *Instr* Peter McClennan, MFA; *Instr* Dick Wray; *Instr* Sandra Parmer Zilker, MFA; *Instr* Charlotte Cosgrove, MFA; *Instr* Don Shaw
Estab 1926. Under the auspices of the Museum of Fine Arts; has a small reference library; pvt; D & E; scholarships; SC 52, LC 6; enrl D 624, E 480, maj 143, Junior School 350
Ent Req: HS dipl preferred
Degrees: 3 yr cert
Tuition: $520 FT, $150 each SC, $100 each Art History; no campus res
Courses: Art History, †Ceramics, Drawing, Handicrafts, History of Art & Archaeology, †Jewelry, †Painting, Photography, †Printmaking, †Sculpture, Papermaking, Visual Fundamentals
Adult Hobby Classes: Enrl 613; tuition $150 each SC
Children's Classes: Enrl 350; tuition $65 per sem (4-17 yrs). Courses—General curriculum incl Clay Sculpture, Design, Drawing, Painting and special classes for advanced teenagers
Summer School: Administrative Dean, Clem Barron; Junior School Dean, Norma R Ory. Enrl 332 adult, 451 Junior School; tuition $115 (adult) for term of 6 wks and $45 (junior) for term of 4 wks beginning June 9. Courses—same as regular session except Art History

HOUSTON BAPTIST COLLEGE, Dept of Art,* 7502 Fondren Rd, 77074. Tel 713-774-7661. *Dean* Gary M Horton
Estab 1963; den; D & E; scholarships; SC 7, LC 9; enrl D 1300, maj 35
Ent Req: HS dipl, ent exam
Degrees: BA & BS
Tuition: $100 per sem hr
Courses: Art Education, Ceramics, Drawing, Graphic Arts, History of Art & Archaeology, Painting, Sculpture, Teacher Training

RICE UNIVERSITY, Dept of Art and Art History, PO Box 1892, 77001. Tel 713-527-4815. *Chmn* W M Widrig, PhD; *Prof* Katherine T Brown, MFA; *Prof* William A Camfield, PhD; *Prof* C A Boterf, MFA; *Prof* Neil Havens, MA; *Prof* Geoffrey Winningham, MFA; *Assoc Prof* Basilios Poulos, MFA; *Assoc Prof* George Smith, MFA; *Asst Prof* Marty Barnes, MFA; *Asst Prof* Karin Broker, MFA; *Asst Prof* Marion Grayson, PhD; *Asst Prof* John S Hallam, PhD; *Prof Emeritus* John O'Neil, MFA; *Prof Emeritus* David G Parsons, MS; *Prof Emeritus* Philip Oliver Smith, PhD; *Lectr* Brian Huberman; *Lectr* Peter T Brown, MFA; *Vis Lectr* Bertrand Davezac, PhD; *Vis Lectr* Thomas McEvilley, PhD
Estab 1912, dept estab 1966-67; pvt; D; scholarships; SC 27, LC 31, GC (BFA) 7; enrl D 125, non-maj 75, maj 50, grad 2 (BFA)
Ent Req: HS dipl, CEEB, evaluations of HS counselors and teachers, interview
Degrees: BA 4 yrs, BFA 5 yrs, MA(Art, Classical Archaeology)
Tuition: $2700 and $140 fees per yr, $1350 and $70 fees per sem, grad $2700 for first six sem; PT $125 per hr and $50 registration fees; campus res—room & board $2190
Courses: Art History, Constructions, Drawing, Film, History of Art & Archaeology, Painting, Photography, Printmaking, Sculpture, Theatre Arts, Video
Adult Hobby Classes: Tuition $300 per class. Courses—Photography

SAN JACINTO COLLEGE NORTH, Art Dept, 77049. Tel 713-458-4050. *Chmn* Dana John Steinheimer, MFA; *Instructor* Robert McCoy, MA; *Instructor* David Parker, AA
Estab 1972; pub; D & E; scholarships; SC 16, LC 1; enrl D 73, E 38, non-maj 77, maj 73
Ent Req: HS dipl
Degrees: AA 2 yrs
Tuition: Res—undergrad $96 per yr, $48 per 12 hrs, $25 for 6 hrs; nonres—undergrad $400 per yr, $200 per sem, $120 per 6 hrs; no campus res
Courses: †Advertising Design, Calligraphy, Commercial Art, Drawing, Fashion Arts, Graphic Arts, Graphic Design, Illustration, Interior Design, Lettering, Painting, Photography, Sculpture, Textile Design, 2-D Design, 3-D Design, †Studio Art
Adult Hobby Classes: Enrl 29; tuition $45 - $50 per 60 hrs. Courses—Oil Painting, Illustration, Photography
Children's Classes: Enrl 15, tuition $35 per 2 wks. Courses—Awareness Workshop
Summer School: Dir, Dana John Steinheimer. Enrl 30 - 50; tuition $48 - $60. Courses—varies beginning May

TEXAS SOUTHERN UNIVERSITY, Art Dept,* 3201 Wheeler Ave, 77004. Tel 713-527-7011. *Head Dept* Dr John T Biggers
Estab 1949; pub; D & E; scholarships; SC 31, LC 12, GC 4; enrl maj 85, other 100
Ent Req: HS dipl
Degrees: BFA and B(Art Educ) 5 yrs
Tuition: $412 annual tuition
Courses: Weaving
Summer School: Dir, Joseph Jones, Jr. Enrl 100; for a term of 6 wks beginning June. Courses—Art Appreciation in Educational Program, Advanced crafts for Teachers, Basic Art for Elementary Teachers, Exhibition: Mural Painting in School, Problems in Art Education, Problems in Secondary Art Education, Research Projects

UNIVERSITY OF HOUSTON, Dept of Art,* 77004. Tel 713-749-2601. *Chmn* George R Bunker, BA. Instrs: FT 29, PT 7
Estab 1927; pub; D & E; scholarships; enrl D 600 maj
Ent Req: HS dipl, SAT
Degrees: BA, BFA, MFA
Tuition: Res—$4 per sem cr hr; nonres—$40 per sem cr hr; campus res available
Courses: Art History, Ceramics, †Drawing, Goldsmithing, Illustration, †Jewelry, †Painting, †Photography, †Printmaking, †Sculpture, Silversmithing, Video, †Graphic Communications, †Environmental Design

UNIVERSITY OF SAINT THOMAS, Art Dept, 3812 Montrose Blvd, 77006. Tel 713-524-3719, Ext 317. *Chmn* Nancy L Jircik, MA; *Prof* Early Staley, MA; *Assoc Prof* Jack Boynton, MA; *Adjunct Prof* Susan Smith, MA; *Adjunct Prof* Robert Graham, MA; *Adjunct Prof* David Gray; *Adjunct Prof* Gary Huntoon
Den; D & E; scholarships; SC 15, LC 7; enrl E 30, maj 44
Ent Req: HS dipl
Degrees: BA 4 yrs
Tuition: $100 per credit hr PT, $1250 per sem FT; campus res available
Courses: Art History, Ceramics, Commercial Art, Drawing, Film, Graphic Arts, History of Art & Archaeology, Painting, Photography, Sculpture, Video
Adult Hobby Classes: Enrl 46; tuition $120 per sem hr. Courses—Art History, Drawings, Fundamentals, Painting, Photography, Watercolor
Summer School: Chmn Art Dept, Nancy Jircik. Enrl 30; tuition $240 for term of 6 wks beginning June 1. Courses—Ceramics, Drawing, Painting, Photography

HUNTSVILLE

SAM HOUSTON STATE UNIVERSITY, Art Dept, 77341. Tel 713-294-1315. *Dept Head* Darryl Patrick, PhD; *Prof* Gene M Eastman, MFA; *Prof* L Gaddis Geeslin, MFA; *Prof* Gene E Jackson, MFA; *Prof* Stanley E Lea, MFA; *Prof* Charles A Pebworth, MA; *Prof* Harry J Ahysen, MFA; *Assoc Prof* Evelyn E Anderson, MFA; *Assoc Prof* William J Breitenbach, MFA; *Assoc Prof* Jimmy H Barker, MFA; *Assoc Prof* Kenneth L Zonker, MA
Estab 1879, dept estab 1936; pub; D; SC 37, LC 9, GC 12; enrl D 844, non-maj 100, maj 190, grad 15
Ent Req: HS dipl, ACT or SAT
Degrees: BA, BFA 4 yrs, MFA 2 yrs
Tuition: Res—$264 per 16 hrs; nonres—$840 per 16 hrs; campus res—room & board $616 per yr
Courses: †Advertising Design, †Art Education, Art History, †Ceramics, †Drawing, †Handicrafts, Illustration, †Painting, †Printmaking, †Sculpture, Fibers
Summer School: Chmn, Darryl Patrick. Enrl varies; tuition $107 per term of 6 wks beginning May 30th and July 6. Courses—Art Educ, Art History, Ceramics, Crafts, Drawing, Painting. Courses offered in Pueble Mexico second term

HURST

TARRANT COUNTY JUNIOR COLLEGE, Art Dept, Northeast Campus, 76053. Tel 817-281-7860. *Assoc Prof* Richard Hlad, MA; *Asst Prof* Martha Gordon, MFA; *Instructor* Roger Tufts, MEd
Estab 1967, dept estab 1968; pub; D & E; SC 19, LC 3; enrl D 250, E 200, non-maj 150, maj 200
Ent Req: HS dipl, GED, admission by individual approval
Degrees: AA and AAS 2 yrs
Tuition: Res—$4 per hr, minimum $25 per sem; nonres—of county $3 per sem hr added to res fee, others $40 per sem hr, aliens $40 per sem hr with $200 minimum fee; no campus res
Courses: Advertising Design, Art Appreciation, Art Education, Art History, Ceramics, Collages, Constructions, Drawing, Jewelry, Mixed Media, Painting, Photography, Printmaking, Sculpture, Weaving, Papermaking
Adult Hobby Classes: Enrl 20; for 7 wks. Courses—Drawing, Oil-Acrylic, Tole Painting
Children's Classes: Enrl 20; 7 wks. Courses—Cartooning, Drawing, Painting
Summer School: Enrl 20; tuition as above for term of 6 wks beginning July. Courses—Art Appreciation, Art Education, Ceramics, Design, Drawing, Painting, Photography

KILGORE

KILGORE COLLEGE, Dept Art and Art Education,* Fine Arts, 1100 Broadway, 75662. Tel 214-984-8531. *Chmn Art Dept* Gary Q Frields, MFA; *Instr* Jeanne E Velde, MA
Estab 1935; D & E; scholarships; SC 7, LC 3; enrl D 75, E 25, non-maj 25, maj 50
Ent Req: HS dipl
Degrees: AA
Tuition: District res—$4 per sem hr; non-district res—$7 per sem hr; non-state res—$23 per sem hr
Courses: †Advertising Design, †Art Education, †Art History, †Commercial Art, Costume Design & Construction, †Drawing, †Fashion Arts, Graphic Arts, Graphic Design, History of Art & Archaeology, Lettering, Mixed Media, Painting, Photography, †Sculpture, Theatre Arts

KINGSVILLE

TEXAS A & I UNIVERSITY, Art Dept, Box 157, 78363. Tel 512-595-2619. *Chmn* Dr Richard Scherpereel
Estab 1925, dept estab 1930; pub; D & E; SC 21, LC 5, GC 2; enrl D 700, non-maj 300, maj 400, art maj 150, grad 20
Ent Req: HS dipl
Degrees: BFA and BA 4 yr
Tuition: Res $280 per sem; nonres $800 per sem
Courses: Advertising Design, Art Education, Art History, Ceramics, Drawing, Graphic Arts, Painting, Printmaking, Sculpture, Teacher Training
Adult Hobby Classes: Courses offered
Summer School: Courses—full schedule

LAKE JACKSON

BRAZOSPORT COLLEGE, Art Dept,* 500 College Dr, 77566. Tel 409-265-6131.
Fine Arts Dept Chmn Richard Wilcher; *Assoc Prof* J Lynn Hayers, MFA; *Assoc Prof* Charles Harding, BA
Estab 1968; pub; D & E; scholarships; SC 10, LC 3; enrl D 50
Ent Req: HS dipl or GED
Degrees: AA 2 yrs
Tuition: In district—$60 per sem; out-of-district—$75 per sem
Courses: Art History, Ceramics, Drawing, History of Art & Archaeology, Mixed Media, Painting, Sculpture, Stage Design, Theatre Arts, Art Appreciation
Adult Hobby Classes: Courses—Ceramics, Painting, Weaving

LEVELLAND

SOUTH PLAINS COLLEGE, Creative Arts Dept, College Ave, 79336. Tel 806-894-9611, Ext 281. *Chmn* Don Stroud. Instrs: FT 3
Estab 1958; pub; D & E; SC 1, LC 5; enrl D 230, E 100, maj 175
Ent Req: HS dipl
Degrees: AA 2 yrs
Tuition: In-dist $4 per sem hr; out-of-dist $4 per sem hr; out-of-state $20 per sem hr; foreign $14 per sem hr
Courses: Advertising Design, Art History, Ceramics, Commercial Art, Drafting, Drawing, Graphic Arts, Graphic Design, Lettering, Painting, Photography, Sculpture, Teacher Training
Adult Hobby Classes: Enrl varies; tuition same as above. Courses—China Painting, Flower Arranging, Gift Wrapping, Oil Painting, Photography, Tole Painting

LUBBOCK

LUBBOCK CHRISTIAN COLLEGE, Art Dept,* 5601 W 19th St, 79407. Tel 806-792-3221. *Chmn* J Lee Roberts
Scholarships offered
Degrees: BA
Tuition: $1285 annual tuition
Courses: Advertising Design, Art Education, Art History, Calligraphy, Ceramics, Design, Drawing, Jewelry, Painting, Printmaking, Sculpture, Textile Design, Weaving

TEXAS TECH UNIVERSITY, Dept of Art, 79409. Tel 806-742-3825. *Interim Chmn* Terry Morrow, MS; *Interim Asst Chmn* Kim Smith, PhD; *Prof* Frank Cheatham, MFA; *Prof* Don Durland, MA; *Prof* Verne Funk, MFA; *Prof* Hugh Gibbons, MA; *Prof* Reid Hastie, PhD; *Prof* Jim Howze, MS; *Prof* Lynwood Kreneck, MFA; *Prof* Bill Lockhart, DED; *Prof* Francis Stephen, MFA; *Assoc Prof* Eugene Alesch, PhD; *Assoc Prof* Bill Bagley, MFA; *Assoc Prof* Peggy Bright, MA; *Assoc Prof* Ken Dixon, MFA; *Assoc Prof* Edna Glenn, MA; *Assoc Prof* Leslie Leupp, MFA; *Assoc Prof* Gene Mittler, PhD; *Assoc Prof* Marvin Moon, PhD; *Assoc Prof* John Queen, MFA; *Assoc Prof* Nancy Reed, PhD; *Assoc Prof* Betty Street, MS; *Assoc Prof* James Hanna, MA; *Assoc Prof* Sara Waters, MFA; *Asst Prof* Chris Burton, MFA; *Asst Prof* Karen Greenebaum, MA; *Asst Prof* Margaret Nagy, MFA; *Asst Prof* Kim Smith, PhD; *Asst Prof* Jeffrey Bowman, MS
Estab 1925, dept estab 1967; pub; D & E; scholarships; SC 80 undergrad, 23 grad, LC 27 undergrad, 17 grad; enrl D 1475 non-maj 700, maj 750, Grad 25
Ent Req: HS dipl, SAT or ACT test
Degrees: BA, BFA, and BSE 4 yr, MAE 36 hrs, MFA 60 hrs minimum, PhD 54 hrs beyond MA minimum
Tuition: Variable for res and nonres; campus residence available
Courses: †Art Education, †Art History, †Ceramics, †Drawing, Film, Graphic Design, †Illustration, †Interior Design, †Jewelry, Lettering, Mixed Media, †Painting, †Photography, †Printmaking, †Sculpture, Textile Design, Video, †Design Communication, †Enameling, Metals, Weaving
Children's Classes: Art Project for talented high school students
Summer School: Same as academic yr

MARSHALL

WILEY COLLEGE, Dept of Fine Arts, Roseborough Springs Rd, 75670. Tel 214-938-8341. *Head Dept* R Ronald O'Neal; *Assoc Prof* C L Violette
Estab 1873; den; D & E; scholarships; SC 16, LC 2; enrl D 56
Ent Req: HS dipl
Degrees: No art major
Tuition: $50 per hr, plus special fees; campus res—$500-$794 per yr
Courses: Advertising Design, Art Education, Art History, Ceramics, Commercial Art, Drawing, Fashion Arts, Graphic Arts, Graphic Design, Painting, Theatre Arts, Decoupage, Enameling
Summer School: Dir, Dr David R Houston. Tuition $50 per hr for term of 8 wks beginning June. Courses—as required

MESQUITE

EASTFIELD COLLEGE, Humanities Division, Art Dept, 3737 Motley, 75150. Tel 214-324-7132
Degrees: AA
Tuition: $8 - $10 per cr hr
Courses: Art Appreciation, Art History, Ceramics, Design, Drawing, Jewelry, Painting, Sculpture

MIDLAND

MIDLAND COLLEGE, Art Dept, 79701. Tel 915-684-7851. *Chmn* Stan Jacobs, PhD; *Instr* John Harmon, MFA; *Instr* Warren Taylor, MFA
Estab 1972; pub; D & E; scholarships; SC 28, LC 4; enrl D 70, E 80, non-maj 125, maj 25
Ent Req: HS dipl
Degrees: AA and AAA 2 yrs
Tuition: Res—undergrad $48 per 12 hrs plus $36 fee; nonres—undergrad $200 per 12 hrs plus $36 fee; no campus res
Courses: †Advertising Design, Aesthetics, Art Education, Art History, †Ceramics, Collages, †Commercial Art, Constructions, Drafting, †Drawing, Fashion Arts, Film, Graphic Arts, Graphic Design, Handicrafts, Illustration, Interior Design, †Jewelry, Lettering, Mixed Media, †Painting, †Photography, †Printmaking, †Sculpture, †Silversmithing, Stage Design, Teacher Training
Adult Hobby Classes: Tuition $20 per 6 wks. Courses—Drawing, Painting
Summer School: Same as regular term

NACOGDOCHES

STEPHEN F AUSTIN STATE UNIVERSITY, Art Dept, Box 3001, 75962. Tel 409-569-4804. *Chmn* Jon D Wink, MFA
Estab 1923; pub; D & E; SC 28, LC 11, GC 11; enrl D 461, non-maj 150, maj 150, grad 20
Ent Req: HS dipl, ACT score 18
Degrees: BFA 4 yrs, MFA 2 yrs, MA 1 yr
Tuition: Res—undergrad $60 per 15 hr, grad $50 per 12 hr; nonres—undergrad $600 per 15 hr, grad $480 per 12 hr; campus residence available
Courses: Advertising Design, Art Education, Art History, Ceramics, Commercial Art, Drawing, Graphic Arts, Graphic Design, Illustration, Jewelry, Lettering, Mixed Media, Painting, Printmaking, Sculpture, Cinematography

ODESSA

UNIVERSITY OF TEXAS OF PERMIAN BASIN, Art Discipline, 79762. Tel 915-367-2133. *Chmn* Stanley Marcus, EdD
Estab 1972; pub; D; scholarships; SC 45, LC 10; enrl non-maj 10, maj 30
Degrees: BA
Tuition: Campus residency available
Courses: Ceramics, Commercial Art, Painting, Printmaking, Sculpture
Summer School: Courses—varied

PARIS

PARIS JUNIOR COLLEGE, Art Dept, 2400 Clarksville St, 75460. Tel 214-785-7661, Ext 459. *Chmn* Ray E Karrer
Estab 1924; pub; D & E; scholarships; SC 12, LC 3; enrl D 63, E 21, non-maj 18, maj 22, others 24
Ent Req: None
Degrees: AA 2 yrs
Tuition: $7 per hour plus $70 fee
Courses: Art Education, †Ceramics, †Drawing, †Painting, †Photography, †Sculpture, Art Appreciation, Design
Adult Hobby Classes: Courses—Watercolor, Fibers, Painting
Children's Classes: Courses—Art Prepatory

PASADENA

SAN JACINTO COLLEGE, Art Dept,* 8060 Spencer Highway, 77505. Tel 713-476-1830. *Div Chmn Fine Arts* Jerry Callahan
Estab 1961; pub; D & E; SC 5, LC 1; enrl D 230, E 45, non-maj 120, maj 155
Ent Req: HS dipl, GED or individual approval
Degrees: AA and AS 2 yrs
Tuition: In district—$48 per sem; res—$168 per sem; nonres—$200 per sem
Courses: Advertising Design, Calligraphy, Commercial Art, Drafting, Drawing, Graphic Arts, Graphic Design, Interior Design, Lettering, Painting, Photography, Sculpture, Theatre Arts
Summer School: Enrl 25; tuition $25 for term of 6 wks beginning June 5th. Courses—Design, Painting Workshop

PLAINVIEW

WAYLAND BAPTIST UNIVERSITY, Dept of Art, Division of Christian Communication Arts, Box 249, 1900 W Seventh, 79072. Tel 806-296-5521. *Chmn* Dr John Stamper
Den; D & E; scholarships; SC 15, LC 2; enrl D 81, E 24, maj 10
Ent Req: HS dipl, ent exam
Degrees: BA and BS 4 yrs
Tuition: $35 per sem hr
Adult Hobby Classes: Courses—Painting, Art Appreciation, Watercolor
Children's Classes: Courses offered through Llano Estarado Museum on Campus
Summer School: Courses—vary each term

ROCKPORT

SIMON MICHAEL SCHOOL OF FINE ARTS, 510 E King, PO Box 1283, 78382. Tel 512-729-6233. *Head Dept* Simon Michael. Instrs: FT 1
Estab 1947; pvt; enrl professionals and beginners
Degrees: None
Ent Req: None
Courses: Drawing, Landscape Architecture, Mixed Media, Painting, Sculpture
Summer School: Enrl varies; tuition varies for each 1 wk workshop. Courses—Travel Art Workshop in USA and Europe

SAN ANGELO

ANGELO STATE UNIVERSITY, Art and Music Dept, ASU Station, 76909. Tel 915-942-2085. *Coordr* Dr Robert Prestiano; *Chmn Art and Music* Dr Charles Robison, PhD
Estab 1963, dept estab 1976; pub; D & E; SC 15, LC 9; enrl D 400 (art), E 50, non-maj 320, maj 80
Ent Req: HS dipl
Degrees: BA(Art) and BA(Art) and Teaching Certification
Tuition: Res—$14 per sem hr; nonres $50 per sem hr; campus res—room and board $486 per sem
Courses: Architecture, Art Education, Art History, Ceramics, Commercial Art, Drawing, Graphic Arts, Painting, Printmaking, Sculpture, Stage Design, Creative Design, History of Contemporary Art, History of Italian Renaissance, Greek and Roman Art, Intaglio Processes
Summer School: Tuition as above for term of 10 wks beginning June 1. Courses—Art History, Introduction to Art, Studio Courses incl Design and Drawing

SAN ANTONIO

INCARNATE WORD COLLEGE, Art Dept,* 4301 Broadway, 78201. Tel 512-828-1261, Ext 234. *Prof* B C O'Halloran, PhD; *Prof* William B Reilly, MFA; *Assoc Prof* Eloise Stoker, MA
Estab 1881, dept estab 1964; den; D; scholarships; SC 14, LC 9; enrl D 195, non-maj 120, maj 75
Ent Req: HS dipl, ent exam
Degrees: BA 4 yrs
Tuition: $113 per sem hr

OUR LADY OF THE LAKE UNIVERSITY, Dept of Art, 411 SW 24 St, 78285. Tel 512-434-6711. *Dean* Sr Isabel Ball, PhD; *Prof* Sr M Tharsilla Fuchs, MA; *Asst Prof* Sr Jule Adele Espey, PhD; *Asst Prof* Sr Dorcas Mladenka, MA. Instrs: FT 1, PT 3
Estab 1911, dept estab 1920; den; D & E; scholarships; SC 12, LC 3; enrl non-maj 62, maj 8
Ent Req: HS dipl, completion of GED tests, 35 on each test or average of 45 on tests
Degrees: BA(Art)
Tuition: Undergrad $110 per sem hr cr; grad $115 per hr cr; English as a foreign language program $1437 per sem, campus res—room & board $1134.38
Courses: Art Education, Art History, Design, Drawing, Graphic Arts, Painting, Photography, Printmaking, Cinema, Practicum in Art, Problems
Adult Hobby Classes: Courses offered

SAINT MARY'S UNIVERSITY OF SAN ANTONIO, Dept of Fine Arts, 78284. Tel 512-436-3319. *Dir* Sharon McMahon. Instrs: FT 4, PT 2
Estab 1852; pvt; D & E; SC 10, LC 20; enrl D 60, maj 58
Ent Req: HS dipl or GED, ent exam
Degrees: BA 4-5 yrs
Tuition: $125 per sem hr, $15 lab fee per course; campus res—room & board $1350-$1620 per sem
Courses: Art Education, Drawing, Film, Graphic Design, History of Art & Archaeology, Painting, Photography, Sculpture, Teacher Training, Theatre Arts
Adult Hobby Classes: Enrl 75-100; tuition $25. Courses—vary
Summer School: Courses—vary

SAN ANTONIO ART INSTITUTE, 6000 N New Braunfels, PO Box 6092, 78209. Tel 512-824-0531. *Dean* Howard Smagula, MFA; *Dir* George Parrino, MFA; *Instr* Carl Embrey, MFA; *Instr* Reginald M Rowe, MFA; *Instr* Louis Turner, BFA; *Instr* Ronald Wyffels, MFA
D & E; scholarships
Ent Req: None
Tuition: $150 per sem; no campus res
Courses: Art History, Calligraphy, Ceramics, Collages, Design, Drawing, Painting, Printmaking, Sculpture, Life Drawing, Critique
Adult Hobby Classes: Enrl 350; tuition $150 for 16 weeks
Children's Classes: Enrl 100; tuition $64 per 10 wks for ages 6—10 yrs. Courses-Ceramics
Summer School: Regular courses offered

SAN ANTONIO COLLEGE, Art & Advertising Dept, 1300 San Pedro Ave, 78284. Tel 512-733-2894. *Chmn* Mel Casas. Instrs: FT 11, PT 16
Estab 1955; pub; D & E; SC 32, LC 3; enrl D 1000-1300, E 250-450
Ent Req: HS dipl, ent exam
Degrees: AA and AS 2 yrs
Tuition: $14 per sem hr res; no campus res
Courses: Advertising Design, Architecture, Art Education, Display, Drawing, History of Art & Archaeology, Illustration, Industrial Design, Jewelry, Lettering, Painting, Photography, Sculpture
Summer School: Dir, Mel Cases. Enrl 250; tuition $14 per sem hr for 6 wks. Courses—Advertising Art, Design, Drawing, Printing

TRINITY UNIVERSITY, Dept of Art,* 715 Stadium Dr, 78284. Tel 512-736-7216. *Chmn & Prof* Robert E Tiemann, MFA; *Prof* Philip J Evett, PhD; *Prof* Glenn N Patton, PhD; *Prof* Elizabeth Ridenhower, MA; *Prof* Jim Stoker, MA; *Prof* William A Bristow, MFA; *Assoc Prof* Henry B Graham, PhD; *Asst Prof* Letha E McIntire, PhD
Estab 1869; pvt; D & E; SC 39, LC 20; enrl D 144, E 30, non-maj 50, maj 90
Ent Req: HS dipl, CEEB, SAT, 3 achievement tests
Degrees: BA 4 yrs
Tuition: $2300 per sem; campus res available
Courses: Art Education, †Art History, Commercial Art, Drawing, Graphic Arts, History of Art & Archaeology, Interior Design, Painting, Photography, Printmaking, Sculpture, Stage Design, Theatre Arts, Video, †Studio Art
Adult Hobby Classes: Courses offered by Department of Continuing Educ
Summer School: Dir, Dept of Continuing Educ. Tuition $114 per hr. Courses—vary

UNIVERSITY OF TEXAS AT SAN ANTONIO, Division of Art and Design, FM 1604, 78285. Tel 512-691-4352. *Div Dir* James Broderick, MA; *Prof* Ronald Binks, MFA; *Prof* Charles Field, MFA; *Prof* Jacinto Quirarte, PhD; *Assoc Prof* Stephen Reynolds, MFA; *Assoc Prof* Judith Sobre, PhD; *Asst Prof* Michael Bigger, MFA; *Asst Prof* Kent Rush, MFA; *Asst Prof* Dennis Olsen, MA; *Vis Prof* Luis Muro, BA; *Vis Asst Prof* Catherine Lee, MFA; *Adjunct Asst Prof* Robert Mullen, PhD
Pub; D & E; scholarships; SC 31, LC 25, GC 17; enrl maj 200, grad 35
Ent Req: HS dipl, ACT, grad, GRE
Degrees: BFA 4 yrs, MFA 2 yrs
Tuition: $50 per sem (12 hrs or under); no campus res
Courses: Art History, Ceramics, Drawing, Painting, Photography, Printmaking, Sculpture
Summer School: Tuition $25 per sem. Courses—Art History, Ceramics, Drawing, Painting, Photography, Printmaking, Sculpture

SAN MARCOS

PALOMAR COLLEGE, Art Dept, 1140 W Mission Rd, 92069. Tel 714-744-1150, Ext 2304. *Chmn* Val Sanders, MA; *Assoc Prof* Harry E Bliss, MFA; *Assoc Prof* George D Durrant, MA; *Assoc Prof* James C Hulbert, BPA; *Assoc Prof* Frank Jones, MFA; *Assoc Prof* Anthony J Lugo, MA; *Assoc Prof* Barry C Reed, MFA; *Assoc Prof* James T Saw, MA; *Assoc Prof* Louise Kirtland, MA; *Assoc Prof* Rita A White, MA; *Assoc Prof* Russell W Baldwin, MA; *Assoc Prof* Everett L Peck, BA
Estab 1950; pub; D & E; schol; SC 31, LC 4; enrl D 775, E 200
Ent Req: Ent exam
Degrees: AA 2 yr
Tuition: None; no campus res
Courses: Art History, †Ceramics, Collages, †Commercial Art, †Drawing, Graphic Arts, Graphic Design, Handicrafts, Illustration, †Jewelry, Lettering, †Painting, †Printmaking, Sculpture, †Silversmithing, Glassblowing, Life Drawing, Stained Glass, 2-D and 3-D Design
Summer School: Courses—basic courses except commercial art and graphic design

SOUTHWEST TEXAS STATE UNIVERSITY, Dept of Art, 78666. Tel 512-245-2611. *Dean* Ralph Harrel; *Chmn* Brian G Row, MFA
Estab 1903, dept estab 1916; pub; D & E; scholarships; SC 31, LC 7, GC 6; enrl D 1600, E 100, non-maj 1300, maj 300
Ent Req: HS dipl, ACT, SAT
Degrees: BS(Secondary Educ), BS(Educ all-level) and BFA(Commercial & Studio) 4 yrs
Tuition: Res $448 per year; nonres $1538 per year; campus res—room & board $1926 per year
Courses: Advertising Design, †Art Education, Art History, †Ceramics, †Commercial Art, †Drawing, Graphic Arts, Graphic Design, Illustration, †Jewelry, Lettering, †Painting, †Printmaking, †Sculpture, Teacher Training, †Textile Design, Video
Summer School: Chmn, Brian Row. Two 6 week terms

SEGUIN

TEXAS LUTHERAN COLLEGE, Dept of Visual Arts, 78155. Tel 512-379-4161, Ext 58. *Chmn* Harold W Hill. Instrs: FT 2
Estab 1923; den; D ; SC 18, LC 3; enrl 1000, maj 30
Ent Req: HS dipl
Degrees: BA(Art) 4 yrs
Tuition: Campus residency available
Courses: Advertising Design, Art Education, Art History, Ceramics, Drawing, Painting, Printmaking, Sculpture, Teacher Training, Design, Introduction to Visual Arts, Watercolor
Adult Hobby Classes: Classes—Art History, Design, Introduction to Visual Arts, Watercolor

SHERMAN

AUSTIN COLLEGE, Art Dept, 75090. Tel 214-892-9101, Ext 251. *Chmn* Carl R Neidhardt, PhD; *Asst Prof* Joseph Havel, MFA; *Asst Prof* Judy Miller, MFA
Estab 1848; pvt; D; scholarships; SC 9, LC 5, GC 8; enrl D 350, maj 55, grad 2
Ent Req: Ent exam plus acceptance by admission committee
Degrees: BA 4 yrs, MA 5 yrs
Tuition: $4600 per yr, $2300 per sem, $550 per course; room & board $2260
Courses: Art Education, Art History, Ceramics, Drawing, Graphic Design, Painting, Photography, Printmaking, Sculpture

TEMPLE

TEMPLE JUNIOR COLLEGE, Art Dept,* 2600 S First, 76501. Tel 817-773-9961. *Chmn* Wayne Toone; *Instr* Michael Donahue, MFA
Estab 1926; pub; D & E; SC 4, LC 2; enrl D 100, E 15, non-maj 85, maj 15
Ent Req: HS dipl, ACT or SAT
Degrees: AA 2 yrs
Tuition: District res—$43 per sem hr; non-district res—$47 per sem hr; non-state res—$62 per sem hr; campus res available
Courses: Art Appreciation, Art History, Art Education, Drawing, Graphic Design, Painting, Printmaking, Sculpture, Figure Drawing
Adult Hobby Classes: Enrl 15 per class; tuition $19 per 8 sessions. Courses—Arts & Crafts, Calligraphy, Drawing

TEXARKANA

TEXARKANA COMMUNITY COLLEGE, Art Dept, 2500 N Robinson Rd, 75501. Tel 214-838-4541. *Chmn* William Caver
Estab 1927; D & E; scholarships
Ent Req: HS dipl
Tuition: District res--$130 for 15 cr hrs; out of district res--$175 for 15 cr hrs

Courses: Art Education, Ceramics, Drafting, Drawing, Painting, Printmaking, Sculpture, Teacher Training, Weaving
Summer School: Dir, Rolfe Wylie. Enrl 20; tuition $47. Courses--Drawing & Ceramics

TYLER

TYLER JUNIOR COLLEGE, Art Program, Box 6117, 75701. Tel 214-531-2200. *Coordr* Charles J Cavanaugh Jr
Scholarships offered
Degrees: AA
Courses: Art Appreciation, Art Education, Art History, Ceramics, Design, Drawing, Handicrafts, Interior Design, Painting, Sculpture
Adult Hobby Classes: Courses offered

UNIVERSITY OF TEXAS AT TYLER, Dept of Art, 3900 University Blvd, 75701. Tel 214-566-1471, Ext 289. *Chmn* William B Stephens, EdD; *Assoc Prof* Kenneth Casstevens, EdD; *Assoc Prof* Donald Van Horn, MFA
Estab 1973; pub; D & E; scholarships; SC 28, LC 6, GC 11
Ent Req: AA degree or 60 hrs of college study
Degrees: BA and BFA
Tuition: Res—$173 per sem; nonres—$323 per sem
Courses: Aesthetics, †Art Education, †Art History, Ceramics, Drawing, Graphic Arts, Graphic Design, History of Art & Archaeology, Interior Design, Mixed Media, Painting, Photography, Printmaking, Sculpture, Teacher Training, †Studio Art
Summer School: Dir, William B Stephens. Tuition res $76, nonres $151. Courses—vary

VICTORIA

VICTORIA COLLEGE, 2200 Red River, 77901. Tel 512-573-3291. *Head Dept* Larry Shook, MA; *Vis Prof* Nancy Bandy
Estab 1925; pub; D & E; SC 9, LC 3; enrl D 100, E 40, non-maj 40, maj 100
Ent Req: HS dipl
Tuition: Res—$100 per sem; nonres—$200 per sem; no campus res
Courses: Art Education, Art History, Commercial Art, Display, Drafting, Drawing, Graphic Design, Printmaking, Sculpture, Teacher Training
Summer School: Courses—as above

WACO

BAYLOR UNIVERSITY, Dept of Fine Arts, 76798. Tel 817-755-1867. *Chmn* Harold C Simmons, PhD; *Instr* Paul Z Kemp, MFA; *Instr* John D McClanahan, MFA; *Instr* Berry J Klingman, MFA; *Instr* Terry M Roller, MA; *Instr* Hilda S Smith; *Instr* Charles J Isoline, MA; *Instr* William M Jensen, PhD; *Instr* Vernie M Logan, MFA
Estab 1845, dept estab 1870; den; D & E; scholarships; SC 60, LC 26, GC 12; enrl D 600, E 20, non-maj 490, maj 110
Ent Req: HS dipl, ent exam, ACT tests
Degrees: AB, BS(Art Educ) and BFA 4 yrs
Tuition: $2910 per yr, $97 per sem; campus res—room & board $2370
Courses: †Art Education, †Art History, †Ceramics, Drawing, Graphic Arts, Handicrafts, †Painting, Photography, Sculpture, †Art Therapy, †Communication Design, Two and Three-Dimensional Design
Summer School: Dean, William Cooper. Enrl 75; tuition $97 per cr hr for term of 6 wks beginning May 28 & July 9. Courses—Art Education, Art History, Ceramics, Communication Design, Crafts, Design, Painting

MCLENNAN COMMUNITY COLLEGE, Fine Arts Dept, 1400 College, 76708. Tel 817-756-6551. *Chmn* William R Haskett
Estab 1965; pub; D & E; SC 8, LC 3; enrl D 35, non-maj 20, maj 40
Ent Req: HS dipl
Degrees: AA 2 yrs
Tuition: Res—$168 per yr; nonres—$900 per yr; no campus res
Courses: Art History, Drawing, Painting, Photography, Sculpture, Art Appreciation, Color, Design, Problems in Contemporary Art
Adult Hobby Classes: Tuition depends on the class. Courses—Ceramics, Drawing, Jewelry, Painting, Sculpture, Stained Glass
Summer School: Tuition $42. Courses—Design, Drawing

WEATHERFORD

WEATHERFORD COLLEGE, Dept of Humanities and Art, Park Ave, 76086. Tel 817-594-5471, Ext 32. *Head Dept of Art* Myrlan Coleman, MA & MFA
Estab 1856, dept estab 1959; pub; D & E; SC 10, LC 4; enrl D 58, non-maj 30, maj 16, others 12
Ent Req: HS dipl
Degrees: AA
Courses: Intermedia, Mixed Media, Painting
Summer School: Term May 24 and July 10

WHARTON

WHARTON COUNTY JUNIOR COLLEGE, Art Dept,* 911 Boling Highway, 77488. Tel 713-532-4560, Ext 52. *Chmn* Bruce F Turner, PhD; *Instructor* Morna Nation, MFA
Pub; D & E; SC 8, LC 2; enrl D 90, E 15
Ent Req: HS dipl, GED
Degrees: 2 yrs
Tuition: District res—$4 per sem hr; non-district—$6.25 per sem hr; non-state res—$42.25 per sem hr
Courses: Art Education, Art History, Ceramics, Drawing, History of Art & Archaeology, Painting, Sculpture, Teacher Training

WICHITA FALLS

MIDWESTERN STATE UNIVERSITY, Dept of Art, 3400 Taft Blvd, 76308. Tel 817-692-6611, Ext 4304. *Chmn* Larry Hilman Davis, MFA
Estab 1926; pub; D & E; SC 20-30, LC 406; enrl D 300 per sem, E 30-50 per sem, non-maj 60, maj 125, others 10
Ent Req: HS dipl, ACT, SAT
Degrees: BA, BFA and BSE 4 yrs
Tuition: $1167 per sem
Courses: †Advertising Design, †Art Education, †Art History, †Ceramics, †Commercial Art, †Drawing, †Goldsmithing, †Graphic Arts, †Graphic Design, Handicrafts, †Jewelry, †Painting, †Photography, †Printmaking, †Sculpture, †Silversmithing, Fibers

UTAH

CEDAR CITY

SOUTHERN UTAH STATE COLLEGE, Dept of Art,* 84720. Tel 801-586-9481, 586-7700. *Chmn* Richard Adams. Instrs: FT 4, PT 2
Estab 1897; pub; D & E; scholarships; SC 29, LC 6; enrl D 300, E 80, maj 60, minors 45
Ent Req: HS dipl ent exam
Degrees: BA and BS 4 yrs
Tuition: $245 per quarter
Courses: Advertising Design, Art Education, Ceramics, Commercial Art, Drawing, Graphic Arts, Graphic Design, History of Art & Archaeology, Illustration, Lettering, Painting, Sculpture, Teacher Training

EPHRAIM

SNOW COLLEGE, Art Dept,* 150 E College Ave, 84627. Tel 801-283-4021. *Chmn* Osrael Allred
Scholarships offered
Degrees: AA, AAS
Tuition: Res—$300 per yr; nonres—$750 per yr
Courses: Art Appreciation, Ceramics, Design, Drawing, Handicrafts, Interior Design, Jewelry, Painting, Photography, Sculpture

LOGAN

UTAH STATE UNIVERSITY
—Dept of Landscape Architecture Environmental Planning, 84322. Tel 801-750-3471. *Head* Jerry W Fuhriman. Instrs: FT 6, PT 3
Tuition: Res—$51 per cr qtr; nonres—$113 per cr qtr
Courses: †Landscape Architecture, †Town & Regional Planning
—Dept of Art, 84322. Tel 801-750-3460. *Head* Dr Ray W Hellberg, PhD; *Prof* R T Clark, MFA; *Instr* Alan Bennett, MFA
Estab 1890; D & E; scholarships; enrl D 340, maj 340, grad 24
Ent Req: HS dipl, HS transcript, ACT
Degrees: BS, BA, BFA, MFA and MA
Tuition: Res—$918 per 15 cr hrs in 3 qtrs; nonres—$2358 per 15 cr hrs in 3 qtrs; campus res available
Courses: †Advertising Design, †Art Education, †Ceramics, †Drawing, †Graphic Arts, †Illustration, †Painting, †Photography, †Printmaking, †Sculpture
Adult Hobby Classes: Courses—Various
Summer School: Head, Prof R T Clark. 4 wk session. Courses—Ceramics, Ceramic Handbuilding, Ceramic Wheelthrow, Drawing, Individual Projects, Landscape Painting, Painting, Photography, Printmaking Studio, Sculpture, Watercolor

OGDEN

WEBER STATE COLLEGE, Art Dept,* 84408. Tel 801-626-6762. *Chmn* David N Cox, MFA; *Prof* Arthur R Adelmann, MFA; *Prof* Dale W Bryner, MFA; *Prof* James R McBeth, MFA; *Prof* Richard J VanWagoner, MFA; *Assoc Prof* Fred Rabe, MA; *Assoc Prof* Doyle Strong, BA; *Asst Prof* Susan Makov, MFA; *Asst Prof* Barbara Schulman, MFA
Estab 1933, dept estab 1937; pub; D & E; scholarships; SC 66, LC 17; enrl D 2464, E 694, non-maj 700, maj 251
Ent Req: HS dipl, ACT
Degrees: AAS 2 yr, BA, BS 2 yr
Tuition: Res—$235 per yr; nonres—$595 per yr; campus res available
Courses: Advertising Design, †Art Education, Art History, Ceramics, †Commercial Art, Drawing, Film, †Graphic Arts, †Graphic Design, †Illustration, Jewelry, Lettering, Painting, †Photography, Printmaking, Sculpture, Silversmithing, Teacher Training, Textile Design
Summer School: Dir, David N Cox. Tuition $235 for term of 8 wks beginning June 15

PROVO

BRIGHAM YOUNG UNIVERSITY, Dept of Art, C-502 HFAC, 84602. Tel 801-378-4266. *Chmn* Franz M Johansen, MA. Instrs: FT 22, PT 5
Estab 1875, dept estab 1893; den; D & E; scholarships; SC 50; enrl E 1975, maj 352, grad 30
Ent Req: HS dipl or ACT
Degrees: BA and BFA 4 yrs, MFA 2 yrs and MA 1 1/2 yrs
Tuition: Undergrad $1340 per yr, $670 per sem, PT $68 per cr hr, grad $1520 per yr, $760 per sem, PT $77 per cr hr; nonchurch member—undergrad $2010 per yr,

$1005 per sem, PT $102 per cr hr, grad $2280 per yr, $1140 per sem, PT $116 per cr hr; campus res—room & board $2080
Courses: †Art Education, †Art History, †Ceramics, †Drawing, †Painting, †Printmaking, †Sculpture, Teacher Training
Children's Classes: Children's Art Workshop
Summer School: Courses same as regular session

SAINT GEORGE

DIXIE COLLEGE, Art Dept,* 84770. Tel 801-673-4811, Ext 297. *Dean Div Fine & Performing Arts* C Paul Anderson. Instrs: FT 3
Estab 1911; pub; D & E; scholarships; SC 24, LC 7, GC 1; enrl D 400, maj 30
Ent Req: HS dipl, ACT
Degrees: AA and AS 2 yrs
Tuition: Res—$157 per quarter; nonres—$503 per quarter
Courses: Advertising Design, Art Education, Art History, Ceramics, Commercial Art, Costume Design & Construction, Drafting, Drawing, Film, Illustration, Interior Design, Painting, Photography, Printmaking, Sculpture, Teacher Training, Textile Design, Theatre Arts, Video, Life Drawing, Portrait Drawing, Three Dimensional Design
Adult Hobby Classes: Enrl 20; tuition $50 per quarter. Courses—Ceramics, Oil Painting, Wood Carving
Summer School: Courses—Basic Design, Basic Drawing, Oil Painting

SALT LAKE CITY

UNIVERSITY OF UTAH, Art Dept, AAC 161, 84112. Tel 801-581-8678. *Chmn & Prof* Paul H Davis, MFA; *Prof* Dorothy Bearnson, MA; *Prof* Angelo Caravaglia, TC; *Prof* Robert S Olpin, PhD; *Prof* Alvin Gittins, BA; *Prof* Frank Anthony Smith, MFA; *Prof* V Douglas Snow, MFA; *Prof* Lennox Tierney; *Prof* Edward Maryon, MFA; *Prof* McRay Magleby, BA; *Assoc Prof* Robert Kleinschmidt, MFA; *Assoc Prof* Richard Johnston, MFA; *Asst Prof* Sheila Muller, MA; *Asst Prof* Brian Patrick, MFA; *Asst Prof* David Pendell, MFA; *Asst Prof* Nathan Winters, PhD; *Asst Prof* Raymond Morales, BA; *Emeritus Prof* George S Dibble, MA
Estab 1850, dept estab 1888; pub; D & E; scholarships; SC 79, LC 57, GC 27; enrl D 3624, E 465, non-maj 1347, maj 350, grad 10
Ent Req: HS dipl
Degrees: BA and BFA 4 yrs, MA and MFA 2 yrs
Tuition: Res $363 for 16 hrs per quarter, $428 for 21 hrs per quarter; nonres—$1033 for 16 hrs per quarter, $1241 for 21 hrs per quarter; campus res available
Courses: Advertising Design, Art Education, †Art History, †Ceramics, Commercial Art, Drawing, Film, Goldsmithing, Graphic Arts, †Graphic Design, †Handicrafts, Illustration, Jewelry, †Painting, Photography, †Printmaking, †Sculpture, †Silversmithing, Teacher Training, Fibers

UTAH TECHNICAL COLLEGE AT SALT LAKE, Commercial Art Dept,* 4600 S Redwood Rd, PO Box 31808, 84131. Tel 801-967-4111. *Dean School Trades & Industry* Walter L White, MA; *Instr* Ralph Huddlestone, BA; *Instr* Grant M Hulet, MA; *Instr* I Douglas Jordan, BA; *Instr* Joseph Lema, BA; *Instr* Allen Reinhold, MA; *Instr* Lois Snyder, MA; *Instr* Fred Van Dyke, BA
Pub; D & E; scholarships; SC 44, LC 7; enrl D 123, E 10, non-maj 81, maj 42
Ent Req: HS dipl or equivalent, aptitude test
Degrees: Certificate, Diploma, AS
Tuition: Res—$45 per cr hr; nonres—$115 per cr hr; no campus res
Courses: Advertising Design, Art Education, †Commercial Art, Drawing, Fashion Arts, Graphic Arts, †Graphic Design, †Illustration, †Lettering, Photography
Summer School: Dean, James Schnirel. Enrl 30; tuition $145 for term of 10 wks beginning June. Courses—Aesthetics, Drawing, Lettering, Media and Techniques

WESTMINSTER COLLEGE, Dept of Art,* 1840 S 13th East, 84105. Tel 801-484-7651, Ext 66. *Chmn Fine Arts Program* Catherine Kuzminski; *Chmn Arts & Letters* Jay Lees; *Assoc Prof* Gordon McBride. Instrs: FT 2, PT 5
Estab 1875; pvt; D; scholarships; SC 25, LC 2; enrl D 900-1000, maj 25
Ent Req: HS dipl, ent exam acceptable, HS grade point average
Degrees: BA and BS 4 yrs
Tuition: $1590 per sem
Courses: Art Education, Art History, Ceramics, Drawing, Jewelry, Painting, Photography, Sculpture, Teacher Training, Weaving

VERMONT

BENNINGTON

BENNINGTON COLLEGE, Visual Arts Division, 05201. Tel 802-442-5401. *Pres* Michael Hooker. Instrs: FT E 70
Estab 1932; pvt; scholarships
Degrees: AB 4 yrs and MA 2 yrs
Tuition: 13,560 including room & board per yr
Courses: †Architecture, Art History, †Ceramics, †Drawing, †Painting, †Photography, †Sculpture, †Graphics, †Visual Arts

BURLINGTON

UNIVERSITY OF VERMONT, Dept of Art, College of Arts & Sciences, 304 Williams Hall, 05405. Tel 802-656-2014. *Chairperson* Barbara M Zucker. Instrs: 16
Pub; D & E; enrl 7400
Degrees: BA and BS 4 yrs
Tuition: Res—$78 per credit hr; nonres $212 per credit hr
Courses: Art Education, Art History, Ceramics, Drawing, Film, Painting, Photography, Printmaking, Sculpture, Video, Design, Fine Metals
Adult Hobby Classes: College of Continuing Education
Summer School: Dir, Lynne Ballard. Two 9 wk sessions beginning in May

CASTLETON

CASTLETON STATE COLLEGE, Art Dept, 05735. Tel 802-468-5611. *Head Dept* Charles R Anderson, BFA; *Asst Prof* Warren Kimble, BFA; *Asst Prof* William Ramage, MFA; *Instructor* Rita Bernatowicz, MFA; *Instructor* Susan Smith, MFA
Estab 1787; Pub; D & E; SC 31, LC 3, GC varies; enrl D 1400, E 1000, non-maj 300, maj 79, grad 5
Ent Req: HS dipl, ACT, SAT, CEEB
Degrees: BA and BS 4 yrs, A/SBA 2 yrs (business with art concentration)
Tuition: Res—undergrad & grad $1250 per yr, $625 per sem, $52 per cr; nonres—undergrad & grad $3050 per yr, $1525 per sem, $127 per cr; campus res—room & board $2396
Courses: Advertising Design, Art Education, Art History, Calligraphy, Commercial Art, Costume Design & Construction, Drawing, Graphic Arts, Graphic Design, Handicrafts, Illustration, Lettering, Painting, Photography, Printmaking, Sculpture, Teacher Training, Theatre Arts, Color Design, Professional Studio Arts, Typography
Summer School: Dir, Dr Jill Ellsworth. Courses—Calligraphy, Crafts, Drawing, Lettering, Painting, Photography, Watercolor

JOHNSON

JOHNSON STATE COLLEGE, Dept Fine Arts, 05656. Tel 802-635-2356. *Assoc Prof* Peter Heller, BFA; *Asst Prof* Jon Batdorff, MFA; *Asst Prof* Peter Moriarty, MFA; *Instr* Judith L Ott, MA; *Lectr* Jeff Goss, BFA
Estab 1828; pub; D & E; SC 30, LC 6; enrl D 308, non-maj 188, maj 120
Ent Req: HS dipl
Degrees: BA and BFA 4 yrs, K-12 teaching cert
Tuition: Res—undergrad $1530 per yr, $765 per sem; nonres—undergrad $3560 per yr, $1780 per sem; campus res—room & board $1470 per yr
Courses: Art Education, Art History, Ceramics, Drawing, Mixed Media, Painting, Photography, Sculpture, †Studio Art
Children's Classes: Gifted and talented prog for high school students
Summer School: Enrl 40; tuition res—$75 per cr hr, nonres—$105 per cr hr for term of 6 wks beginning June. Courses—Mixed Media, Painting, Sculpture

MIDDLEBURY

MIDDLEBURY COLLEGE, Dept of Art, Johnson Building, 05753. Tel 802-388-3711, Ext 5234. *Chmn* John M Hunisak. Instrs: FT 7
Estab 1800; pvt; D; SC 5, LC 22; enrl maj 60, others 500 per term
Ent Req: Exam and cert
Degrees: AB
Tuition: $11,800 per yr includes campus res
Courses: Art History, Drawing, Painting, Printmaking, Sculpture, Design

NORTHFIELD

NORWICH UNIVERSITY, Dept of Philosophy, Religion and Fine Arts, College St, 05663. Tel 802-229-0522, Ext 228. *Chair & Assoc Prof* Harold Krauth, PhD; *Assoc Prof* Brian Webb, PhD; *Assoc Prof* Earl Feckter, MFA; *Asst Prof* Dean Perkins, PhD; *Asst Prof* Robert McKay, PhD; *Asst Prof* James Bennett
Pvt; D & E; D 65 (studio art), E 8, non-maj 126
Ent Req: HS dipl
Degrees: AA
Tuition: Campus residency available
Courses: Art Education, Art History, Drawing, Painting, Photography, Printmaking, Design
Adult Hobby Classes: Chairperson, Harold Krauth, PhD

PLAINSFIELD

GODDARD COLLEGE, Visual Arts Dept, 05667. Tel 802-454-8311. *Head* Diane Tetrault
Estab 1938; pvt; D & E
Degrees: BA 4 yr, MA 1-2 yr
Tuition: Res—undergrad $8900 per yr, $4450 per sem; nonres—undergrad and grad $3900 per yr, $1950 per sem; campus res available
Courses: †Art Education, †Art History, †Ceramics, †Collages, †Conceptual Art, †Drawing, †Graphic Arts, †Graphic Design, †Painting, †Photography, †Printmaking, †Sculpture, †Stage Design, †Teacher Training, †Theatre Arts, †Video, †Weaving, †Etching

POULTNEY

GREEN MOUNTAIN COLLEGE, Dept of Art, 05764. Tel 802-287-9313. *Chmn & Prof* Donald Royce-Roll
Estab 1834; pvt; W; enrl maj 25
Degrees: AA 2 yrs
Tuition: $5700 per yr with room & board
Courses: Art History, Ceramics, Design, Drawing, Graphic Design, Illustration, Painting, Photography, Printmaking, Sculpture, Graphic Design Studio, Fine Art Studio

STOWE

WRIGHT SCHOOL OF ART, Box 2000, 05672. Tel 802-253-4305. *Dir* Stanley Marc Wright. Instrs: FT 2
Estab 1949; SC 5, LC 4; enrl 50
Tuition: $40 per wk
Courses: Painting
Children's Classes: Four Mon PM $5 per lesson, June to Sept. Courses—Drawing, Painting
Summer School: June - Sept

WINOOSKI

ST MICHAEL'S COLLEGE, Fine Arts Dept, 56 College Parkway, 05404. Tel 802-655-2000, Ext 2449. *Prof* Donald A Rathgeb, MFA; *Asst Prof* Roy Kennedy; *Asst Prof* Lance Richbourg, MFA
Estab 1903, dept estab 1965; den; D & E; SC 8, LC 3
Ent Req: HS dipl
Degrees: BA 4 yrs
Tuition: $5929; campus res—room & board $2500
Courses: Art History, Calligraphy, Drawing, Graphic Arts, Painting, Sculpture, Stage Design, Theatre Arts, Art Theory
Summer School: Dir Alan Stockton. Tuition $275 for term of 6 weeks beginning last week in June. Courses—Drawing, Painting

VIRGINIA

ANNANDALE

NORTHERN VIRGINIA COMMUNITY COLLEGE, Art Dept, 8333 Little River Turnpike, 22003. Tel 703-323-3115. *Chmn Humanities Div* Dr Eltse B Carter
Pub; D & E; scholarships; enrl D 589, E 200
Ent Req: Open admis
Degrees: AA(Fine Arts), AA(Art Educ) and AA(Art History) 2 yrs
Tuition: Res—undergrad $13.50 per cr; nonres—undergrad $58 per cr; no campus res
Courses: Aesthetics, †Art Education, †Art History, Drafting, Drawing, Graphic Design, Interior Design, Painting, Printmaking, Sculpture, Stage Design, Theatre Arts, †Fine Arts
Summer School: Chmn Humanities Div, Dr Eltse B Carter. Tuition same as regular session; 2 five week D sessions and 1 ten week E session during Summer. Courses—varied, incl study abroad

ARLINGTON

MARYMOUNT COLLEGE OF VIRGINIA, Arts & Sciences Division,* Old Dominion & N Glebe Rd, 22207. Tel 703-522-5600. *Chmn* Robert Draghi, PhD; *Assoc Prof* Pamela Stoessell, MFA; *Asst Prof* Andrew Monje
Estab 1950; pvt; D & E; SC 14, LC 20
Ent Req: HS dipl, SAT results, letter of recommendation
Degrees: BA 4 yrs, AA 2 yrs
Tuition: $2300 per sem; campus res available
Courses: Advertising Design, Art History, Ceramics, †Commercial Art, Design, Drafting, Drawing, †Fashion Arts, Handicrafts, †Industrial Design, Painting, Sculpture, Textile Design, Clothing Design & Construction, †Studio Arts
Adult Hobby Classes: Courses—any course in fine arts
Summer School: Dir, Alice S Mandanis. Tuition $1600 per summer sem, for term of 5 wks beginning May

ASHLAND

RANDOLPH-MACON COLLEGE, Art Dept,* 23005. Tel 804-798-8372. *Chmn* Jon D Longaker, BA; *Artist in Res* Raymond Berg, MFA; *Vis Instr* John Temple Witt, MFA
Sch estab 1830, dept estab 1953; pvt; D; SC 4, LC 4; enrl D 200, non-maj 200
Degrees: BA & BS 4 yrs
Tuition: $5500 annual tuition; campus res available
Courses: Art History, Drawing, Painting

BLACKSBURG

VIRGINIA POLYTECHNIC INSTITUTE AND STATE UNIVERSITY, Dept of Art, 24061. Tel 703-961-5547. *Head Dept* Victor Huggins; *Instructor* Steve Bickley, MFA; *Instructor* Robert Graham, MFA; *Instructor* Leslye Bloom, PhD; *Instructor* Carol Burch-Brown, MFA; *Instructor* Dean Carter, MFA; *Instructor* David Crane, MFA; *Instructor* Robert Fields, MFA; *Instructor* Maryann Harman, MA; *Instructor* Ray Kass, MFA; *Instructor* Derek Myers, MFA; *Instructor* Jerrie Pike, PhD; *Instructor* Pat Mathews, Phd; *Instructor* Al Sarvis, MFA; *Instructor* Catherine Soussloff, PhD. Instrs: FT 16
Estab 1969; pub; SC 25, LC 12
Degrees: BA 4 yrs
Tuition: $975
Courses: Art Education, Art History, Ceramics, Drawing, Graphic Design, Jewelry, Painting, Printmaking, Sculpture, Design, Studio Art, Watercolor
Summer School: Head Dept, Victor Huggins. Tui proportional to acad yr for two 8 wk terms beginning May and July. Courses—same as above, study abroad program in England & Scotland

BRIDGEWATER COLLEGE

BRIDGEWATER COLLEGE, Art Dept, 22812. Tel 703-828-2501. *Chmn* Paul M Kline
Scholarships
Courses: Art Appreciation, Art History, Design, Drawing, Painting, Printmaking, Sculpture

BRISTOL

VIRGINIA INTERMONT COLLEGE, Fine Arts Dept,* Moore St, 24201. Tel 703-669-6101. *Chmn* Stephen J Hamilton, MFA; *Faculty* Marvin L Tadlock, MFA; *Faculty* James McLendon, BFA; *Faculty* Christine M Walters, MFA
Estab 1884; den; D & E; scholarships; SC 15, LC 4; enrl D 35, non-maj 110
Ent Req: HS dipl, review of work
Degrees: BA(Art) and BA(Art Educ) 4 yrs, AA 2 yrs
Tuition: $3350 per sem

BUENA VISTA

SOUTHERN SEMINARY JUNIOR COLLEGE, 24416. Tel 703-261-6181. *Chmn* Leroy U Rudasill Jr, MA
Estab 1867; pvt; D; SC 10, LC 5; enrl D 185, non-maj 175, maj 10
Ent Req: HS dipl, SAT or ACT
Degrees: AA, AS and AFA 2 yrs
Tuition: Res—undergrad $7300 per yr; nonres—undergrad $4850 per yr
Courses: Art Education, Art History, Ceramics, Display, Drawing, Graphic Arts, Handicrafts, Interior Design, Jewelry, Painting, Photography, Printmaking, Sculpture, Macrame
Summer School: Dir, Joseph L Carter. Enrl 30; tuition $100 per cr hr for 4 wk term beginning May 10 - June 10

CHARLOTTESVILLE

UNIVERSITY OF VIRGINIA, McIntire Dept of Art, Fayerweather Hall, 22903. Tel 804-924-3057, 924-3541. *Chmn* Malcolm Bell. Instrs: FT 20
Estab 1819, dept estab 1951; pub; D; scholarships; SC 21, LC 21, GC 14; enrl D 1175, maj 100, grad 27 res, 18 non-res
Ent Req: HS dipl
Degrees: BA(Studio and Art History), MA(Art History) and PhD(Art History)
Courses: Art History, Drawing, Graphic Arts, Graphic Design, Painting, Photography, Printmaking, Sculpture, Design, Watercolor
Summer School: Enrl 15; tuition varies. Courses—Art History, Studio Art

DANVILLE

AVERETT COLLEGE, Art Dept,* W Main St, 24541. Tel 804-793-7811. *Coordr* Maud F Gatewood, MA; *Assoc Prof* Robert Marsh, MFA; *Asst Prof* Richard Gantt, MFA; *Asst Prof* Diane Kendrick, MFA
Estab 1859, dept estab 1930; pvt; D & E; scholarships; SC 13, LC 5; enrl D 1000, non-maj 250, maj 25
Ent Req: HS dipl
Degrees: AB
Tuition: $100 per sem hr, $1725 per term; campus res available
Courses: Advertising Design, Art Education, Art History, Ceramics, Commercial Art, Drawing, Fashion Arts, History of Art & Archaeology, Illustration, Jewelry, Lettering, Painting, Printmaking, Sculpture, Teacher Training, Textile Design
Summer School: Two 4 wk sessions

FAIRFAX

GEORGE MASON UNIVERSITY, Dept of Art, 22030. Tel 703-323-2076. *Chmn* Carol C Mattusch, PhD. Instrs: FT 7, PT 7
Estab 1948, dept estab 1981; pub; D & E; SC 16, LC 15; enrl non-maj 200, maj 130
Ent Req: HS dipl, SAT or CEEB
Degrees: BA
Tuition: $690 for 12-17 sem hrs
Courses: Art Education, †Art History, Drafting, Drawing, Film, Graphic Arts, History of Art & Archaeology, Painting, Printmaking, Sculpture, Stage Design, Theatre Arts, †Studio Art
Summer School: Courses—Art Appreciation, Studio Arts

FARMVILLE

LONGWOOD COLLEGE, Dept of Art, Pine St, 23901. Tel 804-392-9359. *Head Dept* Barbara L Bishop, MFA
Estab 1839, dept estab 1932; pub; D & E; scholarships; SC 59, LC 15; enrl non-maj 450 per sem, maj 95 per sem
Ent Req: HS dipl
Degrees: BA(Art Educ), BS(Art Educ) 4 yrs, BFA(Studio, Art History) 4 yrs
Courses: †Advertising Design, †Art Education, †Art History, Ceramics, Display, †Drawing, Goldsmithing, Illustration, Jewelry, Lettering, Museum Staff Training, †Painting, Photography, †Printmaking, †Sculpture, †Teacher Training, Basic Design, †Crafts, Fibers, Stained Glass, Three Dimensional Design, Wood Design
Summer School: Art Dept Head, Barbara L Bishop. Tuition varies. Courses—vary, primarily craft studios and workshops

FREDERICKSBURG

MARY WASHINGTON COLLEGE, Art Dept, 22401. Tel 703-899-4339. *Chmn & Prof* Barbara Meyer, PhD; *Prof* Paul C Muick, PhD; *Prof* Cornelia Oliver, PhD; *Prof* John Lamph, MFA; *Assoc Prof* Joseph DiBella, MFA; *Asst Prof* Joseph Dreiss, PhD; *Asst Prof* Mary Belle Pendleton, PhD; *Artist-in-Res* Lorene Nickel, MFA
Estab 1904; pub; D & E; scholarships; SC 18, LC 20; enrl maj 50
Ent Req: HS dipl, ent exam
Degrees: BA and BS 4 yrs
Tuition: Campus residency available
Courses: †Art History, Ceramics, Drawing, Graphic Arts, Painting, Photography, Printmaking, Sculpture, †Studio Art

HAMPTON

HAMPTON INSTITUTE, Art Dept,* 23668. Tel 804-727-5416. *Chmn Art* Benedict Donahue. Instrs: FT 8, PT 4
Estab 1869; pvt; D; scholarships; SC 22, LC 7, GC 9; enrl maj 69, others 300, grad 5
Ent Req: HS grad
Degrees: BA, BS
Tuition: $1565 annual tuition; campus res available
Courses: Art Education, Art History, Ceramics, Commercial Art, Jewelry, Painting, Photography, Design, Metalwork
Summer School: Courses—Advanced Workshop in Ceramics, Art Educ Methods, Art Methods for the Elementary School, Basic Design, Ceramics, Commercial Art, Design, Drawing and Composition, Graphics, Metalwork & Jewelry, Painting, Understanding the Arts

HARRISONBURG

JAMES MADISON UNIVERSITY, Dept of Art, School of Fine Arts & Communication, 22807. Tel 703-433-6216. *Head Dept* Jay D Kain, PhD; *Prof* Martha B Caldwell, PhD; *Prof* Jerry L Coulter, MFA; *Prof* J David Diller, PhD; *Assoc Prof* Kenneth J Beer, MA; *Assoc Prof* James Crable, MFA; *Assoc Prof* Rebecca Humphrey, MFA; *Assoc Prof* Philip James, EdD; *Assoc Prof* Kenneth Szmagaj, MFA; *Assoc Prof* Barbara Lewis, MFA; *Assoc Prof* Ronald Wyancko, MFA; *Assoc Prof* Kathleen Arthur, PhD; *Assoc Prof* Gary Chatelain, MFA; *Assoc Prof* Jack McCaslin, MFA; *Assoc Prof* Masako Miyata, MFA; *Assoc Prof* Alan Tschudi, MFA; *Assoc Prof* Steve Zapton, MFA; *Asst Prof* Robert Bersson, PhD; *Asst Prof* Michael Brodsky, MFA; *Asst Prof* Algar Dole, MFA; *Asst Prof* Barbara Wolanin, PhD; *Instr* Stuart Downs, MA
Estab 1908; pub; D & E; scholarships; SC 31, LC 21, GC 22; enrl D & E 1254, maj 184, GS 12
Ent Req: HS dipl, graduates must submit portfolio, undergrads selected largely on academic merit
Degrees: BA(Art History), BS and BFA(Studio) 4 yrs, MAT 1 1/2 to 2 yrs, MFA 60 credit hours
Tuition: Res—undergrad $830 per sem; nonres—undergrad $1295 per sem; campus res—room and board $1169 per sem
Courses: Advertising Design, Aesthetics, †Art Education, †Art History, †Ceramics, Drafting, †Drawing, Goldsmithing, †Graphic Design, †Jewelry, †Interior Design, Museum Staff Training, †Painting, †Photography, †Printmaking, †Sculpture, Silversmithing, †Textile Design, Computer Graphics, Design, Papermaking, Stained Glass, Typography, Watercolor
Adult Hobby Classes: Tuition $110 for 1-3 cr hr. Courses—Summer workshop, all beginning courses
Children's Classes: Enrl 260; tuition $18 for 6 sessions
Summer School: Dir, Dr Elizabeth Finlayson. Enrl 150; tuition res—undergrad $26 per cr hr

HOLLINS

HOLLINS COLLEGE, Art Dept, 24020. Tel 703-362-6486. *Chmn Dept* Nancy Dahlstrom
Estab 1842; pvt; D; scholarships; SC 13; enrl D 380, maj 55
Ent Req: HS dipl
Degrees: BA 4 yrs
Courses: Aesthetics, †Art History, Drawing, †History of Art & Archaeology, Museum Staff Training, †Painting, †Photography, †Printmaking, †Sculpture, †Teacher Training

LEXINGTON

WASHINGTON AND LEE UNIVERSITY, Dept of Fine Arts, 24450. Tel 703-463-9111, Ext 190, 351. *Head Dept* Dr Albert C Gordon, PhD; *Head Art Division* Dr Pamela H Simpson, PhD; *Prof* I-Hsiung Ju, MA; *Prof* Mario Pellicciaro, MA; *Prof* Dr Herman W Taylor Jr, PhD; *Prof* Dr Gerard Maurice Doyon, PhD; *Asst Prof* Larry M Steme, MFA; *Instr* Debra A Rindge, MA
Estab 1742, dept 1920; pvt; D; scholarships; SC 14, LC 26; enrl D 1200 (in col) non-maj 200, maj 4-6
Ent Req: HS dipl, SAT, 3 CEEB, one English CEEB plus essay on skills in English, English composition test; entrance requirements most rigorous in English; required of all, including art majors
Degrees: BA 4 yrs
Tuition: $5800 per yr; campus res—room & board and tuition average cost $9300 per yr
Courses: Drawing, History of Art & Archaeology, Museum Staff Training, Painting, Printmaking, Sculpture, Study Art Abroad—Taiwan, Greece, France

LYNCHBURG

LYNCHBURG COLLEGE, Art Dept, 24501. Tel 804-845-9071, Ext 295. *Chmn* Thelma L Twery, MEd; *Asst Prof* S Elizabeth LaCour, MFA; *Asst Prof* Virginia Irby Davis, MEd; *Asst Prof* Richard G Pumphrey, MFA
Estab 1903, dept estab 1948; pvt; D & E; SC 26, LC 16, GC 2; enrl D 400, E 50, non-maj 410, maj 40
Ent Req: HS dipl
Degrees: BA and BS 4 yrs
Tuition: Res—undergrad $8100 per yr; nonres—undergrad $5350; campus residency available
Courses: Aesthetics, Art Appreciation, Art Education, Art History, Ceramics, Design, Drawing, Painting, Photography, Printmaking, Sculpture, Teacher Training, Art for Therapy, Art for Communication, Crafts, History of Architecture
Summer School: Courses—Art Education, Art History and Appreciation, Photography

RANDOLPH-MACON WOMAN'S COLLEGE

RANDOLPH-MACON WOMAN'S COLLEGE, Dept of Art, 24503. Tel 804-846-7392, Ext 289. *Chmn* Elliott R Twery. Instrs: FT 3-4
Estab 1891; pvt, W; D; scholarships; SC 18, LC 15; enrl maj 35, others 305
Degrees: BA 4 yrs
Tuition: $9580 incl room & board
Courses: Architecture, †Art History, Ceramics, †Drawing, Film, †Painting, †Printmaking, †Sculpture, American Art, Art Survey, Design
Summer School: Dir, Dr John Justice. Enrl 30; 4 wk term. Courses—various

MCLEAN

MCLEAN ARTS CENTER, Art Dept, 1437 Emerson Ave, 22101. Tel 703-790-0861, 356-3048. *Head Dept* John Bryans
Estab 1955; pvt; D & E; SC 1; enrl D 37, E 6
Tuition: Adults $80 for ten lessons; children $45 for ten lessons
Courses: Drawing, Painting
Adult Hobby Classes: Enrl 28; tuition $80 per 10 lessons. Courses—Drawing, Painting (emphasis on watercolor)
Children's Classes: Enrl 15; tuition $45 per 10 lessons. Courses—Drawing, Painting

NEWPORT NEWS

CHRISTOPHER NEWPORT COLLEGE, Arts & Communications, 50 Shoe Lane, 23606. Tel 804-599-7073. *Head Dept* Dr Rita Hubbard; *Dir of Art* David Alexick, PhD; *Prof* B Anglin, MA; *Prof* James Hines, PhD; *Prof* Bruno Koch, PhD; *Prof* Jon Petruchyk, MFA; *Prof* Charles Riccillo; *Prof* C Brockett, PhD
Estab 1974; pub; D & E; SC 19, LC 4; enrl D 250, E 60, non-maj 200, maj 100
Ent Req: HS dipl, admis committee approval
Degrees: BA and BS 4 yrs
Tuition: Res—undergrad $450 per sem, nonres—undergrad $600 per sem; no campus res
Courses: Aesthetics, Art Education, Art History, Calligraphy, Ceramics, Collages, Commercial Art, Costume Design & Construction, Drawing, Graphic Arts, Illustration, Lettering, Mixed Media, Painting, Photography, Sculpture, Stage Design, Theatre Arts
Summer School: Dir, Dr Barry Woods. Enrl 25; tuition $300. Courses—Ceramics, Drawing, Painting

NORFOLK

NORFOLK STATE COLLEGE, Fine Arts Dept, 23504. Tel 804-623-8844. *Head Dept* Rod A Taylor, PhD
Estab 1935; pub; D & E; SC 50, LC 7; enrl D 355, E 18, non-maj 200, maj 155
Ent Req: HS dipl
Degrees: BA(Art Educ), BA(Fine Arts) and BA(Graphic Design) 4 yrs, MA and MFA in Visual Studies
Courses: History of Art & Archaeology, Jewelry, Lettering, Mixed Media, †Painting, Photography, Printmaking, Sculpture, Teacher Training
Adult Hobby Classes: Enrl 30. Courses—Ceramics, Crafts
Children's Classes: Enrl 45; tuition none. Courses—all areas

OLD DOMINION UNIVERSITY, Art Dept, 23508. Tel 804-440-4047. *Chmn* Vic Pickett
Scholarships
Tuition: Res—$587 per sem, nonres—$1085 per sem
Courses: Color, Fiber, 2-D & 3-D Design
Adult Hobby Classes: Enrl 50; tuition $40 for 8 wks. Courses—Drawing, Painting
Children's Classes: Enrl 25; tuition $40 for 8 wks. Courses—Drawing, Painting
Summer School: Dir, Vic Pickett. Enrl 200; tuition $57 per cr hr, 4 & 8 wk sessions. Courses—Varied studio & art history courses

VIRGINIA WESLEYAN COLLEGE, Art Dept of the Humanities Division,* Wesleyan Dr, 23502. Tel 804-461-3232. *Prof* R E Neil Britton; *Assoc Prof* Barclay Sheaks, BFA; *Adjunct Asst Prof* Myrna Andursky, MA; *Adjunct Asst Prof* Diane Scillia, PhD
Pvt, den; D & E; scholarships; SC 21, LC 8; enrl E 20
Ent Req: HS dipl, SAT
Degrees: BA(Liberal Arts) 4 yrs
Tuition: $4100 per yr; campus res available
Courses: Art Appreciation, Art Education, Art History, Ceramics, Collages, Conceptual Art, Constructions, Drawing, Art Appreciation, Graphic Arts, Handicrafts, Jewelry, Mixed Media, Painting, Photography, Printmaking, Sculpture, Teacher Training, Weaving, Fabric Enrichment

PETERSBURG

RICHARD BLAND COLLEGE, Art Dept,* Rte 1, Box 77A, 23803. Tel 804-732-0111. *Pres* Clarence Maze Jr, PhD
Estab 1960, dept estab 1963; pub; D & E; SC 3, LC 3; enrl D 73
Ent Req: HS dipl, SAT, recommendation of HS counselor
Degrees: AA(Fine Arts) 2 yrs
Courses: Art History, Drawing, Painting, Sculpture, Art Appreciation, Basic Design
Adult Hobby Classes: Courses—Interior Design, Yoga

VIRGINIA STATE UNIVERSITY, Fine & Commercial Art, 23803. Tel 804-520-6328. *Head Dept* Dr A D Macklin, EdD; *Assoc Prof* Michael Gilliatt, EdD; *Asst Prof* Eugene Vango, MFA; *Asst Prof* Doris Woodson, MFA; *Asst Prof* Valery Gates, MFA; *Instructor* Charles Flynn, MA
Estab 1882, dept estab 1935; pub; D & E; SC 16, LC 6, GC 2; enrl D 400, E 60, non-maj 302, maj 98
Ent Req: HS dipl
Degrees: BFA(Art Educ) and BFA(Commercial Art and Design) 4 yrs
Tuition: Res—undergrad and grad $738 per yr; nonres—undergrad and grad $1500 per yr; campus res—room & board $764

Courses: †Advertising Design, Aesthetics, †Art Education, Ceramics, Drawing, History of Art & Archaeology, Jewelry, Lettering, Jewelry, Lettering, Painting, Printmaking, Sculpture
Adult Hobby Classes: Enrl 20; tuition $165 per course. Courses—Batik, Ceramics, Jewelry, Macrame, Painting, Printmaking, Sculpture, Crafts
Summer School: Dir, Dr M McCall. Enrl 20; tuition $55 per cr for term of 12 wks, beginning May 21. Courses—Basic Art, Ceramics, Crafts, Jewelry

PORTSMOUTH

TIDEWATER COMMUNITY COLLEGE, Art Dept, St Route 135, 23703. Tel 804-484-2121. *Asst Prof* Harriette C F Laskin, MEd; *Instr* William G Stobo Jr, BFA
Estab 1968; pub; D & E; SC 12, LC 3; enrl D 120, E 180, non-maj 190, maj 110
Ent Req: HS dipl
Degrees: AA(Fine Arts), AAS(Media Arts) 2 yrs
Tuition: Res—$13.50 per cr hr, nonres—$58 per cr hr; no campus res
Courses: †Advertising Design, Art History, Ceramics, Drawing, Illustration, Lettering, Painting, Photography, Printmaking
Adult Hobby Classes: Offered through Continuing Educ Div
Children's Classes: Offered through Continuing Educ Div
Summer School: Asst Prof, H Laskin. Enrl 15 per course; tuition $128 for term of 10 wks beginning June. Courses—Art History, Ceramics, Design, Drawing, Painting, Photography

RADFORD

RADFORD UNIVERSITY, Art Dept, PO Box 5791, 24142. Tel 703-731-5475.
Chmn Dr G Lynn Gordon, DEd; *Prof* Dr Paul W Frets, DA; *Prof* Dr Noel G Lawson, PhD; *Assoc Prof* Dr Fred Thyed, DEd; *Assoc Prof* Jerry H Krebs, MFA; *Assoc Prof* Felicia Lewandowski, PhD; *Asst Prof* Pam F Lawson, MFA; *Asst Prof* Ed LeShock; *Asst Prof* Dr Helieda Salam, PhD; *Instructor* James Morris
Estab 1910, dept estab 1936; pub; D & E; scholarships; SC 52, LC 12, GC 26; enrl D 1971, E 18, non-maj 978, maj 191, grad 28, others 15
Ent Req: HS dipl, SAT
Degrees: BA, BS (non-teaching) and BS (teaching) 4 yrs, BFA & MS 1 yr, MFA Studio 2 yrs
Tuition: Res—$3909 per yr, $1303 per quarter, $42 per quarter hr; nonres—$4659 per yr, $1553 per quarter, $62 per quarter; out-of-state $750 per yr, $250 per quarter, $45 per quarter hr; campus residency available
Courses: Advertising Design, Architecture, †Art Education, †Art History, Calligraphy, Ceramics, Drawing, Graphic Arts, Graphic Design, Handicrafts, History of Art & Archaeology, Illustration, Jewelry, Lettering, Painting, Photography, Printmaking, Sculpture, Silversmithing, Teacher Training, Textile Design, Enameling, Metalsmithing, Raku, Weaving
Adult Hobby Classes: Tuition $42 per hr
Summer School: Dir, Dr Lentzcner. Enrl 421; tuition as above. Courses—all labs plus Art Appreciation, Art Education

RICHMOND

J SARGEANT REYNOLDS COMMUNITY COLLEGE, Humanities & Social Science Division,* 1651 E Parham Rd, PO Box 12084, 23241. Tel 804-264-2792. *Chmn* Arthur L Dixon
Tuition: Res—$342 per yr; nonres—$1140 per yr
Courses: Art Appreciation, Art History, Ceramics, Drawing, Handicrafts, Photography

UNIVERSITY OF RICHMOND, Dept of Art, 23173. Tel 804-285-6000. *Chmn & Prof* Charles W Johnson Jr, PhD; *Assoc Prof* Demetrios Mavroudis, EdD; *Instr* Anne P Oppenhimer, MA; *Instr* Mark Scala, MFA
Pvt; D & E; SC 29, LC 15
Ent Req: HS dipl, CEEB
Degrees: BA and BS 4 yrs
Tuition: Res—$4410 per yr
Courses: Art Education, Art History, Ceramics, Design, Drawing, Graphic Arts, Graphic Design, Painting, Printmaking, Sculpture
Summer School: Dir, Dr Max Graeber

VIRGINIA COMMONWEALTH UNIVERSITY, School of the Arts, 325 N Harrison St, 23284. Tel 804-257-1700. *Dean* Murry N DePillars. Instrs: FT 141, PT 24
Estab 1838; pub; D & E; scholarships, fels and grad assistantships; enrl 2064 (art), 19,000 (total)
Ent Req: Portfolio
Degrees: BFA, BM and BME 4 yrs, MA, MFA, MAE, MM and MME 2 yrs
Tuition: Res—undergrad $1298, grad $902; nonres—undergrad $2538, grad $1577; art fees approx $50 each sem
Courses: Art Education, Art History, Ceramics, Fashion Arts, Interior Design, Jewelry, Painting, Photography, Printmaking, Sculpture, Theatre Arts, Communication Arts & Design, Fabric Design, Furniture Design
Children's Classes: Summer school offerings
Summer School: Dir Rozanne Epps. Courses 3 - 9 wks, most art disciplines

ROANOKE

VIRGINIA WESTERN COMMUNITY COLLEGE, Commercial Art, Fine Art & Photography,* 3095 Colonial Ave SW, PO Box 14195, 24015. Tel 703-982-7200.
Chmn Div Human Dr Clarence C Mays Jr, EdD; *Asst Prof* Margaret G Ferris, MS; *Asst Prof* Rudolph H Hotheinz, MAE
Pub; D & E; SC 11, LC 2
Ent Req: HS dipl
Degrees: AA 2 yrs
Tuition: Res—$13.50 per cr hr; nonres—$58 per cr hr
Adult Hobby Classes: Courses—Oil Painting, Stained Glass, Watercolor

SALEM

ROANOKE COLLEGE, Art Dept, Olin Hall, High St, 24153. Tel 703-389-2351, Ext 359 or 260. *Chairperson Fine Arts* Dr Karen Adams, PhD; *Assoc Prof* John Brust, MFA; *Asst Prof* Scott Hardwig, MFA; *Instructor* Elizabeth Stephens-Koesters, MFA
Estab 1842, dept estab 1930; den; D; SC 16, LC 8; enrl D 130, non-maj 120, maj 40
Ent Req: HS dipl, SAT or ACT, 13 academic credits—2 English, 3 social sciences, 3 humanities, 2 math, 2 science, 1 interdisciplinary
Degrees: BA 4 yrs
Tuition: Campus residence available
Courses: Advertising Design, Art Education, Art History, Ceramics, Costume Design & Construction, Drawing, Graphic Design, Painting, Photography, Printmaking, Sculpture, Stage Design, Theatre Arts
Adult Hobby Classes: Enrl 25; tuition $75 per sem. Courses—Painting, Watercolor
Children's Classes: Courses—Ceramics
Summer School: Dir, Dr Art Puotinen. Courses—Art History

STAUNTON

MARY BALDWIN COLLEGE, Dept of Art,* Frederick and New Streets, 24401. Tel 703-885-0811, Ext 394. *Head Dept* Ulysse Desportes, Dr Univ of Paris
Estab 1842; pvt; D & E; scholarships; SC 16, LC 18; enrl D 173, E 32, non-maj 172, maj 33, others 4 non-credit
Ent Req: HS dipl
Degrees: BA 4 yrs
Tuition: $8850 annual tuition
Courses: Drawing, Film, Graphic Arts, Graphic Design, Handicrafts, History of Art & Archaeology, Illustration, Interior Design, Lettering, Mixed Media, Museum Staff Training, Painting, Photography, Printmaking, Sculpture, Stage Design, Teacher Training, Theatre Arts, Video, Art for the Exceptional Child, Art Therapy, Fabric Arts, Historical Preservation, Weaving

SWEET BRIAR

SWEET BRIAR COLLEGE, Art History Dept and Art Studio Dept, 24595. Tel 804-381-6125. *Chmn Art Hist Dept* Aileen H Lang, PhD; *Chmn Studio Art* Loren Oliver, MFA; *Asst Prof* Christopher L Litcombe, PhD; *Asst Prof* Roberta Perry, MFA; *Asst Prof* Diane D Moran, PhD; *Vis Lectr* Charles Worsham, MA
Estab 1901, dept estab 1930; pvt; D; scholarships; SC 19, LC 19; enrl D 375 per term, maj 32
Ent Req: HS dipl, col boards
Degrees: BA 4 yrs
Tuition: $9650 incl room and board
Courses: Architecture, †Art History, Ceramics, Drawing, Graphic Arts, History of Art & Archaeology, Mixed Media, Painting, Photography, Printmaking, Sculpture, Teacher Training, †Theatre Arts, Decorative Arts, †Studio Art
Adult Hobby Classes: Courses—Modern Art, Fibre Art History, Graphic Design

WILLIAMSBURG

COLLEGE OF WILLIAM AND MARY, Dept of Fine Arts,* 23185. Tel 804-253-4000. *Chmn* Jerold R Lapp; *Prof* James D Kornwolf, PhD; *Assoc Prof* Henry Coleman, MA; *Assoc Prof* Paul Helfrich, MFA; *Assoc Prof* Marlene Jack, MFA; *Assoc Prof* Miles Chappell, PhD; *Asst Prof* Barbara Watkinson, PhD; *Asst Prof* W D Barnes, MFA; *Lectr* W D Houghland, AIA
Estab 1693, dept estab 1936; pub; D; SC 20, LC 22; enrl D 5000, non-maj 693, maj 64
Ent Req: HS dipl
Degrees: BA 4 yrs
Tuition: Res—$787 per sem; nonres—$2004 per sem; campus res available
Courses: †Architecture, †Art History, †Ceramics, †Drawing, †Graphic Arts, †Painting, †Sculpture
Summer School: Dir, Zeddie Bowen. Courses—Art History, Design, Painting, Sculpture

WISE

CLINCH VALLEY COLLEGE OF THE UNIVERSITY OF VIRGINIA, Performing Arts Dept,* 24293. Tel 703-328-2431. *Assoc Prof* Betty J Gilliam, MFA
Estab 1954, dept estab 1980; pub; D & E; scholarships; SC 9, LC 4
Ent Req: HS dipl, SAT or ACT
Degrees: BA and BS 4 yrs
Tuition: Res—$432 per sem; nonres—$720 per sem
Courses: Art Education, Art History, Ceramics, Costume Design & Construction, Drafting, Drawing, Film, History of Art & Archaeology, Painting, Photography, Sculpture, Stage Design, Teacher Training, Theatre Arts, Stained glass
Adult Hobby Classes: Tuition $30 per hr
Summer School: Dir, Dr George E Culbertson. Tuition $30 per sem hr for two terms of five wks beginning June and July

WASHINGTON

AUBURN

GREEN RIVER COMMUNITY COLLEGE, Art Dept, 1240-12401 SE 320th, 98002. Tel 206-833-9111. *Chmn & Instr* Dr Bernie Bleha, EdD; *Instr* Robert Short, MFA; *Instr* Margaret Von Wrangel, MFA; *Instr* Elayne Levensky, MFA
Estab 1965; pub; D & E; SC 31, LC 4; enrl D 330, E 120
Ent Req: HS dipl or 18 yrs old
Degrees: AA 2 yr
Tuition: Res—undergrad $193.66 per quarter; nonres—undergrad $761.66 per quarter
Courses: Art History, Ceramics, Drawing, Painting, Photography, Weaving, Design, Stained Glass
Summer School: Dir, Bruce Haulman. Tuition $193.66. Courses—Ceramics, Drawing, Painting, Photography

BELLEVUE

BELLEVUE COMMUNITY COLLEGE, Arts Dept, 3000 Landerholm Circle, SE, 98007. Tel 206-641-2341. *Division Chmn* Gary Glocklin
Estab 1966; pub; D & E; SC 15, LC 5; enrl 300, maj 50
Degrees: AA 2 yrs
Courses: Art History, Design, Drawing, Painting, Photography, Sculpture, Textile Design
Adult Hobby Classes: Enrl 600. Courses—Ceramics, Design, Drawing, Jewelry, Painting, Photography, Sculpture

BELLINGHAM

WESTERN WASHINGTON UNIVERSITY, Art Dept, College of Fine and Performing Arts, 98225. Tel 206-676-3660. *Chmn* Gene Vike, MFA. Instrs: FT 15
Estab 1899; pub; D & E; scholarships; enrl D 1500, E 200
Ent Req: HS dipl, ent exam
Degrees: BA, BA(Educ), BFA and MEd 4 yrs
Tuition: Res—$339 per qtr; nonres—$1162 per qtr
Courses: †Art History, †Ceramics, †Drawing, †Graphic Design, †Painting, †Sculpture, †Fibers, †Metals
Adult Hobby Classes: Enrl 200. Courses—Ceramics, Drawing, Fibers, Painting, Sculpture
Summer School: Dir, Mary Robinson. Enrl 3500; tuition $314 FT for 6 & 9 wk courses. Courses—Ceramics, Drawing, Fibers, Painting, Sculpture

BREMERTON

OLYMPIC COLLEGE, Art Dept, 98310. Tel 206-478-4511, Ext 4866. *Chmn* Polly N Zanetta; *Instructor* Kenneth V Crow, MA; *Instructor* LaDeane V Tate, MA; *Instructor* Mel R Wallis, MA
Estab 1946; pub; D & E; scholarships; LC 3; enrl D 125, E 75
Ent Req: HS dipl
Degrees: AA and ATA 2 yrs, cert
Tuition: Res—undergrad $155 per quarter, $19.35 per cr; nonres—undergrad $761.50 per quarter, $60 per cr; no campus res
Courses: Art History, Ceramics, Drawing, Jewelry, Painting, Photography, Printmaking, Sculpture, Stained Glass
Adult Hobby Classes: Courses—Calligraphy, Painting

CHENEY

EASTERN WASHINGTON UNIVERSITY, Dept of Art, 99004. Tel 509-359-2493. *Chmn* Robert J Lloyd
Estab 1886; pub; D; scholarships; SC 58, LC 21, GC 18; enrl D 600, non-maj 200, maj 200, GS 20
Ent Req: Appropriate evidence of ability to succeed academically
Degrees: BA, BEd and BFA 4 yrs, MA and MEd 1 to 2 yrs

ELLENSBURG

CENTRAL WASHINGTON UNIVERSITY, Dept of Art, 98926. Tel 509-963-2665. *Chmn* George Stillman. Instrs: 13
Estab 1891; pub; D; enrl maj 250, others 7134
Ent Req: GPA 2
Degrees: BA, MA and MFA 4-5 yrs
Tuition: FT $289 9 hrs or more, PT $29 per quarter hr; campus residency available
Courses: Art Education, Art History, Commercial Art, Drawing, Jewelry, Painting, Photography, Printmaking, Sculpture, Design, Pottery

EVERETT

EVERETT COMMUNITY COLLEGE, Art Dept, 801 Wetmore Ave, 98201. Tel 206-259-7151. *Chmn* Lowell Hanson
Degrees: AA
Courses: Art Appreciation, Art History, Calligraphy, Ceramics, Design, Drawing, Painting, Photography, Printmaking, Textile Design, Weaving, Stained Glass
Summer School: Courses—Ceramics, Design, Drawing

LONGVIEW

LOWER COLUMBIA COLLEGE, 1600 Maple, PO Box 68, 98632. Tel 206-577-2300. *Instructor* Rosemary Powelson, MFA
Estab 1934; pub; D & E; scholarships; SC 36, LC 8; enrl D 180, E 61
Ent Req: Open admis
Degrees: AAS 2 yrs
Tuition: Res—undergrad $603 per yr, $19.10 per hr; nonres—undergrad $2507 per yr, $152.80 per hr; no campus res
Courses: Art History, Calligraphy, Ceramics, Drawing, Graphic Arts, Painting, Printmaking, Sculpture, Photography, Design
Adult Hobby Classes: Courses—Matting & Framing, Relief Woodcuts, Floral Design, Recreational Photography

MOSES LAKE

BIG BEND COMMUNITY COLLEGE, Art Dept, 98857. Tel 509-762-5351. *Chmn* Stephen Tse, MFA
Estab 1962; pub; D & E; SC 8, LC 1; enrl D 325, E 60, maj 10-15
Ent Req: HS dipl
Degrees: AA 2 yrs
Tuition: Res—undergrad $580.50 per yr, $193.50 per quarter, $19.35 PT; nonres—undergrad $2284.50 per yr, $716.50 per quarter, $76.15 PT; campus residency available
Courses: Art History, Ceramics, Drawing, Graphic Arts, Lettering, Painting, Basic Design
Adult Hobby Classes: Enrl 15. Courses—Drawing
Summer School: Dir, Mike Lang. Enrl 30; tuition $19.35 per cr hr. Courses—Drawing, Painting, Pottery

MOUNT VERNON

SKAGIT VALLEY COLLEGE, Dept of Art, 2405 College Way, 98273. Tel 206-428-1261. *Chmn* Orville K Chatt. Instrs: FT 2, PT 6
Estab 1926; pub; D & E; scholarships; SC 32, LC 1; enrl D 2500, E 3500
Ent Req: Open
Degrees: AA 2 yrs
Tuition: Res—$198 per quarter full time; nonres—$761 per quarter full time
Courses: Ceramics, Drawing, Handicrafts, Jewelry, Painting, Photography, Art Appreciation, Design
Adult Hobby Classes: Four nights a week
Summer School: Dir, Bert Williamson

OLYMPIA

ST MARTINS COLLEGE, Art Dept, 98503. Tel 206-491-4700. *Chmn* Ronald Hurst
Degrees: BFA
Courses: Art Appreciation, Art History, Ceramics, Design, Drawing, Painting, Printmaking

PASCO

COLUMBIA BASIN COLLEGE, Art Dept,* 2600 N 20th Ave, 99302. Tel 509-547-0511. *Chmn Performing Arts Div* Ted Neth, MFA; *Faculty* Morse Glary, MFA
Scholarships offered
Degrees: AA and AS offered
Tuition: Res—$178.50; nonres—$684.50
Courses: Advertising Design, Art Appreciation, Art History, Calligraphy, Ceramics, Design, Drawing, Interior Design, Jewelry, Painting, Photography, Printmaking, Sculpture, Stage Design, Video, Stained Glass

PULLMAN

WASHINGTON STATE UNIVERSITY, Fine Arts Dept,* 99164. Tel 509-335-3564. *Chmn* Ross Coates, PhD. Instrs: FT 11
Estab 1890, dept estab 1925; pub; D & E; scholarships; SC 29, LC 13, GC 25; enrl D 1593, E 131, maj 220, GS 25
Ent Req: HS dipl
Degrees: BA(Fine Arts) 4 yrs, MFA 2 yrs
Tuition: Res—$654; nonres—$1812

SEATTLE

CORNISH INSTITUTE, 710 East Roy, 98102. Tel 206-323-1400. *Pres* Melvin Strauss. Instrs: FT 32, PT 93
Estab 1914; pvt; D & E; scholarships; SC 57, LC 6; enrl non-maj 126 PT, maj 409 FT
Ent Req: HS dipl, portfolio review, fine arts, design, personal interview
Degrees: BFA
Courses: Art History, Conceptual Art, Drafting, Drawing, Graphic Arts, †Graphic Design, Illustration, †Interior Design, Lettering, †Painting, Photography, †Printmaking, †Sculpture
Summer School: Eight wk course beginning July - August

THE DESIGN SCHOOLS, Art Institute of Seattle, 905 East Pine St, 98122. Tel 206-322-0596. *Pres* Jess D Cauthorn; *Instructor* William Cumming; *Instructor* Fred Griffin, BFA; *Instructor* Gail Merrick; *Instructor* Marilyn Nordell, BFA; *Instructor* James Scott, BFA; *Instructor* Tom Price; *Instructor* Nan Cauthorn; *Instructor* Jim Richardson; *Instructor* John Hansen; *Instructor* David Mercer; *Instructor* Anita Griffin; *Instructor* Gail Sullivan; *Instructor* John Hillding; *Instructor* David Daniouth; *Instructor* Sam Dimico

Estab 1946; pvt; D; SC 2; enrl D 320
Ent Req: HS dipl, portfolio approval
Degrees: Prof dipl
Tuition: $1050 per quarter for 8 quarters
Courses: Advertising Design, Commercial Art, Fashion Arts, Film, Graphic Arts, Graphic Design, Illustration, Lettering, Video
Summer School: Enrl 150; tuition $1050 per term of 12 wks beginning July 9

NORTH SEATTLE COMMUNITY COLLEGE, Art Dept, Humanities Division, 9300 Burke Ave N, 98103. Tel 206-634-4513. *Actg Chmn Dept* Elroy Christenson, MFA; *Instructor* John Constantine, MFA; *Instructor* David J Harris, MFA
Estab 1970; pub; D & E; scholarships; SC 27, LC 7; enrl D 150, E 65
Ent Req: HS dipl
Degrees: AA 2 yr, AFA, CFA 2 yr
Tuition: Res—$186.50 per quarter; nonres—$754.50 per quarter; no campus res
Courses: Art History, Calligraphy, Drawing, History of Art & Archaeology, Interior Design, Jewelry, Painting, Photography, Printmaking, Sculpture
Adult Hobby Classes: Drawing, Painting
Summer School: Tuition $152.50 for term of 8 wks beginning June 20.
Courses—Drawing, Introduction to Art

SEATTLE CENTRAL COMMUNITY COLLEGE, Humanities - Social Sciences Division,* 1718 Broadway, 98122. Tel 206-587-4164. *Chmn* Julie Y Hunger
Estab 1970; pub; D & E; scholarships; SC 15, LC 5; enrl D 70, E 50
Ent Req: HS dipl, ent exam
Degrees: AA 2 yrs
Tuition: Res—$186.50 annual tuition; nonres—$754.50 annual tuition; no campus res
Courses: Art History, Painting, Sculpture
Summer School: Courses—Art History, Painting, Sculpture

SEATTLE PACIFIC UNIVERSITY, Art Dept, Third Ave W & W Bertona, 98119. Tel 206-281-2079. *Chmn* Michael Caldwell
Scholarships & fellowships
Courses: Art Appreciation, Art Education, Ceramics, Design, Drawing, Fashion Arts, Film, Handicrafts, Industrial Design, Interior Design, Jewelry, Printmaking, Sculpture, Textile Design, Weaving

SEATTLE UNIVERSITY, Fine Arts Dept, Division of Art, 12th & Madison, 98122. Tel 206-626-6336. *Chmn* William John Summers; *Prof* Nickolas J Damascus, MFA; *Prof* Marvin T Herard, MFA; *Prof* Val Laigo, MFA
D; scholarships
Ent Req: HS dipl and entrance exam
Degrees: BA program offered
Summer School: Chmn, William John Summers. Courses—same as regular session

SHORELINE COMMUNITY COLLEGE, Humanities Division, 16101 Greenwood Ave N, 98133. Tel 206-546-4741. *Chmn* Denzil Walters; *Prof* John Kirk, MFA; *Prof* Mike Larson, BA; *Prof* Denis Ostermeyer, MFA; *Prof* Chris Simons, MFA; *Prof* Willy Clark, PhD; *Prof* Morry Hendrickson, MA; *Prof* Brian Edwards, MA
Estab 1964; pub; D & E; SC 9, LC Art History Survey; enrl D 5500
Ent Req: HS dipl, col ent exam
Degrees: AA and AFA
Tuition: Res—undergrad $190 per quarter, $19 per quarter hr; nonres—undergrad $758 per quarter, $75.80 per quarter hr; no campus res
Courses: †Advertising Design, Art History, Ceramics, †Commercial Art, Drawing, Illustration, Lettering, Painting, Photography, Sculpture, Stage Design, Theatre Arts, †Visual Communications Technology
Summer School: Term of 4 wks June 23-July 22. Courses—Ceramics, Design, Drawing, Photography

UNIVERSITY OF WASHINGTON, School of Art, DM-10, 98195. Tel 206-543-0970. *Dir* Richard Arnold
Estab 1878; pub; D & E; scholarships; SC 113, LC 84, GC 30; enrl D & E 2459, maj 796, grad 90
Ent Req: Must meet university admission req
Degrees: BFA 4 yrs, BA 4 yrs, MA, PhD and MFA
Tuition: Res—undergrad $434, grad $628; nonres—undergrad $1206, grad $1562; campus res—room & board $2050 for double
Courses: †Art History, †Ceramics, Drawing, †Graphic Design, †Industrial Design, Jewelry, †Painting, †Photography, †Printmaking, †Sculpture, Silversmithing, Video, †General Art, †Metal Design

SPOKANE

GONZAGA UNIVERSITY, Dept of Art,* School of Arts and Sciences, E 502 Boone Ave, 99258. Tel 509-328-4220, Ext 3211. *Chmn* Robert Gilmore; *Assoc Prof* R Gilmore. Instrs: FT 3, PT 3
Estab 1962; pvt; D & E; SC 20, LC 5, GC 12; enrl D 250 incl maj 50, grad 8, others 80
Ent Req: HS dipl
Degrees: BA 4 yrs, grad cert in art
Tuition: $2625 per sem; campus res available
Courses: Art Education, Ceramics, Drawing, History of Art & Archaeology, Painting, Printmaking, Sculpture, Teacher Training
Summer School: Dir, Bud Hazel. Term of 6 wks beginning June.
Courses—Ceramics, Drawing, Painting, Printmaking, 19th & 20th Century Art History

SPOKANE FALLS COMMUNITY COLLEGE, Creative & Performing Arts, 99204. Tel 509-459-3710. *Supvr* Donald Nepean; *Dept Chmn* Jo Fyfe
Estab 1963; pub; D & E; scholarships; SC 41, LC 5; enrl D 600, E 200
Ent Req: HS dipl, GED
Degrees: AAA 3 yrs, and AA 2 yrs
Tuition: Res—$191 per quarter; nonres—$759 per quarter; no campus res

Courses: †Advertising Design, Architecture, Art History, Calligraphy, Ceramics, †Commercial Art, †Display, Drawing, Illustration, †Interior Design, Jewelry, Lettering, Mixed Media, Painting, †Photography, Printmaking, Sculpture, Weaving, Intro to Art, Vol Design, Weaving
Adult Hobby Classes: Enrl 35; tuition $25.60 for 6 week term.
Courses—Bannermaking, Drawing, Watercolor, Weaving
Summer School: Courses offered

WHITWORTH COLLEGE, Art Dept,* Hawthorne Rd, 99251. Tel 509-466-1000. *Fine Arts Dept Chmn* Richard Evan; *Prof* Pauline Haas, MFA; *Assoc Prof* Walter Grosvenor, MAT; *Asst Prof* Gordon Wilson, MFA; *Instr* Henry Lyman; *Instr* Shelley Rothschild; *Instr* Mardis Thoreson. Instrs: FT 6
Pvt; D & E; scholarships; SC 18, LC 3
Ent Req: HS dipl
Degrees: BA and BS 4 yrs, MA, MAT & MEd 2 yrs
Tuition: $5120 per yr
Courses: Batik, Textile Arts

TACOMA

FORT STEILACOOM COMMUNITY COLLEGE, Fine Arts Dept, 9401 Far West Dr, 98498. Tel 206-964-6716. *Chmn* Hal Buckner, MFA. Instrs: FT 3, PT 1
Estab 1966, dept estab 1972; pub; D & E; SC 20, LC 5; enrl D 3500
Ent Req: Ent exam
Degrees: AA 2 yrs; AFA
Tuition: $190 per term; no campus res
Courses: Art Education, Ceramics, Drafting, Drawing, Fashion Arts, Film, Interior Design, Painting, Photography, Printmaking, Sculpture, Stage Design, Theatre Arts
Adult Hobby Classes: Courses vary
Summer School: Dir, Walt Boyden. Tuition $19 per cr hr. Courses—Ceramics, Drawing, Painting. Tour Italy June 20 - July 15, 1984

PACIFIC LUTHERAN UNIVERSITY, Dept of Art, School of the Arts, 98447. Tel 206-531-6900. *Chmn* Dennis Cox, MFA; *Prof* Ernst Schwidder, MFA; *Prof* David Keyes, MA; *Prof* Lars Kittleson, MFA; *Prof* George Roskos, MA; *Prof* Walt Tomsic, MFA; *Prof* Tom Torrens, MFA
Estab 1890, dept estab 1960; den; D & E; scholarships; SC 20, LC 12; enrl D 1000, E 50, maj 50
Ent Req: HS dipl, Washington Pre-College Test or ACT
Degrees: BA, BAEd and BFA 4 yrs
Tuition: $177 per hr; campus res—room and board $2200 per sem
Courses: †Advertising Design, Architecture, †Art Education, Art History, †Ceramics, †Commercial Art, †Design, †Drawing, †Film, †Graphic Arts, †Graphic Design, Handicrafts, †Illustration, †Jewelry, Mixed Media, †Painting, †Photography, †Printmaking, †Sculpture, †Fibers, †Stained Glass
Summer School: Dean, Dr Richard Mor. Enrl 100; tuition $120 per sem hr.
Courses—Ceramics, Fibers, Painting, Photography, Stained Glass

TACOMA COMMUNITY COLLEGE, Art Dept,* 5900 12th St, 98465. Tel 206-756-5070. *Art Dept Chmn* Frank Dippolito, MFA
Estab 1965; pub; D & E; scholarships; SC 35, LC 1; enrl D & E 1500
Degrees: AAS and Associate in Liberal Arts 2 yrs
Tuition: Res—$191 per quarter; nonres—$759 per quarter
Courses: Photography, Printmaking, Sculpture, Stage Design

UNIVERSITY OF PUGET SOUND, Art Dept, 1500 N Warner St, 98416. Tel 206-756-3348. *Chmn* Ron Fields. Instrs: FT 7, PT 1
Estab 1935; den; D & E; SC 41, LC 11, GC 23; enrl maj 25, undergrad 400
Ent Req: HS grad
Degrees: BA 4 yrs
Tuition: $5870 per yr, $2935 per sem; campus res—room & board $2810 per yr
Courses: Art History, Ceramics, Drawing, Painting, Printmaking, Sculpture, Teacher Training, Oriental Art, Studio Design, Watercolor
Summer School: Dir, Ron Fields. Enrl 15 per class; tuition $490 per unit for 4 week course. Courses—Art Education, Art History, Batik, Ceramics, Drawing, Watercolor

VANCOUVER

CLARK COLLEGE, Art Dept, 1800 E McLaughlin Blvd, 98663. Tel 206-694-6521. *Dept Coordr* Warren Dunn, MAT; *Instr* Roger Baker, MFA; *Instr* Richard J Stensrude, MAT; *Instr* Joan Henson, MAT
Estab 1933, dept estab 1947; pub; D & E; scholarships; SC 87, LC 3; enrl D 300, E 400
Ent Req: Open door
Degrees: Assoc of Arts and Science, Assoc of Applied Science, and Assoc of General Studies 2 yrs
Tuition: Res—$17.30 per cr hr, $155.70 (9 cr); $173 (10 cr); nonres—$67.90 per cr, $611.10 (9 cr), $679 (10 cr)
Courses: Art History, Calligraphy, Ceramics, Drafting, Drawing, Fashion Arts, Graphic Arts, Graphic Design, Handicrafts, History of Art & Archaeology, Illustration, Interior Design, Jewelry, Lettering, Painting, Photography, Printmaking, Sculpture, Stage Design, Theatre Arts, Video
Adult Hobby Classes: Enrl 20; tuition $38.70 per 2 credit course. Courses—Painting
Children's Classes: Enrl 30; tuition $38.70 for summer qtr. Courses—Children's art
Summer School: Dir, Doug Nosler. Enrl 100; tuition $19.35 per credit.
Courses—Art Appreciation, Calligraphy, Ceramics, Drawing, Photography

WALLA WALLA

WALLA WALLA COMMUNITY COLLEGE, Art Dept, 500 Tausick Way, 99362. Tel 509-527-4212. *Instr* Bill Piper; *Instr* Melissa Webster
Scholarships offered
Degrees: AA offered
Courses: Art Appreciation, Ceramics, Design, Drawing, Handicrafts, Photography, Printmaking, Sculpture

WHITMAN COLLEGE, Art Dept,* 345 Boyer Ave, 99362. Tel 509-527-5111.
Chmn Paul E Dewey
Pvt; D; SC 15, LC 8; enrl D 225, maj 10
Ent Req: HS dipl, ent exam
Degrees: BA 4 yrs
Tuition: $6380 per yr
Courses: Aesthetics, Art Education, Ceramics, Drawing, History of Art &
Archaeology, Painting, Sculpture, Stage Design

WENATCHEE

WENATCHEE VALLEY COLLEGE, Art Dept, 1300 Fifth St, 98801. Tel 509-662-
1651. *Chmn Div of Humanities* Daryl Dietrich, MA; *Instructor* Ruth Allan, MFA;
Instructor Robert Graves, MFA
Estab 1939; pub; D & E; scholarships; LC 4; enrl D 550, E 200, maj 45
Ent Req: HS dipl, open door policy
Degrees: AA 2 yrs
Tuition: Res—undergrad $419 per yr, $173 per quarter, $15.15 per cr hr;
nonres—undergrad $2037 per yr, $697 per quarter; campus residency available
Courses: Art History, Ceramics, Collages, Drawing, Graphic Arts, Interior Design,
Jewelry, Lettering, Painting, Printmaking, Silversmithing
Summer School: Dir, Dr Jim Flint

YAKIMA

YAKIMA VALLEY COLLEGE, Art Dept, S 16th Ave & Nob Hill Blvd, 98908. Tel
509-575-2350. *Dir* Robert A Fisher; *Fac* Herb Blisard
Scholarships offered
Degrees: AA & AS offered
Tuition: Res $193.50 per quarter
Courses: Advertising Design, Art Appreciation, Art History, Calligraphy, Ceramics,
Design, Drawing, Handicrafts, Jewelry, Painting, Photography, Printmaking,
Sculpture

WEST VIRGINIA

ATHENS

CONCORD COLLEGE, Art Dept, 24712. Tel 304-384-3115. *Prof* Maynard R
Coiner, MFA; *Assoc Prof* Gerald C Arrington, MFA; *Asst Prof* Sheila M Chipley,
EdD; *Instructor* Marc O Plummer, MFA
Estab 1872, dept estab 1925; pub; D & E; scholarships; SC 32, LC 3; enrl non-maj
200, maj 75, D 75
Ent Req: HS dipl
Degrees: BA and BS 4 yrs
Tuition: Res—$377 per sem; campus res—room and board $1055 per sem;
nonres—$1062 per sem; campus res—room and board available
Courses: †Advertising Design, †Art Education, †Art History, Calligraphy,
†Ceramics, Collages, †Commercial Art, Constructions, Drawing, Graphic Arts,
Graphic Design, Handicrafts, History of Art & Archaeology, Illustration, Jewelry,
Lettering, †Painting, Printmaking, Sculpture, Teacher Training
Adult Hobby Classes: Enrl varies; tuition based on part-time rates. Courses—Vary
Children's Classes: Enrl varies; tuition none for 4 week sessions. Courses vary
Summer School: Tuition res—$291; nonres—$926 for term of 5 wks beginning June.
Courses—varied

BETHANY

BETHANY COLLEGE, Art Dept,* 26032. Tel 304-829-7000. *Chmn* Walter L
Kornowski, MFA; *Head Dept* David J Judy; *Asst Prof* Wesley Wagner; *Lectr* Peter
West
Estab 1840, dept estab 1958; den; D; scholarships; SC 27, LC 7; enrl D 136, non-
maj 106, maj 30
Ent Req: HS dipl
Degrees: BA and BS 4 yrs
Tuition: $5910 annual tuition; campus res available
Courses: †Advertising Design, †Art Education, Art History, Calligraphy, Ceramics,
Drawing, Illustration, Jewelry, Lettering, Mixed Media, Painting, Photography,
Printmaking, Sculpture
Summer School: Dir, Joseph M Kurey. Tuition $160 per hr for two 5 wk summer
terms and an 11 wk independent study period. Courses—Independent Studies,
Seminars, Tutorials

BLUEFIELD

BLUEFIELD STATE COLLEGE, Art Dept,* 24701. Tel 304-325-7102. *Chmn*
Phyllis J Thompson; *Prof* Allen A Jonas, MFA
Estab 1895; pub; D & E; scholarships; SC 14, LC 4; enrl D 125, E 40, non-maj 150,
maj 10, others 5
Ent Req: HS dipl, 18 yrs old
Degrees: BA, BS, BS(Educ) and BS(Engineering Technology) 4 yrs
Tuition: Res—$297 per sem; nonres—$897 per sem
Courses: †Art Education, Art History, Ceramics, Drawing, Painting, Photography,
Printmaking, Sculpture, Teacher Training
Adult Hobby Classes: Courses—Drawing, Painting, Photography, Silk-screen
Children's Classes: Enrl 10-15; tuition $10 per session. Courses—general art;
occasional special program for advanced students
Summer School: Enrl 15-20; term of 5 wks beginning June/July. Courses—Art Educ
& Appreciation (workshops on occasion)

BUCKHANNON

WEST VIRGINIA WESLEYAN COLLEGE, Dept of Fine Arts, College Avenue,
26201. Tel 304-473-8049. *Chmn* Michael Thiedeman; *Instr* William Oldaker; *Instr*
Stephen Tinelli
Estab 1890; den; D & E; SC 16, LC 6; enrl non-maj 120, maj 20, grad 2
Ent Req: HS dipl, ent exam
Degrees: BA and MA(Teaching)
Tuition: $1970 per sem
Courses: Teacher Training, Theatre Arts
Summer School: Dir, Dr Kenneth B Welliver. Enrl 25; tuition $85 per cr hr for
three 4 wk terms. Courses—Art History, Studio Arts

CHARLESTON

UNIVERSITY OF CHARLESTON (Formerly Morris Harvey College), Art Dept,*
2300 MacCorkle Ave SE, 25304. Tel 304-346-9471. *Coordr* Henry C Keeling.
Instrs: FT 2, PT 3
Estab 1888; pvt; D & E; enrl maj 35, others 150
Ent Req: Usual col req
Degrees: 4 yr
Tuition: $1675 per sem
Courses: Art Education, Art History, Ceramics, Painting, Printmaking, Sculpture,
Advanced Studio, Art Appreciation, Color Theory, Design
Summer School: Tuition $60 per sem hr for sessions of 3 wks beginning May 26,
June 16, July 7, July 28

ELKINS

DAVIS AND ELKINS COLLEGE, Dept of Art,* 26241. Tel 304-636-1900, Ext
254. *Chmn* Jesse F Reed; *Div Arts* Margaret P Goddin. Instrs: FT 1, PT 3
Den; D; scholarships; SC 15, LC 5; enrl maj 3
Ent Req: HS dipl
Degrees: AA & AS 2 yrs, BA 2 yrs
Tuition: $4370 annual tuition; campus res available
Courses: Art Education, Art History, Drawing, Graphic Arts, Painting, Photography,
Sculpture, Teacher Training, Weaving, Pottery
Adult Hobby Classes: Enrl 90
Summer School: Augusta Heritage Arts Workshop. Courses—Appalachian crafts,
Folkcarving, Treenware, Woodworking, Coopering, Basketry, Chairbottoming,
Toymaking, Musical Instrument Construction & Repair, Bushcraft, Pottery, Clay
Prospecting, Calligraphy, Papermaking, Stained Glass, Music, Dance, Folklore

FAIRMONT

FAIRMONT STATE COLLEGE, Art Dept, 26554. Tel 304-367-4000. *Chairperson*
Dr Leta Carson; *Prof* James Brooks, MFA; *Prof* Dr Stephen Smigocki, PhD; *Prof*
Barry Snyder, MFA; *Assoc Prof* John Clovis, MFA
Pub; D & E; scholarships; enrl D maj 35, non-maj 15
Ent Req: HS dipl
Degrees: BA(Art Educ) and BS(Graphics, Fine Arts) 4 yrs
Tuition: Res—undergrad $149 per sem, $16 per cr hr; nonres—undergrad $599 per
sem, $54 per cr hr; campus residency available
Courses: †Art Education, Art History, Ceramics, Design, Drawing, Graphic Arts,
Painting, Photography, Printmaking, Sculpture, Commercial Design
Adult Hobby Classes: Two - three times a wk for 16 wks. Courses—same as above
Children's Classes: Enrl 30; tuition $60 per 10 wk term. Courses—general art
Summer School: Enrl 25; 4 wks per session. Courses—Art Education, Drawing,
Design, Painting, Art Appreciation

GLENVILLE

GLENVILLE STATE COLLEGE, Dept of Art, High St, 26351. Tel 304-462-7361,
Ext 186. *Prof* Charles C Scott, MFA; *Asst Prof* James W Rogers, MFA; *Instructor*
George D Harper, MFA
Estab 1872, dept estab 1952; pub; D & E; scholarships; SC 25, LC 3; enrl D 128, E
42, non-maj 14, maj 55
Ent Req: HS dipl
Degrees: AB 4 yrs
Tuition: Res—undergrad $444 per yr, $222 per sem; nonres—undergrad $1444 per
yr, $722 per sem; campus residency available
Courses: Art Education, Art History, †Ceramics, Drawing, Graphic Arts, Jewelry,
Lettering, †Painting, Photography, Printmaking, Sculpture, Textile Design, Weaving
Summer School: Prof, Charles C/Scott

HUNTINGTON

MARSHALL UNIVERSITY, Dept of Art, 16th St and Third Ave, 25701. Tel 304-
696-6760. Instrs: FT 9
Estab 1903; pub; enrl maj incl grad 200
Ent Req: HS grad
Degrees: BFA and MA in art educ and studio 4 yrs
Tuition: Res—$423.25 per sem; nonres—$1198.25; campus residency available
Courses: Art Education, Ceramics, Painting, Printmaking, Sculpture, Weaving,
Communications Design
Summer School: Tuition $192 for 6 sem hrs, nonres $582 for 5 wk terms

INSTITUTE

WEST VIRGINIA STATE COLLEGE, Art Dept, 25112. Tel 304-766-3196. *Chmn* Dr Paul Nuchims
D & E; scholarships; SC 26, LC 11
Ent Req: HS dipl
Degrees: AB(Art) and BSEd(Art) 4 yrs
Tuition: Res $381; nonres $1066
Courses: Art Education, Art History, Ceramics, Design, Drawing, Graphic Design, Painting, Photography, Printmaking, Teacher Training, Fibers, Computer Graphics, Figure Drawing, Appalachian Art
Summer School: Dir, Dr Paul Nuchims. Enrl 50. Courses—Art Education, Basic Studios, Art Appreciation

KEYSER

POTOMAC STATE COLLEGE, Dept of Art, Mineral St at Fort Ave, 26726. Tel 304-788-3011, Ext 262. *Chmn* Edward M Wade, MA
College estab 1953, dept estab 1974; pub; D & E; SC 8, LC 2; enrl D 160, non-maj 150, others 10
Ent Req: HS dipl
Degrees: AA, AAS
Tuition: Res—undergrad $320 per academic year, $21.25 per hour; nonres—undergrad $955 per academic year, $74.25 per hour
Courses: Art Education, Art History, Drawing, Painting, Sculpture, Visual Foundation
Summer School: Dir, Edward Wade. Enrl 10-20; tuition res—undergrad $77.25 per 3 hrs, nonres—undergrad $236.25 per 3 hrs for 5 wk term beginning June 1.

MONTGOMERY

WEST VIRGINIA INSTITUTE OF TECHNOLOGY, Creative Arts Dept, 25136. Tel 304-442-3257. *Head Dept* Arthur Ray Pierce
Estab 1896; pub; scholarships; enrl 3500 (total)
Ent Req: HS grad
Degrees: AS, BA and BS 2-4 yrs
Courses: Ceramics, Painting, Art Appreciation, Design

MORGANTOWN

WEST VIRGINIA UNIVERSITY, Division of Art, Creative Arts Center, 26506. Tel 304-293-3140. *Chmn* Gary Edson, MFA; *Prof* Robert Anderson, MFA; *Prof* Ying Kit Chan, MFA; *Prof* Urban Couch, MFA; *Prof* Victoria Fergus, MA; *Prof* David Faber, MFA; *Prof* Ben Freedman, MA; *Prof* Clifford Harvey, BFA; *Prof* Alison Helm, MFA; *Prof* Margaret Rajam, PhD; *Prof* Bernie Schultz, PhD; *Prof* Eve Small, MFA; *Prof* William Thomas, PhD; *Prof* John Thompson, MA
Estab 1867, dept estab 1950; pub; D & E; enrl D 250, maj 250, grad 30
Ent Req: HS dipl
Degrees: BA(Art Educ) and BFA 4 yrs, MA(Art) and MFA(Art) 2-4 yrs; grad degrees
Tuition: Res—undergrad $545 per sem, grad $575; nonres—undergrad $1470 per sem, grad $1570; campus residency available
Courses: †Art Education, Art History, †Ceramics, Drawing, †Graphic Design, †Painting, †Printmaking, †Sculpture, Basic Design
Adult Hobby Classes: Courses—Art History, Drawing, Painting, Printmaking
Children's Classes: Childrens Saturday Art Studio (ages 6 - 13)
Summer School: Courses—Art History, Drawing, Graphic Design, Painting, Printmaking

PARKERSBURG

PARKERSBURG COMMUNITY COLLEGE, Art Dept, Route 5 Box 167-A, 26101. Tel 304-424-8000. *Chmn* Ed Pitner, MA
Estab 1961, dept estab 1973; pub; D & E; scholarships; SC 25, LC 5; enrl D 120, E 80, non-maj 125, maj 8
Ent Req: HS dipl plus diagnostic tests in reading, math and English
Degrees: AA 2 yrs
Tuition: Res—$20 per hr; nonres—$73 per hr
Courses: Art History, Ceramics, Drawing, Painting, Photography, Printmaking, Bronze Castings, Wood Carvings
Adult Hobby Classes: Enrl 20; tuition $15 for 2 wks. Courses—Painting, Photography, Wood Carving
Children's Classes: Enrl 40; tuition $15 for 2 wks. Courses—Ceramics, Painting
Summer School: Dir, Roger Allen. Tuition $60 for 2 four wk sessions. Courses—Painting

SALEM

SALEM COLLEGE, Art Dept, 26426. Tel 304-782-5233. *Chmn* Harold Reed
Estab 1888; pvt; D & E; scholarships
Ent Req: HS dipl
Degrees: AA 2 yrs, BA 4 yrs
Tuition: $2036.50 per sem
Courses: Art Appreciation, †Art Education, Ceramics, Commercial Art, Drawing, Graphic Arts, Handicrafts, Painting, Photography, Printmaking, Sculpture, †Teacher Training, †Art Therapy, †Heritage Arts
Adult Hobby Classes: Enrl 20; tuition $2036.50 full time. Courses—Art Appreciation, Commercial Art, Color & Design, Decorative Arts, Drawing, Heritage Crafts, Painting
Children's Classes: Workshop Experiences
Summer School: Dir, Sam Warner. Enrl 10; tuition $60 per cr hr per 6 wk session. Classes May 14 - June 8

SHEPHERDSTOWN

SHEPHERD COLLEGE, Art Dept, 25443. Tel 304-876-2511, Ext 294. *Chmn* Dr R L Jones. Instrs: FT 6, PT 3
Estab 1872; pub; D; scholarships; SC 16, LC 7; enrl maj 110
Ent Req: HS dipl
Degrees: AA and AS, BA, BA(Educ) and BS 4 yrs
Tuition: $366 per yr; campus res $1787 per yr
Courses: Art Education, Art History, Ceramics, Commercial Art, Drawing, Graphic Arts, Handicrafts, Jewelry, Lettering, Painting, Photography, Sculpture, Teacher Training, Aesthetic Criticism, Applied Design, Art Therapy, Design
Adult Hobby Classes: Enrl 30; tuition $25 per hr. Courses—Drawing, Painting, Sculpture
Children's Classes: Enrl 35; tuition $20 per course. Courses—Crafts, Drawing
Summer School: Dir, R L Jones. Enrl 60; tuition $25 per hr. Courses—Drawing

WEST LIBERTY

WEST LIBERTY STATE COLLEGE, Art Dept, 26074. Tel 304-336-8019. *Chairperson* Nancy E Tirone, MS & MA; *Prof* Ernest D Comiskey, MFA; *Prof* Bernie K Peace, MFA; *Prof* Karen Rychlewski, MFA; *Assoc Prof* R Paul Padgett, MFA
Estab 1836; pub; D & E; scholarships; SC 40, LC 6; enrl D 855, E 140, non-maj 900, maj 90, others 12
Ent Req: HS dipl, score of 14 on ACT test or upper three fourths of HS class
Degrees: BA and BS 4 yrs
Tuition: Res—undergrad $470 per yr, $235 per sem, approx $20 per cr hr; nonres—undergrad $1470 per yr, $735 per sem, approx $78 per cr hr; campus residency available
Courses: Advertising Design, †Art Education, Art History, Ceramics, †Commercial Art, Drawing, Film, Graphic Arts, Graphic Design, History of Art & Archaeology, Illustration, Jewelry, Lettering, Painting, Photography, Printmaking, Sculpture, Stage Design, Theatre Arts, Weaving, Studio crafts
Summer School: Dir, Alfred R de Jaager. Tuition res $15 per sem hr, nonres $53 per sem hr. Courses—Art Education, Drawing, Painting, Special Education

WISCONSIN

APPLETON

LAWRENCE UNIVERSITY, Dept of Art, 54911. Tel 414-735-6621, 735-6645. *Chmn* Arthur Thrall. Instrs: FT 3
Estab 1847; SC 8, LC 17
Ent Req: HS performance, CEEB scores, recommendation
Degrees: BA 4 yrs
Tuition: $9390 includes room and board per 3 term yr
Courses: Art Education, Photography, Art History, Drawing, Painting, Photography, Printmaking, Metalwork, Studio Ceramics, 3D Design

BELOIT

BELOIT COLLEGE, Dept of Art,* 53511. Tel 608-365-3391, Ext 677 and 678. *Head Dept & Assoc Prof* Sally A Kovach, MFA; *Prof* Richard W P Olson, MFA; *Assoc Prof* Michael A Simon; *Asst Prof* Debra Mancoff, PhD; *Asst Prof* Debora Donato, MFA; *Adjunct Prof* L W Williams II, PhD. Instrs: FT 4
Estab 1847; pvt; D & E; SC 14, LC 10; enrl maj 30, gen col enrl 1026
Ent Req: Top third of class, 3 yrs foreign language, 4 yrs English, SAT or ACT
Degrees: BA, BS & MAT 4 yrs
Tuition: $3459 per term; campus res available
Courses: †Art History, Ceramics, Drawing, Graphic Arts, Museum Staff Training, Painting, Photography, Printmaking, Sculpture, American Art, Far Eastern Art, Modern Art, Modern Architecture, Renaissance Art, †Studio Art
Children's Classes: Enrl 20; both terms $5-$10

DE PERE

SAINT NORBERT COLLEGE, Art Dept, 54115. *Head Dept* J Vanden Burgt. Instrs: FT 4
Estab 1898; pvt den; D; SC 19, LC 5; enrl D 60, maj 60
Ent Req: HS dipl, ent exam
Degrees: BA 4 yrs
Tuition: $3920 per yr; campus res $1700-$2000 includes room & board
Courses: Aesthetics, Art Education, Art History, Ceramics, Drawing, Graphic Arts, Graphic Design, Illustration, Jewelry, Painting, Photography, Sculpture, Teacher Training
Summer School: Dir, John Giovannini. Terms of 3 or 5 wks beginning June. Courses—Art Education, Ceramics, Drawing, History of Art, Painting, Sculpture

EAU CLAIRE

UNIVERSITY OF WISCONSIN-EAU CLAIRE, Dept of Art, Park and Garfield Aves, 54701. Tel 715-836-3277. *Chmn* Charles Campbell. Instrs: FT 17, PT 1
Estab 1916; pub; D & E; scholarships; SC 31, LC 12; enrl maj 260
Ent Req: HS dipl, ent exam
Degrees: BA and BFA 4 yrs
Tuition: Res $560 per sem, nonres $1785 per sem
Courses: Advertising Design, Art Education, Art History, Ceramics, Drawing, Painting, Printmaking, Sculpture, Fibers, Metalsmithing
Adult Hobby Classes: Courses: Ceramics, Painting
Summer School: Dir, C Campbell. Enrl 100. Courses—Art History, Ceramics, Drawing, Painting, Sculpture, Watercolor

FOND DU LAC

MARIAN COLLEGE, Art Dept, 45 S National Ave (Mailing add: 678 Western Ave, Fond Du Lac, WI 54935). Tel 414-923-7602, Ext 7622. *Coordr* Sr Mary Neff, MA; *Chmn Arts & Letters* Henry L Lindborg, PhD; *Prof* Julienne Rompf, MFA; *Prof* Sr Jean Brenner, MA
Estab 1936; pvt; E; scholarships; SC 20, LC 12; enrl D 107, E 35, maj 6
Ent Req: HS dipl, ACT or SAT
Degrees: BA and BA(Art Educ) 4 yrs
Tuition: $1750 per yr, $875 per sem; campus residency available
Courses: †Art Education, †Fine Arts
Adult Hobby Classes: Workshops, summer sessions, continuing education
Children's Classes: In Relationship with Art Education
Summer School: Workshops, credit art courses

GREEN BAY

UNIVERSITY OF WISCONSIN-GREEN BAY, Visual Arts Dept,* Col of Creative Communication, North Nicolet Rd, 54302. Tel 414-465-2121. *Head Dept* Robert Pum; *Concentration Chmn* Robert J Bauer. Instrs: FT 7, PT 4
EStab 1970; pub; D & E; SC 29, LC 3; enrl D 5500
Ent Req: HS dipl, ent exam
Degrees: BA and BS 4 yrs
Tuition: Res—$926 per yr; nonres—$3065 per yr
Courses: Aesthetics, Art Education, Ceramics, Drawing, Graphic Arts, Jewelry, Painting, Photography, Printmaking, Sculpture, Stage Design, Teacher Training, Textile Design, Theatre Arts, Styles
Summer School: Courses—vary

KENOSHA

CARTHAGE COLLEGE, Art Dept,* 2001 Alfred Dr, 53141. Tel 414-551-8500. *Instr* Phillipp Powell, MFA; *Chmn* Edwin Kalke, MFA
Scholarships offered
Degrees: BA
Tuition: $2432.50 per term
Courses: Advertising Design, Art Education, Art History, Ceramics, Design, Drawing

UNIVERSITY OF WISCONSIN-PARKSIDE, Art Discipline, Fine Arts Division, Box 2000, 53140. Tel 414-553-2457. *Coordr of Art Program* Douglas DeVinny, MFA; *Assoc Prof* Rollin Jansky, MS; *Assoc Prof* John Satre Murphy, MFA; *Assoc Prof* Dennis Bayuzick, MFA; *Assoc Prof* David V Holmes, MFA
Estab 1965; pub; D & E; SC 25, LC 6
Ent Req: HS dipl
Tuition: Res—undergrad $491 per sem, $52.75 per hr; nonres—undergrad $1657 per sem, $150 per hr; no campus res
Courses: Aesthetics, Art Education, Art History, Ceramics, Drawing, Film, Jewelry, Painting, Printmaking, Sculpture, Teacher Training, Textile Design, Art Metals, Life Modeling
Summer School: Tuition $42.25 res, $132.25 nonres per cr hr for term of 8 wks beginning mid June. Courses—vary from summer to summer

LA CROSSE

UNIVERSITY OF WISCONSIN-LA CROSSE, Art Dept, 1725 State St, 54601. Tel 608-785-8230. *Chmn* William Fiorini
Estab 1905; pub; D & E; scholarships; SC 25, LC 5; enrl (univ) 7600
Ent Req: HS dipl
Degrees: BA and BS 4 yrs
Courses: Art Education, Ceramics, Drawing, Graphic Arts, History of Art & Archaeology, Jewelry, Painting, Sculpture, Theatre Arts, Blacksmithing, Crafts
Adult Hobby Classes: Courses—Blacksmithing, Ceramics, Outreach Jewelry
Summer School: Courses—various

VITERBO COLLEGE, Art Dept, 815 S Ninth, 54601. Tel 608-784-0040. *Chmn* Sr Carlene Unser, MA; *Assoc Prof* Tim Crane, MFA; *Asst Prof* Jim Knipe, MFA; *Instructor* Diane Crane; *Instructor* Jan Knipe, MFA; *Artist in Res* Carl Oltuid; *Artist in Res* Joyce Lyon
Estab 1890; pvt; D & E; SC 10-12, LC 6; enrl D 55, maj 55
Degrees: BA and BAEd 4 yrs
Tuition: $1990 per yr; campus res—room & board $1285
Courses: Advertising Design, †Art Education, Art History, Ceramics, Commercial Art, Costume Design & Construction, Drawing, Graphic Arts, Illustration, Painting, Photography, Printmaking, Sculpture, Teacher Training, Theatre Arts, Fibers, Weaving
Summer School: Tuition $40 per sem hr. Courses—summer catalog sent on request

WESTERN WISCONSIN TECHNICAL INSTITUTE, Graphics Division, Sixth & Vine Sts, 54601. Tel 608-785-9178. *Chmn* Torval E Hendrickson, MA
Estab 1911; dept estab 1964; pub; D & E; scholarships; SC & LC 16; enrl D 130, E 145, non-maj 132, maj 143
Ent Req: HS dipl or GED
Degrees: AAS 2 yrs
Courses: Advertising Design, †Commercial Art, Display, Drafting, Drawing, Film, †Graphic Arts, Graphic Design, Illustration, Intermedia, Lettering, Mixed Media, Painting, Photography, Stage Design, Video
Adult Hobby Classes: Enrl 264; tuition $13 per cr. Courses—Color Photo Printing, Home Movie Making, Painting, Photography
Summer School: Dir, T E Hendrickson. Courses—varied

MADISON

EDGEWOOD COLLEGE, Art Dept,* 855 Woodrow St, 53711. Tel 608-257-4861, Ext 207. *Assoc Prof* Ruella Bouchonville; *Asst Prof* Sr Elizabeth Devine; *Instr* Sr M Stephanie Stauder
Estab 1941; den; D & E; institutional grants based on financial needs; SC 20, LC 4; enrl D & E 500 (total), non-maj 70, maj 20
Ent Req: HS dipl, ACT
Degrees: BA or BS 4 yrs
Tuition: $3800 annual tuition; campus res available
Courses: Art Education, Art History, Ceramics, Drawing, Graphic Arts, Graphic Design, Lettering, Painting, Photography, Printmaking, Sculpture, Teacher Training
Summer School: Dir, Dr Joseph Schmiedicke. Tuition $110 per cr. Courses—varied

MADISON AREA TECHNICAL COLLEGE, Communication Arts, 211 N Carroll St, 53703. Tel 608-266-5002. *Chmn* Charles M Haycock, MA
Estab 1911; pub; D & E; scholarships; SC 45, LC 12; enrl D 5300, E 23,000 (part-time)
Ent Req: HS dipl
Degrees: AA 2 yrs commercial art-layout-design
Adult Hobby Classes: Enrl 1000. Courses—same as regular session

UNIVERSITY OF WISCONSIN, MADISON
—**Dept of Art,** School of Education, 6241 Humanities Bldg, 455 N Park, 53706. Tel 608-262-1660. *Chmn* N Wayne Taylor. Instrs: FT 40, PT 18
Estab 1911; pub; scholarships and fels; SC 47, LC 2, GC 19; enrl maj 850
Degrees: BS(Art, Art Educ), BFA, MA(Art, Art Educ), MFA, PhD(Art Educ)
Courses: Art Education, Ceramics, Drawing, Graphic Design, Painting, Photography, Sculpture, Art Metal, Computer Art, Etching, Glassblowing, Lithography, Non-Static Forms, Photo-Offset, Relief Printing, Serigraphy, Stage Design and Lighting, Typography, Woodworking
Summer School: Three wk intersession, 8 wk session
—**Dept of Art History,** College of Letters and Science, 800 University Ave, 53706. Tel 608-263-2340. *Art History Dept Chmn* James M Dennis
Estab 1848, dept estab 1925; pub; D; scholarships; enrl 2372, maj 61, grad 24
Ent Req: HS dipl
Degrees: BA, MA, PhD
Tuition: Res grad—$104.75 per cr; nonres grad—$317 per cr
Courses: †Art History, Graphic Production Technique, Print Illustration
Summer School: Dir, James M Dennis. Tuition res—grad $98 per cr, nonres—grad $293 per cr; term of 8 wks beginning June 19. Courses—American Art & Architecture, Ancient to Medieval Art, Renaissance to Modern Art, Modern European Art

MANITOWOC

SILVER LAKE COLLEGE, Art Dept, 2406 S Alverno Rd, 54220. Tel 414-684-6691. *Assoc Prof* Sr Andree Du Charme, MA; *Instr* Sr Karen Kappell, MA; *Instr* Sr Mariella Eroman, MFA
Estab 1936, dept estab 1959; pvt; D & E; SC 21, LC 6; enrl D 50, E 10, non-maj 25, maj 25
Ent Req: HS dipl, ACT or SAT
Degrees: AA(Commercial Art) 2 yrs, BS or BA(Studio Art) and BS or BA(Art Educ) 4 yrs
Tuition: Res and nonres—undergrad $3600 per yr, $1800 per sem
Courses: Aesthetics, †Art Education, Art History, Calligraphy, Ceramics, †Commercial Art, Drawing, Graphic Arts, Graphic Design, Jewelry, Lettering, Mixed Media, Painting, Photography, Printmaking, Sculpture, Teacher Training, Textile Design
Children's Classes: Enrl 100; tuition $10-$25 per 6 wk term. Courses—Clay, Drawing, Fibers, Photography, Sculpture, Painting, Graphics
Summer School: Dir, Sr Carol Diederich. Enrl 350; tuition $75 per cr per 6 wk terms beginning June 18. Courses—various

MARINETTE

UNIVERSITY OF WISCONSIN CENTER-MARINETTE COUNTY, Art Dept, Bay Shore, 54143. Tel 715-735-7477. *Head Dept* James La Malfa, MFA
Estab 1850, dept estab 1946; pub; D & E; scholarships
Ent Req: HS dipl
Degrees: AA 2 yrs
Tuition: Res—undergrad $465 per sem; nonres—undergrad $1631 per sem
Courses: Art History, Ceramics, Drawing, Painting, Photography, Printmaking, Sculpture, Survey of Art, Watercolor
Summer School: Dir, William A Schmidtke. Tuition $35 per cr for term of 6 wks beginning June 12. Courses—Beginning and Advanced Photography plus courses in other disciplines

MENOMONIE

UNIVERSITY OF WISCONSIN-STOUT, Art Dept, 54751. Tel 715-232-1141. *Head Dept* Gene Bloedorn, MFA; *Prof* James MccCormick, MFA; *Prof* Orazio Fumagalli, PhD; *Prof* Todd Boppel, MFA; *Assoc Prof* Doug Cumming, MFA; *Assoc Prof* John Perri, MFA; *Assoc Prof* William Schulman, ABD; *Assoc Prof* Charles Wimmer, MFA; *Assoc Prof* Robb Wilson, MFA; *Assoc Prof* Eddie Wong, MFA; *Asst Prof* Alan Gamache, MFA; *Asst Prof* Humphrey Gilbert, MFA; *Asst Prof* Sherman Iverson, MFA; *Asst Prof* Dion Manriquez, MFA; *Asst Prof* Rob Price, MFA; *Instructor* Ron Verdon, MFA; *Instructor* Claudia Smith, MA; *Lecturer* Paul DeLong, MFA; *Lecturer* Susan Hunt, MFA; *Lecturer* Daniel Laurence, MFA; *Lecturer* Hal Newton; *Lecturer* Edward Stevens, BA; *Lecturer* Patricia Zontelli, MFA; *Lecturer* Alan Kraning, MFA; *Lecturer* Magdalena Laszkiewicz, BFA; *Specialist* Mary Hovind, BS
Estab 1893, dept estab 1965; pub; E; SC 60, LC 6; enrl D 24, non-maj 1200, maj 450
Ent Req: HS dipl

Degrees: BA(Art) and BS(Art Educ) 4 yrs, emphasis interior or industrial design 4 yrs
Tuition: Res—undergrad $505.15 per sem, $42.09 per cr hr, grad $601.15 per sem, $50.09 per cr hr; nonres—undergrad $1630.65 per sem, grad $1753.15 per sem; campus res—room & board $878 per yr
Courses: †Art Education, Art History, Ceramics, Design, Drawing, †Graphic Design, †Industrial Design, †Interior Design, Painting, Printmaking, Sculpture, Silversmithing, †Art Period Courses, Art Metals, †Blacksmithing, Fashion Illustration
Children's Classes: Courses—Sat classes in Art (Media changes and Drama)
Summer School: Enrl varies with class; tuition res—undergrad $252.57, grad $120.23; nonres—grad $271.77, undergrad $350.63 for term of 8 wks beginning June 1 through August 6. Courses—Art Metals, Ceramics, Drawing, Design, Printmaking, Painting, Sculpture

MEQUOW

CONCORDIA COLLEGE, Art Dept, 53092. Tel 414-243-5700. *Chmn* William L Chandler, MS
Estab 1881, dept estab 1971; den; D & E; SC 6, LC 1; enrl non-maj 100, maj 5
Ent Req: HS dipl
Degrees: AA 2 yrs, BA 2 yrs
Tuition: $1650 per sem, $135 per hr; campus res—room & board $950 per sem
Courses: Art History, Drawing, Handicrafts, Painting, Sculpture, Design
Adult Hobby Classes: Courses available in art and other areas
Summer School: Terms of 5 wks. Courses—Drawing & Painting (outdoors)

MILWAUKEE

ALVERNO COLLEGE, Art Dept, 3401 S 39 St, 53215. Tel 414-647-3873. *Chmn Art Dept* Julie Knotek
Estab 1948; pvt, W only in degree program; D & E; scholarships; SC 20, LC 5; enrl D 200, E 50, maj 35
Ent Req: GPA, class rank and ACT or SAT
Degrees: BA 4 yrs (or 128 cr)
Tuition: $2350 per yr; campus res—room and board $1100 per yr
Courses: Art Education, Ceramics, Drawing, Handicrafts, History of Art & Archaeology, Painting, Printmaking, Sculpture, Stage Design, Teacher Training, Art Therapy, Enameling (Cloisonne), General Crafts, Introduction to Visual Art, Metal Working, Weaving
Summer School: Term June to August. Courses—Art Education, Studio Art

CARDINAL STRITCH COLLEGE, Art Dept, 53217. Tel 414-352-5400, Ext 331. *Head Dept* Sr M Thomasita Fessler, MFA; *Prof* Irene Kilmurry, MS; *Prof* Claudia M Gorecki, MS; *Assoc Prof* John Tryba, MAE; *Assoc Prof* Mildred Tryba, MA; *Asst Prof* Sr Madonna Balestrieri, MA; *Instr* Christine Buth-Furness; *Lectr* Timothy Alber; *Lectr* Sr Jeanne Moynihan
Estab 1937; den; D & E; scholarships; SC 29, LC 17; enrl maj 98
Ent Req: HS dipl, ent exam
Degrees: AA, BA, BFA, BA(Commercial Art), BA(Education)
Tuition: Undergrad $1995 per sem, $125 per cr hr; grad $125 per cr hr; campus res room & board $1075-1150 per sem
Courses: Aesthetics, †Art Education, Art History, Calligraphy, Ceramics, Commercial Art, Constructions, Costume Design & Construction, Drawing, Handicrafts, Illustration, Jewelry, Lettering, Mixed Media, Painting, Photography, Printmaking, Sculpture, Textile Design, Design, Typography, Weaving
Adult Hobby Classes: Enrl 200; tuition $40-$60 per 8-12 wk session. Courses—Enameling & Jewelry Design, Interior Design, Mixed Media, Painting, Photography, Basic Drawing, Watercolor, Chinese Brush Painting, Wood Carving
Children's Classes: Enrl 100; tuition $40 per child per 12 classes. Courses—traditional media plus various crafts
Summer School: Dir, Sr Thomasita. Tuition $125 per cr per 6 wk term of 6 wks beginning June 19th. Courses—Composition, Drawing, Sculpture, Summer Foreign Tour (possible col cr)

MILWAUKEE AREA TECHNICAL COLLEGE, Graphic & Applied Arts Division, 53203. Tel 414-278-6252. *Head Dept* Ralph R Thomas, MFA, *Instructor* Howard Austin, BA; *Instructor* William Bonifay, BS; *Instructor* Mary Anna Brooks, MFA; *Instructor* William Crandall, MA; *Instructor* Joseph O'Lugosz, BFA; *Instructor* Geraldine Geischer, MA; *Instructor* Chris Hansen, BFA; *Instructor* Hans Krommenhoek, MFA; *Instructor* Donald O'Connell, BFA; *Instructor* J Strachota, MS
Estab 1912, dept estab 1958; pub; D & E; financial aid; enrl D 240, E 150
Ent Req: HS dipl
Degrees: AA 2 yrs
Tuition: $1200 per yr, $300 per sem; tuition and fees approx $16 per cr; no campus res
Courses: †Advertising Design, Calligraphy, Ceramics, †Commercial Art, Display, Drawing, †Film, Graphic Design, Illustration, †Jewelry, Lettering, †Photography, Silversmithing
Adult Hobby Classes: Tuition $12 per cr

MILWAUKEE CENTER FOR PHOTOGRAPHY, 207 E Buffalo St, 53202. Tel 414-273-1699. *Pres* Richard Riebel; *Treas* Richard Meeusen; *Secy* Curtis Carter; *Dir* Murray Weiss
Estab 1975; enrl 200
Degrees: AA(photography) 3 yrs
Tuition: Assoc degree $2000 per yr; workshops $160-$180 sem
Adult Hobby Classes: Enrl 140; tuition $160-$180. Courses—basic & advanced photography workshops
Summer School: Dir, Murray Weiss. Enrl 80; tuition $160-$180 per 3-6 wk term. Courses—same as adult

MILWAUKEE INSTITUTE OF ART AND DESIGN (Formerly Milwaukee School of the Arts), 207 N Milwaukee St, 53202. Tel 414-276-7889. *Dir* Terrence J Coffman, BFA; *Chmn Foundations Dept* Charles Vansen, MFA; *Chmn Fine Arts* Ron Bitticks, MFA; *Chmn Design Dept* Steve Quinn, BFA; *Chmn Academics* Jim Slauson, MA. Instrs: FT 11, PT 28
Estab 1974; pvt; D & E; scholarships; enrl D 333, E 20, maj 353
Ent Req: HS dipl, portfolio, letter of intent
Degrees: BFA and MSA 4 yrs
Tuition: $2900 per year, $1450 per sem
Courses: †Advertising Design, Art History, †Drawing, †Illustration, †Industrial Design, †Interior Design, †Painting, Photography, †Printmaking, †Sculpture
Adult Hobby Classes: Enrl 20; tuition $145 per course. Courses—Advertising, Art History, Drawing, Illustration, Interior Design, Painting, Photography, Printmaking, Sculpture
Summer School: Courses—Art History, Basic Design, Drawing, Painting, Photography, Sculpture

MOUNT MARY COLLEGE, Art Dept, 2900 N Menomonee River Parkway, 53222. Tel 414-258-4810. *Chmn* Sr Rosemarita Huebner, MFA; *Prof* Sr M Remy Revor, MFA; *Prof* Sr M Arthur Bresina, MA, OTR; *Asst Prof* Angelee Fuchs, MA; *Asst Prof* Joseph Rozman, MFA; *Asst Prof* Joan Woodside, PhD; *Asst Prof* Charles Kaiser, MA; *Asst Prof* Deirdre Lee Kozlowski, MS; *Asst Prof* Sr Patrick Flannigan, MFA; *Instructor* Robert Curtis, MFA; *Instructor* Pamela Steffan, MA; *Instructor* Harry Wirth, MA; *Instructor* Jane Mihas, MA; *Instructor* Geraldine Wind, PhD; *Instructor* Sr Carla Huebner, MS; *Instructor* Terri Weiss, MA; *Instructor* Candace Walton
Estab 1913, dept estab 1929; den; D & E; scholarships; SC 22, LC 12; enrl D 200, E 30, non-maj 50, maj 200
Ent Req: HS dipl
Degrees: BA 4 yrs
Tuition: $3900 per yr, $1950 per sem; campus res available; board $910-$1190 per yr
Courses: Art Education, Art History, Calligraphy, Ceramics, Costume Design & Construction, Drafting, Drawing, Fashion Arts, Film, Graphic Arts, Graphic Design, Handicrafts, Illustration, Interior Design, Jewelry, Occupational Therapy, Painting, Photography, Printmaking, Sculpture, Silversmithing, Stage Design, Teacher Training, Textile Design, Weaving, Art Internship, Art Therapy, Enameling, Fiber Arts
Children's Classes: Enrl 120; tuition $35 per 2 wks for 6 wks term
Summer School: Dir, Sr Luetta Wolf. Enrl 120; tuition $80 per cr for term of 6 wks beginning June. Courses—Art Therapy, Art Metal, Art Education, Ceramics, Design, Drawing, Fiber Arts, Portraiture, Photography, Watercolor

UNIVERSITY OF WISCONSIN-MILWAUKEE, Dept of Art, School of Fine Arts, 53201. Tel 414-963-4200. *Dean* Robert W Corrigan. Instrs: FT 36, PT 6 Scholarships; enrl maj 860
Degrees: BS(Art), BS(Art Educ), BFA(Art), BFA with teachers cert, MA(Art), MS(Art Educ), MFA(Art), MFA with teachers cert
Tuition: Res—undergrad $620 per sem
Courses: Art Education, Ceramics, Drawing, Painting, Photography, Printmaking, Sculpture, Design, Fibers, Metals, Visual Communication
Summer School: Dir, Charles Kraus. Enrl 300; tuition $60 per cr undergrad res. Courses—Art Education, Drawing, Painting, Photography, Metals, Sculpture

OSHKOSH

UNIVERSITY OF WISCONSIN-OSHKOSH, Dept of Art, 54901. Tel 414-424-2222. *Chmn* David W Hodge. Instrs: FT 24
Estab 1871; pub; D & E; scholarships for grad students; SC 56, LC 14, GC 31; enrl D 10,500, E 2500, maj 300, grad 15, minors 50
Ent Req: HS dipl
Degrees: BA, BAE and BS(Art) 4 yrs, BFA 82 cr
Courses: Advertising Design, Art Education, Art History, Ceramics, Commercial Art, Drawing, Graphic Arts, Jewelry, Lettering, Painting, Photography, Sculpture, Teacher Training, Textile Design, Museology, Woodcraft

PLATTEVILLE

UNIVERSITY OF WISCONSIN-PLATTEVILLE, Dept of Fine Art,* Art Bldg 212B, 53818. Tel 608-342-1781. *Chmn* Roger Gottschalk. Instrs: FT 8
Estab 1866; pub; D & E; SC 30, LC 5, GC 3; enrl maj 105
Ent Req: HS dipl, ent exam
Degrees: BA and BS 4 yrs
Tuition: Res—$550; nonres—$1700
Summer School: Dir, Harold Hutchinson. Enrl 2200; term of 8 wks beginning June. Courses—same as regular session

RICE LAKE

UNIVERSITY OF WISCONSIN, Dept of Art, College Dr, 54868. Tel 715-234-8176. *Assoc Prof* Don Ruedy, MFA; *Lecturer* Allan Selvuss, watercolor
Pub; D & E; scholarships; SC 8, LC 2; enrl D 63, E 10, non-maj 57, maj 16
Ent Req: HS dipl
Degrees: AA & AS 2 yrs
Tuition: Res—$873 per year, $436.50 per sem, $36.50 per cr hr; nonres—$2124 per year, $1562 per sem, $130.25 per cr hr; no campus res
Courses: Art History, Calligraphy, Drawing, Jewelry, Lettering, Painting, Printmaking, Stage Design, Theatre Arts
Adult Hobby Classes: Enrl 20. Courses—Art History, Design, Drawing, Painting
Children's Classes: Enrl 30; tuition $40 for 2 weeks in summer

RIPON

RIPON COLLEGE, Art Dept, 54971. Tel 414-748-8110. *Chmn* Olimpia Ogilvie.
Instrs: FT 3
Estab 1851; pvt; D; scholarships and financial aid; SC 13, LC 8; enrl maj 20
Ent Req: Grad from accredited secondary school, SAT or ACT is recommended, but not required
Degrees: AB 4 yrs
Tuition: $8592 comprehensive fee
Courses: Art History, Drawing, Mixed Media, Painting, Printmaking, Design

RIVER FALLS

UNIVERSITY OF WISCONSIN-RIVER FALLS, Art Dept, 54022. Tel 715-425-3266. *Chmn* Dr John Buschen
Estab 1874, major estab 1958; pub; D; scholarships; SC 26, LC 18; enrl non-maj 400, maj 170
Ent Req: HS dipl
Degrees: BA, BS(Educ), BFA and BS(Liberal Arts) 4 yrs
Tuition: $352 per qtr
Courses: Aesthetics, †Art Education, Art History, Ceramics, Costume Design & Construction, Drawing, Film, Graphic Design, History of Art & Archaeology, Jewelry, Painting, Photography, Printmaking, Sculpture, Silversmithing, Textile Design, Glass Blowing, Fibers, Stained Glass
Summer School: Dir, Dr Roger Swanson. Enrl 1600; tuition $42 per cr for 2 4 week sessions. Courses—Clay, Fibers, Glass, Painting, Printmaking, Sculpture

STEVENS POINT

UNIVERSITY OF WISCONSIN-STEVENS POINT, Dept of Art, Col of Fine Arts, 2100 Main St, 54481. Tel 715-346-2669. *Head Dept* Henry M Runke, MFA; *Prof* Norman Keats, MFA; *Prof* Herbert Sandmann, MFA; *Prof* Richard Schneider, MFA; *Prof* Daniel Fabiano, MFA; *Assoc Prof* Gary Hagen, MFA; *Assoc Prof* David L Smith, PhD; *Assoc Prof* Jerome Gallagher; *Asst Prof* Mark Brueggeman, MFA; *Asst Prof* Wayne Halverson, MA; *Asst Prof* Stephen Hankin, MFA; *Asst Prof* Lisa Aronson
Estab 1894; pub; D & E; enrl D 866, non-maj 666, maj 200
Ent Req: HS dipl
Degrees: BA(Fine Arts), BS(Art Educ), BS(Fine Arts) & BFA(Art-Professional)
Tuition: Campus residency available
Courses: Architecture, †Art Education, Art History, Ceramics, Drawing, Goldsmithing, Graphic Arts, Graphic Design, Jewelry, Lettering, Painting, Printmaking, Sculpture, Silversmithing, Teacher Training, Fiber Arts, Leather, Wood
Children's Classes: Art Workshop
Summer School: Dir, O E Radke. Term of 8 wks beginning June 14. Courses—Art Education, Design, Drawing, Layout & Lettering, Papermaking

SUPERIOR

UNIVERSITY OF WISCONSIN-SUPERIOR, Programs in the Visual Arts, 54880. Tel 715-394-8391. *Chmn & Prof* Mel Olsen, MFA; *Prof* James Grittner, MFA; *Prof* William Morgan, MFA; *Prof* Marjorie Whitsitt, PhD; *Assoc Prof* Leonard Petersen, MFA; *Assoc Prof* Doug Spradlin, MFA; *Asst Prof* Anthony Pfeiffer, MFA; *Lectr* Marlene Nordstrom, MA; *Lectr* Patricia Spencer, MA; *Lectr* Pope Wright, MA
Estab 1896, dept estab 1930; pub; D & E; scholarships; enrl D 250, E 100-125, non-maj 250, maj 150, grad 30
Ent Req: HS dipl
Degrees: BS, BS(Photography), BS(Art Therapy) and BFA 4 yrs, BFA with cert 5 yrs, MA 5-6 yrs
Tuition: Res—undergrad $355.33 per qtr, grad $453; nonres—undergrad $1154.33 per qtr, grad $1319.33 per qtr; campus residency available
Courses: Advertising Design, †Art Education, †Art History, †Ceramics, Collages, Conceptual Art, †Costume Design & Construction, Drawing, †Film, †Graphic Arts, †Handicrafts, †Jewelry, Mixed Media, †Occupational Therapy, †Painting, †Photography, †Printmaking, †Sculpture, †Silversmithing, †Stage Design, †Teacher Training, †Textile Design, Theatre Arts, Video, Surface Design
Adult Hobby Classes: Courses—Batik, Ceramics, Crafts, Drawing, Fibers, Metalwork, Painting, Photography, Spinning, Stained Glass
Children's Classes: Summer session only
Summer School: Tuition varies for term of 8 wks beginning June 12th. Courses—All studios

WAUKESHA

CARROLL COLLEGE, Art Dept, 100 N East Ave, 53186. Tel 414-547-1211, Ext 191. *Chairperson* Marceil Pultorak, MA; *Asst Prof* Philip Krejcarek, MFA; *Lectr* Kathe Kurz, BA; *Lectr* Thomas Selle, MFA; *Vis Prof* Peggy Farrell, graphics
Estab 1846; pvt; D & E; scholarships; SC 21, LC 4; enrl D 1100, E 350
Ent Req: HS dipl, SAT or ACT
Degrees: BA
Tuition: $5330 annual tuition
Courses: Museum Staff Training, Sculpture, †Stage Design, †Teacher Training, Textile Design, †Theatre Arts, †Video, Sculpture, Stage Design, Teacher Training, Textile Design, Theatre Arts, Video, †Pre-Architecture; †Commercial Art; †Weaving
Adult Hobby Classes: Enrl 10 per session. Courses—Photographing Your Own Work
Children's Classes: New program
Summer School: Dir, Dr Gary Stevens. Enrl varies; tuition $200 for term of 6 wks. Courses—Drawing, Graphics, Photography

WHITEWATER

UNIVERSITY OF WISCONSIN-WHITEWATER, Dept of Art, College of the Arts, 53190. Tel 414-472-1324. *Dean* Robert Garwell. Instrs: FT 15, PT 1
Estab 1868; pub; D & E; SC 41, LC 18; enrl D 270, maj 200
Ent Req: HS dipl
Degrees: BA and BS(Art, Art Educ, Art History), BFA 4 yrs
Tuition: Res $545 per sem; nonres $1743 per sem; campus residency $1630
Courses: Advertising Design, †Art Education, †Art History, Ceramics, Commercial Art, Drawing, Graphic Arts, Graphic Design, Illustration, Jewelry, Painting, Photography, Sculpture, Teacher Training, Textile Design, Weaving, Film Animation
Summer School: Tuition res—$43,45 per credit, nonres $140.45 per credit for term of 4 & 8 wks beginning June. Courses—Ceramics, Drawing & Painting

WYOMING

CASPER

CASPER COLLEGE, 125 College Dr, 82601. Tel 307-268-2110. *Actg Head* Lynn R Munns, MFA; *Instructor* Richard Eckhardt-Jacobi, MFA; *Instructor* Linda Lee Ryan, MFA; *Instructor* Wilhelm Ossa, MFA; *Instructor* James L Gaither, MED
Pub; D & E; scholarships; LC 2; enrl D 3870
Ent Req: HS dipl
Degrees: AA 2 yrs
Tuition: Res—undergrad $190 per sem; nonres—undergrad $640 per sem; campus res—room & board $865-$915
Courses: Advertising Design, Aesthetics, Art History, Ceramics, Collages, †Commercial Art, Drafting, Drawing, †Handicrafts, Illustration, Jewelry, †Painting, Photography, †Sculpture, Silversmithing, Textile Design, Theatre Arts, Video
Adult Hobby Classes: Tuition $17 per cr hr. Courses—Ceramics, Fiber Art, Jewelry, Metalsmithing, Paintings, Watercolor
Summer School: Dir, Barbara Crews. Enrl 100; tuition $17 per hr. Courses—Ceramics, Drawing, Jewelry, Painting

CHEYENNE

LARAMIE COUNTY COMMUNITY COLLEGE, Division of Humanities,* 1400 E College Dr, 82007. Tel 307-634-5853, Ext 132. *Div Chmn* Thomas Neal, MA
Estab 1969; pub; D & E; scholarships; SC 19, LC 3; enrl D 80, E 180, non-maj 150, maj 10
Ent Req: HS dipl
Degrees: AA
Tuition: Res—$198 per sem; nonres—$459 per sem
Courses: Art History, Ceramics, Drafting, Drawing, Graphic Arts, Graphic Design, Jewelry, Painting, Photography, Sculpture, Silversmithing, Stage Design, Theatre Arts, Watercolor, Welded Sculpture

LARAMIE

UNIVERSITY OF WYOMING, Art Dept, PO Box 3138, University Station, 82071. Tel 307-766-3269. *Head Dept* James T Forrest, MS. Instrs: FT 8, PT 2
Estab 1886, dept estab 1946; pub; D; scholarships; SC 23, LC 6, GC 13; enrl D 120, non-maj 600, maj 120 grad 21
Ent Req: HS dipl
Degrees: BA, BS and BFA 4 yrs, MFA 3 yrs, MA and MAT 2 yrs
Tuition: Res—$716; nonres—$2226
Adult Hobby Classes: Courses offered
Summer School: Courses offered

POWELL

NORTHWEST COMMUNITY COLLEGE, 82435. Tel 307-764-6507. *Head Dept* John Banks, MA; *Instructor* Ken Fulton; *Instructor* John Giarrizzo
Estab 1946, dept estab 1952; pub; D & E; scholarships; SC 12, LC 4; enrl D 130, E 222, non-maj 317, maj 35
Ent Req: HS dipl, nonres ACT
Degrees: AA 2 yrs
Tuition: Res—undergrad $150 per sem, $13 per cr; nonres—undergrad $425 per sem, $40 per cr; campus res—room & board $1800
Courses: †Advertising Design, †Art Education, Ceramics, †Commercial Art, Drawing, †Graphic Arts, Handicrafts, †Jewelry, Lettering, †Painting, †Photography, †Printmaking, Sculpture, Silversmithing, Leather, Weaving
Adult Hobby Classes: Basic Painting, Ceramics, Drawing, Tole, Watercolor

RIVERTON

CENTRAL WYOMING COLLEGE, Art Center, 82501. Tel 307-856-9291. *Head Dept* Willis R Patterson, MFA; *Instructor* Dave Young, MFA; *Instructor* Press Stephens, MA; *Instructor* Sallie Wesaw, MFA; *Instructor* Nancy Miracle, MA
Estab 1966; pub; D & E; scholarships; SC 20, LC 2; enrl D 300, E 500, non-maj 50, maj 15, others 20
Ent Req: HS dipl, GED
Degrees: AA 2 yrs
Tuition: $336 per yr, $156 per sem, $12 per hr; special workshop fees variable; campus res—room & board $1138
Courses: Ceramics, Constructions, Drafting, Drawing, Handicrafts, Jewelry, Mixed Media, Painting, Photography, Printmaking, Sculpture, Silversmithing, Stage Design, Textile Design, Interior Design, Bronze Casting, Fiber Arts, Lapidary, Stained Glass, Stone/Wood Carving, Weaving

Adult Hobby Classes: Tuition $10 per hr. Courses—Figure Drawing, Macrame, Tole Painting, Pottery, Stained Glass, Landscape Painting
Children's Classes: Tuition variable. Courses—Crafts, Drawing, Music, Painting, Pottery, Sculpture, Theatre
Summer School: Dir, Mohammed Waheed. Enrl 150; tuition varies; term varies. Courses—special workshops as scheduled plus pottery and painting

ROCK SPRINGS

WESTERN WYOMING COLLEGE, Art Dept, 82901. Tel 307-382-2121, Ext 152. *Head Dept* Florence McEwin. Instrs: FT 2, PT 4
Estab 1959; pub; D & E; scholarships; SC 12, LC 1; enrl D 125, E 40, maj 20
Ent Req: HS dipl
Degrees: AA 2 yrs
Tuition: $17.50 per cr hr
Courses: Ceramics, Drawing, Graphic Arts, Handicrafts, History of Art & Archaeology, Painting, Photography, Sculpture, Theatre Arts
Adult Hobby Classes: Enrl 100. Courses—Crafts, Drawing, Painting, Pottery
Summer School: Dir, Dr David Katnra

SHERIDAN

SHERIDAN COLLEGE, Art Dept, 82801. Tel 307-674-6446. *Chmn* Richard Martinsen; *Instr* James Lawson; *Instr* Danna Hildebrand. Instrs: 3
Estab 1951; pub; D & E; scholarships; enrl maj 10
Ent Req: HS dipl
Degrees: AA, AS and AAS 2 yrs
Tuition: $204
Courses: Art Appreciation, Ceramics, Drawing, Graphic Arts, Painting, Photography, Sculpture, Design, Etching, Pottery, Silk Screen
Adult Hobby Classes: Enrl 40-60; tuition varies. Courses—Drawing, Painting, Pottery, Stained Glass
Children's Classes: Enrl 10-15; tuition varies. Courses—Pottery
Summer School: Enrl 10-15; tuition varies. Courses—Painting, Pottery

TORRINGTON

EASTERN WYOMING COLLEGE, Art Dept, 3200 West C St, 82240. Tel 307-532-7111. *Head Dept* Sue Milner. Instrs: FT 1, PT 2
Estab 1948; pub; D & E; scholarships; SC 3, LC 1; enrl D 60, E 50, maj 2
Ent Req: Varied
Degrees: AA and AAS 2 yrs
Tuition: Res—full time $150 per sem; non-res—full time $250 per sem
Courses: Ceramics, Drawing, Graphic Arts, History of Art & Archaeology, Painting, Photography, Sculpture
Adult Hobby Classes: Painting Workshops
Children's Classes: Enrl 50; 8 wks in summer. Courses—general subjects
Summer School: Enrl 18; term of 8 wks noncredit. Courses—Outdoor Sketching

PUERTO RICO

MAYAGUEZ

UNIVERSITY OF PUERTO RICO, MAYAGUEZ, Dept of Humanities, 00708. Tel 809-832-4040, Ext 3156 & 3160. *Dir* James L Ruzicka. Instrs: FT 6
Estab 1970; pub; D; SC 20, LC 15; enrl 402, maj 42
Ent Req: HS dipl
Degrees: BA(Art Theory) and BA(Plastic Arts) 4 yrs
Courses: Seminar in Romanesque Art

PONCE

CATHOLIC UNIVERSITY OF PUERTO RICO, Dept of Fine Arts,* 00732. Tel 809-844-4150. *Head Dept* P Pompilio Alvarez, MFA; *Prof* Ana Basso Bruno, MFA; *Prof* Mahir Laracuente, MM; *Prof* Adrian N Ramirez, MA; *Prof* Hufty E Rawson, BFA; *Prof* Julio Micheli, MFA
Estab 1948, dept estab 1964; den; D; scholarships; SC 22, LC 4; enrl D 50 maj

Ent Req: HS dipl
Degrees: BA 4 yrs
Tuition: $45 per cr hr; campus res available
Courses: Advertising Design, Aesthetics, Art Education, Art History, †Ceramics, Conceptual Art, Constructions, Drawing, Graphic Design, †Painting, †Printmaking, †Sculpture

RIO PIEDRAS

UNIVERSITY OF PUERTO RICO, Dept of Fine Arts,* Ponce de Leon Ave (Mailing add: 21847 Rio Piedras, Rio Piedras, PR 00931). *Head Dept* Luis Hernandez Cruz; *Instructor* John Balossi, MA; *Instructor* Juan Jose Barragan Banda, PhD; *Instructor* Magdalana Ferdinandy, PhD; *Instructor* Jose Buscaglia Guillermety, MA; *Instructor* Susana Herrero, MA; *Instructor* Federico Berreda Y Monge, PhD; *Instructor* Luis Hernandez Cruz,MA
Estab 1902, dept estab 1950; pub; D; scholarships; enrl D 200, maj 45
Ent Req: HS dipl
Degrees: BA 4 yrs
Tuition: $85 per yr; campus res available
Courses: Art History, Painting, Printmaking, Video

SAN GERMAN

INTER AMERICAN UNIVERSITY OF PUERTO RICO, Dept of Art, 00753. Tel 809-892-1095. *Dir* Jaime Carrero, MS; *Assoc Prof* Genoveva Ramirez de Comas, MS; *Auxiliary Prof* V Jaime Asencio-hijo, MA; *Auxiliary Prof* Paul Vivoni, MA; *Auxiliary Prof* Joyce Anne Wlodarczyk, MFA; *Instructor* Jose B Alvarez, BA; *Instructor* Fernando Santiago, MA; *Instructor* Beatriz Nazario de Sanabria, BA
Estab 1912, dept estab 1947; pvt; D; scholarships; SC 20, LC 12; enrl D 135, maj ,135
Ent Req: HS dipl, college board, presentation of portfolio
Degrees: BA 4 yrs
Tuition: Res—undergrad $50 per cr, grad $70 per cr; campus res available
Courses: †Art Education, Art History, Calligraphy, †Ceramics, Drawing, †Graphic Arts, Handicrafts, †Painting, †Photography, †Sculpture, Experimental Design in Native Media, Leather, Macrame, Metals
Adult Hobby Classes: Enrl 15; tuition $45 per course. Courses—Photography, Pottery
Summer School: Courses—Art Appreciation, Basic & Advanced & Color Photography, Painting, Theatre Workshops

SAN JUAN

INSTITUTE OF PUERTO RICAN CULTURE, Escuela de Artes Plasticas, School of Fine Arts, El Morro Grounds (Mailing add: Institute of Puerto Rican Culture, Box 4184, San Juan, PR 00905). Tel 809-725-1522. *Dir Fine Arts* Maria E Somoza
Estab 1971; pub; D; scholarships; SC 38, LC 12, GC 10; enrl D 160
Ent Req: HS dipl, ent exam
Degrees: BA 4 yrs
Tuition: None
Courses: †Sculpture, Teacher Training
Adult Hobby Classes: Enrl 137; tuition $3 per cr. Courses—Sculpture, Graphic, Painting
Summer School: Courses—Basic Drawing, Painting, Sculpture

VIRGIN ISLANDS

CHRISTANSTED SAINT CROIX

SAINT CROIX SCHOOL OF THE ARTS, INC, PO Box 1086, 00820. Tel 809-772-3767. *Executive Dir* Dorothy F Raedler; *Assoc Dir* Barabara B C Nelthropp. Instrs: PT 12
Estab 1970; pvt; D; scholarships; SC 75-85; enrl D 100
Ent Req: Recommendation
Courses: Ceramics, Design, Drawing, Painting, Creative Crafts; Woodcrafting
Children's Classes: 12 yrs & older courses same as above & 8 wk visual-performing arts workshops for 6-15 yr olds
Summer School: 8 week visual-performing arts workshops, ages 6-15

Art Schools In Canada

ALBERTA

BANFF

BANFF CENTRE SCHOOL OF FINE ARTS,* PO Box 1020, T0L 0C0. Tel 403-762-6148. *Dir Banff Centre* Dr D S R Leighton; *Manager School Fine Arts* Neil Armstrong; *Art Dept Head* Terry Johnson; *Ceramics Dept Head* Les Manning; *Fibre Dept Coordr* Inese Birstins; *Photography Dept Head* Hubert Hohn. Instrs: 37
Estab 1933 for summer study, winter cycle prog began 1979; scholarships; enrl winter 135, summer 902
Ent Req: Resume, slides of work, post-secondary art training at a university or art school and/or professional experience in field
Adult Hobby Classes: Tuition $240 per term, $480 per yr

CALGARY

ALBERTA COLLEGE OF ART, Southern Alberta Institute of Technology, 1301 16th Ave NW, T2M 0L4. Tel 403-284-8651. *Head Alberta Col Art* Arthur Meads; *Academic Supv* Howard Price; *Business Mgr* Larry Dennis; *Prog Coordr Found* Stefanie Dumanowski; *Prog Coordr Textiles* Wendy Toogood; *Prog Coordr Ceramics & Glass* Walter Drohan; *Prog Coordr Jewelry & Chmn* Orland Larson; *Prog Coordr Sculpture* Wally May; *Prog Coordr Painting* Wayne Giles; *Prog Coordr Printmaking* Gary Olson; *Prog Coordr Visual Communications & Photographic Arts* Keith Thomson
Estab 1926; pub; D & E; scholarships; SC approx 250, LC 14, GC 7; enrl D 650, E 500, non-maj 240, maj 350, others 60
Ent Req: HS dipl, admis test
Degrees: 4 yr dipl
Tuition: $455 per yr
Courses: Ceramics, Drawing, Jewelry, Painting, Photography, Printmaking, Sculpture, Textile Design, Glass, Visual Communications
Adult Hobby Classes: Enrl 500; tuition varies per course. Courses—Ceramics, Art Fundamentals, Drawing, Jewelry, Painting, Printmaking, Sculpture, Glass, Textiles, Watercolour
Children's Classes: Enrl 140; tuition $90 for 24 wks. Courses—Painting for Teenagers, Ceramics, Mixed Media, Painting, Puppetry, Sculpture

MOUNT ROYAL COLLEGE, Dept Interior Design, 4825 Richard Rd SW, T3E 6K6. Tel 403-240-6100. *Chmn* Don McLeod. Instrs: FT 5, PT 10
Estab 1910; pub; D & E; scholarships; SC 12, LC 17
Ent Req: HS dipl
Degrees: 2 yr dipl
Tuition: $300 per sem
Courses: Design, History of Art & Archaeology, Sculpture, Stage Design, Business Principles & Practices, Graphic Presentation, History of Furniture, Technical Design & Drafting

UNIVERSITY OF CALGARY, Dept of Art,* 2500 University Dr, T2N 1N4. Tel 403-284-5252. *Head* J Polzer; *Dean Faculty Fine Arts* L A Robertson. Instrs: FT 28, PT 7
Estab 1965; pub; D & E; SC 25, LC 10, GC 12; enrl D 167, E 58, all maj
Ent Req: HS dipl
Degrees: BA(Art History), BA Honours(Art History), BFA(Art)
Courses: Art Education, Art History, Ceramics, Graphic Arts, Graphic Design, Painting, Photography, Sculpture
Summer School: Dir, L Cromwell. Two terms of 6 wks, May-July. Courses—Art History, Ceramics, Design, Drawing, Graphics, Painting

EDMONTON

UNIVERSITY OF ALBERTA, Dept of Art and Design, 112 St & 88 Ave, T6G 2C9. Tel 403-432-3261. *Chmn* Jorge Frascara
Estab 1908, dept estab 1946; pub; D & E; SC 51, LC 42, grad 23; enrl D 151, grad 15-20
Ent Req: HS dipl, portfolio
Degrees: BFA 4 yrs, MA & MVA 2 yrs
Tuition: Res—undergrad $770 per yr, grad $964 per yr; nonres—grad $230 per course; campus res available
Courses: †Art History, †Graphic Design, †Industrial Design, †Painting, †Printmaking, †Sculpture
Summer School: Dir, Mr Carswell

LETHBRIDGE

UNIVERSITY OF LETHBRIDGE, Dept of Art, 4401 University Dr, T1K 3M4. Tel 403-329-2691. *Assoc Prof* Larry E Weaver, MFA; *Assoc Prof* Herbert A Hicks, MFA; *Assoc Prof* Charles Crane, MA; *Assoc Prof* Pauline McGeorge, MFA; *Assoc Prof* Carl Granzow, MFA; *Assoc Prof* Bill McCarroll, MFA; *Asst Prof* Jeffrey Spalding, MFA
Estab 1967; pub; D & E; scholarships; SC 26, LC 9
Ent Req: HS dipl
Degrees: BA and BFA 4 yrs
Courses: †Art Education, Art History, †Ceramics, Conceptual Art, Constructions, Drawing, History of Art & Archaeology, Mixed Media, †Painting, Photography, †Printmaking, †Sculpture, Theatre Arts, Video

RED DEER

RED DEER COLLEGE, Dept of Art and Design,* 56 Ave & 32 St, T4N 5H5. Tel 403-342-3300. *Pres* Dr W G Forbes. Instrs: FT 5, PT 2
Estab 1973; pub; D & E; enrl max 40 first yr students, 12 second yr
Ent Req: HS dipl, portfolio
Degrees: Dipl, BFA 2 yrs
Courses: Art History, Ceramics, Commercial Art, Drawing, Painting, Photography, Printmaking, Sculpture, Fundamentals of Visual Communication

BRITISH COLUMBIA

NELSON

DAVID THOMPSON UNIVERSITY CENTRE, Visual Arts Dept, 820 Tenth St, V1L 3C7. *Dept Head* Ric Gomez; *Instr* C Dawn, MA & MFA; *Instr* E H Underhill, PhD; *Instr* A Bain, MFA; *Instr* D J Evans, MFA; *Instr* S Kresta, Dipl; *Instr* G Mackie, Dipl; *Instr* S Stevenson, MA; *Instr* M Zmur, Dipl; *Instr* I Irwin; *Instr* N Wade, MFA
Estab 1960. Co-sponsored by Selkirk College and University of Victoria; pub; D & E; enrl D 165, E 40, maj 35
Ent Req: HS dipl, portfolio
Tuition: Res $250 per sem
Courses: Advertising Design, Art Education, Art History, †Ceramics, Collages, Commercial Art, Conceptual Art, Constructions, Display, Drawing, †Applied Design

VANCOUVER

EMILY CARR COLLEGE OF ART & DESIGN, 1399 Johnston St, V6H 3R9. Tel 604-687-2345. *Prin* Robin C Mayor; *Dir Student Services* Thomas W Kowall; *Dean Instruction* Tom Hudson
Estab 1925; pub; D & E; SC 20, LC 8; enrl 500, maj 300, grad 9
Ent Req: HS dipl plus presentation of folio of art work
Degrees: 4 yr dipl
Tuition: $620 per yr
Courses: Art History, Ceramics, Conceptual Art, Design, Drawing, Film, Graphic Design, Photography, Printmaking, Sculpture, Video, Animation, Interdisciplinary Studies
Adult Hobby Classes: Enrl 886; tuition $100 per 3 months. Courses—Fine Art, Design
Summer School: Dir, Isabel Spalding. Enrl 200; tuition $150-$250 per 4 wks term. Courses—Fine Arts, Design

UNIVERSITY OF BRITISH COLUMBIA
—**Dept of Fine Arts,** 6333 Memorial Rd, V6T 1W5. Tel 604-228-5650. *Head* James O Caswell, PhD; *Prof* Roy Kiyooka; *Prof* Alan Sawyer, PhD; *Prof* Geoffrey Smedley, DFA; *Prof* George Knox, PhD; *Assoc Prof* Richard Prince; *Assoc Prof* Mary Morehart, PhD; *Assoc Prof* Debra Pincus, PhD; *Assoc Prof* W Herbert Gilbert, BA; *Assoc Prof* Marvin Cohodas, PhD; *Assoc Prof* Rhodri Windsor-Liscombe, PhD; *Asst Prof* Penelope Brownell, PhD; *Asst Prof* Moritaka Matsumoto, PhD; *Asst Prof* Barbara Z Sungur, MFA; *Asst Prof* Wendy Dobereiner, MA; *Asst Prof* Serge Guilbaut, PhD; *Asst Prof* David H Solkin, PhD; *Asst Prof* Judith Williams, BA; *Asst Prof* Joanna Woods-Marsden, PhD; *Asst Prof* Robert Young, BA; *Instr* I Marc Pessin, MA; *Instr* Doreen E Walker, MA
Courses: Art History, Drawing, Painting, †Photography, †Printmaking, Sculpture, Western, Asian, †Indigenous Arts of the Americas

—**School of Architecture,** V6T 1W5. Tel 604-228-2779. *Dir* Douglas Shadbolt.
Instrs: FT 14
Estab 1946; pub
Degrees: BArchit, MArchit, 3 yrs
Tuition: $1252 per session
Courses: Architecture

VANCOUVER COMMUNITY COLLEGE, LANGARA CAMPUS, Dept of Fine
Arts, 100 W 49th Ave, V5Y 2Z6. Tel 604-324-5511. *Chmn Dept* Michael Minot,
Dipl Art; *Instr* Catherine Broderick-Lockhart, MFA; *Instr* Gordon Caruso, Dipl Art;
Instr Gerald Formosa, Dipl Art; *Instr* Don Hutchinson, Dipl Art; *Instr* Barry
Holmes, Nat Dipl
Estab 1970; pub; D & E; scholarships; SC 7, LC 1; enrl D 160
Ent Req: HS dipl, portfolio
Degrees: 2 yr Fine Arts Dipl
Tuition: $200-$250 per sem, plus $5 material fees per each $25; no campus res
Courses: Ceramics, Design, Drawing, Painting, Printmaking, Sculpture
Adult Hobby Classes: Enrl 20 per class; tuition $60 per sem. Courses—Design,
Drawing

VICTORIA

UNIVERSITY OF VICTORIA
—**Dept of Visual Arts,** PO Box 1700, V8W 2Y2. Tel 604-721-8011. *Chmn & Prof* R
Brener, Post Dipl, AD; *Prof* P Martin Bates, Dipl Royale, RCA; *Prof* D Harvey,
ATD, RCA; *Prof* D Morton, RCA; *Assoc Prof* M Baden, MA; *Assoc Prof* G
Tiessen, MFA; *Asst Prof* G Curry, MFA; *Asst Prof* F Douglas; *Asst Prof* J Irwin,
MFA; *Asst Prof* N Wade, BFA
Estab 1963; pub; D; enrl 210, maj 18, hons 16
Ent Req: HS dipl
Degrees: BFA, MFA
Tuition: Campus res available
Courses: †Drawing, †Painting, †Photography, †Printmaking, †Sculpture
Summer School: Courses—Drawing, Painting, Printmaking
—**Dept of History in Art,** V8W 2Y2. Tel 604-721-7941. *Chmn* Charles R Wicke,
PhD; *Prof* Siri Gunasinghe, Doctorate; *Prof* S Anthony Welch, PhD; *Prof* Alan
Gowans, PhD; *Asst Prof* John L Osborne, PhD; *Asst Prof* Judith Patt, PhD; *Asst
Prof* Elizabeth Tumasonis, PhD; *Lecturer* M Phil; *Lecturer* Barrie McLean; *Lecturer*
Martin Segger
LC 52, grad 16
Degrees: BA(Art History), MA(Art History)
Tuition: Undergrad—$465 per term, grad—$585 per term
Courses: Art and Architecture from Ancient to Modern Times in the Western
World; Pre-Columbian Americas; The Near East; South and Southeast Asia; The Far
East
Summer School: July 5 - Aug 17

MANITOBA

WINNIPEG

UNIVERSITY OF MANITOBA
—**School of Art,** R3T 2N2. Tel 204-474-9303. *Dir* Charles W Scott, MFA; *Chmn
Drawing* Alex Bruning, MA; *Chmn Painting* Don Reichert, BFA; *Chmn Ceramics*
Robert W Archambeau, MFA; *Chmn Sculpture* Gordon Reeve, MFA; *Chmn
Photography* David McMillan, MFA; *Chmn Graphic Design* Edward Dore, BFA;
Chmn Printmaking Arnold Saper, MFA; *Chmn Art History* Marilyn Baker, PhD;
Chmn Foundations Richard Williams, MFA
Estab 1950; pub; D; SC 35, LC 16; enrl D 420
Ent Req: HS dipl and portfolio
Degrees: BFA 3 yrs, BFA (Art History) 3 yrs, BFA Honors 4 yrs, BFA Honors (Art
History) 4 yrs, Dipl in Art 4 yrs
Tuition: Varies per yr; campus res available
Courses: †Art History, †Ceramics, †Drawing, †Graphic Design, †Painting,
†Photography, †Printmaking, †Sculpture
Adult Hobby Classes: Courses offered
Summer School: Dir, Charles W Scott. Term of 6 wks. Courses—Studio & Art
History Courses
—**Faculty of Architecture,** R3T 2N2. Tel 204-474-9286. *Dean* Harlyn Thompson;
Assoc Dean M Carvalho; *Head Environmental Studies* Rory Fonseca; *Head
Landscape Archit* Alexander Rattray; *Head Dept Interior Design* Michael Cox;
Head Dept City Planning Earl Levin
Estab 1913; pub; scholarships; enrl Environmental Studies 218, Archit 110, Interior
Design 284, City Planning 72, Landscape 60
Ent Req: Senior matriculation or Bachelor for particular subject
Degrees: Interior Design 4 yrs, Archit, Landscape Archit and City Planning 6 yrs
Courses: Architecture, Interior Design, Landscape Architecture, City Planning,
Environmental Studies

NEW BRUNSWICK

EDMUNDSTON

SAINT-LOUIS-MAILLET, Dept of Visual Arts,* E3V 2S8. Tel 506-735-8804.
Chief Robert LaFlamme
Estab 1946, dept estab 1968; pub; D & E; scholarships; SC 12, LC 1; enrl D 20, E
11, non-maj 25, maj 6

Ent Req: HS dipl
Degrees: BA(Fine Arts) 4 yrs
Tuition: $620 per yr; campus res—room & board $475 per yr
Courses: Art History, Ceramics, Drawing, Painting, Sculpture
Children's Classes: Enrl 60; tuition $20 per sem. Courses—Painting

FREDERICTON

NEW BRUNSWICK CRAFT SCHOOL AND CENTRE, PO Box 6000, E3B 5H1.
Tel 506-453-2305. *Dir of Craft* George F Fry; *Dir of Studies* Anne Fox
Estab 1946; pub; D; enrl 70 plus PT
Ent Req: HS dipl, transcript, questionnaire and interview
Degrees: 3 yr dipl
Tuition: New Brunswick students $520 plus materials; others $950 plus materials; no
campus res
Courses: Art History, †Ceramics, Design, Costume Design & Construction, Drawing,
†Jewelry, †Photography, †Silversmithing, †Textile Design, †Enameling, Colour,
†Wood
Summer School: Enrl 1000; tuition $5 for 1 day beginning July through Aug.
Courses—Crafts

UNIVERSITY OF NEW BRUNSWICK, Art Education Section,* Faculty of
Education, PO Box 4400, E3B 5A3. Tel 506-453-4995. *Dir Art Centre* Bruno
Bobak; *Dean Art Faculty* Peter G Kepros
Tuition: Res—$950 per yr
Courses: Art Appreciation, Printmaking, †Art Education for Elementary Teachers,
Crafts for Schools, Pottery and Clay Sculpture
Adult Hobby Classes: Pottery
Summer School: Pottery, Crafts and Children's Art

MONCTON

UNIVERSITE DE MONCTON, Department of Visual Arts, E1A 3E9. Tel 506-
858-4033. Instrs: 7
Estab 1967; pub; D & E; SC 7, LC 3; enrl D 80, E 40, grad 10
Ent Req: HS dipl
Degrees: BA(Fine Arts) 4 yrs
Courses: Aesthetics, Art Education, †Ceramics, Drawing, Graphic Arts, †Graphic
Design, †History of Art & Archaeology, †Painting, †Photography, †Printmaking,
Sculpture, †Teacher Training
Adult Hobby Classes: Evening only

SACKVILLE

MOUNT ALLISON UNIVERSITY, Fine Arts Dept, E0A 3C0. Tel 506-536-2040,
Ext 492. *Head Dept* Virgil Hammock, MFA; *Prof* David Silverberg, BA; *Prof* John
Asimakos; *Assoc Prof* M J A Crooker, MA; *Assoc Prof* Thomas Henderson, MFA;
Assoc Prof Rebecca Burke, MFA; *Asst Prof* Thaddeus Holownia; *Asst Prof* Jean
Maddison, MFA
Estab 1858; pub; D & E; SC 17, LC 5; enrl 80
Ent Req: HS dipl
Degrees: BFA 4 yrs
Tuition: Campus residence available
Courses: †Art History, †Drawing, Intermedia, †Painting, †Photography,
†Printmaking, †Sculpture
Summer School: Courses—Adult Workshop, Art Criticism, High School Workshop,
Photography, Painting, Sculpture

NOVA SCOTIA

ANTIGONISH

ST FRANCIS XAVIER UNIVERSITY, Fine Arts Dept,* B2Q 1C0. Tel 902-863-
3300. *Assoc Prof* T Roach; *Instr* Dr J Grant
Courses: Art History, Drawing, Painting, Composition & Painting, General Studies I
& II

HALIFAX

NOVA SCOTIA COLLEGE OF ART AND DESIGN, 5163 Duke St, B3J 3J6. Tel
902-422-7381. *Pres* Garry Neill Kennedy, MFA; *Dean* Alan Barkley, MFA; *Chmn
Craft Div* Joyce Chown, MFA; *Chmn Studio Div* Gerald Ferguson, MFA; *Chmn
Art Educ Div* Harold Pearse, MA; *Chmn Art History Div* Dennis Young, BA;
Chmn Design Div Frank Fox, ARCA; *Chmn MFA Div* Eric Cameron, BA
Estab 1887; pvt; D & E; SC 67, LC 31, GC 8 each sem; enrl 500, grad 17
Ent Req: HS dipl, portfolio or project
Degrees: BFA, BD(Environmental Planning or Graphic Design) and BA(Art Educ),
MFA and MA(Art Educ)
Tuition: $740 per sem; Visa students $1397; no campus res
Courses: Art Education, Art History, Ceramics, Drawing, Graphic Arts, Graphic
Design, Jewelry, Mixed Media, Painting, Photography, Printmaking, Sculpture,
Textile Design, Video, Environmental Planning, Weaving
Adult Hobby Classes: Tuition $10-$80 per sem. Courses—Ceramics, Drawing,
Fabrics, Jewelry, Painting, Photography, Spinning & Dyeing
Children's Classes: Tuition none. Courses—Art
Summer School: Dean, Alan Barkley. Tuition $740 ($1347 Visa students) for term
of 14 wks beginning May 15. Half sessions offered

TECHNICAL UNIVERSITY OF NOVA SCOTIA (Formerly Nova Scotia Technical College), Faculty of Architecture, Spring Garden Rd, PO Box 1000, B3J 2X4. Tel 902-429-8300. *Dean* E Baniassao, PhD; *Asst Dean* K Hurley; *Instructor* O Biskaps; *Instructor* F Eppell; *Instructor* A Frost; *Instructor* A Wilkie; *Instructor* S Hamed; *Instructor* A Jackson; *Instructor* J Love; *Instructor* M Macalik; *Instructor* P Manning; *Instructor* P McAleer; *Instructor* A Penny; *Instructor* D Procos; *Instructor* M Poulton; *Instructor* M Rubinger; *Instructor* G Wanzel
Estab 1911, faculty estab 1961; pvt; D; scholarships; enrl approx 200, maj 200, grad 2
Ent Req: Previous 2 yrs at univ
Degrees: BArchit 4 yrs, MArchit 1 yr minimum
Tuition: $1250 per year; differential for foreign students
Courses: Art Education, Art History, Constructions, Drafting, Photography
Summer School: Three terms per yr

WOLFVILLE

ACADIA UNIVERSITY, Art Dept, B0P 1X0. Tel 902-542-2201. *Chmn* Michael Coyne, MFA; *Prof* Ian James, MFA
Scholarships
Tuition: $1110
Courses: Art History, Drawing, Painting

ONTARIO

CORNWALL

ST LAWRENCE COLLEGE, Dept of Visual and Creative Arts,* K6H 5R8. Tel 613-933-6080. *Chmn* Dora Campbell; *Instr* Robert Blair; *Instr* Robert Taillefer; *Instr* Robin Wall, BFA
Estab 1967, dept estab 1969; pub; D & E
Ent Req: Hs dipl and portfolio
Degrees: Diploma(Visual & Creative Arts) 3 yrs
Tuition: Res—grad $495; campus res—room $450
Courses: Art History, Ceramics, Commercial Art, Drawing, †Graphic Design, Illustration, Jewelry, Mixed Media, †Painting, †Photography, Printmaking, Sculpture, Silversmithing

DOWNSVIEW

YORK UNIVERSITY, Dept of Visual Arts, Fine Arts Bldg, 4700 Keele St, M3J 1P3. Tel 416-667-3241. *Chairperson* Andrew M Tomcik. Instrs: FT 28, PT 13
Estab 1969; pub; D & E; scholarships; SC 53, LC 17; enrl D over 400, maj 400, others approx 120
Ent Req: HS dipl, interview and portfolio evaluation
Degrees: BA(Hons), BFA(Hons) 4 yrs, MA, MFA
Tuition: Res—$1035; nonres—$2055
Courses: Design, Drawing, Graphic Arts, Painting, Photography, Sculpture, Experimental Directions
Children's Classes: Enrl 30; tuition $5 for 8 wks
Summer School: Chairperson, Andrew W Tomcik. Enrl 100; tuition $41 per cr for 6 wk course. Courses—Art History - Italy, Drawing, Matrix, Painting

GUELPH

UNIVERSITY OF GUELPH, Fine Art Dept, Gordon St, N1G 2W1. Tel 519-824-4120, Ext 2413. *Chmn* George Todd, PhD
Estab 1966; pub; D; SC 30, LC 30; enrl 959, maj 250
Ent Req: HS dipl
Degrees: BA 3 yrs, BA(Hons) 4 yrs
Tuition: Res—undergrad $524 per sem; nonres—undergrad $1350 per sem; campus res available
Courses: Art History, Drawing, Painting, Printmaking, Sculpture

HAMILTON

MCMASTER UNIVERSITY, Dept of Art and Art History,* 1280 Main St W, L8S 4L8. Tel 416-525-9140, ext 4417. *Chmn Dept* G Wallace. Instrs: FT 10
Estab 1934; SC 12, LC 29; enrl 85
Degrees: BA(Studio and Art History), Hons BA(Studio and Art History) 3-4 yrs
Tuition: $1014 per yr; campus res available
Courses: †Art History, †Studio Art Program
Summer School: Summer evening classes May to Aug; summer days July to Aug

KINGSTON

QUEEN'S UNIVERSITY, Dept of Art, K7L 3N6. Tel 613-547-6172. *Head Dept* Bruce Laughton. Instrs: FT 16, PT 5
Estab 1932; pub; D & E; SC 16, LC 25
Ent Req: Grade XIII
Degrees: BA 3 yrs, BA(Hons) and BFA 4 yrs, MA(Conservation), MA(Art History)
Tuition: University admission and fees apply; campus residence available
Courses: Art History, Drawing, Painting, Printmaking, Sculpture, Design
Adult Hobby Classes: Evening classes available
Summer School: Courses offered

LONDON

UNIVERSITY OF WESTERN ONTARIO, Dept of Visual Arts, N6A 5K7. Tel 519-679-2440. *Chmn* D deKergommeaux. Instrs: FT 12, PT 2
Estab 1967; pub; D & E; SC 11, LC 15; enrl maj 160
Ent Req: HS dipl, portfolio and/or interview
Degrees: BA 3 yrs, BA(Hons) and BFA 4 yrs
Tuition: $783
Courses: Drawing, †History of Art & Archaeology, Museum Staff Training, †Painting, †Photography, †Printmaking, †Sculpture
Summer School: Enrl limited; term of 6 wks beginning July. Courses—Visual Arts

OTTAWA

CARLETON UNIVERSITY, Dept of Art History,* Colonel By Dr, K1S 5B6. Tel 613-231-7156. *Chmn* Dr M Marshall. Instrs: FT 5, PT 5
Estab 1964; D & E; scholarships; SC 2, LC 25, GC 3; enrl D over 700, maj 135
Ent Req: HS dipl
Degrees: BA 6 Hons 3-4 yrs
Courses: History of Art & Archaeology
Summer School: Chmn, Dr M Marshall. Courses—Art History

REXDALE

HUMBER COLLEGE OF APPLIED ARTS AND TECHNOLOGY, Creative and Communication Arts Division,* Humber College Blvd, PO Box 1900, M9W 5L7. Tel 416-675-3111. *Dean* Larry Holmes
Estab 1967; pub; D & E; SC 300, LC 75, GC 6; enrl grad 50, PT 25
Ent Req: HS dipl, mature student status, one yr of employment plus 19 yrs of age
Degrees: None, 2 & 3 yr dipl courses
Tuition: $490 per yr
Courses: Ceramics, Drafting, Drawing, Film, Graphic Arts, Graphic Design, History of Art & Archaeology, Industrial Design, Interior Design, Landscape Architecture, Painting, Photography, Furniture Design, Packaging Design, TV Production
Adult Hobby Classes: Enrl 210. Beginning classes in most of regular courses
Summer School: Dean Creative Arts, Larry Holmes. Term of 10-16 wks beginning May and June. Courses—Beginning and advanced classes in most of regular courses

SOUTHAMPTON

SOUTHAMPTON ART SCHOOL, 20 Albert St, N0H 2L0. *Dir* Edna Johnson; *Instr* Herbert Ariss; *Instr* Corbett Gray; *Instr* Roly Fenivick
Estab 1958 as a summer school; pub; D, July and Aug
Tuition: Adults $70 per wk; students (14-18) $50 per wk; children (10-13) $20 per wk, half days only; no campus res
Courses: Art Education, Drawing, Mixed Media, Painting

THUNDER BAY

LAKEHEAD UNIVERSITY, Dept of Fine Art,* Oliver Rd, P7B 5E1. Tel 807-345-2121. *Dean of Faculty of Arts* Ernest Robert Zimmerman; *Lectr* Mark Nisenholt, MFA. Instrs: FT 1, PT 7
Estab 1965, dept estab 1976; pub; D & E
Ent Req: HS dipl, portfolio
Degrees: BA, Honours BA, MA
Tuition: Res—undergrad $1007.50 per yr, PT $195 per course; non-res—undergrad $2222.50 per yr, $365 per course; campus res—room & board $2268
Courses: Art History, Ceramics, Drawing, Painting, Printmaking, Theatre Arts
Adult Hobby Classes: Credit and non-credit courses vary from session to session
Summer School: Credit and non-credit courses vary from session to session

TORONTO

GEORGE BROWN COLLEGE OF APPLIED ARTS AND TECHNOLOGY, Box 1015, Station B, M5T 2T9. Tel 416-967-1212. *Chmn* E K Walker. Instrs: FT 11, PT 9
Estab 1970; D & E; enrl D 300, E 800
Ent Req: HS grade 12 dipl, entr exam
Degrees: 3 yr dipl
Courses: Advertising Design, Calligraphy, Commercial Art, Drawing, Graphic Design, Illustration, Painting, Air Brush Techniques, Cartooning, Marker Rendering Techniques, Photo Retouching, Soapstone Carving, Watercolor

ONTARIO COLLEGE OF ART, 100 McCaul St, M5T 1W1. Tel 416-977-5311. *Pres* Norman B Hathaway, KLJ & AOCA & MGDC; *Registrar* Robert T Begley, HBSc & MSc; *Assoc Registrar* Mary Brimicombe, ADMS; *Business Adminr* John Stewart, BASc & MBA & MPA & PENG; *Dir Information Services* Ruth Hammond, APR; *Financial Aid Officer* Suzanne Coxon, BA; *Chmn Dept Foundation Studies* David Hall-Humpherson, AOCA; *Chmn Dept Commun & Design* Beresford Mitchell, AOCA; *Chmn Dept Design* Joan Burt, BArch, MRAIC; *Chmn Dept Experimental Art* Gustav Weisman, OSA & RCA; *Actg Chmn Dept Fine Art* Dainis Miezats, AOCA & CSPWC; *Chmn Dept Photo & Electric Arts* Richard Hill, PhilM; *Actg Chmn Dept Lib Arts Studies* Arturo Nagel, MFA; *Chmn Dept Technol Studies* Michael Harmes, NDD; *Chmn Industrial Design* Claude Gidman, BA & ACD; *Sr Advisor* Mary Egan Haines, BID, AXA
Estab 1876; pub; D & E; scholarships; SC approx 450; enrl D 1300, E 2000, grad 25, summer 900
Ent Req: HS dipl, interview
Degrees: Diplomia AOCA 4 yrs
Tuition: $964 per yr; $131 per course; yearly fees for applicants outside Canada $4222; no campus res
Courses: †Advertising Design, Art History, †Ceramics, Collages, †Commercial Art, Conceptual Art, Display, †Drawing, Film, †Graphic Arts, †Graphic Design, History

of Art & Archaeology, †Illustration, †Industrial Design, †Interior Design, Jewelry, Mixed Media, †Painting, Photography, †Printmaking, Silversmithing, Stage Design, †Textile Design, Video, Animation, Batik, Color, Composition, †Corporate Design, Costume Illustration, Design Management, †Editorial Design, †Environmental Design, †Experimental Arts, Foundry, †Glass, Holography, Light, Materials and Processes, Metal Work, Moldmaking, †Multimedia Printing, Packaging, †Photo/Electric Arts, Plastics, Systems Design, Typography, Watercolour, Woodworking, Product Design, Systems Design, Typography, Woodworking
Adult Hobby Classes: Enrl 2000; tuition $131 per course for 3 hrs per wk for 30 weeks. Courses—Advertising Design, Art History, Ceramics, Color, Corporate Design, Drawing, Editorial Design, Environmental Design, Glass, Graphics, History of Ceramics & Glass, History of Furniture, Illustration, Industrial Design, Painting, Photography, Printmaking, Sculpture, Textiles, Typography, Watercolor, Woodworking
Summer School: Registrar, R T Begley. Enrl 900; tuition $131 per course for term of 3 wks (5 days a week) or 15 wks (2 evenings a week) beginning May. Courses—Advertising Design, Art History, Ceramics, Color, Corporate Design, Drawing, Editorial Design, Environmental, Glass, Graphics, History of Ceramics & Glass, History of Furniture, Illustration, Industrial Design, Painting, Photography, Printmaking, Sculpture, Textiles, Typography, Watercolor, Woodworking

TORONTO ART THERAPY INSTITUTE, 216 St Clair Ave W, M4V 1R2. Tel 416-921-4374. *Executive Dir* Martin Fischer, MD & DPsych; *Senior Art Therapist* Gilda S Grossman, MSWD; *Chmn Educ Committee* Morton Manilla, PhD; *Lectr* Guiliana Katz, PhD
Estab 1968; D & E
Degrees: Dipl, BA and MA(Art Therapy) through affiliation with other US colleges; graduate level certificate program in art therapy
Adult Hobby Classes: Enrl 6-12; tuition $30 per session. Courses—workshops
Children's Classes: Enrl 6-12; tuition $15 per session. Courses—workshops

TORONTO SCHOOL OF ART, * 225 Brunswick Ave, M5S 2M6. Tel 416-921-3986. *Dir* Barbara Barrett, BA
Estab 1969; pvt; D & E; scholarships; enrl D & E 200
Ent Req: None
Tuition: No campus res
Courses: Drawing, Graphic Arts, Illustration, Mixed Media, Painting, Photography, Printmaking, Sculpture

UNIVERSITY OF TORONTO
—**Dept of Fine Art,** * Sidney Smith Hall, M5S 1A1. Tel 416-978-6272. *Chmn* R P Welsh. Instrs: FT 14, PT 4
Estab 1934; pub; LC, GC
Degrees: BA, MA, PhD
Tuition: Campus res available
Courses: Art Appreciation, Art History, Design, Drawing, Painting, Printmaking
—**School of Architecture,** * 230 College St, M5S 1A1. Tel 416-978-5038. *Dir* Blanche Lemco van Ginkel, MCP; *Assoc Prof* John Hall, OSA CSGA
Estab 1948; pub; D; SC 5, LC 33, GC 11; enrl 299, non-maj 6, maj 293, grad 13
Ent Req: HS dipl, portfolio of work and interview
Degrees: BArchit 5 yrs, MArchit 1 yr for Studio (minimum 2 yrs for research)
Tuition: Campus res available
Courses: Architecture, Drawing, Photography
—**Dept of Landscape Architecture,** * 230 College St, M5S 1A1. Tel 416-978-3103. *Chmn* William Rock Jr, MLA; *Assoc Prof* Edward Fife, MLA; *Assoc Prof* John Danahy, BLA; *Assoc Prof* Gerald Englar, MLA; *Asst Prof* Madis Pihlak, MCP; *Asst Prof* James Belisle, MArch; *Asst Prof* Mark Lindhult, BSc; *Asst Prof* Fidenzio Salvatori, MLA
Estab 1827, dept estab 1965; pub; D; scholarships; enrl 160, maj 140
Ent Req: Grad 13 dipl
Degrees: BLA 4 yr
Tuition: Non-res—undergrad $1163; campus res available
Courses: Aesthetics, Architecture, Art History, Constructions, Drafting, Drawing, Film, Graphic Arts, Landscape Architecture, Landscape Architecture Technology, Landscape Planning, Planting Design

WATERLOO

UNIVERSITY OF WATERLOO, Fine Arts Dept, 200 University Ave W, N2L 3G1. Tel 519-885-4280. *Dean* R K Banks; *Chmn Dept* A M Urquhart, BFA; *Prof* Virgil Burnett, MA; *Prof* Nancy-Lou Patterson, MA; *Assoc Prof* Don MacKay, MFA; *Assoc Prof* Jan Uhde, PhD; *Asst Prof* Basia Irland, MFA; *Asst Prof* Eve Kliman, PhD; *Asst Prof* Art Green, BFA
Estab 1958, dept estab 1968; pub; D & E; SC 32, LC 27; enrl maj 75
Ent Req: HS dipl
Degrees: BA 3 yrs, BA(Hons) 4 yrs
Tuition: $783 per yr; campus res available
Courses: Art History, Calligraphy, Ceramics, Drawing, Film, Illustration, Painting, Photography, Printmaking, Sculpture
Summer School: Enrl 30. Courses—Painting, Drawing, Sculpture

WINDSOR

UNIVERSITY OF WINDSOR, School of Visual Arts, Huron Church Rd at College, N9B 3P4. Tel 519-253-4232, Ext 359. *Dir* Robert C Ferraro. Instrs: FT 10, PT 5
Estab 1960; pub; D & E; scholarships; SC 22, LC 18; enrl D 138, E approx 65, maj 170, others 33
Ent Req: HS dipl grade 13, adult
Degrees: BA 3 yrs, BA(Hons) and BFA 4 yrs, MFA 2 yrs
Tuition: 607 per sem
Courses: Art History, Drawing, Painting, Printmaking, Sculpture
Summer School: Dir, Robert C Ferraro. Enrl 100; tuition $110 per sem for term of 6 wks beginning July. Courses—Art Fundamentals, Art History, Drawing, Painting, Ceramics, Printmaking

PRINCE EDWARD ISLAND

CHARLOTTETOWN

HOLLAND COLLEGE, School of Visual Arts, Burns Ave, West Royalty, C1E 1H7. Tel 902-566-2401. *Dir* Henry Purdy
Estab 1977; scholarships; enrl D 100
Tuition: $425 per yr
Courses: Commercial Art, Photography, Fabric Art, Leather, Pottery, Weaving, Wood
Adult Hobby Classes: Tuition $425 per yr. Courses—Commercial Design, Fabric Arts, Leather, Photography, Pottery, Leather, Weaving, Wood
Summer School: Dir, Henry Purdy. Tuition $75 for one week. Courses—Drawing, Painting, Papermaking, Weaving, Wood

QUEBEC

MONTREAL

CONCORDIA UNIVERSITY, Faculty of Fine Arts, 1395 Dorchester W, H3G 2M5. Tel 514-879-4384. *Dean Faculty Fine Arts* Anthony Emery
D & E
Ent Req: HS dipl, CEGEP dipl Prov of Quebec
Degrees: BFA, BA, post-BFA Dipl in Art Educ & Art Therapy, full-time leading to teaching cert, MA(Art Educ), MFA(Studio or Art History), PhD(Art Educ)
Courses: †Art Education, †Art History, †Graphic Design, Painting, Photography, Sculpture, †Theatre Arts, †Art Therapy, †Cinema Design, †Crafts, †Music
Adult Hobby Classes: Courses offered
Children's Classes: Sat morning classes
Summer School: Courses offered

MCGILL UNIVERSITY
—**Department of Art History,** 853 Sherbrooke West, H3A 2T6. Tel 514-392-4977. *Chmn* R Bertos, PhD; *Prof* G Galavaris, PhD; *Assoc Prof* R Bergmann, PhD; *Assoc Prof* T Glen, PhD; *Asst Prof* Mark A Cheetham
Pvt; D; teaching assistantships; SC 2, LC 7, GC 4, seminars 2
Ent Req: HS dipl or CEGEP Dipl
Degrees: BA 3 yrs, MA 2 yrs, PhD 2 yrs
Tuition: Varies; campus res available
Courses: Drawing, †History of Art & Archaeology, Painting
—**School of Architecture,** * 3484 University St, H3A 2T6. *Dir* Derek Drummond. Instrs: FT 10, PT 9
Estab 1896; fels; SC 12, LC 7
Ent Req: Ent exam
Degrees: BArchit 6 yrs
Courses: Art History, Drawing, Architectural Design, History of Architecture

UNIVERSITE DE MONTREAL, Dept of Art History,* 3150 Jean-Brillant, CP 6128, Succursale A, H3C 3J7. Tel 514-343-6182. *Prof* Nicole Dubreuil-Blondin, Doctorate; *Dir Dept Art History* Lise Lamarche
Dept estab 1961; pvt; D & E; SC 20, LC 70, GC 10; enrl D 270, non-maj 113, maj 106, grad 80, others 151
Ent Req: HS dipl
Degrees: BA
Tuition: Campus res available

UNIVERSITE DU QUEBEC A MONTREAL, Famille des Arts,* CP 8888, succursale A, H3C 3P8. Tel 514-282-3182. *Recteur* Claude Pichette
Estab 1969
Ent Req: 2 yrs after HS
Degrees: Baccalaureat specialise 3 yrs; Master Degrees in Visual Arts; programs in Environmental Design, Graphic Design, History of Art, Visual Arts (engraving, sculpture, painting)
Courses: Drawing, Painting, Teacher Training, Architectural Drafting, Ceramic Sculpture, Design, Etching and Engraving, Graphic Techniques, Modeling, Mural Painting, Scenography
Adult Hobby Classes: Certificate in visual arts available
Children's Classes: Saturday courses

QUEBEC

UNIVERSITE LAVAL CITE UNIVERSITAIRE, School of Visual Arts,* Faculte des Arts, G1K 7P4. Tel 418-656-7631. *Dir Visual Arts* Bernard Jasmin; *Faculty Dean of Arts* Jean Charles Blouin
Estab 1970; pub; D; enrl 300
Ent Req: 2 yrs col
Degrees: BA(Arts Plastiques or Communication Graphique)
Tuition: Res—undergrad $534-$684 per yr, $20 per quarter
Courses: Drawing, Film, Graphic Arts, Graphic Design, Illustration, Painting, Photography, Sculpture, Engraving, Lithography, Silk Screen, Stained Glass, Tapestry

TROIS RIVIERES

UNIVERSITY OF QUEBEC, TROIS RIVIERES, Fine Arts Section,* 3351 boul des Forges, PO Box 500, G9A 5H7. Tel 817-379-1740. *Dir* Christian Demers; *Dir Module d'arts plastiques* Pierre Landry
Estab 1969; pub; D & E; SC 12, LC 8, GC 28; enrl D 150, E 100
Ent Req: Ent exam or DEC

Degrees: Specialized BA(Fine Arts)
Courses: Aesthetics, Art Education, Ceramics, Drafting, Drawing, Graphic Arts, History of Art & Archaeology, Painting, Sculpture, Art Administration, Basic Design, Glass, Weaving
Adult Hobby Classes: Enrl 100. Courses—Painting, Weaving
Summer School: Dir, Henri-Georges St-Louis. Course of 3 wks

SASKATCHEWAN

REGINA

UNIVERSITY OF REGINA
—**Dept of Visual Arts,** S4S 0A2. Tel 306-584-4872. *Acting Head* J Sures. Instrs: FT 8
Pub; enrl 308
Ent Req: HS grad
Degrees: 2 yr cert, BA 3 yrs, BFA 4 yrs, MFA 2 yrs
Tuition: $118 per 4 cr hr course
Courses: Art History, Ceramics, Drawing, Painting, Printmaking, Sculpture

—**Dept of Art Education,*** Faculty of Education, S4S 0A2. Tel 306-584-4546. *Dean of Art* R R Robinson; *Assoc Dean Col Fine Arts* R J W Swales. Instrs: FT 9
Estab 1965; pub; D & E; scholarships; LC 6; enrl D 160, E 20, maj 10
Ent Req: HS dipl, matriculation or degree for maj in art
Degrees: BFA(Visual Arts), cert in Visual Arts
Tuition: $24.50 per cr hr
Courses: Aesthetics, Art Education
Children's Classes: Sat
Summer School: Exten Courses, H Kindred; Dean Educ, Dr Toombs. Term of 3 to 6 wks beginning May

SASKATOON

UNIVERSITY OF SASKATCHEWAN, Dept of Art & Art History, S7N 0W0. Tel 306-343-4528. *Head* Paul C Hamilton. Instrs: FT 12, PT 1
Estab 1936; pub; D; scholarships; SC, LC, GC; enrl approx 880, BFA prog 130, grad 5
Ent Req: HS grad
Degrees: BA 3 yrs, BAHons(Art History), BA(Advanced) 4 yrs, BFA 4 yrs, MA(Studio Art), BEd(Art)
Tuition: $204 per class; 5 classes per acad yr, 1 class during intersession and 1 class during summer school
Courses: Art Education, Art History, Drawing, Painting, Photography, Printmaking, Sculpture, Survey Studio
Summer School: Emma Lake Campus and Saskatoon Campus. Courses—vary per yr

III ART INFORMATION

Major Museums Abroad

Major Art Schools Abroad

State Arts Councils

Directors and Supervisors of Art Education
in School Systems

Art Magazines

Newspapers Carrying Art Notes
and Their Critics

Scholarships and Fellowships

Open Exhibitions

Traveling Exhibition Booking Agencies

Major Museums Abroad

ARGENTINA

BUENOS AIRES

M **CENTRO DE ARTE Y COMMUNICACION,** Center of Art and Communication, Elpidio Gonzalez 4070, 1407. Tel 566-8046, 566-8066. *Pres* Jorge Glusberg
Collections: Catalogs and bulletins on every art exhibition and seminars held by the Center in Argentina and abroad; 150 motion pictures on art, architecture; photograph collection of 7000 Latin American art works; collection of 5000 slides; 600 video-tapes

M **ESCUELA SUPERIOR DE BELLAS ARTES ERNESTO DE LA CARCOVA,** National Superior School of Fine Arts Ernesto de la Carcova, Sculpture Museum, Avda Costanera Sur Esq Brasil, 1107. *Dir* Mario Vanarelli
Collections: Reproductions of world sculpture through the ages: Egyptian, Gothic, Greek, Renaissance, Roman, Romanic, including Michelangelo's David and Moses

M **MUSEO DE ARTE MODERNO,** Teatro General San Martin, Corrientes 1530. Tel 49-4796. *Dir* Guillermo Whitelow
Collections: Latin American paintings, especially Argentine, and contemporary schools

M **MUSEO DE BELLAS ARTES DE LA BOCA,** Pedro Mendoza 1835
Collections: Painting, sculpture, engravings, and maritime museum

M **MUSEO MUNICIPAL DE ARTE ESPANOL ENRIQUE LARRETA,** Obligado 2139 y Juramento 2291. Tel 784-4040. *Dir* Isabel Padilla y de Bordon
Collections: 13th - 16th century wood carvings, gilt objects and painted panels, paintings of Spanish School of 16th and 17th centuries, tapestries, furniture

M **MUSEO NACIONAL DE ARTE DECORATIVO,** National Museum of Decorative Art, Av del Libertador 1902. Tel 83 09 14. *Dir* Dr Federico Aldao
Collections: European and South American works; furniture, sculptures and tapestries

M **MUSEO NACIONAL DE BELLAS ARTES,** National Museum of Fine Arts, Avda Libertador 1473. Tel 83-8814. *Dir* Samuel F Oliver
Collections: Argentine and American paintings; European paintings 16th - 20th centuries; sculpture

CORDOBA

M **MUSEO PROVINCIAL DE BELLES ARTES EMILIO A CARAFFA,** Avenida Hipolito Irigoyen 651, 5000. Tel 22 33 45. *Dir* Carlos Matias Funes
Collections: Provincial art centre, including art library and archives; Argentine and foreign paintings, sculptures, drawings and engravings

ROSARIO

M **ARTE DECORATIVO FIRMA Y ODILO E,** Sta Fe 148, 2000. Tel 62544. *Dir* Beatriz Joyenechea de Tietjen
Collections: Paintings of Goya, Greco, Gerard, Glanderkoetinn, van der Eckhout, Giordano, Murillo, Magnow; silver; 19th century English tapestry; 20th century crystal

M **MUSEO MUNICIPAL DE BELLAS ARTES JUAN B CASTAGNINO,** Municipal Museum of Fine Arts, Br Orono Av Pellegrini. Tel 27310. *Dir* Horacio E Correas
Collections: American and European paintings and sculpture from 16th Century to contemporary, includes works by Jose de Ribera, Goya, El Greco, Valdes Leal and Titian; complete collection of Argentine art from 19th century to present

SANTA FE

M **MUSEO DE BELLAS ARTE ROSA GALISTEO DE RODRIGUEZ,** 4 de Enero 1510, 3000. *Dir* Nydia Pereyra Salva de Impini
Collections: Contemporary Argentine and modern art

TANDIL

M **MUSEO MUNICIPAL DE BELLAS ARTES,** Chacabuco 357. *Dir* E Valor
Collections: Paintings of classical, impressionist, cubist and modern schools

AUSTRALIA

ADELAIDE

M **ART GALLERY OF SOUTH AUSTRALIA,** North Terrace. Tel 08-223-7200. *Dir* David Thomas
Collections: SE Asian textiles; Costume Collection; representative selection of Australian and European paintings and sculpture; large collection of ceramics, drawings, glass, prints and silver; extensive South Australian Historical Collection; SE Asian ceramics; coins, furniture and medals

CANBERRA

M **AUSTRALIAN NATIONAL GALLERY,** *Dir* James Mollison
Collections: 70,000 piece collection— Pollock's Blue Poles, Australian art since 1788, international art since 1950, aboriginal and Pre-Columbian work and art from Asia, Oceania and Africa

HOBART

M **TASMANIAN MUSEUM AND ART GALLERY,** 5 Argyle St, GPO Box 1164M, Tasmania 7001. Tel 002-232696. *Dir* D R Gregg
Collections: Australian and Tasmanian contemporary art; Tasmanian 19th century paintings; photography

LAUNCESTON

M **QUEEN VICTORIA MUSEUM AND ART GALLERY,** Wellington St, Tasmania 7250. Tel 003-31 6777. *Dir* C B Tassell
Collections: Colonial Period (1803 - 1900); contemporary work, visual art collections, relating to Australia; pure and applied art; Tasmanian history; Tasmanian and general anthropology; Tasmanian botany, geology, palaeontology and zoology

MELBOURNE

M **NATIONAL GALLERY OF VICTORIA,** 180 St Kilda Rd, 3004. Tel 03-62-7411. *Dir* Open; *Secy* R P Nolan
Collections: Asian art; Australian art; Tribal art; antiquities, ceramics, costumes, glass, metalwork, old master and modern drawings, paintings, prints and sculpture, textiles, woodwork

PERTH

M **ART GALLERY OF WESTERN AUSTRALIA,** Administration Centre, 47 James St, 6000. Tel 328-7233. *Dir* W F Ellis
Collections: Antique and modern silver; Australian aboriginal artifacts; bronzes, ceramics, glass and pottery, gold and furniture, oils, prints and drawings, sculptures, watercolours

SOUTH BRISBANE

M **QUEENSLAND ART GALLERY,** Queensland Cultural Centre, 160 Anne St, 4101. Tel 292138. *Dir* Raoul Mellish
Collections: Predominantly Australian art, paintings and drawings; European paintings and sculpture, including works by leading Impressionists

SYDNEY

M **ART GALLERY OF NEW SOUTH WALES,** Art Gallery Rd, Domain, 2000. Tel 02-211-2100. *Dir* Edmund Capon
Collections: Australian Aboriginal, including notable burial posts and bark paintings; Australian art; contemporary tapestries, Lurcat and Matisse; decorative arts - British pewter 17th - 18th centuries; English porcelain 18th century and Victorian; European painting and sculpture; Albers, Bonnard, Boudin, Madox Brown, Burne-Jones, Constable, Corot, Danby, Davie, Etty, Fantin-Latour, Fildes, John Gibson, Gore, Hayden, Hepworth, Hogarth, Leger, Leighton, Morris Louis, Monet, Moore, Nash, Ben Nicholson, Pasmore, R E Pine, Pissarro, Poynter, Reynolds, Sickert, Stomer, Strozzi, Sutherland, Tiepolo, Turner, Van Bijlert, Van Bloemen, Wilson, Zadkine; Japanese Ceramics and Woodcuts; Melanesian; Oriental Art - Chinese bronzes and ceramics; Persian ceramics; Persian and Indian miniatures; primitive art; prints and drawings - a good systematic collection, including Callot, Canaletto, Constable, Durer, Goya, Mantegna, Matisse, Meryon, Munch, Picasso, Piranesi, Rembrandt, Turner, Whistler; Thai sculpture; Tibetan, Japanese and Chinese paintings

M **MUSEUM OF APPLIED ARTS AND SCIENCES,** 659-695 Harris St, Broadway, 2007. Tel 02-211-3911. *Dir* L G Sharp
Collections: Asian arts; †ceramics, costume, glass, ivory, metalwork, numismatics, ship models and textiles

AUSTRIA

LINZ

M **WOLFGANG-GURLITT-MUSEUM,** Neue Galerie der Stadt Linz, Blutenstrabe 15, A-4020. Tel 0732-340 55. *Dir* Peter Baum
Collections: 19th and 20th century paintings, drawings, sculptures and prints; about 550 paintings and small sculptures; 2600 graphics

SALZBURG

M **SALTZBURGER MUSEUM CAROLINO AUGUSTEUM,** Salzburg Museum, Museumsplatz 6, Postfach 525, A-5010. Tel 43 1 45, 41 1 37. *Dir Ethnology, History of Civilization, Arts and Crafts* Dr Freidrike Prodinger
Collections: Baroque, 19th century, modern art, coins, furniture, historical chambers, medieval art, prints and drawings, Prehistoric and Roman archaeology

M **SALZBURGER LANDESSAMMLUNGEN-RESIDENZGALERIE,** Residenzplatz 1, A-5010. Tel (06222) 41561/2270. *Dir* Dr Edmund Blechinger
Collections: European paintings, 16th - 20th centuries

VIENNA

M **GEMALDEGALERIE DER AKADEMIE DER BILDENDEN KUNSTE IN WIEN,** Art Gallery of the Academy of Fine Arts, Schillerplatz 3, A-1010. Tel 0222 57 95 16. *Dir* Dr Heribert R Hutter
Collections: Prince Liechtenstein; Paintings of the 12th - 18th centuries - Hieronymus Bosch, Hans Baldung Grien; 17th century Dutch (Rembrandt, Ruisdael, van Goyen, Jan Both and others); Flemish, (Rubens, Jordaens, van Dyck), Guardi, Magnasco, Tiepolo, W von Wurzbach

M **GRAPHISCHE SAMMLUNG ALBERTINA,** Albertina Graphic Art Collection, Augustinerstrasse 1. Tel 52-4232, 5769. *Dir* Dr Walter Koschatzky Study Room open Mon - Thurs 1 - 4 PM, cl during July & Aug, Exhibition Mon, Tues & Thurs 10 AM - 4 PM, Wed 10 AM - 6 PM, Fri 10 AM - 2 PM, Sat & Sun 10 AM - 1 PM. Estab 1796. Average Annual Attendance: 80,000
Collections: Drawings (44,000), watercolors and prints of all schools 14th - 20th centuries; sketchbooks, miniatures and posters. This is one of the largest (1,800,000) and best print collections in Europe
Exhibitions: Vienna Graphic Biennial Exhibition

M **KUNSTHISTORISCHES MUSEUM,** Museum of Fine Arts, 1 Burgring 5, A-1010. *Dir* Dr Friderike Klauner
Collections: Schloss Ambras Collection; Egyptian and Oriental Collections; antiques, ceramics, historical carriages and costumes, jewelry, old music instruments, paintings, tapestries, weapons

M **MUSEUM MODERNER KUNST,** Museum of Modern Art, Schweizergarten, III. *Dir* Dr Dieter Ronte
Under the Museum Moderner Kunst, 2 houses are maintained: Palais Liechtenstein contains modern classics and the latest trends in modern art
Collections: Works of the 20th century: Archipenko, Arp, Barlach, Beckman, Boeckl, Bonnard, Delaunay, Ernst, Gleizes, Hofer, Hoflehner, Jawlensky, Kandinsky, Kirchner, Klee, Kokoschka, Laurens, Leger, Marc, Matisse, Miro, Moore, Munch, Nolde, Picasso, Rodin, Rosso, Wotruba and others

M **OSTERREICHISCHE GALERIE,** Austrian Gallery, Prinz Eugen-Str 27, Postfach 134, A 1037. Tel 72 64 21, 73 44 14. *Dir* Dr Hans Aurenhammer
Collections: Austrian Gallery of 19th and 20th Century Art; Museum of Austrian Baroque Art; Museum of Austrian Medieval Art
M **Museum mittelalterlicher osterreichischer Kunst,** Orangerie des Belvedere, Vienna III
Collections: Austrian medieval paintings and sculptures, especially 14th - 16th century
M **Osterreichisches Barockmuseum,** Unteres Belvedere, Vienna III
Collections: Austrian Baroque art (paintings and sculptures)
M **Osterreichische Galerie des XIX und XX Jahrhunderts,** Oberes Belvedere, Vienna III
Collections: 19th - 20th century Austrian paintings and sculptures

M **Gustinus Ambrosi-Museum,** Vienna II
Collections: Sculpture by G Ambrosi (1893-1975)

M **OSTERREICHISCHES MUSEUM FUR ANGEWANDTE KUNST,** Stubenrign 5
Collections: Ceramics, glass, metal, oriental tapestry, porcelain, textile

BELGIUM

ANTWERP

M **INTERNATIONAAL CULTUREEL CENTRUM,** International Cultural Centre, Meir 50. Tel 031-31-91-81, 31-91-82. *Dir* Florent Bex

M **KONINKLIJK MUSEUM VOOR SCHONE KUNSTEN,** Royal Museum of Fine Arts, Leopold de Waelplein, 2000. Tel 38 78 01-09, 38 58 75. *Deputy Dir* L Wuyts
Collections: Five Centuries of Flemish Painting: Jordaens, Memling, Metsijs, Rubens, Van Dyck, Van Eyck, Van der Weyden; Masterpieces (4000); Survey of Western Painting: Fouquet, Hals, Simone Martini, Ruysdaels, Titiaan, Van Goyen; important works of De Braekeleer, Ensor, Leys, Permeke, Smits and Wouters

M **KUNSTHISTORISCHE MUSEA,** Lange Gasthuisstraat 19, B-2000. Tel 32-42-37. *Cur* Hans Nieuwdorp
M **Rubenshuis,** Wapper 9-11, Antwerp. Tel 32-47-51
Collections: Reconstruction of Rubens' house and studio; original 17th century portico and pavilion; paintings by P P Rubens, his collaborators and pupils; 17th century furnishings
L **Rubenianum,** Kolveniersstraat 20, Antwerp. Tel 32-39-20. *Dir* R A D'Hulst; *Dir* Frans Baudouin
Documentation centre for the study of 17th century Flemish art; library and photo archives
Publications: Corpus Rubenianum Ludwig Burchard
M **Openluchtmuseum voor Beeldhouwkunst (Middelheim),** Middelheimlaan 61, 2020 Antwerp. *Asst Keeper* Marie-Rose Bentein-Stoelen
Collections: Contemporary sculpture, including Rodin, Baillol, Zadkine, Marini, Manzu, Gargallo, Moore, exhibited in a large park; biennial exhibitions devoted to modern sculpture
M **Museum Smidt van Gelder,** Belgielei 91, Antwerp. Tel 39-06-52. *Asst Keeper* Clara Vanderhenst
Collections: Famous collection of Chinese and European porcelains, Dutch 17th century paintings, and of 18th century French furniture
M **Museum Mayer van den Bergh,** Lange Gasthuisstraat 19, Antwerp. Tel 32-42-37. *Cur* Hans Nieuwdorp
Collections: Unique collection of paintings, including Breughel, Metsys, Aertsen, Mostaert, Bronzino, Heda, de Vos, and medieval sculpture, ivories

M **MUSEUM MAYER VAN DEN BERGH,** Lange Gasthuisstraat 19, B-2020. Tel 031-324237. *Cur* Hans M J Nieuwdorp
Collections: Antique pottery and sculpture; applied arts; ceramics and porcelain; decorative arts, ivories and illuminated manuscripts of the Middle Ages; European painting 13th - 18th century, expecially Flemish 15th - 16th century; Flemish sculpture 14th - 16th century; furniture; numismatics; painted windows; prints; textiles

M **MUSEUM PLANTIN-MORETUS,** Plantin-Moretus Museum, Vrijdagmarkt 22, B-2000. Tel 00-32-37-330688, 322455. *Dir* Dr Francine de Nave
Collections: Designs, moulds, printing presses, punches and matrices, wood blocks and copper plates

M **MUSEUM SMIDT VAN GELDER,** Smidt van Gelder Museum, Belgielei 91, 2000. Tel 03-39 06 52, 39 10 90. *Chief Asst* Maria Snoeckx
Collections: Museum arranged as an 18th century artistic living house with 18th century French furniture and paintings, Dutch paintings from the 17th, 18th and 19th centuries, tapestries and most important: 18th century Chinese and European porcelains

M **OPENLUCHTMUSEUM VOOR BEELDHOUWKUNST, MIDDELHEIM,** Open Air Museum for Sculpture Middelheim, Middelheimlaan 61, 2020. Tel 031-27 15 34. *Cur* F Baudouin
Collections: Contemporary sculpture, medals, drawings and graphics by sculptors

M **STEDELIJK PRENTENKABINET,** Municipal Gallery of Graphic Arts, Vrijdagmarkt 23. Tel 031-322455. *Dir* Dr L Voet
Collections: Antwerp iconographic collection; modern drawings: J Ensor, F Jespers, H Leys, W Vaes, Rik Wouters; modern engravings: Cantre, Ensor, Maserel, J Minne, W Vaes; old drawings: Jordaens, E and A Quellin, Rubens, Schut, Van Dyck; old engravings: Galle, Goltzius, Hogenbergh, W Hollar, Jegher, Wiericx, etc

BRUGES

M **STEDELYKE MUSEA,** City Museums, Dyver, 12, 8000. Tel 33 99 11. *Dir* Dr Valentin Vermeersch
Collections: Arentshuis - paintings, porcelain, furniture of the 18th and 19th century; Groeningemuseum - Flemish paintings and modern art; Gruuthusemuseum - furniture, numismatics, sculpture, tapestries, textile art; Museum voor Volkskunde - Folklore

BRUSSELS

M MUSEES ROYAUX D'ART ET D'HISTOIRE, Royal Museums of Art and History, 10 Parc du Cinquantenaire, 1040. Tel 733 96 10. *Cur* Rene de Roo
Collections: American archaeology; Belgium, Egyptian, Far Eastern, Greek, Oriental, Roman and classical art; Medieval, Renaissance and modern art - ceramics, furniture, glass, lace, silver, tapestries, textiles, silver; ethnography; folklore

M MUSEES ROYAUX DES BEAUX-ARTS DE BELGIQUE, Royal Museums of Fine Arts of Belgium, rue du Musee 9. Tel 02-513 96 30. *Dir* Philippe Roberts-Jones
Collections: Medieval, Renaissance and Modern Paintings, Drawings and Sculpture
M Musee d'Art Ancien, rue de la Regence 3, Brussels
Collections: Painting and drawings (15th - 19th centuries) and old and modern sculpture
M Musee d'Art Moderne, rue de la Regence 3, Brussels
Collections: Paintings, drawings and sculpture (19th - 20th centuries), temporary exhibitions
M Musee Constantin Meunier, rue de l'Abbaye 59, Brussels
Collections: Paintings, drawings and sculptures by Constanin Meunier, the artist's house and studio
M Musee Wiertz, rue Vautier 62, Brussels
Collections: Paintings by Antoine Wiertz

M MUSEUM ERASMUS, Rue du Chapitre 31, B-1070. Tel 521 13 83. *Cur* J P Van den Branden
Collections: Documents, paintings, early editions and manuscripts relating to Erasmus and other humanists of the 16th century

LIEGE

M MUSEES D'ARCHEOLOGIE ET D'ARTS DECORATIFS, Liege Museums of Archeology and Decorative Arts, 13 Quai de Maastricht, 4000. *Dir* Joseph Philippe
Collections: Musee Ansembourg - 18th century decorative arts of Liege, housed in a mansion of the same period; Musee Curtius - archaeology; decorative arts from prehistory to 18th century; Musee du Verre - history and art of glass
M Musee Curtius, Liege
The museum is the headquarters of the Archaeological Institute of Liege
Collections: Prehistory, Romano-Belgian and Frankish, Liege coins, decorative arts (from the Middle Ages to the 19th century); Annexes: Roman Hypocaust, Place Saint-Lambert, Liege; lapidary collection in Palais de Justice
M Musee d'Ansembourg, 114 Feronstree, Liege
Collections: 18th century decorative arts of Liege; reconstituted interiors
M Musee du Verre, Liege
Headquarters of the Association internationale pour l'histoire du Verre
Collections: All the main centres of production, from the earliest times to the 20th century, are represented
Publications: Annales, bulletin

VERVIERS

M MUSEES COMMUNAUX BEAUX-ARTS ET ARCHEOLOGIE, Community Museum of Fine Arts and Archaeology, rue Renier 17. Tel 087-331695. *Cur* V Bronowski
Collections: Ancient and modern painting and sculpture, ceramics, folk arts, furniture, graphic arts, regional archaeology, Roman antiquities

BOLIVIA

LA PAZ

M MUSEO NACIONAL DE ARQUEOLOGIA, National Museum, Calle Tihuanacu 93, Casilla oficial 64. Tel 29624. *Dir* Gregorio Cordero Miranda
Collections: Anthropology, archaeology, colonial art, ethnology, folklore, Lake Titicaca District Exhibitions, traditional native arts and crafts

BRAZIL

OURO PRETO

M MUSEU DA INCONFIDENCIA, History of Democratic Ideals and Culture in Minas Gerais, Praca Tiradentes, 139, 35,400. Tel 332. *Dir* Rui Mourao
Collections: Objects related to the 1789 Revolutionaries of Minas Gerais (the Inconfidentes); †furniture, painting, sacred arts, silver, †wood carvings

RIO DE JANEIRO

M MUSEU DE ARTE MODERNA, Museum of Modern Art, Av Beira Mar, Box 44, ZC-39. Tel 231-1871. *Executive Dir* Helosia Aleixo Lustosa
Collections: Large portion of collection destroyed by fire in 1978

M MUSEU NACIONAL DE BELAS ARTES, Ave Rio Branco 199. *Dir* Dr Alcidio Mafra deSouza
Collections: 19th and 20th century Brazilian art, works by outstanding painters; †foreign collections - works by Dutch, English, French, German, Italian, Portuguese and Spanish masters; masterpieces of Foreign Collection: Dutch School - Eight Brazilian Landscapes by Frans Post; French School - 20 Paintings by Eugene Boudin, Ventania (Storm) by Alfred Sisley; Italian School: Portrait of the Cardinal Amadei by Giovanni Battista Gaulli, Baciccia; Sao Caetano (circa 1730) by Giambattista Tiepolo; Graphic Art Department: Prints and drawings by Annibale Carracci, Chagall, Daumier, Durer, Toulouse Lautrec, Picasso, Guido Reni, Renoir, Tiepolo, etc

SAO PAULO

M MUSEU DE ARTE DE SAO PAULO, Sao Paulo Art Museum, Ave Paulista 1578. *Dir* P M Bardi
Collections: Representative works by Portinari and Laser Segall; †ancient and modern paintings and sculptures: American, 19th - 20th Centuries; Brazilian, 17th - 20th Centuries; British, 18th - 20th Centuries; Dutch, Flemish and German, 15th - 20th Centuries; French, 16th - 20th Centuries; Italian, 13th - 20th Centuries; Spanish and Portuguese, 16th - 19th Centuries

BULGARIA

PAZARDZIK

M STANISLAV DOSPEVSKY MUSEUM, B G Dimitrov 50. *Dir* C Radulov
Collections: House where the painter lived and worked, containing documents, personal effects and an exhibition of paintings and icons

CHILE

SANTIAGO

M MUSEO DE ARTE COLONIAL DE SAN FRANCISCO, Alameda Bernardo O'Higgins 834. *Dir* Joaquin Gandarillas Infante
Collections: 16th - 19th century art; includes the most important collection of 17th century paintings in Chile; the life of St Francis depicted in 42 pictures; other religious works of art, furniture

M MUSEO DE ARTE POPULAR AMERICANO, Art of the American Peoples Museum, Casilla 10-D, Univ of Chile. Tel 2 01 28. *Dir* Patricio Court del Pedregal
Collections: Araucarian silver; Popular Art of the American Peoples

M MUSEO NACIONAL DE BELLAS ARTES, National Museum of Fine Arts, Parque Forestal s/n, Casilla 3209. *Dir* Nena Ossa
Collections: Baroque, Chilean and Spanish paintings; sculpture

REPUBLIC OF CHINA

TAIPEI

M NATIONAL PALACE MUSEUM, Shih-Lin, Wai Shuang Hsi, 111. Tel 881-2021 4. *Dir* Dr Chiang Fu-tsung
Collections: Bronzes, calligraphy, carved lacquer, Ch'ing dynasty court and governmental documents, embroidery, enamelware, jades, miniature crafts, oracle bones, painting, porcelain, pottery, rare and old books, tapestry, writing implements

CYPRUS

NICOSIA

M CYPRUS MUSEUM, PO Box 2024. Tel 40-2189. *Dir of Antiquities* V Karageorghis
Collections: Bronze cauldron from Salamis; middle and late Bronze-age geometric, archaic, Classical, Hellenistic and Graeco-Roman pottery; Mycenaean vases; Neolithic stone tools and vessels; sculpture including the fine Arsos Head, the Aphrodite of Soli, and the bronze Statue of Septimus Sevarus; silver trays from Lambousa; terra cotta figurines from Ayia Irini; bronzes, coins, early bronze-age pottery, glass, jewelry, lamps, sanctuary and ploughing models, and other minor works of art

CZECHOSLOVAKIA

BRATISLAVA

M **SLOVENSKA NARODNA GALERIA,** Slovak National Gallery, Razusovo
nabrezie 2. Tel 301 93, 300 37, 300 94. *Dir* Dr Stefan Mruskovic
Collections: Applied arts (1400); European and Slovak painting (4500), Dutch,
Flemish and Italian; graphics and drawings (17,000); Institic art (700); sculpture
(1700)

LITOMERICE

M **SEVEROCESKA GALERIE VYTVARNEHO UMENI,** Michalska 7. Tel 23 38.
Dir Berta Velesikova
Collections: Art of the 19th Century; Baroque Art of the 17th - 18th Centuries;
contemporary art; Gothic Art of the 13th - 16th Centuries; special collections of
naive paintings and sculpture; Renaissance paintings and sculptures of the 15th -
16th Centuries

PRAGUE

M **NARODNI GALERIE V PRAGUE,** National Gallery of Prague, Hradcanske
Namesti 15, 1 Hradcany. Tel 35 24 41-3, 53 44 57-8. *Pres* Dr Jiri Kotalik
Collections: Czech sculpture of the 19th and 20th century; French and
European art of the 19th and 20th century; old Czech art; old European art;
graphic art, modern art

M **STATNI ZIDOVSKE MUZEUM,** State Jewish Museum, 110 01 Jachymova 3.
Tel 633-74-76. *Dir* Otakar Petrik
Collections: Historical archival materials of Bohemian and Moravian Jewish
religious communities; library of ancient books with a collection of Hebrew
Manuscripts; children's drawings and works of painters from the concentration
camp Terezin; silver liturgical objects; textiles from Synagogues of historic
interest

M **UMELECKOPRUMYSLOVE MUZEUM,** Museum of Decorative Arts,
ul.17.listopadu 2. Tel 630 34;661 44 to 46;662 55 to 57;641 13. *Pres* Dr E Poche
Collections: Collections of glass, ceramics, china, furniture, textiles, tapestries,
goldsmith, silversmith, iron, ivory, clocks, prints, posters, photography,
contemporary design

PROVINCES

M **MORAVSKA GALERIE V BRNE,** Moravian Gallery at Brno, Husova ulice 14,
66 226. Tel 20 1511, 24 809. *Art Historian & Dir* Jiri Hlusicka
Collections: Applied Art Collection - ceramics, furniture, glass, graphic design,
jewelry, photography, textiles; Fine Art Collection - graphic art, painting,
sculpture since 14th century to present; Oriental Art Collection; (over 100,000
pieces in collections)

DENMARK

AALBORG

M **NORDJYLLANDS KUNSTMUSEUM,** Art Museum of Northern Jutland,
Kong Christians Alle 50. Tel 13 80 88. *Dir* Else Bulaw
Collections: Collection of graphics, painting and sculpture from this century,
Danish and international. Main museum for the Cobra movement

AARHUS

M **ARHUS KUNSTMUSEUM,** Arhus Art Museum, Vennelystparken, 8000. Tel
06-135255. *Dir* Jens Erik Sorensen
Collections: Danish Art - painting, sculpture, graphic arts, 1750 to present;
European Art, mostly recent graphics; some outstanding works from the 19th
and 20th centuries; photograph collection

CHARLOTTENLUND

M **ORDRUPGAARDSAMLINGEN,** Vilvordevej 110, 2920. Tel 01 641183. *Dir*
Hanne Finsen
Collections: Wilhelm Hansen Collection; paintings by Cezanne, Corot, Courbet,
Degas, Delacroix, Degas, Gauguin, Manet, Pissarro, Renoir, Sisley, and other
French and Danish artists from the 19th century and the beginning of the 20th
century

COPENHAGEN

L **DET KONGELIGE DANSKE KUNSTAKADEMI BIBLIOTEK,** 1 Kongens
Nytoru, K 1050. *Dir* Hakon Lund

M **KOBENHAVNS BYMUSEUM,** Copenhagen City Museum, Vesterbrogade 59,
1620. Tel 01 210772. *Cur* Steffen Linvald
Collections: Photographs 1850 to present; topographical drawings, paintings and
prints

M **KUNSTINDUSTRIMUSEET,** The Danish Museum of Decorative Art,
Bredgade 68, 1260. Tel 14 94 52. *Pres* C B Andersen
Collections: Chinese and Japanese art and handicrafts; European decorative
art from the Middle Ages to present - bookbindings, carpets and tapestries,
furniture, jewelry, porcelain and pottery, silverware and textiles

M **NATIONALMUSEET,** National Museum, Prinsens Palae, Frederiksholms Kanal
12. Tel 01-13 44 11. *Dir* Dr Olaf Olsen

M **NY CARLSBERG GLYPTOTHEK,** Carlsberg Gallery, Dantes Plads, 1556. *Dir*
Flemming Johansen
Collections: Danish and French Paintings and Sculptures from 19th Century;
Egyptian, Etruscan, Greek and Roman Sculpture

STATENS MUSEUM FOR KUNST Royal Museum of Fine Arts
M **Department of Painting and Sculpture,** Solvgade 1307 K. Tel 01 11 21 26. *Dir*
Lars Rostrup Boyesen
Collections: Contains the main collection of Danish paintings and sculpture; a
number of works by other 19th and 20th century Scandinavian artists; J Rump
Collection of Modern French Art; about 1000 paintings by Old Masters of the
Italian, Flemish, Dutch and German Schools (chiefly derived from the Old Royal
Collections, which was organized as an art gallery in the 1760s)
Publications: Kunstmusets Aarsskrift, annually; exhibition catalogues
M **Den Kongelige Kobberstiksamling,** Department of Prints and Drawings,
Solvgade K1307. Tel 01 11 21 26. *Keeper* Erik Fischer
Collections: N A Abildgaard (drawings); Povl Christensen, one-man show;
Danish Drawings of All Times; Greenlandic Prints and Drawings from Older
Times; Palle Nielsen - Orfeus Under Way; Posada (prints); 10 Years'
Acquisitions, 1969-79, (prints and drawings); Three Young Danish Draughtsmen:
Birthe Kronkvist, Karin Birgitte Lund and Erling Jorgensen; one-man show; The
print room includes about 300,000 Danish and foreign prints and drawings
L **Library,** Solvgade, K1307
Reference library
Library Holdings: Vols 50,000
Collections: W Gernsheim's Corpus Photographicum of Drawings; 20th Century
Illustrated Books, mainly French with original prints

M **THORVALDSEN MUSEUM,** Porthusgade 2, 1213 K. Tel 01 121532. *Dir* Dr
Dyveke Helsted
Collections: Greek, Etruscan and Roman bronzes, gems, marbles and vases; 19th
century European paintings and drawings; sculpture and drawings by
Thorvaldsen

HUMLEBAEK

M **LOUISIANA MUSEUM OF MODERN ART,** Gammel Strandvej 13, 3050.
Tel 03-190719. *Dir* Knud W Jensen
Collections: Modern art from 1950, including sculpture—Arp, Max Bill, Calder,
Cesar, Max Ernst, Gabo, Giacometti, Ipousteguy, Kienholz, Laurens, Henry
Moore, Richier, Sekine, Tinguely; painting—Albers, Alechinsky, Bacon,
Corneille, Dine, Dubuffet, Fontana, Sam Francis, Herbin, Hundertwasser, Jorn,
Kelly, Klein, Lichtenstein, Louis, Morley, Noldand, Tapies, Warhol;
Activities: Concerts; cinema; theatre

ECUADOR

QUITO

M **MUSEO DE ARTE COLONIAL,** Apdo 25-55 Calle Cuenca Mejia. *Dir* Carlos
A Rodriguez T
Collections: Many examples of art from the Esuela Quitena of the colonial
epoch - 17th and 18th centuries, 19th century art and some contemporary art

M **NATIONAL MUSEUM OF COLONIAL ART OF THE CASA DE LA
CULTURA EDUCATORIANA,** Calles Cuenca y Mejia 915, 2555. Tel 212-297.
Dir Carlos Rodriquez
Collections: Collections date from the 18th century

EGYPT

ALEXANDRIA

M **GRECO-ROMAN MUSEUM,** Museum St. *Dir* Dr Henry Riad
Collections: Exhibits from the Coptic, Greek and Roman eras

CAIRO

M **COPTIC MUSEUM,** Masr Ateeka. *Dir* Mounir Basta
Collections: Architecture, bone, ebony, frescos, glass, icons, ivory, manuscripts,
metalwork, pottery, sculpture, textiles, woodcarvings

M **EGYPTIAN MUSEUM,** Midan-el-Tahrir Kasr El-Nil. *Dir* Mohammed Mohsen
Collections: Ancient Egyptian Art - Pahraonic, Hellenistic and Roman
Periods; Complete sets of Jewelry, Papyrus and Coins from tombs - Hemaka,
Tutankhamen, Yuya and Thuya

ENGLAND

BATH

M **AMERICAN MUSEUM IN BRITAIN,** Claverton Manor, BA2 7BD. *Dir & Cur* Ian McCallum

BIRMINGHAM

M **BIRMINGHAM MUSEUMS AND ART GALLERY,** Chamberlain Square, B3 3DH. Tel 021 235-2834
Collections: Branch Museums Collections; applied arts - ceramics, costume, silver, textiles; paintings and drawings from 15th century to present including important collection of pre-Raphaelite works

BRIGHTON

M **ROYAL PAVILION, ART GALLERY AND MUSEUMS,** Church St, BN1 1UE. Tel 273-603005. *Dir* John Morley
Collections: Magnificent interiors in Chinese, with regency furniture and works of art of the period
M **Brighton Art Gallery and Museum,** Church St, Brighton
Collections: Early and modern paintings, watercolors, prints and drawings; English pottery and porcelain, including the Willett Collection; decorative art and furniture of Art Nouveau and Art Deco periods; ethnography and archaeology; musical instruments; Brighton history
M **Royal Pavilion,** Brighton
Collections: Once the marine palace of King George IV and other monarchs (1787-1846); interior decorations restored and original furniture
M **Preston Manor,** Preston Park
Collections: Furnished Georgian house, rebuilt 1738, and re-modelled 1905; home of the Stanford family for nearly 200 years; illustrates the way of life of a rich family before the First World War
M **Grange Art Gallery and Museum,** Rottingdean
Collections: Toys, Sussex folk-life, Rudyard Kiplingiana

BRISTOL

M **CITY ART GALLERY,** Queen's Rd, BS8 1RL. TeL 272 299971. *Dir* A D P Wilson
Collections: Bristol porcelain and glass; English pottery, porcelain, silver, glass, furniture; paintings, drawings, sculpture, British and Continental 13th - 20th century; Schiller Collection of Oriental ceramics, glass and metalwork

CAMBRIDGE

M **UNIVERSITY OF CAMBRIDGE,** Fitzwilliam Museum, Trumpington St, CB2 1RB. *Dir* A M Jaffe
Collections: European ceramics; Oriental works of art; antiquities, arms and armour, coins, drawings, furniture, illuminated manuscripts, manuscripts, paintings, prints, sculpture, textiles

DONCASTER

M **DONCASTER MUSEUM AND ART GALLERY,** Chequer Rd, DN1 2AE. Tel 0302-62095, 60814. *Dir* John Barwick
Collections: European painting, ceramics and glass, silver and jewelry

HANLEY

M **STOKE-ON-DISTRICT COUNCIL,** City Museum and Art Gallery, Broad St, ST1 4HS. Tel 29611, Ext 2258. *In Charge* David Rodgers
Collections: One of the finest collections of English ceramics in the world, pre-eminent in Staffordshire ware

KENDAL

M **ABBOT HALL ART GALLERY & MUSEUM OF LAKELAND LIFE & INDUSTRY,** Cumbria LA9 5AL. *Dir* M E Burkett
Collections: Gallery provides changing exhibitions of local and international interest; houses permanent collections of 18th century furniture, paintings and objects d'art; modern paintings; sculpture; drawings; museum features working and social life of the area

LEEDS

M **LEEDS ART GALLERIES,** Temple Newsam House, L515 0AT. Tel 0532 647321, 641358. *Dir* Robert Rowe
Collections: Art Gallery - Old Masters and modern paintings, prints, sculpture and watercolours; Temple Newsman - County House ceramics, paintings, silver, tapestries circa 1500 - 1800; Lutherton Hall - 19th century decorative arts, contemporary fashion, modern crafts, Oriental ceramics

LEICESTER

M **LEICESTERSHIRE MUSEUMS, ART GALLERIES AND RECORDS SERVICE,** Leicestershire Museum and Art Gallery, 96 New Walk, LE1 6TD. Tel 0533-554100. *Dir of Museums and Art Galleries* Patrick J Boylan
Collections: Major special collections include British art, German Impressionism and Expressionism (largest public collection in Britain); European art from Renaissance to present; Oriental decorative arts; contemporary art

LINCOLN

M **LINCOLN CITY AND COUNTY MUSEUM,** Broadgate, LN2 1NN. Tel 522 27980. *Dir* Antony J H Gunstone; *Keeper* A J White
Collections: Natural history, archaeological and historical collections relating to Lincolnshire; large collection of Roman antiquities from Lincoln; fine collection of armour and arms
M **Museum of Lincolnshire Life,** Burton Rd, Lincoln. *Keeper* Mrs C M Wilson
Collections: Displays illustrating the social, agricultural and industrial history of Lincolnshire over the last three centuries
M **Usher Art Gallery,** Lindum Rd, Lincoln. *Keeper* R H Wood
Collections: Exhibits the Usher collection of watches, miniatures, porcelain; special collection of works by Peter De Wint and a general collection of paintings, sculpture and decorative art objects; extensive collection of coins and tokens from Lincolnshire

LIVERPOOL

M **WALKER ART GALLERY,** Merseyside County Council, William Brown St, L38 EL. Tel 051-227-5234. *Dir* Timothy J Stevens
Collections: European drawings, painting, prints, sculpture, watercolors 1300 - present, including notable collections of Italian and Netherlandish painting 1300 - 1600, 19th century British painting

LONDON

M **BRITISH MUSEUM,** Great Russell St, WC1B 3DG. *Dir* D M Wilson
Collections: Egyptian, Greek and Roman Prehistoric and Romano-British, Western Asiatic; coins and medals; prints and drawings; Oriental ethnography

M **COURTAULD INSTITUTE GALLERIES,** Woburn Square. Tel 580 1015. *Dir* Dr Dennis Farr
Collections: Samuel Courtauld Collection of French Impressionist and Post-Impressionist Paintings (Cezanne, Degas, Gauguin, Manet, Monet, Pissarro, Renoir, Seurat, Sisley, Toulouse-Lautrec, Van Gogh); The Roger Fry Collection of French and English, Early 20th Century; The Gambier-Parry Collection of Old Master Paintings and other works of art (mainly Italian Primitives, 14th and 15th century, Fra Angelico, Bernardo Daddi, Lorenzo Monaco, Verrocchi); The Lord Lee of Fareham Collection of European Old Master Paintings (Botticelli, Cranach, Rubens, Simon Martni, Veronese, to Gainsborough and Goya)

M **DULWICH PICTURE GALLERY,** College Rd. *Dir* G A Waterfield
Collections: Alleyn; Bourgeois; Cartwright; Linley; Fairfax Murray; collections from 1626 onwards, gallery 1815

M **NATIONAL GALLERY,** Trafalgar Square, WC2N 5DN. Tel 01-839-2231. *Dir* Michael Levey
Collections: Principal schools, British, Dutch, Early Netherlandish, French, German, Italian; Western European painting circa 1300 to circa 1900

M **NATIONAL PORTRAIT GALLERY,** St Martin's Place, WG2H 0HE. Tel 01-930-1552. *Dir* John Hayes
Collections: National Collection of portraits from Tudor times to present, including sculpture and photographs; caricatures, drawings, miniatures, photographs; printings, sculpture, watercolours

M **QUEEN'S GALLERY,** Buckingham & St James's Palace, Lord Chamberlain's Office, SW1. Tel 930-3007. *Registrar* M E Bishop

M **SOUTH LONDON ART GALLERY,** Peckham Rd, SE5 8UH. *Cur* K A Doughty
Collections: Contemporary British art; 20th century original prints; paintings of the Victorian period; topographical paintings and drawings of local subjects

M **TATE GALLERY,** Millbank, SW1P 4RG. Tel 821 1313, Recorded Info 821 7128. *Dir* Alan Bowness
Collections: Works of Blake, Hogarth, Turner and the Pre-Raphaelites; British painting from the 16th century to present; modern foreign painting from Impressionism onward; modern sculpture (5500 works in collections and 4000 prints)

M **VICTORIA AND ALBERT MUSEUM,** Cromwell Rd, SW7 2RL. Tel 589 6371. *Dir* Dr Roy Strong
Collections: Collections of fine and applied arts of all countries, periods and styles, including Oriental art. European collections are mostly post-classical, architectural details, art of the book, bronzes, calligraphs, carpets, ceramics, clocks, costumes, cutlery, drawings, embroideries, enamels, engravings, fabrics, furniture, glass, gold and silversmiths' work, ironwork, ivories, jewelry, lace, lithographs, manuscripts, metalwork, miniatures, musical instruments, oil

paintings, posters, pottery and porcelain, prints, sculpture, stained glass, tapestries, theatre art, vestments, watches, watercolors, woodwork

M **Apsley House,** London
Opened to the public 1952
Collections: Paintings, silver, porcelain, orders and decorations, and personal relics of the first Duke of Wellington

M **Bethnal Green Museum of Childhood,** London. *Officer-in-Charge* Anthony Burton
Collections: British painting and art objects, ceramics, costumes, textiles, furniture and toys

M **Ham House,**
Collections: Country house built in 1610 and enlarged by Elizabeth, Duchess of Lauderdale; contains much of the original furniture and interior ornament

M **Osterley Park House,**
Collections: 16th century house remodelled by Robert Adam

M **WALLACE COLLECTION,** Hertford House, Manchester Square, W1M 6BN. Tel 01-935-0687, 8. *Dir* J A S Ingamells
Collections: European and Oriental arms and armour; French furniture; Sevres porcelain; paintings and works of art of all European schools, especially the French in the 18th century; goldsmiths' work, miniatures, sculpture

M **WELLINGTON MUSEUM,** Apsley House, 149 Piccadilly, W1V 9FA. Tel 0904-23839. *Officer in Charge* H V T Percival
Collections: Furniture, medals, military orders, paintings, sculpture, services of porcelain, silver plate, snuff boxes, swords, and other personal relics of the first Duke of Wellington

MANCHESTER

M **MANCHESTER CITY ART GALLERIES,** Mosley St. *Dir* T P P Clifford
Collections: British art 17th century; English costume, enamels, silver; Thomas Greg Collection of English Pottery; Old Master and Dutch 17th century painting; pre-Raphaelite painting; Royal Lancastrian pottery; Tylecote Collection of Glass

M **UNIVERSITY OF MANCHESTER,** Whitworth Art Gallery, Whitworth Park, M15 6ER. *Dir* C R Dodwell
Collections: British drawings and watercolors; contemporary British paintings and sculpture; Old Master and modern prints; textiles, wallpapers

NEWCASTLE

M **TYNE AND WEAR COUNTY COUNCIL MUSEUMS,** Laing Art Gallery and Museum, Higham Place. Tel 0632 27734. *Dir of County Museums* J M A Thompson
Collections: British oil paintings circa 1750-1979; British prints and watercolours; British (especially local) ceramics, costume, glass, pewter, silver, etc, of all periods

OXFORD

M **MUSEUM OF MODERN ART OXFORD,** 30 Pembroke St. Tel 0865 722733. *Dir of Museum* David Elliott

M **OXFORD UNIVERSITY,** Ashmolean Museum of Art and Archaeology, Beaumont St, OX1 2PH. *Dir* D T Piper
Collections: British, European, Egyptian, Mediterranean and Near Eastern archaeology; Chinese bronzes; Chinese and Japanese porcelain, painting and lacquer; Dutch, English, Flemish, French and Italian oil paintings; English silver; European ceramics; Hope Collection of Engraved Portraits; Indian sculpture and painting; Islamic pottery and metalwork; Old Master and modern drawings, watercolors and prints; Tibetan art; casts from the antique, coins and medals of all countries and periods, miniatures, sculpture and bronzes

PLYMOUTH

M **PLYMOUTH CITY MUSEUM AND ART GALLERY,** Drake Circus, PL4 8AJ. Tel 0752-68000, Ext 4378. *Dir* J Barber
Collections: The Clarendon Loan Collection of portraits of 16th and 17th century English worthies; Cookworthy's Plymouth and Bristol porcelain; Cottonian Collection of Old Master and English bronzes, drawings, paintings, prints and engravings, early printed books and manuscripts including medieval books of hours (2), watercolours; Dorothy Doughty Royal Worcester Porcelain Figures Collection; Eddystone Lighthouse Slat English, Continental and Oriental ceramics; general collections of paintings and drawings with Stanhope Forbes, James Northcote, William Payne, Samuel Prout, Joshua Reynolds and contemporary artists; silver with special reference to Plymouth Hallmarked Pieces

SHEFFIELD

M **SHEFFIELD CITY MUSEUM,** Weston Park, Yorks S10 2TP. Tel 742-734781, 2. *Dir* Open
Estab 1875
Collections: Sheffield silver, Old Sheffield plate, British and European cutlery, coins and medals, ceramics, local archaeology, natural sciences, local geology

M **Abbeydale Industrial Hamlet,** Abbeydale Rd South, Sheffield
Collections: An 18th century scytheworks with Huntsman type crucible steel furnace, tilt-hammers, grinding-shop and hand forges

M **Bishops' House,** Meersbrook Park, Sheffield
Collections: A late 15th century timber-framed domestic building with 16th - 17th century additions

M **Graves Art Gallery,** Surrey St, Sheffield. *Dir* Julian Spalding
Collections: English, Italian Renaissance and Netherlands paintings

SOUTHAMPTON

M **SOUTHAMPTON ART GALLERY,** Dept Leisure Services, Civic Centre, Hampshire S09 4XF. Tel 23855
Collections: Continental Old Masters; French 19th and 20th century school; British painting from the 18th century to present

SOUTHPORT

M **SEFTON METROPOLITAN BOROUGH,** Atlinson Art Gallery, Lord St, PR8 IDH. Tel 71 33133, Ext 129. *Librn & Arts Services Officer* R E Marston
Collections: British art - local, contemporary and historic; British 18th, 19th and 20th century oils; Chinese ceramics; 18th century English glass; Roman coins; drawings, prints, sculpture and watercolours

WOLVERHAMPTON

M **CENTRAL ART GALLERY,** Lichfield St, WV1 1DU. *Cur* Peter Vigurs
Collections: Contemporary British and American art; 18th century British paintings; 19th and 20th century British paintings and watercolors; Oriental applied art and weapons

TOTNES

L **DARTINGTON COLLEGE OF ARTS,** Library and Resources Centre, TQ9 6EJ. *Librn* Timothy B Giles
Collections: Collection associated with the arts and the handicapped; Dartington Collection of ethnic and folk artefacts, with emphasis on textiles, some musical instruments; The Dartington Hall Trust collection of paintings including some by Rabindranath Tagore and Mark Tobey

YORK

M **YORK CITY ART GALLERY,** Exhibition Square, U01 2EW. Tel 0904-13839. *Cur* Richard Green
Collections: British and European paintings from 1350 to present, including the Lycett Green Collection of Old Masters; Modern Stoneware Pottery; paintings and drawings by York artists, notably William Etty; watercolors, drawings and prints, mostly local topography

ETHIOPIA

ADDIS ABABA

M **UNIVERSITY OF ADDIS ABABA,** Museum of the Institute of Ethiopian Studies, Entoto St, PO Box 1176. Tel 110844, Ext 352. *Dir* Dr Richard Pankurst
Collections: 1350 crosses, the oldest circa 11th - 12th centuries; 6000 pieces in ethnological collections; 395 paintings, the oldest circa 15th century

FINLAND

HELSINKI

M **SUOMEN KANSALLISMUSEO,** National Museum of Finland, Mannerheimintie, PO Box 913, 10. Tel 40251. *Dir* Osmo Vuoristo
Collections: Ethnographical Department with Finnish, Finno-Ugrian and Comparative Ethnographical Collections; Finnish Historical Department with a Collection of Coins and Medals; Prehistoric Department with Finnish and Comparative Collections

TURKU

M **TURUN TAIDEMUSEO,** Turku Art Museum, Puolalanpuisto 20100. Tel 921-330954, 921-330960. *Dir* Erik Bergh
Collections: 19th and 20th century Finnish art, drawings, paintings, prints and sculpture; 19th and 20th centuries international print collection

FRANCE

ALENCON

M **MUSEE DES BEAUX-ARTS ET DE LA DENTELLE,** rue Charles Aveline, 61000
Collections: 17th - 19th century French, Dutch and Flemish paintings; 16th - 19th century French, Italian and Dutch drawings; 16th - 20th century Alencon, Flemish, Italian and Eastern European lace

ANGERS

M **MUSEE DES BEAUX-ARTS,** Museum of Fine Arts, 10 rue du Musee, 49000. *Cur* Viviane Huchard
Collections: Belgian, Dutch, Italian and Spanish painters of the 17th and 18th centuries; French painters of the 17th and 18th centuries - Boucher, Chardin, Fragonard, Greuze, Lancret, Pater, de Troy; French painters of the 19th century - Delacroix, Gerard, Gericult, Ingres; works of David d'Angers - busts, bas-relief, medallions, statues and statuettes; contemporary French artists; paintings - Primitive Art of various schools

AVIGNON

M **MUSEE DU PETIT PALAIS,** Place du Palais des Papes, 84000. *Chief Cur* Georges de Loye
Collections: Italian paintings covering the period from 14th - 16th century; Medieval sculpture from Avignon from 12th - 15th century; paintings of the Avignon school of 14th - 15th centuries

DIJON

M **MUSEE DES BEAUX-ARTS DE DIJON,** Museum of Fine Arts, Place de la Sainte-Chapelle, 21000. *Cur* Pierre Georgel
Collections: Furniture, objects of art, paintings and sculpture

FONTAINEBLEAU

M **MUSEE NATIONAL DU CHATEAU DE FONTAINEBLEAU,** National Museum of Fontainebleau, 77300. Tel 422 27 40. *Cur* Jean-Pierre Samoyault
Collections: 16th - 19th century paintings, furniture and interiors

GRENOBLE

M **MUSEE DES BEAUX-ARTS,** place de Verdun, 38000. *Cur* Pierre Gaudibert
Collections: 16th, 17th and 18th century paintings; French, Spanish, Flemish schools; modern collection; Egyptology collection

LILLE

M **MUSEE DES BEAUX-ARTS DE LILLE,** Museum of Fine Arts, Place de la Republique, 59000. *Chief Cur* Herve Oursel
Collections: Western European art from 15th - 20th centuries - ceramics, coins, medals, objects of art and sculptures

LYON

M **MUSEE DES BEAUX-ARTS, PALAIS SAINT PIERRE,** Museum of Fine Arts, 20 Place des Terreaux, 69001. Tel 28-07-66. *Chief Cur* Madeleine Rocher-Jauneau
Collections: Ancient, Medieval and modern sculpture; Egyptian, Greek and Roman antiquities; French art since the Middle Ages; French, Hispano-Moorish, Italian and Oriental ceramics; Gothic and Renaissance art; Islamic art; modern art and murals by Purvis de Chavannes; Painting of the Lyonnaise School since the 17th century; paintings of the French, Flemish, Dutch, Italian and Spanish Schools; coins, drawings, furniture, local painters and prints

NEUILLY

M **MUSEUM OF WOMEN,** 12 rue de Centre
Collections: Collection made over a 40-year period to glorify womanhood

ORLEANS

M **MUSEE DES BEAUX-ARTS,** Museum of Fine Arts, 1 Place de la Republique, 45000. Tel 38 53 39 22. *Cur-Dir* David OJalvo
Collections: Baugin; Boucher; Deruet (les quatre elements); French Paintings of the 16th - 20th Centuries; Fragonard; Foreign Schools of the 16th - 18th Centuries; Gauguin; La Hyre; Le Nain; Pastels of the 18th Century; Portraits by Corregio, Perronneau, Velasquez, etc; Hubert Robert; Sculpture of the 16th - 20th Centuries; Vouet; Watteau

PARIS

L **ECOLE NLE SUPERIEURE DES BEAUX-ARTS,** La Bibliotheque, 17, quai Malaquais, 75272. *Dir* Jean Musy

M **INSTITUT DE FRANCE,** Musee Conde, Chantilly, 60500. Tel 151 4 457 0362. *Asst to Museum* Amelie Lefebure
Collections: Ceramics, manuscripts, mobiles and paintings

M **MUSEE COGNACQ-JAY,** Cognacq-Jay Museum, 25 Boulevard des Capucines, 75002. Tel 742 3471. *Dir* Therese Burollet
Collections: Art of silversmiths; drawings by Fragonard, Watteau; 18th century works of art; paintings of Boucher, Fragonard, Tiepolo; Quentin de la Tour pastels; sculpture by Lemoyne, Clodion, Falconet, Houdon; miniatures

M **MUSEE D'ART MODERNE DE LA VILLE DE PARIS,** 11 Ave du President Wilson. Tel 723-61-27. *Dir* Suzanne Page
Collections: All art movements from 1900

M **MUSEE DE CLUNY,** Cluny Museum, 6 Place Paul Painleve (V). Tel 325-6200. *Dir* Alain Erlande Brandenburg
Collections: Enamels, furniture, ivories, sculptures and tapestries of the Middle Ages

M **MUSEE DU JEU DE PAUME,** Gallery of Impressionists, Place de la Concorde, 750001. Tel 260 12 07. *Chief Cur* Helen Adhimar
Collections: Impressionists

M **MUSEE DU LOUVRE,** Louvre Museum, Palais du Louvre, Place du Carrousel, 75041. Tel 260 39 26. *Dir* M Andre Chabaud
Collections: Islamic art; Edmond de Rothschild Collection; antiquities, decorative arts, drawings, paintings, sculpture

M **MUSEE DU PETIT PALAIS,** Municipal Museum, Champs-Elysees. Tel 265-99-21, 265-12-73. *Chief Cur* Cacan de Bissy
Collections: Chinese collections; drawings and paintings of the 17th, 18th and 19th centuries; Egyptian, Etruscan and Greek antiquities; furniture, porcelains, tapestries of Sevres and Saxe; objets d'art Art Nouvian and of the Middle Ages and Renaissance; Roman bronzes, ceramics and coins

M **MUSEE MARMOTTAN,** 2 rue Louis Boilly, 160. Tel 224 07 02. *Keeper of Art* M Yves Brayer
Collections: Marmottan; Michel Monet; Donop de Monchy

M **MUSEE NATIONAL D'ART MODERNE,** Centre National d'Art et de Culture Georges Pompidou, Place Beaubourg-rue Staint Merri, 75191. *Dir* Dominique Bozo
Collections: Twentieth century movements in painting and sculpture including: Abstraction, Avant-Garde, Cubism, Expressionism, Fauvism, Futurism, Hyperrealism, Pop Art

M **MUSEE NATIONAL DES MONUMENTS FRANCAIS,** National Museum of French Sculpture and Murals, Palais de Chaillot, Place du Trocadero, 75116. Tel 727 97 27, 727 35 74. *Cur* Philippe Chapu
Collections: Full scale casts of the principal French monuments and sculpture from the beginning of Christianity to the 19th century; full scale reproductions of Medieval murals

M **UNION CENTRALE DES ARTS DECORATIFS,** Central Union of Decorative Arts, 107 rue des Rivoli, 75001. Tel 260 32 14. *Pres* Robert Brunhammer
Collections: Dubuffet bequest; home decor of the French Middle Ages; Oriental art; paper paints, tapestry, textiles

REIMS

M **MUSEE SAINT-DENIS,** 8 rue Chanzy, 51100. Tel 47 28 44. *Cur* Francois Pomarede
Collections: 25 Paintings by Corot; 10 Designs by Cranach; French Paintings of the 19th Century; Paintings on Canvas of the 15th - 16th Centuries; 17 - 18th Century Paintings; Ceramics

RENNES

M **MUSEE DES BEAUX-ARTS,** 20, quai Emile Zola. Tel 16-99 30 83 87. *Cur* Nicole Barbier
Collections: Egyptian, Greek and Roman archeology; drawings, paintings and sculptures from 15th - 20th centuries

STRASBOURG

M **MUSEE DE L'OEUVRE NOTRE DAME,** Cathedral Museum, 3 Place du Chateau. Tel 32 06 39. *In Charge* Hans Zumstein
Collections: 15th Century Rooms - Alsatian paintings, sculptures, stained glass. Gothic Rooms - originals of the 13th century sculptures from the Cathedral; Drawings of the Cathedral, 13th - 15th centuries; meeting room of the Lodge of Stonemasons and Stonecutters (1580). Houses dating from 14th, 16th and 17th centuries. Renaissance Rooms - graphic arts and illustration of books produced at Strasbourg from 1500 - 1600; paintings, drawings by Hans Baldung Grien; rooms devoted to Renaissance furniture and sculpture; still-life room; development of gold and silverware in Strasbourg from 15th - 19th centuries. Romanesque Rooms - sculptures of the 11th and 12th Centuries; stained glass windows from Strasbourg's former Romanesque Cathedral. Rooms of Medieval archaeology; glass collection

M **MUSEE DES BEAUX-ARTS,** Museum of Fine Arts, Chateau des Rohan, 2 Place du Chateau, 67000. Tel 32-48-95. *Conservation* Jean Faviere
Collections: Paintings of the chief European schools, 14th - 19th century, from Giotto to modern times; works by Boucher, Chardin, Corot, Corregio, De Hoogh, El Greco, Fragonard, Goya, Guardi, Filippino Lippi, Lucas of Leyden, Marmion, Memling, Rubens, Tassel, Tiepolo, Tintoretto, Valentin, Van Dyck, van Heemskerk, Veronese, Vouet, Watteau, Zurbaran

TOULOUSE

M **MUSEE DES AUGUSTINS,** Museum of Augustins, 2 ter rue Alsace-Lorraine. Tel 23 11 44. *Cur* Denis Milhau
Collections: Gothic, Modern and Romanesque sculpture of Languedoc; paintings of the 16th - 20th centuries, Flemish, French, Italian and Spanish

TOURS

M **MUSEE DES BEAUX-ARTS,** Museum of Fine Arts, 18 Place Francais Sicard, 37000. Tel 05 68 73. *Chief Conservator* Mrs M N Pinot de Villechenon
Collections: Ancient and modern tapestries; furniture: Chollot, Demoulin; French school of 18th century: Boucher, Lancret, Largilliere, Peronneau; Italian paintings of 13th to 16th century: Mantegna; 17th century paintings; Rembrandt, Rubens, Van Goyen; 19th century paintings: Boulanger, Cazin, Chasseriau, Degas, Delacroix, Monet; sculptures: Bourdelle, Houdon, Lemoyne

VERSAILLES

M **MUSEE NATIONAL DU CHATEAU DE VERSAILLES,** National Museum of the Chateau of Versailles, Palais de Versailles, 78000. Tel 950 58 32. *Cur* Pierre Lemoine
Collections: Furniture, paintings and objects of art contained in the Royal Apartments; paintings of the 16th - 19th centuries contained in the History Museum of France

FEDERAL REPUBLIC OF GERMANY

AACHEN

M **SUERMONDT-LUDWIG-MUSEUM DER STADT AACHEN,** Wilehlmstrasse 18, 5100. Tel 0241-472580. *Dir* Dr Ernst-Gunther Grimme
Collections: Paintings from the Middle Ages to the Baroque; portraits from Middle Ages to present; sculpture from the Roman to Baroque; graphic art (ceramics, textiles)

BERLIN

M **BRUCKE MUSEUM,** Bussardsteig 9, 33. *Dir* Dr L Reidemeister
Collections: German expressionism, paintings, sculptures & graphic art of the Brucke group

M **STAATLICHE MUSEEN PREUSSISCHER KULTURBESITZ,** State Museums, Foundation for Prussian Cultural Treasures, Stauffenbergstrasse 41, 30. Tel 2666. *Dir* Dr Stephan Waetzoldt
—**Department of Sculpture,** *Dir* Dr Peter Bloch
Collections: †Late antiquity to classicism, among others Donatello, Riemenschneider
—**Department of Prints and Drawings,** *Dir* Dr Fedja Anzelewsky
Collections: †300,000 drawings, prints and illustrated books of all epochs of European art; greatest collection of Durer drawings, Bruegel and Rembrandt
—**Museum of Ethnology,** *Dir* Dr Kurt Krieger
Collections: †300,000 items of different cultures; Africa, East Asia (China, Tibet), Europe and North America; ancient America, ceramics, gold; Department of Oceania, houses, masks, ships; South Asia, masks, string puppets
—**Museum of Indian Art,** *Dir* Dr Herbert Hartel
Collections: †Central Asiatic frescoes of the early middle ages from Turfan and Indian sculpture
—**Museum of Far Eastern Art,** *Dir* Dr Beatrix von Rague
Collections: Paintings and ceramics of China and Japan
—**Museum of Islamic Art and Antiquities,** *Dir* Dr Klaus Brisch
Collections: †Book design, ceramics, ebony, glass, metal, stucco and tapestry from Near East, North Africa and Spain
—**Museum of German Ethnology,** *Dir* Dr Theodor Kohlmann
Collections: Folklore objects from German speaking population in Europe, beginning in the 17th century

BONN

M **RHEINISCHES LANDESMUSEUM BONN,** Rhineland Museum, Colmantstrasse 14-16, D 5300. Tel 0228-63 21 58. *Dir* Dr Christoph B Ruger
Collections: Art from the Middle Ages until today; Frankish period; medieval archaeology; prehistoric times; Roman period; coins

M **STADTISHCES KUNSTMUSEUM BONN,** Art Museum of the City of Bonn, Rathausgasse 7, 5300. Tel 773686, 772440. *Dir* Dr Dierk Stemmler

Collections: Art of the 20th century, especially August Macke and the Rhenish expressionists; German art since 1945; graphic arts

BREMEN

M **KUNSTHALLE BREMEN,** Bremen Art Gallery, Am Wall 207, 2800. Tel 32 47 85. *Dir* Dr Gunter Busch
Collections: Coins and medals up to the end of the 19th century; 18th and 19th century Japanese drawings and prints; European paintings, Middle Ages to modern, especially French and German art of the 19th century (drawings, sculpture and prints); 17th - 20th century plastic collections

BRUNSWICK

M **HERZOG ANTON ULRICH-MUSEUM,** Medieval Section: Burg Dankwarderode, Museumstrasse 1, Braunschweig D-33. Tel 0531 1551, 0531 1552. *Dir* Ruediger Klessman
Collections: Chinese lacquers; Egyptian, Greek and Roman antiquities; European paintings of the 15th - 18th centuries; European Renaissance and Baroque decorative art, including bronzes, clocks, French 16th century enamels, furniture, glass, Italian majolica, ivory and wood carvings, laces, porcelain, waxes; illustrated books; Medieval art; prints and drawings from the 15th century to present

COLOGNE

MUSEEN DER STADT KOLN Cologne City Museums,
M **Kunstgewerbemuseum der Stadt Koln,** Eigelsteinturburg. Tel 0221-2213860. *Dir* Prof Brigitte Klesse
Collections: Ceramics, furniture, glass, textiles
M **Wallraf-Richartz-Museum, Museum Ludwig,** An der Rechtschule. Tel 221-23-72. *General Dir* Dr Gerhard Bott
Collections: Museum Ludwig: Painting and sculpture from 1900 to present, especially Expressionism and contemporary art. Wallraf-Richartz-Museum: Painting from 13th century to 1900, especially old Cologne painting and Netherlandish painting; 19th century sculpture
M **Romisch-Germanisches Museum,** Roncalliplatz. Tel 221-45-90, 221-44-38
Collections: Early and pre-historic discoveries; gold ornaments of the era of migrating tribes; Roman excavations; glass and industrial arts
L **Romisch-Germanisches Museum Bibliothek,** Roncalliplatz. *Dir* Dr Hugo Borger
M **Rautenstrach-Joest-Museum,** Ubierring 45. Tel 31-10-65, 31-10-66
Collections: Culture and art of the non-European peoples
L **Rautenstrach-Joest-Museum Bibliothek,** Ubierring 45
M **Kolnisches Stadtmuseum im Zeughaus,** Cologne City Museum, Zeughaustrasse 1. Tel 221-23-52
Collections: Graphic arts of Cologne and the Rhineland; national development and history; photograph collection of the Rhineland (145,000 prints); trade and industrial arts of Cologne religious and rural art and culture
M **Kunstgewerbemuseum,** Arts and Crafts Museum, Overstolzenhaus, Rheingasse 8-12. Tel 221-9521. *Dir* Dr Brigitte Klesse
Collections: European applied arts from the Middle Ages to present, some holdings in Islamic arts
M **Museum fur Ostasiatische Kunst,** Museum of East Asian Art (Mailing add: Universitatstrasse 100, 5000, Hahnenturburg, Rudolfplatz). Tel 221-38-63. *Dir* Dr Roger Goepper
Collections: Art of China, Korea and Japan, especially Buddhist art from Japan; Chinese bronzes; Japanese lacquers; Korean ceramics
M **Schnutgen-Museum,** Cacilienstrasse 19. Tel 221-23-20, 221-23-11. *Dir* Dr Anton Legner
Collections: Religious art, early Middle Ages to Baroque
M **Kunsthalle,** Cologne Art Gallery (Mailing add: Joset-Haubrich-Hof 1). Tel 221-23-35. *Dir* Helmut R Leppier

DUSSELDORF

M **KONSERVATOR DER KUNSTDENKMALER,** von Nordrhein - Westfalen, Volkinger Str 49. Tel 4000 303 53 53. *Dir* Dr Paul Memmesheimer
Collections: Paintings of the 20th century starting from Fauvism, Expressionism and Cubism, it represents the main streams of contemporary art

L **STAATLICHE KUNSTAKODEMIE DUSSELDORF - BIBLIOTHEK,** Eiskellerstr 1, D-4000. *Dir* Norbert Kricke
Collections: Archive on the Academy's actions

M **STADTISCHE KUNSTHALLE,** City Art Gallery, Grabbeplatz 4, Postfach 1120, 4000. Tel 36 57 83. *Dir* Jurgen Harten

FRANKFURT

M **LIEBIEGHAUS, MUSEUM ALTER PLASTIK,** Museum of Sculpture, Schaumainkai 71. Tel 611-63 89 07. *Dir* Dr Herbert Beck
Collections: Sculpture from ancient times to the Middle Ages

M **MUSEUM FUR KUNSTANDWERK,** Museum of Arts and Crafts, Schaumainkai 15, 6. Tel 212 4037. *Dir* Annaliese Ohm
Collections: Bronzes, ceramics, furniture, glass, iron work, manuscripts, pewter, silverwork, textiles

M **STADELSCHES KUNSTINSTITUT,** Staedel Art Institute, Durerstrasse 2, D-6000. *Dir* Dr Klaus Gallwitz

Collections: European schools from the 14th - 20th centuries; 19th and 20th century romantics, French Impressionists and modern paintings, drawings, prints; Old Masters; Dutch and Flemish - Hals, Jordaens, Rembrandt, Rubens, Vermeer; Early Netherland - Master of Flemalle, Bosch, Bouts, van der Goes, van der Weyden, van Eyck; German - Altdorfer, Durer, Holbein; Italian - Fra Angelico, Bellini, Botticelli, Pontormo, Tiepolo

HAMBURG

M **HAMBURGER KUNSTHALLE**, Hamburg Art Museum, Glockengiesserwall 2. Tel 24 82 51. *Dir* Dr Werner Hoffman
Collections: Ancient coins; Masterworks of painting from 14th century to present, including Arp, Beckmann, Bertram, Boucher, Cranach, Dubuffet, Francke, Friedrich, Graubner, Hockney, Jones, Kandinsky, Klee, Kokoschka, Leger, Liebermann, Calude Lorrain, Manet, Menzel, Munch, Nolde, Olitzki, Picasso, Rembrandt, Runge, Tiepolo; medals from 15th - 20th centuries; prints and drawings from 14th - 20th centuries; recent schools of Western art for paintings and sculptures; sculpture of 19th and 20th centuries, including Arp, Barlach, Calder, Caro, Carpeaux, Giacometti, Grase, Hildebrand, Kolbe, Lehmbruck, Luginbuhl, Maillol, Marini, Moore, Nachi, Paolozzi, Man Ray, Rickey, Rodin, Schadow, Segal, Uhlmann

HANNOVER

M **KESTNER-MUSEUM**, Trammplatz 3. Tel 1 68 21 20, 1 68 21 27. *Dir* Dr Peter Munro
Collections: Ancient, medieval and modern coins and medals; Egyptian, Greek, Etruscan and Roman art objects and medieval art; handicrafts, illuminated manuscripts and incunabula of the 15th - 20th centuries

KARLSRUHE

M **STAATLICHE KUNSTHALLE**, State Art Gallery, Hans Thoma Strasse 2-6, D 7500. Tel 071-135355. *Dir* Dr Horst Vey
Collections: 15th - 20th Century German Painting and Graphics; 16th - 20th Century Dutch, Flemish and French Paintings and Graphics

KASSEL

M **STAATLICHE KUNSTSAMMLUNGEN KASSEL**, Schloss Wilhelmshohe, 3500. *Dir* Dr Ulrich Schmidt
Collections: Department of classical antiquities, gallery of 15th - 18th century old master paintings, collection of drawings and engravings

MUNICH

O **BAYERISCHEN STAATSGEMALDESAMMLUNGEN**, Bavarian State Galleries of Art, Barerstr 29, 8000. Tel 089 55911. *Dir* Dr E Steingraber

M **BAYERISCHES NATIONALMUSEUM**, Bavarian National Museum, Prinzregentenstrasse 3, 8000. Tel 2168-1. *General Dir* L Kriss-Rettenbeck
Collections: European art from 900 - 1850, decorative arts, paintings, sculpture; Meissen porcelain; bronze, ceramics, clocks, folk art, furniture, glass, ivory, metalwork, stained glass, tapestries

M **MUISKA-MUSEUM**, Metzstrsse 31, D-8000. Tel 089-453280. *Pres* Gisela von Frankenberg
Collections: Gisela von Frankenberg's Collection of Kowlawole's Motion-Art, consisting of paintings, sculptures, drawings and big-size photographs of antique art; plus a self-developed Sun-Computer of universal signs as key

M **STAATLICHE GRAPHISCHE SAMMLUNG**, National Graphic Collection, Meiserstr 10, D-8000. Tel 089 5591-341. *Dir* Dr Dieter Kuhrmann
Collections: American, English, French, German, Italian and Netherlandish prints and drawings

M **STAATLICHE SAMMLUNG AEGYPTISCHER KUNST**, State Collection of Egyptian Art, Residenz, Hofgartenstr, Meiserstr 10, D-8,2. Tel 089 55 91 350. *Dir* Dr Dietrich Wildung

M **STADTISCHE GALLERIE IM LANBACHHAUS**, Lenbach House City Gallery, Luisenstrasse 33, 2. Tel 52 1041-43. *Dir* Dr Armin Zweite
Collections: Art Nouveau; The Blue Rider and Kandinsky and Klee; paintings of the 19th century (Munich school); Kirbin Archives; Neue Sachlichkeit; Franz von Lenbach, his paintings and private collection of art objects; contemporary art, prints and drawings, 19th and 20th centuries

NUREMBERG

L **BIBLIOTHEK DER AKADEMIE DER BILDENDEN KUNSTE IN NURNBERG**, Bingstr 60. *Pres* Gunther Voglsamer

M **GERMANISCHES NATIONAL MUSEUM**, Germanic National Museum, Kornmarkt 1, 85. Tel 20 39 71. *Chief Dir* Dr Arno Schonberger
Collections: Ancient historical objects, archives, coins, furniture, graphics, instruments, musical instruments, paintings, sculpture, textiles, toys, weapons

STUTTGART

M **STAATSGALERIE STUTTGART**, Konrad-Adenauer-Strasse 32, 1 7000. Tel 0711-212-5108. *Dir* Prof P Beye
Collections: European Art 14th - 20th Century; International Art of the 20th Century

GHANA

ACCRA

M **GHANA NATIONAL MUSEUM**, Barnes Rd, PO Box 3343. Tel 021-21633, 021-21635. *Dir* Prof R B Nunoo
Collections: Archaeology: Materials showing the sequence culture in the whole of Africa, also materials obtained from sites in Ghana, such as Ahinsan, Asebu, Beifikrom, Dawu, Efutu, Twifu Hemang, indicating Stone and Iron Ages; Art: Contemporary Ghanaian graphics, metal products, painting and sculpture; Ethnographic: Materials on Chieftaincy and other traditional institutions, festivals, rites, traditional occupations

L **Library,*** Barnes Rd, PO Box 3343. *Librn* Ramsay F K Abaze
Open for reference to staff, visiting researchers and students
Collections: African Archaeology and Studies

GREECE

ATHENS

M **BENAKI MUSEUM**, 1, odos Koumbari, 138. Tel 3612694, 3611617. *Dir* Dr Angleos Delivorrias
Collections: Ancient Greek Art, chiefly jewelry; Byzantine and post-Byzantine Art, Icons and minor crafts; Collections of Islamic Art and Chinese Porcelain; Greek Popular Art and Historical Relics; Greek Historical Archives

M **BYZANTINE MUSEUM**, Vassilissis Sofias Ave 22. Tel 711-027. *Dir Ephore of Byzantine Antiquities* Paul Lazaridis
Collections: Byzantine icons, ceramics, marbles, metalwork; Post-Byzantine icons, ceramics, marbles, metalwork; icons enlarged by the Loverdos Collection

M **MUSEUM FOR THE MOTHER**,
Collections: Greek & International Society Collection; homemade toys of twigs

M **NATIONAL PINAKOTHIKI AND ALEXANDER SOUTZOS MUSEUM**, 50, av Vass Constantinoulos. Tel 711-010. *Dir* Dr Dimitrious Papastamos
Collections: Engravings, including Dürer, Goya, Rembrandt; 14th - 20th century European painting, including Caravaggio, El Greco, Jordaens, Mondrian, Picasso, Poussin and Tiepolo; 17th - 20th century Greek engravings, paintings and sculpture; impressionist, post-impressionist and contemporary drawings

GUATEMALA

GUATEMALA CITY

M **MUSEO NACIONAL DE ARTE MODERNO**, Edif No 6, Finca La Aurora, Zona 13. *Dir* J Oscar Barrientos
Collections: Paintings, sculpture, engravings, drawings

HONG KONG

M **HONG KONG MUSEUM OF ART**, City Hall. Tel 5-224127. *Cur* L C S Tam
Collections: Chinese antiquities including comprehensive collection of Chinese pottery from the Neolithic to the Q'ing (Ch'ing) Period, and other minor arts such as cloissone, lacquer, bronze and enamelled wares; Chinese Paintings with a specialization of Cantonese artists; historical collection of paintings, prints and drawings of Hong Kong, Macau and China; local and contemporary art

HUNGARY

BUDAPEST

M **MAGYAR NEMZETI GALERIA,** Hungarian National Gallery, Budavari Palota, 1250 Budapest, PO Box 31. Tel 160-100. *Dir* Dr Lorand Bereczky
Collections: Ancient Hungarian art, Contemporary Hungarian Collection, Hungarian graphic art, Modern Hungarian paintings and sculpture; Medal cabinet; naive art

M **SZEPMUVESZET MUSEUM,** Museum of Fine Arts, Dozsa Gyorgy ut 41, 1396. Tel 429-759. *Dir-General* Dr Klara Garas
Collections: Egyptian, Greek and Roman antiquities; modern paintings and sculpture, 19th - 20th century; old pictures, 13th - 18th century; old sculpture, 4th - 18th century; prints and drawings, 14th - 20th century

KECSKEMET

M **MAGYAR NAIV MUVESZEK MUZEUMA,** Gaspar Au II, 6000. *Cur* Agnes Kalman
Collections: Exhibitions of works of Hungarian primitive painters and sculptors

ICELAND

REYKJAVIK

M **LISTASAFN EINARS JONSSONAR,** National Einar Jonsson Gallery, Eiriksgata, PO Box 1051, 121. Tel 1-37-97. *Dir* Olafur Kvaran
Collections: Sculpture and paintings

M **THJODMINJASAFN,** National Museum of Iceland, Sudurgata, PO Box 1439. Tel 1-67-79, 1-32-64. *Dir* Filkand Thor Magnusson
Collections: Archaeological and ethnological artifacts, Icelandic antiquities, portraits, numismatics

INDIA

BARODA

M **BARODA MUSEUM AND PICTURE GALLERY,** Gujarat 390005. *Dir* S K Bhowmik
Collections: Indian archeology; prehistoric and historic; Indian art: ancient, medieval and modern; numismatic collections; modern Indian paintings; industrial art; Asiatic and Egyptian collections; Greek, Roman, European civilizations and art; European paintings; ethnology, zoology, geology, economic botany

M **MUSEUM AND PICTURE GALLERY,** Sayaji Park. Tel 64-605, 63-609. *Dir* Dr S K Bhowmik
Collections: Ancient, Medieval and modern Indian art; Asiatic and Egyptian collections; coins; European, Greek and Roman civilizations and art; European paintings; Indian archaeology, prehistoric and historic; modern paintings; Natural History and Ethnological Collection

CALCUTTA

M **INDIAN MUSEUM,** 27 Jawaharlal Nehru Rd, 700016. Tel 23-98-55. *Dir* Dr Sunil C Ray
Collections: Bronzes and bronze figures, ceramic, coins, copper and stone implements of prehistoric and proto-historic origin, crystal, gold and silver ornaments, ivory, jade, metalware, miniature paintings, papiermache, steatite objects, stone sculptures, stucco figures, terracotta objects, textiles, woodcarvings, tribal and regional objects including sets of cultural objects represented by garments, headdress, ornaments, weapons, utensils, etc

NEW DELHI

M **CRAFTS MUSEUM,** All India Handicrafts Board, Bhairon Rd, Pragati Maidan
Collections: Indian traditional crafts, folk & tribal arts; folk craft

M **LALIT KALA AKADEMI,** National Academy of Art, Rabindra Bhavan, Ferozeshan Rd, 110001. Tel 387241. *Chmn* Karl J Khandalavala
Collections: Permanent collection of graphics, paintings and sculpture

M **NATIONAL GALLERY OF MODERN ART,** Jaipur House, Dr Zakir Husain Rd, 110003. Tel 38-2835, 38-4560, 38-4640. *Dir* Dr L P Sihare
Collections: Indian contemporary paintings, sculptures and graphics. These are displayed in a chronological order as far as possible so as to give a bird's eye view of the evolution of modern Indian art since 1857

M **NATIONAL MUSEUM OF INDIA,** Janpath 11. Tel 38-5441, 38-5444. *Dir* N R Bannerjee
Collections: Arabic, Indian, Persian, Sanskrit language manuscripts; Central Asian antiquities and murals; Museum Conservation Laboratory; Pre-

Columbian and Western Art Collection; prehistoric Indus Valley culture; arms, bronzes, coins, decorative arts, technology, miniatures and drawings, mural paintings, sculptures (stone and terra cottas) from 3rd century BC to 18th century

IRAN

TEHERAN

M **TEHERAN MUSEUM OF CONTEMPORARY ART,**
Collections: Modern Western art works

IRAQ

BAGHDAD

M **BABYLON MUSEUM,** *Dir-Gen of Antiquities* Dr Isa Salmon
Collections: Models, pictures and paintings of the remains at Babylon; the museum is situated amongst the ruins

IRELAND

DUBLIN

M **HUGH LANE MUNICIPAL GALLERY OF MODERN ART,** Charlemont House, Parnell Square, 1. Tel 01-741903. *Cur* Ethna Waldron
Collections: Works of Irish artist Jack B Yeats; 19th century French works; works by contemporary painters

M **NATIONAL GALLERY OF IRELAND,** Merrion Square W, 2. Tel 01 767571. *Dir* Homan Potterton
Collections: American, British, Dutch, Flemish, French, German, Greek, Italian, Irish, Russian, and Spanish art

M **NATIONAL MUSEUM OF IRELAND,** Kildare St, 2. Tel 76 55 21. *Dir* A B O'Riordain
Collections: Art and Industrial Division; Irish Antiquities Division; Irish Folklife Division; Natural History Division

RATHKEALE

L **IRISH INTERNATIONAL ARTS CENTRE,** Castle Matrix Library, *Librn* Denise Economos
Collections: Original prints of the great masters from Durer and Rembrandt to modern times

ISRAEL

BEIT-SHEAN

M **MUNICIPALITY OF BEIT-SHEAN,** Municipal Beit-Shean-Museum, PO Box 301. Tel 065-86221. *Dir* Eizenberg Arie
Collections: Ceramic archaeological items, mosaic floors, statues, showing boxes

HAIFA

M **MUSEUM OF ANCIENT ART,** 26 Shabbetai Levy St. *Dir* Dr J Elgavish
Collections: Ancient Haifa; ancient coins from Israel; antiquities from the excavations of Shikmona from the 18th century BC until 7th century AD; Biblical, Cypriote and Greek pottery; Coptic textiles; Egyptian collection; Jewish and provincial coins; objects from the sea of Haifa; oil lamps from Israel; Roman glass from Israel; Roman portraits from Fayum; Roman portrait paintings from Egypt

M **MUSEUM OF JAPANESE ART,** 89, Hanassi Ave. Tel 04-83554. *Dir* Eli Lancman

M **MUSEUM OF MODERN ART,** 26 Shabbetai Levi St. Tel 04-52 32 55. *Dir* Gabriel Tadmor
Collections: Special collection of paintings by the late M Shemi Hall. Israel paintings, sculpture, drawings and prints; modern American, French, German and English paintings; reproductions; posters

JERUSALEM

M ALEXANDER MONASTERY MUSEUM,
Collections: Roman Antiquities

M ISRAELI ART MUSEUM,
Collections: Artwork of Israeli citizens

M ISRAEL MUSEUM, Hakirya, PO Box 1299, 91000. Tel 02-636231. *Dir* Dr
Martin Weyl
Collections: Ancient Glass; Archaeological Wing; 18th Century English Dining
Room; 18th Century French Period Room; 18th Century Venetian Room;
Judaica; Pre-Columbian; Billy Rose Art Garden; Shrine of the Book (housing the
Dead Sea Scrolls); Youth Wing; ethnography, impressionist and post-
impressionist, old masters
M Bezaiel National Art Museum, Jerusalem. *Chief Cur* Yonna Yapou
Lending libraryof reproductions and slides
Collections: Jewish ceremonial art, ethnological objects, paintings, sculptures,
drawings and prints
M Billy Rose Art Garden, Jerusalem
Collections: Modern European, American and Israeli sculpture and Reuven
Lipchitz collection of Jacques Lipchitz's bronze sketches
M Bronfman Biblical and Archaeological Museum, Jerusalem. *Chief Cur* Yael
Israeli
Collections: Collection of archaeology of Israel from earliest times to Islamic and
Crusader periods; material found in excavations since 1948; neighbouring cultures
from Iran to Italy
M Ruth Youth Wing, Jerusalem. *Chief Cur* Mrs Ayala Gordon
Permanent and travelling educational exhibitions
Collections: 55 classes in painting, sculpture, drama, movement
L Shrine of the Book, Jerusalem. *Cur* Magen Broshi
D Samuel and Jeanne H Gottesman Center for Biblical MSS
Collections: Houses the Dead Sea Scrolls (discovered in Qumran) and
manuscripts from adjacent sites on western shore of the Dead Sea, Masada and
Nahal Hever
L Library, Jerusalem. *Librn* Carmela Teichman
Library Holdings: Vols 65,000; Other — Exhibition catalogs

M L A MAYER MEMORIAL INSTITUTE FOR ISLAMIC ART,
Collections: Metalwork; ceramics; jewelry; carpets; textiles from various
periods & lands

M SAINT ANNE'S MUSEUM, Monastery of the White Fathers
Collections: Material from the Hellenist & Crusader periods

SAFAD

M GLICENSTEIN MUSEUM, *Dir* Isaac Lichtenstein
Collections: Paintings and sculptors of the late Hanoch Glicenstein; Bernard
Shapiro Collection; exhibitions of various artists

TEL AVIV

M DIASPORA MUSEUM, Tel Aviv University
Collections: Chronicles 2500 yrs of Jewish life around the world

M HAARETZ MUSEUM, University St, Ramat Aviv, PO Box 17068, 61170. Tel
03-415244-248. *Dir General Haaretz Museum* J Caleff
Collections: Ancient glass; historical documents of Tel Aviv-Yafo; Jewish
costumes; Jewish ritual and secular art objects; ceramics, coins, prehistoric
finds, scientific and technical apparatus, traditional work tools and methods
L Central Library, University St, Ramat Aviv, PO Box 17068. *Librn* Ernest
Heinemann
M Alphabet Museum, *Dir* Mrs Z Suchowolski
Collections: Documentary exhibition on the development of the alphabets
M Ceramics Museum, *Cur* Mrs Uzza Zevulun
Collections: Pottery in service of men and demonstrating the significance of
pottery in the study of human history

M MUSEUM OF ETHNOGRAPHY AND FOLKLORE,
Collections: Jewish popular art & costumes

M TEL AVIV MUSEUM, 27-29 Shaul Hamelech Blvd. Tel 257361. *Dir & Chief*
Cur Marc Scheps
Collections: Abstract expressionism and abstract art in America—Albers,
Baziotes, Frankenthaler, Louis, Noland, Pollock, Pousette d'Art; Comprehensive
Collection of Jewish Art including Maurycy Gottlieb, Jozef Israels;
Cubism—Archipenko, Gris, Leger, Picasso; Dada and Surrealism—Arp, Dali, de
Chirico, Ernst, Janco, Masson, Matta, Miro, Picabia, Tanguy; European and
American modern art—Impressionism and Post-Impressionism including Corot,
Degas, Ensor, Monet, Pissarro, Renoir, Signac; Expressionism—Heckel,
Kokoschka, Nolde, Pechstein, Rouault, Schmidt-Rottluff; Fauvism—Derain,
Dufy, Matisse, Vlaminck; 19th and 20th century sculpture including Bourdelle,
Caro, Cesar, Degas, Epstein, Lipchitz, Moore, Rodin, Zadkine; Old Masters:
Works of English, Italian, French, Dutch Schools 16th - 18th century; School of
Paris—Chagall, Friesz, Kisling, Modigliani, Pascin, Soutine, Utrillo

ITALY

BARI

M PINACOTECA PROVINCIALE, Via Spalato 19. *Dir* Dr Pina Belli D'Elia
Collections: Apulian, Venetian and Neapolitan paintings and sculpture from 11th
- 19th century

BERGAMO

M GALLERIA DELL' ACCADEMIA CARRARA, Piazza Giacomo Carrara 82/A.
Dir Dr F Rossi
Collections: Paintings by: Bellini, Raffaello, Pisanello, Mantegna, Botticelli, Beato
Angelico, Previtali, Tiepolo, Durer, Brueghel, Van Dyck

BOLOGNA

M PINACOTECA NAZIONALE, via Belle Arti 56. *Dir* Prof Andrea Emiliani
Collections: 14th - 18th century Bolognese paintings and other Italian schools;
German and Italian engravings

FLORENCE

M GALLERIA D'ARTE MODERNA, Palazzo Pitti, Piazza Pitti. *Dir* Dr Sandra
Pinto
Collections: Paintings and sculptures of the 19th and 20th centuries

M GALLERIA DEGLI UFFIZI, Uffizi Gallery, Piazzale degli Iffizi, 50125. Tel 21-
83-41, 45. *Dir* Prof Luciano Berti
Collections: Finest collection of Florentine Renaissance painting in the world.
Antique statues, famous drawing collection, miniatures, tapestries, unique and
complete collection of artists' self-portraits, ranging from the 16th - 20th
century, which was begun in the 17th century by Cardinale Leopoldo de'
Medici, and continued by his successors

M GALLERIA DELL' ACCADEMIA, Via Ricasoli 60
Collections: Michelangelo's statues in Florence and works of art of 13th -19th
century masters, mostly Tuscan

M GALLERIA PALATINA, Palatine Gallery, Palazzo Pitti, Piazza Pitti, 1, 50125.
Tel 26 06 95, 27 03 23. *Dir* Dr Marco Chiarini
Collections: Paintings from 15th - 18th centuries, Andrea del Sarto, Raffaello,
Tiziano

M MUSEO DEGLI ARGENTI, Palazzo Pitti. *Dir* Dr Kirsten Aschengreen
Piacenti
Collections: Summer state apartments of the Medici Grand Dukes; gold, silver,
enamel, objets d'art, hardstones, ivory, amber, cameos and jewels, principally
from the 15th to the 18th centuries

M MUSEO DELLA CASA BUONARROTI, Via Ghibellina 70
Collections: Works by Michelangelo and others

M MUSEO DI SAN MARCO, Piazzo San Marco. Tel 055-210741. *Dir* Dr Giorgio
Bonsanti
Collections: Fro Angelico frescoes and panels; 16th century paintings; 15th
century frescoes; illuminated manuscripts 13th - 16th century

GENOA

M GALLERIA DI PALAZZO BIANCO, White Palace Gallery, via Garibaldi II.
Tel 010-28 26 41. *Dir* Dr Arch Vincenzo Oddi
Collections: Paintings by Genoese and Flemish Masters and other schools;
sculpture and tapestries

LUCCA

M MUSEO DI VILLA GUINIGI, Villa Guinigi, Via della Quarquonia. *Dir* Dr
Clara Baracchini
Collections: Roman and late Roman sculptures and mosaics; Romanesque,
Gothic, Renaissance and Neoclassical sculpture; paintings from 12th to 18th
century including Fra Bartolomeo and Vasari; wood inlays, textiles, medieval
goldsmiths' art

M MUSEO NAZIONALE DI VILLA GUINIGI, National Museum of Villa
Guinigi, via della Quarquonia, 55100. Tel 460-33. *Dir* Dr Clara Barrahini
Collections: Ancient textiles; Gothic, Neoclassical, Romanesque and Renaissance
sculpture; Medieval goldsmiths' art; Old Master paintings, 12th - 18th century;
Roman and late Roman sculptures and mosaics; wooden inlays and sculptures

M PINACOTECA NAZIONALE, National Picture Gallery, piazza Napoleone. Tel
0583 55570. *Dir* Dr Clara Baracchini
Collections: Paintings from churches and palaces of the city and territory, also
from the Medici family and the Tuscan, Venetian, French and Flemish Schools;
photographs

MANTUA

M GALLERIA E MUSEO DEL PALAZZO DUCALE, Gallery and Museum of the Palazzo Ducale, Piazza Sordello, 46100. Tel 369 167, 320 568. *Dir* Dr Ilaria Toesca Bertelli
Collections: Classical antiquities and sculpture; Egyptian antiquities; Medieval, Renaissance and Baroque sculpture; Numismatic Collection; Prehistorical relics from Mantuan Territory

MILAN

M GALLERIA D'ARTE MODERNA E PADIGLIONE D'ARTE CONTEMPORANEA, Villa Reale, Via Palestro 16. *Dir* Dr Mercedes Garberi
Collections: Painting and sculpture from Neo-Classical period to present day, includes the Grassi Collection and Museo Marino Marini (c 200 sculptures, portraits, paintings, drawings and etchings by Marini)

M MUSEO D'ARTE ANTICA, Museum of Ancient Art, Castello Sforzesco. *Dir* Dr Mercedes Garberi
Collections: Paintings including works by Bellini, Brauianbino, Foppa, Guiadi, Lippi, Lotto, Mantegna, Tiepolo, Tintoretto and others; sculpture from early Middle Ages to 16th century mostly concerning Lombard art, including masterpieces like Michelangelo's Pieta-Rondanini; ancient and contemporary drawings, with a very important group of Boccioni works
M Civiche Raccolte de Arte Applicata, Collection of Minor Arts, Piazza Castello, 21022. Tel 02 803071
Collections: Armor, bronzes, ceramics, coins, costumes, ironworks, ivories, mobiles, musical insturments, porcelains, sculpture, textiles
M Racolta delle Stampe Achille Bertarelli, Bertarelli Collection of Engravings, Castello Sforzesco. *Dir* Dr Clelia Alberici
M Raccolte Archaeologiche e Numismatiche, Collection of Archeology and Coins, Castello Sforzesco & Corse Magenta 15. *Dir* Dr Ermanno Arslan
Collections: Castello Sforzesco: Ancient Egyptian, antique and modern coins, prehistoric and later; Corso Magenta: Etruscan, Greek and Roman Collections
M Museo di Milano, Museum of Milan, Vedi Sant'Andrea 6. *Dir* Dr Ermanno Arslan
Collections: Paintings of Milan subjects of the 19th century

M MUSEO POLDI PEZZOLI, Via A Manzoni 12. *Dir* Dr Alessandra Mottola Molfino
Collections: Paintings from 14th - 18th centuries; armor, tapestries, rugs, jewelry, porcelain, glass, textiles, furniture, clocks and watches

M PINACOTECA AMBROSIANA, Ambrosian Picture Gallery, Piazza Pio XI, 2, 20123. Tel 02-800146. *Dir* Dr Angelo Paredi
Collections: Botticelli, Caravaggio, Leonardo, Rapheal, Titian

M PINACOTECA DI BRERA, Via Brera 28. Tel 808-387. *Dir* Dr Carlo Bertelli
Collections: Pictures of all schools, especially Lombard and Venetian; paintings by Mantegna, Bellini, Crivelli, Lotto, Titian, Veronese, Tintoretto, Tiepolo, Foppa, Bergognone, Luini, Piero della Francesca, Bramante, Raphael, Caravaggio, Rembrandt, Van Dyck, Rubens; also 20th century works, mostly Italian

MODENA

M GALLERIA, MUSEO E MEDAGLIERE ESLENSE, Este Gallery and Museum, Palazzo dei Musei, Piazza S Agostino 109. Tel 22-21-45
Collections: Bronzes, coins, drawings, medals, minor arts, paintings, prints and sculptures, most from the Este family

NAPLES

M MUSEO CIVICO GAETANO FILANGIERI, Via Duomo 288. *Dir* Francesco Acton di Leporano
Collections: Paintings, furniture, archives, photographs, library of 15,000 vols, and coin collection of Neapolitan history

M MUSEO E GALLERIE NAZIONALI DI CAPODIMONTE, *Dir* Prof Raffaello Causa
Collections: Paintings from 13th to 18th centuries; paintings and sculptures of 19th century; collection of arms and armor; medals and bronzes of the Renaissance; porcelain

M MUSEO NAZIONALE DI SAN MARTINO, National Museum, Piazzele San Martino, 80100. Tel 37-70-05. *Dir* Dr Teodore Fittipaldi
Collections: Works of art from Farnese, Borgia and Noia Collections, and works recovered from excavations in Southern Italy, particularly in Pompeii and Herculaneum. A foremost collection of ancient bronzes, wall paintings and mosaics; 17th century pictures and paintings; 13th - 17th century sculpture, majolicas and porcelains; section of modern prints, paintings and engravings

PADUA

M MUSEO CIVICO DI PADUA, Municipal Museum, Piazza del Santo, 10. Tel 2-31-06, 2-27-13. *Dir* Prof Giovanni Gorini
Collections: Archaeological Museum; Art Gallery - bronzes, ceramics, industrial arts, painting, sculpture; Bottacin Museum - Greco-Roman, Italian, Paduan, Venetian, Napoleonic coins and medals; Gallery of Pictures; Lapidary Collection

PARMA

M GALLERIA NAZIONALE, Palazzo della Pilotta. *Supt* Prof Eugenio Riccomini
Collections: Paintings from 13th to 19th centuries, including works by Correggio, Parmigianino, Cima, Greco, Piazzetta, Tiepolo, Holbein, Van Dyck, Mor, Nattier, and several painters of the school of Parma; also a modern art section

PERUGIA

M GALLERIA NAZIONALE DELL'UMBRIA, Umbrian National Gallery, Corso Vannucci Palazzo, dei Prior. Tel 075 233 85, 207 12. *Dir* Dr Francesco Santi
Collections: Furniture of the Renaissance; jewels (Umbria-Siena) 13th and 14th centuries; paintings from the Umbrian School from the 13th - 18th centuries; 13th, 14th and 15th century sculpture

PISA

M MUSEO NAZIONALE DI SAN MATTEO, Convento di San Matteo, Lungarno Mediceo. *Dir* Dr Antonino Caleca
Collections: Sculptures by the Pisanos and their school; important collection of the Pisan school of the 13th and 14th centuries, and paintings of the 15th, 16th, and 17th centuries; ceramics; coins and medals

ROME

L AMERICAN ACADEMY IN ROME LIBRARY, Via Angelo Masina 5, 00153. *Dir* John H D'Arms
Collections: Oliver Strunk Collection (musicology); Fototeca (photographs of archaeological sites in Italy, eastern Mediterranian and North Africa); rare books and manuscripts (general Renaissance art and architecture)

M GALLERIA BORGHESE, Borghese Gallery, Villa Borghese. Tel 85-85-77. *Dir* Sara Staccioli
Collections: Baroque and Classical sculptures - G Bernini, Canova; paintings by Caravaggio, Antonello da Messina, Andrea del Sarto, Lorenzo di Credi, Domenichino, Dosso Dossi, Raffaello, Tiziano, Veronese

M GALLERIA DORIA PAMPHILJ, Dorian Gallery, Piazza del Collegio Romano l/a, 00186. *Dir* Dr Eduard A Safarik
Collections: Paintings by Caravaggio, Carracci, Correggio, Filippo Lippi, Lorrain, del Piombo, Titian, Velazquez

M GALLERIA NAZIONALE D'ARTE ANTICA - PALAZZO BARBERINI, National Gallery in Barberini Palace, Via Quattro Fontane 13, 00. Tel 06-4750184. *Dir* Dr Giuseppina Magnanimi
Collections: Italian and Flemish paintings from 12th - 18th century

M GALLERIA NAZIONALE DI ROMA, Palazzo Barberini, Via Quattro Fontane 13. *Dir* Prof Dante Bernini
Collections: 12th - 18th century Italian and European paintings, Baroque architecture; Corsini collection at Palazzo Corsini, Via della Lungara 10

M INSTITUTO NAZIONALE PER LA GRAFICA, Via Della Lungara, 230, 00165. *Dir* M Catelli Isola
Collections: Drawings, engravings

M MUSEI CAPITOLINI, Museum of Sculpture, Piazza del Campidoglio 1471, 00186. Tel 67 97 034, 67 82 862. *Dir* Carlo Pietrangeli
Collections: Ancient sculptures, bronzes, paintings, pottery, tapestry and other works of art

M MUSEO NAZIONALE ROMANO, National Museum of Rome, piazza delle Finanze 1. Tel 06 46-05-30, 46-08-56. *Dir* Dr A La Regina
Collections: Archaelogical collection; glass; Greek Hellenistic and Roman bronzes and sculpture; numismatics; pictures and mosaics

SASSARI

M MUSEO NAZIONALE G A SANNA, G A Sanna National Museum, via Roma 64, Viale Umberto 89, 01700. Tel 27-22-03. *Dir* Dr F Nicosia
Collections: Archeological Collections; Picture Gallery with Medieval and Modern Art; Collection of Sardinian Ethnography; sculptures

TURIN

M ARMERIA REALE, Piazza Castello 191 (Mailing add: Soprintendenza per i Beni Artistici e Storici, Via Accademia delle Scienze 5, 10123). *Pres* Giovanni Romano
Collections: Archaeological arms; arms and armours from 13th - 18th century; arms of the 19th and 20th century; Oriental arms; Collection of the last Savoia: Carlo Alberto, Vittorio Emanuele II and III, Umberto I

M GALLERIA SABAUDA, Soprintendenza per i Beni Artistici e Storici, Via Accademia delle Scienze 5, 10123. Tel 011-542 888. *Dir* Giovanna Galante Garrone
Collections: G Ceruti portraits; Aimone Ducc painting; Flemish Masters; French Masters; Collection Gualino; Italian Masters I until the 16th century; Italian Masters II, including 16th century Venetian painters, until the 18th century; Piedmontese Masters; tapestry

M **MUSEO CIVICO DI TORINO,** Municipal Museum, via Magenta 31, 10100. Tel 516-416, 54.18.2. *Dir* Dr Anna Serena Fava
  Collections: Antique and modern art from 4th - 20th enturies; coins, paintings; sculpture

VATICAN CITY

M **MONUMENTI MUSEI E GALLERIE PONTIFICIE,** Vatican Museums and Galleries, Tel 06 698 3332. *Dir General* Carlo Pietrangeli
  Collections: Byzantine, medieval and modern art; Classical sculpture; early Christian inscriptions; mosaics
  Publications: For all except Missionary Museum: Bollettino dei Monumenti, Musei, Gallerie Pontificie
M **Museo Pio Clementino,** Vatican City. *Cur* Dr Georg Daltrop
  Founded by Pope Clement XIV (1770-74), and enlarged by his successor, Pius VI; exhibits include the Apollo of Belvedere, the Apoxyomenos by Lysippus, the Laocoon Group, the Meleager of Skopas, the Apollo Sauroktonous by Praxiteles; the original Vatican Museum was begun with the Apollo—already in possession of Pope Julius II when he was still a Cardinal, at the end of the 15th century—and the Laocoon Group, foundj in 1506
M **Museo Sacro,** Vatican City
  Founded in 1756 by Pope Benedict XIV; administered by the Apostolic Vatican Library; contains objects of liturgical art, historical relics and curios from the Lateran, objects of palaeolithic, medieval and Renaissance minor arts, paintings of the Roman era
M **Museo Profano,** Vatican City
  Founded in 1767 by Pope Clement XIII; administered by the Apostolic Vatican Library; bronze sculptures and minor arts of the classical era
M **Museo Chiaramonti e Braccio Nuovo**
  Founded by Pope Pivs VII at the beginning of the 19th century, to house the many new findings excavated at that period; exhibits include the statues of the Nile, of Demosthenes and of the Augustus of Primaporta
M **Museo Gregoriano Etrusco,** Vatican City. *Cur* Francesco Roncalli
  Founded by Pope Gregory XVI in 1837; contains objects from the Tomba Regolini Galassi of Cerveteri, the Mars of Todi, bronzes, terracottas and jewellery, and Greek vases from Etruscan tombs
M **Museo Gregoriano Egizio,** Vatican City. *Cur* Gianfranco Nolli
  Inaugurated by Pope Gregory XVI in 1839; contains Egyptian papyri, mummies, sarcophagi and statues, including statue of Queen Tuia (1300 BC)
M **Museo Gregoriano Profano,** Vatican City
  Founded by Gregory XVI in 1844 and housed in the Lateran Palace, it was transferred to a new building in the Vatican and opened to the public in 1970; Roman sculptures from the Pontifical States; portrait-statue of Sophocles, the Marsyas of the Myronian group of Athena and Marsyas, the Flavian reliefs from the Palace of the Apostolic Chancery
M **Museo Pio Cristiano,** Vatican City
  Founded by Pius IX in 1854 and housed in the Lateran Palace; transferred to a new building in the Vatican and opened to the public in 1970; large collection of sarcophagi; Latin and Greek inscriptions from Christian cemeteries and basilicas; the Good Shepherd
M **Museo Missionario Etnologico,** Vatican City. *Cur* P J Penkowski
  Founded by Pius XI in 1926 and housed in the Lateran Palace; transferred to a new building in the Vatican and opened to the public in 1973; ethnographical collections from all over the world
  Publications: Annali
M **Pinacoteca Vaticana,** Vatican City. *Cur* Dr Fabrizio Mancinelli
  Inaugurated by Pope Pius XI in 1932; includes paintings by Fra Angelico, Raphael, Leonardo da Vinci, Titian and Caravaggio, and the Raphael Tapestries
M **Collezione d'Arte Religiosa Moderna,** Vatican City. *Cur* Dr Mario Ferrazza
  Inaugurated in 1973; paintings, sculptures and drawings offered to the Pope by over 200 artists and donors
M **Cappelle, Sale e Gallerie Affrescate,** Vatican City
  Chapel of Beato Angelico (or Niccolo V, 1448-1450); Sistine Chapel constructed for Sixtus IV (1471-1484); Borgia Apartment: decorated by Pinturicchio; Chapel of Urbano VIII (1625-1644); rooms and loggias decorated by Raphael; Gallery of the Maps (1580-83)

JAPAN

HIROSHIMA

M **ITSUKUSHIMA JINJA HOMOTSUKAN,** Miyajima-cho, Saeki-gun. *Cur &
Chief Priest* Motosada Nozaka
  Collections: 2,500 exhibits of paintings, calligraphy, sutras, swords, and other ancient weapons

KURASHIKI

M **OHARA BIJITSUKAN,** Ohara Museum of Art, 1-1-15 Chuo. Tel 0864-22-0005. *Cur* Shin-ichiro Foujita
  Collections: Ancient Egyptian, Persian and Turkish ceramics and sculpture; modern American and European paintings and sculpture; modern Japanese oil paintings, pottery, sculpture and textiles

KYOTO

M **KYOTO KOKURITSU KINDAI BIJUTSUKAN,** National Museum of Modern Art, Kyoto, Enshoji-cho, Okazaki, Sakyo-ku. *Dir* Michiaki Kawakita
  Collections: Kawakatsu Collection which consists of 25 pieces of pottery by Kanjiro Kawai; ceramic works by artists abroad, contemporary print works in Japan and Japanese artists who are active abroad, contemporary sculptures, handicrafts works by contemporary artists, paintings by the artists who have been active in Kyoto mainly

M **KYOTO-SHI BIJUTSUKAN,** Okazaki Park, Sakyo-ku. *Dir* T Fujikawa
  Collections: Contemporary fine arts objects, including 514 Japanese pictures (of which 215 are oils), 39 Japanese sculptures, 86 decorative arts exhibits and 24 Japanese prints

NARA

M **HORYUJI,** Aza Horyuji, Ikaruga-cho Ikoma-gun
  Collections: A large number of Buddhist images and paintings; the buildings date from the Asuka, Nara, Heian, Kamakura, Ashikaga, and Tokugawa periods

M **NARA KOKURITSU HAKUBUTSUKAN,** Nara National Museum, 50 Noborioji-cho, 630. Tel 0742-22-7771. *Dir* Bunsaku Kurata
  Collections: Art objects of Buddhist art, mainly of Japan, including applied arts and archaeological relics, calligraphs, paintings, sculptures, 6th - 14th century

OKAYAMA

M **OHARA BIJITSUKAN,** 1-1-15 Chuo, Kurashiki-city. *Cur* S Fujita
  Collections: Ceramics and sculptures from Egypt, Persia and Turkey; European paintings and sculpture of nineteenth and twentieth centuries; gallery of Japanese paintings; arts and crafts

SHIZUOKA

M **MOA MUSEUM OF ART,** 26-2 Momoyama, Atami 413. *Dir* Yoji Yoshioka
  Collections: Oriental fine arts; paintings, ceramics, lacquers and sculptures

TOKYO

M **BRIDGESTONE BIJUTSUKAN,** Bridgestone Museum of Art, 10-1, 1-chome, Kyobashi Chuo-ku. Tel 563-0241. *Executive Dir* Yasuo Kamon
  Collections: Foreign bronze wares, glass wares and pottery from ancient times to early modern times; foreign original prints from 17th century to present; foreign paintings, mainly Impressionism and after; foreign sculptures from ancient time to present; Japanese Western style paintings late 19th century to present

M **NATIONAL MUSEUM OF WESTERN ART,** Kokuritsu Seiyo Bijutsukan, Ueno Park, Taito-ku. Tel 03-828-5131. *Dir* Seiro Mayekawa
  Collections: Many works of European art from the 14th - 20th century; Matsukata Collection contains 300 paintings, 63 sculptures, including 12 Monet, 3 Renoir and 53 Rodin; Old Master paintings, including Cranach, Barna da Siena, El Greco, Magnasco, Patinir, Rubens, Tintoretto, Joos van Cleve, Van der Weyden

M **NEZU ART MUSEUM,** 6-5 Minami-aoyama, Minato-ku. *Dir* Hisao Sugahara
  Collections: Kaichiro Nezu's private collection, including 7,195 paintings, calligraphy, sculpture, swords, ceramics, lacquer-ware, archeological exhibits; 173 items designated as national treasures

M **NIHON MINGEI KAN,** Japanese Folk Art Museum, 861 Kamaba Meguro-ku. Tel 4-3-33
  Collections: 20,000 objects of folk-craft art from all parts of the world

M **TOKYO KOKURITSU HAKUBUTSUKAN,** 13-9 Ueno Park, Daito-ku. *Dir* Sei Saito
  Collections: Largest art museum in Japan; 86,000 objects of Eastern fine arts, including paintings, calligraphpy, sculpture, metal work, ceramic art, textiles, lacquer ware, archeological exhibits

M **TOKYO KOKURITSU KINDAI BUJUTSUKAN,** National Museum of Modern Art, Tokyo, 3 Kitanomaru Koen, Chiyoda-ku 102. Tel 03 214 2561, 214 2565. *Dir* Shigeo Chiba
  Collections: 19 Calligraphies, 114 drawings, 605 Japanese-style paintings, 861 oil paintings, 1135 prints, 219 sculptures, 65 watercolours
M **Crafts Gallery,** 1 Kitanomaru Koen, Chiyoda-ku 102. Tel 03 211-7781. *Chief Crafts Gallery* Nobuhiko Sugihara
  Collections: 178 Ceramics; 198 dyeing and weaving; 96 lacquer ware; 50 metal works

M **TOKYO NATIONAL UNIVERSITY OF FINE ARTS & MUSIC ART MUSEUM,** Daito-ku, Ueno Park
  Collections: Paintings, sculptures & industrial art of Japan, China & Korea

M **TOKYO-TO BIJUTSUKAN,** Tokyo Metropolitan Art Museum, Ueno Park 8, Taito-ku. Tel 03-823-6921. *Dir* Kazuaki Kudo
  Collections: Contemporary crafts, paintings and sculptures

WAKAYAMA

M **KOYASAN REIHOKAN,** Koyasan Koya-cho, Ito-gun. *Cur* Dr Chikyo Yamamoto
  Collections: 50,000 exhibits, including Buddhist paintings and images, sutras and old documents, some of them registered National Treasures and Important Cultural Properties

KOREA

SEOUL

M **NATIONAL MUSEUM OF KOREA,** Kyong Bok Palace, 1 Sejongro, Chongro-ku. Tel 72-9295. *Dir-General* Sunu Choi
Collections: Bronze wares, Buddhist sculptures, calligraphy, ceramics, paintings and pottery (historical and artistic materials)

LEBANON

BEIRUT

M **AMERICAN UNIVERSITY OF BEIRUT,** Archaeological Museum, Tel 340740, Ext 2523. *Dir* Dr Leila Badre
Collections: Bronze and Iron Age Near Eastern Pottery Collections; bronze figurines, weapons and implements of the Bronze Age Near East; Graeco-Roman imports of pottery from Near East sites; Palaeolithic-Neolithic Flint Collection; Palmyrene funerary sculpture; Phoenician Glass Collection; pottery collection of Islamic periods; substantial coin collection

M **DAHESHITE MUSEUM AND LIBRARY,** POB 202. *Dir* Dr A S M Dahesh
Collections: Aquarelles, gouaches, original paintings, engravings, sculptures in marble, bronze, ivory and wood carvings

M **MUSEE NATIONAL,** National Museum of Lebanon, rue de Damas. Tel 401-00-440. *Dir* Emir Maurice Chehab
Collections: Anthropological sarcophagi of the Greco-Persian period; Byzantine mosaics; ceramics and wainscoting of the Arabic period; Dr C Ford Collection of 25 sarcophagi of the Greek and Helenistic epoch; goblets, mosaics, relief and sarcophagi of the Greco-Roman period; jewelry and statues of the Phoenician period; jewelry in gold of the Arabic, Byzantine and Roman periods; monies in gold, silver and bronze of the Arabic, Byzantine, Helenistic, Phoenician and Roman periods; objects and statues of the Prehistoric period; sarcophagus of Ahiram 13th century BC, depicting the prototype of the whole modern alphabet

MALTA

VALLETTA

M **NATIONAL MUSEUM OF FINE ARTS,** South St. *Dir* Marius J Zerafa
Collections: European art from 14th century to modern times; collection of works by Mattia Preti; collection of historical objects and coins connected with the Nights of Malta

MEXICO

GUADALAJARA

M **MUSEO DEL ESTADO DE JALISCO,** National Museum,
Collections: Archaeological discoveries; early Mexican objects; folk art and costumes

M **MUSEO-TALLER JOSE CLEMENTE OROZCO,** Calle Aurelio Aceves 27, Sector Juarez, Jalisco 44100. *Dir* Margarita V de Orozco
Collections: Paintings and sketches by the artist

MEXICO CITY

M **MUSEO DE ARTE MODERNO,** Museum of Modern Art, Chapultepec Paseo de la Reforma, y Gandhi, 5. Tel 553 63 13. *Dir* Fernando Gamboa
Collections: Contemporary Art 1950-1973; First Six Decades of 20th Century Mexican Painting; Jose Maria Velasco - Academic Bridge to 20th Century Mexican Painting; International Works; Mexican and foreign

M **MUSEO DE SAN CARLOS,** Puente de Alvarado 50, 1. Tel 903-535-1256. *Dir* Graciela Reyes Retana
Collections: English, Flemish, French, German, Hungarian, Italian, Polish, Netherlandish and Spanish paintings from 14th - 19th centuries; 19th century Mexican sculpture
L **Library,*** Puente de Alvarado No 50, 06030
Collections: European painting of the 14th-19th centuries

M **MUSEO NACIONAL DE ANTROPOLOGIA,** National Museum of Anthropology, Ave Paseo de la Reforma y Gandhi S/N, 10. Tel 553-62-66. *Dir* Tgnacio Bernal
Collections: Archaeological and ethnographical

M **MUSEO NACIONAL DE ARTES E INDUSTRIAS POPULARES,** National Museum of Crafts and Popular Industries, Av Juarez No 44, 1. *Dir* Teresa Pomar
Collections: Major permanent collections of Mexican popular arts and crafts with emphasis on native pottery, textiles and lacquer

M **MUSEO NACIONAL DE HISTORIA,** National Hisotrical Museum, Castillo de Chapultepec. *Dir* Felipe Lacouture
Collections: The history of Mexico from the Spanish Conquest to the 1917 Constitution, through collections of ceramics, costumes, documents, European and Oriental China, flags and banners, furniture, jewelry, personal objects, murals by the Mexican painters Gonzalez Camarena, O'Gorman, Clemente Orozco and Siqueiros, paintings, silverware, uniforms. The Alcazar shows apartments of some of the 19th century governors of the country

M **PINACOTECA NACIONAL DE SAN DIEGO,** Dr Mora 7, 1 DF. *Dir* Carmen M de Andrade
Collections: Under auspices of Instituto Nacional de Bellas Artes; paintings of the colonial era in Mexico

PUEBLA

M **MUSEO DE ARTE—JOSE LUIS BELLO Y GONZALES,** Museum of Art, Ave 3, Poniente 302. Tel 41-94-75. *Dir* Alicia Torres de Araujo
Open daily 10 AM - 5 PM. $.15. Estab 1944. Average Annual Attendance: 25, 500
Collections: Agustin Arrieta; Chinese porcelain; European and Mexican furniture with marquetry; European porcelain; Puebla's ceramic (Talavera) lace; bronzes, calamine, coopers, crystal, enamels, engraving, forged irons, ivories, miniatures, pictures, religious ornaments, sculptures, watches
Activities: Tours; individual paintings & original objects of art to Mexican Official Institutions; museum shop sells books

M **MUSEO DE ARTE JOSE LUIS BELLO Y GONZALEZ,** Avenida 3 Poniente 302, Puebla. *Dir* Alicia Torres de Araujo
Collections: Ivories; porcelain; wrought iron; furniture; clocks; watches; musical instruments; Mexican, Chinese and European paintings, sculptures, pottery, vestments, tapestries, ceramics, miniatures

SAN MIGUEL DE ALLENDE

L **INSTITUTO ALLENDE LIBRARY,** Instituto Allende. Tel 2 02 89. *Dir* Stirling Dickinson

TOLUCA

M **MUSEO DE LAS BELLAS ARTES,** Calle de Santos Degollado 102, Mexico. *Dir* Prof Jose M Caballero-Barnard
Collections: Paintings; sculptures; Mexican colonial art

NETHERLANDS

ALKMAAR

M **STEDELIJK MUSEUM ALKMAAR,** Alkmaar Municipal Museum, Doelenstraat 3. *Dir* Dr J J H Jeurissen
Collections: Archaeological items, dolls and other toys, modern sculpture, paintings, silver, tiles

AMSTERDAM

M **REMBRANDT-HUIS MUSEUM,** Rembrandthouse Museum, Jodenbreestraat 4-6, 1011 NK. Tel 020-24 94 86. *Cur* Eva Ornstein-van Slooten
Collections: Almost complete collection of Rembrandt's etchings; 8 drawings by Rembrandt; drawings by Rembrandt's pupils; paintings by Rembrandt's pupils and teachers

M **RIJKSMUSEUM,** State Museum, Stadhouderskade 42 (Mailing add: Hobbemastraat 21, PO Box 50673, 1007 DD). *Dir General* Dr S H Levie
Collections: Asiatic art; Dutch history; Dutch paintings 15th - 19th centuries; prints and drawings from all parts of the world, sculpture and applied art

M **RIJKSMUSEUM VINCENT VAN GOGH,** Vincent Van Gogh State Museum, Paulus Potterstraat 7 1071 CX. Tel 020-764881. *Dir* Dr J van der Wolk
Collections: Drawings and paintings by Vincent van Gogh and contemporaries; prints and letters by Vincent van Gogh

M **STEDLIJK MUSEUM-AMSTERDAM,** Municipal Museum, Paulus Potterstraat 13, PO Box 5082 1007 AB. Tel 020-73 21 66. *Dir* E L L de Wilde
Collections: Applied art and design - especially bibliophile editions, ceramics, furniture (Rietveld), glass, photography, posters, textiles, typography; Cezanne; Chagall; Dutch art 1850 to present; European and American tendencies after 1960 (Colorfield Painting, Conceptual Art, Pop Art, Nouveau Realisme, Zero); European Expressionism; international paintings and sculptures dating from 1850 to present; Monet; paintings by Cobra-group, Dubuffet, Malevich, Matisse, Mondrian; Printroom - drawings, graphic art, especially Werkman, Cobra; van Gogh Collection

ARNHEM

M **GEMEENTEMUSEUM ARNHEM,** Municipal Museum of Arnhem, Utrechtseweg 87, 6000 IT. Tel 085-431841. *Dir* Dr L Brandt Corstius
Collections: Chinese Porcelain 15th - 18th Centuries; Delftware; Dutch Painting 17th - 20th Century (new realism); drawings and prints of the 18th - 20th Centuries; Provincial Archaeology and History; Silverware of the 18th - 19th Centuries; Tin Dutch 15th - 19th Centuries; Topographical and Historical Maps of the Province of Gelderland

DELFT

M STEDELIJK MUSEUM HET PRINSENHOF, Het Prinsenhof State Museum, St Agathaplein 1. Tel 015-13111, Ext 2336. *Dir* Dr R A Leeuw
Collections: Delft silver, Delftica, tapestries and †ware; Dutch art of the 15th, 16th, 17th and 18th centuries; collection of paintings of Orange-Nassau family, especially William the Silent and the 80-year war

EINDHOVEN

M MUNICIPAL VAN ABBEMUSEUM, Eindhoven Municipal Museum, Bilderdijklaan 10, PO Box 235, 5611 NH. Tel 040-448555, Ext 2199. *Dir* R H Fuchs
Collections: Collection ranges from Cubism to the latest trends in art (conceptual art, etc); concept art, Lissitzky Collection, Postpainterly Abstraction, neoconstructivism, specialities

ENSCHEDE

M RIJKSMUSEUM TWENTHE TE ENSCHEDE, Lasondersingel 129. *Dir* Dr Al Hulshoff
Collections: Prehistoric finds of eastern Netherlands, local history and paintings, collection of art from middle ages to c 1930

GRONINGEN

M GRONINGEN MUSEUM VOOR STAD EN LAND, Groningen Museum, Praediniussingel 59. Tel 17 29 29. *Dir* Dr F Haks
Collections: Paintings and drawings from the 16th - 20th Century, mainly Dutch, including Hofstede de Groot Collection, 17th Century and Veendorp Collection, second-half 19th Century; European ceramics; Oriental ceramics; local archaeology and history; silver

HAARLEM

M TEYLERS MUSEUM, Spaarne 16 (Mailing add: Damstraat 21, 2011 HA). Tel 023-32 01 97. *Board of Trustees* H E Stenfert Kroese; *Cur Art* J H van Borssum Buisman; *Cur Palaeontology & Mineralogy* Dr J H C Walenkamp; *Cur Numismatics* Dr H E van Gelder; *Cur Library* J G de Bruijn
Collections: Drawings 16th - 19th century Dutch, Italian and French School; 19th century Dutch paintings; cabinet of coins and medals, historical physical instruments, minerals and fossils

THE HAGUE

M HAAGS GEMEENTEMUSEUM, Municipal Museum of The Hague, Stadhouderslaan 41, 2517 HV, PO Box 72, 2501 CB. Tel 070-51 41 81. *Dir* Dr T van Velzen
Collections: Ancient Decorative Arts Collection includes Chinese pottery and porcelain, Delft pottery, Islamic pottery, Italian and Spanish majolica; ancient Indonesian art; Art of the Ancient World: Coptic textiles, Greek pottery, terracottas; Dutch artists: Jongkind, van Gogh, Weissenbruch; Dutch Colonial furniture; Dutch period rooms 1680-1780; Egyptian, Roman, Islamic, Venetian and Dutch glass; German Expressionists: living Dutch artists, Escher, Heyboer, Mondiran, Werkman; Hague procelain 1776-1784; Hague silver 17th - 19th century; Modern Art Collection includes decorative arts, paintings and sculpture of the 19th and 20th century; objects in Bronze and Dutch pewter; largest collection of works (257) by Piet Mondrian, van Doesburg and other members of the Stijl group; recent trends: Karel Appel, Constant, Visser and Westerik; foreign artists, notably: Bonington, Monet, Redon; Expressionist: Kirchner, Kokoschka, Lissitsky, Picasso; paintings by Bacon, Kitaj, Vasarely; sculptures by Arp, Lipchitz, Moore. Printroom: large collection of prints and drawings of Dutch and foreign masters of the 19th and 20th century, notably: Bresdin, Toulouse Lautrec, Redon

M KONINKLIJK KABINET VAN SCHILDERIJEN, Royal Picture Gallery, Kneuterdijk 6. Tel 46 92 44. *Dir* H R Hoetink
Collections: Paintings of the Dutch and Flemish Masters of the 15th, 16th, 17th and 18th Centuries

M MUSEUM BREDIUS, Prinsegracht 6, 2512 GA The Hague. *Dir* Dr T Van Velzen
Collections: 17th century Dutch art, including paintings and drawings by Rembrandt, van Ruysdael, Jan Steen, Adriaen van Ostade

HERTOGENBOSCH

M NOORDBRABANTS MUSEUM, Bethaniestraat 4, 5211 LJ. Tel 073-13 87 12. *Dir* Dr M M A van Boven
Collections: All collections have an emphasis on local history: archaeology, arts and crafts 1500-1800, coins and medals, painting and sculpture 1500-1900, religious art

HOORN

M WESTFRIES MUSEUM, Huis Verloren, Kerkstraat 10. *Dir* W A Braasem
Collections: 17th and 18th century paintings, prints, oak panelling, glass, pottery, furniture, costumes, interiors; objects of trade, navigation and business; folk art; historical objects from Hoorn and West Friesland; West Friesland naive painting; prehistoric finds

LEERDAM

M NATIONAAL GLASMUSEUM, Lingedijk 28, 4142 LD. Tel 4-7102. *Pres* J Colporaal
Collections: Antique, machine-made and packaging glass; handmade serial glass; unique pieces

LEEUWARDEN

M FRIES MUSEUM, Turfmarkt 24, 8911 KT. Tel 05100-23001. *Dir* Dr C Boschma
Collections: Archaeology, ceramics, costumes, folk art, historical items, painting, prints and drawings, sculpture, silver, textiles

LEIDEN

M STEDELIJK MUSEUM DE LAKENHAL, Leyden Municipal Museum, Oude Singel 28-32, 2312 RA. Tel 071 144044. *Dir* M L Wurfbain
Collections: Paintings (Lucas van Leyden, Rembrandt, Steen, van Goyen, and others - 2000 items); sculpture (medieval, 17th - 20th Century); arms, ceramics, furniture, glass, period rooms, pewter, silver, tiles

MUIDEN

M MUIDERSLOT RIJKSMUSEUM, *Dir* S P Baron Bentinck
Collections: 13th century castle furnished in early 17th century style; paintings, tapestries, furniture and armory

NIJMEGEN

M NIJMEEGS MUSEUM COMMANDERIE VAN SAINT JAN, Franse Plaats 3, 6511 VS. Tel 80-229193. *Dir* Dr G T M Lemmens
Collections: Art and history of Nijmegen and region: Middle Ages - 20th Century; modern international art

OTTERLO

M RIJKSMUSEUM KROLLER-MULLER, Kroller-Muller State Museum, National Park de Hoge Veluwe, 6730 AA. Tel 08382-241. *Dir* Dr R W D Oxenaar
Collections: Van Gogh Collection (278 works); 19th and 20th century art - drawings, paintings, sculptures, sculpture garden, sculptor drawings

ROTTERDAM

M MUSEUM BOYMANS-VAN BEUNINGEN, Mathenesserlaan 18-20, PO Box 2277, 3000 CG. Tel 36 05 00. *Dir* Dr W A L Beeren
Collections: Heronimus Bosch's The Prodigal Son; Pieter Breughel's The Tower of Babel; Italian and French paintings from the 15th - 19th centuries and contemporary paintings and objects; Rembrandt's Portrait of Rembrandt's Son Titus; 21 paintings by Rubens; Hubert and Jan van Eyck's The Three Marys at the Open Sepulchre; paintings of the Netherlands from the brothers van Eyck to Vincent van Gogh; works by Salvador Dali, Jim Dine, Kandinsky, Oscar Kokoschka, Franz Marc, Rene Margritte, Andy Warhol, and others; ceramics, furniture, glass, lace, old and modern drawings and graphic art, pewter, silver

NEW ZEALAND

AUCKLAND

M AUCKLAND CITY ART GALLERY, Kitchener St, PO Box 5449, 1. Tel 792 020. *Head of Department* Grant Kirby
Collections: American and Australian paintings; general collection of European paintings and sculpture from 12th century on; historical and contemporary European prints and drawings; historical and contemporary New Zealand painting, sculpture and prints; International and New Zealand photography

L UNIVERSITY OF AUCKLAND, Fine Arts Library, School of Fine Arts, 20 Whitaker Place, 1. Tel 31 897. *Dir* Jolyon D Saunders
Collections: Quoin Club Collection

DUNEDIN

M DUNEDIN PUBLIC ART GALLERY, Logan Park. *Dir* F H Dickinson
Collections: 15th - 19th century European paintings; New Zealand paintings from 1875; Australian paintings 1900-60; British watercolors; portraits and landscapes; ancillary collections of furniture, ceramics, glass, silver, oriental rugs

INVERCARGILL

M ANDERSON PARK ART GALLERY, Myross Bush Rd, Waikiwi, PO Box 755. *Pres* K A Ballinger
Collections: Contemporary New Zealand art

NAPIER

M HAWKES BAY ART GALLERY AND MUSEUM, Herschel St, PO Box 429.
Tel 57781
Collections: Antiques; Maori artifacts; New Zealand painting and sculpture

WANGANUI

M SARJEANT GALLERY, Queens Park, Box 637. Tel 57052. *Dir* W H Milbank
Collections: European works; local works; New Zealand collection of paintings;
photographic works (based around Denton Collection); sculpture and applied arts

WELLINGTON

M NATIONAL ART GALLERY OF NEW ZEALAND, Buckle St. Tel 859 703.
Dir L H Bieringa
Collections: Australian, British, European and New Zealand art; Sir Harold
Beauchamp Collection of early English drawings, illustrations and watercolors;
Sir John Illott Collection of graphics; Nan Kivell Collection of British original
prints; Monrad Collection of early European graphics; National Collection of
New Zealand drawings; small collection of Old Master drawings; Archdeacon
Smythe Collection; John Weeks Collection; Harold Wright Collection of graphics

NORWAY

BERGEN

M VESTLANDSKE KUNSTINDUSTRIMUSEUM, Western Norway Museum of
Applied Art, Nordal Brunsgate 9, 5000. Tel 05-21 51 08. *Museum Dir* Peter M
Anker
Collections: Antique Bergen silver; Chinese arts from the Renaissance to
modern times; contemporary Norwegian and European ceramics; The General
Munthe Collection of Chinese Art; collections of old European arts and crafts;
The Anna B and William H Singer Collection of art and antiquities; furniture,
glass, metalwork, textiles

LILLEHAMMER

M LILLEHAMMER BYS MALERISAMLING, Lillehammer Art Museum,
Kirkegaten 69, 2600. Tel 062 51944. *Chief Executive* Ole Ronning Johannesen
Collections: Norwegian paintings, sculpture and graphic art from 19th and 20th
centuries

OSLO

M CITY OF OSLO ART COLLECTION, Munch Museum, Toyengaten 53
(Mailing add: PO Box 2812, Kampen 5). *Dir* Alf Boe
Collections: Paintings, prints and drawings of Edvard Munch; works by the
Sculptor Gustav Vigeland (Nobelsgt 32); contemporary paintings (donated by
Rolf E Stenersen); decorations, monuments and sculptures belonging to the city
of Oslo

M KUNSTINDUSTRIMUSEET I OSLO, Oslo Museum of Applied Art, St Olavs
Gate 1. Tel 02-203578. *Dir* Lauritz Opstad
Collections: Ceramics, furniture, glass, silver, textiles, old and modern

M NASJONALGALLERIET, Universitetsgaten 13, 1. *Dir* Knut Berg
Collections: Norwegian paintings and sculpture; Old European paintings; icon
collection; examples, especially of modern French, Danish and Swedish art; a
collection of prints and drawings; a small collection of Greek and Roman
sculptures

M NORSK FOLKEMUSEUM, Norwegian Folk Museum, Bygdoy, 2. Tel 55 80
90. *Dir* Halvard Björkvik
Collections: The Lappish section provides an insight into the ancient culture of
the Lapps. The Open Air Museum totals about 170 old buildings, all original.
Among them are the Stave Church from Hallingdal; farmsteads from different
districts of the country; single buildings of particular interest; The Old Town -
17th, 18th and 19th century town houses. Urban Collections - Norwegian town
interiors from the Renaissance to the present; Henrik Ibsen's study; the first
Parliament Hall of Norway (1814); post-Renaissance costumes; other collections
include peasant art and furniture; post-medieval church art; woven tapestries;
tools and techniques of old Norwegian farming; toys and dolls; modern primitive
musical instruments

M NORSK SJOFARTSMUSEUM, Norwegian Maritime Museum, Bygodoynes
37. Tel 55 63 95. *Dir* Sven Molaug
Collections: The Polarship Gjoa; archives pertaining to maritime history;
instruments, paintings, photographs of ships, ship models, tools and other items
pertaining to maritime collections; special exhibitions of small crafts

L STATENS KUNSTAKADEMI BIBLIOTEKET, Uranienborgsvn 2, 2. *Librn*
Tamiko Kauakami Nielsen

M UNIVERSITETETS SAMLING AV NORDISKE OLDSAKER, University
Museum of National Antiquities, Frederiksgate 2. Tel 416300. *Dir* Dr Sverre
Marstrander
Collections: Church art and profane objects from the Medieval Age; material
from the Norwegian Stone, Bronze and Iron Ages

PAKISTAN

KARACHI

M NATIONAL MUSEUM OF PAKISTAN, Burns Garden. Tel 5-51-08. *Supt of
Museum* Taswir Husain Hamidi
Collections: Specimen of calligraphy, large collection of coins and miniature
paintings spreading from 6th century BC to 19th century AD; ethnological
material from the various regions of Pakistan; gold jewelry from Taxila; Gradhara
sculptures in stone, stucco and terra-cotta; Hindu sculptures in stone; Islamic
period glass, pottery, scientific instruments and carpets; manuscripts, largely of
Muslim period; prehistoric and protohistoric period material from the Indus
Valley sites

LAHORE

M LAHORE FORT MUSEUM, *Supt Archaeology* Ahmad Nabi Khan
Collections: Mughal Gallery: Mughal paintings, coins, calligraphy, mss, faience,
carving; Sikh Gallery: arms and armor, paintings and art of Sikh period; Sikh
Painting Gallery: oil paintings from the Princess Bamba Collection

M LAHORE MUSEUM, Shahrah-E-Quaid-E-Azam. *Dir* Dr Saifur Rahman Dar
Collections: Coins Room; Ethnological I, II and III - Fabrics and Clay Models;
Fagir; Gandhara; Hindu; Islamic; Jain Temple; Pakistan movement; Sadequain's
paintings; arms, calligraphy and miscellaneous, contemporary paintings, miniature
paintings, pre-historic and proto-historic, stamps and medals

PESHAWAR

M PESHAWAR MUSEUM, Grand Trunk Rd. *Dir* Prof Fidaullah Sehrai
Collections: Architectural pieces and minor antiquities; mainly sculptures of the
Grandhara School containing images of Buddha, Bodhisattvas, Buddhist deities,
reliefs illustrating the life of the Buddha and Jataka stories

RAWALPINDI

M ART GALLERY SOCIETY OF CONTEMPORARY ART, Rawalpindi Gallery
of Modern Art, 25 Civil Lines. Tel 6 27 27. *Executive Dir* Zubeida Agha
Collections: Thirty-three paintings by top Pakistani and foreign artists;
permanent collection is not on view due to lack of space

TAXILA

M ARCHAEOLOGICAL MUSEUM, Rawalpindi, Taxila District. *Custodian* A A
Farooq
Collections: Antiquities from Taxila Sites ranging from 7th Century BC to 5th
Century AD; gold and silver ornaments; pottery; sculptures of stone and stucco
of Ganhara and Indo-Afghan School

PERU

LIMA

M MUSEO DE ARTE, Museum of Art, Paseo Colon 125. Tel 32 62 42. *Dir* Dr
Arturo G Seminario
Collections: Colonial painting; pre-Inca and Inca collections; Republic paintings;
carvings, ceramics, furniture, metals, modern paintings, religious art, sculpture,
textiles

M MUSEO NACIONAL DE LA CULTURA PERUANA, National Museum of
Peruvian Culture, Avenida Alfonso Ugarte 650, Apdo 3048. Tel 23 58 92. *Dir*
Dr Rosalia Avalos de Matos
Collections: Ethnography of Amazonic tribes; ethnology, folklore, popular art

PHILIPPINES

MANILA

M LOPEZ MEMORIAL MUSEUM, 10 Lancaster Ave. Tel 80-16-29, 80-51-96.
Dir Celso G Cabrera
Collections: De Muluccis Insulis by Maximilianus Transylvanus (1954); rare
Philippine imprints from early 17th century: Laureano Atlas, Juan Correa,
Nicolas de la Cruz Bagay, Raymundo Magysa, Pinpin and other printers; 13,000
Filipiniana titles; 14th - 15th century artifacts recovered in the Calatagan burial
sites, consists chiefly of a few Annamese and Siamese pieces, beads, Filipino
earthenwares and porcelain of Chinese origin; Luna and Hidalgo paintings;
Relacion de las Islas Filipinas by Jesuit Pedro Chiroino (1604); 90 priceless
letters of Rizal to his mother and sisters; †Spanish and early American period -
albums of pictures, maps, microfilms, old periodicals and woodcuts; travel
literature by Gemelli Careri, Dampier, Hakluyt, La Perouse, Linschoten,
Navarrete, Purchas and others

M UNIVERSITY OF SANTO TOMAS, Santo Tomas Museum, Calle Espana. Tel 47-22-31, Ext 269
Collections: Archaeology, cultural and historical items; Chinese trade pottery; coins; ethnology of the Philippines; medals; Philippine art; shells; stamps

POLAND

CRACOW

L CENTRAL LIBRARY OF THE ACADEMY OF FINE ARTS, ul Smilensk 9, 30-035. *Dir* Anna Pankowicz
Collections: 44,250 photographs, posters, prints

M MUZEUM NARODOWE W KRAKOWIE, National Museum in Cracow, ul Manifestu Lipcowego 12. Tel 227-33, 227-63. *Dir* Tadeusz Chruscick
Collections: National Museum in Cracow consists of several departments with various collections. The Director and Administration seat is in the Palace of E Hutten Czapski. The Emeryk Hutten Czapski Department, ul Manifestu Lipcowego 12 - graphics 120,000, numismatic collections 250,000, old books 45,000. Department of Textiles, ul Smolensk 9. Szolayski House, pl Szczepanski 9 - department of arms and armour, Far Eastern Art, icons. Gallery of Polish painting and sculpture of the 16th - 18th Centuries, Gallery of Polish painting and sculpture of the 19th - 20th Centuries. Czartoryski Collection

M PANSTWOWE ZBIORY SZTUKI NA WAWELU, Wawel State Collections of Art, Wawel 5. *Dir* Dr Jerzy Szablowski
Collections: Italian Renaissance furniture; King Sigismund Augustus 16th Century Collection of Flemish Tapestries; Oriental carpets and tents; Polish, Western-European and Oriental weapons; Royal Treasury; Western-European and Oriental pottery; Western European painting; banners, crown jewels, gold objects, historical relics

LODZ

M MUZEUM SZTUKI, Wieckowskiego 36. Tel 397-90. *Dir* Ryszard Stanislawski
Collections: Paintings of Karol Hiller, Wladyslaw Strzeminski; sculptures of Katarzyna Kobro

WROCLAW

M MINISTRY OF CULTURE AND ART, Museum of Architecture in Wroclaw, Bernardynska nr 5, 50-156. Tel 871-336 75. *Dir* Prof Olgierd Czerner
Collections: Elements of architecture, drawings, graphics, memorials of architects, objects of artistic craftsmanship, pictures, projects, sketches

M MUZEUM NARODOWE, 50-153 Wroclaw. *Dir* Leszek Itman
Collections: Medieval art; Polish painting of the 18th, 19th and 20th centuries; European painting, decorative arts, prints, ethnography and history relating to Silesia; numismatics

M MUZEUM NARODOWE WE WROCLAWIU, National Museum, Place Powstancow Warszawy 5, 50-153. Tel 3 88 39. *Dir* Dr Leszek Itman
Collections: Contemporary art, photography, painting and sculpture; Decorative Hunters Arms 16th - 18th Centuries; Foreign paintings 16th - 19th Centuries, Medieval Art 14th - 16th Centuries; Polish painting 18th - 20th Centuries; Silesian Art 16th - 18th Centuries; Silesian stone carvings 12th - 16th Centuries

PORTUGAL

EVORA

M MUSEU DE EVORA, Largo do Conde de Vila Flor. *Dir* Maria Alice L Tavares Chico
Collections: Paintings: large collection of 16th century Flemish and Portuguese works; 17th century works; local prehistoric tools and Roman art and archeology; sculpture from middle ages to the 19th century; 18th century Portuguese furniture and silver

LAMEGO

M MUSEU DE LAMEGO, *Dir* Abel Montenegro Florido
Collections: Important collection of 16th century Brussels tapestries; Portuguese painting of 16th and 18th centuries; sculpture; religious ornaments

LISBON

M MUSEU CALOUSTE GULBENKIAN, Ave de Berne. Tel 76 50 61. *Dir* Marie Teresa Gomes Ferrevra

M MUSEU NACIONAL DE ARTE ANTIGA, National Museum of Ancient Art, Rua das Janelas Verdes. Tel 664151, 672725. *Dir* Maria Alice Beaumont
Collections: Foreign art - ceramic, goldsmith art, painting and sculpture; Oriental art of Portuguese influence; ornamental art - ceramics, furniture, goldsmith art and textiles; Persian carpets; Portuguese art - paintings from the 15th - 19th centuries; sculpture 13th - 18th centuries

M MUSEU NACIONAL DE ARTE CONTEMPORANEA, National Museum of Contemporary Art, Rua Serpa Pinto 6. Tel 36 80 28. *Dir* Maria de Lourdes Bartholo
Collections: Contemporary painting and sculpture

OPORTO

M MUSEU NACIONAL DE SOARES DOS REIS, National Museum of Soares Dos Reis, Palacio dos Carrancas, Rua de D Manuel II. Tel 27110. *Dir* Maria Emilia Amaral Teixeira
Collections: Furniture, glass, goldsmith, jewelry, old and modern paintings, porcelain, pottery, sculpture

REPUBLIC OF SINGAPORE

SINGAPORE

M NATIONAL MUSEUM ART GALLERY, Stamford Rd, 0617. Tel 326077, 321281. *Dir* Christopher Hooi
Collections: Paintings and sculptures by artists of Singapore and Southeast Asia

REPUBLIC OF SOUTH AFRICA

CAPE PROVINCE

M MICHAELIS COLLECTION, Old Town House, Greenmarket Square. Tel 048 43 40 15. *Dir* W H Gravett
Collections: Dutch and Flemish graphic art and paintings of the 16th - 18th centuries

CAPE TOWN

M SOUTH AFRICAN NATIONAL GALLERY, Government Ave, PO Box 2420, 8000. *Dir* Dr Raymund H van Niekerk
Collections: South African art 19th and 20th century and European art 15th - 20th century, including drawings, paintings, prints, sculptures and watercolours

DURBAN

M DURBAN ART GALLERY, City Hall, Smith St, PO Box 4085, 4000. *Cur* E S J Addleson
Collections: Chinese ceramics; Dutch and Flemish 17th century; French 19th century; Sevres ceramics; South African; Victorian; contemporary art

JOHANNESBURG

M JOHANNESBURG ART GALLERY, Joubert Park. Tel 725-3130. *Dir* Mrs P A Senior
Collections: Approximately 2500 prints from Durer to present; 17th Century Dutch; 19th Century French; 19th Century English; South African; international modern art; small collection of ceramics and textiles

KIMBERLEY

M WILLIAM HUMPHREYS ART GALLERY, Civic Centre, PO Box 885. Tel 0531-28031. *Cur* Mrs R J Holloway
Collections: Representative collection of Dutch, English, Flemish and French Old Masters; collection of South African works of art

PIETERMARITZBURG

M TATHAM ART GALLERY, 2nd Floor City Hall, Commerical Rd, PO Box 321. Tel 27031, Ext 127. *Cur* Lorna Ferguson
Collections: 19th and 20th Century English and French paintings and sculpture; 19th and 20th Century English graphics; modern European graphics; South African painting and sculpture 1920-1940; the Whitwell bequest

PORT ELIZABETH

M KING GEORGE VI ART GALLERY, One Park Dr, 6001. Tel 041-28589. *Dir* Clayton S Holliday
Collections: English painting; international graphics; Oriental ceramics and miniatures; South African art

PRETORIA

M PRETORIA ART MUSEUM, Arcadia Park (on Park St), Transvaal. Tel 444271. *Dir* Dr A J Werth
Collections: American and European graphics, mostly 20th Century; 17th Century Dutch Art; 19th and 20th Century South African

ROMANIA

BUCHAREST

M MUZEUL DE ARTA AL RSR, Str Stirbei Voda 1. *Dir* Dr Alexandru Cebuc
Collections: Medieval Romanian art (9th - 18th century); National Gallery: National, Old Romanian, modern & contemporary works of art; Universal Gallery: paintings, sculptures, European decorative arts & Oriental art; graphic art & prints
M Sectia de arta brincoveneasca, Str Donca Simo 18
Collections: Old Romanian art
M Sectia de Arta Feudala D Minovici, Str Dr N Minovici 3
Collections: Foreign decorative art collection

CLUJ-NAPOCA

M MUZEUL DE ARTA CLUJ-NAPOCA, Museum of Art, Piata Libertatii 30. Tel 951-26952, 951-26953. *Dir* Alexandra Rus
Collections: Decorative arts; European and Romanian art, including graphics, paintings and sculpture of the 15th - 20th centuries

M MUZEUL ETNOGRAFIC AL TRANSILVANIEI, Str 30 Decembrie 21. Tel (951) 12344. *Dir* Tiberiu Graur
Collections: Over 53,000 exhibits with special emphasis on Transylvanian traditional occupations; primitive people; Ethnographical Park, the first open-air museum in Romania is a special section of the Ethnographic Museum

SCOTLAND

DUNDEE

M DUNDEE MUSEUMS AND ART GALLERY, Albert Square, DD1 1DA. Tel 0382-25492. *Dir* James D Boyd
Collections: 18th, 19th and 20th Century Scottish and English paintings; 17th Century Venetian and Flemish works; varied selection of watercolors and prints from the 18th - 20th Century

EDINBURGH

M NATIONAL GALLERY OF SCOTLAND, The Mound, EH2 2EL. *Dir* Colin Thompson
Collections: Drawings, paintings, prints and sculpture, 14th - 19th Centuries

M ROYAL SCOTTISH MUSEUM, Chambers St. Tel 031 225 7534. *Dir* Dr Norman Tebble
Collections: Collections of the Decorative Arts of the World

GLASGOW

M GLASGOW MUSEUMS AND ART GALLERIES, Kelvingrove Art Gallery and Museum, Argyll St, G3 8AG. Tel 041 334 1134. *Dir* Alasdair A Auld
Collections: Archaeology; British and Scottish art (especially the Scottish Colourists); Decorative Art Collection of ceramics, glass, jewelry, silver (especially Scottish); ethnography; Fine Art Collection representing the Dutch, Flemish, French and Italian Schools; history; natural history

SPAIN

BARCELONA

M MUSEO DE ARTE CATALUNA, Museum of Ancient Art, Parque de Montjuich Palacio Nacional. Tel 2-23-18 24. *Cur* M Carmen Farie Sanpera
Collections: Baroque and Renaissance paintings; Catalan Gothic and Romanesque paintings and sculpture

M MUSEO DE ARTE MODERNO, Museum of Modern Art, Palacio de la Ciudadela. Tel 319 57 30. *Dir* Juan Barbeta Antones
Collections: Modern art

M MUSEO PICASSO, Calle Montcada 15-17. Tel 3196310. *Dir* Rosa Maria Subirana
Collections: Pablo Picasso, 1890-1972: paintings, sculpture, drawings and engravings, including the series Las Meninas and the artist's donation, in 1970 of 940 works of art

BILBAO

M MUSEO DE BELLAS ARTES, Museum of Fine Arts, Parque de Dona Casilda de Iturriza. *Dir* Crisanto De Lasterra
Collections: Basque modern and contemporary art; Classical Gothic, Renaissance and Romanesque Art; general contemporary art; 12th century Romantic art; traditional Spanish 12th century art

MADRID

M MUSEO CERRALBO, Ventura Rodriguez 17, 8. *Dir* Consuelo Sanz-Pastor Pierola
Collections: Paintings; drawings; engravings; porcelain arms; carpets; coins; furniture; includes paintings by: El Greco, Ribera, Titian, Van Dyck and Tintoretto

M MUSEO DEL PRADO, Calle de Felipe IV. *Dir* Xavier de Salas
Collections: Paintings by: Botticelli, Rembrandt, Velazquez, El Greco, Goya, Murillo, Raphael, Bosch, Van der Weyden, Zurbaran, Van Dyck, Tiepolo, Ribalta, Rubens, Titian, Veronese, Tintoretto, Moro, Juanes, Menendez, Poussin, Ribera; classical and Renaissance sculpture; jewels and medals

M MUSEO LAZARO GALDIANO, Calle Serrano 122. Tel 2616084. *Dir* D Enrique Pardo Canalis
Collections: 50,000 items: Italian, Spanish and Flemish Renaissance paintings; primitives; Golden Age 18th - 19th century Spanish paintings; 17th century Dutch paintings; English 18th century collection

M MUSEO ROMANTICO, Museum of the Romantic Epoch, San Mateo 13, 4. Tel 448-10-45, 448-10-71
Collections: Books, decorations, furniture and paintings of the Spanish Romantic period

M PATRIMONIO NACIONAL, Calle de Bailen, Spain
Estab 1940 to administer former Crown property; it is responsible for all the museums situated in Royal Palaces & properties & is governed by an administrative council
Publications: Guides to all the Museums
M Palacio Real de Madrid,
Also maintains armoury, coach museum & 300,000 volume library
Collections: Special room devoted to 16th-18th century tapestries, clocks, paintings & porcelain from the Royal Palaces & Pharmacy
M Palacio Real de Aranjuez, Aranjuez
Collections: Former Royal Palace rich in 18th century art
M Monasterio de San Lorenzo de El Escorial, El Escorial
Built by Juan de Herrera & contains many famous works by international artists of the 16th & 18th century from royal residences
M Alcazar de Sevilla, Seville
Collections: Royal residence
M Museum-Monasterio de las Huelgas, Burgos
Founded by Alfonso VIII in the 9th century
M Museo-Monasterio de Tordesillas, Valladolid
Collections: 14th century art
M Museo de la Encarnacion,
Collections: Monastic life in the 16th & 17th centuries
M Museo de las Descalzas Reales,
Collections: Showing monastic life in the 16th & 17th centuries
M Palacio de Rlofrio, Segovia
Founded 18th century
Collections: Notable furniture & paintings of Spanish romantic movement
M Palacio de la Granja de San Ildefonso, Segovia
Collections: Gardens & fountains in imitation of Versailles, tapestry museum
M Museo de Pedralbes, Barcelona
Collections: 19th century royal residence; replicas of modern royal residences
M Castillo de Bellver, Majorca
Collections: Royal palace; small museum of the 18th century

TOLEDO

M CASA DEL GRECO: FUNDACIONES VEGA INCLAN, *Cur* Maria Elena Gomez-Moreno
Collections: Artist's paintings and those of his followers; 16th century furniture
M Museo del Greco,
Collections: El Greco's paintings, including portraits of Christ and the apostles and other 16th and 17th century paintings

M CASA Y MUSEO DEL GRECO, El Greco's House and Museum, Calle de Samuel Levi. Tel 22 40 46
Collections: Furniture, objects of the period, paintings of El Greco, including the series of Christ and the Apostles; other paintings of various periods, 15th - 18th Century

SWITZERLAND 449

SRI LANKA

COLOMBO

M **COLOMBO NATIONAL MUSEUM,** Albert Crescent, PO Box 854. Tel 94767.
Dir Dr P de Silva
Collections: Antiquities of Sri Lanka; rare books and palm leaf manuscripts of Sri Lanka

SWEDEN

GOTHENBURG

M **GOTEBORG KONSTMUSEUM,** Gothenburg Art Gallery, Gotaplatsen 412 56.
Tel 031-189537. *Dir* Karl-Gustaf Heden
Collections: French Art 1800-1945; Old Masters, especially Dutch and Flemish 17th century; Scandinavian art, 17th century to present; contemporary art (international collection of prints and drawings); collections include drawings, prints and watercolours circa 45,000, paintings 2400, sculptures 550

M **ROHSSKA KONSTSLOJDMUSEET,** Rohss Museum of Arts and Crafts, 37-39 Vasgatan, S-41137. Tel 031-188930. *Dir* Jan Brunius
Collections: The Falk Simon Bequest of Old Silver; bookbindings, ceramics, furniture, glass, metalworks, textile

LUND

M **GALERIE ST PETRI ARCHIVE OF EXPERIMENTAL & MARGINAL ART,** PO Box 1507
Collections: Unlimited Expression

STOCKHOLM

M **KUNGL MYNTKABINETTET STATENS MUSEUM FOR MYNT MEDALJ OCH PENNINGHISTORIA,** Royal Coin Cabinet, National Museum of Monetary History, Storgatan 41, PO Box 5405, S-114 84. Tel 08-63 07 70.
Keeper Ulla Westermark
Collections: Bank notes (40,000), coins (400,000), medals (35,000). The collections range over the entire world and all periods

M **NATIONALMUSEUM,** 103 24. *Supt* P Bjurstrom
Collections: 6672 paintings, icons and miniatures; 4492 sculptures, including antiquities; 197,000 drawings and prints; 28,000 numbers of applied art; collections of several royal castles with 7440 works of art

M **NORDISKA MUSEET,** Scandinavian Museum, Djurgarden, S-115 21. Tel 63 08-63. *Dir* Dr Sune Zachrisson
Collections: Costumes, folk art, handcrafts, period furnishings; approximately one million exhibits

M **OSTASIATISKA MUSEET,** Museum of Far Eastern Antiquities, Skeppsholmen, PO Box 163 81, 103 27. Tel 08 244200. *Dir* Bo Gyllensvard
Collections: Approximately 110,000 objects in the permanent collection including Chinese art from Neolithic times to present, Buddhist sculpture, bronzes, painting and porcelain, Stone-age pottery; Indian, Japanese and Korean Art

M **STATENS HISTORISKA MUSEUM,** Museum of National Antiquities, Storgatan 41, PO Box 5405, S 114 84. *Dir* Olov Isaksson
Collections: Prehistory, medieval art, wooden sculpture, gold and silver treasures up to 16th Century

M **STOCKHOLMS STADSMUSEUM,** Ryssgarden Slussen. *Dir* Bjorn Hallerdt
Collections: 48,000 items, including the Lohe Treasure, naive 19th century paintings of Josabeth Sjoberg and armed 15th century vessel; 1,000,000 photographs; 2,000 paintings; 30,000 drawings; sketches; engravings

SWITZERLAND

AARAU

M **AARGAUER KUNSTHAUS,** Aargauer - Platz, 5000. *Dir* Heiny Widmer
Collections: Swiss painting and sculpture from 1750 to the present day; Caspar Wolf paintings (1735-1783) the first painter of the Alps; landscape painter Adolf Staebli and Auberjonois, Bruhmann, Amiet, G Giacometti, Hodler, Meyer-Amden, Louis Soutter, Vallotton

BASEL

M **KUNSTMUSEUM BASEL,** Offentliche Kunstsammlung, St Albangraben 16, CH-4010. Tel (061) 22-08-28. *Dir* Dr Christian Geelhaar
Collections: Pictures from 15th century to present day, notably by Witz, Holbein and contemporary painters; collection includes Grunewald, Greco, Rembrandt; 16th - 17th century Netherlandish painting, Cezanne, Gauguin and Van Gogh; large collection of cubist art; sculptures by Rodin and 20th century artists; American art since 1945; German and Swiss masters

M **MUSEUM FUR VOLKERKUNDE UND SCHWEIZERISCHES MUSEUM FUR VOLKSKUNDE BASEL,** Museum of Ethnological Collections and Folklore, Augustinergasse 2-Munsterplatz 20, PO Box 1048, 4001. Tel 061 25 82 82. *Dir* Dr Gerhard Baer
Collections: Africa, America, Asia, Melanesia, Polynesia, Switzerland; collection of textiles

M **OFFENTLICHE KUNSTSAMMLUNG-KUNSTMUSEUM BASEL,** Museum of Fine Arts, St Albangraben 16, CH-4010. Tel 22 08 28. *Dir* Dr Franz Meyer
Collections: American painting since 1945; 16th and 17th Century Dutch paintings; 15th and 16th Century paintings, including Konrad Witz, Grunewald, Holbein and others; 19th and 20th Century paintings from Corot to present; prints and drawings from Upper Rhine, German and Swiss Masters; sculptures by Rodin and 20th Century artists

BERN

M **KUNSTMUSEUM BERN,** Museum of Fine Arts Berne, Hodlerstrasse 12, CH 3011. Tel 22-09-44. *Dir* Dr Hugo Wagner
Collections: Dutch and contemporary artists; French and other European Masters of the 19th and 20th Centuries; Italian Masters; collection of Paul Klee works of 2600 items; Niklaus Manuel; Foundation Hermann and Margrit Rupf, important Cubist collection; Swiss Baroque Masters; Swiss 19th and 20th Century Masters; 20,000 drawings and engravings; illustrations

CHUR

M **BUNDNER KUNSTMUSEUM CHUR** (Formerly Bunder Art Museum), The Grisons Museum of Art, Postplatz, 7000. Tel 22 17 63. *Dir* Hans Hartmann
Collections: Augusto, Alberto Giacometti, Giovanni, Angelika Kauffmann, E L Kirchner, plastic art, 19th and 20th centuries, Swiss painting

GENEVA

L **SCHOOL OF FINE ARTS LIBRARY,** 9, bd Helvetique, 1205. Tel 022-29 05 10. *In Charge* Jean Luc Zppinger

LA CHAUX DE FONDS

M **MUSEE DES BEAUX-ARTS ET SOCIETE DES AMIS DES ARTS,** Museum of Fine Arts, 33 Rue des Musees, 2300. Tel 039 22 12 50. *Dir & Cur* Paul Seylaz
Collections: Works of local artists as Leopold Robert a le Corbusier and contemporaries; Swiss works of the 19th and 20th Centuries; contemporary art including English, French, German, Italian, Japanese and Polish

LIGORNETTO

M **MUSEO VELA,** CH 6853. Tel 091 74 32 68, 031 61 92 77

SAINT GALLEN

M **HISTORISCHES MUSEUM,** Historical Museum, Musemstrasse 50, 9000. *Cur* Dr Louis Specker
Collections: Burgundian Standards of 1476; costumes, ethnology, furniture, glass and glass painting, graphics, period rooms, pewter, porcelain, textiles, weapons

SCHAFFHAUSEN

M **MUSEUM ZU ALLERHEILIGEN,** All Saints' Museum, Klosterplatz, CH-8200. *Dir* Dr Max Freivogel
Collections: Industrial art; 19th century; prehistoric; Roman

SOLOTHURN

M **KUNSTMUSEUM SOLOTHURN,** Solothurn Art Museum, Werkhofstrasse 30.
Conservator Andre Kamber
Collections: Large collection of Frank Buschser and Otto Grölicher; Holbein d J: Solothurner Madonna 1522; Meister des Paradiesgärtleins: Madonna in den Erdbeeren, um 1425; 20th Century Swiss Art; Cuno Amiet, B Luginbuhl, Alois Carigiet, Franz Eggenschwiler, Max Gubler, Ferdinand Hodler, Schang Hutter, Rolf Iseli, Bernhard Luthi, Manuboules, Otto Morach, Robert Muller, Meret Oppenehim, Dieter Roth, Heinz Schwarz, Rolf Spinnler, Spoerri, Hans Stocker, J Tinguely, Andre Thomkins, Valloton, Karl Walser, Oscar Wiggli

WINTERTHUR

M **KUNSTMUSEUM,** Museumstrasse 52. Tel (052) 84-51-62. *Cur* Dr Rudolf Koella
Collections: Swiss painting and sculpture from 18th century to present day; French, Italian and German painting and sculpture of 19th and 20th centuries, including Monet, Degas, Picasso, Gris, Leger, Klee, Schlemmer, Schwitters, Arp, Kandinsky, Renoir, Bonnard, Maillol, Van Gogh, Rodin, Brancusi, Morandi, Giacometti, de Stael; drawings and prints

ZURICH

M **KUNSTHAUS ZURICH,** Museum of Fine Arts, Heimplatz 1, Box 8024, CH-8001. Tel 01 32 67 65. *Dir* Dr F Baumanu
Collections: Alberto Giacometti-Foundation; medieval and modern sculptures; paintings 15th - 20th centuries, mainly 19th and 20th

M **MUSEUM RIETBERG ZURICH,** Gablerstrasse 14 & 15, CH-8002. Tel 202 45 28. *Dir* Dr Eberhard Fischer
Collections: African art; Chinese Painting; Baron von der Heydt Collection; Japanese Sculpture
L **Library,*** Gablerstrasse 14 & 15
Collections: Baron von der Heydt; Library of Prof Osvald Siren and others

M **SCHWEIZERISCHES LANDESMUSEUM,** Swiss National Museum, Museumstrasse 2, PO Box 2760, CH-8023. Tel 01-221 10 10. *Dir* Dr Hugo Schneider
Collections: Ancient crafts and trades, banners, ceramics, clocks and watches, coins, costumes, excavations, farming implements, furniture, glassware, goldsmith's art, interiors, jewelry, medals, military items, musical instruments, nonferrous metals, paintings, prints and drawings, pewter, prehistory and ancient history, stained glass, statuary, textiles, uniforms, weapons

SYRIA

DAMASCUS

M **NATIONAL MUSEUM OF DAMASCUS,** Reda Saeed St. *General Dir* Dr Afif Bahnassi
Collections: Ancient, Byzantine, Greek, Islamic, Modern, Oriental, Prehistoric and Roman art

TUNISIA

LE BARDO

M **MUSEE NATIONAL DU BARDO,** Bardo National Museum, Tel 261-002. *Dir* Ennaifer Mongi
Collections: Medieval and modern art, modern Islamic art; Greek and Roman antiquities; Roman mosaics

TURKEY

ISTANBUL

M **ISTANBUL ARKEOLOJI MUZELERI,** Archaeological Museums of Istanbul, Sultanahmet. Tel 279069, 279070. *Dir* Necati Dobenay
Collections: Architectural pieces, coins and cuneiform tablets from 6000 BC - 1500 AD, glass, inscriptions, metal, portraits, sarcophagi, statues

M **TOPKAPI SARAY MUSEUM,** Sultanahmed. Tel 28 3546-47. *Dir* Afif Sureyya
Collections: Chinese and Japanese porcelains; miniatures and portraits of Sultans; Alay Kiosk exhibit of Kenan Ozbel; Sami Ozgiritli's collection of furniture; Sultan's costumes; Turkish embroideries; calligraphy, clocks and watches, holy relics, rugs, throne room, tiled kiosk

M **TURK VE ISLAM ESERLERI MUZESI,** Museum of Turkish and Islamic Art, Suleymaniye, 6 Sifahane St. Tel 22 1888. *Dir* Can Kerametli
Collections: Books with miniatures and illumination; fermans and monograms of the Sultans, and other monuments of Islamic art; metalwork and ceramics; old Korans; the oldest Turkish carpets; sculpture in stone and stucco; wood carvings

URUGUAY

MONTEVIDEO

M **MUSEO NACIONAL DE ARTES PLASTICAS,** National Museum of Fine Arts, Tomas Giribaldi 2283, Parque Rodo. Tel 43 800. *Dir* Angel Kalenberg
Collections: Rafael Barradas, Juan Manuel Blanes, Jose Cuneo, Alfredo de Simone, Pedro Figari, Torres Garcia, Carlos Gonzalez, Carlos Federico Saez; 4217 ceramics, drawings, engravings, paintings and sculptures

USSR

LENINGRAD

M **STATE HERMITAGE MUSEUM,** M Dvortsovaya naberezhnaya 34. *Dir* B B Piotrovsky
Collections: Richest collection in Soviet Union of the art of prehistoric, ancient Eastern, Graeco - Roman and medieval times; preserves over 2,600,000 objects d'art, including 40,000 drawings, 500,000 engravings; works by Leonardo de Vinci, Raphael, Titian, Rubens and Rembrandt

MOSCOW

M **STATE MUSEUM OF ORIENTAL ART,** ul Obukha, 16. *Dir* Dr H Popov
Collections: Art of the Republics of Soviet Orient; Chinese art; monuments of art of Japan, India, Vietnam, Korea, Mongolia, Iran and other countries of the East

TALLINN

L **LIBRARY OF THE ESTONIAN STATE ART INSTITUTE,** Tartu maantee 1. *Head of Library* E Mutt
Collections: Books designed by graphic art students

VENEZUELA

CARACAS

M **MUSEO DE BELLAS ARTES,** Museum of Fine Arts, Parque Sucre, Los Caobos 105. Tel 54 37 92. *Dir* Miguel G Arroyo
Collections: Chinese and European porcelain; Egyptian art; European painting; Latin American paintings and sculpture, including primitives; pre-Columbian art; Venezuelan painting from the end of the 19th century to the present; drawings and prints

WALES

CARDIFF

M **NATIONAL MUSEUM OF WALES,** Cathays Park, CF1 3NP. Tel 0222-397951. *Dir* Douglas A Bassett
Collections: Davis Collection includes British paintings and drawings; French art of the 19th century including Renoir's La Parisienne (1874), and major works by Bonnard, Cezanne, Corot, Daumier, Manet, Millet, Monet, Pisarro, van Gogh; Old Masters, including the History of Aaneas, The Four Rubens Tapestry Cartoons, and works by Batoni, Canaletto, Cima, Constable, Gaulli, Guercino, Turner, Richard Wilson; De Winton Collection in continental porcelain; Jackson Collection of silver, containing many rarities (in the National Museum), and the Mostyn Ewer and Dish (Bruges circa 1540); Nance Collection specializes in pottery and porcelain of Swansea and Nantgarw; Pyke Thompson Collection includes ceramics, enamels, prints and watercolours by great artists of the early 19th century - Colman, Cox, De Wint, Girtin, Turner, and later artists including Holman Hunt and Rossetti

NEWPORT

M **NEWPORT MUSEUM AND ART GALLERY,** John Frost Square. Tel 0633-840064. *In Charge* Cefni Barnett
Collections: Art Gallery: ceramics and other applied art objects; early English watercolours; oil paintings by British artists; prints and drawings. Museum: geology; local archaeology (especially Roman); natural and social history

YUGOSLAVIA

BELGRADE

M **MUSEUM OF MODERN ART,** USCE SAVE BB, 11070. Tel 011-326-544. *Dir* Miodrag B Protic
Collections: Drawings, foreign collection of prints, new media, painting, prints, sculpture and tapestry

LJUBLJANA

M **MODERNA GALERIJA,** Modern Art Gallery, Tomsiceva 14, 6100. Tel 061-21-709. *Dir* Zoran Krzisnik
Collections: Slovene painting; sculpture and graphic art from 1900 to present

M **NARODNA GALERIJA,** National Art Gallery, Prezihova ulica 1-pp 432, 61001. Tel 21-765, 21-249. *Dir* Dr Anica Cevc
Collections: Copies of medieval frescoes; Foreign Masters from the 14th Century to the beginning of the 20th Century; Slovenian sculptures and paintings from the 13th to the beginning of the 20th Century

ZAGREB

M **GALERIJE GRADA ZAGREBA,** City Art Galleries, Katarinin trg 2, 41000. Tel 041 424 490. *Dir* Dr Boris Kelemen
Collections: Photograph collection

M **STROSSMAYEROVA GALERIJA STARIH MAJSTORA JUGOSLAVENSKE AKADEMIJE ZNANOSTI I UMJETNOSTI,** Strossmayer's Gallery of Old Masters of the Yugoslavia Academy of Sciences and Arts, Zrinjski trg 11, 41000. Tel 441-849. *Dir* Prof Vinko Zlamalik
Collections: Paintings and sculpture with emphasis on 15th - 16th Century Austrian painting, 16th - 18th Century Dutch and Flemish School, 18th - 20th Century French School, 16th Century German Art, Italian School from Renaissance to 18th Century

ZIMBABWE

SALISBURY

M **NATIONAL GALLERY OF ZIMBABWE RHODESIA,** PO Box 8155, Causeway. Tel 2 05 41. *Acting Dir* C M Till
Collections: African traditional and local contemporary sculpture and paintings; ancient and modern European paintings and sculpture; tapestries

Major Art Schools Abroad

ARGENTINA

BUENOS AIRES

ESCUELA NACIONAL DE BELLAS ARTES MANUEL BELGRANO, National School of Fine Arts Manuel Belgrano, Venceslao Villafane 1342. *Dir* Maria L San Martin

ESCUELA SUPERIOR DE BELLAS ARTES DE LA NACION ERNESTO DE LA CARCOVA, National Superior School of Fine Arts Ernesto de la Carcova, 1701 Tristan Achaval Rodriguez, Avenda Costanera Sur esquina Brasil. Tel 31-5144, 31-4419. *Rector* Jorge E Lezama

AUSTRALIA

BALLARAT

BALLARAT COLLEGE OF ADVANCED EDUCATION, School of the Arts, Gear Ave

DARLINGHURST

SCHOOL OF ART & DESIGN, Department of Technical Education, Forbes St, 2010. Tel 310266. *Head* Don Mitchell

LAUNCESTON

TASMANIAN COLLEGE OF ADVANCED EDUCATION, PO Box 1214, Tasmania 7250. *Head Art Dept* D R Tanton

MELBOURNE

VICTORIAN COLLEGE OF THE ARTS (Formerly National Gallery of Victoria Art School), School of Art, 234 St Kilda Rd, 3004. Tel 62-5061. *Dir* T Lenton Parr

RED HILL

ROYAL AUSTRALIAN INSTITUTE OF ARCHITECTS, 2A Mugga Way, ACT 2603. *Dir* D C R Bailey

SYDNEY

SYDNEY COLLEGE OF ADVANCED EDUCATION, School of Art, 200 Cumberland St, The Rocks

SYDNEY COLLEGE OF THE ARTS, 58 Allen St, PO Box 226, New South Whales 2037. *Principal* J Baily

UNIVERSITY OF SYDNEY, NSW 2006. Telex 20056; Tel 692-1122

AUSTRIA

SALZBURG

INTERNATIONAL SUMMER ACADEMY OF FINE ARTS, Kaigasse 2, PO Box 18, A-5010. *Pres* Dr Wieland Schmied

VIENNA

HOCHSCHULE FUR ANGEWANDTE KUNST IN WIEN, University of Applied Art in Vienna, Stubenring 3, A-1011. Tel 0222-72 21 91. *Rector* Oswald Oberhuber

BELGIUM

ANTWERP

NATIONAAL HOGAR INSTITUUT EN KONIN KLIJKE ACADEMIE VOOR SCHON KUNSTEN, 31 Mutsaertstraat, 2000. Tel 03-232-41-61. *Dir* L T VanLooij

NATIONAAL HOGER INSTITUUT VOOR BOUWKUNST EN STEDEBOUW, National Higher Institute of Architecture and Town Planning, Mutsaertstraat 31, 2000. Tel 32 41 61. *Dir* J De Mol

BRUSSELS

ACADEMIE ROYALE DES BEAUX-ARTS, Royal Academy of Fine Arts, Brussels, 144 ru du Midi, B-1000. Tel 512-73-23, 512-85-50. *Dir* F Vanhemelryck

ECOLE NATIONALE SUPERIEURE DES ARTS VISUELS, Higher School of Visual Arts, 21 abbaye de la Cambre, B1-1050. *Dir* Joseph Noiret

INSTITUT SUPERIEUR D'ARCHITECTURE VICTOR HORTA, 144 rue du Midi, B-1000. Tel 513-59-68. *Dir* Richard Vandendaele

NAMUR

ECOLE DES BEAUX-ARTS, 20 rue des Lombard, 5000. *Dir* M Rogister

BRAZIL

RIO DE JANEIRO

ESCULA DE ARTES VISUAIS, 414 Rua Jardim Botanico, Parque Lage, 22461. *Dir* Ruben Breitman

BULGARIA

SOFIA

NIKOLAJ PAVLOVIC HIGHER INSTITUTE OF FINE ARTS, rue Sipka 1. Tel 88-17-01. *Rector* V Minekov

REPUBLIC OF CHINA

TAIPEI

NATIONAL TAIWAN ACADEMY OF ARTS, 59 Ta-Kwan Rd, Sec I, Pan-chiao Park. Tel 220. *Pres* T L Chang

COLOMBIA

BOGOTA

UNIVERSIDAD JAVERIANA, Javeriana University Faculty of Architecture and Design, Carrera 7, 40-62. Tel 2455102, 2458983. *Acad Dean* Pedro P Polo Verano, BA(Archit)

CZECHOSLOVAKIA

HVIEZDOSLAVOVO NAM

VYSOKA SKOLA VYTVARNYCH UMENI, 814, 37 Bratislava. *Rector* Jan Kulich

PRAGUE

AKADEMIE VYTVARNYCH UMENI, Academy of Fine Arts, U Akademie 4. Tel 37-31-46. *Rector* Milos Axman

VYSOKA SKOLA UMELECKOPRUMYSLOVA, Academy of Applied Arts, nam Krasnoarmejcu 80, 1. *Rector* Jan Simota

DENMARK

AARHUS

SCHOOL OF ARCHITECTURE IN AARHUS, Norreport 20, 8000. Tel 06-13-08-22. *Rector* Nils-Ole Lund

COPENHAGEN

DEN GRAFISKI HOJSKOLE, Graphic College of Denmark, Glentevej 67, 2400. *Dir* Leif Monies

DET KONGELIGE DANSKE KUNSTAKADEMI, The Royal Danish Academy of Fine Arts, Kongens Nytorv 1, 1050 K. *Dir School Archit* Prof H Bertram

DOMINICAN REPUBLIC

SANTO DOMINGO

DIRECCION GENERAL DE BELLAS ARTES, *Dir* Jose Delmonte Peguero

ENGLAND

BIRMINGHAM

CITY OF BIRMINGHAM POLYTECHNIC, Art and Design Centre, Perry Barr, B42 2SU. Tel 356-6911. *Dean Art & Design* P L Field

BRIGHTON

BRIGHTON POLYTECHNIC, Faculty of Art and Design, Grand Parade, BN2 4AT. Tel 0273-604141. *Dean Faculty* R Plummer, ARCA

CHELTENHAM

GLOUCESTERSHIRE COLLEGE OF ART & DESIGN, Gloucester & Brunswick Rd. *Principal* James Martin

FARNHAM

WEST SURREY COLLEGE OF ART & DESIGN, Falkner Rd. Tel 0251-722441. *Principal* L W Stappani

LEICESTER

LEICESTER POLYTECHNIC, Faculty of Art and Design, The Newark, PO Box 143, LE1 PBH. Tel 0533-551551. *Head School Fine Art* John Hoskin

LONDON

CENTRAL SCHOOL OF ART AND DESIGN, Southampton Row, WC1B 4AP. Tel 01-405-1825. *Principal* T H Pannell

CHELSEA SCHOOL OF ART, Manresa Rd, SW3 6LS. Tel 01-352-4846. *Principal* John Barnicoat

CITY AND GUILDS OF LONDON ART SCHOOL, Southampton, WC1B 4AP. *Principal* T Pannell

ROYAL ACADEMY SCHOOLS, Burlington House, Piccadilly, W1V ODS. Tel 01-734-9052, Sch Ext 40. *Cur* Walter Woodington, RP & RBA

ROYAL COLLEGE OF ART, Kensington Gore, SW7 2EU. Tel 01-584-5020. *Rector* Dr Lionel March

SAINT MARTINS SCHOOL OF ART, 107-111 Charing Cross Rd, WC2H 0DU. Tel 01-437-0058. *Principal* Ian Simpson

SCHILLER COLLEGE EUROPE AT LONDON, Wickham Court, West Wickham Kent, BR4 9HH. Tel 01-777-8069. *Dir* M Rugg

SLADE SCHOOL OF FINE ART, University College London, Gower St, WC1E6 BT. *Dir* Lawrence Gowing

MANCHESTER

MANCHESTER POLYTECHNIC, Faculty of Art and Design, Cavendish St, All Saints, M15 6BR. Tel 061-228 6171. *Dept Head Fine Art* D Hensler

NEW CROSS

UNIVERSITY OF LONDON, Goldsmiths' College, Lewisham Way, SE 14 6NW. *Dean* P K Steel

NOTTINGHAM

TRENT POLYTECHNIC, School of Art and Design, Burton Street, NG1 4BU. Tel 0602-48248. *Dean Art & Design* R D Archer

FINLAND

HELSINKI

SUOMEN TAIDEAKATE MIAN KOULO, 0100. *Rector* Jaakko Sievanen

FRANCE

FONTAINEBLEAU

AMERICAN SCHOOL OF ART, Palace of Fontainebleau, 77305. Tel 422-25-39. *Dir* M Tournon-Branly

LOCOSTE

SARAH LAWRENCE COLLEGE, Village des Arts en France du Sarah Lawrence College, (Mailing Add: Foreign Studies Office, Bronxville, NY 10708), 10708. Tel 90-75-82-07. *Dir* Bernard Pfriem

PARIS

ECOLE DU LOUVRE, School of the Louvre, 34 quai du Louvre, 75001. Tel 260-3926. *Principal* H Landais

ECOLE NATIONALE SUPERIEURE DES ARTS DECORATIFS, National College of Decorative Arts, 31 rue d'Ulm, 75005. Tel 326-90-61. *Dir* M Tourliere

ECOLE NATIONALE SUPERIEURE DES BEAUX-ARTS, National College of Fine Arts, 17, quai Malaquais, 75006. Tel 260-34-57. *Dir* Francois Wehrlin

ECOLE SPECIALE D'ARCHITECTURE, 254 blvd Raspail, 75014. *Dir* J F De Moncuit de Boiscuille

SCHILLER COLLEGE, EUROPE UNIVERSITY, Art Department, 103 rue de Lille, 67000. Tel 551-2893. *Dir* D Halmberg

UNIVERSITE DE PARIS I A LA PANTHEON-SORBONNE, 12 Place du Pantheon, 75231. Tel 329-21-40. *Dir* P Huot

VILLENEUVE D'ASCQ

UNITE PEDAGOGIQUE D'ARCHITECTURE DE LILLE, rue Verte, quartier de l'Hotel de Ville, 59650. *Dir* Gerard Engrand

FEDERAL REPUBLIC OF GERMANY

BERLIN

HOCHSCHULE DER KUNSTE BERLIN, 10 Ernst Reuter Platz, 1000. *Pres* Ulrich Roloff

DUSSELDORF

STAATLICHE KUNSTAKADEMIE, DUSSELDORF, Hochschule fur Bildende Kunste, Eiskellerstrasse 1, 4000. Tel 329334. *Dir* Irmin Kamp

HAMBURG

HOCHSCHULE FUR BILDENDE KUNSTE, College of Fine Arts, 2000 Hamburg 76, Lerchenfeld. Tel 22811. *Pres* Dr Carl D Vogel

HEIDELBERG

SCHILLER COLLEGE-EUROPE, Fine Arts Department, 6900 Heidelberg, Friedrich-Ebert-Anlage 4, 69. Tel 06221-12046. *Dir* J K Clark

KARLSRUHE

STAATLICHE AKADEMIE DER BILDENDEN KUNSTE, State Academy of Fine Arts, Reinhold-Frank-Strasse 81-83, 75. Tel 84-30-38. *Rector* Klaus Arnold

MUNICH

AKADEMIE DER BILDENDEN KUNSTE, Academy of Fine Arts, Akademiestr 2. Tel 39 40 57. *Pres* Rudolf Seitz

NUREMBERG

AKADEMIE DER BILDENDEN KUNSTE IN NURNBERG, Academy of Fine Arts in Nuremberg, Bingstrasse 60, 8500. Tel 0911-40 50 61. *Pres* G Voglsamer

STUTTGART

STAATLICHE AKADEMIE DER BILDENDEN KUNSTE, State Academy of Fine Arts, Am Weissenhof 1, 7. Tel 25-10-51. *Rector* Dr Wolfgang Kermer

GREECE

ATHENS

ATHENS CENTRE FOR THE CREATIVE ARTS, 48 Archimidous St, Pangrati

PAROS CYCLADES

AEGEAN SCHOOL OF FINE ARTS, Tel Aspisia Sarris 0284-21737. *Dir* Brett Taylor, MFA

INDIA

BARODA

MAHARAJA SAYAJIRAO UNIVERSITY OF BARODA, Faculty of Fine Arts, University Rd, Pushpa-Baug, Gujarat 390002. Tel 64721, 64238. *Dean Faculty Fine Arts* J D Patel

BOMBAY

ACADEMY OF ARCHITECTURE, Plot 278, Shankar Ghaneker Marg, 400025. *Principal* C K Gumaste

MYSORE

SRI VARALAKSHMI ACADEMIES OF FINE ARTS, Chamaraja Double Rd. *Pres* T Shama Rao

IRELAND

DUBLIN

NATIONAL COLLEGE OF ART AND DESIGN, Kildare St, 2. Tel 682911. *Dir* Noel Sheridan

ROYAL INSTITUTE OF THE ARCHITECTS OF IRELAND, 8 Merrion Square, 2. *Pres* Anthony Reddy

ISRAEL

JERUSALEM

BEZALEL ACADEMY OF ARTS & DESIGN, 10 Shmuel Hanagid St. Tel 02-225111. *Dir* Ran Shechori

YEROHAM

RAMAT HANEGEV COLLEGE, Dept of Art & Design, Tel 057-80575. *Pres & Prof* Dr Menahem Alexenberg

ITALY

BOLOGNA

ACCADEMIA DI BELLE ARTI E LICEO ARTISTICO, Academy of Fine Arts, via Belle Arti 54, 40126. Tel 237-961. *Prof* E Pasqualini

FLORENCE

ACCADEMIA DI BELLE ARTI E LICEO ARTISTICO, via Ricasoli 66, 50122. *Dir* Luigi Biagi

FORTMAN STUDIOS, Via Fiesolana 34, 50122. *Dir* Leo Forte

ROSARY COLLEGE, Graduate School of Fine Arts at Schifanoia Villa, via Boccaccio, 123, 50133. Tel 055-576-195. *Dean* Sr Mary Ewens

MILAN

ACCADEMIA DI BELLE ARTI, Academy of Fine Arts of Brera, Palazzo di Brera, via Brera 28, 20121. Tel 871-379. *Pres* Filippo Tartaglia

NAPLES

ACCADEMIE DE BELLE ARTI E LICEO ARTISTICO, Academy of Fine Arts, via S M Constantinopoli 107-A, 80138. *Dir* Constanza Lorenzetti

PERUGIA

ACCADEMIA DI BELLE ARTI, Academy of Fine Arts, Piazza San Francesco 5, 06100. *Dir* Giorgio Ascani Nuvolo

RAVENNA

ACCADEMIA DE BELLE ARTI, Academy of Fine Arts, Loggetta Lombardesca, Via Roma 13, 48100. Tel 23935. *Dir* C Spadoni

ROME

ACCADEMIA DE BELLE ARTIE LICEO ARTISTICO, Academy of Fine Arts, via Ripetta 222, 00186. Tel 688-834, 688-861. *Dir* Marcello Avenali

AMERICAN ACADEMY IN ROME, Via Angelo Masina 5, 00153. Tel 588-653. *Dir* Sophie Consagra

BRITISH SCHOOL AT ROME, Via Gramsci 61, 00197. *Dir* David Whitehouse, PhD

INSTITUTO CENTRALE DEL RESTAURO, Central Institute for the Restoration of Works of Art, Piazza San Francesco di Paola 9, 00186. Tel 475-11-42. *Dir* Dott G Urbani

VENICE

ACCADEMIA DI BELLE ARTI, Academy of Fine Arts, 1050 Campo della Carita. *Dir* Nedo Fiorentin

JAPAN

KANAZAWA CITY

KANAZAWA BIJUTSU KOGEI DAIGAKU, Kanazawa College of Fine & Industrial Arts, 11-1, Kodachino 5-chome, 920. Tel 62-35-32. *Pres* Mamoru Osawa

KYOTO

KYOTO CITY UNIVERSITY OF FINE ARTS, School of Art, 13-6 Kutsakake-Cho, Ohe, Higashiyama-ku, Nishi Kyo-Ku 810-11. Tel 561-71-41. *Dir* Takeshi Umehara

TOKYO

TAMA ART UNIVERSITY, 3-15-34 Kaminage, Setagaya-Ku. *Pres* Y Naito

TOKYO NATIONAL UNIVERSITY OF FINE ARTS, Ueno Park, Daito-Ku

MEXICO

MEXICO CITY

ESCUELA NACIONAL DE ARTES PLASTICAS, National School of Plastic Arts, Calle Academia 22. Tel 522-06-30. *Master Plastic Arts* Roberto Garibay Sida
Courses: Engraving

SAN MIGUEL DE ALLENDE

INSTITUTO ALLENDE, Allende Institute, Tel 2-01-90. *Pres* Stirling Dickinson

MOROCCO

TETOUAN

ECOLE NATIONALE DES BEAUX ARTS, Ave Mohamed V, Cite Scolaire BP 89. *Dir* Mohammed M Serghini

NETHERLANDS

AMSTERDAM

GERRIT RIETVELD ACADEMIE, Fred Roeskestraat 96, 1076 ED. Tel 72-04-06. *Dir* Simon H den Hartog

RIJKSAKADEMIE VAN BEELDENDE KUNSTEN, State Academy of Fine Arts, PO Box 5508, 1007. Tel 79-78-11

BREDA

ACADEMIE VOOR BEELDENDE KUNSTEN ST JOOST, 18 St Janstraat. *Dir* J Peeters

GRONINGEN

AKADEMIE VOOR BEELDENDE KUNSTEN AKADEMIE MINERVA, 23 Schoolhalm. *Dir* A van Hijum

THE HAGUE

KONINKLIJKE ACADEMIE VAN BEELDENDE KUNSTEN, Royal Academy of Fine Arts, Prinsessegracht 4, 2514. Tel 070-643835. *Dir* J J Beljon

STICHTING DE VRIJE ACADEMIE VOOR BEELDENDE KUNSTEN, Foundation The Free Academy for Fine Arts, De Vrye Academie Psychopolis, De Gheynstraat 129, PO Box 61390, 2506 AJ. Tel 63-89-68. *Dir* George Lampe

HERTOGENBOSCH

KONINKLIJKE AKADEMIE VOOR KUNST EN VORMGEVING, 2 Pettelaarseweg. *Dir* A C P van den Berg

ROTTERDAM

ACADEMIE VAN BEELDENDE KUNSTEN, Academy of Fine Arts, Blaak 10, 3011. Tel 3110-366244, Ext 31. *Pres* Dr D F Nijhoff

NEW ZEALAND

AUCKLAND

UNIVERSITY OF AUCKLAND, School of Fine Arts, 20 Whitaker Place. *Dean* Jolyon D Saunders

NORWAY

OSLO

STATENS HANDVERKS-OG KUNSTINDUSTISKOLE, Sullevalsvn. *Principal* F Wildhagen

STATENS KUNSTAKADEMI, Uranienborgvien 2. *Rector* Ludvig Eikaas

PERU

LIMA

ESCUELA NACIONAL SUPERIOR DE BELLAS ARTES, 681 Ancash. *Dir* Juan Manuel Ugarte Elespupu

POLAND

CRACOW

AKADEMIA SZTUK PIEKNYCH, Academy of Fine Arts, Pac Matekji 13, 31-157. Tel 22-24-50. *Rector* Wlodzimierz Kunc

GDANSK

PANSTWOWA WYZSZA SZKOLA SZTUK PLASTYCZNYCH, 6 Targ Weglowy, 80-836. Tel 31-28-01. *Rector* Franciszek Duszenko

LODZ

PANSTWOWA WYZSZA SZKOLA SZTUK PLASTYCZNYCH, Higher School of Art and Design, 121 Wojska Polskiego St, 91-726. Tel 728-88. *Rector* Krystyn Zielinski

WARSAW

AKADEMIA SZTUK PIEKNYCH, Academy of Fine Arts, Krakowskie Przedmiescie 5, 00-068. Tel 26-19-72. *Rector* Juliusz Bursze

WROCLAW

PANSTWOWA WYZSZA SZKOLA SZTUK PLASTYCZYNCH, 3-4 Plac Polski, 850-156. *Rector* R Kominek

PORTUGAL

LISBON

ESCOLA SUPERIOR DE BELAS ARTES, School of Fine Arts, Largo da Biblioteca Publica, 1200. *Dir* Joaquin M Correia

OPORTO

ESCOLA SUPERIOR DE BELAS ARTES, Au Rodrigues de Freitas. *Dir* Carlos Ramos

SCOTLAND

DUNDEE

DUNCAN OF JORDANSTONE COLLEGE OF ART, Perth Rd. *Principal* M Lacome

EDINBURGH

EDINBURGH COLLEGE OF ART, Lauriston Place, EH3 9DF. Tel 031-229 9311. *Principal* Gavin T N Ross

GLASGOW

GLASGOW SCHOOL OF ART, 167 Renfrew St, G3 6RQ. *Dir* Anthony E Jones

REPUBLIC OF SOUTH AFRICA

PORT ELIZABETH

PORT ELIZABETH TECHNIKON, Department of Art and Design of the Port, Private Bag 6011, 6000. *Head Dept* G H H Nesbit

SPAIN

BARCELONA

ESCUELA SUPERIOR DE BELLAS ARTES SAN JORGE, Calle Europa, Cuidad Universitaria, 14

MADRID

ESCUELA NACIONAL DE ARTES GRAFICAS, Madrid School of Graphic Arts, Calle Jesus Maestro, 3. Tel 234-51-26. *Dir* Luis Gimeno Soldevilla

INSTITUTO DE ARTE DIEGO VELAZQUEZ, Duque de Medinaceli 4, 14. *Dir* Elisa Bermejo

SEVILLE

ESCUELA SUPERIOR DE BELLAS ARTES DE SANTA ISABEL DE HUNGRIA DE SEVILLE, Seville School of Fine Arts, Calle Gonzalo Bilbao 7-9. *Dir* Jose Hernandez Diaz

VALENCIA

ESCUELA SUPERIOR DE BELLAS ARTES DE SAN CARLOS, Valencia School of Fine Arts, Calle del Museo 2. *Dir* Daniel De Nueda Llisiona

SWEDEN

STOCKHOLM

KONSTFACKSKOLAN, National College of Art & Design, Valhallvaegan 191, PO Box 27116, 102 52. *Principal* Gunilla Lagerbielke

KONSTHOGSKOLAN, College of Fine Arts, Fredsgatan 12, Box 16 317, 103 26. *Principal* Georg Suttmer

SWITZERLAND

GENEVA

ECOLES D'ART DE GENEVE, Geneva Schools of Art, 1205
—**Ecole Superieure D'Art Visuel,** Higher School of Visual Arts, 9, bd Helvetique, Geneva, Switzerland 1205. Tel 29-05-10. *Dir* M Michel Rappo
—**Ecole des Arts Decoratifs,** School of Decorative Arts, 15, bd James-Fazy, Switzerland. Tel 31-37-57. *Dir* M Michel Rappo

LAUSANNE

ECOLE CANTONALE DES BEAUX-ARTS ET D'ART APPLIQUE, Ave de l'Elysee 4, 1006. *Dir* J Monnien

LAUSANNE COLLEGE OF ART AND DESIGN, Ave Elysee 4, 1006. Tel 27-75-23. *Principal* Jaques Monnier

TURKEY

ISTANBUL

ISTANBUL DEVLET GUZEL SANATLAR AKADEMISI, Findikli. *Pres* Orhan Shahiler

USSR

EREVAN

EREVAN INSTITUTE OF FINE ARTS & THEATRE, Armenian SSR

LENINGRAD

LENINGRAD I E REPIN INSTITUTE OF ARTS, V-34 Universitetskaya Naberezhnaya. *Rector* V M Oreshnikov

MOSCOW

MOSCOW V I SURIKOV STATE ART INSTITUTE, 30 Tovarishchesky Pereulok. *Dir* N V Tomsky

RIGA

LATVIAN SOCIAL SOVIET REPUBLIC STATE ACADEMY OF ARTS, 13 Bulo Kommunaru. *Rector* Edgars Iltners

TALLINN

ESTONIAN SOVIET SOCIALIST REPUBLIC STATE ART INSTITUTE, Tartu Maantee 1, 200001. *Rector* J Vares

VENEZUELA

CARACAS

ESCUELA DE ARTES VISUALES CRISTOBAL ROJAS, 10 bis Avda Lecuna-Este. *Dir* Carmen Julia Negronde Valery

State Arts Councils

NATIONAL ENDOWMENT FOR THE ARTS REGIONAL REPRESENTATIVES

California, Alaska & Pacific Islands

Virginia Torres
3500 White House Place
Los Angeles, CA 90004
213-385-3990
(AK, CA, HI, Guam, America Samoa, Northern Marianas)

Great Lakes

Bertha Masor
4200 Marine Drive
Chicago, IL 50513
312-782-7858
(IL, IN, MI, OH, WI)

Mid-Atlantic & Mid-South States

Adrian King
P.O. Box 8941
Washington, DC 20003
(DC, DE, KY, MD, NJ, NC, PA, SC, TN, VA, WV)

Northeast States & Caribbean

John Wessel
Two Columbus Circle
New York, NY 10019
212-257-9760
(CT, MA, ME, NH, NY, PR, RI, VT, VI)

Plains States

Romalyn Tilghman
P.O. Box 22489
Kansas City, MO 64113
(AR, IA, KS, MN, MO, NE, ND, OK, SD)

Southern & Gulf States

Robert E. Hollister
P.O. Box 54346
Atlanta, GA 30308
406-627-9757
(AL, FL, GA, LA, MS, TX)

Western States

Terry Melton
601 Belmont Avenue E., Apt. F-6
Seattle, WA 98102
(AZ, CO, ID, NV, NM, UT, WY)

REGIONAL ORGANIZATIONS

Affiliated State Arts Agencies of the Upper Midwest

David Fraher, Executive Director
528 Hennepin Avenue, Suite 302
Minneapolis, MN 44503

612-871-6392
(IA, MN, ND, SD, WI)

The Arts Council of Hawaii

Karl K. Ichida, Executive Director
P.O. Box 50225
Honolulu, HI 96850
(HI)

Consortium of Pacific Arts & Culture

Agana, Guam 96910
(AK, American Samoa, CA, Guam, Mariana Islands)

Great Lakes Arts Alliance

Gregory Gibson, Executive Director
11424 Bellflower Road
Cleveland, OH 44106
216-229-1098
(IL, IN, MI, OH)

Mid-American Arts Alliance

Henry Moran, Executive Director
20 W. Ninth St., Suite 550
Kansas City, MO 64105
816-421-1388
(AR, KS, MO, NE, OK)

Mid-Atlantic Arts Consortium

Sandra Lorentcen, Executive Director
11 E. Chase St., Suite 7-B
Baltimore, MD 21202
301-685-1400
(DE, DC, MD, NJ, NY, PA, VA, WV)

New England Foundation for the Arts, Inc.

Marcia Noebels, Acting Executive Director
25 Mount Auburn St.
Cambridge, MA 02138
617-492-2914
(CT, ME, MA, NH, RI, VT)

Southern Arts Federation

James Backas, Executive Director
1401 Peachtree St., Suite 122
Atlanta, GA 30309
404-874-7244
(AL, FL, GA, KY, LA, MS, NC, SC, TN)

Western States Arts Foundation

Bill Jamison, Executive Director
141 E. Palace Ave.
Sante Fe, NM 87501
505-988-1166
(AZ, CO, ID, MT, NV, NM, OR, UT, WA, WY)

STATE ART AGENCIES

Alabama State Council on the Arts and Humanities

Lamar Rainer, Chairman
P.O. Box 340
Elba, AL 36323
205-897-2252

M. J. Zakrzewski, Executive Director
114 N. Hull St.
Montgomery, AL 36130
205-832-6758

Alaska State Council on the Arts

Robert Miller, Chairman
8240 Resurrection Dr.
Anchorage, AK 99504
907-337-8876

Chris D'Arcy, Actg. Executive Director
619 Warehouse Ave., Suite 220
Anchorage, AK 99501
907-279-1558

Arizona Commission on the Arts

Richard Whitney, Chairman
201 N. Central, #3300
Phoenix, AZ 85073
602-258-5330

Adrienne Hirsch, Executive Director
2024 N. Seventh St., Suite 201
Phoenix, AZ 85006
602-255-5882

Arkansas Arts Council

Candace Burton, Chairman
912 South 22nd
Arkadelphia, AR 71923
501-246-4531

Carolyn Staley, Executive Director
Continental Bldg, Suite 500
Little Rock, AR 72201
501-371-2539

California Arts Council

Consuelo Santos Killans, Chairman
2064 Alameda Way
San Jose, CA 95726
408-984-5340

Marilyn Ryan, Executive Director
1901 Broadway, Suite A
Sacramento, CA 95818
916-445-1530

Colorado Council on the Arts and Humanities

Lucien Wulsin, Chairman
1380 Lawrence St.
Denver, CO 80202
303-573-7181

Ellen Pierce, Executive Director
770 Pennsylvania St.
Denver, CO 80203
303-866-2617

Connecticut Commission on the Arts

Susan Kelly, Chairman
86 Bloomfield Ave.
Hartford, CT 06105
203-233-4885

Gary Young, Executive Director
340 Capitol Ave.
Hartford, CT 06106
203-566-4770

Delaware State Arts Council

Judy Hoopes, Chairman
104 Brookmeadow Rd.
West Farm

Wilmington, DE 19807
302-652-5618

Ann Houseman, Administrator
State Office Bldg.
Wilmington, DE 19801
302-571-3540

DC Commission on the Arts And Humanities

Peggy Cooper Cafritz, Chairman
2900 44th St. NW
Washington, DC 20016
202-244-1966

Mildred Bautista, Executive Director
420 7th St., NW, 2nd Floor
Washington, DC 20004
202-724-5613

Arts Council of Florida

Jack Clark, Chairman
P.O. Box 190
Ocala, FL 32678
904-732-3121

Chris Doolin, Executive Director
Dept. of State, The Capitol
Tallahassee, FL 32304
904-487-2980

Georgia Council for the Arts and Humanities

Rosemary Stiefel, Chairman
880 Clifton Rd., NE
Atlanta, GA 30307
404-373-3582

Frank Ratka, Executive Director
2082 E. Exchange Pl., Suite 100
Tucker, GA 30084
404-656-3967

Hawaii State Foundation on Culture and the Arts

Naomi Morita, Chairman
82 Makalani St.
P.O. Box 4160
Hilo, HI 96720
808-961-7351

Sarah Richards, Executive Director
355 Merchant St., Suite 202
Honolulu, HI 96813
808-548-4145

Idaho Commission on the Arts

Annette Park, Chairman
901 Balsam
Boise, ID 83706
208-345-9921

Joan Lolmaugh, Executive Director
304 W. State St.
Boise, ID 83720
208-334-2119

Illinois Arts Council

David Connor, Chairman
301 SW Adams
Peoria, IL 61631
309-674-7781

Carl Petrick, Executive Director
111 N. Wabash Ave., Suite 700
Chicago, IL 60602
312-793-6750

Indiana Arts Commission

Stuart L. Main, Chairman
Lafayette National Bank
P.O. Box 780
Lafayette, IN 47902
317-423-8397

Thomas Schorgl, Actg. Executive Director
155 E. Market St.
Indianapolis, IN 46204
317-232-1268

Iowa Arts Council

Don Singer, Chairman
320 Lillian Lane
Waterloo, IA 50701
319-235-4638

Sam Grabarski, Executive Director
State Capitol Bldg.
Des Moines, IA 50319
515-281-4451

Kansas Arts Commission

Ruth Browne, Chairman
1603 Fifth St.
Clay Center, KS 67432
913-632-2814

John Reed, Executive Director
112 W. Sixth St.
Topeka, KS 66603
913-296-3335

Kentucky Arts Council

Albert P. Smith, Chairman
Editor and Publisher
The Sentinel-Echo
115 W. Fifth St.
London, KY 40701
606-878-7400

Nash Cox, Executive Director
Berry Hill
Frankfort, KY 40601
502-564-3757

Louisiana State Arts Council

Naomi Marshall, Chairman
21 Maryland Dr.
New Orleans, LA 70124
504-552-9884

Al Head, Executive Director
P.O. Box 44247
Baton Rouge, LA 70804
504-925-3934

Maine State Commission on the Arts and Humanities

John Scarcelli, Chairman
64 High St.
Farmington, ME 04938
207-778-3501

Alden C. Wilson, Executive Director
55 Capital St.
State House Station 25
Augusta, ME 04333
207-289-2724

Maryland State Arts Council

Dr. Gerald W. Johnson, Chairman
1221 Coulbourne Mill Rd.
Rustic Acres
Salisbury, MD 21801
301-651-2200

Hank Johnson, Executive Director
15 W. Mulberry
Baltimore, MD 21201
301-685-6740

Massachusetts Council on the Arts and Humanities

Vernon R. Alden, Chairman
J. Hancock Tower, 49th Floor
200 Clarendon St.
Boston, MA 02116
617-727-0767

Anne Hawley, Executive Director
One Ashburton Pl.
Boston, MA 02108
617-727-3668

Michigan Council for the Arts

Dr. Oscar Remick, Actg. Chairman
President, Alma College
Alma, MI 48801

E. Ray Scott, Executive Director
1200 Sixth Ave.
Executive Plaza
Detroit, MI 48226
313-256-3735

Minnesota State Arts Board

Katherine Murphy, Chairman
3139 S. Rivershore Dr.
Moorhead, MN 56560
218-233-4504

G. James Olsen, Executive Director
432 Summit Ave.
Saint Paul, MN 55102
612-297-2603

Mississippi Arts Commission

Dr. Aubrey K. Lucas, Chairman
Southern Station, Box 5001
Hattiesburg, MS 39406
601-266-5001

Lida Rogers, Executive Director
301 N. Lamar St.
P.O. Box 1341
Jackson, MS 39205
601-354-7336

Missouri Arts Council

Mrs. Talbot MacCarthy, Chairman
6 Robin Hill Lane
St. Louis, MO 63124

Rick Simoncelli, Executive Director
111 N. Seventh St., Suite 105
St. Louis, MO 63101
314-444-6845

Montana Arts Council

Jessica Stickney, Chairman
2206 Main St.
Miles City, MT 59301
406-232-1100

David Nelson, Executive Director
1280 S. Third St. W.
Missoula, MT 59801
406-543-8286

Nebraska Arts Council

Lavon Crosby, Chairman
3720 S. 40th St.
Lincoln, NE 68506
402-488-1700

Robin Tryloff, Executive Director
1313 Farnam-on-the-Mall
Omaha, NE 68102
402-554-2122

Nevada State Council on the Arts

Royal Orser, Chairman
1917 View Dr.
Elko, NV 89801
702-738-5530

Jacqueline Belmont, Executive Director
329 Flint St.
Reno, NV 89502
702-784-6231

New Hampshire Commission on the Arts

Barbara J. Dunfey, Chairman
14 Wood Knoll Dr.
North Hampton, NH 03862
603-964-9821

Robb Hankins, Executive Director
Phenix Hall
40 N. Main St.
Concord, NH 03301
603-271-2789

New Jersey State Council on the Arts

Clement A. Price, Chairman
82 Fairmont Terrace
East Orange, NJ 07018
201-648-5414

Jeffrey Kesper, Executive Director
109 W. State St.
Trenton, NJ 08608
609-292-6130

New Mexico Arts Division

Consuelo Thompson, Chairman
Drawer JJ
Espanola, NM 87532
505-753-3076

Bernard Lopez, Executive Director
113 Lincoln
Santa Fe, NM 87503
505-827-2061

New York State Council on the Arts

Kitty Hart, Chairman
80 Centre St.
New York, NY 10013
212-587-4595

Mary Hays, Executive Director
80 Centre St.
New York, NY 10013
212-587-4597

North Carolina Arts Council

Michael Newman, Chairman
Newman, Calloway, Johnson & Winfree
635 W. 4th St.
Box 2475
Winston-Salem, NC 27102
919-724-1503

Mary Regan, Executive Director
Dept. of Cultural Resources
Raleigh, NC 27611
919-733-2821

North Dakota Council on the Arts

Susan Freeman, Chairman
1215 S. Eighth St.
Fargo, ND 58103
701-235-4384

Donna Evenson, Executive Director
Black Bldg., Suite 811
Fargo, ND 58105
701-237-8962

Ohio Arts Council

John Henle, Chairman
5704 Olentangy Blvd.
Worthington, OH 43085
614-885-7810

Wayne Lawson, Executive Director
727 E. Main St.
Columbus, OH 43205
614-466-2613

Oklahoma State Arts Council

William Horton, Chairman
P.O. Box 1603

Shawnee, OK 74801
405-521-2931

Betty Price, Executive Director
Jim Thorpe Bldg., Room 640
Oklahoma City, OK 73105
405-521-2931

Oregon Arts Commission

Marythea Grebner, Chairman
Southern Oregon State College
1250 Siskiyou Blvd.
Ashland, OR 97520
503-482-6361

Peter deC Hero, Executive Director
835 Summer St. NE
Salem, OR 97301
503-378-3625

Pennsylvania Council on the Arts

Diana R. Rose, Chairman
1035 Devon Rd.
Pittsburgh, PA 15213
412-682-1708

June Arey, Executive Director
Finance Bldg., Room 216
Harrisburg, PA 17120
717-787-6883

Rhode Island State Council on the Arts

Daniel Lecht, Chairman
Rhode Island Lithograph Corp.
P.O. Box 1267
Pawtucket, RI 02862
401-725-1500

Christina A. White, Executive Director
312 Wickenden St.
Providence, RI 02903
401-277-3880

South Carolina Arts Commission

Thomas M. Creech, Chairman
First Federal Savings
P.O. Box 408
Greenville, SC 29602
803-271-722

Scott Sanders, Executive Director
1800 Gervais Street
Columbia, SC 29201
803-758-3442

South Dakota Arts Council

Margaret Quintal, Chairman
1520 N. Ridge Rd.
Mitchell, SD 57301
605-996-6592

Charlotte Carver, Executive Director
108 W. 11th St.
Sioux Falls, SD 57102
605-339-6646

Tennessee Arts Commission

Nellie McNeill, Chairman
3632 Orebank Rd.
Kingsport, TN 37664
615-926-4242

Arthur L. Keeble, Executive Director
505 Deaderick St., Suite 1700
Nashville, TN 37219
615-741-1701

Texas Commission on the Arts

Hugo V. Neuhaus Jr., Chairman
13406 First International Plaza
Houston, TX 77002
713-757-7312

Richard Huff, Executive Director
P.O. Box 13406 Capitol Station
Austin, TX 78711
512-475-6593

Utah Arts Council

JoAnn Freed, Chairman
846 E. Capitol Blvd.
Salt Lake City, UT 84103
801-363-8474

Ruth Draper, Executive Director
617 East South Temple St.
Salt Lake City, UT 84102
801-828-3291

Vermont Council on the Arts

Michael A. Weinberger, Chairman
39 Central St.
Woodstock, VT 05091
802-828-3291

Ellen McCulloch-Lovell, Executive Director
136 State St.
Montpelier, VT 05602
802-828-3291

Virginia Commission for the Arts

Robert E. Lee IV, Chairman
A Smith & Bowman Distellery
Sunset Hills, VA 22090
703-471-4555

Peggy Baggett, Executive Director
400 E. Grace St., 1st Floor
Richmond, VA 23219
804-786-4492

Washington State Arts Commission

Wallie Funk, Chairman
212 First Ave. S.
Seattle, WA 98104
206-622-4791

Michael Croman, Executive Director
Mail Stop GH-11
Olympia, WA 98504
206-753-3860

West Virginia Arts and Humanities Division

Kay Goodwin, Chairman
One Vail Dr.
Ripley, WV 25271
304-372-8737

James B. Andrews, Executive Director
Dept. of Culture & History
Capitol Complex
Charleston, WV 25305
304-348-0240

Wisconsin Arts Board

Father J. Thomas Finucan, Chairman
St. Stanislaus Church
838 Fremont St.
Stevens Point, WI 54481
715-344-3970
Marvin Weaver, Executive Director
123 W. Washington Ave.

Madison, WI 53702
608-266-0190

Wyoming Council on the Arts

John Freeman, Chairman
1703 S. 17th St.
Laramie, WY 82070
307-766-5496

David Fraher, Executive Director
Equality State Bank Bldg., 2nd Floor
Cheyenne, WY 82002
307-777-7742

American Samoa Arts Council

Palauni M. Tuiasosopo, Chairman
Office of the Governor
Pago Pago, AS 96799
633-4115

Matilda Lolotai, Executive Director
P.O. Box 1540
Office of the Governor
Pago Pago, AS 96799
633-4347

Insular Arts Council of Guam

Marilyn Abalos, Chairman
4 Chichirica
Dededo, GU 96912
632-9615

Annie Benavente Stone, Executive Director
P.O. Box 2950
Agana, GU 96910
477-7413

Commonwealth of the Northern Mariana Islands

Jose Rios, Chairman
Mayor of Saipan
Saipan, CM 96950
677-7230

Ana Teregeyo, Executive Director
Dept. of Community & Cultural Affairs
Saipan, CM 96950
677-7230

Institute of Puerto Rican Culture

Carlos Sanz, Chairman
Apartado Postal 4184
San Juan, PR 00905
809-723-2115

Leticia del Rosario, Executive Director
Apartado Postal 4184
San Juan, PR 00905
809-723-2115

Virgin Islands Council on the Arts

Mary Holter, Chairman
P.O. Box 91
Cruz Bay, St John, VI 00830
809-776-6342

Stephen J. Bostic, Executive Director
Caravelle Arcade
Christiansted, St Croix, VI 00820
809-773-3075

Directors and Supervisors of Art Education in School Systems

An asterisk (*) indicates no specific supervisor.

ALABAMA

Dr. John B. Hall
Visual Arts Specialist
State Department of Education
111 Coliseum Boulevard
Montgomery, Alabama 36109
205-261-2749

ALASKA

*

ARIZONA

Mr. Raymond G. Van Diest
Fine Arts Specialist
Arizona Department of Education
1535 W. Jefferson Street
Phoenix, Arizona 85007
602-255-5233

ARKANSAS

Ms. Brenda Turner
Specialist, Art Education
State Department of Education
Education Building Room 3058
Little Rock, Arkansas 72201
501-371-2525 or 501-371-2526

CALIFORNIA

Frank Summers, Consultant
Miguel Muto, Consultant
Arts and Humanities Education
California State Department of Education
721 Capitol Mall
Sacramento, California 95814
916-322-4015

COLORADO

Dr. Jerry Villars, Consultant
Colorado Department of Education
303 West Colfax Avenue
Denver, Colorado 80204
303-534-8871

CONNECTICUT

Dr. Robert J. Saunders
Art Education Consultant
State Department of Education
P. O. Box 2219
Hartford, Connecticut 06115
203-566-4736

DELAWARE

Mr. James R. Gervan
State Supervisor of Art and Music
Department of Public Instruction
Townsend Building
P. O. Box 1402

Dover, Delaware 19902
302-736-4885

DISTRICT OF COLUMBIA

Ms. Renee Watson
Director & Supervisor of Art
Instructional Services Center
Lingdon Elementary School
20th & Evarts Streets, N.E.
Washington, DC 20018
202-576-7813

FLORIDA

Mr. Charles Mooney, Art Consultant
Knott Building
State Department of Education
Tallahassee, Florida 32301
904-488-1701

GEORGIA

Ms. Ruth Gassett
Consultant, Art Education
Art & Humanities Unit
1954 Twin Towers East
Atlanta, Georgia 30334
404-656-7520

HAWAII

Mr. Stanley Yamamoto
Educational Specialist
189 Lunalilo Home Road
Room 1201
Honolulu, Hawaii 96825
808-395-7814

IDAHO

Mr. Bert A. Burda
Fine Arts Representative
Len B. Jordan Office Building
State Department of Education
650 West State Street
Boise, Idaho 83720
208-334-2281

ILLINOIS

*

INDIANA

Ms. Ann Pimberman, Art Consultant
Division of Curriculum
State Department of Education
Room 229 State House
Indianapolis, Indiana 46204
317-927-0111

IOWA

Dr. Laura Magee
Consultant, Arts Education
Curriculum Division
Department of Public Instruction
Grimes State Office Building
Des Moines, Iowa 50319
515-281-3160

KANSAS

Mr. Ray Linder
Education Program Specialist
State Department of Education
120 E Tenth Avenue
Topeka, Kansas 66612
913-296-3201

KENTUCKY

Mrs. Ruth West, Program Manager
Division of Program Development
Kentucky Department of Education
Capitol Plaza Tower
Frankfort, Kentucky 40601
502-564-2672

LOUISIANA

Mrs. Myrtle Kerr
State Supervisor of Art & Humanities
P. O. Box 44064
Baton Rouge, Louisiana 70804
504-342-3393

MAINE

Ms. Caroline Sturtevant
Director, Division of Curriculum
State of Maine
Department of Educational and Cultural Services
Station 23
Augusta, Maine 04333
207-289-2541

MARYLAND

Mr. James Tucker, Jr.
Specialist in the Arts
Maryland State Department of Education
200 W. Baltimore St.
Baltimore, Maryland 21201
301-659-2312

MASSACHUSETTS

Ms. Roselyn Frank
Director, Office for Gifted & Talented
State Department of Education
1385 Hancock Street
Quincy, Massachusetts 02169
617-770-7564

MICHIGAN

Ms. Julie Nichol
Fine Arts Specialist
Michigan Department of Education
Box 30008
Lansing, Michigan 48909
517-373-1484

MINNESOTA

Ms. Mary Honetschager
Arts Education Consultant
Minnesota Department of Education
Capitol Square Building
St. Paul, Minnesota 55101
612-296-4074

MISSISSIPPI

Ms. Sandra Nicola
Art Education Consultant
Mississippi State Dept. of Education
P. O. Box 711
Jackson, Mississippi 39205
601-354-6876

MISSOURI

*

MONTANA

Mrs. Janet Athwal
Art Education Consultant
Office of Public Instruction
State Capitol
Helena, Montana 59620
406-444-4442

NEBRASKA

Mrs. Sheila Brown
Fine Arts Coordinator
Department of Education
301 Centennial Mall South
Lincoln, Nebraska 68509
402-471-4337

NEVADA

Ms. Pat Weninger
Elementary Education Consultant
Nevada Department of Education
Capitol Complex
400 W. King Street
Carson City, Nevada 89710
702-885-3136

NEW HAMPSHIRE

*

NEW JERSEY

Ms. Florence Cookie
Arts Education Coordinator
New Jersey Department of Education
Division of General Academic Education
225 W. State Street, CN500
Trenton, New Jersey 08625
609-292-1544

NEW MEXICO

Ms. Vicki Breen
Director of Visual Arts
New Mexico State Dept. of Education
Education Building
300 Don Gasper
Santa Fe, New Mexico 87503
505-827-6635

NEW YORK

Mr. E. Andrew Mills
Administrator, Arts, Music & Humanities Unit
State Department of Education
Room 681, EBA
Albany, New York 12234
518-474-8779

NORTH CAROLINA

Mr. Doc McCulloch
State Art Consultant
Division of Cultural Arts
State Dept. of Public Instruction
Raleigh, North Carolina 27611
919-733-7467

NORTH DAKOTA

Ms. Patricia Herbel
Assistant Director of Curriculum
Fine Arts & Music
Dept. of Public Instruction
Capitol Building
Bismarck, North Dakota 58505
701-224-2269

OHIO

Mr. Jerry Tollifson, Art Education Consultant
Division of Elementary & Secondary Education
Ohio Departments Building
Room 1005, 65 South Front Street
Columbus, Ohio 43215
614-466-2407

OKLAHOMA

Mr. Charles Mohr, Administrator
Arts-in-Education Program
State Department of Education
2500 N. Lincoln
Oklahoma City, Oklahoma 73105
405-521-3034

OREGON

Dr. Delmer Aebischer
Fine Arts Specialist
State Department of Education
700 Pringle Parkway, S.E.
Salem, Oregon 97310
503-378-3617

PENNSYLVANIA

Mr. Clyde M. McGeary, Chief
Division of Arts & Sciences
Department of Education
Box 911
Harrisburg, Pennsylvania 17108
717-783-6746

RHODE ISLAND

Mr. Ken Fish, Consultant
Division of Program Development
Department of Education
Roger Williams Building
22 Hayes Street
Providence, Rhode Island 02908
401-277-2821

SOUTH CAROLINA

Dr. Thomas Hatfield
State Art Consultant
South Carolina Dept. of Education
801 Rutledge Building
Columbia, South Carolina 29201
803-758-2652

SOUTH DAKOTA

Dr. Joyce Levin
Director of Curriculum
Division of Elementary and Secondary Education
Kneip Building
Pierre, South Dakota 57501
605-773-4693

TENNESSEE

Mr. Beasley Overbey
Arts Specialist
Department of Education
1130 Menzler Road
Nashville, Tennessee 37210
615-741-7054

TEXAS

Ms. Jeanne Rollins
Art Education Specialist
Div. of Curriculum Development
Texas Education Agency
201 East 11th Street
Austin, Texas 78701
512-475-3823

UTAH

Dr. Charles B. Stubbs
State Specialist in Art Education
Utah State Office of Education
250 E. 5th South
Salt Lake City, Utah 84111
801-533-6040 (office)
801-943-7313 (home)

VERMONT

Mr. Donn McCafferty
Chief of Resources Education
Department of Education
Montpelier, Vermont 05602
802-828-3124

VIRGINIA

Mr. Baylor E. Nichols
Associate Director of Art Education
Department of Education
Box 6Q
Richmond, Virginia 23216
804-225-2053

WASHINGTON

Becca Duran
Supervisor of Arts & Music Education
Superintendent of Public Instruction
Old Capitol Building, FG-11
Olympia, Washington 98504
206-753-7389

WEST VIRGINIA

Mr. Richard W. Layman
Coordinator of Art
West Virginia Dept. of Education
Capitol Complex, Building 6, Room 330
Charleston, West Virginia 25305
304-348-7805 (office)
304-586-3032 (home)

WISCONSIN

Vacant

WYOMING

Ms. Sue Holt
Language Arts Coordinator
Hathaway Building
Cheyenne, Wyoming 82002
307-777-6238

SELECTED SCHOOL DISTRICTS

Birmingham City Schools

Patricia Cataldo
Art Consultant
Birmingham Board of Educ
P O Box 10007
Birmingham, AL 35202

Jefferson County Board of Education

Dr Mary Lee
Art Consultant
1009 North 21 St
Birmingham, AL 35203

Tuscaloosa City Schools

Mrs Ronna Lasser
Art Teacher - Coordr, Elementary
1100 21st St E
Tuscaloosa, AL 35041

Mesa Public Schools

Dr Edna Gilbert
Creative Arts Dir
Mesa Unified District
14 W Second Ave
Mesa, AZ 85202

Phoenix Elementary District 1

Del Bohlmeyer
Dir Fine Arts
125 E Lincoln
Phoenix, AZ 85004

Phoenix Union High School District

June LeSueur
General Education Supervisor
2526 W Osborn
Phoenix, AZ 85017

Prescott Elementary Schools

Dr Robert Browne
Asst Supervisor for Educ Servs
P O Box 1231
Prescott, AZ 85302

Tucson Public Schools

Molly Hughes
Dir of Fine Arts
Lee Instructional Center
2025 E Winsette St
Tucson, AZ 85719

Alameda Unified School District

Olivia Krause
Supervisor of Art Education
400 Grand St
Alameda, CA 94501

Alhambra City Schools

Ann Wollen
Art Consultant
15 W Alhambra Rd
Alhambra, CA 91801

Alum Rock Union Elementary School District

Leroy G Wiens
Coordr of Fine Arts
Alum Rock Elem School Dist
2930 Gay Ave
San Jose, CA 95127

Bakersfield City School District

Mary K Mueller
Consultant Art Education
Education Center
1300 Baker St
Bakersfield, CA 93305

Baldwin Park Unified School District

Kathryn McIlreath
Art Specialist
Baldwin Park USD
3699 N Holly Ave
Baldwin Park, CA 91706

Berkeley Unified School District

Herbert Constant
Chairman
Art, Industry & Design
Berkeley High School
Berkeley, CA 94704

Campbell Elementary School District

Marcia Wells
Art Consultant
155 N Third St
Campbell, CA 95008

Campbell Union High School District

Robert Capitolo
District Supervisor of Art
3235 Union Ave
San Jose, CA 95124

Compton Union High School District

Leonard F Fisher
District Curriculum Asst
417 W Alondar Blvd
Compton, CA 90220

Danville Unified School District

Arthur H Dougherty
Fine Arts Coordr
599 Old Orchard Dr
Danville, CA 94526

Escondido Union High School District

Rex Hamilton
Fine Arts Specialist
Fifth & Maple
Escondido, CA 92025

Fresno City Unified School District

Kay Tollady
Fine Arts Coordr
Education Center Tulare M
3132 E Fairmont
Fresno, CA 93721

Fullerton Elementary School District

Gelsomina Barton
Fine Arts Coordr
1401 W Valencia Dr
Fullerton, CA 92633

Garden Grove Unified School District

Bernard M Jones Jr
Art Specialist
10331 Stanford Ave
Garden Grove, CA 92640

Glendale Unified School District

Eleanor Schaubel
Arts Coordr
223 N Jackson St
Glendale, CA 91206

Hudson School District

Kay Cuthbert
Consultant
Hacienda LaPuente Unified School District
P O Box 1217
LaPuente, CA 91749

La Mesa-Spring Valley School District

Jean Ashour
Art Coordr

Maryland Avenue School
5400 Maryland Ave
La Mesa, CA 92041

Long Beach Unified School District

Sherry E Swan
Art Education
701 Locust Ave
Long Beach, CA 90813
Tel 213-436-9931

Los Angeles Unified School District

Fara Wexler
Instructional Specialist, Art
Instructional Planning Div A-327
Administrative Offices
450 N Grand
Los Angeles, CA 90015
Tel 213-625-6000

Montebello Unified School District

Mrs Jewel Bishop Starkey
Consultant, Art
123 S Montebello Blvd
Montebello, CA 90640

Moreno Valley Unified School District

Susan Moehring
Art Dept Chairman
Moreno Valley High School
13911 Perris Blvd
Sunnymead, CA 92388

Mount Diablo Unified School District

James E Snowden
Curriculum Specialist in Art &
Industrial Education
1936 Carlotta Dr
Concord, CA 94519

Newport-Mesa Unified School District

Jenean Romberg
Newport-Mesa School District
1601 Sixteenth St
Newport Beach, CA 92660

Novato Unified School District

Lee Hilton
Curriculum Specialist, Art
1015 Seventh St
Novato, CA 94947

Oakland Unified School District

Stanley H Cohen
Art Specialist
1025 Second Ave
Oakland, CA 94606

Ocean View School District

Karen Keller
Coordr Learning Resources
Rose Clark
Resource Teacher, Art
16940 B St
Huntington Beach, CA 92647

Palo Alto Unified School District

Kathryn M Alexander
Art Consultant
25 Churchill Ave
Palo Alto, CA 94306

Pasadena City Unified School District

Norman E Schmidt
Dir Program/Art Education
Linda Davis
Asst Superintendant
351 S Hudson
Pasadena, CA 91109

San Diego Unified School District

Dr Leven C Leatherbuty
Kay Wagner
Curriculum Specialist
Art Education
San Diego Unified School Dist
4100 Normal St
San Diego, CA 92103
Tel 619-298-8120

San Jose Unified School District

Caroline Kelso
Superintendant of Middle & High School
Educ, San Jose Unified School Dist
1605 Park Ave
San Jose, CA 95126

San Lorenzo Unified School District

Thomas R Phillips
Music & Fine Arts Coordr
15510 Usher St
San Lorenzo, CA 94580

San Mateo City School District

Richard Sperisen, Coordr
Art Educ/School Design
San Mateo County Office of Educ
333 Main St
Redwood, CA 94063

San Mateo Union High School District

Gregg MacGibbon
Art Curriculum Council Chairman
Crestmoor High School
300 Piedmont Ave
San Bruno, CA 94066

Santa Barbara High School District

Janice Y Lorber
Art Dept
700 E Anapamu St
Santa Barbara, CA 93103
Tel 805-063-4331

Santa Clara Unified School District

Janet E Tellefsen
Coordr of Childrens Art
P O Box 397
Santa Clara, CA 95052

Santa Monica Unified School District

Richard Wagnon
Fine Arts Supervisor
Joan F Vaupen
Art Specialist
Santa Monica-Malibu USD
1723 Fourth St
Santa Monica, CA 90402

Sweetwater Union High School District

Frank Buzga
District Art Committee Chmn
Sweetwater Union High School Dist
1130 Fifth Ave
Chula Vista, CA 92011

Ventura Unified School District

John Bay
Dir of Educational Programs & Material
120 E Santa Clara
Ventura, CA 93001

Adams County, School District 12

Dr Norma Goecke
Music & Art Subject Specialty
11285 Highline Dr
Northglen, CO 80233

Aurora Public School

Pat Brown
Art Consultant
Aurora Hills Middle School
1009 S Uvalda
Aurora, CO 80012

Arapahoe County School District 6

Joe Grundemann
Art Chairman
North Elementary
1907 Powers
Littleton, CO 80120

Boulder Valley Public School District

Carol Warlock
Content Area Resource Teacher, Art
Boulder Valley Schools
P O Box 9011
Boulder, CO 80301

Colorado Springs Public Schools, District 11

Don Green
Supervisor
Art Education
1115 N El Paso St
Colorado Springs, CO 80903

Jefferson County School District R-1

Larry T Schultz
Coordr of Art
1209 Quail St
Lakewood, CO 80215

Poudra School District R-1

Lynn Lutkin
Art Coordr
Poudra School District R-1
2407 La Porte Ave
Fort Collins, CO 80521

Bristol Public Schools

Barbara J Grasso
Art Dept Head
Board of Education
129 Church St
Bristol, CT 06010

East Hartford Board of Education

Richard A Sterner
Supervisor/Fine & Performing Arts
110 Long Hill Dr
East Hartford, CT 06108

Fairfield School System

Peter Clarke
Art Coordr
c/o Andrew Warde High School
Fairfield, CT 06430

Greenwich Board of Education

Harold L Krevolin
Coordr Art/Music
290 Greenwich Ave
Greenwich, CT 06830

Hartford Public Schools

Paul J Dilworth
Coordr
William Dixon
Asst Coordr
Dept of the Arts
249 High St
Hartford, CT 06103

Meriden Public Schools

John Oblon
Fine Arts

Board of Education
398 Liberty St
Meriden, CT 06450

Milford Public Schools

Frank J Vespi
Dept Head
Elementary Art Dept
Toulson Bldg
River St
Milford, CT 06460

New Canaan Public Schools

Anne Howden
Chariman Art K-12
Center School
76 South Ave
New Canaan, CT 06840

New Haven Public Schools

Oyarma Tate
Supervisor of Art & Music
765 Elm St
New Haven, CT 06511

Norwalk Public Schools

Dr Donald Rogers
Art Supervisor
Board of Education Offices
105 Main St
Norwalk, CT 06852

Stamford Public Schools

John C Nerreau
Coordr of Art
Hoyt School
1500 High Ridge Rd
Stamford, CT 06903

Alachua County School System

Janice Bice
Art Supervisor
1817 E University Ave
Gainesville, FL 32601
Tel 904-373-5192

Bay County School System

Mary Weaver
Bay County Art Contact
5205 W Highway 98
Panama City, FL 32402

Brevard County School System

June Hinckley
Fine Arts Resource Teacher
1274 S Florida Ave
Rockledge, FL 32955
Tel 305-631-1913

Broward County School System

Betty Lou Sheridan
Supervisor of Art
6650 Griffin Rd
Davie, FL 33314
Tel 305-765-6026

Clay County School System

Jay Alligood
Clay County School Board
P O Box 488
Green Cove Springs, FL 32043
Tel 904-284-3041

Dade County School System

Jackie Hinchey
Consultant, Art Educ
Lindsey Hopkins Bldg

1410 Second Ave
Miami, FL 33132
Tel 305-350-3752

Duval County School Board

Nellie Lynch
Art Supervisor
1701 Prudential Dr
Jackson, FL 32207

Escambia County School Board

Mary Jo Burgess
Supervisor of Art
5402 Lillian Highway
Pensacola, FL 32506

Hillsborough County Board of Public Instruction

Dorothy Kennedy
Supervisor Art & Humanities
901 E Kennedy Blvd
Tampa, FL 33602

Indian River County School System

Gary Brady
2031 13th St
Vero Beach, FL 32960
Tel 305-569-0367

Lee County Public Schools

Margaret A Bare
Coordr of Fine Arts
2266 Second St
Fort Myers, FL 33901

Leon County School System

Lucille Williams
Virginia Laurence
Program Specialists
2757 W Pensacola St
Tallahassee, FL 32304
Tel 904-576-8111

Manatee County School Systems

Sue Barker Sullivan
Art Coordr
P O Box 9069
Bradenton, FL 33506

Okaloosa County School System

Collis V Porter
Art Supervisor
120 Lowery Place
Fort Walton Beach, FL 32548

Orange County School System

Dr Jane Rivell
Supervisor Fine Arts
P O Box 271
Orlando, FL 32802
Tel 305-422-3200

Pinellas County School System

Phyllis M Thurston
Art Supervisor
205 Fourth St SW
Largo, FL 33540
Tel 813-585-9951

Polk County School Board

Joe P Mitchell
Coordr of Art Instruction
P O Box 391
Bartow, FL 33830

St Lucie County School Board

Reed C Owens
Asst Superintendant
2929 Delaware Ave
Fort Pierce, FL 33450

Sarasota County School Board

Dr Ed Santana
Fine Arts Coordr
2418 Hatton St
Sarasota, FL 33577

Volusia County Board of Public Instruction

Dorothy Johnson
Art Supervisor
P O Box 19190
Daytona Beach, FL 32015

Atlanta Public Schools

David Walker
Instructional Servs Ctr
2930 Forrest Hill Dr, SW
Atlanta, GA 30315
Tel 404-659-3381

Callaway Educational Association

Carolyn Ann Page
Art Dir
Dallis St
LaGrange, GA 30240

Clark County School District

Jane D Deason
Visual Art Supervisor
Box 1708
Athens, Ga 30601

Clayton County Schools

Martha Ellen Stilwell
Curriculum Coordr, Art, Music
155 Smith St
Jonesboro, GA 30236

De Kalb County Schools

Sara Jo Sirmans
Supervisor of Art
3770 N Decatur Rd
Decatur, GA 30033

Eastman Public Schools

Earl W Woodward
Arts Supervisor, Title III
Cultural Enrichment Project
Eastman, GA 31023

Macon Public Schools

J Elizabeth McElroy
Art Supervisor, Area 4
Hunt School
990 Shurling Dr
Macon, GA 31201

Peach City Schools

Jead D Pervis
Art Consultant
Fort Valley High School
Knox Valley, GA 31031

Walton County Public Schools

Mrs Perry Nelle Darby
Art Specialist
Monroe Area Comprehensive High School
Bryant Rd
Monroe, GA 30655

Kamehameha Schools

Lee Ables
Chmn Art Dept
The Kamehameha Schools
Kapalama Heights
Honolulu, HI 96817

Arlington Township High School District 214

Edward Fischer
District Coordr Arts, Music & Student
Teaching
Township High School Dist 214
799 W Kensington Rd
Mount Prospect, IL 60056

Champaign County Schools

Julia Triplett
Educational Consultant
200 S Fredrick
Rantoul, IL 61866

Chicago Public Schools

Helen M Joyner
Art Dir
Joyce E Karamas
Art Coordr
228 N LaSalle St
Chicago, IL 60601

Danville Community Consolidated School District 118

William B Handley
Dir Fine Arts
516 N Jackson St
Danville, IL 61832

District 65 Schools, Evanston

Tom Harris
Dir Fine Arts
3701 Davis St
Skokie, IL 60076

District 15 Schools, Palatine

Robert Brehler
Art Chairperson
505 S Quentin Rd
Palatine, IL 60067

Elgin Public Schools, District U-46

George Hore
Dir Art Educ & Music
355 E Chicago
Elgin, IL 60120

Rockford Public Schools

Debra E Gibson
Art Coordr
Board of Education
201 S Madison St
Rockford, IL 61101

Waukegan Unit School District 60

Dr Henry Levy
Supervisor Art & Music
Unit School District 60
Lincoln Ctr
1201 N Sheridan Rd
Waukegan, IL 60085

Anderson Community School Corporation

Henry Case
Supervisor/Consultant Art
30 W 11th St
Anderson, IN 46016

Crown Point Community School Corporation

Cordelia Sykes
Supervisor/Consultant Art
200 E North St
Crown Point, IN 46307

Duneland School Corporation

Helen Sayer
Supervisor/Consultant Art
700 W Porter Ave
Chesterton, IN 46304

Evansville-Vanderburgh School Corporation

Harry Friley
Supervisor/Consultant Art
One SE Ninth St
Evansville, IN 47708

Gary Community School Corporation

Arnold Williams
Supervisor/Consultant Art
620 E 10th Place
Gary, IN 46402

Indianapolis Public Schools

Ted Moore
Constance Palmer
Supervisor/Consultant Art
120 E Walnut St
Indianapolis, IN 46204

Kokomo-Center Township Consolidated Schools

James Osborne
Supervisor/Consultant Art
100 W Lincoln Rd
PO Box 2188
Kokomo, IN 46902

Muncie Community School Corporation

Doris B Stewart
Supervisor/Consultant Art
328 E Washington St
Muncie, IN 47305

North Lawrence Community Schools

Carolyn Asner
Supervisor/Consultant Art
PO Box 729
Bedford, IN 47421

Penn-Harris-Madison School Corporations

Wilbur Eslinger
Supervisor/Consultant Art
55900 Bittersweet Rd
Mishawaka, IN 46544

School City of East Chicago

Jensen Watts
Supervisor/Consultant Art
210 E Columbus Dr
East Chicago, IN 46312

Vincennes Community School Corporation

Anita Gainey, Carla Anderson,
Frances Shrout
Supervisor/Consultant Art
PO Box 1267
Vincennes, IN 47591

Cedar Rapids Community School District

Paula S Prescott
Elementary Art Project Leader
James Erbe
Secondary Arts Project Leader
4141 Johnson Ave NW
Cedar Rapids, IA 52405

Davenport Community School District

Lars H Souder
Coordr Art Education
1001 Harrison
Davenport, IA 52803

Des Moines Independent Community School District

Fred C Hiatt
Art Education Supervisor
1800 Grand Ave
Des Moines, IA 50307

Sioux City Community School District

Robert J Patnaud
Division Head
Art Dept
1221 Pierce St
Sioux City, IA 51105

Shawnee Mission Public School District 512

Dr David Circle
Supervisor of Fine Arts
7230 Belinder Rd
Shawnee Mission, KS 66208

Unified School District 500, Kansas City

Herman Gerber
Dir Art Education
625 Minnesota Ave
Kansas City, KS 66101

Unified School District 501, Topeka Public Schools

Donna D Pauler
Instructional Specialist Art (K-12)
Supervisor of Art
624 W 24th
Topeka, KS 66611

Unified School District Wichita, 259

William W King
Dir of Art Educ
640 N Emporia
Wichita, KS 67214

Jefferson County Public Schools

Norma E Brown
Lead Specialist Art
Durrett Educational Ctr
4409 Preston Highway
Louisville, KY 40213

Caddo Parish School System

Rachel Dunn
Supervisor of Related Arts Educ
1961 Midway
PO Box 32000
Shreveport, LA 71130

Calcasieu Parish School System

Daniel Vidrine
Supervisor
1732 Kirkman St
Lake Charles, LA 70601

East Baton Rouge Parish School System

Kenneth Tollos
Supervisor of Art
PO Box 2950
East Baton Rouge, LA 70821

New Orleans Public Schools

Shirley Corey
Supervisor Comprehensive Arts
Lakeview Annex
5931 Milne St
New Orleans, LA 70124

Ouachita Parish School System

Louise Norris
Arts Coordr
PO Box 1642
Monroe, LA 71201

Allegany County Board of Education

Harry E Mandell
Supervisor of Art
108 Washington St
Cumberland, MD 21502

Anne Arundel County Public Schools

Elizabeth Grimaldis
Coordr Art
2644 Riva Rd
Annapolis, MD 21401

Baltimore City Public Schools

Richard Micherdzinski
Coordr of Art
West Baltimore Middle School
181 N Bend Rd
Baltimore, MD 21229

Baltimore County Public Schools

Henry Jones
Specialist in Art
6901 Charles St
Towson, MD 21204

Calvert County Public Schools

Roberta Greer
Supervisor Instruction
Dares Beach Rd
Prince Frederick, MD 20678

Caroline County Board of Education

Morgan E Williams
Dir Staff Develop
Law Building, 112 Market St
Denton, MD 21629

Carroll County Public Schools

Glenn W Patterson
Supervisor Music & Art
55 N Court St
Westminster, MD 21157

Cecil County Public Schools

Carmelo Palazzo
Specialist Instruction
Fine Arts, Library Media
Booth St Ctr
Elkton, MD 21921

Charles County Board of Education

Dr Ann Richardson
Supervisor of Art
La Plata, MD 20646

Dorchester County Board of Education

Dr W Robert Tolley
Supervisor of Curriculum, Art
700 Glasgow St
PO Box 619
Cambridge, MD 21613

Frederick County Board of Education

Carroll H Kehne Jr
Curriculum Specialist Art Education
115 E Church St
Frederick, MD 21701

Garrett County Board of Education

Robert F Rodeheaver
Dir Secondary Education
40 S Fourth St
PO Box 313
Oakland, MD 21550

Harford County Board of Education

Joseph C Cooney
Supervisor of Art
45 E Gordon St
Bel Air, MD 21014

Howard County Board of Education

Charles Wagner
Supervisor of Art
10910 Route 108
Ellicott City, MD 21043

Kent County Public Schools

Raymond E Clarke
Kent County Public Schools
Washington Ave
Chestertown, MD 21620

Montgomery County Board of Education

Irene Glaser
Supervisor of Elementary Art
850 Hungerford Dr
Rockville, MD 20850

Prince George's County Board of Education

Dr Leroy Gaskin
Supervisor of Art
Northern Area Office
Elaine Wallace
Southern Area Office
7711 Livingston Rd
Oxon Hill, MD 20745

Queen Anne's County Board of Education

Jean S Wood
Supervisor of Instruction
Chesterfield Ave
PO Box C
Centreville, MD 21617

Saint Mary's County Public Schools

George F Thorne
Supervisor Art
Loveville, MD 20656

Somerset County Public Schools

Jack C Morgan
Supervisor Secondary Education
Westover Annes
Westover, MD 21871

Talbot County Public Schools

John Obitz
Supervisor Instruction
PO Box 1029
Washington St
Easton, MD 21601

Washington County Board of Education

Lee Weaver
Coordr Visual Arts
823 Commonwealth Ave
Hagerstown, MD 21740

Wicomico County Board of Education

Thomas Zimmerman
Supervisor of Art & Music
PO Box 1538
Long Ave & Mount Hermon Rd
Salisbury, MD 21801

Worchester County Board of Education

Dr Melvin Ross
Supervisor of Instruction
PO Box 130
Snow Hill, MD 21863

Boston Public Schools

Donald Brown
Dir Fine Arts
26 Court St
Boston, MA 02108

Brockton Public Schools

Tom Richards
Art Dept Head, K-12
43 Crescent St
Brockton, MA 02401

Cambridge School Dept

Rita W Ritterbush
Dir Art
459 Broadway
Cambridge, MA 02138

Fall River Public Schools

Jean Gagnon
Dir Fine Arts
417 Rock St
Fall River, MA 02720

Lowell Public Schools

Thomas McGuire
Dir of Art
Lowell Public Schools
Lowell, MA 01853

New Bedford Public Schools

Raymond G Bisaillon
Art Education Dir
County St Admin Bldg
455 County St
New Bedford, MA 02740

Springfield Public Schools

Teresa Bailey
Supervisor of Art
195 State St
Springfield, MA 01103

Worcester Public Schools

Loukia S Bitzas
Dir Music & Art
Worcester Public Schools
20 Irving St, Rm 35
Worcester, MA 01609

Ann Arbor Public Schools

Ruth L Beatty
Coordr Art
Lakewood School
344 Gralake
Ann Arbor, MI 48103
Tel 313-994-2200

Battle Creek Public Schools

Max D Misner
Dir of Art
Willard Library Bldg
Battle Creek, MI 49016

Bay City Public Schools

Jane D Miller
Coordr
Bay City Public Schools
Bay City, MI 48706

Benton Harbor Public Schools

Charles Murray
Art Dept Chmn
870 Colfax Ave
Benton Harbor, MI 49022

City of Pontiac School District

Otha Whitcomb
Art Specialist
Franklin Elementary School
661 Franklin Rd
Pontiac, MI 48513

Dearborn Public Schools

Marlene Lewis
Elementary Consultant
18700 Audette
Dearborn, MI 48124

Detroit Public Schools

James Jennings
Supervisor
Dept Art Education
842 Schools Ctr
5057 Woodward
Detroit, MI 48202

East Detroit Public Schools

Robert Slebodnik
Asst Principal
15501 Couzens
East Detroit, MI 48021
Tel 313-445-4410

Farmington Public Schools

Beverly L Ellis
Elementary Arts Consultant
Farmington Public Schools
32500 Shiawassee
Farmington, MI 48204

Flint Board of Education

Judy Avitts
Art Consultant
Fine Arts
Flint Community Schools
923 E Kearsley St
Flint, MI 48502

Garden City Public Schools

Donald L Beatty
Deputy Superintendent
Garden City Public Schools
1333 Radcliff St
Garden City, MI 48135

Grand Rapids Public Schools

Verlyn Matusko
Supervisor of Art
Grand Rapids Public Schools
143 Bostwick, NE
Grand Rapids, MI 49503
Tel 616-456-4700

Kalamazoo Public Schools

Doris M Miller
Coordr Elementary Art
Continuing Educ Ctr
Art Office 226
714 S Westridge
Kalamazoo, MI 49007

Lansing School District

Peggy King
Art Coordr
5815 Wise Rd
Lansing, MI 48910

Midland Public Schools

James Hopfensperger
Coordr Art
Midland Public Schools
600 E Carpenter St
Midland, MI 48640

Portage Public Schools

Al Kushner
Chmn
Art Dept
Portage Public Schools
5808 Oregon St
Portage, MI 49002

Port Huron Area School District

Laurence R Manz
Dir
Art Educ
2720 Riverside Dr
Port Huron, MI 48060

Roseville Public Schools

Paula Rollet
Chairperson
Art Dept
Secondary Schools
Brablec High School
Roseville, MI 48066

Saginaw City School District

Richard A Foulds
Dir Fine Arts
Art Educ
550 Millard St
Saginaw, MI 48607

Wayne Community School District

Susan Price
Coordr Visual Arts
3712 William St
Wayne, MI 48184

Anoka-Hennepin Independence School District 11

Jean Thurston
Art Coordr
Educational Service Ctr
1129 Hanson Blvd
Anoka, MN 55303

Independent School District 281, Robbinsdale Area

Robert Mendenhall
Art Coordr
4148 Winnetka Ave N
Minneapolis, MN 55427

Independent School District 624, White Bear Lake

Franklin J Zeller
Art Coordr
Bellaire Elementary School
White Bear Lake, MN 55110

Independent School District 625, Saint Paul

Rosa Smith
Humanities Coordr
Saint Paul Public Schools
360 Colborne
Saint Paul, MN 55102

Osseo Senior High School District

Candy Gordon
Art Coordr
11200 93rd Ave N
Osseo, MN 55369

Rochester, District 535

Kenneth Bauman
Elementary Art Consultant
463 Northern Heights Dr, NE
Rochester, MN 55901

Saint Louis Park Public Schools

Robert Anderson
Dept Chmn
Art Education
6425 W 33rd St
Saint Louis Park, MN 55426

Jackson Public Schools

Bernada Mason
Elementary Curriculum Coordr
712 S President St
Jackson, MS 39205

Ferguson-Florissant School District

Arthur B Kennon
Elementary Art Consultant
655 January Ave
Ferguson, MO 63135

Independence School District

Louis H Braley
Art Consultant
Truman High School
3301 S Noland
Independence, MO 64055

Kansas City Public Schools

Leonard Pryor
District Coordr
Fine & Performing Arts
1211 McGee St, Rm 802
Kansas City, MO 64106

North Kansas City

Katherine Smith
Elementary Art Supervisor
Truman Burton
Dir Secondary Educations
2000 NE 46th St
Kansas City, MO 64116

Ritenour Consolidated School District

Dr Paul Doerrer
Asst Superintendant
2420 Woodson Rd
Saint Louis County, MO 63114

School District of Saint Joseph

Nadine Lueker
Fine Arts Supervisor
School District of Saint Joseph
Tenth & Felix St
Saint Joseph, MO 64501

Saint Louis Public Schools

Billie Phillips
Supervisor of Art
5910 Clifton
Saint Louis, MO 63109

School District 1, Great Falls

James D Poor
Supervisor of Art
1100 Fourth St S
Great Falls, MT 59403

School District 2, Billings

Les Heins
Dir Art Education
101-Tenth St W
Billings, MT 59102

Lincoln Public Schools

Roger Dean Van Deventer
Art Consultant K-12
Public School Administration Bldg
720 S 22nd St
Lincoln, NE 68510

Omaha Public Schools

Gerald Pabst
Art Coordr
3902 Davenport St
Omaha, NE 68131

Las Vegas Public Schools

Ralph Cadwalder
Assoc Superintendent for Secondary Educ
2832 E Flamingo Rd
Las Vegas, NV 87121

Washoe County Public Schools

Alice Taylor
Elementary Curriculum Coordr
Washoe County School District
425 E Ningh St
Reno, NV 89520

Manchester School Union 37

Russell Poehlman
Dir of Art
88 Lowell St
Manchester, NH 03101

Elizabeth Public Schools

Eddie Smith
Coordr Art Education
500 N Broad St
Elizabeth, NJ 07202

Newark Public Schools

Fred Ranson
Dir Fine Arts & Media
Newark Board of Education
Two Cedar St
Newark, NJ 07102

Paterson Board of Education

Frank Napier
Superintendant
33 Church St
Paterson, NJ 07505

Public Schools of Jersey City

Anthony S Guadadiello
241 Erie St
Jersey City, NJ 07302

Trenton Public Schools

Carol Belt
Art Specialist
Trenton Board of Education
Art Ctr
Clinton Ave
Trenton, NJ 08609

Las Vegas City Schools

Judy Rominger
Art Teacher
Robertson High School
Las Vegas, NM 87701

Albany Public Schools

Linda Chalmers
Chairperson Art Dept
Elemenary Level
Livingston Middle School
Northern Blvd
Albany, NY 12207
Frank Knoll
Supervisor of Art
Albany High School
700 Washington Ave
Albany, NY 12203

Binghamton City School District

D Menichello
Chmn Art Dept
31 Main St
Binghamton, NY 13905

Buffalo Public Schools

Lena B Priore
Supervisor of Art
911 Abbott Rd
Buffalo, NY 14220

City School District of Elmira

Thomas Snyder
Supervisor of Art
951 Hoffman St
Elmira 14905

Community School District of New Rochelle

William Livesey
Dept Chairperson
Isaac High School
270 Center St
New Rochelle, NY 10801

Levittown Union Free School District

Dr Hermon Sirois
Asst Superintendant for Instruction
Memorial Education Ctr
Abby Lane
Levittown, NY 11756

Mount Vernon Public Schools

Dr C Andrew Randall
Supervisor of Music & Art
Education Ctr
165 N Columbus Ave
Mt Vernon, NY 10553

New York City Public Schools

Marcia Friedmutter
Dir Art
Cultural Arts Unit
131 Livingston St
Brooklyn, NY 11201

Rochester City School District

Burt A Towne
Dir Arts & Humanities
13 Fitzhugh St S
Rochester, NY 14614

Schenectady Public Schools

William O'Connor
Dir Art
108 Brandywine Ave
Schenectady, NY 12307

School District of Niagara Falls

Gerard Franciosa
Supervisor of Adult Education
24th Street School
Niagra Falls, NY 14303

Sewanhaka Central District 2

Ronald Lopez
Art Coordr
555 Ridge Rd
Elmont
Long Island, NY 11003

Smithtown Public Schools

Ira Schultz
Art Coordr
High School West
Central Rd
Smithtown, NY 11787

White Plains Public Schools

Dr Ronald Topping
Program Coordr
Home Side Lane
White Plains, NY 10605

Yonkers Public Schools

Dr Donohue
Superintendant of Curriculum
145 Palmer Rd
Yonkers, NY 10701

Charlotte-Mecklenburg Schools

Deborah Cooper
Visual Arts Specialist
701 E Second St
Charlotte, NC 28202

Durham City Schools

Karen Hall
Cultural Arts
PO Box 2246
Durham, NC 27702

Fort Bragg Schools

Claudia J Sailor
Cultural Arts Supervisor
For Bragg Schools
PO Box 70089
Fort Bragg, NC 28307

Greensboro Public Schools

Carl O Foster
Cultural Arts Specialist
Drawer V
Greensboro, NC 27402

Wake County Public School System

Rose Melvin
Supervisor Visual Arts
PO Box 28041
Raleigh, NC 27603

Wayne County Schools

Agnes Jensen
Dir Secondary Education
Peggy Massingill
Dir Elementary Education
Wayne County Schools
301 N Herman St, Box GG
Goldsboro, NC 27503

Winston-Salem/Forsyth County Schools

Antony Swider
Coordr Art Education
PO Box 2513
Winston-Salem, NC 27102

Fargo Public Schools

Gene Okerlund
Cultural Resources Dir
Creative Arts Studio
1430 Seventh St S
Fargo, ND 58103

Akron Public Schools

Brian B Heard
Dir Art Education
Miller Staff Develop Ctr
65 Steiner
Akron, OH 44308

Cincinnati Public Schools

Donald P Sowell
Instructional Consultant
Art Education
230 E Ninth St
Cincinnati, OH 45202

Cleveland Public Schools

Robert Woide
Dir Visual Arts
1380 E Sixth St
Cleveland, OH 44114

Columbus Public Schools

Martin F Russell
Dir Unified Arts
Alum Crest Instructional Ctr
2200 Winslow Dr
Columbus, OH 43206

Dayton Public Schools

Armand Martino
Supervisor of Art
Dayton Board of Education
Service Bldg
4280 N Western Ave
Dayton, OH 45427

Kettering City School District

W Fred Von Gruenigen
Art Coordr
Kettering City School District
3490 Far Hills Ave
Kettering, OH 45429

Lima City School District

Joan Hebden
Dir Art
515 S Calumet Ave
Lima, OH 45804

Mansfield City Schools

Mel Coleman
Curriculum Dir
53 W Fourth St
Mansfield, OH 44902

Mentor Public Schools

Ken J Kary
Art Coordr
Mentor High School
6477 Center St
Mentor, OH 44060

Parma City Schools

Wanda Ullman
Coordr Art
6726 Ridge Rd
Parma, OH 44129

Toledo Public Schools

Mildred Sorensen
Toledo Board of Education
Manhattan & Elm
Toledo, OH 43608

Warren City Schools

James G Friend
Supervising Teacher of Art
261 Monroe St, NW
Warren, OH 44482

Washington Local Schools

Marti Osnowitz
Dept Chair
560 Clegg
Toledo, OH 43613

Willoughby-Eastlake City Schools

Uarda Overbaugh
Art Consultant
Edison Elementary School
5288 Karen Isle Dr
Willoughby, OH 44094

Youngstown City Schools

Robert Yalch
Supervisor Art
20 W Wood St
Youngstown, OH 44503

Enid Public Schools, Independent 57

Eldon Ames
Consultant
611 W Wabash
Enid, OK 73701

Tulsa Public Schools

Gary Goree
Supervisor of Art
Education Service Ctr
PO Box 45208
Tulsa, OK 74145

Beaverton School District 48

Louise Finley
Specialist Curriculum Servs
PO Box 200
Beaverton, OR 97005

David Douglas School District

George Hahn
Dept Chmn
1500 SE 130 Ave
Portland, OR 97233

Eugene Public Schools, District 4J

Martha Harris
Curriculum Coordr
200 N Monroe
Eugene, OR 97402

Portland Public Schools

Peggy Viscar
Art Education Coordr
3830 S E 14th St
Portland, OR 97202

Salem Public Schools, District 24J

Don Walton
Art Resource Teacher
1309 Ferry St, NE
Salem, OR 97308

Abington School District

Louis S Mohollen
Supervisor of Art
Abington School District
1841 Susquehanna
Abington, PA 19001

Allentown Public Schools

Barbara J Fischer
Fine Arts Coordr
31 S Penn St
Allentown, PA 18105

Altoona Area School District

Darwin Bistline
Supervisor of Art & Music
Fifth Ave & 15 St
Altoona, PA 16602

Armstrong School District

Charles Milton Hanna
Dept Chmn
Fourth & Tenth
Ford City, PA 16226

Bethlehem School District

Carl Langkamer
Curriculum Specialist, Art & Music
Education Ctr
1516 Sycamore St
Bethlehem, PA 18017

Bristol Township Public Schools

Joseph Pavone
Dept Chmn
63 Manor Circle
Bristol, PA 19007

Chambersburg Area School District

Velda Beuens
Elementary Art Dept Chmn
511 S Sixth St
Chambersburg, PA 17201

Chester Upland School District

Maureen M Roberts
Dir Fine Arts
Chester Upland School District
18th & Melrose
Chester, PA 19013

Council Rock School District

Thomas Ritenbaugh
Art Coordr
Council Rock School District
Swamp Rd
Newtown, PA 18940

Cumberland Valley School District

Gene Van Dyke
Supervisor of Art
6746 Carlisle Pike
Mechanicsburg, PA 17055

Erie School District

Paul G Grack
Coordr Fine Arts
1511 Peach St
Erie, PA 16501

Greater Johnstown School District

Sara Jane Stewart
Supervisor of Art
Chestnut Bldg
501-509 Chestnut St
Johnstown, PA 15906

Harrisburg City School District

Barbara McGeary
Art Supervisor
Harrisburg Arts Magnet School
Riverside Bldg
3219 Green St
Harrisburg, PA 17102

Hazelton Area School District

Albert Sarkas
Surpervisor of Art
Hazelton Area School District
Church & Walnut St
Hazelton, PA 18201

Neshaminy School District

Dr Henry Pearlberg
Supervisor of Fine Arts
2001 Old Lincoln Highway
Langhorne, PA 19047

New Castle Public Schools

Jesse W Badger
Dir Art Education
Administration Bldg
North & East Sts
New Castle, PA 16101

Norristown Area School District

Carol Johnson
Instructional Leader in Art
Norristown High School
1900 Eagle Dr
Norristown, PA 19403

North Penn State District

Jacqueline Thomas
Art Dept Chairperson
400 Penn St
Lansdale, PA 19446

Pennsbury School District

Dave Denick
Art Coordr
3705 Hood Blvd
Fairless Hills, PA 19054

Pittsburgh Public Schools

Terry Stakpole
Dir Arts & Educations
Board of Public Education
341 S Bellefield Ave
Pittsburgh, PA 15213

Reading School District

Earl G McLane
Dir Art
Administration Bldg
Eighth & Washington St
Reading, PA 19601

School District of Lancaster

Albert B Minnich
Dir Art & Industrial Arts
225 W Orange St
Lancaster, PA 17604

School District of Philadelphia

Harry Bonelli
Dir Art Education
Board of Education
21 & Parkway
Philadephia, PA 19103

State College Area School District

Marty Vaughn
Art Coordr
650 Westerly Parkway
State College, PA 18601

Upper Darby School District

Judson G Snyder
District Art Supervisor
Lansdowne Ave & School Lane
Upper Darby, PA 19084

Warren County School District

James Hill
Elementary Art Supervisor
Market Street Elementary School
Market & Second Sts
Warren, PA 16365

West Chester Area School District

Dr Leland N Gage
Art Supervisor
Administration Ctr
320 N Church
West Chester, PA 19380

West Shore School District

Elaine Wilson
Art Supervisor
1000 Hummel Ave
Lemoyne, PA 17043

Wilkes-Barre School District

Andrew Palencar
Art Supervisor
730 S Main St
Wilkes-Barre, PA 18711

Williamsport Area School District

Dr June E Baskin
Supervisor of Art
Transeau Educational Ctr
845 Park Ave
Williamsport, PA 17701

York City School District

Dr Ronald Toomey
Dir Fine Arts
329 S Lindbergh Ave
York, PA 17405

Pawtucket School Department

Robert Venditto
Art Dir
Administration Bldg
Park Place
Pawtucket, RI 02860

Providence School System

Karen Lee Carroll
Arts Coordr
Hope High School
324 Hope St
Providence, RI 02906

Warick School Department

Rene T Velleneuve
Dept Head
Elementary Art
Box 507 Conimicut Sta
34 Warwick Lake Ave
Warwick, RI 02889

Charleston County School District

Sherman McCauley
Fine Arts Consultant
Charleston County School District
Charleston, SC 29401

Darlington County

June McCauley
Art Supervisor
Saint John's High School
Darlington, SC 29532

Florence School District 1

Barbara W Terry
Coordr
109 W Pine St
Florence, SC 29501

Greenville County School District

Robert Strother
Art Consultant
301 Camperdown Way
Box 2848
Greenville, SC 29602

Richmond School District 1

Betty Gibert
Art Coordr
1616 Richland St
Columbia, SC 29201

Spartanburg County School District 6

Mary Lou Hightower
Art Coordr
1493 W O Ezel Blvd
Spartanburg, SC 29301

Spartanburg County School District 7

Betty Jane Bramlett
Art Coordr
Spartanburg City Schools
PO Box 970
Spartanburg, SC 29304

Rapid City Public Schools

Eric Peters
Art Supervisor
Cheyenne-Eagle Butte High School
Eagle Butte, SD 57625

Chattanooga Public Schools

Scott Sanders
Art Resource Teacher
1161 40th St
Chattanooga, TN 37409

Knoxville City Schools

Mitchell Van Metre
Supervisor of Art
101 E Fifth Ave
Knoxville, TN 37917

Memphis City Schools

Betty Pittman
Art Supervisor
Memphis City Schools
2597 Avery Ave
Memphis, TN 38112

Metropolitan Nashville Davidson County Public Schools

Jean Coleman
Supervisor
Art Education
2601 Bransford Ave
Nashville, TN 37204

Abilene Public Schools

Scott Darr
Art Consultant
Abilene Independent School District
PO Box 981
Abilene, TX 79604

Amarillo Independent School District

Richard Ross
Dir of Art Education
910 W Eighth St
Amarillo, TX 79101

Austin Independent School District

Sherilyn Howze
Art Coordr
Austin Indep School District, Secondary
6100 Guadalupe
Austin, TX 78752

Carrollton-Farmers Independent School District

Joan Burk
Art Consultant
PO Box 186
Carrollton, TX 75006

Corpus Christi Independent School District

Ola Underhill
Art Consultant
PO Drawer 110
Corpus Christi, TX 78403

Dallas Independent School District

Jack Brockette
Art Consultant
3700 Ross Ave
Dallas, TX 75204

El Paso Independent School District

Jeanne Weitz
Dept of Fine Arts
2231 Arizona Ave
El Paso, TX 79930

Fort Worth Independent School District

Jo Mosley
Dir Art Education
3210 W Lancaster St
Fort Worth, TX 76107

Houston Independent School District

Annette Watson
Dir Art Education

Houston Independent School District, Secondary
3830 Richmond Ave
Houston, TX 77027

Irving Independent School District

Irene Norman
Art Consultant
901 O'Connor
Irving, TX 75061

Lubbock Independent School District

Zonalynn Stevens
Art Consultant
1628 19th St
Lubbock, TX 79401

North East Independent School District

Mrs Jerry Frey
Art Consultant
Art Education
10333 Broadway
San Antonio, TX 78286

Northside Independent School District

Juanita Lautum
Art Consultant
5900 Evers Rd
San Antonio, TX 78238

Pasadena Independent School District

Katherine Reid
Supervisor of Art
3010 Bayshore Dr
Pasadena, TX 77502

Plaino Independent School District

Linda Williams
Art Consultant
1517 Ave H
Plaino, TX 75074

San Angelo Independent School District

Velma Jo Whitfield
Art Supervisor
100 N Magdalen St
San Angelo, TX 76901

San Antonio Independent School District

Elizabeth Kefauver
Art Consultant
141 La Cava St
San Antonio, TX 78210

Spring Branch Independent School District

Jennifer D Gerlach
Art Coordr
Spring Branch Indep School District
955 Campbell Rd
Houston, TX 77024

Ysleta Independent School District

George Saucier
Art Consultant
8445 Valdestino
El Paso, TX 79907

Davis County School District

Ivan E Cornia
Art Supervisor
45 E State St
Farmington, UT 84025

Jordan School District

George A Welch
Consultant of Fine Arts
9361 S 400 East
Sandy, UT 84070

Salt Lake City Public Schools

Margaret Richards
Education Specialist
Salt Lake City Board of Education
440 E First South
Salt Lake City, UT 84111

Barre City Schools

Janet Jacobs
Coordr Curriculum & Instruction
Barre City Schools
Barre City, VT 15641

Alexandria City Schools

Roy Smith
Curriculum Specialist
3801 W Braddock Rd
PO Box 3009
Alexandrai, VA 22302
Tel 703-998-2160

Arlington County Schools

Larry Bohnert
Specialist Music & Art
1426 N Quincy St
Arlington, VA 22207
Tel 704-558-2011

Chesapeake City Schools

Thomas Felton
Supervisor Art
PO Box 15204
Chesapeake, VA 23320
Tel 804-547-0153

Chesterfield County Schools

Gail Nichols
Art Consultant
School Admin Bldg
Chesterfield, VA 23832
Tel 804-748-1384

Fairfax County Schools

Dr Beverly Heinle
Art Specialist
Masonville Instructional Ctr
3705 Crest Dr
Annandale, VA 22003
Tel 703-698-7500

Hampton City Schools

Dr James Steele
Dir Art & Music
Administration Ctr
1819 Nickerson Blvd
Hampton, VA 23663
Tel 804-851-8411

Henrico County Schools

W Randolph Cheatham
Coordr of Art
201 E Nine Mile Rd
PO Box 40
Highland Springs, VA 23075
Tel 804-737-3498

Newport News

Lee Montgomery
Supervisor of Art
12465 Warwick Blvd
Newport News, VA 23606
Tel 804-599-8714

Norfolk City Schools

Kay Baker
Dir Art Education
800 E City Hall Ave
Norfolk, VA 23510

Portsmouth City Schools

Wilhemenia Smith
Art Specialist
3000 North St
Portsmouth, VA 23704
Tel 804-393-8885

Prince William County Schools

Gary DiVecchia
PO Box 389
Manassas, VA 22110
Tel 703-791-7270

Richmond City Schools

Sam Banks
Coordr Arts & Humanities Ctr
815 N 35th St
Richmond, VA 23223
Tel 804-780-5062

Roanoke City Schools

Leslie Willett
Supervisor Art & Humanities
PO Box 13145
Roanoke, VA 24031
Tel 703-981-2876

Virginia Beach City Schools

Stephena Runyan
Art Coordr
School Admin Bldg
2512 George Mason Dr
PO Box 6038
Virginia Beach, VA 23456
Tel 804-427-4871

Bellevue School District

Dr Jill Matthies
Area Dir Instruction
310 102nd Ave NE
Bellevue, WA 98004

Bellingham School District

Barbara Kelly
Curriculum Dir
Box 878
Bellingham, WA 98227

Bremerton School District

Gerald Johnson
Supervisor, Curriculum
300 N Montgomery
Bremerton, WA 98312

Clover Park School District

James D Blanchard
Supervisor Art Education
10020 Gravelly Lake Dr, SW
Tacoma, WA 98499

Edmonds School District

Bill Anderson
Program Mgr Music & Fine Arts
3800 196th SW
Lynnwood, WA 98036

Everett School District

Ken Kraintz
Supervisor, Fine Arts
4730 Colby Ave
PO Box 2089
Everett, WA 98203

Evergreen School District

Merry Cammack
Curriculum Coordr
12905 NE 29th St
Vancouver, WA 98662

Federal Way School District

Sue Greenleaf
Art Coordr
Totem Junior High School
26630 40th Ave S
Kent, WA 98032

Highline School District

Jerry Bayne
Fine Arts Coordr
15675 Ambaum Blvd SW
Box 66100
Seattle, WA 98166

Kennewick School District

Joan Butler
Coordr Curriculum
200 S Dayton St
Kennewick, WA 99336

Kent School District

Neal Porter
Dir Music & Art
12033 SE 256th
Kent, WA 98031

Lake Washington School District

Roger Long
Curriculum & Program Develop
10903 NE 53rd
PO Box 619
Kirkland, WA 98033

Puyallup School District

Debbie Ross
Art Coordr
Governor John Rogers High School
12801 86th Ave E
Puyallup, WA 98373

Renton School District

Margaret Rose Anderson
Specialist Fine Arts
435 Main Ave S
Renton, WA 98055

Seattle School District

Robert Cathey
Arts Consultant
815 Fourth Ave N
Seattle, WA 98109

Spokane School District

Bob Gregg
Coordr Art
N 200 Bernard
Spokane, WA 99201

Tacoma School District

Charlotte Burke
Teacher, Fine Arts
PO Box 1357
Tacoma, WA 98401

Vancouver School District

C Adair Hilligoss
Creative Arts Coordr
605 N Devine Rd
Vancouver, WA 98661

Yakima School District

Nick Mason
Dir Performing Art
104 N Fourth Ave
Yakima, WA 98902

Cabell County Public Schools

Libby K Caligan
Dir Art
620-20th St
Huntington, WV 25709

Kanawha County Schools

Ruby Stanfield Hall
Consultant Art K-12
200 Elizabeth St
Charleston, WV 25311

Marion County Board of Education

Nancy Harry
Supervisor of Art
200 Gaston Ave
PO Box 712
Fairmont, WV 26554

Monongalia County Schools

Wayne L Miller
Art Consultant
Monongalia County Schools
263 Prairie Ave
Morgantown, WV 26505

Madison Metropolitan School District

Frank C Lindl
Fine Arts Coordr
545 W Dayton St
Madison, WI 53703

Milwaukee Public Schools

Dr Kent Anderson
Curriculum Specialist
PO Drawer 10K
Milwaukee, WI 53201

Racine Unified Schools

Dr Nancy Hunt
Dir Art Education K-12
2200 Northwestern Ave
Racine, WI 53404

Laramie County School District 1

Michael Beeman
Art Coordr
2810 House Ave
Cheyenne, WY 82001

Art Magazines

A for Annuals; M for Monthlies; W for Weeklies; Q for Quarterlies

African Arts (Q)—John Povey, Ed; African Studies Center, University of California, 405 Hilgard Ave, Los Angeles, CA 90024. Yearly $16.00

Afterimage (9 Issues)—Nathan Lyons, Ed; Visual Studies Workshop Inc, 31 Prince St, Rochester, NY 14607.   Yearly $22.00

American Art Journal (Q)—Jane Van N. Turano, Ed; Kennedy Galleries, 40 W. 57th St, Fifth Floor, New York, NY 10019.   Yearly $25.00

American Artist (M)—M. Stephen Doherty, Ed; Marlene Schiller, Mg. Ed; 1515 Broadway, New York, NY 10036.   Yearly $17.50

American Craft (Bi-M)—Lois Moran, Ed; 401 Park Ave S, New York, NY 10016.   Yearly $29.50

American Indian Art Magazine (Q)—Roanne Goldfein, Ed; American Indian Art Inc, 7333 E. Monterey Way #5, Scottsdale, AZ 85251. Yearly $16.00

American Journal of Archaeology (Q)—Brunilde Ridgway, Ed; Archaeological Institute of America, Bryn Mawr College, Bryn Mawr, PA 19010.   Yearly $25.00

American Journal of Art Therapy (Q)—Claire A. Levy, Ed; 6010 Broad Branch Rd NW, Washington, DC 20015.   Yearly $12.00

Antiques (M)—Wendell Garrett, Ed; 551 Fifth Ave, New York, NY 10176.   Yearly $38.00

Appollo (M)—Denys Sutton, Ed; PO Box 47, Hollywood, CA 91603. Yearly $88.00

Archaeology (Bi-M)—Phyllis Pollak Katz, Ed; Archaeological Institute of America, 53 Park Pl, New York, NY 10007.   Yearly $18.00

Architectural Digest (M)—George Oestreich, Pub; 5900 Wilshire Blvd, Los Angeles, CA 90036.   Yearly $36.00

Archives of American Art, Smithsonian (Q)—NMAA, PG Eight & F Sts, NW, Washington, DC 20560.   Membership $35.00

Art & Antiques (Bi-M)—Mary Jean Madigan, Ed; 1515 Broadway, New York, NY 10036.   Yearly $21.00

Art & Auction (10 Issues)—Stuart Greenstar, Ed; 250 W. 57th St, New York, NY 10019.   US $36.00

Art & the Law (Q)—Arlene Shuler, Ed; Volunteer Lawyers for the Arts, 1560 Broadway, New York, NY 10036.   Yearly $20.00

Art Business News (M)—Vicki Wray, Ed; 2135 Summer St, Stamford, CT 06905.   Yearly $18.00

Art Contemporary (Q)—Carl E. Loeffler, Ed; PO Box 3123 Rincon Annex, San Francisco, CA 94119.   Yearly $12.00.

Art Direction (M)—Don Barron, Ed; 10 E. 39th St, New York, NY 10016.   Yearly $18.00

Art Education (Bi-M)—John J. Mahlmann, Ed; National Art Education Association, 1916 Association Dr, Reston, VA 22091. Yearly $50.00

Artforum (M)—Ingrid Sischy, Ed; 205 Mulberry St, New York, NY 10012.   Yearly $36.00

Art Gallery (Bi-M)—Jay Jacobs, Ed; Main St, Ivoryton, CT 06442. Yearly $25.00

Art in America (11 Issues)—Elizabeth C. Baker, Ed; 850 Third Ave, New York, NY 10022.   Yearly $34.95

Art Index (Q)—David Patten, Ed; The H.W. Wilson Co, 950 University Ave, New York, NY 10452.   Subscription on service basis

Art International (Bi-M)—James Fitzsimmons, Ed. & Publ; Via Maraini 17-A, 6900 Lugano, Switzerland

Art Journal (Q)—College Art Assn. of America; 16 East 52nd St, New York, NY 10022.   Yearly $12.00 (non-members)

Art Material Trade News (M)—Erwin E. Feldman, Pub; Syndicate Magazines Inc, 390 5th Ave, New York, NY 10018.   Yearly $23.00

Artnews (M)—Milton Esterow, Pub; 122 E. 42nd St, New York, NY 10017.   Yearly $22.00

Art Product News—Terry L. Gardner, Ed; 4040 W 10th St, PO Box 22575, Indianapolis, IN 46222.   Yearly $12.00

Art Research News (Q); 46 E. 70th St, New York, NY 10021. Membership

Artscanada (Bi-M)—Anne Trueblood Brodzky, Ed; 3 Church St, Toronto, Ontario, M5E 1M2.   Yearly $25.00

Arts Magazine (10 Issues)—Richard Martin, Ed; 23 East 26th St, New York, NY 10010.   Yearly $33.00

Artweek (44 Issues)—Cecile N. McCann, Ed; 1305 Franklin St, Oakland, CA 94612.   Yearly $16.00

Artworkers News (10 Issues)—Daniel Grant, Ed; Foundation for the Community of Artists, 280 Broadway, Suite 412, New York, NY 10007. Yearly $12.00

Black Art: An International Quarterly (Q)—Val Spaulding, Ed; 137-55 Southgate St, Jamaica, NY 11413.   Yearly $12.00

Bulletin of the Cleveland Museum of Art, The (M)—Merald E. Wrolstad, Ed; 11150 East Blvd. at University Circle, Cleveland, OH 44106.   Yearly $10.00

Bulletin of the Detroit Institute of Art (Q)—Andrea Belloli, Ed; 5200 Woodward Ave, Detroit, MI 48202.   Yearly $6.00

Ceramics Monthly (M)—William Hunt, Ed; Professional Publications, Inc, Box 12448, Columbus, OH 43212.   Yearly $14.00

Communication Arts (Bi-M)—Richard S. Coyne, Ed; 410 Sherman Ave, (PO Box 10300), Palo Alto, CA 94303.   Yearly $36.00

Connoisseur, The (M)—Philip Herrera, Ed; 224 W 57th St, New York, NY 10019.   Yearly $12.95

Contemporary Art-Southeast (61 Issues)—John English, Ed; 3317 Piedmont Rd, Atlanta, GA 30305.   Yearly $12.00

Gazette des Beaux-Arts (10 Issues)—Jean Adhemar, Ed; Imprimerie Louis-Jean, 05002 Gap Cedex, France.   Yearly 350 FF

Glass Studio (M)—Maureen Michelson, PO Box 23383, Portland OR 97223.   Yearly $18.00

Goodfellow Review of Crafts (Bi-M)—Christa Malone, Ed; Box 4520, Berkeley, CA 94704.   Single $1.50

Graphics Design: USA (M)—Valerie Stuart & Margie Imershein, Ed; 120 E. 56th St, New York, NY 10022.   Yearly $20.00

Graphis: International Journal for Graphic & Applied Art (Bi-M)—Walter Herdig, Ed; 107 Dufourstrasse, Zurick, Switzerland.   Yearly $59.00

High Performance (Q)—Linda Frye Burnham, Ed; 240 S. Broadway, Los Angeles, CA 90012.   Yearly $15.00

Illustrator (Bi-A)—Dr. Don L. Jardine, Ed; 500 South Fourth St, Minneapolis, MN 55415.   Yearly $4.00

Industrial Design Magazine (Bi-M)—David Ellingson, Ed; 330 W. 42nd St, New York, NY 10036.   Yearly $30.00

Interior Design (M)—Sherman R. Emery, Ed; 850 3rd Ave, New York, NY 10022.   Yearly $34.95

Italix, The Calligraphic Quarterly (Q)—William F. Haywood, Ed; PO Box 279, Fair Lawn, NJ 07410.   Yearly $10.00

Journal of Canadian Art History (Semi-A)—Donald Andrus, Ed; 1395 ouest, Dorchester, Montreal, PQ H3G 2M5, Canada.   Yearly $10.00

Master Drawings (Q)—Felice Stempfle, Ed; Master Drawings Association Inc, 33 E. 36th St, New York, NY 10016.   Yearly $25.00

Metropolitan Museum of Art Bulletin (Q)—Joan Holt, Ed; Fifth Ave at 82nd St, New York, NY 10028.   Yearly $14.00

MFA Bulletin of the Museum of Fine Arts, Boston (A)—465 Huntington Ave, Boston, MA 02115.   Yearly $3.00

Museum News (Bi-M)—Ellen C. Hicks, Ed; American Association of Museums, 1055 Thomas Jefferson Ave, NW, Washington, DC 20020.   Yearly $18.00

National Sculpture Review (Q)—Michael Lantz, Ed; 15 East 26th St, New York, NY 10010.   Yearly $7.00

New Art Examiner (10 Issues)—Jane Addams Allen, Ed; New Art Association, 230 E. Ohio St, Chicago, IL 60611.   Yearly $15.00

Nit & Wit Cultural Arts Magazine (Bi-M)—Leonard Dominguez, Ed; 2745 N. Clark, Chicago, IL 60614.   Two years $13.00

Ocular (Q)—Eric Schwartz, Ed; 1549 Platte St, Denver, CO 80202.   Yearly $14.00

Ornament Magazine (Q)—Robert K. Liu, Ed; 1221 S. LaCienega, Los Angeles, CA 90035.   Yearly $18.00

Philadelphia Museum of Art Bulletin—George H Marcus, Ed; 26 & Parkway, Philadelphia, PA 19101.   Yearly $8.00

Portfolio: The Magazine of the Fine Arts (Bi-M)—Denise Martin, Ed; 271 Madison Ave, New York, NY 10016.   Yearly $18.00

Print (Bi-M)—Martin Fox, Ed; 355 Lexington Ave, New York, NY 10017.   Yearly $29.00

Progressive Architecture (M)—James Murphy, Ed; 1111 Chester Ave, Cleveland, OH 44114   Yearly $25.00

School Arts Magazine (M Sept-May)—David Baker, Ed; 50 Portland St, Worcester, MA 01608.   Yearly $14.00

Society of Architectural Historians Journal (Q)—Naomi Miller, Ed; 1700 Walnut St, Room 716, Philadelphia, PA 19103.   Membership

Southwest Art (M)—Susan Hallsten McGarry, Ed; 9 Greenway Plaza, Houston, TX 77046.   Yearly $27.50

Stained Glass (Q)—Dr Norman L. Temme, Ed; 1125 Willmington Ave, St Louis, MO 63111.   Yearly $15.00

Studio International (Q)—Jasia Reichardt, Ed; Studio Trust, 25 Denmark St, London WC2H 8NJ, England.   Yearly $34.00

Sunshine Artists, USA (M)—J. L. Wahl, Ed; 501 N Virginia Ave, Winter Park, FL 32789.   Yearly $18.00

Technology & Conservation of Art, Architecture, & Antiquities (Q)—S. E. Schur, Ed; One Emerson Pl, Boston, MA 02114.   Yearly $12.00

Today's Art & Graphics (M)—Erwin E Feldman, Pub; Syndicate Magazines Inc, 390 5th Ave, New York, NY 10018.   Yearly $12.00

Umbrella (Bi-M)—Judith A. Hoffberg, Ed; Astro Artz, 240 S Broadway, Los Angeles, CA 90012.   Yearly $20.00

Washington International Artsletter (10 Issues)—Daniel Millsaps, Ed. & Publ; PO Box 9005, Washington, DC 20003.   Yearly $48.00

Women Artists News (Bi-M)—Cynthia Navaretta, Ed; Midmarch Assoc, PO Box 3304, Grand Central Station, New York, NY 10163.   Yearly $12.00

Newspapers Carrying Art Notes and Their Critics

ALABAMA

Birmingham News—Tom Harper
Birmingham Post-Herald—Sandy Amann
Crimson-White—Jamie Sturterant
Florence Times—Jo Ann Nicoll
Gadsden Times—M. D. Garmon
The Huntsville Times—Alan Moore
Lanett Valley Times-News—Stan Hamby
Montgomery Advertiser—M. P. Wilkerson

ALASKA

Anchorage Times—Nancy Cain Schmidt

ARIZONA

Arizona Daily Star, Tucson—Jacqi Tully
Arizona Republic, Phoenix—Wendy Govier
Bisbee Daily Review—Bob Wicks
Flagstaff Arizona Daily Sun—Paul Sweitzer
Mesa Tribune—Pat McElfresh
The Phoenix Gazette—Kyle Lawson
Scottsdale Daily Progress—John Swan
Tucson Citizen—Joel Rochon

ARKANSAS

Arkansas Gazette, Little Rock—Charles Kaufman
Batesville Guard—Josephine Jones
Blytheville Courier News—Gloria White
Ft. Smith Southwest Times-Record—Frances Somers
Newport Daily Independent—Betty Richolson
Paragould Daily Press—Mark Lashley
Rogers Daily-Sunday News—Jerry Hiett
Springdale News—Mike Gauldin

CALIFORNIA

Alameda Times Star—Ken Kofman
Antioch Daily Ledger—Anthony Sorci
Berkeley Independent and Gazette—Bill Haigwood
Beverly Hills Courier—March Schwartz
Brawley News—Margaret Silva-Chairez
Brentwood Post—Juliet Schoen
Chico News and Review—Robert Speer
Concord Transcript—Brooks Kuehl
Corning Daily Observer—Mari Petty
The Daily Democrat—Alan Fishleder
Davis Enterprise—Del McColm
The Desert Sun—Bruce Fessier
El Centro Imperial Valley Press—Margaret Chairez
Evening Press-Enterprise—T. E. Foreman
Fairfield Daily Republic—Ruth Smith
Fremont Argus—Sharon LaMarche
Fresno Bee—David Hale
Fullerton Daily News Tribune—Holly Bridges
The Hanford Sentinel—Ruth J. Gomes
La Habra-Brea Daily Star Progress—Barbara Corbin Giasone
Livermore Tri Valley Herald and News—Sally Tockey
Long Beach Independent—Pat DeLuna
Los Angeles Daily Racing Form—Pierre Bellocq
Los Angeles Herald Examiner—Gene Cannoy
Los Angeles Times—Charles Champlin

Madera Daily Tribune—Pat Arnold
Martinez News Gazette—Robert V. Osmond
Marysville Appeal Democrat—Stanley G. Gelling
Modesto Bee—Leo Stutzin
Monterey Peninsula Herald—Irene Lagorio
Morning Press-Enterprise—T. E. Foreman
Napa Register—Bernice Dunn
North Shore Shopper—Juliet Schoen
Novato Advance—Anne Dolcini
The Oakland Tribune—Charles Shere
Oceanside Blade-Tribune—Angela Mack
Ojai Valley News, Inc—David Claffradini
Palisadian-Post—Juliet Schoen
Palo Alto Peninsula Times Tribune—Gay Morris
Palos Verdes Peninsula News—Richard Esposito
Pasadena Star-News—Mary Cox
Porterville Recorder—Willeta Regan
Press-Enterprise—T. E. Foreman
Press-Telegram—Al Rudis
Richmond Independent and Gazette—Bill Haigwood
Sacramento Bee—Ralph Frattura
Sacramento Union—Richard Simon
San Bernardino Sun—Ray Cooklis
San Diego Daily Transcript—Rod Riggs
San Francisco Chronicle—Tom Albright
San Mateo Times—Mary Helen McAllister
San Pedro News-Pilot—Marc Stern
Santa Barbara News & Review—David Rubien
Santa Barbara News-Press—Joan Crowder
Santa Paula Daily Chronicle—Elaine Fulton
Santa Rosa Press Democrat—Michael Geniella
Turlock Daily Journal—Carl Baggese
Ukiah Daily Journal—Dan McKee
Vallejo Times-Herald—Ginny McPartland
Ventura County Star-Free Press—Rita Moran
Walnut Creek Contra Costa Times—Carol Fowler
Wave Newspapers—Jeri Love
Weaverville Weekly Trinity Journal—Patricia Hamilton

COLORADO

Boulder Daily Camera—Patty Burnett
Colorado Daily—Jennifer Heath
Colorado Springs Sun—Susan Stern
Colorado Transcript—Richard Frost
Denver Post—James Mills
Ft. Morgan Times—Carol Rudnik
Pueblo Star Journal—Margie Wood
Rocky Mountain News, Denver—Keith Raether

CONNECTICUT

American—Teresa Rousseau
The Bridgeport Post & Sunday Post—Betty Tyler
Bristol Press—Linda Smith
Connecticut Daily Campus—Victoria Geibel & Warren Taylor
Danbury News-Times—Jean Buoy
The Greenwich Time—Dorothy Friedman
The Hartford Courant—Malcohn Johnson
Lakeville Journal—Tara Ransom
The New Britain Herald—Judith W. Brown
New Haven Advocate—Heleri Ziou
New Haven Register—Don Rabin
Scribe—Steve Cioffi

Waterbury American (Republican, Sunday Republican)—
  Terri Rousseau
Yale Daily News—Andrea Carroll & Adam Blair

DISTRICT OF COLUMBIA

Air Line Pilot—Robert Hughes
American Teacher—Charles Glendinning
Service Employee—Cynthia Reymer
Washington Post—Paul Richard

FLORIDA

Anna Maria Islander-Longboat Islander—Barbara Forster
Clearwater Sun—Vaughn Hughes
Florida Times-Union, Jacksonville—Clayton Powers
Fort Lauderdale News—Roger Hurlburt
Gainesville Sun—Diane Chun
Hallandale Digest, Inc—Florence Gould
Hollywood Sun-Tattler—Jack Gold
Miami News—Bernie Oelze
Oldsmar Herald—Pat Masterson
Orlando Sentinel—Mark Williams
Palatka Daily News—Ruth Elibeck
Palm Beach Daily News, West Palm Beach—Millie Wolff

GEORGIA

Albany Herald—Louise O. Whiting
Athens Daily News—Masie Underwood
The Atlanta Journal—Clyde Burnett
Augusta Herald—Jack Keller
Banner Herald—Masie Underwood
Banner-Herald & Daily News—Masie Underwood
Cartersville Daily Tribune News—Diane Bagley
Columbus Enquirer—Don Coker
Columbus Times—Carol Gardes
Roswell North Fulton Today—Caffilene Allen
Waycross Journal Herald—Dorothy Smith

HAWAII

The Honolulu Advertiser—Ronn Ronck
KaLeo O Hawaii-The Voice of Hawaii—Jane Betsacon
The Star Bulletin, Honolulu—Ronn Ronck

IDAHO

Coeur d'Alene Press—Clyde Bentley
Idaho Falls Post-Register—Sally Bailey
The Idaho State Journal, Pocatello—Paul Beebe
Lewiston Morning Tribune—Ladd Hamilton
Sunday Journal—Paul Beebe
Times-News, Twin Falls—Bob De Lashmutt

ILLINOIS

Alton Telegraph—Walt Sharp
Arlington Heights Daily Herald—Pamela Thomas
Bloomington Daily Pantagraph—Tony Holloway
Centralia Evening & Sunday Sentinel—Judith Joy
Chicago La Raza Publications, Ltd—Hugo Salinas
The Chicago Sun-Times—Ray W. Kopriva
Chicago Tribune—Alan G. Artner
Daily Courier-News—David Stamps
Decatur Herald & Review—Judy McCormick
Des Plaines Daily Herald—Pamela Thomas
DeKalb Daily Chronicle—Char Digregorio
Dixon Evening Telegraph—Lenny Ingrassia
El Manona Daily—Chris Montes De Oca
Elk Grove Village Daily Herald—Pamela Thomas
The Herald Whig, Quincy—Dave Parks
Hoffman Estates-Schaumburg Daily Herald—
  Pamela Thomas
The Journal—Ray Bachar
Lincoln Courier—William L. Martinie
Moline Daily Dispatch—William McElwain
Mount Prospect-Prospect Heights Daily Herald—Pamela Thomas
Northern Star—W. Thomas Evans
Palatine-Inverness Daily Herald—Pamela Thomas
Register Journal—Steve Snider
The Register-Mail—Robert Harrison
Rockford Register-Republic—David Zimmerman
Rolling Meadows Daily Herald—Pamela Thomas

Watseka Iroquois County Daily Times Republic—
  Bernadine Smith
Wheeling Daily Herald—Pamela Thomas

INDIANA

Bedford Times-Mail—Eleanor Himebaugh
Columbia City Post & Commercial-Mail—Raymond Porter
Columbus Republic—Jim Gilmore
Connersville News-Examiner—Dick Konstanzer
Crawfordsville Journal-Review—Alberta White
Elkhart Truth—Bettie East
Evansville Press—John Smith
Evening World—Joyce J. McDonald & Nancy A. Kirk
The Giveaway—Roger Moon
Huntington Herald Press—David Schultz
Indianapolis News—Marion Simon Garmel
Indianapolis Star—Donn Fry
Monticello Daily Herald-Journal—Jeff Fisher
The Muncie Star—Bruce A. Douglas
News-Sentinel, Fort Wayne—Sharon Little
Shelbyville News—Joan Rehme
Tribune-Star—Howard Stevens
Warsaw Times-Union—Liz Cutler
Washington Times-Herald—Wanita Tetreault

IOWA

Burlington Hawk Eye—Bob Wilson
Centerville Iowegian—Gladys DePuy
Des Moines Register—Nicholas G. Baldwin
Des Moines Tribune—Nicholas G. Baldwin
Iowa City Daily Iowan—John Voland
Muscatine Journal—Gil Dietz
Newton Daily News—Paul Lane
Oelwein Daily Register—Solveig Larson
Sioux City Journal—Jane Hunwardsen
Spencer Daily Reporter Weekender—Carolyn Buller
Washington Evening Journal—Martin A. Chebuhar
Waterloo Courier—Phyllis Singer

KANSAS

Concordia Blade-Empire—Christine Tyler
The Daily Reporter, Independence—Georgia High
Dodge City Daily Globe—Carla Stroud
Eureka Herald—Richard W. Clasen
The High Plains Journal—Jim Brown
The Hutchinson News—Millie Addison
Junction City Daily Union—Jolana Montgomery
Larned Tiller & Toiler—Leslie Zygmond
Lawrence Journal World—Chuck Twardy
Liberal Southwest Daily Times—Ester Groves
Manhattan Mercury—Dr. Donald Mrozek
Newton Kansan—Joe Sullens
Norton Daily Telegram—Mary Beth Boyd
Pratt Tribune—Mrs. El Vena W. Barnes
Russell Daily News—Pauline Sturgeon
Salina Journal—Carol Lichti
The Wichita Eagle-Beacon—Bob Curtright

KENTUCKY

Ashland Daily Independent—Jan Salmon
The Courier-Journal—Sarah Lansdell
Elizabethtown News-Enterprise—Patti Denton
Hopkinsville Kentucky New Era—B. Ray Glenn
Middlesboro Daily News—Tom Dekle
Murray Ledger and Times—Walt Apperson
Paducah Sun—Ron Clark
Richmond Register—Helen Winburn
Winchester Sun—William S. Blakeman

LOUISIANA

Alexandria Daily Town Talk—Phyllis Price
Bastrop Daily Enterprise—Ben Johnston
Crowley Post-Signal—Harold Gonzales
Denham Springs-Livingston Parish News—Chuck Davis
Hammond Daily Star—Joan Davis
Minden Press-Herald—Terri Herrin
News-Star—Cindy Greene
The Shreveport Journal—Ron Rice
Slidell Daily Times—Larry Baudot

The State Times, Baton Rouge—Jean McMullen
States-Item New Orleans—Alberta Collier
The Times Picayune, New Orleans—Roger Green
The Times—Lane Crockett

MAINE

Bangor Daily News—Robert H. Newall
Evening Journal—Marilyn Hackett
Portland Evening Express—Robert S. Niss
The Evening Gazette—Gerard Goggins
Worcester Telegram—Peter Donker

MARYLAND

The Annapolis Evening Capital—Eric Smith
Baltimore Sun—Edward McKee
Columbia Flier—Geoffrey Himes
The Diamondback—David Mills
Daily & Sunday Times, Salisbury—Dick Fleming
Hagerstown Daily Mail—Harry Warner

MASSACHUSETTS

The Berkshire Eagle, Pittsfield—Charles Bonenti
Boston Hellenic Chronicle—Steve Nikas
Boston Herald American—Robert Garrett
The Boston Phoenix—Kit Rachlis
Brockton Enterprise-Times—Jacqueline Asplundh
The Christian Science Monitor, Boston—Theodore Wolft
Bistib Oist-Gazette—John Brenner
Daily Collegian—Jim Moran
Daily News—William Poleri
Framingham South Middlesex News—Virginia Lucier
Haverhill Gazette—Robert J. Gabloski
Holyoke Transcript-Telegram—Ruth Danckert
Lawrence Eagle Tribune—Leo Chabot
The Lowell Sun—Ann Schecter
Medford Daily Mercury—J. William Breslin
New Bedford Standard-Times—Rosalina Mello
Old Colony Memorial—Tim Miller
Post-Gazette—John Brenner
Republican—Robin Karson
Springfield Morning Union—Robin Karson
Taunton Daily Gazette—Gaylord Wyman
The Daily Free Press—Susan Fall, Iver Rose
The Daily Times and Chronicle—Mary A. Haggerty
The Register
The Tech—Dave Staw
West Springfield Record—Marie A. Coburn

MICHIGAN

Alpena News—Betty Werth
Bay City Times—Gay McGee
Benton Harbor-St Joseph Herald-Palladium—Arlys Derrick
Big Rapids Pioneer—Jim Bruskotter
Canton Eagle—S. Bachand
Daily Tribune—Steve Finlay
Detroit Free Press—Dick Mayer
Enquirer and News, Battle Creek—Nancy Crawley
The Flint Journal—James E. Harvey
Grand Rapids Press—Bernice Winslow Mancewicz
Holland Sentinel—Martha Ayres
Jackson Citizen Patriot—Julie Bugal
Kalamazoo Gazette—Verne Berry
Ludington Daily News—Paul Peterson
Macomb Daily, Mount Clemens—Robert Russell
Muskegon Chronicle—John Allen
The Saginaw News—Janet I. Martineau
Towne Courier—Melissa Kaplan

MINNESOTA

Austin Daily Herald—Judy McDermott
Dispatch—David Hawley
Hibbing Tribune—Doreen Lindahl
Minneapolis Star—Kent Gardner
Minneapolis Tribune—Robert Lundegaard
Minnesota Daily—Mike Curti
Red Wing Republican Eagle—Arlin Albrecht
St. Paul Pioneer Press—David Hawley
West Central Tribune—John Tradup

Winona Daily News—Lucy Eckberg
Worthington Daily Globe—Bob Artley

MISSISSIPPI

Biloxi South Mississippi Sun/Daily Herald—Jerry Kinser
Clarion Ledger, Jackson—Bill Nichols
Greenville Delta Democrat-Times—Susie James
McComb Enterprise-Journal—Charles M. Dunagin
Meridian Star—Homer Cook
Mississippi Press—Chuck Brooks
The Daily Mississippian—Ben Herring
Tupelo Daily Journal—Joe Rutherford

MISSOURI

Brookfield Daily News-Bulletin—Barbara Huff
Columbia Missourian—Ruth D'Arcy
Excelsior Springs Daily Standard—Sheila Woods
Farmington Evening Press—James Wooldridge
Independence Examiner—Charles Burke
Jefferson City Capital News—Steve Schrader
The Kansas City Star—Donald Hoffman
Leader & Press—Bill Tatum
National Catholic Reporter—Michael Farrell
Neosho Daily News—Harlan Stark
News & Tribune—Steve Schrader
News Press—Kevin Douglas
St. Joseph News Press—Geralyn Migielicz
Parsons Sun—Linda Fraser
Post-Tribune—Steve Schrader
St. Joseph Gazette—Geralyn Migielicz
St. Louis Post-Dispatch—Frank Peters
Springfield Daily News—Bill Tatum
Sunday News & Leader—Bill Tatum
West Plains Daily Quill—Frank L Martin

MONTANA

Billings Gazette—Christene Myers
Havre Daily News—Eileen Pavlish
Missoula Missoulian—Mea Andrews
The Montana Standard, Butte—Andrea McCormick

NEBRASKA

Kearney Daily Hub—Catherine Roberts
McCook Daily Gazette—Jack Rogers
Omaha World-Herald—Peg Jones
West Omaha Sun—Mary T. Smith

NEVADA

Carson City Nevada Appeal—Val Edwards
Fargo-Moorhead Forum—Janna Anderson
Las Vegas Review-Journal—Brad Peterson
Las Vegas Sun—Stephen Lesnick
The North Las Vegas Valley Times—Doyle May
Reno Evening Gazette & Nevada State Journal—Velda Morby

NEW HAMPSHIRE

The Dartmouth—Jessica Rosenberg

NEW JERSEY

The Beachcomber—Elizabeth Buchholz
Bridgeton Evening News—Mitch Mendelson
Daily Record, Morristown—Marion Filler
The Daily Sunday Register, Red Bank—Hildegarde Fontaine
Homes News, New Brunswick—Doris E. Brown
Newark Star-Ledger—Eileen Watkins
Pascack Valley News—Jane Bailey
The Record, Hackensack—Bill Newton
Suburban Trends—Molly Petrollo
Sunday Record—Bill Newton
Woodbury Gloucester County Times—Susan Caulfield

NEW MEXICO

The Albuquerque Journal—Tom Jacobs
The Albuquerque Tribune—Ollie Reed
Carlsbad Current-Argus—Sharon Nymeyer

Clovis News-Journal—Sharen Hart
Farmington Daily Times—Tim Farrell
Grants Daily Beacon—Sue Winsor
Hobbs Daily News-Sun—Sharon Hendrix
The New Mexican, Santa Fe—Anne Hillerman
Roswell Daily Record—Dianne Neil
The Taos News—Joanne Forman

NEW YORK

Albany Times Union—Fred Lebrun
Batavia Daily News—Marilyn Pfalzer
The Black American—J. Weiss
Buffalo Courier-Express—Richard Huntington
The Buffalo Evening News—Anthony Bannon, Terry Doran
The China Post—Wing Lee
Columbia Daily Spectator—Mike Tubridg
Corning Leader—James Gill
Evening Press—Bruce Estes
Herkimer Evening Telegram—David Colburn
Long-Island Traveler/Watchman—Dave Mack
Mt. Vernon Daily Argus—Kathie Beals
The New York Times—Hilton Kramer
The News, New York—C. Walker
The News World—Joan Sealy
North County News—Elaine Winterstein
Nyack Journal-News—John Cornell
Pawling (N.Y.) News-Chronicle—David Willis
Peekskill Star—John L. Murphy
Pipe Dream—Barry Scholl, Dylana Lembitz
Port Chester Daily Item—Sydney Stanton
The Post-Standard, Syracuse—Gordon Muck
Poughkeepsie Journal—Jeffrey Borak
Press and Sun-Bulletin—Renee Nester
The Record—Joseph Wojcik
Saratogian, Saratoga Springs—Bethany Hicok
Schenectady Gazette—Peg Churchill
The Spectrum—M. Faust
Staten Island Advance—Michael Fressola
Staten Island Register—Richard Ryan
Sunday Herald American—Tim Atseff
Sunday Record—Doug DeLisle
Syracuse Herald-Journal—Herbert Redell
Tarrytown Daily News—Kathy Beals
Times Record, Troy—Doug DeLisle
Washington Square News—Janet Rosen
Woodside Herald—Stephen Schur, Steven Tannenbaum
Yonkers Herald Statesman—Elaine Bissell

NORTH CAROLINA

Asheville Citizen-Times—Tony Brown
The Chapel Hill Newspaper—Charles Horton
The Charlotte News—Larry Toppman
The Daily Reflector, Greenville—Jerry S. Raynor
The Durham Sun—Susan Broili
Elizabeth City Daily Advance—Bessie Culpepper
The Greensboro Record—Abe D. Jones, Jr.
Goldsboro News-Argus—Marilyn Shaw
Hendersonville Times-News—Tucker Veach
Kinston Daily Free Press—Kathy Koonce
Lenoir News-Topic—Ann Robinson
Lumberton Robesonian—Lee Hamilton
Mocksville Davie County Enterprise-Record—Robin Fergusson
The Mountaineer—Ann Janeway
The News and Observer, Raleigh—Jim Buie
Salisbury Evening Post—Debbie Moose
Statesville Record & Landmark—Burwell Whittington
Shelby Star—Brenda Crosby
Sunday Post—Debbie Moose
Sunday Telegram—H. Otto
Tryon Daily Bulletin—Marjorie B. Vining
Washington Daily News—Jeanne England
Winston-Salem Journal & Sentinel—Jim Stanley

NORTH DAKOTA

Dickinson Press—Linda Sailer
Fargo Forum—Janna Anderson
Jamestown Sun—J. P. Furst

OHIO

Akron Beacon Journal—Clyde Morris
The Athens Messenger—Carol James
Beavercreek Daily News—Betty Chandler
Celina Daily Standard—Bob Bricker
Chardon Geauga Times Leader—David C. Lange
Cincinnati Post—B. J. Foreman
Cleveland Plain Dealer—Helen Borsick
Cleveland Press—Tom Muray
Columbus Citizen-Journal—Matthew Herban, III
Daily Kent Stater—Mike Scott
The Daily Times—Mike Deaterla
Dayton Daily News—Betty Dietz Krebs
Dayton Journal Herald—Richard Schwarze
Delphos Daily Herald—Esther Bielawski
Fostoria Review Times—Steve Wolfrom
Galion Inquirer—Steve Stokes
Kent-Ravenna Record-Courier—Everett Stoddors
Lorain Journal—Howard Gollop
The Louisville Herald—Paul M. Clapper
Martins Ferry-Bellaire Times-Leader—Maria Sticco
News-Herald, Willoughby—Steve Zemanek
Painesville Telegraph—James Baron
The Post—Teresa Kramer
Sandusky Register—Jackie Keller
Sidney Daily News—Margie Wuebker
Sunday Messenger—Carol James
The Times Recorder, Zanesville—David Shinn
The Toledo Blade—Boris Nelson
Troy Daily News—Marj Hildebrand
Wapakoneta Daily News—Grace Shaull
Warren Tribune Chronicle—Richard Logan
Youngstown Vindicator—Clyde Singer

OKLAHOMA

Bartlesville Examiner Enterprise—Jim Wood
Blackwell Journal-Tribune—Charles Abbott
Claremore Progress—Brenda Crawford-Clark
The Daily Oklahoman, Oklahoma City—Joy Donovan
Elk City Daily News—Jo Ann Medders
Lawton Constitution—L. R. Thompson
Morning Press, Lawton—L. R. Thompson
Muskogee Daily Phoenix & Times Democrat—Joan Morrison
Oklahoma City Times—Joy Donovan
Pryor Daily Times—Ron Grimsley
Sayre Journal—Peggy Goochey
Seminole Producer—Beverly Bostic
Sunday Constitution—L. R. Thompson
Sunday Oklahoman—Joy Donovan
The Tulsa Tribune—Ellis Widner
The Tulsa World—David MacKenzie

OREGON

Eugene Register Guard—Charlie Nye
Grants Pass Daily Courier—Ruth Acklen
Medford Mail Tribune—Bert Fox
Ontario Daily Argus Observer—Larry Hoffman
Oregon City Enterprise-Courier—Joan Humbert
The Oregon Journal, Portland—Andy Rocchia
Willamette Week—Barry Johnson
World, Coos Bay—Katie Muldoon

PENNSYLVANIA

Allentown Call-Chronicle—Albert Hofammann
Altoona Mirror—David S. Love
Bradford Era — M. T. Cleary
Brookville American—Joe McLaughlin
Campus Voice—Nancy Barg
The Daily Intelligencer, Doylestown—Donald P. Davis
Elizabethtown Chronicle—Michael Escobar
The Evening Times—Nellie Brewster
Greensburg Tribune Review—Gary Hixon
Huntingdon Daily News—Lynn Streightiff
Johnstown Tribune Democrat—John Coleman
King of Prussia Today's Post—Valerie Newitt
Levittown Bucks County Courier Times—Amy Waters
Lewistown Sentinel—Bill Mahon
Lock Haven Express—Charles R. Ryan
Norristown Times Herald—Thomas J. McIntyre
Philadelphia Evening & Sunday Bulletin—Nessa R. Forman
Philadelphia Guide Newspapers, Inc.—Linda Muller

Philadelphia Inquirer—Victoria Donahoe
Philadelphia New Observer—Donald Wright
Philadelphia News Gleaner Publications—Preston Morotz
Philadelphia Welcomat, Inc.—Christine Woodside
Philipsburg Daily Journal—Barbara G. Yoder
Pitt News—Leslie Van Buskirk
The Pittsburgh Post-Gazette—Donald Miller
Pittsburgh Press—Nat Youngblood
The Scranton Times—Robert E. Blasko
The Scrantonian—Mrs. Gene Brislin
The Scranton Tribune—Mrs. Gene Brislin
Sunday Bulletin—Nessa Forman
Sunday Times—Robert Blasko
Tarentum-New Kensington-Vandergrift-Valley News—
  Debra Duncan
The Courier-Express—Connie Waite
Towanda Daily Review—Dennis Irvine
Uniontown Herald-Standard—Nancy Hyde

SOUTH CAROLINA

Anderson Independent-Mall—Betty Martin
Beaufort Gazette—Debbie Radford
Columbia Black News—Connie Wiley
Florence Morning News—Ralph Kaney
Gamecock—Mike Fisher
Greenville News, Greenville—Deb Moore
Myrtle Beach Sun News—Meredith Crews
Orangeburg Times and Democrat—Joyce W. Milkie
The Pickens Sentinel—Joyce Barrett
The Press and Standard—Katrena McCall
The State, Columbia—Martha Beaver

SOUTH DAKOTA

The Daily Republic—Gerald H. Putjenter
Yankton Press & Dakotan—Dean Vik

TENNESSEE

The Athens Daily Post-Athenian Co—Allene Sykes
Chattanooga News-Free Press—Samuel A. Hunter
The Commercial Appeal, Memphis—Donald LaBadie
The Daily Herald—Linda Walters
Elizabethton Star—Rozella Hardin
Greeneville Sun—Robert Sykes
Jackson Sun—Delores Ballard
Johnson City Press Chronicle—Roger Hendrix
Knoxville News-Sentinel—Frank Jordan
The Leaf-Chronicle, Clarksville—Max Moss
Lebanon Democrat—Virginia Vickers Braun
Morristown Citizen Tribune—Carolyn Walter
Murfreesboro Daily News Journal—Pat Matson
Nashville Banner—Caroline Bartholomew
The Nashville Tennessean—Clara Hieronymus
The Oak Ridger, Oak Ridge—Jonell Schmitt

TEXAS

Abilene Reporter-News—Bill Whitaker
Amarillo Daily News—Bette Thompson
The Austin American Statesman—Kathryn McKenna
Big Spring Herald—Richard Horn
Brazosport Facts—Robert Dansby
Caller-Times, Corpus Christi—Maurice Schmidt
Childress Index—Mrs. Morris Higley
Courier Times-Morning Telegraph—Sam Nash
Dallas Morning News—Delores Brown
Dallas Times Herald—Bill Marvel
Del Rio News-Herald—Ima Joe Fleetwood
Denison Herald—John Clift
El Paso Herald Post—Betty Ligon
Express & News—Ben Downing
Fort Worth Star-Telegram—Larry Swindell
Gonzales Inquirer—Pearl Robertson
The Houston Chronicle—Ann Holmes
The Houston Post—Martha Liebrum
Kerrville Daily Times—Rick Rhodes
Mid-Cities Daily News—Bob Francis
Midland Reporter Telegram—Georgia Temple
Nacogdoches Daily Sentinel—Larry Ingle
The Odessa American—Charlotte McCarroll
Orange Leader—Laura Haynes
Pasadena Citizen—Allan Kimball

Pecos Enterprise—Larry Hunter
Plainview Herald—Myrna Smith
Port Arthur News—Denny Angelle
Record News—Martha Steimel
Richardson Daily News—David Matustik
San Angelo Standard Times—Kandis Gatewood
San Antonio Express—Ben King
The San Antonio Light—Glenn Tucker
San Antonio News—Bob Dale
San Marcos Daily Record—Rowe Ray
Sunday Sentinel—Larry Ingle
Terrell Tribune—Mary Said
Times—Gretchen Ray
Times—Martha Steimel
Waco Tribune-Herald—Bob Darden
Waxahachie Daily Light—Sandra Minatra

UTAH

Logan Herald Journal—Edith Morgan
Provo Daily Herald—Renee Nelson
Salt Lake Tribune, Salt Lake City—Helen Forsberg
Spectrum—Melody Trude & Chris Dangerfield
Tooele Transcript—David Anderson

VERMONT

The Bennington Banner—Dennis Redmond
Brattleboro Reformer—Greg Worden
St. Albans Messenger—Cathy Brauner

VIRGINIA

Bristol Herald Courier—Angela Mallicote
Covington Virginian—Horton P. Beirne
Fredericksburg Free Lance-Star—Earle M. Copp
Herald Courier & Virginia-Tennessean—Angela Mallicote
Hopewell News—Va Dail
The Ledger-Star, Norfolk—Teresa Annas
Lynchburg News—Cecil Mullans
Marion Smyth County News—Larry Leathers
The Richmond News Leader—Roy Proctor
Richmond Times-Dispatch—Robert Merritt
The Roanoak Times—Ann Weinstein
Waynesboro News-Virginian—Pat Cook

WASHINGTON

Aberdeen Daily World—Betty Butler
Bellingham Herald—Joan Connell
Ellensburg Daily Record—Joy McGiffin
The Herald—Nancy Erickson
Moses Lake Columbia Basin Daily—Bill Cockshott
Pazifische Rundschau—Baldwin Ackermann
The Seattle Times—Deloris Tarzan
The Seattle Weekly—Ann Senechal
Skagit Valley Herald—L. P. Wood
Tacoma News Tribune—Myron L. Thompson
Vancouver Columbian—Victoria Salter
Wenatchee Daily World—David Kraft

WEST VIRGINIA

The Advertiser, Huntington—Estelle Belanger
Bluefield Daily Telegraph—June Grubb
The Charleston Daily Mail—John Hudkins
The Charleston Gazette—Jay Friedericks
The Evening Journal—Richard Fazenbaker
The Huntington Herald Dispatch—Estelle Belanger

WISCONSIN

Bay Viewer—Dale Ruppert
Bog Viewer—Dale Ruppert
Capital Times, Madison—Carol Riordan
Chippewa Falls Chippewa Herald-Telegram—Howard Meier
Cudohy St. Frances Free Press—Dale Ruppert
Green Bay Press-Gazette—Warren Gerds
Journal-Press—Dale Ruppert
Kenosha News—Elaine Edwards
Leader & Telegram—John Price
The Milwaukee Journal—James M. Auer & Dom Noth
The Milwaukee Sentinel—Dean Jensen
The Post Crescent, Appleton—Carol Hanson

Racine Journal Times—Karen Tancill
South Town Advertiser News—Dale Ruppert
Superior Evening Telegram—Finley Stalvig
The Suburbanite—Dale Ruppert
Voice Journal—Dale Ruppert
Waukesha Freeman—Marilyn Hinkens
Wausau Daily Herald—Mary Beth Marklein
Wisconsin State Journal, Madison—Donald K. Davies

WYOMING

Riverton Ranger—Carolyn B. Tyler
Rock Springs Daily Rocket-Miner—Charles E. Richardson
Sunday Tribune Eagle—Dick Moody
Wyoming Eagle, Cheyenne—Dick Moody
Wyoming State Tribune—Dick Moody

Scholarships and Fellowships

OFFERED BY	AMOUNT	OPEN TO	DURATION	WHEN OFFERED
Abilene Fine Arts Museum, 8015 Mockingbird, Abilene, TX 79605	$500	College bound high school senior; college student in Taylor County	100 credit hrs	Annually
Alberta College of Art, Southern Alberta Institute of Technology, 1301 16th Ave NW, Calgary, AB T2M OL4, Canada	$7500 (total)	Students registered in A.C.A. programmes	One year	Annually
Allied Artists of America, 15 Gramercy Park S, New York, NY 10003	$12,000	Rotating scholarship for any student attending that year's specified art school through Maxwell Arts Club	One year	Annually, December
Lyman Allyn Museum, 625 Williams St, New London, CT 06320	$55 for children's classes	Needy children	One year	Annually
Amarillo Art Center, 2200 S. Van Buren, Amarillo, TX 79178	Variable		Each semester	
American Academy and Institute of Arts and Letters, 633 W. 155th St, New York, NY 10032	5 awards of $5000 each	Painters, sculptors, graphic artists (cannot be applied for)		Annually
American Academy in Rome, 41 E. 56th St, New York, NY 10021	$5400 and up, plus room, meals, travel, study of studio; stipend varies, according to fellowship from $5000-$15,000	Citizens of the U.S.	One year	Annually, deadline Nov. 15
American Academy of Art, 220 State St, Chicago, IL 60604	$16,000	High school seniors and currently enrolled AAA students	One or more school semesters	Bi-annually
American Antiquarian Society, 185 Salisbury St, Worcester, MA 01609	Up to $1833 per month (NEH Fellowships)	Qualified scholars in American history and culture to 1877	Six months-one year	Annually
	Haven & Peterson Fellowships, up to $1800	Qualified scholars in American history & culture to 1877 & open to grad students at work on dissertations	One-three months	Annually
	Boni Fellowship, up to $1250	Qualified scholar working in general field of early American bibliography or printing and publishing history	One-two months	Annually
	Hiatt Fellowship, up to $1200	Open to graduate students working in general field of early American bibliography or printing & publishing history	Minimum 6 weeks	Annually
American Numismatic Society, Broadway at 155th St, New York, NY 10032	$900	Students who have completed one year graduate study in classics, archaeology, history, art history and related fields		deadline March 1
	$3500	Individuals who have completed the ANS Graduate Seminar & general examinations for the doctorate		Deadline March 1
American Oriental Society, Secretary, 329 Sterling Memorial Library, Yale Station, New Haven, CT 06520	The American Oriental Society Fellowship Award for the Study of Chinese Painting—$5000	Students who have completed 3 years of Chinese language study at a recognized university, or the equivalant, and all the requirements for a PhD in Chinese painting studies, except for travel, the written dissertation and its defense	One year	July 1st to June 30th
	Louise Wallace Hackney Fellowship for the Study of Chinese Art—$5000	Post-Doctoral and Doctoral students who are U.S. citizens	One year	July 1st to June 30th
American Scandinavian Foundation, Exchange Division, 127 E. 73rd St, New York, NY 10021	$500-$6000	Applicants with an undergraduate degree (unrestricted fields) for Denmark, Finland, Iceland, Norway and Sweden	Up to one year	Annually

OFFERED BY	AMOUNT	OPEN TO	DURATION	WHEN OFFERED
American Watercolor Society, 14 E. 90th St, New York, NY 10028	Variable	Art schools and colleges for award to outstanding students of watercolor painting	One year	Annually
Arizona Commission on the Arts, 2024 N. Seventh St, Suite 201, Phoenix, AZ 85006	Visual Art Fellowship, $2500 (2)	Residents of Arizona, over 18; students are not eligible	One year	Annually
	Performing Arts Fellowship $3000 (1)	Same as above	One year	Annually
	Writers Fellowship, up to $3000 (2)	Same as above	One year	Annually
Arkansas Arts Center, MacArthur Park, PO Box 2137, Little Rock, AR 72203	Varies as to class	Qualified applicant	By semesters	
Arkansas State University, Dept of Art, State University, AR 72467	$100-$500 range, full or partial tuition grants up to 10 each semester	Entering and current undergraduates	One semester	Each semester
Arrowmont School of Arts and Crafts, Parkway, Box 567, Gatlinburg, TN 37738	$150-$250 (12-15)	Needy students	One or two weeks	Spring and summer
	Assistantships covering room and board and class tuition in exchange for work (14)	Students with experience in particular medium	Two to six weeks	Spring and summer
Art Association of Richmond, McGuire Memorial Hall, 350 Whitewater Blvd, Richmond, IN 47374	Variable	Richmond high school senior studying art	One year	Annually
Art Dealers Association of America, Inc, 575 Madison Ave, New York, NY 10022	$20,000	Doctoral student in art history at American University	Two years	Annually
Art Institute of Boston, 700 Beacon St, Boston, MA 02215	$50 to $1125	Accepted or enrolled students at the Art Institute	One-three years	Annually
Art Institute of Chicago, Michigan Ave. at Adams St, Chicago, IL 60603	Variable	Undergrads	Academic year	Annually
	Variable	Undergrads and students at large	Academic year	Annually
	Variable	Undergrads and grads and certificate students	Academic year	Annually
	Variable	Undergrads and grads and certificate students	Academic year	Annually
Art Institute of Ft. Lauderdale, 3000 E. Las Olas Blvd, Ft. Lauderdale, FL 33316	Variable	Graduating high school seniors	Two years	Annually
Art Institute of Philadelphia, 1622 Chestnut St, Philadelphia, PA 19103	$57,070	High school graduates	Two years	Annually
	$11,130	Continuing students	One quarter	Quarterly
Art Institute of Pittsburgh, 526 Penn Ave, Pittsburgh, PA 15222	$1270	Current students	One quarter	Quarterly
Artists Foundation Inc, 110 Broad St, Boston, MA 02110	$5000	Massachusetts resident over 18 years of age. Students not eligible.		Annually
Artpark, Box 371, Lewiston, NY 14092	Three week residence	Artists of all media	Three weeks during the summer	Deadline Nov.
	Sculpture project funding	Sculptors of all media	Variable	Deadline Nov.
Art Students League of New York, 215 W. 57th St, New York, NY 10019	Tuition $7000 Traveling Scholarships (2)	League students	One year	Annually
Atlanta College of Art, 1280 Peachtree St. NE, Atlanta, GA 30309	Variable	Serious art students	Term	Annually
Atlantic Christian College, Art Department, Wilson, NC 27893	Determined by Art Faculty	All art students	Determined by Art Faculty	Anytime during the year
Austin College Art Dept, Sherman, TX 75090	$500	Incoming freshmen and transfer students	Four years	Annually
Ball State University, 2000 University Ave, Muncie, IN 47306	$3310 graduate assistantship academic year (tuition waived)		One year (renewable)	Annually

OFFERED BY	AMOUNT	OPEN TO	DURATION	WHEN OFFERED
	$3800 doctoral fellowship academic year (tuition waived) $490 summer session		One year (renewable)	Annually
Bassist College, 2000 SW Fifth Ave, Portland, OR 97201	Variable	Students	One and two years	Annually
F. Lammot Belin Arts Scholarship, Waverly Community House, Waverly, PA 18471	$8000	Exceptional ability in chosen field. Must be a U.S. citizen. Preference given to residents of Abingtons or Pocono Northeastern Region		Annually, deadline Dec. 15
Bennington College, Bennington, VT 05201	$10,750 (tuition remission)	Qualified graduate applicants who will in exchange for their assistantships, work in the studios	Two year	Annually
Berry College, Art Department, Mt. Berry, GA 30149	Varies	Freshman art majors	One year	Semi-annually
Birmingham-Bloomfield Art Association, 1516 S. Cranbrook Rd, Birmingham, MI 48009	Full, dependent upon course cost	Local high school art students	Per term	Per term (variable)
Bob Jones University, School of Fine Arts, Wade Hampton Blvd, Greenville, SC 29614	$70 to $210 per month	Undergraduate students with demonstrated financial need and satisfactory school record. Campus work assignment required.	One semester (renewable)	Semi-annually
Bradley University, Peoria, IL 61625	Undergraduate merit scholarships $650; 6 graduate assistantships of approximately $1200 each	Any student in or entering the art program	One year, two year, four year	Annually
W. Braun Co, Wolf and Mary Braun Fund, 260 Fifth Ave, New York, NY 10001	Variable	Through all accredited schools in the U.S. and Canada		Annually
Brewton-Parker College, Art Dept, Box 202, Mt. Vernon, GA 30445	Variable	Freshmen art majors, dormitory students preferred	One year	Each quarter
Brigham Young University, Harris Fine Arts Center, Provo, UT 84602	Tuition	Qualified freshmen applicants, transfer students and continuing students	One year	Annually
Brooklyn Museum Art School, 188 Eastern Pkwy, Brooklyn, NY 11238	Max Beckmann Memorial Scholarships covering tuition and registration fees (20)	College art majors and professional art school students completing their undergraduate studies	One year	Deadline: Apr. 30
	Robert Smithson Memorial Scholarships covering tuition and registration fees (5)	College art majors and professional art school students completing their undergraduate studies	One year	Deadline: Apr. 30
Bucknell University, Dept of Art, Lewisburg, PA 17837	$2500 plus tuition	Registered graduate students	One year, renewable	Annually
California College of Arts and Crafts, 5212 Broadway, Oakland, CA 94618	Variable. Scholarships, loans, grants	Grants & loans, open to all students	One year	Annually
California Institute of the Arts/School of Art and Design, 24700 McBean Pkwy, Valencia, CA 91355	Variable	Everyone	One year	Annually
California State University, Chico, Art Department, Chico, CA 95929	Varies	Art students	One year	Annually
California State University, Hayward, Art Dept, Hayward, CA 94542	Variable	Any art student	One year	
Campbellsville College, Fine Arts Div, Campbellsville, KY 42718	Varied	All applicants who can show proficiency	Four years (renewable)	Semi-annually
Canadian Scandinavian Foundation, McGill Univ, 805 Sherbrook St. W, Montreal, PQ H3G 3G1	Brucebo scholarship, 5,000 SEK for travel, food stipend & cottage use	Talented, young Canadian artist-painter	Two months in Gotland	Annually
	Swedish Institute Bursary Grant	Canadian citizens wishing to pursue studies/research in Scandinavia	four-eight months	Annually
	CSF Special Travel Grants, $1000	Same as above		Annually
	Sylwia Weldon Scholarship for Norway $1000-$1500	Same as above		Annually
Cardinal Stritch College, Art Dept, 6801 N. Yates Rd, Milwaukee, WI 53217	$200 (2)	Art concentrators of present undergraduate students of freshmen, sophomore, and junior status	One year (may apply a second year)	Annually
	$1500 (4)	Talented art students in four year programs	Four years if requirements made	Annually

OFFERED BY	AMOUNT	OPEN TO	DURATION	WHEN OFFERED
Carrizo Art & Craft Workshops, Drawer A, Ruidoso, NM 88345	Tuition plus meals and lodging	Young adults & adults	One and two weeks	Year-round
The Catholic University of America, Dept of Art, Office of Financial Aid, Michigan Ave, Washington, DC 20064	Variable	All applicants		Annually
Cazenovia College, Cazenovia, NY 13035	$100-$1000	Advertising Design majors	Academic year (renewable)	Annually
	$100-$1000	Art majors	Academic year (renewable)	Annually
	$100-1000	Interior Design majors	Academic year (renewable)	Annually
Centenary College of Louisiana, Department of Art, Centenary Blvd, Shreveport, LA 71104	Variable	Outstanding students	One year	Annually
Center for Creative Studies, College of Art and Design, 245 E. Kirby St, Detroit, MI 48202	Varies	Current students and high school seniors	One year	Annually
Center for the Media Arts, 226 W. 26th, New York, NY 10001	$5000	High school seniors	One year	Annually
Central Wyoming College, Art Center, Riverton, WY 82501	Tuition and fees	Anyone with artistic potential regardless of age, race, or sex	One year	Annually and by semester
Chadron State College, Division of Fine Arts, Chadron, NE 69337	Up to full in-state tuition for first year; $100 each semester for subsequent years	No restrictions		Annually
Charles River Creative Arts Program, 56 Centre St, Dover, MA 02030	Variable	Those needing financial aid (local)		Annually to boys and girls 8-15
Charles Stewart Mott Community College, Fine Arts Division, 1401 E. Court St, Flint, MI 48503	Up to $450	Current art students		Annually
Chautauqua Institution Summer School, Box 28, Chautauqua, NY 14722	$6000	Any non-professionals	One summer	Annually
Cheyenne Artist Guild Inc, 1010 E. 16th St, Cheyenne, WY 82001	$300 scholarship for student entering art course in college of choice, plus $100 for art supplies	Senior high school students of Cheyenne only	One year	Annually
	$200 scholarship for student in art profile, plus $50 for art supplies	Senior high school students of Cheyenne only	One year	Annually
Cintas Fellowship Program, Institute of International Education, 809 United Nations Plaza, New York, NY 10017	$6000	Professional artists who are Cuban or of Cuban lineage. Intended for young professionals who have completed their academic and technical training	One year	Annually
Cleveland Institute of Art, 11141 East Boulevard, Cleveland, OH 44106	Variable	Qualified students	One year	Annually
Cleveland State University, Department of Art, Euclid Ave. at E. 24th St, Cleveland, OH 44115	Tuition (part or full)	Incoming high school students, transfer students, and continuing full time studio art majors based on merit. State residents only	One year	Annually
Coe College, Art Department, 1221 First Ave. NE, Cedar Rapids, IA 52402	Variable—Minimum of $3000 awarded	Incoming freshmen students	One to four years	Annually
Colby Community College, Art Department, 1255 S. Range, Colby, KS 67701	$100 up to full tuition and fees	Any applicant, juried portfolio	Two years	Annually
Colby-Sawyer College, New London, NH 03257	Variable	Upperclass students	One year	Annually
College of Mt. Saint Joseph, Art Department, Mt. Saint Joseph, OH 45051	Full tuition Scholastic Art Scholarship	High school graduates	One year (renewable)	Annually
	$500 Fine Arts Scholarship	High school graduates	One year (renewable)	Annually
College of New Rochelle, School of Arts & Sciences, New Rochelle, NY 10801	Variable	Incoming freshman with portfolio	Four years renewable	Annually
College of St. Benedict, Benedict Arts Center, St. Joseph, MN 56374	$350-$500 per year	Incoming art majors and present art majors	One to four years	Annually

OFFERED BY	AMOUNT	OPEN TO	DURATION	WHEN OFFERED
College of St. Catherine, Visual Arts Dept, 2004 Randolph, St. Paul, MN 55105	Variable	Art majors	One year	Annually
College of Saint Mary, 1901 S. 72nd St, Omaha, NE 68124	$1000 per year	High school graduates	One year	Annually
The College of the School of the Ozarks, Department of Art, Point Lookout, MO 65616	Full tuition, room and board work-study scholarships	All applicants, preference to need, academic standing, and geographic location	Four years, or until degree completion	Each semester
Colorado Institute of Art, 200 E. Ninth Ave, Denver, CO 80203	Full or part tuition	In-school institute students	One year, one quarter	Annually & quarterly
Columbia University, School of the Arts, 615 Dodge, New York, NY 10027	Variable	All registered students in competition		Annually
Columbus College, Dept of Art, Algonquin Dr, Columbus, GA 31907	Variable	Entering and undergraduate art majors	3 quarters	Annually, Spring quarter for the coming Fall
Committee for Hispanic Arts & Research, PO Box 12865, Austin, TX 78711	$500	Hispanic artists	One year	Bi-annually
Compton Community College, Art Department, 1111 E. Artesia Blvd, Compton, CA 90221	$100	Art majors	One semester	Fall and Spring
Concordia College, Art Department, 920 S. Eighth, Moorehead, MN 56560	Variable	Entering freshmen and upper classmen	One year	Annually
Coppini Academy of Fine Arts, 115 Melrose Pl, San Antonio, TX 78212	Variable			Annually
Corcoran School of Art, 17th & New York Ave. NW, Washington, DC 10006	William Wilson Corcoran Scholarship	Students from area high schools	Summer course	Annually in Apr.
	Rohsheim Memorial Award	Outstanding first year students	One semester	Annually in May
	Kenneth Stubbs Memorial Award	Outstanding drawing students	One semester	Annually in May
	Mary Lay Thom Sculpture Prize	Outstanding sculpture students	One semester	Annually in May
	Eugene Weisz Memorial Scholarship	Outstanding painting students	One semester	Annually in May
	Sarah Pickens Roberts Memorial Award	Student whose work is judged most promising	One semester	Annually in May
	Cash prizes in Final Annual Graduation Exhibition	Prize-winning students		Annually in May
	Corcoran School of Art Scholarships	Outstanding students enrolled in the Degree or Diploma program	One academic year	Annually in May
Cornell College, Mt. Vernon, IA 52314	$1000-full tuition	Selected on recommendation of Art Dept.	Four years if student remains art major & 3.0 GPA	Annually to freshmen
Cornish Institute 710 E. Roy, Seattle, WA 98102	Variable amounts, tuition scholarships	Registered full-time students	One year	Annually
Cottey College, Fine Arts Division, Nevada, MO 64772	$600	Students interested in art who are attending Cottey College	One year (renewable)	Annually
	$400 (Harry Chew Memorial Scholarship)	Students interested in art who are attending Cottey College	One year (renewable)	Annually
Cranbrook Academy of Art, Bloomfield Hills, MI 48013	Varies, partial tuition grants	Students enrolled in Architecture, Ceramics, Design, Fiber, Metalsmithing, Painting, Photography, Printmaking, and Sculpture at Cranbrook Academy of Art	One year	Annually
Creighton University, Fine Arts Dept, 2500 California St, Omaha, NE 68178	Variable	All freshmen either by audition or portfolio	Four years	Annually
C. W. Post Center of Long Island University, Art Department, Northern Blvd, Greenvale, NY 11548	Variable	Graduate assistants		Semi-annually
Dean Junior College, Visual and Performing Arts Department, 99 Main St, Franklin, MA 02038	Variable	Full-time students	One year	Annually

OFFERED BY	AMOUNT	OPEN TO	DURATION	WHEN OFFERED
Delta State University, Art Department, Box D-2, Cleveland, MS 38733	Smith-Patterson Award ($100)	Senior art students with 3.5 or above average & high attainment in studio work		Annually
	Maxine Boggan Holcombe Scholarship ($100)	Junior art education major with scholarship & accomplishment in studio work		Annually
	Malcolm Norwood Scholarship ($300)	Entering freshman student who is an art major at DSU and shows outstanding art work in the annual Crosstie Festival		Annually
	Departmental Scholarship ($2000)	Freshmen & upper class students with submission of portfolio & transcript of high school or college record		Annually
Denison University, Granville, OH 43023	Vail Scholarships in the Arts-$1000	Prospective freshmen who have been accepted for admission. Awarded on the basis of portfolio and general academic ability	Renewable in the sophomore year and open competitively to juniors and seniors	Annually, deadline March 1
The Design Schools, Art Institute of Houston, 3600 Yoakum Blvd, Houston, TX 77006	$12,000	High school seniors		Annually
Detroit Artists Market, 1452 Randolph St, Detroit, MI 48226	Variable	Any qualified student who is attending the specific school whose turn it is to receive the scholarship; given on rotating basis to Center for Creative Studies, Wayne State University and Cranbrook Academy of Art	One year	Annually
Dickinson State College, Department of Art, Dickinson, ND 58601	$500 TMI Systems Design Corporation Scholarship	Any art or business student	One year	Annually
	$100 Tom Niemitalo Memorial Art Scholarship	Any art major or minor	One year	Annually
	$100 DSC Alumni Foundation Scholarships	Freshmen	One year	Annually
	$100 Clinton A. Sheffield Memorial Art Scholarship	Art students	One year	Annually
Drake University, Des Moines, IA 50311	Variable	Art majors	One year (renewable)	Annually
Dumbarton Oaks Research Library and Collections, 1703 32nd St. NW, Washington, DC 20007	Variable	Graduate students and post-doctoral scholars	One year	Annually
Dunedin Fine Arts & Cultural Center, 1143 Michigan Blvd, Dunedin, FL 33528	Variable	Students sixth grade and above with sincere interest and/or talent and financial need; some collegiate assistance available	5, 8 and 10 weeks depending upon length of class	Year round, per quarter
East Tennessee State University, Carroll Reece Museum, Johnson City, TN 37614	$2000	High school seniors, college students & other persons from the region wishing to continue their art education	One year	Annually
Edinboro University of Pennsylvania, Dept of Art, Edinboro, PA 16444	$3400 & tuition (16)	MFA students	One year (renewable)	Annually
Education Council of the Graphic Arts Industry, Inc, Graphic Arts Technical Center, 4615 Forbes Ave, Pittsburgh, PA 15213	Varies	Students currently enrolled in undergraduate graphic arts program & high school seniors		Annually, deadline: high school Jan. 15, undergrads Mar. 15
Emmanuel College, 400 The Fenway, Boston, MA 02115	$21,200	Full time women students	Four years	Annually
Emily Carr College of Art Design, Charles H. Scott Gallery, 1399 Johnston St, Vancouver, BC V6H 3R9, Canada	$50-$2000	Full time students	One year	Semi-annually
Essex Institute, 132 Essex St, Salem, MA 01970	Variable	Graduate students in American studies	One year	Annually
Fairmont State College, Art Dept, Fairmont, WV 26554	Freshmen aid	All freshmen art students	One year	Annually
	Tuition	Art education majors	Four years	Annually

OFFERED BY	AMOUNT	OPEN TO	DURATION	WHEN OFFERED
Fashion & Art Institute of Dallas, 2829 W. Northwest Hwy, Dallas, TX 75220	$500-$4200	High school seniors	24 months	Semi-annually
Fashion Institute of Technology, 227 W. 27th St, New York, NY 10001	Variable	All students who qualify	Renewable	Annually
Harriet FeBland Art Workshop, 245 E. 63rd St. (408), New York, NY 10021	Tuition for one semester	Winners of the FeBland Group Annual Exhibition Scholarship Award	Semester	Annually
Felician College, 3800 W. Peterson, Chicago, IL 60659	$500	Seniors	One year	Semi-annually
Fiberworks Center for the Textile Arts, 1940 Bonita, Berkeley, CA 94704	$5000	MFA students	Two years	Annually
Findlay College, Art Department, 1000 N. Main St, Findlay, OH 45840	Variable	All students	One year (renewable)	Annually
Flint Institute of Arts, DeWaters Art Center, 1120 E. Kearsley St, Flint, MI 48503	Partial non-credit Full & partial non-credit	Gifted children Financial & Merit; Children & Adults	One semester Term	Prior to each term
Florida Gulf Coast Art Center, 222 Ponce de Leon Blvd, Clearwater, FL 33516	$100 per term	Adult members/children (membership not required)	Quarter (10 weeks)	
Florida State University, School of Visual Arts, Art Dept, Tallahassee, FL 32306	Assistantships $2400 Fellowships $4200-$5000 Stripends $1600 Visual Arts Fellowships-$6000 University Fellowships-$6000	Graduate students in art Graduate students in art history Undergraduates	9 months One year One year One year Four years	Annually Annually Annually Annually Annually
Fort Hays State University, Hays, KS 67601	$15,300 $2000	Graduate Assistantships Undergraduate Scholarships	One year One year	Annually Annually
Frank Phillips College, Art Dept, PO Box 5118, Borger, TX 79007	Variable	Any full time art student	One semester	Annually
Franklin and Marshall College, Art Dept, Lancaster, PA 17604	Variable	Students with pronounced talent		Annually
Friends of Photography, PO Box 500, Carmel, CA 93921	Variable	Photographer who has demonstrated excellence in and commitment to the field of creative photography	One year	Annually
Friends University, Art Department, 2100 University Ave, Wichita, KS 67213	$400 and up	All art majors	One to four years if grades & work standards are maintained	Annually
Furman University, Dept of Art, Greenville, SC 29613	Mattie Hipp Cunningham Scholarship $1350	Art major selected by the faculty of Art Department	One year (can be repeated in unusual circumstances)	Once every third year
The Gallery/Stratford, 54 Romeo St, Stratford, ON N5A 4S9, Canada	$200	Graduating high school students from Perth County who wish further visual arts education	One year	Annually
Georgetown College, Georgetown, KY 40324	$250-$450 plus financial aid on a need basis & academic scholarships	All graduates of accredited secondary schools. A portfolio is required for an art grant but not for admission to the program	As long as academic progress is being made	Semi-annually
Grand Canyon College, Art Department, 3300 W. Camelback Rd, Phoenix, AZ 85061	Up to $700	Studio art majors	One year (renewable)	Annually
Grants for Graduate Study Abroad. Write: Study Abroad Programs, Institute of International Education, 809 United Nations Plaza, New York, NY 10017		Note: People in the arts may apply for any of these awards (Fulbright-Hays and Foreign Governments, ITT International Fellowships, Lusk Memorial Fellowships, Kade Memorial Fellowships), but they must be affiliated with an educational institute abroad while pursuing their studies.		One academic year
Greenwich House Pottery, 16 Jones St, New York, NY 10014	Tuition	Adults and children with talent, currently attending Greenwich House Pottery	One semester (renewable)	Semi-annually
John Simon Guggenheim Memorial Foundation, 90 Park Ave, New York, NY 10016	Adjusted to needs of fellows	Citizens or permanent residents of U.S., Canada, other American states, Caribbean, Phillippines, and French, Dutch, and British possessions in Western Hemisphere, normally 30 to 45 years of age	One year	Annually
Guild of Creative Art, 620 Broad St. Shrewbury, NJ 07701	$75 or one term	Members	One term	Annually

OFFERED BY	AMOUNT	OPEN TO	DURATION	WHEN OFFERED
The Hagley Museum, PO Box 3630, Wilmington, DE 19807	$4600 per year for the first two years & $5000 the second two years, full tuition, travel fund; also $1200 is available to married students with dependent children	Students enrolled as MA candidates		Deadline Feb. 1
Harding University, Department of Art, Box 938, Searcy, AR 72143	Variable	Art majors	One semester	Each semester
Harford Community College, Humanities Division, 401 Thomas Run Rd, Bel Air, MD 21014	$50	Student matriculating in an art program	One year	Annually
Hastings College, Art Department, Hastings, NE 68901	$400-$800	All art majors	Four years	Annually
Herron School of Art, Indiana University-Purdue University at Indianapolis, 1701 N. Pennsylvania St, Indianapolis, IN 46202	Scholarships, total per year $6000. Also various financial aid available through Indiana University	Any student	One year	Annually
Historic Deerfield, Inc, Box 321, Deerfield, MA 01342	Full, partial, and tuition Fellowships	Men and women of undergraduate status	June 18-Aug. 18	Annually
Holland College School of Visual Arts, 50 Burns Ave, Charlottetown, Prince Edward Island C1E 1H7, Canada	$500	Craft program students	One year	Annually
Hope College, Art Department, De Pree Art Center, Holland, MI 49423	$1600 total shared between four separate scholarships	Art majors	One year	Annually
Howard University Department of Art, College of Fine Arts, Sixth and Fairmont Sts. NW, Washington, DC 20001	Up to $2000	Students	One year	Annually
Huntington Library and Art Gallery, San Marino, CA 91108	Variable	Art historians in the fields of the collection (not to candidates for advanced degrees)	One to five months	Annually. Applications received Oct. 1-Dec. 31 for awards beginning the following June
	NEH Fellowships up to $1667 per month	Same as above	Six to twelve months	
Idyllwild School of Music & The Arts, PO Box 38, Idyllwild, CA 92349	$100-$175 per week scholarships & work study	Music, art, drama & dance students	Two, four, six & eight weeks	Summers
Incorporated E. A. Abbey Scholarships for Mural Painting in the USA, 1083 Fifth Ave, New York NY 10028	$6000 scholarship for study in mural painting in U.S. and abroad	U.S. citizens not more than 35 years of age	One year	Biennially
Indiana State University, Department of Art, Terre Haute, IN 47809	$2100	MFA, MS, MA	One year	Annually
	Tuition free	BFA Freshmen	Four years	Annually
	$2000 travel grant	BFA Juniors and Seniors	One summer	Annually
Indiana University, School of Fine Arts, 123 Fine Arts Bldg, Bloomington, IN 47405	$2500	Beginning graduates	One year	Annually
Indian Hills Community College, Ottumwa Campus, Dept. of Art, Grandview at Elm, Ottumwa, IA 52501	$1000	Full-time students in art	One year	Annually
Institute of American Indian Arts Museum, 1369 Cerrillos Rd, Santa Fe, NM 87501	Full tuition & board	Any Native American pursuing a career & or training in arts & crafts, creative writing or museum training	Two years	Quarterly
International Museum of Photography at George Eastman House, 900 East Ave, Rochester, NY 14607	Variable internship		One year	Annually
Jacksonville State University, Art Department, Jacksonville, AL 36265	$350	Graduating high school students	One year	Annually
James Madison University, School of Fine Arts and Communication, Dept of Art, Harrisonburg, VA 22807	$1000-$4000	Art majors with an interest in architecture	One year (renewable)	Annually
	$1000-$4000	Undergraduate art major who plans to enter the career of architecture (no architecture program available)	One year (renewable)	Annually
Jamestown College, Art Department, Jamestown, ND 58401	$1000	Entering freshmen art majors	One year (renewable to total of $4000)	Annually

OFFERED BY	AMOUNT	OPEN TO	DURATION	WHEN OFFERED
John C. Calhoun State Community College, Box 2216, Hwy. 31 North, Decatur, AL 35602	Full tuition (2); sponsored by the Decatur Art Guild	Art majors and visual communication majors	Each quarter	Quarterly
	Full tuition (7) College Scholarships	Art & visual communication majors	One year	Annually
The Johns Hopkins School of Medicine, Department of Art as Applied to Medicine, 624 N. Broadway, Baltimore, MD 21205	$5000	Students enrolled in graduate program	One year	Semi-annually
Johnson Atelier, Technical Institute of Sculpture, 60 Ward Ave Extension, Mercerville, NJ 08619	$4800	Accepted students	One year	Annually
Junior College of Albany, Dept of Fine Arts, 74 New Scotland Ave, Albany, NY 12208	Tuition for one semester at the American School in Paris. (Bocour Award)	Professional art students who are JCA Fine Arts majors and have completed their freshman year. (Apply to Nance Goren, Chairman, 140 New Scotland Ave, New Albany, NY 12208)	One semester	Fall semester
Kansas City Art Institute, 4415 Warwick Blvd, Kansas City, MO 64111	Variable	Demonstrated need, some on merit	One year	Annually
Kansas State University, Department of Art, Manhattan, KS 66506	Variable scholarship awards	Freshmen-senior undergraduates	One year	Annually
Kappa Pi International Honorary Art Fraternity, Box 7843 Midfield, Birmingham, AL 35228	$200, $300 & $500	Active student members only	One year	Annually
Kearney State College, School of Fine Arts & Humanities, Art Department, Kearney, NE 68847	$200 tuition waiver (25)	Entering freshmen	One year	Annually
Kent State University, School of Art, New Art Bldg, Kent, OH 44242	$4000, which includes tuition and most fees (22)	Graduate assistants	One year	Annually, Mar.-Sept.
	Ranging from full tuition and fees to partial remissions (15)	Students	One year	Annually, Fall semester, Spring semester
Lahaina Arts Society, 649 Wharf St, Lahaina, HI 96761	$1000 per year	High school seniors	One year	Annually
Lake Michigan College, Art Department, 2755 E. Napier Ave, Benton Harbor, MI 49022	Full tuition (for 15 semester hrs)	Art majors	One year	Annually
Lindenwood Colleges, Art Department, St. Charles, MO 63301	Variable	Basis of merit & financial need	One year	Annually & semi-annually
Loch Haven Art Center, Inc, 2416 N. Mills Ave, Orlando, FL 32803	Varies (class tuition)	Qualified Applicants	Eight-week classes	Each quarter
Los Angeles County Museum of Art, 5905 Wilshire Blvd, Los Angeles, CA 90036	Variable	Artists under 35 years of age	One year	Annually
Louisiana Tech University, School of Art & Architecture, PO Box 6277, Tech Sta, Ruston, LA 71270	$4000	Graduate MFA assistantships	Two-three years	Annually
Lycoming College, Williamsport, PA 17701	Up to full tuition	All students eligible if qualify for need or academic status	One year, renewable	Annually
The MacDowell Colony, 100 High St, Peterborough, NH 03458	Professional writers, composers, visual artists and filmmakers are provided room, board and the use of an individual studio for seasonal residencies. Accepted applicants contributed on self-determined basis	Nationals of any country	Average residency is 5-7 weeks	Deadlines: Jan. 15 for summer; April 15 for fall; July 15 for winter; Oct. 15 for spring
Manatee Junior College, Department of Art, 26th St. W, Bradenton, FL 33505	Variable	Students majoring in art	One year	Annually
Manitoba Association of Architects, 100 Osborne St. S, Second Floor, Winnipeg, MB R3L 1Y5	$300 (2)	Architecture students enrolled at the University of Manitoba only	One year	Annually
McMurry College, Art Department, Sayles Blvd & S. 14th St, Abilene, TX 79697	$3000	Art students who show special ability	One year	Annually
McPherson College, Art Department, 1600 E. Euclid, McPherson, KS 67460	Variable	Entering students who plan to major in art	One year (renewable if student does satisfactory work to total of $1600)	Annually

OFFERED BY	AMOUNT	OPEN TO	DURATION	WHEN OFFERED
Maple Woods Community College, Art & Art History Department, 2601 NE Barry Rd, Kansas City, MO 646156	Variable	All students	One semester	Annually
Marion Art Center, 80 Pleasant, Box 602, Marion, MA 02738	$500	High school seniors	One year	Annually
Maryland College of Art & Design, 10500 Georgia Ave, Silver Spring, MD 20902	Up to $1500	Degree-seeking students	One year	Annually
Marymount College, Tarrytown, NY 10591	Variable	Any incoming freshman who expresses an interest in studio art, interior design; portfolio required	One year (renewable for four years)	Annually
The Memphis Academy of Arts, Overton Park, Memphis, TN 38112	$15,000-$50,000	High school graduates and college transfers	One year	Annually
Mercyhurst College, Dept of Art, 501 E. 38th St, Erie, PA 16501	Open	All freshmen art applicants	One year, renewable	Annually
Mesa College, Grand Junction, CO 81501	Tuition scholarships (4)		One year	Annually
Mesa Community College, Dept of Art, 1833 W. Southern Ave, Mesa, AZ 85202	$4000	Area students	One year or semester	Annually (spring)
Metropolitan Museum of Art, The Main Bldg, Fifth Ave. at 82nd St, New York, NY 10028	Variable	Scholars researching art historical fields relating to Metropolitan Museum of Art collections	One year	Deadline Jan. 15. Awards letters sent on Mar. 1
Midland College, Art Dept, Midland, TX 79701	Full tuition and fees	Full time student (12hrs) art major, at least 6 credits per semester	One semester continuing for one additional semester	Semi-annually
	$100 per semester	Any student in art	One semester	Semi-annually
Miles Community College, Art Department, 2715 Dickinson St, Miles City, MT 59301	$180	Drama and visual art students	One year	Annually
Millikin University, Art Department, 1184 W. Main, Decatur, IL 62522	$500-$1000	Qualified students	Four years	Annually
Mills College, Art Department, 5000 MacArthur Blvd, P.O. Box 9975, Oakland, CA 94613	Variable	Mills graduate students		Annually
	Eleanor Crum Award in Ceramics	Graduating MFA's		Annually
	Catherine Morgan Trefethen Award	Graduating students		Annually
	Aurelia Henry Reinhardt Faculty Purse	Graduating seniors for further study		Annually
Milwaukee Center for Photography, 207 E. Buffalo St, Milwaukee, WI 53202	$500 per semester	Second semester students		Semi-annually
Milwaukee Institute of Art & Design, 207 N. Milwaukee St, Milwaukee, WI 53202	Varied	Full-time students attending one or more semesters-based on merit and performance	One year	Annually
Minot Art Association, Minot Art Gallery, Box 325, Minot, ND 58701	$200 to attend the International Art Camp at Peace Gardens, ND	High school students (2)	One week	Annually
Mississippi University for Women, Columbus, MS 39701	$100-$2000	Undergraduates	One year & longer	Annually
Missouri Southern State College, Art Department, Newman & Duquesne Rds, Joplin, MO 64801	Variable	Top quality students with art skills and financial needs	One year	Annually
Missouri Western State College, Art Department, 4525 Downs Dr, St. Joseph, MO 64507	Variable	Any qualifying student majoring in art	By semester	By semester
Mitchell Community College, Art Department, E. Broad St, Statesville, NC 28677	Full tuition (2)	Full time students-one high school (competition and recommendation); one sophomore already enrolled	One year	Annually
Montana State University, School of Art, Bozeman, MT 59715	$5700	Graduate students	10 months	Annually-April

OFFERED BY	AMOUNT	OPEN TO	DURATION	WHEN OFFERED
Montalvo Center for the Arts, Montalvo Rd, P.O. Box 158, Saratoga, CA 95070	Varied	Qualified artists with specific projects	Three months (may be extended an additional three months)	
Montclair Art Museum, Art School, 3 S. Mountain Ave, PO Box 1582, Montclair, NJ 07042	Adults $80 Children $50	Adults & children	One year	Fall & Spring
Montclair State College, School of Fine and Performing Arts, Fine Arts Dept, Upper Montclair, NJ 07043	$3000	Qualified graduate students	One year	Annually
Monterey Peninsula Museum of Art, 559 Pacific St, Monterey, CA 93940	$500 per semester (3)	Local college students	One semester with a possible renewal	Semi-annually
Mount Holyoke College, South Hadley, MA 01075	Varied	Graduates of MHC	One year, renewable	Annually
Mount Saint Clare College, Art Department, 400 N. Bluff, Clinton, IA 52732	Varied	Incoming freshmen and students already enrolled	One year; renewable if work merits it	Annually
Mulvane Art Center, Washburn University, Art & Theater Arts Dept, Topeka, KS 66621	$8000	Qualified students	One year plus	Annually
Municipal Art Society of Baltimore City, 135 E. Baltimore St, Baltimore, MD 21202	$3000	Graduate students	One year	Annually
Murray State University, Art Department, 15th St, Murray KY 42071	$100 to $250 (one to five given)	Incoming freshmen		Annually
	$200 (Clara M Eagle Scholarship)	Freshmen, sophomores or juniors majoring in art at Murray State University		Annually
	Deans Full Tuition Scholarship	Freshmen majoring in art	Four years	Annually
Museum of Early Southern Decorative Arts Summer Institute, PO Box 10310, Winston-Salem, NC 27108	Fellowship for partial tuition	Graduate students in history, art history, preservation, museum studies; museum personnel	June-July (four weeks)	Annually
National Endowment for the Arts, 2401 E. Street NW, Washington, DC 20506	Variable	Conceptual/Performance		Deadline Jan. 15
	Variable	Painting		Deadline Feb. 4
	Variable	Video		Deadline Jan. 15
	Variable	Printmaking/Drawing/Artists Books		Deadline Mar. 4
National Gallery of Art, c/o Dr. Douglas Lewis, National Gallery Plaza, Washington, DC 20565	David E. Finley Fellowship	Ph.D. candidates	Two years plus eight months at the National Gallery	Annually (deadline Nov. 30)
	Samuel H. Kress Fellowships (2)	Ph.D. candidates	Two academic years (one at the National Gallery)	Annually (deadline Nov. 30)
	Chester Dale Fellowships (4)	Ph.D. candidates	One academic year	Annually (deadline Nov. 30)
	Robert H. and Clarice Smith Fellowship	Ph.D. candidates or holders	Two academic years	Annually (deadline Nov. 30)
National League of American Pen Women, 1300 17th St, NW, Washington, DC 20036	$500 & $1000	Pen Arts Grant to a deserving Pen Woman, Mature Women Scholarship		Biennial
Nazareth College of Rochester, Art Department, 4245 East Ave, Rochester, NY 14610	Variable	Qualified high school graduates	One year	Annually
New Brunswick Craft School, Box 6000, Fredericton, NB E3B 5H1, Canada	$1500	Second year student who speaks French & excels in chosen medium	One-half year	Annually
New Mexico State University, Art Department, Box 3572, Las Cruces, NM 88003	$2550-$5770 (graduate assistantships)	Graduate students	One-two years	Annually
New York Institute of Technology, Fine Arts Dept, Wheatley Rd, Old Westbury, NY 11568	Variable	High school seniors	One year, renewable	Annually
New York School of Interior Design, 155 E. 56th St, New York, NY 10022	$1300 maximum per term	All students	One semester (renewable)	Annually

OFFERED BY	AMOUNT	OPEN TO	DURATION	WHEN OFFERED
New York State College of Ceramics at Alfred University (SUNY), Harder Hall, Alfred, NY 14802	$500 (2) Additional aid up to one half tuition based on need	Incoming freshmen	One year-renewable	Annually
New York Studio School of Drawing, Painting & Sculpture, 8 W. Eighth St, New York, NY 10011	$400-$3600	Students enrolled for one year who qualify on the basis of need by semester	One year	Annually
Northeastern Oklahoma A&M College, Art Dept, Miami, OK 74354	Tuition	Art majors	One year	Annually
Northeastern Illinois University, Art Department, St. Louis at Bryn Mawr Ave, Chicago, IL 60625	$690 (2 terms)	Board of Governers Talent Scholarships available to gifted art students	Two terms	Annually
Northeastern Oklahoma State University, Division of Arts & Letters, Tahlequah, OK 74464	Varied	Undergraduates	One semester, subject to continuation	
Northeast Missouri State University, Division of Fine Arts, Kirksville, MO 63501	Varying amounts	High school seniors; other awards available to junior college graduates	One year (renewable)	Annually
Northern Illinois University, Department of Art, DeKalb, IL 60115	Jack Arends Scholarship-about $500	Art majors with 3.0 overall grade point average, one year residence at NIU, portfolio, and 3 recommendations (2 from NIU Art Department)	One year	Annually
	James P. Bates Memorial Scholarship-about $500	Rotated among majors in the various areas of the Art Department	One year	Annually
	Richard Keefer Scholarship-about $500	Art majors-rotated among four areas-Art History and Art Education; Drawing, Painting & Printmaking; Crafts & Sculpture; Design & Photography	One year	Annually
	NIU Tuition Waiver-tuition fee for Illinois residents	Accepted or continuing art majors with 2.5 overall grade point average and 3.0 art grade point average, portfolio and recommendations	Renewable for four years with maintenance of 12 hour course load	Annually
	John X. Koznarek Memorial Scholarship-about $250	Accepted or enrolled majors in studio art. Portfolio and three recommendations	One year	Annually
	Cora B. Miner Scholarship-about $400	Preferably to student from DeKalb County with interest in realistic art	One year	Annually
	Frances E. Gates Memorial Scholarship-about $200	Preferably a graduate student specializing in watercolor	One year	Annually
Northern Michigan University, c/o Prof Cinelli, Marquette, MI 49855	$320	Sophomore art and design majors who have been majors in NMU Art Dept at least one semester	Renewable	Annually
Northern Montana College, Department of Art, 611 16th St, Havre, MT 59501	$100	An art major or minor who has demonstrated high art ability and who is in need of financial aid	No limit established	Annually
North Park College, Fine Arts Division, 5125 N. Spaulding, Chicago, IL 60625	$300	Sophomore art majors	One year	Annually
	$500	Junior art majors	One year	Annually
	Lydia Poole Award-amount varies	Any art major	One year	Every two years
Northwest Community College, Powell, WY 82435	Maximum $500 per person per year	All students, portfolio required	One year	Semi-annually
Northwestern College, Art Department, Orange City, IA 51041	$100	Art majors upon acceptance of portfolio	One year	Annually
Northwest Nazarene College, Art Department, Holly at Dewey, Nampa, ID 83651	$750 (4)	Fine arts majors	One year	Annually
Oberlin College, Department of Art, Oberlin, OH 44074	$4725 plus tuition remission (3-4 graduate assistantships)	Graduates with BA degrees who qualify	One year (renewable)	Annually
Occidental College, Art Department, 1600 Campus Rd, Los Angeles, CA 90041	Varied	Art majors who can demonstrate financial need	Renewable for four years	Annually
Ocean City School of Art-Ocean City Cultural Arts Center, 409 Wesley Ave, Ocean City, NJ 08226	Varied	Members and students of the Art Center	One semester	Each semester

OFFERED BY	AMOUNT	OPEN TO	DURATION	WHEN OFFERED
Ohio State University, Dept of History of Art, 100 Hayes Hall, Columbus, OH 43210	$4590 for first year students, to $5310 for fifth year students, plus tuition waiver for teaching associatships	Students who demonstrate accomplishment and evidence of potential excellence in teaching scholarship and/or research in History of Art	Up to 22 quarters	Annually
	University fellowship of $600 per month plus tuition waiver	First year students	One year	Annually
Ohio State University, Graduate School, Department of Art Education, Columbus, OH 43210	$4800 plus tuition	All MA and PhD candidates (special minority fellowships are also awarded)	One calendar year (renewable for three years)	Annually, deadline Feb.
Ohio University, School of Art, College of Fine Arts, Athens, OH 45701	Tuition scholarship, graduate teaching assistantships	Undergraduate students and graduates	One year (renewable)	Annually
Oklahoma City University, NW 23rd at N. Blackwelder, Oklahoma City, OK 73106	$1000-$1250	Junior & senior art majors	One year	Annually
Oklahoma State Tech, 4th and Mission, Okmulgee, OK 74447	Commercial Art Scholarships, $300 up to full tuition, books, and student acitivity fees	Any competitive high school senior. Award is based on cumulative grade point average and ACT scores	From two trimesters to entire duration of program of study	Annually, deadline April 1
Old Dominion University, Norfolk, VA 23508	$800	Studio majors	One year	Annually
Ontario College of Art, 100 McCaul St, Toronto, ON M5T 1W1, Canada	Variable	Ontario College of Art students only	One year	Annually
Oregon School of Arts and Crafts, 8245 SW Barnes Rd, Portland, OR 97225	Variable	Students in financial need	Per term	Per term-deadline for application, one week prior to each term
Oregon College of Art, 30 S. First St, Ashland, OR 97520	Variable	High school and college transfer students-based on competitive art work	Academic year	Annually
Otis Art Institute of Parsons School of Design, 2401 Wilshire Blvd, Los Angeles, CA 90057	Variable	Students enrolled at Otis in the BFA or MFA degree programs	Academic year	Annually
Our Lady of the Lake University, 411 SW 24th St, San Antonio, TX 78285	Variable	Majors in art	Variable	Annually
Pacific Northwest College of Art, 1219 SW Park St, Portland, OR 97205	Variable	Enrolled students	One school year	Annually
Palomar College,* San Marcos, CA 92069	$75 Lake San Marcos Art League Award	Returning sophomore majoring in art		June
	$50 Catherine Ann (Tim) Sawday Memorial Scholarship	Deserving student majoring in art or science		June
	$100 San Dieguito Art Guild Scholarship	Graduate planning to pursue a career in painting		June
	$150 Fallbrook Art Association	Fallbrook resident, full time art student at a two year community college		June
	$150 Showcase of the Arts-Evelyn Surface Memorial	Two awards-one for art student returning to Palomar and one for a graduating art student going on to a 4-year institution		June
	Ivie Frances Wickam Scholarships $1500-$5000	Current women graduates of Palomar College who are evident of financial need, evidence of scholastic record; preference is given to art and/or education students		June
Pan American University, Department of Art, Edinburg, TX 78539	$250-$300 per semester	Entering Freshmen or art majors with 2.5 average (4.00 system), 30 hours completed study	One year	Annually
Parsons School of Design, 65 Fifth Ave, New York, NY 10011	Varied	All financially eligible, matriculated students in the BFA and MFA programs	Academic year	Annually, apply by Mar. 1
Pasadena City College, Art Department, 1570 E. Colorado Blvd, Pasadena, CA 91106	$1000 (2)	Art majors completing seven courses at PCC with a college-wide GPA of 2.5 & art GPA of 3.25		Annually
Penland School of Crafts, Penland, NC 28765	Tuition and partial room and board waived for work scholarships	Applications must include a resume and slides of recent work	Two and three week summer workshops	Annually, deadline April 1
Pennsylvania Academy of the Fine Arts, Broad & Cherry Sts, Philadelphia, PA 19102	Scholastic Magazine Art Award (1), one year tuition	High school seniors	One year	Annually

OFFERED BY	AMOUNT	OPEN TO	DURATION	WHEN OFFERED
	National Honors Society (2) half tuition	High school seniors in National Honor Society	One year	Annually
	Full and half tuition scholarships	2nd, 3rd & 4th year Academy students	One year	Annually
	Cresson European Travel Scholarship and tuition-$3300	3rd, 4th year Academy students	Three months	Annually
	Schiedt & Ware Travel Scholarship-$2000	3rd, 4th year Academy students	Three months	Annually
Peoria Art Guild, 1831 N. Knoxville Ave, Peoria, IL 61603	$27-$45	Children, adults & students who would benefit from artistic instruction, but who would be otherwise unable to attend college art classes	8-10 weeks	4 times each year
Philadelphia College of Art, Broad & Pine Sts, Philadelphia, PA 19102	$4000	High school students, all incoming freshmen	One year	Annually
Place des Arts, 1120 Brunette Ave, Coquitlam, BC V3K 3M2, Canada	Up to $400 through the Coquitlam Fine Arts Council	Any artist living within the area	One year	Annually
The Ponca City Art Association, Box 1394, 819 E. Central, Ponca City, OK 74602	$650	Local art student	One year	Annually
The Pontiac Art Center, 47 Williams St, Pontiac, MI 48053	Varied	All	Ten-week terms	All-year
Portage & District Arts Centre, Box 215, Portage la Prairie, MMB R1N 3B5, Canada	$500	Canadians or landed immigrants, residents of Portage and full time student in visual or performing arts program	One year	Annually
Portland School of Art, 97 Spring St, Portland, ME 04101	Variable	All students	One year (renewable)	Annually
Portland State University, Dept of Art & Architecture, PO Box 751, Portland, OR 97207	Varied	Art major with 20 hrs in art at time of application. Good accumulative GPA and portfolio also required	Academic year	Annually-Spring
Pratt Graphics Center, extension of Pratt Institute, 160 Lexington Ave, New York, NY 10016	Tuition up to a period of one year	Talented artists; the Margaret Lowengrund Scholarship Fund and the Albert Christ-Janer Memorial Scholarship Fund are for American citizens & foreign nationals.	Up to one year	Sept. through July
Presbyterian College, Fine Arts Dept, Clinton, SC 29325	$300	All art students	One year	Annually
Princeton Art Association, Rosedale Rd, PO Box 3019, Princeton, NJ 08540	Varies-approximately $60	Students interested in art	Eight weeks	Four semesters a year
Providence Art Club, II Thomas St, Providence, RI 02903	Varied	Rhode Island School of Design students	One year	Annually
Radford University, PO Box 5791, Radford, VA 24142	Dr. G. Lynn Gordon Scholarship, varies	Undergraduates and graduates	Academic year	Annually
Rensselaer County Historical Society, 59 Second St, Troy NY 12180	Volunteer summer museum intern program	Juniors & seniors with art history, history majors & some museum training	Ten weeks	Annually
Rhode Island School of Design, Two College St, Providence, RI 02903	Variable	Accepted degree candidates on undergraduate & graduate level based on financial need	One year	Annually
Rice University, 6100 S. Main, Houston, TX 77005	Varied	Candidates of the Master of Arts degree in Art History and Classical Archaeology	One year, renewable	Annually
Ricks College, Department of Art, Rexburg, ID 83440	Varied	Art majors	One year	
Ringling School of Art & Design, 1111 27th St, Sarasota, FL 33580	$250-$1000	All Ringling students	One year, some semester grants	Annually
Rocky Mountain School of Art, 1441 Ogden St, Denver CO 80218	$10,000 commercial & fine art scholarships (2)	High school seniors	Three years	Annually-Spring

OFFERED BY	AMOUNT	OPEN TO	DURATION	WHEN OFFERED
	$700 quarterly (Work Study Scholarship)	4 students every 2 years	Two years	
Rosary College, Director of Foreign Studies, River Forest, IL 60305	$500-$1000 each (15)	Nationals of U.S. for study in Florence, Italy, for study in painting, printmaking and art history at Rosary Graduate School of Art, Villa Schifanoia, to men and women qualified for graduate study in fine arts who hold BA or equivilent and have knowledge of Italian	One-two years	Academic year & summer
Salmagundi Club, 47 Fifth Ave, New York, NY 10003	Varied	Qualified applicants, artists under 30 years of age, three examples of work to be submitted for approval by committee	Four years	
Sam Houston State University, Art Department, Huntsville, TX 77340	$4600 (teaching fellowship)	Art majors with BFA or equivalent, with 60 or more hours in art	One year (renewable)	Annually
	$600 (3 art scholarship)	Sophomore or above, art major with artistic aptitude and ability	One year	Annually
San Antonio Art Institute, 6000 N. New Braunfels, PO Box 6092, San Antonio, TX 78209	Full & partial tuition	All students	One semester	Each semester
San Diego State University, College of Professional Studies & Fine Arts, Dept of Art, San Diego, CA 92182	Isabel Kraft Sculpture Scholarship, $3000	Sculpture students		Fall
	Ellsworth Scholarship $500	Painting & sculpture undergraduates		Fall or spring
	Skowhegan Scholarship, summer fees paid for Skowhegan School of Painting & Sculpture in Skowhegan, ME	Seniors in painting & sculpture		Spring
San Francisco Art Institute, 800 Chestnut St, San Francisco, CA 91433	Tuition scholarships	Undergraduate and graduate students with demonstrated financial need	Academic year	Semi-annually
San Jacinto College North, Dept of Art, Houston, TX 77015	Varies upon need (North Shore Area Art League Scholarship); also full tuition & book scholarships	Any full-time student	Fall and Spring	Annually; tuition & book scholarships, each semester
Santa Cruz Art League, Inc, 526 Broadway, Santa Cruz, CA 95060	$500	High school students in Santa Cruz County		Annually in February
Santa Rosa Junior College, Dept of Art, 1501 Mendocino Ave, Santa Rosa, CA 95401	Majorie Kerr Schaffer Memorial Funds	Talented painting student	Spring	
	Pat Maggiora Memorial Funds	Graduating sophomore who is talented in oil painting	Spring	
	Elizabeth Fay Evans Memorial Funds	Second year painting student	Spring	
	Charles Cherney Memorial	Art students	Spring	
	Paul & Lucile Kelley Memorial	Art students	Spring	
	Anonimous donations	Art students	Spring	
Saskatchewan Association of Architects, 101-701 Broadway Ave, Saskatoon, SK S7J 1E8, Canada	$2000	Full time students pursuing a degree in architecture at a Canadian university, previous recipients not eligible, permanent residents		Annually
Scholastic Awards, Scholastic Inc. 730 Broadway, New York, NY 10003	Variable	High school seniors only; talented in art or photography; qualify by portfolio and high school record	One year	Annually
The School of Fashion Design, 136 Newbury St, Boston, MA 02116	$1000	All full time students	One year	Annually
School of Fine Arts, 38660 Mentor Ave, Willoughby, OH 44094	Tuition	Talent plus need	One year	Annually
School of the Art Institute of Chicago, Columbus Dr. at Jackson Blvd, Chicago, IL 60603	$500-$5500	Full-time degree students in need and undergraduate degree students with merit, regardless of need	One year, renewable upon updated application	Annually
School of the Associated Arts, 344 Summit Ave, St Paul, MN 55102	Variable	Advanced students	One year	Annually
School of the Museum of Fine Arts, 230 The Fenway, Boston, MA 02115	$150 to $4000 per year	All diploma or degree matriculating students determined eligible by CCS/ACT needs analysis	Academic year	Annually

OFFERED BY	AMOUNT	OPEN TO	DURATION	WHEN OFFERED
	$95,000 awarded in varying amounts (approx 15 annually)	Graduates of the School of the Museum of Fine Arts	Flexible (average one year)	Annually
The School of the Ozarks, Department of Art, Point Lookout, MO 65726	Full tuition, room and board, Work/Study Grant	Preference to scholarship, financial need, geographic location	Four years	Annually
School of Visual Arts, 209 E. 23rd St, New York, NY 10010	$697,000		Four year BFA, two year MFA	Annually
Sculpture Center Gallery & School, 167 E. 69th St, New York, NY 10021	$1500	Qualified students	One year	Annually
Seaton Hill College, Greensburg, PA 15601	$700 toward tuition	Incoming freshmen art majors	One year	Annually
Shasta College, Art Department, 1605 Old Oregon Trail, PO Box 6006, Redding, CA 96099	Variable	Art students		
Skowhegan School of Painting and Sculpture, Skowhegan, ME 04976	Full scholarships $3000 (6)	Qualified art students 18 years of age and over, portfolio review	Nine weeks July and August	Annually
	Partial scholarships (34)	Qualified art students 18 years of age and over, portfolio review	Nine weeks July and August	Annually
Smithsonian Institute, Office of Fellowships & Grants, Washington, DC 20560	$18,000 plus allowances	Post-doctoral scholars in American art history, Oriental art history and African art	Six months to one year	Deadline Jan. 15
	$11,000 plus allowances	Doctoral candidates in American art history, Oriental art history and African art	Six months to one year	Deadline Jan. 15
	First Ladies Fellowship	Predoctoral or postdoctoral scholars for the study of costume in America. Research plans, information about the intended use of the Smithsonian Collections use and references will be asked for		Deadline Jan. 15
	Freer Gallery Internship	Interns must have working knowledge of one or more of the pertinent Oriental languages & submit a proposal relevant to the Freer collections		
	Hirshhorn Museum & Sculpture Garden Internship	College juniors & seniors who have completed at least 12 semester hours in art history.	Ten weeks	Deadline March 1
		Graduate student internships are available for students in accredited art history graduate programs	One Semester	Deadline March 1
	National Museum of African Art Internship	People enrolled in undergraduate & graduate programs of study & for people interested in exploring museum professions		
	National Museum of American Art Internship	Museum training for college senior graduate students, in art history, studio art and American studies	Nine weeks, commence in June	Deadline Feb. 15
	National Portrait Gallery Internship		Three months	
	Harold P. Stern Memorial Fund at Freer Gallery	Selection of recipients is by invitation only & is based upon outstanding scholarly achievements in the field of Japanese art		
	Sidney & Celia Siegel Fellowship Program at Cooper-Hewitt	Applicants with two years of college education, preference given to those without previous museum experience	Ten weeks	Deadline April 1
Society of Architectural Historians, 1700 Walnut St, Suite 716, Philadelphia, PA 19103	One or two given to participate in annual tour	Outstanding students engaged in graduate work in architecture, architectural history, city planning or urban history, landscape history or landscape design & current member of the Society of Architectural Historians		Annually
	Alice Davis Hitchock Book Award			Annually
	Founders' Award	Student must be engaged in graduate study that involves some aspect of the history of architecture		Annually
Southampton College of C. W. Post Center, Long Island University, Fine Arts Division, Southampton, NY 11968	$1000-$4000	Undergraduates incoming & transfer students	Four years	Annually

OFFERED BY	AMOUNT	OPEN TO	DURATION	WHEN OFFERED
South Carolina Arts Commission, 1800 Gervais St, Columbia, SC 29201	$5000 (6)	Visual arts (2), crafts (1), film/video (1), performing arts (1), literary arts (1)	One year	Annually
South Dakota State University, Memorial Art Center, Medary Ave. at Harvey Dunn St, Brookings, SD 57006	$50-$300	Incoming freshman	Varies	Annually
Southeastern Center for Contemporary Art, 2721 Robinhood Rd, Winston-Salem, NC 27106	Varied	Southeastern artists	For their use	Every two years
Southern Baptist College, Humanities-Art Department, College City, AR 72476	$200	High school seniors and others seeking admittance, by portfolio	One semester (renewable)	Semi-annually
	Variable	Most outstanding art student		Annually
Southern Illinois University, Carbondale, School of Art, Carbondale, IL 62901	$100,000	Graduating seniors, entering freshmen, graduate students, some continuing undergraduates	One year	Annually
Southern Illinois University, Edwardsville, Department of Art and Design, School of Fine Arts and Communications, Edwardsville, IL 62026	Tuition	Graduate students accepted for admission	One year	Annually
Southern Oregon State College, Art Department, 1250 Siskiyou Blvd, Ashland, OR 97520	$4000	Art major	One year	Annually
	$500	Masters candidate with art history emphasis	One year	Annually
Southern Utah State College, Department of Art, Cedar City, UT 84720	Tuition	Residents of Utah and nonresidents	One year	Annually and quarterly
	$519	Freshmen, sophomores, juniors and seniors	One year	Annually
South Florida Art Institute of Hollywood, 1301 S. Ocean Dr, Hollywood, FL 33019	$8000 yearly	Elementary, senior and junior high school graduates	One, two and four years	Annually
	$3000	Senior citizens	One, two and four years	Annually
Southwestern Michigan College, Cherry Grove Rd, Dowagiac, MI 49047	Varied	Art students	One year	Annually
Southwest Missouri State University, Department of Art, 901 S. National, Springfield, MO 65804	$150-$650 (5)	Art majors currently enrolled	One year	Annually
	$360 (2)	Entering freshmen	One year	Annually
Springfield Art Center, 107 Cliff Park Rd, Springfield, OH 45501	$25-$100	Children, some adults, by semester	Ten weeks	Each semester
Springfield College, 263 Alden St, Springfield, MA 01109	Variable	Qualified students based on financial need	One year	Annually
State University Center, Department of Art and Art History, Binghamton, NY 13901	Variable	Art history graduate students	One year	Annually
Stephen F. Austin State University, Art Dept, Box 13001, Nacogdoches, TX 75962	$4725	Graduates	Six semesters for MFA candidates, four semesters for MA candidates	Annually
Sterling College, Art Department, Sterling, KS 67579	Varied	Any art students with 3.5 grade average	One year, renewable	Annually
Margaret Woodbury Strong Museum, One Manhattan Sq, Rochester, NY 14607	H. J. Swinney Museum Studies Internship Program	Graduate students who aspire to a career in the museum profession	Nine months	
Sul Ross State University, Art Dept, Alpine, TX 79830	$400	Entering art major	One year	Annually
Summer Arts Institute, New Jersey School of the Arts, Carriage House, Douglass Campus of Rutgers University, New Brunswick, NJ 08903	$100-$1500	Accepted talented high school students with demonstrated or potential talent in the arts	Summer	Annually

OFFERED BY	AMOUNT	OPEN TO	DURATION	WHEN OFFERED
Summervail Workshop for Art & Critical Studies, PO Box 117, Minturn, CO 81645	$185 per week plus room & supplies	Any interested student	One week workshops	Each summer
	Studio Manager Positions & students assistantships in exchange for work	Any interested student on approval of work	Three day symposia	Each summer
Sunbury Shores Arts and Nature Centre, Inc, 139 Water St, PO Box 100, St. Andrews, NB EOG 2X0, Canada	Approx $400 each; all costs covered	New Brunswick residents ages 15-23 inclusive	Two or three weeks varying with art course	Annually, for July and Aug. Submit application by Mar. 31
Swain School of Design, 19 Hawthorn, New Bedford, MA 02740	$200-$1000	All students	One year	Annually
Syracuse University, School of Art, 203 Crouse College, Syracuse, NY 13210	$1000 for undergraduates, partial & full tuition scholarships for graduates, $5900 fellowships for graduates, half & full assistantships for graduates		One year	Annually
Tarrant County Junior College, Northeast Campus, Department of Art, 828 Harwood Rd, Hurst, TX 76053	$50 tuition award (3)	Art students at freshman-sophomore levels	One semester	Semi-annually
	$130 tuition award (3)	High School seniors	Two semesters	Annually, April
Texarkana College, Art Department, Texarkana, TX 75501	$100	Art majors	One year	Annually
Texas Southern University,* Department of Art, 3201 Wheeler Ave, Houston, TX 77004	$2000	All art students with completion of one year's course work in art at TSU may apply	Four years	Annually
Texas State Technical Institute, PO Box 11016, Amarillo, TX 79111	$150	Continuing students	One or two quarters	Semi-annually
Thousand Islands Craft School, 314 John St, Clayton, NY 13624	$75-$150	Students interested in pottery, weaving, carving, early American decoration, photography, painting or jewelry	One-two weeks	Annually in July & Aug.
Tobe-Coburn School for Fashion Careers, 686 Broadway, New York, NY 10012	$1000-$1500	Students of the school		Annually
Toledo Museum of Art, PO Box 1013, Toledo, OH 43697	Variable ($7000 total)	Students interested in art through Toledo Museum of Art	One year	Annually
Margaret Fort Trahern Gallery, Austin Peay State University, Art Department, Clarksville, TN 37040	Variable	High school art seniors in central Tennessee	One year	Annually
Traphagen School of Fashion, 257 Park Ave. S, New York, NY 10010	$5000 Famous Alumni Scholarships	Second year students	One year	Annually
	$2915 School Art League, New York City Scholarship	First year students		Annually
	$2915 National Scholastic Magazine Scholarship	First year students		Annually
	$5830	First year students (two years) Flemington Fur Co. Competition (open to high school juniors and seniors in NY, NJ, CT, DE, MD and PA)		Annually
	Above scholarships are renewable upon performance each year			
Tucson Museum of Art, Attn: M. E. Thompson, 235 W. Alameda, Tucson, AZ 85701	Varied	Talented needy and minority students for TMA school classes only	One year	Annually
Tufts University, Fine Arts Dept, 11 Talbot Ave, Medford, MA 02155	$13,800	Graduate students	One year	Annually
Tusculum College, Fine Arts Dept, Box 48, Greenville, TN 37743	Varied	Students in upper 40% of their class who show leadership talent, art talent	One year	Annually
Tyler School of Art of Temple University, Beech & Penrose, Elkins Park, PA 19126	$400-$2400	Freshmen, transfers & graduate students	One year	Annually
Ukrainian Culture & Educational Centre, 184 Alexander Ave. E, Winnipeg, MB R3B 0L6, Canada	$600	Students enrolled in an accredited course in museology or fine arts or archival science at any accredited university	One year	Annually

OFFERED BY	AMOUNT	OPEN TO	DURATION	WHEN OFFERED
U.S. Government Grants for Graduate Study Abroad under the Fulbright-Hays Act. Write: Study Abroad Programs, Institute of International Education, 809 United Nations Plaza, New York, NY 10017	Variable	Graduate students who are U.S. citizens with B.A. degree or in the creative and performing arts, 4 years of professional study and/or experience, and who have a knowledge of the language of the country for which the application is made.	One year	Annually
University of Alabama, Dept of Art, Huntsville, AL 35899	Varied	Art major with 2.0 average on 3.0 scale	One year	Annually
University of Alaska at Anchorage,* Dept of Art, 2533 Providence Ave, Anchorage, AK 99504	$250 plus state aid	All art students		Annually
	$300 Alumni Scholarship	All students	One semester	Semesterly
	$500 Muriel Hannah Memorial Scholarship	Native students and students who have shown demonstrated ability in art	Academic year	Annually
University of Arizona, Faculty of Fine Arts, Department of Art, Tucson, AZ 85721	Variable	Students enrolled in art program at UA	One year	Annually
University of Arkansas, Art Dept, Fayetteville, AR 72701	$300 assistantships plus tuition	Graduate students	Two years or more	Annually
	$100-$300 scholarships	Sophomore, junior or senior art students enrolled in the Art Department at the University of Arkansas	One year	Annually
University of California, Department of Art History, Santa Barbara, CA 93106	Variable	Graduate students approved by Art History Department chairman. MA and PhD candidates are also eligible for consideration for departmental Kress Foundation and Art Affiliate Awards	Academic year	Annually
University of Chicago, Cochrane-Woods Art Center, 5540 S Greenwood, Chicago, IL 60637	Variable	The best qualified entering and continuing graduate students	One year	Annually
University of Colorado, Boulder, Fine Arts Department, Boulder, CO 80309	In-state tuition (5)	Undergraduates	One year	Annually
	$2500 plus tuition waiver	Graduate students	One year	Annually
	Maria Elkin Award-$200	Fine arts student	Academic year	
	Eve Drewelowe Award-half resident tuition	Student majoring in painting with preference given to female students	Academic year	Annually (renewable)
	Susan Irey Byrne Award-$500	Student majoring in jewelry with preference given to female students	Academic year	Annually
	Emma Strain Memorial Award-$240	Student majoring in painting	Academic year	Annually
University of Connecticut, Art Dept, Storrs, CT 06268	$2000	Freshmen & advanced majors	One year	Annually
University of Denver, School of Art, University Park, Denver, CO 80208	$20,000	Graduate & undergraduate students	One year	Semi-annually
University of Hartford, Hartford Art School,* 200 Bloomfield Ave, West Hartford, CT 06117	$1000	Competition scholarship award	One year, renewable	Annually
University of Idaho, Department of Art & Architecture, Moscow, ID 83843	Variable	All majors in art, undergraduate and graduate, based on ability alone	One year	Annually
	$400 (Commemorative Art Scholarship)	Upper division undergraduates in art, based on need and ability		Annually in the Spring for Fall semester
University of Illinois, Urbana-Champaign, College of Fine and Applied Arts, 110 Architecture Bldg, 608 E. Lorado Taft Dr, Champaign, IL, 61820	Kate Neal Kinley Memorial Fellowship-$4500	Graduates of the College of Fine and Applied Arts of the University of Illinois, Urbana-Champaign and to graduates of similar institutions of equal educational standing. Preference is given to applicants under 25 years of age	One academic year	Annually
University of Iowa, School of Art and Art History, Iowa City, IA 52242	Graduate College Scholarships up to $2000	All scholarships listed available to graduate students and some undergraduate students	One year (renewable)	Annually

OFFERED BY	AMOUNT	OPEN TO	DURATION	WHEN OFFERED
	Paula P. Grahame Scholarship up to $1500			
	Kress Foundation Fellowship in Art History $3500, Travel Grants to $1200			
	Assistantship $6000 (half-time)			
University of Kansas, Department of Art and Music Education and Music Therapy, 311 Bailey Hall, Lawrence, KS 66045	Variable	Undergraduates in Art Education and graduate students in Art Education	One academic year (renewable)	Annually
University of Lethbridge, Department of Art, 4401 University Dr, Lethbridge, AB, Canada	Variable	Qualified students		Annually
	Art Department Faculty $100	Full-time second/third year student - art major; outstanding accomplishment in an area of Studio Art over at least one full year at the University		Annually
	George Varzari Sculpture Award $100	Full-time student currently enrolled in a sculpture course at the University of Lethbridge - outstanding in area of sculpture. Works sculpted during current academic year		
University of Louisville, Allen R. Hite Art Institute, Louisville, KY 40208	$10,000	High seniors under grads or grads in art or art history through scholastic art competition	One or two semesters	Annually
University of Michigan, Ann Arbor, History of Art Dept, Ann Arbor, MI 48109	Charles L. Freer Scholarship in Oriental Art, amounts vary to $5000	Graduate students in Oriental art	One year	Annually
	Charles L. Freer Fellowships in Oriental Art, amounts vary to $3000	Advanced graduate students in Oriental art, residence at Freer Gallery, Washington, DC	Half year	Annually
	Samuel H. Kress Foundation Scholarship and Fellowship, amounts vary to $6000	Advanced graduate students	One year	Annually
	Graduate Fellowships offered by Horace H. Rackham School of Graduate Studies, amounts vary to $4000	Graduate students	One year	Annually
	Rackham Predoctoral Fellowship, $5000	Predoctoral student	One year	Annually
	Humanities Prize, First Year Fellowship, $6000 plus tuition & fees	Beginning graduate students	Three years	Annually
	Teaching Fellowships up to $6500	Graduate students of the second year & beyond	One year	Annually
University of Minnesota, Duluth, Department of Art, 317 Humanities Bldg, Duluth, MN 55812	Assistantships and/or associateships	Graduate students	One year	Annually
	$150 scholarships (4)	Undergraduate	Summer session only	
	$100 awards (4)	Outstanding new freshmen art majors	Fall quarter only	
	$600 scholarships (11)	Undergraduate and/or graduate	One year	Annually
University of Minnesota, Minneapolis, Art History, 27 Pleasant St. SE, 108 Jones Hall, Minneapolis, MN 55455	$500-$6000	Graduate students	One year	Annually
University of Minnesota, Minneapolis, Department of Studio Art, Minneapolis, MN 55455	$600-$2700		One year	Winter or Spring
University of Mississippi, Department of Art, Fine Arts Center, University, MS 38677	$2600 for half time; $5300 full assistantship (5-6 available), plus $1200 out-of-state fees	Graduate students in art (MFA, MA)	Nine months	Annually
University of Nebraska-Lincoln, Department of Art, Woods Hall, Lincoln, NE 68588	Thomas Coleman Memorial Scholarship in Printmaking $200	Outstanding graduate and undergraduate student in prints		Annually
	Francis Vreeland Award in Art $1600	Outstanding graduate and undergraduate students in studio art		Annually
	Jean R. Faulkner Freshman Art Scholarship $800	Identified creative potential during first year of study		Annually

OFFERED BY	AMOUNT	OPEN TO	DURATION	WHEN OFFERED
	Jean R. Faulkner Student Exhibition Recognition Award, 6 awards of $100 each	Outstanding achievement by students represented in annual undergraduate exhibition		Annually
	E. Evelyn Peterson Memorial Fine Arts Scholarships $10,000	Outstanding students, sophomore and above, with high potential in art		Annually
	Ruth Ann Sack Memorial Scholarship in Photography and Painting, $100 awards	Outstanding upper division students in photography and painting		Annually as income available
University of Nevada, Department of Art, 4505 Maryland Parkway, Las Vegas, NV 89154	$1000	Entering freshmen only	Four years, renewable upon demonstration of satisfactory progress	Annually
University of New Mexico, College of Fine Arts, Albuquerque, NM 87131	Beaumont Newhall Fellowship $500	Graduate photo students	One year	Annually
	Charles Mattox Award-$400	Art students	One year	Annually
	Cheryl Conniff Carroll Award-$400	Art students	One year	Annually
	Bainbridge Bunting Memorial Scholarship-$5000	Art students	One year	Annually
	Hilmer G. Olson Award-$200	Art students	One year	Annually
	Native American Womens Art Scholarships-$1000	Navajo or AIPC women enrolled in MFA program	One year	Annually
University of North Carolina-Chapel Hill, Department of Art, 101 Art Classroom Bldg 079A, Chapel Hill, NC 27514	Emily Pollard Fellowship, $2000-$5000	Graduate students only	One year	Annually
	Samuel H. Kress Fellowship $6000			
University of North Carolina, Dept of Art & Music, University Heights, Asheville, NC 28804	Variable	Outstanding student majoring in art with financial need	One year	Annually
University of Notre Dame, Graduate School, Art, Art History & Design Dept. Notre Dame, IN 46556	Tuition $6270 Stipend $4200	Teaching assistants chosen by faculty	Up to two years	Annually
University of Oregon, School of Architecture and Applied Arts, Dept of Fine and Applied Arts, Eugene, OR 97403	Varied	Students with one year residence	One year	Annually
University of Pittsburgh, Henry Clay Frick Fine Arts Dept, Pittsburgh, PA 15260	$5450-TA, $5775-TF, $6000-Mellon Tuition scholarships	Fine arts graduate students (art history)	One year, renewable	Annually
University of Science & Arts of Oklahoma, Arts Dept, Chickaska, OK 73018	$1200	Incoming freshmen	One year	Annually
University of South Dakota, Art Dept, CFA 179, Vermillion, SD 57069	Freshment Scholarships-$200 (5)			Annually
	Oscar Howe Scholarship-$750	Outstanding art student		Annually
	A B Gunderson Scholarship-$750 (1)	Senior		Annually
	Graduate Assistantships-$3200			Annually
University of Southern California, School of Fine Arts, Watt Hall 103, University Park, Los Angeles, CA 90007	Variable	Fine arts majors	One year	Annually
	$6000-J. Paul Getty Memorial Scholarship	Graduate student, Art History	One year	Annually
	Graduate teaching assistantships (tuition credit and stipend)-contact School of Fine Arts	Graduate students, Art History and Studio Art	One to three years	Annually
	Museum Studies Fellowships-contact School of Fine Arts	Graduate students, Museum Studies Program	One to three years	Annually
	Graduate Fellowships-contact USC Graduate School, ADM 353, USC, Los Angeles, CA 90007	Graduate students	Generally one to three years	Annually
University of Southern Mississippi, Box 5033, Hattiesburg, MS 39401	Grad assistantship, $200-$500 & $3800	Scholarships to undergrads, assistantships to grads	9 months	Annually

OFFERED BY	AMOUNT	OPEN TO	DURATION	WHEN OFFERED
University of Tennessee, Dept of Art, 1715 Volunteer Blvd, Knoxville, TN 37996	$2000 graduate, $1000 undergraduate, $50-$300 undergraduate	Currently enrolled art majors	One, two or three quarters & one year	Annually
University of Texas at Austin, Department of Art, 23rd and San Jacinto, Austin, TX 78712	Scholarships, fellowships and grants in varying amounts; student assistantships; all levels teaching assistantships, varying amounts	Undergraduates & graduate students for terms announced		Semi-annually
University of Texas at San Antonio, Division of Art & Design, San Antonio, TX 78284	$200-$500	Graduate MFA applicants	One year	Each fall term
University of Utah, Art Dept AAC 161, Salt Lake City, UT 84112	Varied	Docents	One year	Annually
University of Washington, School of Art, DM-10, Seattle, WA 98195	Varied	Art majors	One year and quarterly	Annually and quarterly
University of Waterloo, Waterloo, ON N2L 3G1, Canada	$1000	First year entrance students	One year	Annually
	$450	Third year students	One year	Annually
University of Windsor, School of Visual Arts, Huron Church Road at College, Windsor, ON, N9B 3P4, Canada	Variable	Fine arts students, other university students	One year	Annually
University of Wisconsin-Eau Claire, Dept of Art, Park and Garfield Aves, Eau Claire, WI 54701	Variable	Qualified students	One year	Annually
University of Wisconsin-Milwaukee, Art History Dept, PO Box 413, Mitchell Hall 151, Milwaukee WI 53201	$5700 and $4278; also small cash grants to specific research projects	All students		Semi-annually
University of Wisconsin-Superior, Superior, WI 54880	Varied	Candidates with Bachelors degree and competitive portfolio	Academic year	Annually Deadline Mar. 15
	Varied	Undergrads, based upon class rank or portfolio. Must have a high school diploma or equivalent		
University of Wyoming, Art Dept, PO Box 3138, University Station, Laramie, WY 82071	$13,000	Continuing art majors	One year	Annually
Valley City State College, College St, Art Department, Valley City, ND 58072	$100-$500	Any full time art major	One year	Annually
Ventura College, Fine Arts Division, 4667 Telegraph Rd, Ventura CA 93003	Variable	Ventura College Art Students only		Annually
Vincennes University, Art Dept, 1002 N. First St, Vincennes, IN 47591	$4500		One year	Semi-annually
Virginia Museum of Fine Arts, Boulevard & Grove, Richmond, VA 23221	Student $2000, Graduate $4000, VM Professional $2500, VCA Professional $8000	Virginians who have lived in the state for at least five of the last ten years	One year	Annually, Deadline Mar. 5
Waldorf College, Art Department, Forest City, IA 50436	$250 up	Art majors, based on ability & need	Two year	Annually
Washington and Lee University, Dept of Fine Arts, Lexington, VA 24450	Varies according to need	Art majors, college men only	One year (renewable up to four years)	Annually
Wayland Baptists University, Division of Christian Communication Arts, Box 249, 1900 W. Seventh, Plainview, TX 79072	Variable	Everyone majoring or minoring in art	Two semesters	Annually
	Ted Bell Memorial Art Award, $25-$200	Everyone minoring in art	Semester	Annually
Weber State College, Art Department 2001, Ogden, UT 84408	Tuition waiver	All art majors	One year	Annually
Webster College, 470 E. Lockwood, St Louis, MO 63119	Varied	Freshmen-senior art majors	One year	Semi-annually
Wenatchee Valley College, Art Dept, 1300 5th St, Wenatchee, WA 98801	$371 (3 quarters) (4)	Best qualified applicants		

OFFERED BY	AMOUNT	OPEN TO	DURATION	WHEN OFFERED
Wesleyan College, Forsyth Rd, Macon, GA 31297	Varied	Any female who has made application and submits a portofolio	Until student leaves Wesleyan	Annually, before June
Western Illinois University Art Department, West Adams, Macomb, IL 61455	Varied	Graduate applicants with required credentials	One to one and a half years plus summer	Annually or semi-annually
	Varied	Students matriculating or new students with outstanding records or portfolios	Varies with availability	Annually or semi-annually
Western Michigan University, Art Department, Kalamazoo, MI 45004	$300 (College of Fine Arts), $100-$500 (Dept), $4000 total	All students majoring in art	One year	Annually
Western Montana College, Art Dept, 710 S. Atlantic, Dillon, MT 59725	$100	A promising art student in second, third or fourth year at WMC	One year	Annually
	$1000 (16)	Any promising art student	One year	Annually
Western Wyoming College Art Department, Rock Springs, WY 82901	Tuition	High school graduates with strong interest in the arts	One semester	Annually
West Georgia College, Art Department, Carrollton, GA 30117	$4000	Art majors	One year	Annually
	Andre Scholarship-$400	Art majors	One year	Annually
West Liberty State College, Art Dept, Hall of Fine Arts, West Liberty, WV 26074	Tuition scholarship	Graduating high school seniors who plan to be art majors at WLSC	Four years	Annually
West Shore Community College, Div. of Humanities of Fine Arts, 3000 N. Stiles Rd, Scottville, MI 49454	Tuition	Qualified full-time talented art students	One year	Annually
West Texas State University, Department of Art, Box 207, WT Station, Canyon, TX 79016	Up to $500	High School seniors, transfer students and graduate students	One year	Annually
West Virginia University, Division of Art, Morgantown, WV 26506	$2592	MFA degree students	One year (renewable)	Annually
Whitney Museum of American Art, Independent Study Program, 384 Broadway, 4th floor, New York, NY 10013	$3300 Helena Rubenstein Fellowships (10) & tuition $900	Students of outstanding academic achievement	Two semesters	Annually
	$900 and full tuition available studio program (15)	Graduates and advanced undergraduates	One semester	Biannually
Williams College, Department of Art, Williamstown, MA 01267	$3000 Hubbard Hutchinson Memorial Scholarship	Williams senior for two years of graduate work	Two years at $3000 a year	Annually
	Florence & Horace Mayer Scholarship	Williams student majoring in art or music	One year (may be extended second year)	Annually
	Edith Weston Andrews Scholarship	Williams student majoring in art or music	One year (may be extended second year)	Annually
	Beatrice Stone Scholarship	Williams student majoring in art or music	One year (may be extended second year)	Annually
William Woods College, Fulton, MO 65251	$1000	Art majors	One year	Annually
Windward Artists Guild, PO Box 851, Kailua, HI 96734	$100	High school students of Windward Oahu		Annually
Henry Francis du Pont Winterthur Museum, Winterthur, DE 19735	Variable	Graduate students in art conservation, connoisseurship, American culture, and American art history	Two or three years	Annually
	NEH Research Fellowships variable to $15,000	Scholars of American material culture	Six-eleven months	Annually
	$1000 short-term residential fellowships	Scholars of American material culture	One-two months	Annually
Wittenberg University, Art Dept, Crabill Art Center, Springfield, OH 45501	Variable	All art students	One year	Annually
Catherine Lorillard Wolfe Art Club, 802 Broadway, New York, NY 10003	Variable	Art Students League and National School of Design students	One year	Annually
Woodstock School of Art, PO Box 338, Woodstock, NY 12498	Variable	All who qualify by reason of merit and need	Five months	Annually

OFFERED BY	AMOUNT	OPEN TO	DURATION	WHEN OFFERED
Worcester Craft Center, 25 Sagamore Rd, Worcester, MA 01605	Varies	Second year students in professional craft studio program	One year	Annually
	Varies	Second year students in professional craft studio program	One year	Annually
Wright State University, Dept of Art and Art History, Dayton, OH 45435	Variable, $350 minimum	Art majors	Variable, one year minimum	Annually
Helene Wurlitzer Foundation of New Mexico, Box 545, Taos, NM 87571	Resident program provides free studio rent (12)	Any artist in all media & allied fields, creative, not interpretive	Six months	
Yale Center for British Art, Yale University, 1080 Chapel St, PO Box 2120 Yale Station, New Haven, CT 06520	Short term visiting fellowships	Established scholars in the field of British art history		
	Andrew W Mellon Fellowship, $7000 plus travel	Predoctoral candidate from the United Kingdom	One year	
	Graduate fellowship $7000	Predoctoral candidate from Yale to spend one year in the United Kingdom		
Yale University, School of Art, 180 York St, New Haven, CT 06520	Variable	Eligible MFA students	Academic year	Annually, deadline Mar. 1
Yard School of Art, 99 S. Fullerton Ave, Montclair, NJ, 07042	$350	Talented physically handicapped talented children	One year	Anytime
Young Harris College, Department of Art, Young Harris, GA 30582	$420 (4)	Art majors	One year	Annually
Joseph Young/Art in Architecture, 7917½ W Norton Ave, Los Angeles, CA 90046	Tuition-free grant	Qualified students who enroll and study with Joseph Young	One year	Annually
Xavier University, Dept of Art, Cincinnati, OH 45206	$1760-$4200	Graduating high school seniors	Four years	Annually

Open Exhibitions

National, Regional and State-Wide

ALABAMA

BIRMINGHAM BIENNIAL, Birmingham. Biennial, Sept-Nov. All visual art. Open to Ala, Ga, La, Miss, SC artists. Juried, $5000 in cash awards. Entry slides due Jan 15. For further information write Kathleen O'Brien, Birmingham Art Assoc, 2000 Eighth Ave, North, Birmingham, AL 32203.

ALASKA

ALL ALASKA JURIED ART EXHIBITION. Anchorage, annual, Feb. All graphic media (including photography) and sculpture. Open to Alaska residents only. Cash awards. No fee. Limit four entries. Anchorage Historical & Fine Arts Museum, 121 W Seventh Ave, Anchorage, AK 99501.

EARTH, FIRE AND FIBRE statewide juried craft annual. Anchorage, Oct-Nov. All craft media. Open to Alaska residents only. Cash awards. No fee. Limit four entries. Anchorage Historical and Fine Arts Museum, 121 W Seventh Ave, Anchorage, AK 99501.

ARIZONA

ANNUAL NORTHLIGHT SOUTHWEST GALLERY FOUR CORNERS EXHIBITION, Tempe. Annual, Jan-Feb. Photographs. Open to artists in AZ, CO, UT, NM, and TX. Juried, purchase awards. Fee $15 per portfolio. Entries due Nov. For further information write Northlight Gallery, Arizona State University, Art Dept, Tempe, AZ 85281.

CONTEMPORARY REALISM, Scottsdale. Oct-Nov. Paintings & sculpture. Open to Ariz, Calif, Colo, NMex & Tex artists. Juried, cash awards. Fee $20 per 4 slides. Entry slides due Aug 15. For further information write Lee Brotherton, Leslie Levy Gallery, 7141 Main St, Scottsdale, AZ 85251.

DOUGLAS ART ASSOCIATION TWO FLAGS ART FESTIVAL. Annual. Juried show is now international. Open to artists of any country. Fee $7.50 per entry. Limit two entries. Cash awards $1500. Deadline Mar 27. Show opens Apr 6 and ends May 7, 1984. Acceptable media are painting, drawing, graphics, batik, and mixed media. No photography. For further information write Douglas Art Association, Box 3552, Douglas, AZ 85607.

HEARD MUSEUM GUILD, Phoenix. Annual, Nov. All original arts & crafts. Open to Indians of NAm, Indian students & those of Indian descent. Cash awards & ribbons. Fee 20% comn. Entry forms & work due Oct. For further information write Chmn, Heard Museum Guild Indian Arts & Crafts Exhibit, 22 E Monte Vista Rd, Phoenix, AZ 85004.

SCOTTSDALE ARTS FESTIVAL, Scottsdale. Annual, March. Any media. Juried. Entry slides due Dec 1. For further information write Scottsdale Center for the Arts, 7383 Scottsdale Mall, Scottsdale, AZ 85251.

ARKANSAS

ARKANSAS ARTS CENTER DELTA ART EXHIBITION, Little Rock. Annual, Oct-Nov. All paintings & sculpture (not over 500 pounds). Open to artists born in or residing in Ark, La, Miss, Mo, Okla, Tenn & Tex. Juried by slides, $2000 First Award, $3000 purchase awards. Fee $7.50 per entry, limit two. For further information write Townsend Wolfe, The Arkansas Arts Center, MacArthur Park, PO Box 2137, Little Rock, AR 72203.

ARKANSAS ARTS CENTER PRINTS, DRAWINGS & CRAFTS EXHIBITION, Little Rock. Annual, May-June. Prints in all media; drawings in all media; photographs in color and/or monochrome; crafts in metal, clay, textile, glass, wood, plastics & combined media. Open to artists born in or residing in Ark, La, Miss, Mo, Okla, Tenn & Tex. Juried by object, awards & $2000 purchase prizes. Fee $7.50 for each entry, limit two. Dates for entry cards and work due to be announced. For further information write Townsend Wolfe, Director, the Arkansas Arts Center, MacArthur Park, PO Box 2137, Little Rock, AR 72203.

ARKANSAS ARTS CENTER TOYS DESIGNED BY ARTISTS EXHIBITION, Little Rock. Annual, Dec-Jan. Toys in all media. Open to all artists residing in the U.S. $1000 in purchase awards. Fee $7.50 per entry, limit 3. Jury. Dates for entry cards and work due to be announced. For further information write Townsend Wolfe, Director, The Arkansas Arts Center, MacArthur Park, PO Box 2137, Little Rock, AR 72203.

CALIFORNIA

ALL-CALIFORNIA BIENNIAL COMPETITION, Riverside. Biennial, Feb-Mar. Drawings, graphics, mixed media, paintings, photography, prints, textiles & water colors. Open to Calif artists. Juried, cash & one person exhibit awards. Fee $5 per entry, limit 3. Entry slides due Jan 4. For further information write Riverside Art Center & Museum, 3425 7th St, Riverside, CA 92501.

ALL MEDIA JURIED COMPETITION, Brea. Annual, Oct-Nov. All media. Juried, $1600 in cash awards. Fee $5 members, $10 nonmembers. Entries due Sept 30. For further information write OCAA, PO Box 3279, Fullerton, CA 92634.

ALL MEDIA JURIED EXHIBITION, San Diego. Annual, Sept-Oct. All media. Open to San Diego County artists. Juried, $400 in awards & three-person exhibits. Fee $5 per entry, limit 3. Entries due Sept 3. For further information write Graduate School for Community Development, 568 Fifth Ave, San Diego, CA 92101.

ANNUAL ART EXHIBIT, Santa Paula. Annual, Aug. Oil, water color, pastel, graphics & prints. Juried, $1200 in cash awards. Fee $5 per entry, limit 4. Entries due July 30. For further information write Santa Paula Area Chamber of Commerce, PO Box 1, Santa Paula, CA 93060.

ANNUAL JURIED EXHIBITION, San Diego. Annual, Oct. Drawings, graphics, mixed media, painting, photography, prints, sculpture & water color. Open to Calif artists. Juried, $1700 in awards. Fee $15, limit 2. Entries due Sept 13. For further information write San Diego Art Institute, 1449 El Prado, Balboa Park, San Diego, CA 92101.

BRANDON 83 SMALL WORKS, Fallbrook. Nov. Drawings, mixed media, painting, photography, prints, sculpture & water color. Juried, $1000 in awards. Fee $5 per entry, $10 for 3 entries. Entries due Oct 29. For further information write Brandon Gallery, 119 N Main St, Fallbrook, CA 92028.

BURBANK ART EXHIBITION, Burbank. Annual, Sept. Drawing, graphics, mixed media, painting, photography, prints, sculpture & water color. $2000 cash & purchase awards. Fee $5 per entry nonmembers, $3 per entry members. Entries due Sept 2. Creative Arts Center, PO Box 6459, Burbank, CA 91510.

CALIFORNIA WOMEN ARTISTS, San Luis Obispo. Mar. Painting, water color, photography, prints, graphics & sculpture. Open to Calif women. Juried, 3 purchase awards. Fee $10, limit 5. Entry slides due Jan 1. For further information write Fine Arts Committee, ASI, Calif Polytech State Univ, San Luis Obispo, CA 93407.

CENTRAL CALIFORNIA BIENNIAL COMPETITIVE 83, Pacific Grove. Biennial, Feb-Mar. Painting, water color, graphics, textile, sculpture & mixed media. Open to Montery, San Luis Obispo, Santa Clara, Santa Cruz & San Benito County artists. Juried, $1000 in cash awards. Fee $7.50, limit 2. Entry slides due Dec 31. For further information write Pacific Grove Art Center, PO Box 633, Pacific Grove, CA 93950.

CONTEMPORARY AMERICAN FIBERS, Redding. Mar-Apr. Fiber arts & textiles. Open to US artists. Juried, $1500 in awards. Fee $4 per entry, limit 3. Entry slides due Feb 1. For further information write John Harper, Redding Museum, PO Box 427, Redding, CA 96099.

CREATIVE ARTS CENTER JURIED EXHIBITION, Chico. Oct-Nov. Ceramics, drawing, mixed media, painting, prints, sculpture, textiles, water color & glass. Open to Calif artists. Juried, $500 in cash & purchase awards. Fee $5 per entry, limit 2. Entry slides due Sept 12. For further information write Rob Wilson, Creative Arts Center, PO Box 824, Chico, CA 95927.

DELONGPRE SHOW, Hollywood. Nov. Drawings, graphics, mixed media, paintings, photography & water color using Hollywood imagery. Open to continental US artists. Juried, $1000 in purchase awards & certificates of merit. Fee $5 per entry. Entry slides due Sept 30. For further information write Delonpre Show, c/o Hollywood Heritage, PO Box 2586, Hollywood, CA 90078.

DIABLO ART ASSOCIATION, Walnut Creek. Oct. Oils, acrylics, water color & mixed media. Juried, cash awards. Fee $5, limit 3. Entries due Sept 23. For further information write Diablo Art Association, Box 4124, Walnut Creek, CA 94596.

EASTBAY WATERCOLOR SOCIETY, Moraga. Annual, July-Aug. Watermedia on paper. Juried. Fee $6 per entry non-members, $4.50 per entry members, limit 2. Entries due July 9. For further information write Marianne Brown, 245 Rheem Blvd, Moraga, CA 94556.

EIGHTH NATIONAL EXHIBITION, Los Angeles. Mar-Apr. Prints. Open to US & Canada artists. Juried, $4000 in purchase awards. Fee $15 non-members, $10 members. Entries due Dec 15. For further information write LA Printmaking Society, Klein Art Dept, LA Valley College, 5800 Fulton Ave, Van Nuys, CA 91401.

EVIDENCE OF LIGHT, Santa Ana. Oct-Nov. Photography. Juried, purchase awards. Fee $5 per entry. Entries due Oct 11. For further information write Evidence of Light, Santa Ana College, 17th at Bristol, Santa Ana, CA 92706.

FAIRFIELD VISUAL ARTS COMMITTEE, Fairfield. Nov. All media. Juried, $1500 in cash & purchase awards. Fee $3.50 per entry. Entries due Nov 14. For further information write Fairfield Community Center, 1000 Kentucky St, Fairfield, CA 94533.

FIBERWORKS, CENTER FOR THE TEXTILE ARTS, Berkeley. Textile or related. Juried, awards. For further information write to Fiberworks, Center for the Textile Arts, 1940 Bonita, Berkeley, CA 94704.

FIRST OPEN GRAPHICS COMPETITION, El Granada. Annual, Nov-Dec. Graphics. Juried. Fee $5 per entry. Entries due Nov 2. For further information write Coastal Arts League, PO Box 1322, El Granada, CA 94038.

GOLD COUNTRY 1983, Auburn. Nov. Drawings, graphics, paintings, sculpture, water color, ceramics & textile. Juried, $600 in awards. Fee $5 per entry, limit 3. Entries due Nov 5. For further information write Placer Arts League, Gallery One, PO Box 3386, Auburn, CA 95603

INK AND CLAY, Pomona. Annual, for California artists only. Prints, drawings, ceramic ware or sculpture. Juried, purchase awards. Fee $8 for one or two entries. For further information write Art Department, California State Polytechnic University, 3801 W Temple Ave, Pomona, CA 91768.

MODERN ROMANCES: IMAGERY OF MEN & WOMEN TOGETHER IN BAY AREA PAINTING, Arcata. Jan-Feb. Painting & water color. Open to San Francisco Bay Area artists. Entry slides due Sept 17. For further information write Suzaan Boettger, 562 Merritt Ave, Oakland, CA 94610.

MOUNT SAN JACINTO JURIED OPEN, San Jacinto. Jan-Feb. Paintings. Open to Calif, Ore, Ariz, Nev & Baja Calif artists. Juried, $2500 in awards. Fee $10 per piece, limit 2. Entries due Nov 12. For further information write Carolyn Kaneshiro, MSJC Art Dept, 21400 Highway 79, San Jacinto, CA 92383.

OLIVE HYDE ART GALLERY ANNUAL TEXTILE COMPETITION. Annual, May 2-June 3. Textiles. Open to any artist working in predominately fiber media. Juried, awards. Fee $4 per item, limit 3. Work must be hand delivered. For further information write Olive Hyde Art Gallery, City of Fremont, Community Services Department, PO Box 5006, Fremont, CA 94538.

OPEN FINE ARTS COMPETITION, Costa Mesa. Annual, Sept. Ceramics, drawing, graphics, mixed media, painting, photography, prints, sculpture & water color. Juried, $1000 in cash awards. Fee $5 per entry, $3 per entry Costa Mesa Art League, limit 3. Entries due Sept 12. For further information write CMAL, PO Box 1727, Costa Mesa, CA 92626.

OPEN JURIED SHOW, Sacramento. Annual, Nov. All media. Open to Calif & Nev artists. Juried, $5 per entry. Entries due Oct 30. For further information write Robert Ransom, 8920 Glen Alder, Sacramento, CA 95826.

ORANGE COUNTY ART ASSOCIATION, Brea. Annual, Oct 5-Nov 12. All media, contemporary emphasis. Open to all artists. Juried, 3 or more cash prizes. Fee members $5 each entry, non-member $10 each entry. Entries due Sept 15. For further information write to OCAA, 2036 N Main, Santa Ana, CA 92706.

PACIFIC ART GUILD ANNUAL FALL EXHIBIT, Los Angeles. Annual, Oct-Nov. Drawing, graphics, mixed media, painting, prints, water color with 48 inch max. Juried, $550 in cash awards. Fee $4.50 per entry. Entries due Oct 17. For further information write Pacific Art Guild, PO Box 90404, Los Angeles, CA 90009.

PACIFIC RIM, USE, JURIED PRINT SHOW, Rancho Palos Verdes. Dec-Jan. Prints. Open to Alaska, Calif, Hawaii, Ore & Wash artists. Juried, $1000 in awards. Fee $12, limit 2. Entry slides due Oct 7. For further information write Palos Verdes Art Center, 5504 W Crestridge Rd, Rancho Palos Verdes, CA 90274.

JAMES D PHELAN ART AWARD IN VIDEO, San Francisco. Open to Calif born video artists between 20 & 40 years of age. $10,000 in cash awards. Entries due Aug 31. For further information write Phelan Art Award in Video, 1111 - 17th St, San Francisco, CA 94107.

PHOTOGRAPHY JURIED ART EXHIBITION, San Diego. Annual, Nov-Dec. Photography. Open to San Diego County artists. Juried, $400 in awards. Fee $5 per entry, limit 3. Entries due Oct 29. For further information write Graduate School for Community Development, 568 5th Ave, San Diego, CA 92101.

PLACEMENT/DISPLACEMENT, Aptos. Mar. Three-dimensional art no larger than 48 inches any direction. Open to north Calif artists. Juried. Fee $5 for 3 slides. Entry slides due Jan 14. For further information write Cabrillo College Gallery, 6500 Soquel Dr, Aptos, CA 95003.

RELIGIOUS ART FESTIVAL, Sacramento. Annual, Oct. All media. Juried, $1200 in awards. Fee $3.50 per entry, limit 3. Entries due Oct 15. For further information write Saint Johns Lutheran Church, 1701 L St, Sacramento, CA 95814.

SADDLEBACK COLLEGE ART GALLERY PHOTOGRAPHY EXHIBITION, Mission Viejo. Nov-Dec. Photography. Open to San Diego to Santa Barbara artists. Juried, purchase & cash awards. Fee $5 per entry, limit 3. Entries due Oct 30. For further information write William Riley, Saddleback College, 2800 Marguerite Parkway, Mission Viejo, CA 92692.

SAN BERNARDINO ART ASSOCIATION INLAND EXHIBITION. Annual, Oct. Oil, acrylic, watercolor, mixed, collage, graphics (no sculpture or photography). Open to all California artists. Cash awards & purchase awards. Fee $5 per entry, limit 3, 30% comn. Entry cards & work due Sept 29. For further information write San Bernardino Art Association, PO Box 2272, San Bernardino, CA 92406.

SAN FRANCISCO ANNUAL ARTS FESTIVAL. Open to artists of the nine Bay Area counties. For further information write Claire Isaacs, Arts Commission—City and County of San Francisco, 45 Hyde St, San Francisco, CA 94102.

SANTA CRUZ ART LEAGUE. Annual, Apr. Oil, watercolor & mixed media, representational art only. Open to all Calif residents. Jury. Fee $5 per entry, limit three in each medium. For further information write Santa Cruz Art League, 526 Broadway, Santa Cruz, CA 95060.

TRADITIONAL ARTISTS ANNUAL EXHIBITION, Redlands. Annual, Nov-Dec. Representational painting, watercolor, drawing, graphics, sculpture. To be held in San Bernardino County Museum. Juried. Fee $5 per entry, limit 3. For further information write Exhibition Chairman, San Bernardino County Museum, 2022 Orange Tree Lane, Redlands, CA 92373.

2-D NATIONAL 83, San Pedro. Apr-May. 2-D, with max 50 inches including frame. Open to North American artists. Juried, $500 in purchase awards. Fee $5, limit 3. Entry slides due Feb 1. For further information write Angels Gate Cultural Center, 3701 S Gaffey St, San Pedro, CA 90731.

UCLA NATIONAL STUDENT PRINT EXHIBITION, Los Angeles. Mar-Apr. All prints, non-silver photo media & Xerox. Open to US currently enrolled grad or undergrad students. Juried, $500 in awards. Fee $8 for 2 slides. Entry slides due Jan 21. For further information write National Student Print Exhibition, Art Dept, UCLA, 405 Hilgard, Los Angeles, CA 90024.

VESSELS AESTHETIC 1983, Taft. Mar. Ceramics, must allude to vessels form. Juried, purchase merit awards. Fee $7.50. Entry slides due Jan 6. For further information write Jack Mettier, Dir, Taft College Art Gallery, 505 Kern St, Taft, CA 93268.

VISIONARY ART SHOW, San Jose. Annual, Oct. Painting & graphics (metaphysical, spiritual, fantasy, futurist & mystical). Juried, $250 in awards. Fee $5 per entry, limit 5. Entries due Oct 7. For further information write Second Annual Visionary Art, PO Box 997, San Jose, CA 95108.

WCA MEMBERSHIP EXHIBITION, Belmont. Annual, Sept-Nov. All media. Open to Women's Caucus for Art members. Juried, cash awards. Hanging fee $10 per entry. Entry slides due July 22. For further information write Annual Juried Membership, Jeri Robertson, 4536 Grove #1, Oakland, CA 94609.

WCA MEMBERSHIP EXHIBITION, Emeryville. Feb. Drawings, graphics, mixed media, painting, photography, prints, sculpture, textiles & water colors. Open to north Calif WCA members. Juried. Fee $20 for membership. Entries due Jan 7. For further information write WCA, PO Box 8224, Emeryville, CA 94662.

COLORADO

ARTISTS ALPINE HOLIDAY & FESTIVAL, Ouray. Annual, Aug. Painting, sculpture, mixed media, graphics, fiber & photography. Open to US artists. Cash awards & ribbons. Fee $4 per entry. For further information write Ouray County Arts Assoc, PO Box 167, Ouray, CO 81427.

ARTS 82, Boulder. Annual, Oct-Nov. All media. Open to Colo artists. Juried, cash awards & prizes. Fee $12 non-members, $8 members. Entries due June 5. For further information write Boulder Center for the Visual Arts, 1750 13th St, Boulder, CO 80302.

BLACK CANYON ART EXHIBIT, Hotchkiss. June. Oil, graphics, water color & mixed media. Judged, cash awards. Fee $6 per artist, limit 2 paintings & 1 special area. For further information write North Fork Council on Arts & Humanities, Box 686, Hotchkiss, CO 81419.

BRUSH & PALETTE CLUB NATIONAL ART EXHIBITION, Grand Junction. Annual, July-Aug. Oil, water color, mixed, pastel & graphics. Open to all artists. Cash & purchase awards. Fee $6 per entry, limit 2. Entries due July 1. For further information write Brush & Palette, Box 3632, Grand Junction, CO 81502.

CHILDREN'S DIABETES ART COMPETITION, Denver. Annual, May-June. Open to Colo artists. Juried, $5000 in cash awards. Entry slides due Apr 30. For further information write Sally Chase, Coordr, Children's Diabetes Foundation, 700 Delaware, Denver, CO 80204.

COLORADO SPRINGS FINE ARTS EXHIBITION, Colorado Springs. Aug-Sept. Printing, drawings, water color, mixed media & sculpture. Open to Colo artists. Fee $5 per entry, limit 3. Entries due June 17. For further information write Colorado Springs Fine Arts Center, 30 W Dale St, Colorado Springs, CO 80903.

COPPER MOUNTAIN FINE ARTS FESTIVAL, Copper Mountain. Sept 1. Painting, photography & sculpture. Juried. Fee $35 indoor, $25 outdoor. Entries due July 1. For further information write Copper Mountain Resort, PO Box 3003, Copper Mountain, CO 80443.

EAGLES: OUR HERITAGE-PAST & FUTURE, Denver. Sept-Oct. Painting, drawing, sculpture, woodcarving, prints, photography & mixed media. Fee $10, limit 3. For further information write White Face Bear, Ltd, A Wildlife Gallery, 605 Ogden St, Denver, CO 80218.

FINE ARTS LEAGUE, NATIONAL ART SHOW, La Junta. May. Photography, graphics, sculpture & photography. Juried. Fee $6 non-members, $4 members, limit 2. Entries due Apr 24. For further information write Fine Arts League, PO Box 55, La Junta, CO 81050.

FOOTHILLS ART CENTER/ENERGY ART EXHIBITION, Golden. Annual, held March 20 - April 24. Painting, sculpture, drawings, photography, fibers, prints, paper. Open to artists in US, Canada, Mexico. Juried, $15,000 cash awards. Fee $10 per entry, limit of 3, by colored slides. Entries due Jan 4. For further information write to Foothills Art Center, 809 15th St, Golden, CO 80401.

GILPIN COUNTY ARTS ASSOCIATION EXHIBITION, Central City. June-Sept. Painting, sculpture, crafts & photography. Open to Colo artists. Fee $6 per entry. For further information write Gilpin County Arts Assoc, Box 98, Central City, CO 80427.

LONGMONT REGIONAL SPRING ART SHOW, Longmont. Juried, ribbons & cash awards. Limit 3. Entries due May 1. For further information write Sandy Schlagel, 1444 Sumac, Longmont, CO 80501.

WESTERN ART RENDEZVOUS, Littleton. Annual, Oct-Nov. Drawing, painting, graphics, sculpture & photography. Open to Colo residents. Limit 3. Entries due Sept 30. For further information write Mountain Side Art Guild, 1681 S Deframe Court, Lakewood, CO 80228.

WESTERN SLOPE NATIONAL ART EXHIBITION, Montrose. Apr-May. Oil, water media, graphics, sculpture & photography. Juried, cash & purchase awards. Fee $4 & 15% per item, limit 3. Entries due Apr 10. For further information write Gallery Artists, PO Box 2044, Montrose, CO 81402.

CONNECTICUT

CELEBRATION OF AMERICAN CRAFTS, New Haven. Annual, Nov-Dec. Crafts. Open to US artists. Juried. Entries due Aug 1. For further information write Creative Arts Workshop, 80 Audubon St, New Haven, CT 06511.

HUDSON VALLEY ART ASSOCIATION, INC, White Plains. Annual, first week of May. School of realism only; oil, watercolors, graphics, sculpture, pastels. Open to all artists, over 18 years, in this school of art. Double juried show, juried for selection and prizes, monetary and gold medals (not in pastels) in each media. Fee $20 (fee subject to change). Entries due week prior to exhibition. For further information write Joan Rudman, 274 Quarry Road, Stamford, CT 06903.

NEW HAVEN PAINT AND CLAY CLUB. Annual, Mar-Apr. Oil, watercolor, acrylic, graphics & sculpture. Open to artists from the New England states & NY. Prizes & purchase awards. Fee $8 for first entry, $6 for second, 15% comn. Entry cards & work due Mar 2. For further information write NHP & C Club Secretary, 51 Trumbull St, New Haven, CT 06510.

SILVERMINE GUILD CENTER FOR THE ARTS NATIONAL PRINT EXHIBITION, New Canaan. Biennial Oct-Nov. All print media. Open to all artists. Jury, purchase prizes. Fee $12 first entry, $6 second entry, two works per artist allowed. For further information write Exhib Secy, Silvermine Guild Center for the Arts 1037 Silvermine Rd, New Canaan, CT 06840.

SLATER MEMORIAL MUSEUM, Norwich. Annual, Mar-Apr. Sculpture, painting, drawing and prints. Open to all resident Conn artists. Jury, prizes. Fee $6 per piece, limit two; sculpture limited to 200 pounds. For further information write The Slater Memorial Museum, 108 Crescent St. Norwich, CT 06360.

WINTONBURY ART LEAGUE, Bloomfield. Annual, Jun. Painting, drawings, sculpture, graphics, photography & mixed media. Juried, cash & purchase awards. Fee $6 for one entry, $10 for 2. Entries due May 27. For further information write Wintonbury Art League, 9 Fox Chase Rd, Bloomfield, CT 06002.

DELAWARE

DELAWARE ART MUSEUM'S CONTEMPORARY CRAFTS EXHIBITION, Wilmington. Biennial, Dec-Jan. Ceramics, fibers, metals, plastics, wood, leather, and glass; must be original designs executed by the entrants. Open to craftsmen in Delaware and Northeastern US (includes Md, DC, NJ, Pa, NY, and New England). Juried by slides, with cash prizes awarded by judges and purchase prize made by the Museum. Fee; limit of three works per person. For further information contact Lial A Jones, Education Department, Delaware Art Museum, 2301 Kentmere Parkway, Wilmington, DE 19806. Phone: (302) 571-9594.

DISTRICT OF COLUMBIA

ANNUAL EXHIBITION, MINIATURE SOCIETY OF WASHINGTON, DC. Annual, Nov. Painting, graphics, sculpture, carving, & non-traditional, 5 x 8 inches, including frame, sculpture limited to 8 inches. Cash awards. Fee, nonmembers, $15 for 3 entries. Entries due first week of Sept. For further information write Margaret Wisdon, 5812 Massachusetts Ave, NW, Washington, DC 20816.

GOLDEN AGE OF FLIGHT, Washington. Apr-Sept. All 2-D except photography. Juried, $10,000 in awards. No fee. Entries due Dec 17. For further information write Golden Age of Flight Art Contest, National Air & Space Museum, Smithsonian Institution, Washington, DC 20560.

FLORIDA

BOYNTON'S G.A.L.A. (Great American Love Affair), Boynton Beach. Annual, held first weekend in Mar. Paintings, sculpture, drawings, graphics, photography, contemporary crafts. Open to all original artwork, professional. Juried, submit three slides, over $3000 in prizes and ribbons. Fee $45. Entries due February 15. For further information write Eleanor Krusell, PO Box 232, Boynton, FL 33425.

FLORIDA GULF COAST ANNUAL JURIED COMPETITION, Clearwater. Annual. Media & details change annually. For further information write Florida Gulf Coast Art Center, 222 Ponce de Leon Blvd, Belleair, FL 33516.

GLASS THAT WORKS, Miami. May-July. Functional glass. Juried, $2750 in awards. Fee $100 for manufacturers & design firms, $50 for professionals & nonprofessional, $10 students. Entries due Nov 30. For further information write Intercon Arts Inc, 4225 Lennox Dr, Miami, FL 33133.

HALIFAX ART FESTIVAL, Ormond Beach. Nov. Painting, oil, acrylic, watercolor, drawing, graphics, crafts, sculpture, jewelry, photography & ceramics. $8900 in cash awards. Fee $50, limit 3 slides per category. Entries due Aug 8. For further information write Museum of Arts & Science Guild, Halifax Art Festival, Artist Contact, Box 504, Ormond Beach, FL 32074.

MIAMI BEACH OUTDOOR FESTIVAL OF THE ARTS, Miami Beach. Annual, Feb. All media. $25,000 in awards. Fee $125. Entry slides due Dec 1. For further information write Miami Beach Fine Arts Board, PO Bin O, Miami Beach, FL 33119.

SOCIETY OF THE FOUR ARTS EXHIBITION OF CONTEMPORARY AMERICAN PAINTINGS, Palm Beach. Annual, Dec. Oils, watercolor, drawings, mixed, & flat collages completed since Jan. Open to artists residing in the US. $6000 cash awards. Fee $5, limit 2 entries (fee refunded if entry accepted); comn 10%. Specific dates on which entry cards & work are due are announced in prospectus available upon request in Sept. For further information write The Society of the Four Arts, Four Arts Plaza, Palm Beach, FL 33480.

TRANSPARENT WATERCOLOR SHOW, Panama City. Annual, Feb. $2000 in cash awards. Fee $5 per entry non-member, $4 per entry members. Entries due Jan. 31. For further information write Marina Auditorium, 10 Harrison Ave, Panama City, FL 32401.

GEORGIA

ATLANTA PLAYHOUSE THEATRE AND GEORGIA TECH STUDENT INTERNATIONAL DOGWOOD FESTIVAL ART SHOW, Atlanta. Annual, Mar-Apr (Atlanta Dogwood Festival). Any hanging work of art suitable; oils, tempera, drawings, graphics, sculptures, collages, textiles, sculpture, and photography. Open to all artists in the US/international. Juried by slides, judged for awards, with purchase awards and prizes. Fee $10. Entries due February. For further information write Ida S Borochoff, Artistic Director, Atlanta Playhouse Theatre, Ltd, 3450 Old Plantation Rd NW, Atlanta, GA 30327.

NCECA JURIED MEMBERS' EXHIBITION, Atlanta. Feb-Mar. Ceramics. Open to NCECA members. Juried. Entry slides due Nov 15. For further information write Lenny Dowhie, Indiana State Univ, Evansville, Art Dept, 8600 University Blvd, Evansville, IN 47712.

WESLEYAN INTERNATIONAL EXHIBITION OF PRINTS & DRAWINGS, Macon. Jan-Feb. All print & drawings media including collage, no photography. Open to US, Mexico & Canada artists. Juried, $5000 in purchase awards. Fee $12, limit 3. Entry slides due Oct 29. For further information write Linda Bitley, Museum of Arts & Sciences, 4182 Forsyth Rd, Macon, GA 31210.

HAWAII

ARTISTS OF HAWAII, Honolulu. Annual, Dec. All-media. Open to all artists residing in Hawaii. Juried. Fee $3 per entry, limited to three. Slide entries due by Oct 14. For further information write Selden Washington, Asst Dir, Honolulu Academy of Arts, 900 S Beretania St, Honolulu, HI 96814.

1983 PACIFIC STATES PRINT & DRAWING EXHIBITION, Hilo. Mar-Apr. Print & drawing, no photography or offset. Open to Hawaii, Alaska, Wash, Ore & Calif artists. Juried, $2000 in purchase awards. Fee $15, limit 2. Entries due Feb 18. For further information write William Ledenthal, Student Activities Council, Univ Hawaii, Hilo, 1400 Kapiolani St, Hilo, HI 96720.

IDAHO

WORLD OF ART, Pocatello. Oct. Fine arts. Juried. Fee $45. For further information write Don Palmer, PO Box 339, Stanton, CA 90680.

ILLINOIS

ART INSTITUTE OF CHICAGO, Chicago & Vicinity Artists Exhibition. Annual, alternating painting/sculpture & work on paper, not over 9x5x4 (3-D) & 10x6 (2-D). Open to artists, 18 & over, legal residents of 130 mile radius of Chicago. Juried, awards. No fee. For further information write 20th Century Painting & Sculpture Dept, The Art Institute of Chicago, Michigan & Adams, Chicago, IL 60603.

19TH BRADLEY NATIONAL PRINT & DRAWING EXHIBITION, Peoria. Feb-Mar. Prints & drawings. Open to US artists. Juried, $3000 in purchase awards. Fee $12, limit 3. Entries due Dec 1. For further information write Ruth Fraser, 19th Bradley National, Division of Art, Bradley Univ, Peoria, IL 61625.

NORTH SHORE ART LEAGUE NEW HORIZONS IN ART, Chicago. Biennial, May. Painting, sculpture, graphics, photog. Open to Ill artists. Cash awards, purchase awards & ribbons. Fee 20% comn. Entry cards & work due April 2. For further information write North Shore Art League, 620 Lincoln Ave, Winnetka, IL 60093.

7TH NATIONAL WATERCOLOR EXHIBITION, Springfield. Apr-June. Water colors. Open to US artists. Juried, purchase & merit awards. Entry slides due Feb 1. For further information write Springfield Art Assoc Gallery, 700 N Fourth St, Springfield, IL 62702.

SOCIETY OF TYPOGRAPHIC ARTS, STA 100, Chicago. Annual. Books, brochures, announcements, invitations, stationery, annual reports, house organs, calendars, catalogs, posters, manuals, corporate graphics, packages, logos and trademarks. Fee $15 per entry for non members, $10 per entry for members. Entry due April 1. For further information write STA 100, Society of Typographic Arts, 233 E Ontario, Suite 301, Chicago, IL 60611.

INDIANA

BALL STATE UNIVERSITY DRAWING & SMALL SCULPTURE SHOW, Muncie. Annual, Sept-Oct. Drawings & small sculpture. Open to all artists in the United States. One judge, awards. Sculptures judged preliminarily by slides which are due around June 1. Drawings must be sent to the Art Gallery for judging. Due end of July; actual date varies slightly from year to year also. For further information & prospectus write Art Gallery, Ball State University, Muncie, IN 47306.

EVANSVILLE MUSEUM OF ARTS & SCIENCE MID-STATES ART EXHIBITION. Annual, Nov. Painting, sculpture, watercolor, graphic arts, collage & mobiles (no photographs). Open to artists within a radius of 200 miles from Evansville or any resident of the State of Indiana. Juried, awards. Handling fee is $8 for one entry. Entries due in Sept. For further information write Art Comt, Evansville Museum of Arts & Science, 411 SE Riverside Dr, Evansville, IN 47713.

EVANSVILLE MUSEUM OF ARTS & SCIENCE MID-STATES CRAFT EXHIBITION. Annual, Feb. Ceramics, textiles, metal work, wood, enamel, glass & others. Open to artists within a radius of 200 miles from Evansville or any resident of the State of Indiana. Juried, awards. Fee $5 for two objects or less. Entries due Jan. For further information write Craft Comt, Evansville Museum of Arts & Science, 411 SE Riverside Dr, Evansville, IN 47713.

INDIANAPOLIS MUSEUM OF ART, INDIANA ARTISTS EXHIBITION. Biennial, June-July, 1985. Painting & sculpture, works on paper, textiles, wood, glass, ceramics, metalwork, and mixed media. Open to past or present Indiana residents. Preliminary review of slides. Juried, awards. Fee $5 per artist. For further information write Registrar, Indianapolis Museum of Art, 1200 W 38th St, Indianapolis, IN 46208.

WABASH VALLEY EXHIBITION, Terre Haute. Annual, March. All media. Open to artists within a 160 mile radius of Terre Haute. Juried, approx $8000 in prize money, including several Gallery acquisition awards. Fee $5 for first entry, $4 for second entry, $3 for third entry, limit of three. Entries due Feb 14. For further information write Curator, The Sheldon Swope Art Gallery, 25 S Seventh St, Terre Haute, IN 47807.

IOWA

A BANNER YEAR, Ames. Mar-July. Textile & fiber. Open to US, Canada & Mexico artists. Juried. Fee $10 for 1 entry, $15 for 2, limit 2. Entries due Sept 6. For further information write Banner Year, College of Design, Iowa State Univ, Ames, IA 50011.

DES MOINES ART CENTER ANNUAL, Des Moines. Annual, spring. Paintings, drawings, prints, sculpture, crafts. Open to anyone living in Iowa above high school age. Juried, best work $250, best ceramic work $250, adult $100 & student $50 in painting, sculpture, prints, drawings & crafts. No fee. For further information write Des Moines Art Center, Greenwood Park, Des Moines, IA 50312.

IOWA CRAFTS ANNUAL, Mason City. Annual, Oct-Nov-Dec. Open to any and all craft media, such as clay, fiber, metals, and others. Open to all artists, craftspersons residing within the State of Iowa. Juried by submission of the work, up to $1200 in cash awards. No fee. Entry deadline three weeks prior to opening of show. For further information write Richard Leet, Director, Charles H MacNider Museum, 303 Second St SE, Mason City, IA 50401.

PAPER/FIBER VI, Iowa City. Apr. Work using paper and/or fiber. Open to US artists. Juried, $2500 in awards. Fee $10. Entry slides due Feb 1. For further information write Arts Center, 129 E Washington, Iowa City, IA 52240.

SIOUX CITY ART CENTER. Sioux City. Biennial, fall. All media. Open to residents of IA, NE, MN, SD, MO, IL, KS. One-man jury, up to $2500 in purchase & cash awards. Entries due Sept-Oct. For further information write Dir, Sioux City Art Center, 513 Nebraska St, Sioux City, IA 51101.

KANSAS

KACA 3 PLUS, Wichita. Feb-Mar. Open to current & former Kans residents. Cash & honor awards; selected works will travel to Paraguay. Fee $7.50, limit 5. Entries due Nov 12. For further information write Glenice L Matthews, Kansas Artist-Craftsmen Assoc, 3 Plus Exhibit, Wichita Art Assoc, 9112 E Central, Wichita, KS 67206.

KANSAS 8TH NATIONAL SMALL PAINTING, DRAWING & PRINT EXHIBITION, Hays. Feb-Apr. Drawings, paintings & prints. Open to US artists. Juried, $2000 in awards. Fee $10, 84 inch max length. Entry slides due Dec 15. For further information write Dr Zoran Stevanov, Art Dept, Ft Hays State Univ, Hays, KS 67601.

KANSAS WATERCOLOR SOCIETY TRI-STATE EXHIBITION, Wichita. Annual, Mar-Apr. Primarily transparent aqucous on paper. Open to all artists living in KS, MO, OK. Approx $15,000 in cash, patron, patron-purchase awards. For further information write Tim Rigg, Pres, Kansas Watercolor Society, 2516 Reva, Wichita, KS 67207.

KENTUCKY

ALICE LLOYD COLLEGE PAPER WORKS ART EXHIBITION, Pippa Passes. Annual, Mar-Apr. Works on or of paper, no photography. Open to US, Canada, Mexico & Puerto Rico artists. Juried, purchase & exhibition awards. Entry slides due Feb 7. For further information write Alice Lloyd College 4th Annual, Art Dept. Pippa Passes, KY 41844.

J B SPEED ART MUSEUM EIGHT-STATE ANNUAL, Louisville. Annual, Sept. In annual rotation in following order: graphics, painting, sculpture, crafts. Open to artists in Kentucky, Indiana, Ohio, Illinois, Missouri, Tennessee, Virginia, West Virginia. Juried, no special awards, purchase commitments. No fee. Entries due August 2. For further information write Dr Kelly Scott Reed, J B Speed Art Museum, PO Box 8345, Louisville, KY 40208.

KENTUCKY WATERCOLOR SOCIETY AQUEOUS, Louisville. Aug-Oct. Watercolor. Open to artists over 18. Cash & purchase awards. Fee $15 non-members, $7.50 members. Entries due May 31. For further information write Aline Barker, 2714 Wendell Ave, Louisville, KY 40205.

MAGIC SILVER SHOW, Murray State University, Murray. Annual, Jan-Feb. All light sensitive media, photography, black/white & color. Open internationally. Juried, cash awards. Fee $5 per print, limit 5 prints. Entries due Nov 1. For further information write to Michael Johnson, Magic Silver Show, Art Dept, Murray State University, Murray, KY 42071.

LOUISIANA

LOUISIANA WATERCOLOR SOCIETY ANNUAL INTERNATIONAL EXHIBIT, New Orleans. Annual, Mar-Apr. Water color. Juried, $900 cash & purchase awards. Fee $7, limit 3. Entry slides due Jan 8. For further information write Louisiana Watercolor Society, 320 Vincent Ave, New Orleans, LA 70005.

NATIONAL WOMEN'S ART EXHIBITION, New Orleans. May-Nov. Crafts, drawings, graphics, mixed media, painting, photography, sculpture, textiles & water colors. Open to US women artists. Juried. Fee $10 for 3 slides. Entries due Nov 14. For further information write WITM Inc, PO Box 51809, New Orleans, LA 70151.

NEW ORLEANS MUSEUM OF ART. Triennial, fall. Focus on contemporary art by professional artists from thirteen-state region of Southeastern US. Single juror, purchase awards. No fee. For further information write New Orleans Triennial, New Orleans Museum of Art, PO Box 19123, Lelong Ave, City Park, New Orleans, LA 70179.

RIVER ROAD SHOW, Baton Rouge. Annual, June. All original work. Open to US artists. Juried, cash & ribbon awards. Fee $10 per slide non-member, $7.50 per slide members. Entries due Apr 10. For further information write Sylvia Bankston, Guild Gallery, 7371 Florida Blvd, Baton Rouge, LA 70806.

SPAR NATIONAL ART SHOW, Shreveport. Nov-Dec. Open to US artists. Juried, $1500 in awards. Fee $10 for 3 entries, $10 each additional entry. Entry slides due Sept 1. For further information write Jan Van Horn, Shreveport Regional Art Council, 800 Snow St, Shreveport, LA 71101.

MARYLAND

BALTIMORE MUSEUM OF ART BIENNIAL EXHIBITION. Biennial, during odd years. Painting, sculpture (slides or photographs of work not acceptable). Open to artists currently residing in MD. Juried, prizes & awards. No fee. Entries due as announced, usually 3 months before exhibition. For further information write Robin Greene, MD Biennial Coordr, Baltimore Museum of Art, Art Museum Dr, Baltimore, MD 21218.

BALTIMORE WATERCOLOR SOCIETY MID-ATLANTIC WATERCOLOR EXHIBIT, Baltimore. Annual, May. Watercolor. Open to Md, Va, Del, Pa & DC artists. Cash & purchase awards. Fee $5. Entries due Apr 24. For further information write Mary Ruth Buchness, 600 Oak Hill Rd, Cantonsville, MD 21228.

CUMBERLAND VALLEY ANNUAL PHOTOGRAPHIC SALON, Hagerstown. Annual, Feb. Photographs. Open to residents & former residents of the Cumberland Valley region. Juried, prizes & awards. Fee $2, limit 4. Entries due Jan 16. For further information write Washington County Museum of Fine Arts, PO Box 423, Hagerstown, MD 21740.

CUMBERLAND VALLEY ARTISTS ANNUAL EXHIBITION, Hagerstown. Annual, June. Open media. Open to residents & former residents of the Cumberland Valley region. Juried, prizes & awards. Fee $10. Entries due May 15. For further information write Washington County Museum of Fine Arts, PO Box 423, Hagerstown, MD 21740.

EUGENE KORMENDY SCULPTURE COMPETITION, Hillcrest Heights. Annual. Sculpture. Open to professional sculptors 35 years & younger. $5000 in cash awards. Entries due Feb 18. For further information write Paul VI Institute, Kormendy Awards Comt, Suite 118, 3847 Branch Ave, Hillcrest Heights, MD 20748.

LAUREL ARTS GUILD, Laurel. Annual, May. All original 2-D works except photography. Open to Md, Pa, Del, Va & DC artists. Juried, cash awards. Fee commission of 25%, limit 2. Entries due Apr 24. For further information write Clara J Walsh, Montpelier Cultural Arts Center, 9209 Twin Hill Lane, Laurel, MD 20708.

SMALL RELIGIOUS SCULPTURE COMPETITION, Hillcrest Heights. Annual. Sculpture. Open to all sculptors. $3000 in cash awards. Entries due Apr 7. For further information write Paul VI Institute, Kormendy Awards Comt, Suite 118, 3847 Branch Ave, Hillcrest Heights, MD 20748.

MASSACHUSETTS

BOSTON PRINTMAKERS. Annual, location & dates change yearly. All print media. Open to all American and Canadian printmakers. Juried, awards. For further information write Mrs S M Rantz, Secy, 299 High Rock St, Dept A, Needham, MA 02192.

NATIONAL GREEK ARTISTS EXHIBIT, Springfield. Annual, June. All media. Open to Greek American artists. Juried, cash & prize awards. Fee $10. Entry slides due May 2. For further information write James W Shenas, Dir, Greek Cultural Center, 8 Palmfield St, Springfield, MA 01104.

YANKEE GENERAL OF FINE ARTS SPRING SHOW, Gloucester. Apr-June. All media. Juried, cash & ribbon awards. Fee $15. Entries due Apr 1. For further information write Ruth A Brown, 275 E Main St E, Gloucester, MA 01930.

MICHIGAN

MICHIGAN—THE PLACE & THE LAKE, Grand Rapids. Oct. All media. Juried, $2000 in cash & purchase awards. Fee $10. Entry slides due Sept 6. For further information write Norma Rhoda, Bergsma Gallery, Grand Plaza Hotel, Concourse Level, Peart at Monroe, Grand Rapids, MI 49503.

MID-MICHIGAN ANNUAL EXHIBITION, Midland. Annual, fall. All media & mixed media (painting, drawing, prints, sculpture, plastics, ceramics, textiles, jewelry, enameling, metalwork, woodwork, photography). Open to Mich artists 18 years and over, only original work completed within the past 2 yrs. Juried, prizes, & awards. Fee $15 per artist, limit three entries; $10 fee for MAC members. Entries due Jan. For further information write the Midland Art Council of Midland Center for the Arts, Inc, 1801 West St. Andrews, Midland, MI 48640.

SMALL SCULPTURE EXHIBITION, Mount Pleasant. Feb-Mar. Sculpture. Juried, $1200 in awards. Fee $10, limit 2. Entries due Nov 17. For further information write Dir, Univ Art Gallery, Central Michigan Univ, Mount Pleasant, MI 48859.

MINNESOTA

ANNUAL PHOTOGRAPHY COMPETITION & EXHIBITION, Northfield. Annual, Apr-May. Black & white & color prints. Cash awards. Northfield Arts Guild, Box 21, Northfield, MN 55057.

WHITE BEAR ARTS COUNCIL & LAKEWOOD COMMUNITY COLLEGE NORTHERN LIGHTS, White Bear Lake. Bi-annual, Mar-Apr. Paintings, sculpture, drawings, no prints. Open to artists in MN, WI, IA, ND, SD. Juried, prizes, ribbons, money awards & purchase awards. Fee $5 first entry, $3 second entry, two entries per artist. Entries due approximately two weeks before show, date to be decided. For further information write White Bear Arts Council, Box 8715, White Bear Lake, MN 55110.

MISSOURI

PAPER IN PARTICULAR, Columbia. Annual, Jan-Feb. Works on or of paper. Juried. Entry slides due Nov 15. For further information

write Sidney Larson, Chmn Art Dept, Columbia College, 10th & Rogers, Columbia, MO 65201.

PHOTOSPIVA 83, Joplin. Nov-Dec. All photography processes. Open to US artists. Juried, $1000 in cash awards. Fee $5 for first entry, $2 per additional entry; limit 4. Entries due Oct 28. For further information write Spiva Art Center, Newman & Duquesne Roads, Joplin, MO 64801.

ST LOUIS WATERCOLOR COMPETITION, St Louis. Apr-May. Open to artists in 200 mile radius of St Louis. Fee $10 non-members, limit 2. Entries due Apr 18. For further information write St Louis Artists Guild, 227 E Lakewood Ave, St Louis, MO 63119.

WATERCOLOR USA, Springfield. Annual, late spring, early summer. Any aquamedia (paint composed of water-soluble pigment) executed on paper or a paper-like support. Open to living, adult artists, 18 years of age or older, residing in the US. Juried, approximately $8000-$10,000 in cash, purchase awards and patron purchases. Handling fee $10. Entry deadline varies from year to year. For further information write William C Landwehr, Dir, Springfield Art Museum, 1111 E Brookside Dr, Springfield, MO 65807.

YOUNG ARTISTS COMPETITION, St Louis. June. All media. Open to artists 15-21 years old in a 200 mile radius of St Louis. Fee $5 non-members, limit 3. Entries due June 13. For further information write St Louis Artists Guild, 227 E Lockwood Ave, St Louis, MO 63119.

NEBRASKA

ART IN THE PARK, Kearney. Annual, July. Juried. Fee $16. For further information write Larry Peterson, Art Dept, Kearney State College, Kearney, NE 68847.

CAST CLAY, Omaha. Apr-May. Cast clay. Open to US artists. Fee $10, limit 10 slides. Entry slides due Mar 11. For further information write Craftsmen's Gallery, 511 South 11 St, Omaha, NE 68102.

JOSLYN ART MUSEUM BIENNIAL, Omaha. Biennial, held in even-numbered yrs, late winter or spring. All media. Open to artists in Colo, Iowa, Kans, Mo, Nebr, SDak & Wyo. Juried, awards. Entries due as announced. For further information write Joslyn Biennial, Joslyn Art Museum, 2200 Dodge St, Omaha, NE 68102.

NPVAG NATIONAL JURIED ART SHOW, Scottsbluff. Apr. All media. Juried, cash awards. Fee $8 per entry adult, $2 per entry youth. Entries due Apr 1. For further information write North Platte Valley Artists Guild, 106 E 18th St, Box 1041, Scottsbluff, NE 69361.

NEVADA

LAS VEGAS NATIONAL, Las Vegas. Nov. Painting. Open to US artists. Juried, cash awards. Fee $7 per entry, limit 3. Entry slides due Sept 15. For further information write Las Vegas Art Museum, 3333 W Washington Ave, Las Vegas, NV 89107.

NEW JERSEY

ALLIED ARTISTS OF AMERICA INC, Teaneck. Annual, Dec. Oil, acrylics, water media, sculpture, pastel. Open to all artists. Juried, over $11,000 in cash awards, plus medals. Fee $10 for one slide, 20% comn. Slides & entry cards due Oct 12. For further information write (enclose long self-addressed stamped envelope) Sybil D'Orsl, Corres Secy, 699 Wendel Pl, Teaneck, NJ 07666.

BOARDWALK INDIAN SUMMER ART SHOW, Atlantic City. Annual, Sept. All media. $3000 in awards. For further information write Florence Miller, Dir, 205 N Montpelier Ave, Atlantic City, NJ 08401.

GARDEN STATE WATERCOLOR SOCIETY, Princeton. Annual, Sept-Oct. Original works in water colors. Entries due Sept 10. For further information write Dagmar H Tribble, 12 Battle Rd, Princeton, NJ 08540.

HUNTERDON ART CENTER NATIONAL PRINT EXHIBITION, Clinton. Annual, Mar-Apr. All print media except monotype. Open to all artists in the US. Juried, purchase awards. Fee $15 for one or two prints includes insurance & return of work. For further information write A S Marsh, Hunterdon Art Center, 7 Center St, Clinton, NJ 08809.

NATIONAL DRAWING 1983, Trenton. Apr. Drawings. Open to US artists. Juried, $3000 in purchase awards. Fee $10 for 2 entries. Entry slides due Dec 31. For further information write Trenton State College, Hillwood Lakes CN 550, Trenton, NJ 08625.

NEW JERSEY WATER COLOR SOCIETY, East Hanover. Annual, Nov-Dec. Open to NJ artists. Juried. Entries due Oct 29. For further information write Nabisco Brands USA Gallery, River Rd & De Forest Ave, East Hanover, NJ 07631.

OPEN JURIED ART EXHIBITION, Paramus. Nov-Jan. All media. Juried, $1000 in awards. For further information write Bergen Museum of Art & Science, Ridgewood & Fairview Ave, Paramus, NJ 07652.

RED BANK FESTIVAL OF ARTS, Red Bank. Annual, Sept. Juried. Entries due Sept 6. For further information write Red Bank Festival of Arts, 5 Broad St, Red Bank, NJ 07701.

RUTGERS NATIONAL UNIQUE WORKS ON PAPER, Camden. Mar-Apr. Works on paper surface traditional or experimental techniques, excluding print & photography. Open to US artists. Juried, $5000 in purchase awards. Entry slides due Oct 14. For further information write Stedman Art Gallery, Rutgers Univ, Camden, NJ 08102.

SUMMIT ART CENTER JURIED SHOW, Summit. Jan-Feb. All media. Juried, $1500 in awards. Fee $10, limit 1. Entries due Jan 7. For further information write Summit Art Center, 68 Elm St, Summit, NJ 07901.

WESTFIELD ART ASSOCIATION, Westfield. Annual, Mar. Watercolor, graphics. Open to members of Westfield Art Association. Juried, prizes & cash awards. For further information write Sydney Spence, 2159 Bayberry Lane, Westfield, NJ 07090.

NEW MEXICO

DAILY BREAD; ART FROM FEMALE EXPERIENCE, Albuquerque. Nov-Dec. All media. Open to NMex women artists. Juried, cash awards. Fee $3 per entry, limit 3. Entry slides due Oct 28. For further information write Daily Bread; Art from Female Experience, PO Box 40151, Albuquerque, NM 87196.

MUSEUM OF NEW MEXICO, Santa Fe. Biennial, Jan-Apr. All media. Open to artists of NMex, Ariz, Colo, Utah, Okla & Tex. Juried, awards. For further information write Museum of Fine Arts, PO Box 2087, Santa Fe, NM 87503.

NATIONAL WARM GLASS SHOW, Albuquerque. Mar-Apr. Warm or slumped glass. Open to US artists. Juried. Fee $5, limit 3. Entry slides due Jan 28. For further information write ASA Gallery, Box 25, SUB, Univ of New Mexico, Albuquerque, NM 87131.

NATIONAL WESTERN SMALL PAINTING SHOW, Bosque Farms. Annual, June-July. Oil, acrylic, water color, drawing, mixed media, western art. Open to US artists. Juried, cash, purchase & ribbon awards. Fee $10 per entry, limit 3. Entries due May 10. For further information write Natl Western Small Painting Show, Bosque Art Gallery, 655 S Bosque Loop, Bosque Farms, NM 87068.

NEW MEXICO ART LEAGUE SMALL PAINTING SHOW, Albuquerque. Annual, Feb. All media. Open to all artists. Juried, prizes. Fee $8 per entry, limit two. Entry cards and work due Jan 20. For further information write New Mexico Art League, 3407 Juan Tabo NE, Albuquerque, NM 87111.

SEVEN STATE PHOTOGRAPHIC REGIONAL, Albuquerque. Nov-Dec. All photographic processes. Open to Calif, Nev, Ariz, Colo, NMex, Tex & Okla artists. Juried, $10,000 in awards. Entries due Nov 10. For further information write ASA Gallery, Box 25, SUB, Univ of New Mexico, Albuquerque, NM 87131.

NEW YORK

ALL ON PAPER 83, Buffalo. Dec-Jan. All works on or of paper, no photography. Open to US artists. Juried, $1000 in awards. Fee $10, limit 2. Entry slides due Oct 15. For further information write AOP 83, AAO Gallery, 698 Main St, Buffalo, NY 14202.

AMERICAN SOCIETY OF CONTEMPORARY ARTISTS, New York. Annual, Nov. Graphics, painting & sculpture. Juried, awards. For further information write Edith Abrams, Pres, 2820 Ave J, Brooklyn, NY 11210.

AMERICAN WATERCOLOR SOCIETY, New York. Annual, Apr. Watercolor, watermedia. Juried, cash awards with medals. Handling fee $10. Submission by slides. For further information write The American Watercolor Society, 14 E 90 St, New York, NY 10028.

AMERICAN WORKS ON PAPER EXHIBITION, Rochester. Annual, June-Aug. All media. Open to US artists. Juried, $1000 in cash & purchase awards. Fee $8 per entry, limit 3. Entry slides due Apr 22. For further information write American Works on Paper, John Haldoupis, Dir, Zaner Gallery, 100-T Alexander St, Rochester, NY 14620.

AUDUBON ARTISTS, New York. Annual, Mar-Apr, at National Arts Club. Oil, aquamedia, sculpture, graphics. Juried, awards $7000 and ten medals. Fee $10. Slides due Feb 1. For further information write Audubon Artists, 225 W 34th St, Suite 1510, New York, NY 10001.

CHAUTAUQUA ART ASSOCIATION GALLERIES, Chautauqua Institution 27th National Juried Show, Celoron. June 22-July 13. Oil, acrylic, watercolor, drawing, prints, mixed media, photography, small sculpture. Open to US artists. Juried by slides, $6000 in cash & purchase awards. Fee $8 for 1 entry, $12 for 2 & 25% commission. Entry slides due Apr 2. For further information write, Dir, CAA, Box 518 Dept D, Celoron, NY 14720.

COOPERSTOWN ART ASSOCIATION NATIONAL EXHIBITION. Annual, July-Aug. Painting, graphics, sculpture & crafts (no photography). Open to any adult in the US. Over $7000 in prizes. Fee $10 each entry, 20% comn. Mailed entries due in the hands of agent by June 14. Hand delivered entries June 22. For further information write Cooperstown Art Association, 22 Main St, Cooperstown, NY 13326.

EVERSON MUSEUM OF ART, REGIONAL SYRACUSE BIENNIAL, Syracuse, NY. Biennial, Nov-Jan. Painting, prints, drawing, collage, photographs, sculpture, ceramics, fiber. Open to artists over 18 years of age who reside in NY. Fee for non-members. For further information write Everson Museum of Art, Public Info Dept, 401 Harrison St, Syracuse, NY 13202.

FIBER NATIONAL, Dunkirk. Nov. Textiles, all fiber work. Open to US artists. Fee $800, limit 3. Entry slides due Sept 20. For further information write Access to the Arts, 600 Central Ave, Dunkirk, NY 14048.

HUDSON VALLEY ART ASSOCIATION, White Plains. Annual, Apr-May. Oil, watercolor, sculpture, graphics, pastels, acrylics. Open to all artists over 18 years of age. Juried, Cash, medal & ribbon awards. Fee $20 plus 10% commission. For further information write Richard C Pionk, Secy, 1349 Lexington Ave, New York, NY 10028.

IEEE CENTENNIAL ART CONTEST, New York. Oil, watercolor, acrylic & mixed media. Juried, $7000 in awards. Fee $2 per slide. Entries due Aug 31. For further information write Joan Izzo, Centennial Asst, 15th Floor, 345 E 47th St, New York, NY 10017.

NATIONAL ACADEMY OF DESIGN, New York. Annual, Feb-Mar. Oil, sculpture, watercolors, graphics. Open to all artists. Juried, awards. Receive in Jan. No fee. For further information write (requesting prospectus) National Academy of Design, 1083 Fifth Ave, New York, NY 10028.

NATIONAL ARTS CLUB OPEN WATERCOLOR EXHIBITION, New York. Annual, Feb. Watercolor only. Open to all. Juried, cash awards, material awards, one-man show awards. Fee $15. For information write Moses Worthman, AWS, 3027 Brighton Fifth St, Brooklyn, NY 11235.

NATIONAL SCULPTURE SOCIETY, New York. Annual, Feb. Sculpture only. Open to all American sculptors on a juried basis. Jury prizes & awards. No fee. Write for prospectus approx Jan 1. For further information write National Sculpture Society, 15 E 26th St, New York, NY 10010.

NATIONAL SOCIETY OF PAINTERS IN CASEIN & ACRYLIC, New York. Annual, Mar. Casein and acrylic. Open to all artists. Juried, $3200 cash awards & medals. Fee $10. Slides due Jan 15. For further information write Lily Shuff, 155 West 68th St, New York, NY 10023.

PRATT GRAPHICS CENTER INTERNATIONAL, MINIATURE PRINT COMPETITION & EXHIBITION, New York. Biennial, spring. Original prints, no photographs. Juried, approx $1000 in purchase prizes & awards. Fee $5 first entry, $2 each additional. Entries due Jan 15, 1985. For further information write Pratt Graphics Center, 160 Lexington Ave, New York, NY 10016.

SMALL WORKS NATIONAL, Rochester. Annual, Nov-Dec. Painting, watercolor, prints, drawings, mixed media, photography & sculpture. Open to US artists 18 years & older. Juried, cash & purchase awards. Fee $8 for 1 entry, $10 for 2. Entry slides due Sept 16. For further information write Small Works National, John Haldoupis, Dir, Zaner Gallery, 100-C Alexander St, Rochester, NY 14620.

CATHERINE LORILLARD WOLFE ART CLUB, INC, ANNUAL OPEN EXHIBITION, New York. Annual, Oct 7-29. Open to women artists working in traditional manner. Oil, watercolor, pastels, graphics, sculpture. Cash awards. Fee $10 member, $15 non-member. All works juried by slides due Aug 10. For further information send self addressed stamped envelope to Troukie DeBevoisa, 13 Hayton Rd, RD No 4, Lebanon, NJ 08833.

NORTH CAROLINA

ASSOCIATED ARTISTS OF SOUTHPORT, Southport. Annual, July. All media. Juried. Fee $10. Entries due June 17. For further information write June G Brown, 122 Caswell Beach Rd, Southport, NC 28461.

NORTH CAROLINA PRINT & DRAWING SOCIETY ANNUAL EASTERN US PRINT EXHIBITION. Annual, Dec. Open to artists in states east of Mississippi River. All printmaking media, no photos. Juried, purchase awards. Entries due mid-Oct. For further information write North Carolina Print & Drawing Society, 110 E Seventh St, Charlotte, NC 28202.

NORTH CAROLINA ARTISTS EXHIBITION, Raleigh. Triennial, Apr-June 1984. All media. Open to current North Carolina residents. For further information write Curatorial Dept, North Carolina Museum of Art, 2110 Blue Ridge Blvd, Raleigh, NC 27611.

SHELBY ART LEAGUE, Shelby. Annual, Oct. Juried, $4000 in awards. For further information write Shelby Art League, Box 601, Shelby, NC 28150.

SOUTHEASTERN CENTER FOR CONTEMPORARY ART, Winston-Salem. Annual NEA/SECCA Southeastern Artists Fellowship Competition. Media as specified. Open to all artists, 18 years & older, residing in the eleven southeastern states & Washington, DC. Juried. For further information write Southeastern Center for Contemporary Art, 750 Marguerite Dr, Winston-Salem, NC 27106.

NORTH DAKOTA

NATIONAL ART EXHIBIT, Valley City. Biennial, Apr 1985. All fine arts & crafts. Open to all artists. Cash & purchase awards. Fee $10 limit 2. Entries due Feb 28. For further information write Stretch Rogers, Box 1319VCSC, Valley City, ND 58072.

NORTH DAKOTA PRINT & DRAWING EXHIBITION, Grand Forks. Annual, Apr. All prints & drawings. Open to all US artists. Juried, purchase awards. Fee $10. Entries due Mar 1. For further information write North Dakota Annual, Visual Arts Dept, University of North Dakota, Grand Forks, ND 58202.

OHIO

ALTERNATIVES 1983, Athens. All media using photography processes. Open to US artists. Juried, $1000 in cash & purchase awards. Fee $5 per slide, limit 10. Entry slides due Dec 1. For further information write Alternatives 1983, PO Box 775, Athens, OH 45701.

BUTLER INSTITUTE OF AMERICAN ART NATIONAL MID-YEAR SHOW, Youngstown. Annual, July-Aug. Oil, acrylic, transparent & opaque watercolor, gouache, casein, tempera, alkyd or mixed paint media. No pastels or 3-D work. Open to artists of the US. Juried, awards. Fee $10 for 1-3 slides. Entry slides due Mar 20. For further information write the Butler Institute of American Art, 524 Wick Ave, Youngstown, OH 44502.

ELECTROSTATICS INTERNATIONAL, Cleveland. Jan-Feb. Electrostatics, copy art, Xerography. Juried. Fee $5 for 5 slides, limit 5. Entries due Oct 14. For further information write A Aitken, Image Resource Center, One Playhouse Sq #106, 1375 Euclid Ave, Cleveland, OH 44115.

OHIO CERAMIC, SCULPTURE & CRAFT SHOW, Youngstown. Annual, Jan-Feb. Ceramic, enamel, sculpture, fiber, jewelery and craft. Open to present & former Ohio residents. Jury, purchase awards. Entry fee. Entries due Dec 12. For further information write Butler Institute of American Art, 524 Wick Ave, Youngstown, OH 44502.

STEUBENVILLE ART ASSOCIATION, Steubenville. Annual, May. All media. Purchase awards. Fee $5. Entry slides due Apr 9. For further information write Albert Wilson, 608 Carnegie St, Steubenville, OH 43952.

SUMMERFAIR, Cincinnati. Annual, June. Juried exhibition & sale. All fine arts & crafts. Over $5000 in cash awards. Fee $60. Entries due March 1. For further information write Summerfair Dept AAD, PO Box 3277, Cincinnati, OH 45201.

OREGON

SUNRIVER ART COMPETITION, Sunriver. Annual, Feb. All media. Open to Ore artists. Juried, $1750 in awards. No fee. Entry slides due Jan 8. For further information write Sunriver Properties Oregon Ltd, Admin Office, Sunriver, OR 97702.

WILLIAMETTE VALLEY JURIED EXHIBITION, Corvallis. Annual, Nov. Non-functional media. Open to Willamette Valley artists. Juried, cash awards. No fee, limit 2. Entries due Oct 27. For further information write Corvallis Arts Center, 700 SW Madison Ave, Corvallis, OR 97333.

PENNSYLVANIA

ANNUAL INTERNATIONAL COMPETITION, Philadelphia. Annual, fall. Prints and photographs. Juried, purchase & other awards (over $9000). Purchase prizes offered to the Permanent Collection of the Philadelphia Museum of Art (and other museums). Fee $15 (covers 1 yr membership in club, catalogue, return postage). Entries due early Oct. For further information write to Ofelia Garcia, Dir, The Print Club, 1614 Latimer St, Philadelphia, PA 19103.

CARNEGIE INSTITUTE THREE RIVERS ARTS FESTIVAL, Pittsburgh. Annual, June 8-24. Painting, sculpture, crafts, photography, film, video, banners. Open to all artist living in PA, OH, WV, NY, MD & DC. Juried visual arts & artists market. Fee $15. Entry slides due Mar 17. For further information write Three Rivers Arts Festival, 4400 Forbes Ave, Pittsburgh, PA 15213.

ERIE ART CENTER/CLAY NATIONAL. Biennial, Feb-Mar. Open to all US artists. Juried, prizes & purchase awards. Fee $5 per entry-slides only. For prospectus write Clay National, Erie Art Center, 338 W Sixth St, Erie, PA 16507.

HAZELTON ART LEAGUE REGIONAL ART EXHIBIT, Hazelton. Annual, Apr-May. Paintings, sculpture, drawings & graphics. Open to artists within 100 miles of Hazelton. Juried, cash & purchase awards. Fee. For further information write E Ruth Howe, 438 W Broad St, Hazelton, PA 18201.

NATIONAL PRINT COMPETITION, Edinboro. Bi-annual, Mar-Apr. Print (except mono-prints & photography). Open to US artists. Juried, $3000 in purchase awards. Fee $16, limit 2. Entries due Feb 22. For further information write Print Competition 83, Edinboro State College, Art Dept, Edinboro, PA 16444.

PHOTONATIONAL, Erie. Mar-Apr. Photography. Open to US artists. Juried, $5000 in purchase awards. Fee $7 per entry. Entries due Nov 1. For further information write Erie Art Center, 338 W Sixth St, Erie, PA 16507.

WASHINGTON & JEFFERSON COLLEGE NATIONAL PAINTING SHOW, Washington. Annual, Mar-Apr. All painting. Open to any US artist, 18 yrs old. Prizes & purchase awards. Fee $5 for each slide entry. Entry cards & slides due Jan, work due Mar. For further information write Paul B Edwards, Art Dept, Washington & Jefferson College, Washington, PA 15301.

WCA NATIONAL JURIED EXHIBITION, Bethlehem. Mar-Apr. All media. Open to US Women's Caucus for Art members. Juried, $3000 in awards. Fee $5, limit 3. Entry slides due Nov 1. For further information write Le High Univ Art Galleries, GU #17, Bethlehem, PA 18015.

RHODE ISLAND

PROVIDENCE ART CLUB. Three open shows every year, scheduled at different times & varied from season to season; for instance, an open small sculpture show, an open drawing or print show, or perhaps a painting or craft show. For further information write Mrs Tore Dalenius, Providence Art Club, 11 Thomas St, Providence, RI 02903.

SOUTH CAROLINA

CLEMSON NATIONAL JURIED PRINT & DRAWING EXHIBITION, Clemson. Feb-Mar. Works on paper except photography. Open to US artists. Juried, $2500 cash & purchase awards. Fee $10, limit 3. Entries due Nov 3. For further information write Clemson National Print & Drawing Exhibit, Rudolph E Lee Gallary, College of Architecture, Clemson Univ, Clemson, SC 29631.

MURRELLS INLET OUTDOOR ARTS & CRAFTS FESTIVAL INC, Murrells Inlet. Annual, Apr. All media. Open to US & Canadian artists. Juried, cash, ribbon & purchase awards. Fee $60. Entries due Apr 10. For further information write Wilma D Martin, Dir, PO Box 231, Murrells Inlet, SC 29576.

RED CLOUD INDIAN ART SHOW, Pine Ridge. June-Aug. Paintings, graphics, mixed media, 3-D work. Open to any tribal member of the native people of North America. Juried, $3500 in merit & purchase awards. Entries due May 22. For further information write Red Cloud Indian Art Show, Red Cloud Indian School, Pine Ridge, SD 57770.

TENNESSEE

ART SOUTH, Memphis. Biennial, Feb-Mar, even numbered years. Paintings, sculpture. Open to artists residing in the southern USA. Juried, awards. Entry fee. For further information write Dir, Memphis State University Gallery CFA 142, Memphis, TN 38152.

PAPER AND CLAY EXHIBITION, Memphis. Biennial, Feb-Mar, odd years. Drawing, prints, cast paper, ceramics, mixed media including paper and clay. Juried, awards. Fee. For further information write Paper and Clay Show, Art Dept, Memphis State Univ, Memphis, TN 38152.

THE FIGURE: NEW FORM, NEW FUNCTION, Gatlinburg. Nov-Jan. All 2-D & 3-D media not exceeding 8 ft. Open to US artists. Juried, cash & purchase awards. Fee $10, limit 3. Entry slides due Sept 10. For further information write Figure Exhibition, Arrowmont School of Arts & Crafts, Box 567, Gatlinburg, TN 37738.

TEXAS

ABILENE FINE ARTS MUSEUM. Annual, June. Painting only. Open to Texas artists. Juried. Prizes awarded. For further information write Abilene Fine Arts Museum, 801 S Mockingbird, Abilene TX 79605.

THE AMARILLO COMPETITION. Biennial, Dec. Any two-dimensional work. Open to all artists in Tex, NMex, Okla, Colo, Kans, Louisiana & Ark. Juried, purchase prizes and awards variable. Fee $12 per 5 entries. Entries due Oct. For further information write Curator of Art, Amarillo Art Center, Box 447, Amarillo, TX 79178.

ANNUAL JURIED EXHIBITION, Houston. Annual, Jan-Feb. Photography. Juried, $500 in awards. Fee $5, limit 5 slides. Entries due Oct 28. For further information write Houston Center for Photography, 1435 W Alabama, Houston, TX 77006.

COLLEGE OF THE MAINLAND NATIONAL COMPETITION, Texas City. Mar-Apr. Paintings & drawings not in excess of 24 inches. Open to US artists. Juried, $1500 in cash & purchase awards. Fee $5 per slide, limit 3. Entry slides due Jan 10. For further information write College of the Mainland National Competition 1983, 8001 Palmer Highway, Texas City, TX 77591.

EL PASO MUSEUM OF ART NATIONAL SUN CARNIVAL. Biennial, Dec. All painting. Open to any US citizen residing in the US and its territories. Juried, purchase awards. For further information write Bill Rakocy, Curator of Collections, El Paso Museum of Art, 1211 Montana, El Paso, TX 79902.

HILL COUNTRY ARTS FOUNDATION ANNUAL JURIED ART EXHIBITION. Annual, Apr. All media painting & sculpture. Open to all persons residing in US. Juried, $1000 awards (total). Fee $5 per entry, limit 3. Entry slides due Feb 29. For further information write Hill Country Arts Foundation, PO Box 176, Ingram, TX 78025.

HILL COUNTRY ARTS FOUNDATION ANNUAL GRAPHICS/PHOTOGRAPHY EXHIBIT. Sept. All media graphics and photography. Open to all persons residing in the US. Juried, $1000 total awards. Fee $5 per entry, limit three. Entries due Aug. 11. For further

information write Hill Country Arts Foundation, PO Box 176, Ingram, TX 78025.

PERSONAL MYTHOLOGY, Austin. Feb-Mar. Drawing, mixed media, painting. Open to US artists. Juried, $1000 in awards. Fee $5 per entry. Entry slides due Jan 3. For further information write Trinity House Gallery, 4705 Glissman, Austin TX 78702.

PHOTO/FLOW, Arlington. Annual, Nov-Dec. Photography & photography related. Open to US artists. Juried, cash awards. Fee $15 for 3 entries, $5 for each additional entry, limit 5. Entry slides due Sept 28. For further information write Photo/Flow, Univ Tex, Arlington, Box 19089, Arlington, TX 76019.

RIO GRANDE VALLEY ARTS & CRAFTS EXPOSITION, Brownsville. Annual, Nov. All media. Open to all artists & craftsmen. For further information write Brownsville Art League, Attn: Tencha Sloss, PO Box 3404, Brownsville, TX 78520.

TEXAS FINE ARTS ASSOCIATION ANNUAL EXHIBITION, Austin. Annual, Apr-May. All media. Open to all artists residing in US. Jury, prizes, cash awards & purchase awards of approximately $5000. Fee for each entry is $10 for non-members, $5 for members. Slides due Jan, work due Apr. For further information write Texas Fine Arts Association, PO Box 5023, Austin, TX 78763.

2-DIMENSIONS, El Paso. Jan-Feb. Drawing, mixed media, painting, photography. Open to US, Canada & Mexico artists. Juried, $40,000 in purchase awards. Fee $10 for 3 entries. Entries due Nov 15. For further information write R Walz, Dept of Art, Univ Texas, El Paso, TX 79968.

WORKS ON PAPER ANNUAL EXHIBITION, San Marcos. Annual, Nov. Media on or of paper. Open to all artists. Juried. Fee $15 per 2 entries. Slide entry deadline mid-Sept. For further information write Eric C Weller, Art Dept, Southwest Texas State Univeristy, San Marcos, TX 78666.

WHAT'S NEW IN CLAY, Houston. June-July. Clay. Open to US artists. Juried. Fee $15. Entries due May 7. For further information write Univ Houston, Fine Arts Dept, 4800 Calhoun, Houston, TX 77004.

UTAH

CEDAR CITY ART COMMITTEE, Cedar City. Annual, Apr. Juried, min of $500 cash prizes. Fee $10. Entries due Jan 1. Preliminary adjudication by slides. For further information write Cedar City Art Committee, Iron County School District, PO Box 879, Cedar City, UT 84720.

UTAH DESIGNER CRAFTSMAN, Salt Lake City. Feb-May. Metal, clay, wood, fibers, glass & plastic. Open to past & present residents of Utah. Juried, cash awards. Fee $10 for membership, limit 3 entries. Entry slides due Dec 10. For further information write UDC, PO Box 27532, Salt Lake City, UT 84127.

UTAH STATEWIDE COMPETITION AND EXHIBIT, Salt Lake City. Annual, June-Labor Day. Crafts, graphics, painting, photography, sculpture, watercolor. Open to residents of Utah. 15 $200 cash awards, up to $5000 for purchase awards. Entries due approx May 15 (varies each year). For further information write Utah Arts Council, 617 E South Temple, Salt Lake City, UT 84102.

VIRGINIA

GRANBY MALL ARTS & CRAFTS FESTIVAL, Norfolk. Annual, Sept. $5000 in purchase awards & $2300 in cash awards. For further information write Arts Festival, Branby Mall, Norfolk, VA 23510.

LITURGICAL ART IN ARCHITECTURE EXHIBIT, Alexandria. Annual, Oct. Metal, wood, ceramics, glass, textile, print, painting, drawing, paper & mixed media. Juried, publication awards. Fee $20 non-members, $10 members, limit 2. Entry slides due Sept 2. For further information write Sally A. Ewin, IFRAA, 1777 Church St NW, Washington, DC 20036.

SUMI-E SOCIETY OF AMERICA EXHIBITION, New York, NY. Spring. Oriental brush painting only; subjects must be original. Open to all artists. Jury, prizes. Fee $20 for non-members, limit two. For further information write Elizabeth Robinson, 7102 Westbury Rd, McLean, VA 22101.

WEST VIRGINIA

ALLEGHENY INTERNATIONAL MINIATURE ART EXHIBITION, Pipestem. Aug. All media except photography & sculpture. Open to artists over 18. Juried, cash & ribbon awards. Fee $5 per entry, limit 5. Entries due July 15. For further information write Deborah Griffith, The Studio, Pipestem, WV 25979.

EVANS RUN ART ASSOCIATION INC REGIONAL ART, Martinsburg. Annual. Original fine art, no sculpture or photography. Open to artists within 100 miles of Martinsburg. Juried, cash & ribbon awards. Fee $5 per entry, limit 2 in each media. Entries due Apr 16. For further information write B T McCormack Rt 2, Box 4547, Kearneysville, WV 25430.

HUNTINGTON GALLERIES—EXHIBITION 280. Mar-Apr. Open to artists above high school age, living within 280 miles of Huntington. Jury, awards. Fee. Work due Jan. For further information write Exhibition 280, Program Coordinator, Huntington Galleries, 2033 McCoy Rd, Huntington, WV 25701.

WISCONSIN

LAKEFRONT FESTIVAL OF ARTS, Milwaukee. Annual. June. Multi-media. Open to professional artists and craftsmen from across the country. Juried, $7500 in prizes. Fee $12. Entries due Jan 15. For further information write Milwaukee Art Museum, 750 N Lincoln Memorial Dr, Milwaukee, WI 53202.

ON/OF PAPER COMPETITION, Superior. Jan-Feb. Any media on or of paper. Fee $10, limit 3. Entries due Dec 12. For further information write On/Of Paper, Holden Fine Arts 3102, Univ of Wisconsin, Superior, WI 54880.

WYOMING

AMERICAN NATIONAL MINIATURE SHOW, Laramie. Oct. All media except photography. Cash awards. Entries due Sept 16. For further information write ANMS Chairman, 603½ Ivinson, Laramie, WY 82070.

AUDUBON WILDLIFE ART SHOW, Lander. Annual, Sept. Entries due Sept 1. For further information write Audubon Art Show, Box 701, Lander, WY 82520.

WORLD OF ART, Cheyenne. Annual, Nov. All media. Juried. Fee $40. For further information write Don Plamer, PO Box 339, Stanton, CA 90680.

BRITISH COLUMBIA

MUSEUM OF NORTHERN BRITISH COLUMBIA, PRINCE RUPERT MUSEUM ART GALLERY, Prince Rupert. Rotating shows in all media. Gallery is open throughout the year. Bookings required at least on year in advance of show. For further information write Museum Art Gallery, Box 669, Prince Rupert, BC V8J 3S1, Canada.

ONTARIO

CRAFT FOCUS 1, Toronto. Any craft medium. Open to Ontario residents. All works must have been completed after Jan 1, 1982. Juried. Fee $15 members, $25 non-members per 3 slides. Entry slides due Feb 1. For further information write Ontario Crafts Council, 346 Dundas St W, Toronto, ON M5T 1G5, Canada.

FIREWORKS, Toronto. May-June. Open to Canada & US artists. Juried, $2000 in awards. Fee $5, limit 3. Entries due Sept 16. For further information write Cynthia Root, 8 Edenbrook Hill, Islington, ON M9W 3Z6, Canada.

SOUTHWEST 44, Windsor. Annual, March. All media. Open to artists of the southwestern Ont region. Jury prizes. Entries due Feb 10. For further information write The Art Gallery of Windsor, 445 Riverside Dr W, Windsor, ON N9A 6T8, Canada.

Traveling Exhibition Booking Agencies

ALBERTA FOUNDATION, 4th Floor, Beaver House, 10158 103 St, Edmonton, AB T5J OX6 Canada. Contact art program director.
Exhibits—Bridging the Gap; Human Aspects; Four Seasons; Abstracts; John Snow; Illingworth Kerr: At the Circus; Portraits; Art & Imagination; Look Around You. No rental fee. These exhibits travel only in Alberta.

AMARILLO ART CENTER, 2200 S Van Buren, Box 447, Amarillo, TX 79178. Tel 806-372-8356. *Dir* David Turner.
Exhibits—American Images, photographs from the Farm Security Administration. Martin Schreiber.
Cowboys—The Dying Breed. 80 black and white contemporary photographs. Posters and brochures available. Rental fee $500.
Russell Lee—Photographs Retrospective, Surveys of His Work. Starting Jan 1983. Rental fee $1000, brochures available.

AMERICAN CRAFT MUSEUM, 44 W 53rd St, New York, NY 10019. *Coordr of Circulating Exhibitions* Sherry De Leon.
Exhibits—The Robot Exhibit: History, Fantasy & Reality. Robots from every walk of life—toys, historical and recent, personal robots, commercial & one-of-a-kind, industrial & experimental robots, & artists' versions—circulate in this exhibit. Video, explanatory texts & photos trace the appearance & evolution of robots. Rental fee $5500, shipping prorated.
Art to Wear. A survey of the best of today's new handmade clothing using every sort of fiber technique. There are about 45 garments by 25 artists. Rental fee $3000 including transportation by van.

THE AMERICAN FEDERATION OF ARTS, 41 E 65th St, New York, NY 10021. Tel 212-988-7700. *Dir* Wilder Green.
Organizes approximately 20 art exhibitions and file programs per year, which are circulated in the US and abroad—painting, sculpture, graphic arts, photography, design, crafts and film. Exhibitions and catalogues organized by AFA with guest curators for museums, colleges, schools and art centers.
Exhibits—Kanban: Shop Signs of Japan, an unusual show of an art form never before seen in this country.
A selection of watercolors from the permenent collection of Yale Center for British Art, Yale University.

AMERICAN WATERCOLOR SOCIETY, 14 E 90th St, New York, NY 10028. *Chmn Traveling Exhibitions* Dale Meyers.
Exhibits—One exhibition of fifty paintings is selected by the Jury of Awards from our annual exhibitions for a one-year circuit. The exhibition is framed. Many prizewinners from the annual are included. The framed show weighs about 1200 pounds. The AWS annuals are all juried, member and non-member, and are held each April in New York. Requests cannot be considered until the following September. Rental fee of $100 per week (two week minimum) booking. Exhibiting organizations pay on-going shipping. AWS carries limited insurance during the circuit. Two of the Annual Exhibition Catalogs (containing traveling exhibition listings and itineraries) are provided, plus publicity information and several black and white photographs of prize winning paintings.

ANCHORAGE HISTORICAL AND FINE ARTS MUSEUM, 121 W Seventh Ave, Anchorage, AK 99501. *Dir* R L Shalkop.
Circulation of exhibitions in Alaska only. No rental fee; transportation variable. No catalogs available.

ARAPAHOE COMMUNITY COLLEGE, Colorado Gallery of the Arts, 5900 S Santa Fe Dr, Littleton, CO 80120. *Cur* Sally L Perisho.
Exhibits—Wind, Sun & Science: Art of the Southwest American Indians; 4000 Years of Hats. Rental fees are to be determined.

ARIZONA COMMISSION OF THE ARTS, 2024 N Seventh St, Suite 201, Phoenix, AZ 85006. *Visual Arts Coordr* Rex Gulbranson.
Rental Fees: In-state, 4 week booking-$250 plus one way shipping; out-of-state, $450 plus shipping both ways.

THE ARKANSAS ARTS CENTER, State Services Program, PO Box 2137, Little Rock, AR 72203. *Dir Programs* Bill Atkins; *Asst Dir Programs* Theresa Spragins.
Exhibits—23 exhibitions from the Arkansas Arts Center Foundation Collection. Available year-round for scheduled 3 week rental periods. Rental fee $120. Shipping fee $100.

ART CENTER OF BATTLE CREEK, 265 E Emmett St, Battle Creek, MI 49017. *Cur* Linda Poirier.
Exhibits—Watercolor Artists of Michigan; The Land, as Seen by Michigan Artists; How the Artist Draws; The Print, Varieties & Techniques by Michigan Artists. Rental Fees $35-$60 for 4 weeks. Shipping fees are adjustable.

ART IN ARCHITECTURE, 7917 ½ W Norton Ave, Los Angeles, CA 90046. *Exec Dir* Millicent Young
Exhibit—Joseph Young's Triforium. 50 working drawings, photographs and technical studies outlining the designing, prefabrication and construction of the City of Los Angeles million dollar art symbol. Completed in 1975 by Joseph Young, one of America's most controversial architectural artists, the 60 ft high Triforium is the world's first major permanent polyphonoptic sculpture that was built between 1969 and 1975. Rental fee for 30 days $900, plus airfreight costs and insurance from previous exhibitor; exhibition can be accompanied by personal presentation by artist.

THE ART MUSEUM ASSOCIATION OF AMERICA, 270 Sutter St, San Francisco, CA 94108. *Exhibition Program Dir* Harold B Nelson; *Cur* Terri Cohn.
Exhibits—40 touring exhibitions including: Marsden Hartley; Contemporary American Wood Sculpture; West Coast Realist; Edward Steichen Portraits; Mark Tobey Prints; Emotional Impact; Anxious Interiors; Disarming Images. Rental fees $800-$9000. Shipping fees prorated. Catalogs available.

ART MUSEUM, THE COLLEGE OF WOOSTER, University St, Wooster, OH 44691. *Asst to Dir* Phyllis Clark.
Exhibits—Lalanne & Bracquemond; 16th & 17th century printmakers of Northern Europe; 18th century printmakers of Italy. Rental fees and travel arrangements to be negotiated at time of reservations.

ASSOCIATED AMERICAN ARTISTS, 663 Fifth Ave, New York, NY 10022. *Dir* Sylvan Cole.
Original prints in all media by artists of many countries. Etchings, lithographs, woodcuts, serigraphs, intaglios, stencils, in black and white, and color.
Group Exhibitions—Discerning Eye.
One-Man Shows—John Taylor Arms, Mario Avati, Milton Avery, Thomas Hart Benton, Frederico Castellon, Fritz Eichenberg, Armin Landeck, John Muench.
Private and public organizations and institutions having facilities for the care of the fine prints eligible. Rental fees from $100 to $250. For additional information, please write or call 212-755-4211.

ASSOCIATION OF SCIENCE-TECHNOLOGY CENTERS (ASTC), 1016 16th St, NW, Washington, DC 20036. *Traveling Exhibitions* Wendy Pollock, Karen Sugerman & Ellen Horositz.
Exhibits—Museum quality exhibitions on science, technology, science art, natural history, and related subjects. Exhibition formats included

are photography shows, art work and artifact collections and "hands-on" exhibits emphasizing viewer participation. Offerings include: Colors of the Chemist, 20 abstract images & participatory displays about the science & art of instant color film; A Delicate Wilderness, 65 historic photographs of the Canadian frontier by Elliot Barnes; Looking at the Light-interactive displays about mirrors, lenses & light; Maps & Minds, 114 colorful panels that trace the history of mapmaking from ancient times to the present; Weavers of Water, Weavers of Light, 50 color photographs of the microscopic inhabitants of ponds, puddles & lakes. Rental fees are charged for exhibitions, & exhibitors are responsible for the cost of inbound shipping unless otherwise specified. Shipping arrangements are made by ASTC. ASTC Traveling Exhibition Service Catalog available free; call 202-452-0655.

BALTIMORE MUSEUM OF ART, Art Museum Drive, Traveling Exhibitions, Baltimore, MD 21218. *Dir of Educ* Susan S Badder.
Exhibits—Chagall's Exodus; Equitable Bank Photographic Survey of Maryland; Images of Christianity; In the Image of Woman; Mandarin Squares; Mindscapes: Prints by R B Kitaj; The Pliant Reed: Baskets of the Southwest; To Open Eyes (Josef Albers). Rental fee $200 per four week booking; includes transportation, installation, insurance & printed brochures. Catalogs available.

BALZEKAS MUSEUM OF LITHUANIAN CULTURE, 4012 Archer Ave, Chicago, IL 60632. *Pres* Stanley Balzekas, Jr.
Six small portable cases which include history, maps, and some memorabilia on Lithuania dating back 300 years. Rental fee is $150 plus transportation.

BRADLEY UNIVERSITY, Division of Art, Peoria, IL 61625. *Visual Arts Cur* Micheal O'Brien.
Exhibits—Bradley National Print and Drawing Biannual Show, 1983.

BURCHFIELD ART CENTER, State University of New York College at Buffalo, 1300 Elmwood Ave, Buffalo, NY 14222. Tel 716-878-6011. *Dir* Edna M Lindemann.
Exhibits—Charles Burchfield on loan from the permanent collection); Charles Cary Rumsey 1879-1922; Bruce Kurland: Insight Into Still Life; Henry Varnum Poor 1887-1970; Buffalo Society of Artists; The Nevelsons of Western New York. Exhibition catalogs available.

CALIFORNIA STATE COLLEGE, SAN BERNARDINO, 5500 State College Parkway, San Bernardino, CA 92407. *Chmn* Julius Kaplan.
Exhibits—New American Photographs 1982-1983. Rental fee $300. Shipping fee depends on distance. Catalog available.

CENTER FOR CREATIVE PHOTOGRAPHY, 843 E University Blvd, Tucson, AZ 85719. Contact cur of exhibitions.
Exhibits—Ansel Adams: A Survey, 40 framed prints personally selected by Adams to represent his long and distinguished career in photography. 100 running feet. Rental fee $750 per month.
Ansel Adams—Photographs of the Southwest: 1928-1968. 100 framed prints. This exhibition is a landmark as it culminates 40 years of work by Adams in the southwest states. 200 running feet. Rental fee $1500 per month.
Barbara Crane—Photographs from 1948-1980. 100 framed prints ranging from black/white view camera combination imagery to small color Polaroids. Exhibition catalog available at $17.50 each and with a 40% discount to renting institutions. (25 complimentary copies). 200 runing feet. Rental fee $750 per month.
W Eugene and Aileen Smith-Minamata, the photoessay. 65 framed prints. Selection from W Eugene Smith's last and most fulfilling work on the industrial poisoning of the Japanese fishing village. Exhibition catalog available at $3 each and with a 40% discount to renting institutions. (30 complimentary copies). 150 running feet. Rental fee $950 per month.
Jerry Uelsmann, A Retrospective, 1956-1981. Surveys Uelsmann's contribution through 100 prints. 100 framed prints. Exhibition catalogs $39.95. 250 running feet. Rental fee $950 per month.

THE CHRYSLER MUSEUM, Olney Road and Mowbray Arch, Norfolk, VA 23510. *Chief Cur* Thomas W Sokolowski.
Exhibits—Andre Kertesz, Master of Photography & Taste in American Glass. Rental fees & shipping negotiable.

CLEMSON UNIVERSITY, College of Architecture, Rudolph Lee Gallery, PO Box 992, Clemson, SC 29631. *Coordinator of Educational Media and Exhibits* Tom Dimond.

COLORADO STATE UNIVERSITY, Office of Cultural Programs, Lory Student Center, Fort Collings, CO 80523. *Assoc Dir for Programs* Miriam B Harris.
Exhibits—Colorado International Invitational Poster Exhibition. Rental fee $2500. Shipping fees are costs to next touring exhibition site. Exhibition held in odd-numbered years, exhibition available for tour subsequent two years following opening at CSU.

CORNING MUSEUM OF GLASS, Corning, NY 14831. Tel 607-937-5371.
Exhibits—Pressed Glass 1825-1925.

COUNCIL OF AMERICAN INDIAN ARTISTS, Box 5474, New York, NY 10163. *Exec Dir* David McCord.
Exhibits—Occasionally arrange shows of contemporary American Indian art. Rental fee is negotiable and shipping fees vary.

THE DETROIT INSTITUTE OF ARTS, 5200 Woodward Ave, Detroit MI 48202. Contact Dr. Frederick Cummings. Rental and shipping fees vary.

DIAMOND M MUSEUM, PO Box 1149, Snyder, TX 79549. *Assoc Dir* Janet R Parker.
Exhibits—"Art From the Diamond M." There are no rental fees. Shipping fees are at cost. Exhibits only in West Texas.

EDO COMPREHENSIVE EXHIBITION SERVICES, 453 Sycamore Rd, Santa Monica, CA 90402. Contact William Osmun. Tel 213-454-8041.
Exhibits—Earthworks-Land Reclamation as Sculpture; Artist's Quilt, Collection of Ludy Strauss; The Plan of St Gall: A Carolingian Master Plan for Monastic Settlements. . . ; Eva Hesse, A Retrospective of the Drawings; Matisse Prints 1903-1929. Rental fees $3000-$4000. Catalogues available.

ERIE ART MUSEUM, 411 State St, Erie, PA 16501.*Registrar* Linda DeVane-Williams.
Exhibits—Photonational; Clay National; Take a Good Look; Daumier Lithographs; Art of the Comic Book. Rental fee $500. Shipping fee varies.

ESMARK, INC, 55 E Monroe St, Chicago, IL 60603. *Asst Mgr Corporate Affairs* Elizabeth Skalla.
Exhibits—Esmark Collection of Currier & Ives ongoing nationwide tour.

FIBERWORKS, CENTER FOR THE TEXTILE ARTS, 1940 Bonita, Berkely, CA 94704. *Dir* J Weldon Smith.
Exhibits—Contemporary Textile Arts. Fees vary.

FLORIDA ARTIST GROUP, INC, 601 Apalachicola Rd, Venice, FL 33595. *Pres* Anne Atz.
Jury chosen Annual Exhibition of Members Show (34—45 entries) is available following the Spring Exhibition (May). Also, from the local areas other traveling exhibitions are available throughout the year (includes paintings, graphics, sculpture, assemblages). No rental fees; Galleries & museums responsible for transportation expense.

FREEDMAN GALLERY-ALBRIGHT COLLEGE, 13th & Exeter Sts, Reading, PA 19603. Tel 215-921-2381, Ext 347. *Dir* Judith Tannenbaum.
Exhibits—Public Art: Recent Developments. Rental fee $1500 plus shipping. Catalogs available.

FRENCH CULTURAL SERVICES, Exhibitions Dept, 972 Fifth Ave, New York, NY 10021. Tel 212-570-4400.
Exhibits—Photography, documentary & art exhibits available. No rental fees, but one way shipping cost paid by exhibitor. Catalogs available.

GALERIE RESTIGOUCHE GALLERY, 39 Andrew St, PO Box 674, Campbellton, NB E3N 3H1, Canada. *Dir & Curator* Paul Soucy.
Exhibits—Couleurs d'Acadie-Color photographs of brightly painted houses phenomena. 120 running feet. No rental fee. Borrower pays cost of transportation both ways. Catalog available.

GALLERY ASSOCIATION OF NEW YORK STATE, Box 345, Hamilton, NY 13346. Tel 315-824-2510. Contact Janice Oresman.
Exhibits—Twentieth Century American Watercolor. Approximately 40 artists from various periods in this century will be represented.

GIBBES ART GALLERY, 135 Meeting St, Charleston, SC 29401. *Cur* Paul Figueroa.
Exhibits—Japanese Prints; Photographs; Contemporary Prints. Rental fee $250-$1000. Shipping fee one way.

THE SOLOMON R GUGGENHEIM MUSEUM, 1071 Fifth Ave, New York, NY 10128. *Cur* Vivian Barnett.
Exhibits—Concentrations of Individual Artists; European Painting & Sculpture; Modern Sculpture; European Sources of American Abstraction; American Abstract Painting and Works on Paper from the

1930's & 1940's; Postwar American Painting, Postwar European Painting; Post War Art; Latin American Art; Works on Paper. Borrowing institutions will remain responsible for shipping, insurance, packing & other charges.

HALLMARK CARDS, INC, Hallmark Collections, 25th & McGeem, Kansas City, MO 64108. *Mgr Collections & Archives* Sally Hope.
Exhibits—Edward Weston: One Hundred Photographs, catalogue $10; Saul Steinberg Drawings & Watercolors, poster $8; Andre Kertesz: Form & Feeling, poster $6; Portraits from the Hallmark Photographic Collection; Photographic Abstraction; Lewis Hine; Harry Callahan, catalogue $10.

HIBEL MUSEUM OF ART, PO Box 10607, Riviera Beach, FL 33404. Tel 305-848-9633. *Trustee* Andy Plotkin.
Exhibits—From as little as one piece to as many as one hundred or more in the following categories: Paintings, original stone lithographs, porcelain lithographs, collector plates, candlescreens, and drawings (rarely shown to the public). Support materials available include: Posters, catalogues, brochures & press materials, museum gift items, films & slide shows, invitations for opening.

HILLWOOD ART GALLERY, C W Post Center, Long Island University, Greenvale, NY 11548. *Dir* Dr Judith K VanWagner.
Exhibits—Majorie Strider, 1970-1980; Floored; Futurism & Photography; Michele Stuart: A Decade of Work. Rental fee $1500-$4500. Shipping fees are incoming.

HOCKADAY CENTER FOR THE ARTS, Second Ave East at Third St, Kalispell, MT 59901. Tel 406-755-5268. *Dir* Magee Ferguson.
Exhibits—Calligraphers West; Fish-An Exhibit; Northern Rockies Photography. Rental fee $500. Shipping fee paid outgoing.

HUNTERDON ART CENTER, Seven Center St, Clinton, NJ 08809. *Exec Dir* Linda Constant Buki.
Exhibits—Hunterdon Art Center Permanent Collection of Prints. Rental and shipping fees vary.

HUNTSVILLE MUSEUM OF ART, 700 Monroe St, Huntsville, AL 35801. *Cur* Bruce Hiles.
Exhibits—Serial Imagery, 36 prints from the collection of the Huntsville Museum of Art. Rental fee $500. Shipping fee varies.

INDIAN ARTS & CRAFTS BOARD, US Dept of the Interior, Rm 4004, Washington, DC 20240. *Cur* Rosemary Ellison.
Exhibits—Contemporary Sioux Quillwork; Contemporary Southern Plains Indian Metalwork. Rental & shipping fees vary.

INDIANA UNIVERSITY SCHOOL OF FINE ARTS, 123 Fine Arts Bldg, Indiana University, Bloomington, IN 47405. Contact Starr Varner.
Exhibits—Graduate Student Printmaking: 40 Works From 15 Years of MFA Students. Rental fee $250 (includes 15 catalogues). Shipping fee is one way freight.

INSTITUTE OF AMERICAN INDIAN ARTS MUSEUM, 1369 Cerrillos Rd, Santa Fe, NM 87501. Tel 505-988-6281. *Dir* Charles Dailey.
Exhibits—One With the Earth. This exhibit is composed of 110 items including beadwork, ceramics, sculpture, rugs, basketry and paintings. The exhibit is composed of both traditional Indian art forms and contemporary art. Rental fee $1000 for a 6-8 week exhibit. Exhibitor pays transportation. Herdboys of Lesotho: The Coming of Manhood. These selections include black and white and color photographs by Nancy Dahl. 31 black and white and color photographs, 1 title, 1 map and 1 general statement. Rental fee $50. Transportation both ways.
New Directions—Paintings in this exhibit are typical of the development art styles of young Indian people at the Institute of American Indian Arts in the past 20 years. Based on the solid foundations of the old Santa Fe Indian School under Dorothy Dunn, the evolution of painting style has reached out for new directions. Exhibit contains 30 paintings & 1 title. Rental fee $50 and transportation both ways.
Years of Change—Continuing the tradition of the great Native American artists and yet striving in new directions, many of today's Institute of American Indian Arts students are being recognized as valid and innovative contributors to the contemporary Indian art scene. All works are drawn from the museum collection. Exhibit contains 36 paintings, 1 title & 1 statement. Rental fee $50 and return transportation.

INTERNATIONAL EXHIBITIONS FOUNDATION, 1729 H St, NW, Suite 310, Washington, DC 20006. *Pres* Mrs John A Pope.
Exhibits—20th Century Masters: The Thyssen-Bornemisza Collection. The paintings span a 70-year interval & examine a variety of periods that flourished in the wake of Impressionism & before & after the two World Wars. Exhibition catalogue $15.

INTERNATIONAL MUSEUM OF PHOTOGRAPHY AT GEORGE EASTMAN HOUSE, 900 East Ave, Rochester, NY 14607. *Dir Marketing Services* Susan Kramarsky.
Exhibits—10-15 photographic exhibitions circulated internationally. Rental fee $200-$5000.

THE INTERNORTH ART FOUNDATION, 2223 Dodge St, Omaha, NE 68102. *Executive Dir* James J Finnegan.
In 1984 an exhibition in connection with sesquicentennial of Maximilian's journey is planned.

JAMESTOWN COMMUNITY COLLEGE, 525 Falconer St, Jamestown, NY 14701. *Dir* Michael E Campbell.
Exhibits—Albert's Dream, ceramic doll sculpture; WORKS, acrylic paintings & bronze sculpture; Acrylic Impressionistic Paintings & Ceramic Sculpture. Rental & shipping fees vary.

JOHN C CALHOUN STATE COMMUNITY COLLEGE, The Art Gallery, Room 237 Fine Arts Bldg, Highway 31 N, Decatur, AL 35602. *Dir* Helen Austin.

KALAMAZOO INSTITUTE OF ARTS, 315 S Park St, Kalamazoo, MI 49007. *Dir* Thomas Kayser; *Asst for Exhibitions* Helen Sheridan.
Exhibits—The Revitalized Print. Rental fee $500. Shipping as arranged.

KANSAS STATE UNIVERSITY, Art Building, Manhattan, KS 66506. *Asst Cur* Jessica Reichman.
Exhibits—The Photography of Gordon Parks from the Kansas State University permanent collection. Rental fees vary.

KERN COUNTY MUSEUM, 3801 Chester Ave, Bakersfield, CA 93301. *Asst Dir & Cur* Diana Seider.
Exhibits—Hard Times in the Promised Land: Photographs & quotes by dustbowl migrants to Kern County during the 1930s. No rental fee. Shipping paid by exhibitor.

KITCHENER-WATERLOO ART GALLERY, 101 Queen St N, Kitchener, ON N2H 6P7 Canada. *Cur* Jennifer C Watson.
Exhibits—Abstract Art; Animal Images; Artists & Media, printmaking; A J Casson; Group of Seven; A Y Jackson; Our Heritage; W J Phillips; Art: A Study of Flowers; Progression Proof, Silkscreen; Recording the Canadian Landscape; Albert H Robinson: The Mature Years. These exhibits only available in Waterloo region.

LATITUDE 53 SOCIETY OF ARTISTS, 9749 111 St, Edmonton, AB T5K 1J7 Canada. *Pres* Trudie Heiman.
Exhibits—Issues in Clay-Western Canadian Sculpture; J A Irvine Photographic Collection; ANNPAC Poster Show.

LONG BEACH MUSEUM OF ART, 2300 E Ocean Blvd, Long Beach, CA 90803. Tel 213-439-2119. Contact Kent Smith.
Exhibits—Passion & Precision: The Photographer & Grand Prix Racing, 1895-1985. 100 photographs. This exhibition will commemorate the 90th anniversary of the first automobile race and pay tribute to approximately twenty major photographers who have devoted a significant portion of their careers to photographing motor racing. Rental fee $3000. 350 running ft.

MENDEL ART GALLERY, 950 Spadina Crescent E, PO Box 569, Saskatoon, SK S7K 3L6 Canada. *Extension Coordr* Grant Arnold.
Exhibits—Nationally touring-Prime Time Video; Eli Bornstein: Selected Works 1958-1982; Otto Rogers: A Survey 1958-1982; Joe Fafard: Dear Vincent; Wynnona Mulcaster: A Survey 1973-1983; Simon Read/Selected Works.
Provincially touring-Christian Knudsen: Paintings; Stanely Brunst: Radical Painter; Robert Vincent: Selected Works. Catalogues & brochures available with all exhibitions.

MEMORIAL UNIVERSITY OF NEWFOUNDLAND, Art Gallery, Arts & Culture Centre, St John's, NF A1C 5S7 Canada. *Cur* Patricia Grattan.
Exhibits—Contemporary art; folk art; traditional craft of Newfoundland & Labrador. Rental & shipping fees vary.

MIDTOWN GALLERIES, INC, 11 E 57th St, New York, NY 10022. *Dir* Mrs Alan D Gruskin.
Exhibitions arranged for group or one man shows of drawings, watercolors, oils by contemporary American artists. Available to museums, universities, colleges and art centers. Inquiries invited.

THE MUSEUM OF CARTOON ART, Comly Ave, Rye Brook, NY 10573. *Dir* Brian Walker.
Exhibit—Cartoons in America. The cartoons in the collection were

reproduced from woodcuts, engravings, lithographs, original art and printed pages. Cartoons were selected for their effective and timely reflection of following social themes: Settling the Land, The American Character, The Melting Pot, American Ingenuity, In Defense of Freedom, The Rights of the People, The American Dream, Social Problems, Great American Pastimes. Rental fee $1000 for two weeks; special rates for nonprofit organizations.

MUSEUM OF HOLOGRAPHY, 11 Mercer St, New York, NY 10013. Tel 212-840-1540. *Traveling Exhibitions Serv* Paul D Barefoot.
Exhibits—Through the Looking Glass-An exhibition of three-dimensional images made with lasers. Based on the museum's inaugural exhibition of the same name and includes more than 30 examples of state-of-the-art holography, selected for artistic and technical merit. It is the first major and largest exhibition of holography available for wide circulation and provides a thorough introduction to this new art form made with lasers. Rental fee $1500 per week (4 week minimum), plus transportation expense. Camera-ready artwork of catalog provided.

MUSEUM OF MODERN ART, 11 W 53rd St, New York, NY 10019.
Exhibition Program: *Coordinator of Exhibitions* Richard L Palmer; *Assoc Coordr* Caroline Jones.
A number of exhibitions directed by members of the Museum's curatorial staff are offered to other qualified museums on a participating basis. These exhibitions are generally either full-scale projects or reduced versions of shows initially presented at The Museum of Modern Art. Although exhibitions are not necessarily available at all times in all media, the traveling program does cover the entire range of the Museum's New York program-painting, sculpture, drawings, prints, photography, architecture and design. Participating fees usually begin at $750 for smaller exhibitions and range up to several thousand dollars for major exhibitions. Tour participants are also asked to cover prorated transport costs.
International Program: *Dir, International Prog* Waldo Rasmussen; *Assoc Dir* Elizabeth Streibert.
The primary function of the program is to encourage cultural exchange in all the visual arts on a broad international level. Exhibitions of painting, sculpture, drawings, prints, photography, architecture, design, and film are circulated by the Museum to foreign countries under the auspices of The International Council of The Museum of Modern Art. Rental fee plus transportation from preceding exhibitor. Programs with overseas libraries and visiting foreign specialists.
Circulating Film Library: *Librarian* William Sloan.
Films and programs are drawn from the Museum's international archive of films as well as being distributed on behalf of independent producers; these are made available for rental and, in some cases, for lease. The films exemplify or illustrate the history, development, sale and technical diversity of the motion picture. Programming assistance is available upon request. Rental or lease fee plus shipping and handling costs. Catalogues and supplements list more than 900 titles ranging from films of the 1890's to recent independent productions.

MUSEUM OF NEON ART, 704 Traction Ave, Los Angeles, CA 90013. *Dir* Lili Lakich.
Exhibits—Ladies of the Night: Neon/Electric Images of Women; The Neon Jungle. Rental fee $15,000. Shipping fee $8000-$10,000.

MUSEUM OF THE AMERICAN INDIAN/HEYE FOUNDATION, Broadway at 155th St, New York, NY 10032. *Registrar* David Fawcett.
Exhibits—Iroquois Silver—This is an exhibition of silver ornaments & utilitarian objects of the Iroquois people. It is due to travel to several museums in New York State including Indian museums: The schedule for this exhibition is being handled by the Gallery Associations of New York State. Tel 315-824-2510. Catalog.
Star Gods of the Ancient Americas—The first exhibition of its kind, is designed to express the unity of art, religion, astronomy, and seasonal cycles in ancient American thought. Visual components include artifacts from North, Middle, and South American and photographs. Opens Nov 1982.
Glimpses of Algonkian Culture: Indians of Southern New York State. This exhibition provides a brief introduction to three culturally related Algonkian groups: the Metoac, the Delaware and the Mohican.
Native American Painting: Selections from the Museum of the American Indian. This exhibition is a rare showing of some of the finest works on paper & canvas by North American Indians in the Museum's large & newly-recataloged collections. Drawings in ledger books, and paintings from the famed Studio in Santa Fe and from Oklahoma document the development of Indian styles and techniques to the present day. The exhibition is presented in two parts, each containing some fifty works.
With Eagle Glance: Indian Photographic Images 1868-1931. Exhibition of original photographic prints in the private collection of War-

ren Adelson & Ira Spanierman. The images are principally of Plains Indians including several well-known personages such as Geronimo, American Horse, and a delegation of Crow leaders who visited Washington, DC in 1868. Also included are images of some of the cowboys who replaced the Indians as lords of the plains.
Exhibition catalogs with all exhibits.

NASSAU COUNTY MUSEUM OF FINE ART, PO Box D, Roslyn, NY 11576. *Dir* Thomas A Saltzman.
Exhibits—Arthur Leipzig: Jewish Life Around the World. Exhibit contains 133 photographs & 10 educational panels. Rental fee $1000. Shipping fees vary.

NATIONAL FILM BOARD, Still Photography Division, Tunney's Pasture, Ottawa, ON, K1A ON1, Canada. Tel 613-992-1920 *Exec Producer* Martha Langford.
The Still Photography Division exhibits the work of contemporary Canadian photographers. Over 100 traveling exhibitions. No rental fee. Transportation inside Canada, the exhibitor shares the carriers' charges with the NFB; outside Canada, the exhibitor is responsible for transportation costs. Catalogue available.

NATIONAL WATERCOLOR SOCIETY, 390 S Hauser Blvd, #7C, Los Angeles, CA 90036. *Second VPres* Madeline Haase.
Exhibits—Travel shows are juried from the Annual Exhibitions and from the All-Membership Shows. Works are aquamedia on paper. Current shows are framed, under plexi. The approximate number of works in each show is 20-25. Double shows of approximately 45 works are possible when requested long enough in advance. NWS travel shows are available only to museums and galleries with adequate security and supervision. Commercial galleries are not eligible. National Watercolor Society requires that exhibiting galleries provide insurance during the exhibit and pay transportation and in-transit insurance one way. No other fee is charged. A limited number of the Annual Exhibition catalogs are available for a nominal fee.

NEW BRUNSWICK MUSEUM, 277 Douglas Ave, Saint John, NB E2K 1E5 Canada. *Dir* Dr Alan McNairn.
Exhibits—Fire! Fire!; New Brunswick Endangered Species; Samplers; New Brunswick Scenes and Settlements, pictoral.

NEW HARMONY GALLERY OF CONTEMPORARY ART, Owen Block, Main St, New Harmony, IN 47631. *Dir* Jonathan Soard.
Exhibits—Making It In Paper, an Indian Mill Twinrocker hand-made paper; New Harmony Imprints; Hand-lithographs & Intaglios produced by New Harmony Print Workshop.

NEW ORLEANS MUSEUM OF ART, PO Box 19123, City Park, New Orleans, LA 70179. *Assoc Cur* Paul Tarver.
Exhibits—The Photographers of Mother St Croix, photographs by Leslie Gill; Photography in Louisiana, Elizabeth Catlett; Sculpture & Graphics, Clarence John Laughlin & Edward Weston; The Third World of Photography, Early Views of the Vieux Carre; Paintings by William Woodward. Rental fees $200-$1200. One-way transportation. Catalogues and posters available for certain exhibitions.

NEWPORT HARBOR ART MUSEUM, 850 San Clemente Dr, Newport Beach, CA 92660. *Director* Kevin E Consey; *Curator of Exhibitions and Collections* Paul Schimmel.
Organizes and circulates exhibitions of the art of our time, with the emphasis on American art of the last 30 years. Exhibitions are usually circulated by letter directly to other art institutions, but inquiries are always encouraged from any museum looking for exhibitions dealing with painting, sculpture and photography, with an emphasis on modern and contemporary art.

NINE ONE ONE, 911 E Pine, Seattle, WA 98122. *Dir* Jill Medredow.
Exhibits—Local artists. No rental fee. Shipping costs vary.

NORTH GEORGIA COLLEGE, Fine Arts Dept, Dahlonega, GA 30597. *Head Fine Arts* Robert L Owens.
Exhibits—Recent Works. Rental fee $150 each. Shipping fees at cost.

OCTAGON CENTER FOR THE ARTS, 427 Douglas, Ames, IA 50010. *Dir* Martha Benson.
Exhibits—Women in Clay: The Ongoing Tradition. (Available 6/84-12/85). Rental fee $2000. Shipping fee $500.

OHIO FOUNDATION ON THE ARTS, 440 Dublin Ave, Columbus, OH 43216. Tel 614-221-4300. *Dir* Craig McDaniel.
Exhibits—New Masks, contemporary American artists' masks; The Last Laugh, contemporary humor in visual art.

OHIO STATE UNIVERSITY GALLERY OF FINE ART, Hopkins Hall, Rm 240, 128 N Oval Mall, Columbus, OH 43210. *Dir* Jonathan Green.
Exhibits—A Center for the Visual Arts: The Ohio State University Competition; James Friedman Travelling Exhibit: Color Photographs 1979-1982. Rental fee vary. Shipping fees paid for by exhibitors.

OHIO UNIVERSITY, Trisolini Gallery, 48 E Union St, Athens, OH 45701. *Dir* Henry H Lin.
Exhibits—Trisolini Print Project; Young New York Artists from Brooke Alexander, Inc, paintings & sculpture; The Colomon Collection, primitive New Guinea art: Chicago Artists, paintings.

OLD BERGEN ART GUILD, 43 W 33rd St, Bayonne, NJ 07002. Tel 201-437-3599 *Dir* William D Gorman; *Assoc Dir* Jan Gary.
Over 70 group and one-man traveling exhibits—Oils, watercolors, caseins and graphics in all styles by contemporary American artists. Available to museums, art centers, universities, colleges, and libraries. No fee, except for one-way express charge. Send stamped, addressed envelope for free catalog.

OHIO FOUNDATION ON THE ARTS, INC, PO Box 2572, Columbus, OH 43216. *Dir* Maureen McCormick.
Exhibits—20-30 available each year. Rental & shipping fees vary.

OWATONNA ARTS CENTER, PO Box 134, Owatonna, MN 55060. *Cur* Silvan Durben.
Exhibits—The Marianne Young World Costume Collection. This collection includes 98 garments from 25 countries and is complete with accessories such as hats, jewelry, gloves and boots. The collection includes caftans, saris, coats, kimonos and French originals. Examples of the gowns in the collection include: a dress from South Africa made completely of white ostrich feathers; a long gown from Pakistan covered with mirrors held in place by embroidery; a bright blue poncho cape from Bali (used in formal dances) which is painted in gold, yellow and shocking pink; a wine-red caracul skin coat from Afghanistan is embroidered in gold with black caracul edging. The costumes, all in her own petite size, were collected by Marianne Young during 50 years of travel. Rental fee is $400; transportation is negotiable. Brochure available on request.

THE PHILLIPS COLLECTION, 1600 21st St NW, Washington, DC 20009. *Dir* Laughlin Phillips.
Exhibits—Arthur Dove & Duncan Phillips: Artists & Patron (1981); George Braque: The Late Paintings 1940-1963 (1982); Morris Graves: Vision of the Inner Eye (1983).

PHOENIX ART MUSEUM, 1625 N Central Ave, Phoenix, AZ 85004. *Asst Cur* Susan Gordon.
Exhibits—Jay Dusard: The North American Cowboy, painting. Rental fee varies. Chinese Cloisonne: The Claque Collection. Rental fee $4500. Chinese Ceramics: The Wong Collection, blue & white. Rental fee $3000.

PRATT GRAPHICS CENTER, 160 Lexington Ave, New York, NY 10016. *Dir* Andrew Stasik. Tel: 201-685-3169.
Exhibition of graphic arts—original prints, available to art schools, universities, art associations. Current shows—Prints USA: 1982; 9th International Miniature Print Exhibition; Prints by Major 20th century artists; Artists and Fables; Contemporary Serigraphs; New Directions in Printmaking; The Collagraph-A New Print Medium; Contemporary American Fine Arts Posters;Puerto Rican Graphics; Animals in Prints; The Butcher, the Baker, the Candlestick Maker; Images of Labor; Daumier: A Century Tribute; Minimum rental fee.

PURDUE UNIVERSITY, Creative Arts Dept, West Lafayette, IN 47907. *Dir* Mona Berg.
Exhibits—National Cone Box Show, miniature ceramic competition winners. No rental fee. Shipping fee dependant on distance.

ROTHMANS OF PALL MALL CANADA LIMITED, 1500 Don Mills Rd, Toronto, ON M3B 3L1 Canada. Tel 416-449-5525. Contact Alan R Hanlon.
Exhibits—Contemporary Canadian paintings, prints, drawings and Eskimo sculpture. Approx 350 works. Works from the collection available for circulating exhibitions to major public institutions in Canada. Presently circulating is American Accents, consisting of 46 works by 21 artists, the most important collection of American Contemporary Art ever to be shown in Canadian Museums in several decades.

SANFORD MUSEUM AND PLANETARIUM, 117 East Willow, Cherokee, IA 51012. Tel: 712-225-3922. *Dir* J Terry Walker.
Virginia Herrick Quilt Block Exhibit—a large collection of quilt block patterns (some common and uncommon); Oscillons—electronic abstractions by Ben Laposky, photographs of works completed by one of the pioneers of computer art in North America and the world; Midwest Indians and Frontier Photography, early photographs of Indians connected with Iowa and the surrounding states, 1869 - 1900. Rental fee plus shipping charges to be paid by exhibitor.

ST JOHN'S MUSEUM OF ART, 114 Orange St, Wilmington, NC 28401. *Dir* Alan Aiches.
Exhibits—Steffen Thomas: The Freedon of the Figure. Rental fee $6000. Shipping fee prorated.

SMITHSONIAN INSTITUTION TRAVELING EXHIBITION SERVICE (SITES), Washington, DC 20560. *Dir* Peggy A Loar; *Asst Dir* Antonio Diez.
100 Exhibitions—Architecture, cultural history, decorative arts, design, environment, paintings, prints & drawings, photography, science & technology. Available to educational, scientific, cultural and on occasion, commercial institutions. Educational materials and program activities supplement the exhibits. Catalogs, posters and brochures accompany specific exhibits. Annual catalog "Update" available to exhibitors on request. Quarterly newsletter "Siteline" available now.

SPERTUS MUSEUM OF JUDAICA, 618 S Michigan Ave, Chicago, IL 60605. *Museum Registrar* Mary Larkin.
Exhibits—Faith & Forum: Synagogue Architecture in Illinois. Photographic essay consisting of 145 black and white photographs. Rental fee of $1250 (including insurance) for 3 month exhibit. Catalogs included (selling price $10) Transportation charges extra.
Garden of the Generations: Gan Hadorot. Illustrated time-line wall-hung panels. Three 60"x213" panels. Rental fee $300 (including insurance) for 3 month exhibit. Transportation charges extra.
The Jews of Sandor. Photographic essay detailing the lives of the Jews of Sandor, an agrarian village in Iraqi Kurdistan. Original photographs were found in the collection of the Field Museum of Natural History. 25 photographs, 1 lead photograph, 1 map panel, 1 synagogue floor plan. Rental fee of $250 (including insurance) for 3 month exhibit. Catalogs included (selling price $1.50, additional catalogs $1). Transportation charges extra.
The Jews of Yemen. Photographic essay of sudden flight of the Jews from Yeman/Aden to Israel and unfamiliar aspect of Jewish culture. Photographs were taken in Aden and Israel during the period 1949-1950 in the course of Operation Magic Carpet. 71 photographs, 1 map, 8 panels explanatory copy, 1 eight-track cartridge of Yemenite dance music. Rental fee of $750 (including insurance) for 3 month exhibit. Catalogs available (selling price $12 minus 40% discount). Transportation charges extra. Also Film of Boi Temen Dance Festival, rental fee $50.
Kaddish: Memorial to the Six Million. Eight etchings/aquatints by Mauricio Lasansky depicting his memorial to the six million victims of the Holocaust. Rental fee $150 (including insurance) for 3 month exhibit. Transportation charges additional.
David Bennett: Illustrations to the Bible. This exhibit consists of 9 color linoleum-cut prints depicting the Story of Joseph. It includes a print of Abraham & Isaac, edition of 50, which can be sold. 9 prints, 50 running feet. Rental fee $250 (including insurance). Transportation charges extra.
Andy Warhol: 10 Jews of the 20th Century. This exhibit consists of Andy Warhol's outstanding collection. The series highlights prominent Jews who have influenced contemporary life. Taken from existing photographs, Warhol's unique silkscreens capture the mood of each subject in a dynamic presentation. 10 framed print 52 x 40 in. 58 running feet. Rental fee $150 (includes insurance) for 3 month exhibit. Transportation charges additional.

TEXAS FINE ARTS ASSOCIATION, 3809 W 35th St, PO Box 5023 Austin, TX 78703. *In Charge* Beverly Petty.
Approximately 6 exhibitions containing 19-20 paintings each. Travel throughout Texas only. Rental fee $175, plus outgoing freight. Catalogs and biographic material available.

UNIVERSITY OF CALIFORNIA, California Museum of Photography, Riverside, CA 92521. *Cur* Edward W Earle.
Exhibits—The Orient Viewed: China & Japan in Stereographs. Rental fee $25 for four week exhibit. Shipping fees vary. This exhibit is available June 1984.

UNIVERSITY OF NEW MEXICO, Dept of Art, Albuquerque, NM 87131. Tel 505-277-5861.
Exhibits—Print Collection; Photographs Collection.

UNIVERSITY OF NOTRE DAME, THE SNITE MUSEUM OF ART, Notre Dame, IN 46556. Contact Director of Museum.
Exhibits—Cartoons by John McCutcheon; Everett McNear: Chicago Artist; Fritz Kaeser: Photographer: Ivan Mestrovic. Rental fee $250, Mestrovic $2000. Shipping fees one way. Catalogues available at min-

imal charge for Kaeser & Mestrovic; brochures available for McCutcheon & McNear.

UNIVERSITY OF SOUTH DAKOTA, Vermillion, SD 57069. *Dir* John A Day.
Exhibits—Works from permanent collection: Contemporary Prints/ Drawings; Oscar Howe Paintings. Rental fee is cost plus $100-$500 depending on size of show.

UNIVERSITY OF SOUTHERN COLORADO, University Gallery, 2200 N Bonforte Blvd, Pueblo, CO 81001. *Dir* Robert Hench.
Exhibits—Colorado Drawings I, 1983-85; Charles Waldo Love Drawings, 1983-84; Orman Collection selections available. No rental fee.

UNIVERSITY OF TENNESSEE, Department of Art, 1715 Volunteer Blvd, Knoxville, TN 37996. *Dir* Sam Yates.
Exhibits—Walter Hollis Stevens Paintings; 50 Years of TVA Architecture; Ten Contemporary Printmakers; Southern Abstraction. Five Painters. Rental & shipping fees vary. Catalogs and/or posters included.

UNIVERSITY OF WISCONSIN-GREEN BAY, Lawton Gallery, Nicolet Dr, Green Bay, WI 54301. *Cur* Karon Winzenz.
Exhibits—Contemporary Fibers/Fabrics; Contemporary Photography. Midwest Photography Invitationals, Biennial. Rental fee $350-$700. Shipping fees under $400.

UTAH ARTS COUNCIL, 617 E South Temple, Salt Lake City, UT 84102. Tel 801-533-5757.
Exhibits—The exhibition program is designed to provide traveling exhibitions to a statewide audience. Approximately twenty exhibitions are available which vary in size and subject matter. They include works from the permanent collections of the Utah Arts Council, the Utah Museum of Fine Arts and from special collections contributed by organizations and individuals. Exhibitions are scheduled for one month and are free of charge. The may be booked by museums, college and public galleries, community groups or institutions such as libraries, schools, or other non-profit organizations. The Visual Arts staff transports the exhibitions and supervises installation.

VAN ARSDALE ASSOCIATES, INC, PO Box 1965, Winter Park, FL 32790. *Pres* Dorothy T Van Arsdale.
Exhibits—Approx 20 exhibitions of painting, sculpture, drawings, prints, photographs, textiles, both foreign and American, usually about 25 to 50 pieces. Rental fees from $240 to $600 for 4-week booking period. The exhibitor is responsible for outgoing shipping. Annual catalog available plus occasional exhibition catalogs.

WASHINGTON PROJECT FOR THE ARTS, 1227 G St NW, Washington, DC 20005. Tel: 202-347-8304. *Exec Dir* Jock Reynolds.

Exhibits—Assorted exhibitions of experimental and contemporary artists. Washington based and across the county.

WASHINGTON STATE UNIVERSITY, Museum of Art, Pullman, WA 99164. *Dir* Sanford S Shaman. *Secy* Margaret Johnson
Wide range of two-dimensional art objects. Each exhibit includes approx 20-40 art works ranging from works on paper to sculptural objects. Rental fee available on request. Catalogs for certain exhibits.

WESTERN WASHINGTON UNIVERSITY, Bellingham, WA 98225. *Pres* George Thomas.
Exhibits—American Photographs 1970-1980; Works on Paper 1945-1975. Rental fee $200-$2000.

WHITNEY MUSEUM OF AMERICAN ART, 945 Madison Ave, New York, NY 10021. *Registrar* Nancy A McGary.
Exhibits—Vary

THE WINNIPEG ART GALLERY, 300 Memorial Blvd, Winnipeg, MB, R3C 1V1 Canada. *Assoc Cur Extension Servs* Donald DeGrow.
Exhibits—Salvador Dali: "Aliyah"; A Wilderness Alternative: Photographs by Dave O'Hara; Transformation of Vision: The Works of H Eric Bergman; White on White; Baker Lake Prints & Print Drawing 1970-1976; Latitudes & Parallels: A Focus on Contemporary Canadian Photography; Manitoba Juried Photography Exhibition; Manitoba Graphics: Contemporary Canadian Graphics; Sketchbook: Watercolours by Nicolas Howard McGachen. Rental fees vary depending on the exhibition & include insurance. Transporation costs vary depending on the show. Catalogues & brochures may also be included.

LEIGH YAWKEY WOODSON ART MUSEUM, Franklin & 12th Sts, Wausau, WI 54401. *Dir* David J Wagner; *Office Mgr* Marcia Theel; *Cur Exhibitions* Andrew McGivern.
Exhibits—Selections from the McMichael Canadian Collection. Fifty paintings by Canada's Group of Seven. Rental fee $1000 plus insurance & one-way freight. Catalog available. Contact LYWAM Tel 715-845-7010.
Americans in Glass 1984. Contemporary American studio glass. Exclusive European museum tour, July 1984-1986. Catalog available.
Rembrandt's Etchings. 70 works from the Vienna Art Society. Rental fee $3000 plus insurance & one-way freight. Brochure & posters available.

WORCHESTER CRAFT CENTER, 25 Sagamore Rd, Worchester, MA 01605. *Exec Dir* Cyrus D Lipsitt.
Exhibits—Fabric Constructions: The Art Quilt. Rental fee $1500. Precious Objects: Metals. Rental fee $1200. Shipping fees are cost to next exhibit.

IV INDEXES

Organization

Personnel

Subject

Organization Index

Schools are indicated by "S".

Abilene Christian University, Art Dept, Abilene TX (S)
Abilene Fine Arts Museum, Abilene TX
Abraham Baldwin Agricultural College, Art & Humanities Dept, Tifton GA (S)
Academy of Art College, San Francisco CA (S)
Academy of the Arts, Easton MD
Academy of the Museum of Conceptual Art, San Francisco CA
Acadian House Museum, Saint Martinville LA
Acadia University, Art Dept, Wolfville NS (S)
Louise Sloss Ackerman Fine Arts Library, see San Francisco Museum of Modern Art, San Francisco CA
The Ackland Art Museum, see University of North Carolina, Chapel Hill NC
Actual Art Foundation, New York NY
Adams National Historic Site, Quincy MA
Adams State College, Dept of Visual Arts, Alamosa CO (S)
Adams State College, Library, Alamosa CO
Adamy's Plastics and Mold-Making Workshops, Larchmont NY (S)
Addison Gallery of American Art, see Phillips Academy, Andover MA
Adelphi University, Fine Arts Library, Garden City NY
Adelphi University, Dept of Art and Art History, Garden City NY (S)
Adirondack Historical Association, Adirondack Museum, Blue Mountain Lake NY
Adirondack Lakes Center for the Arts, Blue Mountain Lake NY
Adrian College, Art Dept, Adrian MI (S)
Advocates for the Arts, Los Angeles CA
African American Historical and Cultural Society, San Francisco CA
African-American Institute, New York NY
Afro-American Historical and Cultural Museum, Philadelphia PA
Afro Arts Cultural Centre, Inc, African Arts Museum & Gallery, New York NY
Agecroft Association, Richmond VA
Ages of Man Fellowship, Amenia NY
Agnes Scott College, Dept of Art, Decatur GA (S)
Aims Community College, Program for Design & Creative Studies, Greeley CO (S)
A I R Gallery, New York NY
Akron Art Museum, Akron OH
Alabama A & M University, Art Education Dept, Huntsville AL (S)
Alabama Department of Archives and History Museum, Montgomery AL
Alabama Museum of Photography, Birmingham AL
Alabama State University, Art Dept, Montgomery AL (S)
Alaska Artists' Guild, Anchorage AK
Alaska Arts Southeast, Inc, Sitka AK
Alaska Association for the Arts, Fairbanks AK
Alaska State Museum, Juneau AK
Albany Institute of History and Art, Albany NY
Albany Museum of Art, Albany GA
Alberta Art Foundation, Edmonton AB

Alberta College of Art, Southern Alberta Institute of Technology, Calgary AB (S)
Alberta College of Art Gallery, Calgary AB
Alberta College of Art Library, see Southern Alberta Institute of Technology, Calgary AB
Alberta Society of Artists, Calgary AB
Albertus Magnus College, Art Dept, New Haven CT (S)
Albion College, Bobbitt Visual Arts Center, Albion MI
Albion College, Dept of Visual Arts, Albion MI (S)
Albrecht Art Museum, Saint Joseph MO
Albright College, Dept of Art, Reading PA (S)
Albright College, Freedman Gallery, Reading PA
Albright-Knox Art Gallery, see The Buffalo Fine Arts Academy, Buffalo NY
Albuquerque Museum of Art, History and Science, Albuquerque NM
Alcan Smelters and Chemicals Limited, Montreal PQ
Alcorn State University, Dept of Fine Arts, Lorman MS (S)
Aldrich Museum of Contemporary Art, Ridgefield CT
Alexander School of Painting, San Diego CA (S)
Alexandria Museum Visual Art Center, see Central Louisiana Art Association, Alexandria LA
Alice Lloyd College, Art Dept, Pippa Passes KY (S)
Allan Hancock College, Fine Arts Dept, Santa Maria CA (S)
Allegany Community College, Cumberland MD (S)
Allegheny College, Bowman, Megahan and Penelec Galleries, Meadville PA
Allegheny College, Art Dept, Meadville PA (S)
Charlotte W Allen Memorial Art Gallery Library, see University of Rochester, Rochester NY
Allen County Community College, Art Dept, Iola KS (S)
Allen County Public Library, Fine Arts Dept, Fort Wayne IN
Allen Memorial Art Museum, see Oberlin College, Oberlin OH
Allentown Art Museum, Allentown PA
Robert Allerton Library, see Honolulu Academy of Arts, Honolulu HI
Allied Artists of America, Inc, New York NY
Allied Arts Council of Lethbridge, Bowman Arts Center, Lethbridge AB
Allied Arts Council of the Yakima Valley, Yakima WA
Allied Arts of Seattle, Inc, Seattle WA
Charles Allis Art Museum, Milwaukee WI
Allison Mansion, see Marian College, Indianapolis IN
Lyman Allyn Museum, New London CT
Alma College, Dept of Art and Design, Alma MI (S)
Alverno College, Art Dept, Milwaukee WI (S)
Alverno College Gallery, Milwaukee WI
Alvin Community College, Art Dept, Alvin TX (S)
Amarillo Art Center, Amarillo TX
Amarillo Art Center Association, see Amarillo Art Center, Amarillo TX
Amarillo College, Art Dept, Amarillo TX (S)

American Abstract Artists, New York NY
American Academy and Institute of Arts and Letters, New York NY
American Academy in Rome, New York NY (S)
American Academy of Art, Chicago IL (S)
American Antiquarian Society, Worcester MA
American Artists Professional League, Inc, New York NY
American Association of Museums, Washington DC
American Association of University Women, Washington DC
American Baptist Historical Society, Rochester NY
American Ceramic Society, Columbus OH
American Classical College, Albuquerque NM (S)
American Color Print Society, Philadelphia PA
American Committee for South Asian Art, Evanston IL
American Committee for South Asian Art, see Denison University Art Gallery, Granville OH
American Council for the Arts, New York NY
American Craft Council Museum, New York NY
The American Federation of Arts, Miami FL
The American Federation of Arts, New York NY
American Fine Arts Society, New York NY
American Institute for Conservation of Historic and Artistic Works (AIC), Washington DC
American Institute of Architects, Washington DC
American Institute of Architects Foundation, Washington DC
American Institute of Graphic Arts, New York NY
American Jewish Historical Society, Waltham MA
American Life Foundation & Study Institute, American Research Library, Watkins Glen NY
American Museum of Natural History, New York NY
American Numismatic Association Museum, Colorado Springs CO
American Numismatic Society, New York NY
American Portrait Society, Seal Beach CA
American River College, Dept of Art, Sacramento CA (S)
American Scandinavian Foundation Gallery, New York NY
American Society for Aesthetics, Greenvale NY
American Society of Artists, Inc, Chicago IL
American Society of Bookplate Collectors and Designers, Alhambra CA
American Society of Contemporary Artists, Brooklyn NY
American Swedish Historical Foundation and Museum, Philadelphia PA
American Swedish Institute, Minneapolis MN
American University, Watkins Art Gallery, Washington DC
American University, Dept of Art, Washington DC (S)
American Watercolor Society, New York NY
Amerind Foundation, Inc, Dragoon AZ
AmeriTrust Company, Cleveland OH
Amherst College, Mead Art Museum, Amherst MA
Amherst College, Dept of Fine Arts, Amherst MA (S)
Anacostia Neighborhood Museum, Washington DC

Anchorage Historical and Fine Arts Museum, Cook Inlet Historical Society, Anchorage AK
Ancilla College, Art Dept, Donaldson IN (S)
Anderson College, Art Dept, Anderson IN (S)
Anderson County Arts Council, Anderson SC
Anderson Fine Arts Center, Anderson IN
Anderson Gallery, see Virginia Commonwealth University, Richmond VA
Anderson House Museum, see Society of the Cincinnati, Washington DC
Anderson Learning Center, see Nasson College, Springvale ME
And-Or, Resources in Contemporary Arts, Seattle WA
Andrew-Safford House, see Essex Institute, Salem MA
Andrews University, Art Dept, Berrien Springs MI (S)
Angelo State University, Houston Harte University Center, San Angelo TX
Angelo State University, Art and Music Dept, San Angelo TX (S)
Anglo-American Art Museum, see Louisiana State University, Baton Rouge LA
Anna Maria College, Saint Luke's Gallery, Paxton MA
Anna Maria College, Dept of Art, Paxton MA (S)
Ann Arbor Art Association, Ann Arbor MI
Anoka Ramsey Community College, Art Dept, Coon Rapids MN (S)
Antelope Valley College, Art Dept, Division of Fine Arts, Lancaster CA (S)
Antioch College, Noyes, Read and Grey Galleries, Yellow Springs OH
Antioch College, Dept of Art, Yellow Springs OH (S)
Antiquarian and Numismatic Society of Montreal, see Chateau de Ramezay, Montreal PQ
Antonelli Institute of Art & Photography, Professional Photography, Commercial Art & Interior Design, Plymouth Meeting PA (S)
Appalachian State University, Dept of Art, Boone NC (S)
Appaloosa Museum, Inc, Moscow ID
Aquinas College, Art Dept, Grand Rapids MI (S)
Arapahoe Community College, Colorado Gallery of the Arts, Littleton CO
Arbor Lodge State Historical Park, see Game and Parks Commission, Nebraska City NE
Archaeological Institute of America, Boston MA
Archbishop Alter Library, see College of Mount Saint Joseph on the Ohio, Mount Saint Joseph OH
The Architectural League, New York NY
Archive of Contemporary Latin American Art, see Museum of Modern Art of Latin America, Washington DC
Archive of Old Spanish Missions, Diocese of Monterey, see Carmel Mission and Gift Shop, Carmel CA
Archives of American Art, Smithsonian Institution, New York NY
Arco Center for Visual Art, Los Angeles CA
Arizona Artist Guild, Phoenix AZ
The Arizona Bank, Phoenix AZ
Arizona Commission on the Arts, Phoenix AZ
Arizona State University, Tempe AZ
Arizona State University, Tempe AZ (S)
Arizona Watercolor Association, Phoenix AZ
Arkansas Arts Center, Little Rock AR
Arkansas Arts Center, Little Rock AR (S)
Arkansas State University, Dept of Art, State University AR (S)
Arkansas State University Art Gallery, Jonesboro, Jonesboro AR
Arkansas Tech University, Dept of Art, Russellville AR (S)
Arkansas Territorial Restoration, Little Rock AR
Arlington County Department of Public Libraries, Fine Arts Section, Arlington VA
Armstrong Gallery, see Cornell College, Mount Vernon IA
Armstrong Museum of Art and Archaeology, see Olivet College, Olivet MI
Armstrong State College, Fine Arts Dept, Savannah GA (S)
Arnot Art Museum, Elmira NY

Arrott Art Gallery, see New Mexico Highlands University, Las Vegas NM
Arrowmont School of Arts and Crafts, Gatlinburg TN (S)
Arrow Rock State Historic Site, Arrow Rock MO
Art Academy of Cincinnati, Cincinnati OH (S)
Art Association of Harrisburg, School and Galleries, Harrisburg PA
Art Association of Jacksonville, David Strawn Art Gallery, Jacksonville IL
Art Association of Richmond, Richmond IN
Art Association School, Spartanburg SC (S)
Art Barn, Greenwich CT
The Art Center, Mount Clemens MI
The Art Center, Waco TX
Art Center Association, Louisville KY
Art Center College of Design, Pasadena CA (S)
Art Center College of Design, James Lemont Fogg Memorial Library, Pasadena CA
Art Center, Inc, South Bend IN
Art Center of Battle Creek, Battle Creek MI
Art Centre of New Jersey, East Orange NJ (S)
Art Commission of the City of New York, New York NY
Art Complex Museum at Duxbury, Duxbury MA
Art Dealers Association of America, Inc, New York NY
Art Directors Club, Inc, New York NY
Artemisa Gallery, Chicago IL
Art Gallery of Brant, Inc, Brantford ON
Art Gallery of Greater Victoria, Victoria BC
Art Gallery of Hamilton, Hamilton ON
Art Gallery of Nova Scotia, Halifax NS
Art Gallery of Ontario, Toronto ON
Art Gallery of Peterborough, Peterborough ON
Art Gallery of Windsor, Windsor ON
Art Guild of Burlington, Arts for Living Center, Burlington IA
Art in Architecture, Los Angeles CA (S)
Art in Architecture, Joseph Young Library, Los Angeles CA
Art Information Center, Inc, New York NY
Art Institute of Atlanta, Atlanta GA (S)
The Art Institute of Boston, Gallery West, Gallery East, Boston MA
Art Institute of Boston, Boston MA (S)
Art Institute of Chicago, Chicago IL
Art Institute of Fort Lauderdale, Fort Lauderdale FL (S)
Art Institute of Fort Lauderdale, Fort Lauderdale FL
Art Institute of Houston, see The Design Schools, Houston TX (S)
Art Institute of Philadelphia, Philadelphia PA (S)
Art Institute of Philadelphia Library, Philadelphia PA
Art Institute of Pittsburgh, Pittsburgh PA (S)
Art Institute of Pittsburgh Gallery, Pittsburgh PA
Art Institute of Seattle, see The Design Schools, Seattle WA (S)
Art Instruction Schools, Minneapolis MN (S)
Artist-Craftsmen of New York, New York NY
Artists Association of Nantucket, Kenneth Taylor Gallery, Nantucket MA
Artists' Cooperative Gallery, Omaha NE
Artists Equity Association, Inc, Washington DC
Artists' Fellowship, Inc, New York NY
Artists Gallery, Vancouver BC
Artists Guild Inc of New York, New York NY
Artists Guild of Chicago, Chicago IL
Artists Space Gallery, see Committee for the Visual Arts, Inc, New York NY
Artists Technical Institute, New York NY
Artist Studio Centers, Inc, New York NY (S)
Artists Welfare Fund, Inc, see New York Artists Equity Association, Inc, New York NY
Art League, Alexandria VA
Art League of Houston, Houston TX
Art League of Manatee County, Bradenton FL
Art Libraries Society-North America, Iowa City IA
Art Libraries Society-North America, Tucson AZ
Art Life Studios, New York NY (S)
Art Metropole, Toronto ON
The Art Museum Association of America, San Francisco CA
The Art Museum of Santa Cruz County, Santa Cruz CA
Art Museum of South Texas, Corpus Christi TX

Art PAC, Washington DC
Art Patrons League of Mobile, Mobile AL
Artrain, Inc, Detroit MI
Art Research Center, Kansas City MO
Art Restoration Technical Inst, New York NY (S)
Artrium Inc, Santa Rosa CA
Arts and Crafts Association of Meriden Inc, Gallery, Meriden CT
Arts and Crafts Center of Pittsburgh, Pittsburgh PA
Arts and Education Council of Greater Saint Louis, Saint Louis MO
Arts and Humanities Council of Tuscaloosa County, Inc, Tuscaloosa AL
Arts and Letters Club of Toronto, Toronto ON
Arts and Science Center, Nashua NH (S)
Arts and Science Museum, Statesville NC
Arts & Business Council, New York NY
Arts Center of the Ozarks Gallery, see Council of Ozark Artists and Craftsmen, Inc, Springdale AR
Arts Club of Chicago Gallery, Chicago IL
Arts Club of Washington, James Monroe House, Washington DC
Arts Council, Inc, Winston-Salem NC
Arts Council of Hawaii, Honolulu HI
Arts Council of Spartanburg County, Inc, Spartanburg Arts Center, Spartanburg SC
Arts Council of the Mid-Columbia Region, Richland WA
Arts Council of Topeka, Topeka KS
Arts for Living Center, see Art Guild of Burlington, Burlington IA
Arts Place II, see Oklahoma Art Center, Oklahoma City OK
Art Students League of New York, New York NY
Art Students League of New York, New York NY (S)
Asbury College, Student Center Gallery, Wilmore KY
Asbury College, Art Dept, Wilmore KY (S)
Asheville Art Museum, Asheville NC
Ashland College, Art Dept, Ashland OH (S)
Ashland College Arts and Humanities Gallery, Ashland OH
Ashland Oil, Inc, Russell KY
Ashtabula Arts Center, Ashtabula OH
Asian Art Museum of San Francisco, Avery Brundage Collection, San Francisco CA
Asian Collection, see Saint John's University, Jamaica NY
Asia Society, Inc, Gallery, New York NY
Aspen Center for Visual Arts, Aspen CO
Assembly House, see Essex Institute, Salem MA
Associated Artists of New Jersey, Pittstown NJ
Associated Artists of Pittsburgh Arts and Crafts Center, Pittsburgh PA
Associated Artists of Winston-Salem, Winston-Salem NC
Associates of the Art Commission, Inc, see Art Commission of the City of New York, New York NY
Association des Musees Canadiens, see Canadian Museums Association, Ottawa ON
Association for the Preservation of Virgina Antiquities, Richmond VA
Association of American Editorial Cartoonists, Harrison AR
Association of Architectural Librarians, Washington DC
Association of Artist-Run Galleries, New York NY
Association of Art Museum Directors, Savannah GA
Association of Canadian Industrial Designers, Ontario, Toronto ON
Association of Collegiate Schools of Architecture, Washington DC
Association of Hispanic Art, New York NY
Association of Honolulu Artists, Honolulu HI
Association of Medical Illustrators, Midlothian VA
Assumption College, Dept of Fine Arts and Music, Worcester MA (S)
Johnson Atelier Technical Institute of Sculpture, Mercerville NJ (S)
Ateneo Puertorriqueno, San Juan PR
The Athenaeum, see Northern Virginia Fine Arts Association, Alexandria VA
Athenaeum Music and Arts Library, see Library Association of La Jolla, La Jolla CA
Athenaeum of Philadelphia, Philadelphia PA

Atkins Museum of Fine Art, Kansas City MO
Lee Atkyns Studio-Gallery, Duncansville PA
Atlanta Area Technical School, Dept of
Commercial Art, Atlanta GA (S)
Atlanta College of Art, Atlanta GA (S)
Atlanta College of Art Library, Atlanta GA
Atlanta Museum, Atlanta GA
Atlanta Public Library, Fine Arts Dept, Atlanta GA
Atlantic Christian College, Case Art Gallery,
Wilson NC
Atlantic Christian College, Art Dept, Wilson NC
(S)
Atlantic Gallery, New York NY
Attleboro Museum, Center for the Arts, Attleboro
MA
Atwater Kent Museum, Philadelphia PA
Atwood Center Gallery Lounge, see Saint Cloud
State University, Saint Cloud MN
Auburn University, Dept of Art, Auburn AL (S)
Auburn University at Montgomery, Art Dept,
Montgomery AL (S)
Eleanor Dean Audigier Art Collection, see
University of Tennessee, Knoxville TN
Audubon Artists, Inc, New York NY
John James Audubon Museum, see Audubon State
Park, Henderson KY
Audubon State Park, John James Audubon
Museum, Henderson KY
Audubon Wildlife Sanctuary, Audubon PA
Auerbach Art Library, see Wadsworth Atheneum,
Hartford CT
Augsburg College, Art Dept, Minneapolis MN (S)
Augusta College, Dept of Fine Arts, Augusta GA
(S)
Augustana College, Art Dept, Rock Island IL (S)
Augustana College, Centennial Hall Gallery, Rock
Island IL
Augustana College, Art Dept, Sioux Falls SD (S)
Augustana College, Center for Western Studies,
Sioux Falls SD
Augusta Richmond County Museum, Augusta GA
Auraria Higher Education Center, Denver CO
Auraria Library Gallery, see Auraria Higher
Education Center, Denver CO
Aurora College, Art Dept, Aurora IL (S)
Austin Arts Center, see Trinity College, Hartford
CT
Austin College, Ida Green Gallery, Sherman TX
Austin College, Art Dept, Sherman TX (S)
Austin Community College, Dept of Commercial
Art & Fine Arts, RDV Campus, Austin TX (S)
Austin Peay State University, Margaret Fort
Trahern Gallery, Clarksville TN
Austin Peay State University, Dept of Art,
Clarksville TN (S)
Averett College, Art Dept, Danville VA (S)
Avery Architectural and Fine Arts Library, see
Columbia University, New York NY
Milton Avery Graduate School of the Arts, see
Bard College, Annandale-on-Hudson NY (S)
Avila College, Art Division, Dept of Performing
and Visual Art, Kansas City MO (S)
Avila College, Thornhill Art Gallery, Kansas City
MO
Azusa Pacific University, College of Liberal Arts,
Art Dept, Azusa CA (S)
Bacone College Museum, Muskogee OK
Leo Baeck Institute, New York NY
Bakersfield College, Art Dept, Bakersfield CA (S)
Baker University, Dept of Art, Baldwin City KS (S)
Balboa Art Conservation Center, San Diego CA
Baldwin Hotel Museum Annex, see Klamath
County Museum, Klamath Falls OR
Raymond E Baldwin Museum, see Connecticut
State Library, Hartford CT
Baldwin-Wallace College, Art Gallery, Berea OH
Baldwin-Wallace College, Dept of Art, Berea OH
(S)
Ball State University, Muncie IN
Ball State University, Art Dept, Muncie IN (S)
Baltimore Museum of Art, Baltimore MD
Balzekas Museum of Lithuanian Culture, Chicago
IL
Banff Centre, Walter Phillips Gallery, Banff AB
Banff Centre School of Fine Arts, Banff AB (S)
Bank of America, Concourse Gallery, San Francisco
CA
Bank of Maryville, Maryville TN

Bank of Mississippi, Tupelo MS
Bank of Oklahoma, Tulsa OK
Edward M Bannister Gallery, see Rhode Island
College, Providence RI
Baptist College at Charleston, Dept of Art,
Charleston SC (S)
Barat College, Dept of Art, Lake Forest IL (S)
Barber-Scotia College, Art Dept, Concord NC (S)
Dr Jose C Barbosa Museum and Library, see
Institute of Puerto Rican Culture, San Juan PR
Bard College, William Cooper Procter Art Center,
Annandale-on-Hudson NY
Bard College, Milton Avery Graduate School of the
Arts, Annandale-on-Hudson NY (S)
Barnard College, see Columbia University, New
York NY (S)
The Barn Gallery, see Ogunquit Art Association,
Ogunquit ME
Justina M Barnicke Gallery, see University of
Toronto, Toronto ON
John D Barrow Art Gallery, Skaneateles NY
Barry University, Dept of Art, Miami Shores FL (S)
Bartow-Pell Mansion Museum and Garden, New
York NY
Basilian Fathers, Mundare AB
Bassist College, Collections Library, Portland OR
Bass Museum of Art, Miami Beach FL
Bates College, Treat Gallery, Lewiston ME
Bates College, Art Dept, Lewiston ME (S)
Baxter Art Gallery, see California Institute of
Technology, Pasadena CA
Bay Area Art Conservation Guild, Oakland CA
Baycrafters, Inc, Bay Village OH
Bay De Noc Community College, Art Dept,
Escanaba MI (S)
Baylor University, Dept of Fine Arts, Waco TX (S)
Baylor University, Waco TX
Bayonne Free Public Library, Art Dept, Bayonne
NJ
Bay Path Junior College, Dept of Art, Longmeadow
MA (S)
Beaumont Art Museum, Beaumont TX
Beaumont Arts Council, Beaumont TX
Beaumont Gallery, see Maryville College Saint
Louis, Saint Louis MO
Beaverbrook Art Gallery, Fredericton NB
Beaver College, Richard Eugene Fuller Gallery of
Art, Glenside PA
Beaver College, Dept of Fine Arts, Glenside PA (S)
Kenneth C Beck Center for the Cultural Arts,
Lakewood OH
Bedford Gallery, see Longwood College, Farmville
VA
Beebe Summer House, see Essex Institute, Salem
MA
Beeghly Library, see Ohio Wesleyan University,
Delaware OH
Belhaven College, Art Dept, Jackson MS (S)
Cecelia Coker Bell Gallery, Hartsville SC
Belle Grove Plantation, Middletown VA
Belleville Area College, Art Dept, Belleville IL (S)
Bellevue Art Museum, see Pacific Northwest Arts
and Crafts Association, Bellevue WA
Bellevue College, Art Dept, Bellevue NE (S)
Bellevue Community College, Arts Dept, Bellevue
WA (S)
Bell Gallery, see Brown University, Providence RI
Bellingrath Gardens and Home, Theodore AL
Belmont, The Gari Melchers Memorial Gallery, see
Mary Washington College, Fredericksburg VA
Beloit College, Wright Museum of Art, Beloit WI
Beloit College, Dept of Art, Beloit WI (S)
Elmer Belt Library of Vinciana, see University of
California, Los Angeles, Los Angeles CA
Bemidji State University, Art Dept, Bemidji MN
(S)
Benedict College, Visual Art Studies, Columbia SC
(S)
Benedictine College, Art Dept, Atchison KS (S)
Bennington College, Visual Arts Division,
Bennington VT (S)
Bennington Museum, Bennington VT
Benson & Hedges (Canada) Inc, Montreal PQ
William Benton Museum of Art, see University of
Connecticut, Storrs CT
Berea College, Art Department Gallery, Berea KY
Berea College, Art Dept, Berea KY (S)

Bergen Community College, Fine Arts Dept,
Paramus NJ (S)
Bergen Museum of Art & Science, Paramus NJ
Bergstrom Mahler Museum, Neenah WI
Berkeley Art Center, Berkeley CA
Berkeley Public Library, Berkeley CA
Berks Art Alliance, Reading PA
Berkshire Athenaeum, Pittsfield MA
Berkshire Community College, Dept Fine Arts,
Pittsfield MA (S)
Berkshire Museum, Pittsfield MA
Bernard M Baruch College of the City University of
New York, Art Dept, New York NY (S)
Berry College, Art Dept, Mount Berry GA (S)
Berry College, Moon Gallery, Mount Berry GA
Bertha V B Lederer Gallery, see State University of
New York College at Geneseo, Geneseo NY
Jesse Besser Museum, Alpena MI
Bethany College, Art Dept, Bethany WV (S)
Bethany College, Lindsborg KS
Bethany College, Art Dept, Lindsborg KS (S)
Bethany Lutheran College, Art Dept, Mankato MN
(S)
Bethany Nazarene College, Art Dept, Bethany OH
(S)
Bethel College, Dept of Art, North Newton KS (S)
Bethel College, Mennonite Library and Archives,
North Newton KS
Bethel College, Dept of Art, Saint Paul MN (S)
Beverly Hills Public Library, Fine Arts Library,
Beverly Hills CA
Beverly Historical Society, Cabot, Hale and Balch
House Museums, Beverly MA
Beyond Baroque Foundation, Venice CA
Biblical Arts Center, Dallas TX
Bibliotheque Centrale de Pret de L'Outaouais et des
Laurentides Inc, Hull PQ
Bierce Library, see North Dakota Museum of Art,
Grand Forks ND
Big Bend Community College, Art Dept, Moses
Lake WA (S)
Biloxi Art Association, Gallery, Biloxi MS
Biola University, Art Dept, La Mirada CA (S)
Birmingham-Bloomfield Art Association,
Birmingham MI
Birmingham-Bloomfield Art Association,
Birmingham MI (S)
Birmingham Museum of Art, Birmingham AL
Birmingham Public Library, Art and Music
Department, Birmingham AL
Birmingham Southern College, Doris Wainwright
Kennedy Art Center, Birmingham AL
Birmingham-Southern College, Art Dept,
Birmingham AL (S)
Bishop Hill State Historic Site, Bishop Hill IL
Bismarck Junior College, Art Dept, Bismarck ND
(S)
Blackader-Lauterman Library of Architecture and
Art, see McGill University, Montreal PQ
Black Artists Association Arts Center, see
Roosevelt Public Library , Roosevelt NY
Blackburn College, Dept of Art, Carlinville IL (S)
Black Hawk College, Art Dept, Moline IL (S)
Blackhawk Mountain School of Art, Black Hawk
CO (S)
Blackhawk Mountain School of Art Gallery,
Blackhawk CO
Black Hills Art Center, Little Gallery, Spearfish SD
Black Hills State College, Art Dept, Spearfish SD
(S)
Blacksburg Regional Art Association, Blacksburg
VA
Blackstone Valley Campus Art Gallery, see
Community College of Rhode Island, Warwick
RI
Blackwell Library, Art Department, see Salisbury
State College, Salisbury MD
Sarah Campbell Blaffer Gallery, see University of
Houston, Houston TX
Blair Museum of Lithophanes and Carved Waxes,
Toledo OH
Margaret Day Blake Library, see Skowhegan School
of Painting and Sculpture, Skowhegan ME
Blanden Memorial Art Museum, Fort Dodge IA
Blatchley Gallery, see College of Idaho, Caldwell
ID
Mary & Leigh Block Gallery, see Northwestern
University, Evanston IL

Bloomsburg University, Dept of Art, Bloomsburg PA (S)

Bloomsburg University of Pennsylvania, Haas Gallery of Art, Bloomsburg PA

Blount Inc, Montgomery AL

Bluefield State College, Art Dept, Bluefield WV (S)

Blue Lake Community School of Arts, Visual Arts Dept, Muskegon MI (S)

Blue Mountain College, Art Dept, Blue Mountain MS (S)

Blue Mountain Community College, Fine Arts Dept, Pendleton OR (S)

Ernest Blumenschein Home, see Kit Carson Memorial Foundation, Taos NM

B'nai B'rith Klutznick Museum, Washington DC

Bobbitt Visual Arts Center, see Albion College, Albion MI

Bob Jones University, Greenville SC

Bob Jones University, School of Fine Arts, Greenville SC (S)

Boca Raton Center for the Arts, Inc, Boca Raton FL

Richard W Bock Sculpture Collection, see Greenville College, Greenville IL

Boehm Gallery, see Palomar Community College, San Marcos CA

Boise Gallery of Art, Boise ID

Boise State University, Art Dept, Boise ID (S)

William Bonifas Fine Art Center Gallery, Escanaba MI

Daniel Boone Regional Library, Art Dept, Columbia MO

Boothbay Region Art Foundation, Inc, Brick House Gallery, Boothbay Harbor ME

Boston Architectural Center, Boston MA

Boston Art Commission of the City of Boston, Boston MA

Boston Athenaeum, Boston MA

Boston Center for Adult Education, Boston MA (S)

Boston College, Fine Arts Dept, Newton MA (S)

The Bostonian Society, Old State House, Boston MA

Boston Printmakers, Needham MA

Boston Public Library, Boston MA

Boston University, School of Visual Arts, Boston MA (S)

Muriel Isabel Bostwick Library, see Art Gallery of Hamilton, Hamilton ON

Boulder Center for the Visual Arts, Boulder CO

Boulder Public Library and Gallery, Dept of Fine Arts Gallery, Boulder CO

Bowdoin College, Museum of Art & Peary-MacMillan Arctic Museum, Brunswick ME

Bowdoin College, Art Dept, Brunswick ME (S)

Bower's Museum, Santa Ana CA

Bowie State College, Dept of Fine and Performing Arts, Bowie MD (S)

Bowling Green State University, Fine Arts Gallery, Bowling Green OH

Bowling Green State University, School of Art, Bowling Green OH (S)

Bowling Green State University, Art Dept, Huron OH (S)

Bowman Arts Center, see Allied Arts Council of Lethbridge, Lethbridge AB

Bowman, Megahan and Penelec Galleries, see Allegheny College, Meadville PA

Bowne House, Flushing NY

Bradford College, Creative Arts Division, Bradford MA (S)

The Bradford Museum, Niles IL

Bradley University, Hartman Center Gallery, Peoria IL

Bradley University, Division of Art, Peoria IL (S)

Brainerd Art Gallery, see State University of New York College at Potsdam, Potsdam NY

Braithwaite Fine Arts Gallery, see Southern Utah State College, Cedar City UT

Brandeis University, Dept of Fine Arts, Waltham MA (S)

Brandeis University, Rose Art Museum, Waltham MA

Brand Library and Art Center, Glendale CA

Brandon Allied Arts Center Library, see Brandon Allied Arts Council, Brandon MB

Brandon Allied Arts Council, Brandon MB

Brandt Painting Workshops, Corona Del Mar CA (S)

Brandywine River Museum, Chadds Ford PA

Brant Historical Society, Brant County Museum, Brantford ON

Brattleboro Museum and Art Center, Brattleboro VT

Braun Research Library, see Southwest Museum, Los Angeles CA

Brazosport College, Art Dept, Lake Jackson TX (S)

Brea Civic Cultural Center Gallery, Brea CA

Breezewood Foundation Museum and Garden, Monkton MD

Anne Bremer Memorial Library, see San Francisco Art Institute, San Francisco CA

Brenau College, Art Dept, Gainesville GA (S)

Brentwood Art Center, Los Angeles CA (S)

Brescia College, Art Gallery, Owensboro KY

Brescia College, Dept of Art, Owensboro KY (S)

Brevard Art Center and Museum, Inc, Melbourne FL

Brevard College, Division of Fine Arts, Brevard NC (S)

Brevard College, Coltrane Art Center, Brevard NC

Brewton-Parker College, Visual Arts, Mount Vernon GA (S)

Briar Cliff College, Art Dept, Sioux City IA (S)

Brick Store Museum, Kennebunk ME

Bridgeport Art League, Bridgeport CT

Bridgewater College, Art Dept, Bridgewater College VA (S)

Bridgewater State College, Art Dept, Bridgewater MA (S)

Margaret M Bridwell Art Library, see University of Louisville, Louisville KY

Brigham City Museum-Gallery, Brigham City UT

Brigham Young University, Provo UT

Brigham Young University, Dept of Art, Provo UT (S)

Brigham Young University, Hawaii Campus, Division of Fine Arts, Laie HI (S)

Bradford Brinton Memorial Ranch Museum, Big Horn WY

Bristol Art Museum, Bristol RI

Bristol Campus Center, see Hamilton College, Clinton NY

Brockton Art Museum, Brockton MA

Brockton Public Library System, Municipal Art Gallery, Brockton MA

Saidye Bronfman Centre, Montreal PQ

Silas Bronson Library, Art, Music & Theatre Dept, Waterbury CT

Bronx Community College, Music & Art Dept, Bronx NY (S)

Bronx Museum of the Arts, Bronx NY

Bronxville Public Library, Bronxville NY

Brookdale Community College, Art Dept, Lincroft NJ (S)

Brookfield Craft Center, Inc Gallery, Brookfield CT

Brookgreen Gardens, Murrells Inlet SC

Brookline Art Society, Brookline MA

Brooklyn College, Art & Art History Dept, Brooklyn NY (S)

Brooklyn Museum, Brooklyn NY

Brooklyn Museum Art School, Brooklyn NY (S)

Brooklyn Public Library, Art and Music Division, Brooklyn NY

Brooks Institute Photography Library, Santa Barbara CA

Broome County Historical Library, see Roberson Center for the Arts and Sciences, Binghamton NY

Jay R Broussard Memorial Galleries, Division of the Arts, Baton Rouge LA

Annmary Brown Memorial, see Brown University, Providence RI

Brown County Art Gallery Association Inc, Nashville IN

Armstrong Browning Library, see Baylor University, Waco TX

Jean Brown Archive, see Tyringham Institute, Tyringham MA

John Brown House, see Rhode Island Historical Society, Providence RI

Orlando Brown House, see Liberty Hall Museum, Frankfort KY

Brownson Art Gallery, see Manhattanville College, Purchase NY

Brownsville Art League Museum, Brownsville TX

Topham Brown Gallery, see Vernon Art Association, Vernon BC

Brown University, Providence RI

Brown University, Dept of Art, Providence RI (S)

The Bruce Museum, Greenwich CT

Avery Brundage Collection, see Asian Art Museum of San Francisco, San Francisco CA

Brunnier Gallery Museum, see Iowa State University, Ames IA

Richard F Brush Art Gallery, see St Lawrence University, Canton NY

Bryn Mawr College, Art and Archaeology Library, Bryn Mawr PA

Bryn Mawr College, Dept of the History of Art, Bryn Mawr PA (S)

Bucknell University, Center Gallery, Lewisburg PA

Bucknell University, Dept of Art, Lewisburg PA (S)

Bucks County Community College, Fine Arts Dept, Newton PA (S)

Bucks County Community College, Hicks Art Center, Newtown PA

Bucks County Historical Society, Mercer Museum, Doylestown PA

Buffalo and Erie County Public Library, Buffalo NY

Buffalo Bill Memorial Association, Cody WY

The Buffalo Fine Arts Academy, Albright-Knox Art Gallery, Buffalo NY

Buffalo Museum of Science, Research Library, Buffalo NY

Buffalo Society of Artists, Williamsville NY

Ruth Bunker Memorial Library, see Dacotah Prairie Museum, Aberdeen SD

Burbank Public Library, Warner Research Collection, Burbank CA

Burchfield Art Center, Buffalo NY

Bureau of Museums and Historic Sites, see Division of Historical and Cultural Affairs, Dover DE

Thomas Burke Memorial Washington State Museum, see University of Washington, Seattle WA

Burlington County College, Fine Arts Dept, Pemberton NJ (S)

Burlington County Historical Society, Burlington NJ

Burlington Northern, Inc, Saint Paul MN

Burnaby Art Gallery, Burnaby BC

Burpee Art Museum, see Rockford Art Association, Rockford IL

Burroughs Wellcome Company, Research Triangle Park NC

Buscaglia-Castellani Art Gallery, see Niagara University, Niagara Falls NY

Busch-Reisinger Museum, see Harvard University, Cambridge MA

Bush Barn Art Center, see Salem Art Association, Salem OR

Bush-Holley House, see Historical Society of the Town of Greenwich, Inc, Cos Cob CT

Bush House, see Salem Art Association, Salem OR

Buten Museum of Wedgwood, Merion PA

Butera School of Art, Boston MA (S)

Butler County Community College, Art Dept, El Dorado KS (S)

Butler Institute of American Art, Youngstown OH

Butler Museum of American Indian Art, Eugene OR

Butte College, Dept of Fine & Performing Arts, Oroville CA (S)

Butte College, Dept of Art, Oroville CA (S)

Butte Silver Bow Arts Chateau, Butte MT

Byrne Memorial Library, see Saint Xavier College, Chicago IL

Cabot, Hale and Balch House Museums, see Beverly Historical Society, Beverly MA

Cabrillo College, Visual Arts Division, Aptos CA (S)

Cabrini College, Dept of Fine Arts, Radnor PA (S)

Foster Caddell's Art School, Voluntown CT (S)

Joseph A Cain Memorial Art Gallery, see Del Mar College, Corpus Christi TX

Caldwell College, Art Gallery, Caldwell NJ

Caldwell College, Art Dept, Caldwell NJ (S)

California Baptist College, Art Dept, Riverside CA (S)

California College of Arts and Crafts, Meyer Library, Oakland CA

California College of Arts and Crafts, Oakland CA (S)

California Historical Society, San Francisco CA
California Institute of Technology, Baxter Art Gallery, Pasadena CA
California Institute of the Arts, School of Art, Valencia CA (S)
California Institute of the Arts Library, Valencia CA
California Lutheran College, Art Dept, Thousand Oaks CA (S)
California Museum of Science and Industry, Los Angeles CA
California Polytechnic State University at San Luis Obispo, Art Dept, San Luis Obispo CA (S)
California State College Bakersfield, Fine Arts Dept, Bakersfield CA (S)
California State College, San Bernardino, Art Dept, San Bernardino CA (S)
California State College San Bernardino, College Art Galleries, San Bernardino CA
California State College, Stanislaus, Art Dept, Turlock CA (S)
California State College, Stanislaus, Turlock CA
California State Polytechnic University, Pomona, Art Dept, Pomona CA (S)
California State University, Chico, Art Gallery, Chico CA
California State University, Chico, Art Dept, Chico CA (S)
California State University, Dominguez Hills, Art Dept, Carson CA (S)
California State University, Fresno, Art Dept, Fresno CA (S)
California State University Fullerton, Art Gallery, Visual Arts Center, Fullerton CA
California State University, Fullerton, Art Dept, Fullerton CA (S)
California State University, Hayward, University Art Gallery, Hayward CA
California State University, Hayward, Art Dept, Hayward CA (S)
California State University, Long Beach, Long Beach CA (S)
California State University, Long Beach, Long Beach CA
California State University, Los Angeles, Fine Arts Gallery, Los Angeles CA
California State University, Los Angeles, Art Dept, Los Angeles CA (S)
California State University, Northridge, Art Gallery, Northridge CA
California State University, Northridge, Dept of Art-Two Dimensional Media, Northridge CA (S)
California State University, Sacramento, Dept of Art, Sacramento CA (S)
California State University, Sacramento, Library, Humanities Reference and Media Services Center, Sacramento CA
California University of Pennsylvania, Dept of Art, California PA (S)
Eleanor Calvert Memorial Library, see Kitchener-Waterloo Art Gallery, Kitchener ON
Calvert Marine Museum, Solomons MD
Calvin College, Art Dept, Grand Rapids MI (S)
Calvin College Center Art Gallery, Grand Rapids MI
Cambridge Art Association, Cambridge MA
Cambridge Public Library and Gallery, Cambridge ON
Camden County College, Dept of Art, Blackwood NJ (S)
Cameron University, Art Dept, Lawton OK (S)
Grace Campbell Gallery, see John M Cuelenaere Library, Prince Albert SK
Campbell Museum, Camden NJ
Campbellsville College, Fine Arts Division, Campbellsville KY (S)
Campus Martius Museum and Ohio River Museum, see The Ohio Historical Society, Inc, Marietta OH
Canadian Artists' Representation, Le Front Des Artistes Canadians, Toronto ON
Canadiana Sport Art Collection, National Sport and Recreation Centre Inc, Ottawa ON
Canadian Conference of the Arts, Ottawa ON
Canadian Consulate General Dept of External Affairs, 49th Parallel Centre for Contemporary Canadian Art, New York NY

Canadian Crafts Council, Canadien de l'Artisanat, Ottawa ON
Canadian Guild of Crafts, Quebec, see Guilde Canadienne des Metiers d'Art, Quebec, Montreal PQ
Canadian Museums Association, Association des Musees Canadiens, Ottawa ON
Canadian Society for Education Through Art, Regina SK
Canadian Society of Painters in Watercolour, Toronto ON
Canadien de l'Artisanat, see Canadian Crafts Council, Ottawa ON
Canajoharie Library and Art Gallery, Canajoharie NY
Canton Art Institute, Canton OH
Canton Art Institute, Canton OH (S)
Cape Ann Historical Association, Gloucester MA
Cape Cod Community College, Art Dept, West Barnstable MA (S)
Cape School of Art, Provincetown MA (S)
Capital University, Schumacher Gallery, Columbus OH
Capital University, Art Dept, Columbus OH (S)
Caravan House Galleries, see Caravan of East and West, Inc, New York NY
Caravan of East and West, Inc, Caravan House Galleries, New York NY
Cardinal Stritch College, Milwaukee WI
Cardinal Stritch College, Art Dept, Milwaukee WI (S)
Carlen House, see Museum of the City of Mobile, Mobile AL
Carleton College, Dept of Art & Art History, Northfield MN (S)
Carleton University, Dept of Art History, Ottawa ON (S)
Carlow College, Art Dept, Pittsburgh PA (S)
Carlson Gallery, Bridgeport CT
Carlson Tower Gallery, see North Park College, Chicago IL
Carmel Art Institute, School of Painting, Carmel CA (S)
Carmel Mission and Gift Shop, Carmel CA
Carnegie Center of the Arts, Walla Walla WA
Carnegie Institute, Museum of Art, Pittsburgh PA
Carnegie Library of Pittsburgh, Pittsburgh PA
Carnegie-Mellon University, Pittsburgh PA
Carnegie-Mellon University, College of Fine Arts, Pittsburgh PA (S)
Carolina Art Association, Gibbes Art Gallery, Charleston SC
Carrizo Art and Craft Workshops, Ruidoso NM (S)
Carroll College, Art Dept, Waukesha WI (S)
Carson County Square House Museum, Panhandle TX
Kit Carson Memorial Foundation, Taos NM
Carson-Newman College, Art Dept, Jefferson City TN (S)
Amon Carter Museum, Fort Worth TX
Amon Carter Museum Library, see Amon Carter Museum, Fort Worth TX
Carthage College, Art Dept, Kenosha WI (S)
Cartoonists Guild, New York NY
George Washington Carver & The Oaks, see Tuskegee Institute National Historic Site, Tuskegee AL
Casa Amesti, Monterey CA
Casa Blanca Museum, see Institute of Puerto Rican Culture, San Juan PR
Cascade County Historical Society Museum, Great Falls MT
Case Art Gallery, see Atlantic Christian College, Wilson NC
Case Western Reserve University, Dept of Art, Cleveland OH (S)
Casper College, Casper WY (S)
Castle Gallery, see College of New Rochelle, New Rochelle NY
Castleton State College, Art Dept, Castleton VT (S)
Catan-Rose Institute of Art, Forest Hills NY (S)
The Cathedral Museum, New York NY
Catholic Historical Society of Saint Paul, Saint Paul MN
Catholic University of America, Humanities Division, Mullen Library, Washington DC
Catholic University of America, Washington DC (S)

Catholic University of Puerto Rico, Dept of Fine Arts, Ponce PR (S)
Catonsville Community College, Art Dept, Catonsville MD (S)
Cayuga Museum of History and Art, Auburn NY
Cazenovia College, Chapman Art Center Gallery, Cazenovia NY
Cazenovia College, Center for Art & Design Studies, Cazenovia NY (S)
Cedar Crest College, Art Dept, Allentown PA (S)
Cedar Grove, see Philadelphia Museum of Art, Philadelphia PA
Cedar Rapids Museum of Art, Cedar Rapids IA
Centenary College, Art Dept, Hackettstown NJ (S)
Centenary College of Louisiana, Dept of Art, Shreveport LA (S)
Centenary College of Louisiana, Meadows Museum of Art, Shreveport LA
Centennial Hall Gallery, see Augustana College, Rock Island IL
Center for Arts Information, New York NY
Center for Creative Photography, see University of Arizona, Tucson AZ
Center for Creative Studies__College of Art and Design, Detroit MI
Center for Creative Studies - College of Art & Design Library, Detroit MI
Center for Inter-American Relations Art Gallery, New York NY
Center for Western Studies, see Augustana College, Sioux Falls SD
Center Gallery, Madison WI
Central Academy of Commercial Art, Cincinnati OH (S)
Central College, Art Dept, Pella IA (S)
Central Community College - Platte Campus, Creative and Social Cluster, Columbus NE (S)
Central Connecticut State University, Art Dept Museum, New Britain CT
Central Connecticut State University, Dept of Art, New Britain CT (S)
Central Florida Community College, Humanities Dept, Ocala FL (S)
Central Florida Community College Art Collection, Ocala FL
Central Iowa Art Association, Inc, Marshalltown IA
Central Library, Art Division, see Mississauga Library System, Mississauga ON
Central Louisiana Art Association, Alexandria Museum Visual Art Center, Alexandria LA
Central Michigan University, Dept of Art, Mount Pleasant MI (S)
Central Michigan University, Art Gallery, Mount Pleasant MI
Central Missouri State University, Art Dept Gallery, Warrensburg MO
Central Missouri State University, Art Dept, Warrensburg MO (S)
Central Oregon Community College, Dept of Art, Bend OR (S)
Central Piedmont Community College, Art Division, Charlotte NC (S)
Central State University, Art Dept, Edmond OK (S)
Central State University, Dept of Art, Wilberforce OH (S)
Central Washington University, Sarah Spurgeon Gallery, Ellensburg WA
Central Washington University, Dept of Art, Ellensburg WA (S)
Central Wyoming College, Art Center, Riverton WY (S)
Centre Cultural de Shawinigan, Shawinigan PQ
Centre Culturel de Trois Rivieres, Trois Rivieres PQ
Centre Hill Mansion, Petersburg VA
Centro Ceremonial de Caguana, see Institute of Puerto Rican Culture, San Juan PR
Cerritos College, Art Dept, Norwalk CA (S)
Chabot College, Humanities Division, Hayward CA (S)
Chadron State College, Arts Gallery, Chadron NE
Chadron State College, Division of Fine Arts, Chadron NE (S)
Chaffee Art Gallery, see Rutland Area Art Association, Inc, Rutland VT
Chaffey Community College, Art Dept, Alta Loma CA (S)

Chalet of the Golden Fleece, New Glarus WI
Chamberlayne Junior College, Dept of Applied
Arts, Boston MA (S)
Stephen Chan Library of Fine Arts, see New York
University, New York NY
Chapman Art Center Gallery, see Cazenovia
College, Cazenovia NY
Chapman College, Art Dept, Orange CA (S)
Chappell Memorial Library and Art Gallery,
Chappell NE
Charles River Creative Arts Program, Dover MA
(S)
Charles Stewart Mott Community College, Fine
Arts Division, Flint MI (S)
Charleston Museum, Charleston SC
The Chase Manhattan Bank, NA, New York NY
Chateau de Ramezay, Antiquarian and Numismatic
Society of Montreal, Montreal PQ
Chatham College, Art Gallery, Pittsburgh PA
Chatham College, Dept of Art, Pittsburgh PA (S)
Chatham Cultural Centre, Chatham ON
Chattanooga State Technical Community College,
Advertising Arts Dept, Chattanooga TN (S)
Chautauqua Art Association Galleries, Chautauqua
NY
Chautauqua Institution, The Art Center,
Chautauqua NY (S)
Cheltenham Art Centre, Cheltenham PA (S)
Chemeketa Community College, Dept of
Humanities & Communications, Salem OR (S)
Anne Bunce Cheney Library, see University of
Hartford, West Hartford CT
Cherokee National Historical Society, Inc,
Tahlequah OK
Chesapeake Bay Maritime Museum, Saint Michaels
MD
Chester County Historical Society, West Chester
PA
Chesterwood, Stockbridge MA
Cheyney University of Pennsylvania, Dept of Art,
Cheyney PA (S)
Chicago Architecture Foundation, Chicago IL
Chicago Historical Society, Chicago IL
Chicago Public Library, Art Section, Fine Arts
Division, Chicago IL
Chicano-Latino Arts Resource Library, see Galeria
de la Raza, San Francisco CA
Chief Plenty Coups State Monument Museum,
Pryor MT
The Children's Aid Society, Lower Westside
Center, New York NY (S)
Children's Art Centre, Boston MA
Children's Art Foundation, Santa Cruz CA
China House Gallery, see China Institute in
America, New York NY
China Institute in America, China House Gallery,
New York NY
China Trade Museum, Milton MA
Chinese Culture Foundation, Chinese Culture
Center Gallery, San Francisco CA
Chinqua-Penn Plantation House, see University of
North Carolina at Greensboro, Reidsville NC
Chipola Junior College, Division of Fine Arts and
Humanities, Marianna FL (S)
Chowan College, Division of Art, Murfreesboro NC
(S)
Christopher Newport College, Arts &
Communications, Newport News VA (S)
Chronicle-Tribune Art Gallery, see Taylor
University, Upland IN
Jean Outland Chrysler Library, see Chrysler
Museum, Norfolk VA
Chrysler Museum, Norfolk VA
Chung-Cheng Art Gallery, see Saint John's
University, Jamaica NY
Church of Jesus Christ of Latter-Day Saints,
Museum of Church History and Art, Salt Lake
City UT
Ciba-Geigy Corporation, Art Collection, Ardsley
NY
Cincinnati Art Club, Cincinnati OH
Cincinnati Art Museum, Cincinnati OH
Cincinnati Institute of Fine Arts, Cincinnati OH
Citibank, NA, New York NY
Citrus College, Art Dept, Azusa CA (S)
City College of New York, Art Dept, New York
NY (S)

City College of New York, Cohen Art Library,
New York NY
City College of San Francisco, Art Dept, San
Francisco CA (S)
City Colleges of Chicago, Chicago IL (S)
City of Brampton Public Library, Art Gallery,
Brampton ON
City of Holyoke Museum-Wistariahurst, Holyoke
MA
City of Los Angeles, Cultural Affairs Dept, Los
Angeles CA
City University of New York, PhD Program in Art
History, New York NY (S)
Civic Fine Arts Association Museum, Sioux Falls
SD
Clackamas Community College, Art Dept, Oregon
City OR (S)
Claflin College, Dept of Art, Orangeburg SC (S)
Claremore College, Art Dept, Claremore OK (S)
Clarion University, Hazel Sandford Gallery, Clarion
PA
Clarion University of Pennsylvania, Dept of Art,
Clarion PA (S)
Clark College, Dept of Art, Atlanta GA (S)
Clark College, Art Dept, Vancouver WA (S)
Clark County Historical Society, Springfield OH
Clark County Library District, Las Vegas NV
Clarke College, Dept of Art, Dubuque IA (S)
Clark Humanities Museum, see Scripps College,
Claremont CA
Sterling and Francine Clark Art Institute,
Williamstown MA
Clark University, Little Center Gallery, Worcester
MA
Clark University, Dept of Visual & Performing Arts,
Worcester MA (S)
Wilson W Clark Memorial Library, see University
of Portland, Portland OR
Classical School Gallery, Albuquerque NM
Claypool-Young Art Gallery, see Morehead State
University, Morehead KY
Clemson University, Clemson SC
Clemson University, College of Liberal Arts,
Clemson SC (S)
Cleveland Art Association, see Cleveland Institute
of Art, Cleveland OH
Cleveland Institute of Art, Cleveland OH
Cleveland Institute of Art, Cleveland OH (S)
Cleveland Museum of Art, Cleveland OH
Cleveland Public Library, Fine Arts & Special
Collections Dept, Cleveland OH
Cleveland State Community College, Dept of Art,
Cleveland TN (S)
Cleveland State University, Art Dept, Cleveland
OH (S)
Cleveland State University, Library - Art Services,
Cleveland OH
Henry Clews Memorial, see University of
Pennsylvania, Philadelphia PA
Clifford Memorial Library, see University of
Evansville, Evansville IN
Clinch Valley College of the University of Virginia,
Performing Arts Dept, Wise VA (S)
Clinton Art Association Gallery, Clinton IA
Clinton Community College, Humanities Art Dept,
Plattsburgh NY (S)
Clinton Historical Museum Village, Clinton NJ
Cliveden, Philadelphia PA
The Cloisters, see Metropolitan Museum of Art,
New York NY
Jessie L Clough Art Memorial for Teaching, see
Southwestern At Memphis, Memphis TN
Clowes Fund Collection, see Indianapolis Museum
of Art, Indianapolis IN
Coahoma Junior College, Art Education & Fine
Arts Dept, Clarksdale MS (S)
Cochise College, Art Dept, Douglas AZ (S)
Cochise College, Charles Di Peso Library, Douglas
AZ
Cody Country Art League, Cody WY
Coe College, Gordon Fennell Gallery & Marvin
Cone Gallery, Cedar Rapids IA
Coe College, Dept of Art, Cedar Rapids IA (S)
Coffeyville Community College, Art Dept,
Coffeyville KS (S)
Coffman Union Gallery, see University of
Minnesota, Minneapolis MN

Cohen Art Library, see City College of New York,
New York NY
Coker College, Art Dept, Hartsville SC (S)
Francis Colburn Gallery, see University of
Vermont, Burlington VT
Colburn Gallery, see Kenyon College, Gambier OH
Colby College, Art Dept, Waterville ME (S)
Colby Community College, Visual Arts Dept, Colby
KS (S)
Colby Museum of Art, Waterville ME
Colby-Sawyer College, Art Dept, New London NH
(S)
Coleman Library, see Tougaloo College, Tougaloo
MS
Colgate University, Dept of Fine Arts, Hamilton
NY (S)
Colgate University, Picker Art Gallery, Hamilton
NY
College Art Association of America, New York NY
College Art Gallery, see Drew University, Madison
NJ
College Misericordia, Art Dept, Dallas PA (S)
College of Boca Raton, Art & Commercial Art
Dept, Boca Raton FL (S)
College of Charleston, Fine Arts Dept, Charleston
SC (S)
College of DuPage, Humanities Division, Glen
Ellyn IL (S)
College of Eastern Utah, Gallery East, Price UT
College of Great Falls, Dept of Art, Great Falls MT
(S)
College of Idaho, Blatchley Gallery, Caldwell ID
College of Lake County, Art Dept, Grayslake IL
(S)
College of Marin, Art Gallery, Kentfield CA
College of Marin, Dept of Art, Kentfield CA (S)
College of Mount Saint Joseph, Art Dept, Mount
Saint Joseph OH (S)
College of Mount Saint Joseph on the Ohio, Studio
San Giuseppe, Mount Saint Joseph OH
College of Mount Saint Vincent, Fine Arts Dept,
Riverdale NY (S)
College of New Rochelle, Castle Gallery, New
Rochelle NY
College of New Rochelle School of Arts and
Sciences, Undergraduate Art Dept, New Rochelle
NY (S)
College of Notre Dame, Dept of Art, Belmont CA
(S)
College of Notre Dame of Maryland, Art Dept,
Baltimore MD (S)
College of Saint Benedict, Art Dept, Saint Joseph
MN (S)
College of Saint Benedict, Art Gallery, Saint Joseph
MN
College of Saint Catherine, Visual Arts Dept, Saint
Paul MN (S)
College of Saint Elizabeth, Mahoney Library,
Convent Station NJ
College of Saint Elizabeth, Art Dept, Convent
Station NJ (S)
College of Saint Francis, Creative Art Dept, Joliet
IL (S)
College of Saint Mary, Art Dept, Omaha NE (S)
College of Saint Rose, Art Gallery, Albany NY
College of Saint Rose, Division of Art, Albany NY
(S)
College of Saint Teresa, Art Dept, Winona MN (S)
College of Saint Thomas, Dept of Art History, Saint
Paul MN (S)
College of San Mateo, Art, Commercial Art &
Photo Art, San Mateo CA (S)
College of San Mateo Library, Art Division, San
Mateo CA
College of Santa Fe, Visual Art Division, Santa Fe
NM (S)
College of Southern Idaho, Art Gallery, Twin Falls
ID
College of Southern Idaho, Art Dept, Twin Falls ID
(S)
College of Southern Idaho, Herrette Museum, Twin
Falls ID
College of Staten Island, Performing & Creative
Arts Dept, Staten Island NY (S)
College of the Americas, Museum of the Americas,
Brookfield VT
College of the Canyons, Art Dept, Valencia CA (S)

College of the Desert, Art Dept, Palm Desert CA (S)
College of the Holy Cross, Dept Visual Arts, Worcester MA (S)
College of the Ozarks, Dept of Art, Clarksville AR (S)
College of the Ozarks Library, Clarksville AR
College of the Redwoods, Art Dept, Eureka CA (S)
College of the Sequoias, Art Dept, Visalia CA (S)
College of the Siskiyous, Art Dept, Weed CA (S)
College of William and Mary, Joseph & Margaret Muscarelle Museum of Art, Williamsburg VA
College of William and Mary, Dept of Fine Arts, Williamsburg VA (S)
College of Wooster, Dept of Art, Wooster OH (S)
College of Wooster Art Center Museum, Wooster OH
Colonel Black Mansion, Ellsworth ME
Colonial Architecture Museum, see Institute of Puerto Rican Culture, San Juan PR
Colonial Williamsburg Foundation, Williamsburg VA
Colorado College, Dept of Art, Colorado Springs CO (S)
Colorado Gallery of the Arts, see Arapahoe Community College, Littleton CO
Colorado Historical Society, State Museum, Denver CO
Colorado Institute of Art, Denver CO (S)
Colorado Mountain College, Fine Arts Gallery, Breckenridge CO
Colorado Mountain College, Summervail Workshop for Art & Critical Studies, Vail CO (S)
Colorado Springs Fine Arts Center, Colorado Springs CO
Colorado State University, Dept of Art, Fort Collins CO (S)
Colorado Women's College, Lyle True Gallery, Denver CO
Colorado Women's College, Dept of Art, Denver CO (S)
Harold S Colton Memorial Library, see Museum of Northern Arizona, Flagstaff AZ
Coltrane Art Center, see Brevard College, Brevard NC
Columbia Art Association, see Columbia Museums of Art and Science, Columbia SC
Columbia Basin College, Art Dept, Pasco WA (S)
Columbia College, Art Dept, Chicago IL (S)
Columbia College, Dept of Physical Creative and Performing Arts, Columbia CA (S)
Columbia College, Art Dept, Columbia MO (S)
Columbia College, Dept of Art, Columbia SC (S)
Columbia College, see Columbia University, New York NY (S)
Columbia County Historical Society, Kinderhook NY
Columbia Museums of Art and Science, Columbia SC
Columbia River Maritime Museum, Astoria OR
Columbia State Community College, Dept of Art, Columbia TN (S)
Columbia University, Avery Architectural and Fine Arts Library, New York NY
Columbia University, New York NY (S)
Columbus and Lowndes County Historical Society Museum, Columbus MS
Columbus Chapel, Boal Mansion and Museum, Boalsburg PA
Columbus College, Dept of Art Fine Arts Hall, Columbus GA (S)
Columbus College, Experimental Gallery, Columbus GA
Columbus College of Art and Design, Columbus OH (S)
Columbus College of Art and Design, Packard Library, Columbus OH
Columbus Cultural Arts Center, Columbus OH
Columbus Museum of Art, Columbus OH
Columbus Museum of Arts and Sciences, Columbus GA
Committee for Hispanic Arts & Research, Austin TX
Committee for the Visual Arts, Inc, New York NY
Community Arts Council of Chilliwack, Chilliwack BC
Community Arts Council of Vancouver, Vancouver BC

Community College of Allegheny County, Fine Arts Dept, West Mifflin PA (S)
Community College of Allegheny County, Boyce Campus, Art Dept, Monroeville PA (S)
Community College of Baltimore, Art Gallery, Baltimore MD
Community College of Baltimore, Dept of Fine & Applied Arts, Liberty Campus, Baltimore MD (S)
Community College of Rhode Island, Art Department Gallery, Warwick RI
Community College of Rhode Island, Dept of Art, Warwick RI (S)
Community College of the Finger Lakes, Visual & Performing Arts Dept, Canandaigua NY (S)
Community Council for the Arts, Kinston NC
Community Gallery of Lancaster County, Lancaster PA
Compton Community College, Compton CA (S)
Margaret Hutchinson Compton Gallery, see Massachusetts Institute of Technology, Cambridge MA
Concord Antiquarian Society Museum, Concord MA
Concord Art Association, Concord MA
Concord College, Art Dept, Athens WV (S)
Concordia College, Bronxville NY (S)
Concordia College, Art Dept, Mequow WI (S)
Concordia College, Art Dept, Moorhead MN (S)
Concordia College, Art Dept, Saint Paul MN (S)
Concordia College, Koenig Art Gallery, Seward NE
Concordia College, Art Dept, Seward NE (S)
Concordia College Wisconsin, Fine Arts Galleries, Mequon WI
Concordia Historical Institute, Saint Louis MO
Concordia Lutheran College, Dept of Fine Arts, Austin TX (S)
Concordia University, Art Gallery, Montreal PQ
Concordia University, Faculty of Fine Arts, Montreal PQ (S)
Concourse Gallery, see Bank of America, San Francisco CA
Conejo Valley Art Museum, Thousand Oaks CA
Confederate Museum, see Louisiana Historical Association, New Orleans LA
Confederation Centre Art Gallery and Museum, Charlottetown PE
Confederation of American Indians, New York NY
Congressional Arts Caucus, Washington DC
Connecticut College, New London CT (S)
Connecticut Historical Commission, Sloane-Stanley Museum, Kent CT
Connecticut Historical Society, Hartford CT
Connecticut State Library, Raymond E Baldwin Museum, Hartford CT
Connecticut Valley Historical Museum, Springfield MA
Connecticut Women Artist, Inc, Glastonbury CT
Contemporary Arts Center, Cincinnati OH
Contemporary Arts Center, Honolulu HI
Contemporary Arts Museum, Houston TX
Contemporary Art Workshop, Chicago IL
Contemporary Art Workshop, Chicago IL (S)
Contemporary Crafts Association and Gallery, Portland OR
Contra Costa College, Dept of Art, San Pablo CA (S)
Converse College, Art Dept, Spartanburg SC (S)
Converse College, Milliken Art Gallery, Spartanburg SC
Cooke County College, Fine Arts Dept, Gainesville TX (S)
Cooke County College Library, Art Dept, Gainesville TX
Cookeville Art Center, see Cumberland Art Society, Cookeville TN
Cook Inlet Historical Society, see Anchorage Historical and Fine Arts Museum, Anchorage AK
Cooper-Hewitt Museum, Smithsonian Institution, New York NY
Cooperstown Art Association, Cooperstown NY
Cooper Union for the Advancement of Science & Art, Library, New York NY
Cooper Union School of Art, New York NY (S)
Coos Art Museum, Coos Bay OR
Coos Art Museum, Coos Bay OR (S)
Copper Village Museum & Arts Center, Anaconda MT

Coppini Academy of Fine Arts, San Antonio TX
Coppin State College, Art Dept, Baltimore MD (S)
Coquille Valley Art Association, Coquille OR
Corcoran Museum, Washington DC
Corcoran School of Art, Washington DC (S)
Lovis Corinth Memorial Foundation, Inc, New York NY
Cork Gallery, see Lincoln Center for the Performing Arts, New York NY
Cornell College, Armstrong Gallery, Mount Vernon IA
Cornell College, Art Dept, Mount Vernon IA (S)
George D and Harriet W Cornell Fine Arts Center Museum, see Rollins College, Winter Park FL
Cornell University, Herbert F Johnson Museum of Art, Ithaca NY
Cornell University, Ithaca NY (S)
Corning Community College, Division of Humanities, Corning NY (S)
Corning Museum of Glass, Corning NY
Cornish Gallery, see Cornish Institute, Seattle WA
Cornish Institute, Seattle WA (S)
Cornish Institute, Cornish Gallery, Seattle WA
Coronado School of Fine Arts, Coronado CA (S)
Corporate Council for the Arts, Seattle WA
Corpus Christi State University, Weil Art Gallery, Corpus Christi TX
Cortland County Historical Society, Suggett House Museum, Cortland NY
Cortland Free Library, Art Gallery, Cortland NY
Cosanti Foundation, Scottsdale AZ
Cottey College, Fine Arts Division, Nevada MO (S)
Council of American Artist Societies, New York NY
Council of Delaware Artists, Newark DE
Council of Ozark Artists and Craftsmen, Inc, Arts Center of the Ozarks Gallery, Springdale AR
County College of Morris, Art Dept, Randolph NJ (S)
Courtney Art Gallery, see Jersey City State College, Jersey City NJ
Cowboy Artists of America, Kansas City MO
Cowboy Artists of America Museum, Kerrville TX
Cheney Cowles Memorial Museum, see Eastern Washington State Historical Society, Spokane WA
Craft and Folk Art Museum, Los Angeles CA
Craft Center Museum, Wilton CT
Craft Resource Centre, see Ontario Crafts Council, Toronto ON
Crafts Guild Art School for the Deaf, Holland MI (S)
Cranbrook Academy of Art, Bloomfield Hills MI (S)
Cranbrook Academy of Art Museum, Bloomfield Hills MI
William W Crapo Gallery, see Swain School of Design, New Bedford MA
Creative Arts Guild, Dalton GA
Creative School of Design Library, Cuyahoga Falls OH
Creative Time, New York NY
Creek Council House and Museum, Okmulgee OK
Creighton University, Fine and Performing Arts Dept, Omaha NE (S)
Creighton University Art Gallery, Omaha NE
Crocker Art Museum, Sacramento CA
Crocker National Bank, San Francisco CA
Crook County Museum and Art Gallery, Sundance WY
Crowder College, Dept of Art, Neosho MO (S)
Crowninshield-Bentley House, see Essex Institute, Salem MA
John M Cuelenaere Library, Grace Campbell Gallery, Prince Albert SK
Cuesta College, Art Dept, San Luis Obispo CA (S)
Cuesta College Library, Art Dept, San Luis Obispo CA
Irene Cullis Gallery, see Greensboro College, Greensboro NC
Cultural Art Center of Ocean City, Ocean City NJ
Cultural Council Foundation, Fourteen Sculptors Gallery, New York NY
Culver-Stockton College, Division of Fine Arts, Canton MO (S)
Cumberland Art Society, Cookeville Art Center, Cookeville TN

Eastern Montana College, Art Dept, Billings MT (S)

Eastern New Mexico University, Art & Library Gallery, Portales NM

Eastern New Mexico University, Dept of Art, Portales NM (S)

Eastern Oregon State College, Arts & Humanities Dept, La Grande OR (S)

Eastern Washington State Historical Society, Cheney Cowles Memorial Museum, Spokane WA

Eastern Washington University, Dept of Art, Cheney WA (S)

Eastern Wyoming College, Art Dept, Torrington WY (S)

Eastfield College, Humanities Division, Art Dept, Mesquite TX (S)

East Los Angeles College, Art Dept, Monterey Park CA (S)

East Mississippi Junior College, Art Dept, Scooba MS (S)

East Stroudsburg State College, Art Dept, East Stroudsburg PA (S)

East Tennessee State University, Johnson City TN

East Tennessee State University, Fine Arts Dept, Johnson City TN (S)

East Texas State University, Art Dept Gallery, Commerce TX

East Texas State University, Dept of Art, Commerce TX (S)

East Windsor Historical Society Inc, Scantic Academy Museum, East Windsor CT

Eccles Community Art Center, Ogden UT

Eckerd College, Art Dept, Saint Petersburg FL (S)

Ecole des Arts Visuels de L'Universite Laval, see L'Universite Laval, Quebec PQ

Edgewood College, Art Dept, Madison WI (S)

Edgewood College, DeRicci Gallery, Madison WI

Edinboro University of Pennsylvania, Art Dept, Edinboro PA (S)

Edison Community College, Gallery of Fine Art, Fort Myers FL

Edison Community College, Dept of Fine and Performing Arts, Fort Myers FL (S)

Edmonton Art Gallery, Edmonton AB

Edmonton Public Library, Foyer Gallery and Photography Gallery, Edmonton AB

Edmundson Art Foundation, Inc, Des Moines Art Center, Des Moines IA

Education Alliance Art School, New York NY (S)

Edward-Dean Museum of Decorative Arts, see Riverside County Art and Cultural Center, Cherry Valley CA

Egner Fine Arts Center, see Findlay College, Findlay OH

Dwight D Eisenhower Presidential Library, Abilene KS

El Camino College, Division of Fine Arts, Los Angeles CA (S)

El Camino College Art Gallery, Torrance CA

Elder Gallery, see Nebraska Wesleyan University, Lincoln NE

Electronic Arts Intermix, Inc, New York NY

Eleutherian Mills-Hagley Foundation, see Hagley Museum, Wilmington DE

Eleutherian Mills Historical Library, see Hagley Museum, Wilmington DE

Elgin Community College, Fine Arts Dept, Elgin IL (S)

Eli Lilly and Company, Indianapolis IN

Elizabeth City State University, Dept of Art, Elizabeth City NC (S)

Elizabeth Seton College, Art Dept, Yonkers NY (S)

Anton Elli, Cincinnati OH (S)

Elliot Museum, see Historical Society of Martin County, Stuart FL

Ellsworth Community College, Dept of Fine Arts, Iowa Falls IA (S)

Elmhurst College, Art Dept, Elmhurst IL (S)

Elmira College, Hamilton Art Gallery, Elmira NY

Elmira College, Art Dept, Elmira NY (S)

El Molino Viejo, see California Historical Society, San Francisco CA

Elms College, Dept of Fine Arts, Chicopee MA (S)

El Museo del Barrio, New York NY

El Paso Museum of Art, El Paso TX

Elvehjem Museum of Art, see University of Wisconsin, Madison WI

Embarcadero Center Inc, San Francisco CA

Emerald Empire Arts Association, Springfield OR

Fred L Emerson Gallery, see Hamilton College, Clinton NY

Emery Galleries, see Xavier University, Cincinnati OH

Emily Carr College of Art & Design, Vancouver BC (S)

Emily Carr College of Art & Design, The Charles H Scott Gallery, Vancouver BC

Emmanuel College, Art Dept, Boston MA (S)

Emmanuel Gallery, see Auraria Higher Education Center, Denver CO

Emma Willard School Arts Division, Troy NY (S)

Emory University, Art History Dept, Atlanta GA (S)

Emporia State University, Dept of Art, Emporia KS (S)

Emporia State University, Norman R Eppink Art Gallery, Emporia KS

Endicott College, Art Dept, Beverly MA (S)

Englewood Library, Fine Arts Dept, Englewood NJ

Norman R Eppink Art Gallery, see Emporia State University, Emporia KS

Max Epstein Archive, see University of Chicago, Chicago IL

Equitable Life Assurance Society, New York NY

Erie Art Museum, Erie PA

Erie County Library System, Art Dept, Erie PA

Erie Historical Museum, Erie PA

Erskine College, Dept of Art, Due West SC (S)

Escuela de Artes Plasticas, see Institute of Puerto Rican Culture, San Juan PR (S)

Escuela de Artes Plasticas Galleria, see Institute of Puerto Rican Culture, San Juan PR

Wharton Esherick Museum, Paoli PA

Eskimo Museum, Churchill MB

Essex Art Association, Inc, Essex CT

Essex Institute, Salem MA

Estevan National Exhibition Centre Inc, Estevan SK

Agnes Etherington Art Centre, see Queen's University, Kingston ON

Evans Research Library, see Florence Museum, Florence SC

Evanston Art Center, Evanston IL

Evansville Museum of Arts and Science, Evansville IN

Everett Community College, Art Dept, Everett WA (S)

Evergreen House, see Johns Hopkins University, Baltimore MD

Evergreen State College, Evergreen Galleries, Olympia WA

Everhart Museum of Natural History, Science and Art, Scranton PA

Everson Museum of Art, Syracuse NY

Exchange National Bank of Chicago, Chicago IL

Experimental Gallery, see Columbus College, Columbus GA

Exploratorium, San Francisco CA

Henry Failing Art and Music Dept, see Multnomah County Library, Portland OR

Fairbanks Gallery, see Oregon State University, Corvallis OR

Fairbanks Museum and Planetarium, Saint Johnsbury VT

Fairfield Art Association, see Fairfield Public Library and Museum, Fairfield IA

Fairfield Historical Society, Fairfield CT

Fairfield Public Library and Museum, Fairfield Art Association, Fairfield IA

Fairfield University, Fine Arts Dept, Fairfield CT (S)

Fairleigh Dickinson University, Fine Arts Dept, Teaneck NJ (S)

Fairmont State College, Art Dept, Fairmont WV (S)

Fairmount Park Art Association, Philadelphia PA

Fair Street Museum, see Nantucket Historical Association, Nantucket MA

Falkirk Community Cultural Center, San Rafael CA

Farmers' Museum, Inc, see New York State Historical Association, Cooperstown NY

Farmington Art Guild, Farmington CT

Farmington Valley Arts Center, Avon CT

William A Farnsworth Library and Art Museum, Rockland ME

Fashion & Art Institute of Dallas, Dallas TX (S)

Fashion Institute of Technology, Art & Design Division, New York NY (S)

Fashion Institute of Technology, Galleries, New York NY

Faulkner Memorial Art Wing, see Santa Barbara Public Library, Santa Barbara CA

Favell Museum of Western Art & Indian Artifacts, Klamath Falls OR

Fayette Art Museum, Fayette AL

Fayette Bank and Trust Company, Uniontown PA

Fayetteville Museum of Art, Inc, Fayetteville NC

Fayetteville State University, Division of Humanitites and Fine Arts, Fayetteville NC (S)

Feather River Community College, Art Dept, Quincy CA (S)

Harriet FeBland Art Workshop, New York NY (S)

Federal Reserve Bank of Boston, Boston MA

Federal Reserve Bank of Minneapolis, Minneapolis MN

Federal Reserve Bank of Richmond, Richmond VA

Federated Arts Associations of New Jersey, Inc, Westfield NJ

Federated Arts Council of Richmond, Inc, Richmond VA

Federation of Modern Painters and Sculptors, New York NY

Feldman Fine Arts & Audio Visual Dept, see Norfolk Public Library, Norfolk VA

Felician College, Art Dept, Chicago IL (S)

Fenimore House, see New York State Historical Association, Cooperstown NY

Gordon Fennell Gallery & Marvin Cone Gallery, see Coe College, Cedar Rapids IA

Ferguson Library, Stamford CT

Ferris State College, Commercial Art Dept, Big Rapids MI (S)

Fetherston Foundation, Packwood House Museum, Lewisburg PA

Fiberworks, Center for the Textile Arts, Berkeley CA

Field Museum of Natural History, Chicago IL

55 Mercer, New York NY

The Filson Club, Louisville KY

Findlay College, Egner Fine Arts Center, Findlay OH

Findlay College, Art Dept, Findlay OH (S)

Fine Arts Association, School of Fine Arts, Willoughby OH

Fine Arts Center of Clinton, Clinton IL

Fine Arts Club, Second Crossing Gallery, Valley City ND

Fine Arts Museum of the South, Mobile AL

Fine Arts Museums of San Francisco, M H de Young Memorial Museum and California Palace of the Legion of Honor, San Francisco CA

Firehouse Gallery, see Leatherstocking Brush & Palette Club Inc, Cooperstown NY

Firehouse Gallery, see Nassua Community College, Garden City NY

First and Merchants National Bank, Richmond VA

First Commercial Bank in Little Rock, Little Rock AR

First Interstate Bank of Arizona, Tucson AZ

First Interstate Bank of Fort Collins, Fort Collins CO

The First National Bank of Chicago, Chicago IL

First National Bank of Florida, Tampa FL

First Security Bank of Idaho, Boise ID

First Street Forum, Saint Louis MO

Jonathan Fisher Memorial, Inc, see Parson Fisher House, Blue Hill ME

Fisher Scientific Company, Fisher Collection of Alchemical and Historical Pictures, Pittsburgh PA

Fisk University, Division of Humanities & Fine Arts, Nashville TN (S)

Fisk University Museum of Art, Nashville TN

Fitchburg Art Museum, Fitchburg MA

Five Civilized Tribes Museum, Muskogee OK

Flagler College, Visual Arts Dept, Saint Augustine FL (S)

Henry Morrison Flagler Museum, Palm Beach FL

Flamingo Gallery, see Clark County Library District, Las Vegas NV

Flathead Valley Art Association & Art Gallery, see Hockaday Center for the Arts, Kalispell MT

Thomas Gilcrease Institute of American History and Art, Tulsa OK
The Gilman Paper Company, New York NY
Genevieve and Donald Gilmore Art Center, see Kalamazoo Institute of Arts, Kalamazoo MI
Gilpin County Arts Association, Central City CO
Adam & Sophie Gimbel Library, see Parsons School of Design, New York NY
Glassboro State College, Dept of Art, Glassboro NJ (S)
Alfred C Glassell School of Art, Houston TX (S)
Glenbow Museum, Calgary AB
Glendale College, Dept of Fine Arts, Glendale CA (S)
Glendale Federal Savings, Glendale CA
Glendinning Gallery, see Utah Arts Council, Salt Lake City UT
Glenville State College, Dept of Art, Glenville WV (S)
Glessner House, see Chicago Architecture Foundation, Chicago IL
Gloucester County College, Liberal Arts Dept, Sewell NJ (S)
Charles B Goddard Center for the Visual and Performing Arts, Ardmore OK
Goddard College, Visual Arts Dept, Plainsfield VT (S)
Godwin-Ternbach Museum, Flushing NY
Goetz Art School, Bedford Hills NY (S)
Gogebic Community College, Art Dept, Ironwood MI (S)
Golden State Mutual Life, Los Angeles CA
Golden West College, Arts, Humanities and Social Sciences Institute, Huntington Beach CA (S)
Goldman Fine Arts Gallery, see Judaic Museum of the Jewish Community Center, Rockville MD
Goldsboro Art Center, Goldsboro NC (S)
Goldstein Gallery, see University of Minnesota, Saint Paul MN
Morris Goldstein Library, see Judah L Magnes Museum, Berkeley CA
Robert Goldwater Library of Primitive Art, see Metropolitan Museum of Art, New York NY
Gonzaga University, Dept of Art, Spokane WA (S)
Gonzaga University, Ad Art Gallery, Spokane WA
Donald B Gordon Memorial Library, see Palm Beach County Parks and Recreation Department, Delray Beach FL
Gordon Junior College, Art Dept, Barnesville GA (S)
Goshen College, Art Dept, Goshen IN (S)
Goucher College, Art Dept, Towson MD (S)
Goucher College, Kraushaar Auditorium Lobby Gallery, Towson MD
Government Employees Insurance Company, Chevy Chase MD
Governors State University, College of Arts & Science, Art Dept, Park Forest South IL (S)
Grace College, Dept of Art, Winona Lake IN (S)
Graceland College, Art Dept, Lamoni IA (S)
Grambling State University, Art Dept, Grambling LA (S)
Grand Canyon College, Art Dept, Phoenix AZ (S)
Grande Prairie College Gallery, Grande Prairie AB
Grand Marais Art Colony, Grand Marais MN (S)
Grand Prairie Arts Council, Inc, Arts Center of the Grand Prairie, Stuttgart AR
Grand Rapids Art Museum, Grand Rapids MI
Grand Rapids Junior College, Art Dept, Grand Rapids MI (S)
Grand Rapids Public Library, Music & Art Dept, Grand Rapids MI
Grand Valley State Colleges, Art Dept, Allendale MI (S)
Grand View College, Art Dept, Des Moines IA (S)
Gray Art Gallery, see East Carolina University, Greenville NC
Grayson County College, Art Dept, Denison TX (S)
Greater Hartford Community College, Humanities Division & Art Dept, Hartford CT (S)
Greater Lafayette Museum of Art, see Lafayette Art Association, Lafayette IN
Great Lakes Historical Society, Vermilion OH
Greenfield Community College, Art Dept, Greenfield MA (S)
Green Hill Center for North Carolina Art, Greensboro NC

Ida Green Gallery, see Austin College, Sherman TX
Green Mountain College, Dept of Art, Poultney VT (S)
Green River Community College, Art Dept, Auburn WA (S)
Greensboro Artists' League, Greensboro NC
Greensboro College, Dept of Art, Division of Fine Arts, Greensboro NC (S)
Greensboro College, Irene Cullis Gallery, Greensboro NC
Greenville College, Richard W Bock Sculpture Collection, Greenville IL
Greenville College, Division of Language, Literature & Fine Arts, Greenville IL (S)
Greenville County Museum of Art, Greenville SC
Greenville County Museum of Art, Museum School of Art, Greenville SC (S)
Greenville Museum of Art, Greenville NC
Greenville Technical College, Art History Dept, Greenville SC (S)
The Greenwich Art Society Inc, Greenwich CT
Greenwich House Pottery, New York NY (S)
Grey Art Gallery and Study Center, see New York University, New York NY
Grinnell College, Dept of Art, Grinnell IA (S)
Florence Griswold Museum, see Lyme Historical Society, Old Lyme CT
Grolier Club Library, New York NY
Grossmont College, Art Dept, El Cajon CA (S)
Grossmont Community College Gallery, El Cajon CA
M Grumbacher Inc, New York NY
Grunwald Center for the Graphic Arts, see University of California, Los Angeles, Los Angeles CA
Guadalupe Historic Foundation, Santuario de Guadalupe, Santa Fe NM
John Simon Guggenheim Memorial Foundation, New York NY
Solomon R Guggenheim Museum, New York NY
Guilde Canadienne des Metiers d'Art, Quebec, Canadian Guild of Crafts, Quebec, Montreal PQ
Guild Hall of East Hampton, Inc, Museum Section, East Hampton NY
Guild of Book Workers, New York NY
Guild of Boston Artists, Boston MA
Guild of Creative Art, Shrewsbury NJ (S)
Guilford Technical Community College, Commercial Art Dept, Jamestown NC (S)
Gulf Coast Community College, Division of Fine Arts, Panama City FL (S)
Jessica Gund Memorial Library, see Cleveland Institute of Art, Cleveland OH
Emery A Gunnin Architectural Library, see Clemson University, Clemson SC
Gunston Hall Plantation, Lorton VA
Gustavus Adolphus College, Art Dept, Saint Peter MN (S)
Haas Gallery of Art, see Bloomsburg University of Pennsylvania, Bloomsburg PA
Haber School of Sculpture, Roslyn NY (S)
Hagerstown Junior College, Art Dept, Hagerstown MD (S)
The Haggin Museum, Stockton CA
Hagley Museum, Eleutherian Mills-Hagley Foundation, Wilmington DE
Hale Hoikeike, see Maui Historical Society, Wailuku HI
Hallmark Cards, Inc, Kansas City MO
Hall of Fame of the Trotter, Goshen NY
Stan Hywet Hall Foundation, Inc, Akron OH
Hallwalls Gallery, New York NY
Hamilton Art Gallery, see Elmira College, Elmira NY
Hamilton College, Fred L Emerson Gallery, Clinton NY
Hamilton College, Art Dept, Clinton NY (S)
Hamline University, Art Dept, Saint Paul MN (S)
Hamline University Learning Center Gallery, Saint Paul MN
Hammond Castle Museum, Gloucester MA
Hammond-Harwood House Association, Inc, Annapolis MD
Hammond Museum, Museum of the Humanities, North Salem NY
Hampshire County Public Library, Romney WV
Hampton Center for Arts and Humanities, Hampton VA

Hampton Institute, College Museum, Hampton VA
Hampton Institute, Art Dept, Hampton VA (S)
John Hancock Warehouse, see Society for the Preservation of Historic Landmarks, York ME
Hancock Shaker Village, Inc, Pittsfield MA
Hancock Shaker Village Library, see Hancock Shaker Village, Inc, Pittsfield MA
Handforth Gallery, see Tacoma Public Library, Tacoma WA
Hannibal La Grange College, Art Dept, Hannibal MO (S)
Hanover College, Dept of Art, Hanover IN (S)
Dane G Hansen Memorial Museum, Logan KS
Harcum Junior College, Dept of Fine Arts, Bryn Mawr PA (S)
Harding University, Dept of Art, Searcy AR (S)
Hardin-Simmons University, Art Dept, Abilene TX (S)
Harford Community College, Humanities Division, Bel Air MD (S)
Harkness Memorial State Park, Waterford CT
Harlow Gallery, see Kennebec Valley Art Association, Hallowell ME
Harrington Institute of Interior Design, Chicago IL (S)
Harrington Institute of Interior Design, Design Library, Chicago IL
Harrisburg Area Community College, Division of Communication and the Arts, Harrisburg PA (S)
Harrison County Historical Museum, Marshall TX
Harris School of Art, Inc, Franklin TN (S)
Houston Harte University Center, see Angelo State University, San Angelo TX
Hartford Art School of the University of Hartford, West Hartford CT (S)
Hartford Public Library, Hartford CT
Hartland Art Council, Hartland MI
Hartman Center Gallery, see Bradley University, Peoria IL
Hart Nautical Museum, see Massachusetts Institute of Technology, Cambridge MA
Hartnell College, Art and Photography Dept, Salinas CA (S)
Hartnell College Gallery, Salinas CA
Stephen H Hart Library, see Colorado Historical Society, Denver CO
Hartwick College, Art Dept, Oneonta NY (S)
Hartwick College Fine Art Gallery, Oneonta NY
William S Hart Museum, Newhall CA
Harvard University, Cambridge MA
Harvard University, Dept of Fine Arts, Cambridge MA (S)
Harvard University, Dumbarton Oaks Research Library and Collections, Washington DC
Harwood Foundation of the University of New Mexico, Taos NM
Haskell Indian Junior College, Art Dept, Lawrence KS (S)
Hasting Gallery, see Springfield College, Springfield MA
Hastings College, Art Dept, Hastings NE (S)
Hastings County Museum, Belleville ON
Hastings Museum, Hastings NE
Haverford College, Fine Arts Dept, Haverford PA (S)
Haverhill Public Library, Art Dept, Haverhill MA
Hawaii State Library, Fine Arts-Audiovisual Section, Honolulu HI
Hayden Library Art Dept, see Arizona State University, Tempe AZ
Jean P Haydon Museum, Pago Pago, American Samoa PI
Haystack Mountain School of Crafts, Deer Isle ME (S)
Haystack Mountain School of Crafts Gallery, Deer Isle ME
Hayward Area Forum of the Arts, Son Gallery, Hayward CA
Headley-Whitney Museum, Lexington KY
Heard Museum, Phoenix AZ
Hearst Art Gallery, see Saint Mary's College of California, Moraga CA
Hebrew Union College, Gallery of Art and Artifacts, Cincinnati OH
Hebrew Union College, Skirball Museum, Los Angeles CA
Heckscher Museum, Huntington NY
Heidelberg College, Dept of Art, Tiffin OH (S)

Harry D Hendren Gallery, see Lindenwood College, Saint Charles MO

Jack R Hennesey Art Galleries, see Saint Clair County Community College, Port Huron MI

Henry Art Gallery, see University of Washington, Seattle WA

Henry Ford Community College, Art Dept, Dearborn MI (S)

Henry Street Settlement Arts for Living Center, New York NY (S)

Gertrude Herbert Memorial Institute of Art, Augusta GA

Herbert H Lehman College, Art Dept, Bronx NY (S)

Heritage Center, Inc, Pine Ridge SD

Heritage Museum and Gallery, see Lake County Civic Center Association, Inc, Leadville CO

Heritage Plantation of Sandwich, Sandwich MA

Herkimer County Community College, Humanities Division, Herkimer NY (S)

Grover M Hermann Fine Arts Center, see Marietta College, Marietta OH

Hermitage Foundation Museum, Norfolk VA

Herrette Museum, see College of Southern Idaho, Twin Falls ID

Herron School of Art, Indiana University-Purdue University, Indianapolis, Indianapolis IN (S)

Herron School of Art Gallery, see Indiana University - Purdue University at Indianapolis, Indianapolis IN

Hershey Museum of American Life, Hershey PA

Hesston College, Hesston KS (S)

Heublein Inc, Farmington CT

Heward-Washington House, see Charleston Museum, Charleston SC

Hewitt Memorial Library, see Washington State Historical Society, Tacoma WA

Hewlett-Woodmere Public Library, Hewlett NY

Hibbing Community College, Art Dept, Hibbing MN (S)

Edna Hibel Art Foundation, Hibel Museum of Art, Riviera Beach FL

Hickory Museum of Art, Inc, Hickory NC

Hicks Art Center, see Bucks County Community College, Newtown PA

Higgins Armory Museum, Worcester MA

Highland Community College, Freeport IL (S)

High Museum of Art, Atlanta GA

High Plains Museum, McCook NE

High Point College, Fine Arts Dept, High Point NC (S)

Hill Country Arts Foundation, Ingram TX

Hill Junior College, Fine Arts Dept, Hillsboro TX (S)

Hillsborough Community College, Fine Arts Dept, Tampa FL (S)

Hillsdale College, Art Dept, Hillsdale MI (S)

Hill-Stead Museum, Farmington CT

Hillwood Museum, see Marjorie Merriweather Post Foundation of DC, Washington DC

Hillyer Art Library, see Smith College, Northampton MA

Hilson Gallery, see Deerfield Academy, Deerfield MA

Hinds Junior College, Dept of Art, Raymond MS (S)

Hinds Junior College District, Marie Hull Gallery, Raymond MS

Hiram College, Art Dept, Hiram OH (S)

Hirshhorn Museum and Sculpture Garden, Washington DC

Hispanic Society of America, Museum, New York NY

Historical Society of Bloomfield, Bloomfield NJ

Historical Society of Delaware, Wilmington DE

Historical Society of Kent County, Chestertown MD

Historical Society of Martin County, Elliot Museum, Stuart FL

Historical Society of Old Newbury, Cushing House Museum, Newburyport MA

Historical Society of Pennsylvania, Philadelphia PA

Historical Society of the Town of Greenwich, Inc, Bush-Holley House, Cos Cob CT

Historical Society of York County, York PA

Historic Cherry Hill, Albany NY

Historic Deerfield Inc, Deerfield MA

Historic Landmarks Foundation of Indiana, Morris-Butler House, Indianapolis IN

Historic New Orleans Collection, Kemper and Leila Williams Foundation, New Orleans LA

Historic Pensacola Preservation Board, West Florida Museum of History, Pensacola FL

Historic Saint Augustine Preservation Board, Saint Augustine FL

Allen R Hite Art Institute, see University of Louisville, Louisville KY (S)

Allen R Hite Art Institute Gallery, see University of Louisville, Louisville KY

Hobart and William Smith Colleges, Art Dept, Geneva NY (S)

Hockaday Center for the Arts, Flathead Valley Art Association & Art Gallery, Kalispell MT

Hoffberger School of Painting, see Maryland Institute, Baltimore MD (S)

Hoffman Gallery, see Oregon School of Arts and Crafts, Portland OR

Hofstra University, Emily Lowe Gallery, Hempstead NY

Hofstra University, Hempstead NY (S)

Holland College, School of Visual Arts, Charlottetown PE (S)

Holland College, School of Visual Arts Library & Gallery, West Royalty PE

Hollins College, Art Dept, Hollins VA (S)

Hollywood Art Center School, Hollywood CA (S)

Hollywood Art Museum, Hollywood FL

Holman Gallery, see Trenton State College, Trenton NJ

The Holtzman Art Gallery, see Towson State University, Towson MD

Holy Names College, Art Dept, Oakland CA (S)

Holyoke Community College, Dept of Art, Holyoke MA (S)

Honeywell Inc, Minneapolis MN

Honolulu Academy of Arts, Honolulu HI

Honolulu Academy of Arts, Studio Program, Honolulu HI (S)

Honolulu Community College, Honolulu HI (S)

Hood College, Dept of Art, Frederick MD (S)

Hood Museum of Art, Hanover NH

Hoosier Salon Patrons Association, Hoosier Salon Art Gallery, Indianapolis IN

Herbert Hoover Presidential Library & Museum, West Branch IA

Hope College, Art Dept, Holland MI (S)

Hope College, De Pree Art Center & Gallery, Holland MI

Hopewell Museum, Hopewell NJ

Hopi Cultural Center, Second Mesa AZ

Horner Museum, see Oregon State University, Corvallis OR

Houghton College, Art Dept, Houghton NY (S)

Housatonic Community College, Housatonic Museum of Art, Bridgeport CT

Housatonic Community College, Art Dept, Bridgeport CT (S)

House of Happy Walls, see Jack London State Historic Park, Glen Ellen CA

Houston Antique Museum, Chattanooga TN

Houston Baptist College, Dept of Art, Houston TX (S)

Houston Baptist University, Museum of American Architecture and Decorative Arts, Houston TX

Houston Public Library, Houston TX

Howard College, Art Dept, Big Spring TX (S)

Howard Payne University, Dept of Art, Brownwood TX (S)

Howard University, Gallery of Art, Washington DC

Howard University, Art Dept, Washington DC (S)

Howe Architecture Library, see Arizona State University, Tempe AZ

Oscar Howe Art Center, Mitchell SD

Hoyt Institute of Fine Arts, New Castle PA

Hubbell Trading Post, Ganado AZ

Hudson River Museum, Yonkers NY

Hudson Valley Art Association, White Plains NY

Marie Hull Gallery, see Hinds Junior College District, Raymond MS

Humber College of Applied Arts and Technology, Creative and Communication Arts Division, Rexdale ON (S)

Humboldt State University, College of Creative Arts & Humanities, Arcata CA (S)

Humbolt Arts Council, Eureka CA

Hunter College, Art Dept, New York NY (S)

Hunterdon Art Center, Clinton NJ

Hunter Museum of Art, Chattanooga TN

Huntingdon College, Dept of Visual and Performing Arts, Montgomery AL (S)

Archer M Huntington Art Gallery, see University of Texas at Austin, Austin TX

Huntington College, Art Dept, Huntington IN (S)

Huntington Free Library and Reading Room, Depository Library for the Museum of the American Indian, Bronx NY

Huntington Galleries, Huntington WV

Huntington Library, Art Gallery and Botanical Gardens, San Marino CA

Hunt Library, see Carnegie-Mellon University, Pittsburgh PA

Huntsville Art League and Museum Association Inc, Huntsville AL

Huntsville Museum of Art, Huntsville AL

William Morris Hunt Memorial Library, see Museum of Fine Arts, Boston MA

Huron College, Art Dept, Huron SD (S)

Hussian School of Art, Inc, Commercial Art Dept, Philadelphia PA (S)

Hutchinson Art Association, Hutchinson KS

Hutchinson Community Junior College, Art Dept, Hutchinson KS (S)

Hyde Collection, Glens Falls NY

Idaho State University, John B Davis Gallery of Fine Art, Pocatello ID

Idaho State University, Dept of Art, Pocatello ID (S)

Idyllwild School of Music and the Arts, see University of Southern California, Idyllwild CA (S)

Illinois Bell, Chicago IL

Illinois Benedictine College, Fine Arts Dept, Lisle IL (S)

Illinois Central College, Fine Arts Dept, East Peoria IL (S)

Illinois Institute of Technology, Chicago IL (S)

Illinois State Library, Springfield IL

Illinois State Museum of Natural History and Art, Springfield IL

Illinois State University, Normal IL

Illinois State University, Art Dept, Normal IL (S)

Illinois Valley Community College, Div of Humanities and Fine Arts, Oglesby IL (S)

Illinois Wesleyan University, Merwin Gallery, Bloomington IL

Illinois Wesleyan University, School of Art, Bloomington IL (S)

Imhoff Art Gallery, Saint Walburg SK

Imperial Calcasieu Museum, Lake Charles LA

Imperial Valley College, Art Dept, Imperial CA (S)

INA Corporation, Philadelphia PA

Incarnate Word College, Art Dept, San Antonio TX (S)

Independence Museum, see Ladies Library and Art Association, Independence KS

Independence National Historical Park, Philadelphia PA

Independent Curators Incorporated, New York NY

Index of American Design, see National Gallery of Art, Washington DC

Index of Christian Art, see Princeton University, Princeton NJ

Indiana Central University, Leah Ransburg Art Gallery, Indianapolis IN

Indiana Central University, Fine Arts Dept, Indianapolis IN (S)

Indianapolis Marion County Public Library, Art Dept, Indianapolis IN

Indianapolis Museum of Art, Indianapolis IN

Indian Arts & Crafts Association, Albuquerque NM

Indiana State Museum, Indianapolis IN

Indiana State University, Turman Gallery, Terre Haute IN

Indiana State University, Terre Haute IN (S)

Indiana State University, Evansville, Art Dept, Evansville IN (S)

Indiana University, Bloomington IN

Indiana University at South Bend, Fine Arts Dept, South Bend IN (S)

Indiana University, Bloomington, School of Fine Arts, Bloomington IN (S)

Indiana University East, Arts & Science Dept, Richmond IN (S)

The Macgregor Gallery, Nelson BC
McGroarty Cultural Art Center, Cultural Affairs Dept, City of Los Angeles, Tujunga CA (S)
McIntire Dept of Art, see University of Virginia, Charlottesville VA (S)
McIntosh Art Gallery, see University of Western Ontario, London ON
Mackenzie Art Gallery, see University of Regina, Regina SK
R Tait McKenzie Memorial Museum, see Mississippi Valley Conservation Authority, Almonte ON
McKinney Library, see Albany Institute of History and Art, Albany NY
McKissick Museums, Columbia SC
Carrie McLain Museum, Nome AK
The Robert McLaughlin Gallery, Oshawa ON
McLean Arts Center, Art Dept, McLean VA (S)
McLean County Art Association, Arts Center, Bloomington IL
McLennan Community College, Fine Arts Dept, Waco TX (S)
McMaster University, Art Gallery, Hamilton ON
McMaster University, Dept of Art and Art History, Hamilton ON (S)
McMichael Canadian Collection, Kleinburg ON
MacMurray College, Art Dept, Jacksonville IL (S)
McMurry College, Ryan Fine Arts Center, Abilene TX
McMurry College, Art Dept, Abilene TX (S)
Marion Koogler McNay Art Museum, San Antonio TX
McNeese State University, Dept of Visual Arts, Lake Charles LA (S)
Charles H MacNider Museum, Mason City IA
Macomb County Community College, Art Dept, Warren MI (S)
McPherson College, Art Dept, McPherson KS (S)
McPherson College Gallery, McPherson KS
Madison Area Technical College, Communication Arts, Madison WI (S)
Madison Art Center, Madison WI
Madison County Historical Society, Cottage Lawn, Oneida NY
Madison Public Library, Art & Music Division, Madison WI
Madonna College, Art Dept, Livonia MI (S)
Judah L Magnes Museum, Berkeley CA
Mahoney Library, see College of Saint Elizabeth, Convent Station NJ
Maine Art Gallery, Old Academy, see Lincoln County Cultural and Historical Association, Wiscasset ME
Maine Coast Artists, Rockport ME
Maine Historical Society, Portland ME
Maine Maritime Museum, Bath ME
Maine Photographic Workshops, Rockport ME
Maine Photographic Workshops, Rockport ME (S)
Main Line Center of the Arts, Haverford PA
Mainline Center of the Arts, Haverford PA (S)
Maitland Art Center, Maitland FL
Malcolm X College, see City Colleges of Chicago, Chicago IL (S)
Malden Bridge School of Art, Malden Bridge NY (S)
Malden Public Library, Art Dept & Gallery, Malden MA
Malone College, Dept of Art, Canton OH (S)
Maltwood Art Museum and Gallery, see University of Victoria, Victoria BC
Man and His World, see Pavilion of Humour, Montreal PQ
Manatee Junior College, Dept of Art, Bradenton FL (S)
Manchester City Library, Manchester NH
Manchester College, Art Dept, North Manchester IN (S)
Manchester Community College, Fine Arts Dept, Manchester CT (S)
Manchester Historic Association, Manchester NH
Manchester Institute of Arts and Sciences, Manchester NH (S)
Manchester Institute of Arts and Sciences Gallery, Manchester NH
Mandeville Art Gallery, see University of California-San Diego, La Jolla CA
Manhattan College, School of Arts and Sciences, Bronx NY (S)

Manhattan Laboratory Museum, New York NY
Manhattan Psychiatric Center's Sculpture Garden, New York NY
Manhattanville College, Brownson Art Gallery, Purchase NY
Manhattanville College, Art Dept, Purchase NY (S)
Joseph Manigault House, see Charleston Museum, Charleston SC
Manitoba Association of Architects, Winnipeg MB
Manitoba Historical Society, Dalnavert - MacDonald House Museum, Winnipeg MB
Manitoba Society of Artists, Winnipeg MB
Mankato Area Vocational-Technical Institute, Commercial and Technical Art Dept, North Mankato MN (S)
Mankato State University, Art Dept, Mankato MN (S)
Mankato State University, Nichols Gallery, Mankato MN
Mansfield Fine Arts Guild, Mansfield Art Center, Mansfield OH
Mansfield State College, Art Dept, Mansfield PA (S)
Maple Woods Community College, Dept of Art and Art History, Kansas City MO (S)
Marblehead Arts Association, Inc, Marblehead MA
Marblehead Historical Society, Marblehead MA
Jacque Marchais Center of Tibetan Arts, Inc, Staten Island NY
Marian College, Art Dept, Fond Du Lac WI (S)
Marian College, Art Dept, Indianapolis IN (S)
Marian College, Allison Mansion, Indianapolis IN
John Mariani Art Gallery, see University of Northern Colorado, Greeley CO
Marietta College, Grover M Hermann Fine Arts Center, Marietta OH
Marietta College, Art Dept, Marietta OH (S)
The Marine Corporation, Milwaukee WI
Marine Corps Museum, Art Unit, Washington DC
Mariners Museum, Newport News VA
Marin Society of Artists Inc, Ross CA
Marion Art Center, Marion MA
Marion College, Art Dept, Marion IN (S)
Maritime Art Association, Fredericton MB
Marquette University, Museum of Art, Milwaukee WI
Marshall University, Dept of Art, Huntington WV (S)
Mars Hill College, Art Dept, Mars Hill NC (S)
Martin Memorial Library, York PA
Martin Museum of Art, see Baylor University, Waco TX
Mary Baldwin College, Dept of Art, Staunton VA (S)
Marycrest College, Art Dept, Davenport IA (S)
Marygrove College, Dept of Art and Art History, Detroit MI (S)
Maryhill Museum of Art, Goldendale WA
Maryland College of Art and Design, Silver Spring MD (S)
Maryland College of Art and Design Library, Silver Spring MD
Maryland Historical Society Museum, Baltimore MD
Maryland Institute, College of Art Galleries, Baltimore MD
Maryland Institute, College of Art, Baltimore MD (S)
Maryland Museum of African Art, Columbia MD
Marylhurst College, Art Dept, Marylhurst OR (S)
Marymount College, Art Dept, Salina KS (S)
Marymount College, Art Dept, Tarrytown NY (S)
Marymount College of Virginia, Arts & Sciences Division, Arlington VA (S)
Marymount Manhattan College, Fine Arts Dept, New York NY (S)
Marymount Manhattan College Gallery, New York NY
Maryville College, Fine Arts Center Gallery, Maryville TN
Maryville College, Division of Fine Arts, Art Section, Maryville TN (S)
Maryville College Saint Louis, Beaumont Gallery, Saint Louis MO
Maryville College, St Louis, Art Division, Saint Louis MO (S)
Mary Washington College, Art Dept, Fredericksburg VA (S)

Mary Washington College, Belmont, The Gari Melchers Memorial Gallery, Fredericksburg VA
Marywood College, Art Dept, Scranton PA (S)
Mason City Public Library, Mason City IA
Mason County Museum, Maysville KY
Mason Gross School of the Arts, see Rutgers, the State University of New Jersey, New Brunswick NJ (S)
Massachusetts College of Art, Boston MA (S)
Massachusetts Historical Society, Boston MA
Massachusetts Institute of Technology, Cambridge MA (S)
Massachusetts Institute of Technology, Cambridge MA
Massillon Museum, Massillon OH
Masur Museum of Art, see Twin City Art Foundation, Monroe LA
William Hammond Mathers Museum, see Indiana University, Bloomington IN
Mattatuck Historical Society Museum, Mattatuck Museum, Waterbury CT
Mattatuck Museum, see Mattatuck Historical Society Museum, Waterbury CT
Maude Kerns Art Center School, Eugene OR (S)
Maui Community College, Art Dept, Kahului HI (S)
Maui Community College Library, Kahului HI
Maui Historical Society, Hale Hoikeike, Wailuku HI
Frederic R Mayer Art Center & Lamont Gallery, see Phillips Exeter Academy, Exeter NH
Mayer School of Fashion Design, Art Dept, New York NY (S)
Mayville State College Gallery, Mayville ND
Mead Art Museum, see Amherst College, Amherst MA
Meadow Brook Art Gallery, see Oakland University, Rochester MI
Meadows Collection Fine Arts Library, see Southern Methodist University, Dallas TX
Meadows Museum, see Southern Methodist University, Dallas TX
Meadows Museum of Art, see Centenary College of Louisiana, Shreveport LA
Meadville Council on the Arts, Meadville PA
Medicine Hat Museum Art Gallery, National Exhibition Centre, Medicine Hat AB
Medicine Hat Public Library, Medicine Hat AB
Melvin Art Gallery, see Florida Southern College, Lakeland FL
Memorial Hall, see Pocumtuck Valley Memorial Association, Deerfield MA
Memorial Union Art Gallery, see Oregon State University, Corvallis OR
Memorial Union Gallery, see Arizona State University, Tempe AZ
Memorial University of Newfoundland, Art Gallery, Saint John's NF
Memphis Academy of Arts, Memphis TN
Memphis Academy of Arts, Memphis TN (S)
Memphis Brooks Museum of Art, Memphis TN
Memphis-Shelby County Public Library and Information Center, Dept of Art, Music and Recreation, Memphis TN
Memphis State University, Dept of Art, Memphis TN (S)
Memphis State University, Memphis TN
Mendel Art Gallery and Civic Conservatory, Saskatoon SK
Mendocino Art Center, Gallery, Mendocino CA
Mendocino Art Center, Inc, Mendocino CA (S)
Mennonite Library and Archives, see Bethel College, North Newton KS
Merced College, Arts Division, Merced CA (S)
Mercer County Community College Gallery, Trenton NJ
Mercer Museum, see Bucks County Historical Society, Doylestown PA
Mercer University, Art Dept, Macon GA (S)
Mercy College of Detroit, Art Dept, Detroit MI (S)
Mercyhurst College, Dept of Art, Erie PA (S)
Meredith College, Art Dept, Raleigh NC (S)
Meredith Contemporary Art Gallery, Baltimore MD
Meriam Library, see California State University, Chico, Chico CA
Meridian Museum of Art, Meridian MS
Merrick Art Gallery, New Brighton PA

National Trust for Historic Preservation, Washington DC

National Watercolor Society, Lakewood CA

Native American Center for the Living Arts, Niagara Falls NY

Natural History Museum of Los Angeles County, Los Angeles CA

Navajo Nation Library, see Navajo Tribal Museum, Window Rock AZ

Navajo Tribal Museum, Window Rock AZ

Naval Amphibious Museum, Norfolk VA

Naval Historical Center, United States Navy Memorial Museum, Washington DC

Navarro College, Art Dept, Corsicana TX (S)

Nazareth College of Rochester, Art Dept, Rochester NY (S)

Nebraska Art Association, see University of Nebraska, Lincoln, Lincoln NE

Nebraska Arts Council Library, Omaha NE

Nebraska Wesleyan University, Elder Gallery, Lincoln NE

Nebraska Wesleyan University, Art Dept, Lincoln NE (S)

Nebraska Western College, Division of Language and Arts, Scottsbluff NE (S)

Richard L Nelson Gallery, see University of California, Davis CA

Bjarne Ness Gallery, see SVACA - Sheyenne Valley Arts and Crafts Association, Fort Ransom ND

Neuberger Museum, see State University of New York at Purchase, Purchase NY

Neville Public Museum, Green Bay WI

Newark Museum, Newark NJ

Newark Public Library, Art & Music Dept, Newark NJ

Newark School of Fine and Industrial Art, Newark NJ (S)

New Bedford Free Public Library, Art Dept, New Bedford MA

New Bedford Whaling Museum, see Old Dartmouth Historical Society, New Bedford MA

Newberry College, Dept of Art, Newberry SC (S)

New Britain Museum of American Art, New Britain CT

New Brunswick Craft School and Centre, Fredericton NB (S)

New Brunswick Craft School and Centre Gallery, Fredericton NB

New Brunswick Museum, Saint John NB

Newburyport Maritime Society, Custom House Maritime Museum, Newburyport MA

New College of the University of South Florida, Fine Arts Dept, Humanities Division, Sarasota FL (S)

Sophie H Newcomb Memorial College, see Tulane University, New Orleans LA (S)

New England Center for Contemporary Art, Brooklyn CT

New England College, Visual Arts Dept, Henniker NH (S)

New England School of Art & Design, Boston MA (S)

New England Watercolor Society, Scituate MA

Newfoundland Museum, Saint John's NF

The New Gallery of Contemporary Art, Cleveland OH

New Hampshire Art Association, Inc, Manchester NH

New Hampshire Historical Society, Concord NH

The New Harmony Gallery of Contemporary Art, New Harmony IN

New Haven Colony Historical Society, New Haven CT

New Haven Paint and Clay Club, Inc, New Haven CT

New Jersey Historical Society Museum, Newark NJ

New Jersey State Museum, Trenton NJ

New Jersey Watercolor Society, South Orange NJ

New Mexico Art League, Gallery, Albuquerque NM

New Mexico Highlands University, Arrott Art Gallery, Las Vegas NM

New Mexico Highlands University, Division of Fine Arts, Las Vegas NM (S)

New Mexico Junior College, Arts, Business & Humanities Division, Hobbs NM (S)

New Mexico State University, Art Gallery, Las Cruces NM

New Mexico State University, Art Dept, Las Cruces NM (S)

New Muse Community Museum of Brooklyn, Inc, Brooklyn NY

New Museum, New York NY

New Orleans Academy of Fine Arts Gallery, New Orleans LA

New Orleans Museum of Art, New Orleans LA

Newport Art Museum and Art Association, Newport RI

Newport Art Museum School, Newport RI (S)

Newport Harbor Art Museum, Newport Beach CA

Newport Historical Society, Newport RI

New Rochelle Art Association, see New Rochelle Public Library, New Rochelle NY

New Rochelle Public Library, Art Section, New Rochelle NY

New School for Social Research, Adult Education Division, New York NY (S)

New School for Social Research Art Center Gallery, New York NY

New York Academy of Art, New York NY (S)

New York Artists Equity Association, Inc, New York NY

New York City Department of Cultural Affairs, City Gallery, New York NY

New York City Technical College, Namm Hall Library and Learning Resource Center, Brooklyn NY

New York City Technical College of the City University of New York, Dept of Art and Advertising Design, Brooklyn NY (S)

New York Historical Society, New York NY

New York Institute of Photography, New York NY (S)

New York Institute of Technology, Fine Arts Dept, Old Westbury NY (S)

New York Institute of Technology Gallery, Old Westbury NY

New York Public Library, New York NY

New York School of Interior Design, New York NY (S)

New York School of Interior Design Library, New York NY

New York Society of Architects, New York NY

New York State College of Ceramics at Alfred University, Scholes Library of Ceramics, Alfred NY

New York State College of Ceramics at Alfred University, Division of Art & Design, Alfred NY (S)

New York State College of Human Ecology, see Cornell University, Ithaca NY (S)

New York State Historical Association, Cooperstown NY

New York State Library, Manuscripts and Special Collections, Albany NY

New York State Museum, Albany NY

New York State Office of Parks, Recreation & Historical Preservation, Mills Mansion State Historical Site, Staatsburg NY

New York Studio School of Drawing, Painting and Sculpture, New York NY (S)

New York University, New York NY

New York University, Institute of Fine Arts, New York NY (S)

Nexus Gallery, see Foundation for Today's Art, Philadelphia PA

Elizabet Ney Museum, Austin TX

Niagara County Community College, Fine Arts Division, Sanborn NY (S)

Niagara County Community College Art Gallery, Sanborn NY

Niagara University, Fine Arts Dept, Niagara Falls NY (S)

Niagara University, Buscaglia-Castellani Art Gallery, Niagara Falls NY

Nicholls State University, Dept of Art, Thibodaux LA (S)

Nichols Gallery, see Mankato State University, Mankato MN

The Nickle Arts Museum, see University of Calgary, Calgary AB

Nicolaysen Art Museum, Casper WY

Nobles County Art Center Gallery, Worthington MN

Harry Nohr Art Gallery, see University of Wisconsin, Platteville WI

No Man's Land Historical Society Museum, Goodwell OK

Nook Farm Research Library, see Mark Twain Memorial, Hartford CT

Nordstrand Visual Arts Gallery, see Wayne State College, Wayne NE

Norfolk Public Library, Feldman Fine Arts & Audio Visual Dept, Norfolk VA

Norfolk State College, Fine Arts Dept, Norfolk VA (S)

Normandale Community College, Art Dept, Bloomington MN (S)

Northampton County Area Community College, Art Dept, Bethlehem PA (S)

North Arkansas Community College, Art Dept, Harrison AR (S)

North Canton Public Library, Little Art Gallery, North Canton OH

North Carolina Agricultural and Technical State University, Art Dept, Greensboro NC (S)

North Carolina Art Society, Raleigh NC

North Carolina Central University, Museum of Art, Durham NC

North Carolina Central University, Art Dept, Durham NC (S)

North Carolina Museum of Art, Raleigh NC

North Carolina Museums Council, Wilmington NC

North Carolina State University, Harrye Lyons Design Library, Raleigh NC

North Carolina State University at Raleigh, School of Design, Raleigh NC (S)

North Carolina Wesleyan, Dept of Art, Rocky Mount NC (S)

North Central College, Dept of Art, Naperville IL (S)

North Central Michigan College, Art Dept, Petoskey MI (S)

North Country Museum of Arts, Park Rapids MN

North Dakota Museum of Art, Grand Forks ND

North Dakota State School of Science, Dept of Art, Wahpeton ND (S)

North Dakota State University, Memorial Union Art Gallery, Fargo ND

Northeastern Illinois University, North River Community Gallery, Chicago IL

Northeastern Illinois University, Art Dept, Chicago IL (S)

Northeastern Junior College, Dept of Art, Sterling CO (S)

Northeastern Nevada Historical Society Museum, Elko NV

Northeastern Oklahoma A & M College, Art Dept, Miami OK (S)

Northeastern Oklahoma State University, Tahlequah OK (S)

Northeastern University, Dept of Art, Boston MA (S)

Northeast Louisiana University, Dept of Art, Monroe LA (S)

Northeast Mississippi Junior College, Art Dept, Booneville MS (S)

Northeast Missouri State University, Art Dept, Kirksville MO (S)

Northeast Technical Community College, Dept of Art, Norfolk NE (S)

Northern Arizona University, Art Gallery, Flagstaff AZ

Northern Arizona University, Art Dept, Flagstaff AZ (S)

Northern Illinois University, Swen Parson Gallery and Gallery 200, De Kalb IL

Northern Illinois University, Dept of Art, De Kalb IL (S)

Northern Kentucky University, Fine Arts Dept, Highland Heights KY (S)

Northern Kentucky University Gallery, Highland Heights KY

Northern Michigan University, Lee Hall Gallery, Marquette MI

Northern Michigan University, Dept of Art and Design, Marquette MI (S)

Northern Montana College, Dept of Art and Languages, Havre MT (S)

Northern State College, Art Dept, Aberdeen SD (S)

Northern Virginia Community College, Art Dept, Annandale VA (S)

Northern Virginia Fine Arts Association, The Athenaeum, Alexandria VA

North Florida Junior College, Dept Humanities & Art, Madison FL (S)
North Georgia College, Fine Arts Dept, Dahlonega GA (S)
North Hennepin Community College, Art Gallery, Brooklyn Park MN
North Hennepin Community College, Art Dept, Minneapolis MN (S)
North Idaho College, Art Dept, Coeur D'Alene ID (S)
North Iowa Area Community College, Dept of Art, Mason City IA (S)
Northland Pioneer College, Art Dept, Holbrook AZ (S)
North Park College, Carlson Tower Gallery, Chicago IL
North Park College, Art Dept, Chicago IL (S)
Northport-East Northport Public Library, Northport NY
North River Community Gallery, see Northeastern Illinois University, Chicago IL
North Seattle Community College, Art Dept, Seattle WA (S)
North Shore Art League, Winnetka IL
North Shore Art League, Winnetka IL (S)
North Shore Arts Association, Inc, Art Gallery, Gloucester MA
North Shore Community Arts Center, Great Neck NY (S)
North Texas State University, Art Gallery, Denton TX
North Texas State University, Art Dept, Denton TX (S)
North View Gallery, see Portland Community College, Portland OR
Northwest Community College, Powell WY (S)
Northwestern College, Te Paske Gallery of Rowenhorst, Orange City IA
Northwestern College, Art Dept, Orange City IA (S)
Northwestern Connecticut Community College, Fine Arts Dept, Winsted CT (S)
Northwestern Michigan College, Mark Osterlin Library, Traverse City MI
Northwestern Michigan College, Art Dept, Traverse City MI (S)
Northwestern Oklahoma State University, Art Dept, Alva OK (S)
Northwestern State University of Louisiana, Dept of Art, Natchitoches LA (S)
Northwestern University, Evanston IL
Northwestern University, Evanston, Evanston IL (S)
Northwest Missouri State University, DeLuce Gallery, Maryville MO
Northwest Missouri State University, Dept of Art, Maryville MO (S)
Northwest Nazarene College, Art Dept, Nampa ID (S)
Northwood Institute, Alden B Dow Creativity Center, Midland MI (S)
Norton Gallery and School of Art, West Palm Beach FL
R W Norton Art Gallery, Shreveport LA
Norwegian-American Museum, see Vesterheim, Decorah IA
Norwich Free Academy, Slater Memorial Museum & Converse Art Gallery, Norwich CT
Norwich University, Dept of Philosophy, Religion and Fine Arts, Northfield VT (S)
Notre Dame College, Art Dept, Manchester NH (S)
Nova Scotia Association of Architects, Halifax NS
Nova Scotia College of Art and Design, Halifax NS (S)
Nova Scotia College of Art and Design, Anna Leonowens Gallery, Halifax NS
Nova Scotia Museum, W D Lawrence House, Halifax NS
Noyes, Read and Grey Galleries, see Antioch College, Yellow Springs OH
Nutana Collegiate Institute, Memorial Library and Art Gallery, Saskatoon SK
Oakland City College, Division of Fine Arts, Oakland City IN (S)
Oakland Community College, Humanities Dept, Farmington Hills MI (S)
Oakland Museum, Art Dept, Oakland CA

Oakland Public Library, Art, Music & Recreation Section, Oakland CA
Oakland University, Meadow Brook Art Gallery, Rochester MI
Oakland University, Dept of Art and Art History, Rochester MI (S)
Oak Ridge Community Art Center & Museum of Fine Arts, Oak Ridge TN
Oakton Community College, Art & Architecture Dept, Des Plains IL (S)
Oakville Galleries, Oakville ON
Oatlands of the National Trust, Inc, Leesburg VA
Oberlin College, Allen Memorial Art Museum, Oberlin OH
Oberlin College, Dept of Art, Oberlin OH (S)
Occidental College, Art Dept, Los Angeles CA (S)
Occidental College Gallery, Los Angeles CA
Ocean City Arts Center, Ocean City NJ (S)
Ocean County College, Humanities Dept, Toms River NJ (S)
Octagon Center for the Arts, Ames IA
Oglebay Institute Mansion Museum, Wheeling WV
Ogunquit Art Association, The Barn Gallery, Ogunquit ME
Ogunquit Art Center, Ogunquit ME
Ohio Dominican College, Art Dept, Columbus OH (S)
The Ohio Foundation on the Arts, Inc, Columbus OH
Ohio Historical Society, Columbus OH
The Ohio Historical Society, Inc, Campus Martius Museum and Ohio River Museum, Marietta OH
Ohio Northern University, Dept of Art, Ada OH (S)
Ohio State University, Columbus OH
Ohio State University, Columbus OH (S)
Ohio University, Gallery of Fine Arts, Athens OH
Ohio University, School of Art, Athens OH (S)
Ohio University Belmont County Campus, Art Dept, Saint Clairsville OH (S)
Ohio University-Chillicothe Campus, Fine Arts & Humanities Division, Chillicothe OH (S)
Ohio Wesleyan University, Dept of Fine Arts Gallery, Delaware OH
Ohio Wesleyan University, Fine Arts Dept, Delaware OH (S)
Ojai Valley Art Center, Ojai CA
Okaloosa-Walton Junior College, Dept of Fine and Performing Arts, Niceville FL (S)
Okefenokee Heritage Center, Inc, Waycross GA
Oklahoma Art Center, Oklahoma City OK
Oklahoma Art Center Annex and Art School, Oklahoma City OK (S)
Oklahoma Baptist University, Art Dept, Shawnee OK (S)
Oklahoma Center for Science and Art, Kirkpatrick Center, Oklahoma City OK
Oklahoma Christian College, Art Dept, Oklahoma City OK (S)
Oklahoma City University, Art Dept, Oklahoma City OK (S)
Oklahoma Historical Society, Central Museum, Oklahoma City OK
Oklahoma Museum of Art, Oklahoma City OK
Oklahoma State University, Graphic Arts Dept, Okmulgee OK (S)
Oklahoma State University, Gardiner Art Gallery, Stillwater OK
Oklahoma State University, Art Dept, Stillwater OK (S)
Olana State Historic Site, Hudson NY
Old Barracks Museum, Trenton NJ
Old Dartmouth Historical Society, New Bedford Whaling Museum, New Bedford MA
Old Dominion University, Art Dept, Norfolk VA (S)
Old Dominion University Gallery, Norfolk VA
Old Gaol Museum, York ME
Old Post Office Museum, see Pittsburgh History and Landmarks Foundation, Pittsburgh PA
Old Salem Inc, Museum of Early Southern Decorative Arts, Winston-Salem NC
Old School House, see Society for the Preservation of Historic Landmarks, York ME
Old State House, Hartford CT
Olin Art Gallery, see Washington & Jefferson College, Washington PA

Olive-Harvey College, see City Colleges of Chicago, Chicago IL (S)
Olivet College, Armstrong Museum of Art and Archaeology, Olivet MI
Olivet College, Art Dept, Olivet MI (S)
Olivet Nazarene College, Dept of Art, Kankakee IL (S)
Olympic College, Art Dept, Bremerton WA (S)
Omaha Children's Museum, Inc, Omaha NE
The One Club for Art & Copy, New York NY
One Step Beyond, Brattleboro VT
Ontario Association of Art Galleries, Toronto ON
Ontario College of Art, Toronto ON (S)
Ontario College of Art, Gallery 76, Toronto ON
Ontario Crafts Council, Toronto ON
Open Space Gallery, Photography at Open Space, Victoria BC
Oral Roberts University, Fine Arts Dept, Tulsa OK (S)
Orange Coast College, Division of Fine Arts, Costa Mesa CA (S)
Orange County Center for Contemporary Art, Santa Ana CA
Orange County Community College, Art Dept, Middletown NY (S)
Orange County Community of Museums and Galleries, Goshen NY
Orchard Lake School Galeria, Orchard Lake MI
Oregon College of Art, Ashland OR (S)
Oregon Historical Society, Portland OR
Oregon School of Arts and Crafts, Portland OR (S)
Oregon School of Arts and Crafts, Hoffman Gallery, Portland OR
Oregon State University, Corvallis OR
Oregon State University, Dept of Art, Corvallis OR (S)
Organization of Independent Artists, New York NY
Oshkosh Public Museum, Oshkosh WI
Mark Osterlin Library, see Northwestern Michigan College, Traverse City MI
Otero Junior College, Art Dept, La Junta CO (S)
Otis Art Institute of Parsons School of Design, Los Angeles CA (S)
Otis Art Institute of Parsons School of Design Gallery, Los Angeles CA
Ottawa Public Library, Fine Arts Dept, Ottawa ON
Ottawa University, Dept of Art, Ottawa KS (S)
Otterbein College, Dept of Visual Arts, Westerville OH (S)
Ouachita Baptist University, Dept of Art, Arkadelphia AR (S)
Our Lady of the Lake University, Dept of Art, San Antonio TX (S)
Owatonna Arts Center, Owatonna MN
Owen Library, see University of Utah, Salt Lake City UT
Owens Art Gallery, see Mount Allison University, Sackville NB
Owensboro Museum of Fine Art, Owensboro KY
Owens-Corning Fiberglas Corporation, Toledo OH
Oxbow Center for the Arts, Saugatuck MI (S)
Ozaukee Art Center, see Wisconsin Fine Arts Association, Inc, Cedarburg WI
Pace University, Art and Music Dept, New York NY (S)
Pace University, Dept of Art & Design, Pleasantville NY (S)
Pace University, Dyson College Arts & Science, White Plains NY (S)
Pace University Gallery, Briarcliff Manor NY
Pacific - Asia Museum, Pasadena CA
Pacific Basin School of Textile Arts, Berkeley CA (S)
Pacific Grove Art Center, Pacific Grove CA
Pacific Lutheran University, Dept of Art, Tacoma WA (S)
Pacific Northwest Arts and Crafts Association, Bellevue Art Museum, Bellevue WA
Pacific Northwest Bell, Seattle WA
Pacific Northwest College of Art, Portland OR (S)
Pacific Union College, Art Dept, Angwin CA (S)
Pacific University, Old College Hall, Pacific University Museum, Forest Grove OR
Pacific University in Oregon, Dept of Fine Arts, Forest Grove OR (S)
Packard Library, see Columbus College of Art and Design, Columbus OH

Packwood House Museum, see Fetherston Foundation, Lewisburg PA
Paducah Art Guild, Paducah KY
Paier College of Art, Inc, Hamden CT (S)
Paine Art Center and Arboretum, Oshkosh WI
Paine Webber Inc, New York NY
Paint 'N Palette Club, Anamosa IA
Palace of Governors, see Museum of New Mexico, Santa Fe NM
Palette and Chisel Academy of Fine Arts Gallery, Chicago IL
Paley Design Center, see Philadelphia College of Textiles and Science, Philadelphia PA
Palisades Interstate Park Commission, Senate House State Historic Site, Kingston NY
Palm Beach County Parks and Recreation Department, Morikami Museum of Japanese Culture, Delray Beach FL
Palm Beach Junior College, Dept of Art, Lake Worth FL (S)
Donald B Palmer Museum, see Springfield Free Public Library, Springfield NJ
Palm Springs Desert Museum, Inc, Palm Springs CA
Palo Alto Cultural Center, Palo Alto CA
Palo Alto Junior Museum, Palo Alto CA
Palomar College, Art Dept, San Marcos TX (S)
Palomar Community College, Boehm Gallery, San Marcos CA
Palos Verdes Art Center, Rancho Palos Verdes CA
Pan American University, Art Dept, Edinburg TX (S)
Panhandle-Plains Historical Society Museum, Canyon TX
Papercraft Corporation, Pittsburgh PA
Paris Gibson Square, Great Falls MT
Paris Junior College, Art Dept, Paris TX (S)
Park College, Dept of Art, Parkville MO (S)
Parkersburg Art Center, Parkersburg WV
Parkersburg Community College, Art Dept, Parkersburg WV (S)
Parrish Art Museum, Southampton NY
Parson Fisher House, Jonathan Fisher Memorial, Inc, Blue Hill ME
Swen Parson Gallery and Gallery 200, see Northern Illinois University, De Kalb IL
Parsons School of Design, Adam & Sophie Gimbel Library, New York NY
Parsons School of Design, New York NY (S)
The Parthenon, Nashville TN
Pasadena City College, Art Gallery, Pasadena CA
Pasadena City College, Art Dept, Pasadena CA (S)
Pasadena Public Library, Fine Arts Dept, Pasadena CA
Passaic County Community College, Division of Humanities, Paterson NJ (S)
Passaic County Historical Society, Lambert Castle Museum, Paterson NJ
Patrick Henry State Junior College, Art Dept, Monroeville AL (S)
Pattee Library, see Pennsylvania State University, University Park PA
Patterson Homestead, Dayton OH
Patterson Library & Art Gallery, Westfield NY
Pavilion of Humour, Man and His World, Montreal PQ
Joan Whitney Payson Gallery of Art, see Westbrook College, Portland ME
George Peabody Library, see Johns Hopkins University, Baltimore MD
Peabody Museum of Salem, Salem MA
Peace College, Art Dept, Raleigh NC (S)
Peace Museum, Chicago IL
Peale Museum, Baltimore MD
Pearl River Junior College, Fine Arts Dept, Poplarville MS (S)
Katherine Pearman Memorial Library, see Rockford Art Association, Rockford IL
Peirce-Nichols House, see Essex Institute, Salem MA
Pemaquid Group of Artists, Pemaquid Point ME
Pembroke State University, Art Dept, Pembroke NC (S)
Pen and Brush, Inc, New York NY
Pence Gallery, Davis CA
Peninsula Fine Arts Center, Newport News VA
Penland School of Crafts, Penland NC (S)

Pennsylvania Academy of the Fine Arts, Galleries, Philadelphia PA
Pennsylvania Academy of the Fine Arts, Philadelphia PA (S)
Pennsylvania Department of Education, Arts in Education Program, Harrisburg PA
Pennsylvania Farm Museum of Landis Valley, Lancaster PA
Pennsylvania Historical and Museum Commission, Harrisburg PA
Pennsylvania State University, University Park PA
Pennsylvania State University at New Kensington, Depts of Art & Architecture, New Kensington PA (S)
Pennsylvania State University, Capitol Campus, Dept of Humanities, Middletown PA (S)
Pennsylvania State University, Fayette Campus, Dept of Art, Uniontown PA (S)
Pennsylvania State University, University Park, University Park PA (S)
Penn Valley Community College, Art Dept, Kansas City MO (S)
William Penn Memorial Museum, see Pennsylvania Historical and Museum Commission, Harrisburg PA
Penobscot Marine Museum, Searsport ME
Pensacola Junior College, Dept of Visual Arts, Pensacola FL (S)
Pensacola Junior College, Visual Arts Gallery, Pensacola FL
Pensacola Museum of Art, Pensacola FL
Peoria Art Guild, Peoria IL
Peoria Historical Society, Peoria IL
Pepperdine University, Seaver College, Dept of Art, Malibu CA (S)
Peppers Art Center and Gallery, see University of Redlands, Redlands CA
PepsiCo Inc, Purchase NY
Dorothy W Perkins Slide Library, see University of Massachusetts, Amherst, Amherst MA
Elizabeth Perkins House, see Society for the Preservation of Historic Landmarks, York ME
Peru State College, Art Dept, Peru NE (S)
Peters Valley Inc Craft Center Library, Layton NJ
Petzinger Memorial Library, see The Haggin Museum, Stockton CA
Pfeiffer College, Art Program, Misenheimer NC (S)
Phelps County Historical Society Museum, Holdrege NE
Philadelphia Art Alliance, Philadelphia PA
Philadelphia Art Commission, Philadelphia PA
Philadelphia College of Art, Philadelphia PA
Philadelphia College of Art, Philadelphia PA (S)
Philadelphia College of Textiles and Science, School of Textiles, Philadelphia PA (S)
Philadelphia College of Textiles and Science, Paley Design Center, Philadelphia PA
Philadelphia Community College, Dept of Fine Arts, Philadelphia PA (S)
Philadelphia Maritime Museum, Philadelphia PA
Philadelphia Museum of Art, Philadelphia PA
Philadelphia Sketch Club Inc, Philadelphia PA
Philbrook Art Center, Tulsa OK
Philip Morris Incorporated, New York NY
Philipse Manor Hall State Historic Site, Yonkers NY
Phillips Academy, Addison Gallery of American Art, Andover MA
The Phillips Collection, Washington DC
Phillips County Community College, Dept of English and Fine Arts, Helena AR (S)
Phillips County Museum, Helena AR
Phillips Exeter Academy, Frederic R Mayer Art Center & Lamont Gallery, Exeter NH
Frank Phillips, Woolaroc Museum, Bartlesville OK
James Duncan Phillips Library, see Essex Institute, Salem MA
Phillips Library, see Peabody Museum of Salem, Salem MA
Phillips University, Grace Phillips Johnson Art Gallery, Enid OK
Phillips University, Dept of Art, Enid OK (S)
Walter Phillips Gallery, see Banff Centre, Banff AB
Phoenix Art Museum, Phoenix AZ
Phoenix College, Dept of Art and Photography, Phoenix AZ (S)
Phoenix School of Design Library, see Pratt Institute, New York NY

Photographers Gallery, Saskatoon SK
Piatt Castles, West Liberty OH
Picker Art Gallery, see Colgate University, Hamilton NY
Timothy Pickering Library, see Wenham Historical Association and Museum, Inc, Wenham MA
Piedmont College, Art Dept, Demorest GA (S)
Pierce College, Art Dept, Woodland Hills CA (S)
Pikeville College, Fine Arts Dept, Pikeville KY (S)
The Pillsbury Company, Minneapolis MN
Pimeria Alta Historical Society, Nogales AZ
Pinckney Brothers Museum, Orangeburg SC
Pine Castle Center of the Arts, Inc, Orlando FL
Pine Manor College, Visual Arts Dept, Chestnut Hill MA (S)
Pioneer Museum & Art Center, see Plains Indians & Pioneer Historical Foundation, Woodward OK
Pioneer Town, Wimberley TX
Pittsburgh History and Landmarks Foundation, Old Post Office Museum, Pittsburgh PA
Pittsburgh National Bank, Pittsburgh PA
Pittsburgh Plan for Art Gallery, Gallery 407, Pittsburgh PA
Pittsburgh State University, Art Dept, Pittsburg KS (S)
Pitzer College, Dept of Art, Claremont CA (S)
Place des Arts, Coquitlam BC
Plainfield Public Library, Plainfield NJ
Plains Art Museum, Moorhead MN
Plains Indians & Pioneer Historical Foundation, Pioneer Museum & Art Center, Woodward OK
Plainsman Museum, Aurora NE
Henry B Plant Museum, see University of Tampa, Tampa FL
Plastic Club, Art Club for Women, Philadelphia PA
Playboy Enterprises, Inc, Chicago IL
Please Touch Museum, Philadelphia PA
Plumas County Museum, Quincy CA
Plum Tree Fine Arts Program, Pilar NM (S)
Plymouth Antiquarian Society, Plymouth MA
Plymouth State College, Herbert H Lamson Library, Plymouth NH
Plymouth State College, Art Dept, Plymouth NH (S)
Pocumtuck Valley Memorial Association, Memorial Hall, Deerfield MA
Pointe Claire Cultural Centre, Pointe Claire PQ
Point Park College, Performing Arts Dept, Pittsburgh PA (S)
Polish Museum of America, Chicago IL
Polk Community College, Division of Communications and Fine Arts, Winter Haven FL (S)
Polk Public Museum, Lakeland FL
Polynesian Cultural Center, Laie HI
Pomona College, Art Dept, Claremont CA (S)
Ponca City Art Association, Ponca City OK
Ponca City Cultural Center & Museum, Ponca City OK
Ponca City Library, Art Dept, Ponca City OK
Ponce Art Museum, see Museo de Arte de Ponce, Ponce PR
Pontiac Art Center, Pontiac MI (S)
Pontiac Art Center, Pontiac MI
Pope-Leighey House, Mount Vernon VA
Portage and District Arts Council, Portage la Prairie MB
Port Chester Public Library, Fine Arts Dept, Port Chester NY
Dana Porter Arts Library, see University of Waterloo, Waterloo ON
Porterville College, Dept of Fine Arts, Porterville CA (S)
Portland Art Association, Portland OR
Portland Center for the Visual Arts, Portland OR
Portland Children's Museum, Portland OR
Portland Community College, North View Gallery, Portland OR
Portland Community College, Visual & Performing Arts Dept, Portland OR (S)
Portland Museum of Art, Portland ME
Portland Public Library, Art Dept, Portland ME
Portland School of Art, Portland ME (S)
Portland School of Art Library, Portland ME
Portland State University, Portland OR
Portland State University, Dept of Art and Architecture, Portland OR (S)

Salt Lake City Public Library, Fine Arts Department and Atrium Gallery, Salt Lake City UT

Salve Regina - The Newport College, Art Dept, Newport RI (S)

Samford University, Art Dept, Birmingham AL (S)

Sam Houston State University, Art Dept, Huntsville TX (S)

Sampson Art Gallery, see Thiel College, Greenville PA

San Angelo Art Club, Helen King Kendall Memorial Art Gallery, San Angelo TX

San Antonio Art Institute, San Antonio TX (S)

San Antonio Art League, San Antonio TX

San Antonio College, Art & Advertising Dept, San Antonio TX (S)

San Antonio Museum Association, Inc, San Antonio TX

San Antonio Public Library, Dept of Fine Arts, San Antonio TX

San Bernardino Art Association, Inc, San Bernardino CA

San Bernardino County Museum and Satellites, Fine Arts Institute, Redlands CA

San Bernardino Valley College, Art Dept, San Bernardino CA (S)

San Carlos Cathedral, Monterey CA

Hazel Sandford Gallery, see Clarion University, Clarion PA

San Diego Maritime Museum, San Diego CA

San Diego Mesa College, Fine Arts Dept, San Diego CA (S)

San Diego Museum of Art, San Diego CA

San Diego Public Library, Art & Music Section, San Diego CA

San Diego State University, Art Gallery, San Diego CA

San Diego State University, Dept of Art, San Diego CA (S)

Birger Sandzen Memorial Gallery, see Bethany College, Lindsborg KS

San Fernando Valley Historical Society, Mission Hills CA

San Francisco Academy of Comic Art, Library, San Francisco CA

San Francisco Art Institute, San Francisco CA

San Francisco Art Institute, San Francisco CA (S)

San Francisco Camerawork, San Francisco CA

San Francisco City and County Art Commission, San Francisco CA

San Francisco Museum of Modern Art, San Francisco CA

San Francisco Public Library, Art and Music Dept, San Francisco CA

San Francisco State University, Art Dept, San Francisco CA (S)

San Francisco State University, J Paul Leonard Library, San Francisco CA

Sangamon State University, Creative Arts Program, Springfield IL (S)

Sangre De Cristo Arts & Conference Center, Pueblo CO

San Jacinto College, Art Dept, Pasadena TX (S)

San Jacinto College North, Art Dept, Houston TX (S)

San Joaquin Delta College, Art Dept, Stockton CA (S)

San Jose City College, School of Fine Arts, San Jose CA (S)

San Jose Institute of Contemporary Art, San Jose CA

San Jose Museum of Art, San Jose CA

San Jose State University, San Jose CA

San Jose State University, Art Dept, San Jose CA (S)

San Juan Community College, Art Dept, Farmington NM (S)

San Mateo County Arts Council, Belmont CA

Santa Ana College, Art Dept, Santa Ana CA (S)

Santa Barbara City College, Fine Arts Dept, Santa Barbara CA (S)

Santa Barbara Contemporary Arts Forum, Santa Barbara CA

Santa Barbara Museum of Art, Santa Barbara CA

Santa Barbara Public Library, Faulkner Memorial Art Wing, Santa Barbara CA

Santa Cruz Art Center, Santa Cruz CA

Santa Cruz Art League, Inc, Santa Cruz CA

Santa Cruz Public Library, Art, Music, Film Dept, Santa Cruz CA

Santa Cruz Valley Art Association, see Tubac Center of the Arts, Tubac AZ

Santa Fe Workshops of Contemporary Art, Santa Fe NM (S)

Santa Monica College Art Gallery, Santa Monica CA

Santa Rosa Junior College, Art Dept, Santa Rosa CA (S)

Santa Rosa Junior College Art Gallery, Santa Rosa CA

Santuario de Guadalupe, see Guadalupe Historic Foundation, Santa Fe NM

Sarah Lawrence College, Dept of Art, Bronxville NY (S)

Sarah Lawrence College Library, Esther Raushenbush Library, Bronxville NY

Sarasota Art Association, Sarasota FL

Sarnia Public Library, Art Gallery, Sarnia ON

Saskatchewan Arts Board, Regina SK

Saskatchewan Association of Architects, Saskatoon SK

Saskatchewan Power Corporation, Gallery on the Roof, Regina SK

Savannah State College, Dept of Fine Arts, Savannah GA (S)

Savery Art Gallery, see Talladega College, Talladega AL

Saving & Preserving Arts & Cultural Environments, Los Angeles CA

Sawhill Gallery, see James Madison University, Harrisonburg VA

Sawtooth Center for Visual Design, Winston-Salem NC (S)

Sawyer Library, see Williams College, Williamstown MA

Scalamandre Museum of Textiles, New York NY

Scantic Academy Museum, see East Windsor Historical Society Inc, East Windsor CT

Lee Scarfone Gallery, see University of Tampa, Tampa FL

Rudolph Schaeffer School of Design, San Francisco CA (S)

Schenectady County Historical Society, Schenectady NY

Schenectady Museum, Schenectady NY

Taras H Schevchenko Museum and Memorial Park Foundation, Oakville ON

Scholes Library of Ceramics, see New York State College of Ceramics at Alfred University, Alfred NY

Maude Schollenberger Memorial Library, see Wichita Art Association Inc, Wichita KS

Schomburg Center for Research in Black Culture, see New York Public Library, New York NY

Schoolcraft College, Dept of Art, Livonia MI (S)

School of American Research, Santa Fe NM

The School of Fashion Design, Boston MA (S)

School of Fine Arts, Visual Arts Dept, Willoughby OH (S)

School of Nations Museum, see Principia College, Elsah IL

School of the Art Institute of Chicago, Chicago IL (S)

School of the Art Institute of Chicago Library, Chicago IL

School of the Associated Arts, Saint Paul MN (S)

School of the Associated Arts Galleries, Saint Paul MN

School of the Museum of Fine Arts, Boston MA (S)

School of the Ozarks, Dept of Art, Point Lookout MO (S)

School of the Wichita Art Association, Wichita KS (S)

School of Visual Arts, New York NY (S)

School of Visual Arts Library, New York NY

Schuler School of Fine Arts, Baltimore MD (S)

Schumacher Gallery, see Capital University, Columbus OH

Schuyler-Hamilton House, Morristown NJ

Schuyler Mansion State Historic Site, Albany NY

Science Museums of Charlotte, Inc, Discovery Place, Charlotte NC

Agnes Scott College, Dalton Gallery, Decatur GA

Scott Explorers Library, see Martin & Osa Johnson Safari Museum, Chanute KS

Scottsdale Artists' League, Scottsdale AZ

Scottsdale Center for the Arts, Scottsdale AZ

The Charles H Scott Gallery, see Emily Carr College of Art & Design, Vancouver BC

Lucy Scribner Library, see Skidmore College, Saratoga Springs NY

Scripps College, Art Dept, Claremont CA (S)

Scripps College, Clark Humanities Museum, Claremont CA

William and Elaine Scripture Memorial Library, see Rome Historical Society, Rome NY

Sculptors Guild, Inc, New York NY

Sculptor's Society of Canada, Toronto ON

Sculpture Center, New York NY

Sculpture Center Gallery & School, New York NY (S)

Seafirst Corporation, Corporate Affairs Dept, Seattle WA

Joseph E Seagram & Sons, Inc, New York NY

Sears Roebuck and Company, Chicago IL

Seattle Art Museum, Seattle WA

Seattle Central Community College, Humanities - Social Sciences Division, Seattle WA (S)

Seattle Pacific University, Art Dept, Seattle WA (S)

Seattle University, Fine Arts Dept, Division of Art, Seattle WA (S)

Seattle Weaver's Guild, Seattle WA

Second Crossing Gallery, see Fine Arts Club, Valley City ND

Second Street Gallery, Charlottesville VA

Security Pacific National Bank, Los Angeles CA

Seigfred Gallery, see Ohio University, Athens OH

Selsor Gallery of Art, see Martin & Osa Johnson Safari Museum, Chanute KS

Senate House State Historic Site, see Palisades Interstate Park Commission, Kingston NY

Seneca Falls Historical Society Museum, Seneca Falls NY

Seton Hall University, Student Center Art Gallery, South Orange NJ

Seton Hall University, Dept of Art and Music, South Orange NJ (S)

Seton Hill College, Dept of Art, Greensburg PA (S)

Sewall Art Gallery, see Rice University, Houston TX

Seward County Community College, Art Dept, Liberal KS (S)

Shadows-on-the-Teche, New Iberia LA

Shaker Museum, Old Chatham NY

Shaker Museum, Poland Spring ME

Martin C Shallenberger Art Library, see Sweet Briar College, Sweet Briar VA

Sharadin Art Gallery, see Kutztown University, Kutztown PA

Sharon Arts Center, Peterborough NH (S)

Ella Sharp Museum, Jackson MI

Shasta Community College, Art Dept, Fine Arts Division, Redding CA (S)

Shelburne Museum, Shelburne VT

Sheldon Art Museum, Archaeological & Historical Society, Middlebury VT

Sheldon Jackson College, Sheldon Jackson Museum, Sitka AK

Sheldon Library, see Saint Paul's School, Concord NH

Sheldon Memorial Art Gallery, see University of Nebraska, Lincoln, Lincoln NE

Sheldon Museum and Cultural Center, Haines AK

Sheldon Swope Art Gallery, Terre Haute IN

Shepherd College, Art Dept, Shepherdstown WV (S)

Sheridan College, Art Dept, Sheridan WY (S)

Sheridan College of Applied Arts and Technology, Visual Arts Library, Oakville ON

Sheridan College School of Applied Arts and Technology, School of Crafts and Design Library, Mississauga ON

Sherman Art Library, see Hood Museum of Art, Hanover NH

C C Sherrod Library, see East Tennessee State University, Johnson City TN

Shippensburg State College, Art Dept, Shippensburg PA (S)

Shippensburg University, Kauffman Gallery, Shippensburg PA

Ships of The Sea Museum, Savannah GA

Shirley Plantation, Charles City VA

Shoreline Community College, Humanities Division, Seattle WA (S)

Southwest Museum, Los Angeles CA
Southwest Texas State University, Dept of Art, San Marcos TX (S)
Spartanburg Arts Center, see Arts Council of Spartanburg County, Inc, Spartanburg SC
Spartanburg County Art Association, Spartanburg SC
Special Libraries Association, Museum, Arts and Humanities Division, New York NY
Spectrum, Friends of Fine Art, Inc, Toledo OH
J B Speed Art Museum, Louisville KY
Spencer Collection, see New York Public Library, New York NY
Kenneth and Helen Spencer Art Reference Library, see Atkins Museum of Fine Art, Kansas City MO
Spencer Museum of Art, see University of Kansas, Lawrence KS
Spertus Museum of Judaica, Chicago IL
Spirit of '76 Museum, Southern Lorain County Historical Society, Wellington OH
Spiva Art Center, Inc, Joplin MO
Spokane Falls Community College, Creative & Performing Arts, Spokane WA (S)
Spokane Public Library, Art Dept, Spokane WA
Spoon River College, Art Dept, Canton IL (S)
Laura A Sprague Art Gallery, see Joliet Junior College, Joliet IL
Spring Arbor College, Art Dept, Spring Arbor MI (S)
Springfield Art Association of Edwards Place, Springfield IL
Springfield Art Center, Springfield OH
Springfield Art Center, Springfield OH (S)
Springfield Art & Historical Society, Springfield VT
Springfield Art League, Springfield MA
Springfield Art Museum, Springfield MO
Springfield City Library, Art & Music Dept, Springfield MA
Springfield College, Hasting Gallery, Springfield MA
Springfield College, Dept of Visual and Performing Arts, Springfield MA (S)
Springfield College in Illinois, Dept of Art, Springfield IL (S)
Springfield Free Public Library, Donald B Palmer Museum, Springfield NJ
Spring Hill College, Fine Arts Dept, Mobile AL (S)
Springville Museum of Art, Springville UT
Spruance Library, see Bucks County Historical Society, Doylestown PA
Sarah Spurgeon Gallery, see Central Washington University, Ellensburg WA
E R Squibb & Sons, Inc, Princeton NJ
Squires Art Gallery, see Virginia Polytechnic Institute and State University, Blacksburg VA
The Stained Glass Association of America, Saint Louis MO
Herbert S Stamats Library, see Cedar Rapids Museum of Art, Cedar Rapids IA
Stamford Museum and Nature Center, Stamford CT
The Standard Oil Company (Ohio), Cleveland OH
Stanford University, Museum of Art & Art Gallery, Stanford CA
Stanford University, Dept of Art, Stanford CA (S)
Edmund Stanley Library Gallery, see Friends University, Wichita KS
Stanley-Whitman House, Farmington, Farmington CT
Stark Museum of Art, Orange TX
Star-Spangled Banner Flag House Association, Baltimore MD
State Art Museum of Florida, John & Mable Ringling Museum of Art, Sarasota FL
State Capitol Museum, Olympia WA
State Historical Society of Missouri, Columbia MO
State Historical Society of Wisconsin, Madison WI
Staten Island Institute of Arts and Sciences, Staten Island NY
State University College, Dept of Art, Fredonia NY (S)
State University of New York, Myers Fine Arts and Rockwell Kent Galleries, Plattsburgh NY
State University of New York, Agricultural and Technical College, Art Dept, Cobleskill NY (S)
State University of New York at Albany, University Art Gallery, Albany NY

State University of New York at Albany, Art Dept, Albany NY (S)
State University of New York at Binghamton, University Art Gallery, Binghamton NY
State University of New York at Binghamton, Dept Of Art & Art History, Binghamton NY (S)
State University of New York at Buffalo, Lockwood Memorial Library, Buffalo NY
State University of New York at Farmingdale, Advertising Art Design Dept, Farmingdale NY (S)
State University of New York at New Paltz, College Art Gallery, New Paltz NY
State University of New York at Oswego, Tyler Art Gallery, Oswego NY
State University of New York at Purchase, Neuberger Museum, Purchase NY
State University of New York at Stony Brook, Art Gallery, Stony Brook NY
State University of New York at Stony Brook, Art Dept, Stony Brook NY (S)
State University of New York, Buffalo, Dept of Art and Art History, Buffalo NY (S)
State University of New York College at Brockport, Dept of Art, Brockport NY (S)
State University of New York College at Buffalo, Fine Arts Dept, Buffalo NY (S)
State University of New York College at Cortland, Art Slide Library, Cortland NY
State University of New York College at Cortland, Art Dept, Cortland NY (S)
State University of New York College at Fredonia, M C Rockefeller Arts Center Gallery, Fredonia NY
State University of New York College at Geneseo, Bertha V B Lederer Gallery, Geneseo NY
State University of New York College at Geneseo, Dept of Art, Geneseo NY (S)
State University of New York College at New Paltz, New Paltz NY (S)
State University of New York College at Old Westbury, Fine Arts Dept, Old Westbury NY (S)
State University of New York College at Oneonta, Dept of Art, Oneonta NY (S)
State University of New York College at Oneonta, Art Gallery & Sculpture Court, Oneonta NY
State University of New York College at Oswego, Art Dept, Oswego NY (S)
State University of New York College at Potsdam, Brainerd Art Gallery, Potsdam NY
State University of New York College at Potsdam, Dept of Fine Arts, Potsdam NY (S)
State University of New York College at Purchase, Purchase NY (S)
Stedman Art Gallery, see Rutgers University, Camden NJ
T C Steele State Memorial, Nashville IN
Stephen F Austin State University, Art Dept, Nacogdoches TX (S)
Stephen F Austin State University, Art Gallery, Nacogdoches TX
Stephens College, Lewis James & Nellie Stratton Davis Art Gallery, Columbia MO
Stephens College, Art Dept, Columbia MO (S)
Sterling College, Art Dept, Sterling KS (S)
Stetson University, Art Gallery, De Land FL
Stetson University, Art Dept, De Land FL (S)
Florine Stettheimer Library, see Fisk University Museum of Art, Nashville TN
Stevenson Academy of Traditional Painting, Sea Cliff NY (S)
Stevenson Union Art Gallery, see Southern Oregon College, Ashland OR
Stillman College, Stillman Art Gallery and Art Dept, Tuscaloosa AL (S)
Stony Plain Multicultural Centre, Stony Plain AB
Store Front Museum, Jamaica NY
Storm King Art Center, Mountainville NY
Stout Reference Library, see Indianapolis Museum of Art, Indianapolis IN
Stowe-Day Foundation, Hartford CT
Stoxen Library, see Dickinson State College, Dickinson ND
Stradling Museum of the Horse, Inc, Patagonia AZ
Strasburg Museum, Strasburg VA
Stratford Art Association, Gallery Stratford, Stratford ON

Stratton Library, see Sheldon Jackson College, Sitka AK
David Strawn Art Gallery, see Art Association of Jacksonville, Jacksonville IL
Gilbert Stuart Birthplace, Saunderstown RI
Studio Academy School of Advertising Art and Design Inc, Omaha NE (S)
Studio Museum in Harlem, New York NY
Studio San Giuseppe, see College of Mount Saint Joseph on the Ohio, Mount Saint Joseph OH
Studio School of Art and Design, Philadelphia PA (S)
Sturdivant Hall, Selma AL
Suffolk County Community College, Art Dept, Selden NY (S)
Suggett House Museum, see Cortland County Historical Society, Cortland NY
Sullivan County Community College, Division of Commercial Art and Photography, Loch Sheldrake NY (S)
Sul Ross State University, Dept of Art, Alpine TX (S)
Sumi-E Society of America, Annandale VA
Summit Art Center, Inc, Summit NJ
Sumter Gallery of Art, Sumter SC
Sunbury Shores Arts and Nature Centre, Inc, Saint Andrews NB
Sunrise Foundation, Inc, Sunrise Museums, Charleston WV
Sun Valley Center for the Arts and Humanities, Dept of Fine Art, Sun Valley ID (S)
Suomi College, Fine Arts Dept, Hancock MI (S)
Supplementary Educational Center, Art Gallery, Salisbury NC
The Supreme Court of the United States Museum, Washington DC
Surface Design Association, Inc, Fayetteville TN
Surrey Art Gallery, Surrey BC
Surry Community College, Art Dept, Dobson NC (S)
SVACA - Sheyenne Valley Arts and Crafts Association, Bjarne Ness Gallery, Fort Ransom ND
Swain School of Design, William W Crapo Gallery, New Bedford MA
Swain School of Design, New Bedford MA (S)
Swarthmore College, Friends Historical Library, Swarthmore PA
Swarthmore College, Dept of Art, Swarthmore PA (S)
Swedish American Museum Association of Chicago, Chicago IL
Sweet Briar College, Martin C Shallenberger Art Library, Sweet Briar VA
Sweet Briar College, Art History Dept and Art Studio Dept, Sweet Briar VA (S)
Sweetwater Community Fine Arts Center, Rock Springs WY
Swirbul Library Gallery, see Adelphi University, Garden City NY
Synagogue Art and Architectural Library, see Union of American Hebrew Congregations, New York NY
Syracuse University, Syracuse NY
Syracuse University, Syracuse NY (S)
Tabor Opera House Museum, Leadville CO
Tacoma Art Museum, Tacoma WA
Tacoma Community College, Art Dept, Tacoma WA (S)
Tacoma Public Library, Handforth Gallery, Tacoma WA
Taft College, Division of Performing Arts, Taft CA (S)
Lorado Taft Midway Studios, see University of Chicago, Chicago IL
Taft Museum, Cincinnati OH
Talladega College, Savery Art Gallery, Talladega AL
Tallahassee Community College, Art Dept, Tallahassee FL (S)
Tallahassee Junior Museum, Tallahassee FL
Tamarind Institute, see University of New Mexico, Albuquerque NM (S)
Tampa Museum, Tampa FL
Tangeman Fine Arts Gallery, see University of Cincinnati, Cincinnati OH
Taos Art Association Inc, Stables Art Center, Taos NM

Tarble Arts Center, see Eastern Illinois University, Charleston IL
Tarrant County Junior College, Art Dept, Northeast Campus, Hurst TX (S)
Tattoo Art Museum, San Francisco CA
Edward P Taylor Audio-Visual Centre, see Art Gallery of Ontario, Toronto ON
Edward P Taylor Reference Library, see Art Gallery of Ontario, Toronto ON
Elizabeth Prewitt Taylor Memorial Library, see Arkansas Arts Center, Little Rock AR
Kenneth Taylor Gallery, see Artists Association of Nantucket, Nantucket MA
Taylor University, Chronicle-Tribune Art Gallery, Upland IN
Taylor University, Art Dept, Upland IN (S)
Technical University of Nova Scotia, Faculty of Architecture, Halifax NS (S)
Telfair Academy of Arts and Sciences Inc, Savannah GA
Temple Junior College, Art Dept, Temple TX (S)
Temple Museum of Jewish Religious Art, Cleveland OH
Temple University, Philadelphia PA
Temple University, Tyler School of Art, Philadelphia PA (S)
Tennent Art Foundation Gallery, Honolulu HI
Tennessee Botanical Gardens and Fine Arts Center, Education Dept, Nashville TN (S)
Tennessee Botanical Gardens and Fine Arts Center, Inc, Nashville TN
Tennessee Historical Society, Nashville TN
Tennessee State Museum, Nashville TN
Tennessee Valley Art Association and Center, Tuscumbia AL
Tennessee Wesleyan College, Dept of Art, Athens TN (S)
Te Paske Gallery of Rowenhorst, see Northwestern College, Orange City IA
Terra Museum of American Art, Evanston IL
Territorial Statehouse, see Utah Natural Resources & Energy, Parks & Recreation, Fillmore UT
Sandor Teszler Library Gallery, see Wofford College, Spartanburg SC
Texarkana Community College, Art Dept, Texarkana TX (S)
Texas A and I University, Art Gallery, Kingsville TX
Texas A & I University, Art Dept, Kingsville TX (S)
Texas A & M University, College of Architecture and Environmental Design, College Station TX (S)
Texas A & M University, University Art Exhibits, College Station TX
Texas Christian University, Student Center Gallery, Fort Worth TX
Texas Christian University, Art & Art History Dept, Fort Worth TX (S)
Texas Lutheran College, Dept of Visual Arts, Seguin TX (S)
Texas Ranger Hall of Fame and Museum, Waco TX
Texas Southern University, Art Dept, Houston TX (S)
Texas Southmost College, Fine Arts Dept, Brownsville TX (S)
Texas State Technical Institute, Dept of Commercial Art, Amarillo TX (S)
Texas Tech University, Dept of Art, Lubbock TX (S)
Texas Tech University Museum, Lubbock TX
Texas Wesleyan College, Dept of Art, Fort Worth TX (S)
Texas Woman's University, Dept of Art, Denton TX (S)
Texas Woman's University Art Gallery, Denton TX
Textile Museum, Washington DC
Thiel College, Sampson Art Gallery, Greenville PA
Thiel College, Dept of Art, Greenville PA (S)
The Third National Bank and Trust Company, Dayton OH
Thomas College Gallery, Waterville ME
Thomas County Community College, Humanities Division, Thomasville GA (S)
Thomas More College, TM Gallery, Fort Mitchell KY
Thomas More College, Art Dept, Fort Mitchell KY (S)

James H Thomason Library, see Presbyterian College, Clinton SC
Nancy Thompson Library, see Kean College of New Jersey, Union NJ
Tom Thomson Memorial Gallery and Museum of Fine Art, Owen Sound ON
Thorne-Sagendorph Art Gallery, see Keene State College, Keene NH
Thornhill Art Gallery, see Avila College, Kansas City MO
Thornton Community College, Art Dept, South Holland IL (S)
Harry Thornton Library, see Pensacola Museum of Art, Pensacola FL
Thousand Islands Craft School & Textile Museum, Clayton NY (S)
Tidewater Community College, Art Dept, Portsmouth VA (S)
Louis Comfort Tiffany Foundation, New York NY
Tift College, Dept of Art, Forsyth GA (S)
Times Mirror Company, Los Angeles CA
Timken Art Gallery, San Diego CA
Tippecanoe County Historical Museum, Lafayette IN
Tobe-Coburn School for Fashion Careers, New York NY (S)
Frank T Tobey Gallery, see Memphis Academy of Arts, Memphis TN
Toledo Artists' Club, Toledo OH
Toledo Federation of Art Societies, Toledo OH
Toledo Museum of Art, Toledo OH
Toledo Museum of Art, School of Design, Toledo OH (S)
Tome Parish Museum, Tome NM
Tomoka State Park Museum, Ormond Beach FL
Tongass Historical Society Museum, Ketchikan AK
Topeka Public Library, Fine Arts Dept & Gallery of Fine Arts, Topeka KS
Toronto Art Therapy Institute, Toronto ON (S)
Toronto School of Art, Toronto ON (S)
Torrey Gallery, see University of Maine at Machias, Machias ME
Tougaloo College, Tougaloo MS
Tougaloo College, Art Dept, Tougaloo MS (S)
Tower Gallery, see Mount Mary College, Milwaukee WI
Towson State University, Dept of Art, Baltimore MD (S)
Towson State University, Towson MD
Tracey-Warner School, Philadelphia PA (S)
Margaret Fort Trahern Gallery, see Austin Peay State University, Clarksville TN
Transco Energy Company Inc, Houston TX
Transylvania University, Morlan Gallery, Lexington KY
Transylvania University, Studio Arts Dept, Lexington KY (S)
Traphagen School of Fashion, Museum Collection, New York NY
Traphagen School of Fashion, New York NY (S)
Treasure Valley Community College, Art Dept, Ontario OR (S)
Treat Gallery, see Bates College, Lewiston ME
Trenton State College, Art Dept, Trenton NJ (S)
Trenton State College, Holman Gallery, Trenton NJ
Trinity College, Austin Arts Center, Hartford CT
Trinity College, Dept of Fine Arts, Hartford CT (S)
Trinity College, Art Dept, Washington DC (S)
Trinity College Library, Washington DC
Trinity University, Dept of Art, San Antonio TX (S)
Triton College, School of Arts & Sciences, River Grove IL (S)
Triton Museum of Art, Santa Clara CA
Troy State University, Dept of Art, Troy AL (S)
Lyle True Gallery, see Colorado Women's College, Denver CO
Truett-McConnell College, Arts Dept, Cleveland GA (S)
Truman College, see City Colleges of Chicago, Chicago IL (S)
Harry S Truman Library and Museum, Independence MO
Truro Center for the Arts at Castle Hill, Inc, Truro MA (S)
The Trustees of Reservations, The Mission House, Stockbridge MA
Tryon Palace Restoration Complex, New Bern NC

Tubac Center of the Arts, Santa Cruz Valley Art Association, Tubac AZ
Tucson Museum of Art, Tucson AZ
Tucson Museum of Art School, Tucson AZ (S)
Tufts University, Gallery Eleven, Medford MA
Tufts University, Fine Arts Dept, Medford MA (S)
Tulane University, New Orleans LA (S)
Tulane University, New Orleans LA
Tulsa Junior College, Art Dept, Tulsa OK (S)
Tunxis Community College, Graphic Design Dept, Farmington CT (S)
Turman Gallery, see Indiana State University, Terre Haute IN
Turner House Museum, Hattiesburg MS
The Turner Museum, Denver CO
Tusculum College, Fine Arts Dept, Greeneville TN (S)
Tuskegee Institute, Art Dept, Tuskegee Institute AL (S)
Tuskegee Institute National Historic Site, George Washington Carver & The Oaks, Tuskegee AL
Mark Twain Memorial, Hartford CT
Mark Twain Birthplace Museum, Stoutsville MO
Tweed Arts Group, Plainfield NJ
Tweed Museum of Art, see University of Minnesota, Duluth MN
22 Wooster Gallery, New York NY
Twin City Art Foundation, Masur Museum of Art, Monroe LA
Tyler Art Gallery, see State University of New York at Oswego, Oswego NY
Tyler Junior College, Art Program, Tyler TX (S)
Tyler Museum of Art, Tyler TX
Tyler School of Art, see Temple University, Philadelphia PA (S)
Tyler School of Art-Galleries, see Temple University, Philadelphia PA
Tyringham Art Galleries, Tyringham MA
Tyringham Institute, Jean Brown Archive, Tyringham MA
Ukiyo-e Society of America, Inc, New York NY
Ukrainian Cultural and Educational Centre Museum, Winnipeg MB
Ukrainian Institute of America, Inc, New York NY
Ukrainian Museum, New York NY
Ukrainian Museum of Canada, Edmonton AB
Ukrainian National Museum and Library, Chicago IL
Edwin A Ulrich Museum, Hyde Park NY
Edwin A Ulrich Museum of Art, see Wichita State University, Wichita KS
Ulster County Community College, Dept of Visual Arts, Stone Ridge NY (S)
Ulster County Community College, Visual Arts Gallery, Stone Ridge NY
Umberto Romano School of Creative Art, New York NY (S)
Umpqua Community College, Fine & Performing Arts Dept, Roseburg OR (S)
Unaffiliated Artists File, see Committee for the Visual Arts, Inc, New York NY
Union College, Art Dept, Barbourville KY (S)
Union College, Dept of the Arts, Schenectady NY (S)
Union County Public Library Gallery, Monroe NC
Union Gallery, see San Jose State University, San Jose CA
Union of American Hebrew Congregations, Synagogue Art and Architectural Library, New York NY
Union University, Dept of Art, Jackson TN (S)
Unitarian Universalist Association, see Religious Arts Guild, Boston MA
United Methodist Church Commission on Archives and History, Madison NJ
United Methodist Historical Society, Lovely Lane Museum, Baltimore MD
United Missouri Bancshares, Inc, Kansas City MO
United States Capitol Museum, Washington DC
United States Commission of Fine Arts, Washington DC
United States Committee of the International Association of Art, Inc, Washington DC
United States Department of the Interior, Indian Arts and Crafts Board, Washington DC
United States Figure Skating Hall of Fame and Museum, Colorado Springs CO

University of New Brunswick, Art Centre, Fredericton NB
University of New Hampshire, University Art Galleries, Durham NH
University of New Hampshire, Dept of the Arts, Durham NH (S)
University of New Haven, Dept of Humanities, Fine & Performing Arts, West Haven CT (S)
University of New Mexico, Albuquerque NM
University of New Mexico, Albuquerque NM (S)
University of New Orleans, Fine Arts Gallery, New Orleans LA
University of New Orleans, Dept of Fine Arts, New Orleans LA (S)
University of North Alabama, Dept of Art, Florence AL (S)
University of North Carolina, Chapel Hill NC
University of North Carolina at Asheville, Dept of Art and Music, Asheville NC (S)
University of North Carolina at Chapel Hill, Art Dept, Chapel Hill NC (S)
University of North Carolina at Greensboro, Weatherspoon Art Gallery, Greensboro NC
University of North Carolina at Greensboro, Art Dept, Greensboro NC (S)
University of North Carolina at Greensboro, Chinqua-Penn Plantation House, Reidsville NC
University of North Carolina at Wilmington, Dept of Creative Arts - Division of Art, Wilmington NC (S)
University of North Carolina-Charlotte, Creative Arts Dept, Charlotte NC (S)
University of North Dakota, Visual Arts Dept, Grand Forks ND (S)
University of North Dakota-Williston Center, Interior Design Dept, Williston ND (S)
University of Northern Colorado, Dept of Visual Arts, Greeley CO (S)
University of Northern Colorado, John Mariani Art Gallery, Greeley CO
University of Northern Iowa, Gallery of Art, Cedar Falls IA
University of Northern Iowa, Dept of Art, Cedar Falls IA (S)
University of North Florida, Dept of Fine Arts, Jacksonville FL (S)
University of Notre Dame, Notre Dame IN
University of Notre Dame, Dept of Art, Art History & Design, Notre Dame IN (S)
University of Oklahoma, Norman OK
University of Oklahoma, School of Art, Norman OK (S)
University of Oregon, Eugene OR
University of Oregon, Dept of Fine & Applied Arts, Eugene OR (S)
University of Pennsylvania, University Museum of Archaeology & Anthropology, Philadelphia PA
University of Pennsylvania, Graduate School of Fine Arts, Philadelphia PA (S)
University of Pittsburgh, Pittsburgh PA
University of Pittsburgh, Pittsburgh PA (S)
University of Pittsburgh at Johnstown, Dept of Fine Arts, Johnstown PA (S)
University of Portland, Wilson W Clark Memorial Library, Portland OR
University of Puerto Rico, Dept of Fine Arts, Rio Piedras PR (S)
University of Puerto Rico, Museum of Archaeology, History and Art, Rio Piedras PR
University of Puerto Rico, Mayaguez, Dept of Humanities, Mayaguez PR (S)
University of Puget Sound, Kittredge Art Gallery, Tacoma WA
University of Puget Sound, Art Dept, Tacoma WA (S)
University of Quebec, Trois Rivieres, Fine Arts Section, Trois Rivieres PQ (S)
University of Redlands, Peppers Art Center and Gallery, Redlands CA
University of Redlands, Dept of Art, Redlands CA (S)
University of Regina, Mackenzie Art Gallery, Regina SK
University of Regina, Regina SK (S)
University of Rhode Island, Dept of Art, Kingston RI (S)
University of Rhode Island Gallery, Kingston RI

University of Richmond, Dept of Art, Richmond VA (S)
University of Rochester, Rochester NY
University of Rochester, Dept of Fine Arts, Rochester NY (S)
University of Saint Thomas, Art Dept, Houston TX (S)
University of San Diego, Founders' Gallery, San Diego CA
University of San Diego, Art Dept, San Diego CA (S)
University of Santa Clara, de Saisset Museum, Santa Clara CA
University of Santa Clara, Fine Arts Dept, Santa Clara CA (S)
University of Saskatchewan, Gordon Snelgrove Art Gallery, Saskatoon SK
University of Saskatchewan, Dept of Art & Art History, Saskatoon SK (S)
University of Science and Arts of Oklahoma, Arts Dept, Chickasha OK (S)
University of Sherbrooke Cultural Center, Art Gallery, Sherbrooke PQ
University of South Alabama, Ethnic American Slide Library, Mobile AL
University of South Alabama, Dept of Art, Mobile AL (S)
University of South Carolina, Dept of Art, Columbia SC (S)
University of South Carolina at Aiken, Arts & Letters, Aiken SC (S)
University of South Carolina Spartanburg, Library Art Gallery, Spartanburg SC
University of South Dakota, Dept of Art, Vermillion SD (S)
University of South Dakota Art Galleries, Vermillion SD
University of South Dakota, Springfield, Springfield SD (S)
University of Southern California, Idyllwild School of Music and the Arts, Idyllwild CA (S)
University of Southern California, School of Fine Arts, Los Angeles CA (S)
University of Southern California, Los Angeles CA
University of Southern Colorado, School of Liberal Arts, Pueblo CO
University of Southern Colorado, Belmont Campus, Dept of Art, Pueblo CO (S)
University of Southern Maine, Art Dept, Gorham ME (S)
University of Southern Mississippi, Dept of Art, Hattiesburg MS (S)
University of South Florida, Art Galleries, Tampa FL
University of South Florida, Art Dept, Tampa FL (S)
University of Southwestern Louisiana, Lafayette LA
University of Southwestern Louisiana, School of Art and Architecture, Lafayette LA (S)
University of Tampa, Tampa FL
University of Tampa, Dept of Art, Tampa FL (S)
University of Tennessee, Knoxville TN
University of Tennessee at Chattanooga, Dept of Art, Chattanooga TN (S)
University of Tennessee at Chattanooga Art Gallery, Chattanooga TN
University of Tennessee, Knoxville, Dept of Art, Knoxville TN (S)
University of Texas, Austin TX (S)
University of Texas at Arlington, University Art Gallery, Arlington TX (S)
University of Texas at Arlington, Dept of Art, Arlington TX (S)
University of Texas at Austin, Austin TX
University of Texas at El Paso, El Paso TX
University of Texas at El Paso, Dept of Art, El Paso TX (S)
University of Texas at San Antonio, Division of Art and Design, San Antonio TX (S)
University of Texas at Tyler, Dept of Art, Tyler TX (S)
University of Texas of Permian Basin, Art Discipline, Odessa TX (S)
University of the District of Columbia, Art Dept, Washington DC (S)
University of the Pacific, University Center Gallery, Stockton CA

University of the Pacific, Dept of Art, Stockton CA (S)
University of the South, Dept of Fine Arts, Sewanee TN (S)
University of the South Gallery of Fine Arts, Sewanee TN
University of Toledo, Dept of Art, Art Education and Art History, Toledo OH (S)
University of Toronto, Erindale Campus Art Gallery, Mississauga ON
University of Toronto, Toronto ON
University of Toronto, Toronto ON (S)
University of Tulsa, Dept of Art, Tulsa OK (S)
University of Utah, Utah Museum of Fine Arts, Salt Lake City UT
University of Utah, Art Dept, Salt Lake City UT (S)
University of Vermont, Robert Hull Fleming Museum, Burlington VT
University of Vermont, Dept of Art, Burlington VT (S)
University of Victoria, Maltwood Art Museum and Gallery, Victoria BC
University of Victoria, Victoria BC (S)
University of Virginia, Charlottesville VA
University of Virginia, McIntire Dept of Art, Charlottesville VA (S)
University of Washington, School of Art, Seattle WA (S)
University of Washington, Seattle WA
University of Waterloo, Waterloo ON
University of Waterloo, Fine Arts Dept, Waterloo ON (S)
University of Western Ontario, McIntosh Art Gallery, London ON
University of Western Ontario, Dept of Visual Arts, London ON (S)
University of West Florida, Art Gallery, Pensacola FL
University of West Florida, Faculty of Art, Pensacola FL (S)
University of Windsor, School of Visual Arts, Windsor ON (S)
University of Wisconsin, Madison WI
University of Wisconsin, Milwaukee WI
University of Wisconsin, Allen Priebe Gallery, Oshkosh WI
University of Wisconsin, Harry Nohr Art Gallery, Platteville WI
University of Wisconsin, Dept of Art, Rice Lake WI (S)
University of Wisconsin, Gallery 101, River Falls WI
University of Wisconsin Center-Marinette County, Art Dept, Marinette WI (S)
University of Wisconsin-Eau Claire, Dept of Art, Eau Claire WI (S)
University of Wisconsin, Green Bay, Lawton Gallery, Green Bay WI
University of Wisconsin-Green Bay, Visual Arts Dept, Green Bay WI (S)
University of Wisconsin-La Crosse, Art Dept, La Crosse WI (S)
University of Wisconsin, Madison, Madison WI (S)
University of Wisconsin-Milwaukee, Dept of Art, Milwaukee WI (S)
University of Wisconsin-Oshkosh, Dept of Art, Oshkosh WI (S)
University of Wisconsin-Parkside, Art Discipline, Kenosha WI (S)
University of Wisconsin-Platteville, Dept of Fine Art, Platteville WI (S)
University of Wisconsin-River Falls, Art Dept, River Falls WI (S)
University of Wisconsin-Stevens Point, Dept of Art, Stevens Point WI (S)
University of Wisconsin-Stout, Gallery 209, Menomonie WI
University of Wisconsin-Stout, Art Dept, Menomonie WI (S)
University of Wisconsin-Superior, Programs in the Visual Arts, Superior WI (S)
University of Wisconsin-Whitewater, Dept of Art, Whitewater WI (S)
University of Wyoming, Art Museum, Laramie WY
University of Wyoming, Art Dept, Laramie WY (S)
Uris Library, see Metropolitan Museum of Art, New York NY

Western Oklahoma State College, Art Dept, Altus OK (S)
Western Oregon State College, Creative Arts Dept, Visual Arts, Monmouth OR (S)
Western Oregon State College Gallery, Monmouth OR
Western Reserve Historical Society, Cleveland OH
Western State College, Quigley Hall Art Gallery, Gunnison CO
Western State College of Colorado, Dept of Art, Gunnison CO (S)
Western Washington University, Art Dept, Bellingham WA (S)
Western Wisconsin Technical Institute, Graphics Division, La Crosse WI (S)
Western Wyoming College, Art Dept, Rock Springs WY (S)
Westfield Athenaeum, Jasper Rand Art Museum, Westfield MA
Westfield State College, Art Dept, Westfield MA (S)
West Florida Museum of History, see Historic Pensacola Preservation Board, Pensacola FL
West Georgia College, Art Dept, Carrollton GA (S)
West Hills College, Fine Arts Dept, Coalinga CA (S)
West Hills Unitarian Fellowship, Portland OR
Westinghouse Electric Corporation, Pittsburgh PA
West Liberty State College, Art Dept, West Liberty WV (S)
Westmar College, Mock Memorial Art Gallery, LeMars IA
Westmar College, Art Dept, LeMars IA (S)
Westminster College, Art Dept, New Wilmington PA (S)
Westminster College, Dept of Art, Salt Lake City UT (S)
Westminster College Art Gallery, New Wilmington PA
Westmoreland County Museum of Art, Greensburg PA
Westover, Charles City VA
West Point Museum, see United States Military Academy, West Point NY
West Shore Community College, Division of Humanities and Fine Arts, Scottville MI (S)
West Texas State University, Art Dept, Canyon TX (S)
West Valley College, Art Dept, Saratoga CA (S)
West Virginia Institute of Technology, Creative Arts Dept, Montgomery WV (S)
West Virginia State College, Art Dept, Institute WV (S)
West Virginia University, Morgantown WV
West Virginia University, Division of Art, Morgantown WV (S)
West Virginia Wesleyan College, Dept of Fine Arts, Buckhannon WV (S)
Weyerhaeuser Library, see Macalester College Galleries, Saint Paul MN
Wharton County Junior College, Art Dept, Wharton TX (S)
Whatcom Museum of History and Art, Bellingham WA
Wheaton College, Norton MA
Wheaton College, Art Dept, Norton MA (S)
Wheaton College, Dept of Art, Wheaton IL (S)
Mary Cabot Wheelwright Research Library, see Wheelwright Museum, Santa Fe NM
Wheelwright Museum, Santa Fe NM
Whistler House and Parker Gallery, see Lowell Art Association, Lowell MA
Whitefield House Museum, see Moravian Historical Society, Nazareth PA
White Gallery, see Portland State University, Portland OR
White House, Washington DC
Percy H Whiting Art Center, Fairhope AL
Whitman College, Art Dept, Walla Walla WA (S)
Whitney Gallery of Western Art, see Buffalo Bill Memorial Association, Cody WY
Whitney Museum of American Art, New York NY
Whitney Museum of American Art, Fairfield County, Stamford CT
Whittier College, Dept of Art, Whittier CA (S)
Whittier Fine Arts Gallery, see Friends University, Wichita KS
Whitworth College, Art Dept, Spokane WA (S)

Peter and Catharine Whyte Foundation, Peter Whyte Gallery, Banff AB
Wichita Art Association Inc, Wichita KS
Wichita Art Museum, Wichita KS
Wichita Art Museum, see Kansas Watercolor Society, Wichita KS
Wichita Falls Museum and Art Center, Wichita Falls TX
Wichita Public Library, Wichita KS
Wichita State University, Edwin A Ulrich Museum of Art, Wichita KS
Wichita State University, Division of Art, Wichita KS (S)
Widener University, Alfred O Deshong Museum, Chester PA
Albert H Wiggin Gallery (Prints), see Boston Public Library, Boston MA
Frederick S Wight Art Gallery, see University of California, Los Angeles, Los Angeles CA
Wilber Czech Museum, Wilber NE
Wilberforce University, Art Dept, Wilberforce OH (S)
Wilbour Library of Egyptology, see Brooklyn Museum, Brooklyn NY
Wilderness Park Museum, see El Paso Museum of Art, El Paso TX
Wildfowl Art Museum, see Salisbury State College, Salisbury MD
Wiley College, Dept of Fine Arts, Marshall TX (S)
Wilfrid Laurier University, Concourse Gallery, Waterloo ON
Wilkes Art Gallery, North Wilkesboro NC
Wilkes College, Sordoni Art Gallery, Wilkes-Barre PA
Wilkes College, Dept of Art, Wilkes-Barre PA (S)
Wilkes Community College, Arts and Science Division, Wilkesboro NC (S)
Willamette University, George Putnam University Center, Salem OR
Willard House and Clock Museum, Inc, Grafton MA
Willard Library, Dept of Fine Arts, Evansville IN
Willet Stained Glass Studios, Philadelphia PA (S)
William Carey College, Art Dept, Hattiesburg MS (S)
William Jewell College, Art Dept, Liberty MO (S)
William Paterson College, Art Dept, Wayne NJ (S)
William Penn College, Art Dept, Oskaloosa IA (S)
Williams College, Museum of Art, Williamstown MA
Williams College, Dept of Art, Williamstown MA (S)
Kemper and Leila Williams Foundation, see Historic New Orleans Collection, New Orleans LA
Morris R Williams Center for the Arts, see Lafayette College, Easton PA
Williamsport Area Community College, Dept of Engineering and Design, Williamsport PA (S)
William Woods College, Art Gallery, Fulton MO
William Woods-Westminster Colleges, Art Dept, Fulton MO (S)
Willis Library, Humanities Division, see North Texas State University, Denton TX
Willmar Community College, Willmar MN (S)
Wilmington College, Art Dept, Wilmington OH (S)
Wilmington Trust Company, Wilmington DE
Woodrow Wilson Birthplace Foundation, Staunton VA
Woodrow Wilson House, Washington DC
Wine Museum of San Francisco, San Francisco CA
Wingate College, Division of Fine Arts, Wingate NC (S)
Winnipeg Art Gallery, Winnipeg MB
Winnipeg Sketch Club, Winnipeg MB
Winona State University, Art Dept, Winona MN (S)
Winston-Salem State University, Art Dept, Winston-Salem NC (S)
Winterthur in Odessa, see Winterthur Museum and Gardens, Winterthur DE
Winterthur Museum and Gardens, Winterthur DE
Winthrop College, Dept of Art, Rock Hill SC (S)
Winthrop College Gallery of Art, Rock Hill SC
Wisconsin Fine Arts Association, Inc, Ozaukee Art Center, Cedarburg WI
Witte Memorial Museum, see San Antonio Museum Association, Inc, San Antonio TX

Wittenberg University, Art Dept, Springfield OH (S)
Witter Gallery, Storm Lake IA
Wofford College, Sandor Teszler Library Gallery, Spartanburg SC
Catharine Lorillard Wolfe Art Club, Inc, New York NY
Women Artists News Archive, see Midmarch Associates, New York NY
Women in the Arts Foundation, Inc, New York NY
Women's Art Registry of Minnesota Gallery, Minneapolis MN
Women's City Club of Cleveland, Gallery, Cleveland OH
Women's Interart Center, Inc, Interart de St Amand Gallery, New York NY
Wood Art Gallery, Montpelier VT
Woodbury University, Professional Arts Division, Los Angeles CA (S)
Woodlawn Plantation, Mount Vernon VA
Woodmere Art Museum, Philadelphia PA
Leigh Yawkey Woodson Art Museum, Inc, Wausau WI
Woodstock Art Gallery, Woodstock ON
Woodstock School of Art, Inc, New York NY (S)
Woolaroc Museum, see Frank Phillips, Bartlesville OK
Wooster Community Art Center, Danbury CT
Worcester Art Center, see Lawrence University, Appleton WI
Worcester Art Museum, Worcester MA
Worcester Craft Center, Worcester MA (S)
Worcester Craft Center Gallery, Worcester MA
Worcester State College, Arts & Humanities, Worcester MA (S)
World Heritage Museum, see University of Illinois, Champaign IL
John Wornall House Museum, see Jackson County Historical Society, Independence MO
Wright College, see City Colleges of Chicago, Chicago IL (S)
Fielding L Wright Art Center, see Delta State University, Cleveland MS
Frank Lloyd Wright Association, Oak Park IL
Wright Museum of Art, see Beloit College, Beloit WI
Wright School of Art, Stowe VT (S)
Wright State University, Dayton OH
Wright State University, Dept of Art & Art History, Dayton OH (S)
Wustum Art Library, see The Racine Art Association, Inc, Racine WI
Charles A Wustum Museum of Fine Arts, see The Racine Art Association, Inc, Racine WI
Wyoming State Art Gallery, Cheyenne WY
Xavier University, Emery Galleries, Cincinnati OH
Xavier University of Louisiana, Dept of Fine Arts, New Orleans LA (S)
Xerox Corporation, Art Collection, Stamford CT
Yaddo, Saratoga Springs NY (S)
Yager Museum, see Hartwick College Fine Art Gallery, Oneonta NY
Yakima Valley College, Art Dept, Yakima WA (S)
Yale Center for British Art, see Yale University, New Haven CT
Yale University, New Haven CT
Yale University, New Haven CT (S)
Yankton College, Durand Art Collection, Yankton SD
Yankton College, Dept of Art, Yankton SD (S)
Yard School of Art, Montclair NJ (S)
Yarmouth County Historical Society, Yarmouth County Museum, Yarmouth NS
Yavapai College, Art Dept, Prescott AZ (S)
Yellowstone Art Center, Billings MT
Yeshiva University, Museum, New York NY
Yonkers Public Library, Fine Arts Dept, Yonkers NY
York College, Art Dept, York NE (S)
York College of Pennsylvania, Dept of Humanities and Fine Arts, York PA (S)
York College of the City University of New York, Fine and Performing Arts, Jamaica NY (S)
York Institute Museum, Saco ME
York University, Art Gallery, Downsview ON
York University, Dept of Visual Arts, Downsview ON (S)
Yosemite Collections, Yosemite National Park CA

Personnel Index

Individuals affiliated with art schools are indicated by "S".

Aaboe, Anne, *Business Mgr,* University of California, University Art Museum, Berkeley CA

Aach, Herb, *Pres,* Artists Technical Institute, New York NY

Aakhus, Michael, *Asst Prof,* Indiana State University, Evansville, Art Dept, Evansville IN (S)

Aaron, Richard, *Finances,* Orange County Center for Contemporary Art, Santa Ana CA

Abatelli, Carol, *Slide & Picture,* Cooper Union for the Advancement of Science & Art, Library, New York NY

Abbe, Elizabeth, *Librn,* Connecticut Historical Society, Library, Hartford CT

Abbe, Ronald, *Faculty,* Housatonic Community College, Art Dept, Bridgeport CT (S)

Abberger, Nancy, *Secy & Dir of Gallery Activities,* Morse Gallery of Art, Winter Park FL

Abbey, Rita Deanin, *Prof,* University of Nevada, Las Vegas, Dept of Art, Las Vegas NV (S)

Abegglen, Linda M, *Dir of Development & Public Relations,* China Trade Museum, Milton MA

Abeles, Sigmund, *Prof,* University of New Hampshire, Dept of the Arts, Durham NH (S)

Abelman, Arthur F, *Pres,* Sculpture Center, New York NY

Aberle, Peter, *Asst Prof,* Denison University, Dept of Art, Granville OH (S)

Abid, Ann B, *Librn,* Saint Louis Art Museum, Richardson Memorial Library, Saint Louis MO

Abraham, Richard, *Instructor,* Central Community College - Platte Campus, Creative and Social Cluster, Columbus NE (S)

Abrahamson, Roy E, *Academic Area Head,* Southern Illinois University, School of Art, Carbondale IL (S)

Abrams, Edith L, *Pres,* American Society of Contemporary Artists, Brooklyn NY

Abrams, Jack, *Instr,* Wayne Art Center, Wayne PA (S)

Abrams, Jean, *Instr,* Mississippi Delta Junior College, Dept of Fine Arts, Moorhead MS (S)

Abrams, Joseph R, *Chmn,* Mississippi Delta Junior College, Dept of Fine Arts, Moorhead MS (S)

Acker, Brenda, *Registrar,* Oshkosh Public Museum, Oshkosh WI

Acker, Vernon, *Prof,* Eastern New Mexico University, Dept of Art, Portales NM (S)

Ackerman, Andrew, *Dir of Education,* Jewish Museum, New York NY

Ackerman, Frank, *Chief of Exhib,* Natural History Museum of Los Angeles County, Los Angeles CA

Ackerman, Gerald, *Prof,* Pomona College, Art Dept, Claremont CA (S)

Ackerman, James S, *Chmn Dept,* Harvard University, Dept of Fine Arts, Cambridge MA (S)

Ackerman, Robert, *Dean,* Drew University, College Art Gallery, Madison NJ

Ackerman, Rudy S, *Chmn Dept,* Moravian College, Dept of Art, Bethlehem PA (S)

Acomb, Merlin, *Exhibition Designer & Preparator,* University of Vermont, Robert Hull Fleming Museum, Burlington VT

Acorn, Eleanor, *Head Librn,* John M Cuelenaere Library, Grace Campbell Gallery, Prince Albert SK

Acorn, John Thomson, *Head Dept,* Clemson University, College of Liberal Arts, Clemson SC (S)

Acosta, Efeyinwa, *Educ Coordr,* Jamaica Center for the Performing & Visual Arts, Inc, Jamaica Arts Center, Jamaica NY

Adair, Charlene, *Secy,* Five Civilized Tribes Museum, Muskogee OK

Adamchick, Kathryn, *Cur Education & Community Servs,* Queens Museum, Flushing NY

Adams, Anne, *Registrar,* Amon Carter Museum, Fort Worth TX

Adams, Ansel, *Chmn,* The Friends of Photography, Carmel CA

Adams, Bebo, *Business Mgr,* Canton Art Institute, Canton OH (S)

Adams, Betty, *Asst Prof,* Saint Mary's College, Art Dept, Raleigh NC (S)

Adams, Bryding, *Cur Decorative Arts,* Birmingham Museum of Art, Birmingham AL

Adams, Carol, *Dir,* Lincoln County Cultural and Historical Association, Lincoln County Museum, Wiscasset ME

Adams, Celeste, *Cur Oriental Art,* Museum of Fine Arts, Houston, Houston TX

Adams, Charles, *Chmn Dept,* Central Florida Community College, Humanities Dept, Ocala FL (S)

Adams, Clinton, *Dir,* University of New Mexico, Tamarind Institute, Albuquerque NM (S)

Adams, David, *Library Asst,* Metropolitan Museum of Art, The Cloisters Library, New York NY

Adams, Fletcher, *Secy,* New England Watercolor Society, Scituate MA

Adams, Fletcher, *Dir,* George Vesper School of Art, Boston MA (S)

Adams, Henry, *Cur Fine Arts,* Carnegie Institute, Museum of Art, Pittsburgh PA

Adams, Idie, *Ceramic Coordr,* Butte College, Dept of Fine & Performing Arts, Oroville CA (S)

Adams, James R C, *Head Dept,* Manchester College, Art Dept, North Manchester IN (S)

Adams, J Franklin, *Assoc Prof,* Tulane University, Sophie H Newcomb Memorial College, New Orleans LA (S)

Adams, Jill, *Secy,* Waterloo Art Association, Eleventh Street Gallery, Waterloo IA

Adams, Joy, *Instructor,* State University of New York College at Potsdam, Dept of Fine Arts, Potsdam NY (S)

Adams, June Miller, *Asst Cur,* Southern Utah State College, Braithwaite Fine Arts Gallery, Cedar City UT

Adams, Karen, *Chairperson Fine Arts,* Roanoke College, Art Dept, Salem VA (S)

Adams, Kenneth D, *Admin Asst,* Canton Art Institute, Canton OH

Adams, Lillian, *Art Dir,* Port Chester Public Library, Fine Arts Dept, Port Chester NY

Adams, Lowell, *Dir,* Oklahoma Art Center, Oklahoma City OK

Adams, Margaret B, *Dir & Cur,* Presidio of Monterey Army Museum, Monterey CA

Adams, Mary Kathryn, *Assoc Dir,* Oklahoma Art Center, Oklahoma City OK

Adams, Nicholas, *Chmn Dept,* Lehigh University, Dept of Art and Architecture, Bethlehem PA (S)

Adams, Phyllis, *Exec Dir,* Lansing Art Gallery, Lansing MI

Adams, Richard, *Chmn,* Southern Utah State College, Dept of Art, Cedar City UT (S)

Adams, Robert, *Assoc Prof,* Alabama A & M University, Art Education Dept, Huntsville AL (S)

Adams, Roger J, *Head Dept,* Nazareth College of Rochester, Art Dept, Rochester NY (S)

Adams, Roxana, *Field Services,* Alaska State Museum, Juneau AK

Adams, Sandra, *Asst Prof,* Notre Dame College, Art Dept, Manchester NH (S)

Adams, Shelby, *Instr,* Illinois Central College, Fine Arts Dept, East Peoria IL (S)

Adams, Stan, *Instr,* Illinois Central College, Fine Arts Dept, East Peoria IL (S)

Adams, Wesley A, *Deputy Dir Finance & Administration,* Winterthur Museum and Gardens, Winterthur DE

Adams, William R, *Dir,* Historic Saint Augustine Preservation Board, Saint Augustine FL

Adamson, Jeremy, *Cur of Art,* Glenbow Museum, Calgary AB

Adamson, Jim, *Instructor,* Sierra College, Art Dept, Rocklin CA (S)

Adamy, George E, *Dir,* Adamy's Plastics and Mold-Making Workshops, Larchmont NY (S)

Adcoch, Craig, *Asst Prof,* Florida State University, Art History Dept, Tallahassee FL (S)

Addington, Aldon, *Assoc Prof,* Southern Illinois University, School of Art, Carbondale IL (S)

Addison, B Kent, *Prof,* Maryville College, St Louis, Art Division, Saint Louis MO (S)

Addison, Elizabeth, *Mgr Marketing Public Relations,* Art Gallery of Ontario, Toronto ON

Addison, Lynne, *Registrar,* Hudson River Museum, Yonkers NY

Addiss, Stephen, *Adjunct Cur Japanese Art,* New Orleans Museum of Art, New Orleans LA

Addiss, Stephen, *Grad Advisor,* University of Kansas, Kress Foundation Dept of Art History, Lawrence KS (S)

Adelman, Charles, *Asst Prof,* University of Northern Iowa, Dept of Art, Cedar Falls IA (S)

Adelman, Everett, *Instr,* Munson-Williams-Proctor Institute, School of Art, Utica NY (S)

Adelmann, Arthur R, *Prof,* Weber State College, Art Dept, Ogden UT (S)

Adfelstadt, Eric, *Vis Lectr,* California State College, Stanislaus, Art Dept, Turlock CA (S)

Adkins, Cary, *Assoc Prof,* Grand Canyon College, Art Dept, Phoenix AZ (S)

Adleman, Susan I, *Secy,* Annie S Kemerer Museum, Bethlehem PA

Adlin, Nelson, *Prof,* Community College of Baltimore, Dept of Fine & Applied Arts, Liberty Campus, Baltimore MD (S)

Aehle, Michael, *Asst Prof,* Saint Louis Community College at Florissant Valley, Dept of Art, Ferguson MO (S)

Agard, James, *Chmn,* Gettysburg College, Dept of Art, Gettysburg PA (S)

Agee, Sheila, *Asst Dir,* South Dakota State University, South Dakota Memorial Art Center, Brookings SD

Agnew, L Jack, *Prof,* Sullivan County Community College, Division of Commercial Art and Photography, Loch Sheldrake NY (S)

Agostini, Peter, *Instr,* New York Studio School of Drawing, Painting and Sculpture, New York NY (S)

Agueros, Jack, *Dir,* El Museo del Barrio, New York NY

Ahearn, Maureen, *Dir,* Keene State College, Thorne-Sagendorph Art Gallery, Keene NH

Ahmad, Sufi, *Assoc Prof,* Saint Francis College, Art Dept, Fort Wayne IN (S)

Ahmuty, Raynor, *VPres,* Providence Art Club, Providence RI

Aho, Charles, *Adjunct Instr,* Le Moyne College, Art Dept, Syracuse NY (S)

Ahrenkilde, Sven, *Asst to the Dir,* Rochester Institute of Technology, Technical & Education Center of the Graphic Arts, Rochester NY (S)

Ahrens, Kent, *Dir,* Everhart Museum of Natural History, Science and Art, Scranton PA

Ahysen, Harry J, *Prof,* Sam Houston State University, Art Dept, Huntsville TX (S)

Aiches, Alan, *Dir,* Saint John's Museum of Art, Wilmington NC

Aidlin, Jerome, *Prof,* Cleveland Institute of Art, Cleveland OH (S)

Aiken, O S, *Treas,* Florence Museum, Florence SC

Aikin, Roger, *Instr,* Creighton University, Fine and Performing Arts Dept, Omaha NE (S)

Aikman, John, *Instructor,* Linn Benton Community College, Fine & Applied Art Dept, Albany OR (S)

Ainslie, Michael, *Pres,* National Trust for Historic Preservation, Washington DC

Aird, David, *Dir,* Musee Historique de Vaudreuil, Vaudreuil Historical Museum, Vaudreuil PQ

Aistars, John, *Dir Art Prog,* Cazenovia College, Chapman Art Center Gallery, Cazenovia NY

Aistars, John, *Chmn,* Cazenovia College, Center for Art & Design Studies, Cazenovia NY (S)

Akamura, Frank, *Prof,* Napa College, Art Dept, Napa CA (S)

Akers, Adela, *Prof,* Temple University, Tyler School of Art, Philadelphia PA (S)

Akin, Dennis, *Prof,* Dickinson College, Fine Arts Dept, Carlisle PA (S)

Akin, Omer, *Head,* Carnegie-Mellon University, Dept of Architecture, Pittsburgh PA (S)

Albacete, Manuel J, *Assoc Dir,* Canton Art Institute, Canton OH

Albacete, Manuel J, *Assoc Dir,* Canton Art Institute, Canton OH (S)

Alber, Timothy, *Lectr,* Cardinal Stritch College, Art Dept, Milwaukee WI (S)

Albert, Jerry, *Asst,* Tucson Museum of Art, Library, Tucson AZ

Albrams, Susan, *Assoc Registrar,* Hofstra University, Emily Lowe Gallery, Hempstead NY

Albrecht, Cheryl C, *Dir,* College of Mount Saint Joseph on the Ohio, Archbishop Alter Library, Mount Saint Joseph OH

Albrecht, Joseph H, *Pres,* Kenneth C Beck Center for the Cultural Arts, Lakewood OH

Albrecht, Sterling, *Dir Libraries,* Brigham Young University, Harold B Lee Library, Provo UT

Albrich, E, *Librn,* Queen's University, Art & Music Library, Kingston ON

Alcorn-Kunc, Kathryn, *Chmn,* Central State University, Art Dept, Edmond OK (S)

Alden, Gary Wade, *Exec Dir,* Balboa Art Conservation Center, San Diego CA

Alden, Sondra, *Dir,* Martin & Osa Johnson Safari Museum, Chanute KS

Alderette, R, *Instructor,* Golden West College, Arts, Humanities and Social Sciences Institute, Huntington Beach CA (S)

Aldern, Robert J, *Chmn,* Augustana College, Art Dept, Sioux Falls SD (S)

Aldrich, Jane, *Asst Dir,* The Racine Art Association, Inc, Racine WI

Aldrich, Jonathan, *Instructor,* Portland School of Art, Portland ME (S)

Aldrich, Larry, *Founder & Pres,* Soho Center for Visual Artists, New York NY

Alesch, Eugene, *Assoc Prof,* Texas Tech University, Dept of Art, Lubbock TX (S)

Alexander, Barbara, *Asst Prof,* University of Alaska, Dept of Art, Fairbanks AK (S)

Alexander, Barbara, *Asst Dir & Registrar,* California Institute of Technology, Baxter Art Gallery, Pasadena CA

Alexander, James, *Asst Prof,* University of Alabama in Birmingham, Dept of Art, Birmingham AL (S)

Alexander, Joy, *Cur,* University of Michigan, Slide and Photograph Collection, Ann Arbor MI

Alexander, Lorraine, *Pres,* Cheltenham Art Centre, Cheltenham PA (S)

Alexander, Mark, *Cur,* Eastern Illinois University, Tarble Arts Center, Charleston IL

Alexander, Ronald J, *Head Dept,* Northeast Louisiana University, Dept of Art, Monroe LA (S)

Alexander, Sharon, *Secy,* University of Minnesota, Tweed Museum of Art, Duluth MN

Alexander, Shizuko, *Instructor,* Daytona Beach Community College, Dept of Performing and Visual Arts, Daytona Beach FL (S)

Alexander, William C, *Vis Prof,* Victor Valley College, Art Dept, Victorville CA (S)

Alexandrides, Rita, *Registrar,* Everson Museum of Art, Syracuse NY

Alexick, David, *Dir of Art,* Christopher Newport College, Arts & Communications, Newport News VA (S)

Alfano, Domenic, *Adjunct Instr,* New York Institute of Technology, Fine Arts Dept, Old Westbury NY (S)

Alford, Constance, *Asst Prof,* Alcorn State University, Dept of Fine Arts, Lorman MS (S)

Alfredson, Alfred, *Pres,* Palette and Chisel Academy of Fine Arts Gallery, Chicago IL

Algar, James Nelson, *Recording Secy,* Monterey Peninsula Museum of Art, Monterey CA

Alhilali, Neda, *Chmn Dept,* Scripps College, Art Dept, Claremont CA (S)

Ali, Hakim, *Dir William Grant Still Community Arts Center,* City of Los Angeles, Cultural Affairs Dept, Los Angeles CA

Alibrandi, Gaetano, *Instr,* Danforth Museum School, Framingham MA (S)

Alinder, James, *Exec Dir,* The Friends of Photography, Carmel CA

Alkema, Chester, *Prof,* Grand Valley State Colleges, Art Dept, Allendale MI (S)

Alkin, Roger C, *Dir,* Creighton University Art Gallery, Omaha NE

Allaben, Craig, *Gallery Mgr,* University of Massachusetts, Amherst, University Gallery, Amherst MA

Allan, Gerald, *Basic Studies,* Minneapolis College of Art and Design, Minneapolis MN (S)

Allan, Janet, *Secy,* Lahaina Arts Society, Art Organization, Lahaina HI

Allan, Ruth, *Instructor,* Wenatchee Valley College, Art Dept, Wenatchee WA (S)

Allan, Ruth, *Pres,* Wenatchee Valley College, Gallery 76, Wenatchee WA

Allara, Pamela, *Asst Prof,* Tufts University, Fine Arts Dept, Medford MA (S)

Allen, Bruce, *Asst Prof,* Centenary College of Louisiana, Dept of Art, Shreveport LA (S)

Allen, Carl M, *Dir Gallery,* Ashland College Arts and Humanities Gallery, Ashland OH

Allen, Carol, *Secy,* Muttart Gallery Associates, Calgary AB

Allen, Frederick E, *Assoc Dean,* Butte College, Dept of Fine & Performing Arts, Oroville CA (S)

Allen, Frederick E, *Assoc Dean,* Butte College, Dept of Art, Oroville CA (S)

Allen, F Robert, *Instructor,* Saint Louis Community College at Meramec, Art Dept, Saint Louis MO (S)

Allen, Gwen, *Secy,* Plainsman Museum, Aurora NE

Allen, J, *Libr Tech,* Sheridan College of Applied Arts and Technology, Visual Arts Library, Oakville ON

Allen, James A, *Prof,* Daemen College, Art Dept, Amherst NY (S)

Allen, J Clyff, *Dir & Preparator,* Brigham Young University, B F Larsen Gallery, Provo UT

Allen, Jean, *Secy,* Brattleboro Museum and Art Center, Brattleboro VT

Allen, Jean S, *Instr,* Haskell Indian Junior College, Art Dept, Lawrence KS (S)

Allen, Jere H, *Assoc Prof,* University of Mississippi, Dept of Art, University MS (S)

Allen, Jules, *Lectr,* Queensborough Community College, Dept of Art and Design, Bayside NY (S)

Allen, Karyn Elizabeth, *Cur Art,* University of Calgary, The Nickle Arts Museum, Calgary AB

Allen, Kay, *Dir,* Gertrude Herbert Memorial Institute of Art, Augusta GA

Allen, Kay, *Admin Asst,* University of Southern California, Fisher Gallery, Los Angeles CA

Allen, Kristi, *Adminr,* Rocky Mountain School of Art, Denver CO (S)

Allen, Laura Graves, *Actg Cur of Anthropology,* Museum of Northern Arizona, Flagstaff AZ

Allen, Lisa, *Instructor,* Portland School of Art, Portland ME (S)

Allen, Margaret, *Membership Secy,* Los Angeles Institute of Contemporary Art, Los Angeles CA

Allen, Margaret, *Fine Arts Reference Librn,* Grace A Dow Memorial Library, Fine Arts Dept, Midland MI

Allen, Margery, *Asst Dir Reference Division,* Metropolitan Toronto Library Board, Fine Art Dept, Toronto ON

Allen, Mary L, *Asst Dir,* Gunston Hall Plantation, Lorton VA

Allen, Nancy S, *Librn,* Museum of Fine Arts, Boston MA

Allen, Nancy S, *Librn,* Museum of Fine Arts, William Morris Hunt Memorial Library, Boston MA

Allen, Paul F, *Asst Prof,* Concordia College, Art Dept, Moorhead MN (S)

Allen, Reginald, *Cur of Gilbert & Sullivan Coll,* Pierpont Morgan Library, New York NY

Allen, Timothy S, *Dir,* Central Louisiana Art Association, Alexandria Museum Visual Art Center, Alexandria LA

Allen, Van S, *Academic Dean,* Tougaloo College, Art Collection, Tougaloo MS

Allen, William, *Chmn Dept of Art,* Arkansas State University Art Gallery, Jonesboro AR

Allen, William, *Chmn Dept,* Arkansas State University, Dept of Art, State University AR (S)

Allentuck, Marcia E, *Prof,* City University of New York, PhD Program in Art History, New York NY (S)

Alley, James, *Instructor,* Interlochen Arts Academy, Dept of Visual Art, Interlochen MI (S)

Alley, Jon, *Instructor,* Bucks County Community College, Fine Arts Dept, Newton PA (S)

Alley, Perry, *Treas,* Hudson Valley Art Association, White Plains NY

Allgood, C H, *Dir Exhib,* Memphis State University, University Gallery, Memphis TN

Allgood, Pat, *Cur Exhibits,* Texas Tech University Museum, Lubbock TX

Alling, Clarence, *Gallery Dir,* Waterloo Municipal Galleries, Waterloo IA

Allison, Clement, *Prof,* Tusculum College, Fine Arts Dept, Greeneville TN (S)

Allison, Glenn, *Cur,* University of British Columbia, Fine Arts Gallery, Vancouver BC

Allison, Michael, *Cur,* Southern Alleghenies Museum of Art, Loretto PA

Allison, Patricia, *VPres,* Woodmere Art Museum, Philadelphia PA

Allison, Zoe, *VPres & Gallery Coordr,* Columbus College, Experimental Gallery, Columbus GA

Allman, Anne, *Asst Prof,* School of the Ozarks, Dept of Art, Point Lookout MO (S)

Allo, Tony, *Asst Prof,* Indian River Community College, Fine Art Dept, Fort Pierce FL (S)

Allodi, M, *Asst Cur,* Royal Ontario Museum, Canadiana Gallery, Toronto ON

Allred, Osrael, *Chmn,* Snow College, Art Dept, Ephraim UT (S)

Allred, Rayma, *Office Mgr,* Springville Museum of Art, Springville UT

Allumbaugh, James, *Chmn Art Ed,* East Texas State University, Dept of Art, Commerce TX (S)

Allyn, Robert, *Pres,* Owatonna Arts Center, Owatonna MN

Almaguer, Regina, *Art Coordr,* San Francisco City and County Art Commission, San Francisco CA

Almquist, Robert, *Discipline Coordr,* Lewis-Clark State College, Art Dept, Lewiston ID (S)

Alpert, Diane L, *Cur,* Western Kentucky University, Kentucky Museum, Bowling Green KY

Alsdorf, James W, *First VPres,* Arts Club of Chicago Gallery, Chicago IL

Alsdorf, James W, *Pres,* Art Institute of Chicago, Antiquarian Society, Chicago IL

Alston, Robert, *Dir,* Southern Oregon College, Central Art Gallery, Ashland OR

Alston, Robert, *Chmn Dept Art,* Southern Oregon State College, Dept of Art, Ashland OR (S)

Alt, Gordon, *Asst Admin,* Pope-Leighey House, Mount Vernon VA

Alt, Gordon, *Asst Adminr,* Woodlawn Plantation, Mount Vernon VA

Alterman, Deborah, *Library Dir,* Moore College of Art Gallery, Library, Philadelphia PA

Altman, Elizabeth, *Educ Dir,* Washington County Museum of Fine Arts, Hagerstown MD

Altman, Patricia B, *Cur of Textiles & Folk Art,* University of California, Los Angeles, Museum of Cultural History, Los Angeles CA

Altschuler, Judy, *Admin Asst,* University of California, Santa Barbara, University Art Museum, Santa Barbara CA

Altshuler, Linda, *Assoc Dir,* B'nai B'rith Klutznick Museum, Washington DC

Alvare, Carlos J, *Prof,* Lehigh University, Dept of Art and Architecture, Bethlehem PA (S)

Alvarez, Jose B, *Instructor,* Inter American University of Puerto Rico, Dept of Art, San German PR (S)

Alvarez, P Pompilio, *Head Dept,* Catholic University of Puerto Rico, Dept of Fine Arts, Ponce PR (S)

Alviti, John V, *Exec Dir,* Atwater Kent Museum, Philadelphia PA

Alway, Richard, *Warden,* University of Toronto, Justina M Barnicke Gallery, Toronto ON

Ambasz, Emilio, *Pres,* The Architectural League, New York NY

Ambrose, Gail, *Recording Secy,* South County Art Association, Kingston RI

Ambrose, Gordon, *Caretaker & Watchman,* Moose Jaw Art Museum and National Exhibition Centre, History Museum, Moose Jaw SK

Ambrosia, Katherine, *Shop Mgr,* Carmel Mission and Gift Shop, Carmel CA

Ambrosino, Thomas, *Instructor,* Sullivan County Community College, Division of Commercial Art and Photography, Loch Sheldrake NY (S)

Amendola, Sal, *Instr,* Joe Kubert School of Cartoon and Graphic Art Inc, Dover NJ (S)

Amerson, L Price, *Dir,* University of California, Richard L Nelson Gallery, Davis CA

Ames, Kenneth L, *Advanced Studies Chmn,* Winterthur Museum and Gardens, Winterthur DE

Ames, Madge, *Treas,* Kennebec Valley Art Association, Harlow Gallery, Hallowell ME

Ames, M M, *Dir,* University of British Columbia, Museum of Anthropology, Vancouver BC

Ames, Samuel B, *Asst Prof,* Rhode Island College, Art Dept, Providence RI (S)

Ames Petersen, Nancy, *Dir,* Timken Art Gallery, San Diego CA

Amino, Eriko, *Slide Cur,* School of Visual Arts Library, New York NY

Amiot, Theresa, *Chmn Dept,* Elms College, Dept of Fine Arts, Chicopee MA (S)

Ammons, Betty, *Asst Librn,* United Methodist Historical Society, Library, Baltimore MD

Amoroso, L Louis, *Sr VPres,* AmeriTrust Company, Cleveland OH

Amos, Emma, *Asst Prof,* Rutgers, the State University of New Jersey, Mason Gross School of the Arts, New Brunswick NJ (S)

Amrhein, John K, *Univ Librn,* Kutztown University, Rohrbach Library, Kutztown PA

Amundson, Dale, *Dir Exhib,* University of Manitoba, Gallery III, Winnipeg MB

Amyx, Cuet, *Instructor,* Cuesta College, Art Dept, San Luis Obispo CA (S)

Ananian, Elissa, *Prof,* Salem State College, Art Dept, Salem MA (S)

Anawalt, Patricia, *Consulting Cur of Costumes & Textiles,* University of California, Los Angeles, Museum of Cultural History, Los Angeles CA

Andersen, Jeffrey W, *Dir,* Lyme Historical Society, Florence Griswold Museum, Old Lyme CT

Andersen, Marion, *Secy,* Mid-America Arts Alliance, Kansas City MO

Anderson, A Douglas, *Dir Educational Services,* University of Nebraska, Lincoln, Sheldon Memorial Art Gallery, Lincoln NE

Anderson, Albert A, *Chmn Dept,* Clark University, Dept of Visual & Performing Arts, Worcester MA (S)

Anderson, Arthur, *Assoc Prof,* York College of the City University of New York, Fine and Performing Arts, Jamaica NY (S)

Anderson, Arvie, *Pres,* Winnipeg Sketch Club, Winnipeg MB

Anderson, Berneal, *Registrar,* Joslyn Art Museum, Omaha NE

Anderson, Betsy, *Lectr,* Saint Joseph's University, Fine Arts Dept, Philadelphia PA (S)

Anderson, Betsy, *Gallery Co-Dir,* Art League, Alexandria VA

Anderson, Cathleen, *Registrar,* Cornell University, Herbert F Johnson Museum of Art, Ithaca NY

Anderson, Charles R, *Head Dept,* Castleton State College, Art Dept, Castleton VT (S)

Anderson, C Paul, *Dean Div Fine & Performing Arts,* Dixie College, Art Dept, Saint George UT (S)

Anderson, Daniel J, *Head Ceramic,* Southern Illinois University at Edwardsville, Dept of Art and Design, Edwardsville IL (S)

Anderson, David, *Dir Education,* The Design Schools, Art Institute of Houston, Houston TX (S)

Anderson, Dean, *Chmn,* Dulin Gallery of Art, Knoxville TN

Anderson, Dennis, *VPres,* Muttart Gallery Associates, Calgary AB

Anderson, Donald B, *Pres Board Trustees,* Roswell Museum and Art Center, Roswell NM

Anderson, Donald R, *Dir,* University of Louisville, Allen R Hite Art Institute, Louisville KY (S)

Anderson, Dorothea, *Cur,* Plymouth Antiquarian Society, Plymouth MA

Anderson, Ellen, *Instructor,* Saint Mary's College, Art Dept, Raleigh NC (S)

Anderson, Eric, *Faculty,* University of North Carolina-Charlotte, Creative Arts Dept, Charlotte NC (S)

Anderson, Evelyn E, *Assoc Prof,* Sam Houston State University, Art Dept, Huntsville TX (S)

Anderson, Frank J, *Dir,* Wofford College, Sandor Teszler Library Gallery, Spartanburg SC

Anderson, Ian A, *Actg Exec Dir,* United States Figure Skating Hall of Fame and Museum, Colorado Springs CO

Anderson, James C, *Cur,* University of Louisville, University of Louisville Photographic Archives, Louisville KY

Anderson, James P, *Faculty,* Saint Ambrose College, Art Dept, Davenport IA (S)

Anderson, James R, *Asst Prof,* Florida State University, Art Education Dept, Tallahassee FL (S)

Anderson, Jane, *VPres,* Floyd County Museum, New Albany IN

Anderson, Jeffrey C, *Asst Prof,* George Washington University, Dept of Art, Washington DC (S)

Anderson, Jerry, *Chmn,* University of California, Irvine, Studio Art Dept, Irvine CA (S)

Anderson, J M, *Pres,* Sunbury Shores Arts and Nature Centre, Inc, Saint Andrews NB

Anderson, Joan, *Cataloger,* California Institute of the Arts Library, Valencia CA

Anderson, John, *Dir,* College of Idaho, Blatchley Gallery, Caldwell ID

Anderson, Kay, *Adjunct Instr,* University of Northern Iowa, Dept of Art, Cedar Falls IA (S)

Anderson, Laurie, *Head Public Services,* Ponca City Library, Art Dept, Ponca City OK

Anderson, Leon, *Assoc Prof,* Saint Louis Community College at Forest Park, Fine Arts Dept, Saint Louis MO (S)

Anderson, Lowell, *Cur Decorative Arts,* Illinois State Museum of Natural History and Art, Springfield IL

Anderson, Maynard, *Prof,* Wartburg College, Dept of Art, Waverly IA (S)

Anderson, Nancy B, *Dir,* Museum of Arts and Sciences, Inc, Macon GA

Anderson, Neil, *Prof,* Bucknell University, Dept of Art, Lewisburg PA (S)

Anderson, Pat, *Pres & Dir,* Revelstoke Art Group, Revelstoke BC

Anderson, Patricia, *Assoc Cur American Art,* University of Rochester, Memorial Art Gallery, Rochester NY

Anderson, Patricia, *Dir Library,* Englewood Library, Fine Arts Dept, Englewood NJ

Anderson, Patricia M, *Cur Education,* Bowdoin College, Museum of Art & Peary-MacMillan Arctic Museum, Brunswick ME

Anderson, Patricia McGraw, *Dir,* University of Maine at Augusta Gallery, Augusta ME

Anderson, Paul L, *Cur Exhib & Sites,* Church of Jesus Christ of Latter-Day Saints, Museum of Church History and Art, Salt Lake City UT

Anderson, Peter, *Vis Assoc Prof,* Rochester Institute of Technology, School of Photographic Arts & Sciences, Rochester NY (S)

Anderson, Richard E, *Pres,* Aldrich Museum of Contemporary Art, Ridgefield CT

Anderson, Robert, *Prof,* West Virginia University, Division of Art, Morgantown WV (S)

Anderson, Ross C, *Pres,* Montgomery Museum of Fine Arts, Montgomery AL

Anderson, Ruth, *Public Information Officer,* University of British Columbia, Museum of Anthropology, Vancouver BC

Anderson, Ruth Ann, *Gallery Dir,* Orange County Center for Contemporary Art, Santa Ana CA

Anderson, Susan, *Asst Cur Costume and Textiles,* Philadelphia Museum of Art, Philadelphia PA

Anderson, Thomas Duneway, *Regent,* Mount Vernon Ladies' Association of the Union, Mount Vernon VA

Anderson, W T, *Chmn,* Humboldt State University, College of Creative Arts & Humanities, Arcata CA (S)

Anderton, Birgitta, *Conservator Textiles,* Fine Arts Museums of San Francisco, M H de Young Memorial Museum and California Palace of the Legion of Honor, San Francisco CA

Andraka, Judith, *Lectr,* Trinity College, Art Dept, Washington DC (S)

Andrea, Martha, *Instr,* Colby-Sawyer College, Art Dept, New London NH (S)

Andrejevic, Milet, *Instr,* New York Academy of Art, New York NY (S)

Andres, Glenn, *Asst Dir,* Middlebury College, Johnson Gallery, Middlebury VT

Andrew, David S, *Chmn,* University of New Hampshire, Dept of the Arts, Durham NH (S)

Andrews, James C, *Dir,* Rensselaer County Historical Society, Library, Troy NY

Andrews, Jean, *Pres,* Boothbay Region Art Foundation, Inc, Brick House Gallery, Boothbay Harbor ME

Andrews, John F, *Dir Research Activities,* Folger Shakespeare Library, Washington DC

Andrews, Jon Philip, *In Charge Art Coll,* Westinghouse Electric Corporation, Pittsburgh PA

Andrews, Mary, *Librn,* Peter and Catharine Whyte Foundation, Peter Whyte Gallery Library, Banff AB

Andrews, Nancy, *Librn,* San Diego Museum of Art, Art Reference Library, San Diego CA

Andrews, Stephenson B, *Cur,* Association for the Preservation of Virgina Antiquities, Richmond VA

Ashton, Robin, *Chief Conservator*, Montreal Museum of Fine Arts, Montreal PQ

Ashworth, Jo, *Pres*, Middletown Fine Arts Center, Middletown OH

Ashworth, Judie, *Supvr Guest Relations*, Franklin Mint Museum, Franklin Center PA

Asia, Caroli, *Admin Dir & Asst Cur*, Intermuseum Conservation Association, Oberlin OH

Asihene, Emmanuel V, *Chmn Dept*, Clark College, Dept of Art, Atlanta GA (S)

Asimakos, John, *Prof*, Mount Allison University, Fine Arts Dept, Sackville NB (S)

Atherly, Mary, *Registrar & Secy*, Iowa State University, Brunnier Gallery Museum, Ames IA

Atherton, Charles H, *Secy*, United States Commission of Fine Arts, Washington DC

Atkins, Bill, *Asst to Dir*, Arkansas Arts Center, Little Rock AR

Atkins, Bill, *Asst to Dir*, Arkansas Arts Center, Little Rock AR (S)

Atkins, Gregg T, *Coordr*, College of San Mateo Library, Art Division, San Mateo CA

Atkins, Hannah, *Coordr Sanamu African Gallery*, Oklahoma Center for Science and Art, Kirkpatrick Center, Oklahoma City OK

Atkins, Suzi, *Membership Coordr*, Fort Worth Art Museum, Fort Worth TX

Atkinson, David, *Dir Operations*, Owensboro Museum of Fine Art, Owensboro KY

Atkinson, Tracy, *Dir*, Wadsworth Atheneum, Hartford CT

Atkyns, Lee, *Dir*, Lee Atkyns Studio-Gallery, Duncansville PA

Attenborough, Debra, *Cur of Education*, Rodman Hall Arts Centre, Saint Catharines ON

Atwood, Raymond R, *Instructor*, Iowa Central Community College, Dept of Art, Fort Dodge IA (S)

Atz, Anne, *Pres*, Florida Artist Group Inc, Venice FL

Aubry, Diane, *Asst*, Musee du Quebec, Bibliotheque des Art, Quebec PQ

Auchstetter, RosAnn, *Reference-Visual Arts Specialist*, State University of New York at Purchase, Library, Purchase NY

Audrus, Lisa, *Asst Prof*, Portland State University, Dept of Art and Architecture, Portland OR (S)

Auerbach, Seymour, *Prof*, Catholic University of America, Dept of Architecture and Planning, Washington DC (S)

Auger, Genevieve, *Dir Exhibitions*, Musee du Seminaire de Quebec, Quebec PQ

Augspurger, Roger, *Head Dept*, Central Community College - Platte Campus, Creative and Social Cluster, Columbus NE (S)

August, Sandra, *Prof*, Cleveland Institute of Art, Cleveland OH (S)

Augusztiny, Roxana, *Registrar*, University of Washington, Thomas Burke Memorial Washington State Museum, Seattle WA

Aunspaugh, Richard, *Chmn*, Young Harris College, Dept of Art, Young Harris GA (S)

Auping, Michael, *Cur Contemporary Art*, State Art Museum of Florida, John & Mable Ringling Museum of Art, Sarasota FL

Aurand, Charles H, *Dean College Creative Arts*, Northern Arizona University, Art Gallery, Flagstaff AZ

Aurbach, Michael, *Instr*, Hamilton College, Art Dept, Clinton NY (S)

Ausfeld, Margaret, *Actg Cur*, Montgomery Museum of Fine Arts, Montgomery AL

Austin, Helen C, *Instr*, John C Calhoun State Community College, Art Dept, Decatur AL (S)

Austin, Helen C, *Dir*, John C Calhoun State Community College, Art Gallery, Decatur AL

Austin, Howard, *Instructor*, Milwaukee Area Technical College, Graphic & Applied Arts Division, Milwaukee WI (S)

Austin, Richard, *Secy*, Nantucket Historical Association, Fair Street Museum, Nantucket MA

Austin, Robert, *Asst Prof*, Kent State University, Stark Campus, School of Art, Canton OH (S)

Austin, Ted L, *Head Art Dept*, University of Mary Hardin-Baylor, Dept of Fine Arts, Belton TX (S)

Austin, William, *Cur Exhibits*, Institute of the Great Plains, Museum of the Great Plains, Lawton OK

Auth, Susan, *Cur Classical*, Newark Museum, Newark NJ

Authier, David, *Lectr*, California State Polytechnic University, Pomona, Art Dept, Pomona CA (S)

Autio, Rudy, *Prof*, University of Montana, Dept of Art, Missoula MT (S)

Auvil, Kenneth, *Graduate Program Coordr*, San Jose State University, Art Dept, San Jose CA (S)

Avakian, John, *Chmn*, Mount Ida Junior College, Art Dept, Newton Center MA (S)

Avant, Joanne, *Registrar*, The Haggin Museum, Stockton CA

Avara, Emma, *Bus Mgr*, Amarillo Art Center, Amarillo TX

Avdzej, Tamara, *Acquisitions Librn*, Kean College of New Jersey, Nancy Thompson Library, Union NJ

Avens, Irene, *Art Librn*, Godwin-Ternbach Museum, Paul Klapper Library, Flushing NY

Averill, Jill, *Instructor*, Northwestern Michigan College, Art Dept, Traverse City MI (S)

Averill, Norman, *Instr*, Northwestern Michigan College, Art Dept, Traverse City MI (S)

Aversperg, Ruth, *Cultural Dir*, Pointe Claire Cultural Centre, Pointe Claire PQ

Avery, Millie, *VPres*, Copper Village Museum & Arts Center, Anaconda MT

Avery, Virginia, *Pres*, National League of American Pen Women, Washington DC

Avgikos, Jan, *Visual Coll Cur*, Atlanta College of Art Library, Atlanta GA

Axelrod, Felice, *Public Affairs*, Museum of the City of New York, New York NY

Axthelm, Kenneth, *Chief AV Division*, Brooklyn Public Library, Art and Music Division, Brooklyn NY

Ay, Aimee L, *Registrar*, Potsdam Public Museum, Potsdam NY

Ayers, Laura E, *Gallery Dir*, Sumter Gallery of Art, Sumter SC

Ayers, L Philip, *Asst Prof*, Indiana University, Bloomington, School of Fine Arts, Bloomington IN (S)

Ayot, Barbara, *Secy*, Saint Louis Artists' Guild, Saint Louis MO

Azusenis, Helen V, *Planning & Research*, Cleveland Public Library, Fine Arts & Special Collections Dept, Cleveland OH

Azzolina, Ronald, *Sr VPres*, Security Pacific National Bank, Los Angeles CA

Baas, Jacob C, *VPres*, Springfield Art Center, Springfield OH

Baas, Jacquelynn, *Chief Cur*, Hood Museum of Art, Hanover NH

Babcock, Dick, *VPres*, Ravalli County Museum, Hamilton MT

Babcock, Lindy, *Instructor*, Saginaw Valley State College, Dept of Art and Design, University Center MI (S)

Baber, Lance, *Chmn Art Educ*, Herron School of Art, Indiana University-Purdue University, Indianapolis, Indianapolis IN (S)

Babineau-Simenauer, Suzanne, *Cur*, New York University, Photographic Archive, New York NY

Babineau-Simenauer, Suzanne, *Cur*, Institute of Fine Arts, Slide Collection, New York NY

Bach, Christine, *Library Asst*, North Carolina State University, Harrye Lyons Design Library, Raleigh NC

Bachinsky, Vladimir, *Instructor*, Woodstock School of Art, Inc, New York NY (S)

Backlund, Caroline, *Chmn Bd*, Art Libraries Society-North America, Tucson AZ

Backlund, Caroline H, *Reader Services Librn*, National Gallery of Art, Library, Washington DC

Bacon, Eleanor, *Pres*, Toledo Federation of Art Societies, Toledo OH

Bacon, Mardges, *Asst Prof*, Trinity College, Dept of Fine Arts, Hartford CT (S)

Bacon, Margaret, *Assoc Prof*, Daemen College, Art Dept, Amherst NY (S)

Bacon, Wallace, *Pres Board*, Harwood Foundation of the University of New Mexico, Taos NM

Bacot, H Parrott, *Dir & Cur*, Louisiana State University, Anglo-American Art Museum, Baton Rouge LA

Bacot, Jules de R, *Faculty*, North Florida Junior College, Dept Humanities & Art, Madison FL (S)

Badder, Susan S, *Dir Education*, Baltimore Museum of Art, Baltimore MD

Baden, Linda, *Editor*, Indiana University, Art Museum, Bloomington IN

Baden, M, *Assoc Prof*, University of Victoria, Dept of Visual Arts, Victoria BC (S)

Badier, Julie O, *Assoc Prof*, Western Maryland College, Art Dept, Westminster MD (S)

Baer, Roger, *Coordr Graphic Design*, Iowa State University, Dept of Art and Design, Ames IA (S)

Baetjer, Katharine, *Cur & Admin European Paintings*, Metropolitan Museum of Art, New York NY

Bageris, John, *Chmn Fine Arts Dept*, Art Institute of Boston, Boston MA (S)

Baggett, William C, *Chmn*, University of Southern Mississippi, Dept of Art, Hattiesburg MS (S)

Bagley, Bill, *Assoc Prof*, Texas Tech University, Dept of Art, Lubbock TX (S)

Bagnatori, Paola, *Dir of Educ*, Museo Italo Americano, San Francisco CA

Bahauddeen, Muneer, *Asst Preparator*, University of Chicago, David and Alfred Smart Gallery, Chicago IL

Bahling, Eugene, *Chmn Crafts*, Edinboro University of Pennsylvania, Art Dept, Edinboro PA (S)

Bahr, David, *Assoc Prof*, Community College of Baltimore, Dept of Fine & Applied Arts, Liberty Campus, Baltimore MD (S)

Bahus, Mary, *Sales Mgr*, Walters Art Gallery, Baltimore MD

Baier, Georgia, *Asst to Dir*, Beaumont Art Museum, Beaumont TX

Baigell, Matthew, *Prof*, Rutgers, the State University of New Jersey, Graduate Program in Art History, New Brunswick NJ (S)

Bailey, Betty, *Corresp Secy*, Monterey Peninsula Museum of Art, Monterey CA

Bailey, Bruce E, *Exec Dir*, Saint Bernard Foundation and Monastery, Miami Beach FL

Bailey, Forrest, *Conservator*, Atkins Museum of Fine Art, Kansas City MO

Bailey, Jann, *Education Officer*, Art Gallery of Peterborough, Peterborough ON

Bailey, J Terry, *Honorary Cur Burmese Coll*, Denison University Art Gallery, Granville OH

Bailey, Linda, *Membership*, University of Kansas, Spencer Museum of Art, Lawrence KS

Bailey, Nolan, *Asst Prof*, Northwestern State University of Louisiana, Dept of Art, Natchitoches LA (S)

Bailey, Rebecca, *Instr*, Peace College, Art Dept, Raleigh NC (S)

Bailey, Robert J, *Dir Historic Preservation*, Mississippi Department of Archives and History, State Historical Museum, Jackson MS

Bailey, Roger, *Assoc Prof*, Saint Lawrence University, Dept of Fine Arts, Canton NY (S)

Bailey, Walter J, *Chmn*, Baker University, Dept of Art, Baldwin City KS (S)

Bailey, Willis, *Cur Oriental Art*, Zanesville Art Center, Zanesville OH

Bailin, Hella, *Treas*, Associated Artists of New Jersey, Pittstown NJ

Bain, A, *Instr*, David Thompson University Centre, Visual Arts Dept, Nelson BC (S)

Bain-Smith, Pricilla, *Cur*, Phillips University, Grace Phillips Johnson Art Gallery, Enid OK

Bain-Smith, Pricilla, *Assoc Prof*, Phillips University, Dept of Art, Enid OK (S)

Bair, Miles, *Dir*, Illinois Wesleyan University, School of Art, Bloomington IL (S)

Baird, Genevieve, *VPres*, Bay Area Art Conservation Guild, Oakland CA

Baird, John, *Photographer*, Art Research Center, Kansas City MO

Baird, Josiah, *Art Dept Chmn*, Elizabeth City State University, Dept of Art, Elizabeth City NC (S)

Baird, Mary Jane, *Instructor*, Delta State University, Dept of Art, Cleveland MS (S)

Baird, Thomas P, *Prof*, Trinity College, Dept of Fine Arts, Hartford CT (S)

Bajko, Daria, *Admin Dir*, Ukrainian Museum, New York NY

Baker, Bernard W, *Chmn*, California State University, Dominguez Hills, Art Dept, Carson CA (S)

Baker, Bill, *Librn,* Norfolk Public Library, Feldman Fine Arts & Audio Visual Dept, Norfolk VA

Baker, Carolyn, *Member,* The Loading Dock Gallery, Boston MA

Baker, Cassandra, *Executive Dir,* Arts Council of Spartanburg County, Inc, Spartanburg Arts Center, Spartanburg SC

Baker, David R, *Instr,* Southwestern Michigan College, Communications-Humanitites Dept, Dowagiac MI (S)

Baker, Don, *Head Librn,* Willard Library, Dept of Fine Arts, Evansville IN

Baker, Edward R, *Division Dean,* Orange Coast College, Division of Fine Arts, Costa Mesa CA (S)

Baker, Gary, *Prof,* Polk Community College, Division of Communications and Fine Arts, Winter Haven FL (S)

Baker, Howard H, *Chmn,* United States Senate Commission on Art and Antiquities, Washington DC

Baker, James, *Assoc Prof,* Providence College, Art and Art History Dept, Providence RI (S)

Baker, John W, *Chmn,* Francis Marion College, Fine & Applied Arts Dept, Florence SC (S)

Baker, June, *Cur,* Santa Cruz Art League, Inc, Santa Cruz CA

Baker, Loren, *Instr,* Roberts Wesleyan College, Fine Arts Division, Art Dept, Rochester NY (S)

Baker, Marg, *Secy,* South Peace Art Society, Dawson Creek Art Gallery, Dawson Creek BC

Baker, Marilyn, *Chmn Art History,* University of Manitoba, School of Art, Winnipeg MB (S)

Baker, Martha B, *Dir,* Wilkes Art Gallery, North Wilkesboro NC

Baker, Mary, *Assoc Dean,* Cleveland State Community College, Dept of Art, Cleveland TN (S)

Baker, Robert, *VPres,* The Friends of Photography, Carmel CA

Baker, Robert, *Cur Mammalogy & Living Tissues,* Texas Tech University Museum, Lubbock TX

Baker, Roger, *Instr,* Clark College, Art Dept, Vancouver WA (S)

Baker, Sherry, *Secy & Coordr,* Community Arts Council of Chilliwack, Chilliwack BC

Baker, Tom, *Asst Preparator and Designer,* University of Kentucky, Art Museum, Lexington KY

Baker, T R, *Assoc Prof,* Arkansas State University, Dept of Art, State University AR (S)

Baker, William, *Cur of Military History,* Tennessee State Museum, Nashville TN

Baker, William, *Dir Div Humanities,* Philadelphia Community College, Dept of Fine Arts, Philadelphia PA (S)

Bakes, Alan, *Chmn Board,* Visual Arts Ontario, Toronto ON

Bakker, Dirk, *Photographer,* Detroit Institute of Arts, Detroit MI

Bakovych, A, *Asst Prof,* Northern Arizona University, Art Dept, Flagstaff AZ (S)

Balakier, Ann, *Instr,* University of South Dakota, Dept of Art, Vermillion SD (S)

Balanis, Beverly, *Volunteer Coordr,* Palo Alto Cultural Center, Palo Alto CA

Balch, Grace, *Cur,* Columbus and Lowndes County Historical Society Museum, Columbus MS

Balderacchi, Arthur, *Assoc Prof,* University of New Hampshire, Dept of the Arts, Durham NH (S)

Balderson, Lance, *Instr,* Ocean City Arts Center, Ocean City NJ (S)

Baldwin, DeWitt C, *Pres College,* Earlham College, Leeds Gallery, Richmond IN

Baldwin, Harold L, *Cur,* Middle Tennessee State University, Photographic Gallery, Murfreesboro TN

Baldwin, Robert A, *Assoc Prof,* Vanderbilt University, Dept of Fine Arts, Nashville TN (S)

Baldwin, Russell W, *Gallery Dir,* Palomar Community College, Boehm Gallery, San Marcos CA

Baldwin, Russell W, *Assoc Prof,* Palomar College, Art Dept, San Marcos TX (S)

Bale, Denise, *Travel Publications Specialist,* Utah Travel Council, Salt Lake City UT

Balen, Samuel T, *Executive Dir,* National Council of Architectural Registration Boards, Washington DC

Bales, Richard, *Asst to Dir Music,* National Gallery of Art, Washington DC

Balestrieri, Madonna, *Asst Prof,* Cardinal Stritch College, Art Dept, Milwaukee WI (S)

Balf, Oliver, *Painting,* Montserrat School of Visual Art, Beverly MA (S)

Balken, Debra, *Cur Art,* Berkshire Museum, Pittsfield MA

Balken, William R, *Registrar,* University of Utah, Utah Museum of Fine Arts, Salt Lake City UT

Balkman, Kathy, *Art Dir,* Federal Reserve Bank of Minneapolis, Minneapolis MN

Ball, Isabel, *Dean,* Our Lady of the Lake University, Dept of Art, San Antonio TX (S)

Ball, Joyce, *University Librn,* California State University, Sacramento, Library, Humanities Reference and Media Services Center, Sacramento CA

Ball, Kathy, *Registrar,* Lafayette Natural History Museum, Planetarium and Nature Station, Lafayette LA

Ball, Lucile, *Librn,* University of Miami, Reference Library, Coral Gables FL

Ball, Stephen, *VChmn,* Fraunces Tavern Museum, New York NY

Ballance, Stephen, *Instructor,* Northwestern Michigan College, Art Dept, Traverse City MI (S)

Ballantine, Barbara, *Admin Asst,* Decatur House, Washington DC

Ballard, Ann, *Children's Librn,* Lee County Library, Tupelo MS

Ballard, Carol, *Coordr Cultural Affairs,* Blount Inc, Montgomery AL

Ballard, L William, *VChmn,* Walter Cecil Rawls Museum, Courtland VA

Ballard, Thomas H, *Dir,* Plainfield Public Library, Plainfield NJ

Ballay, Joseph, *Head,* Carnegie-Mellon University, Dept of Design, Pittsburgh PA (S)

Ballentine, Don M, *Head Dept,* Atlanta Area Technical School, Dept of Commercial Art, Atlanta GA (S)

Ballinger, Barbara, *Clerical Asst,* Ball State University, Architecture Library, Muncie IN

Ballinger, James K, *Dir,* Phoenix Art Museum, Phoenix AZ

Ballon, Joan, *Asst Prof,* Florida State University, Art Dept, Tallahassee FL (S)

Balogh, Anthony, *Instructor,* Madonna College, Art Dept, Livonia MI (S)

Balogh, Christa, *Instr,* Southeastern Community College, Dept of Fine and Performing Arts, Whiteville NC (S)

Balossi, John, *Instructor,* University of Puerto Rico, Dept of Fine Arts, Rio Piedras PR (S)

Balsiger, B, *Instructor,* Indiana University of Pennsylvania, Dept of Art and Art Education, Indiana PA (S)

Balthaser, Susan, *Admin Asst,* Museum of Our National Heritage, Lexington MA

Balzekas, Stanley, *Pres,* Balzekas Museum of Lithuanian Culture, Chicago IL

Banasiak, John, *Asst Prof,* University of South Dakota, Dept of Art, Vermillion SD (S)

Banda, Juan Jose Barragan, *Instructor,* University of Puerto Rico, Dept of Fine Arts, Rio Piedras PR (S)

Bandy, Mary Lea, *Dir Dept Film,* Museum of Modern Art, New York NY

Bandy, Nancy, *Vis Prof,* Victoria College, Victoria TX (S)

Bandy, Ronald, *Chmn Two-Dimensional Studies,* Bowling Green State University, School of Art, Bowling Green OH (S)

Baniassao, E, *Dean,* Technical University of Nova Scotia, Faculty of Architecture, Halifax NS (S)

Banister, Amy, *Dir Communications,* Contemporary Arts Center, Cincinnati OH

Banister, Amy, *Dir Communications,* Contemporary Arts Center, Library, Cincinnati OH

Banks, Brenda, *Librn,* Edmonton Art Gallery, Library, Edmonton AB

Banks, John, *Head Dept,* Northwest Community College, Powell WY (S)

Banks, Paul N, *Pres,* American Institute for Conservation of Historic and Artistic Works (AIC), Washington DC

Banks, R K, *Dean,* University of Waterloo, Fine Arts Dept, Waterloo ON (S)

Banowicz, Mary Kay, *Instr,* Mount Marty College, Art Dept, Yankton SD (S)

Bantel, Linda, *Assoc Cur,* Pennsylvania Academy of the Fine Arts, Galleries, Philadelphia PA

Bantle, Pat, *Gallery Shop Dir,* Ann Arbor Art Association, Ann Arbor MI

Bapst, Sarah, *Asst Prof,* University of North Carolina at Chapel Hill, Art Dept, Chapel Hill NC (S)

Baptie, Sue M, *Dir,* Vancouver City Archives and Library, Vancouver BC

Baptist, Francis C, *Prof,* Clarion University of Pennsylvania, Dept of Art, Clarion PA (S)

Barbash, Steven, *Asst Prof,* State University of New York College at Cortland, Art Dept, Cortland NY (S)

Barbeau, Lynn, *Cur,* Macdonald Stewart Art Centre, Guelph ON

Barbeau, R, *Secy,* Musee d'Art de Saint-Laurent, Saint-Laurent PQ

Barber, Ardis I, *Pres,* Dahl Fine Arts Center, Rapid City SD

Barber, Jall, *Faculty,* Columbia College, Dept of Physical Creative and Performing Arts, Columbia CA (S)

Barber, Ronald L, *Dir,* Museum of the Philadelphia Civic Center, Philadelphia PA

Barber, William D, *Dir,* Region of Peel Museum and Art Gallery, Brampton ON

Barbu, Leona, *Secy,* Saint Mary's Romanian Orthodox Church, Romanian Ethnic Museum, Cleveland OH

Bard, Joellen, *Exec Dir,* Association of Artist-Run Galleries, New York NY

Barde, Alex, *Assoc Prof,* Pittsburg State University, Art Dept, Pittsburg KS (S)

Bardes, Leo N, *Dir Fine Arts,* College of San Mateo, Art, Commercial Art & Photo Art, San Mateo CA (S)

Barefoot, Paul D, *Dir Traveling Exhibitions,* Museum of Holography, New York NY

Baremore, R E, *Dir,* Louisiana State Exhibit Museum, Shreveport LA

Baren, Anne H, *Adminr,* Katonah Gallery, Katonah NY

Barensfeld, Mark, *Instructor,* Art Academy of Cincinnati, Cincinnati OH (S)

Barger, Jan, *Instr,* Arkansas Arts Center, Little Rock AR (S)

Barilleaux, Rene Daul, *Cur Collection,* Museum of Holography, New York NY

Barilleaux, Rene P, *Cur Collections & Exhibitions,* Museum of Holography, New York NY

Barker, Jimmy H, *Assoc Prof,* Sam Houston State University, Art Dept, Huntsville TX (S)

Barker, Norman, *VPres,* Los Angeles County Museum of Art, Los Angeles CA

Barker, R Mildred, *Cur Manuscripts,* Shaker Museum, Poland Spring ME

Barkley, Alan, *Dean,* Nova Scotia College of Art and Design, Halifax NS (S)

Barkley, Alan, *Dean,* Nova Scotia College of Art and Design, Anna Leonowens Gallery, Halifax NS

Barletta, Barbara, *Asst Prof,* University of Florida, Dept of Art, Gainesville FL (S)

Barley, Mary L, *Chmn,* Howard College, Art Dept, Big Spring TX (S)

Barlow, Lois, *Instructor,* Dunedin Fine Arts and Cultural Center, Dunedin FL (S)

Barnard, Robert, *Prof,* University of North Carolina at Chapel Hill, Art Dept, Chapel Hill NC (S)

Barnes, Barry R, *Head Dept,* College of the Siskiyous, Art Dept, Weed CA (S)

Barnes, Becky, *Pres,* Seattle Weaver's Guild, Seattle WA

Barnes, Carl F, *Prof,* Oakland University, Dept of Art and Art History, Rochester MI (S)

Barnes, Gary, *Asst Prof,* Arkansas Tech University, Dept of Art, Russellville AR (S)

Barnes, Jairus B, *Dir History Museum,* Western Reserve Historical Society, Cleveland OH

Barnes, Kathy Chan, *Festivals Committee Dir,* American Society of Artists, Inc, Chicago IL

Barnes, Marty, *Asst Prof,* Rice University, Dept of Art and Art History, Houston TX (S)

Barnes, Patricia P, *Registrar,* Montclair Art Museum, Museum Art Classes, Montclair NJ (S)

Barnes, Raymond S, *Asst Prof,* Muhlenberg College, Dept of Art, Allentown PA (S)

Barnes, Robert, *Prof,* Indiana University, Bloomington, School of Fine Arts, Bloomington IN (S)

Barnes, Russell, *Dir Development,* Museum of Contemporary Art, Chicago IL

Barnes, Sharron, *Assoc Prof,* Gulf Coast Community College, Division of Fine Arts, Panama City FL (S)

Barnes, Susan, *Cataloger,* Mount Angel Abbey & Seminary Library, Saint Benedict OR

Barnes, Ted, *Instructor,* Ouachita Baptist University, Dept of Art, Arkadelphia AR (S)

Barnes, Thomas, *Asst Prof,* University of Alabama, Art Dept, Tuscaloosa AL (S)

Barnes, W D, *Asst Prof,* College of William and Mary, Dept of Fine Arts, Williamsburg VA (S)

Barnett, Alison, *Travel Development Specialist,* Utah Travel Council, Salt Lake City UT

Barnett, Ed Willis, *Pres & Cur,* Alabama Museum of Photography, Birmingham AL

Barnett, John D, *Asst Cur,* United States Navy, Combat Art Gallery, Washington DC

Barnett, Loretta, *Instr,* Colby-Sawyer College, Art Dept, New London NH (S)

Barnett, Vivian Endicott, *Cur,* Solomon R Guggenheim Museum, New York NY

Barnette, James, *Instructor,* Southeastern Oklahoma State College, Art Dept, Durant OK (S)

Barnhart, Ruth, *Instr,* Coos Art Museum, Coos Bay OR (S)

Barnitz, Downing, *Dir,* Florida Southern College, Melvin Art Gallery, Lakeland FL

Barnitz, Downing, *Coordr Dept,* Florida Southern College, Art Dept, Lakeland FL (S)

Barnum, Amy, *Librn,* New York State Historical Association, Library, Cooperstown NY

Barnum, Robert, *Asst Prof,* Saint Francis College, Art Dept, Fort Wayne IN (S)

Barr, David, *Prof,* Macomb County Community College, Art Dept, Warren MI (S)

Barr, Donald, *Assoc Prof,* School of the Ozarks, Dept of Art, Point Lookout MO (S)

Barr, Jeannot, *VPres,* Dallas Public Library, Dallas Print and Drawing Society, Dallas TX

Barr, Linda, *Librn & Archivist,* McMichael Canadian Collection, Library, Kleinburg ON

Barraclough, Dennis, *Assoc Prof,* Daemen College, Art Dept, Amherst NY (S)

Barrager, Roberta, *Assoc Prof,* Pierce College, Art Dept, Woodland Hills CA (S)

Barrett, Barbara, *Dir,* Toronto School of Art, Toronto ON (S)

Barrett, Bill, *Pres,* Sculptors Guild, Inc, New York NY

Barrett, Maureen, *Secy,* Sierra Nevada Museum of Art, Reno NV

Barrett, Nancy, *Cur Photography,* New Orleans Museum of Art, New Orleans LA

Barrett, Robert, *Dir,* Fresno Arts Center, Fresno CA

Barrett, Terry, *Asst Prof,* Ohio State University, Dept of Art Education, Columbus OH (S)

Barrett, Thomas R, *Dir Art Center,* Saint Paul's School, Art Center in Hargate, Concord NH

Barrett, Timothy, *Instr,* Oxbow Center for the Arts, Saugatuck MI (S)

Barrett, William, *Lecturer,* Columbia University, School of the Arts, Division of Painting & Sculpture, New York NY (S)

Barrett, William O, *Dean,* Corcoran School of Art, Washington DC (S)

Barrick, Ken, *Prof,* New Mexico State University, Art Dept, Las Cruces NM (S)

Barrie, Brooke, *Acad Dir,* Johnson Atelier Technical Institute of Sculpture, Mercerville NJ (S)

Barrie, Dennis, *Dir,* Contemporary Arts Center, Cincinnati OH

Barrie, Dennis, *Dir,* Archives of American Art, Midwest Area Center, New York NY

Barrish, A Jos, *Asst Prof,* University of Dayton, Fine Arts Division, Dayton OH (S)

Barrish, Esther, *Assoc Prof,* Jersey City State College, Art Dept, Jersey City NJ (S)

Barron, Clem, *Admin Dean,* Alfred C Glassell School of Art, Houston TX (S)

Barron, Deana, *Asst to Dir,* First Street Forum, Saint Louis MO

Barron, Ida, *VPres,* Key West Art and Historical Society, Key West FL

Barron, Roslyn, *Assoc Prof,* University of Massachusetts at Boston, Art Dept, Boston MA (S)

Barrows, Candi, *Secy,* University of Vermont, Robert Hull Fleming Museum, Burlington VT

Barrows, Julie B, *Dir & Cur,* Danbury Scott-Fanton Museum and Historical Society, Inc, Library, Danbury CT

Barsch, Virginia, *Prof,* Moorhead State University, Dept of Art, Moorhead MN (S)

Bartel, Marvin, *Prof,* Goshen College, Art Dept, Goshen IN (S)

Bartels, Carl, *Prof,* Springfield College, Dept of Visual and Performing Arts, Springfield MA (S)

Barter, Judith, *Cur,* Amherst College, Mead Art Museum, Amherst MA

Barth, Charles, *Prof,* Mount Mercy College, Art Dept, Cedar Rapids IA (S)

Barth, Frances, *Faculty,* Sarah Lawrence College, Dept of Art, Bronxville NY (S)

Barth, Miles, *Cur of Coll,* International Center of Photography, New York NY

Bartholomew, Gail, *Reference,* Maui Community College Library, Kahului HI

Bartholomew, Terese Tse, *Cur Indian Art,* Asian Art Museum of San Francisco, Avery Brundage Collection, San Francisco CA

Bartko, George, *Assoc Prof,* Saint Louis Community College at Florissant Valley, Dept of Art, Ferguson MO (S)

Bartle, Dorothy Budd, *Cur Coins,* Newark Museum, Newark NJ

Bartlebaugh, Eloise, *Tour Coordr,* The Bradford Museum, Niles IL

Bartlett, Christopher, *Dir,* Towson State University, The Holtzman Art Gallery, Towson MD

Bartlett, Christopher, *Prof,* Maryland College of Art and Design, Silver Spring MD (S)

Bartlett, Jack, *Head,* Mississippi State University, Art Dept, Mississippi State MS (S)

Bartlett, Lewis C, *Photographer,* University of Georgia, Dept of Art Visual Center, Athens GA

Bartley, Joseph F, *Pres,* Peoria Historical Society, Peoria IL

Bartley, Margaret, *Asst Librn,* Boston Architectural Center, Memorial Library, Boston MA

Bartner, Howard C, *Instr,* Johns Hopkins University, School of Medicine, Dept of Art as Applied to Medicine, Baltimore MD (S)

Bartolomucci, Margaret, *First Asst Music and Arts Services,* Berkshire Athenaeum, Pittsfield MA

Barton, Brigid S, *Dir,* University of Santa Clara, de Saisset Museum, Santa Clara CA

Barton, Brigid S, *Asst Prof,* University of Santa Clara, Fine Arts Dept, Santa Clara CA (S)

Barton, James, *Asst Dir,* Johnson Atelier Technical Institute of Sculpture, Mercerville NJ (S)

Barton, Ruth, *Reference Librn,* Detroit Public Library, Fine Arts Dept, Detroit MI

Bartsch, Martha, *Instructor,* Pace University, Dept of Art & Design, Pleasantville NY (S)

Baruzzi, Peter B, *Chmn,* Skidmore College, Dept of Art, Saratoga Springs NY (S)

Basch, Odile, *Mgr Cultural Affairs,* Philip Morris Incorporated, New York NY

Bascom, Mansfield, *Dir,* Wharton Esherick Museum, Paoli PA

Bascom, Ruth E, *Pres,* Wharton Esherick Museum, Paoli PA

Basile, Ken, *Dir,* Salisbury State College, Wildfowl Art Museum, Salisbury MD

Basiuk, Emil, *Pres,* Ukrainian National Museum and Library, Chicago IL

Baspuin, Gertrude, *Administrative Asst,* Midwest Museum of American Art, Elkhart IN

Bassett, Hilary D, *Dir Midland Art Council,* Midland Center for the Arts, Midland MI (S)

Bassett, Jerry, *Exhib Coordr,* University of South Florida, Art Galleries, Tampa FL

Bassett, Mary, *Librn,* Brandywine River Museum, Library, Chadds Ford PA

Bassham, Ben, *Div Coordr Art History,* Kent State University, School of Art, Kent OH (S)

Bassist, Donald H, *Pres,* Bassist College, Collections Library, Portland OR

Bastian, Duane, *Faculty,* University of Toledo, Dept of Art, Art Education and Art History, Toledo OH (S)

Bata-Hyde, Patti, *School Coordr,* Oklahoma Art Center Annex and Art School, Oklahoma City OK (S)

Batchelor, Anthony, *Chmn,* Art Academy of Cincinnati, Cincinnati OH (S)

Batchelor, Elizabeth, *Conservator,* Cincinnati Art Museum, Cincinnati OH

Batdorff, Jon, *Asst Prof,* Johnson State College, Dept Fine Arts, Johnson VT (S)

Bates, Craig D, *Cur Ethnography,* Yosemite Collections, Yosemite National Park CA

Bates, Dorothy, *Instructor,* Charles Stewart Mott Community College, Fine Arts Division, Flint MI (S)

Bates, Pattsy L L, *Instr,* Middlesex Community College, Fine Arts Dept, Middletown CT (S)

Bates, P Martin, *Prof,* University of Victoria, Dept of Visual Arts, Victoria BC (S)

Batis, Robert, *Dir,* Charles B Goddard Center for the Visual and Performing Arts, Ardmore OK

Batkin, Jonathan, *Actg Cur Taylor Mus,* Colorado Springs Fine Arts Center, Colorado Springs CO

Bator, John S, *Instr,* Lincoln University, Dept Fine Arts, Jefferson City MO (S)

Batson, Gayle, *Instr,* Arkansas Arts Center, Little Rock AR (S)

Battenfield, Jackie, *Dir,* Rotunda Gallery, Brooklyn NY

Battisti, Eugenio, *Evan Pugh Prof,* Pennsylvania State University, University Park, Dept of Art History, University Park PA (S)

Batty, Ellen, *Circulation Librn,* Athenaeum of Philadelphia, Philadelphia PA

Batzka, Stephen, *Assoc Prof,* Manchester College, Art Dept, North Manchester IN (S)

Baucher, Heline, *Guide,* Musee des Augustines de l'Hotel Dieu of Quebec, Quebec PQ

Baudains, Linton, *Chmn Art Committee,* Alcan Smelters and Chemicals Limited, Montreal PQ

Bauer, Ann, *Dir,* Vermilion County Museum Society, Danville IL

Bauer, Liz, *Cur,* Hubbell Trading Post, Ganado AZ

Bauer, Marlene, *Instructor,* Marylhurst College, Art Dept, Marylhurst OR (S)

Bauer, Richard G, *Dir,* Capital University, Schumacher Gallery, Columbus OH

Bauer, Robert J, *Concentration Chmn,* University of Wisconsin-Green Bay, Visual Arts Dept, Green Bay WI (S)

Bauerle, Babette, *Library Asst,* Bryn Mawr College, Art and Archaeology Library, Bryn Mawr PA

Baugh, Susan, *Photographer Asst,* Georgia State University, Art Dept, Visual Resource Library & Reading Room, Atlanta GA

Bauman, Margaret, *Dir,* Carnegie-Mellon University, Forbes Street Gallery, Pittsburgh PA

Bauman, Patricia, *Pres,* G G Drayton Club, Salem OH

Bauman, Thomas, *VPres,* G G Drayton Club, Salem OH

Baumann, Edward, *Assoc Prof,* University of Missouri, Art History and Archaeology Dept, Columbia MO (S)

Baumann, Richard, *Cur Renaissance & Modern Art,* University of Missouri, Museum of Art and Archaeology, Columbia MO

Baur, John I H, *Consultant,* Terra Museum of American Art, Evanston IL

Bavolack, Marie, *Lectr,* Tunxis Community College, Graphic Design Dept, Farmington CT (S)

Bavolar, Thomas A, *Treas,* New Jersey Watercolor Society, South Orange NJ

Bavor, Nancy C, *Registrar & Asst Cur,* Stanford University, Museum of Art & Art Gallery, Stanford CA

Baxter, Jane, *Cur Collections,* Santa Barbara Museum of Art, Santa Barbara CA

Baxter, Joseph, *Treas,* Woodmere Art Museum, Philadelphia PA

Baxter, Paula, *Assoc Librn Reference,* Museum of Modern Art, Library, New York NY

Baxter, Terrell, *Mgr Museum Shop,* Philadelphia Museum of Art, Philadelphia PA

Bay, Sonja, *Librn,* Solomon R Guggenheim Museum, Library, New York NY

Bayard, Ivy, *Librn,* Temple University, Tyler School of Art Library, Philadelphia PA

Bayer, Jeffrey J, *Chmn Art & Art History Dept,* University of Alabama in Huntsville, School of Arts, Humanities & Science, Huntsville AL (S)

Bayer, Jeffrey J, *Deputy Dir,* University of Alabama in Huntsville, Gallery of Art, Huntsville AL

Bayersdorfer, Frederick S, *Dir,* Portsmouth Museums, Community Arts Center Division, Portsmouth VA

Bayless, Diane, *Asst Registrar,* Sheldon Swope Art Gallery, Terre Haute IN

Bayless, Stephen, *Prof,* Georgia Southern College, Dept of Art, Statesboro GA (S)

Bayley, Christopher T, *Secy,* Corporate Council for the Arts, Seattle WA

Bayliss, George, *Pres,* National Association of Schools of Art and Design, Reston VA

Bayliss, George V, *Dean School,* University of Michigan, Ann Arbor, School of Art, Ann Arbor MI (S)

Baymiller, Joanna, *Deputy Dir Planning & Development,* Minnesota Museum of Art, Saint Paul MN

Bayreuther, Joanne, *Development Mgr,* Portland Museum of Art, Portland ME

Bayuzick, Dennis, *Assoc Prof,* University of Wisconsin-Parkside, Art Discipline, Kenosha WI (S)

Baz, Douglas, *Faculty,* Sarah Lawrence College, Dept of Art, Bronxville NY (S)

Beach, Dorothy, *Librn,* Trinity College Library, Washington DC

Beach, Robert M, *Dir,* Tome Parish Museum, Tome NM

Beale, Arthur, *Dir Conservation,* Harvard University, William Hayes Fogg Art Museum, Cambridge MA

Beale, H B, *Treas,* Chester County Historical Society, West Chester PA

Beale, Rebecca, *Secy,* Walter Cecil Rawls Museum, Courtland VA

Beale, Richard, *Chairman Exhibitions Committee,* State University of New York College at Geneseo, Bertha V B Lederer Gallery, Geneseo NY

Beale, William, *Dir,* College of Southern Idaho, Library, Twin Falls ID

Beall, Mary, *Head Programming Dept,* Englewood Library, Fine Arts Dept, Englewood NJ

Beals, Robert J, *Pres,* American Ceramic Society, Columbus OH

Beals, Stuart, *Instructor,* Johnson County Community College, Humanities Division, Overland Park KS (S)

Beam, Philip C, *Emeritus Prof,* Bowdoin College, Art Dept, Brunswick ME (S)

Beaman, Hope S, *Treasurer,* Greensboro Artists' League, Greensboro NC

Beaman, John R, *Pres,* Greensboro Artists' League, Greensboro NC

Beamer, Karl, *Asst Prof,* Bloomsburg University, Dept of Art, Bloomsburg PA (S)

Bean, Carole, *Instr,* Creighton University, Fine and Performing Arts Dept, Omaha NE (S)

Bean, Christopher, *Public Service,* Sweet Briar College, Martin C Shallenberger Art Library, Sweet Briar VA

Bean, Jacob, *Cur Drawings,* Metropolitan Museum of Art, New York NY

Bean, Sharon, *Museum Shop Adminr,* Buten Museum of Wedgwood, Merion PA

Beans, Geraldine, *Second VPres,* Arizona Watercolor Association, Phoenix AZ

Bear, James A, *Cur-Dir,* Monticello, Thomas Jefferson Memorial Foundation, Charlottesville VA

Beard, Rick, *Assoc Dir,* Hudson River Museum, Yonkers NY

Bearden, Jacqueline, *Library Dir,* Saint Augustine Historical Society, Library, Saint Augustine FL

Beardman, John, *Assoc Prof,* Oakland University, Dept of Art and Art History, Rochester MI (S)

Beardsley, Jack, *Second VPres,* Spectrum, Friends of Fine Art, Inc, Toledo OH

Beardsley, Jimmie, *Actg Administrator,* Rudolph Schaeffer School of Design, San Francisco CA (S)

Beardsley, Rosemary, *VPres,* Wayne Art Center, Wayne PA

Beardsley, Theodore S, *Dir,* Hispanic Society of America, Museum, New York NY

Bearer, Kathleen, *Community Outreach Coordr,* Southern Alleghenies Museum of Art, Loretto PA

Bearnson, Dorothy, *Prof,* University of Utah, Art Dept, Salt Lake City UT (S)

Beasley, Richard, *Prof,* Northern Arizona University, Art Dept, Flagstaff AZ (S)

Beattie, Brent, *Chief Preparator,* Burnaby Art Gallery, Burnaby BC

Beatty, Norman G, *VPres Media & Government Relations,* Colonial Williamsburg Foundation, Williamsburg VA

Beatty, Reen, *Secy,* Spectrum, Friends of Fine Art, Inc, Toledo OH

Beauchamp, Douglas, *Instructor,* Umpqua Community College, Fine & Performing Arts Dept, Roseburg OR (S)

Beauchamp, Toni, *Asst Dir,* University of Houston, Sarah Campbell Blaffer Gallery, Houston TX

Beaudette, Margaret, *Assoc Prof,* Elizabeth Seton College, Art Dept, Yonkers NY (S)

Beaudoin-Ross, Jacqueline, *Cur Costume,* McGill University, McCord Museum, Montreal PQ

Beck, Martha, *Dir,* The Drawing Center, New York NY

Beck, Mary, *Executive Dir,* Hoosier Salon Patrons Association, Hoosier Salon Art Gallery, Indianapolis IN

Beckelman, John, *Chmn Art Dept,* Coe College, Gordon Fennell Gallery & Marvin Cone Gallery, Cedar Rapids IA

Beckelman, John, *Chmn,* Coe College, Dept of Art, Cedar Rapids IA (S)

Becker, Adele, *Corresponding Secy,* Buffalo Society of Artists, Williamsville NY

Becker, S Johanna, *Chmn,* College of Saint Benedict, Art Dept, Saint Joseph MN (S)

Beckerdite, Luke, *Research Assoc,* Old Salem Inc, Museum of Early Southern Decorative Arts, Winston-Salem NC

Beckley, Kelly, *Pres,* Maude I Kerns Art Center, Henry Korn Gallery, Eugene OR

Beckley, R, *Tres,* Association of Collegiate Schools of Architecture, Washington DC

Beckman, Frederick S, *Chmn,* University of Notre Dame, Dept of Art, Art History & Design, Notre Dame IN (S)

Beckwith, Claudia, *Head Collections Management & Security,* Greenville County Museum of Art, Greenville SC

Bedard, Robert J, *Treas,* Art PAC, Washington DC

Bednarz, Phyllis, *Treasurer,* East Windsor Historical Society Inc, Scantic Academy Museum, East Windsor CT

Beebe, Brian, *VPres,* Santa Barbara Contemporary Arts Forum, Santa Barbara CA

Beebe, Marjorie H, *Dir,* Galleries of the Claremont Colleges, Claremont CA

Beeby, Tom, *Dir School Architecture,* University of Illinois at Chicago, College of Architecture, Art and Urban Planning, Chicago IL (S)

Beekman, Robert S, *VPres,* New York Historical Society, New York NY

Beer, Kenneth J, *Assoc Prof,* James Madison University, Dept of Art, Harrisonburg VA (S)

Beers, George, *Dean of Fine Arts,* De Anza College, Art Dept, Cupertino CA (S)

Begert, Jane, *Assoc Dir,* Portland Museum of Art, Portland ME

Begland, Mary Ann, *Asst Prof,* Rochester Institute of Technology, School of Art and Design, Rochester NY (S)

Begley, John, *Exec Dir,* Art Center Association, Louisville KY

Begley, John P, *Dir,* The New Harmony Gallery of Contemporary Art, New Harmony IN

Begley, Robert T, *Registrar,* Ontario College of Art, Toronto ON (S)

Beglo, Jo, *Reference and Coll Development Librn - Fine Arts and Architecture,* University of Waterloo, Dana Porter Arts Library, Waterloo ON

Begman, Bea, *Treas,* New York Artists Equity Association, Inc, New York NY

Begos, Jane D, *Interpretive Programs Asst,* John Jay Homestead State Historic Site, Katonah NY

Behl, Wolfgang, *Prof,* Hartford Art School of the University of Hartford, West Hartford CT (S)

Behm, Kim, *Adjunct Instr,* University of Northern Iowa, Dept of Art, Cedar Falls IA (S)

Behnken, William, *Secy,* Audubon Artists, Inc, New York NY

Behrens, Fred, *Head Dept,* Columbia State Community College, Dept of Art, Columbia TN (S)

Behrens, Vic, *Lectr,* McMurry College, Art Dept, Abilene TX (S)

Beiersdorfer, Ann, *Dir,* Xavier University, Emery Galleries, Cincinnati OH

Beighley, Lucy, *Pres,* Evanston Art Center, Evanston IL

Beil, Eloise, *Librn,* Staten Island Institute of Arts and Sciences, Library, Staten Island NY

Beilmann, Eric, *Lectr,* Rochester Institute of Technology, School of Art and Design, Rochester NY (S)

Beim, Elizabeth, *Development Officer,* Museum of the American Indian, New York NY

Beitzel, Ross, *Head,* Gloucester County College, Liberal Arts Dept, Sewell NJ (S)

Belasco, Ruth, *Asst Prof,* Spring Hill College, Fine Arts Dept, Mobile AL (S)

Belding, Camilla, *Exec Secy,* Pen and Brush, Inc, New York NY

Beldon, Jeanne, *Development,* Allentown Art Museum, Allentown PA

Belfi, John, *Instr,* Joe Kubert School of Cartoon and Graphic Art Inc, Dover NJ (S)

Belfort-Chalat, Jacqueline, *Dir,* Le Moyne College, Art Dept, Syracuse NY (S)

Belisle, James, *Asst Prof,* University of Toronto, Dept of Landscape Architecture, Toronto ON (S)

Bell, Barbara, *Registrar,* Huntsville Museum of Art, Huntsville AL

Bell, Byron, *Treas,* National Institute for Architectural Education, New York NY

Bell, Eugene, *Instr,* Cuyahoga Valley Art Center, Cuyahoga Falls OH (S)

Bell, Eunice, *Asst to Dir,* Cultural Art Center of Ocean City, Ocean City NJ

Bell, James B, *Dir,* New York Historical Society, New York NY

Bell, Janis, *Asst Prof,* Kenyon College, Art Dept, Gambier OH (S)

Bell, Kathy, *Instructor,* Bob Jones University, School of Fine Arts, Greenville SC (S)

Bell, Leslie B, *Assoc Prof,* Saint Ambrose College, Art Dept, Davenport IA (S)

Bell, Lucille, *Secy Bd of Dir,* New Muse Community Museum of Brooklyn, Inc, Brooklyn NY

Bell, Malcolm, *Chmn,* University of Virginia, McIntire Dept of Art, Charlottesville VA (S)

Bell, Mary, *Asst Librn,* The Buffalo Fine Arts Academy, Art Reference Library, Buffalo NY

Bell, Michael S, *Dir,* Midland Art Council, Midland MI

Bell, Patrick, *Museum Technician,* Brockton Art Museum, Brockton MA

Bell, Robert, *Instructor,* Umpqua Community College, Fine & Performing Arts Dept, Roseburg OR (S)

Bell, Timothy G, *Library Asst,* Santa Cruz Public Library, Art, Music, Film Dept, Santa Cruz CA

Bell, Trevor, *Prof,* Florida State University, Art Dept, Tallahassee FL (S)

Bell, Valerie Jackson, *Cur Exhibits,* Saint Augustine Historical Society, Oldest House and Museums, Saint Augustine FL

Bellah, Don, *Chmn,* Northwestern Oklahoma State University, Art Dept, Alva OK (S)

Bellavance, Leslie, *Instr,* Oxbow Center for the Arts, Saugatuck MI (S)

Beller, Yvonne, *Pres,* Marin Society of Artists Inc, Ross CA

Bellerby, Greg, *Chief Cur of Contemporary Art,* Art Gallery of Greater Victoria, Victoria BC

Bellingham, Susan, *Special Coll Librn,* University of Waterloo, Dana Porter Arts Library, Waterloo ON

Belous, Russell, *Chief Cur,* Historic Pensacola Preservation Board, West Florida Museum of History, Pensacola FL

Belson, Anne M, *In Charge Art Collection,* Federal Reserve Bank of Boston, Boston MA

Belz, Carl I, *Dir,* Brandeis University, Rose Art Museum, Waltham MA

Bemis, Hal L, *Pres,* Philadelphia Art Alliance, Philadelphia PA

Bemis, Schuyler, *Coordr Exhibitions,* Saint Anselm College, Manchester NH

Bemrends, Gin, *Secy,* Singing River Art Association Inc, L & N Railroad Depot Gallery, Pascagoula MS

Ben-Amos, Paula, *African Section Keeper of Coll,* University of Pennsylvania, University Museum of Archaeology & Anthropology, Philadelphia PA

Benbow, Kathy, *Secy,* Hill Country Arts Foundation, Ingram TX

Bencetic, Steve, *Prof,* Mansfield State College, Art Dept, Mansfield PA (S)

Bench, Laura, *Asst Prof,* Seton Hill College, Dept of Art, Greensburg PA (S)

Benckenstein, Eunice R, *VChmn,* Stark Museum of Art, Orange TX

Bendall, Louise, *Dir Development,* Virginia Museum, Danville Museum of Fine Arts and History, Danville VA

Bendel, D, *Head,* Northern Arizona University, Art Dept, Flagstaff AZ (S)

Bendel, Don, *Vis Prof,* Victor Valley College, Art Dept, Victorville CA (S)

Bendel, Rebecca, *Cur of Education,* Tyler Museum of Art, Tyler TX

Bender, Betty W, *Dir,* Spokane Public Library, Art Dept, Spokane WA

Bender, Jeff, *Lectr,* University of Evansville, Art Dept, Evansville IN (S)

Bender, Richard, *Dean Environmental Design,* University of California, Berkeley, College of Environmental Design, Berkeley CA (S)

Bender, Richard, *VPres,* New York Society of Architects, New York NY

Benedetti, Brian, *Instructor,* College Misericordia, Art Dept, Dallas PA (S)

Benedetti, Joan M, *Museum Librn,* Craft and Folk Art Museum, Library-Media Resource Center, Los Angeles CA

Benedict, Mary Jane, *Librn,* J B Speed Art Museum, Art Reference Library, Louisville KY

Benet, Hugh, *Pres,* Star-Spangled Banner Flag House Association, Baltimore MD

Bengtz, Lillian E, *Assoc Dir,* Art Complex Museum at Duxbury, Duxbury MA

Benham, Sarah, *Gallery Dir,* Swain School of Design, William W Crapo Gallery, New Bedford MA

Benio, Pauleve, *Instructor,* Adrian College, Art Dept, Adrian MI (S)

Benivegna, Vito, *Dept Head,* Belleville Area College, Art Dept, Belleville IL (S)

Benjamin, Carl, *Prof,* Pomona College, Art Dept, Claremont CA (S)

Benjamin, Lloyd W, *Chmn,* University of Arkansas at Little Rock, Dept of Art, Little Rock AR (S)

Bennardo, Frank, *Pres,* Boca Raton Center for the Arts, Inc, Boca Raton FL

Bennet, Anna, *Cur Textiles,* Fine Arts Museums of San Francisco, M H de Young Memorial Museum and California Palace of the Legion of Honor, San Francisco CA

Bennett, Alan, *Instr,* Utah State University, Dept of Art, Logan UT (S)

Bennett, Archie, *Instr,* Surry Community College, Art Dept, Dobson NC (S)

Bennett, Carl D, *Chmn Dept Humanities & Fine Arts,* Saint Andrews Presbyterian College, Art Program, Laurinburg NC (S)

Bennett, David, *Dept Head, Advertising Design,* The Design Schools, Art Institute of Houston, Houston TX (S)

Bennett, Don, *Chmn,* San Joaquin Delta College, Art Dept, Stockton CA (S)

Bennett, James, *Asst Prof,* Norwich University, Dept of Philosophy, Religion and Fine Arts, Northfield VT (S)

Bennett, K Sharon, *Librn,* Charleston Museum, Library, Charleston SC

Bennett, Leonie S, *Head,* Lasell Junior College, Art Dept, Auburndale MA (S)

Bennett, Paul, *Dir,* Stratford Art Association, Gallery Stratford, Stratford ON

Benning, Veronica, *Instructor,* Portland School of Art, Portland ME (S)

Benoit, Diane, *Instructor,* Atlanta College of Art, Atlanta GA (S)

Benoon, M D, *Faculty,* Humboldt State University, College of Creative Arts & Humanities, Arcata CA (S)

Bensch, Chris, *Cur of Decorative Arts,* Munson-Williams-Proctor Institute, Museum of Art, Utica NY

Bensen, James Q, *Secy,* The National Art Museum of Sport, New Haven CT

Benson, Anita, *Instructor,* Monterey Peninsula College, Art Dept, Monterey CA (S)

Benson, Barbara E, *Dir Libr,* Historical Society of Delaware, Library, Wilmington DE

Benson, Eugenia, *Fine Arts,* Silas Bronson Library, Art, Music & Theatre Dept, Waterbury CT

Benson, Jack, *Prof,* University of Massachusetts, Amherst, Art History Program, Amherst MA (S)

Benson, Kathryn, *Lectr,* McMurry College, Art Dept, Abilene TX (S)

Benson, Martha, *Dir,* Octagon Center for the Arts, Ames IA

Benson, Skip, *Wood Design,* California College of Arts and Crafts, Oakland CA (S)

Bentley, Eden R, *Librn,* Johnson Atelier Technical Institute of Sculpture, Library, Mercerville NJ

Bentley, T Keilor, *Dir,* Mount Allison University, Owens Art Gallery, Sackville NB

Bentz, Harry D, *Chmn Art Dept,* Shippensburg State College, Art Dept, Shippensburg PA (S)

Berard, Guy, *Prof,* Saint Lawrence University, Dept of Fine Arts, Canton NY (S)

Berch, Helen, *Education Cur,* Dacotah Prairie Museum, Ruth Bunker Memorial Library, Aberdeen SD

Berendsen, Olga, *Dir Prog,* Rutgers, the State University of New Jersey, Graduate Program in Art History, New Brunswick NJ (S)

Berezin, Ellen R, *Cur of Education,* Worcester Art Museum, Worcester MA

Berg, Kathy L, *Librn,* Worcester Art Museum, Library, Worcester MA

Berg, Mona, *Gallery Dir,* Purdue University Galleries, West Lafayette IN

Berg, Niels, *VPres,* Ages of Man Fellowship, Amenia NY

Berg, Raymond, *Artist in Res,* Randolph-Macon College, Art Dept, Ashland VA (S)

Berg, Ronald, *Academic Dean,* Concordia College Wisconsin, Fine Arts Galleries, Mequon WI

Berge, Louise, *Assoc Cur for Classical Art,* Art Institute of Chicago, Chicago IL

Bergeman, Rich, *Instructor,* Linn Benton Community College, Fine & Applied Art Dept, Albany OR (S)

Berger, Howard R, *Pres,* Monmouth Museum and Cultural Center, Lincroft NJ

Berger, Jerry A, *Asst Dir & Cur Collections,* University of Wyoming, Art Museum, Laramie WY

Berger, M, *Sr Library Asst,* McGill University, Blackader-Lauterman Library of Architecture and Art, Montreal PQ

Berger, Patricia, *Cur Chinese Art,* Asian Art Museum of San Francisco, Avery Brundage Collection, San Francisco CA

Berger, Richard, *Chmn Sculpture Dept,* San Francisco Art Institute, San Francisco CA (S)

Berger, Sally, *Board Pres,* Chicago Public Library, Cultural Center, Chicago IL

Berger-Hughes, Mary Lee, *Exec Asst,* Textile Museum, Washington DC

Bergeron, Suzanne, *Secy to Dir,* Bowdoin College, Museum of Art & Peary-MacMillan Arctic Museum, Brunswick ME

Bergfeld, Mary Ann, *Assoc Prof,* Saint Xavier College, Dept of Art, Chicago IL (S)

Bergh, Helen, *Cur of Education,* Dacotah Prairie Museum, Lamont Gallery, Aberdeen SD

Bergin, Robert P, *Treas,* John Simon Guggenheim Memorial Foundation, New York NY

Bergman, Edward A, *Pres,* Art Institute of Chicago, Print and Drawing Club, Chicago IL

Bergman, Joseph, *Assoc Prof,* Siena Heights College, Studio Angelico Art Dept, Adrian MI (S)

Bergman, Robert P, *Dir,* Walters Art Gallery, Baltimore MD

Bergmann, R, *Assoc Prof,* McGill University, Department of Art History, Montreal PQ (S)

Berkey, Erna L, *VPres,* Kenneth C Beck Center for the Cultural Arts, Lakewood OH

Berkhofer, George H, *Executive Dir & Cur Museum,* Clark County Historical Society, Springfield OH

Berkley, Robert J, *Dir,* Nasson College, Anderson Learning Center, Art Dept, Springvale ME

Berkowitz, Rita, *Head Art Dept,* The School of Fashion Design, Boston MA (S)

Berkowitz, Roger M, *Chief Cur & Cur Decorative Arts,* Toledo Museum of Art, Toledo OH

Berland, John, *Prof,* Colorado State University, Dept of Art, Fort Collins CO (S)

Berleant, Arnold, *Secy-Treas,* American Society for Aesthetics, Greenvale NY

Berlo, Janet, *Asst Prof,* University of Missouri-Saint Louis, Art Dept, Saint Louis MO (S)

Berman, Bernard, *Pres Board Trustees,* Allentown Art Museum, Allentown PA

Berman, Janis, *Dir,* California Museum of Science and Industry, Los Angeles CA

Berman, Nancy, *Dir,* Hebrew Union College, Skirball Museum, Los Angeles CA

Bermingham, Peter, *Dir & Chief Cur,* University of Arizona, Museum of Art, Tucson AZ

Bernal, Rudy, *Preparator,* University of Chicago, David and Alfred Smart Gallery, Chicago IL

Bernatowicz, Rita, *Instructor,* Castleton State College, Art Dept, Castleton VT (S)

Berner, Jeff, *Instructor,* Rudolph Schaeffer School of Design, San Francisco CA (S)

Bernstein, JoAnne G, *Prof Art & Chmn Dept,* Mills College, Art Dept, Oakland CA (S)

Bernstein, Lawrence A, *Assoc Prof,* Southern Illinois University, School of Art, Carbondale IL (S)

Bernstein, Roberta, *Asst Prof,* State University of New York at Albany, Art Dept, Albany NY (S)

Bernstock, Judith, *Vis Asst Prof,* Cornell University, Dept of the History of Art, Ithaca NY (S)

Beroza, Barbara L, *Registrar,* Yosemite Collections, Yosemite National Park CA

Berreth, David, *Dir,* Miami University Art Museum, Oxford OH

Berrin, Kathleen, *Cur African Oceania & the Americas,* Fine Arts Museums of San Francisco, M H de Young Memorial Museum and California Palace of the Legion of Honor, San Francisco CA

Berry, Betty, *Chmn,* Ouachita Baptist University, Dept of Art, Arkadelphia AR (S)

Berry, Cindy, *Journal Editor,* Los Angeles Institute of Contemporary Art, Los Angeles CA

Berry, Ethan, *Gallery Dir,* Montserrat School of Visual Art, Beverly MA (S)

Berry, Jim, *Pres,* Association of American Editorial Cartoonists, Harrison AR

Berry, Joy, *Ref Librn,* California Historical Society, Schubert Hall Library, San Francisco CA

Berry, Nancy, *Cur of Education,* Southern Methodist University, Meadows Museum, Dallas TX

Berry, Walter, *Instructor,* Columbia College, Art Dept, Columbia MO (S)

Bershen, Gabrielle, *Asst Cur,* University of Colorado Art Galleries, Boulder CO

Bersson, Robert, *Asst Prof,* James Madison University, Dept of Art, Harrisonburg VA (S)

Bertin, Margaret, *Public Information Officer,* National Museum of African Art, Washington DC

Bertoia, Roberto, *Asst Prof,* Cornell University, Dept of Art, Ithaca NY (S)

Bertolo, Diane, *Asst to Dir,* Hallwalls Gallery, New York NY

Bertos, R, *Chmn,* McGill University, Department of Art History, Montreal PQ (S)

Berube, Claude, *Pres,* La Societe des Decorateurs-Ensembliers du Quebec, Interior Decorators' Society of Quebec, Montreal PQ

Best, Jonathan, *Assoc Prof,* Wesleyan University, Art Dept, Middletown CT (S)

Betak, Henry, *Assoc Prof,* University of Alabama, Art Dept, Tuscaloosa AL (S)

Betancourt, Philip, *Actg Dean,* Temple University, Tyler School of Art-Galleries, Philadelphia PA

Betancourt, Philip, *Actg Dean,* Temple University, Tyler School of Art, Philadelphia PA (S)

Beth, Dana, *Asst Librn,* Saint Louis Art Museum, Richardson Memorial Library, Saint Louis MO

Bethany, Adeline, *Chmn Dept,* Cabrini College, Dept of Fine Arts, Radnor PA (S)

Bethel, Audrey, *Dir,* Arts and Crafts Center of Pittsburgh, Pittsburgh PA

Betsch, William E, *Chmn,* University of Miami, Dept of Art & Art History, Coral Gables FL (S)

Betteley, Roy D R, *Dir,* Marjorie Merriweather Post Foundation of DC, Hillwood Museum, Washington DC

Bettenbender, John, *Dean,* Rutgers, the State University of New Jersey, Mason Gross School of the Arts, New Brunswick NJ (S)

Betti, Claudia, *Basic Drawing Coordr,* North Texas State University, Art Dept, Denton TX (S)

Bettinson, Brenda, *Chmn,* Pace University, Dyson College Arts & Science, White Plains NY (S)

Bettinson, Brenda, *Chmn,* Pace University, Dept of Art & Design, Pleasantville NY (S)

Betts, Katheleen, *Conservator,* Society of the Cincinnati, Anderson House Museum, Washington DC

Betts, Thomas W, *Prof,* Lakeland Community College, Visual Arts Dept, Mentor OH (S)

Bevan, Maria Elena, *Circulation Supvr,* Art Center College of Design, James Lemont Fogg Memorial Library, Pasadena CA

Bevans, Pandy, *Instr,* Mainline Center of the Arts, Haverford PA (S)

Bevington, Maida, *Admin Asst,* Stan Hywet Hall Foundation, Inc, Akron OH

Beymer, Allan, *Chmn,* Merced College, Arts Division, Merced CA (S)

Bianchi, Robert, *Assoc Cur Egyptian & Classical Art,* Brooklyn Museum, Brooklyn NY

Bibler, Richard, *Instructor,* Monterey Peninsula College, Art Dept, Monterey CA (S)

Bibler, Robert, *Instructor,* Chemeketa Community College, Dept of Humanities & Communications, Salem OR (S)

Bice, Megan, *Cur,* Sarnia Public Library, Art Gallery, Sarnia ON

Bickel, John, *VPres Program Planning,* Cedar Rapids Museum of Art, Cedar Rapids IA

Bickford, Christopher P, *Dir,* Connecticut Historical Society, Library, Hartford CT

Bickley, Steve, *Instructor,* Virginia Tech, Dept of Art, Blacksburg VA (S)

Biddle, Livingston, *Chmn,* National Endowment for the Arts, Washington DC

Biedenharn, Jack, *Asst Prof,* Indian River Community College, Fine Art Dept, Fort Pierce FL (S)

Biek, Mary, *Instr,* Southwestern Michigan College, Communications-Humanitites Dept, Dowagiac MI (S)

Bieler, Joanne, *Information Officer,* Newfoundland Museum, Saint John's NF

Bienemann, Bruce, *Dir,* Sioux City Art Center, Sioux City IA

Bierer, Sandra, *Dir & Education Dir,* Merrick Art Gallery, New Brighton PA

Bierman, Sissy, *Secy,* Safety Harbor Museum of History and Fine Arts, Safety Harbor FL

Biers, Jane C, *Cur Ancient Art,* University of Missouri, Museum of Art and Archaeology, Columbia MO

Biers, William R, *Prof,* University of Missouri, Art History and Archaeology Dept, Columbia MO (S)

Bigazzi, Anna, *Library Asst,* University of Hartford, Anne Bunce Cheney Library, West Hartford CT

Bigger, Michael, *Asst Prof,* University of Texas at San Antonio, Division of Art and Design, San Antonio TX (S)

Biggers, John T, *Head Dept,* Texas Southern University, Art Dept, Houston TX (S)

Biggerstaff, Donald, *Chmn of Board,* Association of Medical Illustrators, Midlothian VA

Biggs, Mary Elizabeth, *Secy,* Annie S Kemerer Museum, Bethlehem PA

Bigler, Steve, *Assoc Prof,* University of Northern Iowa, Dept of Art, Cedar Falls IA (S)

Bigus, Richard, *Asst Prof,* University of Northern Iowa, Dept of Art, Cedar Falls IA (S)

Bilaitis, Richard J, *Chmn,* Wayne State University, Dept of Art and Art History, Detroit MI (S)

Bilaitis, Richard J, *Dir,* Wayne State University, Community Arts Gallery, Detroit MI

Bilicke, M Angelene, *Head Dept,* Ancilla College, Art Dept, Donaldson IN (S)

Bilinski, Donald, *Dir,* Polish Museum of America, Chicago IL

Billian, Cathey, *Publicity & Marketing,* Just Above Midtown Gallery, Inc, New York NY

Billings, Loren, *Exec Dir,* Museum, Fine Arts Research & Holographic Center, Chicago IL

Billings, Robert, *Secy,* Museum, Fine Arts Research & Holographic Center, Chicago IL

Billings, Robert H, *Humanities & Fine Arts Chmn,* Los Angeles Harbor College, Art Dept, Wilmington CA (S)

Binford, Anne, *Instr,* Transylvania University, Studio Arts Dept, Lexington KY (S)

Bingham, Brenda, *Pres,* Montclair Art Museum, Montclair NJ

Bingham, Russell, *Assoc Cur,* Edmonton Art Gallery, Edmonton AB

Binks, Ronald, *Prof,* University of Texas at San Antonio, Division of Art and Design, San Antonio TX (S)

Biorn, Sarah, *VPres,* Galesburg Civic Art Center, Galesburg IL

Bippes, Bill, *Dir,* Spring Arbor College, Art Dept, Spring Arbor MI

Birch, James A, *Cur Education,* Cleveland Museum of Art, Cleveland OH

Bird, Robert, *Asst Prof,* Trenton State College, Art Dept, Trenton NJ (S)

Birdsall, James, *Treas,* Owatonna Arts Center, Owatonna MN

Birke, Judy, *Dir,* Munson Gallery, New Haven CT

Birkett, William H, *Assoc Prof,* Rochester Institute of Technology, School of Printing, Rochester NY (S)

Birmingham, Doris A, *Asst Prof,* New England College, Visual Arts Dept, Henniker NH (S)

Birmingham, John, *Exhibition Designer,* University of Maryland, College Park, Art Gallery, College Park MD

Birmingham, Meg, *Asst Cur Education,* Beaumont Art Museum, Beaumont TX

Birney, Ann E, *Librn,* Joslyn Art Museum, Art Reference Library, Omaha NE

Birnie, Adelaide R, *Bursar,* Montclair Art Museum, Montclair NJ

Birstins, Inese, *Fibre Dept Coordr,* Banff Centre School of Fine Arts, Banff AB (S)

Bisaillon, Blaise, *Dir,* Forbes Library, Northampton MA

Bisaillon, Ed, *Dir,* Hastings Museum, Hastings NE

Bischoff, Elmer N, *Prof,* University of California, Berkeley, College of Letters & Sciences, Berkeley CA (S)

Bishop, Barbara L, *Dir,* Longwood College, Bedford Gallery, Farmville VA

Bishop, Barbara L, *Head Dept,* Longwood College, Dept of Art, Farmville VA (S)

Bishop, Budd Harris, *Dir,* Columbus Museum of Art, Columbus OH

Bishop, Carol, *Div Chmn Fine & Applied Art,* Solano Community College, Dept of Fine & Applied Art, Suisun City CA (S)

Bishop, Marjorie, *VPres,* Gallery North, Setauket NY

Bishop, Michael, *Instr,* California State University, Chico, Art Dept, Chico CA (S)

Bishop, Robert, *Dir,* Museum of American Folk Art, New York NY

Bishop, Samuel, *Assoc Prof,* Northeastern University, Dept of Art, Boston MA (S)

Bishop, Steve, *Asst Prof,* Murray State University, Art Dept, Murray KY (S)

Biskaps, O, *Instructor,* Technical University of Nova Scotia, Faculty of Architecture, Halifax NS (S)

Bitley, Linda, *Cur,* Museum of Arts and Sciences, Inc, Macon GA

Bitticks, Ron, *Chmn Fine Arts,* Milwaukee Institute of Art and Design, Milwaukee WI (S)

Bivens, Carol D, *Downtown Gallery Curator,* Roanoke Museum of Fine Arts, Roanoke VA

Bivins, John, *Publications Dir,* Old Salem Inc, Museum of Early Southern Decorative Arts, Winston-Salem NC

Bivins, Richard A, *Dept Head,* Oklahoma State University, Art Dept, Stillwater OK (S)

Bixenman, Betty, *Chmn Dept Fashion Design,* Woodbury University, Professional Arts Division, Los Angeles CA (S)

Bixler, Harvey R, *Cur,* Liberty Hall Museum, Frankfort KY

Bjone, Helen, *VPres,* SVACA - Sheyenne Valley Arts and Crafts Association, Bjarne Ness Gallery, Fort Ransom ND

Bjorkland, Marilyn, *Registrar,* Minneapolis Institute of Arts, Minneapolis MN

Bjorklund, Carol Morrow, *Dir,* North Dakota State University, Memorial Union Art Gallery, Fargo ND

Black, Craig C, *Dir,* Natural History Museum of Los Angeles County, Los Angeles CA

Black, Jack, *Board Chmn,* Fayette Art Museum, Fayette AL

Black, James R, *Instr,* Schoolcraft College, Dept of Art, Livonia MI (S)

Black, Patti Carr, *Dir State Historical Museum,* Mississippi Department of Archives and History, State Historical Museum, Jackson MS

Black, Peggy, *Asst Dir,* Kimball Art Center, Park City UT

Blackaby, James, *Chief Cur,* Bucks County Historical Society, Mercer Museum, Doylestown PA

Blackbeard, Bill, *Dir,* San Francisco Academy of Comic Art, Library, San Francisco CA

Blackburn, A Kimberlin, *VPres,* Tweed Arts Group, Plainfield NJ

Blackburn, Bob, *Intrepretations & Publications,* Oklahoma Historical Society, Central Museum, Oklahoma City OK

Blackburn, Gary, *Instr Music,* Auburn University at Montgomery, Art Dept, Montgomery AL (S)

Blackburn, Robert, *Dir,* Printmaking Workshop, New York NY

Blackburn, Robert, *Adjunct Assoc Prof,* Columbia University, School of the Arts, Division of Painting & Sculpture, New York NY (S)

Blackburn, Vonda, *Exec Dir,* Associated Artists of Winston-Salem, Winston-Salem NC

Blackford, Jan, *Treas,* Green Hill Center for North Carolina Art, Greensboro NC

Blackhurst, Phillip, *Chmn,* University of Kansas, Dept of Art, Lawrence KS (S)

Blackie, Eleanor, *Secy,* Yarmouth County Historical Society, Yarmouth County Museum, Yarmouth NS

Blackley, Terrence, *Chmn Division Fine Arts,* Fullerton College, Division of Fine Arts, Fullerton CA (S)

Blackmun, Barbara, *Instructor,* San Diego Mesa College, Fine Arts Dept, San Diego CA (S)

Blackstock, Susan, *Art Adminr,* Leanin Tree Museum of Western Art, Boulder CO

Blackwell, Barbara, *Assoc Cur,* Cornell University, Herbert F Johnson Museum of Art, Ithaca NY

Blackwell, Eileen, *Secy,* Florence Museum, Florence SC

Blackwell, J V, *Prof,* University of Nebraska at Omaha, Dept of Art, Omaha NE (S)

Blackwood, C Roy, *Asst Prof,* Southeastern Louisiana University, Dept of Visual Arts, Hammond LA (S)

Blackwood, Stephanie K, *Administrative Mgr,* Ohio State University, Gallery of Fine Art, Columbus OH

Blade, Timothy T, *Cur Decorative Arts,* University of Minnesota, Goldstein Gallery, Saint Paul MN

Bladen, Ronald, *Instr,* New York Studio School of Drawing, Painting and Sculpture, New York NY (S)

Blades, Nancy C, *Museum Hist Specialist,* Tryon Palace Restoration Complex, New Bern NC

Bladon, Patty, *Cur Education,* Memphis Brooks Museum of Art, Memphis TN

Blain, Brad, *Dir,* Kitchener-Waterloo Art Gallery, Kitchener ON

Blain, Brad, *Pres,* Ontario Association of Art Galleries, Toronto ON

Blain, Paul, *Extension Cur & Education Officer,* Kitchener-Waterloo Art Gallery, Kitchener ON

Blain, Sandra J, *Dir,* Arrowmont School of Arts and Crafts, Gatlinburg TN (S)

Blain, Wilfred, *Admin Officer,* Ottawa Public Library, Fine Arts Dept, Ottawa ON

Blair, Carl, *Instructor,* Bob Jones University, School of Fine Arts, Greenville SC (S)

Blair, Laurel G, *Cur,* Blair Museum of Lithophanes and Carved Waxes, Toledo OH

Blair, Mary, *Pres,* Brattleboro Museum and Art Center, Brattleboro VT

Blair, Nora, *Library Asst,* Vancouver Art Gallery, Library, Vancouver BC

Blair, Robert, *Instr,* St Lawrence College, Dept of Visual and Creative Arts, Cornwall ON (S)

Blaisdell, Phillip, *Instr,* Joe Kubert School of Cartoon and Graphic Art Inc, Dover NJ (S)

Blake, Brooke, *Pres Board of Trustees,* The American Federation of Arts, New York NY

Blake, Hortense, *Dir,* Clinton Art Association Gallery, Clinton IA

Blakely, George C, *Asst Prof,* Florida State University, Art Dept, Tallahassee FL (S)

Blanchard, Henry J, *Dir,* Centre Cultural de Shawinigan, Shawinigan PQ

Blanchard, Jerry, *Maintenance Dir,* USS North Carolina Battleship Memorial, Wilmington NC

Blandy, Douglas, *Chmn Art Educ,* Bowling Green State University, School of Art, Bowling Green OH (S)

Blanton, Jackson L, *Art Coordr,* Federal Reserve Bank of Richmond, Richmond VA

Blanton, Paul L, *Head Dept,* Idaho State University, Dept of Art, Pocatello ID (S)

Blaskovich, Mary, *Dir,* Copper Village Museum & Arts Center, Anaconda MT

Blatherwick, Mary, *Programme Coordr,* Sunbury Shores Arts and Nature Centre, Inc, Saint Andrews NB

Blayney, Gail, *Asst Dir,* Museum of Northern British Columbia, Library, Prince Rupert BC

Bledsoe, Jane K, *Administrative Dir,* California State University, Long Beach, University Art Museum, Long Beach CA

Bleecker, Margaret, *Cur Coll,* Connecticut Valley Historical Museum, Springfield MA

Bleha, Bernie, *Chmn & Instr,* Green River Community College, Art Dept, Auburn WA (S)

Blevins, James R, *Chmn,* Indiana State University, Evansville, Art Dept, Evansville IN (S)

Blevins, Lois, *Secy,* Fort Missoula Historical Museum, Missoula MT

Blisard, Herb, *Fac,* Yakima Valley College, Art Dept, Yakima WA (S)

Bliss, Harry E, *Assoc Prof,* Palomar College, Art Dept, San Marcos TX (S)

Bliss, Margaret, *Lectr,* Tunxis Community College, Graphic Design Dept, Farmington CT (S)

Blistern, Burton, *Dir,* Saint John's College, Art Gallery, Annapolis MD

Blitzer, Charles, *Asst Secy for Art & History,* Smithsonian Institution, Washington DC

Blizard, William, *Chmn Dept,* Springfield College, Dept of Visual and Performing Arts, Springfield MA (S)

Bloch, E Maurice, *Dir & Cur,* University of California, Los Angeles, Grunwald Center for the Graphic Arts, Los Angeles CA

Bloch, Milton J, *Dir,* Mint Museum of Art, Charlotte NC

Block, Bart, *Asst Program Coordr,* Texas A & M University, Memorial Student Center Arts Committee, College Station TX

Block, R M, *Chief Librn,* Medicine Hat Public Library, Medicine Hat AB

Blocker, Martha G, *Head Librn,* Indianapolis Museum of Art, Stout Reference Library, Indianapolis IN

Blocksma, Robin, *Assoc Cur Art,* Ella Sharp Museum, Jackson MI

Blodgett, David, *Adjunct Lectr,* Indiana University at South Bend, Fine Arts Dept, South Bend IN (S)

Bloedorn, Gene, *Head Dept,* University of Wisconsin-Stout, Art Dept, Menomonie WI (S)

Blom, Billie, *Executive Secy,* Missoula Museum of the Arts, Missoula MT

Blomstrann, Lois L, *Asst to Dir,* New Britain Museum of American Art, New Britain CT

Bloom, Leslye, *Instructor,* Virginia Tech, Dept of Art, Blacksburg VA (S)

Bloom, Rosalind, *Instr,* Rosemont College, Division of the Arts, Rosemont PA (S)

Bloomberg, Louise, *Dir,* University of Massachusetts, Amherst, Dorothy W Perkins Slide Library, Amherst MA

Bloomer, Carolyn, *Lectr,* University of North Carolina at Chapel Hill, Art Dept, Chapel Hill NC (S)

Bloomer, Jerry M, *Librn,* R W Norton Art Gallery, Library, Shreveport LA

Blosser, John, *Head Dept,* Hesston College, Hesston KS (S)

Blosser, Nicholas, *Instr,* Mount Vernon Nazarene College, Art Dept, Mount Vernon OH (S)

Blouin, Jean Charles, *Faculty Dean of Arts,* Universite Laval Cite Universitaire, School of Visual Arts, Quebec PQ (S)

Blouin, Patrick, *Pres,* Royal Architectural Institute of Canada, Ottawa ON

Blount, Alice, *Cur Geology,* Newark Museum, Newark NJ

Blovits, Larry, *Assoc Prof,* Aquinas College, Art Dept, Grand Rapids MI (S)

Blow, David, *Advertising Design Coordr,* North Texas State University, Art Dept, Denton TX (S)

Bloy, James, *Chmn,* Maryville College, Division of Fine Arts, Art Section, Maryville TN (S)

Bloy, James Albert, *Chmn,* Maryville College, Fine Arts Center Gallery, Maryville TN

Blum, Ivan, *Advisor to Board,* Orange County Center for Contemporary Art, Santa Ana CA

Blum, Susan, *Admin Asst,* Virginia Beach Arts Center, Virginia Beach VA

Blum, Zevi, *Assoc Prof,* Cornell University, Dept of Art, Ithaca NY (S)

Blume, Peter F, *Cur,* Allentown Art Museum, Allentown PA

Blumenthal, Arthur R, *Dir,* University of Maryland, College Park, Art Gallery, College Park MD

Blumenthal, Elizabeth, *Instr,* Johns Hopkins University, School of Medicine, Dept of Art as Applied to Medicine, Baltimore MD (S)

Blumenthal, Lyn, *Video Data Bank,* School of the Art Institute of Chicago Library, Chicago IL

Blumrich, Stephen, *Editor Surface Design Journal,* Surface Design Association, Inc, Fayetteville TN

Blundell, Harry, *Dir of Theatre,* Council of Ozark Artists and Craftsmen, Inc, Arts Center of the Ozarks Gallery, Springdale AR

Blundell, Kathi, *Prog Dir,* Council of Ozark Artists and Craftsmen, Inc, Arts Center of the Ozarks Gallery, Springdale AR

Blunk, Robert, *Prof,* Pittsburg State University, Art Dept, Pittsburg KS (S)

Bly, Isaiah, *Business Mgr,* Afro Arts Cultural Centre, Inc, African Arts Museum & Gallery, New York NY

Bly, Simon, *Exec Dir,* Afro Arts Cultural Centre, Inc, African Arts Museum & Gallery, New York NY

Blyer, Verna R, *Administrative Secy,* Canton Art Institute, Canton OH (S)

Boardman, Gerard, *Librn,* South Street Seaport Museum, Library, New York NY

Boardman, Kathryn A, *Asst Cur,* New York State Historical Association, Farmers' Museum, Inc, Cooperstown NY

Boatman, Laura, *Secy,* Polk Public Museum, Lakeland FL

Boaz, William, *Instructor,* Chapman College, Art Dept, Orange CA (S)

Bob, Murray L, *Dir,* James Prendergast Library Association, Jamestown NY

Bobak, Bruno, *Dir Art Centre,* University of New Brunswick, Art Education Section, Fredericton NB (S)

Bobak, Bruno, *Dir,* University of New Brunswick, Art Centre, Fredericton NB

Bober, Phyllis B, *Prof,* Bryn Mawr College, Dept of the History of Art, Bryn Mawr PA (S)

Bobick, Bruce, *Chmn,* West Georgia College, Art Dept, Carrollton GA (S)

Bockstoce, John R, *Cur Ethnology,* Old Dartmouth Historical Society, New Bedford Whaling Museum, New Bedford MA

Bockwith, Wendy, *Instructor,* La Roche College, Division of Graphics, Design, Pittsburgh PA (S)

Bocz, George, *Assoc Prof,* Florida State University, Art Dept, Tallahassee FL (S)

Bodem, Dennis R, *Dir,* Jesse Besser Museum, Alpena MI

Bodenhousen, Gary, *Instr,* Georgia Southern College, Dept of Art, Statesboro GA (S)

Bodine, Paul, *Asst Prof,* Eastern Illinois University, School of Fine Arts, Charleston IL (S)

Boegen, Anne, *Coordr Work with Children and Young Adults,* Miami-Dade Public Library, Miami FL

Boehmer, Ron, *Art Coordr,* Lynchburg Fine Arts Center Inc, Lynchburg VA

Boelke, W, *Dept Chmn,* Western Connecticut State University, School of Arts & Sciences, Danbury CT (S)

Boelts, Jackson, *Coordr Graphic Design,* University of Arizona, Dept of Art, Tucson AZ (S)

Boender, Liselotto, *Library Asst,* Emily Carr College of Art & Design, Library, Vancouver BC

Boesch, William, *Librn,* Portsmouth Athenaeum NR, Inc 1817, Library, Portsmouth NH

Boeve, Edgar G, *Assoc Prof,* Calvin College, Art Dept, Grand Rapids MI (S)

Bogdanovitch, George, *Dir,* Denison University Art Gallery, Granville OH

Bogdanovitch, George, *Prof,* Denison University, Dept of Art, Granville OH (S)

Bogdanowicz, Ingrid, *Lecturer,* Marycrest College, Art Dept, Davenport IA (S)

Boggs, Arlene A, *Librn,* Illinois State University, Museum Library, Normal IL

Boggs, David B, *Dir of Gallery,* University of Maine at Machias, Torrey Gallery, Machias ME

Bogle, Jon Robert, *Chmn Dept,* Lycoming College, Art Dept, Williamsport PA (S)

Bogusky, Alf, *Dir,* Southern Alberta Art Gallery, Lethbridge AB

Bohar, Ruth, *Asst Prof,* University of Missouri-Saint Louis, Art Dept, Saint Louis MO (S)

Bohaska, David J, *Registrar,* Calvert Marine Museum, Solomons MD

Bohen, Barbara E, *Dir,* University of Illinois, World Heritage Museum, Champaign IL

Bohlsen, Darrell, *Exec Dir,* Southwest Craft Center, Ursuline & Villita Galleries, San Antonio TX

Bohn, Anita, *Meseum Educator,* Illinois State University, University Museums, Normal IL

Bohnert, Thomas, *Instructor,* Charles Stewart Mott Community College, Fine Arts Division, Flint MI (S)

Boileau, Andree, *Mgr,* Musee Historique de Vaudreuil, Vaudreuil Historical Museum, Vaudreuil PQ

Boisseau, Catherine C, *Dir,* Fairfield Historical Society, Fairfield CT

Bokovec, Emily, *Asst Prof,* Kent State University, Stark Campus, School of Art, Canton OH (S)

Boland, Dory, *Secy,* Bristol Art Museum, Bristol RI

Boland, Lucye, *Asst Dir & Registrar,* Danbury Scott-Fanton Museum and Historical Society, Inc, Library, Danbury CT

Boland, Robert M, *Chmn Dept,* Berkshire Community College, Dept Fine Arts, Pittsfield MA (S)

Bolas, Gerald D, *Dir,* Washington University, Gallery of Art, Saint Louis MO

Bowman, Brook, *Conservator,* Church of Jesus Christ of Latter-Day Saints, Museum of Church History and Art, Salt Lake City UT

Bowman, David, *Chmn Basic Arts,* Moore College of Art, Philadelphia PA (S)

Bowman, Donald, *Co-Pres,* Pemaquid Group of Artists, Pemaquid Point ME

Bowman, Jeanne, *Art Dir,* Hill Country Arts Foundation, Ingram TX

Bowman, Jeffrey, *Asst Prof,* Texas Tech University, Dept of Art, Lubbock TX (S)

Bowman, Ken, *Instr,* Blackhawk Mountain School of Art, Black Hawk CO (S)

Bowman, Leah, *Prof,* School of the Art Institute of Chicago, Chicago IL (S)

Bowman, Leslie, *Asst Cur of Decorative Arts,* Los Angeles County Museum of Art, Los Angeles CA

Bowman, Robert, *Pres Bd Trustees,* Silvermine Guild Center for the Arts, Galleries, New Canaan CT

Bowman, Roger, *Asst Prof,* William Woods-Westminster Colleges, Art Dept, Fulton MO (S)

Bowman, Russell, *Chief Cur,* Milwaukee Art Museum, Milwaukee WI

Bowman, Stanley, *Chmn Dept,* Cornell University, Dept of Art, Ithaca NY (S)

Bowne, James D, *Deputy Dir,* Huntsville Museum of Art, Huntsville AL

Bowron, Edgar Peters, *Dir,* North Carolina Museum of Art, Raleigh NC

Bows, Albert, *Pres Bd of Directors,* High Museum of Art, Atlanta GA

Bowsfield, Blaire L, *Secy,* Lloydminster Barr Colony Museum Committee, Lloydminster SK

Box, Harold, *Dean,* University of Texas, School of Architecture, Austin TX (S)

Boyce, Gerald G, *Dir,* Indiana Central University, Leah Ransburg Art Gallery, Indianapolis IN

Boyce, Gerald G, *Chmn Dept,* Indiana Central University, Fine Arts Dept, Indianapolis IN (S)

Boyce, Joel Lynn, *Coordr,* Umpqua Community College, Fine & Performing Arts Dept, Roseburg OR (S)

Boyce, Robert, *Asst Prof,* Berea College, Art Dept, Berea KY (S)

Boyce, William G, *Dir,* University of Minnesota, Tweed Museum of Art, Duluth MN

BoyceHarper, Ann, *Asst Dir Admin,* Baltimore Museum of Art, Baltimore MD

Boyd, Don, *Asst Prof,* South Dakota State University, Dept of Visual Arts, Brookings SD (S)

Boyd, James, *Dir Photography,* Art Institute of Fort Lauderdale, Fort Lauderdale FL (S)

Boyd, Judith, *Public Relation Dir,* Morris Museum of Arts and Sciences, Morristown NJ

Boyd, Karen W, *Prof,* Murray State University, Art Dept, Murray KY (S)

Boyd, Willard L, *Pres,* Field Museum of Natural History, Chicago IL

Boyd, William L, *Asst Prof,* Alabama A & M University, Art Education Dept, Huntsville AL (S)

Boydstun, Helen, *Secy,* Museum of the Southwest, Midland TX

Boyens, Charles, *Assoc Prof,* Jersey City State College, Art Dept, Jersey City NJ (S)

Boyer, Barbara, *Asst Prof,* Ohio State University, Dept of Art Education, Columbus OH (S)

Boyer, Irene, *Librn,* Springfield Art Association of Edwards Place, Michael Victor II Art Library, Springfield IL

Boyer, Jack K, *Executive Dir,* Kit Carson Memorial Foundation, Taos NM

Boyer, Patricia, *Cur Prints & Drawings,* Rutgers University, Jane Voorhees Zimmerli Art Museum, New Brunswick NJ

Boyer, Ruth, *Textiles,* California College of Arts and Crafts, Oakland CA (S)

Boyer-Root, Jean, *Pres,* Rogue Valley Art Association, Medford OR

Boyle, Ruth, *Bookstore Mgr,* Laguna Beach Museum of Art, Laguna Beach CA

Boyle, Terry, *Secy,* Wayne Art Center, Wayne PA

Boyle, William J S, *Exec Dir,* Visual Arts Ontario, Toronto ON

Boyne, Walter J, *Dir,* National Air and Space Museum, Washington DC

Boynton, Jack, *Assoc Prof,* University of Saint Thomas, Art Dept, Houston TX (S)

Boynton, Wyman P, *VPres,* John Paul Jones House, Portsmouth NH

Boysen, Bill H, *Crafts Area Head,* Southern Illinois University, School of Art, Carbondale IL (S)

Boyt, Richard, *Instructor,* Crowder College, Dept of Art, Neosho MO (S)

Brabant, Edward A, *Prof,* Rochester Institute of Technology, School of Printing, Rochester NY (S)

Brackbill, Eleanor, *Coordr of Musuem Education,* State University of New York at Purchase, Neuberger Museum, Purchase NY

Brackney, Kathryn S, *Librn,* Georgia Institute of Technology, College of Architecture Library, Atlanta GA

Brackney, William H, *Exec Dir,* American Baptist Historical Society, Rochester NY

Bradbury, Barbara, *Treasurer,* The Greenwich Art Society Inc, Greenwich CT

Bradbury, Ellen, *Cur Fine Arts,* Museum of New Mexico, Santa Fe NM

Braden, James, *Dir,* Utah Travel Council, Salt Lake City UT

Braden, Jan, *Cur Educ,* Joslyn Art Museum, Omaha NE

Bradford, Colleen H, *Chmn,* Brigham City Museum-Gallery, Brigham City UT

Bradford, Roberta, *Asst Librn,* Stowe-Day Foundation, Library, Hartford CT

Bradley, Barbara, *Dir Illustration,* Academy of Art College, San Francisco CA (S)

Bradley, Douglas, *Cur,* University of Notre Dame, Snite Museum of Art, Notre Dame IN

Bradley, E Ross, *Consultant Exposure Programs,* Department of Culture, Government of the Province of Alberta, Beaver House Gallery, Edmonton AB

Bradley, Jessica, *Asst Cur Contemporary Art,* National Gallery of Canada, Ottawa ON

Bradley, Linda S, *Asst Prof,* Florida State University, Art Education Dept, Tallahassee FL (S)

Bradley, Sarah, *Asst Dir Gallery,* Asia Society, Inc, Gallery, New York NY

Bradley-Johnson, Gayle V, *Gallery Dir,* North Park College, Carlson Tower Gallery, Chicago IL

Bradley-Johnson, Gayle V, *Prof,* North Park College, Art Dept, Chicago IL (S)

Bradlyn, Betty, *Cur Education,* Alaska State Museum, Juneau AK

Bradman, Susan, *Pres,* Burlington County Historical Society, Burlington NJ

Bradshaw, Larry, *Assoc Prof,* University of Nebraska at Omaha, Dept of Art, Omaha NE (S)

Bradshaw, William T, *Chmn,* University of California, Riverside, Program in Art, Riverside CA (S)

Bradway, Wallace, *Museum Registrar,* Art Institute of Chicago, Chicago IL

Brady, Carolyn, *Business Mgr,* Freeport Area Arts Council, Freeport Art Museum, Freeport IL

Bragen, Joan, *Corp Program Dir,* DeCordova and Dana Museum and Park, Lincoln MA

Brager, Beverly, *Supervisor,* Madison Public Library, Art & Music Division, Madison WI

Bragg, Nicholas B, *Exec Dir,* Reynolda House, Inc, Winston-Salem NC

Braham, Susan, *Dir of Education,* Brockton Art Museum, Brockton MA

Braig, Kathryn B, *Asst to Librn,* Mariners Museum, Library, Newport News VA

Bramblke, Frank, *Cur Art,* Museum of Art, Science and Industry, Bridgeport CT

Brand, Barbara A, *Admin,* Hammond-Harwood House Association, Inc, Annapolis MD

Brand, Ginna, *Dir Education,* The New Gallery of Contemporary Art, Cleveland OH

Brandon, Elinore, *Chmn Illustration,* Fashion Institute of Technology, Art & Design Division, New York NY (S)

Brandon, Reiko, *Cur Textile Coll,* Honolulu Academy of Arts, Honolulu HI

Brandon, Stephen, *Chmn,* Armstrong State College, Fine Arts Dept, Savannah GA (S)

Brandson, Lorraine, *Asst Cur,* Eskimo Museum, Churchill MB

Brandt, Rex, *Co-Dir,* Brandt Painting Workshops, Corona Del Mar CA (S)

Brannon, Revelie, *Cur,* Clemson University, Fort Hill, Clemson SC

Branson, Edward V, *Instr,* Yavapai College, Art Dept, Prescott AZ (S)

Brantigan, Lisa, *Lectr,* Oakland University, Dept of Art and Art History, Rochester MI (S)

Brassieur, Charles R, *Cur Asst,* Acadian House Museum, Saint Martinville LA

Brassill, Jo Ann, *Prof,* University of Southern Colorado, Belmont Campus, Dept of Art, Pueblo CO (S)

Bratesman, Marion, *Dir Public Relations,* Hood Museum of Art, Hanover NH

Bratley, Carol A, *Commissioner,* Boston Art Commission of the City of Boston, Boston MA

Brauer, David, *Art Historian,* Alfred C Glassell School of Art, Houston TX (S)

Brauer, Fred, *Chmn Div,* Concordia College, Art Dept, Saint Paul MN (S)

Brauer, James, *Assoc Prof,* Concordia College, Bronxville NY (S)

Brauer, Richard, *Dir,* Valparaiso University, University Art Galleries and Collections, Valparaiso IN

Braufman, Sheila B, *Admin Asst,* Triton Museum of Art, Library, Santa Clara CA

Braun, Mary, *Registrar,* University of Chicago, David and Alfred Smart Gallery, Chicago IL

Braun, Suzan, *Assoc Prof,* Eastern Illinois University, School of Fine Arts, Charleston IL (S)

Braunlein, John H, *Museum Cur,* Historical Society of Delaware, Old Town Hall Museum, Wilmington DE

Braunr, A James, *Dean,* San Francisco State University, Art Dept, San Francisco CA (S)

Braunschweiger, Louise, *Dir Southern Calif,* California Historical Society, San Francisco CA

Bravakis, Olivia, *Asst Cur,* Wood Art Gallery, Montpelier VT

Braver, Audrey Daniels, *Dir,* Washington Headquarters Association, Morris-Jumel Mansion, New York NY

Braverman, Ben, *Cur Education,* Minnesota Museum of Art, Saint Paul MN

Bravo, M, *Faculty,* Humboldt State University, College of Creative Arts & Humanities, Arcata CA (S)

Braxton, Anne, *Art Librn,* Ohio University, Fine Arts Library, Athens OH

Bray, Jim, *Prof,* Phillips University, Dept of Art, Enid OK (S)

Braybrooke, Valerie V, *Dir,* Fort Wayne Museum of Art, Fort Wayne IN

Brazil, Judy, *Instructor,* Johnson County Community College, Humanities Division, Overland Park KS (S)

Brazile, Orella R, *Librn,* Southern University Library, Shreveport LA

Brealey, John M, *Conservator Paintings,* Metropolitan Museum of Art, New York NY

Brechner, Michael, *Preparator,* University of Kentucky, Art Museum, Lexington KY

Breed, Charles A, *Prof,* Delta College, Art Dept, University Center MI (S)

Breeskin, Adelyn D, *Sr Curatorial Advisor,* National Museum of American Art, Washington DC

Breitenbach, William J, *Assoc Prof,* Sam Houston State University, Art Dept, Huntsville TX (S)

Breithaupt, E M, *Dir,* Ripon College Art Gallery, Ripon WI

Breitman, Ellen, *Cur Education,* Newport Harbor Art Museum, Newport Beach CA

Brekke, Michael, *Instructor,* Atlanta College of Art, Atlanta GA (S)

Brener, R, *Chmn & Prof,* University of Victoria, Dept of Visual Arts, Victoria BC (S)

Brennan, Linda C, *Asst Cur,* Plumas County Museum, Quincy CA

Brennan, Margaret, *Cur,* Gananoque Historical Museum, Gananoque ON

Brennan, Margaret, *Pres,* Museum of Ossining Historical Society, Ossining NY

Brennan, Nancy, *Dir,* Peale Museum, Baltimore MD

Brennan, Robert H, *Chmn,* University of Bridgeport, Art Dept, Bridgeport CT (S)

Brennan, Ruth, *Exec Dir,* Dahl Fine Arts Center, Rapid City SD

Brennan, Thomas G, *Librn,* Newport Historical Society, Library, Newport RI

Brennan, T Patrick, *Cur,* Oglebay Institute Mansion Museum, Wheeling WV

Brennen, Ray R, *Secy,* Annie S Kemerer Museum, Bethlehem PA

Brenner, Estelle, *Assoc Prof,* Community College of Baltimore, Dept of Fine & Applied Arts, Liberty Campus, Baltimore MD (S)

Brenner, Jean, *Prof,* Marian College, Art Dept, Fond Du Lac WI (S)

Brenner, M Diane, *Museum Archivist,* Anchorage Historical and Fine Arts Museum, Archives, Anchorage AK

Brennian, Hugh, *Chmn,* Lynnwood Arts Centre, Simcoe ON

Bresina, M Arthur, *Prof,* Mount Mary College, Art Dept, Milwaukee WI (S)

Breslow, Elaine, *Dir Development,* Pennsylvania Academy of the Fine Arts, Galleries, Philadelphia PA

Breth, Linda, *Cur Education,* Niagara University, Buscaglia-Castellani Art Gallery, Niagara Falls NY

Brettell, Richard R, *Cur European Painting & Sculpture,* Art Institute of Chicago, Chicago IL

Bretz, Robert, *Librn,* Visual Studies Workshop, Research Center, Rochester NY

Breunig, Robert, *Chief Cur,* Heard Museum, Phoenix AZ

Brevard, Elise, *Coll & Registrar,* Mississippi Museum of Art, Jackson MS

Brezzo, Stephen, *Secy,* Balboa Art Conservation Center, San Diego CA

Brezzo, Steven L, *Dir,* San Diego Museum of Art, San Diego CA

Brian, Fred, *Instructor,* Illinois Wesleyan University, School of Art, Bloomington IL (S)

Briand, Fernand, *Admin Asst,* Musee d'Art Contemporain, Montreal PQ

Brice, John R, *Dir,* Art Center, Inc, South Bend IN

Brickman, Ernest, *Pres,* Association of Honolulu Artists, Honolulu HI

Bridgeford, Robert G, *Dir,* Portland Children's Museum, Portland OR

Bridges, Fowin C, *Dir,* Alabama Department of Archives and History Museum, Montgomery AL

Briggs, David, *Instr,* Wilkes Community College, Arts and Science Division, Wilkesboro NC (S)

Briggs, Linda, *Chmn Dept of Interior Design,* New England School of Art & Design, Boston MA (S)

Briggs, Lorraine, *Adjunct Instr,* Maryville College, St Louis, Art Division, Saint Louis MO (S)

Briggs, Mignon, *Pres,* Art Gallery of Windsor, Windsor ON

Briggs, Peter, *Cur Coll,* University of New Mexico, University Art Museum, Albuquerque NM

Bright, Ann, *Exec Secy,* Brown County Art Gallery Association Inc, Nashville IN

Bright, Jane, *Secy,* Paducah Art Guild, Paducah KY

Bright, Peggy, *Assoc Prof,* Texas Tech University, Dept of Art, Lubbock TX (S)

Brigl, Bob, *Assoc Exhib,* Western Kentucky University, Kentucky Museum, Bowling Green KY

Brigman, Donna, *Secy,* Kansas Watercolor Society, Wichita Art Museum, Wichita KS

Briley, John B, *Mgr,* The Ohio Historical Society, Inc, Campus Martius Museum and Ohio River Museum, Marietta OH

Brill, Margaret, *Prof,* Corning Community College, Division of Humanities, Corning NY (S)

Brill, Robert H, *Research Scientist,* Corning Museum of Glass, Corning NY

Brill, Wayne, *Instructor,* Interlochen Arts Academy, Dept of Visual Art, Interlochen MI (S)

Brim, Trudy, *Secy,* McLean County Art Association, Arts Center, Bloomington IL

Brimicombe, Mary, *Assoc Registrar,* Ontario College of Art, Toronto ON (S)

Brincard, Marie Therese, *Dir Art Exhibitions Programs,* African-American Institute, New York NY

Bringle, Edwina, *Faculty,* University of North Carolina-Charlotte, Creative Arts Dept, Charlotte NC (S)

Brink, Bertil, *Chmn,* Bakersfield College, Art Dept, Bakersfield CA (S)

Brink, Richard L, *Chmn Dept,* Hastings College, Art Dept, Hastings NE (S)

Brinkerhoff, Dericksen M, *Chmn,* University of California, Riverside, Art History Dept, Riverside CA (S)

Brinson, Harold, *Pres,* Southern Arkansas University, Art Dept Gallery & Magale Art Gallery, Magnolia AR

Brisson, Robert A, *Treas,* New York Society of Architects, New York NY

Bristol, Lillian, *Coordr Public Relations,* Montclair Art Museum, Montclair NJ

Bristow, James, *Business Adminr,* Winnipeg Art Gallery, Winnipeg MB

Bristow, William A, *Prof,* Trinity University, Dept of Art, San Antonio TX (S)

Bristowe, C Gordon G, *Asst Dir Admin & Facilities,* Royal Ontario Museum, Toronto ON

Britt, Arthur L, *Dir,* Alabama State University, Art Dept, Montgomery AL (S)

Britt, Nelson C, *Exec Dir,* Springfield Art Association of Edwards Place, Springfield IL

Britt, Sam Glenn, *Assoc Prof,* Delta State University, Dept of Art, Cleveland MS (S)

Britton, Clark, *Chmn Graphic Design,* Wichita State University, Division of Art, Wichita KS (S)

Britton, R E Neil, *Prof,* Virginia Wesleyan College, Art Dept of the Humanities Division, Norfolk VA (S)

Brizendine, Curtis, *Asst Prof,* Swarthmore College, Dept of Art, Swarthmore PA (S)

Broad, Deborah, *Asst Prof,* Moorhead State University, Dept of Art, Moorhead MN (S)

Broad, Eli, *Chmn,* The Museum of Contemporary Art, Los Angeles CA

Broadhurst, Mary Jane, *Secy,* Lafayette Natural History Museum, Planetarium and Nature Station, Lafayette LA

Brocewell, Shirley, *Business Mgr,* University of Regina, Mackenzie Art Gallery, Regina SK

Brock, Robert W, *Chmn,* State University of New York College at Buffalo, Fine Arts Dept, Buffalo NY (S)

Brockett, C, *Prof,* Christopher Newport College, Arts & Communications, Newport News VA (S)

Broderick, Herbert, *Asst Prof,* Herbert H Lehman College, Art Dept, Bronx NY (S)

Broderick, James, *Div Dir,* University of Texas at San Antonio, Division of Art and Design, San Antonio TX (S)

Broderick-Lockhart, Catherine, *Instr,* Vancouver Community College, Langara Campus, Dept of Fine Arts, Vancouver BC (S)

Brodeur, Danyelle, *Coordr,* Dorval Cultural Centre, Dorval PQ

Brodie, Robert G, *Pres,* Vancouver Art Gallery, Vancouver BC

Brodsky, Eugene, *Vis Artist,* University of North Carolina at Chapel Hill, Art Dept, Chapel Hill NC (S)

Brodsky, Michael, *Asst Prof,* James Madison University, Dept of Art, Harrisonburg VA (S)

Brodsky, Stanley, *Prof,* C W Post Center of Long Island University, School of the Arts, Greenvale NY (S)

Brody, Arthur W, *Assoc Prof,* University of Alaska, Dept of Art, Fairbanks AK (S)

Brody, Catherine T, *Chief Librn,* New York City Technical College, Namm Hall Library and Learning Resource Center, Brooklyn NY

Brody, Myron, *Coordr,* Avila College, Art Division, Dept of Performing and Visual Art, Kansas City MO (S)

Broekema, Andrew J, *Dean, College of the Arts,* Ohio State University, Gallery of Fine Art, Columbus OH

Broekema, Andrew J, *Dean Col,* Ohio State University, College of the Arts, Columbus OH (S)

Brohel, Edward R, *Dir,* State University of New York, Myers Fine Arts and Rockwell Kent Galleries, Plattsburgh NY

Brokaw, Dorothy, *Adminr,* Maryhill Museum of Art, Goldendale WA

Broker, Karin, *Asst Prof,* Rice University, Dept of Art and Art History, Houston TX (S)

Bromberg, Anne R, *Cur Educ,* Dallas Museum of Fine Arts, Dallas TX

Broner, Robert, *Pres,* Society of American Graphic Artists, New York NY

Bronikowski, Helen, *Member,* The Loading Dock Gallery, Boston MA

Bronkema, Jim, *Executive Dir,* Embarcadero Center Inc, San Francisco CA

Bronson, A A, *Head Publications,* Art Metropole, Toronto ON

Bronson, Marty, *Dir,* Fashion Institute of Technology, Galleries, New York NY

Bronstien, Colleen, *Asst Dir,* Studio School of Art and Design, Philadelphia PA (S)

Bronzan, Sharon, *Dir,* Portland Community College, North View Gallery, Portland OR

Broocks, Steven, *Cur and Dir,* Freeport Area Arts Council, Freeport Art Museum, Freeport IL

Broodwell, Caroyln, *Prof,* Napa College, Art Dept, Napa CA (S)

Brooke, Anna, *Librn,* Hirshhorn Museum and Sculpture Garden, Library, Washington DC

Brooke, David S, *Dir,* Sterling and Francine Clark Art Institute, Williamstown MA

Brooker, Alice, *Librn,* Springfield Art Museum, Library, Springfield MO

Brookhart, Doris I, *Head Dept,* John Brown University, Art Dept, Siloam Springs AR (S)

Brookhouse, Jon, *Chairperson Dept,* Suomi College, Fine Arts Dept, Hancock MI (S)

Brooks, James, *Instructor,* Bob Jones University, School of Fine Arts, Greenville SC (S)

Brooks, James, *Prof,* Fairmont State College, Art Dept, Fairmont WV (S)

Brooks, John B, *Cur Crafts & Education,* Pennsylvania Farm Museum of Landis Valley, Lancaster PA

Brooks, John H, *Assoc Dir,* Sterling and Francine Clark Art Institute, Williamstown MA

Brooks, Kathleen, *Registrar & Cur,* Biblical Arts Center, Dallas TX

Brooks, Mary Anna, *Instructor,* Milwaukee Area Technical College, Graphic & Applied Arts Division, Milwaukee WI (S)

Brooks, Susan, *Instr,* Ocean City Arts Center, Ocean City NJ (S)

Brooks, Wendell, *Asst Prof,* Trenton State College, Art Dept, Trenton NJ (S)

Broshar, Robert C, *First VPres,* American Institute of Architects, Washington DC

Bross, John, *Instructor,* Greenfield Community College, Art Dept, Greenfield MA (S)

Brothers, Betty, *Prof & Chairperson,* College of Mount Saint Joseph, Art Dept, Mount Saint Joseph OH (S)

Brothers, Darrell W, *Chmn,* Thomas More College, Art Dept, Fort Mitchell KY (S)

Brotter, Raplh, *Chmn,* Queens Museum, Flushing NY

Broude, Norma, *Assoc Prof,* American University, Dept of Art, Washington DC (S)

Broudo, J David, *Head Dept,* Endicott College, Art Dept, Beverly MA (S)

Brough, Richard, *Prof,* University of Alabama, Art Dept, Tuscaloosa AL (S)

Brougham, Elizabeth J, *Dir,* Artists' Cooperative Gallery, Omaha NE

Brouillard, Pierre, *Dir,* Chateau de Ramezay, Antiquarian and Numismatic Society of Montreal, Montreal PQ

Brouillet, Johanne, *Exhibition Staff,* University of Sherbrooke Cultural Center, Art Gallery, Sherbrooke PQ

Broun, Elizabeth, *Asst Dir & Chief Cur,* National Museum of American Art, Washington DC

Brouwer, Bert, *Dir,* Indiana State University, Turman Gallery, Terre Haute IN

Brovard, Inge, *Dir Marketing & Development,* Hudson River Museum, Yonkers NY

Browing, Louis, *Dir,* Mason County Museum, Maysville KY

Brown, Ann, *Gallery Dir,* Marian Osborne Cunningham Art Gallery, Bakersfield CA

Brown, Ann Barton, *Cur Coll,* Brandywine River Museum, Chadds Ford PA

Brown, Barbara, *Treas,* Dallas Public Library, Dallas Print and Drawing Society, Dallas TX

Brown, Bennie, *Librn & Archivist,* Gunston Hall Plantation, Library, Lorton VA

Brown, Beverly, *Instr,* Community College of Baltimore, Dept of Fine & Applied Arts, Liberty Campus, Baltimore MD (S)

Brown, Bruce R, *Assoc Prof,* Monroe Community College, Art Dept, Rochester NY (S)

Brown, C, *Chmn Fine Arts,* Fashion Institute of Technology, Art & Design Division, New York NY (S)

Brown, Carole R, *Asst Prof,* Elmhurst College, Art Dept, Elmhurst IL (S)

Brown, David Alan, *Cur Early Italian Painting,* National Gallery of Art, Washington DC

Brown, David R, *Pres,* American Institute of Graphic Arts, New York NY

Brown, Dick, *Exten Head,* Topeka Public Library, Fine Arts Dept & Gallery of Fine Arts, Topeka KS

Brown, Dion K, *Dir,* Polk Community College, Division of Communications and Fine Arts, Winter Haven FL (S)

Brown, Dudley, *Pres,* Arts Club of Washington, James Monroe House, Washington DC

Brown, Edward, *Museum Dir,* Atlantic Christian College, Case Art Gallery, Wilson NC

Brown, Edward, *Chmn,* Atlantic Christian College, Art Dept, Wilson NC (S)

Brown, Elizabeth, *Pres,* Western Canada Art Association Inc, Southern Alberta Art Gallery, Lethbridge AB

Brown, Elizabeth, *Dir,* College of Mount Saint Joseph on the Ohio, Studio San Giuseppe, Mount Saint Joseph OH

Brown, Elizabeth B, *Librn,* Montgomery Museum of Fine Arts, Library, Montgomery AL

Brown, Ellsworth H, *Dir,* Chicago Historical Society, Chicago IL

Brown, Frances R, *Chmn,* Five Civilized Tribes Museum, Library, Muskogee OK

Brown, Gaye L, *Dir Publications,* Worcester Art Museum, Worcester MA

Brown, Gerald F, *Executive Dir,* Paint 'N Palette Club, Anamosa IA

Brown, Harvley, *VPres,* Columbus and Lowndes County Historical Society Museum, Columbus MS

Brown, Heather, *Secy,* Sunbury Shores Arts and Nature Centre, Inc, Saint Andrews NB

Brown, Jack Perry, *Librn,* Cleveland Museum of Art, Library, Cleveland OH

Brown, James M, *Dir,* Society of the Four Arts, Palm Beach FL

Brown, J Carter, *Dir,* National Gallery of Art, Washington DC

Brown, J Carter, *Chmn,* United States Commission of Fine Arts, Washington DC

Brown, Jean, *Dir,* Tyringham Institute, Library, Tyringham MA

Brown, Joan, *Prof,* University of California, Berkeley, College of Letters & Sciences, Berkeley CA (S)

Brown, Joan, *Lending Dept,* Newark Museum, Newark NJ

Brown, John M, *General Mgr,* Bellingrath Gardens and Home, Theodore AL

Brown, Joseph E, *Assoc Prof,* Rochester Institute of Technology, School of Printing, Rochester NY (S)

Brown, Katharine L, *Dir,* Woodrow Wilson Birthplace Foundation, Staunton VA

Brown, Katherine T, *Prof,* Rice University, Dept of Art and Art History, Houston TX (S)

Brown, Kenneth David, *Head Dept,* Newberry College, Dept of Art, Newberry SC (S)

Brown, Kevin, *Visual Arts Coordr,* Jay R Broussard Memorial Galleries, Division of the Arts, Baton Rouge LA

Brown, Laurie, *Pres,* Brevard Art Center and Museum, Inc, Melbourne FL

Brown, Leonard, *Dir,* Tyringham Institute, Jean Brown Archive, Tyringham MA

Brown, Lora P, *Dir,* Mills House Visual Arts Complex, Garden Grove CA

Brown, Marilyn R, *Asst Prof,* Tulane University, Sophie H Newcomb Memorial College, New Orleans LA (S)

Brown, Michael, *Assoc Cur,* Museum of Fine Arts, Houston, Houston TX

Brown, Mildred B, *Pres,* Paint 'N Palette Club, Anamosa IA

Brown, Milton W, *Res Prof,* City University of New York, PhD Program in Art History, New York NY (S)

Brown, Myrtle, *Library Technician,* Charleston Museum, Library, Charleston SC

Brown, Nadya, *Asst Prof,* Murray State University, Art Dept, Murray KY (S)

Brown, Paul, *Adjunct Asst Prof,* Columbia University, School of the Arts, Division of Painting & Sculpture, New York NY (S)

Brown, Peter T, *Lectr,* Rice University, Dept of Art and Art History, Houston TX (S)

Brown, Quincalee, *Exec Dir,* American Association of University Women, Washington DC

Brown, Raymond B, *Chmn,* University of California, Los Angeles, Dept of Art, Design & Art History, Los Angeles CA (S)

Brown, Reynolds, *Adjunct Instructor,* Auburn University at Montgomery, Art Dept, Montgomery AL (S)

Brown, Robert, *Chmn,* Lincoln Memorial University, Division of Fine Arts, Harrogate TN (S)

Brown, Robert, *Dir,* Archives of American Art, New England Area Center, New York NY

Brown, Robert W, *Prof,* Glendale College, Dept of Fine Arts, Glendale CA (S)

Brown, Sandra, *Asst Prof,* Southwest Baptist University, Art Dept, Bolivar MO (S)

Brown, Steve, *Deputy Dir,* Virginia Museum of Fine Arts, Richmond VA

Brown, Susan, *Asst Dir,* University of Minnesota, University Art Museum, Minneapolis MN

Brown, Susan, *Instructor,* Southeastern Oklahoma State College, Art Dept, Durant OK (S)

Brown, Susan, *Dir Education,* Please Touch Museum, Philadelphia PA

Brown, Terry, *Dir,* Society of Illustrators, New York NY

Brown, Thack, *In Charge Art Coll,* Burroughs Wellcome Company, Research Triangle Park NC

Brown, Theodore M, *Prof,* Cornell University, Dept of the History of Art, Ithaca NY (S)

Brown, Thomas, *Chmn,* Quincy College, Dept of Art, Quincy IL (S)

Brown, Warren D, *Asst Dean Faculty & Assoc Prof,* Southwestern College, Art Dept, Winfield KS (S)

Brown, William, *Gallery Coordr,* University of Evansville, Krannert Gallery, Evansville IN

Brown, William, *Cur Glass,* Zanesville Art Center, Zanesville OH

Brown, William, *Asst Prof,* University of Evansville, Art Dept, Evansville IN (S)

Brown, William, *Area Coordr,* Northern Illinois University, Dept of Art, De Kalb IL (S)

Brown, William Archie, *Lecturer,* Emory University, Art History Dept, Atlanta GA (S)

Brown, William W, *Secy,* Mattatuck Historical Society Museum, Mattatuck Museum, Waterbury CT

Brown, W L Lyons, *Pres Board Governor,* J B Speed Art Museum, Louisville KY

Brown, Yvonne S, *Asst Division Chief,* Chicago Public Library, Art Section, Fine Arts Division, Chicago IL

Browne, Joseph P, *Dir,* University of Portland, Wilson W Clark Memorial Library, Portland OR

Browne, Norman, *Chmn Elem Art Educ,* Pan American University, Art Dept, Edinburg TX (S)

Brownell, Penelope, *Asst Prof,* University of British Columbia, Dept of Fine Arts, Vancouver BC (S)

Brown-Lee, Barbara, *Cur Education & Acting Cur Decorative Arts,* Milwaukee Art Museum, Milwaukee WI

Brownlee, Richard S, *Dir,* State Historical Society of Missouri, Columbia MO

Brownlee, Richard S, *Librn,* State Historical Society of Missouri, Library, Columbia MO

Brownold, Emily, *Dir,* University of Tampa, Henry B Plant Museum, Tampa FL

Browns, Charles C, *Actg Co-Dir,* Fairbanks Museum and Planetarium, Saint Johnsbury VT

Brozovich, Tom J, *Instr,* American River College, Dept of Art, Sacramento CA (S)

Brubaker, Ann, *Dir,* Atkins Museum of Fine Art, Junior Gallery and Creative Arts Center, Kansas City MO

Brubaker, Joseph, *Equipment Technician,* California State University Fullerton, Art Gallery, Visual Arts Center, Fullerton CA

Brucciani, Vicki, *Pres Emeritus,* DuPage Art League, Wheaton IL

Bruce, Chris, *Facilities Mgr,* University of Washington, Henry Art Gallery, Seattle WA

Bruce, Dan, *Asst Cur,* Kelowna Centennial Museum and National Exhibit Centre, Kelowna BC

Bruce, Gale, *Instructor Arts & Crafts,* Palo Alto Junior Museum, Palo Alto CA

Bruce, Janet, *Dir,* Jackson County Historical Society, John Wornall House Museum, Independence MO

Bruce, Tim, *Asst Prof,* Wright State University, Dept of Art & Art History, Dayton OH (S)

Bruder, Harold J, *Chmn,* Queens College, Art Dept, Flushing NY (S)

Brueggeman, Mark, *Asst Prof,* University of Wisconsin-Stevens Point, Dept of Art, Stevens Point WI (S)

Bruhn, Thomas P, *Cur of Collections,* University of Connecticut, William Benton Museum of Art, Storrs CT

Bruker, David, *Exhibit Preparator,* Indiana University, William Hammond Mathers Museum, Bloomington IN

Brumbaugh, R Nickey, *Head Dept,* Coker College, Art Dept, Hartsville SC (S)

Brumbaugh, Thomas B, *Prof,* Vanderbilt University, Dept of Fine Arts, Nashville TN (S)

Brumgardt, John R, *Dir,* Museum of Western Colorado Archives, Grand Junction CO

Brunelle, Edelgard, *Cur,* Pence Gallery, Davis CA

Bruner, Paul, *Assoc Prof,* Rutgers, the State University of New Jersey, Mason Gross School of the Arts, New Brunswick NJ (S)

Bruni, Stephen, *Asst Dir,* Delaware Art Museum, Wilmington DE

Bruning, Alex, *Chmn Drawing,* University of Manitoba, School of Art, Winnipeg MB (S)

Brunkus, Richard, *Assoc Prof,* Albion College, Dept of Visual Arts, Albion MI (S)

Brunner, Christal, *Reference Librn,* Mexico-Audrain County Library, Mexico MO

Brunner, Helen M, *Coordr Research Center,* Visual Studies Workshop, Research Center, Rochester NY

Bruno, Ana Basso, *Prof,* Catholic University of Puerto Rico, Dept of Fine Arts, Ponce PR (S)

Bruno, Vincent J, *Chmn,* University of Texas at Arlington, Dept of Art, Arlington TX (S)

Brunson, Dean, *VPres,* Eccles Community Art Center, Ogden UT

Brush, Gloria, *Asst Prof,* University of Minnesota, Duluth, Art Dept, Duluth MN (S)

Brush, Leif, *Assoc Prof,* University of Minnesota, Duluth, Art Dept, Duluth MN (S)

Brush, Pati, *Field Representative,* Lansing Art Gallery, Lansing MI

Brust, Constance, *Business Mgr,* Plains Art Museum, Main Gallery, Moorhead MN

Brust, John, *Assoc Prof,* Roanoke College, Art Dept, Salem VA (S)

Brutger, James H, *Assoc Prof,* University of Minnesota, Duluth, Art Dept, Duluth MN (S)

Brutuan, Cheryl A, *Asst Cur,* The Buffalo Fine Arts Academy, Albright-Knox Art Gallery, Buffalo NY

Brutus, Mare, *Recording Secy,* American Watercolor Society, New York NY

Bruya, Marilyn, *Asst Prof,* University of Montana, Dept of Art, Missoula MT (S)

Bruzelius, Caroline, *Asst Prof,* Duke University, Dept of Art, Durham NC (S)

Bryan, A Wesley, *VPres Finance,* Philadelphia Museum of Art, Philadelphia PA

Bryan, Dana, *Naturalist,* Tallahassee Junior Museum, Tallahassee FL

Bryan, Jack, *Chmn,* Cameron University, Art Dept, Lawton OK (S)

Bryans, John, *Head Dept,* McLean Arts Center, Art Dept, McLean VA (S)

Bryant, Billy J, *Head Dept,* Northwestern State University of Louisiana, Dept of Art, Natchitoches LA (S)

Bryant, Debra, *A V Coordr,* New Orleans Museum of Art, New Orleans LA

Bryant, Elizabeth, *Instr,* Danforth Museum School, Framingham MA (S)

Bryant, Olen, *Instructor,* Austin Peay State University, Dept of Art, Clarksville TN (S)

Bryant, Susan, *Instructor,* Austin Peay State University, Dept of Art, Clarksville TN (S)

Bryk, Donald, *Music & Art Librn,* Queensborough Community College Library, Bayside NY

Bryner, Dale W, *Prof,* Weber State College, Art Dept, Ogden UT (S)

Brynteson, Susan, *Dir Libraries,* University of Delaware, Morris Library, Newark DE

Bucci, Andrew, *Vis Artist,* Delta State University, Dept of Art, Cleveland MS (S)

Bucek, Anthony J, *Instr,* Agnes Scott College, Dept of Art, Decatur GA (S)

Buchan, David, *Bookstore Mgr,* Art Metropole, Toronto ON

Buchanan, D Harvey, *Chmn,* Case Western Reserve University, Dept of Art, Cleveland OH (S)

Buchanan, James V, *Development Dir,* Columbus Museum of Art, Columbus OH

Buchanan, John E, *Exec Dir,* Lakeview Museum of Arts and Sciences, Peoria IL

Buchanan, Peggy, *Registrar,* Southern Methodist University, Meadows Gallery, Dallas TX

Buchanan, Sidney, *Prof,* University of Nebraska at Omaha, Dept of Art, Omaha NE (S)

Buchanan, William C, *Asst Prof,* Western Carolina University, Dept of Art, Cullowhee NC (S)

Bucher, Francois, *Prof,* Florida State University, Art History Dept, Tallahassee FL (S)

Bucher, O, *Dir,* Santa Barbara City College, Fine Arts Dept, Santa Barbara CA (S)

Buchholz, Regina, *Prof,* Loyola Marymount University, Dept of Art & Art Hist, Los Angeles CA (S)

Buchwald, Howard, *Lecturer,* Columbia University, School of the Arts, Division of Painting & Sculpture, New York NY (S)

Buck, Charles, *VPres,* Boca Raton Center for the Arts, Inc, Boca Raton FL

Buck, Robert T, *Dir,* Brooklyn Museum, Brooklyn NY

Buckley, Kerry, *Development Officer,* San Diego Museum of Art, San Diego CA

Buckley, Margaret, *Librn,* Edmundson Art Foundation, Inc, Des Moines Art Center Library, Des Moines IA

Buckley, R F, *Assoc Prof,* Florida International University, Visual Arts Dept, Miami FL (S)

Buckman, Richard, *Chairperson Dept,* Saint Louis Community College at Florissant Valley, Dept of Art, Ferguson MO (S)

Buckner, Hal, *Chmn,* Fort Steilacoom Community College, Fine Arts Dept, Tacoma WA (S)

Bucl, Marcia, *Program Asst,* Farmington Valley Arts Center, Avon CT

Buda, Frank, *Supervisory Park Technician,* Longfellow National Historic Site, Cambridge MA

Budahl, Lee P, *Assoc Prof,* Western Carolina University, Dept of Art, Cullowhee NC (S)

Buell, Pamela, *Cur Asian Art,* Indiana University, Art Museum, Bloomington IN

Buening, Helen, *Chmn,* Benedictine College, Art Dept, Atchison KS (S)

Buerger, Janet, *Assoc Cur Photography Coll,* International Museum of Photography at George Eastman House, Rochester NY

Buettgenbach, Gary, *Asst Cur,* Wichita State University, Edwin A Ulrich Museum of Art, Wichita KS

Buettner, Stewart, *Chmn of Dept,* Lewis and Clark College, Dept of Art, Portland OR (S)

Buffington, Rod, *Asst Prof,* Eastern Illinois University, School of Fine Arts, Charleston IL (S)

Bugge, Jeannette, *Secy,* Portland Center for the Visual Arts, Portland OR

Buhalis, Nicholas, *Instructor,* Woodstock School of Art, Inc, New York NY (S)

Buhler, Curt F, *Research Fellow for Texts Emeritus,* Pierpont Morgan Library, New York NY

Buhlinger, Ernest, *Secy,* Bassist College, Collections Library, Portland OR

Buick, Glen, *Secy,* Alberta Art Foundation, Edmonton AB

Buitron, Diana M, *Cur of Greek and Roman Art,* Walters Art Gallery, Baltimore MD

Bujnowski, Donald, *Pres,* Surface Design Association, Inc, Fayetteville TN

Bujnowski, Donald G, *Prof,* Rochester Institute of Technology, School for American Craftsmen, Rochester NY (S)

Buki, Linda Constant, *Exec Dir,* Hunterdon Art Center, Clinton NJ

Buki, Zoltan, *Cur Fine Arts,* New Jersey State Museum, Trenton NJ

Bukowski, William, *Head of Dept,* Bethany Lutheran College, Art Dept, Mankato MN (S)

Buksbaum, Ronald, *Asst Prof,* Greater Hartford Community College, Humanities Division & Art Dept, Hartford CT (S)

Buley, Barbara J, *Assoc Prof,* Centenary College, Art Dept, Hackettstown NJ (S)

Bulger, Margaret Ann, *Folklife Adminr,* Florida Folklife Programs, White Springs FL

Bull, Douglas S, *Assoc Prof,* Monroe Community College, Art Dept, Rochester NY (S)

Bullard, Diane, *Bookkeeper,* Dahl Fine Arts Center, Rapid City SD

Bullard, E John, *Dir,* New Orleans Museum of Art, New Orleans LA

Bullock, Ray E, *Dir,* Taylor University, Chronicle-Tribune Art Gallery, Upland IN

Bullock, Ray E, *Chmn,* Taylor University, Art Dept, Upland IN (S)

Bullock, Robert S, *Chmn Dept,* Azusa Pacific University, College of Liberal Arts, Art Dept, Azusa CA (S)

Bullock, Starmanda, *Dir,* Howard University, Gallery of Art, Washington DC

Bullock, Starmanda, *Head Dept,* Howard University, Art Dept, Washington DC (S)

Bult, Sandra, *Cur Collection,* Chesapeake Bay Maritime Museum, Library, Saint Michaels MD

Bumbeck, David M, *Dir,* Middlebury College, Johnson Gallery, Middlebury VT

Bumgardner, Georgia B, *Cur Graphic Arts,* American Antiquarian Society, Worcester MA

Bumgarner, Bette, *Exhib Designer,* Calvert Marine Museum, Solomons MD

Bumpass, Terry, *Instr,* New Mexico Junior College, Arts, Business & Humanities Division, Hobbs NM (S)

Bunce, Frederick, *Chmn Art Dept,* Indiana State University, Turman Gallery, Terre Haute IN

Bunce, Fredrick W, *Chmn,* Indiana State University, Dept of Art, Terre Haute IN (S)

Bunce, William, *Dir,* University of Wisconsin, Kohler Art Library, Madison WI

Bunch, Nona, *Asst,* Diamond M Foundation Museum, Snyder TX

Buncher, Isabelle, *Secy,* Galesburg Civic Art Center, Galesburg IL

Bunker, George R, *Chmn,* University of Houston, Dept of Art, Houston TX (S)

Bunker, John S, *Assoc Dir,* Jacksonville Art Museum, Jacksonville FL

Bunnell, Peter C, *Pres,* The Friends of Photography, Carmel CA

Bunse, Don, *Prof,* University of Montana, Dept of Art, Missoula MT (S)

Burant, Jim, *Collections Mgr,* Public Archives of Canada, Picture Division, Ottawa ON

Burback, William, *Dir Education,* Museum of Fine Arts, Boston MA

Burben, Michael, *Instructor,* Montclair Art Museum, Museum Art Classes, Montclair NJ (S)

Burcaw, Ellis, *VPres,* Appaloosa Museum, Inc, Moscow ID

Burch, Devery, *Registrar,* Amarillo Art Center, Amarillo TX

Burch, J Lindsey, *Asst Prof,* Johns Hopkins University, School of Medicine, Dept of Art as Applied to Medicine, Baltimore MD (S)

Burch, Marlyn, *Pres,* Arts Council of Topeka, Topeka KS

Burch-Brown, Carol, *Instructor,* Virginia Tech, Dept of Art, Blacksburg VA (S)

Burchenal, Margaret, *Education Dir,* Portland Museum of Art, Portland ME

Burchett, Debra, *Dir Develop,* Los Angeles Institute of Contemporary Art, Los Angeles CA

Burchett, Jayme, *Assoc Prof,* School of the Ozarks, Dept of Art, Point Lookout MO (S)

Burchett, Kenneth E, *Prof & Chmn,* School of the Ozarks, Dept of Art, Point Lookout MO (S)

Burckhardt, Rudy, *Lectr,* University of Pennsylvania, College Arts & Science, Philadelphia PA (S)

Burda, Edward, *Registrar,* Southern Alleghenies Museum of Art, Loretto PA

Burdayron, Linda, *Animator,* Dorval Cultural Centre, Dorval PQ

Burden, Jeff, *Instr,* Southwestern Michigan College, Communications-Humanitites Dept, Dowagiac MI (S)

Burden, Shirley, *VPres,* Southern California Contemporary Art Galleries of the Los Angeles Art Association, Los Angeles CA

Burdick, Marjorie Z, *Secy,* University of Florida, University Gallery, Gainesville FL

Burdick, Vanroy R, *Asst Librn,* California College of Arts and Crafts, Meyer Library, Oakland CA

Bureau, Betti, *Treas Board of Dir,* Lake County Civic Center Association, Inc, Heritage Museum and Gallery, Leadville CO

Burford, James, *Dept Chmn,* Mount Vernon College, Art Dept, Washington DC (S)

Burg, Anne, *Children's Instructor,* Montclair Art Museum, Museum Art Classes, Montclair NJ (S)

Burgart, Herbert, *Pres,* Ringling School of Art and Design, Sarasota FL (S)

Burger, Gary C, *Dir,* Berkshire Museum, Pittsfield MA

Burgess, James L, *Chmn & Assoc Prof,* Salisbury State College, Art Dept, Salisbury MD (S)

Burgess, Larry E, *Cur,* Lincoln Memorial Shrine, Redlands CA

Burggraf, Ray, *Assoc Prof,* Florida State University, Art Dept, Tallahassee FL (S)

Burghardt, James H, *Librn,* Multnomah County Library, Henry Failing Art and Music Dept, Portland OR

Burgis, G C, *Dir,* City of Brampton Public Library, Art Gallery, Brampton ON

Burgt, J Vanden, *Head Dept,* Saint Norbert College, Art Dept, De Pere WI (S)

Burhans, Dicey Taylor, *Cur Pre-Columbian Art,* University of Virginia, Art Museum, Charlottesville VA

Burhans, Ira, *Instructor,* Dunedin Fine Arts and Cultural Center, Dunedin FL (S)

Burk, C William, *Dir,* Southern Oregon Historical Society, Jacksonville Museum, Jacksonville OR

Burk, George, *Cur,* Nasson College, Anderson Learning Center, Art Dept, Springvale ME

Burke, Bobbye, *Secy,* Print Club, Philadelphia PA

Burke, Dan, *Visual Arts Coordr,* Utah Arts Council, Glendinning Gallery, Salt Lake City UT

Burke, Dan, *Dept Chmn,* Mercyhurst College, Dept of Art, Erie PA (S)

Burke, Daniel, *Dir,* La Salle College Art Museum, Philadelphia PA

Burke, Gay, *Assoc Prof,* University of Alabama, Art Dept, Tuscaloosa AL (S)

Burke, Holly, *Secy,* Adirondack Lakes Center for the Arts, Blue Mountain Lake NY

Burke, James, *Prof,* Louisiana State University, School of Art, Baton Rouge LA (S)

Burke, James D, *Dir,* Saint Louis Art Museum, Saint Louis MO

Burke, Jean, *Secy,* Visual Arts Ontario, Toronto ON

Burke, Kelly, *Instructor,* Boston Center for Adult Education, Boston MA (S)

Burke, Rebecca, *Assoc Prof,* Mount Allison University, Fine Arts Dept, Sackville NB (S)

Burke, William J, *Assoc Prof,* Florida International University, Visual Arts Dept, Miami FL (S)

Cahill, Patricia, *Publicist,* Museum of Fine Arts, Springfield MA

Cahn, Martha, *Public Relations,* Hunterdon Art Center, Clinton NJ

Cahoon, Herbert, *Cur Autograph Manuscripts,* Pierpont Morgan Library, New York NY

Cain, Anne, *Head Reference,* Pasadena Public Library, Fine Arts Dept, Pasadena CA

Cain, James, *Head Dept,* Edison Community College, Gallery of Fine Art, Fort Myers FL

Cairns, R Christopher, *Chmn,* Haverford College, Fine Arts Dept, Haverford PA (S)

Cairns, Roger, *Assoc Prof,* Montgomery County Community College, Communicating Arts Dept, Blue Bell PA (S)

Calabrese, John A, *Asst Prof,* Texas Woman's University, Dept of Art, Denton TX (S)

Calabro, Richard, *Prof,* University of Rhode Island, Dept of Art, Kingston RI (S)

Calcagno, Nick, *Chmn,* Northeastern Oklahoma A & M College, Art Dept, Miami OK (S)

Calcagno, Philip M, *Fine Arts Librn,* Southern Illinois University, Lovejoy Library, Edwardsville IL

Calden, Lisa C, *Registrar,* University of Wisconsin, Elvehjem Museum of Art, Madison WI

Calder, A W, *Pres,* Providence Art Club, Providence RI

Calder, Jacqueline, *Cur,* Historic Cherry Hill, Albany NY

Calderwood, Kathy, *Assoc Prof,* Nazareth College of Rochester, Art Dept, Rochester NY (S)

Calderwood, Roger D, *Cur,* Victoria Society of Maine, Victoria Mansion and Morse Libby Mansion, Portland ME

Caldwell, B, *Faculty,* Truett-McConnell College, Arts Dept, Cleveland GA (S)

Caldwell, C, *Assoc Prof,* Northern Arizona University, Art Dept, Flagstaff AZ (S)

Caldwell, John, *Adjunct Cur Contemporary Art,* Carnegie Institute, Museum of Art, Pittsburgh PA

Caldwell, Martha B, *Prof,* James Madison University, Dept of Art, Harrisonburg VA (S)

Caldwell, Michael, *Chmn,* Seattle Pacific University, Art Dept, Seattle WA (S)

Caldwell, Ruby, *Asst Librn,* Amarillo Art Center, Library, Amarillo TX

Caldwell, Sherry, *Coordr of Tennessee State Museum Association Inc,* Tennessee State Museum, Nashville TN

Cale, David, *Assoc Prof,* Amarillo College, Art Dept, Amarillo TX (S)

Calhoun, Jim, *Music Librn,* Dallas Public Library, Fine Arts Division, Dallas TX

Calhoun, Larry, *Chmn Art Dept,* MacMurray College, Art Dept, Jacksonville IL (S)

Calhoun, Ralph E, *Instructor,* Guilford Technical Community College, Commercial Art Dept, Jamestown NC (S)

Calinescu, Adriana, *Cur Ancient Art,* Indiana University, Art Museum, Bloomington IN

Calisch, Douglas, *Asst Prof,* Wabash College, Art Dept, Crawfordsville IN (S)

Calkins, Robert G, *Pres,* International Center of Medieval Art, Inc, New York NY

Calkins, Robert G, *Prof,* Cornell University, Dept of the History of Art, Ithaca NY (S)

Callahan, Diane, *Spec Instr,* Southwest Baptist University, Art Dept, Bolivar MO (S)

Callahan, Jerry, *Div Chmn Fine Arts,* San Jacinto College, Art Dept, Pasadena TX (S)

Callahan, Katherine, *Pres,* Coquille Valley Art Association, Coquille OR

Callahan, Sharon G, *Coordr Public Relations,* Currier Gallery of Art, Manchester NH

Callan, Ann, *Librn,* Fort Lauderdale Museum of the Arts, Library, Fort Lauderdale FL

Callas, Connie, *Secy,* Pacific Grove Art Center, Pacific Grove CA

Callaway, Steven, *Asst to Dir,* Mills House Visual Arts Complex, Garden Grove CA

Callmann, Ellen, *Prof,* Muhlenberg College, Dept of Art, Allentown PA (S)

Callner, Richard, *Prof,* State University of New York at Albany, Art Dept, Albany NY (S)

Callow, Bette Ray, *Asst Librn,* Memphis Academy of Arts, G Pillow Lewis Memorial Library, Memphis TN

Calluori-Holcombe, Anna, *Dir,* Illinois Wesleyan University, Merwin Gallery, Bloomington IL

Calman, Wendy, *Assoc Prof,* Indiana University, Bloomington, School of Fine Arts, Bloomington IN (S)

Calmes, Michael, *Dir of Development and Public Relations,* Brockton Art Museum, Brockton MA

Calmins, Laura, *Cur European Decorative Arts & Sculpture,* Fine Arts Museums of San Francisco, M H de Young Memorial Museum and California Palace of the Legion of Honor, San Francisco CA

Calvert, C C, *Dir,* Mason County Museum, Maysville KY

Calvert, Janice, *Asst to Dir,* Region of Peel Museum and Art Gallery, Brampton ON

Camak, Helen, *Pres,* Anderson County Arts Council, Anderson SC

Camarata, Martin, *Prof,* California State College, Stanislaus, Art Dept, Turlock CA (S)

Camarigg, Elizabeth, *Art Librn,* Mason City Public Library, Mason City IA

Camber, Diane W, *Dir,* Bass Museum of Art, Miami Beach FL

Cameron, Ben, *Assoc Prof,* Columbia College, Art Dept, Columbia MO (S)

Cameron, Brooke, *Chmn,* University of Missouri, Art Dept, Columbia MO (S)

Cameron, Debbie, *Office Mgr,* Mount Saint Vincent University, Art Gallery, Halifax NS

Cameron, Duncan F, *Dir,* Glenbow Museum, Calgary AB

Cameron, Eric, *Chmn MFA Div,* Nova Scotia College of Art and Design, Halifax NS (S)

Cameron, John B, *Chmn Dept,* Oakland University, Dept of Art and Art History, Rochester MI (S)

Camfield, William A, *Prof,* Rice University, Dept of Art and Art History, Houston TX (S)

Camille, Cerise, *Asst Prof,* University of Alabama in Birmingham, Dept of Art, Birmingham AL (S)

Camon, Robert, *Pres,* National Assembly of Local Arts Agencies, Washington DC

Camp, Edward, *Prof,* Manatee Junior College, Dept of Art, Bradenton FL (S)

Camp, Kenneth, *Chmn,* Illinois Central College, Fine Arts Dept, East Peoria IL (S)

Camp, Orton P, *Pres,* Mattatuck Historical Society Museum, Mattatuck Museum, Waterbury CT

Camp, R, *Instructor,* Golden West College, Arts, Humanities and Social Sciences Institute, Huntington Beach CA (S)

Campbell, Andrew, *VPres,* Afro Arts Cultural Centre, Inc, African Arts Museum & Gallery, New York NY

Campbell, Charles, *Chmn,* University of Wisconsin-Eau Claire, Dept of Art, Eau Claire WI (S)

Campbell, David, *Public Info Officer,* Heard Museum, Phoenix AZ

Campbell, Donald, *Instructor,* Colby-Sawyer College, Art Dept, New London NH (S)

Campbell, Dora, *Chmn,* St Lawrence College, Dept of Visual and Creative Arts, Cornwall ON (S)

Campbell, Francis D, *Librn,* American Numismatic Society, Library, New York NY

Campbell, Frank, *Music Cur,* New York Public Library, Shelby Cullom Davis Museum, Library & Museum of the Performing Arts, New York NY

Campbell, Gretna, *Instr,* New York Studio School of Drawing, Painting and Sculpture, New York NY (S)

Campbell, Jacqueline Simone, *Asst Prof,* University of North Alabama, Dept of Art, Florence AL (S)

Campbell, Laurence Brasey, *Chmn,* Judson College, Division of Fine Arts, Marion AL (S)

Campbell, Mary, *Asst Prof,* Jersey City State College, Art Dept, Jersey City NJ (S)

Campbell, Mary, *VPres,* Ann Arbor Art Association, Ann Arbor MI

Campbell, Mary L, *Librn,* Robert W Ryerss Library and Museum, Library, Philadelphia PA

Campbell, Mary S, *Executive Dir,* Studio Museum in Harlem, New York NY

Campbell, M L, *Registrar & Conservator,* Rome Historical Society, Rome Information and Cultural Center, Rome NY

Campbell, Nancy, *Asst Prof,* Mount Holyoke College, Art Dept, South Hadley MA (S)

Campbell, Paul R, *Dir,* Rhode Island Historical Society, Library, Providence RI

Campbell, Sara, *Cur,* Norton Simon Museum, Pasadena CA

Campbell, Sharon, *Head Exhibitions & Education,* Greenville County Museum of Art, Greenville SC

Campbell, Sharon W, *Dir,* Greenville County Museum of Art, Museum School of Art, Greenville SC (S)

Campbell, Susan, *Slide Librn,* Center for Creative Studies - College of Art & Design Library, Detroit MI

Campbell, Walter A, *Prof,* Rochester Institute of Technology, School of Printing, Rochester NY (S)

Campolli, Eleanor, *Assoc Prof,* Jersey City State College, Art Dept, Jersey City NJ (S)

Camurati, Al, *VPres,* National Art League Inc, Douglaston NY

Canady, R, *VPres & Secy,* The Turner Museum, Denver CO

Canale, Joan, *Admin Assoc,* New York Public Library, Shelby Cullom Davis Museum, Library & Museum of the Performing Arts, New York NY

Canavan, John J, *Pres,* Springfield City Library, Art & Music Dept, Springfield MA

Canby, Jeanny Vorys, *Cur of Egyptian and Ancient Near Eastern Art,* Walters Art Gallery, Baltimore MD

Cancannon, Ann Worth, *Dir,* Art Center of Battle Creek, Battle Creek MI

Cancel, Luis R, *Dir,* Bronx Museum of the Arts, Bronx NY

Candau, Eugenie, *Librn,* San Francisco Museum of Modern Art, Louise Sloss Ackerman Fine Arts Library, San Francisco CA

Canedy, Norman, *Prof,* University of Minnesota, Minneapolis, Art History, Minneapolis MN (S)

Canepa, Jack, *Assoc Prof,* Webster College, Art Dept, Webster Groves MO (S)

Caner, John E Z, *Dir Henry Gallery Association,* University of Washington, Henry Art Gallery, Seattle WA

Canfield, Barbara, *Pres,* Hutchinson Art Association, Hutchinson KS

Cangialosi, Russell, *Chmn,* Los Angeles City College, Dept of Art, Los Angeles CA (S)

Cann, Constance, *In Charge Art Coll,* First and Merchants National Bank, Richmond VA

Canning, Thomas, *Librn,* West Virginia University, Creative Arts Center Library, Morgantown WV

Cannon, Chris, *Financial Officer,* Albany Museum of Art, Albany GA

Cannon, Daniel G, *Exec Dir,* National Art Education Association, Reston VA

Cannuli, Richard, *Instructor,* Villanova University, Dept of Art and Art History, Villanova PA (S)

Cano, Margarita, *Public Relations Coordr,* Miami-Dade Public Library, Miami FL

Cansino, Felicia, *Art Coordr,* Crocker National Bank, San Francisco CA

Cantin, Barry, *Library Asst,* New Orleans Museum of Art, Felix J Dreyfous Library, New Orleans LA

Cantini, Virgil D, *Chmn,* University of Pittsburgh, Dept of Studio Arts, Pittsburgh PA (S)

Cantler, Anne S, *Chmn House Committee,* National Society of Colonial Dames of the State of Maryland, Mount Clare Mansion, Baltimore MD

Cantone, Grace, *Prof,* Adelphi University, Dept of Art and Art History, Garden City NY (S)

Cantor, Dorothy, *Educ Dir,* Mattatuck Historical Society Museum, Mattatuck Museum, Waterbury CT

Cantrell, Gary, *Performing Arts Librn,* Adelphi University, Fine Arts Library, Garden City NY

Cantrell, Jacques, *Librn,* MPK Omega Co, Mike Kiefer Bio-Art Museum, Amarillo TX

Canzani, Joseph V, *Pres,* Columbus College of Art and Design, Columbus OH (S)

Capa, Cornell, *Executive Dir,* International Center of Photography, New York NY

Capen, Elizabeth, *VPres,* Old State House, Hartford CT

Capen, Judith, *Asst Prof,* Catholic University of America, Dept of Architecture and Planning, Washington DC (S)

Capen, Lloyd, *Treas,* Haystack Mountain School of Crafts Gallery, Deer Isle ME

Capizzo, Barbara, *Pres,* Artists Association of Nantucket, Kenneth Taylor Gallery, Nantucket MA

Caplan, Jerry, *Chmn,* Chatham College, Dept of Art, Pittsburgh PA (S)

Caplan, Jerry L, *Co-Dir,* Chatham College, Art Gallery, Pittsburgh PA

Caplow, Harriet, *Prof,* Indiana State University, Dept of Humanities, Terre Haute IN (S)

Caponi, Anthony, *Head Dept,* Macalester College, Dept of Art, Saint Paul MN (S)

Capozzi, John, *Art Cur,* Saint Bonaventure University Art Collection, Saint Bonaventure NY

Cappuccio, Thomas, *Prof,* Northern Michigan University, Dept of Art and Design, Marquette MI (S)

Capson, Evelyn, *Librn,* Boca Raton Center for the Arts, Inc, Library of the Center, Boca Raton FL

Caraco, Edward P, *Cur European Paintings,* New Orleans Museum of Art, New Orleans LA

Caravaglia, Angelo, *Prof,* University of Utah, Art Dept, Salt Lake City UT (S)

Carboni, Tamra, *Chief Cur Education,* Louisiana Department of Culture, Recreation and Tourism, Louisiana State Museum, New Orleans LA

Carbonneau, R J, *Pres of Board,* The Racine Art Association, Inc, Racine WI

Carbotti, Richard, *Instructor,* Roger Williams College, Art Dept, Bristol RI (S)

Carbotti, Richard, *Instr,* Salve Regina - The Newport College, Art Dept, Newport RI (S)

Carchman, JoAnn, *Dir Community Services,* Princeton University, Art Museum, Princeton NJ

Carden, Micki, *Asst Dir,* Miami-Dade Public Library, Miami FL

Cardiff, Gene, *Cur Natural History,* San Bernardino County Museum and Satellites, Fine Arts Institute, Redlands CA

Cardinale, Robert L, *Dir,* Boston University, Program in Artisanry, Boston MA (S)

Cardon, Patrick D, *VDir Cur,* Brooklyn Museum, Brooklyn NY

Carew, Eileen, *Exhibitions Coordr,* Danforth Museum of Art, Framingham MA

Carew, Roberta, *Admin Asst,* Valentine Museum, Richmond VA

Carey, John T, *Prof Emeritus,* University of West Florida, Faculty of Art, Pensacola FL (S)

Carey, Martha, *Asst Cur Research,* The Phillips Collection, Washington DC

Carey, Philip, *Cur Exhibitions & Design,* Roberson Center for the Arts and Sciences, Binghamton NY

Cargile, Ellen, *Instr,* Fort Lewis College, Art Dept, Durango CO (S)

Carlano, Marianne, *Cur Textile & Costumes,* Wadsworth Atheneum, Hartford CT

Carlberg, Norman, *Dir,* Maryland Institute, Rinehart School of Sculpture, Baltimore MD (S)

Carlbon, Larry, *VPres,* Hunterdon Art Center, Clinton NJ

Carleton, Samuel B, *Dir,* Imperial Calcasieu Museum, Lake Charles LA

Carley, O, *Assoc Prof,* Northern Arizona University, Art Dept, Flagstaff AZ (S)

Carling, Philip C, *First VPres,* Monmouth Museum and Cultural Center, Lincroft NJ

Carlisle, Dianna, *Cur,* Mississippi Valley Conservation Authority, R Tait McKenzie Memorial Museum, Almonte ON

Carlisle, Roger, *Asst Prof,* Arkansas State University, Dept of Art, State University AR (S)

Carlozzi, Annette DiMeo, *Cur,* Laguna Gloria Art Museum, Austin TX

Carlsen, Charles, *Biology Lab,* Exploratorium, San Francisco CA

Carlsen, Clifford, *Chmn,* Metropolitan Arts Commission, Portland OR

Carlsgaard, Lynn, *Asst Prof,* Northern State College, Art Dept, Aberdeen SD (S)

Carlson, Donna, *Admin Asst,* Art Dealers Association of America, Inc, New York NY

Carlson, Eleanor, *Chairperson Music Dept,* Southeastern Massachusetts University, College of Visual and Performing Arts, North Dartmouth MA (S)

Carlson, Eric, *Coordr,* State University of New York College at Purchase, Dept of Art History, Purchase NY (S)

Carlson, Richard B, *Admin,* Hudson River Museum, Yonkers NY

Carlson, Victor I, *Cur Prints & Drawings,* Baltimore Museum of Art, Baltimore MD

Carlton, Dale, *Instructor,* Rudolph Schaeffer School of Design, San Francisco CA (S)

Carmean, E A, *Cur 20th Century Art,* National Gallery of Art, Washington DC

Carmichael, Donald R, *Dir,* Eastern Illinois University, Tarble Arts Center, Charleston IL

Carmichael, Jae, *Pres,* National Watercolor Society, Lakewood CA

Carmichael, Mary E, *Head Dept,* Erskine College, Dept of Art, Due West SC (S)

Carmichael, Wade, *Exhib Design Coordr,* Indiana State Museum, Indianapolis IN

Carmin, James H, *Librn,* University of Oregon, School of Architecture and Allied Arts Library, Eugene OR

Carmine, Val, *Secy,* Community Council for the Arts, Kinston NC

Carneghi, Donna, *Admn Asst,* San Jose Museum of Art, San Jose CA

Carner, G C, *Dir,* University of Southwestern Louisiana, School of Art and Architecture, Lafayette LA (S)

Carnes, Griffiths C, *Dir,* Cowboy Artists of America Museum, Kerrville TX

Carney, Harold E, *Assoc Prof,* Tulane University, Sophie H Newcomb Memorial College, New Orleans LA (S)

Carney, Karen, *Librn,* Simon's Rock of Bard College, Library, Great Barrington MA

Carniel, Angelo, *Assoc Prof,* East Stroudsburg State College, Art Dept, East Stroudsburg PA (S)

Carpenter, Bruce, *VPres,* Western Illinois University, Macomb IL

Carpenter, Gilbert F, *Dir,* University of North Carolina at Greensboro, Weatherspoon Art Gallery, Greensboro NC

Carpenter, Laura, *Education Coordr,* Southeastern Center for Contemporary Art, Winston-Salem NC

Carpenter, Willard C, *Chmn,* Southern Arkansas University, Dept of Art, Magnolia AR (S)

Carpenter, Willard C, *Chmn Art Dept,* Southern Arkansas University, Art Dept Gallery & Magale Art Gallery, Magnolia AR

Carpentier, Paul, *Conservator & Ethnographer,* Musee du Quebec, Quebec PQ

Carpentier, Paul, *Chief Canadian Centre for Folk Culture Studies,* National Museum of Man, Ottawa ON

Carr, Amelia, *Instructor,* Lake Forest College, Dept of Art, Lake Forest IL (S)

Carr, Betty, *Secy,* Saint Augustine Art Association Gallery, Saint Augustine FL

Carr, Carolyn Kinder, *Cur of Art,* Akron Art Museum, Akron OH

Carr, Diane, *Secy,* Springfield Art Museum, Springfield MO

Carr, Frances A, *Archivist,* Shaker Museum, Poland Spring ME

Carr, Margaret S, *Museum Secy,* East Tennessee State University, Carroll Reece Museum, Johnson City TN

Carraway, Clyde L, *Exec Dir,* Alaska Arts Southeast, Inc, Sitka AK

Carr-Black, Patti, *Dir,* Mississippi State Historical Museum, Jackson MS

Carrere, Ernest A, *Pres of Board,* New Orleans Museum of Art, New Orleans LA

Carrero, Jaime, *Dir,* Inter American University of Puerto Rico, Dept of Art, San German PR (S)

Carr-Harris, Ian, *Dir,* Ontario College of Art, Library-Audiovisual Centre, Toronto ON

Carrillo, Alfred, *Asst Prof,* Pierce College, Art Dept, Woodland Hills CA (S)

Carris, Henry, *Pres & Co-founder,* Rutland Area Art Association, Inc, Chaffee Art Gallery, Rutland VT

Carroll, M, *Asst Dir Operations,* National Museum of Man, Ottawa ON

Carroll, Margaret D, *Asst Prof,* Wellesley College, Art Dept, Wellesley MA (S)

Carroll, Richard S, *Dir,* State Art Museum of Florida, John & Mable Ringling Museum of Art, Sarasota FL

Carroll, Robert, *Vis Prof,* Cleveland Institute of Art, Cleveland OH (S)

Carroon, Robert G, *Dir,* Litchfield Historical Society, Litchfield CT

Carrott, Richard G, *Prof,* University of California, Riverside, Art History Dept, Riverside CA (S)

Carson, Leta, *Chairperson,* Fairmont State College, Art Dept, Fairmont WV (S)

Carson, Mearl, *Supv,* Palo Alto Junior Museum, Palo Alto CA

Carstens, Jon, *Chmn,* Pacific Union College, Art Dept, Angwin CA (S)

Carswell, John, *Cur,* University of Chicago, Oriental Institute, Chicago IL

Carter, Charles Hill, *Owner,* Shirley Plantation, Charles City VA

Carter, Curtis, *Secy,* Milwaukee Center for Photography, Milwaukee WI (S)

Carter, Curtis L, *Dir,* Marquette University, Museum of Art, Milwaukee WI

Carter, Dean, *Instructor,* Virginia Tech, Dept of Art, Blacksburg VA (S)

Carter, Eltse B, *Chmn Humanities Div,* Northern Virginia Community College, Art Dept, Annandale VA (S)

Carter, Jerry, *Pres,* International Association of Contemporary Mosaicists, Silver Spring MD

Carter, John S, *Exec Dir,* Maine Maritime Museum, Bath ME

Carter, Kate, *Assoc Dir,* Maine Photographic Workshops, Rockport ME

Carter, Lynn, *Dir,* American Scandinavian Foundation Gallery, New York NY

Carter, Rand, *Chmn,* Hamilton College, Art Dept, Clinton NY (S)

Carter, Robert, *Cur Exhibitions,* Museum of the Philadelphia Civic Center, Philadelphia PA

Carter, Robert, *Chmn,* Jamestown College, Art Dept, Jamestown ND (S)

Carter, Warrick, *Chmn,* Governors State University, College of Arts & Science, Art Dept, Park Forest South IL (S)

Carter, Yvonne, *Assoc Prof,* University of the District of Columbia, Art Dept, Washington DC (S)

Cartmell, Robert, *Assoc Prof,* State University of New York at Albany, Art Dept, Albany NY (S)

Cartwright, Carroll L, *Treasurer,* The American Federation of Arts, New York NY

Cartwright, Guenther, *Asst Prof,* Rochester Institute of Technology, School of Photographic Arts & Sciences, Rochester NY (S)

Cartwright, Rick, *Asst Prof,* Saint Francis College, Art Dept, Fort Wayne IN (S)

Caruso, Gordon, *Instr,* Vancouver Community College, Langara Campus, Dept of Fine Arts, Vancouver BC (S)

Carvalho, M, *Assoc Dean,* University of Manitoba, Faculty of Architecture, Winnipeg MB (S)

Carver, Mary E, *Cur Asst & Registrar,* J B Speed Art Museum, Louisville KY

Carver, Melvin, *Prof,* North Carolina Central University, Art Dept, Durham NC (S)

Casa, Frank, *Chmn Dept,* Central Connecticut State University, Dept of Art, New Britain CT (S)

Casas, Mel, *Chmn,* San Antonio College, Art & Advertising Dept, San Antonio TX (S)

Cascio, Georgia, *Cur Exhibits,* Schenectady Museum, Schenectady NY

Casebier, Rodney, *Instructor,* William Woods-Westminster Colleges, Art Dept, Fulton MO (S)

Casey, Grace, *Executive Dir,* New Hampshire Art Association, Inc, Manchester NH

Casey, Jack, *Executive Secy,* San Antonio Art League, San Antonio TX

Casey, James B, *Head Librn,* Ohio Historical Society, Archives-Library Division, Columbus OH

Casey, Jean, *Reference,* Mason City Public Library, Mason City IA

Casher, Theodore P, *Instructor,* Dean Junior College, Visual and Performing Art Dept, Franklin MA (S)

Cashman, Norine D, *Cur,* Brown University, Slide & Photo Collection, Providence RI

Caskey, Robert, *Instructor,* Charles Stewart Mott Community College, Fine Arts Division, Flint MI (S)

Cason, Robert A, *Museum Cur,* Alabama Department of Archives and History Museum, Montgomery AL

Casper, Dorothy, *Secy,* Museo Italo Americano, San Francisco CA

Casper, Geraldine, *Cur,* Bergstrom Mahler Museum, Neenah WI

Cass, David B, *Assoc Cur,* Sterling and Francine Clark Art Institute, Williamstown MA

Cassel, Barbara, *In Charge Art Coll,* Glendale Federal Savings, Glendale CA

Cassell, William, *VPres,* Madison County Historical Society, Cottage Lawn, Oneida NY

Cassels-Brown, R, *Librn,* Saint Paul's School, Sheldon Library, Concord NH

Cassidy, Victor, *Secy,* N.A.M.E. Gallery, Chicago IL

Cassill, Carroll, *Prof,* Cleveland Institute of Art, Cleveland OH (S)

Cassino, Barbara, *Assoc Prof,* University of Northern Iowa, Dept of Art, Cedar Falls IA (S)

Cassino, Michael, *Prof,* Adrian College, Art Dept, Adrian MI (S)

Cassone, John, *Assoc Prof,* Los Angeles Harbor College, Art Dept, Wilmington CA (S)

Casstevens, Kenneth, *Assoc Prof,* University of Texas at Tyler, Dept of Art, Tyler TX (S)

Cast, David, *Assoc Prof,* Bryn Mawr College, Dept of the History of Art, Bryn Mawr PA (S)

Castellani, John A, *Resident Dir,* Mount Vernon Ladies' Association of the Union, Mount Vernon VA

Castellano, Virginia, *Dir,* Guadalupe Historic Foundation, Santuario de Guadalupe, Santa Fe NM

Castile, Rand, *Dir,* Japan Society, Inc, Japan House Gallery, New York NY

Castillo, Pepe, *Co-Dean of Fine Arts School,* El Museo del Barrio, New York NY

Castleberry, May, *Librn,* Whitney Museum of American Art, Library, New York NY

Castleman, Riva, *Dir Prints & Illustrated Books,* Museum of Modern Art, New York NY

Casto-Landolt, Belinda, *Cur,* Red Rock State Park Museum, Church Rock NM

Caswell, James O, *Head,* University of British Columbia, Dept of Fine Arts, Vancouver BC (S)

Catalano, Kathleen, *Cur,* Longfellow National Historic Site, Cambridge MA

Cataldi, Pat, *Cur,* United States Figure Skating Hall of Fame and Museum, Colorado Springs CO

Catan, Paul, *Pres,* Rensselaer Newman Foundation Chapel and Cultural Center, Troy NY

Catan-Rose, Richard, *Dir,* Catan-Rose Institute of Art, Forest Hills NY (S)

Cate, Phillip Dennis, *Dir,* Rutgers University, Jane Voorhees Zimmerli Art Museum, New Brunswick NJ

Cater, Tarja, *Administration Officer,* International Association of Contemporary Mosaicists, Silver Spring MD

Cathcart, Linda L, *Dir,* Contemporary Arts Museum, Houston TX

Cathey, Donna, *Administrator,* Newport Harbor Art Museum, Newport Beach CA

Catron, Patricia D'Arcy, *Dir,* Springfield Art Center, Springfield OH

Catron, Patricia D'Arcy, *Dir,* Springfield Art Center, Springfield OH (S)

Catterall, John, *Dept Head & Prof,* New Mexico State University, Art Dept, Las Cruces NM (S)

Catterall, John, *Dir Art,* Montana State University, School of Art, Bozeman MT (S)

Caulk, Douglas, *Museum Mgr,* State University of New York at Purchase, Neuberger Museum, Purchase NY

Causey, Dorothy, *Registrar,* Edison Community College, Gallery of Fine Art, Fort Myers FL

Cauthen, Gene, *Dir Fine Arts Gallery,* Mount Wachusett Community College, Art Galleries, Gardner MA

Cauthorn, Jess D, *Pres,* The Design Schools, Art Institute of Seattle, Seattle WA (S)

Cauthorn, Nan, *Instructor,* The Design Schools, Art Institute of Seattle, Seattle WA (S)

Cavalieri, Corliss, *Community Outreach Coordr,* Southern Alleghenies Museum of Art, Loretto PA

Cavalli, Robert, *Pres Board of Dir,* Lake County Civic Center Association, Inc, Heritage Museum and Gallery, Leadville CO

Cavanagh, Carroll J, *Secy & Gen Counsel,* National Gallery of Art, Washington DC

Cavanaugh, Charles J, *Coordr,* Tyler Junior College, Art Program, Tyler TX (S)

Cavanaugh, Marianne L, *Librn,* Kalamazoo Institute of Arts, Library, Kalamazoo MI

Cavano, Betty, *VPres,* Cleveland Museum of Art, Print Club of Cleveland, Cleveland OH

Caver, William, *Chmn,* Texarkana Community College, Art Dept, Texarkana TX (S)

Caviness, Madeline, *VPres,* International Center of Medieval Art, Inc, New York NY

Caviness, Madeline H, *Prof,* Tufts University, Fine Arts Dept, Medford MA (S)

Cawood, Hobart G, *Supt,* Independence National Historical Park, Philadelphia PA

Caya, Ronald F, *Dir,* Scottsdale Center for the Arts, Scottsdale AZ

Caya, Ronald F, *Dir,* Scottsdale Artists' League, Scottsdale AZ

Cazort, Mimi, *Cur Drawings,* National Gallery of Canada, Ottawa ON

Cebular, Janet, *Instr,* Mainline Center of the Arts, Haverford PA (S)

Cecere, James G, *Chmn Dept,* Mansfield State College, Art Dept, Mansfield PA (S)

Cederholm, Theresa D, *Coordr Art & Architecture,* Boston Public Library, Fine Arts Dept, Boston MA

Cellini, Nicholas, *Fine Arts Librn,* Beverly Hills Public Library, Fine Arts Library, Beverly Hills CA

Centofanti, Louis M, *Assoc Prof,* Niagara University, Fine Arts Dept, Niagara Falls NY (S)

Cerniglia, Alice, *Asst Cur,* Sierra Nevada Museum of Art, Reno NV

Cerny, Charlene, *Cur American & Latin American Coll,* Museum of New Mexico, Museum of International Folk Art, Santa Fe NM

Cerny, Katarina, *Cur,* American Swedish Historical Foundation and Museum, Philadelphia PA

Cervantes, James, *Cur Military History,* Heritage Plantation of Sandwich, Sandwich MA

Cervene, Richard, *Prof,* Grinnell College, Dept of Art, Grinnell IA (S)

Chafee, Richard, *Asst Prof,* Connecticut College, Dept of Art History, New London CT (S)

Chaffee, Tom, *Assoc Prof,* Arkansas State University, Dept of Art, State University AR (S)

Challinor, David, *Asst Secy Science,* Smithsonian Institution, Washington DC

Chalmers, E Laurence, *Pres,* Art Institute of Chicago, Chicago IL

Chalmers, Joan, *Secy,* Canadian Crafts Council, Conseil Canadien de l'Artisanat, Ottawa ON

Chaloupek, Pat, *VPres,* Keokuk Art Center, Keokuk IA

Chamber, Don, *Chairperson Div Creative Arts,* Monterey Peninsula College, Art Dept, Monterey CA (S)

Chamberlain, Anne, *Pres,* Art Information Center, Inc, New York NY

Chamberlain, Ken, *Head Librn,* Emily Carr College of Art & Design, Library, Vancouver BC

Chamberlain, Owen, *Dept Chmn,* Portland Community College, Visual & Performing Arts Dept, Portland OR (S)

Chamberlain, Peter, *Asst Prof,* Elmira College, Art Dept, Elmira NY (S)

Chamberlin, Marsha, *Executive Dir,* Ann Arbor Art Association, Ann Arbor MI

Chamberlin, Wesley, *Faculty,* San Francisco State University, Art Dept, San Francisco CA (S)

Chambers, Gerald, *Adj Prof,* Washington and Jefferson College, Art Dept, Washington PA (S)

Chambers, Thomas A, *Dean,* Golden West College, Arts, Humanities and Social Sciences Institute, Huntington Beach CA (S)

Chambliss, George, *Exec Dir Jekyll Island,* Jekyll Island Authority Museum, Jekyll Island GA

Chambliss, Judith, *Curriculum Dir,* Oregon School of Arts and Crafts, Hoffman Gallery, Portland OR

Chan, Ying Kit, *Prof,* West Virginia University, Division of Art, Morgantown WV (S)

Chandler, William L, *Chmn,* Concordia College, Art Dept, Mequow WI (S)

Chandler, William L, *Cur,* Concordia College Wisconsin, Fine Arts Galleries, Mequon WI

Chang, F Ming, *Assoc Prof,* Seton Hall University, Dept of Art and Music, South Orange NJ (S)

Chang, John R, *Deputy Dir,* Vancouver City Archives and Library, Vancouver BC

Chanlatte, Luis A, *Cur Archaeology,* University of Puerto Rico, Museum of Archaeology, History and Art, Rio Piedras PR

Channin, Richard, *Assoc Prof,* University of Pittsburgh at Johnstown, Dept of Fine Arts, Johnstown PA (S)

Chao, Paul, *Assoc Librn,* Seton Hall University, Library, South Orange NJ

Chapin, Leslie A, *Treas,* Westfield Athenaeum, Jasper Rand Art Museum, Westfield MA

Chaplin, George, *Dir Studio Arts Program,* Trinity College, Austin Arts Center, Hartford CT

Chaplin, George, *Dir,* Trinity College, Dept of Fine Arts, Hartford CT (S)

Chapman, Allan D, *Museum Librn,* Metropolitan Museum of Art, Robert Goldwater Library of Primitive Art, New York NY

Chapman, Christopher, *Pres,* Royal Canadian Academy of Arts, Toronto ON

Chapman, Dollie, *Instr,* Woodbury University, Professional Arts Division, Los Angeles CA (S)

Chapman, Hugh M, *Secy,* Columbia Museums of Art and Science, Columbia Art Association, Columbia SC

Chapp, Belena, *Asst Dir,* Purdue University Galleries, West Lafayette IN

Chappell, Miles, *Assoc Prof,* College of William and Mary, Dept of Fine Arts, Williamsburg VA (S)

Chappell, Sally Kitt, *Prof,* DePaul University, Dept of Art, Chicago IL (S)

Charest, Olivier, *Cur,* Pavilion of Humour, Man and His World, Montreal PQ

Charland, William, *Prof,* New Mexico State University, Art Dept, Las Cruces NM (S)

Charles, Charles, *Assoc Prof,* University of North Florida, Dept of Fine Arts, Jacksonville FL (S)

Charles, Peter, *Fac,* Georgetown University, Dept of Fine Arts, Washington DC (S)

Charley, Alfred B, *Assoc Prof,* Clarion University of Pennsylvania, Dept of Art, Clarion PA (S)

Charnow, Elliott, *Chmn,* Chabot College, Humanities Division, Hayward CA (S)

Charshee, Pamela Ford, *Cur,* National Society of Colonial Dames of the State of Maryland, Mount Clare Mansion, Baltimore MD

Charters, Cynthia, *Cur & Registrar,* University of California, Richard L Nelson Gallery, Davis CA

Chase, David, *Pres Board of Trustees,* Museum of Northern Arizona, Flagstaff AZ

Chase, Guy M, *Dir & Cur,* Greenville College, Richard W Bock Sculpture Collection, Greenville IL

Chase, Guy M, *Asst Prof,* Greenville College, Division of Language, Literature & Fine Arts, Greenville IL (S)

Chase, Stuart, *Asst to Dir,* Museum of the Southwest, Midland TX

Chase, Stuart A, *Asst to Dir,* Museum of the Southwest, Midland TX

Chase, W T, *Head Conservator & Technical Laboratory,* Freer Gallery of Art, Washington DC

Chasson, Timothy R, *Asst Prof,* Grinnell College, Dept of Art, Grinnell IA (S)

Chasteen, James, *Pres,* John C Calhoun State Community College, Art Gallery, Decatur AL

Chatelain, Gary, *Assoc Prof,* James Madison University, Dept of Art, Harrisonburg VA (S)

Chatt, Orville K, *Chmn,* Skagit Valley College, Dept of Art, Mount Vernon WA (S)

Chatterjee, Sankar, *Cur Paleontology,* Texas Tech University Museum, Lubbock TX

Chatton, Mildred, *Asst,* San Jose Museum of Art, Library, San Jose CA

Cheatham, Frank, *Prof,* Texas Tech University, Dept of Art, Lubbock TX (S)

Chee, Chen-Khee, *Asst Prof,* University of Minnesota, Duluth, Art Dept, Duluth MN (S)

Cheetham, Mark A, *Asst Prof,* McGill University, Department of Art History, Montreal PQ (S)

Cheevers, James W, *Senior Cur,* United States Naval Academy Museum, Annapolis MD

Chegwidden, Dennis, *Prof,* Hutchinson Community Junior College, Art Dept, Hutchinson KS (S)

Chelimsky, Oscar, *Assoc Prof,* Maryland College of Art and Design, Silver Spring MD (S)

Chellstrop, Marjorie, *Instructor,* Madonna College, Art Dept, Livonia MI (S)

Chen, Phil, *Instr,* Oxbow Center for the Arts, Saugatuck MI (S)

Chenevert, Edward V, *Dir,* Portland Public Library, Art Dept, Portland ME

Cheney, Iris, *Prof,* University of Massachusetts, Amherst, Art History Program, Amherst MA (S)

Cheney, Liana, *Chairperson Dept,* University of Lowell, Dept of Art, Lowell MA (S)

Cheng, Jane, *Cataloger,* Atkins Museum of Fine Art, Kenneth and Helen Spencer Art Reference Library, Kansas City MO

Chepp, Mark, *Cur,* University of Wisconsin, University Art Museum, Milwaukee WI

Chernow, Burt, *Dir,* Housatonic Community College, Housatonic Museum of Art, Bridgeport CT

Chernow, Burt, *Faculty,* Housatonic Community College, Art Dept, Bridgeport CT (S)

Cherrier, Patricia, *Sr Secy,* Hood Museum of Art, Hanover NH

Cherrington, Beth, *Secy,* French Art Colony, Inc, Gallipolis OH

Cherry, E, *Secy,* Association of Collegiate Schools of Architecture, Washington DC

Cherry, Schroeder, *Cur Education,* Studio Museum in Harlem, New York NY

Cherry, Terry, *Staff,* East Mississippi Junior College, Art Dept, Scooba MS (S)

Cheshire, Craig, *Prof,* Portland State University, Dept of Art and Architecture, Portland OR (S)

Cheshire, U T Richard, *Pres,* University of Tampa, Lee Scarfone Gallery, Tampa FL

Chesterman, Karen, *Bd of Dirs Pres,* Sioux City Art Center, Sioux City IA

Chetham, Charles, *Dir & Chief Cur,* Smith College, Museum of Art, Northampton MA

Chevalier, Renee, *Admin Asst,* Columbia Museums of Art and Science, Columbia SC

Chevian, Margaret, *Asst,* Providence Public Library, Art and Music Dept, Providence RI

Chew, Paul A, *Dir,* Westmoreland County Museum of Art, Greensburg PA

Chiang, Vivian, *Admin,* Chinese Culture Foundation, Chinese Culture Center Gallery, San Francisco CA

Chiba-Cohen, Judith, *Cur European Coll,* Museum of New Mexico, Museum of International Folk Art, Santa Fe NM

Chickanzeff, Sharon, *Head Librn,* Parsons School of Design, Adam & Sophie Gimbel Library, New York NY

Chieffo, Beverly, *Instructor,* Albertus Magnus College, Art Dept, New Haven CT (S)

Chieffo, Clifford, *Prof,* Georgetown University, Dept of Fine Arts, Washington DC (S)

Chieffo, Clifford T, *Cur,* Georgetown University, Art and History Museum, Washington DC

Chieffo, Patricia H, *Assoc Cur,* Georgetown University, Art and History Museum, Washington DC

Chieffo, Patricia H, *Chief Office Intern Programs,* National Museum of American Art, Washington DC

Chiego, William J, *Chief Cur,* North Carolina Museum of Art, Raleigh NC

Child, Kent, *Gallery Advisor & Humanities Division Dir,* Gavilan College, Art Gallery, Gilroy CA

Child, Kent, *Fine Arts Dept Chmn,* Gavilan College, Art Dept, Gilroy CA (S)

Childs, Bruce, *Instructor,* Austin Peay State University, Dept of Art, Clarksville TN (S)

Childs, David A, *VPres,* Historical Society of Martin County, Elliot Museum, Stuart FL

Childs, Elizabeth, *Cur of General Coll,* Valentine Museum, Richmond VA

Childs, Ellen, *Lectr,* Tunxis Community College, Graphic Design Dept, Farmington CT (S)

Childs, Robert V, *Collections Mgr,* University of California, Los Angeles, Museum of Cultural History, Los Angeles CA

Childs, Suse C, *Librn,* Metropolitan Museum of Art, The Cloisters Library, New York NY

Chilla, Benigna, *Instr,* Berkshire Community College, Dept Fine Arts, Pittsfield MA (S)

Chillman, Helen, *Slide & Photograph,* Yale University, Art and Architecture Library, New Haven CT

Chilton, W P, *Pres of Board,* Hermitage Foundation Museum, Norfolk VA

Chimy, Myron, *Dir,* Basilian Fathers, Mundare AB

Chin, Cecilia, *Chief Librn,* National Museum of American Art, Library of the National Museum of American Art and the National Portrait Gallery, Washington DC

Chin, Wanda W, *Coordr Exhibits & Exhibits Designer,* University of Alaska, Museum, Fairbanks AK

Chinn, Louise, *Assoc Dir Dept Publications,* Museum of Modern Art, New York NY

Chipley, Sheila M, *Asst Prof,* Concord College, Art Dept, Athens WV (S)

Chism, Robert H, *Instr,* Butler County Community College, Art Dept, El Dorado KS (S)

Chlebak, George F, *Chmn,* Kansas Wesleyan University, Art Dept, Salina KS (S)

Chmel, Patrick, *Chmn,* Rider College, Dept of Fine Arts, Lawrenceville NJ (S)

Chmura, Helen, *Chmn Fine Arts,* Lourdes College, Art Dept, Sylvania OH (S)

Choate, Jerry, *Instructor,* Northeastern Oklahoma State University, Tahlequah OK (S)

Choate, Randall, *Adjunct Instr,* Maryville College, St Louis, Art Division, Saint Louis MO (S)

Choban, Irving, *Pres,* Long Island Historical Society, Brooklyn NY

Chodkowski, Henry J, *Prof,* University of Louisville, Allen R Hite Art Institute, Louisville KY (S)

Chotowski, Henry, *Asst Prof,* Florida State University, Art Dept, Tallahassee FL (S)

Chouinard, Denis, *VPres,* La Societe des Decorateurs-Ensembliers du Quebec, Interior Decorators' Society of Quebec, Montreal PQ

Chouteau, Thomas F, *Faculty,* Saint Ambrose College, Art Dept, Davenport IA (S)

Chow, Ming Wu, *Instr,* Arkansas Arts Center, Little Rock AR (S)

Chown, Joyce, *Chmn Craft Div,* Nova Scotia College of Art and Design, Halifax NS (S)

Choy, Terence T, *Prof,* University of Alaska, Dept of Art, Fairbanks AK (S)

Chrisman, Diane S, *Deputy Dir Public Services,* Buffalo and Erie County Public Library, Buffalo NY

Christensen, Chris, *VPres,* Eccles Community Art Center, Ogden UT

Christensen, Cynthia, *Asst to Dir,* Joslyn Art Museum, Omaha NE

Christensen, John, *Instr,* Taft College, Division of Performing Arts, Taft CA (S)

Christensen, Robert C, *Dir Education & Special Programs,* Charles H MacNider Museum, Mason City IA

Christensen, Ruth, *Librn,* Southwest Museum, Braun Research Library, Los Angeles CA

Christensen, V A, *Dir,* Spiva Art Center, Inc, Joplin MO

Christensen, Valerie, *Cur & Registrar,* Presidential Museum, Odessa TX

Christenson, Elroy, *Actg Chmn Dept,* North Seattle Community College, Art Dept, Seattle WA (S)

Christenson, John, *Instr,* Mount San Jacinto College, Art Dept, San Jacinto CA (S)

Christian, Martha, *Instr,* Southwestern at Memphis, Dept of Art, Memphis TN (S)

Christianson, John, *Dir in Charge of Academic Relations,* Vesterheim, Norwegian-American Museum, Decorah IA

Christie, H, *Chmn Display Design,* Fashion Institute of Technology, Art & Design Division, New York NY (S)

Christie, Robert, *Gallery Supv,* University of Saskatchewan, Gordon Snelgrove Art Gallery, Saskatoon SK

Christin, J J, *Secy,* Rockwell International Corporation Trust, Pittsburgh PA

Christison, Florence, *Dir,* New Mexico Art League, Gallery, Albuquerque NM

Christoph, Peter, *Manuscripts and Special Coll,* New York State Library, Manuscripts and Special Collections, Albany NY

Christy, Anita, *Asst Dir,* China Institute in America, China House Gallery, New York NY

Chrysler, Walter P, *Chairman Board of Trustees,* Chrysler Museum, Norfolk VA

Chu, Petra Ten-Doesschate, *Dir,* Seton Hall University, Student Center Art Gallery, South Orange NJ

Chu, Petra Ten-Doesschate, *Chmn,* Seton Hall University, Dept of Art and Music, South Orange NJ (S)

Chumley, Gail, *Dir Office Operations,* Memphis Brooks Museum of Art, Memphis TN

Chumley, Jere, *Assoc Prof,* Cleveland State Community College, Dept of Art, Cleveland TN (S)

Chung, Jongsoon P, *Instructor,* Albertus Magnus College, Art Dept, New Haven CT (S)

Chung, Robert Y, *Asst Prof,* Rochester Institute of Technology, School of Printing, Rochester NY (S)

Church, Elsa K, *Librn,* Schenectady County Historical Society, Library, Schenectady NY

Church, Jack, *Pres,* Key West Art and Historical Society, Key West FL

Church, Jean, *Instr,* Illinois Valley Community College, Div of Humanities and Fine Arts, Oglesby IL (S)

Church, John, *Instructor,* Interlochen Arts Academy, Dept of Visual Art, Interlochen MI (S)

Churches, Roger, *Chmn,* Loma Linda University, La Sierra Campus, Art Dept, Riverside CA (S)

Churchill, Angiola, *Chmn,* New York University, Dept of Art Education & Division of Creative Arts, New York NY (S)

Churchill, Angiola, *Co-Chmn,* International Center for Advanced Studies in Art, New York NY

Churdar, Janice, *Staff Supv,* Bob Jones University, Greenville SC

Cialdella, Gary, *Head Photography Dept,* Kalamazoo Institute of Arts, Artcenter School, Kalamazoo MI (S)

Cianfoni, Emilio, *Chief Conservator,* Vizcaya Museum and Gardens, Miami FL

Ciarrochi, Ray, *Adjunct Asst Prof,* Columbia University, School of the Arts, Division of Painting & Sculpture, New York NY (S)

Ciccone, Amy Navratil, *Librn,* Chrysler Museum, Jean Outland Chrysler Library, Norfolk VA

Ciccone, Oscar, *Co-Dean of Fine Arts School,* El Museo del Barrio, New York NY

Cicotello, Louis M, *Chmn,* University of Missouri-Kansas City, Dept of Art and Art History, Kansas City MO (S)

Ciganko, Richard, *Chmn,* State University of New York College at New Paltz, Art Education Dept, New Paltz NY (S)

Cikovsky, Nicholas, *Cur American Art,* National Gallery of Art, Washington DC

Cinelli, Michael J, *Head Dept,* Northern Michigan University, Dept of Art and Design, Marquette MI (S)

Cipot, Carol, *Exec Secy,* Society of Medalists, Danbury CT

Clabaugh, John, *Asst Prof,* Nebraska Wesleyan University, Art Dept, Lincoln NE (S)

Claff, Mark, *Pres,* China Trade Museum, Milton MA

Claffey, Debra, *Coordr,* The Loading Dock Gallery, Boston MA

Clahassey, Patricia, *Assoc Prof,* College of Saint Rose, Division of Art, Albany NY (S)

Clain-Stefanelli, Elvira, *Art Advisory Board,* Society of Medalists, Danbury CT

Clamer, Carol, *Coordr,* Muse Art Gallery, Philadelphia PA

Clancy, Patrick, *Facilities Mgr & Exhibitions Cur,* Arts Council, Inc, Winston-Salem NC

Clapp, Anne de C, *Chmn,* Wellesley College, Art Dept, Wellesley MA (S)

Clapp, Robert T, *Secy,* Providence Athenaeum, Library, Providence RI

Clarien, Gary, *Workshop Supv,* Palo Alto Cultural Center, Palo Alto CA

Clark, Alson, *Librn,* University of Southern California, Architecture and Fine Arts Library, Los Angeles CA

Clark, A McFadyen, *Chief Canadian Ethnology Service,* National Museum of Man, Ottawa ON

Clark, Andrea, *Registrar,* Norton Simon Museum, Pasadena CA

Clark, Andrea, *Library Resources,* Oklahoma Historical Society, Central Museum, Oklahoma City OK

Clark, A William, *Prof,* Fairleigh Dickinson University, Fine Arts Dept, Teaneck NJ (S)

Clark, Bede, *Instructor,* Dunedin Fine Arts and Cultural Center, Dunedin FL (S)

Clark, Bob, *Head Dept,* Southwestern Technical College, Commercial Art and Advertising Design Dept, Sylva NC (S)

Clark, Carol, *Cur Paintings,* Amon Carter Museum, Fort Worth TX

Clark, Carroll S, *Ed-in-Chief,* National Museum of American Art, Washington DC

Clark, Gary F, *Asst Prof,* Bloomsburg University, Dept of Art, Bloomsburg PA (S)

Clark, Howard, *Instr,* Oxbow Center for the Arts, Saugatuck MI (S)

Clark, James M, *Chmn,* Blackburn College, Dept of Art, Carlinville IL (S)

Clark, Jane, *Dir Educ,* South Street Seaport Museum, New York NY

Clark, John B, *Dir,* The Bruce Museum, Greenwich CT

Clark, Kathryn, *Instr,* Oxbow Center for the Arts, Saugatuck MI (S)

Clark, Leslie, *Instructor,* Rudolph Schaeffer School of Design, San Francisco CA (S)

Clark, M, *Chmn,* Concord Antiquarian Society Museum, Library, Concord MA

Clark, Madge, *Asst to Dir & Public Relations,* Dixon Gallery and Gardens, Memphis TN

Clark, Margot, *Assoc Prof,* University of New Hampshire, Dept of the Arts, Durham NH (S)

Clark, Mark A, *Cur Decorative Arts,* Chrysler Museum, Norfolk VA

Clark, Mary Ellen, *Business Mgr,* Owensboro Museum of Fine Art, Owensboro KY

Clark, Mel Kauila, *Assoc Prof,* Park College, Dept of Art, Parkville MO (S)

Clark, Nichols, *Dir,* Phillips Exeter Academy, Frederic R Mayer Art Center & Lamont Gallery, Exeter NH

Clark, Peter P, *Registrar,* National Baseball Hall of Fame and Museum, Inc, Art Collection, Cooperstown NY

Clark, Phyllis Blair, *Asst Mus Dir,* College of Wooster Art Center Museum, Wooster OH

Clark, Richard, *Cur Design,* United States Military Academy, West Point Museum, West Point NY

Clark, Robert Sterling, *Vis Prof,* Williams College, Dept of Art, Williamstown MA (S)

Clark, R T, *Prof,* Utah State University, Dept of Art, Logan UT (S)

Clark, Sharon, *Asst to Dir,* University of Miami, Lowe Art Museum, Coral Gables FL

Clark, Sterling, *Asst Chmn Photography,* Art Institute of Fort Lauderdale, Fort Lauderdale FL (S)

Clark, Sylvia, *Head Dept,* Drexel University, Dept of Design, Philadelphia PA (S)

Clark, Vicky A, *Cur Education,* Carnegie Institute, Museum of Art, Pittsburgh PA

Clark, Willy, *Prof,* Shoreline Community College, Humanities Division, Seattle WA (S)

Clarke, Allan, *Exhibits Officer,* Newfoundland Museum, Saint John's NF

Clarke, Jude, *Cur,* Vernon Art Association, Topham Brown Gallery, Vernon BC

Clarke, Robert, *Instructor,* Mohawk Valley Community College, Advertising Design and Production, Utica NY (S)

Clarke, Ruth Anne, *Museum Asst,* Historical Society of Delaware, Old Town Hall Museum, Wilmington DE

Clarke-Hazlett, Janet, *Librn,* Vassar College Art Gallery, Art Library, Poughkeepsie NY

Clarke-Spater, Susan, *Dir,* Pimeria Alta Historical Society, Nogales AZ

Clark-Langager, Sarah, *Cur Painting & Sculpture,* Munson-Williams-Proctor Institute, Museum of Art, Utica NY

Clarkson, John D, *Cur Art and Dir Acquisition,* West Virginia University, Creative Arts Center and Gallery, Morgantown WV

Clasby-LeTellier, Kathleen, *VPres,* Lewistown Art Center, Lewistown MT

Claxton-Oldfield, Patricia, *Librn,* The Robert McLaughlin Gallery, Library, Oshawa ON

Clay, Calvin, *Pres,* Art Patrons League of Mobile, Mobile AL

Clay, Langdon F, *Asst Dir,* University of Rochester, Memorial Art Gallery, Rochester NY

Clayson, Hollis, *Asst Prof,* Northwestern University, Evanston, Dept of Art History, Evanston IL (S)

Clayton, Foster, *Registrar,* Kimbell Art Museum, Fort Worth TX

Clayton, John M, *University Archivist & Dir Permanent Coll,* University of Delaware, University Art Collections, Newark DE

Clayton, Ronald, *Asst Prof,* Arkansas State University, Dept of Art, State University AR (S)

Clayton, William, *Art Librn,* University of Georgia, University of Georgia Libraries, Athens GA

Clayton, Wini, *Head Dept,* Allegany Community College, Cumberland MD (S)

Clearwater, James, *Asst Dir,* New York University, Grey Art Gallery and Study Center, New York NY

Cleary, John R, *Asst Prof,* Salisbury State College, Art Dept, Salisbury MD (S)

Cleary, John R, *Gallery Dir,* Salisbury State College, College Gallery, Salisbury MD

Cleary, Manon, *Prof,* University of the District of Columbia, Art Dept, Washington DC (S)

Cleary, Suzanne, *Education Dir,* Philipse Manor Hall State Historic Site, Yonkers NY

Clemans, H, *Instructor,* Golden West College, Arts, Humanities and Social Sciences Institute, Huntington Beach CA (S)

Clement, Adele, *Secy,* Essex Art Association, Inc, Essex CT

Clement, Claudia, *Librn,* And-Or, Resources in Contemporary Arts, Seattle WA

Clement, Constance, *Asst Dir Education & Information,* Yale University, Yale Center for British Art, New Haven CT

Clemente, Vincent, *Instr,* Munson-Williams-Proctor Institute, School of Art, Utica NY (S)

Clementi, Anthony, *Asst Prof,* New York Institute of Technology, Fine Arts Dept, Old Westbury NY (S)

Clemmer, Edwin L, *Prof,* Adams State College, Dept of Visual Arts, Alamosa CO (S)

Clemmer, John, *Chmn,* Tulane University, Sophie H Newcomb Memorial College, New Orleans LA (S)

Clemmer, John, *Chmn & Dir Galleries,* Tulane University, Dept Art Newcomb Col Art Galleries, New Orleans LA

Clervi, Paul, *Assoc Prof,* William Woods-Westminster Colleges, Art Dept, Fulton MO (S)

Clervi, Paul, *Dir,* William Woods College, Art Gallery, Fulton MO

Cleveland, M, *Asst Prof,* Kearney State College, Dept of Art, Kearney NE (S)

Cleveland, R Earl, *Chmn Dept,* Carson-Newman College, Art Dept, Jefferson City TN (S)

Clewell, E B, *Cur,* Moravian Historical Society, Whitefield House Museum, Nazareth PA

Clewley, Susan, *Gallery Shop Mgr,* Madison Art Center, Madison WI

Clifford, Christina, *Librn,* San Diego Public Library, Art & Music Section, San Diego CA

Clifford, Deborah P, *Pres,* Sheldon Art Museum, Archaeological & Historical Society, Middlebury VT

Clifford, Ethel, *Admin Asst,* Haystack Mountain School of Crafts Gallery, Deer Isle ME

Clifford, Kenneth, *Assoc Prof,* Mississippi State University, Art Dept, Mississippi State MS (S)

Clifr, Arlene L, *Dir,* Fisk University, Division of Humanities & Fine Arts, Nashville TN (S)

Cline, Fred A, *Librn,* Asian Art Museum of San Francisco, Library, San Francisco CA

Cline, Kay, *Museum on Wheels Dir,* Monterey Peninsula Museum of Art, Monterey CA

Clingman, Allen, *Pres,* Community Arts Council of Vancouver, Vancouver BC

Clinkscales, Joyce M, *Librn,* University of Arkansas, Fine Arts Library, Fayetteville AR

Clisby, Roger D, *Chief Cur,* Crocker Art Museum, Sacramento CA

Close, Patrick, *Dir,* Photographers Gallery, Library, Saskatoon SK

Cloud, Susan, *Secy,* Verde Valley Art Association, Inc, Jerome AZ

Cloudsley, Donald, *Deputy Dir Support Services,* Buffalo and Erie County Public Library, Buffalo NY

Clough, Charles, *VPres,* Hallwalls Gallery, New York NY

Clough, Jeffory, *Asst Librn,* Portland School of Art Library, Portland ME

Clovis, John, *Assoc Prof,* Fairmont State College, Art Dept, Fairmont WV (S)

Clowes, Allen W, *Cur,* Indianapolis Museum of Art, Clowes Fund Collection, Indianapolis IN

Clute, Elizabeth, *Asst to Dir,* National Museum of Racing, Inc, Saratoga Springs NY

Coates, Ann S, *Cur Slides,* University of Louisville, Slide Collection, Louisville KY

Coates, James, *Asst Prof,* University of Lowell, Dept of Art, Lowell MA (S)

Coates, Ross, *Chmn,* Washington State University, Fine Arts Dept, Pullman WA (S)

Cobb, Henry Ives, *VChmn,* Museum of Modern Art, New York NY

Cobb, Whitfield, *VPres,* Blacksburg Regional Art Association, Blacksburg VA

Cocaougher, Robert L, *Assoc Prof,* University of North Florida, Dept of Fine Arts, Jacksonville FL (S)

Cochran, Malcolm, *Exhibitions Designer & Asst Cur,* Hood Museum of Art, Hanover NH

Cockerline, Neil C, *Cur,* Anderson Fine Arts Center, Anderson IN

Cocordas, Elaine J, *Dir Exhibitions,* Philadelphia College of Art, Philadelphia PA

Coddington, Dabney M, *Communications Specialist,* Tryon Palace Restoration Complex, New Bern NC

Codell, Julie F, *Asst Prof,* University of Montana, Dept of Art, Missoula MT (S)

Coe, Henry H R, *Chmn,* Buffalo Bill Memorial Association, Cody WY

Coe, Mildred M, *Exec Dir,* Hickory Museum of Art, Inc, Hickory NC

Coe, William R, *Am Section Cur,* University of Pennsylvania, University Museum of Archaeology & Anthropology, Philadelphia PA

Coelho, Tony, *Treas,* Congressional Arts Caucus, Washington DC

Coes, Kent Day, *Historian,* Artists' Fellowship, Inc, New York NY

Cofer, Alene N, *Assoc Dir,* Mariners Museum, Newport News VA

Coffey, Bettye, *Clerical Hostess,* Red River Valley Museum, Vernon TX

Coffey, John W, *Cur,* Bowdoin College, Museum of Art & Peary-MacMillan Arctic Museum, Brunswick ME

Coffey, Steve, *Visual Arts Dir,* Brewton-Parker College, Visual Arts, Mount Vernon GA (S)

Coffey, Susan C, *Research Cur,* Norton Simon Museum, Pasadena CA

Coffin, David R, *Prof,* Princeton University, Dept of Art and Archaeology, Princeton NJ (S)

Coffman, Michael, *Program Developer,* Jacksonville Museum of Arts and Sciences, Jacksonville FL

Coffman, Terrence J, *Dir,* Milwaukee Institute of Art and Design, Milwaukee WI (S)

Cogan, Marshall S, *Chmn,* American Council for the Arts, New York NY

Cogan, Sam C, *Asst Dir,* California Museum of Science and Industry, Los Angeles CA

Coghlan, Gladys, *Librn,* Bennington Museum, Library, Bennington VT

Cogswell, James, *Asst Prof,* Florida State University, Art Dept, Tallahassee FL (S)

Cogswell, Margaret P, *Chief Office Public Programs,* National Museum of American Art, Washington DC

Cohan, Allan L, *Coordr,* Ulster County Community College, Visual Arts Gallery, Stone Ridge NY

Cohan, Jack, *Dir Jorgensen Auditorium,* University of Connecticut, Jorgensen Gallery, Storrs CT

Cohan, Zara, *Gallery Dir,* Kean College of New Jersey, Union NJ

Cohen, Allan, *Head Dept,* Ulster County Community College, Dept of Visual Arts, Stone Ridge NY (S)

Cohen, Janet, *Adjunct Instr,* New York Institute of Technology, Fine Arts Dept, Old Westbury NY (S)

Cohen, Marcia, *Instructor,* Atlanta College of Art, Atlanta GA (S)

Cohen, Mark, *Adjunct Prof,* Wilkes College, Dept of Art, Wilkes-Barre PA (S)

Cohen, Nancy, *Instr,* Mainline Center of the Arts, Haverford PA (S)

Cohen, Sylvia S, *Development Dir,* Arapahoe Community College, Colorado Gallery of the Arts, Littleton CO

Cohenour, Barbara, *Instr,* Claremore College, Art Dept, Claremore OK (S)

Cohn, Anna R, *Dir,* B'nai B'rith Klutznick Museum, Washington DC

Cohn, Marjorie, *Assoc Conservator,* Harvard University, William Hayes Fogg Art Museum, Cambridge MA

Cohn, Shelley, *Deputy Dir,* Arizona Commission on the Arts, Phoenix AZ

Cohnstaedt, Joy, *Executive Dir,* Saskatchewan Arts Board, Regina SK

Cohodas, Marvin, *Assoc Prof,* University of British Columbia, Dept of Fine Arts, Vancouver BC (S)

Coin, Gregory, *Adminr,* New Jersey Historical Society Museum, New Jersey Historical Society at Morven, Newark NJ

Coiner, Maynard R, *Prof,* Concord College, Art Dept, Athens WV (S)

Coit, J Knox, *Actg Dir,* Dubuque Art Association, Old Jail Gallery, Dubuque IA

Coke, Charles V, *Assoc Prof,* Northwestern State University of Louisiana, Dept of Art, Natchitoches LA (S)

Coker, Alyce, *Assoc Prof,* University of Minnesota, Duluth, Art Dept, Duluth MN (S)

Coker, Robert R, *Treas,* Brookgreen Gardens, Murrells Inlet SC

Colarusso, Corrine, *Instructor,* Atlanta College of Art, Atlanta GA (S)

Colburn, Richard, *Asst Prof,* University of Northern Iowa, Dept of Art, Cedar Falls IA (S)

Colby, Bill D, *Dir,* University of Puget Sound, Kittredge Art Gallery, Tacoma WA

Colby, Tracy B, *Head Fiber & Fabric,* Southern Illinois University at Edwardsville, Dept of Art and Design, Edwardsville IL (S)

Colchado, Jose, *Art Educ Coordr,* San Jose State University, Art Dept, San Jose CA (S)

Cole, Bruce, *Prof,* Indiana University, Bloomington, School of Fine Arts, Bloomington IN (S)

Cole, Charles, *Pres of Board of Trustees,* Western Colorado Center for the Arts, Inc, Grand Junction CO

Cole, David C, *Cur,* Fort George G Meade Museum, Fort Meade MD

Cole, Elise, *Cur Art Education,* Ella Sharp Museum, Jackson MI

Cole, Elizabeth, *Faculty,* University of Toledo, Dept of Art, Art Education and Art History, Toledo OH (S)

Cole, Howson W, *Librn,* Virginia Historical Society, Library, Richmond VA

Cole, Jeanette, *Adjunct Instr,* Franklin and Marshall College, Art Dept, Lancaster PA (S)

Cole, Michael, *Artist,* San Bernardino County Museum and Satellites, Fine Arts Institute, Redlands CA

Cole, Robert A, *Assoc Prof,* Rochester Institute of Technology, School of Art and Design, Rochester NY (S)

Cole, Sylvan, *Board Dir Member,* Art Information Center, Inc, New York NY

Coleburn, Sue, *Bookstore Mgr,* Brandywine River Museum, Chadds Ford PA

Coleman, C Allen, *Co-Dir,* New York University, 80 Washington Square East Galleries, New York NY

Coleman, Elizabeth A, *Cur Costumes & Textiles,* Brooklyn Museum, Brooklyn NY

Coleman, Henry, *Assoc Prof,* College of William and Mary, Dept of Fine Arts, Williamsburg VA (S)

Coleman, Herbert, *Head,* Mississippi Valley State University, Fine Arts Dept, Itta Bena MS (S)

Coleman, Loring W, *VPres,* Concord Art Association, Concord MA

Coleman, Myrlan, *Head Dept of Art,* Weatherford College, Dept of Humanities and Art, Weatherford TX (S)

Coleman, Oliver, *Undergrad Coordr,* University of Georgia, Franklin College of Arts and Sciences, Dept of Art, Athens GA (S)

Coleman, R Colleen, *In Charge,* Sheldon Swope Art Gallery, Research Library, Terre Haute IN

Coleman, Thomas, *Prof,* Indiana University, Bloomington, School of Fine Arts, Bloomington IN (S)

Colemon, Catherine, *Asst Librn,* Wadsworth Atheneum, Auerbach Art Library, Hartford CT

Coley, Betty A, *Librn,* Baylor University, Armstrong Browning Library, Waco TX

Coley, Philip, *Assoc Prof,* Auburn University at Montgomery, Art Dept, Montgomery AL (S)

Colin, Ralph F, *Admin VPres & Counsel,* Art Dealers Association of America, Inc, New York NY

Colker, Ed, *Dean,* State University of New York College at Purchase, Division of Visual Arts, Purchase NY (S)

Coll, Eduardo Morales, *Pres,* Ateneo Puertorriqueno, San Juan PR

Colleck, Philip, *VPres,* National Antique and Art Dealers Association of America, New York NY

Collens, David R, *Dir,* Storm King Art Center, Mountainville NY

Collett, Joan, *Librn,* Saint Louis Public Library, Saint Louis MO

Collette, Alfred T, *Dir,* Syracuse University, Art Collection, Syracuse NY

Colley, Christine, *Assoc Prof,* Vanderbilt University, Dept of Fine Arts, Nashville TN (S)

Collier, Glenn W, *Secy,* Springfield Art Center, Springfield OH

Collier, Natalee, *Head Performing Arts Dept,* Long Beach Public Library, Long Beach CA

Collier, Ralph, *Pres,* Campbell Museum, Camden NJ

Collier, Ric, *Dir,* Art Museum of South Texas, Corpus Christi TX

Collier, Will, *Instr,* Santa Rosa Junior College, Art Dept, Santa Rosa CA (S)

Collingnon, Frederick, *Chmn City & Regional Planning,* University of California, Berkeley, College of Environmental Design, Berkeley CA (S)

Collings, Anita, *Instr,* Ocean City Arts Center, Ocean City NJ (S)

Collins, Alan, *Prof,* Loma Linda University, La Sierra Campus, Art Dept, Riverside CA (S)

Collins, Allison, *Dir,* New Orleans Academy of Fine Arts Gallery, New Orleans LA

Collins, Barbara H, *Asst Dir,* Old Dartmouth Historical Society, New Bedford Whaling Museum, New Bedford MA

Collins, Dana, *Instr,* Illinois Valley Community College, Div of Humanities and Fine Arts, Oglesby IL (S)

Collins, David, *Asst Dir & General Adminr,* Newark Museum, Newark NJ

Collins, David M, *Adminr,* Frick Collection, New York NY

Collins, Gen, *Secy,* Seneca Falls Historical Society Museum, Seneca Falls NY

Collins, Harvey A, *Chmn Dept,* Olivet Nazarene College, Dept of Art, Kankakee IL (S)

Collins, Joel, *Asst Prof,* Mount Union College, Dept of Art, Alliance OH (S)

Collins, J Stephen, *Chairperson Div,* Modesto Junior College, Arts Humanities and Speech Division, Modesto CA (S)

Collins, J W, *Pres,* Bank of Mississippi, Tupelo MS

Collins, Kathleen, *Secy,* Imperial Calcasieu Museum, Gibson Library, Lake Charles LA

Collins, Kathleen, *Asst Prof,* Rochester Institute of Technology, School of Photographic Arts & Sciences, Rochester NY (S)

Collins, Lizetta, *Adjunct Instructor,* Auburn University at Montgomery, Art Dept, Montgomery AL (S)

Collins, M Regina, *Chmn,* Mount Mary College, Tower Gallery, Milwaukee WI

Collins, Reba Neighbors, *Dir,* Will Rogers Memorial and Museum, Claremore OK

Collins, Steve, *Technical Asst,* Art Research Center, Kansas City MO

Collins, Susan, *Asst Dir,* Westerly Public Library, Westerly RI

Collins, Timothy, *VPres,* Sierra Nevada Museum of Art, Reno NV

Collinson, Helen, *Cur,* University of Alberta, Ring House Gallery, Edmonton AB

Coll Vidal, Rosa G, *Pres,* Museo Historico de Puerto Rico Inc, Santurce PR

Colson, Chester, *Prof,* Wilkes College, Dept of Art, Wilkes-Barre PA (S)

Colt, Rosemary, *Secy,* Providence Athenaeum, Providence RI

Colvert, Richard, *Secy,* Charles B Goddard Center for the Visual and Performing Arts, Ardmore OK

Colvig, Richard, *Sr Librn in Charge,* Oakland Public Library, Art, Music & Recreation Section, Oakland CA

Colvin, Richard D, *Exhibits Designer,* Rollins College, George D and Harriet W Cornell Fine Arts Center Museum, Winter Park FL

Colwill, Stiles T, *Cur,* Maryland Historical Society Museum, Baltimore MD

Colyer, Darrell, *Exhib Coordr,* University of Alberta, Ring House Gallery, Edmonton AB

Combs, Kenneth I, *Chmn Div,* Pacific University in Oregon, Dept of Fine Arts, Forest Grove OR (S)

Combton, Kathleen, *Asst Cur,* Alberta College of Art Gallery, Calgary AB

Comer, Eugenia, *Assoc Prof,* Augusta College, Dept of Fine Arts, Augusta GA (S)

Comer, Fred, *Exec Dir,* Iowa State Education Association, Salisbury House, Des Moines IA

Comerford, Susan, *Instructor,* Umpqua Community College, Fine & Performing Arts Dept, Roseburg OR (S)

Comiskey, Ernest D, *Prof,* West Liberty State College, Art Dept, West Liberty WV (S)

Compasso, Isabel, *Lectr,* Tunxis Community College, Graphic Design Dept, Farmington CT (S)

Comport, Jean, *First Asst Fine Arts Department,* Detroit Public Library, Fine Arts Dept, Detroit MI

Compton, Beverley C, *Pres,* Municipal Art Society of Baltimore City, Baltimore MD

Compton, John C, *Assoc Prof,* Rochester Institute of Technology, School of Photographic Arts & Sciences, Rochester NY (S)

Compton, Julie M, *Head Fine Arts Department,* Atlanta Public Library, Fine Arts Dept, Atlanta GA

Comstock, Jane, *Adjunct Prof,* University of Colorado at Denver, Dept of Fine Arts, Denver CO (S)

Comtois, George, *Dir,* Manchester Historic Association, Manchester NH

Conant, Howard, *Dept Head,* University of Arizona, Dept of Art, Tucson AZ (S)

Conant, Rita, *Secy,* John Paul Jones House, Portsmouth NH

Conaway, Beverly, *VPres,* West Hills Unitarian Fellowship, Portland OR

Conaway, James, *Exhib Dir,* Hamline University Learning Center Gallery, Saint Paul MN

Conaway, James, *Prof,* Hamline University, Art Dept, Saint Paul MN (S)

Concannon, Ann, *Dir,* Art Center of Battle Creek, Michigan Art & Artist Archives, Battle Creek MI

Concholar, Dan, *Dir,* Art Information Center, Inc, New York NY

Condax, Philip, *Dir Technology Coll,* International Museum of Photography at George Eastman House, Rochester NY

Condon, E Jane, *Dir,* Canadian Artists' Representation, Le Front Des Artistes Canadiens, Toronto ON

Condon, Richard, *Registrar & Cur MacMillan Arctic Museum,* Bowdoin College, Museum of Art & Peary-MacMillan Arctic Museum, Brunswick ME

Cone, S Reid, *Exec Dir,* Community Council for the Arts, Kinston NC

Conesa, Lilliam, *Supv Processing Center,* Miami-Dade Public Library, Miami FL

Conforti, Anna, *Secy,* Vassar College Art Gallery, Poughkeepsie NY

Conger, Amy, *Coordr,* Corpus Christi State University, Weil Art Gallery, Corpus Christi TX

Conger, Clement E, *Cur,* Department of State, Diplomatic Reception Rooms, Washington DC

Conger, Clement E, *Cur,* White House, Washington DC

Conger, William, *Chmn Dept & Prof,* DePaul University, Dept of Art, Chicago IL (S)

Conklin, Jo-Ann, *Registrar,* University of Iowa, Museum of Art, Iowa City IA

Conley, Alston Stoney, *Instr,* Danforth Museum School, Framingham MA (S)

Conley, B, *Instructor,* Golden West College, Arts, Humanities and Social Sciences Institute, Huntington Beach CA (S)

Conlon, F S, *Dir,* USS North Carolina Battleship Memorial, Wilmington NC

Conn, Donald J, *Museum Mgr,* The Bostonian Society, Old State House, Boston MA

Conn, Jack T, *Pres Board Trustees,* Oklahoma Historical Society, Central Museum, Oklahoma City OK

Conn, Richard, *Cur Native Arts Department,* Denver Art Museum, Frederic H Douglas Library, Denver CO

Connell, Stephen, *Assoc Prof,* University of Montana, Dept of Art, Missoula MT (S)

Connelly, James L, *Assoc Prof,* University of Kansas, Kress Foundation Dept of Art History, Lawrence KS (S)

Connelly, Linda M, *Historic Site Manager II,* John Jay Homestead State Historic Site, Katonah NY

Conner, Ann Louise, *Assoc Prof,* University of North Carolina at Wilmington, Dept of Creative Arts - Division of Art, Wilmington NC (S)

Conner, Mary Rebecca, *Assoc Prof,* Saint Mary College, Art Dept, Leavenworth KS (S)

Conner, Will, *General Mgr,* Mid-America Arts Alliance, Kansas City MO

Conners, Gary M, *Store Supv,* Church of Jesus Christ of Latter-Day Saints, Museum of Church History and Art, Salt Lake City UT

Connett, Dee M, *Chairperson & Assoc Prof,* Friends University, Art Dept, Wichita KS (S)

Connolly, Agnes R, *Auditor,* Solomon R Guggenheim Museum, New York NY

Connolly, Bruce E, *Dir,* New York State College of Ceramics at Alfred University, Scholes Library of Ceramics, Alfred NY

Connolly, Felicia, *Office Admin,* Wenham Historical Association and Museum, Inc, Wenham MA

Connolly, John, *Chmn,* College of Notre Dame of Maryland, Art Dept, Baltimore MD (S)

Connor, Russell, *Head, Public Educ,* Whitney Museum of American Art, New York NY

Connors, Jeanne, *Assoc Prof,* Community College of Allegheny County, Boyce Campus, Art Dept, Monroeville PA (S)

Conovey, Robin, *Instr,* Ocean City Arts Center, Ocean City NJ (S)

Conrad, Geoffrey W, *Dir,* Indiana University, William Hammond Mathers Museum, Bloomington IN

Conrad, John, *Instructor,* San Diego Mesa College, Fine Arts Dept, San Diego CA (S)

Conrad, Rene, *VPres,* San Mateo County Arts Council, Belmont CA

Conrad, Sadie, *Secy,* Kelowna Centennial Museum and National Exhibit Centre, Kelowna BC

Conrad, Theodore, *VPres,* Jersey City Museum Association, Jersey City NJ

Conrads, Margaret, *Research Cur,* Hudson River Museum, Yonkers NY

Conragan, A Kirk, *Dir,* Josephine D Randall Junior Museum, San Francisco CA

Conrey, Kathie, *Cultural Arts Mgr,* Brea Civic Cultural Center Gallery, Brea CA

Consagra, Sophie, *Pres,* American Academy in Rome, New York NY (S)

Consey, Kevin E, *Dir,* San Antonio Museum Association, Inc, San Antonio Museum of Art, San Antonio TX

Consey, Kevin E, *Dir,* Newport Harbor Art Museum, Newport Beach CA

Console, Carmen, *Instr,* Studio School of Art and Design, Philadelphia PA (S)

Constable, Giles, *Dir,* Harvard University, Dumbarton Oaks Research Library and Collections, Washington DC

Constans, Mary, *Prof,* Portland State University, Dept of Art and Architecture, Portland OR (S)

Constantine, Greg, *Prof,* Andrews University, Art Dept, Berrien Springs MI (S)

Constantine, John, *Instructor,* North Seattle Community College, Art Dept, Seattle WA (S)

Contes, Anna, *Instructor,* Woodstock School of Art, Inc, New York NY (S)

Contigulia, Georgiana, *Cur of Decorative & Fine Arts,* Colorado Historical Society, State Museum, Denver CO

Contini, Anita, *Exec Dir,* Creative Time, New York NY

Contino, Francis, *Treas,* Peale Museum, Baltimore MD

Conviser, Rebecca, *Asst Prof,* Marymount College, Art Dept, Tarrytown NY (S)

Conway, Connie, *Floor Mgr,* Omaha Children's Museum, Inc, Omaha NE

Conway, Don, *Chmn Dept Interior Design,* Woodbury University, Professional Arts Division, Los Angeles CA (S)

Conway, Wallace, *Cur Exhibits,* New Jersey State Museum, Trenton NJ

Conwill, Kinshasha, *Deputy Dir,* Studio Museum in Harlem, New York NY

Conyers, Wayne, *Instructor,* McPherson College, Art Dept, McPherson KS (S)

Cook, Alexander B, *VPres,* Great Lakes Historical Society, Vermilion OH

Cook, Barbara, *Asst,* Providence Public Library, Art and Music Dept, Providence RI

Cook, Christopher C, *Dir,* Phillips Academy, Addison Gallery of American Art, Andover MA

Cook, Douglas, *Head Dept Theatre and Film,* Pennsylvania State University, University Park, College of Arts and Architecture, University Park PA (S)

Cook, Gary A, *Asst Prof,* Wake Forest University, Dept of Art, Winston-Salem NC (S)

Cook, John, *Asst Prof,* Bloomsburg University, Dept of Art, Bloomsburg PA (S)

Cook, John F, *Dir,* Bloomsburg University of Pennsylvania, Haas Gallery of Art, Bloomsburg PA

Cook, Julia A, *Exec Dir,* Custer County Art Center, Miles City MT

Cook, Lloyd, *Program Chmn,* Texas State Technical Institute, Dept of Commercial Art, Amarillo TX (S)

Cook, Mary, *Museum Secy,* University of Oklahoma, Museum of Art, Norman OK

Cook, Nancy, *Controller,* Museum of Contemporary Art, Chicago IL

Cook, Norma, *Membership Secy,* Ella Sharp Museum, Jackson MI

Cook, Ralph, *Prof,* Shorter College, Art Dept, Rome GA (S)

Cook, Ruth, *Asst,* Lincoln National Life Foundation, Inc, Louis A Warren Lincoln Library and Museum, Fort Wayne IN

Cook, Sterling, *Cur,* Miami University Art Museum, Oxford OH

Cook, W H, *Admin VPres,* Transco Energy Company Inc, Houston TX

Cooke, Constance B, *Dir,* Queens Borough Public Library, Art and Music Division, Jamaica NY

Cooke, Janet, *Instructor,* Montclair Art Museum, Museum Art Classes, Montclair NJ (S)

Cooke, Marlis, *Departmental Secy,* University of Alberta, Ring House Gallery, Edmonton AB

Cooke, Robert T, *Assoc Prof,* Rutgers, the State University of New Jersey, Mason Gross School of the Arts, New Brunswick NJ (S)

Cooke, Sarah, *Archivist,* Tippecanoe County Historical Museum, Lafayette IN

Cooke, S Tucker, *Chmn,* University of North Carolina at Asheville, Dept of Art and Music, Asheville NC (S)

Cook-Endres, Barbara, *Secy,* Manitoba Society of Artists, Winnipeg MB

Cookingham, Robert M, *Actg Assoc Dir,* California State University, Chico, Meriam Library, Chico CA

Coolidge, Daniel J, *Chmn Trustees,* Longfellow's Wayside Inn, South Sudbury MA

Coolidge, Hope, *Librn,* Isabella Stewart Gardner Museum, Library, Boston MA

Coolidge, Nancy R, *Admin Dir,* Society for the Preservation of New England Antiquities, Boston MA

Coon, A W, *VPres of the Board,* R W Norton Art Gallery, Shreveport LA

Coones, R C, *Instructor,* Northeastern Oklahoma State University, Tahlequah OK (S)

Cooney-Crawford, Kristen, *In Charge,* Soho Center for Visual Artists, Library, New York NY

Cooper, Bobby, *Div Head,* Utica Junior College, Humanities Division, Utica MS (S)

Cooper, Diana, *Reference Librn,* University of British Columbia, Fine Arts Division Library, Vancouver BC

Cooper, Gloria, *Registrar,* Terra Museum of American Art, Evanston IL

Cooper, Helen, *Cur American Painting,* Yale University, Art Gallery, New Haven CT

Cooper, Janice, *Business Mgr,* Texas Tech University Museum, Lubbock TX

Cooper, Ken, *Community Services Dir,* Gavilan College, Art Gallery, Gilroy CA

Cooper, Mario, *Pres,* American Watercolor Society, New York NY

Cooper, Michael, *Instructor,* De Anza College, Art Dept, Cupertino CA (S)

Cooper, Monty, *Communications Mgr,* Edmonton Art Gallery, Edmonton AB

Cooper, Ora, *Instr,* University of Judaism, Dept of Continuing Education, Los Angeles CA (S)

Cooper, Shoshanah G, *Asst Dir,* Museum of Holography, New York NY

Cooper, Willard, *Chmn Dept & Prof,* Centenary College of Louisiana, Dept of Art, Shreveport LA (S)

Cooper, Willard, *Cur,* Centenary College of Louisiana, Meadows Museum of Art, Shreveport LA

Coopersmith, Georgia, *Gallery Dir,* State University of New York College at Potsdam, Brainerd Art Gallery, Potsdam NY

Cope, Johnnye Louise, *Humanities Librn,* North Texas State University, Willis Library, Humanities Division, Denton TX

Cope, Mary, *Chief Reference Div,* City College of New York, Cohen Art Library, New York NY

Copeland, Betty D, *Chmn,* Texas Woman's University, Dept of Art, Denton TX (S)

Copeland, Karen, *Education Coordr,* Pacific - Asia Museum, Pasadena CA

Copeland, Lee G, *Dean,* University of Pennsylvania, Graduate School of Fine Arts, Philadelphia PA (S)

Coplan, Robin, *Dir,* Maryland Institute, College of Art Galleries, Baltimore MD

Copland, Leslie, *Dir,* Maude I Kerns Art Center, Henry Korn Gallery, Eugene OR

Copland, Leslie, *Dir,* Maude Kerns Art Center School, Eugene OR (S)

Copley, Claire, *Secy,* Committee for the Visual Arts, Inc, New York NY

Coppage, Carol B, *Exec Dir,* Northwood Institute, Alden B Dow Creativity Center, Midland MI (S)

Corbeil, John W, *Assoc Prof,* Pierce College, Art Dept, Woodland Hills CA (S)

Corbelletti, Raniero, *Head Dept Archit,* Pennsylvania State University, University Park, College of Arts and Architecture, University Park PA (S)

Corbett, Dennis, *Asst Program Dir,* Association of Artist-Run Galleries, New York NY

Corbett, Kathy, *Cur Education,* Missouri Historical Society, Saint Louis MO

Corbett, Ray, *Pres,* Yarmouth County Historical Society, Yarmouth County Museum, Yarmouth NS

Corbett, Roy G, *Asst Dir Admin,* Walters Art Gallery, Baltimore MD

Corbin, George, *Chmn,* Herbert H Lehman College, Art Dept, Bronx NY (S)

Corbin, Tarrence, *Instr,* Arkansas Arts Center, Little Rock AR (S)

Corcoran, Frank, *Asst Dir Pub Prog,* National Museum of Man, Ottawa ON

Cordes, Christopher, *Asst Prof,* University of Rhode Island, Dept of Art, Kingston RI (S)

Corey, Constance, *Acting Asst Librn,* Arizona State University, Hayden Library Art Dept, Tempe AZ

Corey, L, *Pres,* Museum of the Historical Society of Early American Decoration, Albany NY

Corey, Liz, *Admin Asst,* Pacific - Asia Museum, Pasadena CA

Corey, Peter L, *Dir,* Sheldon Jackson College, Sheldon Jackson Museum, Sitka AK

Corinth, Thomas, *Secy,* Lovis Corinth Memorial Foundation, Inc, New York NY

Cormack, Malcolm, *Cur Paintings,* Yale University, Yale Center for British Art, New Haven CT

Cormier, George Anne, *Slide Libm,* San Antonio Museum Association, Inc, Ellen S Quillin Memorial Library, San Antonio TX

Cormier, Robert, *Commissioner,* Boston Art Commission of the City of Boston, Boston MA

Cormier, Robert J, *Pres,* Guild of Boston Artists, Boston MA

Cornelius, Phil, *Area Chmn Ceramics,* Pasadena City College, Art Dept, Pasadena CA (S)

Cornell, Dorothy, *Dir,* River Vale Public Library, Art Dept, River Vale NJ

Cornell, Thomas B, *Prof,* Bowdoin College, Art Dept, Brunswick ME (S)

Cornett, J, *Asst Prof,* Northern Arizona University, Art Dept, Flagstaff AZ (S)

Cornett, James W, *Cur Natural Science,* Palm Springs Desert Museum, Inc, Palm Springs CA

Corning, Mary L, *Librn,* Wenham Historical Association and Museum, Inc, Timothy Pickering Library, Wenham MA

Corr, Jim, *Dir,* Western Montana College, Art Gallery, Dillon MT

Corr, Martha, *Museum Shop Mgr,* Virginia Museum, Danville Museum of Fine Arts and History, Danville VA

Correia, Peter, *Asst Prof,* Ulster County Community College, Dept of Visual Arts, Stone Ridge NY (S)

Correro, Guido, *Prof,* Herkimer County Community College, Humanities Division, Herkimer NY (S)

Corrigan, David J, *Cur,* Connecticut State Library, Raymond E Baldwin Museum, Hartford CT

Corrigan, Paul J, *Instructor,* Modesto Junior College, Arts Humanities and Speech Division, Modesto CA (S)

Corrigan, Robert W, *Dean,* University of Wisconsin-Milwaukee, Dept of Art, Milwaukee WI (S)

Corsberg, Dorothy, *Div Chmn Humanities,* Northeastern Junior College, Dept of Art, Sterling CO (S)

Corser, James, *Business Mgr,* Fort Worth Art Museum, Fort Worth TX

Corwin, Norman, *Instructor,* University of Southern California, Idyllwild School of Music and the Arts, Idyllwild CA (S)

Cory, Ken, *Librn,* Western Montana College, Library, Dillon MT

Cosgrove, Charlotte, *Instr,* Alfred C Glassell School of Art, Houston TX (S)

Cosgrove, J, *Instructor,* Aurora College, Art Dept, Aurora IL (S)

Cosgrove, Robert, *Vis Lecturer,* North Central College, Dept of Art, Naperville IL (S)

Costa, C, *Secy,* National Association of Women Artists, Inc, New York NY

Costantini, Mary, *Chmn Dept,* Caldwell College, Art Dept, Caldwell NJ (S)

Costanzo, Nancy, *Assoc,* Elms College, Dept of Fine Arts, Chicopee MA (S)

Costello, Kathleen, *Public Relations,* Newport Harbor Art Museum, Newport Beach CA

Costello, Michael J, *Dir,* Silvermine Guild School of the Arts, New Canaan CT (S)

Costigan, Constance C, *Asst Prof,* George Washington University, Dept of Art, Washington DC (S)

Cota, Julie, *Secy,* University of Maine at Orono, Art Collection, Orono ME

Cote, Alan, *Instructor,* Bard College, Milton Avery Graduate School of the Arts, Annandale-on-Hudson NY (S)

Cote, Andre, *Dean,* Barry University, Dept of Art, Miami Shores FL (S)

Cote, Jean-Guy, *Pres Board Dir & Pres Executive Committee,* Le Musee Regional de Rimouski, Rimouski PQ

Cote, Philip, *Chmn Holoyoke Historical Commission,* City of Holyoke Museum-Wistariahurst, Holyoke MA

Cotharn, Ruth Helen, *Admin Asst,* Lufkin Historical and Creative Arts Center, Lufkin TX

Cotherman, Steven R, *Dir Wyo State Art Gallery,* Wyoming State Art Gallery, Cheyenne WY

Cothren, Michael, *Asst Prof,* Swarthmore College, Dept of Art, Swarthmore PA (S)

Cotner, Lloyd, *Asst Prof,* Williamsport Area Community College, Dept of Engineering and Design, Williamsport PA (S)

Cotter, Jacqueline, *Instr,* Mainline Center of the Arts, Haverford PA (S)

Couch, Urban, *Cur CAC Galleries,* West Virginia University, West Virginia University Galleries, Morgantown WV

Couch, Urban, *Prof,* West Virginia University, Division of Art, Morgantown WV (S)

Coughin, Marge, *Dir Special Events,* American Society of Artists, Inc, Chicago IL

Coughlin, Caroline M, *Assoc Dir,* Drew University, Art Dept Library, Madison NJ

Coulling, Stanley H, *Executive Dir,* Oglebay Institute Mansion Museum, Wheeling WV

Coulter, Jerry L, *Prof,* James Madison University, Dept of Art, Harrisonburg VA (S)

Couper, James M, *Assoc Prof,* Florida International University, Visual Arts Dept, Miami FL (S)

Court, Elizabeth, *Conservator,* Balboa Art Conservation Center, San Diego CA

Courtemanche, Susan, *Asst Dir Development & Membership,* Worcester Art Museum, Worcester MA

Courtney, David, *Dir,* Florida Atlantic University, Ritter Art Gallery, Boca Raton FL

Courtney, Howard, *Pres,* Peoria Art Guild, Peoria IL

Courtney, Kathleen, *Lectr,* Mount Marty College, Art Dept, Yankton SD (S)

Courtney, Keith, *Community Relations,* Art Gallery of Hamilton, Hamilton ON

Courvoisier, Lois, *Librn,* Crocker Art Museum, Research Library, Sacramento CA

Couture, Marie, *Chmn Dept,* Rivier College, Art Dept, Nashua NH (S)

Coverstone, Jean L, *Head Dept,* Grace College, Dept of Art, Winona Lake IN (S)

Covert, Diane, *Instructor,* Avila College, Art Division, Dept of Performing and Visual Art, Kansas City MO (S)

Covert, George, *Photo Archivist,* Seneca Falls Historical Society Museum, Seneca Falls NY

Covey, Martha, *Library Asst,* University of Colorado Art Galleries, Art and Architecture Library, Boulder CO

Covington, George M, *Pres,* Art Institute of Chicago, Auxiliary Board, Chicago IL

Covington, Joseph F, *Dir Education,* North Carolina Museum of Art, Raleigh NC

Covington-Vogl, Laurel, *Assoc Prof,* Fort Lewis College, Art Dept, Durango CO (S)

Covinton, Patricia B, *Undergrad Admissions,* Southern Illinois University, School of Art, Carbondale IL (S)

Cowan, Catherine M, *Librn,* Vancouver Art Gallery, Library, Vancouver BC

Cowden, Dorothy, *Dir,* University of Tampa, Lee Scarfone Gallery, Tampa FL

Cowden, Dorothy, *Dir,* University of Tampa, Dept of Art, Tampa FL (S)

Cowen, Keay, *Pres,* Lewistown Art Center, Lewistown MT

Cowles, Charles, *Cur,* Seattle Art Museum, Modern Art Pavilion, Seattle WA

Cowles, Gardner, *VChmn,* Museum of Modern Art, New York NY

Cowles, Sharon, *Secy,* Gallery North, Setauket NY

Cowley, Edward, *Prof,* State University of New York at Albany, Art Dept, Albany NY (S)

Cox, Abbe Rose, *Instr,* Surry Community College, Art Dept, Dobson NC (S)

Cox, Allyn, *Secy,* Art Commission of the City of New York, Associates of the Art Commission, Inc, New York NY

Cox, Beverly, *Cur Exhib,* National Portrait Gallery, Washington DC

Cox, David N, *Chmn,* Weber State College, Art Dept, Ogden UT (S)

Cox, Dennis, *Chmn,* Pacific Lutheran University, Dept of Art, Tacoma WA (S)

Cox, DiAnn, *Instructor,* Anton Elli, Cincinnati OH (S)

Cox, Donald M, *VPres,* The American Federation of Arts, New York NY

Cox, Kathryn D, *Registrar,* Frick Art Museum, Pittsburgh PA

Cox, Lauren, *Asst Coordr,* Prince George Art Gallery, Prince George BC

Cox, Lynn W, *Registrar,* Montgomery Museum of Fine Arts, Montgomery AL

Cox, Marvel, *Instructor,* Sioux City Art Center, Sioux City IA (S)

Cox, Michael, *Head Dept Interior Design,* University of Manitoba, Faculty of Architecture, Winnipeg MB (S)

Cox, Pat, *First VPres,* National Watercolor Society, Lakewood CA

Cox, Peter, *VPres,* Artists' Fellowship, Inc, New York NY

Cox, Shirley Ann, *Coordr Education,* Church of Jesus Christ of Latter-Day Saints, Museum of Church History and Art, Salt Lake City UT

Coxon, Suzanne, *Financial Aid Officer,* Ontario College of Art, Toronto ON (S)

Coxwell, Roy, *Chmn of the Board,* Desert Caballeros Western Museum, Wickenburg AZ

Coxwell, Teen, *VPres,* Santa Barbara Contemporary Arts Forum, Santa Barbara CA

Coyle, Jack, *Registrar,* University of California, University Art Museum, Berkeley CA

Coyne, Michael, *Chmn,* Acadia University, Art Dept, Wolfville NS (S)

Cozzi, Ciriaco, *Pres,* Provincetown Art Association and Museum, Provincetown MA

Cozzie, Anthony F, *Dir,* Roswell P Flower Memorial Library, Art Gallery, Watertown NY

Crabb, Patrick, *Instructor,* Santa Ana College, Art Dept, Santa Ana CA (S)

Crabb, Ted, *Dir & Secy,* University of Wisconsin, Memorial Union Gallery, Madison WI

Crable, James, *Assoc Prof,* James Madison University, Dept of Art, Harrisonburg VA (S)

Crabtree, Donna, *VPres,* DuPage Art League, Wheaton IL

Crabtree, G F, *Exec Dir,* Presidential Museum, Odessa TX

Craft, Douglas, *Prof,* College of New Rochelle School of Arts and Sciences, Undergraduate Art Dept, New Rochelle NY (S)

Craig, Albert K, *Librn,* Alabama Department of Archives and History Museum, Library, Montgomery AL

Craig, Christina, *Asst Prof,* Trenton State College, Art Dept, Trenton NJ (S)

Craig, Lois A, *Assoc Dean,* Massachusetts Institute of Technology, School of Architecture and Planning, Cambridge MA (S)

Craig, Susan V, *Librn,* University of Kansas, Murphy Library of Art History, Lawrence KS

Craig, W Frederick, *Chmn Management Division,* Rochester Institute of Technology, School of Printing, Rochester NY (S)

Craighead, Robert S, *Cur Astronomy,* Hastings Museum, Hastings NE

Crain, John W, *Dir,* Dallas Historical Society, Dallas TX

Cramer, D L, *Pres,* Society of Illustrators, New York NY

Cramer, Michael, *Treas,* Saint Louis Artists' Guild, Saint Louis MO

Crandall, Charles C, *Chmn,* Iowa Western Community College, Art Dept, Council Bluffs IA (S)

Crandall, James, *Prof,* Pierce College, Art Dept, Woodland Hills CA (S)

Crandall, William, *Instructor,* Milwaukee Area Technical College, Graphic & Applied Arts Division, Milwaukee WI (S)

Crane, Barbara, *Prof,* School of the Art Institute of Chicago, Chicago IL (S)

Crane, Charles, *Assoc Prof,* University of Lethbridge, Dept of Art, Lethbridge AB (S)

Crane, David, *Instructor,* Virginia Tech, Dept of Art, Blacksburg VA (S)

Crane, Diane, *Instructor,* Viterbo College, Art Dept, La Crosse WI (S)

Crane, James, *Prof,* Eckerd College, Art Dept, Saint Petersburg FL (S)

Crane, Ruth, *Registrar,* Fairbanks Museum and Planetarium, Saint Johnsbury VT

Crane, Tim, *Assoc Prof,* Viterbo College, Art Dept, La Crosse WI (S)

Crane, Tim, *Dir,* Viterbo College Art Gallery, La Crosse WI

Crary, Miner D, *Chairman Board Trustees,* Heckscher Museum, Huntington NY

Crask, R M, *Coordr Fine Arts & Assoc Prof,* Jefferson Community College, Fine Arts, Louisville KY (S)

Craven, David, *Asst Prof,* State University of New York College at Cortland, Art Dept, Cortland NY (S)

Craven, Jayne, *Head Art & Music Department,* Public Library of Cincinnati and Hamilton County, Art and Music Dept, Cincinnati OH

Craven, Roy C, *Dir,* University of Florida, University Gallery, Gainesville FL

Crawford, James, *Instr,* California State University, Chico, Art Dept, Chico CA (S)

Crawford, J J, *Pres,* Strasburg Museum, Strasburg VA

Crawford, Robert, *Dir,* Ridgewood School of Art and Design, Ridgewood NJ (S)

CrawfordVolk, Mary, *Asst Prof,* Tufts University, Fine Arts Dept, Medford MA (S)

Crawley, Richard, *Pres,* Taos Art Association Inc, Stables Art Center, Taos NM

Crayne, J Robert, *Chmn Dept,* Slippery Rock University of Pennsylvania, Dept of Art, Slippery Rock PA (S)

Creamer, George, *Visiting Artists,* Mount Holyoke College, Art Dept, South Hadley MA (S)

Creasy, Peg, *Instr,* Illinois Central College, Fine Arts Dept, East Peoria IL (S)

Crebbs, Jan, *Public Relations & Media,* Tucson Museum of Art, Tucson AZ

Creel, Dana S, *Pres,* Sleepy Hollow Restorations Inc, Tarrytown NY

Crelly, William R, *Prof,* Emory University, Art History Dept, Atlanta GA (S)

Crenascol, Louis de, *Prof,* Seton Hall University, Dept of Art and Music, South Orange NJ (S)

Crenshaw, Karen B, *Conservator,* Carnegie Institute, Museum of Art, Pittsburgh PA

Crespo, Michael, *Assoc Prof,* Louisiana State University, School of Art, Baton Rouge LA (S)

Cress, George, *Dir,* University of Tennessee at Chattanooga Art Gallery, Chattanooga TN

Cress, George, *Head,* University of Tennessee at Chattanooga, Dept of Art, Chattanooga TN (S)

Creswell, Pearl, *Asst to Cur,* Fisk University Museum of Art, Nashville TN

Crew, Roger T, *Archivist,* Mariners Museum, Library, Newport News VA

Crews, Polly, *Dir,* Fort Smith Art Center, Fort Smith AR

Crider, Deann, *Registrar,* United States Figure Skating Hall of Fame and Museum, Colorado Springs CO

Cridge, Edmund, *Head Instructional Media Services,* University of Alaska, Elmer E Rasmuson Library, Fairbanks AK

Crilley, Sue, *Cur Cultural History,* New Jersey State Museum, Trenton NJ

Crimmings, Gerald, *Chmn Fine Arts,* Moore College of Art, Philadelphia PA (S)

Crimson, Linda, *Adjunct Lectr,* Indiana University at South Bend, Fine Arts Dept, South Bend IN (S)

Crisp, Lynn, *Library Asst,* North Carolina State University, Harrye Lyons Design Library, Raleigh NC

Crispen, Jean L, *Admin Secy,* Fruitlands Museums, Harvard MA

Crispino, Luigi, *Chmn Dept,* Franklin College, Art Dept, Franklin IN (S)

Cristovich, William, *Pres,* Louisiana Department of Culture, Recreation and Tourism, Louisiana State Museum, New Orleans LA

Critchfield, Sue, *Librn,* Museum of New Mexico, Museum of Fine Arts Library, Santa Fe NM

Crocker, Elli, *Instr,* Danforth Museum School, Framingham MA (S)

Crockett, Ted, *Treas,* Salisbury State College, Wildfowl Art Museum, Salisbury MD

Croft, Michael, *VPres,* Society of North American Goldsmiths, Milwaukee WI

Croft, Michael, *Coordr Three-Dimensional Areas,* University of Arizona, Dept of Art, Tucson AZ (S)

Croft, Rebecca, *Head Information Center,* Lexington Public Library, Skydome Gallery, Lexington KY

Croke, Carolyn, *Chief Librn,* Woodstock Art Gallery, Woodstock ON

Cromer, Jim, *Chmn Art Educ,* University of South Carolina, Dept of Art, Columbia SC (S)

Cromwell, Jarvis, *Secy,* New York Historical Society, New York NY

Cromwell-Lacy, Sherry, *Dir Exhibitions,* Kansas City Art Institute, Charlotte Crosby Kemper Gallery, Kansas City MO

Croneberger, Robert, *Dir,* Memphis-Shelby County Public Library and Information Center, Dept of Art, Music and Recreation, Memphis TN

Cronin, Mervell T, *Treas,* Attleboro Museum, Center for the Arts, Attleboro MA

Cronk, Frank A, *Dept Chmn,* University of Idaho, College of Art & Architecture, Moscow ID (S)

Cronk, Frank A, *Faculty,* Idaho State University, Dept of Art, Pocatello ID (S)

Crontz, Jean, *Registrar,* Central Academy of Commercial Art, Cincinnati OH (S)

Croog, Elizabeth A, *Assoc Secy & Assoc Gen Counsel,* National Gallery of Art, Washington DC

Crooker, M J A, *Assoc Prof,* Mount Allison University, Fine Arts Dept, Sackville NB (S)

Crosby, LaVon, *Chmn,* Nebraska Arts Council Library, Omaha NE

Crosby, Peter, *Secy,* Fairbanks Museum and Planetarium, Saint Johnsbury VT

Crosby, Ranice W, *Dir Emeritus,* Johns Hopkins University, School of Medicine, Dept of Art as Applied to Medicine, Baltimore MD (S)

Crosby, Thomas M, *Chmn Board,* Walker Art Center, Minneapolis MN

Crosman, Christopher, *Cur Education,* The Buffalo Fine Arts Academy, Albright-Knox Art Gallery, Buffalo NY

Cross, F K, *Dir,* Attleboro Museum, Center for the Arts, Attleboro MA

Cross, Frank Moore, *Dir,* Harvard University, Harvard Semitic Museum, Cambridge MA

Cross, Leroy, *Instr,* Cuyahoga Valley Art Center, Cuyahoga Falls OH (S)

Cross, Ruth C, *Secy,* University of Virginia, Art Museum, Charlottesville VA

Crossin, Alan, *Chmn Management Committee,* Manitoba Historical Society, Dalnavert - MacDonald House Museum, Winnipeg MB

Crossman, Rodney, *Instr,* Marion College, Art Dept, Marion IN (S)

Crotchett, Susan I, *Instructor,* Greenville College, Division of Language, Literature & Fine Arts, Greenville IL (S)

Croton, Fred, *General Mgr,* City of Los Angeles, Cultural Affairs Dept, Los Angeles CA

Croton, Lynn, *Asst Prof,* C W Post Center of Long Island University, School of the Arts, Greenvale NY (S)

Crouch, D E, *Faculty,* Western Illinois University, College of Fine Arts, Macomb IL (S)

Crouch, Elizabeth, *Actg Dir,* Grand Rapids Art Museum, Grand Rapids MI

Crouse, Michael G, *Asst Prof,* University of Alabama in Huntsville, School of Arts, Humanities & Science, Huntsville AL (S)

Crouse, Michael G, *Dir,* University of Alabama in Huntsville, Gallery of Art, Huntsville AL

Crow, Charles, *Pres,* Mexico-Audrain County Library, Mexico MO

Crow, Kenneth V, *Instructor,* Olympic College, Art Dept, Bremerton WA (S)

Crowder, Charles, *Dir Music,* The Phillips Collection, Washington DC

Crowe, Ann, *Instructor,* Atlanta College of Art, Atlanta GA (S)

Crowe, Edith, *Art Reference Librn,* San Jose State University, Robert D Clark Library, San Jose CA

Crowe, M, *Lectr,* Chamberlayne Junior College, Dept of Applied Arts, Boston MA (S)

Crowell, Bruce, *Dean,* Mesa College, Art Dept, Grand Junction CO (S)

Crowley, Pat, *Dir,* Texas Christian University, Student Center Gallery, Fort Worth TX

Crowley, William, *Cur,* Adirondack Historical Association, Adirondack Museum, Blue Mountain Lake NY

Crown, Carol, *Chmn Dept,* Memphis State University, Dept of Art, Memphis TN (S)

Crown, Patricia, *Assoc Prof,* University of Missouri, Art History and Archaeology Dept, Columbia MO (S)

Crown, Roberta, *Exec Coordr,* Women in the Arts Foundation, Inc, New York NY

Crown, William, *Treas,* Florida Gulf Coast Art Center, Inc, Clearwater FL

Croydon, Michael, *Prof,* Lake Forest College, Dept of Art, Lake Forest IL (S)

Croydon, Monika, *Slide Librn,* Southern Alberta Institute of Technology, Alberta College of Art Library, Calgary AB

Crozier, John, *Librn,* Santa Barbara Museum of Art, Library, Santa Barbara CA

Crozier, William, *Prof,* Oregon State University, Dept of Art, Corvallis OR (S)

Cruise, James E, *Dir,* Royal Ontario Museum, Toronto ON

Crumet, Helen, *Main Gallery Chairperson,* Licking County Art Association Gallery, Newark OH

Cruz, Ada P, *Admin Asst,* Museum of Holography, New York NY

Cruz, Luis Hernandez, *Instructor,* University of Puerto Rico, Dept of Fine Arts, Rio Piedras PR (S)

Cruz, Patricia, *Develop Dir,* Studio Museum in Harlem, New York NY

Csyri, Charles, *Prof,* Ohio State University, Dept of Art Education, Columbus OH (S)

Cubbs, Joanne, *Assoc Cur Exhibitions,* John Michael Kohler Arts Center, Sheboygan WI

Cucci, Alfred, *Art Dir,* Studio Museum in Harlem, New York NY

Culbertson, Margaret, *Librn,* University of Houston, Franzheim Architecture Library, Houston TX

Cullen, Frances, *Dir,* Georgia State University, Art Dept, Visual Resource Library & Reading Room, Atlanta GA

Cullen, Ronald, *VPres,* Canton Art Institute, Canton OH

Cullen, William H, *Treas,* Monterey Peninsula Museum of Art, Monterey CA

Culley, Lou Ann, *Assoc Prof,* Kansas State University, Art Dept, Manhattan KS (S)

Culley, Paul T, *Head Technical Ref & ILL,* New York State College of Ceramics at Alfred University, Scholes Library of Ceramics, Alfred NY

Cullimore, Mary Joanne, *Asst Prof,* Dominican College of San Rafael, Art Dept, San Rafael CA (S)

Cullison, William R, *Cur,* Tulane University, University Art Collection, New Orleans LA

Culver, Michael, *Cur,* Museum of Art of Ogunquit, Ogunquit ME

Cumming, Doug, *Assoc Prof,* University of Wisconsin-Stout, Art Dept, Menomonie WI (S)

Cumming, Glen E, *Dir,* Art Gallery of Hamilton, Hamilton ON

Cumming, Robert, *Assoc Prof,* Hartford Art School of the University of Hartford, West Hartford CT (S)

Cumming, William, *Instructor,* The Design Schools, Art Institute of Seattle, Seattle WA (S)

Cummings, Douglas, *Coordr Indian Gallery,* Oklahoma Center for Science and Art, Kirkpatrick Center, Oklahoma City OK

Cummings, Frederick J, *Dir,* Detroit Institute of Arts, Detroit MI

Cummings, Hildegard, *Cur of Education,* University of Connecticut, William Benton Museum of Art, Storrs CT

Cummings, Mary, *Dir,* Missoula Museum of the Arts, Missoula MT

Cummings, Paul, *Adjunct Cur, Drawings,* Whitney Museum of American Art, New York NY

Cummings, Paul, *Pres,* The Drawing Society, New York NY

Cummings, Terri, *Cur Education,* Corpus Christi State University, South Texas Artmobile, Corpus Christi TX

Cummins, Karen, *Asst Dir,* New Jersey State Museum, Trenton NJ

Cuneo, Robert, *Assoc Prof,* University of Bridgeport, Art Dept, Bridgeport CT (S)

Cunningham, Carole A, *Registrar,* University of Michigan, Museum of Art, Ann Arbor MI

Cunningham, Francis, *Co-Dir,* New York Academy of Art, New York NY (S)

Cunningham, Jackie, *Asst Cur Collections,* Albuquerque Museum of Art, History and Science, Albuquerque NM

Cunningham, John, *Pres,* Carmel Art Institute, School of Painting, Carmel CA (S)

Cunningham, Karlene, *Area Chairperson Apparel Arts,* Pasadena City College, Art Dept, Pasadena CA (S)

Cunningham, Linda, *Chmn Dept,* Franklin and Marshall College, Art Dept, Lancaster PA (S)

Curfman, John, *Prof,* Colorado State University, Dept of Art, Fort Collins CO (S)

Curfman, Robert, *Vis Prof,* Marion College, Art Dept, Marion IN (S)

Curler, Dawna, *Programs Dir,* Southern Oregon Historical Society, Jacksonville Museum, Jacksonville OR

Curran, Darryl, *Pres,* Los Angeles Center For Photographic Studies, Los Angeles CA

Curran, Joan Wadleigh, *Asst Prof,* Trenton State College, Art Dept, Trenton NJ (S)

Current, Ira B, *Assoc Prof,* Rochester Institute of Technology, School of Photographic Arts & Sciences, Rochester NY (S)

Currie, Elizabeth M, *Coordr Exhibition,* New York Historical Society, New York NY

Currie, William, *Dir,* Hallwalls Gallery, New York NY

Currier, Prescott, *Pres,* Lincoln County Cultural and Historical Association, Wiscasset ME

Curry, G, *Asst Prof,* University of Victoria, Dept of Visual Arts, Victoria BC (S)

Curtis, George H, *Asst Dir,* Harry S Truman Library and Museum, Independence MO

Curtis, Howard W, *Dir,* Haverhill Public Library, Art Dept, Haverhill MA

Curtis, Matilda, *Instructor,* Guilford Technical Community College, Commercial Art Dept, Jamestown NC (S)

Curtis, Nelson, *Chmn,* Idaho State University, Dept of Art, Pocatello ID (S)

Curtis, Robert, *Pres-Elect,* National Art Education Association, Reston VA

Curtis, Robert, *Instructor,* Mount Mary College, Art Dept, Milwaukee WI (S)

Curtis, Roger, *Treas,* North Shore Arts Association, Inc, Art Gallery, Gloucester MA

Curtis, Samuel L, *Prof,* Cheyney University of Pennsylvania, Dept of Art, Cheyney PA (S)

Curtis, Sandra J, *Area Collector,* Archives of American Art, Texas Area Center: Museum of Fine Arts, New York NY

Curtis, Verna, *Assoc Cur,* Milwaukee Art Museum, Milwaukee WI

Curtis, Walter D, *Asst Prof,* University of Arkansas, Art Dept, Fayetteville AR (S)

Curtis, Winifred, *Secy,* North Shore Arts Association, Inc, Art Gallery, Gloucester MA

Cushing, John D, *Librn,* Massachusetts Historical Society, Library, Boston MA

Cushing, Stanley E, *Librn,* Guild of Book Workers, Library, New York NY

Cusick, Jessica, *Project Dir,* Public Art Fund, Inc, New York NY

Cutler, Anthony, *Prof,* Pennsylvania State University, University Park, Dept of Art History, University Park PA (S)

Cutler, Jerry, *Asst Prof,* University of Florida, Dept of Art, Gainesville FL (S)

Cutler, Jo Ann, *Educ Dir,* Omaha Children's Museum, Inc, Omaha NE

Cyr, Paul, *Dept Head Genealogy & Whaling Coll,* New Bedford Free Public Library, Art Dept, New Bedford MA

Cywin, Allison, *Cur,* Newport Art Museum and Art Association, Newport RI

Czarnecki, James G, *Chmn Dept,* University of Nebraska at Omaha, Dept of Art, Omaha NE (S)

Czarniecki, M J, *Dir,* Minnesota Museum of Art, Saint Paul MN

Czestochowski, Joseph, *Dir,* Cedar Rapids Museum of Art, Cedar Rapids IA

Czichos, Raymond L, *Dir,* Pioneer Town, Wimberley TX

Czlonka, Judith, *Dir Exhibition Series,* Beyond Baroque Foundation, Venice CA

Czuma, Stanislaw, *Cur Indian Art,* Cleveland Museum of Art, Cleveland OH

Dabash, Adrian G, *Assoc Prof,* Providence College, Art and Art History Dept, Providence RI (S)

Daboll, Lisa, *Faculty,* North Idaho College, Art Dept, Coeur D'Alene ID (S)

daCosta-Nunes, Hedy, *Instructor,* Monmouth College, Dept of Art, West Long Branch NJ (S)

Daggett, Clark, *Secy,* Historic Cherry Hill, Albany NY

Dahl, Ronald, *Chmn Fine Arts,* Minneapolis College of Art and Design, Minneapolis MN (S)

Dahlquist, Marcy, *Chmn Communications,* Minneapolis Institute of Arts, Minneapolis MN

Dahlstrom, Irving, *Pres,* American Swedish Institute, Minneapolis MN

Dahlstrom, Nancy, *Chmn Dept,* Hollins College, Art Dept, Hollins VA (S)

Dailey, Charles, *Dir,* Institute of American Indian Arts Museum, Santa Fe NM

Dailey, Charles A, *Dir,* Institute of American Indian Arts, Santa Fe NM (S)

Daily, Tina, *Instructor,* Umpqua Community College, Fine & Performing Arts Dept, Roseburg OR (S)

Daitzman, Eleanor, *Exec Dir,* Main Line Center of the Arts, Haverford PA

Daitzman, Eleanor, *Admin Exec Dir,* Mainline Center of the Arts, Haverford PA (S)

Dake, Dennis, *Coordr Art Educ,* Iowa State University, Dept of Art and Design, Ames IA (S)

Dale, Libby, *Community Relations Officer,* First Interstate Bank of Fort Collins, Fort Collins CO

Dale, Ron, *Asst Prof,* University of Mississippi, Dept of Art, University MS (S)

Dalenius, Majory, *Gallery Secy,* Providence Art Club, Providence RI

Dalich, Mildred, *Secy,* Cascade County Historical Society Museum, Great Falls MT

Dalkey, Fred, *Staff,* Sacramento City College, Art Dept, Sacramento CA (S)

Dallavis, Olive Louise, *Pres,* Avila College, Thornhill Art Gallery, Kansas City MO

Dalling, W Harvey, *Cur,* Kings County Historical Society and Museum, Hampton NB

Dalton, Jean, *Pres,* Connecticut Women Artist, Inc, Glastonbury CT

Dalton, Mary L, *Business Mgr,* Midland Art Council, Midland MI

Daly, Charles, *Prof,* College of New Rochelle School of Arts and Sciences, Undergraduate Art Dept, New Rochelle NY (S)

Daly, Sally, *Secy,* Farmington Valley Arts Center, Avon CT

Dalzotto, Eugene, *Prof,* Bemidji State University, Art Dept, Bemidji MN (S)

Damascus, Nickolas J, *Prof,* Seattle University, Fine Arts Dept, Division of Art, Seattle WA (S)

D'Amato, Juliana, *Prof,* Albertus Magnus College, Art Dept, New Haven CT (S)

D'Ambrosio, Margaret, *Assoc Librn,* American Numismatic Society, Library, New York NY

Damon, T A, *Dir,* Naval Historical Center, United States Navy Memorial Museum, Washington DC

Damron, John, *Recording Secy,* American Artists Professional League, Inc, New York NY

Dana, Emilie, *Curatorial Asst,* Harvard University, Busch-Reisinger Museum, Cambridge MA

Danahy, John, *Assoc Prof,* University of Toronto, Dept of Landscape Architecture, Toronto ON (S)

Danderson, Hale, *Asst Prof,* University of Northern Iowa, Dept of Art, Cedar Falls IA (S)

Dandignac, Pat, *Editor-in-Chief American Craft Magazine,* American Craft Council, New York NY

Dane, William J, *Supv Art & Music Department,* Newark Public Library, Art & Music Dept, Newark NJ

Danforth, Charles D, *Chmn Div,* University of Maine at Augusta, Division of Arts and Humanities, Augusta ME (S)

D'Angelo, Olga, *Cur Asst,* State University of New York at Purchase, Neuberger Museum, Purchase NY

Dangremond, David W, *Dir,* Bennington Museum, Bennington VT

Daniel, Betty, *Library Records,* Washington University, Art and Architecture Library, Saint Louis MO

Daniel, James, *VPres,* Virginia Museum, Danville Museum of Fine Arts and History, Danville VA

Daniel, Vesta, *Asst Chairperson Dept,* Northern Illinois University, Dept of Art, De Kalb IL (S)

Daniels, Beverley, *Dir,* The One Club for Art & Copy, New York NY

Daniels, Chester J, *Senior Technologist,* Rochester Institute of Technology, Technical & Education Center of the Graphic Arts, Rochester NY (S)

Daniels, Dan, *In Charge Art Coll & Dir Public Relations,* M Grumbacher Inc, New York NY

Daniels, Frank A, *Pres,* North Carolina Art Society, Raleigh NC

Daniels, Gene, *Visiting Prof,* Adams State College, Dept of Visual Arts, Alamosa CO (S)

Daniels, John, *Assoc Dir Programs,* State Art Museum of Florida, John & Mable Ringling Museum of Art, Sarasota FL

Danielson, Phyllis I, *Pres,* Kendall School of Design, Grand Rapids MI (S)

Danilov, Victor J, *Pres,* Museum of Science and Industry, Chicago IL

Daniouth, David, *Instructor,* The Design Schools, Art Institute of Seattle, Seattle WA (S)

Danner, Katharine, *Dir,* Southern Oregon College, Stevenson Union Art Gallery, Ashland OR

Danninger, Nan, *Program & Volunteer Coordr,* Mingei International Inc, Mingei International Museum of World Folk Art, La Jolla CA

Danoff, I Michael, *Dir,* Akron Art Museum, Akron OH

Danowski, Mathew, *Editing Post Production Facility,* Electronic Arts Intermix, Inc, New York NY

Dantzic, Cynthia, *Chmn,* Long Island University, Brooklyn Center Art Dept, Brooklyn NY (S)

Danyi, M Consilia, *Instructor,* Ancilla College, Art Dept, Donaldson IN (S)

Danzig, Sarah, *Second VPres,* North Shore Art League, Winnetka IL

Danziger, Fred, *Instr,* Wayne Art Center, Wayne PA (S)

Danzker, Jo-Anne Birnie, *Cur,* Vancouver Art Gallery, Vancouver BC

Dardi, Virgil D, *Chmn,* Museo Italo Americano, San Francisco CA d'Argence, Rene-Yvon Lefebvre, *Dir & Chief Cur,* Asian Art Museum of San Francisco, Avery Brundage Collection, San Francisco CA

Darien, Gwen, *Fiscal Administrator,* Institute for Art & Urban Resources, Project Studios One, Long Island City NY

D'Arista, Robert, *Chmn,* American University, Watkins Art Gallery, Washington DC

D'Arista, Robert, *Asst Prof,* American University, Dept of Art, Washington DC (S)

Darke, Jayne, *Public Information,* South Carolina Arts Commission, Columbia SC

Darling, Alberta, *Communications & Marketing,* Milwaukee Art Museum, Milwaukee WI

Darling, Janina, *Asst Prof,* Eastern Illinois University, School of Fine Arts, Charleston IL (S)

Darling, Sharon, *Cur Decorative Arts,* Chicago Historical Society, Chicago IL

Darnell, Polly C, *Librn,* Sheldon Art Museum, Library, Middlebury VT

Daro, Hazel E, *Admin Asst,* University of Alaska, Museum, Fairbanks AK

Darr, Alan, *Cur European Sculpture & Decorative Art,* Detroit Institute of Arts, Detroit MI

Darriau, Jean-Paul, *Assoc Prof,* Indiana University, Bloomington, School of Fine Arts, Bloomington IN (S)

Darst, Lise, *Museum Cur,* Rosenberg Library, Galveston TX

Dattel, Michael, *Dir Advertising/Graphic Design,* Academy of Art College, San Francisco CA (S)

Daub, Eugene, *Instr,* Mainline Center of the Arts, Haverford PA (S)

Daube, Leon, *Pres,* Charles B Goddard Center for the Visual and Performing Arts, Ardmore OK

Daubert, Debra, *Cataloger,* Oshkosh Public Museum, Oshkosh WI

Daugherty, Charles, *Assoc Prof,* Pomona College, Art Dept, Claremont CA (S)

Daugherty, Marshall, *Chmn,* Mercer University, Art Dept, Macon GA (S)

Daugherty, Michael, *Prof,* Louisiana State University, School of Art, Baton Rouge LA (S)

Daughters, Horace C, *Treas,* Cincinnati Art Club, Cincinnati OH

D'Avanzo, Suzanne H, *Asst Prof,* Providence College, Art and Art History Dept, Providence RI (S)

Davenport, Diane, *Head Art & Music Dept,* Berkeley Public Library, Berkeley CA

Davenport, Patricia, *Cur Educ,* El Paso Museum of Art, El Paso TX

Davenport, Thomas, *Chmn Design Studies,* Bowling Green State University, School of Art, Bowling Green OH (S)

Davenport, William H, *Oceanian Section Cur,* University of Pennsylvania, University Museum of Archaeology & Anthropology, Philadelphia PA

Davezac, Bertrand, *Vis Lectr,* Rice University, Dept of Art and Art History, Houston TX (S)

Davezac, Shehira, *Lectr,* Indiana University, Bloomington, School of Fine Arts, Bloomington IN (S)

Davi, Susan A, *Reference Librn (Art & Art History),* University of Delaware, Morris Library, Newark DE

Davidhazy, Andrew, *Assoc Prof,* Rochester Institute of Technology, School of Photographic Arts & Sciences, Rochester NY (S)

Davidock, Peter, *Registrar,* National Gallery of Art, Washington DC

Davidson, Bernice, *Research Cur,* Frick Collection, New York NY

Davidson, Gail, *Asst Prof,* C W Post Center of Long Island University, School of the Arts, Greenvale NY (S)

Davidson, John, *VPres,* Brattleboro Museum and Art Center, Brattleboro VT

Davidson, Marilyn, *Cur Education,* Huntington Galleries, Huntington WV

Davidson, Sandra, *Dir,* Wheaton College, Watson Gallery, Norton MA

Davies, Barbara, *Secy,* Pacific Grove Art Center, Pacific Grove CA

Davies, Harry, *Chmn,* Adelphi University, Dept of Art and Art History, Garden City NY (S)

Davies, Hugh M, *Dir,* La Jolla Museum of Contemporary Art, La Jolla CA

Davies, Judith, *Asst Prof,* Wellesley College, Art Dept, Wellesley MA (S)

Davies, Tames, *Pres,* Montserrat School of Visual Art, Beverly MA (S)

Davies, Thomas L, *Instr,* Rosemont College, Division of the Arts, Rosemont PA (S)

Davila, Arturo V, *Dir,* University of Puerto Rico, Museum of Archaeology, History and Art, Rio Piedras PR

Davis, Ann Marie, *Co-Dir,* Tyringham Art Galleries, Tyringham MA

Davis, Arney M, *Pres,* Hill Country Arts Foundation, Ingram TX

Davis, Art, *Asst Prof,* Grace College, Dept of Art, Winona Lake IN (S)

Davis, Audrey L, *Dir,* McGroarty Cultural Art Center, Cultural Affairs Dept, City of Los Angeles, Tujunga CA (S)

Davis, Ben, *Video Chmn,* Atlanta College of Art, Atlanta GA (S)

Davis, Caecilia W, *Assoc Prof,* Tulane University, Sophie H Newcomb Memorial College, New Orleans LA (S)

Davis, Carol, *Admin Asst,* Walter Cecil Rawls Museum, Courtland VA

Davis, Charles B, *Pres,* Federated Arts Council of Richmond, Inc, Richmond VA

Davis, Colonius, *Prof,* Southampton College of Long Island University, C W Post Center Fine Arts Division, Southampton NY (S)

Davis, Cynthia, *VPres,* Second Street Gallery, Charlottesville VA

Davis, Darwin R, *Dir,* Saint Joseph Art Association Inc, Krasl Art Center, Saint Joseph MI

Davis, David, *Division Chmn,* Fordham University, Art Dept, New York NY (S)

Davis, Dick C E, *VChmn,* Nebraska Arts Council Library, Omaha NE

Davis, Donald, *Co-Dir,* Tyringham Art Galleries, Tyringham MA

Davis, Don F, *Chmn Dept,* Southern Illinois University at Edwardsville, Dept of Art and Design, Edwardsville IL (S)

Davis, Dorri, *Secy,* Keokuk Art Center, Keokuk IA

Davis, Dustin P, *Head,* Frostburg State College, The Stephanie Ann Roper Gallery, Frostburg MD

Davis, Dustin P, *Head Dept,* Frostburg State College, Dept of Art and Art Education, Frostburg MD (S)

Davis, Elizabeth Phraner, *Pres,* Gallery North, Setauket NY

Davis, Euan G, *Chmn,* Walter Cecil Rawls Museum, Courtland VA

Davis, Gary, *Co-Dir,* Tyringham Art Galleries, Tyringham MA

Davis, Gordon, *Dir,* Illinois State University, University Museums, Normal IL

Davis, Gordon A, *Dir,* Illinois State University, Center for the Visual Arts Gallery, Normal IL

Davis, Ilse, *Libr Technician,* University of Oklahoma, School of Architecture Library, Norman OK

Davis, Jack, *Dept Chmn,* Beaver College, Richard Eugene Fuller Gallery of Art, Glenside PA

Davis, Jack, *Chmn,* Beaver College, Dept of Fine Arts, Glenside PA (S)

Davis, Jack R, *Chmn,* Oklahoma City University, Art Dept, Oklahoma City OK (S)

Davis, J Hornor, *Exec Dir,* Sunrise Foundation, Inc, Sunrise Museums, Charleston WV

Davis, Jim, *Head Dept,* East Texas State University, Dept of Art, Commerce TX (S)

Davis, Joan C, *Dir,* Bob Jones University, Greenville SC

Davis, Joann, *Office Mgr,* Polk Public Museum, Lakeland FL

Davis, Joyce, *Instructor,* Florida Southern College, Art Dept, Lakeland FL (S)

Davis, J R Leighton, *Dir & Cur,* St Mary's University, Art Gallery, Halifax NS

Davis, Kate, *Registrar,* Edmonton Art Gallery, Edmonton AB

Davis, Keith F, *Cur,* Hallmark Cards, Inc, Hallmark Collections, Kansas City MO

Davis, Larry Hilman, *Chmn,* Midwestern State University, Dept of Art, Wichita Falls TX (S)

Davis, Lawrence A, *Acad Dean,* University of Arkansas at Pine Bluff, Art Dept, Pine Bluff AR (S)

Davis, Lee Baxter, *Chmn Graphics,* East Texas State University, Dept of Art, Commerce TX (S)

Davis, Lenore, *Treasurer,* Surface Design Association, Inc, Fayetteville TN

Davis, Linda, *Pres,* Clark County Historical Society, Springfield OH

Davis, Lois, *Secy,* Art Gallery of Peterborough, Peterborough ON

Davis, Mary, *Secy,* Louisiana Department of Culture, Recreation and Tourism, Louisiana State Museum, New Orleans LA

Davis, Mary B, *Librn,* Huntington Free Library and Reading Room, Depository Library for the Museum of the American Indian, Bronx NY

Davis, M Chace, *Pres,* Peale Museum, Baltimore MD

Davis, Nancy K, *Asst Prof,* Texas Woman's University, Dept of Art, Denton TX (S)

Davis, Paul, *Instructor,* Saginaw Valley State College, Dept of Art and Design, University Center MI (S)

Davis, Paul H, *Chmn & Prof,* University of Utah, Art Dept, Salt Lake City UT (S)

Davis, Randy, *Program Coordr,* Portland Center for the Visual Arts, Portland OR

Davis, Richard, *Sculpture Coordr,* North Texas State University, Art Dept, Denton TX (S)

Davis, Robert, *Dir Div Fine Arts,* Shasta Community College, Art Dept, Fine Arts Division, Redding CA (S)

Davis, Robert S, *Pres,* Providence Athenaeum, Library, Providence RI

Davis, Roy, *Asst Dir,* Montclair Art Museum, Montclair NJ

Davis, Susan, *VPres,* Actual Art Foundation, New York NY

Davis, Susan, *Pres,* Riverside Art Center and Museum, Riverside CA

Davis, Trudy, *Librn,* Woodrow Wilson Birthplace Foundation, Library, Staunton VA

Davis, Virginia Irby, *Asst Prof,* Lynchburg College, Art Dept, Lynchburg VA (S)

Davis, Wes, *Dir,* Angelo State University, Houston Harte University Center, San Angelo TX

Davis, William, *VPres,* Art League of Houston, Houston TX

Davis, William D, *Interim Dir,* Pennsylvania State University, Museum of Art, University Park PA

Davis, Willis Bing, *Chmn,* Central State University, Dept of Art, Wilberforce OH (S)

Davis, W M, *VPres,* New England School of Art & Design, Boston MA (S)

Daw, Robert H, *Fine Arts Dept Head,* Topeka Public Library, Fine Arts Dept & Gallery of Fine Arts, Topeka KS

Dawalt, Kent, *Assoc Prof,* Indiana University, Bloomington, School of Fine Arts, Bloomington IN (S)

Dawkins, Jimmie, *Assoc Prof,* Alabama A & M University, Art Education Dept, Huntsville AL (S)

Dawn, C, *Instr,* David Thompson University Centre, Visual Arts Dept, Nelson BC (S)

Dawson, Belle, *Program,* Alaska Artists' Guild, Anchorage AK

Dawson, Bess, *Dir,* Mississippi Art Colony, Meridian MS

Dawson-Tibbitts, Cory, *Asst Cur Exhibitions,* Lakeview Museum of Arts and Sciences, Peoria IL

Day, Caroline, *Secy,* Lubbock Art Association, Inc, Lubbock TX

Day, Edith H, *Chmn,* North Florida Junior College, Dept Humanities & Art, Madison FL (S)

Day, Elmer, *Vis Prof,* Kent State University, Stark Campus, School of Art, Canton OH (S)

Day, Gary, *Asst Prof,* University of Nebraska at Omaha, Dept of Art, Omaha NE (S)

Day, Holliday T, *Cur American Art,* Joslyn Art Museum, Omaha NE

Day, J Dennis, *Dir,* Salt Lake City Public Library, Fine Arts Department and Atrium Gallery, Salt Lake City UT

Day, John A, *Dir,* University of South Dakota Art Galleries, Vermillion SD

Day, John A, *Dean,* University of South Dakota, Dept of Art, Vermillion SD (S)

Dayal, Hermona, *Cur,* Tougaloo College, Art Collection, Tougaloo MS

Dayton, Gary, *Cur Coll,* Roberson Center for the Arts and Sciences, Binghamton NY

Deal, Georgia, *Instr,* Munson-Williams-Proctor Institute, School of Art, Utica NY (S)

Deal, Joe M, *Asst Prof,* University of California, Riverside, Program in Art, Riverside CA (S)

de Alcuaz, Marie, *Cur,* University of Southern California, Fisher Gallery, Los Angeles CA

Dean, Doug, *Asst Dir,* Southwestern School of Art, Albuquerque NM (S)

Dean, Lina, *Instructor,* Interlochen Arts Academy, Dept of Visual Art, Interlochen MI (S)

Dean, Richard, *Asst Prof,* Dean Junior College, Visual and Performing Art Dept, Franklin MA (S)

DeAngelis, Joseph B, *Senior Adviser,* Pennsylvania Department of Education, Arts in Education Program, Harrisburg PA

DeAngelus, Michele, *Cur,* Kaufman & Broad, Inc, Los Angeles CA

Dear, Adelaide, *Secy,* Jersey City Museum Association, Jersey City NJ

Dearborn, Mona, *Keeper Catalog of American Portraits,* National Portrait Gallery, Washington DC

DeArcangelis, Gloria, *Asst Prof,* Vanderbilt University, Dept of Fine Arts, Nashville TN (S)

Deardorf, Catherine, *Membership,* Blanden Memorial Art Museum, Fort Dodge IA

Dearth, Robert, *Dir Office Cultural Affairs Oakland Univ,* Oakland University, Meadow Brook Art Gallery, Rochester MI

De Baecke, Maggie, *Dir,* Studio School of Art and Design, Philadelphia PA (S)

De Bauche, Lynne, *Asst Cur,* Benedict College, Visual Art Studies, Columbia SC (S)

DeBeradinis, Jack, *Business Mgr,* Institute of Contemporary Art, Boston MA

De Bruin, Joan, *Dir Education,* Junior Arts Center, Los Angeles CA

Debs, Barbara Knowles, *Pres,* Manhattanville College, Brownson Art Gallery, Purchase NY

de Callatay, Xavier, *Instr,* New York Academy of Art, New York NY (S)

De Carlo, Mary Ann, *Secy,* Long Island Graphic Eye Gallery, Port Washington NY

DeCato, Carolyn Clark, *Registrar,* Walker Art Center, Minneapolis MN

de Cecilia, Janet, *Asst Prof,* New York Institute of Technology, Fine Arts Dept, Old Westbury NY (S)

de Chero, Peter, *Chmn,* National Assembly of State Arts Agencies, Washington DC

Decker, David O, *Assoc Prof,* University of Maine, Art Dept, Orono ME (S)

Decker, Geri, *Librn,* University of Notre Dame, Architecture Library, Notre Dame IN

DeConcini, Barbara, *Academic Chmn,* Atlanta College of Art, Atlanta GA (S)

Dedrick, Philip, *Chmn Dept Fine Arts,* Rockford College, Dept of Fine Arts, Rockford IL (S)

Dee, Elaine Evans, *Cur Drawings & Prints,* Cooper-Hewitt Museum, Smithsonian Institution, New York NY

Dee, Ivan, *Librn,* Museum, Fine Arts Research & Holographic Center, David Wender Library, Chicago IL

Deeley, Florence, *Instr,* Ocean City Arts Center, Ocean City NJ (S)

Deemer, Jean, *Instr,* Cuyahoga Valley Art Center, Cuyahoga Falls OH (S)

Deering, Ronald F, *Cur,* Southern Baptist Seminary Museum, Louisville KY

Deering, Winifred, *Dir,* Roger Deering Studio - Gallery, Kennebunkport ME

Deese, Rupert, *Instructor,* Cuesta College, Art Dept, San Luis Obispo CA

Deetz, James J, *Dir,* University of California, R H Lowie Museum of Anthropology, Berkeley CA

de Fato, Elizabeth, *Librn,* Seattle Art Museum, Library, Seattle WA

DeFazio, Raymond, *Assoc Prof,* Seton Hill College, Dept of Art, Greensburg PA (S)

DeFeo, Jay, *Asst Prof,* Mills College, Art Dept, Oakland CA (S)

DeFrancesco, John, *Asst Prof,* College of Saint Teresa, Art Dept, Winona MN (S)

Degen, Jeff, *Instructor,* Rudolph Schaeffer School of Design, San Francisco CA (S)

De Geneste, Saundra, *Asst Prof,* Trenton State College, Art Dept, Trenton NJ (S)

DeGenevieve, Barbara, *In Charge Photography,* University of Illinois, Urbana-Champaign, School of Art and Design, Champaign IL (S)

de Graffenried, Gaines, *Cur,* Texas Ranger Hall of Fame and Museum, Waco TX

de Grassi, Leonard, *Prof,* Glendale College, Dept of Fine Arts, Glendale CA (S)

DeGroat, George, *Extended Education Service,* Monterey Peninsula Museum of Art, Monterey CA

Dehimer, B, *Librn,* Rome Historical Society, William and Elaine Scripture Memorial Library, Rome NY

Dehoney, Martyvonne, *Chmn Art Dept,* Drew University, College Art Gallery, Madison NJ

Dehoney, Martyvonne, *Chmn Dept,* Drew University, Art Dept, Madison NJ (S)

Deib, Anette, *Cur,* Stony Plain Multicultural Centre, Stony Plain AB

Deighton, Edwin J, *Asst Dir,* University of Oklahoma, Museum of Art, Norman OK

Deitch, Dora, *Reference Librn,* Detroit Public Library, Fine Arts Dept, Detroit MI

DeJong, J D, *Prof,* Central College, Art Dept, Pella IA (S)

deKergommeaux, D, *Chmn,* University of Western Ontario, Dept of Visual Arts, London ON (S)

Dekker, Mary, *Cur,* Falkirk Community Cultural Center, San Rafael CA

Delabano, Barney, *Cur Exhibitions,* Dallas Museum of Fine Arts, Dallas TX

De La Cruz, Luis, *Technical Supervisor,* Newport Harbor Art Museum, Newport Beach CA

Delafield, David, *Emeritus Prof,* University of Northern Iowa, Dept of Art, Cedar Falls IA (S)

Delaiti, Nancy, *Assoc Prof,* Berkshire Community College, Dept Fine Arts, Pittsfield MA (S)

DeLaittre, Barbara M, *Pres,* Minneapolis Institute of Arts, Friends of the Institute, Minneapolis MN

Delaney, Barry Leo, *Cur of Art,* Staten Island Institute of Arts and Sciences, Staten Island NY

Delaney, Caldwell, *Dir,* Museum of the City of Mobile, Mobile AL

Delaney, Jan, *Coordr Gallery Services & Mem Secy,* London Regional Art Gallery, London ON

Delaney, Robert O, *Pres,* Art Institute of Chicago, Woman's Board, Chicago IL

DeLap, Amy, *Instr,* Vincennes University Junior College, Art Dept, Vincennes IN (S)

de la Torre, David, *Development Dir,* Triton Museum of Art, Santa Clara CA

Delbo, Jose, *Instr,* Joe Kubert School of Cartoon and Graphic Art Inc, Dover NJ (S)

Delehanty, Suzanne, *Dir,* State University of New York at Purchase, Neuberger Museum, Purchase NY

Delisle, Georges, *Dir,* Public Archives of Canada, Picture Division, Ottawa ON

Dell, Roger, *Cur Gallery Program,* Honolulu Academy of Arts, Honolulu HI

Della-Piana, Alissa, *Illustration,* Montserrat School of Visual Art, Beverly MA (S)

Dellaripa, Filomena, *Instructor,* Samuel S Fleisher Art Memorial, Philadelphia PA (S)

Deller, Harris, *Assoc Prof,* Southern Illinois University, School of Art, Carbondale IL (S)

Delluva, Patricia, *Registrar,* Allentown Art Museum, Allentown PA

DeLong, David G, *Chmn Div Urban Design,* Columbia University, Graduate School of Architecture and Planning, New York NY (S)

DeLong, Paul, *Lecturer,* University of Wisconsin-Stout, Art Dept, Menomonie WI (S)

De Longa, Leonard, *Prof,* Mount Holyoke College, Art Dept, South Hadley MA (S)

de Looper, Willem, *Cur,* The Phillips Collection, Washington DC

DeLorme, Carmen, *Animator,* Musee d'Art de Joliette, Joliette PQ

Delorme-toupin, Carmen, *In Charge,* Musee d'Art de Joliette, Library, Joliette PQ

De Lotbinier-Harwood, Susanne, *Coordr,* Powerhouse Gallery, Montreal PQ

Deltry, Mary, *Instr,* Ocean City Arts Center, Ocean City NJ (S)

Deluca, Ben J, *Executive Dir,* Hammond Castle Museum, Gloucester MA

deLuca, E P, *Chmn Division Fine Arts, Language, Literature,* Peace College, Art Dept, Raleigh NC (S)

DeLuca, Richard, *Cur Educ,* Roberson Center for the Arts and Sciences, Binghamton NY

DelValle, Helen, *VPres,* American Society of Artists, Inc, Chicago IL

Delvin, Robert C, *Fine Arts Librn,* Illinois Wesleyan University, Slide Library, Bloomington IL

Delworth, Kirby, *Staff Librn,* Carnegie Library of Pittsburgh, Pittsburgh PA

Delz, William, *Chmn,* Herkimer County Community College, Humanities Division, Herkimer NY (S)

Demansky, Edward, *Asst Prof,* East Stroudsburg State College, Art Dept, East Stroudsburg PA (S)

DeMars, Billie, *Secy,* Gilpin County Arts Association, Central City CO

Dembrowski, Valerie F, *Controller,* Southwest Museum, Los Angeles CA

DeMelim, John, *Prof,* Rhode Island College, Art Dept, Providence RI (S)

de Menil, John, *Dir,* Rice University, Institute for the Arts, Rice Museum, Houston TX

Demers, Christian, *Dir,* University of Quebec, Trois Rivieres, Fine Arts Section, Trois Rivieres PQ (S)

Demetrion, James T, *Dir,* Edmundson Art Foundation, Inc, Des Moines Art Center, Des Moines IA

D'Emilio, Sandra, *Cur,* Museum of New Mexico, Museum of Fine Arts, Santa Fe NM

de Monchaux, John, *Dean,* Massachusetts Institute of Technology, School of Architecture and Planning, Cambridge MA (S)

DeMont, Beverly, *Pres,* North Shore Arts Association, Inc, Art Gallery, Gloucester MA

de Montebello, Philippe, *Dir,* Metropolitan Museum of Art, New York NY

DeMoss, Max, *Instr,* Mount San Jacinto College, Art Dept, San Jacinto CA (S)

DeMots, Lois, *Instructor,* Siena Heights College, Studio Angelico Art Dept, Adrian MI (S)

DeMoulpied, Deborah, *Asst Prof,* University of Maine, Art Dept, Orono ME (S)

Dempsey, Bruce H, *Dir,* Jacksonville Art Museum, Jacksonville FL

Dempsey, H A, *Chief Cur,* Glenbow Museum, Calgary AB

Dempsey, James H, *Pres,* Cleveland Museum of Art, Cleveland OH

Dempsey, John P, *Assoc Prof,* University of Alabama in Huntsville, School of Arts, Humanities & Science, Huntsville AL (S)

de Narvaez, Martha M, *Cur of Mss & Rare Bks,* Hispanic Society of America, Library, New York NY

Denby, Greg, *Preparatorial,* University of Notre Dame, Snite Museum of Art, Notre Dame IN

Denenberg, Beverly, *Cur,* California Historical Society, San Francisco CA

Dengate, James, *Cur of Numismatics,* University of Illinois, World Heritage Museum, Champaign IL

Denison, Cara D, *Cur Drawings and Prints,* Pierpont Morgan Library, New York NY

Denker, Bert, *Decorative Arts Photographic Coll,* Winterthur Museum and Gardens, Library, Winterthur DE

Denman, R, *Dir & Cur,* Museum of Northern British Columbia, Prince Rupert Museum Art Gallery, Prince Rupert BC

Denman, Ron, *Dir,* Museum of Northern British Columbia, Library, Prince Rupert BC

Dennard, William, *Instr,* Alfred C Glassell School of Art, Houston TX (S)

Dennett, Bernie, *Dept Head,* Ray-Vogue College of Design, Chicago IL (S)

Denney, Dave A, *Cur of Exhibits & Design,* The Haggin Museum, Stockton CA

Denning, Catherine, *Cur,* Brown University, Annmary Brown Memorial, Providence RI

Denning, Dennis, *Chmn,* Marymount College, Art Dept, Salina KS (S)

Dennis, David, *Installation Coordr,* University of Iowa, Museum of Art, Iowa City IA

Dennis, Gail, *Cur Education,* Historical Society of York County, York PA

Dennis, James M, *Art History Dept Chmn,* University of Wisconsin, Madison, Dept of Art History, Madison WI (S)

Dennis, Larry, *Business Mgr,* Alberta College of Art, Southern Alberta Institute of Technology, Calgary AB (S)

Dennis, Terry, *Instructor,* Rochester Community College, Art Dept, Rochester MN (S)

Dennis, Thomas L, *Supv of Maintenance,* Frick Art Museum, Pittsburgh PA

Dennis, Warren C, *Chmn,* Appalachian State University, Dept of Art, Boone NC (S)

Dennison, Keith E, *Dir,* The Haggin Museum, Stockton CA

Denny, Paul, *Prof,* Phillips University, Dept of Art, Enid OK (S)

Denny, Robert F, *Secy,* Guild Hall of East Hampton, Inc, Museum Section, East Hampton NY

Denny, Walter B, *Assoc Prof,* University of Massachusetts, Amherst, Art History Program, Amherst MA (S)

Densham, Robert, *Assoc Prof,* California Polytechnic State University at San Luis Obispo, Art Dept, San Luis Obispo CA (S)

Denton, Cynthia, *Secy,* Lewistown Art Center, Lewistown MT

Denton, Lynn, *Lectr,* Saint Joseph's University, Fine Arts Dept, Philadelphia PA (S)

Denton, Mark L, *Asst Dean,* Tulane University, School of Architecture, New Orleans LA (S)

Denton, Spencer, *Dir,* Five Civilized Tribes Museum, Muskogee OK

Deorr, Rose Marie, *Asst Dean Admin,* Rochester Institute of Technology, College of Fine and Applied Arts, Rochester NY (S)

de Paul-Schweitzer, Mary, *In Charge,* Marian College, Allison Mansion, Indianapolis IN

dePencier, H, *Cur Asst,* Royal Ontario Museum, Canadiana Gallery, Toronto ON

Depentu, Ronald, *Adjunct Asst Prof,* Le Moyne College, Art Dept, Syracuse NY (S)

dePeyster, James A, *VPres,* Society of the Four Arts, Palm Beach FL

DePietro, Anne Cohen, *Assoc Cur,* Heckscher Museum, Huntington NY

DePillars, Murry N, *Dean,* Virginia Commonwealth University, School of the Arts, Richmond VA (S)

DePopolo, Margaret, *Librn,* Massachusetts Institute of Technology, Rotch Library of Architecture and Planning, Cambridge MA

DeProspero, Al, *Prof,* Delaware County Community College, Communications and Humanities House, Media PA (S)

Deragon, Rick, *Special Cur & Registrar,* Monterey Peninsula Museum of Art, Monterey CA

Deranyi, Sylvia, *Librn,* New Brunswick Craft School and Centre Gallery, Library, Fredericton NB

Derbes, Anne, *Asst Prof,* Hood College, Dept of Art, Frederick MD (S)

Der Deridn, Curistine, *Store Mgr,* Museum of Contemporary Art, Chicago IL

Dern, James, *Secy,* Canajoharie Library and Art Gallery, Canajoharie NY

Deroko, Joan, *Gift Shop Mgr,* Studio Museum in Harlem, New York NY

de Rolon, Rosalind, *Ed & Coordr Public Information,* Fort Worth Art Museum, Fort Worth TX

DeRoux, Kenneth, *Cur Visual Arts,* Alaska State Museum, Juneau AK

Derrevere, William, *Instr,* Tulsa Junior College, Art Dept, Tulsa OK (S)

DeRuiter, Garret, *Prof,* Eastern Illinois University, School of Fine Arts, Charleston IL (S)

de Sanabria, Beatriz Nazario, *Instructor,* Inter American University of Puerto Rico, Dept of Art, San German PR (S)

de Savoye, Janni, *Exec Asst,* Visual Arts Ontario, Toronto ON

des Grange, Jane, *Dir,* Hartwick College Fine Art Gallery, Yager Museum, Oneonta NY

Deshaies, Arthur E, *Prof,* Florida State University, Art Dept, Tallahassee FL (S)

Deshaies, Ruth Dryden, *Chmn Art Prog,* Tallahassee Community College, Art Dept, Tallahassee FL (S)

Desir, Dorothy, *Asst Cur,* Just Above Midtown Gallery, Inc, New York NY

DeSisso, Janet, *Asst Dir,* Store Front Museum, Jamaica NY

DesJardins, Andrea, *Librn,* The Art Institute of Boston, Library, Boston MA

DesJardins, Andrea, *Cataloger,* The Bostonian Society, Library, Boston MA

DesJardins, Deedee Andrea, *Librn,* Brockton Art Museum, Library, Brockton MA

Desloover, Rose E, *Assoc Prof,* Marygrove College, Dept of Art and Art History, Detroit MI (S)

Desmarais, Charles, *Dir,* University of California, California Museum of Photography, Riverside CA

Desmond, Kathleen, *Asst Prof,* Ohio State University, Dept of Art Education, Columbus OH (S)

De Sota, Raoul, *Assoc Prof,* Los Angeles City College, Dept of Art, Los Angeles CA (S)

Despard, Douglas C, *Pres,* Monterey History and Art Association, Monterey CA

Desportes, Ulysse, *Head Dept,* Mary Baldwin College, Dept of Art, Staunton VA (S)

DesRosiers, Roger, *Dean School,* Washington University, School of Fine Arts, Saint Louis MO (S)

Dessureault, Pierre, *Producer,* National Film Board of Canada, Still Photography Division, Ottawa ON

D'Estout, Marc, *Asst Dir,* Triton Museum of Art, Santa Clara CA

de Swinton, Elizabeth, *Cur Oriental Art,* Worcester Art Museum, Worcester MA

de Temple, Jean, *Asst Dir,* Ottawa Public Library, Fine Arts Dept, Ottawa ON

Deter, Sue F, *Registrar,* University of Virginia, Art Museum, Charlottesville VA

Detheux, Jean, *Instr,* New York Studio School of Drawing, Painting and Sculpture, New York NY (S)

Detmers, Bill, *Assoc Prof,* Louisiana State University, School of Art, Baton Rouge LA (S)

Detweiler, Kelly, *Asst Prof,* University of Santa Clara, Fine Arts Dept, Santa Clara CA (S)

Deussen, Paul W, *Chmn Dept Art,* Michigan State University, Kresge Art Center Gallery, East Lansing MI

Deussen, Paul W, *Chmn Dept,* Michigan State University, Dept of Art, East Lansing MI (S)

Deutsch, Sanna, *Registrar,* Honolulu Academy of Arts, Honolulu HI

Devaney, Anne, *Asst Prof,* Sangamon State University, Creative Arts Program, Springfield IL (S)

DeVecsey, Esther, *Dir,* Rice University, Sewall Art Gallery, Houston TX

DeViejo, Isadora Rose, *Cur Applied Arts,* Hispanic Society of America, Museum, New York NY

Devine, Elizabeth, *Asst Prof,* Edgewood College, Art Dept, Madison WI (S)

Devine, Marge Duffy, *Scribe,* National Cartoonists Society, Brooklyn NY

Devine, Mary Ann, *Chmn,* University of Judaism, Dept of Continuing Education, Los Angeles CA (S)

Devine, Sue, *Cur,* Museum of the Southwest, Midland TX

DeVinny, Douglas, *Coordr of Art Program,* University of Wisconsin-Parkside, Art Discipline, Kenosha WI (S)

Devlin, Harry, *Pres,* Associated Artists of New Jersey, Pittstown NJ

Devlin, Richard, *Chmn Dept,* Carlow College, Art Dept, Pittsburgh PA (S)

Devon, Marjorie, *Asst Dir,* University of New Mexico, Tamarind Institute, Albuquerque NM (S)

DeVore, James, *Chmn,* Ohio Northern University, Dept of Art, Ada OH (S)

DeVore, Richard, *Prof,* Colorado State University, Dept of Art, Fort Collins CO (S)

Dew, James, *Prof,* University of Montana, Dept of Art, Missoula MT (S)

Dew, Roderick, *Librn,* Colorado Springs Fine Arts Center, Library, Colorado Springs CO

Dewdney, Eric, *Coordr Cultural Services,* Cambridge Public Library and Gallery, Cambridge ON

Dewey, Paul E, *Chmn,* Whitman College, Art Dept, Walla Walla WA (S)

Dewey, Priscilla B, *Dir,* Charles River Creative Arts Program, Dover MA (S)

Dewey, Richard, *Librn Aga Khan Program for Islamic Architecture,* Massachusetts Institute of Technology, Rotch Library of Architecture and Planning, Cambridge MA

Dewey, Talbot, *Dir,* Charles River Creative Arts Program, Dover MA (S)

Dewey, Tom, *Assoc Prof,* University of Mississippi, Dept of Art, University MS (S)

deWinter, Patrick M, *Cur Early Western Art,* Cleveland Museum of Art, Cleveland OH

de Wit, Wim, *Cur Architectural & Printed Collections,* Chicago Historical Society, Chicago IL

DeWitt, Martin, *Dir,* Rockford Art Association, Burpee Art Museum, Rockford IL

DeWolfe, Christopher, *VPres,* Art Gallery of Windsor, Windsor ON

Dey, Penny, *Administrator,* Artists Association of Nantucket, Kenneth Taylor Gallery, Nantucket MA

Dhaemers, Robert, *Prof,* Mills College, Art Dept, Oakland CA (S)

d'Harnoncourt, Anne, *The George D Widener Dir,* Philadelphia Museum of Art, Philadelphia PA

Diage, Katherine, *Dir,* University of California, University Art Gallery, Riverside CA

Diao, David, *Instructor,* Bard College, Milton Avery Graduate School of the Arts, Annandale-on-Hudson NY (S)

Dibble, George S, *Emeritus Prof,* University of Utah, Art Dept, Salt Lake City UT (S)

Dibble, Thomas Reilly, *Dir,* Southern Vermont Art Center, Manchester VT

DiBella, Joseph, *Assoc Prof,* Mary Washington College, Art Dept, Fredericksburg VA (S)

Dibert, Rita, *Asst Prof,* Pomona College, Art Dept, Claremont CA (S)

DiCicco, John, *Asst Prof,* Providence College, Art and Art History Dept, Providence RI (S)

Dickenhof, John, *Area Chmn Crafts,* Pasadena City College, Art Dept, Pasadena CA (S)

Dickenson, Sara, *Prof,* Southern University in New Orleans, Art Dept, New Orleans LA (S)

Dickenson, Victoria, *Chief Cur,* Newfoundland Museum, Saint John's NF

Dickerson, Jane E, *Secy,* Historical Society of Martin County, Elliot Museum, Stuart FL

Dickey, Susan J, *Cur Coll,* Indiana State Museum, Indianapolis IN

Dickey, Terry P, *VPres,* Alaska Association for the Arts, Fairbanks AK

Dickey, Terry P, *Coordr Pub Servs & Educ,* University of Alaska, Museum, Fairbanks AK

Dickinson, David, *Asst Prof,* Rochester Institute of Technology, School of Art and Design, Rochester NY (S)

Dickinson, Nancy, *Assoc Cur,* Brown University, Bell Gallery, Providence RI

Dickinson, Susan, *Executive Secy,* Rodman Hall Arts Centre, Saint Catharines ON

Dickson, David W D, *Pres,* Montclair State College, Gallery One, Upper Montclair NJ

Dickson, Janet S, *Cur Education,* Yale University, Art Gallery, New Haven CT

Dickson, Lois, *Dir of Design,* Prudential Insurance Collection, Newark NJ

DiCostanza, C, *Faculty,* Humboldt State University, College of Creative Arts & Humanities, Arcata CA (S)

Didriksen, Martha, *Pres,* Quincy Art Center, Quincy IL

Diduk, Barbara, *Asst Prof,* Dickinson College, Fine Arts Dept, Carlisle PA (S)

Dieckman, Suzanne, *Instr,* Creighton University, Fine and Performing Arts Dept, Omaha NE (S)

Dieckman, Virginia, *Dir,* Edna Hibel Art Foundation, Hibel Museum of Art, Riviera Beach FL

Diehl, George K, *Chmn Dept Fine Arts,* La Salle College, Dept of Fine Arts, Philadelphia PA (S)

Diehl, Mary, *2nd VPres,* Lahaina Arts Society, Art Organization, Lahaina HI

Diehl, Robert B, *Dir Building Servs,* Museum of Science and Industry, Chicago IL

Diehn, Gwen, *Admin Asst to Dir,* University of Notre Dame, Snite Museum of Art, Notre Dame IN

Diehr, James T, *Chmn Dept,* Austin Peay State University, Dept of Art, Clarksville TN (S)

Diener, Bert, *Pres,* New York Artists Equity Association, Inc, New York NY

Diener, Paul W, *Chmn Fine Arts,* York College of Pennsylvania, Dept of Humanities and Fine Arts, York PA (S)

Dierfeldt, Jerome, *Exhib Specialist,* Hastings Museum, Hastings NE

Dieruf, Thomas, *Pres,* Art Center Association, Louisville KY

Dieter, Joseph, *Lectr,* Johns Hopkins University, School of Medicine, Dept of Art as Applied to Medicine, Baltimore MD (S)

Dieterly, Richard, *Secy,* Hunterdon Art Center, Clinton NJ

Dietrich, Bruce L, *Dir,* Reading Public Museum and Art Gallery, Reading PA

Dietrich, Daryl, *Chmn Div of Humanities,* Wenatchee Valley College, Art Dept, Wenatchee WA (S)

Dietrich, Dorothy, *Cur Exhibits,* Schenectady Museum, Schenectady NY

Dietsch, Elaine, *Registrar,* Santa Barbara Museum of Art, Santa Barbara CA

Dietz, Charles, *Dir,* Zanesville Art Center, Zanesville OH

Dietz, Judy, *Acting Registrar,* Art Gallery of Nova Scotia, Halifax NS

Dietz, Ulysses G, *Cur Decorative Arts,* Newark Museum, Newark NJ

DiGiusto, Gerald, *Prof,* State University of New York College at Cortland, Art Dept, Cortland NY (S)

Di Julio, Max, *Prog Dir,* Loretto Heights College, Dept of Art, Denver CO (S)

Dileo, Fame, *Gallery Coordr,* Trenton State College, Holman Gallery, Trenton NJ

DiLillo, Connie, *Division Chair,* Lincoln College, Art Dept, Lincoln IL (S)

Dill, Lesley, *Children's Instructor,* Montclair Art Museum, Museum Art Classes, Montclair NJ (S)

Dillenbeck, Mildred, *Dir,* Frederic Remington Art Museum, Ogdensburg NY

Diller, J David, *Prof,* James Madison University, Dept of Art, Harrisonburg VA (S)

Dillingham, Judith, *Librn,* Anderson Fine Arts Center, Library, Anderson IN

Dillon, Brad, *VPres,* Hutchinson Art Association, Hutchinson KS

Dillon, John, *Asst Prof,* Chadron State College, Division of Fine Arts, Chadron NE (S)

Dillon, John, *Prof,* University of Alabama in Birmingham, Dept of Art, Birmingham AL (S)

Dillon, Mildred, *VPres,* American Color Print Society, Philadelphia PA

Dillon, Virginia, *Circulation Dept Head,* Wichita Public Library, Wichita KS

Dillow, Nancy, *Chief Cur,* Winnipeg Art Gallery, Winnipeg MB

Dills, Keith, *Assoc Prof,* California Polytechnic State University at San Luis Obispo, Art Dept, San Luis Obispo CA (S)

Dilworth, J Richardson, *Chmn Bd Trustees,* Metropolitan Museum of Art, New York NY

DiMattia, Ernest A, *Dir,* Ferguson Library, Stamford CT

DiMattio, Vincent, *Assoc Prof,* Monmouth College, Dept of Art, West Long Branch NJ (S)

Dimico, Sam, *Instructor,* The Design Schools, Art Institute of Seattle, Seattle WA (S)

Dimond, Thomas, *Assoc Prof Art,* Eastern Oregon State College, Arts & Humanities Dept, La Grande OR (S)

Dimond, Tom, *Coordr Educational Media & Exhib,* Clemson University, Rudolph E Lee Gallery, Clemson SC

Dimor, Phillip, *Dept Head AV,* New Bedford Free Public Library, Art Dept, New Bedford MA

Dinda, Richard, *Chmn,* Concordia Lutheran College, Dept of Fine Arts, Austin TX (S)

Dineen, Diane, *Librn,* Mississauga Library System, Central Library, Art Division, Mississauga ON

Dines, Nicholas, *Dir MLA Prog,* University of Massachusetts, Amherst, Dept Landscape Architecture & Regional Planning, Amherst MA (S)

Dingler, John, *Preparator,* University of California, University Art Gallery, Riverside CA

Dings, Marjorie, *Membership & Publicity,* Wellesley College, Museum, Wellesley MA

Dinkelspiel, Edgar N, *Pres,* Long Branch Historical Museum, Long Branch NJ

Dinneen, Marie de Sales, *Assoc Prof,* Regis College, Dept of Art, Weston MA (S)

Dinsmore, Grant, *Instructor,* La Roche College, Division of Graphics, Design, Pittsburgh PA (S)

Dinsmore, John N, *Prof,* Kearney State College, Dept of Art, Kearney NE (S)

Dion, Kerry, *Astist-in-Residence,* Sierra Nevada Museum of Art, Reno NV

DiPaolo, John, *Chmn Drawing & Painting,* De Young Museum Art School, San Francisco CA (S)

Dipietro, David A, *Instr,* Pennsylvania State University, Fayette Campus, Dept of Art, Uniontown PA (S)

Dippolito, Frank, *Art Dept Chmn,* Tacoma Community College, Art Dept, Tacoma WA (S)

Dirks, John, *Asst Dir,* Museum of Art of Ogunquit, Ogunquit ME

Dirr, Kathyann, *Registrar & Educational Officer,* Hall of Fame of the Trotter, Goshen NY

DiSalvi, Margaret, *Librn,* Newark Museum, Library, Newark NJ

Dishman, Sue, *Secy,* Arts and Science Museum, Statesville NC

DiTeresa, Neil, *Prof,* Berea College, Art Dept, Berea KY (S)

Dittman, Reidar, *Prof,* Saint Olaf College, Art Dept, Northfield MN (S)

Dittman, Thelma, *Registrar,* Canton Art Institute, Canton OH (S)

Divelbess, Diane, *Prof,* California State Polytechnic University, Pomona, Art Dept, Pomona CA (S)

Divelbiss, Maggie, *Assoc Dir,* Sangre De Cristo Arts & Conference Center, Pueblo CO

Dively, Charlotte Lyeth, *Chmn,* Artrain, Inc, Detroit MI

Divers, Dorothy, *Assoc Prof,* Saint Olaf College, Art Dept, Northfield MN (S)

Dix, Marilyn, *Asst to Dir,* Print Club, Philadelphia PA

Dixon, Aimee, *Instr,* Arkansas Arts Center, Little Rock AR (S)

Dixon, Arthur L, *Chmn,* J Sargeant Reynolds Community College, Humanities & Social Science Division, Richmond VA (S)

Dixon, Bob, *Asst Prof,* Sangamon State University, Creative Arts Program, Springfield IL (S)

Dixon, Daniel, *Dir Museum Programs,* Manhattan Laboratory Museum, New York NY

Dixon, F Eugene, *Pres,* Philadelphia Art Commission, Philadelphia PA

Dixon, Gerald, *VPres,* No Man's Land Historical Society Museum, Goodwell OK

Dixon, Howard, *Pres,* Nobles County Art Center Gallery, Worthington MN

Dixon, Jenny, *Exec Dir,* Public Art Fund, Inc, New York NY

Dixon, John, *Adjunct Assoc,* Wright State University, Dept of Art & Art History, Dayton OH (S)

Dixon, John W, *Prof,* University of North Carolina at Chapel Hill, Art Dept, Chapel Hill NC (S)

Dixon, Joycelyn, *Staff Specialist,* Pacific Northwest Bell, Seattle WA

Dixon, Ken, *Assoc Prof,* Texas Tech University, Dept of Art, Lubbock TX (S)

Dixon, Laurinda, *Prof,* Syracuse University, Dept of Fine Arts, Syracuse NY (S)

Dixon, Stewart, *Pres,* Chicago Historical Society, Chicago IL

Dixon, Yvonne, *Asst Prof,* Trinity College, Art Dept, Washington DC (S)

Doak, Banton S, *Assoc Prof,* Florida Southern College, Art Dept, Lakeland FL (S)

Doak, Gale L, *Asst Prof,* Florida Southern College, Art Dept, Lakeland FL (S)

Doan, Arthur M, *Pres,* Pimeria Alta Historical Society, Nogales AZ

Doanto, James, *Instructor,* Antonelli Institute of Art & Photography, Professional Photography, Commercial Art & Interior Design, Plymouth Meeting PA (S)

Dobb, Theodore C, *Librn,* Simon Fraser University, Library, Burnaby BC

Dobbins, Nancy, *Hostess,* Baylor University, Armstrong Browning Library, Waco TX

Dobbs, Gigi, *Program Development Dir,* The Art Museum Association of America, San Francisco CA

Dobbs, Jim, *Lectr,* California State Polytechnic University, Pomona, Art Dept, Pomona CA (S)

Dobbs, John, *Assoc Prof,* John Jay College of Criminal Justice, Dept of Art, Music and Philosophy, New York NY (S)

Dobe, William, *Asst Prof,* Notre Dame College, Art Dept, Manchester NH (S)

Dobereiner, Wendy, *Asst Prof,* University of British Columbia, Dept of Fine Arts, Vancouver BC (S)

Dobkin, John, *Dir,* National Academy School of Fine Arts, New York NY (S)

Dobkin, John H, *Dir,* National Academy of Design, New York NY

Dobrea, Jean, *VPres,* Saint Mary's Romanian Orthodox Church, Romanian Ethnic Museum, Cleveland OH

Dobrowolski, Fred, *Lectr,* Notre Dame College, Art Dept, Manchester NH (S)

Dobrowolsky, Stanley, *Secy,* Taras H Schevchenko Museum and Memorial Park Foundation, Oakville ON

Dockerg, Floyd, *Instr,* Cleveland State Community College, Dept of Art, Cleveland TN (S)

Docktor, Gail C, *Public Information Coordr,* Fine Arts Museums of San Francisco, M H de Young Memorial Museum and California Palace of the Legion of Honor, San Francisco CA

Doctorow, Erica, *Head Fine Arts Library,* Adelphi University, Fine Arts Library, Garden City NY

Dodd, Jerry, *Co-Dir,* East Texas State University, Art Dept Gallery, Commerce TX

Dodd, Jerry, *Chmn Sculpture,* East Texas State University, Dept of Art, Commerce TX (S)

Dodd, John, *VPres,* Huntsville Art League and Museum Association Inc, Huntsville AL

Dodderidge, Richard W, *Interim Pres,* Kansas City Art Institute, Kansas City MO (S)

Dodds, Nancy, *Public Relations,* Alberta College of Art Gallery, Calgary AB

Dodds, Robert J, *Pres,* Pittsburgh Plan for Art Gallery, Gallery 407, Pittsburgh PA

Dodge, Robert, *Instructor,* Bucks County Community College, Fine Arts Dept, Newton PA (S)

Dodsworth, Barbara, *Instructor,* Elizabeth Seton College, Art Dept, Yonkers NY (S)

Dodworth, Allen, *Dir,* Western Colorado Center for the Arts, Inc, Grand Junction CO

Doe, Donald Bartlett, *Asst Dir,* University of Nebraska, Lincoln, Sheldon Memorial Art Gallery, Lincoln NE

D'Oench, Ellen, *Adjunct Prof,* Wesleyan University, Art Dept, Middletown CT (S)

D'Oench, Ellen G, *Cur,* Wesleyan University, Davison Art Center, Middletown CT

Doerfler, Roy D, *Instructor,* Nebraska Western College, Division of Language and Arts, Scottsbluff NE (S)

Doering, Colette, *Assoc Prof,* Avila College, Art Division, Dept of Performing and Visual Art, Kansas City MO (S)

Doerzbach, Cindy, *Cur,* Salisbury State College, Wildfowl Art Museum, Salisbury MD

Driggers, Jeff, *Art and Music Dept Librn,* Jacksonville Public Library, Art and Music Dept, Jacksonville FL

Drisch, Diane, *Registrar,* Indiana University, Art Museum, Bloomington IN

Driscoll, Rev Jeremy, *Acquisitions Librn,* Mount Angel Abbey & Seminary Library, Saint Benedict OR

Droege, Anthony, *Prof,* Indiana University at South Bend, Fine Arts Dept, South Bend IN (S)

Droege, John, *Assoc Prof,* Bridgewater State College, Art Dept, Bridgewater MA (S)

Drohan, Walter, *Prog Coordr Ceramics & Glass,* Alberta College of Art, Southern Alberta Institute of Technology, Calgary AB (S)

Droll, Donald, *Pres,* Committee for the Visual Arts, Inc, New York NY

Droll, Donald, *Asst Dir,* University of North Carolina at Greensboro, Weatherspoon Art Gallery, Greensboro NC

Dronberger, Jane, *Prof,* Hutchinson Community Junior College, Art Dept, Hutchinson KS (S)

Druick, Douglas, *Cur Prints,* National Gallery of Canada, Ottawa ON

Drumm, Nelde, *Secy,* Fitchburg Art Museum, Fitchburg MA

Drummond, Derek, *Dir,* McGill University, School of Architecture, Montreal PQ (S)

Drummond, Herbert W, *Humanities Reference Librn,* California State University, Sacramento, Library, Humanities Reference and Media Services Center, Sacramento CA

Drury, Frank, *Special Services Librn,* University of Portland, Wilson W Clark Memorial Library, Portland OR

Dryden, J E, *Sr Archivist,* Department of Culture, Government of the Province of Alberta, Provincial Archives of Alberta, Edmonton AB

Dryer, A L, *Resident Potter,* Strasburg Museum, Strasburg VA

Dryfhout, John H, *Supt & Chief Cur,* Saint-Gaudens National Historic Site, Cornish NH

D'Souza, Nativity, *General Mgr,* Fine Arts Museums of San Francisco, The Museum Society, San Francisco CA

Du Bois, Alan, *Asst Dir,* Museum of Fine Arts of Saint Petersburg, Florida, Inc, Saint Petersburg FL

DuBois, William W, *Asst Prof,* Rochester Institute of Technology, School of Photographic Arts & Sciences, Rochester NY (S)

DuBon, David, *Cur Medieval and Renaissance Decorative Arts,* Philadelphia Museum of Art, Philadelphia PA

Dubreuil-Blondin, Nicole, *Prof,* Universite de Montreal, Dept of Art History, Montreal PQ (S)

Duce, Scott, *Asst Prof,* Wesleyan College, Art Dept, Macon GA (S)

Duchac, Kenneth F, *Dir,* Brooklyn Public Library, Art and Music Division, Brooklyn NY

Ducham, Robert, *Exhibit Designer,* Okefenokee Heritage Center, Inc, Waycross GA

Du Charme, Andree, *Assoc Prof,* Silver Lake College, Art Dept, Manitowoc WI (S)

Duchesneau, Guy P E, *Mgr,* Society of the Montreal Military and Maritime Museum, Saint Helen's Island Museum, Montreal PQ

Duckett, Jo, *Education Coordr,* Science Museums of Charlotte, Inc, Discovery Place, Charlotte NC

Duckworth, T A, *Pres,* Leigh Yawkey Woodson Art Museum, Inc, Wausau WI

Dudics, Kitty, *Instructor,* Del Mar College, Dept of Art, Corpus Christi TX (S)

Dudley, David, *Dir Upper Midwest Conservation Assoc,* Minneapolis Institute of Arts, Minneapolis MN

Dudley, Janice Stafford, *Secy,* MacArthur Memorial Museum, Norfolk VA

Dudley, Peter, *Instructor,* Greenfield Community College, Art Dept, Greenfield MA (S)

Duea, Edward, *Mgr,* Arts Club of Washington, James Monroe House, Washington DC

Dueck, Cathy, *Secy,* Ukrainian Cultural and Educational Centre Museum, Winnipeg MB

Duensing, Sally, *Professional Internship Prog,* Exploratorium, San Francisco CA

Duerksen, George L, *Chmn Dept,* University of Kansas, Dept of Art, Music Education and Music Therapy, Lawrence KS (S)

Duff, James H, *Dir,* Brandywine River Museum, Chadds Ford PA

Duffek, Robert, *Instructor,* Mohawk Valley Community College, Advertising Design and Production, Utica NY (S)

Duffy, Brian R, *Instr,* Villa Maria College of Buffalo, Art Dept, Buffalo NY (S)

Duffy, Mary, *Admin Asst,* Museum of Holography, Reference Library, New York NY

Duffy, Val, *Dir Education,* William A Farnsworth Library and Art Museum, Library, Rockland ME

Duffy, Valerie N, *Dir Education,* William A Farnsworth Library and Art Museum, Rockland ME

DuFort, Robert, *Instr,* Schoolcraft College, Dept of Art, Livonia MI (S)

Dufour, Lydia A, *Cur Iconography,* Hispanic Society of America, Museum, New York NY

Dufour, M Calude, *Pres,* La Societe des Arts de Chicoutimi, Chicoutimi PQ

Dufour, Paul, *Prof,* Louisiana State University, School of Art, Baton Rouge LA (S)

Dugan, Alan, *Instructor,* Truro Center for the Arts at Castle Hill, Inc, Truro MA (S)

Dugan, George, *Assoc Prof,* State University of New York College at Cortland, Art Dept, Cortland NY (S)

Dugas, Juge Jacques, *VPres,* Musee d'Art de Joliette, Joliette PQ

Dugdale, James, *Instructor,* Joliet Junior College, Fine Arts Dept, Joliet IL (S)

Duggan, Jane E, *Asst,* Providence Public Library, Art and Music Dept, Providence RI

Duggan, Lynn, *Asst Prof,* Nazareth College of Rochester, Art Dept, Rochester NY (S)

Duhme, H Richard, *Head Sculpture,* Chautauqua Institution, The Art Center, Chautauqua NY (S)

Duke, Carl F, *Head Dept,* Pensacola Junior College, Dept of Visual Arts, Pensacola FL (S)

Duke, Sylvia, *Instr,* Coos Art Museum, Coos Bay OR (S)

Dumanowski, Stefanie, *Prog Coordr Found,* Alberta College of Art, Southern Alberta Institute of Technology, Calgary AB (S)

Dummer, Nancy N, *Admin Asst,* John Michael Kohler Arts Center, Library, Sheboygan WI

Dunaway, Bob A, *Chmn,* Hinds Junior College, Dept of Art, Raymond MS (S)

Dunaway, Sherry R, *Asst Dir-Registrar,* University of Texas at Arlington, University Art Gallery, Arlington TX

Dunaway, Suzann, *Asst to the Dir,* Mills College, Art Gallery, Oakland CA

Dunbar, Burton L, *Secy-Treasurer,* Midwest Art History Society, Madison WI

Dunbar, Frank, *Secy Board of Trustees,* Royal Ontario Museum, Toronto ON

Dunbar, Philip H, *Museum Cur,* Connecticut Historical Society, Hartford CT

Dunbeck, Helen, *Adminr,* Museum of Contemporary Art, Chicago IL

Duncan, Carol, *Prof Art History,* Ramapo College of New Jersey, School of Contemporary Arts, Mahwah NJ (S)

Duncan, Donald, *Assoc Prof,* Ohio State University, Dept of Art Education, Columbus OH (S)

Duncan, J Russell, *Pres,* Norton Gallery and School of Art, West Palm Beach FL

Duncan, Marianna, *Develop Coordr,* Lufkin Historical and Creative Arts Center, Lufkin TX

Duncan, Richard, *Assoc Prof,* Florida International University, Visual Arts Dept, Miami FL (S)

Dungan, Margaret, *Admin,* Please Touch Museum, Philadelphia PA

Dunifon, Don, *Prof,* Wittenberg University, Art Dept, Springfield OH (S)

Dunkelman, Martha, *Assoc Prof,* Wright State University, Dept of Art & Art History, Dayton OH (S)

Dunkle, Alvin, *Dir,* Thiel College, Sampson Art Gallery, Greenville PA

Dunlap, Barbara, *Special Collections & Archives,* City College of New York, Cohen Art Library, New York NY

Dunlap, Ellen S, *Dir,* The Rosenbach Museum and Library, Philadelphia PA

Dunlevy, Raymond, *Dept Chmn,* California University of Pennsylvania, Dept of Art, California PA (S)

Dunlop, Hank, *Interior Architecture Design,* California College of Arts and Crafts, Oakland CA (S)

Dunn, David W, *Dir,* Fetherston Foundation, Packwood House Museum, Lewisburg PA

Dunn, McChesney S, *Assoc Dir,* Southeastern Center for Contemporary Art, Winston-Salem NC

Dunn, Nancy, *Gallery Dir,* Frog Hollow Craft Center, Middlebury VT

Dunn, Roger, *Asst Prof,* Bridgewater State College, Art Dept, Bridgewater MA (S)

Dunn, Sandra, *Information Services Officer,* Ontario Crafts Council, Craft Resource Centre, Toronto ON

Dunn, Tom, *Instr,* Azusa Pacific University, College of Liberal Arts, Art Dept, Azusa CA (S)

Dunn, Warren, *Dept Coordr,* Clark College, Art Dept, Vancouver WA (S)

Dunne, Jane, *Exec Dir,* Society of Typographic Arts, Chicago IL

Dunnigan, Mary C, *Librn,* University of Virginia, Fiske Kimball Fine Arts Library, Charlottesville VA

DunSeith, Marie, *Mgr Development,* Art Gallery of Ontario, Toronto ON

Dunstane, Laura Mae, *Custodian,* West Baton Rouge Museum, Port Allen LA

Dunwiddie, Charlotte, *Pres,* National Sculpture Society, New York NY

Duplaix, Sally, *Exec Dir,* Providence Athenaeum, Providence RI

Dupree, Barbara, *Lectr,* Centenary College of Louisiana, Dept of Art, Shreveport LA (S)

Durante, Joanne, *Secy,* Women's City Club of Cleveland, Gallery, Cleveland OH

Durham, David, *Chmn Dept,* Saint Louis Community College at Meramec, Art Dept, Saint Louis MO (S)

Durham, Jimmie, *Exec Dir,* Foundation for the Community of Artists, New York NY

Durkee, Stephen, *Prof,* Framingham State College, Art Dept, Framingham MA (S)

Durken, Silvan A, *Cur,* Owatonna Arts Center, Owatonna MN

Durkin, Frederic J, *VPres,* Everson Museum of Art, Syracuse NY

Durland, Don, *Prof,* Texas Tech University, Dept of Art, Lubbock TX (S)

Duross, Ann Marie, *Public Information Coordr,* State University of New York at Purchase, Neuberger Museum, Purchase NY

Durrant, George D, *Assoc Prof,* Palomar College, Art Dept, San Marcos TX (S)

Dursum, Brian, *Registrar & Cur Oriental Art,* University of Miami, Lowe Art Museum, Coral Gables FL

Dusch, Peggy, *Asst Head,* Carnegie Library of Pittsburgh, Pittsburgh PA

Dusek, Bernard W, *Prof,* California Polytechnic State University at San Luis Obispo, Art Dept, San Luis Obispo CA (S)

Dusendschon, Noel, *Prof,* Indiana University-Purdue University, Dept of Fine Arts, Fort Wayne IN (S)

Dutro, Leroy, *Mgr de Young Bookshop,* Fine Arts Museums of San Francisco, The Museum Society, San Francisco CA

Dutt-Justice, Mary Anne, *Pres,* Wayne Art Center, Wayne PA

Dutton, Richard, *Dept Head,* Indian Hills Community College, Ottumwa Campus, Dept of Art, Ottumwa IA (S)

Dutton, Richard H, *Head Dept,* Indian Hills Community College, Dept of Art, Centerville IA (S)

Duty, Michael, *Dir,* The Rockwell Museum, Corning NY

Duval, Cynthia, *Cur Decorative Arts,* State Art Museum of Florida, John & Mable Ringling Museum of Art, Sarasota FL

Duvall, A, *VPres,* Museum of the Historical Society of Early American Decoration, Albany NY

Duvigneaud, Diane, *Prof Emeritus,* North Central College, Dept of Art, Naperville IL (S)

Dvidson, Perry, *Pres,* Chautauqua Art Association Galleries, Chautauqua NY

Dvorak, Anna, *Librn,* North Carolina Museum of Art, Reference Library, Raleigh NC

D'Vorzon, Berenice, *Assoc Prof,* Wilkes College, Dept of Art, Wilkes-Barre PA (S)

Dworkin, Ellen, *Asst Librn,* Brand Library and Art Center, Glendale CA

Dwyer, Eugene J, *Asst Prof,* Kenyon College, Art Dept, Gambier OH (S)

Dwyer, Kathy L, *Exec Dir,* Federated Arts Council of Richmond, Inc, Richmond VA

Dwyer, Marilyn, *Museum Receptionist & Shop Mgr,* Bowdoin College, Museum of Art & Peary-MacMillan Arctic Museum, Brunswick ME

Dwyer, Melva J, *Head Librn,* University of British Columbia, Fine Arts Division Library, Vancouver BC

Dwyer, Rob, *Dir,* Quincy Society of Fine Arts, Quincy IL

Dyer, E May, *Chmn,* Lock Haven State College, Art Dept, Lock Haven PA (S)

Dyer, M Wayne, *Asst Prof,* East Tennessee State University, Fine Arts Dept, Johnson City TN (S)

Dykes, Stephen E, *Deputy Dir Admin,* Fine Arts Museums of San Francisco, M H de Young Memorial Museum and California Palace of the Legion of Honor, San Francisco CA

Dynneson, Donald, *Prof,* Concordia College, Art Dept, Seward NE (S)

Dyson, Jack R, *Cur,* Kit Carson Memorial Foundation, Kit Carson Home and Museum, Taos NM

Dyson, Robert H, *Dir & Near East Section Cur,* University of Pennsylvania, University Museum of Archaeology & Anthropology, Philadelphia PA

Dzuba, Ethelwyn, *Education Coordr,* Estevan National Exhibition Centre Inc, Estevan SK

Dzus, Theodore, *Pres,* Ukrainian Institute of America, Inc, New York NY

Eades, Luis E, *Assoc Chmn,* University of Colorado, Boulder, Dept of Fine Arts, Boulder CO (S)

Eads, Hannah, *Asst Prof,* Eastern Illinois University, School of Fine Arts, Charleston IL (S)

Eagen, Christopher T, *Dir,* University of Cincinnati, Tangeman Fine Arts Gallery, Cincinnati OH

Eager, George, *Asst Dir,* Museum of the American Indian, New York NY

Eager, Gerald, *Prof,* Bucknell University, Dept of Art, Lewisburg PA (S)

Eakins, E, *Pres Board of Trustees,* Burnaby Art Gallery, Burnaby BC

Eakins, Joyce, *Dir,* Colorado Women's College, Lyle True Gallery, Denver CO

Eakins, Joyce, *Instr,* Colorado Women's College, Dept of Art, Denver CO (S)

Ealer, William, *Asst Prof,* Williamsport Area Community College, Dept of Engineering and Design, Williamsport PA (S)

Eames, Owen, *VPres,* Washington Art Association, Washington Depot CT

Earle, Edward W, *Cur,* University of California, California Museum of Photography, Riverside CA

Earls-Solari, Bonnie, *Cur,* Bank of America, Concourse Gallery, San Francisco CA

Eason, Laurie, *Dir,* Palo Alto Cultural Center, Palo Alto CA

Eason, Robert, *Theatre Librn,* Dallas Public Library, Fine Arts Division, Dallas TX

East, Dennis, *Division Chief,* Ohio Historical Society, Archives-Library Division, Columbus OH

Eastman, Gene M, *Prof,* Sam Houston State University, Art Dept, Huntsville TX (S)

Eaton, Casindania P, *Librn,* American Academy and Institute of Arts and Letters, Library, New York NY

Eaton, John, *Executive Dir,* Georgia Volunteer Lawyers for the Arts, Inc, Atlanta GA

Eaton, Juanita, *Secy,* Kingsport Fine Arts Center, Kingsport TN

Ebel, Helen, *Secy,* Portage and District Arts Council, Portage la Prairie MB

Ebeling, Klaus, *Prof,* Jefferson Community College, Art Dept, Watertown NY (S)

Eber, Marian, *Admin Analyst,* University of California, Los Angeles, Frederick S Wight Art Gallery, Los Angeles CA

Eberdt, Clarice, *Prof Emeritus,* Marycrest College, Art Dept, Davenport IA (S)

Ebert, D, *Instructor,* Golden West College, Arts, Humanities and Social Sciences Institute, Huntington Beach CA (S)

Ebie, William D, *Asst Dir,* Roswell Museum and Art Center, Roswell NM

Ebitz, David, *Asst Prof,* University of Maine, Art Dept, Orono ME (S)

Eble, Bernard, *Chmn Memorial Hall Committee,* Louisiana Historical Association, Confederate Museum, New Orleans LA

Eccles, Vera, *Pres,* Eccles Community Art Center, Ogden UT

Echevarria, Carmen, *Asst Prof,* Saint Mary College, Art Dept, Leavenworth KS (S)

Echeverria, Felipe, *Assoc Prof,* University of Northern Iowa, Dept of Art, Cedar Falls IA (S)

Ecke, Tsen Yu-ho, *Consultant for Chinese Art,* Honolulu Academy of Arts, Honolulu HI

Eckersley, T C, *Chmn,* State University of New York College at Oswego, Art Dept, Oswego NY (S)

Eckert, John, *Asst Prof,* Eckerd College, Art Dept, Saint Petersburg FL (S)

Eckert, W Dean, *Chmn,* Lindenwood College, Harry D Hendren Gallery, Saint Charles MO

Eckert, W Dean, *Chmn Dept,* Lindenwood Colleges, Art Dept, Saint Charles MO (S)

Eckes, Harold, *Dir,* Los Angeles Trade-Technical College Library, Art Dept, Los Angeles CA

Eckhardt-Jacobi, Richard, *Instructor,* Casper College, Casper WY (S)

EdBorg, Judy A, *American Artisans Dir,* American Society of Artists, Inc, Chicago IL

Eddey, Roy, *VDir Finance & Personnel,* Brooklyn Museum, Brooklyn NY

Eddy, Edith, *Asst Mgr,* Mission San Luis Rey Museum, San Luis Rey CA

Eddy, Warren S, *Dir,* Cortland Free Library, Art Gallery, Cortland NY

Edelson, Brenda, *Dir Programs,* Baltimore Museum of Art, Baltimore MD

Edelson, Gilbert S, *Secy & Treasurer,* Art Dealers Association of America, Inc, New York NY

Edelstein, J M, *Chief Librn,* National Gallery of Art, Library, Washington DC

Edelstein, Teri J, *Dir,* Mount Holyoke College Art Museum, South Hadley MA

Edens, Marjorie, *Historian-Newsletter Editor,* Southern Oregon Historical Society, Jacksonville Museum, Jacksonville OR

Edge, Kippy, *Chmn Art Committee,* Angelo State University, Houston Harte University Center, San Angelo TX

Edgerton, Samuel Y, *Dir Grad Program,* Williams College, Dept of Art, Williamstown MA (S)

Edie, Richard, *Prof,* South Dakota State University, Dept of Visual Arts, Brookings SD (S)

Edkins, Barbara, *Librn,* Peabody Museum of Salem, Phillips Library, Salem MA

Edland, Svein, *Cur Exhibits,* Loveland Museum and Gallery, Loveland CO

Edlhauser, June M, *Coordr Fine Arts,* Milwaukee Public Library, Art, Music & Recreation Dept, Milwaukee WI

Edmond, Pierre, *Secy,* Musee Historique de Vaudreuil, Vaudreuil Historical Museum, Vaudreuil PQ

Edmondson-Haney, Kristine, *Asst Prof,* University of Massachusetts, Amherst, Art History Program, Amherst MA (S)

Edmonston, Paul, *Grad Coordr,* University of Georgia, Franklin College of Arts and Sciences, Dept of Art, Athens GA (S)

Edmunds, Sheila, *Division Chmn,* Wells College, Dept of Art & Art History, Aurora NY (S)

Edmundson, Gerald, *Assoc Prof,* East Tennessee State University, Fine Arts Dept, Johnson City TN (S)

Edmundson, Gerald G, *Dir Exhibitions,* East Tennessee State University, Elizabeth Slocum Gallery, Johnson City TN

Edmundson, Margaret, *Head Fine Arts Department,* Salt Lake City Public Library, Fine Arts Department and Atrium Gallery, Salt Lake City UT

Edson, Gary, *Chmn Art Dept,* West Virginia University, West Virginia University Galleries, Morgantown WV

Edson, Gary, *Chmn,* West Virginia University, Division of Art, Morgantown WV (S)

Edwards, Beverly, *Dir Museum School,* Brockton Art Museum, Brockton MA

Edwards, Brian, *Prof,* Shoreline Community College, Humanities Division, Seattle WA (S)

Edwards, Charleen K, *Managing Editor,* Corning Museum of Glass, Corning NY

Edwards, Ella Yates, *Librn,* Atlanta Public Library, Fine Arts Dept, Atlanta GA

Edwards, James, *Cur Exhibits,* Art Museum of South Texas, Corpus Christi TX

Edwards, Jonathan, *Facilities Tech,* Washington University, Gallery of Art, Saint Louis MO

Edwards, Laverne, *Instructor,* Rudolph Schaeffer School of Design, San Francisco CA (S)

Edwards, Lella Lee, *VPres,* Art League, Alexandria VA

Edwards, Marcia, *Pres,* Fort Smith Art Center, Fort Smith AR

Edwards, Mary Jane, *Assoc Prof,* Nazareth College of Rochester, Art Dept, Rochester NY (S)

Edwards, Olga, *Exhibitis Chmn,* Huntsville Art League and Museum Association Inc, Huntsville AL

Edwards, Paul B, *Chmn,* Washington & Jefferson College, Olin Art Gallery, Washington PA

Edwards, Paul B, *Chmn Art Dept,* Washington and Jefferson College, Art Dept, Washington PA (S)

Edwards, William T, *Assoc Prof,* Clarion University of Pennsylvania, Dept of Art, Clarion PA (S)

Efland, Arthur, *Prof,* Ohio State University, Dept of Art Education, Columbus OH (S)

Egan, Albert T, *VPres,* Nantucket Historical Association, Fair Street Museum, Nantucket MA

Egan, Mildred, *Librn,* Watkins Institute, Library, Nashville TN

Egan, William C, *Pres,* Everson Museum of Art, Syracuse NY

Eggers, Barbara, *VPres,* Artrium Inc, Santa Rosa CA

Egherman, Davida, *Professional Training Coordr,* The Art Museum Association of America, San Francisco CA

Egherman, Ronald, *Assoc Dir,* University of California, University Art Museum, Berkeley CA

Egleston, Robert, *Cur,* New Haven Colony Historical Society, New Haven CT

Eglinski, Edmund, *Assoc Prof,* University of Kansas, Kress Foundation Dept of Art History, Lawrence KS (S)

Egnew, Louise, *Second VPres,* Toledo Federation of Art Societies, Toledo OH

Ehrenthal, Michael, *VPres,* National Council on Art in Jewish Life, New York NY

Ehrhardt, Ursula M, *Asst Prof,* Salisbury State College, Art Dept, Salisbury MD (S)

Ehrlich, Martha, *Asst Prof,* Murray State University, Art Dept, Murray KY (S)

Ehrlich, Nancy, *Dir,* Jackson County Historical Society, Research Library and Archives, Independence MO

Ehrlichman, Donald, *Chmn Three-Dimensional Studies,* Bowling Green State University, School of Art, Bowling Green OH (S)

Ehrmann, Donald, *President,* Florida Gulf Coast Art Center, Inc, Clearwater FL

Eicher, Joanne B, *Head Dept,* University of Minnesota, Dept of Design, Housing & Apparel, Saint Paul MN (S)

Eichler, Leonard, *Registrar & Preparator,* Syracuse University, Joe and Emily Lowe Art Gallery, Syracuse NY

Eick, Lawrence E, *Cur,* Missoula Museum of the Arts, Missoula MT

Eickhorst, William, *Asst Prof,* Missouri Western State College, Art Dept, Saint Joseph MO (S)

Eickhorst, William, *Chmn Department of Art,* Missouri Western State College, Fine Arts Gallery, Saint Joseph MO

Eickoff, Harold, *Pres,* Trenton State College, Holman Gallery, Trenton NJ

Eide, Joel S, *Dir Art Gallery,* Northern Arizona University, Art Gallery, Flagstaff AZ

Eide, John, *Instructor,* Portland School of Art, Portland ME (S)

Eidelberg, Martin, *Prof,* Rutgers, the State University of New Jersey, Graduate Program in Art History, New Brunswick NJ (S)

Eifert, Donald A, *Pres,* Society of Medalists, Danbury CT

Eige, G Eason, *Cur Collections,* Huntington Galleries, Huntington WV

Eigenbrodt, Susan, *Prof,* Western New Mexico University, College of Arts and Letters, Art Dept, Silver City NM (S)

Einhorn, Benjamin, *Chairperson,* New York City Technical College of the City University of New York, Dept of Art and Advertising Design, Brooklyn NY (S)

Eirk, Katherine, *Secy,* American Institute for Conservation of Historic and Artistic Works (AIC), Washington DC

Eis, Ruth, *Cur,* Judah L Magnes Museum, Berkeley CA

Eisenman, Alvin, *Prof,* Yale University, School of Art, New Haven CT (S)

Eisenman, Michael, *Asst Prof,* University of Pennsylvania, College Arts & Science, Philadelphia PA (S)

Eisentrager, James, *ViceChmn Dept,* University of Nebraska at Lincoln, Dept of Art, Lincoln NE (S)

Eisman, Hy, *Instr,* Joe Kubert School of Cartoon and Graphic Art Inc, Dover NJ (S)

Eisner, William S, *Dir Technical Services,* Rochester Institute of Technology, Technical & Education Center of the Graphic Arts, Rochester NY (S)

Eisterhold, Gerard, *Graphic Designer,* Art Research Center, Kansas City MO

Eitner, Lorenz, *Dir,* Stanford University, Museum of Art & Art Gallery, Stanford CA

Eitner, Lorenz, *Chmn Dept Art,* Stanford University, Dept of Art, Stanford CA (S)

Ekdahl, Janis, *Asst Dir,* Museum of Modern Art, Library, New York NY

Ekedal, Ellen, *Dir,* Loyola Marymount University, Art Gallery, Los Angeles CA

Eknoian, Gerald, *Instructor,* De Anza College, Art Dept, Cupertino CA (S)

Ekstrom, Ann Kathryn, *Bookshop,* University of Kansas, Spencer Museum of Art, Lawrence KS

Ela, Janet, *Cur Coll,* Madison Art Center, Madison WI

Ela, Patrick, *Executive Dir,* Craft and Folk Art Museum, Los Angeles CA

Elam, Leslie A, *Dir & Secy,* American Numismatic Society, New York NY

Elder, William Voss, *Cur Decorative Arts,* Baltimore Museum of Art, Baltimore MD

Elderfield, John, *Dir Drawings,* Museum of Modern Art, New York NY

Eldred, Dale, *Chmn Sculpture,* Kansas City Art Institute, Kansas City MO (S)

Eldredge, Bruce B, *Exec Dir,* Frederic Remington Art Museum, Ogdensburg NY

Eldredge, Charles C, *Dir,* National Museum of American Art, Washington DC

Eldridge, Jan, *Instructor,* Solano Community College, Dept of Fine & Applied Art, Suisun City CA (S)

Eley, L, *Library Asst,* University of Regina, Fine Arts Library, Regina SK

Elfrank, James, *Library Dir,* North Canton Public Library, Little Art Gallery, North Canton OH

Elfvin, John T, *VPres,* The Buffalo Fine Arts Academy, Albright-Knox Art Gallery, Buffalo NY

Elgart, Ruth, *Instr,* Mainline Center of the Arts, Haverford PA (S)

Elias, Clifford E, *Secy,* Merrimack Valley Textile Museum, North Andover MA

Elias, Margery M, *Assoc,* Dezign House III, Cleveland OH

Elias, Ramon J, *Dir,* Dezign House III, Cleveland OH

Eliet, Leslie Ann, *Registrar,* Colgate University, Picker Art Gallery, Hamilton NY

Eliscur, Frank, *Art Advisory Board,* Society of Medalists, Danbury CT

Elkington, Richard N, *Chmn,* Providence College, Art and Art History Dept, Providence RI (S)

Elks, Hazel Hulbert, *Library Dir,* Free Public Library of Elizabeth, Fine Arts Dept, Elizabeth NJ

Ellard, Bob, *Pres,* Saskatchewan Association of Architects, Saskatoon SK

Ellgren, Heidi, *Asst Treas,* Hall of Fame of the Trotter, Goshen NY

Elliot, Catherine, *Exhib Coordr,* University of Western Ontario, McIntosh Art Gallery, London ON

Elliot, Mary Gene, *Cur,* Atlanta Museum, Atlanta GA

Elliott, Edward, *Chief Security,* Portland Museum of Art, Portland ME

Elliott, Gerald A, *Dept Head,* Lenoir Community College, Art Dept, Kinston NC (S)

Elliott, James, *Dir,* University of California, University Art Museum, Berkeley CA

Elliott, J H, *Dir,* Atlanta Museum, Atlanta GA

Elliott, Joan, *Special Collections,* Willard Library, Dept of Fine Arts, Evansville IN

Elliott, Joseph, *Asst Prof,* Muhlenberg College, Dept of Art, Allentown PA (S)

Elliott, Patricia, *Chmn Fine & Performing Arts Dept,* Marymount Manhattan College, Fine Arts Dept, New York NY (S)

Elliott, Rosamond D, *VPres,* Rhode Island Watercolor Society, Pawtucket RI

Ellis, Anita, *Cur Decorative Arts,* Cincinnati Art Museum, Cincinnati OH

Ellis, Donald, *Dir of Exhib,* University of Manitoba, Faculty of Architecture Exhibition Centre, Winnipeg MB

Ellis, George R, *Dir,* Honolulu Academy of Arts, Honolulu HI

Ellis, Jack D, *Dir,* Morehead State University, Library, Morehead KY

Ellis, J Theodore, *Pres,* Gilpin County Arts Association, Central City CO

Ellis, Robert H, *Cur,* Kendall Whaling Museum, Sharon MA

Ellison, Rosemary, *Acting Cur,* Museum of the Plains Indian, Browning MT

Ellison, Rosemary, *Cur,* Southern Plains Indian Museum, Anadarko OK

Ellstrom, Shelly, *Dir,* Minot Art Gallery, Minot Art Association, Minot ND

Ellsworth, Linda V, *Historian,* Historic Pensacola Preservation Board, West Florida Museum of History, Pensacola FL

El-Omami, Anne, *Cur Educ,* Joslyn Art Museum, Omaha NE

Elrod, James, *Head,* California Institute of the Arts Library, Valencia CA

Elsas, Ellen, *Instr,* University of Alabama in Birmingham, Dept of Art, Birmingham AL (S)

Elving, Christine, *Mgr,* Artists Gallery, Vancouver BC

Ely, Clara, *Dir,* Brownsville Art League Museum, Brownsville TX

Ely, Georgette, *Store Mgr,* Millicent Rogers Museum, Taos NM

Ely, Robert V, *VPres,* Roswell Museum and Art Center, Roswell NM

Elyjiw, Zenon A, *Senior Technologist,* Rochester Institute of Technology, Technical & Education Center of the Graphic Arts, Rochester NY (S)

Elzea, Rowland P, *Assoc Dir & Chief Cur,* Delaware Art Museum, Wilmington DE

Emanuel, Martin, *Instructor,* Atlanta College of Art, Atlanta GA (S)

Emanuelli, Sharon, *Sr Curator,* Craft and Folk Art Museum, Los Angeles CA

Embrey, Carl, *Instr,* San Antonio Art Institute, San Antonio TX (S)

Emeny, Frederick, *Trustee,* Hill-Stead Museum, Farmington CT

Emerick, Judon, *Chmn Dept,* Pomona College, Art Dept, Claremont CA (S)

Emerson, Dawn, *Registrar,* Seneca Falls Historical Society Museum, Seneca Falls NY

Emerson, John M, *Pres,* Canadian Society for Education Through Art, Toronto ON

Emerson, Judy, *Cur,* Appaloosa Museum, Inc, Moscow ID

Emerson, Roberta Shinn, *Dir,* Huntington Galleries, Huntington WV

Emerson, William R, *Dir,* Franklin D Roosevelt Library and Museum, Hyde Park NY

Emery, Alan R, *Dir,* National Museums of Canada, National Museum of Natural Sciences, Ottawa ON

Emery, Anthony, *Dean Faculty Fine Arts,* Concordia University, Faculty of Fine Arts, Montreal PQ (S)

Emmerich, Carl, *Prof,* Eastern Illinois University, School of Fine Arts, Charleston IL (S)

Emmert, Christine, *VPres,* Gilpin County Arts Association, Central City CO

Emont-Scott, Deborah R, *Sanders Sosland Cur 20th Century Art,* Atkins Museum of Fine Art, Kansas City MO

Emori, Jerilyn, *Public Relations Coordr,* University of California, California Museum of Photography, Riverside CA

Emrich, Jeanette, *Registrar,* Florida Gulf Coast Art Center, Inc, Clearwater FL

Endress, Lawerence, *Instr,* Saint Francis College, Art Dept, Fort Wayne IN (S)

Eng, James, *Asst Prof,* Framingham State College, Art Dept, Framingham MA (S)

Eng, James, *Instr,* Danforth Museum School, Framingham MA (S)

Engdahl, David A, *Prof,* Rochester Institute of Technology, School of Photographic Arts & Sciences, Rochester NY (S)

Engel, Betty, *Chief Conservator,* Balboa Art Conservation Center, San Diego CA

Engel, Charlene, *Asst Prof,* Moravian College, Dept of Art, Bethlehem PA (S)

Engel, Helen Vanden, *Music Librn,* Grand Rapids Public Library, Music & Art Dept, Grand Rapids MI

Engeman, Richard H, *Librn,* Southern Oregon Historical Society, Library, Jacksonville OR

Engerman, Jeanne, *Asst Librn,* Washington State Historical Society, Hewitt Memorial Library, Tacoma WA

Englar, Gerald, *Assoc Prof,* University of Toronto, Dept of Landscape Architecture, Toronto ON (S)

Engle, G W, *Adminr,* Colorado Springs Fine Arts Center, Colorado Springs CO

Engle, Mary, *Art Dept Chairperson,* Northern Montana College, Dept of Art and Languages, Havre MT (S)

Englehardt, Jas A, *Faculty,* Idaho State University, Dept of Art, Pocatello ID (S)

Englehart, Stanton, *Prof,* Fort Lewis College, Art Dept, Durango CO (S)

Engleman, Lothar K, *Prof,* Rochester Institute of Technology, School of Photographic Arts & Sciences, Rochester NY (S)

Engler, Christine, *Recording Secy,* Society of American Graphic Artists, New York NY

English, Christopher, *Gallery Dir,* N.A.M.E. Gallery, Chicago IL

English, Joseph G, *Adminr,* National Gallery of Art, Washington DC

English, Lloyd C, *Chmn,* Western Oklahoma State College, Art Dept, Altus OK (S)

Engman, Robert M, *Prof,* University of Pennsylvania, College Arts & Science, Philadelphia PA (S)

Enniz, Bruce, *Secy,* Montana Historical Society, Helena MT

Enos, M, *Lectr,* Chamberlayne Junior College, Dept of Applied Arts, Boston MA (S)

Ens, Dennis, *VPrincipal,* Nutana Collegiate Institute, Memorial Library and Art Gallery, Saskatoon SK

Ensor, John H, *Treasurer,* Star-Spangled Banner Flag House Association, Baltimore MD

Entin, Daniel, *Exec Dir,* Nicholas Roerich Museum, New York NY

Entwistle, Barbara J, *Admim Asst,* William A Farnsworth Library and Art Museum, Rockland ME

Enyeart, James, *Dir,* University of Arizona, Center for Creative Photography, Tucson AZ

Epke, William P, *Dir Corporate Support,* Equitable Life Assurance Society, New York NY

Eppell, F, *Instructor,* Technical University of Nova Scotia, Faculty of Architecture, Halifax NS (S)

Eppridge, Theresa, *Asst Prof,* College of New Rochelle School of Arts and Sciences, Undergraduate Art Dept, New Rochelle NY (S)

Epstein, Ann, *Asst Prof,* Duke University, Dept of Art, Durham NC (S)

Epstein, Lee, *VPres,* Art Directors Club, Inc, New York NY

Epstein, Robert, *Chmn Ceramics,* Corcoran School of Art, Washington DC (S)

Epting, Marion, *Instr,* California State University, Chico, Art Dept, Chico CA (S)

Epting, Marion A, *Chmn,* California State University, Chico, Art Dept, Chico CA (S)

Erbes, Roslyn, *Prof,* Indiana State University, Dept of Humanities, Terre Haute IN (S)

Erdle, Robert, *Painting and Drawing Coordr,* North Texas State University, Art Dept, Denton TX (S)

Erdman, David V, *Publications Dir,* New York Public Library, Shelby Cullom Davis Museum, Library & Museum of the Performing Arts, New York NY

Erdossy, Alan, *Dir,* Sharon Arts Center, Peterborough NH (S)

Erf, Greg, *Copy Center,* Visual Studies Workshop, Rochester NY

Erhard, P D, *Faculty,* Andrews University, Art Dept, Berrien Springs MI (S)

Erickson, Lynda, *Art Libr Asst,* Old Dominion University Gallery, Art Library, Norfolk VA

Eriksson-Rylander, Joyce, *Dir,* Cambridge Art Association, Cambridge MA

Erney, Richard A, *Dir,* State Historical Society of Wisconsin, Madison WI

Eroman, Mariella, *Instr,* Silver Lake College, Art Dept, Manitowoc WI (S)

Ertas, Adnan, *Instructor,* College of DuPage, Humanities Division, Glen Ellyn IL (S)

Ertman, Earl L, *Head Dept,* University of Akron, University Galleries, Akron OH

Ertman, Earl L, *Dept Head,* University of Akron, Dept of Art, Akron OH (S)

Esau, Erika, *Librn,* Kimbell Art Museum, Fort Worth TX

Esbensen, Leonard, *Asst Prof,* Mount Saint Mary's College, Art Dept, Los Angeles CA (S)

Escott, Charles, *Chmn,* West Valley College, Art Dept, Saratoga CA (S)

Escott, Louise, *Pres,* DuPage Art League, Wheaton IL

Eshelman, Paul, *Vis Lecturer,* North Central College, Dept of Art, Naperville IL (S)

Eshelman, Ralph E, *Dir,* Calvert Marine Museum, Solomons MD

Eshoo, Robert, *Supv Currier Art Center,* Currier Gallery of Art, Manchester NH

Eshoo, Virginia, *Coordr Membership,* Currier Gallery of Art, Manchester NH

Eskind, Andrew, *Dir Interdept Services,* International Museum of Photography at George Eastman House, Rochester NY

Eskind, Robert, *Registrar,* Museum of the Philadelphia Civic Center, Philadelphia PA

Esko, Claudia, *Cur Education,* Birmingham Museum of Art, Birmingham AL

Espey, Jule Adele, *Asst Prof,* Our Lady of the Lake University, Dept of Art, San Antonio TX (S)

Esposito, Cecilia, *Asst to Dir,* Hyde Collection, Glens Falls NY

Esquibel, George A, *Instructor,* Sacramento City College, Art Dept, Sacramento CA (S)

Esslinger, Claudia, *Asst Prof,* Denison University, Dept of Art, Granville OH (S)

Estabrook, Reed, *Assoc Prof,* University of Northern Iowa, Dept of Art, Cedar Falls IA (S)

Estabrook, Reed, *Chmn Photography,* Kansas City Art Institute, Kansas City MO (S)

Esterly, Freda Mulcahy, *Museum Lectr,* Staten Island Institute of Arts and Sciences, Staten Island NY

Estes, James, *Instr,* Alfred C Glassell School of Art, Houston TX (S)

Estes, Jim, *Assoc Prof,* Missouri Western State College, Art Dept, Saint Joseph MO (S)

Estes, Rosemary, *Archivist,* Old Salem Inc, Library, Winston-Salem NC

Etchart, Pat, *Pres of Board,* Yellowstone Art Center, Billings MT

Ethier, L, *Pres,* Musee d'Art de Saint-Laurent, Saint-Laurent PQ

Etier, Marc, *Vis Prof,* East Central University, Art Dept, Ada OK (S)

Etter, Juanita, *Asst Mgr,* The Ohio Historical Society, Inc, Campus Martius Museum and Ohio River Museum, Marietta OH

Ettinger, Gary, *Business Mgr,* Portland Art Association, Portland OR

Eubank, Douglas E, *Prof,* Chowan College, Division of Art, Murfreesboro NC (S)

Euell, Julian T, *Dir & Chief Exec Officer,* Oakland Museum, Art Dept, Oakland CA

Eugene, Robert, *Adminr,* Princeton Antiques Bookservice, Art Marketing Reference Library, Atlantic City NJ

Eulich, Muriel, *Adjunct Instr,* Maryville College, St Louis, Art Division, Saint Louis MO (S)

Euster, Joanne, *Dir,* San Francisco State University, J Paul Leonard Library, San Francisco CA

Evan, Richard, *Fine Arts Dept Chmn,* Whitworth College, Art Dept, Spokane WA (S)

Evans, Bruce H, *Dir,* Dayton Art Institute, Dayton OH

Evans, Connie, *Dir Stables Gallery,* Taos Art Association Inc, Stables Art Center, Taos NM

Evans, Constance, *Assoc Prof,* Southampton College of Long Island University, C W Post Center Fine Arts Division, Southampton NY (S)

Evans, David, *Chairperson,* William Penn College, Art Dept, Oskaloosa IA (S)

Evans, Deborah L, *Dir,* Annie S Kemerer Museum, Bethlehem PA

Evans, D J, *Instr,* David Thompson University Centre, Visual Arts Dept, Nelson BC (S)

Evans, Donald, *Assoc Prof,* Vanderbilt University, Dept of Fine Arts, Nashville TN (S)

Evans, Donald W, *Pres,* Quapaw Quarter Association, Inc, Villa Marre, Little Rock AR

Evans, Dorinda, *Asst Prof,* Emory University, Art History Dept, Atlanta GA (S)

Evans, Dorothy, *Membership Secy,* University of California, California Museum of Photography, Riverside CA

Evans, Elaine A, *Cur Coll,* University of Tennessee, Frank H McClung Museum, Knoxville TN

Evans, Fydella, *Registrar,* Percy H Whiting Art Center, Fairhope AL

Evans, Howard M, *Dir,* Haystack Mountain School of Crafts Gallery, Deer Isle ME

Evans, Howard M, *Dir,* Haystack Mountain School of Crafts, Deer Isle ME (S)

Evans, Jane Turnbull, *Coordr Education & Extension,* University of Regina, Mackenzie Art Gallery, Regina SK

Evans, Nancy Goyne, *Registrar,* Winterthur Museum and Gardens, Winterthur DE

Evans, Peggy, *Treasurer,* French Art Colony, Inc, Gallipolis OH

Evans, Robert J, *Head Art Section & Cur of Art,* Illinois State Museum of Natural History and Art, Springfield IL

Evans, Robert W, *Dir,* State University of New York at Purchase, Library, Purchase NY

Evans, Sharon, *Pres,* N.A.M.E. Gallery, Chicago IL

Evans, William, *Basic Design Coordr,* North Texas State University, Art Dept, Denton TX (S)

Evans-Elsner, Emily, *Librn,* Portland Art Association, Museum Library, Portland OR

Evanson, Charles, *Executive Dir,* J K Ralston Museum and Art Center, Willo Ralston Library for Historical Research, Sidney MT

Evarts, Wilbur, *Executive Dir,* Paint 'N Palette Club, Anamosa IA

Evelyn, Douglas E, *Deputy Dir,* National Museum of American History, Smithsonian Institution, Washington DC

Even, Robert L, *Chmn Dept,* Northern Illinois University, Swen Parson Gallery and Gallery 200, De Kalb IL

Even, Robert L, *Chmn Dept Art,* Northern Illinois University, Dept of Art, De Kalb IL (S)

Everets, Pam, *Pres,* Farmington Art Guild, Farmington CT

Everett, Dorothy, *Guide Supervisor,* Legislative Building Art Gallery, Regina SK

Everett, Len, *Treas,* Allied Artists of America, Inc, New York NY

Everett, Len G, *VPres,* Audubon Artists, Inc, New York NY

Everson, Vicki S, *Dir,* Paris Gibson Square, Great Falls MT

Evett, Philip J, *Prof,* Trinity University, Dept of Art, San Antonio TX (S)

Ewing, Dan, *Chmn Dept,* Hobart and William Smith Colleges, Art Dept, Geneva NY (S)

Ewing, Lauren, *Assoc Prof,* Rutgers, the State University of New Jersey, Mason Gross School of the Arts, New Brunswick NJ (S)

Ewing, Reid, *Pres,* Morse Gallery of Art, Winter Park FL

Ewing, William, *Dir Exhib,* International Center of Photography, New York NY

Exon, Randall L, *Asst Prof,* Swarthmore College, Dept of Art, Swarthmore PA (S)

Eyerly, Pauline, *Cur Education,* Portland Art Association, Portland Art Museum, Portland OR

Eynard, Pat, *Cur,* Louisiana Historical Association, Confederate Museum, New Orleans LA

Eyre, Pat, *Media Dir,* Utah Travel Council, Salt Lake City UT

Eyrich, Ruth, *Correspondence Secy,* National Watercolor Society, Lakewood CA

Faber, David, *Prof,* West Virginia University, Division of Art, Morgantown WV (S)

Fabiano, Daniel, *Prof,* University of Wisconsin-Stevens Point, Dept of Art, Stevens Point WI (S)

Fabrycki, William, *Instructor,* Joliet Junior College, Fine Arts Dept, Joliet IL (S)

Faccenda, Phil, *VPres,* Cascade County Historical Society Museum, Great Falls MT

Facci, Domenico, *Exec Officer,* Audubon Artists, Inc, New York NY

Facci, Domenico, *VPres,* National Sculpture Society, New York NY

Faccinto, Victor, *Gallery Dir,* Wake Forest University, Dept of Art, Winston-Salem NC (S)

Faddis, George, *Cur,* Rockport Art Association, Rockport MA

Faddis, Helen, *Secy,* Rockport Art Association, Rockport MA

Fagaly, William A, *Asst Dir for Art,* New Orleans Museum of Art, New Orleans LA

Fagen, Henry, *Chmn Dept,* Converse College, Art Dept, Spartanburg SC (S)

Fagen, Henry, *Dir,* Converse College, Milliken Art Gallery, Spartanburg SC

Faggioli, Renzo, *Ceramist-in-Residence,* Moravian College, Dept of Art, Bethlehem PA (S)

Fagin, Barbara, *Program Coordr,* Oklahoma Museum of Art, Oklahoma City OK

Fahnstrom, Dale E, *Chmn,* Illinois Institute of Technology, Institute of Design, Chicago IL (S)

Fahringer, Anita, *Asst Librn,* University of Pennsylvania, John and Ada Lewis Memorial Library, Philadelphia PA

Fahy, Everett, *Dir,* Frick Collection, New York NY

Fair, Barry, *Registrar,* London Regional Art Gallery, London ON

Fairbanks, Jonathan, *Cur American Decorative Arts,* Museum of Fine Arts, Boston MA

Fairbanks, Justin, *Instr,* Eastern Arizona College, Thatcher AZ (S)

Fairbanks, Ortho R, *Coordr,* Northland Pioneer College, Art Dept, Holbrook AZ (S)

Fairbanks, Theresa, *Conservator Paper,* Yale University, Yale Center for British Art, New Haven CT

Fairchild-Foy, Sally, *Regent,* Schuyler-Hamilton House, Morristown NJ

Faircloth, Norman D, *Head,* Guilford Technical Community College, Commercial Art Dept, Jamestown NC (S)

Fairfield, Douglas, *Instr,* Blue Lake Community School of Arts, Visual Arts Dept, Muskegon MI (S)

Fairfield, Douglas A, *Asst Cur,* Muskegon Museum of Art, Muskegon MI

Falbo, Edna, *Treasurer,* National League of American Pen Women, Washington DC

Falcone, Tony, *Assoc Dir,* Southwest Arts Foundation, Houston TX

Fales, Haliburton, *Pres,* Pierpont Morgan Library, New York NY

Faleski, Denise, *Asst Prof,* College Misericordia, Art Dept, Dallas PA (S)

Falgoust, Hymel G, *Prof,* Southeastern Louisiana University, Dept of Visual Arts, Hammond LA (S)

Falk, David, *Secy,* Rochester Historical Society, Rochester NY

Falk, Jane E, *Asst Registrar,* Walker Art Center, Minneapolis MN

Falk, Jane E, *Consult,* Tattoo Art Museum, San Francisco CA

Falk, Lorne, *Cur,* Banff Centre, Walter Phillips Gallery, Banff AB

Falk, Robert, *Historic Site Asst,* Schuyler Mansion State Historic Site, Albany NY

Falkner, Avery, *Instr,* Pepperdine University, Seaver College, Dept of Art, Malibu CA (S)

Falls, David, *Installations Officer,* University of Western Ontario, McIntosh Art Gallery, London ON

Fames, William C W, *Chmn of Board,* Salmagundi Club, New York NY

Fana, Maria, *Instructor,* Boston Center for Adult Education, Boston MA (S)

Fane, Diana, *Cur African, Oceanic & New World Cultures,* Brooklyn Museum, Brooklyn NY

Fanelli, Deborah, *Instructor,* Wake Forest University, Dept of Art, Winston-Salem NC (S)

Fannin, Bill, *Cur,* Missouri State Museum, Jefferson City MO

Farber, Lola, *Head of Education,* Colorado Historical Society, State Museum, Denver CO

Farese, Mary Anne, *Chairwoman,* Fairleigh Dickinson University, Fine Arts Dept, Teaneck NJ (S)

Faries, Molly, *Assoc Prof,* Indiana University, Bloomington, School of Fine Arts, Bloomington IN (S)

Farinella, Paul J, *Pres,* Munson-Williams-Proctor Institute, Museum of Art, Utica NY

Farley, Authur Leonard, *Prof,* Mississippi State University, Art Dept, Mississippi State MS (S)

Farley, Harold, *Dir,* Naval Amphibious Museum, Norfolk VA

Farley, Laine, *Art Selector,* University of California, Library, Riverside CA

Farmer, Barthwell, *Chmn Art History,* Edinboro University of Pennsylvania, Art Dept, Edinboro PA (S)

Farmer, Betsy, *Instructor,* Shippensburg State College, Art Dept, Shippensburg PA (S)

Farmer, Frank, *Installation Coordr,* Committee for the Visual Arts, Inc, New York NY

Farmer, J David, *Dir,* University of California, Santa Barbara, University Art Museum, Santa Barbara CA

Farmer, Terrance, *Instructor,* Springfield College in Illinois, Dept of Art, Springfield IL (S)

Farnam, Anne, *Cur,* Essex Institute, Salem MA

Farquharson, Alexander, *Instructor,* Boston Center for Adult Education, Boston MA (S)

Farr, Dorothy, *Cur,* Queen's University, Agnes Etherington Art Centre, Kingston ON

Farr, Frederick S, *Chmn Monterey Council,* Casa Amesti, Monterey CA

Farrar, Elaine W, *Instr,* Yavapai College, Art Dept, Prescott AZ (S)

Farrar, Ross, *Assoc Dir,* Museum of Fine Arts, Boston MA

Farrell, Bill, *Prof,* School of the Art Institute of Chicago, Chicago IL (S)

Farrell, Eugene, *Sr Conservator of Science,* Harvard University, William Hayes Fogg Art Museum, Cambridge MA

Farrell, Michael, *Asst to Dir,* Hermitage Foundation Museum, Norfolk VA

Farrell, Peggy, *Vis Prof,* Carroll College, Art Dept, Waukesha WI (S)

Farrell-Ward, Lorna, *Cur,* Vancouver Art Gallery, Vancouver BC

Farrington, Mitzi, *Treasurer,* Safety Harbor Museum of History and Fine Arts, Safety Harbor FL

Faryniak, Karen, *Instructor,* Mohawk Valley Community College, Advertising Design and Production, Utica NY (S)

Fash, William L, *Dean,* Georgia Institute of Technology, College of Architecture, Atlanta GA (S)

Fast, L W, *Principal,* Nutana Collegiate Institute, Memorial Library and Art Gallery, Saskatoon SK

Fast, Stanley P, *Site Admin,* Mark Twain Birthplace Museum, Stoutsville MO

Faster, Donna, *Instructor,* Northeast Technical Community College, Dept of Art, Norfolk NE (S)

Fasulo, Marijo, *Asst Dir,* State University of New York at Albany, University Art Gallery, Albany NY

Fatzer, Jill, *Chief Reference Librn,* University of Delaware, Morris Library, Newark DE

Faudie, Fred, *Assoc Prof,* University of Lowell, Dept of Art, Lowell MA (S)

Faul, Karene, *Assoc Prof,* College of Saint Rose, Division of Art, Albany NY (S)

Faulds, W Rod, *Admin Dir,* Brattleboro Museum and Art Center, Brattleboro VT

Faulkner, Mary, *Second VPres,* Florida Artist Group Inc, Venice FL

Faunce, Sarah, *Cur European & Contemporary Paintings & Sculpture,* Brooklyn Museum, Brooklyn NY

Fausett, Dean, *Pres,* National Society of Mural Painters, Inc, New York NY

Favata, Alexa A, *Asst Dir,* University of South Florida, Art Galleries, Tampa FL

Favell, Gene H, *Pres,* Favell Museum of Western Art & Indian Artifacts, Klamath Falls OR

Favell, Winifred L, *VPres & Treas,* Favell Museum of Western Art & Indian Artifacts, Klamath Falls OR

Fawcett, David, *Registrar,* Museum of the American Indian, New York NY

Fawcett, Linda, *Instructor,* Hardin-Simmons University, Art Dept, Abilene TX (S)

Fawcett, W Peyton, *Librn,* Field Museum of Natural History, Library, Chicago IL

Fawkes, Judith, *Lectr,* Lewis and Clark College, Dept of Art, Portland OR (S)

Fawthrop, Bob, *Cur,* East Windsor Historical Society Inc, Scantic Academy Museum, East Windsor CT

Fawthrop, Terri, *VPres,* East Windsor Historical Society Inc, Scantic Academy Museum, East Windsor CT

Faxon, Susan, *Performing Arts Coordr,* Hampton Center for Arts and Humanities, Hampton VA

Fay, Alden, *Asst Coordr,* Luna County Historical Society, Inc, Deming Luna Mimbres Museum, Deming NM

Fay, Joe, *Adjunct Asst Prof,* University of Southern California, School of Fine Arts, Los Angeles CA (S)

Fay, Peter, *Head Librn,* John F Kennedy Center for the Performing Arts, Performing Arts Library, Washington DC

Fazzini, Richard, *Cur Egyptian & Classical Art,* Brooklyn Museum, Brooklyn NY

Fears, Eileen, *Asst Prof,* California State Polytechnic University, Pomona, Art Dept, Pomona CA (S)

Featherstone, David, *Exec Assoc,* The Friends of Photography, Carmel CA

FeBland, Harriet, *Dir,* Harriet FeBland Art Workshop, New York NY (S)

Feckter, Earl, *Assoc Prof,* Norwich University, Dept of Philosophy, Religion and Fine Arts, Northfield VT (S)

Feddema, Bruce, *Vis Lecturer,* North Central College, Dept of Art, Naperville IL (S)

Federighi, Christine, *Assoc Prof,* University of Miami, Dept of Art & Art History, Coral Gables FL (S)

Feeder, James, *Dir,* San Jose State University, Union Gallery, San Jose CA

Feelings, Muriel, *Education,* Afro-American Historical and Cultural Museum, Philadelphia PA

Feeney, John, *Historic Site Mgr,* New York State Office of Parks, Recreation & Historical Preservation, Mills Mansion State Historical Site, Staatsburg NY

Feeney, Maura, *Registrar,* Connecticut Historical Society, Hartford CT

Feeny, Lawrence, *Assoc Prof,* Mississippi University for Women, Division of Fine & Performing Arts, Columbus MS (S)

Fees, Paul, *Cur Buffalo Bill Museum,* Buffalo Bill Memorial Association, Cody WY

Feher, Joseph, *Senior Cur & Cur Graphic Arts,* Honolulu Academy of Arts, Honolulu HI

Feher, Joseph, *Cur,* Honolulu Academy of Arts, Studio Program, Honolulu HI (S)

Feidscher, Sharla, *Dir Public Affairs,* Please Touch Museum, Philadelphia PA

Feidt, Thorp, *Art History,* Montserrat School of Visual Art, Beverly MA (S)

Feigenbaum, Rita, *Registrar,* Jewish Museum, New York NY

Feiman, Debi, *Exec Dir,* Organization of Independent Artists, New York NY

Fein, Ruth B, *Pres,* American Jewish Historical Society, Waltham MA

Feinberg, Jean F, *Asst Cur,* Wesleyan University, Ezra and Cecile Zilkha Galleries, Middletown CT

Feinblatt, Ebria, *Sr Cur of Prints and Drawings,* Los Angeles County Museum of Art, Los Angeles CA

Feingold, Joseph, *VPres,* New York Society of Architects, New York NY

Feld, Norma, *Asst Librn,* International Museum of Photography at George Eastman House, Library, Rochester NY

Felder, Paul, *Asst Prof,* Lehigh University, Dept of Art and Architecture, Bethlehem PA (S)

Feldhaus, Fran, *Instr,* California State University, Chico, Art Dept, Chico CA (S)

Feldman, Arthur M, *Dir,* Spertus Museum of Judaica, Chicago IL

Feldman, Bruce, *Instr,* Mainline Center of the Arts, Haverford PA (S)

Feldman, Eugene P, *Dir Publications,* DuSable Museum of African American History, Chicago IL

Feldman, Joel B, *Asst Prof,* Southern Illinois University, School of Art, Carbondale IL (S)

Feldman, Nan, *Instr,* Danforth Museum School, Framingham MA (S)

Felker, Froun, *Pres,* Cumberland Art Society, Cookeville Art Center, Cookeville TN

Fell, Kathleen, *Instr,* Ocean City Arts Center, Ocean City NJ (S)

Fellman, Sandi, *Asst Prof,* Rutgers, the State University of New Jersey, Mason Gross School of the Arts, New Brunswick NJ (S)

Felter, James Warren, *Dir,* Simon Fraser University, Simon Fraser Gallery, Burnaby BC

Felter, Susan, *Asst Prof,* University of Santa Clara, Fine Arts Dept, Santa Clara CA (S)

Feltus, A E, *Assoc Prof,* American University, Dept of Art, Washington DC (S)

Fender, Roy, *Prof,* Western Maryland College, Art Dept, Westminster MD (S)

Fenivick, Roly, *Instr,* Southampton Art School, Southampton ON (S)

Fenn, Dan H, *Dir,* National Archives and Records Service, John F Kennedy Library and Museum, Dorchester MA

Fennimore, Patricia, *Head Childrens Department,* Springfield Free Public Library, Donald B Palmer Museum, Springfield NJ

Fenno, John, *Pres,* Canajoharie Library and Art Gallery, Canajoharie NY

Fensch, Charles, *Dept Chmn,* University of Texas at El Paso, El Paso TX

Fensch, Charles, *Head Dept,* University of Texas at El Paso, Dept of Art, El Paso TX (S)

Fenton, T, *Dir,* Edmonton Art Gallery, Edmonton AB

Fentress, Elizabeth C, *Executive Dir,* North Carolina Art Society, Raleigh NC

Ferber, Elise V H, *Head Art Information Service,* National Gallery of Art, Washington DC

Ferber, Linda, *Cur American Paintings & Sculpture,* Brooklyn Museum, Brooklyn NY

Ferdinandy, Magdalena, *Instructor,* University of Puerto Rico, Dept of Fine Arts, Rio Piedras PR (S)

Ference, Cynthia K, *Dir,* Green Hill Center for North Carolina Art, Greensboro NC

Fergerson, Robert, *Lectr,* Trinity College, Art Dept, Washington DC (S)

Fergeson, Norris J, *Cur,* Marion Koogler McNay Art Museum, San Antonio TX

Fergus, Victoria, *Prof,* West Virginia University, Division of Art, Morgantown WV (S)

Ferguson, Carra, *Prof,* Georgetown University, Dept of Fine Arts, Washington DC (S)

Ferguson, Charles, *Trustee,* Hill-Stead Museum, Farmington CT

Ferguson, Charles B, *Dir,* New Britain Museum of American Art, New Britain CT

Ferguson, Charles C, *Chmn,* Macdonald Stewart Art Centre, Guelph ON

Ferguson, Gerald, *Chmn Studio Div,* Nova Scotia College of Art and Design, Halifax NS (S)

Ferguson, John, *Instructor,* Saint Louis Community College at Meramec, Art Dept, Saint Louis MO (S)

Ferguson, John S, *VPres,* Everson Museum of Art, Syracuse NY

Ferguson, Ken, *Business Mgr,* Art Gallery of Windsor, Windsor ON

Ferguson, Ken, *Vis Prof,* Victor Valley College, Art Dept, Victorville CA (S)

Ferguson, Kenneth, *Chmn Crafts,* Kansas City Art Institute, Kansas City MO (S)

Ferguson, Magee, *Dir,* Hockaday Center for the Arts, Flathead Valley Art Association & Art Gallery, Kalispell MT

Ferguson, Magee, *Coordr,* University of Northern Colorado, John Mariani Art Gallery, Greeley CO

Ferguson, Marie D, *Adminr,* Dayton Art Institute, Dayton OH

Ferguson, Nancy, *Pres,* Marblehead Arts Association, Inc, Marblehead MA

Ferguson, Robert, *Asst Cur,* Jersey City Museum Association, Jersey City NJ

Ferguson, Rodney, *Asst Prof,* Southern University in New Orleans, Art Dept, New Orleans LA (S)

Ferguson, Van, *Rare Books Librn,* Rosenberg Library, Galveston TX

Ferguson, William Russell, *Assoc Reference Librn,* Frick Art Reference Library, New York NY

Fergusson, Frances, *Assoc Prof,* University of Massachusetts at Boston, Art Dept, Boston MA (S)

Fergusson, Peter J, *Prof,* Wellesley College, Art Dept, Wellesley MA (S)

Fern, Alan, *Dir,* National Portrait Gallery, Washington DC

Fernandez, Rafael A, *Cur Prints & Drawings,* Sterling and Francine Clark Art Institute, Williamstown MA

Ferng, Hou-Ran, *Librn,* Saint John's University, Asian Collection, Jamaica NY

Ferrario, Paula, *Serials and Rare Books,* Washington University, Art and Architecture Library, Saint Louis MO

Ferraro, Robert C, *Dir,* University of Windsor, School of Visual Arts, Windsor ON (S)

Ferren, Rae, *Assoc Cur,* Guild Hall of East Hampton, Inc, Museum Section, East Hampton NY

Ferrerri, Kathy, *Asst to Dir,* College of New Rochelle, Castle Gallery, New Rochelle NY

Ferris, Margaret G, *Asst Prof,* Virginia Western Community College, Commercial Art, Fine Art & Photography, Roanoke VA (S)

Ferris, Robert, *Education Officer,* Public Archives of Canada, Laurier House, Ottawa ON

Ferris, Scott, *Cur,* Plains Art Museum, Main Gallery, Moorhead MN

Ferro, Patricia, *Pres,* Santa Cruz Art League, Inc, Santa Cruz CA

Ferrulli, Helen, *Dir Education,* Indianapolis Museum of Art, Indianapolis IN

Fertitta, Angelo, *Chmn Gallery,* The Art Institute of Boston, Gallery West, Gallery East, Boston MA

Fessler, Donald R, *Pres,* Blacksburg Regional Art Association, Blacksburg VA

Fessler, M Thomasita, *Head Dept,* Cardinal Stritch College, Art Dept, Milwaukee WI (S)

Feszczak, Zenon L, *Dir Design,* Museum of the Philadelphia Civic Center, Philadelphia PA

Fetchko, Peter, *Dir,* Peabody Museum of Salem, Salem MA

Fetter, Dian, *Chmn Dept,* Catonsville Community College, Art Dept, Catonsville MD (S)

Fiandaca, Fred, *Asst Prof,* Framingham State College, Art Dept, Framingham MA (S)

Fichner-Rathus, Lois, *Asst Prof,* Trenton State College, Art Dept, Trenton NJ (S)

Fichter, Robert W, *Assoc Prof,* Florida State University, Art Dept, Tallahassee FL (S)

Ficken, Dale, *Assoc Prof,* Fort Hays State University, Dept of Art, Hays KS (S)

Fickle, Dorothy H, *Asst Cur Southeast Asian & Indian Art,* Atkins Museum of Fine Art, Kansas City MO

Fidler, Spencer, *Prof,* New Mexico State University, Art Dept, Las Cruces NM (S)

Fiehler, Joann E, *Asst Prof,* University of Dayton, Fine Arts Division, Dayton OH (S)

Field, Charles, *Prof,* University of Texas at San Antonio, Division of Art and Design, San Antonio TX (S)

Field, M Theophane, *Chmn,* Sacred Heart College, Dept of Art, Belmont NC (S)

Field, Natalie, *Historian,* Ella Sharp Museum, Jackson MI

Field, Philip, *Chmn Printmaking,* Pan American University, Art Dept, Edinburg TX (S)

Field, Richard S, *Cur Prints, Drawings & Photographs,* Yale University, Art Gallery, New Haven CT

Fields, Robert, *Instructor,* Virginia Tech, Dept of Art, Blacksburg VA (S)

Fields, Ron, *Chmn,* University of Puget Sound, Art Dept, Tacoma WA (S)

Fields, Shirley F, *Cur,* Florida Atlantic University, Ritter Art Gallery, Boca Raton FL

Fierke, Margaret, *Chmn Printmaking, Painting and Drawing,* Herron School of Art, Indiana University-Purdue University, Indianapolis, Indianapolis IN (S)

Fife, Edward, *Assoc Prof,* University of Toronto, Dept of Landscape Architecture, Toronto ON (S)

Fifield, Mary L, *Assoc Prof,* Saint Louis Community College at Forest Park, Fine Arts Dept, Saint Louis MO (S)

Figone, Richard P, *Pres,* Museo Italo Americano, San Francisco CA

Figueroa, Paul C, *Cur Education,* Carolina Art Association, Gibbes Art Gallery, Charleston SC

Fikaris, Peter, *Prof,* North Park College, Art Dept, Chicago IL (S)

File, M Jeanne, *Prof,* Daemen College, Art Dept, Amherst NY (S)

Filipczak, Zirka Z, *Chmn Dept,* Williams College, Dept of Art, Williamstown MA (S)

Filkosky, Josefa, *Chairperson,* Seton Hill College, Dept of Art, Greensburg PA (S)

Fillos, Debra A, *Cur & Librn,* Lyme Historical Society, Florence Griswold Museum, Old Lyme CT

Filson, Ronald C, *Dean,* Tulane University, School of Architecture, New Orleans LA (S)

Finch, Martin, *Pres,* Association of Medical Illustrators, Midlothian VA

Finch, Robert, *Instr,* Mainline Center of the Arts, Haverford PA (S)

Findkoglu, Zeki, *Assoc Prof,* University of the District of Columbia, Art Dept, Washington DC (S)

Findlay, James A, *Dir,* Rhode Island School of Design, Library, Providence RI

Findley, Jerry, *Asst Dir,* Southern Oregon College, Stevenson Union Art Gallery, Ashland OR

Fine, Jud, *Asst Prof,* University of Southern California, School of Fine Arts, Los Angeles CA (S)

Fineberg, Stephen, *Assoc Prof,* Knox College, Dept of Art, Galesburg IL (S)

Finegan, Don, *Prof,* University of Northern Iowa, Dept of Art, Cedar Falls IA (S)

Finger, H Ellis, *Center Dir,* Lafayette College, Morris R Williams Center for the Arts, Easton PA

Fingesten, Peter, *Chmn,* Pace University, Art and Music Dept, New York NY (S)

Fink, Bertram, *Assoc Prof,* Hillsdale College, Art Dept, Hillsdale MI (S)

Fink, Eleanor E, *Chief Office of Research Support,* National Museum of American Art, Washington DC

Fink, Herbert L, *Prof,* Southern Illinois University, School of Art, Carbondale IL (S)

Fink, Jack, *Prof,* Nassau Community College, Art Dept, Garden City NY (S)

Fink, Joanne, *Instr,* Mainline Center of the Arts, Haverford PA (S)

Fink, Lois M, *Cur Research & Fellowships,* National Museum of American Art, Washington DC

Finkel, Kenneth, *Cur of Prints,* Library Company of Philadelphia, Dept of Art, Philadelphia PA

Finkel, Rose Brein, *Instr,* Mainline Center of the Arts, Haverford PA (S)

Finkelpearl, Katherine D, *Librn,* Wellesley College, Art Library, Wellesley MA

Finkelpearl, Thomas, *Publicity Dir,* Institute for Art & Urban Resources, Project Studios One, Long Island City NY

Finley, Carolina F, *Cur,* Wilkes Art Gallery, North Wilkesboro NC

Finley, Gregg, *Chief Cur,* New Brunswick Museum, Saint John NB

Finn, Joe, *VPres,* Waterworks Gallery, Salisbury NC

Finston, Arlene Renee, *Instr,* Mainline Center of the Arts, Haverford PA (S)

Fiorello, Joseph, *Prof,* Cape Cod Community College, Art Dept, West Barnstable MA (S)

Fiorentino, Francis, *Instr,* Munson-Williams-Proctor Institute, School of Art, Utica NY (S)

Fiori, Dennis, *Dir,* Concord Antiquarian Society Museum, Concord MA

Fiorini, William, *Chmn,* University of Wisconsin-La Crosse, Art Dept, La Crosse WI (S)

Firestone, Evan R, *Chmn Dept,* Iowa State University, Dept of Art and Design, Ames IA (S)

Fisch, Arline M, *Pres,* Society of North American Goldsmiths, Milwaukee WI

Fisch, Robert W, *Cur Arms,* United States Military Academy, West Point Museum, West Point NY

Fischer, Alice S, *Executive Secy,* Fine Arts Museums of San Francisco, The Museum Society, San Francisco CA

Fischer, Barbara, *Children's Room Dept Head,* Wichita Public Library, Wichita KS

Fischer, Billie, *Instr,* Kalamazoo College, Art Dept, Kalamazoo MI (S)

Fischer, Henry G, *Lila Acheson Wallace Research Cur Egyptology,* Metropolitan Museum of Art, New York NY

Fischer, Joseph, *Instr,* Marian College, Art Dept, Indianapolis IN (S)

Fischer, Martin, *Executive Dir,* Toronto Art Therapy Institute, Toronto ON (S)

Fischer, Nanette G, *Pres,* Lemoyne Center for the Visual Arts, Tallahassee FL

Fish, Aaron, *Educational Liaison,* Bergen Museum of Art & Science, Paramus NJ

Fish, James H, *Dir,* Springfield City Library, Art & Music Dept, Springfield MA

Fish, Jeanne, *Pres,* Humbolt Arts Council, Eureka CA

Fisher, Alleene Lowery, *Dir,* Crafts Guild Art School for the Deaf, Holland MI (S)

Fisher, B C, *Owner,* Westover, Charles City VA

Fisher, Frederick J, *Dir,* Hyde Collection, Glens Falls NY

Fisher, F S, *Mgr,* Westover, Charles City VA

Fisher, James, *Dir,* Elizabet Ney Museum, Austin TX

Fisher, James, *Registrar,* Fort Worth Art Museum, Fort Worth TX

Fisher, Jay M, *Assoc Cur Prints, Drawings & Photographs,* Baltimore Museum of Art, Baltimore MD

Fisher, Jennifer, *Performing Arts Coordr,* St Mary's University, Art Gallery, Halifax NS

Fisher, Jocelyn, *Pres,* Beyond Baroque Foundation, Venice CA

Fisher, John C, *Secy,* Louisiana State University, Anglo-American Art Museum, Baton Rouge LA

Fisher, John J, *Journal Ed,* American Society for Aesthetics, Greenvale NY

Fisher, June, *Asst Chmn Fashion,* Art Institute of Fort Lauderdale, Fort Lauderdale FL (S)

Fisher, Kenneth, *Pres of Board,* Seattle Art Museum, Seattle WA

Fisher, Mac, *Instructor,* Samuel S Fleisher Art Memorial, Philadelphia PA (S)

Fisher, Marna, *Educ Coordr,* Saint Joseph Art Association Inc, Krasl Art Center, Saint Joseph MI

Fisher, Miriam, *Pres,* Fetherston Foundation, Packwood House Museum, Lewisburg PA

Fisher, Nora, *Cur Textiles,* Museum of New Mexico, Museum of International Folk Art, Santa Fe NM

Fisher, Richard, *Instr,* Framingham State College, Art Dept, Framingham MA (S)

Fisher, Robert A, *Dir,* Yakima Valley College, Art Dept, Yakima WA (S)

Fisher, Suzanne, *Division Head,* Public Library of Columbus and Franklin County, Humanities, Fine Arts and Recreation Division, Columbus OH

Fisher-Page, Margot, *Dir,* Oakville Galleries, Oakville ON

Fishman, Louise, *Adjunct Asst Prof,* Columbia University, School of the Arts, Division of Painting & Sculpture, New York NY (S)

Fisk, Ann, *Dir,* Rockport Art Association, Rockport MA

Fiske, Patricia L, *Actg Dir,* Textile Museum, Washington DC

Fiske, Timothy, *Assoc Dir,* Minneapolis Institute of Arts, Minneapolis MN

Fister, Patricia, *Research Fellow Japanese Art,* New Orleans Museum of Art, New Orleans LA

Fitch, Diane, *Asst Prof,* Wright State University, Dept of Art & Art History, Dayton OH (S)

Fitch, George, *Fine Arts Coordr,* Tunxis Community College, Graphic Design Dept, Farmington CT (S)

Fitzgerald, Anita, *Instructor,* Cazenovia College, Center for Art & Design Studies, Cazenovia NY (S)

Fitzgerald, Dori B, *Membership & Education Coordr,* Roanoke Museum of Fine Arts, Roanoke VA

Fitzgerald, Kevin, *Asst Librn,* Atlanta College of Art Library, Atlanta GA

Fitzgerald, Oscar, *Assoc Dir,* Naval Historical Center, United States Navy Memorial Museum, Washington DC

Fitzgerald, Richard, *Dir,* League of New Hampshire Craftsmen, Concord Gallery, Concord NH

Fitzgerald, Richard F, *Chmn Fine Arts Div,* Florida Keys Community College, Art Dept, Key West FL (S)

Fitzgerald, Susan, *Membership Specialist,* Minnesota Museum of Art, Saint Paul MN

Fitzgibbon, Cecelia, *Manager Conferences & Membership,* American Council for the Arts, New York NY

Fitzpatrick, Philip, *Instructor,* Lamar University, Art Dept, Beaumont TX (S)

Fitzpatrick, Robert, *Pres,* California Institute of the Arts, School of Art, Valencia CA (S)

Flack, C E, *Admin Asst,* Rome Historical Society, Rome Information and Cultural Center, Rome NY

Flagg, Morgan, *VPres,* Monterey Peninsula Museum of Art, Monterey CA

Flagg, Thomas J, *Dean,* Howard University, Art Dept, Washington DC (S)

Flake, Peter, *Chmn,* Catholic University of America, Dept of Architecture and Planning, Washington DC (S)

Flam, Jack, *Prof,* City University of New York, PhD Program in Art History, New York NY (S)

Flanagan, E Michael, *Dir,* Northern Illinois University, Swen Parson Gallery and Gallery 200, De Kalb IL

Flanagan, Jeanne, *Dir,* College of Saint Rose, Art Gallery, Albany NY

Flanagan, Lisa, *Asst Dir Finance,* Harvard University, William Hayes Fogg Art Museum, Cambridge MA

Flanery, Rick, *Instructor,* Salem College, Art Dept, Winston-Salem NC (S)

Flannery, Louis, *Chief Librn,* Oregon Historical Society, Library, Portland OR

Flannigan, Patrick, *Asst Prof,* Mount Mary College, Art Dept, Milwaukee WI (S)

Flateman, Ira, *Dir,* Silvermine Guild Center for the Arts, Galleries, New Canaan CT

Flavin, Patricia, *Librn,* Long Island Historical Society, Library, Brooklyn NY

Fleck, D, *In Charge of Collection,* Knight Publishing Company, Charlotte NC

Fleck, Paul, *Pres,* Arts and Letters Club of Toronto, Toronto ON

Fleck, Paul D, *Dir,* Ontario College of Art, Gallery 76, Toronto ON

Fleck, Rudolf, *Asst Prof,* Loyola Marymount University, Dept of Art & Art Hist, Los Angeles CA (S)

Flecky, Michael, *Asst Prof,* Creighton University, Fine and Performing Arts Dept, Omaha NE (S)

Fleharty, Kathy, *Treas,* Lewistown Art Center, Lewistown MT

Fleischer, Roland E, *Prof,* Pennsylvania State University, University Park, Dept of Art History, University Park PA (S)

Fleming, Glynda, *VPres,* New Mexico Art League, Gallery, Albuquerque NM

Fleming, Mark, *Exhibition Coordr,* Parkersburg Art Center, Parkersburg WV

Fleming, Park, *Instr,* Arkansas Arts Center, Little Rock AR (S)

Fleminger, Susan, *Dir,* Henry Street Settlement Arts for Living Center, New York NY (S)

Fletcher, Donald B, *Pres,* Redwood Library and Athenaeum, Newport RI

Fletcher, Stephen J, *Photography,* California Historical Society, Schubert Hall Library, San Francisco CA

Fletcher, Veeva, *Cur,* Desert Caballeros Western Museum, Wickenburg AZ

Flewelling, Margo, *Exec Asst,* New Brunswick Museum, Saint John NB

Flewwelling, Morris, *Dir,* Red Deer and District Museum and Archives, Exhibition Centre, Red Deer AB

Flick, Robert, *Assoc Prof,* University of Southern California, School of Fine Arts, Los Angeles CA (S)

Flickenger, Paul, *Instr,* West Shore Community College, Division of Humanities and Fine Arts, Scottville MI (S)

Flint, Janet Altic, *Cur Graphic Arts,* National Museum of American Art, Washington DC

Floberg, John F, *Chmn Contributions,* The Firestone Tire & Rubber Company, Akron OH

Floberg, Richard, *Assoc Prof,* Rochester Institute of Technology, School of Photographic Arts & Sciences, Rochester NY (S)

Flodstrom, Sven, *Pres,* Swedish American Museum Association of Chicago, Chicago IL

Flom, K Christine, *Cur,* Hartwick College Fine Art Gallery, Oneonta NY

Flood, James W, *Dept Chmn,* Towson State University, Dept of Art, Baltimore MD (S)

Florenza, Blanche, *Secy,* Art Directors Club, Inc, New York NY

Florian, Florence H, *Art Reference,* United States Capitol Museum, Art Reference Library, Washington DC

Florio, R A, *Exec Dir,* Art Students League of New York, New York NY (S)

Florio, Rosina A, *Exec Dir & Dir Libr,* Art Students League of New York, New York NY

Flowers, H D, *Chairperson Dept,* Bowie State College, Dept of Fine and Performing Arts, Bowie MD (S)

Flowers, Randolph, *Instructor,* Del Mar College, Dept of Art, Corpus Christi TX (S)

Flowers, Thomas E, *Chmn,* Furman University, Dept of Art, Greenville SC (S)

Floyd, Margaret, *Chmn Fine Arts Dept,* Tufts University, Fine Arts Dept, Medford MA (S)

Fluegel, Jane, *Dir Development,* The Drawing Center, New York NY

Flumiani, C M, *Pres,* Classical School Gallery, Albuquerque NM

Flumiani, C M, *Dir,* American Classical College, Albuquerque NM (S)

Flynn, Barbara, *Head Audio-visual Center,* Chicago Public Library, Cultural Center, Chicago IL

Flynn, Charles, *Instructor,* Virginia State University, Fine & Commercial Art, Petersburg VA (S)

Flynn, James, *Dir,* Chief Plenty Coups State Monument Museum, Pryor MT

Flynt, Henry N, *Pres,* Historic Deerfield Inc, Deerfield MA

Focht, Kay, *Museum Dir,* Las Vegas Art Museum, Las Vegas NV

Fogle, Charles, *Instr,* Arkansas Arts Center, Little Rock AR (S)

Fohlman, Lynette, *Iowa State Center Cur,* Iowa State University, Brunnier Gallery Museum, Ames IA

Fohrman, Darcie, *Cur Exhib,* San Diego Museum of Art, San Diego CA

Folda, Jaroslav, *Chmn,* University of North Carolina at Chapel Hill, Art Dept, Chapel Hill NC (S)

Foley, Bob, *Librn,* Banff Centre, School of Fine Arts Library, Banff AB

Foley, Kathy Kelsey, *Dir,* Northwestern University, Mary & Leigh Block Gallery, Evanston IL

Foley, Suzanne, *Dir,* University of Wisconsin, University Art Museum, Milwaukee WI

Foley, Suzanne, *Chief Cur,* San Francisco Museum of Modern Art, San Francisco CA

Folgarait, Leonard, *Asst Prof,* Vanderbilt University, Dept of Fine Arts, Nashville TN (S)

Folkama, Ellen E, *Asst Archivist,* MacArthur Memorial Museum, Library & Archives, Norfolk VA

Folsom, Karl L, *Preparator,* Wine Museum of San Francisco, San Francisco CA

Foltin, Bela, *Head Fine Arts Office,* University of Georgia, University of Georgia Libraries, Athens GA

Folwell, Elizabeth, *Dir,* Adirondack Lakes Center for the Arts, Blue Mountain Lake NY

Fondaw, Ron, *Asst Prof,* University of Miami, Dept of Art & Art History, Coral Gables FL (S)

Fong, Lawrence, *Registrar,* University of Arizona, Center for Creative Photography, Tucson AZ

Fong, Wen, *Chmn Prog Chinese and Japanese Art and Archaeology,* Princeton University, Dept of Art and Archaeology, Princeton NJ (S)

Fonseca, Rory, *Head Environmental Studies,* University of Manitoba, Faculty of Architecture, Winnipeg MB (S)

Fontaine, Sue, *Public Relations Dir,* New York Public Library, Shelby Cullom Davis Museum, Library & Museum of the Performing Arts, New York NY

Fontana, Leslie, *Instr,* Ocean City Arts Center, Ocean City NJ (S)

Fontein, Jan, *Dir,* Museum of Fine Arts, Boston MA

Foote, Vincent M, *Dir Product Design Prog,* North Carolina State University at Raleigh, School of Design, Raleigh NC (S)

Footlick, Diane, *Memberships,* Museum of Fine Arts of Saint Petersburg, Florida, Inc, Saint Petersburg FL

Forbes, Anne, *Instr,* Danforth Museum School, Framingham MA (S)

Forbes, Donna M, *Dir,* Yellowstone Art Center, Billings MT

Forbes, H A Crosby, *Cur,* China Trade Museum, Milton MA

Forbes, James, *Dir Development,* Atkins Museum of Fine Art, Kansas City MO

Forbes, Wayne, *Instr,* Illinois Central College, Fine Arts Dept, East Peoria IL (S)

Forbes, W G, *Pres,* Red Deer College, Dept of Art and Design, Red Deer AB (S)

Force, Debra J, *Dir & Cur,* INA Corporation, Philadelphia PA

Force, Roland W, *Dir,* Museum of the American Indian, New York NY

Ford, Beth M, *Instructor,* Florida Southern College, Art Dept, Lakeland FL (S)

Ford, Harry X, *Pres,* California College of Arts and Crafts, Oakland CA (S)

Ford, Howard, *Dir,* Sarnia Public Library, Art Gallery, Sarnia ON

Ford, Sharon, *Instructor,* Santa Ana College, Art Dept, Santa Ana CA (S)

Ford, Walter B, *Pres,* Detroit Institute of Arts, Founders Society, Detroit MI

Forde, E C, *Chmn,* California State University, Los Angeles, Art Dept, Los Angeles CA (S)

Foreman, Mary D, *Dir,* Percy H Whiting Art Center, Fairhope AL

Forest, Michel, *Technician,* Musee d'Art de Joliette, Joliette PQ

Forester, Alice, *VPres,* Leigh Yawkey Woodson Art Museum, Inc, Wausau WI

Foreyta, R, *Asst Dean,* Kansas State University, College of Architecture and Design, Manhattan KS (S)

Forgang, David M, *Chief Cur,* Yosemite Collections, Yosemite National Park CA

Forge, Andrew, *Prof,* Yale University, School of Art, New Haven CT (S)

Forker, Lee R, *Treasurer,* The Bostonian Society, Old State House, Boston MA

Forlier, John, *Dir,* Department of Culture, Government of the Province of Alberta, Provincial Museum of Alberta, Edmonton AB

Formo, Peter L, *VPres,* Amerind Foundation, Inc, Dragoon AZ

Formosa, Gerald, *Instr,* Vancouver Community College, Langara Campus, Dept of Fine Arts, Vancouver BC (S)

Forrest, James T, *Dir,* University of Wyoming, Art Museum, Laramie WY

Forrest, James T, *Head Dept,* University of Wyoming, Art Dept, Laramie WY (S)

Forrest, James Taylor, *Dir,* Bradford Brinton Memorial Ranch Museum, Big Horn WY

Forrest, Kevin, *Community Program Officer,* University of Regina, Mackenzie Art Gallery, Regina SK

Forrester, Vivian, *House Mgr,* University of North Carolina at Greensboro, Chinqua-Penn Plantation House, Reidsville NC

Forry, Richard R, *Administrator,* Arrow Rock State Historic Site, Arrow Rock MO

Forsha, Lynda, *Cur,* La Jolla Museum of Contemporary Art, La Jolla CA

Forster-Hahn, Francoise, *Prof,* University of California, Riverside, Art History Dept, Riverside CA (S)

Forsyth, Ilene, *VPres,* International Center of Medieval Art, Inc, New York NY

Forte, Joseph C, *Faculty,* Sarah Lawrence College, Dept of Art, Bronxville NY (S)

Fortriede, Steven, *Public Services Mgr,* Allen County Public Library, Fine Arts Dept, Fort Wayne IN

Fortson, Kay, *Pres,* Kimbell Art Museum, Fort Worth TX

Fosco, Peter J, *VPres,* Chicago Public Library, Cultural Center, Chicago IL

Foss, Carolynn A, *Registrar,* Norwich Free Academy, Slater Memorial Museum & Converse Art Gallery, Norwich CT

Foss, Jeremy, *Chmn Fine Arts, 2D,* Massachusetts College of Art, Boston MA (S)

Foss, Scottie, *Cur Education,* Loch Haven Art Center, Inc, Orlando FL

Foster, April, *Instructor,* Art Academy of Cincinnati, Cincinnati OH (S)

Foster, Arthur J, *Secy,* American Fine Arts Society, New York NY

Foster, Betty, *Educational Chmn,* Huntsville Art League and Museum Association Inc, Huntsville AL

Foster, Bill, *Dir,* Portland Art Association, Northwest Film Study Center, Portland OR

Foster, David, *Chmn Art Dept,* Lake Tahoe Community College, Art Dept, South Lake Tahoe CA (S)

Foster, Doris, *Visual Arts Coordr,* Fine Arts Association, School of Fine Arts, Willoughby OH

Foster, Doris, *Visual Arts Coordr & Gallery Dir,* School of Fine Arts, Visual Arts Dept, Willoughby OH (S)

Foster, Elaine, *Prof,* Jersey City State College, Art Dept, Jersey City NJ (S)

Foster, G W, *Secy,* Hoosier Salon Patrons Association, Hoosier Salon Art Gallery, Indianapolis IN

Foster, Joan, *Exec Dir,* Ontario Crafts Council, Toronto ON

Foster, Kathleen, *Head Cur,* Pennsylvania Academy of the Fine Arts, Galleries, Philadelphia PA

Foster, Linda, *School Mgr,* DeCordova and Dana Museum and Park, Lincoln MA

Foster, Mark, *Vis Asst Prof,* Rochester Institute of Technology, School of Art and Design, Rochester NY (S)

Foster, Mary Sue, *Chmn Art Educ,* Wichita State University, Division of Art, Wichita KS (S)

Foster, Nancy, *Registrar,* Manitoba Historical Society, Dalnavert - MacDonald House Museum, Winnipeg MB

Foster, Nick, *Vis Prof,* Drew University, Art Dept, Madison NJ (S)

Foster, Phyllis, *Museum Cur,* Herbert Hoover Presidential Library & Museum, West Branch IA

Foster, R, *Cur,* Lloydminster Barr Colony Museum Committee, Lloydminster SK

Foster, Roger W, *VPres,* Fitchburg Art Museum, Fitchburg MA

Foti, Silvana, *Asst Prof,* Methodist College, Art Dept, Fayetteville NC (S)

Fotis, Koula, *VPres,* Civic Fine Arts Association Museum, Sioux Falls SD

Fouche, Ruth C, *In Charge of Art Coll,* Bank of Maryville, Maryville TN

Foulks, Renee, *Instr,* Keystone Junior College, Fine Arts Dept, Factoryville PA (S)

Fowler, Albert W, *Assoc Dir,* Swarthmore College, Friends Historical Library, Swarthmore PA

Fowler, Harriet, *Cur,* University of Kentucky, Art Museum, Lexington KY

Fowler, Jon H, *Dir Dept,* Missouri Southern State College, Dept Fine Art, Joplin MO (S)

Fowler, Margaret, *Education Coordr & Registrar,* Star-Spangled Banner Flag House Association, Library, Baltimore MD

Fowler, Michael, *Assoc Prof,* York College, Art Dept, York NE (S)

Fox, Anne, *Dir of Studies,* New Brunswick Craft School and Centre, Fredericton NB (S)

Fox, Frank, *Chmn Design Div,* Nova Scotia College of Art and Design, Halifax NS (S)

Fox, Hugh R, *Asst Prof,* Rochester Institute of Technology, School of Printing, Rochester NY (S)

Fox, Janice L, *Researcher-in-Residence,* Missouri Historical Society, Library, Saint Louis MO

Fox, Jan Marshall, *Art Coordr,* University of Wisconsin, Memorial Union Gallery, Madison WI

Fox, John, *Asst Prof,* Community College of the Finger Lakes, Visual & Performing Arts Dept, Canandaigua NY (S)

Fox, Katie, *Asst Cur,* Salisbury State College, Wildfowl Art Museum, Salisbury MD

Fox, Louis, *Gallery Dir,* University of Redlands, Peppers Art Center and Gallery, Redlands CA

Fox, Mabert E, *Secy,* Washington County Museum of Fine Arts, Hagerstown MD

Fox, Marie, *Conservator,* Balboa Art Conservation Center, San Diego CA

Fox, Mary, *Dir,* Burnaby Art Gallery, Burnaby BC

Fox, Michael J, *Dir,* Heard Museum, Phoenix AZ

Fox, Randall, *Supt,* Game and Parks Commission, Arbor Lodge State Historical Park, Nebraska City NE

Fox, Thurman O, *Dir Museum,* State Historical Society of Wisconsin, Madison WI

Fox, Vicki Reikes, *Education Coordr,* Danforth Museum of Art, Framingham MA

Foxworth, Carolyn, *Asst Dir Public Affairs,* Dallas Museum of Fine Arts, Dallas TX

Fraenkel, Richard, *Prof,* University of Rhode Island, Dept of Art, Kingston RI (S)

Francell, Larry, *Dir Operations,* Dallas Museum of Fine Arts, Dallas TX

Francell, Larry, *Dir,* Wichita Falls Museum and Art Center, Wichita Falls TX

Francis, Cortez, *Chmn,* Manatee Junior College, Dept of Art, Bradenton FL (S)

Francis, Nancy E, *Librn,* Kitchener-Waterloo Art Gallery, Eleanor Calvert Memorial Library, Kitchener ON

Francis, Ronald, *Chmn Imaging & Photographic Sciences,* Rochester Institute of Technology, School of Photographic Arts & Sciences, Rochester NY (S)

Francis, Tom, *Painting Chmn,* Atlanta College of Art, Atlanta GA (S)

Francke, Oscar, *Cur Entomology,* Texas Tech University Museum, Lubbock TX

Franco, Barbara, *Cur of Collection & Exhibition Coordr,* Museum of Our National Heritage, Lexington MA

Francoeur, Vickie, *Asst Prof,* East Tennessee State University, Fine Arts Dept, Johnson City TN (S)

Francolini, Edward, *Pres,* Society of Scribes, Ltd, New York NY

Frandrup, Dennis, *Asst Prof,* College of Saint Benedict, Art Dept, Saint Joseph MN (S)

Frandsen, Doris, *VPres & Dir Exhib,* Waterloo Art Association, Eleventh Street Gallery, Waterloo IA

Frank, David, *Prof,* Mississippi University for Women, Division of Fine & Performing Arts, Columbus MS (S)

Frank, Denise, *Asst Prof,* Chattanooga State Technical Community College, Advertising Arts Dept, Chattanooga TN (S)

Frank, Herbert, *Pres Board of Dir,* Maryhill Museum of Art, Goldendale WA

Frank, Richard, *Cur Education,* Norton Gallery and School of Art, West Palm Beach FL

Frank, Stuart M, *Dir,* Kendall Whaling Museum, Sharon MA

Frankel, Dextra, *Dir,* California State University Fullerton, Art Gallery, Visual Arts Center, Fullerton CA

Frankel, J, *Head Dept,* Dutchess Community College, Dept of Visual Arts, Poughkeepsie NY (S)

Frankel, Jerome, *Chmn Visual Art,* Dutchess Community College, Dept of Visual Arts, Poughkeepsie NY (S)

Frankel, Robert, *Dir,* Delaware Art Museum, Wilmington DE

Frankenbach, Susan, *Asst Dir,* University of New Hampshire, University Art Galleries, Durham NH

Franklin, Carolyn, *Catalog Librn,* San Francisco Art Institute, Anne Bremer Memorial Library, San Francisco CA

Franklin, Elizabeth, *Asst,* Tucson Museum of Art, Library, Tucson AZ

Franklin, Hardy R, *Dir Libr,* Public Library of the District of Columbia, Art Division, Washington DC

Frankston, Leon, *Prof,* Nassau Community College, Art Dept, Garden City NY (S)

Frantz, Barry, *Chmn Fine Arts Div,* Cuesta College, Art Dept, San Luis Obispo CA (S)

Frantz, James H, *Conservator Objects,* Metropolitan Museum of Art, New York NY

Frantz, John C, *Dir,* San Francisco Public Library, Art and Music Dept, San Francisco CA

Frantz, Susanne, *Cur Exhibitions,* Tucson Museum of Art, Tucson AZ

Franza, R D, *Pres,* Art Students League of New York, New York NY

Frappier, Gilles, *Dir,* Ottawa Public Library, Fine Arts Dept, Ottawa ON

Frascara, Jorge, *Chmn,* University of Alberta, Dept of Art and Design, Edmonton AB (S)

Fraser, A Ian, *Research Cur,* Indianapolis Museum of Art, Clowes Fund Collection, Indianapolis IN

Fraser, A Ian, *Chmn Art History,* Herron School of Art, Indiana University-Purdue University, Indianapolis, Indianapolis IN (S)

Fraser, Jan, *Dir,* Sid W Richardson Foundation, Collection of Western Art, Fort Worth TX

Fraser, M, *Chmn of Board,* University of Victoria, Maltwood Art Museum and Gallery, Victoria BC

Fraser, Marilee, *Department Head Community Relations,* Eli Lilly and Company, Indianapolis IN

Fraser, Nancy, *VPres,* Kennebec Valley Art Association, Harlow Gallery, Hallowell ME

Fraser, Ted, *Cur,* Art Gallery of Windsor, Windsor ON

Frauchiger, Fritz A, *Dir,* Arco Center for Visual Art, Los Angeles CA

Fraunfelter, George, *Adj Cur Geology,* Southern Illinois University, University Museum, Carbondale IL

Frazar, Stanton M, *Dir,* Historic New Orleans Collection, Kemper and Leila Williams Foundation, New Orleans LA

Fraze, Denny, *Chmn,* Amarillo College, Art Dept, Amarillo TX (S)

Frazer, Alan D, *Cur,* New Jersey Historical Society Museum, Newark NJ

Frazer, John, *Chmn,* Wesleyan University, Art Dept, Middletown CT (S)

Frazer, Margaret E, *Cur Medieval Art,* Metropolitan Museum of Art, New York NY

Frazier, Clifton T, *Assoc Prof,* Rochester Institute of Technology, School of Printing, Rochester NY (S)

Frazier, Gillian, *Instr,* Danforth Museum School, Framingham MA (S)

Frazier, William, *Exhib Coordr,* University of Houston, Sarah Campbell Blaffer Gallery, Houston TX

Freckleton, W E, *Pres,* Southwest Arts Foundation, Houston TX

Frederick, Kavin, *Adjunct Lectr,* Manhattan College, School of Arts and Sciences, Bronx NY (S)

Fredericks, Edward H C, *Exec Dir,* San Diego Maritime Museum, San Diego CA

Fredericks, Marshall M, *First VPres,* Brookgreen Gardens, Murrells Inlet SC

Fredericksen, Burton, *Cur Paintings,* J Paul Getty Museum, Malibu CA

Frederickson, Burdette M, *Development Dir,* Joslyn Art Museum, Omaha NE

Fredrick, Charles, *Assoc Prof,* California State Polytechnic University, Pomona, Art Dept, Pomona CA (S)

Fredrick, Gene, *Chmn Printmaking,* Corcoran School of Art, Washington DC (S)

Free, Robert M, *Asst Dir,* University of Washington, Thomas Burke Memorial Washington State Museum, Seattle WA

Freed, Denise Lisiecki, *Head Printmaking Dept,* Kalamazoo Institute of Arts, Artcenter School, Kalamazoo MI (S)

Freed, Donald E, *Pres,* New York Society of Architects, New York NY

Freedberg, S J, *Chief Cur,* National Gallery of Art, Washington DC

Freedman, Ben, *Prof,* West Virginia University, Division of Art, Morgantown WV (S)

Freedman, Jacob B, *Executive Dir,* Prospect Hospital, Bronx NY

Freehling, Stanley M, *Pres,* Arts Club of Chicago Gallery, Chicago IL

Freel, Mirle E, *Dir Arts Dept,* Southwestern Community College, Art Dept, Creston IA (S)

Freeman, Dallas, *Dept Head,* Iowa Lakes Community College, Dept of Art, Estherville IA (S)

Freeman, David, *Assoc Prof,* Winthrop College, Dept of Art, Rock Hill SC (S)

Freeman, Gary, *Chmn Sculpture,* Herron School of Art, Indiana University-Purdue University, Indianapolis, Indianapolis IN (S)

Freeman, Jeff, *Asst Prof,* University of South Dakota, Dept of Art, Vermillion SD (S)

Freeman, John, *Treas,* Erie Art Museum, Erie PA

Freeman, John Crosby, *Dir,* American Life Foundation & Study Institute, American Research Library, Watkins Glen NY

Freeman, Larry, *Cur Decorative Arts Libr,* American Life Foundation & Study Institute, American Research Library, Watkins Glen NY

Freeman, Louis, *Chmn,* Central Piedmont Community College, Art Division, Charlotte NC (S)

Freeman, Mark, *Pres,* National Society of Painters in Casein and Acrylic, Inc, New York NY

Freeman, Nan B, *Asst Prof,* Wellesley College, Art Dept, Wellesley MA (S)

Freeman, Rob, *Gallery Technician,* Macdonald Stewart Art Centre, Guelph ON

Freeman, Ruth, *Cur,* American Life Foundation & Study Institute, American Research Library, Watkins Glen NY

Freeman, Tina, *Adjunct Cur Photography,* New Orleans Museum of Art, New Orleans LA

Freeman, W E, *Dir,* Charleston Museum, Charleston SC

Freer, Harvey, *Dir Coll,* Maryhill Museum of Art, Goldendale WA

Freer, Raymond A, *Chmn,* Anderson College, Art Dept, Anderson IN (S)

Freggiaro, Diane, *Librn & Archivist,* The Haggin Museum, Stockton CA

Fregin, Nancy J, *Pres,* American Society of Artists, Inc, Chicago IL

Freiser, Michael, *Mgr of Museum Shop,* Jewish Museum, New York NY

Freitag, Sally, *Registrar,* Worcester Art Museum, Worcester MA

Freitag, Wolfgang , *Librn,* Harvard University, Fine Arts Library, Cambridge MA

Freitas, Marilyn, *Cur,* Schenectady County Historical Society, Schenectady NY

Frel, Jiri, *Cur Antiquities,* J Paul Getty Museum, Malibu CA

Frel, Jiri, *Adjunct Prof,* University of Southern California, School of Fine Arts, Los Angeles CA (S)

Frem, Barbara, *Chmn Ceramics,* East Texas State University, Dept of Art, Commerce TX (S)

French, La Wanda, *Supervisor,* Ponca City Cultural Center & Museum, Ponca City OK

French, Ron, *Dir,* Anton Elli, Cincinnati OH (S)

French, Stephen, *Assoc Chair, Studio,* San Jose State University, Art Dept, San Jose CA (S)

Freshley, Katherine T, *Librn,* Textile Museum, Arthur D Jenkins Library, Washington DC

Frets, Paul W, *Prof,* Radford University, Art Dept, Radford VA (S)

Fretwell, Jacqualene, *Librn,* Saint Augustine Historical Society, Oldest House and Museums, Saint Augustine FL

Freudenheim, Tom L, *Dir,* Worcester Art Museum, Worcester MA

Freund, David, *Assoc Prof Photography,* Ramapo College of New Jersey, School of Contemporary Arts, Mahwah NJ (S)

Frew, Rachel, *Libr Asst,* University of North Carolina, Art Library, Chapel Hill NC

Frey, Barbara, *Co-Dir,* East Texas State University, Art Dept Gallery, Commerce TX

Frey, Mary, *Instructor,* Hartford Art School of the University of Hartford, West Hartford CT (S)

Friary, Donald R, *Executive Dir & Secy,* Historic Deerfield Inc, Deerfield MA

Frick, Arthur C, *Dept Head,* Wartburg College, Dept of Art, Waverly IA (S)

Frick, Henry Clay, *Pres,* Frick Collection, New York NY

Fridley, Pat, *Secy,* Alaska Artists' Guild, Anchorage AK

Fridley, Russell W, *Dir,* Minnesota Historical Society, Saint Paul MN

Fried, Howard, *Chmn Performance & Video Dept,* San Francisco Art Institute, San Francisco CA (S)

Friedberg, Arthur L, *Exec Dir,* American Ceramic Society, Columbus OH

Friedman, Alice T, *Asst Prof,* Wellesley College, Art Dept, Wellesley MA (S)

Friedman, Betty, *Executive Dir,* Farmington Valley Arts Center, Avon CT

Friedman, Estelle, *Instructor,* Santa Ana College, Art Dept, Santa Ana CA (S)

Friedman, Joan, *Cur Rare Books,* Yale University, Yale Center for British Art, New Haven CT

Friedman, John, *Chmn Photography,* De Young Museum Art School, San Francisco CA (S)

Friedman, Lowell, *Chmn of the Board,* Fine Arts Museum of the South, Mobile AL

Friedman, Martin, *Dir,* Walker Art Center, Minneapolis MN

Friedman, Mildred S, *Cur Design,* Walker Art Center, Minneapolis MN

Friedrich, Heiner, *VPres,* Dia Art Foundation, Inc, New York NY

Frields, Gary Q, *Chmn Art Dept,* Kilgore College, Dept Art and Art Education, Kilgore TX (S)

Friesen, Paul, *Assoc Prof,* Bethel College, Dept of Art, North Newton KS (S)

Frinta, Mojimir, *Art Historian,* State University of New York at Albany, Art Dept Slide Library, Albany NY

Frinta, Mojimir, *Prof,* State University of New York at Albany, Art Dept, Albany NY (S)

Frisbee, Edward, *Pres,* Historic Cherry Hill, Albany NY

Frisbee, John L, *Dir,* Lyndhurst, Tarrytown NY

Frisch, Susan, *Program Asst,* Chesterwood, Library, Stockbridge MA

Frith, Don, *In Charge Ceramics, Glass & Metal,* University of Illinois, Urbana-Champaign, School of Art and Design, Champaign IL (S)

Fritzmann, Frank J, *Gallery Coordr,* Northeastern Illinois University, North River Community Gallery, Chicago IL

Froelich, Susan, *Exhibit Gallery Dir,* Ann Arbor Art Association, Ann Arbor MI

Frohock, Edith, *Prof,* University of Alabama in Birmingham, Dept of Art, Birmingham AL (S)

Froiland, Sven G, *Executive Dir,* Augustana College, Center for Western Studies, Sioux Falls SD

Frombach, Ernest, *Prof,* Mansfield State College, Art Dept, Mansfield PA (S)

Fromer, Seymour, *Dir,* Judah L Magnes Museum, Berkeley CA

Fronmuller, Regina Marie, *Head Dept,* Springfield College in Illinois, Dept of Art, Springfield IL (S)

Fronton, Andre, *Registrar,* National Gallery of Canada, Ottawa ON

Frontz, Stephanie, *Librn,* University of Rochester, Charlotte W Allen Memorial Art Gallery Library, Rochester NY

Frontz, Stephanie J, *Librarian,* University of Rochester, Fine Arts Library, Rochester NY

Frost, A, *Instructor,* Technical University of Nova Scotia, Faculty of Architecture, Halifax NS (S)

Frost, F Daniel, *Pres,* Los Angeles County Museum of Art, Los Angeles CA

Frost, J William, *Dir,* Swarthmore College, Friends Historical Library, Swarthmore PA

Frost, Rosalie, *Librn,* Concord Antiquarian Society Museum, Library, Concord MA

Frudakis, Zenos, *Instr,* Wayne Art Center, Wayne PA (S)

Frueh, Joanna, *Asst Prof,* Oberlin College, Dept of Art, Oberlin OH (S)

Fruhan, Catherine, *Asst Prof,* College of Wooster, Dept of Art, Wooster OH (S)

Fry, Doris H, *Cur,* Museum of the Historical Society of Early American Decoration, Albany NY

Fry, George, *Dir of Crafts,* New Brunswick Craft School and Centre Gallery, Fredericton NB

Fry, George, *VPres,* Canadian Crafts Council, Conseil Canadien de l'Artisanat, Ottawa ON

Fry, George F, *Dir of Craft,* New Brunswick Craft School and Centre, Fredericton NB (S)

Fryberger, Betsy G, *Cur of Prints & Drawings,* Stanford University, Museum of Art & Art Gallery, Stanford CA

Frye, Irene S, *Asst Cur,* Hispanic Society of America, Library, New York NY

Fu, Shen, *Cur Chinese Art,* Freer Gallery of Art, Washington DC

Fuchs, Angelee, *Asst Prof,* Mount Mary College, Art Dept, Milwaukee WI (S)

Fuchs, M Tharsilla, *Prof,* Our Lady of the Lake University, Dept of Art, San Antonio TX (S)

Fudge, John R, *Chmn,* University of Colorado at Denver, Dept of Fine Arts, Denver CO (S)

Fuerstein, Carol, *Ed,* Solomon R Guggenheim Museum, New York NY

Fuerstein, Saul, *Preparator,* Solomon R Guggenheim Museum, New York NY

Fugitt, Patricia J, *Asst Dir,* Corpus Christi State University, Weil Art Gallery, Corpus Christi TX

Fuglie, Gordon, *Cur Asst,* University of California, Los Angeles, Grunwald Center for the Graphic Arts, Los Angeles CA

Fuhriman, Jerry W, *Head,* Utah State University, Dept of Landscape Architecture Environmental Planning, Logan UT (S)

Fujita, Kenji, *Program Coordr,* Committee for the Visual Arts, Inc, New York NY

Fullam, Alice F, *Head Art and Music Dept,* Free Public Library, Art and Music Dept, Trenton NJ

Fuller, Donald R, *Pres,* Hickory Museum of Art, Inc, Hickory NC

Fuller, Richard, *Assoc Prof,* Wilkes College, Dept of Art, Wilkes-Barre PA (S)

Fulton, Jack, *Chmn Photography Dept,* San Francisco Art Institute, San Francisco CA (S)

Fulton, Judith F, *Pres,* Community Gallery of Lancaster County, Lancaster PA

Fulton, Ken, *Instructor,* Northwest Community College, Powell WY (S)

Fulton, Marianne, *Asst Cur Photography Coll,* International Museum of Photography at George Eastman House, Rochester NY

Fulton, William Duncan, *Pres,* Amerind Foundation, Inc, Dragoon AZ

Fumagalli, Orazio, *Prof,* University of Wisconsin-Stout, Art Dept, Menomonie WI (S)

Fumasi, Eddie L, *Cur Asst,* Arco Center for Visual Art, Los Angeles CA

Fundingsland, Marilyn, *Asst Dir,* North Dakota Museum of Art, Grand Forks ND

Funk, Dan, *Vis Prof,* Nebraska Wesleyan University, Art Dept, Lincoln NE (S)

Funk, Robert, *Instructor,* Springfield College, Dept of Visual and Performing Arts, Springfield MA (S)

Funk, Roger, *Chmn Design,* Kansas City Art Institute, Kansas City MO (S)

Funk, Tom, *Prof,* Ocean County College, Humanities Dept, Toms River NJ (S)

Funk, Verne, *Prof,* Texas Tech University, Dept of Art, Lubbock TX (S)

Furches, Harry, *Assoc Prof,* Murray State University, Art Dept, Murray KY (S)

Furk, Brent Funder, *Lecturer,* Mississippi State University, Art Dept, Mississippi State MS (S)

Furlong, Terry, *Financial Coordr,* Women in the Arts Foundation, Inc, New York NY

Furlong-Gardner, Dorothy, *Instructor,* Southeastern Louisiana University, Dept of Visual Arts, Hammond LA (S)

Furman, Evelyn E, *Cur,* Tabor Opera House Museum, Leadville CO

Furmicola, John, *Instr,* Rosemont College, Division of the Arts, Rosemont PA (S)

Furstenberg, James H, *Cur Program Development,* Honolulu Academy of Arts, Honolulu HI

Furtak, Rosemary, *Librn,* Walker Art Center, Staff Reference Library, Minneapolis MN

Fury, Joseph M, *Cur Educ,* Davenport Municipal Art Gallery, Davenport IA

Fusco, Peter, *Cur of European Sculpture,* Los Angeles County Museum of Art, Los Angeles CA

Futernick, Robert, *Conservator Paper,* Fine Arts Museums of San Francisco, M H de Young Memorial Museum and California Palace of the Legion of Honor, San Francisco CA

Fyfe, Jo, *Dept Chmn,* Spokane Falls Community College, Creative & Performing Arts, Spokane WA (S)

Gabel, Marlene, *Dir,* Contemporary Crafts Association and Gallery, Portland OR

Gabhart, Ann, *Dir,* Wellesley College, Museum, Wellesley MA

Gabhart, Ann R, *Lecturer,* Wellesley College, Art Dept, Wellesley MA (S)

Gabriel, Robert A, *Exec Dir,* Brevard Art Center and Museum, Inc, Melbourne FL

Gabryl, Belynda, *Instr,* Salve Regina - The Newport College, Art Dept, Newport RI (S)

Gadd, Emily, *Slide Cur,* Montana State University, Creative Arts Library, Bozeman MT

Gaddis, Paul O, *Pres,* University of Pennsylvania, Henry Clews Memorial, Philadelphia PA

Gadson, James, *Assoc Prof,* University of North Carolina at Chapel Hill, Art Dept, Chapel Hill NC (S)

Gaffney, Gary, *Instructor,* Art Academy of Cincinnati, Cincinnati OH (S)

Gaffney, Richard W, *Chmn,* Wagner College, Dept of Art, Staten Island NY (S)

Gage, Robert, *Chairperson,* Waubonsee Community College, Fine Arts Dept, Sugar Grove IL (S)

Gaglio, Nicholas, *VPres,* Palm Beach County Parks and Recreation Department, Morikami Museum of Japanese Culture, Delray Beach FL

Gagne, Jocelyne, *Secy,* Pavilion of Humour, Man and His World, Montreal PQ

Gagne, W Arthur, *Admin,* Worcester Art Museum, Worcester MA

Gagnier, Bruce, *Dean,* New York Studio School of Drawing, Painting and Sculpture, New York NY (S)

Gagnon, Carolle, *Dir,* Musee du Seminaire de Quebec, Quebec PQ

Gagnon, Claire, *Conservator,* Musee des Augustines de l'Hotel Dieu of Quebec, Quebec PQ

Gagnon, Luc, *Exhib & Research,* Musee d'Art de Saint-Laurent, Saint-Laurent PQ

Gahran, Hazel Ward, *Mgr Museum Shop,* Kauai Museum, Lihue HI

Gahran, Robert, *Researcher,* Kauai Museum, Lihue HI

Gaines, C T, *Prof,* Presbyterian College, Fine Arts Dept, Clinton SC (S)

Gaines, Edith B, *Dir Annual Programs,* Art Institute of Chicago, Chicago IL

Gaines, Ervin J, *Dir,* Cleveland Public Library, Fine Arts & Special Collections Dept, Cleveland OH

Gaines, George H, *Chmn,* Georgia College, Art Dept, Milledgeville GA (S)

Gaines, William, *Programs Dir,* Virginia Museum of Fine Arts, Richmond VA

Gaither, Edmund B, *Dir,* Museum of the National Center of Afro-American Artists, Boston MA

Gaither, James L, *Instructor,* Casper College, Casper WY (S)

Galantic, Ivan, *Assoc Prof,* Tufts University, Fine Arts Dept, Medford MA (S)

Galavaris, G, *Prof,* McGill University, Department of Art History, Montreal PQ (S)

Galban, Victoria S, *Asst Cur Research,* Metropolitan Museum of Art, Robert Lehman Collection Library, New York NY

Galembo, Phyllis, *Assoc Prof,* State University of New York at Albany, Art Dept, Albany NY (S)

Galis, Diana, *Asst Prof,* Franklin and Marshall College, Art Dept, Lancaster PA (S)

Gall, Sally, *Coordr Special Projects,* Contemporary Arts Museum, Houston TX

Gallagher, Cynthia, *Adjunct Instr,* New York Institute of Technology, Fine Arts Dept, Old Westbury NY (S)

Gallagher, Jean, *Asst Prof,* University of Tennessee at Chattanooga, Dept of Art, Chattanooga TN (S)

Gallagher, Jerome, *Assoc Prof,* University of Wisconsin-Stevens Point, Dept of Art, Stevens Point WI (S)

Gallagher, Marsha, *Cur Material Culture,* Joslyn Art Museum, Omaha NE

Gallagher, Pat, *Dir,* Oklahoma Art Center, Arts Place II, Oklahoma City OK

Gallanos, Alma, *Asst Instr,* Stevenson Academy of Traditional Painting, Sea Cliff NY (S)

Gallant, Nissan, *VPres,* Art Centre of New Jersey, East Orange NJ (S)

Galliani, Joe, *Administrator Editor,* American Portrait Society, Seal Beach CA

Gallo, Frank, *In Charge Sculpture,* University of Illinois, Urbana-Champaign, School of Art and Design, Champaign IL (S)

Galloway, Gail, *Cur,* The Supreme Court of the United States Museum, Washington DC

Galloway, Helen, *Assoc Prof,* Saint Mary's College, Art Dept, Winona MN (S)

Galloway, John, *Pres,* Hartland Art Council, Hartland MI

Galloway, Patricia, *Dir Special Projects,* Mississippi Department of Archives and History, State Historical Museum, Jackson MS

Galloway, R Dean, *Dir,* California State College, Stanislaus, Vasche Library, Turlock CA

Gallup, Andy, *Exhibits Technician,* Institute of the Great Plains, Museum of the Great Plains, Lawton OK

Galvin, Susan, *Treas,* Hill-Stead Museum, Farmington CT

Gamache, Alan, *Asst Prof,* University of Wisconsin-Stout, Art Dept, Menomonie WI (S)

Gamble-Depew, Linda, *Business Mgr,* Montana Historical Society, Helena MT

Gandy, Cheri, *VPres,* Redding Museum and Art Center, Redding CA

Gang, Pamela L, *Program Coordr,* Adirondack Lakes Center for the Arts, Blue Mountain Lake NY

Gangemi, Carol, *Chmn Advertising Design,* Moore College of Art, Philadelphia PA (S)

Gans, Lucy, *Asst Prof,* Lehigh University, Dept of Art and Architecture, Bethlehem PA (S)

Gant, Sally, *Educ Coordr,* Old Salem Inc, Museum of Early Southern Decorative Arts, Winston-Salem NC

Gantt, Richard, *Asst Prof,* Averett College, Art Dept, Danville VA (S)

Ganzel, Paula, *Installationist,* Arizona State University, University Art Collections, Tempe AZ

Garballey, Jim, *Head Sign Painting,* Butera School of Art, Boston MA (S)

Garcia, Donna Marie, *District Adminr,* Kauai Regional Library, Lihue HI

Garcia, Frieda, *Exec Dir,* Children's Art Centre, Boston MA

Garcia, Hector, *Assoc Prof,* Indiana University-Purdue University, Dept of Fine Arts, Fort Wayne IN (S)

Garcia, Jane Lee, *Pres of Board,* Bronx Museum of the Arts, Bronx NY

Garcia, Ofelia, *Dir,* Print Club, Philadelphia PA

Garcia, Salvador, *Asst Cur,* Galeria de la Raza, Studio 24, San Francisco CA

Gardner, Allan R, *Instructor,* Portland School of Art, Portland ME (S)

Gardner, Byron, *Prof,* Portland State University, Dept of Art and Architecture, Portland OR (S)

Gardner, Charles, *Chmn Photography,* Moore College of Art, Philadelphia PA (S)

Gardner, Cyril, *Instr,* Mainline Center of the Arts, Haverford PA (S)

Gardner, Doll, *Fine Arts Chmn,* West Hills Unitarian Fellowship, Portland OR

Gardner, Elizabeth E, *Cur European Paintings,* Metropolitan Museum of Art, New York NY

Gardner, Frederick, *Head, Public Services,* California Institute of the Arts Library, Valencia CA

Gardner, Jack, *Admin,* Clark County Library District, Las Vegas NV

Gardner, Janet, *Dir,* Spoon River College, Art Dept, Canton IL (S)

Gardner, Nina, *Registrar,* Manchester Institute of Arts and Sciences, Manchester NH (S)

Gardner, Norman, *Second VPres,* Kent Art Association, Inc, Kent CT

Gardner, Robert, *Planetarium Dir,* Sunrise Foundation, Inc, Sunrise Museums, Charleston WV

Gardner, William F, *Faculty,* North Florida Junior College, Dept Humanities & Art, Madison FL (S)

Garfield, Alan, *Chmn,* Marycrest College, Art Dept, Davenport IA (S)

Garfius, Robert, *Dean,* University of California, Irvine, Studio Art Dept, Irvine CA (S)

Gargan, R, *Secy,* Dartmouth Heritage Museum, Dartmouth NS

Garhart, Martin, *Assoc Prof,* Kenyon College, Art Dept, Gambier OH (S)

Gariepy, Luce, *Asst,* Musee du Quebec, Bibliotheque des Art, Quebec PQ

Garipoli, Rosemarie, *Dir of Development,* Jewish Museum, New York NY

Garneau, Alma, *Admin Services Mgr,* Edmonton Art Gallery, Edmonton AB

Garner, Gretchen, *Chairperson,* Saint Xavier College, Dept of Art, Chicago IL (S)

Garner, Marilyn, *Treas,* Eccles Community Art Center, Ogden UT

Garoza, Valdis, *Asst Prof,* Marietta College, Art Dept, Marietta OH (S)

Garr, Greta, *Instr,* Wayne Art Center, Wayne PA (S)

Garrard, Mary D, *Prof,* American University, Dept of Art, Washington DC (S)

Garratt, Leanne, *Secy,* Saskatchewan Power Corporation, Gallery on the Roof, Regina SK

Garret, Rolland, *VPres,* Montclair State College, Gallery One, Upper Montclair NJ

Garrett, Alexandra, *VPres,* Beyond Baroque Foundation, Venice CA

Garrison, Douglas, *Office Mgr,* Birmingham-Bloomfield Art Association, Birmingham MI

Garrison, Jim, *Instructor,* Mesa Community College, Dept of Art & Photography, Mesa AZ (S)

Garrison, J Ritchie, *Dir of Education,* Historic Deerfield Inc, Deerfield MA

Garrison, Lisa, *Museum Education Dir,* Manhattan Laboratory Museum, New York NY

Garside, A La Moyne, *Chmn,* Brigham Young University, Hawaii Campus, Division of Fine Arts, Laie HI (S)

Garte, Edna J, *Asst Prof,* University of Minnesota, Duluth, Art Dept, Duluth MN (S)

Garten, Clifford, *Instructor,* Hamline University, Art Dept, Saint Paul MN (S)

Garthwaite, Ernest, *Asst Prof,* York College of the City University of New York, Fine and Performing Arts, Jamaica NY (S)

Garvan, Beatrice, *Cur American Decorative Arts,* Philadelphia Museum of Art, Philadelphia PA

Garver, Stockton, *Chmn Art History,* Wichita State University, Division of Art, Wichita KS (S)

Garver, Thomas H, *Dir,* Madison Art Center, Madison WI

Garvey, Timothy, *Instructor,* Illinois Wesleyan University, School of Art, Bloomington IL (S)

Garvey, William, *Pres,* Erie Historical Museum, Erie PA

Garvin, Bruce, *Treas,* Danforth Museum of Art, Framingham MA

Garvin, James L, *Cur,* New Hampshire Historical Society, Concord NH

Garwell, Robert, *Dean,* University of Wisconsin-Whitewater, Dept of Art, Whitewater WI (S)

Gary, Rudy, *Head Operations,* Greenville County Museum of Art, Greenville SC

Garza, Lynne, *Asst Librn & Reference,* Detroit Institute of Arts, Research Library, Detroit MI

Garzio, Angelo, *Prof,* Kansas State University, Art Dept, Manhattan KS (S)

Garzon-Blanco, Armando, *Art Dept Head,* Nicholls State University, Dept of Art, Thibodaux LA (S)

Gascon, France, *Dir of Exhib,* Musee d'Art Contemporain, Montreal PQ

Gaskill, Diane, *Vis Lecturer,* North Central College, Dept of Art, Naperville IL (S)

Gaskin, Leroy, *Cur Ceramics & Sculpture,* Smith-Mason Gallery and Museum, Washington DC

Gasparro, Frank, *Instructor,* Samuel S Fleisher Art Memorial, Philadelphia PA (S)

Gastellum, L Edward, *Supt,* Hubbell Trading Post, Ganado AZ

Gater, Helen, *Assoc Librn,* Arizona State University, Hayden Library Art Dept, Tempe AZ

Gates, Carole C, *Instr,* Villa Maria College of Buffalo, Art Dept, Buffalo NY (S)

Gates, Elaine, *Assoc Prof,* Hood College, Dept of Art, Frederick MD (S)

Gates, H I, *Assoc Prof,* George Washington University, Dept of Art, Washington DC (S)

Gates, Jay, *Asst Dir & Samuel Sosland Cur American Art,* Atkins Museum of Fine Art, Kansas City MO

Gates, Kathryn, *Registrar,* Portland Art Association, Portland Art Museum, Portland OR

Gates, Thomas, *Library Asst,* University of Southern California, Architecture and Fine Arts Library, Los Angeles CA

Gates, Tom, *Chmn Art History,* De Young Museum Art School, San Francisco CA (S)

Gates, Valery, *Asst Prof,* Virginia State University, Fine & Commercial Art, Petersburg VA (S)

Gatewood, Maud F, *Coordr,* Averett College, Art Dept, Danville VA (S)

Gathman, Jan D, *Instr,* University of North Dakota-Williston Center, Interior Design Dept, Williston ND (S)

Gatley, Ian, *Assoc Prof Art,* Eastern Oregon State College, Arts & Humanities Dept, La Grande OR (S)

Gatrall, Carol, *Pres,* Art Barn, Greenwich CT

Gatty, Arthur, *Dir Governor's School for the Arts,* Pennsylvania Department of Education, Arts in Education Program, Harrisburg PA

Gaudiere, Millicent Hall, *Adminr,* Association of Art Museum Directors, Savannah GA

Gaudreau, Therest Marie, *Acquisitions,* Trinity College Library, Washington DC

Gaughan, Tom, *Instructor,* Samuel S Fleisher Art Memorial, Philadelphia PA (S)

Gaugler, William, *Assoc Chair, Art History,* San Jose State University, Art Dept, San Jose CA (S)

Gaul, Elaine, *Registrar,* Indiana University, William Hammond Mathers Museum, Bloomington IN

Gauvreau, Robert G, *Instructor,* Modesto Junior College, Arts Humanities and Speech Division, Modesto CA (S)

Gavin, Carney E S, *Cur,* Harvard University, Harvard Semitic Museum, Cambridge MA

Gawron, Carol, *Supv Traveling Libraries,* Miami-Dade Public Library, Miami FL

Gay, Robert, *Instr,* Waynesburg College, Dept of Fine Arts, Waynesburg PA (S)

Gay, Zan, *Librn,* University of Miami, Reference Library, Coral Gables FL

Gaydos, Tim, *Instructor,* Montclair Art Museum, Museum Art Classes, Montclair NJ (S)

Gayle, Margot, *Secy,* Art Commission of the City of New York, New York NY

Gazda, Elaine K, *Assoc Cur,* University of Michigan, Kelsey Museum of Ancient and Medieval Archaeology, Ann Arbor MI

Gazetas, Mary, *Mgr Cultural & Heritage Servs,* Richmond Arts Centre, Richmond BC

Gealt, Adelheid, *Cur Western Art to 1800,* Indiana University, Art Museum, Bloomington IN

Gealt, Barry, *Assoc Prof,* Indiana University, Bloomington, School of Fine Arts, Bloomington IN (S)

Geanakos, James, *Intern,* Clark University, Little Center Gallery, Worcester MA

Gear, Josephine, *Dir,* State University of New York at Binghamton, University Art Gallery, Binghamton NY

Geary-Furniss, Judy, *Assoc Dir,* Lakeview Museum of Arts and Sciences, Peoria IL

Gebb, Wayne, *Faculty,* Midway College, Art Dept, Midway KY (S)

Gedeun, Lucinda H, *Asst to Dir,* University of California, Los Angeles, Grunwald Center for the Graphic Arts, Los Angeles CA

Geer, Suvan, *Dir,* Orange County Center for Contemporary Art, Santa Ana CA

Geeslin, L Gaddis, *Prof,* Sam Houston State University, Art Dept, Huntsville TX (S)

Gehrke, Richard A, *Gallery Dir,* New Mexico State University, Art Gallery, Las Cruces NM

Gehrm, Barbara, *Secy,* Salisbury State College, Wildfowl Art Museum, Salisbury MD

Geibert, Ron, *Asst Prof,* Wright State University, Dept of Art & Art History, Dayton OH (S)

Geil, Marian, *Pres Board of Dir,* Copper Village Museum & Arts Center, Anaconda MT

Geiman, Robert H, *Dir,* University of Alaska, Elmer E Rasmuson Library, Fairbanks AK

Geimzer, Eugene, *Asst Prof,* Loyola University of Chicago, Fine Arts Dept, Chicago IL (S)

Geis, Mary Christina, *Dir,* Georgian Court College Gallery, Lakewood NJ

Geis, Mary Christina, *Head Dept,* Georgian Court College, Dept of Art, Lakewood NJ (S)

Geischer, Geraldine, *Instructor,* Milwaukee Area Technical College, Graphic & Applied Arts Division, Milwaukee WI (S)

Geisinger, Christine, *Pres,* Witter Gallery, Storm Lake IA

Geisinger, William, *Instructor,* De Anza College, Art Dept, Cupertino CA (S)

Geisler, Paula, *Art Dir,* New Mexico Highlands University, Arrott Art Gallery, Las Vegas NM

Geissinger, Michael A, *Asst Prof,* Rochester Institute of Technology, School of Photographic Arts & Sciences, Rochester NY (S)

Geist, Sidney, *Instr,* New York Studio School of Drawing, Painting and Sculpture, New York NY (S)

Gelburd, Gail, *Dir,* Hofstra University, Emily Lowe Gallery, Hempstead NY

Geldin, Sherri, *Admin,* The Museum of Contemporary Art, Los Angeles CA

Gelfand, Dan, *Instructor,* Woodstock School of Art, Inc, New York NY (S)

Gelinas, Andre A, *Pres,* Fitchburg Art Museum, Fitchburg MA

Gellman, Lola B, *Prof,* Queensborough Community College, Dept of Art and Design, Bayside NY (S)

Gelman, Janet, *Cur Education,* Museum of Fine Arts, Springfield MA

Gelman, Janet, *Cur Education,* George Walter Vincent Smith Art Museum, Springfield MA

Gelston, Judy, *Secy,* Skaneateles Library Association, Skaneateles NY

Geltner, Frank, *Asst Dir,* University of Oregon, Aperture: Photo Gallery, Eugene OR

Gely, Mimi, *Dir,* Prince George Art Gallery, Prince George BC

Gemmill, John K, *Pres,* New Hampshire Historical Society, Concord NH

Genaro, Ann, *Secy to Dir,* National Museum of Racing, Inc, Saratoga Springs NY

Genette, John, *Exec Dir,* Allied Arts Council of the Yakima Valley, Yakima WA

Genter, Anne S, *Secy,* Pittsburgh History and Landmarks Foundation, Old Post Office Museum, Pittsburgh PA

Gentle, Thom, *Secy-Treas & Dir,* Intermuseum Conservation Association, Oberlin OH

Gentry, James, *Dir,* Southern Highland Handicraft Guild, Folk Art Center, Asheville NC

George, Raymond, *Vis Instr,* Munson-Williams-Proctor Institute, School of Art, Utica NY (S)

George, Tom, *Chmn,* Salisbury State College, Wildfowl Art Museum, Salisbury MD

Georgias, Andrew, *Assoc Prof,* Glendale College, Dept of Fine Arts, Glendale CA (S)

Georgion, Tyrone, *Chmn,* State University of New York, Buffalo, Dept of Art and Art History, Buffalo NY (S)

Gerald, Terry, *Adminr,* Mexican Museum, San Francisco CA

Gerard, John, *Cur of Coll,* Cranbrook Academy of Art Museum, Bloomfield Hills MI

Gerard, Lou, *Secy,* Pacific Northwest Arts and Crafts Association, Bellevue Art Museum, Bellevue WA

Gerardia, Helen, *Treas,* Society of American Graphic Artists, New York NY

Gerardine, M, *Dir,* Caldwell College, Art Gallery, Caldwell NJ

Gerber, Jack, *Pres,* Pennsylvania Academy of the Fine Arts, Fellowship of the Pennsylvania Academy of the Fine Arts, Philadelphia PA

Gerber, John H, *Head Division,* Culver-Stockton College, Division of Fine Arts, Canton MO (S)

Gerdts, Abigail Booth, *Archivist,* National Academy of Design, Fine Arts Archives, New York NY

Gerdts, William H, *Chmn Exec Committee,* City University of New York, PhD Program in Art History, New York NY (S)

Gerena, Victor M, *Dir,* Institute of Puerto Rican Culture, Museo de Bellas Artes, San Juan PR

Germain, Jean-Pierre, *Dir General,* Bibliotheque Centrale de Pret de L'Outaouais et des Laurentides Inc, Hull PQ

Gern, Jess W, *Chmn,* Western State College, Quigley Hall Art Gallery, Gunnison CO

Gerrier, Arthur J, *Manuscripts Asst,* Maine Historical Society, Library, Portland ME

Gerrish, Richard, *Galleries Mgr,* Galleries of the Claremont Colleges, Claremont CA

Gerson, Paula, *Treas,* International Center of Medieval Art, Inc, New York NY

Gertjejansen, Doyle, *Chmn,* University of New Orleans, Dept of Fine Arts, New Orleans LA (S)

Gettinger, Ed, *Head Dept,* University of South Dakota, Springfield, Springfield SD (S)

Gettinger, Edmond, *Lectr,* Mount Marty College, Art Dept, Yankton SD (S)

Getty, Nilda C, *Prof,* Colorado State University, Dept of Art, Fort Collins CO (S)

Getty, Ron, *Cur of Cultural History,* Glenbow Museum, Calgary AB

Gevins, Jack, *Instructor,* Bucks County Community College, Fine Arts Dept, Newton PA (S)

Geyelin, Peter, *Development Dir,* Please Touch Museum, Philadelphia PA

Geyer, Eddie Joyce, *Vol Coordr,* Saint Augustine Historical Society, Oldest House and Museums, Saint Augustine FL

Geyer, George E, *Instructor,* Santa Ana College, Art Dept, Santa Ana CA (S)

Ghaemi, Anita, *Asst Cur,* University of Chicago, Oriental Institute, Chicago IL

Ghannam, Edward, *Assoc Prof,* University of Miami, Dept of Art & Art History, Coral Gables FL (S)

Glazer, Steve, *Chmn,* Saint Mary-of-the-Woods College, Art Dept, Saint Mary-of-the-Woods IN (S)

Gleason, Margaret, *VPres,* Triton Museum of Art, Santa Clara CA

Gleason, Ronald, *VPres,* The Art Museum Association of America, San Francisco CA

Gleason, Thomas J, *Asst Dir,* Biblical Arts Center, Dallas TX

Gleeman, E L, *Instr,* Normandale Community College, Art Dept, Bloomington MN (S)

Gleeson, Larry, *Art History Coordr,* North Texas State University, Art Dept, Denton TX (S)

Gleeson, M, *Executive Dir,* Artists Guild of Chicago, Chicago IL

Glen, T, *Assoc Prof,* McGill University, Department of Art History, Montreal PQ (S)

Glendinning, Peter, *Instructor,* Michigan State University, Leland Summer Art School, Leland MI (S)

Glenn, Barbara, *Assoc Prof,* Bethel College, Dept of Art, Saint Paul MN (S)

Glenn, Constance W, *Dir,* California State University, Long Beach, University Art Museum, Long Beach CA

Glenn, Dixie, *Instr,* University of Kansas, Dept of Art, Music Education and Music Therapy, Lawrence KS (S)

Glenn, Dixie, *Instr,* Blackhawk Mountain School of Art, Black Hawk CO (S)

Glenn, Edna, *Assoc Prof,* Texas Tech University, Dept of Art, Lubbock TX (S)

Glenn, Karin, *Secy,* Wichita State University, Edwin A Ulrich Museum of Art, Wichita KS

Glenn, Ralph, *Instructor,* Madonna College, Art Dept, Livonia MI (S)

Glickman, Rhoda, *Exec Dir,* Congressional Arts Caucus, Washington DC

Glidden, Germain G, *Pres,* The National Art Museum of Sport, New Haven CT

Glidden, Germain G, *Dir,* National Art Museum of Sports, Inc, New York NY

Glier, Nancy, *Business Mgr,* Contemporary Arts Center, Cincinnati OH

Glisson, Frank, *Dir Exhibits,* California Museum of Science and Industry, Los Angeles CA

Globus, Dorothy Twining, *Exhib Coordr,* Cooper-Hewitt Museum, Smithsonian Institution, New York NY

Glocklin, Gary, *Division Chmn,* Bellevue Community College, Arts Dept, Bellevue WA (S)

Glosser, Mary Sue, *Cur Arts Educ Servs,* Hood Museum of Art, Hanover NH

Glover, Beverly, *Admin,* Oklahoma Museum of Art, Oklahoma City OK

Glover, Ellen, *Treas,* Blacksburg Regional Art Association, Blacksburg VA

Glover, Lisa, *Librn,* American Council for the Arts, Library, New York NY

Glover, Lou Ann, *First VPres,* Spectrum, Friends of Fine Art, Inc, Toledo OH

Glover, Tom, *Asst Prof,* Amarillo College, Art Dept, Amarillo TX (S)

Gluhman, Joseph W, *Head Dept,* Western Kentucky University, Art Dept, Bowling Green KY (S)

Gluth, J E, *Dir Admin Services,* Heublein Inc, Farmington CT

Gnat, Raymond, *Dir,* Indianapolis Marion County Public Library, Art Dept, Indianapolis IN

Goad, Albert W, *Chmn,* Ashland College Arts and Humanities Gallery, Ashland OH

Goad, Albert W, *Chmn,* Ashland College, Art Dept, Ashland OH (S)

Goald, Robert, *Instr,* Community College of Baltimore, Dept of Fine & Applied Arts, Liberty Campus, Baltimore MD (S)

Gobar, Anne, *Dir,* Headley-Whitney Museum, Lexington KY

Godbolt, Fred B, *Pres Emeritus,* Kelly-Griggs House Museum, Red Bluff CA

Goddin, Margaret P, *Div Arts,* Davis and Elkins College, Dept of Art, Elkins WV (S)

Godfrey, Jane, *Bookshop Mgr,* The Phillips Collection, Washington DC

Godfrey, Judy, *Programs Dir,* Centenary College of Louisiana, Meadows Museum of Art, Shreveport LA

Godlewski, Henry, *Asst Prof,* Mohawk Valley Community College, Advertising Design and Production, Utica NY (S)

Godlewski, Susan Glover, *Assoc Librn & Head Reference Dept,* Art Institute of Chicago, Ryerson and Burnham Libraries, Chicago IL

Goebel, Heather, *Arts Unit Mgr,* Fort Worth Public Library, Fine Arts Section, Fort Worth TX

Goehl, George, *First VPres,* Brown County Art Gallery Association Inc, Nashville IN

Goehlich, John, *Dept Head,* Ray-Vogue College of Design, Chicago IL (S)

Goelet, Robert G, *Pres,* New York Historical Society, New York NY

Goelet, Robert G, *Pres,* American Museum of Natural History, New York NY

Goering, Jackie, *VPres,* Alaska Association for the Arts, Fairbanks AK

Goering, Karen, *Cur Art,* Missouri Historical Society, Saint Louis MO

Goetemann, Gordon, *Prof,* College of Saint Benedict, Art Dept, Saint Joseph MN (S)

Goetz, Edith, *Instructor,* Goetz Art School, Bedford Hills NY (S)

Goetz, Richard V, *Dir,* Goetz Art School, Bedford Hills NY (S)

Goetz, Robert C, *Treas,* National Gallery of Art, Washington DC

Goff, Barbara, *Clerk,* Detroit Public Library, Fine Arts Dept, Detroit MI

Goff, Lila J, *Asst to Dir for Libraries and Museum Coll,* Minnesota Historical Society, Saint Paul MN

Goff, Lloyd Lozes, *Secy,* National Society of Mural Painters, Inc, New York NY

Goffen, Rona, *Assoc Prof,* Duke University, Dept of Art, Durham NC (S)

Gogel, Ken, *Prof,* University of Northern Iowa, Dept of Art, Cedar Falls IA (S)

Goggin, Nan, *Instructor,* Delta State University, Dept of Art, Cleveland MS (S)

Gohman, Angela, *Instr,* Huntington College, Art Dept, Huntington IN (S)

Gohn, Randy, *Dir,* Doshi Center for Contemporary Art, Harrisburg PA

Goist, David, *Conservator,* North Carolina Museum of Art, Raleigh NC

Gokhale, Shakuntala, *Librn,* Fort Worth Public Library, Fine Arts Section, Fort Worth TX

Gold, Catherine, *Educational Officer,* Queen's University, Agnes Etherington Art Centre, Kingston ON

Gold, Harvey, *Dir Admin & Finance,* Pennsylvania Academy of the Fine Arts, Galleries, Philadelphia PA

Gold, Marvin, *Pres,* Erie Art Museum, Erie PA

Gold, Rubin, *Instructor,* Boston Center for Adult Education, Boston MA (S)

Goldberg, Elizabeth, *Dir,* Gallery North, Setauket NY

Goldberg, Joshua, *Cur of Education,* University of Arizona, Museum of Art, Tucson AZ

Goldblatt, Dan, *Public Relations & Events Coordr,* Virginia Beach Arts Center, Virginia Beach VA

Golden, Morton, *Deputy Dir Admin,* Los Angeles County Museum of Art, Los Angeles CA

Golden, Morton J, *Dir,* Palm Springs Desert Museum, Inc, Palm Springs CA

Goldfarb, Hilliard, *Asst Prof,* Case Western Reserve University, Dept of Art, Cleveland OH (S)

Goldfinger, Eliot, *Instr,* New York Academy of Art, New York NY (S)

Goldin, Leon, *Prof,* Columbia University, School of the Arts, Division of Painting & Sculpture, New York NY (S)

Golding, Robert D, *Instructor,* Antonelli Institute of Art & Photography, Professional Photography, Commercial Art & Interior Design, Plymouth Meeting PA (S)

Goldman, Amy, *Vis Asst Prof,* University of Southern California, School of Fine Arts, Los Angeles CA (S)

Goldman, Cheryl, *Instructor,* Rhode Island College, Art Dept, Providence RI (S)

Goldman, Harvey, *Coordr Gallery,* Southeastern Massachusetts University, College of Visual and Performing Arts, North Dartmouth MA (S)

Goldman, Nancy, *Film Librn,* University of California, Pacific Film Archive, Berkeley CA

Goldman, Stewart, *Chmn,* Art Academy of Cincinnati, Cincinnati OH (S)

Goldrach, Alain, *Conservator Paintings,* Museum of Fine Arts, Boston MA

Goldsberry, Max R, *Chmn Human & Fine Arts,* Garden City Community Junior College, Art Dept, Garden City KS (S)

Goldsmith, Christopher, *Exec Dir,* Milwaukee Art Museum, Milwaukee WI

Goldsmith, W, *Secy,* Society of Typographic Arts, Chicago IL

Goldsmith, Zina, *Gallery Dir,* Beaver College, Richard Eugene Fuller Gallery of Art, Glenside PA

Goldstein, Alan, *Instructor,* Bucks County Community College, Fine Arts Dept, Newton PA (S)

Goldstein, Howard, *Chmn Dept,* Trenton State College, Art Dept, Trenton NJ (S)

Goldstein, Howard, *Dir,* Trenton State College, Holman Gallery, Trenton NJ

Goldstein, Linda, *Registrar,* Rice University, Institute for the Arts, Rice Museum, Houston TX

Goldstein, Milton, *Prof,* Adelphi University, Dept of Art and Art History, Garden City NY (S)

Goldstein, Nathan, *Chmn Found Dept,* Art Institute of Boston, Boston MA (S)

Goldstein, Roger, *Assoc Prof,* C W Post Center of Long Island University, School of the Arts, Greenvale NY (S)

Goldstein, Sidney M, *Chief Cur,* Corning Museum of Glass, Corning NY

Goldstein, Vivian, *Trustee,* Foundation for Today's Art, Nexus Gallery, Philadelphia PA

Goldston, James M, *Chmn,* Museum of Oriental Cultures, Corpus Christi TX

Goldwater, Marge, *Cur,* Walker Art Center, Minneapolis MN

Goldworm, Judith, *Asst to Dir,* Lehigh University Art Galleries, Bethlehem PA

Goler, Robert, *Cur Collection,* Fraunces Tavern Museum, New York NY

Golfman, Eleanor, *Pres,* Manitoba Society of Artists, Winnipeg MB

Golojuch, Janice, *Instructor,* Salisbury State College, Art Dept, Salisbury MD (S)

Golub, Lenore, *Asst Cur,* Hofstra University, Emily Lowe Gallery, Hempstead NY

Golub, Leon, *Actg Dean,* Rutgers, the State University of New Jersey, Mason Gross School of the Arts, New Brunswick NJ (S)

Gomes, Manuel, *Pres,* Wallingford Art League, Wallingford CT

Gomez, Ric, *Dept Head,* David Thompson University Centre, Visual Arts Dept, Nelson BC (S)

Gomez, Roberto, *Assoc Prof,* Compton Community College, Compton CA (S)

Gomez-Sicre, Jose, *Dir,* Museum of Modern Art of Latin America, Washington DC

Gonchar, Nancy, *Coordr Exhib,* Visual Studies Workshop, Rochester NY

Gondek, Thomas, *Chmn-Foundation,* Kendall School of Design, Grand Rapids MI (S)

Gong, William, *Secy,* Chinese Culture Foundation, Chinese Culture Center Gallery, San Francisco CA

Gonzales, Alex, *Instructor,* Monterey Peninsula College, Art Dept, Monterey CA (S)

Gonzales, Camille, *Technical Asst,* Santa Monica College Art Gallery, Santa Monica CA

Gonzalez, Xavier, *Instructor,* Truro Center for the Arts at Castle Hill, Inc, Truro MA (S)

Good, Merrie, *Second VPres & Mgr,* The Chase Manhattan Bank, NA, New York NY

Goodale, Carol S, *Educ Coordr,* Pontiac Art Center, Pontiac MI

Goodbody, James B, *Pres,* Portland School of Art, Portland ME (S)

Goode Bryant, Linda, *Executive Dir,* Just Above Midtown Gallery, Inc, New York NY

Goodfriend, Pennelope, *Public Relations,* Organization of Independent Artists, New York NY

Goodheart, John, *Prof,* Indiana University, Bloomington, School of Fine Arts, Bloomington IN (S)

Goodhue, Beverly, *Education Coordr,* Lynnwood Arts Centre, Simcoe ON

Goodhue, Timothy, *Registrar,* Yale University, Yale Center for British Art, New Haven CT

Goodlett, Henry, *Pres,* Central Florida Community College Art Collection, Ocala FL

Goodman, Bernard, *Asst Supt,* Independence National Historical Park, Philadelphia PA

Goodman, Janis, *Lectr,* Trinity College, Art Dept, Washington DC (S)

Goodman, Marilyn J S, *Executive Dir,* Philadelphia Art Alliance, Philadelphia PA

Goodman, Rina, *Dir,* Ward-Nasse Gallery, New York NY

Goodman, Sherry B, *Special Asst to Pres,* Museum of Science and Industry, Chicago IL

Goodman, Susan, *Chief Cur,* Jewish Museum, New York NY

Goodnough, Joan, *Adminr Asst to Dir,* Moose Jaw Art Museum and National Exhibition Centre, History Museum, Moose Jaw SK

Goodpaster, Gracie, *Pres,* Pence Gallery, Davis CA

Goodrich, Margaret, *Librn,* Denver Art Museum, Frederic H Douglas Library, Denver CO

Goodridge, James, *Lectr,* University of Evansville, Art Dept, Evansville IN (S)

Goodridge, Laurence W, *Instructor,* Art Academy of Cincinnati, Cincinnati OH (S)

Goodspeed, Barbara, *First VPres,* Kent Art Association, Inc, Kent CT

Goodwin, Catherine L, *Pres,* Lowell Art Association, Whistler House and Parker Gallery, Lowell MA

Goodwin, David, *Asst Prof,* Coe College, Dept of Art, Cedar Rapids IA (S)

Goodwin, Deborah L, *Cur,* Cape Ann Historical Association, Gloucester MA

Goodwin, J, *Extension Officer,* Mendel Art Gallery and Civic Conservatory, Saskatoon SK

Goodwin, John, *Dir,* Art Metropole, Toronto ON

Goodyear, Frank H, *Pres,* Pennsylvania Academy of the Fine Arts, Galleries, Philadelphia PA

Goodyear, John, *Prof,* Rutgers, the State University of New Jersey, Mason Gross School of the Arts, New Brunswick NJ (S)

Goosey, Jim, *Construction Specialist,* Montana State University, Museum of the Rockies, Bozeman MT

Goossen, Eugene C, *Prof,* City University of New York, PhD Program in Art History, New York NY (S)

Gorder, Kenneth, *VChmn,* Nicolaysen Art Museum, Casper WY

Gordh, Bill, *Performance Coordr,* Franklin Furnace Archive, Inc, New York NY

Gordin, Sidney, *Prof,* University of California, Berkeley, College of Letters & Sciences, Berkeley CA (S)

Gordon, Albert C, *Head Dept,* Washington and Lee University, Dept of Fine Arts, Lexington VA (S)

Gordon, Albert C, *Dir,* Washington and Lee University, Gallery of DuPont Hall, Lexington VA

Gordon, Alden R, *Asst Prof,* Trinity College, Dept of Fine Arts, Hartford CT (S)

Gordon, Amorita, *Cur & Registrar,* Lauren Rogers Library and Museum of Art, Laurel MS

Gordon, Anne, *Women's VPres,* Art Students League of New York, New York NY

Gordon, Anne W, *Librn,* University of Pittsburgh, Henry Clay Frick Fine Arts Library, Pittsburgh PA

Gordon, Betsy, *Instr,* Patrick Henry State Junior College, Art Dept, Monroeville AL (S)

Gordon, Christina, *Admin Asst,* Beaumont Art Museum, Beaumont TX

Gordon, Dana, *Exec Dir of Bd,* Washington Women's Arts Center, Washington DC

Gordon, Geri, *Gallery Co-Dir,* Art League, Alexandria VA

Gordon, Glenn, *Public Relations,* University of Regina, Mackenzie Art Gallery, Regina SK

Gordon, G Lynn, *Chmn,* Radford University, Art Dept, Radford VA (S)

Gordon, Irene, *Lectr,* John Jay College of Criminal Justice, Dept of Art, Music and Philosophy, New York NY (S)

Gordon, John, *Instructor,* Sioux City Art Center, Sioux City IA (S)

Gordon, John S, *Dean,* University of Southern California, School of Fine Arts, Los Angeles CA (S)

Gordon, Joy L, *Dir,* Danforth Museum of Art, Framingham MA

Gordon, Lewis, *Asst Prof,* Saint Joseph's University, Fine Arts Dept, Philadelphia PA (S)

Gordon, Linda, *Public Relations Officer,* Whitney Museum of American Art, New York NY

Gordon, Martha, *Asst Prof,* Tarrant County Junior College, Art Dept, Northeast Campus, Hurst TX (S)

Gordon, Pat, *Member,* The Loading Dock Gallery, Boston MA

Gore, Jefferson A, *Cur Fine Arts,* Reading Public Museum and Art Gallery, Reading PA

Gore, Ken, *VPres,* North Shore Arts Association, Inc, Art Gallery, Gloucester MA

Gore, Kenneth L, *VPres,* Guild of Boston Artists, Boston MA

Gore, Michael, *Exec Dir,* Belle Grove Plantation, Middletown VA

Gore, Sam, *Head Dept,* Mississippi College, Art Dept, Clinton MS (S)

Gore, Tom, *Cur,* Open Space Gallery, Photography at Open Space, Victoria BC

Gorecki, Claudia M, *Prof,* Cardinal Stritch College, Art Dept, Milwaukee WI (S)

Goren, Nance, *Chairperson,* Junior College of Albany, Fine Arts Division, Albany NY (S)

Gorewitz, Rubin L, *Pres,* Organization of Independent Artists, New York NY

Goring, Kaui, *Secy,* Maui Historical Society, Hale Hoikeike, Wailuku HI

Gormally, Tom, *Asst Cur,* Wichita State University, Edwin A Ulrich Museum of Art, Wichita KS

Gorman, Bradford, *Asst to Dir,* Art Gallery of Hamilton, Hamilton ON

Gorman, James, *Assoc Prof,* Vincennes University, Art Dept, Vincennes IN (S)

Gorman, William D, *Dir,* Allied Artists of America, Inc, New York NY

Gorman, William D, *First VPres,* American Watercolor Society, New York NY

Gormley, Tom, *Instr,* University of Miami, Dept of Art & Art History, Coral Gables FL (S)

Gorove, Margaret, *Chmn,* University of Mississippi, Dept of Art, University MS (S)

Gorove, Margaret, *Dir,* University of Mississippi, University Gallery, University MS

Gorse, George, *Asst Prof,* Pomona College, Art Dept, Claremont CA (S)

Gorton, Tonda, *Arts Services Coordr,* Arizona Commission on the Arts, Phoenix AZ

Gosley, G S, *Dir,* Dartmouth Heritage Museum, Dartmouth NS

Gosner, Kenneth, *Cur Zoology,* Newark Museum, Newark NJ

Goss, James, *Dir of Museums & Cur Ethnology,* Texas Tech University Museum, Lubbock TX

Goss, Jeff, *Lectr,* Johnson State College, Dept Fine Arts, Johnson VT (S)

Gostin, Arlene, *Chairperson Educ,* Philadelphia College of Art, Philadelphia PA (S)

Gotlob, Mark, *Assoc Dir & Admin,* State Art Museum of Florida, John & Mable Ringling Museum of Art, Sarasota FL

Gott, Wesley A, *Chmn,* Southwest Baptist University, Art Dept, Bolivar MO (S)

Gottlieb, Gerald, *Cur Early Chldren's Books,* Pierpont Morgan Library, New York NY

Gottschalk, Roger, *Chmn,* University of Wisconsin-Platteville, Dept of Fine Art, Platteville WI (S)

Gottselig, Len, *Librn,* Glenbow Museum, Library, Calgary AB

Gottwald, Bruce C, *Pres,* Virginia Museum of Fine Arts, Richmond VA

Goudie, Harland J, *Chmn,* Knox College, Dept of Art, Galesburg IL (S)

Goudreault, Sylvain, *Tech Dir,* Centre Cultural de Shawinigan, Shawinigan PQ

Goughnour, David, *Instructor,* Iowa Lakes Community College, Dept of Art, Estherville IA (S)

Gould, Philip, *Faculty,* Sarah Lawrence College, Dept of Art, Bronxville NY (S)

Goulette, Michele, *Extension Cur,* Art Gallery of Windsor, Windsor ON

Gouma-Peterson, Thalia, *Prof,* College of Wooster, Dept of Art, Wooster OH (S)

Gourentech, Jacqueline, *Asst Prof,* Wesleyan University, Art Dept, Middletown CT (S)

Gourley, Hugh J, *Dir,* Colby Museum of Art, Waterville ME

Govier, Victor M, *Exhib Program Dir,* Anacostia Neighborhood Museum, Washington DC

Gowans, Alan, *Prof,* University of Victoria, Dept of History in Art, Victoria BC (S)

Gower, Dorothy, *VPres,* Vernon Art Association, Topham Brown Gallery, Vernon BC

Graber, Oileg, *Aga Khan Prof Islamic Art,* Harvard University, Dept of Fine Arts, Cambridge MA (S)

Graburn, Richard K, *Dir,* University of Calgary, The Nickle Arts Museum, Calgary AB

Grado, Angelo John, *Pres,* American Artists Professional League, Inc, New York NY

Grady, Dennis, *Vis Asst Prof,* University of Southern California, School of Fine Arts, Los Angeles CA (S)

Grady, Marguerite, *Asst Librn,* Stanford University, Art Library, Stanford CA

Graeser, James, *1st VChmn Bd,* Coos Art Museum, Coos Bay OR

Graff, Leslie F, *Dir Visual Arts,* Department of Culture, Government of the Province of Alberta, Beaver House Gallery, Edmonton AB

Graff, Terry, *Education Cur,* Art Gallery of Windsor, Windsor ON

Graft, James, *Dir of Educ,* Colorado Institute of Art, Denver CO (S)

Graham, Anne, *Coordr Jewelry,* University of Delaware, Dept of Art, Newark DE (S)

Graham, Conrad, *Registrar,* McGill University, McCord Museum, Montreal PQ

Graham, Douglas, *Pres & Treas,* The Turner Museum, Denver CO

Graham, Edward W, *Cur & Dir,* Audubon Wildlife Sanctuary, Audubon PA

Graham, Henry B, *Assoc Prof,* Trinity University, Dept of Art, San Antonio TX (S)

Graham, Hugh C, *VPres,* United States Figure Skating Hall of Fame and Museum, Colorado Springs CO

Graham, Julie, *Executive Member,* 22 Wooster Gallery, New York NY

Graham, Mark, *Instructor,* State University of New York College at Cortland, Art Dept, Cortland NY (S)

Graham, Mary E, *Librn,* Heard Museum, Library, Phoenix AZ

Graham, Michael Tom, *Chmn Dept,* American University, Dept of Art, Washington DC (S)

Graham, Robert, *Instructor,* Virginia Tech, Dept of Art, Blacksburg VA (S)

Graham, Robert, *Adjunct Prof,* University of Saint Thomas, Art Dept, Houston TX (S)

Grainger, Nessa, *Pres,* New Jersey Watercolor Society, South Orange NJ

Gralapp, Marcelee, *Library Dir,* Boulder Public Library and Gallery, Dept of Fine Arts Gallery, Boulder CO

Gramberg, Liliana, *Head Dept & Prof,* Trinity College, Art Dept, Washington DC (S)

Gramer, Kevin, *Asst Dir & Cur,* Dacotah Prairie Museum, Lamont Gallery, Aberdeen SD

Granata, Angelo, *Dir,* University of Alabama, Moody Gallery of Art, University AL

Granata, Angelo, *Prof,* University of Alabama, Art Dept, Tuscaloosa AL (S)

Granda, Julio, *Asst Prof,* Berkshire Community College, Dept Fine Arts, Pittsfield MA (S)

Grandy, Stuart, *Pres,* Arts and Crafts Association of Meriden Inc, Gallery, Meriden CT

Granne, Regina, *Instructor,* Bard College, Milton Avery Graduate School of the Arts, Annandale-on-Hudson NY (S)

Grant, Carol, *Secy,* Octagon Center for the Arts, Ames IA

Grant, Charles, *Dir,* Sunbury Shores Arts and Nature Centre, Inc, Saint Andrews NB
Grant, Ellsworth, *VPres,* Stowe-Day Foundation, Hartford CT
Grant, Ford A, *Dir,* Thomas College Gallery, Waterville ME
Grant, Frank R, *Dir,* Fort Missoula Historical Museum, Missoula MT
Grant, Geraldine, *Animator,* Galerie Restigouche Gallery, Campbellton NB
Grant, Gregor, *Actg Head Restoration & Conservation Lab,* National Gallery of Canada, Ottawa ON
Grant, J, *Instr,* St Francis Xavier University, Fine Arts Dept, Antigonish NS (S)
Grant, Jerry V, *Dir,* Hancock Shaker Village, Inc, Pittsfield MA
Grant, Susan K, *Instructor,* Texas Woman's University, Dept of Art, Denton TX (S)
Granzow, Carl, *Assoc Prof,* University of Lethbridge, Dept of Art, Lethbridge AB (S)
Grasso, Mary Ann, *Dir,* Burbank Public Library, Warner Research Collection, Burbank CA
Grattan, Patricia, *Cur,* Memorial University of Newfoundland, Art Gallery, Saint John's NF
Graubart, Maria K, *Librn,* Currier Gallery of Art, Library, Manchester NH
Graves, Jane, *Fine Arts Librn,* Skidmore College, Lucy Scribner Library, Saratoga Springs NY
Graves, K, *Instructor,* Grand Canyon College, Art Dept, Phoenix AZ (S)
Graves, Robert, *Instructor,* Wenatchee Valley College, Art Dept, Wenatchee WA (S)
Gravis, Betty, *VPres,* Marian Osborne Cunningham Art Gallery, Bakersfield CA
Gray, Carol, *Pres,* Council of Delaware Artists, Newark DE
Gray, Corbett, *Instr,* Southampton Art School, Southampton ON (S)
Gray, David, *Adjunct Prof,* University of Saint Thomas, Art Dept, Houston TX (S)
Gray, Deborah, *Lectr,* California State Polytechnic University, Pomona, Art Dept, Pomona CA (S)
Gray, Donald, *Asst Dir,* University of Northern Iowa, Art and Music Section Library, Cedar Falls IA
Gray, Donald F, *Chmn,* Community College of Rhode Island, Art Department Gallery, Warwick RI
Gray, Donald F, *Chmn,* Community College of Rhode Island, Dept of Art, Warwick RI (S)
Gray, Lorena, *Secy,* Paint 'N Palette Club, Anamosa IA
Gray, Marlene, *Publicity Dir,* Museum of Our National Heritage, Lexington MA
Gray, Noel, *Prof,* Chadron State College, Division of Fine Arts, Chadron NE (S)
Gray, Patsy E, *Librn,* Huntsville Museum of Art, Reference Library, Huntsville AL
Gray, Phyllis A, *Chief Librn,* Miami Beach Public Library, Miami Beach FL
Gray, Robert, *Pres,* Prescott Fine Arts Association, Prescott AZ
Gray, Suzanne, *VPres,* Chautauqua Art Association Galleries, Chautauqua NY
Gray Nelson, Jane, *Librn,* Fine Arts Museums of San Francisco, Library, San Francisco CA
Grayson, Helen, *Pres,* Main Line Center of the Arts, Haverford PA
Grayson, Marion, *Asst Prof,* Rice University, Dept of Art and Art History, Houston TX (S)
Graze, Sue, *Assoc Cur Contemporary Art,* Dallas Museum of Fine Arts, Dallas TX
Grazier, Deborah Davis, *Admin Asst,* Southern Alleghenies Museum of Art, Loretto PA
Greathouse, W S, *Pres & Dir,* Charles and Emma Frye Art Museum, Seattle WA
Greeley, Elizabeth, *Secy,* New Haven Paint and Clay Club, Inc, New Haven CT
Greeley, Mary, *Dir,* Oregon School of Arts and Crafts, Portland OR
Greeley, Mary, *Executive Dir,* Oregon School of Arts and Crafts, Hoffman Gallery, Portland OR
Green, Alfred E, *Assoc Prof,* Texas Woman's University, Dept of Art, Denton TX (S)
Green, Allan, *Dept Head,* Union College, Art Dept, Barbourville KY (S)

Green, Art, *Asst Prof,* University of Waterloo, Fine Arts Dept, Waterloo ON (S)
Green, Brent, *Head Dept,* Abilene Christian University, Art Dept, Abilene TX (S)
Green, Charles, *Dir,* Museum of Cartoon Art, Port Chester NY
Green, Elwood, *Museum Dir,* Native American Center for the Living Arts, Niagara Falls NY
Green, Frank L, *Librn,* Washington State Historical Society, Hewitt Memorial Library, Tacoma WA
Green, Harriet, *Registrar,* Columbia Museums of Art and Science, Columbia SC
Green, James, *Cur of Printed Books,* Library Company of Philadelphia, Dept of Art, Philadelphia PA
Green, Jane Whipple, *Dir,* Federated Art Associations of New Jersey, Inc, Westfield NJ
Green, John T, *Pres,* Lafayette Natural History Museum, Planetarium and Nature Station, Lafayette LA
Green, Jonathan, *Dir,* Ohio State University, Gallery of Fine Art, Columbus OH
Green, Kathleen, *Public Relations,* Whatcom Museum of History and Art, Bellingham WA
Green, Lane, *Dir,* Tallahassee Junior Museum, Tallahassee FL
Green, Lila, *Instr,* Danforth Museum School, Framingham MA (S)
Green, Michael, *Admin,* The Phillips Collection, Washington DC
Green, Michael, *Assoc Prof,* College of Southern Idaho, Art Dept, Twin Falls ID (S)
Green, Mike, *Gallery Dir,* College of Southern Idaho, Art Gallery, Twin Falls ID
Green, Nancy W, *Librn,* American Numismatic Association Museum, Library, Colorado Springs CO
Green, Peter, *Pres,* Southern Alberta Art Gallery, Lethbridge AB
Green, Phil, *Chmn Filmmaking Dept,* San Francisco Art Institute, San Francisco CA (S)
Green, Richard, *Instr,* John C Calhoun State Community College, Art Dept, Decatur AL (S)
Green, Richard, *Cur,* John C Calhoun State Community College, Art Gallery, Decatur AL
Green, Rowland, *Treas,* Prince George Art Gallery, Prince George BC
Green, Stanley, *Instructor,* Harding University, Dept of Art, Searcy AR (S)
Green, Wilder, *Dir,* The American Federation of Arts, New York NY
Green, Wilder, *VPres,* The Drawing Society, New York NY
Greenberg, Deborah J, *Public Affairs Coordr,* Solomon R Guggenheim Museum, New York NY
Greenberg, Ted A, *Registrar,* Judah L Magnes Museum, Berkeley CA
Greenbert, Pearl, *Instr Art Educ,* Kean College of New Jersey, Fine Arts Dept, Union NJ (S)
Greene, Adele, *Vice Chmn,* American Craft Council, New York NY
Greene, Anne, *Dir,* Art Association School, Spartanburg SC (S)
Greene, Brant, *Program Dir,* Saint Cloud State University, Atwood Center Gallery Lounge, Saint Cloud MN
Greene, Casey, *Dir Libr & Archives,* Dallas Historical Society, Dallas TX
Greene, D, *Admin Mgr,* Association of Collegiate Schools of Architecture, Washington DC
Greene, James, *VPres,* Burlington County Historical Society, Burlington NJ
Greene, Jane Fackler, *Head,* Birmingham Public Library, Art and Music Department, Birmingham AL
Greene, J Craig, *Chmn,* Meredith College, Art Dept, Raleigh NC (S)
Greene, Jon S, *Head Librn,* University of California, Los Angeles, Architecture and Urban Planning Library, Los Angeles CA
Greene, Judith, *Exec Secy,* Lizzadro Museum of Lapidary Art, Elmhurst IL
Greene, Ryland W, *Prof,* Cedar Crest College, Art Dept, Allentown PA (S)
Greene, Stephen, *Prof,* Temple University, Tyler School of Art, Philadelphia PA (S)

Greenebaum, Karen, *Asst Prof,* Texas Tech University, Dept of Art, Lubbock TX (S)
Greenfeather, Randy, *Exec Dir,* The Indian Museum, Wichita KS
Greenfield, Gerald, *Chairperson Photography & Film,* Philadelphia College of Art, Philadelphia PA (S)
Greenfield, Joan A, *Instr,* Woodbury University, Professional Arts Division, Los Angeles CA (S)
Greenfield, Sylvia R, *Assoc Prof,* Southern Illinois University, School of Art, Carbondale IL (S)
Greenfield, Valerie, *Cur,* Alberta College of Art Gallery, Calgary AB
Greenhill, Sharon, *Dir Planning,* Laguna Gloria Art Museum, Austin TX
Greenleaf, Floyd, *Chmn Arts & Letters,* Southern Missionary College, Art Dept, Collegedale TN (S)
Greenlee, Jean, *Interim Dir,* Fort Wayne Fine Arts Foundation, Inc, Fort Wayne IN
Greenquist, Steven, *Asst Prof,* Augusta College, Dept of Fine Arts, Augusta GA (S)
Greenspan, Sheila, *Education & Extension Officer,* Art Gallery of Hamilton, Hamilton ON
Greenwold, Mark, *Assoc Prof,* State University of New York at Albany, Art Dept, Albany NY (S)
Greenwood, Bette, *Instr,* Wayne Art Center, Wayne PA (S)
Greenwood, David, *Program Dir,* Oxbow Center for the Arts, Saugatuck MI (S)
Greenwood, Louise, *Asst,* York University, Art Gallery, Downsview ON
Greenwood, Michael, *Cur of Art,* York University, Art Gallery, Downsview ON
Greenwood, William, *Instr,* Wayne Art Center, Wayne PA (S)
Greenwood, William, *Instructor,* Woodstock School of Art, Inc, New York NY (S)
Greer, Dwaine, *Coordr Art Educ,* University of Arizona, Dept of Art, Tucson AZ (S)
Greer, Joy, *In Charge Art Coll & Program,* First Commercial Bank in Little Rock, Little Rock AR
Gregerman, Marjorie, *Asst Prof,* Johns Hopkins University, School of Medicine, Dept of Art as Applied to Medicine, Baltimore MD (S)
Gregersen, Thomas, *Asst Cur,* Palm Beach County Parks and Recreation Department, Morikami Museum of Japanese Culture, Delray Beach FL
Gregg, Richard N, *Dir,* Allentown Art Museum, Allentown PA
Gregorian, Vartan, *Pres,* New York Public Library, New York NY
Gregory, Eleann Ann, *Asst Prof,* West Texas State University, Art Dept, Canyon TX (S)
Gregory, Fred, *Instructor,* Atlanta College of Art, Atlanta GA (S)
Gregory, G W, *Pres,* Skaneateles Library Association, Skaneateles NY
Gregory, Joan, *Head,* University of North Carolina at Greensboro, Art Dept, Greensboro NC (S)
Gregory, Lynn, *Rentals Coordinator,* Sangre De Cristo Arts & Conference Center, Pueblo CO
Gregory, Rona, *Coll Librn,* Massachusetts Institute of Technology, Rotch Library of Architecture and Planning, Cambridge MA
Greh, Bill, *Instructor,* Montclair Art Museum, Museum Art Classes, Montclair NJ (S)
Greimel, Karl H, *Dean,* Lawrence Institute of Technology, School of Architecture, Southfield MI (S)
Greischar, Donna, *Pres of Board,* Oshkosh Public Museum, Oshkosh WI
Greisinger, Pamela, *Instructor,* Daytona Beach Community College, Dept of Performing and Visual Arts, Daytona Beach FL (S)
Grennan, Joan, *Friends of the Art Gallery Exec Dir,* Vassar College Art Gallery, Poughkeepsie NY
Grenwis, Martina, *Secy,* Cleveland Museum of Art, Print Club of Cleveland, Cleveland OH
Greogry, Diane, *Asst Prof,* Murray State University, Art Dept, Murray KY (S)
Grese, David F, *Faculty,* Idaho State University, Dept of Art, Pocatello ID (S)
Gresham, Paul A, *Instructor,* Oklahoma State University, Graphic Arts Dept, Okmulgee OK (S)

Greyman, Marcia, *Gallery Dir,* Lexington Public Library, Skydome Gallery, Lexington KY

Gribbon, Deborah, *Cur,* Isabella Stewart Gardner Museum, Boston MA

Griffin, Anita, *Instructor,* The Design Schools, Art Institute of Seattle, Seattle WA (S)

Griffin, Dan W, *Dir,* Meridian Museum of Art, Meridian MS

Griffin, Fred, *Instructor,* The Design Schools, Art Institute of Seattle, Seattle WA (S)

Griffin, Gary, *Assoc Prof,* Rochester Institute of Technology, School for American Craftsmen, Rochester NY (S)

Griffin, John T, *Pres,* Five Civilized Tribes Museum, Muskogee OK

Griffin, Linda, *Picture Specialist,* San Diego Public Library, Art & Music Section, San Diego CA

Griffin, Linda, *Bookmobile Librn,* Mexico-Audrain County Library, Mexico MO

Griffin, Penny, *Asst Prof,* Salem College, Art Dept, Winston-Salem NC (S)

Griffin, Tommy L, *Designer-Preparator,* University of Oregon, Museum of Art, Eugene OR

Griffis, Larry L, *Dir,* Bethany College, Birger Sandzen Memorial Gallery, Lindsborg KS

Griffith, Debbie, *Display Coordr,* Kelowna Centennial Museum and National Exhibit Centre, Kelowna BC

Griffith, Dennison W, *Exec Dir,* The Ohio Foundation on the Arts, Inc, Columbus OH

Griffith, Fuller O, *Asst Prof,* George Washington University, Dept of Art, Washington DC (S)

Griffith, Julius, *Pres,* Canadian Society of Painters in Watercolour, Toronto ON

Griffith, Marion, *Gallery Dir,* Sculpture Center Gallery & School, New York NY (S)

Griffith, Robert, *Asst Prof,* University of Lowell, Dept of Art, Lowell MA (S)

Griffith, Roberta, *Chmn,* Hartwick College, Art Dept, Oneonta NY (S)

Griffith, Sheryl, *Catalog Librn,* Franklin D Roosevelt Library and Museum, Library, Hyde Park NY

Griffith, Thomas, *Instr,* California State University, Chico, Art Dept, Chico CA (S)

Grigsby, Robert E, *Pres,* Rehoboth Art League, Inc, Rehoboth Beach DE

Grill-Sferlazzo, Tina, *Coordr Patrons & Friends,* Brandeis University, Rose Art Museum, Waltham MA

Grima, Kathleen P, *Executive Dir,* Red River Valley Museum, Vernon TX

Grimald, Mary Ellen, *Historic Site Asst,* Schuyler Mansion State Historic Site, Albany NY

Grimes, William C, *Gallery Asst,* Indiana University - Purdue University at Indianapolis, Herron School of Art Gallery, Indianapolis IN

Grimm, Albert, *VPres,* Spirit of '76 Museum, Southern Lorain County Historical Society, Wellington OH

Grimm, Amy, *Shop Asst,* Madison Art Center, Madison WI

Grimm, Raymond, *Prof,* Portland State University, Dept of Art and Architecture, Portland OR (S)

Grinnell, Nancy W, *Librn,* Art Complex Museum at Duxbury, Library, Duxbury MA

Grippi, Salvatore, *Prof,* Ithaca College, Fine Art Dept, Ithaca NY (S)

Grissom, Eugene E, *Prof,* University of Florida, Dept of Art, Gainesville FL (S)

Griswold, A B, *Pres,* Breezewood Foundation Museum and Garden, Monkton MD

Griswold, Scott, *Instr,* Ocean City Arts Center, Ocean City NJ (S)

Grittner, James, *Prof,* University of Wisconsin-Superior, Programs in the Visual Arts, Superior WI (S)

Grizzell, Kenneth, *Prof,* University of South Dakota, Dept of Art, Vermillion SD (S)

Groble, K, *VPres,* Society of Typographic Arts, Chicago IL

Groce, Susan, *Asst Prof,* University of Maine, Art Dept, Orono ME (S)

Groch, Marilyn, *Admin Asst,* Beyond Baroque Foundation, Venice CA

Groff, John, *Registrar,* Philadelphia Maritime Museum, Philadelphia PA

Grogan, Kevin, *Dir Fine Arts Ctr,* Tennessee Botanical Gardens and Fine Arts Center, Education Dept, Nashville TN (S)

Grogan, Kevin, *Dir Fine Arts Center,* Tennessee Botanical Gardens and Fine Arts Center, Inc, Nashville TN

Gronberg, Erli, *Asst Prof Interior Design,* Kendall School of Design, Grand Rapids MI (S)

Groome, Les, *Secy General,* Canadian Society for Education Through Art, Toronto ON

Grootkerk, Paul, *Asst Prof,* Mississippi State University, Art Dept, Mississippi State MS (S)

Grosch, William E, *Assoc Prof,* Clarion University of Pennsylvania, Dept of Art, Clarion PA (S)

Grose, Virginia M, *VPres,* South Carolina National Bank, Columbia SC

Gross, Chaim, *Treasurer,* Sculptors Guild, Inc, New York NY

Gross, Charles M, *Prof,* University of Mississippi, Dept of Art, University MS (S)

Gross, Kenneth R, *Dir,* Birmingham-Bloomfield Art Association, Birmingham MI

Gross, Kenneth R, *Executive Dir,* Birmingham-Bloomfield Art Association, Birmingham MI (S)

Gross, Laurence F, *Cur,* Merrimack Valley Textile Museum, North Andover MA

Gross, Louis, *Prof,* Glendale College, Dept of Fine Arts, Glendale CA (S)

Gross, Margarete K, *Picture Coll Librn,* Chicago Public Library, Art Section, Fine Arts Division, Chicago IL

Gross, Sandra, *Cur,* Atwater Kent Museum, Philadelphia PA

Grossberg, Jacob, *Instructor,* Bard College, Milton Avery Graduate School of the Arts, Annandale-on-Hudson NY (S)

Grossman, Albert G, *Asst Dir Operations & Finance,* Cleveland Museum of Art, Cleveland OH

Grossman, Audley M, *Cur Performing Arts,* Detroit Institute of Arts, Detroit MI

Grossman, Barbara, *Lectr,* Tunxis Community College, Graphic Design Dept, Farmington CT (S)

Grossman, Gilda S, *Senior Art Therapist,* Toronto Art Therapy Institute, Toronto ON (S)

Grossman, Oscar, *Treas,* Southern California Contemporary Art Galleries of the Los Angeles Art Association, Los Angeles CA

Grossman, Sheldon, *Cur Northern & Later Italian Painting,* National Gallery of Art, Washington DC

Grosvenor, Walter, *Assoc Prof,* Whitworth College, Art Dept, Spokane WA (S)

Grote, Mark, *Chmn,* Loyola University of New Orleans, Dept of Visual Arts, New Orleans LA (S)

Grove, Belle, *Pres,* Belle Grove Plantation, Middletown VA

Grove, Jerome L, *Pres,* Center for Creative Studies__College of Art and Design, Detroit MI (S)

Growdon, Marcia Cohn, *Dir,* Sierra Nevada Museum of Art, Reno NV

Growe, Bruce, *Asst Prof,* University of Alabama, Art Dept, Tuscaloosa AL (S)

Grubar, Francis S, *Prof,* George Washington University, Dept of Art, Washington DC (S)

Grube, Dick Dewayne, *Dir,* National Infantry Museum, Fort Benning GA

Grubel, Fred, *Exec Dir,* Leo Baeck Institute, New York NY

Gruber, Doris, *Periodicals,* Trinity College Library, Washington DC

Gruber, Richard, *Lectr,* Southwestern at Memphis, Dept of Art, Memphis TN (S)

Gruenwald, Larry, *Technician,* University of Minnesota, Tweed Museum of Art, Duluth MN

Grum, Franc, *Richard S Hunter Prof,* Rochester Institute of Technology, School of Photographic Arts & Sciences, Rochester NY (S)

Grunberg, Stephanie, *Cur of Education,* Rutgers University, Jane Voorhees Zimmerli Art Museum, New Brunswick NJ

Grundy, J Owen, *Pres,* Jersey City Museum Association, Jersey City NJ

Grunebaum, Gabriele H, *VPres,* Ukiyo-e Society of America, Inc, New York NY

Gruner, Charles J, *Dir Lecture & Demonstration Service,* American Society of Artists, Inc, Chicago IL

Grunewald, Max, *Pres,* Leo Baeck Institute, New York NY

Gruninger, Pamela, *Dir,* Whitney Museum of American Art, Fairfield County, Stamford CT

Grupp, Carl A, *Assoc Prof,* Augustana College, Art Dept, Sioux Falls SD (S)

Grusheski, Edward, *Cur Education,* Museum of the Philadelphia Civic Center, Philadelphia PA

Guadagno, Carmelo, *Photographer,* Solomon R Guggenheim Museum, New York NY

Gualtieri, Gregory, *Registrar of Collections,* Southern Oregon Historical Society, Jacksonville Museum, Jacksonville OR

Gualtieri, Joseph P, *Dir,* Norwich Free Academy, Slater Memorial Museum & Converse Art Gallery, Norwich CT

Guarisco, Molly, *Secy,* University of New Orleans, Fine Arts Gallery, New Orleans LA

Gubelmann, Walter S, *Pres,* Society of the Four Arts, Palm Beach FL

Gudmundsen, F Tor, *Instructor,* Woodstock School of Art, Inc, New York NY (S)

Guenther, Bruce, *Assoc Cur,* Seattle Art Museum, Modern Art Pavilion, Seattle WA

Guenthler, John R, *Assoc Prof,* Indiana University Southeast, Fine Arts Dept, New Albany IN (S)

Guerin, Charles, *Cur Fine Arts Coll & Exhib,* Colorado Springs Fine Arts Center, Colorado Springs CO

Guernsey, David T, *Exec Dir,* Ships of The Sea Museum, Savannah GA

Guerra, Mary Ellen, *Research Assoc, Art Theft Archive,* International Foundation for Art Research, Inc, New York NY

Guertin, Joseph, *Instructor,* Portland School of Art, Portland ME (S)

Guest, Tim, *Cur,* Art Metropole, Toronto ON

Guest, Tim, *Archivist,* Art Metropole, Library, Toronto ON

Guffin, Raymond L, *Assoc Prof,* Stillman College, Stillman Art Gallery and Art Dept, Tuscaloosa AL (S)

Guglielmo, Cindy, *Admin Asst,* Woodrow Wilson House, Washington DC

Guheen, Elizabeth, *Dir,* Montana State University, Fine Arts Gallery, Bozeman MT

Guilbaut, Serge, *Asst Prof,* University of British Columbia, Dept of Fine Arts, Vancouver BC (S)

Guild, Rebecca A, *Mgr,* Gibson Society, Inc, Gibson House Museum, Boston MA

Guilfoile, William J, *Public Relations,* National Baseball Hall of Fame and Museum, Inc, Art Collection, Cooperstown NY

Guillaume, Harry, *Emeritus Prof,* University of Northern Iowa, Dept of Art, Cedar Falls IA (S)

Guillermety, Jose Buscaglia, *Instructor,* University of Puerto Rico, Dept of Fine Arts, Rio Piedras PR (S)

Guilmain, Jacques, *Prof,* State University of New York at Stony Brook, Art Dept, Stony Brook NY (S)

Guip, David, *Faculty,* University of Toledo, Dept of Art, Art Education and Art History, Toledo OH (S)

Guiwits, Bruce, *Instruct,* Blue Mountain Community College, Fine Arts Dept, Pendleton OR (S)

Gulbranson, Rex, *Visual Arts Coordr,* Arizona Commission on the Arts, Phoenix AZ

Guldin, Mark F, *Dean,* Rochester Institute of Technology, College of Graphic Arts and Photography, Rochester NY (S)

Gulkin, Harry, *Executive Dir,* Saidye Bronfman Centre, Montreal PQ

Gummere, Judy, *Circulation Head,* Lake Forest Library, Fine Art Dept, Lake Forest IL

Gumz, Kimberlie, *Librn,* University of Notre Dame, Catalog Library, Notre Dame IN

Gunasinghe, Siri, *Prof,* University of Victoria, Dept of History in Art, Victoria BC (S)

Gunderson, Barry, *Chmn,* Kenyon College, Art Dept, Gambier OH (S)

Gunderson, Jeff, *Librn*, San Francisco Art Institute, Anne Bremer Memorial Library, San Francisco CA

Gunn, Steve, *Supt of Grounds*, University of North Carolina at Greensboro, Chinqua-Penn Plantation House, Reidsville NC

Gunnion, Vernon S, *Cur Collections*, Pennsylvania Farm Museum of Landis Valley, Lancaster PA

Gunter, Frank, *In Charge Painting*, University of Illinois, Urbana-Champaign, School of Art and Design, Champaign IL (S)

Gunter, Maynard, *Asst Prof*, University of Northern Iowa, Dept of Art, Cedar Falls IA (S)

Gunther, Charles F, *Dir Education*, Toledo Museum of Art, Toledo OH

Gunther, Charles F, *Asst Dir*, Toledo Museum of Art, School of Design, Toledo OH (S)

Guraedy, J Bruce, *Head Dept*, East Central Junior College, Art Dept, Decatur MS (S)

Gurney, Susan, *Asst Librn*, National Museum of American Art, Library of the National Museum of American Art and the National Portrait Gallery, Washington DC

Gurr, Steve, *Chmn*, Georgia Southwestern College, Art Dept, Americus GA (S)

Gury, Albert, *Instr*, Mainline Center of the Arts, Haverford PA (S)

Guske, Jennifer, *Instructor*, Marylhurst College, Art Dept, Marylhurst OR (S)

Gusman, Annie, *Chmn Illustration Dept*, Art Institute of Boston, Boston MA (S)

Gussow, Roy, *VPres*, New York Artists Equity Association, Inc, New York NY

Gussow, Roy, *Adjunct Prof*, Columbia University, School of the Arts, Division of Painting & Sculpture, New York NY (S)

Gustafson, Dwight, *Dean*, Bob Jones University, School of Fine Arts, Greenville SC (S)

Gustafson, Louise, *Pres*, Arts Council of the Mid-Columbia Region, Richland WA

Gustafson, R David, *Chmn*, Rock Valley College, Dept of Art, Rockford IL (S)

Gustavson, Robert E, *Executive Dir*, Corporate Council for the Arts, Seattle WA

Gustin, Mickey, *Actg Exec Dir*, King County Arts Commission, Seattle WA

Gustow, Hazel, *Library Dir*, Philadelphia College of Art, Library, Philadelphia PA

Gutekunst, B, *Head Humanities Division*, Catholic University of America, Humanities Division, Mullen Library, Washington DC

Gutenschwager, Mary, *Chmn*, Saint Louis University, Art & Art History Dept, Saint Louis MO (S)

Guthman, Sandra, *Pres*, Art Institute of Chicago, Society for Contemporary Arts, Chicago IL

Guthrie, Jill, *Publication Ed*, Princeton University, Art Museum, Princeton NJ

Guthrie-McNaughton, Isabella, *Librn*, Royal Ontario Museum, Library, Toronto ON

Gutierrez, Armando, *Pres*, Committee for Hispanic Arts & Research, Austin TX

Gutridge, Delbert R, *Registrar*, Cleveland Museum of Art, Cleveland OH

Gutterman, Sue, *AV Coordr*, Saint Mary's College, Cushwa-Leighton Library, Notre Dame IN

Guy, Phyllis, *Cur*, Henry Morrison Flagler Museum, Palm Beach FL

Guzman, Diane, *Librn*, Brooklyn Museum, Wilbour Library of Egyptology, Brooklyn NY

Gwinn, John, *Instr*, Mainline Center of the Arts, Haverford PA (S)

Haag, John, *Pres*, Ojai Valley Art Center, Ojai CA

Haak, Lori, *Secy*, Madison Art Center, Madison WI

Haarer, Ann, *Chmn Dept*, College of Saint Elizabeth, Art Dept, Convent Station NJ (S)

Haas, Charles W, *Asst Prof*, Monroe Community College, Art Dept, Rochester NY (S)

Haas, Edward F, *Chief Cur*, Louisiana Department of Culture, Recreation and Tourism, Louisiana Historical Center Library, New Orleans LA

Haas, Elizabeth, *Pres*, The Greenwich Art Society Inc, Greenwich CT

Haas, Pauline, *Prof*, Whitworth College, Art Dept, Spokane WA (S)

Haber, Mortimer N, *Dir*, Haber School of Sculpture, Roslyn NY (S)

Haberland, Jody, *Head*, Arlington County Department of Public Libraries, Fine Arts Section, Arlington VA

Haberman, David, *Assoc Prof*, Cuyahoga Community College, Dept of Art, Cleveland OH (S)

Haberman, Lynne Allen, *Tamarind Master Printer & Studio Mgr*, University of New Mexico, Tamarind Institute, Albuquerque NM (S)

Habershaw, David, *VPres*, Bristol Art Museum, Bristol RI

Habst, Gail J, *Communications Officer*, Visual Arts Ontario, Toronto ON

Hachey, Paul A, *Asst Cur*, Beaverbrook Art Gallery, Fredericton NB

Hachey, Vivian, *Sales Mgr*, New Brunswick Museum, Saint John NB

Hack, Janet S, *Graphics Designer*, Hall of Fame of the Trotter, Goshen NY

Hack, Rosalinda I, *Chief Fine Arts Division*, Chicago Public Library, Art Section, Fine Arts Division, Chicago IL

Hacker, Robert G, *Paul & Louise Miller Prof*, Rochester Institute of Technology, School of Printing, Rochester NY (S)

Hacker, Susan, *Asst Prof*, Webster College, Art Dept, Webster Groves MO (S)

Hackett, Joan, *Art Education Cur*, Museum of Art, Science and Industry, Bridgeport CT

Hackley, Martha, *Mgr Sales & Info*, Frick Collection, New York NY

Hackman, Deanna, *Secy*, Conejo Valley Art Museum, Thousand Oaks CA

Hackstead, Carmon, *Cur*, Grande Prairie College Gallery, Grande Prairie AB

Haddah, Farid A, *Asst Prof*, New England College, Visual Arts Dept, Henniker NH (S)

Haddaway, William R, *Art Librn*, Dallas Public Library, Fine Arts Division, Dallas TX

Hadley, Rollin van N, *Dir*, Isabella Stewart Gardner Museum, Boston MA

Hadson, Carol J, *Public Information*, Schenectady Museum, Schenectady NY

Hadwin, Millie, *Dir*, Ella Sharp Museum, Jackson MI

Hadzi, Martha Leeb, *Prof*, Mount Holyoke College, Art Dept, South Hadley MA (S)

Haff, Elizebeth, *Cur*, Brockton Art Museum, Brockton MA

Haffner, Gloria, *VPres*, DuPage Art League, Wheaton IL

Hafif, Marcia, *Faculty*, Sarah Lawrence College, Dept of Art, Bronxville NY (S)

Hagan, Jane, *Librn*, Brand Library and Art Center, Glendale CA

Hagan, Kay, *Instructor*, Saint Louis Community College at Meramec, Art Dept, Saint Louis MO (S)

Hagelberger, Richard, *Assoc Prof*, Wittenberg University, Art Dept, Springfield OH (S)

Hageman, Lee, *Chmn Dept Art*, Northwest Missouri State University, DeLuce Gallery, Maryville MO

Hageman, Lee, *Chmn Dept*, Northwest Missouri State University, Dept of Art, Maryville MO (S)

Hagen, Gary, *Assoc Prof*, University of Wisconsin-Stevens Point, Dept of Art, Stevens Point WI (S)

Hager, Hellmut, *Head Dept Art History*, Pennsylvania State University, University Park, College of Arts and Architecture, University Park PA (S)

Hager, Michael W, *Dir*, Montana State University, Museum of the Rockies, Bozeman MT

Hagerbaumer, Ruby, *Curatorial Asst*, Joslyn Art Museum, Omaha NE

Hagerman, Carol, *VPres*, DuPage Art League, Wheaton IL

Hagerty, Harriet M, *Recording Secy*, Pen and Brush, Inc, New York NY

Haggerstone, Wyn, *Dir*, Revelstoke Art Group, Revelstoke BC

Haggerty, Gerard, *Dir Visual Arts Program*, Bowdoin College, Art Dept, Brunswick ME (S)

Hagler, Michael, *Cur Exhibitions & Designs*, Atkins Museum of Fine Art, Kansas City MO

Haglich, Bianca, *Prof*, Marymount College, Art Dept, Tarrytown NY (S)

Hagloch, Jenny, *Cur*, Salem Art Association, Salem OR

Hagy, Ruth K, *Cur*, Chester County Historical Society, West Chester PA

Hahn, Cynthia J, *Asst Prof*, Florida State University, Art History Dept, Tallahassee FL (S)

Hahn, Elisabeth L, *Asst Registrar*, Independent Curators Incorporated, New York NY

Haight, Donald A, *Pres*, Academy of Art College, San Francisco CA (S)

Haight, Giuliana Nardelli, *Exec Dir*, Museo Italo Americano, San Francisco CA

Hail, Christopher, *Asst Librn*, Harvard University, Frances Loeb Library, Cambridge MA

Haimson, Jean, *Office Mgr*, Palo Alto Cultural Center, Palo Alto CA

Haines, Mary Egan, *Sr Advisor*, Ontario College of Art, Toronto ON (S)

Hair, Norman J, *Chmn*, Gulf Coast Community College, Division of Fine Arts, Panama City FL (S)

Hairston, Guy, *Exec Dir*, Tennessee Botanical Gardens and Fine Arts Center, Inc, Nashville TN

Hajduczok, Lydia, *Public Relations*, Ukrainian Museum, New York NY

Hakala, Sue, *Coordr*, Galeria Mesa, Cultural Activities Dept, Mesa AZ

Hakkinen, Elisabeth S, *Dir Sheldon Museum*, Sheldon Museum and Cultural Center, Haines AK

Halaby, Samia A, *Executive Member*, 22 Wooster Gallery, New York NY

Halbreich, Kathy, *Dir Exhib*, Massachusetts Institute of Technology, MIT Committee on Visual Arts (Hayden Gallery and MIT Permanent Collection), Cambridge MA

Halbrook, Anne-Mieke, *Head Librn*, J Paul Getty Museum, Research Library, Malibu CA

Hale, Alison B, *Secy*, Ages of Man Fellowship, Amenia NY

Hale, David, *Instr*, Colby-Sawyer College, Art Dept, New London NH (S)

Hale, Dorothy, *Dir*, Klamath Falls Art Association, Klamath Art Gallery, Klamath Falls OR

Hale, Elizabeth F, *Librn*, Society of the Montreal Military and Maritime Museum, MacDonald-Steward Library, Montreal PQ

Hale, George N, *Treas*, California Historical Society, San Francisco CA

Hale, Joan, *Recording Secy*, Arizona Artist Guild, Phoenix AZ

Hale, Nathan Cabot, *Pres*, Ages of Man Fellowship, Amenia NY

Hale, Perri, *Asst Prof*, Herbert H Lehman College, Art Dept, Bronx NY (S)

Hale, Reuben, *Chmn*, Palm Beach Junior College, Dept of Art, Lake Worth FL (S)

Halem, Henry, *Grad Coordr*, Kent State University, School of Art, Kent OH (S)

Hales, Andrea, *Slide Cur*, University of Southern California, Architecture and Fine Arts Library, Los Angeles CA

Haletsky, John, *Cur*, University of Miami, Lowe Art Museum, Coral Gables FL

Halfen, Bea, *Registrar*, Paine Art Center and Arboretum, Oshkosh WI

Halkin, Theodore, *Prof*, School of the Art Institute of Chicago, Chicago IL (S)

Hall, Barbara, *Assoc Cur*, University of Chicago, Oriental Institute, Chicago IL

Hall, David, *Recordings Cur*, New York Public Library, Shelby Cullom Davis Museum, Library & Museum of the Performing Arts, New York NY

Hall, Doug, *Instructor*, Kirkwood Community College, Dept of Fine Arts, Cedar Rapids IA (S)

Hall, Elton W, *Cur Coll*, Old Dartmouth Historical Society, New Bedford Whaling Museum, New Bedford MA

Hall, F Whitney, *Chief Administrative Officer*, Fine Arts Museums of San Francisco, M H de Young Memorial Museum and California Palace of the Legion of Honor, San Francisco CA

Hall, Gilbert W, *Actg Chmn*, Ohio State University, Dept of Art, Columbus OH (S)

Hall, Howard A, *Assoc Prof*, Southwestern Oregon Community College, Visual Arts Dept, Coos Bay OR (S)

Hall, Hugh M, *Lectr,* University of Pennsylvania, College Arts & Science, Philadelphia PA (S)

Hall, Jackie, *Executive Dir,* Lincoln Community Arts Council, Lincoln NE

Hall, Janice, *Cur of Coll,* Putnam Museum, Davenport IA

Hall, Jean, *Secy,* University of Chicago, David and Alfred Smart Gallery, Chicago IL

Hall, John, *Assoc Prof,* University of Toronto, School of Architecture, Toronto ON (S)

Hall, Marjorie N, *Asst to the Dir & Registrar,* Berkshire Museum, Pittsfield MA

Hall, Mark, *Instructor,* MacMurray College, Art Dept, Jacksonville IL (S)

Hall, Martha, *Readers' Services Librn,* Philadelphia College of Art, Library, Philadelphia PA

Hall, Mary-Anne, *Docent,* Norwich Free Academy, Slater Memorial Museum & Converse Art Gallery, Norwich CT

Hall, Michael D, *Head Sculpture Dept,* Cranbrook Academy of Art, Bloomfield Hills MI (S)

Hall, Rick, *Instructor,* College of Marin, Dept of Art, Kentfield CA (S)

Hall, Robert, *Cur,* Fisk University Museum of Art, Nashville TN

Hall, Robert, *Cur,* Fisk University, Division of Humanities & Fine Arts, Nashville TN (S)

Hall, Robert, *Chmn,* Flagler College, Visual Arts Dept, Saint Augustine FL (S)

Hall, Susanne, *Cur Education,* Hickory Museum of Art, Inc, Hickory NC

Hall, Virginius C, *Assoc Dir,* Virginia Historical Society, Richmond VA

Hall, Walter, *Asst Prof,* Hartford Art School of the University of Hartford, West Hartford CT (S)

Hall, William, *VPres,* Everson Museum of Art, Syracuse NY

Hallahan, John J, *City Library Dir,* Manchester City Library, Manchester NH

Hallam, John S, *Asst Prof,* Rice University, Dept of Art and Art History, Houston TX (S)

Hallenberg, Heather M, *Asst Cur Taft Museum,* Taft Museum, Cincinnati OH

Haller, Douglas M, *Photography,* California Historical Society, Schubert Hall Library, San Francisco CA

Hallett, Robert, *Art Dept Chmn,* Citrus College, Art Dept, Azusa CA (S)

Hall-Humpherson, David, *Chmn Dept Foundation Studies,* Ontario College of Art, Toronto ON (S)

Hallmark, Donald P, *Librn,* Greenville College, Research Library, Greenville IL

Halloran, Dennis H, *Dir,* Agecroft Association, Richmond VA

Hall-Smith, Arthur, *Assoc Prof,* George Washington University, Dept of Art, Washington DC (S)

Halm, Robert J, *Assoc Prof,* Iowa Central Community College, Dept of Art, Fort Dodge IA (S)

Halpin, Jerome, *Cataloger,* Adams State College, Library, Alamosa CO

Halpin, Marjorie M, *Cur Ethnology,* University of British Columbia, Museum of Anthropology, Vancouver BC

Halter, Ellen F, *Asst Prof,* Concordia College, Bronxville NY (S)

Halula, Theresa, *Gallery Dir,* California State University, Hayward, University Art Gallery, Hayward CA

Halverson, Edith, *Admin Asst,* Ferguson Library, Stamford CT

Halverson, Wayne, *Asst Prof,* University of Wisconsin-Stevens Point, Dept of Art, Stevens Point WI (S)

Ham, F Gerald, *Archivist,* State Historical Society of Wisconsin, Archives, Madison WI

Hamann, Carol, *VPres,* New York Artists Equity Association, Inc, New York NY

Hamann, Marilyn, *Chmn,* University of Kentucky, Dept of Art, Lexington KY (S)

Hambrick, Robert T, *VPres,* Hickory Museum of Art, Inc, Hickory NC

Hamburger, Sydney K, *Cur,* Academy of the Arts, Easton MD

Hamed, S, *Instructor,* Technical University of Nova Scotia, Faculty of Architecture, Halifax NS (S)

Hamilton, Charles, *VPres & Dir Education,* Art Institute of Philadelphia, Philadelphia PA (S)

Hamilton, Esley, *Adjunct Instr,* Maryville College, St Louis, Art Division, Saint Louis MO (S)

Hamilton, John, *Cur Exhibits,* Museum of Our National Heritage, Lexington MA

Hamilton, Katie, *Instr,* Marian College, Art Dept, Indianapolis IN (S)

Hamilton, Lucy, *Program Advisor,* University of Tennessee, University of Tennessee Exhibits Committee, Knoxville TN

Hamilton, Paul C, *Head,* University of Saskatchewan, Dept of Art & Art History, Saskatoon SK (S)

Hamilton, Reed, *Pres,* Doshi Center for Contemporary Art, Harrisburg PA

Hamilton, Rosie, *Pres,* West Hills Unitarian Fellowship, Portland OR

Hamilton, Shirley, *Pres,* Allied Arts Council of Lethbridge, Bowman Arts Center, Lethbridge AB

Hamilton, Stephen J, *Chmn,* Virginia Intermont College, Fine Arts Dept, Bristol VA (S)

Hamlett, Dale, *Assoc Prof,* Eastern New Mexico University, Dept of Art, Portales NM (S)

Hamm, Donna, *Cur Educ,* Art Museum of South Texas, Corpus Christi TX

Hamm, Jack, *Artists-in-Residence,* Dallas Baptist College, Dept of Art, Dallas TX (S)

Hamm, Russ, *Chmn,* College of Lake County, Art Dept, Grayslake IL (S)

Hamma, Kenneth, *Asst Prof,* University of Southern California, School of Fine Arts, Los Angeles CA (S)

Hammack, Louis, *Head Technical Services,* Art Institute of Chicago, Ryerson and Burnham Libraries, Chicago IL

Hammell, Rebecca J, *Museum Cur,* Historical Society of Delaware, George Read II House, Wilmington DE

Hammer, Alfred E, *Dean,* Hartford Art School of the University of Hartford, West Hartford CT (S)

Hammett, Kate, *Public Relations Dir,* Oklahoma Art Center, Oklahoma City OK

Hammill, Earl W, *Treasurer,* The Racine Art Association, Inc, Racine WI

Hammock, Virgil, *Head Dept,* Mount Allison University, Fine Arts Dept, Sackville NB (S)

Hammon, Margaret, *Dir,* Muckenthaler Cultural Center, Fullerton CA

Hammond, Jack, *Instr,* Maryland College of Art and Design, Silver Spring MD (S)

Hammond, Lyman E, *Dir,* MacArthur Memorial Museum, Norfolk VA

Hammond, Natalie Hays, *Dir,* Hammond Museum, Museum of the Humanities, North Salem NY

Hammond, Ruth, *Dir Information Services,* Ontario College of Art, Toronto ON (S)

Hample, Henry, *Office Mgr,* Santa Cruz Art Center, Santa Cruz CA

Hampshire, Nancy E, *Instructor,* Providence College, Art and Art History Dept, Providence RI (S)

Hampton, Grace, *Chmn,* Jackson State University, Dept of Art, Jackson MS (S)

Hamrick, John E, *Pres,* San Diego Maritime Museum, San Diego CA

Hanamura, Robertt, *Dir,* Hayward Area Forum of the Arts, Son Gallery, Hayward CA

Hanchrow, Grace M, *Asst Dir for Development,* Montgomery Museum of Fine Arts, Montgomery AL

Hancox, William J, *Executive Dir,* Confederation Centre Art Gallery and Museum, Charlottetown PE

Hand, John, *Cur Northern European Painting,* National Gallery of Art, Washington DC

Hand, Ronald, *Preparator,* Pennsylvania State University, Museum of Art, University Park PA

Handleman, David, *Pres Meadow Brook Gallery Assocs,* Oakland University, Meadow Brook Art Gallery, Rochester MI

Handy, Barbara, *Cur Material Culture,* Colorado Historical Society, State Museum, Denver CO

Handy, Susan, *Museum Shop Mgr,* Rhode Island School of Design, Museum of Art, Providence RI

Haner, Paul F, *Conservator,* Worcester Art Museum, Worcester MA

Hanes, James, *Asst Prof,* La Salle College, Dept of Fine Arts, Philadelphia PA (S)

Hanes, Paula, *Adjunct Instr,* University of Northern Iowa, Dept of Art, Cedar Falls IA (S)

Haney, Gary, *Asst Dir,* Association of Collegiate Schools of Architecture, Washington DC

Haney, Jeffrey, *Dir Development,* Colorado Springs Fine Arts Center, Colorado Springs CO

Hanford, Marie, *Exec Secy,* Iroquois County Historical Museum, Watseka IL

Hanft, Margie, *Film Librn,* California Institute of the Arts Library, Valencia CA

Hanhardt, John G, *Cur, Film & Video,* Whitney Museum of American Art, New York NY

Hankel, Wayne, *Pres,* SVACA - Sheyenne Valley Arts and Crafts Association, Bjarne Ness Gallery, Fort Ransom ND

Hankin, Stephen, *Asst Prof,* University of Wisconsin-Stevens Point, Dept of Art, Stevens Point WI (S)

Hanks, J C, *Registrar Art,* Texas A & M University, University Art Exhibits, College Station TX

Hanks, Rome, *Instructor,* Lycoming College, Art Dept, Williamsport PA (S)

Hanlon, Alan R, *Dir Rothmans Art Program,* Rothmans of Pall Mall Canada Limited, Toronto ON

Hanna, Beth L, *Dir,* Brant Historical Society, Brant County Museum, Brantford ON

Hanna, James, *Assoc Prof,* Texas Tech University, Dept of Art, Lubbock TX (S)

Hanna, Martha, *Producer,* National Film Board of Canada, Still Photography Division, Ottawa ON

Hannan, William, *Assoc Prof,* Black Hawk College, Art Dept, Moline IL (S)

Hannen, Frank, *Cur,* National Infantry Museum, Fort Benning GA

Hannibal, Joe, *Chmn,* California State Polytechnic University, Pomona, Art Dept, Pomona CA (S)

Hanniford, Sultana, *Pres,* Lyme Art Association, Inc, Old Lyme CT

Hansard, William, *Assoc Prof,* University of Massachusetts at Boston, Art Dept, Boston MA (S)

Hansell, Stephen, *Tech Coordr,* Ashtabula Arts Center, Ashtabula OH

Hansen, Arthur, *Treas,* Jersey City Museum Association, Jersey City NJ

Hansen, Chris, *Instructor,* Milwaukee Area Technical College, Graphic & Applied Arts Division, Milwaukee WI (S)

Hansen, James L, *Prof,* Portland State University, Dept of Art and Architecture, Portland OR (S)

Hansen, John, *Instructor,* The Design Schools, Art Institute of Seattle, Seattle WA (S)

Hansen, Roland, *Head Readers Services,* School of the Art Institute of Chicago Library, Chicago IL

Hanson, Hardy, *Prof,* University of California, Santa Cruz, Board of Studies in Art, Santa Cruz CA (S)

Hanson, Lowell, *Chmn,* Everett Community College, Art Dept, Everett WA (S)

Hanson, Robert, *Instr,* Pacific Northwest College of Art, Portland OR (S)

Hanzelin, Fred L, *Chmn,* Thornton Community College, Art Dept, South Holland IL (S)

Har, Lorraine, *Chmn Textile Design,* Fashion Institute of Technology, Art & Design Division, New York NY (S)

Haralson, Carol, *Graphic Designer & Publications Editor,* Philbrook Art Center, Tulsa OK

Harasimowicz, Alan, *Exhibits Designer,* Southern Illinois University, University Museum, Carbondale IL

Harbour, John W, *Exec Dir,* Sleepy Hollow Restorations Inc, Tarrytown NY

Harby, William, *Pres,* The Loading Dock Gallery, Boston MA

Hard, Michael W, *Treas,* Amerind Foundation, Inc, Dragoon AZ

Hardberger, Linda M, *Librn,* San Antonio Museum Association, Inc, Ellen S Quillin Memorial Library, San Antonio TX

Hardeny, Suzanne, *Assoc Prof,* Seton Hill College, Dept of Art, Greensburg PA (S)

Hardiman, George W, *In Charge Art Educ,* University of Illinois, Urbana-Champaign, School of Art and Design, Champaign IL (S)

Harding, Charles, *Assoc Prof,* Brazosport College, Art Dept, Lake Jackson TX (S)

Harding, Mary P, *Dir,* Society for the Preservation of Historic Landmarks, York ME

Hardwig, Scott, *Asst Prof,* Roanoke College, Art Dept, Salem VA (S)

Hardy, David, *Gallery Supt & Preparator,* University of Utah, Utah Museum of Fine Arts, Salt Lake City UT

Hardy, Robert, *Dir,* Cypress College, Fine Arts Gallery, Cypress CA

Haren, John Van, *Dept Head,* Eastern Michigan University, Ford Gallery, Ypsilanti MI

Hargensen, H Lynne, *Faculty,* Idaho State University, Dept of Art, Pocatello ID (S)

Hargett, Marty, *Assoc Prof,* Lincoln College, Art Dept, Lincoln IL (S)

Hargrove, June E, *Assoc Prof,* Cleveland State University, Art Dept, Cleveland OH (S)

Hargrove, Kathryn, *Cur,* Bates College, Treat Gallery, Lewiston ME

Harington, Charles J, *Coordr,* Chadron State College, Arts Gallery, Chadron NE

Harkins, Thomas, *Catalogue Librn,* Stowe-Day Foundation, Library, Hartford CT

Harkness, Mary Lou, *Librn,* University of South Florida, Library, Tampa FL

Harlow, Ann, *Dir,* Saint Mary's College of California, Hearst Art Gallery, Moraga CA

Harlow, Bonnie K, *Registrar & Cur Collections,* Saint Joseph Museum, Saint Joseph MO

Harman, Maryann, *Instructor,* Virginia Tech, Dept of Art, Blacksburg VA (S)

Harman, Robert, *Rights & Reproductions,* Pennsylvania Academy of the Fine Arts, Galleries, Philadelphia PA

Harmes, Michael, *Chmn Dept Technol Studies,* Ontario College of Art, Toronto ON (S)

Harmon, Harry W, *Secy,* American Institute of Architects, Washington DC

Harmon, Jean, *Asst Prof,* Missouri Western State College, Art Dept, Saint Joseph MO (S)

Harmon, John, *Instr,* Midland College, Art Dept, Midland TX (S)

Harnack, Curtis, *Exec Dir,* Yaddo, Saratoga Springs NY (S)

Harnick, Sarah-Ann, *Asst Dir Student Activities,* Rider College Art Gallery, Lawrenceville NJ

Haroldsson, Andrea, *Graphic Designer,* Brockton Art Museum, Brockton MA

Harper, Evelyne, *Treas,* Ogunquit Art Association, The Barn Gallery, Ogunquit ME

Harper, George D, *Instructor,* Glenville State College, Dept of Art, Glenville WV (S)

Harper, Grady, *Prof,* Northwestern State University of Louisiana, Dept of Art, Natchitoches LA (S)

Harper, John, *Arts Cur,* Redding Museum and Art Center, Redding CA

Harper, Paula, *Assoc Prof,* University of Miami, Dept of Art & Art History, Coral Gables FL (S)

Harper, Prudence O, *Chmn Ancient Near Eastern Art,* Metropolitan Museum of Art, New York NY

Harper, Robert L, *Head Librn,* California College of Arts and Crafts, Meyer Library, Oakland CA

Harper, Robert W, *Dir,* Lightner Museum, Saint Augustine FL

Harper, William C, *Assoc Prof,* Florida State University, Art Dept, Tallahassee FL (S)

Harpole, Patricia, *Chief Reference Librn,* Minnesota Historical Society, Library, Saint Paul MN

Harrard, Jennifer, *Secy,* Burnaby Art Gallery, Burnaby BC

Harrel, Ralph, *Dean,* Southwest Texas State University, Dept of Art, San Marcos TX (S)

Harrell, Telathia, *Secy,* Virginia Beach Arts Center, Virginia Beach VA

Harriman, Cynthia Wills, *Secy,* Portsmouth Athenaeum NR, Inc 1817, Portsmouth NH

Harrington, Alice, *Co-Dir,* Art Association of Jacksonville, David Strawn Art Gallery, Jacksonville IL

Harrington, Charles J, *Chmn Div,* Chadron State College, Division of Fine Arts, Chadron NE (S)

Harrington, Elaine, *Cur,* Chicago Architecture Foundation, Glessner House, Chicago IL

Harrington, Jack, *Co-Dir,* Art Association of Jacksonville, David Strawn Art Gallery, Jacksonville IL

Harrington, Karen, *Instructor,* Northeast Technical Community College, Dept of Art, Norfolk NE (S)

Harrington, Patrick, *Exec Dir,* Landmark Society of Western New York, Inc, Wenrich Memorial Library, New York NY

Harrington, Patrick, *Dir,* Landmark Society of Western New York, Inc, Rochester NY

Harrington, Ruthanne, *Lectr,* Notre Dame College, Art Dept, Manchester NH (S)

Harrington, Tomas, *Cur Coll,* Hancock Shaker Village, Inc, Pittsfield MA

Harris, Albert F, *Admin Asst,* Portsmouth Museums, Community Arts Center Division, Portsmouth VA

Harris, Allyn O, *Gallery Dir,* Community College of Baltimore, Art Gallery, Baltimore MD

Harris, Allyn O, *Prof,* Community College of Baltimore, Dept of Fine & Applied Arts, Liberty Campus, Baltimore MD (S)

Harris, A Peter, *Dir,* Rodman Hall Arts Centre, Saint Catharines ON

Harris, Barbara, *Pres,* Artrium Inc, Santa Rosa CA

Harris, Beatrice, *Dean,* Yard School of Art, Montclair NJ (S)

Harris, Conley, *Assoc Prof,* University of New Hampshire, Dept of the Arts, Durham NH (S)

Harris, David J, *Instructor,* North Seattle Community College, Art Dept, Seattle WA (S)

Harris, Dorothy, *Chairperson,* Jersey City State College, Art Dept, Jersey City NJ (S)

Harris, Gene E, *Cur,* Brandywine River Museum, Chadds Ford PA

Harris, Guy, *Pres,* Singing River Art Association Inc, L & N Railroad Depot Gallery, Pascagoula MS

Harris, Harmon, *Public Relations,* Historical Society of Pennsylvania, Philadelphia PA

Harris, J Carver, *Mgr,* Saint Augustine Historical Society, Library, Saint Augustine FL

Harris, Jean C, *Prof,* Mount Holyoke College, Art Dept, South Hadley MA (S)

Harris, Jeanne, *Assoc Cur Oriental Art,* Atkins Museum of Fine Art, Kansas City MO

Harris, John M, *Dir,* Tippecanoe County Historical Museum, Lafayette IN

Harris, Judith, *Program Dir,* Alaska Arts Southeast, Inc, Sitka AK

Harris, Mac, *Museums & Historical Sites,* Oklahoma Historical Society, Central Museum, Oklahoma City OK

Harris, Macil, *Gift Shop Mgr,* The Indian Museum, Wichita KS

Harris, Pat, *Instructor,* Umpqua Community College, Fine & Performing Arts Dept, Roseburg OR (S)

Harris, Paul Rogers, *Dir,* The Art Center, Waco TX

Harris, Robert, *Prof,* Smith College, Art Dept, Northampton MA (S)

Harris, Susan, *Asst Prof,* University of Evansville, Art Dept, Evansville IN (S)

Harris, Wilhelmina S, *Supt,* Adams National Historic Site, Quincy MA

Harrison, Anthony, *Sr Lecturer,* Columbia University, School of the Arts, Division of Painting & Sculpture, New York NY (S)

Harrison, Catherine R, *Asst Dir,* Tom Thomson Memorial Gallery and Museum of Fine Art, Owen Sound ON

Harrison, Cheryl, *Asst Prof,* Brevard College, Division of Fine Arts, Brevard NC (S)

Harrison, Darrell, *Operations Coordr,* Science Museums of Charlotte, Inc, Discovery Place, Charlotte NC

Harrison, David, *Assoc Prof,* Converse College, Art Dept, Spartanburg SC (S)

Harrison, Ed, *Pres Bd of Governors,* Natural History Museum of Los Angeles County, Los Angeles CA

Harrison, Eliza C, *Dir,* Hershey Museum of American Life, Hershey PA

Harrison, Helen A, *Consultant Cur,* Guild Hall of East Hampton, Inc, Museum Section, East Hampton NY

Harrison, Julia, *Cur of Ethnology,* Glenbow Museum, Calgary AB

Harrison, Loretta, *Asst Dir,* Oregon State University, Horner Museum, Corvallis OR

Harrison, Richard D, *Pres,* Oklahoma Art Center, Oklahoma City OK

Harrob, Terry, *Instructor,* Anton Elli, Cincinnati OH (S)

Harroff, William, *Librn,* Oklahoma State University, Architecture Library, Stillwater OK

Harrover, May, *Librn,* Millicent Rogers Museum, Library, Taos NM

Harrow, Arthur, *Pres,* Artists' Fellowship, Inc, New York NY

Harsh, Lester, *Pres,* High Plains Museum, McCook NE

Harsh, William, *Asst Prof,* Assumption College, Dept of Fine Arts and Music, Worcester MA (S)

Hart, Allen M, *Dir,* The Children's Aid Society, Lower Westside Center, New York NY (S)

Hart, Barbara A, *Admin Officer,* National Portrait Gallery, Washington DC

Hart, E J, *Adminr & Head Archivist,* Peter and Catharine Whyte Foundation, Peter Whyte Gallery, Banff AB

Hart, Katherine, *Registrar & Cur Asst,* University of California, Los Angeles, Frederick S Wight Art Gallery, Los Angeles CA

Hart, Lyn, *Libr,* Johns Hopkins University, George Peabody Library, Baltimore MD

Hart, Nathaniel, *Chmn,* University of Minnesota, Morris, Humanities Division, Morris MN (S)

Hart, Robert A, *Dir,* Santa Barbara Public Library, Faulkner Memorial Art Wing, Santa Barbara CA

Hart, Robert G, *Gen Mgr,* United States Department of the Interior, Indian Arts and Crafts Board, Washington DC

Hart, Vincent, *Lectr,* Georgian Court College, Dept of Art, Lakewood NJ (S)

Hartgen, Vincent A, *Emeritus Prof,* University of Maine, Art Dept, Orono ME (S)

Harthorn, Sandy, *Cur,* Boise Gallery of Art, Boise ID

Hartigan, Grace, *Dir,* Maryland Institute, Hoffberger School of Painting, Baltimore MD (S)

Hartke, Mary, *Secy,* Iroquois County Historical Museum, Watseka IL

Hartman, Eleanor C, *Librn,* Los Angeles County Museum of Art, Library, Los Angeles CA

Hartman, George, *Supt,* Toledo Museum of Art, Toledo OH

Hartman, Jim, *Asst State Historic Preservation Officer for History,* Colorado Historical Society, State Museum, Denver CO

Hartman, Robert, *Prof,* University of California, Berkeley, College of Letters & Sciences, Berkeley CA (S)

Hartman, Russell P, *Cur,* Navajo Tribal Museum, Window Rock AZ

Hartman, Steve, *Cur,* Museum of Arts and Sciences, Inc, Macon GA

Hartman, Terry L, *Instructor,* Modesto Junior College, Arts Humanities and Speech Division, Modesto CA (S)

Hartman, Thomas, *Design Dir,* University of California, Los Angeles, Frederick S Wight Art Gallery, Los Angeles CA

Hartmann, Barbara, *Coordr,* Edmonton Public Library, Foyer Gallery and Photography Gallery, Edmonton AB

Hartwell, Carroll T, *Cur Photography,* Minneapolis Institute of Arts, Minneapolis MN

Hartwell, Janice E, *Assoc Prof,* Florida State University, Art Dept, Tallahassee FL (S)

Hartwig, Cleo, *Executive VPres,* Sculptors Guild, Inc, New York NY

Hartzell, Helen, *Gift Shop,* Westmoreland County Museum of Art, Greensburg PA

Harvath, John, *Head, Fine Arts & Recreation,* Houston Public Library, Houston TX

Harvey, Archer St Clair, *Asst Prof,* Rutgers, the State University of New Jersey, Graduate Program in Art History, New Brunswick NJ (S)

Harvey, Bunny, *Asst Prof,* Wellesley College, Art Dept, Wellesley MA (S)

Harvey, Clifford, *Prof,* West Virginia University, Division of Art, Morgantown WV (S)

Harvey, D, *Prof,* University of Victoria, Dept of Visual Arts, Victoria BC (S)

Harvey, Edgar, *Chmn,* Sioux Falls College, Dept of Art, Sioux Falls SD (S)

Harvey, Georgia, *Registrar,* Hebrew Union College, Skirball Museum, Los Angeles CA

Harvey, Karen J, *Librn,* Smith College, Hillyer Art Library, Northampton MA

Harvey, Linda, *Asst Cur,* Regina Public Library, Dunlop Art Gallery, Regina SK

Harvey, Loyd, *Chmn Finance Committee,* Virginia Museum, Danville Museum of Fine Arts and History, Danville VA

Harvey, Wayne H, *Pres,* Schenectady County Historical Society, Schenectady NY

Harwick, Joanne, *Assoc Prof,* Fort Hays State University, Dept of Art, Hays KS (S)

Harwig, Mike, *Exhibitions Coordr,* Independent Curators Incorporated, New York NY

Hasbury, S, *Art Documentalist,* National Gallery of Canada, Library, Ottawa ON

Haschka, Jonathan, *Artist-in-Res,* Creighton University, Fine and Performing Arts Dept, Omaha NE (S)

Hasen, Irwin, *Instr,* Joe Kubert School of Cartoon and Graphic Art Inc, Dover NJ (S)

Hasfjord, Nellie N, *Dir,* Adams State College, Library, Alamosa CO

Haskell, Barbara, *Cur,* Whitney Museum of American Art, New York NY

Haskell, Eric, *Pres,* Scripps College, Clark Humanities Museum, Claremont CA

Haskett, William R, *Chmn,* McLennan Community College, Fine Arts Dept, Waco TX (S)

Haskin, Myra, *Corresp Secy,* Main Line Center of the Arts, Haverford PA

Haslam, Anne Marie, *Librn,* Delaware Art Museum, Library, Wilmington DE

Hassan, Gaylord, *Coordr of Cultural Arts,* New Muse Community Museum of Brooklyn, Inc, Brooklyn NY

Hasselbach, Gloria, *Instructor,* Goldsboro Art Center, Goldsboro NC (S)

Hassell, John F, *Pres,* Charleston Museum, Charleston SC

Hassenpflug, Earl, *Chmn,* Otterbein College, Dept of Visual Arts, Westerville OH (S)

Hassrick, Peter H, *Dir,* Buffalo Bill Memorial Association, Cody WY

Hastie, Reid, *Prof,* Texas Tech University, Dept of Art, Lubbock TX (S)

Hastings, Charlotte, *Executive Member,* 22 Wooster Gallery, New York NY

Haswell, Hollee, *Librn,* Sleepy Hollow Restorations Inc, Library, Tarrytown NY

Hatch, John, *Prof,* University of New Hampshire, Dept of the Arts, Durham NH (S)

Hatfield, Gene, *Asst Prof,* University of Central Arkansas, Art Dept, Conway AR (S)

Hathaway, Carol J, *Coordr,* Roger Williams College, Art Dept, Bristol RI (S)

Hathaway, Janice, *Asst Prof,* Mississippi University for Women, Division of Fine & Performing Arts, Columbus MS (S)

Hathaway, Norman B, *Pres,* Ontario College of Art, Toronto ON (S)

Hathaway, Walter M, *Dir,* Columbia Museums of Art and Science, Columbia SC

Hatley, George B, *Secy,* Appaloosa Museum, Inc, Moscow ID

Hatmaker, Paul, *Treas,* Strasburg Museum, Strasburg VA

Hauck, Alice H, *Asst Prof,* Providence College, Art and Art History Dept, Providence RI (S)

Hauck, Darthe C, *Membership Coordr,* Historical Society of Pennsylvania, Philadelphia PA

Hauge, Lila, *Dir,* Mayville State College Gallery, Mayville ND

Hauge, Paul, *Communication Design Chmn,* Art Center College of Design, Pasadena CA (S)

Haugerud, James S, *Registrar,* United States Senate Commission on Art and Antiquities, Washington DC

Haught, Mary, *Secy,* State University of New York College at Potsdam, Brainerd Art Gallery, Potsdam NY

Haupin, Louise, *Coordr Crafts,* Cornell University, Herbert F Johnson Museum of Art, Ithaca NY

Haupt, Shirley, *Prof,* University of Northern Iowa, Dept of Art, Cedar Falls IA (S)

Haury, David A, *Archivist,* Bethel College, Mennonite Library and Archives, North Newton KS

Hausen, Rena, *Editor,* Midmarch Associates, Women Artists News Archive, New York NY

Hauser, Reine, *Coordr,* Soho Center for Visual Artists, Soho 20, New York NY

Hauser, Robert A, *Museum Conservator,* Merrimack Valley Textile Museum, North Andover MA

Hausman, Jerome J, *Academy VPres,* Massachusetts College of Art, Boston MA (S)

Hausmann, Albert Charles, *Asst Prof,* University of North Alabama, Dept of Art, Florence AL (S)

Hausrath, Joan, *Prof,* Bridgewater State College, Art Dept, Bridgewater MA (S)

Havas, Edwin, *Instructor,* Montclair Art Museum, Museum Art Classes, Montclair NJ (S)

Havas, Edwin, *Asst Prof,* Seton Hall University, Dept of Art and Music, South Orange NJ (S)

Havas, Sandy, *Dir,* Eccles Community Art Center, Ogden UT

Havel, Joseph, *Asst Prof,* Austin College, Art Dept, Sherman TX (S)

Havel, Lynn B, *Instr,* Butler County Community College, Art Dept, El Dorado KS (S)

Havens, Arlene, *Exhib Coordr,* Palos Verdes Art Center, Rancho Palos Verdes CA

Havens, Neil, *Prof,* Rice University, Dept of Art and Art History, Houston TX (S)

Havens, Walter, *Admin,* Favell Museum of Western Art & Indian Artifacts, Klamath Falls OR

Haver, Ronald, *Dir of Film Programs,* Los Angeles County Museum of Art, Los Angeles CA

Haverty, Grace, *Secy,* DuPage Art League, Wheaton IL

Haviland, David S, *Dean,* Rensselaer Polytechnic Institute, School of Architecture, Troy NY (S)

Havis, C Kenneth, *Gallery Dir,* North Texas State University, Art Gallery, Denton TX

Hawes, Louis, *Prof,* Indiana University, Bloomington, School of Fine Arts, Bloomington IN (S)

Hawkes, Elizabeth, *Assoc Cur & Cur John Sloan Archives,* Delaware Art Museum, Wilmington DE

Hawkes, Mary, *Secy,* Pocumtuck Valley Memorial Association, Memorial Hall, Deerfield MA

Hawkins, Ashton, *VPres, Secy & Counsel,* Metropolitan Museum of Art, New York NY

Hawkins, Clarence, *Instr,* Marian College, Art Dept, Indianapolis IN (S)

Hawkins, John, *Chmn & Prof,* Queensborough Community College, Dept of Art and Design, Bayside NY (S)

Hawkins, Laura, *Office Mgr,* Northeastern Nevada Historical Society Museum, Elko NV

Hawkins, Lewis, *Asst Prof,* Maryland College of Art and Design, Silver Spring MD (S)

Hawley, Henry, *Chief Cur Later Western Art,* Cleveland Museum of Art, Cleveland OH

Haworth, Stephen K, *Asst Prof,* University of West Florida, Faculty of Art, Pensacola FL (S)

Hawthorne, Robins, *VPres,* Octagon Center for the Arts, Ames IA

Haxthausen, Charles W, *Cur,* Harvard University, Busch-Reisinger Museum, Cambridge MA

Hay, Dick, *Pres,* Lincoln Community Arts Council, Lincoln NE

Hayano, Carl, *Grad Coordr,* Northern Illinois University, Dept of Art, De Kalb IL (S)

Hayashi, Masumi, *Asst Prof,* Cleveland State University, Art Dept, Cleveland OH (S)

Haycock, Charles M, *Chmn,* Madison Area Technical College, Communication Arts, Madison WI (S)

Haycock, Everett, *Prof,* Ohio Wesleyan University, Fine Arts Dept, Delaware OH (S)

Haydu, John R, *Asst Prof,* Central Missouri State University, Art Dept, Warrensburg MO (S)

Hayers, J Lynn, *Assoc Prof,* Brazosport College, Art Dept, Lake Jackson TX (S)

Hayes, Bonnie, *Asst Prof,* Beaver College, Dept of Fine Arts, Glenside PA (S)

Hayes, George M, *Asst Prof,* Shorter College, Art Dept, Rome GA (S)

Hayes, Lorraine, *Libr Technician,* Institute of American Indian Arts Museum, Library, Santa Fe NM

Hayes, Richard, *Dir of Permanent Collection,* Thiel College, Sampson Art Gallery, Greenville PA

Hayes, Tricia N, *Membership & Volunteer Coordr,* Bennington Museum, Bennington VT

Haymaker, James, *Dir,* Pfeiffer College, Art Program, Misenheimer NC (S)

Hayman, E Sherman, *Coordr,* Muse Art Gallery, Philadelphia PA

Haynes, James, *Treas,* Maui Historical Society, Hale Hoikeike, Wailuku HI

Hays, Audrey G, *Head,* Norfolk Public Library, Feldman Fine Arts & Audio Visual Dept, Norfolk VA

Hayslip, Ellwyn, *Head Dept,* Plymouth State College, Art Dept, Plymouth NH (S)

Hayter, Stanley William, *Board Dir Member,* Art Information Center, Inc, New York NY

Hayton, Greg, *Chief Librn,* Cambridge Public Library and Gallery, Cambridge ON

Hayward, Jane, *Cur,* Metropolitan Museum of Art, The Cloisters, New York NY

Haywood, Robert E, *Exec Dir,* Waterworks Gallery, Salisbury NC

Hazard, George S, *Dir,* Columbus and Lowndes County Historical Society Museum, Columbus MS

Hazelgrove, Nancy, *Cur,* University of Toronto, Erindale Campus Art Gallery, Mississauga ON

Hazen, W E, *Faculty,* Andrews University, Art Dept, Berrien Springs MI (S)

Hazlehurst, F Hamilton, *Dir,* Vanderbilt University, Art Gallery, Nashville TN

Hazlehurst, F Hamilton, *Chmn,* Vanderbilt University, Dept of Fine Arts, Nashville TN (S)

Hazlitt, Donald, *Lecturer,* Columbia University, School of the Arts, Division of Painting & Sculpture, New York NY (S)

Head, Albert B, *Div of the Arts Exec Dir,* Jay R Broussard Memorial Galleries, Division of the Arts, Baton Rouge LA

Head, Carolyn, *Secy,* Old Salem Inc, Museum of Early Southern Decorative Arts, Winston-Salem NC

Head, John, *Asst Prof,* Rochester Institute of Technology, School of Photographic Arts & Sciences, Rochester NY (S)

Head, Robert W, *Chmn,* Murray State University, Clara M Eagle Gallery, Murray KY

Head, Robert W, *Chmn,* Murray State University, Art Dept, Murray KY (S)

Headrick, Maggie, *Treas,* Buffalo Society of Artists, Williamsville NY

Heald, Betty, *Dir Exhibitions,* Ohio Wesleyan University, Dept of Fine Arts Gallery, Delaware OH

Heald, Betty, *Assoc Prof,* Ohio Wesleyan University, Fine Arts Dept, Delaware OH (S)

Healey, Ruth, *Gallery Dir,* Russell Sage College, New Gallery, Troy NY

Heard, J, *Instructor,* Golden West College, Arts, Humanities and Social Sciences Institute, Huntington Beach CA (S)

Hearn, Thomas, *VPres,* University of Alabama, Visual Arts Gallery, Birmingham AL

Hearst, Judy Smith, *VPres,* D-Art, A Visual Arts Center for Dallas, Dallas TX

Heasley, Charles, *Asst Prof,* State University of New York College at Cortland, Art Dept, Cortland NY (S)

Heath, Anne, *Chmn General Studies,* California State University, Northridge, Dept of Art-Two Dimensional Media, Northridge CA (S)

Heath, Terrence, *Dir,* Winnipeg Art Gallery, Winnipeg MB

Hebert, Al, *Prof,* Macomb County Community College, Art Dept, Warren MI (S)

Hecht, David B, *Treasurer,* Long Island Graphic Eye Gallery, Port Washington NY

Hecht, David B, *Co-Pres,* Long Beach Art Association, Long Beach NY

Heckencamp, Linda, *Ceramics,* Chautauqua Institution, The Art Center, Chautauqua NY (S)

Hecker, Frances E, *Head,* Tulane University, Architecture Library, New Orleans LA

Heckler, Margaret, *Secy,* Congressional Arts Caucus, Washington DC

Heckler, Mark, *Chmn,* Siena College, Fine Arts Dept, Londonville NY (S)

Heckman, Steve, *Chmn Fine Arts & Communication,* Seward County Community College, Art Dept, Liberal KS (S)

Hecksher, Morrison H, *Cur American Decorative Art,* Metropolitan Museum of Art, New York NY

Hedberg, Gregory, *Chief Cur,* Wadsworth Atheneum, Hartford CT

Hedberg-Duff, Judith, *Instr,* Coos Art Museum, Coos Bay OR (S)

Hedges, Tammy L, *Dir,* Lewistown Art Center, Lewistown MT

Hedin, Thomas F, *Assoc Prof,* University of Minnesota, Duluth, Art Dept, Duluth MN (S)

Hedrick, Basil C, *Dir,* University of Alaska, Museum, Fairbanks AK

Heefner, William F, *Pres,* Bucks County Historical Society, Mercer Museum, Doylestown PA

Heelis, Sharon Lyn, *Art Gallery Secy,* Brigham Young University, B F Larsen Gallery, Provo UT

Heepke, Carol, *Cur Education,* San Diego Museum of Art, San Diego CA

Heffernan, Ildiko, *Dir,* University of Vermont, Robert Hull Fleming Museum, Burlington VT

Heffner, Jane E, *Development Officer,* Whitney Museum of American Art, New York NY

Heflin, Patricia, *Staff Asst,* Department of State, Diplomatic Reception Rooms, Washington DC

Hegarty, Kevin, *Dir,* Tacoma Public Library, Handforth Gallery, Tacoma WA

Hegarty, Melinda, *Instr,* Eastern Illinois University, School of Fine Arts, Charleston IL (S)

Hehman, Jennifer, *Asst Librn,* Indiana University - Purdue University at Indianapolis, Art Library, Indianapolis IN

Heide, Cynthia, *Dir of Corporate Affairs,* Benson & Hedges (Canada) Inc, Montreal PQ

Heidel, Frederick H, *Prof,* Portland State University, Dept of Art and Architecture, Portland OR (S)

Heideman, Margaret L, *Board Pres,* Art Gallery of Peterborough, Peterborough ON

Heidman, Susan, *Asst Prof,* Smith College, Art Dept, Northampton MA (S)

Heikenen, Patricia S, *Supvr Information,* Minnesota Museum of Art, Saint Paul MN

Heil, Harry, *Dir,* Western State College, Quigley Hall Art Gallery, Gunnison CO

Heilbron, Louis H, *Pres,* California Historical Society, San Francisco CA

Heilman, Donna, *Pres,* Fort Missoula Historical Museum, Missoula MT

Heim, Suzanne M, *Dir & Cur,* Godwin-Ternbach Museum, Flushing NY

Heiman, Trudie, *Pres,* Latitude 53 Society of Artists, Edmonton AB

Hein, Max, *Instr,* Santa Rosa Junior College, Art Dept, Santa Rosa CA (S)

Heinicke, Janet, *Chairperson Dept,* Simpson College, Art Dept, Indianola IA (S)

Heinicke, Janet, *Head Art Dept,* Simpson College Art Gallery, Indianola IA

Heinmiller, Carl, *VPres,* Sheldon Museum and Cultural Center, Haines AK

Heinrich, Adrienne, *Pres,* Associated Artists of Pittsburgh Arts and Crafts Center, Pittsburgh PA

Heintz, David, *Film-Video,* California College of Arts and Crafts, Oakland CA (S)

Heinz, T A, *Librn,* Frank Lloyd Wright Association, Library, Oak Park IL

Heipp, Richard, *Asst Prof,* University of Florida, Dept of Art, Gainesville FL (S)

Heisch, John, *Dir Reference Library,* Oklahoma Historical Society, Library, Oklahoma City OK

Heischman, Robert, *Assoc Prof,* Rochester Institute of Technology, School of Art and Design, Rochester NY (S)

Heiss, Alanna, *Exec Dir,* Institute for Art & Urban Resources, Project Studios One, Long Island City NY

Heisser, Geralyn, *Education Cur,* Seneca Falls Historical Society Museum, Seneca Falls NY

Heit, Dorothea, *Vis Prof,* Oral Roberts University, Fine Arts Dept, Tulsa OK (S)

Heiting, John R, *Assoc Dir & Cur of Collections,* McKissick Museums, Columbia SC

Hektner, Vernon E, *Dean,* North Dakota State School of Science, Dept of Art, Wahpeton ND (S)

Held, Jon, *First Asst,* Dallas Public Library, Fine Arts Division, Dallas TX

Held, Roger, *Chmn,* Elmira College, Art Dept, Elmira NY (S)

Held, Shirley, *Coordr Crafts,* Iowa State University, Dept of Art and Design, Ames IA (S)

Helfet, Tessa, *Cur,* Norton Simon Museum, Pasadena CA

Helfrich, Paul, *Assoc Prof,* College of William and Mary, Dept of Fine Arts, Williamsburg VA (S)

Hellberg, Ray W, *Head,* Utah State University, Dept of Art, Logan UT (S)

Hellebrand, Nancy, *Instructor,* Bucks County Community College, Fine Arts Dept, Newton PA (S)

Heller, Angelica, *VPres,* The National Art Museum of Sport, New Haven CT

Heller, Barbara, *Gallery Mgr,* The Society of Arts and Crafts, Boston MA

Heller, John, *Prof,* Bridgewater State College, Art Dept, Bridgewater MA (S)

Heller, Jules, *Dean College of Fine Arts,* Arizona State University, School of Art, Tempe AZ (S)

Heller, Peter, *Assoc Prof,* Johnson State College, Dept Fine Arts, Johnson VT (S)

Heller, Reinhold, *Actg Dir,* University of Chicago, David and Alfred Smart Gallery, Chicago IL

Heller, Reinhold, *Chmn,* University of Chicago, Dept of Art History and Committee on Art and Design, Chicago IL (S)

Heller, Tobie, *Librn,* Palm Beach County Parks and Recreation Department, Donald B Gordon Memorial Library, Delray Beach FL

Heller, Tom, *Assoc Cur,* Newport Harbor Art Museum, Newport Beach CA

Heller, Vivian, *Admin Asst,* University of Chicago, David and Alfred Smart Gallery, Chicago IL

Hellerstine, Marjorie, *Chmn Critical Studies,* Massachusetts College of Art, Boston MA (S)

Hellier, Bob, *Preparator,* Tampa Museum, Tampa FL

Hellman, Dorothy E, *Dir,* Traphagen School of Fashion, New York NY (S)

Helm, Alison, *Prof,* West Virginia University, Division of Art, Morgantown WV (S)

Helmholz, Robert, *Asst Dir Development,* Cincinnati Art Museum, Cincinnati OH

Helsell, Charles, *Cur,* University of Minnesota, University Art Museum, Minneapolis MN

Helseth, William, *Instr,* Chattanooga State Technical Community College, Advertising Arts Dept, Chattanooga TN (S)

Helton, Michael, *Prof,* North Carolina Central University, Art Dept, Durham NC (S)

Hembroff, John, *Development Officer,* Seattle Art Museum, Seattle WA

Hemdahl-Owen, Ann, *Assoc Prof,* Jefferson Community College, Fine Arts, Louisville KY (S)

Hemmens, George, *Dir School Urban Planning,* University of Illinois at Chicago, College of Architecture, Art and Urban Planning, Chicago IL (S)

Hempel, Gordon, *Secy,* Artists Guild of Chicago, Chicago IL

Hemus, Sharon, *Special Events Coordr,* San Diego Museum of Art, San Diego CA

Hench, Robert, *Gallery Dir,* University of Southern Colorado, School of Liberal Arts, Pueblo CO

Hench, Robert, *Assoc Prof,* University of Southern Colorado, Belmont Campus, Dept of Art, Pueblo CO (S)

Hendershot, Jim, *Asst Prof,* Saint John's University, Art Dept, Collegeville MN (S)

Henderson, Eugene, *First VPres,* Hoosier Salon Patrons Association, Hoosier Salon Art Gallery, Indianapolis IN

Henderson, John T, *Pres,* Jefferson Community College, Art Dept, Watertown NY (S)

Henderson, Jon M, *Mgr Library Services,* Hallmark Cards, Inc, Creative Library, Kansas City MO

Henderson, J T, *Cur,* Woodstock Art Gallery, Woodstock ON

Henderson, J Welles, *Pres,* Philadelphia Maritime Museum, Philadelphia PA

Henderson, Lana T, *Chmn,* North Carolina Central University, Art Dept, Durham NC (S)

Henderson, Maren, *Assoc Prof,* California State Polytechnic University, Pomona, Art Dept, Pomona CA (S)

Henderson, Michael, *Historic Site Mgr,* Acadian House Museum, Saint Martinville LA

Henderson, Robbin, *Dir & Cur,* Berkeley Art Center, Berkeley CA

Henderson, Robert Morton, *Chief,* New York Public Library, Shelby Cullom Davis Museum, Library & Museum of the Performing Arts, New York NY

Henderson, Theresa, *Pres,* Contemporary Arts Center, Cincinnati OH

Henderson, Thomas, *Assoc Prof,* Mount Allison University, Fine Arts Dept, Sackville NB (S)

Hendley, Bert, *Pres Board Dir,* Zanesville Art Center, Zanesville OH

Hendrick, Barbara, *Mgr Bookshop,* Long Beach Museum of Art, Long Beach CA

Hendricks, Barkley L, *Assoc Prof,* Connecticut College, Dept of Art, New London CT (S)

Hendricks, Bartlett, *Cur Science,* Berkshire Museum, Pittsfield MA

Hendricks, James, *Chmn,* Mount Vernon Nazarene College, Art Dept, Mount Vernon OH (S)

Hendrickson, Hope Coppage, *Staff,* Cliveden, Philadelphia PA

Hendrickson, Morry, *Prof,* Shoreline Community College, Humanities Division, Seattle WA (S)

Hendrickson, Peggy, *Secy,* University of Minnesota, Tweed Museum of Art, Duluth MN

Hendrickson, Ted, *Instructor,* Connecticut College, Dept of Art, New London CT (S)

Hendrickson, Torval E, *Chmn,* Western Wisconsin Technical Institute, Graphics Division, La Crosse WI (S)

Henes, Ernst L, *Museum Dir,* Spirit of '76 Museum, Southern Lorain County Historical Society, Wellington OH

Henes, Margaret, *Secy,* Spirit of '76 Museum, Southern Lorain County Historical Society, Wellington OH

Hengst, Timothy, *Asst Prof,* Johns Hopkins University, School of Medicine, Dept of Art as Applied to Medicine, Baltimore MD (S)

Henisch, Heinz, *Prof,* Pennsylvania State University, University Park, Dept of Art History, University Park PA (S)

Henkel, Margot A, *Executive Dir,* New York Society of Architects, New York NY

Henkin, Joe, *Pres,* Civic Fine Arts Association Museum, Sioux Falls SD

Hennessey, William, *Dir,* University of Kentucky, Art Museum, Lexington KY

Hennig, Barbara A C, *Adm인r,* Fayetteville Museum of Art, Inc, Fayetteville NC

Henning, Darrell, *Cur,* Vesterheim, Norwegian-American Museum, Decorah IA

Henning, Edward B, *Chief Cur Modern Art,* Cleveland Museum of Art, Cleveland OH

Henning, Louise, *Reference Librn,* University of Wisconsin, Kohler Art Library, Madison WI

Henning, Robert, *Cur Exhibitions,* Santa Barbara Museum of Art, Santa Barbara CA

Henning, Roni, *Master Printer,* New York Institute of Technology, Fine Arts Dept, Old Westbury NY (S)

Henning, Virginia, *Cur,* Chalet of the Golden Fleece, New Glarus WI

Henning, William T, *Cur Collections,* Hunter Museum of Art, Chattanooga TN

Henriksen, Harry C, *Cur Exhibits,* University of Illinois, Museum of Natural History, Champaign IL

Henry, Anneliese, *Secy,* Second Street Gallery, Charlottesville VA

Henry, Clarice, *Art Librn,* Hewlett-Woodmere Public Library, Hewlett NY

Henry, Diane V, *A V Librn,* Public Library of the District of Columbia, Audiovisual Division, Washington DC

Henry, Fred, *Asst Prof,* Southern Arkansas University, Dept of Art, Magnolia AR (S)

Henry, Fred, *Assoc Prof,* Southern Arkansas University, Art Dept Gallery & Magale Art Gallery, Magnolia AR

Henry, Jean, *Dir & Cur,* Drexel University Museum, Philadelphia PA

Henry, John B, *Dir Coll & Exhibitions,* Mississippi Museum of Art, Jackson MS

Henry, Joseph, *Asst Dir & VPres,* Art Center College of Design, Pasadena CA (S)

Henry, Margaret, *Exec Dir,* Association of Medical Illustrators, Midlothian VA

Henry, Michael, *Chmn & Prof,* Prairie State College, Art Dept, Chicago Heights IL (S)

Henry, Nancy, *Public Information,* Museum of the American Indian, New York NY

Henry, Penelope, *Librn,* Parrish Art Museum, Aline B Saarinen Library, Southampton NY

Henry, Sara, *Asst Prof,* Drew University, Art Dept, Madison NJ (S)

Henry, William, *Educ Dir,* Parrish Art Museum, Southampton NY

Hensche, Henry, *Dir,* Cape School of Art, Provincetown MA (S)

Hensel, Sandra, *Dir Public Relations & Special Events,* Akron Art Museum, Akron OH

Henselmann, Caspar, *Vis Artist,* University of North Carolina at Chapel Hill, Art Dept, Chapel Hill NC (S)

Henshall, Barbara, *Cur,* Martin & Osa Johnson Safari Museum, Chanute KS

Hensler, Ruth, *Instructor,* Saint Louis Community College at Meramec, Art Dcpt, Saint Louis MO (S)

Hensley, Fred Owen, *Head,* University of North Alabama, Dept of Art, Florence AL (S)

Hensley, Paul B, *Archivist,* Winterthur Museum and Gardens, Library, Winterthur DE

Henson, Joan, *Instr,* Clark College, Art Dept, Vancouver WA (S)

Hentchel, Fred, *Instr,* Illinois Central College, Fine Arts Dept, East Peoria IL (S)

Hentz, Christopher, *Assoc Prof,* Louisiana State University, School of Art, Baton Rouge LA (S)

Henze, F E, *Secy,* Rome Historical Society, Rome Information and Cultural Center, Rome NY

Hepburn, Charles M, *Dean of Studies,* College of Great Falls, Dept of Art, Great Falls MT (S)

Hepburn, Tony, *Head Dept,* New York State College of Ceramics at Alfred University, Division of Art & Design, Alfred NY (S)

Hepler, Paul, *Dir,* State University of New York College at Geneseo, Bertha V B Lederer Gallery, Geneseo NY

Hepler, Paul, *Chmn,* State University of New York College at Geneseo, Dept of Art, Geneseo NY (S)

Heppell, Shirley, *Librn,* Cortland County Historical Society, Kellogg Memorial Reading Room, Cortland NY

Herard, Marvin T, *Prof,* Seattle University, Fine Arts Dept, Division of Art, Seattle WA (S)

Herbert, Sharon, *Assoc Cur,* University of Michigan, Kelsey Museum of Ancient and Medieval Archaeology, Ann Arbor MI

Herbold, LuAnn, *Recording Secy,* North Shore Art League, Winnetka IL

Herdeg, John A, *Pres Trustees,* Winterthur Museum and Gardens, Winterthur DE

Heredia, Ruben, *Vis Prof,* Butte College, Dept of Fine & Performing Arts, Oroville CA (S)

Herger, Dorothy, *Instructor,* Solano Community College, Dept of Fine & Applied Art, Suisun City CA (S)

Hering, Michael J, *Mgr Coll,* School of American Research, Santa Fe NM

Herman, Lloyd E, *Dir,* National Museum of American Art, Renwick Gallery, Washington DC

Hermann, Arthur, *Dir,* University of California, Memorial Union Art Gallery, Davis CA

Hermann, Robert R, *Chmn,* Arts and Education Council of Greater Saint Louis, Saint Louis MO

Hermant, Sydney M, *Chmn Board of Trustees,* Royal Ontario Museum, Toronto ON

Hernandez, Jo Farb, *Dir,* Triton Museum of Art, Santa Clara CA

Hernandez, Sam, *Asst Prof,* University of Santa Clara, Fine Arts Dept, Santa Clara CA (S)

Hernandez, San R, *Chmn,* University of Santa Clara, Fine Arts Dept, Santa Clara CA (S)

Hernandez Cruz, Luis, *Head Dept,* University of Puerto Rico, Dept of Fine Arts, Rio Piedras PR (S)

Herod, Dave D, *Senior Cur Anthropologist,* University of California, R H Lowie Museum of Anthropology, Berkeley CA

Heron, Reginald, *Assoc Prof,* Indiana University, Bloomington, School of Fine Arts, Bloomington IN (S)

Herper, Paul, *Dean,* Pratt Institute, School of Architecture, Brooklyn NY (S)

Herr, Marcianne, *Cur of Education,* Akron Art Museum, Akron OH

Herrero, Susana, *Instructor,* University of Puerto Rico, Dept of Fine Arts, Rio Piedras PR (S)

Herrick, Daniel, *VPres Finance,* Metropolitan Museum of Art, New York NY

Herrick, Fred R, *Dir,* Springfield Art & Historical Society, Springfield VT

Herring, Jack W, *Dir,* Baylor University, Armstrong Browning Library, Waco TX

Herrington, Thomas E, *Chief Preparator,* New Orleans Museum of Art, New Orleans LA

Herrmann, Arthur D, *Pres,* Columbus Museum of Art, Columbus OH

Herrold, David, *Asst Prof,* DePauw University, Art Dept, Greencastle IN (S)

Hershberg, Israel, *Instr,* New York Academy of Art, New York NY (S)

Hershberger, Abner, *Chmn,* Goshen College, Art Dept, Goshen IN (S)

Herskowitz, Sylvia A, *Dir,* Yeshiva University, Museum, New York NY

Hert, Judith R, *Humanities Div Chmn,* San Bernardino Valley College, Art Dept, San Bernardino CA (S)

Hertel, C H, *Prof Art,* Pitzer College, Dept of Art, Claremont CA (S)

Hertz, Richard, *Academic Studies Dept Chmn,* Art Center College of Design, Pasadena CA (S)

Hertzberg, David, *Asst Cur,* Vizcaya Museum and Gardens, Miami FL

Hertzi, Joseph R, *Gallery Dir,* Canton Art Institute, Canton OH

Hertzi, Joseph R, *Dir,* Canton Art Institute, Canton OH (S)

Hertzman, Gay M, *Asst Dir,* North Carolina Museum of Art, Raleigh NC

Herzberg, Lois, *Librn II,* Yonkers Public Library, Fine Arts Dept, Yonkers NY

Herzbrun, Helene M, *Prof,* American University, Dept of Art, Washington DC (S)

Hess, Honee, *Cur of Education,* University of Iowa, Museum of Art, Iowa City IA

Hess, Joyce, *Art Librn,* University of Texas at Austin, Fine Arts Library, Austin TX

Hess, Stanley W, *Librn,* Atkins Museum of Fine Art, Kenneth and Helen Spencer Art Reference Library, Kansas City MO

Hesslein, Shirley, *Librn,* State University of New York at Buffalo, Lockwood Memorial Library, Buffalo NY

Hester, Warren, *Pres,* Coppini Academy of Fine Arts, San Antonio TX

Heth, Susan, *Registrar,* University of Alberta, Ring House Gallery, Edmonton AB

Hetzel, Peter, *Asst Prof,* Catholic University of America, Dept of Architecture and Planning, Washington DC (S)

Heugh, Nancy, *Assoc Conservator of Paper,* Atkins Museum of Fine Art, Kansas City MO

Heuler, Henry J, *Assoc Prof,* University of West Florida, Faculty of Art, Pensacola FL (S)

Heuler, Judith A, *Asst Prof,* University of West Florida, Faculty of Art, Pensacola FL (S)

Heuser, Lorraine, *Catalog Librn,* Moore College of Art Gallery, Library, Philadelphia PA

Hewitt, Clarissa, *Assoc Prof,* California Polytechnic State University at San Luis Obispo, Art Dept, San Luis Obispo CA (S)

Hewitt, Duncan A, *Chmn,* University of Southern Maine, Art Dept, Gorham ME (S)

Hewitt, Linda V, *Asst Dir,* Isabella Stewart Gardner Museum, Boston MA

Hewitt, Mary Jane, *Dir,* The Museum of African American Art, Santa Monica CA

Heyd, William D, *Admin Asst,* Arts Council of Hawaii, Honolulu HI

Heyduck, Bill, *Prof,* Eastern Illinois University, School of Fine Arts, Charleston IL (S)

Heyl, H Elizabeth, *Secy,* Burlington County Historical Society, Burlington NJ

Heyman, Ellen H, *Assoc Prof,* Clinton Community College, Humanities Art Dept, Plattsburgh NY (S)

Heyman, Therese, *Sr Cur Prints & Photographs,* Oakland Museum, Art Dept, Oakland CA

Heywood, Thomas J, *Treasurer,* National Assembly of Local Arts Agencies, Washington DC

Hiatt, DeAnn, *Dir Public Relations,* Colorado Springs Fine Arts Center, Colorado Springs CO

Hibbard, James, *Prof,* Portland State University, Dept of Art and Architecture, Portland OR (S)

Hibbs, Vivian A, *Cur Archaeology,* Hispanic Society of America, Museum, New York NY

Hibel, William, *VPres,* Edna Hibel Art Foundation, Hibel Museum of Art, Riviera Beach FL

Hickenbotham, Kathleen, *Lectr,* Mount Marty College, Art Dept, Yankton SD (S)

Hickey, Margaret, *Chmn Design,* Massachusetts College of Art, Boston MA (S)

Hickey, Maureen, *Dir of Art Education,* Berkshire Museum, Pittsfield MA

Hicklin, Barbara Roe, *Pres,* Alberta Society of Artists, Calgary AB

Hickman, Theresa, *Mem Secy,* Norton Gallery and School of Art, West Palm Beach FL

Hicks, D W, *Pres,* Frontier Times Museum, Bandera TX

Hicks, Ellen C, *Ed,* American Association of Museums, Washington DC

Hicks, Herbert A, *Assoc Prof,* University of Lethbridge, Dept of Art, Lethbridge AB (S)

Hicks, John, *Planetarium Dir,* Museum of the Southwest, Library, Midland TX

Hicks, Kathryn, *Dir,* University of South Carolina Spartanburg, Library Art Gallery, Spartanburg SC

Hicks, Leon, *Assoc Prof,* Webster College, Art Dept, Webster Groves MO (S)

Hicks, Louis, *Cur,* Elizabet Ney Museum, Austin TX

Hicks, Margaret, *Dir,* Navarro College, Art Dept, Corsicana TX (S)

Hicks, Ron, *Instructor,* Johnson County Community College, Humanities Division, Overland Park KS (S)

Hicks, Steve, *Chmn,* Oklahoma Baptist University, Art Dept, Shawnee OK (S)

Hickson, Howard, *Dir,* Northeastern Nevada Historical Society Museum, Elko NV

Hider, William A, *Treas,* Everson Museum of Art, Syracuse NY

Hidge, Phillip, *Prof,* Wilmington College, Art Dept, Wilmington OH (S)

Hiebert, Kenneth, *Chairperson Graphic Design,* Philadelphia College of Art, Philadelphia PA (S)

Hiers, C J, *Head,* Auburn University, Dept of Art, Auburn AL (S)

Hiesinger, Kathryn B, *Cur European Decorative Arts after 1700,* Philadelphia Museum of Art, Philadelphia PA

Hiester, Jan, *Registrar,* Charleston Museum, Charleston SC

Hietbrink, Elaine, *Secy,* South Dakota State University, South Dakota Memorial Art Center, Brookings SD

Higa, Yosh, *Assoc Prof,* Southampton College of Long Island University, C W Post Center Fine Arts Division, Southampton NY (S)

Higdon, Elizabeth, *Asst Prof,* Duke University, Dept of Art, Durham NC (S)

Higgins, John J, *Dir of Finance,* Museum of Fine Arts, Boston MA

Higham, Del P, *Actg Acad Dean,* Tunxis Community College, Graphic Design Dept, Farmington CT (S)

Highfill, Karen, *Librn,* Institute of American Indian Arts Museum, Library, Santa Fe NM

Hight, C, *Pres,* Association of Collegiate Schools of Architecture, Washington DC

Hight, Eleanor M, *Asst Dir,* Wellesley College, Museum, Wellesley MA

Hightower, Caroline, *Exec Dir,* American Institute of Graphic Arts, New York NY

Hightower, John B, *Pres,* South Street Seaport Museum, New York NY

Hiigel, Lewis E, *Dean Div,* El Camino College, Division of Fine Arts, Los Angeles CA (S)

Hild, Robert, *Head Dept,* Westminster College, Art Dept, New Wilmington PA (S)

Hildebrand, Danna, *Instr,* Sheridan College, Art Dept, Sheridan WY (S)

Hildebrand, Terry, *Supvr Plant & Security,* Minnesota Museum of Art, Saint Paul MN

Hildebrandt, Greg, *Instr,* Joe Kubert School of Cartoon and Graphic Art Inc, Dover NJ (S)

Hildenbrand, William F, *Executive Secy,* United States Senate Commission on Art and Antiquities, Washington DC

Hildreth, Joseph, *Assoc Prof,* State University of New York College at Potsdam, Dept of Fine Arts, Potsdam NY (S)

Hile, Jeanette, *Asst Prof,* Seton Hall University, Dept of Art and Music, South Orange NJ (S)

Hileman, Jayne, *Asst Prof,* Saint Xavier College, Dept of Art, Chicago IL (S)

Hiles, Bruce, *Cur of Exhibitions,* Huntsville Museum of Art, Huntsville AL

Hilke, Mary, *Exec Secy & Cur,* Koochiching County Historical Society Museum, International Falls MN

Hilker, Gordon, *Dir,* United States International University, School of Performing and Visual Arts, San Diego CA (S)

Hill, Charles, *Cur Canadian Art,* National Gallery of Canada, Ottawa ON

Hill, Esther, *Faculty,* University of North Carolina-Charlotte, Creative Arts Dept, Charlotte NC (S)

Hill, Harold W, *Chmn,* Texas Lutheran College, Dept of Visual Arts, Seguin TX (S)

Hill, James Berry, *Secy,* National Antique and Art Dealers Association of America, New York NY

Hill, John W, *Pres,* Concord Art Association, Concord MA

Hill, Larry, *Treas,* Vernon Art Association, Topham Brown Gallery, Vernon BC

Hill, Loyd, *Pres,* Waterworks Gallery, Salisbury NC

Hill, Maralys, *Librn,* Mingei International Inc, Reference Library, La Jolla CA

Hill, Marie, *Secy,* Vernon Art Association, Topham Brown Gallery, Vernon BC

Hill, Nicholas, *Head Art Dept,* Bethany College, Art Dept, Lindsborg KS (S)

Hill, Peter, *Prof,* University of Nebraska at Omaha, Dept of Art, Omaha NE (S)

Hill, Randy, *Pres,* Keokuk Art Center, Keokuk IA

Hill, Richard, *Drawing Chmn,* Atlanta College of Art, Atlanta GA (S)

Hill, Richard, *Chmn Dept Photo & Electric Arts,* Ontario College of Art, Toronto ON (S)

Hill, Sherri, *Art Gallery & Craft Center Coordr,* Youngstown State University, Kilcawley Center Art Gallery, Youngstown OH

Hill, S Richardson, *Pres,* University of Alabama, Visual Arts Gallery, Birmingham AL

Hill, Steven, *Instructor,* Avila College, Art Division, Dept of Performing and Visual Art, Kansas City MO (S)

Hill, Tim, *VPres,* The Friends of Photography, Carmel CA

Hill, William M, *Dir,* Santa Monica College Art Gallery, Santa Monica CA

Hillabold, Nancy, *Cur,* University of Regina, Slide Library, Regina SK

Hillain-Ligon, D Regina, *Cur,* Maryland Museum of African Art, Columbia MD

Hillbruner, Fred, *Asst Dir & Head Technical Services,* School of the Art Institute of Chicago Library, Chicago IL

Hillding, John, *Instructor,* The Design Schools, Art Institute of Seattle, Seattle WA (S)

Hiller, Jack, *Chmn,* Valparaiso University, University Art Galleries and Collections, Valparaiso IN

Hilliard, Elbert R, *Dir,* Mississippi Department of Archives and History, State Historical Museum, Jackson MS

Hilliard, Glenn, *Pres,* Liberty Life Insurance Company, Greenville SC

Hilligoss, Martha, *Chief Art Dept,* Saint Louis Public Library, Saint Louis MO

Hillix, Virginia, *Education Consultant,* Art Research Center, Kansas City MO

Hillman, Arthur, *Instructor,* Simon's Rock of Bard College, Studio Arts Dept, Great Barrington MA (S)

Hillman, Elizabeth, *Cur,* South Peace Art Society, Dawson Creek Art Gallery, Dawson Creek BC

Hillman, Raymond, *Librn,* The Haggin Museum, Petzinger Memorial Library, Stockton CA

Hills, Patricia, *Adjunct Cur, 18th & 19th Century Art,* Whitney Museum of American Art, New York NY

Hilpert, Renee L, *Instructor,* Rudolph Schaeffer School of Design, San Francisco CA (S)

Hilt, Lyda, *Librn Genealogical Section,* Tippecanoe County Historical Museum, Alameda McCollough Library, Lafayette IN

Hilton, Alison, *Fac,* Georgetown University, Dept of Fine Arts, Washington DC (S)

Hilton, Jennifer, *Instr,* Oxbow Center for the Arts, Saugatuck MI (S)

Hilton, Ken, *Dir Electronics,* Museum, Fine Arts Research & Holographic Center, Chicago IL

Hilton, Russell, *Dir System Development,* Museum, Fine Arts Research & Holographic Center, Chicago IL

Hilty, Thomas, *Dir Grad Studies,* Bowling Green State University, School of Art, Bowling Green OH (S)

Hime, Gary D, *Asst Librn,* Wichita Public Library, Wichita KS

Himel, Margaret, *Fac,* Georgetown University, Dept of Fine Arts, Washington DC (S)

Hinckley, William P, *Pres,* Parson Fisher House, Jonathan Fisher Memorial, Inc, Blue Hill ME

Hindle, Sarah K, *Pres,* Concord Antiquarian Society Museum, Concord MA

Hinds, Patricia, *Fine Arts Coordr,* Antelope Valley College, Art Dept, Division of Fine Arts, Lancaster CA (S)

Hindson, Bradley T, *Assoc Prof,* Rochester Institute of Technology, School of Photographic Arts & Sciences, Rochester NY (S)

Hine, Lela M, *Cur & Registrar,* Hermitage Foundation Museum, Norfolk VA

Hines, Adrienne G, *Chmn,* Federated Arts Council of Richmond, Inc, Richmond VA

Hines, Claire, *Librn,* Brownsville Art League Museum, Brownsville TX

Hines, Felrath, *Chief Conservator,* Hirshhorn Museum and Sculpture Garden, Washington DC

Hines, James, *Prof,* Christopher Newport College, Arts & Communications, Newport News VA (S)

Hines, Norman, *Assoc Prof,* Pomona College, Art Dept, Claremont CA (S)

Hines, Norman, *Instr,* Illinois Central College, Fine Arts Dept, East Peoria IL (S)

Hingston, Rebecca, *Financial Officer,* Portland Museum of Art, Portland ME

Hinken, Susan, *Technical Services Librn,* University of Portland, Wilson W Clark Memorial Library, Portland OR

Hinkhouse, Jim, *Prof,* Fort Hays State University, Dept of Art, Hays KS (S)

Hinkle, John, *Pres,* Creative Arts Guild, Dalton GA

Hinkle, Joseph, *Secy,* China Trade Museum, Milton MA

Hinks, Avis, *Secy,* Jesse Besser Museum, Alpena MI

Hinojosa, Gloria Selene, *First Asst,* Houston Public Library, Houston TX

Hinson, Tom E, *Cur Contemporary Art,* Cleveland Museum of Art, Cleveland OH

Hinton, Sam, *VPres,* Mingei International Inc, Mingei International Museum of World Folk Art, La Jolla CA

Hios, Theo, *VPres,* Federation of Modern Painters and Sculptors, New York NY

Hippel, Bruce, *Instr,* Ocean City Arts Center, Ocean City NJ (S)

Hipperson, Gayl, *Actg Head Natural Sciences,* New Brunswick Museum, Saint John NB

Hirano, M, *Assoc Prof,* American University, Dept of Art, Washington DC (S)

Hire, Herman M, *Dir,* University of Southwestern Louisiana, University Art Museum, Lafayette LA

Hirota, Norma, *Art Specialist,* Hawaii State Library, Fine Arts-Audiovisual Section, Honolulu HI

Hirsch, Adrienne, *Executive Dir,* Arizona Commission on the Arts, Phoenix AZ

Hirsch, Barron, *Chmn Dept,* Saginaw Valley State College, Dept of Art and Design, University Center MI (S)

Hirsch, Betty Wurth, *Dir,* China Trade Museum, Milton MA

Hirschfeld, Susan B, *Asst Cur,* Solomon R Guggenheim Museum, New York NY

Hirschl, Milton, *Prof,* Pierce College, Art Dept, Woodland Hills CA (S)

Hirschl, Norman, *Pres,* Art Dealers Association of America, Inc, New York NY

Hirsh, Sharon, *Chairperson & Assoc Prof,* Dickinson College, Fine Arts Dept, Carlisle PA (S)

Hirshen, Sanford, *Chmn Architecture,* University of California, Berkeley, College of Environmental Design, Berkeley CA (S)

Hirshler, Eric E, *Prof,* Denison University, Dept of Art, Granville OH (S)

Hirst, Larry, *Instructor,* Delta State University, Dept of Art, Cleveland MS (S)

Hissinson, Genevra, *Asst to Dir Special Events,* National Gallery of Art, Washington DC

Hitch, Henry C, *Pres,* No Man's Land Historical Society Museum, Goodwell OK

Hitchcock, D Michael, *Assoc Prof,* George Washington University, Dept of Art, Washington DC (S)

Hitchcock, P, *Chmn,* California State University, Sacramento, Dept of Art, Sacramento CA (S)

Hitchings, Gladys, *Librn,* Davenport Municipal Art Gallery, Art Reference Library, Davenport IA

Hitchings, Sinclair H, *Keeper of Prints,* Boston Public Library, Albert H Wiggin Gallery (Prints), Boston MA

Hite, Madeline D, *Cur Education,* Division of Historical and Cultural Affairs, Bureau of Museums and Historic Sites, Dover DE

Hitner, Chuch, *Coordr Painting & Drawing,* University of Arizona, Dept of Art, Tucson AZ (S)

Hittman, Suzanne, *Development Officer,* Pacific Northwest Arts and Crafts Association, Bellevue Art Museum, Bellevue WA

Hively, Mignon, *Head Dept,* Otero Junior College, Art Dept, La Junta CO (S)

Hix, Charles, *Dean,* Texas A & M University, College of Architecture and Environmental Design, College Station TX (S)

Hixon, Nancy S, *Registrar,* University of Houston, Sarah Campbell Blaffer Gallery, Houston TX

Hlad, Richard, *Assoc Prof,* Tarrant County Junior College, Art Dept, Northeast Campus, Hurst TX (S)

Hluszok, Zenon, *Archivist,* Ukrainian Cultural and Educational Centre Museum, Winnipeg MB

Hnatkowsky, V, *Chmn of Pub Rel,* Ukrainian Institute of America, Inc, New York NY

Ho, Abraham P, *Cur,* Saint John's University, Chung-Cheng Art Gallery, Jamaica NY

Ho, Rosa, *Dir & Cur,* Surrey Art Gallery, Surrey BC

Ho, Wai-Kam, *Sr Research Cur Chinese Art,* Cleveland Museum of Art, Cleveland OH

Hoadley, Bruce, *Instructor,* Truro Center for the Arts at Castle Hill, Inc, Truro MA (S)

Hoar, Bill, *Asst Prof,* Northern State College, Art Dept, Aberdeen SD (S)

Hoar, Joan, *Volunteer Coordr,* Philbrook Art Center, Tulsa OK

Hoare, Gabriel Mary, *Assoc Prof,* Webster College, Art Dept, Webster Groves MO (S)

Hobbs, Constance, *Instructor,* University of North Carolina at Wilmington, Dept of Creative Arts - Division of Art, Wilmington NC (S)

Hobbs, Franklin W, *First Regent,* Gunston Hall Plantation, Lorton VA

Hobbs, Joe F, *Dir,* University of Oklahoma, School of Art, Norman OK (S)

Hobbs, Robert C, *Dir,* University of Iowa, Museum of Art, Iowa City IA

Hobbs, Robert D, *Prof,* Clarion University of Pennsylvania, Dept of Art, Clarion PA (S)

Holownia, Thaddeus, *Asst Prof,* Mount Allison University, Fine Arts Dept, Sackville NB (S)

Holst, Lise, *Asst Cur & Registrar,* Williams College, Museum of Art, Williamstown MA

Holston, Frank, *Prof,* Community College of Baltimore, Dept of Fine & Applied Arts, Liberty Campus, Baltimore MD (S)

Holt, Alison, *Asst Libr,* Art Center College of Design, James Lemont Fogg Memorial Library, Pasadena CA

Holt, Jane B, *Hostess,* Centre Hill Mansion, Petersburg VA

Holt, Laura, *Anthropology Librn,* Museum of New Mexico, Library, Santa Fe NM

Holt, R J, *Dir,* Chesapeake Bay Maritime Museum, Saint Michaels MD

Holt, Sue, *Instructor,* Dunedin Fine Arts and Cultural Center, Dunedin FL (S)

Holtgrewe, Douglas, *Asst Prof,* Elmira College, Art Dept, Elmira NY (S)

Holton, Dorothy, *Gallery Shop Mgr,* Carolina Art Association, Gibbes Art Gallery, Charleston SC

Holton, Mark, *Cur,* Confederation Centre Art Gallery and Museum, Charlottetown PE

Holton, Susan, *Librn,* American Institute of Architects, Library, Washington DC

Holubar, Michael, *Technical Services Supvr,* Madison Art Center, Madison WI

Holverson, John, *Dir,* Portland Museum of Art, Portland ME

Holzrichter, Elmer, *Prof,* Kearney State College, Dept of Art, Kearney NE (S)

Homan, Carol, *Cataloguer,* Philadelphia Museum of Art, Library, Philadelphia PA

Homan, Ralph, *Instructor,* College of the Sequoias, Art Dept, Visalia CA (S)

Homes, Philip C, *Executive Dir,* Peters Valley Inc Craft Center Library, Layton NJ

Hommel, William L, *Dir Kirkpatrick Ctr,* Oklahoma Center for Science and Art, Kirkpatrick Center, Oklahoma City OK

Honan, Margot, *Asst Cur of Manuscripts,* Colorado Historical Society, State Museum, Denver CO

Honczarenko, M, *Secy,* Ukrainian Institute of America, Inc, New York NY

Honig, Mervin, *VPres,* Allied Artists of America, Inc, New York NY

Honig, Sylvia, *Asst Prof,* Trenton State College, Art Dept, Trenton NJ (S)

Hoobler, James A, *Exec Dir,* Tennessee Historical Society, Nashville TN

Hood, Gail, *Instructor,* Southeastern Louisiana University, Dept of Visual Arts, Hammond LA (S)

Hood, Gary, *Cur,* Wichita State University, Edwin A Ulrich Museum of Art, Wichita KS

Hood, Graham S, *Dir & Cur Coll,* Colonial Williamsburg Foundation, Williamsburg VA

Hood, Harry, *Pres,* Madison County Historical Society, Cottage Lawn, Oneida NY

Hood, Mary Bryan, *Dir,* Owensboro Museum of Fine Art, Owensboro KY

Hood, Paul, *Development Dir,* Virginia Museum of Fine Arts, Richmond VA

Hood, Richard, *Pres,* American Color Print Society, Philadelphia PA

Hood, William, *Assoc Prof,* Oberlin College, Dept of Art, Oberlin OH (S)

Hoogs, Barbara F, *Keeper, Lending Center,* Honolulu Academy of Arts, Honolulu HI

Hook, Charles E, *Asst Prof,* Florida State University, Art Dept, Tallahassee FL (S)

Hooker, Kathy Lennonx, *Chief,* New York Public Library, Schomburg Center for Research in Black Culture, New York NY

Hooker, Michael, *Pres,* Bennington College, Visual Arts Division, Bennington VT (S)

Hooks, Earl J, *Dir,* Fisk University Museum of Art, Nashville TN

Hooper, Rosemary, *Coordr Printmaking,* University of Delaware, Dept of Art, Newark DE (S)

Hooper-Cowan, Aileen, *Cur of Collections,* Sculptor's Society of Canada, Toronto ON

Hooten, Joseph, *Instructor,* Long Beach City College, Dept of Art, Long Beach CA (S)

Hoover, Bobbye, *Admin Asst,* Museum of Fine Arts of Saint Petersburg, Florida, Inc, Saint Petersburg FL

Hoover, Don, *Asst Cur Educ,* El Paso Museum of Art, El Paso TX

Hoover, Richard L, *Treas,* The Stained Glass Association of America, Saint Louis MO

Hopcraft, Timothy, *Controller,* Art Gallery of Ontario, Toronto ON

Hope, Sally, *Mgr, Collections & Archives,* Hallmark Cards, Inc, Hallmark Collections, Kansas City MO

Hope, Samuel, *Exec Dir,* National Association of Schools of Art and Design, Reston VA

Hope-Smith, Page, *Arts Centre Coordr,* Richmond Arts Centre, Richmond BC

Hopkins, Elizabeth, *VPres,* San Bernardino County Museum and Satellites, Fine Arts Institute, Redlands CA

Hopkins, Henry T, *Dir,* San Francisco Museum of Modern Art, San Francisco CA

Hopkins, Joe, *Chmn,* Sullivan County Community College, Division of Commercial Art and Photography, Loch Sheldrake NY (S)

Hopkins, Joseph W, *Exhib Coordr,* University of Tennessee, Frank H McClung Museum, Knoxville TN

Hopkins, Kenneth R, *Dir,* State Capitol Museum, Olympia WA

Hopkins, Melissa, *Membership Mgr,* University of Rochester, Memorial Art Gallery, Rochester NY

Hopkins, Miles B, *VPres,* Star-Spangled Banner Flag House Association, Baltimore MD

Hopkins, Susan, *Instr,* Ocean City Arts Center, Ocean City NJ (S)

Hopper, Deborah, *Asst to Librn,* Saint Louis Art Museum, Richardson Memorial Library, Saint Louis MO

Hopper, James, *Chmn,* Mount Union College, Dept of Art, Alliance OH (S)

Hopper, Kerry, *Preparator & Bldg Mgr,* Beaumont Art Museum, Beaumont TX

Hopper, Pamela, *Public Information Asst,* Memphis Brooks Museum of Art, Memphis TN

Hopton, Leslie, *Museum Educator,* Kelowna Centennial Museum and National Exhibit Centre, Kelowna BC

Horbach, C Frederick, *Prof,* Cumberland County College, Humanities Dept, Vineland NJ (S)

Horman, Elizabeth, *VPres,* New York Artists Equity Association, Inc, New York NY

Horn, Augustine, *Faculty,* Saint Gregory's College, Dept of Art, Shawnee OK (S)

Horn, Bruce, *Assoc Dir,* Northern Arizona University, Art Dept, Flagstaff AZ (S)

Horn, Roni, *Asst Prof,* Colgate University, Dept of Fine Arts, Hamilton NY (S)

Horn, Samuel, *Secy,* New York Society of Architects, New York NY

Hornaday, Richard, *Instr,* California State University, Chico, Art Dept, Chico CA (S)

Horne, Catherine W, *Asst Archivist & Cur Exhibitions,* McKissick Museums, Columbia SC

Horne, Walter G, *Chmn Photography Plates & Press Division,* Rochester Institute of Technology, School of Printing, Rochester NY (S)

Horning, Jerome, *Instr,* Creighton University, Fine and Performing Arts Dept, Omaha NE (S)

Hornstein, Sara, *Assoc Prof,* Dowling College, Dept of Art, Oakdale NY (S)

Horowitz, Marvin, *Assoc Prof,* New York Institute of Technology, Fine Arts Dept, Old Westbury NY (S)

Horrell, Jeffrey L, *Librn,* Hood Museum of Art, Sherman Art Library, Hanover NH

Horrocks, Sandra, *Public Relations Mgr,* Philadelphia Museum of Art, Philadelphia PA

Horse Capture, George P, *Cur Plains Indian Museum,* Buffalo Bill Memorial Association, Cody WY

Horsey, Ann, *Cur Coll,* Division of Historical and Cultural Affairs, Bureau of Museums and Historic Sites, Dover DE

Horsfield, Kate, *Video Data Bank,* School of the Art Institute of Chicago Library, Chicago IL

Horste, Kathryn, *Asst Prof,* Colgate University, Dept of Fine Arts, Hamilton NY (S)

Hortenburg, Larry, *Instructor,* Austin Peay State University, Dept of Art, Clarksville TN (S)

Hortenbury, Larry, *Dir,* Austin Peay State University, Margaret Fort Trahern Gallery, Clarksville TN

Hortian, Serena, *Dir,* Scalamandre Museum of Textiles, New York NY

Horton, Alfred F, *Assoc Prof,* Rochester Institute of Technology, School of Printing, Rochester NY (S)

Horton, Christopher, *Assoc Prof,* Hartford Art School of the University of Hartford, West Hartford CT (S)

Horton, Frank L, *Dir,* Old Salem Inc, Museum of Early Southern Decorative Arts, Winston-Salem NC

Horton, Gary M, *Dean,* Houston Baptist College, Dept of Art, Houston TX (S)

Horton, James I, *Assoc Prof,* Rochester Institute of Technology, School of Printing, Rochester NY (S)

Horuitz, Suzanne, *Trustee,* Foundation for Today's Art, Nexus Gallery, Philadelphia PA

Horvat, Krisjohn O, *Asst Prof,* Rhode Island College, Art Dept, Providence RI (S)

Horvath, David, *Asst Cur,* University of Louisville, University of Louisville Photographic Archives, Louisville KY

Hoskins, Alice, *Education Officer,* Art Gallery of Nova Scotia, Halifax NS

Hosley, William, *Decorative Arts, Assoc Cur,* Wadsworth Atheneum, Hartford CT

Hosmer, Ken, *Art Dir,* Carrizo Art and Craft Workshops, Ruidoso NM (S)

Hossler, Marguerite H, *Instr,* Woodbury University, Professional Arts Division, Los Angeles CA (S)

Hostetter, David, *Cur of Planetarium,* Lafayette Natural History Museum, Planetarium and Nature Station, Lafayette LA

Hostetter, Eric, *Asst Prof,* Indiana University, Bloomington, School of Fine Arts, Bloomington IN (S)

Hotchkiss, Horace L, *Cur,* Winterthur Museum and Gardens, Winterthur in Odessa, Winterthur DE

Hotheinz, Rudolph H, *Asst Prof,* Virginia Western Community College, Commercial Art, Fine Art & Photography, Roanoke VA (S)

Houck, Pat, *Public Relations,* French Art Colony, Inc, Gallipolis OH

Houde, Jean-Luc, *Asst Dir,* Centre Cultural de Shawinigan, Shawinigan PQ

Houeman, Alice, *Conservator,* Alaska State Museum, Juneau AK

Hough, Katherine Plake, *Cur Art,* Palm Springs Desert Museum, Inc, Palm Springs CA

Hough, Melissa, *Asst Cur,* INA Corporation, Philadelphia PA

Houghland, W D, *Lectr,* College of William and Mary, Dept of Fine Arts, Williamsburg VA (S)

Houglum, John, *Instructor,* Dunedin Fine Arts and Cultural Center, Dunedin FL (S)

Houk, Joseph E, *Dean,* Pace University, Dyson College Arts & Science, White Plains NY (S)

Houk, Mary Margaret, *Dir,* Brevard College, Jones Library, Brevard NC

Houlihan, Patrick T, *Dir,* Southwest Museum, Los Angeles CA

Houllahan, Roberta, *Instructor,* Rhode Island College, Art Dept, Providence RI (S)

House, William, *Actg Chmn Industrial Design,* Center for Creative Studies_College of Art and Design, Detroit MI (S)

Housego, Paul, *Permanent Collection,* Art Metropole, Toronto ON

Housel, Jim, *Pres,* Ladies Library and Art Association, Independence Museum, Independence KS

Houseman, Ann, *Actg Division Dir,* Division of Historical and Cultural Affairs, Bureau of Museums and Historic Sites, Dover DE

Houser, Caroline, *Asst Prof,* Smith College, Art Dept, Northampton MA (S)

Houser, Constance, *Secy,* Gaston County Museum of Art & History, Dallas NC

Housman, Russell, *Prof,* Nassau Community College, Art Dept, Garden City NY (S)

Houston, Blanche V, *Cataloguer,* Frick Art Reference Library, New York NY

Houston, Oliver C, *Chmn Fine Arts,* Graceland College, Art Dept, Lamoni IA (S)

Houze, Herbert, *Cur Winchester Arms Museum,* Buffalo Bill Memorial Association, Cody WY

Hoven, Tore, *Mgr,* Seattle Art Museum, Modern Art Pavilion, Seattle WA

Hover, Jesse, *Chairperson,* City College of San Francisco, Art Dept, San Francisco CA (S)

Hovind, Mary, *Specialist,* University of Wisconsin-Stout, Art Dept, Menomonie WI (S)

Hovland, Jody, *VPres,* Iowa City, Johnson County Arts Council, Iowa City IA

Howard, Cecil, *Prof,* Western New Mexico University, College of Arts and Letters, Art Dept, Silver City NM (S)

Howard, Charles H, *Librn,* Penobscot Marine Museum, Library, Searsport ME

Howard, Cordelia, *Dir Libr Servs,* Long Beach Public Library, Long Beach CA

Howard, Jan, *Cur Prints & Drawings,* University of Kansas, Spencer Museum of Art, Lawrence KS

Howard, Jane B, *Asst Prof,* Indian River Community College, Fine Art Dept, Fort Pierce FL (S)

Howard, Jean, *Instructor,* Johnson County Community College, Humanities Division, Overland Park KS (S)

Howard, Jonas A, *Coordr & Prof,* Indiana University Southeast, Fine Arts Dept, New Albany IN (S)

Howard, Kathryn, *Photographer,* Art Research Center, Kansas City MO

Howard, Paul, *Asst Prof,* Coe College, Dept of Art, Cedar Rapids IA (S)

Howard, Robert, *Prof,* University of North Carolina at Chapel Hill, Art Dept, Chapel Hill NC (S)

Howat, John K, *Chmn American Art Dept,* Metropolitan Museum of Art, New York NY

Howdle, Bruce, *Vis Prof,* Victor Valley College, Art Dept, Victorville CA (S)

Howe, Eunice, *Asst Prof,* University of Southern California, School of Fine Arts, Los Angeles CA (S)

Howe, James, *Chmn Art Dept,* Kean College of New Jersey, Union NJ

Howe, James, *Chmn Fine Arts Dept,* Kean College of New Jersey, Fine Arts Dept, Union NJ (S)

Howe, Katherine, *Asst Dir Administration & Assoc Cur,* Museum of Fine Arts, Houston, Houston TX

Howe, Raymond, *Cur Education,* New Jersey State Museum, Trenton NJ

Howe, Robert L, *Deputy Dir Admin,* Museum of Modern Art, New York NY

Howell, Bob, *Assoc Prof,* Hardin-Simmons University, Art Dept, Abilene TX (S)

Howell, Charles, *Cur Entomology,* San Bernardino County Museum and Satellites, Fine Arts Institute, Redlands CA

Howell, Joseph, *Secy & Registrar,* Zanesville Art Center, Zanesville OH

Howell, Joseph, *Librn,* Zanesville Art Center, Library, Zanesville OH

Howell, Robert D, *Assoc Prof,* California Polytechnic State University at San Luis Obispo, Art Dept, San Luis Obispo CA (S)

Howell, Sally, *Dir,* Willamette University, George Putnam University Center, Salem OR

Howett, John, *Chmn & Prof,* Emory University, Art History Dept, Atlanta GA (S)

Howk, Cynthia, *Res Coordr,* Landmark Society of Western New York, Inc, Wenrich Memorial Library, New York NY

Howkins, Mary Ball, *Asst Prof,* Rhode Island College, Art Dept, Providence RI (S)

Howland, Cindy, *Treas,* Redding Museum and Art Center, Redding CA

Howland, Ed, *Pres,* Redding Museum and Art Center, Redding CA

Howlett, Denver, *Grants & Memorial Liaison,* Indiana State Museum, Indianapolis IN

Howlett, Dorn, *Chmn Art Educ,* Edinboro University of Pennsylvania, Art Dept, Edinboro PA (S)

Howrigan, Roger, *Instr,* Saint Thomas Aquinas College, Art Dept, Sparkhill NY (S)

Howsare, Susan, *Asst Prof,* Waynesburg College, Dept of Fine Arts, Waynesburg PA (S)

Howze, Jim, *Prof,* Texas Tech University, Dept of Art, Lubbock TX (S)

Howze, William, *Dir Special Programs,* Amon Carter Museum, Fort Worth TX

Hoyman, Lisa, *Childrens Room,* Mason City Public Library, Mason City IA

Hruska, Dorothy Irene, *Co-Dir & Museologist,* LeSueur County Historical Society Museum, Elysian MN

Hruska, James E, *Dir & Secy,* LeSueur County Historical Society Museum, Elysian MN

Hruska, Robert J, *Asst Dir & Cur Anthropology,* Oshkosh Public Museum, Oshkosh WI

Hubbard, John D, *Prof,* Northern Michigan University, Dept of Art and Design, Marquette MI (S)

Hubbard, Marguerite B, *Cur Museum,* Franklin D Roosevelt Library and Museum, Hyde Park NY

Hubbard, Rita, *Head Dept,* Christopher Newport College, Arts & Communications, Newport News VA (S)

Hubbard, William, *VPres,* Pocumtuck Valley Memorial Association, Memorial Hall, Deerfield MA

Hubbell, Robert Fleet, *Pres,* American Portrait Society, Seal Beach CA

Hubbs, Nina, *Head, Installation & Design,* University of California, University Art Museum, Berkeley CA

Huber, Gerard, *Coordr Grad Programs,* East Texas State University, Dept of Art, Commerce TX (S)

Huber, R, *Instructor,* Golden West College, Arts, Humanities and Social Sciences Institute, Huntington Beach CA (S)

Huber, Robert L, *Asst to Chmn Fine and Performing Arts,* Ocean County College, Humanities Dept, Toms River NJ (S)

Huber, Tallie, *Asst Development Mgr,* Sangre De Cristo Arts & Conference Center, Pueblo CO

Huberman, Brian, *Lectr,* Rice University, Dept of Art and Art History, Houston TX (S)

Hubley, Loretta, *Instructor,* Madonna College, Art Dept, Livonia MI (S)

Hucker, Robert, *Treas,* Amarillo Art Center, Amarillo Art Center Association, Amarillo TX

Huddlestone, Ralph, *Instr,* Utah Technical College at Salt Lake, Commercial Art Dept, Salt Lake City UT (S)

Hudon, Paul, *Assoc Cur,* Merrimack Valley Textile Museum, North Andover MA

Hudson, Donna M, *Secy,* Lynchburg Fine Arts Center Inc, Lynchburg VA

Hudson, Judy, *Cur Art,* Valley National Bank of Arizona, Phoenix AZ

Hudson, Nancy, *Asst Dir,* Clark County Library District, Las Vegas NV

Hudson, Ralph M, *VPres,* Kappa Pi International Honorary Art Fraternity, Birmingham AL

Hudson, Tom, *Dean Instruction,* Emily Carr College of Art & Design, Vancouver BC (S)

Huebner, Carla, *Instructor,* Mount Mary College, Art Dept, Milwaukee WI (S)

Huebner, Gregory, *Chmn,* Wabash College, Art Dept, Crawfordsville IN (S)

Huebner, Rosemarita, *Chmn,* Mount Mary College, Art Dept, Milwaukee WI (S)

Huemer, Frances, *Prof,* University of North Carolina at Chapel Hill, Art Dept, Chapel Hill NC (S)

Huenefeld, Wesley, *Pres,* Plainsman Museum, Aurora NE

Huether, David, *Instructor,* Dickinson State College, Dept of Art, Dickinson ND (S)

Huey, Joyce, *Dir Support Services,* South Carolina Arts Commission, Columbia SC

Huey, Norma, *Exec Dir,* Women's City Club of Cleveland, Gallery, Cleveland OH

Huff, Caroline, *Chmn,* Prince George's Community College, Art Dept, Largo MD (S)

Huff, Clyde A, *Chmn,* Ladies Library and Art Association, Independence Museum, Independence KS

Huff, James, *Cur Talladega Art Collection,* Talladega College, Savery Art Gallery, Talladega AL

Huff, John, *Interior Design,* University of Georgia, Franklin College of Arts and Sciences, Dept of Art, Athens GA (S)

Huff, Robert, *Chmn Dept,* Miami-Dade Community College Campuses, Art Dept, Miami FL (S)

Huffington, Roy, *Chmn Society Board of Trustees,* Asia Society, Inc, Gallery, New York NY

Huffman, Brenda, *Asst Prof,* Hartford Art School of the University of Hartford, West Hartford CT (S)

Huffman, Kathy, *Cur,* Long Beach Museum of Art, Long Beach CA

Huffman, Lorilee, *Registrar,* Southern Illinois University, University Museum, Carbondale IL

Huffstot, John, *Assoc Cur & Graphics Designer,* University of Missouri, Museum of Art and Archaeology, Columbia MO

Huggins, Victor, *Head Art Dept,* Virginia Polytechnic Institute and State University, University Art Gallery, Blacksburg VA

Huggins, Victor, *Head Dept,* Virginia Tech, Dept of Art, Blacksburg VA (S)

Hughes, Danny R, *Asst Executive Dir,* Arts Council of Spartanburg County, Inc, Spartanburg Arts Center, Spartanburg SC

Hughes, Gary, *Actg Head Canadian History,* New Brunswick Museum, Saint John NB

Hughes, Inez H, *Dir,* Harrison County Historical Museum, Marshall TX

Hughes, John, *Assoc Prof,* Missouri Western State College, Art Dept, Saint Joseph MO (S)

Hughes, John T, *Gallery Coordr,* Missouri Western State College, Fine Arts Gallery, Saint Joseph MO

Hughes, Max, *Vice Chmn,* Salisbury State College, Wildfowl Art Museum, Salisbury MD

Hughes, Phillip Samuel, *Under Secy,* Smithsonian Institution, Washington DC

Hughes, Polly, *Prof,* Western New Mexico University, College of Arts and Letters, Art Dept, Silver City NM (S)

Hughes, William J, *Chmn,* Blue Mountain Community College, Fine Arts Dept, Pendleton OR (S)

Hughson, John, *Chmn,* State University College, Dept of Art, Fredonia NY (S)

Hughston, Milan R, *Asst Librn,* Amon Carter Museum, Amon Carter Museum Library, Fort Worth TX

Hui, Ka Kwong, *Assoc Prof,* Rutgers, the State University of New Jersey, Mason Gross School of the Arts, New Brunswick NJ (S)

Huisman, Carl J, *Assoc Prof,* Calvin College, Art Dept, Grand Rapids MI (S)

Hulbert, Bette, *Cur Collections,* Alaska State Museum, Juneau AK

Hulbert, James C, *Assoc Prof,* Palomar College, Art Dept, San Marcos TX (S)

Hulet, Grant M, *Instr,* Utah Technical College at Salt Lake, Commercial Art Dept, Salt Lake City UT (S)

Hulick, Diana, *Asst Prof,* University of Maine, Art Dept, Orono ME (S)

Hulick, Diana Emery, *Cur,* University of Maine at Orono, Art Collection, Orono ME

Hulitar, Philip, *Vpres,* Society of the Four Arts, Palm Beach FL

Hull, David, *Principal Librn,* National Maritime Museum, Library, San Francisco CA

Hull, Elizabeth, *Instructor,* Roger Williams College, Art Dept, Bristol RI (S)

Hull, Joan C, *Pres & Exec Dir,* New Jersey Historical Society Museum, Newark NJ

Hull, Julana, *Instructor,* Claremore College, Art Dept, Claremore OK (S)

Hull, Thomas V, *Chmn,* Special Libraries Association, Museum, Arts and Humanities Division, New York NY

Hull, Vida, *Instructor,* Shippensburg State College, Art Dept, Shippensburg PA (S)

Hulstrunk, Alfred, *Cur Education,* Schenectady Museum, Schenectady NY

Hultin, Leola, *Secy,* Coquille Valley Art Association, Coquille OR

Humelsine, Carlisle H, *VPres,* National Gallery of Art, Washington DC

Hummel, Charles F, *Deputy Dir Collections,* Winterthur Museum and Gardens, Winterthur DE

Hummel, Lisa, *Registrar,* Virginia Museum of Fine Arts, Richmond VA

Hummer, Philip W, *VPres,* Chicago Historical Society, Chicago IL

Humphery, Rosemary, *Admin Asst,* Ashtabula Arts Center, Ashtabula OH

Humphrey, David R, *Dean,* Florida School of the Arts, Visual Arts, Palatka FL (S)

Humphrey, Don, *Chief Cur,* Museum of New Mexico, Museum of Fine Arts, Santa Fe NM

Humphrey, Rebecca, *Assoc Prof,* James Madison University, Dept of Art, Harrisonburg VA (S)

Humphrey, Rita S, *Admin Asst,* Baylor University, Armstrong Browning Library, Waco TX

Humphreys, Bill, *Secy,* Salisbury State College, Wildfowl Art Museum, Salisbury MD

Humphreys, Glenn E, *Ref Librn,* California Historical Society, Schubert Hall Library, San Francisco CA

Hunger, Julie Y, *Chmn,* Seattle Central Community College, Humanities - Social Sciences Division, Seattle WA (S)

Hungerford, Constance Cain, *Chairperson Dept Art,* Swarthmore College, Dept of Art, Swarthmore PA (S)

Hunisak, John M, *Chmn,* Middlebury College, Dept of Art, Middlebury VT (S)

Hunsberger, Charles W, *Dir,* Clark County Library District, Las Vegas NV

Hunt, Carol, *Registrar,* Putnam Museum, Davenport IA

Hunt, Carole, *Secy,* Strasburg Museum, Strasburg VA

Hunt, David, *Cur Western Art,* Joslyn Art Museum, Omaha NE

Hunt, David, *Assoc Prof,* Fort Lewis College, Art Dept, Durango CO (S)

Hunt, Diana K, *Admin,* Art Institute of Pittsburgh Gallery, Resource Center, Pittsburgh PA

Hunt, Dot, *Library Asst,* North Carolina State University, Harrye Lyons Design Library, Raleigh NC

Hunt, Gordon, *Pres,* Art Guild of Burlington, Arts for Living Center, Burlington IA

Hunt, Hal, *Chmn Interior Design & Dec,* Traphagen School of Fashion, New York NY (S)

Hunt, James, *Head Dept,* Washburn University of Topeka, Dept of Art, Topeka KS (S)

Hunt, James R, *Head Librn,* Public Library of Cincinnati and Hamilton County, Art and Music Dept, Cincinnati OH

Hunt, John P, *Executive Secy,* Marblehead Historical Society, Marblehead MA

Hunt, Marilyn Berling, *Program Coordr,* University of California, Memorial Union Art Gallery, Davis CA

Hunt, Mark A, *Museum Dir,* Kansas State Historial Society Museum, Topeka KS

Hunt, R J, *Dir,* Washburn University, Mulvane Art Center, Topeka KS

Hunt, Susan, *Lecturer,* University of Wisconsin-Stout, Art Dept, Menomonie WI (S)

Hunter, Beth, *Cur Special Programs,* Missouri State Museum, Jefferson City MO

Hunter, Bruce, *First VPres,* Community Arts Council of Vancouver, Vancouver BC

Hunter, Carolyn, *Art Librn,* Public Library of Charlotte and Mecklenburg County, Charlotte NC

Hunter, J, *Chief Librn,* National Gallery of Canada, Library, Ottawa ON

Hunter, Jean, *Supvr Personnel,* Minnesota Museum of Art, Saint Paul MN

Hunter, John, *Art & Theatre Arts Chmn,* Washburn University of Topeka, Dept of Art, Topeka KS (S)

Hunter, John, *Asst Prof,* Cleveland State University, Art Dept, Cleveland OH (S)

Hunter, Lawrence B, *Grad Coordr,* San Diego State University, Dept of Art, San Diego CA (S)

Hunter, Ralph, *Prof,* Napa College, Art Dept, Napa CA (S)

Hunter, Sam, *Prof,* Princeton University, Dept of Art and Archaeology, Princeton NJ (S)

Hunter, Sylvia, *2nd VChmn,* Fine Arts Museums of San Francisco, The Museum Society, San Francisco CA

Hunter, Terry K, *Instructor,* South Carolina State College, Art Program, Orangeburg SC (S)

Huntoon, Gary, *Adjunct Prof,* University of Saint Thomas, Art Dept, Houston TX (S)

Hurley, D, *Lectr,* Chamberlayne Junior College, Dept of Applied Arts, Boston MA (S)

Hurley, K, *Asst Dean,* Technical University of Nova Scotia, Faculty of Architecture, Halifax NS (S)

Hurley, Paul, *Chairperson,* Harrisburg Area Community College, Division of Communication and the Arts, Harrisburg PA (S)

Hurley, Zenobia, *Librn,* Department of Culture, Government of the Province of Alberta, Visual Arts Library, Edmonton AB

Hurst, Ronald, *Chmn,* St Martins College, Art Dept, Olympia WA (S)

Hurt, James, *Instr,* Cottey College, Fine Arts Division, Nevada MO (S)

Hurtig, Judith, *Pres,* Iowa City, Johnson County Arts Council, Iowa City IA

Hurtig, Martin, *Dir School Art & Design,* University of Illinois at Chicago, College of Architecture, Art and Urban Planning, Chicago IL (S)

Hurwich, Ariel, *Asst Cur,* Yeshiva University, Museum, New York NY

Hurwitz, Sidney, *Pres,* Boston Printmakers, Needham MA

Husband, Elizabeth F, *Secy,* Amerind Foundation, Inc, Dragoon AZ

Huskey, Susan, *Instructor,* Dunedin Fine Arts and Cultural Center, Dunedin FL (S)

Husten, Amy, *Registrar,* Louisiana Department of Culture, Recreation and Tourism, Louisiana State Museum, New Orleans LA

Huston, Bea, *Pres,* Cedar Rapids Museum of Art, Cedar Rapids IA

Huston, Perry, *Conservator,* Kimbell Art Museum, Fort Worth TX

Huston, Perry C, *VPres,* American Institute for Conservation of Historic and Artistic Works (AIC), Washington DC

Hutchens, Holly, *VPres,* American Committee for South Asian Art, Evanston IL

Hutchens, Holly B, *Cur,* University of Chicago, Max Epstein Archive, Chicago IL

Hutchens, James, *Asst Prof,* Ohio State University, Dept of Art Education, Columbus OH (S)

Hutchins, Barbara M, *Executive Secy,* Religious Arts Guild, Unitarian Universalist Association, Boston MA

Hutchins, Frank L, *Pres,* Southern Vermont Art Center, Manchester VT

Hutchins, Jane, *Textile Conservator,* Merrimack Valley Textile Museum, North Andover MA

Hutchinson, Don, *Instr,* Vancouver Community College, Langara Campus, Dept of Fine Arts, Vancouver BC (S)

Hutchinson, Janet, *Dir,* Historical Society of Martin County, Elliot Museum, Stuart FL

Hutchinson, Louise D, *Historian,* Anacostia Neighborhood Museum, Washington DC

Hutchison, Jane C, *Pres,* Midwest Art History Society, Madison WI

Hutchner, Steve, *Instr,* Colorado Women's College, Dept of Art, Denver CO (S)

Hutslar, Don, *Actg Head History,* Ohio Historical Society, Columbus OH

Hutson, Bill, *Instr,* Creighton University, Fine and Performing Arts Dept, Omaha NE (S)

Hutter, Alice, *Member,* The Loading Dock Gallery, Boston MA

Hutton, Virginia, *Chmn,* Midway College, Art Dept, Midway KY (S)

Hutton, William, *Sr Cur,* Toledo Museum of Art, Toledo OH

Hyatt, Gordon, *Secy,* Municipal Art Society of New York, New York NY

Hyatt, John D, *Librn,* Rosenberg Library, Galveston TX

Hyde, T Budge, *Head Art Dept,* Greenfield Community College, Art Dept, Greenfield MA (S)

Hyer, Christine D, *Develop Officer,* University of Rochester, Memorial Art Gallery, Rochester NY

Hyland, Alice M, *Asst Prof,* Southwestern at Memphis, Dept of Art, Memphis TN (S)

Hyland, Alice Merrill, *Cur,* Southwestern At Memphis, Jessie L Clough Art Memorial for Teaching, Memphis TN

Hyland, Douglas, *Dir,* Memphis Brooks Museum of Art, Memphis TN

Hyland, Douglas, *Asst Prof,* Southwestern at Memphis, Dept of Art, Memphis TN (S)

Hyland, John W, *Chmn,* American Academy in Rome, New York NY (S)

Hyleck, Walter, *Assoc Prof,* Berea College, Art Dept, Berea KY (S)

Hylton, Kevin, *Executive Member,* 22 Wooster Gallery, New York NY

Hylton, Zola, *Recording Secy,* Marian Osborne Cunningham Art Gallery, Bakersfield CA

Hynes, William, *Instructor,* Shippensburg State College, Art Dept, Shippensburg PA (S)

Hynes, William, *Dir,* Shippensburg University, Kauffman Gallery, Shippensburg PA

Hysell, David M, *Prof,* Rhode Island College, Art Dept, Providence RI (S)

Hyslin, Richard, *Chmn Dept,* Pan American University, Art Dept, Edinburg TX (S)

Hysong, Joe, *Instructor,* Monterey Peninsula College, Art Dept, Monterey CA (S)

Iacono, Domenic J, *Cur Coll,* Syracuse University, Art Collection, Syracuse NY

Iakovidis, Spyros, *Mediterranean Section Cur,* University of Pennsylvania, University Museum of Archaeology & Anthropology, Philadelphia PA

Ianco-Starrels, Josine, *Dir Municipal Art Gallery,* City of Los Angeles, Cultural Affairs Dept, Los Angeles CA

Ichida, Karl K, *Exec Dir,* Arts Council of Hawaii, Honolulu HI

Iguchi, Yashiro, *Conservator Asiatic Art,* Museum of Fine Arts, Boston MA

Ikeda, Yoshiro, *Assoc Prof,* Kansas State University, Art Dept, Manhattan KS (S)

Iler, Henry, *Prof,* Georgia Southern College, Dept of Art, Statesboro GA (S)

Iles, Bill R, *Chmn,* McNeese State University, Dept of Visual Arts, Lake Charles LA (S)

Illies, Madeleine, *Reserve Supv,* Washington University, Art and Architecture Library, Saint Louis MO

Illigen, Karolina, *Instr,* Danforth Museum School, Framingham MA (S)

Immaculatium, Cor, *Chairperson Dept,* Marywood College, Art Dept, Scranton PA (S)

Ingalls, Hunter, *Instructor,* West Texas State University, Art Dept, Canyon TX (S)

Ingersoll, Jonathan, *Asst Prof,* Saint Mary's College of Maryland, Arts and Letters Division, Saint Mary's City MD (S)

Ingham, David, *Controller,* Seattle Art Museum, Seattle WA

Ingolia, Jane, *Galleries,* University of South Florida, Art Galleries, Tampa FL

Ingram, Marilyn, *Cur Education,* Kimbell Art Museum, Fort Worth TX

Ingram, Martin, *Lectr,* University of Pennsylvania, College Arts & Science, Philadelphia PA (S)

Inlow, Terry, *Asst Prof,* Wilmington College, Art Dept, Wilmington OH (S)

Inman, Virginia, *Museum Shop Mgr,* M Flint Institute of Arts, Flint MI

Insalaco, Thomas F, *Assoc Prof,* Community College of the Finger Lakes, Visual & Performing Arts Dept, Canandaigua NY (S)

Inwood, Bart, *Instructor,* Anton Elli, Cincinnati OH (S)

Ipock, Grace C, *Registrar,* Tryon Palace Restoration Complex, New Bern NC

Irby, Frank, *Instr,* Pacific Northwest College of Art, Portland OR (S)

Irby, Judith, *Admin Asst,* Art Dealers Association of America, Inc, New York NY

Ireland, Martha, *Cur,* Princeton Antiques Bookservice, Art Marketing Reference Library, Atlantic City NJ

Iriberry, Mildred G, *Asst Librn & Cat,* Brooklyn Museum, Art Reference Library, Brooklyn NY

Irland, Basia, *Asst Prof,* University of Waterloo, Fine Arts Dept, Waterloo ON (S)

Irvin, Roberta W, *Pres,* Southeastern Center for Contemporary Art, Winston-Salem NC

Irving, Joan, *Co-Dir,* Brandt Painting Workshops, Corona Del Mar CA (S)

Irving, Mark, *Coordr Public Relations,* New Muse Community Museum of Brooklyn, Inc, Brooklyn NY

Irving, Norbert, *Assoc Prof,* Atlantic Christian College, Art Dept, Wilson NC (S)

Irwin, Arthur, *Coordr Professional Art,* City College of San Francisco, Art Dept, San Francisco CA (S)

Irwin, I, *Instr,* David Thompson University Centre, Visual Arts Dept, Nelson BC (S)

Irwin, J, *Asst Prof,* University of Victoria, Dept of Visual Arts, Victoria BC (S)

Isaacs, Claire N, *Dir Cultural Affairs,* San Francisco City and County Art Commission, San Francisco CA

Isaacson, Alice, *Pres,* Green Hill Center for North Carolina Art, Greensboro NC

Isaacson, Gene, *Asst Supt & VPres Acad Affairs,* Santa Ana College, Art Dept, Santa Ana CA (S)

Isaacson, Joel, *Chmn,* University of Michigan, Ann Arbor, Dept of History of Art, Ann Arbor MI (S)

Isaacson, M, *Faculty,* Humboldt State University, College of Creative Arts & Humanities, Arcata CA (S)

Isaacson, Marcia, *Asst Prof,* University of Florida, Dept of Art, Gainesville FL (S)

Isca, Kay Lynn, *Head Fine Arts Dept,* Allen County Public Library, Fine Arts Dept, Fort Wayne IN

Iselin, Lewis, *Pres,* Louis Comfort Tiffany Foundation, New York NY

Isermann, Jim, *Program Coordr,* Los Angeles Contemporary Exhibitions, Inc, Los Angeles CA

Ishikawa, Joseph, *Dir of Gallery,* Michigan State University, Kresge Art Center Gallery, East Lansing MI

Isman, Bonnie, *Dir,* Jones Library, Inc, Amherst MA

Isoline, Charles J, *Instr,* Baylor University, Dept of Fine Arts, Waco TX (S)

Ison, Susan, *Dir,* Loveland Museum and Gallery, Loveland CO

Israel, Eliot, *Pres,* Roosevelt Public Library, Black Artists Association Arts Center, Roosevelt NY

Italiano, J N, *Assoc Prof,* College of the Holy Cross, Dept Visual Arts, Worcester MA (S)

Italiano, Lisa, *Asst Cur Education,* Museum of Fine Arts, Springfield MA

Italiano, Lisa, *Asst Cur Education,* George Walter Vincent Smith Art Museum, Springfield MA

Iten, Thomas, *Chmn Applied Photography,* Rochester Institute of Technology, School of Photographic Arts & Sciences, Rochester NY (S)

Itter, William, *Prof,* Indiana University, Bloomington, School of Fine Arts, Bloomington IN (S)

Ittmann, John, *Cur Prints & Drawings,* Minneapolis Institute of Arts, Minneapolis MN

Iutzi-Johnson, Roy D, *Dir,* Carrie McLain Museum, Nome AK

Iverson, Sherman, *Asst Prof,* University of Wisconsin-Stout, Art Dept, Menomonie WI (S)

Ives, Colta, *Cur in Charge,* Metropolitan Museum of Art, Dept of Prints & Photographs, New York NY

Ivins, Mildred, *Chmn Fashion Illustration,* Moore College of Art, Philadelphia PA (S)

Ivory, Paul W, *Dir,* Chesterwood, Stockbridge MA

Izquierdo, Manuel, *Instr,* Pacific Northwest College of Art, Portland OR (S)

Izzo, Alan, *Asst Dir,* San Bernardino County Museum and Satellites, Fine Arts Institute, Redlands CA

Jachimowicz, Elizabeth, *Cur Costumes,* Chicago Historical Society, Chicago IL

Jack, Ann L, *Dir,* College of Marin, Art Gallery, Kentfield CA

Jack, Marlene, *Assoc Prof,* College of William and Mary, Dept of Fine Arts, Williamsburg VA (S)

Jack, Meredith M, *Prof,* Lamar University, Art Dept, Beaumont TX (S)

Jackel, Wendy, *Recording Secy,* New York Artists Equity Association, Inc, New York NY

Jackson, A, *Instructor,* Golden West College, Arts, Humanities and Social Sciences Institute, Huntington Beach CA (S)

Jackson, A, *Instructor,* Technical University of Nova Scotia, Faculty of Architecture, Halifax NS (S)

Jackson, Anke, *Asst to Dir,* Parrish Art Museum, Southampton NY

Jackson, Arnold, *Secy,* American Society of Artists, Inc, Chicago IL

Jackson, B, *Secy-Registrar,* University of Victoria, Maltwood Art Museum and Gallery, Victoria BC

Jackson, Bev, *Asst Admin,* Favell Museum of Western Art & Indian Artifacts, Klamath Falls OR

Jackson, Carolyn A, *Instructor,* Treasure Valley Community College, Art Dept, Ontario OR (S)

Jackson, Dana, *Conservator,* Vesterheim, Norwegian-American Museum, Decorah IA

Jackson, Don, *Dean,* Howard Payne University, Dept of Art, Brownwood TX (S)

Jackson, Frank D, *Slide Librn,* University of Georgia, Dept of Art Visual Center, Athens GA

Jackson, Gay, *Public Relations,* Huntington Galleries, Huntington WV

Jackson, Gene E, *Prof,* Sam Houston State University, Art Dept, Huntsville TX (S)

Jackson, Gloria, *Asst Librn,* Museum of Our National Heritage, Lexington MA

Jackson, Herb, *Dir,* Davidson College Art Gallery, Davidson NC

Jackson, Herb, *Chmn,* Davidson College, Art Dept, Davidson NC (S)

Jackson, Jack, *Art Librn,* Boston Athenaeum, Boston MA

Jackson, James F, *Asst Cur,* University of Wyoming, Art Museum, Laramie WY

Jackson, Kathleen, *Secy,* State University of New York at Oswego, Tyler Art Gallery, Oswego NY

Jackson, Martin, *Instructor,* Samuel S Fleisher Art Memorial, Philadelphia PA (S)

Jackson, Milton, *Div Chmn,* James H Faulkner State Jr College, Bay Minette AL (S)

Jackson, P, *Faculty,* Western Illinois University, College of Fine Arts, Macomb IL (S)

Jackson, Paula S, *Public Relations,* Indianapolis Museum of Art, Indianapolis IN

Jackson, Robert M, *Dept Chmn,* Treasure Valley Community College, Art Dept, Ontario OR (S)

Jackson, Rosemary H, *Dir,* Museum of Holography, New York NY

Jackson, Steve, *Photo Technician,* Montana State University, Museum of the Rockies, Bozeman MT

Jackson, Virginia, *Public Relations,* Indiana University, Art Museum, Bloomington IN

Jackson, Ward, *Archivist,* Solomon R Guggenheim Museum, New York NY

Jackson, William, *Chmn Art Dept,* Simon's Rock of Bard College, Great Barrington MA

Jackson, William, *Chairperson Studio Arts Dept,* Simon's Rock of Bard College, Studio Arts Dept, Great Barrington MA (S)

Jackson, William M, *Adminr,* Solomon R Guggenheim Museum, New York NY

Jacob, Mary Jane, *Chief Cur,* Museum of Contemporary Art, Chicago IL

Jacob, Ray, *Gallery Dir,* Orange County Center for Contemporary Art, Santa Ana CA

Jacobi, Angela, *Registrar,* University of Wisconsin, University Art Museum, Milwaukee WI

Jacobowitz, Ellen, *Assoc Cur Prints,* Philadelphia Museum of Art, Philadelphia PA

Jacobs, Carmel, *Head Dept,* Mount Saint Clare College, Art Dept, Clinton IA (S)

Jacobs, Charles M, *Cur,* Historic Landmarks Foundation of Indiana, Morris-Butler House, Indianapolis IN

Jacobs, David, *Chmn,* Hofstra University, Dept of Fine Arts, Hempstead NY (S)

Jacobs, Ellen, *Assoc Prof,* Florida International University, Visual Arts Dept, Miami FL (S)

Jacobs, Jack, *Pres,* Grand Prairie Arts Council, Inc, Arts Center of the Grand Prairie, Stuttgart AR

Jacobs, John R, *Chmn Dept,* Rio Hondo College, Fine Arts Dept, Whittier CA (S)

Jacobs, Joseph, *Dir,* Bucknell University, Center Gallery, Lewisburg PA

Jacobs, Joyce, *Instr,* Georgian Court College, Dept of Art, Lakewood NJ (S)

Jacobs, Martha, *Vol Dir,* Omaha Children's Museum, Inc, Omaha NE

Jacobs, Nancy, *Library Asst,* New Orleans Museum of Art, Felix J Dreyfous Library, New Orleans LA

Jacobs, Peter A, *Chmn,* Colorado State University, Dept of Art, Fort Collins CO (S)

Jacobs, Stan, *Chmn,* Midland College, Art Dept, Midland TX (S)

Jacobs, Stephen P, *Assoc Dean,* Tulane University, School of Architecture, New Orleans LA (S)

Jacobsen, Florence S, *Arts & Sites Dir,* Church of Jesus Christ of Latter-Day Saints, Museum of Church History and Art, Salt Lake City UT

Jacobsen, Harlan, *VPres,* Paint 'N Palette Club, Anamosa IA

Jacobsen, Lolli, *Dir Textile Arts,* Mendocino Art Center, Inc, Mendocino CA (S)

Jacobsen, Michael, *Art History,* University of Georgia, Franklin College of Arts and Sciences, Dept of Art, Athens GA (S)

Jacobsen, Robert, *Cur Oriental Arts,* Minneapolis Institute of Arts, Minneapolis MN

Jacobson, Lee, *Instructor,* Chemeketa Community College, Dept of Humanities & Communications, Salem OR (S)

Jacobson, Lori, *Cur Coll,* McAllen International Museum, McAllen TX

Jacobson, S, *Faculty,* Humboldt State University, College of Creative Arts & Humanities, Arcata CA (S)

Jacobson, Selma, *Second VPres, Archivist & Board of Dir,* Swedish American Museum Association of Chicago, Chicago IL

Jacobson, Thora E, *Dir,* Philadelphia Museum of Art, Samuel S Fleisher Art Memorial, Philadelphia PA

Jacobson, Thora E, *Dir,* Samuel S Fleisher Art Memorial, Philadelphia PA (S)

Jacobson, Timothy, *Editor,* Chicago Historical Society, Chicago IL

Jacoby, R B , *VPres,* Mississippi Art Colony, Meridian MS

Jacoby, Thomas J, *Head,* University of Connecticut, Art and Design Library, Storrs CT

Jacole, John R, *Chair Fine Arts,* Rio Hondo College Art Gallery, Whittier CA

Jacquard, Jerry, *Prof,* Indiana University, Bloomington, School of Fine Arts, Bloomington IN (S)

Jacques, Michael, *Assoc Prof,* Emmanuel College, Art Dept, Boston MA (S)

Jaeger, Ernest, *Secy,* Tweed Arts Group, Plainfield NJ

Jaeger, Susan, *Public Relations Dir,* DeCordova and Dana Museum and Park, Lincoln MA

Jaenike, Vaughn, *Dean,* Eastern Illinois University, School of Fine Arts, Charleston IL (S)

Jaffe, Hilde W, *Dean,* Fashion Institute of Technology, Art & Design Division, New York NY (S)

Jaffe, John G, *Dir,* Sweet Briar College, Martin C Shallenberger Art Library, Sweet Briar VA

Jaffe, Richard, *VPres,* Print Club, Philadelphia PA

Jaffe, Sondra, *Dir Public Relations,* Bronx Museum of the Arts, Bronx NY

Jaffe, Steven, *Co-Chairperson Painting & Drawing,* Philadelphia College of Art, Philadelphia PA (S)

Jahos, Catherine, *Program Adminr,* Monmouth Museum and Cultural Center, Lincroft NJ

Jakob, Fred, *Supt,* Frick Collection, New York NY

Jalonen, Nancy, *Exec Dir,* San Mateo County Arts Council, Belmont CA

James, Earl, *Dir,* Decatur House, Washington DC

James, Earl, *Dir,* Woodrow Wilson House, Washington DC

James, George, *Chmn Dept,* California State University, Fullerton, Art Dept, Fullerton CA (S)

James, Ian, *Prof,* Acadia University, Art Dept, Wolfville NS (S)

James, Kathleen, *Assoc Cur,* Brown University, Slide & Photo Collection, Providence RI

James, Philip, *Assoc Prof,* James Madison University, Dept of Art, Harrisonburg VA (S)

James, Sally, *Chmn,* Bemidji State University, Art Dept, Bemidji MN (S)

James, Ted, *Assoc Dir Art,* Joslyn Art Museum, Omaha NE

Jameson, Colin, *VPres,* Key West Art and Historical Society, Key West FL

Jamieson, Charles F, *Prof,* Maryville College, St Louis, Art Division, Saint Louis MO (S)

Jamieson, Gail, *Chmn,* Phoenix College, Dept of Art and Photography, Phoenix AZ (S)

Janes, Gail, *Educ Head,* Tacoma Art Museum, Tacoma WA

Janick, Richard, *Instructor,* Monterey Peninsula College, Art Dept, Monterey CA (S)

Janis, Eugenia P, *Prof,* Wellesley College, Art Dept, Wellesley MA (S)

Jankowski, Edward, *Asst Prof,* Monmouth College, Dept of Art, West Long Branch NJ (S)

Jansa, Dolores A, *Secy,* Southwest Arts Foundation, Houston TX

Jansen, Catherine, *Instructor,* Bucks County Community College, Fine Arts Dept, Newton PA (S)

Jansen, Hans, *Cur,* Yankton College, Durand Art Collection, Yankton SD

Jansky, Rollin, *Assoc Prof,* University of Wisconsin-Parkside, Art Discipline, Kenosha WI (S)

Janson, Anthony F, *Senior Cur,* Indianapolis Museum of Art, Indianapolis IN

Janzen, Paul, *Coordr,* Wenatchee Valley College, Gallery 76, Wenatchee WA

Jaramillo, Gloria, *Cur of Collections,* Mexican Museum, San Francisco CA

Jardine, Don, *Assoc Dir,* Art Instruction Schools, Minneapolis MN (S)

Jareckie, Stephen B, *Cur Photography,* Worcester Art Museum, Worcester MA

Jarmusch, Ann, *Dir Exhibitions,* Temple University, Tyler School of Art-Galleries, Philadelphia PA

Jaroche, Barbara, *Faculty,* Sarah Lawrence College, Dept of Art, Bronxville NY (S)

Jarvis, Liz, *Public Programs & Vol,* Buten Museum of Wedgwood, Merion PA

Jascob, Charles, *Instructor,* De Anza College, Art Dept, Cupertino CA (S)

Jaskevich, Jane, *Prof,* Polk Community College, Division of Communications and Fine Arts, Winter Haven FL (S)

Jasmin, Bernard, *Dir Visual Arts,* Universite Laval Cite Universitaire, School of Visual Arts, Quebec PQ (S)

Jedrey, Micheline, *Assoc Librn,* Massachusetts Institute of Technology, Rotch Library of Architecture and Planning, Cambridge MA

Jeffords, James, *VChmn,* Congressional Arts Caucus, Washington DC

Jeffress, Charles, *Assoc Prof,* Louisiana College, Dept of Art, Pineville LA (S)

Jeffries, William W, *Dir,* United States Naval Academy Museum, Annapolis MD

Jekyll, Robert, *VChmn Board,* Visual Arts Ontario, Toronto ON

Jellison, Carolyn, *Secy,* Art Association of Richmond, Richmond IN

Jendrzejewski, Amy Delap, *Assoc Prof,* Vincennes University, Art Dept, Vincennes IN (S)

Jendrzejewski, Andrew, *Chmn & Assoc Prof,* Vincennes University, Art Dept, Vincennes IN (S)

Jendrzejewski, Andrew, *Chmn,* Vincennes University Junior College, Art Dept, Vincennes IN (S)

Jenkins, Arthur D, *Pres,* Textile Museum, Washington DC

Jenkins, Basil W R, *Dir,* Francis E Fowler Jr Foundation Museum, Beverly Hills CA

Jenkins, Betty, *Recording Secy,* Toledo Federation of Art Societies, Toledo OH

Jenkins, Donald, *Dir,* Portland Art Association, Portland Art Museum, Portland OR

Jenkins, Jack, *Asst Prof,* Rochester Institute of Technology, School of Printing, Rochester NY (S)

Jenkins, Norma P H, *Librn,* Corning Museum of Glass, Library, Corning NY

Jenkins, Suzanne, *Registrar,* National Portrait Gallery, Washington DC

Jenkins, Virginia, *Dir,* Central Michigan University, Art Gallery, Mount Pleasant MI

Jenkinson, Pamela, *Public Information Officer,* Los Angeles County Museum of Art, Los Angeles CA

Jenkner, Ingrid, *Cur,* Macdonald Stewart Art Centre, Guelph ON

Jenneman, Eugene A, *Asst Dir,* Jesse Besser Museum, Alpena MI

Jennerjahn, W P, *Prof,* Adelphi University, Dept of Art and Art History, Garden City NY (S)

Jennings, Charles W, *Assoc Prof,* California Polytechnic State University at San Luis Obispo, Art Dept, San Luis Obispo CA (S)

Jennings, DeAnn, *Instructor,* Los Angeles Harbor College, Art Dept, Wilmington CA (S)

Jennings, Edward, *Cur,* Talladega College, Savery Art Gallery, Talladega AL

Jennings, Garnett, *Programming,* Huntsville Art League and Museum Association Inc, Huntsville AL

Jennings, Gwen, *Admin Dir,* Pacific Basin School of Textile Arts, Berkeley CA (S)

Jennings, James W, *Exec VPres & Dir,* Virginia Museum, Danville Museum of Fine Arts and History, Danville VA

Jennings, W Croft, *Chmn Museum Commission,* Columbia Museums of Art and Science, Columbia SC

Jensen, Carl, *Asst Prof,* University of Southern Colorado, Belmont Campus, Dept of Art, Pueblo CO (S)

Jensen, Dorothy, *Registrar & Public Information,* Beaumont Art Museum, Beaumont TX

Jensen, Inger, *Program Adminr,* Pacific Basin School of Textile Arts, Berkeley CA (S)

Jensen, James, *Asst Prof,* Loyola University of Chicago, Fine Arts Dept, Chicago IL (S)

Jensen, James F, *Cur Western Art & Publications Ed,* Honolulu Academy of Arts, Honolulu HI

Jensen, Janet M, *Dir,* Peoria Art Guild, Peoria IL

Jensen, Margaret P, *Head Fine Arts Library,* University of Michigan, Fine Arts Library, Ann Arbor MI

Jensen, Paul G, *Pres,* Thomas College Gallery, Waterville ME

Jensen, Robert, *Graphic Designer,* Walker Art Center, Minneapolis MN

Jensen, Robert, *Instructor,* Rudolph Schaeffer School of Design, San Francisco CA (S)

Jensen, Robert A, *Dir & Assoc Prof,* Calvin College, Art Dept, Grand Rapids MI (S)

Jensen, William M, *Instr,* Baylor University, Dept of Fine Arts, Waco TX (S)

Jensen, William M, *Dir,* Baylor University, Martin Museum of Art, Waco TX

Jergens, Robert, *Prof,* Cleveland Institute of Art, Cleveland OH (S)

Jessiman, John, *Prof,* State University of New York College at Cortland, Art Dept, Cortland NY (S)

Jessop, Gerald, *Dir,* Moose Jaw Art Museum and National Exhibition Centre, History Museum, Moose Jaw SK

Jessup, Kathryn C, *Asst Dir,* University of Arizona, Museum of Art, Tucson AZ

Jessup, Robert, *Asst Prof,* Cornell University, Dept of Art, Ithaca NY (S)

Jeter, Edith, *Librn,* Valentine Museum, Library, Richmond VA

Jevnikar, Jana, *Assoc Dir,* Center for Arts Information, New York NY

Jewell-Vitale, Thomas, *Chmn,* Loras College, Dept of Art, Dubuque IA (S)

Jiggetts, Joseph, *Chmn Bd of Dir,* New Muse Community Museum of Brooklyn, Inc, Brooklyn NY

Jile, Michael, *Asst Prof,* Fort Hays State University, Dept of Art, Hays KS (S)

Jimison, Ray, *Treas,* Gaston County Museum of Art & History, Dallas NC

Jipson, James W, *Assoc Prof,* Villa Maria College of Buffalo, Art Dept, Buffalo NY (S)

Jircik, Nancy L, *Chmn,* University of Saint Thomas, Art Dept, Houston TX (S)

Joachim, Harold, *Cur Prints & Drawings,* Art Institute of Chicago, Chicago IL

Joe, Henry, *Actg Chmn & Assoc Prof,* Knox College, Dept of Art, Galesburg IL (S)

Joel, Abraham, *Head Conservator,* Detroit Institute of Arts, Detroit MI

Joffe-Bouska, Marcia, *Board Dir,* Artists' Cooperative Gallery, Omaha NE

Johansen, Franz M, *Chmn Art Acquisitions Committee,* Brigham Young University, B F Larsen Gallery, Provo UT

Johansen, Franz M, *Chmn,* Brigham Young University, Dept of Art, Provo UT (S)

John, Ken, *Cur,* Lightner Museum, Saint Augustine FL

John, Paul, *Exhibit Specialist,* Bower's Museum, Santa Ana CA

Johnes, Marjorie, *Head Cataloguer,* Saint Mary's College, Cushwa-Leighton Library, Notre Dame IN

Johns, Forrest L, *Head Dept,* Oklahoma State University, Graphic Arts Dept, Okmulgee OK (S)

Johnson, Ann, *Periodicals Librn,* Saint Mary's College, Cushwa-Leighton Library, Notre Dame IN

Johnson, Barbara M, *Dir,* Union County Public Library Gallery, Monroe NC

Johnson, Benita, *Conservator,* University of California, Los Angeles, Museum of Cultural History, Los Angeles CA

Johnson, Bill, *Building & Grounds,* Museum of the Southwest, Midland TX

Johnson, Brooks, *Cur of Photography,* Chrysler Museum, Norfolk VA

Johnson, Bruce L, *Dir,* California Historical Society, Schubert Hall Library, San Francisco CA

Johnson, Byron, *Cur of History,* Albuquerque Museum of Art, History and Science, Albuquerque NM

Johnson, C Clayton, *Pres,* Southern Ohio Museum Corporation, Southern Ohio Museum & Cultural Center, Portsmouth OH

Johnson, Charles W, *Chmn & Prof,* University of Richmond, Dept of Art, Richmond VA (S)

Johnson, Chris, *Photography,* California College of Arts and Crafts, Oakland CA (S)

Johnson, Dale, *Asst Prof,* Olivet College, Art Dept, Olivet MI (S)

Johnson, Dale R, *Prof,* Bethel College, Dept of Art, Saint Paul MN (S)

Johnson, David, *Staff,* Benedict College, Visual Art Studies, Columbia SC (S)

Johnson, David, *Chairperson,* Indiana State University, Dept of Humanities, Terre Haute IN (S)

Johnson, David B, *Chmn,* William Jewell College, Art Dept, Liberty MO (S)

Johnson, Dennis, *Instr,* Moravian College, Dept of Art, Bethlehem PA (S)

Johnson, Diana, *Treas,* Print Council of America, Boston MA

Johnson, Dolores, *Dir Development,* Walker Art Center, Minneapolis MN

Johnson, Don, *Instructor,* Cochise College, Art Dept, Douglas AZ (S)

Johnson, Edith, *Treas,* Swedish American Museum Association of Chicago, Chicago IL

Johnson, Edna, *Dir,* Southampton Art School, Southampton ON (S)

Johnson, Eileen, *Cur Archaeology & Lubbock Lake Site Dir,* Texas Tech University Museum, Lubbock TX

Johnson, Elizabeth, *Cur Collections,* University of British Columbia, Museum of Anthropology, Vancouver BC

Johnson, Ellen H, *Honorary Cur Modern Art,* Oberlin College, Allen Memorial Art Museum, Oberlin OH

Johnson, Eric, *Asst Prof,* California Polytechnic State University at San Luis Obispo, Art Dept, San Luis Obispo CA (S)

Johnson, Evert A, *Cur Art,* Southern Illinois University, University Museum, Carbondale IL

Johnson, Gayle C, *VPres,* Chautauqua Art Association Galleries, Chautauqua NY

Johnson, George, *Exhib Designer,* University of California, Los Angeles, Museum of Cultural History, Los Angeles CA

Johnson, Gerald C, *Assoc Prof,* University of Colorado at Denver, Dept of Fine Arts, Denver CO (S)

Johnson, Haynes, *Pres,* Stamford Museum and Nature Center, Stamford CT

Jones, Lial A, *Dir,* Delaware Art Museum, Downtown Gallery, Wilmington DE

Jones, Lora W, *Dir Community Affairs,* E R Squibb & Sons, Inc, Princeton NJ

Jones, Lucille, *VPres,* DuPage Art League, Wheaton IL

Jones, Maedine, *Asst Cur,* Plains Indians & Pioneer Historical Foundation, Pioneer Museum & Art Center, Woodward OK

Jones, Margaret, *Children's Librn,* Mexico-Audrain County Library, Mexico MO

Jones, Marilyn, *Instructor,* William Jewell College, Art Dept, Liberty MO (S)

Jones, Marvin H, *Assoc Prof,* Cleveland State University, Art Dept, Cleveland OH (S)

Jones, Mary, *Education Officer,* University of Regina, Mackenzie Art Gallery, Regina SK

Jones, Melissa, *Cur of Education,* Gaston County Museum of Art & History, Dallas NC

Jones, Mike, *Animal Cur,* Tallahassee Junior Museum, Tallahassee FL

Jones, Nancy, *Programs Dir,* California Historical Society, San Francisco CA

Jones, Pat, *Secy,* Huntsville Art League and Museum Association Inc, Huntsville AL

Jones, Paul, *Pres Board Trustees,* Zanesville Art Center, Zanesville OH

Jones, Richard L, *Chmn,* Russell Sage College, Visual and Performing Arts Dept, Troy NY (S)

Jones, R L, *Chmn,* Shepherd College, Art Dept, Shepherdstown WV (S)

Jones, Sally, *Coordr of Museum Information,* Tennessee State Museum, Nashville TN

Jones, Samuel W, *Dir,* Audubon State Park, John James Audubon Museum, Henderson KY

Jones, Susan, *Art Coordr,* Community Council for the Arts, Kinston NC

Jones, V Stephen, *Asst to Dir,* Hickory Museum of Art, Inc, Hickory NC

Jones, Wallace, *Finance,* Plastic Club, Art Club for Women, Philadelphia PA

Jones, Warren E, *Vice Chmn Board Trustees,* McMichael Canadian Collection, Kleinburg ON

Jones, Wilbur, *Dir Admin,* African-American Institute, New York NY

Jonitis, Aldona, *Chmn,* State University of New York at Stony Brook, Art Dept, Stony Brook NY (S)

Joost-Gaugier, Christiane L, *Prof,* New Mexico State University, Art Dept, Las Cruces NM (S)

Jordan, Catherine, *Executive Dir,* Women's Art Registry of Minnesota Gallery, Minneapolis MN

Jordan, I Douglas, *Instr,* Utah Technical College at Salt Lake, Commercial Art Dept, Salt Lake City UT (S)

Jordan, Jack, *Head Dept,* Southern University in New Orleans, Art Dept, New Orleans LA (S)

Jordan, Jim, *Head Dept,* South Dakota State University, Dept of Visual Arts, Brookings SD (S)

Jordan, Jim, *Film Dept Chmn,* Art Center College of Design, Pasadena CA (S)

Jordan, Jim M, *Chmn,* Dartmouth College, Dept of Art, Hanover NH (S)

Jordan, Julia, *Dir,* Rocky Mount Arts and Crafts Center, Rocky Mount NC

Jordan, Marie, *Slide Librn,* Art Center College of Design, James Lemont Fogg Memorial Library, Pasadena CA

Jordan, Mary, *Cur Collections,* Mississippi State Historical Museum, Jackson MS

Jordan, William, *Deputy Dir,* Kimbell Art Museum, Fort Worth TX

Jorgensen, Sandra, *Chairperson Art Dept,* Elmhurst College, Art Dept, Elmhurst IL (S)

Jorgenson, Dean Dale, *Head Div Fine Arts,* Northeast Missouri State University, Art Dept, Kirksville MO (S)

Jorgenson, Lynn, *Executive Dir,* The Art Museum Association of America, San Francisco CA

Jorman, John, *Treas,* Salt Lake Art Center, Salt Lake City UT

Joseph, Andrea, *Assoc Prof,* Portland State University, Dept of Art and Architecture, Portland OR (S)

Joseph, Philip, *Chmn,* Miami University, Art Dept, Hamilton OH (S)

Joseph, Raymond, *VPres,* Lansing Art Gallery, Lansing MI

Josephs, Cynthia A, *Library and Museum Dir,* Springfield Free Public Library, Donald B Palmer Museum, Springfield NJ

Josephson, Ken, *Prof,* School of the Art Institute of Chicago, Chicago IL (S)

Joslyn, Cathie, *Asst Prof,* Clarion University of Pennsylvania, Dept of Art, Clarion PA (S)

Jovine, Marcel, *Art Advisory Board,* Society of Medalists, Danbury CT

Jowers, Bryan, *Asst Prof,* Northwestern State University of Louisiana, Dept of Art, Natchitoches LA (S)

Joy, Suellen, *Asst Dir,* Art Center Association, Louisville KY

Joyal, Me Serge, *VPres,* Musee d'Art de Joliette, Joliette PQ

Joyaux, Alain, *Dir,* Ball State University, Art Gallery, Muncie IN

Joyce, Karen P, *Treas,* Adirondack Lakes Center for the Arts, Blue Mountain Lake NY

Joyce, Kathleen, *Assoc Prof,* Rocky Mountain College, Art Dept, Billings MT (S)

Joyner, Charles, *Dir Design Fundamentals,* North Carolina State University at Raleigh, School of Design, Raleigh NC (S)

Joyner, Marjorie Hake, *Librn,* Ball State University, Architecture Library, Muncie IN

Ju, I-Hsiung, *Prof,* Washington and Lee University, Dept of Fine Arts, Lexington VA (S)

Judd, A F, *Prom Dir,* USS North Carolina Battleship Memorial, Wilmington NC

Judge, Joseph M, *Cur,* MacArthur Memorial Museum, Norfolk VA

Judkins, Helen, *Art Gallery Dir,* Pointe Claire Cultural Centre, Pointe Claire PQ

Judson, J Richard, *Prof,* University of North Carolina at Chapel Hill, Art Dept, Chapel Hill NC (S)

Judson, William, *Cur Film and Video,* Carnegie Institute, Museum of Art, Pittsburgh PA

Judy, David J, *Head Dept,* Bethany College, Art Dept, Bethany WV (S)

Juergensen, Virginia, *Assoc Prof,* Mohawk Valley Community College, Advertising Design and Production, Utica NY (S)

Jule, Walter, *Pres,* Printing and Drawing Council of Canada, Dept Art & Design, Edmonton AB

Julian, Joanne, *Head Dept,* College of the Canyons, Art Dept, Valencia CA (S)

Julian, Margot, *Registrar,* Millicent Rogers Museum, Taos NM

Juliano, Marilynn Briggs, *Instr,* Mainline Center of the Arts, Haverford PA (S)

Julio, Pat T, *Dept Head,* Western State College, Quigley Hall Art Gallery, Gunnison CO

Jumonville, Florence, *Head Librn,* Historic New Orleans Collection, Library, New Orleans LA

Jung, Michael, *Chmn Dept,* Denison University, Dept of Art, Granville OH (S)

Juristo, Michelle S, *Cur,* University of South Florida, Art Galleries, Tampa FL

Jurkowski, Joseph, *Prof,* West Shore Community College, Division of Humanities and Fine Arts, Scottville MI (S)

Jussel, Christian, *Treas,* National Antique and Art Dealers Association of America, New York NY

Juszczyk, James, *Exhibition Chair,* American Abstract Artists, New York NY

Kabriel, J Ronald, *Asst Prof,* Catholic University of America, Dept of Architecture and Planning, Washington DC (S)

Kacena, Carolyn, *Actg Librn,* California State University Fullerton, Library, Fullerton CA

Kach, Claire, *Head, Art & Music Division,* Queens Borough Public Library, Art and Music Division, Jamaica NY

Kachel, Harold S, *Museum Dir,* No Man's Land Historical Society Museum, Goodwell OK

Kachel, Joan Overton, *Cur & Secy,* No Man's Land Historical Society Museum, Goodwell OK

Kachline, Clifford, *Historian,* National Baseball Hall of Fame and Museum, Inc, Art Collection, Cooperstown NY

Kachor, Sophia, *Exec Dir,* Ukrainian Cultural and Educational Centre Museum, Winnipeg MB

Kacurak, Karen, *Co-Dir,* Carnegie-Mellon University, Forbes Street Gallery, Pittsburgh PA

Kadis, Averil, *Chief Public Relations Division,* Enoch Pratt Free Library of Baltimore City, Baltimore MD

Kaericher, John, *Chmn Dept,* Northwestern College, Art Dept, Orange City IA (S)

Kaeyman, Jadee, *VPres,* Farmington Valley Arts Center, Avon CT

Kagan, Datsie, *Secy,* Farmington Art Guild, Farmington CT

Kagan, Larry, *Chmn,* Rensselaer Polytechnic Institute, Dept of Art, Troy NY (S)

Kaganoff, Nathan M, *Librn,* American Jewish Historical Society, Lee M Friedman Memorial Library, Waltham MA

Kagle, Joe L, *Dir,* Southeast Arkansas Arts and Science Center, Pine Bluff AR

Kahao, Mary Jane, *Pres & Dir Art,* West Baton Rouge Museum, Port Allen LA

Kahler, David, *Pres Bd Trustees,* Milwaukee Art Museum, Milwaukee WI

Kahler, Richard F, *Pres,* Rome Historical Society, Rome Information and Cultural Center, Rome NY

Kahmeyer, Ray, *Prof,* Bethany College, Art Dept, Lindsborg KS (S)

Kahn, Deborah, *Asst Prof,* Indiana University, Bloomington, School of Fine Arts, Bloomington IN (S)

Kahn, Elizabeth, *Asst Prof,* Saint Lawrence University, Dept of Fine Arts, Canton NY (S)

Kahn, Herbert, *Cur,* Exchange National Bank of Chicago, Chicago IL

Kahn, H Peter, *Prof,* Cornell University, Dept of the History of Art, Ithaca NY (S)

Kahute, Robert M, *Asst Prof,* Rochester Institute of Technology, School of Art and Design, Rochester NY (S)

Kain, Jay D, *Head Dept,* James Madison University, Dept of Art, Harrisonburg VA (S)

Kaiser, Charles, *Asst Prof,* Mount Mary College, Art Dept, Milwaukee WI (S)

Kaiser, Kay, *Secy,* Art League, Alexandria VA

Kaiser, Michael, *Instr Commercial Art,* Honolulu Community College, Honolulu HI (S)

Kaish, Luise, *Chmn,* Columbia University, School of the Arts, Division of Painting & Sculpture, New York NY (S)

Kajitani, Nobuko, *Conservator Textiles,* Metropolitan Museum of Art, New York NY

Kakas, Christopher, *Asst Prof,* University of Alabama, Art Dept, Tuscaloosa AL (S)

Kakis, Juris, *Asst Prof,* Ohio Dominican College, Art Dept, Columbus OH (S)

Kakudo, Yoshiko, *Cur Japanese Art,* Asian Art Museum of San Francisco, Avery Brundage Collection, San Francisco CA

Kalb, Marty J, *Chair,* Ohio Wesleyan University, Dept of Fine Arts Gallery, Delaware OH

Kalb, Marty J, *Chmn,* Ohio Wesleyan University, Fine Arts Dept, Delaware OH (S)

Kalke, Edwin, *Chmn,* Carthage College, Art Dept, Kenosha WI (S)

Kamansky, David, *Dir,* Pacific - Asia Museum, Pasadena CA

Kamerling, Leonard J, *Coordr Alaska Heritage Film Project,* University of Alaska, Museum, Fairbanks AK

Kaminsky, Lauren, *Cur,* Historical Society of the Town of Greenwich, Inc, Bush-Holley House, Cos Cob CT

Kaminsky, Vera, *Coordr Fibers,* University of Delaware, Dept of Art, Newark DE (S)

Kamm, Keith, *Bibliographer,* Athenaeum of Philadelphia, Philadelphia PA

Kammermeyer, Michael J, *Chmn,* California State University, Long Beach, Design Dept, Long Beach CA (S)

Kammersgard, Lisa, *Asst Gallery Dir,* San Mateo County Arts Council, Belmont CA

Kampen, Mike, *Faculty,* University of North Carolina-Charlotte, Creative Arts Dept, Charlotte NC (S)

Kampen, Natalie, *Assoc Prof,* University of Rhode Island, Dept of Art, Kingston RI (S)

Kan, Michael, *Deputy Dir & Cur Ethnographic Art,* Detroit Institute of Arts, Detroit MI

Kane, Helen E, *Office Mgr,* Everhart Museum of Natural History, Science and Art, Scranton PA

Kane, Jean DuVal, *Dir Coll,* Valentine Museum, Richmond VA

Kane, John, *Art Preparator,* University of Nevada, Las Vegas, Art Gallery, Las Vegas NV

Kane, Katherine, *Head of Public Service & Access,* Colorado Historical Society, State Museum, Denver CO

Kane, Mary Ann, *VPres,* Cortland County Historical Society, Suggett House Museum, Cortland NY

Kane, Patricia, *Cur American Decorative Arts,* Yale University, Art Gallery, New Haven CT

Kane, Susan, *Asst Prof,* Oberlin College, Dept of Art, Oberlin OH (S)

Kaneko, James S, *Chmn,* American River College, Dept of Art, Sacramento CA (S)

Kaneko, John H, *Instr,* American River College, Dept of Art, Sacramento CA (S)

Kaneko, Jun, *Head Ceramics Dept,* Cranbrook Academy of Art, Bloomfield Hills MI (S)

Kaneshiro, Carolyn, *Instr,* Mount San Jacinto College, Art Dept, San Jacinto CA (S)

Kaneshiro, Robin, *Preparator,* Berkeley Art Center, Berkeley CA

Kangas, Gene, *Assoc Prof,* Cleveland State University, Art Dept, Cleveland OH (S)

Kangas, James, *Head Art, Music & Drama Dept,* Flint Public Library, Fine Arts Dept, Flint MI

Kaniaris, Peter, *Asst Prof,* Albion College, Dept of Visual Arts, Albion MI (S)

Kannel, Bea, *Dir Volunteers,* Stan Hywet Hall Foundation, Inc, Akron OH

Kaplan, Donna, *Corresp Secy,* Seattle Weaver's Guild, Seattle WA

Kaplan, Helene, *Dir Educ,* Octagon Center for the Arts, Ames IA

Kaplan, Jerome, *Chairperson Printmaking,* Philadelphia College of Art, Philadelphia PA (S)

Kaplan, Jo Parker, *Develoment Dir,* Lemoyne Center for the Visual Arts, Tallahassee FL

Kaplan, Julius, *Chmn Dept,* California State College, San Bernardino, Art Dept, San Bernardino CA (S)

Kaplan, Julius, *Chmn Art Dept,* California State College San Bernardino, College Art Galleries, San Bernardino CA

Kaplan, Lester, *Exec Dir,* Judaic Museum of the Jewish Community Center, Goldman Fine Arts Gallery, Rockville MD

Kaplan, Paul H D, *Asst Prof,* Wake Forest University, Dept of Art, Winston-Salem NC (S)

Kaplan, Stanley, *Prof,* Nassau Community College, Art Dept, Garden City NY (S)

Kaplan Lane, Barbara, *Dir Public Information,* Jewish Museum, New York NY

Kaplowitz, Kenneth, *Asst Prof,* Trenton State College, Art Dept, Trenton NJ (S)

Kapp, Kenneth A, *Cur,* Kauai Museum, Lihue HI

Kappell, Karen, *Instr,* Silver Lake College, Art Dept, Manitowoc WI (S)

Kaprielian, Walter, *Pres,* Art Directors Club, Inc, New York NY

Karasch, Barrie, *Secy,* Brookfield Craft Center, Inc Gallery, Brookfield CT

Karatzas, Steven, *Chmn Dept,* Linfield College, Art Dept, McMinnville OR (S)

Karberg, Richard, *Prof,* Cuyahoga Community College, Dept of Art, Cleveland OH (S)

Karcheski, Walter J, *Assoc Cur & Librn,* Higgins Armory Museum, Worcester MA

Karcheski, Walter J, *Librn,* Higgins Armory Museum, Library, Worcester MA

Kardon, Janet, *Dir,* University of Pennsylvania, Institute of Contemporary Art, Philadelphia PA

Karlowicz, T M, *Faculty,* Western Illinois University, College of Fine Arts, Macomb IL (S)

Karlstrom, Paul, *Dir,* Archives of American Art, M H de Young Memorial Museum, New York NY

Karolyi, Janet, *Secy,* California State University, Chico, Art Gallery, Chico CA

Karow, Betty, *Librn,* Milwaukee Art Museum, Library, Milwaukee WI

Karp, Marilynn, *Faculty Dir,* New York University, 80 Washington Square East Galleries, New York NY

Karpen, John E, *Assoc Prof,* Rochester Institute of Technology, School of Photographic Arts & Sciences, Rochester NY (S)

Karpiscak, Lee, *Assoc Cur,* University of Arizona, Museum of Art, Tucson AZ

Karraker, Jack, *Chmn Dept,* Kearney State College, Dept of Art, Kearney NE (S)

Karrer, Ray E, *Chmn,* Paris Junior College, Art Dept, Paris TX (S)

Karsina, James, *Assoc Prof,* Aquinas College, Art Dept, Grand Rapids MI (S)

Karsmizki, Ken, *Cur History,* Montana State University, Museum of the Rockies, Bozeman MT

Karterud, Arvin, *Cur,* Lyman Allyn Museum, New London CT

Kartzinel, Wayne, *Dir,* Westchester Community College, Westchester Art Workshop, White Plains NY (S)

Karver, Sherry, *Instr,* California State University, Chico, Art Dept, Chico CA (S)

Kary, Norman, *Facility Chmn,* D-Art, A Visual Arts Center for Dallas, Dallas TX

Kasakaitis, Jurgis, *Head Librn,* Balzekas Museum of Lithuanian Culture, Research Library, Chicago IL

Kasal, Robert, *Head Dept,* Portland State University, Dept of Art and Architecture, Portland OR (S)

Kasper, Edward J, *Pres,* New Haven Paint and Clay Club, Inc, New Haven CT

Kasper, Janice, *Teacher,* Penobscot Marine Museum, Searsport ME

Kasprzak, Constance, *Dir Display & Design,* Museum, Fine Arts Research & Holographic Center, Chicago IL

Kass, Emily, *Interim Dir,* University of New Mexico, University Art Museum, Albuquerque NM

Kass, Emily, *Dir,* University of New Mexico, Jonson Gallery, Albuquerque NM

Kass, Ray, *Instructor,* Virginia Tech, Dept of Art, Blacksburg VA (S)

Kass, Tom, *Deputy Dir,* Rudolph Schaeffer School of Design, San Francisco CA (S)

Kassebaum, J Philip, *Pres Board,* Carolina Art Association, Gibbes Art Gallery, Charleston SC

Kassiday, Sharlene, *Instructor,* Joliet Junior College, Fine Arts Dept, Joliet IL (S)

Kassoy, Bernard, *Instructor,* Harriet FeBland Art Workshop, New York NY (S)

Kassoy, Hortense, *Instructor,* Harriet FeBland Art Workshop, New York NY (S)

Kastin, Judith B, *Treasurer,* Society of Scribes, Ltd, New York NY

Katauskas, Joseph, *VPres,* Balzekas Museum of Lithuanian Culture, Chicago IL

Katsaros, Aliki, *Asst to the Dir,* Fitchburg Art Museum, Fitchburg MA

Katsiff, Bruce, *Chairperson,* Bucks County Community College, Hicks Art Center, Newtown PA

Katsiff, Bruce, *Chairperson Dept,* Bucks County Community College, Fine Arts Dept, Newton PA (S)

Katsourides, Andrew, *Asst Prof,* Central Missouri State University, Art Dept, Warrensburg MO (S)

Katz, Alice A, *Head,* University of Illinois, Chicago, Health Science Center, Dept of Biocommunication Arts, Chicago IL (S)

Katz, Guiliana, *Lectr,* Toronto Art Therapy Institute, Toronto ON (S)

Katz, Karl, *Consultant Film & Television,* Metropolitan Museum of Art, New York NY

Katz, Marshall P, *Pres,* Papercraft Corporation, Pittsburgh PA

Katz, Melvin, *Prof,* Portland State University, Dept of Art and Architecture, Portland OR (S)

Katz, Robert, *Prof,* University of Maine at Augusta, Division of Arts and Humanities, Augusta ME (S)

Katz, Theodore, *Chief Div Educ,* Philadelphia Museum of Art, Philadelphia PA

Katzenberg, Dena, *Cur Textiles,* Baltimore Museum of Art, Baltimore MD

Katzive, David H, *Pres,* The Art Museum Association of America, San Francisco CA

Kauders, Audrey, *Assoc Dir Admin,* Joslyn Art Museum, Omaha NE

Kaufman, Barbara, *Asst Prof,* Seton Hall University, Dept of Art and Music, South Orange NJ (S)

Kaufman, Barbara W, *Cur Exhib,* Seton Hall University, Student Center Art Gallery, South Orange NJ

Kaufman, Glen, *Fabric Design,* University of Georgia, Franklin College of Arts and Sciences, Dept of Art, Athens GA (S)

Kaufman, Irving, *Dir Grad Studies,* City College of New York, Art Dept, New York NY (S)

Kaufman, Jane, *Chief Cataloguer,* Harvard University, Fine Arts Library, Cambridge MA

Kaufman, Lillian, *Pres,* Koochiching County Historical Society Museum, International Falls MN

Kaufman, Robert, *Librn,* Cooper-Hewitt Museum, Smithsonian Institution, New York NY

Kaufman, Susan, *Dir,* University of the South Gallery of Fine Arts, Sewanee TN

Kaul, Marlin, *Prof,* Bemidji State University, Art Dept, Bemidji MN (S)

Kaulback, Peggy, *Education,* Butler Institute of American Art, Youngstown OH

Kaven, Dennis, *Assoc Prof,* Grand View College, Art Dept, Des Moines IA (S)

Kavin, Paul E, *Dir,* Dunedin Fine Arts and Cultural Center, Dunedin FL (S)

Kay, Stan, *Instr,* Joe Kubert School of Cartoon and Graphic Art Inc, Dover NJ (S)

Kay, Terrence, *Dir Education,* Museum, Fine Arts Research & Holographic Center, Chicago IL

Kaya, Douglas, *Instr,* Leeward Community College, Arts and Humanities Division, Pearl City HI (S)

Kayser, Marilyn, *Pres Bd of Mgrs,* University of Rochester, Memorial Art Gallery, Rochester NY

Kayser, Robert, *Asst Prof,* Rochester Institute of Technology, School of Photographic Arts & Sciences, Rochester NY (S)

Kayser, Thomas A, *Exec Dir,* Kalamazoo Institute of Arts, Genevieve and Donald Gilmore Art Center, Kalamazoo MI

Keane, Richard, *Prof,* School of the Art Institute of Chicago, Chicago IL (S)

Keane, Terry, *Cur of Exhib,* Tyler Museum of Art, Tyler TX

Kearney, John, *Dir,* Contemporary Art Workshop, Chicago IL

Kearney, John W, *Dir,* Contemporary Art Workshop, Chicago IL (S)

Kearney, Lynn, *Admin Dir,* Contemporary Art Workshop, Chicago IL (S)

Kearns, Jerry L, *Head Reference Section,* Library of Congress, Washington DC

Kearns, Lola, *Dir Arts in Special Education Project,* Pennsylvania Department of Education, Arts in Education Program, Harrisburg PA

Kearsc, Dieter Morris, *Dir Planning & Development,* New Museum, New York NY

Keating, Patrick, *Chmn Dept,* Northeast Technical Community College, Dept of Art, Norfolk NE (S)

Keats, Norman, *Prof,* University of Wisconsin-Stevens Point, Dept of Art, Stevens Point WI (S)

Keaveney, Sydney Starr, *Art and Architecture Librn,* Pratt Institute Library, Art & Architecture Dept, Brooklyn NY

Keay, Robert, *Installation Mgr,* Canadian Consulate General Dept of External Affairs, 49th Parallel Centre for Contemporary Canadian Art, New York NY

Kebrle, John, *Pres,* The Stained Glass Association of America, Saint Louis MO

Kee, Lorna, *Chief Education & Cultural Affairs Div,* National Museum of Man, Ottawa ON

Keech, John, *Asst Prof,* Arkansas State University, Dept of Art, State University AR (S)

Keefe, Gerald, *VPres,* Florida Gulf Coast Art Center, Inc, Clearwater FL

Keefe, Jean, *Head Public Information,* J Paul Getty Museum, Malibu CA

Keefe, John W, *Cur Decorative Arts,* New Orleans Museum of Art, New Orleans LA

Keegan, Daniel T, *Instr,* Graceland College, Art Dept, Lamoni IA (S)

Keeler, David B, *Chief Office of Design & Construction,* National Museum of American Art, Washington DC

Keeley, Shelagh, *Cur Asst,* York University, Art Gallery, Downsview ON

Keeling, Henry C, *Coordr,* University of Charleston, Art Dept, Charleston WV (S)

Keeling, Jon, *Instructor,* Anton Elli, Cincinnati OH (S)

Keen, Betty, *Registrar,* Birmingham Museum of Art, Birmingham AL

Keen, Karen, *Instructor,* Bob Jones University, School of Fine Arts, Greenville SC (S)

Keene, Catherine, *Dir,* Passaic County Historical Society, Lambert Castle Museum, Paterson NJ

Keene, Paul, *Instructor,* Bucks County Community College, Fine Arts Dept, Newton PA (S)

Keener, Scott, *Secy,* University of North Carolina at Greensboro, Weatherspoon Art Gallery, Greensboro NC

Keener, William G, *Assoc Dir,* Ohio Historical Society, Columbus OH

Keeney, Allen L, *Dir,* Sweetwater Community Fine Arts Center, Rock Springs WY

Keens, William, *Dir,* American Council for the Arts, New York NY

Kefalos, Roberta, *Public Information,* Carolina Art Association, Gibbes Art Gallery, Charleston SC

Keillor, Frank, *Pres,* Pacific Grove Art Center, Pacific Grove CA

Keim, Rebecca, *Asst Dir for Outreach,* University of Minnesota, University Art Museum, Minneapolis MN

Keiser, Dale, *Second VPres,* Toledo Artists' Club, Toledo OH

Keith, Marie C, *Asst Librn & Indexer of Photographs,* Frick Art Reference Library, New York NY

Keithlambert, D, *Dept Chmn,* Gaston College, Art Dept, Dallas NC (S)

Kelder, Diane, *Prof,* City University of New York, PhD Program in Art History, New York NY (S)

Kelder, Diane, *Chmn,* College of Staten Island, Performing & Creative Arts Dept, Staten Island NY (S)

Kelen, Erwin A, *VPres,* Walker Art Center, Minneapolis MN

Kelleher, Bradford D, *VPres & Publisher,* Metropolitan Museum of Art, New York NY

Kelleher, Gregory, *Pres,* Ogunquit Art Association, The Barn Gallery, Ogunquit ME

Keller, Carol, *Cur,* Auraria Higher Education Center, Auraria Library Gallery, Denver CO

Keller, Douglas, *Head Dept,* Coffeyville Community College, Art Dept, Coffeyville KS (S)

Keller, Emily, *Cur,* Brea Civic Cultural Center Gallery, Brea CA

Keller, Harold, *Prof,* Fairleigh Dickinson University, Fine Arts Dept, Teaneck NJ (S)

Keller, John, *Asst Prof,* Harding University, Dept of Art, Searcy AR (S)

Keller, Judith, *Cur of Prints and Drawings,* University of Texas at Austin, Archer M Huntington Art Gallery, Austin TX

Keller, Marie, *Assoc Cur,* The Drawing Center, New York NY

Keller, Marjorie, *Dir Exhibition,* University of Rhode Island Gallery, Kingston RI

Keller, Marjorie, *Assoc Prof,* University of Rhode Island, Dept of Art, Kingston RI (S)

Keller, Steven, *Asst Dean,* Hartford Art School of the University of Hartford, West Hartford CT (S)

Keller, William B, *Head Librn,* Maryland Historical Society Museum, Library, Baltimore MD

Kelley, Cecilia, *Instr,* Schoolcraft College, Dept of Art, Livonia MI (S)

Kelley, Clarence, *Asst Cur Asian Art,* Dayton Art Institute, Dayton OH

Kelley, Donald C, *Art Gallery Dir,* Boston Athenaeum, Boston MA

Kelley, Fred, *Museum Shop Mgr,* Pennsylvania Academy of the Fine Arts, Galleries, Philadelphia PA

Kelley, Geraldine, *Prog Educational-Community Services Coordr,* Southern Illinois University, University Museum, Carbondale IL

Kelley, Helen, *Prof,* California Polytechnic State University at San Luis Obispo, Art Dept, San Luis Obispo CA (S)

Kelley, Michael, *Vis Prof,* Minneapolis College of Art and Design, Minneapolis MN (S)

Kelley, Peter E, *Actg Chmn,* Pratt Institute, Pratt-Phoenix School of Design, New York NY (S)

Kelley, Regina, *Instructor,* Portland School of Art, Portland ME (S)

Kelley, Robert, *Administrator,* Virginia Beach Arts Center, Virginia Beach VA

Kellogg, Seth, *VChmn,* Verde Valley Art Association, Inc, Jerome AZ

Kellum, Barbara, *Asst Prof,* Smith College, Art Dept, Northampton MA (S)

Kelly, Ann, *Archivist-Librn,* Shaker Museum, Emma B King Library, Old Chatham NY

Kelly, Ardie L, *Librn,* Mariners Museum, Library, Newport News VA

Kelly, Cathie, *Asst Prof,* University of Nevada, Las Vegas, Dept of Art, Las Vegas NV (S)

Kelly, Charlotte, *Cur Slide & Photograph Library & Art History Teaching Coll,* University of Delaware, University Art Collections, Newark DE

Kelly, Cherie, *Instructor,* Southwestern School of Art, Albuquerque NM (S)

Kelly, Claire, *Asst Prof,* Portland State University, Dept of Art and Architecture, Portland OR (S)

Kelly, Clyde, *Prof,* Los Angeles City College, Dept of Art, Los Angeles CA (S)

Kelly, D J, *Faculty,* Western Illinois University, College of Fine Arts, Macomb IL (S)

Kelly, Elinor, *Librn,* Eastern Washington State Historical Society, Library, Spokane WA

Kelly, James, *Chief Cur of Collections,* Tennessee State Museum, Nashville TN

Kelly, Liam, *Actg Dir,* Boston Public Library, Central Library, Boston MA

Kelly, Margaret, *Recording Secy,* Florida Artist Group Inc, Venice FL

Kelly, Maurus, *Pastor Reverend,* Mission San Miguel Museum, San Miguel CA

Kelly, Michael, *Librn & Archivist,* Buffalo Bill Memorial Association, Harold McCracken Research Library, Cody WY

Kelly, Mike, *Vis Prof,* Oral Roberts University, Fine Arts Dept, Tulsa OK (S)

Kelly, Missy, *Development Officer,* Oklahoma Museum of Art, Oklahoma City OK

Kelly, Pamela, *Library Asst In Charge of Circulation & Reserve,* Sheldon Jackson College, Stratton Library, Sitka AK

Kelly, Perry, *Assoc Prof,* Western Carolina University, Dept of Art, Cullowhee NC (S)

Kelly, Robert, *Instructor,* Bard College, Milton Avery Graduate School of the Arts, Annandale-on-Hudson NY (S)

Kelly, Semey, *Public Relations,* Dalhousie University, Art Gallery, Halifax NS

Kelly, Vincent N, *Instr,* Yavapai College, Art Dept, Prescott AZ (S)

Kelly, William, *Assoc Prof,* Bemidji State University, Art Dept, Bemidji MN (S)

Kelly-Quinlan, Linda, *Exhib Dir,* Fredericton National Exhibition Centre, Fredericton NB

Kemp, Betty R, *Dir,* Lee County Library, Tupelo MS

Kemp, Paul Z, *Instr,* Baylor University, Dept of Fine Arts, Waco TX (S)

Kemp, Sheldon, *Field Representative,* Lansing Art Gallery, Lansing MI

Kemp, Weston D, *Assoc Prof,* Rochester Institute of Technology, School of Photographic Arts & Sciences, Rochester NY (S)

Kemper, R Crosby, *Chmn,* United Missouri Bancshares, Inc, Kansas City MO

Kempf, Elizabeth, *Instr,* Wayne Art Center, Wayne PA (S)

Kenamore, Jane, *Cur Special Coll,* Rosenberg Library, Galveston TX

Kendall, Donald M, *Chmn,* PepsiCo Inc, Purchase NY

Kendall, Meredith, *Business Asst,* Hood Museum of Art, Hanover NH

Kendall, M M, *Secy,* Mason County Museum, Maysville KY

Kendall, Thomas, *Asst Dir Art Center School,* Kalamazoo Institute of Arts, Artcenter School, Kalamazoo MI (S)

Kendall, William, *Asst Prof,* Bridgewater State College, Art Dept, Bridgewater MA (S)

Kendon, Jennifer Doran, *Admin Officer,* University of British Columbia, Museum of Anthropology, Vancouver BC

Kendra, A Walter, *Dir,* Central Connecticut State University, Art Dept Museum, New Britain CT

Kendrick, Diane, *Asst Prof,* Averett College, Art Dept, Danville VA (S)

Kendrick, Marvin, *Assoc Prof,* Hartford Art School of the University of Hartford, West Hartford CT (S)

Keneklis, James, *Business Mgr,* Brockton Art Museum, Brockton MA

Kenfield, John F, *Assoc Prof,* Rutgers, the State University of New Jersey, Graduate Program in Art History, New Brunswick NJ (S)

Kennard, Clande L, *Assoc Prof,* Southwestern University, Art Dept, Georgetown TX (S)

Kennedy, Barbara, *Financial Mgr,* Oklahoma Museum of Art, Oklahoma City OK

Kennedy, Carol Jean, *Education Coordr,* Arizona Commission on the Arts, Phoenix AZ

Kennedy, Garry Neill, *Pres,* Nova Scotia College of Art and Design, Halifax NS (S)

Kennedy, Garry Neill, *Pres,* Nova Scotia College of Art and Design, Anna Leonowens Gallery, Halifax NS

Kennedy, Gene, *Dir,* Grossmont Community College Gallery, El Cajon CA

Kennedy, Harriet F, *Asst Dir,* Museum of the National Center of Afro-American Artists, Boston MA

Kennedy, James E, *Head,* University of South Alabama, Ethnic American Slide Library, Mobile AL

Kennedy, James E, *Chmn,* University of South Alabama, Dept of Art, Mobile AL (S)

Kennedy, Jane G, *Membership Dir,* Institute of Contemporary Art, Boston MA

Kennedy, Janet, *Asst Prof,* Indiana University, Bloomington, School of Fine Arts, Bloomington IN (S)

Kennedy, Joan, *Asst to Dir,* DeCordova and Dana Museum and Park, Lincoln MA

Kennedy, Judy, *Dept of Education,* Columbia Museums of Art and Science, Columbia SC

Kennedy, Patrick, *Instr,* Orange County Community College, Art Dept, Middletown NY (S)

Kennedy, Robert, *Prof,* North Carolina Central University, Art Dept, Durham NC (S)

Kennedy, Roger G, *Dir,* National Museum of American History, Smithsonian Institution, Washington DC

Kennedy, Ronald, *Assoc Prof,* Southeastern Louisiana University, Dept of Visual Arts, Hammond LA (S)

Kennedy, Roy, *Asst Prof,* St Michael's College, Fine Arts Dept, Winooski VT (S)

Kennedy, Sharmon, *Prog Dir,* Farmington Art Guild, Farmington CT

Kenney, Marilyn, *Secy,* Penobscot Marine Museum, Searsport ME

Kenney, Rose, *Dir,* Oak Ridge Community Art Center & Museum of Fine Arts, Oak Ridge TN

Kennington, Sarah J, *Registrar,* University of California, Los Angeles, Museum of Cultural History, Los Angeles CA

Kennon, Arthur, *Ed,* Kappa Pi International Honorary Art Fraternity, Birmingham AL

Kenny, Edith, *Chmn Dept,* Marygrove College, Dept of Art and Art History, Detroit MI (S)

Kenny, Ellen, *Dir,* College of New Rochelle, Castle Gallery, New Rochelle NY

Kent, A Atwater, *Chmn of Board of Trustees,* Atwater Kent Museum, Philadelphia PA

Kent, A Atwater, *Treasurer,* Atwater Kent Museum, Philadelphia PA

Kent, Charles I, *Pres,* Lancaster County Art Association, Lancaster PA

Kent, David, *Dir Performing Arts,* Southeast Arkansas Arts and Science Center, Pine Bluff AR

Kent, Renee, *Slide Librn,* Sarah Lawrence College Library, Esther Raushenbush Library, Bronxville NY

Kent, Sheman, *Dir Omniplex,* Oklahoma Center for Science and Art, Kirkpatrick Center, Oklahoma City OK

Kenyon, Richard A, *Chmn,* Rhode Island College, Art Dept, Providence RI (S)

Keogh, Mary, *Board Dir,* Artists' Cooperative Gallery, Omaha NE

Keough, Maureen, *Pres,* Springfield Art League, Springfield MA

Kepes, Katherine, *Staff Librn,* Carnegie Library of Pittsburgh, Pittsburgh PA

Kepros, Peter G, *Dean Art Faculty,* University of New Brunswick, Art Education Section, Fredericton NB (S)

Kern, Norval C, *Prof,* Trenton State College, Art Dept, Trenton NJ (S)

Kernan, Kerri, *Chmn,* Texas A & M University, Memorial Student Center Arts Committee, College Station TX

Kerns, Ed, *Dept Head,* Lafayette College, Dept of Art, Easton PA (S)

Kerr, Dennis, *Lectr,* Saint Joseph's University, Fine Arts Dept, Philadelphia PA (S)

Kerr, Donald, *Chmn Dept,* Grand Valley State Colleges, Art Dept, Allendale MI (S)

Kerr, Myrtle, *Treas,* Kappa Pi International Honorary Art Fraternity, Birmingham AL

Kerr, Robert, *Asst Dean,* Rochester Institute of Technology, College of Fine and Applied Arts, Rochester NY (S)

Kerr, Warren, *Pres,* Klamath Falls Art Association, Klamath Art Gallery, Klamath Falls OR

Kerri, Gwendolyn, *Secy,* Memorial University of Newfoundland, Art Gallery, Saint John's NF

Kerridge, Barbara, *Center Administrator,* Lafayette College, Morris R Williams Center for the Arts, Easton PA

Kerslake, Kenneth A, *Prof,* University of Florida, Dept of Art, Gainesville FL (S)

Kersting, Irene, *Admin Asst,* Albuquerque Museum of Art, History and Science, Albuquerque NM

Kertess, Klaus, *Cur,* Parrish Art Museum, Southampton NY

Kesler, Karen, *Executive Dir,* Mendocino Art Center, Gallery, Mendocino CA

Kesler, Karen A, *Executive Dir,* Mendocino Art Center, Inc, Mendocino CA (S)

Kessler, Fred, *Secy,* Fetherston Foundation, Packwood House Museum, Lewisburg PA

Kessler, Herbert L, *Chmn,* Johns Hopkins University, Dept of the History of Art, Baltimore MD (S)

Kessler-Post, Nancy, *Librn,* Museum of the City of New York, Library, New York NY

Kester, Lee, *Gift Shop Mgr,* Paine Art Center and Arboretum, Oshkosh WI

Kester, Susanne, *Media Resources Coordr,* Hebrew Union College, Skirball Museum, Los Angeles CA

Kesterson-Bollen, Sharon, *Asst Prof,* College of Mount Saint Joseph, Art Dept, Mount Saint Joseph OH (S)

Ketchum, James R, *Cur,* United States Senate Commission on Art and Antiquities, Washington DC

Ketner, David, *Prof,* University of Rhode Island, Dept of Art, Kingston RI (S)

Ketner, Joseph D, *Cur & Registrar,* Washington University, Gallery of Art, Saint Louis MO

Ketsimpalis, Tom, *Cur Education,* Loveland Museum and Gallery, Loveland CO

Kettle, James, *Pres,* Hopewell Museum, Hopewell NJ

Kettler, Kerwin E, *Academic Dean,* New York School of Interior Design, New York NY (S)

Kettlewell, James, *Adjunct Cur,* Hyde Collection, Glens Falls NY

Kettner, David, *Co-Chairperson Painting & Drawing,* Philadelphia College of Art, Philadelphia PA (S)

Kettner, Pat, *Treas,* Manitoba Society of Artists, Winnipeg MB

Keuz, Frances T, *Asst Prof,* University of Nebraska at Omaha, Dept of Art, Omaha NE (S)

Key, Margaret A, *Registrar,* Bower's Museum, Santa Ana CA

Keyes, David, *Prof,* Pacific Lutheran University, Dept of Art, Tacoma WA (S)

Keyes, Richard, *Instructor,* Long Beach City College, Dept of Art, Long Beach CA (S)

Keyes, Richard D, *Head Dept Art,* Long Beach City College, Dept of Art, Long Beach CA (S)

Keyser, William A, *Crafts Chmn,* Rochester Institute of Technology, School for American Craftsmen, Rochester NY (S)

Keziere, Russell, *Vanguard Ed,* Vancouver Art Gallery, Vancouver BC

Khalidi, Omar, *Librn Aga Khan Program for Islamic Architecture,* Massachusetts Institute of Technology, Museum, Cambridge MA

Kiah, Virginia J, *Dir & Founder,* Kiah Museum, Savannah GA

Kibler, Robert, *Asst Prof,* Glendale College, Dept of Fine Arts, Glendale CA (S)

Kidd, George, *Pres,* Art Gallery of Greater Victoria, Victoria BC

Kiefer, Catherine Rudy, *Exec Secy,* Frick Art Museum, Pittsburgh PA

Kiefer, June, *VPres,* MPK Omega Co, Mike Kiefer Bio-Art Museum, Amarillo TX

Kiefer, Micheal P, *Librn,* Amarillo Art Center, Library, Amarillo TX

Kiefer, Mike, *Pres,* MPK Omega Co, Mike Kiefer Bio-Art Museum, Amarillo TX

Kiel, Martha, *Instructor,* Hardin-Simmons University, Art Dept, Abilene TX (S)

Kieschnick, William F, *Pres,* The Museum of Contemporary Art, Los Angeles CA

Kietzman, K M, *Dept Head,* College of Saint Francis, Creative Art Dept, Joliet IL (S)

Kietzman, William, *Slide & ILL Librn,* Plymouth State College, Herbert H Lamson Library, Plymouth NH

Kievets, Dennis, *Chmn,* Hiram College, Art Dept, Hiram OH (S)

Kihl, Elizabeth, *Librn,* Washington Art Association, Library, Washington Depot CT

Kihlstedt, Folke T, *Assoc Prof,* Franklin and Marshall College, Art Dept, Lancaster PA (S)

Kilbourne, John D, *Dir,* Society of the Cincinnati, Anderson House Museum, Washington DC

Kilbride, D, *Commercial Artist,* Saskatchewan Power Corporation, Gallery on the Roof, Regina SK

Kilby, Claudia, *Vice Dir,* Orange County Center for Contemporary Art, Santa Ana CA

Kilinski, Karl, *Chmn Art History,* Southern Methodist University, Division of Art and Art History, Dallas TX (S)

Kilmurry, Irene, *Prof,* Cardinal Stritch College, Art Dept, Milwaukee WI (S)

Kim, Carol A, *Asst Cur,* China Trade Museum, Milton MA

Kimble, Warren, *Asst Prof,* Castleton State College, Art Dept, Castleton VT (S)

Kimbrell, Leonard B, *Prof,* Portland State University, Dept of Art and Architecture, Portland OR (S)

Kimelman, Kate, *Asst Cur,* Stanford University, Museum of Art & Art Gallery, Stanford CA

Kimes, Don, *Program Dir,* New York Studio School of Drawing, Painting and Sculpture, New York NY (S)

Kimmel, Kent N, *Assoc Prof,* Salisbury State College, Art Dept, Salisbury MD (S)

Kinard, John R, *Dir,* Anacostia Neighborhood Museum, Washington DC

Kinch, Bruce, *Co-Chmn Photography Dept,* Art Institute of Boston, Boston MA (S)

Kindraka, Monica, *Cur,* Cedar Rapids Museum of Art, Cedar Rapids IA

King, Ann, *Asst Dir,* Utah Travel Council, Salt Lake City UT

King, Anthony G, *Dir,* Washington State Historical Society, Tacoma WA

King, Barbara N, *Secy,* Kenneth C Beck Center for the Cultural Arts, Lakewood OH

King, Barry, *Education Officer,* New Brunswick Museum, Saint John NB

King, Bruce, *Asst Dir,* Valentine Museum, Richmond VA

King, Charles H, *Cataloger,* National Museum of American Art, Library of the National Museum of American Art and the National Portrait Gallery, Washington DC

King, Duane, *Exec Dir,* Cherokee National Historical Society, Inc, Tahlequah OK

King, Jack, *Assoc Prof,* Augusta College, Dept of Fine Arts, Augusta GA (S)

King, James, *Pres,* Red River Valley Museum, Vernon TX

King, Jeanne, *Instructor,* Cazenovia College, Center for Art & Design Studies, Cazenovia NY (S)

King, John, *Head Art Education,* Edmonton Art Gallery, Edmonton AB

King, Karen, *Dir Development,* California Museum of Science and Industry, Los Angeles CA

King, Kendall, *VPres,* Marin Society of Artists Inc, Ross CA

King, Lucille, *Office Mgr,* Ponca City Art Association, Ponca City OK

King, Lyndel, *Dir,* University of Minnesota, University Art Museum, Minneapolis MN

King, Lyndel, *Secy,* The Art Museum Association of America, San Francisco CA

King, Maureen, *Secy,* Cypress College, Fine Arts Gallery, Cypress CA

King, Max, *Graphic Designer,* Craft and Folk Art Museum, Los Angeles CA

King, Shirley, *Admin Asst,* Midland Art Council, Midland MI

King, Wayne C, *Business Mgr,* Columbus Museum of Art, Columbus OH

King, Wendy H, *Admin Asst,* Museo Italo Americano, Library, San Francisco CA

King, Wilma, *Staff,* Benedict College, Visual Art Studies, Columbia SC (S)

Kinginger, Polly, *First VPres,* Berks Art Alliance, Reading PA

Kingsbury, Barbara, *Chmn Dept of Interior Design,* New England School of Art & Design, Boston MA (S)

Kingsley, Elizabeth, *Pres,* Historical Society of Bloomfield, Bloomfield NJ

Kingsley, Leonard E, *Pres,* Fine Arts Museums of San Francisco, M H de Young Memorial Museum and California Palace of the Legion of Honor, San Francisco CA

Kingsley, Robert, *Asst Prof,* DePauw University, Art Dept, Greencastle IN (S)

Kingston, Ray, *Chmn,* Utah Arts Council, Glendinning Gallery, Salt Lake City UT

Kington, L Brent, *Dir,* Southern Illinois University, School of Art, Carbondale IL (S)

Kinkay, Tony, *Assoc Prof,* Montgomery County Community College, Communicating Arts Dept, Blue Bell PA (S)

Kinnaird, Robert B, *Dir,* Kentucky Historical Society, Old State Capitol & Annex, Frankfort KY

Kinnarid, Richard, *Prof,* University of North Carolina at Chapel Hill, Art Dept, Chapel Hill NC (S)

Kinne, Carol, *Lecturer,* Colgate University, Dept of Fine Arts, Hamilton NY (S)

Kinney, Dale, *Chmn Dept & Assoc Prof,* Bryn Mawr College, Dept of the History of Art, Bryn Mawr PA (S)

Kinney, David, *Cur Education,* Hunterdon Art Center, Clinton NJ

Kinney, Marjorie, *Librn,* Kansas City Public Library, Art & Music Department, Kansas City MO

Kinney, Mary T, *Dean,* Columbus College of Art and Design, Columbus OH (S)

Kinoshita, Gene, *VPres,* Royal Canadian Academy of Arts, Toronto ON

Kinrade, Lee Newton, *Head Design Dept,* Winnipeg Art Gallery, Winnipeg MB

Kinsella, Doris, *Asst Dean,* Hartford Art School of the University of Hartford, West Hartford CT (S)

Kinsella, M, *Asst Prof,* Kearney State College, Dept of Art, Kearney NE (S)

Kinsinger, Patti, *Exhib Coordr,* Public Library of Columbus and Franklin County, Humanities, Fine Arts and Recreation Division, Columbus OH

Kinsman, Robert D, *Dir,* Sheldon Swope Art Gallery, Terre Haute IN

Kintzler, David, *Asst Dir,* Housatonic Community College, Housatonic Museum of Art, Bridgeport CT

Kintzler, David, *Chmn,* Housatonic Community College, Art Dept, Bridgeport CT (S)

Kiper, Carol, *Vis Prof,* Oral Roberts University, Fine Arts Dept, Tulsa OK (S)

Kipilii, Mary Lu, *Head AV Unit,* Hawaii State Library, Fine Arts-Audiovisual Section, Honolulu HI

Kirby, Kent, *Chmn,* Alma College, Dept of Art and Design, Alma MI (S)

Kirby, Peggy Jo, *Registrar,* North Carolina Museum of Art, Raleigh NC

Kirk, John, *Prof,* Shoreline Community College, Humanities Division, Seattle WA (S)

Kirk, Lloyd H, *In Charge Collection,* Honeywell Inc, Minneapolis MN

Kirk, Muriel S, *Coordr,* Museum of Fine Arts of Saint Petersburg, Florida, Inc, Art Reference Library, Saint Petersburg FL

Kirkey, Brian, *Coordr Summer Institute,* Visual Studies Workshop, Rochester NY

Kirking, Clayton C, *Librn,* Phoenix Art Museum, Art Research Library, Phoenix AZ

Kirkland, Kent, *Pres,* Springfield Art & Historical Society, Springfield VT

Kirkland, Sara, *VPres,* Singing River Art Association Inc, L & N Railroad Depot Gallery, Pascagoula MS

Kirkman, Dale, *Pres,* Phillips County Museum, Helena AR

Kirkpatrick, James, *Treasurer,* Ukiyo-e Society of America, Inc, New York NY

Kirkpatrick, John E, *Pres, Board Governors,* Oklahoma Center for Science and Art, Kirkpatrick Center, Oklahoma City OK

Kirkpatrick, Nancy, *Adminr,* Hirshhorn Museum and Sculpture Garden, Washington DC

Kirkpatrick, Nancy, *Head Slide Librn,* Art Institute of Chicago, Ryerson and Burnham Libraries, Chicago IL

Kirkpatrick, Susan, *Dir,* San Jose Institute of Contemporary Art, San Jose CA

Kirn, Mary Em, *Chmn Dept,* Augustana College, Art Dept, Rock Island IL (S)

Kirn, Mary Em, *Head Art Dept,* Augustana College, Centennial Hall Gallery, Rock Island IL

Kirsch, Edith, *Asst Prof,* Colorado College, Dept of Art, Colorado Springs CO (S)

Kirtland, Louise, *Assoc Prof,* Palomar College, Art Dept, San Marcos TX (S)

Kiser, Kimmerly, *Asst Prof,* Wright State University, Dept of Art & Art History, Dayton OH (S)

Kiskadden, Robert M, *Asst Dean & Grad Coordr,* Wichita State University, Division of Art, Wichita KS (S)

Kisselof, Margaret, *Dir,* Roosevelt Public Library , Black Artists Association Arts Center, Roosevelt NY

Kistner, Cynthia, *Adjunct Instr,* Maryville College, St Louis, Art Division, Saint Louis MO (S)

Kitao, T Kaori, *Prof,* Swarthmore College, Dept of Art, Swarthmore PA (S)

Kitchner, Landon, *Dir,* Johnson County Community College, Humanities Division, Overland Park KS (S)

Kittle, Barbara, *Librn,* University of Arizona, Museum of Art Library, Tucson AZ

Kittleson, Gloria, *Asst Dir Auxillary Activities,* Minnesota Museum of Art, Saint Paul MN

Kittleson, Lars, *Prof,* Pacific Lutheran University, Dept of Art, Tacoma WA (S)

Kitzing, Erna, *Bookeeper,* Springfield Free Public Library, Donald B Palmer Museum, Springfield NJ

Kiyooka, Roy, *Prof,* University of British Columbia, Dept of Fine Arts, Vancouver BC (S)

Kizik, Roger, *Preparator,* Brandeis University, Rose Art Museum, Waltham MA

Klahn, David, *Assoc Dean,* Ohio University, School of Arts, Athens OH (S)

Klassen, John, *Dir,* Massillon Museum, Massillon OH

Klaven, Marvin L, *Dir,* Millikin University, Kirkland Gallery, Decatur IL

Klaven, Marvin L, *Chmn Art Dept,* Millikin University, Art Dept, Decatur IL (S)

Kledis, Jarel, *Dir,* Westmar College, Mock Library Art Dept, LeMars IA

Kleeman, Richard, *Head Dept,* Allegheny College, Art Dept, Meadville PA (S)

Klein, Charles, *Pres,* Desert Caballeros Western Museum, Wickenburg AZ

Klein, Elliot, *Media Coordr,* San Mateo County Arts Council, Belmont CA

Klein, Henry, *Chmn,* Los Angeles Valley College, Art Dept, Van Nuys CA (S)

Klein, Leanne, *Librn,* Minnesota Museum of Art, Library, Saint Paul MN

Klein, Paul, *Second VPres Exhibitions,* Arizona Artist Guild, Phoenix AZ

Klein, Ruth Murray, *Chmn,* Please Touch Museum, Philadelphia PA

Klein, Stephanie, *Librn & Archivist,* Missouri Historical Society, Library, Saint Louis MO

Klein, Victor L, *Pres,* Birmingham-Bloomfield Art Association, Birmingham MI

Kleinbauer, Eugene, *Prof,* Indiana University, Bloomington, School of Fine Arts, Bloomington IN (S)

Kleiner, Diana, *Dir Undergrad Studies,* Yale University, Dept of the History of Art, New Haven CT (S)

Kleinfeldt, Kendal, *Staff Site Interpreter,* Patterson Homestead, Dayton OH

Kleinsasser, Jerome, *Chmn,* California State College Bakersfield, Fine Arts Dept, Bakersfield CA (S)

Kleinschmidt, Robert, *Assoc Prof,* University of Utah, Art Dept, Salt Lake City UT (S)

Kleinsmith, Gene, *Chmn Dept,* Victor Valley College, Art Dept, Victorville CA (S)

Klemm, Jean Agnes, *Assoc Prof,* Siena Heights College, Studio Angelico Art Dept, Adrian MI (S)

Klemm, Jeannine, *Dir,* Siena Heights College, Little Gallery, Studio Angelico, Adrian MI

Klemm, Jeannine, *Chairperson Dept,* Siena Heights College, Studio Angelico Art Dept, Adrian MI (S)

Klemmer, Virginia, *Gallery Dir,* Sarasota Art Association, Sarasota FL

Klenk, William, *Prof,* University of Rhode Island, Dept of Art, Kingston RI (S)

Kleppe, Shirley, *First VPres,* Arizona Artist Guild, Phoenix AZ

Kliman, Eve, *Asst Prof,* University of Waterloo, Fine Arts Dept, Waterloo ON (S)

Klimiades, Mario N, *Librn,* Amerind Foundation, Inc, Fulton-Hayden Memorial Library, Dragoon AZ

Kline, Paul M, *Chmn,* Bridgewater College, Art Dept, Bridgewater College VA (S)

Kline, Richard, *Chmn Dept,* Central Michigan University, Dept of Art, Mount Pleasant MI (S)

Klingaman, David B, *Pres,* Rensselaer County Historical Society, Hart-Cluett Mansion, 1827, Troy NY

Klingman, Berry J, *Instr,* Baylor University, Dept of Fine Arts, Waco TX (S)

Klinkon, Heinz, *Vis Asst Prof,* Rochester Institute of Technology, School of Art and Design, Rochester NY (S)

Klish, Renee, *Registrar,* United States Military Academy, West Point Museum, West Point NY

Klobe, Tom, *Dir,* University of Hawaii at Manoa, Art Gallery, Honolulu HI

Klonis, Stewart, *Pres,* American Fine Arts Society, New York NY

Klopfer, M, *Art Ed,* Lovis Corinth Memorial Foundation, Inc, New York NY

Kluba, William, *Lectr,* Tunxis Community College, Graphic Design Dept, Farmington CT (S)

Kluge, Gordon, *Chmn Printamking Dept,* San Francisco Art Institute, San Francisco CA (S)

Kluge, Janice, *Asst Prof,* University of Alabama in Birmingham, Dept of Art, Birmingham AL (S)

Klukas, Arnold, *Asst Prof,* Oberlin College, Dept of Art, Oberlin OH (S)

Klyberg, Albert T, *Dir,* Rhode Island Historical Society, Providence RI

Knachel, Philip A, *Acting Dir,* Folger Shakespeare Library, Washington DC

Knaub, Donald E, *Dir,* Huntsville Museum of Art, Huntsville AL

Knauber, Ann, *Membership Coordr,* Fine Arts Museums of San Francisco, The Museum Society, San Francisco CA

Knaus, Tracy, *Secy,* Fetherston Foundation, Packwood House Museum, Lewisburg PA

Knecht, John, *Asst Prof,* Colgate University, Dept of Fine Arts, Hamilton NY (S)

Knecht, Samuel, *Acting Dir,* Hillsdale College, Art Dept, Hillsdale MI (S)

Kneisel, Joyce, *Research Asst,* Burbank Public Library, Warner Research Collection, Burbank CA

Kneisel, Stephen, *Asst Supv,* Newark Museum, Junior Museum, Newark NJ

Knepper, Ben, *Exhib Preparator,* Ohio State University, Gallery of Fine Art, Columbus OH

Knepper, John R, *Pres,* Art Institute of Pittsburgh Gallery, Pittsburgh PA

Knepper, John R, *Pres,* Art Institute of Pittsburgh, Pittsburgh PA (S)

Knight, John H, *Chmn,* Illinois Valley Community College, Div of Humanities and Fine Arts, Oglesby IL (S)

Knight, Katie, *Asst Prof,* Saint Louis Community College at Forest Park, Fine Arts Dept, Saint Louis MO (S)

Knight, Mary Ann, *Head Dept Music and Arts Services,* Berkshire Athenaeum, Pittsfield MA

Knight, T L, *Faculty,* Humboldt State University, College of Creative Arts & Humanities, Arcata CA (S)

Knights, T, *Assoc Prof,* Northern Arizona University, Art Dept, Flagstaff AZ (S)

Knipe, Jan, *Instructor,* Viterbo College, Art Dept, La Crosse WI (S)

Knipe, Jim, *Asst Prof,* Viterbo College, Art Dept, La Crosse WI (S)

Knisley, Rhoda, *Prof,* Spring Arbor College, Art Dept, Spring Arbor MI (S)

Knodel, Gerhardt, *Head Fiber Dept,* Cranbrook Academy of Art, Bloomfield Hills MI (S)

Knoop, Cary, *Prof,* Eastern Illinois University, School of Fine Arts, Charleston IL (S)

Knop, Chris, *Registrar,* Philbrook Art Center, Tulsa OK

Knopka, Susan, *Instructor,* Solano Community College, Dept of Fine & Applied Art, Suisun City CA (S)

Knotek, Julie, *Chmn Art Dept,* Alverno College, Art Dept, Milwaukee WI (S)

Knott, Elen, *Development Asst,* Reynolda House, Inc, Winston-Salem NC

Knott, Irene, *First Asst Music and Arts Services,* Berkshire Athenaeum, Pittsfield MA

Knott, Robert, *Prof,* Wake Forest University, Dept of Art, Winston-Salem NC (S)

Knowles, Penny, *Cur Education,* Santa Barbara Museum of Art, Santa Barbara CA

Knowlton, Kenn, *Instructor,* Art Academy of Cincinnati, Cincinnati OH (S)

Knox, George, *Prof,* University of British Columbia, Dept of Fine Arts, Vancouver BC (S)

Knox, Northrup R, *VPres,* The Buffalo Fine Arts Academy, Albright-Knox Art Gallery, Buffalo NY

Knox, Seymour H, *Chmn,* The Buffalo Fine Arts Academy, Albright-Knox Art Gallery, Buffalo NY

Knudson, Craig, *Chmn,* Ellsworth Community College, Dept of Fine Arts, Iowa Falls IA (S)

Knudson, Elizabeth, *Librn,* University of Utah, Owen Library, Salt Lake City UT

Knuth, Priscilla, *Managing Editor,* Oregon Historical Society, Library, Portland OR

Knutson, Norman, *Chmn Art Dept,* Adrian College, Art Dept, Adrian MI (S)

Ko, Anthony, *Chmn 2-D Area,* Edinboro University of Pennsylvania, Art Dept, Edinboro PA (S)

Koberg, William, *Preparator,* The Phillips Collection, Washington DC

Kobrynich, Bill, *Dir Interior Design,* Art Institute of Fort Lauderdale, Fort Lauderdale FL (S)

Koch, Bruno, *Prof,* Christopher Newport College, Arts & Communications, Newport News VA (S)

Koch, Cynthia, *Dir,* Old Barracks Museum, Trenton NJ

Koch, George, *Pres,* Artists Equity Association, Inc, Washington DC

Koch, George, *Pres,* United States Committee of the International Association of Art, Inc, Washington DC

Koch, Robert, *Prof,* Princeton University, Dept of Art and Archaeology, Princeton NJ (S)

Kocher, E G, *Cur,* West Bend Gallery of Fine Arts, West Bend WI

Kocher, Robert, *Prof,* Coe College, Dept of Art, Cedar Rapids IA (S)

Kochka, Al, *Dir,* Sangre De Cristo Arts & Conference Center, Pueblo CO

Kockritz, Susan, *VPres,* Balboa Art Conservation Center, San Diego CA

Kodera, Louisa McDonald, *Asst Prof,* Mount Holyoke College, Art Dept, South Hadley MA (S)

Koehler, Karen, *Cur Asst,* University of Massachusetts, Amherst, University Gallery, Amherst MA

Koehler, Paul J, *Asst Prof,* Augustana College, Art Dept, Sioux Falls SD (S)

Koel, Ottilia, *Librn & Manuscripts Cur,* New Haven Colony Historical Society, Research Library, New Haven CT

Koenig, Audrey, *Cur Adminr & Registrar,* Newark Museum, Newark NJ

Koenig, Robert j, *Dir,* Montclair Art Museum, Montclair NJ

Koeninger, Kay, *Cur Coll,* Galleries of the Claremont Colleges, Claremont CA

Koerber, Louis V, *VPres,* Star-Spangled Banner Flag House Association, Baltimore MD

Koerlin, Ernest, *Assoc Prof,* Wright State University, Dept of Art & Art History, Dayton OH (S)

Kogel, Albert, *Instructor,* Cochise College, Art Dept, Douglas AZ (S)

Kohl, Joyce, *Asst Prof,* University of Southern California, School of Fine Arts, Los Angeles CA (S)

Kohler, Ruth, *Dir,* John Michael Kohler Arts Center, Sheboygan WI

Kohler, Sandra, *Instr,* Mainline Center of the Arts, Haverford PA (S)

Kohlschreiber, Molly Haines, *Instr,* Victor Valley College, Art Dept, Victorville CA (S)

Kohn, Bernard A, *Treas,* American Color Print Society, Philadelphia PA

Kohn, David M, *Exec Dir,* Long Island Historical Society, Brooklyn NY

Kohring, Dagmar, *Development,* Harvard University, Busch-Reisinger Museum, Cambridge MA

Kolarik, Ruth, *Asst Prof,* Colorado College, Dept of Art, Colorado Springs CO (S)

Kolb, Nancy D, *Asst Exec Dir,* Pennsylvania Historical and Museum Commission, Harrisburg PA

Koldoff, Patsy, *Cur,* First Interstate Bank of Arizona, Tucson AZ

Kolhoff, Florence, *VPres,* Cumberland Art Society, Cookeville Art Center, Cookeville TN

Kolinski, Kris, *Instr,* Highland Community College, Freeport IL (S)

Kologie, Lucille, *Instructor,* Southwestern School of Art, Albuquerque NM (S)

Kolok, William, *Asst Prof,* Kentucky Wesleyan College, Dept Art, Owensboro KY (S)

Kolowrat, Elizabeth, *Museum Educ,* Pennsylvania Academy of the Fine Arts, Galleries, Philadelphia PA

Kolt, Ingrid, *Education & Events Coordr,* Surrey Art Gallery, Surrey BC

Komac, Dennis, *Dir,* San Diego State University, Art Gallery, San Diego CA

Komechak, Michael E, *Head,* Illinois Benedictine College, Fine Arts Dept, Lisle IL (S)

Komives, Ralph, *Head Dept,* Stephens College, Art Dept, Columbia MO (S)

Komizes, Ralph, *Actg Dir,* Stephens College, Lewis James & Nellie Stratton Davis Art Gallery, Columbia MO

Konopka, Joseph, *VPres,* Associated Artists of New Jersey, Pittstown NJ

Konrad, Anton, *Conservator,* Museo de Arte de Ponce, Ponce Art Museum, Ponce PR

Koons, Darrel, *Instructor,* Bob Jones University, School of Fine Arts, Greenville SC (S)

Koons, Kathy, *Office Mgr,* Civic Fine Arts Association Museum, Sioux Falls SD

Koontz, Sondra, *State-Wide Film Service,* Wichita Public Library, Wichita KS

Koop, Rebecca, *Instructor,* William Jewell College, Art Dept, Liberty MO (S)

Kooperman, Evelyn, *Librn,* San Diego Public Library, Art & Music Section, San Diego CA

Koozer, Don, *Art Library Supervisor,* University of Oklahoma, Art Library, Norman OK

Kopf, Vicki S, *Cur,* Southeastern Center for Contemporary Art, Winston-Salem NC

Kopley, Elizabeth, *Development,* Newark Museum, Newark NJ

Kopp, Marilyn, *Secy,* Hickory Museum of Art, Inc, Hickory NC

Koppeis, Francis, *Innkeeper,* Longfellow's Wayside Inn, South Sudbury MA

Koras, George, *Prof,* State University of New York at Stony Brook, Art Dept, Stony Brook NY (S)

Korbutiak, Christine, *Educ/Extension Coordr,* Ukrainian Cultural and Educational Centre Museum, Winnipeg MB

Kordich, Diane D, *Assoc Prof,* Northern Michigan University, Dept of Art and Design, Marquette MI (S)

Korey, Marie E, *Rare Book Librn,* Free Library of Philadelphia, Rare Book Dept, Philadelphia PA

Korf, Kumi, *Lecturer,* Ithaca College, Fine Art Dept, Ithaca NY (S)

Korman, Bette, *Founder & Exec Dir,* Manhattan Laboratory Museum, New York NY

Kornegay, Julia, *Dir,* Louisburg College, Art Gallery, Louisburg NC

Kornhauser, Stephen, *Head Conservator,* Wadsworth Atheneum, Hartford CT

Kornitnik, Mary, *Finance Officer,* Sweetwater Community Fine Arts Center, Rock Springs WY

Kornowski, Walter L, *Chmn,* Bethany College, Art Dept, Bethany WV (S)

Kornwolf, James D, *Chmn Fine Arts Dept,* College of William and Mary, Joseph & Margaret Muscarelle Museum of Art, Williamsburg VA

Kornwolf, James D, *Prof,* College of William and Mary, Dept of Fine Arts, Williamsburg VA (S)

Koroscik, Judith, *Asst Prof,* Ohio State University, Dept of Art Education, Columbus OH (S)

Korper, Olga, *VPres,* Professional Art Dealers Association of Canada, Toronto ON

Korshak, Yvonne, *Assoc Prof,* Adelphi University, Dept of Art and Art History, Garden City NY (S)

Kortum, Karl, *Chief Cur,* National Maritime Museum, San Francisco CA

Korzenik, Diana, *Chmn Art Educ,* Massachusetts College of Art, Boston MA (S)

Kosan, Julius T, *Assoc Prof,* Bowling Green State University, Art Dept, Huron OH (S)

Kosche, Eugene R, *Cur History,* Bennington Museum, Bennington VT

Koshalek, Richard, *Dir,* The Museum of Contemporary Art, Los Angeles CA

Koshute, Joseph, *Art Dir,* Patterson Library & Art Gallery, Westfield NY

Kosik, Edwin M, *Chmn Trustees,* Everhart Museum of Natural History, Science and Art, Scranton PA

Koslosky, Robert, *Assoc Prof,* Bloomsburg University, Dept of Art, Bloomsburg PA (S)

Koss, Gene H, *Assoc Prof,* Tulane University, Sophie H Newcomb Memorial College, New Orleans LA (S)

Kosuge, Michihiro, *Assoc Prof,* Portland State University, Dept of Art and Architecture, Portland OR (S)

Kotik, Charlotte, *Consultant Cur Prints & Drawings,* Brooklyn Museum, Brooklyn NY

Kotin, David B, *Head Canadian History Department,* Metropolitan Toronto Library Board, Canadian History Dept, Toronto ON

Koursaros, Harry G, *Assoc Prof,* Albright College, Dept of Art, Reading PA (S)

Koutroulis, Aris, *Chmn Fine Arts,* Center for Creative Studies__College of Art and Design, Detroit MI (S)

Kovach, Ruth Ann, *Chmn Dept,* Waldorf College, Art Dept, Forest City IA (S)

Kovach, Sally A, *Head Dept & Assoc Prof,* Beloit College, Dept of Art, Beloit WI (S)

Kovacs, B Jeanne, *Secy,* Wallingford Art League, Wallingford CT

Kovacs, Katherine M, *Archivist,* Corcoran Museum, Washington DC

Kowal, Calvin, *Instructor,* Art Academy of Cincinnati, Cincinnati OH (S)

Kowalek, Jon W, *Dir,* Tacoma Art Museum, Tacoma WA

Kowalke, Kit, *Dept Head,* Honolulu Community College, Honolulu HI (S)

Kowall, Thomas W, *Dir Student Services,* Emily Carr College of Art & Design, Vancouver BC (S)

Kowalski, Dennis, *Instr,* Oxbow Center for the Arts, Saugatuck MI (S)

Kowalski, Lee, *Public Relations,* Vernon Art Association, Topham Brown Gallery, Vernon BC

Kowalski, Libby, *Prof,* State University of New York College at Cortland, Art Dept, Cor⁺land NY (S)

Kowalski, Onoosh, *Instr,* Marian College, Art Dept, Indianapolis IN (S)

Kowski, Robert, *Chmn Dept,* Greensboro College, Dept of Art, Division of Fine Arts, Greensboro NC (S)

Kowski, Robert, *Asst Prof,* Greensboro College, Irene Cullis Gallery, Greensboro NC

Kozloff, Arielle P, *Cur Ancient Art,* Cleveland Museum of Art, Cleveland OH

Kozlowski, Deirdre Lee, *Asst Prof,* Mount Mary College, Art Dept, Milwaukee WI (S)

Kozlowski, Ronald S, *Dir,* Public Library of Charlotte and Mecklenburg County, Charlotte NC

Kozuch, Roberta, *Asst Prof,* Loyola University of Chicago, Fine Arts Dept, Chicago IL (S)

Kozuszek, Larry, *Prof,* Saint Louis Community College at Florissant Valley, Dept of Art, Ferguson MO (S)

Kpenig, Robert J, *Dir,* Montclair Art Museum, Museum Art Classes, Montclair NJ (S)

Kraemer, Pat, *Instructor,* Rochester Community College, Art Dept, Rochester MN (S)

Kraft, Ann, *Development Assoc,* Solomon R Guggenheim Museum, New York NY

Kraft, Regina, *Assoc Prof,* Elizabeth Seton College, Art Dept, Yonkers NY (S)

Krainak, Paul, *Instr,* Oxbow Center for the Arts, Saugatuck MI (S)

Krakel, Dean, *Exec Dir,* National Cowboy Hall of Fame and Western Heritage Center, Oklahoma City OK

Kramer, Edith, *Cur Film,* University of California, Pacific Film Archive, Berkeley CA

Kramer, Gerald, *Assoc Prof,* Cuyahoga Community College, Dept of Art, Cleveland OH (S)

Kramer, Leslie, *Dir,* Elmira College, Hamilton Art Gallery, Elmira NY

Kramer, Leslie, *Instructor,* Elmira College, Art Dept, Elmira NY (S)

Kramer, Margia, *Asst Prof,* Hartford Art School of the University of Hartford, West Hartford CT (S)

Kramer, Steve, *Instr,* Ellsworth Community College, Dept of Fine Arts, Iowa Falls IA (S)

Kramer, Trudy, *Dir,* Parrish Art Museum, Southampton NY

Krammers, Barry, *Instructor,* Biola University, Art Dept, La Mirada CA (S)

Krane, Susan, *Cur,* The Buffalo Fine Arts Academy, Albright-Knox Art Gallery, Buffalo NY

Kraning, Alan, *Lecturer,* University of Wisconsin-Stout, Art Dept, Menomonie WI (S)

Krashes, Barbara, *VPres,* Federation of Modern Painters and Sculptors, New York NY

Krass, Jeffrey, *Cur,* Dia Art Foundation, Inc, New York NY

Kratsas, James R, *Cur Fine Art,* Kansas State Historical Society Museum, Topeka KS

Kratsas, Martha D, *Asst Museum Dir,* Kansas State Historical Society Museum, Topeka KS

Kraus, Russell C, *Dir,* Rochester Institute of Technology, School of Photographic Arts & Sciences, Rochester NY (S)

Krause, Bonnie, *Cur History,* Southern Illinois University, University Museum, Carbondale IL

Krause, Carolyn, *Publications Coordr,* Contemporary Arts Center, Cincinnati OH

Krause, Lawrence, *Prof,* Cleveland Institute of Art Cleveland OH (S)

Krause, Leanne, *Bookstore Mgr,* Museum of Holography, New York NY

Krause, Martin F, *Asst Cur Prints & Drawings,* Indianapolis Museum of Art, Indianapolis IN

Krauss, James A, *Assoc Prof,* Oakton Community College, Art & Architecture Dept, Des Plains IL (S)

Krauss, Rosalind, *Prof,* City University of New York, PhD Program in Art History, New York NY (S)

Krausz, Peter Thomas, *Cur,* Saidye Bronfman Centre, Montreal PQ

Krauth, Harold, *Chair & Assoc Prof,* Norwich University, Dept of Philosophy, Religion and Fine Arts, Northfield VT (S)

Krawetz, Sandra, *Public Relations Coordr,* Toledo Museum of Art, Toledo OH

Kray, Robert, *Asst Prof,* Luzerne County Community College, Commercial Art Dept, Nanticoke PA (S)

Kraywinkel, Howard, *Dir Museum Photography,* Art Institute of Chicago, Chicago IL

Krebs, Harry, *Assoc Prof,* Dickinson College, Fine Arts Dept, Carlisle PA (S)

Krebs, Jerry H, *Assoc Prof,* Radford University, Art Dept, Radford VA (S)

Krebs, Rose, *Assoc Prof,* C W Post Center of Long Island University, School of the Arts, Greenvale NY (S)

Kree, Kirsten, *Instructor,* Montclair Art Museum, Museum Art Classes, Montclair NJ (S)

Kreeger, David Lloyd, *Pres,* Corcoran Museum, Washington DC

Kreger, Philip, *Chief of Exhibits,* Tennessee State Museum, Nashville TN

Kreider, Robert, *Dir,* Bethel College, Mennonite Library and Archives, North Newton KS

Kreisberg, Luisa, *Dir Public Information,* Museum of Modern Art, New York NY

Kreiter, James W, *Cur Art,* Neville Public Museum, Green Bay WI

Krejcarek, Philip, *Asst Prof,* Carroll College, Art Dept, Waukesha WI (S)

Krekler, Judith, *Instructor,* Anton Elli, Cincinnati OH (S)

Kremgold, David, *Asst Prof,* University of Florida, Dept of Art, Gainesville FL (S)

Kreneck, Lynwood, *Prof,* Texas Tech University, Dept of Art, Lubbock TX (S)

Krens, Thomas, *Dir,* Williams College, Museum of Art, Williamstown MA

Kresta, S, *Instr,* David Thompson University Centre, Visual Arts Dept, Nelson BC (S)

Krier, Maureen, *Head of the Library Committee,* Danforth Museum of Art, Library, Framingham MA

Krimstein, Jordan, *Instr,* Blackhawk Mountain School of Art, Black Hawk CO (S)

Krinsky, Carol, *First VPres,* Society of Architectural Historians, Philadelphia PA

Krinsky, Maxine, *Instr,* Mainline Center of the Arts, Haverford PA (S)

Krinsky, Maxine, *Instr,* Wayne Art Center, Wayne PA (S)

Kristof, Jane, *Assoc Prof,* Portland State University, Dept of Art and Architecture, Portland OR (S)

Krochman-Marks, Kay, *Asst Music & Fine Arts Librn,* Southern Methodist University, Fine Arts Library, Dallas TX

Kroeker, Leon, *Head Dept,* Oral Roberts University, Fine Arts Dept, Tulsa OK (S)

Kroll, Morton, *Dir,* King County Arts Commission, Seattle WA

Krommenhoek, Hans, *Instructor,* Milwaukee Area Technical College, Graphic & Applied Arts Division, Milwaukee WI (S)

Kronenberg, John L, *Assoc Dean,* Rochester Institute of Technology, College of Graphic Arts and Photography, Rochester NY (S)

Kronewetter, Justin, *Prof,* Ohio Wesleyan University, Fine Arts Dept, Delaware OH (S)

Kronstedt, Richard, *Dir,* Minneapolis College of Art and Design, Library and Media Center, Minneapolis MN

Kroop, Bernie, *Instructional Asst,* Sullivan County Community College, Division of Commercial Art and Photography, Loch Sheldrake NY (S)

Kropf, Joan, *Cur,* Salvador Dali Foundation Museum, Saint Petersburg FL

Krudo, Shlomo, *VPres,* Artists Guild of Chicago, Chicago IL

Krueger, Donald W, *Dir,* Clark University, Little Center Gallery, Worcester MA

Krueger, Donald W, *Dir Studio Art Program,* Clark University, Dept of Visual & Performing Arts, Worcester MA (S)

Krueger, Gene, *Chmn County Museum Board,* J K Ralston Museum and Art Center, Sidney MT

Krueger, Joan, *Exhibition Coordr,* Artrain, Inc, Detroit MI

Krueger, Lise, *Admin Officer,* National Film Board of Canada, Still Photography Division, Ottawa ON

Krueger, Lothar, *Prof Emeritus,* University of Arkansas, Art Dept, Fayetteville AR (S)

Krueger, Pamela, *Dir,* Laurentian University, Museum and Arts Centre, Sudbury ON

Kruetzman, William E, *Technician,* J B Speed Art Museum, Louisville KY

Krug, Harry E, *Chairperson & Prof,* Pittsburg State University, Art Dept, Pittsburg KS (S)

Krug, Kersti, *Asst Dir Finance & Admin,* National Gallery of Canada, Ottawa ON

Krule, Bernard K, *Assoc Prof,* Oakton Community College, Art & Architecture Dept, Des Plains IL (S)

Krulik, Barbara, *Asst,* National Academy of Design, New York NY

Krupp, Delia Schalansky, *Slide Cur,* California State University, Sacramento, Library, Humanities Reference and Media Services Center, Sacramento CA

Kruse, Donald, *Assoc Prof,* Indiana University-Purdue University, Dept of Fine Arts, Fort Wayne IN (S)

Kruse, Gerald, *Assoc Prof,* South Dakota State University, Dept of Visual Arts, Brookings SD (S)

Krush, Beth, *Chmn Illustration,* Moore College of Art, Philadelphia PA (S)

Krutza, June, *Prof,* Eastern Illinois University, School of Fine Arts, Charleston IL (S)

Krych, Lesia, *Librn,* Art Institute of Philadelphia Library, Philadelphia PA

Kryzsko, Karen, *Head Dept & Assoc Prof,* Saint Mary's College, Art Dept, Winona MN (S)

Kuan, Baulu, *Assoc Prof,* College of Saint Benedict, Art Dept, Saint Joseph MN (S)

Kubert, Joe, *Pres,* Joe Kubert School of Cartoon and Graphic Art Inc, Dover NJ (S)

Kubly, Don, *Pres & Dir,* Art Center College of Design, Pasadena CA (S)

Kubris, Valdes, *Assoc Prof,* New York Institute of Technology, Fine Arts Dept, Old Westbury NY (S)

Kuch, Harry G, *Pres,* Woodmere Art Museum, Philadelphia PA

Kuchar, Kathleen, *Prof,* Fort Hays State University, Dept of Art, Hays KS (S)

Kuchel, Konrad G, *Coordr Exhibition Loans,* The American Federation of Arts, New York NY

Kuchler, LaVerne, *Actg Librn,* Contemporary Crafts Association and Gallery, Library, Portland OR

Kuchta, Ronald A, *Dir,* Everson Museum of Art, Syracuse NY

Kucklick, Elizabeth T, *Program Consultant,* Xerox Corporation, Art Collection, Stamford CT

Kuczynski, John D, *Art Dept Chmn & Prof,* Pierce College, Art Dept, Woodland Hills CA (S)

Kudlawiec, Dennis P, *Chmn,* Livingston University, Division of Fine Arts, Livingston AL (S)

KudronKulh, Georgeann, *Dir of Educ,* Edmundson Art Foundation, Inc, Des Moines Art Center, Des Moines IA

Kuehn, Claire, *Archivist & Librn,* Panhandle-Plains Historical Society Museum, Library, Canyon TX

Kuehn, Gary, *Assoc Prof,* Rutgers, the State University of New Jersey, Mason Gross School of the Arts, New Brunswick NJ (S)

Kuehne, R E, *VPres,* Orange County Community of Museums and Galleries, Goshen NY

Kuehne, Richard E, *Dir Museum,* United States Military Academy, West Point Museum, West Point NY

Kuflik, Louise, *Secy,* Guild of Book Workers, New York NY

Kugler, Jamie, *Children's Program,* Palo Alto Cultural Center, Palo Alto CA

Kugler, Richard C, *Dir,* Old Dartmouth Historical Society, New Bedford Whaling Museum, New Bedford MA

Kuhl, Condon, *Chairperson Dept,* Drake University, Art Dept, Des Moines IA (S)

Kuhn, Annette, *Adminr,* Art Commission of the City of New York, New York NY

Kuhn, Marylou, *Chmn,* Florida State University, Art Education Dept, Tallahassee FL (S)

Kuiper, John, *Dir Film Coll,* International Museum of Photography at George Eastman House, Rochester NY

Kujawski, Mary, *Cur of Educ,* University of Michigan, Museum of Art, Ann Arbor MI

Kumnick, Charles, *Asst Prof,* Trenton State College, Art Dept, Trenton NJ (S)

Kun, Authur E, *Assoc Prof,* Tulane University, Sophie H Newcomb Memorial College, New Orleans LA (S)

Kuniholm, Hope, *Librn Intern,* Cornell University, Herbert F Johnson Museum Library, Ithaca NY

Kunkel, Jerry W, *Chmn,* University of Colorado, Boulder, Dept of Fine Arts, Boulder CO (S)

Kunkle-Miller, Carole, *Lectr,* Carlow College, Art Dept, Pittsburgh PA (S)

Kuntz, David L, *Cur Exhibitions,* Illinois State University, Center for the Visual Arts Gallery, Normal IL

Kuntz, Jospeh, *Cur Decorative Arts & Assoc Cur European Decorative Arts,* Atkins Museum of Fine Art, Kansas City MO

Kunze, Steve, *Lectr,* Azusa Pacific University, College of Liberal Arts, Art Dept, Azusa CA (S)

Kuo, James K Y, *Prof,* Daemen College, Art Dept, Amherst NY (S)

Kuony, John H, *Dir,* Oshkosh Public Museum, Oshkosh WI

Kupfer, Marcia, *Asst Prof,* Northwestern University, Evanston, Dept of Art History, Evanston IL (S)

Kupferberg, Kenneth, *Treas,* Bowne House, Flushing NY

Kuretsky, Susan D, *Chmn Art Dept,* Vassar College, Art Dept, Poughkeepsie NY (S)

Kurka, Donald F, *Head Art Dept,* University of Tennessee, Knoxville, Dept of Art, Knoxville TN (S)

Kuronen, Dennis, *Asst Prof,* Beaver College, Dept of Fine Arts, Glenside PA (S)

Kurriger, Patricia, *Instructor,* College of DuPage, Humanities Division, Glen Ellyn IL (S)

Kurth, E J, *Pres,* Heritage Center, Inc, Pine Ridge SD

Kurtich, John, *Prof,* School of the Art Institute of Chicago, Chicago IL (S)

Kurtz, Judith, *Coordr Museum Programs & Public Relations,* University of Utah, Utah Museum of Fine Arts, Salt Lake City UT

Kurtz, Stephen G, *Principal,* Phillips Exeter Academy, Frederic R Mayer Art Center & Lamont Gallery, Exeter NH

Kuruna, Daniel L, *Chmn Dept,* Western Illinois University, College of Fine Arts, Macomb IL (S)

Kurutz, K D, *Cur Education,* Crocker Art Museum, Sacramento CA

Kurz, Kathe, *Lectr,* Carroll College, Art Dept, Waukesha WI (S)

Kusaba, Yoshio, *Instr,* California State University, Chico, Art Dept, Chico CA (S)

Kushner, Robert B, *Assoc Prof,* Rochester Institute of Technology, School of Photographic Arts & Sciences, Rochester NY (S)

Kushnir, Gail, *Vis Instr,* Judson College, Division of Fine Arts, Elgin IL (S)

Kusnerz, P A, *Librn,* University of Michigan, Art & Architecture Library, Ann Arbor MI

Kuspit, Donald, *Prof,* State University of New York at Stony Brook, Art Dept, Stony Brook NY (S)

Kutsky, Irene, *Assoc Prof,* College of New Rochelle School of Arts and Sciences, Undergraduate Art Dept, New Rochelle NY (S)

Kuwayama, George, *Sr Cur of Far Eastern Art,* Los Angeles County Museum of Art, Los Angeles CA

Kuykendall, Karen Tucker, *Cur Education,* Florida Gulf Coast Art Center, Inc, Clearwater FL

Kuyoth-Smith, Connie, *Bookkeeper,* Western Colorado Center for the Arts, Inc, Grand Junction CO

Kuyper, Joan, *Dir,* Bergen Museum of Art & Science, Paramus NJ

Kuzminski, Catherine, *Chmn Fine Arts Program,* Westminster College, Dept of Art, Salt Lake City UT (S)

Kwan, Mona Worthington, *Dir,* Santa Barbara Contemporary Arts Forum, Santa Barbara CA

Kysar, Lola, *Treas,* Coquille Valley Art Association, Coquille OR

Laakso, David, *Prof,* Cape Cod Community College, Art Dept, West Barnstable MA (S)

Laatsch, Gary, *Instructor,* Saginaw Valley State College, Dept of Art and Design, University Center MI (S)

Lab, Walter F, *Instructor,* Modesto Junior College, Arts Humanities and Speech Division, Modesto CA (S)

LaBante, Linelle, *Prof,* College of Notre Dame of Maryland, Art Dept, Baltimore MD (S)

Labaw, Patricia J, *Secy,* Princeton Art Association, Princeton NJ

LaBelle, Marguerite, *Assoc Prof,* Jersey City State College, Art Dept, Jersey City NJ (S)

Laber, Philip, *Olive DeLuce Art Gallery Coll Cur,* Northwest Missouri State University, DeLuce Gallery, Maryville MO

Laborde, Diane, *Cur of Natural Science,* Lafayette Natural History Museum, Planetarium and Nature Station, Lafayette LA

Labot, Tony, *Preparator,* Academy of the Museum of Conceptual Art, San Francisco CA

La Buz, Ronald, *Instructor,* Mohawk Valley Community College, Advertising Design and Production, Utica NY (S)

Lac, Renata, *Dir,* A I R Gallery, New York NY

Lachman-Kalitzki, Eva, *Founder,* International Society For the Study of Expressionism, Cincinnati OH

Lackey, Lea, *Instructor,* Salem College, Art Dept, Winston-Salem NC (S)

Lacock, Roger, *VPres of Board & Pres,* The Racine Art Association, Inc, Racine WI

LaCosta Burke, Jeannie, *Instr,* Vincennes University Junior College, Art Dept, Vincennes IN (S)

LaCour, S Elizabeth, *Asst Prof,* Lynchburg College, Art Dept, Lynchburg VA (S)

Lacouture, Jay, *Chairperson,* Salve Regina - The Newport College, Art Dept, Newport RI (S)

Lada, Sophia, *Cur,* Ukrainian Cultural and Educational Centre Museum, Winnipeg MB

Ladely, Dan, *Dir Sheldon Film Theatre,* University of Nebraska, Lincoln, Sheldon Memorial Art Gallery, Lincoln NE

Lader, Melvin P, *Asst Prof,* George Washington University, Dept of Art, Washington DC (S)

Ladis, Andrew, *Asst Prof,* Vanderbilt University, Dept of Fine Arts, Nashville TN (S)

Ladish, Mary, *Cur Asst,* Marquette University, Museum of Art, Milwaukee WI

Ladnier, Paul, *Instr,* University of North Florida, Dept of Fine Arts, Jacksonville FL (S)

Ladoucuer, Philip A, *Asst to Registrar,* Syracuse University, Art Collection, Syracuse NY

LaFantasie, Glenn, *Ed, Roger Williams Corresp,* Rhode Island Historical Society, Providence RI

Lafferty, Anna, *Graphic Design Coordr,* Tunxis Community College, Graphic Design Dept, Farmington CT (S)

LaFlamme, Robert, *Chief,* Saint-Louis-Maillet, Dept of Visual Arts, Edmundston NB (S)

Lafo, Rachel, *Cur,* DeCordova and Dana Museum and Park, Lincoln MA

LaFollette, Curtis K, *Assoc Prof,* Rhode Island College, Art Dept, Providence RI (S)

Lafon, Dee J, *Chmn,* East Central University, Art Dept, Ada OK (S)

LaFond, Louise, *Assoc Prof,* Colorado College, Dept of Art, Colorado Springs CO (S)

LaFond, Robert, *Registrar,* Princeton University, Art Museum, Princeton NJ

La Ford, Gene, *Instructor,* Springfield College, Dept of Visual and Performing Arts, Springfield MA (S)

Lafortune, F, *Chief Librn,* Musee du Quebec, Bibliotheque des Art, Quebec PQ

LaFrance, Michael, *VPres,* LeSueur County Historical Society Museum, Elysian MN

Lagimodiere, Claudette, *Head Educ & Public Programs,* Winnipeg Art Gallery, Winnipeg MB

Lagoria, Georgianna, *Asst Dir,* University of Santa Clara, de Saisset Museum, Santa Clara CA

Lahaye, Francois, *Dir,* Centre Culturel de Trois Rivieres, Trois Rivieres PQ

Lai, Waihang, *Faculty,* Kauai Community College, Dept of Art, Lihue HI (S)

Laigo, Val, *Prof,* Seattle University, Fine Arts Dept, Division of Art, Seattle WA (S)

Laing, C, *Asst Dir Finance & Admin,* National Museum of Man, Ottawa ON

Laing, Michele, *Reference Librn,* University of Manitoba, Library, Winnipeg MB

Lake, Jerry L, *Assoc Prof,* George Washington University, Dept of Art, Washington DC (S)

Lake, Mary M, *Dir,* Peninsula Fine Arts Center, Newport News VA

Lakeman, Oscar, *Member,* The Loading Dock Gallery, Boston MA

Laker, Philip, *Asst Prof,* Northwest Missouri State University, Dept of Art, Maryville MO (S)

Lakich, Lili, *Dir,* Museum of Neon Art, Los Angeles CA

Lally, Franca P, *Asst Dir,* Caravan of East and West, Inc, Caravan House Galleries, New York NY

Lally, John, *Gallery Dir,* Caravan of East and West, Inc, Caravan House Galleries, New York NY

Lalonde, Marcel, *Dir,* Saint Joseph's Oratory, Montreal PQ

La Malfa, James, *Head Dept,* University of Wisconsin Center-Marinette County, Art Dept, Marinette WI (S)

Lamarche, Lise, *Dir Dept Art History,* Universite de Montreal, Dept of Art History, Montreal PQ (S)

La Marea, Howard, *Assoc Prof,* C W Post Center of Long Island University, School of the Arts, Greenvale NY (S)

Lamarre, Blanche, *Lectr,* Notre Dame College, Art Dept, Manchester NH (S)

Lamb, Barbara, *Asst to Dir,* California State University Fullerton, Art Gallery, Visual Arts Center, Fullerton CA

Lamb, Kurt H, *Dir,* Mexico-Audrain County Library, Mexico MO

Lambert, Anne, *Cur Education,* University of Wisconsin, Elvehjem Museum of Art, Madison WI

Lambert, Don, *Exec Dir,* Arts Council of Topeka, Topeka KS

Lambert, Molly, *Gallery Dir,* Fiberworks, Center for the Textile Arts, Berkeley CA

Lambert, Nancy Sifferd, *Librn,* Yale University, Art and Architecture Library, New Haven CT

Lambert, Rose, *Librn,* Louisiana Department of Culture, Recreation and Tourism, Louisiana Historical Center Library, New Orleans LA

Lambert, William E, *Chmn,* Del Mar College, Dept of Art, Corpus Christi TX (S)

Lamb-Wanacha, Diane, *Lectr,* College of Mount Saint Vincent, Fine Arts Dept, Riverdale NY (S)

Lamia, Stephen, *Cur,* McMaster University, Art Gallery, Hamilton ON

Lamkin, John Patrick, *Dir,* Plum Tree Fine Arts Program, Pilar NM (S)

Lamont, Bridget, *Dir,* Illinois State Library, Springfield IL

Lamothe, Donal, *Chmn,* Assumption College, Dept of Fine Arts and Music, Worcester MA (S)

Lamoureux, Richard E, *Asst Prof,* Assumption College, Dept of Fine Arts and Music, Worcester MA (S)

Lamp, Frederick, *Assoc Cur Art of Africa, Americas, Oceania,* Baltimore Museum of Art, Baltimore MD

Lampe, William, *Preparator,* University of Minnesota, University Art Museum, Minneapolis MN

Lamph, John, *Prof,* Mary Washington College, Art Dept, Fredericksburg VA (S)

Lancaster, Jan, *Asst Cur Research,* The Phillips Collection, Washington DC

Lancaster, Zoe, *VPres,* Surface Design Association, Inc, Fayetteville TN

Lance, Kathleen, *Cataloger & Branch Coordr,* Sweet Briar College, Martin C Shallenberger Art Library, Sweet Briar VA

Land, Norman, *Assoc Prof,* University of Missouri, Art History and Archaeology Dept, Columbia MO (S)

Landa, Robin, *Chmn,* Elizabeth Seton College, Art Dept, Yonkers NY (S)

Landau, Ellen G, *Asst Prof,* Case Western Reserve University, Dept of Art, Cleveland OH (S)

Landau, Laureen, *Instructor,* Sacramento City College, Art Dept, Sacramento CA (S)

Landau, Zuki, *Chief Librn,* School of Visual Arts Library, New York NY

Landes, Bernard, *Gallery Dir,* Jewish Community Center, Center Lobby Gallery, Long Beach CA

Landis, Ellen J, *Cur of Art,* Albuquerque Museum of Art, History and Science, Albuquerque NM

Landon, R Kirk, *Pres Board Trustees,* Metropolitan Museum and Art Center, Coral Gables FL

Landrum, Ney C, *Dir,* Tomoka State Park Museum, Ormond Beach FL

Landry, Dorothy, *Asst Custodian,* West Baton Rouge Museum, Port Allen LA

Landry, Pierre, *Dir Module d'arts plastiques,* University of Quebec, Trois Rivieres, Fine Arts Section, Trois Rivieres PQ (S)

Landsmark, Theodore C, *Dean Grad & Continuing Educ,* Massachusetts College of Art, Boston MA (S)

Land-Weber, E, *Faculty,* Humboldt State University, College of Creative Arts & Humanities, Arcata CA (S)

Landwehr, William C, *Dir,* Quincy Art Center, Library, Quincy IL

Landwehr, William C, *Dir,* Springfield Art Museum, Springfield MO

Lane, C Gardner, *Dir,* Penobscot Marine Museum, Searsport ME

Lane, Jean, *Prof,* Jersey City State College, Art Dept, Jersey City NJ (S)

Lane, John R, *Dir,* Carnegie Institute, Museum of Art, Pittsburgh PA

Lane, Mark, *Dir,* San Antonio Museum Association, Inc, Witte Memorial Museum, San Antonio TX

Lane, Suzette, *Asst Cur,* Cornell University, Herbert F Johnson Museum Library, Ithaca NY

Lane, William, *Gallery Dir,* Rio Hondo College Art Gallery, Whittier CA

Lang, Aileen H, *Chmn Art Hist Dept,* Sweet Briar College, Art History Dept and Art Studio Dept, Sweet Briar VA (S)

Lang, Doug, *Chmn Academic Studies,* Corcoran School of Art, Washington DC (S)

Lang, James, *Asst Prof,* La Salle College, Dept of Fine Arts, Philadelphia PA (S)

Lang, Richard, *Dir,* Wheelwright Museum, Santa Fe NM

Lang, Thomas, *Assoc Prof,* Webster College, Art Dept, Webster Groves MO (S)

Lang, Veloris, *Chmn Dept,* Glendale College, Dept of Fine Arts, Glendale CA (S)

Langdon, Janice, *Instructor,* Rudolph Schaeffer School of Design, San Francisco CA (S)

Lange, Patricia, *Libr Asst,* University of Maryland, College Park, Art Library, College Park MD

Lange, Robert H, *Chmn Board of Governors,* Kansas City Art Institute, Charlotte Crosby Kemper Gallery, Kansas City MO

Lange, Yvonne, *Dir,* Museum of New Mexico, Museum of International Folk Art, Santa Fe NM

Langevin, Ann, *Exten Admin,* Clark County Library District, Las Vegas NV

Langford, Martha, *Executive Producer,* National Film Board of Canada, Still Photography Division, Ottawa ON

Langham, Marcia, *Instructor,* Young Harris College, Dept of Art, Young Harris GA (S)

Langland, Harold, *Prof,* Indiana University at South Bend, Fine Arts Dept, South Bend IN (S)

Langley, Pepper, *Master Woodcarver,* Calvert Marine Museum, Solomons MD

Langlykke, Peter, *Dir,* Hudson River Museum, Yonkers NY

Langmuir, Jane, *Pres,* Providence Athenaeum, Providence RI

Lanier, David, *Prof,* University of the District of Columbia, Art Dept, Washington DC (S)

Lankford, Louis, *Asst Prof,* Ohio State University, Dept of Art Education, Columbus OH (S)

Lanmon, Dwight P, *Dir,* Corning Museum of Glass, Corning NY

Lanning, Dixie M, *Librn,* Bethany College, Library, Lindsborg KS

Lansbury, Edgar, *Cur,* Nicholas Roerich Museum, New York NY

Lansdown, Robert R, *Dir,* Frank Phillips, Woolaroc Museum, Bartlesville OK

Lansner, Ruth, *Secy,* Ukiyo-e Society of America, Inc, New York NY

Lantzy, Donald M, *Dean,* Syracuse University, College of Visual and Performing Arts, Syracuse NY (S)

Lao, Lincoln, *Chairperson Dept Art,* Schoolcraft College, Dept of Art, Livonia MI (S)

Lapaglia, Nancy, *Chmn Art,* City Colleges of Chicago, Daley College, Chicago IL (S)

LaPalme, Robert, *Dir,* Pavilion of Humour, Man and His World, Montreal PQ

Lapidus, Marshall A, *Asst Librn,* Sterling and Francine Clark Art Institute, Clark Art Institute Library, Williamstown MA

Lapierre, Raymond C, *Pres,* Musee d'Art de Joliette, Joliette PQ

LaPlante, Betty, *Secy,* Syracuse University, Joe and Emily Lowe Art Gallery, Syracuse NY

LaPlantz, D M, *Faculty,* Humboldt State University, College of Creative Arts & Humanities, Arcata CA (S)

LaPointe, Madeleine, *Library Technician,* Sheridan College School of Applied Arts and Technology, School of Crafts and Design Library, Mississauga ON

Laporte, Norbert, *Dir,* William Bonifas Fine Art Center Gallery, Escanaba MI

Lapp, Jerold R, *Chmn,* College of William and Mary, Dept of Fine Arts, Williamsburg VA (S)

Lapp, Maurice, *Instr,* Santa Rosa Junior College, Art Dept, Santa Rosa CA (S)

Lapsansky, Phillip, *Chief of Reference,* Library Company of Philadelphia, Dept of Art, Philadelphia PA

Laracuente, Mahir, *Prof,* Catholic University of Puerto Rico, Dept of Fine Arts, Ponce PR (S)

Laraway, E S, *Dir,* John Paul Jones House, Portsmouth NH

Larisch, Kathleen, *Program Adminr,* Pacific Basin School of Textile Arts, Berkeley CA (S)

Larise, Stephen, *Tech Asst,* State University of New York at Stony Brook, Art Gallery, Stony Brook NY

Lark, Tom, *Cur of Collections,* Albuquerque Museum of Art, History and Science, Albuquerque NM

Larkin, Alan, *Assoc Prof,* Indiana University at South Bend, Fine Arts Dept, South Bend IN (S)

Larkin, Amy, *Performing Arts Coordr,* King County Arts Commission, Seattle WA

Larkin, Anna C, *Dir,* Academy of the Arts, Easton MD

Larkin, Frank Y, *VPres,* Museum of Modern Art, New York NY

Larkin, James S, *VPres,* Alabama Museum of Photography, Birmingham AL

Larkin, Mary, *Cur Collections,* Spertus Museum of Judaica, Chicago IL

Larkin, Teri, *Admin Asst to Dir,* University of Notre Dame, Snite Museum of Art, Notre Dame IN

Larmer, Oscar V, *Prof,* Kansas State University, Art Dept, Manhattan KS (S)

Larochelle, Pierre, *Dir,* L'Universite Laval, Ecole des Arts Visuels de L'Universite Laval, Quebec PQ

LaRoux, Leonard, *Asst Prof,* College of Saint Rose, Division of Art, Albany NY (S)

Larow, Magdalen, *Prof,* Nazareth College of Rochester, Art Dept, Rochester NY (S)

Larrick, Tim, *Public Information Officer,* San Diego Museum of Art, San Diego CA

Larsen, Dinah W, *Coordr Ethnology,* University of Alaska, Museum, Fairbanks AK

Larsen, Jack Lenor, *Vice Chmn,* American Craft Council, New York NY

Larsen, Maria, *Cur & Registrar,* Shaker Museum, Old Chatham NY

Larsen, Patric, *Assoc Prof,* University of Central Arkansas, Art Dept, Conway AR (S)

Larsen, Richard, *Chmn,* Lloydminster Barr Colony Museum Committee, Lloydminster SK

Larsen, Tom, *VPres,* University of Nebraska, Lincoln, Nebraska Art Association, Lincoln NE

Larsen, William, *Librn,* Southwest Craft Center, Library, San Antonio TX

Larsen-Martin, Susan, *Assoc Prof,* University of Southern California, School of Fine Arts, Los Angeles CA (S)

Larson, Mary, *Library Technician,* University of Colorado Art Galleries, Art and Architecture Library, Boulder CO

Larson, Mike, *Prof,* Shoreline Community College, Humanities Division, Seattle WA (S)

Larson, Orland, *Prog Coordr Jewelry & Chmn,* Alberta College of Art, Southern Alberta Institute of Technology, Calgary AB (S)

Larson, Sidney, *Cur,* State Historical Society of Missouri, Columbia MO

Larson, Sidney, *Instructor,* Columbia College, Art Dept, Columbia MO (S)

Larson, William, *Prof,* Temple University, Tyler School of Art, Philadelphia PA (S)

LaSalle, Barbara, *Registrar,* Brooklyn Museum, Brooklyn NY

Lasansky, Leonardo, *Prof,* Hamline University, Art Dept, Saint Paul MN (S)

Lasansky, William, *Head Dept,* Bucknell University, Dept of Art, Lewisburg PA (S)

Lasar, Steven, *VPres,* Washington Art Association, Washington Depot CT

Lasch, Robert, *Pres,* Tubac Center of the Arts, Santa Cruz Valley Art Association, Tubac AZ

Laska, David, *VPres,* National Society of Painters in Casein and Acrylic, Inc, New York NY

Laska, Linda, *Dir Classes,* The Greenwich Art Society Inc, Greenwich CT

Laske, Lyle, *Prof,* Moorhead State University, Dept of Art, Moorhead MN (S)

Laskin, Harriette C F, *Asst Prof,* Tidewater Community College, Art Dept, Portsmouth VA (S)

Laskin, Myron, *Cur European Art,* National Gallery of Canada, Ottawa ON

Lassonde, Barbara, *Asst Librn,* Minneapolis Institute of Arts, Art Reference Library, Minneapolis MN

Laszkiewicz, Magdalena, *Lecturer,* University of Wisconsin-Stout, Art Dept, Menomonie WI (S)

Lathrop, Peri, *Secy,* Nicolaysen Art Museum, Casper WY

Latimer, Beverly D, *Dir,* Lafayette Natural History Museum, Planetarium and Nature Station, Lafayette LA

Latimer, Linda, *Public Information Coordr,* Columbus Museum of Art, Columbus OH

Latka, Nick, *Instructor,* University of Southern Colorado, Belmont Campus, Dept of Art, Pueblo CO (S)

Latoie, Leon, *Dir,* Musee Kateri Tekakwitha, Cahughnawaga PQ

Latoszek, Ania, *Head Historical Interpreter,* Dundurn Castle, Hamilton ON

Latour, Ira, *Instr,* California State University, Chico, Art Dept, Chico CA (S)

Latta, George, *Emeritus Prof,* William Woods-Westminster Colleges, Art Dept, Fulton MO (S)

Lattimore, Walter, *Asst Prof,* University of the District of Columbia, Art Dept, Washington DC (S)

Lattin, Bill, *Pres,* Tongass Historical Society Museum, Ketchikan AK

Latton, Susan, *Coordr Membership & Outreach,* University of Wisconsin, Elvehjem Museum of Art, Madison WI

Latzko, Walter, *Admin Asst,* Hall of Fame of the Trotter, Goshen NY

Lau, Edwin F, *Pres,* The Museum, Greenwood SC

Laufer, Marilyn, *Educ Cur,* Sioux City Art Center, Sioux City IA

Laughlin, Thomas C, *Registrar,* Museum of Fine Arts of Saint Petersburg, Florida, Inc, Saint Petersburg FL

Laughner, Charles, *Pres,* Laughner Brothers, Inc, Indianapolis IN

Laughton, Bruce, *Head Dept,* Queen's University, Dept of Art, Kingston ON (S)

Lauitt, Edward, *First VPres,* Society for Folk Arts Preservation, Inc, New York NY

Laurence, Daniel, *Lecturer,* University of Wisconsin-Stout, Art Dept, Menomonie WI (S)

Laurent, John, *Prof,* University of New Hampshire, Dept of the Arts, Durham NH (S)

Laurette, Patrick, *Asst Cur,* Art Gallery of Nova Scotia, Halifax NS

Lauriana, Sister Mary, *Art Dir,* Felician College, Art Dept, Chicago IL (S)

Laurin, Ulric, *VPres,* Musee d'Art de Joliette, Joliette PQ

Lauten, Elodie, *Cultural Asst,* Canadian Consulate General Dept of External Affairs, 49th Parallel Centre for Contemporary Canadian Art, New York NY

Lauvao, Fa'ailoilo, *Cur,* Jean P Haydon Museum, Pago Pago, American Samoa PI

Lauver, James, *Asst Prof,* Northern State College, Art Dept, Aberdeen SD (S)

LaVallee, Adrienne, *Program & Education Coordr,* Manchester Institute of Arts and Sciences Gallery, Manchester NH

Lavallee, Adrienne, *Program Coordr,* Manchester Institute of Arts and Sciences, Manchester NH (S)

Lavallee, G, *VPres,* Musee d'Art de Saint-Laurent, Saint-Laurent PQ

Lavelle, Diana, *Asst Cur Education,* Sarnia Public Library, Art Gallery, Sarnia ON

Lavey, Mary, *Adjunct Prof,* Adams State College, Dept of Visual Arts, Alamosa CO (S)

Law, Aaron, *Chmn Visual Communications,* Herron School of Art, Indiana University-Purdue University, Indianapolis, Indianapolis IN (S)

Law, R B, *Faculty,* Western Illinois University, College of Fine Arts, Macomb IL (S)

Lawall, David B, *Cur,* University of Virginia, Art Museum, Charlottesville VA

Lawerence, Ray, *Treas,* Lubbock Art Association, Inc, Lubbock TX

Lawhorn, James C, *Adminr,* Huntington Galleries, Huntington WV

Lawn, Robert, *Chmn & Prof,* Nassau Community College, Art Dept, Garden City NY (S)

Lawner, Ruth, *Publishing Editor,* University of Kansas, Spencer Museum of Art, Lawrence KS

Lawrence, Amy, *Dir,* Advocates for the Arts, Los Angeles CA

Lawrence, Camille, *Instructor,* Davidson County Community College, Language-Fine Arts Dept, Lexington NC (S)

Lawrence, Charles D, *Cur,* United States Navy, Combat Art Gallery, Washington DC

Lawrence, Cynthia, *Asst Prof,* Rutgers, the State University of New Jersey, Graduate Program in Art History, New Brunswick NJ (S)

Lawrence, David, *Head Dept,* San Bernardino Valley College, Art Dept, San Bernardino CA (S)

Lawrence, Dierdre, *Librn,* Brooklyn Museum, Brooklyn NY

Lawrence, Jacob, *Board Dir Member,* Art Information Center, Inc, New York NY

Lawrence, John, *Cur,* Historic New Orleans Collection, Kemper and Leila Williams Foundation, New Orleans LA

Lawrence, John D, *Head Dept,* La Grange College, Lamar Dudd Art Center, La Grange GA (S)

Lawrence, Katherine, *Asst to Dir,* Dixon Gallery and Gardens, Memphis TN

Lawrence, Robert M, *Pres,* American Institute of Architects, Washington DC

Lawrence, Robert S, *Instr,* Cottey College, Fine Arts Division, Nevada MO (S)

Lawrence, Sally, *Actg Dir,* Pacific Northwest College of Art, Portland OR (S)

Lawrie, Irene L, *Registrar,* Lightner Museum, Saint Augustine FL

Laws, Bill, *First VPres,* The Stained Glass Association of America, Saint Louis MO

Lawson, Edward P, *Chief Education Dept*, Hirshhorn Museum and Sculpture Garden, Washington DC

Lawson, Elizabeth K, *Membership Assoc*, Solomon R Guggenheim Museum, New York NY

Lawson, James, *Instr*, Sheridan College, Art Dept, Sheridan WY (S)

Lawson, John, *Corresp Secy*, San Bernardino Art Association, Inc, San Bernardino CA

Lawson, Noel G, *Prof*, Radford University, Art Dept, Radford VA (S)

Lawson, Pam F, *Asst Prof*, Radford University, Art Dept, Radford VA (S)

Lawton, Jim, *Instructor*, Michigan State University, Leland Summer Art School, Leland MI (S)

Lawton, Maria, *Dir*, Boca Raton Center for the Arts, Inc, Boca Raton FL

Lawton, Mary S, *Chmn Fine Arts Dept*, Loyola University of Chicago, Fine Arts Dept, Chicago IL (S)

Lawton, Thomas, *Dir*, Freer Gallery of Art, Washington DC

Layton, Gloria, *Pres*, Octagon Center for the Arts, Ames IA

Lazar, Arthur, *Lectr*, Lake Forest College, Dept of Art, Lake Forest IL (S)

Lazar, Howard, *Coordr Street Artist Program*, San Francisco City and County Art Commission, San Francisco CA

Lazarus, Alan H, *Chmn*, William Paterson College, Art Dept, Wayne NJ (S)

Lazarus, Diane Gail, *Dir*, Evanston Art Center, Evanston IL

Lazarus, Eleanor, *Actg Dir & Asst Dir for Educ*, DeCordova and Dana Museum and Park, Lincoln MA

Lazarus, Fred, *Pres*, Maryland Institute, College of Art Galleries, Baltimore MD

Lazarus, Fred, *Pres*, Maryland Institute, College of Art, Baltimore MD (S)

Lazarus, Mark, *Asst Prof*, South Dakota State University, Dept of Visual Arts, Brookings SD (S)

Lazerek, John, *Treas*, Mystic Art Association, Inc, Mystic CT

Lazzaro, Claudia, *Asst Prof*, Cornell University, Dept of the History of Art, Ithaca NY (S)

Lazzaro, Richard, *Chmn*, University of Wisconsin, Art Dept Gallery, Madison WI

L/Bunse, Dale, *Faculty*, Columbia College, Dept of Physical Creative and Performing Arts, Columbia CA (S)

Lea, K, *Supvr*, Lethbridge Community College Gallery, Lethbridge AB

Lea, Stanley E, *Prof*, Sam Houston State University, Art Dept, Huntsville TX (S)

Leach, David, *Assoc Prof*, Wright State University, Dept of Art & Art History, Dayton OH (S)

Leach, Frederick D, *Prof*, Hamline University, Art Dept, Saint Paul MN (S)

Leach, Mark, *Cur*, Paris Gibson Square, Great Falls MT

Leach, Maurice D, *Librn*, Washington and Lee University, Art Dept Library, Lexington VA

Leach, Pamela, *Office Mgr*, San Jose Museum of Art, San Jose CA

Leach, Richard, *Prof*, Albion College, Dept of Visual Arts, Albion MI (S)

Leader, Garnet R, *Pres*, Kappa Pi International Honorary Art Fraternity, Birmingham AL

Leadingham, Jo, *Gallery Coordr*, Kentucky State University, Jackson Hall Gallery, Frankfort KY

Leaf, Roy, *Exec Dir*, Skowhegan School of Painting and Sculpture, Skowhegan ME (S)

Leahy, John Louise, *Assoc Prof*, Marygrove College, Dept of Art and Art History, Detroit MI (S)

Leake, James C, *Secy*, Cherokee National Historical Society, Inc, Tahlequah OK

Leaney, David, *Pres Bd Trustees*, Stratford Art Association, Gallery Stratford, Stratford ON

Leary, Edward F, *Dir*, Boston University, School of Visual Arts, Boston MA (S)

Leary, Thomas, *Chmn Dept*, Salem State College, Art Dept, Salem MA (S)

Leavitt, Thomas W, *Dir*, Merrimack Valley Textile Museum, North Andover MA

Leavitt, Thomas W, *Dir*, Cornell University, Herbert F Johnson Museum of Art, Ithaca NY

Leavitt, Thomas W, *Prof*, Cornell University, Dept of the History of Art, Ithaca NY (S)

LeBaron, John, *Chmn Dept*, Santa Rosa Junior College, Art Dept, Santa Rosa CA (S)

Lebeck, Steven, *Coordr Graphic Design*, Florida School of the Arts, Visual Arts, Palatka FL (S)

LeBlanc, Stephen, *Cur*, Southwest Museum, Los Angeles CA

Lebowitz, Stephanie, *Asst Dir*, Atlantic Gallery, New York NY

Lecavalier, Fernand, *Pastor & Dir*, Musee de la Basilique Notre-Dame, Montreal PQ

Lechner, Hadrian, *Asst Prof*, Rochester Institute of Technology, School of Photographic Arts & Sciences, Rochester NY (S)

Lechtzin, Stanley, *Prof*, Temple University, Tyler School of Art, Philadelphia PA (S)

LeClair, Charles, *Instructor*, Truro Center for the Arts at Castle Hill, Inc, Truro MA (S)

Ledbetter, Roseanne, *Secy*, Western Illinois University, Macomb IL

LeDuc, Paul, *Artistic Cur*, Saint Joseph's Oratory, Montreal PQ

Lee, Catherine, *Vis Asst Prof*, University of Texas at San Antonio, Division of Art and Design, San Antonio TX (S)

Lee, Christopher G, *Dir*, Columbus Chapel, Boal Mansion and Museum, Boalsburg PA

Lee, Ellen W, *Assoc Cur Painting & Sculpture*, Indianapolis Museum of Art, Indianapolis IN

Lee, Emory, *Exec VPres*, Chinese Culture Foundation, Chinese Culture Center Gallery, San Francisco CA

Lee, Esther, *Asst Head Art & Music Division*, Queens Borough Public Library, Art and Music Division, Jamaica NY

Lee, Hyosoo, *Technical Services Librn*, Cleveland Institute of Art, Jessica Gund Memorial Library, Cleveland OH

Lee, Jean, *Coordr Public Programs*, Evansville Museum of Arts and Science, Evansville IN

Lee, Jean Gordon, *Cur Far Eastern Art*, Philadelphia Museum of Art, Philadelphia PA

Lee, Kyung, *Assoc Prof*, Philadelphia Community College, Dept of Fine Arts, Philadelphia PA (S)

Lee, Marielou, *Admin Secy*, Davenport Municipal Art Gallery, Davenport IA

Lee, Mathilde Boal, *Pres*, Columbus Chapel, Boal Mansion and Museum, Boalsburg PA

Lee, Robert E, *Dir of Library*, University of Western Ontario, The D B Weldon Library, London ON

Lee, Robert J, *Assoc Prof*, Marymount College, Art Dept, Tarrytown NY (S)

Lee, Vera, *Asn Pres*, Biloxi Art Association, Gallery, Biloxi MS

Lee, William B, *Dir*, Bower's Museum, Santa Ana CA

Lee, Wynn, *Dir & Cur*, Mark Twain Memorial, Hartford CT

Leean, Arch, *Assoc Prof*, Saint Olaf College, Art Dept, Northfield MN (S)

Lee-Bevier, Kip, *Dir of Visitor Services*, Wine Museum of San Francisco, San Francisco CA

Leece, Curtis, *Instructor*, Saginaw Valley State College, Dept of Art and Design, University Center MI (S)

Leedy, Sheery, *Asst Prof*, University of Northern Iowa, Dept of Art, Cedar Falls IA (S)

Leedy, Walter C, *Assoc Prof*, Cleveland State University, Art Dept, Cleveland OH (S)

Leek, Thomas A, *Dir*, Southern Utah State College, Braithwaite Fine Arts Gallery, Cedar City UT

Leen, Mary, *Librn*, The Bostonian Society, Library, Boston MA

Leeper, John P, *Librn*, Marion Koogler McNay Art Museum, Reference Library, San Antonio TX

Leeper, John Palmer, *Dir*, Marion Koogler McNay Art Museum, San Antonio TX

Lees, Gary P, *Dir Dept & Assoc Prof*, Johns Hopkins University, School of Medicine, Dept of Art as Applied to Medicine, Baltimore MD (S)

Lees, Jay, *Chmn Arts & Letters*, Westminster College, Dept of Art, Salt Lake City UT (S)

Lee-Smith, Hughie, *Pres*, Audubon Artists, Inc, New York NY

Leet, Richard E, *Dir*, Charles H MacNider Museum, Mason City IA

Leete, William, *Prof*, University of Rhode Island, Dept of Art, Kingston RI (S)

Leete, William C, *Exhib Coordr*, Northern Michigan University, Lee Hall Gallery, Marquette MI

Leete, William C, *Assoc Prof*, Northern Michigan University, Dept of Art and Design, Marquette MI (S)

Lee-Whitman, Leanna, *Asst Cur*, INA Corporation, Philadelphia PA

LeFevre, Geraldine, *Asst Dir*, San Antonio Public Library, Dept of Fine Arts, San Antonio TX

Leff, Jay C, *Pres*, Fayette Bank and Trust Company, Uniontown PA

LeFrancois, G, *Asst Dir Education & Program Development*, Brooklyn Museum Art School, Brooklyn NY (S)

Legault, Sylvie, *Treas*, La Societe des Decorateurs-Ensembliers du Quebec, Interior Decorators' Society of Quebec, Montreal PQ

Legentil, Danielle, *Exhib & Research*, Musee d'Art de Saint-Laurent, Saint-Laurent PQ

Lehman, Arnold L, *Dir*, Baltimore Museum of Art, Baltimore MD

Lehman, Arnold L, *Dir*, Metropolitan Museum and Art Center, Library, Coral Gables FL

Lehman, Mark, *Asst Prof*, Trenton State College, Art Dept, Trenton NJ (S)

Lehman, Robert, *Cur*, Parrish Art Museum, Southampton NY

Lehrer, Leonard, *Dir*, Arizona State University, School of Art, Tempe AZ (S)

Lehrer, Susan Frisch, *Asst Dir*, Chesterwood, Stockbridge MA

Leib, Arlene, *Chmn*, University of Toronto, Erindale Campus Art Gallery, Mississauga ON

Leibert, Peter, *Chmn*, Connecticut College, Dept of Art, New London CT (S)

Leichty, Erle, *Akkadian Cur*, University of Pennsylvania, University Museum of Archaeology & Anthropology, Philadelphia PA

Leider, Karen, *Cataloger*, Trinity College Library, Washington DC

Leidig, Andree, *Asst Dir*, Kirkland Art Center, Clinton NY

Leifer, Elizabeth, *Instr*, Suomi College, Fine Arts Dept, Hancock MI (S)

Leighton, D S R, *Dir Banff Centre*, Banff Centre School of Fine Arts, Banff AB (S)

Leininger, Michael, *Reference Librn*, Massachusetts Institute of Technology, Museum, Cambridge MA

Leippe, Harry M, *Prof*, New Mexico Highlands University, Division of Fine Arts, Las Vegas NM (S)

Leipzig, Arthur, *Prof*, C W Post Center of Long Island University, School of the Arts, Greenvale NY (S)

Leisher, William, *Head Conservation*, Los Angeles County Museum of Art, Los Angeles CA

Leisure, Hoyt B, *VPres*, Los Angeles County Museum of Art, Los Angeles CA

Leith, Christine, *Div Chmn*, Emma Willard School Arts Division, Troy NY (S)

Lekberg, Barbara, *VPres*, Sculpture Center, New York NY

Lem, Wu Chien, *Asst Prof*, University of South Dakota, Dept of Art, Vermillion SD (S)

Lema, Joseph, *Instr*, Utah Technical College at Salt Lake, Commercial Art Dept, Salt Lake City UT (S)

Lemay, Charles, *Lectr*, Notre Dame College, Art Dept, Manchester NH (S)

Lemberg, Milton, *Treas*, Arizona Watercolor Association, Phoenix AZ

Lemecha, Vera, *Dir*, Nova Scotia College of Art and Design, Anna Leonowens Gallery, Halifax NS

Lemmenes, Audley G, *VPres & Dir Business Affairs*, Museum of Science and Industry, Chicago IL

Lemmerman, Harold, *Dir*, Jersey City State College, Courtney Art Gallery, Jersey City NJ

Lemmerman, Harold, *Prof*, Jersey City State College, Art Dept, Jersey City NJ (S)

Lemmon, Robert J, *Treas,* Muttart Gallery Associates, Calgary AB

Lemon, Robert, *Chmn,* Rollins College, Dept of Art, Main Campus, Winter Park FL (S)

Lemp, Frank J, *Dir,* Ottawa University, Dept of Art, Ottawa KS (S)

Lenderman, Max L, *Assoc Prof,* Rochester Institute of Technology, School for American Craftsmen, Rochester NY (S)

Lenertz, John, *Instructor,* School of the Associated Arts, Saint Paul MN (S)

Lennig, Arthur, *Assoc Prof,* State University of New York at Albany, Art Dept, Albany NY (S)

Lennon, Timothy, *Conservator,* Art Institute of Chicago, Chicago IL

Lent, Donald, *Chmn,* Bates College, Art Dept, Lewiston ME (S)

Leon, Bruno, *Dean,* University of Detroit, School of Architecture, Detroit MI (S)

Leon, Clinton J, *Instr,* Haskell Indian Junior College, Art Dept, Lawrence KS (S)

Leon, Dennis, *Sculpture,* California College of Arts and Crafts, Oakland CA (S)

Leonard, Albert, *Assoc Prof,* University of Missouri, Art History and Archaeology Dept, Columbia MO (S)

Leonard, Marion K, *Museum Dir,* Connecticut Historical Commission, Sloane-Stanley Museum, Kent CT

Leoshko, Janice, *Treasurer,* American Committee for South Asian Art, Evanston IL

Leoshko, Janice, *Vis Prof,* Denison University, Dept of Art, Granville OH (S)

Lepine, Micheline, *Technical Asst to Dir,* Burchfield Art Center, Buffalo NY

LePore, Kathy, *Asst Librn,* Robert W Ryerss Library and Museum, Library, Philadelphia PA

Lequire, Stephen, *Asst Prof,* University of North Carolina at Wilmington, Dept of Creative Arts - Division of Art, Wilmington NC (S)

Lerand, Laura, *Secy,* Visual Arts Ontario, Toronto ON

Lergier, Clara S, *Librn,* Ateneo Puertorriqueno, Library, San Juan PR

Lerner, Abram, *Dir,* Hirshhorn Museum and Sculpture Garden, Washington DC

Lerner, Alexandra, *Trustee,* Foundation for Today's Art, Nexus Gallery, Philadelphia PA

Lerner, Martin, *Cur Far Eastern Art,* Metropolitan Museum of Art, New York NY

Lerner, Susan, *Communications Coordr,* Pacific - Asia Museum, Pasadena CA

Leroux, Jack, *Business Administrator,* The Robert McLaughlin Gallery, Oshawa ON

Leshko, Jaroslaw, *Assoc Prof,* Smith College, Art Dept, Northampton MA (S)

LeShock, Ed, *Asst Prof,* Radford University, Art Dept, Radford VA (S)

Lesko, Diane, *Co-Dir,* Lycoming College Gallery, Williamsport PA

Lesko, Diane M, *Asst Prof,* Lycoming College, Art Dept, Williamsport PA (S)

Lessard, Elizabeth, *Librn,* Manchester Historic Association, Library, Manchester NH

Lessey, Harriet, *Asst Exec Dir Bd,* Washington Women's Arts Center, Washington DC

Lessick, Helen, *Instructor,* Marylhurst College, Art Dept, Marylhurst OR (S)

Lester, Laura, *Public Info Officer,* The Phillips Collection, Washington DC

Lester, William Carey, *Assoc Prof,* Delta State University, Dept of Art, Cleveland MS (S)

LeSueur, Marc, *Art History,* California College of Arts and Crafts, Oakland CA (S)

Letchworth, Francis, *Museum Artist,* Frank Phillips, Woolaroc Museum, Bartlesville OK

Lethert, Helen M, *Dir Public Relations,* Art Institute of Chicago, Chicago IL

Letourneau, Fernande, *VPres,* Musee Historique de Vaudreuil, Vaudreuil Historical Museum, Vaudreuil PQ

Lettenstrom, Dean R, *Prof,* University of Minnesota, Duluth, Art Dept, Duluth MN (S)

Lettes, Susan, *Lectr,* University of Pennsylvania, College Arts & Science, Philadelphia PA (S)

Lettieri, Robin, *Dir,* Port Chester Public Library, Fine Arts Dept, Port Chester NY

Leupp, Leslie, *Assoc Prof,* Texas Tech University, Dept of Art, Lubbock TX (S)

LeVant, Howard, *Asst Prof,* Rochester Institute of Technology, School of Photographic Arts & Sciences, Rochester NY (S)

Levensky, Elayne, *Instr,* Green River Community College, Art Dept, Auburn WA (S)

Levenson, Harvey R, *Chairperson,* La Roche College, Division of Graphics, Design, Pittsburgh PA (S)

LeVeque, Ann, *Museum Cur,* Rhode Island Historical Society, Providence RI

Leverette, Carlton, *Assoc Prof,* Community College of Baltimore, Dept of Fine & Applied Arts, Liberty Campus, Baltimore MD (S)

Levin, Carol, *Secy,* Atlantic Gallery, New York NY

Levin, Cecelia, *Cur Educ,* Asian Art Museum of San Francisco, Avery Brundage Collection, San Francisco CA

Levin, Earl, *Head Dept City Planning,* University of Manitoba, Faculty of Architecture, Winnipeg MB (S)

Levin, Gail, *Assoc Cur, Hopper Collection,* Whitney Museum of American Art, New York NY

Levin, Linda, *Asst Dir,* Johnson Atelier Technical Institute of Sculpture, Mercerville NJ (S)

Levin, Ruth, *Registrar,* Bennington Museum, Bennington VT

Levine, David, *Pres,* Art Commission of the City of New York, Associates of the Art Commission, Inc, New York NY

Levine, David, *Actg State Archivist,* Ohio Historical Society, Archives-Library Division, Columbus OH

Levine, Edward M, *Dean,* East Carolina University, School of Art, Greenville NC (S)

Levine, Gillian, *Cur,* Institute of Contemporary Art, Boston MA

Levine, Julius S, *Assoc Prof,* Catholic University of America, Dept of Architecture and Planning, Washington DC (S)

LeVine, Newton, *Assoc Prof Architecture,* Ramapo College of New Jersey, School of Contemporary Arts, Mahwah NJ (S)

Levine, Phyllis, *Public Information Dir,* International Center of Photography, New York NY

Levine, Richard, *Dir,* The American Foundation for the Arts, Miami FL

Levine, Sam, *Treasurer,* National Council on Art in Jewish Life, New York NY

Levine, Steven, *Assoc Prof,* Bryn Mawr College, Dept of the History of Art, Bryn Mawr PA (S)

Levinson, Robert A, *Chmn Board of Governors,* Brooklyn Museum, Brooklyn NY

Levitan, Greta, *Dir Exhibits,* Please Touch Museum, Philadelphia PA

Levitt, Isabell, *Prof,* North Carolina Central University, Art Dept, Durham NC (S)

Levra, Ray, *Instructor,* Cochise College, Art Dept, Douglas AZ (S)

Levy, David C, *Executive Dean,* Parsons School of Design, New York NY (S)

Levy, Irvin L, *VPres,* The American Federation of Arts, New York NY

Levy, Jane, *Librn,* Judah L Magnes Museum, Morris Goldstein Library, Berkeley CA

Levy, M B, *Chmn Dept,* Purdue University, Lafayette, Dept of Creative Arts, Art & Design Section, West Lafayette IN (S)

Levy, Paul, *Chmn Graphic Design,* Corcoran School of Art, Washington DC (S)

Levy, S Arthur, *Librn,* Buten Museum of Wedgwood, Library, Merion PA

Levy, Suzanne, *Cur Education,* Fort Worth Art Museum, Fort Worth TX

Lew, Eileen, *Chmn Children's Classes,* De Young Museum Art School, San Francisco CA (S)

Lew, Robert F, *Real Estate Adminr,* Pittsburgh National Bank, Pittsburgh PA

Lewallen, Connie, *Assoc Cur Matrix,* University of California, University Art Museum, Berkeley CA

Lewandowski, Edmund D, *Chmn,* Winthrop College, Dept of Art, Rock Hill SC (S)

Lewandowski, Edmund D, *Dir,* Winthrop College Gallery of Art, Rock Hill SC

Lewandowski, Felicia, *Assoc Prof,* Radford University, Art Dept, Radford VA (S)

Lewin, Jacqueline, *Cur Hist & Librn,* Saint Joseph Museum, Saint Joseph MO

LeWinter, Stephen S, *Asst Prof,* University of Tennessee at Chattanooga, Dept of Art, Chattanooga TN (S)

Lewis, A B, *Cur Millington-Barnard Coll,* University of Mississippi, University Museums, Oxford MS

Lewis, Albert J, *Instructor,* San Diego Mesa College, Fine Arts Dept, San Diego CA (S)

Lewis, Arnold, *Dir,* College of Wooster Art Center Museum, Wooster OH

Lewis, Arnold, *Chmn,* College of Wooster, Dept of Art, Wooster OH (S)

Lewis, Barbara, *Assoc Prof,* James Madison University, Dept of Art, Harrisonburg VA (S)

Lewis, Carolyn K, *Asst Prof,* University of New Orleans, Dept of Fine Arts, New Orleans LA (S)

Lewis, Dave, *Exec Dir,* Indian Arts & Crafts Association, Albuquerque NM

Lewis, Dawson, *Development Officer,* Your Heritage House, Inc, Detroit MI

Lewis, D E, *Chmn Board,* Glenbow Museum, Calgary AB

Lewis, Dorothy, *Librn,* Southern University, Art and Architecture Library, Baton Rouge LA

Lewis, Douglas, *Cur Sculpture,* National Gallery of Art, Washington DC

Lewis, Elma, *Artistic Dir,* Museum of the National Center of Afro-American Artists, Boston MA

Lewis, Jack R, *Chmn Fine Arts,* Georgia Southwestern College, Art Gallery, Americus GA

Lewis, James E, *Dir,* Morgan State University Gallery of Art, Baltimore MD

Lewis, James Edward, *Dir,* Morgan State University, Dept of Art, Baltimore MD (S)

Lewis, Jerry, *Chmn Dept,* Joliet Junior College, Fine Arts Dept, Joliet IL (S)

Lewis, Julius, *Pres,* Art Institute of Chicago, Old Masters Society, Chicago IL

Lewis, Louise, *Dir,* California State University, Northridge, Art Gallery, Northridge CA

Lewis, Louise L, *Assoc Prof,* Gulf Coast Community College, Division of Fine Arts, Panama City FL (S)

Lewis, Lucy, *Instructor,* University of Southern California, Idyllwild School of Music and the Arts, Idyllwild CA (S)

Lewis, Marcia, *Instructor,* Long Beach City College, Dept of Art, Long Beach CA (S)

Lewis, Mariam, *Secy,* Chautauqua Art Association Galleries, Chautauqua NY

Lewis, Mark, *Chmn,* Point Park College, Performing Arts Dept, Pittsburgh PA (S)

Lewis, Michael, *Prof,* University of Maine, Art Dept, Orono ME (S)

Lewis, Monty, *Dir,* Coronado School of Fine Arts, Coronado CA (S)

Lewis, Raeford W, *Instr,* Central Missouri State University, Art Dept, Warrensburg MO (S)

Lewis, Ralph M, *Dir,* Rosicrucian Egyptian Museum and Art Gallery, San Jose CA

Lewis, Robert, *Treasurer,* Cleveland Museum of Art, Print Club of Cleveland, Cleveland OH

Lewis, Sally, *Secy,* Santa Barbara Contemporary Arts Forum, Santa Barbara CA

Lewis, Sally, *Recording Secy,* Key West Art and Historical Society, Key West FL

Lewis, Samella, *Cur,* The Museum of African American Art, Santa Monica CA

Lewis, Stanley, *Instr,* New York Studio School of Drawing, Painting and Sculpture, New York NY (S)

Lewis, Susan, *Chief Librn,* Boston Architectural Center, Memorial Library, Boston MA

Lewis, Toby, *Dir of Sales,* The New Gallery of Contemporary Art, Cleveland OH

Lewis, Virginia E, *Dir,* Frick Art Museum, Pittsburgh PA

Lewis, Wally, *Dept Head, Photography,* The Design Schools, Art Institute of Houston, Houston TX (S)

Lewis, William, *Div Coordr Art Educ,* Kent State University, School of Art, Kent OH (S)

Lewitin, Marguerite A L, *Pres,* Women's Interart Center, Inc, Interart de St Amand Gallery, New York NY

Lewitzky, Bella, *Instructor,* University of Southern California, Idyllwild School of Music and the Arts, Idyllwild CA (S)

Leys, Dale, *Assoc Prof,* Murray State University, Art Dept, Murray KY (S)

Li, Chu-tsing, *Res Cur Far Eastern Art,* Atkins Museum of Fine Art, Kansas City MO

Li, Chu-tsing, *Prof,* University of Kansas, Kress Foundation Dept of Art History, Lawrence KS (S)

Liakos, J Dimitri, *Area Coordr,* Northern Illinois University, Dept of Art, De Kalb IL (S)

Libby, Gary, *VPres,* Southwest Arts Foundation, Houston TX

Libby, Gary Russell, *Dir,* Museum of Arts and Sciences, Cuban Museum, Planetarium, Daytona Beach FL

Libeskind, Daniel, *Head Architecture Dept,* Cranbrook Academy of Art, Bloomfield Hills MI (S)

Libhart, Myles, *Program Dir,* United States Department of the Interior, Indian Arts and Crafts Board, Washington DC

Libin, Laurence, *Cur Musical Instruments,* Metropolitan Museum of Art, New York NY

Licht, Ira, *Dir,* University of Miami, Lowe Art Museum, Coral Gables FL

Lichtenfels, Lynn, *Cur,* Elizabet Ney Museum, Austin TX

Liddell, Raymond A, *Exec Dir,* Archaeological Institute of America, Boston MA

Liddle, Nancy, *Dir,* State University of New York at Albany, University Art Gallery, Albany NY

Lidh, William R, *Assoc Prof,* Western Carolina University, Dept of Art, Cullowhee NC (S)

Lidtke, Thomas D, *Executive Dir & Librn,* West Bend Gallery of Fine Arts, West Bend WI

Lieberman, Lorna, *Doll Cur,* Wenham Historical Association and Museum, Inc, Wenham MA

Lieberman, William S, *Chmn Twentieth Century Art,* Metropolitan Museum of Art, New York NY

Liebman, Steven, *Instr,* Hamilton College, Art Dept, Clinton NY (S)

Lien, Lary, *Chairperson Dept,* Interlochen Arts Academy, Dept of Visual Art, Interlochen MI (S)

Lierheimer, Violet, *Acquisitions Librn,* Mexico-Audrain County Library, Mexico MO

Lierley, Mary, *Asst Prof,* Kearney State College, Dept of Art, Kearney NE (S)

Liese, Ted, *VPres,* Prescott Fine Arts Association, Prescott AZ

Lifschitz, Edward, *Cur Education,* National Museum of African Art, Washington DC

Lifson, Hank, *Dir Gallery & Chmn Dept of Art,* Cornell College, Armstrong Gallery, Mount Vernon IA

Lifson, Hugh, *Head Dept,* Cornell College, Art Dept, Mount Vernon IA (S)

Ligammari, Joseph, *Manager Marketing,* American Council for the Arts, New York NY

Light, Frank, *Pres,* Emerald Empire Arts Association, Springfield OR

Lignell, Ellen, *Library Dir,* Kansas City Art Institute, Library, Kansas City MO

Ligo, Larry L, *Assoc Prof,* Davidson College, Art Dept, Davidson NC (S)

Ligon, Claude M, *Dir,* Maryland Museum of African Art, Columbia MD

Lile, Jill, *Instr,* Creighton University, Fine and Performing Arts Dept, Omaha NE (S)

Lilley, Mary C, *Exec Dir,* Pontiac Art Center, Pontiac MI (S)

Lilley, Mary C, *Exec Dir,* Pontiac Art Center, Pontiac MI

Lillich, Meredith, *Prof,* Syracuse University, Dept of Fine Arts, Syracuse NY (S)

Lilly, Dick, *Executive Dir,* Allied Arts of Seattle, Inc, Seattle WA

Lilly, Edward G, *VPres,* North Carolina Art Society, Raleigh NC

Lillys, William, *Head Museum Education,* Los Angeles County Museum of Art, Los Angeles CA

Lilyquist, Christine, *Cur Egyptian Art,* Metropolitan Museum of Art, New York NY

Lim, Lucy, *Executive Dir,* Chinese Culture Foundation, Chinese Culture Center Gallery, San Francisco CA

Limbaugh, Marty, *Asst to Dir,* Fresno Arts Center, Fresno CA

Limondjian, Hilde, *Program Mgr Concerts & Lectures,* Metropolitan Museum of Art, New York NY

Limonte, Naomi, *Secy,* American Color Print Society, Philadelphia PA

Limpert, John, *Dir Membership & Development,* Museum of Modern Art, New York NY

Lin, Henry H, *Dir,* Ohio University, Gallery of Fine Arts, Athens OH

Lin, Henry H, *Dean,* Ohio University, School of Art, Athens OH (S)

Linard, Laura, *Cur Special Coll,* Chicago Public Library, Cultural Center, Chicago IL

Lincer, Catherin, *Libr Dir,* Cochise College, Charles Di Peso Library, Douglas AZ

Lindabury, Jean, *VChmn,* Princeton Art Association, Princeton NJ

Lindberg, E Theodore, *Dir,* Emily Carr College of Art & Design, The Charles H Scott Gallery, Vancouver BC

Lindborg, Henry L, *Chmn Arts & Letters,* Marian College, Art Dept, Fond Du Lac WI (S)

Lindeman, Kathryn B, *Writer & Editor,* Smithsonian Institution, Washington DC

Lindemann, Edna M, *Dir,* Burchfield Art Center, Buffalo NY

Lindemann, Hans K, *Owner & Founder,* Museum of American Treasures, National City CA

Lindemann, Shirley, *Cur,* Museum of American Treasures, National City CA

Linden, Barbara, *Facilities Mgr,* Massachusetts Institute of Technology, Museum, Cambridge MA

Lindenheim, Diane, *Instructor,* Bucks County Community College, Fine Arts Dept, Newton PA (S)

Linder, Ronald F, *Instr,* Mainline Center of the Arts, Haverford PA (S)

Linder, Ronald F, *Instr,* Rosemont College, Division of the Arts, Rosemont PA (S)

Lindgren, Bernice, *Treas,* Phelps County Historical Society Museum, Holdrege NE

Lindgren, Don, *Pres,* Phelps County Historical Society Museum, Holdrege NE

Lindgren, Racthel, *Comptroller,* La Jolla Museum of Contemporary Art, La Jolla CA

Lindhult, Mark, *Asst Prof,* University of Toronto, Dept of Landscape Architecture, Toronto ON (S)

Lindner, Harry, *Instructor,* Northeast Technical Community College, Dept of Art, Norfolk NE (S)

Lindo, Arthur, *Public Relations Mgr,* Brooklyn Museum, Brooklyn NY

Lindquist, Evan, *Prof,* Arkansas State University, Dept of Art, State University AR (S)

Lindquist, Kenneth H, *Dir,* Arnot Art Museum, Elmira NY

Lindsay, Betsey, *Instr,* Pacific Northwest College of Art, Portland OR (S)

Lindsay, G Carroll, *Planning & Program Develop Dir,* New York State Museum, Albany NY

Lindsay, Henry, *Chmn Div Fine Arts,* Howard Payne University, Dept of Art, Brownwood TX (S)

Lindsey, Anne, *Assoc Prof,* University of Tennessee at Chattanooga, Dept of Art, Chattanooga TN (S)

Lindstrom, Bill, *Dir,* Maui Community College Library, Kahului HI

Linehan, James, *Asst Prof,* University of Maine, Art Dept, Orono ME (S)

Linehan, J E, *Asst Prof,* Saint Andrews Presbyterian College, Art Program, Laurinburg NC (S)

Linehan, Thomas, *Asst Prof,* Ohio State University, Dept of Art Education, Columbus OH (S)

Linerode, Darla, *Asst Education Dir,* Memphis Brooks Museum of Art, Memphis TN

Lineweaver, Ann, *VPres,* Green Hill Center for North Carolina Art, Greensboro NC

Lingen, Joan, *Chmn,* Clarke College, Dept of Art, Dubuque IA (S)

Linhares, Philip, *Graduate Studies,* California College of Arts and Crafts, Oakland CA (S)

Linhares, Philip E, *Dir,* Mills College, Art Gallery, Oakland CA

Link, Howard A, *Cur Asian Art & Keeper of Ukiyo-e Center,* Honolulu Academy of Arts, Honolulu HI

Link, John, *Chairperson Dept,* Western Michigan University, Dept of Art, Kalamazoo MI (S)

Link, John, *Chairperson,* Western Michigan University, Gallery II, Kalamazoo MI

Linn, Suellen, *Library Dir,* Lake Placid Center for Music, Drama & Art, Nettie Marie Jones Fine Arts Library, Lake Placid NY

Linn, Winona, *Secy,* Ravalli County Museum, Hamilton MT

Linnehan, Genevieve, *Asst Dir,* Tampa Museum, Tampa FL

Linsky, Robert, *Chmn Dept of Graphic Design,* New England School of Art & Design, Boston MA (S)

Lint, Doug, *VPres,* Southern Alberta Art Gallery, Lethbridge AB

Lintault, M Joan, *Assoc Prof,* Southern Illinois University, School of Art, Carbondale IL (S)

Lintault, Roger, *Instructor,* California State College, San Bernardino, Art Dept, San Bernardino CA (S)

Linton, Margot, *Membership Dir,* The American Federation of Arts, New York NY

Lipfert, Nathan, *Asst Cur,* Maine Maritime Museum, Bath ME

Lipinski, Marlene, *Coordr Graphics,* Columbia College, Art Dept, Chicago IL (S)

Lipinsky, Lino S, *Cur,* John Jay Homestead State Historic Site, Katonah NY

Lipnick, Robert, *Asst Prof,* Marycrest College, Art Dept, Davenport IA (S)

Lipofsky, Marvin, *Glass,* California College of Arts and Crafts, Oakland CA (S)

Lipowicz, Edward, *Cur,* Canajoharie Library and Art Gallery, Canajoharie NY

Lipp, Frederick, *Prof,* Rochester Institute of Technology, School of Art and Design, Rochester NY (S)

Lippert, Catherine Beth, *Assoc Cur Decorative Arts,* Indianapolis Museum of Art, Indianapolis IN

Lippincott, Miriam, *Publicity,* Rockport Art Association, Rockport MA

Lippman, Irvin, *Public Affairs Coordr,* Amon Carter Museum, Fort Worth TX

Lippman, Judith, *Dir,* Meredith Contemporary Art Gallery, Baltimore MD

Lippman, Mandy, *Asst Dir,* Meredith Contemporary Art Gallery, Baltimore MD

Lips, Pleter, *Instr,* Berkshire Community College, Dept Fine Arts, Pittsfield MA (S)

Lipscomb, H Bernard, *Instr Interior Design,* Kean College of New Jersey, Fine Arts Dept, Union NJ (S)

Lipsitt, Cyrus D, *Executive Dir,* Worcester Craft Center Gallery, Worcester MA

Lipsitt, Cyrus D, *Exec Dir,* Worcester Craft Center, Worcester MA (S)

Lis, Edward, *Instr,* Wayne Art Center, Wayne PA (S)

Lisanti, Dominic A, *Business Adminr,* Newark Museum, Newark NJ

Lisk, Paddy, *VPres,* Lexington Art League, Inc, Lexington KY

Lispcome, Brenda C, *Coordr of Art,* Stillman College, Stillman Art Gallery and Art Dept, Tuscaloosa AL (S)

Liss, Allen, *Cur Anthropology,* Charleston Museum, Charleston SC

Liss, Eve, *Secy,* Yeshiva University, Museum, New York NY

Lister, Cynthia, *VPres,* Print Club, Philadelphia PA

Lister, Peter, *Instr,* Rosemont College, Division of the Arts, Rosemont PA (S)

Liston, Helen, *VPres,* Alaska Artists' Guild, Anchorage AK

Litalo, Darlene Y, *Asst to Dir,* Nicolaysen Art Museum, Casper WY

Litcombe, Christopher L, *Asst Prof,* Sweet Briar College, Art History Dept and Art Studio Dept, Sweet Briar VA (S)

Little, Kenneth D, *Registrar,* University of Arizona, Museum of Art, Tucson AZ

Little, Robert, *Cur Decorative Arts,* Montreal Museum of Fine Arts, Montreal PQ

Little, Warren M, *Dir,* Higgins Armory Museum, Worcester MA

Littlefield, Doris B, *Cur Coll,* Vizcaya Museum and Gardens, Miami FL

Littlefield, F Lee, *Asst Prof,* Southern Illinois University, School of Art, Carbondale IL (S)

Littman, Robert R, *Dir,* New York University, Grey Art Gallery and Study Center, New York NY

Livengood, James, *Executive Secy,* Marblehead Arts Association, Inc, Marblehead MA

Liverant, Gigi H, *Secy,* Connecticut Women Artist, Inc, Glastonbury CT

Livesay, Thomas A, *Asst Dir Admin,* Dallas Museum of Fine Arts, Dallas TX

Livingston, Barbara, *VPres,* Paducah Art Guild, Paducah KY

Livingston, Jane, *Assoc Dir,* Corcoran Museum, Washington DC

Livingston, Margery, *Chmn,* San Francisco State University, Art Dept, San Francisco CA (S)

Lizza, Richard, *Asst Prof,* University of Tennessee at Chattanooga, Dept of Art, Chattanooga TN (S)

Lizzadro, John S, *Dir,* Lizzadro Museum of Lapidary Art, Elmhurst IL

Llewellyn, Frederick, *Dir,* Forest Lawn Museum, Glendale CA

Llewellyn, Jane E, *Mgr,* Forest Lawn Museum, Glendale CA

Lloyd, Norman, *Exhibition Preparator,* Muckenthaler Cultural Center, Fullerton CA

Lloyd, Robert J, *Chmn,* Eastern Washington University, Dept of Art, Cheney WA (S)

Lloyd, R Scott, *Admin Asst, Educational Servs,* Museum of Holography, New York NY

Lloyd, Timothy L, *Chmn,* Carleton College, Dept of Art & Art History, Northfield MN (S)

Lloyd, Tom, *Dir & Cur,* Store Front Museum, Jamaica NY

Loader, Kevin, *Admin Dir,* Farmington Art Guild, Farmington CT

Loar, Steve, *Asst Prof,* Rochester Institute of Technology, School of Art and Design, Rochester NY (S)

Locatelli, Paul, *Academic VPres,* University of Santa Clara, de Saisset Museum, Santa Clara CA

Locey, Jean, *Asst Prof,* Cornell University, Dept of Art, Ithaca NY (S)

Lochapelle, Pierre, *Dir,* Musee du Quebec, Quebec PQ

Lochiatto, Anna, *Instr,* Danforth Museum School, Framingham MA (S)

Lochridge, Katherine, *Dir,* Heckscher Museum, Huntington NY

Lochtefeld, John, *Prof,* Marymount College, Art Dept, Tarrytown NY (S)

Lock, Earl, *Dir,* University of Nebraska at Omaha, Art Gallery, Omaha NE

Lock, Earl W, *Dir,* Paducah Art Guild, Paducah KY

Lockart, Robert, *Instr,* Blackhawk Mountain School of Art, Black Hawk CO (S)

Locke, John A, *Asst Prof,* Ulster County Community College, Dept of Visual Arts, Stone Ridge NY (S)

Locker, David, *Asst Librn,* Willard Library, Dept of Fine Arts, Evansville IN

Lockhart, Anne I, *Cur of Western Art,* University of Michigan, Museum of Art, Ann Arbor MI

Lockhart, Bill, *Prof,* Texas Tech University, Dept of Art, Lubbock TX (S)

Lockhart, L, *Head Security,* Glenbow Museum, Calgary AB

Lockpez, Inverna, *Dir,* Intar Latin American Gallery, New York NY

Lockpez, Inverna, *Cur,* Women's Interart Center, Inc, Interart de St Amand Gallery, New York NY

Lockwood, Gerri, *Secy,* Museum of Fine Arts, Springfield MA

Lodge, Judith, *Asst Prof,* College of Saint Rose, Division of Art, Albany NY (S)

Loeb, Alex M, *Pres,* Mississippi Art Colony, Meridian MS

Loeb, Jean R, *Secy & Treas,* Mississippi Art Colony, Meridian MS

Loebelsohn, Carol, *Chmn Fashion Illustration,* Traphagen School of Fashion, New York NY (S)

Loeffler, Carl E, *Pres,* La Mamelle Inc, San Francisco CA

Loehr, Thomas, *Asst Prof,* Spring Hill College, Fine Arts Dept, Mobile AL (S)

Loerke, William, *Prof,* Catholic University of America, Dept of Architecture and Planning, Washington DC (S)

Loertscher, Pamela, *Secy,* Midland Art Council, Midland MI

Loescher, Robert, *Prof,* School of the Art Institute of Chicago, Chicago IL (S)

Loeser, Herta, *Co-Pres,* The Society of Arts and Crafts, Boston MA

Loew, Michael, *Instr,* New York Studio School of Drawing, Painting and Sculpture, New York NY (S)

Loewenstein, Mel J, *Exec Dir,* Arts and Education Council of Greater Saint Louis, Saint Louis MO

Lofgren, John Z, *Dir,* American Swedish Institute, Minneapolis MN

Lofstrom, Mark, *Public Relations Officer,* Honolulu Academy of Arts, Honolulu HI

Loftis, Lynnea, *Asst Dir,* Ella Sharp Museum, Jackson MI

Logan, Anne-Marie, *Librn,* Yale University, Reference Library, New Haven CT

Logan, David, *Assoc Prof,* East Tennessee State University, Fine Arts Dept, Johnson City TN (S)

Logan, James, *Dir,* Tom Thomson Memorial Gallery and Museum of Fine Art, Owen Sound ON

Logan, Jill, *Res Coordr,* Salvador Dali Foundation Museum, Saint Petersburg FL

Logan, J Thomas, *Chmn,* Metropolitan State College, Art Dept, Denver CO (S)

Logan, Lowell, *VPres,* Southern Arkansas University, Art Dept Gallery & Magale Art Gallery, Magnolia AR

Logan, Martha, *Secy,* Ohio State University, Gallery of Fine Art, Columbus OH

Logan, Tom, *Dir,* Monterey Peninsula Museum of Art, Monterey CA

Logan, Vernie M, *Instr,* Baylor University, Dept of Fine Arts, Waco TX (S)

Logan, Vernie M, *Cur,* Baylor University, Martin Museum of Art, Waco TX

Logue, Kathleen B, *Instr,* Mainline Center of the Arts, Haverford PA (S)

Lohden, Bernardine, *Gift Shop,* Rome Art and Community Center, Rome NY

Loizeaux, Dan, *Chmn Dept,* Propersi Galleries and School of Art Inc, Greenwich CT (S)

Lokensgard, Lynn, *Instructor,* Lamar University, Art Dept, Beaumont TX (S)

Loll, Carole, *Registrar,* Ella Sharp Museum, Jackson MI

Lombard, Maggie, *Dir Sales Shop,* Colorado Springs Fine Arts Center, Colorado Springs CO

Lombardi, Nancy, *Prog Dir Art,* Lansing Community College, Performing and Creative Arts Dept, Lansing MI (S)

Lombardo, Dan, *Cur,* Jones Library, Inc, Amherst MA

Lomeo, Charlotte, *Public Services Officer,* Arizona State University, University Art Collections, Tempe AZ

Loncke, Julia, *Office Mgr,* Lynnwood Arts Centre, Simcoe ON

London, Laurence, *Managing Dir,* Charles B Goddard Center for the Visual and Performing Arts, Ardmore OK

Lonergan, Mary Ann, *Instructor,* Briar Cliff College, Art Dept, Sioux City IA (S)

Long, Charles, *Museum Consultant,* San Antonio Art League, San Antonio TX

Long, Charles, *Public Information Officer,* Fine Arts Museums of San Francisco, M H de Young Memorial Museum and California Palace of the Legion of Honor, San Francisco CA

Long, Clarence W, *Pres Board of Trustees,* Indianapolis Museum of Art, Indianapolis IN

Long, Ellen, *Dept Head,* Ray-Vogue College of Design, Chicago IL (S)

Long, John M, *Dean School of Fine Arts,* Troy State University, Dept of Art, Troy AL (S)

Long, Julia, *Reference,* Saint Mary's College, Cushwa-Leighton Library, Notre Dame IN

Long, Laurel, *Instructor,* Cazenovia College, Center for Art & Design Studies, Cazenovia NY (S)

Long, Melba LeGrande, *Assoc Prof,* Converse College, Art Dept, Spartanburg SC (S)

Long, Nancy, *Gallery Mgr & Public Relations,* Morse Gallery of Art, Winter Park FL

Long, Noyes C, *Asst Dean,* Appalachian State University, Dept of Art, Boone NC (S)

Long, Randy, *Asst Prof,* Indiana University, Bloomington, School of Fine Arts, Bloomington IN (S)

Long, Rose-Carol, *Prof,* City University of New York, PhD Program in Art History, New York NY (S)

Long, Walter K, *Dir,* Cayuga Museum of History and Art, Auburn NY

Long, William, *Secy,* Central Louisiana Art Association, Alexandria Museum Visual Art Center, Alexandria LA

Longaker, Jon D, *Chmn,* Randolph-Macon College, Art Dept, Ashland VA (S)

Longen, Leonarda, *Prof Emeritus,* Mount Marty College, Art Dept, Yankton SD (S)

Longland, Jean R, *Cur,* Hispanic Society of America, Library, New York NY

Longnecker, Martha, *Pres,* Mingei International Inc, Mingei International Museum of World Folk Art, La Jolla CA

Longstreet, Marguerite, *Secy,* Willard House and Clock Museum, Inc, Grafton MA

Longstreet, Stephen, *Pres,* Southern California Contemporary Art Galleries of the Los Angeles Art Association, Los Angeles CA

Longsworth, Charles R, *Pres,* Colonial Williamsburg Foundation, Williamsburg VA

Longtin, Barbara C, *Asst Dir,* Muscatine Art Center, Muscatine IA

Loomis, Ormond H, *Dir,* Florida Folklife Programs, White Springs FL

Loomis, Tom, *Assoc Prof,* Mansfield State College, Art Dept, Mansfield PA (S)

Looney, M O, *Pres,* Missouri Western State College, Fine Arts Gallery, Saint Joseph MO

Looney, Robert F, *Head,* Free Library of Philadelphia, Print and Picture Dept, Philadelphia PA

Lopez, Donald, *Deputy Dir,* National Air and Space Museum, Washington DC

Lopez, Jesse, *Production Mgr,* Rice University, Institute for the Arts, Rice Museum, Houston TX

LoPresti, Maryellen, *Librn,* North Carolina State University, Harrye Lyons Design Library, Raleigh NC

Loranth, Alice N, *Head Fine Arts & Special Coll Dept,* Cleveland Public Library, Fine Arts & Special Collections Dept, Cleveland OH

Lord, Catherine, *Dean,* California Institute of the Arts, School of Art, Valencia CA (S)

Lord, Eileen, *Prof,* University of Bridgeport, Art Dept, Bridgeport CT (S)

Lord, Florence S, *Coordr,* Kenyon College, Colburn Gallery, Gambier OH

Lord, Robert, *Chmn Committee,* Old Gaol Museum, York ME

Lore, Angela, *Admin Asst,* National Gallery of Art, Washington DC

Lorence, Kay, *Dir,* Coos Art Museum, Coos Bay OR

Lorenz, Melinda, *Cur Exhibitions,* Galleries of the Claremont Colleges, Claremont CA

Lorenzana, Katherine Harper, *Asst Prof,* Loyola Marymount University, Dept of Art & Art Hist, Los Angeles CA (S)

Lorenzi, Linda, *Cur Exhibits & Sales,* Riverside Art Center and Museum, Riverside CA

Lorey, Denise, *Museum Shop,* Joslyn Art Museum, Omaha NE

Lorfano, Pauline D, *Chmn,* National League of American Pen Women, Washington DC

Lyke, Linda, *Dir,* Occidental College Gallery, Los Angeles CA

Lykins, Jere, *Asst Prof,* Berry College, Art Dept, Mount Berry GA (S)

Lyle, Charles T, *Exec Dir,* Historical Society of Delaware, Old Town Hall Museum, Wilmington DE

Lyman, David H, *Founder & Dir,* Maine Photographic Workshops, Rockport ME

Lyman, David H, *Founder & Dir,* Maine Photographic Workshops, Rockport ME (S)

Lyman, Henry, *Instr,* Whitworth College, Art Dept, Spokane WA (S)

Lyman, Thomas W, *Prof,* Emory University, Art History Dept, Atlanta GA (S)

Lynagh, Patricia, *Ref Librn,* University of Maryland, College Park, Art Library, College Park MD

Lynagh, Patricia, *Media Center Librn,* Cleveland Institute of Art, Jessica Gund Memorial Library, Cleveland OH

Lynch, John, *Instructor,* Columbia College, Art Dept, Columbia MO (S)

Lynch, Kenneth, *Pres,* Craft Center Museum, Wilton CT

Lynch, Ronald, *Program Dir,* Institute for Art & Urban Resources, Project Studios One, Long Island City NY

Lynde, Donna, *Instr,* Cottey College, Fine Arts Division, Nevada MO (S)

Lynds, Clyde, *Board Member,* Actual Art Foundation, New York NY

Lyon, Elizabeth T, *Cur,* Centre Hill Mansion, Petersburg VA

Lyon, Joyce, *Artist in Res,* Viterbo College, Art Dept, La Crosse WI (S)

Lyon, Pat, *Business Mgr,* Pacific Northwest Arts and Crafts Association, Bellevue Art Museum, Bellevue WA

Lyons, Joan, *Coordr Print Shop,* Visual Studies Workshop, Rochester NY

Lyons, Lynda, *Exploratorium Mgr,* University of California, Los Angeles, Exploratorium, University Student Union, Los Angeles CA

Lyons, Nathan, *Dir,* Visual Studies Workshop, Rochester NY

Lystra, Doni, *Pres,* Ann Arbor Art Association, Ann Arbor MI

Lytle, Richard, *Prof,* Yale University, School of Art, New Haven CT (S)

Maag, Albert, *Dir,* Capital University, Art Library, Columbus OH

Maakestad, John, *Prof,* Saint Olaf College, Art Dept, Northfield MN (S)

Maass, R Andrew, *Dir,* Tucson Museum of Art, Tucson AZ

MacAdam, Barbara, *Asst Cur,* Hood Museum of Art, Hanover NH

Macalik, M, *Instructor,* Technical University of Nova Scotia, Faculty of Architecture, Halifax NS (S)

MacArthur, William C, *Instr,* American River College, Dept of Art, Sacramento CA (S)

Macaulay, Thomas, *Assoc Prof,* Wright State University, Dept of Art & Art History, Dayton OH (S)

MacBee, Henrietta, *Registrar,* Bowdoin College, Museum of Art & Peary-MacMillan Arctic Museum, Brunswick ME

MacBeth, Deborah, *Librn,* Navajo Tribal Museum, Navajo Nation Library, Window Rock AZ

MacCarthy, Douglas B, *Pres,* First Street Forum, Saint Louis MO

MacCluskey, Tom, *Instr,* Colorado Women's College, Dept of Art, Denver CO (S)

Macdonald, Anne, *Exec Dir,* Community Arts Council of Vancouver, Vancouver BC

MacDonald, Bruce, *Vis Lectr,* Tufts University, Fine Arts Dept, Medford MA (S)

MacDonald, Bruce K, *Dean,* School of the Museum of Fine Arts, Boston MA (S)

MacDonald, C A, *Pres,* Litchfield Historical Society, Litchfield CT

MacDonald, George, *Dir,* National Museum of Man, Ottawa ON

MacDonald, George F, *Dir, National Museum of Man,* National Museums of Canada, Ottawa ON

MacDonald, Judy, *Registrar,* Confederation Centre Art Gallery and Museum, Charlottetown PE

Macdonald, Robert R, *Dir,* Louisiana Department of Culture, Recreation and Tourism, Louisiana State Museum, New Orleans LA

MacDougall, E Bruce, *Head,* University of Massachusetts, Amherst, Dept Landscape Architecture & Regional Planning, Amherst MA (S)

MacDougall, Elisabeth B, *Dir Studies,* Harvard University, Garden Library, Washington DC

MacEachran, David F, *Assoc Prof,* New England College, Visual Arts Dept, Henniker NH (S)

MacEachron, David, *Pres Japan Society,* Japan Society, Inc, Japan House Gallery, New York NY

MacFarlane, D, *Asst Slide Librn,* York University, Fine Arts Slide Library, Downsview ON

MacGillivray, Vera, *Dir,* Fine Arts Center of Clinton, Clinton IL

MacGregor, Nancy, *Pres,* National Art Education Association, Reston VA

MacGregor, Nancy, *Assoc Prof,* Ohio State University, Dept of Art Education, Columbus OH (S)

Machek, Frank, *Gallery Dir,* Albion College, Bobbitt Visual Arts Center, Albion MI

Machek, Frank, *Chmn Dept Visual Arts,* Albion College, Dept of Visual Arts, Albion MI (S)

Mack, Angela, *Asst Cur,* Carolina Art Association, Gibbes Art Gallery, Charleston SC

Mack, James, *Chmn Humanities,* City Colleges of Chicago, Loop College, Chicago IL (S)

Mack, Laura, *Librn,* Museum of Holography, Reference Library, New York NY

Mack, Rodger, *Dir,* Syracuse University, College of Visual and Performing Arts, Syracuse NY (S)

MacKay, Allan, *Dir & Cur,* Mendel Art Gallery and Civic Conservatory, Saskatoon SK

MacKay, Don, *Assoc Prof,* University of Waterloo, Fine Arts Dept, Waterloo ON (S)

MacKellar, Linda, *Faculty,* Midway College, Art Dept, Midway KY (S)

MacKenzie, Warren, *Chmn Dept,* University of Minnesota, Minneapolis, Dept of Studio Art, Minneapolis MN (S)

Mackey, Karl A, *Managing Dir,* Kenneth C Beck Center for the Cultural Arts, Lakewood OH

MacKichan, Margaret, *Vis Prof,* Nebraska Wesleyan University, Art Dept, Lincoln NE (S)

Mackie, Deryl, *Cur Fine Arts,* Afro-American Historical and Cultural Museum, Philadelphia PA

Mackie, G, *Instr,* David Thompson University Centre, Visual Arts Dept, Nelson BC (S)

MacKillop, Rod, *Faculty,* University of North Carolina-Charlotte, Creative Arts Dept, Charlotte NC (S)

Macklin, A D, *Head Dept,* Virginia State University, Fine & Commercial Art, Petersburg VA (S)

Macknight, H, *Recording Secy,* Lyceum Club and Women's Art Association of Canada, Toronto ON

MacLaughlin, Joseph S, *Exec Dir,* Old State House, Hartford CT

MacLeish, A Bruce, *Assoc Cur,* New York State Historical Association, Fenimore House, Cooperstown NY

Macmaster, W T, *Assoc Dir,* Rome Historical Society, Rome Information and Cultural Center, Rome NY

MacNeil, Wendy S, *Asst Prof,* Wellesley College, Art Dept, Wellesley MA (S)

MacNeille, Jeanette C, *Exec Dir,* Alaska Association for the Arts, Fairbanks AK

MacNutt, Glenn, *VPres,* New England Watercolor Society, Scituate MA

Macomber, William B, *Pres,* Metropolitan Museum of Art, New York NY

Mac Pherson, Thomas, *Cur,* Benedict College, Visual Art Studies, Columbia SC (S)

MacTaggart, Alan, *Chmn,* Lander College, Dept of Fine Arts, Greenwood SC (S)

Madden, Charles F, *Admin,* Webster College, Loretto-Hilton Center Gallery, Saint Louis MO

Madden, J Robert, *Prof,* Lamar University, Art Dept, Beaumont TX (S)

Madden, Lois, *Executive Secy,* Art Center Association, Louisville KY

Maddison, Jean, *Asst Prof,* Mount Allison University, Fine Arts Dept, Sackville NB (S)

Maddox, Donna, *Dept Head,* Columbus College, Experimental Gallery, Columbus GA

Maddox, Donna L, *Chair,* Columbus College, Dept of Art Fine Arts Hall, Columbus GA (S)

Maddox, Gene, *Instructor,* College of the Sequoias, Art Dept, Visalia CA (S)

Maddox, Jerrold, *Dir School Visual Arts,* Pennsylvania State University, University Park, College of Arts and Architecture, University Park PA (S)

Mader, Daniel, *Prof,* College of Mount Saint Joseph, Art Dept, Mount Saint Joseph OH (S)

Madigan, Richard A, *Dir,* Norton Gallery and School of Art, West Palm Beach FL

Madonia, Ann C, *Cur,* Davenport Municipal Art Gallery, Davenport IA

Madrigal, August, *Prof,* University of Bridgeport, Art Dept, Bridgeport CT (S)

Madsen, Viggo Holm, *Pres,* Long Island Graphic Eye Gallery, Port Washington NY

Madson, Donald A, *Asst Dir,* Morris Museum of Arts and Sciences, Morristown NJ

Maeda, R, *Chmn,* Brandeis University, Dept of Fine Arts, Waltham MA (S)

Magavern, Samuel D, *Pres,* The Buffalo Fine Arts Academy, Albright-Knox Art Gallery, Buffalo NY

Magavern, William J, *Treas,* The Buffalo Fine Arts Academy, Albright-Knox Art Gallery, Buffalo NY

Magee, Eileen, *Program Coordr,* Athenaeum of Philadelphia, Philadelphia PA

Maggio, Ron, *Instructor,* Springfield College, Dept of Visual and Performing Arts, Springfield MA (S)

Magill, Betty, *Secy,* Ball State University, Art Gallery, Muncie IN

Magill, Peggy, *Public Relations,* Dayton Art Institute, Dayton OH

Magill, Vera, *Secy,* Quincy Art Center, Quincy IL

Maginnis, Ann, *Librn,* Corcoran Museum, Library, Washington DC

Maginnis, Hayden, *Dir,* McMaster University, Art Gallery, Hamilton ON

Magleby, McRay, *Prof,* University of Utah, Art Dept, Salt Lake City UT (S)

Magnan, Oscar, *Dir,* Saint Peter's College, Art Gallery, Jersey City NJ

Magnan, Oscar G, *Chmn,* Saint Peter's College, Fine Arts Dept, Jersey City NJ (S)

Magnuson, Richard C, *Chmn Board Trustees,* Minnesota Museum of Art, Saint Paul MN

Magnusson, Paul, *Pres,* Portland Center for the Visual Arts, Portland OR

Magoon, Charles, *Resident Cur,* Waterville Historical Association, Redington Museum, Waterville ME

Magowan, Robert A, *VPres,* Society of the Four Arts, Palm Beach FL

Magri, P, *Instr,* Chamberlayne Junior College, Dept of Applied Arts, Boston MA (S)

Maguire, Diana, *Sales Desk Mgr,* Allentown Art Museum, Allentown PA

Maguire, William, *Assoc Prof,* Florida International University, Visual Arts Dept, Miami FL (S)

Mahe, John, *Cur,* Historic New Orleans Collection, Kemper and Leila Williams Foundation, New Orleans LA

Maher, James B, *Librn,* Brooks Institute Photography Library, Santa Barbara CA

Mahler, R, *Chmn,* Oakville Galleries, Oakville ON

Mahnke, K Y, *Instr,* Presbyterian College, Fine Arts Dept, Clinton SC (S)

Mahon, Jean, *Corresponding Secy,* Art Guild of Burlington, Arts for Living Center, Burlington IA

Mahoney, Charles A, *Pres,* New England Watercolor Society, Scituate MA

Mahoney, Eugene, *Dir,* Game and Parks Commission, Arbor Lodge State Historical Park, Nebraska City NE

Mahoney, Michael, *Chmn Dept Fine Arts,* Trinity College, Austin Arts Center, Hartford CT

Mahoney, Michael R T, *Chmn,* Trinity College, Dept of Fine Arts, Hartford CT (S)

Mahoney, William, *Dir,* Columbia University, Teachers Col Program in Art & Education, New York NY (S)

Mahy, Gordon, *Assoc Prof,* Mars Hill College, Art Dept, Mars Hill NC (S)

Maier, Manfred, *Vis Prof,* Ball State University, Art Dept, Muncie IN (S)

Mailey, Jean, *Cur Textile Study Room,* Metropolitan Museum of Art, New York NY

Main, Claire, *Admin Asst,* Amarillo Art Center, Amarillo TX

Maine, Virginia, *Treas,* Coos Art Museum, Coos Bay OR

Maines, Clark, *Assoc Prof,* Wesleyan University, Art Dept, Middletown CT (S)

Maione, Orlando, *Pres,* Triton Museum of Art, Santa Clara CA

Maize, Shirley, *Dir,* Tennessee Valley Art Association and Center, Tuscumbia AL

Majeske, Robert, *Instr,* Illinois Central College, Fine Arts Dept, East Peoria IL (S)

Majeski, Thomas H, *Prof,* University of Nebraska at Omaha, Dept of Art, Omaha NE (S)

Majoli, Pauline, *Prof,* Loyola Marymount University, Dept of Art & Art Hist, Los Angeles CA (S)

Makov, Susan, *Asst Prof,* Weber State College, Art Dept, Ogden UT (S)

Makow, Yoram, *Prof,* California State Polytechnic University, Pomona, Art Dept, Pomona CA (S)

Malak, Gregory, *Cur,* Will Rogers Memorial and Museum, Claremore OK

Malarky, Louise, *VPres,* Middletown Fine Arts Center, Middletown OH

Malcolm, Christian, *Dir Programs,* American Scandinavian Foundation Gallery, New York NY

Malgeri, Dina G, *Librn,* Malden Public Library, Art Dept & Gallery, Malden MA

Malia, Peter J, *Managing Editor,* Connecticut Historical Society, Hartford CT

Malizia, Dominic, *Instr,* Danforth Museum School, Framingham MA (S)

Mallman-Law, Joyce, *Public Information,* Glenbow Museum, Calgary AB

Mallory, Nina, *Assoc Prof,* State University of New York at Stony Brook, Art Dept, Stony Brook NY (S)

Malm, Eric S, *Secy,* Brookgreen Gardens, Murrells Inlet SC

Malmgren, Lynn C, *Dir,* American Swedish Historical Foundation and Museum, Philadelphia PA

Malmquist, A Keith, *Prof,* Bemidji State University, Art Dept, Bemidji MN (S)

Malone, Carolyn, *Asst Prof,* University of Southern California, School of Fine Arts, Los Angeles CA (S)

Malone, Delores, *Secy,* Fine Arts Museums of San Francisco, M H de Young Memorial Museum and California Palace of the Legion of Honor, San Francisco CA

Malone, Mike, *VPres,* Montana Historical Society, Helena MT

Malone, Robert R, *Head Printmaking,* Southern Illinois University at Edwardsville, Dept of Art and Design, Edwardsville IL (S)

Maloney, Patricia, *Asst Prof,* Washington and Jefferson College, Art Dept, Washington PA (S)

Maloney, Stephanie J, *Dir,* University of Louisville, Allen R Hite Art Institute, Louisville KY

Maloney, Vickie L, *Asst Dir,* University of Washington, Henry Art Gallery, Seattle WA

Malpass, Leslie, *Pres,* Western Illinois University, Macomb IL

Maluen, Fred, *Coordr Interior Design,* Iowa State University, Dept of Art and Design, Ames IA (S)

Mancoff, Debra, *Asst Prof,* Beloit College, Dept of Art, Beloit WI (S)

Mandel, Gerry, *Pres,* Children's Art Foundation, Santa Cruz CA

Mandle, Roger, *Dir,* Toledo Museum of Art, Toledo OH

Mandolini, Ann, *Cur of Education,* Putnam Museum, Davenport IA

Manetta, Edward, *Chmn,* Saint John's University, Dept of Fine Arts, Jamaica NY (S)

Mangels, John D, *Treas,* Corporate Council for the Arts, Seattle WA

Mangiamele, Leslie, *Instr,* Arkansas Arts Center, Little Rock AR (S)

Mangiaracina, Bernarnd, *Instructor,* Bucks County Community College, Fine Arts Dept, Newton PA (S)

Mangulis, Ingrida, *Prof,* Salem State College, Art Dept, Salem MA (S)

Mangum, William, *Prof,* Salem College, Art Dept, Winston-Salem NC (S)

Manhart, Marcia, *Actg Dir,* Philbrook Art Center, Tulsa OK

Manheim, Emily M, *VPres,* National Antique and Art Dealers Association of America, New York NY

Manilla, Morton, *Chmn Educ Committee,* Toronto Art Therapy Institute, Toronto ON (S)

Maniscalco, Nelson R, *Chmn,* Cedar Crest College, Art Dept, Allentown PA (S)

Manley, Joan D, *VPres,* The Friends of Photography, Carmel CA

Mann, Elaine E, *Dir,* National Museum of Racing, Inc, Saratoga Springs NY

Mann, Jack, *Asst Prof,* Wittenberg University, Art Dept, Springfield OH (S)

Mann, Joan, *Editor & Public Information,* King County Arts Commission, Seattle WA

Mann, S Lee, *Chmn,* University of Kansas, Dept of Design, Lawrence KS (S)

Mann, Virginia, *Chief Registrar,* Fine Arts Museums of San Francisco, M H de Young Memorial Museum and California Palace of the Legion of Honor, San Francisco CA

Mann, Vivian, *Cur of Judaica,* Jewish Museum, New York NY

Mannering, William, *Treas,* Annie S Kemerer Museum, Bethlehem PA

Mannes, Edythe E, *Admin Asst,* Laguna Beach Museum of Art, Laguna Beach CA

Mannheimer, Marc, *Asst Prof,* Bradford College, Creative Arts Division, Bradford MA (S)

Mannikka, Eleanor, *Assoc Cur,* University of Michigan, Slide and Photograph Collection, Ann Arbor MI

Manning, Carder, *Chmn,* Penn Valley Community College, Art Dept, Kansas City MO (S)

Manning, Doris, *Secy,* The New Harmony Gallery of Contemporary Art, New Harmony IN

Manning, Larry, *Instructor,* Jefferson Davis State Junior College, Art Dept, Brewton AL (S)

Manning, Les, *Ceramics Dept Head,* Banff Centre School of Fine Arts, Banff AB (S)

Manning, P, *Instructor,* Technical University of Nova Scotia, Faculty of Architecture, Halifax NS (S)

Manning, Reuben, *Chmn,* Langston University, Art Dept, Langston OK (S)

Manning, Robert F, *Prof,* Manchester Community College, Fine Arts Dept, Manchester CT (S)

Manns, Suzanne, *Instr,* Alfred C Glassell School of Art, Houston TX (S)

Manriquez, Dion, *Asst Prof,* University of Wisconsin-Stout, Art Dept, Menomonie WI (S)

Mansfield, Patricia, *Secy,* Surface Design Association, Inc, Fayetteville TN

Manship, John, *Pres,* Rockport Art Association, Rockport MA

Mansmann, Betsy, *Exec Dir,* Northern Virginia Fine Arts Association, The Athenaeum, Alexandria VA

Manson, Martha L, *Cur,* San Jose Museum of Art, San Jose CA

Mantie, Eugene, *Audiovisual Media Coordr,* National Portrait Gallery, Washington DC

Mantin, Regina, *Asst Cur Art,* New Brunswick Museum, Saint John NB

Manton, Jill, *Art Coordr,* San Francisco City and County Art Commission, San Francisco CA

Manuella, Frank, *Chmn Advertising Design,* Pan American University, Art Dept, Edinburg TX (S)

Manusos, Mary, *Gallery Dir,* Ohio University, Seigfred Gallery, Athens OH

Maounis, John, *Photograph Librarian,* National Maritime Museum, San Francisco CA

Mapes, Jean, *Registrar,* Philadelphia College of Textiles and Science, Paley Design Center, Philadelphia PA

Mapp, Thomas, *Dir,* University of Chicago, Lorado Taft Midway Studios, Chicago IL

Maradiaga, Ralph, *Co-Dir,* Galeria de la Raza, Studio 24, San Francisco CA

Marak, L B, *Faculty,* Humboldt State University, College of Creative Arts & Humanities, Arcata CA (S)

Marakas, Ted, *Chmn Div,* Baldwin-Wallace College, Dept of Art, Berea OH

Marandel, J Patrice, *Cur European Paintings,* Detroit Institute of Arts, Detroit MI

Marantz, Kenneth A, *Chmn Dept,* Ohio State University, Dept of Art Education, Columbus OH (S)

Marble, Fran, *Librn,* Allied Arts Council of the Yakima Valley, Warehouse Library, Yakima WA

Marcellus, Robert, *Instructor,* College of the Sequoias, Art Dept, Visalia CA (S)

Marchant, Sylvia L, *Head Development & Interpretive Programs,* Greenville County Museum of Art, Greenville SC

Marchard, Andre, *Chief Cur,* Musee du Quebec, Quebec PQ

Marche, Marie, *Public Relations Dir,* Boca Raton Center for the Arts, Inc, Boca Raton FL

Marchini, Julie, *Asst Dir,* Montclair State College, Gallery One, Upper Montclair NJ

Marconi, Nello, *Chief Design & Production,* National Portrait Gallery, Washington DC

Marcou, George T, *Assoc Prof,* Catholic University of America, Dept of Architecture and Planning, Washington DC (S)

Marcus, Evelyn, *Asst to Exhibitions Designer,* Hood Museum of Art, Hanover NH

Marcus, James, *Treasurer,* Guild Hall of East Hampton, Inc, Museum Section, East Hampton NY

Marcus, Janet, *Education Cur,* Craft and Folk Art Museum, Los Angeles CA

Marcus, Peter, *Chairperson Two-Dimensional Dept,* Washington University, School of Fine Arts, Saint Louis MO (S)

Marcus, Richard, *Librn & Dir,* Spertus Museum of Judaica, Library, Chicago IL

Marcus, Stanley, *Chmn,* University of Texas of Permian Basin, Art Discipline, Odessa TX (S)

Marcus, Terry, *Librn,* Institute of Art & Design, Library, Milwaukee WI

Marcusen, Richard B, *Instr,* Yavapai College, Art Dept, Prescott AZ (S)

Marcy, Jean F, *Librn,* Saint Johnsbury Athenaeum, Saint Johnsbury VT

Marden, Fred, *VPres,* Brookfield Craft Center, Inc Gallery, Brookfield CT

Marder, Tod, *Asst Prof,* Rutgers, the State University of New Jersey, Graduate Program in Art History, New Brunswick NJ (S)

Marein, Shirley, *Assoc Prof,* New York Institute of Technology, Fine Arts Dept, Old Westbury NY (S)

Mares, E A, *Cur of Education,* Albuquerque Museum of Art, History and Science, Albuquerque NM

Marfuta, Barbara, *Office Mgr,* Brevard Art Center and Museum, Inc, Melbourne FL

Margolius, Philip N, *Pres,* Judaic Museum of the Jewish Community Center, Goldman Fine Arts Gallery, Rockville MD

Margosian, Lucille, *Chmn,* Laney College, Art Dept, Oakland CA (S)

Margulies, Phyllis, *Educ Coordr,* Metropolitan Museum and Art Center, Coral Gables FL

Margulies, Stephen, *Cur Asst,* University of Virginia, Art Museum, Charlottesville VA

Mariasy, Richard, *Treas,* Spectrum, Friends of Fine Art, Inc, Toledo OH

Marie, Bernadette, *Archivist,* Saint Mary's College, Cushwa-Leighton Library, Notre Dame IN

Marinaro, Louis, *Exhib Dir,* University of Michigan, Slusser Gallery, Ann Arbor MI

Marincola, Paula, *Asst Dir,* University of Pennsylvania, Institute of Contemporary Art, Philadelphia PA

Marino, Olivia, *Cur Education,* Philbrook Art Center, Tulsa OK

Marino, T J, *Dean,* New York Institute of Photography, New York NY (S)

Marinosci, Angelo, *Asst Prof,* Salve Regina - The Newport College, Art Dept, Newport RI (S)

Marion, Florence, *Whistler House Dir,* Lowell Art Association, Whistler House and Parker Gallery, Lowell MA

Marion, Jane, *Treas,* Keokuk Art Center, Keokuk IA

Marioni, Tom, *Dir,* Academy of the Museum of Conceptual Art, San Francisco CA

Maris, Arno, *Chmn Dept,* Westfield State College, Art Dept, Westfield MA (S)

Mark, Berger, *Prof,* Rutgers, the State University of New Jersey, Mason Gross School of the Arts, New Brunswick NJ (S)

Mark, Joseph, *Instructor,* Williamsport Area Community College, Dept of Engineering and Design, Williamsport PA (S)

Markham, Susan, *Cur Educ Service,* Hancock Shaker Village, Inc, Pittsfield MA

Markle, Greer, *Head Dept,* Sun Valley Center for the Arts and Humanities, Dept of Fine Art, Sun Valley ID (S)

Markman, Ronald, *Prof,* Indiana University, Bloomington, School of Fine Arts, Bloomington IN (S)

Marks, Arthur, *Prof,* University of North Carolina at Chapel Hill, Art Dept, Chapel Hill NC (S)

Marks, D Patti, *Asst Mgr,* Chicago Architecture Foundation, ArchiCenter, Chicago IL

Marks, Graham, *Asst Prof,* Rochester Institute of Technology, School for American Craftsmen, Rochester NY (S)

Marks, Nancy, *Asst to Dir,* University of Wisconsin, Allen Priebe Gallery, Oshkosh WI

Marks, Robert C, *Dean,* Harrington Institute of Interior Design, Chicago IL (S)

Markson, Eileen, *Head Librn,* Bryn Mawr College, Art and Archaeology Library, Bryn Mawr PA

Markson, Teri, *Library Asst (Books),* University of California, Art Dept Library, Davis CA

Markwell, Judith, *Gallery Coordr,* El Camino College Art Gallery, Torrance CA

Marlais, Michael, *Instr,* Colby College, Art Dept, Waterville ME (S)

Marlin, William, *Chmn Dept,* Camden County College, Dept of Art, Blackwood NJ (S)

Marling, Karal Ann, *Chmn,* University of Minnesota, Minneapolis, Art History, Minneapolis MN (S)

Marlow, Jessie, *Clerical Hostess,* Red River Valley Museum, Vernon TX

Marohn, Pat, *Dir,* Tubac Center of the Arts, Santa Cruz Valley Art Association, Tubac AZ

Maronde, Doreen, *Head Dept,* Kirkwood Community College, Dept of Fine Arts, Cedar Rapids IA (S)

Marquardt, Emil, *Sr Secy,* Florida Gulf Coast Art Center, Inc, Clearwater FL

Marriner, Ernest C, *Librn,* Waterville Historical Association, Redington Museum, Waterville ME

Marriott, William, *Foundation,* University of Georgia, Franklin College of Arts and Sciences, Dept of Art, Athens GA (S)

Marron, Donald B, *VPres,* Museum of Modern Art, New York NY

Marron, Donald B, *Pres,* Paine Webber Inc, New York NY

Mars, Marilyn, *Executive Dir,* Second Street Gallery, Charlottesville VA

Mars, Robert E, *VPres Admin Affairs,* Art Institute of Chicago, Chicago IL

Marsh, Allan Thomas, *Chmn,* Montgomery College, Dept of Art, Rockville MD (S)

Marsh, Anne Steele, *Secy,* Associated Artists of New Jersey, Pittstown NJ

Marsh, E Thomas, *Prof,* University of Louisville, Allen R Hite Art Institute, Louisville KY (S)

Marsh, Gloria, *Library Technician,* Art Gallery of Ontario, Edward P Taylor Reference Library, Toronto ON

Marsh, Helen, *Art Dir,* Westerly Public Library, Westerly RI

Marsh, Robert, *Assoc Prof,* Averett College, Art Dept, Danville VA (S)

Marsh, Sheila J, *Media Servs Libr,* California State University, Sacramento, Library, Humanities Reference and Media Services Center, Sacramento CA

Marsh, Stephen, *Instructor,* Daytona Beach Community College, Dept of Performing and Visual Arts, Daytona Beach FL (S)

Marshall, Ann, *Cur Coll,* Heard Museum, Phoenix AZ

Marshall, Gordon, *Asst Librn,* Library Company of Philadelphia, Dept of Art, Philadelphia PA

Marshall, Howard, *Adj Prof,* University of Missouri, Art History and Archaeology Dept, Columbia MO (S)

Marshall, Joseph W, *Librn,* Franklin D Roosevelt Library and Museum, Library, Hyde Park NY

Marshall, M, *Chmn,* Carleton University, Dept of Art History, Ottawa ON (S)

Marshall, Paul, *Secy,* Colonel Black Mansion, Ellsworth ME

Marshall, Richard, *Assoc Cur, Exhibitions,* Whitney Museum of American Art, New York NY

Marshall, Thomas, *Assoc Prof,* Atlantic Christian College, Art Dept, Wilson NC (S)

Marshman, Robert B, *Assoc Prof,* University of West Florida, Faculty of Art, Pensacola FL (S)

Marston, Edgar J, *Pres Board of Trustees,* La Jolla Museum of Contemporary Art, La Jolla CA

Marston, Rose, *Instr,* Danforth Museum School, Framingham MA (S)

Marter, Joan, *Asst Prof,* Rutgers, the State University of New Jersey, Graduate Program in Art History, New Brunswick NJ (S)

Martin, Anette, *Museum Aide,* Carrie McLain Museum, Nome AK

Martin, Bernice, *Dir Operations,* Museum of Science and Industry, Chicago IL

Martin, C Max, *Park Mgr,* Utah Natural Resources & Energy, Parks & Recreation, Territorial Statehouse, Fillmore UT

Martin, Don, *Asst Prof,* Flagler College, Visual Arts Dept, Saint Augustine FL (S)

Martin, Edean, *Visual Arts Dir,* Mid-America Arts Alliance, Kansas City MO

Martin, Ellen, *Asst Dir,* University of Northern Colorado, John Mariani Art Gallery, Greeley CO

Martin, Frederick, *Secy,* John D Barrow Art Gallery, Skaneateles NY

Martin, Gene, *Dir,* Daniel Boone Regional Library, Art Dept, Columbia MO

Martin, Gloria, *Lectr,* Notre Dame College, Art Dept, Manchester NH (S)

Martin, Irene, *Acting Dir,* Southern Methodist University, Meadows Gallery, Dallas TX

Martin, Jane, *Dir,* Saint Mary's Romanian Orthodox Church, Romanian Ethnic Museum, Cleveland OH

Martin, John, *Prof,* Wesleyan University, Art Dept, Middletown CT (S)

Martin, John H, *Deputy Dir Admin,* Corning Museum of Glass, Corning NY

Martin, John R, *Prof,* Princeton University, Dept of Art and Archaeology, Princeton NJ (S)

Martin, John Rupert, *VPres,* College Art Association of America, New York NY

Martin, Joseph, *Dir,* National Museums of Canada, National Gallery of Canada, Ottawa ON

Martin, Joseph, *Dir,* National Gallery of Canada, Ottawa ON

Martin, Karin, *Museum Secy,* Beaumont Art Museum, Beaumont TX

Martin, Laura B, *Asst Dir,* Roberson Center for the Arts and Sciences, Binghamton NY

Martin, Leo J, *Asst Dir,* Loyola University of Chicago, Martin D'Arcy Gallery of Art, Chicago IL

Martin, Lonna, *Office Secy,* Charles B Goddard Center for the Visual and Performing Arts, Ardmore OK

Martin, Loretta, *Asst Cur Coll,* El Paso Museum of Art, El Paso TX

Martin, Mary Abbe, *Public Information,* Walker Art Center, Minneapolis MN

Martin, Michel, *Conservator Contemporary Art,* Musee du Quebec, Quebec PQ

Martin, Ray, *Prof,* School of the Art Institute of Chicago, Chicago IL (S)

Martin, Robert, *Treas,* Toledo Federation of Art Societies, Toledo OH

Martin, Roger, *Design,* Montserrat School of Visual Art, Beverly MA (S)

Martin, Rosanne, *Slide Librn,* Montclair State College, Slide Library, Upper Montclair NJ

Martin, Suzanne, *Secy,* The Society of Arts and Crafts, Boston MA

Martin, Thomas, *Asst Prof,* New York Institute of Technology, Fine Arts Dept, Old Westbury NY (S)

Martin, Tony, *Dir,* Idaho State University, John B Davis Gallery of Fine Art, Pocatello ID

Martin, Vernon, *Dept Head,* Hartford Public Library, Hartford CT

Martinez, Albert, *Dir,* Ghost Ranch Living Museum, Abiquiu NM

Martinez, Bernice P, *Librn,* Harwood Foundation of the University of New Mexico, Library, Taos NM

Martinez, Dan, *Instr,* Mount San Jacinto College, Art Dept, San Jacinto CA (S)

Martinez, Edward W, *Chmn Dept,* University of Nevada, Reno, Art Dept, Reno NV (S)

Martinez, Ferdinand, *Lectr,* Aquinas College, Art Dept, Grand Rapids MI (S)

Martinez, Manual, *Instructor,* Cochise College, Art Dept, Douglas AZ (S)

Martin-Felton, Zora, *Education Program Dir,* Anacostia Neighborhood Museum, Washington DC

Martinsen, Richard, *Chmn,* Sheridan College, Art Dept, Sheridan WY (S)

Martinson, Robert, *Librn,* Housatonic Community College, Library, Bridgeport CT

Martz, James, *Librn,* Dickinson State College, Stoxen Library, Dickinson ND

Martz, Mary J, *Handicapped Services Coordr,* Junior Arts Center, Los Angeles CA

Marus, Lilian, *Executive Secy,* National Institute for Architectural Education, New York NY

Marvin, James C, *Dir,* Topeka Public Library, Fine Arts Dept & Gallery of Fine Arts, Topeka KS

Marvin, Miranda C, *Assoc Prof,* Wellesley College, Art Dept, Wellesley MA (S)

Marx, Gary, *Cur of Exhibits,* Anchorage Historical and Fine Arts Museum, Cook Inlet Historical Society, Anchorage AK

Marxhausen, Benjamin W, *Assoc Prof,* Concordia College, Art Dept, Saint Paul MN (S)

Marxhausen, Reinhold P, *Prof,* Concordia College, Art Dept, Seward NE (S)

Maryon, Edward, *Prof,* University of Utah, Art Dept, Salt Lake City UT (S)

Marzahn, Bruce, *Dir,* Daemen College, Daemen Gallery, Amherst NY

Marzahn, Bruce, *Assoc Prof,* Daemen College, Art Dept, Amherst NY (S)

Marzio, Peter C, *Dir,* Museum of Fine Arts, Houston, Houston TX

Marzo, Janet, *Cur,* Nassua Community College, Firehouse Gallery, Garden City NY

Masel, Marjorie, *Instr,* College of Saint Benedict, Art Dept, Saint Joseph MN (S)

Masin, Phil, *Instructor,* William Jewell College, Art Dept, Liberty MO (S)

Masler, Marilyn, *Registrar,* Memphis Brooks Museum of Art, Memphis TN

Masling, Annette, *Librn,* The Buffalo Fine Arts Academy, Art Reference Library, Buffalo NY

Mason, Benjamin, *Dir,* Shelburne Museum, Shelburne VT

Mason, Bonnie C, *Program & Public Relations Coordr,* Miami University Art Museum, Oxford OH

Mason, Charles E, *Honorary Cur of Prints,* Boston Athenaeum, Boston MA

Mason, Daniel, *Department Head,* Bethany College, Mingenback Art Center, Lindsborg KS

Mason, Elizabeth, *Prof,* Harding University, Dept of Art, Searcy AR (S)

Mason, Francis S, *Asst Dir,* Pierpont Morgan Library, New York NY

Mason, Glenn, *Dir,* Eastern Washington State Historical Society, Cheney Cowles Memorial Museum, Spokane WA

Mason, Helen S, *Dir,* Smith-Mason Gallery and Museum, Washington DC

Mason, Molly, *Asst Prof,* Tulane University, Sophie H Newcomb Memorial College, New Orleans LA (S)

McAlister, Roger Cornell, *Chmn Dept,* Lane Community College, Art and Applied Design Dept, Eugene OR (S)

McAllister, Gerry, *Dir,* University of California-San Diego, Mandeville Art Gallery, La Jolla CA

McAndrew, Dennis A, *Cur of Education,* Huntsville Museum of Art, Huntsville AL

McArt, Craig J, *Prof,* Rochester Institute of Technology, School of Art and Design, Rochester NY (S)

McArthur, Kenneth S, *Managing Dir,* Eva Brook Donly Museum, Simcoe ON

McAvity, John G, *Executive Dir,* Canadian Museums Association, Association des Musees Canadiens, Ottawa ON

McBeth, James R, *Prof,* Weber State College, Art Dept, Ogden UT (S)

McBoggs, Mayo, *Assoc Prof,* Converse College, Art Dept, Spartanburg SC (S)

McBratney-Stapleton, Deborah, *Executive Dir,* Anderson Fine Arts Center, Anderson IN

McBride, Alexander T, *Chmn Dept,* Juniata College, Dept of Art, Huntingdon PA (S)

McBride, Delbert J, *Cur,* State Capitol Museum, Olympia WA

McBride, Gordon, *Assoc Prof,* Westminster College, Dept of Art, Salt Lake City UT (S)

McBride, Peggy, *Reference Librn,* University of British Columbia, Fine Arts Division Library, Vancouver BC

McCabe, Judith, *Sales Mgr,* Portland Museum of Art, Portland ME

McCabe, Maureen, *Assoc Prof,* Connecticut College, Dept of Art, New London CT (S)

McCafferty, Jay, *Instructor,* Los Angeles Harbor College, Art Dept, Wilmington CA (S)

McCaffrey, Rosanne, *Cur & Syst Dir,* Historic New Orleans Collection, Kemper and Leila Williams Foundation, New Orleans LA

McCain, Deborah, *Pres,* Katonah Gallery, Katonah NY

McCall, L A, *Board Pres,* Florence Museum, Florence SC

McCallig, Patrick, *VPres,* Museum, Fine Arts Research & Holographic Center, Chicago IL

McCann, David, *Registrar,* Fine Arts Museum of the South, Mobile AL

McCarren, Paul, *Instructor,* Georgetown University, Dept of Fine Arts, Washington DC (S)

McCarroll, Bill, *Assoc Prof,* University of Lethbridge, Dept of Art, Lethbridge AB (S)

McCarroll, B J, *Gallery Dir,* University of Lethbridge, Art Gallery, Lethbridge AB

McCarron, John, *Cur Capricorn Asunder Gallery,* San Francisco City and County Art Commission, San Francisco CA

McCarthy, Dennis, *Prof,* Benedictine College, Art Dept, Atchison KS (S)

McCarthy, Gerard, *Program Dir,* Creative Time, New York NY

McCarthy, John R, *Treas,* Artists' Fellowship, Inc, New York NY

McCarthy, Paul, *Head Alaska & Polar Regions Collections,* University of Alaska, Elmer E Rasmuson Library, Fairbanks AK

McCarty, Gayle, *Dir,* Hinds Junior College District, Marie Hull Gallery, Raymond MS

McCarty, Mary, *Grad Division Chair,* School of the Art Institute of Chicago, Chicago IL (S)

McCarty, Michael, *Instructor,* Utica Junior College, Humanities Division, Utica MS (S)

McCarty, Timothy L, *Asst Dir,* University of Minnesota, Paul Whitney Larson Gallery, Saint Paul MN

McCaslin, Jack, *Assoc Prof,* James Madison University, Dept of Art, Harrisonburg VA (S)

McCaulay, Janet, *Mgr Community Arts Center,* Fort Wayne Fine Arts Foundation, Inc, Fort Wayne IN

McCauley, Gardiner R, *Executive Dir,* Montalvo Center for the Arts, Saratoga CA

McCausland, Samuel B, *Instructor,* Central Academy of Commercial Art, Cincinnati OH (S)

MccCormick, James, *Prof,* University of Wisconsin-Stout, Art Dept, Menomonie WI (S)

McChesney, Clif, *Instructor,* Michigan State University, Leland Summer Art School, Leland MI (S)

McClain, Bruce A, *Chmn,* Gustavus Adolphus College, Art Dept, Saint Peter MN (S)

McClain, Sam, *Treasurer,* Alaska Artists' Guild, Anchorage AK

McClanahan, John D, *Instr,* Baylor University, Dept of Fine Arts, Waco TX (S)

McClary, Larry, *Drawing,* California College of Arts and Crafts, Oakland CA (S)

McCleary, Mary, *Dir,* Stephen F Austin State University, Art Gallery, Nacogdoches TX

McCleary, Peter, *Chmn Grad Group,* University of Pennsylvania, Dept of Architecture, Philadelphia PA (S)

McClecny, Charles, *Chmn 3-D Area,* Edinboro University of Pennsylvania, Art Dept, Edinboro PA (S)

McClendon, Max, *Instructor,* Southeastern Oklahoma State College, Art Dept, Durant OK (S)

McClennan, Peter, *Instr,* Alfred C Glassell School of Art, Houston TX (S)

McClenney, Cheryl, *Asst Dir Program,* Philadelphia Museum of Art, Philadelphia PA

McCloud, Darlene, *Dir,* Municipal Art Society of New York, Information Exchange, New York NY

McCloy, Norah, *Music Librn,* Banff Centre, School of Fine Arts Library, Banff AB

McClung, Millard, *Assoc Dir,* Oregon Historical Society, Portland OR

McClure, Nell, *Asst Cur Education,* Minnesota Museum of Art, Saint Paul MN

McCluskey, John, *Lectr,* Bucknell University, Dept of Art, Lewisburg PA (S)

McCollum, Michael L, *Assoc Prof,* University of Nevada, Las Vegas, Dept of Art, Las Vegas NV (S)

McComb, Ron, *Librn,* Cornish Institute, Library, Seattle WA

McCombs, Bruce, *Asst Prof,* Hope College, Art Dept, Holland MI (S)

McCommons, R, *Executive Dir,* Association of Collegiate Schools of Architecture, Washington DC

McConahay, Janis, *Instr,* Heidelberg College, Dept of Art, Tiffin OH (S)

McConathy, Deirdre, *Instructor,* University of Illinois, Chicago, Health Science Center, Dept of Biocommunication Arts, Chicago IL (S)

McCone, Michael, *Deputy Dir,* San Francisco Museum of Modern Art, San Francisco CA

McConnell, Michael, *Assoc Prof,* University of New Hampshire, Dept of the Arts, Durham NH (S)

McConson, Marcus A, *Dir & Librn,* American Antiquarian Society, Library, Worcester MA

McConville, Rebecca, *Dir Admissions,* Ringling School of Art and Design, Sarasota FL (S)

McCord, David, *Exec Dir,* Confederation of American Indians, Council of American Indian Artists, New York NY

McCord, Marie M, *Prof,* Oakland City College, Division of Fine Arts, Oakland City IN (S)

McCorison, Marcus A, *Dir,* American Antiquarian Society, Worcester MA

McCorkle, Helen, *Treasurer,* Gallery North, Setauket NY

McCormick, Charles James, *Chmn,* Georgetown College, Art Dept, Georgetown KY (S)

McCormick, James, *Chmn,* Georgetown College Gallery, Georgetown KY

McCormick, John, *Assoc Prof,* Delta College, Art Dept, University Center MI (S)

McCormick, Maureen, *Dir Touring Exhibitions Program,* The Ohio Foundation on the Arts, Inc, Columbus OH

McCourt, Mike, *Art Cur,* Montana Historical Society, Library, Helena MT

McCoy, Elinor Sue, *Cur Educational Services,* University of Utah, Utah Museum of Fine Arts, Salt Lake City UT

McCoy, Evelyn, *Sr Dir,* Arkansas Arts Center, Little Rock AR

McCoy, Evelyn, *Dir,* Arkansas Arts Center, Elizabeth Prewitt Taylor Memorial Library, Little Rock AR

McCoy, Garnett, *Sr Cur,* Archives of American Art, Washington Center, New York NY

McCoy, Katherine, *Exec VPres,* Industrial Designers Society of America, McLean VA

McCoy, Katherine, *Assoc Head Design Dept,* Cranbrook Academy of Art, Bloomfield Hills MI (S)

McCoy, L Frank, *Chmn,* University of Montevallo, College of Fine Arts, Montevallo AL (S)

McCoy, Michael, *Assoc Head Design Dept,* Cranbrook Academy of Art, Bloomfield Hills MI (S)

McCoy, Nancy, *Asst Dir,* Woodrow Wilson House, Washington DC

McCoy, Robert, *Instructor,* San Jacinto College North, Art Dept, Houston TX (S)

McCoy, Robin, *Instr,* Ocean City Arts Center, Ocean City NJ (S)

McCoy, Sally, *Instructor,* La Roche College, Division of Graphics, Design, Pittsburgh PA (S)

McCracken, Patrick, *Cur,* The Art Center, Waco TX

McCracken, Peggie, *Cur Kirkpatrick Ctr,* Oklahoma Center for Science and Art, Kirkpatrick Center, Oklahoma City OK

McCrady, Howard, *VPres,* Phoenix Art Museum, Phoenix AZ

McCready, Eric, *Dir,* University of Texas at Austin, Archer M Huntington Art Gallery, Austin TX

McCready, Reyburn R, *Librn,* University of Oregon, School of Architecture and Allied Arts Library, Eugene OR

McCredie, James R, *Dir,* New York University, Institute of Fine Arts, New York NY (S)

McCroskey, Nancy, *Asst Prof,* Indiana University-Purdue University, Dept of Fine Arts, Fort Wayne IN (S)

McCue, Harry, *Chmn,* Ithaca College, Fine Art Dept, Ithaca NY (S)

McCuistion, Fred, *Pres,* Council of Ozark Artists and Craftsmen, Inc, Arts Center of the Ozarks Gallery, Springdale AR

McCulley, Clyde E, *Dir,* Munson-Williams-Proctor Institute, School of Art, Utica NY (S)

McCulloch-Lovell, Ellen, *Secy,* National Assembly of State Arts Agencies, Washington DC

McCullough, Joseph, *Pres,* Cleveland Institute of Art, Cleveland OH

McCullough, Joseph, *Pres,* Cleveland Institute of Art, Cleveland OH (S)

McCullum, Ann M, *Secy,* Victoria Society of Maine, Victoria Mansion and Morse Libby Mansion, Portland ME

McCune, Ellis E, *Pres,* California State University, Hayward, University Art Gallery, Hayward CA

McCutchen, Kathryn, *Cur Asst,* Department of State, Diplomatic Reception Rooms, Washington DC

McDade, George C, *Faculty,* Monroe Community College, Art Dept, Rochester NY (S)

McDaniel, Craig, *Dir,* Southern Ohio Museum Corporation, Southern Ohio Museum & Cultural Center, Portsmouth OH

McDaniel, Jean Robertson, *Dir,* Southern Ohio Museum Corporation, Southern Ohio Museum & Cultural Center, Portsmouth OH

McDermand, Robert V, *Coordr Public Services,* Plymouth State College, Herbert H Lamson Library, Plymouth NH

McDermott, Mary Ellen, *Prof,* Cleveland Institute of Art, Cleveland OH (S)

McDonald, Arthur W, *Chmn,* College of Charleston, Fine Arts Dept, Charleston SC (S)

McDonald, Carolyn R, *Registrar,* Illinois State University, Center for the Visual Arts Gallery, Normal IL

McDonald, Dianne, *Publicity & General Asst,* Virginia Museum, Danville Museum of Fine Arts and History, Danville VA

McDonald, Robert, *Coordr Art,* Cape Cod Community College, Art Dept, West Barnstable MA (S)

McDonald, Robert, *Dir,* The Art Museum of Santa Cruz County, Santa Cruz CA

McDonnell, Gordon, *Asst Dir,* Yellowstone Art Center, Billings MT

McDonnell, Maureen, *Instr,* Seton Hill College, Dept of Art, Greensburg PA (S)

McDonough, Eileen, *Assoc Dean,* Barry University, Dept of Art, Miami Shores FL (S)

McLaughlin, Victor, *Pres,* Oak Ridge Community Art Center & Museum of Fine Arts, Oak Ridge TN

McLean, Barbara, *Dir Development,* The New Gallery of Contemporary Art, Cleveland OH

McLean, Barrie, *Lecturer,* University of Victoria, Dept of History in Art, Victoria BC (S)

McLean, Harriet, *Exec Dir,* Boston Center for Adult Education, Boston MA (S)

McLean, Peter, *Assoc Prof,* Hartford Art School of the University of Hartford, West Hartford CT (S)

McLelland, Patricia, *Pres,* Canadian Crafts Council, Conseil Canadien de l'Artisanat, Ottawa ON

McLendon, James, *Faculty,* Virginia Intermont College, Fine Arts Dept, Bristol VA (S)

McLendon, Marty, *Chmn,* Northeast Mississippi Junior College, Art Dept, Booneville MS (S)

McLennan, Bill, *Graphic Designer, Photographer,* University of British Columbia, Museum of Anthropology, Vancouver BC

McLeod, Don, *Chmn,* Mount Royal College, Dept Interior Design, Calgary AB (S)

McLeod, Phyllis A, *Dir,* Fayetteville Museum of Art, Inc, Fayetteville NC

McLeod, Robert W, *Recording Secy,* Lowell Art Association, Whistler House and Parker Gallery, Lowell MA

Mcllink, Machteld, *Pres,* Archaeological Institute of America, Boston MA

McMahan, Robert, *Prof,* Antelope Valley College, Art Dept, Division of Fine Arts, Lancaster CA (S)

McMahon, James, *Prof,* Manatee Junior College, Dept of Art, Bradenton FL (S)

McMahon, Sharon, *Dir,* Saint Mary's University of San Antonio, Dept of Fine Arts, San Antonio TX (S)

McMahon, Therese M, *Gallery Asst,* Arco Center for Visual Art, Los Angeles CA

McManus, G Louis, *Supt,* Sterling and Francine Clark Art Institute, Williamstown MA

McManus, James, *Instr,* California State University, Chico, Art Dept, Chico CA (S)

McManus, James W, *Gallery Dir,* California State University, Chico, Art Gallery, Chico CA

McManus, Kathleen, *Installations,* College of Wooster Art Center Museum, Wooster OH

McMenomy, Robert, *Instructor,* Long Beach City College, Dept of Art, Long Beach CA (S)

McMichael, Robert, *Dir,* McMichael Canadian Collection, Kleinburg ON

McMillan, Adell, *Dir,* University of Oregon, Aperture: Photo Gallery, Eugene OR

McMillan, Alma, *Shops Mgr,* Sunrise Foundation, Inc, Sunrise Museums, Charleston WV

McMillan, Collin, *Chmn,* Confederation Centre Art Gallery and Museum, Charlottetown PE

McMillan, David, *Chmn Photography,* University of Manitoba, School of Art, Winnipeg MB (S)

McMillan, Kenneth L, *Assoc Prof,* University of North Florida, Dept of Fine Arts, Jacksonville FL (S)

McMillan, Konrad, *Instr,* Taft College, Division of Performing Arts, Taft CA (S)

McMillan, R Bruce, *Dir,* Illinois State Museum of Natural History and Art, Springfield IL

McMillan, Rosemary D, *Secy,* Sierra Arts Foundation, Reno NV

McMillion, James E, *Prof,* Rochester Institute of Technology, School of Photographic Arts & Sciences, Rochester NY (S)

McMorris, Penny, *Cur,* Owens-Corning Fiberglas Corporation, Toledo OH

McNairn, Alan, *Dir,* New Brunswick Museum, Saint John NB

McNally, Dennis, *Asst Prof,* Saint Joseph's University, Fine Arts Dept, Philadelphia PA (S)

McNally, Sheila, *Prof,* University of Minnesota, Minneapolis, Art History, Minneapolis MN (S)

McNamara, Thomas, *Controller,* Museum of the City of New York, New York NY

McNamara, Victor D, *Asst Cur,* Presidio of Monterey Army Museum, Monterey CA

McNamara, Walter, *Gallery Cur,* University of Nevada, Reno, Reno NV

McNamee, Harriet, *Cur,* Towson State University, Roberts Gallery, Towson MD

McNaught, William, *Dir,* Archives of American Art, New York Area Center, New York NY

McNaughton, James W, *Prof,* Indiana State University, Evansville, Art Dept, Evansville IN (S)

McNaughton, Patrick, *Assoc Prof,* Indiana University, Bloomington, School of Fine Arts, Bloomington IN (S)

McNealy, Earnest, *Assoc Prof,* Claflin College, Dept of Art, Orangeburg SC (S)

McNealy, Terry A, *Librn,* Bucks County Historical Society, Spruance Library, Doylestown PA

McNeil, David K, *Dir,* Chatham Cultural Centre, Chatham ON

McNeil, Donald B, *Art Cur,* General Mills, Inc, Minneapolis MN

McNeill, Lloyd, *Assoc Prof,* Rutgers, the State University of New Jersey, Mason Gross School of the Arts, New Brunswick NJ (S)

McNutt, James, *Asst Prof,* University of Alabama, Art Dept, Tuscaloosa AL (S)

McPhail, Donald W, *Pres,* Print Club, Philadelphia PA

McPhail, Edna, *Pres,* South Peace Art Society, Dawson Creek Art Gallery, Dawson Creek BC

McPheeters, E Keith, *Dean,* Auburn University, Dept of Art, Auburn AL (S)

McPhersom, Heather, *Asst Prof,* University of Alabama in Birmingham, Dept of Art, Birmingham AL (S)

McPherson, C R, *VPres,* Wilmington Trust Company, Wilmington DE

McQuay, Paul L, *Dir Dept,* Williamsport Area Community College, Dept of Engineering and Design, Williamsport PA (S)

McQuillan, Frances, *Instructor,* Montclair Art Museum, Museum Art Classes, Montclair NJ (S)

McQuiston, William, *Dir,* Rensselaer Newman Foundation Chapel and Cultural Center, Troy NY

McRae, Donald C, *Dean Col,* University of New Mexico, College of Fine Arts, Albuquerque NM (S)

McRae, Marylee, *Gallery Coordr,* The Marine Corporation, Milwaukee WI

McRae, R G, *Head Dept,* Valdosta State College, Dept of Art, Valdosta GA (S)

McRae, R S, *Head Art Dept,* Valdosta State College, Art Gallery, Valdosta GA

McRaven, Donald B, *Assoc Prof,* Moorhead State University, Dept of Art, Moorhead MN (S)

McRoberts, Jerry, *Assoc Prof,* Eastern Illinois University, School of Fine Arts, Charleston IL (S)

McRoberts, Michele, *Instructor,* Roger Williams College, Art Dept, Bristol RI (S)

McSheffrey, Gerald R, *Dean,* Arizona State University, College of Architecture, Tempe AZ (S)

McVaugh, Robert, *Asst Prof,* Colgate University, Dept of Fine Arts, Hamilton NY (S)

McVity, Patsy B, *Cur,* Concord Art Association, Concord MA

McWayne, Barry J, *Coordr Photog,* University of Alaska, Museum, Fairbanks AK

McWhinney, Madeline, *Asst Dir Operations,* Whitney Museum of American Art, New York NY

McWhorter, Jean, *Supervisor,* Richland Art Workshop, Columbia SC (S)

McWhorter, Mark, *Instructor,* Indian Hills Community College, Dept of Art, Centerville IA (S)

McWhorter, Mark, *Instructor,* Indian Hills Community College, Ottumwa Campus, Dept of Art, Ottumwa IA (S)

McWilliams, David Jackson, *Dir,* La Casa del Libro, Library, San Juan PR

Mead-Desehenes, Mary, *Instr,* Danforth Museum School, Framingham MA (S)

Meader, Robert F W, *Librn,* Hancock Shaker Village, Inc, Hancock Shaker Village Library, Pittsfield MA

Meadows, Donald F, *Library Bd Dir,* Metropolitan Toronto Library Board, Fine Art Dept, Toronto ON

Meadows, Lorena D, *Secy,* Morgan State University Gallery of Art, Baltimore MD

Meadows, Patricia B, *Pres,* D-Art, A Visual Arts Center for Dallas, Dallas TX

Meadows, Patricia B, *Program Dir,* D-Art, A Visual Arts Center for Dallas, Dallas TX

Meads, Arthur, *Head Alberta Col Art,* Alberta College of Art, Southern Alberta Institute of Technology, Calgary AB (S)

Meakin, Alexander C, *Pres,* Great Lakes Historical Society, Vermilion OH

Meals, Joseph, *VPres,* Cleveland Museum of Art, Print Club of Cleveland, Cleveland OH

Meany, Phillip, *Assoc Prof,* University of Minnesota, Duluth, Art Dept, Duluth MN (S)

Meany, Phillip, *Assoc Prof,* University of Minnesota, Duluth, Art Dept, Duluth MN (S)

Mear, Margaret, *Asst Prof,* Saint Mary's College, Art Dept, Winona MN (S)

Mecham, John, *Cur Herpetology & Ichthyology,* Texas Tech University Museum, Lubbock TX

Medina, Dennis, *Museum Cur,* Dwight D Eisenhower Presidential Library, Abilene KS

Medley, Ronald, *Dept Head,* Allen County Community College, Art Dept, Iola KS (S)

Medlock, Rudy, *Head Art Dept,* Asbury College, Student Center Gallery, Wilmore KY

Meehan, William, *Chmn,* DePauw University, Art Dept, Greencastle IN (S)

Meek, A J, *Assoc Prof,* Louisiana State University, School of Art, Baton Rouge LA (S)

Meek, Carol, *Pres,* Lubbock Art Association, Inc, Lubbock TX

Meeker, Barbara M, *Chmn Art Committee,* Purdue University Calumet, Bicentennial Library Gallery, Hammond IN

Meeker, David Olan, *Exec VPres,* American Institute of Architects, Washington DC

Meeks, Francis, *Treasurer,* Kenai Historical Society Inc, Kenai Community Historical Center, Kenai AK

Meeks, Roger, *Pres,* Kenai Historical Society Inc, Kenai Community Historical Center, Kenai AK

Meens, A, *Chmn,* Art Gallery of Brant, Inc, Brantford ON

Meeusen, Richard, *Treas,* Milwaukee Center for Photography, Milwaukee WI (S)

Megan, Ralph, *Executive Dir,* Quapaw Quarter Association, Inc, Preservation Resource Center, Little Rock AR

Megorden, Winston, *Instr,* California State University, Chico, Art Dept, Chico CA (S)

Meidinger, Sandy, *Asst,* Custer County Art Center, Miles City MT

Meinhardt, Nevin, *Dir Advertising Design,* Art Institute of Fort Lauderdale, Fort Lauderdale FL (S)

Meinig, Laurel, *Executive Dir,* First Street Forum, Saint Louis MO

Meinwald, Dan, *Registrar & Cur,* University of California, California Museum of Photography, Riverside CA

Meixner, Laura, *Asst Prof,* Cornell University, Dept of the History of Art, Ithaca NY (S)

Meizner, Karen L, *Head Cataloger,* Atkins Museum of Fine Art, Kenneth and Helen Spencer Art Reference Library, Kansas City MO

Mejer, Robert Lee, *Gallery Dir,* Quincy College, Art Gallery, Quincy IL

Mekas, Adolfas, *Dir Program,* Bard College, Milton Avery Graduate School of the Arts, Annandale-on-Hudson NY (S)

Mekkawi, Mod, *Librn,* Howard University, Architecture & Planning Library, Washington DC

Melber, Robert, *Cur Antique Auto Museum,* Heritage Plantation of Sandwich, Sandwich MA

Melberg, Jerald, *Cur of Exhib,* Mint Museum of Art, Charlotte NC

Melby, David, *Lectr,* Saint Mary College, Art Dept, Leavenworth KS (S)

Melchert, James S, *Chmn,* University of California, Berkeley, College of Letters & Sciences, Berkeley CA (S)

Meline, Elva, *Cur,* San Fernando Valley Historical Society, Mission Hills CA

Melion, Walter, *Asst Prof,* Duke University, Dept of Art, Durham NC (S)

Mellinger, Sydney S, *Librn,* Lake Forest Library, Fine Art Dept, Lake Forest IL

Mellon, Paul, *Chmn Board of Trustees,* National Gallery of Art, Washington DC

Mellown, Robert, *Assoc Prof,* University of Alabama, Art Dept, Tuscaloosa AL (S)

Melnyk, Nadia, *Secy,* Ukrainian Cultural and Educational Centre Museum, Winnipeg MB

Melson, Claudia F, *Cur Registration,* Division of Historical and Cultural Affairs, Bureau of Museums and Historic Sites, Dover DE

Melton, Nancy, *Assoc Dir,* Mariners Museum, Newport News VA

Melton, Willard, *Instructor,* Sacramento City College, Art Dept, Sacramento CA (S)

Meltzer, Stephen, *Asst Prof,* University of Southern California, School of Fine Arts, Los Angeles CA (S)

Melvin, Douglas, *Faculty,* North Central Michigan College, Art Dept, Petoskey MI (S)

Melvin, Edwards, *Prof,* Rutgers, the State University of New Jersey, Mason Gross School of the Arts, New Brunswick NJ (S)

Menapace, Ralph C, *Pres,* Municipal Art Society of New York, New York NY

Menard, Andre, *Dir,* Musee d'Art Contemporain, Montreal PQ

Menard, Lloyd, *Prof,* University of South Dakota, Dept of Art, Vermillion SD (S)

Mendelson, Haim, *Pres,* Federation of Modern Painters and Sculptors, New York NY

Mendenhall, Bethany, *Assoc Librn,* J Paul Getty Museum, Research Library, Malibu CA

Mendenhall, Jan, *Pres,* Allied Arts Council of the Yakima Valley, Yakima WA

Mendenhall, John, *Assoc Prof,* California Polytechnic State University at San Luis Obispo, Art Dept, San Luis Obispo CA (S)

Mendenhall, Pam, *Dept Head, Interior Design,* The Design Schools, Art Institute of Houston, Houston TX (S)

Mendez, Charles, *Instr,* Maryland College of Art and Design, Silver Spring MD (S)

Mendro, Donna, *Recordings Librn,* Dallas Public Library, Fine Arts Division, Dallas TX

Menger, Linda, *Asst Prof,* Delta College, Art Dept, University Center MI (S)

Menges, Edward, *Prof,* Saint Louis Community College at Florissant Valley, Dept of Art, Ferguson MO (S)

Menn, Richard J, *Cur,* Carmel Mission and Gift Shop, Carmel CA

Menschel, Robert B, *Chmn,* Guild Hall of East Hampton, Inc, Museum Section, East Hampton NY

Mentzer, Robert, *Pres,* Licking County Art Association Gallery, Newark OH

Menzies, Neal, *Library Dir,* Otis Art Institute of Parsons School of Design Gallery, Library, Los Angeles CA

Mercer, David, *Instructor,* The Design Schools, Art Institute of Seattle, Seattle WA (S)

Merchant, John, *Instr,* Lakeland Community College, Visual Arts Dept, Mentor OH (S)

Mercier, Guy, *Educatives Services,* Musee du Quebec, Quebec PQ

Merendino, Janice, *Instr,* Rosemont College, Division of the Arts, Rosemont PA (S)

Merkel, Bernadette, *Chmn,* Rochester Institute of Technology, School of Art and Design, Rochester NY (S)

Merkel, Robert, *Pres,* Monroe City-County Fine Arts Council, Monroe MI

Merrell, C Phelps, *Supt,* Norton Gallery and School of Art, West Palm Beach FL

Merriam, Gail, *Chmn,* Fine Arts Museums of San Francisco, The Museum Society, San Francisco CA

Merrick, Gail, *Instructor,* The Design Schools, Art Institute of Seattle, Seattle WA (S)

Merrick, Robert S, *Trustee,* Merrick Art Gallery, New Brighton PA

Merrill, Lawrence, *Lectr,* Nazareth College of Rochester, Art Dept, Rochester NY (S)

Merrill, Nancy O, *Cur Glass,* Chrysler Museum, Norfolk VA

Merrill, Ross, *Conservator,* National Gallery of Art, Washington DC

Merritt, Douglas, *Dir,* University of North Carolina at Greensboro, Chinqua-Penn Plantation House, Reidsville NC

Merritt, Raymond, *Liberal Arts,* Minneapolis College of Art and Design, Minneapolis MN (S)

Merritt, Richard, *Assoc Prof,* University of New Hampshire, Dept of the Arts, Durham NH (S)

Merrow, Sharon, *Membership Secy,* William A Farnsworth Library and Art Museum, Rockland ME

Merson, Bob, *Pres,* Meridian Museum of Art, Meridian MS

Mertens, Joan R, *Cur Greek & Roman Art,* Metropolitan Museum of Art, New York NY

Mertes, Charles, *Gallery Dir,* Westmar College, Mock Memorial Art Gallery, LeMars IA

Mesler, James, *Asst Dir Operations,* Queens Museum, Flushing NY

Mesmer, Richard E, *Secy,* The Stained Glass Association of America, Saint Louis MO

Messer, Thomas M, *Dir,* Solomon R Guggenheim Museum, New York NY

Messersmith, Fred, *Dir,* Stetson University, Art Gallery, De Land FL

Messersmith, Fred, *Head Dept,* Stetson University, Art Dept, De Land FL (S)

Messineo, Len, *Art & Music Dept Head,* Wichita Public Library, Wichita KS

Meszaros, Imre, *Librn,* Washington University, Art and Architecture Library, Saint Louis MO

Metcalf, C E, *Executive Dir,* Oklahoma Historical Society, Central Museum, Oklahoma City OK

Metcalf, William E, *Chief Cur,* American Numismatic Society, New York NY

Metcalfe, Dorothy, *Information Officer,* Vancouver Art Gallery, Vancouver BC

Metcalfe, Elizabeth, *Adjunct Instr,* Maryville College, St Louis, Art Division, Saint Louis MO (S)

Metcoff, Don, *Librn,* American Society of Artists, Inc, Library, Chicago IL

Metraux, M, *Cur,* York University, Fine Arts Slide Library, Downsview ON

Metsopoulos, Marian J, *Exec Dir,* Foothills Art Center, Inc, Golden CO

Metsopoulos, Marian J, *Exec Dir,* Foothills Art Center, Inc, Golden CO (S)

Mettier, Jack, *Chmn Div,* Taft College, Division of Performing Arts, Taft CA (S)

Metz, Carolyn J, *Dir Visual Resources & Servs,* Indianapolis Museum of Art, Visual Resources & Services, Indianapolis IN

Metz, Rinda, *Asst Prof,* Ohio Wesleyan University, Fine Arts Dept, Delaware OH (S)

Metzger, Ann, *Pres,* Saint Louis Artists' Guild, Saint Louis MO

Metzger, Judy, *Asst Librn,* Long Island Historical Society, Library, Brooklyn NY

Metzger, Robert, *Art Dir,* Stamford Museum and Nature Center, Stamford CT

Metzker, Dale, *Asst Prof,* Williamsport Area Community College, Dept of Engineering and Design, Williamsport PA (S)

Meunier, Brian A, *Asst Prof,* Swarthmore College, Dept of Art, Swarthmore PA (S)

Mew, T J, *Chmn,* Berry College, Art Dept, Mount Berry GA (S)

Mew, T J, *Chmn,* Berry College, Moon Library, Mount Berry GA

Meyberg, Nancy, *Coordr,* Santa Cruz Art Center, Santa Cruz CA

Meyer, Barbara, *Chmn & Prof,* Mary Washington College, Art Dept, Fredericksburg VA (S)

Meyer, Charles E, *Dir,* Bradley University, Division of Art, Peoria IL (S)

Meyer, Eileen, *Second VPres,* Marian Osborne Cunningham Art Gallery, Bakersfield CA

Meyer, Elisabeth, *Asst Prof,* Cornell University, Dept of Art, Ithaca NY (S)

Meyer, Fred, *Prof,* Rochester Institute of Technology, School of Art and Design, Rochester NY (S)

Meyer, Helen L, *Secy,* Bergen Museum of Art & Science, Paramus NJ

Meyer, Inga, *Pres,* New Rochelle Public Library, New Rochelle Art Association, New Rochelle NY

Meyer, Irving, *Chmn Trustee Committee,* George Walter Vincent Smith Art Museum, Springfield MA

Meyer, Joan L, *Head Technical Servs & Ref Dept,* Springfield Free Public Library, Donald B Palmer Museum, Springfield NJ

Meyer, Otto, *VPres,* The Friends of Photography, Carmel CA

Meyer, Robert, *Chmn Division,* Sierra College, Art Dept, Rocklin CA (S)

Meyer, Ruth K, *Dir Taft Musuem,* Taft Museum, Cincinnati OH

Meyer, Ursula, *Prof Emeritus,* Herbert H Lehman College, Art Dept, Bronx NY (S)

Meyers, Dale, *Active Honorary Pres,* American Watercolor Society, New York NY

Meyers, Dan, *Dir Development,* International Museum of Photography at George Eastman House, Rochester NY

Meyers, Francis, *Prof,* Cleveland Institute of Art, Cleveland OH (S)

Meyers, Mary, *Librn,* Cowboy Artists of America Museum, Library, Kerrville TX

Meyers, Ronald, *Ceramics,* University of Georgia, Franklin College of Arts and Sciences, Dept of Art, Athens GA (S)

Mezzatesta, Michael, *Assoc Cur European Art,* Kimbell Art Museum, Fort Worth TX

Michael, Carola, *Pres,* Queens Museum, Flushing NY

Michael, J R, *Pres,* Safety Harbor Museum of History and Fine Arts, Safety Harbor FL

Michael, Simon, *Head Dept,* Simon Michael School of Fine Arts, Rockport TX (S)

Michaelides, C, *Dean School,* Washington University, School of Architecture, Saint Louis MO (S)

Michaels, Marion, *Dean School Liberal Arts,* Auburn University at Montgomery, Art Dept, Montgomery AL (S)

Michaels, Rebecca, *Programs Coordr,* Anderson County Arts Council, Anderson SC

Michaely, Alina, *Dir Fine Arts,* Saidye Bronfman Centre, Montreal PQ

Michala, Mollie, *Lecturer,* Emory University, Art History Dept, Atlanta GA (S)

Michalak, Thomas J, *Dir of University Libraries,* Carnegie-Mellon University, Hunt Library, Pittsburgh PA

Michalik, Chester, *Assoc Prof,* Smith College, Art Dept, Northampton MA (S)

Michaux, Henry G, *Assoc Prof,* South Carolina State College, Art Program, Orangeburg SC (S)

Michel, Delbert, *Chmn,* Hope College, Art Dept, Holland MI (S)

Micheli, Julio, *Prof,* Catholic University of Puerto Rico, Dept of Fine Arts, Ponce PR (S)

Michels, Eileen, *Secy,* Society of Architectural Historians, Philadelphia PA

Michlosky, Pamela, *Business Mgr,* The Rockwell Museum, Corning NY

Mick, Cheryl, *Admin Dir,* D-Art, A Visual Arts Center for Dallas, Dallas TX

Micka, David P, *Cultural Affairs Committee,* Springfield College, Hasting Gallery, Springfield MA

Mickelson, Duane, *Instr,* Concordia College, Art Dept, Moorhead MN (S)

Mickenberg, David, *Dir,* Oklahoma Museum of Art, Oklahoma City OK

Miclau, Daniel, *Pres,* Saint Mary's Romanian Orthodox Church, Romanian Ethnic Museum, Cleveland OH

Midani, Akram, *Dean,* Carnegie-Mellon University, College of Fine Arts, Pittsburgh PA (S)

Middaugh, Robert, *Cur,* The First National Bank of Chicago, Chicago IL

Middlekauff, Robert, *Dir,* Huntington Library, Art Gallery and Botanical Gardens, San Marino CA

Middlesworth-Kohn, Vicki, *Asst Cur Educ,* Western Kentucky University, Kentucky Museum, Bowling Green KY

Miele, John, *Dir Fashion Illustration,* Art Institute of Fort Lauderdale, Fort Lauderdale FL (S)

Mier, Norman, *Dept Head,* Ray-Vogue College of Design, Chicago IL (S)

Miezats, Dainis, *Actg Chmn Dept Fine Art,* Ontario College of Art, Toronto ON (S)

Mihailovic, Olivera, *Cur,* University of Chicago, Art Slide Collection, Chicago IL

Mihal, Milan, *Assoc Prof,* Vanderbilt University, Dept of Fine Arts, Nashville TN (S)

Mihas, Jane, *Instructor,* Mount Mary College, Art Dept, Milwaukee WI (S)

Mijares, Maria, *Exhibit Chair,* Tweed Arts Group, Plainfield NJ

Mikus, Eleanore, *Assoc Prof,* Cornell University, Dept of Art, Ithaca NY (S)

Milan, George, *Dir Performing Arts Division,* City of Los Angeles, Cultural Affairs Dept, Los Angeles CA

Miles, Christine, *Dir,* Fraunces Tavern Museum, New York NY

Miles, David, *Faculty,* Ohio University Belmont County Campus, Art Dept, Saint Clairsville OH (S)

Miles, Grady Garfield, *Prof,* Barber-Scotia College, Art Dept, Concord NC (S)

Miles, Linda, *Cur Education,* Institute of the Great Plains, Museum of the Great Plains, Lawton OK

Miley, Les, *Chmn Art Dept,* University of Evansville, Krannert Gallery, Evansville IN

Miley, Leslie, *Dept Head,* University of Evansville, Art Dept, Evansville IN (S)

Miley, Mimi, *Cur Educ,* Allentown Art Museum, Allentown PA

Milford, Frovies, *Chmn of Trustees,* John D Barrow Art Gallery, Skaneateles NY

Milhoan, Randy, *Dir,* Colorado Mountain College, Summervail Workshop for Art & Critical Studies, Vail CO (S)

Milkovich, Michael, *Dir,* Museum of Fine Arts of Saint Petersburg, Florida, Inc, Saint Petersburg FL

Millar, James S, *Treas,* Portsmouth Athenaeum NR, Inc 1817, Portsmouth NH

Millard, Charles, *Chief Cur,* Hirshhorn Museum and Sculpture Garden, Washington DC

Millener, Linda, *Pres,* Brookfield Craft Center, Inc Gallery, Brookfield CT

Miller, A, *Vol Librn,* Vizcaya Museum and Gardens, Library, Miami FL

Miller, Arch M, *Chmn,* University of Rochester, Dept of Fine Arts, Rochester NY (S)

Miller, Ardyce L, *Instructor,* Bismarck Junior College, Art Dept, Bismarck ND (S)

Miller, Barbara, *Chmn,* Maui Community College, Art Dept, Kahului HI (S)

Miller, Bill, *VPres,* Morse Gallery of Art, Winter Park FL

Miller, Bob, *Assoc Dir Exhibit Design,* Exploratorium, San Francisco CA

Miller, Bobbie, *Cur Entomology & Registrar,* San Bernardino County Museum and Satellites, Fine Arts Institute, Redlands CA

Miller, Burnett, *Cur,* La Jolla Museum of Contemporary Art, La Jolla CA

Miller, Carol, *Specialist,* Galeria Mesa, Cultural Activities Dept, Mesa AZ

Miller, Carol, *Museum Asst,* Arizona State University, University Art Collections, Tempe AZ

Miller, Danny, *Instr,* Haskell Indian Junior College, Art Dept, Lawrence KS (S)

Miller, David, *Dir,* Skidmore College, Art Gallery, Saratoga Springs NY

Miller, Donald, *Secy,* National Sculpture Society, New York NY

Miller, Edward C, *Assoc Prof,* Rochester Institute of Technology, School of Art and Design, Rochester NY (S)

Miller, Eleanor, *Secy,* Boothbay Region Art Foundation, Inc, Brick House Gallery, Boothbay Harbor ME

Miller, Elinor S, *Chmn,* Saint Mary's College of Maryland, Arts and Letters Division, Saint Mary's City MD (S)

Miller, Harriet S, *Exec Dir,* Palos Verdes Art Center, Rancho Palos Verdes CA

Miller, Helga, *Librn,* Winnipeg Sketch Club, Library, Winnipeg MB

Miller, H Ray, *Dir,* Riverside Art Center and Museum, Riverside CA

Miller, Irene K, *Librn,* Fairfield Historical Society, Library, Fairfield CT

Miller, J Brough, *Prof,* Texas Woman's University, Dept of Art, Denton TX (S)

Miller, Jean J, *Art Librn,* University of Hartford, Anne Bunce Cheney Library, West Hartford CT

Miller, John, *Vis Prof,* Minneapolis College of Art and Design, Minneapolis MN (S)

Miller, John Franklin, *Exec Dir,* Stan Hywet Hall Foundation, Inc, Akron OH

Miller, John P, *Preparator,* Vassar College Art Gallery, Poughkeepsie NY

Miller, Joseph, *Dir Grad Studies,* Catholic University of America, Dept of Architecture and Planning, Washington DC (S)

Miller, J Robert, *Lectr,* McMurry College, Art Dept, Abilene TX (S)

Miller, Judy, *Asst Prof,* Austin College, Art Dept, Sherman TX (S)

Miller, Julia, *Asst Prof,* State University of New York College at Potsdam, Dept of Fine Arts, Potsdam NY (S)

Miller, Kenneth R, *Exec VPres,* Mitchell Museum, Mount Vernon IL

Miller, K R, *Dir,* Mitchell Museum, Library, Mount Vernon IL

Miller, Laurence, *Dir,* Laguna Gloria Art Museum, Austin TX

Miller, Lawrence K, *Pres,* Hancock Shaker Village, Inc, Pittsfield MA

Miller, Lee Anne, *Dean,* Cooper Union School of Art, New York NY (S)

Miller, Lenore D, *Cur,* George Washington University, The Dimock Gallery, Washington DC

Miller, Louisa, *VPres,* Kenai Historical Society Inc, Kenai Community Historical Center, Kenai AK

Miller, Margaret A, *Dir,* University of South Florida, Art Galleries, Tampa FL

Miller, Marie Celeste, *Vis Assoc Prof,* Aquinas College, Art Dept, Grand Rapids MI (S)

Miller, Marion G, *Assoc Prof,* Mount Holyoke College, Art Dept, South Hadley MA (S)

Miller, Marjorie, *Art Librn,* Fashion Institute of Technology, Library, New York NY

Miller, Marlene, *Instructor,* Bucks County Community College, Fine Arts Dept, Newton PA (S)

Miller, Marlene, *Instr,* Illinois Central College, Fine Arts Dept, East Peoria IL (S)

Miller, Martha, *Dir of Interior Design,* Academy of Art College, San Francisco CA (S)

Miller, Mary, *Asst Librn,* Minneapolis College of Art and Design, Library and Media Center, Minneapolis MN

Miller, Maryan, *Mgr Sales-Rental Gallery,* Lakeview Museum of Arts and Sciences, Peoria IL

Miller, Mary M, *Librn,* Springfield Art Center, Library, Springfield OH

Miller, Meg, *Exec Dir,* Wayne Art Center, Wayne PA (S)

Miller, Nancy, *Cur,* Brandeis University, Rose Art Museum, Waltham MA

Miller, Robert, *Dept Head,* Ray-Vogue College of Design, Chicago IL (S)

Miller, Ruby, *Secy,* Mitchell Museum, Mount Vernon IL

Miller, Rus A, *Pres,* Pocumtuck Valley Memorial Association, Memorial Hall, Deerfield MA

Miller, Ruth, *Instr,* New York Studio School of Drawing, Painting and Sculpture, New York NY (S)

Miller, Samual C, *Dir,* Newark Museum, Newark NJ

Miller, Sandy, *Exhibition Officer,* Mount Saint Vincent University, Art Gallery, Halifax NS

Miller, Thom, *Theatre Coordr,* Ashtabula Arts Center, Ashtabula OH

Miller, Valerie, *Dir,* Gibbes Art Gallery School, Charleston SC (S)

Miller, Virginia, *Pres,* Portage and District Arts Council, Portage la Prairie MB

Miller, Wade, *Special Projects,* Just Above Midtown Gallery, Inc, New York NY

Miller, William, *VPres,* University of Nebraska, Lincoln, Nebraska Art Association, Lincoln NE

Miller, William B, *Dir,* Presbyterian Historical Society, Philadelphia PA

Miller, William B, *Librn,* Presbyterian Historical Society, Art Library, Philadelphia PA

Miller, William B, *Pres Historical Society,* Waterville Historical Association, Redington Museum, Waterville ME

Miller, William P, *Deputy Dir,* Jamaica Center for the Performing & Visual Arts, Inc, Jamaica Arts Center, Jamaica NY

Miller-Keller, Andrea, *Cur Matrix,* Wadsworth Atheneum, Hartford CT

Millett, Robert W, *Chairperson Div,* Utica College of Syracuse University, Division of Humanities, Utica NY (S)

Milley, John C, *Chief Museum Operations,* Independence National Historical Park, Philadelphia PA

Millin, Aimee, *Secy,* Canadian Society of Painters in Watercolour, Toronto ON

Milloff, Mark, *Instr,* Berkshire Community College, Dept Fine Arts, Pittsfield MA (S)

Mills, Anne, *Secy,* University of Notre Dame, Snite Museum of Art, Notre Dame IN

Mills, Betty, *Cur Historic Textiles & Costumes,* Texas Tech University Museum, Lubbock TX

Mills, David, *Asst Dir,* Newfoundland Museum, Saint John's NF

Mills, Fred V, *Chmn Art Dept,* Illinois State University, Art Dept, Normal IL (S)

Mills, James, *Assoc Prof,* East Tennessee State University, Fine Arts Dept, Johnson City TN (S)

Mills, Jane, *Secy,* Columbia County Historical Society, Kinderhook NY

Mills, John, *Cur Peter Matteson Tavern,* Bennington Museum, Bennington VT

Mills, Lawrence, *Chmn,* Central College, Art Dept, Pella IA (S)

Mills, Majorie, *First VPres,* San Bernardino Art Association, Inc, San Bernardino CA

Mills, Margaret M, *Exec Dir,* American Academy and Institute of Arts and Letters, New York NY

Mills, Richard, *Asst Prof,* Auburn University at Montgomery, Art Dept, Montgomery AL (S)

Mills, Robert, *Pres,* Galesburg Civic Art Center, Galesburg IL

Mills, Ruth B, *Dir,* Art Association of Richmond, Richmond IN

Mills, Sally, *Cur,* Vassar College Art Gallery, Poughkeepsie NY

Millson-Martula, Chris, *Dir,* Saint Xavier College, Byrne Memorial Library, Chicago IL

Millstein, Barbara, *Assoc Cur Sculpture Garden,* Brooklyn Museum, Brooklyn NY

Millstone, David, *Dir & Pres,* Millhouse-Bundy Performing & Fine Arts Center, Waitsfield VT

Millstone, Linde, *VPres,* Millhouse-Bundy Performing & Fine Arts Center, Waitsfield VT

Millward, Ruth, *Prof,* Louisiana State University, School of Art, Baton Rouge LA (S)

Milne, Mary, *Asst Coordr,* Powerhouse Gallery, Montreal PQ

Milne, Norman F, *Clerk,* Currier Gallery of Art, Manchester NH

Milner, Jane, *Instr,* Mainline Center of the Arts, Haverford PA (S)

Milner, Sue, *Head Dept,* Eastern Wyoming College, Art Dept, Torrington WY (S)

Milnes, Robert W, *Chmn Art Dept,* Edinboro University of Pennsylvania, Art Dept, Edinboro PA (S)

Milosevich, Joe, *Instructor,* Joliet Junior College, Fine Arts Dept, Joliet IL (S)

Milosevich, Joe B, *Gallery Dir,* Joliet Junior College, Laura A Sprague Art Gallery, Joliet IL

Milota, Edward, *Design Chief,* New Brunswick Museum, Saint John NB

Milrany, Donna J, *Dir,* Portland Center for the Visual Arts, Portland OR

Milrod, Linda J, *Dir,* Dalhousie University, Art Gallery, Halifax NS

Mimms, Robert D, *Sr Exhibit Specialist,* United States Naval Academy Museum, Annapolis MD

Mims, Hazel, *Secy,* Fine Arts Museum of the South, Mobile AL

Mims, Thomas E, *Assoc Prof,* University of North Alabama, Dept of Art, Florence AL (S)

Mineo, Ronald, *Dir,* Art Life Studios, New York NY (S)

Miner, Jane Clary, *Pres,* Buffalo Society of Artists, Williamsville NY

Miner, Laura Lynn, *In Charge Art Coll,* Citibank, NA, New York NY

Minges, Sarita, *VPres,* Community Council for the Arts, Kinston NC

Minivielle, Shereen H, *Dir,* Shadows-on-the-Teche, New Iberia LA

Minnaugh, Patricia, *Chmn Fine Arts Dept,* Barry University, Dept of Art, Miami Shores FL (S)

Mino, Yutaka, *Cur Oriental Art,* Indianapolis Museum of Art, Indianapolis IN

Minogve, Eileen, *Asst Dir,* Northport-East Northport Public Library, Northport NY

Minot, Michael, *Chmn Dept,* Vancouver Community College, Langara Campus, Dept of Fine Arts, Vancouver BC (S)

Minter, Barbara, *Secy,* Art League of Houston, Houston TX

Minter-Dowd, Christine, *Dir,* DAR Museum, National Society Daughters of the American Revolution, Washington DC

Mintich, Mary, *Assoc Prof,* Winthrop College, Dept of Art, Rock Hill SC (S)

Miotke, Anne, *Instructor,* Art Academy of Cincinnati, Cincinnati OH (S)

Mira, Evalyn, *Dir,* Zigler Museum, Jennings LA

Mira, Ivan, *Dir,* Zigler Museum, Jennings LA

Mirabile, Kathleen, *Pres,* Manchester Historic Association, Manchester NH

Miracle, Nancy, *Instructor,* Central Wyoming College, Art Center, Riverton WY (S)

Miraglia, Anthony J, *Chairperson Fine Art,* Southeastern Massachusetts University, College of Visual and Performing Arts, North Dartmouth MA (S)

Miranda, Grace, *Center Adminr,* Muckenthaler Cultural Center, Fullerton CA

Miseho, Ivan R, *Instr,* Orange County Community College, Art Dept, Middletown NY (S)

Misfeldt, Willard, *Chmn Art History,* Bowling Green State University, School of Art, Bowling Green OH (S)

Mishkin, Gail M, *Asst Cur,* George Washington University, The Dimock Gallery, Washington DC

Miss, Mary, *VPres,* Committee for the Visual Arts, Inc, New York NY

Miss, Mary, *Faculty,* Sarah Lawrence College, Dept of Art, Bronxville NY (S)

Mitchel, Irene, *Prof,* East Stroudsburg State College, Art Dept, East Stroudsburg PA (S)

Mitchell, Alex F, *Chmn Dept,* Lake Forest College, Dept of Art, Lake Forest IL (S)

Mitchell, Beresford, *Chmn Dept Commun & Design,* Ontario College of Art, Toronto ON (S)

Mitchell, Brenda, *Registrar,* Akron Art Museum, Akron OH

Mitchell, C, *Instructor,* Golden West College, Arts, Humanities and Social Sciences Institute, Huntington Beach CA (S)

Mitchell, Dolores, *Instr,* California State University, Chico, Art Dept, Chico CA (S)

Mitchell, Douglas, *Prof,* Cape Cod Community College, Art Dept, West Barnstable MA (S)

Mitchell, Jeannette, *Librn,* Portsmouth Athenaeum NR, Inc 1817, Portsmouth NH

Mitchell, Jeannie, *Instructor,* Springfield College in Illinois, Dept of Art, Springfield IL (S)

Mitchell, Jean S, *Office Mgr,* Cliveden, Philadelphia PA

Mitchell, Judith L, *In Charge Art Coll,* The Third National Bank and Trust Company, Dayton OH

Mitchell, Kathleen, *Visiting Lecturer,* Texas Woman's University, Dept of Art, Denton TX (S)

Mitchell, Kathy, *Member Secy,* Beaumont Art Museum, Beaumont TX

Mitchell, Kenneth Eugene, *Head Dept,* Colby Community College, Visual Arts Dept, Colby KS (S)

Mitchell, Kevin, *Research Asst,* University of Alabama, Visual Arts Gallery, Birmingham AL

Mitchell, M F, *Pres,* Mendel Art Gallery and Civic Conservatory, Saskatoon SK

Mitchell, Muriel, *Chmn,* Bay Path Junior College, Dept of Art, Longmeadow MA (S)

Mitchell, Ramona, *Lectr,* Lake Forest College, Dept of Art, Lake Forest IL (S)

Mitchell, Richard, *Chmn Dept,* Youngstown State University, Art Dept, Youngstown OH (S)

Mitchell, Robert, *Business Mgr,* Society of North American Goldsmiths, Milwaukee WI

Mitchell, Robin, *Registrar,* University of Kentucky, Art Museum, Lexington KY

Mitchell, Ronald T, *Instr,* West Hills College, Fine Arts Dept, Coalinga CA (S)

Mitchell, Stanley A, *Prof,* Chowan College, Division of Art, Murfreesboro NC (S)

Mitchell, Suzanne, *Cur Oriental Art,* Detroit Institute of Arts, Detroit MI

Mitchell, Timothy, *Assoc Prof,* University of Kansas, Kress Foundation Dept of Art History, Lawrence KS (S)

Mitnic, Larry, *Chairperson Architectural Studies,* Philadelphia College of Art, Philadelphia PA (S)

Mitsanas, D, *Faculty,* Humboldt State University, College of Creative Arts & Humanities, Arcata CA (S)

Mitsuda, Mary, *Asst Dir Publications,* Contemporary Arts Center, Honolulu HI

Mittelberger, Ernest G, *Dir,* Wine Museum of San Francisco, San Francisco CA

Mittelgluck, Eugene L, *Dir,* New Rochelle Public Library, Art Section, New Rochelle NY

Mittler, Gene, *Assoc Prof,* Texas Tech University, Dept of Art, Lubbock TX (S)

Miyata, Masako, *Assoc Prof,* James Madison University, Dept of Art, Harrisonburg VA (S)

Miyata, Wayne A, *Faculty,* Kauai Community College, Dept of Art, Lihue HI (S)

Miyazaki, Hiroshi, *Instructor,* San Diego Mcsa College, Fine Arts Dept, San Diego CA (S)

Mize, Dianne, *Dept Head,* Piedmont College, Art Dept, Demorest GA (S)

Mladenka, Dorcas, *Asst Prof,* Our Lady of the Lake University, Dept of Art, San Antonio TX (S)

Moazur, Tom, *Instr,* Creighton University, Fine and Performing Arts Dept, Omaha NE (S)

Mocek, Betty Ann, *Instr,* College of Saint Teresa, Art Dept, Winona MN (S)

Mochizuki, Tomie, *Librn,* Japan Society, Inc, Library, New York NY

Mochon, Anne, *Asst Prof,* Tufts University, Fine Arts Dept, Medford MA (S)

Mocsanyi, Paul, *Dir,* New School for Social Research Art Center Gallery, Collectors Institute of the New School, New York NY

Modden, John, *Education Coordr,* Tallahassee Junior Museum, Tallahassee FL

Mode, Carol A, *Program Coordr Educ,* Tennessee Botanical Gardens and Fine Arts Center, Education Dept, Nashville TN (S)

Mode, Robert L, *Assoc Prof,* Vanderbilt University, Dept of Fine Arts, Nashville TN (S)

Model, Elisabeth, *Secy,* Federation of Modern Painters and Sculptors, New York NY

Moehring, Eugene P, *Cur Exhibits,* Southern Illinois University, University Museum, Carbondale IL

Moeller, Gary E, *Dir,* Claremore College, Art Dept, Claremore OK (S)

Moeny, Christine E, *Reference & Special Coll Librn,* Adams State College, Library, Alamosa CO

Moes, Robert, *Cur Oriental Art,* Brooklyn Museum, Brooklyn NY

Moeser, James, *Dean,* University of Kansas, School of Fine Arts, Lawrence KS (S)

Moffett, Charles S, *Cur Painting,* Fine Arts Museums of San Francisco, M H de Young Memorial Museum and California Palace of the Legion of Honor, San Francisco CA

Moffett, Kenworth, *Cur Contemporary Art,* Museum of Fine Arts, Boston MA

Moffett, William, *Instr,* Wilkes Community College, Arts and Science Division, Wilkesboro NC (S)

Moffett, W L, *Faculty,* Western Illinois University, College of Fine Arts, Macomb IL (S)

Moffitt, Beth, *Coordr of Art,* University of New Haven, Dept of Humanities, Fine & Performing Arts, West Haven CT (S)

Moffitt, John, *Prof,* New Mexico State University, Art Dept, Las Cruces NM (S)

Mofford, Juliet, *Educator,* Old Gaol Museum, York ME

Mogoon, Charles, *Resident Cur,* Waterville Historical Association, Redington Museum, Waterville ME

Mohan, Nancy, *Education,* Hastings County Museum, Belleville ON

Moisan, Micheline, *Assoc Cur Dept Prints and Drawings,* Montreal Museum of Fine Arts, Montreal PQ

Moldenhauer, R, *Business Mgr,* Mendel Art Gallery and Civic Conservatory, Saskatoon SK

Moldovan, George, *Assoc Prof,* East Tennessee State University, Fine Arts Dept, Johnson City TN (S)

Moldroski, Al, *Assoc Prof,* Eastern Illinois University, School of Fine Arts, Charleston IL (S)

Molen, Larry Ter, *VPres Develop & Public Relations,* Art Institute of Chicago, Chicago IL

Molina, Samuel B, *Asst Prof,* George Washington University, Dept of Art, Washington DC (S)

Molloy, Ellen, *Adminr,* The Trustees of Reservations, The Mission House, Stockbridge MA

Molloy, Terry, *Chmn,* Verde Valley Art Association, Inc, Jerome AZ

Molner, Frank, *Instructor,* Santa Ana College, Art Dept, Santa Ana CA (S)

Mominee, John, *Dir,* University of Wisconsin, Harry Nohr Art Gallery, Platteville WI

Monaco, Theresa, *Assoc Prof,* Emmanuel College, Art Dept, Boston MA (S)

Monaghan, Kathleen M, *Public Relations,* Santa Barbara Museum of Art, Santa Barbara CA

Monaghan, Susan, *Asst to the Dir,* Ann Arbor Art Association, Ann Arbor MI

Monahan, Michael, *Undergraduate Advisor,* California State University, Chico, Art Dept, Chico CA (S)

Monahan, Michael, *Instr,* California State University, Chico, Art Dept, Chico CA (S)

Mondrus, Martin, *Prof,* Glendale College, Dept of Fine Arts, Glendale CA (S)

Mondschein, Natalie, *Admin Secy,* Washington University, Gallery of Art, Saint Louis MO

Monge, Federico Berreda Y, *Instructor,* University of Puerto Rico, Dept of Fine Arts, Rio Piedras PR (S)

Mongrain, Jeff, *Fine Arts Chairperson,* Valley City State College, Art Dept, Valley City ND (S)

Monheimer, Richard, *Science Service Division Dir,* New York State Museum, Albany NY

Monje, Andrew, *Asst Prof,* Marymount College of Virginia, Arts & Sciences Division, Arlington VA (S)

Monkhouse, Christopher, *Cur Decorative Arts,* Rhode Island School of Design, Museum of Art, Providence RI

Monkhouse, Valerie, *Dir, Library Servs,* National Museums of Canada, Library, Ottawa ON

Monkman, Betty C, *Registrar & Assoc Cur,* White House, Washington DC

Monnich, Theodore, *Cur,* Craft Center Museum, Wilton CT

Monroe, Arthur, *Registrar,* Oakland Museum, Art Dept, Oakland CA

Monroe, Betty Iverson, *Assoc Prof,* Northwestern University, Evanston, Dept of Art History, Evanston IL (S)

Monroe, Dan, *Deputy Dir,* Alaska State Museum, Juneau AK

Monroe, Michael, *Cur,* National Museum of American Art, Renwick Gallery, Washington DC

Monroe, Paula, *Secy,* McLean County Art Association, Arts Center, Bloomington IL

Monroe, P Jensen, *Supv Museum Prog,* The Rockwell Museum, Corning NY

Monroe, P S, *Second VPres,* San Bernardino Art Association, Inc, San Bernardino CA

Monroe, Ruth E, *Dir,* Westmar College, Art Dept, LeMars IA (S)

Monsma, Marvin, *Librn,* Calvin College Center Art Gallery, Library, Grand Rapids MI

Monson, Richard D, *Chair Dept,* Central Missouri State University, Art Dept, Warrensburg MO (S)

Montano, Salvatore, *Instr,* New York Academy of Art, New York NY (S)

Monteferrante, Sally, *Instr,* Community College of Baltimore, Dept of Fine & Applied Arts, Liberty Campus, Baltimore MD (S)

Montgomery, Joseph, *Instr,* James H Faulkner State Jr College, Bay Minette AL (S)

Montgomery, Katherine, *Chmn,* Davidson County Community College, Language-Fine Arts Dept, Lexington NC (S)

Montgomery, L A D, *Treas,* Pennsylvania Academy of the Fine Arts, Fellowship of the Pennsylvania Academy of the Fine Arts, Philadelphia PA

Montgomery, Renee, *Registrar,* Los Angeles County Museum of Art, Los Angeles CA

Montgomery, Robert P, *Chmn,* John Jay College of Criminal Justice, Dept of Art, Music and Philosophy, New York NY (S)

Montgomery, Rose, *Registrar,* Texas Tech University Museum, Lubbock TX

Montgomery, Sue B, *Assoc Prof,* Oral Roberts University, Fine Arts Dept, Tulsa OK (S)

Monthan, G, *Assoc Prof,* Northern Arizona University, Art Dept, Flagstaff AZ (S)

Monti, Laura, *In Charge,* Boston Public Library, Rare Book & Manuscripts Dept, Boston MA

Montileaux, Paulette, *Museum Asst,* Sioux Indian Museum, Rapid City SD

Montoya, Malaquias, *Ethnic Art Studies,* California College of Arts and Crafts, Oakland CA (S)

Montplaisir, Isabelle, *Librn,* Musee d'Art Contemporain, Bibliotheque, Montreal PQ

Montverde, Mildred, *Assoc Prof,* University of Southern Colorado, Belmont Campus, Dept of Art, Pueblo CO (S)

Moody, Barbara, *Foundation Project,* Montserrat School of Visual Art, Beverly MA (S)

Moody, James W, *Dir,* Historic Pensacola Preservation Board, West Florida Museum of History, Pensacola FL

Moon, Caroline, *Museum Coordr,* Iowa State Education Association, Salisbury House, Des Moines IA

Moon, Marvin, *Assoc Prof,* Texas Tech University, Dept of Art, Lubbock TX (S)

Moon, Robert G, *Cur,* Plumas County Museum, Quincy CA

Moone, Charles L, *Prof,* University of Colorado at Denver, Dept of Fine Arts, Denver CO (S)

Mooney, Brent, *Head Marketing Dept,* Winnipeg Art Gallery, Winnipeg MB

Mooney, James E, *Dir,* Historical Society of Pennsylvania, Philadelphia PA

Mooney, Tom, *Office Mgr,* Cherokee National Historical Society, Inc, Tahlequah OK

Moore, Anne, *Cur Education,* Ball State University, Art Gallery, Muncie IN

Moore, Bevette, *Registrar,* Northeastern Nevada Historical Society Museum, Elko NV

Moore, Brian, *Preparator,* Ball State University, Art Gallery, Muncie IN

Moore, Charles E, *Installation Supervisor,* East Tennessee State University, Carroll Reece Museum, Johnson City TN

Moore, Craig, *Prof,* Taylor University, Art Dept, Upland IN (S)

Moore, Diane, *Exec Dir,* Art Directors Club, Inc, New York NY

Moore, Donald Everett, *Acting Chmn,* Mitchell Community College, Visual Art Dept, Statesville NC (S)

Moore, Doyle, *In Charge Graphic Design,* University of Illinois, Urbana-Champaign, School of Art and Design, Champaign IL (S)

Moore, Elanie, *Instr,* Mount San Jacinto College, Art Dept, San Jacinto CA (S)

Moore, George S, *Pres,* Hispanic Society of America, Museum, New York NY

Moore, Jack, *Cur Exhib,* Indiana State Museum, Indianapolis IN

Moore, Jack L, *Assoc Prof,* Motlow State Community College, Art Dept, Tullahoma TN (S)

Moore, James, *Div Head,* Campbellsville College, Fine Arts Division, Campbellsville KY (S)

Moore, James C, *Dir,* Albuquerque Museum of Art, History and Science, Albuquerque NM

Moore, Jerry, *Exhibits Coordr,* McAllen International Museum, McAllen TX

Moore, Jerry C, *Assoc Dean,* University of Kansas, School of Fine Arts, Lawrence KS (S)

Moore, Jimmy, *Pres,* Community Council for the Arts, Kinston NC

Moore, John, *Prof,* Temple University, Tyler School of Art, Philadelphia PA (S)

Moore, John F, *Treas,* Southwest Arts Foundation, Houston TX

Moore, Kathleen, *Asst to Art Librn,* University of Louisville, Margaret M Bridwell Art Library, Louisville KY

Moore, Kathleen, *Asst Supt,* Game and Parks Commission, Arbor Lodge State Historical Park, Nebraska City NE

Moore, Lawrence, *Expansion Arts Coordr,* Arizona Commission on the Arts, Phoenix AZ

Moore, Louise, *Secy & Registrar,* Western Colorado Center for the Arts, Inc, Grand Junction CO

Moore, M, *Special Projects Researcher,* Latitude 53 Society of Artists, Edmonton AB

Moore, Marie, *Librn,* Canajoharie Library and Art Gallery, Library, Canajoharie NY

Moore, Mark, *Clerk,* Santa Cruz Public Library, Art, Music, Film Dept, Santa Cruz CA

Moore, Michael R, *Head,* Purdue University Calumet Campus, Dept of Creative Arts, Hammond IN (S)

Moore, Olga, *Chmn,* Rutgers University, Camden, Art Dept, Camden NJ (S)

Moore, Roger Allan, *Asst Treasurer & Clerk,* The Bostonian Society, Old State House, Boston MA

Moore, Russell J, *Dir,* Long Beach Museum of Art, Long Beach CA

Moore, Russell J, *Exec Dir,* San Jose Museum of Art, San Jose CA

Moore, Sally, *Instructor,* Southwestern Technical College, Commercial Art and Advertising Design Dept, Sylva NC (S)

Moore, Turner, *Secy,* Star-Spangled Banner Flag House Association, Baltimore MD

Moorhead, Robert, *Cur,* Deerfield Academy, Hilson Gallery, Deerfield MA

Mooslin, Nancy, *Secy,* Orange County Center for Contemporary Art, Santa Ana CA

Moppett, G, *Asst Cur,* Mendel Art Gallery and Civic Conservatory, Saskatoon SK

Morache, Peggy L, *Business Mgr,* Bennington Museum, Bennington VT

Morain, Patrick, *Instructor,* Saint Louis Community College at Meramec, Art Dept, Saint Louis MO (S)

Morais, LeRoy, *Assoc Prof,* University of Maryland Baltimore County, Visual Arts Dept, Catonsville MD (S)

Morales, Amapola, *Dir Harlem Youth Bd Program,* Manhattan Laboratory Museum, New York NY

Morales, Luis M Rodriquez, *Exec Dir,* Institute of Puerto Rican Culture, Instituto de Cultura Puertorriquena, San Juan PR

Morales, Martha, *Exec Secy,* American Institute for Conservation of Historic and Artistic Works (AIC), Washington DC

Morales, Raymond, *Asst Prof,* University of Utah, Art Dept, Salt Lake City UT (S)

Moran, Ann, *Recording Secy,* Lyme Art Association, Inc, Old Lyme CT

Moran, Diane D, *Asst Prof,* Sweet Briar College, Art History Dept and Art Studio Dept, Sweet Briar VA (S)

Moran, Henry, *Executive Dir,* Mid-America Arts Alliance, Kansas City MO

Moran, Jose, *Instructor,* California State College, San Bernardino, Art Dept, San Bernardino CA (S)

Moran, Lois, *Executive Dir of Council,* American Craft Council, New York NY

Morandi, Thomas, *Assoc Prof Art,* Eastern Oregon State College, Arts & Humanities Dept, La Grande OR (S)

Moreau, Keith, *Gallery Mgr,* Mississauga Library System, Mississauga ON

Morehart, Mary, *Assoc Prof,* University of British Columbia, Dept of Fine Arts, Vancouver BC (S)

Morehouse, Dorothy V, *Dir,* Monmouth Museum and Cultural Center, Lincroft NJ

Morel, Sylvie, *Chief Nat Prog Div,* National Museum of Man, Ottawa ON

Moreland, David L, *Faculty,* Idaho State University, Dept of Art, Pocatello ID (S)

Morello, Samuel E, *Chmn Dept,* Charles Stewart Mott Community College, Fine Arts Division, Flint MI (S)

Morentz, Barry, *VPres,* Society of Scribes, Ltd, New York NY

Morey, Mark, *Cur Education,* Amarillo Art Center, Amarillo TX

Morgan, Andrew, *Prof,* University of Miami, Dept of Art & Art History, Coral Gables FL (S)

Morgan, Charlene, *Admin Asst,* Ontario Association of Art Galleries, Resource Centre, Toronto ON

Morgan, Charles, *Printmaking,* University of Georgia, Franklin College of Arts and Sciences, Dept of Art, Athens GA (S)

Morgan, Connie, *Office Admin,* West Hills Unitarian Fellowship, Portland OR

Morgan, Dahlia, *Gallery Dir & Lecturer,* Florida International University, Visual Arts Dept, Miami FL (S)

Morgan, Edward A, *Pres Board Trustees,* Huntington Free Library and Reading Room, Depository Library for the Museum of the American Indian, Bronx NY

Morgan, Helen, *Assoc Prof,* South Dakota State University, Dept of Visual Arts, Brookings SD (S)

Morgan, Jane, *Secy,* Prescott Fine Arts Association, Prescott AZ

Morgan, Jane Hale, *Library Dir,* Detroit Public Library, Fine Arts Dept, Detroit MI

Morgan, Jim, *Instructor,* Goldsboro Art Center, Goldsboro NC (S)

Morgan, Linda D, *Instructional Media Specialist,* McKissick Museums, Art Library, Columbia SC

Morgan, M, *Faculty,* Humboldt State University, College of Creative Arts & Humanities, Arcata CA (S)

Morgan, Madel, *Dir Archives & Library,* Mississippi Department of Archives and History, State Historical Museum, Jackson MS

Morgan, Mavera, *Prof,* University of the District of Columbia, Art Dept, Washington DC (S)

Morgan, Nancy, *Asst Dir,* Northern Virginia Fine Arts Association, The Athenaeum, Alexandria VA

Morgan, Nigel, *Dir,* Princeton University, Index of Christian Art, Princeton NJ

Morgan, Richard, *Programs Cur,* Charles Allis Art Museum, Milwaukee WI

Morgan, Robert C, *Asst Prof,* Rochester Institute of Technology, School of Art and Design, Rochester NY (S)

Morgan, William, *Prof,* University of Wisconsin-Superior, Programs in the Visual Arts, Superior WI (S)

Morgan, W P, *Dir & Cur,* Regina Public Library, Dunlop Art Gallery, Regina SK

Morganstern, Anne M, *Actg Chmn Dept,* Ohio State University, Dept of the History of Art, Columbus OH (S)

Morgenstein, Susan W, *Dir,* Judaic Museum of the Jewish Community Center, Goldman Fine Arts Gallery, Rockville MD

Morgret, Phyllis, *Cur Collections,* College of Southern Idaho, Herrette Museum, Twin Falls ID

Moriarty, Kim, *Admin Asst,* Children's Art Centre, Boston MA

Moriarty, Peter, *Asst Prof,* Johnson State College, Dept Fine Arts, Johnson VT (S)

Morin, France, *Dir,* Canadian Consulate General Dept of External Affairs, 49th Parallel Centre for Contemporary Canadian Art, New York NY

Morin, M Jeanne, *Guide,* Musee des Augustines de l'Hotel Dieu de Quebec, Quebec PQ

Morin, Rachel, *Guide,* Musee des Augustines de l'Hotel Dieu de Quebec, Quebec PQ

Morningstar, William, *Asst Prof,* Berea College, Art Dept, Berea KY (S)

Morr, Lynell A, *Librn,* State Art Museum of Florida, Art Research Library, Sarasota FL

Morrill, Hope, *Curatorial Registrar,* Montclair Art Museum, Montclair NJ

Morrin, Peter, *Cur of 20th Century Art,* High Museum of Art, Atlanta GA

Morris, Daniel, *Chmn,* Waynesburg College, Dept of Fine Arts, Waynesburg PA (S)

Morris, Donald, *Cur,* Olivet College, Armstrong Museum of Art and Archaeology, Olivet MI

Morris, Doris, *VPres,* DuPage Art League, Wheaton IL

Morris, Gwin, *Pres,* Harrison County Historical Museum, Marshall TX

Munoz, Teresa, *Assoc Prof,* Loyola Marymount University, Dept of Art & Art Hist, Los Angeles CA (S)

Munro, Alan, *Dir,* Alaska State Museum, Juneau AK

Munsch, Gene, *Conservator Furniture,* Fine Arts Museums of San Francisco, M H de Young Memorial Museum and California Palace of the Legion of Honor, San Francisco CA

Munson, Richard, *Chmn,* University of Northern Colorado, Dept of Visual Arts, Greeley CO (S)

Munyer, Edward A, *Asst Dir,* Illinois State Museum of Natural History and Art, Springfield IL

Munzenrider, Claire, *Conservator,* Museum of New Mexico, Museum of International Folk Art, Santa Fe NM

Munzer, Annette, *Cur Collections,* Tucson Museum of Art, Tucson AZ

Murakishi, Steve, *Head Printmaking Dept,* Cranbrook Academy of Art, Bloomfield Hills MI (S)

Murata, Hiroshi, *Assoc Prof,* Trenton State College, Art Dept, Trenton NJ (S)

Murchie, John, *Dir,* Nova Scotia College of Art and Design, Library, Halifax NS

Murdock, Lynn, *Librn,* Berkeley Public Library, Berkeley CA

Murdock, Robert A, *Exec Dir,* Association for the Preservation of Virgina Antiquities, Richmond VA

Murdock, Robert M, *Chief Cur,* Walker Art Center, Minneapolis MN

Murdock, William, *Dir,* Pace University Gallery, Arts Building Library, Briarcliff Manor NY

Murgrave, Shirley, *Prof,* University of Alabama, Art Dept, Tuscaloosa AL (S)

Muro, George, *Head,* Allan Hancock College, Fine Arts Dept, Santa Maria CA (S)

Muro, Luis, *Vis Prof,* University of Texas at San Antonio, Division of Art and Design, San Antonio TX (S)

Murphy, Cheryl, *Pres,* Colorado Institute of Art, Denver CO (S)

Murphy, Christine Marie, *Assoc Prof,* College of Mount Saint Vincent, Fine Arts Dept, Riverdale NY (S)

Murphy, Christus, *Member,* The Loading Dock Gallery, Boston MA

Murphy, Donn, *Prof,* Georgetown University, Dept of Fine Arts, Washington DC (S)

Murphy, James J, *Chairperson Studio Art,* Florida State University, Art Dept, Tallahassee FL (S)

Murphy, John Cullen, *Pres,* National Cartoonists Society, Brooklyn NY

Murphy, John Satre, *Assoc Prof,* University of Wisconsin-Parkside, Art Discipline, Kenosha WI (S)

Murphy, J P, *Chmn,* Rockland Community College, Graphic Arts & Advertising Tech Dept, Suffern NY (S)

Murphy, Kenneth, *Instructor,* Mohawk Valley Community College, Advertising Design and Production, Utica NY (S)

Murphy, Marilyn, *Asst Prof,* Vanderbilt University, Dept of Fine Arts, Nashville TN (S)

Murphy, Marissa, *Asst Dir,* Thomas More College, TM Gallery, Fort Mitchell KY

Murphy, Mary-Kate, *Librn,* Maine Historical Society, Library, Portland ME

Murphy, Patrick, *Asst Prof,* Williamsport Area Community College, Dept of Engineering and Design, Williamsport PA (S)

Murphy, Rivers C, *Prof,* Northwestern State University of Louisiana, Dept of Art, Natchitoches LA (S)

Murray, Ann H, *Chmn Dept,* Wheaton College, Art Dept, Norton MA (S)

Murray, Donald R, *Assoc Prof,* Malone College, Dept of Art, Canton OH (S)

Murray, Don E, *Assoc Prof,* University of Florida, Dept of Art, Gainesville FL (S)

Murray, Gale, *Asst Prof,* Colorado College, Dept of Art, Colorado Springs CO (S)

Murray, I, *Librn,* McGill University, Blackader-Lauterman Library of Architecture and Art, Montreal PQ

Murray, James, *Assoc Prof,* Mount Saint Mary's College, Art Dept, Los Angeles CA (S)

Murray, Joan, *Dir,* The Robert McLaughlin Gallery, Oshawa ON

Murray, John, *Associate Dir Fine Arts Dept,* New York Institute of Technology Gallery, Old Westbury NY

Murray, John, *Chmn,* New York Institute of Technology, Fine Arts Dept, Old Westbury NY (S)

Murray, L, *Chief Cur Canadian War Museum,* National Museum of Man, Ottawa ON

Murray, L Carol, *Registrar,* Baltimore Museum of Art, Baltimore MD

Murray, L F, *Cur,* National Museums of Canada, Canadian War Museum, Ottawa ON

Murray, Marsha, *Lectr,* McMurry College, Art Dept, Abilene TX (S)

Murray, Morag, *Asst Cur,* Wheaton College, Watson Gallery, Norton MA

Murray, Neale, *Chmn Dept,* North Park College, Art Dept, Chicago IL (S)

Murray, Richard N, *Dir,* Archives of American Art, Smithsonian Institution, New York NY

Murray, Stephen, *Dir,* Indiana University, Bloomington, School of Fine Arts, Bloomington IN (S)

Murray, Suzanne, *Admin Asst,* Burchfield Art Center, Buffalo NY

Murray, Tim, *Dir,* Brevard College, Coltrane Art Center, Brevard NC

Murray, Timothy G, *Prof,* Brevard College, Division of Fine Arts, Brevard NC (S)

Murrow, Nila West, *Head Dept,* Bethany Nazarene College, Art Dept, Bethany OH (S)

Musgrove, Stephen W, *Asst Dir,* Mint Museum of Art, Charlotte NC

Must, Raymond, *Assoc Prof,* Wright State University, Dept of Art & Art History, Dayton OH (S)

Must, Rose, *Secy,* Lafayette Natural History Museum, Planetarium and Nature Station, Lafayette LA

Muth, Tom J, *Asst Dir,* Topeka Public Library, Fine Arts Dept & Gallery of Fine Arts, Topeka KS

Muysson, William, *Assoc Cur,* Queen's University, Agnes Etherington Art Centre, Kingston ON

Myer, John Randolph, *Head Dept,* Massachusetts Institute of Technology, School of Architecture and Planning, Cambridge MA (S)

Myers, Adele, *Instr,* Saint Thomas Aquinas College, Art Dept, Sparkhill NY (S)

Myers, Cate, *Dean of Faculty,* Manhattanville College, Brownson Art Gallery, Purchase NY

Myers, Derek, *Instructor,* Virginia Tech, Dept of Art, Blacksburg VA (S)

Myers, Fred A, *Dir,* Thomas Gilcrease Institute of American History and Art, Tulsa OK

Myers, Gay, *Conservator,* Lyman Allyn Museum, New London CT

Myers, Jack, *Instr,* Pacific Northwest College of Art, Portland OR (S)

Myers, John, *Asst Prof,* University of North Carolina at Wilmington, Dept of Creative Arts - Division of Art, Wilmington NC (S)

Myers, Legh, *Secy,* Sculptors Guild, Inc, New York NY

Myers, Lynn R, *Chief Cur,* McKissick Museums, Columbia SC

Myers, Mary L, *Cur,* Metropolitan Museum of Art, Dept of Prints & Photographs, New York NY

Myers, Robert, *Instr,* Ellsworth Community College, Dept of Fine Arts, Iowa Falls IA (S)

Myers, Trent, *Cur Exhibitions,* Madison Art Center, Madison WI

Myers, V, *Secy,* Macdonald Stewart Art Centre, Guelph ON

Myers, William, *Head Manuscripts,* Ohio Historical Society, Archives-Library Division, Columbus OH

Myron, Robert, *Chmn,* Hofstra University, Dept of Art History, Hempstead NY (S)

Naab, Michael, *Dir,* Columbia River Maritime Museum, Astoria OR

Nabers, Ned, *Assoc Prof,* Vanderbilt University, Dept of Fine Arts, Nashville TN (S)

Nadel, Joshua, *Prof,* University of Maine at Augusta, Division of Arts and Humanities, Augusta ME (S)

Naef, Weston J, *Cur Photography,* Metropolitan Museum of Art, Dept of Prints & Photographs, New York NY

Naeve, Milo M, *Cur American Art,* Art Institute of Chicago, Chicago IL

Naftulin, Lawrence, *Dir Development,* Historical Society of Pennsylvania, Philadelphia PA

Nagatzni, Patrick, *Asst Prof,* Loyola Marymount University, Dept of Art & Art Hist, Los Angeles CA (S)

Nagel, Arturo, *Actg Chmn Dept Lib Arts Studies,* Ontario College of Art, Toronto ON (S)

Nagel, John, *Instructor,* Saint Louis Community College at Meramec, Art Dept, Saint Louis MO (S)

Nagel, Paul C, *Dir,* Virginia Historical Society, Richmond VA

Nagel, Stewart, *Assoc Prof,* Bloomsburg University, Dept of Art, Bloomsburg PA (S)

Nager, Arthur, *Assoc Prof,* University of Bridgeport, Art Dept, Bridgeport CT (S)

Nagle, Ron, *Asst Prof,* Mills College, Art Dept, Oakland CA (S)

Nagy, Margaret, *Asst Prof,* Texas Tech University, Dept of Art, Lubbock TX (S)

Nagy, Martin W, *Pres,* Spectrum, Friends of Fine Art, Inc, Toledo OH

Nair, Vijay, *Librn,* Adirondack Historical Association, Library, Blue Mountain Lake NY

Najarian, Hovak, *Chmn,* College of the Desert, Art Dept, Palm Desert CA (S)

Nakazato, Hitoshi, *Asst Prof,* University of Pennsylvania, College Arts & Science, Philadelphia PA (S)

Nama, George, *VPres,* Society of American Graphic Artists, New York NY

Namer, Rosella, *Librn,* Viterbo College Art Gallery, Zoeller Fine Arts Library, La Crosse WI

Nance, Archie L, *VPres,* The Fort Worth National Bank, Fort Worth TX

Nance, William W, *Asst Prof,* Alabama A & M University, Art Education Dept, Huntsville AL (S)

Nance-Sasser, Steven, *Instructor,* Marylhurst College, Art Dept, Marylhurst OR (S)

Nantais-Picher, Lise, *Exec Asst,* Musee du Quebec, Quebec PQ

Naos, Theodore, *Assoc Prof,* Catholic University of America, Dept of Architecture and Planning, Washington DC (S)

Narad, Regina L, *Admin Asst,* Westmoreland County Museum of Art, Greensburg PA

Nartker, John, *Prof,* College of Mount Saint Joseph, Art Dept, Mount Saint Joseph OH (S)

Nasby, Judith, *Dir,* Macdonald Stewart Art Centre, Guelph ON

Nasca, Veronica, *Secy,* Museum of Cartoon Art, Port Chester NY

Nasgaard, Roald, *Chief Cur,* Art Gallery of Ontario, Toronto ON

Nash, Steven A, *Asst Dir & Chief Cur,* Dallas Museum of Fine Arts, Dallas TX

Nason, James, *Cur Ethnology & Anthropology,* University of Washington, Thomas Burke Memorial Washington State Museum, Seattle WA

Nason, Kirk, *Systems Analyst,* American Portrait Society, Seal Beach CA

Naspo, Diana, *Instructor,* Montclair Art Museum, Museum Art Classes, Montclair NJ (S)

Nathanson, Carol, *Assoc Prof,* Wright State University, Dept of Art & Art History, Dayton OH (S)

Nation, Morna, *Instructor,* Wharton County Junior College, Art Dept, Wharton TX (S)

Naujoks, Robert, *Dir,* Mount Mercy College, McAuley Gallery, Cedar Rapids IA

Naujoks, Robert, *Asst Prof,* Mount Mercy College, Art Dept, Cedar Rapids IA (S)

Naumann, Helen, *Vis Lecturer,* North Central College, Dept of Art, Naperville IL (S)

Naumer, Helmuth J, *Exec Dir,* San Antonio Museum Association, Inc, San Antonio TX

Nauss, Oscar, *Chmn of Trustees,* Yarmouth County Historical Society, Yarmouth County Museum, Yarmouth NS

Nava, John, *Dept Chmn,* University of Redlands, Peppers Art Center and Gallery, Redlands CA

Nava, John R, *Assoc Prof Art,* University of Redlands, Dept of Art, Redlands CA (S)

Navaretton, Cynthia, *Exec Dir,* Midmarch Associates, Women Artists News Archive, New York NY

Navone, Edward, *Asst Dir,* Washburn University, Mulvane Art Center, Topeka KS

Navrat, Dennis Edward, *Co-Dir,* Dickinson State College, Mind's Eye Gallery, Dickinson ND

Navrat, Dennis Edward, *Prof,* Dickinson State College, Dept of Art, Dickinson ND (S)

Nawrocki, Thomas, *Prof,* Mississippi University for Women, Division of Fine & Performing Arts, Columbus MS (S)

Naylor, Geoffrey J, *Prof,* University of Florida, Dept of Art, Gainesville FL (S)

Nazarevicz, W, *VPres,* Ukrainian Institute of America, Inc, New York NY

Neaher, Nancy C, *Vis Asst Prof,* Cornell University, Dept of the History of Art, Ithaca NY (S)

Neal, Berna E, *Head,* University of Maryland, College Park, Architecture Library, College Park MD

Neal, Thomas, *Div Chmn,* Laramie County Community College, Division of Humanities, Cheyenne WY (S)

Near, Pinkney, *Chief Cur,* Virginia Museum of Fine Arts, Richmond VA

Neary, Patrick, *Cur Exhib,* Heard Museum, Phoenix AZ

Needham, Harry T, *Exec VPres and Dir,* Desert Caballeros Western Museum, Wickenburg AZ

Needham, Paul, *Cur Printed Books and Bindings,* Pierpont Morgan Library, New York NY

Needle, Bill, *Chairperson,* Southeast Missouri State University, Dept of Art, Cape Girardeau MO (S)

Neely, Esther, *Gallery Cur,* University of Minnesota, Paul Whitney Larson Gallery, Saint Paul MN

Neely, Mark E, *Dir,* Lincoln National Life Foundation, Inc, Louis A Warren Lincoln Library and Museum, Fort Wayne IN

Neff, George, *Chmn Dept,* Glassboro State College, Dept of Art, Glassboro NJ (S)

Neff, Mary, *Coordr,* Marian College, Art Dept, Fond Du Lac WI (S)

Neff, William B, *Secy Treas,* Special Libraries Association, Museum, Arts and Humanities Division, New York NY

Neidhardt, Carl R, *Dir,* Austin College, Ida Green Gallery, Sherman TX

Neidhardt, Carl R, *Chmn,* Austin College, Art Dept, Sherman TX (S)

Neil, J M, *Dir,* Nicolaysen Art Museum, Casper WY

Neil, Milton, *Instr,* Joe Kubert School of Cartoon and Graphic Art Inc, Dover NJ (S)

Neill, Mary G, *Cur Oriental Art,* Yale University, Art Gallery, New Haven CT

Neils, Jenifer, *Asst Prof,* Case Western Reserve University, Dept of Art, Cleveland OH (S)

Neiman, Steven, *Secy,* Doshi Center for Contemporary Art, Harrisburg PA

Neiswender, Barbara, *Asst Dir for Develop,* New Orleans Museum of Art, New Orleans LA

Nelsen, Kenneth, *Asst Prof,* Northwest Missouri State University, Dept of Art, Maryville MO (S)

Nelson, Art, *Ceramics,* California College of Arts and Crafts, Oakland CA (S)

Nelson, Burton R, *Cur Exhib,* Hastings Museum, Hastings NE

Nelson, Dan, *Asst Dir,* Bradford Brinton Memorial Ranch Museum, Big Horn WY

Nelson, Dean E, *Chief Bureau of Museums and Historic Sites,* Division of Historical and Cultural Affairs, Bureau of Museums and Historic Sites, Dover DE

Nelson, Diane, *Correspondence Secy,* Association of Medical Illustrators, Midlothian VA

Nelson, Doris Helen, *Exec Dir,* Salem Art Association, Salem OR

Nelson, Harold B, *Exhibition Prog Dir,* The Art Museum Association of America, San Francisco CA

Nelson, James, *Dir & Cur,* Yuma Fine Arts Association, Yuma Art Center, Yuma AZ

Nelson, James, *Dir,* Jacksonville Public Library, Art and Music Dept, Jacksonville FL

Nelson, Jane, *Chmn Dept,* Missouri Western State College, Art Dept, Saint Joseph MO (S)

Nelson, Jean, *Lectr,* Notre Dame College, Art Dept, Manchester NH (S)

Nelson, Jeffrey, *Prof,* Butte College, Dept of Fine & Performing Arts, Oroville CA (S)

Nelson, Joyce, *Mgr Tweed Museum Gift Shop,* University of Minnesota, Tweed Museum of Art, Duluth MN

Nelson, Kirk, *Cur Art & Decorative Arts,* Bennington Museum, Bennington VT

Nelson, Lawrence R, *Coordr Fine & Performing Arts,* Chipola Junior College, Division of Fine Arts and Humanities, Marianna FL (S)

Nelson, Lila, *Textiles Cur,* Vesterheim, Norwegian-American Museum, Decorah IA

Nelson, Marion, *Prof,* University of Minnesota, Minneapolis, Art History, Minneapolis MN (S)

Nelson, Marion John, *Dir,* Vesterheim, Norwegian-American Museum, Decorah IA

Nelson, Ms Kennedy B, *Dir,* Pittsburgh Plan for Art Gallery, Gallery 407, Pittsburgh PA

Nelson, Naomi, *Education,* Afro-American Historical and Cultural Museum, Philadelphia PA

Nelson, Osea, *Asst Dir,* Bradford Brinton Memorial Ranch Museum, Big Horn WY

Nelson, Richard, *Asst Cur,* Muskegon Museum of Art, Muskegon MI

Nelson, Robert, *VPres,* Missouri Western State College, Fine Arts Gallery, Saint Joseph MO

Nelson, Susan, *Asst Prof,* Indiana University, Bloomington, School of Fine Arts, Bloomington IN (S)

Nelson, Vernon H, *Asst Treas,* Annie S Kemerer Museum, Bethlehem PA

Nelson-Kise, James, *Pres,* Philadelphia Museum of Art, Samuel S Fleisher Art Memorial, Philadelphia PA

Nelthropp, Barabara B C, *Assoc Dir,* Saint Croix School of the Arts, Inc, Christansted Saint Croix VI (S)

Nemet, Thomas, *Pres,* Jamaica Center for the Performing & Visual Arts, Inc, Jamaica Arts Center, Jamaica NY

Nemethy, Vicky, *Asst Dir,* Saint Joseph Art Association Inc, Krasl Art Center, Saint Joseph MI

Nemeti, Gail, *Exec Dir,* Art Barn, Greenwich CT

Nemiroff, Diana, *Asst Cur Contemporary Art,* National Gallery of Canada, Ottawa ON

Nepean, Donald, *Supvr,* Spokane Falls Community College, Creative & Performing Arts, Spokane WA (S)

Nerison, Jane, *Secy,* Middletown Fine Arts Center, Middletown OH

Nerney, Michael F, *Pres,* Adirondack Lakes Center for the Arts, Blue Mountain Lake NY

Nesbit, Doug, *Public Information Officer,* Western Kentucky University, Kentucky Museum, Bowling Green KY

Nesbitt, John J, *Treas,* Wayne Art Center, Wayne PA

Nesgih, Deane, *Instr,* Maryland College of Art and Design, Silver Spring MD (S)

Nesler, Tina, *Bus Mgr,* Sierra Nevada Museum of Art, Reno NV

Ness, Gary C, *Dir,* Ohio Historical Society, Columbus OH

Nestor, Linda, *Asst Prof,* College of Santa Fe, Visual Art Division, Santa Fe NM (S)

Neth, Ted, *Chmn Performing Arts Div,* Columbia Basin College, Art Dept, Pasco WA (S)

Netsky, Ron, *Asst Prof,* Nazareth College of Rochester, Art Dept, Rochester NY (S)

Nettles, Beatrice, *Assoc Prof,* Rochester Institute of Technology, School of Photographic Arts & Sciences, Rochester NY (S)

Neubert, George W, *Dir,* University of Nebraska, Lincoln, Sheldon Memorial Art Gallery, Lincoln NE

Neuman, Robert M, *Asst Prof,* Florida State University, Art History Dept, Tallahassee FL (S)

Neumann, J E, *Faculty,* Western Illinois University, College of Fine Arts, Macomb IL (S)

Neumann, Lynn, *Adminr,* Library Association of La Jolla, Athenaeum Music and Arts Library, La Jolla CA

Neumann, Timothy C, *Cur & Dir,* Pocumtuck Valley Memorial Association, Memorial Hall, Deerfield MA

Neuroth, Karl O, *Chmn Fine Arts,* Keystone Junior College, Fine Arts Dept, Factoryville PA (S)

Nevadomi, Kenneth, *Assoc Prof,* Cleveland State University, Art Dept, Cleveland OH (S)

Nevelson, Louise, *VPres,* Federation of Modern Painters and Sculptors, New York NY

Nevins, Christopher B, *Cur,* Fairfield Historical Society, Fairfield CT

Nevins, Jerome, *Prof,* Albertus Magnus College, Art Dept, New Haven CT (S)

Nevling, Lorin I, *Dir,* Field Museum of Natural History, Chicago IL

Newberg, Alan K, *Head,* Eastern Montana College, Art Dept, Billings MT (S)

Newberry, Susan, *Dir Education,* Newark Museum, Newark NJ

Newbold, Theodore T, *Actg Dir,* Philadelphia Maritime Museum, Philadelphia PA

Newbold, Theodore T, *Pres,* Fairmount Park Art Association, Philadelphia PA

Newcomber, F K, *Cur,* Schuyler-Hamilton House, Morristown NJ

Newell, Cain, *Secy,* National Council on Art in Jewish Life, New York NY

Newell, Elizabeth, *Cur Education & Dir,* Connecticut Valley Historical Museum, Springfield MA

Newell, Larry, *Chmn,* Pearl River Junior College, Fine Arts Dept, Poplarville MS (S)

Newell, Lyn, *Instr,* Berkshire Community College, Dept Fine Arts, Pittsfield MA (S)

Newkirk, Sara, *Pres,* Floyd County Museum, New Albany IN

Newland, Joseph N, *Editor of Publications,* University of Washington, Henry Art Gallery, Seattle WA

Newman, Barbara, *Instructor,* Boston Center for Adult Education, Boston MA (S)

Newman, Carol Kaufman, *Educ Dir,* Yeshiva University, Museum, New York NY

Newman, Daniel, *Prof,* Rutgers, the State University of New Jersey, Mason Gross School of the Arts, New Brunswick NJ (S)

Newman, Elias, *Exec Officer,* New York Artists Equity Association, Inc, Artists Welfare Fund, Inc, New York NY

Newman, Jerry, *Prof,* Lamar University, Art Dept, Beaumont TX (S)

Newman, John, *Faculty,* Sarah Lawrence College, Dept of Art, Bronxville NY (S)

Newman, Naomi, *Board Member,* Actual Art Foundation, New York NY

Newman, Richard, *Chmn,* Bradford College, Creative Arts Division, Bradford MA (S)

Newman, Ruth D, *Co-Dir,* New York University, 80 Washington Square East Galleries, New York NY

Newman, Sasha, *Assoc Cur,* The Phillips Collection, Washington DC

Newmark, Susan W, *Coordr,* Hebrew Union College, Gallery of Art and Artifacts, Cincinnati OH

Newmeyer-Hill, Sarah, *Admin Officer,* Freer Gallery of Art, Washington DC

Newquist, Laurence W, *Pres,* Kent Art Association, Inc, Kent CT

Newton, Douglas, *Chmn Primitive Art,* Metropolitan Museum of Art, New York NY

Newton, Earle W, *Pres,* College of the Americas, Museum of the Americas, Brookfield VT

Newton, Earle W, *Dir,* College of the Americas, Library, Brookfield VT

Newton, Hal, *Lecturer,* University of Wisconsin-Stout, Art Dept, Menomonie WI (S)

Newton, Harold, *Instructor,* Williamsport Area Community College, Dept of Engineering and Design, Williamsport PA (S)

Ng, W Tin, *Exec Dir,* Alberta Art Foundation, Edmonton AB

Nichelson, Jack C, *Prof,* University of Florida, Dept of Art, Gainesville FL (S)

Nichlin-Pommer, Linda, *Distinguished Prof,* City University of New York, PhD Program in Art History, New York NY (S)

Nicholas, Myra J, *Reference Librn,* Santa Barbara Public Library, Faulkner Memorial Art Wing, Santa Barbara CA

Nichols, Adele, *Dir,* Kennebec Valley Art Association, Harlow Gallery, Hallowell ME

Nichols, Arthur Ray, *Corresp Secy,* Pen and Brush, Inc, New York NY

Nichols, David, *Artist-In-Res,* Western Carolina University, Dept of Art, Cullowhee NC (S)

Nichols, Earl, *Coordr Japanese Gallery,* Oklahoma Center for Science and Art, Kirkpatrick Center, Oklahoma City OK

Nichols, E E, *Chmn Painting,* Pan American University, Art Dept, Edinburg TX (S)

Nichols, Frank, *Assoc Prof,* Fort Hays State University, Dept of Art, Hays KS (S)

Nichols, Malcolm, *Instructor,* San Diego Mesa College, Fine Arts Dept, San Diego CA (S)

Nichols, Ned, *Dir,* Fayette Art Museum, Fayette AL

Nichols, Ray, *Coordr Graphic Design,* University of Delaware, Dept of Art, Newark DE (S)

Nichols, Walter, *Prof,* Mount Saint Mary's College, Fine Arts Dept, Emmitsburg MD (S)

Nichols, William, *Instr,* Wilkes Community College, Arts and Science Division, Wilkesboro NC (S)

Nicholson, Freda, *Chief Exec Officer,* Science Museums of Charlotte, Inc, Discovery Place, Charlotte NC

Nicholson, Joan, *Deputy Dir-NY,* American Academy in Rome, New York NY (S)

Nicholson, Joanna, *Chmn,* Fairfield University, Fine Arts Dept, Fairfield CT (S)

Nicholson, Thomas D, *Dir,* American Museum of Natural History, New York NY

Nickel, Helmut, *Cur Arms & Armor,* Metropolitan Museum of Art, New York NY

Nickel, Lorene, *Artist-in-Res,* Mary Washington College, Art Dept, Fredericksburg VA (S)

Nickel, Peter, *Adjunct Instr,* Southwestern University, Art Dept, Georgetown TX (S)

Nickol, Michael, *VPres,* Midwest Museum of American Art, Elkhart IN

Nicola, Suzanne, *Executive Dir,* Pine Castle Center of the Arts, Inc, Orlando FL

Nicolaysen, Jon C, *Chmn Board,* Nicolaysen Art Museum, Casper WY

Nielsen, Helen, *Secy,* New Mexico Art League, Gallery, Albuquerque NM

Nielsen, Larry, *Cur,* Harold Warp Pioneer Village Foundation, Minden NE

Nielsen, Nina, *VPres,* The Society of Arts and Crafts, Boston MA

Nielsen, Thomas L, *Instr Pottery,* Red Rocks Community College, Human Resources & Services Division, Golden CO (S)

Nienhuis, Pamela, *Cur,* Spartanburg County Art Association, Spartanburg SC

Niergarten-Smith, Beej, *Dir,* Laumeier Sculpture Park, Saint Louis MO

Nieves, Miguel A, *Librn,* Institute of Puerto Rican Culture, Library, San Juan PR

Niewald, Wilbur, *Chmn Painting & Printmaking,* Kansas City Art Institute, Kansas City MO (S)

Nihart, F B, *Deputy Dir,* Marine Corps Museum, Art Unit, Washington DC

Nikirk, Robert, *Librn,* Grolier Club Library, New York NY

Nilsson, Jo H, *Photography & Slide Librn,* Seattle Art Museum, Library, Seattle WA

Nimocks, Susan, *Dir,* McDowel House and Apothecary Shop, Danville KY

Nims, Florence W, *Dir,* Ogunquit Art Center, Ogunquit ME

Nisenholt, Mark, *Lectr,* Lakehead University, Dept of Fine Art, Thunder Bay ON (S)

Niswonger, Gary, *Chairperson Art Dept,* Smith College, Art Dept, Northampton MA (S)

Nitsch, Paul Arlyn, *Artists-in-Res,* Queens College, Art Dept, Charlotte NC (S)

Nix, W Robert, *Art Education,* University of Georgia, Franklin College of Arts and Sciences, Dept of Art, Athens GA (S)

Nixon, Carlis, *Instructor,* Linn Benton Community College, Fine & Applied Art Dept, Albany OR (S)

Nobel, Robert, *Chief Cur,* Museum of the Philadelphia Civic Center, Philadelphia PA

Noble, Joseph Veach, *Pres,* Brookgreen Gardens, Murrells Inlet SC

Noble, Joseph Veach, *Dir,* Museum of the City of New York, New York NY

Noble, N N, *Asst Prof,* Presbyterian College, Fine Arts Dept, Clinton SC (S)

Nock, Walter J, *Museum Specialist,* United States Military Academy, West Point Museum, West Point NY

Nodal, Al, *Dir,* Otis Art Institute of Parsons School of Design Gallery, Los Angeles CA

Noe, Jerry, *Assoc Prof,* University of North Carolina at Chapel Hill, Art Dept, Chapel Hill NC (S)

Noel, Barbara H, *Dean Col,* Southeastern Massachusetts University, College of Visual and Performing Arts, North Dartmouth MA (S)

Noenning, Anita, *Pres,* Bay Area Art Conservation Guild, Oakland CA

Noerdlinger, Janau, *Instr,* Blackhawk Mountain School of Art, Black Hawk CO (S)

Noffke, Gary, *Jewelry & Metalwork,* University of Georgia, Franklin College of Arts and Sciences, Dept of Art, Athens GA (S)

Noga, Joseph L, *Coordr Grad Program,* Rochester Institute of Technology, School of Printing, Rochester NY (S)

Nohrr, Philip, *Secy,* Brevard Art Center and Museum, Inc, Melbourne FL

Nolan, John F, *Pres,* Massachusetts College of Art, Boston MA (S)

Nolan, Liesel, *Head Art and Architecture Library,* University of Colorado Art Galleries, Art and Architecture Library, Boulder CO

Nolan, Margaret P, *Chief Librn,* Metropolitan Museum of Art, Photograph and Slide Library, New York NY

Nolan, Pat, *VPres,* Craft Center Museum, Wilton CT

Nolan, Patricia E, *Special Arts Services Dir,* American Society of Artists, Inc, Chicago IL

Nolan, William, *Foundation Chmn,* Atlanta College of Art, Atlanta GA (S)

Nolf, Richard A, *Dir,* Saint Joseph Museum, Saint Joseph MO

Nollman, Ellen A, *Librn,* Freer Gallery of Art, Library, Washington DC

Nomecos, Mary, *Instr,* Studio School of Art and Design, Philadelphia PA (S)

Nonn, Thomas I, *Chmn,* Kingsborough Community College, Dept of Art, Brooklyn NY (S)

Noon, Patrick, *Cur Prints & Drawings,* Yale University, Yale Center for British Art, New Haven CT

Nordberg, Linda, *VPres,* Katonah Gallery, Katonah NY

Nordberg, Paul C, *Instr,* Pierce College, Art Dept, Woodland Hills CA (S)

Nordell, Marilyn, *Instructor,* The Design Schools, Art Institute of Seattle, Seattle WA (S)

Nordland, Gerald, *Dir,* Milwaukee Art Museum, Milwaukee WI

Nordmeyer, Jim, *Instructor,* Dunedin Fine Arts and Cultural Center, Dunedin FL (S)

Nordrum, Douglas A, *Exec Dir,* The Art Center, Mount Clemens MI

Nordstom, Ken, *Instructor,* Iowa Lakes Community College, Dept of Art, Estherville IA (S)

Nordstrom, Marlene, *Lectr,* University of Wisconsin-Superior, Programs in the Visual Arts, Superior WI (S)

Nordstrom, Vereen Ann, *Secy,* Swedish American Museum Association of Chicago, Chicago IL

Norick, Frank A, *Asst Dir,* University of California, R H Lowie Museum of Anthropology, Berkeley CA

Norman, Karen, *Educ Coordr,* Arkansas Territorial Restoration, Little Rock AR

Norman, Stuart, *Exec Dir,* Greensboro Artists' League, Greensboro NC

Norris, Andrea, *Chief Cur,* University of Texas at Austin, Archer M Huntington Art Gallery, Austin TX

Norris, Randy, *Head Dept,* Yankton College, Dept of Art, Yankton SD (S)

Norris, Sarah, *Librn,* Tacoma Art Museum, Reference Library, Tacoma WA

Norris, Shannon, *Secy,* Community Arts Council of Vancouver, Vancouver BC

Norris, Trevor, *Designer,* University of Southern California, Fisher Gallery, Los Angeles CA

North, John, *Dir Learning Resources Center,* Ryerson Polytechnical Institute Library, Toronto ON

North, Kenda, *Lectr,* University of California, Riverside, Program in Art, Riverside CA (S)

Northcutt, John, *Archaeologist,* Institute of the Great Plains, Museum of the Great Plains, Lawton OK

Northington, David, *Cur Botany,* Texas Tech University Museum, Lubbock TX

Northup, Albert Dale, *Chmn Fine Art Dept,* Saint Clair County Community College, Art Dept, Port Huron MI (S)

Northup, Marjorie, *Cur of Education,* Reynolda House, Inc, Winston-Salem NC

Norton, C D, *Pres,* Lighthouse Gallery, Tequesta FL

Norton, Marti, *Cur Education,* Paine Art Center and Arboretum, Oshkosh WI

Norton, Paul, *Prof,* University of Massachusetts, Amherst, Art History Program, Amherst MA (S)

Norton, Richard W, *Pres of the Board,* R W Norton Art Gallery, Shreveport LA

Norwood, Malcolm M, *Chmn Dept,* Delta State University, Fielding L Wright Art Center, Cleveland MS

Norwood, Malcolm M, *Chmn,* Delta State University, Dept of Art, Cleveland MS (S)

Norwood, Nancy, *Media Center,* Visual Studies Workshop, Rochester NY

Nosanow, Barbara Shissler, *Asst Dir, Museum Programs,* National Museum of American Art, Washington DC

Nothern, Tamara, *Cur Ethnographic & Archeological Collections,* Hood Museum of Art, Hanover NH

Nottage, Mary Ellen Hennessey, *Cur of Decorative Art,* Kansas State Historial Society Museum, Topeka KS

Novak, Allen, *AV Librn,* Ringling School of Art Library, Sarasota FL

Novak, Philip, *Asst Dir,* Stamford Museum and Nature Center, Stamford CT

Novelli, Martin, *Assoc Dean Academic Affairs,* Philadelphia College of Art, Philadelphia PA (S)

Nowack, P, *Dean Applied Arts,* Ryerson Polytechnical Institute Library, Toronto ON

Noyes, Marie E, *Asst to Dir,* Norwich Free Academy, Slater Memorial Museum & Converse Art Gallery, Norwich CT

Nozkowski, Tom, *Pres,* 55 Mercer, New York NY

Nozynski, John H, *Dir,* Tampa Museum, Tampa FL

Nuchims, Paul, *Chmn,* West Virginia State College, Art Dept, Institute WV (S)

Nugent, Bob, *Gallery Dir,* Sonoma State University Art Gallery, Rohnert Park CA

Nugent, Kristina Rice, *Chmn,* Miracosta College, Art Dept, Oceanside CA (S)

Nugent, Patricia, *Instr,* Rosemont College, Division of the Arts, Rosemont PA (S)

Nunn, Gil, *Photo Technician,* Institute of the Great Plains, Museum of the Great Plains, Lawton OK

Nunn, Willie, *Specialist,* Elizabet Ney Museum, Austin TX

Nunnelley, Robert, *Prof,* Fairleigh Dickinson University, Fine Arts Dept, Teaneck NJ (S)

Nusbaum, Daniel C, *Chmn,* Mount Saint Mary's College, Fine Arts Dept, Emmitsburg MD (S)

Nutini, Teo, *Dir,* Ashland Oil, Inc, Russell KY

Nutter, Coral, *Comptroller,* Huntington Galleries, Huntington WV

Nutter, Daniel L, *Dir,* Southwestern College, Memorial Library - Art Dept, Winfield KS

Nutzle, Futzie, *Vis Prof,* Victor Valley College, Art Dept, Victorville CA (S)

Nuzum, Thomas, *Instructor,* Charles Stewart Mott Community College, Fine Arts Division, Flint MI (S)

Nyburg, Mary, *Pres,* Haystack Mountain School of Crafts Gallery, Deer Isle ME

Nyce, Fletcher E, *Secy,* Cincinnati Institute of Fine Arts, Cincinnati OH

Nyerges, Michael, *Dir,* Patterson Library & Art Gallery, Westfield NY

Nygren, Edward J, *Cur,* Corcoran Museum, Washington DC

Oagley, Howard, *Prof,* University of Evansville, Art Dept, Evansville IN (S)

Oak, Jacquelyn, *Registrar,* Museum of Our National Heritage, Lexington MA

Oakes, Arthur, *Assoc Prof,* University of Alabama, Art Dept, Tuscaloosa AL (S)

Oakes, John Warren, *Dir,* Western Kentucky University, University Gallery, Bowling Green KY

Oakley, Rhoda, *Prof,* University of Maine at Augusta, Division of Arts and Humanities, Augusta ME (S)

Oberhausen, Judy, *Cur,* Art Center, Inc, South Bend IN

O'Biso, Carol, *Registrar,* The American Federation of Arts, New York NY

O'Brian, Ellen Morrison, *Gallery Dir,* Biloxi Art Association, Gallery, Biloxi MS

O'Brien, Denise G, *Admin,* Pointe Claire Cultural Centre, Pointe Claire PQ

O'Brien, Diane, *Studio School Coordr,* Midland Art Council, Midland MI

O'Brien, Elzino, *Instr,* The School of Fashion Design, Boston MA (S)

O'Brien, JoAnn, *Chmn,* College of New Rochelle School of Arts and Sciences, Undergraduate Art Dept, New Rochelle NY (S)

O'Brien, Kerry, *Cur,* Old Gaol Museum, York ME

O'Brien, Marcia E, *Dir Office of Cultural Development,* Nassau County Museum of Fine Art, Roslyn NY

O'Brien, Maureen C, *Assoc Dir & Cur Affairs,* Parrish Art Museum, Southampton NY

O'Brien, Mern, *Registrar,* Dalhousie University, Art Gallery, Halifax NS

O'Brien, Paddy, *Asst Dir & Cur,* London Regional Art Gallery, London ON

O'Brien, Robert B, *Chmn of the Board,* New Jersey Historical Society Museum, Newark NJ

O'Bryan, Lorene, *Treas,* Brattleboro Museum and Art Center, Brattleboro VT

Ochiai, Hisako, *Educational Dir,* Museum of Oriental Cultures, Corpus Christi TX

Ockenga, Starr, *Dir,* Massachusetts Institute of Technology, Creative Photography Gallery, Cambridge MA

O'Connell, Charles, *Pres,* Attleboro Museum, Center for the Arts, Attleboro MA

O'Connell, Donald, *Instructor,* Milwaukee Area Technical College, Graphic & Applied Arts Division, Milwaukee WI (S)

O'Connell, Kenneth R, *Prof,* University of Oregon, Dept of Fine & Applied Arts, Eugene OR (S)

O'Connor, David, *Egyptian Section Assoc Cur,* University of Pennsylvania, University Museum of Archaeology & Anthropology, Philadelphia PA

O'Connor, Elizabeth, *Deputy Chair,* City College of New York, Art Dept, New York NY (S)

O'Connor, George, *Pres,* Montana Historical Society, Helena MT

O'Connor, John A, *Assoc Prof,* University of Florida, Dept of Art, Gainesville FL (S)

O'Connor, M E, *Dir,* Bayonne Free Public Library, Art Dept, Bayonne NJ

O'Connor, Stanley J, *Prof,* Cornell University, Dept of the History of Art, Ithaca NY (S)

O'Connor, Thom, *Prof,* State University of New York at Albany, Art Dept, Albany NY (S)

O'Daniel, D Patrick, *Pres Bd Dir,* Evansville Museum of Arts and Science, Evansville IN

Odell, Cay, *Gallery Dir,* Saint Augustine Art Association Gallery, Saint Augustine FL

Odevseff, Barbara, *Registrar,* Wichita Art Museum, Wichita KS

Odom, Patt, *Head,* Jackson County Junior College, Art Dept, Gautier MS (S)

O'Donal, Rory, *Executive Dir,* Ontario Association of Art Galleries, Toronto ON

O'Donnell, Ellen, *Dir,* Provincetown Art Association and Museum, Provincetown MA

O'Donnell, Patricia Chapin, *Dir,* Philadelphia College of Textiles and Science, Paley Design Center, Philadelphia PA

Oedel, William T, *Cur,* Historical Society of Pennsylvania, Philadelphia PA

Oehlschlaeger, Frank, *Asst Prof,* Notre Dame College, Art Dept, Manchester NH (S)

Oestreich, Nelson E, *Dir,* Westminster College Art Gallery, New Wilmington PA

Oettel, Russell L, *Chmn Dept,* Indiana University-Purdue University, Dept of Fine Arts, Fort Wayne IN (S)

Offenbacher, Hurley, *Construction Mgr,* National Gallery of Art, Washington DC

Offner, Elliot, *Prof,* Smith College, Art Dept, Northampton MA (S)

O'Gara, Gordon C, *Asst Dir Administration & Business,* Palm Springs Desert Museum, Inc, Palm Springs CA

Ogard, Elvira, *Secy,* Guadalupe Historic Foundation, Santuario de Guadalupe, Santa Fe NM

Ogden, Carolyn Cron, *Dir,* Carnegie Center of the Arts, Walla Walla WA

Ogilvie, Olimpia, *Chmn,* Ripon College, Art Dept, Ripon WI (S)

Ogle, Debra, *Asst Cur,* Oklahoma Museum of Art, Oklahoma City OK

Ogle, Philip, *Instructor,* School of the Associated Arts, Saint Paul MN (S)

O'Gorman, James F, *Prof,* Wellesley College, Art Dept, Wellesley MA (S)

O'Halloran, B C, *Prof,* Incarnate Word College, Art Dept, San Antonio TX (S)

O'Hara, Arthur N, *Business Mgr,* Great Lakes Historical Society, Vermilion OH

O'Hara, Bruce, *Photographer,* Tougaloo College, Art Collection, Tougaloo MS

O'Hara, Bruce, *Asst Prof,* Tougaloo College, Art Dept, Tougaloo MS (S)

O'Hara, Donal J, *Prof,* University of Bridgeport, Art Dept, Bridgeport CT (S)

O'Hara, Edward, *Librn,* Manhattanville College, Manhattanville Library, Purchase NY

O'Hara, J, *Instr,* Northern Arizona University, Art Dept, Flagstaff AZ (S)

O'Hare, Marita, *Executive Dir,* The Architectural League, New York NY

O'Hare, Timothy, *Div Chmn,* College of Great Falls, Dept of Art, Great Falls MT (S)

O'Hayes, Patrick, *Secy,* Newport Historical Society, Newport RI

Ohe, John, *Registrar,* Kern County Museum, Bakersfield CA

O'Hear, James, *Asst Chmn & Dir Undergrad Studies,* Catholic University of America, Dept of Architecture and Planning, Washington DC (S)

O'Hern, Dianne, *Asst Prof,* Southern Arkansas University, Dept of Art, Magnolia AR (S)

O'Hern, Dianne, *Asst Prof,* Southern Arkansas University, Art Dept Gallery & Magale Art Gallery, Magnolia AR

Ohlin, Betty E, *Asst Prof,* Rhode Island College, Art Dept, Providence RI (S)

Ohman, Richard, *Asst Prof,* Ohio University-Chillicothe Campus, Fine Arts & Humanities Division, Chillicothe OH (S)

Oikawa-Picante, Teri, *Conservator Painting,* Fine Arts Museums of San Francisco, M H de Young Memorial Museum and California Palace of the Legion of Honor, San Francisco CA

Okada, Connie, *Librn,* University of Washington, Art Library, Seattle WA

O'Kane, Michael, *Technician,* State University of New York at Binghamton, University Art Gallery, Binghamton NY

O'Keefe, Michael, *Asst Prof,* Oklahoma Christian College, Art Dept, Oklahoma City OK (S)

O'Keeffe, Judith, *Educator,* Burnaby Art Gallery, Burnaby BC

O'Kelley, Doramae, *Chmn Education Dept,* Dayton Art Institute, Dayton OH

Oklinetzky, Sam, *Dir,* University of Oklahoma, Museum of Art, Norman OK

Oko, Andrew J, *Cur History Coll,* Art Gallery of Hamilton, Muriel Isabel Bostwick Library, Hamilton ON

Okoomian, Carolyn, *Cur Childrens Museum,* Sunrise Foundation, Inc, Sunrise Museums, Charleston WV

Olander, William, *Actg Dir,* Oberlin College, Allen Memorial Art Museum, Oberlin OH

Olbrantz, John, *Dir,* Pacific Northwest Arts and Crafts Association, Bellevue Art Museum, Bellevue WA

Oldach, Linda, *Asst Librn,* Mount Wachusett Community College, Library, Gardner MA

Oldaker, William, *Instr,* West Virginia Wesleyan College, Dept of Fine Arts, Buckhannon WV (S)

Oldenburg, Richard E, *Dir Museum,* Museum of Modern Art, New York NY

Oldham, Bert, *Art Dept Chmn,* Shasta Community College, Art Dept, Fine Arts Division, Redding CA (S)

Oldham, Ellen, *Keeper,* Boston Public Library, Rare Book & Manuscripts Dept, Boston MA

Olds, C C, *Prof,* Bowdoin College, Art Dept, Brunswick ME (S)

O'Leary, Dennis, *Dir,* Boise Gallery of Art, Boise ID

O'Leary, Jay, *Division Chmn of Fine Arts,* Wayne State College, Nordstrand Visual Arts Gallery, Wayne NE

O'Leary, Jay, *Div Chmn,* Wayne State College, Art Dept, Wayne NE (S)

O'Leary, John, *Vis Artist,* Temple University, Tyler School of Art, Philadelphia PA (S)

Olejarz, Harold, *Board of Dir,* Cultural Council Foundation, Fourteen Sculptors Gallery, New York NY

Oleksy, Francis, *Pres Board of Trustees,* Anderson Fine Arts Center, Anderson IN

Olenik, Janet, *Instr,* Glendale College, Dept of Fine Arts, Glendale CA (S)

Olin, Ferris, *Art Librn,* Rutgers University, Art Library, New Brunswick NJ

Oliver, Celia Y, *Registrar,* Shelburne Museum, Shelburne VT

Oliver, Cornelia, *Prof,* Mary Washington College, Art Dept, Fredericksburg VA (S)

Oliver, F Duane, *Asst Prof,* Western Carolina University, Dept of Art, Cullowhee NC (S)

Oliver, John A, *Dir,* Flint Public Library, Fine Arts Dept, Flint MI

Oliver, Loren, *Chmn Studio Art,* Sweet Briar College, Art History Dept and Art Studio Dept, Sweet Briar VA (S)

Oliver, Michael, *Asst Prof,* Friends University, Art Dept, Wichita KS (S)

Oliver, Robert, *Dir,* Arizona Watercolor Association, Phoenix AZ

Oliver, Victor, *Preparator,* Oakland Museum, Art Dept, Oakland CA

Olivier, Kate, *Assoc Conservator,* Harvard University, William Hayes Fogg Art Museum, Cambridge MA

Ollman, Arthur, *Pres,* San Francisco Camerawork, San Francisco CA

Olmstead, Laura, *Registrar,* George Walter Vincent Smith Art Museum, Springfield MA

Olmstead, Philip, *Pres,* Seneca Falls Historical Society Museum, Seneca Falls NY

Olney, Susan Faxon, *Dir,* University of New Hampshire, University Art Galleries, Durham NH

O'Looney, James, *Asst Prof,* Mohawk Valley Community College, Advertising Design and Production, Utica NY (S)

Olpin, Robert S, *Dir,* University of Utah, Owen Library, Salt Lake City UT

Olpin, Robert S, *Prof,* University of Utah, Art Dept, Salt Lake City UT (S)

Olsen, Dennis, *Asst Prof,* University of Texas at San Antonio, Division of Art and Design, San Antonio TX (S)

Olsen, Frederick L, *Instr,* Mount San Jacinto College, Art Dept, San Jacinto CA (S)

Olsen, James T, *Asst Prof,* Dana College, Art Dept, Blair NE (S)

Olsen, Janice, *Dir Handforth Gallery,* Tacoma Public Library, Handforth Gallery, Tacoma WA

Olsen, Mel, *Chmn & Prof,* University of Wisconsin-Superior, Programs in the Visual Arts, Superior WI (S)

Olsen, Paul, *Asst Prof,* Mississippi University for Women, Division of Fine & Performing Arts, Columbus MS (S)

Olsen, Sandra H, *Dir,* Niagara University, Buscaglia-Castellani Art Gallery, Niagara Falls NY

Olsen, Stanley W, *Dir,* Museum of the United States, Washington DC

Olsen, Steven L, *Research Supv,* Church of Jesus Christ of Latter-Day Saints, Museum of Church History and Art, Salt Lake City UT

Olsen, Valerie L, *Chief Cur Collections,* New Orleans Museum of Art, New Orleans LA

Olson, Edna M, *Secy of Board,* The Racine Art Association, Inc, Racine WI

Olson, Gary, *Prog Coordr Printmaking,* Alberta College of Art, Southern Alberta Institute of Technology, Calgary AB (S)

Olson, George, *Prof,* College of Wooster, Dept of Art, Wooster OH (S)

Olson, Gerald, *Dir,* Dixie College, Southwestern Utah Art Gallery, Saint George UT

Olson, Janis, *Registrar,* Whatcom Museum of History and Art, Bellingham WA

Olson, Joann, *Librn,* Miami University Art Museum, Library, Oxford OH

Olson, Joseph, *Prof,* Georgia Southern College, Dept of Art, Statesboro GA (S)

Olson, Kathi, *Cur,* Fort Missoula Historical Museum, Missoula MT

Olson, Martina, *Arts & Crafts Dir,* Yugtarvik Regional Museum, Bethel AK

Olson, Paul, *Fine Arts Chmn,* Oakland City College, Division of Fine Arts, Oakland City IN (S)

Olson, Paulette, *Executive Secy,* Society of Architectural Historians, Philadelphia PA

Olson, Richard D, *Bibliographer,* Northwestern University, Art Library, Evanston IL

Olson, Richard W P, *Prof,* Beloit College, Dept of Art, Beloit WI (S)

Olsson, Helen, *Libr Asst,* Newark Museum, Library, Newark NJ

Olszewski, Edward J, *Assoc Prof,* Case Western Reserve University, Dept of Art, Cleveland OH (S)

Olszewski, Michael, *Chmn Textile Design,* Moore College of Art, Philadelphia PA (S)

Oltuid, Carl, *Artist in Res,* Viterbo College, Art Dept, La Crosse WI (S)

Oltvedt, Carl, *Asst Prof,* Moorhead State University, Dept of Art, Moorhead MN (S)

O'Lugosz, Joseph, *Instructor,* Milwaukee Area Technical College, Graphic & Applied Arts Division, Milwaukee WI (S)

Olvera, John, *Interior Design Coordr,* North Texas State University, Art Dept, Denton TX (S)

Olvera, Karen, *Slide Librn,* North Texas State University, Art Slide Library, Denton TX

Olynyk, Betty, *Secy,* Revelstoke Art Group, Revelstoke BC

O'Malley, Dennis M, *Coordr,* Rhode Island College, Edward M Bannister Gallery, Providence RI

O'Malley, Leslie C, *Dir,* Cortland County Historical Society, Suggett House Museum, Cortland NY

O'Malley, Lynda W, *Cur & Caretaker,* South County Art Association, Kingston RI

O'Malley, William, *Instructor,* Charles Stewart Mott Community College, Fine Arts Division, Flint MI (S)

Oman, Richard G, *Cur Coll,* Church of Jesus Christ of Latter-Day Saints, Museum of Church History and Art, Salt Lake City UT

Omar, Margit, *Assoc Prof,* University of Southern California, School of Fine Arts, Los Angeles CA (S)

O'Meara, Virginia, *Assoc Prof,* Maryville College, St Louis, Art Division, Saint Louis MO (S)

Omelia, John F, *Asst Prof,* Manhattan College, School of Arts and Sciences, Bronx NY (S)

O'Neal, R Ronald, *Head Dept,* Wiley College, Dept of Fine Arts, Marshall TX (S)

O'Neil, John, *Prof Emeritus,* Rice University, Dept of Art and Art History, Houston TX (S)

Oneil, John, *Chmn,* University of South Carolina, Dept of Art, Columbia SC (S)

O'Neili, Robert, *Prof,* Lamar University, Art Dept, Beaumont TX (S)

O'Neil, Jim, *Treas,* Art Guild of Burlington, Arts for Living Center, Burlington IA

Onken, Michael O, *Grad Studies,* Southern Illinois University, School of Art, Carbondale IL (S)

Onorato, Ronald, *Chmn,* University of Rhode Island, Dept of Art, Kingston RI (S)

Onyile, Onyile, *Instr,* University of Northern Iowa, Dept of Art, Cedar Falls IA (S)

Opar, Barbara A, *Architecture Librn,* Syracuse University, Ernest Stevenson Bird Library, Syracuse NY

Oppenheimer, Frank, *Dir,* Exploratorium, San Francisco CA

Oppenheimer, Jesse, *Pres,* Marion Koogler McNay Art Museum, San Antonio TX

Oppenhimer, Anne P, *Instr,* University of Richmond, Dept of Art, Richmond VA (S)

Oppermann, Kathleen, *Admin Asst,* Chesterwood, Stockbridge MA

Oppler, Ellen, *Prof,* Syracuse University, Dept of Fine Arts, Syracuse NY (S)

Orchard, Harry F, *Fine Arts Cur,* Morris Museum of Arts and Sciences, Morristown NJ

Orchard, Sharon, *Librn,* Coquille Valley Art Association, Library, Coquille OR

O'Rear, Edward C, *Chmn,* Liberty Hall Museum, Frankfort KY

O'Reilly, Priscilla, *Registrar,* Historic New Orleans Collection, Kemper and Leila Williams Foundation, New Orleans LA

Orenstein, Phil, *Assoc Prof,* Rutgers, the State University of New Jersey, Mason Gross School of the Arts, New Brunswick NJ (S)

Ormond, Mark, *Cur,* Metropolitan Museum and Art Center, Coral Gables FL

O'Rourke, Alice, *Pres,* Edgewood College, DeRicci Gallery, Madison WI

O'Rourke, James, *Dir & Secy Board Dir,* Plains Art Museum, Main Gallery, Moorhead MN

Orr, Agnes, *Volunteer,* Redding Museum and Art Center, Museum Research Library, Redding CA

Orr, William, *Cur Manuscripts,* Joslyn Art Museum, Omaha NE

Orr-Cahall, Christina, *Chief Cur Art,* Oakland Museum, Art Dept, Oakland CA

Orr-McMahon, Kim, *Asst Prof,* Bryn Mawr College, Dept of the History of Art, Bryn Mawr PA (S)

Ortbals, John, *Asst Prof,* Saint Louis Community College at Florissant Valley, Dept of Art, Ferguson MO (S)

Orth, Fredrick, *Dir,* San Diego State University, Art Gallery, San Diego CA

Orth, Fredrick, *Chmn,* San Diego State University, Dept of Art, San Diego CA (S)

Ortiz, Rafael, *Assoc Prof,* Rutgers, the State University of New Jersey, Mason Gross School of the Arts, New Brunswick NJ (S)

Ortman, George, *Head Painting Dept,* Cranbrook Academy of Art, Bloomfield Hills MI (S)

Ortner, Frederick, *Asst Prof,* Knox College, Dept of Art, Galesburg IL (S)

Orton, Colin, *Cur Numismatics,* University of Calgary, The Nickle Arts Museum, Calgary AB

Ory, Norma R, *Dean Junior School,* Alfred C Glassell School of Art, Houston TX (S)

Osborn, Don, *Chmn Exhibits,* Arkansas State University Art Gallery, Jonesboro, Jonesboro AR

Osborn, Don, *Asst Prof,* Arkansas State University, Dept of Art, State University AR (S)

Osborn, Elaine, *Museum Publicity Agent,* Bower's Museum, Santa Ana CA

Osborn, Jane Ellen, *Dir,* Parkersburg Art Center, Parkersburg WV

Osborne, Addis M, *Asst Dir & Designer,* Museum of Our National Heritage, Lexington MA

Osborne, Carol, *Assoc Dir & Cur Coll,* Stanford University, Museum of Art & Art Gallery, Stanford CA

Osborne, John L, *Asst Prof,* University of Victoria, Dept of History in Art, Victoria BC (S)

Osbun, Jack, *Assoc Prof,* Wittenberg University, Art Dept, Springfield OH (S)

Osgood, William B, *Chmn,* Boston Art Commission of the City of Boston, Boston MA

Osler, William, *Secy,* Arts and Letters Club of Toronto, Toronto ON

Osman, Randolph, *Gallery Dir,* East Carolina University, Gray Art Gallery, Greenville NC

Ossa, Wilhelm, *Instructor,* Casper College, Casper WY (S)

Ostermeyer, Denis, *Prof,* Shoreline Community College, Humanities Division, Seattle WA (S)

Ostiguy, Jean-Rene, *Research Cur Canadian Art,* National Gallery of Canada, Ottawa ON

Ostrow, Mindy, *Asst Dir,* State University of New York at Oswego, Tyler Art Gallery, Oswego NY

Ostrow, Stephen E, *Exec Dir,* Portland Art Association, Portland OR

Ostwald, Bruce, *Asst Prof,* Hartford Art School of the University of Hartford, West Hartford CT (S)

Oswald, April A, *Asst Art Librn,* University of Chicago, Art Library, Chicago IL

Oswald, Genevieve, *Dance Cur,* New York Public Library, Shelby Cullom Davis Museum, Library & Museum of the Performing Arts, New York NY

Oswald, Louis, *VPres,* Plainsman Museum, Aurora NE

Otan, Valerie, *Outreach Coordr,* Richmond Art Center, Richmond CA

Otis, Helen K, *Conservator Prints & Drawings,* Metropolitan Museum of Art, New York NY

O'Toole, Judith H, *Dir,* Wilkes College, Sordoni Art Gallery, Wilkes-Barre PA

Otremba, Geraldine M, *Deputy Dir of Operations & Center Liaison with the Library of Congress,* John F Kennedy Center for the Performing Arts, Performing Arts Library, Washington DC

Ott, Judith L, *Instr,* Johnson State College, Dept Fine Arts, Johnson VT (S)

Ott, Wendell, *Dir,* Roswell Museum and Art Center, Roswell NM

Ottaviano, Scotty, *Instructor,* Cazenovia College, Center for Art & Design Studies, Cazenovia NY (S)

Ottemiller, William, *VPres,* Seneca Falls Historical Society Museum, Seneca Falls NY

Ottensmeyer, David J, *Chief Executive Officer,* Lovelace Medical Foundation, Art Collection, Albuquerque NM

Otto, Jane, *Secy,* Fine Arts Museums of San Francisco, The Museum Society, San Francisco CA

Otto, Martha, *Head Archaeology,* Ohio Historical Society, Columbus OH

Otton, William G, *Dir,* Laguna Beach Museum of Art, Laguna Beach CA

Oughton, Larry, *Assoc Prof,* Delta College, Art Dept, University Center MI (S)

Ourecky, Irma, *Pres,* Wilber Czech Museum, Wilber NE

Outterbridge, John, *Dir Watts Towers Arts Center,* City of Los Angeles, Cultural Affairs Dept, Los Angeles CA

Ovellette, David, *Dir Galleries,* Florida School of the Arts, Visual Arts, Palatka FL (S)

Overby, Osmund, *Second VPres,* Society of Architectural Historians, Philadelphia PA

Overby, Osmund, *Prof,* University of Missouri, Art History and Archaeology Dept, Columbia MO (S)

Overland, Carlton E, *Cur Coll,* University of Wisconsin, Elvehjem Museum of Art, Madison WI

Overstrom, Sandra, *Cur,* Jordan Historical Museum of The Twenty, Jordan ON

Overtom, George W, *Pres,* Art Institute of Chicago, Textile Society, Chicago IL

Overvoorde, Chris Stoffel, *Assoc Prof,* Calvin College, Art Dept, Grand Rapids MI (S)

Owczarski, Marian, *Dir,* Orchard Lake School Galeria, Orchard Lake MI

Owen, Thomas G, *Dean,* Jacksonville University, Dept of Art, Jacksonville FL (S)

Owens, George A, *Pres,* Tougaloo College, Art Collection, Tougaloo MS

Owens, Gwendolyn, *Assoc Cur,* Cornell University, Herbert F Johnson Museum of Art, Ithaca NY

Owens, Helen McKenzie, *Pres,* Kelly-Griggs House Museum, Red Bluff CA

Owens, John, *Pres,* Arts and Humanities Council of Tuscaloosa County, Inc, Tuscaloosa AL

Owens, Robert L, *Chmn,* North Georgia College, Fine Arts Dept, Dahlonega GA (S)

Owings, Erma L, *Dir,* Ravalli County Museum, Hamilton MT

Ownbey, Ronald B, *Chmn,* Mount San Antonio College, Art Dept, Walnut CA (S)

Ownby, Joanna, *Registrar & Asst Cur,* Crocker Art Museum, Sacramento CA

Owooh, Ruby M, *Mus Dir,* Afro Arts Cultural Centre, Inc, African Arts Museum & Gallery, New York NY

Oxman, M, *Assoc Prof,* American University, Dept of Art, Washington DC (S)

Oxnam, Robert, *Pres,* Asia Society, Inc, Gallery, New York NY

Ozdogan, Turker, *Assoc Prof,* George Washington University, Dept of Art, Washington DC (S)

Ozegovic, Jack, *Instructor,* Northwestern Michigan College, Art Dept, Traverse City MI (S)

Ozura, Jane, *Reference Librn,* University of Portland, Wilson W Clark Memorial Library, Portland OR

Paar, Marge, *Instructor,* Springfield College, Dept of Visual and Performing Arts, Springfield MA (S)

Paasche, Norman, *Assoc Prof,* Lewis and Clark College, Dept of Art, Portland OR (S)

Pace, Gary, *Museum Guide,* The Parthenon, Nashville TN

Pace, Lorenzo, *Executive Member,* 22 Wooster Gallery, New York NY

Pace, Stephen, *Assoc Prof,* American University, Dept of Art, Washington DC (S)

Pachter, Marc, *Asst Dir for History & Public Programs,* National Portrait Gallery, Washington DC

Packard, Daniel, *Prof,* University of South Dakota, Dept of Art, Vermillion SD (S)

Packard, Georgeann, *Executive Member,* 22 Wooster Gallery, New York NY

Packard, Helen, *Secy,* Toledo Artists' Club, Toledo OH

Padden, Barbara K, *Head Art & Music Dept,* Multnomah County Library, Henry Failing Art and Music Dept, Portland OR

Paddison, Sara, *Instructor,* Goldsboro Art Center, Goldsboro NC (S)

Paddock, Eric, *Cur of Photographs,* Colorado Historical Society, State Museum, Denver CO

Padgett, James, *Advisor,* Wilberforce University, Art Dept, Wilberforce OH (S)

Padgett, Michael, *Gallery Dir,* University of Wisconsin, Gallery 101, River Falls WI

Padgett, R Paul, *Assoc Prof,* West Liberty State College, Art Dept, West Liberty WV (S)

Padgham, Ronald E, *Chmn Fine Arts,* Rochester Institute of Technology, School of Art and Design, Rochester NY (S)

Pagano, Neil, *VPres,* The New Harmony Gallery of Contemporary Art, New Harmony IN

Page, Addison Franklin, *Dir & Cur,* J B Speed Art Museum, Louisville KY

Page, A N, *Acting Pres,* Salisbury State College, College Gallery, Salisbury MD

Page, Clarence, *Dir Air Space Museum,* Oklahoma Center for Science and Art, Kirkpatrick Center, Oklahoma City OK

Page, Elizabeth, *Coordr Programs & Special Events,* Worcester Art Museum, Worcester MA

Page, Greg, *Asst Prof,* Cornell University, Dept of Art, Ithaca NY (S)

Page, John, *Prof,* University of Northern Iowa, Dept of Art, Cedar Falls IA (S)

Page, John F, *Dir & Secy,* New Hampshire Historical Society, Concord NH

Page, Marcia, *Registrar,* Craft and Folk Art Museum, Los Angeles CA

Page, Richard C, *Dir Botanical Gardens,* Tennessee Botanical Gardens and Fine Arts Center, Education Dept, Nashville TN (S)

Paggie, Michael, *Office Mgr,* Madison Art Center, Madison WI

Pahl, James H, *Asst Dir,* Museum of New Mexico, Museum of International Folk Art, Santa Fe NM

Paier, Edward T, *Pres,* Paier College of Art, Inc, Hamden CT (S)

Paige, J M, *Asst Dir,* Art Gallery of Greater Victoria, Library, Victoria BC

Paige, Robert, *Assoc Prof,* Philadelphia Community College, Dept of Fine Arts, Philadelphia PA (S)

Paikowsky, Sandra, *Cur,* Concordia University, Art Gallery, Montreal PQ

Paine, Stephen D, *Commissioner,* Boston Art Commission of the City of Boston, Boston MA

Paine, Thelma, *Dept Head Reference,* New Bedford Free Public Library, Art Dept, New Bedford MA

Paine, Wesley M, *Dir,* The Parthenon, Nashville TN

Painter, Jerry E, *Instructor,* Guilford Technical Community College, Commercial Art Dept, Jamestown NC (S)

Paisley, Eldon, *Maintenance Chief,* New Brunswick Museum, Saint John NB

Pajaud, William, *Correspondence Secy & Dir Program Advisor,* Golden State Mutual Life, Los Angeles CA

Pakan, William A, *Dir,* Rochester Institute of Technology, School of Printing, Rochester NY (S)

Pal, Pratapaditya, *Adjunct Prof,* University of Southern California, School of Fine Arts, Los Angeles CA (S)

Palca, Doris, *Head Publications,* Whitney Museum of American Art, New York NY

Palchick, Bernard S, *Chmn Dept,* Kalamazoo College, Art Dept, Kalamazoo MI (S)

Palen, Jennie M, *Treas,* Pen and Brush, Inc, New York NY

Paley, Irving, *Dir Public Relations,* Museum of Science and Industry, Chicago IL

Paley, William S, *Chmn of Board,* Museum of Modern Art, New York NY

Palezynski, John J, *Secy,* Westfield Athenaeum, Jasper Rand Art Museum, Westfield MA

Palijczuk, Wasyl, *Gallery Dir,* Western Maryland College, Gallery One, Westminster MD

Palijczuk, Wasyl, *Head Dept,* Western Maryland College, Art Dept, Westminster MD (S)

Palladino-Craig, Allys, *Dir,* Florida State University, Art Gallery, Tallahassee FL

Pallas, James, *Prof,* Macomb County Community College, Art Dept, Warren MI (S)

Palmer, Anne, *Adminr,* Akron Art Museum, Akron OH

Palmer, Jane, *Asst Prof,* Lake Erie College-Garfield Senior College, Art Dept, Painesville OH (S)

Palmer, Lawman F, *Asst Prof,* University of North Alabama, Dept of Art, Florence AL (S)

Palmer, Merrill J, *Chmn,* University of North Florida, Dept of Fine Arts, Jacksonville FL (S)

Palmer, Richard, *Coordr Exhib,* Museum of Modern Art, New York NY

Palmer, R K, *Chmn Div,* Frank Phillips College, Art Dept, Borger TX (S)

Palmer, Robert, *Assoc Prof,* Cleveland Institute of Art, Cleveland OH (S)

Palusky, Robert, *Instr,* Hamilton College, Art Dept, Clinton NY (S)

Panadero, Marjorie, *Assoc Cur,* University of Michigan, Slide and Photograph Collection, Ann Arbor MI

Panas, Leo, *Assoc Prof,* University of Lowell, Dept of Art, Lowell MA (S)

Panasiuk, Fred, *Controller,* Columbia Museums of Art and Science, Columbia SC

Panciera, David J, *Dir,* Westerly Public Library, Westerly RI

Pancoast, Virginia, *Research Assoc, Authentication Service,* International Foundation for Art Research, Inc, New York NY

Panczenko, Russell, *Asst Dir,* Williams College, Museum of Art, Williamstown MA

Pandolfi, Rosemary, *Cataloger,* School of Visual Arts Library, New York NY

Pankow, David P, *Asst Prof,* Rochester Institute of Technology, School of Printing, Rochester NY (S)

Panosian, Stephen, *Prof,* Salem State College, Art Dept, Salem MA (S)

Pantin, Graciela, *Dir,* Galeria Venezuela, New York NY

Panyard, Gerry, *Instructor,* Madonna College, Art Dept, Livonia MI (S)

Panzera, Anthony, *Instr,* New York Academy of Art, New York NY (S)

Paoletti, John T, *Prof,* Wesleyan University, Art Dept, Middletown CT (S)

Paone, Peter, *VPres,* Print Club, Philadelphia PA

Papageorge, Maria, *Prog Coordr,* International Council of Museums Committee of the American Association of Museums, Washington DC

Papageorge, Tod, *Prof,* Yale University, School of Art, New Haven CT (S)

Papier, Maurice A, *Head Dept,* Saint Francis College, Art Dept, Fort Wayne IN (S)

Papo, Iso, *Head,* Pine Manor College, Visual Arts Dept, Chestnut Hill MA (S)

Papp, L Roy, *Treas,* Phoenix Art Museum, Phoenix AZ

Pappas, George C, *Chmn,* College of the Sequoias, Art Dept, Visalia CA (S)

Pappas, Marilyn, *Chmn Fine Arts, 3D,* Massachusetts College of Art, Boston MA (S)

Paquin, Diane, *Dir Museum,* Le Musee Regional de Rimouski, Rimouski PQ

Paradis, Guy, *Conservator Drawing,* Musee du Quebec, Quebec PQ

Paradis, H James, *Chmn, Ceramics & Sculpture,* Saint Mary's College, Moreau Gallery Three, Notre Dame IN

Paradis, H James, *Chmn,* Saint Mary's College, Dept of Art, Notre Dame IN (S)

Paradis, Magella, *Cur,* Musee du Seminaire de Quebec, Quebec PQ

Paras, Vicky, *Admin Asst,* The New Gallery of Contemporary Art, Cleveland OH

Paratore, Philip, *Prof,* University of Maine at Augusta, Division of Arts and Humanities, Augusta ME (S)

Parcher, Mrytle, *Treas,* Fitchburg Art Museum, Fitchburg MA

Pardee, Hearne, *Asst Prof,* Colby College, Art Dept, Waterville ME (S)

Pardington, Ralph, *Instructor,* College of Santa Fe, Visual Art Division, Santa Fe NM (S)

Pardo, Mary, *Instructor,* Dickinson College, Fine Arts Dept, Carlisle PA (S)

Pardue, Diana, *Asst Cur,* Heard Museum, Phoenix AZ

Pare, Jean-Pierre, *Asst to Archivist,* Musee du Seminaire de Quebec, Quebec PQ

Parente, R A, *Chmn Art Dept,* Anna Maria College, Saint Luke's Gallery, Paxton MA

Parente, Ralph, *Chmn Dept,* Anna Maria College, Dept of Art, Paxton MA (S)

Parfenoff, Michael S, *Dir,* Blackhawk Mountain School of Art Gallery, Blackhawk CO

Parfenoff, Michael S, *Pres,* Blackhawk Mountain School of Art, Black Hawk CO (S)

Parham, Shirley, *Education,* Afro-American Historical and Cultural Museum, Philadelphia PA

Paris, Kay, *Exec Dir,* Beaumont Art Museum, Beaumont TX

Parish, Kay S, *Admin Asst,* Hunter Museum of Art, Chattanooga TN

Park, Heo, *Librn,* Berkeley Public Library, Berkeley CA

Park, Leland, *Librn,* Davidson College Art Gallery, Library, Davidson NC

Park, Marlene, *Prof,* John Jay College of Criminal Justice, Dept of Art, Music and Philosophy, New York NY (S)

Parke, David L, *Assoc Dir,* New York State Historical Association, Farmers' Museum, Inc, Cooperstown NY

Parker, Alan, *Assoc Prof,* Tift College, Dept of Art, Forsyth GA (S)

Parker, Ara Rose, *Video Distribution Mgr,* Art Metropole, Toronto ON

Parker, Barry, *Chairperson Sculpture,* Philadelphia College of Art, Philadelphia PA (S)

Parker, Bart, *Prof,* University of Rhode Island, Dept of Art, Kingston RI (S)

Parker, Carol, *Asst Prof,* Muhlenberg College, Dept of Art, Allentown PA (S)

Parker, Cheryl Ann, *Asst Dir,* Blanden Memorial Art Museum, Fort Dodge IA

Parker, C J, *Head Dept,* Peace College, Art Dept, Raleigh NC (S)

Parker, David, *Instructor,* San Jacinto College North, Art Dept, Houston TX (S)

Parker, David W, *Head Div,* Chowan College, Division of Art, Murfreesboro NC (S)

Parker, Harry S, *Dir,* Dallas Museum of Fine Arts, Dallas TX

Parker, James, *Cur European Sculpture & Decorative Arts,* Metropolitan Museum of Art, New York NY

Parker, Jane H, *Public Relations,* McAllen International Museum, McAllen TX

Parker, Janet R, *Assoc Dir,* Diamond M Foundation Museum, Snyder TX

Parker, June, *Pres,* Prince George Art Gallery, Prince George BC

Parker, Lucile, *Chmn,* William Carey College, Art Dept, Hattiesburg MS (S)

Parker, Mason, *Dir,* Mount Wachusett Community College, Library, Gardner MA

Parker, Nancy, *Visual Arts Coordr,* Hampton Center for Arts and Humanities, Hampton VA

Parker, Paul E, *Pres,* Washington Headquarters Association, Morris-Jumel Mansion, New York NY

Parker, Paul L, *Pres,* Minnesota Historical Society, Saint Paul MN

Parker, Peter J, *Chief of Manuscripts,* Historical Society of Pennsylvania, Philadelphia PA

Parker, Russell A, *Assoc Prof,* Cumberland College, Dept of Art, Williamsburg KY (S)

Parker, S M, *Faculty,* Western Illinois University, College of Fine Arts, Macomb IL (S)

Parker, Steve, *Pres,* Maui Historical Society, Hale Hoikeike, Wailuku HI

Parker, Thomas, *Chmn Dept,* Drury College, Art, Art History and Architecture Dept, Springfield MO (S)

Parker, Thomas W, *Dir,* The Bostonian Society, Old State House, Boston MA

Parker, Tim Ann, *Asst Head,* University of Connecticut, Art and Design Library, Storrs CT

Parker, William, *Chmn Board of Trustees,* Visual Studies Workshop, Rochester NY

Parke-Taylor, Michael, *Cur Exhibitions,* University of Regina, Mackenzie Art Gallery, Regina SK

Parkhurst, Charles, *Co-Dir,* Williams College, Museum of Art, Williamstown MA

Parkhurst, Martha, *Dir Membership & Development,* Baltimore Museum of Art, Baltimore MD

Parkins, Rob W, *Chmn of the Bd,* Bass Museum of Art, Miami Beach FL

Parkinson, John, *VPres & Treas,* Museum of Modern Art, New York NY

Parkinson, Mike, *Library Supv,* Alberta College of Art Gallery, Library, Calgary AB

Parks, Ann B, *Asst Dir,* Landmark Society of Western New York, Inc, Wenrich Memorial Library, New York NY

Parks, Susan, *Registrar,* Florida State University, Art Gallery, Tallahassee FL

Parks-Kirby, Carie, *Asst Prof,* Alma College, Dept of Art and Design, Alma MI (S)

Parmalee, Paul, *Dir,* University of Tennessee, Frank H McClung Museum, Knoxville TN

Parman, Sue, *Program Consult,* Angelo State University, Houston Harte University Center, San Angelo TX

Parrino, George, *Dir,* San Antonio Art Institute, San Antonio TX (S)

Parris, Nina, *Chief Cur,* Columbia Museums of Art and Science, Columbia SC

Parris, Peggy, *Instructor,* Sioux City Art Center, Sioux City IA (S)

Parrish, David, *Registrar,* Wadsworth Atheneum, Hartford CT

Parrish, LaRayne, *Cur,* Wheelwright Museum, Santa Fe NM

Parry, Pamela, *Registrar,* Norton Gallery and School of Art, West Palm Beach FL

Parry, Pamela Jeffcott, *Exec Secy,* Art Libraries Society-North America, Tucson AZ

Parshall, Robert, *Assoc Prof,* University of Illinois, Chicago, Health Science Center, Dept of Biocommunication Arts, Chicago IL (S)

Parsons, David G, *Prof Emeritus,* Rice University, Dept of Art and Art History, Houston TX (S)

Parsons, Jean, *Instructor,* Interlochen Arts Academy, Dept of Visual Art, Interlochen MI (S)

Parsons, June C, *Mgr,* Oklahoma Art Center, Arts Place II, Oklahoma City OK

Parsons, Merribell, *VDir for Education,* Metropolitan Museum of Art, New York NY

Parsons, Norma, *Librn,* Birmingham Public Library, Art and Music Department, Birmingham AL

Parsons, Peggy, *Gift Shop Coordr,* Salisbury State College, Wildfowl Art Museum, Salisbury MD

Parsons, Richard, *Prof,* Lakeland Community College, Visual Arts Dept, Mentor OH (S)

Parsons, Roy, *Dir Development,* Dayton Art Institute, Dayton OH

Parsons, Sheila, *Instr,* Arkansas Arts Center, Little Rock AR (S)

Parton, Ralf, *Prof,* California State College, Stanislaus, Art Dept, Turlock CA (S)

Partridge, Bede, *Head Librn,* Mount Angel Abbey & Seminary Library, Saint Benedict OR

Partridge, Donald B, *Pres,* Philadelphia College of Textiles and Science, School of Textiles, Philadelphia PA (S)

Partridge, Kathleen, *Instructor,* Mohawk Valley Community College, Advertising Design and Production, Utica NY (S)

Paschall, JoAnne, *Dir,* Atlanta College of Art Library, Atlanta GA

Paschke, Edward F, *Chmn Art Dept,* Northwestern University, Evanston, Dept of Art, Evanston IL (S)

Pasditrz, George, *Pres,* Center Gallery, Madison WI

Passage, George W, *Pres,* Mariners Museum, Newport News VA

Patano, Tony, *Coordr Interior Design,* Columbia College, Art Dept, Chicago IL (S)

Pate, Betty, *Asst Prof,* University of Mississippi, Dept of Art, University MS (S)

Patel, Girish, *Visual Communication Chmn,* Atlanta College of Art, Atlanta GA (S)

Patitucci, Joe, *Instr,* American River College, Dept of Art, Sacramento CA (S)

Patnode, J Scott, *Dir,* Gonzaga University, Ad Art Gallery, Spokane WA

Patrick, Brian, *Asst Prof,* University of Utah, Art Dept, Salt Lake City UT (S)

Patrick, Darryl, *Dept Head,* Sam Houston State University, Art Dept, Huntsville TX (S)

Patrick, Peggy, *Asst Dir,* Edmundson Art Foundation, Inc, Des Moines Art Center, Des Moines IA

Patrick, Vernon, *Instr,* California State University, Chico, Art Dept, Chico CA (S)

Patt, Judith, *Asst Prof,* University of Victoria, Dept of History in Art, Victoria BC (S)

Patt, Susan Davis, *Asst Prof,* Loma Linda University, La Sierra Campus, Art Dept, Riverside CA (S)

Pattemore, A, *Secy,* Rodman Hall Arts Centre, Saint Catharines ON

Patten, Barbara, *Chmn,* Spring Hill College, Fine Arts Dept, Mobile AL (S)

Patterson, Belinda C, *Slide Cur,* Memphis State University, Art History Slide Library, Memphis TN

Patterson, Curtis, *Sculpture Chmn,* Atlanta College of Art, Atlanta GA (S)

Patterson, John G, *Pres,* Sarasota Art Association, Sarasota FL

Patterson, Michelle, *Prof,* North Carolina Central University, Art Dept, Durham NC (S)

Patterson, Nancy-Lou, *Prof,* University of Waterloo, Fine Arts Dept, Waterloo ON (S)

Patterson, Russell, *Dir,* Pikeville College, Fine Arts Dept, Pikeville KY (S)

Patterson, Shannon, *Reference Librn,* Adams State College, Library, Alamosa CO

Patterson, Vivian, *Asst Cur,* Williams College, Museum of Art, Williamstown MA

Patterson, Willis R, *Head Dept,* Central Wyoming College, Art Center, Riverton WY (S)

Patton, Glenn N, *Prof,* Trinity University, Dept of Art, San Antonio TX (S)

Patton, Thomas, *Asst Prof,* University of Missouri-Saint Louis, Art Dept, Saint Louis MO (S)

Pauelka, Jeffery J, *Exhibition Program Coordr,* The American Federation of Arts, New York NY

Paukert, Karel, *Chief Cur Musical Arts,* Cleveland Museum of Art, Cleveland OH

Paul, Anne, *Financial Servs,* London Regional Art Gallery, London ON

Paul, Linda D, *Asst VPres,* Indianapolis Museum of Art, Downtown Gallery, Indianapolis IN

Paul, Sherri, *Asst Librn,* Sleepy Hollow Restorations Inc, Library, Tarrytown NY

Paulin, Richard C, *Dir,* University of Oregon, Museum of Art, Eugene OR

Paull, James F, *Dir,* University of the Pacific, University Center Gallery, Stockton CA

Paulsen, Richard, *Asst Prof,* Elmhurst College, Art Dept, Elmhurst IL (S)

Paulson, Alan, *Asst Prof,* Gettysburg College, Dept of Art, Gettysburg PA (S)

Paulson, Barbara, *Reference Librn,* Pierpont Morgan Library, New York NY

Paulson, Peter J, *Dir,* New York State Library, Manuscripts and Special Collections, Albany NY

Paulson, Robert, *Two-Dimensional Area Head,* Southern Illinois University, School of Art, Carbondale IL (S)

Paulson, Suzanne, *Dir of Education,* Laguna Beach Museum of Art, Laguna Beach CA

Paustain, Henry, *Museum Technician & Preparator,* Oberlin College, Allen Memorial Art Museum, Oberlin OH

Pav, John, *Prof,* East Tennessee State University, Fine Arts Dept, Johnson City TN (S)

Pavia, Raymond F, *Secy,* National Institute for Architectural Education, New York NY

Pavlik, John, *Adminr,* Fisher Scientific Company, Fisher Collection of Alchemical and Historical Pictures, Pittsburgh PA

Payne, Jacqueline, *Library Technician,* Sheridan College of Applied Arts and Technology, Visual Arts Library, Oakville ON

Payne, William J, *Dean,* University of Georgia, Franklin College of Arts and Sciences, Dept of Art, Athens GA (S)

Payson, Phillips, *Secy,* Washington Art Association, Washington Depot CT

Payton, Martin F, *Chmn,* Xavier University of Louisiana, Dept of Fine Arts, New Orleans LA (S)

Peace, Bernie K, *Prof,* West Liberty State College, Art Dept, West Liberty WV (S)

Peachy, Burt, *Dean of Fine & Performing Arts,* Santa Ana College, Art Dept, Santa Ana CA (S)

Pearce, Mary L, *Head Dept,* Rehoboth Art League, Inc, Rehoboth Beach DE (S)

Pearce, Mary L, *Exec Secy,* Rehoboth Art League, Inc, Rehoboth Beach DE

Pearse, Harold, *Chmn Art Educ Div,* Nova Scotia College of Art and Design, Halifax NS (S)

Pearson, Clifton, *Head Dept,* Alabama A & M University, Art Education Dept, Huntsville AL (S)

Pearson, Duane, *Superintendent,* Roosevelt-Vanderbilt National Historic Sites, Hyde Park NY

Pearson, Frank C, *Chmn,* Dickinson State College, Dept of Art, Dickinson ND (S)

Pearson, Jim, *Assoc Prof,* Vincennes University, Art Dept, Vincennes IN (S)

Pearson, Jim, *Instr,* Vincennes University Junior College, Art Dept, Vincennes IN (S)

Pearson, John, *Chmn,* Oberlin College, Dept of Art, Oberlin OH (S)

Pearson, Lennart, *Librn,* Presbyterian College, James H Thomason Library, Clinton SC

Pearson, Leonard, *Chairperson Board of Trustees,* Spokane Public Library, Art Dept, Spokane WA

Pearson, Ronald Hayes, *Chmn Board,* Haystack Mountain School of Crafts Gallery, Deer Isle ME

Pease, David, *Dean,* Yale University, School of Art, New Haven CT

Pease, Edmund W, *Admin Officer,* University of Rochester, Memorial Art Gallery, Rochester NY

Pebworth, Charles A, *Prof,* Sam Houston State University, Art Dept, Huntsville TX (S)

Pecchenino, J Ronald, *Chmn Dept,* University of the Pacific, University Center Gallery, Stockton CA

Pecchenino, J Ronald, *Chmn,* University of the Pacific, Dept of Art, Stockton CA (S)

Peck, Everett L, *Assoc Prof,* Palomar College, Art Dept, San Marcos TX (S)

Peck, Judith, *Asst Prof,* Ramapo College of New Jersey, School of Contemporary Arts, Mahwah NJ (S)

Peck, Louis A, *Chmn,* Boise State University, Art Dept, Boise ID (S)

Peck, Margaret, *Asst,* Tucson Museum of Art, Library, Tucson AZ

Peck, William H, *Cur Ancient,* Detroit Institute of Arts, Detroit MI

Pecoraro, Sal, *Instructor,* De Anza College, Art Dept, Cupertino CA (S)

Peden, Melissa, *Secy,* North Carolina Art Society, Raleigh NC

Pedersen, Andrea, *Public Relations Dir,* Creative Time, New York NY

Pedersen, Margaret, *Pres,* Southern Artists Association, Fine Arts Center, Hot Springs AR

Pederson, Ronald, *Chmn Dept,* Aquinas College, Art Dept, Grand Rapids MI (S)

Pedley, John G, *Dir,* University of Michigan, Kelsey Museum of Ancient and Medieval Archaeology, Ann Arbor MI

Pedzich, Joan, *Chief Archivist,* International Museum of Photography at George Eastman House, Library, Rochester NY

Peebles, David, *Pres,* Peninsula Fine Arts Center, Newport News VA

Peebles, Phoebe, *Archivist,* Harvard University, William Hayes Fogg Art Museum, Cambridge MA

Peeno, Sherman L, *Pres,* Cincinnati Art Club, Cincinnati OH

Peeples, Eldora H, *Registrar,* Rollins College, George D and Harriet W Cornell Fine Arts Center Museum, Winter Park FL

Peeps, Claire, *Exec Asst,* The Friends of Photography, Carmel CA

Pegolotti, James, *Dean,* Western Connecticut State University, School of Arts & Sciences, Danbury CT (S)

Peirce, John, *Pres,* Alaska Artists' Guild, Anchorage AK

Peirce, S, *Asst Prof,* Northern Arizona University, Art Dept, Flagstaff AZ (S)

Pekarsky, Mel, *Assoc Prof,* State University of New York at Stony Brook, Art Dept, Stony Brook NY (S)

Peladeau, Marius B, *Dir,* William A Farnsworth Library and Art Museum, Rockland ME

Pelfrey, Robert, *Instructor,* Cuesta College, Art Dept, San Luis Obispo CA (S)

Pelham, Alfred M, *Treas,* Detroit Institute of Arts, Founders Society, Detroit MI

Pelissero, Lauri, *Public Relations,* Laguna Beach Museum of Art, Laguna Beach CA

Pell, John G, *Pres,* Fort Ticonderoga Museum, Ticonderoga NY

Pellaton, Ann, *VPres,* Long Island Graphic Eye Gallery, Port Washington NY

Pellecchia, Linda, *Asst Prof,* Davidson College, Art Dept, Davidson NC (S)

Pellegrini, Francis N, *Dept Chmn,* State University of New York at Farmingdale, Advertising Art Design Dept, Farmingdale NY (S)

Pellerito, Marlene, *Instructor,* Saginaw Valley State College, Dept of Art and Design, University Center MI (S)

Pelletier, Jacqueline, *Chef de Bibliotheque,* Universite de Montreal, Bibliotheque d'Amenagement, Montreal PQ

Pelli, Cesar, *Dean,* Yale University, School of Architecture, New Haven CT (S)

Pellicciaro, Mario, *Prof,* Washington and Lee University, Dept of Fine Arts, Lexington VA (S)

Pellizzi, Philippa, *Pres,* Dia Art Foundation, Inc, New York NY

Pelosini, Elaine, *Instructor,* School of the Associated Arts, Saint Paul MN (S)

Pelton, Richard M, *Pres,* Munson Gallery, New Haven CT

Peltz, Margaret, *Secy,* Fine Arts Center of Clinton, Clinton IL

Pelzel, Thomas O, *Assoc Prof,* University of California, Riverside, Art History Dept, Riverside CA (S)

Pena, Allision H, *Cur of Exhibits,* Lafayette Natural History Museum, Planetarium and Nature Station, Lafayette LA

Pena, Gladys, *Cur,* El Museo del Barrio, New York NY

Penay, Lucinao J, *Assoc Prof,* American University, Dept of Art, Washington DC (S)

Pence, Danny, *Cur Medical Zoology,* Texas Tech University Museum, Lubbock TX

Pence, Nina, *Chmn Exhib,* Klamath Falls Art Association, Klamath Art Gallery, Klamath Falls OR

Pendell, David, *Asst Prof,* University of Utah, Art Dept, Salt Lake City UT (S)

Pendergraft, Norman, *Prof,* North Carolina Central University, Art Dept, Durham NC (S)

Pendergraft, Norman E, *Dir,* North Carolina Central University, Museum of Art, Durham NC

Pendleton, Eldridge H, *Dir,* Old Gaol Museum, York ME

Pendleton, Mary Belle, *Asst Prof,* Mary Washington College, Art Dept, Fredericksburg VA (S)

Penegar, Lucy, *VPres,* Gaston County Museum of Art & History, Dallas NC

Penhallow, David, *Cur,* Kauai Museum, Lihue HI

Peniston, Robert C, *Dir,* Washington and Lee University, Lee Chapel and Museum, Lexington VA

Pennella, Lisa, *Slide Librn,* Munson-Williams-Proctor Institute, Art Reference Library, Utica NY

Pennington, Mary Anne, *Exec Dir,* Greenville Museum of Art, Greenville NC

Penny, A, *Instructor,* Technical University of Nova Scotia, Faculty of Architecture, Halifax NS (S)

Penny, Karen, *Asst Program Coordr,* Texas A & M University, Memorial Student Center Arts Committee, College Station TX

Pepe, Marie Huper, *Chmn,* Agnes Scott College, Dept of Art, Decatur GA (S)

Pepich, Bruce W, *Dir,* The Racine Art Association, Inc, Racine WI

Pepich, Bruce W, *Dir,* The Racine Art Association, Inc, Charles A Wustum Museum of Fine Arts, Racine WI

Pepich, Bruce W, *Dir,* The Racine Art Association, Inc, Wustum Art Library, Racine WI

Pepper, Choral C, *Dir,* Kimball Art Center, Park City UT

Peppin, Nancy, *Cur Education,* Sierra Nevada Museum of Art, Reno NV

Percey, Roland, *Area Chmn Photography,* Pasadena City College, Art Dept, Pasadena CA (S)

Percy, Ann, *Assoc Cur Drawings,* Philadelphia Museum of Art, Philadelphia PA

Percy, Rolan, *Dir,* Pasadena City College, Art Gallery, Pasadena CA

Perdairs, Peter, *Instructor,* Avila College, Art Division, Dept of Performing and Visual Art, Kansas City MO (S)

Perez, Sandy, *Secy,* North Country Museum of Arts, Park Rapids MN

Perfect, Stephan, *Instr,* Saint Francis College, Art Dept, Fort Wayne IN (S)

Perisho, Sally L, *Dir,* Arapahoe Community College, Colorado Gallery of the Arts, Littleton CO

Perkins, Allison, *Cur Educ,* Joslyn Art Museum, Omaha NE

Perkins, Barbara, *Cur,* State University of New York at Binghamton, University Art Gallery, Binghamton NY

Perkins, Dean, *Asst Prof,* Norwich University, Dept of Philosophy, Religion and Fine Arts, Northfield VT (S)

Perkins, Elizabeth, *Cur,* Kentucky Historical Society, Old State Capitol & Annex, Frankfort KY

Perkins, Harry, *Secy,* New Haven Colony Historical Society, New Haven CT

Perkins, Helen D, *VPres,* Stowe-Day Foundation, Hartford CT

Perkins, Margaret, *Assoc Cur of Education,* University of Arizona, Museum of Art, Tucson AZ

Perkins, Mary Louise, *Dir,* Brandon Allied Arts Council, Brandon MB

Perkins, Tim, *Media Center Dir,* Minneapolis College of Art and Design, Library and Media Center, Minneapolis MN

Perlin, Ruth R, *Head Extension Prog Development,* National Gallery of Art, Washington DC

Perlis, Ellen, *Instructor,* Umpqua Community College, Fine & Performing Arts Dept, Roseburg OR (S)

Perlman, Bennard B, *Chmn & Prof,* Community College of Baltimore, Dept of Fine & Applied Arts, Liberty Campus, Baltimore MD (S)

Permet, Joe, *Executive Dir,* Jewish Community Center, Center Lobby Gallery, Long Beach CA

Pernish, Paul, *Dept Head,* Contra Costa College, Dept of Art, San Pablo CA (S)

Pernot, M M, *Dir,* Burlington County Historical Society, Burlington NJ

Perreault, John, *Cur Contemporary Art,* Everson Museum of Art, Syracuse NY

Perri, John, *Assoc Prof,* University of Wisconsin-Stout, Art Dept, Menomonie WI (S)

Perrin, Louise H M, *Library Asst,* Historic Deerfield Inc, Henry N Flynt Library, Deerfield MA

Perrine, Rebecca, *Cur Special Coll,* Virginia Historical Society, Richmond VA

Perrot, Paul N, *Asst Secy for Museum Programs,* Smithsonian Institution, Washington DC

Perry, Barbara, *Adjunct Asst Prof,* Le Moyne College, Art Dept, Syracuse NY (S)

Perry, Beverly Cook, *Designer,* Amarillo Art Center, Amarillo TX

Perry, Donald, *Chmn,* Emporia State University, Dept of Art, Emporia KS (S)

Perry, Donald, *Dir,* Emporia State University, Norman R Eppink Art Gallery, Emporia KS

Perry, Doug, *Executive,* Arts and Humanities Council of Tuscaloosa County, Inc, Tuscaloosa AL

Perry, Irene, *Engineering & Science,* Cooper Union for the Advancement of Science & Art, Library, New York NY

Perry, Lallah M, *Asst Prof,* Delta State University, Dept of Art, Cleveland MS (S)

Perry, Roberta, *Asst Prof,* Sweet Briar College, Art History Dept and Art Studio Dept, Sweet Briar VA (S)

Perryman, Tom, *Asst Dir,* Associated Artists of Winston-Salem, Winston-Salem NC

Persily, Terry, *Pres,* Ashtabula Arts Center, Ashtabula OH

Persson, Karin, *Admin Asst,* American Swedish Historical Foundation and Museum, Philadelphia PA

Pertman, Bill, *VPres,* Women's Interart Center, Inc, Interart de St Amand Gallery, New York NY

Pessin, I Marc, *Instr,* University of British Columbia, Dept of Fine Arts, Vancouver BC (S)

Petch, H, *Pres,* University of Victoria, Maltwood Art Museum and Gallery, Victoria BC

Petcoff, Jessie W, *Staff Asst,* Duke University Union Galleries, Durham NC

Peter, Max, *Cur,* College of Idaho, Blatchley Gallery, Caldwell ID

Peterdi, Gabor, *Prof,* Yale University, School of Art, New Haven CT (S)

Peters, F Warren, *Librn,* Detroit Institute of Arts, Research Library, Detroit MI

Peters, H C, *Executive Secy,* Manitoba Association of Architects, Winnipeg MB

Peters, Jean, *Dir Public Relations,* Paine Art Center and Arboretum, Oshkosh WI

Peters, Larry D, *Gallery Dir,* Topeka Public Library, Fine Arts Dept & Gallery of Fine Arts, Topeka KS

Peters, V Paige, *Dir,* Verde Valley Art Association, Inc, Jerome AZ

Peters, Wallace, *Assoc Prof,* Philadelphia Community College, Dept of Fine Arts, Philadelphia PA (S)

Peters, Walter C, *Pres Board Trustees,* Zigler Museum, Jennings LA

Petersen, Carol, *Secy,* Augustana College, Centennial Hall Gallery, Rock Island IL

Petersen, Daniel W, *Instructor,* Modesto Junior College, Arts Humanities and Speech Division, Modesto CA (S)

Petersen, Jetret S, *Secy,* Kenai Historical Society Inc, Kenai Community Historical Center, Kenai AK

Petersen, Leonard, *Assoc Prof,* University of Wisconsin-Superior, Programs in the Visual Arts, Superior WI (S)

Petersen, Wayne L, *Promotion Dir,* Augustana College, Center for Western Studies, Sioux Falls SD

Petersen, Will, *Instr,* Oxbow Center for the Arts, Saugatuck MI (S)

Petersmeyer, J C, *Pres,* Manitoba Association of Architects, Winnipeg MB

Peterson, A E S, *Recording Secy,* Rhode Island Watercolor Society, Pawtucket RI

Peterson, Allan, *Dir,* Pensacola Junior College, Visual Arts Gallery, Pensacola FL

Peterson, Burdette, *Gallery Dir,* Brand Library and Art Center, Glendale CA

Peterson, C D, *Chmn Human & Fine Arts,* Doane College, Dept of Art, Crete NE (S)

Peterson, Dean, *Instr,* College of Saint Rose, Division of Art, Albany NY (S)

Peterson, D R, *Instr,* Normandale Community College, Art Dept, Bloomington MN (S)

Peterson, Frederick, *Coordr,* University of Minnesota, Morris, Humanities Division, Morris MN (S)

Peterson, Genevieve, *Cur and Secy,* Nobles County Art Center Gallery, Worthington MN

Peterson, Glen L, *Chmn,* Yavapai College, Art Dept, Prescott AZ (S)

Peterson, Harold, *Librn,* Minneapolis Institute of Arts, Art Reference Library, Minneapolis MN

Peterson, Helen, *Gallery Hostess,* Copper Village Museum & Arts Center, Anaconda MT

Peterson, James, *Asst Prof,* Franklin and Marshall College, Art Dept, Lancaster PA (S)

Peterson, John D, *Dir,* Morris Museum of Arts and Sciences, Morristown NJ

Peterson, Karin E, *Site Adminr,* Historical Society of Delaware, George Read II House, Wilmington DE

Peterson, Larry D, *Prof,* Kearney State College, Dept of Art, Kearney NE (S)

Peterson, Margaret, *Asst Prof,* Central Missouri State University, Art Dept, Warrensburg MO (S)

Peterson, Martin E, *Cur Paintings,* San Diego Museum of Art, San Diego CA

Peterson, Pauline M, *Reference Librn,* Jones Library, Inc, Amherst MA

Peterson, Richard, *Dir Film & Video,* Walker Art Center, Minneapolis MN

Peterson, Robert O, *Board Chmn,* American Craft Council, New York NY

Peterson, Robert S, *VPres & Dir Admissions,* Art Institute of Fort Lauderdale, Fort Lauderdale FL (S)

Peterson, Roy, *VPres,* Association of American Editorial Cartoonists, Harrison AR

Peterson, Russell D, *Assoc Dean,* College of Lake County, Art Dept, Grayslake IL (S)

Peterson, Stan, *Outreach Coordr,* Richmond Art Center, Richmond CA

Peterson, Susan, *Instructor,* University of Southern California, Idyllwild School of Music and the Arts, Idyllwild CA (S)

Peterson, Willard, *Instr,* Roberts Wesleyan College, Fine Arts Division, Art Dept, Rochester NY (S)

Petheo, Bela, *Assoc Prof,* Saint John's University, Art Dept, Collegeville MN (S)

Petibone, John, *Dir Education,* Hammond Castle Museum, Gloucester MA

Petrash, David, *Dept Head,* Grayson County College, Art Dept, Denison TX (S)

Petrie, Claire, *Reference Librn & Cataloguer,* Parsons School of Design, Adam & Sophie Gimbel Library, New York NY

Petroll, Walter O, *Head of Gardens,* Winterthur Museum and Gardens, Winterthur DE

Petruchyk, Jon, *Prof,* Christopher Newport College, Arts & Communications, Newport News VA (S)

Pettigrew, Kenneth W, *Cur,* Gilbert Stuart Birthplace, Saunderstown RI

Peugh, Benton, *Instructor,* Southwestern College, Art Dept, Winfield KS (S)

Pevitts, Robert, *Chmn,* Kentucky Wesleyan College, Dept Art, Owensboro KY (S)

Peyrat, Jean, *Librn,* Center for Creative Studies - College of Art & Design Library, Detroit MI

Peyton, Lenore, *Dir,* Place des Arts, Coquitlam BC

Peyton, Morgan, *Public Information Dir,* Sunrise Foundation, Inc, Sunrise Museums, Charleston WV

Pfaff, Larry, *Deputy Librn,* Art Gallery of Ontario, Edward P Taylor Reference Library, Toronto ON

Pfeifer, Willialm B, *Assoc Dir,* Sleepy Hollow Restorations Inc, Tarrytown NY

Pfeiffer, Anthony, *Asst Prof,* University of Wisconsin-Superior, Programs in the Visual Arts, Superior WI (S)

Pferd, Kathleen, *Registrar,* Newport Harbor Art Museum, Newport Beach CA

Pfluger, James R, *Asst Dir,* Panhandle-Plains Historical Society Museum, Canyon TX

Pfrehm, Paul, *Asst Prof,* Chadron State College, Division of Fine Arts, Chadron NE (S)

Pharis, Rudolph V, *Exec Dir,* Lufkin Historical and Creative Arts Center, Lufkin TX

Phelan, Andrew, *Actg Dean,* Pratt Institute, School of Art and Design, Brooklyn NY (S)

Phelan, Thomas, *Treasurer,* Rensselaer Newman Foundation Chapel and Cultural Center, Troy NY

Phelan, William, *Assoc Prof,* Southampton College of Long Island University, C W Post Center Fine Arts Division, Southampton NY (S)

Phelps, Brent, *Photography Coordr,* North Texas State University, Art Dept, Denton TX (S)

Phelps, Carolyn, *Visual Arts Asst,* Arkansas Arts Center, Elizabeth Prewitt Taylor Memorial Library, Little Rock AR

Phelps, Jon J, *Union Dir,* Duke University Union Galleries, Union Galleries Committee, Durham NC

Phifer, Matilda, *Instr,* Ocean City Arts Center, Ocean City NJ (S)

Phil, M, *Lecturer,* University of Victoria, Dept of History in Art, Victoria BC (S)

Philbin, Kate, *Dir Education,* Bennington Museum, Bennington VT

Philbrick, Ruth, *Cur,* National Gallery of Art, Photographic Archives, Washington DC

Philippsen, Lola M, *Collection Development & ILL Librn,* Saint Mary's College, Cushwa-Leighton Library, Notre Dame IN

Phillips, Barbara L, *Asst Dir,* Carnegie Institute, Museum of Art, Pittsburgh PA

Phillips, Beverley, *Library Asst,* Winnipeg Art Gallery, Clara Lander Library, Winnipeg MB

Phillips, Carol, *Dir,* University of Regina, Mackenzie Art Gallery, Regina SK

Phillips, Constance, *Academic Dean,* Kendall School of Design, Grand Rapids MI (S)

Phillips, Dick, *Pres Elect,* Art Guild of Burlington, Arts for Living Center, Burlington IA

Phillips, Gema, *Member,* The Loading Dock Gallery, Boston MA

Phillips, Helen, *Asst Prof,* University of Central Arkansas, Art Dept, Conway AR (S)

Phillips, Herbert E, *Dir,* Rochester Institute of Technology, Technical & Education Center of the Graphic Arts, Rochester NY (S)

Phillips, Laughlin, *Dir,* The Phillips Collection, Washington DC

Phillips, Lisa, *Head,* Whitney Museum of American Art, Whitney at Philip Morris, New York NY

Phillips, Miriam, *Secy,* Wharton Esherick Museum, Paoli PA

Phillips, Robert F, *Cur of Contemporary Art,* Toledo Museum of Art, Toledo OH

Phillips, Stephen, *Asst Prof,* Central Missouri State University, Art Dept, Warrensburg MO (S)

Phillpot, Clive, *Dir,* Museum of Modern Art, Library, New York NY

Phipps, Richard, *Chmn,* Capital University, Art Dept, Columbus OH (S)

Pianta, Carol, *Admin Asst,* Tyler Museum of Art, Tyler TX

Piatt, Frances, *Secy & Treas,* Piatt Castles, West Liberty OH

Piatt, William N, *Pres,* Piatt Castles, West Liberty OH

Piazza, Paul M, *Dir,* Colorado Springs Fine Arts Center, Colorado Springs CO

Picaidma, Marilyn, *Chmn,* Marymount College, Art Dept, Tarrytown NY (S)

Picco, Ronald, *Assoc Prof,* College of Santa Fe, Visual Art Division, Santa Fe NM (S)

Piche, Thomas, *Asst to Cur,* Syracuse University, Art Collection, Syracuse NY

Pichette, Claude, *Recteur,* Universite du Quebec a Montreal, Famille des Arts, Montreal PQ (S)

Pick, Joan, *Pres,* West Bend Gallery of Fine Arts, West Bend WI

Pickard-Pritchard, B, *Dir Visual Arts,* Rutgers, the State University of New Jersey, Mason Gross School of the Arts, New Brunswick NJ (S)

Pickett, Vic, *Chmn,* Old Dominion University, Art Dept, Norfolk VA (S)

Pickford, Christopher P, *Dir,* Connecticut Historical Society, Hartford CT

Pickrel, Thomas, *Asst Prof,* University of Missouri-Saint Louis, Art Dept, Saint Louis MO (S)

Piel, Dan, *Assoc Prof,* California Polytechnic State University at San Luis Obispo, Art Dept, San Luis Obispo CA (S)

Piel, William Louis, *Pres,* United Methodist Historical Society, Lovely Lane Museum, Baltimore MD

Piene, Otto, *Dir,* Massachusetts Institute of Technology, Center for Advanced Visual Studies, Cambridge MA (S)

Pierce, Ann, *Instr,* California State University, Chico, Art Dept, Chico CA (S)

Pierce, Ann T, *Dir,* California State University, Chico, Art Gallery, Chico CA

Pierce, Arthur Ray, *Head Dept,* West Virginia Institute of Technology, Creative Arts Dept, Montgomery WV (S)

Pierce, Christopher, *Asst Prof,* Berea College, Art Dept, Berea KY (S)

Pierce, Delilah W, *Cur Painting,* Smith-Mason Gallery and Museum, Washington DC

Pierce, Donald, *Cur Decorative Arts,* High Museum of Art, Atlanta GA

Pierce, Lary, *Asst Prof,* Winthrop College, Dept of Art, Rock Hill SC (S)

Pierce, Margaret S, *Dir Public Relations,* Southern Vermont Art Center, Manchester VT

Pierce, Richard, *Public Affairs Assoc,* Solomon R Guggenheim Museum, New York NY

Pierce, Sally, *Print Dept Cur,* Boston Athenaeum, Boston MA

Pierle, Robert, *Dir Programs,* Mid-America Arts Alliance, Kansas City MO

Pierotti, Ray, *Coordr of Galleries,* Saint Clair County Community College, Jack R Hennesey Art Galleries, Port Huron MI

Pierotti, Ray, *Exec Dir,* Sawtooth Center for Visual Design, Winston-Salem NC (S)

Pierro, Leonard, *Instr Specialized Studio,* Kean College of New Jersey, Fine Arts Dept, Union NJ (S)

Piersol, Dan, *Registrar,* New Orleans Museum of Art, New Orleans LA

Pierson, Dave, *Instructor,* Dunedin Fine Arts and Cultural Center, Dunedin FL (S)

Pierson, Richard, *Dean of Admis,* Clark University, Dept of Visual & Performing Arts, Worcester MA (S)

Pieslak, Dixie, *Lectr,* Azusa Pacific University, College of Liberal Arts, Art Dept, Azusa CA (S)

Pietrezack, Ted, *VPres,* Ontario Association of Art Galleries, Toronto ON

Pietroforte, Alfred, *Instructor,* College of the Sequoias, Art Dept, Visalia CA (S)

Pihlak, Madis, *Asst Prof,* University of Toronto, Dept of Landscape Architecture, Toronto ON (S)

Pike, Jerrie, *Instructor,* Virginia Tech, Dept of Art, Blacksburg VA (S)

Pike, Kermit J, *Librn,* Western Reserve Historical Society, Cleveland OH

Pilat, Peter, *Instructor,* Monterey Peninsula College, Art Dept, Monterey CA (S)

Pilgram, Suzanne, *Instr,* Georgian Court College, Dept of Art, Lakewood NJ (S)

Pilgrim, Dianne H, *Cur Decorative Arts,* Brooklyn Museum, Brooklyn NY (S)

Pilgrim, James, *Dep Dir,* Metropolitan Museum of Art, New York NY

Pili, Enosa, *Executive Dir,* Jean P Haydon Museum, Pago Pago, American Samoa PI

Pillsbury, Edmund P, *Dir,* Kimbell Art Museum, Fort Worth TX

Pinardi, Brenda, *Prof,* University of Lowell, Dept of Art, Lowell MA (S)

Pinardi, Enrico, *Prof,* Rhode Island College, Art Dept, Providence RI (S)

Pinckney, Lawrence R, *Cur,* Pinckney Brothers Museum, Orangeburg SC

Pinckney, Robert E, *Pres,* Pinckney Brothers Museum, Orangeburg SC

Pinckney, S M, *VPres,* Pinckney Brothers Museum, Orangeburg SC

Pincus, Debra, *Assoc Prof,* University of British Columbia, Dept of Fine Arts, Vancouver BC (S)

Pincus-Witten, Robert, *Prof,* City University of New York, PhD Program in Art History, New York NY (S)

Pindell, Howardena, *Assoc Prof,* State University of New York at Stony Brook, Art Dept, Stony Brook NY (S)

Pinedo, Maria V, *Cur & Education Coordinator,* Galeria de la Raza, Studio 24, San Francisco CA

Pinedo, Maria V, *Dir,* Galeria de la Raza, Chicano-Latino Arts Resource Library, San Francisco CA

Pines, Philip A, *Dir,* Hall of Fame of the Trotter, Goshen NY

Pines, Philip A, *Pres,* Orange County Community of Museums and Galleries, Goshen NY

Pinkham, Harold, *Pres,* Beverly Historical Society, Cabot, Hale and Balch House Museums, Beverly MA

Pinkney, Helen, *Assoc Cur Textiles,* Dayton Art Institute, Dayton OH

Pinkney, Helen, *Librn,* Dayton Art Institute, Library, Dayton OH

Pintea, June C, *Admin Asst & Shop Mgr,* Erie Historical Museum, Erie PA

Pinto, John, *Assoc Prof,* Smith College, Art Dept, Northampton MA (S)

Pionk, Richard, *Secy,* Hudson Valley Art Association, White Plains NY

Piper, Bill, *Instr,* Walla Walla Community College, Art Dept, Walla Walla WA (S)

Pirnke, Heinz, *VPres,* Revelstoke Art Group, Revelstoke BC

Pisano, Edward, *Security,* Brooklyn Museum, Brooklyn NY

Pisciotta, Henry, *Fine Arts Librn,* Carnegie-Mellon University, Hunt Library, Pittsburgh PA

Piskoti, James, *Prof,* California State College, Stanislaus, Art Dept, Turlock CA (S)

Pisney, Raymond, *Dir,* Missouri Historical Society, Saint Louis MO

Pistorius, Nancy, *Asst Head Fine Arts Library,* University of New Mexico, Fine Arts Library, Albuquerque NM

Pitman, Ursula, *Exhib Interpreter,* Fitchburg Art Museum, Fitchburg MA

Pitner, Ed, *Chmn,* Parkersburg Community College, Art Dept, Parkersburg WV (S)

Pitre, Marc, *Dir,* Galerie d'art de l'Universite de Moncton, Moncton NB

Pitt, Paul, *Assoc Prof,* Harding University, Dept of Art, Searcy AR (S)

Pitter, Pauline O, *Secy,* Pine Castle Center of the Arts, Inc, Orlando FL

Pittman, Melinda, *Cur,* Rochester Historical Society, Rochester NY

Pitts, Betty, *Exec Secy,* Riverside Art Center and Museum, Riverside CA

Pitts, Terence R, *Cur & Libr Photography Archive,* University of Arizona, Center for Creative Photography, Tucson AZ

Pitts, Terence R, *Librn,* University of Arizona, Photography Library, Tucson AZ

Pitts Rembert, Virginia, *Chmn Dept,* University of Alabama, Art Dept, University AL (S)

Pivovar, Ronald A, *Chmn Dept,* Thiel College, Dept of Art, Greenville PA (S)

Piwonka, R, *Exec Dir,* Columbia County Historical Society, Library, Kinderhook NY

P-Jobb, Andor S, *Assoc Prof,* Clarion University of Pennsylvania, Dept of Art, Clarion PA (S)

Place, Bradley E, *Head Dept,* University of Tulsa, Dept of Art, Tulsa OK (S)

Plagens, Peter, *Prof,* University of North Carolina at Chapel Hill, Art Dept, Chapel Hill NC (S)

Plant, Mary, *Admin Asst,* Community Arts Council of Vancouver, Vancouver BC

Plantz, John, *Treas,* Luna County Historical Society, Inc, Deming Luna Mimbres Museum, Deming NM

Plasentin, Joe, *Instr,* Pepperdine University, Seaver College, Dept of Art, Malibu CA (S)

Platais, Maris, *Secy,* Guild of Boston Artists, Boston MA

Platou, Dode, *Chief Cur,* Historic New Orleans Collection, Kemper and Leila Williams Foundation, New Orleans LA

Platt, Geoffrey, *Executive Dir,* National Assembly of State Arts Agencies, Washington DC

Platt, John H, *Head Librn,* Historical Society of Pennsylvania, Philadelphia PA

Platt, Melanie, *Asn VPres,* Biloxi Art Association, Gallery, Biloxi MS

Platt, Susan, *Asst Prof,* Mills College, Art Dept, Oakland CA (S)

Platter, Allen, *Head,* Southeastern Oklahoma State College, Art Dept, Durant OK (S)

Platts, Mary Kate, *Asn Treas,* Biloxi Art Association, Gallery, Biloxi MS

Platzer, Eryl, *Head Conservation & Registration,* Colorado Historical Society, State Museum, Denver CO

Plewa, Elvira, *Admin Asst,* University of Arizona, Museum of Art, Tucson AZ

Plogman, Berward, *Assoc Prof,* University of Dayton, Fine Arts Division, Dayton OH (S)

Plosky, Charles, *Asst Prof,* Jersey City State College, Art Dept, Jersey City NJ (S)

Plotkin, Theodore, *Pres,* Edna Hibel Art Foundation, Hibel Museum of Art, Riviera Beach FL

Plous, Phyllis, *Cur,* University of California, Santa Barbara, University Art Museum, Santa Barbara CA

Plummer, Carlton, *Prof,* University of Lowell, Dept of Art, Lowell MA (S)

Plummer, John, *Prof,* Princeton University, Dept of Art and Archaeology, Princeton NJ (S)

Plummer, John H, *Cur Medieval and Renaissance Manuscripts,* Pierpont Morgan Library, New York NY

Plummer, Marc O, *Instructor,* Concord College, Art Dept, Athens WV (S)

Plye, Gene, *Assoc Dir,* Morehead State University, Claypool-Young Art Gallery, Morehead KY

Podgajny, Stephen J, *Exec Dir,* York Institute Museum, Saco ME

Podmaniczky, Christine, *Cur,* William A Farnsworth Library and Art Museum, Library, Rockland ME

Podwal, Mark, *VPres,* National Council on Art in Jewish Life, New York NY

Poellnitz, Nathan, *Lectr,* Tunxis Community College, Graphic Design Dept, Farmington CT (S)

Poesch, Jessie J, *Prof,* Tulane University, Sophie H Newcomb Memorial College, New Orleans LA (S)

Poggemeyer, Karen, *Asst Dir,* Eccles Community Art Center, Ogden UT

Pogue, Dwight, *Asst Prof,* Smith College, Art Dept, Northampton MA (S)

Pogue, Larry, *Chmn,* East Central Junior College, Art Dept, Union MO (S)

Pointer, Janice, *Secy Registrar,* North Carolina Central University, Museum of Art, Durham NC

Poirer, Carmelle, *Secy,* Galerie d'art de l'Universite de Moncton, Moncton NB

Poirier, Linda, *Cur,* Art Center of Battle Creek, Battle Creek MI

Pokinski, Deborah, *Instr,* Hamilton College, Art Dept, Clinton NY (S)

Polan, Louise, *Cur Exhib,* Huntington Galleries, Huntington WV

Polch, Karel, *Executive Secy,* Fairmount Park Art Association, Philadelphia PA

Poleskie, Steve, *Prof,* Cornell University, Dept of Art, Ithaca NY (S)

Poletes, George, *Div Dir Fine Arts,* College of Saint Thomas, Dept of Art History, Saint Paul MN (S)

Poling, Clark V, *Assoc Prof,* Emory University, Art History Dept, Atlanta GA (S)

Poling, John, *Pres Chilkat Valley Historical Society,* Sheldon Museum and Cultural Center, Haines AK

Polk, Andrew, *Asst Prof,* Wake Forest University, Dept of Art, Winston-Salem NC (S)

Polkinghorne, Bruce, *VPres,* Koochiching County Historical Society Museum, International Falls MN

Pollan, Pat, *Bookkeeper,* Carson County Square House Museum, Panhandle TX

Pollard, Julie, *Corresponding Secy,* Arizona Watercolor Association, Phoenix AZ

Pollen, Linda, *Member,* The Loading Dock Gallery, Boston MA

Pollini, John, *Archaeological Museum Cur,* Johns Hopkins University, Archaeological Museum, Baltimore MD

Pollitt, Jerome J, *Chmn,* Yale University, Dept of the History of Art, New Haven CT (S)

Pollock, Bettina, *Gallery Shop Asst,* Ann Arbor Art Association, Ann Arbor MI

Polshek, James Stewart, *Dean Architectural Planning,* Columbia University, Graduate School of Architecture and Planning, New York NY (S)

Polster, Joanne, *Librn,* American Craft Council Museum, Library, New York NY

Polster, Joanne, *Head,* American Craft Council, American Craft Council Library, New York NY

Polston, John, *Chmn Fine Arts,* Sinclair Community College, Dept of Art, Dayton OH (S)

Polus, Judith A, *Cur of Education,* Leigh Yawkey Woodson Art Museum, Inc, Wausau WI

Polzer, J, *Head,* University of Calgary, Dept of Art, Calgary AB (S)

Pomeroy, Dan, *Chief Researcher,* Tennessee State Museum, Nashville TN

Pomeroy, Stacy F, *Cur,* Rensselaer County Historical Society, Hart-Cluett Mansion, 1827, Troy NY

Pomfret, Robert F, *Asst Treas,* Rhode Island Watercolor Society, Pawtucket RI

Pond, David, *Pres,* Kingsport Fine Arts Center, Kingsport TN

Pond, Freda, *Recording Coordr,* Women in the Arts Foundation, Inc, New York NY

Poole, Jerry D, *Head Dept,* University of Central Arkansas, Art Dept, Conway AR (S)

Poole, Katherine, *Visual Servs Librn,* Harvard University, Frances Loeb Library, Cambridge MA

Poor, Robert, *Prof,* University of Minnesota, Minneapolis, Art History, Minneapolis MN (S)

Poor-Monteith, Candida, *Instr,* Danforth Museum School, Framingham MA (S)

Pope, John C, *Trustee,* Hill-Stead Museum, Farmington CT

Pope, Melissa, *Public Relations & Education,* Frog Hollow Craft Center, Middlebury VT

Pope, Pat, *Sales Mgr,* Frog Hollow Craft Center, Middlebury VT

Pope, Richard C, *Assoc Prof,* University of Alabama in Huntsville, School of Arts, Humanities & Science, Huntsville AL (S)

Pope-Hennessy, John, *Consultative Chmn European Paintings,* Metropolitan Museum of Art, New York NY

Popovic, Tanya, *Chairperson & Librn,* LeMoyne College, Art Gallery, Syracuse NY

Popovich, Ljubica D, *Assoc Prof,* Vanderbilt University, Dept of Fine Arts, Nashville TN (S)

Popovich, Nancy, *Secy,* Southern Alberta Art Gallery, Lethbridge AB

Popp, Janet E, *Secy,* Capital University, Schumacher Gallery, Columbus OH

Poppenberg, Mary C, *Dir Public Relations,* Carnegie Institute, Museum of Art, Pittsburgh PA

Poppino, Stephen, *Reference Librn,* College of Southern Idaho, Library, Twin Falls ID

Porada, Edith, *Honorary Cur Seals and Tablets,* Pierpont Morgan Library, New York NY

Poras, E Linda, *Dir Education & Public Relations,* Fitchburg Art Museum, Fitchburg MA

Porcelli, Carolyn, *Development Assoc,* Solomon R Guggenheim Museum, New York NY

Poritsky, Raphael, *Lectr,* Cleveland Institute of Art, Cleveland OH (S)

Porps, Ernest O, *Assoc Prof,* University of Colorado at Denver, Dept of Fine Arts, Denver CO (S)

Porten, Virginia B, *Business Mgr,* Roanoke Museum of Fine Arts, Roanoke VA

Porter, Anastasia, *Corresp Secy,* Lowell Art Association, Whistler House and Parker Gallery, Lowell MA

Porter, Charles, *Adjunct Lectr,* Manhattan College, School of Arts and Sciences, Bronx NY (S)

Porter, Daniel R, *Dir,* New York State Historical Association, Fenimore House, Cooperstown NY

Porter, Daniel R, *Dir,* New York State Historical Association, Farmers' Museum, Inc, Cooperstown NY

Porter, David S, *Assoc Prof,* University of North Florida, Dept of Fine Arts, Jacksonville FL (S)

Porter, Dean A, *Dir,* University of Notre Dame, Snite Museum of Art, Notre Dame IN

Porter, Edward, *Pres College,* International Fine Arts College, Miami FL (S)

Porter, Elmer J, *Secy,* Kappa Pi International Honorary Art Fraternity, Birmingham AL

Porter, Elwin, *Dir,* South Florida Art Institute of Hollywood, Hollywood FL (S)

Porter, Glenn, *General Dir,* Hagley Museum, Eleutherian Mills-Hagley Foundation, Wilmington DE

Porter, Glenn, *General Dir,* Hagley Museum, Eleutherian Mills Historical Library, Wilmington DE

Porter, Jeanne Chenault, *Assoc Prof,* Pennsylvania State University, University Park, Dept of Art History, University Park PA (S)

Porter, Jerry C, *Dir,* Museum of the Southwest, Midland TX

Porter, Joseph, *Cur Western History,* Joslyn Art Museum, Omaha NE

Porter, Richard, *Registrar,* Pennsylvania State University, Museum of Art, University Park PA

Porter, Robert, *Manager Publishing,* American Council for the Arts, New York NY

Porter, Walden, *Librn & Registrar,* The Turner Museum, Denver CO

Portland, Jack, *Lectr,* Lewis and Clark College, Dept of Art, Portland OR (S)

Poser, Mimi, *Development and Public Affairs Officer,* Solomon R Guggenheim Museum, New York NY

Posner, David, *Asst Prof,* Georgia Southern College, Dept of Art, Statesboro GA (S)

Posner, Helaine, *Actg Dir & Cur,* University of Massachusetts, Amherst, University Gallery, Amherst MA

Possehl, Gregory L, *Assoc Dir & Asian Cur,* University of Pennsylvania, University Museum of Archaeology & Anthropology, Philadelphia PA

Post, Barbara, *Second VPres,* Berks Art Alliance, Reading PA

Post, William, *Cur Ornithology,* Charleston Museum, Charleston SC

Poster, Amy, *Assoc Cur Oriental Art,* Brooklyn Museum, Brooklyn NY

Postler, Janet W, *Dir & Cur,* Cascade County Historical Society Museum, Great Falls MT

Postler, Klaus, *Dir,* One Step Beyond, Brattleboro VT

Posyniak, Suzanne, *Cur Asst,* Regina Public Library, Dunlop Art Gallery, Regina SK

Posz, A Conrad, *Dir,* Art Instruction Schools, Minneapolis MN (S)

Potoff, Leni, *Conservator,* Solomon R Guggenheim Museum, New York NY

Potoff, Reeva, *Adjunct Asst Prof,* Columbia University, School of the Arts, Division of Painting & Sculpture, New York NY (S)

Potter, G W, *Faculty,* Western Illinois University, College of Fine Arts, Macomb IL (S)

Potter, Ted, *Dir,* Southeastern Center for Contemporary Art, Winston-Salem NC

Pottruff, Richard, *Dir,* Art Gallery of Brant, Inc, Brantford ON

Potts, Charles, *Photography Dept Chmn,* Art Center College of Design, Pasadena CA (S)

Poulet, Anne, *Cur European Decorative Arts & Sculpture,* Museum of Fine Arts, Boston MA

Poulos, Anna, *Chairperson,* College of Saint Teresa, Art Dept, Winona MN (S)

Poulos, Basilios, *Assoc Prof,* Rice University, Dept of Art and Art History, Houston TX (S)

Poulton, M, *Instructor,* Technical University of Nova Scotia, Faculty of Architecture, Halifax NS (S)

Powell, Dan, *Asst Prof,* University of Northern Iowa, Dept of Art, Cedar Falls IA (S)

Powell, David, *Asst Prof,* Bradford College, Creative Arts Division, Bradford MA (S)

Powell, Dolores A Z, *VPres for North Jersey,* Federated Art Associations of New Jersey, Inc, Westfield NJ

Powell, Donald, *Bibliographer,* Tucson Museum of Art, Library, Tucson AZ

Powell, Earl A, *Dir,* Los Angeles County Museum of Art, Los Angeles CA

Powell, Phillipp, *Instr,* Carthage College, Art Dept, Kenosha WI (S)

Powell, William, *Instructor,* Delta State University, Dept of Art, Cleveland MS (S)

Powelson, Rosemary, *Instructor,* Lower Columbia College, Longview WA (S)

Powers, Carolyn, *Asst Prof,* New Mexico Highlands University, Division of Fine Arts, Las Vegas NM (S)

Powers, David F, *Cur,* National Archives and Records Service, John F Kennedy Library and Museum, Dorchester MA

Powers, H Burton, *Pres,* Stowe-Day Foundation, Hartford CT

Powers, JoAnn, *Asst Prof,* C W Post Center of Long Island University, School of the Arts, Greenvale NY (S)

Powers, Judith Boodon, *Managing Dir,* Florida Gulf Coast Art Center, Inc, Clearwater FL

Powers, Judith Boodon, *Managing Dir,* Florida Gulf Coast Art Center, Inc, Clearwater FL (S)

Poynor, Robin, *Asst Prof,* University of Florida, Dept of Art, Gainesville FL (S)

Pozzatti, Rudy, *Prof,* Indiana University, Bloomington, School of Fine Arts, Bloomington IN (S)

Pozzi, Lucio, *Treas,* American Abstract Artists, New York NY

Prabhu, Vas, *Coordr Educ,* Cornell University, Herbert F Johnson Museum of Art, Ithaca NY

Praeger, Sandy, *Docents,* University of Kansas, Spencer Museum of Art, Lawrence KS

Pramuk, Mary Vlcek, *Cur,* West Baton Rouge Museum, Port Allen LA

Pransky, Shirley, *Instructor,* Boston Center for Adult Education, Boston MA (S)

Prasch, Richard, *Prof,* Portland State University, Dept of Art and Architecture, Portland OR (S)

Prather, Marla, *Cur Painting, Sculpture & Decorative Art,* University of Kansas, Spencer Museum of Art, Lawrence KS

Pratt, Gail, *Fund Development,* Honolulu Academy of Arts, Honolulu HI

Pratt, Jean A, *Instr,* American River College, Dept of Art, Sacramento CA (S)

Pratt, Laura C, *Head Librn,* Maryland College of Art and Design Library, Silver Spring MD

Pratt, Sandy, *Dir,* Klamath County Museum, Klamath Falls OR

Pratt, Vernon, *Asst Prof,* Duke University, Dept of Art, Durham NC (S)

Pratt, William C, *Dir,* Twin City Art Foundation, Masur Museum of Art, Monroe LA

Preble, Michael, *Cur Collections,* Portland Museum of Art, Portland ME

Preisner, Olga, *Cur,* Pennsylvania State University, Museum of Art, University Park PA

Preiss, Rod W, *Asst Dir,* Jacque Marchais Center of Tibetan Arts, Inc, Staten Island NY

Prekop, Martin, *Undergrad Division Chmn,* School of the Art Institute of Chicago, Chicago IL (S)

Prendeville, Jet M, *Art Librn,* Rice University, Art Library, Houston TX

Prentiss, Bard, *Chmn,* State University of New York College at Cortland, Art Dept, Cortland NY (S)

Prentiss, Margo, *Secy Registrar,* Albrecht Art Museum, Saint Joseph MO

Prescott, Margaret, *Asst Librn,* Baltimore Museum of Art, E Kirkbride Miller Art Research Library, Baltimore MD

Pressing, Kirk L, *Supv Central Services,* Milwaukee Public Library, Art, Music & Recreation Dept, Milwaukee WI

Pressly, Nancy, *Chief Cur of Art,* San Antonio Museum Association, Inc, San Antonio Museum of Art, San Antonio TX

Prestiano, Robert, *Coordr,* Angelo State University, Art and Music Dept, San Angelo TX (S)

Preston, Herbert R, *VPres,* Star-Spangled Banner Flag House Association, Baltimore MD

Preszler, Robert E, *Cur,* Washington County Museum of Fine Arts, Hagerstown MD

Price, Allison, *Gallery Dir,* Vanderbilt University, Art Gallery, Nashville TN

Price, B Byron, *Dir,* Panhandle-Plains Historical Society Museum, Canyon TX

Price, Charles, *Prof,* Connecticut College, Dept of Art History, New London CT (S)

Price, Geraldine, *Adv Dir,* Santa Fe Workshops of Contemporary Art, Santa Fe NM (S)

Price, Howard, *Academic Supv,* Alberta College of Art, Southern Alberta Institute of Technology, Calgary AB (S)

Price, Joan, *Supervisor Art Education,* City College of New York, Art Dept, New York NY (S)

Price, L, *Faculty,* Humboldt State University, College of Creative Arts & Humanities, Arcata CA (S)

Price, Larry, *Librn,* Berkshire Athenaeum, Pittsfield MA

Price, Marcia, *Pres,* Salt Lake Art Center, Salt Lake City UT

Price, Michael, *Head Dept,* Hamline University, Art Dept, Saint Paul MN (S)

Price, Priscilla B, *Registrar,* Corning Museum of Glass, Corning NY

Price, Ramon, *Art Cur,* DuSable Museum of African American History, Chicago IL

Price, R Bret, *Instructor,* Chapman College, Art Dept, Orange CA (S)

Price, Rita, *First VPres,* North Shore Art League, Winnetka IL

Price, Rob, *Asst Prof,* University of Wisconsin-Stout, Art Dept, Menomonie WI (S)

Price, Sally Irwin, *Dir,* Baycrafters, Inc, Bay Village OH

Price, Tom, *Instructor,* The Design Schools, Art Institute of Seattle, Seattle WA (S)

Prichett, Peter P, *Pres,* Annie S Kemerer Museum, Bethlehem PA

Priest, T, *Asst Prof,* College of the Holy Cross, Dept Visual Arts, Worcester MA (S)

Priester, Mary, *Asst Cur,* Portland Art Association, Portland Art Museum, Portland OR

Primm, Joan, *Cur of Education,* Bower's Museum, Santa Ana CA

Prince, Antoinette, *Co-Dir & Treas,* The Loading Dock Gallery, Boston MA

Prince, Paul, *Designer of Exhib,* University of California, Santa Barbara, University Art Museum, Santa Barbara CA

Prince, R, *Pres,* Rodman Hall Arts Centre, Saint Catharines ON

Prince, Richard, *Assoc Prof,* University of British Columbia, Dept of Fine Arts, Vancouver BC (S)

Prince, Roger O, *Dir,* Wooster Community Art Center, Danbury CT

Prins, Johanna W, *Slide Cur,* Syracuse University, Ernest Stevenson Bird Library, Syracuse NY

Pritchard, Aline, *Art Cur,* Leo Baeck Institute, New York NY

Pritchard, C William, *Mgr Business Operations,* Iowa State Education Association, Salisbury House, Des Moines IA

Privatsky, Benni, *Co-Dir,* Dickinson State College, Mind's Eye Gallery, Dickinson ND

Privitt, Bob, *Instr,* Pepperdine University, Seaver College, Dept of Art, Malibu CA (S)

Privratsky, Grace, *Chmn,* North Country Museum of Arts, Park Rapids MN

Probert, Richard, *Chmn,* Muskingum College, Creative & Performing Arts Dept, New Concord OH (S)

Procaccini, Donald, *Prof,* Emmanuel College, Art Dept, Boston MA (S)

Procos, D, *Instructor,* Technical University of Nova Scotia, Faculty of Architecture, Halifax NS (S)

Proctor, Letitia, *Librn,* Memphis Brooks Museum of Art, Library, Memphis TN

Proctor, Valerie, *Cur,* Public Archives of Canada, Laurier House, Ottawa ON

Prokop, Clifton A, *Assoc Prof,* Keystone Junior College, Fine Arts Dept, Factoryville PA (S)

Prokop, Peter, *Pres & Cur,* Taras H Schevchenko Museum and Memorial Park Foundation, Oakville ON

Prokopoff, Stephen S, *Dir,* University of Illinois, Krannert Art Museum, Champaign IL

Prokos, Nicholas, *Lectr,* Lake Forest College, Dept of Art, Lake Forest IL (S)

Prol, Elbertus, *Cur,* Ringwood Manor House Museum, Ringwood NJ

Prom, James, *Instructor,* Rochester Community College, Art Dept, Rochester MN (S)

Promos, Marianne, *Head Art Dept,* Free Library of Philadelphia, Art Dept, Philadelphia PA

Proper, David R, *Librn,* Historic Deerfield Inc, Henry N Flynt Library, Deerfield MA

Propersi, August, *Dir,* Propersi Galleries and School of Art Inc, Greenwich CT (S)

Propersi, August, *Pres & Dir,* Propersi School of Art Inc Galleries, Greenwich CT

Propersi, Joann, *VPres,* Propersi Galleries and School of Art Inc, Greenwich CT (S)

Propersi, Joann, *VPres,* Propersi School of Art Inc Galleries, Greenwich CT

Propersi, Linda, *Administrative Asst,* Propersi Galleries and School of Art Inc, Greenwich CT (S)

Propersi, Linda, *Admin Asst,* Propersi School of Art Inc Galleries, Greenwich CT

Propersi, Michael, *Office Mgr,* Propersi Galleries and School of Art Inc, Greenwich CT (S)

Propersi, Michael, *Office Mgr,* Propersi School of Art Inc Galleries, Greenwich CT

Proske, Beatrice G, *Cur Emeritus Sculpture,* Hispanic Society of America, Museum, New York NY

Prosperi, Paul, *Treasurer,* Norton Gallery and School of Art, West Palm Beach FL

Pross, Lester F, *Dir,* Berea College, Art Department Gallery, Berea KY

Pross, Lester F, *Chmn,* Berea College, Art Dept, Berea KY (S)

Prosser, Judy, *Archivist-Registrar,* Museum of Western Colorado Archives, Grand Junction CO

Provan, Archibald D, *Assoc Prof,* Rochester Institute of Technology, School of Printing, Rochester NY (S)

Provencher, Alfred, *Chmn,* Monmouth College, Dept of Art, West Long Branch NJ (S)

Provenzano, Jan, *Education Coordr,* Rockford Art Association, Burpee Art Museum, Rockford IL

Provo, Dan, *Cur Anthropology,* Institute of the Great Plains, Museum of the Great Plains, Lawton OK

Pruce, Jerry, *Adjunct Instr,* Maryville College, St Louis, Art Division, Saint Louis MO (S)

Prucha, John J, *VPres,* Everson Museum of Art, Syracuse NY

Prueitt, Hillary, *Public Relations,* Stan Hywet Hall Foundation, Inc, Akron OH

Pruner, Gary L, *Instr,* American River College, Dept of Art, Sacramento CA (S)

Prvry, Chrystyna, *Archivist,* Ukrainian Museum, New York NY

Pryor, Joan S, *Museum Technician,* Tuskegee Institute National Historic Site, George Washington Carver & The Oaks, Tuskegee AL

Puccinelli, Lydia, *Cur Coll,* National Museum of African Art, Washington DC

Pughe, Debra, *Mgr of Exhibitions,* Fine Arts Museums of San Francisco, M H de Young Memorial Museum and California Palace of the Legion of Honor, San Francisco CA

Pujol, Elliott, *Prof,* Kansas State University, Art Dept, Manhattan KS (S)

Pullen, Vicki, *Chmn,* Columbia College, Dept of Art, Columbia SC (S)

Puls, Lucy, *Asst Prof,* Western Carolina University, Dept of Art, Cullowhee NC (S)

Pulsifer, Dorothy, *Asst Prof,* Bridgewater State College, Art Dept, Bridgewater MA (S)

Pulsipher, Brent E, *Instr,* Graceland College, Art Dept, Lamoni IA (S)

Pultorak, Marceil, *Chairperson,* Carroll College, Art Dept, Waukesha WI (S)

Pum, Robert, *Head Dept,* University of Wisconsin-Green Bay, Visual Arts Dept, Green Bay WI (S)

Pumphrey, Richard G, *Asst Prof,* Lynchburg College, Art Dept, Lynchburg VA (S)

Purden, Debi, *Registrar,* Museum of Contemporary Art, Chicago IL

Purdy, Gerald, *Assoc Prof,* University of Southern California, School of Fine Arts, Los Angeles CA (S)

Purdy, Henry, *Dir,* Holland College, School of Visual Arts Library & Gallery, West Royalty PE

Purdy, Henry, *Dir,* Holland College, School of Visual Arts, Charlottetown PE (S)

Purnell, J Hurst, *Pres,* Historical Society of Kent County, Chestertown MD

Purrington, Philip F, *Sr Cur,* Old Dartmouth Historical Society, New Bedford Whaling Museum, New Bedford MA

Pursell, Clay, *Adjunct Instr,* Maryville College, St Louis, Art Division, Saint Louis MO (S)

Purses-Smith, M, *Chmn of Art Committee,* Wilfrid Laurier University, Concourse Gallery, Waterloo ON

Purucker, Karen Noll, *Dir,* Fuller Lodge Art Center, Los Alamos NM

Purvis, Alston, *Assoc Prof,* Boston University, School of Visual Arts, Boston MA (S)

Purvis, Susan, *Instr,* Arkansas Arts Center, Little Rock AR (S)

Puryear, Thomas, *Chairperson Art History,* Southeastern Massachusetts University, College of Visual and Performing Arts, North Dartmouth MA (S)

Pustari, C Joseph, *Dean College Arts & Science,* University of San Diego, Art Dept, San Diego CA (S)

Putka, Robert, *Instr,* Cuyahoga Valley Art Center, Cuyahoga Falls OH (S)

Putnam, Luann, *In Charge,* Central Iowa Art Association, Inc, Art Reference Library, Marshalltown IA

Putnam, Mancy L, *Pres,* Marion Art Center, Marion MA

Putney, Elizabeth, *Assoc Educ,* Old Salem Inc, Museum of Early Southern Decorative Arts, Winston-Salem NC

Pyles, Julian, *Chmn Division Art, Science, Business,* Barber-Scotia College, Art Dept, Concord NC (S)

Pylyshenko, Wolodymyr, *Chmn,* State University of New York College at Brockport, Dept of Art, Brockport NY (S)

Quandt, Elizabeth, *Instr,* Santa Rosa Junior College, Art Dept, Santa Rosa CA (S)

Queen, John, *Assoc Prof,* Texas Tech University, Dept of Art, Lubbock TX (S)

Queen, Louise, *Asst Secy,* United Methodist Church Commission on Archives and History, Madison NJ

Quick, Betsy, *Exhib Coordr,* University of California, Los Angeles, Museum of Cultural History, Los Angeles CA

Quick, Edward R, *Head Registration & Prep,* Joslyn Art Museum, Omaha NE

Quick, Marion, *Co-owner,* Grand Marais Art Colony, Grand Marais MN (S)

Quick, Michael, *Cur of American Art,* Los Angeles County Museum of Art, Los Angeles CA

Quick, Richard, *Dir,* Rahr-West Museum, Manitowoc WI

Quiller, Stephen, *Visiting Prof,* Adams State College, Dept of Visual Arts, Alamosa CO (S)

Quimby, Frank, *Prof,* Salem State College, Art Dept, Salem MA (S)

Quimby, George I, *Dir,* University of Washington, Thomas Burke Memorial Washington State Museum, Seattle WA

Quimby, Ian M G, *Editor Publications Office,* Winterthur Museum and Gardens, Winterthur DE

Quin, Langdon, *Asst Prof,* Cornell University, Dept of Art, Ithaca NY (S)

Quinn, Ann, *Cur of Education,* San Bernardino County Museum and Satellites, Fine Arts Institute, Redlands CA

Quinn, Michael H, *VPres,* Columbia Museums of Art and Science, Columbia SC

Quinn, Michael H, *VPres,* Columbia Museums of Art and Science, Columbia Art Association, Columbia SC

Quinn, Noel, *Asst to Dir,* California State University, Los Angeles, Fine Arts Gallery, Los Angeles CA

Quinn, Steve, *Chmn Design Dept,* Milwaukee Institute of Art and Design, Milwaukee WI (S)

Quinn, William, *Actg Dir,* Kent State University, School of Art, Kent OH (S)

Quinsac, Annie Paul, *Chmn Art History,* University of South Carolina, Dept of Art, Columbia SC (S)

Quintal, Margaret, *Dir,* Oscar Howe Art Center, Mitchell SD

Quirarte, Jacinto, *Prof,* University of Texas at San Antonio, Division of Art and Design, San Antonio TX (S)

Quirk, James, *Assoc Prof,* Northern Michigan University, Dept of Art and Design, Marquette MI (S)

Quirk, Marie S, *Museum Dir,* City of Holyoke Museum-Wistariahurst, Holyoke MA

Quirke, Lillian, *Instructor,* De Anza College, Art Dept, Cupertino CA (S)

Raasch, L, *Dir,* Art Institute of Chicago, Junior Museum, Chicago IL

Rab, Harry, *Asst Prof,* Rochester Institute of Technology, School of Printing, Rochester NY (S)

Rabe, Fred, *Assoc Prof,* Weber State College, Art Dept, Ogden UT (S)

Rabe, Lou, *Asst to Dir,* University of Southwestern Louisiana, University Art Museum, Lafayette LA

Rabe, Michael, *Asst Prof,* Saint Xavier College, Dept of Art, Chicago IL (S)

Rabinovitch, Celia, *Asst Prof,* University of Colorado at Denver, Dept of Fine Arts, Denver CO (S)

Rabis, James, *Librn,* Fairfield Public Library and Museum, Fairfield Art Association, Fairfield IA

Radan, George, *Instr,* Rosemont College, Division of the Arts, Rosemont PA (S)

Radan, George, *Prof,* Villanova University, Dept of Art and Art History, Villanova PA (S)

Radecki, Martin J, *Chief Conservator,* Indianapolis Museum of Art, Indianapolis IN

Radell, Lloyd, *Chmn,* Mercy College of Detroit, Art Dept, Detroit MI (S)

Radell, Sheila, *Childrens Dept Head,* Topeka Public Library, Fine Arts Dept & Gallery of Fine Arts, Topeka KS

Rademacher, Richard J, *Head Librn,* Wichita Public Library, Wichita KS

Radice, Anne-Imelda, *Chief Cur,* United States Capitol Museum, Washington DC

Radke, Gary, *Prof,* Syracuse University, Dept of Fine Arts, Syracuse NY (S)

Radmer, Sue, *Asst Dir,* Municipal Art Society of New York, Information Exchange, New York NY

Radosh, Sondra M, *Asst Dir,* Jones Library, Inc, Amherst MA

Raducha, Joan, *Newsletter Editor,* American Committee for South Asian Art, Evanston IL

Radysh, Jeanne, *Dept Head,* Ray-Vogue College of Design, Chicago IL (S)

Raedeke, Paul, *Dir Photography,* Academy of Art College, San Francisco CA (S)

Raedeler, Dorothy F, *Executive Dir,* Saint Croix School of the Arts, Inc, Christansted Saint Croix VI (S)

Raetsch, Fred, *Secy,* Anderson County Arts Council, Anderson SC

Rafael, Ruth, *Archivist,* Judah L Magnes Museum, Berkeley CA

Raggio, Olga, *Chmn European Sculture & Decorative Arts,* Metropolitan Museum of Art, New York NY

Ragir, John, *Treas,* N.A.M.E. Gallery, Chicago IL

Rago, Juliet, *Prof,* Loyola University of Chicago, Fine Arts Dept, Chicago IL (S)

Ragouzis, Perry, *Coordr Teacher Cert,* Colorado State University, Dept of Art, Fort Collins CO (S)

Raguin, J C, *Assoc Prof,* College of the Holy Cross, Dept Visual Arts, Worcester MA (S)

Rahill, Margaret Fish, *Cur,* Charles Allis Art Museum, Milwaukee WI

Rahja, Virginia, *Dir,* School of the Associated Arts Galleries, Saint Paul MN

Rahja, Virginia, *Dir,* School of the Associated Arts, Saint Paul MN (S)

Rahm, Bob, *Area Chmn Design,* Pasadena City College, Art Dept, Pasadena CA (S)

Raia, Frank, *VPres & Dir Education,* Art Institute of Fort Lauderdale, Fort Lauderdale FL (S)

Raines, D O, *Assoc Prof,* Presbyterian College, Fine Arts Dept, Clinton SC (S)

Raines, Kevin, *Prof,* College of Notre Dame of Maryland, Art Dept, Baltimore MD (S)

Rainwater, Robert, *Keeper of Prints,* New York Public Library, Prints Room, New York NY

Raisanen, Roberta, *Bus Mgr,* Ashtabula Arts Center, Ashtabula OH

Raiselis, Robert, *Asst to Exhibitions Designer,* Hood Museum of Art, Hanover NH

Rait, Eleanor, *Cur Collections,* Hofstra University, Emily Lowe Gallery, Hempstead NY

Raizman, D, *Faculty,* Western Illinois University, College of Fine Arts, Macomb IL (S)

Rajam, Margaret, *Prof,* West Virginia University, Division of Art, Morgantown WV (S)

Rajer, Anton, *Assoc Conservation,* Atkins Museum of Fine Art, Kansas City MO

Rakocy, William, *Cur Coll,* El Paso Museum of Art, El Paso TX

Ralston, Penny, *Pres,* South Arkansas Art Center, El Dorado AR

Ram, Russell, *VPres,* Buffalo Society of Artists, Williamsville NY

Ramage, Andrew, *Chmn & Assoc Prof,* Cornell University, Dept of the History of Art, Ithaca NY (S)

Ramage, William, *Asst Prof,* Castleton State College, Art Dept, Castleton VT (S)

Ramberg, W Dodd, *Prof,* Catholic University of America, Dept of Architecture and Planning, Washington DC (S)

Ramirez, Adrian N, *Prof,* Catholic University of Puerto Rico, Dept of Fine Arts, Ponce PR (S)

Ramirez, Humberto, *Preparator,* Florida State University, Art Gallery, Tallahassee FL

Ramirez, Lisa Mari, *Registrar,* San Jose State University, Union Gallery, San Jose CA

Ramirez de Comas, Genoveva, *Assoc Prof,* Inter American University of Puerto Rico, Dept of Art, San German PR (S)

Ramos, Polly, *Volunteer Coordr,* Metropolitan Museum and Art Center, Coral Gables FL

Ramsaran, Helen, *Assoc Prof,* John Jay College of Criminal Justice, Dept of Art, Music and Philosophy, New York NY (S)

Ramsauer, Joseph, *Assoc Prof,* Black Hawk College, Art Dept, Moline IL (S)

Ramsay, Charles, *Instr,* Oral Roberts University, Fine Arts Dept, Tulsa OK (S)

Ramsay, George, *Chmn & Prof,* Wittenberg University, Art Dept, Springfield OH (S)

Ramsdell, F A, *Secy,* Potsdam Public Museum, Potsdam NY

Ramsey, Robert David, *Chmn,* College of Notre Dame, Dept of Art, Belmont CA (S)

Ramsey, Robert W, *Actg Chmn,* California State University, Long Beach, Art Dept, Long Beach CA (S)

Ranadive, Joan, *Asst Dir,* M Flint Institute of Arts, Flint MI

Rand, Harry Z, *Cur 20th Century Painting & Sculpture,* National Museum of American Art, Washington DC

Rand, Olan A, *Asst Prof,* Northwestern University, Evanston, Dept of Art History, Evanston IL (S)

Randall, Ann K, *Chief Librn,* City College of New York, Cohen Art Library, New York NY

Randall, Genevieve, *Second VPres,* National League of American Pen Women, Washington DC

Randall, Lilian M C, *Cur of Manuscripts and Rare Books,* Walters Art Gallery, Baltimore MD

Randall, Richard H, *Cur of Medieval Art,* Walters Art Gallery, Baltimore MD

Randall, Vicky, *Instructor,* Bethany College, Art Dept, Lindsborg KS (S)

Randazzo, Angelo, *Gallery Dir,* Manchester Institute of Arts and Sciences Gallery, Manchester NH

Randazzo, Angelo, *Exec Dir,* Manchester Institute of Arts and Sciences, Manchester NH (S)

Randel, Jo, *Chmn Bd,* Carson County Square House Museum, Panhandle TX

Randolph, John, *Chmn,* Phillips University, Dept of Art, Enid OK (S)

Randolph, Mary Ellen, *Assoc Prof,* Hood College, Dept of Art, Frederick MD (S)

Rands, Robert L, *Adj Cur Archaeology,* Southern Illinois University, University Museum, Carbondale IL

Raneo, Frank, *Chmn Fashion Illustration,* New England School of Art & Design, Boston MA (S)

Rankaitis, Susan, *Instructor,* Chapman College, Art Dept, Orange CA (S)

Rankin, Allan, *Pres,* Maritime Art Association, Fredericton MB

Rankin, Joseph T, *Cur,* New York Public Library, Spencer Collection, New York NY

Rankin, Joseph T, *Chief,* New York Public Library, Art, Prints and Photographs Division, New York NY

Rankin, Marjorie E, *Dean,* Drexel University, Dept of Design, Philadelphia PA (S)

Rann, V, *VPres,* Madison County Historical Society, Cottage Lawn, Oneida NY

Ransom, Bill, *Asst Prof,* Chattanooga State Technical Community College, Advertising Arts Dept, Chattanooga TN (S)

Ranspach, Ernest, *Faculty,* College of Boca Raton, Art & Commercial Art Dept, Boca Raton FL (S)

Rantoul, Talbot N, *Asst Prof,* Northeastern University, Dept of Art, Boston MA (S)

Raquel, Alba, *Secy,* Museo Historico de Puerto Rico Inc, Santurce PR

Rasbury, Patricia, *Cur of Education,* Tennessee State Museum, Nashville TN

Rash, Dillman A, *Chmn Board of Governors,* J B Speed Art Museum, Louisville KY

Rash, Nancy, *Chmn,* Connecticut College, Dept of Art History, New London CT (S)

Rasmussen, Gerald E, *Dir,* Stamford Museum and Nature Center, Stamford CT

Rasmussen, Keith, *Instructor,* Atlanta College of Art, Atlanta GA (S)

Rasmussen, Marie, *Instructor,* Umpqua Community College, Fine & Performing Arts Dept, Roseburg OR (S)

Rasmussen, Waldo, *Dir International Prog,* Museum of Modern Art, New York NY

Ratcliffe, Jefferson, *Cur,* Sturdivant Hall, Selma AL

Rathbun, Joan Nachbaur, *Dir,* Longview Museum and Arts Center, Longview TX

Rathbun, William Jay, *Asian Art Cur,* Seattle Art Museum, Seattle WA

Rathgeb, Donald A, *Prof,* St Michael's College, Fine Arts Dept, Winooski VT (S)

Rathman, Lois, *Second VPres,* Monmouth Museum and Cultural Center, Lincroft NJ

Ratner, Hindy, *Extension Cur,* University of British Columbia, Museum of Anthropology, Vancouver BC

Ratner, Joanne, *Cur Asst,* Hebrew Union College, Skirball Museum, Los Angeles CA

Ratner, Rhoda, *Librn,* National Museum of American History, Branch Library, Washington DC

Rattner, Carl, *Assoc Prof,* Saint Thomas Aquinas College, Art Dept, Sparkhill NY (S)

Rattray, Alexander, *Head Landscape Archit,* University of Manitoba, Faculty of Architecture, Winnipeg MB (S)

Rauch, Jeanne, *Pres,* Gaston County Museum of Art & History, Dallas NC

Rauch, John V, *Prof,* Northern Michigan University, Dept of Art and Design, Marquette MI (S)

Raudzens, Mark, *Prof,* Salem State College, Art Dept, Salem MA (S)

Rauer, Albert, *Chmn,* Montgomery County Community College, Communicating Arts Dept, Blue Bell PA (S)

Rauf, M De, *Assoc Prof,* Thomas More College, Art Dept, Fort Mitchell KY (S)

Rauf, M deDeo, *Dir,* Thomas More College, TM Gallery, Fort Mitchell KY

Rausch, Charles, *Dir,* University of Minnesota, Paul Whitney Larson Gallery, Saint Paul MN

Rauschenberg, Bradford L, *Research Fellow,* Old Salem Inc, Library, Winston-Salem NC

Rauschenberg, Christopher, *Instructor,* Marylhurst College, Art Dept, Marylhurst OR (S)

Ravence, C, *Assoc Prof,* American University, Dept of Art, Washington DC (S)

Ravenel, Gaillard F, *Chief Design & Installation,* National Gallery of Art, Washington DC

Rawlins, Scott, *Educational Coordr,* Calvert Marine Museum, Solomons MD

Rawls, William A, *Dir Theatre,* Rocky Mount Arts and Crafts Center, Rocky Mount NC

Rawson, G H, *Pres,* Lyceum Club and Women's Art Association of Canada, Toronto ON

Rawson, Hufty E, *Prof,* Catholic University of Puerto Rico, Dept of Fine Arts, Ponce PR (S)

Rawstad, Lockie, *Dir Membership,* Walker Art Center, Minneapolis MN

Ray, Dee, *Secy,* Redding Museum and Art Center, Redding CA

Ray, Glen A, *Coordr Arts,* Old Dominion University Gallery, Norfolk VA

Ray, Gordon N, *Pres,* John Simon Guggenheim Memorial Foundation, New York NY

Ray, Jim, *Dir,* Albrecht Art Museum, Saint Joseph MO

Ray, Lawrence A, *Assoc Prof,* Lambuth College, Dept of Art, Jackson TN (S)

Ray, M Louise, *Letters,* National League of American Pen Women, Washington DC

Ray, Timothy, *Assoc Prof,* Moorhead State University, Dept of Art, Moorhead MN (S)

Ray, Wade, *Dir,* Ray-Vogue College of Design, Chicago IL (S)

Rayburn, Pat, *Pres,* The Dalles Art Association, The Dalles OR

Rayen, James W, *Prof,* Wellesley College, Art Dept, Wellesley MA (S)

Raymond, Glenn T, *Prof,* Grand Rapids Junior College, Art Dept, Grand Rapids MI (S)

Raymond, Kathleen, *Visiting Artist,* Southwestern University, Art Dept, Georgetown TX (S)

Raz, Robert, *Dir Library,* Grand Rapids Public Library, Music & Art Dept, Grand Rapids MI

Razadi-Kazadi, Camille, *A V Librn,* Beverly Hills Public Library, Fine Arts Library, Beverly Hills CA

Rea, W H, *Horticulturist,* Tryon Palace Restoration Complex, New Bern NC

Read, Ronald W, *Media Specialist & Librn,* Church of Jesus Christ of Latter-Day Saints, Museum of Church History and Art, Salt Lake City UT

Reading, Jane, *Pres,* Hunterdon Art Center, Clinton NJ

Ready, Alma D, *Head,* Pimeria Alta Historical Society, Library, Nogales AZ

Reardon, Jean, *Secy,* Newburyport Maritime Society, Custom House Maritime Museum, Newburyport MA

Reardon, J P, *Assoc Prof,* College of the Holy Cross, Dept Visual Arts, Worcester MA (S)

Reardon, Michael J, *Dir,* Blackhawk Mountain School of Art Gallery, Blackhawk CO

Reaves, Wendy W, *Cur Prints,* National Portrait Gallery, Washington DC

Reber, Mick, *Chmn,* Fort Lewis College, Art Dept, Durango CO (S)

Reboli, John P, *Chmn & Assoc Prof,* College of the Holy Cross, Dept Visual Arts, Worcester MA (S)

Rebsamen, Werner, *Assoc Prof,* Rochester Institute of Technology, School of Printing, Rochester NY (S)

Reckert, Carrie, *Mgr Public Relations,* The Bradford Museum, Niles IL

Rector, Lois, *Instructor,* Dunedin Fine Arts and Cultural Center, Dunedin FL (S)

Redd, Richard J *Prof,* Lehigh University, Dept of Art and Architecture, Bethlehem PA (S)

Redding, Julie, *Library Cur,* Beaumont Art Museum, Library, Beaumont TX

Reddix, Roscoe, *Assoc Prof,* Southern University in New Orleans, Art Dept, New Orleans LA (S)

Redfern, Alan, *Chmn Bd,* High Plains Museum, McCook NE

Redford, Marcia, *Dir,* Fort Saskatchewan Municipal Library, Exhibit Room, Fort Saskatchewan AB

Redjinski, Barbara, *Registrar,* Portland Museum of Art, Portland ME

Redman, Lois, *Gallery Asst,* Emily Carr College of Art & Design, The Charles H Scott Gallery, Vancouver BC

Redmond, Charles R, *Secy of Foundation,* Times Mirror Company, Los Angeles CA

Reece, Annie, *Librn,* Concord Antiquarian Society Museum, Library, Concord MA

Reece, Raymond, *Public Services Librn,* University of California, Los Angeles, Art Library, Los Angeles CA

Reed, Alan, *Instructor,* Saint John's University, Art Dept, Collegeville MN (S)

Reed, Barry C, *Assoc Prof,* Palomar College, Art Dept, San Marcos TX (S)

Reed, Carl, *Chmn & Asst Prof,* Colorado College, Dept of Art, Colorado Springs CO (S)

Reed, Charles L, *Actg Dir,* Virginia Museum of Fine Arts, Richmond VA

Reed, David, *Instr,* New York Studio School of Drawing, Painting and Sculpture, New York NY (S)

Reed, Dennis, *Dir,* Los Angeles Valley College, Art Gallery, Van Nuys CA

Reed, Dorothy B, *Registrar,* Plymouth Antiquarian Society, Plymouth MA

Reed, Harold, *Chmn,* Salem College, Art Dept, Salem WV (S)

Reed, Howard B, *Actg Co-Dir,* Fairbanks Museum and Planetarium, Saint Johnsbury VT

Reed, Ida, *Head,* Carnegie Library of Pittsburgh, Pittsburgh PA

Reed, Jesse F, *Chmn,* Davis and Elkins College, Dept of Art, Elkins WV (S)

Reed, Kelly Scott, *Communications Officer,* J B Speed Art Museum, Louisville KY

Reed, Nancy, *Assoc Prof,* Texas Tech University, Dept of Art, Lubbock TX (S)

Reed, Richard S, *Dir,* Fruitlands Museums, Harvard MA

Reed, Robert, *Assoc Prof,* Yale University, School of Art, New Haven CT (S)

Reed, Rosalie, *Registrar,* Yale University, Art Gallery, New Haven CT

Reed, Shirley M, *Dir,* Community Gallery of Lancaster County, Lancaster PA

Reed, Sue W, *Pres,* Print Council of America, Boston MA

Reed, William G, *Pres,* Corporate Council for the Arts, Seattle WA

Reeder, Charles L, *Instr,* Mainline Center of the Arts, Haverford PA (S)

Rees, John, *Dir Auto Museum,* Western Reserve Historical Society, Cleveland OH

Rees, Philip, *Art Librn,* University of North Carolina, Art Library, Chapel Hill NC

Reese, Anne O, *Librn,* Toledo Museum of Art, Library, Toledo OH

Reese, Becky Duval, *Educational Cur,* University of Texas at Austin, Archer M Huntington Art Gallery, Austin TX

Reese, Sharen, *Co-Treas,* Coos Art Museum, Coos Bay OR

Reeve, Gordon, *Chmn Sculpture,* University of Manitoba, School of Art, Winnipeg MB (S)

Reeves, Don, *Cur Coll,* National Cowboy Hall of Fame and Western Heritage Center, Oklahoma City OK

Reeves, John, *Secy,* Canton Art Institute, Canton OH

Regan, Franklin F, *Pres,* Bowne House, Flushing NY

Regan, Patricia, *Publicity Dir,* D-Art, A Visual Arts Center for Dallas, Dallas TX

Reger, Lawrence L, *Dir,* American Association of Museums, Washington DC

Regier, Kathleen J, *Chairperson Dept,* Webster College, Art Dept, Webster Groves MO (S)

Regier, Robert W, *Chmn,* Bethel College, Dept of Art, North Newton KS (S)

Reich, Sheldon, *Coordr Art History,* University of Arizona, Dept of Art, Tucson AZ (S)

Reichart, Deb, *Exec Dir,* Meadville Council on the Arts, Meadville PA

Reichert, Don, *Chmn Painting,* University of Manitoba, School of Art, Winnipeg MB (S)

Reichlin, Elinor, *Librn,* Society for the Preservation of New England Antiquities, Library, Boston MA

Reid, Bryan S, *Secy,* Chicago Historical Society, Chicago IL

Reid, Donna, *Instructor,* Chemeketa Community College, Dept of Humanities & Communications, Salem OR (S)

Reid, Lawry, *Chairperson Dept,* Dean Junior College, Visual and Performing Art Dept, Franklin MA (S)

Reid, Megan, *Dir,* Dacotah Prairie Museum, Ruth Bunker Memorial Library, Aberdeen SD

Reid, R, *Men's VPres,* Art Students League of New York, New York NY

Reid, Richard S, *Dir,* Mary Washington College, Belmont, The Gari Melchers Memorial Gallery, Fredericksburg VA

Reidhaar, James, *Asst Prof,* Indiana University, Bloomington, School of Fine Arts, Bloomington IN (S)

Reids, Ann, *Cur,* Lethbridge Public Library, Art Gallery, Lethbridge AB

Reifel, J Noel, *Div Coordr Painting,* Kent State University, School of Art, Kent OH (S)

Reilly, Jerry M, *Instructor,* Modesto Junior College, Arts Humanities and Speech Division, Modesto CA (S)

Reilly, Patricia, *Asst to Dir,* The One Club for Art & Copy, New York NY

Reilly, William B, *Prof,* Incarnate Word College, Art Dept, San Antonio TX (S)

Reimer, Hennie, *Assoc Prof,* Siena Heights College, Studio Angelico Art Dept, Adrian MI (S)

Reimer, Jean, *Secy,* Marian Osborne Cunningham Art Gallery, Bakersfield CA

Reimer, Nora, *Chmn Board,* Crook County Museum and Art Gallery, Sundance WY

Reimers, William, *Secy,* Art Patrons League of Mobile, Mobile AL

Reina, Charles, *Asst Prof,* Nassau Community College, Art Dept, Garden City NY (S)

Reinhardt, Debbie, *Registrar,* Laumeier Sculpture Park, Saint Louis MO

Reinhardt, Richard, *Chairperson Crafts,* Philadelphia College of Art, Philadelphia PA (S)

Reinhart, Susan, *Assoc Prof,* University of Bridgeport, Art Dept, Bridgeport CT (S)

Reinhold, Allen, *Instr,* Utah Technical College at Salt Lake, Commercial Art Dept, Salt Lake City UT (S)

Reinholtz, Richard, *Assoc Prof,* University of Montana, Dept of Art, Missoula MT (S)

Reinke, Bernnett, *Library Dir,* Dickinson State College, Stoxen Library, Dickinson ND

Reis, William, *Instr,* Salve Regina - The Newport College, Art Dept, Newport RI (S)

Reisinger, Landon C, *Librn,* Historical Society of York County, Library, York PA

Reister, Pamela, *Registrar,* University of Michigan, Kelsey Museum of Ancient and Medieval Archaeology, Ann Arbor MI

Reizen, Sandra, *Secy,* Rensselaer County Historical Society, Hart-Cluett Mansion, 1827, Troy NY

Relkin, Fern, *Second VPres,* Art Centre of New Jersey, East Orange NJ (S)

Rembert, Virginia Pitts, *Prof,* University of Alabama, Art Dept, Tuscaloosa AL (S)

Remington, R Roger, *Prof,* Rochester Institute of Technology, School of Art and Design, Rochester NY (S)

Remsing, Joseph G, *Instructor,* Modesto Junior College, Arts Humanities and Speech Division, Modesto CA (S)

Rendall, Amanda, *Library Asst,* San Francisco Art Institute, Anne Bremer Memorial Library, San Francisco CA

Renforth, John, *Assoc Dir,* Corporate Council for the Arts, Seattle WA

Rennalls, Martin A, *Prof,* Rochester Institute of Technology, School of Photographic Arts & Sciences, Rochester NY (S)

Renner, Emmanuel, *Pres,* College of Saint Benedict, Art Gallery, Saint Joseph MN

Rennich, Marie, *Exec Dir,* Cheltenham Art Centre, Cheltenham PA (S)

Renwick, D, *VPres,* Community Arts Council of Chilliwack, Chilliwack BC

Reoutt, Steve, *Graphic Design,* California College of Arts and Crafts, Oakland CA (S)

Replogle, Rex, *Assoc Prof,* Kansas State University, Art Dept, Manhattan KS (S)

Repplier, Cynthia, *Coordr Education & Visitor Servs,* Brandywine River Museum, Chadds Ford PA

Reppucci, David K, *VPres,* Lowell Art Association, Whistler House and Parker Gallery, Lowell MA

Rerch, Julie, *Dean,* Moore College of Art, Philadelphia PA (S)

Resch, Fran, *Gallery Dir,* Allegheny College, Bowman, Megahan and Penelec Galleries, Meadville PA

Resenberger, Julie, *Secy,* Omaha Children's Museum, Inc, Omaha NE

Resnikoff, Florence, *Metal Arts,* California College of Arts and Crafts, Oakland CA (S)

Ressmeyer, Richard, *Cur Education,* Heritage Plantation of Sandwich, Sandwich MA

Ressmeyer, Richard, *Cur,* Heritage Plantation of Sandwich, Library, Sandwich MA

Restivo, John P, *Dir Services,* Canadiana Sport Art Collection, National Sport and Recreation Centre Inc, Ottawa ON

Retfalvi, A, *Librn,* University of Toronto, Fine Art Library, Toronto ON

Retherford, Elaine, *Third VPres,* Arizona Watercolor Association, Phoenix AZ

Rettig, Jacqueline, *Asst Prof,* Fairleigh Dickinson University, Fine Arts Dept, Teaneck NJ (S)

Reuter, Laurel J, *Dir & Head Cur,* North Dakota Museum of Art, Grand Forks ND

Revor, M Remy, *Prof,* Mount Mary College, Art Dept, Milwaukee WI (S)

Rewald, John, *Distinguished Prof,* City University of New York, PhD Program in Art History, New York NY (S)

Rey, George, *Vis Prof,* Harrisburg Area Community College, Division of Communication and the Arts, Harrisburg PA (S)

Reyes, Lawney, *Corp Art Cur,* Seafirst Corporation, Corporate Affairs Dept, Seattle WA

Reynolds, Allie, *Pres,* National Hall of Fame for Famous American Indians, Anadarko OK

Reynolds, Don L, *Asst Dir & Cur Pony Express Stables,* Saint Joseph Museum, Saint Joseph MO

Reynolds, Dorothy, *Dir,* Safety Harbor Museum of History and Fine Arts, Safety Harbor FL

Reynolds, Gary, *Cur Painting & Sculpture,* Newark Museum, Newark NJ

Reynolds, George K, *VPres,* Peale Museum, Baltimore MD

Reynolds, Harold M, *Asst Prof,* Central Missouri State University, Art Dept, Warrensburg MO (S)

Reynolds, Jamie, *Cur,* Ogunquit Art Association, The Barn Gallery, Ogunquit ME

Reynolds, Robert, *Prof,* California Polytechnic State University at San Luis Obispo, Art Dept, San Luis Obispo CA (S)

Reynolds, Robert, *Cur Geology,* San Bernardino County Museum and Satellites, Fine Arts Institute, Redlands CA

Reynolds, Ron, *Head Dept,* Arkansas Tech University, Dept of Art, Russellville AR (S)

Reynolds, Sally, *Gift Shop Mgr,* Ella Sharp Museum, Jackson MI

Reynolds, Stephen, *Assoc Prof,* University of Texas at San Antonio, Division of Art and Design, San Antonio TX (S)

Reynolds, Ted, *Asst Prof,* University of North Florida, Dept of Fine Arts, Jacksonville FL (S)

Reynolds, Valrae, *Cur Oriental Coll,* Newark Museum, Newark NJ

Rezac, Roslyn, *Coordr,* University of Minnesota, Coffman Union Gallery, Minneapolis MN

Rezelman, Betsy C, *Instructor,* Saint Lawrence University, Dept of Fine Arts, Canton NY (S)

Rezelman, Betsy Cogger, *Dir,* St Lawrence University, Richard F Brush Art Gallery, Canton NY

Rhein, Donna E, *Libm,* Dallas Museum of Fine Arts, Library, Dallas TX

Rhie, Marylin, *Lectr,* Smith College, Art Dept, Northampton MA (S)

Rhodes, David, *Pres,* School of Visual Arts, New York NY (S)

Rhodes, Herbert C, *Dir,* Supplementary Educational Center, Art Gallery, Salisbury NC

Rhodes, Jim, *Adult Serv Dept,* Topeka Public Library, Fine Arts Dept & Gallery of Fine Arts, Topeka KS

Rhodes, Milton, *Pres,* American Council for the Arts, New York NY

Rhodes, Milton, *Pres & Executive Dir,* Arts Council, Inc, Winston-Salem NC

Rhodes, Silas H, *Chmn,* School of Visual Arts, New York NY (S)

Rhodes, Thomas A, *Dir Museum & Historic Preservation,* Jekyll Island Authority Museum, Jekyll Island GA

Ribble, Joanne, *Secy,* Cedar Rapids Museum of Art, Cedar Rapids IA

Ricahrd, Nancy, *Dir Foundation,* University of Southwestern Louisiana, University Art Museum, Lafayette LA

Ricciardi, Dana D, *Registrar,* China Trade Museum, Milton MA

Ricciardi, Dana D, *Archivist,* China Trade Museum, Library and Archives, Milton MA

Riccillo, Charles, *Prof,* Christopher Newport College, Arts & Communications, Newport News VA (S)

Ricciotti, Dominic, *Asst Prof,* University of Arkansas, Art Dept, Fayetteville AR (S)

Rice, Anthony, *Head of Dept,* Wesleyan College, Art Dept, Macon GA (S)

Rice, Danielle, *Cur Education,* Wadsworth Atheneum, Hartford CT

Rice, Edward, *Treas,* Maritime Art Association, Fredericton MB

Rice, Gordon, *Asst Cur,* Surrey Art Gallery, Surrey BC

Rice, James, *Asst Prof,* Dallas Baptist College, Dept of Art, Dallas TX (S)

Rice, Jane G, *Dep Dir,* San Diego Museum of Art, San Diego CA

Rice, Nancy, *Assoc Prof,* Maryville College, St Louis, Art Division, Saint Louis MO (S)

Rice, Nancy N, *Gallery Dir,* Maryville College Saint Louis, Beaumont Gallery, Saint Louis MO

Rice, Norman S, *Dir,* Albany Institute of History and Art, Albany NY

Rice, Pat, *Admin Asst,* Bower's Museum, Santa Ana CA

Rice Bloeme, Allyn, *Libm,* Traphagen School of Fashion, Library, New York NY

Ricehill, Ernest, *Instructor,* Sioux City Art Center, Sioux City IA (S)

Rice-Wichman, Juliet, *Pres,* Kauai Museum, Lihue HI

Rich, Marcia, *Shop Mgr,* Blanden Memorial Art Museum, Fort Dodge IA

Rich, Robert E, *VPres,* The Buffalo Fine Arts Academy, Albright-Knox Art Gallery, Buffalo NY

Rich, Sanford, *Lectr,* Tunxis Community College, Graphic Design Dept, Farmington CT (S)

Richard, Gloria, *Secy,* Galerie Restigouche Gallery, Campbellton NB

Richard, Jack, *Dir,* Richard Gallery and Almond Tea Gallery, Divisions of Studios of Jack Richard, Cuyahoga Falls OH

Richard, Jack, *Dir,* Studios of Jack Richard Creative School of Design, Cuyahoga Falls OH (S)

Richard, Jim, *Prof,* University of New Orleans, Dept of Fine Arts, New Orleans LA (S)

Richards, Bruce, *VPres,* Southern Artists Association, Fine Arts Center, Hot Springs AR

Richards, David, *Public Relations Mgr,* University of Rochester, Memorial Art Gallery, Rochester NY

Richards, Deb, *Registrar,* Dallas Museum of Fine Arts, Dallas TX

Richards, Judith Olch, *Assoc Dir,* Independent Curators Incorporated, New York NY

Richards, Karl, *Prof,* Arkansas State University, Dept of Art, State University AR (S)

Richards, Katherine, *Assoc Libm,* New York Historical Society, Library, New York NY

Richards, Lee, *Prof,* New Mexico State University, Art Dept, Las Cruces NM (S)

Richards, Louise S, *Chief Cur Prints & Drawings,* Cleveland Museum of Art, Cleveland OH

Richards, Matt, *Dir,* One Step Beyond, Brattleboro VT

Richards, Mildred R, *Asst to Dir,* Terra Museum of American Art, Evanston IL

Richards, Milton, *Head Dept,* Mohawk Valley Community College, Advertising Design and Production, Utica NY (S)

Richards, Nancy E, *Cur,* Winterthur Museum and Gardens, Winterthur DE

Richards, Peter, *Artist Coordr,* Exploratorium, San Francisco CA

Richards, Richard, *Prof,* Assumption College, Dept of Fine Arts and Music, Worcester MA (S)

Richards, Rosalyn, *Prof,* Bucknell University, Dept of Art, Lewisburg PA (S)

Richardson, Babs, *Museum Shop Mgr,* Philbrook Art Center, Tulsa OK

Richardson, Brenda, *Asst Dir & Cur Paintings & Sculpture,* Baltimore Museum of Art, Baltimore MD

Richardson, Coma N, *Asst to Pres,* Southwest Arts Foundation, Houston TX

Richardson, Gail, *Libm,* La Jolla Museum of Contemporary Art, Helen Palmer Geisel Library, La Jolla CA

Richardson, Gordon, *Asst Prof,* University of Dayton, Fine Arts Division, Dayton OH (S)

Richardson, James, *Exhibit Preparator,* Ella Sharp Museum, Jackson MI

Richardson, Jim, *Instructor,* The Design Schools, Art Institute of Seattle, Seattle WA (S)

Richardson, John A, *Head Art History,* Southern Illinois University at Edwardsville, Dept of Art and Design, Edwardsville IL (S)

Richardson, Katherine W, *Asst to Dir,* Essex Institute, Salem MA

Richardson, Martha, *Asst Dir,* Archaeological Institute of America, Boston MA

Richardson, Martha, *Fine Arts Dept Head,* Jackson County Junior College, Art Dept, Gautier MS (S)

Richardson, Orin, *Treas,* Huntsville Art League and Museum Association Inc, Huntsville AL

Richardson, Thomas, *Chmn,* Coahoma Junior College, Art Education & Fine Arts Dept, Clarksdale MS (S)

Richardson, Thomas L, *Chmn,* Grambling State University, Art Dept, Grambling LA (S)

Richardson, Wallace, *Pres,* University of Nebraska, Lincoln, Nebraska Art Association, Lincoln NE

Richardt, George, *Pres Board,* The Parthenon, Nashville TN

Richartz, Frederick, *Educ Coordinator,* Lyman Allyn Museum, New London CT

Richbourg, Lance, *Asst Prof,* St Michael's College, Fine Arts Dept, Winooski VT (S)

Richenburg, Robert, *Prof,* Ithaca College, Fine Art Dept, Ithaca NY (S)

Richeter, John, *Pres,* Art Centre of New Jersey, East Orange NJ (S)

Richie, Glynatta, *Business Manager,* Amon Carter Museum, Fort Worth TX

Richman, Gary, *Assoc Prof,* University of Rhode Island, Dept of Art, Kingston RI (S)

Richman, Irwin, *Prof,* Pennsylvania State University, Capitol Campus, Dept of Humanities, Middletown PA (S)

Richmond, Fred, *Chmn Exec Board,* Congressional Arts Caucus, Washington DC

Richmond, William, *Asst Prof,* University of Evansville, Art Dept, Evansville IN (S)

Richter, Mischa, *VPres,* Provincetown Art Association and Museum, Provincetown MA

Rickard, Ted, *Mgr Resource Centre,* Ontario Crafts Council, Toronto ON

Rickard, Ted, *Mgr,* Ontario Crafts Council, Craft Resource Centre, Toronto ON

Rickels, Robert E, *Prof,* Concordia College, Art Dept, Saint Paul MN (S)

Rickers, Karen, *Programme-Publicity Officer,* Chatham Cultural Centre, Chatham ON

Ricketson, Mary Ann, *Dir,* Lake Placid Center for Music, Drama & Art, Fine Arts Gallery, Lake Placid NY

Ricketts, Nancy, *Library Asst In Charge of Interlibrary Loan & Periodicals,* Sheldon Jackson College, Stratton Library, Sitka AK

Riday, George E, *Pres,* Redlands Art Association, Redlands CA

Ridder, Daniel H, *Treas,* Los Angeles County Museum of Art, Los Angeles CA

Riddle, Pamela A, *Development & Membership Officer,* Contemporary Arts Museum, Houston TX

Riddle, Peggy, *Dir Research & Public Programs,* Dallas Historical Society, Dallas TX

Ridenhower, Elizabeth, *Prof,* Trinity University, Dept of Art, San Antonio TX (S)

Rider, Wanda, *First VPres,* National League of American Pen Women, Washington DC

Ridge, A D, *Provincial Archivist,* Department of Culture, Government of the Province of Alberta, Provincial Archives of Alberta, Edmonton AB

Ridge, Michele, *Secy,* Erie Art Museum, Erie PA

Ridge, Michele M, *Dir,* Erie County Library System, Art Dept, Erie PA

Ridington, Thomas, *Asst Prof,* La Salle College, Dept of Fine Arts, Philadelphia PA (S)

Ridley, Gregory, *Assoc Prof,* Fisk University, Division of Humanities & Fine Arts, Nashville TN (S)

Riebel, Richard, *Pres,* Milwaukee Center for Photography, Milwaukee WI (S)

Riedel, Fred, *Coordr Film Circ & Loans,* The American Federation of Arts, New York NY

Rieder, William, *Head Photo Archives,* J Paul Getty Museum, Photo Archives, Malibu CA

Riedinger, Robert J, *Correspondence Secy,* Artists' Fellowship, Inc, New York NY

Rieger, Sonja, *Asst Prof,* University of Alabama in Birmingham, Dept of Art, Birmingham AL (S)

Riel, Pamela, *Educ Coordr,* Manchester Institute of Arts and Sciences Gallery, Manchester NH

Rielly, Barbara, *Pres,* Columbia County Historical Society, Kinderhook NY

Riemer, Terry, *Office Administrator & Asst to Dir,* McKissick Museums, Columbia SC

Ries, Barbara, *Secy,* Augustana College, Center for Western Studies, Sioux Falls SD

Rifai, Maggie, *Admin Asst,* Kentucky Guild of Artists and Craftsmen Inc, Berea KY

Rigby, Bruce, *Asst Prof,* Trenton State College, Art Dept, Trenton NJ (S)

Rigdon, Lois, *Dir,* Art Guild of Burlington, Arts for Living Center, Burlington IA

Rigg, Jim, *Pres,* Kansas Watercolor Society, Wichita Art Museum, Wichita KS

Rigg, Margaret, *Assoc Prof,* Eckerd College, Art Dept, Saint Petersburg FL (S)

Riggins, Lois, *Dir,* Tennessee State Museum, Nashville TN

Riggs, Don, *Chief Libm,* Arizona State University, Hayden Library Art Dept, Tempe AZ

Riggs, Leigh, *Asst Dir,* Community Council for the Arts, Kinston NC

Rights, Edith A, *Libm,* Montclair Art Museum, LeBrun Library, Montclair NJ

Rigsby, Joe, *Asst Prof,* Murray State University, Art Dept, Murray KY (S)

Riley, Carroll L, *Adj Cur Anthropology,* Southern Illinois University, University Museum, Carbondale IL

Riley, Judith, *Registrar,* Corcoran Museum, Washington DC

Rimberg, Andrea, *Pres,* Catharine Lorillard Wolfe Art Club, Inc, New York NY

Rindge, Debora, *Dir,* Washington and Lee University, Gallery of DuPont Hall, Lexington VA

Rindge, Debra A, *Instr,* Washington and Lee University, Dept of Fine Arts, Lexington VA (S)

Rindlisbacher, David, *Asst Prof,* West Texas State University, Art Dept, Canyon TX (S)

Rinehart, Barbara, *Education Coordr,* University of Notre Dame, Snite Museum of Art, Notre Dame IN

Rinehart, Linda, *Pres,* Huntsville Art League and Museum Association Inc, Huntsville AL

Rinehart, Michael, *Librn,* Sterling and Francine Clark Art Institute, Clark Art Institute Library, Williamstown MA

Ringering, Dennis L, *Head Drawing & Painting,* Southern Illinois University at Edwardsville, Dept of Art and Design, Edwardsville IL (S)

Rink, Bernard C, *Library Dir,* Northwestern Michigan College, Mark Osterlin Library, Traverse City MI

Riordan, John, *Prof,* State University of New York College at Potsdam, Dept of Fine Arts, Potsdam NY (S)

Riordan, Mary, *Dir,* Muskegon Museum of Art, Muskegon MI

Riorden, Virginia, *Comptroller,* Sterling and Francine Clark Art Institute, Williamstown MA

Riordon, Bernard, *Cur & Dir,* Art Gallery of Nova Scotia, Halifax NS

Rios, Gilbert, *Chmn Art 3-D Media,* California State University, Northridge, Dept of Art-Two Dimensional Media, Northridge CA (S)

Rios, John, *Prof,* Texas Woman's University, Dept of Art, Denton TX (S)

Rios, Nora, *Asst Dir,* Corpus Christi State University, South Texas Artmobile, Corpus Christi TX

Ripley, S Dillon, *Secy,* Smithsonian Institution, Washington DC

Rippe, Peter, *Executive Dir,* Roanoke Museum of Fine Arts, Roanoke VA

Rippeteau, Bruce, *Asst State Historic Preservation Officer for Archaeology,* Colorado Historical Society, State Museum, Denver CO

Risch, Elaine, *Asst to Art Librn,* Rutgers University, Art Library, New Brunswick NJ

Riseman, Henry, *Dir,* New England Center for Contemporary Art, Brooklyn CT

Riser, Harry, *Pres,* Hoosier Salon Patrons Association, Hoosier Salon Art Gallery, Indianapolis IN

Rishady, Ronald, *Instructor,* University of North Alabama, Dept of Art, Florence AL (S)

Rishel, Joseph, *Cur Paintings before 1900,* Philadelphia Museum of Art, Philadelphia PA

Rishel, Joseph, *Cur,* Philadelphia Museum of Art, Rodin Museum, Philadelphia PA

Rishel, Joseph, *Cur,* Philadelphia Museum of Art, John Johnson Collection, Philadelphia PA

Rising, Joan, *Art Historian,* Greenfield Community College, Art Dept, Greenfield MA (S)

Risley, John, *Prof,* Wesleyan University, Art Dept, Middletown CT (S)

Risley, Mary, *Adjunct Prof,* Wesleyan University, Art Dept, Middletown CT (S)

Riss, Murray, *Asst Prof,* Southwestern at Memphis, Dept of Art, Memphis TN (S)

Risse, Robert, *Assoc Prof,* University of Massachusetts at Boston, Art Dept, Boston MA (S)

Ristine, James D, *Cur Exhibitions,* Minnesota Museum of Art, Saint Paul MN

Ritch, Karen, *Coordr Spec Events & Mem,* The Phillips Collection, Washington DC

Ritch, Sally, *VPres,* Hill Country Arts Foundation, Ingram TX

Ritchie, Ann, *Treas,* American Watercolor Society, New York NY

Ritchie, Charles L, *Board Pres,* Lake Placid Center for Music, Drama & Art, Fine Arts Gallery, Lake Placid NY

Ritchie, Christina, *Video Cur,* Art Metropole, Toronto ON

Ritchie, Steve, *Development Officer,* Portland Art Association, Portland OR

Ritchie, Verna Ford, *Art & Music Librn,* University of Northern Iowa, Art and Music Section Library, Cedar Falls IA

Ritter, Josef, *Instructor,* Cazenovia College, Center for Art & Design Studies, Cazenovia NY (S)

Ritts, Edwin, *Dir,* Asheville Art Museum, Asheville NC

Rivard-Shaw, Nancy, *Cur American Art,* Detroit Institute of Arts, Detroit MI

Rivera, Manuel, *Chmn Fine Arts,* Hartnell College, Art and Photography Dept, Salinas CA (S)

Rizk, Ronald, *Assoc Prof,* University of Southern California, School of Fine Arts, Los Angeles CA (S)

Rizzo, Michael, *Exhibition Technician,* Morris Museum of Arts and Sciences, Morristown NJ

Roach, Jeannetta C, *Librn,* Tougaloo College, Coleman Library, Tougaloo MS

Roach, T, *Assoc Prof,* St Francis Xavier University, Fine Arts Dept, Antigonish NS (S)

Road, Rachel, *Cur of Photography,* Tippecanoe County Historical Museum, Lafayette IN

Robayashi, Shuko, *Instructor,* Rudolph Schaeffer School of Design, San Francisco CA (S)

Robbert, Paul, *Instr,* Oxbow Center for the Arts, Saugatuck MI (S)

Robbins, Daniel, *Chmn,* Union College, Dept of the Arts, Schenectady NY (S)

Robbins, Phyllis Y, *Instr,* American River College, Dept of Art, Sacramento CA (S)

Robbins, Warren M, *Senior Scholar & Founding Dir Emeritus,* National Museum of African Art, Washington DC

Roberds, Gene, *Coordr Fine Art,* Florida School of the Arts, Visual Arts, Palatka FL (S)

Roberson, Suzanne, *Photo Librn,* Albany Institute of History and Art, McKinney Library, Albany NY

Robert, Henry Flood, *Dir,* Joslyn Art Museum, Omaha NE

Roberts, Charles, *VPres,* Erie Art Museum, Erie PA

Roberts, Gene, *Head of Design & Production,* Colorado Historical Society, State Museum, Denver CO

Roberts, George H, *Faculty,* Idaho State University, Dept of Art, Pocatello ID (S)

Roberts, Harriet, *Chmn Interior Design,* Moore College of Art, Philadelphia PA (S)

Roberts, Helene, *Cur Visual Coll,* Harvard University, Fine Arts Library, Cambridge MA

Roberts, Jeffrey P, *Historian,* Atwater Kent Museum, Philadelphia PA

Roberts, J Lee, *Chmn,* Lubbock Christian College, Art Dept, Lubbock TX (S)

Roberts, Kate, *Membership,* Plains Art Museum, Main Gallery, Moorhead MN

Roberts, Laura, *Cur Education,* Rhode Island Historical Society, Providence RI

Roberts, Lois, *Treas,* South Peace Art Society, Dawson Creek Art Gallery, Dawson Creek BC

Roberts, Mary C, *Assoc Prof,* Northwestern State University of Louisiana, Dept of Art, Natchitoches LA (S)

Roberts, Nancy, *VPres,* Omaha Children's Museum, Inc, Omaha NE

Roberts, Patti, *Library Technician,* Ringling School of Art Library, Sarasota FL

Roberts, Paul, *Treas,* Santa Barbara Contemporary Arts Forum, Santa Barbara CA

Roberts, Percival R, *Prof,* Bloomsburg University, Dept of Art, Bloomsburg PA (S)

Roberts, Sally, *Vis Assoc Prof,* Drew University, Art Dept, Madison NJ (S)

Roberts, Selina M, *Dir,* Metropolitan Arts Commission, Portland OR

Roberts, Stephen, *Board Dir,* Artists' Cooperative Gallery, Omaha NE

Roberts, Thom, *Exhibits Coordr,* Science Museums of Charlotte, Inc, Discovery Place, Charlotte NC

Robertshaw, Mary Jane, *Assoc Prof,* College of New Rochelle School of Arts and Sciences, Undergraduate Art Dept, New Rochelle NY (S)

Robertson, Beverly, *Librn,* Metropolitan Museum of Art, Uris Library, New York NY

Robertson, Charles J, *Asst Dir, Museum Resources,* National Museum of American Art, Washington DC

Robertson, David J, *Prof,* Rochester Institute of Technology, School of Photographic Arts & Sciences, Rochester NY (S)

Robertson, Donald, *Assoc Prof,* Northwest Missouri State University, Dept of Art, Maryville MO (S)

Robertson, Donald, *Prof,* Tulane University, Sophie H Newcomb Memorial College, New Orleans LA (S)

Robertson, Emma, *Pres,* Afro Arts Cultural Centre, Inc, African Arts Museum & Gallery, New York NY

Robertson, Jack, *Librn,* Vanderbilt University, Arts Reference Library, Nashville TN

Robertson, Joan E, *Art Cur,* Kemper Group, Long Grove IL

Robertson, Joe Chris, *Chmn,* Mars Hill College, Art Dept, Mars Hill NC (S)

Robertson, J T, *Chmn Board Dir,* Sumter Gallery of Art, Sumter SC

Robertson, Karen, *Dir,* Morgan State University Gallery of Art, Library, Baltimore MD

Robertson, L A, *Dean Faculty Fine Arts,* University of Calgary, Dept of Art, Calgary AB (S)

Robertson, Roderick, *Asst Prof,* Saint Mary's College, Art Dept, Winona MN (S)

Robertson, Struan, *VChmn,* Art Gallery of Nova Scotia, Halifax NS

Robidoux, Omer, *Dir,* Eskimo Museum, Churchill MB

Robins, Corinne, *VPres,* Organization of Independent Artists, New York NY

Robinson, Art, *Business Mgr,* New Brunswick Museum, Saint John NB

Robinson, David, *Dir Education,* Southeast Arkansas Arts and Science Center, Pine Bluff AR

Robinson, Diana, *Asst,* Ohio State University, Fine Arts Library, Columbus OH

Robinson, Don D, *Chmn Dept,* Harding University, Dept of Art, Searcy AR (S)

Robinson, Douglas, *Registrar,* Hirshhorn Museum and Sculpture Garden, Washington DC

Robinson, Duncan, *Dir,* Yale University, Yale Center for British Art, New Haven CT

Robinson, Francis W, *Cur Emeritus Medieval Art,* Detroit Institute of Arts, Detroit MI

Robinson, Franklin, *Dir,* Rhode Island School of Design, Museum of Art, Providence RI

Robinson, George, *Prof,* Bethel College, Dept of Art, Saint Paul MN (S)

Robinson, Grove, *Chmn Dept Art,* Union University, Dept of Art, Jackson TN (S)

Robinson, Gwen, *Admin Asst,* Yuma Fine Arts Association, Yuma Art Center, Yuma AZ

Robinson, Hilda, *Admin Asst,* African American Historical and Cultural Society, San Francisco CA

Robinson, Jontyle, *Asst Prof,* Emory University, Art History Dept, Atlanta GA (S)

Robinson, Joyce, *Dir Educational Prog,* Colorado Springs Fine Arts Center, Colorado Springs CO

Robinson, Lilien F, *Chmn,* George Washington University, Dept of Art, Washington DC (S)

Robinson, Luclare, *Gift Shop Mgr,* Museum of Oriental Cultures, Corpus Christi TX

Robinson, Mary Ann, *Dir,* McPherson College Gallery, McPherson KS

Robinson, Mary Ann, *Chmn,* McPherson College, Art Dept, McPherson KS (S)

Robinson, Orvetta, *Librn,* Illinois State Museum of Natural History and Art, Library, Springfield IL

Robinson, Roger W, *Pres,* Willard House and Clock Museum, Inc, Grafton MA

Robinson, Roger W, *Dir,* Willard House and Clock Museum, Inc, Grafton MA

Robinson, R R, *Dean of Art,* University of Regina, Dept of Art Education, Regina SK (S)

Robinson, Sanger P, *Secretary,* Arts Club of Chicago Gallery, Chicago IL

Robinson, Sarah, *Admin Asst,* Richmond Art Center, Richmond CA

Robinson, Susan, *Chmn,* Loyola Marymount University, Dept of Art & Art Hist, Los Angeles CA (S)

Robinson, William A, *Dir,* University of Houston, Sarah Campbell Blaffer Gallery, Houston TX

Robison, Andrew, *Cur Prints & Drawings,* National Gallery of Art, Washington DC

Robison, Charles, *Chmn Art and Music,* Angelo State University, Art and Music Dept, San Angelo TX (S)

Robison, Vaughan Hill, *Pres,* Montgomery Museum of Fine Arts, Montgomery AL

Robles, Elsa Ortiz, *Exec Dir,* Association of Hispanic Art, New York NY

Roche, Valerie, *Instr,* Creighton University, Fine and Performing Arts Dept, Omaha NE (S)

Rochelle, Myrtle, *VPres,* Lubbock Art Association, Inc, Lubbock TX

Rochette, Edward C, *Exec VPres,* American Numismatic Association Museum, Colorado Springs CO

Rock, John, *Prof,* Oregon State University, Dept of Art, Corvallis OR (S)

Rock, William, *Chmn,* University of Toronto, Dept of Landscape Architecture, Toronto ON (S)

Rockefeller, David, *VChmn,* Museum of Modern Art, New York NY

Rockefeller 3rd, John D, *Pres,* Museum of Modern Art, New York NY

Rockhill, King, *Pres,* Appaloosa Museum, Inc, Moscow ID

Rockmuller, Rebecca, *Actg Dir,* Hewlett-Woodmere Public Library, Hewlett NY

Rod, Donald O, *Dir,* University of Northern Iowa, Art and Music Section Library, Cedar Falls IA

Rodbard, Betty, *Treas,* National Watercolor Society, Lakewood CA

Rode, Meredith, *Prof,* University of the District of Columbia, Art Dept, Washington DC (S)

Rode-Finch, J Dustin, *Instr,* Mainline Center of the Arts, Haverford PA (S)

Rodgers, Brenda, *Instr,* Alcorn State University, Dept of Fine Arts, Lorman MS (S)

Rodgers, Linda, *Pres,* Wayne Art Center, Wayne PA (S)

Rodgers, Ralph G, *Gen Mgr,* Polynesian Cultural Center, Laie HI

Rodrigues, Richard, *Coordr Fine Arts,* City College of San Francisco, Art Dept, San Francisco CA (S)

Rodriguez, Romeo, *Dir,* Committee for Hispanic Arts & Research, Austin TX

Rodriquez, Peter, *Founder & Exec Dir,* Mexican Museum, San Francisco CA

Roe, Albert S, *Prof,* Cornell University, Dept of the History of Art, Ithaca NY (S)

Roe, Ruth, *Librn,* Newport Harbor Art Museum, Library, Newport Beach CA

Roemer, Carol, *Instructor,* Long Beach City College, Dept of Art, Long Beach CA (S)

Roese, Ronnie, *Dir Museum Services,* Dallas Historical Society, Dallas TX

Roeyer, Mark, *Exhib Designer,* University of Kansas, Spencer Museum of Art, Lawrence KS

Rogan, Robert C, *Head Dept,* Lamar University, Art Dept, Beaumont TX (S)

Rogers, Charles B, *Dir,* Rogers House Museum Gallery, Ellsworth KS

Rogers, Frances, *Pres,* Brown County Art Gallery Association Inc, Nashville IN

Rogers, Francis D, *VPres,* Art Commission of the City of New York, Associates of the Art Commission, Inc, New York NY

Rogers, Gina, *Adjunct Instructor,* Texas Woman's University, Dept of Art, Denton TX (S)

Rogers, James W, *Asst Prof,* Glenville State College, Dept of Art, Glenville WV (S)

Rogers, John L, *Assoc Prof,* Aurora College, Art Dept, Aurora IL (S)

Rogers, Judith, *Instructor,* Linn Benton Community College, Fine & Applied Art Dept, Albany OR (S)

Rogers, June, *Treas,* Alaska Association for the Arts, Fairbanks AK

Rogers, Millard F, *Dir,* Cincinnati Art Museum, Cincinnati OH

Rogers, Millard F, *Dir,* Cincinnati Art Museum, Library, Cincinnati OH

Rogers, Nancy, *Art Dir,* Watkins Institute, Nashville TN

Rogers, Riley, *Dir,* Fine Arts Club, Second Crossing Gallery, Valley City ND

Rogers, Robert, *Asst Prof,* Queensborough Community College, Dept of Art and Design, Bayside NY (S)

Rogers, Ruth E, *Mgr,* Rogers House Museum Gallery, Ellsworth KS

Rogers, S, *Instructor,* Golden West College, Arts, Humanities and Social Sciences Institute, Huntington Beach CA (S)

Rogers, Samuel S, *Pres,* Merrimack Valley Textile Museum, North Andover MA

Rogers, Thresa, *Instr,* Community College of Baltimore, Dept of Fine & Applied Arts, Liberty Campus, Baltimore MD (S)

Rogers-Lafferty, Sarah, *Cur,* Contemporary Arts Center, Cincinnati OH

Rogers-Lafferty, Sarah, *Cur,* Contemporary Arts Center, Library, Cincinnati OH

Rogge, Steve, *Dir,* Mason City Public Library, Mason City IA

Rogoff, Anita, *Prof,* Case Western Reserve University, Dept of Art, Cleveland OH (S)

Rogovin, Mark, *Dir,* Peace Museum, Chicago IL

Rohlfing, Christian, *Asst Dir for Coll,* Cooper-Hewitt Museum, Smithsonian Institution, New York NY

Rohling, Mark, *Preparator,* Contemporary Arts Center, Cincinnati OH

Rohm, Robert H, *Prof,* University of Rhode Island, Dept of Art, Kingston RI (S)

Rohn, David, *Vis Instr,* Drew University, Art Dept, Madison NJ (S)

Rohr, Candice, *Secy,* Maude I Kerns Art Center, Henry Korn Gallery, Eugene OR

Rohrabaugh, Teresa, *Dir,* Southwest Missouri State University, University Gallery, Springfield MO

Rohrer, Judith, *Asst Prof,* Wesleyan University, Art Dept, Middletown CT (S)

Rolfing, Sue, *Asst Dir,* Hockaday Center for the Arts, Flathead Valley Art Association & Art Gallery, Kalispell MT

Rolla, Donald D, *Operations Officer,* AmeriTrust Company, Cleveland OH

Roller, Gilbert, *Chmn Fine Arts,* Asbury College, Art Dept, Wilmore KY (S)

Roller, Marion, *Chmn Design Dept,* Traphagen School of Fashion, New York NY (S)

Roller, Terry, *Asst Prof,* Eastern Illinois University, School of Fine Arts, Charleston IL (S)

Roller, Terry M, *Instr,* Baylor University, Dept of Fine Arts, Waco TX (S)

Rollins, Caroline, *Membership, Sales & Publications,* Yale University, Art Gallery, New Haven CT

Rollins, Ken, *Dir,* Polk Public Museum, Lakeland FL

Roloff, Daphne, *Dir of Libraries,* Art Institute of Chicago, Ryerson and Burnham Libraries, Chicago IL

Roloff, John, *Lecturer,* Mills College, Art Dept, Oakland CA (S)

Rom, Cristine, *Special Collection Librn,* Cleveland Institute of Art, Jessica Gund Memorial Library, Cleveland OH

Romancito, Rick, *Museum Asst,* Millicent Rogers Museum, Taos NM

Romano, James, *Assoc Cur Egyptian & Classical Art,* Brooklyn Museum, Brooklyn NY

Romano, Salvatore, *Asst Prof,* Herbert H Lehman College, Art Dept, Bronx NY (S)

Romano, Umberto, *Dir,* Umberto Romano School of Creative Art, New York NY (S)

Rombout, Luke, *Dir,* Vancouver Art Gallery, Vancouver BC

Romeo, Lorraine, *Dir,* Revelstoke Art Group, Revelstoke BC

Romero, Orlando, *Librn,* Museum of New Mexico, Library, Santa Fe NM

Rompf, Julienne, *Prof,* Marian College, Art Dept, Fond Du Lac WI (S)

Roncalli, Rafaele A, *Pres,* Ukiyo-e Society of America, Inc, New York NY

Rooney, Paul M, *Dir,* Buffalo and Erie County Public Library, Buffalo NY

Rooney, Steve, *Adminr,* International Center of Photography, New York NY

Rooney, Thomas, *Assoc Prof,* Catholic University of America, Dept of Art, Washington DC (S)

Roos, Sandra, *General Studies,* California College of Arts and Crafts, Oakland CA (S)

Roosa, Wayne, *Asst Prof,* Bethel College, Dept of Art, Saint Paul MN (S)

Roosevelt, Anna C, *Cur South America,* Museum of the American Indian, New York NY

Root, Joan, *Instr,* New York Academy of Art, New York NY (S)

Root, Margaret C, *Asst Cur,* University of Michigan, Kelsey Museum of Ancient and Medieval Archaeology, Ann Arbor MI

Root, Nile R, *Assoc Prof,* Rochester Institute of Technology, School of Photographic Arts & Sciences, Rochester NY (S)

Root, Nina J, *Chairwoman Library Services,* American Museum of Natural History, Library, New York NY

Roozen, Mary Louise, *In Charge Art Coll,* The Marine Corporation, Milwaukee WI

Ropko, Frederick, *Prof,* University of the District of Columbia, Art Dept, Washington DC (S)

Rorem, Jan, *Assoc Prof,* Black Hawk College, Art Dept, Moline IL (S)

Rorimer, Anne, *Assoc Cur 20th Century Painting & Sculpture,* Art Institute of Chicago, Chicago IL

Rosa, Joyce, *Chmn,* C W Post Center of Long Island University, School of the Arts, Greenvale NY (S)

Rosand, David, *Chmn,* Columbia University, Dept of Art History and Archaeology, New York NY (S)

Rosati, Angelo V, *Prof,* Rhode Island College, Art Dept, Providence RI (S)

Rose, Beatric, *Treas,* Florida Artist Group Inc, Venice FL

Rose, Jack, *Dir Fashion,* Art Institute of Fort Lauderdale, Fort Lauderdale FL (S)

Rose, Larry, *Instructor,* Oklahoma State University, Graphic Arts Dept, Okmulgee OK (S)

Rose, Margaret, *Acquisitions Librn,* Art Center College of Design, James Lemont Fogg Memorial Library, Pasadena CA

Rose, Patricia, *Chmn,* Florida State University, Art History Dept, Tallahassee FL (S)

Roseberry, Helen, *Museum Coordr,* East Tennessee State University, Carroll Reece Museum, Johnson City TN

Rosemarin, Carey, *Executive Member,* 22 Wooster Gallery, New York NY

Rosemfeld, Myra Nan, *Research Cur,* Montreal Museum of Fine Arts, Montreal PQ

Rosen, James M, *Instr,* Santa Rosa Junior College, Art Dept, Santa Rosa CA (S)

Rosen, Michael, *Chmn Architecture,* City Colleges of Chicago, Daley College, Chicago IL (S)

Rosen, Seymour, *Dir,* Saving & Preserving Arts & Cultural Environments, Los Angeles CA

Rosen, Steven W, *Chief Cur,* Columbus Museum of Art, Columbus OH

Rosenbaum, Allen, *Dir,* Princeton University, Art Museum, Princeton NJ

Rosenbaum, Arthur, *Drawing & Painting,* University of Georgia, Franklin College of Arts and Sciences, Dept of Art, Athens GA (S)

Rosenbaum, Joan H, *Dir,* Jewish Museum, New York NY

Rosenbaum-Cooper, Judith, *Coll Development,* Chicago Public Library, Art Section, Fine Arts Division, Chicago IL

Rosenberg, Amy, *Assoc Cur,* University of Michigan, Kelsey Museum of Ancient and Medieval Archaeology, Ann Arbor MI

Rosenberg, Herbert, *Asst Prof,* Jersey City State College, Art Dept, Jersey City NJ (S)

Rosenberg, Howard, *Art Dept Chmn,* University of Nevada, Reno, Reno NV

Rosenberg, Kay, *Asst Prof,* Bradford College, Creative Arts Division, Bradford MA (S)

Rosenberg, Marcia, *School Dir,* Danforth Museum School, Framingham MA (S)

Rosenberg, Mel, *Dept Mgr,* Los Angeles Public Library, Art and Music Dept, Los Angeles CA

Rosenberg, Paul B, *Pres Board of Trustees,* Danforth Museum of Art, Framingham MA

Rosenberg, Rhoda, *Instr,* Danforth Museum School, Framingham MA (S)

Rosenberg, Sondra, *Chmn,* City Colleges of Chicago, Kennedy-King College, Chicago IL (S)

Rosenberger, Pat, *Executive Dir,* Valley Art Center Inc, Clarkston WA

Rosenberger, Wayne, *VPres,* Iroquois County Historical Museum, Watseka IL

Rosenblatt, Arthur, *Dir Education,* National Institute for Architectural Education, New York NY

Rosenblatt, Arthur, *VPres Architecture & Planning,* Metropolitan Museum of Art, New York NY

Rosenblum, Bonnie Levinson, *Dir Education,* Hudson River Museum, Yonkers NY

Rosenfeld, L, *Cur Coll,* Edinboro University of Pennsylvania, Art Dept, Edinboro PA (S)

Rosenfield, John M, *Actg Dir*, Harvard University, William Hayes Fogg Art Museum, Cambridge MA

Rosenman, Barry, *Cur*, Plains Art Museum, Main Gallery, Moorhead MN

Rosenstein, Harris, *Exec Adminr*, Rice University, Institute for the Arts, Rice Museum, Houston TX

Rosenstein, Lynne, *Program Dir*, Jewish Community Center, Center Lobby Gallery, Long Beach CA

Rosensweig, Larry, *Cur*, Palm Beach County Parks and Recreation Department, Morikami Museum of Japanese Culture, Delray Beach FL

Rosenthal, Ann, *Publicist*, Franklin Furnace Archive, Inc, New York NY

Rosenthal, Donald A, *Chief Cur*, University of Rochester, Memorial Art Gallery, Rochester NY

Rosenthal, Gertrude, *Consultant for Western Art*, Honolulu Academy of Arts, Honolulu HI

Rosenthal, Jane, *Prof*, Columbia University, Dept of Art History & Archeology, New York NY

Rosenthal, Jane, *Chmn*, Columbia University, Barnard College, New York NY (S)

Rosenthal, Mark, *Cur 20th Century Art*, Philadelphia Museum of Art, Philadelphia PA

Rosenthal, Nan, *Sr Instructor*, Whitney Museum of American Art, Downtown Branch, New York NY

Rosenzweig, Harry, *Dir*, Montclair State College, Gallery One, Upper Montclair NJ

Rosevear, Carol, *Librn*, New Brunswick Museum, Library, Saint John NB

Roskies, Louise, *Dir Continuing Education & Jewish Studies*, Saidye Bronfman Centre, Montreal PQ

Roskill, Mark, *Prof*, University of Massachusetts, Amherst, Art History Program, Amherst MA (S)

Roskos, George, *Prof*, Pacific Lutheran University, Dept of Art, Tacoma WA (S)

Rosler, Martha, *Asst Prof*, Rutgers, the State University of New Jersey, Mason Gross School of the Arts, New Brunswick NJ (S)

Rosner, June, *Dir*, Marymount Manhattan College Gallery, New York NY

Rosnow, Nancy, *Asst Prof*, New Mexico Highlands University, Division of Fine Arts, Las Vegas NM (S)

Rosoff, Sidney, *Secy*, American Craft Council, New York NY

Rospond, Mary Chris, *Public Relations*, Newark Museum, Newark NJ

Ross, Alex, *Librn*, Stanford University, Art Library, Stanford CA

Ross, Barbara T, *Custodian Prints & Drawings*, Princeton University, Art Museum, Princeton NJ

Ross, David A, *Dir*, Institute of Contemporary Art, Boston MA

Ross, David A, *Exec Dir*, McAllen International Museum, McAllen TX

Ross, Doran H, *Asst Dir & Cur Africa, Oceania & Indonesia*, University of California, Los Angeles, Museum of Cultural History, Los Angeles CA

Ross, Douglas, *Chmn Graduate Committee*, University of Nebraska at Lincoln, Dept of Art, Lincoln NE (S)

Ross, Helen, *Chmn Fine Arts Department*, Montclair State College, Gallery One, Upper Montclair NJ

Ross, Helene, *Chmn*, Montclair State College, Fine Arts Dept, Montclair NJ (S)

Ross, Joanne, *Research Asst*, Visual Studies Workshop, Research Center, Rochester NY

Ross, John, *Adjunct Prof*, Columbia University, School of the Arts, Division of Painting & Sculpture, New York NY (S)

Ross, Johnnie, *Instructor*, Portland School of Art, Portland ME (S)

Ross, Joseph B, *Asst Prof*, Saint Mary's College of Maryland, Arts and Letters Division, Saint Mary's City MD (S)

Ross, Judy, *Asst Prof*, Moravian College, Dept of Art, Bethlehem PA (S)

Ross, Linda, *Instr*, Pennsylvania State University, Capitol Campus, Dept of Humanities, Middletown PA (S)

Ross, Louis, *Asst Prof*, Trenton State College, Art Dept, Trenton NJ (S)

Ross, Mary Anne, *Instructor*, Delta State University, Dept of Art, Cleveland MS (S)

Ross, Novelene, *Cur Education*, Wichita Art Museum, Wichita KS

Ross, Robert, *Gallery Dir*, University of Arkansas, Fine Arts Center Gallery, Fayetteville AR

Ross, Robert, *Asst Prof*, Catholic University of America, Dept of Art, Washington DC (S)

Ross, S, *Faculty*, Humboldt State University, College of Creative Arts & Humanities, Arcata CA (S)

Ross, Sylvia P, *VPres*, Lafayette Natural History Museum, Planetarium and Nature Station, Lafayette LA

Rossen, Susan F, *Editorial Coordr*, Art Institute of Chicago, Chicago IL

Rossetti, Victor, *VPres*, Ashtabula Arts Center, Ashtabula OH

Rossi, David, *Lecturer*, Marycrest College, Art Dept, Davenport IA (S)

Rossi, Diana, *Catalog Asst*, San Francisco Art Institute, Anne Bremer Memorial Library, San Francisco CA

Rossmassler, Louise, *Archivist*, Philadelphia Museum of Art, Library, Philadelphia PA

Rossol, Monona, *Pres*, Artist-Craftsmen of New York, New York NY

Rost, Michael, *Chmn Applied & Fine Arts*, Porterville College, Dept of Fine Arts, Porterville CA (S)

Roster, Laila, *Dir*, Contemporary Arts Center, Honolulu HI

Rostkowski, Steven, *Museum Shop Mgr*, Baltimore Museum of Art, Baltimore MD

Roth, Ann, *Exec Dir*, Frog Hollow Craft Center, Middlebury VT

Roth, Leslie, *Asst Dir*, C W Post College of Long Island University, Hillwood Art Gallery, Greenvale NY

Roth, Suzanne, *Painting & Drawing*, Chautauqua Institution, The Art Center, Chautauqua NY (S)

Rothenberg, Jacob, *Chmn*, City College of New York, Art Dept, New York NY (S)

Rothrock, Ilse S, *Librn*, Kimbell Art Museum, Library, Fort Worth TX

Rothschild, Shelley, *Instr*, Whitworth College, Art Dept, Spokane WA (S)

Rotner, Robert, *Assoc Dir*, Harvard University, William Hayes Fogg Art Museum, Cambridge MA

Roulet, Ann, *Pres*, Cleveland Institute of Art, Cleveland Art Association, Cleveland OH

Roulston, Pat, *Librn*, University of Regina, Art Gallery Resource Centre, Regina SK

Rounds, Earl, *Treas*, Bristol Art Museum, Bristol RI

Rourke, Orland J, *Assoc Prof*, Concordia College, Art Dept, Moorhead MN (S)

Rousc, Jeffrey P, *Registrar*, Westmoreland County Museum of Art, Greensburg PA

Rouse, Terrie, *Cur*, Studio Museum in Harlem, New York NY

Rousek, Marie, *Librn*, College of Saint Elizabeth, Mahoney Library, Convent Station NJ

Roush, Linda, *Asst Dir*, Omaha Children's Museum, Inc, Omaha NE

Roussel, Denis, *Library Technician*, Canadian Museums Association, Museum Documentation Centre, Ottawa ON

Rovetti, Paul F, *Dir*, University of Connecticut, William Benton Museum of Art, Storrs CT

Row, Brian G, *Chmn*, Southwest Texas State University, Dept of Art, San Marcos TX (S)

Rowan, George, *Assoc Prof*, University of New Orleans, Dept of Fine Arts, New Orleans LA (S)

Rowan, Gerald, *Prog Coordr*, Northampton County Area Community College, Art Dept, Bethlehem PA (S)

Rowan, Madeline Bronsdon, *Cur Ethnology & Education*, University of British Columbia, Museum of Anthropology, Vancouver BC

Rowden, Lyn, *Public Programs Specialist*, University of Oklahoma, Museum of Art, Norman OK

Rowe, Ann P, *Asst Cur New World*, Textile Museum, Washington DC

Rowe, Donald, *Dir*, Olivet College, Armstrong Museum of Art and Archaeology, Olivet MI

Rowe, Donald, *Chmn*, Olivet College, Art Dept, Olivet MI (S)

Rowe, Donald F, *Dir*, Loyola University of Chicago, Martin D'Arcy Gallery of Art, Chicago IL

Rowe, M Jessica, *Dir*, Blanden Memorial Art Museum, Fort Dodge IA

Rowe, Reginald M, *Instr*, San Antonio Art Institute, San Antonio TX (S)

Rowe, Sandra, *Lectr*, California State Polytechnic University, Pomona, Art Dept, Pomona CA (S)

Rowe, Susan, *Instructor*, Olivet College, Art Dept, Olivet MI (S)

Rowe, William, *Asst Prof*, Arkansas State University, Dept of Art, State University AR (S)

Rowe, William Thomas, *Assoc Prof*, Saint Mary's College of Maryland, Arts and Letters Division, Saint Mary's City MD (S)

Rowe-Shields, Michele, *Museum Adminr*, Cranbrook Academy of Art Museum, Bloomfield Hills MI

Rowland, Katherine L, *Consultant Special Projects*, Friends of the Arts and Sciences, Hilton Leech Studio, Sarasota FL (S)

Rowley, Kristin, *Head Fibers*, Chautauqua Institution, The Art Center, Chautauqua NY (S)

Rowley, Linda, *Secy*, University of Louisville, Allen R Hite Art Institute Gallery, Louisville KY

Rowley, Susan, *Asst Prof*, Nazareth College of Rochester, Art Dept, Rochester NY (S)

Rowntree, John, *Instructor*, Mohawk Valley Community College, Advertising Design and Production, Utica NY (S)

Roworth, Wendy, *Assoc Prof*, University of Rhode Island, Dept of Art, Kingston RI (S)

Roy, Barbara, *Mgr Cataloging Servs*, Presbyterian Historical Society, Philadelphia PA

Roy, Carmen, *Senior Scientist Canadian Centre for Folk Culture Studies*, National Museum of Man, Ottawa ON

Roy, James, *Chmn*, Saint Cloud State University, Dept of Art, Saint Cloud MN (S)

Roy, Margery, *Sr Admin Asst*, Mount Holyoke College Art Museum, South Hadley MA

Roy, Rob, *Instr*, Suomi College, Fine Arts Dept, Hancock MI (S)

Royce, Diana, *Head Librn*, Stowe-Day Foundation, Library, Hartford CT

Royce-Roll, Donald, *Chmn & Prof*, Green Mountain College, Dept of Art, Poultney VT (S)

Rozelle, Robert V, *Public Relations*, Dallas Museum of Fine Arts, Dallas TX

Rozier, Robert, *Asst Prof*, Alma College, Dept of Art and Design, Alma MI (S)

Rozman, Joseph, *Asst Prof*, Mount Mary College, Art Dept, Milwaukee WI (S)

Rozniatowski, David William, *Chief Librn*, Winnipeg Art Gallery, Clara Lander Library, Winnipeg MB

Rubasamen, Grace, *Gallery Mgr*, Mendocino Art Center, Gallery, Mendocino CA

Rubel, William, *VPres*, Children's Art Foundation, Santa Cruz CA

Rubenstein, Elliott, *Assoc Prof*, Rochester Institute of Technology, School of Photographic Arts & Sciences, Rochester NY (S)

Rubin, Cynthia, *Asst Prof*, Connecticut College, Dept of Art, New London CT (S)

Rubin, David S, *Dir Exhibitions*, San Francisco Art Institute, San Francisco CA

Rubin, James H, *Assoc Prof*, State University of New York at Stony Brook, Art Dept, Stony Brook NY (S)

Rubin, Loretta, *Dir*, Conejo Valley Art Museum, Thousand Oaks CA

Rubin, Mona H, *Dir Finance & Development*, Museum of Holography, New York NY

Rubin, Virginia, *Executive Assoc Dir*, Exploratorium, San Francisco CA

Rubin, William, *Dir Painting & Sculpture Coll*, Museum of Modern Art, New York NY

Rubinger, M, *Instructor*, Technical University of Nova Scotia, Faculty of Architecture, Halifax NS (S)

Rudasill, Leroy U, *Chmn*, Southern Seminary Junior College, Buena Vista VA (S)

Rudberg, Peggy, *Slide Librn,* Minneapolis College of Art and Design, Library and Media Center, Minneapolis MN

Rudd, Amanda S, *Commissioner,* Chicago Public Library, Art Section, Fine Arts Division, Chicago IL

Rudell, Joan Marie, *Dir,* Black Hills Art Center, Little Gallery, Spearfish SD

Rudolph, Wolf, *Assoc Prof,* Indiana University, Bloomington, School of Fine Arts, Bloomington IN (S)

Rudy, Andrea, *Vistors Center Adminr,* Stowe-Day Foundation, Hartford CT

Ruedy, Don, *Assoc Prof,* University of Wisconsin, Dept of Art, Rice Lake WI (S)

Rueschhoff, Philip H, *Prof,* University of Kansas, Dept of Art, Music Education and Music Therapy, Lawrence KS (S)

Ruff, Eric, *Cur,* Yarmouth County Historical Society, Yarmouth County Museum, Yarmouth NS

Ruffer, David G, *Pres,* Albright College, Freedman Gallery, Reading PA

Ruffo, Joseph M, *Head Dept,* University of Northern Iowa, Dept of Art, Cedar Falls IA (S)

Ruffolo, Robert E, *Pres,* Princeton Antiques Bookservice, Art Marketing Reference Library, Atlantic City NJ

Rufo, Christy R, *Pres,* New England School of Art & Design, Boston MA (S)

Rugg, Ruth Ann, *Public Relations Dir,* Kimbell Art Museum, Fort Worth TX

Ruggie, Cathie, *Asst Prof,* Saint Xavier College, Dept of Art, Chicago IL (S)

Ruggles, Janet E, *Conservator,* Balboa Art Conservation Center, San Diego CA

Rugila, Elaine, *Treas,* Monroe City-County Fine Arts Council, Monroe MI

Ruiz, Ben, *Instr,* Joe Kubert School of Cartoon and Graphic Art Inc, Dover NJ (S)

Rumford, Beatrix T, *Dir,* Abby Aldrich Rockefeller Folk Art Center, Williamsburg VA

Runge, Tedd, *Design & Creative Studies Program Coordr,* Aims Community College, Program for Design & Creative Studies, Greeley CO (S)

Runke, Henry M, *Head Dept,* University of Wisconsin-Stevens Point, Dept of Art, Stevens Point WI (S)

Runyon, John M, *Chmn & Prof,* Corning Community College, Division of Humanities, Corning NY (S)

Rupe, Bonnie, *Acquisitions Dept Head,* Wichita Public Library, Wichita KS

Rupert, Carola G, *Dir,* Kern County Museum, Bakersfield CA

Rupp, Cora J, *Pres,* Art League, Alexandria VA

Ruppert, John, *Instructor,* Webster College, Art Dept, Webster Groves MO (S)

Rusak, Halina, *Assoc Librn,* Rutgers University, Art Library, New Brunswick NJ

Rush, Kent, *Asst Prof,* University of Texas at San Antonio, Division of Art and Design, San Antonio TX (S)

Rush, Salee, *Instr,* Mainline Center of the Arts, Haverford PA (S)

Rushing, Byron, *Pres,* Museum of Afro-American History, Boston MA

Rushton, Brian N, *Publications & Marketing Division Head,* Brooklyn Museum, Brooklyn NY

Rushton, Joseph, *Asst Prof,* Ohio Wesleyan University, Fine Arts Dept, Delaware OH (S)

Rusinow, Ellen Maurie, *Instructor,* Boston Center for Adult Education, Boston MA (S)

Rusnell, Wesley A, *Registrar & Cur,* Roswell Museum and Art Center, Roswell NM

Russell, Don, *Coordr Book Distribution,* Visual Studies Workshop, Rochester NY

Russell, H, *Instructor,* Indiana University of Pennsylvania, Dept of Art and Art Education, Indiana PA (S)

Russell, Jennifer, *Asst Dir Program,* Whitney Museum of American Art, New York NY

Russell, John I, *Lectr,* John Jay College of Criminal Justice, Dept of Art, Music and Philosophy, New York NY (S)

Russell, John I, *Exec Dir,* Brookfield Craft Center, Inc Gallery, Brookfield CT

Russell, Kay, *Corresponding Secy,* Gilpin County Arts Association, Central City CO

Russell, Kay, *Chmn Textiles,* De Young Museum Art School, San Francisco CA (S)

Russell, Lester, *Chmn Applied Arts,* Peru State College, Art Dept, Peru NE (S)

Russell, Reba, *Cur,* Dixon Gallery and Gardens, Memphis TN

Russell, Rhonda, *Secy to Dir,* Memphis Brooks Museum of Art, Memphis TN

Russell, Robert, *Assoc Prof,* Pittsburg State University, Art Dept, Pittsburg KS (S)

Russell, Robert, *Assoc Prof,* Jersey City State College, Art Dept, Jersey City NJ (S)

Russell, Robert L, *Exec Dir,* Omaha Children's Museum, Inc, Omaha NE

Russell, Stella, *Prof,* Nassau Community College, Art Dept, Garden City NY (S)

Russell, Thomas, *Instructor,* Roger Williams College, Art Dept, Bristol RI (S)

Russell, Thomas L, *Prof,* Baker University, Dept of Art, Baldwin City KS (S)

Russo, Alexander, *Chairperson,* Hood College, Dept of Art, Frederick MD (S)

Rust, David, *Preparator & Registrar,* Oklahoma Museum of Art, Oklahoma City OK

Rust, Jow Carroll, *Pres,* San Antonio Art League, San Antonio TX

Ruthig, Linda, *Secy,* Cortland County Historical Society, Suggett House Museum, Cortland NY

Rutkowski, Walter E, *Head Department,* Louisiana State University, Dept of Fine Arts Gallery, Baton Rouge LA

Rutkowski, Walter E, *Head Dept,* Louisiana State University, School of Art, Baton Rouge LA (S)

Rutkowsky, Paul, *Asst Prof,* Florida State University, Art Dept, Tallahassee FL (S)

Rutledge, Patricia R, *Librn,* Cincinnati Art Museum, Library, Cincinnati OH

Rutledge, Ruth, *Instr,* Victor Valley College, Art Dept, Victorville CA (S)

Rutsten, G Roslyn, *Coordr,* Hagerstown Junior College, Art Dept, Hagerstown MD (S)

Ruttinger, Jacquelin, *Chmn,* Saint Mary-of-the-Woods College, Art Dept, Saint Mary-of-the-Woods IN (S)

Ruwadi, Raymond, *Clerk & Treas,* Massillon Museum, Massillon OH

Ruyle, Kermit, *Asst Prof,* Saint Louis Community College at Florissant Valley, Dept of Art, Ferguson MO (S)

Ruzicka, Francis A, *Head Dept,* University of Georgia, Franklin College of Arts and Sciences, Dept of Art, Athens GA (S)

Ruzicka, James L, *Dir,* University of Puerto Rico, Mayaguez, Dept of Humanities, Mayaguez PR (S)

Ryals, Bunny, *Faculty,* North Carolina Wesleyan, Dept of Art, Rocky Mount NC (S)

Ryan, David, *Dir,* Fort Worth Art Museum, Fort Worth TX

Ryan, James, *Historic Site Mgr,* Olana State Historic Site, Hudson NY

Ryan, Jeffrey, *Development Officer,* Fraunces Tavern Museum, New York NY

Ryan, Joanne, *Dean of Faculty,* Philadelphia College of Art, Philadelphia PA

Ryan, Joanne, *Dean Academic Affairs,* Philadelphia College of Art, Philadelphia PA (S)

Ryan, Linda Lee, *Instructor,* Casper College, Casper WY (S)

Ryan, Martin, *Assoc Prof,* Monmouth College, Dept of Art, West Long Branch NJ (S)

Ryan, Martin, *Gallery Asst,* Sheldon Swope Art Gallery, Terre Haute IN

Ryan, Noel, *Chief Librn,* Mississauga Library System, Mississauga ON

Rychlewski, Karen, *Prof,* West Liberty State College, Art Dept, West Liberty WV (S)

Ryden, Kenneth G, *Chmn,* Greenville College, Division of Language, Literature & Fine Arts, Greenville IL (S)

Rykowski, Chris, *Instr,* Studio School of Art and Design, Philadelphia PA (S)

Ryland, Stan, *Pres Board Dir,* Plains Art Museum, Main Gallery, Moorhead MN

Ryskamp, Charles, *Dir,* Pierpont Morgan Library, New York NY

Ryuto, Setsuko, *Admin Asst,* The Haggin Museum, Stockton CA

Saavi, Martin, *Second VPres,* Brown County Art Gallery Association Inc, Nashville IN

Sabarsky, Serge, *VPres,* Art Dealers Association of America, Inc, New York NY

Sacher, Pamela, *Instructor,* Greenfield Community College, Art Dept, Greenfield MA (S)

Sachs, Samuel, *Dir,* Minneapolis Institute of Arts, Minneapolis MN

Saddler, Paula, *Admin Asst,* Yale University, Dept of the History of Art, New Haven CT (S)

Sadowski, Jerry, *Instr,* Marygrove College, Dept of Art and Art History, Detroit MI (S)

Saether, Jan, *Chmn Painting Dept,* Venice Sculpture Studio, Inc, Venice CA (S)

Safford, Monique, *Development Asst,* Los Angeles Contemporary Exhibitions, Inc, Los Angeles CA

Safley, Ann, *Staff Librn,* Carnegie Library of Pittsburgh, Pittsburgh PA

Safrin, Robert W, *Deput Dir Public Affairs,* Winterthur Museum and Gardens, Winterthur DE

Sage, Bernita, *Bookkeeper,* Lansing Art Gallery, Lansing MI

Sager, Donald J, *City Librn,* Milwaukee Public Library, Art, Music & Recreation Dept, Milwaukee WI

Sagonic, Livio, *Asst Prof,* Drew University, Art Dept, Madison NJ (S)

Sahlstrand, James, *Dir Art Gallery,* Central Washington University, Sarah Spurgeon Gallery, Ellensburg WA

Saillant, Michele, *Asst,* Rhode Island College, Edward M Bannister Gallery, Providence RI

Sain, Robert, *Dir Development,* The Museum of Contemporary Art, Los Angeles CA

Saint-Clair, Guy, *Dir,* University Club Library, New York NY

Saito, Deborah, *Librn,* Sheldon Jackson College, Stratton Library, Sitka AK

Saitzman, Thomas A, *Dir Museum of Fine Art,* Nassau County Museum of Fine Art, Roslyn NY

Sajbel, Edward R, *Art Dept Chmn,* University of Southern Colorado, School of Liberal Arts, Pueblo CO

Sajbel, Edward R, *Chmn,* University of Southern Colorado, Belmont Campus, Dept of Art, Pueblo CO (S)

Sakaguchi, Ben, *Area Chmn Studio Art,* Pasadena City College, Art Dept, Pasadena CA (S)

Salam, Helieda, *Asst Prof,* Radford University, Art Dept, Radford VA (S)

Salan, Jean, *Asst Dir,* National Museum of African Art, Washington DC

Saler, Karen, *Co-Chairperson Foundation Program,* Philadelphia College of Art, Philadelphia PA (S)

Salinas, Gregory, *Pres,* Guadalupe Historic Foundation, Santuario de Guadalupe, Santa Fe NM

Salisbury, John, *Second VPres,* The Stained Glass Association of America, Saint Louis MO

Salkind, Leni, *Instr,* Baker University, Dept of Art, Baldwin City KS (S)

Salmon, Ray, *Instructor,* Solano Community College, Dept of Fine & Applied Art, Suisun City CA (S)

Salomon, Judith, *Assoc Prof,* Cleveland Institute of Art, Cleveland OH (S)

Saltman, Don, *Pres,* Jewish Community Center, Center Lobby Gallery, Long Beach CA

Saltmarche, Kenneth, *Dir,* Art Gallery of Windsor, Windsor ON

Saltzman, Lee, *VPres,* Brevard Art Center and Museum, Inc, Melbourne FL

Saltzman, Marvin, *Prof,* University of North Carolina at Chapel Hill, Art Dept, Chapel Hill NC (S)

Salvatori, Fidenzio, *Asst Prof,* University of Toronto, Dept of Landscape Architecture, Toronto ON (S)

Salveson, Douglas, *Dir,* Findlay College, Egner Fine Arts Center, Findlay OH

Salwierak, Marian, *Chmn,* Saint Gregory's College, Dept of Art, Shawnee OK (S)

Salyer, Ruth Osgood, *Admin Dir,* Laguna Beach School of Art, Laguna Beach CA (S)

Salzberg, Marvin, *Chmn,* Bronx Community College, Music & Art Dept, Bronx NY (S)

Salzillo, Marjorie, *Instr,* Munson-Williams-Proctor Institute, School of Art, Utica NY (S)

Salzillo, William, *Dir,* Hamilton College, Fred L Emerson Gallery, Clinton NY

Salzillo, William, *Instr,* Hamilton College, Art Dept, Clinton NY (S)

Salzman, Stanley, *Chmn Board,* National Institute for Architectural Education, New York NY

Samaha, Sumayyah, *Executive Member,* 22 Wooster Gallery, New York NY

Samilenko, John M, *Admin Dir,* Ukrainian Institute of America, Inc, New York NY

Sammon, Christine, *Head Librn,* Southern Alberta Institute of Technology, Alberta College of Art Library, Calgary AB

Sammons, Richard, *Instructor,* Bismarck Junior College, Art Dept, Bismarck ND (S)

Sample, George, *Asst Prof,* Central Missouri State University, Art Dept, Warrensburg MO (S)

Samples, R McCartney, *Asst Dir Education & Communication,* Royal Ontario Museum, Toronto ON

Samples, Robert, *Chmn Board,* Metropolitan Cultural Arts Center, Minneapolis MN

Sampson, Rose, *Treas,* Galesburg Civic Art Center, Galesburg IL

Samuel, Evelyn K, *Dir,* New York University, Stephen Chan Library of Fine Arts, New York NY

Samuelson, Jerry, *Dean Sch Arts,* California State University, Fullerton, Art Dept, Fullerton CA (S)

Samuelson, Rich, *Dir & Pres,* Atlantic Gallery, New York NY

Sanberg, Thomas G, *Dir Development,* Museum of Science and Industry, Chicago IL

Sanchez, Beatrice Rivas, *Dean,* Cranbrook Academy of Art, Bloomfield Hills MI (S)

Sanchez, Cynthia, *Asst Cur,* Museum of New Mexico, Museum of Fine Arts, Santa Fe NM

Sand, Viki, *Dir,* Shaker Museum, Old Chatham NY

Sande, Theodore A, *Exec Dir,* Western Reserve Historical Society, Cleveland OH

Sandelin, Lee, *Art Librn,* San Diego State University, Love Library and Art Department Slide Library, San Diego CA

Sanders, Albert E, *Cur Natural History,* Charleston Museum, Charleston SC

Sanders, Gayla, *Lectr,* University of North Carolina at Wilmington, Dept of Creative Arts - Division of Art, Wilmington NC (S)

Sanders, J, *Faculty,* Western Illinois University, College of Fine Arts, Macomb IL (S)

Sanders, Robert, *Cur Herpetology,* San Bernardino County Museum and Satellites, Fine Arts Institute, Redlands CA

Sanders, Scott, *Exec Dir,* South Carolina Arts Commission, Columbia SC

Sanders, Val, *Chmn,* Palomar College, Art Dept, San Marcos TX (S)

Sanderson, Christopher, *Faculty,* Sarah Lawrence College, Dept of Art, Bronxville NY (S)

Sanderson, Douglas, *Secy,* American Abstract Artists, New York NY

Sanderson, Helen G, *Dir Development,* Philbrook Art Center, Tulsa OK

Sanderson, Wiley, *Photographic Design,* University of Georgia, Franklin College of Arts and Sciences, Dept of Art, Athens GA (S)

Sandgren, Erik, *Vis Instructor,* Treasure Valley Community College, Art Dept, Ontario OR (S)

Sandler, Irving, *Assoc Prof,* State University of New York College at Purchase, Dept of Art History, Purchase NY (S)

Sandler, Joan, *Museum Education Community Education,* Metropolitan Museum of Art, New York NY

Sandler, Lucy Freeman, *Pres,* College Art Association of America, New York NY

Sandman, Keith, *Instr,* Munson-Williams-Proctor Institute, School of Art, Utica NY (S)

Sandmann, Herbert, *Prof,* University of Wisconsin-Stevens Point, Dept of Art, Stevens Point WI (S)

Sandok, Flo, *Instructor,* Rochester Community College, Art Dept, Rochester MN (S)

Sands, Betty, *Asst Dir,* Edna Hibel Art Foundation, Hibel Museum of Art, Riviera Beach FL

Sands, John O, *Asst Dir for Coll,* Mariners Museum, Newport News VA

Sandusky, Bill, *Gallery Dir,* Saint Mary's College, Moreau Gallery Three, Notre Dame IN

Sandusky, Giovanna Lenzi, *Gallery Dir,* Saint Mary's College, Moreau Gallery Three, Notre Dame IN

Sandvig, Helen, *Recording Secy,* Seattle Weaver's Guild, Seattle WA

Sandvik, Trond, *Dir Educ,* Tennessee Botanical Gardens and Fine Arts Center, Education Dept, Nashville TN (S)

Sandweiss, Martha, *Cur Photographic Coll,* Amon Carter Museum, Fort Worth TX

Sandy, Tamara, *Asst Dir,* Ward-Nasse Gallery, New York NY

Sanford, Cynthia, *Trustee & Cur,* Jersey City Museum Association, Jersey City NJ

Sanger, Carol A, *Actg Chief Librn,* Queensborough Community College Library, Bayside NY

Sanger, Helen, *Librn,* Frick Art Reference Library, New York NY

Sanguinetti, E F, *Dir,* University of Utah, Utah Museum of Fine Arts, Salt Lake City UT

Sankowsky, Itzhak, *Instr,* Mainline Center of the Arts, Haverford PA (S)

Sano, Emily, *Asst Dir Academic Programs & Servs & Cur Asian Art,* Kimbell Art Museum, Fort Worth TX

SantAmbrogioe, Lucy, *Cur,* Historical Society of Bloomfield, Bloomfield NJ

Santiago, Fernando, *Instructor,* Inter American University of Puerto Rico, Dept of Art, San German PR (S)

Santomasso, Eugene A, *Assoc Prof,* City University of New York, PhD Program in Art History, New York NY (S)

Santos, Adele, *Chmn,* University of Pennsylvania, Dept of Architecture, Philadelphia PA (S)

Sanvels, Linda, *Coordr Art Ed,* Richmond Art Center, Richmond CA

Saper, Arnold, *Chmn Printmaking,* University of Manitoba, School of Art, Winnipeg MB (S)

Sargent, C H, *Dir,* Watkins Institute, Nashville TN

Sargent, William, *Assoc Cur,* China Trade Museum, Milton MA

Saridakis, Dianne, *Registrar,* Art Institute of Philadelphia, Philadelphia PA (S)

Sarner, Amy, *Instr,* Mainline Center of the Arts, Haverford PA (S)

Sarton, Jay, *Cur Roberson Kopernik Observatory,* Roberson Center for the Arts and Sciences, Binghamton NY

Sarvis, Al, *Instructor,* Virginia Tech, Dept of Art, Blacksburg VA (S)

Sasowsky, Norman, *Coordr Art Educ,* University of Delaware, Dept of Art, Newark DE (S)

Sasso, Paul, *Asst Prof,* Murray State University, Art Dept, Murray KY (S)

Satchell, Ernest P, *Chmn,* University of Maryland Eastern Shore, Art Education Dept, Princess Anne MD (S)

Satz, Arthur, *Pres,* New York School of Interior Design, New York NY (S)

Sauberli, Ronald, *Library Asst,* Illinois State Museum of Natural History and Art, Library, Springfield IL

Saul, John V, *Cur & Mgr,* Frontier Times Museum, Bandera TX

Saules, Marilyn, *Cur,* Dundurn Castle, Hamilton ON

Saunders, Andrew, *VPres,* Art Patrons League of Mobile, Mobile AL

Saunders, Boyd, *Chmn Studio,* University of South Carolina, Dept of Art, Columbia SC (S)

Saunders, Eleanor, *Asst Prof,* State University of New York College at Purchase, Dept of Art History, Purchase NY (S)

Saunders, F Wenderoth, *Treas,* Lincoln County Cultural and Historical Association, Maine Art Gallery, Old Academy, Wiscasset ME

Saunders, Joan, *Gallery Coordr,* University of Hartford, Joseloff Gallery, West Hartford CT

Sauthoff, Helga, *Registrar,* Kelowna Centennial Museum and National Exhibit Centre, Kelowna BC

Savage, James, *Dir,* School of Fine Arts, Visual Arts Dept, Willoughby OH (S)

Savage, James J, *Executive Dir,* Fine Arts Association, School of Fine Arts, Willowghby OH

Savage, William W, *Cur Education Museum,* McKissick Museums, Columbia SC

SaVar, Hilda, *Instr,* Rosemont College, Division of the Arts, Rosemont PA (S)

Savinar, Tad, *Instructor,* Marylhurst College, Art Dept, Marylhurst OR (S)

Savini, Richard, *Vis Lectr,* California State College, Stanislaus, Art Dept, Turlock CA (S)

Saw, James T, *Assoc Prof,* Palomar College, Art Dept, San Marcos TX (S)

Sawtelle, Joseph G, *Pres,* Portsmouth Athenaeum NR, Inc 1817, Portsmouth NH

Sawycky, Roman, *Supervising Art Librn,* Free Public Library of Elizabeth, Fine Arts Dept, Elizabeth NJ

Sawyer, Alan, *Prof,* University of British Columbia, Dept of Fine Arts, Vancouver BC (S)

Sawyer, Henry W, *VPres,* Fairmount Park Art Association, Philadelphia PA

Saxon, Maureen, *Admin Asst,* University of Kentucky, Art Museum, Lexington KY

Sayre, C Franklin, *Asst Prof,* Oakland University, Dept of Art and Art History, Rochester MI (S)

Sayre, Eleanor A, *Cur Prints & Drawings,* Museum of Fine Arts, Boston MA

Scafetta, Stafano, *Sr Conservator,* National Museum of American Art, Washington DC

Scaife, Richard M, *Chmn Museum of Art Committee,* Carnegie Institute, Muscum of Art, Pittsburgh PA

Scala, Joseph A, *Dir,* Syracuse University, Joe and Emily Lowe Art Gallery, Syracuse NY

Scala, Mark, *Instr,* University of Richmond, Dept of Art, Richmond VA (S)

Scalamandre, Franco, *Founder & Pres,* Scalamandre Museum of Textiles, New York NY

Scalfe, Gladys, *Music,* National League of American Pen Women, Washington DC

Scannell, Joseph E, *Chmn,* Saint Anselm College, Dept of Fine Arts, Manchester NH (S)

Scannell, J S, *Asst Prof,* College of the Holy Cross, Dept Visual Arts, Worcester MA (S)

Scantlin, Helen, *VPres,* Lahaina Arts Society, Art Organization, Lahaina HI

Scarborough, Cleve K, *Dir,* Hunter Museum of Art, Chattanooga TN

Scarborough, Louis, *Instr,* Joe Kubert School of Cartoon and Graphic Art Inc, Dover NJ (S)

Scarlett, Robert, *Librn,* Memphis Academy of Arts, G Pillow Lewis Memorial Library, Memphis TN

Scarpat, James V, *Business Mgr,* The American Federation of Arts, New York NY

Scarpilta, Salvatore, *Artist-in-Residence,* Maryland Institute, Hoffberger School of Painting, Baltimore MD (S)

Scatena, James A, *1st VPres,* Museo Italo Americano, San Francisco CA

Schaad, Dee, *Asst Prof,* Indiana Central University, Fine Arts Dept, Indianapolis IN (S)

Schaber, Ken, *Assoc Prof,* Lake Michigan College, Dept of Art, Benton Harbor MI (S)

Schaefer, Cindy, *Asst,* Kitchener-Waterloo Art Gallery, Kitchener ON

Schaefer, Fred, *Instructor,* Williamsport Area Community College, Dept of Engineering and Design, Williamsport PA (S)

Schaefer, Ronald, *Chmn,* University of North Dakota, Visual Arts Dept, Grand Forks ND (S)

Schaeffer, Rudolph, *Dir Emeritus,* Rudolph Schaeffer School of Design, San Francisco CA (S)

Schaeffer, William D, *Pres,* Inter-Society Color Council, Natick MA

Schaenfeld, Clar Olin, *Co-Pres,* Long Beach Art Association, Long Beach NY

Schafer, Michael L, *Pres,* Mohawk Valley Community College, Advertising Design and Production, Utica NY (S)

Schaff, Dion, *Chmn,* Worcester State College, Arts & Humanities, Worcester MA (S)

Schaffer, Jo, *Cur,* State University of New York College at Cortland, Art Slide Library, Cortland NY

Schaffer, Joseph, *Development Officer,* Heard Museum, Phoenix AZ

Schaffer, Peter L, *Pres,* National Antique and Art Dealers Association of America, New York NY

Schaffer, Richard, *Asst Registrar,* University of Arizona, Museum of Art, Tucson AZ

Schaller, Bernard, *Dir,* Musee d'Art de Joliette, Joliette PQ

Schaller, Ralph, *Assoc Prof,* Loyola University of Chicago, Fine Arts Dept, Chicago IL (S)

Schalliol, David, *Cur Exhibits,* Indiana University, William Hammond Mathers Museum, Bloomington IN

Schantz, Michael W, *Dir,* Woodmere Art Museum, Philadelphia PA

Schantz, Tom, *Gallery Dir,* Kutztown University, Sharadin Art Gallery, Kutztown PA

Schapp, Rebecca, *Museum Coordr,* University of Santa Clara, de Saisset Museum, Santa Clara CA

Schar, Stuart, *Dir,* Kent State University, School of Art Gallery, Kent OH

Schar, Stuart, *Chmn & Prof,* Kent State University, Art Dept, Warren OH (S)

Scharfenberg, D F, *Faculty,* Western Illinois University, College of Fine Arts, Macomb IL (S)

Schastok, Sara L, *Pres,* American Committee for South Asian Art, Evanston IL

Schatz, Charlotte, *Instructor,* Bucks County Community College, Fine Arts Dept, Newton PA (S)

Schatz, Julius, *Pres,* National Council on Art in Jewish Life, New York NY

Schauer, Rudolph, *Prof,* University of Minnesota, Duluth, Art Dept, Duluth MN (S)

Scheck, Colleen E, *Actg Chmn,* Grand Canyon College, Art Dept, Phoenix AZ (S)

Scheck, James, *VPres Admin,* Philadelphia Art Alliance, Philadelphia PA

Schecter, Jack, *Dir,* University of Judaism, Dept of Continuing Education, Los Angeles CA (S)

Scheele, William F, *Dir & Secy Board,* Columbus Museum of Arts and Sciences, Columbus GA

Scheer, Lisa, *Instructor,* Saint Mary's College of Maryland, Arts and Letters Division, Saint Mary's City MD (S)

Scheer, Malcolm E, *Librn,* New York School of Interior Design Library, New York NY

Scheer, Steven S, *Chmn,* Saint Meinrad College, Dept of Art, Saint Meinrad IN (S)

Schefcik, Jerry, *Visual Art Cur,* Sangre De Cristo Arts & Conference Center, Pueblo CO

Scheffler, Patricia, *Head Librn,* Interlochen Arts Academy Library, Interlochen MI

Scheibe, Paul F, *Managing Dir,* Biblical Arts Center, Dallas TX

Scheidt, Patricia M, *Dir,* Arts Club of Chicago Gallery, Chicago IL

Schell, Deborah, *Librn,* Saginaw Art Museum, Library, Saginaw MI

Schell, Edwin, *Executive Secy,* United Methodist Historical Society, Lovely Lane Museum, Baltimore MD

Schell, Edwin, *Librn,* United Methodist Historical Society, Library, Baltimore MD

Schell, William H, *Dir,* Martin Memorial Library, York PA

Schellin, P Israel, *Lectr,* Mount Saint Mary's College, Art Dept, Los Angeles CA (S)

Schelling, George, *Asst Instr,* Luzerne County Community College, Commercial Art Dept, Nanticoke PA (S)

Schenck, Marvin, *Exhibits Coordr,* Scottsdale Center for the Arts, Scottsdale AZ

Schenk, Joseph B, *Dir,* Okefenokee Heritage Center, Inc, Waycross GA

Scher, Linda E, *Correspondence Secy,* Salmagundi Club, New York NY

Scherer, Herbert G, *Librn,* University of Minnesota, Art Library, Minneapolis MN

Scherpereel, Richard, *Dir,* Texas A and I University, Art Gallery, Kingsville TX

Scherpereel, Richard, *Chmn,* Texas A & I University, Art Dept, Kingsville TX (S)

Scherrer, Ruth, *Registrar,* Pacific - Asia Museum, Pasadena CA

Scherz, Barbara, *Membership & Program Liaison,* Madison Art Center, Madison WI

Schetzsle, Letha, *Registrar & Cur,* Denison University Art Gallery, Granville OH

Schick, Marjorie, *Assoc Prof,* Pittsburg State University, Art Dept, Pittsburg KS (S)

Schienbaum, David, *Instructor,* College of Santa Fe, Visual Art Division, Santa Fe NM (S)

Schier, Peter, *Assoc Prof,* University of Bridgeport, Art Dept, Bridgeport CT (S)

Schier, Werner, *Instr,* Woodbury University, Professional Arts Division, Los Angeles CA (S)

Schiffner, R, *Instructor,* Golden West College, Arts, Humanities and Social Sciences Institute, Huntington Beach CA (S)

Schild, Curt, *Asst Dir & Cur,* Rosicrucian Egyptian Museum and Art Gallery, San Jose CA

Schild, I, *Chmn Photography,* Fashion Institute of Technology, Art & Design Division, New York NY (S)

Schimansky, Donya-Dobrila, *Museum Librn,* Metropolitan Museum of Art, Thomas J Watson Library, New York NY

Schimmel, Caroline F, *Pres,* Guild of Book Workers, New York NY

Schimmel, Paul, *Cur Exhibitions,* Newport Harbor Art Museum, Newport Beach CA

Schimmelman, Janice C, *Asst Prof,* Oakland University, Dept of Art and Art History, Rochester MI (S)

Schinder, Kim S, *Asst to Dir,* Ohio University, Gallery of Fine Arts, Athens OH

Schindle, A, *Faculty,* Western Illinois University, College of Fine Arts, Macomb IL (S)

Schipa, Mary, *Asst Dir,* Millhouse-Bundy Performing & Fine Arts Center, Waitsfield VT

Schipporeit, George, *Chmn Architecture,* Illinois Institute of Technology, College of Architecture, Planning and Design, Dept of Architecture, Chicago IL (S)

Schira, Peter, *Deputy Chmn,* Bronx Community College, Music & Art Dept, Bronx NY (S)

Schirm, David, *Asst Prof,* University of Southern California, School of Fine Arts, Los Angeles CA (S)

Schlageter, Robert W, *Dir,* Cummer Gallery of Art, DeEtte Holden Cummer Museum Foundation, Jacksonville FL

Schlanzky, Gerhard, *Dir Exhibitions,* Museum of Holography, New York NY

Schlawin, Judy, *Asst Prof,* Winona State University, Art Dept, Winona MN (S)

Schlein, Frederick C, *Dir,* The Museum, Greenwood SC

Schleiniger, Ruth, *Asn Recording Secy,* Biloxi Art Association, Gallery, Biloxi MS

Schlesinger, Arthur, *Pres,* American Academy and Institute of Arts and Letters, New York NY

Schlesinger, Stephen L, *Secy,* John Simon Guggenheim Memorial Foundation, New York NY

Schlesinger, Thaleia, *Development Dir,* Institute of Contemporary Art, Boston MA

Schlesselman, F W, *Treas,* Cedar Rapids Museum of Art, Cedar Rapids IA

Schling, Dorothy T, *Dir,* Danbury Scott-Fanton Museum and Historical Society, Inc, Danbury CT

Schloss, Stuart, *Chmn,* Contemporary Arts Center, Cincinnati OH

Schlossberg, Leon, *Asst Prof,* Johns Hopkins University, School of Medicine, Dept of Art as Applied to Medicine, Baltimore MD (S)

Schlosser, Tom, *Chmn Dept,* College of Saint Mary, Art Dept, Omaha NE (S)

Schlump, John, *Prof,* Wittenberg University, Art Dept, Springfield OH (S)

Schluntz, Roger L, *Chmn Archit,* Arizona State University, College of Architecture, Tempe AZ (S)

Schmaljohn, Russell, *Asst Prof,* Northwest Missouri State University, Dept of Art, Maryville MO (S)

Schmid, Frederick, *Dir,* Virginia Beach Arts Center, Virginia Beach VA

Schmidlapp, Judie, *Executive Secy,* Buffalo Bill Memorial Association, Cody WY

Schmidt, Elizabeth H, *Coordr of Educ,* Agecroft Association, Richmond VA

Schmidt, Fred, *Instr,* Arkansas Arts Center, Little Rock AR (S)

Schmidt, Kathleen, *Instructor,* Northeastern Oklahoma State University, Tahlequah OK (S)

Schmidt, Martin F, *Dir,* The Filson Club, Louisville KY

Schmidt, Martin F, *Librn,* The Filson Club, Reference and Research Library, Louisville KY

Schmidt, Marvin, *Dir,* Feather River Community College, Art Dept, Quincy CA (S)

Schmidt, Myron, *Asst Prof,* Dean Junior College, Visual and Performing Art Dept, Franklin MA (S)

Schmidt, Shirley, *Secy,* Hutchinson Art Association, Hutchinson KS

Schmidt, Tom, *Gen Mgr,* University of California, Pacific Film Archive, Berkeley CA

Schmidt, Vince, *Deputy Dir,* Illinois State Library, Springfield IL

Schmit, Patricia, *Dir Publications & Academic Affairs,* Historic New Orleans Collection, Kemper and Leila Williams Foundation, New Orleans LA

Schmits, John W, *Faculty,* Saint Ambrose College, Art Dept, Davenport IA (S)

Schmitt, Helmut, *Dir,* Merritt College, Art Dept, Oakland CA (S)

Schmitt, Jean K, *Cur & Admin Far Eastern Art,* Metropolitan Museum of Art, New York NY

Schmitt, Marilyn, *Assoc Prof,* University of Miami, Dept of Art & Art History, Coral Gables FL (S)

Schmitz, Marie, *Registrar,* Missouri Historical Society, Saint Louis MO

Schmitz, Robert D, *Prof,* Rochester Institute of Technology, School for American Craftsmen, Rochester NY (S)

Schmutzhart, Berthold, *Chmn Sculpture,* Corcoran School of Art, Washington DC (S)

Schnabel, David J, *Chmn Dept,* Pasadena City College, Art Dept, Pasadena CA (S)

Schneer, Valerie, *Librn I,* Yonkers Public Library, Fine Arts Dept, Yonkers NY

Schneffer, Stephen G, *Chmn,* Presbyterian College, Fine Arts Dept, Clinton SC (S)

Schneider, Anne, *Dir,* J K Ralston Museum and Art Center, Sidney MT

Schneider, Cary, *Librn,* National Trust for Historic Preservation, Library, Information Services, Washington DC

Schneider, Elsa, *Education Cur,* Historic New Orleans Collection, Kemper and Leila Williams Foundation, New Orleans LA

Schneider, Emery E, *Chmn Design Composition Division,* Rochester Institute of Technology, School of Printing, Rochester NY (S)

Schneider, Gail K, *Editor & Librn,* Staten Island Institute of Arts and Sciences, Staten Island NY

Schneider, Janet, *Dir,* Queens Museum, Flushing NY

Schneider, Karen, *Librn,* The Phillips Collection, Library, Washington DC

Schneider, Laurie, *Prof,* John Jay College of Criminal Justice, Dept of Art, Music and Philosophy, New York NY (S)

Schneider, Lorraine, *Instr,* Coos Art Museum, Coos Bay OR (S)

Schneider, Richard, *Prof,* University of Wisconsin-Stevens Point, Dept of Art, Stevens Point WI (S)

Schneider, Richard D, *Assoc Prof,* Cleveland State University, Art Dept, Cleveland OH (S)

Schneider, Robert M, *VPres,* Xerox Corporation, Art Collection, Stamford CT

Schneider, Shellie, *VPres,* Long Island Graphic Eye Gallery, Port Washington NY

Schneiderman, Richard S, *Dir & Cur Graphic Art,* University of Georgia, Georgia Museum of Art, Athens GA

Schnell, Julie, *Instructor,* Mississippi State University, Art Dept, Mississippi State MS (S)

Schnell, Ronald, *Chmn Dept,* Tougaloo College, Art Dept, Tougaloo MS (S)

Schnepper, Mary, *Cur of Coll,* Evansville Museum of Arts and Science, Evansville IN

Schnidlapp, Donald, *Asst Prof,* Winona State University, Art Dept, Winona MN (S)

Schnieder, David, *Instr,* Blackhawk Mountain School of Art, Black Hawk CO (S)

Schnorr, Emil, *Adjunct Prof,* Springfield College, Dept of Visual and Performing Arts, Springfield MA (S)

Schnorr, Emil G, *Conservator,* George Walter Vincent Smith Art Museum, Springfield MA

Seabold, Tom, *Dir,* Keokuk Art Center, Keokuk IA

Seager, Pamela L, *Assoc Dir,* California Historical Society, San Francisco CA

Seagrave, Edmund O, *Assoc Dir,* University of Connecticut, Jorgensen Gallery, Storrs CT

Seaker, Janet, *Secy-Treas,* North Carolina Museums Council, Wilmington NC

Seale, Robert, *Treasurer,* Sierra Nevada Museum of Art, Reno NV

Seaman, Anne T, *Librn,* Honolulu Academy of Arts, Robert Allerton Library, Honolulu HI

Seamans, Warren A, *Dir,* Massachusetts Institute of Technology, Museum, Cambridge MA

Searing, Helen, *Prof,* Smith College, Art Dept, Northampton MA (S)

Searle, Annie, *Public Relations Mgr,* Seattle Art Museum, Seattle WA

Searles, David D, *Deputy Chmn,* National Endowment for the Arts, Washington DC

Searles, Rose, *Head Circulation Department,* Springfield Free Public Library, Donald B Palmer Museum, Springfield NJ

Searls, Maryse, *Assoc Prof,* University of New Hampshire, Dept of the Arts, Durham NH (S)

Sears, Anthony R, *Prof,* Rochester Institute of Technology, School of Printing, Rochester NY (S)

Sears, L Dennis, *Instr,* Huntingdon College, Dept of Visual and Performing Arts, Montgomery AL (S)

Sears, Patricia, *Librn,* Birmingham Public Library, Art and Music Department, Birmingham AL

Sears, Patrick H, *Chief Designer,* North Carolina Museum of Art, Raleigh NC

Secor, W Fielding, *VPres,* Mattatuck Historical Society Museum, Mattatuck Museum, Waterbury CT

Seefried, Monique, *Lecturer,* Emory University, Art History Dept, Atlanta GA (S)

Seeley, A Mae, *Dir,* Staten Island Institute of Arts and Sciences, Staten Island NY

Seeley, J, *Assoc Prof,* Wesleyan University, Art Dept, Middletown CT (S)

Seelhorst, R C, *Instructor,* Indiana University of Pennsylvania, Dept of Art and Art Education, Indiana PA (S)

Seelye, Eugene A, *Chmn,* Clarion University of Pennsylvania, Dept of Art, Clarion PA (S)

Seeman, Fred, *Secy,* Actual Art Foundation, New York NY

Seery, Florence, *Programs Asst,* American Scandinavian Foundation Gallery, New York NY

Sefcik, James F, *Dir Public Relations & Development,* Chrysler Museum, Norfolk VA

Segalman, Richard, *Instructor,* Woodstock School of Art, Inc, New York NY (S)

Segerson, Marge, *Librn,* Museum of Arts and Sciences, Library, Daytona Beach FL

Segger, Martin, *Dir & Cur,* University of Victoria, Maltwood Art Museum and Gallery, Victoria BC

Segger, Martin, *Lecturer,* University of Victoria, Dept of History in Art, Victoria BC (S)

Seibels, Cynthia, *Librn,* Kennedy Galleries, Art Library, New York NY

Seibert, Donald C, *Fine Arts Dept Head,* Syracuse University, Ernest Stevenson Bird Library, Syracuse NY

Seidelman, James E, *Exec Dir,* Kentucky Guild of Artists and Craftsmen Inc, Berea KY

Seidelman, James E, *Pres,* Lexington Art League, Inc, Lexington KY

Seidemann, Herman, *Pres Board Dir,* Museum of Northern British Columbia, Prince Rupert Museum Art Gallery, Prince Rupert BC

Seidman, Suzanne, *Cur,* Portsmouth Museums, Community Arts Center Division, Portsmouth VA

Seiz, John, *Instructor,* Springfield College in Illinois, Dept of Art, Springfield IL (S)

Sekerak, Clarence J, *Secy,* Cincinnati Art Club, Cincinnati OH

Selby, Lee, *Chief Visitors Services,* Lightner Museum, Saint Augustine FL

Selby, Pat, *Pres,* Cuyahoga Valley Art Center, Cuyahoga Falls OH (S)

Seley, Beverly, *Assoc Prof,* Grand Valley State Colleges, Art Dept, Allendale MI (S)

Seligman, Thomas K, *Deputy Dir Education & Exhibition,* Fine Arts Museums of San Francisco, M H de Young Memorial Museum and California Palace of the Legion of Honor, San Francisco CA

Seligsohn, Valerie, *Assoc Prof,* Philadelphia Community College, Dept of Fine Arts, Philadelphia PA (S)

Sella, Alvin, *Prof,* University of Alabama, Art Dept, Tuscaloosa AL (S)

Sellars, Beth, *Cur Art,* Eastern Washington State Historical Society, Cheney Cowles Memorial Museum, Spokane WA

Sellars, Judith, *Librn,* Museum of New Mexico, Museum of International Folk Art Library, Santa Fe NM

Selle, Thomas, *Lectr,* Carroll College, Art Dept, Waukesha WI (S)

Sellers, Gail, *Instructor,* Saint Xavier College, Dept of Art, Chicago IL (S)

Selsby, Errol, *Arts Mgr,* Scottsdale Center for the Arts, Scottsdale AZ

Selter, Dan, *Prof & Program Dir,* Transylvania University, Studio Arts Dept, Lexington KY (S)

Seltzer, Phyllis, *Pres,* Cleveland Museum of Art, Print Club of Cleveland, Cleveland OH

Selvar, Jane Cumming, *Dir,* Bronxville Public Library, Bronxville NY

Selvuss, Allan, *Lecturer,* University of Wisconsin, Dept of Art, Rice Lake WI (S)

Selzi, Paul, *Chmn Art Gallery,* Fairfield Public Library and Museum, Fairfield Art Association, Fairfield IA

Semmel, Joan, *Assoc Prof,* Rutgers, the State University of New Jersey, Mason Gross School of the Arts, New Brunswick NJ (S)

Semper, Rob, *Assoc Dir,* Exploratorium, San Francisco CA

Senior, William, *First VPres,* New Jersey Watercolor Society, South Orange NJ

Seniw, N, *Pres,* Ukrainian Museum of Canada, Edmonton AB

Senn, Barbara, *Admin Asst,* Galleries of the Claremont Colleges, Claremont CA

Sennett, Arthur, *Art Department Chmn,* State University of New York College at Potsdam, Brainerd Art Gallery, Potsdam NY

Sennett, Arthur, *Chmn,* State University of New York College at Potsdam, Dept of Fine Arts, Potsdam NY (S)

Senti, Marvel, *Exhibitions,* Hutchinson Art Association, Hutchinson KS

Senungetuk, Ronald, *Dept Head,* University of Alaska, Dept of Art, Fairbanks AK (S)

Sepessy, Joan L, *Asst Librn,* Toledo Museum of Art, Library, Toledo OH

Serenco, Henry, *Assoc Prof,* University of Nebraska at Omaha, Dept of Art, Omaha NE (S)

Serenyi, Peter, *Chmn,* Northeastern University, Dept of Art, Boston MA (S)

Serfaty, Gail F, *Asst Cur,* Department of State, Diplomatic Reception Rooms, Washington DC

Serio, Chris, *Cur,* Arkansas Territorial Restoration, Little Rock AR

Serota, Karen, *Registrar,* Detroit Institute of Arts, Detroit MI

Seto, John, *Cur Oriental Art,* Birmingham Museum of Art, Birmingham AL

Settle, James N, *Dean,* Hunter College, Art Dept, New York NY (S)

Settle-Cooney, Mary, *Asst Dir,* Tennessee Valley Art Association and Center, Tuscumbia AL

Setzer, Barbara, *Admin Asst,* Waterworks Gallery, Salisbury NC

Seventy, Sylvia, *Dir Education,* Fiberworks, Center for the Textile Arts, Berkeley CA

Sever, Ziya, *Chmn,* Alvin Community College, Art Dept, Alvin TX (S)

Severa, Joan, *Cur of Textiles,* State Historical Society of Wisconsin, Madison WI

Severance, Scott, *Dir,* Rome Art and Community Center, Rome NY

Severens, Martha R, *Cur Collections,* Carolina Art Association, Gibbes Art Gallery, Charleston SC

Severson, Daryl J, *Actg Librn,* Albany Institute of History and Art, McKinney Library, Albany NY

Severson, Jack, *Technician,* Regina Public Library, Dunlop Art Gallery, Regina SK

Sevigny, Maurice J, *Dir School Art,* Bowling Green State University, Fine Arts Gallery, Bowling Green OH

Sevigny, Maurice J, *Dir,* Bowling Green State University, School of Art, Bowling Green OH (S)

Sevy, Barbara, *Librn,* Philadelphia Museum of Art, Library, Philadelphia PA

Sevy, Barbara, *Librn,* Philadelphia Museum of Art, Library, Philadelphia PA

Seward, Claude, *Instr,* Orange County Community College, Art Dept, Middletown NY (S)

Seward, Harry, *Chmn,* Mid-America Arts Alliance, Kansas City MO

Sewell, Darrel, *Cur American Art,* Philadelphia Museum of Art, Philadelphia PA

Sewell, Jack, *Cur,* Art Institute of Chicago, Oriental Dept, Chicago IL

Sexton, Irwin, *Dir,* San Antonio Public Library, Dept of Fine Arts, San Antonio TX

Seymour, Larry, *Theatre Dir,* Hill Country Arts Foundation, Ingram TX

Sfirri, Mark, *Instructor,* Bucks County Community College, Fine Arts Dept, Newton PA (S)

Shackelford, Bruce M, *Dir,* Creek Council House and Museum, Okmulgee OK

Shackelford, Elizabeth, *Dir Student Servs,* Atlanta College of Art, Atlanta GA (S)

Shadbolt, Douglas, *Dir,* University of British Columbia, School of Architecture, Vancouver BC (S)

Shadwell, Gail, *Chmn,* Elgin Community College, Fine Arts Dept, Elgin IL (S)

Shafer, Ann, *Admin Asst,* Eastern Illinois University, Tarble Arts Center, Charleston IL

Shafer, Stan, *Assoc Prof,* College of Saint Benedict, Art Dept, Saint Joseph MN (S)

Shafer, Stanley, *Chmn of Art Dept & Gallery Dir,* College of Saint Benedict, Art Gallery, Saint Joseph MN

Shaffer, Ellen, *Cur,* Silverado Museum, Saint Helena CA

Shaffer, Mary, *Art Head,* Northwest Nazarene College, Art Dept, Nampa ID (S)

Shaffer, R, *Assoc Prof,* American University, Dept of Art, Washington DC (S)

Shaffer, Sharon, *Instructor,* Anton Elli, Cincinnati OH (S)

Shaffstall, James W, *Assoc Prof,* Hanover College, Dept of Art, Hanover IN (S)

Shakespeare, Valerie, *Pres,* Actual Art Foundation, New York NY

Shalkop, R L, *Dir,* Anchorage Historical and Fine Arts Museum, Cook Inlet Historical Society, Anchorage AK

Shaman, Sanford S, *Dir,* Washington State University, Museum of Art, Pullman WA

Shanahan, Kathleen, *Instructor,* Columbia College, Art Dept, Columbia MO (S)

Shander, Ira, *Instr,* Studio School of Art and Design, Philadelphia PA (S)

Shane, Audrey, *Cur Documentation,* University of British Columbia, Museum of Anthropology, Vancouver BC

Shaner, Carol, *Exhibits Librn,* Sarah Lawrence College Library, Esther Raushenbush Library, Bronxville NY

Shanewise, Marilyn, *Admin Asst Ctr Western Studies,* Joslyn Art Museum, Omaha NE

Shangraw, Clarence F, *Sr Cur,* Asian Art Museum of San Francisco, Avery Brundage Collection, San Francisco CA

Shankel, Carol, *Public Relations,* University of Kansas, Spencer Museum of Art, Lawrence KS

Shankman, Gary, *Instr,* Maryland College of Art and Design, Silver Spring MD (S)

Shannahan, John W, *Dir,* Connecticut Historical Commission, Sloane-Stanley Museum, Kent CT

Shannon, Joseph, *Chief Exhib,* Hirshhorn Museum and Sculpture Garden, Washington DC

Shannon, Joseph, *Prof,* Trenton State College, Art Dept, Trenton NJ (S)

Shannon, Mary O, *Exec Secy,* Boston Art Commission of the City of Boston, Boston MA

Shannon, Mary R, *Cur,* Rochester Historical Society, Rochester NY

Shapiro, Babe, *Dir,* Maryland Institute, Mount Royal Graduate School of Painting, Baltimore MD (S)

Shapiro, Irving, *Dir*, American Academy of Art, Chicago IL (S)

Shaniro, Michael, *Asst Prmf*, Duke University, Dept of Art, Durham NC (S)Shearman, John, *Chmn Dept*, Princeton University, Dept of Art and Archaeology, Princeton NJ (S)

Sharma, Sue, *Chief Art & Music Division*, Brooklyn Public Library, Art and Music Division, Brooklyn NY

Sharp, Elbert L, *Exhibition Preparator*, Memphis Brooks Museum of Art, Memphis TN

Sharp, Ellen, *Graphic Arts*, Detroit Institute of Arts, Detroit MI

Sharp, James C, *Librn*, Seton Hall University, Library, South Orange NJ

Sharp, Kenton, *Dean*, Montserrat School of Visual Art, Beverly MA (S)

Sharpe, Elizabeth, *Secy*, Canadian Artists' Representation, Le Front Des Artistes Canadiens, Toronto ON

Sharpe, Sara, *Treas*, Plastic Club, Art Club for Women, Philadelphia PA

Sharpe, William, *Bus Officer*, Greensboro Artists' League, Greensboro NC

Sharps, Leslie Ann, *Asst to the Dir*, University of Cincinnati, Tangeman Fine Arts Gallery, Cincinnati OH

Shatto, Gloria, *Pres*, Berry College, Moon Gallery, Mount Berry GA

Shaughnessy, Marie, *Funding*, Alaska Artists' Guild, Anchorage AK

Shaughnessy, Robert, *Prof*, Southampton College of Long Island University, C W Post Center Fine Arts Division, Southampton NY (S)

Shauley, Pam, *Admin Coordr*, Farmington Valley Arts Center, Avon CT

Shaw, Audrey, *Admin Secy*, Association of Canadian Industrial Designers, Ontario, Toronto ON

Shaw, Courtney, *Head Art Library*, University of Maryland, College Park, Art Library, College Park MD

Shaw, Don, *Instr*, Alfred C Glassell School of Art, Houston TX (S)

Shaw, H Allen, *Instructor*, Oklahoma State University, Graphic Arts Dept, Okmulgee OK (S)

Shaw, Luke A, *Assoc Prof*, Coppin State College, Art Dept, Baltimore MD (S)

Shaw, Mary M, *Dir*, Johnson-Humrickhouse Museum, Coshocton OH

Shaw, Meg, *Librn*, University of Kentucky, Art Library, Lexington KY

Shaw, Renata, *Actg Chief*, Library of Congress, Washington DC

Shaw, Robert H, *Chmn*, Texas Southmost College, Fine Arts Dept, Brownsville TX (S)

Shaw, Thomas M, *Asst Prof*, Rutgers, the State University of New Jersey, Graduate Program in Art History, New Brunswick NJ (S)

Shaw, Wayne, *Faculty*, Belleville Area College, Art Dept, Belleville IL (S)

Shaw, Winifred, *Assoc Prof*, University of New Hampshire, Dept of the Arts, Durham NH (S)

Shaw-Adelman, Jean, *Librn*, University of Pennsylvania, John and Ada Lewis Memorial Library, Philadelphia PA

Shay, Edward H, *Assoc Prof*, Southern Illinois University, School of Art, Carbondale IL (S)

Shay, Martin, *Site Adminr*, Missouri State Museum, Jefferson City MO

Shea, David, *Tres*, Hoosier Salon Patrons Association, Hoosier Salon Art Gallery, Indianapolis IN

Shea, Leo G, *VPres*, Birmingham-Bloomfield Art Association, Birmingham MI

Shea, Liliosa, *Assoc Prof*, Notre Dame College, Art Dept, Manchester NH (S)

Sheaks, Barclay, *Assoc Prof*, Virginia Wesleyan College, Art Dept of the Humanities Division, Norfolk VA (S)

Shear, T Leslie, *Chmn Prog in Classical Archaeology*, Princeton University, Dept of Art and Archaeology, Princeton NJ (S)

Shearer, Linda, *Exec Dir*, Committee for the Visual Arts, Inc, New York NY

Shearer, Susan, *Pres*, National Museum of American History, Society For Commercial Archeology, Washington DC

Shearer, Susan, *Information Services Coordr*, National Trust for Historic Preservation, Library, Information Services, Washingtmn DC

Shearouse, Henry G, *Librn*, Denver Public Library, Arts & Recreation Dept, Denver CO

Shearouse, Linda N, *Librn*, Museum of Fine Arts, Houston, Hirsch Library, Houston TX

Shears, Edith D, *Pres*, Toledo Artists' Club, Toledo OH

Sheckter, Bonnie, *Secy*, Printing and Drawing Council of Canada, Dept Art & Design, Edmonton AB

Sheeter, F S, *Pres*, Grolier Club Library, New York NY

Sheets, Billie, *Instructor*, Umpqua Community College, Fine & Performing Arts Dept, Roseburg OR (S)

Sheff, Donald, *Dir*, New York Institute of Photography, New York NY (S)

Sheffield, Alton, *Exec Asst*, Museum of the City of Mobile, Reference Library, Mobile AL

Sheffield, John T, *Treas*, Wichita Art Association Inc, Wichita KS

Sheinberg, Jacqueline, *Coordr Education Services*, State University of New York at Purchase, Neuberger Museum, Purchase NY

Sheingorn, Pamela, *Chmn*, Bernard M Baruch College of the City University of New York, Art Dept, New York NY (S)

Shekore, Mark, *Prof*, Northern State College, Art Dept, Aberdeen SD (S)

Shelby, Lisa, *Coordr of Public Information & Special Educator*, Memphis Brooks Museum of Art, Memphis TN

Sheldon, James L, *Cur Photography*, Phillips Academy, Addison Gallery of American Art, Andover MA

Sheldon, Judy, *Ref Librn*, California Historical Society, Schubert Hall Library, San Francisco CA

Sheldon, Larry, *Preparator & Registrar*, Miami University Art Museum, Oxford OH

Sheley, Wayne M, *Dean*, West Virginia University, West Virginia University Galleries, Morgantown WV

Shellman, Feay, *Actg Dir & Cur*, Telfair Academy of Arts and Sciences Inc, Savannah GA

Shelper, Joseph, *Co-Dir*, Chatham College, Art Gallery, Pittsburgh PA

Shelton, L T, *Cur Coll*, Missouri State Museum, Jefferson City MO

Shenk, Melinda, *Public Relations Coordr*, Ashtabula Arts Center, Ashtabula OH

Shenoi, Suman, *Costume Cur*, University of Minnesota, Goldstein Gallery, Saint Paul MN

Shepard, Brooks, *Pres*, New Haven Colony Historical Society, New Haven CT

Shepard, Charles, *First VPres*, Rochester Historical Society, Rochester NY

Shepard, Fred, *Preparator*, University of Santa Clara, de Saisset Museum, Santa Clara CA

Shepard, Fred, *Prof*, Murray State University, Art Dept, Murray KY (S)

Shepard, Willard, *Secy*, Lyman Allyn Museum, New London CT

Shepherd, Dorothy G, *Research Consultant Textiles & Islamic Art*, Cleveland Museum of Art, Cleveland OH

Shepherd, Elizabeth, *Actg Cur*, Oberlin College, Allen Memorial Art Museum, Oberlin OH

Shepherd, Gyde V, *Actg Asst Dir Public Programs*, National Gallery of Canada, Ottawa ON

Shepherd, Murray, *University Librn*, University of Waterloo, Dana Porter Arts Library, Waterloo ON

Shepler, Martha, *Instructor*, La Roche College, Division of Graphics, Design, Pittsburgh PA (S)

Shepp, James G, *Dir*, Maitland Art Center, Maitland FL

Sheppard, Ileen, *Program Admin*, Queens Museum, Flushing NY

Sheppard, John, *Dir Public Relations*, Brandywine River Museum, Chadds Ford PA

Sheppard, Luvon, *Instr*, Rochester Institute of Technology, School of Art and Design, Rochester NY (S)

Sherburn, Anne, *Development & Public Relations*, Museum of the Smuthuest, Midland T

Sheres, Lisa, *Asst Art Dir*, Southeast Banking Corporation, Miami FL

Sheridan, Helen, *Head Librn*, Kalamazoo Institute of Arts, Library, Kalamazoo MI

Sheriff, Judy, *Young Adult*, Mason City Public Library, Mason City IA

Sheriff, Mary, *Asst Prof*, University of North Carolina at Chapel Hill, Art Dept, Chapel Hill NC (S)

Sherman, Ann, *Asst Prof*, University of Kansas, Dept of Art, Music Education and Music Therapy, Lawrence KS (S)

Sherman, Helen, *Assoc Prof*, Marygrove College, Dept of Art and Art History, Detroit MI (S)

Sherman, Paul T, *Admin Services Librn*, New York City Technical College, Namm Hall Library and Learning Resource Center, Brooklyn NY

Sherman, Sarah, *Head Art Collection*, Northwestern University, Art Library, Evanston IL

Sherman, William A, *Pres*, Newport Historical Society, Newport RI

Shermoe, Raymond, *Executive Dir*, Civic Fine Arts Association Museum, Sioux Falls SD

Sherrill, Frank, *Cur*, Arts and Science Museum, Statesville NC

Sherwood, David J, *Pres*, Newark Museum, Newark NJ

Sherwood, Muriel, *Treasurer*, Kings County Historical Society and Museum, Hampton NB

Sherwood, Richard E, *Chmn*, Los Angeles County Museum of Art, Los Angeles CA

Shestack, Alan, *Dir*, Yale University, Art Gallery, New Haven CT

Shetley, Vernon, *Asst Librn*, M Knoedler & Co, Inc, Library, New York NY

Shewan, Robert, *Chmn*, Roberts Wesleyan College, Fine Arts Division, Art Dept, Rochester NY (S)

Shewkenek, B, *Cur*, Nutana Collegiate Institute, Memorial Library and Art Gallery, Saskatoon SK

Shewmake, Edwin, *Prof*, Salem College, Art Dept, Winston-Salem NC (S)

Shickles, Tim, *Dir & Cur Educ*, Carson County Square House Museum, Panhandle TX

Shickman, Allan, *Asst Prof*, University of Northern Iowa, Dept of Art, Cedar Falls IA (S)

Shield, Jan G, *Asst Prof*, Pacific University in Oregon, Dept of Fine Arts, Forest Grove OR (S)

Shield, Karen, *Cur*, Pacific University, Old College Hall, Pacific University Museum, Forest Grove OR

Shields, C D, *In Charge Art Program*, The Standard Oil Company (Ohio), Cleveland OH

Shields, Dot, *Asst Librn*, University of Michigan, Art & Architecture Library, Ann Arbor MI

Shields, Sarah, *Cur of Library*, Valentine Museum, Library, Richmond VA

Shields, W, *Dir Programs*, Royal Architectural Institute of Canada, Ottawa ON

Shiff, Richard, *Assoc Prof*, University of North Carolina at Chapel Hill, Art Dept, Chapel Hill NC (S)

Shigaki, Betty Jean, *Dir*, Rochester Art Center, Rochester MN

Shikowitz, Joyce, *Asst Prof*, Rochester Institute of Technology, School of Art and Design, Rochester NY (S)

Shimizu, Yoshiake, *Cur Japanese Art*, Freer Gallery of Art, Washington DC

Shindelbower, Daniel N, *Chmn*, Eastern Kentucky University, Art Dept, Richmond KY (S)

Shine, Carolyn R, *Cur Costumes, Textiles, Tribal Arts*, Cincinnati Art Museum, Cincinnati OH

Shipley, Cynthia K, *Coordr Visual Resources & Servs*, Indianapolis Museum of Art, Visual Resources & Services, Indianapolis IN

Shipley, Roger, *Co-Dir*, Lycoming College Gallery, Williamsport PA

Shipley, Roger Douglas, *Assoc Prof*, Lycoming College, Art Dept, Williamsport PA (S)

Shipley, Walter B, *Instr*, Okaloosa-Walton Junior College, Dept of Fine and Performing Arts, Niceville FL (S)

Shireman, Candace, *Supv Art Services*, Cleveland State University, Library - Art Services, Cleveland OH

Shires, Bill, *Instructor,* West Texas State University, Art Dept, Canyon TX (S)

Shirley, Karen, *Project Dir,* Antioch College, Noyes, Read and Grey Galleries, Yellow Springs OH

Shirley, Karen, *Prof,* Antioch College, Dept of Art, Yellow Springs OH (S)

Shirley, Lawrence W, *VPres,* Currier Gallery of Art, Manchester NH

Shirley, Margaret, *Instructor,* Marylhurst College, Art Dept, Marylhurst OR (S)

Shishido, Miles, *Prof,* Pacific University in Oregon, Dept of Fine Arts, Forest Grove OR (S)

Shively, Stephen, *Asst Naturalist,* Lafayette Natural History Museum, Planetarium and Nature Station, Lafayette LA

Shoemaker, Innis H, *Dir,* University of North Carolina, The Ackland Art Museum, Chapel Hill NC

Shoemaker, Stephanie, *Asst Dir,* Newport Art Museum and Art Association, Newport RI

Shoemaker, William S, *Prof,* Rochester Institute of Technology, School of Photographic Arts & Sciences, Rochester NY (S)

Shook, Larry, *Head Dept,* Victoria College, Victoria TX (S)

Shoolroy, Clifton B, *Pres,* Sierra Nevada Museum of Art, Reno NV

Shopmaker, Laurence, *Asst Dir,* State University of New York at Purchase, Neuberger Museum, Purchase NY

Shores, Ken, *Prof,* Lewis and Clark College, Dept of Art, Portland OR (S)

Short, Frank, *Instr,* Montgomery County Community College, Communicating Arts Dept, Blue Bell PA (S)

Short, Robert, *Instr,* Green River Community College, Art Dept, Auburn WA (S)

Short, Tom, *Asst Prof,* Northampton County Area Community College, Art Dept, Bethlehem PA (S)

Shoudy, Charles, *VPres,* Historic Cherry Hill, Albany NY

Showen, E, *Project Mgr,* Association of Collegiate Schools of Architecture, Washington DC

Showman, Richard K, *Ed, Nathanael Green Papers,* Rhode Island Historical Society, Providence RI

Shroff, Piroja, *Art Education,* California College of Arts and Crafts, Oakland CA (S)

Shrott, Gail, *Cur,* University of Delaware, University Gallery, Newark DE

Shrum, L Vance, *Asst to Dir,* Cummer Gallery of Art, DeEtte Holden Cummer Museum Foundation, Jacksonville FL

Shtern, Adele, *Asst Prof,* University of Bridgeport, Art Dept, Bridgeport CT (S)

Shubert, Joseph, *State Librn-Assoc Commissioner for Libraries,* New York State Library, Manuscripts and Special Collections, Albany NY

Shuck, Patrick, *Instructor,* Saint Louis Community College at Meramec, Art Dept, Saint Louis MO (S)

Shuff, Lily, *Secy,* National Society of Painters in Casein and Acrylic, Inc, New York NY

Shuffleburg, David, *Clerk,* Springfield Art & Historical Society, Springfield VT

Shugart, Ruth, *Librn,* Lightner Museum, Library, Saint Augustine FL

Shull, Carl, *Prof,* Eastern Illinois University, School of Fine Arts, Charleston IL (S)

Shuman, Geraldine S, *Museum Coordr,* Hastings Museum, Hastings NE

Shumoke, Josie, *Secy,* Columbus and Lowndes County Historical Society Museum, Columbus MS

Shumway, Floyd M, *Dir,* New Haven Colony Historical Society, New Haven CT

Shust, Maria, *Dir,* Ukrainian Museum, New York NY

Shutze, Phyllis, *Public Relations,* Essex Institute, Salem MA

Shy, Bob, *Asst,* Custer County Art Center, Miles City MT

Sias, James H, *Asst Prof,* Rochester Institute of Technology, School of Art and Design, Rochester NY (S)

Sibley, Donna M, *Museum Guide,* Tomoka State Park Museum, Ormond Beach FL

Sickman, Laurence, *Lectr,* University of Kansas, Kress Foundation Dept of Art History, Lawrence KS (S)

Siddall, Catherine, *Asst Dir,* Oakville Galleries, Oakville ON

Siddens, Vera Jo, *Asst Prof,* University of Northern Iowa, Dept of Art, Cedar Falls IA (S)

Sides, Patricia, *Registrar,* Evansville Museum of Arts and Science, Evansville IN

Sidman, Howard F, *Instructor,* MacMurray College, Art Dept, Jacksonville IL (S)

Sido, Lee T, *Dir,* University of Nevada, Las Vegas, Art Gallery, Las Vegas NV

Sido, Lee T, *Assoc Prof,* University of Nevada, Las Vegas, Dept of Art, Las Vegas NV (S)

Sidrow, Sigred, *Librn,* Jacque Marchais Center of Tibetan Arts, Inc, Library, Staten Island NY

Siebecker, Dorothy, *Cataloger,* Tucson Museum of Art, Library, Tucson AZ

Siebel, Julia, *Secy,* The Friends of Photography, Carmel CA

Siebenheller, William, *Pres,* Staten Island Institute of Arts and Sciences, Staten Island NY

Sieber, Robert N, *Dir,* Pennsylvania Farm Museum of Landis Valley, Lancaster PA

Sieber, Roy, *Assoc Dir,* National Museum of African Art, Washington DC

Sieber, Roy, *Prof,* Indiana University, Bloomington, School of Fine Arts, Bloomington IN (S)

Siedenburg, Joan, *Pres,* Cortland County Historical Society, Suggett House Museum, Cortland NY

Sieg, Robert, *Instructor,* East Central University, Art Dept, Ada OK (S)

Sieger, JoAnne D, *Dir,* Earlham College, Leeds Gallery, Richmond IN

Sieger, JoAnne D, *Chmn Dept,* Earlham College, Art Dept, Richmond IN (S)

Siegfried, Susan, *Asst Prof,* Northwestern University, Evanston, Dept of Art History, Evanston IL (S)

Siekert, John, *VPres,* Art Guild of Burlington, Arts for Living Center, Burlington IA

Sieling, Bryan, *Cur,* Southern Ohio Museum Corporation, Southern Ohio Museum & Cultural Center, Portsmouth OH

Sierra, Emilia, *Clothing Chmn,* Traphagen School of Fashion, New York NY (S)

Siersma, Betsy, *Actg Dir & Registrar,* University of Massachusetts, Amherst, University Gallery, Amherst MA

Sifford, Harlan L, *Librn,* University of Iowa, Art Library, Iowa City IA

Sigg, Franz, *Research Assoc,* Rochester Institute of Technology, Technical & Education Center of the Graphic Arts, Rochester NY (S)

Siggins, Judy, *Asst Dir,* Harvard University, Dumbarton Oaks Research Library and Collections, Washington DC

Sigler, Douglas E, *Assoc Prof,* Rochester Institute of Technology, School for American Craftsmen, Rochester NY (S)

Siglin, Leona, *VPres,* Coquille Valley Art Association, Coquille OR

Sikes, J Davis, *Chmn Div,* Jacksonville University, Dept of Art, Jacksonville FL (S)

Sikora, Corinne, *Pres,* Polk Public Museum, Lakeland FL

Silberstein-Storfer, Muriel R, *Pres,* Art Commission of the City of New York, New York NY

Silbiger, Kathy, *Dir Development & Community Relations,* Madison Art Center, Madison WI

Silbonm, Lynn, *Coordr,* State University of New York at Stony Brook, Art Gallery, Stony Brook NY

Silhan, William A, *Assoc Prof,* University of West Florida, Faculty of Art, Pensacola FL (S)

Siller, N, *Dean Art,* Ryerson Polytechnical Institute Library, Toronto ON

Sills, Joyce, *Assoc Prof,* Rutgers, the State University of New Jersey, Mason Gross School of the Arts, New Brunswick NJ (S)

Silosky, Daniel, *Registrar,* Huntington Galleries, Huntington WV

Silva, Maxine Watter, *Art Program Dir,* College Misericordia, Art Dept, Dallas PA (S)

Silver, Adele Z, *Mgr Public Information & Membership,* Cleveland Museum of Art, Cleveland OH

Silver, Arthur, *Prof,* C W Post Center of Long Island University, School of the Arts, Greenvale NY (S)

Silver, Daniel Jeremy, *Dir,* Temple Museum of Jewish Religious Art, Cleveland OH

Silver, Jonathan, *Instr,* New York Studio School of Drawing, Painting and Sculpture, New York NY (S)

Silver, Julius L, *Prof,* Rochester Institute of Technology, School of Printing, Rochester NY (S)

Silver, Larry, *Chmn Dept,* Northwestern University, Evanston, Dept of Art History, Evanston IL (S)

Silverberg, David, *Prof,* Mount Allison University, Fine Arts Dept, Sackville NB (S)

Silverman, Joy, *Dir,* Los Angeles Contemporary Exhibitions, Inc, Los Angeles CA

Silverman, Lanny, *Cur Education & Public Programming,* Madison Art Center, Madison WI

Silverman, Paul, *University Pres,* University of Maine at Orono, Art Collection, Orono ME

Silverstein, Helen, *Dir Public Affairs & Speical Programs,* Manhattan Laboratory Museum, New York NY

Silvester, Roger, *VPres,* Printing and Drawing Council of Canada, Dept Art & Design, Edmonton AB

Silvestro, Clement M, *Dir & Librn,* Museum of Our National Heritage, Lexington MA

Sim, Richard, *Prof,* Antelope Valley College, Art Dept, Division of Fine Arts, Lancaster CA (S)

Simkin, Phillips, *Assoc Prof,* York College of the City University of New York, Fine and Performing Arts, Jamaica NY (S)

Simmons, Charles B, *Executive Dir,* Henry Morrison Flagler Museum, Palm Beach FL

Simmons, Dale M, *Chmn,* Alberta Art Foundation, Edmonton AB

Simmons, E H, *Dir,* Marine Corps Museum, Art Unit, Washington DC

Simmons, Gail, *Exec Dir,* Artists Equity Association, Inc, Washington DC

Simmons, Harold C, *Chmn,* Baylor University, Dept of Fine Arts, Waco TX (S)

Simmons, John W, *Asst Prof,* Lee College, Dept of Music & Fine Arts, Cleveland TN (S)

Simmons, Ken, *VPres,* African American Historical and Cultural Society, San Francisco CA

Simmons, Michael, *Instr,* California State University, Chico, Art Dept, Chico CA (S)

Simmons, Patricia, *Secy,* Southern Illinois University, University Museum, Carbondale IL

Simmons, Terry K, *Exhib Chmn,* Delta State University, Fielding L Wright Art Center, Cleveland MS

Simmons, Terry K, *Assoc Prof,* Delta State University, Dept of Art, Cleveland MS (S)

Simon, Carol, *Registrar,* Beloit College, Wright Museum of Art, Beloit WI

Simon, C M, *Dir,* Heritage Center, Inc, Pine Ridge SD

Simon, David L, *Chmn Dept,* Colby College, Art Dept, Waterville ME (S)

Simon, Dorothy, *Asst Cur,* Institute of Fine Arts, Slide Collection, New York NY

Simon, Elizabeth, *Asst Prof,* Daemen College, Art Dept, Amherst NY (S)

Simon, Herbert, *Assoc Prof,* Wilkes College, Dept of Art, Wilkes-Barre PA (S)

Simon, Michael A, *Assoc Prof,* Beloit College, Dept of Art, Beloit WI (S)

Simon, Norton, *Pres,* Norton Simon Museum, Pasadena CA

Simon, Robert, *Chmn Academic Studies,* Art Institute of Boston, Boston MA (S)

Simon, Sidney, *Academic Dir,* Skowhegan School of Painting and Sculpture, Skowhegan ME (S)

Simon, Sidney, *Prof,* University of Minnesota, Minneapolis, Art History, Minneapolis MN (S)

Simon, Sonia C, *Asst Prof,* Colby College, Art Dept, Waterville ME (S)

Simon, Sybil C, *Exec Dir,* Arts & Business Council, New York NY

Simonds, M E, *Cur,* Hastings County Museum, Belleville ON

Simonoff, Arnold, *Assoc Prof,* C W Post Center of Long Island University, School of the Arts, Greenvale NY (S)

Simons, Anneke Prins, *Prof,* Jersey City State College, Art Dept, Jersey City NJ (S)

Simons, Chris, *Prof,* Shoreline Community College, Humanities Division, Seattle WA (S)

Simonsen, Vibeke, *Interior Design Consultant,* Champion International Corporation, Stamford CT

Simpson, David, *Prof,* University of California, Berkeley, College of Letters & Sciences, Berkeley CA (S)

Simpson, Derrol, *Pres,* Gananoque Historical Museum, Gananoque ON

Simpson, Glen C, *Assoc Prof,* University of Alaska, Dept of Art, Fairbanks AK (S)

Simpson, James, *Instructor,* Long Beach City College, Dept of Art, Long Beach CA (S)

Simpson, Leslie T, *Dir,* Post Memorial Art Reference Library, Joplin MO

Simpson, Pamela H, *Head Art Division,* Washington and Lee University, Dept of Fine Arts, Lexington VA (S)

Simpson, Patricia M, *Pres Cultural Heritage Board,* City of Los Angeles, Cultural Affairs Dept, Los Angeles CA

Simpson, R Tate, *Secy,* Marblehead Arts Association, Inc, Marblehead MA

Simpson, Ruth D, *Cur Archeaology,* San Bernardino County Museum and Satellites, Fine Arts Institute, Redlands CA

Simpson, Valerie, *Cur Decorative Arts,* New Brunswick Museum, Saint John NB

Simpson, William Kelly, *Cur Egyptian Art,* Museum of Fine Arts, Boston MA

Sims, Carol, *Librn,* National Infantry Museum, Library, Fort Benning GA

Sims, Ester, *Chmn Div Communication & Humanities,* Aims Community College, Program for Design & Creative Studies, Greeley CO (S)

Sims, Judith, *Dir Prog,* Laguna Gloria Art Museum, Austin TX

Sims, Patterson, *Assoc Cur Permanent Collection,* Whitney Museum of American Art, New York NY

Sims, William R, *Chmn Dept,* Cornell University, New York State College of Human Ecology, Ithaca NY (S)

Sinatra, Joan, *Membership Dir,* DeCordova and Dana Museum and Park, Lincoln MA

Sinclair, Jane, *Instructor,* Chapman College, Art Dept, Orange CA (S)

Sinclair, Susan, *Archivist,* Isabella Stewart Gardner Museum, Library, Boston MA

Sindelar, Norma, *Archives Technician,* Saint Louis Art Museum, Richardson Memorial Library, Saint Louis MO

Sing, Susan, *Instr,* Glendale College, Dept of Fine Arts, Glendale CA (S)

Singer, Arnold, *Prof,* Cornell University, Dept of Art, Ithaca NY (S)

Singer, Clyde, *Assoc Dir,* Butler Institute of American Art, Youngstown OH

Singstock, Allen, *Arboretum Mgr,* Paine Art Center and Arboretum, Oshkosh WI

Sintz, Edward F, *Dir,* Miami-Dade Public Library, Miami FL

Sipe, Gary R, *Asst Librn,* Yale University, Art and Architecture Library, New Haven CT

Sipiora, Leonard P, *Dir,* El Paso Museum of Art, El Paso TX

Sires, Paul, *Ceramics,* Chautauqua Institution, The Art Center, Chautauqua NY (S)

Sirignano, Rita, *Executive Asst,* Institute for Art & Urban Resources, Project Studios One, Long Island City NY

Sirna, Jessie, *Program Coordr & Educator,* M Flint Institute of Arts, Flint MI

Siroonian, Harold, *Librn,* McMaster University, Library, Hamilton ON

Sisler, Rebecca, *Executive Dir,* Royal Canadian Academy of Arts, Toronto ON

Sisserson, Helen, *Asst Prof,* Nassau Community College, Art Dept, Garden City NY (S)

Sittenfeld, Paul George, *Pres,* Cincinnati Institute of Fine Arts, Cincinnati OH

Sivers, Cora, *Cur of Marghab Collection,* South Dakota State University, South Dakota Memorial Art Center, Brookings SD

Sizemore, Jean, *Lectr,* Southwestern at Memphis, Dept of Art, Memphis TN (S)

Sjoberg, Ake W, *Babylonian Section Tablet Coll Cur,* University of Pennsylvania, University Museum of Archaeology & Anthropology, Philadelphia PA

Skaggs, Jerry, *Dir,* French Art Colony, Inc, Gallipolis OH

Skaggs, Nettie, *Exec Secy,* Floyd County Museum, New Albany IN

Skaggs, Robert L, *Instr,* Hannibal La Grange College, Art Dept, Hannibal MO (S)

Skaith, Susan, *Secy,* University of Western Ontario, McIntosh Art Gallery, London ON

Skelley, Jack, *Co-Dir Reading Servs,* Beyond Baroque Foundation, Venice CA

Skelley, Robert C, *Prof,* University of Florida, Dept of Art, Gainesville FL (S)

Skidmore, Linda, *Admin Asst,* Art Center of Battle Creek, Battle Creek MI

Skidmore, Steve, *Dir,* Ponca City Library, Art Dept, Ponca City OK

Skiles, Jackie, *Newsletter Editor,* Women in the Arts Foundation, Inc, New York NY

Skillen, Sandra, *Prog Coordr,* Museum of Arts and Sciences, Inc, Macon GA

Skilliter, Lowell, *Treas,* Toledo Artists' Club, Toledo OH

Skinner, Arthur, *Asst Prof,* Eckerd College, Art Dept, Saint Petersburg FL (S)

Skinner, Bill, *Chmn Div of Communications & Arts,* North Arkansas Community College, Art Dept, Harrison AR (S)

Skinner, D E, *Chmn,* Corporate Council for the Arts, Seattle WA

Skinner, Edyth, *Chmn & Prof,* County College of Morris, Art Dept, Randolph NJ (S)

Skinner, Robert, *Prof,* Southampton College of Long Island University, C W Post Center Fine Arts Division, Southampton NY (S)

Skira, Sylvie, *Gallery Dir,* Maine Coast Artists, Rockport ME

Skjelstad, Lucy, *Dir,* Oregon State University, Horner Museum, Corvallis OR

Sklarski, Bonnie, *Prof,* Indiana University, Bloomington, School of Fine Arts, Bloomington IN (S)

Skornicka, Joel, *Dir of Development,* University of Wisconsin, Elvehjem Museum of Art, Madison WI

Skovronsky, Gloria B, *Admin Asst,* California State University, Long Beach, University Art Museum, Long Beach CA

Skuja, Lucija, *Head Music & Art Dept,* Grand Rapids Public Library, Music & Art Dept, Grand Rapids MI

Skurkis, Barry, *Chmn,* North Central College, Dept of Art, Naperville IL (S)

Skvarla, Diane K, *Museum Specialist,* United States Senate Commission on Art and Antiquities, Washington DC

Skye, Ann, *Education Coordr,* The Art Center, Waco TX

Slaaen, Marlaine, *Instr,* University of North Dakota-Williston Center, Interior Design Dept, Williston ND (S)

Slade, Bobbie, *Asn Corresp Secy,* Biloxi Art Association, Gallery, Biloxi MS

Slade, G Richard, *Pres,* Minneapolis College of Art and Design, Minneapolis MN (S)

Slade, Heather, *Staff Site Interpreter,* Patterson Homestead, Dayton OH

Slade, Rona, *Asst Dean,* Corcoran School of Art, Washington DC (S)

Slade, Roy, *Dir Museum,* Cranbrook Academy of Art Museum, Bloomfield Hills MI

Slade, Roy, *Pres,* Cranbrook Academy of Art, Bloomfield Hills MI (S)

Slaffer, Susan, *Public Program Coordr,* Heard Museum, Phoenix AZ

Slane, Kathleen, *Asst Prof,* University of Missouri, Art History and Archaeology Dept, Columbia MO (S)

Slate, Joseph, *Prof,* Kenyon College, Art Dept, Gambier OH (S)

Slater, Van E, *Prof,* Compton Community College, Compton CA (S)

Slattum, Jerry, *Chmn Dept,* California Lutheran College, Art Dept, Thousand Oaks CA (S)

Slaugenhop, Ann, *Secy,* Red River Valley Museum, Vernon TX

Slaughter, Carl, *Vis Prof,* Columbia College, Art Dept, Columbia MO (S)

Slauson, Jim, *Chmn Academics,* Milwaukee Institute of Art and Design, Milwaukee WI (S)

Slavish, Peter J, *Faculty,* Blackburn College, Dept of Art, Carlinville IL (S)

Slaymaker, Sandy, *Instr,* Wayne Art Center, Wayne PA (S)

Slayton, Ronald, *Cur,* Wood Art Gallery, Montpelier VT

Sleadd, M, *Faculty,* Stephens College, Art Dept, Columbia MO (S)

Slee, David W, *Technician,* University of Michigan, Kelsey Museum of Ancient and Medieval Archaeology, Ann Arbor MI

Sleele, Curtis, *Asst Prof,* Arkansas State University, Dept of Art, State University AR (S)

Sleight, Donald , *Chmn,* Niagara County Community College, Fine Arts Division, Sanborn NY (S)

Sleight, Frederick W, *Librn,* Palm Springs Desert Museum, Inc, Library, Palm Springs CA

Slenker, Elizabeth, *Instr,* Saint Thomas Aquinas College, Art Dept, Sparkhill NY (S)

Sloan, John K, *2nd VPres,* Southwest Arts Foundation, Houston TX

Sloane, Eric, *Art Advisory Board,* Society of Medalists, Danbury CT

Slorp, John S, *Pres,* Memphis Academy of Arts, Frank T Tobey Gallery, Memphis TN

Sloshberg, Leah P, *Dir,* New Jersey State Museum, Trenton NJ

Slottman, Helen, *First VPres,* Pen and Brush, Inc, New York NY

Slouffman, Jim, *Dir Education,* Anton Elli, Cincinnati OH (S)

Slusarenko, Kay, *Chairperson,* Marylhurst College, Art Dept, Marylhurst OR (S)

Smagula, Howard, *Dean,* San Antonio Art Institute, San Antonio TX (S)

Small, Carol, *Instr,* Gettysburg College, Dept of Art, Gettysburg PA (S)

Small, Eve, *Prof,* West Virginia University, Division of Art, Morgantown WV (S)

Smallenberg, Harry, *Chmn General Studies,* Center for Creative Studies__College of Art and Design, Detroit MI (S)

Smalley, David, *Prof,* Connecticut College, Dept of Art, New London CT (S)

Smalley, Stephen, *Chmn,* Bridgewater State College, Art Dept, Bridgewater MA (S)

Smar, Joyce, *Supv Music,* Toledo Museum of Art, Toledo OH

Smart, Glenda, *Educ Chmn,* Art Association School, Spartanburg SC (S)

Smedley, Geoffrey, *Prof,* University of British Columbia, Dept of Fine Arts, Vancouver BC (S)

Smemo, Suzanne, *Instr,* Concordia College, Art Dept, Moorhead MN (S)

Smenner, Ray, *Cur Education,* Springfield Art Museum, Springfield MO

Smigocki, Stephen, *Prof,* Fairmont State College, Art Dept, Fairmont WV (S)

Smigrod, Claudia, *Lectr,* Trinity College, Art Dept, Washington DC (S)

Smiley, Becky, *Faculty,* Howard College, Art Dept, Big Spring TX (S)

Smiley, James, *Instructor,* Daytona Beach Community College, Dept of Performing and Visual Arts, Daytona Beach FL (S)

Smiter, Janine, *Chief Information Servs & Public Relations,* National Gallery of Canada, Ottawa ON

Smith, Aj, *Instr,* Arkansas Arts Center, Little Rock AR (S)

Smith, Allen C, *Cur Coll,* Arnot Art Museum, Elmira NY

Smith, Ann, *Dir,* Mattatuck Historical Society Museum, Mattatuck Museum, Waterbury CT

Smith, Arthur, *Prof,* Salem State College, Art Dept, Salem MA (S)

Smith, Barbara, *Asst Dir,* Portland Public Library, Art Dept, Portland ME

Smith, B G, *Supt,* Texas Ranger Hall of Fame and Museum, Waco TX

Smith, B J, *Dir,* Oklahoma State University, Gardiner Art Gallery, Stillwater OK

Smith, Brydon, *Asst Dir Coll & Research,* National Gallery of Canada, Ottawa ON

Smith, Carey, *Asst Framer,* Kalamunda Museum of Western Art, Somers MT

Smith, Carol, *Mgr Museum Shop,* Glenbow Museum, Calgary AB

Smith, Catherine, *Instr,* Cleveland State Community College, Dept of Art, Cleveland TN (S)

Smith, Cecil, *Pres,* Kalamunda Museum of Western Art, Somers MT

Smith, Charles, *Cultural Center Manager,* Hampton Center for Arts and Humanities, Hampton VA

Smith, Claude, *Prof,* Western New Mexico University, College of Arts and Letters, Art Dept, Silver City NM (S)

Smith, Claudia, *Instructor,* University of Wisconsin-Stout, Art Dept, Menomonie WI (S)

Smith, Darold, *Assoc Prof,* West Texas State University, Art Dept, Canyon TX (S)

Smith, David, *Asst Prof,* University of New Hampshire, Dept of the Arts, Durham NH (S)

Smith, David L, *Assoc Prof,* University of Wisconsin-Stevens Point, Dept of Art, Stevens Point WI (S)

Smith, Debbie, *Registrar,* Western Kentucky University, Kentucky Museum, Bowling Green KY

Smith, Donald C, *Prof,* Rhode Island College, Art Dept, Providence RI (S)

Smith, Donald L, *Assoc Prof,* Rochester Institute of Technology, School of Photographic Arts & Sciences, Rochester NY (S)

Smith, Doreen, *Secy,* Alaska Association for the Arts, Fairbanks AK

Smith, Dorothy V, *Publicity,* Leatherstocking Brush & Palette Club Inc, Cooperstown NY

Smith, Douglas, *Photographer,* Southern Oregon Historical Society, Jacksonville Museum, Jacksonville OR

Smith, Douglas Campbell, *Assoc Prof,* Central Oregon Community College, Dept of Art, Bend OR (S)

Smith, Earl E T, *VPres,* Society of the Four Arts, Palm Beach FL

Smith, Elinore, *Slide Librn,* Tucson Museum of Art, Library, Tucson AZ

Smith, Elise, *Faculty,* North Carolina Wesleyan, Dept of Art, Rocky Mount NC (S)

Smith, Elizabeth B, *Asst Prof,* Pennsylvania State University, University Park, Dept of Art History, University Park PA (S)

Smith, Frank Anthony, *Prof,* University of Utah, Art Dept, Salt Lake City UT (S)

Smith, Fred T, *Asst Prof,* University of Minnesota, Minneapolis, Art History, Minneapolis MN (S)

Smith, Gary, *Cur,* Missouri Historical Society, Saint Louis MO

Smith, Gary T, *Dir,* Hartnell College Gallery, Salinas CA

Smith, George, *Assoc Prof,* Rice University, Dept of Art and Art History, Houston TX (S)

Smith, George, *Asst Prof,* University of the District of Columbia, Art Dept, Washington DC (S)

Smith, George Ivan, *Asst Prof,* Portland State University, Dept of Art and Architecture, Portland OR (S)

Smith, George M, *Adminr,* Woodlawn Plantation, Mount Vernon VA

Smith, Gerald, *Dir,* San Bernardino County Museum and Satellites, Fine Arts Institute, Redlands CA

Smith, Gerald D, *Dean,* Huntington College, Art Dept, Huntington IN (S)

Smith, Gladys, *Asst Librn,* Chappell Memorial Library and Art Gallery, Chappell NE

Smith, Greg, *Asst Dir,* Toledo Museum of Art, Toledo OH

Smith, Hilda S, *Instr,* Baylor University, Dept of Fine Arts, Waco TX (S)

Smith, Iras, *Librn,* Fine Arts Museum of the South, Library, Mobile AL

Smith, J, *Faculty,* Western Illinois University, College of Fine Arts, Macomb IL (S)

Smith, Jack, *Div Coordr Crafts,* Kent State University, School of Art, Kent OH (S)

Smith, Jack R, *Dept Head,* Southern Connecticut State College, Dept of Art, New Haven CT (S)

Smith, James E, *Assoc Prof,* Western Carolina University, Dept of Art, Cullowhee NC (S)

Smith, James G E, *Cur North America,* Museum of the American Indian, New York NY

Smith, James L, *Pres,* Waterloo Art Association, Eleventh Street Gallery, Waterloo IA

Smith, James Morton, *Dir,* Winterthur Museum and Gardens, Winterthur DE

Smith, Janet Carl, *Coordr of Programs & Exhibits,* Chicago Public Library, Cultural Center, Chicago IL

Smith, Jean, *Arts & Architecture Librn,* Pennsylvania State University, Pattee Library, University Park PA

Smith, Jo, *Office Mgr,* Marin Society of Artists Inc, Ross CA

Smith, Joan F, *Instr,* Rosemont College, Division of the Arts, Rosemont PA (S)

Smith, John, *Artist-in-Residence,* Trinity College, Dept of Fine Arts, Hartford CT (S)

Smith, John W, *Asst Prof,* University of Arkansas, Art Dept, Fayetteville AR (S)

Smith, Joseph E, *Asst Prof,* Oakland City College, Division of Fine Arts, Oakland City IN (S)

Smith, Joyce, *Pres,* Douglas Art Association, Little Gallery, Douglas AZ

Smith, K, *Secy,* Royal Ontario Museum, Canadiana Gallery, Toronto ON

Smith, Kendall, *Pres,* Lafayette Art Association, Greater Lafayette Museum of Art, Lafayette IN

Smith, Kent, *Asst Cur,* Long Beach Museum of Art, Long Beach CA

Smith, Kim, *Interim Asst Chmn,* Texas Tech University, Dept of Art, Lubbock TX (S)

Smith, Kim, *Asst Prof,* Texas Tech University, Dept of Art, Lubbock TX (S)

Smith, Kirby F, *Public Information Officer,* Pennsylvania Academy of the Fine Arts, Galleries, Philadelphia PA

Smith, La Priel, *Museum Attendant,* Kalamunda Museum of Western Art, Somers MT

Smith, Lester K, *Arts Librn,* Northern Illinois University, Library, De Kalb IL

Smith, Maggie, *Recording Secy,* Kent Art Association, Inc, Kent CT

Smith, Maggie, *Bookstore Mgr,* Salvador Dali Foundation Museum, Saint Petersburg FL

Smith, Margaret Supplee, *Chairwoman,* Wake Forest University, Dept of Art, Winston-Salem NC (S)

Smith, Marie W, *VPres,* Kalamunda Museum of Western Art, Somers MT

Smith, Marilyn, *Admin Asst,* Art Museum of South Texas, Corpus Christi TX

Smith, Marjorie, *Instr,* Arkansas Arts Center, Little Rock AR (S)

Smith, Mark S, *Dir,* Texas Woman's University Art Gallery, Denton TX

Smith, Mark S, *Asst Prof,* Texas Woman's University, Dept of Art, Denton TX (S)

Smith, Marsha, *Art Asst,* Newark Museum, Junior Museum, Newark NJ

Smith, Merrill W, *Visual Coll Librn,* Massachusetts Institute of Technology, Rotch Library of Architecture and Planning, Cambridge MA

Smith, Michael, *Asst Prof,* East Tennessee State University, Fine Arts Dept, Johnson City TN (S)

Smith, Michael H, *Dir,* California Institute of Technology, Baxter Art Gallery, Pasadena CA

Smith, Michael J, *Dir,* Putnam Museum, Davenport IA

Smith, Michael J, *Asst Chmn Dept,* Southern Illinois University at Edwardsville, Dept of Art and Design, Edwardsville IL (S)

Smith, Nan, *Asst Prof,* University of Florida, Dept of Art, Gainesville FL (S)

Smith, Nancy, *Secy,* Lexington Art League, Inc, Lexington KY

Smith, Nancy, *Asst Librn,* University of Southern California, Architecture and Fine Arts Library, Los Angeles CA

Smith, Nancy Bigger, *Dir of Develop,* London Regional Art Gallery, London ON

Smith, Nelson, *Instructor,* Madonna College, Art Dept, Livonia MI (S)

Smith, Patricia, *Business Mgr,* Asheville Art Museum, Asheville NC

Smith, Paul, *Adminr,* Foundation for the Community of Artists, New York NY

Smith, Paul, *VPres,* Louis Comfort Tiffany Foundation, New York NY

Smith, Paul J, *Dir,* American Craft Council Museum, New York NY

Smith, Peter, *Head Publications & Communications,* National Gallery of Canada, Ottawa ON

Smith, Philip Oliver, *Prof Emeritus,* Rice University, Dept of Art and Art History, Houston TX (S)

Smith, R, *Asst Dir,* University Club Library, New York NY

Smith, Raychelle R, *Museum Attendant,* Kalamunda Museum of Western Art, Somers MT

Smith, Richard, *Secy,* Floyd County Museum, New Albany IN

Smith, Rita, *Instr,* Studio School of Art and Design, Philadelphia PA (S)

Smith, Robert, *Pres,* Industrial Designers Society of America, McLean VA

Smith, Robert, *Chairperson Design Dept,* Washington University, School of Fine Arts, Saint Louis MO (S)

Smith, Robert L, *Dir,* Los Angeles Institute of Contemporary Art, Los Angeles CA

Smith, Rockwell L, *Secy,* Kalamunda Museum of Western Art, Somers MT

Smith, Sharon, *Graduate Advisor,* California State University, Chico, Art Dept, Chico CA (S)

Smith, Sharon, *Instr,* California State University, Chico, Art Dept, Chico CA (S)

Smith, Sherry, *Dir Public Information,* Laguna Gloria Art Museum, Austin TX

Smith, Shirley, *Pres Manitoba Historical Society,* Manitoba Historical Society, Dalnavert - MacDonald House Museum, Winnipeg MB

Smith, Stephen L, *Framer,* Kalamunda Museum of Western Art, Somers MT

Smith, Stuart W, *Managing Dir,* Salvador Dali Foundation Museum, Saint Petersburg FL

Smith, Susan, *Instructor,* Castleton State College, Art Dept, Castleton VT (S)

Smith, Susan, *Adjunct Prof,* University of Saint Thomas, Art Dept, Houston TX (S)

Smith, Terrell, *Development,* Marion Koogler McNay Art Museum, San Antonio TX

Smith, Thomas G, *Dir of Environmental Education Dept,* Berkshire Museum, Pittsfield MA

Smith, T Michael, *Sr Registrar,* Church of Jesus Christ of Latter-Day Saints, Museum of Church History and Art, Salt Lake City UT

Smith, Tobi, *Financial Dir,* Los Angeles Institute of Contemporary Art, Los Angeles CA

Smith, Valerie, *Cur,* Committee for the Visual Arts, Inc, New York NY

Smith, Vera S, *Secy,* Sheldon Museum and Cultural Center, Haines AK

Smith, Walter, *Prof,* Pierce College, Art Dept, Woodland Hills CA (S)

Smith, W I, *Dominion Archivist,* Public Archives of Canada, Picture Division, Ottawa ON

Smith, Willard, *Instructor,* College of DuPage, Humanities Division, Glen Ellyn IL (S)

Smith, William, *Cur,* Historical Society of Bloomfield, Bloomfield NJ

Smith, William B, *Pres,* Fine Arts Center of Clinton, Clinton IL

Smith, Yvonne, *Interpretive Programs Asst,* Olana State Historic Site, Hudson NY

Smithers, Margaret, *Instructor,* Southwestern School of Art, Albuquerque NM (S)

Smith-Hurd, Diane, *Instructor,* Art Academy of Cincinnati, Cincinnati OH (S)

Smits, Kathy, *Secy,* Bergstrom Mahler Museum, Neenah WI

Smogor, Robert, *Registrar,* University of Notre Dame, Snite Museum of Art, Notre Dame IN

Smoot, Myrna, *Asst Dir Museum Programs,* Los Angeles County Museum of Art, Los Angeles CA

Smullin, Frank, *Instr,* Duke University, Dept of Art, Durham NC (S)

Smyder, Jean, *Gallery Hostess,* Pemaquid Group of Artists, Pemaquid Point ME

Smyrnios, Arleigh, *Instr,* Kalamazoo Valley Community College, Dept of Art, Kalamazoo MI (S)

Smyser, Mike, *Coordr & Assoc Prof,* Montgomery County Community College, Communicating Arts Dept, Blue Bell PA (S)

Smyth, David, *Lecturer,* Ithaca College, Fine Art Dept, Ithaca NY (S)

Smyth, Estelle, *Exec Secy,* William Bonifas Fine Art Center Gallery, Escanaba MI

Smyth, Frances, *Editor,* National Gallery of Art, Washington DC

Snead, Charles S, *VPres,* Phoenix Art Museum, Phoenix AZ

Sneddeker, Duane, *Cur Special Projects,* Missouri Historical Society, Saint Louis MO

Snell, Joseph W, *Exec Dir,* Kansas State Historial Society Museum, Topeka KS

Snell, Tommy, *Asst Dir,* Pinckney Brothers Museum, Orangeburg SC

Snellenberger, Earl, *Assoc Prof,* Indiana Central University, Fine Arts Dept, Indianapolis IN (S)

Snider, Jenny, *Adjunct Assoc Prof,* Columbia University, School of the Arts, Division of Painting & Sculpture, New York NY (S)

Sninsky, Anna Marie, *Exec Dir,* Associated Artists of Pittsburgh Arts and Crafts Center, Pittsburgh PA

Snoblin, Karl, *Registrar & Prepartor,* Northwestern University, Mary & Leigh Block Gallery, Evanston 1L

Snodgrass, John, *Treas,* Charles B Goddard Center for the Visual and Performing Arts, Ardmore OK

Snook, Cloyde E, *Prof,* Adams State College, Dept of Visual Arts, Alamosa CO (S)

Snooks, A Nancy, *Asst Prof,* Pierce College, Art Dept, Woodland Hills CA (S)

Snow, Maryly, *Librn,* University of California, Architectural Slide Library, Berkeley CA

Snow, N Nicoll, *Pres,* Lockwood-Mathews Mansion Museum, Norwalk CT

Snow, V Douglas, *Prof,* University of Utah, Art Dept, Salt Lake City UT (S)

Snowden, Pennell, *Cur,* Muchnic Foundation and Atchison Art Association, Muchnic Gallery, Atchison KS

Snowden, Sylvia, *Coordr,* Washington Women's Arts Center, Washington DC

Snydacker, Daniel, *Exec Dir,* Newport Historical Society, Newport RI

Snyder, Barry, *Prof,* Fairmont State College, Art Dept, Fairmont WV (S)

Snyder, Dean, *Instr,* Oxbow Center for the Arts, Saugatuck MI (S)

Snyder, Dean, *General Design,* California College of Arts and Crafts, Oakland CA (S)

Snyder, George E, *Business Mgr,* Cincinnati Art Museum, Cincinnati OH

Snyder, James E, *Prof,* Bryn Mawr College, Dept of the History of Art, Bryn Mawr PA (S)

Snyder, Jill, *Admin Asst,* Solomon R Guggenheim Museum, New York NY

Snyder, Lawrence H, *VPres Operations,* Philadelphia Museum of Art, Philadelphia PA

Snyder, Lois, *Instr,* Utah Technical College at Salt Lake, Commercial Art Dept, Salt Lake City UT (S)

Snyder, Mary, *Asst Dir,* Nova Scotia College of Art and Design, Library, Halifax NS

Snyder, Roberta, *Cur,* Muttart Gallery Associates, Calgary AB

Sobczak, J Austin, *Treas,* Jesse Besser Museum, Alpena MI

Sobieszek, Robert, *Dir Photography Coll,* International Museum of Photography at George Eastman House, Rochester NY

Sobocinski, Stanley, *Assoc Prof,* Dean Junior College, Visual and Performing Art Dept, Franklin MA (S)

Sobol, Judith E, *Dir,* Westbrook College, Joan Whitney Payson Gallery of Art, Portland ME

Sobotik, Kent, *Chief Cur,* Dayton Art Institute, Dayton OH

Sobre, Judith, *Assoc Prof,* University of Texas at San Antonio, Division of Art and Design, San Antonio TX (S)

Socha, Dan, *In Charge Printmaking,* University of Illinois, Urbana-Champaign, School of Art and Design, Champaign IL (S)

Sochynsky, Rostyslaw, *Chmn of Membership Committee,* Ukrainian Institute of America, Inc, New York NY

Socolow, Edith, *Assoc Prof,* Harrisburg Area Community College, Division of Communication and the Arts, Harrisburg PA (S)

Soderlund, Jean R, *Cur Peace Collection,* Swarthmore College, Friends Historical Library, Swarthmore PA

Soderman-Olson, Marcie, *Asst Cur Education,* Minnesota Museum of Art, Saint Paul MN

Sodervick, Bruce, *Assoc Prof,* Rochester Institute of Technology, School of Art and Design, Rochester NY (S)

Soeten, Harlan, *Cur,* National Maritime Museum, San Francisco CA

Sokol, David, *Chmn Dept Hist of Architecture & Art,* University of Illinois at Chicago, College of Architecture, Art and Urban Planning, Chicago IL (S)

Sokol, David M, *Cur,* Terra Museum of American Art, Evanston IL

Sokolow, Isobel Folb, *VPres,* New York Artists Equity Association, Inc, New York NY

Sokolowski, Thomas W, *Chief Cur,* Chrysler Museum, Norfolk VA

Solem, John, *Assoc Prof,* California Lutheran College, Art Dept, Thousand Oaks CA (S)

Soleri, Paolo, *Pres,* Cosanti Foundation, Scottsdale AZ

Solimene, Alfonse, *Instr,* New York Academy of Art, New York NY (S)

Solkin, David H, *Asst Prof,* University of British Columbia, Dept of Fine Arts, Vancouver BC (S)

Solley, Thomas T, *Dir,* Indiana University, Art Museum, Bloomington IN

Sollins, Susan, *Exec Dir,* Independent Curators Incorporated, New York NY

Solmssen, Peter, *Pres,* Philadelphia College of Art, Philadelphia PA

Solmssen, Peter, *Pres,* Philadelphia College of Art, Philadelphia PA (S)

Solomon, Bernard, *Assoc Prof,* Georgia Southern College, Dept of Art, Statesboro GA (S)

Solomon, Laurence H, *Dir,* New Bedford Free Public Library, Art Dept, New Bedford MA

Solot, E V, *Faculty,* Western Illinois University, College of Fine Arts, Macomb IL (S)

Soloway, Lynn, *Vis Prof,* Nebraska Wesleyan University, Art Dept, Lincoln NE (S)

Soloway, Reta, *Pres,* Allied Artists of America, Inc, New York NY

Soltan, Joanna, *Cur,* Hammond Castle Museum, Gloucester MA

Soluri, Michael, *Asst Prof,* Rochester Institute of Technology, School of Photographic Arts & Sciences, Rochester NY (S)

Solvick, Shirley, *Chief Fine Arts Department,* Detroit Public Library, Fine Arts Dept, Detroit MI

Somers, Brian, *Instructor,* Claremore College, Art Dept, Claremore OK (S)

Somers, David, *Registrar,* Art Gallery of Hamilton, Hamilton ON

Somerville, Romaine S, *Dir,* Maryland Historical Society Museum, Baltimore MD

Sommer, Frank H, *Head, Library Div,* Winterthur Museum and Gardens, Library, Winterthur DE

Sommerfeld, John F, *Instructor,* Lamar University, Art Dept, Beaumont TX (S)

Somogyi, George J, *Chmn & Prof,* Lakeland Community College, Visual Arts Dept, Mentor OH (S)

Somoza, Maria E, *Dir Fine Arts,* Institute of Puerto Rican Culture, Escuela de Artes Plasticas, San Juan PR (S)

Sonday, Milton, *Cur Textiles,* Cooper-Hewitt Museum, Smithsonian Institution, New York NY

Sonneborn, Sydney R, *Head Dept,* Miles Community College, Dept of Fine Arts and Humanities, Miles City MT (S)

Sonnhalter, Betty, *Secy,* United States Figure Skating Hall of Fame and Museum, Colorado Springs CO

Soos, David, *Instr,* Arkansas Arts Center, Little Rock AR (S)

Soper, Harlan, *Bd of Trustees,* Sioux City Art Center, Sioux City IA

Sopher, Vicki, *Asst Dir,* Decatur House, Washington DC

Sopocko, P, *Instructor,* Golden West College, Arts, Humanities and Social Sciences Institute, Huntington Beach CA (S)

Sorbie, John, *Prof,* Colorado State University, Dept of Art, Fort Collins CO (S)

Soreff, Stephen, *Assoc Prof,* C W Post Center of Long Island University, School of the Arts, Greenvale NY (S)

Sorento, Bruno, *Assoc Prof,* Community College of Allegheny County, Boyce Campus, Art Dept, Monroeville PA (S)

Sorge, Walter, *Prof,* Eastern Illinois University, School of Fine Arts, Charleston IL (S)

Soriano, Doris, *Assoc Dir Adult Servs,* Long Beach Public Library, Long Beach CA

Soriano, Irene, *Cur Applied Arts,* Hispanic Society of America, Museum, New York NY

Sorokow, Janice, *Mgr,* Museum of Fine Arts, Dept of Photographic Services, Boston MA

Sorrells, Harley R, *Cur,* Chief Plenty Coups State Monument Museum, Pryor MT

Soto, Jorge, *Co-Dean of Fine Arts School,* El Museo del Barrio, New York NY

Soucy, Paul, *Dir & Cur,* Galerie Restigouche Gallery, Campbellton NB

Souder, Jim, *Instr,* Studio School of Art and Design, Philadelphia PA (S)

Soule, Robert, *Supt,* Yale University, Art Gallery, New Haven CT

Soules, Marilynn, *Cur,* Dundurn Castle, Hamilton ON

Sourakli, Judy, *Registrar,* University of Washington, Henry Art Gallery, Seattle WA

Sours, Nicole, *Exec Dir,* Oatlands of the National Trust, Inc, Leesburg VA

Sousa, Gene, *Cur,* Millhouse-Bundy Performing & Fine Arts Center, Waitsfield VT

Soussloff, Catherine, *Instructor,* Virginia Tech, Dept of Art, Blacksburg VA (S)

Souter, David H, *VPres,* New Hampshire Historical Society, Concord NH

Southall, Thomas, *Cur Photography,* University of Kansas, Spencer Museum of Art, Lawrence KS

Southall, Thomas, *Assoc Prof,* University of Kansas, Kress Foundation Dept of Art History, Lawrence KS (S)

Southam, Thomas, *Cur of the Coll,* University of Utah, Utah Museum of Fine Arts, Salt Lake City UT

Southard, Edna, *Educ Coordr,* Miami University Art Museum, Oxford OH

Southerland, Louise, *Dolls & Toys,* Luna County Historical Society, Inc, Deming Luna Mimbres Museum, Deming NM

Southerland, Ted, *Coordr,* Luna County Historical Society, Inc, Deming Luna Mimbres Museum, Deming NM

Southworth, Miles F, *Prof,* Rochester Institute of Technology, School of Printing, Rochester NY (S)

Sovik, Edward, *Prof,* Saint Olaf College, Art Dept, Northfield MN (S)

Sowder, Diane, *Instr,* Huntington College, Art Dept, Huntington IN (S)

Spaeth, Eloise, *First VChmn,* Guild Hall of East Hampton, Inc, Museum Section, East Hampton NY

Spaeth, Otto L, *Chmn,* Archives of American Art, Smithsonian Institution, New York NY

Spaid, Gregory P, *Asst Prof,* Kenyon College, Art Dept, Gambier OH (S)

Spakes, Larry, *Artist in Res,* Phillips County Community College, Dept of English and Fine Arts, Helena AR (S)

Spalding, Jeffrey, *Asst Prof,* University of Lethbridge, Dept of Art, Lethbridge AB (S)

Spang, Joseph P, *Cur,* Historic Deerfield Inc, Deerfield MA

Spangenberg, Kristin L, *Cur Prints, Drawings & Photographs,* Cincinnati Art Museum, Cincinnati OH

Sparacino, Michael, *Admin Personnel,* Metropolitan Museum of Art, New York NY

Sparling, Mary, *Dir Art Gallery,* Mount Saint Vincent University, Art Gallery, Halifax NS

Sparshott, Francis, *Pres,* American Society for Aesthetics, Greenvale NY

Spaugh, Sara, *Instr,* Coos Art Museum, Coos Bay OR (S)

Spaulding, Warren, *Secy,* Lincoln County Cultural and Historical Association, Maine Art Gallery, Old Academy, Wiscasset ME

Spaull, Malcolm, *Asst Prof,* Rochester Institute of Technology, School of Photographic Arts & Sciences, Rochester NY (S)

Spear, Judith D, *Dir McLean County Arts Center,* McLean County Art Association, Arts Center, Bloomington IL

Spear, Peggy, *Development Officer,* Pacific - Asia Museum, Pasadena CA

Spear, Richard, *Prof,* Oberlin College, Dept of Art, Oberlin OH (S)

Speare, William E, *Cur Science & Natural History & Planetarium Dir,* Everhart Museum of Natural History, Science and Art, Scranton PA

Spector, Buzz, *VPres,* N.A.M.E. Gallery, Chicago IL

Spector, Henry, *Promotion & Publicity Specialist,* Museum of the Philadelphia Civic Center, Philadelphia PA

Spector, Howard, *Exec Dir,* Los Angeles Center For Photographic Studies, Los Angeles CA

Spector, Jack J, *Prof,* Rutgers, the State University of New Jersey, Graduate Program in Art History, New Brunswick NJ (S)

Speece, Vera, *Chairperson Dept,* Cooke County College, Fine Arts Dept, Gainesville TX (S)

Speer, Mary, *Education Coordr,* McAllen International Museum, McAllen TX

Speerbrecker, Greta, *Treasurer,* Revelstoke Art Group, Revelstoke BC

Speier, Robert W, *Chmn,* Whittier College, Dept of Art, Whittier CA (S)

Speight, Jerry, *Asst Prof,* Murray State University, Art Dept, Murray KY (S)

Speirs, W B, *Asst Provincial Archivist,* Department of Culture, Government of the Province of Alberta, Provincial Archives of Alberta, Edmonton AB

Speller, Randall, *Documentalist,* Art Gallery of Ontario, Edward P Taylor Reference Library, Toronto ON

Spence, Joseph, *Faculty,* University of North Carolina-Charlotte, Creative Arts Dept, Charlotte NC (S)

Spence, Karen, *Library Asst (Slides),* University of California, Art Dept Library, Davis CA

Spencer, Anne, *Cur Ethnology,* Newark Museum, Newark NJ

Spencer, Avery, *Mem Secy,* Berkshire Museum, Pittsfield MA

Spencer, Bea, *Secy,* Owatonna Arts Center, Owatonna MN

Spencer, Harriet S, *Pres,* Walker Art Center, Minneapolis MN

Spencer, Helen, *Tech Serv Head,* Topeka Public Library, Fine Arts Dept & Gallery of Fine Arts, Topeka KS

Spencer, Howard D, *Cur of Coll-Exhib,* Wichita Art Museum, Wichita KS

Spencer, John M, *Bldg Mgr,* Owatonna Arts Center, Owatonna MN

Spencer, John R, *Chmn Dept,* Duke University, Dept of Art, Durham NC (S)

Spencer, Patricia, *Lectr,* University of Wisconsin-Superior, Programs in the Visual Arts, Superior WI (S)

Spencer, R, *VChmn,* Macdonald Stewart Art Centre, Guelph ON

Spencer, Stephanie, *Asst Prof,* Indiana University at South Bend, Fine Arts Dept, South Bend IN (S)

Spencer, Stewart, *Secy,* Fort Wayne Fine Arts Foundation, Inc, Fort Wayne IN

Spencer, Ted, *Cur Exhibits,* National Baseball Hall of Fame and Museum, Inc, Art Collection, Cooperstown NY

Spengler, Peg, *Pres,* North Shore Art League, Winnetka IL

Spengler, Peg, *Pres,* North Shore Art League, Winnetka IL (S)

Spenser, Phyllis, *Cur Museum Coll,* Traphagen School of Fashion, Museum Collection, New York NY

Speraw, James A, *Museum Technician,* Fort George G Meade Museum, Fort Meade MD

Sperber, Barbara, *Administrator,* Queens Museum, Flushing NY

Sperling, Maxine, *Instr,* Wayne Art Center, Wayne PA (S)

Sperr, Portia, *Executive Dir,* Please Touch Museum, Philadelphia PA

Sperry, James, *Head Div,* Huron College, Art Dept, Huron SD (S)

Speyer, A James, *Cur 20th Century Painting & Sculpture,* Art Institute of Chicago, Chicago IL

Spielman, Martha, *Instructor,* Claremore College, Art Dept, Claremore OK (S)

Spigel, Bernice, *Dir,* Creative Arts Guild, Dalton GA

Spillman, Jane Shadel, *Cur American Glass,* Corning Museum of Glass, Corning NY

Spinar, Melvin, *Assoc Prof,* South Dakota State University, Dept of Visual Arts, Brookings SD (S)

Spindler, Erica, *Instructor,* Southeastern Louisiana University, Dept of Visual Arts, Hammond LA (S)

Spinski, Victor, *Coordr Ceramics,* University of Delaware, Dept of Art, Newark DE (S)

Spiro, Stephen B, *Cur,* University of Notre Dame, Snite Museum of Art, Notre Dame IN

Spitzer, Laura, *Fiscal Asst,* Institute for Art & Urban Resources, Project Studios One, Long Island City NY

Spohn, Charles L, *Dean School Fine Arts,* Miami University, Art Dept, Oxford OH (S)

Sponberg, Lars, *Prof,* North Park College, Art Dept, Chicago IL (S)

Sponenberg, Susan, *Coordr,* Luzerne County Community College, Commercial Art Dept, Nanticoke PA (S)

Sponenborgh, Mark, *Chmn,* Oregon State University, Fairbanks Gallery, Corvallis OR

Sponenburgh, Mark, *Chmn,* Oregon State University, Dept of Art, Corvallis OR (S)

Spoo, Corinne H, *Librn,* Paine Art Center and Arboretum, George P Nevitt Library, Oshkosh WI

Spooner, Dave, *Chmn,* Mount Hood Community College, Art Dept, Gresham OR (S)

Sporre, Dennis J, *Chmn,* University of North Carolina at Wilmington, Dept of Creative Arts - Division of Art, Wilmington NC (S)

Spradlin, Doug, *Assoc Prof,* University of Wisconsin-Superior, Programs in the Visual Arts, Superior WI (S)

Sprague, Mary, *Instructor,* Saint Louis Community College at Meramec, Art Dept, Saint Louis MO (S)

Sprague, Norman, *Pres,* Southwest Museum, Los Angeles CA

Spratlin, Samuel A, *Financial Secy,* Berkshire Museum, Pittsfield MA

Spratt, Frederick, *Chmn,* San Jose State University, Art Dept, San Jose CA (S)

Spriggs, Betty, *Talking Books for the Blind,* Wichita Public Library, Wichita KS

Spring, Ernest, *First VPres,* Toledo Artists' Club, Toledo OH

Springer, Frank, *Secy,* National Cartoonists Society, Brooklyn NY

Springer-Roberts, Lynn, *Cur European Decorative Arts,* Art Institute of Chicago, Chicago IL

Springfield, Roschelle, *Programs Coordr,* Lufkin Historical and Creative Arts Center, Lufkin TX

Springman, Charles, *Development Officer,* The American Federation of Arts, New York NY

Spriri, John, *Asst Prof,* Lakeland Community College, Visual Arts Dept, Mentor OH (S)

Spritz, Kenneth P, *Dir External Relations,* Hood Museum of Art, Hanover NH

Sproat, John G, *Pres,* Columbia Museums of Art and Science, Columbia SC

Spurgin, John E, *Chmn,* Mankato State University, Art Dept, Mankato MN (S)

Spurling, Norine, *Recording Secy,* Buffalo Society of Artists, Williamsville NY

Squier, Jack L, *Prof,* Cornell University, Dept of Art, Ithaca NY (S)

Squires, William, *Art Appreciation,* University of Georgia, Franklin College of Arts and Sciences, Dept of Art, Athens GA (S)

Staats, Valerie, *Dir Enterprise & Marketing,* Native American Center for the Living Arts, Niagara Falls NY

Stack, Danial M, *Dean,* International Fine Arts College, Miami FL (S)

Stackhouse, Robert, *Chmn Fine Arts,* Corcoran School of Art, Washington DC (S)

Stacy, Betty, *Librn,* Virginia Museum of Fine Arts, Library, Richmond VA

Staebler, Tom, *VPres & Art Dir,* Playboy Enterprises, Inc, Chicago IL

Staffne, Dennis, *Asst Prof,* Northern Michigan University, Dept of Art and Design, Marquette MI (S)

Stafford, Beverly B, *Librn,* Oregon School of Arts and Crafts, Library, Portland OR

Stafford, F Eugene, *Instructor,* Guilford Technical Community College, Commercial Art Dept, Jamestown NC (S)

Stagg, Deborah, *Tech Servs,* Philadelphia College of Art, Library, Philadelphia PA

Staggs, Marsi, *Pub Relations Dir,* National Cowboy Hall of Fame and Western Heritage Center, Oklahoma City OK

Stahl, Judith R, *Art Dir,* Louisiana State University, Union Art Gallery, Baton Rouge LA

Stair, David, *Treas,* Dulin Gallery of Art, Knoxville TN

Stair, L Caesar, *2nd VChmn,* Dulin Gallery of Art, Knoxville TN

Staiti, Paul J, *Asst Prof,* Mount Holyoke College, Art Dept, South Hadley MA (S)

Staley, Allen, *Dir Grad Studies,* Columbia University, Dept of Art History and Archaeology, New York NY (S)

Staley, Early, *Prof,* University of Saint Thomas, Art Dept, Houston TX (S)

Stallings, Robert L, *Chmn,* Tryon Palace Restoration Complex, New Bern NC

Stalnaker, Budd, *Prof,* Indiana University, Bloomington, School of Fine Arts, Bloomington IN (S)

Stalsworth, Lee, *Chief Photography,* Hirshhorn Museum and Sculpture Garden, Washington DC

Stalzer, Betsy, *Pub Relations,* Salvador Dali Foundation Museum, Saint Petersburg FL

Stambaugh, Rex, *Asst Prof,* Winthrop College, Dept of Art, Rock Hill SC (S)

Stamm, Theresa, *Instr,* Rosemont College, Division of the Arts, Rosemont PA (S)

Stamper, John, *Chmn,* Wayland Baptist University, Dept of Art, Plainview TX (S)

Stampfle, Felice, *Cur Drawings and Prints,* Pierpont Morgan Library, New York NY

Stanczak, Julian, *Prof,* Cleveland Institute of Art, Cleveland OH (S)

Stanczak, Lisa, *Auditorium Mgr & Librn,* University of Notre Dame, Snite Museum of Art, Notre Dame IN

Standley, Ray, *Treas,* Beverly Historical Society, Cabot, Hale and Balch House Museums, Beverly MA

Standring, Timothy, *Asst Prof,* Loyola University of Chicago, Fine Arts Dept, Chicago IL (S)

Stanfill, Sarah, *Chmn,* Liberty Hall Museum, Orlando Brown House, Frankfort KY

Stanis, Elaine-Carol, *Cur of Children's Literature,* Rutgers University, Jane Voorhees Zimmerli Art Museum, New Brunswick NJ

Stanislawski, Barbara, *Coll Mgr,* School of American Research, Library, Santa Fe NM

Stankiewicz, Mary Ann, *Asst Prof,* University of Maine, Art Dept, Orono ME (S)

Stanland, Janice, *Museum Registrar,* Pennsylvania Academy of the Fine Arts, Galleries, Philadelphia PA

Stanley, David, *Asst Prof,* University of Florida, Dept of Art, Gainesville FL (S)

Stanley, Janet L, *Librn,* National Museum of African Art, Branch Library, Washington DC

Stanley, John G, *Chmn Div Fine Arts & Humanities,* Florida Junior College at Jacksonville, South Campus, Art Dept, Jacksonville FL (S)

Stanley, Keith, *Cur Classical Coll,* Duke University Union Galleries, Durham NC

Stanley, Louise, *Vis Artist,* University of North Carolina at Chapel Hill, Art Dept, Chapel Hill NC (S)

Stanley, Robert A, *Prof & Discipline Coordr,* Oakton Community College, Art & Architecture Dept, Des Plains IL (S)

Stanley, Talcott, *Pres,* Hill-Stead Museum, Farmington CT

Stannard, Doreen, *Admin Asst,* Estevan National Exhibition Centre Inc, Estevan SK

Stansbury, George, *Chmn,* University of Mary Hardin-Baylor, Dept of Fine Arts, Belton TX (S)

Stanske, N, *Faculty,* Stephens College, Art Dept, Columbia MO (S)

Stanton, Frank, *Prof,* Saint Louis Community College at Florissant Valley, Dept of Art, Ferguson MO (S)

Staples, Wayne, *Assoc Cur,* Edmonton Art Gallery, Edmonton AB

Stapp, William F, *Cur Photographs,* National Portrait Gallery, Washington DC

Starasta, Betty J, *Faculty,* Spoon River College, Art Dept, Canton IL (S)

Starchild, Adam, *Chmn,* Confederation of American Indians, Council of American Indian Artists, New York NY

Stark, Alan, *Prof,* Treasure Valley Community College, Art Dept, Ontario OR (S)

Stark, David, *Cur of Education,* Munson-Williams-Proctor Institute, Museum of Art, Utica NY

Stark, J W, *Dir Art Exhib and Special Asst to the Pres for Development of Cultural Programs,* Texas A & M University, University Art Exhibits, College Station TX

Stark, Nelda C, *Chmn,* Stark Museum of Art, Orange TX

Stark, Robert, *Asst Dir,* Oregon Historical Society, Portland OR

Starks, Linda, *Secy,* Art Institute of Chicago, Chicago IL

Starn, Wendy, *Cur Educ,* Central Louisiana Art Association, Alexandria Museum Visual Art Center, Alexandria LA

Starner, Donald, *Bus Mgr,* Stan Hywet Hall Foundation, Inc, Akron OH

Starobin, Leslie, *Instr,* Danforth Museum School, Framingham MA (S)

Starr, Daniel, *Assoc Librn Cataloguing,* Museum of Modern Art, Library, New York NY

Starr, Kathy, *Education,* Massillon Museum, Massillon OH

Starr, Kenneth, *Pres,* American Association of Museums, Washington DC

Starr, Lorin, *Membership,* California Historical Society, San Francisco CA

Stars, W K, *Dir,* Duke University Union Galleries, Durham NC

Stars, W K, *Assoc Prof,* Duke University, Dept of Art, Durham NC (S)

Stasik, Andrew, *Dir,* Pratt Institute, Pratt Manhattan Center Gallery, New York NY

Statlander, Raymond, *Asst Prof,* Jersey City State College, Art Dept, Jersey City NJ (S)

Stauder, M Stephanie, *Instr,* Edgewood College, Art Dept, Madison WI (S)

Stauder, M Stephanie, *Art Department Chmn,* Edgewood College, DeRicci Gallery, Madison WI

Stauffacher, Bonnie, *Asst Cur Fine Arts,* Sunrise Foundation, Inc, Sunrise Museums, Charleston WV

Stauffer, Judith M, *Artistic Dir,* Lemoyne Center for the Visual Arts, Tallahassee FL

Stave, James K, *Exhibition Coordr,* The American Federation of Arts, New York NY

Staven, Leland, *Cur,* Agnes Scott College, Dalton Gallery, Decatur GA

Stavropoulos, Theo, *Assoc Prof,* Herbert H Lehman College, Art Dept, Bronx NY (S)

Stayton, Kevin, *Assoc Cur Decorative Arts,* Brooklyn Museum, Brooklyn NY

Steadman, Clinton, *Treas,* Rochester Historical Society, Rochester NY

Steadman, Dan, *Chairperson Division Language & Arts,* Nebraska Western College, Division of Language and Arts, Scottsbluff NE (S)

Steadman, David W, *Dir,* Chrysler Museum, Norfolk VA

Steadman, Thomas, *Asst Prof,* Georgia Southern College, Dept of Art, Statesboro GA (S)

Steakley, Douglas, *Treas,* Society of North American Goldsmiths, Milwaukee WI

Steans, Joan, *Asst Prof,* Jersey City State College, Art Dept, Jersey City NJ (S)

Stearus, Robert, *Dir Performing Arts,* Walker Art Center, Minneapolis MN

Stebbins, Jackie, *Pres,* Lansing Art Gallery, Lansing MI

Stebbins, James F, *Chmn Bd,* Fraunces Tavern Museum, New York NY

Stebbins, Joan, *Secy & Treas,* Western Canada Art Association Inc, Southern Alberta Art Gallery, Lethbridge AB

Stebbins, Joan, *Gallery Asst,* Southern Alberta Art Gallery, Lethbridge AB

Stebbins, Theodore, *Cur American Photography,* Museum of Fine Arts, Boston MA

Stebinger, Patricia, *Instructor,* Marylhurst College, Art Dept, Marylhurst OR (S)

Stedman, Lewis, *Cur Arts & Crafts,* Heritage Plantation of Sandwich, Sandwich MA

Steed, Mary Ann, *Business Mgr,* Sunrise Foundation, Inc, Sunrise Museums, Charleston WV

Steel, Joan, *Librn,* Mendel Art Gallery and Civic Conservatory, Reference Library, Saskatoon SK

Steel, LaVar, *Dir,* College of Southern Idaho, Art Gallery, Twin Falls ID

Steel, LaVar, *Chmn,* College of Southern Idaho, Art Dept, Twin Falls ID (S)

Steel, Virginia Oberlin, *Dir,* Rutgers University, Stedman Art Gallery, Camden NJ

Steele, Craig, *Financial Aid,* Rocky Mountain School of Art, Denver CO (S)

Steele, John, *Assoc Prof,* East Tennessee State University, Fine Arts Dept, Johnson City TN (S)

Steele, Lina, *Cur,* National Gallery of Art, Index of American Design, Washington DC

Steele, Lisa, *Student Servs,* Rocky Mountain School of Art, Denver CO (S)

Steele, Philip J, *Dir,* Rocky Mountain School of Art, Denver CO (S)

Steele, Ray W, *Dir,* C M Russell Museum, Great Falls MT

Steele, Steven, *Asst Dir,* Rocky Mountain School of Art, Denver CO (S)

Steenberg, Gerald W, *Dir Library,* Saint Paul Public Library, Art & Music Dept, Saint Paul MN

Steensland, Ronald, *Dir,* Lexington Public Library, Skydome Gallery, Lexington KY

Stefanko, Micheal, *Chmn Arts Dept,* Community College of Allegheny County, Fine Arts Dept, West Mifflin PA (S)

Steffan, Pamela, *Instructor,* Mount Mary College, Art Dept, Milwaukee WI (S)

Steffens, Dean, *Treas,* Octagon Center for the Arts, Ames IA

Steffens, Louise, *Exec Asst,* The Phillips Collection, Washington DC

Stegeman, Charles, *Prof,* Haverford College, Fine Arts Dept, Haverford PA (S)

Steger, Charles W, *Dean,* Virginia Polytechnic Institute and State University, Architecture Library, Blacksburg VA

Stegman, Richard, *Regional Service Librn,* Clark County Library District, Las Vegas NV

Stegner, George A, *Fine Arts Chmn,* Queens College, Art Dept, Charlotte NC (S)

Steigleder, Linda, *Registrar,* University of Georgia, Georgia Museum of Art, Athens GA

Stein, Claire A, *Executive Dir,* National Sculpture Society, New York NY

Stein, Edwin E, *Dir,* University of Hartford, Joseloff Gallery, West Hartford CT

Stein, Fritz, *Pres,* Mystic Art Association, Inc, Mystic CT

Stein, Judith, *Asst Cur,* Pennsylvania Academy of the Fine Arts, Galleries, Philadelphia PA

Stein, Margaret, *Instructor,* Greenfield Community College, Art Dept, Greenfield MA (S)

Stein, Michael, *Faculty,* Housatonic Community College, Art Dept, Bridgeport CT (S)

Stein, Paul, *Pres,* Summit Art Center, Inc, Summit NJ

Stein, Paul, *Secy,* Ann Arbor Art Association, Ann Arbor MI

Stein, Ray, *Cur Science,* New Jersey State Museum, Trenton NJ

Stein, Susan R, *Dir,* American Institute of Architects Foundation, Washington DC

Stein, Virginia, *Librn,* Eastern Michigan University, Art Dept Book Collection, Ypsilanti MI

Steinberg, Linda, *Instr,* University of Judaism, Dept of Continuing Education, Los Angeles CA (S)

Steinberg, Ronald M, *Prof,* Rhode Island College, Art Dept, Providence RI (S)

Steiner, Chris, *Cur Education,* Beaumont Art Museum, Beaumont TX

Steiner, Sally, *Cur of Education,* California State University, Long Beach, University Art Museum, Long Beach CA

Steiner, Suzanne, *Assoc Chmn,* Carlow College, Art Dept, Pittsburgh PA (S)

Steinfeldt, Cecilia, *Sr Cur,* San Antonio Museum Association, Inc, San Antonio Museum of Art, San Antonio TX

Steinheimer, Dana John, *Chmn,* San Jacinto College North, Art Dept, Houston TX (S)

Steinschulte, Thilo, *VPres,* Central Louisiana Art Association, Alexandria Museum Visual Art Center, Alexandria LA

Steinway, Kate, *Cur Prints & Photogs,* Connecticut Historical Society, Hartford CT

Steiro, Carol, *Cur Coll,* Museum of New Mexico, Museum of International Folk Art, Santa Fe NM

Steketee, Craig, *Chmn Dept,* Biola University, Art Dept, La Mirada CA (S)

Stelfox, Evearad, *Dir,* Dacotah Prairie Museum, Lamont Gallery, Aberdeen SD

Stelzer, Stuart, *Library Dir,* College of the Ozarks Library, Clarksville AR

Steme, Larry M, *Asst Prof,* Washington and Lee University, Dept of Fine Arts, Lexington VA (S)

Stensrude, Richard J, *Instr,* Clark College, Art Dept, Vancouver WA (S)

Stephan, Joanne, *Record Secy,* Berks Art Alliance, Reading PA

Stephanian, C, *Media Dir,* San Francisco Art Institute, Anne Bremer Memorial Library, San Francisco CA

Stephanic, Jeffrey L, *Asst Prof,* George Washington University, Dept of Art, Washington DC (S)

Stephen, Barbara, *Assoc Dir,* Royal Ontario Museum, Toronto ON

Stephen, Francis, *Prof,* Texas Tech University, Dept of Art, Lubbock TX (S)

Stephens, Marjorie, *Registrar,* Brooklyn Museum Art School, Brooklyn NY (S)

Stephens, Michael, *Coordr,* Art Research Center, Kansas City MO

Stephens, Michael, *Cur,* Millicent Rogers Museum, Taos NM

Stephens, Press, *Instructor,* Central Wyoming College, Art Center, Riverton WY (S)

Stephens, Robert, *Instr,* John C Calhoun State Community College, Art Dept, Decatur AL (S)

Stephens, William B, *Chmn,* University of Texas at Tyler, Dept of Art, Tyler TX (S)

Stephens-Koesters, Elizabeth, *Instructor,* Roanoke College, Art Dept, Salem VA (S)

Stephenson, Ann, *Dean Humanities,* Southwestern College, Art Dept, Chula Vista CA

Stephenson, Christie, *Bibliographer,* University of Virginia, Fiske Kimball Fine Arts Library, Charlottesville VA

Stephenson, Robert E, *Librn,* Virginia Polytechnic Institute and State University, Architecture Library, Blacksburg VA

Stepney, P S, *Asst Dir Natural History,* Department of Culture, Government of the Province of Alberta, Provincial Museum of Alberta, Edmonton AB

Sterba, Lynn, *Asst,* University of Houston, Franzheim Architecture Library, Houston TX

Sterling, Cary, *Dir,* Ojai Valley Art Center, Ojai CA

Sterling, William H, *Chmn,* Wilkes College, Dept of Art, Wilkes-Barre PA (S)

Stern, Ellen, *Registrar,* Southeast Arkansas Arts and Science Center, Pine Bluff AR

Stern, Evelyn, *Exec Dir,* Society for Folk Arts Preservation, Inc, New York NY

Stern, M, *Collection Development,* State University of New York at Buffalo, Lockwood Memorial Library, Buffalo NY

Sternal, Thomas, *Chairperson,* Winona State University, Art Dept, Winona MN (S)

Sternberg, Harry, *Instructor,* University of Southern California, Idyllwild School of Music and the Arts, Idyllwild CA (S)

Sterrenburg, Joan, *Prof,* Indiana University, Bloomington, School of Fine Arts, Bloomington IN (S)

Sterritt, James, *Chairperson 3-D Dept,* Washington University, School of Fine Arts, Saint Louis MO (S)

Stetson, Daniel Everett, *Dir,* University of Northern Iowa, Gallery of Art, Cedar Falls IA

Stevanov, Zoran, *Dir of Exhib,* Fort Hays State University, Visual Arts Center, Hays KS

Stevanov, Zoran, *Assoc Prof,* Fort Hays State University, Dept of Art, Hays KS (S)

Steven, Dorothy, *Dir,* Monterey Public Library, Art & Architecture Dept, Monterey CA

Steven, Leland, *Assoc Prof,* Agnes Scott College, Dept of Art, Decatur GA (S)

Stevens, Carol, *Dir Information,* Maine Photographic Workshops, Rockport ME

Stevens, Craig, *Assoc Dir,* Maine Photographic Workshops, Rockport ME

Stevens, Edward, *Lecturer,* University of Wisconsin-Stout, Art Dept, Menomonie WI (S)

Stevens, Edward John, *Dir,* Newark School of Fine and Industrial Art, Newark NJ (S)

Stevens, Elizabeth, *Exec Dir,* Louis Comfort Tiffany Foundation, New York NY

Stevens, Faye, *Secy,* Phelps County Historical Society Museum, Holdrege NE

Stevens, George F, *Secy & Dir,* Oregon State University, Memorial Union Art Gallery, Corvallis OR

Stevens, Joan, *Chmn Academics,* Moore College of Art, Philadelphia PA (S)

Stevens, Joanne, *Treas,* DuPage Art League, Wheaton IL

Stevens, Linda, *Treas,* Orange County Center for Contemporary Art, Santa Ana CA

Stevens, Lynnette, *Periodical Librn,* LeMoyne College, Art Gallery, Syracuse NY

Stevens, Martha, *Cur of Education,* Alaska State Museum, Library, Juneau AK

Stevens, Roger L, *Chmn of the Board of Trustees,* John F Kennedy Center for the Performing Arts, Washington DC

Stevens, Tom, *Pres,* Art Association of Jacksonville, David Strawn Art Gallery, Jacksonville IL

Stevens, Wendell Barry, *Instr,* Alice Lloyd College, Art Dept, Pippa Passes KY (S)

Stevenson, Harold Ransom, *Head Dept,* Stevenson Academy of Traditional Painting, Sea Cliff NY (S)

Stevenson, James, *Dir Art School,* Fine Arts Museums of San Francisco, M H de Young Memorial Museum and California Palace of the Legion of Honor, San Francisco CA

Stevenson, Jim, *Dir,* De Young Museum Art School, San Francisco CA (S)

Stevenson, Joan, *Librn III & Head Department,* Yonkers Public Library, Fine Arts Dept, Yonkers NY

Stevenson, John R, *Pres,* National Gallery of Art, Washington DC

Stevenson, Lori, *Student Dir,* Thiel College, Sampson Art Gallery, Greenville PA

Stevenson, R L, *Fine Arts Coordr,* Savannah State College, Dept of Fine Arts, Savannah GA (S)

Stevenson, Ruth Carter, *Pres,* Amon Carter Museum, Fort Worth TX

Stevenson, S, *Instr,* David Thompson University Centre, Visual Arts Dept, Nelson BC (S)

Stewart, Albert, *Exec Dir,* Richmond Art Center, Richmond CA

Stewart, Ann, *Sr Citizens Coordr,* University of Utah, Utah Museum of Fine Arts, Salt Lake City UT

Stewart, Clara M, *Corresp Secy,* Rhode Island Watercolor Society, Pawtucket RI

Stewart, Dorothy, *VPres,* Florida Artist Group Inc, Venice FL

Stewart, Duncan E, *Dir,* University of West Florida, Art Gallery, Pensacola FL

Stewart, Duncan E, *Assoc Prof,* University of West Florida, Faculty of Art, Pensacola FL (S)

Stewart, F, *VPres Board of Dir,* Museum of Northern British Columbia, Prince Rupert Museum Art Gallery, Prince Rupert BC

Stewart, Frank, *Pres,* Muttart Gallery Associates, Calgary AB

Stewart, James A, *Cur Historic Buildings,* Division of Historical and Cultural Affairs, Bureau of Museums and Historic Sites, Dover DE

Stewart, Jan, *Dean Colllege,* Cornell University, Dept of Art, Ithaca NY (S)

Stewart, Jason, *Preparator,* State University of New York at Albany, University Art Gallery, Albany NY

Stewart, John, *Dean,* University of Montevallo, College of Fine Arts, Montevallo AL (S)

Stewart, John, *Business Adminr,* Ontario College of Art, Toronto ON (S)

Stewart, John A, *Treas,* Rhode Island Watercolor Society, Pawtucket RI

Stewart, Mack, *Secy,* Rensselaer Newman Foundation Chapel and Cultural Center, Troy NY

Stewart, Maureen, *Adminr,* New Museum, New York NY

Stewart, Maurine, *Chmn Dept Art,* Howard Payne University, Dept of Art, Brownwood TX (S)

Stewart, Milo V, *Assoc Dir and Chief Educ,* New York State Historical Association, Fenimore House, Cooperstown NY

Stewart, Priscilla, *Prof,* Manatee Junior College, Dept of Art, Bradenton FL (S)

Stewart, Robert, *Photography Chmn,* Atlanta College of Art, Atlanta GA (S)

Stewart, Robert G, *Cur Paintings & Sculpture,* National Portrait Gallery, Washington DC

Stewart, Sheila, *Chief Cur & Registrar,* Central Louisiana Art Association, Alexandria Museum Visual Art Center, Alexandria LA

Stewart, Wes, *Photographer Technician,* Old Salem Inc, Museum of Early Southern Decorative Arts, Winston-Salem NC

Stewart, William G, *General Manager,* Willet Stained Glass Studios, Philadelphia PA (S)

Stey, James L, *Prof,* Tulane University, Sophie H Newcomb Memorial College, New Orleans LA (S)

Steyaert, John, *Assoc Prof,* University of Minnesota, Minneapolis, Art History, Minneapolis MN (S)

Stiassni, Christine, *Dir,* Museum of Art, Science and Industry, Bridgeport CT

Stibbe, Katherine Campbell, *Pres,* Nicholas Roerich Museum, New York NY

Stidsen, Donald, *Asst Cur Exhibits,* Massachusetts Institute of Technology, Museum, Cambridge MA

Stieglitz, Mary, *Dir,* University of Minnesota, Goldstein Gallery, Saint Paul MN

Stieler, Earl W, *Adminr,* University of Waterloo, Arts Centre Gallery, Waterloo ON

Stiles, Lois Kent, *Chief Art Div,* Public Library of the District of Columbia, Art Division, Washington DC

Stiles, Mary, *Public Information Officer,* Fraunces Tavern Museum, New York NY

Stillman, Damie, *Pres,* Society of Architectural Historians, Philadelphia PA

Stillman, Diane B, *Cur of Education,* Delaware Art Museum, Wilmington DE

Stillman, George, *Dir,* Central Washington University, Sarah Spurgeon Gallery, Ellensburg WA

Stillman, George, *Chmn,* Central Washington University, Dept of Art, Ellensburg WA (S)

Stimson, Sheila, *Friends of Lovejoy Library,* Southern Illinois University, Lovejoy Library, Edwardsville IL

Stimson, William A, *Treas,* Fine Arts Museums of San Francisco, The Museum Society, San Francisco CA

Stine, Richard, *Dir,* Roberson Center for the Arts and Sciences, Binghamton NY

Stiner, Jim, *Dir Public Affairs,* Kohler Company, Kohler WI

Stirnaman, Glen, *Secy,* San Bernardino Art Association, Inc, San Bernardino CA

Stites, Mary Henry, *Secy,* Moravian Historical Society, Whitefield House Museum, Nazareth PA

Stites, M Elizabeth, *Librn,* Maryland College of Art and Design Library, Silver Spring MD

Stitt, Susan, *Dir,* The Museums at Stony Brook, Stony Brook NY

St Jean, George, *Librn,* Monterey History and Art Association, Allen Knight Maritime Museum Library, Monterey CA

St John, Richard, *Chmn Studio Arts,* Wichita State University, Division of Art, Wichita KS (S)

St John, S C, *Controller,* San Francisco Museum of Modern Art, San Francisco CA

St John, Terry, *Asst Cur,* Oakland Museum, Art Dept, Oakland CA

St Lawrence, Frances, *Business Mgr,* Birmingham-Bloomfield Art Association, Birmingham MI

Stobo, William G, *Instr,* Tidewater Community College, Art Dept, Portsmouth VA (S)

Stockly, A Holmes, *Pres,* Victoria Society of Maine, Victoria Mansion and Morse Libby Mansion, Portland ME

Stockly, Elizabeth, *Dir,* Art Center College of Design, James Lemont Fogg Memorial Library, Pasadena CA

Stocksdale, Joy, *Instructor,* Rudolph Schaeffer School of Design, San Francisco CA (S)

Stockwell, Beatrice, *Chmn,* Stanley-Whitman House, Farmington, Farmington CT

Stockwell, Ross, *Instructor,* San Diego Mesa College, Fine Arts Dept, San Diego CA (S)

Stockwell, Sharon, *Instr,* Bethany College, Art Dept, Lindsborg KS (S)

Stoddard, Stanford C, *Chmn of Board,* Detroit Institute of Arts, Founders Society, Detroit MI

Stodola, Betsy, *Pres,* Phoenix Art Museum, Phoenix AZ

Stoessell, Pamela, *Assoc Prof,* Marymount College of Virginia, Arts & Sciences Division, Arlington VA (S)

Stoesser, Elise, *Asst Cur,* Regina Public Library, Dunlop Art Gallery, Regina SK

Stoffa, Michael, *VPres,* Rockport Art Association, Rockport MA

Stoker, Eloise, *Assoc Prof,* Incarnate Word College, Art Dept, San Antonio TX (S)

Stoker, Jim, *Prof,* Trinity University, Dept of Art, San Antonio TX (S)

Stokes, Charlotte, *Asst Prof,* Oakland University, Dept of Art and Art History, Rochester MI (S)

Stokes, Lana, *Asst to Cur,* University of Louisville, Slide Collection, Louisville KY

Stokrocki, Mary Lou, *Asst Prof,* Cleveland State University, Art Dept, Cleveland OH (S)

Stokstad, Marilyn, *Research Cur,* University of Kansas, Spencer Museum of Art, Lawrence KS

Stokstad, Marilyn, *Consult Cur Medieval Art,* Atkins Museum of Fine Art, Kansas City MO

Stokstad, Marilyn, *Prof,* University of Kansas, Kress Foundation Dept of Art History, Lawrence KS (S)

Stolz, Merton P, *Treas,* Providence Athenaeum, Providence RI

Stone, Caroline, *Coordr of Exhibitions,* Memorial University of Newfoundland, Art Gallery, Saint John's NF

Stone, Carolyn, *Chmn Art Education,* Delta State University, Fielding L Wright Art Center, Cleveland MS

Stone, Carolyn Rea, *Prof,* Delta State University, Dept of Art, Cleveland MS (S)

Stone, Catherine, *Gallery Hostess,* Copper Village Museum & Arts Center, Anaconda MT

Stone, Daniel, *Pres,* National Art League Inc, Douglaston NY

Stone, Dorris, *Exec Secy,* Watkins Institute, Nashville TN

Stone, Earl E, *Dir,* Monterey History and Art Association, Allen Knight Maritime Museum, Monterey CA

Stone, Gretchen K, *Cur,* Guild of Boston Artists, Boston MA

Stone, Isabel, *Secy,* Plastic Club, Art Club for Women, Philadelphia PA

Stone, K G, *Pres,* San Bernardino Art Association, Inc, San Bernardino CA

Stone, K Gordon, *Assoc Museum Librn,* Metropolitan Museum of Art, Irene Lewisohn Costume Reference Library, New York NY

Stone, Linda, *Cur Art,* Frank Phillips, Woolaroc Museum, Bartlesville OK

Stone, Michael, *Secy,* Ashtabula Arts Center, Ashtabula OH

Stone, Norma, *Pres Bd of Trustees,* The Art Center, Mount Clemens MI

Stone, Pat, *Instr,* Woodbury University, Professional Arts Division, Los Angeles CA (S)

Stone, Stanley, *1st VPres,* Women's City Club of Cleveland, Gallery, Cleveland OH

Stone, Suzi, *Secy,* Contemporary Arts Center, Cincinnati OH

Stone-Ferrier, Linda, *Asst Prof,* University of Kansas, Kress Foundation Dept of Art History, Lawrence KS (S)

Stoneham, John, *Librn,* Maryland Institute, Library, Baltimore MD

Stonehill, John, *VChmn,* National Institute for Architectural Education, New York NY

Stonum, Paul T, *Executive VPres & Dir,* National Hall of Fame for Famous American Indians, Anadarko OK

Stonum, Sally, *Treas & Secy,* National Hall of Fame for Famous American Indians, Anadarko OK

Stoops, Susan, *Registrar,* Brandeis University, Rose Art Museum, Waltham MA

Storer, C A, *Chmn Board Trustees,* Zigler Museum, Jennings LA

Storey, Jackson Grey, *Pres,* Central Academy of Commercial Art, Cincinnati OH (S)

Story, Jean, *Registrar,* Contemporary Arts Museum, Houston TX

Story, Lewis W, *Interim Dir,* Denver Art Museum, Denver CO

Story, William E, *Dir,* Saginaw Art Museum, Saginaw MI

Stott, Margaret, *Cur Ethnology & Education,* University of British Columbia, Museum of Anthropology, Vancouver BC

Stotz, Virginia, *Instr Art History,* Kean College of New Jersey, Fine Arts Dept, Union NJ (S)

Stoughton, Gen, *Librn,* Oak Ridge Community Art Center & Museum of Fine Arts, Library, Oak Ridge TN

Stoughton, Michael, *Assoc Prof,* University of Minnesota, Minneapolis, Art History, Minneapolis MN (S)

Stout, Kenneth, *Dept Chairperson,* University of Arkansas, Art Dept, Fayetteville AR (S)

Stout, Martha S, *Registrar,* Atkins Museum of Fine Art, Kansas City MO

Stover, Donald L, *American Decorative Arts,* Fine Arts Museums of San Francisco, M H de Young Memorial Museum and California Palace of the Legion of Honor, San Francisco CA

Stover, Edwin L, *Dir School Fine Arts,* San Jose City College, School of Fine Arts, San Jose CA (S)

Stover, Richard, *Division Dean,* Riverside City College, Dept of Art, Riverside CA (S)

Stow, James P, *Pres,* Westfield Athenaeum, Jasper Rand Art Museum, Westfield MA

Stowens, Doris, *Registrar,* American Craft Council Museum, New York NY

Strachota, J, *Instructor,* Milwaukee Area Technical College, Graphic & Applied Arts Division, Milwaukee WI (S)

Strachota, John, *Gallery Dir,* Milwaukee Area Technical College, Kronquist Craft Gallery, Milwaukee WI

Stradling, Anne C, *Dir,* Stradling Museum of the Horse, Inc, Patagonia AZ

Straight, Robert, *Coordr Foundations,* University of Delaware, Dept of Art, Newark DE (S)

Strand, Elizabeth, *Prof,* Concordia College, Art Dept, Moorhead MN (S)

Strandberg, Kevin, *Instructor,* Illinois Wesleyan University, School of Art, Bloomington IL (S)

Strater, Henry, *Dir,* Museum of Art of Ogunquit, Ogunquit ME

Stratton, Marcel C, *Assoc Prof,* Moorhead State University, Dept of Art, Moorhead MN (S)

Straub, Dale, *Prof,* Williamsport Area Community College, Dept of Engineering and Design, Williamsport PA (S)

Straub, Judith S, *Pres,* Academy of the Arts, Easton MD

Strauber, Susan, *Faculty,* Grinnell College, Dept of Art, Grinnell IA (S)

Straus, John W, *VPres,* The American Federation of Arts, New York NY

Strauss, Gordon, *Chmn Bd of Trustees,* Princeton Art Association, Princeton NJ

Strauss, Melvin, *Pres,* Cornish Institute, Seattle WA (S)

Strauss, Rosemary I, *Chmn,* Northern Kentucky University, Fine Arts Dept, Highland Heights KY (S)

Strawbridge, John, *VPres,* Washington Art Association, Washington Depot CT

Strawn, Martha, *Faculty,* University of North Carolina-Charlotte, Creative Arts Dept, Charlotte NC (S)

Strawn, Mel, *Dir,* University of Denver, School of Art, Denver CO (S)

Street, Betty, *Assoc Prof,* Texas Tech University, Dept of Art, Lubbock TX (S)

Streeter, Henry, *Pres,* Wenham Historical Association and Museum, Inc, Wenham MA

Streetman, Evon, *Assoc Prof,* University of Florida, Dept of Art, Gainesville FL (S)

Streetman, John W, *Dir,* Evansville Museum of Arts and Science, Evansville IN

Strehlke, Carl B, *Asst Cur,* Philadelphia Museum of Art, John Johnson Collection, Philadelphia PA

Streng, Barbara, *Admin Asst,* Boise Gallery of Art, Boise ID

Stress, Mildred, *Cur,* Madison County Historical Society, Cottage Lawn, Oneida NY

Striby, James C, *Academic Dean,* Atlanta College of Art, Atlanta GA (S)

Strickland, Eycke, *Lecturer,* Emory University, Art History Dept, Atlanta GA (S)

Strickler, Susan, *Cur American Art,* Worcester Art Museum, Worcester MA

Stringer, John, *Dir Visual Arts Program,* Center for Inter-American Relations Art Gallery, New York NY

Stringer, Mary Evelyn, *Prof,* Mississippi University for Women, Division of Fine & Performing Arts, Columbus MS (S)

Stroebel, Leslie, *Chmn Photographic Technology,* Rochester Institute of Technology, School of Photographic Arts & Sciences, Rochester NY (S)

Stroh, Charles, *Head Dept,* Kansas State University, Art Dept, Manhattan KS (S)

Strohl, Barbara, *Comptroller,* Allentown Art Museum, Allentown PA

Strohm, Robert, *Asst Dir,* Virginia Historical Society, Richmond VA

Strohmaier, Thomas, *Instr,* University of Dayton, Fine Arts Division, Dayton OH (S)

Strohman, Barbara, *Chmn Dept of Art,* Bloomsburg University of Pennsylvania, Haas Gallery of Art, Bloomsburg PA

Strohman, Barbara J, *Chmn Dept,* Bloomsburg University, Dept of Art, Bloomsburg PA (S)

Strombotne, James S, *Prof,* University of California, Riverside, Program in Art, Riverside CA (S)

Strommen, Kim, *Assoc Dean School,* Washington University, School of Fine Arts, Saint Louis MO (S)

Stromsten, Amy, *Asst Prof,* Rutgers, the State University of New Jersey, Mason Gross School of the Arts, New Brunswick NJ (S)

Stronecker, Carol, *Editor of Publications,* Walters Art Gallery, Baltimore MD

Strong, Barbara, *Instructor,* College of the Sequoias, Art Dept, Visalia CA (S)

Strong, Doyle, *Assoc Prof,* Weber State College, Art Dept, Ogden UT (S)

Strong, Susan R, *Head Art Reference & Slide Room & Archivist,* New York State College of Ceramics at Alfred University, Scholes Library of Ceramics, Alfred NY

Strosahl, William, *Second VPres,* American Watercolor Society, New York NY

Strother, Joseph W, *Dir,* Louisiana Tech University, School of Art and Architecture, Ruston LA (S)

Strother, Mary, *Instr,* Normandale Community College, Art Dept, Bloomington MN (S)

Stroud, Don, *Chmn,* South Plains College, Creative Arts Dept, Levelland TX (S)

Stroud, John M, *Cur,* Naval Amphibious Museum, Norfolk VA

Stroud, Peter, *Prof,* Rutgers, the State University of New Jersey, Mason Gross School of the Arts, New Brunswick NJ (S)

Strouse, Norman H, *Dir,* Silverado Museum, Saint Helena CA

Struble, Bradley, *Gallery Display Artist,* Alberta College of Art Gallery, Calgary AB

Strueber, Michael M, *Dir,* Southern Alleghenies Museum of Art, Loretto PA

Strueber, Micheal, *Chmn,* St Francis College, Fine Arts Dept, Loretto PA (S)

Strump, M, *Chmn Jewelry Design,* Fashion Institute of Technology, Art & Design Division, New York NY (S)

Stuart, Donald, *Pres,* Ontario Crafts Council, Toronto ON

Stuart, Joseph, *Dir,* South Dakota State University, South Dakota Memorial Art Center, Brookings SD

Stuart, Joseph, *Prof,* South Dakota State University, Dept of Visual Arts, Brookings SD (S)

Stuart, Kathleen, *Recording Secy,* Arizona Watercolor Association, Phoenix AZ

Stuart, Shaw, *Board of Dir,* Cultural Council Foundation, Fourteen Sculptors Gallery, New York NY

Stuart, Signe, *Asst Prof,* South Dakota State University, Dept of Visual Arts, Brookings SD (S)

Stubblebine, James H, *Prof,* Rutgers, the State University of New Jersey, Graduate Program in Art History, New Brunswick NJ (S)

Stubbs, Maurice, *University Art Cur,* University of Western Ontario, McIntosh Art Gallery, London ON

Stuck, Jack, *Asst Prof,* C W Post Center of Long Island University, School of the Arts, Greenvale NY (S)

Stuckenbruck-Smith, Linda, *Asst Prof,* Texas Woman's University, Dept of Art, Denton TX (S)

Stucker, Richard L, *Assoc Dir,* Hood Museum of Art, Hanover NH

Stuckert, Caroline M, *Dir,* Buten Museum of Wedgwood, Merion PA

Studt, Shirlee A, *Art Librn,* Michigan State University, Art Library, East Lansing MI

Stuhl, Hal, *Pres,* Missouri Historical Society, Saint Louis MO

Stuhlman, Rachel, *Librn,* International Museum of Photography at George Eastman House, Library, Rochester NY

Stuiver, Chitra, *Art Spec,* Hawaii State Library, Fine Arts-Audiovisual Section, Honolulu HI

Stull, Donald L, *Commissioner,* Boston Art Commission of the City of Boston, Boston MA

Stump, Jeanne, *Chairperson,* University of Kansas, Kress Foundation Dept of Art History, Lawrence KS (S)

Stunsaas, Starla, *Instr,* Vincennes University Junior College, Art Dept, Vincennes IN (S)

Sturgell, Jack S, *Dir,* University of Delaware, Student Center Art Gallery, Newark DE

Sturgeon, Mary C, *Asst Chmn Art Hist,* University of North Carolina at Chapel Hill, Art Dept, Chapel Hill NC (S)

Sturges, Hollister, *Cur European Art,* Joslyn Art Museum, Omaha NE

Sturman, Richard, *Pres,* Dubuque Art Association, Old Jail Gallery, Dubuque IA

Sturr, Ed, *Assoc Prof,* Kansas State University, Art Dept, Manhattan KS (S)

Sturzenberger, Doris, *Archivist,* Saint Louis Art Museum, Richardson Memorial Library, Saint Louis MO

Stutman, Ellen, *Instructor,* Boston Center for Adult Education, Boston MA (S)

Stutzman, Mary Lou, *Asst Dir,* Pacific Grove Art Center, Library, Pacific Grove CA

Styron, Thomas W, *Executive Dir,* Greenville County Museum of Art, Greenville SC

Su, Julie C, *Cataloger,* Indianapolis Museum of Art, Stout Reference Library, Indianapolis IN

Suarez, Diana W, *Cur Education,* Hunter Museum of Art, Chattanooga TN

Sudano, G R, *Head Dept,* Purdue University, Lafayette, Dept of Creative Arts, Art & Design Section, West Lafayette IN (S)

Suddith, John T, *Chmn,* Louisiana College, Dept of Art, Pineville LA (S)

Suddock, Barbara, *Newsletter,* Alaska Artists' Guild, Anchorage AK

Sudler, Barbara, *Executive Dir,* Colorado Historical Society, State Museum, Denver CO

Suelflow, August R, *Dir,* Concordia Historical Institute, Saint Louis MO

Suelzer, Maureen, *Instr,* Marian College, Art Dept, Indianapolis IN (S)

Sugarman, Joanne M, *Admin Asst,* Hood Museum of Art, Hanover NH

Sugrue, Kimberly, *Slide Cur,* Wright State University, Dept of Art and Art History Resource Center & Slide Library, Dayton OH

Suhre, Terry, *Cur Asst,* Illinois State Museum of Natural History and Art, Springfield IL

Sullivan, Arthur L, *Dir Landscape Architecture,* North Carolina State University at Raleigh, School of Design, Raleigh NC (S)

Sullivan, Gail, *Instructor,* The Design Schools, Art Institute of Seattle, Seattle WA (S)

Sullivan, Gene, *Chmn,* Framingham State College, Art Dept, Framingham MA (S)

Sullivan, Gerald P, *Lectr,* University of Santa Clara, Fine Arts Dept, Santa Clara CA (S)

Sullivan, James E, *Assoc Prof,* Southern Illinois University, School of Art, Carbondale IL (S)

Sullivan, Jaqueline, *Asst Dir for Admin,* New Orleans Museum of Art, New Orleans LA

Sullivan, Larry, *Librn,* New York Historical Society, New York NY

Sullivan, Larry E, *Librn,* New York Historical Society, Library, New York NY

Sullivan, Margaret, *Research Cur,* University of Illinois, Krannert Art Museum, Champaign IL

Sullivan, Martin E, *Asst Commissioner,* New York State Museum, Albany NY

Sullivan, Max W, *Dir,* University of Texas at Arlington, University Art Gallery, Arlington TX

Sullivan, Milton F, *Prof,* Southern Illinois University, School of Art, Carbondale IL (S)

Sullivan, Patricia, *Asst Librn,* Cornell University, Fine Arts Library, Ithaca NY

Sullivan, Robert D, *Museum Servs Div,* New York State Museum, Albany NY

Sullivan, Ronald Dee, *Assoc Prof,* Del Mar College, Dept of Art, Corpus Christi TX (S)

Sullivan, Rosalie Mercein, *Dir,* James Monroe Law Office - Museum and Memorial Library, Fredericksburg VA

Sullivan, Ruth, *Research Cur,* Kimbell Art Museum, Fort Worth TX

Sullivan, Scott A, *Grad Studies Coordr,* North Texas State University, Art Dept, Denton TX (S)

Sullivan, Sylvia, *Pres,* Conejo Valley Art Museum, Thousand Oaks CA

Sullivant, Wayne, *Artist-in-Residence,* William Woods-Westminster Colleges, Art Dept, Fulton MO (S)

Sulser, Ruth, *Coordr Volunteers,* Museum of Fine Arts, Springfield MA

Sultz, Jan, *Lectr,* Webster College, Art Dept, Webster Groves MO (S)

Sultz, Phil, *Assoc Prof,* Webster College, Art Dept, Webster Groves MO (S)

Sumits, William J, *Chief Photographic Laboratory,* National Gallery of Art, Washington DC

Summer, Eugenia, *Dir of Gallery, Cur of Museum & Permanent Coll,* Mississippi University for Women, Art Gallery and Museum, Columbus MS

Summer, Eugenia, *Head Dept & Prof,* Mississippi University for Women, Division of Fine & Performing Arts, Columbus MS (S)

Summerford, Ben L, *Prof,* American University, Dept of Art, Washington DC (S)

Summers, William John, *Chmn,* Seattle University, Fine Arts Dept, Division of Art, Seattle WA (S)

Summerville, Gabrielle, *Deputy Dir,* Society of the Four Arts, Palm Beach FL

Sumner, Janet, *Recording Secy,* Artists' Fellowship, Inc, New York NY

Sumner, Steven, *Prof,* State University of New York College at Potsdam, Dept of Fine Arts, Potsdam NY (S)

Sumrall, Robert F, *Cur of Ship Models,* United States Naval Academy Museum, Annapolis MD

Sundberg, Ruth M, *Assoc Dir,* Art Center of Battle Creek, Battle Creek MI

Sundbye, Delores A, *Supv Art & Music Dept,* Saint Paul Public Library, Art & Music Dept, Saint Paul MN

Sundet, E S, *Faculty,* Humboldt State University, College of Creative Arts & Humanities, Arcata CA (S)

Sung, Lillian, *Asst Prof,* Central Missouri State University, Art Dept, Warrensburg MO (S)

Sungur, Barbara Z, *Asst Prof,* University of British Columbia, Dept of Fine Arts, Vancouver BC (S)

Sunkel, Robert, *Percival DeLuce Art Gallery Coll Cur,* Northwest Missouri State University, DeLuce Gallery, Maryville MO

Sunkel, Robert, *Assoc Prof,* Northwest Missouri State University, Dept of Art, Maryville MO (S)

Sures, J, *Acting Head,* University of Regina, Dept of Visual Arts, Regina SK (S)

Surkamer, Susie, *Dir Arts Development,* South Carolina Arts Commission, Columbia SC

Surratt, Margaret, *VChmn,* Carson County Square House Museum, Panhandle TX

Surtees, Ursula, *Dir & Cur,* Kelowna Centennial Museum and National Exhibit Centre, Kelowna BC

Sussman, Elisabeth, *Cur,* Institute of Contemporary Art, Boston MA

Sussman, Gary, *Dir,* Sculpture Center Gallery & School, New York NY (S)

Sussman, Gary, *School Dir,* Sculpture Center, New York NY

Suter, Sherwood E, *Dept Chmn & Gallery Dir,* McMurry College, Ryan Fine Arts Center, Abilene TX

Suter, Sherwood E, *Head Dept,* McMurry College, Art Dept, Abilene TX (S)

Sutherland, A J, *Pres Bd,* Timken Art Gallery, San Diego CA

Sutinen, Paul, *Program Asst,* Marylhurst College, Art Dept, Marylhurst OR (S)

Sutter, James, *Prof,* State University of New York College at Potsdam, Dept of Fine Arts, Potsdam NY (S)

Suttman, Paul, *Adjunct Assoc Prof,* Columbia University, School of the Arts, Division of Painting & Sculpture, New York NY (S)

Sutton, B Lee, *Lectr,* Centenary College of Louisiana, Dept of Art, Shreveport LA (S)

Sutton, Judith, *Assoc Dir,* Public Library of Charlotte and Mecklenburg County, Charlotte NC

Sutton, Patricia, *Asst Prof,* Hartford Art School of the University of Hartford, West Hartford CT (S)

Suzor, Mary, *Assoc Cur,* Museum of Fine Arts, Springfield MA

Suzor, Mary E, *Assoc Cur,* George Walter Vincent Smith Art Museum, Springfield MA

Svendsen, Alf, *Prof,* Delaware County Community College, Communications and Humanities House, Media PA (S)

Svendsen, Louise Averill, *Cur Emer,* Solomon R Guggenheim Museum, New York NY

Swaim, Darlene, *Chmn Dept Art,* Mesa Community College, Dept of Art & Photography, Mesa AZ (S)

Swain, Kristin A, *Supv Museum Coll,* The Rockwell Museum, Corning NY

Swain, Robert F, *Dir,* Queen's University, Agnes Etherington Art Centre, Kingston ON

Swain, Shirley, *Dir,* Saint Louis County Historical Society, Duluth MN

Swain, Tim, *Gallery Asst,* Anderson Fine Arts Center, Anderson IN

Swales, R J W, *Assoc Dean Col Fine Arts,* University of Regina, Dept of Art Education, Regina SK (S)

Swank, Scott T, *Deputy Dir Interpretation,* Winterthur Museum and Gardens, Winterthur DE

Swanson, David, *In Charge Art Program,* Lutheran Brotherhood Gallery, Minneapolis MN

Swanson, Mary Virginia, *Exec Asst,* The Friends of Photography, Carmel CA

Swanson, Roy, *Prof,* Hutchinson Community Junior College, Art Dept, Hutchinson KS (S)

Swanson, Thoma, *Chmn,* Albertus Magnus College, Art Dept, New Haven CT (S)

Swanson, Vern G, *Dir,* Springville Museum of Art, Springville UT

Swartz, Henry, *Undergrad Coordr,* North Texas State University, Art Dept, Denton TX (S)

Swearingen, Eugene, *Chmn Executive Committee,* Bank of Oklahoma, Tulsa OK

Sweatt, Lilla, *Slide Cur,* San Diego State University, Love Library and Art Department Slide Library, San Diego CA

Sweeney, Gray, *Assoc Prof,* Grand Valley State Colleges, Art Dept, Allendale MI (S)

Sweeney, James, *Painting,* Montserrat School of Visual Art, Beverly MA (S)

Sweeney, J Craig, *VPres,* Sierra Arts Foundation, Reno NV

Sweeney, Mary Sue, *Dir Programs & Publications & Spec Asst to Dir,* Newark Museum, Newark NJ

Sweeney, Patrick, *Registrar,* Davenport Municipal Art Gallery, Davenport IA

Sweeney, Richard, *Dir,* Public Library of Columbus and Franklin County, Humanities, Fine Arts and Recreation Division, Columbus OH

Sweeney, Robert T, *Chmn,* Amherst College, Dept of Fine Arts, Amherst MA (S)

Sweet, Lonn M, *Chmn,* Northern State College, Art Dept, Aberdeen SD (S)

Sweet, Richard, *VPres,* Attleboro Museum, Center for the Arts, Attleboro MA

Sweet, Sam, *Mgr Dir,* Women's Interart Center, Inc, Interart de St Amand Gallery, New York NY

Sweeting, Sharon, *Bulletin Ed,* Special Libraries Association, Museum, Arts and Humanities Division, New York NY

Swenson, Inga Christine, *Asst Cur Prints,* Smith College, Museum of Art, Northampton MA

Swenson, Ronald, *Dean,* School of the Associated Arts, Saint Paul MN (S)

Swenson, Sandra, *Chmn Art History,* Pan American University, Art Dept, Edinburg TX (S)

Swerdlove, Dorothy, *Theatre Cur,* New York Public Library, Shelby Cullom Davis Museum, Library & Museum of the Performing Arts, New York NY

Swider, Bogdan, *Asst Prof,* Colorado College, Dept of Art, Colorado Springs CO (S)

Swider, Marilyn, *Instr,* Blue Lake Community School of Arts, Visual Arts Dept, Muskegon MI (S)

Swieszkowski, Linda, *Librn,* Montana State University, Creative Arts Library, Bozeman MT

Swift, June M, *Executive Secy,* Saint Joseph Museum, Saint Joseph MO

Swig, Roselyne C, *Pres Commission,* San Francisco City and County Art Commission, San Francisco CA

Swigon, Ted, *Pres,* Polish Museum of America, Chicago IL

Swigon, Theodore J, *Dir Exhibits,* Museum of Science and Industry, Chicago IL

Swimmer, Ross O, *Pres,* Cherokee National Historical Society, Inc, Tahlequah OK

Swinson, William R, *Dir,* Walter Cecil Rawls Museum, Courtland VA

Swinton, Elizabeth, *Asst Prof,* Tufts University, Fine Arts Dept, Medford MA (S)

Swisher, Ann, *Asst Program Coordr,* Oklahoma Museum of Art, Oklahoma City OK

Swope, Susan, *Pres,* San Mateo County Arts Council, Belmont CA

Swords-Steffen, Susan, *Sr Asst Librn,* Saint Xavier College, Byrne Memorial Library, Chicago IL

Swyrydenko, Walter, *Asst Prof*, Lakeland Community College, Visual Arts Dept, Mentor OH (S)

Sykes, Lawrence F, *Prof*, Rhode Island College, Art Dept, Providence RI (S)

Sykora, T A, *Secy*, Great Lakes Historical Society, Vermilion OH

Sylvester, Judith, *Conservator*, Indiana University, William Hammond Mathers Museum, Bloomington IN

Symes, Arthur L, *Dir*, Southern University A & M College, Division of Architecture, Baton Rouge LA (S)

Symns, Edith M, *Dir of Gallery*, Hutchinson Art Association, Hutchinson KS

Synnott, Beatrice, *Secy*, Concord Art Association, Concord MA

Syvinski, Henry, *Instructor*, Villanova University, Dept of Art and Art History, Villanova PA (S)

Szabla, Joanne, *Prof*, Rochester Institute of Technology, School of Art and Design, Rochester NY (S)

Szabo, George, *Cur Robert Lehman Collection*, Metropolitan Museum of Art, New York NY

Szabo, Steve, *Chmn Photography*, Corcoran School of Art, Washington DC (S)

Szameit, Manfred, *Treas*, Civic Fine Arts Association Museum, Sioux Falls SD

Szarkowski, John, *Dir Dept Photography*, Museum of Modern Art, New York NY

Szczepaniak, L, *Slide Librn*, York University, Fine Arts Slide Library, Downsview ON

Szeitz, P R, *Chmn*, Moorhead State University, Dept of Art, Moorhead MN (S)

Szmagaj, Kenneth, *Assoc Prof*, James Madison University, Dept of Art, Harrisonburg VA (S)

Szoke, Andrew, *Asst Prof*, Northampton County Area Community College, Art Dept, Bethlehem PA (S)

Szubski, James, *Dir of Development*, Akron Art Museum, Akron OH

Szuszitzky, Blanche, *Treas*, North Country Museum of Arts, Park Rapids MN

Szynaka, Edward, *Library Dir*, Pasadena Public Library, Fine Arts Dept, Pasadena CA

Tabak, Lisa, *Asst Cur*, Solomon R Guggenheim Museum, New York NY

Tacang, Lee, *Instructor*, De Anza College, Art Dept, Cupertino CA (S)

Tacha, Athena, *Prof*, Oberlin College, Dept of Art, Oberlin OH (S)

Tack, Catherine, *Staff Librn*, Carnegie Library of Pittsburgh, Pittsburgh PA

Tade, George T, *Dean*, Texas Christian University, Art & Art History Dept, Fort Worth TX (S)

Tadlock, Marvin L, *Faculty*, Virginia Intermont College, Fine Arts Dept, Bristol VA (S)

Taff, Cavett, *Cur Exhibits*, Mississippi State Historical Museum, Jackson MS

Tafler, David, *Instr*, Rosemont College, Division of the Arts, Rosemont PA (S)

Tafoya, Guadalupe, *Museum Asst*, Millicent Rogers Museum, Taos NM

Taggart, Ross, *Lectr*, University of Kansas, Kress Foundation Dept of Art History, Lawrence KS (S)

Taggert, Charles, *Dir Resource Develop*, Museum of Fine Arts, Boston MA

Taggert, Cris, *Instructor*, Anton Elli, Cincinnati OH (S)

Tai, Jane S, *Assoc Dir & Exhibition Program Dir*, The American Federation of Arts, New York NY

Tai, Susan, *Asst Cur Oriental Art*, Santa Barbara Museum of Art, Santa Barbara CA

Taillefer, Robert, *Instr*, St Lawrence College, Dept of Visual and Creative Arts, Cornwall ON (S)

Tait, Lane, *Business Mgr*, Hill Country Arts Foundation, Ingram TX

Takach, Mary H, *Dir*, Pensacola Museum of Art, Pensacola FL

Takahara, Takeshi, *Assoc Prof*, Grand Valley State Colleges, Art Dept, Allendale MI (S)

Takeuchi, Arthur S, *Dean*, Illinois Institute of Technology, College of Architecture, Planning and Design, Dept of Architecture, Chicago IL (S)

Talalay, Marjorie, *Dir*, The New Gallery of Contemporary Art, Cleveland OH

Talaswalma, Terrance, *Dir*, Hopi Cultural Center, Second Mesa AZ

Talbot, Charles, *Prof*, Smith College, Art Dept, Northampton MA (S)

Talbot, Howard C, *Dir*, National Baseball Hall of Fame and Museum, Inc, Art Collection, Cooperstown NY

Talbot, Rudolf, *Co-Pres*, The Society of Arts and Crafts, Boston MA

Talbot, William, *Exec Secy*, Washington Art Association, Washington Depot CT

Talbot, William S, *Asst Dir Administration & Assoc Cur Paintings*, Cleveland Museum of Art, Cleveland OH

Talbot, William S, *Pres*, Intermuseum Conservation Association, Oberlin OH

Talbot-Stanaway, Susan, *Education & Registrar*, Plains Art Museum, Main Gallery, Moorhead MN

Talbott, Ronald, *Instr*, Harrisburg Area Community College, Division of Communication and the Arts, Harrisburg PA (S)

Tallman, Carol W, *Librn*, Pennsylvania Historical and Museum Commission, Library, Harrisburg PA

Tamayo, Daisy, *Sr Art Librn*, Free Public Library of Elizabeth, Fine Arts Dept, Elizabeth NJ

Tamerlis, Victor, *Treas*, Sculpture Center, New York NY

Tamplin, Illi-Maria, *Dir*, Art Gallery of Peterborough, Peterborough ON

Tandy, Jean C, *Coordinator Dept Art*, Mount Wachusett Community College, Art Galleries, Gardner MA

Tanenbaum, Marta, *Instr*, Spring Arbor College, Art Dept, Spring Arbor MI (S)

Tang, Carol, *Asst Librn*, University of Pennsylvania, John and Ada Lewis Memorial Library, Philadelphia PA

Tangi, Georgia, *Asst Prof*, Kentucky Wesleyan College, Dept Art, Owensboro KY (S)

Tanier, George, *Treas*, Art Information Center, Inc, New York NY

Tanier, Inger, *Board Dir Member*, Art Information Center, Inc, New York NY

Tanis, Steven, *Coordr Drawing & Painting*, University of Delaware, Dept of Art, Newark DE (S)

Tannenbaum, Judith, *Dir of Gallery*, Albright College, Freedman Gallery, Reading PA

Tanner, Joan, *Pres Bd of Dirs*, Santa Barbara Contemporary Arts Forum, Santa Barbara CA

Tanner, Warren, *Artistic Dir*, Organization of Independent Artists, New York NY

Tanselle, G Thomas, *VPres*, John Simon Guggenheim Memorial Foundation, New York NY

Taplin, Franklin P, *Dir*, Westfield Athenaeum, Jasper Rand Art Museum, Westfield MA

Tapscott, E V, *Supvr*, Houston Baptist University, Museum of American Architecture and Decorative Arts, Houston TX

Taragin, Davira, *Actg Cur Modern Art*, Detroit Institute of Arts, Detroit MI

Tarbox, Gurdon L, *Dir & Librn*, Brookgreen Gardens, Murrells Inlet SC

Tardo, Barbara, *Assoc Prof*, Southeastern Louisiana University, Dept of Visual Arts, Hammond LA (S)

Tarnowski, Thomas, *Instructor*, Johnson County Community College, Humanities Division, Overland Park KS (S)

Tartaglia, Barbara B, *Cur Community Servs*, McKissick Museums, Columbia SC

Tarver, Paul, *Asst Registrar & Cur Travelling Exhibitions*, New Orleans Museum of Art, New Orleans LA

Tasse, M Jeanne, *Dir*, Marietta College, Grover M Hermann Fine Arts Center, Marietta OH

Tate, John, *Asst Art*, Dartmouth Heritage Museum, Dartmouth NS

Tate, LaDeane V, *Instructor*, Olympic College, Art Dept, Bremerton WA (S)

Tate, Louise G, *Pres Cultural Affairs Commission*, City of Los Angeles, Cultural Affairs Dept, Los Angeles CA

Tatham, David, *Chmn*, Syracuse University, Dept of Fine Arts, Syracuse NY (S)

Tatman, Sandra, *Architectural Librn*, Athenaeum of Philadelphia, Philadelphia PA

Tator, Marie A, *Assoc Prof*, Salisbury State College, Art Dept, Salisbury MD (S)

Tatrai, Marilyn, *Registrar*, Rutgers University, Jane Voorhees Zimmerli Art Museum, New Brunswick NJ

Tatum, Jas, *Asst Prof*, Lincoln University, Dept Fine Arts, Jefferson City MO (S)

Taub, Rae Stone, *Secy*, Marin Society of Artists Inc, Ross CA

Taubman, A Alfred, *Pres*, Archives of American Art, Smithsonian Institution, New York NY

Taulbee, Kathryn, *Registrar*, Cincinnati Art Museum, Cincinnati OH

Taurins, Irene, *Registrar*, Philadelphia Museum of Art, Philadelphia PA

Tausig, Micheal, *Dir*, Napa College, Art Dept, Napa CA (S)

Tayler, Neale, *Pres*, Wilfrid Laurier University, Concourse Gallery, Waterloo ON

Taylor, Adelle, *Bookkeeper*, Community Council for the Arts, Kinston NC

Taylor, Ben, *Chmn Museum Committee*, Fairfield Public Library and Museum, Fairfield Art Association, Fairfield IA

Taylor, Brent, *Ceramics Technician*, Victor Valley College, Art Dept, Victorville CA (S)

Taylor, Charles, *Preparator*, Philbrook Art Center, Tulsa OK

Taylor, Donald R, *Dir*, Gunston Hall Plantation, Lorton VA

Taylor, Elizabeth H, *Assoc Dir*, Hammond Museum, Museum of the Humanities, North Salem NY

Taylor, Elmer, *Ceramics Coordr*, North Texas State University, Art Dept, Denton TX (S)

Taylor, Frances, *Executive Dir*, Cultural Art Center of Ocean City, Ocean City NJ

Taylor, George, *VPres*, Plastic Club, Art Club for Women, Philadelphia PA

Taylor, Ginger, *Coordr*, Art League of Houston, Houston TX

Taylor, Herman W, *Prof*, Washington and Lee University, Dept of Fine Arts, Lexington VA (S)

Taylor, Howard J, *Asst Dir*, Philadelphia Maritime Museum, Philadelphia PA

Taylor, Hugh H, *Prof*, Washington and Jefferson College, Art Dept, Washington PA (S)

Taylor, Ira M, *Chmn*, Hardin-Simmons University, Art Dept, Abilene TX (S)

Taylor, J Allyn, *Chmn Board Turstees*, McMichael Canadian Collection, Kleinburg ON

Taylor, James, *Manuscripts & Microfilm*, Winterthur Museum and Gardens, Library, Winterthur DE

Taylor, Joan, *Assoc Prof*, Fairleigh Dickinson University, Fine Arts Dept, Teaneck NJ (S)

Taylor, John A, *Fine Arts Chmn*, Lincoln University, Dept Fine Arts, Jefferson City MO (S)

Taylor, John R, *Pres Bd of Trustees*, Edmundson Art Foundation, Inc, Des Moines Art Center, Des Moines IA

Taylor, Katrina V H, *Cur*, Marjorie Merriweather Post Foundation of DC, Hillwood Museum, Washington DC

Taylor, Lisa, *Dir*, Cooper-Hewitt Museum, Smithsonian Institution, New York NY

Taylor, Mack, *Instructor*, La Roche College, Division of Graphics, Design, Pittsburgh PA (S)

Taylor, Marcia, *Asst Prof*, Trenton State College, Art Dept, Trenton NJ (S)

Taylor, Marilyn S, *Cur Ethnology*, Saint Joseph Museum, Saint Joseph MO

Taylor, Mary C, *Head Dept*, Doane College, Dept of Art, Crete NE (S)

Taylor, Mary Jane, *Dir*, Brenau College, Art Dept, Gainesville GA (S)

Taylor, Michael, *Asst Prof*, Rochester Institute of Technology, School for American Craftsmen, Rochester NY (S)

Taylor, Michael D, *Chairperson Dept*, University of Missouri-Saint Louis, Art Dept, Saint Louis MO (S)

Taylor, Michiko O, *Gallery Administrator*, Lafayette College, Morris R Williams Center for the Arts, Easton PA

Taylor, N Wayne, *Chmn,* University of Wisconsin, Madison, Dept of Art, Madison WI (S)

Taylor, Ora Gordon, *Cur,* Liberty Hall Museum, Orlando Brown House, Frankfort KY

Taylor, Peggy, *Secy,* Humbolt Arts Council, Eureka CA

Taylor, Rene, *Dir,* Museo de Arte de Ponce, Ponce Art Museum, Ponce PR

Taylor, Rod A, *Head Dept,* Norfolk State College, Fine Arts Dept, Norfolk VA (S)

Taylor, Sally, *Admis Asst,* Jacksonville Museum of Arts and Sciences, Jacksonville FL

Taylor, Sarah, *Cur,* Plains Indians & Pioneer Historical Foundation, Pioneer Museum & Art Center, Woodward OK

Taylor, Susan Aaron, *Chmn Crafts,* Center for Creative Studies__College of Art and Design, Detroit MI (S)

Taylor, Susie, *Instructor,* Rudolph Schaeffer School of Design, San Francisco CA (S)

Taylor, Tim, *Chmn Bd of Dir,* Art Gallery of Nova Scotia, Halifax NS

Taylor, Tom, *Coordr Fine Arts,* Columbia College, Art Dept, Chicago IL (S)

Taylor, Veda, *Co-Chmn & Secy,* Valley Art Center Inc, Clarkston WA

Taylor, Warren, *Painting & Drawing,* Chautauqua Institution, The Art Center, Chautauqua NY (S)

Taylor, Warren, *Instr,* Midland College, Art Dept, Midland TX (S)

Taylor, W E, *Dir,* National Museums of Canada, National Museum of Man, Ottawa ON

Taylor, Will, *Cur Art Coll,* Lovelace Medical Foundation, Art Collection, Albuquerque NM

Taylor, William, *Asst Prof,* University of the District of Columbia, Art Dept, Washington DC (S)

Taylor, William A, *Slide Cur,* University of Rochester, Fine Arts Library, Rochester NY

Taylor, William C, *Business Mgr,* Arts Council of Spartanburg County, Inc, Spartanburg Arts Center, Spartanburg SC

Tchakalian, Sam, *Chmn Painting Dept,* San Francisco Art Institute, San Francisco CA (S)

Teahan, John W, *Librn,* Wadsworth Atheneum, Auerbach Art Library, Hartford CT

Tebbens, Marianne, *Instr,* Mainline Center of the Arts, Haverford PA (S)

Tebbens, Marianne, *Instr,* Wayne Art Center, Wayne PA (S)

Teczar, Steven, *Art Division Chmn,* Maryville College, St Louis, Art Division, Saint Louis MO (S)

Teholiz, Leo, *Head Dept,* West Shore Community College, Division of Humanities and Fine Arts, Scottville MI (S)

Teichert, Gayl, *Gallery Clerk,* University of Montana, Gallery of Visual Arts, Missoula MT

Teicholz, Susan, *Assoc Cur Exhibitions,* University of California, University Art Museum, Berkeley CA

Teitgen, Marcia, *Instructor,* Rudolph Schaeffer School of Design, San Francisco CA (S)

Teitz, Richard Stuart, *Dir,* Hood Museum of Art, Hanover NH

Teixeira, Alice, *Secy,* Providence Art Club, Providence RI

Telford, Elizabeth S, *Registrar,* State Art Museum of Florida, John & Mable Ringling Museum of Art, Sarasota FL

Teller, Dee, *VPres,* Owatonna Arts Center, Owatonna MN

Teller, Douglas H, *Prof,* George Washington University, Dept of Art, Washington DC (S)

Teller, Gus, *Deputy Dir Operations,* Fine Arts Museums of San Francisco, M H de Young Memorial Museum and California Palace of the Legion of Honor, San Francisco CA

Tellinghuisen, Richard, *Operations Mgr,* Newport Harbor Art Museum, Newport Beach CA

Temkin, Merle, *Education Program Dir,* Rotunda Gallery, Brooklyn NY

Temme, Norman, *Ed,* The Stained Glass Association of America, Saint Louis MO

Temple, Tom, *Assoc Prof,* Central Oregon Community College, Dept of Art, Bend OR (S)

Tenabe, Gabriel S, *Cur,* Morgan State University Gallery of Art, Baltimore MD

Tenenbaum, Samuel J, *Chmn,* South Carolina Arts Commission, Columbia SC

Tenhaaf, Nell, *Coordr,* Powerhouse Gallery, Montreal PQ

Tennant, Phillip, *Chmn Art Ceramics, Photography, Woodworking & Design,* Herron School of Art, Indiana University-Purdue University, Indianapolis, Indianapolis IN (S)

Tennen, Steven, *Exec Dir,* Jamaica Center for the Performing & Visual Arts, Inc, Jamaica Arts Center, Jamaica NY

Tennent, Elaine, *Dir,* Tennent Art Foundation Gallery, Honolulu HI

Tennent, John H, *VPres,* Bowne House, Flushing NY

Tennent, William, *Cur,* Museum of Western Colorado Archives, Grand Junction CO

Teodorowych, Oksana, *Cur,* Ukrainian National Museum and Library, Chicago IL

Teoli, Alfred, *Assoc Prof,* University of Illinois, Chicago, Health Science Center, Dept of Biocommunication Arts, Chicago IL (S)

Terenzio, Stephanie, *Asst Dir & Cur 20th Century Art,* University of Connecticut, William Benton Museum of Art, Storrs CT

Tereshko, Daniel, *Assoc Prof,* Moravian College, Dept of Art, Bethlehem PA (S)

Terhune, Anne, *Assoc Prof,* College of New Rochelle School of Arts and Sciences, Undergraduate Art Dept, New Rochelle NY (S)

Terra, Daniel J, *Pres,* Terra Museum of American Art, Evanston IL

Terrell, James A, *Chmn,* Southwestern Oklahoma State University, Art Dept, Weatherford OK (S)

Terrill, Evelyn B, *Exhib Chmn,* West Baton Rouge Museum, Port Allen LA

Terrill, Martha, *Cur,* Transco Energy Company Inc, Houston TX

Terrones, Abigail, *Registrar,* University of Minnesota, University Art Museum, Minneapolis MN

Terry, Carol, *VPres,* California Historical Society, San Francisco CA

Terry, George D, *Dir & Archivist,* McKissick Museums, Columbia SC

Tersteeg, William, *Assoc Prof,* Keystone Junior College, Fine Arts Dept, Factoryville PA (S)

Teslow, Pamela, *Cur,* North Country Museum of Arts, Park Rapids MN

Teter, Keith, *Industrial Design Chmn,* Art Center College of Design, Pasadena CA (S)

Tetrault, Diane, *Head,* Goddard College, Visual Arts Dept, Plainsfield VT (S)

Tetreault, Theodore J, *Park Manager,* Harkness Memorial State Park, Waterford CT

Tettleton, Robert L, *Prof,* University of Mississippi, Dept of Art, University MS (S)

Thadani, Dhiru, *Asst Prof,* Catholic University of America, Dept of Architecture and Planning, Washington DC (S)

Thalacker, Donald W, *Dir Arts-in-Arch Program,* General Services Administration, Washington DC

Thaler, Janice M, *Cur,* French Art Colony, Inc, Gallipolis OH

Thalken, Thomas T, *Library Dir,* Herbert Hoover Presidential Library & Museum, West Branch IA

Thames, Marvin E, *Chmn Fine Arts,* Delgado College, Dept of Fine Arts, New Orleans LA (S)

Thane, David, *Secy & Treas,* Saskatchewan Association of Architects, Saskatoon SK

Thatcher, Cherie, *Dir,* Witter Gallery, Storm Lake IA

Thatcher, Margaret, *Treasurer,* Actual Art Foundation, New York NY

Thayer, Russell, *Assoc Prof,* Delta College, Art Dept, University Center MI (S)

Thayn, Florian H, *Art Reference,* United States Capitol Museum, Washington DC

Theel, Marcia M, *Office Mgr,* Leigh Yawkey Woodson Art Museum, Inc, Wausau WI

Theilen, Anne Marie, *Dir Neighborhood Art Program,* San Francisco City and County Art Commission, San Francisco CA

Thein, John, *Instr,* Creighton University, Fine and Performing Arts Dept, Omaha NE (S)

Theis, Andrew, *Instr,* Studio School of Art and Design, Philadelphia PA (S)

Thelin, Valfred, *VPres,* Ogunquit Art Association, The Barn Gallery, Ogunquit ME

Theobald, Sharon A, *Dir,* Lafayette Art Association, Greater Lafayette Museum of Art, Lafayette IN

Theodore, Josephine, *Executive Secy,* University of Utah, Utah Museum of Fine Arts, Salt Lake City UT

Theriault, Lucien, *Pres,* Musee Historique de Vaudreuil, Vaudreuil Historical Museum, Vaudreuil PQ

Theriault, Normand, *Cur Contemporary Canadian Art,* Montreal Museum of Fine Arts, Montreal PQ

Thibault, Claude, *Conservator Ancient Art,* Musee du Quebec, Quebec PQ

Thibeault, Leopold, *Preparator,* Galerie Restigouche Gallery, Campbellton NB

Thibodeau, Dick, *Coordr,* Plum Tree Fine Arts Program, Pilar NM (S)

Thiedeman, Michael, *Chmn,* West Virginia Wesleyan College, Dept of Fine Arts, Buckhannon WV (S)

Thielen, Greg G, *Cur of Coll & Registrar,* Springfield Art Museum, Springfield MO

Thies, Gail, *Cur History,* Cascade County Historical Society Museum, Great Falls MT

Thiras, Antoinette, *Registrar,* Phillips Academy, Addison Gallery of American Art, Andover MA

Thirlby, Ted, *Executive Member,* 22 Wooster Gallery, New York NY

Thomas, Bob, *Dir of Arts & Sciences,* Indian Hills Community College, Ottumwa Campus, Dept of Art, Ottumwa IA (S)

Thomas, Bryn, *Instr,* Studio School of Art and Design, Philadelphia PA (S)

Thomas, C David, *Asst Prof,* Emmanuel College, Art Dept, Boston MA (S)

Thomas, Elaine, *Dept Chmn,* Tuskegee Institute, Art Dept, Tuskegee Institute AL (S)

Thomas, Elaine G, *Dir,* International Correspondence Schools, School of Art, Scranton PA (S)

Thomas, Elizabeth, *Membership Coordr,* Philbrook Art Center, Tulsa OK

Thomas, George, *Dir,* Whatcom Museum of History and Art, Bellingham WA

Thomas, Haywood, *Pres,* Virginia Museum, Danville Museum of Fine Arts and History, Danville VA

Thomas, Homer, *Prof,* University of Missouri, Art History and Archaeology Dept, Columbia MO (S)

Thomas, James, *Deputy Dir Admin,* American Association of Museums, Washington DC

Thomas, James A, *Maintenance,* Tryon Palace Restoration Complex, New Bern NC

Thomas, James E, *Prof,* Rochester Institute of Technology, School of Art and Design, Rochester NY (S)

Thomas, John, *Assoc Prof,* Hanover College, Dept of Art, Hanover IN (S)

Thomas, Leon E, *Pres,* Fairfield Historical Society, Fairfield CT

Thomas, Lewis, *Mgr Legion Bookshop,* Fine Arts Museums of San Francisco, The Museum Society, San Francisco CA

Thomas, Linda, *Registrar,* Museum of Fine Arts, Boston MA

Thomas, Ralph R, *Head Dept,* Milwaukee Area Technical College, Graphic & Applied Arts Division, Milwaukee WI (S)

Thomas, Richard C, *Head Metalsmithing Dept,* Cranbrook Academy of Art, Bloomfield Hills MI (S)

Thomas, Ronald, *Instructor,* Saint Louis Community College at Meramec, Art Dept, Saint Louis MO (S)

Thomas, Sam, *Asst Prof,* Mansfield State College, Art Dept, Mansfield PA (S)

Thomas, Sharon, *Secy,* Loveland Museum and Gallery, Loveland CO

Thomas, Sidney, *Prof,* Syracuse University, Dept of Fine Arts, Syracuse NY (S)

Thomas, Troy, *Asst Prof,* Pennsylvania State University, Capitol Campus, Dept of Humanities, Middletown PA (S)

Tobey, Gene, *Instructor,* Linn Benton Community College, Fine & Applied Art Dept, Albany OR (S)

Tobin, Catharine, *Libr Asst,* Albany Institute of History and Art, McKinney Library, Albany NY

Todaro, Frank, *Building & Grounds Supt,* R W Norton Art Gallery, Shreveport LA

Todd, Diana, *Art Dir,* Floyd County Museum, New Albany IN

Todd, Gene, *Frontier Life,* Luna County Historical Society, Inc, Deming Luna Mimbres Museum, Deming NM

Todd, George, *Chmn,* University of Guelph, Fine Art Dept, Guelph ON (S)

Todd, Hugh, *Librn,* Litchfield Historical Society, Ingraham Memorial Research Library, Litchfield CT

Todd, James, *Chmn Dept,* University of Montana, Dept of Art, Missoula MT (S)

Todd, Richard, *Photographer,* University of California, Los Angeles, Museum of Cultural History, Los Angeles CA

Todd, Ron, *Gallery Dir,* University of New Orleans, Fine Arts Gallery, New Orleans LA

Todd, Ron, *Asst Prof,* University of New Orleans, Dept of Fine Arts, New Orleans LA (S)

Toedetemeir, Terry, *Instr,* Pacific Northwest College of Art, Portland OR (S)

Toensing, Robert E, *Instr,* Anoka Ramsey Community College, Art Dept, Coon Rapids MN (S)

Tokar, Eileen M, *Development Coordr,* Montclair Art Museum, Montclair NJ

Tokarski, Carol, *Executive Dir,* Anderson County Arts Council, Anderson SC

Tolbert, James A, *Chmn Dept,* Linn Benton Community College, Fine & Applied Art Dept, Albany OR (S)

Toledano, Roulhac, *VPres,* Louisiana Department of Culture, Recreation and Tourism, Louisiana State Museum, New Orleans LA

Tolles, Bryant F, *Dir,* Essex Institute, Salem MA

Tolmatch, Elaine, *Registrar,* Montreal Museum of Fine Arts, Montreal PQ

Tomasini, Wallace J, *Dir,* University of Iowa, School of Art and Art History, Iowa City IA (S)

Tomasita, Mary, *Head Department,* Cardinal Stritch College, Milwaukee WI

Tomcik, Andrew M, *Chairperson,* York University, Dept of Visual Arts, Downsview ON (S)

Tomko, George, *Cur,* Rahr-West Museum, Manitowoc WI

Tomory, Will, *Chmn,* Southwestern Michigan College, Communications-Humanitites Dept, Dowagiac MI (S)

Tompkins, Robert S, *Asst Prof,* Rochester Institute of Technology, School of Printing, Rochester NY (S)

Tomsic, Walt, *Prof,* Pacific Lutheran University, Dept of Art, Tacoma WA (S)

Tonelli, Edith A, *Dir,* University of California, Los Angeles, Frederick S Wight Art Gallery, Los Angeles CA

Toner, William H, *Dir,* Maine Historical Society, Portland ME

Tongeren, Herk Van, *Exec Dir,* Johnson Atelier Technical Institute of Sculpture, Mercerville NJ (S)

Tonselle, G T, *Secy,* Grolier Club Library, New York NY

Toogood, Wendy, *Prog Coordr Textiles,* Alberta College of Art, Southern Alberta Institute of Technology, Calgary AB (S)

Toomey, Cheri, *Libr Asst,* Otis Art Institute of Parsons School of Design Gallery, Library, Los Angeles CA

Toon, J, *Historical Resources Librn,* Department of Culture, Government of the Province of Alberta, Provincial Archives of Alberta, Edmonton AB

Toone, Wayne, *Chmn,* Temple Junior College, Art Dept, Temple TX (S)

Toperzer, Tom R, *Assoc Prof,* Bethel College, Dept of Art, Saint Paul MN (S)

Toppan, Muriel L, *Librn,* Walters Art Gallery, Library, Baltimore MD

Torcoletti, Enzo, *VPres,* Saint Augustine Art Association Gallery, Saint Augustine FL

Torcoletti, Enzo, *Assoc Prof,* Flagler College, Visual Arts Dept, Saint Augustine FL (S)

Tornheim, N, *Instructor,* Golden West College, Arts, Humanities and Social Sciences Institute, Huntington Beach CA (S)

Torrens, Tom, *Prof,* Pacific Lutheran University, Dept of Art, Tacoma WA (S)

Torrenti, Thomas, *VPres,* Lyme Art Association, Inc, Old Lyme CT

Torres, Evelyn, *Asst Exec Dir,* Visual Artists and Galleries Association, Inc, VAGA, New York NY

Torrini, Rudolph E, *Chmn Dept,* Fontbonne College, Art Dept, Saint Louis MO (S)

Tostenrud, Don B, *Chmn & Chief Executive Officer,* The Arizona Bank, Phoenix AZ

Toth, Carl, *Head Photography Dept,* Cranbrook Academy of Art, Bloomfield Hills MI (S)

Toth, Judith, *Lectr,* Oakland University, Dept of Art and Art History, Rochester MI (S)

Tottis, James, *Community Coordr,* Artrain, Inc, Detroit MI

Toubes, Xavier, *Lectr,* University of North Carolina at Chapel Hill, Art Dept, Chapel Hill NC (S)

Touhey, Paula, *Cur Education,* Kenosha Public Museum, Kenosha WI

Toupin, Juanita, *Librn,* Montreal Museum of Fine Arts, Library, Montreal PQ

Tourais, Zelie, *Cur Education,* Vizcaya Museum and Gardens, Miami FL

Tovish, Harold, *Prof,* Boston University, School of Visual Arts, Boston MA (S)

Towe, Kelly, *Instructor,* Anton Elli, Cincinnati OH (S)

Tower, Joan, *Instructor,* Bard College, Milton Avery Graduate School of the Arts, Annandale-on-Hudson NY (S)

Townsend, Bernadette, *Libr Technician,* Institute of American Indian Arts Museum, Library, Santa Fe NM

Townsend, Carol A, *Chmn Dept,* Daemen College, Art Dept, Amherst NY (S)

Townsend, Vera, *Chmn,* University of Missouri, Art History and Archaeology Dept, Columbia MO (S)

Townshend, Richard Fraser, *Cur Africa, Oceania & Americas,* Art Institute of Chicago, Chicago IL

Toy, Theresa Snow, *Fine Arts Librn,* Manchester City Library, Manchester NH

Trachtman, Philip, *Pres,* Art Institute of Philadelphia, Philadelphia PA (S)

Tracy, Elizabeth, *Artist-in-Residence,* Trinity College, Dept of Fine Arts, Hartford CT (S)

Tracy, Paul, *Exhibition Preparator Asst,* Memphis Brooks Museum of Art, Memphis TN

Tracy, Regina, *Dir & Cur,* Newburyport Maritime Society, Custom House Maritime Museum, Newburyport MA

Trafford, Hal, *Head Commercial Art,* Butera School of Art, Boston MA (S)

Trager, Neil C, *Dir,* State University of New York at New Paltz, College Art Gallery, New Paltz NY

Trakis, Louis, *Head Dept,* Manhattanville College, Art Dept, Purchase NY (S)

Trank, Lynn, *Prof,* Eastern Illinois University, School of Fine Arts, Charleston IL (S)

Trapp, Claude W, *Pres,* Headley-Whitney Museum, Lexington KY

Trapp, Frank, *Dir,* Amherst College, Mead Art Museum, Amherst MA

Trapp, Roy, *Exhibits Supv,* University of South Florida, Art Galleries, Tampa FL

Trasatti, Peggy, *Programming Coordr,* Clark County Library District, Las Vegas NV

Trask, David S, *Chmn,* Greenville Technical College, Art History Dept, Greenville SC (S)

Trau, Robert A, *Instructor,* Central Academy of Commercial Art, Cincinnati OH (S)

Trauger, John F, *Assoc Prof,* Rochester Institute of Technology, School of Photographic Arts & Sciences, Rochester NY (S)

Trautlein, Donald, *VPres,* Annie S Kemerer Museum, Bethlehem PA

Travis, Betsy, *Asst Dir,* Potsdam Public Museum, Potsdam NY

Travis, David, *Cur Photography,* Art Institute of Chicago, Chicago IL

Treadway, Beth, *Instructor,* Pace University, Dept of Art & Design, Pleasantville NY (S)

Treadway, Beth A, *Gallery Dir,* Pace University Gallery, Briarcliff Manor NY

Treanor, Dennis, *Cur Arts & Crafts,* Josephine D Randall Junior Museum, San Francisco CA

Trechsel, Gail Andrews, *Asst Dir,* Birmingham Museum of Art, Birmingham AL

Tredennick, Dorothy, *Prof,* Berea College, Art Dept, Berea KY (S)

Treese, William R, *Head Arts Library,* University of California, Santa Barbara, Arts Library, Santa Barbara CA

Trefry, Philippe, *Asst,* Musee du Quebec, Bibliotheque des Art, Quebec PQ

Tremblay, Ginette, *Executive Secy,* Musee d'Art de Joliette, Joliette PQ

Tremonto, Roxie, *Prof,* School of the Art Institute of Chicago, Chicago IL (S)

Trent, Robert F, *Cur Exhibitions & Education,* Connecticut Historical Society, Hartford CT

Trepp, George, *Dir,* Long Beach Public Library, Art Dept, Long Beach NY

Tresler, George W, *Pres,* Cody Country Art League, Cody WY

Triano, Anthony, *Asst Prof,* Seton Hall University, Dept of Art and Music, South Orange NJ (S)

Trickey, Karen, *Lectr,* Nazareth College of Rochester, Art Dept, Rochester NY (S)

Triggs, James, *Secy,* Society of American Historical Artists, Stamford CT

Triggs, Stanley, *Cur Photography,* McGill University, McCord Museum, Montreal PQ

Trincere, Yolanda, *Division Dir & Assoc Prof,* Southampton College of Long Island University, C W Post Center Fine Arts Division, Southampton NY (S)

Tripp, Powell, *Chmn Graphic Communication,* Center for Creative Studies__College of Art and Design, Detroit MI (S)

Tripp, Susan G, *Dir Univ Collections,* Johns Hopkins University, Evergreen House, Baltimore MD

Trippe, Jane, *Secy,* Main Line Center of the Arts, Haverford PA

Trissel, James, *Prof,* Colorado College, Dept of Art, Colorado Springs CO (S)

Trivers, Mollie, *Events Coordr,* Scottsdale Center for the Arts, Scottsdale AZ

Trivigno, Pat, *Prof,* Tulane University, Sophie H Newcomb Memorial College, New Orleans LA (S)

Troeger, Betty J, *Asst Prof,* Florida State University, Art Education Dept, Tallahassee FL (S)

Troiani, Don, *Pres,* Society of American Historical Artists, Stamford CT

Trona, Barry, *Assoc Registrar,* Hofstra University, Emily Lowe Gallery, Hempstead NY

Trop, Sandra, *Asst Dir,* Everson Museum of Art, Syracuse NY

Trout, Margot, *Instructor,* Portland School of Art, Portland ME (S)

Trowbridge, Janeth, *Exec Dir,* Rogue Valley Art Association, Medford OR

Troy, Nancy, *Asst Prof,* Northwestern University, Evanston, Dept of Art History, Evanston IL (S)

Truan, George, *Chmn Art Dept,* Texas Southmost College, Fine Arts Dept, Brownsville TX (S)

Truax, Harold A, *Assoc Dean,* Miami University, Art Dept, Oxford OH (S)

Trubner, Henry, *Asian Art Cur,* Seattle Art Museum, Seattle WA

Trudel, Jean, *Dir,* Montreal Museum of Fine Arts, Montreal PQ

True, Leroy H, *Pres,* Nantucket Historical Association, Fair Street Museum, Nantucket MA

Truettner, William H, *Cur 18th & 19th Century Painting & Sculpture,* National Museum of American Art, Washington DC

Trujillo, Rupert A, *Dean,* Harwood Foundation of the University of New Mexico, Taos NM

Trumpy, Sigrid, *Cur of Robinson Coll,* United States Naval Academy Museum, Annapolis MD

Tryba, John, *Assoc Prof,* Cardinal Stritch College, Art Dept, Milwaukee WI (S)

Tryba, Mildred, *Assoc Prof,* Cardinal Stritch College, Art Dept, Milwaukee WI (S)

Utterbach, Rosalie, *Chmn Div,* Woodbury University, Professional Arts Division, Los Angeles CA (S)

Utzinger, Robert C, *Dir Architecture,* Montana State University, School of Architecture, Bozeman MT (S)

Uyemura, Ken, *Prof,* University of Miami, Dept of Art & Art History, Coral Gables FL (S)

Vachon, Auguste, *Special Collections,* Public Archives of Canada, Picture Division, Ottawa ON

Vadeboncoeur, Guy, *Pres,* Canadian Museums Association, Association des Musees Canadiens, Ottawa ON

Vahrenkamp, Linda, *Dir,* Star-Spangled Banner Flag House Association, Baltimore MD

Vajda, Elizabeth, *Head Librn,* Cooper Union for the Advancement of Science & Art, Library, New York NY

Valdes, Karen, *Dir Cur,* Miami-Dade Community College, South Campus, Art Gallery, Miami FL

Valencia, Romolo, *Instr Graphic Arts,* Honolulu Community College, Honolulu HI (S)

Valentin, Jean-Pierre, *Pres,* Professional Art Dealers Association of Canada, Toronto ON

Valentine, Lanci, *Dir Public Affairs,* Art Complex Museum at Duxbury, Duxbury MA

Valentine, Milfred, *Chmn,* Jones County Junior College, Art Dept, Ellisville MS (S)

Valenza, Dan, *Assoc Prof,* University of New Hampshire, Dept of the Arts, Durham NH (S)

Valicenti, Rick, *Pres,* Society of Typographic Arts, Chicago IL

Valk, Will, *Lectr,* Coe College, Dept of Art, Cedar Rapids IA (S)

Valkanas, Alene, *Programming & Publicity Dir,* Museum of Contemporary Art, Chicago IL

Vallari, Richard, *Dir Admissions,* Art Institute of Philadelphia, Philadelphia PA (S)

Valley, Derek R, *Registrar,* State Capitol Museum, Olympia WA

Vallila, Marja, *Asst Prof,* State University of New York at Albany, Art Dept, Albany NY (S)

Valore, Leonard, *VPres Educ,* International Correspondence Schools, School of Art, Scranton PA (S)

Van Auker, Alfred, *Prof,* Pierce College, Art Dept, Woodland Hills CA (S)

Van Bergen, Trudy, *Asst Cur,* Arts and Science Museum, Statesville NC

Van Bodegraven, A, *Treas,* Albright College, Freedman Gallery, Reading PA

vanBuren, Anne, *Prof,* Tufts University, Fine Arts Dept, Medford MA (S)

Van Buskirk, Mazelle, *Lectr,* Indiana University, Bloomington, School of Fine Arts, Bloomington IN (S)

Vance, Alex, *Dir,* Bergstrom Mahler Museum, Neenah WI

Vance, Carl, *Deputy Dir,* Santa Barbara Museum of Art, Santa Barbara CA

Vance, Joseph, *Treas,* Society of Animal Artists, Inc, Bronx NY

Vance, Lavern, *Pres,* Ravalli County Museum, Hamilton MT

Vanco, John, *Exec Dir,* Erie Art Museum, Erie PA

van Damme, B J, *Special Asst Dir,* Brooklyn Museum, Brooklyn NY

Vandeboncoeur, Guy, *Cur,* Society of the Montreal Military and Maritime Museum, Saint Helen's Island Museum, Montreal PQ

Van Deest, Orval, *Chmn,* Dakota State College, Division of Fine and Applied Art, Madison SD (S)

Vandegrift, David, *Assoc Prof,* Marygrove College, Dept of Art and Art History, Detroit MI (S)

Van Der Beck, E Stanley, *Chmn,* University of Maryland Baltimore County, Visual Arts Dept, Catonsville MD (S)

Vanderbilt, Hugh B, *VPres,* Historic Deerfield Inc, Deerfield MA

Vanderhill, Marlene, *Asst Dir,* Calvin College Center Art Gallery, Grand Rapids MI

Van Derhill, Rein, *Exhib Coordr,* Northwestern College, Te Paske Gallery of Rowenhorst, Orange City IA

Vanderhill, Rein, *Asst Prof,* Northwestern College, Art Dept, Orange City IA (S)

VanderHoek, J J, *Pres,* Community Arts Council of Chilliwack, Chilliwack BC

Van Derlans, Paula, *Gallery Asst,* California State University, Los Angeles, Fine Arts Gallery, Los Angeles CA

VanDerpool, Karen, *Instr,* California State University, Chico, Art Dept, Chico CA (S)

Vanderway, Richard, *Education Coordr,* Whatcom Museum of History and Art, Bellingham WA

VanderWeg, Phillip, *Chmn Art Dept,* Middle Tennessee State University, Art Dept, Murfreesboro TN (S)

VanderWerf, Sidney, *Asst Prof,* University of Northern Iowa, Dept of Art, Cedar Falls IA (S)

Vandinburgh, William G, *Executive Dean,* California State University, Hayward, University Art Gallery, Hayward CA

Van Doren, Marcia, *VPres,* Wenatchee Valley College, Gallery 76, Wenatchee WA

VanDuyne, Cecelia, *Recording Secy,* Art Centre of New Jersey, East Orange NJ (S)

Van Dyk, Stephen H, *Librn,* New York Institute of Technology Gallery, Art & Architectural Library, Old Westbury NY

Van Dyke, Andrea, *Communications & Marketing,* Milwaukee Art Museum, Milwaukee WI

Van Dyke, Fred, *Instr,* Utah Technical College at Salt Lake, Commercial Art Dept, Salt Lake City UT (S)

van Everdingen, Arie, *Assoc Prof,* Monmouth College, Dept of Art, West Long Branch NJ (S)

Vanger, Lee, *Librn,* Ships of The Sea Museum, Library, Savannah GA

Van Gilder, Caron, *Exec Dir,* Ashtabula Arts Center, Ashtabula OH

van Ginkel, Blanche Lemco, *Dir,* University of Toronto, School of Architecture, Toronto ON (S)

Vango, Eugene, *Asst Prof,* Virginia State University, Fine & Commercial Art, Petersburg VA (S)

VanGraafeiland, Peter, *Treasurer,* North Carolina Art Society, Raleigh NC

Van Haren, John E, *Head Dept,* Eastern Michigan University, Dept of Art, Ypsilanti MI (S)

Van Horn, Chalmer, *Assoc Prof,* Williamsport Area Community College, Dept of Engineering and Design, Williamsport PA (S)

Van Horn, David, *Prof,* Siena Heights College, Studio Angelico Art Dept, Adrian MI (S)

Van Horn, Donald, *Assoc Prof,* University of Texas at Tyler, Dept of Art, Tyler TX (S)

Van Horn, Henry, *Exec Secy,* Mansfield Fine Arts Guild, Mansfield Art Center, Mansfield OH

Van Horn, Kathleen, *Office Mgr & Bookkeeper,* Alaska Arts Southeast, Inc, Sitka AK

VanHorn, Walter, *Cur of Coll,* Anchorage Historical and Fine Arts Museum, Cook Inlet Historical Society, Anchorage AK

VanLoen, Alfred, *Prof,* C W Post Center of Long Island University, School of the Arts, Greenvale NY (S)

Vann, H D, *Faculty,* Florida College, Division of Art, Temple Terrace FL (S)

Vann, Lowell C, *Chmn,* Samford University, Art Dept, Birmingham AL (S)

Van Niel, Eloise, *Head Fine Arts-Audiovisual Section,* Hawaii State Library, Fine Arts-Audiovisual Section, Honolulu HI

VanRiemsdijk, Adrienne, *VPres,* Canadian Crafts Council, Conseil Canadien de l'Artisanat, Ottawa ON

Van Schaack, Eric, *Chmn,* Colgate University, Dept of Fine Arts, Hamilton NY (S)

Van Scoy, Burton B, *Dir Education,* Brevard Art Center and Museum, Inc, Melbourne FL

Vansen, Charles, *Chmn Foundations Dept,* Milwaukee Institute of Art and Design, Milwaukee WI (S)

Van Tassell, Katherin, *Asst Cur Register,* Minnesota Museum of Art, Saint Paul MN

Van Veen, Felicia, *Treas,* Artists Technical Institute, New York NY

VanVoorst, Philip, *Assoc Prof,* Northwest Missouri State University, Dept of Art, Maryville MO (S)

Van Wagner, Judith K, *Dir,* C W Post College of Long Island University, Hillwood Art Gallery, Greenvale NY

VanWagoner, Richard J, *Prof,* Weber State College, Art Dept, Ogden UT (S)

Van Why, Joseph S, *Dir,* Stowe-Day Foundation, Hartford CT

VanWinkle, William M, *VPres,* Litchfield Historical Society, Litchfield CT

VanZandt, Paul, *Chmn Dept,* Pembroke State University, Art Dept, Pembroke NC (S)

van Zanten, David, *Assoc Prof,* Northwestern University, Evanston, Dept of Art History, Evanston IL (S)

vanZelst, Lambertus, *Dir Research Laboratory,* Museum of Fine Arts, Boston MA

Varner, Lynn Adkins, *Staff Asst,* University of New Mexico, Jonson Gallery, Albuquerque NM

Varnes, Richard, *Dir Media & Programing,* Boulder Public Library and Gallery, Dept of Fine Arts Gallery, Boulder CO

Varnum, Maevernon, *Instr,* Wayne Art Center, Wayne PA (S)

Variano, John L, *Chmn,* Mount Holyoke College, Art Dept, South Hadley MA (S)

Vascovitch, J M, *Chmn Dept,* Chamberlayne Junior College, Dept of Applied Arts, Boston MA (S)

Vasiloff, Susan, *Asst Dir,* University of Tampa, Henry B Plant Museum, Tampa FL

Vaskys, Petras, *Chairperson Crafts,* Philadelphia College of Art, Philadelphia PA (S)

Vaslef, Irene, *Librn,* Harvard University, Library, Washington DC

Vasquez, Leah, *Asst Dir,* University of California, Irvine, Fine Art Gallery, Irvine CA

Vasse, Nancy, *Visual Arts & Exhibits Coordr,* Ashtabula Arts Center, Ashtabula OH

Vasseur, Dominique, *Asst Cur European Painting & Registrar,* Dayton Art Institute, Dayton OH

Vaughan, Thomas, *Dir,* Oregon Historical Society, Portland OR

Vaux, Richard, *Assoc Prof,* Adelphi University, Dept of Art and Art History, Garden City NY (S)

Vazquez, Paul, *Prof,* University of Bridgeport, Art Dept, Bridgeport CT (S)

Veasey, Ruth, *Instr,* Ocean City Arts Center, Ocean City NJ (S)

Veerkamp, Patrick, *Chmn,* Southwestern University, Art Dept, Georgetown TX (S)

Vega, Ed, *Dept Head,* University of Albuquerque, Art Dept, Albuquerque NM (S)

Vega-Rivera, Carmen, *Asst Dir,* Bronx Museum of the Arts, Bronx NY

Vegter-Kubic, Erica, *Dir,* San Jose State University, Art Gallery, San Jose CA

Veinus, P, *Asst Prof,* Northern Arizona University, Art Dept, Flagstaff AZ (S)

Velasquez, Geraldine, *Asst Prof,* Georgian Court College, Dept of Art, Lakewood NJ (S)

Velde, Jeanne E, *Instr,* Kilgore College, Dept Art and Art Education, Kilgore TX (S)

Velick, Susanne, *Secy,* Birmingham-Bloomfield Art Association, Birmingham MI

Vena, Dante, *Chairperson Art Educ,* Southeastern Massachusetts University, College of Visual and Performing Arts, North Dartmouth MA (S)

Venegas, Haydee, *Asst to Dir,* Museo de Arte de Ponce, Ponce Art Museum, Ponce PR

Venet, Keneth, *Readers Services,* Trinity College Library, Washington DC

Vengroff, Linda, *Asst Dir,* Texas Tech University Museum, Lubbock TX

Venner, Tom, *Asst Prof,* Siena Heights College, Studio Angelico Art Dept, Adrian MI (S)

Ventimiglia, John T, *Instructor,* Portland School of Art, Portland ME (S)

Ventura, Anthony, *Second VPres,* New Jersey Watercolor Society, South Orange NJ

Verble, Carol, *Asst Librn,* Missouri Historical Society, Library, Saint Louis MO

Verchomin, J, *Dir,* Ukrainian Museum of Canada, Edmonton AB

Verdon, Ron, *Instructor,* University of Wisconsin-Stout, Art Dept, Menomonie WI (S)

Verdon, Timothy, *Asst Prof,* Florida State University, Art History Dept, Tallahassee FL (S)

Ver Hague, James, *Assoc Prof,* Rochester Institute of Technology, School of Art and Design, Rochester NY (S)

Vermeule, Cornelius C, *Cur Classical Art,* Museum of Fine Arts, Boston MA

Vernon, Ann D, *Dir Education,* Chrysler Museum, Norfolk VA

Vernon, Carol, *Assoc Prof,* Southwestern Oregon Community College, Visual Arts Dept, Coos Bay OR (S)

Vernon, Donald E, *Pres,* Winnipeg Art Gallery, Winnipeg MB

Verre, Philip, *Cur,* Bronx Museum of the Arts, Bronx NY

Versaci, Nancy R, *Dir,* Brown University, Bell Gallery, Providence RI

Verschoyle, Hubert, *Secy,* San Antonio Art League, San Antonio TX

Verstegen, Clare, *Prog Coordr,* Arrowmont School of Arts and Crafts, Gatlinburg TN (S)

Verworn, Charles, *Chief Custodian,* Rodman Hall Arts Centre, Saint Catharines ON

Vesanen, Rocky, *Dir Communications,* Philbrook Art Center, Tulsa OK

Vettoretti, Teresa, *Asst to the Dir,* State University of New York at Purchase, Neuberger Museum, Purchase NY

Vezina, Raymond, *Art Inventory Section,* Public Archives of Canada, Picture Division, Ottawa ON

Viall, Richard, *Pres,* Gilbert Stuart Birthplace, Saunderstown RI

Vicente, Esteban, *Instr,* New York Studio School of Drawing, Painting and Sculpture, New York NY (S)

Vickers, Jack, *Instructor,* Solano Community College, Dept of Fine & Applied Art, Suisun City CA (S)

Vickers, Robert, *Prof,* Hope College, Art Dept, Holland MI (S)

Victor, James, *Instr,* Rosemont College, Division of the Arts, Rosemont PA (S)

Victor, Mary O'Neill, *Dir,* Fine Arts Museum of the South, Mobile AL

Vidnovic, Nick, *Lectr,* University of Pennsylvania, College Arts & Science, Philadelphia PA (S)

Viener, Saul, *Chmn Executive Council,* American Jewish Historical Society, Waltham MA

Viera, Ricardo, *Dir Exhib & Coll,* Lehigh University Art Galleries, Bethlehem PA

Viera, Ricardo, *Assoc Prof,* Lehigh University, Dept of Art and Architecture, Bethlehem PA (S)

Viesulas, Romas, *Prof,* Temple University, Tyler School of Art, Philadelphia PA (S)

Vigiletti, Robert, *Chmn Photography,* Center for Creative Studies—College of Art and Design, Detroit MI (S)

Vigtel, Gudmund, *Dir,* High Museum of Art, Atlanta GA

Viirlaid, Helle, *Registrar,* Vancouver Art Gallery, Vancouver BC

Vike, Gene, *Chmn,* Western Washington University, Art Dept, Bellingham WA (S)

Vilcins, M, *Reference Librn,* National Gallery of Canada, Library, Ottawa ON

Villafine, Josefina, *VPres,* Museo Historico de Puerto Rico Inc, Santurce PR

Villeneuve, Pat, *Dir,* Tucson Museum of Art School, Tucson AZ (S)

Vincent, Ellen, *Academic Dean,* Maryland College of Art and Design, Silver Spring MD (S)

Vincent, Henry, *Treas,* Verde Valley Art Association, Inc, Jerome AZ

Vincent, Joseph G, *Dir,* Rome Historical Society, Rome Information and Cultural Center, Rome NY

Vine, Naomi, *Education Dir,* Museum of Contemporary Art, Chicago IL

Vinograd, Richard, *Asst Prof,* University of Southern California, School of Fine Arts, Los Angeles CA (S)

Vinski, Jerome, *Planetarium,* Newark Museum, Newark NJ

Vint, Virginia H, *Prof,* Winona State University, Art Dept, Winona MN (S)

Vinzani, Jenny, *Instructor,* Vincennes University, Art Dept, Vincennes IN (S)

Violette, C L, *Assoc Prof,* Wiley College, Dept of Fine Arts, Marshall TX (S)

Vislosky, R J, *Instructor,* Indiana University of Pennsylvania, Dept of Art and Art Education, Indiana PA (S)

Visser, Mary, *Adjunct Instr,* Southwestern University, Art Dept, Georgetown TX (S)

Visser, Susan R, *Registrar,* Columbus Museum of Art, Columbus OH

Vitagliano, M, *Assoc Prof,* Chamberlayne Junior College, Dept of Applied Arts, Boston MA (S)

Vito, Denise, *Gallery Asst,* Center for Inter-American Relations Art Gallery, New York NY

Vivoni, Paul, *Auxiliary Prof,* Inter American University of Puerto Rico, Dept of Art, San German PR (S)

Vocelka, Mary, *Librn,* Yosemite Collections, Research Library, Yosemite National Park CA

Voci, Peter, *Instr,* New York Institute of Technology, Fine Arts Dept, Old Westbury NY (S)

Voelkle, William M, *Cur Medieval and Renaissance Manuscripts,* Pierpont Morgan Library, New York NY

Vogler, Cheryl, *Libr Asst,* Saint Louis Art Museum, Richardson Memorial Library, Saint Louis MO

Vogt, Diane L, *Head Librn,* Cranbrook Academy of Art Museum, Library, Bloomfield Hills MI

Vogt, Joel, *Instructor,* Avila College, Art Division, Dept of Performing and Visual Art, Kansas City MO (S)

Vogt, John, *Assoc Prof,* Kansas State University, Art Dept, Manhattan KS (S)

Vogt, Margaret, *Registrar,* Massillon Museum, Massillon OH

Volant, Jacques, *Cur,* Eskimo Museum, Churchill MB

Volk, Hiltraud, *Secy,* Coos Art Museum, Coos Bay OR

Volkert, James, *Art Cur,* Junior Arts Center, Los Angeles CA

Von Bamford, Lawrence, *Asst Chmn,* Colorado State University, Dept of Art, Fort Collins CO (S)

vonBarann, L, *VPres,* Doshi Center for Contemporary Art, Harrisburg PA

von Barann, Lawrence, *Vis Prof,* Harrisburg Area Community College, Division of Communication and the Arts, Harrisburg PA (S)

Von Barghahn, Barbara, *Assoc Prof,* George Washington University, Dept of Art, Washington DC (S)

vonBergen, John, *Instr,* Munson-Williams-Proctor Institute, School of Art, Utica NY (S)

von Bothmer, Dietrich, *Chmn Greek & Roman Art,* Metropolitan Museum of Art, New York NY

vonBujdoss, Nicholas, *Asst Prof,* Smith College, Art Dept, Northampton MA (S)

VonGlan, LeRoy, *Instructor,* Northeast Technical Community College, Dept of Art, Norfolk NE (S)

Von Hennenburg, M, *Prof,* Florida State University, Art History Dept, Tallahassee FL (S)

Von Mengershansen, Cornelia, *Instructor,* University of Southern California, Idyllwild School of Music and the Arts, Idyllwild CA (S)

vonRebhan, Anne, *Slide Librn,* National Gallery of Art, Educational Division Slide Library, Washington DC

vonSchlegell, David, *Assoc Prof,* Yale University, School of Art, New Haven CT (S)

Vontz, Al, *VPres,* Contemporary Arts Center, Cincinnati OH

Von Wrangel, Margaret, *Instr,* Green River Community College, Art Dept, Auburn WA (S)

Voos, William J, *Pres,* Atlanta College of Art, Atlanta GA (S)

Vore, Linda, *Faculty,* Midway College, Art Dept, Midway KY (S)

Voris, Peter, *Prof,* New Mexico State University, Art Dept, Las Cruces NM (S)

Vose, Bill, *Vis Lecturer,* North Central College, Dept of Art, Naperville IL (S)

Voss, Bill, *Instructor,* Mesa Community College, Dept of Art & Photography, Mesa AZ (S)

Voss, Dennis, *Asst Prof,* University of Montana, Dept of Art, Missoula MT (S)

Voss, Jerrold, *Dir,* Ohio State University, School of Architecture, Columbus OH (S)

Voss, Marjorie Anne, *Sr Cur,* Tongass Historical Society Museum, Ketchikan AK

Votaw, Barbara, *Conservator,* Bob Jones University, Greenville SC

Voulkos, Peter H, *Prof,* University of California, Berkeley, College of Letters & Sciences, Berkeley CA (S)

Vournakis, Karen, *Asst Prof,* Colgate University, Dept of Fine Arts, Hamilton NY (S)

Vruwink, J, *Assoc Prof,* Central College, Art Dept, Pella IA (S)

Vuilleumier, Eleanor, *Registrar,* Carnegie Institute, Museum of Art, Pittsburgh PA

Wabnitz, Robert, *Asst Prof,* Rochester Institute of Technology, School of Art and Design, Rochester NY (S)

Wada, Warner W, *Asst Prof Painting,* Ramapo College of New Jersey, School of Contemporary Arts, Mahwah NJ (S)

Wada, Wes, *Assoc Prof,* College of Southern Idaho, Art Dept, Twin Falls ID (S)

Waddel, Carl, *Dean,* Fresno City College, Art Dept, Fresno CA (S)

Waddell, Ann, *Office Coordr,* Pontiac Art Center, Pontiac MI

Waddell, Carol N, *Asst Dir & Librn,* Tippecanoe County Historical Museum, Lafayette IN

Waddell, James, *Dean,* Western New Mexico University, College of Arts and Letters, Art Dept, Silver City NM (S)

Waddell, Roberta, *Cur of Graphic Arts,* Toledo Museum of Art, Toledo OH

Waddington, Susan R, *Head,* Providence Public Library, Art and Music Dept, Providence RI

Wade, Edward M, *Chmn,* Potomac State College, Dept of Art, Keyser WV (S)

Wade, Edwin L, *Cur Non-Western Art,* Philbrook Art Center, Tulsa OK

Wade, Joyce, *Secy,* Pence Gallery, Davis CA

Wade, N, *Instr,* David Thompson University Centre, Visual Arts Dept, Nelson BC (S)

Wade, N, *Asst Prof,* University of Victoria, Dept of Visual Arts, Victoria BC (S)

Wadley, William Bert, *Chmn Dept,* University of the South, Dept of Fine Arts, Sewanee TN (S)

Wadsworth, Dorothy, *Instructor,* Johnson County Community College, Humanities Division, Overland Park KS (S)

Wagle, Kate, *Prof,* New Mexico State University, Art Dept, Las Cruces NM (S)

Wagman, N E, *Prof,* Salem State College, Art Dept, Salem MA (S)

Wagner, Betty L, *Librn,* University of Washington, Architecture, Urban Planning Library, Seattle WA

Wagner, Brian, *Instr,* Rosemont College, Division of the Arts, Rosemont PA (S)

Wagner, Catherine, *Lecturer,* Mills College, Art Dept, Oakland CA (S)

Wagner, David J, *Dir,* Leigh Yawkey Woodson Art Museum, Inc, Wausau WI

Wagner, Joseph, *Prof,* Kent State University, Stark Campus, School of Art, Canton OH (S)

Wagner, Merrill, *Pres,* American Abstract Artists, New York NY

Wagner, Nora, *Education Dir,* Mexican Museum, San Francisco CA

Wagner, Norman, *Printmaking Chmn,* Atlanta College of Art, Atlanta GA (S)

Wagner, Wesley, *Asst Prof,* Bethany College, Art Dept, Bethany WV (S)

Wagoner, David, *Preparator,* University of New Mexico, University Art Museum, Albuquerque NM

Wagstaff, Marge, *Secy,* Reynolda House, Inc, Winston-Salem NC

Wahlman, Maude, *Asst Prof,* University of Mississippi, Dept of Art, University MS (S)

Wailes, Bernard, *European Archives Assoc Cur,* University of Pennsylvania, University Museum of Archaeology & Anthropology, Philadelphia PA

Wait, Newman E, *Pres,* Yaddo, Saratoga Springs NY (S)

Waite, William, *Dir,* Chautauqua Art Association Galleries, Chautauqua NY

Wakerford, Mary, *Admin Asst,* Hofstra University, Emily Lowe Gallery, Hempstead NY

Walbridge, Barbara, *Pres,* Balboa Art Conservation Center, San Diego CA

Walch, John L, *Dir,* Saint Gregory's Abbey and College, Mabee-Gerrer Museum of Art, Shawnee OK

Waldfogel, Melvin, *Prof,* University of Minnesota, Minneapolis, Art History, Minneapolis MN (S)

Waldie, James R, *Pres,* Historical Society of Martin County, Elliot Museum, Stuart FL

Waldman, Diane, *Deputy Dir,* Solomon R Guggenheim Museum, New York NY

Waldman, Loretta, *Artmobile Librn,* Miami-Dade Public Library, Miami FL

Waldorf, Gwendolyn, *Cur of Collections & Exhibitions,* Tallahassee Junior Museum, Tallahassee FL

Waldron, Shirley A, *Publicity Coordr,* Cultural Art Center of Ocean City, Ocean City NJ

Walford, E John, *Chmn,* Wheaton College, Dept of Art, Wheaton IL (S)

Walford, Norman, *Chief of Admin,* Art Gallery of Ontario, Toronto ON

Walker, Alan, *Pres,* Jesse Besser Museum, Alpena MI

Walker, Barbara C, *Chmn,* Southeastern Louisiana University, Dept of Visual Arts, Hammond LA (S)

Walker, Barry, *Assoc Cur Prints & Drawings,* Brooklyn Museum, Brooklyn NY

Walker, Brian, *Dir,* Museum of Cartoon Art, Port Chester NY

Walker, Brooks, *Dir,* Walker Museum, Library, Fairlee VT

Walker, Charles, *Instructor,* De Anza College, Art Dept, Cupertino CA (S)

Walker, Daniel S, *Cur Ancient, Near and Far Eastern Arts,* Cincinnati Art Museum, Cincinnati OH

Walker, Doreen E, *Instr,* University of British Columbia, Dept of Fine Arts, Vancouver BC (S)

Walker, E K, *Chmn,* George Brown College of Applied Arts and Technology, Toronto ON (S)

Walker, Herbert Brooks, *Dir,* Walker Museum, Fairlee VT

Walker, H Kenneth, *Chairperson,* Daytona Beach Community College, Dept of Performing and Visual Arts, Daytona Beach FL (S)

Walker, J Charles, *Div Coordr Design,* Kent State University, School of Art, Kent OH (S)

Walker, Joe, *Chmn,* New Mexico Junior College, Arts, Business & Humanities Division, Hobbs NM (S)

Walker, John, *Chmn,* Community College of the Finger Lakes, Visual & Performing Arts Dept, Canandaigua NY (S)

Walker, Larry, *Head Dept,* Georgia State University, Dept of Art, Atlanta GA (S)

Walker, Marina, *Registrar,* State University of New York at Purchase, Neuberger Museum, Purchase NY

Walker, Mort, *Pres,* Museum of Cartoon Art, Port Chester NY

Walker, Nancy H, *Asst Cur,* Kiah Museum, Savannah GA

Walker, Noel Gahagan, *Asst Dir,* Walker Museum, Fairlee VT

Walker, Patricia, *Instr,* Danforth Museum School, Framingham MA (S)

Walker, Raymond, *Prof,* Jersey City State College, Art Dept, Jersey City NJ (S)

Walker, Roslyn, *Cur,* National Museum of African Art, Washington DC

Walker, Wanda J, *Registrar,* Montana State University, Museum of the Rockies, Bozeman MT

Walker, William B, *Chief Librn,* Metropolitan Museum of Art, New York NY

Walkey, Frederick P, *Dir,* Newport Art Museum and Art Association, Newport RI

Wall, Brent, *Instructor,* Aurora College, Art Dept, Aurora IL (S)

Wall, Brent, *Assoc Prof,* Saint Xavier College, Dept of Art, Chicago IL (S)

Wall, Brian, *Prof,* University of California, Berkeley, College of Letters & Sciences, Berkeley CA (S)

Wall, Constance, *Asst Librn & Cataloguer,* Detroit Institute of Arts, Research Library, Detroit MI

Wall, Robin, *Instr,* St Lawrence College, Dept of Visual and Creative Arts, Cornwall ON (S)

Wallace, Betty, *Dir,* Nebraska Wesleyan University, Elder Gallery, Lincoln NE

Wallace, Betty, *Head Dept,* Nebraska Wesleyan University, Art Dept, Lincoln NE (S)

Wallace, Brenda, *Dir,* London Regional Art Gallery, London ON

Wallace, Bruce, *Assoc Prof,* University of Tennessee at Chattanooga, Dept of Art, Chattanooga TN (S)

Wallace, Carol, *Art & Music Reference Librn,* Kansas City Public Library, Art & Music Department, Kansas City MO

Wallace, Dee, *Librn,* University of Illinois, Ricker Library of Architecture and Art, Champaign IL

Wallace, Elizabeth, *Asst Cur,* Virginia Beach Arts Center, Virginia Beach VA

Wallace, G, *Chmn Dept,* McMaster University, Dept of Art and Art History, Hamilton ON (S)

Wallace, Julia, *Educ Officer,* Art Gallery of Greater Victoria, Victoria BC

Wallace, Leonard R, *Chmn Dept,* Orange County Community College, Art Dept, Middletown NY (S)

Wallace, Richard W, *Prof,* Wellesley College, Art Dept, Wellesley MA (S)

Wallace, Victoria, *Dir,* Northport-East Northport Public Library, Northport NY

Wallach, Sharon, *Gallery Dir,* San Mateo County Arts Council, Belmont CA

Wallens, Nancy G, *Head of Reference,* Lake Forest Library, Fine Art Dept, Lake Forest IL

Waller, A Bret, *Dir,* University of Rochester, Memorial Art Gallery, Rochester NY

Waller, Richard, *Community Gallery Coordr,* Brooklyn Museum, Brooklyn NY

Waller, Susan, *Asst Cur,* Cranbrook Academy of Art Museum, Bloomfield Hills MI

Waller/Zirkle, Merle, *Assoc Prof,* Grinnell College, Dept of Art, Grinnell IA (S)

Walling, Cathleen, *Asst Dir Administration,* University of California, California Museum of Photography, Riverside CA

Wallis, Mel R, *Instructor,* Olympic College, Art Dept, Bremerton WA (S)

Wallschlaeger, Charles A, *Chmn Dept,* Ohio State University, Dept of Industrial Design, Columbus OH (S)

Walpole, Donald, *Assoc Prof,* Saint Meinrad College, Dept of Art, Saint Meinrad IN (S)

Walpuck, Kenneth, *Assoc Prof,* Queensborough Community College, Dept of Art and Design, Bayside NY (S)

Walser, A F, *Pres,* Arts and Science Museum, Statesville NC

Walsh, Albert J, *Coordr Fine & Performing Arts,* Butte College, Dept of Fine & Performing Arts, Oroville CA (S)

Walsh, Anne P, *Asst,* Worcester Art Museum, Library, Worcester MA

Walsh, Bee, *Pres,* San Bernardino County Museum and Satellites, Fine Arts Institute, Redlands CA

Walsh, Breffny A, *Dir,* Rensselaer County Historical Society, Hart-Cluett Mansion, 1827, Troy NY

Walsh, Dawna Hamm, *Asst Prof,* Dallas Baptist College, Dept of Art, Dallas TX (S)

Walsh, Jane, *Archivist,* Newport Art Museum and Art Association, Newport RI

Walsh, Janet, *Corresponding Secy,* American Watercolor Society, New York NY

Walsh, John, *Dir,* J Paul Getty Museum, Malibu CA

Walsh, Justa, *Treasurer,* Hill Country Arts Foundation, Ingram TX

Walsh, Marguerite, *Asst Prof,* New England College, Visual Arts Dept, Henniker NH (S)

Walsh, Nancy, *Museum Shop Mgr,* Bennington Museum, Bennington VT

Walsh, Richard K, *Pres,* Oregon College of Art, Ashland OR (S)

Walsh, Sue, *Asst Cur Decorative Arts,* Dayton Art Institute, Dayton OH

Walsh, Thomas, *Sculpture Area Head,* Southern Illinois University, School of Art, Carbondale IL (S)

Walter, Arnold, *Instr,* West Hills College, Fine Arts Dept, Coalinga CA (S)

Walter, Charles Thomas, *Asst Prof,* Bloomsburg University, Dept of Art, Bloomsburg PA (S)

Walter, David, *Treas,* Princeton Art Association, Princeton NJ

Walter, Elizabeth, *Asst Prof,* University of North Alabama, Dept of Art, Florence AL (S)

Walters, Christine M, *Faculty,* Virginia Intermont College, Fine Arts Dept, Bristol VA (S)

Walters, Denzil, *Chmn,* Shoreline Community College, Humanities Division, Seattle WA (S)

Walters, Don, *Chmn Dept,* Western Montana College, Art Dept, Dillon MT (S)

Walters, Elizabeth J, *Asst Prof,* Pennsylvania State University, University Park, Dept of Art History, University Park PA (S)

Walters, Janet S, *Asst VPres,* Wachovia Bank & Trust Company, NA, Winston-Salem NC

Walters, Louisella, *Dir,* Regis College, L J Walters Jr Gallery, Weston MA

Walters, Louisella, *Prof,* Regis College, Dept of Art, Weston MA (S)

Walters, Sylvia Solochek, *Assoc Prof,* University of Missouri-Saint Louis, Art Dept, Saint Louis MO (S)

Walters, Sylvia Solochek, *Dir,* University of Missouri, Saint Louis, Gallery 210, Saint Louis MO

Waltershausen, George L, *Chmn Dept,* Monmouth College, Dept of Art, Monmouth IL (S)

Walton, Candace, *Instructor,* Mount Mary College, Art Dept, Milwaukee WI (S)

Walton, James M, *Pres,* Carnegie Institute, Museum of Art, Pittsburgh PA

Walton, Jeri, *Sales Shop Manager,* Montana State University, Museum of the Rockies, Bozeman MT

Walton, Thomas, *Asst Prof,* Catholic University of America, Dept of Architecture and Planning, Washington DC (S)

Wands, Bruce, *Instr,* Joe Kubert School of Cartoon and Graphic Art Inc, Dover NJ (S)

Wands, Robert, *Asst Prof,* University of Southern Colorado, Belmont Campus, Dept of Art, Pueblo CO (S)

Wang, Lawrence, *Registrar,* Dixon Gallery and Gardens, Memphis TN

Wanserski, Martin, *Assoc Prof,* University of South Dakota, Dept of Art, Vermillion SD (S)

Wantz, John A, *Instructor,* College of DuPage, Humanities Division, Glen Ellyn IL (S)

Wantz, Justine, *Assoc Prof,* Loyola University of Chicago, Fine Arts Dept, Chicago IL (S)

Wantz, Richard G, *Pres Board of Trustees,* Washington County Museum of Fine Arts, Hagerstown MD

Wanzel, G, *Instructor,* Technical University of Nova Scotia, Faculty of Architecture, Halifax NS (S)

Ward, Barbara, *Conservator,* Vizcaya Museum and Gardens, Miami FL

Ward, Bill, *Prof,* University of Miami, Dept of Art & Art History, Coral Gables FL (S)

Ward, Jan R, *Assoc Prof,* Del Mar College, Dept of Art, Corpus Christi TX (S)

Ward, John L, *Assoc Prof,* University of Florida, Dept of Art, Gainesville FL (S)

Ward, Joseph, *Chmn,* Baptist College at Charleston, Dept of Art, Charleston SC (S)

Ward, Lillie, *Secy,* Afro Arts Cultural Centre, Inc, African Arts Museum & Gallery, New York NY

Ward, Lyle, *Head Dept,* College of the Ozarks, Dept of Art, Clarksville AR (S)

Ward, Mary Sater, *Cur Education,* Montgomery Museum of Fine Arts, Montgomery AL

Ward, Melinda, *Dir Media,* Walker Art Center, Minneapolis MN

Ward, Nina, *Adjunct Instr,* University of Northern Iowa, Dept of Art, Cedar Falls IA (S)

Ward, Phillip A, *Prof,* University of Florida, Dept of Art, Gainesville FL (S)

Ward, Roger, *Lectr,* University of Kansas, Kress Foundation Dept of Art History, Lawrence KS (S)

Ward, Roger B, *Asst Cur European Painting & Sculpture,* Atkins Museum of Fine Art, Kansas City MO

Ward, William, *Instructor,* Philadelphia Maritime Museum, Philadelphia PA

Ward, William E, *Asst in East Indian Art & Museum Designer,* Cleveland Museum of Art, Cleveland OH

Warda, Rebecca M, *Dir,* Widener University, Alfred O Deshong Museum, Chester PA

Wardlaw, George, *Chmn Dept,* University of Massachusetts, Amherst, College of Arts and Sciences, Amherst MA (S)

Wardle, Alfred, *Instr,* Munson-Williams-Proctor Institute, School of Art, Utica NY (S)

Wardwell, Allen, *Dir Gallery,* Asia Society, Inc, Gallery, New York NY

Wardwell, Anne E, *Cur Textiles,* Cleveland Museum of Art, Cleveland OH

Ware, Greg, *Dir,* Reed College Art Gallery, Portland OR

Warehall, Bill, *Instructor,* California State College, San Bernardino, Art Dept, San Bernardino CA (S)

Wareham, Ann Z, *Pres,* Tobe-Coburn School for Fashion Careers, New York NY (S)

Waricher, George, *Instructor,* Shippensburg State College, Art Dept, Shippensburg PA (S)

Waring, Lyn, *Community Arts Coordr,* King County Arts Commission, Seattle WA

Wark, Raymond, *Instr,* Woodbury University, Professional Arts Division, Los Angeles CA (S)

Wark, Robert R, *Cur Art Coll,* Huntington Library, Art Gallery and Botanical Gardens, San Marino CA

Warmus, William, *Asst Cur 20th Century Glass,* Corning Museum of Glass, Corning NY

Warner, Chris, *Cur,* Yellowstone Art Center, Billings MT

Warner, Douglas, *Instructor,* Charles Stewart Mott Community College, Fine Arts Division, Flint MI (S)

Warner, H, *Instructor,* Golden West College, Arts, Humanities and Social Sciences Institute, Huntington Beach CA (S)

Warner, John, *Treas,* Fine Arts Center of Clinton, Clinton IL

Warner, Lewis H, *Pres,* Tracey-Warner School, Philadelphia PA (S)

Warner, Mary, *Prof in Charge,* University of Montana, Gallery of Visual Arts, Missoula MT

Warner, Michael, *Cur,* Whatcom Museum of History and Art, Bellingham WA

Warner, Ronald H, *VChmn,* Arizona Commission on the Arts, Phoenix AZ

Warp, Harold, *Pres,* Harold Warp Pioneer Village Foundation, Minden NE

Warren, Bee, *Librn,* DeCordova and Dana Museum and Park, DeCordova Museum Library, Lincoln MA

Warren, Betty, *Dir,* Malden Bridge School of Art, Malden Bridge NY (S)

Warren, David, *Assoc Dir,* Museum of Fine Arts, Houston, Houston TX

Warren, Lynne, *Asst Cur,* Museum of Contemporary Art, Chicago IL

Warren, Ralph, *Gallery Dir,* Bowling Green State University, School of Art, Bowling Green OH (S)

Warren, Richard J, *Instr,* Okaloosa-Walton Junior College, Dept of Fine and Performing Arts, Niceville FL (S)

Warren, Russell, *Asst Prof,* Davidson College, Art Dept, Davidson NC (S)

Warren, Sarah, *Asst Mgr,* Whitney Museum of American Art, Whitney at Philip Morris, New York NY

Warsager, Susan, *Membership & Tours Coordr,* Spertus Museum of Judaica, Chicago IL

Warshasky, Stanford, *Dir,* Silas Bronson Library, Art, Music & Theatre Dept, Waterbury CT

Warwick, Katherine, *Asst to Dir Public Information,* National Gallery of Art, Washington DC

Washington, Selden, *Asst Dir,* Honolulu Academy of Arts, Honolulu HI

Wasil, Dan, *Cur,* Los Angeles Institute of Contemporary Art, Los Angeles CA

Wasserstein, Susan M, *Public Relations,* Art Dealers Association of America, Inc, New York NY

Watcke, Thomas C, *Head Dept,* Albright College, Dept of Art, Reading PA (S)

Waterhouse, John, *Cur Coll,* Massachusetts Institute of Technology, Hart Nautical Museum, Cambridge MA

Waterhouse, Richard, *Art Coordr,* Okefenokee Heritage Center, Inc, Waycross GA

Waters, Arnold, *Pres,* Fairbanks Museum and Planetarium, Saint Johnsbury VT

Waters, Jerry, *Instructor,* Fisk University, Division of Humanities & Fine Arts, Nashville TN (S)

Waters, Karen J, *Dean,* Texas Wesleyan College, Dept of Art, Fort Worth TX (S)

Waters, Kathryn M, *Asst Prof,* Indiana State University, Evansville, Art Dept, Evansville IN (S)

Waters, Sara, *Assoc Prof,* Texas Tech University, Dept of Art, Lubbock TX (S)

Waterton, E, *Asst Dir Human History,* Department of Culture, Government of the Province of Alberta, Provincial Museum of Alberta, Edmonton AB

Watkins, Ben, *Prof,* Eastern Illinois University, School of Fine Arts, Charleston IL (S)

Watkins, Charles Alan, *Exec Dir,* Erie Historical Museum, Erie PA

Watkins, Ruth, *Prof,* College of Notre Dame of Maryland, Art Dept, Baltimore MD (S)

Watkinson, Barbara, *Asst Prof,* College of William and Mary, Dept of Fine Arts, Williamsburg VA (S)

Watkinson, Patricia, *Cur,* Washington State University, Museum of Art, Pullman WA

Watrous, John, *Instr,* Santa Rosa Junior College, Art Dept, Santa Rosa CA (S)

Watrous, John, *Dir,* Santa Rosa Junior College Art Gallery, Santa Rosa CA

Watrous, L Vance, *VChmn Art Hist,* State University of New York, Buffalo, Dept of Art and Art History, Buffalo NY (S)

Watrous, Rebecca, *Educ Dir,* Historic Cherry Hill, Albany NY

Watson, Clarissa H, *Dir,* Country Art Gallery, Locust Valley NY

Watson, Donna, *Instructor,* Umpqua Community College, Fine & Performing Arts Dept, Roseburg OR (S)

Watson, Herb, *Designer,* University of British Columbia, Museum of Anthropology, Vancouver BC

Watson, Jan, *Asst Prof,* Bradford College, Creative Arts Division, Bradford MA (S)

Watson, Jennifer C, *Cur,* Kitchener-Waterloo Art Gallery, Kitchener ON

Watson, Joseph A, *Assoc Prof,* Rochester Institute of Technology, School of Art and Design, Rochester NY (S)

Watson, Katharine J, *Dir,* Bowdoin College, Museum of Art & Peary-MacMillan Arctic Museum, Brunswick ME

Watson, Lorraine, *Instr,* Ocean City Arts Center, Ocean City NJ (S)

Watson, Mary, *Library Asst,* Georgia Institute of Technology, College of Architecture Library, Atlanta GA

Watson, Scott, *Cur,* Vancouver Art Gallery, Vancouver BC

Watson, Thomas, *Instructor,* Columbia College, Art Dept, Columbia MO (S)

Watson, T M, *Mgr,* Cowboy Artists of America, Kansas City MO

Watson, Wendy, *Chief Cur,* Mount Holyoke College Art Museum, South Hadley MA

Watt, James, *Cur Asiatic,* Museum of Fine Arts, Boston MA

Watt, Virginia J, *Dir,* Guilde Canadienne des Metiers d'Art, Quebec, Canadian Guild of Crafts, Quebec, Montreal PQ

Wattenmaker, Richard J, *Dir,* M Flint Institute of Arts, Flint MI

Watts, Billie Ann, *Secy,* Muckenthaler Cultural Center, Fullerton CA

Watts, Christopher, *Dir,* Cornish Institute, Cornish Gallery, Seattle WA

Watts, Michael, *Asst Prof,* Murray State University, Art Dept, Murray KY (S)

Watts, R Michael, *Gallery Dir,* Murray State University, Clara M Eagle Gallery, Murray KY

Watts, Robert, *Prof,* Rutgers, the State University of New Jersey, Mason Gross School of the Arts, New Brunswick NJ (S)

Watts, Roland S, *Chmn,* Winston-Salem State University, Art Dept, Winston-Salem NC (S)

Waufle, Alan D, *Dir,* Gaston County Museum of Art & History, Dallas NC

Wavell, Joan B, *Adminr,* Rollins College, George D and Harriet W Cornell Fine Arts Center Museum, Winter Park FL

Wax, Bernard, *Dir,* American Jewish Historical Society, Waltham MA

Waxman, Joanne, *Librn,* Portland School of Art Library, Portland ME

Waxman, S, *Secy,* McMaster University, Art Gallery, Hamilton ON

Way, Gordon, *Dir,* Cody Country Art League, Cody WY

Waymeyer, Catherine, *Adjunct Instr,* Maryville College, St Louis, Art Division, Saint Louis MO (S)

Wayne, Sam, *Instructor,* Saint Louis Community College at Meramec, Art Dept, Saint Louis MO (S)

Weaver, Donald E, *Cur of Archaeology,* Museum of Northern Arizona, Flagstaff AZ

Weaver, George, *Chmn of Board,* Chautauqua Art Association Galleries, Chautauqua NY

Weaver, James D, *Dir,* Tyler Museum of Art, Tyler TX

Weaver, Judy, *Administrative Asst,* Montana State University, Museum of the Rockies, Bozeman MT

Weaver, Larry E, *Assoc Prof,* University of Lethbridge, Dept of Art, Lethbridge AB (S)

Weaver, L E, *Chmn Art Dept,* University of Lethbridge, Art Gallery, Lethbridge AB

Weaver, Paula, *Asst Prof,* University of the District of Columbia, Art Dept, Washington DC (S)

Weaver, Robert C, *Photography & Graphic Design,* Southern Illinois University at Edwardsville, Dept of Art and Design, Edwardsville IL (S)

Webb, Beth R, *Mus and Art Librn,* Brigham Young University, Harold B Lee Library, Provo UT

Webb, Brian, *Assoc Prof,* Norwich University, Dept of Philosophy, Religion and Fine Arts, Northfield VT (S)

Webb, Caroline, *Cur Coll,* Old Barracks Museum, Trenton NJ

Webb, Clem, *Adjunct Instructor,* Lamar University, Art Dept, Beaumont TX (S)

Webb, Edward, *Cur Historic Houses,* Charleston Museum, Charleston SC

Webb, L Robert, *VPres,* Adirondack Lakes Center for the Arts, Blue Mountain Lake NY

Webb, Paula, *Publicist,* Rice University, Institute for the Arts, Rice Museum, Houston TX

Webb, Peggy, *Chmn Board of Trustees,* Lee County Library, Tupelo MS

Webb, Robert L, *Librn,* Kendall Whaling Museum, Library, Sharon MA

Webber, David A, *Dir,* Confederation Centre Art Gallery and Museum, Charlottetown PE

Webber, Larry Jan, *Assoc Prof,* Mississippi State University, Art Dept, Mississippi State MS (S)

Webber, Nancy E, *Asst Prof,* Los Angeles Harbor College, Art Dept, Wilmington CA (S)

Webby, Ernest J, *Dir,* Brockton Public Library System, Municipal Art Gallery, Brockton MA

Weber, Arthur, *Dean,* Herron School of Art, Indiana University-Purdue University, Indianapolis, Indianapolis IN (S)

Weber, B M A, *Vis Prof,* California Lutheran College, Art Dept, Thousand Oaks CA (S)

Weber, Bruce, *Cur,* Norton Gallery and School of Art, West Palm Beach FL

Weber, Dorothy M, *Executive Dir,* Visual Artists and Galleries Association, Inc, VAGA, New York NY

Weber, Jean M, *Dir,* Museum of New Mexico, Santa Fe NM

Weber, John, *Assoc Prof,* Elmhurst College, Art Dept, Elmhurst IL (S)

Weber, Joseph A, *Art Education,* Southern Illinois University at Edwardsville, Dept of Art and Design, Edwardsville IL (S)

Weber, Louis, *Assoc Prof,* University of Dayton, Fine Arts Division, Dayton OH (S)

Weber, Mark, *Adjunct Instr,* Maryville College, St Louis, Art Division, Saint Louis MO (S)

Weberg, Lorraine, *Art Librn,* Fashion Institute of Technology, Library, New York NY

Webrand, Sandy, *VPres,* Conejo Valley Art Museum, Thousand Oaks CA

Webre, Steve, *Archives,* Louisiana Department of Culture, Recreation and Tourism, Louisiana Historical Center Library, New Orleans LA

Webster, Barry, *Honourary Secy,* Community Arts Council of Vancouver, Vancouver BC

Webster, Donald B, *Cur,* Royal Ontario Museum, Canadiana Gallery, Toronto ON

Webster, M, *Assoc Prof,* Northern Arizona University, Art Dept, Flagstaff AZ (S)

Webster, Melissa, *Instr,* Walla Walla Community College, Art Dept, Walla Walla WA (S)

Webster, Paul, *Lectr,* Oakland University, Dept of Art and Art History, Rochester MI (S)

Webster, Robert J, *Assoc Prof,* Rochester Institute of Technology, School of Printing, Rochester NY (S)

Webster, Ruth, *Treas,* Cortland County Historical Society, Suggett House Museum, Cortland NY

Wechsler, Jeffrey, *Cur Painting & Sculpture & Asst Dir,* Rutgers University, Jane Voorhees Zimmerli Art Museum, New Brunswick NJ

Weddle, B D, *Mgr,* T C Steele State Memorial, Nashville IN

Wedig, Dale, *Instructor,* Northern Michigan University, Dept of Art and Design, Marquette MI (S)

Weekly, Nancy, *Archivist & Registrar,* Burchfield Art Center, Buffalo NY

Weeks, Dennis W, *Dir,* Saint Joseph's University, Fine Arts Dept, Philadelphia PA (S)

Weeks, Edward F, *Cur Painting & Sculpture,* Birmingham Museum of Art, Birmingham AL

Weeks, James, *Prof,* Boston University, School of Visual Arts, Boston MA (S)

Weer, Barry D, *Cur Art,* Illinois State University, Center for the Visual Arts Gallery, Normal IL

Wees, Beth Carver, *Assoc Cur,* Sterling and Francine Clark Art Institute, Williamstown MA

Wees, J Dustin, *Photograph & Slide Librn,* Sterling and Francine Clark Art Institute, Williamstown MA

Wegner, Pamela, *Prof,* Mount Saint Mary's College, Fine Arts Dept, Emmitsburg MD (S)

Wegner, Susan, *Prof,* Bowdoin College, Art Dept, Brunswick ME (S)

Wehrle, Armin, *Chmn Bd,* Coos Art Museum, Coos Bay OR

Wei, Philip, *Dir Library Services,* Plymouth State College, Herbert H Lamson Library, Plymouth NH

Weidenfeller, Jack, *VPres,* Fort Missoula Historical Museum, Missoula MT

Weidensee, Victor, *Chmn,* Black Hills State College, Art Dept, Spearfish SD (S)

Weidl, Beverly, *Cur,* Hopewell Museum, Hopewell NJ

Weidman, James F, *Development Officer,* Huntington Galleries, Huntington WV

Weidman, Jeffrey, *Art Librn,* Oberlin College, Clarence Ward Art Library, Oberlin OH

Weidmann, Daniel, *Graphic Designer,* Brooklyn Museum, Brooklyn NY

Weidner, H G, *VPres,* Women's City Club of Cleveland, Gallery, Cleveland OH

Weidner, Marsha, *Asst Prof,* Oberlin College, Dept of Art, Oberlin OH (S)

Weiffenbach, Jean-Edith V, *Dir,* University of Colorado Art Galleries, Boulder CO

Weigand, Charles J, *Assoc Prof,* Rochester Institute of Technology, School of Printing, Rochester NY (S)

Weigel, Jan, *Assoc Dir Taft Museum,* Taft Museum, Cincinnati OH

Weikart, Richard, *Pres,* Maryland College of Art and Design, Silver Spring MD (S)

Weil, Norman, *Asst Prof,* Northwest Missouri State University, Dept of Art, Maryville MO (S)

Weil, Rose R, *Exec Secy,* College Art Association of America, New York NY

Weil, Stephen, *Deputy Dir,* Hirshhorn Museum and Sculpture Garden, Washington DC

Weiler, Kay, *Secy,* Art Guild of Burlington, Arts for Living Center, Burlington IA

Weiler, Melody, *Assoc Prof,* Murray State University, Art Dept, Murray KY (S)

Weimer, Ginni, *Art & Architecture,* Cooper Union for the Advancement of Science & Art, Library, New York NY

Weimerskirch, Robert, *Instr,* Alfred C Glassell School of Art, Houston TX (S)

Wein, Frances, *Ed,* National Portrait Gallery, Washington DC

Weinberg, Adam, *Dir Education,* Walker Art Center, Minneapolis MN

Weinberg, Ephraim, *Dir School,* Pennsylvania Academy of the Fine Arts, Galleries, Philadelphia PA

Weinberg, Ephraim, *Dir,* Pennsylvania Academy of the Fine Arts, Philadelphia PA (S)

Weinberg, H Barbara, *Assoc Prof,* City University of New York, PhD Program in Art History, New York NY (S)

Weinbrecht, Ruby, *Chmn Libr Committee,* James Monroe Law Office - Museum and Memorial Library, Library, Fredericksburg VA

Weiner, Elsa, *Gallery Dir,* Moore College of Art Gallery, Philadelphia PA

Weiner, Samuel, *Assoc Prof,* Rutgers, the State University of New Jersey, Mason Gross School of the Arts, New Brunswick NJ (S)

Weingrod, Carmi, *Slide Cur,* University of Oregon, School of Architecture and Allied Arts Library, Eugene OR

Weinhardt, Carl J, *Dir,* Vizcaya Museum and Gardens, Miami FL

Weinheimer, George, *Actg Dir,* Schenectady Museum, Schenectady NY

Weininger, Jennifer B, *Dir Public Information,* Worcester Art Museum, Worcester MA

Weinke, Jane, *Assoc Cur,* Leigh Yawkey Woodson Art Museum, Inc, Wausau WI

Weinland, Richard, *Treas,* Katonah Gallery, Katonah NY

Weinman, Albert, *Art Advisory Board,* Society of Medalists, Danbury CT

Weinraub, Charles, *Pres,* Fort Wayne Fine Arts Foundation, Inc, Fort Wayne IN

Weinrich, Peter H, *Exec Dir,* Canadian Crafts Council, Conseil Canadien de l'Artisanat, Ottawa ON

Weinstein, M, *Treasurer,* Lovis Corinth Memorial Foundation, Inc, New York NY

Weir, Katherine M, *Librn,* Arizona State University, Howe Architecture Library, Tempe AZ

Weir, Stan, *Vis Prof,* Oral Roberts University, Fine Arts Dept, Tulsa OK (S)

Weirich, David, *Instr,* Mount San Jacinto College, Art Dept, San Jacinto CA (S)

Weirich, Nancy, *Librn,* Tippecanoe County Historical Museum, Alameda McCollough Library, Lafayette IN

Weisberg, Ruth, *Prof,* University of Southern California, School of Fine Arts, Los Angeles CA (S)

Weisenburger, Patricia, *Librn,* Kansas State University, Paul Weigel Library, Manhattan KS

Weishaar, Michael, *Local Minister,* Mission San Luis Rey Museum, San Luis Rey CA

Weisl, Edwin L, *Pres,* International Foundation for Art Research, Inc, New York NY

Weisman, Gustav, *Chmn Dept Experimental Art,* Ontario College of Art, Toronto ON (S)

Weisman, Judy, *Chief, Education and Public Programs,* Chicago Historical Society, Chicago IL

Weiss, Art, *Dept Chmn,* California State University, Northridge, Dept of Art-Two Dimensional Media, Northridge CA (S)

Weiss, Art, *Instr,* Woodbury University, Professional Arts Division, Los Angeles CA (S)

Weiss, Esther, *Pres,* Alaska Association for the Arts, Fairbanks AK

Weiss, Gilbert H, *Dir,* Antonelli Institute of Art & Photography, Professional Photography, Commercial Art & Interior Design, Plymouth Meeting PA (S)

Weiss, Harvey, *Asst Prof,* Adelphi University, Dept of Art and Art History, Garden City NY (S)

Weiss, Irwin, *Instr,* Rosemont College, Division of the Arts, Rosemont PA (S)

Weiss, John, *Coordr Photography,* University of Delaware, Dept of Art, Newark DE (S)

Weiss, Murray, *Dir,* Milwaukee Center for Photography, Milwaukee WI (S)

Weiss, Nathan, *Pres,* Kean College of New Jersey, Union NJ

Weiss, Olga, *Research Assoc,* Spertus Museum of Judaica, Chicago IL

Weiss, Terri, *Instructor,* Mount Mary College, Art Dept, Milwaukee WI (S)

Weissen-Flutt, Priscilla, *Dir,* Alverno College Gallery, Milwaukee WI

Weisser, Terry Drayman, *Dir of Conservation Dept,* Walters Art Gallery, Baltimore MD

Weissman, Benjamin, *Co-Dir Reading Series,* Beyond Baroque Foundation, Venice CA

Weissman, Walter, *Pres,* Foundation for the Community of Artists, New York NY

Weisz, Helen, *Instructor,* Bucks County Community College, Fine Arts Dept, Newton PA (S)

Weitman, Grace, *Secy,* Craft Center Museum, Wilton CT

Weitman, Malka, *Public Relations,* Judah L Magnes Museum, Berkeley CA

Weitzel, Robert D, *Dean,* Cleveland Institute of Art, Cleveland OH

Weitzenhoffer, Clara, *VPres,* Timken Art Gallery, San Diego CA

Weitzman, Kurt, *Consultative Cur,* Metropolitan Museum of Art, The Cloisters, New York NY

Welber, Beverly Zisla, *Arts Admin,* Saint Anselm College, Manchester NH

Welch, Bill, *Instructor,* Oklahoma State University, Graphic Arts Dept, Okmulgee OK (S)

Welch, Ileana, *Dir Cultural Heritage,* City of Los Angeles, Cultural Affairs Dept, Los Angeles CA

Welch, John N, *Treas,* Nantucket Historical Association, Fair Street Museum, Nantucket MA

Welch, Josiah, *Pres,* Newburyport Maritime Society, Custom House Maritime Museum, Newburyport MA

Welch, Olga, *Exec Dir,* Cooperstown Art Association, Cooperstown NY

Welch, Paul, *Chmn Dept,* Northwestern Michigan College, Art Dept, Traverse City MI (S)

Welch, Robert B, *Chmn,* Limestone College, Art Dept, Gaffney SC (S)

Welch, S Anthony, *Prof,* University of Victoria, Dept of History in Art, Victoria BC (S)

Welch, Sue C, *Librn,* Schenectady Museum, Library, Schenectady NY

Welch, William F, *Chairman,* Georgia Volunteer Lawyers for the Arts, Inc, Atlanta GA

Welchans, Roger A, *Chmn,* John Carroll University, Dept of Fine Arts, Cleveland OH (S)

Welden, Dan, *VPres,* Society of American Graphic Artists, New York NY

Welden, Larry, *Instructor,* Sacramento City College, Art Dept, Sacramento CA (S)

Weldon Smith, J, *Dir,* Fiberworks, Center for the Textile Arts, Berkeley CA

Wellington, Margot, *Executive Dir,* Municipal Art Society of New York, New York NY

Welliver, Jackie, *Instructor,* Williamsport Area Community College, Dept of Engineering and Design, Williamsport PA (S)

Welliver, Neil G, *Prof,* University of Pennsylvania, College Arts & Science, Philadelphia PA (S)

Wellman, Charles W, *Chmn,* University of Central Florida, Art Dept, Orlando FL (S)

Wells, Augusta, *Secy,* Lighthouse Gallery, Tequesta FL

Wells, Carol B, *Instr,* Villa Maria College of Buffalo, Art Dept, Buffalo NY (S)

Wells, David, *Ref,* Clark County Library District, Las Vegas NV

Wells, Gerald, *Assoc Prof,* Fort Lewis College, Art Dept, Durango CO (S)

Wells, James L, *Cur Graphics,* Smith-Mason Gallery and Museum, Washington DC

Wells, Robert, *Prof,* Northeastern University, Dept of Art, Boston MA (S)

Wells, Rufus, *Asst Prof,* University of the District of Columbia, Art Dept, Washington DC (S)

Wells, Sheila, *Prof,* Rochester Institute of Technology, School of Art and Design, Rochester NY (S)

Wells, Susan Ann, *Dir,* Columbus Cultural Arts Center, Columbus OH

Wells, Suzanne, *Special Exhibitions Coordr,* Philadelphia Museum of Art, Philadelphia PA

Wells, Vern, *Area Chmn Art History,* Pasadena City College, Art Dept, Pasadena CA (S)

Welsh, Genrose, *Staff Asst,* Jackson County Historical Society, John Wornall House Museum, Independence MO

Welsh, Peter, *Cur,* Southwest Museum, Los Angeles CA

Welsh, Robert, *Chmn,* Burlington County College, Fine Arts Dept, Pemberton NJ (S)

Welsh, R P, *Chmn,* University of Toronto, Dept of Fine Art, Toronto ON (S)

Welu, James A, *Chief Cur,* Worcester Art Museum, Worcester MA

Welu, William J, *Chairperson,* Briar Cliff College, Art Dept, Sioux City IA (S)

Weng, Siegfried, *Dir Emeritus,* Evansville Museum of Arts and Science, Evansville IN

Weng, Wan-go H C, *Dir,* China Institute in America, China House Gallery, New York NY

Wenger, Bruce, *Head Art Dept,* Houghton College, Art Dept, Houghton NY (S)

Wenig-Horswell, Judy, *Asst Prof,* Goshen College, Art Dept, Goshen IN (S)

Wentworth, T T, *Dir & Cur,* T T Wentworth, Jr Museum, Pensacola FL

Wentworth, T W, *Deputy Dir & Secy,* T T Wentworth, Jr Museum, Pensacola FL

Wentzell, Judith, *Art Librn,* Portland Public Library, Art Dept, Portland ME

Wenzel, Carol, *Business Mgr,* Historic Deerfield Inc, Deerfield MA

Wenzel-Rideout, Carol R, *Cur Education,* Frederic Remington Art Museum, Ogdensburg NY

Werbel, Lee, *Program Coordr,* Los Angeles Contemporary Exhibitions, Inc, Los Angeles CA

Werberig, Charles C, *Assoc Prof,* Rochester Institute of Technology, School of Photographic Arts & Sciences, Rochester NY (S)

Werfel, Gina, *Asst Prof,* Colby College, Art Dept, Waterville ME (S)

Werger, Art, *Asst Prof,* Wesleyan College, Art Dept, Macon GA (S)

Werk, Horst, *Assoc Prof,* Corning Community College, Division of Humanities, Corning NY (S)

Werle, Thomas, *Asst Prof,* Greater Hartford Community College, Humanities Division & Art Dept, Hartford CT (S)

Werner, Bev, *Asst Dir,* Fine Arts Club, Second Crossing Gallery, Valley City ND

Werner, Don, *Designer,* Museum of the American Indian, New York NY

Werness, Hope B, *Chmn Dept & Gallery Dir,* California State College, Stanislaus, Art Dept, Turlock CA (S)

Wert, Ned O, *Chmn Exhib,* Indiana University of Pennsylvania, Kipp Gallery, Indiana PA

Wertheim, Earl, *Asst Prof,* Sullivan County Community College, Division of Commercial Art and Photography, Loch Sheldrake NY (S)

Wertkin, Gerard C, *Asst Dir,* Museum of American Folk Art, New York NY

Wertz, Andrew W, *Dir,* Hamilton College, Bristol Campus Center, Clinton NY

Wesaw, Sallie, *Instructor,* Central Wyoming College, Art Center, Riverton WY (S)

Wescott, Richard, *Dir,* Augusta Richmond County Museum, Augusta GA

Wesp, Erwin O, *Exhib Chmn,* Coppini Academy of Fine Arts, San Antonio TX

Wessel, Frederick, *Assoc Prof,* Hartford Art School of the University of Hartford, West Hartford CT (S)

Wessels, Henry, *Assoc Prof,* California Polytechnic State University at San Luis Obispo, Art Dept, San Luis Obispo CA (S)

West, Bruce, *Asst Prof,* Lewis and Clark College, Dept of Art, Portland OR (S)

West, Catherine, *Dir,* Clinton Historical Museum Village, Clinton NJ

West, Harvey, *Dir,* University of Washington, Henry Art Gallery, Seattle WA

West, Jean, *Arts Workshop,* Newark Museum, Newark NJ

West, Judith, *Asst Prof,* Florida State University, Art Dept, Tallahassee FL (S)

West, Peter, *Lectr,* Bethany College, Art Dept, Bethany WV (S)

West, Richard V, *Dir,* Santa Barbara Museum of Art, Santa Barbara CA

West, Sharon, *Head Information Access Services,* University of Alaska, Elmer E Rasmuson Library, Fairbanks AK

Westberg, Alma, *Art & Music Librn,* Santa Cruz Public Library, Art, Music, Film Dept, Santa Cruz CA

Westcoat, Bonna, *Asst Prof,* Emory University, Art History Dept, Atlanta GA (S)

Wester, Janie, *Asst Prof,* Oklahoma Baptist University, Art Dept, Shawnee OK (S)

Western, Dominique C, *Cur Exhib,* Division of Historical and Cultural Affairs, Bureau of Museums and Historic Sites, Dover DE

Westervelt, Alice, *Museum Shop Mgr,* Rhode Island School of Design, Museum of Art, Providence RI

Westgard, Cheryl, *Pres,* Dallas Public Library, Dallas Print and Drawing Society, Dallas TX

Westhafer, Dorothy H, *Gallery Dir,* Niagara County Community College Art Gallery, Sanborn NY

Westhusing, James, *Program Asst,* Alaska Arts Southeast, Inc, Sitka AK

Westin, Robert H, *Chmn,* University of Florida, Dept of Art, Gainesville FL (S)

Westin, Sandra, *Public Affairs Officer,* National Portrait Gallery, Washington DC

Westlake, Judith Ann, *Executive Dir,* Doshi Center for Contemporary Art, Harrisburg PA

Westman, Penn, *Treas,* Rockport Art Association, Rockport MA

Westmoreland, Rosamond, *Sr Conservator,* National Portrait Gallery, Washington DC

Weston, Norman B, *VChmn,* Detroit Institute of Arts, Founders Society, Detroit MI

Weston, Robert T, *Art Museum Adminr,* Detroit Institute of Arts, Detroit MI

Weston, Spencer, *Prog Dir,* Afro-American Historical and Cultural Museum, Philadelphia PA

Westwood, Jefferson, *Ctr Dir,* State University of New York College at Fredonia, M C Rockefeller Arts Center Gallery, Fredonia NY

Wetherbee, Ralph H, *Chmn Board,* Springfield Art Center, Springfield OH

Wetzel, David, *Head of Publications,* Colorado Historical Society, State Museum, Denver CO

Weyerhaeuser, Charles A, *Museum Dir,* Art Complex Museum at Duxbury, Duxbury MA

Wheat, Gilbert C, *Chmn Dept,* College of Marin, Dept of Art, Kentfield CA (S)

Wheatley, Kim R, *Music Librn,* Munson-Williams-Proctor Institute, Art Reference Library, Utica NY

Wheeler, Catherine, *Head Public Relations,* Winterthur Museum and Gardens, Winterthur DE

Wheeler, Claire, *Admin Asst,* Shaker Museum, Old Chatham NY

Wheeler, Doris A, *Librn,* Louisiana State University, Design Resource Center, Baton Rouge LA

Wheeler, Jean, *Asst,* San Jose Museum of Art, Library, San Jose CA

Wheeler, Mark, *Pres,* Art Institute of Fort Lauderdale, Fort Lauderdale FL (S)

Wheeler, Robert C, *Assoc Dir,* Minnesota Historical Society, Saint Paul MN

Wheelock, Arthur K, *Cur Dutch & Flemish Painting,* National Gallery of Art, Washington DC

Whetstone, Nita, *Adjunct Instructor,* Auburn University at Montgomery, Art Dept, Montgomery AL (S)

Whipple, Florence, *Exec Secy,* New Brunswick Museum, Saint John NB

Whisnant, Joe, *Cur,* Greensboro Artists' League, Greensboro NC

Whitacre, Steven, *Chmn Found,* Kansas City Art Institute, Kansas City MO (S)

Whitaker, Richard R, *Dean,* University of Illinois at Chicago, College of Architecture, Art and Urban Planning, Chicago IL (S)

Whitcomb, Sylvia C, *Pres,* Colonel Black Mansion, Ellsworth ME

Whitcomb, Therese T, *Dir,* University of San Diego, Founders' Gallery, San Diego CA

White, Anne, *Dir Education,* International Center of Photography, New York NY

White, Barbara, *Business Mgr,* Kimbell Art Museum, Fort Worth TX

White, Barbara, *Asst Prof,* Tufts University, Fine Arts Dept, Medford MA (S)

White, Barbara, *Instructor,* Charles Stewart Mott Community College, Fine Arts Division, Flint MI (S)

White, Blair, *Asst Dir,* Southern Highland Handicraft Guild, Folk Art Center, Asheville NC

White, Christopher, *Gallery Coordr,* Carlson Gallery, Bridgeport CT

White, Cliff, *Pres,* Peter and Catharine Whyte Foundation, Peter Whyte Gallery, Banff AB

White, David O, *Museum Dir,* Connecticut State Library, Raymond E Baldwin Museum, Hartford CT

White, Diane C, *Slide Librn,* University of New Hampshire, Dept of the Arts Slide Library, Durham NH

White, E Alan, *Assoc Prof,* University of Tennessee at Chattanooga, Dept of Art, Chattanooga TN (S)

White, Evelyn, *Art & Slide Librn,* California Institute of the Arts Library, Valencia CA

White, George, *Secy,* Dulin Gallery of Art, Knoxville TN

White, George M, *Architect of the Capitol,* United States Capitol Museum, Washington DC

White, Ian M, *Dir,* Fine Arts Museums of San Francisco, M H de Young Memorial Museum and California Palace of the Legion of Honor, San Francisco CA

White, Lelia, *Dir Library Services,* Oakland Public Library, Art, Music & Recreation Section, Oakland CA

White, Lynda, *Slide Librn,* University of Virginia, Fiske Kimball Fine Arts Library, Charlottesville VA

White, Lynn W, *Arts Mgr,* Scottsdale Center for the Arts, Scottsdale AZ

White, Melvin, *VChmn,* Dulin Gallery of Art, Knoxville TN

White, Nancy P, *Asst Dir,* Spokane Public Library, Art Dept, Spokane WA

White, Nathalia, *Secy,* Pensacola Junior College, Visual Arts Gallery, Pensacola FL

White, Norval, *VPres,* Art Commission of the City of New York, New York NY

White, Paul L, *VPres,* Mystic Art Association, Inc, Mystic CT

White, Rita A, *Assoc Prof,* Palomar College, Art Dept, San Marcos TX (S)

White, Sid, *Dir,* Evergreen State College, Evergreen Galleries, Olympia WA

White, Walter L, *Dean School Trades & Industry,* Utah Technical College at Salt Lake, Commercial Art Dept, Salt Lake City UT (S)

White, William, *Asst Prof,* Jersey City State College, Art Dept, Jersey City NJ (S)

Whitehead, Frances, *Asst Prof,* Indiana University, Bloomington, School of Fine Arts, Bloomington IN (S)

Whitehouse, Jean, *VPres,* Wallingford Art League, Wallingford CT

Whitehouse, Suzanne, *Pres,* Berks Art Alliance, Reading PA

Whitehurst, Deborah, *Museum Special Projects Coordr,* Arizona Commission on the Arts, Phoenix AZ

Whitenack, Michael, *Supv, Visual Art Resources,* University of Oregon, Museum of Art, Eugene OR

Whitesides, Patricia, *Registrar,* Toledo Museum of Art, Toledo OH

Whiteworth, Ilene, *Registrar,* Montgomery Museum of Fine Arts, Montgomery AL

Whitfield, Tony, *Preformance Cur,* Just Above Midtown Gallery, Inc, New York NY

Whitlock, John J, *Dir,* Southern Illinois University, University Museum, Carbondale IL

Whitlow, James, *Instr,* Southwest Art League Seminars, Santa Fe NM (S)

Whitman, Nicholas, *Cur Photography,* Old Dartmouth Historical Society, New Bedford Whaling Museum, New Bedford MA

Whitman, Sue, *Pub Relations Dir,* Norton Gallery and School of Art, West Palm Beach FL

Whitmore, Doris L, *Dir,* Jacksonville Museum of Arts and Sciences, Jacksonville FL

Whitner, Barbara, *Secy,* Waterworks Gallery, Salisbury NC

Whitney, Allota, *Registrar,* Heritage Plantation of Sandwich, Sandwich MA

Whitney, Patrick, *Chmn Design,* Minneapolis College of Art and Design, Minneapolis MN (S)

Whitney, Richard H, *Chmn,* Arizona Commission on the Arts, Phoenix AZ

Whitney, Steve, *Asst Prof,* Coe College, Dept of Art, Cedar Rapids IA (S)

Whitside, Forbes, *Prof,* Oberlin College, Dept of Art, Oberlin OH (S)

Whitsitt, Marjorie, *Prof,* University of Wisconsin-Superior, Programs in the Visual Arts, Superior WI (S)

Whitson, Lynn, *Head Art, Music, Recreation Dept,* Memphis-Shelby County Public Library and Information Center, Dept of Art, Music and Recreation, Memphis TN

Whitten, Lee, *Asst Prof,* Los Angeles City College, Dept of Art, Los Angeles CA (S)

Whittington, Harrell, *Instructor,* Bob Jones University, School of Fine Arts, Greenville SC (S)

Whittington, Jon, *Chmn,* Belhaven College, Art Dept, Jackson MS (S)

Wholley, Jay, *Assoc Prof,* Ramapo College of New Jersey, School of Contemporary Arts, Mahwah NJ (S)

Whyte, Lorna, *Secy,* Gananoque Historical Museum, Gananoque ON

Wicke, Charles R, *Chmn,* University of Victoria, Dept of History in Art, Victoria BC (S)

Wickman, John E, *Dir,* Dwight D Eisenhower Presidential Library, Abilene KS

Wicks, Eugene C, *Dir School,* University of Illinois, Urbana-Champaign, School of Art and Design, Champaign IL (S)

Wicks, Phyllis, *Pres,* Kennebec Valley Art Association, Harlow Gallery, Hallowell ME

Wicks, Robert, *Prof,* Harrisburg Area Community College, Division of Communication and the Arts, Harrisburg PA (S)

Widdicield, Garnette, *Pres,* Arizona Artist Guild, Phoenix AZ

Widman, Harry, *Instr,* Pacific Northwest College of Art, Portland OR (S)

Widrig, W M, *Chmn,* Rice University, Dept of Art and Art History, Houston TX (S)

Wiedemann, Karl T, *Chmn of Board,* Wichita Art Association Inc, Wichita KS

Wiedmann, Dan, *Acting VDir Operations,* Brooklyn Museum, Brooklyn NY

Wiegmann, Richard, *Dir,* Concordia College, Koenig Art Gallery, Seward NE

Wiegmann, Richard, *Prof,* Concordia College, Art Dept, Seward NE (S)

Wiehe, Mary, *Chmn,* Hannibal La Grange College, Art Dept, Hannibal MO (S)

Wier, John, *VPres,* Wilfrid Laurier University, Concourse Gallery, Waterloo ON

Wierwill, Wilma, *Librn,* Telfair Academy of Arts and Sciences Inc, Library, Savannah GA

Wiesendanger, Margaret, *Conservator,* Saint Gregory's Abbey and College, Mabee-Gerrer Museum of Art, Shawnee OK

Wiesendanger, Martin, *Conservator,* Saint Gregory's Abbey and College, Mabee-Gerrer Museum of Art, Shawnee OK

Wiest, Gretchen, *Executive Dir,* National Assembly of Local Arts Agencies, Washington DC

Wiggin, Lewis M, *Secy,* Litchfield Historical Society, Litchfield CT

Wiggins, Art, *In Charge Art Coll,* First National Bank of Florida, Tampa FL

Wiggins, Wilton Hale, *VPres,* Guild of Book Workers, New York NY

Wikander, Lawrence E, *Librn,* Williams College, Sawyer Library, Williamstown MA

Wilcher, Richard, *Fine Arts Dept Chmn,* Brazosport College, Art Dept, Lake Jackson TX (S)

Wilcox, Jeffrey, *Assoc Cur Exhib,* University of Missouri, Museum of Art and Archaeology, Columbia MO

Wilcox, Lawrence, *Instr,* New Mexico Junior College, Arts, Business & Humanities Division, Hobbs NM (S)

Wilcox, Rosalind, *Instr,* Woodbury University, Professional Arts Division, Los Angeles CA (S)

Wilcox, Ruth Rogers, *Correspondence Secy,* Coppini Academy of Fine Arts, San Antonio TX

Wilde, Betty, *Cur Satellite Galleries,* Bronx Museum of the Arts, Bronx NY

Wilde, Wilson, *Chmn,* Old State House, Hartford CT

Wilen, Carl, *Assoc Prof,* Eastern Illinois University, School of Fine Arts, Charleston IL (S)

Wilen, Eve, *Exec Dir,* New York Artists Equity Association, Inc, New York NY

Wiley, Charles, *Prof,* Eastern New Mexico University, Dept of Art, Portales NM (S)

Wiley, Patricia A, *Asst Museums & Special Projects,* Pittsburgh History and Landmarks Foundation, Old Post Office Museum, Pittsburgh PA

Wilhelm, Mary Lou, *Dir,* Cuesta College Library, Art Dept, San Luis Obispo CA

Wilk, Christopher, *Asst Cur,* Brooklyn Museum, Brooklyn NY

Wilk, Sarah, *Asst Prof,* Rutgers, the State University of New Jersey, Graduate Program in Art History, New Brunswick NJ (S)

Wilke, Gerhard M, *Chmn,* Holyoke Community College, Dept of Art, Holyoke MA (S)

Wilkerson, Sally, *Prof,* Berea College, Art Dept, Berea KY (S)

Wilkie, A, *Instructor,* Technical University of Nova Scotia, Faculty of Architecture, Halifax NS (S)

Wilkins, David G, *Dir,* University of Pittsburgh, University Art Gallery, Pittsburgh PA

Wilkinson, Betty F, *Librn,* Art Gallery of Windsor, Reference Library, Windsor ON

Wilkinson, Raymond, *Gen Servs,* Museum of Our National Heritage, Lexington MA

Wilkinson, Vivian, *Chmn,* Mount Aloysius Junior College, Art Dept, Cresson PA (S)

Wilkinson, William D, *Dir,* Mariners Museum, Newport News VA

Wilks, Esther Ross, *Pres,* Lahaina Arts Society, Art Organization, Lahaina HI

Will, Vernon, *Head Conservation,* Ohio Historical Society, Archives-Library Division, Columbus OH

Willard, Anne, *Archivist,* New Haven Colony Historical Society, Research Library, New Haven CT

Willard, David, *Cur,* Boise Gallery of Art, Boise ID

Willard, LeBaron S, *Secy-Treas,* Society of the Four Arts, Palm Beach FL

Willauer, George J, *Pres,* Lyme Historical Society, Florence Griswold Museum, Old Lyme CT

Willcox, Thomas H, *Pres of Board of Trustees,* Chrysler Museum, Norfolk VA

Willers, Karl E, *Asst Mgr,* Whitney Museum of American Art, Downtown Branch, New York NY

Willet, E Crosby, *Pres,* Willet Stained Glass Studios, Philadelphia PA (S)

Williams, Ann, *Asst Prof,* Beaver College, Dept of Fine Arts, Glenside PA (S)

Williams, Ardelia, *Head Dept,* Marion College, Art Dept, Marion IN (S)

Williams, Charlene, *Business Mgr,* Lemoyne Center for the Visual Arts, Tallahassee FL

Williams, Clarence, *VChmn,* Carson County Square House Museum, Panhandle TX

Williams, David, *Registrar,* National Cowboy Hall of Fame and Western Heritage Center, Oklahoma City OK

Williams, Dick, *Instructor,* Iowa Lakes Community College, Dept of Art, Estherville IA (S)

Williams, Edward Bann, *Registrar,* Marion Koogler McNay Art Museum, San Antonio TX

Williams, Ellen R, *Asst Prof,* George Washington University, Dept of Art, Washington DC (S)

Williams, Ethelynn, *Head of Reference,* New Rochelle Public Library, Art Section, New Rochelle NY

Williams, G, *Faculty,* Stephens College, Art Dept, Columbia MO (S)

Williams, Gretchen, *Instr,* Greensboro College, Dept of Art, Division of Fine Arts, Greensboro NC (S)

Williams, H, *Pres,* Moravian Historical Society, Whitefield House Museum, Nazareth PA

Williams, H L, *Prof,* Florida A & M University, Dept of Visual Arts and Humanities, Tallahassee FL (S)

Williams, James A, *Asst Gallery Supt & Preparator,* University of Utah, Utah Museum of Fine Arts, Salt Lake City UT

Williams, Jane, *Agent,* Richard Gallery and Almond Tea Gallery, Divisions of Studios of Jack Richard, Cuyahoga Falls OH

Williams, Janice, *Asst Prof,* Augusta College, Dept of Fine Arts, Augusta GA (S)

Williams, Jay, *Dir,* Edison Community College, Gallery of Fine Art, Fort Myers FL

Williams, John, *Chmn,* University of Pittsburgh, Henry Clay Frick Fine Arts Dept, Pittsburgh PA (S)

Williams, Judith, *Asst Prof,* University of British Columbia, Dept of Fine Arts, Vancouver BC (S)

Williams, Kay P, *Dir,* Tryon Palace Restoration Complex, New Bern NC

Williams, Kenneth, *Graphic Design,* University of Georgia, Franklin College of Arts and Sciences, Dept of Art, Athens GA (S)

Williams, Lawrence, *Prof,* Rochester Institute of Technology, School of Art and Design, Rochester NY (S)

Williams, Lorraine, *Cur Archaeology-Ethnology,* New Jersey State Museum, Trenton NJ

Williams, L W, *Adjunct Prof,* Beloit College, Dept of Art, Beloit WI (S)

Williams, Margaret Click, *Chmn Dept,* Saint Mary's College, Art Dept, Raleigh NC (S)

Williams, Marjorie, *Secy,* Will Rogers Memorial and Museum, Claremore OK

Williams, Martha, *Asst to Dir,* Fine Arts Museums of San Francisco, M H de Young Memorial Museum and California Palace of the Legion of Honor, San Francisco CA

Williams, Mary, *Asst Cur,* University of British Columbia, Fine Arts Gallery, Vancouver BC

Williams, Mary Jane, *Registrar,* Arizona State University, University Art Collections, Tempe AZ

Williams, Maudine B, *Head Librn,* Indiana University - Purdue University at Indianapolis, Art Library, Indianapolis IN

Williams, Norman, *Assoc Prof,* Rochester Institute of Technology, School of Art and Design, Rochester NY (S)

Williams, Paula, *Cur Special Coll,* Institute of the Great Plains, Research Library, Lawton OK

Williams, Paul H, *Prof,* Adams State College, Dept of Visual Arts, Alamosa CO (S)

Williams, Richard, *Instr,* Arkansas Arts Center, Little Rock AR (S)

Williams, Richard, *Chmn Foundations,* University of Manitoba, School of Art, Winnipeg MB (S)

Williams, Richmond T, *Library Dir,* Hagley Museum, Eleutherian Mills Historical Library, Wilmington DE

Williams, Robert, *Instr,* Mankato Area Vocational-Technical Institute, Commercial and Technical Art Dept, North Mankato MN (S)

Williams, Roberta L, *Exec Dir,* Louisville Art Gallery, Louisville KY

Williams, Roger, *Dir,* Art Academy of Cincinnati, Cincinnati OH (S)

Williams, Ron, *Head,* Merced College, Arts Division, Merced CA (S)

Williams, Sheri, *Gallery Chmn,* Texas A & M University, Memorial Student Center Arts Committee, College Station TX

Williams, Stephen R, *Dir,* Museum of Arts and History, Port Huron MI

Williams, Sylvia H, *Dir,* National Museum of African Art, Washington DC

Williams, W, *Assoc Prof,* Northern Arizona University, Art Dept, Flagstaff AZ (S)

Williams, William E, *Asst Prof,* Haverford College, Fine Arts Dept, Haverford PA (S)

Williams, William J, *Chmn Museum Committee,* Taft Museum, Cincinnati OH

Williams, William J, *Instructor,* Columbia College, Art Dept, Columbia MO (S)

Williams, Winifred S, *Assoc Prof,* Texas Woman's University, Dept of Art, Denton TX (S)

Williamson, Donald, *Instr Visual Communications,* Kendall School of Design, Grand Rapids MI (S)

Williamson, James, *Head Education Services,* Art Gallery of Ontario, Toronto ON

Willingham, Helen, *VPres,* Red River Valley Museum, Vernon TX

Willis, Jay, *Assoc Prof,* University of Southern California, School of Fine Arts, Los Angeles CA (S)

Willis, Patricia C, *Cur Literature,* The Rosenbach Museum and Library, Philadelphia PA

Willis, William, *Chmn Art Committee,* North Canton Public Library, Little Art Gallery, North Canton OH

Willis, William H, *Dir,* The Art Institute of Boston, Gallery West, Gallery East, Boston MA

Willis, William H, *Pres,* Art Institute of Boston, Boston MA (S)

Willock, Tom, *Dir,* Medicine Hat Museum Art Gallery, National Exhibition Centre, Medicine Hat AB

Willoughby, Donna E, *Assoc Dean,* Golden West College, Arts, Humanities and Social Sciences Institute, Huntington Beach CA (S)

Willoughby, Karin L, *Cur Geology,* McKissick Museums, Columbia SC

Wills, J Robert, *Dean,* University of Texas, Dept of Art, Austin TX (S)

Willse, Michael D, *Chmn Div,* Rosemont College, Division of the Arts, Rosemont PA (S)

Willson, Beverly, *Dir,* Albany Museum of Art, Albany GA

Willson, Charles, *Editor & Historian American Archives,* National Portrait Gallery, Washington DC

Willson, Valerie, *Instructor,* Marylhurst College, Art Dept, Marylhurst OR (S)

Wilmarth, Susan, *Lecturer,* Columbia University, School of the Arts, Division of Painting & Sculpture, New York NY (S)

Wilmerdiuf, John, *Deputy Dir,* National Gallery of Art, Washington DC

Wilmot, Marjorie, *Recording Secy,* Bowne House, Flushing NY

Wilson, Bob, *Instructor,* Anton Elli, Cincinnati OH (S)

Wilson, Chris, *Assoc Prof,* Atlantic Christian College, Art Dept, Wilson NC (S)

Wilson, Christine, *Dir Public Information,* Mississippi Department of Archives and History, State Historical Museum, Jackson MS

Wilson, Diana, *Art Reference Librn,* Huntington Library, Art Gallery and Botanical Gardens, Art Reference Library, San Marino CA

Wilson, Dianne Penny, *Pub Relations Specialist,* University of Georgia, Georgia Museum of Art, Athens GA

Wilson, Don, *Vis Prof,* Oral Roberts University, Fine Arts Dept, Tulsa OK (S)

Wilson, Duffy, *Dir,* Native American Center for the Living Arts, Niagara Falls NY

Wilson, Ed, *Chmn Dept,* State University of New York at Binghamton, Dept Of Art & Art History, Binghamton NY (S)

Wilson, Forrest, *Prof,* Catholic University of America, Dept of Architecture and Planning, Washington DC (S)

Wilson, Fredric W, *Asst Cur Gilbert & Sullivan Coll,* Pierpont Morgan Library, New York NY

Wilson, Gillian, *Cur Decorative Arts,* J Paul Getty Museum, Malibu CA

Wilson, Gordon, *Asst Prof,* Whitworth College, Art Dept, Spokane WA (S)

Wilson, Jackie, *Actg Dir,* Amarillo Art Center, Amarillo TX

Wilson, Jane, *Educ Dir & Registrar,* Owensboro Museum of Fine Art, Owensboro KY

Wilson, Jane, *Adjunct Prof,* Columbia University, School of the Arts, Division of Painting & Sculpture, New York NY (S)

Wilson, Jay M, *Pres Board of Trustees,* Walters Art Gallery, Baltimore MD

Wilson, J D, *Pres,* Kelowna Centennial Museum and National Exhibit Centre, Kelowna BC

Wilson, Jean S, *Asst Cur,* Arapahoe Community College, Colorado Gallery of the Arts, Littleton CO

Wilson, Joanne, *Gallery Dir,* Waterloo Art Association, Eleventh Street Gallery, Waterloo IA

Wilson, John L, *Pres Board of Trustees,* Hoyt Institute of Fine Arts, New Castle PA

Wilson, John M, *Instr,* Hope College, Art Dept, Holland MI (S)

Wilson, John Montgomery, *Dir,* Hope College, De Pree Art Center & Gallery, Holland MI

Wilson, John R, *Prof,* Butte College, Dept of Fine & Performing Arts, Oroville CA (S)

Wilson, Joyce, *Chmn,* Bellevue College, Art Dept, Bellevue NE (S)

Wilson, Katherine Ann, *Public Relations Officer,* Huntington Library, Art Gallery and Botanical Gardens, San Marino CA

Wilson, Kenneth T, *Assoc Prof,* Bloomsburg University, Dept of Art, Bloomsburg PA (S)

Wilson, Lucy, *Art Librn,* Laney College Library, Art Section, Oakland CA

Wilson, Lucy P, *Business Mgr,* Southeastern Center for Contemporary Art, Winston-Salem NC

Wilson, M, *Chmn,* College of Saint Catherine, Visual Arts Dept, Saint Paul MN (S)

Wilson, Marc, *Lectr,* University of Kansas, Kress Foundation Dept of Art History, Lawrence KS (S)

Wilson, Marc F, *Dir & Cur Oriental Art,* Atkins Museum of Fine Art, Kansas City MO

Wilson, Margaret, *Treas,* Essex Art Association, Inc, Essex CT

Wilson, Martha, *Executive Dir,* Franklin Furnace Archive, Inc, New York NY

Wilson, Nancy, *Instr,* Arkansas Arts Center, Little Rock AR (S)

Wilson, Patsy, *Dir Library Services,* Cooke County College Library, Art Dept, Gainesville TX

Wilson, Robb, *Assoc Prof,* University of Wisconsin-Stout, Art Dept, Menomonie WI (S)

Wilson, Sally D, *Pres & Chmn,* Bristol Art Museum, Bristol RI

Wilson, Stanley, *Prof,* California State Polytechnic University, Pomona, Art Dept, Pomona CA (S)

Wilson, Stephen, *Instr,* California State University, Chico, Art Dept, Chico CA (S)

Wilson, Steve, *Dir,* Institute of the Great Plains, Museum of the Great Plains, Lawton OK

Wilson, Thomas R C, *Pres,* Sierra Arts Foundation, Reno NV

Wilson, Tom Muir, *Assoc Prof,* Rochester Institute of Technology, School of Photographic Arts & Sciences, Rochester NY (S)

Wilson, Wallace, *Assoc Prof,* University of Florida, Dept of Art, Gainesville FL (S)

Wilson, William, *Prof,* State University of New York at Albany, Art Dept, Albany NY (S)

Wilson-Jeronimo, John, *Exec Dir,* National Architectural Accrediting Board, Inc, Washington DC

Wilt, David, *Community Outreach Coordr,* Southern Alleghenies Museum of Art, Museum Extension, Loretto PA

Wilwers, Ed, *Prof,* Arkansas Tech University, Dept of Art, Russellville AR (S)

Wimmer, Charles, *Assoc Prof,* University of Wisconsin-Stout, Art Dept, Menomonie WI (S)

Wimmer, Joyce, *Secy,* The Museum, Greenwood SC

Winans, Martha, *Dir Art Gallery,* Indiana University - Purdue University at Indianapolis, Herron School of Art Gallery, Indianapolis IN

Wind, Geraldine, *Instructor,* Mount Mary College, Art Dept, Milwaukee WI (S)

Winder, F L, *Secy,* Eccles Community Art Center, Ogden UT

Windham, Howard, *Chairperson Design,* Southeastern Massachusetts University, College of Visual and Performing Arts, North Dartmouth MA (S)

Windsor, Jack, *Instr,* California State University, Chico, Art Dept, Chico CA (S)

Windsor-Liscombe, Rhodri, *Assoc Prof,* University of British Columbia, Dept of Fine Arts, Vancouver BC (S)

Wine, Geraldine, *Secy,* G G Drayton Club, Salem OH

Wine, Jerry, *Treasurer,* G G Drayton Club, Salem OH

Wineland, Gene, *Chmn,* Pratt Community College, Art Dept, Pratt KS (S)

Wineman, Nada, *Cur Coll,* Jacksonville Museum of Arts and Sciences, Jacksonville FL

Winer, Donald A, *Cur of Fine Arts,* Pennsylvania Historical and Museum Commission, William Penn Memorial Museum, Harrisburg PA

Winfield, Rodney M, *Prof,* Maryville College, St Louis, Art Division, Saint Louis MO (S)

Wing, James A, *Asst Prof,* Gogebic Community College, Art Dept, Ironwood MI (S)

Wing, Stephen, *Prof,* Mars Hill College, Art Dept, Mars Hill NC (S)

Wingenbach, LeRoy, *Secy Board of Dir,* Lake County Civic Center Association, Inc, Heritage Museum and Gallery, Leadville CO

Wingerter, Robert G, *Pres,* Toledo Museum of Art, Toledo OH

Wink, Jon D, *Chmn,* Stephen F Austin State University, Art Dept, Nacogdoches TX (S)

Winkler, Helen, *VPres,* Dia Art Foundation, Inc, New York NY

Winningham, Geoffrey, *Prof,* Rice University, Dept of Art and Art History, Houston TX (S)

Winsand, Orvill, *Head,* Carnegie-Mellon University, Dept of Art, Pittsburgh PA (S)

Winsett, Merrill, *Chmn of the Board of Trustees,* Amarillo Art Center, Amarillo Art Center Association, Amarillo TX

Winslow, John R, *Chmn Dept,* Catholic University of America, Dept of Art, Washington DC (S)

Winter, Gerald G, *Prof,* University of Miami, Dept of Art & Art History, Coral Gables FL (S)

Winter, John, *Conservation Scientist,* Freer Gallery of Art, Washington DC

Winter, Robert, *Instr,* Lenoir Rhyne College, Dept of Art, Hickory NC (S)

Winter, William, *Pres,* Mississippi State Historical Museum, Jackson MS

Winter, William F, *Pres Board Trustees,* Mississippi Department of Archives and History, State Historical Museum, Jackson MS

Winterich, Douglas, *Cur Education,* Old Barracks Museum, Trenton NJ

Winters, John L, *Assoc Prof,* University of Mississippi, Dept of Art, University MS (S)

Winters, Nathan, *Asst Prof,* University of Utah, Art Dept, Salt Lake City UT (S)

Winzenz, Karon, *Cur Art,* University of Wisconsin, Green Bay, Lawton Gallery, Green Bay WI

Wipfler, Heina, *Asst Prof,* Queensborough Community College, Dept of Art and Design, Bayside NY (S)

Wirtenberg, Pat, *Coordr,* Children's Art Centre, Boston MA

Wirth, Harry, *Instructor,* Mount Mary College, Art Dept, Milwaukee WI (S)

Wirtz, Virginia, *Mus Dir,* Maui Historical Society, Hale Hoikeike, Wailuku HI

Wise, Diane, *Admin Asst,* Reynolda House, Inc, Winston-Salem NC

Wise, Edward, *Secy,* Pemaquid Group of Artists, Pemaquid Point ME

Wise, Howard, *Pres,* Electronic Arts Intermix, Inc, New York NY

Wise, Lawrence, *Chmn of Fine Arts,* New Mexico Highlands University, Arrott Art Gallery, Las Vegas NM

Wise, Loren E, *Chmn,* New Mexico Highlands University, Division of Fine Arts, Las Vegas NM (S)

Wise, R Gordon, *Dir,* Millersville University, Art Dept, Millersville PA (S)

Wise, Suzanne Tanderup, *Cur,* Northwestern University, Mary & Leigh Block Gallery, Evanston IL

Wiseman, James R, *VPres,* Archaeological Institute of America, Boston MA

Wiseman, Robin, *Instructor,* Roger Williams College, Art Dept, Bristol RI (S)

Wismer, Edward, *Head Teaching Staff,* Ocean City Arts Center, Ocean City NJ (S)

Wisniewski, Dale, *Vis Lecturer,* North Central College, Dept of Art, Naperville IL (S)

Wisnosky, John, *Chmn Department Art,* University of Hawaii at Manoa, Art Gallery, Honolulu HI

Wisnosky, John, *Chmn,* University of Hawaii at Manoa, Dept of Art, Honolulu HI (S)

Wistar, Caroline, *Asst Cur,* La Salle College Art Museum, Philadelphia PA

Witgus, Veberly, *Asst Prof,* College of Notre Dame of Maryland, Art Dept, Baltimore MD (S)

Witherow, Dale, *Assoc Prof,* Mansfield State College, Art Dept, Mansfield PA (S)

Withrow, W J, *Dir,* Art Gallery of Ontario, Toronto ON

Witkin, Isaac, *Instr,* New York Studio School of Drawing, Painting and Sculpture, New York NY (S)

Witt, David, *Cur,* Harwood Foundation of the University of New Mexico, Taos NM

Witt, John Temple, *Vis Instr,* Randolph-Macon College, Art Dept, Ashland VA (S)

Witt, Ruth E, *Interim Dir,* University of Missouri, Museum of Art and Archaeology, Columbia MO

Witt, Tom, *Chmn Design Sciences,* Arizona State University, College of Architecture, Tempe AZ (S)

Witter, Robert, *Asst Prof,* City Colleges of Chicago, Malcolm X College, Chicago IL (S)

Wittershiem, John, *Asst Prof,* Siena Heights College, Studio Angelico Art Dept, Adrian MI (S)

Witthoft, Brucia, *Assoc Prof,* Framingham State College, Art Dept, Framingham MA (S)

Wittmann, Harold M, *Asst Dir,* Fine Arts Museum of the South, Mobile AL

Wittmer, Marcilene, *Assoc Prof,* University of Miami, Dept of Art & Art History, Coral Gables FL (S)

Witwick, Deborah, *Public Relations,* Edmonton Art Gallery, Edmonton AB

Witzling, Mara, *Assoc Prof,* University of New Hampshire, Dept of the Arts, Durham NH (S)

Witzmann, Hugh, *Head Dept,* Saint John's University, Art Dept, Collegeville MN (S)

Wixom, William D, *Chmn,* Metropolitan Museum of Art, The Cloisters, New York NY

Wlodarczyk, Joyce Anne, *Auxiliary Prof,* Inter American University of Puerto Rico, Dept of Art, San German PR (S)

Wodiczko, Krystov, *Adjunct Asst Prof,* New York Institute of Technology, Fine Arts Dept, Old Westbury NY (S)

Wohl, Marcia, *Instr,* Mainline Center of the Arts, Haverford PA (S)

Wohlgemuth, Joyce, *Pres,* Cascade County Historical Society Museum, Great Falls MT

Wojcik, Gary, *Asst Prof,* Ithaca College, Fine Art Dept, Ithaca NY (S)

Wolanin, Barbara, *Asst Prof,* James Madison University, Dept of Art, Harrisonburg VA (S)

Wolber, Paul, *Prof,* Spring Arbor College, Art Dept, Spring Arbor MI (S)

Wold, William, *Assoc Prof,* University of South Dakota, Dept of Art, Vermillion SD (S)

Wolf, Arthur H, *Dir,* Millicent Rogers Museum, Taos NM

Wolf, Edwin, *Librn,* Library Company of Philadelphia, Dept of Art, Philadelphia PA

Wolf, John H, *Chmn of the Board,* Woodmere Art Museum, Philadelphia PA

Wolf, Karen, *Instr,* Marian College, Art Dept, Indianapolis IN (S)

Wolf, Marian, *Asst Librn,* Solomon R Guggenheim Museum, Library, New York NY

Wolf, Patricia, *Cur of Education,* Anchorage Historical and Fine Arts Museum, Cook Inlet Historical Society, Anchorage AK

Wolf, Richard, *Chmn,* Eastern Connecticut State College, Art Dept, Willimantic CT (S)

Wolf, Sara, *Librn,* Mint Museum of Art, Library, Charlotte NC

Wolf, Tom, *Dir,* Bard College, William Cooper Procter Art Center, Annandale-on-Hudson NY

Wolfe, Andrew D, *Chmn,* International Museum of Photography at George Eastman House, Rochester NY

Wolfe, Greg, *Chmn,* Art Academy of Cincinnati, Cincinnati OH (S)

Wolfe, John T, *Head Division Humanities & Fine Arts,* Fayetteville State University, Division of Humanitites and Fine Arts, Fayetteville NC (S)

Wolfe, Laurie, *Librn,* Bethel College, Mennonite Library and Archives, North Newton KS

Wolfe, Marika, *Library Asst,* University of California, Architectural Slide Library, Berkeley CA

Wolfe, Marshall, *Pres,* Saint Augustine Art Association Gallery, Saint Augustine FL

Wolfe, Mercy Dobell, *Pres,* Pen and Brush, Inc, New York NY

Wolfe, Michael, *Finance Officer,* Whitney Museum of American Art, New York NY

Wolfe, Townsend, *Exec Dir,* Arkansas Arts Center, Little Rock AR (S)

Wolfe, Townsend D, *Exec Dir,* Arkansas Arts Center, Little Rock AR

Wolfram, William R, *Head Dept,* Concordia College, Art Dept, Seward NE (S)

Wolin, Jeffrey, *Asst Prof,* Indiana University, Bloomington, School of Fine Arts, Bloomington IN (S)

Wolin, Ron, *Executive Dir,* Cartoonists Guild, New York NY

Wollowitz, Charles, *Adjunct Asst Prof,* Le Moyne College, Art Dept, Syracuse NY (S)

Wolock, Barbara, *Asst to Dir,* Hunterdon Art Center, Clinton NJ

Wolsk, Nancy, *Coordr,* Transylvania University, Morlan Gallery, Lexington KY

Wolsk, Nancy, *Instr,* Transylvania University, Studio Arts Dept, Lexington KY (S)

Wolter, Ted, *Asst Dir Kirkland Gallery & Art Prof,* Millikin University, Kirkland Gallery, Decatur IL

Woltereck, Jane D, *Cur,* Star-Spangled Banner Flag House Association, Library, Baltimore MD

Woltman, Robert, *Cur of Exhibits,* Albuquerque Museum of Art, History and Science, Albuquerque NM

Wolynetz, Lubow, *Educational Dir,* Ukrainian Museum, New York NY

Womack, William, *Instr,* Southwestern at Memphis, Dept of Art, Memphis TN (S)

Wong, Alice, *Registrar,* University of California, Santa Barbara, University Art Museum, Santa Barbara CA

Wong, A Y, *Asst Prof,* Lincoln College, Art Dept, Lincoln IL (S)

Wong, Eddie, *Cur,* University of Wisconsin-Stout, Gallery 209, Menomonie WI

Wong, Eddie, *Assoc Prof,* University of Wisconsin-Stout, Art Dept, Menomonie WI (S)

Wong, Michele, *Registrar,* New York University, Grey Art Gallery and Study Center, New York NY

Woo, Kathryn, *Asst Dir Admin,* Smith College, Museum of Art, Northampton MA

Wood, Barbara, *Staff Secy,* Hampton Center for Arts and Humanities, Hampton VA

Wood, Carol, *Admin Asst,* University of Vermont, Robert Hull Fleming Museum, Burlington VT

Wood, Clifford P, *Assoc Humanities Reference Librn,* California State University, Sacramento, Library, Humanities Reference and Media Services Center, Sacramento CA

Wood, Dale D, *Business Mgr,* Paine Art Center and Arboretum, Oshkosh WI

Wood, Dan, *Dept Head,* Vermilion Community College, Art Dept, Ely MN (S)

Wood, Dan D, *Assoc Prof,* Southern Illinois University, School of Art, Carbondale IL (S)

Wood, Derek, *Instr,* Arkansas Arts Center, Little Rock AR (S)

Wood, Dolores, *Secy,* San Angelo Art Club, Helen King Kendall Memorial Art Gallery, San Angelo TX

Wood, Donald C, *Pres,* Danbury Scott-Fanton Museum and Historical Society, Inc, Danbury CT

Wood, Emmett S, *Pres,* Jefferson County Historical Society Museum, Madison IN

Wood, James N, *Dir,* Art Institute of Chicago, Chicago IL

Wood, John J, *Deputy Dir,* Minnesota Historical Society, Saint Paul MN

Wood, Marcia J, *Instr,* Kalamazoo College, Art Dept, Kalamazoo MI (S)

Wood, Marilyn, *Instr,* Normandale Community College, Art Dept, Bloomington MN (S)

Wood, Richard H, *Art Librn,* Wesleyan University, Art Library, Middletown CT

Wood, Susan B, *Dir,* Greenwich House Pottery, New York NY (S)

Woodall, Carmen, *Secy,* Millicent Rogers Museum, Taos NM

Woodbridge, George, *VPres,* Newport Historical Society, Newport RI

Woodburn, Steven, *Adjunct Assoc Prof,* New York Institute of Technology, Fine Arts Dept, Old Westbury NY (S)

Wooden, Howard E, *Dir,* Wichita Art Museum, Wichita KS

Woodfaulk, Karen, *Chmn,* Claflin College, Dept of Art, Orangeburg SC (S)

Woodford, Don, *Instructor,* California State College, San Bernardino, Art Dept, San Bernardino CA (S)

Woodford, Don, *Dir,* California State College San Bernardino, College Art Galleries, San Bernardino CA

Woodham, Jean, *VPres Membership,* Sculptors Guild, Inc, New York NY

Woodhouse, Anne, *Cur Decorative Arts,* State Historical Society of Wisconsin, Madison WI

Woodman, Timothy W, *VPres,* New Hampshire Historical Society, Concord NH

Woodruff, Marian, *Dir Educ,* Currier Gallery of Art, Manchester NH

Woods, Arlene, *Asst Prof,* Salve Regina - The Newport College, Art Dept, Newport RI (S)

Woods, Jackie, *Exec Dir,* New Muse Community Museum of Brooklyn, Inc, Brooklyn NY

Woods, Jean, *Dir,* Washington County Museum of Fine Arts, Hagerstown MD

Woods, Jennifer L, *Chief Conservation,* Library Company of Philadelphia, Dept of Art, Philadelphia PA

Woods, Jim, *Dir,* College of Southern Idaho, Herrette Museum, Twin Falls ID

Woods, Mary N, *Asst Prof,* Pennsylvania State University, University Park, Dept of Art History, University Park PA (S)

Woods, Michael, *Dir Fine Art,* Academy of Art College, San Francisco CA (S)

Woods, Paula, *Cur of Educ,* Tippecanoe County Historical Museum, Lafayette IN

Woods, Shirley, *Asst to Dir,* Montgomery Museum of Fine Arts, Montgomery AL

Woods, Yvette, *Instructor,* Saint Louis Community College at Meramec, Art Dept, Saint Louis MO (S)

Woodside, Joan, *Asst Prof,* Mount Mary College, Art Dept, Milwaukee WI (S)

Woods-Marsden, Joanna, *Asst Prof,* University of British Columbia, Dept of Fine Arts, Vancouver BC (S)

Woodson, B A, *Chmn Art Dept & Prof,* Saint Andrews Presbyterian College, Art Program, Laurinburg NC (S)

Woodson, Doris, *Asst Prof,* Virginia State University, Fine & Commercial Art, Petersburg VA (S)

Woodson, Lynn, *Pres,* South County Art Association, Kingston RI

Woodward, Emily M, *Grants & Accessibility Coordr,* University of California, Los Angeles, Museum of Cultural History, Los Angeles CA

Woodward, Gary, *Assoc Prof,* Kansas State University, Art Dept, Manhattan KS (S)

Woodward, Kessler, *Asst Prof,* University of Alaska, Dept of Art, Fairbanks AK (S)

Woodward, Richard, *Dir Art Servs,* Virginia Museum of Fine Arts, Richmond VA

Woodward, Roland H, *Exec Dir,* Chester County Historical Society, West Chester PA

Woodward, Shirley, *Admin Asst,* Chrysler Museum, Norfolk VA

Woodward, W T, *Asst Prof,* George Washington University, Dept of Art, Washington DC (S)

Woody, Howard, *Instr,* University of South Carolina, Dept of Art, Columbia SC (S)

Woody, Margaret, *Secy,* African American Historical and Cultural Society, San Francisco CA

Woolard, Alice, *Exec Secy,* Licking County Art Association Gallery, Newark OH

Woolf, Burton I, *VPres,* National Assembly of Local Arts Agencies, Washington DC

Woolfolk, Charles, *Assoc Dean,* Rutgers, the State University of New Jersey, Mason Gross School of the Arts, New Brunswick NJ (S)

Woolley, John, *Dir,* Trinity College, Austin Arts Center, Hartford CT

Wooster, Laurence, *Assoc Prof,* Pittsburg State University, Art Dept, Pittsburg KS (S)

Wooters, David A, *Asst Archivist,* International Museum of Photography at George Eastman House, Library, Rochester NY

Workman, Libby, *Dir & Cur,* Houston Antique Museum, Chattanooga TN

Workman, Reginald, *Coordr Music,* New Muse Community Museum of Brooklyn, Inc, Brooklyn NY

Woroch, Stepan, *Board of Dir,* Ukrainian Institute of America, Inc, New York NY

Worrell, Robert, *Chmn,* Ricks College, Dept of Art, Rexburg ID (S)

Worsham, Charles, *Vis Lectr,* Sweet Briar College, Art History Dept and Art Studio Dept, Sweet Briar VA (S)

Worsley, Dorcas, *Librn,* Tucson Museum of Art, Library, Tucson AZ

Worth, Carl, *Cur,* Walnut Creek Civic Arts Department Gallery, Walnut Creek CA

Worth, Peter, *Chief Acad Advisor,* University of Nebraska at Lincoln, Dept of Art, Lincoln NE (S)

Worth, Tim, *Cur,* Manitoba Historical Society, Dalnavert - MacDonald House Museum, Winnipeg MB

Worthen, Bill, *Dir,* Arkansas Territorial Restoration, Little Rock AR

Worthen, W B, *Dir,* Arkansas Territorial Restoration, Library, Little Rock AR

Worthingham, Catherine, *Secy,* San Mateo County Arts Council, Belmont CA

Wortman, Harold R, *Chmn,* Cumberland College, Dept of Art, Williamsburg KY (S)

Wortz, Melinda, *Dir,* University of California, Irvine, Fine Art Gallery, Irvine CA

Wos, Joanna H, *Librn,* American Institute of Architects Foundation, Library, Washington DC

Wost, David, *Instructor,* Sioux City Art Center, Sioux City IA (S)

Wozniak, Joseph, *Asst Prof,* Seton Hall University, Dept of Art and Music, South Orange NJ (S)

Wray, Dick, *Instr,* Alfred C Glassell School of Art, Houston TX (S)

Wray, George T, *Prof,* University of Idaho, College of Art & Architecture, Moscow ID (S)

Wray, George T, *Faculty,* Idaho State University, Dept of Art, Pocatello ID (S)

Wride, Bruce, *Instr,* Mount San Jacinto College, Art Dept, San Jacinto CA (S)

Wright, Alan D, *Pres,* Fine Arts Association, School of Fine Arts, Willoughby OH

Wright, David W, *Registrar,* Pierpont Morgan Library, New York NY

Wright, Gerald D, *Genealogy,* California Historical Society, Schubert Hall Library, San Francisco CA

Wright, Helena, *Librn,* Merrimack Valley Textile Museum, Library, North Andover MA

Wright, Irene, *Bookstore Mgr,* Pacific - Asia Museum, Pasadena CA

Wright, James, *Head Fine Arts Library,* University of New Mexico, Fine Arts Library, Albuquerque NM

Wright, Jana, *Dir of Admissions,* School of the Art Institute of Chicago, Chicago IL (S)

Wright, J Franklin, *Prof,* George Washington University, Dept of Art, Washington DC (S)

Wright, J V, *Chief Archaeological Survey of Canada,* National Museum of Man, Ottawa ON

Wright, Lester D, *Instr,* Graceland College, Art Dept, Lamoni IA (S)

Wright, Mary A, *Dept Head,* San Antonio Public Library, Dept of Fine Arts, San Antonio TX

Wright, Nina, *Pres,* Ruder & Finn Fine Arts, New York NY

Wright, Patricia, *Asst Dir,* Sweet Briar College, Martin C Shallenberger Art Library, Sweet Briar VA

Wright, Philip C, *Cur,* Hill-Stead Museum, Farmington CT

Wright, P J, *Dir,* Butte Silver Bow Arts Chateau, Butte MT

Wright, Pope, *Lectr,* University of Wisconsin-Superior, Programs in the Visual Arts, Superior WI (S)

Wright, Rebecca H, *Admin Asst,* Solomon R Guggenheim Museum, New York NY

Wright, Sally, *Secy,* Art Gallery of Peterborough, Peterborough ON

Wright, Sara, *Business Mgr,* Southeast Arkansas Arts and Science Center, Pine Bluff AR

Wright, Stanley Marc, *Dir,* Wright School of Art, Stowe VT (S)

Wright, Sylvia H, *Librn,* City College of New York, Architecture Library, New York NY

Wright, Thomas, *Treasurer,* Lahaina Arts Society, Art Organization, Lahaina HI

Wright, Vicki C, *Asst to Dir,* University of Maryland, College Park, Art Gallery, College Park MD

Wright, Vincent, *Asst Prof,* C W Post Center of Long Island University, School of the Arts, Greenvale NY (S)

Wright, Virginia L, *Assoc Librn,* Corning Museum of Glass, Library, Corning NY

Wrnacchione, Matthew, *Business Mgr,* Indianapolis Museum of Art, Indianapolis IN

Wrolstad, Merald E, *Chief Editor Museum Publications,* Cleveland Museum of Art, Cleveland OH

Wu, Marshall, *Cur of Asian Art,* University of Michigan, Museum of Art, Ann Arbor MI

Wullschleger, Paul, *Asst Chmn Advertising Design,* Art Institute of Fort Lauderdale, Fort Lauderdale FL (S)

Wurdemann, Helen, *Dir,* Southern California Contemporary Art Galleries of the Los Angeles Art Association, Los Angeles CA

Wurmfeld, Sanford, *Chmn Art Dept,* Hunter College, Art Dept, New York NY (S)

Wurtele, Margaret, *Arts Grants Adminr,* Dayton Hudson Corporation, Minneapolis MN

Wyancko, Ronald, *Assoc Prof,* James Madison University, Dept of Art, Harrisonburg VA (S)

Wyant, Katherine F, *Dir-Cur,* Potsdam Public Museum, Potsdam NY

Wyatt, Stanley, *Dir Evening Session,* City College of New York, Art Dept, New York NY (S)

Wyatt, Susan, *Asst Dir,* Committee for the Visual Arts, Inc, New York NY

Wyckoff, D L, *Dir Development,* New York School of Interior Design, New York NY (S)

Wyffels, Ronald, *Instr,* San Antonio Art Institute, San Antonio TX (S)

Wyle, Edith R, *Prog Dir,* Craft and Folk Art Museum, Los Angeles CA

Wyman, Stephen, *Chmn,* Middlesex County College, Visual Arts Dept, Edison NJ (S)

Wyngaard, Susan E, *Head Librn,* Ohio State University, Fine Arts Library, Columbus OH

Wynn, Ronald, *Chmn Creative Arts,* Western Oregon State College, Creative Arts Dept, Visual Arts, Monmouth OR (S)

Wynne, Brian J, *Exec Dir,* Industrial Designers Society of America, McLean VA

Wynne, Nancy G, *Librn,* Amon Carter Museum, Amon Carter Museum Library, Fort Worth TX

Wyrick, Charles L, *Dir,* Carolina Art Association, Gibbes Art Gallery, Charleston SC

Wyroba, Francis, *Chairperson,* Florida International University, Visual Arts Dept, Miami FL (S)

Wysocki, Sharon, *Admin Asst,* Old Barracks Museum, Trenton NJ

Wyss, Patrick, *Pres Elect,* Dahl Fine Arts Center, Rapid City SD

Yacoe, Donald, *Prof,* C W Post Center of Long Island University, School of the Arts, Greenvale NY (S)

Yager, David, *Chmn,* University of South Florida, Art Dept, Tampa FL (S)

Yager, Jay, *Gallery Dir,* Eastern Michigan University, Ford Gallery, Ypsilanti MI

Yamin, Steven, *Corresponding Secy,* Society of American Graphic Artists, New York NY

Yancey, Benjamin W, *Chmn of Board,* Historic New Orleans Collection, Kemper and Leila Williams Foundation, New Orleans LA

Yanes, Robert, *Cur Permanent Coll,* San Jose State University, Union Gallery, San Jose CA

Yanez, Rene, *Co-Dir,* Galeria de la Raza, Studio 24, San Francisco CA

Yanik, John V, *Assoc Prof,* Catholic University of America, Dept of Architecture and Planning, Washington DC (S)

Yanok, Roxlyn, *Admin Asst to Dir,* Bowdoin College, Museum of Art & Peary-MacMillan Arctic Museum, Brunswick ME

Yao, Win Berta, *Art Specialist,* Arizona State University, Hayden Library Art Dept, Tempe AZ

Yarborough, Charlotte, *Pres,* Fayetteville Museum of Art, Inc, Fayetteville NC

Yarde, Richard, *Assoc Prof,* University of Massachusetts at Boston, Art Dept, Boston MA (S)

Yarden, Elie, *Instructor,* Bard College, Milton Avery Graduate School of the Arts, Annandale-on-Hudson NY (S)

Yarwood, Kim, *Preparator,* Niagara University, Buscaglia-Castellani Art Gallery, Niagara Falls NY

Yassin, Robert A, *Dir,* Indianapolis Museum of Art, Indianapolis IN

Yasuda, Robert, *Assoc Prof,* C W Post Center of Long Island University, School of the Arts, Greenvale NY (S)

Yates, Jean, *Instr,* Santa Rosa Junior College, Art Dept, Santa Rosa CA (S)

Yates, Steve, *Cur,* Museum of New Mexico, Museum of Fine Arts, Santa Fe NM

Yeager, Barbara, *Membership Secy,* Westmoreland County Museum of Art, Greensburg PA

Yeager, Virginia, *Chmn,* Jamestown Community College, Art Dept, Jamestown NY (S)

Yeager, William, *Cur,* Eva Brook Donly Museum, Simcoe ON

Yeates, Michael, *Asst Dir Coll,* Massachusetts Institute of Technology, Museum, Cambridge MA

Yee, Paul, *Cur Coll,* Vancouver City Archives and Library, Vancouver BC

Yegge, Robert, *VPres,* National Assembly of State Arts Agencies, Washington DC

Yelen, Alice Rae, *Principal Cur Education,* New Orleans Museum of Art, New Orleans LA

Yellis, Kenneth A, *Cur Education,* National Portrait Gallery, Washington DC

Yenawine, Bruce, *Dir,* Swain School of Design, William W Crapo Gallery, New Bedford MA

Yenawine, Bruce H, *Pres,* Swain School of Design, New Bedford MA (S)

Yenawine, Philip, *Asst Dir Dept Education,* Museum of Modern Art, New York NY

Yeo, Ronald, *Chief Librn,* Regina Public Library, Art Dept, Regina SK

Yeomans, Edith, *Executive Admin,* Professional Art Dealers Association of Canada, Toronto ON

Yep, Carlos, *Treas,* Community Arts Council of Vancouver, Vancouver BC

Yes, Phyllis A, *Asst Prof,* Lewis and Clark College, Dept of Art, Portland OR (S)

Yess, Mary, *Exec Dir,* Princeton Art Association, Princeton NJ

Yoder, Andy, *Preparator,* The New Gallery of Contemporary Art, Cleveland OH

Yonekura, George T, *Pres,* United States Figure Skating Hall of Fame and Museum, Colorado Springs CO

Yonemura, Ann, *Asst Cur Japanese Art,* Freer Gallery of Art, Washington DC

Yonker, Dolores M, *Chmn,* California State University, Northridge, Art History Dept, Northridge CA (S)

York, Hildreth, *Chmn Dept,* Rutgers University, Newark, Art Dept, Newark NJ (S)

York, Hildreth, *Assoc Prof,* Rutgers, the State University of New Jersey, Graduate Program in Art History, New Brunswick NJ (S)

York, Jeffrey, *Cur Education,* Everson Museum of Art, Syracuse NY

Yoshida, Ray, *Prof,* School of the Art Institute of Chicago, Chicago IL (S)

Yost, Kenneth, *VPres,* Monterey Peninsula Museum of Art, Monterey CA

Youland, Debbie, *Personal Asst & Secy,* Confederation Centre Art Gallery and Museum, Charlottetown PE

Young, Barbara, *Art Librn,* Miami-Dade Public Library, Miami FL

Young, Barbara, *Prof,* California Polytechnic State University at San Luis Obispo, Art Dept, San Luis Obispo CA (S)

Young, Becky, *Lectr,* University of Pennsylvania, College Arts & Science, Philadelphia PA (S)

Young, Betty, *Librn,* Duke University Union Galleries, East Campus Library, Durham NC

Young, Brent, *Assoc Prof,* Cleveland Institute of Art, Cleveland OH (S)

Young, Charles, *Asst Prof,* Calvin College, Art Dept, Grand Rapids MI (S)

Young, Charles, *Instructor,* Austin Peay State University, Dept of Art, Clarksville TN (S)

Young, Charles A, *Head Dept,* University of the District of Columbia, Art Dept, Washington DC (S)

Young, Chloe H, *Sr Cur,* Oberlin College, Allen Memorial Art Museum, Oberlin OH

Young, Christopher R, *Cur Collections & Registrar,* M Flint Institute of Arts, Flint MI

Young, Claire, *Cur,* Clinton Historical Museum Village, Clinton NJ

Young, Daniel, *Chmn,* State University of New York College at Oneonta, Dept of Art, Oneonta NY (S)

Young, Dave, *Instructor,* Central Wyoming College, Art Center, Riverton WY (S)

Young, David, *Head Dept Landscape Archit,* Pennsylvania State University, University Park, College of Arts and Architecture, University Park PA (S)

Young, David, *Head, Programmes & Public Relations,* Royal Ontario Museum, Toronto ON

Young, Deborah, *Traveling Exhib Officer,* Art Gallery of Nova Scotia, Halifax NS

Young, Dennis, *Chmn Art History Div,* Nova Scotia College of Art and Design, Halifax NS (S)

Young, Denny T, *Cur Painting,* Cincinnati Art Museum, Cincinnati OH

Young, Donn L, *Exec Dir,* Paine Art Center and Arboretum, Oshkosh WI

Young, Frances E, *Reference Librn,* Frick Art Reference Library, New York NY

Young, G, *Chmn,* Sarnia Public Library, Art Gallery, Sarnia ON

Young, G E, *Dean Art,* Eastern Oregon State College, Arts & Humanities Dept, La Grande OR (S)

Young, George, *Dir,* Kling Gallery, Philadelphia PA

Young, Gloria A, *Exhibitions & Publications Research,* Philbrook Art Center, Tulsa OK

Young, Jack, *Instr,* Wilkes Community College, Arts and Science Division, Wilkesboro NC (S)

Young, James L, *Dir,* College of Eastern Utah, Gallery East, Price UT

Young, Jane, *Cur,* Surrey Art Gallery, Surrey BC

Young, Jane Anne, *Dir of Education,* University of Virginia, Art Museum, Charlottesville VA

Young, Joseph L, *Dir,* Art in Architecture, Los Angeles CA (S)

Young, Joseph L, *Dir,* Art in Architecture, Joseph Young Library, Los Angeles CA

Young, Joshua A S, *Pres,* The Bostonian Society, Old State House, Boston MA

Young, Kathleen, *Admin Mgr,* San Mateo County Arts Council, Belmont CA

Young, Martie, *Cur Asian Art,* Cornell University, Herbert F Johnson Museum of Art, Ithaca NY

Young, Martie W, *Prof,* Cornell University, Dept of the History of Art, Ithaca NY (S)

Young, Patrick, *Photographer,* University of Michigan, Slide and Photograph Collection, Ann Arbor MI

Young, Retha, *Treas,* Sheldon Museum and Cultural Center, Haines AK

Young, Robert, *Asst Prof,* University of British Columbia, Dept of Fine Arts, Vancouver BC (S)

Young, Sherrill F, *Treas,* Hickory Museum of Art, Inc, Hickory NC

Young, Suzie, *Gallery Asst,* Simon Fraser University, Simon Fraser Gallery, Burnaby BC

Young, Thomas E, *Librn,* Philbrook Art Center, Library, Tulsa OK

Young, Tom, *Instructor,* Greenfield Community College, Art Dept, Greenfield MA (S)

Young, William, *Vis Lectr,* Tufts University, Fine Arts Dept, Medford MA (S)

Young, William Thomas, *Prof,* University of New Orleans, Dept of Fine Arts, New Orleans LA (S)

Young, Willow, *Special Programs Coordr,* Craft and Folk Art Museum, Los Angeles CA

Youngblood, Judy, *Printmaking Coordr,* North Texas State University, Art Dept, Denton TX (S)

Youngblood, Michael S, *Asst Prof,* Southern Illinois University, School of Art, Carbondale IL (S)

Youngers, Peter L, *Head Dept,* Northeastern Junior College, Dept of Art, Sterling CO (S)

Youngman, James E, *Head Dept,* Artist Studio Centers, Inc, New York NY (S)

Yrigoyen, Charles, *Secy,* United Methodist Church Commission on Archives and History, Madison NJ

Yu, Chilin, *Librn,* Columbus College of Art and Design, Packard Library, Columbus OH

Yuhas, Louise, *Chmn,* Occidental College, Art Dept, Los Angeles CA (S)

Yussupoff, Elina, *Secy,* Nicholas Roerich Museum, New York NY

Zabarsky, Melvin, *Prof,* University of New Hampshire, Dept of the Arts, Durham NH (S)

Zabel, Barbara B, *Assoc Prof,* Connecticut College, Dept of Art History, New London CT (S)

Zaborowski, Dennis, *Asst Chmn Studio Art,* University of North Carolina at Chapel Hill, Art Dept, Chapel Hill NC (S)

Zaborowski, Dennis, *Assoc Prof,* University of North Carolina at Chapel Hill, Art Dept, Chapel Hill NC (S)

Zachos, Kimon S, *Pres,* Currier Gallery of Art, Manchester NH

Zadro, Michael, *Chmn,* State University of New York College at New Paltz, Art Studio Dept, New Paltz NY (S)

Zafran, Eric, *Cur European Art,* High Museum of Art, Atlanta GA

Zager, Daniel, *Music Librn,* Pennsylvania State University, Pattee Library, University Park PA

Zagorski, Edward J, *In Charge Industrial Design,* University of Illinois, Urbana-Champaign, School of Art and Design, Champaign IL (S)

Zagorski, Stanislaw, *Prof,* Temple University, Tyler School of Art, Philadelphia PA (S)

Zahner, Mary, *Asst Prof,* University of Dayton, Fine Arts Division, Dayton OH (S)

Zahourek, Jon, *Instr,* New York Academy of Art, New York NY (S)

Zahradnik, Gordon, *Head Dept,* Sterling College, Art Dept, Sterling KS (S)

Zakia, Richard D, *Chmn Fine Arts Photography,* Rochester Institute of Technology, School of Photographic Arts & Sciences, Rochester NY (S)

Zakin, M, *Staff,* Sarah Lawrence College, Dept of Art, Bronxville NY (S)

Zakin, Mikhail, *Instructor,* Truro Center for the Arts at Castle Hill, Inc, Truro MA (S)

Zakoian, Paul, *Sculpture,* Contemporary Art Workshop, Chicago IL (S)

Zakon, Ronnie, *Cur Education,* Rhode Island School of Design, Museum of Art, Providence RI

Zallinger, Rudolph, *Prof,* Hartford Art School of the University of Hartford, West Hartford CT (S)

Zamkoff, B, *Chmn Fashion Design,* Fashion Institute of Technology, Art & Design Division, New York NY (S)

Zamora, Frank, *Assoc Prof,* Biola University, Art Dept, La Mirada CA (S)

Zanetta, Polly N, *Chmn,* Olympic College, Art Dept, Bremerton WA (S)

Zannieri, Nina, *Cur,* Rhode Island Historical Society, Aldrich House, Providence RI

Zanzi, James, *Prof,* School of the Art Institute of Chicago, Chicago IL (S)

Zapton, Steve, *Assoc Prof,* James Madison University, Dept of Art, Harrisonburg VA (S)

Zaruba, Gary E, *Prof,* Kearney State College, Dept of Art, Kearney NE (S)

Zassman, Merye, *Asst Dir,* The Society of Arts and Crafts, Boston MA

Zastoupil, Carol, *Instructor,* Avila College, Art Division, Dept of Performing and Visual Art, Kansas City MO (S)

Zastoupil, Carol, *Dir,* Avila College, Thornhill Art Gallery, Kansas City MO

Zauft, Richard, *Chmn Dept,* University of South Dakota, Dept of Art, Vermillion SD (S)

Zawadi, Ima, *Exec Secy,* New Muse Community Museum of Brooklyn, Inc, Brooklyn NY

Zayas, Ana, *Librn,* Museo de Arte de Ponce, Library, Ponce PR

Zeber, Claudia, *Instr,* Cuyahoga Valley Art Center, Cuyahoga Falls OH (S)

Zehnder, Marvin, *Prof,* Northern Michigan University, Dept of Art and Design, Marquette MI (S)

Zeidenbergs, Olafs, *Dir,* Southern Connecticut State College, Art Gallery, New Haven CT

Zeidler, Jeanne, *Dir,* Hampton Institute, College Museum, Hampton VA

Zeiser, Bruce H, *Treas,* Springfield Art & Historical Society, Springfield VT

Zeitlin, Marilyn, *Dir,* Virginia Commonwealth University, Anderson Gallery, Richmond VA

Zeller, Terry, *Cur Educ,* Texas Tech University Museum, Lubbock TX

Zeller, William, *VPres,* Jesse Besser Museum, Alpena MI

Zelnik, Martin, *Chmn Interior Design,* Fashion Institute of Technology, Art & Design Division, New York NY (S)

Zendejas, R E, *Dir Museum Services,* Colorado Springs Fine Arts Center, Colorado Springs CO

Zeniuk, Jerry, *Faculty,* Sarah Lawrence College, Dept of Art, Bronxville NY (S)

Zentner, Barbara, *Registrar,* University of Oregon, Museum of Art, Eugene OR

Zerban, Dianna, *Secy,* Longview Museum and Arts Center, Longview TX

Zic, Virginia F, *Chmn,* Sacred Heart University, Dept of Art, Bridgeport CT (S)

Ziegler, Arthur P, *Pres,* Pittsburgh History and Landmarks Foundation, Old Post Office Museum, Pittsburgh PA

Zielinski, L Stanley, *Prof,* University of Alaska, Dept of Art, Fairbanks AK (S)

Ziemann, Richard, *Prof,* Herbert H Lehman College, Art Dept, Bronx NY (S)

Ziff, Jerrold, *In Charge Art History,* University of Illinois, Urbana-Champaign, School of Art and Design, Champaign IL (S)

Zilker, Sandra Parmer, *Instr,* Alfred C Glassell School of Art, Houston TX (S)

Zimmer, Dorothy, *Assoc Prof,* Montgomery County Community College, Communicating Arts Dept, Blue Bell PA (S)

Zimmer, Sandra, *Instructor,* Linn Benton Community College, Fine & Applied Art Dept, Albany OR (S)

Zimmerer-McKelvie, Kathy, *Gallery Dir,* University Art Gallery of California State University at Dominguez Hills, Dominguez Hills CA

Zimmerman, D, *Sales Shop Mgr,* Albany Museum of Art, Albany GA

Zimmerman, E E, *VPres,* Heritage Center, Inc, Pine Ridge SD

Zimmerman, Ernest Robert, *Dean of Faculty of Arts,* Lakehead University, Dept of Fine Art, Thunder Bay ON (S)

Zimmerman, Evelyn, *Education Coordr,* League of New Hampshire Craftsmen, Concord Gallery, Concord NH

Zimmerman, Frederick, *Assoc Prof,* State University of New York College at Cortland, Art Dept, Cortland NY (S)

Zimmerman, Gerald, *Asst Division Chief,* Chicago Public Library, Art Section, Fine Arts Division, Chicago IL

Zimmerman, Jerome, *Prof,* C W Post Center of Long Island University, School of the Arts, Greenvale NY (S)

Zimmerman, Leonard, *Pres,* Mid-Hudson Arts and Science Center, Poughkeepsie NY

Zimmerman, Paul, *Prof,* Hartford Art School of the University of Hartford, West Hartford CT (S)

Zimmerman, Phil, *Pres,* Farmington Valley Arts Center, Avon CT

Zimmerman, Philip D, *Exec Dir,* Historical Society of York County, York PA

Zimmerman, Salli, *Assoc Prof,* Nassau Community College, Art Dept, Garden City NY (S)

Zimmerman, Susan, *Asst Prof,* University of Illinois, Chicago, Health Science Center, Dept of Biocommunication Arts, Chicago IL (S)

Zimmermann, Andy, *Member,* The Loading Dock Gallery, Boston MA

Zingrich, Roy, *Adjunct Instr,* Maryville College, St Louis, Art Division, Saint Louis MO (S)

Zink, James, *Dir,* Southeast Missouri State University, Kent Library, Cape Girardeau MO

Zink, Louise, *Treas,* Hutchinson Art Association, Hutchinson KS

Zins, Daniel, *Instructor,* Atlanta College of Art, Atlanta GA (S)

Zinser, Robert E, *Treas,* Springfield Art Center, Springfield OH

Zipin, Martin, *Prof,* Harcum Junior College, Dept of Fine Arts, Bryn Mawr PA (S)

Zippay, Lori, *Distribution,* Electronic Arts Intermix, Inc, New York NY

Zirkle, Louis G, *Chmn Dept,* Grinnell College, Dept of Art, Grinnell IA (S)

Zisla, Harold, *Chmn,* Indiana University at South Bend, Fine Arts Dept, South Bend IN (S)

Zivich, Matthew, *Prof,* Saginaw Valley State College, Dept of Art and Design, University Center MI (S)

Zmur, M, *Instr,* David Thompson University Centre, Visual Arts Dept, Nelson BC (S)

Zobrist, Benedict K, *Dir,* Harry S Truman Library and Museum, Independence MO

Zoeckler, Lyndy, *Tech Svs & Ref Librn,* Otis Art Institute of Parsons School of Design Gallery, Library, Los Angeles CA

Zona, Louis A, *Dir,* Butler Institute of American Art, Youngstown OH

Zonghi, Berta, *Asst Keeper,* Boston Public Library, Rare Book & Manuscripts Dept, Boston MA

Zongker, Lorraine, *Dir Museum Services,* The Indian Museum, Wichita KS

Zonker, Kenneth L, *Assoc Prof,* Sam Houston State University, Art Dept, Huntsville TX (S)

Zontelli, Patricia, *Lecturer,* University of Wisconsin-Stout, Art Dept, Menomonie WI (S)

Zorn, Madalon, *Administrative Asst,* Children's Art Foundation, Santa Cruz CA

Zorn, Peter, *Assoc Prof,* University of Miami, Dept of Art & Art History, Coral Gables FL (S)

Zsako, Julius, *Prof,* Seton Hall University, Dept of Art and Music, South Orange NJ (S)

Zuberec, M, *VPres,* Rodman Hall Arts Centre, Saint Catharines ON

Zuccarini, Ezio, *Instr,* Mainline Center of the Arts, Haverford PA (S)

Zucker, Barbara M, *Chairperson,* University of Vermont, Dept of Art, Burlington VT (S)

Zucker, Mark, *Assoc Prof,* Louisiana State University, School of Art, Baton Rouge LA (S)

Zuckerman, Edith, *Slide Cur,* Temple University, Slide Library, Philadelphia PA

Zuelsdorf, Catherine, *Asst Prof,* University of Alaska, Dept of Art, Fairbanks AK (S)

Zuhn, Cheryl, *Dept Head,* Ray-Vogue College of Design, Chicago IL (S)

Zujkowski, Stan, *Asst Prof,* Mansfield State College, Art Dept, Mansfield PA (S)

Zukowsky, John R, *Cur Dept Architecture,* Art Institute of Chicago, Chicago IL

Zumeta, Julio, *Instructor,* Art Academy of Cincinnati, Cincinnati OH (S)

Zumkehr, John L, *Cur Gallery,* North Canton Public Library, Little Art Gallery, North Canton OH

Zuraw, Cathy, *Head Librn,* Sheridan College School of Applied Arts and Technology, School of Crafts and Design Library, Mississauga ON

Zurawski, Simone, *Asst Prof,* DePaul University, Dept of Art, Chicago IL (S)

Zweck, Jack, *Pres,* Wisconsin Fine Arts Association, Inc, Ozaukee Art Center, Cedarburg WI

Zwick, Leander P, *Pres,* Canton Art Institute, Canton OH

Zytkiewicz, Halina, *Assoc Prof,* Community College of Baltimore, Dept of Fine & Applied Arts, Liberty Campus, Baltimore MD (S)

Zywicki, Joseph B, *Cur Painting & Sculpture,* Chicago Historical Society, Chicago IL

Subject Index

Major subjects are listed first, followed by named collections.

AFRICAN ART

African-American Institute, New York NY
Albion College, Bobbitt Visual Arts Center, Albion MI
Baltimore Museum of Art, Baltimore MD
Bower's Museum, Santa Ana CA
Brandeis University, Rose Art Museum, Waltham MA
Dallas Museum of Fine Arts, Dallas TX
Detroit Institute of Arts, Detroit MI
Edmundson Art Foundation, Inc, Des Moines Art Center, Des Moines IA
Everhart Museum of Natural History, Science and Art, Scranton PA
Everson Museum of Art, Syracuse NY
Fine Arts Museum of the South, Mobile AL
Fisk University Museum of Art, Nashville TN
M Flint Institute of Arts, Flint MI
Florence Museum, Florence SC
Galleries of the Claremont Colleges, Claremont CA
Hampton Institute, College Museum, Hampton VA
Heard Museum, Phoenix AZ
High Museum of Art, Atlanta GA
Hofstra University, Emily Lowe Gallery, Hempstead NY
Hollywood Art Museum, Hollywood FL
Howard University, Gallery of Art, Washington DC
Illinois State University, University Museums, Normal IL
Martin & Osa Johnson Safari Museum, Chanute KS
Loch Haven Art Center, Inc, Orlando FL
Marietta College, Grover M Hermann Fine Arts Center, Marietta OH
Maryland Museum of African Art, Columbia MD
Minneapolis Institute of Arts, Minneapolis MN
Minnesota Museum of Art, Saint Paul MN
Montreal Museum of Fine Arts, Montreal PQ
Muscatine Art Center, Muscatine IA
The Museum, Greenwood SC
Museum of the Philadelphia Civic Center, Philadelphia PA
Museum of the United States, Washington DC
New Muse Community Museum of Brooklyn, Inc, Brooklyn NY
New Orleans Museum of Art, New Orleans LA
North Carolina Central University, Museum of Art, Durham NC
North Carolina Museum of Art, Raleigh NC
North Country Museum of Arts, Park Rapids MN
Norwich Free Academy, Slater Memorial Museum & Converse Art Gallery, Norwich CT
Oklahoma Center for Science and Art, Kirkpatrick Center, Oklahoma City OK
Philbrook Art Center, Tulsa OK
Plains Art Museum, Main Gallery, Moorhead MN
Plains Art Museum, Rourke Art Gallery, Moorhead MN
Portland Art Association, Portland Art Museum, Portland OR
Putnam Museum, Davenport IA
St Lawrence University, Richard F Brush Art Gallery, Canton NY
Schenectady Museum, Schenectady NY

State University of New York at Purchase, Neuberger Museum, Purchase NY
Topeka Public Library, Fine Arts Dept & Gallery of Fine Arts, Topeka KS
University of Delaware, University Art Collections, Newark DE
University of Iowa, Museum of Art, Iowa City IA
University of Kentucky, Art Museum, Lexington KY
University of Maryland, College Park, Art Gallery, College Park MD
University of Miami, Lowe Art Museum, Coral Gables FL
University of Michigan, Museum of Art, Ann Arbor MI
University of Notre Dame, Snite Museum of Art, Notre Dame IN
University of Oklahoma, Museum of Art, Norman OK
University of Oregon, Museum of Art, Eugene OR
University of Santa Clara, de Saisset Museum, Santa Clara CA
University of South Florida, Art Galleries, Tampa FL
University of Wisconsin-Stout, Gallery 209, Menomonie WI
Williams College, Museum of Art, Williamstown MA

AFRO-AMERICAN ART

Afro-American Historical and Cultural Museum, Philadelphia PA
Albany Museum of Art, Albany GA
Anacostia Neighborhood Museum, Washington DC
DuSable Museum of African American History, Chicago IL
Fisk University Museum of Art, Nashville TN
Florence Museum, Florence SC
Hampton Institute, College Museum, Hampton VA
Howard University, Gallery of Art, Washington DC
The Museum of African American Art, Santa Monica CA
Museum of the National Center of Afro-American Artists, Boston MA
New Muse Community Museum of Brooklyn, Inc, Brooklyn NY
Scripps College, Clark Humanities Museum, Claremont CA
Store Front Museum, Jamaica NY
Studio Museum in Harlem, New York NY

AMERICAN INDIAN ART

Amerind Foundation, Inc, Dragoon AZ
Anchorage Historical and Fine Arts Museum, Cook Inlet Historical Society, Anchorage AK
Atlanta Museum, Atlanta GA
Bacone College Museum, Muskogee OK
Bower's Museum, Santa Ana CA
Brandeis University, Rose Art Museum, Waltham MA
The Bruce Museum, Greenwich CT
Butler Institute of American Art, Youngstown OH

Butler Museum of American Indian Art, Eugene OR
Capital University, Schumacher Gallery, Columbus OH
Carmel Mission and Gift Shop, Carmel CA
Cayuga Museum of History and Art, Auburn NY
Chief Plenty Coups State Monument Museum, Pryor MT
Colby Museum of Art, Waterville ME
Colorado Springs Fine Arts Center, Colorado Springs CO
Dacotah Prairie Museum, Lamont Gallery, Aberdeen SD
Denver Art Museum, Denver CO
Desert Caballeros Western Museum, Wickenburg AZ
Evansville Museum of Arts and Science, Evansville IN
Everhart Museum of Natural History, Science and Art, Scranton PA
Favell Museum of Western Art & Indian Artifacts, Klamath Falls OR
Five Civilized Tribes Museum, Muskogee OK
Fruitlands Museums, Harvard MA
Thomas Gilcrease Institute of American History and Art, Tulsa OK
Hampton Institute, College Museum, Hampton VA
Hartwick College Fine Art Gallery, Yager Museum, Oneonta NY
Harwood Foundation of the University of New Mexico, Taos NM
Hastings Museum, Hastings NE
Heard Museum, Phoenix AZ
Heritage Center, Inc, Pine Ridge SD
Heritage Plantation of Sandwich, Sandwich MA
Illinois State University, University Museums, Normal IL
The Indian Museum, Wichita KS
Institute of American Indian Arts Museum, Santa Fe NM
Johnson-Humrickhouse Museum, Coshocton OH
Joslyn Art Museum, Omaha NE
Kelly-Griggs House Museum, Red Bluff CA
Kiah Museum, Savannah GA
Koshare Indian Museum, Inc, La Junta CO
Leanin Tree Museum of Western Art, Boulder CO
Legislative Building Art Gallery, Regina SK
Louisiana Arts and Science Center, Baton Rouge LA
Maryhill Museum of Art, Goldendale WA
Mills College, Art Gallery, Oakland CA
Minneapolis Institute of Arts, Minneapolis MN
Minnesota Museum of Art, Saint Paul MN
Montclair Art Museum, Montclair NJ
Morris Museum of Arts and Sciences, Morristown NJ
Musee d'Art de Saint-Laurent, Saint-Laurent PQ
Museum of Arts and History, Port Huron MI
Museum of Arts and Sciences, Cuban Museum, Planetarium, Daytona Beach FL
Museum of Art, Science and Industry, Bridgeport CT
Museum of Fine Arts, Houston, Houston TX

Museum of New Mexico, Museum of Fine Arts, Santa Fe NM
Museum of Northern Arizona, Flagstaff AZ
Museum of Northern British Columbia, Prince Rupert Museum Art Gallery, Prince Rupert BC
Museum of the American Indian, New York NY
Museum of the Plains Indian, Browning MT
Museum of the Southwest, Midland TX
National Hall of Fame for Famous American Indians, Anadarko OK
Newark Museum, Newark NJ
North Carolina Museum of Art, Raleigh NC
Northern Illinois University, Swen Parson Gallery and Gallery 200, De Kalb IL
Norwich Free Academy, Slater Memorial Museum & Converse Art Gallery, Norwich CT
Oakville Galleries, Oakville ON
Oklahoma Historical Society, Central Museum, Oklahoma City OK
Oregon State University, Horner Museum, Corvallis OR
Oshkosh Public Museum, Oshkosh WI
Philbrook Art Center, Tulsa OK
Frank Phillips, Woolaroc Museum, Bartlesville OK
Plains Art Museum, Main Gallery, Moorhead MN
Plains Art Museum, Rourke Art Gallery, Moorhead MN
Plains Indians & Pioneer Historical Foundation, Pioneer Museum & Art Center, Woodward OK
Ponca City Cultural Center & Museum, Ponca City OK
Portland Art Association, Portland Art Museum, Portland OR
Principia College, School of Nations Museum, Elsah IL
Putnam Museum, Davenport IA
Rahr-West Museum, Manitowoc WI
Redding Museum and Art Center, Redding CA
Red River Valley Museum, Vernon TX
Red Rock State Park Museum, Church Rock NM
The Rockwell Museum, Corning NY
Lauren Rogers Library and Museum of Art, Laurel MS
Millicent Rogers Museum, Taos NM
Roswell Museum and Art Center, Roswell NM
Safety Harbor Museum of History and Fine Arts, Safety Harbor FL
Saint Bonaventure University Art Collection, Saint Bonaventure NY
Saint Francis College, Lakeview Gallery, Fort Wayne IN
Saint Louis Art Museum, Saint Louis MO
Schenectady Museum, Schenectady NY
School of American Research, Santa Fe NM
Sheldon Museum and Cultural Center, Haines AK
Sioux Indian Museum, Rapid City, SD
South Dakota State University, South Dakota Memorial Art Center, Brookings SD
Southern Plains Indian Museum, Anadarko OK
Southwest Museum, Los Angeles CA
Stanford University, Museum of Art & Art Gallery, Stanford CA
Stark Museum of Art, Orange TX
State Capitol Museum, Olympia WA
Stradling Museum of the Horse, Inc, Patagonia AZ
Strasburg Museum, Strasburg VA
Tallahassee Junior Museum, Tallahassee FL
Tomoka State Park Museum, Ormond Beach FL
University of Cincinnati, Tangeman Fine Arts Gallery, Cincinnati OH
University of Miami, Lowe Art Museum, Coral Gables FL
University of Notre Dame, Snite Museum of Art, Notre Dame IN
University of Southern Colorado, School of Liberal Arts, Pueblo CO
Walker Museum, Fairlee VT
T T Wentworth, Jr Museum, Pensacola FL
Whatcom Museum of History and Art, Bellingham WA
Wheelwright Museum, Santa Fe NM
Wichita State University, Edwin A Ulrich Museum of Art, Wichita KS
Yosemite Collections, Yosemite National Park CA

AMERICAN WESTERN ART

Appaloosa Museum, Inc, Moscow ID
Birmingham Museum of Art, Birmingham AL
Brigham Young University, B F Larsen Gallery, Provo UT
Bradford Brinton Memorial Ranch Museum, Big Horn WY
Buffalo Bill Memorial Association, Cody WY
Carson County Square House Museum, Panhandle TX
Amon Carter Museum, Fort Worth TX
Desert Caballeros Western Museum, Wickenburg AZ
Diamond M Foundation Museum, Snyder TX
Favell Museum of Western Art & Indian Artifacts, Klamath Falls OR
Frontier Times Museum, Bandera TX
William S Hart Museum, Newhall CA
Joslyn Art Museum, Omaha NE
Kalamunda Museum of Western Art, Somers MT
Leanin Tree Museum of Western Art, Boulder CO
Marietta College, Grover M Hermann Fine Arts Center, Marietta OH
Mississippi Museum of Art, Jackson MS
National Cowboy Hall of Fame and Western Heritage Center, Oklahoma City OK
R W Norton Art Gallery, Shreveport LA
Pioneer Town, Wimberley TX
The Rockwell Museum, Corning NY
C M Russell Museum, Great Falls MT
Sangre De Cristo Arts & Conference Center, Pueblo CO
Southwest Arts Foundation, Houston TX
Southwest Museum, Los Angeles CA
Stanford University, Museum of Art & Art Gallery, Stanford CA
Stark Museum of Art, Orange TX
Texas Tech University Museum, Lubbock TX
University of Texas at Austin, Archer M Huntington Art Gallery, Austin TX
Wyoming State Art Gallery, Cheyenne WY

ANTHROPOLOGY

Indiana University, William Hammond Mathers Museum, Bloomington IN
Oklahoma Historical Society, Central Museum, Oklahoma City OK
Pennsylvania Historical and Museum Commission, Harrisburg PA
University of Pennsylvania, University Museum of Archaeology & Anthropology, Philadelphia PA
University of Washington, Thomas Burke Memorial Washington State Museum, Seattle WA

ANTIQUITIES - ASSYRIAN

Cincinnati Art Museum, Cincinnati OH
Metropolitan Museum of Art, New York NY
Rosicrucian Egyptian Museum and Art Gallery, San Jose CA
Toledo Museum of Art, Toledo OH
University of Chicago, Oriental Institute, Chicago IL
University of Missouri, Museum of Art and Archaeology, Columbia MO
University of Rochester, Memorial Art Gallery, Rochester NY
Walters Art Gallery, Baltimore MD

ANTIQUITIES - BYZANTINE

Cincinnati Art Museum, Cincinnati OH
Detroit Institute of Arts, Detroit MI
Harvard University, Dumbarton Oaks Research Library and Collections, Washington DC
Metropolitan Museum of Art, New York NY
Newark Museum, Newark NJ
Princeton University, Art Museum, Princeton NJ
University of Chicago, Oriental Institute, Chicago IL
University of Illinois, World Heritage Museum, Champaign IL
University of Missouri, Museum of Art and Archaeology, Columbia MO
Walters Art Gallery, Baltimore MD

ANTIQUITIES - EGYPTIAN

Lyman Allyn Museum, New London CT
Lee Atkyns Studio-Gallery, Duncansville PA
Berkshire Museum, Pittsfield MA
Cincinnati Art Museum, Cincinnati OH
Cleveland Museum of Art, Cleveland OH
Detroit Institute of Arts, Detroit MI
Evansville Museum of Arts and Science, Evansville IN
Fine Arts Museums of San Francisco, M H de Young Memorial Museum and California Palace of the Legion of Honor, San Francisco CA
Freeport Area Arts Council, Freeport Art Museum, Freeport IL
Godwin-Ternbach Museum, Flushing NY
Harvard University, Harvard Semitic Museum, Cambridge MA
Harvard University, William Hayes Fogg Art Museum, Cambridge MA
Johns Hopkins University, Archaeological Museum, Baltimore MD
Metropolitan Museum of Art, New York NY
Milwaukee Art Museum, Milwaukee WI
Mount Holyoke College Art Museum, South Hadley MA
Museum of Fine Arts, Boston MA
Newark Museum, Newark NJ
Princeton University, Art Museum, Princeton NJ
Rosicrucian Egyptian Museum and Art Gallery, San Jose CA
Saint Gregory's Abbey and College, Mabee-Gerrer Museum of Art, Shawnee OK
Saint Louis Art Museum, Saint Louis MO
Toledo Museum of Art, Toledo OH
University of Chicago, Oriental Institute, Chicago IL
University of Illinois, World Heritage Museum, Champaign IL
University of Michigan, Kelsey Museum of Ancient and Medieval Archaeology, Ann Arbor MI
University of Missouri, Museum of Art and Archaeology, Columbia MO
University of North Carolina, The Ackland Art Museum, Chapel Hill NC
University of Rochester, Memorial Art Gallery, Rochester NY
University of Utah, Utah Museum of Fine Arts, Salt Lake City UT
University of Wisconsin, Elvehjem Museum of Art, Madison WI
Walters Art Gallery, Baltimore MD
Worcester Art Museum, Worcester MA

ANTIQUITIES - ETRUSCAN

Metropolitan Museum of Art, New York NY
Newark Museum, Newark NJ
University of Chicago, Oriental Institute, Chicago IL
University of Missouri, Museum of Art and Archaeology, Columbia MO
Vassar College Art Gallery, Poughkeepsie NY
Walters Art Gallery, Baltimore MD

ANTIQUITIES - GREEK

Lyman Allyn Museum, New London CT
Baltimore Museum of Art, Baltimore MD
Beloit College, Wright Museum of Art, Beloit WI
Berkshire Museum, Pittsfield MA
Bowdoin College, Museum of Art & Peary-MacMillan Arctic Museum, Brunswick ME
Chrysler Museum, Norfolk VA
Cincinnati Art Museum, Cincinnati OH
Cleveland Museum of Art, Cleveland OH
Corcoran Museum, Washington DC
Fine Arts Museums of San Francisco, M H de Young Memorial Museum and California Palace of the Legion of Honor, San Francisco CA
Freeport Area Arts Council, Freeport Art Museum, Freeport IL
Isabella Stewart Gardner Museum, Boston MA
J Paul Getty Museum, Malibu CA
Godwin-Ternbach Museum, Flushing NY
Harvard University, William Hayes Fogg Art Museum, Cambridge MA
James Madison University, Sawhill Gallery, Harrisonburg VA

Metropolitan Museum of Art, New York NY
Milwaukee Art Museum, Milwaukee WI
Minneapolis Institute of Arts, Minneapolis MN
Mount Holyoke College Art Museum, South
Hadley MA
Munson-Williams-Proctor Institute, Museum of Art,
Utica NY
Museum of Fine Arts, Boston MA
Museum of Fine Arts, Houston, Houston TX
Newark Museum, Newark NJ
Portland Art Association, Portland Art Museum,
Portland OR
Princeton University, Art Museum, Princeton NJ
Queen's University, Agnes Etherington Art Centre,
Kingston ON
Rhode Island School of Design, Museum of Art,
Providence RI
Saginaw Art Museum, Saginaw MI
Saint Gregory's Abbey and College, Mabee-Gerrer
Museum of Art, Shawnee OK
Santa Barbara Museum of Art, Santa Barbara CA
Seattle Art Museum, Seattle WA
Staten Island Institute of Arts and Sciences, Staten
Island NY
Toledo Museum of Art, Toledo OH
University of Chicago, David and Alfred Smart
Gallery, Chicago IL
University of Illinois, World Heritage Museum,
Champaign IL
University of Kansas, Spencer Museum of Art,
Lawrence KS
University of Michigan, Kelsey Museum of Ancient
and Medieval Archaeology, Ann Arbor MI
University of Michigan, Museum of Art, Ann Arbor
MI
University of Mississippi, University Museums,
Oxford MS
University of Missouri, Museum of Art and
Archaeology, Columbia MO
University of Texas at Austin, Archer M
Huntington Art Gallery, Austin TX
University of Vermont, Robert Hull Fleming
Museum, Burlington VT
University of Wisconsin, Elvehjem Museum of Art,
Madison WI
Vassar College Art Gallery, Poughkeepsie NY
Virginia Museum of Fine Arts, Richmond VA
Walters Art Gallery, Baltimore MD
Williams College, Museum of Art, Williamstown
MA
Yale University, Art Gallery, New Haven CT

ANTIQUITIES - ORIENTAL

Atlanta Museum, Atlanta GA
Cincinnati Art Museum, Cincinnati OH
Detroit Institute of Arts, Detroit MI
Harvard University, William Hayes Fogg Art
Museum, Cambridge MA
Museum of Fine Arts, Springfield MA
Northwestern College, Te Paske Gallery of
Rowenhorst, Orange City IA
Plains Art Museum, Main Gallery, Moorhead MN
Portland Art Association, Portland Art Museum,
Portland OR
Staten Island Institute of Arts and Sciences, Staten
Island NY
Toledo Museum of Art, Toledo OH
University of Illinois, World Heritage Museum,
Champaign IL
Worcester Art Museum, Worcester MA

ANTIQUITIES - PERSIAN

Cincinnati Art Museum, Cincinnati OH
Detroit Institute of Arts, Detroit MI
Metropolitan Museum of Art, New York NY
Munson-Williams-Proctor Institute, Museum of Art,
Utica NY
Plains Art Museum, Main Gallery, Moorhead MN
Plains Art Museum, Rourke Art Gallery, Moorhead
MN
University of Chicago, Oriental Institute, Chicago
IL
University of Missouri, Museum of Art and
Archaeology, Columbia MO
Walters Art Gallery, Baltimore MD

ANTIQUITIES - ROMAN

Lyman Allyn Museum, New London CT
Baltimore Museum of Art, Baltimore MD
Berkshire Museum, Pittsfield MA
Bowdoin College, Museum of Art & Peary-
MacMillan Arctic Museum, Brunswick ME
Chrysler Museum, Norfolk VA
Cincinnati Art Museum, Cincinnati OH
Cleveland Museum of Art, Cleveland OH
Detroit Institute of Arts, Detroit MI
Fine Arts Museums of San Francisco, M H de
Young Memorial Museum and California Palace
of the Legion of Honor, San Francisco CA
Freeport Area Arts Council, Freeport Art Museum,
Freeport IL
Isabella Stewart Gardner Museum, Boston MA
J Paul Getty Museum, Malibu CA
Harvard University, William Hayes Fogg Art
Museum, Cambridge MA
James Madison University, Sawhill Gallery,
Harrisonburg VA
Johns Hopkins University, Archaeological Museum,
Baltimore MD
Metropolitan Museum of Art, New York NY
Milwaukee Art Museum, Milwaukee WI
Minneapolis Institute of Arts, Minneapolis MN
Mount Holyoke College Art Museum, South
Hadley MA
Museum of Fine Arts, Boston MA
Museum of Fine Arts, Houston, Houston TX
Newark Museum, Newark NJ
Princeton University, Art Museum, Princeton NJ
Queen's University, Agnes Etherington Art Centre,
Kingston ON
Rhode Island School of Design, Museum of Art,
Providence RI
Saginaw Art Museum, Saginaw MI
Saint Gregory's Abbey and College, Mabee-Gerrer
Museum of Art, Shawnee OK
Santa Barbara Museum of Art, Santa Barbara CA
Seattle Art Museum, Seattle WA
Staten Island Institute of Arts and Sciences, Staten
Island NY
Toledo Museum of Art, Toledo OH
University of Chicago, David and Alfred Smart
Gallery, Chicago IL
University of Illinois, World Heritage Museum,
Champaign IL
University of Kansas, Spencer Museum of Art,
Lawrence KS
University of Michigan, Kelsey Museum of Ancient
and Medieval Archaeology, Ann Arbor MI
University of Michigan, Museum of Art, Ann Arbor
MI
University of Mississippi, University Museums,
Oxford MS
University of Missouri, Museum of Art and
Archaeology, Columbia MO
University of Texas at Austin, Archer M
Huntington Art Gallery, Austin TX
University of Vermont, Robert Hull Fleming
Museum, Burlington VT
Vassar College Art Gallery, Poughkeepsie NY
Vizcaya Museum and Gardens, Miami FL
Walters Art Gallery, Baltimore MD
Williams College, Museum of Art, Williamstown
MA
Yale University, Art Gallery, New Haven CT

ARCHAEOLOGY

Amerind Foundation, Inc, Dragoon AZ
Augusta Richmond County Museum, Augusta GA
Department of Culture, Government of the
Province of Alberta, Provincial Museum of
Alberta, Edmonton AB
Heard Museum, Phoenix AZ
Hebrew Union College, Skirball Museum, Los
Angeles CA
Institute of the Great Plains, Museum of the Great
Plains, Lawton OK
Lakeview Museum of Arts and Sciences, Peoria IL
Loveland Museum and Gallery, Loveland CO
Museum of Northern Arizona, Flagstaff AZ
National Museum of American History,
Smithsonian Institution, Washington DC
National Museum of Man, Ottawa ON

Native American Center for the Living Arts,
Niagara Falls NY
Oklahoma Historical Society, Central Museum,
Oklahoma City OK
Pennsylvania Historical and Museum Commission,
Harrisburg PA
Frank Phillips, Woolaroc Museum, Bartlesville OK
Ponca City Cultural Center & Museum, Ponca City
OK
Saint Augustine Historical Society, Oldest House
and Museums, Saint Augustine FL
Spertus Museum of Judaica, Chicago IL
State Art Museum of Florida, John & Mable
Ringling Museum of Art, Sarasota FL
University of California, Los Angeles, Museum of
Cultural History, Los Angeles CA
University of Pennsylvania, University Museum of
Archaeology & Anthropology, Philadelphia PA
University of Tennessee, Frank H McClung
Museum, Knoxville TN
Vassar College Art Gallery, Poughkeepsie NY

ARCHITECTURE

Allentown Art Museum, Allentown PA
Art Institute of Chicago, Chicago IL
Athenaeum of Philadelphia, Philadelphia PA
Baltimore Museum of Art, Baltimore MD
Boston Public Library, Albert H Wiggin Gallery
(Prints), Boston MA
Chicago Architecture Foundation, Glessner House,
Chicago IL
Clemson University, Rudolph E Lee Gallery,
Clemson SC
Cooper-Hewitt Museum, Smithsonian Institution,
New York NY
Historic New Orleans Collection, Kemper and Leila
Williams Foundation, New Orleans LA
Hudson River Museum, Yonkers NY
Institute for Art & Urban Resources, Project
Studios One, Long Island City NY
Library of Congress, Washington DC
Maryland Historical Society Museum, Baltimore
MD
Milwaukee Art Museum, Milwaukee WI
Munson-Williams-Proctor Institute, Museum of Art,
Utica NY
Museum of Modern Art, New York NY
Philadelphia Museum of Art, Philadelphia PA
Pope-Leighey House, Mount Vernon VA
State University of New York College at Fredonia,
M C Rockefeller Arts Center Gallery, Fredonia
NY
United States Capitol Museum, Washington DC
University of California, Santa Barbara, University
Art Museum, Santa Barbara CA
Vassar College Art Gallery, Poughkeepsie NY
Westover, Charles City VA

ASIAN ART

Art Gallery of Greater Victoria, Victoria BC
Asian Art Museum of San Francisco, Avery
Brundage Collection, San Francisco CA
Asia Society, Inc, Gallery, New York NY
Berea College, Art Department Gallery, Berea KY
Birmingham Museum of Art, Birmingham AL
Bower's Museum, Santa Ana CA
Breezewood Foundation Museum and Garden,
Monkton MD
Centenary College of Louisiana, Meadows Museum
of Art, Shreveport LA
Cornell University, Herbert F Johnson Museum of
Art, Ithaca NY
Drexel University Museum, Philadelphia PA
Francis E Fowler Jr Foundation Museum, Beverly
Hills CA
Freer Gallery of Art, Washington DC
Honolulu Academy of Arts, Honolulu HI
James Madison University, Sawhill Gallery,
Harrisonburg VA
Los Angeles County Museum of Art, Los Angeles
CA
Memphis Brooks Museum of Art, Memphis TN
Minnesota Museum of Art, Saint Paul MN
Mount Holyoke College Art Museum, South
Hadley MA

Murray State University, Clara M Eagle Gallery, Murray KY
Newark Museum, Newark NJ
New York University, Grey Art Gallery and Study Center, New York NY
Philadelphia Museum of Art, Philadelphia PA
Philbrook Art Center, Tulsa OK
Portland Art Association, Portland Art Museum, Portland OR
Principia College, School of Nations Museum, Elsah IL
Putnam Museum, Davenport IA
Seattle Art Museum, Seattle WA
Tacoma Art Museum, Tacoma WA
University of California, Los Angeles, Museum of Cultural History, Los Angeles CA
University of Iowa, Museum of Art, Iowa City IA
University of Michigan, Museum of Art, Ann Arbor MI
University of Missouri, Museum of Art and Archaeology, Columbia MO
University of San Diego, Founders' Gallery, San Diego CA
Virginia Museum of Fine Arts, Richmond VA

BAROQUE ART

Hartwick College Fine Art Gallery, Oneonta NY
Mint Museum of Art, Charlotte NC
San Diego Museum of Art, San Diego CA
State Art Museum of Florida, John & Mable Ringling Museum of Art, Sarasota FL
University of Miami, Lowe Art Museum, Coral Gables FL
University of Notre Dame, Snite Museum of Art, Notre Dame IN

BRONZES

Atkins Museum of Fine Art, Kansas City MO
Atlanta Museum, Atlanta GA
Baltimore Museum of Art, Baltimore MD
Chesterwood, Stockbridge MA
College of Wooster Art Center Museum, Wooster OH
Concordia College Wisconsin, Fine Arts Galleries, Mequon WI
Corcoran Museum, Washington DC
Diamond M Foundation Museum, Snyder TX
Franklin Mint Museum, Franklin Center PA
Freer Gallery of Art, Washington DC
Frick Collection, New York NY
Godwin-Ternbach Museum, Flushing NY
Hall of Fame of the Trotter, Goshen NY
Harvard University, William Hayes Fogg Art Museum, Cambridge MA
Hermitage Foundation Museum, Norfolk VA
Indianapolis Museum of Art, Indianapolis IN
Leanin Tree Museum of Western Art, Boulder CO
Loyola University of Chicago, Martin D'Arcy Gallery of Art, Chicago IL
National Cowboy Hall of Fame and Western Heritage Center, Oklahoma City OK
National Hall of Fame for Famous American Indians, Anadarko OK
National Museum of Racing, Inc, Saratoga Springs NY
Norton Gallery and School of Art, West Palm Beach FL
Princeton University, Art Museum, Princeton NJ
Frederic Remington Art Museum, Ogdensburg NY
The Rockwell Museum, Corning NY
Rollins College, George D and Harriet W Cornell Fine Arts Center Museum, Winter Park FL
Saint Louis Art Museum, Saint Louis MO
Society of the Cincinnati, Anderson House Museum, Washington DC
Springville Museum of Art, Springville UT
University of Iowa, Museum of Art, Iowa City IA
University of Michigan, Kelsey Museum of Ancient and Medieval Archaeology, Ann Arbor MI
Virginia Museum, Danville Museum of Fine Arts and History, Danville VA
Virginia Museum of Fine Arts, Richmond VA
Vizcaya Museum and Gardens, Miami FL

CALLIGRAPHY

Portland Art Association, Portland Art Museum, Portland OR
Saint John's University, Chung-Cheng Art Gallery, Jamaica NY
George Walter Vincent Smith Art Museum, Springfield MA

CARPETS & RUGS

Department of State, Diplomatic Reception Rooms, Washington DC
Hermitage Foundation Museum, Norfolk VA
Huntington Galleries, Huntington WV
Iowa State Education Association, Salisbury House, Des Moines IA
Portland Art Association, Portland Art Museum, Portland OR
The Rosenbach Museum and Library, Philadelphia PA
Sierra Nevada Museum of Art, Reno NV
George Walter Vincent Smith Art Museum, Springfield MA
Vizcaya Museum and Gardens, Miami FL
Woodmere Art Museum, Philadelphia PA

CARTOONS

Hartwick College Fine Art Gallery, Oneonta NY
Herbert Hoover Presidential Library & Museum, West Branch IA
Kansas State Historial Society Museum, Topeka KS
Pavilion of Humour, Man and His World, Montreal PQ
Harry S Truman Library and Museum, Independence MO

CERAMICS

Albany Institute of History and Art, Albany NY
Albion College, Bobbitt Visual Arts Center, Albion MI
American Swedish Institute, Minneapolis MN
Atkins Museum of Fine Art, Kansas City MO
Baltimore Museum of Art, Baltimore MD
Berea College, Art Department Gallery, Berea KY
Brandeis University, Rose Art Museum, Waltham MA
Buten Museum of Wedgwood, Merion PA
Butler Institute of American Art, Youngstown OH
California State University, Chico, Art Gallery, Chico CA
Calvin College Center Art Gallery, Grand Rapids MI
Charleston Museum, Charleston SC
Chester County Historical Society, West Chester PA
Cleveland Museum of Art, Cleveland OH
College of Saint Benedict, Art Gallery, Saint Joseph MN
Columbus Museum of Art, Columbus OH
Concordia College, Koenig Art Gallery, Seward NE
Cranbrook Academy of Art Museum, Bloomfield Hills MI
Creighton University Art Gallery, Omaha NE
DAR Museum, National Society Daughters of the American Revolution, Washington DC
Drexel University Museum, Philadelphia PA
Erie Art Museum, Erie PA
Essex Institute, Salem MA
Everson Museum of Art, Syracuse NY
Fort Lauderdale Museum of the Arts, Fort Lauderdale FL
Goucher College, Kraushaar Auditorium Lobby Gallery, Towson MD
Harrison County Historical Museum, Marshall TX
Harvard University, William Hayes Fogg Art Museum, Cambridge MA
Haystack Mountain School of Crafts Gallery, Deer Isle ME
Historic Deerfield Inc, Deerfield MA
Honolulu Academy of Arts, Honolulu HI
Indianapolis Museum of Art, Indianapolis IN
Institute of American Indian Arts Museum, Santa Fe NM
Iowa State University, Brunnier Gallery Museum, Ames IA

Jacksonville Art Museum, Jacksonville FL
Lemoyne Center for the Visual Arts, Tallahassee FL
Mercer County Community College Gallery, Trenton NJ
James Monroe Law Office - Museum and Memorial Library, Fredericksburg VA
Mount Saint Vincent University, Art Gallery, Halifax NS
Musee d'Art de Saint-Laurent, Saint-Laurent PQ
The Museum, Greenwood SC
National Museum of American History, Smithsonian Institution, Washington DC
Northwestern College, Te Paske Gallery of Rowenhorst, Orange City IA
Oglebay Institute Mansion Museum, Wheeling WV
Old Salem Inc, Museum of Early Southern Decorative Arts, Winston-Salem NC
Palm Beach County Parks and Recreation Department, Morikami Museum of Japanese Culture, Delray Beach FL
Parrish Art Museum, Southampton NY
Pennsylvania State University, Museum of Art, University Park PA
Philbrook Art Center, Tulsa OK
Phillips County Museum, Helena AR
Portland Art Association, Portland Art Museum, Portland OR
Principia College, School of Nations Museum, Elsah IL
Santa Barbara Museum of Art, Santa Barbara CA
Ella Sharp Museum, Jackson MI
Shelburne Museum, Shelburne VT
George Walter Vincent Smith Art Museum, Springfield MA
Society of the Cincinnati, Anderson House Museum, Washington DC
Southern Alleghenies Museum of Art, Loretto PA
Southern Illinois University, University Museum, Carbondale IL
State University of New York College at Geneseo, Bertha V B Lederer Gallery, Geneseo NY
Syracuse University, Art Collection, Syracuse NY
Toledo Museum of Art, Toledo OH
Triton Museum of Art, Santa Clara CA
United States Naval Academy Museum, Annapolis MD
University of Colorado Art Galleries, Boulder CO
University of Michigan, Museum of Art, Ann Arbor MI
University of Nebraska, Lincoln, Sheldon Memorial Art Gallery, Lincoln NE
University of Santa Clara, de Saisset Museum, Santa Clara CA
University of South Florida, Art Galleries, Tampa FL
University of Washington, Henry Art Gallery, Seattle WA
Vassar College Art Gallery, Poughkeepsie NY
Washburn University, Mulvane Art Center, Topeka KS

COINS & MEDALS

Balzekas Museum of Lithuanian Culture, Chicago IL
Bowdoin College, Museum of Art & Peary-MacMillan Arctic Museum, Brunswick ME
Franklin Mint Museum, Franklin Center PA
Hastings Museum, Hastings NE
Kings County Historical Society and Museum, Hampton NB
Musee du Seminaire de Quebec, Quebec PQ
Museum of the American Indian, New York NY
National Museum of American History, Smithsonian Institution, Washington DC
Newark Museum, Newark NJ
Portland Art Association, Portland Art Museum, Portland OR
Public Archives of Canada, Picture Division, Ottawa ON
Royal Ontario Museum, Canadiana Gallery, Toronto ON
State Art Museum of Florida, John & Mable Ringling Museum of Art, Sarasota FL
University of Calgary, The Nickle Arts Museum, Calgary AB
University of California, Santa Barbara, University Art Museum, Santa Barbara CA

T T Wentworth, Jr Museum, Pensacola FL
Wheaton College, Watson Gallery, Norton MA

COSTUMES

Arapahoe Community College, Colorado Gallery of
  the Arts, Littleton CO
Bassist College, Collections Library, Portland OR
Canton Art Institute, Canton OH
Cincinnati Art Museum, Cincinnati OH
Kelly-Griggs House Museum, Red Bluff CA
Kelowna Centennial Museum and National Exhibit
  Centre, Kelowna BC
Los Angeles County Museum of Art, Los Angeles
  CA
McGill University, McCord Museum, Montreal PQ
Metropolitan Museum and Art Center, Coral
  Gables FL
Metropolitan Museum of Art, New York NY
Museum of New Mexico, Museum of International
  Folk Art, Santa Fe NM
Museum of the City of New York, New York NY
The Museums at Stony Brook, Stony Brook NY
North Texas State University, Art Gallery, Denton
  TX
Please Touch Museum, Philadelphia PA
Potsdam Public Museum, Potsdam NY
Reynolda House, Inc, Winston-Salem NC
Society for the Preservation of Historic Landmarks,
  Old School House, York ME
Southern Illinois University, University Museum,
  Carbondale IL
Traphagen School of Fashion, Museum Collection,
  New York NY
University of Vermont, Robert Hull Fleming
  Museum, Burlington VT
Valentine Museum, Richmond VA

CRAFTS

Albuquerque Museum of Art, History and Science,
  Albuquerque NM
Arizona State University, University Art
  Collections, Tempe AZ
Bucks County Historical Society, Mercer Museum,
  Doylestown PA
College of Saint Benedict, Art Gallery, Saint Joseph
  MN
Confederation Centre Art Gallery and Museum,
  Charlottetown PE
Contemporary Crafts Association and Gallery,
  Portland OR
Craft and Folk Art Museum, Los Angeles CA
Craft Center Museum, Wilton CT
East Tennessee State University, Carroll Reece
  Museum, Johnson City TN
Evansville Museum of Arts and Science, Evansville
  IN
Favell Museum of Western Art & Indian Artifacts,
  Klamath Falls OR
Fine Arts Museum of the South, Mobile AL
Frog Hollow Craft Center, Middlebury VT
Georgetown College Gallery, Georgetown KY
Institute of American Indian Arts Museum, Santa
  Fe NM
Long Beach Museum of Art, Long Beach CA
Carrie McLain Museum, Nome AK
Marietta College, Grover M Hermann Fine Arts
  Center, Marietta OH
Massillon Museum, Massillon OH
Milwaukee Area Technical College, Kronquist Craft
  Gallery, Milwaukee WI
Minnesota Museum of Art, Saint Paul MN
Minot Art Gallery, Minot Art Association, Minot
  ND
Moose Jaw Art Museum and National Exhibition
  Centre, History Museum, Moose Jaw SK
Museum of the Plains Indian, Browning MT
Oakland Museum, Art Dept, Oakland CA
Octagon Center for the Arts, Ames IA
Old Dartmouth Historical Society, New Bedford
  Whaling Museum, New Bedford MA
Principia College, School of Nations Museum,
  Elsah IL
Lauren Rogers Library and Museum of Art, Laurel
  MS
San Diego State University, Art Gallery, San Diego
  CA

Taras H Schevchenko Museum and Memorial Park
  Foundation, Oakville ON
Sioux Indian Museum, Rapid City SD
Southern Plains Indian Museum, Anadarko OK
Southwest Museum, Los Angeles CA
Ukrainian Museum of Canada, Edmonton AB
Worcester Craft Center Gallery, Worcester MA

DECORATIVE ARTS

Albuquerque Museum of Art, History and Science,
  Albuquerque NM
Lyman Allyn Museum, New London CT
Arkansas Arts Center, Little Rock AR
Art Gallery of Greater Victoria, Victoria BC
Art Institute of Chicago, Chicago IL
Athenaeum of Philadelphia, Philadelphia PA
Atlanta Museum, Atlanta GA
Augusta Richmond County Museum, Augusta GA
Baltimore Museum of Art, Baltimore MD
Beloit College, Wright Museum of Art, Beloit WI
Bennington Museum, Bennington VT
Birmingham Museum of Art, Birmingham AL
Bower's Museum, Santa Ana CA
Bowne House, Flushing NY
Canton Art Institute, Canton OH
Carnegie Institute, Museum of Art, Pittsburgh PA
Center for Inter-American Relations Art Gallery,
  New York NY
Charleston Museum, Charleston SC
Chesterwood, Stockbridge MA
Chicago Historical Society, Chicago IL
China Trade Museum, Milton MA
Church of Jesus Christ of Latter-Day Saints,
  Museum of Church History and Art, Salt Lake
  City UT
Cincinnati Art Museum, Cincinnati OH
Cleveland Museum of Art, Cleveland OH
College of the Americas, Museum of the Americas,
  Brookfield VT
Columbia County Historical Society, Kinderhook
  NY
Columbia Museums of Art and Science, Columbia
  SC
Connecticut Valley Historical Museum, Springfield
  MA
Cooper-Hewitt Museum, Smithsonian Institution,
  New York NY
Cranbrook Academy of Art Museum, Bloomfield
  Hills MI
Crocker Art Museum, Sacramento CA
Cummer Gallery of Art, DeEtte Holden Cummer
  Museum Foundation, Jacksonville FL
Currier Gallery of Art, Manchester NH
Department of Culture, Government of the
  Province of Alberta, Provincial Museum of
  Alberta, Edmonton AB
Detroit Institute of Arts, Detroit MI
Division of Historical and Cultural Affairs, Bureau
  of Museums and Historic Sites, Dover DE
Dixon Gallery and Gardens, Memphis TN
Drexel University Museum, Philadelphia PA
El Paso Museum of Art, El Paso TX
Evansville Museum of Arts and Science, Evansville
  IN
William A Farnsworth Library and Art Museum,
  Rockland ME
Fetherston Foundation, Packwood House Museum,
  Lewisburg PA
Fine Arts Museum of the South, Mobile AL
Fine Arts Museums of San Francisco, M H de
  Young Memorial Museum and California Palace
  of the Legion of Honor, San Francisco CA
M Flint Institute of Arts, Flint MI
Francis E Fowler Jr Foundation Museum, Beverly
  Hills CA
J Paul Getty Museum, Malibu CA
Grand Rapids Art Museum, Grand Rapids MI
Gunston Hall Plantation, Lorton VA
The Haggin Museum, Stockton CA
Harvard University, Dumbarton Oaks Research
  Library and Collections, Washington DC
Harvard University, William Hayes Fogg Art
  Museum, Cambridge MA
Hermitage Foundation Museum, Norfolk VA
Hershey Museum of American Life, Hershey PA
High Museum of Art, Atlanta GA

Hispanic Society of America, Museum, New York
  NY
Historical Society of York County, York PA
Historic Cherry Hill, Albany NY
Historic Deerfield Inc, Deerfield MA
Historic Landmarks Foundation of Indiana, Morris-
  Butler House, Indianapolis IN
Honolulu Academy of Arts, Honolulu HI
Hudson River Museum, Yonkers NY
Huntington Galleries, Huntington WV
Huntington Library, Art Gallery and Botanical
  Gardens, San Marino CA
Illinois State Museum of Natural History and Art,
  Springfield IL
Illinois State University, University Museums,
  Normal IL
Independence National Historical Park,
  Philadelphia PA
Indianapolis Museum of Art, Indianapolis IN
Johnson-Humrickhouse Museum, Coshocton OH
Joslyn Art Museum, Omaha NE
Annie S Kemerer Museum, Bethlehem PA
Kendall Whaling Museum, Sharon MA
Lightner Museum, Saint Augustine FL
Litchfield Historical Society, Litchfield CT
Longfellow's Wayside Inn, South Sudbury MA
Long Island Historical Society, Brooklyn NY
Los Angeles County Museum of Art, Los Angeles
  CA
Louisiana Department of Culture, Recreation and
  Tourism, Louisiana State Museum, New Orleans
  LA
Louisiana State University, Anglo-American Art
  Museum, Baton Rouge LA
Luna County Historical Society, Inc, Deming Luna
  Mimbres Museum, Deming NM
L'Universite Laval, Ecole des Arts Visuels de
  L'Universite Laval, Quebec PQ
Macdonald Stewart Art Centre, Guelph ON
McGill University, McCord Museum, Montreal PQ
Madison County Historical Society, Cottage Lawn,
  Oneida NY
Marquette University, Museum of Art, Milwaukee
  WI
Metropolitan Museum of Art, New York NY
Miami University Art Museum, Oxford OH
Minneapolis Institute of Arts, Minneapolis MN
Mint Museum of Art, Charlotte NC
Montreal Museum of Fine Arts, Montreal PQ
Morris Museum of Arts and Sciences, Morristown
  NJ
Munson-Williams-Proctor Institute, Museum of Art,
  Utica NY
Muscatine Art Center, Muscatine IA
Museum of Arts and History, Port Huron MI
Museum of Arts and Sciences, Cuban Museum,
  Planetarium, Daytona Beach FL
Museum of Fine Arts, Boston MA
Museum of Fine Arts, Houston, Houston TX
Museum of Fine Arts of Saint Petersburg, Florida,
  Inc, Saint Petersburg FL
Museum of Our National Heritage, Lexington MA
Museum of the American Indian, New York NY
Museum of the City of New York, New York NY
Museum of the Historical Society of Early
  American Decoration, Albany NY
The Museums at Stony Brook, Stony Brook NY
National Society of Colonial Dames of the State of
  Maryland, Mount Clare Mansion, Baltimore MD
National Trust for Historic Preservation,
  Washington DC
Newark Museum, Newark NJ
Newburyport Maritime Society, Custom House
  Maritime Museum, Newburyport MA
New Jersey Historical Society Museum, Newark NJ
New Jersey State Museum, Trenton NJ
New York State Museum, Albany NY
North Carolina Museum of Art, Raleigh NC
Oberlin College, Allen Memorial Art Museum,
  Oberlin OH
The Ohio Historical Society, Inc, Campus Martius
  Museum and Ohio River Museum, Marietta OH
Old Barracks Museum, Trenton NJ
Old Gaol Museum, York ME
Old Salem Inc, Museum of Early Southern
  Decorative Arts, Winston-Salem NC
Owensboro Museum of Fine Art, Owensboro KY

Southern Alleghenies Museum of Art, Loretto PA
Southern Illinois University, University Museum, Carbondale IL
Springfield Art Museum, Springfield MO
State Art Museum of Florida, John & Mable Ringling Museum of Art, Sarasota FL
State University of New York at Albany, University Art Gallery, Albany NY
State University of New York at Purchase, Neuberger Museum, Purchase NY
State University of New York College at Potsdam, Brainerd Art Gallery, Potsdam NY
Ulster County Community College, Visual Arts Gallery, Stone Ridge NY
United States Naval Academy Museum, Annapolis MD
University of California, Los Angeles, Grunwald Center for the Graphic Arts, Los Angeles CA
University of Colorado Art Galleries, Boulder CO
University of Georgia, Georgia Museum of Art, Athens GA
University of Illinois, Krannert Art Museum, Champaign IL
University of Iowa, Museum of Art, Iowa City IA
University of Louisville, Allen R Hite Art Institute Gallery, Louisville KY
University of Massachusetts, Amherst, University Gallery, Amherst MA
University of Minnesota, University Art Museum, Minneapolis MN
University of Mississippi, University Museums, Oxford MS
University of Missouri, Museum of Art and Archaeology, Columbia MO
University of Nebraska, Lincoln, Sheldon Memorial Art Gallery, Lincoln NE
University of New Mexico, University Art Museum, Albuquerque NM
University of North Carolina, The Ackland Art Museum, Chapel Hill NC
University of North Carolina at Greensboro, Weatherspoon Art Gallery, Greensboro NC
University of Notre Dame, Snite Museum of Art, Notre Dame IN
University of Pittsburgh, University Art Gallery, Pittsburgh PA
University of Southern Colorado, School of Liberal Arts, Pueblo CO
University of South Florida, Art Galleries, Tampa FL
University of Texas at Austin, Archer M Huntington Art Gallery, Austin TX
University of Vermont, Robert Hull Fleming Museum, Burlington VT
University of Washington, Henry Art Gallery, Seattle WA
University of Wisconsin, Allen Priebe Gallery, Oshkosh WI
University of Wisconsin-Stout, Gallery 209, Menomonie WI
Valparaiso University, University Art Galleries and Collections, Valparaiso IN
Vassar College Art Gallery, Poughkeepsie NY
Washington County Museum of Fine Arts, Hagerstown MD
Westminster College Art Gallery, New Wilmington PA
Wheaton College, Watson Gallery, Norton MA
Whitney Museum of American Art, New York NY
Wichita Art Museum, Wichita KS
Williams College, Museum of Art, Williamstown MA

EMBROIDERY

Baltimore Museum of Art, Baltimore MD
Historic Deerfield Inc, Deerfield MA
Ukrainian National Museum and Library, Chicago IL
West Baton Rouge Museum, Port Allen LA

ENAMELS

Loyola University of Chicago, Martin D'Arcy Gallery of Art, Chicago IL

ESKIMO ART

Alaska State Museum, Juneau AK
Anchorage Historical and Fine Arts Museum, Cook Inlet Historical Society, Anchorage AK
Capital University, Schumacher Gallery, Columbus OH
Eskimo Museum, Churchill MB
Johnson-Humrickhouse Museum, Coshocton OH
Kendall Whaling Museum, Sharon MA
Louisiana Arts and Science Center, Baton Rouge LA
Macdonald Stewart Art Centre, Guelph ON
Carrie McLain Museum, Nome AK
Museum of the United States, Washington DC
Portland Art Association, Portland Art Museum, Portland OR
Science Museums of Charlotte, Inc, Discovery Place, Charlotte NC
Winnipeg Art Gallery, Winnipeg MB
Yugtarvik Regional Museum, Bethel AK

ETCHINGS & ENGRAVINGS

Albrecht Art Museum, Saint Joseph MO
Clinton Art Association Gallery, Clinton IA
Delaware Art Museum, Wilmington DE
Lincoln National Life Foundation, Inc, Louis A Warren Lincoln Library and Museum, Fort Wayne IN
Mary Washington College, Belmont, The Gari Melchers Memorial Gallery, Fredericksburg VA
Northwestern College, Te Paske Gallery of Rowenhorst, Orange City IA
Parrish Art Museum, Southampton NY
Portland Art Association, Portland Art Museum, Portland OR
The Rockwell Museum, Corning NY
Saint Gregory's Abbey and College, Mabee-Gerrer Museum of Art, Shawnee OK
State Capitol Museum, Olympia WA
Vassar College Art Gallery, Poughkeepsie NY

ETHNOLOGY

Chief Plenty Coups State Monument Museum, Pryor MT
Department of Culture, Government of the Province of Alberta, Provincial Museum of Alberta, Edmonton AB
Institute of the Great Plains, Museum of the Great Plains, Lawton OK
Kenosha Public Museum, Kenosha WI
Museum of the Philadelphia Civic Center, Philadelphia PA
National Museum of Man, Ottawa ON
Newburyport Maritime Society, Custom House Maritime Museum, Newburyport MA
New York State Museum, Albany NY
Oklahoma Historical Society, Central Museum, Oklahoma City OK
Peabody Museum of Salem, Salem MA
Putnam Museum, Davenport IA
Queen's University, Agnes Etherington Art Centre, Kingston ON
Rhode Island School of Design, Museum of Art, Providence RI
Shelburne Museum, Shelburne VT
Sheldon Jackson College, Sheldon Jackson Museum, Sitka AK
Smith-Mason Gallery and Museum, Washington DC
University of Alaska, Museum, Fairbanks AK
University of Alberta, Ring House Gallery, Edmonton AB
University of Pennsylvania, University Museum of Archaeology & Anthropology, Philadelphia PA
University of Vermont, Robert Hull Fleming Museum, Burlington VT

FOLK ART

Anderson Fine Arts Center, Anderson IN
Balzekas Museum of Lithuanian Culture, Chicago IL
Beyond Baroque Foundation, Venice CA
Bucks County Historical Society, Mercer Museum, Doylestown PA
Cardinal Stritch College, Milwaukee WI
College of the Americas, Museum of the Americas, Brookfield VT
Cortland County Historical Society, Suggett House Museum, Cortland NY
Craft and Folk Art Museum, Los Angeles CA
Department of Culture, Government of the Province of Alberta, Provincial Museum of Alberta, Edmonton AB
Everhart Museum of Natural History, Science and Art, Scranton PA
Frostburg State College, The Stephanie Ann Roper Gallery, Frostburg MD
Galeria de la Raza, Studio 24, San Francisco CA
Heritage Plantation of Sandwich, Sandwich MA
Historical Society of York County, York PA
Illinois State Museum of Natural History and Art, Springfield IL
Indiana University, William Hammond Mathers Museum, Bloomington IN
Kiah Museum, Savannah GA
McAllen International Museum, McAllen TX
Mercer County Community College Gallery, Trenton NJ
Miami University Art Museum, Oxford OH
Mingei International Inc, Mingei International Museum of World Folk Art, La Jolla CA
Monterey Peninsula Museum of Art, Monterey CA
Musee d'Art de Saint-Laurent, Saint-Laurent PQ
Museum of American Folk Art, New York NY
Museum of New Mexico, Museum of International Folk Art, Santa Fe NM
National Museum of Man, Ottawa ON
New York State Historical Association, Fenimore House, Cooperstown NY
Palm Beach County Parks and Recreation Department, Morikami Museum of Japanese Culture, Delray Beach FL
Pennsylvania Historical and Museum Commission, Harrisburg PA
Philadelphia Museum of Art, Philadelphia PA
Reading Public Museum and Art Gallery, Reading PA
Abby Aldrich Rockefeller Folk Art Center, Williamsburg VA
Saint Mary's Romanian Orthodox Church, Romanian Ethnic Museum, Cleveland OH
Shelburne Museum, Shelburne VT
Ukrainian Museum, New York NY
Ukrainian National Museum and Library, Chicago IL
University of California, Los Angeles, Museum of Cultural History, Los Angeles CA
University of Florida, University Gallery, Gainesville FL
University of Rochester, Memorial Art Gallery, Rochester NY
University of San Diego, Founders' Gallery, San Diego CA
University of South Florida, Art Galleries, Tampa FL

FURNITURE

Albany Institute of History and Art, Albany NY
Lyman Allyn Museum, New London CT
Atkins Museum of Fine Art, Kansas City MO
Atlanta Museum, Atlanta GA
Ball State University, Art Gallery, Muncie IN
Baltimore Museum of Art, Baltimore MD
Bennington Museum, Bennington VT
California Historical Society, San Francisco CA
Carnegie Institute, Museum of Art, Pittsburgh PA
Kit Carson Memorial Foundation, Taos NM
Center for Inter-American Relations Art Gallery, New York NY
Charleston Museum, Charleston SC
China Trade Museum, Milton MA
Columbia Museums of Art and Science, Columbia SC

GLASS

GOLD

GRAPHICS

Howard University, Gallery of Art, Washington DC
Huntsville Museum of Art, Huntsville AL
Illinois State Museum of Natural History and Art, Springfield IL
Institute of American Indian Arts Museum, Santa Fe NM
Jewish Museum, New York NY
John C Calhoun State Community College, Art Gallery, Decatur AL
Joslyn Art Museum, Omaha NE
Kalamazoo Institute of Arts, Genevieve and Donald Gilmore Art Center, Kalamazoo MI
La Casa del Libro, Library, San Juan PR
Lehigh University Art Galleries, Bethlehem PA
Louisiana Arts and Science Center, Baton Rouge LA
Louisiana State University, Anglo-American Art Museum, Baton Rouge LA
L'Universite Laval, Ecole des Arts Visuels de L'Universite Laval, Quebec PQ
Judah L Magnes Museum, Berkeley CA
Marion Koogler McNay Art Museum, San Antonio TX
Metropolitan Museum and Art Center, Coral Gables FL
Montgomery Museum of Fine Arts, Montgomery AL
Mount Allison University, Owens Art Gallery, Sackville NB
Muscatine Art Center, Muscatine IA
Museum of Fine Arts, Springfield MA
Museum of Modern Art, New York NY
National Museum of American History, Smithsonian Institution, Washington DC
New Orleans Museum of Art, New Orleans LA
Oberlin College, Allen Memorial Art Museum, Oberlin OH
Owensboro Museum of Fine Art, Owensboro KY
Pennsylvania State University, Museum of Art, University Park PA
Portland Art Association, Portland Art Museum, Portland OR
C W Post College of Long Island University, Hillwood Art Gallery, Greenvale NY
Queen's University, Agnes Etherington Art Centre, Kingston ON
Randolph-Macon Womans College, Maier Museum of Art, Lynchburg VA
Rhode Island School of Design, Museum of Art, Providence RI
Roswell Museum and Art Center, Roswell NM
St Lawrence University, Richard F Brush Art Gallery, Canton NY
San Jose State University, Art Gallery, San Jose CA
San Jose State University, Union Gallery, San Jose CA
Siena Heights College, Little Gallery, Studio Angelico, Adrian MI
Sierra Nevada Museum of Art, Reno NV
Simon Fraser University, Simon Fraser Gallery, Burnaby BC
Norton Simon Museum, Pasadena CA
Smith-Mason Gallery and Museum, Washington DC
State University of New York College at Geneseo, Bertha V B Lederer Gallery, Geneseo NY
Stephens College, Lewis James & Nellie Stratton Davis Art Gallery, Columbia MO
Tryon Palace Restoration Complex, New Bern NC
United States Navy, Combat Art Gallery, Washington DC
University of Alberta, Ring House Gallery, Edmonton AB
University of California, Los Angeles, Grunwald Center for the Graphic Arts, Los Angeles CA
University of Connecticut, William Benton Museum of Art, Storrs CT
University of Georgia, Georgia Museum of Art, Athens GA
University of Kansas, Spencer Museum of Art, Lawrence KS
University of Kentucky, Art Museum, Lexington KY
University of Michigan, Museum of Art, Ann Arbor MI
University of Santa Clara, de Saisset Museum, Santa Clara CA

University of Sherbrooke Cultural Center, Art Gallery, Sherbrooke PQ
University of Utah, Utah Museum of Fine Arts, Salt Lake City UT
University of Wisconsin, University Art Museum, Milwaukee WI
Vancouver Art Gallery, Vancouver BC
Walker Art Center, Minneapolis MN
Wine Museum of San Francisco, San Francisco CA
Winnipeg Art Gallery, Winnipeg MB
Woodmere Art Museum, Philadelphia PA

HISPANIC ART

Intar Latin American Gallery, New York NY

HISTORICAL MATERIAL

Alabama Department of Archives and History Museum, Montgomery AL
Alaska State Museum, Juneau AK
Ateneo Puertorriqueno, San Juan PR
Beverly Historical Society, Cabot, Hale and Balch House Museums, Beverly MA
Brant Historical Society, Brant County Museum, Brantford ON
Brick Store Museum, Kennebunk ME
California Historical Society, History Center Library, San Francisco CA
Casa Amesti, Monterey CA
Chesapeake Bay Maritime Museum, Saint Michaels MD
Clark County Historical Society, Springfield OH
Clinton Historical Museum Village, Clinton NJ
Cliveden, Philadelphia PA
Columbus and Lowndes County Historical Society Museum, Columbus MS
Dacotah Prairie Museum, Lamont Gallery, Aberdeen SD
Eva Brook Donly Museum, Simcoe ON
East Tennessee State University, Carroll Reece Museum, Johnson City TN
Erie Art Museum, Erie PA
Floyd County Museum, New Albany IN
Fort Ticonderoga Museum, Ticonderoga NY
Gananoque Historical Museum, Gananoque ON
Thomas Gilcrease Institute of American History and Art, Tulsa OK
Glenbow Museum, Calgary AB
Great Lakes Historical Society, Vermilion OH
Harrison County Historical Museum, Marshall TX
Historical Society of Bloomfield, Bloomfield NJ
Historical Society of Old Newbury, Cushing House Museum, Newburyport MA
Indiana University, William Hammond Mathers Museum, Bloomington IN
Institute of the Great Plains, Museum of the Great Plains, Lawton OK
John Paul Jones House, Portsmouth NH
Jordan Historical Museum of The Twenty, Jordan ON
Kansas State Historial Society Museum, Topeka KS
Kelowna Centennial Museum and National Exhibit Centre, Kelowna BC
Kentucky Historical Society, Old State Capitol & Annex, Frankfort KY
Klamath County Museum, Klamath Falls OR
Long Branch Historical Museum, Long Branch NJ
Louisiana State Exhibit Museum, Shreveport LA
Loveland Museum and Gallery, Loveland CO
Luna County Historical Society, Inc, Deming Luna Mimbres Museum, Deming NM
Missouri Historical Society, Saint Louis MO
Missouri State Museum, Jefferson City MO
Moravian Historical Society, Whitefield House Museum, Nazareth PA
Muscatine Art Center, Muscatine IA
Museum of Northern British Columbia, Prince Rupert Museum Art Gallery, Prince Rupert BC
Museum of the American Indian, New York NY
National Archives and Records Service, John F Kennedy Library and Museum, Dorchester MA
National Museum of Man, Ottawa ON
Naval Amphibious Museum, Norfolk VA
Newfoundland Museum, Saint John's NF

No Man's Land Historical Society Museum, Goodwell OK
Northeastern Nevada Historical Society Museum, Elko NV
The Ohio Historical Society, Inc, Campus Martius Museum and Ohio River Museum, Marietta OH
Ohio State University, Gallery of Fine Art, Columbus OH
Oklahoma Historical Society, Central Museum, Oklahoma City OK
Old Gaol Museum, York ME
Palo Alto Cultural Center, Palo Alto CA
Phelps County Historical Society Museum, Holdrege NE
Philipse Manor Hall State Historic Site, Yonkers NY
Pittsburgh History and Landmarks Foundation, Old Post Office Museum, Pittsburgh PA
Ringwood Manor House Museum, Ringwood NJ
Rome Historical Society, Rome Information and Cultural Center, Rome NY
Franklin D Roosevelt Library and Museum, Hyde Park NY
Safety Harbor Museum of History and Fine Arts, Safety Harbor FL
Saint Bernard Foundation and Monastery, Miami Beach FL
Saint-Gaudens National Historic Site, Cornish NH
Saint Louis County Historical Society, Duluth MN
Sheldon Art Museum, Archaeological & Historical Society, Middlebury VT
Society of the Montreal Military and Maritime Museum, Saint Helen's Island Museum, Montreal PQ
Southern Oregon Historical Society, Jacksonville Museum, Jacksonville OR
State Historical Society of Wisconsin, Madison WI
Tennessee State Museum, Nashville TN
Ukrainian Museum of Canada, Edmonton AB
United Methodist Historical Society, Library, Baltimore MD
USS North Carolina Battleship Memorial, Wilmington NC
Van Cortlandt Mansion & Museum, Bronx NY
Harold Warp Pioneer Village Foundation, Minden NE
Waterville Historical Association, Redington Museum, Waterville ME
Western Reserve Historical Society, Cleveland OH
Woodrow Wilson Birthplace Foundation, Staunton VA
York Institute Museum, Saco ME

IVORY

The Bruce Museum, Greenwich CT
Diamond M Foundation Museum, Snyder TX
Harvard University, Dumbarton Oaks Research Library and Collections, Washington DC
Iowa State University, Brunnier Gallery Museum, Ames IA
Loyola University of Chicago, Martin D'Arcy Gallery of Art, Chicago IL
Mitchell Museum, Mount Vernon IL
The Museum, Greenwood SC
Oklahoma Center for Science and Art, Kirkpatrick Center, Oklahoma City OK
Rahr-West Museum, Manitowoc WI
Robert W Ryerss Library and Museum, Philadelphia PA
Saint John's University, Chung-Cheng Art Gallery, Jamaica NY
University of Michigan, Kelsey Museum of Ancient and Medieval Archaeology, Ann Arbor MI
University of Santa Clara, de Saisset Museum, Santa Clara CA
Yugtarvik Regional Museum, Bethel AK

JADE

Diamond M Foundation Museum, Snyder TX
Freer Gallery of Art, Washington DC
Harvard University, William Hayes Fogg Art Museum, Cambridge MA
Hermitage Foundation Museum, Norfolk VA
Indianapolis Museum of Art, Indianapolis IN
Mitchell Museum, Mount Vernon IL

Norton Gallery and School of Art, West Palm Beach FL
Roswell Museum and Art Center, Roswell NM
Saint John's University, Chung-Cheng Art Gallery, Jamaica NY
Seattle Art Museum, Seattle WA
Virginia Museum of Fine Arts, Richmond VA
Washington County Museum of Fine Arts, Hagerstown MD

JEWELRY

Baltimore Museum of Art, Baltimore MD
Harvard University, Dumbarton Oaks Research Library and Collections, Washington DC
Haystack Mountain School of Crafts Gallery, Deer Isle ME
Institute of American Indian Arts Museum, Santa Fe NM
Kings County Historical Society and Museum, Hampton NB
James Monroe Law Office - Museum and Memorial Library, Fredericksburg VA
Rollins College, George D and Harriet W Cornell Fine Arts Center Museum, Winter Park FL
Southwestern At Memphis, Jessie L Clough Art Memorial for Teaching, Memphis TN
Taft Museum, Cincinnati OH
Valentine Museum, Richmond VA
Virginia Museum of Fine Arts, Richmond VA

JUDAICA

American Jewish Historical Society, Waltham MA
Leo Baeck Institute, New York NY
B'nai B'rith Klutznick Museum, Library, Washington DC
Hebrew Union College, Skirball Museum, Los Angeles CA
Jewish Community Center, Center Lobby Gallery, Long Beach CA
Jewish Museum, New York NY
Judah L Magnes Museum, Berkeley CA
Spertus Museum of Judaica, Chicago IL
Temple Museum of Jewish Religious Art, Cleveland OH

LACES

Baltimore Museum of Art, Baltimore MD
Cooper-Hewitt Museum, Smithsonian Institution, New York NY
Montreal Museum of Fine Arts, Montreal PQ
Portland Art Association, Portland Art Museum, Portland OR
Washington County Museum of Fine Arts, Hagerstown MD

LATIN AMERICAN ART

Arizona State University, University Art Collections, Tempe AZ
Committee for Hispanic Arts & Research, Austin TX
Institute of Puerto Rican Culture, Museo de Bellas Artes, San Juan PR
Metropolitan Museum and Art Center, Coral Gables FL
University of Florida, University Gallery, Gainesville FL
University of Texas at Austin, Archer M Huntington Art Gallery, Austin TX

MANUSCRIPTS

American Jewish Historical Society, Waltham MA
Archives of American Art, Smithsonian Institution, New York NY
Brigham Young University, B F Larsen Gallery, Provo UT
Chicago Historical Society, Chicago IL
Freer Gallery of Art, Washington DC
Haverhill Public Library, Art Dept, Haverhill MA
Litchfield Historical Society, Ingraham Memorial Research Library, Litchfield CT

Judah L Magnes Museum, Berkeley CA
Ohio State University, Gallery of Fine Art, Columbus OH
Old Gaol Museum, York ME
The Rosenbach Museum and Library, Philadelphia PA
United States Naval Academy Museum, Annapolis MD
University of Michigan, Museum of Art, Ann Arbor MI
Washington County Museum of Fine Arts, Hagerstown MD

MARINE PAINTING

The Bostonian Society, Old State House, Boston MA
Butler Institute of American Art, Youngstown OH
Columbia River Maritime Museum, Astoria OR
Great Lakes Historical Society, Vermilion OH
Kendall Whaling Museum, Sharon MA
Maine Maritime Museum, Bath ME
Massachusetts Institute of Technology, Hart Nautical Museum, Cambridge MA
National Maritime Museum, San Francisco CA
Naval Historical Center, United States Navy Memorial Museum, Washington DC
Newburyport Maritime Society, Custom House Maritime Museum, Newburyport MA
Nova Scotia Museum, W D Lawrence House, Halifax NS
Peabody Museum of Salem, Salem MA
Penobscot Marine Museum, Searsport ME
San Diego Maritime Museum, San Diego CA
US Coast Guard Museum, New London CT
Wichita State University, Edwin A Ulrich Museum of Art, Wichita KS
Yarmouth County Historical Society, Yarmouth County Museum, Yarmouth NS

MEDIEVAL ART

Lyman Allyn Museum, New London CT
Marion Koogler McNay Art Museum, San Antonio TX
Metropolitan Museum of Art, New York NY
Monterey History and Art Association, Allen Knight Maritime Museum, Monterey CA
Museum of Fine Arts, Houston, Houston TX
Rensselaer Newman Foundation Chapel and Cultural Center, Troy NY
Saint Mary's College of California, Hearst Art Gallery, Moraga CA
Toledo Museum of Art, Toledo OH
University of Illinois, Krannert Art Museum, Champaign IL
University of Rochester, Memorial Art Gallery, Rochester NY
University of Vermont, Robert Hull Fleming Museum, Burlington VT
University of Wisconsin, Elvehjem Museum of Art, Madison WI
Vassar College Art Gallery, Poughkeepsie NY
Williams College, Museum of Art, Williamstown MA
Worcester Art Museum, Worcester MA

METALWORK

Freer Gallery of Art, Washington DC
Harvard University, Dumbarton Oaks Research Library and Collections, Washington DC
Maryland Historical Society Museum, Baltimore MD
Musee d'Art de Saint-Laurent, Saint-Laurent PQ
Old Salem Inc, Museum of Early Southern Decorative Arts, Winston-Salem NC
Pioneer Town, Wimberley TX
Principia College, School of Nations Museum, Elsah IL
Saint Clair County Community College, Jack R Hennesey Art Galleries, Port Huron MI
Shaker Museum, Poland Spring ME
Southern Illinois University, University Museum, Carbondale IL

Southwestern At Memphis, Jessie L Clough Art Memorial for Teaching, Memphis TN
United States Naval Academy Museum, Annapolis MD

MEXICAN ART

Center for Inter-American Relations Art Gallery, New York NY
Craft and Folk Art Museum, Los Angeles CA
Davenport Municipal Art Gallery, Davenport IA
El Paso Museum of Art, El Paso TX
Fresno Arts Center, Fresno CA
McAllen International Museum, McAllen TX
Mercer County Community College Gallery, Trenton NJ
Museum of New Mexico, Museum of Fine Arts, Santa Fe NM
Museum of New Mexico, Museum of International Folk Art, Santa Fe NM
Phoenix Art Museum, Phoenix AZ
Redding Museum and Art Center, Redding CA
University of Houston, Sarah Campbell Blaffer Gallery, Houston TX
Wichita Art Museum, Wichita KS

MINIATURES

Carolina Art Association, Gibbes Art Gallery, Charleston SC
National Museum of American Art, Washington DC
New Jersey Historical Society Museum, Newark NJ
New Orleans Museum of Art, New Orleans LA
R W Norton Art Gallery, Shreveport LA
University of Cincinnati, Tangeman Fine Arts Gallery, Cincinnati OH

MOSAICS

Baltimore Museum of Art, Baltimore MD
Harvard University, Dumbarton Oaks Research Library and Collections, Washington DC
Worcester Art Museum, Worcester MA

ORIENTAL ART

Allentown Art Museum, Allentown PA
Lyman Allyn Museum, New London CT
Amherst College, Mead Art Museum, Amherst MA
Art Complex Museum at Duxbury, Duxbury MA
Art Gallery of Greater Victoria, Victoria BC
Art Institute of Chicago, Chicago IL
Asian Art Museum of San Francisco, Avery Brundage Collection, San Francisco CA
Atkins Museum of Fine Art, Kansas City MO
Baltimore Museum of Art, Baltimore MD
Bates College, Treat Gallery, Lewiston ME
Beloit College, Wright Museum of Art, Beloit WI
Berkshire Museum, Pittsfield MA
Blanden Memorial Art Museum, Fort Dodge IA
Boise Gallery of Art, Boise ID
California State University, Chico, Art Gallery, Chico CA
Carnegie Institute, Museum of Art, Pittsburgh PA
Carolina Art Association, Gibbes Art Gallery, Charleston SC
China Institute in America, China House Gallery, New York NY
China Trade Museum, Milton MA
Chrysler Museum, Norfolk VA
City of Holyoke Museum-Wistariahurst, Holyoke MA
Cleveland Museum of Art, Cleveland OH
Colby Museum of Art, Waterville ME
College of William and Mary, Joseph & Margaret Muscarelle Museum of Art, Williamsburg VA
College of Wooster Art Center Museum, Wooster OH
Columbus Museum of Art, Columbus OH
Craft and Folk Art Museum, Los Angeles CA
Cummer Gallery of Art, DeEtte Holden Cummer Museum Foundation, Jacksonville FL
Davenport Municipal Art Gallery, Davenport IA
Dayton Art Institute, Dayton OH
Denver Art Museum, Denver CO
Drexel University Museum, Philadelphia PA

Evansville Museum of Arts and Science, Evansville IN
Everhart Museum of Natural History, Science and Art, Scranton PA
Everson Museum of Art, Syracuse NY
Fine Arts Museum of the South, Mobile AL
M Flint Institute of Arts, Flint MI
Florence Museum, Florence SC
Francis E Fowler Jr Foundation Museum, Beverly Hills CA
Freeport Area Arts Council, Freeport Art Museum, Freeport IL
Fresno Arts Center, Fresno CA
Galleries of the Claremont Colleges, Claremont CA
Isabella Stewart Gardner Museum, Boston MA
Greenville College, Richard W Bock Sculpture Collection, Greenville IL
Hammond-Harwood House Association, Inc, Annapolis MD
Headley-Whitney Museum, Lexington KY
Hermitage Foundation Museum, Norfolk VA
High Museum of Art, Atlanta GA
Hofstra University, Emily Lowe Gallery, Hempstead NY
Honolulu Academy of Arts, Honolulu HI
Indianapolis Museum of Art, Indianapolis IN
Johns Hopkins University, Evergreen House, Baltimore MD
Johnson-Humrickhouse Museum, Coshocton OH
Kenosha Public Museum, Kenosha WI
Memphis Brooks Museum of Art, Memphis TN
Metropolitan Museum and Art Center, Coral Gables FL
Metropolitan Museum of Art, New York NY
Minneapolis Institute of Arts, Minneapolis MN
Musee du Seminaire de Quebec, Quebec PQ
Museum of Fine Arts, Boston MA
Museum of Fine Arts, Houston, Houston TX
Museum of Fine Arts, Springfield MA
Museum of Oriental Cultures, Corpus Christi TX
Museum of the Philadelphia Civic Center, Philadelphia PA
Museum of the Southwest, Midland TX
National Society of Colonial Dames of the State of Maryland, Mount Clare Mansion, Baltimore MD
Newark Museum, Newark NJ
Norwich Free Academy, Slater Memorial Museum & Converse Art Gallery, Norwich CT
Oklahoma Center for Science and Art, Kirkpatrick Center, Oklahoma City OK
Oregon State University, Horner Museum, Corvallis OR
Pacific - Asia Museum, Pasadena CA
Pacific University, Old College Hall, Pacific University Museum, Forest Grove OR
Parrish Art Museum, Southampton NY
Pennsylvania State University, Museum of Art, University Park PA
Philadelphia Museum of Art, Philadelphia PA
Philbrook Art Center, Tulsa OK
Phoenix Art Museum, Phoenix AZ
Plains Art Museum, Main Gallery, Moorhead MN
Portland Art Association, Portland Art Museum, Portland OR
Potsdam Public Museum, Potsdam NY
Princeton University, Art Museum, Princeton NJ
Rhode Island Historical Society, John Brown House, Providence RI
Rhode Island School of Design, Museum of Art, Providence RI
Roswell Museum and Art Center, Roswell NM
Saginaw Art Museum, Saginaw MI
Saint Francis College, Lakeview Gallery, Fort Wayne IN
Saint John's University, Chung-Cheng Art Gallery, Jamaica NY
St Lawrence University, Richard F Brush Art Gallery, Canton NY
Saint Louis Art Museum, Saint Louis MO
San Diego Museum of Art, San Diego CA
Santa Barbara Museum of Art, Santa Barbara CA
Scripps College, Clark Humanities Museum, Claremont CA
Seattle Art Museum, Seattle WA
George Walter Vincent Smith Art Museum, Springfield MA
Society of the Cincinnati, Anderson House Museum, Washington DC

Sonoma State University Art Gallery, Rohnert Park CA
Stanford University, Museum of Art & Art Gallery, Stanford CA
State University of New York at New Paltz, College Art Gallery, New Paltz NY
Taft Museum, Cincinnati OH
Tallahassee Junior Museum, Tallahassee FL
Tucson Museum of Art, Tucson AZ
University of Chicago, David and Alfred Smart Gallery, Chicago IL
University of Florida, University Gallery, Gainesville FL
University of Illinois, Krannert Art Museum, Champaign IL
University of Kansas, Spencer Museum of Art, Lawrence KS
University of Miami, Lowe Art Museum, Coral Gables FL
University of Missouri, Museum of Art and Archaeology, Columbia MO
University of North Carolina at Greensboro, Chinqua-Penn Plantation House, Reidsville NC
University of Notre Dame, Snite Museum of Art, Notre Dame IN
University of Oregon, Museum of Art, Eugene OR
University of Regina, Mackenzie Art Gallery, Regina SK
University of Tampa, Henry B Plant Museum, Tampa FL
University of Vermont, Robert Hull Fleming Museum, Burlington VT
University of Wisconsin, Elvehjem Museum of Art, Madison WI
University of Wisconsin, University Art Museum, Milwaukee WI
Vanderbilt University, Art Gallery, Nashville TN
Vassar College Art Gallery, Poughkeepsie NY
Virginia Museum, Danville Museum of Fine Arts and History, Danville VA
Walker Museum, Fairlee VT
Washington and Lee University, Gallery of DuPont Hall, Lexington VA
Washington County Museum of Fine Arts, Hagerstown MD
Wesleyan University, Davison Art Center, Middletown CT
Widener University, Alfred O Deshong Museum, Chester PA
Williams College, Museum of Art, Williamstown MA
Woodmere Art Museum, Philadelphia PA
Yale University, Art Gallery, New Haven CT

PAINTING - AMERICAN

Abilene Fine Arts Museum, Abilene TX
Albany Institute of History and Art, Albany NY
Alberta College of Art Gallery, Calgary AB
Albrecht Art Museum, Saint Joseph MO
Albright College, Freedman Gallery, Reading PA
Allegheny College, Bowman, Megahan and Penelec Galleries, Meadville PA
Allentown Art Museum, Allentown PA
American University, Watkins Art Gallery, Washington DC
Arizona State University, University Art Collections, Tempe AZ
Arkansas Arts Center, Little Rock AR
Art Complex Museum at Duxbury, Duxbury MA
Art Gallery of Nova Scotia, Halifax NS
Art Gallery of Ontario, Toronto ON
Art Institute of Chicago, Chicago IL
Artists' Cooperative Gallery, Omaha NE
Atlanta Museum, Atlanta GA
Attleboro Museum, Center for the Arts, Attleboro MA
Augusta Richmond County Museum, Augusta GA
Baldwin-Wallace College, Art Gallery, Berea OH
Ball State University, Art Gallery, Muncie IN
Baltimore Museum of Art, Baltimore MD
Bard College, William Cooper Procter Art Center, Annandale-on-Hudson NY
Bates College, Treat Gallery, Lewiston ME
Beaumont Art Museum, Beaumont TX
Beloit College, Wright Museum of Art, Beloit WI
Berea College, Art Department Gallery, Berea KY

Bergstrom Mahler Museum, Neenah WI
Berkshire Museum, Pittsfield MA
Birmingham Museum of Art, Birmingham AL
Blanden Memorial Art Museum, Fort Dodge IA
Boise Gallery of Art, Boise ID
Brandeis University, Rose Art Museum, Waltham MA
Brandywine River Museum, Chadds Ford PA
Brigham Young University, B F Larsen Gallery, Provo UT
Brockton Art Museum, Brockton MA
The Bruce Museum, Greenwich CT
The Buffalo Fine Arts Academy, Albright-Knox Art Gallery, Buffalo NY
Butler Institute of American Art, Youngstown OH
Canton Art Institute, Canton OH
Capital University, Schumacher Gallery, Columbus OH
Cardinal Stritch College, Milwaukee WI
Carnegie Institute, Museum of Art, Pittsburgh PA
Carolina Art Association, Gibbes Art Gallery, Charleston SC
Amon Carter Museum, Fort Worth TX
Chrysler Museum, Norfolk VA
Cincinnati Art Museum, Cincinnati OH
Clemson University, Rudolph E Lee Gallery, Clemson SC
Cleveland Museum of Art, Cleveland OH
Clinton Art Association Gallery, Clinton IA
Colby Museum of Art, Waterville ME
College of Idaho, Blatchley Gallery, Caldwell ID
College of Saint Benedict, Art Gallery, Saint Joseph MN
College of the Americas, Museum of the Americas, Brookfield VT
College of William and Mary, Joseph & Margaret Muscarelle Museum of Art, Williamsburg VA
College of Wooster Art Center Museum, Wooster OH
Colorado Springs Fine Arts Center, Colorado Springs CO
Columbia County Historical Society, Kinderhook NY
Columbia Museums of Art and Science, Columbia SC
Columbus Chapel, Boal Mansion and Museum, Boalsburg PA
Columbus Museum of Art, Columbus OH
Columbus Museum of Arts and Sciences, Columbus GA
Community College of Baltimore, Art Gallery, Baltimore MD
Confederation Centre Art Gallery and Museum, Charlottetown PE
Connecticut Valley Historical Museum, Springfield MA
Coos Art Museum, Coos Bay OR
Corcoran Museum, Washington DC
Cornell University, Herbert F Johnson Museum of Art, Ithaca NY
Country Art Gallery, Locust Valley NY
Creighton University Art Gallery, Omaha NE
Crocker Art Museum, Sacramento CA
Cummer Gallery of Art, DeEtte Holden Cummer Museum Foundation, Jacksonville FL
Currier Gallery of Art, Manchester NH
Dahl Fine Arts Center, Rapid City SD
Dallas Museum of Fine Arts, Dallas TX
Danforth Museum of Art, Framingham MA
DAR Museum, National Society Daughters of the American Revolution, Washington DC
Davenport Municipal Art Gallery, Davenport IA
Dayton Art Institute, Dayton OH
Delaware Art Museum, Wilmington DE
Denver Art Museum, Denver CO
Dezign House III, Cleveland OH
Dickinson State College, Mind's Eye Gallery, Dickinson ND
Dulin Gallery of Art, Knoxville TN
East Carolina University, Gray Art Gallery, Greenville NC
East Tennessee State University, Carroll Reece Museum, Johnson City TN
Edmonton Art Gallery, Edmonton AB
Edmundson Art Foundation, Inc, Des Moines Art Center, Des Moines IA
Wharton Esherick Museum, Paoli PA
Essex Institute, Salem MA

San Jose Museum of Art, San Jose CA
San Jose State University, Union Gallery, San Jose CA
Santa Barbara Museum of Art, Santa Barbara CA
Schenectady Museum, Schenectady NY
Seattle Art Museum, Seattle WA
Ella Sharp Museum, Jackson MI
Shelburne Museum, Shelburne VT
Silverado Museum, Saint Helena CA
Smith College, Museum of Art, Northampton MA
George Walter Vincent Smith Art Museum, Springfield MA
Smith-Mason Gallery and Museum, Washington DC
Society of the Cincinnati, Anderson House Museum, Washington DC
South Dakota State University, South Dakota Memorial Art Center, Brookings SD
Southern Alleghenies Museum of Art, Loretto PA
Southern Illinois University, University Museum, Carbondale IL
Southern Utah State College, Braithwaite Fine Arts Gallery, Cedar City UT
Springfield Art Museum, Springfield MO
Springville Museum of Art, Springville UT
Staten Island Institute of Arts and Sciences, Staten Island NY
State University of New York at Albany, University Art Gallery, Albany NY
State University of New York at New Paltz, College Art Gallery, New Paltz NY
State University of New York at Oswego, Tyler Art Gallery, Oswego NY
State University of New York at Purchase, Neuberger Museum, Purchase NY
State University of New York College at Geneseo, Bertha V B Lederer Gallery, Geneseo NY
State University of New York College at Potsdam, Brainerd Art Gallery, Potsdam NY
Stephens College, Lewis James & Nellie Stratton Davis Art Gallery, Columbia MO
Stetson University, Art Gallery, De Land FL
SVACA - Sheyenne Valley Arts and Crafts Association, Bjarne Ness Gallery, Fort Ransom ND
Syracuse University, Art Collection, Syracuse NY
Tacoma Art Museum, Tacoma WA
Terra Museum of American Art, Evanston IL
Timken Art Gallery, San Diego CA
Toledo Museum of Art, Toledo OH
Tomoka State Park Museum, Ormond Beach FL
Topeka Public Library, Fine Arts Dept & Gallery of Fine Arts, Topeka KS
Triton Museum of Art, Santa Clara CA
Tryon Palace Restoration Complex, New Bern NC
Tucson Museum of Art, Tucson AZ
Edwin A Ulrich Museum, Hyde Park NY
Ulster County Community College, Visual Arts Gallery, Stone Ridge NY
United States Capitol Museum, Washington DC
United States Naval Academy Museum, Annapolis MD
University of Alberta, Ring House Gallery, Edmonton AB
University of Chicago, David and Alfred Smart Gallery, Chicago IL
University of Colorado Art Galleries, Boulder CO
University of Connecticut, William Benton Museum of Art, Storrs CT
University of Delaware, University Art Collections, Newark DE
University of Florida, University Gallery, Gainesville FL
University of Georgia, Georgia Museum of Art, Athens GA
University of Illinois, Krannert Art Museum, Champaign IL
University of Iowa, Museum of Art, Iowa City IA
University of Kansas, Spencer Museum of Art, Lawrence KS
University of Kentucky, Art Museum, Lexington KY
University of Maryland, College Park, Art Gallery, College Park MD
University of Minnesota, Tweed Museum of Art, Duluth MN
University of Minnesota, University Art Museum, Minneapolis MN

University of Nebraska, Lincoln, Sheldon Memorial Art Gallery, Lincoln NE
University of New Mexico, University Art Museum, Albuquerque NM
University of North Carolina, The Ackland Art Museum, Chapel Hill NC
University of North Carolina at Greensboro, Weatherspoon Art Gallery, Greensboro NC
University of Northern Iowa, Gallery of Art, Cedar Falls IA
University of Notre Dame, Snite Museum of Art, Notre Dame IN
University of Pittsburgh, University Art Gallery, Pittsburgh PA
University of Santa Clara, de Saisset Museum, Santa Clara CA
University of Southern California, Fisher Gallery, Los Angeles CA
University of South Florida, Art Galleries, Tampa FL
University of Southwestern Louisiana, University Art Museum, Lafayette LA
University of Texas at Austin, Archer M Huntington Art Gallery, Austin TX
University of Wisconsin, Elvehjem Museum of Art, Madison WI
University of Wisconsin, Memorial Union Gallery, Madison WI
University of Wisconsin, University Art Museum, Milwaukee WI
University of Wisconsin-Stout, Gallery 209, Menomonie WI
Valentine Museum, Richmond VA
Valparaiso University, University Art Galleries and Collections, Valparaiso IN
Vancouver Art Gallery, Vancouver BC
Vassar College Art Gallery, Poughkeepsie NY
Virginia Commonwealth University, Anderson Gallery, Richmond VA
Walker Art Center, Minneapolis MN
Walker Museum, Fairlee VT
Washburn University, Mulvane Art Center, Topeka KS
Washington County Museum of Fine Arts, Hagerstown MD
Westbrook College, Joan Whitney Payson Gallery of Art, Portland ME
Western State College, Quigley Hall Art Gallery, Gunnison CO
Westminster College Art Gallery, New Wilmington PA
Westmoreland County Museum of Art, Greensburg PA
White House, Washington DC
Whitney Museum of American Art, New York NY
Wichita Art Museum, Wichita KS
Wichita State University, Edwin A Ulrich Museum of Art, Wichita KS
Widener University, Alfred O Deshong Museum, Chester PA
Williams College, Museum of Art, Williamstown MA
Winnipeg Art Gallery, Winnipeg MB
Wood Art Gallery, Montpelier VT
Woodmere Art Museum, Philadelphia PA
Worcester Art Museum, Worcester MA
Yale University, Art Gallery, New Haven CT
York Institute Museum, Saco ME
Zigler Museum, Jennings LA

PAINTING - BRITISH

Albany Institute of History and Art, Albany NY
Arnot Art Museum, Elmira NY
Baltimore Museum of Art, Baltimore MD
Bates College, Treat Gallery, Lewiston ME
Beaverbrook Art Gallery, Fredericton NB
Bowdoin College, Museum of Art & Peary-MacMillan Arctic Museum, Brunswick ME
College of the Americas, Museum of the Americas, Brookfield VT
Corcoran Museum, Washington DC
Davenport Municipal Art Gallery, Davenport IA
Delaware Art Museum, Wilmington DE
Dixon Gallery and Gardens, Memphis TN
Gunston Hall Plantation, Lorton VA
Huntington Library, Art Gallery and Botanical Gardens, San Marino CA

Kendall Whaling Museum, Sharon MA
Kitchener-Waterloo Art Gallery, Kitchener ON
Louisiana State University, Anglo-American Art Museum, Baton Rouge LA
Mint Museum of Art, Charlotte NC
Montreal Museum of Fine Arts, Montreal PQ
Museum of Fine Arts, Springfield MA
New Orleans Museum of Art, New Orleans LA
Oklahoma Museum of Art, Oklahoma City OK
Owensboro Museum of Fine Art, Owensboro KY
Pennsylvania State University, Museum of Art, University Park PA
Princeton University, Art Museum, Princeton NJ
The Rosenbach Museum and Library, Philadelphia PA
San Diego Museum of Art, San Diego CA
University of Florida, University Gallery, Gainesville FL
University of Notre Dame, Snite Museum of Art, Notre Dame IN
University of Southern California, Fisher Gallery, Los Angeles CA
University of Utah, Utah Museum of Fine Arts, Salt Lake City UT
Walters Art Gallery, Baltimore MD
Westmoreland County Museum of Art, Greensburg PA
Worcester Art Museum, Worcester MA
Yale University, Yale Center for British Art, New Haven CT

PAINTING - CANADIAN

Kitchener-Waterloo Art Gallery, Kitchener ON
L'Universite Laval, Ecole des Arts Visuels de L'Universite Laval, Quebec PQ
McGill University, McCord Museum, Montreal PQ
Montreal Museum of Fine Arts, Montreal PQ
Provincial Archives of Manitoba, Winnipeg MB

PAINTING - DUTCH

Arnot Art Museum, Elmira NY
Bates College, Treat Gallery, Lewiston ME
Calvin College Center Art Gallery, Grand Rapids MI
Chrysler Museum, Norfolk VA
Sterling and Francine Clark Art Institute, Williamstown MA
Corcoran Museum, Washington DC
Evansville Museum of Arts and Science, Evansville IN
Isabella Stewart Gardner Museum, Boston MA
Kendall Whaling Museum, Sharon MA
Memphis Brooks Museum of Art, Memphis TN
Montreal Museum of Fine Arts, Montreal PQ
Museum of Fine Arts, Springfield MA
San Diego Museum of Art, San Diego CA
Timken Art Gallery, San Diego CA
University of California, Santa Barbara, University Art Museum, Santa Barbara CA
University of Southern California, Fisher Gallery, Los Angeles CA
Worcester Art Museum, Worcester MA

PAINTING - EUROPEAN

Allentown Art Museum, Allentown PA
American University, Watkins Art Gallery, Washington DC
Art Complex Museum at Duxbury, Duxbury MA
Art Gallery of Greater Victoria, Victoria BC
Art Gallery of Ontario, Toronto ON
Ball State University, Art Gallery, Muncie IN
Bates College, Treat Gallery, Lewiston ME
Beloit College, Wright Museum of Art, Beloit WI
Berkshire Museum, Pittsfield MA
Blanden Memorial Art Museum, Fort Dodge IA
Bob Jones University, Greenville SC
Boise Gallery of Art, Boise ID
Bowdoin College, Museum of Art & Peary-MacMillan Arctic Museum, Brunswick ME
Brockton Art Museum, Brockton MA
Brown University, Bell Gallery, Providence RI
The Buffalo Fine Arts Academy, Albright-Knox Art Gallery, Buffalo NY

Carnegie Institute, Museum of Art, Pittsburgh PA
Cincinnati Art Museum, Cincinnati OH
Cleveland Museum of Art, Cleveland OH
Columbia Museums of Art and Science, Columbia SC
Columbus Museum of Art, Columbus OH
Columbus Museum of Arts and Sciences, Columbus GA
Corcoran Museum, Washington DC
Cornell University, Herbert F Johnson Museum of Art, Ithaca NY
Country Art Gallery, Locust Valley NY
Crocker Art Museum, Sacramento CA
Cummer Gallery of Art, DeEtte Holden Cummer Museum Foundation, Jacksonville FL
Currier Gallery of Art, Manchester NH
Dallas Museum of Fine Arts, Dallas TX
Danforth Museum of Art, Framingham MA
Davenport Municipal Art Gallery, Davenport IA
Dayton Art Institute, Dayton OH
Denver Art Museum, Denver CO
Detroit Institute of Arts, Detroit MI
Dezign House III, Cleveland OH
Edmonton Art Gallery, Edmonton AB
Evansville Museum of Arts and Science, Evansville IN
Everhart Museum of Natural History, Science and Art, Scranton PA
Fairbanks Museum and Planetarium, Saint Johnsbury VT
William A Farnsworth Library and Art Museum, Rockland ME
Fine Arts Museums of San Francisco, M H de Young Memorial Museum and California Palace of the Legion of Honor, San Francisco CA
M Flint Institute of Arts, Flint MI
Frick Collection, New York NY
Godwin-Ternbach Museum, Flushing NY
Grand Rapids Art Museum, Grand Rapids MI
Solomon R Guggenheim Museum, New York NY
The Haggin Museum, Stockton CA
Harvard University, Busch-Reisinger Museum, Cambridge MA
Harvard University, William Hayes Fogg Art Museum, Cambridge MA
Headley-Whitney Museum, Lexington KY
Gertrude Herbert Memorial Institute of Art, Augusta GA
High Museum of Art, Atlanta GA
Hirshhorn Museum and Sculpture Garden, Washington DC
Hofstra University, Emily Lowe Gallery, Hempstead NY
Honolulu Academy of Arts, Honolulu HI
Huntington Galleries, Huntington WV
Hyde Collection, Glens Falls NY
Indianapolis Museum of Art, Indianapolis IN
Joslyn Art Museum, Omaha NE
Kendall Whaling Museum, Sharon MA
La Salle College Art Museum, Philadelphia PA
Le Musee Regional de Rimouski, Rimouski PQ
Los Angeles County Museum of Art, Los Angeles CA
Maryhill Museum of Art, Goldendale WA
McMaster University, Art Gallery, Hamilton ON
Marion Koogler McNay Art Museum, San Antonio TX
Merrick Art Gallery, New Brighton PA
Metropolitan Museum of Art, New York NY
Milwaukee Art Museum, Milwaukee WI
Minneapolis Institute of Arts, Minneapolis MN
Mint Museum of Art, Charlotte NC
Mount Holyoke College Art Museum, South Hadley MA
Munson-Williams-Proctor Institute, Museum of Art, Utica NY
Musee d'Art de Joliette, Joliette PQ
Museum of Arts and Sciences, Inc, Macon GA
Museum of Fine Arts, Springfield MA
Museum of Fine Arts, Houston, Houston TX
Muskegon Museum of Art, Muskegon MI
New Orleans Museum of Art, New Orleans LA
New York University, Grey Art Gallery and Study Center, New York NY
North Carolina Museum of Art, Raleigh NC
North Country Museum of Arts, Park Rapids MN
Northwestern College, Te Paske Gallery of Rowenhorst, Orange City IA

R W Norton Art Gallery, Shreveport LA
Oklahoma Museum of Art, Oklahoma City OK
Philadelphia Museum of Art, Philadelphia PA
Philbrook Art Center, Tulsa OK
The Phillips Collection, Washington DC
Portland Art Association, Portland Art Museum, Portland OR
Portland Museum of Art, Portland ME
Princeton University, Art Museum, Princeton NJ
Reading Public Museum and Art Gallery, Reading PA
Frederic Remington Art Museum, Ogdensburg NY
Lauren Rogers Library and Museum of Art, Laurel MS
Rollins College, George D and Harriet W Cornell Fine Arts Center Museum, Winter Park FL
Saginaw Art Museum, Saginaw MI
Saint Gregory's Abbey and College, Mabee-Gerrer Museum of Art, Shawnee OK
Saint Louis Art Museum, Saint Louis MO
San Diego Museum of Art, San Diego CA
Santa Barbara Museum of Art, Santa Barbara CA
Seattle Art Museum, Seattle WA
Shelburne Museum, Shelburne VT
Smith College, Museum of Art, Northampton MA
George Walter Vincent Smith Art Museum, Springfield MA
Southern Illinois University, University Museum, Carbondale IL
State Art Museum of Florida, John & Mable Ringling Museum of Art, Sarasota FL
State University of New York at Purchase, Neuberger Museum, Purchase NY
Taft Museum, Cincinnati OH
Toledo Museum of Art, Toledo OH
Tucson Museum of Art, Tucson AZ
University of Chicago, David and Alfred Smart Gallery, Chicago IL
University of Cincinnati, Tangeman Fine Arts Gallery, Cincinnati OH
University of Connecticut, William Benton Museum of Art, Storrs CT
University of Illinois, Krannert Art Museum, Champaign IL
University of Iowa, Museum of Art, Iowa City IA
University of Kansas, Spencer Museum of Art, Lawrence KS
University of Kentucky, Art Museum, Lexington KY
University of Missouri, Museum of Art and Archaeology, Columbia MO
University of North Carolina, The Ackland Art Museum, Chapel Hill NC
University of North Carolina at Greensboro, Weatherspoon Art Gallery, Greensboro NC
University of Northern Iowa, Gallery of Art, Cedar Falls IA
University of Notre Dame, Snite Museum of Art, Notre Dame IN
University of Oklahoma, Museum of Art, Norman OK
University of Wisconsin, Elvehjem Museum of Art, Madison WI
Vancouver Art Gallery, Vancouver BC
Vanderbilt University, Art Gallery, Nashville TN
Vassar College Art Gallery, Poughkeepsie NY
Virginia Museum of Fine Arts, Richmond VA
Walters Art Gallery, Baltimore MD
Washburn University, Mulvane Art Center, Topeka KS
Washington and Lee University, Gallery of DuPont Hall, Lexington VA
Westbrook College, Joan Whitney Payson Gallery of Art, Portland ME
Westmoreland County Museum of Art, Greensburg PA
Wichita State University, Edwin A Ulrich Museum of Art, Wichita KS
Widener University, Alfred O Deshong Museum, Chester PA
Wilkes College, Sordoni Art Gallery, Wilkes-Barre PA
Williams College, Museum of Art, Williamstown MA
Woodmere Art Museum, Philadelphia PA
Yale University, Art Gallery, New Haven CT
Zigler Museum, Jennings LA

PAINTING - FLEMISH

Arnot Art Museum, Elmira NY
Capital University, Schumacher Gallery, Columbus OH
Chrysler Museum, Norfolk VA
Sterling and Francine Clark Art Institute, Williamstown MA
Clemson University, Fort Hill, Clemson SC
Columbus Chapel, Boal Mansion and Museum, Boalsburg PA
Corcoran Museum, Washington DC
Evansville Museum of Arts and Science, Evansville IN
Frick Art Museum, Pittsburgh PA
Isabella Stewart Gardner Museum, Boston MA
Memphis Brooks Museum of Art, Memphis TN
San Diego Museum of Art, San Diego CA
University of California, Santa Barbara, University Art Museum, Santa Barbara CA
University of Southern California, Fisher Gallery, Los Angeles CA
Virginia Museum of Fine Arts, Richmond VA
Worcester Art Museum, Worcester MA

PAINTING - FRENCH

Arnot Art Museum, Elmira NY
Art Institute of Chicago, Chicago IL
Baltimore Museum of Art, Baltimore MD
Bates College, Treat Gallery, Lewiston ME
Chrysler Museum, Norfolk VA
Sterling and Francine Clark Art Institute, Williamstown MA
Corcoran Museum, Washington DC
Davenport Municipal Art Gallery, Davenport IA
Dixon Gallery and Gardens, Memphis TN
Drexel University Museum, Philadelphia PA
Frick Art Museum, Pittsburgh PA
Isabella Stewart Gardner Museum, Boston MA
Grand Rapids Art Museum, Grand Rapids MI
The Haggin Museum, Stockton CA
Hill-Stead Museum, Farmington CT
Montreal Museum of Fine Arts, Montreal PQ
Museum of Fine Arts, Springfield MA
Norton Gallery and School of Art, West Palm Beach FL
Oklahoma Museum of Art, Oklahoma City OK
Saint Louis Art Museum, Saint Louis MO
Tacoma Art Museum, Tacoma WA
Telfair Academy of Arts and Sciences Inc, Savannah GA
Timken Art Gallery, San Diego CA
University of Notre Dame, Snite Museum of Art, Notre Dame IN
University of Rochester, Memorial Art Gallery, Rochester NY
University of Southern California, Fisher Gallery, Los Angeles CA
Westbrook College, Joan Whitney Payson Gallery of Art, Portland ME
Worcester Art Museum, Worcester MA

PAINTING - GERMAN

Arnot Art Museum, Elmira NY
Columbus Chapel, Boal Mansion and Museum, Boalsburg PA
Davenport Municipal Art Gallery, Davenport IA
Drexel University Museum, Philadelphia PA
Grand Rapids Art Museum, Grand Rapids MI
Metropolitan Museum of Art, New York NY
Milwaukee Art Museum, Milwaukee WI
Saint Louis Art Museum, Saint Louis MO
Telfair Academy of Arts and Sciences Inc, Savannah GA
University of Kansas, Spencer Museum of Art, Lawrence KS

PAINTING - ITALIAN

Arnot Art Museum, Elmira NY
Ball State University, Art Gallery, Muncie IN
Bates College, Treat Gallery, Lewiston ME
Canton Art Institute, Canton OH
Chrysler Museum, Norfolk VA
Sterling and Francine Clark Art Institute,
    Williamstown MA
Classical School Gallery, Albuquerque NM
Columbia Museums of Art and Science, Columbia
    SC
Columbus Chapel, Boal Mansion and Museum,
    Boalsburg PA
Frick Art Museum, Pittsburgh PA
Frick Collection, New York NY
Galleries of the Claremont Colleges, Claremont CA
Isabella Stewart Gardner Museum, Boston MA
Grand Rapids Art Museum, Grand Rapids MI
Howard University, Gallery of Art, Washington DC
Hyde Collection, Glens Falls NY
Indianapolis Museum of Art, Clowes Fund
    Collection, Indianapolis IN
Memphis Brooks Museum of Art, Memphis TN
Museum of Fine Arts, Springfield MA
Parrish Art Museum, Southampton NY
Philbrook Art Center, Tulsa OK
San Diego Museum of Art, San Diego CA
State University of New York College at Potsdam,
    Brainerd Art Gallery, Potsdam NY
Timken Art Gallery, San Diego CA
University of Arizona, Museum of Art, Tucson AZ
University of California, Santa Barbara, University
    Art Museum, Santa Barbara CA
University of Notre Dame, Snite Museum of Art,
    Notre Dame IN
University of Southern California, Fisher Gallery,
    Los Angeles CA
University of Tennessee, Eleanor Dean Audigier
    Art Collection, Knoxville TN
University of Utah, Utah Museum of Fine Arts, Salt
    Lake City UT
Vanderbilt University, Art Gallery, Nashville TN
Vassar College Art Gallery, Poughkeepsie NY
Virginia Museum of Fine Arts, Richmond VA

PAINTING - JAPANESE

Calvin College Center Art Gallery, Grand Rapids
    MI
Cleveland Museum of Art, Cleveland OH
Hofstra University, Emily Lowe Gallery,
    Hempstead NY
Honolulu Academy of Arts, Honolulu HI
Japan Society, Inc, Japan House Gallery, New York
    NY
Johns Hopkins University, Evergreen House,
    Baltimore MD
Kendall Whaling Museum, Sharon MA
New Orleans Museum of Art, New Orleans LA
Palm Beach County Parks and Recreation
    Department, Morikami Museum of Japanese
    Culture, Delray Beach FL
Saint John's University, Chung-Cheng Art Gallery,
    Jamaica NY
Seattle Art Museum, Seattle WA
State University of New York College at Potsdam,
    Brainerd Art Gallery, Potsdam NY

PAINTING - POLISH

Orchard Lake School Galeria, Orchard Lake MI
Polish Museum of America, Chicago IL

PAINTING - RUSSIAN

Concordia College Wisconsin, Fine Arts Galleries,
    Mequon WI
University of Wisconsin, Elvehjem Museum of Art,
    Madison WI

PAINTING - SCANDINAVIAN

American Swedish Historical Foundation and
    Museum, Philadelphia PA
American Swedish Institute, Minneapolis MN

PAINTING - SPANISH

Arnot Art Museum, Elmira NY
Canton Art Institute, Canton OH
Columbus Chapel, Boal Mansion and Museum,
    Boalsburg PA
Montreal Museum of Fine Arts, Montreal PQ
San Diego Museum of Art, San Diego CA
Southern Methodist University, Meadows Museum,
    Dallas TX
Timken Art Gallery, San Diego CA

PERIOD ROOMS

Adams National Historic Site, Quincy MA
Allentown Art Museum, Allentown PA
Atkins Museum of Fine Art, Kansas City MO
Bartow-Pell Mansion Museum and Garden, New
    York NY
Brick Store Museum, Kennebunk ME
Kit Carson Memorial Foundation, Taos NM
Centre Hill Mansion, Petersburg VA
Chateau de Ramezay, Antiquarian and Numismatic
    Society of Montreal, Montreal PQ
Chester County Historical Society, West Chester
    PA
Chicago Architecture Foundation, Glessner House,
    Chicago IL
Cincinnati Art Museum, Cincinnati OH
City of Holyoke Museum-Wistariahurst, Holyoke
    MA
Clemson University, Fort Hill, Clemson SC
Cliveden, Philadelphia PA
Colonel Black Mansion, Ellsworth ME
Concord Antiquarian Society Museum, Concord
    MA
Creek Council House and Museum, Okmulgee OK
Decatur House, Washington DC
Department of State, Diplomatic Reception Rooms,
    Washington DC
Desert Caballeros Western Museum, Wickenburg
    AZ
Division of Historical and Cultural Affairs, Bureau
    of Museums and Historic Sites, Dover DE
Dixon Gallery and Gardens, Memphis TN
Dundurn Castle, Hamilton ON
East Tennessee State University, Carroll Reece
    Museum, Johnson City TN
Essex Institute, Salem MA
Henry Morrison Flagler Museum, Palm Beach FL
Frick Art Museum, Pittsburgh PA
Gananoque Historical Museum, Gananoque ON
Gibson Society, Inc, Gibson House Museum,
    Boston MA
Stan Hywet Hall Foundation, Inc, Akron OH
Hancock Shaker Village, Inc, Pittsfield MA
Historic Cherry Hill, Albany NY
Hopewell Museum, Hopewell NJ
Imperial Calcasieu Museum, Lake Charles LA
Independence National Historical Park,
    Philadelphia PA
Indianapolis Museum of Art, Indianapolis IN
John Jay Homestead State Historic Site, Katonah
    NY
John Paul Jones House, Portsmouth NH
Jordan Historical Museum of The Twenty, Jordan
    ON
Kentucky Historical Society, Old State Capitol &
    Annex, Frankfort KY
Ladies Library and Art Association, Independence
    Museum, Independence KS
Liberty Hall Museum, Frankfort KY
Longfellow National Historic Site, Cambridge MA
Longfellow's Wayside Inn, South Sudbury MA
Loveland Museum and Gallery, Loveland CO
Manitoba Historical Society, Dalnavert -
    MacDonald House Museum, Winnipeg MB
Mattatuck Historical Society Museum, Mattatuck
    Museum, Waterbury CT
Minneapolis Institute of Arts, Minneapolis MN
Monticello, Thomas Jefferson Memorial
    Foundation, Charlottesville VA

Mount Vernon Ladies' Association of the Union,
    Mount Vernon VA
Muchnic Foundation and Atchison Art Association,
    Muchnic Gallery, Atchison KS
Museum of Fine Arts, Boston MA
New York State Historical Association, Farmers'
    Museum, Inc, Cooperstown NY
New York State Office of Parks, Recreation &
    Historical Preservation, Mills Mansion State
    Historical Site, Staatsburg NY
Oatlands of the National Trust, Inc, Leesburg VA
Oglebay Institute Mansion Museum, Wheeling WV
Old Barracks Museum, Trenton NJ
Paine Art Center and Arboretum, Oshkosh WI
Pennsylvania Historical and Museum Commission,
    Harrisburg PA
Peoria Historical Society, Peoria IL
Phelps County Historical Society Museum,
    Holdrege NE
Philadelphia Museum of Art, Philadelphia PA
Public Archives of Canada, Laurier House, Ottawa
    ON
Rhode Island Historical Society, John Brown
    House, Providence RI
Robert W Ryerss Library and Museum,
    Philadelphia PA
Saint Augustine Historical Society, Oldest House
    and Museums, Saint Augustine FL
Saint-Gaudens National Historic Site, Cornish NH
Schuyler-Hamilton House, Morristown NJ
Schuyler Mansion State Historic Site, Albany NY
Seneca Falls Historical Society Museum, Seneca
    Falls NY
Shelburne Museum, Shelburne VT
Sheldon Art Museum, Archaeological & Historical
    Society, Middlebury VT
Society for the Preservation of Historic Landmarks,
    Elizabeth Perkins House, York ME
Stanley-Whitman House, Farmington, Farmington
    CT
State Historical Society of Wisconsin, Madison WI
Sturdivant Hall, Selma AL
Telfair Academy of Arts and Sciences Inc,
    Savannah GA
Tippecanoe County Historical Museum, Lafayette
    IN
The Trustees of Reservations, The Mission House,
    Stockbridge MA
Mark Twain Birthplace Museum, Stoutsville MO
University of the South Gallery of Fine Arts,
    Sewanee TN
Vermilion County Museum Society, Danville IL
Washington Headquarters Association, Morris-
    Jumel Mansion, New York NY
Western Reserve Historical Society, Cleveland OH
Woodrow Wilson House, Washington DC

PEWTER

Albany Institute of History and Art, Albany NY
Essex Institute, Salem MA
Franklin Mint Museum, Franklin Center PA
Historic Deerfield Inc, Deerfield MA
Litchfield Historical Society, Litchfield CT
New Haven Colony Historical Society, New Haven
    CT
Oglebay Institute Mansion Museum, Wheeling WV

PHOTOGRAPHY

Adirondack Historical Association, Adirondack
    Museum, Blue Mountain Lake NY
Alabama Museum of Photography, Birmingham AL
Alberta College of Art Gallery, Calgary AB
Albrecht Art Museum, Saint Joseph MO
Albright College, Freedman Gallery, Reading PA
Albuquerque Museum of Art, History and Science,
    Albuquerque NM
Amarillo Art Center, Amarillo TX
Art Institute of Chicago, Chicago IL
Beaumont Art Museum, Beaumont TX
Berea College, Art Department Gallery, Berea KY
Jesse Besser Museum, Alpena MI
Boston Public Library, Albert H Wiggin Gallery
    (Prints), Boston MA
Carnegie Institute, Museum of Art, Pittsburgh PA
Amon Carter Museum, Fort Worth TX
Cincinnati Art Museum, Cincinnati OH

Clinton Art Association Gallery, Clinton IA
Corcoran Museum, Washington DC
Cornell University, Herbert F Johnson Museum of Art, Ithaca NY
Creighton University Art Gallery, Omaha NE
Crocker Art Museum, Sacramento CA
DuSable Museum of African American History, Chicago IL
Edmonton Art Gallery, Edmonton AB
The Friends of Photography, Carmel CA
Galleries of the Claremont Colleges, Claremont CA
George Washington University, The Dimock Gallery, Washington DC
Grossmont Community College Gallery, El Cajon CA
Guild Hall of East Hampton, Inc, Museum Section, East Hampton NY
Hallmark Cards, Inc, Hallmark Collections, Kansas City MO
Harvard University, William Hayes Fogg Art Museum, Cambridge MA
Haverhill Public Library, Art Dept, Haverhill MA
High Museum of Art, Atlanta GA
Historic New Orleans Collection, Kemper and Leila Williams Foundation, New Orleans LA
Hofstra University, Emily Lowe Gallery, Hempstead NY
Hudson River Museum, Yonkers NY
Illinois State Museum of Natural History and Art, Springfield IL
Institute for Art & Urban Resources, Project Studios One, Long Island City NY
Institute of American Indian Arts Museum, Santa Fe NM
International Center of Photography, New York NY
International Museum of Photography at George Eastman House, Rochester NY
Kalamazoo Institute of Arts, Genevieve and Donald Gilmore Art Center, Kalamazoo MI
Lafayette College, Morris R Williams Center for the Arts, Easton PA
Lehigh University Art Galleries, Bethlehem PA
Library of Congress, Washington DC
Long Island Historical Society, Brooklyn NY
Los Angeles Center For Photographic Studies, Los Angeles CA
Louisiana Arts and Science Center, Baton Rouge LA
Louisiana Department of Culture, Recreation and Tourism, Louisiana State Museum, New Orleans LA
Marquette University, Museum of Art, Milwaukee WI
Meridian Museum of Art, Meridian MS
Merrimack Valley Textile Museum, North Andover MA
Metropolitan Museum of Art, New York NY
Miami-Dade Community College, South Campus, Art Gallery, Miami FL
Middle Tennessee State University, Photographic Gallery, Murfreesboro TN
Midwest Museum of American Art, Elkhart IN
Mills College, Art Gallery, Oakland CA
Minneapolis Institute of Arts, Minneapolis MN
Monterey Peninsula Museum of Art, Monterey CA
MPK Omega Co, Mike Kiefer Bio-Art Museum, Amarillo TX
The Museum, Greenwood SC
Museum, Fine Arts Research & Holographic Center, Chicago IL
Museum of Fine Arts, Houston, Houston TX
Museum of Holography, New York NY
Museum of Modern Art, New York NY
Museum of the City of New York, New York NY
National Film Board of Canada, Still Photography Division, Ottawa ON
National Maritime Museum, San Francisco CA
National Museum of American History, Smithsonian Institution, Washington DC
New Orleans Museum of Art, New Orleans LA
Newport Harbor Art Museum, Newport Beach CA
Oakland Museum, Art Dept, Oakland CA
Ohio Wesleyan University, Dept of Fine Arts Gallery, Delaware OH
Olana State Historic Site, Hudson NY
Open Space Gallery, Photography at Open Space, Victoria BC

Peale Museum, Baltimore MD
Phillips Academy, Addison Gallery of American Art, Andover MA
Photographers Gallery, Saskatoon SK
Plains Art Museum, Main Gallery, Moorhead MN
Polk Public Museum, Lakeland FL
Portland Art Association, Portland Art Museum, Portland OR
Potsdam Public Museum, Potsdam NY
Provincial Archives of Manitoba, Winnipeg MB
Roberson Center for the Arts and Sciences, Binghamton NY
Saint Anselm College, Manchester NH
St Lawrence University, Richard F Brush Art Gallery, Canton NY
Saint Louis Art Museum, Saint Louis MO
San Francisco Museum of Modern Art, San Francisco CA
Silverado Museum, Saint Helena CA
Smith College, Museum of Art, Northampton MA
Society for the Preservation of New England Antiquities, Boston MA
Southern Illinois University, University Museum, Carbondale IL
State Historical Society of Wisconsin, Madison WI
State University of New York at Purchase, Neuberger Museum, Purchase NY
Studio Museum in Harlem, New York NY
Swedish American Museum Association of Chicago, Chicago IL
Ulster County Community College, Visual Arts Gallery, Stone Ridge NY
United Methodist Historical Society, Lovely Lane Museum, Baltimore MD
University of Alaska, Museum, Fairbanks AK
University of Arizona, Center for Creative Photography, Tucson AZ
University of Calgary, The Nickle Arts Museum, Calgary AB
University of California, Los Angeles, Grunwald Center for the Graphic Arts, Los Angeles CA
University of Colorado Art Galleries, Boulder CO
University of Florida, University Gallery, Gainesville FL
University of Iowa, Museum of Art, Iowa City IA
University of Massachusetts, Amherst, University Gallery, Amherst MA
University of Nebraska, Lincoln, Sheldon Memorial Art Gallery, Lincoln NE
University of New Mexico, University Art Museum, Albuquerque NM
University of Notre Dame, Snite Museum of Art, Notre Dame IN
University of Oklahoma, Museum of Art, Norman OK
University of Santa Clara, de Saisset Museum, Santa Clara CA
University of South Florida, Art Galleries, Tampa FL
University of Washington, Henry Art Gallery, Seattle WA
University of West Florida, Art Gallery, Pensacola FL
University of Wisconsin, University Art Museum, Milwaukee WI
Utah Natural Resources & Energy, Parks & Recreation, Territorial Statehouse, Fillmore UT
Valentine Museum, Richmond VA
Virginia Commonwealth University, Anderson Gallery, Richmond VA
Walker Art Center, Minneapolis MN
Wesleyan University, Davison Art Center, Middletown CT
Whatcom Museum of History and Art, Bellingham WA
Yosemite Collections, Yosemite National Park CA

PORCELAIN

Allentown Art Museum, Allentown PA
American Swedish Institute, Minneapolis MN
Atlanta Museum, Atlanta GA
Baltimore Museum of Art, Baltimore MD
Beaverbrook Art Gallery, Fredericton NB
Bellingrath Gardens and Home, Theodore AL
The Bradford Museum, Niles IL
The Bruce Museum, Greenwich CT
China Trade Museum, Milton MA

Sterling and Francine Clark Art Institute, Williamstown MA
College of Wooster Art Center Museum, Wooster OH
Cranbrook Academy of Art Museum, Bloomfield Hills MI
Cummer Gallery of Art, DeEtte Holden Cummer Museum Foundation, Jacksonville FL
Department of State, Diplomatic Reception Rooms, Washington DC
Dixon Gallery and Gardens, Memphis TN
Everson Museum of Art, Syracuse NY
Fort Smith Art Center, Fort Smith AR
Franklin Mint Museum, Franklin Center PA
Frick Art Museum, Pittsburgh PA
Frick Collection, New York NY
Hammond-Harwood House Association, Inc, Annapolis MD
Headley-Whitney Museum, Lexington KY
Hill-Stead Museum, Farmington CT
Herbert Hoover Presidential Library & Museum, West Branch IA
Indianapolis Museum of Art, Indianapolis IN
Jacksonville Art Museum, Jacksonville FL
Lehigh University Art Galleries, Bethlehem PA
Maryland Historical Society Museum, Baltimore MD
Memphis Brooks Museum of Art, Memphis TN
Montreal Museum of Fine Arts, Montreal PQ
Museum of Fine Arts, Boston MA
National Society of Colonial Dames of the State of Maryland, Mount Clare Mansion, Baltimore MD
Parrish Art Museum, Southampton NY
Philadelphia Museum of Art, Philadelphia PA
Frederic Remington Art Museum, Ogdensburg NY
Rhode Island School of Design, Museum of Art, Providence RI
Riverside County Art and Cultural Center, Edward-Dean Museum of Decorative Arts, Cherry Valley CA
The Rosenbach Museum and Library, Philadelphia PA
Robert W Ryerss Library and Museum, Philadelphia PA
Saint John's University, Chung-Cheng Art Gallery, Jamaica NY
Saint Louis Art Museum, Saint Louis MO
Seattle Art Museum, Seattle WA
Ella Sharp Museum, Jackson MI
Ships of The Sea Museum, Savannah GA
Stark Museum of Art, Orange TX
Taft Museum, Cincinnati OH
University of Notre Dame, Snite Museum of Art, Notre Dame IN
University of Tampa, Henry B Plant Museum, Tampa FL
University of Tennessee, Eleanor Dean Audigier Art Collection, Knoxville TN
Virginia Museum, Danville Museum of Fine Arts and History, Danville VA
Virginia Museum of Fine Arts, Richmond VA
Washington and Lee University, Gallery of DuPont Hall, Lexington VA
T T Wentworth, Jr Museum, Pensacola FL
White House, Washington DC
Wichita Art Museum, Wichita KS
Woodmere Art Museum, Philadelphia PA

PORTRAITS

Baltimore Museum of Art, Baltimore MD
Bowdoin College, Museum of Art & Peary-MacMillan Arctic Museum, Brunswick ME
Canton Art Institute, Canton OH
Carolina Art Association, Gibbes Art Gallery, Charleston SC
Everson Museum of Art, Syracuse NY
Huntington Galleries, Huntington WV
Independence National Historical Park, Philadelphia PA
Indianapolis Museum of Art, Indianapolis IN
John Jay Homestead State Historic Site, Katonah NY
Jekyll Island Authority Museum, Jekyll Island GA
Legislative Building Art Gallery, Regina SK
Lincoln National Life Foundation, Inc, Louis A Warren Lincoln Library and Museum, Fort Wayne IN

James Monroe Law Office - Museum and Memorial
Library, Fredericksburg VA
Musee Historique de Vaudreuil, Vaudreuil
Historical Museum, Vaudreuil PQ
New Jersey Historical Society Museum, Newark NJ
R W Norton Art Gallery, Shreveport LA
Oshkosh Public Museum, Oshkosh WI
Parrish Art Museum, Southampton NY
Philipse Manor Hall State Historic Site, Yonkers
NY
Presidential Museum, Odessa TX
Rollins College, George D and Harriet W Cornell
Fine Arts Center Museum, Winter Park FL
Royal Ontario Museum, Canadiana Gallery,
Toronto ON
Shirley Plantation, Charles City VA
Gilbert Stuart Birthplace, Saunderstown RI
Telfair Academy of Arts and Sciences Inc,
Savannah GA
Harry S Truman Library and Museum,
Independence MO
United States Military Academy, West Point
Museum, West Point NY
University of Southern California, Fisher Gallery,
Los Angeles CA
White House, Washington DC

POSTERS

American Jewish Historical Society, Waltham MA
Greenville College, Richard W Bock Sculpture
Collection, Greenville IL
Herbert Hoover Presidential Library & Museum,
West Branch IA
Jersey City Museum Association, Jersey City NJ
Museum of Modern Art, New York NY
New Jersey Historical Society Museum, Newark NJ
Oakville Galleries, Oakville ON
Public Archives of Canada, Picture Division,
Ottawa ON

POTTERY

Allegheny College, Bowman, Megahan and Penelec
Galleries, Meadville PA
Art Association of Jacksonville, David Strawn Art
Gallery, Jacksonville IL
Atkins Museum of Fine Art, Kansas City MO
Beloit College, Wright Museum of Art, Beloit WI
Brevard College, Coltrane Art Center, Brevard NC
Clinton Art Association Gallery, Clinton IA
Creighton University Art Gallery, Omaha NE
Drew University, College Art Gallery, Madison NJ
Freeport Area Arts Council, Freeport Art Museum,
Freeport IL
Grand Rapids Art Museum, Grand Rapids MI
Grossmont Community College Gallery, El Cajon
CA
Harvard University, Dumbarton Oaks Research
Library and Collections, Washington DC
Johnson-Humrickhouse Museum, Coshocton OH
Kenosha Public Museum, Kenosha WI
Litchfield Historical Society, Litchfield CT
Maryland Historical Society Museum, Baltimore
MD
Meridian Museum of Art, Meridian MS
Mount Saint Vincent University, Art Gallery,
Halifax NS
Musee Historique de Vaudreuil, Vaudreuil
Historical Museum, Vaudreuil PQ
R W Norton Art Gallery, Shreveport LA
Peoria Historical Society, Peoria IL
Polk Public Museum, Lakeland FL
Potsdam Public Museum, Potsdam NY
Redding Museum and Art Center, Redding CA
Saint John's Museum of Art, Wilmington NC
San Francisco Museum of Modern Art, San
Francisco CA
Southwestern At Memphis, Jessie L Clough Art
Memorial for Teaching, Memphis TN
Topeka Public Library, Fine Arts Dept & Gallery of
Fine Arts, Topeka KS
University of Michigan, Kelsey Museum of Ancient
and Medieval Archaeology, Ann Arbor MI
University of Washington, Henry Art Gallery,
Seattle WA
Virginia Museum of Fine Arts, Richmond VA
West Baton Rouge Museum, Port Allen LA

PRE-COLUMBIAN ART

Art Association of Jacksonville, David Strawn Art
Gallery, Jacksonville IL
Birmingham Museum of Art, Birmingham AL
Bower's Museum, Santa Ana CA
Brandeis University, Rose Art Museum, Waltham
MA
Center for Inter-American Relations Art Gallery,
New York NY
Colgate University, Picker Art Gallery, Hamilton
NY
College of the Americas, Museum of the Americas,
Brookfield VT
Dallas Museum of Fine Arts, Dallas TX
East Tennessee State University, Carroll Reece
Museum, Johnson City TN
Edison Community College, Gallery of Fine Art,
Fort Myers FL
Harvard University, Dumbarton Oaks Research
Library and Collections, Washington DC
High Museum of Art, Atlanta GA
Hofstra University, Emily Lowe Gallery,
Hempstead NY
Hood Museum of Art, Hanover NH
Illinois State University, University Museums,
Normal IL
Jacksonville Art Museum, Jacksonville FL
Loch Haven Art Center, Inc, Orlando FL
Metropolitan Museum and Art Center, Coral
Gables FL
Minneapolis Institute of Arts, Minneapolis MN
Mint Museum of Art, Charlotte NC
Mount Holyoke College Art Museum, South
Hadley MA
Munson-Williams-Proctor Institute, Museum of Art,
Utica NY
Musee d'Art de Joliette, Joliette PQ
Museum of Fine Arts, Houston, Houston TX
Museum of the American Indian, New York NY
Natural History Museum of Los Angeles County,
Los Angeles CA
Newark Museum, Newark NJ
New Orleans Museum of Art, New Orleans LA
North Carolina Museum of Art, Raleigh NC
Oklahoma Center for Science and Art, Kirkpatrick
Center, Oklahoma City OK
Plains Art Museum, Main Gallery, Moorhead MN
Plains Art Museum, Rourke Art Gallery, Moorhead
MN
Polk Public Museum, Lakeland FL
Portland Art Association, Portland Art Museum,
Portland OR
Princeton University, Art Museum, Princeton NJ
Putnam Museum, Davenport IA
Redding Museum and Art Center, Redding CA
Saint Gregory's Abbey and College, Mabee-Gerrer
Museum of Art, Shawnee OK
Saint Louis Art Museum, Saint Louis MO
Science Museums of Charlotte, Inc, Discovery
Place, Charlotte NC
Southwest Museum, Los Angeles CA
State University of New York at New Paltz,
College Art Gallery, New Paltz NY
Tallahassee Junior Museum, Tallahassee FL
Tucson Museum of Art, Tucson AZ
University of Delaware, University Art Collections,
Newark DE
University of Florida, University Gallery,
Gainesville FL
University of Houston, Sarah Campbell Blaffer
Gallery, Houston TX
University of Illinois, Krannert Art Museum,
Champaign IL
University of Iowa, Museum of Art, Iowa City IA
University of Kentucky, Art Museum, Lexington
KY
University of Miami, Lowe Art Museum, Coral
Gables FL
University of Missouri, Museum of Art and
Archaeology, Columbia MO
University of Notre Dame, Snite Museum of Art,
Notre Dame IN
University of South Florida, Art Galleries, Tampa
FL
Wichita Art Museum, Wichita KS
Williams College, Museum of Art, Williamstown
MA
Worcester Art Museum, Worcester MA

PRIMITIVE ART

Lyman Allyn Museum, New London CT
Anchorage Historical and Fine Arts Museum, Cook
Inlet Historical Society, Anchorage AK
Art Gallery of Greater Victoria, Victoria BC
Art Institute of Chicago, Chicago IL
Bishop Hill State Historic Site, Bishop Hill IL
The Buffalo Fine Arts Academy, Albright-Knox Art
Gallery, Buffalo NY
Capital University, Schumacher Gallery, Columbus
OH
Cornell University, Herbert F Johnson Museum of
Art, Ithaca NY
Field Museum of Natural History, Chicago IL
Fine Arts Museums of San Francisco, M H de
Young Memorial Museum and California Palace
of the Legion of Honor, San Francisco CA
Gallery of Prehistoric Paintings, New York NY
Heritage Plantation of Sandwich, Sandwich MA
Indiana University, Art Museum, Bloomington IN
Maryhill Museum of Art, Goldendale WA
Metropolitan Museum of Art, New York NY
Museum of Fine Arts, Springfield MA
Museum of Fine Arts, Houston, Houston TX
Olivet College, Armstrong Museum of Art and
Archaeology, Olivet MI
Science Museums of Charlotte, Inc, Discovery
Place, Charlotte NC
Seattle Art Museum, Seattle WA
Southwest Museum, Los Angeles CA
Staten Island Institute of Arts and Sciences, Staten
Island NY
State University of New York at New Paltz,
College Art Gallery, New Paltz NY
Stephens College, Lewis James & Nellie Stratton
Davis Art Gallery, Columbia MO
University of Missouri, Museum of Art and
Archaeology, Columbia MO
University of Rochester, Memorial Art Gallery,
Rochester NY

PRINTS

Abilene Fine Arts Museum, Abilene TX
Adirondack Historical Association, Adirondack
Museum, Blue Mountain Lake NY
Albion College, Bobbitt Visual Arts Center, Albion
MI
Albrecht Art Museum, Saint Joseph MO
Albright College, Freedman Gallery, Reading PA
Aldrich Museum of Contemporary Art, Ridgefield
CT
Arizona State University, University Art
Collections, Tempe AZ
Arkansas Arts Center, Little Rock AR
Art Gallery of Brant, Inc, Brantford ON
Art Gallery of Nova Scotia, Halifax NS
Art Institute of Chicago, Chicago IL
Art Museum of South Texas, Corpus Christi TX
Attleboro Museum, Center for the Arts, Attleboro
MA
Augustana College, Centennial Hall Gallery, Rock
Island IL
Leo Baeck Institute, New York NY
Baldwin-Wallace College, Art Gallery, Berea OH
Ball State University, Art Gallery, Muncie IN
Baltimore Museum of Art, Baltimore MD
Bard College, William Cooper Procter Art Center,
Annandale-on-Hudson NY
Bates College, Treat Gallery, Lewiston ME
Baylor University, Martin Museum of Art, Waco
TX
Beaverbrook Art Gallery, Fredericton NB
Beloit College, Wright Museum of Art, Beloit WI
Berea College, Art Department Gallery, Berea KY
Jesse Besser Museum, Alpena MI
Bowdoin College, Museum of Art & Peary-
MacMillan Arctic Museum, Brunswick ME
Brandeis University, Rose Art Museum, Waltham
MA
Brevard College, Coltrane Art Center, Brevard NC
Brigham Young University, B F Larsen Gallery,
Provo UT
Brown University, Bell Gallery, Providence RI
The Buffalo Fine Arts Academy, Albright-Knox Art
Gallery, Buffalo NY
Burnaby Art Gallery, Burnaby BC
Butler Institute of American Art, Youngstown OH

State Art Museum of Florida, John & Mable Ringling Museum of Art, Sarasota FL
Staten Island Institute of Arts and Sciences, Staten Island NY
State University of New York at Albany, University Art Gallery, Albany NY
State University of New York at New Paltz, College Art Gallery, New Paltz NY
State University of New York at Oswego, Tyler Art Gallery, Oswego NY
State University of New York at Purchase, Neuberger Museum, Purchase NY
State University of New York College at Fredonia, M C Rockefeller Arts Center Gallery, Fredonia NY
State University of New York College at Potsdam, Brainerd Art Gallery, Potsdam NY
Stetson University, Art Gallery, De Land FL
Toledo Museum of Art, Toledo OH
Ulster County Community College, Visual Arts Gallery, Stone Ridge NY
United States Naval Academy Museum, Annapolis MD
University of Calgary, The Nickle Arts Museum, Calgary AB
University of California, Los Angeles, Grunwald Center for the Graphic Arts, Los Angeles CA
University of California, Santa Barbara, University Art Museum, Santa Barbara CA
University of Colorado Art Galleries, Boulder CO
University of Delaware, University Art Collections, Newark DE
University of Florida, University Gallery, Gainesville FL
University of Houston, Sarah Campbell Blaffer Gallery, Houston TX
University of Illinois, Krannert Art Museum, Champaign IL
University of Iowa, Museum of Art, Iowa City IA
University of Louisville, Allen R Hite Art Institute Gallery, Louisville KY
University of Maryland, College Park, Art Gallery, College Park MD
University of Massachusetts, Amherst, University Gallery, Amherst MA
University of Minnesota, Tweed Museum of Art, Duluth MN
University of Minnesota, University Art Museum, Minneapolis MN
University of Missouri, Museum of Art and Archaeology, Columbia MO
University of Nebraska, Lincoln, Sheldon Memorial Art Gallery, Lincoln NE
University of New Brunswick, Art Centre, Fredericton NB
University of New Mexico, University Art Museum, Albuquerque NM
University of North Carolina, The Ackland Art Museum, Chapel Hill NC
University of North Carolina at Greensboro, Weatherspoon Art Gallery, Greensboro NC
University of Notre Dame, Snite Museum of Art, Notre Dame IN
University of Pittsburgh, University Art Gallery, Pittsburgh PA
University of Rochester, Memorial Art Gallery, Rochester NY
University of Southern Colorado, School of Liberal Arts, Pueblo CO
University of South Florida, Art Galleries, Tampa FL
University of Texas at Austin, Archer M Huntington Art Gallery, Austin TX
University of Vermont, Robert Hull Fleming Museum, Burlington VT
University of Washington, Henry Art Gallery, Seattle WA
University of West Florida, Art Gallery, Pensacola FL
University of Wisconsin, Memorial Union Gallery, Madison WI
University of Wisconsin, Allen Priebe Gallery, Oshkosh WI
University of Wisconsin, University Art Museum, Milwaukee WI
University of Wisconsin-Stout, Gallery 209, Menomonie WI

Utah Natural Resources & Energy, Parks & Recreation, Territorial Statehouse, Fillmore UT
Valentine Museum, Richmond VA
Valparaiso University, University Art Galleries and Collections, Valparaiso IN
Vanderbilt University, Art Gallery, Nashville TN
Virginia Commonwealth University, Anderson Gallery, Richmond VA
Virginia Museum, Danville Museum of Fine Arts and History, Danville VA
Walker Museum, Fairlee VT
Washburn University, Mulvane Art Center, Topeka KS
Washington County Museum of Fine Arts, Hagerstown MD
Washington State University, Museum of Art, Pullman WA
Wayne State College, Nordstrand Visual Arts Gallery, Wayne NE
Wesleyan University, Davison Art Center, Middletown CT
Western Michigan University, Gallery II, Kalamazoo MI
Western State College, Quigley Hall Art Gallery, Gunnison CO
Westminster College Art Gallery, New Wilmington PA
Westmoreland County Museum of Art, Greensburg PA
Wheaton College, Watson Gallery, Norton MA
White House, Washington DC
Whitney Museum of American Art, New York NY
Wichita Falls Museum and Art Center, Wichita Falls TX
Williams College, Museum of Art, Williamstown MA
Worcester Art Museum, Worcester MA
Yellowstone Art Center, Billings MT

RELIGIOUS ART

Art Complex Museum at Duxbury, Duxbury MA
Leo Baeck Institute, New York NY
Bass Museum of Art, Miami Beach FL
Biblical Arts Center, Dallas TX
Bob Jones University, Greenville SC
Breezewood Foundation Museum and Garden, Monkton MD
The Cathedral Museum, New York NY
Catholic Historical Society of Saint Paul, Saint Paul MN
Church of Jesus Christ of Latter-Day Saints, Museum of Church History and Art, Salt Lake City UT
Concordia Historical Institute, Saint Louis MO
Georgetown University, Art and History Museum, Washington DC
Harvard University, Dumbarton Oaks Research Library and Collections, Washington DC
Institute of Puerto Rican Culture, Dominican Convent Museum, San Juan PR
Institute of Puerto Rican Culture, Museo de Arte Religioso Porta Coeli, San Juan PR
Los Angeles County Museum of Art, Los Angeles CA
Louisiana Arts and Science Center, Baton Rouge LA
Mission San Luis Rey Museum, San Luis Rey CA
Mission San Miguel Museum, San Miguel CA
Moravian Historical Society, Whitefield House Museum, Nazareth PA
Musee d'Art de Joliette, Joliette PQ
Musee Kateri Tekakwitha, Cahughnawaga PQ
National Council on Art in Jewish Life, New York NY
Newark Museum, Newark NJ
Paine Art Center and Arboretum, Oshkosh WI
Rensselaer Newman Foundation Chapel and Cultural Center, Troy NY
Millicent Rogers Museum, Taos NM
Saint Bernard Foundation and Monastery, Miami Beach FL
Saint Mary's College of California, Hearst Art Gallery, Moraga CA
San Carlos Cathedral, Monterey CA
Southern Baptist Seminary Museum, Louisville KY
Timken Art Gallery, San Diego CA
Tome Parish Museum, Tome NM

United Methodist Church Commission on Archives and History, Madison NJ
United Methodist Historical Society, Lovely Lane Museum, Baltimore MD
University of Wisconsin, Elvehjem Museum of Art, Madison WI
University of Wisconsin, University Art Museum, Milwaukee WI
Valparaiso University, University Art Galleries and Collections, Valparaiso IN
Yeshiva University, Museum, New York NY

RENAISSANCE ART

Lyman Allyn Museum, New London CT
Ball State University, Art Gallery, Muncie IN
Baltimore Museum of Art, Baltimore MD
Berea College, Art Department Gallery, Berea KY
Columbia Museums of Art and Science, Columbia SC
El Paso Museum of Art, El Paso TX
M Flint Institute of Arts, Flint MI
Frick Collection, New York NY
Galleries of the Claremont Colleges, Claremont CA
Grand Rapids Art Museum, Grand Rapids MI
Hartwick College Fine Art Gallery, Oneonta NY
Harvard University, Busch-Reisinger Museum, Cambridge MA
Gertrude Herbert Memorial Institute of Art, Augusta GA
Historic Landmarks Foundation of Indiana, Morris-Butler House, Indianapolis IN
Honolulu Academy of Arts, Honolulu HI
Howard University, Gallery of Art, Washington DC
Indianapolis Museum of Art, Clowes Fund Collection, Indianapolis IN
Memphis Brooks Museum of Art, Memphis TN
Mint Museum of Art, Charlotte NC
Montclair State College, Gallery One, Upper Montclair NJ
New Orleans Museum of Art, New Orleans LA
Parrish Art Museum, Southampton NY
Portland Art Association, Portland Art Museum, Portland OR
San Diego Museum of Art, San Diego CA
Taft Museum, Cincinnati OH
University of Arizona, Museum of Art, Tucson AZ
University of Rochester, Memorial Art Gallery, Rochester NY
University of Utah, Utah Museum of Fine Arts, Salt Lake City UT
University of Wisconsin, Elvehjem Museum of Art, Madison WI
Vanderbilt University, Art Gallery, Nashville TN
Virginia Museum of Fine Arts, Richmond VA

RESTORATIONS

Huntington Galleries, Huntington WV

SCRIMSHAW

Heritage Plantation of Sandwich, Sandwich MA
Kendall Whaling Museum, Sharon MA
Old Dartmouth Historical Society, New Bedford Whaling Museum, New Bedford MA
Ships of The Sea Museum, Savannah GA

SCULPTURE

Albany Institute of History and Art, Albany NY
Albright College, Freedman Gallery, Reading PA
American Swedish Institute, Minneapolis MN
Arizona State University, University Art Collections, Tempe AZ
Art Gallery of Nova Scotia, Halifax NS
Art Gallery of Ontario, Toronto ON
Art Institute of Chicago, Chicago IL
Aspen Center for Visual Arts, Aspen CO
Atkins Museum of Fine Art, Kansas City MO
Atlanta Museum, Atlanta GA
Augusta Richmond County Museum, Augusta GA
Leo Baeck Institute, New York NY
Baldwin-Wallace College, Art Gallery, Berea OH
Baltimore Museum of Art, Baltimore MD
Bard College, William Cooper Procter Art Center, Annandale-on-Hudson NY
Bass Museum of Art, Miami Beach FL

Baylor University, Martin Museum of Art, Waco TX

Beaumont Art Museum, Beaumont TX

Beaverbrook Art Gallery, Fredericton NB

Beloit College, Wright Museum of Art, Beloit WI

Bergstrom Mahler Museum, Neenah WI

Berkshire Museum, Pittsfield MA

Birmingham Museum of Art, Birmingham AL

Blanden Memorial Art Museum, Fort Dodge IA

Boise Gallery of Art, Boise ID

Brigham Young University, B F Larsen Gallery, Provo UT

Brookgreen Gardens, Murrells Inlet SC

The Buffalo Fine Arts Academy, Albright-Knox Art Gallery, Buffalo NY

Butler Institute of American Art, Youngstown OH

Calvin College Center Art Gallery, Grand Rapids MI

Canton Art Institute, Canton OH

Capital University, Schumacher Gallery, Columbus OH

Carnegie Institute, Museum of Art, Pittsburgh PA

Amon Carter Museum, Fort Worth TX

Chesterwood, Stockbridge MA

Cincinnati Art Museum, Cincinnati OH

Sterling and Francine Clark Art Institute, Williamstown MA

Cleveland Museum of Art, Cleveland OH

Clinton Art Association Gallery, Clinton IA

College of Saint Benedict, Art Gallery, Saint Joseph MN

College of William and Mary, Joseph & Margaret Muscarelle Museum of Art, Williamsburg VA

College of Wooster Art Center Museum, Wooster OH

Colorado Springs Fine Arts Center, Colorado Springs CO

Columbia County Historical Society, Kinderhook NY

Columbus Museum of Art, Columbus OH

Columbus Museum of Arts and Sciences, Columbus GA

Coos Art Museum, Coos Bay OR

Cornell University, Herbert F Johnson Museum of Art, Ithaca NY

Country Art Gallery, Locust Valley NY

Cranbrook Academy of Art Museum, Bloomfield Hills MI

Creighton University Art Gallery, Omaha NE

Crocker Art Museum, Sacramento CA

Cummer Gallery of Art, DeEtte Holden Cummer Museum Foundation, Jacksonville FL

Delaware Art Museum, Wilmington DE

Del Mar College, Joseph A Cain Memorial Art Gallery, Corpus Christi TX

Drexel University Museum, Philadelphia PA

DuSable Museum of African American History, Chicago IL

Edmundson Art Foundation, Inc, Des Moines Art Center, Des Moines IA

Wharton Esherick Museum, Paoli PA

Essex Institute, Salem MA

Everhart Museum of Natural History, Science and Art, Scranton PA

Everson Museum of Art, Syracuse NY

Fine Arts Museum of the South, Mobile AL

M Flint Institute of Arts, Flint MI

Florida State University, Art Gallery, Tallahassee FL

Fort Lauderdale Museum of the Arts, Fort Lauderdale FL

Fort Wayne Museum of Art, Fort Wayne IN

Freeport Area Arts Council, Freeport Art Museum, Freeport IL

Frick Collection, New York NY

Fruitlands Museums, Harvard MA

Gaston County Museum of Art & History, Dallas NC

Georgetown College Gallery, Georgetown KY

Georgetown University, Art and History Museum, Washington DC

George Washington University, The Dimock Gallery, Washington DC

Goucher College, Kraushaar Auditorium Lobby Gallery, Towson MD

Grand Rapids Art Museum, Grand Rapids MI

Greenville College, Richard W Bock Sculpture Collection, Greenville IL

Solomon R Guggenheim Museum, New York NY

Guild Hall of East Hampton, Inc, Museum Section, East Hampton NY

Hartwick College Fine Art Gallery, Oneonta NY

Harvard University, Dumbarton Oaks Research Library and Collections, Washington DC

Harvard University, William Hayes Fogg Art Museum, Cambridge MA

Heard Museum, Phoenix AZ

Heckscher Museum, Huntington NY

Gertrude Herbert Memorial Institute of Art, Augusta GA

High Museum of Art, Atlanta GA

Hirshhorn Museum and Sculpture Garden, Washington DC

Hispanic Society of America, Museum, New York NY

Historic Landmarks Foundation of Indiana, Morris-Butler House, Indianapolis IN

Honolulu Academy of Arts, Honolulu HI

Housatonic Community College, Housatonic Museum of Art, Bridgeport CT

Howard University, Gallery of Art, Washington DC

Hudson River Museum, Yonkers NY

Hunter Museum of Art, Chattanooga TN

Huntington Library, Art Gallery and Botanical Gardens, San Marino CA

Hyde Collection, Glens Falls NY

Illinois State Museum of Natural History and Art, Springfield IL

Institute for Art & Urban Resources, Project Studios One, Long Island City NY

Institute of American Indian Arts Museum, Santa Fe NM

Iowa State Education Association, Salisbury House, Des Moines IA

Jersey City Museum Association, Jersey City NJ

Joslyn Art Museum, Omaha NE

Kalamazoo Institute of Arts, Genevieve and Donald Gilmore Art Center, Kalamazoo MI

Kent State University, School of Art Gallery, Kent OH

La Jolla Museum of Contemporary Art, La Jolla CA

Laumeier Sculpture Park, Saint Louis MO

Leanin Tree Museum of Western Art, Boulder CO

Lehigh University Art Galleries, Bethlehem PA

Le Musee Regional de Rimouski, Rimouski PQ

Lincoln Memorial Shrine, Redlands CA

Long Beach Museum of Art, Long Beach CA

Long Island Historical Society, Brooklyn NY

Los Angeles County Museum of Art, Los Angeles CA

Loyola University of Chicago, Martin D'Arcy Gallery of Art, Chicago IL

L'Universite Laval, Ecole des Arts Visuels de L'Universite Laval, Quebec PQ

The Robert McLaughlin Gallery, Oshawa ON

Marietta College, Grover M Hermann Fine Arts Center, Marietta OH

Marquette University, Museum of Art, Milwaukee WI

Maryhill Museum of Art, Goldendale WA

Massachusetts Institute of Technology, MIT Committee on Visual Arts (Hayden Gallery and MIT Permanent Collection), Cambridge MA

Marion Koogler McNay Art Museum, San Antonio TX

Memphis Brooks Museum of Art, Memphis TN

Meridian Museum of Art, Meridian MS

Metropolitan Museum and Art Center, Coral Gables FL

Metropolitan Museum of Art, New York NY

Miami-Dade Community College, South Campus, Art Gallery, Miami FL

Miami University Art Museum, Oxford OH

Michigan State University, Kresge Art Center Gallery, East Lansing MI

Middlebury College, Johnson Gallery, Middlebury VT

Midwest Museum of American Art, Elkhart IN

Millhouse-Bundy Performing & Fine Arts Center, Waitsfield VT

Millikin University, Kirkland Gallery, Decatur IL

Minneapolis Institute of Arts, Minneapolis MN

Minnesota Museum of Art, Saint Paul MN

Mint Museum of Art, Charlotte NC

Mississippi Valley Conservation Authority, R Tait McKenzie Memorial Museum, Almonte ON

James Monroe Law Office - Museum and Memorial Library, Fredericksburg VA

Mount Allison University, Owens Art Gallery, Sackville NB

Mount Holyoke College Art Museum, South Hadley MA

MPK Omega Co, Mike Kiefer Bio-Art Museum, Amarillo TX

Munson-Williams-Proctor Institute, Museum of Art, Utica NY

Musee du Quebec, Quebec PQ

Musee Historique de Vaudreuil, Vaudreuil Historical Museum, Vaudreuil PQ

Museum of Art of Ogunquit, Ogunquit ME

Museum of Arts and Sciences, Inc, Macon GA

Museum of Fine Arts, Boston MA

Museum of Fine Arts, Houston, Houston TX

Museum of Fine Arts, Springfield MA

Museum of Fine Arts of Saint Petersburg, Florida, Inc, Saint Petersburg FL

Museum of Modern Art, New York NY

Museum of the United States, Washington DC

Nassau County Museum of Fine Art, Roslyn NY

Nassua Community College, Firehouse Gallery, Garden City NY

National Air and Space Museum, Washington DC

National Museum of American Art, Washington DC

Nebraska Wesleyan University, Elder Gallery, Lincoln NE

Newark Museum, Newark NJ

New Orleans Museum of Art, New Orleans LA

New School for Social Research Art Center Gallery, New York NY

Elizabet Ney Museum, Austin TX

North Carolina Museum of Art, Raleigh NC

Northwestern College, Te Paske Gallery of Rowenhorst, Orange City IA

Norton Gallery and School of Art, West Palm Beach FL

R W Norton Art Gallery, Shreveport LA

Oakland Museum, Art Dept, Oakland CA

Oberlin College, Allen Memorial Art Museum, Oberlin OH

Oklahoma Art Center, Oklahoma City OK

Oklahoma Museum of Art, Oklahoma City OK

Olivet College, Armstrong Museum of Art and Archaeology, Olivet MI

Palm Springs Desert Museum, Inc, Palm Springs CA

Pennsylvania Academy of the Fine Arts, Galleries, Philadelphia PA

Pennsylvania State University, Museum of Art, University Park PA

Philbrook Art Center, Tulsa OK

Phillips Academy, Addison Gallery of American Art, Andover MA

Phoenix Art Museum, Phoenix AZ

Pioneer Town, Wimberley TX

Plains Art Museum, Main Gallery, Moorhead MN

Ponca City Cultural Center & Museum, Ponca City OK

Portland Art Association, Portland Art Museum, Portland OR

Portland Museum of Art, Portland ME

Purdue University Galleries, West Lafayette IN

Queen's University, Agnes Etherington Art Centre, Kingston ON

Red River Valley Museum, Vernon TX

Frederic Remington Art Museum, Ogdensburg NY

Rensselaer Newman Foundation Chapel and Cultural Center, Troy NY

Robert W Ryerss Library and Museum, Philadelphia PA

Saginaw Art Museum, Saginaw MI

Saint Clair County Community College, Jack R Hennesey Art Galleries, Port Huron MI

Saint Johnsbury Athenaeum, Saint Johnsbury VT

Saint John's Museum of Art, Wilmington NC

St Lawrence University, Richard F Brush Art Gallery, Canton NY

Saint Louis Art Museum, Saint Louis MO

Saint Mary's College of California, Hearst Art Gallery, Moraga CA

San Carlos Cathedral, Monterey CA

San Diego Museum of Art, San Diego CA
San Diego State University, Art Gallery, San Diego CA
San Francisco Museum of Modern Art, San Francisco CA
San Jose Museum of Art, San Jose CA
San Jose State University, Union Gallery, San Jose CA
Santa Barbara Museum of Art, Santa Barbara CA
Scottsdale Center for the Arts, Scottsdale AZ
Scripps College, Clark Humanities Museum, Claremont CA
Silverado Museum, Saint Helena CA
Norton Simon Museum, Pasadena CA
Smith-Mason Gallery and Museum, Washington DC
Society of the Cincinnati, Anderson House Museum, Washington DC
Southern Alleghenies Museum of Art, Loretto PA
Southern Illinois University, University Museum, Carbondale IL
Springfield Art Museum, Springfield MO
Stanford University, Museum of Art & Art Gallery, Stanford CA
State Art Museum of Florida, John & Mable Ringling Museum of Art, Sarasota FL
Staten Island Institute of Arts and Sciences, Staten Island NY
State University of New York at Albany, University Art Gallery, Albany NY
State University of New York at Purchase, Neuberger Museum, Purchase NY
State University of New York College at Fredonia, M C Rockefeller Arts Center Gallery, Fredonia NY
State University of New York College at Geneseo, Bertha V B Lederer Gallery, Geneseo NY
State University of New York College at Potsdam, Brainerd Art Gallery, Potsdam NY
Stephens College, Lewis James & Nellie Stratton Davis Art Gallery, Columbia MO
Storm King Art Center, Mountainville NY
Studio Museum in Harlem, New York NY
Tacoma Art Museum, Tacoma WA
Toledo Museum of Art, Toledo OH
Tomoka State Park Museum, Ormond Beach FL
Triton Museum of Art, Santa Clara CA
Tucson Museum of Art, Tucson AZ
Tyringham Art Galleries, Tyringham MA
Ulster County Community College, Visual Arts Gallery, Stone Ridge NY
United States Capitol Museum, Washington DC
United States Naval Academy Museum, Annapolis MD
University of Alberta, Ring House Gallery, Edmonton AB
University of Arizona, Museum of Art, Tucson AZ
University of Calgary, The Nickle Arts Museum, Calgary AB
University of California, Los Angeles, Frederick S Wight Art Gallery, Los Angeles CA
University of Chicago, David and Alfred Smart Gallery, Chicago IL
University of Colorado Art Galleries, Boulder CO
University of Connecticut, William Benton Museum of Art, Storrs CT
University of Delaware, University Art Collections, Newark DE
University of Iowa, Museum of Art, Iowa City IA
University of Kentucky, Art Museum, Lexington KY
University of Maryland, College Park, Art Gallery, College Park MD
University of Michigan, Kelsey Museum of Ancient and Medieval Archaeology, Ann Arbor MI
University of Michigan, Museum of Art, Ann Arbor MI
University of Minnesota, Tweed Museum of Art, Duluth MN
University of Minnesota, University Art Museum, Minneapolis MN
University of Missouri, Museum of Art and Archaeology, Columbia MO
University of Nebraska, Lincoln, Sheldon Memorial Art Gallery, Lincoln NE
University of New Mexico, University Art Museum, Albuquerque NM

University of North Carolina, The Ackland Art Museum, Chapel Hill NC
University of North Carolina at Greensboro, Weatherspoon Art Gallery, Greensboro NC
University of Notre Dame, Snite Museum of Art, Notre Dame IN
University of Pittsburgh, University Art Gallery, Pittsburgh PA
University of San Diego, Founders' Gallery, San Diego CA
University of Santa Clara, de Saisset Museum, Santa Clara CA
University of South Florida, Art Galleries, Tampa FL
University of Tennessee, Eleanor Dean Audigier Art Collection, Knoxville TN
University of Wisconsin, Memorial Union Gallery, Madison WI
University of Wisconsin, University Art Museum, Milwaukee WI
University of Wisconsin-Stout, Gallery 209, Menomonie WI
Valentine Museum, Richmond VA
Vancouver Art Gallery, Vancouver BC
Vassar College Art Gallery, Poughkeepsie NY
Virginia Museum of Fine Arts, Richmond VA
Walker Art Center, Minneapolis MN
Walker Museum, Fairlee VT
Washburn University, Mulvane Art Center, Topeka KS
Washington County Museum of Fine Arts, Hagerstown MD
Westmoreland County Museum of Art, Greensburg PA
Wheaton College, Watson Gallery, Norton MA
White House, Washington DC
Whitney Museum of American Art, New York NY
Wichita Art Museum, Wichita KS
Wichita State University, Edwin A Ulrich Museum of Art, Wichita KS
Widener University, Alfred O Deshong Museum, Chester PA
Wilkes College, Sordoni Art Gallery, Wilkes-Barre PA
Williams College, Museum of Art, Williamstown MA
Winnipeg Art Gallery, Winnipeg MB
Woodmere Art Museum, Philadelphia PA
Yale University, Art Gallery, New Haven CT
York Institute Museum, Saco ME
Zigler Museum, Jennings LA

SILVER

Albany Institute of History and Art, Albany NY
Allentown Art Museum, Allentown PA
Lyman Allyn Museum, New London CT
Baltimore Museum of Art, Baltimore MD
Berea College, Art Department Gallery, Berea KY
Berkshire Museum, Pittsfield MA
Birmingham Museum of Art, Birmingham AL
China Trade Museum, Milton MA
Sterling and Francine Clark Art Institute, Williamstown MA
Currier Gallery of Art, Manchester NH
DAR Museum, National Society Daughters of the American Revolution, Washington DC
Department of State, Diplomatic Reception Rooms, Washington DC
Detroit Institute of Arts, Detroit MI
Essex Institute, Salem MA
Francis E Fowler Jr Foundation Museum, Beverly Hills CA
Frick Art Museum, Pittsburgh PA
Hammond-Harwood House Association, Inc, Annapolis MD
Harvard University, William Hayes Fogg Art Museum, Cambridge MA
Hill-Stead Museum, Farmington CT
Historic Deerfield Inc, Deerfield MA
Huntington Galleries, Huntington WV
Le Musee Regional de Rimouski, Rimouski PQ
Litchfield Historical Society, Litchfield CT
Louisiana State University, Anglo-American Art Museum, Baton Rouge LA
Loyola University of Chicago, Martin D'Arcy Gallery of Art, Chicago IL

Maryland Historical Society Museum, Baltimore MD
McKissick Museums, Columbia SC
Mitchell Museum, Mount Vernon IL
James Monroe Law Office - Museum and Memorial Library, Fredericksburg VA
Montclair Art Museum, Montclair NJ
Musee d'Art de Saint-Laurent, Saint-Laurent PQ
Museum of Arts and Sciences, Cuban Museum, Planetarium, Daytona Beach FL
Museum of Fine Arts, Boston MA
National Society of Colonial Dames of the State of Maryland, Mount Clare Mansion, Baltimore MD
New Haven Colony Historical Society, New Haven CT
R W Norton Art Gallery, Shreveport LA
Portland Art Association, Portland Art Museum, Portland OR
Frederic Remington Art Museum, Ogdensburg NY
Lauren Rogers Library and Museum of Art, Laurel MS
The Rosenbach Museum and Library, Philadelphia PA
San Diego Museum of Art, San Diego CA
Shirley Plantation, Charles City VA
Spertus Museum of Judaica, Chicago IL
United States Naval Academy Museum, Annapolis MD
University of Iowa, Museum of Art, Iowa City IA
University of Santa Clara, de Saisset Museum, Santa Clara CA
University of Tennessee, Eleanor Dean Audigier Art Collection, Knoxville TN
University of Utah, Utah Museum of Fine Arts, Salt Lake City UT
Valentine Museum, Richmond VA
Virginia Museum of Fine Arts, Richmond VA
Yale University, Art Gallery, New Haven CT

SOUTHWESTERN ART

Amerind Foundation, Inc, Dragoon AZ
Colorado Springs Fine Arts Center, Colorado Springs CO
Douglas Art Association, Little Gallery, Douglas AZ
Harwood Foundation of the University of New Mexico, Taos NM
Heard Museum, Phoenix AZ
Northern Arizona University, Art Gallery, Flagstaff AZ
Palm Springs Desert Museum, Inc, Palm Springs CA
Roswell Museum and Art Center, Roswell NM
Yuma Fine Arts Association, Yuma Art Center, Yuma AZ

STAINED GLASS

Art Institute of Chicago, Chicago IL
Corcoran Museum, Washington DC
Higgins Armory Museum, Worcester MA
Jekyll Island Authority Museum, Jekyll Island GA

TAPESTRIES

American Swedish Institute, Minneapolis MN
Baltimore Museum of Art, Baltimore MD
College of Wooster Art Center Museum, Wooster OH
Corcoran Museum, Washington DC
Cummer Gallery of Art, DeEtte Holden Cummer Museum Foundation, Jacksonville FL
Frick Art Museum, Pittsburgh PA
Higgins Armory Museum, Worcester MA
Hill-Stead Museum, Farmington CT
Hyde Collection, Glens Falls NY
Iowa State Education Association, Salisbury House, Des Moines IA
R W Norton Art Gallery, Shreveport LA
Norton Simon Museum, Pasadena CA
Society of the Cincinnati, Anderson House Museum, Washington DC
University of Houston, Sarah Campbell Blaffer Gallery, Houston TX
University of San Diego, Founders' Gallery, San Diego CA

Collections

B G Canton Gallery

Stanford University, Museum of Art & Art Gallery, Stanford CA

Carder Steuben Glass Collection

The Rockwell Museum, Corning NY

Carney Ceramics Collection

Parrish Art Museum, Southampton NY

Emily Carr Collection

Vancouver Art Gallery, Vancouver BC

Carrington Collection of Chinese Art

Rhode Island Historical Society, John Brown House, Providence RI

John H Cassell Collection of Political Cartoons

Hartwick College Fine Art Gallery, Oneonta NY

Cass Wedgewood Collection

Wheaton College, Watson Gallery, Norton MA

Chagall Graphics Collection

San Jose State University, Art Gallery, San Jose CA

Mark Chagall Stained Glass Collection

Art Institute of Chicago, Chicago IL

Conrad Wise Chapman Oils Collection

Valentine Museum, Richmond VA

Child Art Collection

Illinois State University, University Museums, Normal IL

Christian Brothers Collection

Wine Museum of San Francisco, San Francisco CA

Frederic Edwin Church Collection

Olana State Historic Site, Hudson NY

Civil War Collection

Chicago Historical Society, Chicago IL
Historic New Orleans Collection, Kemper and Leila Williams Foundation, New Orleans LA
Jackson County Historical Society, 1859 Marshal's House, Jail & Museum, Independence MO
Kiah Museum, Savannah GA
Library of Congress, Washington DC
Muscatine Art Center, Muscatine IA
Museum of Arts and History, Port Huron MI
Phillips County Museum, Helena AR
Jackson County Historical Society, John Wornall House Museum, Independence MO

Clark European Collection

Corcoran Museum, Washington DC

Laura A Clubb Collection of Paintings

Philbrook Art Center, Tulsa OK

Coe Collection

Coe College, Gordon Fennell Gallery & Marvin Cone Gallery, Cedar Rapids IA

Colburn Gemstone Collection

McKissick Museums, Columbia SC

Colsa Collection

Saint Mary's Romanian Orthodox Church, Romanian Ethnic Museum, Cleveland OH

Cone Collection of French Art

Baltimore Museum of Art, Baltimore MD

Marvin Cone Oils Collection

Coe College, Gordon Fennell Gallery & Marvin Cone Gallery, Cedar Rapids IA

Copeland Collection

Delaware Art Museum, Wilmington DE

Cotter Collection

Saint Mary's College, Moreau Gallery Three, Notre Dame IN

Cowan Collection

The Parthenon, Nashville TN

Craig Collection of Edna Hibel

Edna Hibel Art Foundation, Hibel Museum of Art, Riviera Beach FL

Crozier Collection of Chinese Art

Philadelphia Museum of Art, Philadelphia PA

Cummings Collection

Colby Museum of Art, Waterville ME

Currier and Ives Lithograph Collection

Diamond M Foundation Museum, Snyder TX

Charles Cutts Collection

Sierra Nevada Museum of Art, Reno NV

Cybis Collection

Mercer County Community College Gallery, Trenton NJ

Elise Agnus Daingerfield 18th Century Collection

Baltimore Museum of Art, Baltimore MD

Cyrus Dallin Bronze Collection

Springville Museum of Art, Springville UT

Dana Collection

University of Montana, Gallery of Visual Arts, Missoula MT

Norman Davis Collection of Classical Art

Seattle Art Museum, Seattle WA

D'Berger Collection

University of Santa Clara, de Saisset Museum, Santa Clara CA

Agnes Delano Watercolor and Print Collection

Howard University, Gallery of Art, Washington DC

Maynard Dixon Collection

Brigham Young University, B F Larsen Gallery, Provo UT

F B Doane Collection of Western American Art

Frontier Times Museum, Bandera TX

Dorflinger Glass Collection

Everhart Museum of Natural History, Science and Art, Scranton PA

Doughty Bird Collection

Reynolda House, Inc, Winston-Salem NC

Doughty Porcelain Collection

Parrish Art Museum, Southampton NY

Grace G Drayton Collection

G G Drayton Club, Salem OH

Marie Dressler Collection

Kiah Museum, Savannah GA

Anthony J Drexel Collection of 19th Century Paintings & Sculptures

Drexel University Museum, Philadelphia PA

Driebe Collection of Paintings

Lehigh University Art Galleries, Bethlehem PA

Dunbarton Print Collection

Saint Mary's College, Moreau Gallery Three, Notre Dame IN

Dunnigan Collection of Etchings

Parrish Art Museum, Southampton NY

Harvey Dunn Paintings Collection

South Dakota State University, South Dakota Memorial Art Center, Brookings SD

Holliday Collection of Neo-Impressionist Paintings

Indianapolis Museum of Art, Indianapolis IN

Oliver Wendell Holmes Stereographic Collection

Canton Art Institute, Canton OH

Winslow Homer Collection

Bowdoin College, Museum of Art & Peary-
    MacMillan Arctic Museum, Brunswick ME
Colby Museum of Art, Waterville ME

Winslow Homer Woodcut Collection

State Capitol Museum, Olympia WA

Samuel Houghton Great Basin Collection

Sierra Nevada Museum of Art, Reno NV

J Harry Howard Gemstone Collection

McKissick Museums, Columbia SC

Oscar Howe Collection

University of South Dakota Art Galleries,
    Vermillion SD

Anna C Hoyt Collection of Old Masters

Vanderbilt University, Art Gallery, Nashville TN

Gardiner Greene Hubbard Endowment Collection of Prints

Library of Congress, Washington DC

Winifred Kimball Hudnut Collection

University of Utah, Utah Museum of Fine Arts, Salt
    Lake City UT

Marie Hull Collection

Delta State University, Fielding L Wright Art
    Center, Cleveland MS

J Marvin Hunter Western Americana Collection

Frontier Times Museum, Bandera TX

Charles & Elsa Hutzler Memorial Collection of Contemporary Sculpture

Baltimore Museum of Art, Baltimore MD

International Collection of Child Art

Illinois State University, University Museums,
    Normal IL

Isaacson Porcelain Collection

Seattle Art Museum, Seattle WA

Harry L Jackson Print Collection

Murray State University, Clara M Eagle Gallery,
    Murray KY

Mary Frick Jacobs European Art Collection

Baltimore Museum of Art, Baltimore MD

Japanese Prints

University of Southwestern Louisiana, University
    Art Museum, Lafayette LA

Japanese Woodcut Collection

Oregon State University, Fairbanks Gallery,
    Corvallis OR

Jarves Collection of Italian Paintings

Yale University, Art Gallery, New Haven CT

Jette Collection

Colby Museum of Art, Waterville ME

E Johnson Collection

Saint Louis County Historical Society, Duluth MN

John G Johnson Collection of Old Masters

Philadelphia Museum of Art, Philadelphia PA

S C Johnson & Son Collection

National Museum of American Art, Washington
    DC

F B Johnston Collection

Library of Congress, Washington DC

Harriet Lane Johnston Collection

National Museum of American Art, Washington
    DC

T Catesby Jones Collection of 20th Century European Art

Virginia Museum of Fine Arts, Richmond VA

Sylvan Lehman Joseph Print Collection

Bates College, Treat Gallery, Lewiston ME

Eugene S Juda Memorial Engravings Collection

Albrecht Art Museum, Saint Joseph MO

Vasily Kandinsky Collection

Solomon R Guggenheim Museum, New York NY

William Keith Paintings Collection

Saint Mary's College of California, Hearst Art
    Gallery, Moraga CA

Kelsey Collection

Mercer County Community College Gallery,
    Trenton NJ

Kemper Collection of American Paintings

Albrecht Art Museum, Saint Joseph MO

Kempsmith Collection

Lehigh University Art Galleries, Bethlehem PA

Victor Kiam Painting Collection

New Orleans Museum of Art, New Orleans LA

Darius Kinsey Photograph Collection

Whatcom Museum of History and Art, Bellingham
    WA

Paul Klee Collection

Solomon R Guggenheim Museum, New York NY

Klee Graphics Collection

San Jose State University, Art Gallery, San Jose
    CA

Erin Kohn Doll Collection

Columbia Museums of Art and Science, Columbia
    SC

Kolb Graphics Collection

University of Santa Clara, de Saisset Museum,
    Santa Clara CA

Korean Pottery Collection

Allegheny College, Bowman, Megahan and Penelec
    Galleries, Meadville PA

Kraft-Ball Collection of Roman and Syrian Glass

Ball State University, Art Gallery, Muncie IN

Krannert Memorial Collection

Indiana Central University, Leah Ransburg Art
    Gallery, Indianapolis IN

Samuel H Kress Collection

Allentown Art Museum, Allentown PA
Columbia Museums of Art and Science, Columbia
    SC
El Paso Museum of Art, El Paso TX
High Museum of Art, Atlanta GA
Howard University, Gallery of Art, Washington DC
Memphis Brooks Museum of Art, Memphis TN
North Carolina Museum of Art, Raleigh NC
Philbrook Art Center, Tulsa OK
Portland Art Association, Portland Art Museum,
    Portland OR
Trinity College, Austin Arts Center, Hartford CT
University of Arizona, Museum of Art, Tucson AZ
University of Miami, Lowe Art Museum, Coral
    Gables FL
Vanderbilt University, Art Gallery, Nashville TN

Samuel H Kress Collection of Renaissance Art

Berea College, Art Department Gallery, Berea KY
Honolulu Academy of Arts, Honolulu HI
New Orleans Museum of Art, New Orleans LA

Kress Study Collection

University of Notre Dame, Snite Museum of Art,
    Notre Dame IN

Irma Kruse Collection

Hastings Museum, Hastings NE

Kurdian Collection of Mexican Art

Wichita Art Museum, Wichita KS

Labhard Photography Collection

University of New Mexico, University Art
   Museum, Albuquerque NM

**Mary Andrews Ladd Collection of Japanese
Prints**

Portland Art Association, Portland Art Museum,
   Portland OR

**William S Ladd Collection of Pre-Columbian
Art**

Portland Art Association, Portland Art Museum,
   Portland OR

B Lafon Drawing Collection

Historic New Orleans Collection, Kemper and Leila
   Williams Foundation, New Orleans LA

Norman LaLiberte Collection

Saint Mary's College, Moreau Gallery Three, Notre
   Dame IN

Sylvan and Mary Lang Collection

Marion Koogler McNay Art Museum, San Antonio
   TX

**John D Lankenau Collection of 19th
Century Paintings & Sculptures**

Drexel University Museum, Philadelphia PA

Mauricio Lasansky Print Collection

University of Iowa, Museum of Art, Iowa City IA

Samuel K Lathrop Collection

University of Miami, Lowe Art Museum, Coral
   Gables FL

Latin American Art Collection

Museum of Modern Art of Latin America,
   Washington DC

Latter-Schlesinger Miniature Collection

New Orleans Museum of Art, New Orleans LA

Clarence Laughlin Photograph Collection

Historic New Orleans Collection, Kemper and Leila
   Williams Foundation, New Orleans LA

**Roberta Campbell Lawson Collection of
Indian Artifacts**

Philbrook Art Center, Tulsa OK

Lawther Collection of Ethiopian Crosses

Portland Art Association, Portland Art Museum,
   Portland OR

Layton Collection

Milwaukee Art Museum, Milwaukee WI

Robert Lehman Collection

Metropolitan Museum of Art, New York NY

Dr Louis Levy Collection of American Prints

Memphis Brooks Museum of Art, Memphis TN

**Julius Levy Memorial Collection of Oriental
Art**

Baltimore Museum of Art, Baltimore MD

Lewis Collection of Classical Antiquities

Portland Art Association, Portland Art Museum,
   Portland OR

Lewis-Kneberg Collection

University of Tennessee, Frank H McClung
   Museum, Knoxville TN

Dan Leyrer Photograph Collection

Historic New Orleans Collection, Kemper and Leila
   Williams Foundation, New Orleans LA

Jonas Lie Collection of Panama Canal Oils

United States Military Academy, West Point
   Museum, West Point NY

Liedesdorf Collection of European Armor

United States Military Academy, West Point
   Museum, West Point NY

Jacques Lipchitz Sculpture Collection

Metropolitan Museum and Art Center, Coral
   Gables FL
University of Arizona, Museum of Art, Tucson AZ

Lithophane Collection

Blair Museum of Lithophanes and Carved Waxes,
   Toledo OH

Alain Locke Collection of African Art

Howard University, Gallery of Art, Washington DC

Lockwood-deForest Collection

Mark Twain Memorial, Hartford CT

George A Lucas Collection

Baltimore Museum of Art, Baltimore MD

McCrellis Doll Collection

Rhode Island Historical Society, John Brown
   House, Providence RI

McFadden Collection of Old Masters

Philadelphia Museum of Art, Philadelphia PA

McLanahan Memorial Collection

Baltimore Museum of Art, Baltimore MD

George F McMurray Collection

Trinity College, Austin Arts Center, Hartford CT

**Paul McPharlin Collection of Theatre &
Graphic Arts**

Detroit Institute of Arts, Detroit MI

Ernst Mahler Collection of Germanic Glass

Bergstrom Mahler Museum, Neenah WI

Richard Mandell Collection

McKissick Museums, Columbia SC

Mildred Many Memorial Collection

The Indian Museum, Wichita KS

Marghab Linens Collection

South Dakota State University, South Dakota
   Memorial Art Center, Brookings SD

John Marin Collection

Colby Museum of Art, Waterville ME

Norma & John C Marin Collection

University of Maine at Machias, Torrey Gallery,
   Machias ME

**Markley Collection of Ancient Peruvian
Ceramics**

Pennsylvania State University, Museum of Art,
   University Park PA

Marks Collection of Pre-Columbian Art

East Tennessee State University, Carroll Reece
   Museum, Johnson City TN

Jacob Marks Memorial Collection

Memphis Academy of Arts, Frank T Tobey
   Gallery, Memphis TN

William H Marlatt Collection

Cleveland Museum of Art, Cleveland OH

Fred Dana Marsh Collection

Tomoka State Park Museum, Ormond Beach FL

**Martinez-Canas Collection of Latin
American Paintings**

Metropolitan Museum and Art Center, Coral
   Gables FL

Masonic Collection

Museum of Our National Heritage, Lexington MA

Saidie A May Collection

Baltimore Museum of Art, Baltimore MD

Meissen Porcelain Collection

Cummer Gallery of Art, DeEtte Holden Cummer
Museum Foundation, Jacksonville FL
Virginia Museum of Fine Arts, Richmond VA

Charles M Messer Leica Camera Collection

Miami University Art Museum, Oxford OH

Conger Metcalf Collection

Coe College, Gordon Fennell Gallery & Marvin
Cone Gallery, Cedar Rapids IA

Mexican American Art

Committee for Hispanic Arts & Research, Austin
TX

Michael Silver Collection

University of Utah, Utah Museum of Fine Arts, Salt
Lake City UT

Michener Collection of American Paintings

University of Texas at Austin, Archer M
Huntington Art Gallery, Austin TX

Military Art Collection

Fort George G Meade Museum, Fort Meade MD
National Infantry Museum, Fort Benning GA

Samuel & Tobie Miller Collection

Baltimore Museum of Art, Baltimore MD

Millington-Barnard Collection

University of Mississippi, University Museums,
Oxford MS

**Albert K Mitchell Russell-Remington
Collection**

National Cowboy Hall of Fame and Western
Heritage Center, Oklahoma City OK

Molinari Coin Collection

Bowdoin College, Museum of Art & Peary-
MacMillan Arctic Museum, Brunswick ME

Marianne Moore Archive Collection

The Rosenbach Museum and Library, Philadelphia
PA

Moore Collection

University of Illinois, Krannert Art Museum,
Champaign IL

Grace Moore Collection

University of Tennessee, Frank H McClung
Museum, Knoxville TN

Henry Moore Sculpture Collection

Art Gallery of Ontario, Toronto ON

**Morgenroth Collection of Renaissance
Medals**

University of California, Santa Barbara, University
Art Museum, Santa Barbara CA

Mormon Collection

Church of Jesus Christ of Latter-Day Saints,
Museum of Church History and Art, Salt Lake
City UT

**Howard J Morrison Jr Osteological
Collection**

Kiah Museum, Savannah GA

Morse Collection

Beloit College, Wright Museum of Art, Beloit WI

William Moser Collection of African Art

Fort Wayne Museum of Art, Fort Wayne IN

Motion Pictures

MPK Omega Co, Mike Kiefer Bio-Art Museum,
Amarillo TX

William Sidney Mount Collection

The Museums at Stony Brook, Stony Brook NY

Arnold Mountfort Collection

University of Santa Clara, de Saisset Museum,
Santa Clara CA

Mourot Collection of Meissen Porcelain

Virginia Museum of Fine Arts, Richmond VA

**Roland P Murdock Collection of American
Art**

Wichita Art Museum, Wichita KS

Musical Instruments

Metropolitan Museum of Art, New York NY

**Gwen Houston Naftzger Collection of
Porcelain Birds**

Wichita Art Museum, Wichita KS

**L S and Ida L Naftzger Collection of Prints
and Drawings**

Wichita Art Museum, Wichita KS

**M C Naftzger Collection of Russell
Paintings**

Wichita Art Museum, Wichita KS

Nause & Graff Print Collection

Northern Illinois University, Swen Parson Gallery
and Gallery 200, De Kalb IL

Neuhoff Collection of English Furniture

Columbia Museums of Art and Science, Columbia
SC

Newcomb Pottery Collection

West Baton Rouge Museum, Port Allen LA

Harry T Norton Collection of Glass

Montreal Museum of Fine Arts, Montreal PQ

Alice B Nunn Silver Collection

Portland Art Association, Portland Art Museum,
Portland OR

Frances Oliver Collection of Procelain

Birmingham Museum of Art, Birmingham AL

Olsen Collection

University of Illinois, Krannert Art Museum,
Champaign IL

**Oppenheimer Collection of Gothic and
Medieval Art**

Marion Koogler McNay Art Museum, San Antonio
TX

Oriental Furniture Collection

Atkins Museum of Fine Art, Kansas City MO

Parish Collection of Furniture

Frederic Remington Art Museum, Ogdensburg NY

Parker Lace Collection

Montreal Museum of Fine Arts, Montreal PQ

**Samuel Parrish Collection of Renaissance
Art**

Parrish Art Museum, Southampton NY

J G D'Arcy Paul Collection

Baltimore Museum of Art, Baltimore MD

John Barton Payne Collection

Virginia Museum of Fine Arts, Richmond VA

Peabody Institute Collection

Baltimore Museum of Art, Baltimore MD

Adelaide Pearson Collection

Colby Museum of Art, Waterville ME

**Samuel Pees Contemporary Painting
Collection**

Allegheny College, Bowman, Megahan and Penelec
Galleries, Meadville PA

Pendleton Collection

Kelly-Griggs House Museum, Red Bluff CA

Pendleton House Decorative Arts Collection

Rhode Island School of Design, Museum of Art,
Providence RI

Joseph Pennell Collection

George Washington University, The Dimock Gallery, Washington DC

Pennell Endowment Collection of Prints

Library of Congress, Washington DC

Mel Pfaelzer Surrealist Collection

Northern Illinois University, Swen Parson Gallery and Gallery 200, De Kalb IL

Leonard Pfeiffer Collection

University of Arizona, Museum of Art, Tucson AZ

Phelps Collection

Delaware Art Museum, Wilmington DE

Walter J Phillips Collection

Banff Centre, Walter Phillips Gallery, Banff AB

Phillips Portrait Collection

Parrish Art Museum, Southampton NY

George Phippen Memorial Western Bronze Collection

Desert Caballeros Western Museum, Wickenburg AZ

Duncan Phyfe Furniture Collection

Taft Museum, Cincinnati OH

Albert Pilavin Collection of 20th Century American Arts

Rhode Island School of Design, Museum of Art, Providence RI

Lucile Pillow Porcelain Collection

Montreal Museum of Fine Arts, Montreal PQ

Pitkin Collection of Oriental Art

Beloit College, Wright Museum of Art, Beloit WI

Sylvia Pizitz Collection

Birmingham Museum of Art, Birmingham AL

Poindexter Collection

University of Montana, Gallery of Visual Arts, Missoula MT

William J Pollock Collection of American Indian Art

Colby Museum of Art, Waterville ME

Potlatch Collection

University of Minnesota, Tweed Museum of Art, Duluth MN

Charles Pratt Collection of Chinese Jades

Vassar College Art Gallery, Poughkeepsie NY

Lillian Thomas Pratt Collection of Czarist Jewels

Virginia Museum of Fine Arts, Richmond VA

Elisabeth Severance Prentiss Collection

Cleveland Museum of Art, Cleveland OH

William Henry Price Memorial Collection of Oil Paintings

Oregon State University, Memorial Union Art Gallery, Corvallis OR

Pulsifer Collection of Winslow Homer

Colby Museum of Art, Waterville ME

Putnam Collection

Timken Art Gallery, San Diego CA

Quaker Art Collection

Swarthmore College, Friends Historical Library, Swarthmore PA

Freda & Clara Radoff Mexican Print Collection

University of Houston, Sarah Campbell Blaffer Gallery, Houston TX

Natacha Rambova Egyptian Collection

University of Utah, Utah Museum of Fine Arts, Salt Lake City UT

Rand Collection of American Indian Art

Montclair Art Museum, Montclair NJ

Rasmussen Collection of Eskimo Arts

Portland Art Association, Portland Art Museum, Portland OR

W T Rawleigh Collection

Freeport Area Arts Council, Freeport Art Museum, Freeport IL

Ray American Indian Collection

Red River Valley Museum, Vernon TX

Frederic Remington Collection

Bradford Brinton Memorial Ranch Museum, Big Horn WY
Buffalo Bill Memorial Association, Cody WY
R W Norton Art Gallery, Shreveport LA
St Lawrence University, Richard F Brush Art Gallery, Canton NY

Richards Coin Collection

Hastings Museum, Hastings NE

General Lawrason Riggs Collection

Baltimore Museum of Art, Baltimore MD

Rindisbacher Watercolor Collection

United States Military Academy, West Point Museum, West Point NY

William Ritschel Collection

Monterey Peninsula Museum of Art, Monterey CA

Rives Collection of Palestinian Art

Birmingham Museum of Art, Birmingham AL

David Roberts Collection

Riverside County Art and Cultural Center, Edward-Dean Museum of Decorative Arts, Cherry Valley CA

Roberts Sculpture Collection

Portland Art Association, Portland Art Museum, Portland OR

David Robinson Collection of Antiquities

University of Mississippi, University Museums, Oxford MS

Marion Sharp Robinson Collection

University of Utah, Utah Museum of Fine Arts, Salt Lake City UT

Abby Aldrich Rockefeller Collection of Japanese Art

Rhode Island School of Design, Museum of Art, Providence RI

Robert F Rockwell Foundation Collection

The Rockwell Museum, Corning NY

Rodeo Portrait Collection

National Cowboy Hall of Fame and Western Heritage Center, Oklahoma City OK

Grace Rainey Rogers Collection

Cleveland Museum of Art, Cleveland OH

John Rogers Sculpture Collection

Saginaw Art Museum, Saginaw MI

Roland Art Collection

The Haggin Museum, Petzinger Memorial Library, Stockton CA

Edward Rose Collection of Ceramics

Brandeis University, Rose Art Museum, Waltham MA

Guy Rowe Wax Drawings Collections

Angelo State University, Houston Harte University Center, San Angelo TX

Peter Paul Rubens Collection

State Art Museum of Florida, John & Mable Ringling Museum of Art, Sarasota FL

Charles M Russell Collection

Bradford Brinton Memorial Ranch Museum, Big Horn WY
Buffalo Bill Memorial Association, Cody WY
William S Hart Museum, Newhall CA
R W Norton Art Gallery, Shreveport LA
C M Russell Museum, Great Falls MT

Charles M Russell Paintings

Wichita Art Museum, Wichita KS

Sackler Collection

Metropolitan Museum of Art, New York NY

Saint Joseph Photographic Collection

Albrecht Art Museum, Saint Joseph MO

Wilbur Sandison Photography Collection

Whatcom Museum of History and Art, Bellingham WA

Sandwich Glass Collection

Brockton Art Museum, Brockton MA

Sargent Collection of American Indian Art

Montclair Art Museum, Montclair NJ

Sawhill Artifact Collection

James Madison University, Sawhill Gallery, Harrisonburg VA

Jonathan Sax Print Collection

University of Minnesota, Tweed Museum of Art, Duluth MN

Bertha Schaefer Bequest Collection

University of Nebraska, Lincoln, Sheldon Memorial Art Gallery, Lincoln NE

Eugene Schaefer Collection of Ancient Glass

Newark Museum, Newark NJ

Galka Scheyer Blue Four Collection

Norton Simon Museum, Pasadena CA

Alice F Schott Doll Collection

Santa Barbara Museum of Art, Santa Barbara CA

Schreyvogel Collection

National Cowboy Hall of Fame and Western Heritage Center, Oklahoma City OK

Schuette Woodland Indian Collection

Rahr-West Museum, Manitowoc WI

Schwartz Collection of Chinese Ivories

Rahr-West Museum, Manitowoc WI

Scotese Graphic Collection

Columbia Museums of Art and Science, Columbia SC

Philip Sears Sculpture Collection

Fruitlands Museums, Harvard MA

Seibels Collection

Columbia Museums of Art and Science, Columbia SC

Shaker Collection

Hancock Shaker Village, Inc, Pittsfield MA
Shaker Museum, Old Chatham NY

John L Severance Collection

Cleveland Museum of Art, Cleveland OH

Sharp Collection of Glass

Frederic Remington Art Museum, Ogdensburg NY

Inglis Sheldon-Williams Collection

Regina Public Library, Dunlop Art Gallery, Regina SK

William Ludlow Sheppard Watercolor Collection

Valentine Museum, Richmond VA

David M Shoup Collection of Korean Pottery

Allegheny College, Bowman, Megahan and Penelec Galleries, Meadville PA

Franz W Sichel Collection of Glass

Wine Museum of San Francisco, San Francisco CA

B Simon Lithography Collection

Historic New Orleans Collection, Kemper and Leila Williams Foundation, New Orleans LA

Eric Sloan Collection

Connecticut Historical Commission, Sloane-Stanley Museum, Kent CT

Sloan Collection

Valparaiso University, University Art Galleries and Collections, Valparaiso IN

Helen S Slosberg Collection of Oceanic Art

Brandeis University, Rose Art Museum, Waltham MA

C R Smith Collection of Western American Art

University of Texas at Austin, Archer M Huntington Art Gallery, Austin TX

Smith Painting Collection

Woodmere Art Museum, Philadelphia PA

Smith-Patterson Memorial Collection

Delta State University, Fielding L Wright Art Center, Cleveland MS

Sonnenschein Collection

Cornell College, Armstrong Gallery, Mount Vernon IA

Southeast Asian Artifact Collection

Illinois State University, University Museums, Normal IL

Leon Spilliaert Collection

Metropolitan Museum of Art, New York NY

Benton Spruance Print Collection

Beaver College, Richard Eugene Fuller Gallery of Art, Glenside PA

Anisoara Stan Collection

Saint Mary's Romanian Orthodox Church, Romanian Ethnic Museum, Cleveland OH

Stanford Family Collection

Stanford University, Museum of Art & Art Gallery, Stanford CA

Staples Collection of Indonesian Art

James Madison University, Sawhill Gallery, Harrisonburg VA

John Steele Print Collection

East Tennessee State University, Carroll Reece Museum, Johnson City TN

Stern Collection

Philadelphia Museum of Art, Philadelphia PA

Harold P Stern Collection of Oriental Art

Vanderbilt University, Art Gallery, Nashville TN

Stern-Davis Collection of Peruvian Painting

New Orleans Museum of Art, New Orleans LA

Robert Louis Stevenson Collection

Silverado Museum, Saint Helena CA

Stiegel Glass Collection

Philadelphia Museum of Art, Philadelphia PA

Alfred Stieglitz Collection

Fisk University Museum of Art, Nashville TN

Clyfford Still Collection

San Francisco Museum of Modern Art, San Francisco CA

Thomas D Stimson Memorial Collection of Far Eastern Art

Seattle Art Museum, Seattle WA

Stoddard Collection of Greek Vases

Yale University, Art Gallery, New Haven CT

Ala Story Print Collection

University of California, Santa Barbara, University Art Museum, Santa Barbara CA

Thomas Sully Gallery Collection

Longwood College, Bedford Gallery, Farmville VA

Sully Portrait Collection

United States Military Academy, West Point
Museum, West Point NY

Tabor Collection of Oriental Art

Philbrook Art Center, Tulsa OK

**Robert H Tannahill Collection of
Impressionist & Post Impressionist
Paintings**

Detroit Institute of Arts, Detroit MI

Taylor Collection of Southwestern Art

Colorado Springs Fine Arts Center, Colorado
Springs CO

**Justin K Thannhauser Collection of
Impressionist & Post-Impressionist
Paintings**

Solomon R Guggenheim Museum, New York NY

Thieme Collection of Paintings

Fort Wayne Museum of Art, Fort Wayne IN

Thorne Miniature Collection

Art Institute of Chicago, Chicago IL

Tibetan Art Collection

Jacque Marchais Center of Tibetan Arts, Inc, Staten
Island NY

Louis Comfort Tiffany Collection

Morse Gallery of Art, Winter Park FL

Tiffany Glass Collection

Houston Antique Museum, Chattanooga TN
Johns Hopkins University, Evergreen House,
Baltimore MD
Mark Twain Memorial, Hartford CT

William Toben Memorial Collection

Albrecht Art Museum, Saint Joseph MO

Trees Collection

University of Illinois, Krannert Art Museum,
Champaign IL

Trovwer Silver Collection

University of Utah, Utah Museum of Fine Arts, Salt
Lake City UT

Tucker Porcelain Collection

Philadelphia Museum of Art, Philadelphia PA

J M W Turner Watercolor Collection

Indianapolis Museum of Art, Indianapolis IN
The Turner Museum, Denver CO

**George P Tweed Memorial Collection of
Paintings**

University of Minnesota, Tweed Museum of Art,
Duluth MN

Tyson Collection

Philadelphia Museum of Art, Philadelphia PA

Uhry Print Collection

High Museum of Art, Atlanta GA

Doris Ulmann Photography Collection

Berea College, Art Department Gallery, Berea KY

**Edward Virginus Valentine Sculpture
Collection**

Valentine Museum, Richmond VA

Vanderpoel Collection

Norwich Free Academy, Slater Memorial Museum
& Converse Art Gallery, Norwich CT

**Van Ess Collection of Renaissance and
Baroque Art**

Hartwick College Fine Art Gallery, Oneonta NY

Matthew Vassar Collection

Vassar College Art Gallery, Poughkeepsie NY

James Ven Der Zee Photography Collection

Studio Museum in Harlem, New York NY

Ellis Verink Photograph Collection

Polk Public Museum, Lakeland FL

Voertman Collection

North Texas State University, Art Gallery, Denton
TX

Von Schleinitz Collection

Milwaukee Art Museum, Milwaukee WI

J H Wade Collection

Cleveland Museum of Art, Cleveland OH

Walker Collection of French Impressionists

Corcoran Museum, Washington DC

Cloud Wampler Collection of Oriental Art

Everson Museum of Art, Syracuse NY

**Felix M Warburg Collection of Medieval
Sculpture**

Vassar College Art Gallery, Poughkeepsie NY

Andy Warhol Collection

University of Maryland, College Park, Art Gallery,
College Park MD

Warren Collection of Classical Antiquities

Bowdoin College, Museum of Art & Peary-
MacMillan Arctic Museum, Brunswick ME

**Watkins Collection of American and
European Paintings**

American University, Watkins Art Gallery,
Washington DC

Homer Watson Collection

Kitchener-Waterloo Art Gallery, Kitchener ON

William Watson Collection of Ceramics

Lemoyne Center for the Visual Arts, Tallahassee FL

Samuel Bell Waugh Collection

Edwin A Ulrich Museum, Hyde Park NY

Frederick J Waugh Collection

Edwin A Ulrich Museum, Hyde Park NY

Coulten Waugh Collection

Edwin A Ulrich Museum, Hyde Park NY

**Ulrich Collection of Frederick J Waugh
Paintings**

Wichita State University, Edwin A Ulrich Museum
of Art, Wichita KS

Wax Collection

Blair Museum of Lithophanes and Carved Waxes,
Toledo OH

John Wayne Collection

National Cowboy Hall of Fame and Western
Heritage Center, Oklahoma City OK

**Weatherhead Collection of Contemporary
Graphics**

Fort Wayne Museum of Art, Fort Wayne IN

Wedgwood Collection

Buten Museum of Wedgwood, Merion PA
R W Norton Art Gallery, Shreveport LA

Teresa Jackson Weill Collection

Brandeis University, Rose Art Museum, Waltham
MA

J Alden Weir Collection

Brigham Young University, B F Larsen Gallery,
Provo UT

Ward Wells Anchorage Photo Collection

Anchorage Historical and Fine Arts Museum,
Archives, Anchorage AK

Benjamin West Collection

Bob Jones University, Greenville SC

Maurice Wetheim Collection

Harvard University, William Hayes Fogg Art
Museum, Cambridge MA

Candace Wheeler Collection

Mark Twain Memorial, Hartford CT

James McNeill Whistler Collection

Freer Gallery of Art, Washington DC

White Collection

Baltimore Museum of Art, Baltimore MD
Philadelphia Museum of Art, Philadelphia PA

Elizabeth White Collection

Sumter Gallery of Art, Sumter SC

Whitney Silver Collection

Montclair Art Museum, Montclair NJ

Whittington Memorial Collection

Delta State University, Fielding L Wright Art
Center, Cleveland MS

Bartlett Wicks Collection

University of Utah, Utah Museum of Fine Arts, Salt
Lake City UT

Alfred H Wiggin Collection

Boston Public Library, Albert H Wiggin Gallery
(Prints), Boston MA

Archibald M Willard Paintings Collection

Spirit of '76 Museum, Southern Lorain County
Historical Society, Wellington OH

Will Collection of Paintings & Drawings

Jersey City Museum Association, Jersey City NJ

**Adolph D and Wilkins C Williams
Collection**

Virginia Museum of Fine Arts, Richmond VA

Ralph Wilson Collection

Lehigh University Art Galleries, Bethlehem PA

Wilstach Collection of Old Masters

Philadelphia Museum of Art, Philadelphia PA

W Lloyd Wright Collection

George Washington University, The Dimock
Gallery, Washington DC

Wurtzburger Collection

Baltimore Museum of Art, Baltimore MD

Andrew Wyeth Collection

Brandywine River Museum, Chadds Ford PA
Greenville County Museum of Art, Greenville SC

Mahonri Young Collection of Manuscripts

Brigham Young University, B F Larsen Gallery,
Provo UT

Karl Zerbe Collection of Serigraphs

Lemoyne Center for the Visual Arts, Tallahassee FL

William Woodward Collection

Baltimore Museum of Art, Baltimore MD

Theodore Wores Collection

Triton Museum of Art, Santa Clara CA